THE COMPLETE PARALLEL BIBLE

THE COMPLETE PARALLEL BIBLE

The Complete Parallel

BIBLE

Containing the Old and New Testaments

with the Apocryphal/Deuterocanonical Books

NEW REVISED STANDARD VERSION

REVISED ENGLISH BIBLE

NEW AMERICAN BIBLE

NEW JERUSALEM BIBLE

New York   Oxford

OXFORD UNIVERSITY PRESS

OXFORD UNIVERSITY PRESS

Oxford   New York   Toronto   Delhi   Bombay   Calcutta   Madras   Karachi   Kuala Lumpur
Singapore   Hong Kong   Tokyo   Nairobi   Dar es Salaam   Cape Town   Melbourne   Auckland   Madrid
and associated companies in
Berlin   Ibadan

Printed in the United States of America

1 3 5 7 9 8 6 4 2

Contents

THE OLD TESTAMENT

CONTENTS

THE APOCRYPHAL/DEUTEROCANONICAL BOOKS

THE NEW TESTAMENT

Alphabetical Listing of the Books of the Bible
(Including the Apocryphal / Deuterocanonical Books of the Old Testament)

Acts	2902	2 Kings	772
Additions to Esther	2186	Lamentations	1792
Amos	2008	Letter of Jeremiah (Baruch 6)	2414
Azariah, Prayer of	2420	Leviticus	204
Baruch	2400	Luke	2752
Bel and the Dragon	2434	1 Maccabees	2438
1 Chronicles	838	2 Maccabees	2508
2 Chronicles	904	3 Maccabees	2580
Colossians	3096	4 Maccabees	2622
1 Corinthians	3012	Malachi	2108
2 Corinthians	3044	Manasseh, Prayer of	2578
Daniel	1932	Mark	2706
Deuteronomy	366	Matthew	2632
Ecclesiastes	1432	Micah	2038
Ecclesiasticus (Sirach)	2266	Nahum	2054
Ephesians	3076	Nehemiah	1006
1 Esdras	2560	Numbers	272
2 Esdras	2586	Obadiah	2028
Esther (Hebrew)	1040	1 Peter	3172
Esther (Greek)	2186	2 Peter	3182
Exodus	114	Philemon	3136
Ezekiel	1812	Philippians	3088
Ezra	982	Prayer of Azariah	2420
Galatians	3064	Prayer of Manasseh	2578
Genesis	2	Proverbs	1358
Habakkuk	2062	Psalm 151	2579
Haggai	2080	Psalms	1132
Hebrews	3138	Revelation	3210
Hosea	1970	Romans	2978
Isaiah	1470	Ruth	560
James	3164	1 Samuel	568
Jeremiah	1636	2 Samuel	640
Jeremiah, Letter of (Baruch 6)	2414	Sirach (Ecclesiasticus)	2266
Job	1048	Song of Songs (Song of Solomon)	1454
Joel	1996	Song of the Three Jews	2420
John	2830	Susanna	2428
1 John	3188	1 Thessalonians	3104
2 John	3202	2 Thessalonians	3112
3 John	3204	1 Timothy	3116
Jonah	2032	2 Timothy	3126
Joshua	450	Titus	3132
Jude	3206	Tobit	2120
Judges	504	Wisdom of Solomon	2214
Judith	2152	Zechariah	2086
1 Kings	702	Zephaniah	2070

Alphabetical Listing of the Books of the Bible
(Including the Apocryphal/Deuterocanonical Books of the Old Testament)

Introduction
to the Complete Parallel Bible

With this volume, Oxford University Press publishes the first four-version parallel text of the Bible that includes the Hebrew Scriptures (the Old Testament), the New Testament, and all of the books recognized as deuterocanonical or apocryphal by the Protestant, Anglican, Roman Catholic, and Orthodox communities. It presents these collections of biblical materials in columns to allow the reader to compare passages in one version with the same passages in other versions. The following information is intended to guide the reader to the best use of the volume, and to point out some of its characteristics.

The Translations and Their Backgrounds

The translations included are the New Revised Standard Version (NRSV), the Revised English Bible (REB), the New American Bible (NAB), and the New Jerusalem Bible (NJB). The first two translations are the work of ecumenical committees of scholars, the NRSV in the United States and the REB in Great Britain. These two committees taken together included scholars from Protestant, Anglican, Catholic, Orthodox, and Jewish communities. The NAB and NJB, also the work of committees, were produced primarily by Catholic scholars, again in the United States and Great Britain respectively. The NRSV, NAB, and NJB carry the *imprimatur* indicating the acceptability of the translation for use by Roman Catholics; the REB was sponsored by all of the churches in the British Isles, including the Catholic Church.

The Arrangement of the Translations

For almost all of the biblical texts, across any two-page spread are four columns, each containing the text of one translation. (The exceptions to this arrangement are detailed below.) From left to right, the translations are the NRSV, the REB, the NAB, and the NJB. The reader may therefore compare passages in two ecumenical translations, one (the NRSV) more literal, the other (the REB) freer and more literary; and may then make the same comparison between two Catholic translations, again with the more literal one (the NAB) on the left and the freer one (the NJB) on the right. This assures the widest possible range of translation approaches.

The parallel arrangement is affected by the fact that the different translations can vary in length for any given passage. If the translations were to run without any break, therefore, the parallel arrangement would soon break down. On the other hand, an exact verse-to-verse parallel structure would require continual adjustment in the length of lines in all the translations, producing a misleading impression of versification. The arrangement therefore allows each translation to run consecutively, with realignments taking place at every chapter start, and with each page ending as nearly as possible on the same verse in all translations. This means that the length of the text columns varies, but each translation can be read consecutively and preserves its paragraphing structure.

The one exception to the preservation of paragraph breaks in the translations occurs when a chapter starts in the middle of a paragraph. In this case, the chapters all begin at the same point on the page, but the convention of leaving the first verse of a chapter unnumbered is dropped: the first verse of any chapter that begins in the middle of a paragraph is numbered. (An example occurs on pp. 884-885.)

At several points in the text this four-version arrangement changes because particular books are not represented in all four versions. Notes in the text call attention to these places: within the Hebrew Scriptures (Old Testament) this is the case at the book of Esther. Only the NRSV and REB translate Hebrew Esther, and therefore this book appears in these two translations on both left- and right-hand pages. (See below for a fuller explanation.) The same arrangement occurs for those apocryphal books not part of the Catholic canon: 1 and 2 Esdras and the Prayer of Manasseh.

For the books of 3 and 4 Maccabees and for Psalm 151, which are represented only in the NRSV, that translation appears in all four columns across the two-page spread.

The Order of the Biblical Materials

The order of books of the Bible within the volume follows the order of the NRSV text. There are two reasons for this. The first is that the NRSV is the most complete translation, and therefore appears in the left-hand column on the left-hand page in all instances. The second reason is that, for the books regarded as deuterocanonical or apocryphal in the various Christian traditions, the NRSV text includes a note on the canonical status of the various books in different Christian traditions. These notes appear before the book of Tobit (p. 2120), before the book of 1 Esdras (p. 2560), before the book of 2 Esdras (p. 2586), and before the book of 4 Maccabees (p. 2622).

Following the order of the NRSV text in the arrangement of books has necessarily required rearrangements in the order of the books for the other translations. In most cases this should not lead to any confusion, but a few places deserve comment.

The first, as mentioned above, concerns the book of Esther. The NRSV and REB translations offer two versions of Esther, one a translation of the (shorter) Hebrew text, the other (among the Apocryphal/Deuterocanonical books) a translation of the Greek text with its additional matter. The NAB and NJB translations offer only a translation of the longer version of Esther, based on the Hebrew version with the additions from the Greek text placed in their contexts in the story. Within the Hebrew Scriptures, therefore, the shorter version of Esther appears in only the NRSV and REB translations, beginning on p. 1040. Within the Deuterocanonical and Apocryphal books, its longer version appears in all four translations beginning on p. 2186.

It would have been possible to reproduce, among the Hebrew Scriptures, those portions of Esther from the NAB and NJB translations that were translated directly from Hebrew Esther. The remaining sections, translated from the longer Greek text, could then have been placed next to their corresponding passages in the NRSV and REB translations of Greek Esther, in the Apocryphal/Deuterocanonical books. In the editor's judgment, however, this would have disrupted the NAB and NJB versions of Esther. The arrangement in the present volume keeps all four translations intact, yet allows for paralleling of content. The reader should note, however, — as is stated in a notice at the head of the NAB and NJB versions of Esther, p. 2187 — that the designation ''deuterocanonical'' properly applies only to the additional passages of Esther in those translations.

The book of Baruch appears in slightly different form in the various translations. The NRSV and REB divide it into two parts: Baruch chs 1–5 (also chs 1–5 in the NAB and NJB) and the Letter of Jeremiah (Baruch ch 6 in the NAB and NJB).

The book of Daniel in the Hebrew Scriptures has three Greek additions that have been handled differently by the various translations. In the NRSV and REB, these additional blocks of material appear, separated from their placement in the story of Daniel, in the Apocryphal/Deuterocanonical books. In the NAB and NJB they appear within the book of Daniel, and follow the chapter and verse numbering of the book. In order to present parallel content together, this volume uses the following arrangement in the Apocryphal/Deuterocanonical books:

NRSV AND REB	NAB AND NJB
The Prayer of Azariah and the Song of the Three Young Men	Daniel 3.24–90
Susanna	Daniel 13
Bel and the Dragon	Daniel 14

Notes have been placed in the text, both in the Old Testament and in the Apocryphal/Deuterocanonical sections, to assist the reader. Within the Hebrew Scriptures the NRSV and REB translate only the Hebrew and Aramaic text of Daniel; the NAB and NJB versions of Daniel in that section are thus shortened as well.

This arrangement, unlike the situation with Esther explained above, is not as disruptive to the narrative of Daniel because the Greek additions are clearly differentiated from their contexts in all four translations.

Variations in the Texts of the Different Translations

So much for the arrangement and order of the books themselves. Within any given book there are also choices to be made. In general the NRSV tries to reproduce the text in the order of its established form, that is, as far as possible without rearrangement in verse or chapter order. The REB, NAB, and NJB, to varying degrees, rearrange the order of the text where their translators have reason to believe that they can reconstruct a more likely order for the original text.

The order of chapters and verses within each translation is retained in the present edition, since the arrangement of each is a part of the translators' choices in their presentation of the text. This sometimes requires accommodation in the parallel format, however. In the case of minimal rearrangement in one translation, where only one or a few verses are involved and where they are placed close to their traditional positions, there is generally no disruption in any of the other translations. The reader should, however, note the order of verses in such cases since the comparison between the translations will often be informative.

In cases where a verse or short passage in one translation has been transferred to a more distant point, there is no rearrangement in the other translations, but a notice has been placed within the affected translation, enclosed within double daggers, thus: ‡20.10 see below‡. (An example occurs on p. 1083.)

In the case of major rearrangements in one or more of the translations, the parallel text will sometimes show a gap in the translations, sometimes with an indication enclosed in double daggers of where the text has been relocated. A good example of this appears beginning on p. 1093, in Job chs 25–28, where several of the translations have shifted large sections of the text.

Explanations in the Translators' Footnotes

The translators' footnotes in the present volume also call for some comment. The NRSV and REB translators have provided footnotes to their translations giving textual information (sources of conjectural readings, alternative readings, and literal translations). The NJB also has a skeletal system of footnotes.

The NAB translation in other editions comes with a very full set of explanatory footnotes as part of its standard apparatus. Such a large amount of material could not be included in the present volume, and the Confraternity of Christian Doctrine has granted permission to reproduce the translation without the apparatus. But it was clear that, in the case of footnotes that explained noticeable characteristics of the text—the rearrangement or omission of verses, for instance—the reader would find such information valuable. The current volume therefore provides such material excerpted from the full NAB apparatus. Readers should be aware, however, that the standard NAB text needs to be consulted in order to understand the translators' full arguments.

The reader should also, in cases of textual rearrangement or in areas where verses have been omitted or bracketed in one or more translations, consult the notes to all the translations, since the notes to one translation are likely to have a bearing on the other translations. Sometimes one translation has preferred a rendition that another has put in a footnote; sometimes a note will explain the rationale behind another translation's choice of verse order.

In several cases one or more translations have placed material that is of doubtful textual authority in footnotes or elsewhere in the text, while other translations have left it in the text but with notice of its textual status explained in a footnote. The parallel arrangement in the current volume required adaptation in these instances. In nearly all cases, material appears in the text and not in footnotes; but a notice has been inserted, where necessary, to call attention to the fact that particular translators have doubted the textual status of such passages.

Two major instances of this occur. One is in the book of Sirach, ch 51. Between vv. 12 and 13 of this chapter, the Hebrew version of Sirach inserts 16 verses. The NRSV translation gives these in the body of the text, although set off with rules and printed in italics to call attention to their textual status. The REB and NJB trans-

lations omit them altogether. The NAB includes them in a footnote. In the current edition, these verses appear in the NAB text, but notice of their textual status is given at the occurrence.

The other instance occurs in John 7.53–8.11. This passage, the account of the woman taken in adultery, has long been a textual problem, as is explained in all four translations. The NRSV, the NAB, and the NJB print it within the text but call attention to its status; the REB prints it as an appendix to the gospel. It appears in place in all four translations, but once again with notification of its problems.

Variations in Verse Numbering

The numbering of chapters and verses in the Bible does not go back to the original texts themselves, and in the case of verse numbering particularly is of relatively recent origin. In some cases ancient texts placed their equivalents of chapter and verse divisions in locations different from those indicated by the modern numbering. In the current volume the reader should be aware that every effort has been made to put verses that are parallel in content together, even if they do not carry the same verse number. Particularly in the Psalms, the traditional Catholic verse numbering—followed by the NAB—often differs from that in the other translations.

First Kings chs 4 and 5 (pp. 714-715) provides an example in which the NRSV and REB follow the traditional verse numbering of the King James Version, whereas the NAB and NJB use the Hebrew verse numbering. This means that in this case, the NRSV and REB verses 4.21 through 4.34 are given as parallels to 5.1–14 in the NAB and NJB.

Uses of the Parallel Text

Finally, it may be helpful to readers to include a few words about the usefulness of such a parallel text of the Bible. The uses of such a volume are several:

The volume can be a valuable tool in suggesting the possible range of meanings in a given biblical text. The nuances of the original languages of a text cannot all be reproduced when the text is translated into another language. A careful comparison among different translations can help to overcome this disability in any single translation.

The parallel text can be a significant timesaver when researching passages for classroom or preaching use. Often a particular passage is most effectively presented in a translation other than the one in primary use. This volume will quickly provide the comparison passages that will allow the most effective one to be found.

The texts contained here can provide valuable clues for analysis. In cases where the texts are similar, that is an indication that the scholarly community has attained some consensus on the rendition; in cases where the texts differ, the reader can use that as a clue to areas that would be fruitful for research in commentaries, dictionaries, etc.

Lastly, the value of a parallel edition of such an important literary artifact as the Bible lies in its ability to provoke the reader afresh with the meaning of passages that may have become overly familiar. Most readers find a translation they like and stick to it. Since the present volume allows easy access to alternative renderings, it also allows the reader to encounter even a familiar text as something new.

It is with the hope that readers will find fresh insight for their research and thought within its pages that Oxford University Press has undertaken the publication of this edition.

THE EDITORS

OXFORD UNIVERSITY PRESS

Acknowledgments

The Publisher wishes to thank all those who have contributed to this volume:

Doug and June Gunden and their proofreading team, who proofread and corrected the entire volume and suggested numerous improvements.

Leslie Phillips, who designed it and oversaw the production.

The translation owners, particularly those of the New American Bible and New Jerusalem Bible, who allowed the apparatus of their texts to be modified to fit the parallel format.

Acknowledgments

The Publisher wishes to thank all those who have contributed to this volume.

Doug and Jane Olina extend their proofreading team who proofread and corrected the reproductions and the re-set supporting improvements.

Leslie Phillips, whose agreed it and oversaw the production.

The transcription we are particularly grateful for the New American Bible and the translation Bible, who allowed the apparatus of their texts to be modified to fit the parallel format.

To the Reader

This preface is addressed to you by the Committee of translators, who wish to explain, as briefly as possible, the origin and character of our work. The publication of our revision is yet another step in the long, continual process of making the Bible available in the form of the English language that is most widely current in our day. To summarize in a single sentence: the New Revised Standard Version of the Bible is an authorized revision of the Revised Standard Version, published in 1952, which was a revision of the American Standard Version, published in 1901, which, in turn, embodied earlier revisions of the King James Version, published in 1611.

In the course of time, the King James Version came to be regarded as "the Authorized Version." With good reason it has been termed "the noblest monument of English prose," and it has entered, as no other book has, into the making of the personal character and the public institutions of the English-speaking peoples. We owe to it an incalculable debt.

Yet the King James Version has serious defects. By the middle of the nineteenth century, the development of biblical studies and the discovery of many biblical manuscripts more ancient than those on which the King James Version was based made it apparent that these defects were so many as to call for revision. The task was begun, by authority of the Church of England, in 1870. The (British) Revised Version of the Bible was published in 1881–1885; and the American Standard Version, its variant embodying the preferences of the American scholars associated with the work, was published, as was mentioned above, in 1901. In 1928 the copyright of the latter was acquired by the International Council of Religious Education and thus passed into the ownership of the churches of the United States and Canada that were associated in this Council through their boards of education and publication.

The Council appointed a committee of scholars to have charge of the text of the American Standard Version and to undertake inquiry concerning the need for further revision. After studying the questions whether or not revision should be undertaken, and if so, what its nature and extent should be, in 1937 the Council authorized a revision. The scholars who served as members of the Committee worked in two sections, one dealing with the Old Testament and one with the New Testament. In 1946 the Revised Standard Version of the New Testament was published. The publication of the Revised Standard Version of the Bible, containing the Old and New Testaments, took place on September 30, 1952. A translation of the Apocryphal/Deuterocanonical Books of the Old Testament followed in 1957. In 1977 this collection was issued in an expanded edition, containing three additional texts received by Eastern Orthodox communions (3 and 4 Maccabees and Psalm 151). Thereafter the Revised Standard Version gained the distinction of being officially authorized for use by all major Christian churches: Protestant, Anglican, Roman Catholic, and Eastern Orthodox.

The Revised Standard Version Bible Committee is a continuing body, comprising about thirty members, both men and women. Ecumenical in representation, it includes scholars affiliated with various Protestant denominations, as well as several Roman Catholic members, an Eastern Orthodox member, and a Jewish member who serves in the Old Testament section. For a period of time the Committee included several members from Canada and from England.

Because no translation of the Bible is perfect or is acceptable to all groups of readers, and because discoveries of older manuscripts and further investigation of linguistic features of the text continue to become available, renderings of the Bible have proliferated. During the years following the publication of the Revised Standard Version, twenty-six other English translations and revisions of the Bible were produced by committees and by individual scholars—not to mention twenty-five other translations and revisions of the New Testament alone. One of the latter was the second edition of the RSV New Testament, issued in 1971, twenty-five years after its initial publication.

Following the publication of the RSV Old Testament in 1952, significant advances were made in the discovery and interpretation of documents in Semitic languages related to Hebrew. In addition to the information that had become available in the late 1940s from the Dead Sea texts of Isaiah and Habakkuk, subsequent acquisitions from the same area brought to light many other early copies of all the books of the Hebrew Scriptures (except Esther), though most of these copies are fragmentary. During the same period early Greek manuscript copies of books of the New Testament also became available.

In order to take these discoveries into account, along with recent studies of documents in Semitic languages related to Hebrew, in 1974 the Policies Committee of the Revised Standard Version, which is a standing committee of the National Council of the Churches of Christ in the U.S.A., authorized the preparation of a revision of the entire RSV Bible.

For the Old Testament the Committee has made use of the *Biblia Hebraica Stuttgartensia* (1977; ed. sec. emendata, 1983). This is an edition of the Hebrew and Aramaic text as current early in the Christian era and fixed by Jewish scholars (the "Masoretes") of the sixth to the ninth centuries. The vowel signs, which were added by the Masoretes, are accepted in the main, but where a more probable and convincing reading can be obtained by assuming different vowels, this has been done. No notes are given in such cases, because the vowel points are less ancient and reliable than the consonants. When an alternative reading given by the Masoretes is translated in a footnote, this is identified by the words "Another reading is."

Departures from the consonantal text of the best manuscripts have been made only where it seems clear that errors in copying had been made before the text was standardized. Most of the corrections adopted are based on the ancient versions (translations into Greek, Aramaic, Syriac, and Latin), which were made prior to the time of the work of the Masoretes and which therefore may reflect earlier forms of the Hebrew text. In such instances a footnote specifies the version or versions from which the correction has been derived and also gives a translation of the Masoretic Text. Where it was deemed appropriate to do so, information is supplied in footnotes from subsidiary Jewish traditions concerning other textual readings (the *Tiqqune Sopherim*, "emendations of the scribes"). These are identified in the footnotes as "Ancient Heb tradition."

Occasionally it is evident that the text has suffered in transmission and that none of the versions provides a satisfactory restoration. Here we can only follow the best judgment of competent scholars as to the most probable reconstruction of the original text. Such reconstructions are indicated in footnotes by the abbreviation Cn ("Correction"), and a translation of the Masoretic Text is added.

For the Apocryphal/Deuterocanonical Books of the Old Testament the Committee has made use of a number of texts. For most of these books the basic Greek text from which the present translation was made is the edition of the Septuagint prepared by Alfred Rahlfs and published by the Württemberg Bible Society (Stuttgart, 1935). For several of the books the more recently published individual volumes of the Göttingen Septuagint project were utilized. For the book of Tobit it was decided to follow the form of the Greek text found in codex Sinaiticus (supported as it is by evidence from Qumran); where this text is defective, it was supplemented and corrected by other Greek manuscripts. For the three Additions to Daniel (namely, Susanna, the Prayer of Azariah and the Song of the Three Jews, and Bel and the Dragon) the Committee continued to use the Greek version attributed to Theodotion (the so-called "Theodotion-Daniel"). In translating Ecclesiasticus (Sirach), while constant reference was made to the Hebrew fragments of a large portion of this book (those discovered at Qumran and Masada as well as those recovered from the Cairo Geniza), the Committee generally followed the Greek text (including verse numbers) published by Joseph Ziegler in the Göttingen Septuagint (1965). But in many places the Committee has translated the Hebrew text when this provides a reading that is clearly superior to the Greek; the Syriac and Latin versions were also consulted throughout and occasionally adopted. The basic text adopted in rendering 2 Esdras is the Latin version given in *Biblia Sacra*, edited by Robert Weber (Stuttgart, 1971). This was supplemented by consulting the Latin text as edited by R. L. Bensly (1895) and by Bruno Violet (1910), as well as by taking into account the several Oriental versions of 2 Esdras, namely, the Syriac, Ethiopic, Arabic (two forms, referred to as Arabic 1 and Arabic 2), Armenian, and Georgian versions. Finally, since the Additions

to the Book of Esther are disjointed and quite unintelligible as they stand in most editions of the Apocrypha, we have provided them with their original context by translating the whole of the Greek version of Esther from Robert Hanhart's Göttingen edition (1983).

For the New Testament the Committee has based its work on the most recent edition of *The Greek New Testament,* prepared by an interconfessional and international committee and published by the United Bible Societies (1966; 3rd ed. corrected, 1983; information concerning changes to be introduced into the critical apparatus of the forthcoming 4th edition was available to the Committee). As in that edition, double brackets are used to enclose a few passages that are generally regarded to be later additions to the text, but which we have retained because of their evident antiquity and their importance in the textual tradition. Only in very rare instances have we replaced the text or the punctuation of the Bible Societies' edition by an alternative that seemed to us to be superior. Here and there in the footnotes the phrase, ''Other ancient authorities read,'' identifies alternative readings preserved by Greek manuscripts and early versions. In both Testaments, alternative renderings of the text are indicated by the word, ''Or.''

As for the style of English adopted for the present revision, among the mandates given to the Committee in 1980 by the Division of Education and Ministry of the National Council of Churches of Christ (which now holds the copyright of the RSV Bible) was the directive to continue in the tradition of the King James Bible, but to introduce such changes as are warranted on the basis of accuracy, clarity, euphony, and current English usage. Within the constraints set by the original texts and by the mandates of the Division, the Committee has followed the maxim, ''As literal as possible, as free as necessary.'' As a consequence, the New Revised Standard Version (NRSV) remains essentially a literal translation. Paraphrastic renderings have been adopted only sparingly, and then chiefly to compensate for a deficiency in the English language—the lack of a common gender third person singular pronoun.

During the almost half a century since the publication of the RSV, many in the churches have become sensitive to the danger of linguistic sexism arising from the inherent bias of the English language towards the masculine gender, a bias that in the case of the Bible has often restricted or obscured the meaning of the original text. The mandates from the Division specified that, in references to men and women, masculine-oriented language should be eliminated as far as this can be done without altering passages that reflect the historical situation of ancient patriarchal culture. As can be appreciated, more than once the Committee found that the several mandates stood in tension and even in conflict. The various concerns had to be balanced case by case in order to provide a faithful and acceptable rendering without using contrived English. Only very occasionally has the pronoun ''he'' or ''him'' been retained in passages where the reference may have been to a woman as well as to a man; for example, in several legal texts in Leviticus and Deuteronomy. In such instances of formal, legal language, the options of either putting the passage in the plural or of introducing additional nouns to avoid masculine pronouns in English seemed to the Committee to obscure the historic structure and literary character of the original. In the vast majority of cases, however, inclusiveness has been attained by simple rephrasing or by introducing plural forms when this does not distort the meaning of the passage. Of course, in narrative and in parable no attempt was made to generalize the sex of individual persons.

Another aspect of style will be detected by readers who compare the more stately English rendering of the Old Testament with the less formal rendering adopted for the New Testament. For example, the traditional distinction between *shall* and *will* in English has been retained in the Old Testament as appropriate in rendering a document that embodies what may be termed the classic form of Hebrew, while in the New Testament the abandonment of such distinctions in the usage of the future tense in English reflects the more colloquial nature of the koine Greek used by most New Testament authors except when they are quoting the Old Testament.

Careful readers will notice that here and there in the Old Testament the word LORD (or in certain cases GOD) is printed in capital letters. This represents the traditional manner in English versions of rendering the Divine Name, the ''Tetragrammaton'' (see the notes on Exodus 3.14, 15), following the precedent of the ancient Greek and Latin translators and the long established practice in the reading of the Hebrew Scriptures in the synagogue.

While it is almost if not quite certain that the Name was originally pronounced ''Yahweh,'' this pronunciation was not indicated when the Masoretes added vowel sounds to the consonantal Hebrew text. To the four consonants YHWH of the Name, which had come to be regarded as too sacred to be pronounced, they attached vowel signs indicating that in its place should be read the Hebrew word *Adonai* meaning ''Lord'' (or *Elohim* meaning ''God''). Ancient Greek translators employed the word *Kyrios* (''Lord'') for the Name. The Vulgate likewise used the Latin word *Dominus* (''Lord''). The form ''Jehovah'' is of late medieval origin; it is a combination of the consonants of the Divine Name and the vowels attached to it by the Masoretes but belonging to an entirely different word. Although the American Standard Version (1901) had used ''Jehovah'' to render the Tetragrammaton (the sound of Y being represented by J and the sound of W by V, as in Latin), for two reasons the Committees that produced the RSV and NRSV returned to the more familiar usage of the King James Version. (1) The word ''Jehovah'' does not accurately represent any form of the Name ever used in Hebrew. (2) The use of any proper name for the one and only God, as though there were other gods from whom the true God had to be distinguished, began to be discontinued in Judaism before the Christian era and is inappropriate for the universal faith of the Christian Church.

It will be seen that in the Psalms and in other prayers addressed to God the archaic second person singular pronouns *(thee, thou, thine)* and verb forms *(art, hast, hadst)* are no longer used. Although some readers may regret this change, it should be pointed out that in the original languages neither the Old Testament nor the New makes any linguistic distinction between addressing a human being and addressing the Deity. Furthermore, in the tradition of the King James Version one will not expect to find the use of capital letters for pronouns that refer to the Deity—such capitalization is an unnecessary innovation that has only recently been introduced into a few English translations of the Bible. Finally, we have left to the discretion of the licensed publishers such matters as section headings, cross-references, and clues to the pronunciation of proper names.

This new version seeks to preserve all that is best in the English Bible as it has been known and used through the years. It is intended for use in public reading and congregational worship, as well as in private study, instruction, and meditation. We have resisted the temptation to introduce terms and phrases that merely reflect current moods, and have tried to put the message of the Scriptures in simple enduring words and expressions that are worthy to stand in the great tradition of the King James Bible and its predecessors.

In traditional Judaism and Christianity, the Bible has been more than a historical document to be preserved or a classic of literature to be cherished and admired; it is recognized as the unique record of God's dealings with people over the ages. The Old Testament sets forth the call of a special people to enter into covenant relation with the God of justice and steadfast love and to bring God's law to the nations. The New Testament records the life and work of Jesus Christ, the one in whom ''the Word became flesh,'' as well as describes the rise and spread of the early Christian Church. The Bible carries its full message, not to those who regard it simply as a noble literary heritage of the past or who wish to use it to enhance political purposes and advance otherwise desirable goals, but to all persons and communities who read it so that they may discern and understand what God is saying to them. That message must not be disguised in phrases that are no longer clear, or hidden under words that have changed or lost their meaning; it must be presented in language that is direct and plain and meaningful to people today. It is the hope and prayer of the translators that this version of the Bible may continue to hold a large place in congregational life and to speak to all readers, young and old alike, helping them to understand and believe and respond to its message.

For the Committee,
BRUCE M. METZGER

Abbreviations

The following abbreviations are used for the books of the Bible:

OLD TESTAMENT

Gen	Genesis	2 Chr	2 Chronicles	Dan	Daniel
Ex	Exodus	Ezra	Ezra	Hos	Hosea
Lev	Leviticus	Neh	Nehemiah	Joel	Joel
Num	Numbers	Esth	Esther	Am	Amos
Deut	Deuteronomy	Job	Job	Ob	Obadiah
Josh	Joshua	Ps	Psalms	Jon	Jonah
Judg	Judges	Prov	Proverbs	Mic	Micah
Ruth	Ruth	Eccl	Ecclesiastes	Nah	Nahum
1 Sam	1 Samuel	Song	Song of Solomon	Hab	Habakkuk
2 Sam	2 Samuel	Isa	Isaiah	Zeph	Zephaniah
1 Kings	1 Kings	Jer	Jeremiah	Hag	Haggai
2 Kings	2 Kings	Lam	Lamentations	Zech	Zechariah
1 Chr	1 Chronicles	Ezek	Ezekiel	Mal	Malachi

APOCRYPHAL / DEUTEROCANONICAL BOOKS

Tob	Tobit	Song of Thr	Prayer of Azariah and the Song of the Three Jews
Jdt	Judith		
Add Esth	Additions to Esther (Gk)	Sus	Susanna
Wis	Wisdom	Bel	Bel and the Dragon
Sir	Sirach (Ecclesiasticus)	1 Macc	1 Maccabees
Bar	Baruch	2 Macc	2 Maccabees
1 Esd	1 Esdras	3 Macc	3 Maccabees
2 Esd	2 Esdras	4 Macc	4 Maccabees
Let Jer	Letter of Jeremiah	Pr Man	Prayer of Manasseh

NEW TESTAMENT

Mt	Matthew	Eph	Ephesians	Heb	Hebrews
Mk	Mark	Phil	Philippians	Jas	James
Lk	Luke	Col	Colossians	1 Pet	1 Peter
Jn	John	1 Thess	1 Thessalonians	2 Pet	2 Peter
Acts	Acts of the Apostles	2 Thess	2 Thessalonians	1 Jn	1 John
Rom	Romans	1 Tim	1 Timothy	2 Jn	2 John
1 Cor	1 Corinthians	2 Tim	2 Timothy	3 Jn	3 John
2 Cor	2 Corinthians	Titus	Titus	Jude	Jude
Gal	Galatians	Philem	Philemon	Rev	Revelation

In the NRSV notes to the books of the Old Testament the following abbreviations are used:

Ant.	Josephus, *Antiquities of the Jews*
Aram	Aramaic
Ch, chs	Chapter, chapters
Cn	Correction; made where the text has suffered in transmission and the versions provide no satisfactory restoration but where the Standard Bible Committee agrees with the judgment of competent scholars as to the most probable reconstruction of the original text.
Gk	Septuagint, Greek version of the Old Testament
Heb	Hebrew of the consonantal Masoretic Text of the Old Testament
Josephus	Flavius Josephus (Jewish historian, about A.D. 37 to about 95)
Macc	The book(s) of the Maccabees

Ms(s)   Manuscript(s)
MT   The Hebrew of the pointed Masoretic Text of the Old Testament
OL   Old Latin
Q Ms(s)   Manuscript(s) found at Qumran by the Dead Sea
Sam   Samaritan Hebrew text of the Old Testament
Syr   Syriac Version of the Old Testament
Syr H   Syriac Version of Origen's Hexapla
Tg   Targum
Vg   Vulgate, Latin Version of the Old Testament

Preface to the Revised English Bible

The second half of the twentieth century has produced many new versions of the Bible. One of the pioneers was The New English Bible, which was distinctive inasmuch as it was a new translation from the ancient texts and was officially commissioned by the majority of the British Churches.

The translators themselves were chosen for their ability as scholars, without regard to Church affiliation. Literary advisers read and criticized the translators' drafts.

The translation of the New Testament appeared in 1961. The Old Testament and the Apocrypha were published with a limited revision of the New Testament in 1970; The New English Bible was then complete. Two years later a new impression appeared with some very minor corrections, and The New English Bible has remained substantially as it was first produced until the present day. It has proved to be of great value throughout the English-speaking world and is very widely used.

The debt of the Churches to those who served on the various committees and panels is very considerable and has been gladly acknowledged on many occasions. One name that will always be associated with The New English Bible is that of Dr C.H. Dodd, who as Director from start to finish brought to the enterprise outstanding leadership, sensitivity, and scholarship. It is fitting also to recall with gratitude the roles of Professor Sir Godfrey Driver, Joint Director from 1965, and Professor W. D. McHardy, Deputy Director from 1968.

It was right that The New English Bible in its original form, like any other version, should be subject to critical examination and discussion, and especially the Old Testament, which had not had the advantage of even a limited general revision. From the beginning helpful suggestions and criticisms had come in from many quarters. Moreover the widespread enthusiasm for The New English Bible had resulted in its being frequently used for reading aloud in public worship, the implications of which had not been fully anticipated by the translators. As a result it became desirable to review the translation, and in 1974 the Joint Committee of the Churches decided to set in train what was to become a major revision of the text.

New translators' panels were constituted under the chairmanship of Professor W. D. McHardy, who was appointed Director of Revision. The result of their work is The Revised English Bible, a translation standing firmly in the tradition established by The New English Bible. This substantial revision expresses the mind and conviction of biblical scholars and translators of the 1980s, as The New English Bible expressed the mind of a previous generation of such specialists, and it is fortunate that some distinguished scholars have been able to give their services throughout the entire process. To them we owe a great deal, and to none more than to Professor McHardy, who has served with great devotion throughout and made this a large part of his life's work.

The original initiative for making the New English Bible translation had come from the Church of Scotland in 1946, and a number of other Churches later joined them and formed a committee which was to plan and direct a new translation in contemporary language. The Joint Committee comprised representatives of the Baptist Union of Great Britain and Ireland, the Church of England, the Church of Scotland, the Congregational Church of England and Wales, the Council of Churches for Wales, the Irish Council of Churches, the London Yearly Meeting of the Religious Society of Friends, the Methodist Church of Great Britain, and the Presbyterian Church of England, as well as of the British and Foreign Bible Society and the National Bible Society of Scotland. Roman Catholic representatives later attended as observers.

After publication of the complete translation, there were changes in the composition of the Joint Committee. The Roman Catholic Church entered into full membership, with representatives from the hierarchies of England and Wales, Scotland, and Ireland. Following the union of the Presbyterian Church of England with the Congregational Church as the United Reformed Church, the united church was represented on the Committee. After the review began, the Committee was joined by representatives of the Salvation Army and the Moravian Church.

The progress of the work of the revisers has been regularly reported to meetings of the Joint Committee, taking place once and sometimes twice a year in the Jerusalem Chamber, Westminster Abbey. The Committee has much appreciated the courtesy of the Dean and Chapter in making the Chamber available for these meetings.

Members of the Joint Committee have given guidance and support to the Director of Revision throughout, and have had the opportunity of inspecting drafts as the work on each book approached its final stage, in many cases making detailed comments and criticisms for the consideration of the Director and revisers.

Care has been taken to ensure that the style of English used is fluent and of appropriate dignity for liturgical use, while maintaining intelligibility for worshippers of a wide range of ages and backgrounds. The revisers have sought to avoid complex or technical terms where possible, and to provide sentence structure and word order, especially in the Psalms, which will facilitate congregational reading but will not misrepresent the meaning of the original texts. As the 'you'-form of address to God is now commonly used, the 'thou'-form which was preserved in the language of prayer in The New English Bible has been abandoned. The use of male-oriented language, in passages of traditional versions of the Bible which evidently apply to both genders, has become a sensitive issue in recent years; the revisers have preferred more inclusive gender reference where that has been possible without compromising scholarly integrity or English style.

The headings in the Psalms have been translated from those prefixed in ancient times to the Hebrew Psalms.

The traditional verse numbering of the Authorized (King James) Version is retained in The Revised English Bible for ease of reference. Where the Authorized Version contains passages which are found in the manuscripts on which that version rests, but which are absent from those followed by The Revised English Bible, these passages are reproduced in footnotes, in order to explain gaps in the verse numbering.

A table of measures, weights, and values will be found on page xxix. The ancient terms usually appear in the text, but modern equivalents have been used when it seemed appropriate to do so.

The Joint Committee commends The Revised English Bible to the Churches and to the English-speaking world with due humility, but with confidence that God has yet new light and truth to break forth from his word. The Committee prays that the new version will prove to be a means to that end.

DONALD COGGAN
Chairman of the Joint Committee

Introduction to the Old Testament

The Old Testament consists of a collection of works composed at various times from the twelfth to the second century B.C.E. The books are written in classical Hebrew, except some brief portions (Ezra 4:8—6:18 and 7:12—26; Jeremiah 10:11, and Daniel 2:4—7:28) which are in Aramaic, a closely related and widely used language.

Very few manuscripts survived the destruction of Jerusalem in 70 C.E., and soon after that disaster the Jewish religious leaders set about defining the 'canon' (the scriptures accepted as authoritative) and finally standardizing the text. This was the Massoretic or 'traditional' text.

The original texts were written in a script which represents only a small proportion of the vowel sounds. In order to preserve the correct pronunciation in school and synagogue, and so to fix the meaning of words which could be read in more than one way, the Massoretic editors used vowel signs to modify the consonantal symbols. They were following a continuous tradition of reading the scriptures aloud; over the years errors had crept in, and so on occasion the present revisers, like the translators of The New English Bible, substituted other vowel signs where it seemed necessary.

In one case the Massoretes did not give the true vocalization. The divine name (YHWH in Hebrew characters) was probably pronounced 'Yahweh', but the name was regarded as ineffable, too sacred to be pronounced. The Massoretes, therefore, wrote in the vowel signs of the alternative words *adonai* ('Lord') or *elohim* ('God') to warn readers to use one of these in its place. Where the divine name occurs in the Hebrew text, this has been

signalled in The Revised English Bible by using capital letters for 'LORD' or 'GOD', a widely accepted practice.

It is probable that the Massoretic Text remained substantially unaltered from the second century C.E. to the present time, and this text is reproduced in all Hebrew Bibles. The New English Bible translators used the third edition of R. Kittel's *Biblia Hebraica* (Stuttgart, 1937). A new and thoroughly revised edition, *Biblia Hebraica Stuttgartensia*, appeared in 1967/77, and is the most widely used modern edition. Both these take their text from a manuscript of the early eleventh century C.E. now preserved in Leningrad.

Despite the care used in the copying of the Massoretic Text, it contains errors, in the correction of which there are witnesses to be heard. None of them is throughout superior to the Massoretic Text, but in particular places their evidence may preserve the correct reading.

There are, firstly, Hebrew texts which are outside the Massoretic tradition: the Samaritan text and the Dead Sea Scrolls. The Samaritan text consists only of the Pentateuch (Genesis–Deuteronomy). It must date from a period before the secession of the Samaritans from Judaism (probably no later than the second century B.C.E.), but is preserved only in manuscripts the earliest of which is tentatively assigned to the eleventh century C.E. This is in effect the Hebrew text in Samaritan characters. Translators of the Old Testament may now make use of what are commonly known as the Dead Sea Scrolls, the discovery of which, in 1947 and after, revealed Hebrew manuscripts perhaps a thousand years older than those previously known.

The translators and revisers had in addition to the early Hebrew texts the evidence provided by the ancient versions in other languages. The earliest of these, the Greek translation made in Egypt in the third and second centuries B.C.E. and commonly called the Septuagint, is the major tool for recovering the original Hebrew text. In the early Christian era Lucian produced an edition of the Septuagint. Other Greek versions of the period were those of Aquila, Symmachus, and Theodotion.

When the need for a Latin Bible arose, the Old Latin version was produced by translating the Septuagint. The Vulgate, Jerome's translation into Latin of the Hebrew text, followed towards the end of the fourth century C.E.

As Hebrew had ceased to be commonly understood in Palestine, renderings into Aramaic known as Targums had been produced for synagogue use from the fourth century B.C.E. onwards. The early Christian church in Mesopotamia had its version in Syriac (a form of Aramaic); it is known as the Peshitta, a 'simple' or literal translation.

All these versions contribute in varying degrees to the recovery and understanding of the Hebrew.

Other contributions to the understanding of the Hebrew text have been made by archaeological discoveries and by the study of the cognate Semitic languages. This last method, used by medieval Jewish scholars and also by Christian scholars in the seventeenth and following centuries, has received fresh impetus from the decipherment of texts notably from Ras Shamra in Syria. It is a method which has led to valuable results, but its application demands both skill and particular caution; the revisers have been aware of the dangers of an over-zealous use of it.

The text is not infrequently uncertain and its meaning obscure, and after all the study of the texts and versions, the languages and culture of the ancient Near East, there remain a number of passages where the translator must either leave a blank in his version or, as the New English Bible translators and the present revisers have chosen to do, resort to conjectural emendation of the Hebrew text. This has been done as sparingly as possible, and attention is drawn to such cases in footnotes by the indicator *prob. rdg.*

Where exact identification of specialized terms such as 'Sheol' (the Hebrew word for the underworld) is required, these have been given as transliterations of the Hebrew, but where exact identification is less vital they have been rendered by some word or phrase approaching the original sense. The rendering of the terms for each kind of sacrifice has been revised and standardized in the statements of the Jewish legal codes, whereas they have been translated more freely in parts of the Old Testament where no technical problems are involved and strict consistency is not of overriding importance.

Where no exact equivalent exists for the original Hebrew, a somewhat expanded translation has been provided; on the other hand some abbreviation has been made when the Hebrew text seemed unduly repetitive by the

normal standards of writing in English. Changes such as substituting nouns for pronouns have been made when clarity demanded it.

As elsewhere in The Revised English Bible, the guiding principle adopted has been to seek a fluent and idiomatic way of expressing biblical writing in contemporary English. Much emphasis has been laid on correctness and intelligibility, and at the same time on endeavouring to convey something of the directness and simplicity of the Hebrew original. All those who have been concerned with the production of this translation have done their work in the conviction that the Old Testament has contributed vitally to every tradition of Christian worship and culture, and that an accurate understanding of the Bible of the Jews is essential to the full appreciation of Christian doctrine and the events recorded in the New Testament.

Introduction to the Apocrypha

The term 'Apocrypha', a Greek word meaning 'hidden (things)', was early used in different senses. It was applied to writings which were regarded as so important and precious that they must be hidden from the general public and preserved for initiates, the inner circle of believers. It also came to be applied to writings which were hidden not because they were too good, but because they were not good enough: because, that is, they were secondary, questionable, or heretical. A third usage may be traced to Jerome (*ca.* 342–420 C.E.). He was familiar with the scriptures in their Hebrew as well as their Greek form, and for him apocryphal books were those outside the Hebrew 'canon', the scriptures accepted as authoritative by the Jews.

It is the usage of Jerome that is adopted here. The Apocrypha in this translation consists of fifteen books or parts of books. They are works outside the canon adopted in Palestine; that is they form no part of the Hebrew scriptures, although the original language of some of them was Hebrew. They are all, except The Second Book of Esdras, in the Greek version of the Old Testament made for the Greek-speaking Jews in Egypt and known as the Septuagint. Gentile converts to Christianity overwhelmingly outnumbered those of Jewish origin, and so the Bible in Greek — the international language — with the extra books included in it, came to be adopted as the Bible of the early Church, and many early Christian writers quote them as scripture. With the exception of The First and Second Books of Esdras and The Prayer of Manasseh, the Roman Catholic Church recognizes these writings as part of the Old Testament, and designates them as deuterocanonical, that is added later to the canon. They are included in the Latin Vulgate Bible.

In Greek and Latin manuscripts of the Old Testament these books are dispersed throughout the Old Testament, generally in the places most in accord with their contents, and it was this arrangement which was traditionally followed by the Roman Catholic Church. The practice of collecting them into a separate unit dates back no farther than 1520 C.E., and explains why certain of the items are but fragments; they are passages not found in the Hebrew Bible, and so have been removed from the books in which they occur in the Greek version. To help the reader over this disunity and lack of context, the present revisers have adopted various devices used in The New English Bible: the name of Daniel appears in the titles of the stories of Susanna, and Bel and the Snake, as a reminder that these tales are to be read with The Book of Daniel; a note after the title of The Prayer of Azariah and The Song of the Three indicates that this item is to be found in the third chapter of the Greek form of Daniel; the six additions to the Book of Esther, which are disjointed as printed in older translations of the Apocrypha, are provided with a context by rendering the whole of the Greek version of Esther.

Due weight has been given to the variant readings given in critical editions of the Greek, the text of the ancient versions, and the suggestions of editors and commentators. The texts used for the revision were those edited by H. B. Swete in *The Old Testament in Greek according to the Septuagint*, and A. Rahlfs in his *Septuaginta*. In places these editions include two texts: the present revisers chose to use the Codex Sinaiticus text of Tobit together with the Old Latin version. They used Theodotion's version of the additions to The Book of Daniel, namely The Prayer of Azariah and The Song of the Three, Daniel and Susanna, and Daniel, Bel, and the Snake.

The variant readings given in critical editions of the Greek were consulted throughout, and for Ecclesiasticus constant reference was made to the various forms of the Hebrew text. For The Second Book of Esdras, which apart from a few verses is not extant in Greek, the translation is based on the Latin text of R. L. Bensly's *The Fourth Book of Ezra*.

Alternative readings from Greek manuscripts and the evidence of early translations (*Vss.*, that is Versions) are given, as footnotes, only where they are significant either for text or for meaning. In a few places where the text seems to have suffered in the course of transmission and in its present form is obscure or even unintelligible, a slight change was made in the text and the rendering marked *prob. rdg*. Where an alternative interpretation was thought to deserve serious consideration it was recorded as a footnote with *or* as an indicator.

No attempt has been made to achieve consistency in the treatment of proper names. Familiar English forms have been used, especially when the reference is to well-known Old Testament characters or places.

In The First and Second Books of the Maccabees the dates given are reckoned according to the Greek or Seleucid era. As a help to the reader the nearest dates according to the Christian reckoning have been added at the foot of the page.

This revision of the Apocrypha shares with the rest of The Revised English Bible the aim of providing a rendering which is both faithful and idiomatic, conveying the meaning of the original in language which will be the closest natural equivalent. Every attempt has been made to avoid on the one hand free paraphrase, and on the other a formal fidelity that would result in a rendering which was all too obviously a translation. It is hoped that these documents, valuable in themselves and indispensable for the study of the New Testament, have been made more intelligible and more readily accessible.

Introduction to the New Testament

The Revised English Bible, a revision of The New English Bible, carries forward the aim of its predecessor to provide English-speaking readers with a faithful rendering of the best available Greek text into modern English, incorporating the gains of modern biblical scholarship.

The earliest manuscripts of the books of the New Testament were written down within a generation of their first composition. But the transmission of the text has not been altogether straightforward, and there is no scholarly Greek text of the New Testament which commands universal acceptance at the present time. Those who prepared the first draft of The New English Bible New Testament usually started with the text originally published by Eberhard Nestle at the end of the nineteenth century. The translators considered variant readings on their merits and, having weighed the evidence, selected for translation in each passage the reading which, to the best of their judgement, seemed most likely to represent what the author wrote. In assessing the evidence, the translators took into account (*a*) manuscripts of the New Testament in Greek, (*b*) early translations into other languages, and (*c*) quotations from the New Testament by early Christian writers. These three sources of evidence were referred to as 'witnesses'. The complete text eventually followed was edited by R. V. G. Tasker and published as *The Greek New Testament* (Oxford and Cambridge University Presses, 1964). A notable contribution to New Testament biblical studies after the completion of The New English Bible was the publication of *Novum Testamentum Graece*, edited by Kurt Aland and others (Deutsche Bibelstiftung, Stuttgart, 26th edn 1979), and this was a major point of reference for those engaged in the revision. The translators and revisers have taken into consideration not only the evidence presented in recent editions of the Greek text, but also the work of exegetical and literary scholarship, which is continuing all the time. The revisers have drawn attention in footnotes to variant readings which may result in significant alternative understanding or interpretation of the text, and in particular to those readings which were followed in The New English Bible, but which now seem to the revisers to be less probable than those used in this revision. They are well aware that their judgement is

provisional, but they believe the text they have adopted to be an improvement on that underlying earlier translations.

In accordance with the original decision of the Joint Committee of the Churches, the translators and revisers attempted to use consistently the idiom of contemporary English, employing its natural vocabulary, constructions, and rhythms to convey the meaning of the Greek. The revision has been concerned to avoid archaisms, technical terms, and pretentious language as far as possible. The New English Bible and its revisers adopted the wholesome practice of the translators of the Authorized (King James) Version, who recognized no obligation to render the same Greek word everywhere by the same English word. This version claims to be a translation rather than a paraphrase, observing faithfulness to the meaning of the text without necessarily reproducing grammatical structure or translating word for word.

The revisers are conscious of the limitations and imperfections of their work. Anyone who has tried it will know that it is impossible to make a perfect translation. Only those who have long meditated on the Greek original are aware of the richness and subtlety of meaning that may lie even within what appears to be the most simple of sentences, or know the despair that can attend efforts to bring it out through the medium of a different language. All who have been involved in the work trust that under the providence of Almighty God this revision may build on the achievement of The New English Bible in opening yet further the truth of the scriptures.

Abbreviations of the Books of the Bible and the Apocrypha in Alphabetical Order

ABBREVIATION, LOCATION, TITLE

Acts NT   Acts of the Apostles
Amos OT   Amos
Bar. APOC.   Baruch
Bel & Snake APOC.   Daniel, Bel,
   and the Snake
1 Chr. OT   1 Chronicles
2 Chr. OT   2 Chronicles
Col. NT   Colossians
1 Cor. NT   1 Corinthians
2 Cor. NT   2 Corinthians
Dan. OT   Daniel
Deut. OT   Deuteronomy
Eccles. OT   Ecclesiastes
Ecclus. APOC.   Ecclesiasticus or
   the Wisdom of Jesus
   Son of Sirach
Eph. NT   Ephesians
1 Esd. APOC.   1 Esdras
2 Esd. APOC.   2 Esdras
Esther OT   Esther
Exod. OT   Exodus
Ezek. OT   Ezekiel
Ezra OT   Ezra
Gal. NT   Galatians
Gen. OT   Genesis
Hab. OT   Habakkuk
Hag. OT   Haggai
Heb. NT   Hebrews
Hos. OT   Hosea
Isa. OT   Isaiah

ABBREVIATION, LOCATION, TITLE

Jas. NT   James
Jdt. APOC.   Judith
Jer. OT   Jeremiah
Jn. NT   John
1 Jn. NT   1 John
2 Jn. NT   2 John
3 Jn. NT   3 John
Job OT   Job
Joel OT   Joel
Jonah OT   Jonah
Josh. OT   Joshua
Jude NT   Jude
Judg. OT   Judges
1 Kgs. OT   1 Kings
2 Kgs. OT   2 Kings
Lam. OT   Lamentations
Lev. OT   Leviticus
Lk. NT   Luke
L. of Jer. APOC.   Letter of
   Jeremiah
1 Macc. APOC.   1 Maccabees
2 Macc. APOC.   2 Maccabees
Mal. OT   Malachi
Matt. NT   Matthew
Mic. OT   Micah
Mk. NT   Mark
Nahum OT   Nahum
Neh. OT   Nehemiah
Num. OT   Numbers

ABBREVIATION, LOCATION, TITLE

Obad. OT   Obadiah
1 Pet. NT   1 Peter
2 Pet. NT   2 Peter
Phil. NT   Philippians
Philem. NT   Philemon
Pr. of Az. APOC.   Prayer of
   Azariah
Pr. of Man. APOC.   Prayer of
   Manasseh
Prov. OT   Proverbs
Ps(s). OT   Psalms
Rest of Esth. APOC.   Rest of Esther
Rev. NT   Revelation of John
Rom. NT   Romans
Ruth OT   Ruth
1 Sam. OT   1 Samuel
2 Sam. OT   2 Samuel
S. of S. OT   Song of Songs
S. of Three APOC.   Song of the
   Three
Sus. APOC.   Daniel and Susanna
1 Thess. NT   1 Thessalonians
2 Thess. NT   2 Thessalonians
Ti. NT   Titus
1 Tim. NT   1 Timothy
2 Tim. NT   2 Timothy
Tob. APOC.   Tobit
Wisd. APOC.   Wisdom
Zech. OT   Zechariah
Zeph. OT   Zephaniah

Other Abbreviations and Notes

An explanation of terms, names of ancient versions, etc., as used in footnotes to the text, appears in the Introductions to the Old Testament, the Apocrypha, and the New Testament where appropriate.

Ant.   Flavius Josephus, *Antiquities of the Jews*
Apoc.   Apocrypha
Aq.   Aquila, Greek version of the Hebrew Scriptures
Aram.   Aramaic
B.C.E.   Before the Common Era (= B.C.)
B.J.   Flavius Josephus, *The Jewish War*
ca.   *circa*, approximately
C.E.   Common Era (= A.D.)
cf.   *confer*, compare
ch(s).   chapter(s)
cp.   compare
e.g.   *exempli gratia*, for example

Gk.	Greek (language or version)
Heb.	Hebrew
i.e.	*id est*, that is
Lat.	Latin version
lit.	literally
Lives	Diogenes Laertius, *Lives and Opinions of Eminent Philosophers*
Luc.	Lucian's edition of the Septuagint
mng.	meaning
MS(S).	manuscript(s)
MT	Massoretic Text
n(n).	note(s)
NT	New Testament
om.	omit(s)
or	indicates an alternative interpretation
OT	Old Testament
Pesh.	Peshitta, Syriac version of Hebrew Scriptures
poss.	possible
prob.	probable
rdg	reading
Samar.	Samaritan Pentateuch
Scroll	text derived from the Dead Sea Scrolls
Sept.	Septuagint, Greek version of Hebrew Scriptures (with additional books now included in Apocrypha)
Symm.	Symmachus, Greek version of Hebrew Scriptures
Syr.	Syriac
Targ.	Targum
Tfn.	translators' footnotes
Theod.	Theodotion, Greek version of Hebrew Scriptures
Vg.	Vulgate, Latin version of the Bible
v(v).	verse(s)
Vs(s).	Version(s)
[ ]	In keywords, square brackets enclose words that are included for clarity of reference, but are not themselves the subject of the note.

Measures, Weights, and Values

No precise modern equivalents can be given for the units of measurements, weight, and value used in the ancient world, which themselves varied at different times, in different places, and in different contexts of use. The approximate equivalents given below may be helpful as an indication of the order of magnitude implied by a particular term.

LENGTH

Unit	Approx. equivalent in metres	As read at
hand's breadth	0.075	Ezek. 40:5
span	0.225	1 Sam. 17:4Tfn.
cubit (short) = 6 hand's breadths	0.45	Judg. 3:16Tfn.
cubit (long) = 7 hand's breadths	0.525	2 Chr. 3:3

WEIGHTS AND VALUES

Unit	Approx. equivalent in grammes	As read at
gerah	0.6	Ezek. 45:12
shekel (sacred) = 20 gerahs	12	Lev. 27:25
mina = 50 shekels	600	1 Kgs. 10:17
mina = 60 shekels	720	Ezek. 45:12
talent = 3000 shekels	36000	Exod. 38:25

Mention is made (Gen. 23:16) of a shekel of 'the standard recognized by merchants'; its relationship to the sacred standard is uncertain.

The 'pound' of the New Testament (John 12:3) may be referred to the Roman standard of about 317 grammes.

Related to gold or silver, the weights tabulated above are frequently used as measures of value. In the Old Testament 'beka' (*lit.* half) is used to signify a half-shekel (Exod. 38:26). The 'talent' of the New Testament (Matt. 18:24) evidently signifies a large but not precise monetary value.

COINS

The 'daric' (1 Chr. 29:7) was a gold coin weighing just over 8 grammes, said to have been equivalent to a month's pay for a soldier in the Persian army. What is referred to as a 'drachma' (Neh. 7:70) may have been a silver coin of about 4.4 grammes.

The 'denarius' of the New Testament (Mark 14:5) is said to have been the equivalent of a day's wage for a labourer.

MEASURES OF CAPACITY: DRY MEASURES

Unit	Approx. equivalent in litres	As read at
kab	2.5	2 Kgs. 6:25
omer	4.5	Exod. 16:32
seah	15	1 Sam. 25:18Tfn.
ephah = 10 omers	45	Exod. 16:36
kor = 10 ephahs	450	1 Kgs. 4:22
homer = 10 ephahs	450	Ezek. 45:11

LIQUID MEASURES

Unit	Approx. equivalent in litres	As read at
log	1	Lev. 14:10
hin = 12 log	12	Num. 15:7
bath = 6 hin	72	Ezek. 45:14
kor = 10 bath	720	Ezek. 45:14

Preface to the New American Bible
The Old Testament

On September 30, 1943, His Holiness Pope Pius XII issued his now famous encyclical on scripture studies, *Divino afflante Spiritu*. He wrote: "We ought to explain the original text which was written by the inspired author himself and has more authority and greater weight than any, even the very best, translation whether ancient or modern. This can be done all the more easily and fruitfully if to the knowledge of languages be joined a real skill in literary criticism of the same text."

Early in 1944, in conformity with the spirit of the encyclical, and with the encouragement of Archbishop Cicognani, Apostolic Delegate to the United States, the Bishops' Committee of the Confraternity of Christian Doctrine requested members of The Catholic Biblical Association of America to translate the sacred scriptures from the original languages or from the oldest extant form of the text, and to present the sense of the biblical text in as correct a form as possible.

The first English Catholic version of the Bible, the Douay-Rheims (1582–1609/10), and its revision by Bishop Challoner (1750) were based on the Latin Vulgate. In view of the relative certainties more recently attained by textual and higher criticism, it has become increasingly desirable that contemporary translations of the sacred books into English be prepared in which due reverence for the text and strict observance of the rules of criticism would be combined.

The New American Bible has accomplished this in response to the need of the church in America today. It is the achievement of some fifty biblical scholars, the greater number of whom, though not all, are Catholics. In particular, the editors-in-chief have devoted twenty-five years to this work. The collaboration of scholars who are not Catholic fulfills the directive of the Second Vatican Council, not only that "correct translations be made into different languages especially from the original texts of the sacred books," but that, "with the approval of the church authority, these translations be produced in cooperation with separated brothers" so that "all Christians may be able to use them."

The text of the books contained in *The New American Bible* is a completely new translation throughout. From the original and the oldest available texts of the sacred books, it aims to convey as directly as possible the thought and individual style of the inspired writers. The better understanding of Hebrew and Greek, and the steady development of the science of textual criticism, the fruit of patient study since the time of St. Jerome, have allowed the translators and editors in their use of all available materials to approach more closely than ever before the sense of what the sacred authors actually wrote.

Where the translation supposes the received text—Hebrew, Aramaic, or Greek, as the case may be—ordinarily contained in the best-known editions, as the original or the oldest extant form, no additional remarks are necessary. But for those who are happily able to study the original text of the scriptures at firsthand, a supplementary series of textual notes pertaining to the Old Testament was added originally in an appendix to the typical edition. (It is now obtainable in a separate booklet from The Catholic Biblical Association of America, The Catholic University of America, Washington, DC 20064.) These notes furnish a guide in those cases in which the editorial board judges that the manuscripts in the original languages, or the evidence of the ancient versions, or some similar source, furnish the correct reading of a passage, or at least a reading more true to the original than that customarily printed in the available editions.

The Massoretic text of 1 and 2 Samuel has in numerous instances been corrected by the more ancient manuscripts Samuel a, b, and c from Cave 4 of Qumran, with the aid of important evidence from the Septuagint in both its oldest form and its Lucianic recension. Fragments of the lost Book of Tobit in Aramaic and in Hebrew, recovered from Cave 4 of Qumran, are in substantial agreement with the Sinaiticus Greek recension used for the

translation of this book. The lost original Hebrew text of 1 Maccabees is replaced by its oldest extant form in Greek. Judith, 2 Maccabees, and parts of Esther are also translated from the Greek.

The basic text for the Psalms is not the Massoretic but one which the editors considered closer to the original inspired form, namely the Hebrew text underlying the new Latin Psalter of the Church, the *Liber Psalmorum* (1944[1], 1945[2]). Nevertheless they retained full liberty to establish the reading of the original text on sound critical principles.

The translation of Sirach, based on the original Hebrew as far as it is preserved and corrected from the ancient versions, is often interpreted in the light of the traditional Greek text. In the Book of Baruch the basic text is the Greek of the Septuagint, with some readings derived from an underlying Hebrew form no longer extant. In the deuterocanonical sections of Daniel (3, 24–90; 13, 1—14, 42), the basic text is the Greek text of Theodotion, occasionally revised according to the Greek text of the Septuagint.

In some instances in the Book of Job, in Proverbs, Sirach, Isaiah, Jeremiah, Ezekiel, Hosea, Amos, Micah, Nahum, Habakkuk, and Zechariah there is good reason to believe that the original order of lines was accidentally disturbed in the transmission of the text. The verse numbers given in such cases are always those of the current Hebrew text, though the arrangement differs. In these instances the textual notes advise the reader of the difficulty. Cases of exceptional dislocation are called to the reader's attention by footnotes.

The Books of *Genesis to Ruth* were first published in 1952; the Wisdom Books, *Job to Sirach*, in 1955, the Prophetic Books, *Isaiah to Malachi*, in 1961; and the Historical Books, *Samuel to Maccabees*, in 1969.

The revision of *Job to Sirach* includes changes in strophe division in Job and Proverbs and in titles of principal parts and sections of Wisdom and Ecclesiastes. Corrections in the text of Sirach are made in 39, 27—44, 17 on the basis of the Masada text, and in 51, 13–30 on the basis of the occurrence of this canticle in the Psalms scroll from Qumran Cave 11. In the Psalms, the enumeration found in the Hebrew text is followed instead of the double enumeration, according to both the Hebrew and the Latin Vulgate texts, contained in the previous edition of this book.

In the Prophetic Books *Isaiah to Malachi*, only minor revisions have been made in the structure and wording of the texts.

The spelling of proper names in *The New American Bible* follows the customary forms found in most English Bibles since the Authorized Version.

The work of translating the Bible has been characterized as "the sacred and apostolic work of interpreting the word of God and of presenting it to the laity in translations as clear as the difficulty of the matter and the limitations of human knowledge permit" (A. G. Cicognani, Apostolic Delegate, in *The Catholic Biblical Quarterly*, 6, [1944], 389-90). In the appraisal of the present work, it is hoped that the words of the encyclical *Divino afflante Spiritu* will serve as a guide: "Let all the sons of the church bear in mind that the efforts of these resolute laborers in the vineyard of the Lord should be judged not only with equity and justice but also with the greatest charity; all moreover should abhor that intemperate zeal which imagines that whatever is new should for that very reason be opposed or suspected."

Conscious of their personal limitations for the task thus defined, those who have prepared this text cannot expect that it will be considered perfect; but they can hope that it may deepen in its readers "the right understanding of the divinely given Scriptures," and awaken in them "that piety by which it behooves us to be grateful to the God of all providence, who from the throne of his majesty has sent these books as so many personal letters to his own children" (*Divino afflante Spiritu*).

Preface to the New American Bible
First Edition of the New Testament

The New Testament translation has been approached with essentially the same fidelity to the thought and individual style of the biblical writers as was applied in the Old Testament. In some cases, however, the problem of marked literary peculiarities had to be met. What by any Western standard are the limited vocabularies and stylistic infelicities of the evangelists cannot be retained in the exact form in which they appear in the originals without displeasing the modern ear. A compromise is here attempted whereby some measure of the poverty of the evangelists' expression is kept and placed at the service of their message in its richness. Similarly, the syntactical shortcomings of Paul, his frequent lapses into anacoluthon, and the like, are rendered as they occur in his epistles rather than "smoothed out." Only thus, the translators suppose, will contemporary readers have some adequate idea of the kind of writing they have before them. When the prose of the original flows more smoothly, as in Luke, Acts, and Hebrews, it is reflected in the translation.

The Gospel according to John comprises a special case. Absolute fidelity to his technique of reiterated phrasing would result in an assault on the English ear, yet the softening of the vocal effect by substitution of other words and phrases would destroy the effectiveness of his poetry. Again, resort is had to compromise. This is not an easy matter when the very repetitiousness which the author deliberately employed is at the same time regarded by those who read and speak English to be a serious stylistic defect. Only those familiar with the Greek originals can know what a relentless tattoo Johannine poetry can produce. A similar observation could be made regarding other New Testament books as well. Matthew and Mark are given to identical phrasing twice and three times in the same sentence. As for the rhetorical overgrowth and mixed figures of speech in the letters of Peter, James, and Jude, the translator must resist a powerful compulsion to tidy them up if only to render these letters intelligibly.

Without seeking refuge in complaints against the inspired authors, however, the translators of *The New American Bible* here state that what they have attempted is a translation rather than a paraphrase. To be sure, all translation can be called paraphrase by definition. Any striving for complete fidelity will shortly end in infidelity. Nonetheless, it must be pointed out that the temptation to improve overladen sentences by the consolidation or elimination of multiplied adjectives, or the simplification of clumsy hendiadys, has been resisted here. For the most part, rhetorically ineffective words and phrases are retained in this translation in some form, even when it is clear that a Western contemporary writer would never have employed them.

The spelling of proper names in *The New American Bible* follows the customary forms found in most English Bibles since the Authorized Version.

Despite the arbitrary character of the divisions into numbered verses (a scheme which in its present form is only four centuries old), the translators have made a constant effort to keep within an English verse the whole verbal content of the Greek verse. At times the effort has not seemed worth the result since it often does violence to the original author's flow of expression, which preceded it by so many centuries. If this translation had been prepared for purposes of public reading only, the editors would have foregone the effort at an early stage. But since they never departed from the threefold objective of preparing a translation suitable for liturgical use, private reading, and the purposes of students, the last-named consideration prevailed. Those familiar with Greek should be able to discover how the translators of the New Testament have rendered any given original verse of scripture, if their exegetical or theological tasks require them to know this. At the same time, the fact should be set down here that the editors did not commit themselves in the synoptic gospels to rendering repeated words or phrases identically.

This leads to a final consideration: the Greek text used for the New Testament. Here, punctuation and verse division are at least as important as variant reading. In general, Nestle-Aland's *Novum Testamentum Graece* (25th edition, 1963) was followed. Additional help was derived from *The Greek New Testament* (Aland, Black,

Metzger, Wikgren), produced for the use of translators by the United Bible Societies in 1966. However, the editors did not confine themselves strictly to these texts; at times, they inclined toward readings otherwise attested. The omission of alternative translations does not mean that the translators think them without merit, but only that in every case they had to make a choice.

Poorly attested readings do not occur in this translation. Doubtful readings of some merit appear within brackets; public readers may include such words or phrases, or omit them entirely without any damage to sense. Parentheses are used, as ordinarily in English, as a punctuation device. Material they enclose is in no sense textually doubtful. It is simply thought to be parenthetical in the intention of the biblical author, even though there is no such punctuation mark in Greek. The difficulty in dealing with quotation marks is well known. Since they do not appear in any form in the original text, wherever they occur here they constitute an editorial decision.

Preface to the Revised Edition

The New Testament of *The New American Bible,* a fresh translation from the Greek text, was first published in complete form in 1970, together with the Old Testament translation that had been completed the previous year. Portions of the New Testament had appeared earlier, in somewhat different form, in the provisional Mass lectionary of 1964 and in the *Lectionary for Mass* of 1970.

Since 1970 many different printings of the New Testament have been issued by a number of publishers, both separately and in complete Bibles, and the text has become widely known both in the United States and in other English-speaking countries. Most American Catholics have been influenced by it because of its widespread use in the liturgy, and it has received a generally favorable reception from many other Christians as well. It has taken its place among the standard contemporary translations of the New Testament, respected for its fidelity to the original and its attempt to render this into current American English.

Although the scriptures themselves are timeless, translations and explanations of them quickly become dated in an era marked by rapid cultural change to a degree never previously experienced. The explosion of biblical studies that has taken place in our century and the changing nature of our language itself require periodic adjustment both in translations and in the accompanying explanatory materials. The experience of actual use of the New Testament of *The New American Bible,* especially in oral proclamation, has provided a basis for further improvement. Accordingly, it was decided in 1978 to proceed with a thorough revision of the New Testament to reflect advances in scholarship and to satisfy needs identified through pastoral experience.

For this purpose a steering committee was formed to plan, organize, and direct the work of revision, to engage collaborators, and to serve as an editorial board to coordinate the work of the various revisers and to determine the final form of the text and the explanatory materials. Guidelines were drawn up and collaborators selected in 1978 and early 1979, and November of 1980 was established as the deadline for manuscripts. From December 1980 through September 1986 the editorial board met a total of fifty times and carefully reviewed and revised all the material in order to ensure accuracy and consistency of approach. The editors also worked together with the bishops' ad hoc committee that was appointed by the National Conference of Catholic Bishops in 1982 to oversee the revision.

The threefold purpose of the translation that was expressed in the preface to the first edition has been maintained in the revision: to provide a version suitable for liturgical proclamation, for private reading, and for purposes of study. Special attention has been given to the first of these purposes, since oral proclamation demands special qualities in a translation, and experience had provided insights and suggestions that could lead to improvement in this area.

The primary aim of the revision is to produce a version as accurate and faithful to the meaning of the Greek original as is possible for a translation. The editors have consequently moved in the direction of a formal-equivalence approach to translation, matching the vocabulary, structure, and even word order of the original as

closely as possible in the receptor language. Some other contemporary biblical versions have adopted, in varying degrees, a dynamic-equivalence approach, which attempts to respect the individuality of each language by expressing the meaning of the original in a linguistic structure suited to English, even though this may be very different from the corresponding Greek structure. While this approach often results in fresh and brilliant renderings, it has the disadvantages of more or less radically abandoning traditional biblical and liturgical terminology and phraseology, of expanding the text to include what more properly belongs in notes, commentaries, or preaching, and of tending toward paraphrase. A more formal approach seems better suited to the specific purposes intended for this translation.

At the same time, the editors have wished to produce a version in English that reflects contemporary American usage and is readily understandable to ordinary educated people, but one that will be recognized as dignified speech, on the level of formal rather than colloquial usage. These aims are not in fact contradictory, for there are different levels of language in current use: the language of formal situations is not that of colloquial conversation, though people understand both and may pass from one to the other without adverting to the transition. The liturgy is a formal situation that requires a level of discourse more dignified, formal, and hieratic than the world of business, sport, or informal communication. People readily understand this more formal level even though they may not often use it; our passive vocabulary is much larger than our active vocabulary. Hence this revision, while avoiding archaisms, does not shrink from traditional biblical terms that are easily understood even though not in common use in everyday speech. The level of language consciously aimed at is one appropriate for liturgical proclamation; this may also permit the translation to serve the purposes of devotional reading and serious study.

A particular effort has been made to insure consistency of vocabulary. Always to translate a given Greek word by the same English equivalent would lead to ludicrous results and to infidelity to the meaning of the text. But in passages where a particular Greek term retains the same meaning, it has been rendered in the same way insofar as this has been feasible; this is particularly significant in the case of terms that have a specific theological meaning. The synoptic gospels have been carefully translated so as to reveal both the similarities and the differences of the Greek.

An especially sensitive problem today is the question of discrimination in language. In recent years there has been much discussion about allegations of anti-Jewish expressions in the New Testament and of language that discriminates against various minorities. Above all, however, the question of discrimination against women affects the largest number of people and arouses the greatest degree of interest and concern. At present there is little agreement about these problems or about the best way to deal with them. In all these areas the present translation attempts to display a sensitivity appropriate to the present state of the questions under discussion, which are not yet resolved and in regard to which it is impossible to please everyone, since intelligent and sincere participants in the debate hold mutually contradictory views.

The primary concern in this revision is fidelity to what the text says. When the meaning of the Greek is inclusive of both sexes, the translation seeks to reproduce such inclusivity insofar as this is possible in normal English usage, without resort to inelegant circumlocutions or neologisms that would offend against the dignity of the language. Although the generic sense of *man* is traditional in English, many today reject it; its use has therefore generally been avoided, though it is retained in cases where no fully satisfactory equivalent could be found. English does not possess a gender-inclusive third personal pronoun in the singular, and this translation continues to use the masculine resumptive pronoun after *everyone* or *anyone,* in the traditional way, where this cannot be avoided without infidelity to the meaning.

The translation of the Greek word *adelphos,* particularly in the plural form *adelphoi,* poses an especially delicate problem. While the term literally means *brothers* or other male blood relatives, even in profane Greek the plural can designate two persons, one of either sex, who were born of the same parents. It was adopted by the early Christians to designate, in a figurative sense, the members of the Christian community, who were conscious of a new familial relationship to one another by reason of their adoption as children of God. They are

consequently addressed as *adelphoi*. This has traditionally been rendered into English by *brothers* or, more archaically, *brethren*. There has never been any doubt that this designation includes *all* the members of the Christian community, both male and female. Given the absence in English of a corresponding term that explicitly includes both sexes, this translation retains the usage of *brothers*, with the inclusive meaning that has been tradtionally attached to it in this biblical context.

Since the New Testament is the product of a particular time and culture, the views expressed in it and the language in which they are expressed reflect a particular cultural conditioning, which sometimes makes them quite different from contemporary ideas and concerns. Discriminatory language should be eliminated insofar as possible whenever it is unfaithful to the meaning of the New Testament, but the text should not be altered in order to adjust it to contemporary concerns. This translation does not introduce any changes, expansions, additions to, or subtractions from the text of scripture. It further retains the traditional biblical ways of speaking about God and about Christ, including the use of masculine nouns and pronouns.

The Greek text followed in this translation is that of the third edition of *The Greek New Testament*, edited by Kurt Aland, Matthew Black, Carlo Martini, Bruce Metzger, and Allen Wikgren, and published by the United Bible Societies in 1975. The same text, with a different critical apparatus and variations in punctuation and typography, was published as the twenty-sixth edition of the Nestle-Aland *Novum Testamentum Graece* in 1979 by the Deutsche Bibelstiftung, Stuttgart. This edition has also been consulted. When variant readings occur, the translation, with few exceptions, follows the reading that was placed in the text of these Greek editions, though the occurrence of the principal variants is pointed out in the notes.

The editors of the Greek text placed square brackets around words or portions of words of which the authenticity is questionable because the evidence of textual witnesses is inconclusive. The same has been done in the translation insofar as it is possible to reproduce this convention in English. It should be possible to read the text either with or without the disputed words, but in English it is not always feasible to provide this alternative, and in some passages the bracketed words must be included to make sense. As in the first edition, parentheses do not indicate textual uncertainty, but are simply a punctuation device to indicate a passage that in the editors' judgment appears parenthetical to the thought of the author.

Citations from the Old Testament are placed within quotation marks; longer citations are set off as block quotations in a separate indented paragraph. Insofar as possible, the translation of such Old Testament citations agrees with that of *The New American Bible* Old Testament whenever the underlying Greek agrees with the Hebrew (or, in some cases, the Aramaic or Greek) text from which the Old Testament translation was made. But citations in the New Testament frequently follow the Septuagint or some other version, or were made from memory; hence, in many cases the translation in the New Testament passage will not agree with what appears in the Old Testament.

The New American Bible is a Roman Catholic translation. This revision, however, like the first edition, has been accomplished with the collaboration of scholars from other Christian churches, both among the revisers and on the editorial board, in response to the encouragement of Vatican Council II (*Dei Verbum*, 22). The editorial board expresses gratitude to all who have collaborated in the revision: to all the revisers, consultants, and bishops who contributed to it, to reviewers of the first edition, and to those who voluntarily submitted suggestions. May this translation fulfill its threefold purpose, "so that the word of the Lord may speed forward and be glorified" (2 Thes 3, 1).

The Feast of St. Jerome
September 30, 1986

Collaborators on the Old Testament of the New American Bible

BISHOPS' COMMITTEE OF THE CONFRATERNITY OF CHRISTIAN DOCTRINE

Most Rev. Charles P. Greco, D.D., *Chairman*   Most Rev. Joseph T. McGucken, S.T.D.   Most Rev. Vincent S. Waters, D.D.
Most Rev. Romeo Blanchette, D.D.   Most Rev. Christopher J. Weldon, D.D.

EDITORS IN CHIEF

Rev. Louis F. Hartman, C.SS.R., S.S.L., LING. OR. L., *Chairman*
Rev. Msgr. Patrick W. Skehan, S.T.D., LL.D., *Vice-Chairman*   Rev. Stephen J. Hartdegen, O.F.M., S.S.L., *Secretary*

ASSOCIATE EDITORS AND TRANSLATORS

Rev. Edward P. Arbez, S.S., S.T.D.

Rev. Msgr. Edward J. Byrne, PH.D., S.T.D.

Rev. Edward A. Cerny, S.S., S.T.D.

Rev. James E. Coleran, S.J., S.T.L., S.S.L.

Rev. John J. Collins, S.J., M.A., S.S.L.

Sr. M. Emmanuel Collins, O.S.E., PH.D.

Prof. Frank M. Cross, Jr., PH.D.

Rev. Patrick Cummins, O.S.B., S.T.D.

Rev. Antonine A. DeGuglielmo, O.F.M., S.T.D., S.S.L., S.S. LECT. GEN.

Rev. Alexander A. DiLella, O.F.M., S.T.L., S.S.L., PH.D.

Most Rev. John J. Dougherty, S.T.L., S.S.D.

William A. Dowd, S.J., S.T.D., S.S.L.

Prof. David Noel Freedman, PH.D.

Rev. Michael J. Gruenthaner, S.J., S.T.D., S.S.D.

Rev. Msgr. Maurice A. Hofer, S.S.L.

Rev. Justin Krellner, O.S.B., S.T.D.

Rev. Joseph L. Lilly, C.M., S.T.D., S.S.L.

Rev. Roderick F. MacKenzie, S.J., M.A., S.S.D.

Rev. Edward A. Mangan, C.SS.R., S.S.L.

Rev. Daniel W. Martin, C.M., S.T.L., S.S.L.

Rev. William H. McClellan, S.J.

Rev. James McGlinchey, C.M., S.T.D.

Rev. Frederick Moriarty, S.J., S.S.L., S.T.D.

Rev. Richard T. Murphy, O.P., S.T.D., S.S.D.

Rev. Roland E. Murphy, O. CARM., M.A., S.T.D., S.S.L.

Rev. Msgr. William R. Newton, M.S., S.S.D.

Rev. Eberhard Olinger, O.S.B.

Rev. Charles H. Pickar, O.S.A., S.T.L., S.S.L.

Rev. Christopher Rehwinkel, O.F.M., S.T.D., S.S. LECT. GEN.

Rev. Msgr. John R. Rowan, S.T.D., S.S.L.

Prof. J. A. Sanders, PH.D.

Rev. Edward F. Siegman, C.PP.S., S.T.D., S.S.L.

Rev. Msgr. Matthew P. Stapleton, S.T.D., S.S.L.

Rev. Msgr. John E. Steinmueller, S.T.D., S.S.L.

Rev. John Ujlaki, O.S.B., LITT.D.

Rev. Bruce Vawter, C.M., S.T.L., S.S.D.

Rev. John B. Weisengoff, S.T.D., S.S.L.

Collaborators on the Revised New Testament of the New American Bible

BISHOPS' AD HOC COMMITTEE
Most Rev. Theodore E. McCarrick, D.D.   Most Rev. Richard J. Sklba, D.D.
Most Rev. J. Francis Stafford, D.D.   Most Rev. John F. Whealon, D.D., *Chairman*

BOARD OF EDITORS
Rev. Msgr. Myles M. Bourke   Rev. Francis T. Gignac, S.J., *Chairman*
Rev. Stephen J. Hartdegen, O.F.M., *Secretary*   Rev. Claude J. Peifer, O.S.B.   Rev. John H. Reumann

REVISERS

Rev. Msgr. Myles M. Bourke	Rev. Francis T. Gignac, S.J.	Dr. Paul J. Kobelski
Rev. Frederick W. Danker	Rev. Stephen J. Hartdegen, O.F.M.	Dr. J. Rebecca Lyman
Rev. Alexander A. Di Lella, O.F.M.	Dr. Maurya P. Horgan	Bro. Elliott C. Maloney, O.S.B.
Rev. Charles H. Giblin, S.J.	Rev. John R. Keating, S.J.	Dr. Janet A. Timbie
	Rev. John Knox	

CONSULTANTS
Rev. Joseph Jensen, O.S.B.   Rev. Aidan Kavanagh, O.S.B.   Dr. Marianne Sawicki

DEVELOPMENT MANAGER   Richard J. Nare

WORD PROCESSOR   Suzanna Jordan

Collaborators on the Revised Psalms of the New American Bible

BISHOPS' AD HOC COMMITTEE
Most Rev. Enrique San Pedro, S.J.   Most Rev. Richard Sklba, D.D.   Most Rev. Donald W. Troutman, S.T.D., S.S.L.
Most Rev. Emil A. Wcela   Most Rev. John F. Whealon, S.S.L., *Chairman*

BOARD OF EDITORS
Rev. Richard Clifford, S.J.   Bro. Aloysius Fitzgerald, F.S.C.   Rev. Joseph Jensen, O.S.B.
Rev. Roland Murphy, O. CARM.   Sr. Irene Nowell, O.S.B.   Dr. Judith Sanderson

REVISERS

Prof. Gary Anderson	Bro. Aloysius Fitzgerald, F.S.C.	Dr. Michael Patrick O'Connor
Rev. Michael L. Barré	Rev. Michael D. Guinan, O.F.M.	Rev. Brian J. Peckham, S.J.
Rev. Christopher T. Begg	Rev. William L. Holladay	Prof. Jimmy J. Roberts
Dr. Joseph Blenkinsopp	Rev. William Irwin, C.S.B.	Sr. Eileen M. Schuller, O.S.U.
Rev. Anthony R. Ceresko, O.S.F.S.	Rev. Joseph Jensen, O.S.B.	Dr. Byron E. Shafer
Rev. Richard J. Clifford, S.J.	Rev. John S. Kselman	Prof. Mark S. Smith
Rev. Aelred Cody, O.S.B.	Dr. Conrad E. L'Heureux	Prof. Matitiahu Tsevat
Prof. Michael D. Coogan	Rev. Leo Laberge, O.M.I.	Dr. Eugene C. Ulrich
Rev. Alexander A. Di Lella, O.F.M.	Dr. Paul G. Mosca	Prof. James C. Vanderkam
Dr. Robert A. Di Vito	Rev. Dr. Roland E. Murphy, O. CARM.	Rev. Jerome T. Walsh

ENGLISH CONSULTANTS
Dr. Catherine Dunn   Bro. Daniel Burke, F.S.C.

DEVELOPMENT MANAGER   Richard J. Nare

Abbreviations of Books of the Bible

Acts	Acts of the Apostles	Jb	Job	Nm	Numbers		
Am	Amos	Jdt	Judith	Ob	Obadiah		
Bar	Baruch	Jer	Jeremiah	Phil	Philippians		
1 Chr	1 Chronicles	Jgs	Judges	Phlm	Philemon		
2 Chr	2 Chronicles	Jl	Joel	Prv	Proverbs		
Col	Colossians	Jn	John	Ps(s)	Psalms		
1 Cor	1 Corinthians	1 Jn	1 John	1 Pt	1 Peter		
2 Cor	2 Corinthians	2 Jn	2 John	2 Pt	2 Peter		
Dn	Daniel	3 Jn	3 John	Rom	Romans		
Dt	Deuteronomy	Jon	Jonah	Ru	Ruth		
Eccl	Ecclesiastes	Jos	Joshua	Rv	Revelation		
Eph	Ephesians	Jude	Jude	Sir	Sirach		
Est	Esther	1 Kgs	1 Kings	1 Sm	1 Samuel		
Ex	Exodus	2 Kgs	2 Kings	2 Sm	2 Samuel		
Ez	Ezekiel	Lam	Lamentations	Song(Sg)	Song of Songs		
Ezr	Ezra	Lk	Luke	Tb	Tobit		
Gal	Galatians	Lv	Leviticus	1 Thes	1 Thessalonians		
Gn	Genesis	Mal	Malachi	2 Thes	2 Thessalonians		
Hb	Habakkuk	1 Mc	1 Maccabees	Ti	Titus		
Heb	Hebrews	2 Mc	2 Maccabees	1 Tm	1 Timothy		
Hg	Haggai	Mi	Micah	2 Tm	2 Timothy		
Hos	Hosea	Mk	Mark	Wis	Wisdom		
Is	Isaiah	Mt	Matthew	Zec	Zechariah		
Jas	James	Na	Nahum	Zep	Zephaniah		
		Neh	Nehemiah				

Simple Key to References

Gn 1, 1   refers to the Book of Genesis, chapter 1, verse 1.
Gn 1, 1a   refers to the Book of Genesis, chapter 1, the first part of verse 1.
Gn 1, 1f   refers to the Book of Genesis, chapter 1, verse 1 and the following verse (2).
Gn 1, 1–10   refers to the Book of Genesis, chapter 1, verses 1 to 10 inclusive.
Gn 1, 1–10.14 refers to the Book of Genesis, chapter 1, verses 1 to 10 inclusive and verse 14.
Gn 1, 1–2, 3 refers to the Book of Genesis, chapter 1, verse 1 to chapter 2, verse 3 inclusive.
Gn 1, 1; 2, 3 refers to the Book of Genesis, chapter 1, verse 1 and chapter 2, verse 3.

Abbreviations of Books of the Bible

Simple Key to References

Editor's Foreword

The Bible is not a book but a library, joining together dozens of writings, history, stories, poetry and letters. Almost the only common factor is that they all speak to us of God, revealing his nature, his awesome sovereignty and his tender love.

The Old Testament is normally divided into three sections. The histories (including the Pentateuch, the basic first five books, the great Law of Israel) show God's loving guidance and correction of Israel from nomad beginnings through all the trials and infidelities of the settled civilisation in Palestine. The Wisdom books (including the Psalms, the prayerbook of Israel) express the wisdom of Israel drawn from God for the practical art of living. The prophetic writings gather the warnings and promises of God expressed through those special messengers who strove to keep Israel faithful for the centuries before Christ. By all these means God was forming his people, preparing them for the fulfilment of his purposes in Christ.

The New Testament is best divided into two sections. First come the four gospels, the record of the message of Good News brought by Jesus. Then the letters written by Paul and other apostolic figures to the nascent churches of Mediterranean Christianity, to give them instruction and help to solve their problems, but also to be a source of understanding and guidance for every generation of Christians. The last book of the Bible, the Revelation to John, sums all up in the vision of deliverance from persecution and a glorious establishment of the reign of God in the New Jerusalem.

This Reader's Edition of *The New Jerusalem Bible* is based on the much larger Regular Edition first published in 1985. While the biblical text remains unchanged, the notes have been pared to make the volume more accessible and manageable. There will be questions left unanswered here for which the answer can be found in the Regular Edition.

The translation follows the original Hebrew, Aramaic and Greek texts. For the Old Testament (OT) the 'Massoretic Text' (MT), established in the 8–9th centuries AD by Jewish scholars, is used. Only when this presents insuperable difficulties have emendations or other versions, such as the ancient Greek translation begun in 200 BC at Alexandria, the 'Septuagint' (abbreviated 'LXX'), been used. In certain OT books passages exist only in the LXX version; these passages have been printed in italics. Italics are used also, and in the New Testament (NT) exclusively, to indicate quotations from other books of the Bible. Occasionally the verse-numbering shows a disturbed order; the verse-numbers always follow the MT, but versions or logic may show that another order of printing the verses is preferable. On occasion also a gap may be left (. . .); this indicates an unintelligible word or an incomplete sentence in the original, which scholars have not been able to fill out satisfactorily. Brackets in the OT text indicate that the passage is considered a gloss, an addition or explanation later than the original text. = This sign indicates a parallel passage within the same book. It also can signify simply 'equals'. // indicates a parallel passage within another book.

The work of many devoted scholars has contributed to this Bible: those who produced the parent *Bible de Jérusalem* in 1956, the collaborators on the first English *Jerusalem Bible* (1966), the revisers of the *Bible de Jérusalem* (1973), and those who combined to produce the Regular Edition of *The New Jerusalem Bible* in 1985. The grateful reader might spare a prayer of thanks and blessing on them.

'So now let us begin our narrative, without adding any more to what has been said above; there would be no sense in expanding the preface to the history and curtailing the history itself' (2 Mc 2:32).

HENRY WANSBROUGH
Feast of the Assumption, 1989
Ampleforth Abbey

Books of the Bible in Alphabetical Order of Abbreviations

Ac	Acts	Jg	Judges	Ob	Obadiah
Am	Amos	Jl	Joel	1 P	1 Peter
Ba	Baruch	Jm	James	2 P	2 Peter
1 Ch	1 Chronicles	Jn	John	Ph	Philippians
2 Ch	2 Chronicles	1 Jn	1 John	Phm	Philemon
1 Co	1 Corinthians	2 Jn	2 John	Pr	Proverbs
2 Co	2 Corinthians	3 Jn	3 John	Ps	Psalms
Col	Colossians	Jon	Jonah	Qo	Ecclesiastes/Qoheleth
Dn	Daniel	Jos	Joshua	Rm	Romans
Dt	Deuteronomy	Jr	Jeremiah	Rt	Ruth
Ep	Ephesians	Jude	Jude	Rv	Revelation
Est	Esther	1 K	1 Kings	1 S	1 Samuel
Ex	Exodus	2 K	2 Kings	2 S	2 Samuel
Ezk	Ezekiel	Lk	Luke	Sg	Song of Songs
Ezr	Ezra	Lm	Lamentations	Si	Ecclesiasticus/Ben Sira
Ga	Galatians	Lv	Leviticus	Tb	Tobit
Gn	Genesis	1 M	1 Maccabees	1 Th	1 Thessalonians
Hab	Habakkuk	2 M	2 Maccabees	2 Th	2 Thessalonians
Heb	Hebrews	Mi	Micah	1 Tm	1 Timothy
Hg	Haggai	Mk	Mark	2 Tm	2 Timothy
Ho	Hosea	Ml	Malachi	Tt	Titus
Is	Isaiah	Mt	Matthew	Ws	Wisdom
Jb	Job	Na	Nahum	Zc	Zechariah
Jdt	Judith	Nb	Numbers	Zp	Zephaniah
		Ne	Nehemiah		

Other Abbreviations

OT	Old Testament
NT	New Testament
LXX	The Greek "Septuagint," the earliest translation into Greek of the Hebrew Old Testament, dating from the last two centuries before Christ
Aram.	Aramaic
Gk	Greek
Hebr.	Hebrew
Lit.	Literally
Vulg.	Vulgate, the Latin "popular" translation made by St Jerome in the fourth century AD
ch., chh.	chapter(s)
gloss	an addition to or elaboration of the original text
MS, MSS	manuscript(s)
par.	parallel, a passage where other parallels are also indicated
seq.	and following verse(s)
v., vv.	verse(s)
=	parallel passage within the same book
//	parallel passage in another book

THE COMPLETE PARALLEL BIBLE

The Hebrew Scriptures Commonly Called

THE OLD TESTAMENT

Genesis   Genesis

1 In the beginning when God created*a* the heavens and the earth, 2 the earth was a formless void and darkness covered the face of the deep, while a wind from God*b* swept over the face of the waters. 3 Then God said, "Let there be light"; and there was light. 4 And God saw that the light was good; and God separated the light from the darkness. 5 God called the light Day, and the darkness he called Night. And there was evening and there was morning, the first day.

6 And God said, "Let there be a dome in the midst of the waters, and let it separate the waters from the waters." 7 So God made the dome and separated the waters that were under the dome from the waters that were above the dome. And it was so. 8 God called the dome Sky. And there was evening and there was morning, the second day.

9 And God said, "Let the waters under the sky be gathered together into one place, and let the dry land appear." And it was so. 10 God called the dry land Earth, and the waters that were gathered together he called Seas. And God saw that it was good. 11 Then God said, "Let the earth put forth vegetation: plants yielding seed, and fruit trees of every kind on earth that bear fruit with the seed in it." And it was so. 12 The earth brought forth vegetation: plants yielding seed of every kind, and trees of every kind bearing fruit with the seed in it. And God saw that it was good. 13 And there was evening and there was morning, the third day.

14 And God said, "Let there be lights in the dome of the sky to separate the day from the night; and let them be for signs and for seasons and for days and years, 15 and let them be lights in the dome of the sky to give light upon the earth." And it was so. 16 God made the two great lights— the greater light to rule the day and the lesser light to rule the night — and the stars. 17 God set them in the dome of the sky to give light upon the earth, 18 to rule over the day and over the night, and to separate the light from the darkness. And God saw that it was good. 19 And there was evening and there was morning, the fourth day.

20 And God said, "Let the waters bring forth swarms of living creatures, and let birds fly above the earth across the dome of the sky." 21 So God created the great sea monsters and every living creature that moves, of every kind, with which the waters swarm, and every winged bird of every kind. And God saw that it was good. 22 God blessed them, saying, "Be fruitful and multiply and fill the waters in the seas, and let birds multiply on the earth." 23 And there was evening and there was morning, the fifth day.

24 And God said, "Let the earth bring forth living creatures of every kind: cattle and creeping things and wild animals of the earth of every kind." And it was so. 25 God made the wild animals of the earth of every kind, and the cattle of every kind, and everything that creeps upon the ground of every kind. And God saw that it was good. 26 Then God said, "Let us make humankind*c* in our image, according to our likeness; and let them have dominion over the fish of the sea, and over the birds of the air, and over the cattle, and over all the wild animals of the earth,*d* and over every creeping thing that creeps upon the earth."

27 So God created humankind*c* in his image,
in the image of God he created them;*e*
male and female he created them.

1 In the beginning God created the heavens and the earth. 2 The earth was a vast waste, darkness covered the deep, and the spirit of God hovered over the surface of the water. 3 God said, 'Let there be light,' and there was light; 4 and God saw the light was good, and he separated light from darkness. 5 He called the light day, and the darkness night. So evening came, and morning came; it was the first day.

6 God said, 'Let there be a vault between the waters, to separate water from water.' 7 So God made the vault, and separated the water under the vault from the water above it, and so it was; 8 and God called the vault the heavens. Evening came, and morning came, the second day.

9 God said, 'Let the water under the heavens be gathered into one place, so that dry land may appear'; and so it was. 10 God called the dry land earth, and the gathering of the water he called sea; and God saw that it was good. 11 Then God said, 'Let the earth produce growing things; let there be on the earth plants that bear seed, and trees bearing fruit each with its own kind of seed.' So it was; 12 the earth produced growing things: plants bearing their own kind of seed and trees bearing fruit, each with its own kind of seed; and God saw that it was good. 13 Evening came, and morning came, the third day.

14 God said, 'Let there be lights in the vault of the heavens to separate day from night, and let them serve as signs both for festivals and for seasons and years. 15 Let them also shine in the heavens to give light on earth.' So it was; 16 God made two great lights, the greater to govern the day and the lesser to govern the night; he also made the stars. 17 God put these lights in the vault of the heavens to give light on earth, 18 to govern day and night, and to separate light from darkness; and God saw that it was good. 19 Evening came, and morning came, the fourth day.

20 God said, 'Let the water teem with living creatures, and let birds fly above the earth across the vault of the heavens.' 21 God then created the great sea-beasts and all living creatures that move and swarm in the water, according to their various kinds, and every kind of bird; and God saw that it was good. 22 He blessed them and said, 'Be fruitful and increase; fill the water of the sea, and let the birds increase on the land.' 23 Evening came, and morning came, the fifth day.

24 God said, 'Let the earth bring forth living creatures, according to their various kinds: cattle, creeping things, and wild animals, all according to their various kinds.' So it was; 25 God made wild animals, cattle, and every creeping thing, all according to their various kinds; and he saw that it was good. 26 Then God said, 'Let us make human beings in our image, after our likeness, to have dominion over the fish in the sea, the birds of the air, the cattle, all wild animals on land, and everything that creeps on the earth.'

27 God created human beings in his own image;
in the image of God he created them;
male and female he created them.

---

a Or *when God began to create* or *In the beginning God created*
b Or *while the spirit of God* or *while a mighty wind*   *c* Heb *adam*
d Syr: Heb *and over all the earth*   *e* Heb *him*

1:1–2 **In . . . earth was:** *or* When God began to create the heavens and the earth, 2the earth was.   **1:2 the spirit . . . hovered:** *or* a great wind swept; *or* a wind from God swept.

THE BOOK OF
Genesis

Genesis

1 In the beginning, when God created the heavens and the earth, 2 the earth was a formless wasteland, and darkness covered the abyss, while a mighty wind swept over the waters.

3 Then God said, "Let there be light," and there was light. 4 God saw how good the light was. God then separated the light from the darkness. 5 God called the light "day," and the darkness he called "night." Thus evening came, and morning followed — the first day.

6 Then God said, "Let there be a dome in the middle of the waters, to separate one body of water from the other." And so it happened: 7 God made the dome, and it separated the water above the dome from the water below it. 8 God called the dome "the sky." Evening came, and morning followed — the second day.

9 Then God said, "Let the water under the sky be gathered into a single basin, so that the dry land may appear." And so it happened: the water under the sky was gathered into its basin, and the dry land appeared. 10 God called the dry land "the earth," and the basin of the water he called "the sea." God saw how good it was. 11 Then God said, "Let the earth bring forth vegetation: every kind of plant that bears seed and every kind of fruit tree on earth that bears fruit with its seed in it." And so it happened: 12 the earth brought forth every kind of plant that bears seed and every kind of fruit tree on earth that bears fruit with its seed in it. God saw how good it was. 13 Evening came, and morning followed — the third day.

14 Then God said: "Let there be lights in the dome of the sky, to separate day from night. Let them mark the fixed times, the days and the years, 15 and serve as luminaries in the dome of the sky, to shed light upon the earth." And so it happened: 16 God made the two great lights, the greater one to govern the day, and the lesser one to govern the night; and he made the stars. 17 God set them in the dome of the sky, to shed light upon the earth, 18 to govern the day and the night, and to separate the light from the darkness. God saw how good it was. 19 Evening came, and morning followed — the fourth day.

20 Then God said, "Let the water teem with an abundance of living creatures, and on the earth let birds fly beneath the dome of the sky." And so it happened: 21 God created the great sea monsters and all kinds of swimming creatures with which the water teems, 22 and God blessed them, saying, "Be fertile, multiply, and fill the water of the seas; and let the birds multiply on the earth." 23 Evening came, and morning followed — the fifth day.

24 Then God said, "Let the earth bring forth all kinds of living creatures: cattle, creeping things, and wild animals of all kinds." And so it happened: 25 God made all kinds of wild animals, all kinds of cattle, and all kinds of creeping things of the earth. God saw how good it was. 26 Then God said: "Let us make man in our image, after our likeness. Let them have dominion over the fish of the sea, the birds of the air, and the cattle, and over all the wild animals and all the creatures that crawl on the ground."

27 God created man in his image;
in the divine image he created him;
male and female he created them.

1 In the beginning God created heaven and earth. 2 Now the earth was a formless void, there was darkness over the deep, with a divine wind sweeping over the waters.

3 God said, 'Let there be light,' and there was light. 4 God saw that light was good, and God divided light from darkness. 5 God called light 'day', and darkness he called 'night'. Evening came and morning came: the first day.

6 God said, 'Let there be a vault through the middle of the waters to divide the waters in two.' And so it was. 7 God made the vault, and it divided the waters under the vault from the waters above the vault. 8 God called the vault 'heaven'. Evening came and morning came: the second day.

9 God said, 'Let the waters under heaven come together into a single mass, and let dry land appear.' And so it was. 10 God called the dry land 'earth' and the mass of waters 'seas', and God saw that it was good.

11 God said, 'Let the earth produce vegetation: seed-bearing plants, and fruit trees on earth, bearing fruit with their seed inside, each corresponding to its own species.' And so it was. 12 The earth produced vegetation: the various kinds of seed-bearing plants and the fruit trees with seed inside, each corresponding to its own species. God saw that it was good. 13 Evening came and morning came: the third day.

14 God said, 'Let there be lights in the vault of heaven to divide day from night, and let them indicate festivals, days and years. 15 Let them be lights in the vault of heaven to shine on the earth.' And so it was. 16 God made the two great lights: the greater light to govern the day, the smaller light to govern the night, and the stars. 17 God set them in the vault of heaven to shine on the earth, 18 to govern the day and the night and to divide light from darkness. God saw that it was good. 19 Evening came and morning came: the fourth day.

20 God said, 'Let the waters be alive with a swarm of living creatures, and let birds wing their way above the earth across the vault of heaven.' And so it was. 21 God created great sea-monsters and all the creatures that glide and teem in the waters in their own species, and winged birds in their own species. God saw that it was good. 22 God blessed them, saying, 'Be fruitful, multiply, and fill the waters of the seas; and let the birds multiply on land.' 23 Evening came and morning came: the fifth day.

24 God said, 'Let the earth produce every kind of living creature in its own species: cattle, creeping things and wild animals of all kinds.' And so it was. 25 God made wild animals in their own species, and cattle in theirs, and every creature that crawls along the earth in its own species. God saw that it was good.

26 God said, 'Let us make man in our own image, in the likeness of ourselves, and let them be masters of the fish of the sea, the birds of heaven, the cattle, all the wild animals and all the creatures that creep along the ground.'

27 God created man in the image of himself,
in the image of God he created him,
male and female he created them.

NEW REVISED STANDARD VERSION

28 God blessed them, and God said to them, "Be fruitful and multiply, and fill the earth and subdue it; and have dominion over the fish of the sea and over the birds of the air and over every living thing that moves upon the earth." 29 God said, "See, I have given you every plant yielding seed that is upon the face of all the earth, and every tree with seed in its fruit; you shall have them for food. 30 And to every beast of the earth, and to every bird of the air, and to everything that creeps on the earth, everything that has the breath of life, I have given every green plant for food." And it was so. 31 God saw everything that he had made, and indeed, it was very good. And there was evening and there was morning, the sixth day.

2 Thus the heavens and the earth were finished, and all their multitude. 2 And on the seventh day God finished the work that he had done, and he rested on the seventh day from all the work that he had done. 3 So God blessed the seventh day and hallowed it, because on it God rested from all the work that he had done in creation.

4 These are the generations of the heavens and the earth when they were created.

In the day that the LORD God made the earth and the heavens, 5 when no plant of the field was yet in the earth and no herb of the field had yet sprung up—for the LORD God had not caused it to rain upon the earth, and there was no one to till the ground; 6 but a stream would rise from the earth, and water the whole face of the ground— 7 then the LORD God formed man from the dust of the ground, *f* and breathed into his nostrils the breath of life; and the man became a living being. 8 And the LORD God planted a garden in Eden, in the east; and there he put the man whom he had formed. 9 Out of the ground the LORD God made to grow every tree that is pleasant to the sight and good for food, the tree of life also in the midst of the garden, and the tree of the knowledge of good and evil.

10 A river flows out of Eden to water the garden, and from there it divides and becomes four branches. 11 The name of the first is Pishon; it is the one that flows around the whole land of Havilah, where there is gold; 12 and the gold of that land is good; bdellium and onyx stone are there. 13 The name of the second river is Gihon; it is the one that flows around the whole land of Cush. 14 The name of the third river is Tigris, which flows east of Assyria. And the fourth river is the Euphrates.

15 The LORD God took the man and put him in the garden of Eden to till it and keep it. 16 And the LORD God commanded the man, "You may freely eat of every tree of the garden; 17 but of the tree of the knowledge of good and evil you shall not eat, for in the day that you eat of it you shall die."

18 Then the LORD God said, "It is not good that the man should be alone; I will make him a helper as his partner." 19 So out of the ground the LORD God formed every animal of the field and every bird of the air, and brought them to the man to see what he would call them; and whatever the man called every living creature, that was its name. 20 The man gave names to all cattle, and to the birds of the air, and to every animal of the field; but for the man*g* there was not found a helper as his partner. 21 So the LORD God caused a deep sleep to fall upon the man, and he slept; then he took one of his ribs and closed up its place with flesh. 22 And the rib that the LORD God had taken from the man he made into a woman and brought her to the man. 23 Then the man said,

"This at last is bone of my bones
and flesh of my flesh;
this one shall be called Woman,*h*
for out of Man*i* this one was taken."

REVISED ENGLISH BIBLE

28 God blessed them and said to them, 'Be fruitful and increase, fill the earth and subdue it, have dominion over the fish in the sea, the birds of the air, and every living thing that moves on the earth.' 29 God also said, 'Throughout the earth I give you all plants that bear seed, and every tree that bears fruit with seed: they shall be yours for food. 30 All green plants I give for food to the wild animals, to all the birds of the air, and to everything that creeps on the earth, every living creature.' So it was; 31 and God saw all that he had made, and it was very good. Evening came, and morning came, the sixth day.

2 Thus the heavens and the earth and everything in them were completed. 2 On the sixth day God brought to an end all the work he had been doing; on the seventh day, having finished all his work, 3 God blessed the day and made it holy, because it was the day he finished all his work of creation.

4 THIS is the story of the heavens and the earth after their creation.

When the LORD God made the earth and the heavens, 5 there was neither shrub nor plant growing on the earth, because the LORD God had sent no rain; nor was there anyone to till the ground. 6 Moisture used to well up out of the earth and water all the surface of the ground.

7 The LORD God formed a human being from the dust of the ground and breathed into his nostrils the breath of life, so that he became a living creature. 8 The LORD God planted a garden in Eden away to the east, and in it he put the man he had formed. 9 The LORD God made trees grow up from the ground, every kind of tree pleasing to the eye and good for food; and in the middle of the garden he set the tree of life and the tree of the knowledge of good and evil.

10 There was a river flowing from Eden to water the garden, and from there it branched into four streams. 11 The name of the first is Pishon; it is the river which skirts the whole land of Havilah, where gold is found. 12 The gold of that land is good; gum resin and cornelians are also to be found there. 13 The name of the second river is Gihon; this is the one which skirts the whole land of Cush. 14 The name of the third is Tigris; this is the river which flows east of Asshur. The fourth river is the Euphrates.

15 The LORD God took the man and put him in the garden of Eden to till it and look after it. 16 'You may eat from any tree in the garden', he told the man, 17 'except from the tree of the knowledge of good and evil; the day you eat from that, you are surely doomed to die.' 18 Then the LORD God said, 'It is not good for the man to be alone; I shall make a partner suited to him.' 19 So from the earth he formed all the wild animals and all the birds of the air, and brought them to the man to see what he would call them; whatever the man called each living creature, that would be its name. 20 The man gave names to all cattle, to the birds of the air, and to every wild animal; but for the man himself no suitable partner was found. 21 The LORD God then put the man into a deep sleep and, while he slept, he took one of the man's ribs and closed up the flesh over the place. 22 The rib he had taken out of the man the LORD God built up into a woman, and he brought her to the man. 23 The man said:

'This one at last
is bone from my bones,
flesh from my flesh!
She shall be called woman,
for from man was she taken.'

f Or *formed a man* (Heb *adam*) *of dust from the ground* (Heb *adamah*)
g Or *for Adam*   *h* Heb *ishshah*   *i* Heb *ish*

2:2 **sixth:** *so some Vss.; Heb.* seventh.   2:7 **human being:** *Heb.* adam. **ground:** *Heb.* adamah.   2:12 **gum resin:** *or* bdellium. 2:23 **woman:** *Heb.* ishshah. **man:** *Heb.* ish.

NEW AMERICAN BIBLE

28 God blessed them, saying: "Be fertile and multiply; fill the earth and subdue it. Have dominion over the fish of the sea, the birds of the air, and all the living things that move on the earth." 29 God also said: "See, I give you every seed-bearing plant all over the earth and every tree that has seed-bearing fruit on it to be your food; 30 and to all the animals of the land, all the birds of the air, and all the living creatures that crawl on the ground, I give all the green plants for food." And so it happened. 31 God looked at everything he had made, and he found it very good. Evening came, and morning followed — the sixth day.

2 Thus the heavens and the earth and all their array were completed. 2 Since on the seventh day God was finished with the work he had been doing, he rested on the seventh day from all the work he had undertaken. 3 So God blessed the seventh day and made it holy, because on it he rested from all the work he had done in creation.

4 Such is the story of the heavens and the earth at their creation.

At the time when the LORD God made the earth and the heavens — 5 while as yet there was no field shrub on earth and no grass of the field had sprouted, for the LORD God had sent no rain upon the earth and there was no man to till the soil, 6 but a stream was welling up out of the earth and was watering all the surface of the ground — 7 the LORD God formed man out of the clay of the ground and blew into his nostrils the breath of life, and so man became a living being.

8 Then the LORD God planted a garden in Eden, in the east, and he placed there the man whom he had formed. 9 Out of the ground the LORD God made various trees grow that were delightful to look at and good for food, with the tree of life in the middle of the garden and the tree of the knowledge of good and bad.

10 A river rises in Eden to water the garden; beyond there it divides and becomes four branches. 11 The name of the first is the Pishon; it is the one that winds through the whole land of Havilah, where there is gold. 12 The gold of that land is excellent; bdellium and lapis lazuli are also there. 13 The name of the second river is the Gihon; it is the one that winds all through the land of Cush. 14 The name of the third river is the Tigris; it is the one that flows east of Asshur. The fourth river is the Euphrates.

15 The LORD God then took the man and settled him in the garden of Eden, to cultivate and care for it. 16 The LORD God gave man this order: "You are free to eat from any of the trees of the garden 17 except the tree of knowledge of good and bad. From that tree you shall not eat; the moment you eat from it you are surely doomed to die."

18 The LORD God said: "It is not good for the man to be alone. I will make a suitable partner for him." 19 So the LORD God formed out of the ground various wild animals and various birds of the air, and he brought them to the man to see what he would call them; whatever the man called each of them would be its name. 20 The man gave names to all the cattle, all the birds of the air, and all the wild animals; but none proved to be the suitable partner for the man.

21 So the LORD God cast a deep sleep on the man, and while he was asleep, he took out one of his ribs and closed up its place with flesh. 22 The LORD God then built up into a woman the rib that he had taken from the man. When he brought her to the man, 23 the man said:

"This one, at last, is bone of my bones
 and flesh of my flesh;
This one shall be called 'woman,'
 for out of 'her man' this one has been taken."

NEW JERUSALEM BIBLE

28 God blessed them, saying to them, 'Be fruitful, multiply, fill the earth and subdue it. Be masters of the fish of the sea, the birds of heaven and all the living creatures that move on earth.' 29 God also said, 'Look, to you I give all the seed-bearing plants everywhere on the surface of the earth, and all the trees with seed-bearing fruit; this will be your food. 30 And to all the wild animals, all the birds of heaven and all the living creatures that creep along the ground, I give all the foliage of the plants as their food.' And so it was. 31 God saw all he had made, and indeed it was very good. Evening came and morning came: the sixth day.

2 Thus heaven and earth were completed with all their array. 2 On the seventh day God had completed the work he had been doing. He rested on the seventh day after all the work he had been doing. 3 God blessed the seventh day and made it holy, because on that day he rested after all his work of creating.

4 Such was the story of heaven and earth as they were created.

At the time when Yahweh God made earth and heaven 5 there was as yet no wild bush on the earth nor had any wild plant yet sprung up, for Yahweh God had not sent rain on the earth, nor was there any man to till the soil. 6 Instead, water flowed out of the ground and watered all the surface of the soil. 7 Yahweh God shaped man from the soil of the ground and blew the breath of life into his nostrils, and man became a living being.

8 Yahweh God planted a garden in Eden, which is in the east, and there he put the man he had fashioned. 9 From the soil, Yahweh God caused to grow every kind of tree, enticing to look at and good to eat, with the tree of life in the middle of the garden, and the tree of the knowledge of good and evil.

10 A river flowed from Eden to water the garden, and from there it divided to make four streams. 11 The first is named the Pishon, and this winds all through the land of Havilah where there is gold. 12 The gold of this country is pure; bdellium and cornelian stone are found there. 13 The second river is named the Gihon, and this winds all through the land of Cush. 14 The third river is named the Tigris, and this flows to the east of Ashur. The fourth river is the Euphrates.

15 Yahweh God took the man and settled him in the garden of Eden to cultivate and take care of it. 16 Then Yahweh God gave the man this command, 'You are free to eat of all the trees in the garden. 17 But of the tree of the knowledge of good and evil you are not to eat; for, the day you eat of that, you are doomed to die.'

18 Yahweh God said, 'It is not right that the man should be alone. I shall make him a helper.' 19 So from the soil Yahweh God fashioned all the wild animals and all the birds of heaven. These he brought to the man to see what he would call them; each one was to bear the name the man would give it. 20 The man gave names to all the cattle, all the birds of heaven and all the wild animals. But no helper suitable for the man was found for him. 21 Then, Yahweh God made the man fall into a deep sleep. And, while he was asleep, he took one of his ribs and closed the flesh up again forthwith. 22 Yahweh God fashioned the rib he had taken from the man into a woman, and brought her to the man. 23 And the man said:

This one at last is bone of my bones
 and flesh of my flesh!
She is to be called Woman,
 because she was taken from Man.

NEW REVISED STANDARD VERSION

24 Therefore a man leaves his father and his mother and clings to his wife, and they become one flesh. 25 And the man and his wife were both naked, and were not ashamed.

3 Now the serpent was more crafty than any other wild animal that the LORD God had made. He said to the woman, "Did God say, 'You shall not eat from any tree in the garden'?" 2 The woman said to the serpent, "We may eat of the fruit of the trees in the garden; 3 but God said, 'You shall not eat of the fruit of the tree that is in the middle of the garden, nor shall you touch it, or you shall die.' " 4 But the serpent said to the woman, "You will not die; 5 for God knows that when you eat of it your eyes will be opened, and you will be like God, *j* knowing good and evil." 6 So when the woman saw that the tree was good for food, and that it was a delight to the eyes, and that the tree was to be desired to make one wise, she took of its fruit and ate; and she also gave some to her husband, who was with her, and he ate. 7 Then the eyes of both were opened, and they knew that they were naked; and they sewed fig leaves together and made loincloths for themselves.

8 They heard the sound of the LORD God walking in the garden at the time of the evening breeze, and the man and his wife hid themselves from the presence of the LORD God among the trees of the garden. 9 But the LORD God called to the man, and said to him, "Where are you?" 10 He said, "I heard the sound of you in the garden, and I was afraid, because I was naked; and I hid myself." 11 He said, "Who told you that you were naked? Have you eaten from the tree of which I commanded you not to eat?" 12 The man said, "The woman whom you gave to be with me, she gave me fruit from the tree, and I ate." 13 Then the LORD God said to the woman, "What is this that you have done?" The woman said, "The serpent tricked me, and I ate." 14 The LORD God said to the serpent,

"Because you have done this,
cursed are you among all animals
and among all wild creatures;
upon your belly you shall go,
and dust you shall eat
all the days of your life.
15 I will put enmity between you and the woman,
and between your offspring and hers;
he will strike your head,
and you will strike his heel."
16 To the woman he said,
"I will greatly increase your pangs in childbearing;
in pain you shall bring forth children,
yet your desire shall be for your husband,
and he shall rule over you."
17 And to the man*k* he said,
"Because you have listened to the voice of your wife,
and have eaten of the tree
about which I commanded you,
'You shall not eat of it,'
cursed is the ground because of you;
in toil you shall eat of it all the days of your life;
18 thorns and thistles it shall bring forth for you;
and you shall eat the plants of the field.
19 By the sweat of your face
you shall eat bread
until you return to the ground,
for out of it you were taken;
you are dust,
and to dust you shall return."

j Or *gods*   *k* Or *to Adam*

REVISED ENGLISH BIBLE

24 That is why a man leaves his father and mother and attaches himself to his wife, and the two become one. 25 Both were naked, the man and his wife, but they had no feeling of shame.

3 THE serpent, which was the most cunning of all the creatures the LORD God had made, asked the woman, 'Is it true that God has forbidden you to eat from any tree in the garden?' 2 She replied, 'We may eat the fruit of any tree in the garden, 3 except for the tree in the middle of the garden. God has forbidden us to eat the fruit of that tree or even to touch it; if we do, we shall die.' 4 'Of course you will not die,' said the serpent; 5 'for God knows that, as soon as you eat it, your eyes will be opened and you will be like God himself, knowing both good and evil.' 6 The woman looked at the tree: the fruit would be good to eat; it was pleasing to the eye and desirable for the knowledge it could give. So she took some and ate it; she also gave some to her husband, and he ate it. 7 Then the eyes of both of them were opened, and they knew that they were naked; so they stitched fig-leaves together and made themselves loincloths.

8 The man and his wife heard the sound of the LORD God walking about in the garden at the time of the evening breeze, and they hid from him among the trees. 9 The LORD God called to the man, 'Where are you?' 10 He replied, 'I heard the sound of you in the garden and I was afraid because I was naked, so I hid.' 11 God said, 'Who told you that you were naked? Have you eaten from the tree which I forbade you to eat from?' 12 The man replied, 'It was the woman you gave to be with me who gave me fruit from the tree, and I ate it.' 13 The LORD God said to the woman, 'What have you done?' The woman answered, 'It was the serpent who deceived me into eating it.' 14 Then the LORD God said to the serpent:

'Because you have done this you are cursed alone of all cattle and the creatures of the wild.
'On your belly you will crawl,
and dust you will eat
all the days of your life.
15 I shall put enmity between you and the woman,
between your brood and hers.
They will strike at your head,
and you will strike at their heel.'
16 To the woman he said:
'I shall give you great labour in childbearing;
with labour you will bear children.
You will desire your husband,
but he will be your master.'
17 And to the man he said: 'Because you have listened to your wife and have eaten from the tree which I forbade you,
on your account the earth will be cursed.
You will get your food from it only by labour
all the days of your life;
18 it will yield thorns and thistles for you.
You will eat of the produce of the field,
19 and only by the sweat of your brow will you win your bread
until you return to the earth;
for from it you were taken.
Dust you are, to dust you will return.'

3:5 **God himself:** or *gods.*   3:6 **desirable . . . give:** or *tempting to contemplate.*

NEW AMERICAN BIBLE

24 That is why a man leaves his father and mother and clings to his wife, and the two of them become one body.

25 The man and his wife were both naked, yet they felt no shame.

3 Now the serpent was the most cunning of all the animals that the LORD God had made. The serpent asked the woman, "Did God really tell you not to eat from any of the trees in the garden?" 2 The woman answered the serpent: "We may eat of the fruit of the trees in the garden; 3 it is only about the fruit of the tree in the middle of the garden that God said, 'You shall not eat it or even touch it, lest you die.' " 4 But the serpent said to the woman: "You certainly will not die! 5 No, God knows well that the moment you eat of it your eyes will be opened and you will be like gods who know what is good and what is bad." 6 The woman saw that the tree was good for food, pleasing to the eyes, and desirable for gaining wisdom. So she took some of its fruit and ate it; and she also gave some to her husband, who was with her, and he ate it. 7 Then the eyes of both of them were opened, and they realized that they were naked; so they sewed fig leaves together and made loincloths for themselves.

8 When they heard the sound of the LORD God moving about in the garden at the breezy time of the day, the man and his wife hid themselves from the LORD God among the trees of the garden. 9 The LORD God then called to the man and asked him, "Where are you?" 10 He answered, "I heard you in the garden; but I was afraid, because I was naked, so I hid myself." 11 Then he asked, "Who told you that you were naked? You have eaten, then, from the tree of which I had forbidden you to eat!" 12 The man replied, "The woman whom you put here with me — she gave me fruit from the tree, so I ate it." 13 The LORD God then asked the woman, "Why did you do such a thing?" The woman answered, "The serpent tricked me into it, so I ate it."

14 Then the LORD God said to the serpent:
"Because you have done this, you shall be banned
    from all the animals
    and from all the wild creatures;
  On your belly shall you crawl,
    and dirt shall you eat
    all the days of your life.
15 I will put enmity between you and the woman,
    and between your offspring and hers;
  He will strike at your head,
    while you strike at his heel."
16 To the woman he said:
"I will intensify the pangs of your childbearing;
  in pain shall you bring forth children.
  Yet your urge shall be for your husband,
    and he shall be your master."
17 To the man he said: "Because you listened to your wife and ate from the tree of which I had forbidden you to eat,
"Cursed be the ground because of you!
  In toil shall you eat its yield
  all the days of your life.
18 Thorns and thistles shall it bring forth to you,
  as you eat of the plants of the field.
19 By the sweat of your face
    shall you get bread to eat,
Until you return to the ground,
    from which you were taken;
For you are dirt,
    and to dirt you shall return."

NEW JERUSALEM BIBLE

24 This is why a man leaves his father and mother and becomes attached to his wife, and they become one flesh.

25 Now, both of them were naked, the man and his wife, but they felt no shame before each other.

3 Now, the snake was the most subtle of all the wild animals that Yahweh God had made. It asked the woman, 'Did God really say you were not to eat from any of the trees in the garden?' 2 The woman answered the snake, 'We may eat the fruit of the trees in the garden. 3 But of the fruit of the tree in the middle of the garden God said, "You must not eat it, nor touch it, under pain of death." ' 4 Then the snake said to the woman, 'No! You will not die! 5 God knows in fact that the day you eat it your eyes will be opened and you will be like gods, knowing good from evil.' 6 The woman saw that the tree was good to eat and pleasing to the eye, and that it was enticing for the wisdom that it could give. So she took some of its fruit and ate it. She also gave some to her husband who was with her, and he ate it. 7 Then the eyes of both of them were opened and they realised that they were naked. So they sewed fig-leaves together to make themselves loin-cloths.

8 The man and his wife heard the sound of Yahweh God walking in the garden in the cool of the day, and they hid from Yahweh God among the trees of the garden. 9 But Yahweh God called to the man. 'Where are you?' he asked. 10 'I heard the sound of you in the garden,' he replied. 'I was afraid because I was naked, so I hid.' 11 'Who told you that you were naked?' he asked. 'Have you been eating from the tree I forbade you to eat?' 12 The man replied, 'It was the woman you put with me; she gave me some fruit from the tree, and I ate it.' 13 Then Yahweh God said to the woman, 'Why did you do that?' The woman replied, 'The snake tempted me and I ate.'

14 Then Yahweh God said to the snake, 'Because you have done this,
  Accursed be you
  of all animals wild and tame!
  On your belly you will go
  and on dust you will feed
  as long as you live.
15 I shall put enmity
  between you and the woman,
  and between your offspring and hers;
  it*a* will bruise your head
  and you will strike its heel.'
16 To the woman he said:
  I shall give you intense pain in childbearing,
  you will give birth to your children in pain.
  Your yearning will be for your husband,
  and he will dominate you.
17 To the man he said, 'Because you listened to the voice of your wife and ate from the tree of which I had forbidden you to eat,
  Accursed be the soil because of you!
  Painfully will you get your food from it
  as long as you live.
18 It will yield you brambles and thistles,
  as you eat the produce of the land.
19 By the sweat of your face
  will you earn your food,
  until you return to the ground,
  as you were taken from it.
  For dust you are
  and to dust you shall return.'

---

a 3 Gk reads 'he', suggesting a personal saviour.

NEW REVISED STANDARD VERSION	REVISED ENGLISH BIBLE

NEW REVISED STANDARD VERSION

20 The man named his wife Eve,*l* because she was the mother of all living. 21 And the LORD God made garments of skins for the man*m* and for his wife, and clothed them.

22 Then the LORD God said, "See, the man has become like one of us, knowing good and evil; and now, he might reach out his hand and take also from the tree of life, and eat, and live forever" — 23 therefore the LORD God sent him forth from the garden of Eden, to till the ground from which he was taken. 24 He drove out the man; and at the east of the garden of Eden he placed the cherubim, and a sword flaming and turning to guard the way to the tree of life.

4 Now the man knew his wife Eve, and she conceived and bore Cain, saying, "I have produced*n* a man with the help of the LORD." 2 Next she bore his brother Abel. Now Abel was a keeper of sheep, and Cain a tiller of the ground. 3 In the course of time Cain brought to the LORD an offering of the fruit of the ground, 4 and Abel for his part brought of the firstlings of his flock, their fat portions. And the LORD had regard for Abel and his offering, 5 but for Cain and his offering he had no regard. So Cain was very angry, and his countenance fell. 6 The LORD said to Cain, "Why are you angry, and why has your countenance fallen? 7 If you do well, will you not be accepted? And if you do not do well, sin is lurking at the door; its desire is for you, but you must master it."

8 Cain said to his brother Abel, "Let us go out to the field."*o* And when they were in the field, Cain rose up against his brother Abel, and killed him. 9 Then the LORD said to Cain, "Where is your brother Abel?" He said, "I do not know; am I my brother's keeper?" 10 And the LORD said, "What have you done? Listen; your brother's blood is crying out to me from the ground! 11 And now you are cursed from the ground, which has opened its mouth to receive your brother's blood from your hand. 12 When you till the ground, it will no longer yield to you its strength; you will be a fugitive and a wanderer on the earth." 13 Cain said to the LORD, "My punishment is greater than I can bear! 14 Today you have driven me away from the soil, and I shall be hidden from your face; I shall be a fugitive and a wanderer on the earth, and anyone who meets me may kill me." 15 Then the LORD said to him, "Not so!*p* Whoever kills Cain will suffer a sevenfold vengeance." And the LORD put a mark on Cain, so that no one who came upon him would kill him. 16 Then Cain went away from the presence of the LORD, and settled in the land of Nod,*q* east of Eden.

17 Cain knew his wife, and she conceived and bore Enoch; and he built a city, and named it Enoch after his son Enoch. 18 To Enoch was born Irad; and Irad was the father of Mehujael, and Mehujael the father of Methushael, and Methushael the father of Lamech. 19 Lamech took two wives; the name of the one was Adah, and the name of the other Zillah. 20 Adah bore Jabal; he was the ancestor of those who live in tents and have livestock. 21 His brother's name was Jubal; he was the ancestor of all those who play the lyre and pipe. 22 Zillah bore Tubal-cain, who made all kinds of bronze and iron tools. The sister of Tubal-cain was Naamah.

23 Lamech said to his wives:

"Adah and Zillah, hear my voice;
you wives of Lamech, listen to what I say:
I have killed a man for wounding me,
a young man for striking me.

REVISED ENGLISH BIBLE

20 The man named his wife Eve because she was the mother of all living beings. 21 The LORD God made coverings from skins for the man and his wife and clothed them. 22 But he said, 'The man has become like one of us, knowing good and evil; what if he now reaches out and takes fruit from the tree of life also, and eats it and lives for ever?' 23 So the LORD God banished him from the garden of Eden to till the ground from which he had been taken. 24 When he drove him out, God settled him to the east of the garden of Eden, and he stationed the cherubim and a sword whirling and flashing to guard the way to the tree of life.

4 The man lay with his wife Eve, and she conceived and gave birth to Cain. She said, 'With the help of the LORD I have brought into being a male child.' 2 Afterwards she had another child, Abel. He tended the flock, and Cain worked the land. 3 In due season Cain brought some of the fruits of the earth as an offering to the LORD, 4 while Abel brought the choicest of the firstborn of his flock. The LORD regarded Abel and his offering with favour, 5 but not Cain and his offering. Cain was furious and he glowered. 6 The LORD said to Cain,

'Why are you angry? Why are you scowling?
7 If you do well, you hold your head up;
if not, sin is a demon crouching at the door;
it will desire you, and you will be mastered by it.'
8 Cain said to his brother Abel, 'Let us go out into the country.' Once there, Cain attacked and murdered his brother. 9 The LORD asked Cain, 'Where is your brother Abel?' 'I do not know,' Cain answered. 'Am I my brother's keeper?' 10 The LORD said, 'What have you done? Your brother's blood is crying out to me from the ground. 11 Now you are accursed and will be banished from the very ground which has opened its mouth to receive the blood you have shed. 12 When you till the ground, it will no longer yield you its produce. You shall be a wanderer, a fugitive on the earth.' 13 Cain said to the LORD, 'My punishment is heavier than I can bear; 14 now you are driving me off the land, and I must hide myself from your presence. I shall be a wanderer, a fugitive on the earth, and I can be killed at sight by anyone.' 15 The LORD answered him, 'No: if anyone kills Cain, sevenfold vengeance will be exacted from him.' The LORD put a mark on Cain, so that anyone happening to meet him should not kill him. 16 Cain went out from the LORD's presence and settled in the land of Nod to the east of Eden.

17 Then Cain lay with his wife; and she conceived and gave birth to Enoch. Cain was then building a town which he named Enoch after his son. 18 Enoch was the father of Irad, Irad of Mehujael, Mehujael of Methushael, and Methushael of Lamech.

19 Lamech married two women, one named Adah, the other Zillah. 20 Adah gave birth to Jabal, the ancestor of tent-dwellers who raise flocks and herds. 21 His brother's name was Jubal; he was the ancestor of those who play the harp and pipe. 22 Zillah, the other wife, bore Tubal-cain, the master of all coppersmiths and blacksmiths, and Tubal-cain's sister was Naamah. 23 Lamech said to his wives:

'Adah and Zillah, listen to me;
wives of Lamech, mark what I say:
I kill a man for wounding me,
a young man for a blow.

---

l In Heb *Eve* resembles the word for *living*   *m* Or *for Adam*
n The verb in Heb resembles the word for *Cain*   *o* Sam Gk Syr Compare Vg: MT lacks *Let us go out to the field*   *p* Gk Syr Vg: Heb *Therefore*   *q* That is *Wandering*

3:20 **Eve:** *that is* Life.   4:7 **and you . . . it:** *or* but you must master it.   4:8 **Let us . . . country:** *so Samar.; Heb.* omits. 4:16 **Nod:** *that is* Wandering.

NEW AMERICAN BIBLE

20 The man called his wife Eve, because she became the mother of all the living.

21 For the man and his wife the LORD God made leather garments, with which he clothed them. 22 Then the LORD God said: "See! The man has become like one of us, knowing what is good and what is bad! Therefore, he must not be allowed to put out his hand to take fruit from the tree of life also, and thus eat of it and live forever." 23 The LORD God therefore banished him from the garden of Eden, to till the ground from which he had been taken. 24 When he expelled the man, he settled him east of the garden of Eden; and he stationed the cherubim and the fiery revolving sword, to guard the way to the tree of life.

4 The man had relations with his wife Eve, and she conceived and bore Cain, saying, "I have produced a man with the help of the LORD." 2 Next she bore his brother Abel. Abel became a keeper of flocks, and Cain a tiller of the soil. 3 In the course of time Cain brought an offering to the LORD from the fruit of the soil, 4 while Abel, for his part, brought one of the best firstlings of his flock. The LORD looked with favor on Abel and his offering, 5 but on Cain and his offering he did not. Cain greatly resented this and was crestfallen. 6 So the LORD said to Cain: "Why are you so resentful and crestfallen? 7 If you do well, you can hold up your head; but if not, sin is a demon lurking at the door: his urge is toward you, yet you can be his master."

8 Cain said to his brother Abel, "Let us go out in the field." When they were in the field, Cain attacked his brother Abel and killed him. 9 Then the LORD asked Cain, "Where is your brother Abel?" He answered, "I do not know. Am I my brother's keeper?" 10 The LORD then said: "What have you done! Listen: Your brother's blood cries out to me from the soil! 11 Therefore you shall be banned from the soil that opened its mouth to receive your brother's blood from your hand. 12 If you till the soil, it shall no longer give you its produce. You shall become a restless wanderer on the earth." 13 Cain said to the LORD: "My punishment is too great to bear. 14 Since you have now banished me from the soil, and I must avoid your presence and become a restless wanderer on the earth, anyone may kill me at sight." 15 "Not so!" the LORD said to him. "If anyone kills Cain, Cain shall be avenged sevenfold." So the LORD put a mark on Cain, lest anyone should kill him at sight. 16 Cain then left the LORD's presence and settled in the land of Nod, east of Eden.

17 Cain had relations with his wife, and she conceived and bore Enoch. Cain also became the founder of a city, which he named after his son Enoch. 18 To Enoch was born Irad, and Irad became the father of Mehujael; Mehujael became the father of Methusael, and Methusael became the father of Lamech. 19 Lamech took two wives; the name of the first was Adah, and the name of the second Zillah. 20 Adah gave birth to Jabal, the ancestor of all who dwell in tents and keep cattle. 21 His brother's name was Jubal; he was the ancestor of all who play the lyre and the pipe. 22 Zillah, on her part, gave birth to Tubalcain, the ancestor of all who forge instruments of bronze and iron. The sister of Tubalcain was Naamah. 23 Lamech said to his wives:

"Adah and Zillah, hear my voice;
    wives of Lamech, listen to my utterance:
I have killed a man for wounding me,
    a boy for bruising me.

NEW JERUSALEM BIBLE

20 The man named his wife 'Eve' because she was the mother of all those who live. 21 Yahweh God made tunics of skins for the man and his wife and clothed them. 22 Then Yahweh God said, 'Now that the man has become like one of us in knowing good from evil, he must not be allowed to reach out his hand and pick from the tree of life too, and eat and live for ever!' 23 So Yahweh God expelled him from the garden of Eden, to till the soil from which he had been taken. 24 He banished the man, and in front of the garden of Eden he posted the great winged creatures and the fiery flashing sword, to guard the way to the tree of life.

4 The man had intercourse with his wife Eve, and she conceived and gave birth to Cain. 'I have acquired a man with the help of Yahweh,' she said. 2 She gave birth to a second child, Abel, the brother of Cain. Now Abel became a shepherd and kept flocks, while Cain tilled the soil. 3 Time passed and Cain brought some of the produce of the soil as an offering for Yahweh, 4 while Abel for his part brought the first-born of his flock and some of their fat as well. Yahweh looked with favour on Abel and his offering. 5 But he did not look with favour on Cain and his offering, and Cain was very angry and downcast. 6 Yahweh asked Cain, 'Why are you angry and downcast? 7 If you are doing right, surely you ought to hold your head high! But if you are not doing right, Sin is crouching at the door hungry to get you. You can still master him.' 8 Cain said to his brother Abel, 'Let us go out'; and while they were in the open country, Cain set on his brother Abel and killed him.

9 Yahweh asked Cain, 'Where is your brother Abel?' 'I do not know,' he replied. 'Am I my brother's guardian?' 10 'What have you done?' Yahweh asked. 'Listen! Your brother's blood is crying out to me from the ground. 11 Now be cursed and banned from the ground that has opened its mouth to receive your brother's blood at your hands. 12 When you till the ground it will no longer yield up its strength to you. A restless wanderer you will be on earth.' 13 Cain then said to Yahweh, 'My punishment is greater than I can bear. 14 Look, today you drive me from the surface of the earth. I must hide from you, and be a restless wanderer on earth. Why, whoever comes across me will kill me!' 15 'Very well, then,' Yahweh replied, 'whoever kills Cain will suffer a sevenfold vengeance.' So Yahweh put a mark on Cain, so that no one coming across him would kill him. 16 Cain left Yahweh's presence and settled in the land of Nod, east of Eden.

17 Cain had intercourse with his wife, and she conceived and gave birth to Enoch. He became the founder of a city and gave the city the name of his son Enoch. 18 Enoch fathered Irad, and Irad fathered Mehujael; Mehujael fathered Methushael, and Methushael fathered Lamech. 19 Lamech married two women: the name of the first was Adah and the name of the second Zillah. 20 Adah gave birth to Jabal: he was the ancestor of tent-dwelling herdsmen. 21 His brother's name was Jubal: he was the ancestor of all who play the harp and the pipe. 22 As for Zillah, she gave birth to Tubal-Cain: he was the ancestor of all who work copper and iron. Tubal-Cain's sister was Naamah.

23 Lamech said to his wives:
Adah and Zillah, hear my voice,
    wives of Lamech, listen to what I say:
I killed a man for wounding me,
    a boy for striking me.

NEW REVISED STANDARD VERSION

24 If Cain is avenged sevenfold,
truly Lamech seventy-sevenfold."

25 Adam knew his wife again, and she bore a son and named him Seth, for she said, "God has appointed[r] for me another child instead of Abel, because Cain killed him." 26 To Seth also a son was born, and he named him Enosh. At that time people began to invoke the name of the LORD.

5 This is the list of the descendants of Adam. When God created humankind,[s] he made them[t] in the likeness of God. 2 Male and female he created them, and he blessed them and named them "Humankind"[s] when they were created.

3 When Adam had lived one hundred thirty years, he became the father of a son in his likeness, according to his image, and named him Seth. 4 The days of Adam after he became the father of Seth were eight hundred years; and he had other sons and daughters. 5 Thus all the days that Adam lived were nine hundred thirty years; and he died.

6 When Seth had lived one hundred five years, he became the father of Enosh. 7 Seth lived after the birth of Enosh eight hundred seven years, and had other sons and daughters. 8 Thus all the days of Seth were nine hundred twelve years; and he died.

9 When Enosh had lived ninety years, he became the father of Kenan. 10 Enosh lived after the birth of Kenan eight hundred fifteen years, and had other sons and daughters. 11 Thus all the days of Enosh were nine hundred five years; and he died.

12 When Kenan had lived seventy years, he became the father of Mahalalel. 13 Kenan lived after the birth of Mahalalel eight hundred forty years, and had other sons and daughters. 14 Thus all the days of Kenan were nine hundred and ten years; and he died.

15 When Mahalalel had lived sixty-five years, he became the father of Jared. 16 Mahalalel lived after the birth of Jared eight hundred thirty years, and had other sons and daughters. 17 Thus all the days of Mahalalel were eight hundred ninety-five years; and he died.

18 When Jared had lived one hundred sixty-two years he became the father of Enoch. 19 Jared lived after the birth of Enoch eight hundred years, and had other sons and daughters. 20 Thus all the days of Jared were nine hundred sixty-two years; and he died.

21 When Enoch had lived sixty-five years, he became the father of Methuselah. 22 Enoch walked with God after the birth of Methuselah three hundred years, and had other sons and daughters. 23 Thus all the days of Enoch were three hundred sixty-five years. 24 Enoch walked with God; then he was no more, because God took him.

25 When Methuselah had lived one hundred eighty-seven years, he became the father of Lamech. 26 Methuselah lived after the birth of Lamech seven hundred eighty-two years, and had other sons and daughters. 27 Thus all the days of Methuselah were nine hundred sixty-nine years; and he died.

28 When Lamech had lived one hundred eighty-two years, he became the father of a son; 29 he named him Noah, saying, "Out of the ground that the LORD has cursed this one shall bring us relief from our work and from the toil of our hands." 30 Lamech lived after the birth of Noah five hundred ninety-five years, and had other sons and daughters. 31 Thus all the days of Lamech were seven hundred seventy-seven years; and he died.

32 After Noah was five hundred years old, Noah became the father of Shem, Ham, and Japheth.

REVISED ENGLISH BIBLE

24 If sevenfold vengeance was to be exacted for Cain, for Lamech it would be seventy-sevenfold.'

25 Adam lay with his wife again. She gave birth to a son, and named him Seth, 'for', she said, 'God has granted me another son in place of Abel, because Cain killed him'. 26 Seth too had a son, whom he named Enosh. At that time people began to invoke the LORD by name.

5 THIS is the list of Adam's descendants. On the day when God created human beings he made them in his own likeness. 2 He created them male and female, and on the day when he created them, he blessed them and called them man.

3 Adam was one hundred and thirty years old when he begot a son in his likeness and image, and named him Seth. 4 After the birth of Seth he lived eight hundred years, and had other sons and daughters. 5 He lived nine hundred and thirty years, and then he died.

6 Seth was one hundred and five years old when he begot Enosh. 7 After the birth of Enosh he lived eight hundred and seven years, and had other sons and daughters. 8 He lived nine hundred and twelve years, and then he died.

9 Enosh was ninety years old when he begot Kenan. 10 After the birth of Kenan he lived eight hundred and fifteen years, and had other sons and daughters. 11 He lived nine hundred and five years, and then he died.

12 Kenan was seventy years old when he begot Mahalalel. 13 After the birth of Mahalalel he lived eight hundred and forty years, and had other sons and daughters. 14 He lived nine hundred and ten years, and then he died.

15 Mahalalel was sixty-five years old when he begot Jared. 16 After the birth of Jared he lived eight hundred and thirty years, and had other sons and daughters. 17 He lived eight hundred and ninety-five years, and then he died.

18 Jared was one hundred and sixty-two years old when he begot Enoch. 19 After the birth of Enoch he lived eight hundred years, and had other sons and daughters. 20 He lived nine hundred and sixty-two years, and then he died.

21 Enoch was sixty-five years old when he begot Methuselah. 22 After the birth of Methuselah, Enoch walked with God for three hundred years, and had other sons and daughters. 23 He lived three hundred and sixty-five years. 24 Enoch walked with God, and then was seen no more, because God had taken him away.

25 Methuselah was one hundred and eighty-seven years old when he begot Lamech. 26 After the birth of Lamech he lived for seven hundred and eighty-two years, and had other sons and daughters. 27 He lived nine hundred and sixty-nine years, and then he died.

28 Lamech was one hundred and eighty-two years old when he begot a son. 29 He named him Noah, saying, 'This boy will bring us relief from our work, from the labour that has come upon us because of the LORD's curse on the ground.' 30 After the birth of Noah he lived for five hundred and ninety-five years, and had other sons and daughters. 31 Lamech lived seven hundred and seventy-seven years, and then he died. 32 Noah was five hundred years old when he begot Shem, Ham, and Japheth.

---

[r] The verb in Heb resembles the word for *Seth*   [s] Heb *adam*
[t] Heb *him*

4:25 **Seth:** *that is* Granted.   4:26 **LORD:** *this represents the Hebrew consonants YHWH; see Introduction, p. xxii.*

24 If Cain is avenged sevenfold,
then Lamech seventy-sevenfold."

25 Adam again had relations with his wife, and she gave birth to a son whom she called Seth. "God has granted me more offspring in place of Abel," she said, "because Cain slew him." 26 To Seth, in turn, a son was born, and he named him Enosh.

At that time men began to invoke the LORD by name.

5 This is the record of the descendants of Adam. When God created man, he made him in the likeness of God; 2 he created them male and female. When they were created, he blessed them and named them "man."

3 Adam was one hundred and thirty years old when he begot a son in his likeness, after his image; and he named him Seth. 4 Adam lived eight hundred years after the birth of Seth, and he had other sons and daughters. 5 The whole lifetime of Adam was nine hundred and thirty years; then he died.

6 When Seth was one hundred and five years old, he became the father of Enosh. 7 Seth lived eight hundred and seven years after birth of Enosh, and he had other sons and daughters. 8 The whole lifetime of Seth was nine hundred and twelve years; then he died.

9 When Enosh was ninety years old, he became the father of Kenan. 10 Enosh lived eight hundred and fifteen years after the birth of Kenan, and he had other sons and daughters. 11 The whole lifetime of Enosh was nine hundred and five years; then he died.

12 When Kenan was seventy years old, he became the father of Mahalalel. 13 Kenan lived eight hundred and forty years after the birth of Mahalalel, and he had other sons and daughters. 14 The whole lifetime of Kenan was nine hundred and ten years; then he died.

15 When Mahalalel was sixty-five years old, he became the father of Jared. 16 Mahalalel lived eight hundred and thirty years after the birth of Jared, and he had other sons and daughters. 17 The whole lifetime of Mahalalel was eight hundred and ninety-five years; then he died.

18 When Jared was one hundred and sixty-two years old, he became the father of Enoch. 19 Jared lived eight hundred years after the birth of Enoch, and he had other sons and daughters. 20 The whole lifetime of Jared was nine hundred and sixty-two years; then he died.

21 When Enoch was sixty-five years old, he became the father of Methuselah. 22 Enoch lived three hundred years after the birth of Methuselah, and he had other sons and daughters. 23 The whole lifetime of Enoch was three hundred and sixty-five years. 24 Then Enoch walked with God, and he was no longer here, for God took him.

25 When Methuselah was one hundred and eighty-seven years old, he became the father of Lamech. 26 Methuselah lived seven hundred and eighty-two years after the birth of Lamech, and he had other sons and daughters. 27 The whole lifetime of Methuselah was nine hundred and sixty-nine years; then he died.

28 When Lamech was one hundred and eighty-two years old, he begot a son 29 and named him Noah, saying, "Out of the very ground that the LORD has put under a curse, this one shall bring us relief from our work and the toil of our hands." 30 Lamech lived five hundred and ninety-five years after the birth of Noah, and he had other sons and daughters. 31 The whole lifetime of Lamech was seven hundred and seventy-seven years; then he died.

32 When Noah was five hundred years old, he became the father of Shem, Ham and Japheth.

24 Sevenfold vengeance for Cain,
but seventy-sevenfold for Lamech.

25 Adam had intercourse with his wife, and she gave birth to a son whom she named Seth, 'because God has granted me other offspring', she said, 'in place of Abel, since Cain has killed him.' 26 A son was also born to Seth, and he named him Enosh. This man was the first to invoke the name Yahweh.

5 This is the roll of Adam's descendants:
On the day that God created Adam he made him in the likeness of God. 2 Male and female he created them. He blessed them and gave them the name Man, when they were created.

3 When Adam was a hundred and thirty years old he fathered a son, in his likeness, after his image, and he called him Seth. 4 Adam lived for eight hundred years after the birth of Seth and he fathered sons and daughters. 5 In all, Adam lived for nine hundred and thirty years; then he died.

6 When Seth was a hundred and five years old he fathered Enosh. 7 After the birth of Enosh, Seth lived for eight hundred and seven years, and he fathered sons and daughters. 8 In all, Seth lived for nine hundred and twelve years; then he died.

9 When Enosh was ninety years old he fathered Kenan. 10 After the birth of Kenan, Enosh lived for eight hundred and fifteen years and he fathered sons and daughters. 11 In all, Enosh lived for nine hundred and five years; then he died.

12 When Kenan was seventy years old he fathered Mahalalel. 13 After the birth of Mahalalel, Kenan lived for eight hundred and forty years and he fathered sons and daughters. 14 In all, Kenan lived for nine hundred and ten years; then he died.

15 When Mahalalel was sixty-five years old he fathered Jared. 16 After the birth of Jared, Mahalalel lived for eight hundred and thirty years and he fathered sons and daughters. 17 In all, Mahalalel lived for eight hundred and ninety-five years; then he died.

18 When Jared was a hundred and sixty-two years old he fathered Enoch. 19 After the birth of Enoch, Jared lived for eight hundred years and he fathered sons and daughters. 20 In all, Jared lived for nine hundred and sixty-two years; then he died.

21 When Enoch was sixty-five years old he fathered Methuselah. 22 Enoch walked with God. After the birth of Methuselah, Enoch lived for three hundred years and he fathered sons and daughters. 23 In all, Enoch lived for three hundred and sixty-five years. 24 Enoch walked with God, then was no more, because God took him.

25 When Methuselah was a hundred and eighty-seven years old he fathered Lamech. 26 After the birth of Lamech, Methuselah lived for seven hundred and eighty-two years and he fathered sons and daughters. 27 In all, Methuselah lived for nine hundred and sixty-nine years; then he died.

28 When Lamech was a hundred and eighty-two years old he fathered a son. 29 He gave him the name Noah because, he said, 'Here is one who will give us, in the midst of our toil and the labouring of our hands, a consolation out of the very soil that Yahweh cursed.' 30 After the birth of Noah, Lamech lived for five hundred and ninety-five years and fathered sons and daughters. 31 In all, Lamech lived for seven hundred and seventy-seven years; then he died.

32 When Noah was five hundred years old he fathered Shem, Ham and Japheth.

NEW REVISED STANDARD VERSION

6 When people began to multiply on the face of the ground, and daughters were born to them, 2 the sons of God saw that they were fair; and they took wives for themselves of all that they chose. 3 Then the LORD said, "My spirit shall not abide*u* in mortals forever, for they are flesh; their days shall be one hundred twenty years." 4 The Nephilim were on the earth in those days — and also afterward — when the sons of God went in to the daughters of humans, who bore children to them. These were the heroes that were of old, warriors of renown.

5 The LORD saw that the wickedness of humankind was great in the earth, and that every inclination of the thoughts of their hearts was only evil continually. 6 And the LORD was sorry that he had made humankind on the earth, and it grieved him to his heart. 7 So the LORD said, "I will blot out from the earth the human beings I have created — people together with animals and creeping things and birds of the air, for I am sorry that I have made them." 8 But Noah found favor in the sight of the LORD.

9 These are the descendants of Noah. Noah was a righteous man, blameless in his generation; Noah walked with God. 10 And Noah had three sons, Shem, Ham, and Japheth.

11 Now the earth was corrupt in God's sight, and the earth was filled with violence. 12 And God saw that the earth was corrupt; for all flesh had corrupted its ways upon the earth. 13 And God said to Noah, "I have determined to make an end of all flesh, for the earth is filled with violence because of them; now I am going to destroy them along with the earth. 14 Make yourself an ark of cypress*u* wood; make rooms in the ark, and cover it inside and out with pitch. 15 This is how you are to make it: the length of the ark three hundred cubits, its width fifty cubits, and its height thirty cubits. 16 Make a roof*v* for the ark, and finish it to a cubit above; and put the door of the ark in its side; make it with lower, second, and third decks. 17 For my part, I am going to bring a flood of waters on the earth, to destroy from under heaven all flesh in which is the breath of life; everything that is on the earth shall die. 18 But I will establish my covenant with you; and you shall come into the ark, you, your sons, your wife, and your sons' wives with you. 19 And of every living thing, of all flesh, you shall bring two of every kind into the ark, to keep them alive with you; they shall be male and female. 20 Of the birds according to their kinds, and of the animals according to their kinds, of every creeping thing of the ground according to its kind, two of every kind shall come in to you, to keep them alive. 21 Also take with you every kind of food that is eaten, and store it up; and it shall serve as food for you and for them." 22 Noah did this; he did all that God commanded him.

7 Then the LORD said to Noah, "Go into the ark, you and all your household, for I have seen that you alone are righteous before me in this generation. 2 Take with you seven pairs of all clean animals, the male and its mate; and a pair of the animals that are not clean, the male and its mate; 3 and seven pairs of the birds of the air also, male and female, to keep their kind alive on the face of all the earth. 4 For in seven days I will send rain on the earth for forty days and forty nights; and every living thing that I have made I will blot out from the face of the ground." 5 And Noah did all that the LORD had commanded him.

6 Noah was six hundred years old when the flood of waters came on the earth. 7 And Noah with his sons and his wife and his sons' wives went into the ark to escape the waters of the flood. 8 Of clean animals, and of animals that are not clean, and of birds, and of everything that creeps on the ground, 9 two and two, male and female, went into the ark with Noah, as God had commanded Noah. 10 And after

REVISED ENGLISH BIBLE

6 THE human race began to increase and to spread over the earth and daughters were born to them. 2 The sons of the gods saw how beautiful these daughters were, so they took for themselves such women as they chose. 3 But the LORD said, 'My spirit will not remain in a human being for ever; because he is mortal flesh, he will live only for a hundred and twenty years.'

4 In those days as well as later, when the sons of the gods had intercourse with the daughters of mortals and children were born to them, the Nephilim were on the earth; they were the heroes of old, people of renown.

5 When the LORD saw how great was the wickedness of human beings on earth, and how their every thought and inclination were always wicked, 6 he bitterly regretted that he had made mankind on earth. 7 He said, 'I shall wipe off the face of the earth this human race which I have created — yes, man and beast, creeping things and birds. I regret that I ever made them.' 8 Noah, however, had won the LORD's favour.

9 This is the story of Noah. Noah was a righteous man, the one blameless man of his time, and he walked with God. 10 He had three sons: Shem, Ham, and Japheth. 11 God saw that the world was corrupt and full of violence; 12 and seeing this corruption, for the life of everyone on earth was corrupt, 13 God said to Noah, 'I am going to bring the whole human race to an end, for because of them the earth is full of violence. I am about to destroy them, and the earth along with them. 14 Make yourself an ark with ribs of cypress; cover it with reeds and coat it inside and out with pitch. 15 This is to be its design: the length of the ark is to be three hundred cubits, its breadth fifty cubits, and its height thirty cubits. 16 You are to make a roof for the ark, giving it a fall of one cubit when complete; put a door in the side of the ark, and build three decks, lower, middle, and upper. 17 I am about to bring the waters of the flood over the earth to destroy from under heaven every human being that has the spirit of life; everything on earth shall perish. 18 But with you I shall make my covenant, and you will go into the ark, you with your sons, your wife, and your sons' wives. 19 You are to bring living creatures of every kind into the ark to keep them alive with you, two of each kind, a male and a female; 20 two of every kind of bird, beast, and creeping thing are to come to you to be kept alive. 21 See that you take and store by you every kind of food that can be eaten; this will be food for you and for them.' 22 Noah carried out exactly all God had commanded him.

7 The LORD said to Noah, 'Go into the ark, you and all your household; for you alone in this generation have I found to be righteous. 2 Take with you seven pairs, a male and female, of all beasts that are ritually clean, and one pair, a male and female, of all beasts that are not clean; 3 also seven pairs, males and females, of every bird — to ensure that life continues on earth. 4 For in seven days' time I am going to send rain on the earth for forty days and forty nights, and I shall wipe off the face of the earth every living creature I have made.' 5 Noah did all that the LORD had commanded him. 6 He was six hundred years old when the water of the flood came on the earth.

7 So to escape the flood Noah went into the ark together with his sons, his wife, and his sons' wives. 8–9 And to him on board the ark went one pair, a male and a female, of all beasts, clean and unclean, of birds, and of everything that creeps on the ground, two by two, as God had commanded.

---

u Meaning of Heb uncertain   *v* Or *window*

6:4 **Nephilim:** *or* giants.   6:14 **cover . . . reeds:** *or* make compartments in it.

NEW AMERICAN BIBLE

6 When men began to multiply on earth and daughters were born to them, 2 the sons of heaven saw how beautiful the daughters of man were, and so they took for their wives as many of them as they chose. 3 Then the LORD said: "My spirit shall not remain in man forever, since he is but flesh. His days shall comprise one hundred and twenty years."

4 At that time the Nephilim appeared on earth (as well as later), after the sons of heaven had intercourse with the daughters of man, who bore them sons. They were the heroes of old, the men of renown.

5 When the LORD saw how great was man's wickedness on earth, and how no desire that his heart conceived was ever anything but evil, 6 he regretted that he had made man on the earth, and his heart was grieved.

7 So the LORD said: "I will wipe out from the earth the men whom I have created, and not only the men, but also the beasts and the creeping things and the birds of the air, for I am sorry that I made them." 8 But Noah found favor with the LORD.

9 These are the descendants of Noah. Noah, a good man and blameless in that age, 10 for he walked with God, begot three sons: Shem, Ham and Japheth.

11 In the eyes of God the earth was corrupt and full of lawlessness. 12 When God saw how corrupt the earth had become, since all mortals led depraved lives on earth, 13 he said to Noah: "I have decided to put an end to all mortals on earth; the earth is full of lawlessness because of them. So I will destroy them and all life on earth.

14 "Make yourself an ark of gopherwood, put various compartments in it, and cover it inside and out with pitch. 15 This is how you shall build it: the length of the ark shall be three hundred cubits, its width fifty cubits, and its height thirty cubits. 16 Make an opening for daylight in the ark, and finish the ark a cubit above it. Put an entrance in the side of the ark, which you shall make with bottom, second and third decks. 17 I, on my part, am about to bring the flood [waters] on the earth, to destroy everywhere all creatures in which there is the breath of life; everything on earth shall perish. 18 But with you I will establish my covenant; you and your sons, your wife and your sons' wives, shall go into the ark. 19 Of all other living creatures you shall bring two into the ark, one male and one female, that you may keep them alive with you. 20 Of all kinds of birds, of all kinds of beasts, and of all kinds of creeping things, two of each shall come into the ark with you, to stay alive. 21 Moreover, you are to provide yourself with all the food that is to be eaten, and store it away, that it may serve as provisions for you and for them." 22 This Noah did; he carried out all the commands that God gave him.

7 Then the LORD said to Noah: "Go into the ark, you and all your household, for you alone in this age have I found to be truly just. 2 Of every clean animal, take with you seven pairs, a male and its mate; and of the unclean animals, one pair, a male and its mate; 3 likewise, of every clean bird of the air, seven pairs, a male and a female, and of all the unclean birds, one pair, a male and a female. Thus you will keep their issue alive over all the earth. 4 Seven days from now I will bring rain down on the earth for forty days and forty nights, and so I will wipe out from the surface of the earth every moving creature that I have made." 5 Noah did just as the LORD had commanded him.

6 Noah was six hundred years old when the flood waters came upon the earth. 7 Together with his sons, his wife, and his sons' wives, Noah went into the ark because of the waters of the flood. 8 Of the clean animals and the unclean, of the birds, and of everything that creeps on the ground, 9 [two by two] male and female entered the ark with Noah, just as the LORD had commanded him. 10 As soon as the

NEW JERUSALEM BIBLE

6 When people began being numerous on earth, and daughters had been born to them, 2 the sons of God, looking at the women, saw how beautiful they were and married as many of them as they chose. 3 Yahweh said, 'My spirit cannot be indefinitely responsible for human beings, who are only flesh; let the time allowed each be a hundred and twenty years.' 4 The Nephilim were on earth in those days (and even afterwards) when the sons of God resorted to the women, and had children by them. These were the heroes of days gone by, men of renown.

5 Yahweh saw that human wickedness was great on earth and that human hearts contrived nothing but wicked schemes all day long. 6 Yahweh regretted having made human beings on earth, and was grieved at heart. 7 And Yahweh said, 'I shall rid the surface of the earth of the human beings whom I created — human and animal, the creeping things and the birds of heaven — for I regret having made them.' 8 But Noah won Yahweh's favour.

9 This is the story of Noah:

Noah was a good man, an upright man among his contemporaries, and he walked with God. 10 Noah fathered three sons, Shem, Ham and Japheth. 11 God saw that the earth was corrupt and full of lawlessness. 12 God looked at the earth: it was corrupt, for corrupt were the ways of all living things on earth.

13 God said to Noah, 'I have decided that the end has come for all living things, for the earth is full of lawlessness because of human beings. So I am now about to destroy them and the earth. 14 Make yourself an ark out of resinous wood. Make it of reeds and caulk it with pitch inside and out. 15 This is how to make it: the length of the ark is to be three hundred cubits, its breadth fifty cubits, and its height thirty cubits. 16 Make a roof to the ark, building it up to a cubit higher. Put the entrance in the side of the ark, which is to be made with lower, second and third decks.

17 'For my part I am going to send the flood, the waters, on earth, to destroy all living things having the breath of life under heaven; everything on earth is to perish. 18 But with you I shall establish my covenant and you will go aboard the ark, yourself, your sons, your wife, and your sons' wives along with you. 19 From all living creatures, from all living things, you must take two of each kind aboard the ark, to save their lives with yours; they must be a male and a female. 20 Of every species of bird, of every kind of animal and of every kind of creature that creeps along the ground, two must go with you so that their lives may be saved. 21 For your part, provide yourself with eatables of all kinds, and lay in a store of them, to serve as food for yourself and them.' 22 Noah did this; exactly as God commanded him, he did.

7 Yahweh said to Noah, 'Go aboard the ark, you and all your household, for you alone of your contemporaries do I see before me as an upright man. 2 Of every clean animal you must take seven pairs, a male and its female; of the unclean animals you must take one pair, a male and its female 3 (and of the birds of heaven, seven pairs, a male and its female), to preserve their species throughout the earth. 4 For in seven days' time I shall make it rain on earth for forty days and forty nights, and I shall wipe every creature I have made off the face of the earth.' 5 Noah did exactly as Yahweh commanded him.

6 Noah was six hundred years old when the flood came, the waters over the earth.

7 Noah with his sons, his wife, and his sons' wives boarded the ark to escape the waters of the flood. 8 (Of the clean animals and the animals that are not clean, of the birds and all that creeps along the ground, 9 one pair boarded the ark with Noah, one male and one female, as God had com-

seven days the waters of the flood came on the earth.

11 In the six hundredth year of Noah's life, in the second month, on the seventeenth day of the month, on that day all the fountains of the great deep burst forth, and the windows of the heavens were opened. 12 The rain fell on the earth forty days and forty nights. 13 On the very same day Noah with his sons, Shem and Ham and Japheth, and Noah's wife and the three wives of his sons entered the ark, 14 they and every wild animal of every kind, and all domestic animals of every kind, and every creeping thing that creeps on the earth, and every bird of every kind — every bird, every winged creature. 15 They went into the ark with Noah, two and two of all flesh in which there was the breath of life. 16 And those that entered, male and female of all flesh, went in as God had commanded him; and the LORD shut him in.

17 The flood continued forty days on the earth; and the waters increased, and bore up the ark, and it rose high above the earth. 18 The waters swelled and increased greatly on the earth; and the ark floated on the face of the waters. 19 The waters swelled so mightily on the earth that all the high mountains under the whole heaven were covered; 20 the waters swelled above the mountains, covering them fifteen cubits deep. 21 And all flesh died that moved on the earth, birds, domestic animals, wild animals, all swarming creatures that swarm on the earth, and all human beings; 22 everything on dry land in whose nostrils was the breath of life died. 23 He blotted out every living thing that was on the face of the ground, human beings and animals and creeping things and birds of the air; they were blotted out from the earth. Only Noah was left, and those that were with him in the ark. 24 And the waters swelled on the earth for one hundred fifty days.

8 But God remembered Noah and all the wild animals and all the domestic animals that were with him in the ark. And God made a wind blow over the earth, and the waters subsided; 2 the fountains of the deep and the windows of the heavens were closed, the rain from the heavens was restrained, 3 and the waters gradually receded from the earth. At the end of one hundred fifty days the waters had abated; 4 and in the seventh month, on the seventeenth day of the month, the ark came to rest on the mountains of Ararat. 5 The waters continued to abate until the tenth month; in the tenth month, on the first day of the month, the tops of the mountains appeared.

6 At the end of forty days Noah opened the window of the ark that he had made 7 and sent out the raven; and it went to and fro until the waters were dried up from the earth. 8 Then he sent out the dove from him, to see if the waters had subsided from the face of the ground; 9 but the dove found no place to set its foot, and it returned to him to the ark, for the waters were still on the face of the whole earth. So he put out his hand and took it and brought it into the ark with him. 10 He waited another seven days, and again he sent out the dove from the ark; 11 and the dove came back to him in the evening, and there in its beak was a freshly plucked olive leaf; so Noah knew that the waters had subsided from the earth. 12 Then he waited another seven days, and sent out the dove; and it did not return to him any more.

13 In the six hundred first year, in the first month, the first day of the month, the waters were dried up from the earth; and Noah removed the covering of the ark, and looked, and saw that the face of the ground was drying. 14 In the second month, on the twenty-seventh day of the month, the earth was dry. 15 Then God said to Noah, 16 "Go out of

10 At the end of seven days the water of the flood came over the earth. 11 In the year when Noah was six hundred years old, on the seventeenth day of the second month, that very day all the springs of the great deep burst out, the windows of the heavens were opened, 12 and rain fell on the earth for forty days and forty nights. 13 That was the day Noah went into the ark with his sons, Shem, Ham, and Japheth, his own wife, and his three sons' wives. 14 Wild animals of every kind, cattle of every kind, every kind of thing that creeps on the ground, and winged birds of every kind — 15 all living creatures came two by two to Noah in the ark. 16 Those which came were one male and one female of all living things; they came in as God had commanded Noah, and the LORD closed the door on him.

17 The flood continued on the earth for forty days, and the swelling waters lifted up the ark so that it rose high above the ground. 18 The ark floated on the surface of the swollen waters as they increased over the earth. 19 They increased more and more until they covered all the high mountains everywhere under heaven. 20 The water increased until the mountains were covered to a depth of fifteen cubits. 21 Every living thing that moved on earth perished: birds, cattle, wild animals, all creatures that swarm on the ground, and all human beings. 22 Everything on dry land died, everything that had the breath of life in its nostrils. 23 God wiped out every living creature that existed on earth, man and beast, creeping thing and bird; they were all wiped out over the whole earth, and only Noah and those who were with him in the ark survived.

24 When the water had increased over the earth for a hundred and fifty days,

8 1 God took thought for Noah and all the beasts and cattle with him in the ark, and he caused a wind to blow over the earth, so that the water began to subside. 2 The springs of the deep and the windows of the heavens were stopped up, the downpour from the skies was checked. 3 Gradually the water receded from the earth, and by the end of a hundred and fifty days it had abated. 4 On the seventeenth day of the seventh month the ark grounded on the mountains of Ararat. 5 The water continued to abate until the tenth month, and on the first day of the tenth month the tops of the mountains could be seen.

6 At the end of forty days Noah opened the hatch that he had made in the ark, 7 and sent out a raven; it continued flying to and fro until the water on the earth had dried up. 8 Then Noah sent out a dove to see whether the water on the earth had subsided. 9 But the dove found no place where she could settle because all the earth was under water, and so she came back to him in the ark. Noah reached out and caught her, and brought her into the ark. 10 He waited seven days more and again sent out the dove from the ark. 11 She came back to him towards evening with a freshly plucked olive leaf in her beak. Noah knew then that the water had subsided from the earth's surface. 12 He waited yet another seven days and, when he sent out the dove, she did not come back to him. 13 So it came about that, on the first day of the first month of his six hundred and first year, the water had dried up on the earth, and when Noah removed the hatch and looked out, he saw that the ground was dry. 14 By the twenty-seventh day of the second month the earth was dry, 15 and God spoke to Noah. 16 'Come out of

NEW AMERICAN BIBLE

seven days were over, the waters of the flood came upon the earth.

11 In the six hundredth year of Noah's life, in the second month, on the seventeenth day of the month: it was on that day that

All the fountains of the great abyss burst forth,
and the floodgates of the sky were opened.

12 For forty days and forty nights heavy rain poured down on the earth.

13 On the precise day named, Noah and his sons Shem, Ham and Japheth, and Noah's wife, and the three wives of Noah's sons had entered the ark, 14 together with every kind of wild beast, every kind of domestic animal, every kind of creeping thing of the earth, and every kind of bird. 15 Pairs of all creatures in which there was the breath of life entered the ark with Noah. 16 Those that entered were male and female, and of all species they came, as God had commanded Noah. Then the LORD shut him in.

17 The flood continued upon the earth for forty days. As the waters increased, they lifted the ark, so that it rose above the earth. 18 The swelling waters increased greatly, but the ark floated on the surface of the waters. 19 Higher and higher above the earth rose the waters, until all the highest mountains everywhere were submerged, 20 the crest rising fifteen cubits higher than the submerged mountains. 21 All creatures that stirred on earth perished: birds, cattle, wild animals, and all that swarmed on the earth, as well as all mankind. 22 Everything on dry land with the faintest breath of life in its nostrils died out. 23 The LORD wiped out every living thing on earth: man and cattle, the creeping things and the birds of the air; all were wiped out from the earth. Only Noah and those with him in the ark were left.

8 7, 24 The waters maintained their crest over the earth for one hundred and fifty days, 1 and then God remembered Noah and all the animals, wild and tame, that were with him in the ark. So God made a wind sweep over the earth, and the waters began to subside. 2 The fountains of the abyss and the floodgates of the sky were closed, and the downpour from the sky was held back. 3 Gradually the waters receded from the earth. At the end of one hundred and fifty days, the waters had so diminished 4 that, in the seventh month, on the seventeenth day of the month, the ark came to rest on the mountains of Ararat. 5 The waters continued to diminish until the tenth month, and on the first day of the tenth month the tops of the mountains appeared.

6 At the end of forty days Noah opened the hatch he had made in the ark, 7 and he sent out a raven, to see if the waters had lessened on the earth. It flew back and forth until the waters dried off from the earth. 8 Then he sent out a dove, to see if the waters had lessened on the earth. 9 But the dove could find no place to alight and perch, and it returned to him in the ark, for there was water all over the earth. Putting out his hand, he caught the dove and drew it back to him inside the ark. 10 He waited seven days more and again sent the dove out from the ark. 11 In the evening the dove came back to him, and there in its bill was a plucked-off olive leaf! So Noah knew that the waters had lessened on the earth. 12 He waited still another seven days and then released the dove once more; and this time it did not come back.

13 In the six hundred and first year of Noah's life, in the first month, on the first day of the month, the water began to dry up on the earth. Noah then removed the covering of the ark and saw that the surface of the ground was drying up. 14 In the second month, on the twenty-seventh day of the month, the earth was dry.

15 Then God said to Noah: 16 "Go out of the ark, together

NEW JERUSALEM BIBLE

manded Noah.) 10 Seven days later the waters of the flood appeared on earth.

11 In the six hundredth year of Noah's life, in the second month, and on the seventeenth day of the month, that very day all the springs of the great deep burst through, and the sluices of heaven opened. 12 And heavy rain fell on earth for forty days and forty nights.

13 That very day Noah and his sons Shem, Ham and Japheth boarded the ark, with Noah's wife and the three wives of his sons, 14 and with them every species of wild animal, every species of cattle, every species of creeping things that creep along the ground, every species of bird, everything that flies, everything with wings. 15 One pair of all that was alive and had the breath of life boarded the ark with Noah, 16 and those that went aboard were a male and female of all that was alive, as God had commanded him.

Then Yahweh shut him in.

17 The flood lasted forty days on earth. The waters swelled, lifting the ark until it floated off the ground. 18 The waters rose, swelling higher above the ground, and the ark drifted away over the waters. 19 The waters rose higher and higher above the ground until all the highest mountains under the whole of heaven were submerged. 20 The waters reached their peak fifteen cubits above the submerged mountains. 21 And all living things that stirred on earth perished; birds, cattle, wild animals, all the creatures swarming over the earth, and all human beings. 22 Everything with the least breath of life in its nostrils, everything on dry land, died. 23 Every living thing on the face of the earth was wiped out, people, animals, creeping things and birds; they were wiped off the earth and only Noah was left, and those with him in the ark. 24 The waters maintained their level on earth for a hundred and fifty days.

8 But God had Noah in mind, and all the wild animals and all the cattle that were with him in the ark. God sent a wind across the earth and the waters began to subside. 2 The springs of the deep and the sluices of heaven were stopped up and the heavy rain from heaven was held back. 3 Little by little, the waters ebbed from the earth. After a hundred and fifty days the waters fell, 4 and in the seventh month, on the seventeenth day of the month, the ark came to rest on the mountains of Ararat. 5 The waters gradually fell until the tenth month when, on the first day of the tenth month, the mountain tops appeared.

6 At the end of forty days Noah opened the window he had made in the ark 7 and released a raven, which flew back and forth as it waited for the waters to dry up on earth. 8 He then released a dove, to see whether the waters were receding from the surface of the earth. 9 But the dove, finding nowhere to perch, returned to him in the ark, for there was water over the whole surface of the earth; putting out his hand he took hold of it and brought it back into the ark with him. 10 After waiting seven more days, he again released the dove from the ark. 11 In the evening, the dove came back to him and there in its beak was a freshly-picked olive leaf! So Noah realised that the waters were receding from the earth. 12 After waiting seven more days, he released the dove, and now it returned to him no more.

13 It was in the six hundred and first year of Noah's life, in the first month and on the first of the month, that the waters began drying out on earth. Noah lifted back the hatch of the ark and looked out. The surface of the ground was dry!

14 In the second month, on the twenty-seventh day of the month, the earth was dry.

15 Then God said to Noah, 16 'Come out of the ark, you,

7, 24: This verse belongs to chapter 7 but its contents properly introduce chapter 8.

NEW REVISED STANDARD VERSION

the ark, you and your wife, and your sons and your sons' wives with you. 17 Bring out with you every living thing that is with you of all flesh — birds and animals and every creeping thing that creeps on the earth — so that they may abound on the earth, and be fruitful and multiply on the earth." 18 So Noah went out with his sons and his wife and his sons' wives. 19 And every animal, every creeping thing, and every bird, everything that moves on the earth, went out of the ark by families.

20 Then Noah built an altar to the LORD, and took of every clean animal and of every clean bird, and offered burnt offerings on the altar. 21 And when the LORD smelled the pleasing odor, the LORD said in his heart, "I will never again curse the ground because of humankind, for the inclination of the human heart is evil from youth; nor will I ever again destroy every living creature as I have done.

22   As long as the earth endures,
     seedtime and harvest, cold and heat,
     summer and winter, day and night,
     shall not cease."

9 God blessed Noah and his sons, and said to them, "Be fruitful and multiply, and fill the earth. 2 The fear and dread of you shall rest on every animal of the earth, and on every bird of the air, on everything that creeps on the ground, and on all the fish of the sea; into your hand they are delivered. 3 Every moving thing that lives shall be food for you; and just as I gave you the green plants, I give you everything. 4 Only, you shall not eat flesh with its life, that is, its blood. 5 For your own lifeblood I will surely require a reckoning: from every animal I will require it and from human beings, each one for the blood of another, I will require a reckoning for human life.

6   Whoever sheds the blood of a human,
     by a human shall that person's blood be shed;
    for in his own image
     God made humankind.

7 And you, be fruitful and multiply, abound on the earth and multiply in it."

8 Then God said to Noah and to his sons with him, 9 "As for me, I am establishing my covenant with you and your descendants after you, 10 and with every living creature that is with you, the birds, the domestic animals, and every animal of the earth with you, as many as came out of the ark. w 11 I establish my covenant with you, that never again shall all flesh be cut off by the waters of a flood, and never again shall there be a flood to destroy the earth." 12 God said, "This is the sign of the covenant that I make between me and you and every living creature that is with you, for all future generations: 13 I have set my bow in the clouds, and it shall be a sign of the covenant between me and the earth. 14 When I bring clouds over the earth and the bow is seen in the clouds, 15 I will remember my covenant that is between me and you and every living creature of all flesh; and the waters shall never again become a flood to destroy all flesh. 16 When the bow is in the clouds, I will see it and remember the everlasting covenant between God and every living creature of all flesh that is on the earth." 17 God said to Noah, "This is the sign of the covenant that I have established between me and all flesh that is on the earth."

18 The sons of Noah who went out of the ark were Shem, Ham, and Japheth. Ham was the father of Canaan. 19 These three were the sons of Noah; and from these the whole earth was peopled.

REVISED ENGLISH BIBLE

the ark together with your wife, your sons, and their wives,' he said. 17 'Bring out every living creature that is with you, live things of every kind, birds, beasts, and creeping things, and let them spread over the earth and be fruitful and increase on it.' 18 So Noah came out with his sons, his wife, and his sons' wives, 19 and all the animals, creeping things, and birds; everything that moves on the ground came out of the ark, one kind after another.

20 Noah built an altar to the LORD and, taking beasts and birds of every kind that were ritually clean, he offered them as whole-offerings on it. 21 When the LORD smelt the soothing odour, he said within himself, 'Never again shall I put the earth under a curse because of mankind, however evil their inclination may be from their youth upwards, nor shall I ever again kill all living creatures, as I have just done.

22 'As long as the earth lasts,
    seedtime and harvest, cold and heat,
    summer and winter, day and night,
    they will never cease.'

9 GOD blessed Noah and his sons; he said to them, 'Be fruitful and increase in numbers, and fill the earth. 2 Fear and dread of you will come on all the animals on earth, on all the birds of the air, on everything that moves on the ground, and on all fish in the sea; they are made subject to you. 3 Every creature that lives and moves will be food for you; I give them all to you, as I have given you every green plant. 4 But you must never eat flesh with its life still in it, that is the blood. 5 And further, for your life-blood I shall demand satisfaction; from every animal I shall require it, and from human beings also I shall require satisfaction for the death of their fellows.

6 'Anyone who sheds human blood,
    for that human being his blood will be shed;
   because in the image of God
    has God made human beings.

7 'Be fruitful, then, and increase in number; people the earth and rule over it.'

8 God said to Noah and his sons: 9 'I am now establishing my covenant with you and with your descendants after you, 10 and with every living creature that is with you, all birds and cattle, all the animals with you on earth, all that have come out of the ark. 11 I shall sustain my covenant with you: never again will all living creatures be destroyed by the waters of a flood, never again will there be a flood to lay waste the earth.'

12 God said, 'For all generations to come, this is the sign which I am giving of the covenant between myself and you and all living creatures with you:

13 My bow I set in the clouds
    to be a sign of the covenant
    between myself and the earth.
14 When I bring clouds over the earth,
    the rainbow will appear in the clouds.

15 'Then I shall remember the covenant which I have made with you and with all living creatures, and never again will the waters become a flood to destroy all creation. 16 Whenever the bow appears in the cloud, I shall see it and remember the everlasting covenant between God and living creatures of every kind on earth.' 17 So God said to Noah, 'This is the sign of the covenant which I have established with all that lives on earth.'

18 The sons of Noah who came out of the ark were Shem, Ham, and Japheth; Ham was the father of Canaan. 19 These three were the sons of Noah, and their descendants spread over the whole earth.

---

w Gk: Heb adds *every animal of the earth*

9:7 **rule:** *prob. rdg, cp. 1:28; Heb.* increase.

NEW AMERICAN BIBLE

NEW JERUSALEM BIBLE

with your wife and your sons and your sons' wives. 17 Bring out with you every living thing that is with you — all bodily creatures, be they birds or animals or creeping things of the earth — and let them abound on the earth, breeding and multiplying on it." 18 So Noah came out, together with his wife and his sons and his sons' wives; 19 and all the animals, wild and tame, all the birds, and all the creeping creatures of the earth left the ark, one kind after another.

20 Then Noah built an altar to the LORD, and choosing from every clean animal and every clean bird, he offered holocausts on the altar. 21 When the LORD smelled the sweet odor, he said to himself: "Never again will I doom the earth because of man, since the desires of man's heart are evil from the start; nor will I ever again strike down all living beings, as I have done.

22 As long as the earth lasts,
seedtime and harvest,
cold and heat,
Summer and winter,
and day and night
shall not cease."

9 God blessed Noah and his sons and said to them: "Be fertile and multiply and fill the earth. 2 Dread fear of you shall come upon all the animals of the earth and all the birds of the air, upon all the creatures that move about on the ground and all the fishes of the sea; into your power they are delivered. 3 Every creature that is alive shall be yours to eat; I give them all to you as I did the green plants. 4 Only flesh with its lifeblood still in it you shall not eat. 5 For your own lifeblood, too, I will demand an accounting: from every animal I will demand it, and from man in regard to his fellow man I will demand an accounting for human life.

6 If anyone sheds the blood of man,
by man shall his blood be shed;
For in the image of God
has man been made.

7 Be fertile, then, and multiply; abound on earth and subdue it."

8 God said to Noah and to his sons with him: 9 "See, I am now establishing my covenant with you and your descendants after you 10 and with every living creature that was with you: all the birds, and the various tame and wild animals that were with you and came out of the ark. 11 I will establish my covenant with you, that never again shall all bodily creatures be destroyed by the waters of a flood; there shall not be another flood to devastate the earth." 12 God added: "This is the sign that I am giving for all ages to come, of the covenant between me and you and every living creature with you: 13 I set my bow in the clouds to serve as a sign of the covenant between me and the earth. 14 When I bring clouds over the earth, and the bow appears in the clouds, 15 I will recall the covenant I have made between me and you and all living beings, so that the waters shall never again become a flood to destroy all mortal beings. 16 As the bow appears in the clouds, I will see it and recall the everlasting covenant that I have established between God and all living beings — all mortal creatures that are on earth." 17 God told Noah: "This is the sign of the covenant I have established between me and all mortal creatures that are on earth."

18 The sons of Noah who came out of the ark were Shem, Ham and Japheth. (Ham was the father of Canaan.) 19 These three were the sons of Noah, and from them the whole earth was peopled.

your wife, your sons, and your sons' wives with you. 17 Bring out all the animals with you, all living things, the birds, the cattle and all the creeping things that creep along the ground, for them to swarm on earth, for them to breed and multiply on earth.' 18 So Noah came out with his sons, his wife, and his sons' wives. 19 And all the wild animals, all the cattle, all the birds and all the creeping things that creep along the ground, came out of the ark, one species after another.

20 Then Noah built an altar to Yahweh and, choosing from all the clean animals and all the clean birds he presented burnt offerings on the altar. 21 Yahweh smelt the pleasing smell and said to himself, 'Never again will I curse the earth because of human beings, because their heart contrives evil from their infancy. Never again will I strike down every living thing as I have done.

22 As long as earth endures,
seed-time and harvest,
cold and heat,
summer and winter,
day and night
will never cease.'

9 God blessed Noah and his sons and said to them, 'Breed, multiply and fill the earth. 2 Be the terror and the dread of all the animals on land and all the birds of heaven, of everything that moves on land and all the fish of the sea; they are placed in your hands. 3 Every living thing that moves will be yours to eat, no less than the foliage of the plants. I give you everything, 4 with this exception: you must not eat flesh with life, that is to say blood, in it. 5 And I shall demand account of your life-blood, too. I shall demand it of every animal, and of man. Of man as regards his fellow-man, I shall demand account for human life.

6 He who sheds the blood of man,
by man shall his blood be shed,
for in the image of God
was man created.

7 Be fruitful then and multiply,
teem over the earth and subdue it!'

8 God spoke as follows to Noah and his sons, 9 'I am now establishing my covenant with you and with your descendants to come, 10 and with every living creature that was with you: birds, cattle and every wild animal with you; everything that came out of the ark, every living thing on earth. 11 And I shall maintain my covenant with you: that never again shall all living things be destroyed by the waters of a flood, nor shall there ever again be a flood to devastate the earth.'

12 'And this', God said, 'is the sign of the covenant which I now make between myself and you and every living creature with you for all ages to come: 13 I now set my bow in the clouds and it will be the sign of the covenant between me and the earth. 14 When I gather the clouds over the earth and the bow appears in the clouds, 15 I shall recall the covenant between myself and you and every living creature, in a word all living things, and never again will the waters become a flood to destroy all living things. 16 When the bow is in the clouds I shall see it and call to mind the eternal covenant between God and every living creature on earth, that is, all living things.'

17 'That', God told Noah, 'is the sign of the covenant I have established between myself and all living things on earth.'

18 The sons of Noah who came out of the ark were Shem, Ham and Japheth — Ham being the father of Canaan. 19 These three were Noah's sons, and from these the whole earth was peopled.

NEW REVISED STANDARD VERSION

20 Noah, a man of the soil, was the first to plant a vineyard. 21 He drank some of the wine and became drunk, and he lay uncovered in his tent. 22 And Ham, the father of Canaan, saw the nakedness of his father, and told his two brothers outside. 23 Then Shem and Japheth took a garment, laid it on both their shoulders, and walked backward and covered the nakedness of their father; their faces were turned away, and they did not see their father's nakedness. 24 When Noah awoke from his wine and knew what his youngest son had done to him, 25 he said,

"Cursed be Canaan;
    lowest of slaves shall he be to his brothers."

26 He also said,

"Blessed by the LORD my God be Shem;
    and let Canaan be his slave.
27 May God make space for*x* Japheth,
    and let him live in the tents of Shem;
    and let Canaan be his slave."

28 After the flood Noah lived three hundred fifty years. 29 All the days of Noah were nine hundred fifty years; and he died.

10 These are the descendants of Noah's sons, Shem, Ham, and Japheth; children were born to them after the flood. 2 The descendants of Japheth: Gomer, Magog, Madai, Javan, Tubal, Meshech, and Tiras. 3 The descendants of Gomer: Ashkenaz, Riphath, and Togarmah. 4 The descendants of Javan: Elishah, Tarshish, Kittim, and Rodanim.*y* 5 From these the coastland peoples spread. These are the descendants of Japheth*z* in their lands, with their own language, by their families, in their nations.

6 The descendants of Ham: Cush, Egypt, Put, and Canaan. 7 The descendants of Cush: Seba, Havilah, Sabtah, Raamah, and Sabteca. The descendants of Raamah: Sheba and Dedan. 8 Cush became the father of Nimrod; he was the first on earth to become a mighty warrior. 9 He was a mighty hunter before the LORD; therefore it is said, "Like Nimrod a mighty hunter before the LORD." 10 The beginning of his kingdom was Babel, Erech, and Accad, all of them in the land of Shinar. 11 From that land he went into Assyria, and built Nineveh, Rehoboth-ir, Calah, and 12 Resen between Nineveh and Calah; that is the great city. 13 Egypt became the father of Ludim, Anamim, Lehabim, Naphtuhim, 14 Pathrusim, Casluhim, and Caphtorim, from which the Philistines come.*a*

15 Canaan became the father of Sidon his firstborn, and Heth, 16 and the Jebusites, the Amorites, the Girgashites, 17 the Hivites, the Arkites, the Sinites, 18 the Arvadites, the Zemarites, and the Hamathites. Afterward the families of the Canaanites spread abroad. 19 And the territory of the Canaanites extended from Sidon, in the direction of Gerar, as far as Gaza, and in the direction of Sodom, Gomorrah, Admah, and Zeboiim, as far as Lasha. 20 These are the descendants of Ham, by their families, their languages, their lands, and their nations.

21 To Shem also, the father of all the children of Eber, the elder brother of Japheth, children were born. 22 The descendants of Shem: Elam, Asshur, Arpachshad, Lud, and

REVISED ENGLISH BIBLE

20 Noah, who was the first tiller of the soil, planted a vineyard. 21 He drank so much of the wine that he became drunk and lay naked inside his tent. 22 Ham, father of Canaan, saw his father naked, and went out and told his two brothers. 23 Shem and Japheth took a cloak, put it on their shoulders, and, walking backwards, covered their father's naked body. They kept their faces averted, so that they did not see his nakedness. 24 When Noah woke from his drunkenness and learnt what his youngest son had done to him, 25 he said:

'Cursed be Canaan!
    Most servile of slaves
    shall he be to his brothers.'

26 And he went on:

'Bless, O LORD,
    the tents of Shem;
    may Canaan be his slave.
27 May God extend Japheth's boundaries,
    let him dwell in the tents of Shem,
    may Canaan be his slave.'

28 After the flood Noah lived for three hundred and fifty years; 29 he was nine hundred and fifty years old when he died.

10 These are the descendants of Noah's sons, Shem, Ham, and Japheth, the sons born to them after the flood. 2 The sons of Japheth: Gomer, Magog, Madai, Javan, Tubal, Meshech, and Tiras. 3 The sons of Gomer: Ashkenaz, Riphath, and Togarmah. 4 The sons of Javan: Elishah, Tarshish, Kittim, and Rodanim. 5 From these the peoples of the coasts and islands separated into their own countries, each with their own language, family by family, nation by nation.

6 The sons of Ham: Cush, Mizraim, Put, and Canaan. 7 The sons of Cush: Seba, Havilah, Sabtah, Raamah, and Sabtecha. The sons of Raamah: Sheba and Dedan. 8 Cush was the father of Nimrod, who began to be known on earth for his might. 9 He was outstanding as a mighty hunter — as the saying goes, 'like Nimrod, outstanding as a mighty hunter'. 10 At first his kingdom consisted of Babel, Erech, and Accad, all of them in the land of Shinar. 11 From that land he migrated to Assyria and built Nineveh, Rehoboth-ir, Calah, 12 and Resen, a great city between Nineveh and Calah. 13 From Mizraim sprang the Ludim, Anamites, Lehabites, Naphtuhites, 14 Pathrusites, Casluhites, and the Caphtorites, from whom the Philistines were descended.

15 Canaan was the father of Sidon, who was his eldest son, and Heth, 16 the Jebusites, the Amorites, the Girgashites, 17 the Hivites, the Arkites, the Sinites, 18 the Arvadites, the Zemarites, and the Hamathites. Later the Canaanites spread, 19 and then the Canaanite border ran from Sidon towards Gerar all the way to Gaza; then all the way to Sodom and Gomorrah, Admah, and Zeboyim as far as Lasha. 20 These were the sons of Ham, by families and languages, with their countries and nations.

21 Sons were born also to Shem, elder brother of Japheth, the ancestor of all the sons of Eber. 22 The sons of Shem: Elam, Asshur, Arphaxad, Lud, and Aram. 23 The sons of

---

x Heb *yapht*, a play on *Japheth*   *y* Heb Mss Sam Gk See 1 Chr 1:7: MT *Dodanim*   *z* Compare verses 20, 31. Heb lacks *These are the descendants of Japheth*   *a* Cn: Heb *Casluhim, from which the Philistines come, and Caphtorim*

9:26 **Bless . . . Shem:** *prob. rdg;* Heb. Blessed is the LORD the God of Shem.   9:27 **extend:** *Heb.* japht.   10:2 **Javan:** *or* Greece.   10:4 **Tarshish, Kittim:** *or* Tarshish of the Kittians. **Rodanim:** *so Samar.; Heb.* Dodanim.   10:6 **Mizraim:** *or* Egypt.   10:14 **and the Caphtorites:** *transposed from end of verse; cp. Amos 9:7.*   10:15 **Heth:** *or* the Hittites.

NEW AMERICAN BIBLE

20 Now Noah, a man of the soil, was the first to plant a vineyard. 21 When he drank some of the wine, he became drunk and lay naked inside his tent. 22 Ham, the father of Canaan, saw his father's nakedness, and he told his two brothers outside about it. 23 Shem and Japheth, however, took a robe, and holding it on their backs, they walked backward and covered their father's nakedness; since their faces were turned the other way, they did not see their father's nakedness. 24 When Noah woke up from his drunkenness and learned what his youngest son had done to him, 25 he said:

"Cursed be Canaan!
The lowest of slaves
shall he be to his brothers."

26 He also said:

"Blessed be the LORD, the God of Shem!
Let Canaan be his slave.

27 May God expand Japheth,
so that he dwells among the tents of Shem;
and let Canaan be his slave."

28 Noah lived three hundred and fifty years after the flood. 29 The whole lifetime of Noah was nine hundred and fifty years; then he died.

10 These are the descendants of Noah's sons, Shem, Ham and Japheth, to whom sons were born after the flood.

2 The descendants of Japheth:
Gomer, Magog, Madai, Javan, Tubal, Meschech and Tiras.

3 The descendants of Gomer:
Ashkenaz, Riphath and Togarmah.

4 The descendants of Javan:
Elishah, Tarshish, the Kittim and the Rodanim.

5 These are the descendants of Japheth, and from them sprang the maritime nations, in their respective lands — each with its own language — by their clans within their nations.

6 The descendants of Ham:
Cush, Mizraim, Put and Canaan.

7 The descendants of Cush:
Seba, Havilah, Sabtah, Raamah and Sabteca.
The descendants of Raamah: Sheba and Dedan.

8 Cush became the father of Nimrod, who was the first potentate on earth. 9 He was a mighty hunter by the grace of the LORD; hence the saying, "Like Nimrod, a mighty hunter by the grace of the LORD." 10 The chief cities of his kingdom were Babylon, Erech and Accad, all of them in the land of Shinar. 11 From that land he went forth to Asshur, where he built Nineveh, Rehoboth-Ir and Calah, 12 as well as Resen, between Nineveh and Calah, the latter being the principal city.

13 Mizraim became the father of the Ludim, the Anamim, the Lehabim, the Naphtuhim, 14 the Pathrusim, the Casluhim, and the Caphtorim from whom the Philistines sprang.

15 Canaan became the father of Sidon, his first-born, and of Heth; 16 also of the Jebusites, the Amorites, the Girgashites, 17 the Hivites, the Arkites, the Sinites, 18 the Arvadites, the Zemarites and the Hamathites. Afterward, the clans of the Canaanites spread out, 19 so that the Canaanite borders extended from Sidon all the way to Gerar, near Gaza, and all the way to Sodom, Gomorrah, Admah and Zeboiim, near Lasha.

20 These are the descendants of Ham, according to their clans and languages, by their lands and nations.

21 To Shem also, Japheth's oldest brother and the ancestor of all the children of Eber, sons were born.

22 The descendants of Shem:
Elam, Asshur, Arpachshad, Lud and Aram.

NEW JERUSALEM BIBLE

20 Noah, a tiller of the soil, was the first to plant the vine. 21 He drank some of the wine, and while he was drunk, he lay uncovered in his tent. 22 Ham, father of Canaan, saw his father naked and told his two brothers outside. 23 Shem and Japheth took a cloak and they both put it over their shoulders, and walking backwards, covered their father's nakedness; they kept their faces turned away, and they did not look at their father naked. 24 When Noah awoke from his stupor he learned what his youngest son had done to him, 25 and said:

Accursed be Canaan,
he shall be
his brothers' meanest slave.

26 He added:

Blessed be Yahweh, God of Shem,
let Canaan be his slave!

27 May God make space for Japheth,
may he live in the tents of Shem,
and let Canaan be his slave!

28 After the flood Noah lived three hundred and fifty years. 29 In all, Noah's life lasted nine hundred and fifty years; then he died.

10 These are the descendants of Noah's sons, Shem, Ham and Japheth, to whom sons were born after the flood:

2 Japheth's sons: Gomer, Magog, the Medes, Javan, Tubal, Meshech, Tiras. 3 Gomer's sons: Ashkenaz, Riphath, Togarmah. 4 Javan's sons: Elishah, Tarshish, the Kittim, the Dananites. 5 From these came the dispersal to the islands of the nations.

These were Japheth's sons, in their respective countries, each with its own language, by clan and nation.

6 Ham's sons: Cush, Mizraim, Put, Canaan. 7 Cush's sons: Seba, Havilah, Sabtah, Raamah, Sabteca. Raamah's sons: Sheba, Dedan.

8 Cush fathered Nimrod who was the first potentate on earth. 9 He was a mighty hunter in the eyes of Yahweh, hence the saying, 'Like Nimrod, a mighty hunter in the eyes of Yahweh'. 10 The mainstays of his empire were Babel, Erech and Accad, all of them in the land of Shinar. 11 From this country came Asshur, and he built Nineveh, Rehoboth-Ir, Calah, 12 and Resen between Nineveh and Calah (this being the capital).

13 Mizraim fathered the people of Lud, of Anam, Lehab, Naphtuh, 14 Pathros, Casluh and Caphtor, from which the Philistines came.

15 Canaan fathered Sidon, his first-born, then Heth, 16 and the Jebusites, the Amorites, Girgashites, 17 Hivites, Arkites, Sinites, 18 Arvadites, Zemarites and Hamathites. Later, the Canaanite clans spread out. 19 The Canaanite frontier stretched from Sidon all the way to Gerar near Gaza, and all the way to Sodom, Gomorrah, Admah and Zeboiim near Lesha.

20 These were Ham's sons, by clans and languages, by countries and nations.

21 Shem too fathered sons, being ancestor of all the sons of Eber and Japheth's elder brother.

22 Shem's sons: Elam, Asshur, Arpachshad, Lud, Aram.

NEW REVISED STANDARD VERSION

Aram. 23 The descendants of Aram: Uz, Hul, Gether, and Mash. 24 Arphachshad became the father of Shelah; and Shelah became the father of Eber. 25 To Eber were born two sons: the name of the one was Peleg,*b* for in his days the earth was divided, and his brother's name was Joktan. 26 Joktan became the father of Almodad, Sheleph, Hazarmaveth, Jerah, 27 Hadoram, Uzal, Diklah, 28 Obal, Abimael, Sheba, 29 Ophir, Havilah, and Jobab; all these were the descendants of Joktan. 30 The territory in which they lived extended from Mesha in the direction of Sephar, the hill country of the east. 31 These are the descendants of Shem, by their families, their languages, their lands, and their nations.

32 These are the families of Noah's sons, according to their genealogies, in their nations; and from these the nations spread abroad on the earth after the flood.

11 Now the whole earth had one language and the same words. 2 And as they migrated from the east,*c* they came upon a plain in the land of Shinar and settled there. 3 And they said to one another, "Come, let us make bricks, and burn them thoroughly." And they had brick for stone, and bitumen for mortar. 4 Then they said, "Come, let us build ourselves a city, and a tower with its top in the heavens, and let us make a name for ourselves; otherwise we shall be scattered abroad upon the face of the whole earth." 5 The LORD came down to see the city and the tower, which mortals had built. 6 And the LORD said, "Look, they are one people, and they have all one language; and this is only the beginning of what they will do; nothing that they propose to do will now be impossible for them. 7 Come, let us go down, and confuse their language there, so that they will not understand one another's speech." 8 So the LORD scattered them abroad from there over the face of all the earth, and they left off building the city. 9 Therefore it was called Babel, because there the LORD confused*d* the language of all the earth; and from there the LORD scattered them abroad over the face of all the earth.

10 These are the descendants of Shem. When Shem was one hundred years old, he became the father of Arpachshad two years after the flood; 11 and Shem lived after the birth of Arpachshad five hundred years, and had other sons and daughters.

12 When Arpachshad had lived thirty-five years, he became the father of Shelah; 13 and Arpachshad lived after the birth of Shelah four hundred three years, and had other sons and daughters.

14 When Shelah had lived thirty years, he became the father of Eber; 15 and Shelah lived after the birth of Eber four hundred three years, and had other sons and daughters.

16 When Eber had lived thirty-four years, he became the father of Peleg; 17 and Eber lived after the birth of Peleg four hundred thirty years, and had other sons and daughters.

18 When Peleg had lived thirty years, he became the father of Reu; 19 and Peleg lived after the birth of Reu two hundred nine years, and had other sons and daughters.

20 When Reu had lived thirty-two years, he became the father of Serug; 21 and Reu lived after the birth of Serug two hundred seven years, and had other sons and daughters.

22 When Serug had lived thirty years, he became the father of Nahor; 23 and Serug lived after the birth of Nahor two hundred years, and had other sons and daughters.

24 When Nahor had lived twenty-nine years, he became the father of Terah; 25 and Nahor lived after the birth of Terah one hundred nineteen years, and had other sons and daughters.

26 When Terah had lived seventy years, he became the father of Abram, Nahor, and Haran.

REVISED ENGLISH BIBLE

Aram: Uz, Hul, Gether, and Mash. 24 Arphaxad was the father of Shelah, and Shelah the father of Eber. 25 Eber had two sons: one was named Peleg, because in his time the earth was divided; and his brother's name was Joktan. 26 Joktan was the father of Almodad, Sheleph, Hazarmoth, Jerah, 27 Hadoram, Uzal, Diklah, 28 Obal, Abimael, Sheba, 29 Ophir, Havilah, and Jobab. All these were sons of Joktan. 30 They lived in the eastern hill-country, from Mesha all the way to Sephar. 31 These were the sons of Shem, by families and languages, with their countries and nations.

32 These were the families of the sons of Noah according to their genealogies, nation by nation; and from them came the separate nations on earth after the flood.

11 THERE was a time when all the world spoke a single language and used the same words. 2 As people journeyed in the east, they came upon a plain in the land of Shinar and settled there. 3 They said to one another, 'Come, let us make bricks and bake them hard'; they used bricks for stone, and bitumen for mortar. 4 Then they said, 'Let us build ourselves a city and a tower with its top in the heavens and make a name for ourselves, or we shall be dispersed over the face of the earth.' 5 The LORD came down to see the city and tower which they had built, 6 and he said, 'Here they are, one people with a single language, and now they have started to do this; from now on nothing they have a mind to do will be beyond their reach. 7 Come, let us go down there and confuse their language, so that they will not understand what they say to one another.' 8 So the LORD dispersed them from there all over the earth, and they left off building the city. 9 That is why it is called Babel, because there the LORD made a babble of the language of the whole world. It was from that place the LORD scattered people over the face of the earth.

10 These are the descendants of Shem. Shem was a hundred years old when he begot Arphaxad, two years after the flood. 11 After the birth of Arphaxad he lived five hundred years, and had other sons and daughters. 12 Arphaxad was thirty-five years old when he begot Shelah. 13 After the birth of Shelah he lived four hundred and three years, and had other sons and daughters.

14 Shelah was thirty years old when he begot Eber. 15 After the birth of Eber he lived four hundred and three years, and had other sons and daughters.

16 Eber was thirty-four years old when he begot Peleg. 17 After the birth of Peleg he lived four hundred and thirty years, and had other sons and daughters.

18 Peleg was thirty years old when he begot Reu. 19 After the birth of Reu he lived two hundred and nine years, and had other sons and daughters.

20 Reu was thirty-two years old when he begot Serug. 21 After the birth of Serug he lived two hundred and seven years, and had other sons and daughters.

22 Serug was thirty years old when he begot Nahor. 23 After the birth of Nahor he lived two hundred years, and had other sons and daughters.

24 Nahor was twenty-nine years old when he begot Terah. 25 After the birth of Terah he lived a hundred and nineteen years, and had other sons and daughters.

26 Terah was seventy years old when he begot Abram, Nahor, and Haran.

---

b That is *Division*   *c* Or *migrated eastward*   *d* Heb *balal*, meaning to confuse

10:25 **Peleg:** *that is* Division.   11:1 **the same:** *or* few.
11:9 **Babel:** *that is* Babylon.

NEW AMERICAN BIBLE

23 The descendants of Aram:
Uz, Hul, Gether and Mash.
24 Arpachshad became the father of Shelah, and Shelah became the father of Eber. 25 To Eber two sons were born: the name of the first was Peleg, for in his time the world was divided; and the name of his brother was Joktan.
26 Joktan became the father of Almodad, Sheleph, Hazarmaveth, Jerah, 27 Hadoram, Uzal, Diklah, 28 Obal, Abimael, Sheba 29 Ophir, Havilah and Jobab. All these were descendants of Joktan. 30 Their settlements extended all the way to Sephar, the eastern hill country.
31 These are the descendants of Shem, according to their clans and languages, by their lands and nations.
32 These are the groupings of Noah's sons, according to their origins and by their nations. From these the other nations of the earth branched out after the flood.

11 The whole world spoke the same language, using the same words. 2 While men were migrating in the east, they came upon a valley in the land of Shinar and settled there. 3 They said to one another, "Come, let us mold bricks and harden them with fire." They used bricks for stone, and bitumen for mortar. 4 Then they said, "Come, let us build ourselves a city and a tower with its top in the sky, and so make a name for ourselves; otherwise we shall be scattered all over the earth."
5 The LORD came down to see the city and the tower that the men had built. 6 Then the LORD said: "If now, while they are one people, all speaking the same language, they have started to do this, nothing will later stop them from doing whatever they presume to do. 7 Let us then go down and there confuse their language, so that one will not understand what another says." 8 Thus the LORD scattered them from there all over the earth, and they stopped building the city.
9 That is why it was called Babel, because there the LORD confused the speech of all the world. It was from that place that he scattered them all over the earth.
10 This is the record of the descendants of Shem. When Shem was one hundred years old, he became the father of Arpachshad, two years after the flood. 11 Shem lived five hundred years after the birth of Arpachshad, and he had other sons and daughters.
12 When Arpachshad was thirty-five years old, he became the father of Shelah. 13 Arpachshad lived four hundred and three years after the birth of Shelah, and he had other sons and daughters.
14 When Shelah was thirty years old, he became the father of Eber. 15 Shelah lived four hundred and three years after the birth of Eber, and he had other sons and daughters.
16 When Eber was thirty-four years old, he became the father of Peleg. 17 Eber lived four hundred and thirty years after the birth of Peleg, and he had other sons and daughters.
18 When Peleg was thirty years old, he became the father of Reu. 19 Peleg lived two hundred and nine years after the birth of Reu, and he had other sons and daughters.
20 When Reu was thirty-two years old, he became the father of Serug. 21 Reu lived two hundred and seven years after the birth of Serug, and he had other sons and daughters.
22 When Serug was thirty years old, he became the father of Nahor. 23 Serug lived two hundred years after the birth of Nahor, and he had other sons and daughters.
24 When Nahor was twenty-nine years old, he became the father of Terah. 25 Nahor lived one hundred and nineteen years after the birth of Terah, and he had other sons and daughters.
26 When Terah was seventy years old, he became the father of Abram, Nahor and Haran.

NEW JERUSALEM BIBLE

23 Aram's sons: Uz, Hul, Gether and Mash.
24 Arpachshad fathered Shelah, and Shelah fathered Eber. 25 To Eber were born two sons: the first was called Peleg, because it was in his time that the earth was divided, and his brother was called Joktan. 26 Joktan fathered Almodad, Sheleph, Hazarmaveth, Jerah, 27 Hadoram, Uzal, Diklah, 28 Obal, Abima-El, Sheba, 29 Ophir, Havilah, Jobab; all these were sons of Joktan. 30 They occupied a stretch of country from Mesha all the way to Sephar, the eastern mountain range.
31 These were Shem's sons, by clans and languages, by countries and nations.
32 Such were the clans of Noah's descendants, listed by descent and nation. From them, other nations branched out on earth after the flood.

11 The whole world spoke the same language, with the same vocabulary. 2 Now, as people moved eastwards they found a valley in the land of Shinar where they settled. 3 They said to one another, 'Come, let us make bricks and bake them in the fire.' For stone they used bricks, and for mortar they used bitumen. 4 'Come,' they said, 'let us build ourselves a city and a tower with its top reaching heaven. Let us make a name for ourselves, so that we do not get scattered all over the world.'
5 Now Yahweh came down to see the city and the tower that the people had built. 6 'So they are all a single people with a single language!' said Yahweh. 'This is only the start of their undertakings! Now nothing they plan to do will be beyond them. 7 Come, let us go down and confuse their language there, so that they cannot understand one another.'
8 Yahweh scattered them thence all over the world, and they stopped building the city. 9 That is why it was called Babel, since there Yahweh confused the language of the whole world, and from there Yahweh scattered them all over the world.
10 These are Shem's descendants:
When Shem was a hundred years old he fathered Arpachshad, two years after the flood. 11 After the birth of Arpachshad, Shem lived five hundred years and fathered sons and daughters.
12 When Arpachshad was thirty-five years old he fathered Shelah. 13 After the birth of Shelah, Arpachshad lived four hundred and three years and fathered sons and daughters.
14 When Shelah was thirty years old he fathered Eber. 15 After the birth of Eber, Shelah lived four hundred and three years and fathered sons and daughters.
16 When Eber was thirty-four years old he fathered Peleg. 17 After the birth of Peleg, Eber lived four hundred and thirty years and fathered sons and daughters.
18 When Peleg was thirty years old he fathered Reu. 19 After the birth of Reu, Peleg lived two hundred and nine years and fathered sons and daughters.
20 When Reu was thirty-two years old he fathered Serug. 21 After the birth of Serug, Reu lived two hundred and seven years and fathered sons and daughters.
22 When Serug was thirty years old he fathered Nahor. 23 After the birth of Nahor, Serug lived two hundred years and fathered sons and daughters.
24 When Nahor was twenty-nine years old he fathered Terah. 25 After the birth of Terah, Nahor lived a hundred and nineteen years and fathered sons and daughters.
26 When Terah was seventy years old he fathered Abram, Nahor and Haran.

NEW REVISED STANDARD VERSION

27 Now these are the descendants of Terah. Terah was the father of Abram, Nahor, and Haran; and Haran was the father of Lot. 28 Haran died before his father Terah in the land of his birth, in Ur of the Chaldeans. 29 Abram and Nahor took wives; the name of Abram's wife was Sarai, and the name of Nahor's wife was Milcah. She was the daughter of Haran the father of Milcah and Iscah. 30 Now Sarai was barren; she had no child.

31 Terah took his son Abram and his grandson Lot son of Haran, and his daughter-in-law Sarai, his son Abram's wife, and they went out together from Ur of the Chaldeans to go into the land of Canaan; but when they came to Haran, they settled there. 32 The days of Terah were two hundred five years; and Terah died in Haran.

12 Now the Lord said to Abram, "Go from your country and your kindred and your father's house to the land that I will show you. 2 I will make of you a great nation, and I will bless you, and make your name great, so that you will be a blessing. 3 I will bless those who bless you, and the one who curses you I will curse; and in you all the families of the earth shall be blessed."*e*

4 So Abram went, as the Lord had told him; and Lot went with him. Abram was seventy-five years old when he departed from Haran. 5 Abram took his wife Sarai and his brother's son Lot, and all the possessions that they had gathered, and the persons whom they had acquired in Haran; and they set forth to go to the land of Canaan. When they had come to the land of Canaan, 6 Abram passed through the land to the place at Shechem, to the oak *f* of Moreh. At that time the Canaanites were in the land. 7 Then the Lord appeared to Abram, and said, "To your offspring *g* I will give this land." So he built there an altar to the Lord, who had appeared to him. 8 From there he moved on to the hill country on the east of Bethel, and pitched his tent, with Bethel on the west and Ai on the east; and there he built an altar to the Lord and invoked the name of the Lord. 9 And Abram journeyed on by stages toward the Negeb.

10 Now there was a famine in the land. So Abram went down to Egypt to reside there as an alien, for the famine was severe in the land. 11 When he was about to enter Egypt, he said to his wife Sarai, "I know well that you are a woman beautiful in appearance; 12 and when the Egyptians see you, they will say, 'This is his wife'; then they will kill me, but they will let you live. 13 Say you are my sister, so that it may go well with me because of you, and that my life may be spared on your account." 14 When Abram entered Egypt the Egyptians saw that the woman was very beautiful. 15 When the officials of Pharaoh saw her, they praised her to Pharaoh. And the woman was taken into Pharaoh's house. 16 And for her sake he dealt well with Abram; and he had sheep, oxen, male donkeys, male and female slaves, female donkeys, and camels.

17 But the Lord afflicted Pharaoh and his house with great plagues because of Sarai, Abram's wife. 18 So Pharaoh called Abram, and said, "What is this you have done to me? Why did you not tell me that she was your wife? 19 Why did you say, 'She is my sister,' so that I took her for my wife? Now then, here is your wife, take her, and be gone." 20 And Pharaoh gave his men orders concerning him; and they set him on the way, with his wife and all that he had.

REVISED ENGLISH BIBLE

27 These are the descendants of Terah. Terah was the father of Abram, Nahor, and Haran. Haran was Lot's father. 28 Haran died in the land of his birth, Ur of the Chaldees, during his father's lifetime. 29 Abram and Nahor married wives; Abram's wife was called Sarai, and Nahor's Milcah. She was the daughter of Haran, father of Milcah and Iscah. 30 Sarai was barren; she had no child. 31 Terah took his son Abram, his grandson Lot the son of Haran, and his daughter-in-law Sarai, Abram's wife, and they set out from Ur of the Chaldees for Canaan. But when they reached Harran, they settled there. 32 Terah was two hundred and five years old when he died in Harran.

12 The Lord said to Abram, 'Leave your own country, your kin, and your father's house, and go to a country that I will show you. 2 I shall make you into a great nation; I shall bless you and make your name so great that it will be used in blessings:
3 those who bless you, I shall bless;
those who curse you, I shall curse.
All the peoples on earth
will wish to be blessed as you are blessed.'

4 Abram, who was seventy-five years old when he left Harran, set out as the Lord had bidden him, and Lot went with him. 5 He took his wife Sarai, his brother's son Lot, and all the possessions they had gathered and the dependants they had acquired in Harran, and they departed for Canaan. When they arrived there, 6 Abram went on as far as the sanctuary at Shechem, the terebinth tree of Moreh. (At that time the Canaanites lived in the land.) 7 When the Lord appeared to him and said, 'I am giving this land to your descendants,' Abram built an altar there to the Lord who had appeared to him. 8 From there he moved on to the hill-country east of Bethel and pitched his tent between Bethel on the west and Ai on the east. He built there an altar to the Lord whom he invoked by name. 9 Thus Abram journeyed by stages towards the Negeb.

10 The land was stricken by a famine so severe that Abram went down to Egypt to live there for a time. 11 As he was about to enter Egypt, he said to his wife Sarai, 'I am well aware that you are a beautiful woman, and 12 I know that when the Egyptians see you and think, "She is his wife," they will let you live but they will kill me. 13 Tell them you are my sister, so that all may go well with me because of you, and my life be spared on your account.'

14 When Abram arrived in Egypt, the Egyptians saw that Sarai was indeed very beautiful, 15 and Pharaoh's courtiers, when they saw her, sang her praises to Pharaoh. She was taken into Pharaoh's household, 16 and he treated Abram well because of her, and Abram acquired sheep and cattle and donkeys, male and female slaves, she-donkeys, and camels. 17 But when the Lord inflicted plagues on Pharaoh and his household on account of Abram's wife Sarai, 18 Pharaoh summoned Abram. 'Why have you treated me like this?' he said. 'Why did you not tell me she was your wife? 19 Why did you say she was your sister, so that I took her as a wife? Here she is: take her and go.' 20 Pharaoh gave his men orders, and they sent Abram on his way with his wife and all that belonged to him.

---

e Or *by you all the families of the earth shall bless themselves*
f Or *terebinth*   *g* Heb *seed*

11:32 **two hundred and five:** *or, with Samar.,* one hundred and forty-five.   12:3 **will wish . . . are blessed:** *or* will be blessed because of you.

27 This is the record of the descendants of Terah. Terah became the father of Abram, Nahor and Haran, and Haran became the father of Lot. 28 Haran died before his father Terah, in his native land, in Ur of the Chaldeans. 29 Abram and Nahor took wives; the name of Abram's wife was Sarai, and the name of Nahor's wife was Milcah, daughter of Haran, the father of Milcah and Iscah. 30 Sarai was barren; she had no child.

31 Terah took his son Abram, his grandson Lot, son of Haran, and his daughter-in-law Sarai, the wife of his son Abram, and brought them out of Ur of the Chaldeans, to go to the land of Canaan. But when they reached Haran, they settled there. 32 The lifetime of Terah was two hundred and five years; then Terah died in Haran.

12 The LORD said to Abram: "Go forth from the land of your kinsfolk and from your father's house to a land that I will show you. 2 "I will make of you a great nation,
and I will bless you;
I will make your name great,
so that you will be a blessing.
3 I will bless those who bless you
and curse those who curse you.
All the communities of the earth
shall find blessing in you."

4 Abram went as the LORD directed him, and Lot went with him. Abram was seventy-five years old when he left Haran. 5 Abram took his wife Sarai, his brother's son Lot, all the possessions that they had accumulated, and the persons that they had acquired in Haran, and they set out for the land of Canaan. When they came to the land of Canaan, 6 Abram passed through the land as far as the sacred place at Shechem, by the terebinth of Moreh. (The Canaanites were then in the land.)

7 The LORD appeared to Abram and said, "To your descendants I will give this land." So Abram built an altar there to the LORD who had appeared to him. 8 From there he moved on to the hill country east of Bethel, pitching his tent with Bethel to the west and Ai to the east. He built an altar there to the LORD and invoked the LORD by name. 9 Then Abram journeyed on by stages to the Negeb.

10 There was famine in the land; so Abram went down to Egypt to sojourn there, since the famine in the land was severe. 11 When he was about to enter Egypt, he said to his wife Sarai: "I know well how beautiful a woman you are. 12 When the Egyptians see you, they will say, 'She is his wife'; then they will kill me, but let you live. 13 Please say, therefore, that you are my sister, so that it may go well with me on your account and my life may be spared for your sake." 14 When Abram came to Egypt, the Egyptians saw how beautiful the woman was; 15 and when Pharaoh's courtiers saw her, they praised her to Pharaoh. So she was taken into Pharaoh's palace. 16 On her account it went very well with Abram, and he received flocks and herds, male and female slaves, male and female asses, and camels.

17 But the LORD struck Pharaoh and his household with severe plagues because of Abram's wife Sarai. 18 Then Pharaoh summoned Abram and said to him: "How could you do this to me! Why didn't you tell me she was your wife? 19 Why did you say, 'She is my sister,' so that I took her for my wife? Here, then, is your wife. Take her and be gone!" 20 Then Pharaoh gave men orders concerning him, and they sent him on his way, with his wife and all that belonged to him.

27 These are Terah's descendants:
Terah fathered Abram, Nahor and Haran. Haran fathered Lot. 28 Haran died in the presence of his father Terah in his native land, Ur of the Chaldaeans. 29 Abram and Nahor both married: Abram's wife was called Sarai, Nahor's wife was called Milcah daughter of Haran, father of Milcah and Iscah. 30 Sarai was barren, having no child.

31 Terah took his son Abram, his grandson Lot son of Haran, and his daughter-in-law the wife of Abram, and made them leave Ur of the Chaldaeans to go to the land of Canaan. But on arrival in Haran they settled there.

32 Terah's life lasted two hundred and five years; then he died at Haran.

12 Yahweh said to Abram, 'Leave your country, your kindred and your father's house for a country which I shall show you; 2 and I shall make you a great nation, I shall bless you and make your name famous; you are to be a blessing!
3 I shall bless those who bless you,
and shall curse those who curse you,
and all clans on earth
will bless themselves by you.'

4 So Abram went as Yahweh told him, and Lot went with him. Abram was seventy-five years old when he left Haran. 5 Abram took his wife Sarai, his nephew Lot, all the possessions they had amassed and the people they had acquired in Haran. They set off for the land of Canaan, and arrived there.

6 Abram passed through the country as far as the holy place at Shechem, the Oak of Moreh. The Canaanites were in the country at the time. 7 Yahweh appeared to Abram and said, 'I shall give this country to your progeny.' And there, Abram built an altar to Yahweh who had appeared to him. 8 From there he moved on to the mountainous district east of Bethel, where he pitched his tent, with Bethel to the west and Ai to the east. There he built an altar to Yahweh and invoked the name of Yahweh. 9 Then Abram made his way stage by stage to the Negeb.

10 b There was a famine in the country, and Abram went down to Egypt to stay there for a time, since the famine in the country was severe. 11 When he was about to enter Egypt, he said to his wife Sarai, 'Look, I know you are a beautiful woman. 12 When the Egyptians see you they will say, "That is his wife," and they will kill me but leave you alive. 13 Therefore please tell them you are my sister, so that they may treat me well because of you and spare my life out of regard for you.' 14 When Abram arrived in Egypt the Egyptians did indeed see that the woman was very beautiful. 15 When Pharaoh's officials saw her they sang her praises to Pharaoh and the woman was taken into Pharaoh's household. 16 And Abram was very well treated because of her and received flocks, oxen, donkeys, men and women slaves, she-donkeys and camels. 17 But Yahweh inflicted severe plagues on Pharaoh and his household because of Abram's wife Sarai. 18 So Pharaoh summoned Abram and said, 'What is this you have done to me? Why did you not tell me she was your wife? 19 Why did you say, "She is my sister," so that I took her to be my wife? Now, here is your wife. Take her and go!' 20 And Pharaoh gave his people orders about him; they sent him on his way with his wife and all his possessions.

b 12 12:10seq. = 20; = 26:1–11.

NEW REVISED STANDARD VERSION

13 So Abram went up from Egypt, he and his wife, and all that he had, and Lot with him, into the Negeb. 2 Now Abram was very rich in livestock, in silver, and in gold. 3 He journeyed on by stages from the Negeb as far as Bethel, to the place where his tent had been at the beginning, between Bethel and Ai, 4 to the place where he had made an altar at the first; and there Abram called on the name of the LORD. 5 Now Lot, who went with Abram, also had flocks and herds and tents, 6 so that the land could not support both of them living together; for their possessions were so great that they could not live together, 7 and there was strife between the herders of Abram's livestock and the herders of Lot's livestock. At that time the Canaanites and the Perizzites lived in the land.

8 Then Abram said to Lot, "Let there be no strife between you and me, and between your herders and my herders; for we are kindred. 9 Is not the whole land before you? Separate yourself from me. If you take the left hand, then I will go to the right; or if you take the right hand, then I will go to the left." 10 Lot looked about him, and saw that the plain of the Jordan was well watered everywhere like the garden of the LORD, like the land of Egypt, in the direction of Zoar; this was before the LORD had destroyed Sodom and Gomorrah. 11 So Lot chose for himself all the plain of the Jordan, and Lot journeyed eastward; thus they separated from each other. 12 Abram settled in the land of Canaan, while Lot settled among the cities of the Plain and moved his tent as far as Sodom. 13 Now the people of Sodom were wicked, great sinners against the LORD.

14 The LORD said to Abram, after Lot had separated from him, "Raise your eyes now, and look from the place where you are, northward and southward and eastward and westward; 15 for all the land that you see I will give to you and to your offspring[h] forever. 16 I will make your offspring like the dust of the earth; so that if one can count the dust of the earth, your offspring also can be counted. 17 Rise up, walk through the length and the breadth of the land, for I will give it to you." 18 So Abram moved his tent, and came and settled by the oaks[i] of Mamre, which are at Hebron; and there he built an altar to the LORD.

14 In the days of King Amraphel of Shinar, King Arioch of Ellasar, King Chedorlaomer of Elam, and King Tidal of Goiim, 2 these kings made war with King Bera of Sodom, King Birsha of Gomorrah, King Shinab of Admah, King Shemeber of Zeboiim, and the king of Bela (that is, Zoar). 3 All these joined forces in the Valley of Siddim (that is, the Dead Sea).[j] 4 Twelve years they had served Chedorlaomer, but in the thirteenth year they rebelled. 5 In the fourteenth year Chedorlaomer and the kings who were with him came and subdued the Rephaim in Ashteroth-karnaim, the Zuzim in Ham, the Emim in Shaveh-kiriathaim, 6 and the Horites in the hill country of Seir as far as El-paran on the edge of the wilderness; 7 then they turned back and came to En-mishpat (that is, Kadesh), and subdued all the country of the Amalekites, and also the Amorites who lived in Hazazon-tamar. 8 Then the king of Sodom, the king of Gomorrah, the king of Admah, the king of Zeboiim, and the king of Bela (that is, Zoar) went out, and they joined battle in the Valley of Siddim 9 with King Chedorlaomer of Elam, King Tidal of Goiim, King Amraphel of Shinar, and King Arioch of Ellasar, four kings against five. 10 Now the Valley of Siddim was full of bitumen pits; and as the kings of Sodom and Gomorrah fled, some fell into them, and the rest fled to the hill country.

REVISED ENGLISH BIBLE

13 FROM Egypt Abram went up into the Negeb, he and his wife and all that he possessed, and Lot went with him. 2 Abram had become very rich in cattle and in silver and gold. 3 From the Negeb he journeyed by stages towards Bethel, to the place between Bethel and Ai where he had earlier pitched his tent, 4 and where he had previously set up an altar and invoked the LORD by name. 5 Since Lot, who was travelling with Abram, also possessed sheep and cattle and tents, 6 the land could not support them while they were together. They had so much livestock that they could not settle in the same district, 7 and quarrels arose between Abram's herdsmen and Lot's. (The Canaanites and the Perizzites were then living in the land.) 8 Abram said to Lot, 'There must be no quarrelling between us, or between my herdsmen and yours; for we are close kinsmen. 9 The whole country is there in front of you. Let us part company: if you go north, I shall go south; if you go south, I shall go north.' 10 Lot looked around and saw how well watered the whole plain of Jordan was; all the way to Zoar it was like the Garden of the LORD, like the land of Egypt. This was before the LORD had destroyed Sodom and Gomorrah. 11 So Lot chose all the Jordan plain and took the road to the east. They parted company: 12 Abram settled in Canaan, while Lot settled among the cities of the plain and pitched his tent near Sodom. 13 Now the men of Sodom in their wickedness had committed monstrous sins against the LORD.

14 After Lot and Abram had parted, the LORD said to Abram, 'Look around from where you are towards north, south, east, and west: 15 all the land you see I shall give to you and to your descendants for ever. 16 I shall make your descendants countless as the dust of the earth; only if the specks of dust on the ground could be counted could your descendants be counted. 17 Now go through the length and breadth of the land, for I am giving it to you.' 18 Abram moved his tent and settled by the terebinths of Mamre at Hebron, where he built an altar to the LORD.

14 IN those days King Amraphel of Shinar, King Arioch of Ellasar, King Kedorlaomer of Elam, and King Tidal of Goyim 2 went to war against King Bera of Sodom, King Birsha of Gomorrah, King Shinab of Admah, King Shemeber of Zeboyim, and the king of Bela, which is Zoar. 3 These kings joined forces in the valley of Siddim, which is now the Dead Sea. 4 For twelve years they had been subject to Kedorlaomer, but in the thirteenth year they rebelled. 5 Then in the fourteenth year Kedorlaomer and the kings allied with him came and defeated the Rephaim in Ashteroth-karnaim, the Zuzim in Ham, the Emim in Shaveh-kiriathaim, 6 and the Horites in their hill-country, Seir as far as El-paran on the edge of the wilderness. 7 On their way back they came to En-mishpat, which is now Kadesh, and laid waste all the territory of the Amalekites as well as that of the Amorites who lived in Hazazon-tamar. 8 Then the kings of Sodom, Gomorrah, Admah, Zeboyim, and Bela, which is now Zoar, marched out and drew up their forces against them in the valley of Siddim, 9 against King Kedorlaomer of Elam, King Tidal of Goyim, King Amraphel of Shinar, and King Arioch of Ellasar, four kings against five. 10 Now the valley of Siddim was full of bitumen pits, and when the kings of Sodom and Gomorrah fled, some of their men fell into them, but the rest made their escape to the hills. 11 The four kings captured all the flocks and herds of

---

[h] Heb *seed*　[i] Or *terebinths*　[j] Heb *Salt Sea*

13:10 **the Garden of the LORD:** *or* a wonderful garden.
14:3 **Dead Sea:** *lit.* Salt Sea.

24

NEW AMERICAN BIBLE

13 From Egypt Abram went up to the Negeb with his wife and all that belonged to him, and Lot accompanied him. 2 Now Abram was very rich in livestock, silver and gold. 3 From the Negeb he traveled by stages toward Bethel, to the place between Bethel and Ai where his tent had formerly stood, 4 The site where he had first built the altar; and there he invoked the LORD by name.

5 Lot, who went with Abram, also had flocks and herds and tents, 6 so that the land could not support them if they stayed together; their possessions were so great that they could not dwell together. 7 There were quarrels between the herdsmen of Abram's livestock and those of Lot's. (At this time the Canaanites and the Perizzites were occupying the land.)

8 So Abram said to Lot: "Let there be no strife between you and me, or between your herdsmen and mine, for we are kinsmen. 9 Is not the whole land at your disposal? Please separate from me. If you prefer the left, I will go to the right; if you prefer the right, I will go to the left." 10 Lot looked about and saw how well watered the whole Jordan Plain was as far as Zoar, like the LORD's own garden, or like Egypt. (This was before the LORD had destroyed Sodom and Gomorrah.) 11 Lot, therefore, chose for himself the whole Jordan Plain and set out eastward. Thus they separated from each other; 12 Abram stayed in the land of Canaan, while Lot settled among the cities of the Plain, pitching his tents near Sodom. 13 Now the inhabitants of Sodom were very wicked in the sins they committed against the LORD.

14 After Lot had left, the LORD said to Abram: "Look about you, and from where you are, gaze to the north and south, east and west; 15 all the land that you see I will give to you and your descendants forever. 16 I will make your descendants like the dust of the earth; if anyone could count the dust of the earth, your descendants too might be counted. 17 Set forth and walk about in the land, through its length and breadth, for to you I will give it." 18 Abram moved his tents and went on to settle near the terebinth of Mamre, which is at Hebron. There he built an altar to the LORD.

14 In the days of . . . , Amraphel king of Shinar, Arioch king of Ellasar, Chedorlaomer king of Elam, and Tidal king of Goiim 2 made war on Bera king of Sodom, Birsha king of Gomorrah, Shinab king of Admah, Shemeber king of Zeboiim, and the king of Bela (that is, Zoar). 3 All the latter kings joined forces in the Valley of Siddim (that is, the Salt Sea). 4 For twelve years they had been subject to Chedorlaomer, but in the thirteenth year they rebelled. 5 In the fourteenth year Chedorlaomer and the kings allied with him came and defeated the Rephaim in Ashteroth-karnaim, the Zuzim in Ham, the Emim in Shaveh-kiriathaim, 6 and the Horites in the hill country of Seir, as far as Elparan, close by the wilderness. 7 They then turned back and came to Enmishpat (that is, Kadesh), and they subdued the whole country both of the Amalekites and of the Amorites who dwelt in Hazazon-tamar. 8 Thereupon the king of Sodom, the king of Gomorrah, the king of Admah, the king of Zeboiim, and the king of Bela (that is, Zoar) marched out, and in the Valley of Siddim they went into battle against them: 9 against Chedorlaomer king of Elam, Tidal king of Goiim, Amraphel king of Shinar, and Arioch king of Ellasar — four kings against five. 10 Now the Valley of Siddim was full of bitumen pits; and as the kings of Sodom and Gomorrah fled, they fell into these, while the rest fled to the mountains. 11 The victors seized all the pos-

NEW JERUSALEM BIBLE

13 From Egypt Abram returned to the Negeb with his wife and all he possessed, and Lot with him. 2 Abram was very rich in livestock, silver and gold. 3 By stages he went from the Negeb to Bethel, where he had first pitched his tent, between Bethel and Ai, 4 at the place where he had formerly erected the altar. There Abram invoked the name of Yahweh.

5 Lot, who was travelling with Abram, had flocks and cattle of his own, and tents too. 6 The land was not sufficient to accommodate them both at once, for they had too many possessions to be able to live together. 7 Dispute broke out between the herdsmen of Abram's livestock and those of Lot. (The Canaanites and Perizzites were living in the country at the time.) 8 Accordingly Abram said to Lot, 'We do not want discord between us or between my herdsmen and yours, for we are kinsmen. 9 Is not the whole land open before you? Go in the opposite direction to me: if you take the left, I shall go right; if you take the right, I shall go left.'

10 Looking round, Lot saw all the Jordan plain, irrigated everywhere — this was before Yahweh destroyed Sodom and Gomorrah — like the garden of Yahweh or the land of Egypt, as far as Zoar. 11 So Lot chose all the Jordan plain for himself and moved off eastwards. Thus they parted company: 12 Abram settled in the land of Canaan; Lot settled among the cities of the plain, pitching his tents on the outskirts of Sodom. 13 Now the people of Sodom were vicious and great sinners against Yahweh.

14 Yahweh said to Abram after Lot had parted company from him, 'Look all round from where you are, to north and south, to east and west, 15 for all the land within sight I shall give to you and your descendants for ever. 16 I shall make your descendants like the dust on the ground; when people succeed in counting the specks of dust on the ground, then they will be able to count your descendants too! 17 On your feet! Travel the length and breadth of the country, for I mean to give it to you.'

18 So Abram moved his tent and went to settle at the Oak of Mamre, at Hebron, and there he built an altar to Yahweh.

14 When Amraphel king of Shinar, Arioch king of Ellasar, Chedor-Laomer king of Elam, and Tidal king of the Goiim, 2 made war on Bera king of Sodom, Birsha king of Gomorrah, Shinab king of Admah, Shemeber king of Zeboiim, and the king of Bela (that is, Zoar), 3 all the latter joined forces in the Valley of Siddim (now the Salt Sea). 4 For twelve years they had been under the yoke of Chedor-Laomer, but in the thirteenth year they revolted. 5 In the fourteenth year Chedor-Laomer arrived and the kings who had allied themselves with him. They defeated the Rephaim at Ashteroth-Carnaim, the Zuzim at Ham, the Emim in the Plain of Kiriathaim, 6 the Horites in the mountainous district of Seir near El-Paran, which is on the edge of the desert. 7 Wheeling round, they came to the Spring of Judgement (that is, Kadesh); they conquered all the territory of the Amalekites and also the Amorites who lived in Hazazon-Tamar. 8 Then the kings of Sodom, Gomorrah, Admah, Zeboiim and Bela (that is, Zoar) marched out and engaged them in the Valley of Siddim: 9 Chedor-Laomer king of Elam, Tidal king of the Goiim, Amraphel king of Shinar and Arioch king of Ellasar: four kings against five. 10 Now there were many bitumen wells in the Valley of Siddim, and in their flight the kings of Sodom and Gomorrah fell into them, while the rest fled into the hills. 11 The

14, 1: In the days of . . . : the personal name by which the event is dated has not been preserved.

NEW REVISED STANDARD VERSION

11 So the enemy took all the goods of Sodom and Gomorrah, and all their provisions, and went their way; 12 they also took Lot, the son of Abram's brother, who lived in Sodom, and his goods, and departed.

13 Then one who had escaped came and told Abram the Hebrew, who was living by the oaks *k* of Mamre the Amorite, brother of Eshcol and of Aner; these were allies of Abram. 14 When Abram heard that his nephew had been taken captive, he led forth his trained men, born in his house, three hundred eighteen of them, and went in pursuit as far as Dan. 15 He divided his forces against them by night, he and his servants, and routed them and pursued them to Hobah, north of Damascus. 16 Then he brought back all the goods, and also brought back his nephew Lot with his goods, and the women and the people.

17 After his return from the defeat of Chedorlaomer and the kings who were with him, the king of Sodom went out to meet him at the Valley of Shaveh (that is, the King's Valley). 18 And King Melchizedek of Salem brought out bread and wine; he was priest of God Most High. *l* 19 He blessed him and said,

"Blessed be Abram by God Most High, *l*
   maker of heaven and earth;
   20 and blessed be God Most High, *l*
   who has delivered your enemies into your
         hand!"

And Abram gave him one tenth of everything. 21 Then the king of Sodom said to Abram, "Give me the persons, but take the goods for yourself." 22 But Abram said to the king of Sodom, "I have sworn to the LORD, God Most High, *l* maker of heaven and earth, 23 that I would not take a thread or a sandal-thong or anything that is yours, so that you might not say, 'I have made Abram rich.' 24 I will take nothing but what the young men have eaten, and the share of the men who went with me — Aner, Eshcol, and Mamre. Let them take their share."

15 After these things the word of the LORD came to Abram in a vision, "Do not be afraid, Abram, I am your shield; your reward shall be very great." 2 But Abram said, "O Lord GOD, what will you give me, for I continue childless, and the heir of my house is Eliezer of Damascus?" *m* 3 And Abram said, "You have given me no offspring, and so a slave born in my house is to be my heir." 4 But the word of the LORD came to him, "This man shall not be your heir; no one but your very own issue shall be your heir." 5 He brought him outside and said, "Look toward heaven and count the stars, if you are able to count them." Then he said to him, "So shall your descendants be." 6 And he believed the LORD; and the LORD *n* reckoned it to him as righteousness.

7 Then he said to him, "I am the LORD who brought you from Ur of the Chaldeans, to give you this land to possess." 8 But he said, "O Lord GOD, how am I to know that I shall possess it?" 9 He said to him, "Bring me a heifer three years old, a female goat three years old, a ram three years old, a turtledove, and a young pigeon." 10 He brought him all these and cut them in two, laying each half over against the other; but he did not cut the birds in two. 11 And when birds of prey came down on the carcasses, Abram drove them away.

12 As the sun was going down, a deep sleep fell upon Abram, and a deep and terrifying darkness descended upon him. 13 Then the LORD *n* said to Abram, "Know this for certain, that your offspring shall be aliens in a land that is not theirs, and shall be slaves there, and they shall be oppressed for four hundred years; 14 but I will bring judgment

REVISED ENGLISH BIBLE

Sodom and Gomorrah and all their provisions, and withdrew, 12 carrying off Abram's nephew, Lot, who was living in Sodom, and his flocks and herds.

13 A fugitive brought the news to Abram the Hebrew, who at that time had his camp by the terebinths of Mamre the Amorite. This Mamre was the brother of Eshcol and Aner, allies of Abram. 14 When Abram heard that his kinsman had been taken prisoner, he mustered his three hundred and eighteen retainers, men born in his household, and went in pursuit as far as Dan. 15 Abram and his followers surrounded the enemy by night, routed them, and pursued them as far as Hobah, north of Damascus. 16 He recovered all the flocks and herds and also his kinsman Lot with his flocks and herds, together with the women and all his company. 17 On Abram's return from defeating Kedorlaomer and the allied kings, the king of Sodom came out to meet him in the valley of Shaveh, which is now the King's Valley.

18 THEN the king of Salem, Melchizedek, brought food and wine. He was priest of God Most High, 19 and he pronounced this blessing on Abram:

'Blessed be Abram by God Most High,
   Creator of the heavens and the earth.
   20 And blessed be God Most High,
   who has delivered your enemies into your hand.'

Then Abram gave him a tithe of all the booty.

21 The king of Sodom said to Abram, 'Give me the people, and you can take the livestock.' 22 But Abram replied, 'I lift my hand and swear by the LORD, God Most High, Creator of the heavens and the earth: 23 not a thread or a sandal-thong shall I accept of anything that is yours. You will never say, "I made Abram rich." 24 I shall accept nothing but what the young men have eaten and the share of the men who went with me, Aner, Eshcol, and Mamre; they must have their share.'

15 AFTER this the word of the LORD came to Abram in a vision. He said, 'Do not be afraid, Abram; I am your shield. Your reward will be very great.' 2 Abram replied, 'Lord GOD, what can you give me, seeing that I am childless? The heir to my household is Eliezer of Damascus. 3 You have given me no children, and so my heir must be a slave born in my house.' 4 The word of the LORD came to him: 'This man will not be your heir; your heir will be a child of your own body.' 5 He brought Abram outside and said, 'Look up at the sky, and count the stars, if you can. So many will your descendants be.'

6 Abram put his faith in the LORD, who reckoned it to him as righteousness, 7 and said, 'I am the LORD who brought you out from Ur of the Chaldees to give you this land as your possession.' 8 Abram asked, 'Lord GOD, how can I be sure that I shall occupy it?' 9 The LORD answered, 'Bring me a heifer three years old, a she-goat three years old, a ram three years old, a turtle-dove, and a young pigeon.' 10 Abram brought him all these, cut the animals in two, and set the pieces opposite each other, but he did not cut the birds in half. 11 Birds of prey swooped down on the carcasses, but he scared them away. 12 As the sun was going down, Abram fell into a trance and great and fearful darkness came over him. 13 The LORD said to Abram, 'Know this for certain: your descendants will be aliens living in a land that is not their own; they will be enslaved and held in oppression for four hundred years. 14 But I shall punish the

---

k Or *terebinths*   *l* Heb *El Elyon*   *m* Meaning of Heb uncertain
n Heb *he*

NEW AMERICAN BIBLE

NEW JERUSALEM BIBLE

sessions and food supplies of Sodom and Gomorrah and then went their way, 12 taking with them Abram's nephew Lot, who had been living in Sodom, as well as his possessions.

13 A fugitive came and brought the news to Abram the Hebrew, who was camping at the terebinth of Mamre the Amorite, a kinsman of Eshcol and Aner; these were in league with Abram. 14 When Abram heard that his nephew had been captured, he mustered three hundred and eighteen of his retainers, born in his house, and went in pursuit as far as Dan. 15 He and his party deployed against them at night, defeated them, and pursued them as far as Hobah, which is north of Damascus. 16 He recovered all the possessions, besides bringing back his kinsman Lot and his possessions, along with the women and the other captives.

17 When Abram returned from his victory over Chedorlaomer and the kings who were allied with him, the king of Sodom went out to greet him in the Valley of Shaveh (that is, the King's Valley).

18 Melchizedek, king of Salem, brought out bread and wine, and being a priest of God Most High, he blessed Abram with these words:

19 "Blessed be Abram by God Most High,
    the creator of heaven and earth;
20 And blessed be God Most High,
    who delivered your foes into your hand."

Then Abram gave him a tenth of everything.

21 The king of Sodom said to Abram, "Give me the people; the goods you may keep." 22 But Abram replied to the king of Sodom: "I have sworn to the LORD, God Most High, the creator of heaven and earth, 23 that I would not take so much as a thread or a sandal strap from anything that is yours, lest you should say, 'I made Abram rich.' 24 Nothing for me except what my servants have used up and the share that is due to the men who joined me — Aner, Eshcol and Mamre; let them take their share."

15 Some time after these events, this word of the LORD came to Abram in a vision:

"Fear not, Abram!
I am your shield;
I will make your reward very great."

2 But Abram said, "O Lord GOD, what good will your gifts be, if I keep on being childless and have as my heir the steward of my house, Eliezer?" 3 Abram continued, "See, you have given me no offspring, and so one of my servants will be my heir." 4 Then the word of the LORD came to him: "No, that one shall not be your heir; your own issue shall be your heir." 5 He took him outside and said, "Look up at the sky and count the stars, if you can. Just so," he added, "shall your descendants be." 6 Abram put his faith in the LORD, who credited it to him as an act of righteousness.

7 He then said to him, "I am the LORD who brought you from Ur of the Chaldeans to give you this land as a possession." 8 "O Lord GOD," he asked, "how am I to know that I shall possess it?" 9 He answered him, "Bring me a three-year-old heifer, a three-year-old she-goat, a three-year-old ram, a turtle-dove, and a young pigeon." 10 He brought him all these, split them in two, and placed each half opposite the other; but the birds he did not cut up. 11 Birds of prey swooped down on the carcasses, but Abram stayed with them. 12 As the sun was about to set, a trance fell upon Abram, and a deep, terrifying darkness enveloped him.

13 Then the LORD said to Abram: "Know for certain that your descendants shall be aliens in a land not their own, where they shall be enslaved and oppressed for four hundred years. 14 But I will bring judgment on the nation they

conquerors seized all the possessions of Sodom and Gomorrah, and all their provisions, and made off. 12 They also took Lot (the nephew of Abram) and his possessions and made off; he had been living at Sodom.

13 A survivor came to tell Abram, and Aner the Hebrew, who was living at the Oak of the Amorite Mamre, the brother of Eshcol; these were allies of Abram. 14 When Abram heard that his kinsman had been taken captive, he mustered his retainers born in his own household, numbering three hundred and eighteen, and gave chase as far as Dan. 15 He and his retainers deployed against them under cover of dark, defeated them and pursued them as far as Hobah, north of Damascus. 16 He recaptured all the goods as well as his kinsman Lot and his possessions, together with the women and people.

17 When Abram returned from defeating Chedor-Laomer and the kings who had been on his side, the king of Sodom came to meet him in the Valley of Shaveh (that is, the Valley of the King). 18 Melchizedek king of Salem brought bread and wine; he was a priest of God Most High. 19 He pronounced this blessing:

Blessed be Abram by God Most High,
    Creator of heaven and earth.
And blessed be God Most High
    for putting your enemies into your clutches.

20 And Abram gave him a tenth of everything.

21 The king of Sodom said to Abram, 'Give me the people and take the possessions for yourself.' 22 But Abram replied to the king of Sodom, 'I swear by God Most High, Creator of heaven and earth: 23 not one thread, not one sandal strap, will I take of what is yours, for you to be able to say, "I made Abram rich." 24 For myself, nothing — except what the troops have used up, and the share due to the men who came with me, Eshcol, Aner and Mamre; let them take their share.'

15 c Some time later, the word of Yahweh came to Abram in a vision:

Do not be afraid, Abram!
I am your shield
and shall give you a very great reward.

2 'Lord Yahweh,' Abram replied, 'what use are your gifts, as I am going on my way childless? . . . d 3 Since you have given me no offspring,' Abram continued, 'a member of my household will be my heir.' 4 Then Yahweh's word came to him in reply, 'Such a one will not be your heir; no, your heir will be the issue of your own body.' 5 Then taking him outside, he said, 'Look up at the sky and count the stars if you can. Just so will your descendants be,' he told him. 6 Abram put his faith in Yahweh and this was reckoned to him as uprightness.

7 He then said to him, 'I am Yahweh who brought you out of Ur of the Chaldaeans to give you this country as your possession.' 8 'Lord Yahweh,' Abram replied, 'how can I know that I shall possess it?' 9 He said to him, 'Bring me a three-year-old heifer, a three-year-old she-goat, a three-year-old ram, a turtledove and a young pigeon.' 10 He brought him all these, split the animals down the middle and placed each half opposite the other; but the birds he did not divide. 11 And whenever birds of prey swooped down on the carcases, Abram drove them off.

12 Now, as the sun was on the point of setting, a trance fell on Abram, and a deep dark dread descended on him. 13 Then Yahweh said to Abram, 'Know this for certain, that your descendants will be exiles in a land not their own, and be enslaved and oppressed for four hundred years. 14 But I

c **15** = 17; 12:2-7.   d **15** The remainder of the v. is unintelligible.

on the nation that they serve, and afterward they shall come out with great possessions. 15 As for yourself, you shall go to your ancestors in peace; you shall be buried in a good old age. 16 And they shall come back here in the fourth generation; for the iniquity of the Amorites is not yet complete."

17 When the sun had gone down and it was dark, a smoking fire pot and a flaming torch passed between these pieces. 18 On that day the LORD made a covenant with Abram, saying, "To your descendants I give this land, from the river of Egypt to the great river, the river Euphrates, 19 the land of the Kenites, the Kenizzites, the Kadmonites, 20 the Hittites, the Perizzites, the Rephaim, 21 the Amorites, the Canaanites, the Girgashites, and the Jebusites."

16 Now Sarai, Abram's wife, bore him no children. She had an Egyptian slave-girl whose name was Hagar, 2 and Sarai said to Abram, "You see that the LORD has prevented me from bearing children; go in to my slave-girl; it may be that I shall obtain children by her." And Abram listened to the voice of Sarai. 3 So, after Abram had lived ten years in the land of Canaan, Sarai, Abram's wife, took Hagar the Egyptian, her slave-girl, and gave her to her husband Abram as a wife. 4 He went in to Hagar, and she conceived; and when she saw that she had conceived, she looked with contempt on her mistress. 5 Then Sarai said to Abram, "May the wrong done to me be on you! I gave my slave-girl to your embrace, and when she saw that she had conceived, she looked on me with contempt. May the LORD judge between you and me!" 6 But Abram said to Sarai, "Your slave-girl is in your power; do to her as you please." Then Sarai dealt harshly with her, and she ran away from her.

7 The angel of the LORD found her by a spring of water in the wilderness, the spring on the way to Shur. 8 And he said, "Hagar, slave-girl of Sarai, where have you come from and where are you going?" She said, "I am running away from my mistress Sarai." 9 The angel of the LORD said to her, "Return to your mistress, and submit to her. 10 The angel of the LORD also said to her, "I will so greatly multiply your offspring that they cannot be counted for multitude." 11 And the angel of the LORD said to her,

"Now you have conceived and shall bear a son;
    you shall call him Ishmael,o
    for the LORD has given heed to your affliction.
12 He shall be a wild ass of a man,
    with his hand against everyone,
    and everyone's hand against him;
    and he shall live at odds with all his kin."

13 So she named the LORD who spoke to her, "You are El-roi";p for she said, "Have I really seen God and remained alive after seeing him?"q 14 Therefore the well was called Beer-lahai-roi;r it lies between Kadesh and Bered.

15 Hagar bore Abram a son; and Abram named his son, whom Hagar bore, Ishmael. 16 Abram was eighty-six years old when Hagar bore hims Ishmael.

17 When Abram was ninety-nine years old, the LORD appeared to Abram, and said to him, "I am God Almighty;t walk before me, and be blameless. 2 And I will make my covenant between me and you, and will make you

---

nation whose slaves they are, and afterwards they will depart with great possessions. 15 You yourself will join your forefathers in peace and be buried at a ripe old age. 16 But it will be the fourth generation who will return here, for till then the Amorites will not be ripe for punishment.' 17 The sun went down and it was dusk, and there appeared a smoking brazier and a flaming torch which passed between the divided pieces. 18 That day the LORD made a covenant with Abram, and said, 'I give to your descendants this land from the river of Egypt to the Great River, the river Euphrates, 19 the territory of the Kenites, Kenizzites, Kadmonites, 20 Hittites, Perizzites, Rephaim, 21 Amorites, Canaanites, Girgashites, and Jebusites.'

16 Abram's wife Sarai had borne him no children. She had, however, an Egyptian slave-girl named Hagar, 2 and Sarai said to Abram, 'The LORD has not let me have a child. Take my slave-girl; perhaps through her I shall have a son.' Abram heeded what his wife said; 3 so Sarai brought her slave-girl, Hagar the Egyptian, to her husband and gave her to Abram as a wife. When this happened Abram had been in Canaan for ten years. 4 He lay with Hagar and she conceived; and when she knew that she was pregnant, she looked down on her mistress. 5 Sarai complained to Abram, 'I am being wronged; you must do something about it. It was I who gave my slave-girl into your arms, but since she has known that she is pregnant, she has despised me. May the LORD see justice done between you and me.' 6 Abram replied, 'Your slave-girl is in your hands; deal with her as you please.' So Sarai ill-treated her and she ran away from her mistress.

7 The angel of the LORD came upon Hagar by a spring in the wilderness, the spring on the road to Shur, 8 and he said, 'Hagar, Sarai's slave-girl, where have you come from and where are you going?' She answered, 'I am running away from Sarai my mistress.' 9 The angel of the LORD said to her, 'Go back to your mistress and submit to ill-treatment at her hands.' 10 He also said. 'I shall make your descendants too many to be counted.' 11 The angel of the LORD went on:

'You are with child and will bear a son.
    You are to name him Ishmael,
    because the LORD has heard of your ill-treatment.
12 He will be like the wild ass;
    his hand will be against everyone
    and everyone's hand against him;
    and he will live at odds with all his kin.'

13 Hagar called the LORD who spoke to her by the name El-roi, for she said, 'Have I indeed seen God and still live after that vision?' 14 That is why the well is called Beer-lahai-roi; it lies between Kadesh and Bered. 15 Hagar bore Abram a son, and he named the child she bore him Ishmael. 16 Abram was eighty-six years old when she bore Ishmael.

17 When Abram was ninety-nine years old, the LORD appeared to him and said, 'I am God Almighty. Live always in my presence and be blameless, 2 so that I may make my covenant with you and give you many de-

---

o That is *God hears*   p Perhaps *God of seeing* or *God who sees*
q Meaning of Heb uncertain   r That is *the Well of the Living One who sees me*   s Heb *Abram*   t Traditional rendering of Heb *El Shaddai*

16:11 **Ishmael:** *that is* God heard.   16:13 **El-roi:** *that is* God of a vision. **God . . . live:** *prob. rdg; Heb.* hither.
16:14 **Beer-lahai-roi:** *that is* the Well of the Living One of Vision.

NEW AMERICAN BIBLE

must serve, and in the end they will depart with great wealth. 15 You, however, shall join your forefathers in peace; you shall be buried at a contented old age. 16 In the fourth time-span the others shall come back here; the wickedness of the Amorites will not have reached its full measure until then."

17 When the sun had set and it was dark, there appeared a smoking brazier and a flaming torch, which passed between those pieces. 18 It was on that occasion that the LORD made a covenant with Abram, saying: "To your descendants I give this land, from the Wadi of Egypt to the Great River [the Euphrates], 19 the land of the Kenites, the Kenizzites, the Kadmonites, 20 the Hittites, the Perizzites, the Rephaim, 21 the Amorites, the Canaanites, the Girgashites, and the Jebusites."

16 Abram's wife Sarai had borne him no children. She had, however, an Egyptian maidservant named Hagar. 2 Sarai said to Abram: "The LORD has kept me from bearing children. Have intercourse, then, with my maid; perhaps I shall have sons through her." Abram heeded Sarai's request. 3 Thus, after Abram had lived ten years in the land of Canaan, his wife Sarai took her maid, Hagar the Egyptian, and gave her to her husband Abram to be his concubine. 4 He had intercourse with her, and she became pregnant. When she became aware of her pregnancy, she looked on her mistress with disdain. 5 So Sarai said to Abram: "You are responsible for this outrage against me. I myself gave my maid to your embrace; but ever since she became aware of her pregnancy, she has been looking on me with disdain. May the LORD decide between you and me!" 6 Abram told Sarai: "Your maid is in your power. Do to her whatever you please." Sarai then abused her so much that Hagar ran away from her.

7 The LORD's messenger found her by a spring in the wilderness, the spring on the road to Shur, 8 and he asked, "Hagar, maid of Sarai, where have you come from and where are you going?" She answered, "I am running away from my mistress, Sarai." 9 But the LORD's messenger told her: "Go back to your mistress and submit to her abusive treatment. 10 I will make your descendants so numerous," added the LORD's messenger, "that they will be too many to count. 11 Besides," the LORD's messenger said to her:

"You are now pregnant and shall bear a son;
    you shall name him Ishmael,
For the LORD has heard you,
    God has answered you.
12 He shall be a wild ass of a man,
    his hand against everyone,
    and everyone's hand against him;
In opposition to all his kin
    shall he encamp."

13 To the LORD who spoke to her she gave a name, saying, "You are the God of Vision"; she meant, "Have I really seen God and remained alive after my vision?" 14 That is why the well is called Beer-lahai-roi. It is between Kadesh and Bered.

15 Hagar bore Abram a son, and Abram named the son whom Hagar bore him Ishmael. 16 Abram was eighty-six years old when Hagar bore him Ishmael.

17 When Abram was ninety-nine years old, the LORD appeared to him and said: "I am God the Almighty. Walk in my presence and be blameless. 2 Between you and me I will establish my covenant, and I will multiply you exceedingly."

NEW JERUSALEM BIBLE

shall bring judgement on the nation that enslaves them and after this they will leave, with many possessions. 15 For your part, you will join your ancestors in peace; you will be buried at a happy old age. 16 In the fourth generation they will come back here, for until then the iniquity of the Amorites will not have reached its full extent.'

17 When the sun had set and it was dark, there appeared a smoking firepot and a flaming torch passing between the animals' pieces. 18 That day Yahweh made a covenant with Abram in these terms:

'To your descendants I give this country,
    from the River of Egypt to the Great River,
the River Euphrates, 19 the Kenites, the Kenizzites, the Kadmonites, 20 the Hittites, the Perizzites, the Rephaim, 21 the Amorites, the Canaanites, the Girgashites, and the Jebusites.'

16 e Abram's wife Sarai had borne him no child, but she had an Egyptian slave-girl called Hagar. 2 So Sarai said to Abram, 'Listen, now! Since Yahweh has kept me from having children, go to my slave-girl. Perhaps I shall get children through her.' And Abram took Sarai's advice.

3 Thus, after Abram had lived in the land of Canaan for ten years, Sarai took Hagar her Egyptian slave-girl and gave her to Abram as his wife. 4 He went to Hagar and she conceived. And once she knew she had conceived, her mistress counted for nothing in her eyes. 5 Then Sarai said to Abram, 'This outrage done to me is your fault! It was I who put my slave-girl into your arms but, now she knows that she has conceived, I count for nothing in her eyes. Yahweh judge between me and you!' 6 'Very well,' Abram said to Sarai, 'your slave-girl is at your disposal. Treat her as you think fit.' Sarai accordingly treated her so badly that she ran away from her.

7 The angel of Yahweh found her by a spring in the desert, the spring on the road to Shur. 8 He said, 'Hagar, slave-girl of Sarai, where have you come from, and where are you going?' 'I am running away from my mistress Sarai,' she replied. 9 The angel of Yahweh said to her, 'Go back to your mistress and submit to her.' 10 The angel of Yahweh further said to her, 'I shall make your descendants too numerous to be counted.' 11 Then the angel of Yahweh said to her:

Now, you have conceived and will bear a son,
    and you shall name him Ishmael,
    for Yahweh has heard your cries of distress.
12 A wild donkey of a man he will be,
    his hand against every man, and every man's
      hand against him,
    living his life in defiance of all his kinsmen.

13 Hagar gave a name to Yahweh who had spoken to her, 'You are El Roi,' by which she meant, 'Did I not go on seeing here, after him who sees me?' 14 This is why the well is called the well of Lahai Roi; it is between Kadesh and Bered.

15 Hagar bore Abram a son, and Abram gave his son borne by Hagar the name Ishmael. 16 Abram was eighty-six years old when Hagar bore him Ishmael.

17 f When Abram was ninety-nine years old Yahweh appeared to him and said, 'I am El Shaddai. Live in my presence, be perfect, 2 and I shall grant a covenant between myself and you, and make you very numerous.'

e **16** = 21:8–19.   f **17** = 15.

| NEW REVISED STANDARD VERSION | REVISED ENGLISH BIBLE |

exceedingly numerous." 3 Then Abram fell on his face; and God said to him, 4 "As for me, this is my covenant with you: You shall be the ancestor of a multitude of nations. 5 No longer shall your name be Abram,[u] but your name shall be Abraham;[v] for I have made you the ancestor of a multitude of nations. 6 I will make you exceedingly fruitful; and I will make nations of you, and kings shall come from you. 7 I will establish my covenant between me and you, and your offspring after you throughout their generations, for an everlasting covenant, to be God to you and to your offspring[w] after you. 8 And I will give to you, and to your offspring after you, the land where you are now an alien, all the land of Canaan, for a perpetual holding; and I will be their God."

9 God said to Abraham, "As for you, you shall keep my covenant, you and your offspring after you throughout their generations. 10 This is my covenant, which you shall keep, between me and you and your offspring after you: Every male among you shall be circumcised. 11 You shall circumcise the flesh of your foreskins, and it shall be a sign of the covenant between me and you. 12 Throughout your generations every male among you shall be circumcised when he is eight days old, including the slave born in your house and the one bought with your money from any foreigner who is not of your offspring. 13 Both the slave born in your house and the one bought with your money must be circumcised. So shall my covenant be in your flesh an everlasting covenant. 14 Any uncircumcised male who is not circumcised in the flesh of his foreskin shall be cut off from his people; he has broken my covenant."

15 God said to Abraham, "As for Sarai your wife, you shall not call her Sarai, but Sarah shall be her name. 16 I will bless her, and moreover I will give you a son by her. I will bless her, and she shall give rise to nations; kings of peoples shall come from her." 17 Then Abraham fell on his face and laughed, and said to himself, "Can a child be born to a man who is a hundred years old? Can Sarah, who is ninety years old, bear a child?" 18 And Abraham said to God, "O that Ishmael might live in your sight!" 19 God said, "No, but your wife Sarah shall bear you a son, and you shall name him Isaac.[x] I will establish my covenant with him as an everlasting covenant for his offspring after him. 20 As for Ishmael, I have heard you; I will bless him and make him fruitful and exceedingly numerous; he shall be the father of twelve princes, and I will make him a great nation. 21 But my covenant I will establish with Isaac, whom Sarah shall bear to you at this season next year." 22 And when he had finished talking with him, God went up from Abraham.

23 Then Abraham took his son Ishmael and all the slaves born in his house or bought with his money, every male among the men of Abraham's house, and he circumcised the flesh of their foreskins that very day, as God had said to him. 24 Abraham was ninety-nine years old when he was circumcised in the flesh of his foreskin. 25 And his son Ishmael was thirteen years old when he was circumcised in the flesh of his foreskin. 26 That very day Abraham and his son Ishmael were circumcised; 27 and all the men of his house, slaves born in the house and those bought with money from a foreigner, were circumcised with him.

18 The LORD appeared to Abraham[y] by the oaks[z] of Mamre, as he sat at the entrance of his tent in the heat of the day. 2 He looked up and saw three men standing near him. When he saw them, he ran from the tent entrance to meet them, and bowed down to the ground. 3 He said,

scendants.' 3 Abram bowed low, and God went on, 4 'This is my covenant with you: you are to be the father of many nations. 5 Your name will no longer be Abram, but Abraham; for I shall make you father of many nations. 6 I shall make you exceedingly fruitful; I shall make nations out of you, and kings shall spring from you. 7 I shall maintain my covenant with you and your descendants after you, generation after generation, an everlasting covenant: I shall be your God, yours and your descendants'. 8 As a possession for all time I shall give you and your descendants after you the land in which you now are aliens, the whole of Canaan, and I shall be their God.'

9 God said to Abraham, 'For your part, you must keep my covenant, you and your descendants after you, generation by generation. 10 This is how you are to keep this covenant between myself and you and your descendants after you: circumcise yourselves, every male among you. 11 You must circumcise the flesh of your foreskin, and it will be the sign of the covenant between us. 12 Every male among you in every generation must be circumcised on the eighth day, both those born in your house and any foreigner, not a member of your family but purchased. 13 Circumcise both those born in your house and those you buy; thus your flesh will be marked with the sign of my everlasting covenant. 14 Every uncircumcised male, everyone who has not had the flesh of his foreskin circumcised, will be cut off from the kin of his father; he has broken my covenant.'

15 God said to Abraham, 'As for Sarai your wife, you are to call her not Sarai, but Sarah. 16 I shall bless her and give you a son by her. I shall bless her and she will be the mother of nations; from her kings of peoples will spring.' 17 Abraham bowed low, and laughing said to himself, 'Can a son be born to a man who is a hundred years old? Can Sarah bear a child at ninety?' 18 He said to God, 'If only Ishmael might enjoy your special favour!' 19 But God replied, 'No; your wife Sarah will bear you a son, and you are to call him Isaac. With him I shall maintain my covenant as an everlasting covenant for his descendants after him. 20 But I have heard your request about Ishmael; I have blessed him and I shall make him fruitful. I shall give him many descendants; he will be father of twelve princes, and I shall raise a great nation from him. 21 But my covenant I shall fulfil with Isaac, whom Sarah will bear to you at this time next year.' 22 When he had finished talking with Abraham, God left him.

23 Then Abraham took Ishmael his son, everyone who had been born in his household and everyone he had bought, every male in his household, and that same day he circumcised the flesh of their foreskins as God had commanded him. 24 Abraham was ninety-nine years old when he was circumcised. 25 Ishmael was thirteen years old when he was circumcised. 26 Both Abraham and Ishmael were circumcised on the same day. 27 All the men of Abraham's household, born in the house or bought from foreigners, were circumcised with him.

18 THE LORD appeared to Abraham by the terebinths of Mamre, as he was sitting at the opening of his tent in the heat of the day. 2 He looked up and saw three men standing over against him. On seeing them, he hurried from his tent door to meet them. Bowing low 3 he said, 'Sirs, if

---

u That is *exalted ancestor*   v Here taken to mean *ancestor of a multitude*   w Heb *seed*   x That is *he laughs*   y Heb *him*
z Or *terebinths*

17:5 **Abram:** *that is* High Father. **Abraham:** *that is* Father of Many.
17:15 **Sarai:** *that is* Mockery. **Sarah:** *that is* Princess.
17:19 **Isaac:** *that is* He laughs.

3 When Abram prostrated himself, God continued to speak to him: 4 "My covenant with you is this: you are to become the father of a host of nations. 5 No longer shall you be called Abram; your name shall be Abraham, for I am making you the father of a host of nations. 6 I will render you exceedingly fertile; I will make nations of you; kings shall stem from you. 7 I will maintain my covenant with you and your descendants after you throughout the ages as an everlasting pact, to be your God and the God of your descendants after you. 8 I will give to you and to your descendants after you the land in which you are now staying, the whole land of Canaan, as a permanent possession; and I will be their God."

9 God also said to Abraham: "On your part, you and your descendants after you must keep my covenant throughout the ages. 10 This is my covenant with you and your descendants after you that you must keep: every male among you shall be circumcised. 11 Circumcise the flesh of your foreskin, and that shall be the mark of the covenant between you and me. 12 Throughout the ages, every male among you, when he is eight days old, shall be circumcised, including houseborn slaves and those acquired with money from any foreigner who is not of your blood. 13 Yes, both the houseborn slaves and those acquired with money must be circumcised. Thus my covenant shall be in your flesh as an everlasting pact. 14 If a male is uncircumcised, that is, if the flesh of his foreskin has not been cut away, such a one shall be cut off from his people; he has broken my covenant."

15 God further said to Abraham: "As for your wife Sarai, do not call her Sarai; her name shall be Sarah. 16 I will bless her, and I will give you a son by her. Him also will I bless; he shall give rise to nations, and rulers of peoples shall issue from him." 17 Abraham prostrated himself and laughed as he said to himself, "Can a child be born to a man who is a hundred years old? Or can Sarah give birth at ninety?" 18 Then Abraham said to God, "Let but Ishmael live on by your favor!" 19 God replied: "Nevertheless, your wife Sarah is to bear you a son, and you shall call him Isaac. I will maintain my covenant with him as an everlasting pact, to be his God and the God of his descendants after him. 20 As for Ishmael, I am heeding you: I hereby bless him. I will make him fertile and will multiply him exceedingly. He shall become the father of twelve chieftains, and I will make of him a great nation. 21 But my covenant I will maintain with Isaac, whom Sarah shall bear to you by this time next year." 22 When he had finished speaking with him, God departed from Abraham.

23 Then Abraham took his son Ishmael and all his slaves, whether born in his house or acquired with his money — every male among the members of Abraham's household — and he circumcised the flesh of their foreskins on that same day, as God had told him to do. 24 Abraham was ninety-nine years old when the flesh of his foreskin was circumcised, 25 and his son Ishmael was thirteen years old when the flesh of his foreskin was circumcised. 26 Thus, on that same day Abraham and his son Ishmael were circumcised; 27 and all the male members of his household, including the slaves born in his house or acquired with his money from foreigners, were circumcised with him.

18 The LORD appeared to Abraham by the terebinth of Mamre, as he sat in the entrance of his tent, while the day was growing hot. 2 Looking up, he saw three men standing nearby. When he saw them, he ran from the entrance of the tent to greet them; and bowing to the ground,

3 And Abram bowed to the ground.

God spoke to him as follows, 4 'For my part, this is my covenant with you: you will become the father of many nations. 5 And you are no longer to be called Abram; your name is to be Abraham, for I am making you father of many nations. 6 I shall make you exceedingly fertile. I shall make you into nations, and your issue will be kings. 7 And I shall maintain my covenant between myself and you, and your descendants after you, generation after generation, as a covenant in perpetuity, to be your God and the God of your descendants after you. 8 And to you and to your descendants after you, I shall give the country where you are now immigrants, the entire land of Canaan, to own in perpetuity. And I shall be their God.'

9 God further said to Abraham, 'You for your part must keep my covenant, you and your descendants after you, generation after generation. 10 This is my covenant which you must keep between myself and you, and your descendants after you: every one of your males must be circumcised. 11 You must circumcise the flesh of your foreskin, and that will be the sign of the covenant between myself and you. 12 As soon as he is eight days old, every one of your males, generation after generation, must be circumcised, including slaves born within the household or bought from a foreigner not of your descent. 13 Whether born within the household or bought, they must be circumcised. My covenant must be marked in your flesh as a covenant in perpetuity. 14 The uncircumcised male, whose foreskin has not been circumcised — that person must be cut off from his people: he has broken my covenant.'

15 Furthermore God said to Abraham, 'As regards your wife Sarai, you must not call her Sarai, but Sarah. 16 I shall bless her and moreover give you a son by her. I shall bless her and she will become nations: kings of peoples will issue from her.' 17 Abraham bowed to the ground, and he laughed,g thinking to himself, 'Is a child to be born to a man one hundred years old, and will Sarah have a child at the age of ninety?' 18 Abraham said to God, 'May Ishmael live in your presence! That will be enough!' 19 But God replied, 'Yes, your wife Sarah will bear you a son whom you must name Isaac. And I shall maintain my covenant with him, a covenant in perpetuity, to be his God and the God of his descendants after him. 20 For Ishmael too I grant you your request. I hereby bless him and will make him fruitful and exceedingly numerous. He will be the father of twelve princes, and I shall make him into a great nation. 21 But my covenant I shall maintain with Isaac, whom Sarah will bear you at this time next year.' 22 When he had finished speaking to Abraham, God went up from him.

23 Then Abraham took his son Ishmael, all the slaves born in his household or whom he had bought, in short all the males among the people of Abraham's household, and circumcised their foreskins that same day, as God had said to him. 24 Abraham was ninety-nine years old when his foreskin was circumcised. 25 Ishmael his son was thirteen years old when his foreskin was circumcised. 26 Abraham and his son Ishmael were circumcised on the very same day, 27 and all the men of his household, those born in the household and those bought from foreigners, were circumcised with him.

18 Yahweh appeared to him at the Oak of Mamre while he was sitting by the entrance of the tent during the hottest part of the day. 2 He looked up, and there he saw three men standing near him. As soon as he saw them he ran from the entrance of the tent to greet them, and

g 17 Play on the Hebr. root 'laugh' in the name Isaac, which in fact means 'God will smile'.

NEW REVISED STANDARD VERSION

"My lord, if I find favor with you, do not pass by your servant. 4 Let a little water be brought, and wash your feet, and rest yourselves under the tree. 5 Let me bring a little bread, that you may refresh yourselves, and after that you may pass on — since you have come to your servant." So they said, "Do as you have said." 6 And Abraham hastened into the tent to Sarah, and said, "Make ready quickly three measures[a] of choice flour, knead it, and make cakes." 7 Abraham ran to the herd, and took a calf, tender and good, and gave it to the servant, who hastened to prepare it. 8 Then he took curds and milk and the calf that he had prepared, and set it before them; and he stood by them under the tree while they ate.

9 They said to him, "Where is your wife Sarah?" And he said, "There, in the tent." 10 Then one said, "I will surely return to you in due season, and your wife Sarah shall have a son." And Sarah was listening at the tent entrance behind him. 11 Now Abraham and Sarah were old, advanced in age; it had ceased to be with Sarah after the manner of women. 12 So Sarah laughed to herself, saying, "After I have grown old, and my husband is old, shall I have pleasure?" 13 The LORD said to Abraham, "Why did Sarah laugh, and say, 'Shall I indeed bear a child, now that I am old?' 14 Is anything too wonderful for the LORD? At the set time I will return to you, in due season, and Sarah shall have a son." 15 But Sarah denied, saying, "I did not laugh"; for she was afraid. He said, "Oh yes, you did laugh."

16 Then the men set out from there, and they looked toward Sodom; and Abraham went with them to set them on their way. 17 The LORD said, "Shall I hide from Abraham what I am about to do, 18 seeing that Abraham shall become a great and mighty nation, and all the nations of the earth shall be blessed in him?[b] 19 No, for I have chosen[c] him, that he may charge his children and his household after him to keep the way of the LORD by doing righteousness and justice; so that the LORD may bring about for Abraham what he has promised him." 20 Then the LORD said, "How great is the outcry against Sodom and Gomorrah and how very grave their sin! 21 I must go down and see whether they have done altogether according to the outcry that has come to me; and if not, I will know."

22 So the men turned from there, and went toward Sodom, while Abraham remained standing before the LORD.[d] 23 Then Abraham came near and said, "Will you indeed sweep away the righteous with the wicked? 24 Suppose there are fifty righteous within the city; will you then sweep away the place and not forgive it for the fifty righteous who are in it? 25 Far be it from you to do such a thing, to slay the righteous with the wicked, so that the righteous fare as the wicked! Far be that from you! Shall not the Judge of all the earth do what is just?" 26 And the LORD said, "If I find at Sodom fifty righteous in the city, I will forgive the whole place for their sake." 27 Abraham answered, "Let me take it upon myself to speak to the Lord, I who am but dust and ashes. 28 Suppose five of the fifty righteous are lacking? Will you destroy the whole city for lack of five?" And he said, "I will not destroy it if I find forty-five there." 29 Again he spoke to him, "Suppose forty are found there." He answered, "For the sake of forty I will not do it." 30 Then he said, "Oh do not let the Lord be angry if I speak. Suppose thirty are found there." He answered, "I will not do it, if I find thirty there." 31 He said, "Let me take it upon myself to speak to the Lord. Suppose twenty are found there." He answered, "For the sake of twenty I will not destroy it."

REVISED ENGLISH BIBLE

I have deserved your favour, do not go past your servant without a visit. 4 Let me send for some water so that you may bathe your feet; and rest under this tree, 5 while I fetch a little food so that you may refresh yourselves. Afterwards you may continue the journey which has brought you my way.' They said, 'Very well, do as you say.' 6 So Abraham hurried into the tent to Sarah and said, 'Quick, take three measures of flour, knead it, and make cakes.' 7 He then hastened to the herd, chose a fine, tender calf, and gave it to a servant, who prepared it at once. 8 He took curds and milk and the calf which was now ready, set it all before them, and there under the tree waited on them himself while they ate.

9 They asked him where Sarah his wife was, and he replied, 'She is in the tent.' 10 One of them said, 'About this time next year I shall come back to you, and your wife Sarah will have a son.' Now Sarah was listening at the opening of the tent close by him. 11 Both Abraham and Sarah were very old, Sarah being well past the age of childbearing. 12 So she laughed to herself and said, 'At my time of life I am past bearing children, and my husband is old.' 13 The LORD said to Abraham, 'Why did Sarah laugh and say, "Can I really bear a child now that I am so old?" 14 Is anything impossible for the LORD? In due season, at this time next year, I shall come back to you, and Sarah will have a son.' 15 Because she was frightened, Sarah lied and denied that she had laughed; but he said, 'Yes, you did laugh.'

16 The men set out and looked down towards Sodom, and Abraham went with them to see them on their way. 17 The LORD had thought to himself, 'Shall I conceal from Abraham what I am about to do? 18 He will become a great and powerful nation, and all nations on earth will wish to be blessed as he is blessed. 19 I have singled him out so that he may charge his sons and family after him to conform to the way of the LORD and do what is right and just; thus I shall fulfil for him all that I have promised.' 20 The LORD said, 'How great is the outcry over Sodom and Gomorrah! How grave their deeds must be! 21 I shall go down and see whether their deeds warrant the outcry reaching me. I must know the truth.' 22 When the men turned and went off towards Sodom, Abraham remained standing before the LORD. 23 Abraham drew near him and asked, 'Will you really sweep away innocent and wicked together? 24 Suppose there are fifty innocent in the city; will you really sweep it away, and not pardon the place because of the fifty innocent there? 25 Far be it from you to do such a thing — to kill innocent and wicked together; for then the innocent would suffer with the wicked. Far be it from you! Should not the judge of all the earth do what is just?' 26 The LORD replied, 'If I find in Sodom fifty innocent, I shall pardon the whole place for their sake.' 27 Abraham said, 'May I make so bold as to speak to the Lord, I who am nothing but dust and ashes: 28 suppose there are five short of fifty innocent? Will you destroy the whole city for the lack of five men?' 'If I find forty-five there,' he replied, 'I shall not destroy it.' 29 Abraham spoke again, 'Suppose forty can be found there?' 'For the sake of the forty I shall not do it,' he replied. 30 Then Abraham said, 'Let not my Lord become angry if I speak again: suppose thirty can be found there?' He answered, 'If I find thirty there, I shall not do it.' 31 Abraham continued, 'May I make so bold as to speak to the Lord: suppose twenty can be found there?' He replied, 'For the sake of the twenty I shall not destroy it.' 32 Abraham said, 'Let not my

---

a Heb seahs   b Or and all the nations of the earth shall bless themselves by him   c Heb known   d Another ancient tradition reads while the LORD remained standing before Abraham

18:18 will wish . . . is blessed: or will be blessed because of him.
18:22 Abraham . . . LORD: original reading was probably the LORD remained standing before Abraham.

3 he said: "Sir, if I may ask you this favor, please do not go on past your servant. 4 Let some water be brought, that you may bathe your feet, and then rest yourselves under the tree. 5 Now that you have come this close to your servant, let me bring you a little food, that you may refresh yourselves; and afterward you may go on your way." "Very well," they replied, "do as you have said."

6 Abraham hastened into the tent and told Sarah, "Quick, three seahs of fine flour! Knead it and make rolls." 7 He ran to the herd, picked out a tender, choice steer, and gave it to a servant, who quickly prepared it. 8 Then he got some curds and milk, as well as the steer that had been prepared, and set these before them; and he waited on them under the tree while they ate.

9 "Where is your wife Sarah?" they asked him. "There in the tent," he replied. 10 One of them said, "I will surely return to you about this time next year, and Sarah will then have a son." Sarah was listening at the entrance of the tent, just behind him. 11 Now Abraham and Sarah were old, advanced in years, and Sarah had stopped having her womanly periods. 12 So Sarah laughed to herself and said, "Now that I am so withered and my husband is so old, am I still to have sexual pleasure?" 13 But the LORD said to Abraham: "Why did Sarah laugh and say, 'Shall I really bear a child, old as I am?' 14 Is anything too marvelous for the LORD to do? At the appointed time, about this time next year, I will return to you, and Sarah will have a son." 15 Because she was afraid, Sarah dissembled, saying, "I didn't laugh." But he said, "Yes you did."

16 The men set out from there and looked down toward Sodom; Abraham was walking with them, to see them on their way. 17 The LORD reflected: "Shall I hide from Abraham what I am about to do, 18 now that he is to become a great and populous nation, and all the nations of the earth are to find blessing in him? 19 Indeed, I have singled him out that he may direct his sons and his posterity to keep the way of the LORD by doing what is right and just, so that the LORD may carry into effect for Abraham the promises he made about him." 20 Then the LORD said: "The outcry against Sodom and Gomorrah is so great, and their sin so grave, 21 that I must go down and see whether or not their actions fully correspond to the cry against them that comes to me. I mean to find out."

22 While the two men walked on farther toward Sodom, the LORD remained standing before Abraham. 23 Then Abraham drew nearer to him and said: "Will you sweep away the innocent with the guilty? 24 Suppose there were fifty innocent people in the city; would you wipe out the place, rather than spare it for the sake of the fifty innocent people within it? 25 Far be it from you to do such a thing, to make the innocent die with the guilty, so that the innocent and the guilty would be treated alike! Should not the judge of all the world act with justice?" 26 The LORD replied, "If I find fifty innocent people in the city of Sodom, I will spare the whole place for their sake." 27 Abraham spoke up again: "See how I am presuming to speak to my Lord, though I am but dust and ashes! 28 What if there are five less than fifty innocent people? Will you destroy the whole city because of those five?" "I will not destroy it," he answered, "if I find forty-five there." 29 But Abraham persisted, saying, "What if only forty are found there?" He replied, "I will forbear doing it for the sake of the forty." 30 Then he said, "Let not my Lord grow impatient if I go on. What if only thirty are found there?" He replied, "I will forbear doing it if I can find but thirty there." 31 Still he went on, "Since I have thus dared to speak to my Lord, what if there are no more than twenty?" "I will not destroy it," he answered, "for the sake of the twenty." 32 But he still persisted, "Please, let not my

bowed to the ground. 3 'My lord,' he said, 'if I find favour with you, please do not pass your servant by. 4 Let me have a little water brought, and you can wash your feet and have a rest under the tree. 5 Let me fetch a little bread and you can refresh yourselves before going further, now that you have come in your servant's direction.' They replied, 'Do as you say.'

6 Abraham hurried to the tent and said to Sarah, 'Quick, knead three measures of best flour and make loaves.' 7 Then, running to the herd, Abraham took a fine and tender calf and gave it to the servant, who hurried to prepare it. 8 Then taking curds, milk and the calf which had been prepared, he laid all before them, and they ate while he remained standing near them under the tree.

9 'Where is your wife Sarah?' they asked him. 'She is in the tent,' he replied. 10 Then his guest said, 'I shall come back to you next year, and then your wife Sarah will have a son.' Sarah was listening at the entrance of the tent behind him. 11 Now Abraham and Sarah were old, well on in years, and Sarah had ceased to have her monthly periods. 12 So Sarah laughed to herself, thinking, 'Now that I am past the age of childbearing, and my husband is an old man, is pleasure to come my way again?' 13 But Yahweh asked Abraham, 'Why did Sarah laugh and say, "Am I really going to have a child now that I am old?" 14 Nothing is impossible for Yahweh. I shall come back to you at the same time next year and Sarah will have a son.' 15 Sarah said, 'I did not laugh,' lying because she was afraid. But he replied, 'Oh yes, you did laugh.'

16 From there the men set out and arrived within sight of Sodom, with Abraham accompanying them to speed them on their way. 17 Now Yahweh had wondered, 'Shall I conceal from Abraham what I am going to do, 18 as Abraham will become a great and powerful nation and all nations on earth will bless themselves by him? 19 For I have singled him out to command his sons and his family after him to keep the way of Yahweh by doing what is upright and just, so that Yahweh can carry out for Abraham what he has promised him.' 20 Then Yahweh said, 'The outcry against Sodom and Gomorrah is so great and their sin is so grave, 21 that I shall go down and see whether or not their actions are at all as the outcry reaching me would suggest. Then I shall know.'

22 While the men left there and went to Sodom, Yahweh remained in Abraham's presence. 23 Abraham stepped forward and said, 'Will you really destroy the upright with the guilty? 24 Suppose there are fifty upright people in the city. Will you really destroy it? Will you not spare the place for the sake of the fifty upright in it? 25 Do not think of doing such a thing: to put the upright to death with the guilty, so that upright and guilty fare alike! Is the judge of the whole world not to act justly?' 26 Yahweh replied, 'If I find fifty upright people in the city of Sodom, I will spare the whole place because of them.' 27 Abraham spoke up and said, 'It is presumptuous of me to speak to the Lord, I who am dust and ashes: 28 Suppose the fifty upright were five short? Would you destroy the whole city because of five?' 'No,' he replied, 'I shall not destroy it if I find forty-five there.' 29 Abraham persisted and said, 'Suppose there are forty to be found there?' 'I shall not do it,' he replied, 'for the sake of the forty.' 30 Abraham said, 'I hope the Lord will not be angry if I go on: Suppose there are only thirty to be found there?' 'I shall not do it,' he replied, 'if I find thirty there.' 31 He said, 'It is presumptuous of me to speak to the Lord: Suppose there are only twenty there?' 'I shall not destroy it,' he replied, 'for the sake of the twenty.' 32 He said, 'I trust my

NEW REVISED STANDARD VERSION

32 Then he said, "Oh do not let the Lord be angry if I speak just once more. Suppose ten are found there." He answered, "For the sake of ten I will not destroy it." 33 And the LORD went his way, when he had finished speaking to Abraham; and Abraham returned to his place.

19 The two angels came to Sodom in the evening, and Lot was sitting in the gateway of Sodom. When Lot saw them, he rose to meet them, and bowed down with his face to the ground. 2 He said, "Please, my lords, turn aside to your servant's house and spend the night, and wash your feet; then you can rise early and go on your way." They said, "No; we will spend the night in the square." 3 But he urged them strongly; so they turned aside to him and entered his house; and he made them a feast, and baked unleavened bread, and they ate. 4 But before they lay down, the men of the city, the men of Sodom, both young and old, all the people to the last man, surrounded the house; 5 and they called to Lot, "Where are the men who came to you tonight? Bring them out to us, so that we may know them." 6 Lot went out of the door to the men, shut the door after him, 7 and said, "I beg you, my brothers, do not act so wickedly. 8 Look, I have two daughters who have not known a man; let me bring them out to you, and do to them as you please; only do nothing to these men, for they have come under the shelter of my roof." 9 But they replied, "Stand back!" And they said, "This fellow came here as an alien, and he would play the judge! Now we will deal worse with you than with them." Then they pressed hard against the man Lot, and came near the door to break it down. 10 But the men inside reached out their hands and brought Lot into the house with them, and shut the door. 11 And they struck with blindness the men who were at the door of the house, both small and great, so that they were unable to find the door.

12 Then the men said to Lot, "Have you anyone else here? Sons-in-law, sons, daughters, or anyone you have in the city — bring them out of the place. 13 For we are about to destroy this place, because the outcry against its people has become great before the LORD, and the LORD has sent us to destroy it." 14 So Lot went out and said to his sons-in-law, who were to marry his daughters, "Up, get out of this place; for the LORD is about to destroy the city." But he seemed to his sons-in-law to be jesting.

15 When morning dawned, the angels urged Lot, saying, "Get up, take your wife and your two daughters who are here, or else you will be consumed in the punishment of the city." 16 But he lingered; so the men seized him and his wife and his two daughters by the hand, the LORD being merciful to him, and they brought him out and left him outside the city. 17 When they had brought them outside, they^e said, "Flee for your life; do not look back or stop anywhere in the Plain; flee to the hills, or else you will be consumed." 18 And Lot said to them, "Oh, no, my lords; 19 your servant has found favor with you, and you have shown me great kindness in saving my life; but I cannot flee to the hills, for fear the disaster will overtake me and I die. 20 Look, that city is near enough to flee to, and it is a little one. Let me escape there — is it not a little one? — and my life will be saved!" 21 He said to him, "Very well, I grant you this favor too, and will not overthrow the city of which you have spoken. 22 Hurry, escape there, for I can do nothing until you arrive there." Therefore the city was called Zoar.^f 23 The sun had risen on the earth when Lot came to Zoar.

REVISED ENGLISH BIBLE

Lord become angry if I speak just once more: suppose ten can be found there?' 'For the sake of the ten I shall not destroy it,' said the Lord. 33 When the LORD had finished talking to Abraham, he went away, and Abraham returned home.

19 The two angels came to Sodom in the evening while Lot was sitting by the city gate. When he saw them, he rose to meet them and bowing low 2 he said, 'I pray you, sirs, turn aside to your servant's house to spend the night there and bathe your feet. You can continue your journey in the morning.' 'No,' they answered, 'we shall spend the night in the street.' 3 But Lot was so insistent that they accompanied him into his house. He prepared a meal for them, baking unleavened bread for them to eat.

4 Before they had lain down to sleep, the men of Sodom, both young and old, everyone without exception, surrounded the house. 5 They called to Lot: 'Where are the men who came to you tonight? Bring them out to us so that we may have intercourse with them.' 6 Lot went out into the doorway to them, and, closing the door behind him, 7 said, 'No, my friends, do not do anything so wicked. 8 Look, I have two daughters, virgins both of them; let me bring them out to you, and you can do what you like with them. But do nothing to these men, because they have come under the shelter of my roof.' 9 They said, 'Out of our way! This fellow has come and settled here as an alien, and does he now take it upon himself to judge us? We will treat you worse than them.' They crowded in on Lot and pressed close to break down the door. 10 But the two men inside reached out, pulled Lot into the house, and shut the door. 11 Then they struck those in the doorway, both young and old, with blindness so that they could not find the entrance.

12 The two men said to Lot, 'Have you anyone here, sons-in-law, sons, or daughters, or anyone else belonging to you in the city? Get them out of this place, 13 because we are going to destroy it. The LORD is aware of the great outcry against its citizens and has sent us to destroy it.' 14 So Lot went out and urged his sons-in-law to get out of the place at once. 'The LORD is about to destroy the city,' he said. But they did not take him seriously.

15 As soon as it was dawn, the angels urged Lot: 'Quick, take your wife and your two daughters who are here, or you will be destroyed when the city is punished.' 16 When he delayed, they grabbed his hand and the hands of his wife and two daughters, because the LORD had spared him, and they led him to safety outside the city. 17 After they had brought them out, one said, 'Flee for your lives! Do not look back or stop anywhere in the plain. Flee to the hills or you will be destroyed.' 18 Lot replied, 'No, sirs! 19 You have shown your servant favour, and even more by your unfailing care you have saved my life, but I cannot escape to the hills; I shall be overtaken by the disaster, and die. 20 Look, here is a town, only a small place, near enough for me to get to quickly. Let me escape to this small place and save my life.' 21 He said to him, 'I grant your request: I shall not overthrow the town you speak of. 22 But flee there quickly, because I can do nothing until you are there.' That is why the place was called Zoar. 23 The sun had risen over

---

^e Gk Syr Vg: Heb *he*   ^f That is *Little*   19:22 **Zoar:** *that is* Small.

Lord grow angry if I speak up this last time. What if there are at least ten there?" "For the sake of those ten," he replied, "I will not destroy it."

33 The LORD departed as soon as he had finished speaking with Abraham, and Abraham returned home.

19 The two angels reached Sodom in the evening, as Lot was sitting at the gate of Sodom. When Lot saw them, he got up to greet them; and bowing down with his face to the ground, 2 he said, "Please, gentlemen, come aside into your servant's house for the night, and bathe your feet; you can get up early to continue your journey." But they replied, "No, we shall pass the night in the town square." 3 He urged them so strongly, however, that they turned aside to his place and entered his house. He prepared a meal for them, baking cakes without leaven, and they dined.

4 Before they went to bed, all the townsmen of Sodom, both young and old — all the people to the last man — closed in on the house. 5 They called to Lot and said to him, "Where are the men who came to your house tonight? Bring them out to us that we may have intimacies with them." 6 Lot went out to meet them at the entrance. When he had shut the door behind him, 7 he said, "I beg you, my brothers, not to do this wicked thing. 8 I have two daughters who have never had intercourse with men. Let me bring them out to you, and you may do to them as you please. But don't do anything to these men, for you know they have come under the shelter of my roof." 9 They replied, "Stand back! This fellow," they sneered, "came here as an immigrant, and now he dares to give orders! We'll treat you worse than them!" With that, they pressed hard against Lot, moving in closer to break down the door. 10 But his guests put out their hands, pulled Lot inside with them, and closed the door; 11 at the same time they struck the men at the entrance of the house, one and all, with such a blinding light that they were utterly unable to reach the doorway.

12 Then the angels said to Lot: "Who else belongs to you here? Your sons [sons-in-law] and your daughters and all who belong to you in the city — take them away from it! 13 We are about to destroy this place, for the outcry reaching the LORD against those in the city is so great that he has sent us to destroy it." 14 So Lot went out and spoke to his sons-in-law, who had contracted marriage with his daughters. "Get up and leave this place," he told them; "the LORD is about to destroy the city." But his sons-in-law thought he was joking.

15 As dawn was breaking, the angels urged Lot on, saying, "On your way! Take with you your wife and your two daughters who are here, or you will be swept away in the punishment of the city." 16 When he hesitated, the men, by the LORD's mercy, seized his hand and the hands of his wife and his two daughters and led them to safety outside the city. 17 As soon as they had been brought outside, he was told: "Flee for your life! Don't look back or stop anywhere on the Plain. Get off to the hills at once, or you will be swept away." 18 "Oh, no, my lord!" replied Lot. 19 "You have already thought enough of your servant to do me the great kindness of intervening to save my life. But I cannot flee to the hills to keep the disaster from overtaking me, and so I shall die. 20 Look, this town ahead is near enough to escape to. It's only a small place. Let me flee there — it's a small place, isn't it? — that my life may be saved." 21 "Well, then," he replied, "I will also grant you the favor you now ask. I will not overthrow the town you speak of. 22 Hurry, escape there! I cannot do anything until you arrive there." That is why the town was called Zoar.

23 The sun was just rising over the earth as Lot arrived in

Lord will not be angry if I speak once more: perhaps there will only be ten.' 'I shall not destroy it,' he replied, 'for the sake of the ten.'

33 When he had finished talking to Abraham Yahweh went away, and Abraham returned home.

19 When the two angels reached Sodom in the evening, Lot was sitting at the gate of Sodom. As soon as Lot saw them, he stood up to greet them, and bowed to the ground. 2 'My lords,' he said, 'please come down to your servant's house to stay the night and wash your feet. Then you can make an early start on your journey.' 'No,' they said, 'we shall spend the night in the square.' 3 But he pressed them so much that they went home with him and entered his house. He prepared a meal for them, baking unleavened bread, and they had supper.

4 They had not gone to bed when the house was surrounded by the townspeople, the men of Sodom both young and old, all the people without exception. 5 Calling out to Lot they said, 'Where are the men who came to you tonight? Send them out to us so that we can have intercourse with them.'

6 Lot came out to them at the door and, having shut the door behind him, 7 said, 'Please, brothers, do not be wicked. 8 Look, I have two daughters who are virgins. I am ready to send them out to you, for you to treat as you please, but do nothing to these men since they are now under the protection of my roof.' 9 But they retorted, 'Stand back! This fellow came here as a foreigner, and now he wants to play the judge. Now we shall treat you worse than them.' Then they forced Lot back and moved forward to break down the door. 10 But the men reached out, pulled Lot back into the house with them, and shut the door. 11 And they dazzled those who were at the door of the house, one and all, with a blinding light, so that they could not find the doorway.

12 The men said to Lot, 'Have you anyone else here? Your sons, your daughters and all your people in the city, take them away, 13 for we are about to destroy this place, since the outcry to Yahweh against those in it has grown so loud that Yahweh has sent us to destroy it.' 14 So Lot went off and spoke to his future sons-in-law who were to marry his daughters. 'On your feet!' he said, 'Leave this place, for Yahweh is about to destroy the city.' But his sons-in-law thought he was joking.

15 When dawn broke the angels urged Lot on, 'To your feet! Take your wife and your two daughters who are here, or you will be swept away in the punishment of the city.' 16 And as he hesitated, the men seized his hand and the hands of his wife and his two daughters — Yahweh being merciful to him — and led him out and left him outside the city.

17 When they had brought him outside, he was told, 'Flee for your life. Do not look behind you or stop anywhere on the plain. Flee to the hills or you will be swept away.' 18 'Oh no, my lord!' Lot said to them, 19 'You have already been very good to your servant and shown me even greater love by saving my life, but I cannot flee to the hills, or disaster will overtake me and I shall die. 20 That town over there is near enough to flee to, and is small. Let me flee there — after all it is only a small place — and so survive.' 21 He replied, 'I grant you this favour too, and will not overthrow the town you speak of. 22 Hurry, flee to that one, for I cannot do anything until you reach it.' That is why the town is named Zoar.

23 The sun rose over the horizon just as Lot was entering

19, 12: Since Lot apparently had no sons, a glossator interpreted the term to mean sons-in-law.

NEW REVISED STANDARD VERSION

24 Then the LORD rained on Sodom and Gomorrah sulfur and fire from the LORD out of heaven; 25 and he overthrew those cities, and all the Plain, and all the inhabitants of the cities, and what grew on the ground. 26 But Lot's wife, behind him, looked back, and she became a pillar of salt.

27 Abraham went early in the morning to the place where he had stood before the LORD; 28 and he looked down toward Sodom and Gomorrah and toward all the land of the Plain and saw the smoke of the land going up like the smoke of a furnace.

29 So it was that, when God destroyed the cities of the Plain, God remembered Abraham, and sent Lot out of the midst of the overthrow, when he overthrew the cities in which Lot had settled.

30 Now Lot went up out of Zoar and settled in the hills with his two daughters, for he was afraid to stay in Zoar; so he lived in a cave with his two daughters. 31 And the firstborn said to the younger, "Our father is old, and there is not a man on earth to come in to us after the manner of all the world. 32 Come, let us make our father drink wine, and we will lie with him, so that we may preserve offspring through our father." 33 So they made their father drink wine that night; and the firstborn went in, and lay with her father; he did not know when she lay down or when she rose. 34 On the next day, the firstborn said to the younger, "Look, I lay last night with my father; let us make him drink wine tonight also; then you go in and lie with him, so that we may preserve offspring through our father." 35 So they made their father drink wine that night also; and the younger rose, and lay with him; and he did not know when she lay down or when she rose. 36 Thus both the daughters of Lot became pregnant by their father. 37 The firstborn bore a son, and named him Moab; he is the ancestor of the Moabites to this day. 38 The younger also bore a son and named him Ben-ammi; he is the ancestor of the Ammonites to this day.

20 From there Abraham journeyed toward the region of the Negeb, and settled between Kadesh and Shur. While residing in Gerar as an alien, 2 Abraham said of his wife Sarah, "She is my sister." And King Abimelech of Gerar sent and took Sarah. 3 But God came to Abimelech in a dream by night, and said to him, "You are about to die because of the woman whom you have taken; for she is a married woman." 4 Now Abimelech had not approached her; so he said, "Lord, will you destroy an innocent people? 5 Did he not himself say to me, 'She is my sister'? And she herself said, 'He is my brother.' I did this in the integrity of my heart and the innocence of my hands." 6 Then God said to him in the dream, "Yes, I know that you did this in the integrity of your heart; furthermore it was I who kept you from sinning against me. Therefore I did not let you touch her. 7 Now then, return the man's wife; for he is a prophet, and he will pray for you and you shall live. But if you do not restore her, know that you shall surely die, you and all that are yours."

8 So Abimelech rose early in the morning, and called all his servants and told them all these things; and the men were very much afraid. 9 Then Abimelech called Abraham, and said to him, "What have you done to us? How have I sinned against you, that you have brought such great guilt on me and my kingdom? You have done things to me that ought not to be done." 10 And Abimelech said to Abraham, "What were you thinking of, that you did this thing?" 11 Abraham

REVISED ENGLISH BIBLE

the land as Lot entered Zoar, 24 and the LORD rained down fire and brimstone from the skies on Sodom and Gomorrah. 25 He overthrew those cities and destroyed all the plain, with everyone living and everything growing in the ground. 26 But Lot's wife looked back, and she turned into a pillar of salt.

27 Early next morning Abraham went to the place where he had stood in the presence of the LORD. 28 As he looked over Sodom and Gomorrah and all the wide extent of the plain, he saw thick smoke rising from the earth like smoke from a kiln. 29 Thus it was, when God destroyed the cities of the plain, he took thought for Abraham by rescuing Lot from the total destruction of the cities where he had been living.

30 Because Lot was afraid to stay in Zoar, he went up from there and settled with his two daughters in the hill-country, where he lived with them in a cave. 31 The elder daughter said to the younger, 'Our father is old and there is not a man in the country to come to us in the usual way. 32 Come now, let us ply our father with wine and then lie with him and in this way preserve the family through our father.' 33 That night they gave him wine to drink, and the elder daughter came and lay with him, and he did not know when she lay down and when she got up. 34 Next day the elder said to the younger, 'Last night I lay with my father. Let us ply him with wine again tonight; then you go in and lie with him. So we shall preserve the family through our father.' 35 They gave their father wine to drink that night also; and the younger daughter went and lay with him, and he did not know when she lay down and when she got up. 36 In this way both of Lot's daughters came to be pregnant by their father. 37 The elder daughter bore a son and called him Moab; he was the ancestor of the present-day Moabites. 38 The younger also bore a son, whom she called Ben-ammi; he was the ancestor of the present-day Ammonites.

20 ABRAHAM journeyed by stages from there into the Negeb, and settled between Kadesh and Shur, living as an alien in Gerar. 2 He said of Sarah his wife that she was his sister, and King Abimelech of Gerar had her brought to him. 3 But God came to Abimelech in a dream by night and said, 'You shall die because of this woman whom you have taken; she is a married woman.' 4 Abimelech, who had not gone near her, protested, 'Lord, will you destroy people who are innocent? 5 He told me himself that she was his sister, and she also said that he was her brother. It was in good faith and in all innocence that I did this.' 6 'Yes, I know that you acted in good faith,' God replied in the dream. 'Indeed, it was I who held you back from committing a sin against me. That was why I did not let you touch her. 7 But now send back the man's wife; he is a prophet and will intercede on your behalf, and you will live. But if you do not give her back, I tell you that you are doomed to die, you and all your household.'

8 Next morning Abimelech rose early and called together all his court officials; when he told them the whole story, the men were terrified. 9 Abimelech then summoned Abraham. 'Why have you treated us like this?' he demanded. 'What harm have I done you that you should bring this great sin on me and my kingdom? You have done to me something you ought never to have done.' 10 And he asked, 'What was your purpose in doing this?' 11 Abraham an-

NEW AMERICAN BIBLE | NEW JERUSALEM BIBLE

Zoar; 24 at the same time the LORD rained down sulphurous fire upon Sodom and Gomorrah [from the LORD out of heaven]. 25 He overthrew those cities and the whole Plain, together with the inhabitants of the cities and the produce of the soil. 26 But Lot's wife looked back, and she was turned into a pillar of salt.

27 Early the next morning Abraham went to the place where he had stood in the LORD's presence. 28 As he looked down toward Sodom and Gomorrah and the whole region of the Plain, he saw dense smoke over the land rising like fumes from a furnace.

29 Thus it came to pass: when God destroyed the Cities of the Plain, he was mindful of Abraham by sending Lot away from the upheaval by which God overthrew the cities where Lot had been living.

30 Since Lot was afraid to stay in Zoar, he and his two daughters went up from Zoar and settled in the hill country, where he lived with his two daughters in a cave. 31 The older one said to the younger: "Our father is getting old, and there is not a man on earth to unite with us as was the custom everywhere. 32 Come, let us ply our father with wine and then lie with him, that we may have offspring by our father." 33 So that night they plied their father with wine, and the older one went in and lay with her father; but he was not aware of her lying down or her getting up. 34 Next day the older one said to the younger: "Last night it was I who lay with my father. Let us ply him with wine again tonight, and then you go in and lie with him, that we may both have offspring by our father." 35 So that night, too, they plied their father with wine, and then the younger one went in and lay with him; but again he was not aware of her lying down or her getting up.

36 Thus both of Lot's daughters became pregnant by their father. 37 The older one gave birth to a son whom she named Moab, saying, "From my father." He is the ancestor of the Moabites of today. 38 The younger one, too, gave birth to a son, and she named him Ammon, saying, "The son of my kin." He is the ancestor of the Ammonites of today.

20 Abraham journeyed on to the region of the Negeb, where he settled between Kadesh and Shur. While he stayed in Gerar, 2 he said of his wife Sarah, "She is my sister." So Abimelech, king of Gerar, sent and took Sarah. 3 But God came to Abimelech in a dream one night and said to him, "You are about to die because of the woman you have taken, for she has a husband." 4 Abimelech, who had not approached her, said: "O Lord, would you slay a man even though he is innocent? 5 He himself told me, 'She is my sister,' and she herself also stated, 'He is my brother.' I did it in good faith and with clean hands." 6 God answered him in the dream: "Yes, I know you did it in good faith. In fact, it was I who kept you from sinning against me; that is why I did not let you touch her. 7 Therefore, return the man's wife — as a spokesman he will intercede for you — that your life may be saved. If you do not return her, you can be sure that you and all who are yours will certainly die."

8 Early the next morning Abimelech called all his court officials and informed them of everything that had happened, and the men were horrified. 9 Then Abimelech summoned Abraham and said to him: "How could you do this to us! What wrong did I do to you that you should have brought such monstrous guilt on me and my kingdom? You have treated me in an intolerable way. 10 What were you afraid of," he asked him, "that you should have done such a thing?" 11 "I was afraid," answered Abraham, "because I

Zoar. 24 Then Yahweh rained down on Sodom and Gomorrah brimstone and fire of his own sending. 25 He overthrew those cities and the whole plain, with all the people living in the cities and everything that grew there. 26 But Lot's wife looked back, and was turned into a pillar of salt.

27 Next morning, Abraham hurried to the place where he had stood before Yahweh, 28 and looking towards Sodom and Gomorrah and the whole area of the plain, he saw the smoke rising from the ground like smoke from a furnace.

29 Thus it was that, when God destroyed the cities of the plain, he did not forget Abraham and he rescued Lot from the midst of the overthrow, when he overthrew the cities where Lot was living.

30 After leaving Zoar Lot settled in the hill country with his two daughters, for he dared not stay at Zoar. He lived in a cave, he and his two daughters.

31 The elder said to the younger, 'Our father is an old man, and there is no one here to marry us in the normal way of the world. 32 Come on, let us ply our father with wine and sleep with him. In this way we can preserve the race by our father.' 33 That night they made their father drunk, and the elder slept with her father though he was unaware of her coming to bed or of her leaving. 34 The next day the elder said to the younger, 'Last night, I was the one who slept with our father. Let us make him drunk again tonight, and you go and sleep with him. In this way we can preserve the race by our father.' 35 They made their father drunk that night too, and the younger went and slept with him, though he was unaware of her coming to bed or of her leaving. 36 Both Lot's daughters thus became pregnant by their father. 37 The elder gave birth to a son whom she named Moab; and he is the ancestor of the Moabitesh of our own times. 38 The younger also gave birth to a son whom she named Ben-Ammi; and he is the ancestor of the Bene-Ammon of our own times.

20 iAbraham left there for the region of the Negeb, and settled between Kadesh and Shur. While staying in Gerar, 2 Abraham said of his wife Sarah, 'She is my sister,' and Abimelech the king of Gerar had Sarah brought to him. 3 But God visited Abimelech in a dream one night. 'You are to die,' he told him, 'because of the woman you have taken, for she is a married woman.' 4 Abimelech, however, had not gone near her; so he said, 'Lord, would you kill someone even if he is upright? 5 Did he not tell me himself, "She is my sister"? And she herself said, "He is my brother." I did this with a clear conscience and clean hands.' 6 'Yes, I know,' God replied in the dream, 'that you did this with a clear conscience and I myself prevented you from sinning against me. That was why I did not let you touch her. 7 Now send the man's wife back; for he is a prophet and can intercede on your behalf for your life. But understand that if you do not send her back, this means death for you and all yours.'

8 Early next morning, Abimelech summoned his full court and told them the whole story, at which the people were very much afraid. 9 Then summoning Abraham, Abimelech said to him, 'What have you done to us? What wrong have I done you, for you to bring such guilt on me and on my kingdom? You had no right to treat me like this.' 10 Abimelech then said to Abraham, 'What possessed you to do such a thing?' 11 'Because', Abraham replied, 'I thought

h 19 Popular explanations of the name Moab as 'from my father' and of Ben Ammon as 'son of my kinsman'.
i 20 = 12:10–20; = 26:1–11.

NEW REVISED STANDARD VERSION	REVISED ENGLISH BIBLE

said, "I did it because I thought, There is no fear of God at all in this place, and they will kill me because of my wife. 12 Besides, she is indeed my sister, the daughter of my father but not the daughter of my mother; and she became my wife. 13 And when God caused me to wander from my father's house, I said to her, 'This is the kindness you must do me: at every place to which we come, say of me, He is my brother.' " 14 Then Abimelech took sheep and oxen, and male and female slaves, and gave them to Abraham, and restored his wife Sarah to him. 15 Abimelech said, "My land is before you; settle where it pleases you." 16 To Sarah he said, "Look, I have given your brother a thousand pieces of silver; it is your exoneration before all who are with you; you are completely vindicated." 17 Then Abraham prayed to God; and God healed Abimelech, and also healed his wife and female slaves so that they bore children. 18 For the LORD had closed fast all the wombs of the house of Abimelech because of Sarah, Abraham's wife.

21 The LORD dealt with Sarah as he had said, and the LORD did for Sarah as he had promised. 2 Sarah conceived and bore Abraham a son in his old age, at the time of which God had spoken to him. 3 Abraham gave the name Isaac to his son whom Sarah bore him. 4 And Abraham circumcised his son Isaac when he was eight days old, as God had commanded him. 5 Abraham was a hundred years old when his son Isaac was born to him. 6 Now Sarah said, "God has brought laughter for me; everyone who hears will laugh with me." 7 And she said, "Who would ever have said to Abraham that Sarah would nurse children? Yet I have borne him a son in his old age."

8 The child grew, and was weaned; and Abraham made a great feast on the day that Isaac was weaned. 9 But Sarah saw the son of Hagar the Egyptian, whom she had borne to Abraham, playing with her son Isaac.*g* 10 So she said to Abraham, "Cast out this slave woman with her son; for the son of this slave woman shall not inherit along with my son Isaac." 11 The matter was very distressing to Abraham on account of his son. 12 But God said to Abraham, "Do not be distressed because of the boy and because of your slave woman; whatever Sarah says to you, do as she tells you, for it is through Isaac that offspring shall be named for you. 13 As for the son of the slave woman, I will make a nation of him also, because he is your offspring." 14 So Abraham rose early in the morning, and took bread and a skin of water, and gave it to Hagar, putting it on her shoulder, along with the child, and sent her away. And she departed, and wandered about in the wilderness of Beer-sheba.

15 When the water in the skin was gone, she cast the child under one of the bushes. 16 Then she went and sat down opposite him a good way off, about the distance of a bowshot; for she said, "Do not let me look on the death of the child." And as she sat opposite him, she lifted up her voice and wept. 17 And God heard the voice of the boy; and the angel of God called to Hagar from heaven, and said to her, "What troubles you, Hagar? Do not be afraid; for God has heard the voice of the boy where he is. 18 Come, lift up the boy and hold him fast with your hand, for I will make a great nation of him." 19 Then God opened her eyes and she saw a well of water. She went, and filled the skin with water, and gave the boy a drink.

20 God was with the boy, and he grew up; he lived in the wilderness, and became an expert with the bow. 21 He lived in the wilderness of Paran; and his mother got a wife for him from the land of Egypt.

22 At that time Abimelech, with Phicol the commander of his army, said to Abraham, "God is with you in all that you do; 23 now therefore swear to me here by God that you

swered, 'I said to myself, "There is no fear of God in this place, and I shall be killed for the sake of my wife." 12 She is in fact my sister, my father's daughter though not by my mother, and she became my wife. 13 When God set me wandering from my father's house, I said to her, "There is a duty towards me which you must loyally fulfil: wherever we go, you must say that I am your brother." ' 14 Then Abimelech took sheep and cattle and male and female slaves and gave them to Abraham. He returned Sarah to him 15 and said, 'My country is at your disposal; settle wherever you please.' 16 To Sarah he said, 'I have given your brother a thousand pieces of silver to compensate you for all that has befallen you; you are completely cleared.' 17 Then Abraham interceded with God, and he healed Abimelech, his wife, and his slave-girls, so that they could have children; 18 for the LORD had made every woman in Abimelech's household barren on account of Sarah, Abraham's wife.

21 THE LORD showed favour to Sarah as he had promised, and made good what he had said about her. 2 She conceived and at the time foretold by God she bore a son to Abraham in his old age. 3 The son whom Sarah bore to him Abraham named Isaac, 4 and when Isaac was eight days old Abraham circumcised him, as decreed by God. 5 Abraham was a hundred years old when his son Isaac was born. 6 Sarah said, 'God has given me good reason to laugh, and everyone who hears will laugh with me.' 7 She added, 'Whoever would have told Abraham that Sarah would suckle children? Yet I have borne him a son in his old age.' 8 The boy grew and was weaned, and on the day of his weaning Abraham gave a great feast.

9 Sarah saw the son whom Hagar the Egyptian had borne to Abraham playing with Isaac, 10 and she said to Abraham, 'Drive out this slave-girl and her son! I will not have this slave's son sharing the inheritance with my son Isaac.' 11 Abraham was very upset at this because of Ishmael, 12 but God said to him, 'Do not be upset for the boy and your slave-girl. Do as Sarah says, because it is through Isaac's line that your name will be perpetuated. 13 I shall make a nation of the slave-girl's son, because he also is your child.'

14 Early next morning Abraham took some food and a full water-skin and gave them to Hagar. He set the child on her shoulder and sent her away, and she wandered about in the wilderness of Beersheba. 15 When the water in the skin was finished, she thrust the child under a bush, 16 then went and sat down some way off, about a bowshot distant. 'How can I watch the child die?' she said, and sat there, weeping bitterly. 17 God heard the child crying, and the angel of God called from heaven to Hagar, 'What is the matter, Hagar? Do not be afraid: God has heard the child crying where you laid him. 18 Go, lift the child and hold him in your arms, because I shall make of him a great nation.' 19 Then God opened her eyes and she saw a well full of water; she went to it, filled the water-skin, and gave the child a drink. 20 God was with the child as he grew up. He lived in the wilderness of Paran and became an archer; 21 and his mother got him a wife from Egypt.

22 About that time Abimelech, with Phicol the commander of his army, said to Abraham: 'God is with you in all that you do. 23 Here and now swear to me in the name of God,

g Gk Vg: Heb lacks *with her son Isaac*

|

thought there would surely be no fear of God in this place, and so they would kill me on account of my wife. 12 Besides, she is in truth my sister, but only my father's daughter, not my mother's; and so she became my wife. 13 When God sent me wandering from my father's house, I asked her: 'Would you do me this favor? In whatever place we come to, say that I am your brother.' "

14 Then Abimelech took flocks and herds and male and female slaves and gave them to Abraham; and after he restored his wife Sarah to him, 15 he said, "Here, my land lies at your disposal; settle wherever you please." 16 To Sarah he said: "See, I have given your brother a thousand shekels of silver. Let that serve you as a vindication before all who are with you; your honor has been preserved with everyone." 17 Abraham then interceded with God, and God restored health to Abimelech, that is, to his wife and his maidservants, so that they could bear children; 18 for God had tightly closed every womb in Abimelech's household on account of Abraham's wife Sarah.

21 The LORD took note of Sarah as he had said he would; he did for her as he had promised. 2 Sarah became pregnant and bore Abraham a son in his old age, at the set time that God had stated. 3 Abraham gave the name Isaac to this son of his whom Sarah bore him. 4 When his son Isaac was eight days old, Abraham circumcised him, as God had commanded. 5 Abraham was a hundred years old when his son Isaac was born to him. 6 Sarah then said, "God has given me cause to laugh, and all who hear of it will laugh with me. 7 Who would have told Abraham," she added, "that Sarah would nurse children! Yet I have borne him a son in his old age." 8 Isaac grew, and on the day of the child's weaning Abraham held a great feast.

9 Sarah noticed the son whom Hagar the Egyptian had borne to Abraham playing with her son Isaac; 10 so she demanded of Abraham: "Drive out that slave and her son! No son of that slave is going to share the inheritance with my son Isaac!" 11 Abraham was greatly distressed, especially on account of his son Ishmael. 12 But God said to Abraham: "Do not be distressed about the boy or about your slave woman. Heed the demands of Sarah, no matter what she is asking of you; for it is through Isaac that descendants shall bear your name. 13 As for the son of the slave woman, I will make a great nation of him also, since he too is your offspring."

14 Early the next morning Abraham got some bread and a skin of water and gave them to Hagar. Then, placing the child on her back, he sent her away. As she roamed aimlessly in the wilderness of Beer-sheba, 15 the water in the skin was used up. So she put the child down under a shrub, 16 and then went and sat down opposite him, about a bowshot away; for she said to herself, "Let me not watch to see the child die." As she sat opposite him, he began to cry. 17 God heard the boy's cry, and God's messenger called to Hagar from heaven: "What is the matter, Hagar? Don't be afraid; God has heard the boy's cry in this plight of his. 18 Arise, lift up the boy and hold him by the hand; for I will make of him a great nation." 19 Then God opened her eyes, and she saw a well of water. She went and filled the skin with water, and then let the boy drink.

20 God was with the boy as he grew up. He lived in the wilderness and became an expert bowman, 21 with his home in the wilderness of Paran. His mother got a wife for him from the land of Egypt.

22 About that time Abimelech, accompanied by Phicol, the commander of his army, said to Abraham: "God is with you in everything you do. 23 Therefore, swear to me by God

there would be no fear of God here and that I should be killed for the sake of my wife. 12 Anyway, she really is my sister, my father's daughter though not my mother's, besides being my wife. 13 So when God made me wander far from my father's home I said to her, "There is an act of love you can do me: everywhere we go, say of me that I am your brother." '

14 Abimelech took sheep, cattle, men and women slaves, and presented them to Abraham, and gave him back his wife Sarah. 15 And Abimelech said, 'Look, my land is open to you. Settle wherever you please.' 16 To Sarah he said, 'Look, I am giving your brother a thousand pieces of silver. This will allay suspicions about you, as far as all the people round you are concerned; you have been completely vindicated.' 17 Abraham then interceded with God, and God healed Abimelech, his wife and his slave-girls, so that they could have children, 18 for Yahweh had made all the women of Abimelech's household barren on account of Sarah, Abraham's wife.

21 Yahweh treated Sarah as he had said, and did what he had promised her. 2 Sarah conceived and bore Abraham a son in his old age, at the time God had promised. 3 Abraham named the son born to him Isaac, the son to whom Sarah had given birth. 4 Abraham circumcised his son Isaac when he was eight days old, as God had commanded him. 5 Abraham was a hundred years old when his son Isaac was born to him. 6 Sarah said:

God has given me cause to laugh!
All who hear about this will laugh with me!

7 She added:

Whoever would have told Abraham
that Sarah would nurse children!
Yet I have borne a son in his old age.

8 j The child grew and was weaned, and Abraham gave a great banquet on the day Isaac was weaned. 9 Now Sarah watched the son that Hagar the Egyptian had borne to Abraham, playing with her son Isaac. 10 'Drive away that slave-girl and her son,' she said to Abraham, 'this slave-girl's son is not to share the inheritance with my son Isaac.' 11 This greatly distressed Abraham, because the slave-girl's child too was his son, 12 but God said to him, 'Do not distress yourself on account of the boy and your slave-girl. Do whatever Sarah says, for Isaac is the one through whom your name will be carried on. 13 But the slave-girl's son I shall also make into a great nation, for he too is your child.' 14 Early next morning, Abraham took some bread and a skin of water and, giving them to Hagar, put the child on her shoulder and sent her away.

She wandered off into the desert of Beersheba. 15 When the skin of water was finished she abandoned the child under a bush. 16 Then she went and sat down at a distance, about a bowshot away, thinking, 'I cannot bear to see the child die.' Sitting at a distance, she began to sob. 17 God heard the boy crying, and the angel of God called to Hagar from heaven. 'What is wrong, Hagar?' he asked. 'Do not be afraid, for God has heard the boy's cry in his plight. 18 Go and pick the boy up and hold him safe, for I shall make him into a great nation.' 19 Then God opened Hagar's eyes and she saw a well, so she went and filled the skin with water and gave the boy a drink.

20 God was with the boy. He grew up and made his home in the desert, and he became an archer. 21 He made his home in the desert of Paran, and his mother got him a wife from Egypt.

22 About then, Abimelech and Phicol, the commander of his army, said to Abraham, 'Since God is with you in everything you do, 23 swear to me by God, here and now,

will not deal falsely with me or with my offspring or with my posterity, but as I have dealt loyally with you, you will deal with me and with the land where you have resided as an alien." 24 And Abraham said, "I swear it."

25 When Abraham complained to Abimelech about a well of water that Abimelech's servants had seized, 26 Abimelech said, "I do not know who has done this; you did not tell me, and I have not heard of it until today." 27 So Abraham took sheep and oxen and gave them to Abimelech, and the two men made a covenant. 28 Abraham set apart seven ewe lambs of the flock. 29 And Abimelech said to Abraham, "What is the meaning of these seven ewe lambs that you have set apart?" 30 He said, "These seven ewe lambs you shall accept from my hand, in order that you may be a witness for me that I dug this well." 31 Therefore that place was called Beer-sheba;*h* because there both of them swore an oath. 32 When they had made a covenant at Beer-sheba, Abimelech, with Phicol the commander of his army, left and returned to the land of the Philistines. 33 Abraham*i* planted a tamarisk tree in Beer-sheba, and called there on the name of the Lord, the Everlasting God.*j* 34 And Abraham resided as an alien many days in the land of the Philistines.

22 After these things God tested Abraham. He said to him, "Abraham!" And he said, "Here I am." 2 He said, "Take your son, your only son Isaac, whom you love, and go to the land of Moriah, and offer him there as a burnt offering on one of the mountains that I shall show you." 3 So Abraham rose early in the morning, saddled his donkey, and took two of his young men with him, and his son Isaac; he cut the wood for the burnt offering, and set out and went to the place in the distance that God had shown him. 4 On the third day Abraham looked up and saw the place far away. 5 Then Abraham said to his young men, "Stay here with the donkey; the boy and I will go over there; we will worship, and then we will come back to you." 6 Abraham took the wood of the burnt offering and laid it on his son Isaac, and he himself carried the fire and the knife. So the two of them walked on together. 7 Isaac said to his father Abraham, "Father!" And he said, "Here I am, my son." He said, "The fire and the wood are here, but where is the lamb for a burnt offering?" 8 Abraham said, "God himself will provide the lamb for a burnt offering, my son." So the two of them walked on together.

9 When they came to the place that God had shown him, Abraham built an altar there and laid the wood in order. He bound his son Isaac, and laid him on the altar, on top of the wood. 10 Then Abraham reached out his hand and took the knife to kill*k* his son. 11 But the angel of the Lord called to him from heaven, and said, "Abraham, Abraham!" And he said, "Here I am." 12 He said, "Do not lay your hand on the boy or do anything to him; for now I know that you fear God, since you have not withheld your son, your only son, from me." 13 And Abraham looked up and saw a ram, caught in a thicket by its horns. Abraham went and took the ram and offered it up as a burnt offering instead of his son. 14 So Abraham called that place "The Lord will provide";*l* as it is said to this day, "On the mount of the Lord it shall be provided."*m*

15 The angel of the Lord called to Abraham a second time from heaven, 16 and said, "By myself I have sworn, says the Lord: Because you have done this, and have not withheld your son, your only son, 17 I will indeed bless you,

that you will not break faith with me or with my children and my descendants. As I have kept faith with you, so must you keep faith with me and with the country where you are living.' 24 Abraham said, 'I swear it.'

25 It happened that Abraham had a complaint to make to Abimelech about a well which Abimelech's men had seized. 26 Abimelech said, 'I do not know who did this. Up to this moment you never mentioned it, nor did I hear of it from anyone else.' 27 Then Abraham took sheep and cattle and gave them to Abimelech, and the two of them made a pact. 28 Abraham set seven ewe lambs apart, 29 and when Abimelech asked him why he had done so, 30 he said, 'Accept these seven lambs from me as a testimony on my behalf that I dug this well.' 31 This is why that place was called Beersheba, because there the two of them swore an oath. 32 When they had made the pact at Beersheba, Abimelech departed with Phicol the commander of his army, and returned to the country of the Philistines. 33 Abraham planted a tamarisk tree at Beersheba, and there he invoked the Lord, the Everlasting God, by name. 34 He lived as an alien in the country of the Philistines for many years.

22 Some time later God put Abraham to the test. 'Abraham!' he called to him, and Abraham replied, 'Here I am!' 2 God said, 'Take your one and only son Isaac whom you love, and go to the land of Moriah. There you shall offer him as a sacrifice on one of the heights which I shall show you.' 3 Early in the morning Abraham saddled his donkey, and took with him two of his men and his son Isaac; and having split firewood for the sacrifice, he set out for the place of which God had spoken. 4 On the third day Abraham looked up and saw the shrine in the distance. 5 He said to his men, 'Stay here with the donkey while I and the boy go on ahead. We shall worship there, and then come back to you.'

6 Abraham took the wood for the sacrifice and put it on his son Isaac's shoulder, while he himself carried the fire and the knife. As the two of them went on together, 7 Isaac spoke. 'Father!' he said. Abraham answered, 'What is it, my son?' Isaac said, 'Here are the fire and the wood, but where is the sheep for a sacrifice?' 8 Abraham answered, 'God will provide himself with a sheep for a sacrifice, my son.' The two of them went on together 9 until they came to the place of which God had spoken. There Abraham built an altar and arranged the wood. He bound his son Isaac and laid him on the altar on top of the wood. 10 He reached out for the knife to slay his son, 11 but the angel of the Lord called to him from heaven, 'Abraham! Abraham!' He answered, 'Here I am!' 12 The angel said, 'Do not raise your hand against the boy; do not touch him. Now I know that you are a godfearing man. You have not withheld from me your son, your only son.' 13 Abraham looked round, and there in a thicket he saw a ram caught by its horns. He went, seized the ram, and offered it as a sacrifice instead of his son. 14 Abraham named that shrine 'The Lord will provide'; and to this day the saying is: 'In the mountain of the Lord it was provided.'

15 Then the angel of the Lord called from heaven a second time to Abraham 16 and said, 'This is the word of the Lord: By my own self I swear that because you have done this and have not withheld your son, your only son, 17 I shall

---

h That is *Well of seven* or *Well of the oath*   *i* Heb *He*   *j* Or *the Lord, El Olam*   *k* Or *to slaughter*   *l* Or *will see*; Heb traditionally transliterated *Jehovah Jireh*   *m* Or *he shall be seen*

21:31 **Beersheba:** *that is* Well of Seven *and* Well of an Oath.
21:33 **tamarisk tree:** *or* strip of ground.

NEW AMERICAN BIBLE

at this place that you will not deal falsely with me or with my progeny and posterity, but will act as loyally toward me and the land in which you stay as I have acted toward you." 24 To this Abraham replied, "I so swear."

25 Abraham, however, reproached Abimelech about a well that Abimelech's men had seized by force. 26 "I have no idea who did that," Abimelech replied. "In fact, you never told me about it, nor did I ever hear of it until now."

27 Then Abraham took sheep and cattle and gave them to Abimelech and the two made a pact. 28 Abraham also set apart seven lambs of the flock, 29 and Abimelech asked him, "What is the purpose of these seven ewe lambs that you have set apart?" 30 Abraham answered, "The seven ewe lambs you shall accept from me that thus I may have your acknowledgment that the well was dug by me." 31 This is why the place is called Beer-sheba; the two of them took an oath there. 32 When they had thus made the pact in Beer-sheba, Abimelech, along with Phicol, the commander of his army, left and returned to the land of the Philistines.

33 Abraham planted a tamarisk at Beer-sheba, and there he invoked by name the LORD, God the Eternal. 34 Abraham resided in the land of the Philistines for many years.

22 Some time after these events, God put Abraham to the test. He called to him, "Abraham!" "Ready!" he replied. 2 Then God said: "Take your son Isaac, your only one, whom you love, and go to the land of Moriah. There you shall offer him up as a holocaust on a height that I will point out to you." 3 Early the next morning Abraham saddled his donkey, took with him his son Isaac, and two of his servants as well, and with the wood that he had cut for the holocaust, set out for the place of which God had told him.

4 On the third day Abraham got sight of the place from afar. 5 Then he said to his servants: "Both of you stay here with the donkey, while the boy and I go on over yonder. We will worship and then come back to you." 6 Thereupon Abraham took the wood for the holocaust and laid it on his son Isaac's shoulders, while he himself carried the fire and the knife. 7 As the two walked on together, Isaac spoke to his father Abraham: "Father!" he said. "Yes, son," he replied. Isaac continued, "Here are the fire and the wood, but where is the sheep for the holocaust?" 8 "Son," Abraham answered, "God himself will provide the sheep for the holocaust." Then the two continued going forward.

9 When they came to the place of which God had told him, Abraham built an altar there and arranged the wood on it. Next he tied up his son Isaac, and put him on top of the wood on the altar. 10 Then he reached out and took the knife to slaughter his son. 11 But the LORD's messenger called to him from heaven, "Abraham, Abraham!" "Yes, Lord," he answered. 12 "Do not lay your hand on the boy," said the messenger. "Do not do the least thing to him. I know now how devoted you are to God, since you did not withhold from me your own beloved son." 13 As Abraham looked about, he spied a ram caught by its horns in the thicket. So he went and took the ram and offered it up as a holocaust in place of his son. 14 Abraham named the site Yahweh-yireh; hence people now say, "On the mountain the LORD will see."

15 Again the LORD's messenger called to Abraham from heaven 16 and said: "I swear by myself, declares the LORD, that because you acted as you did in not withholding from me your beloved son, 17 I will bless you abundantly and

NEW JERUSALEM BIBLE

that you will not act treacherously towards me or my kith and kin, but behave with the same faithful love to me and the land of which you are a guest as I have behaved to you.' 24 'Yes,' Abraham replied, 'I swear it.'

25 Abraham then reproached Abimelech about a well that Abimelech's servants had seized. 26 'I do not know who has done this,' Abimelech said. 'You yourself have never mentioned it to me and, for myself, I heard nothing of it till today.' 27 Abraham then took sheep and cattle and presented them to Abimelech, and the two of them made a covenant. 28 Abraham put seven lambs of the flock on one side. 29 'Why have you put these seven lambs on one side?' Abimelech asked Abraham. 30 He replied, 'You must accept these seven lambs from me as evidence that I have dug this well.' 31 This was why the place was called Beersheba k: because there the two of them swore an oath.

32 After they had made a covenant at Beersheba, Abimelech and Phicol, the commander of his army, left and went back to Philistine territory. 33 And Abraham planted a tamarisk at Beersheba and there he invoked the name of Yahweh. 34 Abraham stayed for a long while in Philistine territory.

22 It happened some time later that God put Abraham to the test. 'Abraham, Abraham!' he called. 'Here I am,' he replied. 2 God said, 'Take your son, your only son, your beloved Isaac, and go to the land of Moriah, where you are to offer him as a burnt offering on one of the mountains which I shall point out to you.'

3 Early next morning Abraham saddled his donkey and took with him two of his servants and his son Isaac. He chopped wood for the burnt offering and started on his journey to the place which God had indicated to him. 4 On the third day Abraham looked up and saw the place in the distance. 5 Then Abraham said to his servants, 'Stay here with the donkey. The boy and I are going over there; we shall worship and then come back to you.'

6 Abraham took the wood for the burnt offering, loaded it on Isaac, and carried in his own hands the fire and the knife. Then the two of them set out together. 7 Isaac spoke to his father Abraham. 'Father?' he said. 'Yes, my son,' he replied. 'Look,' he said, 'here are the fire and the wood, but where is the lamb for the burnt offering?' 8 Abraham replied, 'My son, God himself will provide the lamb for the burnt offering.' And the two of them went on together.

9 When they arrived at the place which God had indicated to him, Abraham built an altar there, and arranged the wood. Then he bound his son and put him on the altar on top of the wood. 10 Abraham stretched out his hand and took the knife to kill his son.

11 But the angel of Yahweh called to him from heaven. 'Abraham, Abraham!' he said. 'Here I am,' he replied. 12 'Do not raise your hand against the boy,' the angel said. 'Do not harm him, for now I know you fear God. You have not refused me your own beloved son.' 13 Then looking up, Abraham saw a ram caught by its horns in a bush. Abraham took the ram and offered it as a burnt offering in place of his son. 14 Abraham called this place 'Yahweh provides', and hence the saying today: 'On the mountain Yahweh provides.'

15 The angel of Yahweh called Abraham a second time from heaven. 16 'I swear by my own self, Yahweh declares, that because you have done this, because you have not refused me your own beloved son, 17 I will shower blessings

k 21 Fragments using two explanations of the name as 'Well of the Seven' and 'Well of the Oath'. The story is parallel with 26:15–33.

and I will make your offspring as numerous as the stars of heaven and as the sand that is on the seashore. And your offspring shall possess the gate of their enemies, 18 and by your offspring shall all the nations of the earth gain blessing for themselves, because you have obeyed my voice." 19 So Abraham returned to his young men, and they arose and went together to Beer-sheba; and Abraham lived at Beer-sheba.

20 Now after these things it was told Abraham, "Milcah also has borne children, to your brother Nahor: 21 Uz the firstborn, Buz his brother, Kemuel the father of Aram, 22 Chesed, Hazo, Pildash, Jidlaph, and Bethuel." 23 Bethuel became the father of Rebekah. These eight Milcah bore to Nahor, Abraham's brother. 24 Moreover, his concubine, whose name was Reumah, bore Tebah, Gaham, Tahash, and Maacah.

23 Sarah lived one hundred twenty-seven years; this was the length of Sarah's life. 2 And Sarah died at Kiriath-arba (that is, Hebron) in the land of Canaan; and Abraham went in to mourn for Sarah and to weep for her. 3 Abraham rose up from beside his dead, and said to the Hittites, 4 "I am a stranger and an alien residing among you; give me property among you for a burying place, so that I may bury my dead out of my sight." 5 The Hittites answered Abraham, 6 "Hear us, my lord; you are a mighty prince among us. Bury your dead in the choicest of our burial places; none of us will withhold from you any burial ground for burying your dead." 7 Abraham rose and bowed to the Hittites, the people of the land. 8 He said to them, "If you are willing that I should bury my dead out of my sight, hear me, and entreat for me Ephron son of Zohar, 9 so that he may give me the cave of Machpelah, which he owns; it is at the end of his field. For the full price let him give it to me in your presence as a possession for a burying place." 10 Now Ephron was sitting among the Hittites; and Ephron the Hittite answered Abraham in the hearing of the Hittites, of all who went in at the gate of his city, 11 "No, my lord, hear me; I give you the field, and I give you the cave that is in it; in the presence of my people I give it to you; bury your dead." 12 Then Abraham bowed down before the people of the land. 13 He said to Ephron in the hearing of the people of the land, "If you only will listen to me! I will give the price of the field; accept it from me, so that I may bury my dead there." 14 Ephron answered Abraham, 15 "My lord, listen to me; a piece of land worth four hundred shekels of silver—what is that between you and me? Bury your dead." 16 Abraham agreed with Ephron; and Abraham weighed out for Ephron the silver that he had named in the hearing of the Hittites, four hundred shekels of silver, according to the weights current among the merchants.

17 So the field of Ephron in Machpelah, which was to the east of Mamre, the field with the cave that was in it and all the trees that were in the field, throughout its whole area, passed 18 to Abraham as a possession in the presence of the Hittites, in the presence of all who went in at the gate of his city. 19 After this, Abraham buried Sarah his wife in the cave of the field of Machpelah facing Mamre (that is, Hebron) in the land of Canaan. 20 The field and the cave that is in it passed from the Hittites into Abraham's possession as a burying place.

24 Now Abraham was old, well advanced in years; and the Lord had blessed Abraham in all things. 2 Abraham said to his servant, the oldest of his house, who had charge of all that he had, "Put your hand under my thigh 3 and I will make you swear by the Lord, the God of heaven and earth, that you will not get a wife for my son from the daughters of the Canaanites, among whom I live, 4 but will

bless you abundantly and make your descendants as numerous as the stars in the sky or the grains of sand on the seashore. Your descendants will possess the cities of their enemies. 18 All nations on earth will wish to be blessed as your descendants are blessed, because you have been obedient to me.'

19 Abraham then went back to his men, and together they returned to Beersheba; and there Abraham remained.

20 After this Abraham was told, 'Milcah has borne sons to your brother Nahor: 21 Uz his firstborn, then his brother Buz, and Kemuel father of Aram, 22 and Kesed, Hazo, Pildash, Jidlaph, and Bethuel; 23 and a daughter, Rebecca, has been born to Bethuel.' These eight Milcah bore to Abraham's brother Nahor. 24 His concubine, whose name was Reumah, also bore him sons: Tebah, Gaham, Tahash, and Maacah.

23 Sarah lived to be a hundred and twenty-seven years old, 2 and she died in Kiriath-arba (which is Hebron) in Canaan. Abraham went in to mourn over Sarah and to weep for her. 3 When at last he rose and left the presence of his dead one, he approached the Hittites: 4 'I am an alien and a settler among you,' he said. 'Make over to me some ground among you for a burial-place, that I may bury my dead.' 5 The Hittites answered, 6 'Listen to us, sir: you are a mighty prince among us; bury your dead in the best grave we have. There is not one of us who would deny you his grave or hinder you from burying your dead.'

7 Abraham rose and bowing low to the Hittites, the people of that region, 8 he said to them, 'If you have a mind to help me about the burial, then listen to me: speak to Ephron son of Zohar on my behalf, 9 and ask him to grant me the cave that belongs to him at Machpelah, at the far end of his land. In your presence let him make it over to me for the full price, so that I may take possession of it as a burial-place.' 10 Ephron was sitting with the other Hittites and in the hearing of all who had assembled at the city gate he gave Abraham this answer: 11 'No, sir; hear me: I shall make you a gift of the land and also give you the cave which is on it. In the presence of my people I give it to you; so bury your dead.' 12 Abraham bowed low before the people 13 and said to Ephron in their hearing, 'Do you really mean it? But listen to me—let me give you the price of the land: take it from me, and I shall bury my dead there.' 14 Ephron answered, 15 'Listen, sir: land worth four hundred shekels of silver, what is that between me and you! You may bury your dead there.' 16 Abraham closed the bargain with him and weighed out the amount that Ephron had named in the hearing of the Hittites, four hundred shekels of the standard recognized by merchants.

17 So the plot of land belonging to Ephron at Machpelah to the east of Mamre, the plot, the cave that is on it, with all the trees in the whole area, became the 18 legal possession of Abraham, in the presence of all the Hittites who had assembled at the city gate. 19 After this Abraham buried his wife Sarah in the cave on the plot of land at Machpelah to the east of Mamre, which is Hebron, in Canaan. 20 Thus, by purchase from the Hittites, the plot and the cave on it became Abraham's possession as a burial-place.

24 Abraham was by now a very old man, and the Lord had blessed him in all that he did. 2 Abraham said to the servant who had been longest in his service and was in charge of all he owned, 'Give me your solemn oath: 3 I want you to swear by the Lord, the God of heaven and earth, that you will not take a wife for my son from the women of the Canaanites among whom I am living. 4 You

24:2 **Give . . . oath:** lit. Put your hand under my thigh.

make your descendants as countless as the stars of the sky and the sands of the seashore; your descendants shall take possession of the gates of their enemies, 18 and in your descendants all the nations of the earth shall find blessing — all this because you obeyed my command."

19 Abraham then returned to his servants, and they set out together for Beer-sheba, where Abraham made his home.

20 Some time afterward, the news came to Abraham: "Milcah too has borne sons, to your brother Nahor: 21 Uz, his first-born, his brother Buz, Kemuel (the father of Aram), 22 Chesed, Hazo, Pildash, Jidlaph and Bethuel." 23 Bethuel became the father of Rebekah. These eight Milcah bore to Abraham's brother Nahor. 24 His concubine, whose name was Reumah, also bore children: Tebah, Gaham, Tahash and Maacah.

23 The span of Sarah's life was one hundred and twenty-seven years. 2 She died in Kiriatharba (that is, Hebron) in the land of Canaan, and Abraham performed the customary mourning rites for her. 3 Then he left the side of his dead one and addressed the Hittites: 4 "Although I am a resident alien among you, sell me from your holdings a piece of property for a burial ground, that I may bury my dead wife. 5 The Hittites answered Abraham: "Please, sir, 6 listen to us! You are an elect of God among us. Bury your dead in the choicest of our burial sites. None of us would deny you his burial ground for the burial of your dead." 7 Abraham, however, began to bow low before the local citizens, the Hittites, 8 while he appealed to them: "If you will allow me room for burial of my dead, listen to me! Intercede for me with Ephron, son of Zohar, asking him 9 to sell me the cave of Machpelah that he owns; it is at the edge of his field. Let him sell it to me in your presence, at its full price, for a burial place."

10 Now Ephron was present with the Hittites. So Ephron the Hittite replied to Abraham in the hearing of the Hittites who sat on his town council: 11 "Please, sir, listen to me! I give you both the field and the cave in it; in the presence of my kinsmen I make this gift. Bury your dead!" 12 But Abraham, after bowing low before the local citizens, addressed Ephron in the hearing of these men: 13 "Ah, if only you would please listen to me! I will pay you the price of the field. Accept it from me, that I may bury my dead there." 14 Ephron replied to Abraham, "Please, 15 sir, listen to me! A piece of land worth four hundred shekels of silver — what is that between you and me, as long as you can bury your dead?" 16 Abraham accepted Ephron's terms; he weighed out to him the silver that Ephron had stipulated in the hearing of the Hittites, four hundred shekels of silver at the current market value.

17 Thus Ephron's field in Machpelah, facing Mamre, together with its cave and all the trees anywhere within its limits, was conveyed 18 to Abraham by purchase in the presence of all the Hittites who sat on Ephron's town council. 19 After this transaction, Abraham buried his wife Sarah in the cave of the field of Machpelah, facing Mamre (that is, Hebron) in the land of Canaan. 20 Thus the field with its cave was transferred from the Hittites to Abraham as a burial place.

24 Abraham had now reached a ripe old age, and the LORD had blessed him in every way. 2 Abraham said to the senior servant of his household, who had charge of all his possessions: "Put your hand under my thigh, 3 and I will make you swear by the LORD, the God of heaven and the God of earth, that you will not procure a wife for my son from the daughters of the Canaanites among whom I live,

on you and make your descendants as numerous as the stars of heaven and the grains of sand on the seashore. Your descendants will gain possession of the gates of their enemies. 18 All nations on earth will bless themselves by your descendants, because you have obeyed my command.'

19 Abraham went back to his servants, and together they set out for Beersheba, and Abraham settled in Beersheba.

20 It happened some time later that Abraham received word that Milcah, too, had now borne sons to his brother Nahor: 21 Uz his first-born, Buz his brother, Kemuel father of Aram, 22 Chesed, Hazo, Pildash, Jidlaph, Bethuel 23 (and Bethuel was the father of Rebekah). These were the eight children Milcah gave Nahor, Abraham's brother. 24 He had a concubine named Reumah, and she too had children: Tebah, Gaham, Tahash and Maacah.

23 The length of Sarah's life was a hundred and twenty-seven years. 2 She died at Kiriath-Arba — now Hebron — in the land of Canaan, and Abraham proceeded to mourn and bewail her.

3 Then rising from beside his dead, Abraham spoke to the Hittites, 4 'I am a stranger resident here,' he said. 'Let me have a burial site of my own here, so that I can remove my dead for burial.' 5 The Hittites replied to Abraham, 6 'Please listen to us, my lord, we regard you as a prince of God; bury your dead in the best of our tombs; not one of us would refuse you his tomb for you to bury your dead.' 7 At this, Abraham rose and bowed low to the local people, the Hittites, 8 and pleaded with them as follows, 'If you consent to my removing my dead for burial, you must agree to intercede for me with Ephron son of Zohar, 9 for him to let me have the cave he owns at Machpelah, which is on the edge of his field. Let him sell it to me in your presence at its full price, for a burial site of my own.' 10 Now Ephron was sitting among the Hittites, and Ephron the Hittite answered Abraham in the hearing of the Hittites, of all the inhabitants of his town. 11 'No, my lord, listen to me,' he said. 'I give you the field and the cave in it; I make this gift in the presence of my kinsmen. Bury your dead.'

12 Abraham bowed low to the local people 13 and, in the hearing of the local people, replied to Ephron as follows, 'Be good enough to listen to me. I shall pay the price of the field; accept it from me and I shall bury my dead there.' 14 Ephron replied to Abraham, 15 'Please listen to me, my lord. What is a plot of land for four hundred shekels of silver between me and you? Bury your dead.' 16 Abraham agreed to Ephron's terms, and Abraham weighed out for Ephron the silver he had stipulated in the hearing of the Hittites, namely four hundred shekels of silver, according to the current commercial rate.

17 Thus Ephron's field at Machpelah, facing Mamre — the field and the cave in it and all the trees anywhere within the boundaries of the field — passed 18 into Abraham's possession in the sight of the Hittites, of all the inhabitants of his town. 19 And after this, Abraham buried his wife Sarah in the cave of the field of Machpelah, facing Mamre — now Hebron — in the land of Canaan. 20 And so the field and the cave in it passed from the Hittites into Abraham's possession as a burial site of his own.

24 By now Abraham was an old man, well on in years, and Yahweh had blessed Abraham in every way. 2 Abraham said to the senior servant in his household, the steward of all his property, 'Place your hand under my thigh: 3 I am going to make you swear by Yahweh, God of heaven and God of earth, that you will not choose a wife for my son from the daughters of the Canaanites among whom

go to my country and to my kindred and get a wife for my son Isaac." 5 The servant said to him, "Perhaps the woman may not be willing to follow me to this land; must I then take your son back to the land from which you came?" 6 Abraham said to him, "See to it that you do not take my son back there. 7 The LORD, the God of heaven, who took me from my father's house and from the land of my birth, and who spoke to me and swore to me, 'To your offspring I will give this land,' he will send his angel before you, and you shall take a wife for my son from there. 8 But if the woman is not willing to follow you, then you will be free from this oath of mine; only you must not take my son back there." 9 So the servant put his hand under the thigh of Abraham his master and swore to him concerning this matter.

10 Then the servant took ten of his master's camels and departed, taking all kinds of choice gifts from his master; and he set out and went to Aram-naharaim, to the city of Nahor. 11 He made the camels kneel down outside the city by the well of water; it was toward evening, the time when women go out to draw water. 12 And he said, "O LORD, God of my master Abraham, please grant me success today and show steadfast love to my master Abraham. 13 I am standing here by the spring of water, and the daughters of the townspeople are coming out to draw water. 14 Let the girl to whom I shall say, 'Please offer your jar that I may drink,' and who shall say, 'Drink, and I will water your camels' — let her be the one whom you have appointed for your servant Isaac. By this I shall know that you have shown steadfast love to my master."

15 Before he had finished speaking, there was Rebekah, who was born to Bethuel son of Milcah, the wife of Nahor, Abraham's brother, coming out with her water jar on her shoulder. 16 The girl was very fair to look upon, a virgin, whom no man had known. She went down to the spring, filled her jar, and came up. 17 Then the servant ran to meet her and said, "Please let me sip a little water from your jar." 18 "Drink, my lord," she said, and quickly lowered her jar upon her hand and gave him a drink. 19 When she had finished giving him a drink, she said, "I will draw for your camels also, until they have finished drinking." 20 So she quickly emptied her jar into the trough and ran again to the well to draw, and she drew for all his camels. 21 The man gazed at her in silence to learn whether or not the LORD had made his journey successful.

22 When the camels had finished drinking, the man took a gold nose-ring weighing a half shekel, and two bracelets for her arms weighing ten gold shekels, 23 and said, "Tell me whose daughter you are. Is there room in your father's house for us to spend the night?" 24 She said to him, "I am the daughter of Bethuel son of Milcah, whom she bore to Nahor." 25 She added, "We have plenty of straw and fodder and a place to spend the night." 26 The man bowed his head and worshiped the LORD 27 and said, "Blessed be the LORD, the God of my master Abraham, who has not forsaken his steadfast love and his faithfulness toward my master. As for me, the LORD has led me on the way to the house of my master's kin."

28 Then the girl ran and told her mother's household about these things. 29 Rebekah had a brother whose name was Laban; and Laban ran out to the man, to the spring. 30 As soon as he had seen the nose-ring, and the bracelets on his sister's arms, and when he heard the words of his sister Rebekah, "Thus the man spoke to me," he went to the man; and there he was, standing by the camels at the spring. 31 He said, "Come in, O blessed of the LORD. Why do you stand outside when I have prepared the house and a place for the camels?" 32 So the man came into the house; and Laban

must go to my own country and to my own kindred to find a wife for my son Isaac.' 5 'What if the woman is unwilling to come with me to this country?' the servant asked. 'Must I take your son back to the land you came from?' 6 Abraham said to him, 'On no account are you to take my son back there. 7 The LORD the God of heaven who took me from my father's house and the land of my birth, the LORD who swore to me that he would give this land to my descendants — he will send his angel before you, and you will take a wife from there for my son. 8 If the woman is unwilling to come with you, then you will be released from your oath to me; only you must not take my son back there.' 9 The servant then put his hand under his master Abraham's thigh and swore that oath.

10 The servant chose ten camels from his master's herds and, with all kinds of gifts from his master, he went to Aram-naharaim, to the town where Nahor lived. 11 Towards evening, the time when the women go out to draw water, he made the camels kneel down by the well outside the town. 12 'LORD God of my master Abraham,' he said, 'give me good fortune this day; keep faith with my master Abraham. 13 Here I am by the spring, as the women of the town come out to draw water. 14 I shall say to a girl, "Please lower your jar so that I may drink"; and if she answers, "Drink, and I shall water your camels also," let that be the girl whom you intend for your servant Isaac. In this way I shall know that you have kept faith with my master.'

15 Before he had finished praying, he saw Rebecca coming out with her water-jar on her shoulder. She was the daughter of Bethuel son of Milcah, the wife of Abraham's brother Nahor. 16 The girl was very beautiful and a virgin guiltless of intercourse with any man. She went down to the spring, filled her jar, and came up again. 17 Abraham's servant hurried to meet her and said, 'Will you give me a little water from your jar?' 18 'Please drink, sir,' she answered, and at once lowered her jar on to her hand to let him drink. 19 When she had finished giving him a drink, she said, 'I shall draw water for your camels also until they have had enough.' 20 She quickly emptied her jar into the water trough, and then hurrying again to the well she drew water and watered all the camels.

21 The man was watching quietly to see whether or not the LORD had made his journey successful, 22 and when the camels had finished drinking, he took a gold nose-ring weighing half a shekel, and two bracelets for her wrists weighing ten shekels, also of gold. 23 'Tell me, please, whose daughter you are,' he said. 'Is there room in your father's house for us to spend the night?' 24 She answered, 'I am the daughter of Bethuel son of Nahor and Milcah; 25 we have plenty of straw and fodder and also room for you to spend the night.' 26 So the man bowed down and prostrated himself before the LORD 27 and said, 'Blessed be the LORD the God of my master Abraham. His faithfulness to my master has been constant and unfailing, for he has guided me to the house of my master's kinsman.'

28 The girl ran to her mother's house and told them what had happened. 29–30 Rebecca had a brother named Laban, and, when he saw the nose-ring, and also the bracelets on his sister's wrists, and heard his sister Rebecca's account of what the man had said to her, he hurried out to the spring. When he got there he found the man still standing by the camels. 31 'Come in,' he said, 'you whom the LORD has blessed. Why are you staying out here? I have prepared the house and there is a place for the camels.' 32 The man went

4 but that you will go to my own land and to my kindred to get a wife for my son Isaac." 5 The servant asked him: "What if the woman is unwilling to follow me to this land? Should I then take your son back to the land from which you migrated?" 6 "Never take my son back there for any reason," Abraham told him. 7 "The LORD, the God of heaven, who took me from my father's house and the land of my kin, and who confirmed by oath the promise he then made to me, 'I will give this land to your descendants, — he will send his messenger before you, and you will obtain a wife for my son there. 8 If the woman is unwilling to follow you, you will be released from this oath. But never take my son back there!" 9 So the servant put his hand under the thigh of his master Abraham and swore to him in this undertaking.

10 The servant then took ten of his master's camels, and bearing all kinds of gifts from his master, he made his way to the city of Nahor in Aram Naharaim. 11 Near evening, at the time when women go out to draw water, he made the camels kneel by the well outside the city. 12 Then he prayed: "LORD, God of my master Abraham, let it turn out favorably for me today and thus deal graciously with my master Abraham. 13 While I stand here at the spring and the daughters of the townsmen are coming out to draw water, 14 if I say to a girl, 'Please lower your jug, that I may drink,' and she answers, 'Take a drink, and let me give water to your camels, too,' let her be the one whom you have decided upon for your servant Isaac. In this way I shall know that you have dealt graciously with my master."

15 He had scarcely finished these words when Rebekah (who was born to Bethuel, son of Milcah, the wife of Abraham's brother Nahor) came out with a jug on her shoulder. 16 The girl was very beautiful, a virgin, untouched by man. She went down to the spring and filled her jug. As she came up, 17 the servant ran toward her and said, "Please give me a sip of water from your jug." 18 "Take a drink, sir," she replied, and quickly lowering the jug onto her hand, she gave him a drink. 19 When she had let him drink his fill, she said, "I will draw water for your camels, too, until they have drunk their fill." 20 With that, she quickly emptied her jug into the drinking trough and ran back to the well to draw more water, until she had drawn enough for all the camels. 21 The man watched her the whole time, silently waiting to learn whether or not the LORD had made his errand successful. 22 When the camels had finished drinking, the man took out a gold ring weighing half a shekel, which he fastened on her nose, and two gold bracelets weighing ten shekels, which he put on her wrists. 23 Then he asked her: "Whose daughter are you? Tell me, please. And is there room in your father's house for us to spend the night?" 24 She answered: "I am the daughter of Bethuel the son of Milcah, whom she bore to Nahor. 25 There is plenty of straw and fodder at our place," she added, "and room to spend the night." 26 The man then bowed down in worship to the LORD, 27 saying: "Blessed be the LORD, the God of my master Abraham, who has not let his constant kindness toward my master fail. As for myself also, the LORD has led me straight to the house of my master's brother."

28 Then the girl ran off and told her mother's household about it. 29 Now Rebekah had a brother named Laban. 30 As soon as he saw the ring and the bracelets on his sister Rebekah and heard her words about what the man had said to her, Laban rushed outside to the man at the spring. When he reached him, he was still standing by the camels at the spring. 31 So he said to him: "Come, blessed of the LORD! Why are you staying outside when I have made the house ready for you, as well as a place for the camels?" 32 The

I live 4 but will go to my native land and my own kinsfolk to choose a wife for my son Isaac.' 5 The servant asked him, 'What if the girl does not want to follow me to this country? Should I then take your son back to the country from which you come?' 6 Abraham replied, 'On no account are you to take my son back there. 7 Yahweh, God of heaven and God of earth, who took me from my father's home, and from the land of my kinsfolk, and who promised me on oath, "I shall give this country to your descendants"— he will now send his angel ahead of you, so that you can get a wife for my son from there. 8 If then the girl refuses to follow you, you will be quit of this oath to me. Only do not take my son back there.' 9 And the servant placed his hand under the thigh of his master Abraham, and swore to him that he would do it.

10 The servant took ten of his master's camels and, carrying all kinds of gifts from his master, set out for the city of Nahor in Aram Naharaim. 11 In the evening, at the time when women come out to draw water, he made the camels kneel outside the town near the well. 12 And he said, 'Yahweh, God of my master Abraham, give me success today and show faithful love to my master Abraham. 13 While I stand by the spring as the young women from the town come out to draw water, 14 I shall say to one of the girls, "Please lower your pitcher and let me drink." And if she answers, "Drink, and I shall water your camels too," let her be the one you have decreed for your servant Isaac; by this I shall know you have shown faithful love to my master.'

15 He had not finished speaking when out came Rebekah —who was the daughter of Bethuel son of Milcah, the wife of Abraham's brother Nahor—with a pitcher on her shoulder. 16 The girl was very beautiful, and a virgin; no man had touched her. She went down to the spring, filled her pitcher and came up again. 17 Running towards her, the servant said, 'Please give me a sip of water from your pitcher.' 18 She replied, 'Drink, my lord,' and quickly lowered her pitcher on her arm and gave him a drink. 19 When she had finished letting him drink, she said, 'I shall draw water for your camels, too, until they have had enough.' 20 She quickly emptied her pitcher into the trough, and ran to the well again to draw, and drew for all the camels. 21 All the while, the man stood watching her, not daring to speak, wondering whether Yahweh had made his journey successful or not.

22 When the camels had finished drinking, the man took a gold ring weighing half a shekel, and put it through her nose, and put two bracelets weighing ten gold shekels on her arms, 23 and said, 'Whose daughter are you? Please tell me. Is there room at your father's house for us to spend the night?' 24 She replied, 'I am the daughter of Bethuel, the son whom Milcah bore to Nahor.' 25 And she went on, 'We have plenty of straw and fodder, and room to spend the night.' 26 Then the man bowed down and worshipped Yahweh 27 saying, 'Blessed be Yahweh, God of my master Abraham, for not withholding his faithful love from my master. Yahweh has led me straight to the house of my master's brother.'

28 The girl ran to her mother's house to tell what had happened. 29 Now Rebekah had a brother called Laban, and Laban ran out to the man at the spring. 30 As soon as he had seen the ring and the bracelets his sister was wearing, and had heard his sister Rebekah saying, 'This is what the man said to me,' he went to the man and found him still standing by his camels at the spring. 31 He said to him, 'Come in, blessed of Yahweh, why stay out here when I have cleared the house and made room for the camels?' 32 The man went

NEW REVISED STANDARD VERSION

unloaded the camels, and gave him straw and fodder for the camels, and water to wash his feet and the feet of the men who were with him. 33 Then food was set before him to eat; but he said, "I will not eat until I have told my errand." He said, "Speak on."

34 So he said, "I am Abraham's servant. 35 The LORD has greatly blessed my master, and he has become wealthy; he has given him flocks and herds, silver and gold, male and female slaves, camels and donkeys. 36 And Sarah my master's wife bore a son to my master when she was old; and he has given him all that he has. 37 My master made me swear, saying, 'You shall not take a wife for my son from the daughters of the Canaanites, in whose land I live; 38 but you shall go to my father's house, to my kindred, and get a wife for my son.' 39 I said to my master, 'Perhaps the woman will not follow me.' 40 But he said to me, 'The LORD, before whom I walk, will send his angel with you and make your way successful. You shall get a wife for my son from my kindred, from my father's house. 41 Then you will be free from my oath, when you come to my kindred; even if they will not give her to you, you will be free from my oath.'

42 "I came today to the spring, and said, 'O LORD, the God of my master Abraham, if now you will only make successful the way I am going! 43 I am standing here by the spring of water; let the young woman who comes out to draw, to whom I shall say, "Please give me a little water from your jar to drink," 44 and who will say to me, "Drink, and I will draw for your camels also"—let her be the woman whom the LORD has appointed for my master's son.'

45 "Before I had finished speaking in my heart, there was Rebekah coming out with her water jar on her shoulder; and she went down to the spring, and drew. I said to her, 'Please let me drink.' 46 She quickly let down her jar from her shoulder, and said, 'Drink, and I will also water your camels.' So I drank, and she also watered the camels. 47 Then I asked her, 'Whose daughter are you?' She said, 'The daughter of Bethuel, Nahor's son, whom Milcah bore to him.' So I put the ring on her nose, and the bracelets on her arms. 48 Then I bowed my head and worshiped the LORD, and blessed the LORD, the God of my master Abraham, who had led me by the right way to obtain the daughter of my master's kinsman for his son. 49 Now then, if you will deal loyally and truly with my master, tell me; and if not, tell me, so that I may turn either to the right hand or to the left."

50 Then Laban and Bethuel answered, "The thing comes from the LORD; we cannot speak to you anything bad or good. 51 Look, Rebekah is before you, take her and go, and let her be the wife of your master's son, as the LORD has spoken."

52 When Abraham's servant heard their words, he bowed himself to the ground before the LORD. 53 And the servant brought out jewelry of silver and of gold, and garments, and gave them to Rebekah; he also gave to her brother and to her mother costly ornaments. 54 Then he and the men who were with him ate and drank, and they spent the night there. When they rose in the morning, he said, "Send me back to my master." 55 Her brother and her mother said, "Let the girl remain with us a while, at least ten days; after that she may go." 56 But he said to them, "Do not delay me, since the LORD has made my journey successful; let me go that I may go to my master." 57 They said, "We will call the girl, and ask her." 58 And they called Rebekah, and said to her, "Will you go with this man?" She said, "I will." 59 So they sent away their sister Rebekah and her nurse along with Abraham's servant and his men.

REVISED ENGLISH BIBLE

into the house, while the camels were unloaded and provided with straw and fodder, and water was brought for him and his men to bathe their feet. 33 But when food was set before him, he protested, 'I will not eat until I have delivered my message.' Laban said, 'Let us hear it.'

34 'I am Abraham's servant,' he answered. 35 'The LORD has greatly blessed my master, and he has become a wealthy man: the LORD has given him flocks and herds, silver and gold, male and female slaves, camels and donkeys. 36 My master's wife Sarah in her old age bore him a son, to whom he has assigned all that he has. 37 My master made me swear an oath, saying, "You must not take a wife for my son from the women of the Canaanites in whose land I am living; 38 but go to my father's home, to my family, to get a wife for him." 39 I asked, "What if the woman will not come with me?" 40 He answered, "The LORD, in whose presence I have lived, will send his angel with you and make your journey successful. You are to take a wife for my son from my family and from my father's house; 41 then you will be released from the charge I have laid upon you. But if, when you come to my family, they refuse to give her to you, you will likewise be released from the charge."

42 'Today when I came to the spring, I prayed, "LORD God of my master Abraham, if you will make my journey successful, let it turn out in this way: 43 here I am by the spring; when a young woman comes out to draw water, I shall say to her, 'Give me a little water from your jar to drink.' 44 If she answers, 'Yes, do drink, and I shall draw water for your camels as well,' she is the woman whom the LORD intends for my master's son." 45 Before I had finished praying, I saw Rebecca coming out with her water-jar on her shoulder. She went down to the spring and drew water, and I said to her, "Will you please give me a drink?" 46 At once she lowered her jar from her shoulder and said, "Drink; and I shall water your camels." So I drank, and she also gave the camels water. 47 I asked her whose daughter she was, and she said, "I am the daughter of Bethuel son of Nahor and Milcah." Then I put the ring in her nose and the bracelets on her wrists, 48 and I bowed low in worship before the LORD. I blessed the LORD, the God of my master Abraham, who had led me by the right road to take my master's niece for his son. 49 Now tell me if you mean to deal loyally and faithfully with my master. If not, say so, and I shall turn elsewhere.'

50 Laban and Bethuel replied, 'Since this is from the LORD, we can say nothing for or against it. 51 Here is Rebecca; take her and go. She shall be the wife of your master's son, as the LORD has decreed.' 52 When Abraham's servant heard what they said, he prostrated himself on the ground before the LORD. 53 Then he brought out silver and gold ornaments, and articles of clothing, and gave them to Rebecca, and he gave costly gifts to her brother and her mother. 54 He and his men then ate and drank and spent the night there.

When they rose in the morning, Abraham's servant said, 'Give me leave to go back to my master.' 55 Rebecca's brother and her mother replied, 'Let the girl stay with us for a few days, say ten days, and then she can go.' 56 But he said to them, 'Do not detain me, for it is the LORD who has granted me success. Give me leave to go back to my master.' 57 They said, 'Let us call the girl and see what she says.' 58 They called Rebecca and asked her if she would go with the man, and she answered, 'Yes, I will go.' 59 So they let their sister Rebecca and her maid go with Abraham's

man then went inside; and while the camels were being unloaded and provided with straw and fodder, water was brought to bathe his feet and the feet of the men who were with him. 33 But when the table was set for him, he said, "I will not eat until I have told my tale." "Do so," they replied.

34 "I am Abraham's servant," he began. 35 "The LORD has blessed my master so abundantly that he has become a wealthy man; he has given him flocks and herds, silver and gold, male and female slaves, and camels and asses. 36 My master's wife Sarah bore a son to my master in her old age, and he has given him everything he owns. 37 My master put me under oath, saying: 'You shall not procure a wife for my son among the daughters of the Canaanites in whose land I live; 38 instead, you shall go to my father's house, to my own relatives, to get a wife for my son.' 39 When I asked my master, 'What if the woman will not follow me?' 40 he replied: 'The LORD, in whose presence I have always walked, will send his messenger with you and make your errand successful, and so you will get a wife for my son from my own kindred of my father's house. 41 Then you shall be released from my ban. If you visit my kindred and they refuse you, then, too, you shall be released from my ban.'

42 "When I came to the spring today, I prayed: 'LORD, God of my master Abraham, may it be your will to make successful the errand I am engaged on! 43 While I stand here at the spring, if I say to a young woman who comes out to draw water, Please give me a little water from your jug, 44 and she answers, Not only may you have a drink, but I will give water to your camels, too — let her be the woman whom the LORD has decided upon for my master's son.'

45 "I had scarcely finished saying this prayer to myself when Rebekah came out with a jug on her shoulder. After she went down to the spring and drew water, I said to her, 'Please let me have a drink.' 46 She quickly lowered the jug she was carrying and said, 'Take a drink, and let me bring water for your camels, too.' So I drank, and she watered the camels also. 47 When I asked her, 'Whose daughter are you?' she answered, 'The daughter of Bethuel, son of Nahor, born to Nahor by Milcah.' So I put the ring on her nose and the bracelets on her wrists. 48 Then I bowed down in worship to the LORD, blessing the LORD, the God of my master Abraham, who had led me on the right road to obtain the daughter of my master's kinsman for his son. 49 If, therefore, you have in mind to show true loyalty to my master, let me know; but if not, let me know that, too. I can then proceed accordingly."

50 Laban and his household said in reply: "This thing comes from the LORD; we can say nothing to you either for or against it. 51 Here is Rebekah, ready for you; take her with you, that she may become the wife of your master's son, as the LORD has said." 52 When Abraham's servant heard their answer, he bowed to the ground before the LORD. 53 Then he brought out objects of silver and gold and articles of clothing and presented them to Rebekah; he also gave costly presents to her brother and mother. 54 After he and the men with him had eaten and drunk, they spent the night there.

When they were up the next morning, he said, "Give me leave to return to my master." 55 Her brother and mother replied, "Let the girl stay with us a short while, say ten days; after that she may go." 56 But he said to them, "Do not detain me, now that the LORD has made my errand successful; let me go back to my master." 57 They answered, "Let us call the girl and see what she herself has to say about it." 58 So they called Rebekah and asked her, "Do you wish to go with this man?" She answered, "I do." 59 At this they allowed their sister Rebekah and her nurse to take leave, along with Abraham's servant and his men. 60 Invoking a

to the house, and Laban unloaded the camels. He provided straw and fodder for the camels and water for him and his companions to wash their feet.

33 They offered him food, but he said, 'I will eat nothing before I have said what I have to say.' Laban said, 'Speak.' 34 He said, 'I am Abraham's servant. 35 Yahweh has loaded my master with blessings, and Abraham is now very rich. He has given him flocks and herds, silver and gold, men and women slaves, camels and donkeys. 36 Sarah, my master's wife, bore my master a son in his old age, and he has made over all his property to him. 37 My master made me take this oath, "You are not to choose a wife for my son from the daughters of the Canaanites in whose country I live. 38 Instead, you are to go to my father's home and to my own kinsfolk to choose a wife for my son." 39 I said to my master, "Suppose the girl will not agree to come with me?" 40 and his reply was, "Yahweh, in whose presence I have walked, will send his angel with you and make your journey successful, for you to choose a wife for my son from my own kinsfolk, from my father's house. 41 Then you will be quit of my curse: if you go to my family and they refuse you, you will be quit of my curse." 42 Arriving today at the spring I said, "Yahweh, God of my master Abraham, please grant a successful outcome to the course I propose to take. 43 While I stand by the spring, if a girl comes out to draw water and I say to her, 'Please give me a little water to drink from your pitcher,' 44 if she replies, 'Drink by all means, and I shall draw water for your camels too,' let her be the girl whom Yahweh has decreed for my master's son." 45 I was still saying this in my mind when Rebekah came out, her pitcher on her shoulder. She came down to the spring and drew water. I said to her, "Please give me a drink." 46 Quickly she lowered her pitcher saying, "Drink, and I shall water your camels too." 47 I asked her, "Whose daughter are you?" She replied, "I am the daughter of Bethuel, whom Milcah bore to Nahor." Then I put this ring through her nose and these bracelets on her arms. 48 I bowed down and worshipped Yahweh, and I blessed Yahweh, God of my master Abraham, who had led me by a direct path to choose the daughter of my master's brother for his son. 49 Now tell me whether you are prepared to show constant and faithful love to my master; if not, say so, and I shall know what to do.'

50 Laban and Bethuel replied, 'This is from Yahweh; it is not for us to say yes or no to you. 51 Rebekah is there before you. Take her and go; and let her become the wife of your master's son, as Yahweh has decreed.' 52 On hearing this, Abraham's servant bowed to the ground before Yahweh. 53 He brought out silver and gold ornaments and clothes which he gave to Rebekah; he also gave rich presents to her brother and to her mother.

54 They ate and drank, he and his companions, and spent the night there. Next morning when they were up, he said, 'Let me go back to my master.' 55 Rebekah's brother and mother replied, 'Let the girl stay with us for ten days or so; then she can go.' 56 But he replied, 'Do not delay me, since Yahweh has made my journey successful; let me leave and go back to my master.' 57 They replied, 'Let us call the girl and find out what she has to say.' 58 They called Rebekah and asked her, 'Will you go with this man?' She replied, 'I will.' 59 Accordingly they let their sister Rebekah go, with her nurse, and Abraham's servant and his men. 60 They

NEW REVISED STANDARD VERSION

REVISED ENGLISH BIBLE

60 And they blessed Rebekah and said to her,
"May you, our sister, become
thousands of myriads;
may your offspring gain possession
of the gates of their foes."
61 Then Rebekah and her maids rose up, mounted the camels, and followed the man; thus the servant took Rebekah, and went his way.

62 Now Isaac had come from[n] Beer-lahai-roi, and was settled in the Negeb. 63 Isaac went out in the evening to walk[o] in the field; and looking up, he saw camels coming. 64 And Rebekah looked up, and when she saw Isaac, she slipped quickly from the camel, 65 and said to the servant, "Who is the man over there, walking in the field to meet us?" The servant said, "It is my master." So she took her veil and covered herself. 66 And the servant told Isaac all the things that he had done. 67 Then Isaac brought her into his mother Sarah's tent. He took Rebekah, and she became his wife; and he loved her. So Isaac was comforted after his mother's death.

25 Abraham took another wife, whose name was Keturah. 2 She bore him Zimran, Jokshan, Medan, Midian, Ishbak, and Shuah. 3 Jokshan was the father of Sheba and Dedan. The sons of Dedan were Asshurim, Letushim, and Leummim. 4 The sons of Midian were Ephah, Epher, Hanoch, Abida, and Eldaah. All these were the children of Keturah. 5 Abraham gave all he had to Isaac. 6 But to the sons of his concubines Abraham gave gifts, while he was still living, and he sent them away from his son Isaac, eastward to the east country.

7 This is the length of Abraham's life, one hundred seventy-five years. 8 Abraham breathed his last and died in a good old age, an old man and full of years, and was gathered to his people. 9 His sons Isaac and Ishmael buried him in the cave of Machpelah, in the field of Ephron son of Zohar the Hittite, east of Mamre, 10 the field that Abraham purchased from the Hittites. There Abraham was buried, with his wife Sarah. 11 After the death of Abraham God blessed his son Isaac. And Isaac settled at Beer-lahai-roi.

12 These are the descendants of Ishmael, Abraham's son, whom Hagar the Egyptian, Sarah's slave-girl, bore to Abraham. 13 These are the names of the sons of Ishmael, named in the order of their birth: Nebaioth, the firstborn of Ishmael; and Kedar, Adbeel, Mibsam, 14 Mishma, Dumah, Massa, 15 Hadad, Tema, Jetur, Naphish, and Kedemah. 16 These are the sons of Ishmael and these are their names, by their villages and by their encampments; twelve princes according to their tribes. 17 (This is the length of the life of Ishmael, one hundred thirty-seven years; he breathed his last and died, and was gathered to his people.) 18 They settled from Havilah to Shur, which is opposite Egypt in the direction of Assyria; he settled down[p] alongside of[q] all his people.

19 These are the descendants of Isaac, Abraham's son: Abraham was the father of Isaac, 20 and Isaac was forty years old when he married Rebekah, daughter of Bethuel the Aramean of Paddan-aram, sister of Laban the Aramean. 21 Isaac prayed to the LORD for his wife, because she was barren; and the LORD granted his prayer, and his wife Rebekah conceived. 22 The children struggled together within her; and she said, "If it is to be this way, why do I live?"[r] So she went to inquire of the LORD. 23 And the LORD said to her,

servant and his men. 60 They blessed Rebecca and said to her:
'You are our sister, may you be the mother of
many children;
may your sons possess the cities of their enemies.'
61 Rebecca and her companions mounted their camels to follow the man. So the servant took Rebecca and set out.

62 Isaac meanwhile had moved on as far as Beer-lahai-roi and was living in the Negeb. 63 One evening when he had gone out into the open country hoping to meet them, he looked and saw camels approaching. 64 When Rebecca saw Isaac, she dismounted from her camel, 65 saying to the servant, 'Who is that man walking across the open country towards us?' When the servant answered, 'It is my master,' she took her veil and covered herself. 66 The servant related to Isaac all that had happened. 67 Isaac conducted her into the tent and took her as his wife. So she became his wife, and he loved her and was consoled for the death of his mother.

25 ABRAHAM married another wife, whose name was Keturah. 2 She bore him Zimran, Jokshan, Medan, Midian, Ishbak, and Shuah. 3 Jokshan became the father of Sheba and Dedan. The descendants of Dedan were the Asshurim, Letushim, and Leummim, 4 and the sons of Midian were Ephah, Epher, Enoch, Abida, and Eldaah. All these were descendants of Keturah.

5 Abraham had assigned all that he possessed to Isaac; 6 and he had already in his lifetime made gifts to his sons by his concubines and had sent them away eastwards, to a land of the east, out of his son Isaac's way. 7 Abraham had lived for a hundred and seventy-five years 8 when he breathed his last. He died at a great age, a full span of years, and was gathered to his forefathers. 9 His sons, Isaac and Ishmael, buried him in the cave at Machpelah, on the land of Ephron son of Zohar the Hittite, east of Mamre, 10 the plot which Abraham had bought from the Hittites. There Abraham was buried with his wife Sarah. 11 After the death of Abraham, God blessed his son Isaac, who settled close by Beer-lahai-roi.

12 This is the table of the descendants of Abraham's son Ishmael, whom Hagar the Egyptian, Sarah's slave-girl, bore to him. 13 These are the names of the sons of Ishmael listed in order of their birth: Nebaioth, Ishmael's eldest son, then Kedar, Adbeel, Mibsam, 14 Mishma, Dumah, Massa, 15 Hadad, Tema, Jetur, Naphish, and Kedemah. 16 These are the sons of Ishmael, after whom their hamlets and encampments were named, twelve princes according to their tribes. 17 Ishmael had lived for a hundred and thirty-seven years when he breathed his last. So he died and was gathered to his forefathers. 18 Ishmael's sons inhabited the land from Havilah to Shur, which is east of Egypt on the way to Asshur; he himself had settled to the east of his brothers.

19 This is an account of the descendants of Abraham's son Isaac. Isaac's father was Abraham. 20 When Isaac was forty years old he married Rebecca daughter of Bethuel, the Aramaean from Paddan-aram and sister of Laban the Aramaean. 21 Isaac appealed to the LORD on behalf of his wife because she was childless; the LORD gave heed to his entreaty, and Rebecca conceived. 22 The children pressed on each other in her womb, and she said, 'If all is well, why am I like this?' She went to seek guidance of the LORD, 23 who said to her:

---

[n] Syr Tg: Heb *from coming to*   [o] Meaning of Heb word is uncertain
[p] Heb *he fell*   [q] Or *down in opposition to*   [r] Syr: Meaning of Heb uncertain

24:63 **hoping to meet them:** *Heb. uncertain.*   24:67 **into the tent:** *prob. rdg; Heb. adds* Sarah his mother.

blessing on Rebekah, they said:
"Sister, may you grow
    into thousands of myriads;
And may your descendants gain possession
    of the gates of their enemies!"
61 Then Rebekah and her maids started out; they mounted their camels and followed the man. So the servant took Rebekah and went on his way.

62 Meanwhile Isaac had gone from Beer-lahai-roi and was living in the region of the Negeb. 63 One day toward evening he went out . . . in the field, and as he looked around, he noticed that camels were approaching. 64 Rebekah, too, was looking about, and when she saw him, she alighted from her camel 65 and asked the servant, "Who is the man out there, walking through the fields toward us?" "That is my master," replied the servant. Then she covered herself with her veil.

66 The servant recounted to Isaac all the things he had done. 67 Then Isaac took Rebekah into his tent; he married her, and thus she became his wife. In his love for her Isaac found solace after the death of his mother Sarah.

25 Abraham married another wife, whose name was Keturah. 2 She bore him Zimran, Jokshan, Medan, Midian, Ishbak and Shuah. 3 Jokshan became the father of Sheba and Dedan. The descendants of Dedan were the Asshurim, the Letushim, and the Leummim. 4 The descendants of Midian were Ephah, Epher, Hanoch, Abida and Eldaah. All of these were descendants of Keturah.

5 Abraham deeded everything that he owned to his son Isaac. 6 To his sons by concubinage, however, he made grants while he was still living, as he sent them away eastward, to the land of Kedem, away from his son Isaac.

7 The whole span of Abraham's life was one hundred and seventy-five years. 8 Then he breathed his last, dying at a ripe old age, grown old after a full life; and he was taken to his kinsmen. 9 His sons Isaac and Ishmael buried him in the cave of Machpelah, in the field of Ephron, son of Zohar the Hittite, which faces Mamre, 10 the field that Abraham had bought from the Hittites; there he was buried next to his wife Sarah. 11 After the death of Abraham, God blessed his son Isaac, who made his home near Beer-lahai-roi.

12 These are the descendants of Abraham's son Ishmael, whom Hagar the Egyptian, Sarah's slave, bore to Abraham. 13 These are the names of Ishmael's sons, listed in the order of their birth: Nebaioth (Ishmael's firstborn), Kedar, Adbeel, Mibsam, 14 Mishma, Dumah, Massa, 15 Hadad, Tema, Jetur, Naphish and Kedemah. 16 These are the sons of Ishmael, their names by their villages and encampments; twelve chieftains of as many tribal groups.

17 The span of Ishmael's life was one hundred and thirty-seven years. After he had breathed his last and died, he was taken to his kinsmen. 18 The Ishmaelites ranged from Havilah-by-Shur, which is on the border of Egypt, all the way to Asshur; and each of them pitched camp in opposition to his various kinsmen.

19 This is the family history of Isaac, son of Abraham; Abraham had begotten Isaac. 20 Isaac was forty years old when he married Rebekah, the daughter of Bethuel the Aramean of Paddan-aram and the sister of Laban the Aramean. 21 Isaac entreated the LORD on behalf of his wife, since she was sterile. The LORD heard his entreaty, and Rebekah became pregnant. 22 But the children in her womb jostled each other so much that she exclaimed, "If this is to be so, what good will it do me!" She went to consult the LORD, 23 and he answered her:

blessed Rebekah and said to her:
Sister of ours, from you may there spring
    thousands and tens of thousands!
May your descendants gain possession
    of the gates of their enemies!
61 And forthwith, Rebekah and her maids mounted the camels, and followed the man. The servant took Rebekah and departed.

62 Isaac meanwhile had come back from the well of Lahai Roi and was living in the Negeb. 63 While Isaac was out walking towards evening in the fields, he looked up and saw camels approaching. 64 And Rebekah looked up and saw Isaac. She jumped down from her camel, 65 and asked the servant, 'Who is that man walking through the fields towards us?' The servant replied, 'That is my master.' So she took her veil and covered herself up. 66 The servant told Isaac the whole story. 67 Then Isaac took her into his tent. He married Rebekah and made her his wife. And in his love for her, Isaac was consoled for the loss of his mother.

25 Abraham married another wife whose name was Keturah; 2 and she bore him Zimram, Jokshan, Medan, Midian, Ishbak and Shuah. 3 Jokshan was the father of Sheba and Dedan, and the descendants of Dedan were the Asshurites, the Letushim and the Leummim. 4 The descendants of Midian were Ephah, Epher, Hanoch, Abida and Eldaah. All these were descendants of Keturah.

5 Abraham left all his possessions to Isaac. 6 To the sons of his concubines Abraham made grants during his lifetime, sending them away from his son Isaac eastward, to the Land of the East.

7 The number of years Abraham lived was a hundred and seventy-five. 8 When Abraham had breathed his last, dying at a happy ripe age, old and full of years, he was gathered to his people. 9 His sons Isaac and Ishmael buried him in the cave of Machpelah facing Mamre, in the field of Ephron the Hittite son of Zohar. 10 This was the field that Abraham had bought from the Hittites, and Abraham and his wife Sarah were buried there. 11 After Abraham's death, God blessed his son Isaac. Isaac settled near the well of Lahai Roi.

12 These are the descendants of Ishmael son of Abraham by Hagar, Sarah's Egyptian slave-girl. 13 These are the names of the sons of Ishmael by name and line: Ishmael's first-born was Nebaioth; then Kedar, Adbeel, Mibsam, 14 Mishma, Dumah, Massa, 15 Hadad, Tema, Jetur, Naphish and Kedemah. 16 These are the sons of Ishmael, and these are their names, according to their settlements and encampments, twelve chiefs of as many tribes.

17 The number of years Ishmael lived was one hundred and thirty-seven. When he breathed his last and died, he was gathered to his people. 18 He lived in the territory stretching from Havilah-by-Shur just outside Egypt on the way to Assyria, and he held his own against all his kinsmen.

19 This is the story of Isaac son of Abraham. Abraham fathered Isaac. 20 Isaac was forty years old when he married Rebekah the daughter of Bethuel the Aramaean of Paddan-Aram, and sister of Laban the Aramaean. 21 Isaac prayed to Yahweh on behalf of his wife, for she was barren. Yahweh heard his prayer, and his wife Rebekah conceived. 22 But the children inside her struggled so much that she said, 'If this is the way of it, why go on living?' So she went to consult Yahweh, 23 and Yahweh said to her:

24, 63: He went out: the meaning of the Hebrew term that follows this is obscure.

NEW REVISED STANDARD VERSION

REVISED ENGLISH BIBLE

"Two nations are in your womb,
and two peoples born of you shall be divided;
the one shall be stronger than the other,
the elder shall serve the younger."

24 When her time to give birth was at hand, there were twins in her womb. 25 The first came out red, all his body like a hairy mantle; so they named him Esau. 26 Afterward his brother came out, with his hand gripping Esau's heel; so he was named Jacob.s Isaac was sixty years old when she bore them.

27 When the boys grew up, Esau was a skillful hunter, a man of the field, while Jacob was a quiet man, living in tents. 28 Isaac loved Esau, because he was fond of game; but Rebekah loved Jacob.

29 Once when Jacob was cooking a stew, Esau came in from the field, and he was famished. 30 Esau said to Jacob, "Let me eat some of that red stuff, for I am famished!" (Therefore he was called Edom.t) 31 Jacob said, "First sell me your birthright." 32 Esau said, "I am about to die; of what use is a birthright to me?" 33 Jacob said, "Swear to me first."u So he swore to him, and sold his birthright to Jacob. 34 Then Jacob gave Esau bread and lentil stew, and he ate and drank, and rose and went his way. Thus Esau despised his birthright.

26 Now there was a famine in the land, besides the former famine that had occurred in the days of Abraham. And Isaac went to Gerar, to King Abimelech of the Philistines. 2 The LORD appeared to Isaacv and said, "Do not go down to Egypt; settle in the land that I shall show you. 3 Reside in this land as an alien, and I will be with you, and will bless you; for to you and to your descendants I will give all these lands, and I will fulfill the oath that I swore to your father Abraham. 4 I will make your offspring as numerous as the stars of heaven, and will give to your offspring all these lands; and all the nations of the earth shall gain blessing for themselves through your offspring, 5 because Abraham obeyed my voice and kept my charge, my commandments, my statutes, and my laws."

6 So Isaac settled in Gerar. 7 When the men of the place asked him about his wife, he said, "She is my sister"; for he was afraid to say, "My wife," thinking, "or else the men of the place might kill me for the sake of Rebekah, because she is attractive in appearance." 8 When Isaac had been there a long time, King Abimelech of the Philistines looked out of a window and saw him fondling his wife Rebekah. 9 So Abimelech called for Isaac, and said, "So she is your wife! Why then did you say, 'She is my sister'?" Isaac said to him, "Because I thought I might die because of her." 10 Abimelech said, "What is this you have done to us? One of the people might easily have lain with your wife, and you would have brought guilt upon us." 11 So Abimelech warned all the people, saying, "Whoever touches this man or his wife shall be put to death."

12 Isaac sowed seed in that land, and in the same year reaped a hundredfold. The LORD blessed him, 13 and the man became rich; he prospered more and more until he became very wealthy. 14 He had possessions of flocks and herds, and a great household, so that the Philistines envied him. 15 (Now the Philistines had stopped up and filled with earth all the wells that his father's servants had dug in the days of his father Abraham.) 16 And Abimelech said to Isaac, "Go away from us; you have become too powerful for us."

17 So Isaac departed from there and camped in the valley of Gerar and settled there. 18 Isaac dug again the wells

'Two nations are in your womb,
two peoples going their own ways from birth.
One will be stronger than the other;
the elder will be servant to the younger.'

24 When her time had come, there were indeed twins in her womb. 25 The first to come out was reddish and covered with hairs like a cloak, and they named him Esau. 26 Immediately afterwards his brother was born with his hand grasping Esau's heel, and he was given the name Jacob. Isaac was sixty years old when they were born. 27 As the boys grew up, Esau became a skilful hunter, an outdoor man, while Jacob lived quietly among the tents. 28 Isaac favoured Esau because he kept him supplied with game, but Rebecca favoured Jacob. 29 One day Jacob was preparing broth when Esau came in from the country, exhausted. 30 He said to Jacob, 'I am exhausted; give me a helping of that red broth.' This is why he was called Edom. 31 Jacob retorted, 'Not till you sell me your rights as the firstborn.' 32 Esau replied, 'Here I am at death's door; what use is a birthright to me?' 33 Jacob said, 'First give me your oath!' So he gave him his oath and sold his birthright to Jacob. 34 Then Jacob gave Esau bread and some lentil broth, and he ate and drank and went his way. Esau showed by this how little he valued his birthright.

26 THE land was stricken by a famine — not the earlier famine which happened in Abraham's time — and Isaac went to Abimelech the Philistine king at Gerar. 2 The LORD appeared to Isaac and said, 'Do not go down to Egypt, but stay in this country as I bid you. 3 Stay here and I shall be with you and bless you, for to you and to your descendants I shall give all these lands, so fulfilling the oath which I swore to your father Abraham. 4 I shall make your descendants as numerous as the stars in the heavens, and give them all these lands. All the nations of the earth will wish to be blessed as they are blessed, 5 because Abraham obeyed me and kept my charge, my commandments, statutes, and laws.'

6 Isaac settled in Gerar, and, 7 when the men of the place asked questions about his wife, he told them that she was his sister, for he was afraid to say Rebecca was his wife, in case they murdered him because of her; for she was very beautiful. 8 But when they had been there some considerable time, Abimelech the Philistine king looked down from his window and there was Isaac caressing his wife Rebecca. 9 He summoned Isaac and said, 'So she is your wife! What made you say she was your sister?' Isaac answered, 'I thought I should be put to death because of her.' 10 Abimelech said, 'Why have you treated us like this? One of the people might easily have lain with your wife, and then you would have made us incur guilt.' 11 Abimelech warned all the people that whoever harmed this man or his wife would be put to death.

12 Isaac sowed seed in that land, and the same year he reaped a hundredfold. The LORD had blessed him, 13 and he became more and more wealthy, until he was very prosperous indeed. 14 He had flocks and herds and many slaves, so that the Philistines were envious of him. 15 They stopped up and filled with earth all the wells dug by the slaves in the days of Isaac's father Abraham. 18 Isaac reopened the wells which were dug in the lifetime of his father Abraham and stopped up by the Philistines after his death. He called them by the names which his father had given them.

16 Then Abimelech said to him, 'Go, leave us; you have become too powerful for us.' 17 When Isaac left that place, he encamped in the wadi of Gerar, and stayed there. 19 Then

---

s That is He takes by the heel or He supplants t That is Red
u Heb today v Heb him

25:26 **Jacob:** that is He caught by the heel or He supplanted.
25:30 **Edom:** that is Red. 26:15–19 Verse 18 transposed to follow 15.

"Two nations are in your womb,
> two peoples are quarreling while still within you;
But one shall surpass the other,
> and the older shall serve the younger.

24 When the time of her delivery came, there were twins in her womb. 25 The first to emerge was reddish, and his whole body was like a hairy mantle; so they named him Esau. 26 His brother came out next, gripping Esau's heel; so they named him Jacob. Isaac was sixty years old when they were born.

27 As the boys grew up, Esau became a skillful hunter, a man who lived in the open; whereas Jacob was a simple man, who kept to his tents. 28 Isaac preferred Esau, because he was fond of game; but Rebekah preferred Jacob. 29 Once, when Jacob was cooking a stew, Esau came in from the open, famished. 30 He said to Jacob, "Let me gulp down some of that red stuff; I'm starving." (That is why he was called Edom.) 31 But Jacob replied, "First give me your birthright in exchange for it." 32 "Look," said Esau, "I'm on the point of dying. What good will any birthright do me?" 33 But Jacob insisted, "Swear to me first!" So he sold Jacob his birthright under oath. 34 Jacob then gave him some bread and the lentil stew; and Esau ate, drank, got up, and went his way. Esau cared little for his birthright.

26 There was a famine in the land (distinct from the earlier one that had occurred in the days of Abraham), and Isaac went down to Abimelech, king of the Philistines in Gerar. 2 The LORD appeared to him and said: "Do not go down to Egypt, but continue to camp wherever in this land I tell you. 3 Stay in this land, and I will be with you and bless you; for to you and your descendants I will give all these lands, in fulfillment of the oath that I swore to your father Abraham. 4 I will make your descendants as numerous as the stars in the sky and give them all these lands, and in your descendants all the nations of the earth shall find blessing— 5 this because Abraham obeyed me, keeping my mandate (my commandments, my ordinances and my instructions)."

6 So Isaac settled in Gerar. 7 When the men of the place asked questions about his wife, he answered, "She is my sister." He was afraid, if he called her his wife, the men of the place would kill him on account of Rebekah, since she was very beautiful. 8 But when he had been there for a long time, Abimelech, king of the Philistines, happened to look out of a window and was surprised to see Isaac fondling his wife Rebekah. 9 He called for Isaac and said: "She must certainly be your wife! How could you have said, 'She is my sister'?" Isaac replied, "I thought I might lose my life on her account." 10 "How could you do this to us!" exclaimed Abimelech. "It would have taken very little for one of the men to lie with your wife, and you would have thus brought guilt upon us!" 11 Abimelech therefore gave this warning to all his men: "Anyone who molests this man or his wife shall forthwith be put to death."

12 Isaac sowed a crop in that region and reaped a hundredfold the same year. Since the LORD blessed him, 13 he became richer and richer all the time, until he was very wealthy indeed. 14 He acquired such flocks and herds, and so many work animals, that the Philistines became envious of him. (15 The Philistines had stopped up and filled with dirt all the wells that his father's servants had dug back in the days of his father Abraham.) 16 So Abimelech said to Isaac, "Go away from us; you have become far too numerous for us." 17 Isaac left there and made the Wadi Gerar his regular campsite. (18 Isaac reopened the wells which his

There are two nations in your womb,
> your issue will be two rival peoples.
One nation will have the mastery of the other,
> and the elder will serve the younger.

24 When the time came for her confinement, there were indeed twins in her womb. 25 The first to be born was red, altogether like a hairy cloak; so they named him Esau. 26 Then his brother was born, with his hand grasping Esau's heel; so they named him Jacob.[l] Isaac was sixty years old at the time of their birth. 27 When the boys grew up Esau became a skilled hunter, a man of the open country. Jacob on the other hand was a quiet man, staying at home among the tents. 28 Isaac preferred Esau, for he had a taste for wild game; but Rebekah preferred Jacob.

29 Once, when Jacob was cooking a stew, Esau returned from the countryside exhausted. 30 Esau said to Jacob, 'Give me a mouthful of that red stuff there; I am exhausted' — hence the name given to him, Edom. 31 Jacob said, 'First, give me your birthright in exchange.' 32 Esau said, 'Here I am, at death's door; what use is a birthright to me?' 33 Then Jacob said, 'First give me your oath'; he gave him his oath and sold his birthright to Jacob. 34 Then Jacob gave him some bread and lentil stew; he ate, drank, got up and went away. That was all Esau cared about his birthright.

26 [m]There was a famine in the country — different from the previous famine which took place in the time of Abraham — and Isaac went to Abimelech, the Philistine king at Gerar. 2 Yahweh had appeared to him and said, 'Do not go down to Egypt; stay in the country which I shall point out to you. 3 Remain for the present in that country; I shall be with you and bless you, for I shall give all these countries to you and your descendants in fulfilment of the oath I swore to your father Abraham. 4 I shall make your descendants as numerous as the stars of heaven, and I shall give them all these countries, and all nations on earth will bless themselves by your descendants 5 in return for Abraham's obedience; for he kept my charge, my commandments, my statutes and my laws.' 6 So Isaac stayed at Gerar.

7 When the people of the place asked him about his wife he replied, 'She is my sister,' for he was afraid to say, 'She is my wife,' thinking, 'The people of the place will kill me because of Rebekah, since she is beautiful.' 8 When he had been there some time, Abimelech the Philistine king happened to look out of the window and saw Isaac fondling his wife Rebekah. 9 Abimelech summoned Isaac and said to him, 'Surely she must be your wife! How could you have said, "She is my sister"?' Isaac replied, 'Because I thought I might be killed on her account.' 10 Abimelech said, 'What a thing to do to us! One of the people might easily have slept with your wife. We should have incurred guilt, thanks to you.' 11 Then Abimelech issued this order to all the people: 'Whoever touches this man or his wife will be put to death.'

12 Isaac sowed his crops in that country, and that year he reaped a hundredfold. Yahweh blessed him 13 and the man became rich; he prospered more and more until he was very rich indeed. 14 He acquired flocks and herds and a large retinue. The Philistines began to envy him.

15 [n]The Philistines had blocked up all the wells dug by his father's servants — in the days of his father Abraham — filling them in with earth. 16 Then Abimelech said to Isaac, 'You must leave us, for you have become much more powerful than we are.' 17 So Isaac left; he pitched camp in the Valley of Gerar and there he stayed. 18 Isaac reopened the

---

l **25** Fragments full of word-play: Edom/Esau = red; Seir = hairy; Jacob = heel/supplant.   *m* **26** 26:1seq. = 12:10–20; = 20.
n **26** 26:15seq. = 21:25–31.

NEW REVISED STANDARD VERSION

REVISED ENGLISH BIBLE

of water that had been dug in the days of his father Abraham; for the Philistines had stopped them up after the death of Abraham; and he gave them the names that his father had given them. 19 But when Isaac's servants dug in the valley and found there a well of spring water, 20 the herders of Gerar quarreled with Isaac's herders, saying, "The water is ours." So he called the well Esek,*w* because they contended with him. 21 Then they dug another well, and they quarreled over that one also; so he called it Sitnah.*x* 22 He moved from there and dug another well, and they did not quarrel over it; so he called it Rehoboth,*y* saying, "Now the LORD has made room for us, and we shall be fruitful in the land."

23 From there he went up to Beer-sheba. 24 And that very night the LORD appeared to him and said, "I am the God of your father Abraham; do not be afraid, for I am with you and will bless you and make your offspring numerous for my servant Abraham's sake." 25 So he built an altar there, called on the name of the LORD, and pitched his tent there. And there Isaac's servants dug a well.

26 Then Abimelech went to him from Gerar, with Ahuzzath his adviser and Phicol the commander of his army. 27 Isaac said to them, "Why have you come to me, seeing that you hate me and have sent me away from you?" 28 They said, "We see plainly that the LORD has been with you; so we say, let there be an oath between you and us, and let us make a covenant with you 29 so that you will do us no harm, just as we have not touched you and have done to you nothing but good and have sent you away in peace. You are now the blessed of the LORD." 30 So he made them a feast, and they ate and drank. 31 In the morning they rose early and exchanged oaths; and Isaac set them on their way, and they departed from him in peace. 32 That same day Isaac's servants came and told him about the well that they had dug, and said to him, "We have found water!" 33 He called it Shibah;*z* therefore the name of the city is Beer-sheba*a* to this day.

34 When Esau was forty years old, he married Judith daughter of Beeri the Hittite, and Basemath daughter of Elon the Hittite; 35 and they made life bitter for Isaac and Rebekah.

27

When Isaac was old and his eyes were dim so that he could not see, he called his elder son Esau and said to him, "My son"; and he answered, "Here I am." 2 He said, "See, I am old; I do not know the day of my death. 3 Now then, take your weapons, your quiver and your bow, and go out to the field, and hunt game for me. 4 Then prepare for me savory food, such as I like, and bring it to me to eat, so that I may bless you before I die."

5 Now Rebekah was listening when Isaac spoke to his son Esau. So when Esau went to the field to hunt for game and bring it, 6 Rebekah said to her son Jacob, "I heard your father say to your brother Esau, 7 'Bring me game, and prepare for me savory food to eat, that I may bless you before the LORD before I die.' 8 Now therefore, my son, obey my word as I command you. 9 Go to the flock, and get me two choice kids, so that I may prepare from them savory food for your father, such as he likes; 10 and you shall take it to your father to eat, so that he may bless you before he dies." 11 But Jacob said to his mother Rebekah, "Look, my brother Esau is a hairy man, and I am a man of smooth skin. 12 Perhaps my father will feel me, and I shall seem to be mocking him, and bring a curse on myself and not a blessing." 13 His mother said to him, "Let your curse be on me,

Isaac's slaves dug in the wadi and found a spring of running water, 20 but the shepherds of Gerar quarrelled with Isaac's shepherds, claiming the water as theirs. He called the well Esek, because they made difficulties for him. 21 His men then dug another well, but a quarrel arose over that also, so he called it Sitnah. 22 He moved on from there and dug another well; over that there was no dispute, so he called it Rehoboth, saying, 'Now the LORD has given us room and our people will become more numerous in the land.'

23 From there Isaac went up country to Beersheba; 24 that same night the LORD appeared to him. 'I am the God of your father Abraham,' he said; 'I am with you, so do not be afraid. I shall bless you and give you many descendants for the sake of my servant Abraham.' 25 Isaac built an altar there and invoked the LORD by name. He pitched his tent, and there also his slaves dug a well.

26 Abimelech came to him from Gerar with Ahuzzath his friend and Phicol the commander of his army. 27 Isaac said to them, 'Why have you come here to me? You were ill-disposed towards me and sent me away from your midst.' 28 They answered, 'We have realized that the LORD is with you, and we propose that the two of us should bind each other by oath and make a pact. 29 You are to do us no harm, just as we have in no way molested you. We were always ready to do you a good turn and we let you go away peaceably. Now the LORD has prospered you.' 30 Isaac then gave a feast for them, and they ate and drank. 31 Early next morning they exchanged oaths, and after Isaac bade them farewell, they parted from him in peace. 32 The same day Isaac's slaves came and told him about a well they had dug: 'We have found water,' they told him. 33 He named the well Shibah; this is why the city is called Beersheba to this day.

34 When Esau was forty years old he married Judith daughter of Beeri the Hittite, and Basemath daughter of Elon the Hittite; 35 this was a source of bitter grief to Isaac and Rebecca.

27

WHEN Isaac grew old and his eyes had become so dim that he could not see, he called for his elder son Esau. 'My son!' he said. Esau answered, 'Here I am.' 2 Isaac said, 'Listen now: I am old and I do not know when I may die. 3 Take your hunting gear, your quiver and bow, and go out into the country and get me some game. 4 Then make me a savoury dish, the kind I like, and bring it for me to eat so that I may give you my blessing before I die.'

5 Now Rebecca had been listening as Isaac talked to his son Esau. When Esau went off into the country to hunt game for his father, 6 she said to her son Jacob, 'I have just overheard your father say to your brother Esau, 7 "Bring me some game and make a savoury dish for me to eat so that I may bless you in the presence of the LORD before I die." 8 Listen now to me, my son, and do what I tell you. 9 Go to the flock and pick me out two fine young kids, and I shall make them into a savoury dish for your father, the kind he likes. 10 Then take it in to your father to eat so that he may bless you before he dies.' 11 'But my brother Esau is a hairy man,' Jacob said to his mother Rebecca, 'and my skin is smooth. 12 Suppose my father touches me; he will know that I am playing a trick on him and I shall bring a curse instead of a blessing on myself.' 13 His mother answered, 'Let any

26:20 **Esek:** *that is* Difficulty.   26:21 **Sitnah:** *that is* Enmity.
26:22 **Rehoboth:** *that is* Roominess.   26:33 **Shibah:** *that is* Oath.
Beersheba: *that is* Well of an Oath.   27:5 **for his father:** *so Gk;*
Heb. to bring.

father's servants had dug back in the days of his father Abraham and which the Philistines had stopped up after Abraham's death; he gave them the same names that his father had given them.) 19 But when Isaac's servants dug in the wadi and reached spring water in their well, 20 the shepherds of Gerar quarreled with Isaac's servants, saying, "The water belongs to us!" So the well was called Esek, because they had challenged him there. 21 Then they dug another well, and they quarreled over that one too; so it was called Sitnah. 22 When he had moved on from there, he dug still another well; but over this one they did not quarrel. It was called Rehoboth, because he said, "The LORD has now given us ample room, and we shall flourish in the land."

23 From there Isaac went up to Beer-sheba. 24 The same night the LORD appeared to him and said: "I am the God of your father Abraham. You have no need to fear, since I am with you. I will bless you and multiply your descendants for the sake of my servant Abraham." 25 So he built an altar there and invoked the LORD by name. After he had pitched his tent there, his servants began to dig a well nearby.

26 Abimelech had meanwhile come to him from Gerar, accompanied by Ahuzzath, his councilor, and Phicol, the general of his army. 27 Isaac asked them, "Why have you come to me, seeing that you hate me and have driven me away from you?" 28 They answered: "We are convinced that the LORD is with you, so we propose that there be a sworn agreement between our two sides — between you and us. Let us make a pact with you: 29 you shall not act unkindly toward us, just as we have not molested you, but have always acted kindly toward you and have let you depart in peace. Henceforth, 'The LORD's blessing be upon you!' " 30 Isaac then made a feast for them, and they ate and drank. 31 Early the next morning they exchanged oaths. Then Isaac bade them farewell, and they departed from him in peace.

32 That same day Isaac's servants came and brought him news about the well they had been digging; they told him, "We have reached water!" 33 He called it Shibah; hence the name of the city, Beer-sheba, to this day.

34 When Esau was forty years old, he married Judith, daughter of Beeri the Hittite, and Basemath, daughter of Elon the Hivite. 35 But they became a source of embitterment to Isaac and Rebekah.

27 When Isaac was so old that his eyesight had failed him, he called his older son Esau and said to him, "Son!" "Yes, father!" he replied. 2 Isaac then said, "As you can see, I am so old that I may now die at any time. 3 Take your gear, therefore — your quiver and bow — and go out into the country to hunt some game for me. 4 With your catch prepare an appetizing dish for me, such as I like, and bring it to me to eat, so that I may give you my special blessing before I die."

5 Rebekah had been listening while Isaac was speaking to his son Esau. So when Esau went out into the country to hunt some game for his father, 6 Rebekah said to her son Jacob, "Listen! I overheard your father tell your brother Esau, 7 'Bring me some game and with it prepare an appetizing dish for me to eat, that I may give you my blessing with the LORD's approval before I die.' 8 Now, son, listen carefully to what I tell you. 9 Go to the flock and get me two choice kids. With these I will prepare an appetizing dish for your father, such as he likes. 10 Then bring it to your father to eat, that he may bless you before he dies." 11 "But my brother Esau is a hairy man," said Jacob to his mother Rebekah, "and I am smooth-skinned! 12 Suppose my father feels me? He will think I am making sport of him, and I shall bring on myself a curse instead of a blessing." 13 His

wells dug by the servants of his father Abraham and blocked up by the Philistines after Abraham's death, and he gave them the same names as his father had given them.

19 But when Isaac's servants, digging in the valley, found a well of spring-water there, 20 the herdsmen of Gerar disputed it with Isaac's herdsmen, saying, 'That water is ours!' So Isaac named the well Esek, because they had disputed with him. 21 They dug another well, and there was a dispute over that one too; so he named it Sitnah. 22 Then he left there, and dug another well, and since there was no dispute over this one, he named it Rehoboth, saying, 'Now Yahweh has made room for us to thrive in the country.'

23 From there he went up to Beersheba. 24 Yahweh appeared to him the same night and said:

I am the God of your father Abraham.
Do not be afraid, for I am with you.
I shall bless you and multiply your offspring
for my servant Abraham's sake.

25 There he built an altar and invoked the name of Yahweh. There he pitched his tent, and there Isaac's servants sank a well.

26 o Abimelech came from Gerar to see him, with Ahuzzath his adviser and Phicol the commander of his army. 27 Isaac said to them, 'Why do you come to me since you hate me, and have made me leave you?' 28 'It became clear to us that Yahweh was with you,' they replied, 'and so we thought, "It is time to have a treaty sworn between us, between us and you." So let us make a covenant with you: 29 that you will not do us any harm, since we never molested you but were unfailingly kind to you and let you go away in peace. Henceforth, Yahweh's blessing on you!' 30 He then made them a feast and they ate and drank.

31 Early next morning, they exchanged oaths. Then Isaac bade them farewell and they left him as friends. 32 It happened, the same day, that Isaac's servants brought him news about the well they had been digging. 'We have found water!' they said to him. 33 So he called the well Sheba, and hence the town is named Beersheba to this day.

34 When Esau was forty years old he married Judith daughter of Beeri the Hittite, and Basemath daughter of Elon the Hittite. 35 These were a bitter disappointment to Isaac and Rebekah.

27 When Isaac had grown old, and his eyes were so weak that he could no longer see, he summoned his elder son Esau. 'Son!' he said, and Esau replied, 'Here I am.' 2 He then said, 'Look, I am old and do not know when I may die. 3 Now take your weapons, your quiver and bow; go out into the country and hunt me some game. 4 Make me the kind of appetising dish I like and bring it to me to eat and I shall give you my special blessing before I die.'

5 Rebekah was listening while Isaac was talking to his son Esau. So when Esau went into the country to hunt game for his father, 6 Rebekah said to her son Jacob, 'I have just heard your father saying to your brother Esau, 7 "Bring me some game and make an appetising dish for me to eat and then I shall bless you in Yahweh's presence before I die." 8 Now, son, listen to me and do as I tell you. 9 Go to the flock and bring me back two good kids, so that I can make the kind of special dish your father likes. 10 Then take it to your father for him to eat, so that he may bless you before he dies.' 11 Jacob said to his mother Rebekah, 'Look, my brother Esau is hairy, while I am smooth-skinned. 12 If my father happens to touch me, he will see I am cheating him, and I shall bring a curse down on myself instead of a blessing.'

o 26 26:26seq. = 21:22–33.

my son; only obey my word, and go, get them for me."
14 So he went and got them and brought them to his mother;
and his mother prepared savory food, such as his father
loved. 15 Then Rebekah took the best garments of her elder
son Esau, which were with her in the house, and put them
on her younger son Jacob; 16 and she put the skins of the
kids on his hands and on the smooth part of his neck.
17 Then she handed the savory food, and the bread that she
had prepared, to her son Jacob.

18 So he went in to his father, and said, "My father";
and he said, "Here I am; who are you, my son?" 19 Jacob
said to his father, "I am Esau your firstborn. I have done as
you told me; now sit up and eat of my game, so that you
may bless me." 20 But Isaac said to his son, "How is it that
you have found it so quickly, my son?" He answered, "Because the LORD your God granted me success." 21 Then
Isaac said to Jacob, "Come near, that I may feel you, my
son, to know whether you are really my son Esau or not."
22 So Jacob went up to his father Isaac, who felt him and
said, "The voice is Jacob's voice, but the hands are the
hands of Esau." 23 He did not recognize him, because his
hands were hairy like his brother Esau's hands; so he
blessed him. 24 He said, "Are you really my son Esau?" He
answered, "I am." 25 Then he said, "Bring it to me, that I
may eat of my son's game and bless you." So he brought it
to him, and he ate; and he brought him wine, and he drank.
26 Then his father Isaac said to him, "Come near and kiss
me, my son." 27 So he came near and kissed him; and he
smelled the smell of his garments, and blessed him, and
said,

"Ah, the smell of my son
   is like the smell of a field that the LORD has
     blessed.
28 May God give you of the dew of heaven,
   and of the fatness of the earth,
   and plenty of grain and wine.
29 Let peoples serve you,
   and nations bow down to you.
  Be lord over your brothers,
   and may your mother's sons bow down to you.
  Cursed be everyone who curses you,
   and blessed be everyone who blesses you!"

30 As soon as Isaac had finished blessing Jacob, when
Jacob had scarcely gone out from the presence of his father
Isaac, his brother Esau came in from his hunting. 31 He also
prepared savory food, and brought it to his father. And he
said to his father, "Let my father sit up and eat of his son's
game, so that you may bless me." 32 His father Isaac said to
him, "Who are you?" He answered, "I am your firstborn
son, Esau." 33 Then Isaac trembled violently, and said,
"Who was it then that hunted game and brought it to me,
and I ate it all*b* before you came, and I have blessed him?
— yes, and blessed he shall be!" 34 When Esau heard his
father's words, he cried out with an exceedingly great and
bitter cry, and said to his father, "Bless me, me also, father!" 35 But he said, "Your brother came deceitfully, and
he has taken away your blessing." 36 Esau said, "Is he not
rightly named Jacob?*c* For he has supplanted me these two
times. He took away my birthright; and look, now he has
taken away my blessing." Then he said, "Have you not
reserved a blessing for me?" 37 Isaac answered Esau, "I
have already made him your lord, and I have given him all
his brothers as servants, and with grain and wine I have
sustained him. What then can I do for you, my son?"

curse for you fall on me, my son. Do as I say; go and fetch
me the kids.' 14 So Jacob went and got them and brought
them to his mother, who made them into a savoury dish
such as his father liked. 15 Rebecca then took her elder son's
clothes, Esau's best clothes which she had by her in the
house, and put them on Jacob her younger son. 16 She put
the goatskins on his hands and on the smooth nape of his
neck. 17 Then she handed to her son Jacob the savoury dish
and the bread she had made.

18 He went in to his father and said, 'Father!' Isaac answered, 'Yes, my son; which are you?' 19 Jacob answered,
'I am Esau, your elder son. I have done as you told me.
Come, sit up and eat some of the game I have for you and
then give me your blessing.' 20 Isaac said, 'How did you
find it so quickly, my son?' Jacob answered, 'Because the
LORD your God put it in my way.' 21 Isaac then said to
Jacob, 'Come close and let me touch you, my son, to make
sure that you are my son Esau.' 22 When Jacob came close
to his father, Isaac felt him and said, 'The voice is Jacob's
voice, but the hands are the hands of Esau.' 23 He did not
recognize him, because his hands were hairy like Esau's,
and so he blessed him.

24 He asked, 'Are you really my son Esau?' and when he
answered, 'Yes, I am,' 25 Isaac said, 'Bring me some of the
game to eat, my son, so that I may give you my blessing.'
Jacob brought it to him, and he ate; he brought him wine
also, and he drank it. 26 Then his father said to him, 'Come
near, my son, and kiss me.' 27 So he went near and kissed
him, and when Isaac smelt the smell of his clothes, he
blessed him and said, 'The smell of my son is like the smell
of open country blessed by the LORD.

28 'God give you dew from heaven
   and the richness of the earth,
   corn and new wine in plenty!
29 May peoples serve you
   and nations bow down to you.
  May you be lord over your brothers,
   and may your mother's sons bow down to you.
  A curse on those who curse you,
   but a blessing on those who bless you!'

30 Isaac finished blessing Jacob, who had scarcely left his
father's presence when his brother Esau came in from hunting. 31 He too prepared a savoury dish and brought it to his
father. He said, 'Come, father, eat some of the game I have
for you, and then give me your blessing.' 32 'Who are you?'
his father Isaac asked him. 'I am Esau, your elder son,' he
replied. 33 Then Isaac, greatly agitated, said, 'Then who
was it that hunted game and brought it to me? I ate it just
before you came in, and I blessed him, and the blessing will
stand.' 34 When Esau heard this, he lamented loudly and
bitterly. 'Father, bless me too,' he begged. 35 But Isaac
said, 'Your brother came full of deceit and took your blessing.' 36 'He is not called Jacob for nothing,' said Esau.
'This is the second time he has supplanted me. He took
away my right as the firstborn, and now he has taken away
my blessing. Have you kept back any blessing for me?'
37 Isaac answered, 'I have made him lord over you and set
all his brothers under him. I have bestowed upon him grain
and new wine for his sustenance. What is there left that I

---

b Cn: Heb *of all*   *c* That is *He supplants* or *He takes by the heel*   27:36 **Jacob:** *that is* He caught by the heel *or* He supplanted.

NEW AMERICAN BIBLE

mother, however, replied: "Let any curse against you, son, fall on me! Just do as I say. Go and get me the kids."

14 So Jacob went and got them and brought them to his mother; and with them she prepared an appetizing dish, such as his father liked. 15 Rebekah then took the best clothes of her older son Esau that she had in the house, and gave them to her younger son Jacob to wear; 16 and with the skins of the kids she covered up his hands and the hairless parts of his neck. 17 Then she handed her son Jacob the appetizing dish and the bread she had prepared.

18 Bringing them to his father, Jacob said, "Father!" "Yes?" replied Isaac. "Which of my sons are you?" 19 Jacob answered his father: "I am Esau, your first-born. I did as you told me. Please sit up and eat some of my game, so that you may give me your special blessing." 20 But Isaac asked, "How did you succeed so quickly, son?" He answered, "The LORD, your God, let things turn out well with me." 21 Isaac then said to Jacob, "Come closer, son, that I may feel you, to learn whether you really are my son Esau or not." 22 So Jacob moved up closer to his father. When Isaac felt him, he said, "Although the voice is Jacob's, the hands are Esau's." 23 (He failed to identify him because his hands were hairy, like those of his brother Esau; so in the end he gave him his blessing.) 24 Again he asked him, "Are you really my son Esau?" "Certainly," he replied. 25 Then Isaac said, "Serve me your game, son, that I may eat of it and then give you my blessing." Jacob served it to him, and Isaac ate; he brought him wine, and he drank. 26 Finally his father Isaac said to him, "Come closer, son, and kiss me." 27 As Jacob went up and kissed him, Isaac smelled the fragrance of his clothes. With that, he blessed him, saying,

> "Ah, the fragrance of my son
> is like the fragrance of a field
> that the LORD has blessed!

> 28 "May God give to you
> of the dew of the heavens
> And of the fertility of the earth
> abundance of grain and wine.

> 29 "Let peoples serve you,
> and nations pay you homage;
> Be master of your brothers,
> and may your mother's sons bow down to you.

> Cursed be those who curse you,
> and blessed be those who bless you."

30 Jacob had scarcely left his father, just after Isaac had finished blessing him, when his brother Esau came back from his hunt. 31 Then he too prepared an appetizing dish with his game, and bringing it to his father, he said, "Please, father, eat some of your son's game, that you may then give me your special blessing." 32 "Who are you?" his father Isaac asked him. "I am Esau," he replied, "your first-born son." 33 With that, Isaac was seized with a fit of uncontrollable trembling. "Who was it, then," he asked, "that hunted game and brought it to me? I finished eating it just before you came, and I blessed him. Now he must remain blessed!" 34 On hearing his father's words, Esau burst into loud, bitter sobbing. "Father, bless me too!" he begged. 35 When Isaac explained, "Your brother came here by a ruse and carried off your blessing," 36 Esau exclaimed, "He has been well named Jacob! He has now supplanted me twice! First he took away my birthright, and now he has taken away my blessing." Then he pleaded, "Haven't you saved a blessing for me?" 37 Isaac replied: "I have already appointed him your master, and I have assigned to him all his kinsmen as his slaves; besides, I have enriched him with grain and wine. What then can I do for you, son?" 38 But

NEW JERUSALEM BIBLE

13 But his mother replied, 'On me be the curse, my son! Just listen to me; go and fetch me the kids.' 14 So he went to fetch them and brought them to his mother, and she made the kind of special dish his father liked. 15 Rebekah took her elder son Esau's best clothes, which she had at home, and dressed her younger son Jacob in them, 16 covering his arms and the smooth part of his neck with the skins of the kids. 17 She then handed the special dish and the bread she had made to her son Jacob.

18 He went to his father and said, 'Father!' 'Yes?' he replied. 'Which of my sons are you?' 19 Jacob said to his father, 'I am Esau your first-born; I have done as you told me. Please sit up and eat some of the game I have brought and then give me your soul's blessing.' 20 Isaac said to his son, 'Son, how did you succeed so quickly?' He replied, 'Because Yahweh your God made things go well for me.' 21 Isaac said to Jacob, 'Come closer, son, so that I can feel you and be sure whether you really are my son Esau or not.' 22 Jacob went closer to his father Isaac, who felt him and said, 'The voice is Jacob's voice but the arms are the arms of Esau!' 23 He did not recognise him since his arms were hairy like his brother Esau's, and so he blessed him. 24 He said, 'Are you really my son Esau?' And he replied, 'I am.' 25 Isaac said, 'Serve it to me, so that I can eat my son's game and give you my special blessing.' He served it to him and he ate; he offered him wine, and he drank. 26 His father Isaac said to him, 'Come closer, and kiss me, son.' 27 He went closer and kissed his father, who sniffed the smell of his clothes. Then he blessed him, saying:

> Ah, the smell of my son
> is like the smell of a fertile field
> which Yahweh has blessed.
> 28 May God give you
> dew from heaven,
> and the richness of the earth,
> abundance of grain and wine!
> 29 Let peoples serve you
> and nations bow low before you!
> Be master of your brothers;
> let your mother's other sons bow low before
>   you!
> Accursed be whoever curses you
> and blessed be whoever blesses you!

30 As soon as Isaac had finished blessing Jacob, and just as Jacob was leaving his father Isaac, his brother Esau returned from hunting. 31 He too made an appetising dish and brought it to his father, 'Father, please eat some of your son's game and then give me your special blessing.' 32 His father Isaac asked, 'Who are you?' 'I am your first-born son, Esau,' he replied. 33 At this Isaac was seized with a violent trembling and said, 'Who was it, then, that went hunting and brought me the game? I finished eating it just before you came; I blessed him, and now blessed he will remain!' 34 On hearing his father's words, Esau cried out loudly and bitterly and said to his father, 'Father, bless me too!' 35 But he replied, 'Your brother came by fraud and took your blessing.' 36 Esau said, 'His name should be Jacob right enough, for he has now supplanted me twice. First he took my birthright, and look, now he has gone and taken my blessing! But', he added, 'have you not kept a blessing for me?' 37 Isaac replied to Esau, 'I have already made him your master; I have given him all his brothers as servants, I have given him grain and wine to sustain him. So what can I do for you, son?' 38 Esau said to his father, 'Can you bless

NEW REVISED STANDARD VERSION

38 Esau said to his father, "Have you only one blessing, father? Bless me, me also, father!" And Esau lifted up his voice and wept.

39 Then his father Isaac answered him:
"See, away from*d* the fatness of the earth shall
> your home be,
> and away from*e* the dew of heaven on high.
40 By your sword you shall live,
> and you shall serve your brother;
> but when you break loose, *f*
> you shall break his yoke from your neck."

41 Now Esau hated Jacob because of the blessing with which his father had blessed him, and Esau said to himself, "The days of mourning for my father are approaching; then I will kill my brother Jacob." 42 But the words of her elder son Esau were told to Rebekah; so she sent and called her younger son Jacob and said to him, "Your brother Esau is consoling himself by planning to kill you. 43 Now therefore, my son, obey my voice; flee at once to my brother Laban in Haran, 44 and stay with him a while, until your brother's fury turns away — 45 until your brother's anger against you turns away, and he forgets what you have done to him; then I will send, and bring you back from there. Why should I lose both of you in one day?"

46 Then Rebekah said to Isaac, "I am weary of my life because of the Hittite women. If Jacob marries one of the Hittite women such as these, one of the women of the land, what good will my life be to me?"

28 Then Isaac called Jacob and blessed him, and charged him, "You shall not marry one of the Canaanite women. 2 Go at once to Paddan-aram to the house of Bethuel, your mother's father; and take as wife from there one of the daughters of Laban, your mother's brother. 3 May God Almighty*g* bless you and make you fruitful and numerous, that you may become a company of peoples. 4 May he give to you the blessing of Abraham, to you and to your offspring with you, so that you may take possession of the land where you now live as an alien — land that God gave to Abraham." 5 Thus Isaac sent Jacob away; and he went to Paddan-aram, to Laban son of Bethuel the Aramean, the brother of Rebekah, Jacob's and Esau's mother.

6 Now Esau saw that Isaac had blessed Jacob and sent him away to Paddan-aram to take a wife from there, and that as he blessed him he charged him, "You shall not marry one of the Canaanite women," 7 and that Jacob had obeyed his father and his mother and gone to Paddan-aram. 8 So when Esau saw that the Canaanite women did not please his father Isaac, 9 Esau went to Ishmael and took Mahalath daughter of Abraham's son Ishmael, and sister of Nebaioth, to be his wife in addition to the wives he had.

10 Jacob left Beer-sheba and went toward Haran. 11 He came to a certain place and stayed there for the night, because the sun had set. Taking one of the stones of the place, he put it under his head and lay down in that place. 12 And he dreamed that there was a ladder*h* set up on the earth, the top of it reaching to heaven; and the angels of God were ascending and descending on it. 13 And the LORD stood beside him*i* and said, "I am the LORD, the God of Abraham your father and the God of Isaac; the land on which you lie I will give to you and to your offspring; 14 and your offspring shall be like the dust of the earth, and you shall spread abroad to the west and to the east and to the north and to the south; and all the families of the earth shall be blessed*j* in you and in your offspring. 15 Know that I am

REVISED ENGLISH BIBLE

can do for you, my son?' 38 Esau asked, 'Had you then only one blessing, father? Bless me, too, my father.' Esau wept bitterly, 39 and his father Isaac answered:

'Your dwelling will be far from the richness
> of the earth,
> far from the dew of heaven above.
40 By your sword you will live,
> and you will serve your brother.
> But the time will come when you grow
> restive
> and break his yoke from your neck.'

41 Esau harboured a grudge against Jacob because of the blessing which his father had given him, and he said to himself, 'The time of mourning for my father will soon be here; then I am going to kill my brother Jacob.' 42 When Rebecca was told what her elder son Esau was planning, she called Jacob, her younger son, and said to him, 'Your brother Esau is threatening to kill you. 43 Now, my son, listen to me. Be off at once to my brother Laban in Harran, 44 and stay with him for a while until your brother's anger cools. 45 When it has died down and he has forgotten what you did to him, I will send and fetch you back. Why should I lose you both in one day?'

46 Rebecca said to Isaac, 'I am weary to death of Hittite women! If Jacob marries a Hittite woman like those who live here, my life will not be worth living.'

28 So Isaac called Jacob, and after blessing him, gave him these instructions: 'You are not to marry a Canaanite woman. 2 Go now to the home of Bethuel, your mother's father, in Paddan-aram, and there find a wife, one of the daughters of Laban, your mother's brother. 3 May God Almighty bless you; may he make you fruitful and increase your descendants until they become a community of nations. 4 May he bestow on you and your offspring the blessing given to Abraham, that you may possess the land where you are now living, and which God assigned to Abraham!' 5 Then Isaac sent Jacob away, and he went to Paddan-aram to Laban, son of Bethuel the Aramaean and brother of Rebecca, the mother of Jacob and Esau.

6 Esau learnt that Isaac had given Jacob his blessing and had sent him away to Paddan-aram to find a wife there, that when he blessed him he had forbidden him to marry a Canaanite woman, 7 and that Jacob had obeyed his father and mother and gone to Paddan-aram. 8 Seeing that his father disliked Canaanite women, 9 Esau went to Ishmael and, in addition to his other wives, married Mahalath sister of Nebaioth and daughter of Abraham's son Ishmael.

10 Jacob set out from Beersheba and journeyed towards Harran. 11 He came to a certain shrine and, because the sun had gone down, he stopped for the night. He took one of the stones there and, using it as a pillow under his head, he lay down to sleep. 12 In a dream he saw a ladder, which rested on the ground with its top reaching to heaven, and angels of God were going up and down on it. 13 The LORD was standing beside him saying, 'I am the LORD, the God of your father Abraham and the God of Isaac. This land on which you are lying I shall give to you and your descendants. 14 They will be countless as the specks of dust on the ground, and you will spread far and wide, to west and east, to north and south. All the families of the earth will wish to be blessed as you and your descendants are blessed. 15 I

---

d Or *See, of*   *e* Or *and of*   *f* Meaning of Heb uncertain
g Traditional rendering of Heb *El Shaddai*   *h* Or *stairway* or *ramp*
i Or *stood above it*   *j* Or *shall bless themselves*

28:13 **beside him:** or above it.

NEW AMERICAN BIBLE

Esau urged his father, "Have you only that one blessing, father? Bless me too!" Isaac, however, made no reply; and Esau wept aloud. ³⁹ Finally Isaac spoke again and said to him:

"Ah, far from the fertile earth
shall be your dwelling;
far from the dew of the heavens above!
⁴⁰ "By your sword you shall live,
and your brother you shall serve;
But when you become restive,
you shall throw off his yoke from your neck."

⁴¹ Esau bore Jacob a grudge because of the blessing his father had given him. He said to himself, "When the time of mourning for my father comes, I will kill my brother Jacob." ⁴² When Rebekah got news of what her older son Esau had in mind, she called her younger son Jacob and said to him: "Listen! Your brother Esau intends to settle accounts with you by killing you. ⁴³ Therefore, son, do what I tell you: flee at once to my brother Laban in Haran, ⁴⁴ and stay with him a while until your brother's fury subsides ⁴⁵ [until your brother's anger against you subsides] and he forgets what you did to him. Then I will send for you and bring you back. Must I lose both of you in a single day?"

⁴⁶ Rebekah said to Isaac: "I am disgusted with life because of the Hittite women. If Jacob also should marry a Hittite woman, a native of the land, like these women, what good would life be to me?"

28 Isaac therefore called Jacob, greeted him with a blessing, and charged him: "You shall not marry a Canaanite woman! ² Go now to Paddan-aram, to the home of your mother's father Bethuel, and there choose a wife for yourself from among the daughters of your uncle Laban. ³ May God Almighty bless you and make you fertile, multiply you that you may become an assembly of peoples. ⁴ May he extend to you and your descendants the blessing he gave to Abraham, so that you may gain possession of the land where you are staying, which he assigned to Abraham." ⁵ Then Isaac sent Jacob on his way; he went to Paddan-aram, to Laban, son of Bethuel, the Aramean, and brother of Rebekah, the mother of Jacob and Esau.

⁶ Esau noted that Isaac had blessed Jacob when he sent him to Paddan-aram to get himself a wife, charging him, as he gave him his blessing, not to marry a Canaanite woman, ⁷ and that Jacob had obeyed his father and mother and gone to Paddan-aram. ⁸ Esau realized how displeasing the Canaanite women were to his father Isaac, ⁹ so he went to Ishmael, and in addition to the wives he had, married Mahalath, the daughter of Abraham's son Ishmael and sister of Nebaioth.

¹⁰ Jacob departed from Beer-sheba and proceeded toward Haran. ¹¹ When he came upon a certain shrine, as the sun had already set, he stopped there for the night. Taking one of the stones at the shrine, he put it under his head and lay down to sleep at that spot. ¹² Then he had a dream: a stairway rested on the ground, with its top reaching to the heavens; and God's messengers were going up and down on it. ¹³ And there was the LORD standing beside him and saying: "I, the LORD, am the God of your forefather Abraham and the God of Isaac; the land on which you are lying I will give to you and your descendants. ¹⁴ These shall be as plentiful as the dust of the earth, and through them you shall spread out east and west, north and south. In you and your descendants all the nations of the earth shall find blessing. ¹⁵ Know

NEW JERUSALEM BIBLE

only once, father? Father, bless me too.' Isaac remained silent, and Esau began to weep aloud. ³⁹ Then his father Isaac spoke again and said:

'Far from the richness of the earth
and the dew of heaven above,
your home will be.
⁴⁰ By your sword you will live,
and your brother will you serve.

But when you win your freedom, you will shake his yoke off your neck.'

⁴¹ Esau hated Jacob because of the blessing his father had given him, and Esau said to himself, 'The time to mourn for my father will soon be here. Then I shall kill my brother Jacob.' ⁴² When the words of Esau, her elder son, were repeated to Rebekah, she sent for her younger son Jacob and said to him, 'Look, your brother Esau means to take revenge and kill you. ⁴³ Now, son, listen to me; go at once and take refuge with my brother Laban in Haran. ⁴⁴ Stay with him a while, until your brother's fury cools, ⁴⁵ until your brother's anger is diverted from you and he forgets what you have done to him. Then I shall send someone to bring you back. I do not want to lose you both on one day!'

⁴⁶ Rebekah said to Isaac, 'The Hittite women sicken me to death. If Jacob were to marry a Hittite woman like these, one of the local women, what would there be left in life for me?'

28 So Isaac summoned Jacob and blessed him; and he gave him this order: 'You are not to marry any of the Canaanite women. ² Go off to Paddan-Aram, the home of Bethuel your mother's father, and there choose a wife for yourself from the daughters of Laban your mother's brother. ³ May El Shaddai bless you; may he make you fruitful and make you multiply so that you become a group of nations. ⁴ May he grant you the blessing of Abraham, you and your descendants after you, so that one day you may own the country where you are now living as a stranger — which God gave to Abraham.' ⁵ Then Isaac sent Jacob away, and Jacob went to Paddan-Aram, to Laban son of Bethuel the Aramaean and brother of Rebekah the mother of Jacob and Esau.

⁶ When Esau saw that Isaac had blessed Jacob and sent him to Paddan-Aram to choose a wife there, and that in blessing him he had given him this order: 'You are not to choose a wife from the Canaanite women,' ⁷ and that, in obedience to his father and mother, Jacob had gone to Paddan-Aram, ⁸ Esau then realised how much his father Isaac disapproved of the Canaanite women. ⁹ So Esau went to Ishmael and chose for a wife, in addition to the wives he had, Mahalath daughter of Abraham's son Ishmael and sister of Nebaioth.

¹⁰ Jacob left Beersheba and set out for Haran. ¹¹ When he had reached a certain place, he stopped there for the night, since the sun had set. Taking one of the stones of that place, he made it his pillow and lay down where he was. ¹² He had a dream: there was a ladder, planted on the ground with its top reaching to heaven; and God's angels were going up and down on it. ¹³ And there was Yahweh, standing beside him and saying, 'I, Yahweh, am the God of Abraham your father, and the God of Isaac. The ground on which you are lying I shall give to you and your descendants. ¹⁴ Your descendants will be as plentiful as the dust on the ground; you will spread out to west and east, to north and south, and all clans on earth will bless themselves by you and your descendants. ¹⁵ Be sure, I am with you; I shall keep you safe

57

with you and will keep you wherever you go, and will bring you back to this land; for I will not leave you until I have done what I have promised you." 16 Then Jacob woke from his sleep and said, "Surely the LORD is in this place — and I did not know it!" 17 And he was afraid, and said, "How awesome is this place! This is none other than the house of God, and this is the gate of heaven."

18 So Jacob rose early in the morning, and he took the stone that he had put under his head and set it up for a pillar and poured oil on the top of it. 19 He called that place Bethel;*k* but the name of the city was Luz at the first. 20 Then Jacob made a vow, saying, "If God will be with me, and will keep me in this way that I go, and will give me bread to eat and clothing to wear, 21 so that I come again to my father's house in peace, then the LORD shall be my God, 22 and this stone, which I have set up for a pillar, shall be God's house; and of all that you give me I will surely give one tenth to you."

29 Then Jacob went on his journey, and came to the land of the people of the east. 2 As he looked, he saw a well in the field and three flocks of sheep lying there beside it; for out of that well the flocks were watered. The stone on the well's mouth was large, 3 and when all the flocks were gathered there, the shepherds would roll the stone from the mouth of the well, and water the sheep, and put the stone back in its place on the mouth of the well.

4 Jacob said to them, "My brothers, where do you come from?" They said, "We are from Haran." 5 He said to them, "Do you know Laban son of Nahor?" They said, "We do." 6 He said to them, "Is it well with him?" "Yes," they replied, "and here is his daughter Rachel, coming with the sheep." 7 He said, "Look, it is still broad daylight; it is not time for the animals to be gathered together. Water the sheep, and go, pasture them." 8 But they said, "We cannot until all the flocks are gathered together, and the stone is rolled from the mouth of the well; then we water the sheep."

9 While he was still speaking with them, Rachel came with her father's sheep; for she kept them. 10 Now when Jacob saw Rachel, the daughter of his mother's brother Laban, and the sheep of his mother's brother Laban, Jacob went up and rolled the stone from the well's mouth, and watered the flock of his mother's brother Laban. 11 Then Jacob kissed Rachel, and wept aloud. 12 And Jacob told Rachel that he was her father's kinsman, and that he was Rebekah's son; and she ran and told her father.

13 When Laban heard the news about his sister's son Jacob, he ran to meet him; he embraced him and kissed him, and brought him to his house. Jacob*l* told Laban all these things, 14 and Laban said to him, "Surely you are my bone and my flesh!" And he stayed with him a month.

15 Then Laban said to Jacob, "Because you are my kinsman, should you therefore serve me for nothing? Tell me, what shall your wages be?" 16 Now Laban had two daughters; the name of the elder was Leah, and the name of the younger was Rachel. 17 Leah's eyes were lovely,*m* and Rachel was graceful and beautiful. 18 Jacob loved Rachel; so he said, "I will serve you seven years for your younger daughter Rachel." 19 Laban said, "It is better that I give her to you than that I should give her to any other man; stay with me." 20 So Jacob served seven years for Rachel, and they seemed to him but a few days because of the love he had for her.

21 Then Jacob said to Laban, "Give me my wife that I may go in to her, for my time is completed." 22 So Laban gathered together all the people of the place, and made a feast. 23 But in the evening he took his daughter Leah and

shall be with you to protect you wherever you go, and I shall bring you back to this land. I shall not leave you until I have done what I have promised you.'

16 When Jacob woke from his sleep he said, 'Truly the LORD is in this place, and I did not know it.' 17 He was awestruck and said, 'How awesome is this place! This is none other than the house of God; it is the gateway to heaven.' 18 Early in the morning, when Jacob awoke, he took the stone on which his head had rested, and set it up as a sacred pillar, pouring oil over it. 19 He named that place Beth-el; but the earlier name of the town was Luz. 20 Jacob made this vow: 'If God will be with me, if he will protect me on my journey and give me food to eat and clothes to wear, 21 so that I come back safely to my father's house, then the LORD shall be my God, 22 and this stone which I have set up as a sacred pillar shall be a house of God. And of all that you give me, I shall allot a tenth part to you.'

29 JACOB, continuing his journey, came to the land of the eastern tribes. 2 There he saw a well in the open country with three flocks of sheep lying beside it, because flocks were watered from that well. Over its mouth was a huge stone, 3 and all the herdsmen used to gather there and roll it off the mouth of the well and water the flocks; then they would replace the stone over the well. 4 Jacob said to them, 'Where are you from, my friends?' 'We are from Harran,' they replied. 5 He asked them if they knew Laban the grandson of Nahor. They answered, 'Yes, we do.' 6 'Is he well?' Jacob asked; and they answered, 'Yes, he is well, and there is his daughter Rachel coming with the flock.' 7 Jacob said, 'It is still broad daylight, and not yet time for penning the sheep. Water the flocks and then go and let them graze.' 8 But they replied, 'We cannot, until all the herdsmen have assembled and the stone has been rolled away from the mouth of the well; then we can water our flocks.' 9 While he was talking to them, Rachel arrived with her father's flock, for she was a shepherdess. 10 Immediately Jacob saw Rachel, the daughter of Laban his mother's brother, with Laban's flock, he went forward, rolled the stone off the mouth of the well and watered Laban's sheep. 11 He kissed Rachel, and was moved to tears. 12 When he told her that he was her father's kinsman, Rebecca's son, she ran and told her father. 13 No sooner had Laban heard the news of his sister's son Jacob, than he hurried to meet him, embraced and kissed him, and welcomed him to his home. Jacob told Laban all that had happened, 14 and Laban said, 'Yes, you are my own flesh and blood.'

After Jacob had stayed with him for a whole month, 15 Laban said to him, 'Why should you work for me for nothing simply because you are my kinsman? Tell me what wage you would settle for.' 16 Now Laban had two daughters: the elder was called Leah, and the younger Rachel. 17 Leah was dull-eyed, but Rachel was beautiful in both face and figure, and 18 Jacob had fallen in love with her. He said, 'For your younger daughter Rachel I would work seven years.' 19 Laban replied, 'It is better that I should give her to you than to anyone else; stay with me.'

20 When Jacob had worked seven years for Rachel, and they seemed like a few days because he loved her, 21 he said to Laban, 'I have served my time. Give me my wife that I may lie with her.' 22 Laban brought all the people of the place together and held a wedding feast. 23 In the evening he

k That is House of God   *l* Heb He   *m* Meaning of Heb uncertain   28:19 **Beth-el:** *that is* House of God.   29:5 **grandson:** *lit.* son.

that I am with you; I will protect you wherever you go, and bring you back to this land. I will never leave you until I have done what I promised you."

16 When Jacob awoke from his sleep, he exclaimed, "Truly, the LORD is in this spot, although I did not know it!" 17 In solemn wonder he cried out: "How awesome is this shrine! This is nothing else but an abode of God, and that is the gateway to heaven!" 18 Early the next morning Jacob took the stone that he had put under his head, set it up as a memorial stone, and poured oil on top of it. 19 He called that site Bethel, whereas the former name of the town had been Luz.

20 Jacob then made this vow: "If God remains with me, to protect me on this journey I am making and to give me enough bread to eat and clothing to wear, 21 and I come back safe to my father's house, the LORD shall be my God. 22 This stone that I have set up as a memorial stone shall be God's abode. Of everything you give me, I will faithfully return a tenth part to you."

29 After Jacob resumed his journey, he came to the land of the Easterners. 2 Looking about, he saw a well in the open country, with three droves of sheep huddled near it, for droves were watered from that well. A large stone covered the mouth of the well. 3 Only when all the shepherds were assembled there could they roll the stone away from the mouth of the well and water the flocks. Then they would put the stone back again over the mouth of the well.

4 Jacob said to them, "Friends, where are you from?" "We are from Haran," they replied. 5 Then he asked them, "Do you know Laban, son of Nahor?" "We do," they answered. 6 He inquired further, "Is he well?" "He is," they answered; "and here comes his daughter Rachel with his flock." 7 Then he said: "There is still much daylight left; it is hardly the time to bring the animals home. Why don't you water the flocks now, and then continue pasturing them?" 8 "We cannot," they replied, "until all the shepherds are here to roll the stone away from the mouth of the well; only then can we water the flocks."

9 While he was still talking with them, Rachel arrived with her father's sheep; she was the one who tended them. 10 As soon as Jacob saw Rachel, the daughter of his uncle Laban, with the sheep of his uncle Laban, he went up, rolled the stone away from the mouth of the well, and watered his uncle's sheep. 11 Then Jacob kissed Rachel and burst into tears. 12 He told her that he was her father's relative, Rebekah's son, and she ran to tell her father. 13 When Laban heard the news about his sister's son Jacob, he hurried out to meet him. After embracing and kissing him, he brought him to his house. Jacob then recounted to Laban all that had happened, 14 and Laban said to him, "You are indeed my flesh and blood."

After Jacob had stayed with him a full month, 15 Laban said to him: "Should you serve me for nothing just because you are a relative of mine? Tell me what your wages should be." 16 Now Laban had two daughters; the older was called Leah, the younger Rachel. 17 Leah had lovely eyes, but Rachel was well formed and beautiful. 18 Since Jacob had fallen in love with Rachel, he answered Laban, "I will serve you seven years for your younger daughter Rachel." 19 Laban replied, "I prefer to give her to you rather than to an outsider. Stay with me." 20 So Jacob served seven years for Rachel, yet they seemed to him but a few days because of his love for her.

21 Then Jacob said to Laban, "Give me my wife, that I may consummate my marriage with her, for my term is now completed." 22 So Laban invited all the local inhabitants and gave a feast. 23 At the nightfall he took his daughter Leah

wherever you go, and bring you back to this country, for I shall never desert you until I have done what I have promised you.' 16 Then Jacob awoke from his sleep and said, 'Truly, Yahweh is in this place and I did not know!' 17 He was afraid and said, 'How awe-inspiring this place is! This is nothing less than the abode of God, and this is the gate of heaven!' 18 Early next morning, Jacob took the stone he had used for his pillow, and set it up as a pillar, pouring oil over the top of it. 19 He named the place Bethel, but before that the town had been called Luz.

20 Jacob then made this vow, 'If God remains with me and keeps me safe on this journey I am making, if he gives me food to eat and clothes to wear, 21 and if I come home safe to my father's home, then Yahweh shall be my God. 22 This stone I have set up as a pillar is to be a house of God, and I shall faithfully pay you a tenth part of everything you give me.'

29 Continuing his journey, Jacob reached the Land of the Easterners. 2 And there, out in the open, he saw a well with three flocks of sheep lying beside it; this well was used for watering the flocks. Now the stone on the mouth of the well was a large one, 3 and only when all the flocks had collected there, did they roll the stone off the mouth of the well and water the sheep; then they would replace the stone over the mouth of the well. 4 Jacob said to the shepherds, 'Friends, where are you from?' They replied, 'We are from Haran.' 5 He asked them, 'Do you know Laban son of Nahor?' They replied, 'We do.' 6 Then he asked them, 'Is he well?' 'He is,' they replied, 'and here comes his daughter Rachel with the flock.' 7 Then he said, 'But it is still broad daylight, not the time to round up the animals. Why don't you water the sheep and take them back to graze?' 8 To which, they replied, 'We can't, until all the shepherds have assembled to roll the stone off the mouth of the well; then we can water the sheep.'

9 He was still talking to them, when Rachel arrived with her father's flock, for she was a shepherdess. 10 As soon as Jacob saw Rachel, his uncle Laban's daughter, with his uncle Laban's flock, he went up and, rolling the stone off the mouth of the well, watered his uncle Laban's sheep. 11 Then Jacob kissed Rachel and burst into tears. 12 He told Rachel he was her father's kinsman and Rebekah's son, and she ran to tell her father. 13 As soon as he heard her speak of his sister's son Jacob, Laban ran to greet him, embraced him, kissed him and took him to his house. Jacob told Laban everything that had happened, 14 and Laban said to him, 'You are indeed my bone and flesh!'

After Jacob had been staying with him for a month, 15 Laban said to Jacob, 'Just because you are my kinsman, why should you work for me for nothing? Tell me what wages you want.' 16 Now Laban had two daughters, the elder named Leah, and the younger Rachel. 17 Leah had lovely eyes, but Rachel was shapely and beautiful, 18 and Jacob had fallen in love with Rachel. So his answer was, 'I shall work for you for seven years in exchange for your younger daughter Rachel.' 19 Laban replied, 'It is better for me to give her to you than to a stranger; stay with me.'

20 So Jacob worked for seven years for Rachel, and they seemed to him like a few days because he loved her so much. 21 Then Jacob said to Laban, 'Give me my wife, for my time is up and I should like to go to her.' 22 Laban gathered all the people of the place together, and gave a banquet. 23 But when night came, he took his daughter Leah

brought her to Jacob; and he went in to her. 24(Laban gave his maid Zilpah to his daughter Leah to be her maid.) 25When morning came, it was Leah! And Jacob said to Laban, "What is this you have done to me? Did I not serve with you for Rachel? Why then have you deceived me?" 26Laban said, "This is not done in our country — giving the younger before the firstborn. 27Complete the week of this one, and we will give you the other also in return for serving me another seven years." 28Jacob did so, and completed her week; then Laban gave him his daughter Rachel as a wife. 29(Laban gave his maid Bilhah to his daughter Rachel to be her maid.) 30So Jacob went in to Rachel also, and he loved Rachel more than Leah. He served Laban*n* for another seven years.

31 When the LORD saw that Leah was unloved, he opened her womb; but Rachel was barren. 32Leah conceived and bore a son, and she named him Reuben;*o* for she said, "Because the LORD has looked on my affliction; surely now my husband will love me." 33She conceived again and bore a son, and said, "Because the LORD has heard*p* that I am hated, he has given me this son also"; and she named him Simeon. 34Again she conceived and bore a son, and said, "Now this time my husband will be joined*q* to me, because I have borne him three sons"; therefore he was named Levi. 35She conceived again and bore a son, and said, "This time I will praise*r* the LORD"; therefore she named him Judah; then she ceased bearing.

30

When Rachel saw that she bore Jacob no children, she envied her sister; and she said to Jacob, "Give me children, or I shall die!" 2Jacob became very angry with Rachel and said, "Am I in the place of God, who has withheld from you the fruit of the womb?" 3Then she said, "Here is my maid Bilhah; go in to her, that she may bear upon my knees and that I too may have children through her." 4So she gave him her maid Bilhah as a wife; and Jacob went in to her. 5And Bilhah conceived and bore Jacob a son. 6Then Rachel said, "God has judged me, and has also heard my voice and given me a son"; therefore she named him Dan.*s* 7Rachel's maid Bilhah conceived again and bore Jacob a second son. 8Then Rachel said, "With mighty wrestlings I have wrestled*t* with my sister, and have prevailed"; so she named him Naphtali.

9 When Leah saw that she had ceased bearing children, she took her maid Zilpah and gave her to Jacob as a wife. 10Then Leah's maid Zilpah bore Jacob a son. 11And Leah said, "Good fortune!" so she named him Gad.*u* 12Leah's maid Zilpah bore Jacob a second son. 13And Leah said, "Happy am I! For the women will call me happy"; so she named him Asher.*v*

14 In the days of wheat harvest Reuben went and found mandrakes in the field, and brought them to his mother Leah. Then Rachel said to Leah, "Please give me some of your son's mandrakes." 15But she said to her, "Is it a small matter that you have taken away my husband? Would you take away my son's mandrakes also?" Rachel said, "Then he may lie with you tonight for your son's mandrakes." 16When Jacob came from the field in the evening, Leah went out to meet him, and said, "You must come in to me; for I have hired you with my son's mandrakes." So he lay with her that night. 17And God heeded Leah, and she con-

took his daughter Leah and brought her to Jacob, and he lay with her. 24At the same time Laban gave his slave-girl Zilpah to his daughter Leah. 25But when morning came, there was Leah! Jacob said to Laban, 'What is this you have done to me? It was for Rachel I worked. Why have you played this trick on me?' 26Laban answered, 'It is against the custom of our country to marry off the younger sister before the elder. 27Go through with the seven days' feast for the elder, and the younger shall be given you in return for a further seven years' work.' 28Jacob agreed, and completed the seven days for Leah.

Then Laban gave Jacob his daughter Rachel to be his wife; 29and to serve Rachel he gave his slave-girl Bilhah. 30Jacob lay with Rachel also; he loved her rather than Leah, and he worked for Laban for a further seven years. 31When the LORD saw that Leah was unloved, he granted her a child, but Rachel remained childless. 32Leah conceived and gave birth to a son; and she called him Reuben, for she said, 'The LORD has seen my humiliation, but now my husband will love me.' 33Again she conceived and had a son and said, 'The LORD, hearing that I am unloved, has given me this child also'; and she called him Simeon. 34She conceived again and had a son and said, 'Now that I have borne him three sons my husband will surely be attached to me.' So she called him Levi. 35Once more she conceived and had a son, and said, 'Now I shall praise the LORD'; therefore she named him Judah. Then for a while she bore no more children.

30

When Rachel found that she bore Jacob no children, she became jealous of her sister and complained to Jacob, 'Give me sons, or I shall die!' 2Jacob said angrily to Rachel, 'Can I take the place of God, who has denied you children?' 3'Here is my slave-girl Bilhah,' she replied. 'Lie with her, so that she may bear sons to be laid upon my knees, and through her I too may build up a family.' 4When she gave him her slave-girl Bilhah as a wife, Jacob lay with her, 5and she conceived and bore him a son. 6Then Rachel said, 'God has given judgement for me; he has indeed heard me and given me a son'; so she named him Dan. 7Rachel's slave-girl Bilhah conceived again and bore Jacob another son. 8Rachel said, 'I have devised a fine trick against my sister, and it has succeeded' so she named him Naphtali.

9When Leah found that she had stopped bearing children, she took her slave-girl Zilpah and gave her to Jacob as a wife, 10and Zilpah, Leah's slave-girl, bore Jacob a son. 11Leah said, 'Good fortune has come,' and she named him Gad. 12Zilpah bore Jacob another son, 13and Leah said, 'Happiness has come, for women will call me happy'; so she named him Asher.

14Once at the time of the wheat harvest when Reuben was out in the open country he found some mandrakes and brought them to Leah his mother. Rachel asked Leah for some of her son's mandrakes, 15but Leah said, 'Is it not enough to have taken away my husband, that you should take these mandrakes as well?' Rachel said, 'Very well, in exchange for your son's mandrakes let Jacob sleep with you tonight.' 16In the evening, when Jacob came in from the country Leah went out to meet him. 'You are to sleep with me tonight,' she told him. 'I have hired you with my son's mandrakes.' He slept with her that night, 17and God heard

---

n Heb *him*   *o* That is *See, a son*   *p* Heb *shama*   *q* Heb *lawah*
r Heb *hodah*   *s* That is *He judged*   *t* Heb *niphtal*   *u* That is
Fortune   *v* That is *Happy*

29:32 **Reuben:** *that is* See, a son.   29:33 **Simeon:** *that is*
Hearing.   29:34 **Levi:** *that is* Attachment.   29:35 **Judah:** *that is* Praise.   30:6 **Dan:** *that is* He has given judgement.
30:8 **Naphtali:** *that is* Trickery.   30:11 **Gad:** *that is* Good
Fortune.   30:13 **Asher:** *that is* Happy.

and brought her to Jacob, and Jacob consummated the marriage with her. 24 (Laban assigned his slave girl Zilpah to his daughter Leah as her maidservant.) 25 In the morning Jacob was amazed: it was Leah! So he cried out to Laban: "How could you do this to me! Was it not for Rachel that I served you? Why did you dupe me?" 26 "It is not the custom in our country," Laban replied, "to marry off a younger daughter before an older one. 27 Finish the bridal week for this one, and then I will give you the other too, in return for another seven years of service with me."

28 Jacob agreed. He finished the bridal week for Leah, and then Laban gave him his daughter Rachel in marriage. 29 (Laban assigned his slave girl Bilhah to his daughter Rachel as her maidservant.) 30 Jacob then consummated his marriage with Rachel also, and he loved her more than Leah. Thus he remained in Laban's service another seven years.

31 When the LORD saw that Leah was unloved, he made her fruitful, while Rachel remained barren. 32 Leah conceived and bore a son, and she named him Reuben; for she said, "It means, 'The LORD saw my misery; now my husband will love me.'" 33 She conceived again and bore a son, and said, "It means, 'The LORD heard that I was unloved,' and therefore he has given me this one also"; so she named him Simeon. 34 Again she conceived and bore a son, and she said, "Now at last my husband will become attached to me, since I have now borne him three sons"; that is why she named him Levi. 35 Once more she conceived and bore a son, and she said, "This time I will give grateful praise to the LORD"; therefore she named him Judah. Then she stopped bearing children.

30 When Rachel saw that she failed to bear children to Jacob, she became envious of her sister. She said to Jacob, "Give me children or I shall die!" 2 In anger Jacob retorted, "Can I take the place of God, who has denied you the fruit of the womb?" 3 She replied, "Here is my maidservant Bilhah. Have intercourse with her, and let her give birth on my knees, so that I too may have offspring, at least through her." 4 So she gave him her maidservant Bilhah as a consort, and Jacob had intercourse with her. 5 When Bilhah conceived and bore a son, 6 Rachel said, "God has vindicated me; indeed he has heeded my plea and given me a son." Therefore she named him Dan. 7 Rachel's maidservant Bilhah conceived again and bore a second son, 8 and Rachel said, "I engaged in a fateful struggle with my sister, and I prevailed." So she named him Naphtali.

9 When Leah saw that she had ceased to bear children, she gave her maidservant Zilpah to Jacob as a consort. 10 So Jacob had intercourse with Zilpah, and she conceived and bore a son. 11 Leah then said, "What good luck!" So she named him Gad. 12 Then Leah's maidservant Zilpah bore a second son to Jacob; 13 and Leah said, "What good fortune!" — meaning, "Women call me fortunate." So she named him Asher.

14 One day, during the wheat harvest, when Reuben was out in the field, he came upon some mandrakes which he brought home to his mother Leah. Rachel asked Leah, "Please let me have some of your son's mandrakes." 15 Leah replied, "Was it not enough for you to take away my husband, that you must now take my son's mandrakes too?" "Very well, then!" Rachel answered. "In exchange for your son's mandrakes, Jacob may lie with you tonight." 16 That evening, when Jacob came home from the fields, Leah went out to meet him. "You are now to come in with me," she told him, "because I have paid for you with my son's mandrakes." So that night he slept with her, 17 and God heard

and brought her to Jacob, and he slept with her. 24 (Laban gave his slave-girl Zilpah to his daughter Leah as her slave.) 25 When morning came, it was Leah! So Jacob said to Laban, 'What have you done to me? Did I not work for you for Rachel? Why then have you tricked me?' 26 Laban replied, 'It is not the custom in our place to marry off the younger before the elder. 27 Finish this marriage week and I shall give you the other one too in return for your working for me for another seven years.' 28 Jacob agreed and, when he had finished the week, Laban gave him his daughter Rachel as his wife. 29 (Laban gave his slave-girl Bilhah to his daughter Rachel as her slave.) 30 So Jacob slept with Rachel too, and he loved Rachel more than Leah. He worked for Laban for another seven years.

31 When Yahweh saw that Leah was unloved, he opened her womb, while Rachel remained barren. 32 Leah conceived and gave birth to a son whom she named Reuben, meaning 'Yahweh has seen my misery'; and she said, 'Now my husband will love me.' 33 Conceiving again, she gave birth to a son and said, 'Yahweh heard that I was unloved, and so he has given me this one too'; and she named him Simeon. 34 Again she conceived and gave birth to a son, and said, 'This time my husband will become attached to me, because I have borne him three sons.' Accordingly, she named him Levi. 35 Again she conceived and gave birth to a son, and said, 'Now I shall praise Yahweh!' Accordingly, she named him Judah. Then she had no more children.

30 Rachel, seeing that she herself gave Jacob no children, became jealous of her sister. And she said to Jacob, 'Give me children, or I shall die!' 2 This made Jacob angry with Rachel, and he retorted, 'Am I in the position of God, who has denied you motherhood?' 3 So she said, 'Here is my slave-girl, Bilhah. Sleep with her and let her give birth on my knees; through her, then, I too shall have children!' 4 So she gave him her slave-girl Bilhah as concubine. Jacob slept with her, 5 and Bilhah conceived and gave birth to a son by Jacob. 6 Then Rachel said, 'God has done me justice; yes, he has heard my prayer and given me a son.' Accordingly she named him Dan. 7 Again Rachel's slave-girl Bilhah conceived and gave birth to a second son by Jacob. 8 Then Rachel said, 'I have fought a fateful battle with my sister, and I have won!' So she named him Naphtali.

9 Now Leah, seeing that she had ceased to bear children, took her slave-girl Zilpah and gave her to Jacob as concubine. 10 So Leah's slave-girl Zilpah gave birth to a son by Jacob. 11 Then Leah exclaimed, 'What good fortune!' So she named him Gad. 12 Leah's slave-girl Zilpah gave birth to a second son by Jacob. 13 Then Leah said, 'What blessedness! Women will call me blessed!' So she named him Asher.

14 One day, at the time of the wheat harvest, Reuben found some mandrakesp in the field and brought them to his mother Leah. Rachel said to Leah, 'Please give me some of your son's mandrakes.' 15 Leah replied, 'Is it not enough to have taken my husband, without your taking my son's mandrakes as well?' So Rachel said, 'Very well, he can sleep with you tonight in return for your son's mandrakes.' 16 When Jacob came back from the fields that night, Leah went out to meet him and said, 'You must come to me, for I have hired you at the price of my son's mandrakes.' So he slept with her that night. 17 God heard Leah, and she con-

p 30 The Hebr. name is similar to 'love'; and it was considered an aphrodisiac by the ancients.

ceived and bore Jacob a fifth son. 18 Leah said, "God has given me my hire[w] because I gave my maid to my husband"; so she named him Issachar. 19 And Leah conceived again, and she bore Jacob a sixth son. 20 Then Leah said, "God has endowed me with a good dowry; now my husband will honor[x] me, because I have borne him six sons"; so she named him Zebulun. 21 Afterwards she bore a daughter, and named her Dinah.

22 Then God remembered Rachel, and God heeded her and opened her womb. 23 She conceived and bore a son, and said, "God has taken away my reproach"; 24 and she named him Joseph,[y] saying, "May the LORD add to me another son!"

25 When Rachel had borne Joseph, Jacob said to Laban, "Send me away, that I may go to my own home and country. 26 Give me my wives and my children for whom I have served you, and let me go; for you know very well the service I have given you." 27 But Laban said to him, "If you will allow me to say so, I have learned by divination that the LORD has blessed me because of you; 28 name your wages, and I will give it." 29 Jacob said to him, "You yourself know how I have served you, and how your cattle have fared with me. 30 For you had little before I came, and it has increased abundantly; and the LORD has blessed you wherever I turned. But now when shall I provide for my own household also?" 31 He said, "What shall I give you?" Jacob said, "You shall not give me anything; if you will do this for me, I will again feed your flock and keep it: 32 let me pass through all your flock today, removing from it every speckled and spotted sheep and every black lamb, and the spotted and speckled among the goats; and such shall be my wages. 33 So my honesty will answer for me later, when you come to look into my wages with you. Every one that is not speckled and spotted among the goats and black among the lambs, if found with me, shall be counted stolen." 34 Laban said, "Good! Let it be as you have said." 35 But that day Laban removed the male goats that were striped and spotted, and all the female goats that were speckled and spotted, every one that had white on it, and every lamb that was black, and put them in charge of his sons; 36 and he set a distance of three days' journey between himself and Jacob, while Jacob was pasturing the rest of Laban's flock.

37 Then Jacob took fresh rods of poplar and almond and plane, and peeled white streaks in them, exposing the white of the rods. 38 He set the rods that he had peeled in front of the flocks in the troughs, that is, the watering places, where the flocks came to drink. And since they bred when they came to drink, 39 the flocks bred in front of the rods, and so the flocks produced young that were striped, speckled, and spotted. 40 Jacob separated the lambs, and set the faces of the flocks toward the striped and the completely black animals in the flock of Laban; and he put his own droves apart, and did not put them with Laban's flock. 41 Whenever the stronger of the flock were breeding, Jacob laid the rods in the troughs before the eyes of the flock, that they might breed among the rods, 42 but for the feebler of the flock he did not lay them there; so the feebler were Laban's, and the stronger Jacob's. 43 Thus the man grew exceedingly rich, and had large flocks, and male and female slaves, and camels and donkeys.

Leah's prayer, so that she conceived and bore a fifth son to Jacob. 18 Leah said, 'God has rewarded me, because I gave my slave-girl to my husband'; so she named him Issachar. 19 Leah conceived again and bore a sixth son. 20 She said, 'God has endowed me with a noble dowry. Now my husband will honour me like a princess, because I have borne him six sons'; so she named him Zebulun. 21 Later she bore a daughter whom she named Dinah. 22 Then God took thought for Rachel; he heard her prayer and gave her a child. 23 After she conceived and bore a son, she said, 'God has taken away my humiliation.' 24 She named him Joseph, saying, 'May the Lord add another son to me!'

25 After Rachel had given birth to Joseph, Jacob said to Laban, 'Send me on my way, for I want to return to my own home and country. 26 Give me my wives and children for whom I have served you, and I shall go; you know what service I have rendered you.' 27 Laban answered, 'I should like to say this—I have become prosperous and the LORD has blessed me through you. 28 So now tell me what wages I owe you, and I shall give you them.' 29 'You know how I have served you,' replied Jacob, 'and how your herds have prospered under my care. 30 The few you had when I came have increased beyond measure, and wherever I went the LORD brought you blessings. But is it not time for me to make provision for my family?' 31 Laban said, 'Then what shall I give you?' 'Nothing at all,' answered Jacob; 'I will tend your flocks and be in charge of them as before, if you will do what I suggest. 32 I shall go through your flocks today and pick out from them every black lamb, and all the brindled and the spotted goats, and they will be my wages. 33 This is a fair offer, and it will be to my own disadvantage later on, when we come to settling my wages: any goat amongst mine that is not spotted or brindled and any lamb that is not black will have been stolen.' 34 Laban agreed: 'Let it be as you say.'

35 But that same day Laban removed the he-goats that were striped and brindled and all the spotted and brindled she-goats, all that had any white on them, and every ram that was black, and he handed them over to his sons. 36 Then he put a distance of three days' journey between himself and Jacob, while Jacob was tending the rest of Laban's flocks. 37 So Jacob took fresh rods of poplar, almond, and plane trees, and peeled off strips of bark, exposing the white of the rods. 38 He fixed the peeled rods upright in the troughs at the watering-places where the flocks came to drink, so that they were facing the she-goats that were in heat when they came to drink. 39 They mated beside the rods and gave birth to young that were striped and spotted and brindled. 40 The rams Jacob separated, and let the ewes run only with such of the rams in Laban's flocks as were striped and black; and thus he built up flocks for himself, which he did not add to Laban's sheep. 41 As for the goats, whenever the more vigorous were in heat, he set the rods in front of them at the troughs so that they mated beside the rods. 42 He did not put them there for the weaker goats, and in this way the weaker came to be Laban's and the stronger Jacob's. 43 So Jacob's wealth increased more and more until he possessed great flocks, as well as male and female slaves, camels, and donkeys.

30:18 **Issachar:** *that is* Reward.   30:20 **Zebulun:** *that is* Prince.
30:24 **Joseph:** *that is* May he add.   30:32 **from them:** *so Gk;*
Heb. adds every spotted and brindled sheep and.

---

[w] Heb *sakar*   [x] Heb *zabal*   [y] That is *He adds*

her prayer; she conceived and bore a fifth son to Jacob. ¹⁸Leah then said, "God has given me my reward for having let my husband have my maidservant"; so she named him Issachar. ¹⁹Leah conceived again and bore a sixth son to Jacob; ²⁰and she said, "God has brought me a precious gift. This time my husband will offer me presents, now that I have borne him six sons"; so she named him Zebulun. ²¹Finally, she gave birth to a daughter, and she named her Dinah.

²²Then God remembered Rachel; he heard her prayer and made her fruitful. ²³She conceived and bore a son, and she said, "God has removed my disgrace." ²⁴So she named him Joseph, meaning, "May the LORD add another son to this one for me!"

²⁵After Rachel gave birth to Joseph, Jacob said to Laban: "Give me leave to go to my homeland. ²⁶Let me have my wives, for whom I served you, and my children, too, that I may depart. You know very well the service that I have rendered you." ²⁷Laban answered him: "If you will please. . . .

"I have learned through divination that it is because of you that God has blessed me. ²⁸So," he continued, "state what wages you want from me, and I will pay them." ²⁹Jacob replied: "You know what work I did for you and how well your livestock fared under my care; ³⁰the little you had before I came has grown into very much, since the LORD's blessings came upon you in my company. Therefore I should now do something for my own household as well." ³¹"What should I pay you?" Laban asked. Jacob answered: "You do not have to pay me anything outright. I will again pasture and tend your flock, if you do this one thing for me: ³²go through your whole flock today and remove from it every dark animal among the sheep and every spotted or speckled one among the goats. Only such animals shall be my wages. ³³In the future, whenever you check on these wages of mine, let my honesty testify against me: any animal in my possession that is not a speckled or spotted goat, or a dark sheep, got there by theft!" ³⁴"Very well," agreed Laban. "Let it be as you say."

³⁵That same day Laban removed the streaked and spotted he-goats and all the speckled and spotted she-goats, all those with some white on them, as well as the fully dark-colored sheep; these he left . . . in charge of his sons. ³⁶Then he put a three days' journey between himself and Jacob, while Jacob continued to pasture the rest of Laban's flock.

³⁷Jacob, however, got some fresh shoots of poplar, almond and plane trees, and he made white stripes in them by peeling off the bark down to the white core of the shoots. ³⁸The rods that he had thus peeled he then set upright in the watering troughs, so that they would be in front of the animals that drank from the troughs. When the animals were in heat as they came to drink, ³⁹the goats mated by the rods, and so they brought forth streaked, speckled and spotted kids. ⁴⁰The sheep, on the other hand, Jacob kept apart, and he set these animals to face the streaked or fully dark-colored animals of Laban. Thus he produced special flocks of his own, which he did not put with Laban's flock. ⁴¹Moreover, whenever the hardier animals were in heat, Jacob would set the rods in the troughs in full view of these animals, so that they mated by the rods; ⁴²but with the weaker animals he would not put the rods there. So the feeble animals would go to Laban, but the sturdy ones to Jacob. ⁴³Thus the man grew increasingly prosperous, and he came to own not only large flocks but also male and female servants and camels and asses.

ceived and gave birth to a fifth son by Jacob. ¹⁸Then Leah said, 'God has given me my reward for giving my slave-girl to my husband.' So she named him Issachar. ¹⁹Again Leah conceived and gave birth to a sixth son by Jacob, ²⁰and said, 'God has given me a fine gift; now my husband will bring me presents, for I have borne him six sons.' So she named him Zebulun. ²¹Later she gave birth to a daughter and named her Dinah.

²²Then God remembered Rachel; he heard her and opened her womb. ²³She conceived and gave birth to a son, and said, 'God has taken away my disgrace!' ²⁴She named him Joseph, saying, 'May Yahweh add another son for me!'

²⁵When Rachel had given birth to Joseph, Jacob said to Laban, 'Release me and let me go home to my own country. ²⁶Give me my wives for whom I have worked for you, and my children, and let me go. You are well aware how long I have worked for you.' ²⁷Laban replied, 'If I have done what pleases you . . . I have learnt by divination that Yahweh has blessed me because of you. ²⁸So name your wages,' he added, 'and I will pay.' ²⁹He replied, 'You know how hard I have worked for you, and how your stock has fared in my charge. ³⁰The little you had before I came has increased enormously, and Yahweh has blessed you wherever I have been. When am I to provide for my own household too?' ³¹Laban said, 'How much am I to pay you?' Jacob replied, 'You need not pay me anything. I shall change my mind and go on tending your flock, if you do this one thing for me.

³²'Go through your entire flock today and remove every black animal among the sheep, and every speckled or spotted one among the goats. These will be my wages, ³³and my uprightness will answer for me later: when you come to check my wages, every goat I have that is not speckled or spotted, and every sheep that is not black will count as stolen by me.' ³⁴Laban replied, 'Good, just as you say.' ³⁵That same day he removed the striped and speckled he-goats and all the spotted and speckled she-goats, every one that had white on it, and all the black sheep, and entrusted these to his sons. ³⁶Then he put a three days' journey between himself and Jacob, while Jacob grazed the rest of Laban's flock.

³⁷Jacob then got fresh shoots from poplar, almond and plane trees, and peeled them in white strips, laying bare the white part of the shoots. ³⁸He set up the shoots he had peeled in front of the animals, in the troughs, in the water-holes where the animals came to drink. Since they mated when they came to drink, ³⁹the goats thus mated in front of the shoots and so the goats produced striped, spotted and speckled young. ⁴⁰The ewes, on the other hand, Jacob kept apart and made these face whatever was striped or black in Laban's flock. Thus he built up droves of his own which he did not put with Laban's flocks. ⁴¹Furthermore, whenever the sturdier animals were mating, Jacob put the shoots where the animals could see them, in the troughs, so that they would mate in front of the shoots. ⁴²But when the animals were feeble, he did not put them there; so Laban got the feeble, and Jacob the sturdy. ⁴³Thus the man grew extremely rich, and came to own large flocks, men and women slaves, camels and donkeys.

31 Now Jacob heard that the sons of Laban were saying, "Jacob has taken all that was our father's; he has gained all this wealth from what belonged to our father." 2 And Jacob saw that Laban did not regard him as favorably as he did before. 3 Then the LORD said to Jacob, "Return to the land of your ancestors and to your kindred, and I will be with you." 4 So Jacob sent and called Rachel and Leah into the field where his flock was, 5 and said to them, "I see that your father does not regard me as favorably as he did before. But the God of my father has been with me. 6 You know that I have served your father with all my strength; 7 yet your father has cheated me and changed my wages ten times, but God did not permit him to harm me. 8 If he said, 'The speckled shall be your wages,' then all the flock bore speckled; and if he said, 'The striped shall be your wages,' then all the flock bore striped. 9 Thus God has taken away the livestock of your father, and given them to me.

10 During the mating of the flock I once had a dream in which I looked up and saw that the male goats that leaped upon the flock were striped, speckled, and mottled. 11 Then the angel of God said to me in the dream, 'Jacob,' and I said, 'Here I am!' 12 And he said, 'Look up and see that all the goats that leap on the flock are striped, speckled, and mottled; for I have seen all that Laban is doing to you. 13 I am the God of Bethel,ᶻ where you anointed a pillar and made a vow to me. Now leave this land at once and return to the land of your birth.'" 14 Then Rachel and Leah answered him, "Is there any portion or inheritance left to us in our father's house? 15 Are we not regarded by him as foreigners? For he has sold us, and he has been using up the money given for us. 16 All the property that God has taken away from our father belongs to us and to our children; now then, do whatever God has said to you."

17 So Jacob arose, and set his children and his wives on camels; 18 and he drove away all his livestock, all the property that he had gained, the livestock in his possession that he had acquired in Paddan-aram, to go to his father Isaac in the land of Canaan.

19 Now Laban had gone to shear his sheep, and Rachel stole her father's household gods. 20 And Jacob deceived Laban the Aramean, in that he did not tell him that he intended to flee. 21 So he fled with all that he had; starting out he crossed the Euphrates,ᵃ and set his face toward the hill country of Gilead.

22 On the third day Laban was told that Jacob had fled. 23 So he took his kinsfolk with him and pursued him for seven days until he caught up with him in the hill country of Gilead. 24 But God came to Laban the Aramean in a dream by night, and said to him, "Take heed that you say not a word to Jacob, either good or bad."

25 Laban overtook Jacob. Now Jacob had pitched his tent in the hill country, and Laban with his kinsfolk camped in the hill country of Gilead. 26 Laban said to Jacob, "What have you done? You have deceived me, and carried away my daughters like captives of the sword. 27 Why did you flee secretly and deceive me and not tell me? I would have sent you away with mirth and songs, with tambourine and lyre. 28 And why did you not permit me to kiss my sons and my daughters farewell? What you have done is foolish. 29 It is in my power to do you harm; but the God of your father spoke to me last night, saying, 'Take heed that you speak to Jacob neither good nor bad.' 30 Even though you had to go because you longed greatly for your father's house, why did you steal my gods?" 31 Jacob answered Laban, "Because I was afraid, for I thought that you would take your daughters from me by force. 32 But anyone with whom you find

31 JACOB learnt that Laban's sons were saying, 'Jacob has taken everything that our father had, and all his wealth has come from our father's property.' 2 He noticed also that Laban was not so well disposed to him as he had once been. 3 The LORD said to Jacob, 'Go back to the land of your fathers and to your kindred; I shall be with you,' 4 and Jacob sent word to Rachel and Leah to come out to where his flocks were in the country. 5 He said to them, 'I have been noticing that your father is not so friendly to me as once he was. But the God of my father has been with me. 6 You yourselves know I have served your father to the best of my ability, 7 yet he has cheated me and changed my wages ten times over. But God did not let him do me any harm. 8 If your father said, "The spotted ones are to be your wages," then all the flock bore spotted young; and if he said, "The striped ones are to be your wages," then all the flock bore striped young. 9 It is God who has taken away your father's livestock and given them to me. 10 In the season when the flocks were in heat, I had a dream in which I saw that the he-goats which were mating were striped and spotted and dappled. 11 The angel of God called to me in the dream, "Jacob!" and I replied, "Here I am!" 12 He said, "See what is happening: all the he-goats mating are striped and spotted and dappled, for I have seen all that Laban has been doing to you. 13 I am the God of Bethel where you anointed a sacred pillar and made a vow to me. Now leave this country at once and return to your native land." ' 14 Rachel and Leah answered him, 'We no longer have any share in our father's house. 15 Does he not look on us as strangers, now that he has sold us and used the money paid for us? 16 All the wealth which God has saved from our father's clutches is surely ours and our children's. Now do whatever God has told you to do.' 17 At once Jacob put his sons and his wives on camels, 18 and he drove off all the cattle and other livestock which he had acquired in Paddan-aram, to go to his father Isaac in Canaan.

19 When Laban had gone to shear his sheep, Rachel stole the household gods belonging to her father. 20 Jacob hoodwinked Laban the Aramaean and kept his departure secret; 21 he fled with all that he possessed, and soon was over the Euphrates and on the way to the hill-country of Gilead. 22 Three days later, when Laban heard that Jacob had fled, 23 he took his kinsmen with him and pursued Jacob for seven days until he caught up with him in the hill-country of Gilead. 24 But God came to Laban the Aramaean in a dream by night and said to him, 'Be careful to say nothing to Jacob, not a word.'

25 When Laban caught up with him, Jacob had pitched his tent in the hill-country of Gilead, and Laban encamped with his kinsmen in the same hill-country. 26 Laban said to Jacob, 'What have you done? You have deceived me and carried off my daughters as though they were captives taken in war. 27 Why did you slip away secretly without telling me? I would have set you on your way with songs and the music of tambourines and harps. 28 You did not even let me kiss my daughters and their children. In this you behaved foolishly. 29 I have it in my power to harm all of you, but last night the God of your father spoke to me; he told me to be careful to say nothing to you, not one word. 30 I expect that really you went away because you were homesick and pining for your father's house; but why did you steal my gods?'

31 Jacob answered, 'I was afraid; I thought you would take your daughters from me by force. 32 Whoever is found

---

ᶻ Cn: Meaning of Heb uncertain   ᵃ Heb *the river*

31:13 **the God of Bethel:** *or* the God Bethel.

NEW AMERICAN BIBLE

31 Jacob learned that Laban's sons were saying, "Jacob has taken everything that belonged to our father, and he has accumulated all this wealth of his by using our father's property." 2 Jacob perceived, too, that Laban's attitude toward him was not what it had previously been. 3 Then the LORD said to Jacob, "Return to the land of your fathers, where you were born, and I will be with you."

4 So Jacob sent for Rachel and Leah to meet him where he was in the field with his flock. 5 There he said to them: "I have noticed that your father's attitude toward me is not as it was in the past; but the God of my father has been with me. 6 You well know what effort I put into serving your father; 7 yet your father cheated me and changed my wages time after time. God, however, did not let him do me any harm. 8 Whenever your father said, 'The speckled animals shall be your wages,' the entire flock would bear speckled young; whenever he said, 'The streaked animals shall be your wages,' the entire flock would bear streaked young. 9 Thus God reclaimed your father's livestock and gave it to me. 10 Once, in the breeding season, I had a dream in which I saw mating he-goats that were streaked, speckled and mottled. 11 In the dream God's messenger called to me, 'Jacob!' 'Here!' I replied. 12 Then he said, 'Note well. All the he-goats in the flock, as they mate, are streaked, speckled and mottled, for I have seen all the things that Laban has been doing to you. 13 I am the God who appeared to you in Bethel, where you anointed a memorial stone and made a vow to me. Up, then! Leave this land and return to the land of your birth.' "

14 Rachel and Leah answered him: "Have we still an heir's portion in our father's house? 15 Are we not regarded by him as outsiders? He not only sold us; he has even used up the money that he got for us! 16 All the wealth that God reclaimed from our father really belongs to us and our children. Therefore, do just as God has told you." 17 Jacob proceeded to put his children and wives on camels, 18 and he drove off with all his livestock and all the property he had acquired in Paddan-aram, to go to his father Isaac in the land of Canaan.

19 Now Laban had gone away to shear his sheep, and Rachel had meanwhile appropriated her father's household idols. 20 Jacob had hoodwinked Laban the Aramean by not telling him of his intended flight. 21 Thus he made his escape with all that he had. Once he was across the Euphrates, he headed for the highlands of Gilead.

22 On the third day, word came to Laban that Jacob fled. 23 Taking his kinsmen with him, he pursued him for seven days until he caught up with him in the hill country of Gilead. 24 But that night God appeared to Laban the Aramean in a dream and warned him. "Take care not to threaten Jacob with any harm."

25 When Laban overtook Jacob, Jacob's tents were pitched in the highlands; Laban also pitched his tents there, on Mount Gilead. 26 "What do you mean," Laban demanded of Jacob, "by hoodwinking me and carrying off my daughters like war captives? 27 Why did you dupe me by stealing away secretly? You should have told me, and I would have sent you off with merry singing to the sound of tambourines and harps. 28 You did not even allow me a parting kiss to my daughters and grandchildren! What you have now done is a senseless thing. 29 I have it in my power to harm all of you; but last night the God of your father said to me, 'Take care not to threaten Jacob with any harm!' 30 Granted that you had to leave because you were desperately homesick for your father's house, why did you steal my gods?" 31 "I was frightened," Jacob replied to Laban, "at the thought that you might take your daughters away from me by force. 32 But as for your gods, the one you find them with shall not remain

NEW JERUSALEM BIBLE

31 Jacob learned that Laban's sons were saying, 'Jacob has taken everything that belonged to our father; it is at our father's expense that he has acquired all this wealth,' 2 and Jacob also saw that Laban's manner towards him was not as it had been in the past. 3 Yahweh said to Jacob, 'Go back to the land of your ancestors, where you were born, and I shall be with you.' 4 So Jacob had Rachel and Leah called to the fields where his flocks were, 5 and he said to them, 'I can see that your father's manner towards me is not as it was in the past, but the God of my father has been with me. 6 You yourselves know that I have worked for your father with all my might, 7 and that your father has tricked me, changing my wages ten times over, and yet God has not allowed him to harm me. 8 Whenever he said, "The spotted ones will be your wages," all the animals produced spotted young; whenever he said, "The striped ones will be your wages," all the animals produced striped young. 9 Thus God has reclaimed your father's livestock and given it to me. 10 Once, when the animals were on heat, I suddenly saw in a dream that the he-goats covering the females were striped or spotted or piebald. 11 In the dream the angel of God called to me, "Jacob!" I said, "Here I am." 12 He said, "Now take note: all the he-goats covering the females are striped or spotted or piebald — for I too have noted all the things that Laban has been doing to you, 13 I am the God who appeared to you at Bethel, where you poured oil on a pillar and made a vow to me. On your feet, then, leave this country and return to the land of your birth." '

14 In answer Rachel and Leah said to him, 'Are we still likely to inherit anything from our father's estate? 15 Does he not think of us as outsiders now? For not only has he sold us, but he has completely swallowed up the money he got for us. 16 All the wealth that God has reclaimed from our father belonged to us and our children in any case. So do whatever God has told you.'

17 Forthwith, Jacob put his children and his wives on camels, 18 and drove off all his livestock — with all the possessions he had acquired, the livestock belonging to him which he had acquired in Paddan-Aram — to go to his father Isaac in Canaan. 19 Laban was away, shearing his sheep; Rachel in the meanwhile had appropriated the household idols belonging to her father, 20 and Jacob had outwitted Laban the Aramaean so that he would not be forewarned of his flight. 21 Thus he got away with all he had. He was soon across the River and heading for Mount Gilead.

22 Three days later Laban was told that Jacob had fled. 23 Taking his brothers with him, he pursued him for seven days and overtook him at Mount Gilead. 24 But God appeared to Laban the Aramaean in a dream that night and said to him, 'On no account say anything whatever to Jacob.' 25 Laban caught up with Jacob, who had pitched his tent in the hills; and Laban pitched camp on Mount Gilead.

26 Laban said to Jacob, 'What do you mean by outwitting me and then carrying off my daughters like prisoners of war? 27 Why did you flee in secret, stealing away without letting me know, so that I could send you on your way rejoicing, with songs and the music of tambourines and harps? 28 You did not even let me kiss my sons and daughters. You have behaved like a fool. 29 It is in my power to harm you, but the God of your father said to me last night, "On no account say anything whatever to Jacob." 30 Now it may be you really went because you had such a longing for your father's house, but why did you steal my gods?'

31 Jacob answered Laban, 'I was afraid, thinking you were going to snatch your daughters from me. 32 But whoever is found in possession of your gods shall not remain

NEW REVISED STANDARD VERSION

your gods shall not live. In the presence of our kinsfolk, point out what I have that is yours, and take it." Now Jacob did not know that Rachel had stolen the gods.*b*

33 So Laban went into Jacob's tent, and into Leah's tent, and into the tent of the two maids, but he did not find them. And he went out of Leah's tent, and entered Rachel's. 34 Now Rachel had taken the household gods and put them in the camel's saddle, and sat on them. Laban felt all about in the tent, but did not find them. 35 And she said to her father, "Let not my lord be angry that I cannot rise before you, for the way of women is upon me." So he searched, but did not find the household gods.

36 Then Jacob became angry, and upbraided Laban. Jacob said to Laban, "What is my offense? What is my sin, that you have hotly pursued me? 37 Although you have felt about through all my goods, what have you found of all your household goods? Set it here before my kinsfolk and your kinsfolk, so that they may decide between us two. 38 These twenty years I have been with you; your ewes and your female goats have not miscarried, and I have not eaten the rams of your flocks. 39 That which was torn by wild beasts I did not bring to you; I bore the loss of it myself; of my hand you required it, whether stolen by day or stolen by night. 40 It was like this with me: by day the heat consumed me, and the cold by night, and my sleep fled from my eyes. 41 These twenty years I have been in your house; I served you fourteen years for your two daughters, and six years for your flock, and you have changed my wages ten times. 42 If the God of my father, the God of Abraham and the Fear*c* of Isaac, had not been on my side, surely now you would have sent me away empty-handed. God saw my affliction and the labor of my hands, and rebuked you last night."

43 Then Laban answered and said to Jacob, "The daughters are my daughters, the children are my children, the flocks are my flocks, and all that you see is mine. But what can I do today about these daughters of mine, or about their children whom they have borne? 44 Come now, let us make a covenant, you and I; and let it be a witness between you and me." 45 So Jacob took a stone, and set it up as a pillar. 46 And Jacob said to his kinsfolk, "Gather stones," and they took stones, and made a heap; and they ate there by the heap. 47 Laban called it Jegar-sahadutha:*d* but Jacob called it Galeed.*e* 48 Laban said, "This heap is a witness between you and me today." Therefore he called it Galeed, 49 and the pillar*f* Mizpah,*g* for he said, "The LORD watch between you and me, when we are absent one from the other. 50 If you ill-treat my daughters, or if you take wives in addition to my daughters, though no one else is with us, remember that God is witness between you and me."

51 Then Laban said to Jacob, "See this heap and see the pillar, which I have set between you and me. 52 This heap is a witness, and the pillar is a witness, that I will not pass beyond this heap to you, and you will not pass beyond this heap and this pillar to me, for harm. 53 May the God of Abraham and the God of Nahor"—the God of their father—"judge between us." So Jacob swore by the Fear*c* of his father Isaac, 54 and Jacob offered a sacrifice on the height and called his kinsfolk to eat bread; and they ate bread and tarried all night in the hill country.

55*h* Early in the morning Laban rose up, and kissed his grandchildren and his daughters and blessed them; then he departed and returned home.

---

b Heb *them*   *c* Meaning of Heb uncertain   *d* In Aramaic *The heap of witness*   *e* In Hebrew *The heap of witness*   *f* Compare Sam: MT lacks *the pillar*   *g* That is *Watchpost*   *h* Ch 32.1 in Heb

REVISED ENGLISH BIBLE

in possession of your gods shall die for it. In the presence of our kinsmen as witnesses, identify anything I have that is yours, and take it back.' Jacob did not know that Rachel had stolen the gods. 33 Laban went into Jacob's tent and Leah's tent and that of the two slave-girls, but he found nothing. After coming from Leah's tent he went into Rachel's. 34 In the mean time Rachel had taken the household gods and put them in the camel-bag and was sitting on them. Laban went through the whole tent but found nothing. 35 Rachel said, 'Do not take it amiss, father, that I cannot rise in your presence: the common lot of woman is upon me.' So for all his searching, Laban did not find the household gods.

36 Jacob heatedly took Laban to task. 'What have I done wrong?' he exclaimed. 'What is my offence, that you have come after me in hot pursuit 37 and have gone through all my belongings? Have you found a single article belonging to your household? If so, set it here in front of my kinsmen and yours, and let them decide between the two of us. 38 In all the twenty years I have been with you, your ewes and she-goats have never miscarried. I have never eaten rams from your flocks. 39 I have never brought to you the carcass of any animal mangled by wild beasts, but I bore the loss myself. You demanded that I should pay compensation for anything stolen by day or by night. 40 This was the way of it: the heat wore me down by day and the frost by night; I got no sleep. 41 For twenty years I have been in your household. I worked fourteen years for you to win your two daughters and six years for your flocks, and you changed my wages ten times over. 42 If the God of my father, the God of Abraham and the Fear of Isaac, had not been with me, you would now have sent me away empty-handed. But God saw my labour and my hardships, and last night he delivered his verdict.'

43 Laban answered Jacob, 'The daughters are my daughters, the children are my children, the flocks are my flocks; all you see is mine. But what am I to do now about my daughters and the children they have borne? 44 Come, let us make a pact, you and I, and let there be a witness between us.' 45 So Jacob chose a great stone and set it up as a sacred pillar. 46 Then he told his kinsmen to gather stones, and they took them and built a cairn, and beside the cairn they ate together. 47 Laban called it Jegar-sahadutha, and Jacob called it Gal-ed. 48 'This cairn', said Laban, 'is a witness today between you and me.' That was why it was named Gal-ed; 49 it was also named Mizpah, for Laban said, 'May the LORD watch between you and me when we are absent from one another. 50 If you ill-treat my daughters or take other wives besides them, then though no one is there as a witness, God will be the witness between us.'

51 Laban said to Jacob, 'Here is this cairn, and here the pillar which I have set up between us. 52 Both cairn and pillar are witnesses that I am not to pass beyond this cairn to your side with evil intent, and you must not pass beyond this cairn and this pillar to my side with evil intent. 53 May the God of Abraham and the God of Nahor judge between us.' Jacob swore this oath in the name of the Fear of Isaac, the God of his father. 54 He slaughtered an animal for sacrifice there in the hill-country, and summoned his kinsmen to the feast. They ate together and spent the night there.

55 Laban rose early in the morning, kissed his daughters and their children, gave them his blessing, and then returned to his home.

31:47 **Jegar-sahadutha:** *Aram. for* Cairn of Witness. **Gal-ed:** *Heb. for* Cairn of Witness.   31:49 **Mizpah:** *that is* Watch-tower.   31:53 **between us:** *so Gk; Heb.* adds the God of their father.   31:55 *In Heb. 32:1.*

alive! If, with my kinsmen looking on, you identify anything here as belonging to you, take it." Jacob, of course, had no idea that Rachel had stolen the idols.

33 Laban then went in and searched Jacob's tent and Leah's tent, as well as the tents of the two maidservants; but he did not find the idols. Leaving Leah's tent, he went into Rachel's. 34 Now Rachel had taken the idols, put them inside a camel cushion, and seated herself upon them. When Laban had rummaged through the rest of her tent without finding them, 35 Rachel said to her father, "Let not my lord feel offended that I cannot rise in your presence; a woman's period is upon me." So, despite his search, he did not find his idols.

36 Jacob, now enraged, upbraided Laban. "What crime or offense have I committed," he demanded, "that you should hound me so fiercely? 37 Now that you have ransacked all my things, have you found a single object taken from your belongings? If so, produce it here before your kinsmen and mine, and let them decide between us two.

38 "In the twenty years that I was under you, no ewe or she-goat of yours ever miscarried, and I have never feasted on a ram of your flock. 39 I never brought you an animal torn by wild beasts; I made good the loss myself. You held me responsible for anything stolen by day or night. 40 How often the scorching heat ravaged me by day, and the frost by night, while sleep fled from my eyes! 41 Of the twenty years that I have now spent in your household, I slaved fourteen years for your two daughters and six years for your flock, while you changed my wages time after time. 42 If my ancestral God, the God of Abraham and the Awesome One of Isaac, had not been on my side, you would now have sent me away empty-handed. But God saw my plight and the fruits of my toil, and last night he gave judgment."

43 Laban replied to Jacob: "The women are mine, their children are mine, and the flocks are mine; everything you see belongs to me. But since these women are my daughters, I will now do something for them and for the children they have borne. 44 Come, then, we will make a pact, you and I; the LORD shall be a witness between us."

45 Then Jacob took a stone and set it up as a memorial stone. 46 Jacob said to his kinsmen, "Gather some stones." So they got some stones and made a mound; and they had a meal there at the mound. 47 Laban called it Jegarsahadutha, but Jacob named it Galeed. 48 "This mound," said Laban, "shall be a witness from now on between you and me." That is why it was named Galeed— 49 and also Mizpah, for he said: "May the LORD keep watch between you and me when we are out of each other's sight. 50 If you mistreat my daughters, or take other wives besides my daughters, remember that even though no one else is about, God will be witness between you and me."

51 Laban said further to Jacob: "Here is this mound, and here is the memorial stone that I have set up between you and me. 52 This mound shall be witness, and this memorial stone shall be witness, that, with hostile intent, neither may I pass beyond this mound into your territory nor may you pass beyond it into mine. 53 May the God of Abraham and the god of Nahor [their ancestral deities] maintain justice between us!" Jacob took the oath by the Awesome One of Issac. 54 He then offered a sacrifice on the mountain and invited his kinsmen to share in the meal. When they had eaten, they passed the night on the mountain.

32 Early the next morning, Laban kissed his grandchildren and his daughters goodbye; then he set out on his journey back home, 2 while Jacob continued on his own

alive. In the presence of our brothers, examine for yourself what I have, and take what is yours.' Now Jacob did not know that Rachel had appropriated them. 33 Laban went into Jacob's tent, and then into Leah's tent and the tent of the two slave-girls, but he found nothing. He came out of Leah's tent and went into Rachel's. 34 Now Rachel had taken the household idols and put them inside a camel cushion, and was sitting on them. Laban went through everything in the tent but found nothing. 35 Then Rachel said to her father, 'Do not look angry, because I cannot rise in your presence, for I am as women are from time to time.' Laban searched but did not find the idols.

36 Then Jacob lost his temper and took Laban to task. And Jacob said to Laban, 'What is my offence, what is my crime, for you to have hounded me like this? 37 You have gone through all my belongings; have you found anything belonging to your household? Produce it here in the presence of my brothers and yours, and let them decide between the two of us. 38 In all the twenty years I was under you, your ewes and your she-goats never miscarried, and I never ate rams from your flock. 39 Those mauled I never brought back to you, but bore the loss myself. You demanded compensation from me, whether the animal was stolen in daylight or at night. 40 In the daytime the heat devoured me, and frost at night; I never had a good night's sleep. 41 It was like this for the twenty years I spent in your household. Fourteen years I slaved for you for your two daughters, and six years for your flock, since you changed my wages ten times over. 42 If the God of my father, the God of Abraham, the Kinsman of Isaac, had not been with me, you would have sent me away empty-handed. But God saw my plight and my labours, and last night he delivered judgement.'

43 Laban replied to Jacob, 'These daughters are my daughters and these children are my children, this livestock is my livestock: everything you see belongs to me. But what can I do today about my daughters here or about the children they have borne? 44 So come, let us make a pact, you and me . . . ,q and let that serve as a witness between us.'

45 Jacob then took a stone and set it up as a memorial. 46 Jacob said to his kinsmen, 'Collect some stones,' and gathering some stones they made a cairn. They had a meal there, on the cairn, and 47 Laban called it Jegar-Sahadutha while Jacob called it Galeed. 48 Laban said, 'May this cairn be a witness between us today.' That is why he named it Galeed, 49 and also Mizpah, because he said, 'Let Yahweh act as watchman between us when we are no longer in sight of each other. 50 If you ill-treat my daughters or marry other women besides my daughters, even though no one be with us, remember: God is witness between us.' 51 Then Laban said to Jacob, 'Here is this cairn I have thrown up between us, and here the pillar. 52 This cairn is a witness, and the pillar is a witness, that I am not to cross to your side of this cairn and you are not to cross to my side of this cairn and pillar, with hostile intent. 53 May the God of Abraham and the god of Nahor judge between us.' Then Jacob swore by the Kinsman of his father Isaac. 54 He offered a sacrifice on the mountain and invited his kinsmen to the meal. They ate the meal, and passed the night on the mountain.

32 Early next morning, Laban kissed his grandchildren and daughters and blessed them. Then Laban left to return home. 2 While Jacob was going on his way, angels of

q 31 Some words have probably fallen out of the text at this point.

NEW REVISED STANDARD VERSION	REVISED ENGLISH BIBLE

NEW REVISED STANDARD VERSION

32 Jacob went on his way and the angels of God met him; 2 and when Jacob saw them he said, "This is God's camp!" So he called that place Mahanaim.*i*

3 Jacob sent messengers before him to his brother Esau in the land of Seir, the country of Edom, 4 instructing them, "Thus you shall say to my lord Esau: Thus says your servant Jacob, 'I have lived with Laban as an alien, and stayed until now; 5 and I have oxen, donkeys, flocks, male and female slaves; and I have sent to tell my lord, in order that I may find favor in your sight.'"

6 The messengers returned to Jacob, saying, "We came to your brother Esau, and he is coming to meet you, and four hundred men are with him." 7 Then Jacob was greatly afraid and distressed; and he divided the people that were with him, and the flocks and herds and camels, into two companies, 8 thinking, "If Esau comes to the one company and destroys it, then the company that is left will escape."

9 And Jacob said, "O God of my father Abraham and God of my father Isaac, O LORD who said to me, 'Return to your country and to your kindred, and I will do you good,' 10 I am not worthy of the least of all the steadfast love and all the faithfulness that you have shown to your servant, for with only my staff I crossed this Jordan; and now I have become two companies. 11 Deliver me, please, from the hand of my brother, from the hand of Esau, for I am afraid of him; he may come and kill us all, the mothers with the children. 12 Yet you have said, 'I will surely do you good, and make your offspring as the sand of the sea, which cannot be counted because of their number.'"

13 So he spent that night there, and from what he had with him he took a present for his brother Esau, 14 two hundred female goats and twenty male goats, two hundred ewes and twenty rams, 15 thirty milch camels and their colts, forty cows and ten bulls, twenty female donkeys and ten male donkeys. 16 These he delivered into the hand of his servants, every drove by itself, and said to his servants, "Pass on ahead of me, and put a space between drove and drove." 17 He instructed the foremost, "When Esau my brother meets you, and asks you, 'To whom do you belong? Where are you going? And whose are these ahead of you?' 18 then you shall say, 'They belong to your servant Jacob; they are a present sent to my lord Esau; and moreover he is behind us.'" 19 He likewise instructed the second and the third and all who followed the droves, "You shall say the same thing to Esau when you meet him, 20 and you shall say, 'Moreover your servant Jacob is behind us.'" For he thought, "I may appease him with the present that goes ahead of me, and afterwards I shall see his face; perhaps he will accept me." 21 So the present passed on ahead of him; and he himself spent that night in the camp.

22 The same night he got up and took his two wives, his two maids, and his eleven children, and crossed the ford of the Jabbok. 23 He took them and sent them across the stream, and likewise everything that he had. 24 Jacob was left alone; and a man wrestled with him until daybreak. 25 When the man saw that he did not prevail against Jacob, he struck him on the hip socket; and Jacob's hip was put out of joint as he wrestled with him. 26 Then he said, "Let me go, for the day is breaking." But Jacob said, "I will not let you go, unless you bless me." 27 So he said to him, "What is your name?" And he said, "Jacob." 28 Then the man *j* said, "You shall no longer be called Jacob, but Israel,*k* for you have striven with God and with humans,*l* and have prevailed." 29 Then Jacob asked him, "Please tell me your name." But he said, "Why is it that you ask my name?" And there he blessed him. 30 So Jacob called the place Peniel,*m*

REVISED ENGLISH BIBLE

32 As Jacob continued his journey he was met by angels of God. 2 When he saw them, Jacob exclaimed, 'This is the company of God,' and he called that place Mahanaim.

3 Jacob sent messengers ahead of him to his brother Esau to the district of Seir in Edomite territory, 4 instructing them to say to Esau, 'My lord, your servant Jacob sends this message: I have been living with Laban and have stayed there till now. 5 I have acquired oxen, donkeys, and sheep, as well as male and female slaves, and I am sending to tell you this, my lord, so that I may win your favour.' 6 The messengers returned to Jacob and said, 'We went to your brother Esau and he is already on the way to meet you with four hundred men.' 7 Jacob, much afraid and distressed, divided the people with him, as well as the sheep, cattle, and camels, into two companies. 8 He reasoned that, if Esau should come upon one company and destroy it, the other might still survive.

9 Jacob prayed, 'God of my father Abraham, God of my father Isaac, LORD at whose bidding I came back to my own country and to my kindred, and who promised me prosperity, 10 I am not worthy of all the true and steadfast love which you have shown to me your servant. The last time I crossed the Jordan, I owned nothing but the staff in my hand; now I have two camps. 11 Save me, I pray, from my brother Esau, for I am afraid that he may come and destroy me; he will spare neither mother nor child. 12 But you said, "I shall make you prosper and your descendants will be like the sand of the sea, beyond all counting."'

13 After spending the night there Jacob chose a gift for his brother Esau from the herds he had with him: 14 two hundred she-goats, twenty he-goats, two hundred ewes and twenty rams, 15 thirty milch-camels with their young, forty cows and ten young bulls, twenty she-donkeys and ten donkeys. 16 He put each drove into the charge of a servant and said, 'Go on ahead of me, and leave gaps between one drove and the next.' 17 To the first servant he gave these instructions: 'When my brother Esau meets you and asks who your master is and where you are going and who owns these animals you are driving, 18 you are to say, "They belong to your servant Jacob, who sends them as a gift to my lord Esau; he himself is coming behind us."' 19 He gave the same instructions to the second, to the third, and to all the drovers, telling each to say the same thing to Esau when they met him. 20 And they were to add, 'Your servant Jacob is coming behind us.' Jacob thought, 'I shall appease him with the gift that I have sent on ahead, and afterwards, when we come face to face, perhaps he will receive me kindly.' 21 So Jacob's gift went on ahead of him, while he himself stayed that night at Maheneh.

22 During the night Jacob rose, and taking his two wives, his two slave-girls, and his eleven sons, he crossed the ford of Jabbok. 23 After he had sent them across the wadi with all that he had, 24 Jacob was left alone, and a man wrestled with him there till daybreak. 25 When the man saw that he could not get the better of Jacob, he struck him in the hollow of his thigh, so that Jacob's hip was dislocated as they wrestled. 26 The man said, 'Let me go, for day is breaking,' but Jacob replied, 'I will not let you go unless you bless me.' 27 The man asked, 'What is your name?' 'Jacob,' he answered. 28 The man said, 'Your name shall no longer be Jacob but Israel, because you have striven with God and with mortals, and have prevailed.' 29 Jacob said, 'Tell me your name, I pray.' He replied, 'Why do you ask my name?' but he gave him his blessing there. 30 Jacob called

---

i Here taken to mean *Two camps*   *j* Heb *he*   *k* That is *The one who strives with God* or *God strives*   *l* Or *with divine and human beings*   *m* That is *The face of God*

32:2 **Mahanaim:** *that is* Two Companies.   32:24 **till daybreak:** *or at* daybreak.   32:28 **Israel:** *that is* God strove.

68

NEW AMERICAN BIBLE	NEW JERUSALEM BIBLE

way. Then God's messengers encountered Jacob. 3When he saw them he said, "This is God's encampment." So he named that place Mahanaim.

4Jacob sent messengers ahead to his brother Esau in the land of Seir, the country of Edom, 5with this message: "Thus shall you say to my lord Esau: 'Your servant Jacob speaks as follows: I have been staying with Laban and have been detained there until now. 6I own cattle, asses and sheep, as well as male and female servants. I am sending my lord this information in the hope of gaining your favor.' " 7When the messengers returned to Jacob, they said, "We reached your brother Esau. He is now coming to meet you, accompanied by four hundred men."

8Jacob was very much frightened. In his anxiety, he divided the people who were with him, as well as his flocks, herds, and camels, into two camps. 9"If Esau should attack and overwhelm one camp," he reasoned, "the remaining camp may still survive." 10Then he prayed, "O God of my father Abraham and God of my father Isaac! You told me, O LORD, 'Go back to the land of your birth, and I will be good to you.' 11I am unworthy of all the acts of kindness that you have loyally performed for your servant: although I crossed the Jordan here with nothing but my staff, I have now grown into two companies. 12Save me, I pray, from the hand of my brother Esau! Otherwise I fear that when he comes he will strike me down and slay the mothers and children. 13You yourself said, 'I will be very good to you, and I will make your descendants like the sands of the sea, which are too numerous to count.' "

14After passing the night there, Jacob selected from what he had with him the following presents for his brother Esau: 15two hundred she-goats and twenty he-goats; two hundred ewes and twenty rams; 16thirty milch camels and their young; forty cows and ten bulls; twenty she-asses and ten he-asses. 17He put these animals in charge of his servants, in separate droves, and he told the servants, "Go on ahead of me, but keep a space between one drove and the next." 18To the servant in the lead he gave this instruction: "When my brother Esau meets you, he may ask you, 'Whose man are you? Where are you going? To whom do these animals ahead of you belong?' 19Then you shall answer, 'They belong to your brother Jacob, but they have been sent as a gift to my lord Esau; and Jacob himself is right behind us.' " 20He gave similar instructions to the second servant and the third and to all the others who followed behind the droves, namely: "Thus and thus shall you say to Esau, when you reach him; 21and be sure to add, 'Your servant Jacob is right behind us.' " For Jacob reasoned, "If I first appease him with gifts that precede me, then later, when I face him, perhaps he will forgive me." 22So the gifts went on ahead of him, while he stayed that night in the camp.

23In the course of that night, however, Jacob arose, took his two wives, with the two maidservants and his eleven children, and crossed the ford of the Jabbok. 24After he had taken them across the stream and had brought over all his possessions, 25Jacob was left there alone. Then some man wrestled with him until the break of dawn. 26When the man saw that he could not prevail over him, he struck Jacob's hip at its socket, so that the hip socket was wrenched as they wrestled. 27The man then said, "Let me go, for it is daybreak." But Jacob said, "I will not let you go until you bless me." 28"What is your name?" the man asked. He answered, "Jacob." 29Then the man said, "You shall no longer be spoken of as Jacob, but as Israel, because you have contended with divine and human beings and have prevailed." 30Jacob then asked him, "Do tell me your name, please." He answered, "Why should you want to know my name?" With that, he bade him farewell. 31Jacob named the place

God encountered him, 3and on seeing them he said, 'This is God's camp,' and he named the place Mahanaim.

4Jacob sent messengers ahead of him to his brother Esau in Seir, the open country of Edom, 5with these instructions, 'Say this to my lord Esau, "Here is the message of your servant Jacob: I have been staying with Laban and have been delayed there until now, 6and I own oxen, beasts of burden and flocks, and men and women slaves. I send news of this to my lord in the hope of winning your favour." ' 7The messengers returned to Jacob and told him, 'We went to your brother Esau, and he is already on his way to meet you; there are four hundred men with him.'

8Jacob was greatly afraid and distressed. He divided the people with him, and the flocks and cattle, into two camps, 9thinking, 'If Esau comes to one of the camps and attacks it, the remaining camp may be able to escape.' 10Jacob said, 'God of my father Abraham, and God of my father Isaac, Yahweh who told me, "Go back to your native land and I will be good to you," 11I am unworthy of all the faithful love and constancy you have shown your servant. I had only my staff when I crossed this Jordan, and now I have grown into two camps. 12I implore you, save me from my brother Esau's clutches, for I am afraid that he may come and attack me, mothers and children alike. 13Yet it was you who said, "I shall be very good to you, and make your descendants like the sand of the sea, which is too numerous to count." ' 14Then Jacob passed that night there.

From what he had with him he chose a gift for his brother Esau: 15two hundred she-goats and twenty he-goats, two hundred ewes and twenty rams, 16thirty camels in milk with their calves, forty cows and ten bulls, twenty female donkeys and ten male. 17He put them in the charge of his servants, in separate droves, and told his servants, 'Go ahead of me, leaving a space between each drove and the next.' 18He gave the leading man this order: 'When my brother Esau meets you and asks, "Whose man are you? Where are you going? Whose are those animals that you are driving?" 19you will answer, "Your servant Jacob's. They are a gift sent to my lord Esau. And Jacob himself is just behind us." ' 20He gave the same order to the second and the third, and to all who were following the droves. 'That is what you must say to Esau when you find him. 21And you must add, "Your servant Jacob himself is just behind us." ' For he thought, 'If I conciliate him by sending a gift in advance, perhaps he will be well inclined towards me when I face him.' 22The gift went ahead of him, but he himself spent that night in the camp.

23That same night he got up and, taking his two wives, his two slave-girls and his eleven children, crossed the ford of the Jabbok. 24After he had taken them across the stream, he sent all his possessions over too. 25And Jacob was left alone.

Then someone wrestled with him until daybreak 26who, seeing that he could not master him, struck him on the hip socket, and Jacob's hip was dislocated as he wrestled with him. 27He said, 'Let me go, for day is breaking.' Jacob replied, 'I will not let you go unless you bless me.' 28The other said, 'What is your name?' 'Jacob,' he replied. 29He said, 'No longer are you to be called Jacob,r but Israel since you have shown your strength against God and men and have prevailed.' 30Then Jacob asked, 'Please tell me your name.' He replied, 'Why do you ask my name?' With that, he blessed him there.

r**32** = 35:10.

69

NEW REVISED STANDARD VERSION	REVISED ENGLISH BIBLE

saying, "For I have seen God face to face, and yet my life is preserved." 31 The sun rose upon him as he passed Penuel, limping because of his hip. 32 Therefore to this day the Israelites do not eat the thigh muscle that is on the hip socket, because he struck Jacob on the hip socket at the thigh muscle.

33 Now Jacob looked up and saw Esau coming, and four hundred men with him. So he divided the children among Leah and Rachel and the two maids. 2 He put the maids with their children in front, then Leah with her children, and Rachel and Joseph last of all. 3 He himself went on ahead of them, bowing himself to the ground seven times, until he came near his brother.

4 But Esau ran to meet him, and embraced him, and fell on his neck and kissed him, and they wept. 5 When Esau looked up and saw the women and children, he said, "Who are these with you?" Jacob said, "The children whom God has graciously given your servant." 6 Then the maids drew near, they and their children, and bowed down; 7 Leah likewise and her children drew near and bowed down; and finally Joseph and Rachel drew near, and they bowed down. 8 Esau said, "What do you mean by all this company that I met?" Jacob answered, "To find favor with my lord." 9 But Esau said, "I have enough, my brother; keep what you have for yourself." 10 Jacob said, "No, please; if I find favor with you, then accept my present from my hand; for truly to see your face is like seeing the face of God—since you have received me with such favor. 11 Please accept my gift that is brought to you, because God has dealt graciously with me, and because I have everything I want." So he urged him, and he took it.

12 Then Esau said, "Let us journey on our way, and I will go alongside you." 13 But Jacob said to him, "My lord knows that the children are frail and that the flocks and herds, which are nursing, are a care to me; and if they are overdriven for one day, all the flocks will die. 14 Let my lord pass on ahead of his servant, and I will lead on slowly, according to the pace of the cattle that are before me and according to the pace of the children, until I come to my lord in Seir."

15 So Esau said, "Let me leave with you some of the people who are with me." But he said, "Why should my lord be so kind to me?" 16 So Esau returned that day on his way to Seir. 17 But Jacob journeyed to Succoth,n and built himself a house, and made booths for his cattle; therefore the place is called Succoth.

18 Jacob came safely to the city of Shechem, which is in the land of Canaan, on his way from Paddan-aram; and he camped before the city. 19 And from the sons of Hamor, Shechem's father, he bought for one hundred pieces of moneyo the plot of land on which he had pitched his tent. 20 There he erected an altar and called it El-Elohe-Israel.p

34 Now Dinah the daughter of Leah, whom she had borne to Jacob, went out to visit the women of the region. 2 When Shechem son of Hamor the Hivite, prince of the region, saw her, he seized her and lay with her by force. 3 And his soul was drawn to Dinah daughter of Jacob; he loved the girl, and spoke tenderly to her. 4 So Shechem spoke to his father Hamor, saying, "Get me this girl to be my wife."

5 Now Jacob heard that Shechemq had defiled his daughter Dinah; but his sons were with his cattle in the field, so Jacob held his peace until they came. 6 And Hamor the father of Shechem went out to Jacob to speak with him,

the place Peniel, 'because', he said, 'I have seen God face to face yet my life is spared'. 31 The sun rose as Jacob passed through Penuel, limping because of his hip. 32 That is why to this day the Israelites do not eat the sinew that is on the hollow of the thigh, because the man had struck Jacob on that sinew.

33 Jacob looked up and there was Esau coming with four hundred men. He divided the children between Leah and Rachel and the two slave-girls. 2 He put the slave-girls and their children in front, Leah with her children next, and Rachel and Joseph in the rear. 3 He himself went on ahead of them, bowing low to the ground seven times as he approached his brother. 4 Esau ran to meet him and embraced him; he threw his arms round him and kissed him, and they both wept. 5 When Esau caught sight of the women and children, he asked, 'Who are these with you?' Jacob replied, 'The children whom God has graciously given to your servant.' 6 The slave-girls came near, each with her children, and they bowed low; 7 then Leah with her children came near and bowed low, and lastly Joseph and Rachel came and bowed low also. 8 Esau asked, 'What was all that company of yours that I met?' 'It was meant to win favour with you, my lord,' was the answer. 9 Esau said, 'I have more than enough. Keep what you have, my brother.' 10 But Jacob replied, 'No, please! If I have won your favour, then accept, I pray, this gift from me; for, as you see, I come into your presence as into that of a god, and yet you receive me favourably. 11 Accept this gift which I bring you; for God has been gracious to me, and I have all I want.' Thus urged, Esau accepted it.

12 Esau said, 'Let us set out, and I shall go at your pace.' 13 But Jacob answered him, 'You must know, my lord, that the children are small; the flocks and herds are suckling their young and I am concerned for them, and if they are overdriven for a single day, my beasts will all die. 14 I beg you, my lord, to go on ahead, and I shall move by easy stages at the pace of the livestock I am driving and the pace of the children, until I come to my lord in Seir.' 15 Esau said, 'Let me detail some of my men to escort you,' but he replied, 'There is no reason why my lord should be so kind.' 16 That day Esau turned back towards Seir, 17 while Jacob set out for Succoth; there he built himself a house and made shelters for his cattle. Therefore he named that place Succoth.

18 So having journeyed from Paddan-aram, Jacob arrived safely at the town of Shechem in Canaan and pitched his tent to the east of it. 19 The piece of land where he had pitched his tent he bought from the sons of Hamor, Shechem's father, for a hundred sheep. 20 He erected an altar there and called it El-elohey-israel.

34 Dinah, the daughter whom Leah had borne to Jacob, went out to visit women of the district, 2 and Shechem, son of Hamor the Hivite, the local prince, saw her. He took her, lay with her, and violated her. 3 But Shechem was deeply attached to Jacob's daughter Dinah; he loved the girl and sought to win her affection. 4 Shechem said to Hamor his father, 'You must get me this girl as my wife.' 5 When Jacob learnt that his daughter Dinah had been dishonoured, his sons were with the herds in the open country, so he held his peace until they came home. 6 Meanwhile Shechem's father Hamor came out to Jacob to talk the matter over with him. 7 When they heard the news Jacob's sons

n That is *Booths*   o Heb *one hundred qesitah*   p That is *God, the God of Israel*   q Heb *he*

32:30 **Peniel:** *that is* Face of God (*elsewhere* Penuel).
33:17 **Succoth:** *that is* Shelters.   33:19 **sheep:** *or* pieces of money.   33:20 **El-elohey-israel:** *that is* God the God of Israel.

NEW AMERICAN BIBLE

Peniel, "Because I have seen God face to face," he said, "yet my life has been spared."

32 At sunrise, as he left Penuel, Jacob limped along because of his hip. 33 That is why, to this day, the Israelites do not eat the sciatic muscle that is on the hip socket, inasmuch as Jacob's hip socket was struck at the sciatic muscle.

33 Jacob looked up and saw Esau coming, accompanied by four hundred men. So he divided his children among Leah, Rachel and the two maidservants, 2 putting the maids and their children first, Leah and her children next, and Rachel and Joseph last. 3 He himself went on ahead of them, bowing to the ground seven times, until he reached his brother. 4 Esau ran to meet him, embraced him, and flinging himself on his neck, kissed him as he wept. 5 When Esau looked about, he saw the women and children. "Who are these with you?" he asked. Jacob answered, "They are the children whom God has graciously bestowed on your servant." 6 Then the maidservants and their children came forward and bowed low; 7 next, Leah and her children came forward and bowed low; lastly, Rachel and her children came forward and bowed low. 8 Then Esau asked, "What did you intend with all those droves that I encountered?" Jacob answered, "It was to gain my lord's favor." 9 "I have plenty," replied Esau; "you should keep what is yours, brother." 10 "No, I beg you!" said Jacob. "If you will do me the favor, please accept this gift from me, since to come into your presence is for me like coming into the presence of God, now that you have received me so kindly. 11 Do accept the present I have brought you; God has been generous toward me, and I have an abundance." Since he so urged him, Esau accepted.

12 Then Esau said, "Let us break camp and be on our way; I will travel alongside you." 13 But Jacob replied: "As my lord can see, the children are frail. Besides, I am encumbered with the flocks and herds, which now have sucklings; if overdriven for a single day, the whole flock will die. 14 Let my lord, then, go on ahead of me, while I proceed more slowly at the pace of the livestock before me and at the pace of my children, until I join my lord in Seir." 15 Esau replied, "Let me at least put at your disposal some of the men who are with me." But Jacob said, "For what reason? Please indulge me in this, my lord." 16 So on the same day that Esau began his journey back to Seir, 17 Jacob journeyed to Succoth. There he built a home for himself and made booths for his livestock. That is why the place was called Succoth.

18 Having thus come from Paddan-aram, Jacob arrived safely at the city of Shechem, which is in the land of Canaan, and he encamped in sight of the city. 19 The plot of ground on which he had pitched his tent he bought for a hundred pieces of bullion from the descendants of Hamor, the founder of Shechem. 20 He set up a memorial stone there and invoked "El, the God of Israel."

34 Dinah, the daughter whom Leah had borne to Jacob, went out to visit some of the women of the land. 2 When Shechem, son of Hamor the Hivite, who was chief of the region, saw her, he seized her and lay with her by force. 3 Since he was strongly attracted to Dinah, daughter of Jacob, indeed was really in love with the girl, he endeavored to win her affection. 4 Shechem also asked his father Hamor, "Get me this girl for a wife."

5 Meanwhile, Jacob heard that Shechem had defiled his daughter Dinah; but since his sons were out in the fields with his livestock, he held his peace until they came home. 6 Now Hamor, the father of Shechem, went out to discuss the matter with Jacob, 7 just as Jacob's sons were coming in

NEW JERUSALEM BIBLE

31 Jacob named the place Peniel, 'Because I have seen God face to face,' he said, 'and have survived.' 32 The sun rose as he passed Peniel, limping from his hip. 33 That is why to this day the Israelites do not eat the thigh sinew which is at the hip socket: because he had struck Jacob at the hip socket on the thigh sinew.

33 Looking up, Jacob saw Esau coming and with him four hundred men. He then divided the children between Leah, Rachel and the two slave-girls. 2 He put the slave-girls and their children in front, with Leah and her children following, and Rachel and Joseph behind. 3 He himself went ahead of them and bowed to the ground seven times, until he reached his brother. 4 But Esau ran to meet him, took him in his arms, threw himself on his neck and wept as he kissed him. 5 Then looking up he saw the women and children. 'Who are these with you?' he asked. Jacob answered, 'The children whom God has bestowed on your servant.' 6 The slave-girls then came up with their children, and they all bowed low. 7 Then Leah too came up with her children, and they all bowed low. Finally Rachel and Joseph came up and bowed low.

8 Esau asked, 'What was the purpose of that whole camp I just met?' 'To win my lord's favour,' he replied. 9 'Brother, I have plenty,' Esau answered, 'keep what is yours.' 10 Jacob protested, 'No, if I have won your favour, please accept the gift I offer, for in fact I have come into your presence as into the presence of God, since you have received me kindly. 11 So accept the gift I have brought for you, since God has been generous to me and I have all I need.' And he urged him, and Esau accepted.

12 Esau said, 'Let us break camp and move off; I shall go beside you.' 13 But Jacob replied, 'As my lord knows, the children are weak, and the sheep and cows which have calved make it hard for me. If they are driven too hard, even for one day, the whole drove will die. 14 May it please my lord to go on ahead of his servant. For my part, I shall move at a slower pace, to suit the flock I am driving and the children, until I join my lord in Seir.' 15 Esau then said, 'At least let me leave you some of the people who are with me.' 'What for?' Jacob asked. 'Please indulge me, my lord!' 16 So that day Esau turned back towards Seir, 17 but Jacob made his way to Succoth, where he built himself a house and made shelters for his livestock; that is why the place was given the name of Succoth.

18 Jacob arrived safely at the town of Shechem in Canaanite territory, on his return from Paddan-Aram. He encamped opposite the town 19 and for one hundred pieces of silver he bought from the sons of Hamor father of Shechem the piece of land on which he had pitched his tent. 20 There he erected an altar which he called 'El, God of Israel'.

34 Dinah, who was Jacob's daughter by Leah, went out to visit some of the women of that region. 2 Shechem son of Hamor the Hivite, headman of the region, saw her, seized her and forced her to sleep with him. 3 He was captivated by Dinah daughter of Jacob; he fell in love with the girl and tried to win her heart. 4 Accordingly Shechem said to his father Hamor, 'Get me this girl; I want to marry her.' 5 Meanwhile, Jacob had heard how his daughter Dinah had been dishonoured, but since his sons were out in the countryside with his livestock, Jacob said nothing until they came back.

6 Hamor father of Shechem was visiting Jacob to discuss the matter with him, 7 when Jacob's sons returned from the

NEW REVISED STANDARD VERSION

7 just as the sons of Jacob came in from the field. When they heard of it, the men were indignant and very angry, because he had committed an outrage in Israel by lying with Jacob's daughter, for such a thing ought not to be done.

8 But Hamor spoke with them, saying, "The heart of my son Shechem longs for your daughter; please give her to him in marriage. 9 Make marriages with us; give your daughters to us, and take our daughters for yourselves. 10 You shall live with us; and the land shall be open to you; live and trade in it, and get property in it." 11 Shechem also said to her father and to her brothers, "Let me find favor with you, and whatever you say to me I will give. 12 Put the marriage present and gift as high as you like, and I will give whatever you ask me; only give me the girl to be my wife."

13 The sons of Jacob answered Shechem and his father Hamor deceitfully, because he had defiled their sister Dinah. 14 They said to them, "We cannot do this thing, to give our sister to one who is uncircumcised, for that would be a disgrace to us. 15 Only on this condition will we consent to you: that you will become as we are and every male among you be circumcised. 16 Then we will give our daughters to you, and we will take your daughters for ourselves, and we will live among you and become one people. 17 But if you will not listen to us and be circumcised, then we will take our daughter and be gone."

18 Their words pleased Hamor and Hamor's son Shechem. 19 And the young man did not delay to do the thing, because he was delighted with Jacob's daughter. Now he was the most honored of all his family. 20 So Hamor and his son Shechem came to the gate of their city and spoke to the men of their city, saying, 21 "These people are friendly with us; let them live in the land and trade in it, for the land is large enough for them; let us take their daughters in marriage, and let us give them our daughters. 22 Only on this condition will they agree to live among us, to become one people: that every male among us be circumcised as they are circumcised. 23 Will not their livestock, their property, and all their animals be ours? Only let us agree with them, and they will live among us." 24 And all who went out of the city gate heeded Hamor and his son Shechem; and every male was circumcised, all who went out of the gate of his city.

25 On the third day, when they were still in pain, two of the sons of Jacob, Simeon and Levi, Dinah's brothers, took their swords and came against the city unawares, and killed all the males. 26 They killed Hamor and his son Shechem with the sword, and took Dinah out of Shechem's house, and went away. 27 And the other sons of Jacob came upon the slain, and plundered the city, because their sister had been defiled. 28 They took their flocks and their herds, their donkeys, and whatever was in the city and in the field. 29 All their wealth, all their little ones and their wives, all that was in the houses, they captured and made their prey. 30 Then Jacob said to Simeon and Levi, "You have brought trouble on me by making me odious to the inhabitants of the land, the Canaanites and the Perizzites; my numbers are few, and if they gather themselves against me and attack me, I shall be destroyed, both I and my household." 31 But they said, "Should our sister be treated like a whore?"

35 God said to Jacob, "Arise, go up to Bethel, and settle there. Make an altar there to the God who appeared to you when you fled from your brother Esau."

REVISED ENGLISH BIBLE

came home from the country; they were distressed and very angry, because in lying with Jacob's daughter Shechem had done what the Israelites hold to be an intolerable outrage. 8 Hamor appealed to them: 'My son Shechem is in love with this girl; I beg you to let him have her as his wife. 9 Let us ally ourselves in marriage; you give us your daughters, and you take ours. 10 If you settle among us, the country is open before you; make your home in it, move about freely, and acquire land of your own.' 11 Shechem said to the girl's father and brothers, 'I am eager to win your favour and I shall give whatever you ask. 12 Fix the bride-price and the gift as high as you like, and I shall give whatever you ask; only, give me the girl in marriage.'

13 Jacob's sons replied to Shechem and his father Hamor deceitfully, because Shechem had violated their sister Dinah: 14 'We cannot do this,' they said; 'we cannot give our sister to a man who is uncircumcised, for we look on that as a disgrace. 15 Only on one condition can we give our consent: if you follow our example and have every male among you circumcised, 16 we shall give you our daughters and take yours for ourselves. We will then live among you, and become one people with you. 17 But if you refuse to listen to us and be circumcised, we shall take the girl and go.' 18 Their proposal appeared satisfactory to Hamor and his son Shechem; 19 and the young man, who was held in respect above anyone in his father's house, did not hesitate to do what they had said, because his heart had been captured by Jacob's daughter.

20 Hamor and Shechem went to the gate of their town and addressed their fellow-townsmen: 21 'These men are friendly towards us,' they said; 'let them live in our country and move freely in it. The land has room enough for them. Let us marry their daughters and give them ours. 22 But on this condition only will these men agree to live with us as one people: every male among us must be circumcised as they are. 23 Their herds, their livestock, and all their chattels will then be ours. We need only agree to their condition, and then they are free to live with us.' 24 All the able-bodied men agreed with Hamor and his son Shechem, and every able-bodied male among them was circumcised. 25 Then two days later, while they were still in pain, two of Jacob's sons, Simeon and Levi, full brothers to Dinah, after arming themselves with swords, boldly entered the town and killed every male. 26 They cut down Hamor and his son Shechem and took Dinah from Shechem's house and went off. 27 Jacob's other sons came in over the dead bodies and plundered the town which had brought dishonour on their sister. 28 They seized flocks, cattle, donkeys, whatever was inside the town and outside in the open country; 29 they carried off all the wealth, the women, and the children, and looted everything in the houses.

30 Jacob said to Simeon and Levi, 'You have brought trouble on me; you have brought my name into bad odour among the people of the country, the Canaanites and the Perizzites. My numbers are few; if they combine against me and attack, I shall be destroyed, I and my household with me.' 31 They answered, 'Is our sister to be treated as a common whore?'

35 GOD said to Jacob, 'Go up now to Bethel and, when you have settled there, erect an altar to the God who appeared to you when you fled from your brother Esau.'

from the fields. When they heard the news, the men were shocked and seethed with indignation. What Shechem had done was an outrage in Israel; such a thing could not be tolerated.

8 Hamor appealed to them, saying, "My son Shechem has his heart set on your daughter. Please give her to him in marriage. 9 Intermarry with us; give your daughters to us, and take our daughters for yourselves. 10 Thus you can live among us. The land is open before you; you can settle and move about freely in it, and acquire landed property here." 11 Then Shechem, too, appealed to Dinah's father and brothers: "Do me this favor, and I will pay whatever you demand of me. 12 No matter how high you set the bridal price, I will pay you whatever you ask; only give me the maiden in marriage."

13 Jacob's sons replied to Shechem and his father Hamor with guile, speaking as they did because their sister Dinah had been defiled. 14 "We could not do such a thing," they said, "as to give our sister to an uncircumcised man; that would be a disgrace for us. 15 We will agree with you only on this condition, that you become like us by having every male among you circumcised. 16 Then we will give you our daughters and take yours in marriage; we will settle among you and become one kindred people with you. 17 But if you do not comply with our terms regarding circumcision, we will take our daughter and go away."

18 Their proposal seemed fair to Hamor and his son Shechem. 19 The young man lost no time in acting in the matter, since he was deeply in love with Jacob's daughter. Moreover, he was more highly respected than anyone else in his clan. 20 So Hamor and his son Shechem went to their town council and thus presented the matter to their fellow townsmen: 21 "These men are friendly toward us. Let them settle in the land and move about in it freely; there is ample room in the country for them. We can marry their daughters and give our daughters to them in marriage. 22 But the men will agree to live with us and form one kindred people with us only on this condition, that every male among us be circumcised as they themselves are. 23 Would not the livestock they have acquired — all their animals — then be ours? Let us, therefore, give in to them, so that they may settle among us."

24 All the able-bodied men of the town agreed with Hamor and his son Shechem, and all the males, including every able-bodied man in the community, were circumcised. 25 On the third day, while they were still in pain, Dinah's full brothers Simeon and Levi, two of Jacob's sons, took their swords, advanced against the city without any trouble, and massacred all the males. 26 After they had put Hamor and his son Shechem to the sword, they took Dinah from Shechem's house and left. 27 Then the other sons of Jacob followed up the slaughter and sacked the city in reprisal for their sister Dinah's defilement. 28 They seized their flocks, herds and asses, whatever was in the city and in the country around. 29 They carried off all their wealth, their women, and their children, and took for loot whatever was in the houses.

30 Jacob said to Simeon and Levi: "You have brought trouble upon me by making me loathsome to the inhabitants of the land, the Canaanites and the Perizzites. I have so few men that, if these people unite against me and attack me, I and my family will be wiped out." 31 But they retorted, "Should our sister have been treated like a harlot?"

35

God said to Jacob: "Go up now to Bethel. Settle there and build an altar there to the God who appeared to you while you were fleeing from your brother

countryside and heard the news; the men were outraged and infuriated that Shechem had insulted Israel by sleeping with Jacob's daughter — a thing totally unacceptable. 8 Hamor reasoned with them as follows, 'My son Shechem's heart is set on your daughter. Please allow her to marry him. 9 Intermarry with us; give us your daughters and take our daughters for yourselves. 10 We can live together, and the country will be open to you, for you to live in, and move about in, and acquire holdings.' 11 Then Shechem addressed the girl's father and brothers, 'Grant me this favour, and I will give you whatever you ask. 12 Demand as high a bride-price from me as you please, and I will pay as much as you ask. Only let me marry the girl.'

13 Jacob's sons gave Shechem and his father Hamor a crafty answer, speaking as they did because he had dishonoured their sister Dinah. 14 'We cannot do this,' they said to them. 'To give our sister to an uncircumcised man would be a disgrace for us. 15 We can agree only on one condition: that you become like us by circumcising all your males. 16 Then we will give you our daughters, taking yours for ourselves; and we will stay with you to make one nation. 17 But if you will not agree to our terms about being circumcised, we shall take our daughter and go.' 18 Hamor and Shechem son of Hamor were pleased with what they heard. 19 The young man did not hesitate about doing this, for he was deeply in love with Jacob's daughter. Moreover he was the most respected member of his entire family.

20 Hamor and his son Shechem went to the gate of their town and spoke to their fellow-townsmen as follows, 21 'These men are friendly; let them settle in the region and move about freely in it; there is plenty of room here for them; we shall marry their daughters and give our daughters to them. 22 But these men will agree to settle with us and become a single nation only on this condition: that all our males be circumcised like them. 23 Will not the livestock they own, all their animals, become ours? Then let us give our assent to this, so that they can settle with us.' 24 All the citizens of the town agreed to the proposal made by Hamor and his son Shechem, and all the males were circumcised.

25 Now on the third day, when the men were still in pain, Jacob's two sons Simeon and Levi, Dinah's brothers, each took his sword and advanced unopposed against the town and slaughtered all the males. 26 They killed Hamor and his son Shechem with the sword, removed Dinah from Shechem's house and came away. 27 When Jacob's other sons came on the slain, they pillaged the town in reprisal for the dishonouring of their sister. 28 They seized their flocks, cattle, donkeys, everything else in the town and in the countryside, 29 and all their possessions. They took all their children and wives captive and looted everything to be found in the houses.

30 Jacob said to Simeon and Levi, 'You have done me an ill turn by bringing me into bad odour with the people of the region, the Canaanites and the Perizzites. I have few men, whereas they will unite against me to defeat me and destroy me and my family.' 31 They retorted, 'Should our sister be treated like a whore?'

35

God said to Jacob, 'Move on, go to Bethel and settle there. Make an altar there for the God who appeared to you when you were fleeing from your brother Esau.'

NEW REVISED STANDARD VERSION

2 So Jacob said to his household and to all who were with him, "Put away the foreign gods that are among you, and purify yourselves, and change your clothes; 3 then come, let us go up to Bethel, that I may make an altar there to the God who answered me in the day of my distress and has been with me wherever I have gone." 4 So they gave to Jacob all the foreign gods that they had, and the rings that were in their ears; and Jacob hid them under the oak that was near Shechem.

5 As they journeyed, a terror from God fell upon the cities all around them, so that no one pursued them. 6 Jacob came to Luz (that is, Bethel), which is in the land of Canaan, he and all the people who were with him, 7 and there he built an altar and called the place El-bethel,r because it was there that God had revealed himself to him when he fled from his brother. 8 And Deborah, Rebekah's nurse, died, and she was buried under an oak below Bethel. So it was called Allon-bacuth.s

9 God appeared to Jacob again when he came from Paddan-aram, and he blessed him. 10 God said to him, "Your name is Jacob; no longer shall you be called Jacob, but Israel shall be your name." So he was called Israel. 11 God said to him, "I am God Almighty:t be fruitful and multiply; a nation and a company of nations shall come from you, and kings shall spring from you. 12 The land that I gave to Abraham and Isaac I will give to you, and I will give the land to your offspring after you." 13 Then God went up from him at the place where he had spoken with him. 14 Jacob set up a pillar in the place where he had spoken with him, a pillar of stone; and he poured out a drink offering on it, and poured oil on it. 15 So Jacob called the place where God had spoken with him Bethel.

16 Then they journeyed from Bethel; and when they were still some distance from Ephrath, Rachel was in childbirth, and she had hard labor. 17 When she was in her hard labor, the midwife said to her, "Do not be afraid; for now you will have another son." 18 As her soul was departing (for she died), she named him Ben-oni;u but his father called him Benjamin.v 19 So Rachel died, and she was buried on the way to Ephrath (that is, Bethlehem), 20 and Jacob set up a pillar at her grave; it is the pillar of Rachel's tomb, which is there to this day. 21 Israel journeyed on, and pitched his tent beyond the tower of Eder.

22 While Israel lived in that land, Reuben went and lay with Bilhah his father's concubine; and Israel heard of it.

Now the sons of Jacob were twelve. 23 The sons of Leah: Reuben (Jacob's firstborn), Simeon, Levi, Judah, Issachar, and Zebulun. 24 The sons of Rachel: Joseph and Benjamin. 25 The sons of Bilhah, Rachel's maid: Dan and Naphtali. 26 The sons of Zilpah, Leah's maid: Gad and Asher. These were the sons of Jacob who were born to him in Paddan-aram.

27 Jacob came to his father Isaac at Mamre, or Kiriath-arba (that is, Hebron), where Abraham and Isaac had resided as aliens. 28 Now the days of Isaac were one hundred eighty years. 29 And Isaac breathed his last; he died and was gathered to his people, old and full of days; and his sons Esau and Jacob buried him.

REVISED ENGLISH BIBLE

2 Jacob said to his household and to all who were with him, 'Get rid of the foreign gods which you have; then purify yourselves, and put on fresh clothes. 3 We are to set off for Bethel, so that I can erect an altar there to the God who answered me when I was in distress; he has been with me wherever I have gone.' 4 They handed over to Jacob all the foreign gods in their possession and the ear-rings they were wearing, and he buried them under the terebinth tree near Shechem. 5 As they moved off, the towns round about were panic-stricken, so that they were unable to pursue Jacob's sons. 6 Jacob and all the people with him came to Luz, that is Bethel, in Canaan. 7 There he built an altar, and called the place El-bethel, because it was there that God had revealed himself to him when he was fleeing from his brother. 8 Rebecca's nurse Deborah died and was buried under the oak below Bethel, and Jacob called it Allon-bakuth.

9 God appeared again to Jacob after his return from Paddan-aram, and blessed him. 10 God said: 'Jacob is now your name, but it is going to be Jacob no longer: your name is to be Israel.'

So Jacob was called Israel. 11 God said to him:

'I am God Almighty.

Be fruitful and increase:

a nation, a host of nations will come from you;

kings also will descend from you.

12 The land I gave to Abraham and Isaac I give to you;

and to your descendants also I shall give this land.'

13 When God left him, 14 Jacob raised a sacred pillar of stone in the place where God had spoken with him, and he offered a drink-offering on it and poured oil over it. 15 Jacob called the place where God had spoken with him Bethel.

16 They moved from Bethel, and when there was still some distance to go to Ephrathah, Rachel went into labour and her pains were severe. 17 While they were on her, the midwife said, 'Do not be afraid, for this is another son for you.' 18 Then with her last breath, as she was dying, she named him Ben-oni, but his father called him Benjamin. 19 So Rachel died and was buried by the side of the road to Ephrathah, that is Bethlehem. 20 Over her grave Jacob set up a sacred pillar; and to this day it is known as the Pillar of Rachel's Grave. 21 Then continuing his journey Israel pitched his tent on the other side of Migdal-eder. 22 While Israel was living in that district, Reuben lay with his father's concubine Bilhah; and Israel came to hear of it.

The sons of Jacob were twelve. 23 The sons of Leah: Jacob's firstborn Reuben, then Simeon, Levi, Judah, Issachar, and Zebulun. 24 The sons of Rachel: Joseph and Benjamin. 25 The sons of Rachel's slave-girl Bilhah: Dan and Naphtali. 26 The sons of Leah's slave-girl Zilpah: Gad and Asher. These were Jacob's sons, born to him in Paddan-aram. 27 Jacob came to his father Isaac at Mamre near Kiriath-arba, that is Hebron, where Abraham and Isaac had stayed. 28 Isaac was a hundred and eighty years old when he breathed his last. 29 He died and was gathered to his father's kin at this very great age, and his sons Esau and Jacob buried him.

---

r That is God of Bethel   s That is Oak of weeping   t Traditional rendering of Heb El Shaddai   u That is Son of my sorrow
v That is Son of the right hand or Son of the South

35:7 El-bethel: that is God of Bethel.   35:8 Allon-bakuth: that is Oak of Weeping.   35:18 Ben-oni: that is Son of my Grief. Benjamin: that is Son of the Right Hand or Son of Good Luck.

NEW AMERICAN BIBLE

NEW JERUSALEM BIBLE

Esau." 2 So Jacob told his family and all the others who were with him: "Get rid of the foreign gods that you have among you; then purify yourselves and put on fresh clothes. 3 We are now to go up to Bethel, and I will build an altar there to the God who answered me in my hour of distress and who has been with me wherever I have gone." 4 They therefore handed over to Jacob all the foreign gods in their possession and also the rings they had in their ears. 5 Then, as they set out, a terror from God fell upon the towns round about, so that no one pursued the sons of Jacob.

6 Thus Jacob and all the people who were with him arrived in Luz [that is, Bethel] in the land of Canaan. 7 There he built an altar and named the place Bethel, for it was there that God had revealed himself to him when he was fleeing from his brother.

8 Death came to Rebekah's nurse Deborah; she was buried under the oak below Bethel, and so it was called Allon-bacuth.

9 On Jacob's arrival from Paddan-aram, God appeared to him again and blessed him. 10 God said to him:

"You whose name is Jacob
shall no longer be called Jacob,
but Israel shall be your name."

Thus he was named Israel. 11 God also said to him:

"I am God Almighty;
be fruitful and multiply.
A nation, indeed an assembly of nations,
shall stem from you,
and kings shall issue from your loins.
12 The land I once gave
to Abraham and Isaac
I now give to you;
And to your descendants after you
will I give this land."

13 Then God departed from him. 14 On the site where God had spoken with him, Jacob set up a memorial stone, and upon it he made a libation and poured out oil. 15 Jacob named the site Bethel, because God had spoken with him there.

16 Then they departed from Bethel: but while they still had some distance to go on the way to Ephrath, Rachel began to be in labor and to suffer great distress. 17 When her pangs were most severe, her midwife said to her, "Have no fear! This time, too, you have a son." 18 With her last breath — for she was at the point of death — she called him Ben-oni; his father, however, named him Benjamin. 19 Thus Rachel died; and she was buried on the road to Ephrath [that is, Bethlehem]. 20 Jacob set up a memorial stone on her grave, and the same monument marks Rachel's grave to this day.

21 Israel moved on and pitched his tent beyond Migdal-eder. 22 While Israel was encamped in that region, Reuben went and lay with Bilhah, his father's concubine. When Israel heard of it, he was greatly offended.

The sons of Jacob were now twelve. 23 The sons of Leah: Reuben, Jacob's first-born, Simeon, Levi, Judah, Issachar, and Zebulun; 24 the sons of Rachel: Joseph and Benjamin; 25 the sons of Rachel's maid Bilhah: Dan and Naphtali; 26 the sons of Leah's maid Zilpah: Gad and Asher. These are the sons of Jacob who were born to him in Paddan-aram.

27 Jacob went home to his father Isaac at Mamre, in Kiriath-arba [that is, Hebron], where Abraham and Isaac had stayed. 28 The lifetime of Isaac was one hundred and eighty years; 29 then he breathed his last. After a full life, he died as an old man and was taken to his kinsmen. His sons Esau and Jacob buried him.

2 Jacob said to his family and to all who were with him, 'Get rid of the foreign gods you have with you; cleanse yourselves, and change your clothes. 3 We must move on and go to Bethel. There I shall make an altar for the God who heard me when I was in distress, and gave me his help on the journey I made.' 4 They gave Jacob all the foreign gods in their possession, and the earrings that they were wearing. Jacob buried them under the oak tree near Shechem. 5 They broke camp; a divine terror struck the towns round about, and no one pursued the sons of Jacob.

6 When Jacob arrived at Luz in Canaan — that is, Bethel — and all the people with him, 7 he built an altar there and named the place El-Bethel, since it was there that God had appeared to him when he was fleeing from his brother.

8 Deborah, who had been Rebekah's nurse, died and was buried below Bethel, under the oak tree; so they named it the Oak of Tears.

9 God again appeared to Jacob on his return from Paddan-Aram, and blessed him. 10 God said to him, 'Your name is Jacob,ˢ but from now on you will be called not Jacob but Israel.' Thus he came by the name Israel.

11 God said to him, 'I am El Shaddai. Be fruitful and multiply. A nation, indeed an assembly of nations, will descend from you, and kings will issue from your loins. 12 The country which I gave to Abraham and Isaac, I now give to you; and this country I shall give to your descendants after you.' 13 Then God went up from him.

14 Jacob raised a monument at the spot where he had spoken to him, a standing-stone, on which he made a libation and poured oil. 15 Jacob named the place Bethel where God had spoken to him.

16 They left Bethel, and while they were still some distance from Ephrath, Rachel went into labour, and her pains were severe. 17 When her labour was at its hardest, the midwife said to her, 'Do not worry, this is going to be another boy.' 18 At the moment when she breathed her last, for she was dying, she named him Ben-Oni. His father, however, named him Benjamin. 19 So Rachel died and was buried on the road to Ephrath, now Bethlehem. 20 Jacob raised a monument on her grave, that same monument of Rachel's Tomb which is there today.

21 Israel left and pitched his tent beyond Migdal-Eder. 22 While Israel was living in that district, Reuben went and slept with Bilhah his father's concubine, and Israel found out.

The sons of Jacob were now twelve. 23 The sons of Leah: Jacob's eldest son Reuben, then Simeon, Levi, Judah, Issachar and Zebulun. 24 The sons of Rachel: Joseph and Benjamin. 25 The sons of Bilhah, Rachel's slave-girl: Dan and Naphtali. 26 The sons of Zilpah, Leah's slave-girl: Gad and Asher. These were the sons born to Jacob in Paddan-Aram.

27 Jacob came home to his father Isaac at Mamre, at Kiriath-Arba — now Hebron — where Abraham and Isaac had stayed. 28 Isaac was one hundred and eighty years old 29 when he breathed his last. He died and was gathered to his people, an old man who had enjoyed his full span of life. His sons Esau and Jacob buried him.

35, 19: Bethlehem: the gloss comes from a later tradition that identified the site with Bethlehem, also called Ephrath or Ephratha (Jos 15, 59; Ru 4, 11; Mi 5, 1).

ˢ 35 = 32:29.

NEW REVISED STANDARD VERSION

36 These are the descendants of Esau (that is, Edom). 2 Esau took his wives from the Canaanites: Adah daughter of Elon the Hittite, Oholibamah daughter of Anah son[w] of Zibeon the Hivite, 3 and Basemath, Ishmael's daughter, sister of Nebaioth. 4 Adah bore Eliphaz to Esau; Basemath bore Reuel; 5 and Oholibamah bore Jeush, Jalam, and Korah. These are the sons of Esau who were born to him in the land of Canaan.

6 Then Esau took his wives, his sons, his daughters, and all the members of his household, his cattle, all his livestock, and all the property he had acquired in the land of Canaan; and he moved to a land some distance from his brother Jacob. 7 For their possessions were too great for them to live together; the land where they were staying could not support them because of their livestock. 8 So Esau settled in the hill country of Seir; Esau is Edom.

9 These are the descendants of Esau, ancestor of the Edomites, in the hill country of Seir. 10 These are the names of Esau's sons: Eliphaz son of Adah the wife of Esau; Reuel, the son of Esau's wife Basemath. 11 The sons of Eliphaz were Teman, Omar, Zepho, Gatam, and Kenaz. 12 (Timna was a concubine of Eliphaz, Esau's son; she bore Amalek to Eliphaz.) These were the sons of Adah, Esau's wife. 13 These were the sons of Reuel: Nahath, Zerah, Shammah, and Mizzah. These were the sons of Esau's wife, Basemath. 14 These were the sons of Esau's wife Oholibamah, daughter of Anah son[x] of Zibeon: she bore to Esau Jeush, Jalam, and Korah.

15 These are the clans[y] of the sons of Esau. The sons of Eliphaz the firstborn of Esau: the clans[y] Teman, Omar, Zepho, Kenaz, 16 Korah, Gatam, and Amalek; these are the clans[y] of Eliphaz in the land of Edom; they are the sons of Adah. 17 These are the sons of Esau's son Reuel: the clans[y] Nahath, Zerah, Shammah, and Mizzah; these are the clans[y] of Reuel in the land of Edom; they are the sons of Esau's wife Basemath. 18 These are the sons of Esau's wife Oholibamah: the clans[y] Jeush, Jalam, and Korah; these are the clans[y] born of Esau's wife Oholibamah, the daughter of Anah. 19 These are the sons of Esau (that is, Edom), and these are their clans.[y]

20 These are the sons of Seir the Horite, the inhabitants of the land: Lotan, Shobal, Zibeon, Anah, 21 Dishon, Ezer, and Dishan; these are the clans[y] of the Horites, the sons of Seir in the land of Edom. 22 The sons of Lotan were Hori and Heman; and Lotan's sister was Timna. 23 These are the sons of Shobal: Alvan, Manahath, Ebal, Shepho, and Onam. 24 These are the sons of Zibeon: Aiah and Anah; he is the Anah who found the springs[z] in the wilderness, as he pastured the donkeys of his father Zibeon. 25 These are the children of Anah: Dishon and Oholibamah daughter of Anah. 26 These are the sons of Dishon: Hemdan, Eshban, Ithran, and Cheran. 27 These are the sons of Ezer: Bilhan, Zaavan, and Akan. 28 These are the sons of Dishan: Uz and Aran. 29 These are the clans[y] of the Horites: the clans[y] Lotan, Shobal, Zibeon, Anah, 30 Dishon, Ezer, and Dishan; these are the clans[y] of the Horites, clan by clan[a] in the land of Seir.

31 These are the kings who reigned in the land of Edom, before any king reigned over the Israelites. 32 Bela son of Beor reigned in Edom, the name of his city being Dinhabah. 33 Bela died, and Jobab son of Zerah of Bozrah succeeded him as king. 34 Jobab died, and Husham of the land of the

REVISED ENGLISH BIBLE

36 THIS is an account of the descendants of Esau, that is Edom. 2 Esau took Canaanite women in marriage: Adah daughter of Elon the Hittite and Oholibamah daughter of Anah son of Zibeon the Horite, 3 and Basemath, Ishmael's daughter, sister of Nebaioth.

4 Adah bore Eliphaz to Esau; Basemath bore Reuel, 5 and Oholibamah bore Jeush, Jaalam, and Korah. These were Esau's sons, born to him in Canaan. 6 Esau took his wives, his sons and daughters and all the members of his household, his livestock, all the animals, and all the possessions he had acquired in Canaan, and went to the district of Seir out of the way of his brother Jacob, 7 because they had so much stock that they could not live together. The region where they were staying could not support them because of the numbers of their livestock. 8 So Esau lived in the hill-country of Seir. (Esau is Edom.)

9 This is an account of the descendants of Esau father of the Edomites in the hill-country of Seir.

10 These are the names of the sons of Esau: Eliphaz was the son of Esau's wife Adah. Reuel was the son of Esau's wife Basemath. 11 The sons of Eliphaz were Teman, Omar, Zepho, Gatam, and Kenaz. 12 Timna was the concubine of Esau's son Eliphaz, and she bore Amalek to him. These are the descendants of Esau's wife Adah. 13 These are the sons of Reuel: Nahath, Zerah, Shammah, and Mizzah. These were the descendants of Esau's wife Basemath. 14 These were the sons of Esau's wife Oholibamah daughter of Anah son of Zibeon: she bore him Jeush, Jaalam, and Korah.

15 These are the chiefs descended from Esau. The sons of Esau's eldest son Eliphaz: Teman, Omar, Zepho, Kenaz, 16 Korah, Gatam, Amalek. These are the chiefs descended from Eliphaz in Edom. These are the descendants of Adah. 17 These are the sons of Esau's son Reuel who were chiefs: Nahath, Zerah, Shammah, Mizzah. These are the chiefs descended from Reuel in Edom. These are the descendants of Esau's wife Basemath. 18 These are the sons of Esau's wife Oholibamah: chief Jeush, chief Jaalam, chief Korah. These are the chiefs born to Oholibamah daughter of Anah and wife of Esau. 19 These are the sons of Esau, that is Edom, and these are their chiefs.

20 These are the sons of Seir the Horite, the original inhabitants of the land: Lotan, Shobal, Zibeon, Anah, 21 Dishon, Ezer, and Dishan. These are the chiefs of the Horites, the sons of Seir in Edom. 22 The sons of Lotan were Hori and Hemam, and Lotan had a sister named Timna. 23 These are the sons of Shobal: Alvan, Manahath, Ebal, Shepho, and Onam. 24 These are the sons of Zibeon: Aiah and Anah. He is the Anah who found hot springs in the wilderness while he was tending the donkeys of his father Zibeon. 25 These are the children of Anah: Dishon and Oholibamah daughter of Anah. 26 These are the children of Dishon: Hemdan, Eshban, Ithran, and Cheran. 27 These are the sons of Ezer: Bilhan, Zavan, and Akan. 28 These are the sons of Dishan: Uz and Aran.

29 These are the chiefs descended from the Horites: Lotan, Shobal, Zibeon, Anah, 30 Dishon, Ezer, Dishan. These are the chiefs that were descended from the Horites according to their clans in the district of Seir.

31 These are the kings who ruled over Edom before there were kings in Israel: 32 Bela son of Beor became king in Edom, and his city was named Dinhabah; 33 when he died, he was succeeded by Jobab son of Zerah of Bozrah.

36:2 son: so Samar.; Heb. daughter. **Horite:** prob. rdg (cp. verses 20,21); Heb. Hivite. 36:6 **of Seir:** so Syriac; Heb. omits. 36:14 **son of Zibeon:** so Samar.; Heb. daughter of Zibeon. 36:24 **hot springs:** Heb. word of uncertain meaning.

w Sam Gk Syr: Heb daughter   x Gk Syr: Heb daughter   y Or chiefs   z Meaning of Heb uncertain   a Or chief by chief

36 These are the descendants of Esau [that is, Edom]. 2 Esau took his wives from among the Canaanite women: Adah, daughter of Elon the Hittite; Oholibamah, granddaughter through Anah of Zibeon the Hivite; 3 and Basemath, daughter of Ishmael and sister of Nebaioth. 4 Adah bore Eliphaz to Esau; Basemath bore Reuel; 5 and Oholibamah bore Jeush, Jalam and Korah. These are the sons of Esau who were born to him in the land of Cannan.

6 Esau took his wives, his sons, his daughters, and all the members of his household, as well as his livestock comprising various animals and all the property he had acquired in the land of Canaan, and went to the land of Seir, out of the way of his brother Jacob. 7 Their possessions had become too great for them to dwell together, and the land in which they were staying could not support them because of their livestock. 8 So Esau settled in the highlands of Seir. [Esau is Edom.] 9 These are the descendants of Esau, ancestor of the Edomites, in the highlands of Seir.

10 These are the names of Esau's sons: Eliphaz, son of Esau's wife Adah; and Reuel, son of Esau's wife Basemath. 11 The sons of Eliphaz were Teman, Omar, Zepho, Gatam and Kenaz. 12 (Esau's son Eliphaz had a concubine Timna, and she bore Amalek to Eliphaz.) These are the descendants of Esau's wife Adah. 13 The sons of Reuel were Nahath, Zerah, Shammah and Mizzah. These are the descendants of Esau's wife Basemath. 14 The descendants of Esau's wife Oholibamah — granddaughter through Anah of Zibeon — whom she bore to Esau were Jeush, Jalam and Korah.

15 The following are the clans of Esau's descendants. The descendants of Eliphaz, Esau's first-born: the clans of Teman, Omar, Zepho, Kenaz, 16 Korah, Gatam and Amalek. These are the clans of Eliphaz in the land of Edom; they are descended from Adah. 17 The descendants of Esau's son Reuel: the clans of Nahath, Zerah, Shammah and Mizzah. These are the clans of Reuel in the land of Edom; they are descended from Esau's wife Basemath. 18 The descendants of Esau's wife Oholibamah: the clans of Jeush, Jalam and Korah. These are the clans of Esau's wife Oholibamah, daughter of Anah. 19 Such are the descendants of Esau [that is, Edom] according to their clans.

20 The following are the descendants of Seir the Horite, the original settlers in the land: Lotan, Shobal, Zibeon, Anah, 21 Dishon, Ezer and Dishan; they are the Horite clans descended from Seir, in the land of Edom. 22 Lotan's descendants were Hori and Hemam, and Lotan's sister was Timna. 23 Shobal's descendants were Alvan, Mahanath, Ebal, Shepho and Onam. 24 Zibeon's descendants were Aiah and Anah. (He is the Anah who found water in the desert while he was pasturing the asses of his father Zibeon.) 25 The descendants of Anah were Dishon and Oholibamah, daughter of Anah. 26 The descendants of Dishon were Hemdan, Eshban, Ithran and Cheran. 27 The descendants of Ezer were Bilhan, Zaavan and Akan. 28 The descendants of Dishan were Uz and Aran. 29 These are the Horite clans: the clans of Lotan, Shobal, Zibeon, Anah, 30 Dishon, Ezer and Dishan; they were the clans of the Horites, clan by clan, in the land of Seir.

31 The following are the kings who reigned in the land of Edom before any king reigned over the Israelites. 32 Bela, son of Beor, became king in Edom; the name of his city was Dinhabah. 33 When Bela died, Jobab, son of Zerah, from Bozrah, succeeded him as king. 34 When Jobab died, Hu-

36 These are the descendants of Esau, that is, Edom. 2 Esau chose his wives from the women of Canaan: Adah daughter of Elon the Hittite, Oholibamah daughter of Anah, son of Zibeon the Horite, 3 Basemath daughter of Ishmael and sister of Nebaioth. 4 Adah bore Eliphaz to Esau, Basemath bore Reuel, 5 Oholibamah bore Jeush, Jalam and Korah. These were the sons of Esau born to him in Canaan.

6 Esau took his wives, his sons and daughters, all the members of his household, his livestock, all his cattle and all the goods he had acquired in Canaan and left for Seir, away from his brother Jacob. 7 For they had acquired too much to live together. The land in which they were at that time could not support them both because of their livestock. 8 That is why Edom settled in the mountainous region of Seir. Esau is Edom.

9 These are the descendants of Esau, ancestor of Edom, in the mountainous region of Seir.

10 These are the names of Esau's sons: Eliphaz son of Esau's wife Adah, and Reuel son of Esau's wife Basemath. 11 The sons of Eliphaz were: Teman, Omar, Zepho, Gatam and Kenaz. 12 Eliphaz son of Esau had Timna for concubine and she bore him Amalek. These were the sons of Esau's wife Adah.

13 These were the sons of Reuel: Nahath, Zerah, Shammah and Mizzah. These were the sons of Esau's wife Basemath.

14 And these were the sons of Esau's wife Oholibamah daughter of Anah, son of Zibeon: she bore him Jeush, Jalam and Korah.

15 These are the chieftains of Esau.

The descendants of Eliphaz, Esau's eldest son: the chieftains of Teman, Omar, Zepho, Kenaz, 16 Gatam and Amalek. These are the chieftains of Eliphaz in Edom and are descended from Adah.

17 The descendants of Esau's son Reuel: the chieftains of Nahath, Zerah, Shammah and Mizzah. These are the chieftains of Reuel in Edom and are descended from Esau's wife Basemath.

18 The descendants of Esau's wife Oholibamah: the chieftains of Jeush, Jalam and Korah. These are the chieftains of Esau's wife Oholibamah daughter of Anah.

19 These were the sons of Esau — that is, Edom — and these are their chieftains.

20 These are the sons of Seir the Horite, natives of the country: Lotan, Shobal, Zibeon, Anah, 21 Dishon, Ezer and Dishan; these were the Horite chieftains descended from Seir, in Edom. 22 The sons of Lotan were Hori and Hemam, and Lotan's sister was Timna. 23 These are the sons of Shobal: Alvan, Manahath, Ebal, Shepho and Onam. 24 These are the sons of Zibeon: Aiah, Anah — the Anah who found the hot springs in the desert while pasturing his father Zibeon's donkeys. 25 These are the children of Anah: Dishon, and Oholibamah daughter of Anah. 26 These are the sons of Dishon: Hemdan, Eshban, Ithran and Cheran. 27 These are the sons of Ezer: Bilhan, Zaavan and Akan. 28 These are the sons of Dishan: Uz and Aran.

29 These are the Horite chieftains: the chieftains of Lotan, Shobal, Zibeon, Anah, 30 Dishon, Ezer and Dishan. These are the chieftains of the Horites, by their clans, in Seir.

31 These are the kings who reigned in Edom before an Israelite king. 32 In Edom reigned Bela son of Beor; his city was called Dinhabah. 33 Bela died and Jobab son of Zerah, from Bozrah, succeeded. 34 Jobab died and Husham from

NEW REVISED STANDARD VERSION	REVISED ENGLISH BIBLE

Temanites succeeded him as king. 35 Husham died, and Hadad son of Bedad, who defeated Midian in the country of Moab, succeeded him as king, the name of his city being Avith. 36 Hadad died, and Samlah of Masrekah succeeded him as king. 37 Samlah died, and Shaul of Rehoboth on the Euphrates succeeded him as king. 38 Shaul died, and Baal-hanan son of Achbor succeeded him as king. 39 Baal-hanan son of Achbor died, and Hadar succeeded him as king, the name of his city being Pau; his wife's name was Mehetabel, the daughter of Matred, daughter of Me-zahab.

40 These are the names of the clans*b* of Esau, according to their families and their localities by their names: the clans*b* Timna, Alvah, Jetheth, 41 Oholibamah, Elah, Pinon, 42 Kenaz, Teman, Mibzar, 43 Magdiel, and Iram; these are the clans*b* of Edom (that is, Esau, the father of Edom), according to their settlements in the land that they held.

37 Jacob settled in the land where his father had lived as an alien, the land of Canaan. 2 This is the story of the family of Jacob.

Joseph, being seventeen years old, was shepherding the flock with his brothers; he was a helper to the sons of Bilhah and Zilpah, his father's wives; and Joseph brought a bad report of them to their father. 3 Now Israel loved Joseph more than any other of his children, because he was the son of his old age; and he had made him a long robe with sleeves.*c* 4 But when his brothers saw that their father loved him more than all his brothers, they hated him, and could not speak peaceably to him.

5 Once Joseph had a dream, and when he told it to his brothers, they hated him even more. 6 He said to them, "Listen to this dream that I dreamed. 7 There we were, binding sheaves in the field. Suddenly my sheaf rose and stood upright; then your sheaves gathered around it, and bowed down to my sheaf." 8 His brothers said to him, "Are you indeed to reign over us? Are you indeed to have dominion over us?" So they hated him even more because of his dreams and his words.

9 He had another dream, and told it to his brothers, saying, "Look, I have had another dream: the sun, the moon, and eleven stars were bowing down to me." 10 But when he told it to his father and to his brothers, his father rebuked him, and said to him, "What kind of dream is this that you have had? Shall we indeed come, I and your mother and your brothers, and bow to the ground before you?" 11 So his brothers were jealous of him, but his father kept the matter in mind.

12 Now his brothers went to pasture their father's flock near Shechem. 13 And Israel said to Joseph, "Are not your brothers pasturing the flock at Shechem? Come, I will send you to them." He answered, "Here I am." 14 So he said to him, "Go now, see if it is well with your brothers and with the flock; and bring word back to me." So he sent him from the valley of Hebron.

He came to Shechem, 15 and a man found him wandering in the fields; the man asked him, "What are you seeking?" 16 "I am seeking my brothers," he said; "tell me, please, where they are pasturing the flock." 17 The man said, "They have gone away, for I heard them say, 'Let us go to Dothan.'" So Joseph went after his brothers, and found them at Dothan. 18 They saw him from a distance, and before he came near to them, they conspired to kill him. 19 They said to one another, "Here comes this dreamer. 20 Come now, let us kill him and throw him into one of the pits; then we shall say that a wild animal has devoured him, and we shall see what will become of his dreams." 21 But when Reuben

34 When Jobab died, he was succeeded by Husham the Temanite. 35 When Husham died, he was succeeded by Hadad son of Bedad, who defeated Midian in Moabite country. His city was named Avith. 36 When Hadad died, he was succeeded by Samlah of Masrekah. 37 When Samlah died, he was succeeded by Saul of Rehoboth-on-the-Euphrates. 38 When Saul died, he was succeeded by Baal-hanan son of Akbor. 39 When Baal-hanan died, he was succeeded by Hadar. His city was named Pau; his wife's name was Mehetabel daughter of Matred a woman of Me-zahab.

40 These are the names of the chiefs descended from Esau, according to their families and places: Timna, Alvah, Jetheth, 41 Oholibamah, Elah, Pinon, 42 Kenaz, Teman, Mibzar, 43 Magdiel, and Iram: all chiefs of Edom according to their settlements in the land which they possessed. (Esau is the father of the Edomites.)

37 JACOB settled in Canaan, the country in which his father had made his home, 2 and this is an account of Jacob's descendants.

When Joseph was a youth of seventeen, he used to accompany his brothers, the sons of Bilhah and Zilpah, his father's wives, when they were in charge of the flock, and he told tales about them to their father. 3 Because Joseph was a child of his old age, Israel loved him best of all his sons, and he made him a long robe with sleeves. 4 When his brothers saw that their father loved him best, it aroused their hatred and they had nothing but harsh words for him.

5 Joseph had a dream, and when he told it to his brothers, their hatred of him became still greater. 6 He said to them, 'Listen to this dream I had. 7 We were out in the field binding sheaves, when all at once my sheaf rose and stood upright, and your sheaves gathered round and bowed in homage before my sheaf.' 8 His brothers retorted, 'Do you think that you will indeed be king over us and rule us?' and they hated him still more because of his dreams and what he had said. 9 Then he had another dream, which he related to his father and his brothers. 'Listen!' he said. 'I have had another dream, and in it the sun, the moon, and eleven stars were bowing down to me.' 10 When he told his father and his brothers, his father took him to task: 'What do you mean by this dream of yours?' he asked. 'Are we to come and bow to the ground before you, I and your mother and your brothers?' 11 His brothers were jealous of him, but his father did not forget the incident.

12 Joseph's brothers had gone to herd their father's flocks at Shechem. 13 Israel said to him, 'Your brothers are herding the flocks at Shechem; I am going to send you to them.' Joseph answered, 'I am ready to go.' 14 Israel told him to go and see if all was well with his brothers and the flocks, and to bring back word to him. So Joseph was sent off from the vale of Hebron and came to Shechem, where 15 a man met him wandering in the open country and asked him what he was looking for. 16 'I am looking for my brothers,' he replied. 'Can you tell me where they are herding the flocks?' 17 The man said, 'They have moved from here; I heard them speak of going to Dothan.' Joseph went after his brothers and came up with them at Dothan. 18 They saw him in the distance, and before he reached them, they plotted to kill him. 19 'Here comes that dreamer,' they said to one another. 20 'Now is our chance; let us kill him and throw him into one of these cisterns; we can say that a wild beast has devoured him. Then we shall see what becomes of his dreams.'

36:39 **a woman of Me-zahab:** *or* daughter of Me-zahab.   37:3 **a long . . . sleeves:** *or* an ornamental robe.   37:9 **his father and:** *so Gk; Heb. omits.*

b Or *chiefs*   *c* Traditional rendering (compare Gk): *a coat of many colors;* Meaning of Heb uncertain

sham, from the land of the Temanites, succeeded him as king. He defeated the Midianites in the country of Moab; the name of his city was Avith. 35 When Husham died, Hadad, son of Bedad, succeeded him as king. 36 When Hadad died, Samlah, from Masrekah, succeeded him as king. 37 When Samlah died, Shaul, from Rehoboth-on-the-River, succeeded him as king. 38 When Shaul died, Baal-hanan, son of Achbor, succeeded him as king. 39 When Baal-Hanan died, Hadar succeeded him as king; the name of his city was Pau. (His wife's name was Mehetabel; she was the daughter of Matred, son of Mezahab.)

40 The following are the names of the clans of Esau individually according to their subdivisions and localities: the clans of Timna, Alvah, Jetheth, 41 Oholibamah, Elah, Pinon, 42 Kenaz, Teman, Mibzar, 43 Magdiel and Iram. These are the clans of the Edomites, according to their settlements in their territorial holdings. [Esau was the father of the Edomites.]

37 Jacob settled in the land where his father had stayed, the land of Canaan. 2 This is his family history. When Joseph was seventeen years old, he was tending the flocks with his brothers; he was an assistant to the sons of his father's wives Bilhah and Zilpah, and he brought his father bad reports about them.

3 Israel loved Joseph best of all his sons, for he was the child of his old age; and he had made him a long tunic. 4 When his brothers saw that their father loved him best of all his sons, they hated him so much that they would not even greet him.

5 Once Joseph had a dream, which he told to his brothers: 6 "Listen to this dream I had. 7 There we were, binding sheaves in the field, when suddenly my sheaf rose to an upright position, and your sheaves formed a ring around my sheaf and bowed down to it." 8 "Are you really going to make yourself king over us?" his brothers asked him. "Or impose your rule on us?" So they hated him all the more because of his talk about his dreams.

9 Then he had another dream, and this one, too, he told to his brothers. "I had another dream," he said; "this time, the sun and the moon and eleven stars were bowing down to me." 10 When he also told it to his father, his father reproved him. "What is the meaning of this dream of yours?" he asked, "Can it be that I and your mother and your brothers are to come and bow to the ground before you?" 11 So his brothers were wrought up against him but his father pondered the matter.

12 One day, when his brothers had gone to pasture their father's flocks at Shechem, 13 Israel said to Joseph, "Your brothers, you know, are tending our flocks at Shechem. Get ready; I will send you to them." "I am ready," Joseph answered. 14 "Go then," he replied; "see if all is well with your brothers and the flocks, and bring back word." So he sent him off from the valley of Hebron. When Joseph reached Shechem, 15 a man met him as he was wandering about in the fields. "What are you looking for?" the man asked him. 16 "I am looking for my brothers," he answered. "Could you please tell me where they are tending the flocks?" 17 The man told him, "They have moved on from here; in fact, I heard them say, 'Let us go on to Dothan.' " So Joseph went after his brothers and caught up with them in Dothan. 18 They noticed him from a distance, and before he came up to them, they plotted to kill him. 19 They said to one another: "Here comes that master dreamer! 20 Come on, let us kill him and throw him into one of the cisterns here; we could say that a wild beast devoured him. We shall then see what comes of his dreams."

the land of the Temanites succeeded. 35 Husham died and Hadad son of Bedad succeeded; he defeated the Midianites in Moab, and his city was called Avith. 36 Hadad died and Samlah of Masrekah succeeded. 37 Samlah died and Shaul of Rehoboth-ha-Nahar succeeded. 38 Shaul died and Baal-Hanan son of Achbor succeeded. 39 Baal-Hanan died and Hadad succeeded; his city was called Pau and his wife's name was Mehetabel daughter of Matred, from Mezahab.

40 These are the names of the chieftains of Esau — according to their clans and localities: the chieftains of Timna, Alvah, Jetheth, 41 Oholibamah, Elah, Pinon, 42 Kenaz, Teman, Mibzar, 43 Magdiel and Iram. These are the chieftains of Edom, as settled in the territory which they own. Esau was Edom's ancestor.

37 But Jacob settled in the land where his father had stayed, the land of Canaan.

2 This is the story of Joseph.

Joseph was seventeen years old. As he was young, he was shepherding the flock with his brothers, with the sons of his father's wives, Bilhah and Zilpah; and Joseph brought his father bad reports about them.

3 Jacob loved Joseph more than all his other sons, for he was the son of his old age, and he had a decorated tunic made for him. 4 But his brothers, seeing how much more his father loved him than all his other sons, came to hate him so much that they could not say a civil word to him.

5 Now Joseph had a dream, and he repeated it to his brothers, who then hated him more than ever. 6 'Listen', he said, 'to the dream I had. 7 We were binding sheaves in the field, when my sheaf suddenly rose and stood upright, and then your sheaves gathered round and bowed to my sheaf.' 8 'So you want to be king over us,' his brothers retorted, 'you want to lord it over us?' And they hated him even more, on account of his dreams and of what he said. 9 He had another dream which he recounted to his brothers. 'Look, I have had another dream,' he said. 'There were the sun, the moon and eleven stars, bowing down to me.' 10 He told his father and brothers, and his father scolded him. 'A fine dream to have!' he said to him. 'Are all of us then, myself, your mother and your brothers, to come and bow to the ground before you?' 11 His brothers held it against him, but his father pondered the matter.

12 His brothers went to pasture their father's flock at Shechem. 13 Then Israel said to Joseph, 'Your brothers are with the flock at Shechem, aren't they? Come, I am going to send you to them.' 'I am ready,' he replied. 14 He said to him, 'Go and see how your brothers and the flock are doing, and bring me word.' He sent him from the valley of Hebron, and Joseph arrived at Shechem.

15 A man found him wandering in the countryside and asked him, 'What are you looking for?' 16 'I am looking for my brothers,' he replied. 'Please tell me where they are pasturing their flock.' 17 The man answered, 'They have moved on from here; indeed I heard them say, "Let us go to Dothan." ' So Joseph went after his brothers and found them at Dothan.

18 They saw him in the distance, and before he reached them they made a plot to kill him. 19 'Here comes that dreamer,' they said to one another. 20 'Come on, let us kill him now and throw him down one of the storage-wells; we can say that some wild animal has devoured him. Then we shall see what becomes of his dreams.'

NEW REVISED STANDARD VERSION

REVISED ENGLISH BIBLE

heard it, he delivered him out of their hands, saying, "Let us not take his life." 22 Reuben said to them, "Shed no blood; throw him into this pit here in the wilderness, but lay no hand on him"—that he might rescue him out of their hand and restore him to his father. 23 So when Joseph came to his brothers, they stripped him of his robe, the long robe with sleeves*d* that he wore; 24 and they took him and threw him into a pit. The pit was empty; there was no water in it.

25 Then they sat down to eat; and looking up they saw a caravan of Ishmaelites coming from Gilead, with their camels carrying gum, balm, and resin, on their way to carry it down to Egypt. 26 Then Judah said to his brothers, "What profit is it if we kill our brother and conceal his blood? 27 Come, let us sell him to the Ishmaelites, and not lay our hands on him, for he is our brother, our own flesh." And his brothers agreed. 28 When some Midianite traders passed by, they drew Joseph up, lifting him out of the pit, and sold him to the Ishmaelites for twenty pieces of silver. And they took Joseph to Egypt.

29 When Reuben returned to the pit and saw that Joseph was not in the pit, he tore his clothes. 30 He returned to his brothers, and said, "The boy is gone; and I, where can I turn?" 31 Then they took Joseph's robe, slaughtered a goat, and dipped the robe in the blood. 32 They had the long robe with sleeves*d* taken to their father, and they said, "This we have found; see now whether it is your son's robe or not." 33 He recognized it, and said, "It is my son's robe! A wild animal has devoured him; Joseph is without doubt torn to pieces." 34 Then Jacob tore his garments, and put sackcloth on his loins, and mourned for his son many days. 35 All his sons and all his daughters sought to comfort him; but he refused to be comforted, and said, "No, I shall go down to Sheol to my son, mourning." Thus his father bewailed him. 36 Meanwhile the Midianites had sold him in Egypt to Potiphar, one of Pharaoh's officials, the captain of the guard.

38 It happened at that time that Judah went down from his brothers and settled near a certain Adullamite whose name was Hirah. 2 There Judah saw the daughter of a certain Canaanite whose name was Shua; he married her and went in to her. 3 She conceived and bore a son; and he named him Er. 4 Again she conceived and bore a son whom she named Onan. 5 Yet again she bore a son, and she named him Shelah. She*e* was in Chezib when she bore him. 6 Judah took a wife for Er his firstborn; her name was Tamar. 7 But Er, Judah's firstborn, was wicked in the sight of the LORD, and the LORD put him to death. 8 Then Judah said to Onan, "Go in to your brother's wife and perform the duty of a brother-in-law to her; raise up offspring for your brother." 9 But since Onan knew that the offspring would not be his, he spilled his semen on the ground whenever he went in to his brother's wife, so that he would not give offspring to his brother. 10 What he did was displeasing in the sight of the LORD, and he put him to death also. 11 Then Judah said to his daughter-in-law Tamar, "Remain a widow in your father's house until my son Shelah grows up"—for he feared that he too would die, like his brothers. So Tamar went to live in her father's house.

12 In course of time the wife of Judah, Shua's daughter, died; when Judah's time of mourning was over,*f* he went up to Timnah to his sheepshearers, he and his friend Hirah the Adullamite. 13 When Tamar was told, "Your father-in-law is going up to Timnah to shear his sheep," 14 she put off

21 When Reuben heard, he came to his rescue, urging them not to take his life. 22 'Let us have no bloodshed,' he said. 'Throw him into this cistern in the wilderness, but do him no injury.' Reuben meant to rescue him from their clutches in order to restore him to his father. 23 When Joseph reached his brothers, they stripped off the long robe with sleeves which he was wearing, 24 picked him up, and threw him into the cistern. It was empty, with no water in it.

25 They had sat down to eat when, looking up, they saw an Ishmaelite caravan coming on the way down to Egypt, with camels carrying gum tragacanth and balm and myrrh. 26 Judah said to his brothers, 'What do we gain by killing our brother and concealing his death? 27 Why not sell him to these Ishmaelites? Let us do him no harm, for after all, he is our brother, our own flesh and blood'; his brothers agreed. 28 Meanwhile some passing Midianite merchants drew Joseph up out of the cistern and sold him for twenty pieces of silver to the Ishmaelites; they brought Joseph to Egypt. 29 When Reuben came back to the cistern, he found Joseph had gone. He tore his clothes 30 and going to his brothers he said, 'The boy is not there. Whatever shall I do?'

31 Joseph's brothers took the long robe with sleeves, and dipped it in the blood of a goat which they had killed. 32 After tearing the robe, they brought it to their father and said, 'Look what we have found. Do you recognize it? Is this your son's robe or not?' 33 Jacob recognized it. 'It is my son's,' he said. 'A wild beast has devoured him. Joseph has been torn to pieces.' 34 Jacob tore his clothes; he put on sackcloth and for many days he mourned his son. 35 Though his sons and daughters all tried to comfort him, he refused to be comforted. He said, 'No, I shall go to Sheol mourning for my son.' Thus Joseph's father wept for him. 36 The Midianites meanwhile had sold Joseph in Egypt to Potiphar, one of Pharaoh's court officials, the captain of the guard.

38 ABOUT that time Judah parted from his brothers, and heading south he pitched his tent in company with an Adullamite named Hirah. 2 There he saw Bathshua the daughter of a Canaanite and married her. He lay with her, 3 and she conceived and bore a son, whom she called Er. 4 She conceived again and bore a son, whom she called Onan. 5 Once more she conceived and bore a son whom she called Shelah, and she was at Kezib when she bore him. 6 Judah found a wife for his eldest son Er; her name was Tamar. 7 But Judah's eldest son Er was wicked in the LORD's sight, and the LORD took away his life. 8 Then Judah told Onan to sleep with his brother's wife, to do his duty as the husband's brother and raise up offspring for his brother. 9 But Onan knew that the offspring would not count as his; so whenever he lay with his brother's wife, he spilled his seed on the ground so as not to raise up offspring for his brother. 10 What he did was wicked in the LORD's sight, and the LORD took away his life also. 11 Judah said to his daughter-in-law Tamar, 'Remain as a widow in your father's house until my son Shelah grows up'; for he was afraid that Shelah too might die like his brothers. So Tamar went and stayed in her father's house.

12 Time passed, and Judah's wife Bathshua died. When he had finished mourning, he and his friend Hirah the Adullamite went up to Timnath at sheep-shearing. 13 When Tamar was told that her fatherin-law was on his way to shear his sheep at Timnath, 14 she took off her widow's clothes,

37:35 **Sheol:** *or* the underworld.   38:5 **and she was:** *so Gk; Heb.* and he shall be.   38:14,21 **where . . . forks:** *or* by the gate of Enaim; *cp. Gk.*

d See note on 37.3   *e* Gk: Heb *He*   *f* Heb *when Judah was comforted*

NEW AMERICAN BIBLE

21 When Reuben heard this, he tried to save him from their hands, saying, "We must not take his life. 22 Instead of shedding blood," he continued, "just throw him into that cistern there in the desert; but don't kill him outright." His purpose was to rescue him from their hands and restore him to his father. 23 So when Joseph came up to them, they stripped him of the long tunic he had on; 24 then they took him and threw him into the cistern, which was empty and dry.

25 They then sat down to their meal. Looking up, they saw a caravan of Ishmaelites coming from Gilead, their camels laden with gum, balm and resin to be taken down to Egypt. 26 Judah said to his brothers: "What is to be gained by killing our brother and concealing his blood? 27 Rather, let us sell him to these Ishmaelites, instead of doing away with him ourselves. After all, he is our brother, our own flesh." His brothers agreed. 28 They sold Joseph to the Ishmaelites for twenty pieces of silver.

Some Midianite traders passed by, and they pulled Joseph up out of the cistern and took him to Egypt. 29 When Reuben went back to the cistern and saw that Joseph was not in it, he tore his clothes, 30 and returning to his brothers, he exclaimed: "The boy is gone! And I — where can I turn?" 31 They took Joseph's tunic, and after slaughtering a goat, dipped the tunic in its blood. 32 They then sent someone to bring the long tunic to their father, with the message: "We found this. See whether it is your son's tunic or not." 33 He recognized it and exclaimed: "My son's tunic! A wild beast has devoured him! Joseph has been torn to pieces!" 34 Then Jacob rent his clothes, put sackcloth on his loins, and mourned his son many days. 35 Though his sons and daughters tried to console him, he refused all consolation, saying, "No, I will go down mourning to my son in the nether world." Thus did his father lament him.

36 The Midianites, meanwhile, sold Joseph in Egypt to Potiphar, a courtier of Pharaoh and his chief steward.

38 About that time Judah parted from his brothers and pitched his tent near a certain Adullamite named Hirah. 2 There he met the daughter of a Canaanite named Shua, married her, and had relations with her. 3 She conceived and bore a son, whom she named Er. 4 Again she conceived and bore a son, whom she named Onan. 5 Then she bore still another son, whom she named Shelah. They were in Chezib when he was born.

6 Judah got a wife named Tamar for his first-born, Er. 7 But Er, Judah's first-born, greatly offended the LORD; so the LORD took his life. 8 Then Judah said to Onan, "Unite with your brother's widow, in fulfillment of your duty as brother-in-law, and thus preserve your brother's line." 9 Onan, however, knew that the descendants would not be counted as his; so whenever he had relations with his brother's widow, he wasted his seed on the ground, to avoid contributing offspring for his brother. 10 What he did greatly offended the LORD, and the LORD took his life too. 11 Thereupon Judah said to his daughter-in-law Tamar, "Stay as a widow in your father's house until my son Shelah grows up" — for he feared that Shelah also might die like his brothers. So Tamar went to live in her father's house.

12 Years passed, and Judah's wife, the daughter of Shua, died. After Judah completed the period of mourning, he went up to Timnah for the shearing of his sheep, in company with his friend Hirah the Adullamite. 13 When Tamar was told that her father-in-law was on his way up to Timnah to shear his sheep, 14 she took off her widow's garb, veiled

NEW JERUSALEM BIBLE

21 But Reuben heard, and he saved him from their clutches. 'We must not take his life,' he said. 22 'Shed no blood,' said Reuben to them, 'throw him down that well out in the desert, but do not kill him yourselves' — intending to save him from them and to restore him to his father. 23 So, when Joseph reached his brothers, they pulled off his tunic, the decorated tunic which he was wearing, 24 and catching hold of him, threw him into the well. The well was empty, with no water in it. 25 They then sat down to eat.

Looking up, they saw a group of Ishmaelites who were coming from Gilead, their camels laden with gum tragacanth, balsam and resin, which they were taking to Egypt. 26 Then Judah said to his brothers, 'What do we gain by killing our brother and covering up his blood? 27 Come, let us sell him to the Ishmaelites, then we shall not have laid hands on him ourselves. After all, he is our brother, and our own flesh.' His brothers agreed.

28 Now some Midianite merchants were passing, and they pulled Joseph out of the well. They sold Joseph to the Ishmaelites for twenty shekels of silver, and these men took Joseph to Egypt. 29 When Reuben went back to the well, there was no sign of Joseph. Tearing his clothes, 30 he went back to his brothers. 'The boy has gone,' he said. 'What am I going to do?'

31 They took Joseph's tunic and, slaughtering a goat, dipped the tunic in the blood. 32 Then they sent off the decorated tunic and had it taken to their father, with the message, 'This is what we have found. Do you recognise it as your son's tunic or not?' 33 He recognised it and cried, 'My son's tunic! A wild animal has devoured him! Joseph has been torn to pieces!' 34 Tearing his clothes and putting sackcloth round his waist, Jacob mourned his son for many days. 35 All his sons and daughters tried to comfort him, but he refused to be comforted. 'No,' he said, 'I will go down to Sheol in mourning and join my son.' Thus his father wept for him.

36 Meanwhile the Midianites had sold him in Egypt to Potiphar, one of Pharaoh's officials and commander of the guard.

38 It happened at about that time that Judah left his brothers, to go down and settle with a certain Adullamite called Hirah. 2 There Judah saw the daughter of a Canaanite called Shua. He made her his wife and slept with her. 3 She conceived and gave birth to a son whom she named Er. 4 She conceived again and gave birth to a son whom she named Onan. 5 Yet again she gave birth to a son whom she named Shelah. She was at Chezib when she gave birth to him.

6 Judah took a wife for his first-born Er, and her name was Tamar. 7 But Er, Judah's first-born, offended Yahweh, and Yahweh killed him. 8 Then Judah said to Onan, 'Take your brother's wife, and do your duty as her brother-in-law, to maintain your brother's line.' 9 But Onan, knowing that the line would not count as his, spilt his seed on the ground every time he slept with his brother's wife, to avoid providing offspring for his brother. 10 What he did was offensive to Yahweh, who killed him too. 11 Then Judah said to his daughter-in-law Tamar, 'Go home as a widow to your father, until my son Shelah grows up,' for he was thinking, 'He must not die like his brothers.' So Tamar went home to her father.

12 A long time passed, and then Shua's daughter, the wife of Judah, died. After Judah had been comforted he went up to Timnah for the shearing of his sheep, he and his friend Hirah the Adullamite. 13 When Tamar was told, 'Look, your father-in-law is going up to Timnah for the shearing of his sheep,' 14 she changed out of her widow's clothes,

her widow's garments, put on a veil, wrapped herself up, and sat down at the entrance to Enaim, which is on the road to Timnah. She saw that Shelah was grown up, yet she had not been given to him in marriage. 15 When Judah saw her, he thought her to be a prostitute, for she had covered her face. 16 He went over to her at the road side, and said, "Come, let me come in to you," for he did not know that she was his daughter-in-law. She said, "What will you give me, that you may come in to me?" 17 He answered, "I will send you a kid from the flock." And she said, "Only if you give me a pledge, until you send it." 18 He said, "What pledge shall I give you?" She replied, "Your signet and your cord, and the staff that is in your hand." So he gave them to her, and went in to her, and she conceived by him. 19 Then she got up and went away, and taking off her veil she put on the garments of her widowhood.

20 When Judah sent the kid by his friend the Adullamite, to recover the pledge from the woman, he could not find her. 21 He asked the townspeople, "Where is the temple prostitute who was at Enaim by the wayside?" But they said, "No prostitute has been here." 22 So he returned to Judah, and said, "I have not found her; moreover the townspeople said, 'No prostitute has been here.' " 23 Judah replied, "Let her keep the things as her own, otherwise we will be laughed at; you see, I sent this kid, and you could not find her."

24 About three months later Judah was told, "Your daughter-in-law Tamar has played the whore; moreover she is pregnant as a result of whoredom." And Judah said, "Bring her out, and let her be burned." 25 As she was being brought out, she sent word to her father-in-law, "It was the owner of these who made me pregnant." And she said, "Take note, please, whose these are, the signet and the cord and the staff." 26 Then Judah acknowledged them and said, "She is more in the right than I, since I did not give her to my son Shelah." And he did not lie with her again.

27 When the time of her delivery came, there were twins in her womb. 28 While she was in labor, one put out a hand; and the midwife took and bound on his hand a crimson thread, saying, "This one came out first." 29 But just then he drew back his hand, and out came his brother; and she said, "What a breach you have made for yourself!" Therefore he was named Perez.g 30 Afterward his brother came out with the crimson thread on his hand; and he was named Zerah.h

39 Now Joseph was taken down to Egypt, and Potiphar, an officer of Pharaoh, the captain of the guard, an Egyptian, bought him from the Ishmaelites who had brought him down there. 2 The LORD was with Joseph, and he became a successful man; he was in the house of his Egyptian master. 3 His master saw that the LORD was with him, and that the LORD caused all that he did to prosper in his hands. 4 So Joseph found favor in his sight and attended him; he made him overseer of his house and put him in charge of all that he had. 5 From the time that he made him overseer in his house and over all that he had, the LORD blessed the Egyptian's house for Joseph's sake; the blessing of the LORD was on all that he had, in house and field. 6 So he left all that he had in Joseph's charge; and, with him there, he had no concern for anything but the food that he ate.

Now Joseph was handsome and good-looking. 7 And after a time his master's wife cast her eyes on Joseph and said, "Lie with me." 8 But he refused and said to his master's

covered her face with a veil, and then sat where the road forks on the way to Timnah. She did this because she saw that although Shelah was now grown up she had not been given to him as a wife. 15 When Judah saw her he thought she was a prostitute, for she had veiled her face. 16 He turned to her where she sat by the roadside and said, 'Let me lie with you,' not realizing she was his daughter-in-law. She said, 'What will you give to lie with me?' 17 He answered, 'I shall send you a young goat from my flock.' She said, 'I agree, if you will give me a pledge until you send it.' 18 He asked what pledge he should give her, and she replied, 'Your seal and its cord, and the staff which you are holding.' He handed them over to her and lay with her, and she became pregnant. 19 She then rose and went home, where she took off her veil and put on her widow's clothes again.

20 Judah sent the goat by his friend the Adullamite in order to recover the pledge from the woman, but he could not find her. 21 When he enquired of the people of that place, 'Where is that temple-prostitute, the one who was sitting where the road forks?' they answered, 'There has been no temple-prostitute here.' 22 So he went back to Judah and reported that he had failed to find her and that the men of the place had said there was no such prostitute there. 23 Judah said, 'Let her keep the pledge, or we shall be a laughing-stock. After all, I did send the kid, even though you could not find her.'

24 About three months later Judah was told that his daughter-in-law Tamar had played the prostitute and got herself pregnant. 'Bring her out,' ordered Judah, 'so that she may be burnt.' 25 But as she was being brought out, she sent word to her father-in-law. 'The father of my child is the man to whom these things belong,' she said. 'See if you recognize whose they are, this seal, the pattern of the cord, and the staff.' 26 Judah identified them and said, 'She is more in the right than I am, because I did not give her to my son Shelah.' He did not have intercourse with her again.

27 When her time was come, she was found to have twins in her womb, 28 and while she was in labour one of them put out a hand. The midwife took a scarlet thread and fastened it round the wrist, saying, 'This one appeared first.' 29 No sooner had he drawn back his hand, than his brother came out and the midwife said, 'What! You have broken out first!' So he was named Perez. 30 Soon afterwards his brother was born with the scarlet thread on his wrist, and he was named Zerah.

39 WHEN Joseph was taken down to Egypt by the Ishmaelites, he was bought from them by an Egyptian, Potiphar, one of Pharaoh's court officials, the captain of the guard. 2 Joseph prospered, for the LORD was with him. He lived in the house of his Egyptian master, 3 who saw that the LORD was with him and was giving him success in all that he undertook. 4 Thus Joseph won his master's favour, and became his attendant. Indeed, his master put him in charge of his household, and entrusted him with everything he had. 5 From the time that he put Joseph in charge of his household and all his property, the LORD blessed the household through Joseph; the LORD's blessing was on all that was his in house and field. 6 Potiphar left it all in Joseph's care, and concerned himself with nothing but the food he ate.

Now Joseph was handsome in both face and figure, 7 and after a time his master's wife became infatuated with him. 'Come, make love to me,' she said. 8 But Joseph refused.

g That is A breach   h That is Brightness; perhaps alluding to the crimson thread

38:29 Perez: that is Breaking out.   38:30 Zerah: that is Scarlet.

her face by covering herself with a shawl, and sat down at the entrance to Enaim, which is on the way to Timnah; for she was aware that, although Shelah was now grown up, she had not been given to him in marriage. 15 When Judah saw her, he mistook her for a harlot, since she had covered her face. 16 So he went over to her at the roadside, and not realizing that she was his daughter-in-law, he said, "Come, let me have intercourse with you." She replied, "What will you pay me for letting you have intercourse with me?" 17 He answered, "I will send you a kid from the flock." "Very well," she said, "provided you leave a pledge until you send it." 18 Judah asked, "What pledge am I to give you?" She answered, "Your seal and cord, and the staff you carry." So he gave them to her and had intercourse with her, and she conceived by him. 19 When she went away, she took off her shawl and put on her widow's garb again.

20 Judah sent the kid by his friend the Adullamite to recover the pledge from the woman; but he could not find her. 21 So he asked the men of the place, "Where is the temple prostitute, the one by the roadside in Enaim?" But they answered, "There has never been a temple prostitute here." 22 He went back to Judah and told him, "I could not find her; and besides, the men of the place said there was no temple prostitute there." 23 "Let her keep the things," Judah replied; "otherwise we shall become a laughingstock. After all, I did send her the kid, even though you were unable to find her."

24 About three months later, Judah was told that his daughter-in-law Tamar had played the harlot and was now with child from her harlotry. "Bring her out," cried Judah; "she shall be burned." 25 But as they were bringing her out, she sent word to her father-in-law, "It is by the man to whom these things belong that I am with child. Please verify," she added, "whose seal and cord and whose staff these are." 26 Judah recognized them and said, "She is more in the right than I am, since I did not give her to my son Shelah." But he had no further relations with her.

27 When the time of her delivery came, she was found to have twins in her womb. 28 While she was giving birth, one infant put out his hand; and the midwife, taking a crimson thread, tied it on his hand, to note that this one came out first. 29 But as he withdrew his hand, his brother came out; and she said, "What a breach you have made for yourself!" So he was called Perez. 30 Afterward his brother came out; he was called Zerah.

39 When Joseph was taken down to Egypt, a certain Egyptian (Potiphar, a courtier of Pharaoh and his chief steward) bought him from the Ishmaelites who had brought him there. 2 But since the LORD was with him, Joseph got on very well and was assigned to the household of his Egyptian master. 3 When his master saw that the LORD was with him and brought him success in whatever he did, 4 he took a liking to Joseph and made him his personal attendant; he put him in charge of his household and entrusted to him all his possessions. 5 From the moment that he put him in charge of his household and all his possessions, the LORD blessed the Egyptian's house for Joseph's sake; in fact, the LORD's blessing was on everything he owned, both inside the house and out. 6 Having left everything he owned in Joseph's charge, he gave no thought, with Joseph there, to anything but the food he ate.

Now Joseph was strikingly handsome in countenance and body. 7 After a time, his master's wife began to look fondly at him and said, "Lie with me." 8 But he refused. "As long

wrapped a veil around her to disguise herself, and sat down at the entrance to Enaim, which is on the way to Timnah; for she saw that, although Shelah was grown up, she had not been given to him as his wife.

15 Judah, seeing her, took her for a prostitute, since her face was veiled. 16 Going up to her on the road, he said, 'Here, let me sleep with you.' He did not know that she was his daughter-in-law. 'What will you give me for sleeping with you?' she asked. 17 'I will send you a kid from the flock,' he said. 'Agreed, if you give me a pledge until you send it,' she replied. 18 'What pledge shall I give you?' he asked. 'Your seal and cord and the staff you are holding,' she replied. He gave them to her and slept with her, and she conceived by him. 19 Then she got up and left him and, taking off her veil, resumed her widow's weeds.

20 Judah sent the kid by his friend the Adullamite, to recover the pledge from the woman. But he did not find her. 21 He enquired from the men of the place, 'Where is the prostitute who was by the roadside at Enaim?' 'There has been no prostitute there,' they answered. 22 So returning to Judah he said, 'I did not find her. What is more, the men of the place told me there had been no prostitute there.' 23 'Let her keep the things,' Judah said, 'or we shall become a laughing-stock. At least I sent her this kid, even though you did not find her.'

24 About three months later, Judah was told, 'Your daughter-in-law has played the harlot; furthermore, she is pregnant, as a result of her misconduct.' 'Bring her out,' Judah ordered, 'and let her be burnt alive!' 25 But as she was being led off, she sent word to her father-in-law, 'It was the owner of these who made me pregnant. Please verify', she said, 'whose seal and cord and staff these are.' 26 Judah recognised them and said, 'She was right and I was wrong, since I did not give her to my son Shelah.' He had no further intercourse with her.

27 When the time for her confinement came, there were twins in her womb! 28 During the delivery, one of them put out a hand, and the midwife caught it and tied a scarlet thread to it, indicating that this was the first to arrive. 29 Whereupon, he drew back his hand, and out came his brother. Then she said, 'What a breach you have opened for yourself!' So he was named Perez. 30 Then his brother came out with the scarlet thread on his hand, so he was named Zerah.

39 Now Joseph had been taken down into Egypt. Potiphar the Egyptian, one of Pharaoh's officials and commander of the guard, bought him from the Ishmaelites who had taken him down there. 2 Yahweh was with Joseph, and everything he undertook was successful. He lodged in the house of his Egyptian master, 3 and when his master saw how Yahweh was with him and how Yahweh made everything he undertook successful, 4 he was pleased with Joseph and made him his personal attendant; and his master put him in charge of his household, entrusting him with all his possessions. 5 And from the time he put him in charge of his household and all his possessions, Yahweh blessed the Egyptian's household out of consideration for Joseph; Yahweh's blessing extended to all his possessions, both household and estate. 6 So he left Joseph to handle all his possessions, and with him there, concerned himself with nothing beyond the food he ate.

Now Joseph was well built and handsome, 7 and it happened some time later that his master's wife cast her eyes on Joseph and said, 'Sleep with me.' 8 But he refused.

NEW REVISED STANDARD VERSION

wife, "Look, with me here, my master has no concern about anything in the house, and he has put everything that he has in my hand. 9 He is not greater in this house than I am, nor has he kept back anything from me except yourself, because you are his wife. How then could I do this great wickedness, and sin against God?" 10 And although she spoke to Joseph day after day, he would not consent to lie beside her or to be with her. 11 One day, however, when he went into the house to do his work, and while no one else was in the house, 12 she caught hold of his garment, saying, "Lie with me!" But he left his garment in her hand, and fled and ran outside. 13 When she saw that he had left his garment in her hand and had fled outside, 14 she called out to the members of her household and said to them, "See, my husband*i* has brought among us a Hebrew to insult us! He came in to me to lie with me, and I cried out with a loud voice; 15 and when he heard me raise my voice and cry out, he left his garment beside me, and fled outside." 16 Then she kept his garment by her until his master came home, 17 and she told him the same story, saying, "The Hebrew servant, whom you have brought among us, came in to me to insult me; 18 but as soon as I raised my voice and cried out, he left his garment beside me, and fled outside."

19 When his master heard the words that his wife spoke to him, saying, "This is the way your servant treated me," he became enraged. 20 And Joseph's master took him and put him into the prison, the place where the king's prisoners were confined; he remained there in prison. 21 But the LORD was with Joseph and showed him steadfast love; he gave him favor in the sight of the chief jailer. 22 The chief jailer committed to Joseph's care all the prisoners who were in the prison, and whatever was done there, he was the one who did it. 23 The chief jailer paid no heed to anything that was in Joseph's care, because the LORD was with him; and whatever he did, the LORD made it prosper.

40 Some time after this, the cupbearer of the king of Egypt and his baker offended their lord the king of Egypt. 2 Pharaoh was angry with his two officers, the chief cupbearer and the chief baker, 3 and he put them in custody in the house of the captain of the guard, in the prison where Joseph was confined. 4 The captain of the guard charged Joseph with them, and he waited on them; and they continued for some time in custody. 5 One night they both dreamed — the cupbearer and the baker of the king of Egypt, who were confined in the prison — each his own dream, and each dream with its own meaning. 6 When Joseph came to them in the morning, he saw that they were troubled. 7 So he asked Pharaoh's officers, who were with him in custody in his master's house, "Why are your faces downcast today?" 8 They said to him, "We have had dreams, and there is no one to interpret them." And Joseph said to them, "Do not interpretations belong to God? Please tell them to me."

9 So the chief cupbearer told his dream to Joseph, and said to him, "In my dream there was a vine before me, 10 and on the vine there were three branches. As soon as it budded, its blossoms came out and the clusters ripened into grapes. 11 Pharaoh's cup was in my hand; and I took the grapes and pressed them into Pharaoh's cup, and placed the cup in Pharaoh's hand." 12 Then Joseph said to him, "This is its interpretation: the three branches are three days; 13 within three days Pharaoh will lift up your head and restore you to your office; and you shall place Pharaoh's cup in his hand, just as you used to do when you were his cupbearer. 14 But remember me when it is well with you; please do me the kindness to make mention of me to Pharaoh, and so get me out of this place. 15 For in fact I was

REVISED ENGLISH BIBLE

'Think of my master,' he said; 'he leaves the management of his whole house to me; he has trusted me with all he has. 9 I am as important in this house as he is, and he has withheld nothing from me except you, because you are his wife. How can I do such a wicked thing? It is a sin against God.' 10 Though she kept on at Joseph day after day, he refused to lie with her or be in her company.

11 One day when he came into the house to see to his duties, and none of the household servants was there indoors, 12 she caught him by his loincloth, saying, 'Come, make love to me,' but he left the loincloth in her hand and ran from the house. 13 When she saw that he had left his loincloth and run out of the house, 14 she called to her servants, 'Look at this! My husband has brought in a Hebrew to bring insult on us. He came in here to rape me, but I gave a loud scream. 15 When he heard me scream and call for help, he ran out, leaving his loincloth behind.' 16 She kept it by her until his master came home, 17 and then she repeated her tale: 'That Hebrew slave you brought in came to my room to make me an object of insult. 18 But when I screamed for help, he ran out of the house, leaving his loincloth behind.' 19 Joseph's master was furious when he heard his wife's account of what his slave had done to her. 20 He had Joseph seized and thrown into the guardhouse, where the king's prisoners were kept; and there he was confined. 21 But the LORD was with Joseph and kept faith with him, so that he won the favour of the governor of the guardhouse. 22 Joseph was put in charge of the prisoners, and he directed all their work. 23 The governor ceased to concern himself with anything entrusted to Joseph, because the LORD was with him and gave him success in all that he did.

40 Some time after these events it happened that the king's cupbearer and the royal baker gave offence to their lord, the king of Egypt. 2 Pharaoh was displeased with his two officials, his chief cupbearer and chief baker, 3 and put them in custody in the house of the captain of the guard, in the guardhouse where Joseph was imprisoned. 4 The captain appointed Joseph as their attendant, and he waited on them.

They had been in prison in the guardhouse for some time, 5 when one night the king's cupbearer and his baker both had dreams, each with a meaning of its own. 6 Coming to them in the morning, Joseph saw that they looked dispirited, 7 and asked these officials in custody with him in his master's house, why they were so downcast that day. 8 They replied, 'We have each had a dream, but there is no one to interpret them.' Joseph said to them, 'All interpretation belongs to God. Why not tell me your dreams?' 9 So the chief cupbearer told Joseph his dream: 'In my dream', he said, 'there was a vine in front of me. 10 On the vine there were three branches, and as soon as it budded, it blossomed and its clusters ripened into grapes. 11 I plucked the grapes and pressed them into Pharaoh's cup which I was holding, and then put the cup into Pharaoh's hand.' 12 Joseph said to him, 'This is the interpretation. The three branches are three days: 13 within three days Pharaoh will raise your head and restore you to your post; then you will put the cup into Pharaoh's hand as you used to do when you were his cupbearer. 14 When things go well with you, remember me and do me the kindness of bringing my case to Pharaoh's notice; help me to get out of this prison. 15 I was carried off by force

|

as I am here," he told her, "my master does not concern himself with anything in the house, but has entrusted to me all he owns. 9He wields no more authority in this house than I do, and he has withheld from me nothing but yourself, since you are his wife. How, then, could I commit so great a wrong and thus stand condemned before God?" 10Although she tried to entice him day after day, he would not agree to lie beside her, or even stay near her.

11One such day, when Joseph came into the house to do his work, and none of the household servants were then in the house, 12she laid hold of him by his cloak, saying, "Lie with me!" But leaving the cloak in her hand, he got away from her and ran outside. 13When she saw that he had left his cloak in her hand as he fled outside, 14she screamed for her household servants and told them, "Look! my husband has brought in a Hebrew slave to make sport of us! He came in here to lie with me, but I cried out as loud as I could. 15When he heard me scream for help, he left his cloak beside me and ran away outside."

16She kept the cloak with her until his master came home. 17Then she told him the same story: "The Hebrew slave whom you brought here broke in on me, to make sport of me. 18But when I screamed for help, he left his cloak beside me and fled outside." 19As soon as the master heard his wife's story about how his slave had treated her, he became enraged. 20He seized Joseph and threw him into the jail where the royal prisoners were confined.

But even while he was in prison, 21the LORD remained with Joseph; he showed him kindness by making the chief jailer well-disposed toward him. 22The chief jailer put Joseph in charge of all the prisoners in the jail, and everything that had to be done there was done under his management. 23The chief jailer did not concern himself with anything at all that was in Joseph's charge, since the LORD was with him and brought success to all he did.

40 Some time afterward, the royal cupbearer and baker gave offense to their lord, the king of Egypt. 2Pharaoh was angry with his two courtiers, the chief cupbearer and the chief baker, 3and he put them in custody in the house of the chief steward (the same jail where Joseph was confined). 4The chief steward assigned Joseph to them, and he became their attendant.

After they had been in custody for some time, 5the cupbearer and the baker of the king of Egypt who were confined in the jail both had dreams on the same night, each dream with its own meaning. 6When Joseph came to them in the morning, he noticed that they looked disturbed. 7So he asked Pharaoh's courtiers who were with him in custody in his master's house, "Why do you look so sad today?" 8They answered him, "We have had dreams, but there is no one to interpret them for us." Joseph said to them, "Surely, interpretations come from God. Please tell the dreams to me."

9Then the chief cupbearer told Joseph his dream. "In my dream," he said, "I saw a vine in front of me, 10and on the vine were three branches. It had barely budded when its blossoms came out, and its clusters ripened into grapes. 11Pharaoh's cup is in my hand; so I took the grapes, pressed them out into his cup, and put it in Pharaoh's hand." 12Joseph said to him: "This is what it means. The three branches are three days; 13within three days Pharaoh will lift up your head and restore you to your post. You will be handing Pharaoh his cup as you formerly used to do when you were his cupbearer. 14So if you will still remember, when all is well with you, that I was here with you, please do me the favor of mentioning me to Pharaoh, to get me out of this place. 15The truth is that I was kidnaped from the

'Look,' he said to his master's wife, 'with me here, my master does not concern himself with what happens in the house, having entrusted all his possessions to me. 9He himself wields no more authority in this house than I do. He has exempted nothing from me except yourself, because you are his wife. How could I do anything so wicked, and sin against God?' 10Although she spoke to Joseph day after day, he would not agree to sleep with her or be with her.

11But one day when Joseph came into the house to do his work, and none of the men of the household happened to be indoors, 12she caught hold of him by his tunic and said, 'Sleep with me.' But he left the tunic in her hand, took to his heels and got out. 13When she saw that he had left the tunic in her hands as he ran out, 14she called her servants and said to them, 'Look at this! My husband brought in a Hebrew to make a fool of me! He burst in on me, but I screamed, 15and when he heard me scream, he left his tunic beside me and ran out of the house.'

16She kept his tunic by her until his master came home. 17Then she told him the same tale, 'The Hebrew slave you brought to us burst in on me to make a fool of me. 18But when I screamed, he left his tunic beside me and ran away.' 19When his master heard his wife say, 'This was how your slave treated me,' he became furious. 20Joseph's master had him arrested and committed to the gaol where the king's prisoners were kept.

And there in gaol he stayed. 21But Yahweh was with Joseph. He showed him faithful love and made him popular with the chief gaoler. 22The chief gaoler put Joseph in charge of all the prisoners in the gaol, making him responsible for everything done there. 23The chief gaoler did not bother about anything put in his charge, since Yahweh was with him, and Yahweh made everything he undertook successful.

40 It happened some time later that the king of Egypt's cup-bearer and his baker offended their master the king of Egypt. 2Pharaoh was angry with his two officials, the chief cup-bearer and the chief baker, 3and put them in custody in the house of the commander of the guard, in the gaol where Joseph was a prisoner. 4The commander of the guard assigned Joseph to them to attend to their wants, and they remained in custody for some time.

5Now both of them had dreams on the same night, each with its own meaning for the cup-bearer and the baker of the king of Egypt, who were prisoners in the gaol. 6When Joseph came to them in the morning, he saw that they looked gloomy, 7and he asked the two officials who were in custody with him in his master's house, 'Why these sad looks today?' 8They replied, 'We have each had a dream, but there is no one to interpret it.' 'Are not interpretations God's business?' Joseph asked them. 'Tell me about them.'

9So the chief cup-bearer described his dream to Joseph, telling him, 'In my dream there was a vine in front of me. 10On the vine were three branches; no sooner had it budded than it blossomed, and its clusters became ripe grapes. 11I had Pharaoh's cup in my hand; I picked the grapes and squeezed them into Pharaoh's cup, and put the cup into Pharaoh's hand.' 12'This is what it means,' Joseph told him. 'The three branches are three days. 13In another three days Pharaoh will lift up your head by restoring you to your position. Then you will hand Pharaoh his cup, as you did before, when you were his cup-bearer. 14But be sure to remember me when things go well with you, and keep faith with me by kindly reminding Pharaoh about me, to get me out of this house. 15I was kidnapped from the land of the

stolen out of the land of the Hebrews; and here also I have done nothing that they should have put me into the dungeon."

16 When the chief baker saw that the interpretation was favorable, he said to Joseph, "I also had a dream: there were three cake baskets on my head, 17 and in the uppermost basket there were all sorts of baked food for Pharaoh, but the birds were eating it out of the basket on my head." 18 And Joseph answered, "This is its interpretation: the three baskets are three days; 19 within three days Pharaoh will lift up your head — from you! — and hang you on a pole; and the birds will eat the flesh from you."

20 On the third day, which was Pharaoh's birthday, he made a feast for all his servants, and lifted up the head of the chief cupbearer and the head of the chief baker among his servants. 21 He restored the chief cupbearer to his cupbearing, and he placed the cup in Pharaoh's hand; 22 but the chief baker he hanged, just as Joseph had interpreted to them. 23 Yet the chief cupbearer did not remember Joseph, but forgot him.

41 After two whole years, Pharaoh dreamed that he was standing by the Nile, 2 and there came up out of the Nile seven sleek and fat cows, and they grazed in the reed grass. 3 Then seven other cows, ugly and thin, came up out of the Nile after them, and stood by the other cows on the bank of the Nile. 4 The ugly and thin cows ate up the seven sleek and fat cows. And Pharaoh awoke. 5 Then he fell asleep and dreamed a second time; seven ears of grain, plump and good, were growing on one stalk. 6 Then seven ears, thin and blighted by the east wind, sprouted after them. 7 The thin ears swallowed up the seven plump and full ears. Pharaoh awoke, and it was a dream. 8 In the morning his spirit was troubled; so he sent and called for all the magicians of Egypt and all its wise men. Pharaoh told them his dreams, but there was no one who could interpret them to Pharaoh.

9 Then the chief cupbearer said to Pharaoh, "I remember my faults today. 10 Once Pharaoh was angry with his servants, and put me and the chief baker in custody in the house of the captain of the guard. 11 We dreamed on the same night, he and I, each having a dream with its own meaning. 12 A young Hebrew was there with us, a servant of the captain of the guard. When we told him, he interpreted our dreams to us, giving an interpretation to each according to his dream. 13 As he interpreted to us, so it turned out; I was restored to my office, and the baker was hanged."

14 Then Pharaoh sent for Joseph, and he was hurriedly brought out of the dungeon. When he had shaved himself and changed his clothes, he came in before Pharaoh. 15 And Pharaoh said to Joseph, "I have had a dream, and there is no one who can interpret it. I have heard it said of you that when you hear a dream you can interpret it." 16 Joseph answered Pharaoh, "It is not I; God will give Pharaoh a favorable answer." 17 Then Pharaoh said to Joseph, "In my dream I was standing on the banks of the Nile; 18 and seven cows, fat and sleek, came up out of the Nile and fed in the reed grass. 19 Then seven other cows came up after them, poor, very ugly, and thin. Never had I seen such ugly ones in all the land of Egypt. 20 The thin and ugly cows ate up the first seven fat cows, 21 but when they had eaten them no one would have known that they had done so, for they were still as ugly as before. Then I awoke. 22 I fell asleep a second time *j* and I saw in my dream seven ears of grain, full and good, growing on one stalk, 23 and seven ears, withered,

from the land of the Hebrews, and here I have done nothing to deserve being put into this dungeon.'

16 When the chief baker saw that the interpretation given by Joseph had been favourable, he said to him, 'I too had a dream, and in my dream there were three baskets of white bread on my head. 17 In the top basket there was every kind of food such as a baker might prepare for Pharaoh, but the birds were eating out of the top basket on my head.' 18 Joseph answered, 'This is the interpretation. The three baskets are three days; 19 within three days Pharaoh will raise your head off your shoulders and hang you on a tree, and the birds of the air will devour the flesh off your bones.'

20 The third day was Pharaoh's birthday and he gave a banquet for all his officials. He had the chief cupbearer and the chief baker brought up where they were all assembled. 21 The cupbearer was restored to his position, and he put the cup into Pharaoh's hand; 22 but the baker was hanged. All went as Joseph had said in interpreting the dreams for them. 23 The cupbearer, however, did not bear Joseph in mind; he forgot him.

41 Two years later Pharaoh had a dream: he was standing by the Nile, 2 when there came up from the river seven cows, sleek and fat, and they grazed among the reeds. 3 Presently seven other cows, gaunt and lean, came up from the river, and stood beside the cows on the river bank. 4 The cows that were gaunt and lean devoured the seven cows that were sleek and fat. Then Pharaoh woke up. 5 He fell asleep again and had a second dream: he saw seven ears of grain, full and ripe, growing on a single stalk. 6 Springing up after them were seven other ears, thin and shrivelled by the east wind. 7 The thin ears swallowed up the seven ears that were full and plump. Then Pharaoh woke up and found it was a dream.

8 In the morning Pharaoh's mind was so troubled that he summoned all the dream-interpreters and wise men of Egypt, and told them his dreams; but there was no one who could interpret them for him. 9 Then Pharaoh's chief cupbearer spoke up. 'Now I must mention my offences,' he said: 10 'Pharaoh was angry with his servants, and imprisoned me and the chief baker in the house of the captain of the guard. 11 One night we both had dreams, each requiring its own interpretation. 12 We had with us there a young Hebrew, a slave of the captain of the guard, and when we told him our dreams he interpreted them for us, giving each dream its own interpretation. 13 Things turned out exactly as the dreams had been interpreted to us: I was restored to my post, the other was hanged.'

14 Pharaoh thereupon sent for Joseph, and they hurriedly brought him out of the dungeon. After he had shaved and changed his clothes, he came in before Pharaoh, 15 who said to him, 'I have had a dream which no one can interpret. I have heard that you can interpret any dream you hear.' 16 Joseph answered, 'Not I, but God, can give an answer which will reassure Pharaoh.' 17 Then Pharaoh said to him: 'In my dream I was standing on the bank of the Nile, 18 when there came up from the river seven cows, fat and sleek, and they grazed among the reeds. 19 After them seven other cows came up that were in poor condition, very gaunt and lean; in all Egypt I have never seen such gaunt creatures. 20 These lean, gaunt cows devoured the first cows, the seven fat ones. 21 They were swallowed up, but no one could have told they were in the bellies of the others, which looked just as gaunt as before. Then I woke up. 22 In another dream I saw seven ears of grain, full and ripe, growing on a single stalk. 23 Springing up after them were seven other

j Gk Syr Vg: Heb lacks *I fell asleep a second time*

NEW AMERICAN BIBLE

land of the Hebrews, and here I have not done anything for which I should have been put into a dungeon."

16 When the chief baker saw that Joseph had given this favorable interpretation, he said to him: "I too had a dream. In it I had three wicker baskets on my head; 17 in the top one were all kinds of bakery products for Pharaoh, but the birds were pecking at them out of the basket on my head." 18 Joseph said to him in reply: "This is what it means. The three baskets are three days; 19 within three days Pharaoh will lift up your head and have you impaled on a stake, and the birds will be pecking the flesh from your body."

20 And in fact, on the third day, which was Pharaoh's birthday, when he gave a banquet to all his staff, with his courtiers around him, he lifted up the heads of the chief cupbearer and chief baker. 21 He restored the chief cupbearer to his office, so that he again handed the cup to Pharaoh; 22 but the chief baker he impaled—just as Joseph had told them in his interpretation. 23 Yet the chief cupbearer gave no thought to Joseph; he had forgotten him.

41 After a lapse of two years, Pharaoh had a dream. He saw himself standing by the Nile, 2 when up out of the Nile came seven cows, handsome and fat; they grazed in the reed grass. 3 Behind them seven other cows, ugly and gaunt, came up out of the Nile; and standing on the bank of the Nile beside the others, 4 the ugly, gaunt cows ate up the seven handsome, fat cows. Then Pharaoh woke up.

5 He fell asleep again and had another dream. He saw seven ears of grain, fat and healthy, growing on a single stalk. 6 Behind them sprouted seven ears of grain, thin and blasted by the east wind; 7 and the seven thin ears swallowed up the seven fat, healthy ears. Then Pharaoh woke up, to find it was only a dream.

8 Next morning his spirit was agitated. So he summoned all the magicians and sages of Egypt and recounted his dreams to them; but no one could interpret his dreams for him. 9 Then the chief cupbearer spoke up and said to Pharaoh: "On this occasion I am reminded of my negligence. 10 Once, when Pharaoh was angry, he put me and the chief baker in custody in the house of the chief steward. 11 Later, we both had dreams on the same night, and each of our dreams had its own meaning. 12 There with us was a Hebrew youth, a slave of the chief steward; and when we told him our dreams, he interpreted them for us and explained for each of us the meaning of his dream. 13 And it turned out just as he had told us: I was restored to my post, but the other man was impaled."

14 Pharaoh therefore had Joseph summoned, and they hurriedly brought him from the dungeon. After he shaved and changed his clothes, he came into Pharaoh's presence. 15 Pharaoh then said to him: "I had certain dreams that no one can interpret. But I hear it said of you that the moment you are told a dream you can interpret it." 16 "It is not I," Joseph replied to Pharaoh, "but God who will give Pharaoh the right answer."

17 Then Pharaoh said to Joseph: "In my dream, I was standing on the bank of the Nile, 18 when up from the Nile came seven cows, fat and well-formed; they grazed in the reed grass. 19 Behind them came seven other cows, scrawny, most ill-formed and gaunt. Never have I seen such ugly specimens as these in all the land of Egypt! 20 The gaunt, ugly cows ate up the first seven fat cows. 21 But when they had consumed them, no one could tell that they had done so, because they looked as ugly as before. Then I woke up. 22 In another dream, I saw seven ears of grain, fat and healthy, growing on a single stalk. 23 Behind them

NEW JERUSALEM BIBLE

Hebrews in the first place, and even here I have done nothing to warrant being put in the dungeon.'

16 The chief baker, seeing that the interpretation had been favourable, said to Joseph, 'I too had a dream; there were three wicker trays on my head. 17 In the top tray there were all kinds of pastries for Pharaoh, such as a baker might make, and the birds were eating them off the tray on my head.' 18 Joseph replied as follows, 'This is what it means: the three trays are three days. 19 In another three days Pharaoh will lift up your head by hanging you on a gallows, and the birds will eat the flesh off your bones.'

20 And so it happened; the third day was Pharaoh's birthday and he gave a banquet for all his officials. Of his officials he lifted up the head of the chief cup-bearer and the chief baker, 21 the chief cup-bearer by restoring him to his cup-bearing, so that he again handed Pharaoh his cup; 22 and by hanging the chief baker, as Joseph had explained to them. 23 But the chief cup-bearer did not remember Joseph; he had forgotten him.

41 Two years later it happened that Pharaoh had a dream: there he was, standing by the Nile, 2 and there, coming up from the Nile, were seven cows, sleek and fat, and they began to feed among the rushes. 3 And then seven other cows, wretched and lean, came up from the Nile, behind them; and these went over and stood beside the other cows on the bank of the Nile. 4 The wretched and lean cows ate the seven sleek and fat cows. Then Pharaoh woke up.

5 He fell asleep and dreamed a second time: there, growing on one stalk, were seven ears of grain, full and ripe. 6 And then sprouting, behind them, came seven ears of grain, meagre and scorched by the east wind. 7 The scanty ears of grain swallowed the seven full and ripe ears of grain. Then Pharaoh woke up; it had been a dream.

8 In the morning Pharaoh, feeling disturbed, had all the magicians and wise men of Egypt summoned to him. Pharaoh told them his dream, but there was no one to interpret it for Pharaoh. 9 Then the chief cup-bearer addressed Pharaoh, 'Today, I recall having been at fault. 10 When Pharaoh was angry with his servants, he put myself and the chief baker in custody in the house of the commander of the guard. 11 We had a dream on the same night, he and I, and each man's dream had a meaning for himself. 12 There was a young Hebrew with us, one of the slaves belonging to the commander of the guard. We told our dreams to him and he interpreted them for us, telling each of us what his dream meant. 13 It turned out exactly according to his interpretation: I was restored to my position, but the other man was hanged.'

14 Then Pharaoh had Joseph summoned, and they hurried him from the dungeon. He shaved and changed his clothes, and presented himself before Pharaoh. 15 Pharaoh said to Joseph, 'I have had a dream, and there is no one to interpret it. But I have heard it said of you that you can interpret a dream the instant you hear it.' 16 'Not I,' Joseph replied to Pharaoh, 'God will give Pharaoh a favourable answer.'

17 So Pharaoh told Joseph, 'In my dream there I was, standing on the bank of the Nile. 18 And there were seven cows, fat and sleek, coming up out of the Nile, and they began to feed among the rushes. 19 And then seven other cows came up, behind them, starved, very wretched and lean; I have never seen such poor cows in all Egypt. 20 The lean and wretched cows ate up the first seven fat cows. 21 But when they had eaten them up, it was impossible to tell they had eaten them, for they looked as wretched as ever. Then I woke up. 22 And then again in my dream, there, growing on one stalk, were seven ears of grain, beautifully ripe; 23 but then sprouting up behind them came

| NEW REVISED STANDARD VERSION | REVISED ENGLISH BIBLE |

thin, and blighted by the east wind, sprouting after them; 24 and the thin ears swallowed up the seven good ears. But when I told it to the magicians, there was no one who could explain it to me."

25 Then Joseph said to Pharaoh, "Pharaoh's dreams are one and the same; God has revealed to Pharaoh what he is about to do. 26 The seven good cows are seven years, and the seven good ears are seven years; the dreams are one. 27 The seven lean and ugly cows that came up after them are seven years, as are the seven empty ears blighted by the east wind. They are seven years of famine. 28 It is as I told Pharaoh; God has shown to Pharaoh what he is about to do. 29 There will come seven years of great plenty throughout all the land of Egypt. 30 After them there will arise seven years of famine, and all the plenty will be forgotten in the land of Egypt; the famine will consume the land. 31 The plenty will no longer be known in the land because of the famine that will follow, for it will be very grievous. 32 And the doubling of Pharaoh's dream means that the thing is fixed by God, and God will shortly bring it about. 33 Now therefore let Pharaoh select a man who is discerning and wise, and set him over the land of Egypt. 34 Let Pharaoh proceed to appoint overseers over the land, and take one-fifth of the produce of the land of Egypt during the seven plenteous years. 35 Let them gather all the food of these good years that are coming, and lay up grain under the authority of Pharaoh for food in the cities, and let them keep it. 36 That food shall be a reserve for the land against the seven years of famine that are to befall the land of Egypt, so that the land may not perish through the famine."

37 The proposal pleased Pharaoh and all his servants. 38 Pharaoh said to his servants, "Can we find anyone else like this—one in whom is the spirit of God?" 39 So Pharaoh said to Joseph, "Since God has shown you all this, there is no one so discerning and wise as you. 40 You shall be over my house, and all my people shall order themselves as you command; only with regard to the throne will I be greater than you." 41 And Pharaoh said to Joseph, "See, I have set you over all the land of Egypt." 42 Removing his signet ring from his hand, Pharaoh put it on Joseph's hand; he arrayed him in garments of fine linen, and put a gold chain around his neck. 43 He had him ride in the chariot of his second-in-command; and they cried out in front of him, "Bow the knee!"k Thus he set him over all the land of Egypt. 44 Moreover Pharaoh said to Joseph, "I am Pharaoh, and without your consent no one shall lift up hand or foot in all the land of Egypt." 45 Pharaoh gave Joseph the name Zaphenath-paneah; and he gave him Asenath daughter of Potiphera, priest of On, as his wife. Thus Joseph gained authority over the land of Egypt.

46 Joseph was thirty years old when he entered the service of Pharaoh king of Egypt. And Joseph went out from the presence of Pharaoh, and went through all the land of Egypt. 47 During the seven plenteous years the earth produced abundantly. 48 He gathered up all the food of the seven years when there was plentyl in the land of Egypt, and stored up food in the cities; he stored up in every city the food from the fields around it. 49 So Joseph stored up grain in such abundance—like the sand of the sea—that he stopped measuring it; it was beyond measure.

50 Before the years of famine came, Joseph had two sons, whom Asenath daughter of Potiphera, priest of On, bore to him. 51 Joseph named the firstborn Manasseh,m "For," he said, "God has made me forget all my hardship and all my father's house." 52 The second he named

ears, blighted, thin, and shrivelled by the east wind. 24 The thin ears swallowed up the seven ripe ears. When I spoke to the dream-interpreters, no one could tell me the meaning.'

25 Joseph said to Pharaoh, 'Pharaoh's dreams are both the same; God has told Pharaoh what he is about to do. 26 The seven good cows are seven years, and the seven good ears of grain are seven years—it is all one dream. 27 The seven lean and gaunt cows that came up after them are seven years, and so also are the seven empty ears of grain blighted by the east wind; there are going to be seven years of famine. 28 It is as I have told Pharaoh: God has let Pharaoh see what he is about to do. 29 There are to be seven years of bumper harvests throughout Egypt. 30 After them will come seven years of famine; so that the great harvests in Egypt will all be forgotten, and famine will ruin the country. 31 The good years will leave no trace in the land because of the famine that follows, for it will be very severe. 32 That Pharaoh has dreamed this twice means God is firmly resolved on this plan, and very soon he will put it into effect.

33 'Let Pharaoh now look for a man of vision and wisdom and put him in charge of the country. 34 Pharaoh should take steps to appoint commissioners over the land to take one fifth of the produce of Egypt during the seven years of plenty. 35 They should collect all food produced in the good years that are coming and put the grain under Pharaoh's control as a store of food to be kept in the towns. 36 This food will be a reserve for the country against the seven years of famine which will come on Egypt, and so the country will not be devastated by the famine.'

37 The plan commended itself both to Pharaoh and to all his officials, 38 and Pharaoh asked them, 'Could we find another man like this, one so endowed with the spirit of God?' 39 To Joseph he said, 'Since God has made all this known to you, no one has your vision and wisdom. 40 You shall be in charge of my household, and all my people will respect your every word. Only in regard to the throne shall I rank higher than you.' 41 Pharaoh went on, 'I hereby give you authority over the whole land of Egypt.' 42 He took off his signet ring and put it on Joseph's finger; he had him dressed in robes of fine linen, and hung a gold chain round his neck. 43 He mounted him in his viceroy's chariot and men cried 'Make way!' before him. Thus Pharaoh made him ruler over all Egypt 44 and said to him, 'I am the Pharaoh, yet without your consent no one will lift hand or foot throughout Egypt.' 45 Pharaoh named him Zaphenath-paneah, and he gave him as his wife Asenath daughter of Potiphera priest of On. Joseph's authority extended over the whole of Egypt.

46 Joseph was thirty years old at the time he entered the service of Pharaoh king of Egypt. When he left the royal presence, he made a tour of inspection through the land. 47 During the seven years of plenty when there were abundant harvests, 48 Joseph gathered all the food produced in Egypt then and stored it in the towns, putting in each the food from the surrounding country. 49 He stored the grain in huge quantities; it was like the sand of the sea, so much that he stopped measuring: it was beyond all measure.

50 Before the years of famine came, two sons were born to Joseph by Asenath daughter of Potiphera priest of On. 51 He named the elder Manasseh, 'for', he said, 'God has made me forget all my troubles and my father's family'.

---

k Abrek, apparently an Egyptian word similar in sound to the Hebrew word meaning to kneel   l Sam Gk: MT the seven years that were   m That is Making to forget

41:43 **Make way:** Egyptian word of uncertain meaning.
41:51 **Manasseh:** that is Causing to forget.

sprouted seven ears of grain, shriveled and thin and blasted by the east wind; 24 and the seven thin ears swallowed up the seven healthy ears. I have spoken to the magicians, but none of them can give me an explanation."

25 Joseph said to Pharaoh: "Both of Pharaoh's dreams have the same meaning. God has thus foretold to Pharaoh what he is about to do. 26 The seven healthy cows are seven years, and the seven healthy ears are seven years — the same in each dream. 27 So also, the seven thin, ugly cows that came up after them are seven years, as are the seven thin, wind-blasted ears; they are seven years of famine. 28 It is just as I told Pharaoh: God has revealed to Pharaoh what he is about to do. 29 Seven years of great abundance are now coming throughout the land of Egypt; 30 but these will be followed by seven years of famine, when all the abundance in the land of Egypt will be forgotten. When the famine has ravaged the land, 31 no trace of the abundance will be found in the land because of the famine that follows it — so utterly severe will that famine be. 32 That Pharaoh had the same dream twice means that the matter has been reaffirmed by God and that God will soon bring it about.

33 "Therefore, let Pharaoh seek out a wise and discerning man and put him in charge of the land of Egypt. 34 Pharaoh should also take action to appoint overseers, so as to regiment the land during the seven years of abundance. 35 They should husband all the food of the coming good years, collecting the grain under Pharaoh's authority, to be stored in the towns for food. 36 This food will serve as a reserve for the country against the seven years of famine that are to follow in the land of Egypt, so that the land may not perish in the famine."

37 This advice pleased Pharaoh and all his officials. 38 "Could we find another like him," Pharaoh asked his officials, "a man so endowed with the spirit of God?" 39 So Pharaoh said to Joseph: "Since God has made all this known to you, no one can be as wise and discerning as you are. 40 You shall be in charge of my palace, and all my people shall dart at your command. Only in respect to the throne shall I outrank you. 41 Herewith," Pharaoh told Joseph, "I place you in charge of the whole land of Egypt." 42 With that, Pharaoh took off his signet ring and put it on Joseph's finger. He had him dressed in robes of fine linen and put a gold chain about his neck. 43 He then had him ride in the chariot of his vizier, and they shouted "Abrek!" before him.

Thus was Joseph installed over the whole land of Egypt. 44 "I, Pharaoh, proclaim," he told Joseph, "that without your approval no one shall move hand or foot in all the land of Egypt." 45 Pharaoh also bestowed the name of Zaphnathpaneah on Joseph, and he gave him in marriage Asenath, the daughter of Potiphera, priest of Heliopolis. 46 Joseph was thirty years old when he entered the service of Pharaoh, king of Egypt.

After Joseph left Pharaoh's presence, he traveled throughout the land of Egypt. 47 During the seven years of plenty, when the land produced abundant crops, 48 he husbanded all the food of these years of plenty that the land of Egypt was enjoying and stored it in the towns, placing in each town the crops of the fields around it. 49 Joseph garnered grain in quantities like the sands of the sea, so vast that at last he stopped measuring it, for it was beyond measure.

50 Before the famine years set in, Joseph became the father of two sons, born to him by Asenath, daughter of Potiphera, priest of Heliopolis. 51 He named his first-born Manasseh, meaning, "God has made me forget entirely the sufferings I endured at the hands of my family"; 52 and the

seven ears of grain, withered, meagre and scorched by the east wind. 24 Then the shrivelled ears of grain swallowed the seven ripe ears of grain. I have told the magicians, but no one has given me the answer.'

25 Joseph said to Pharaoh, 'Pharaoh's dreams are one and the same: God has revealed to Pharaoh what he is going to do. 26 The seven fine cows are seven years and the seven ripe ears of grain are seven years; it is one and the same dream. 27 The seven gaunt and lean cows coming up behind them are seven years, as are the seven shrivelled ears of grain scorched by the east wind: there will be seven years of famine. 28 It is as I have told Pharaoh: God has revealed to Pharaoh what he is going to do. 29 Seven years are coming, bringing great plenty to the whole of Egypt, 30 but seven years of famine will follow them, when all the plenty in Egypt will be forgotten, and famine will exhaust the land. 31 The famine that is to follow will be so very severe that no one will remember what plenty the country used to enjoy. 32 The reason why Pharaoh had the same dream twice is that the event is already determined by God, and God will shortly bring it about.

33 'Pharaoh should now find someone intelligent and wise to govern Egypt. 34 Pharaoh should take action and appoint supervisors for the country, and impose a tax of one-fifth on Egypt during the seven years of plenty. 35 They will collect all the food produced during these good years that are coming, and store the grain under Pharaoh's authority, putting it in the towns and keeping it. 36 This food will form a reserve for the country against the seven years of famine which are coming on Egypt, so that the country will not be destroyed by the famine.'

37 Pharaoh and all his ministers approved of what he had said. 38 Then Pharaoh asked his ministers, 'Can we find anyone else endowed with the spirit of God, like him?' 39 So Pharaoh said to Joseph, 'Since God has given you knowledge of all this, there can be no one as intelligent and wise as you. 40 You shall be my chancellor, and all my people shall respect your orders; only this throne shall set me above you.' 41 Pharaoh said to Joseph, 'I hereby make you governor of the whole of Egypt.' 42 Pharaoh took the ring from his hand and put it on Joseph's. He dressed him in robes of fine linen and put a gold chain round his neck. 43 He made him ride in the best chariot he had after his own, and they shouted 'Abrek!' ahead of him. Thus he became governor of the whole of Egypt.

44 Pharaoh said to Joseph, 'Although I am Pharaoh, no one is to move hand or foot without your permission throughout Egypt.' 45 Pharaoh named Joseph Zaphenath-Paneah, and gave him Asenath daughter of Potiphera, priest of On, to be his wife. And Joseph began to journey all over Egypt.

46 Joseph was thirty years old when he entered the service of Pharaoh king of Egypt. After leaving Pharaoh's presence, Joseph travelled throughout the length and breadth of Egypt. 47 During the seven years of plenty, the soil yielded generously. 48 He collected all the food of the seven years while there was an abundance in Egypt, and stored the food in the towns, placing in each the food from the surrounding countryside. 49 Joseph gathered in grain like the sand of the sea, in such quantity that he gave up keeping count, since it was past accounting.

50 Before the year of famine came, two sons were born to Joseph: Asenath daughter of Potiphera, priest of On, bore him these. 51 Joseph named the first-born Manasseh, 'Because', he said, 'God has made me completely forget my hardships and my father's House.' 52 He named the second

NEW REVISED STANDARD VERSION

Ephraim,[n] "For God has made me fruitful in the land of my misfortunes."

53 The seven years of plenty that prevailed in the land of Egypt came to an end; 54 and the seven years of famine began to come, just as Joseph had said. There was famine in every country, but throughout the land of Egypt there was bread. 55 When all the land of Egypt was famished, the people cried to Pharaoh for bread. Pharaoh said to all the Egyptians, "Go to Joseph; what he says to you, do." 56 And since the famine had spread over all the land, Joseph opened all the storehouses,[o] and sold to the Egyptians, for the famine was severe in the land of Egypt. 57 Moreover, all the world came to Joseph in Egypt to buy grain, because the famine became severe throughout the world.

42 When Jacob learned that there was grain in Egypt, he said to his sons, "Why do you keep looking at one another? 2 I have heard," he said, "that there is grain in Egypt; go down and buy grain for us there, that we may live and not die." 3 So ten of Joseph's brothers went down to buy grain in Egypt. 4 But Jacob did not send Joseph's brother Benjamin with his brothers, for he feared that harm might come to him. 5 Thus the sons of Israel were among the other people who came to buy grain, for the famine had reached the land of Canaan.

6 Now Joseph was governor over the land; it was he who sold to all the people of the land. And Joseph's brothers came and bowed themselves before him with their faces to the ground. 7 When Joseph saw his brothers, he recognized them, but he treated them like strangers and spoke harshly to them. "Where do you come from?" he said. They said, "From the land of Canaan, to buy food." 8 Although Joseph had recognized his brothers, they did not recognize him. 9 Joseph also remembered the dreams that he had dreamed about them. He said to them, "You are spies; you have come to see the nakedness of the land!" 10 They said to him, "No, my lord; your servants have come to buy food. 11 We are all sons of one man; we are honest men; your servants have never been spies." 12 But he said to them, "No, you have come to see the nakedness of the land!" 13 They said, "We, your servants, are twelve brothers, the sons of a certain man in the land of Canaan; the youngest, however, is now with our father, and one is no more." 14 But Joseph said to them, "It is just as I have said to you; you are spies! 15 Here is how you shall be tested: as Pharaoh lives, you shall not leave this place unless your youngest brother comes here! 16 Let one of you go and bring your brother, while the rest of you remain in prison, in order that your words may be tested, whether there is truth in you; or else, as Pharaoh lives, surely you are spies." 17 And he put them all together in prison for three days.

18 On the third day Joseph said to them, "Do this and you will live, for I fear God: 19 if you are honest men, let one of your brothers stay here where you are imprisoned. The rest of you shall go and carry grain for the famine of your households, 20 and bring your youngest brother to me. Thus your words will be verified, and you shall not die." And they agreed to do so. 21 They said to one another, "Alas, we are paying the penalty for what we did to our brother; we saw his anguish when he pleaded with us, but we would not listen. That is why this anguish has come upon us." 22 Then Reuben answered them, "Did I not tell you not to wrong the boy? But you would not listen. So now there comes a reckoning for his blood." 23 They did not know that Joseph understood them, since he spoke with them through an interpreter. 24 He turned away from them

REVISED ENGLISH BIBLE

52 He named the second Ephraim, 'for', he said, 'God has made me fruitful in the land of my hardships'. 53 When the seven years of plenty in Egypt came to an end, 54 the seven years of famine began, as Joseph had predicted. There was famine in every country, but there was food throughout Egypt. 55 When the famine came to be felt through all Egypt, the people appealed to Pharaoh for food and he ordered them to go to Joseph and do whatever he told them. 56 When the whole land was in the grip of famine, Joseph opened all the granaries and sold grain to the Egyptians, for the famine was severe. 57 The whole world came to Egypt to buy grain from Joseph, so severe was the famine everywhere.

42 WHEN Jacob learnt that there was grain in Egypt, he said to his sons, 'Why do you stand staring at each other? 2 I hear there is grain in Egypt. Go down there, and buy some for us to keep us alive and save us from starving to death.' 3 So ten of Joseph's brothers went down to buy grain from Egypt, 4 but Jacob did not let Joseph's brother Benjamin go with them, for fear that he might come to harm.

5 Thus the sons of Israel went with everyone else to buy grain because of the famine in Canaan. 6 Now Joseph was governor of the land, and it was he who sold the grain to all its people. Joseph's brothers came and bowed to the ground before him, 7 and when he saw his brothers he recognized them but, pretending not to know them, he greeted them harshly. 'Where do you come from?' he demanded. 'From Canaan to buy food,' they answered. 8 Although Joseph had recognized his brothers, they did not recognize him. 9 He remembered the dreams he had had about them and said, 'You are spies; you have come to spy out the weak points in our defences.' 10 'No, my lord,' they answered; 'your servants have come to buy food. 11 We are all sons of one man. We are honest men; your servants are not spies.' 12 'No,' he maintained, 'it is to spy out our weaknesses that you have come.' 13 They said, 'There were twelve of us, my lord, all brothers, sons of one man back in Canaan; the youngest is still with our father, and one is lost.' 14 But Joseph insisted, 'As I have already said to you: you are spies. 15 This is how you will be put to the test: unless your youngest brother comes here, I swear by the life of Pharaoh you shall not leave this place. 16 Send one of your number to fetch your brother; the rest of you will remain in prison. Thus your story will be tested to see whether you are telling the truth. If not, then by the life of Pharaoh you must be spies.' 17 With that he kept them in prison for three days.

18 On the third day Joseph said to them, 'Do what I say and your lives will be spared, for I am a godfearing man: 19 if you are honest men, only one of you brothers shall be kept in prison, while the rest of you may go and take grain for your starving households; 20 but you must bring your youngest brother to me. In this way your words will be proved true, and you will not die.'

21 They consented, and among themselves they said, 'No doubt we are being punished because of our brother. We saw his distress when he pleaded with us and we refused to listen. That is why this distress has come on us.' 22 Reuben said, 'Did I not warn you not to do wrong to the boy? But you would not listen, and now his blood is on our heads, and we must pay.' 23 They did not know that Joseph understood, since he had used an interpreter. 24 Joseph turned

---

[n] From a Hebrew word meaning *to be fruitful*   [o] Gk Vg Compare Syr: Heb *opened all that was in* (or, *among*) *them*

41:52 **Ephraim:** *that is* Fruit.   41:56 **the granaries:** *so Gk; Heb.* which was in them.

second he named Ephraim, meaning, "God has made me fruitful in the land of my affliction."

53 When the seven years of abundance enjoyed by the land of Egypt came to an end, 54 the seven years of famine set in, just as Joseph had predicted. Although there was famine in all the other countries, food was available throughout the land of Egypt. 55 When hunger came to be felt throughout the land of Egypt and the people cried to Pharaoh for bread, Pharaoh directed all the Egyptians to go to Joseph and do whatever he told them. 56 When the famine had spread throughout the land, Joseph opened all the cities that had grain and rationed it to the Egyptians, since the famine had gripped the land of Egypt. 57 In fact, all the world came to Joseph to obtain rations of grain, for famine had gripped the whole world.

42 When Jacob learned that grain rations were available in Egypt, he said to his sons: "Why do you keep gaping at one another? 2 I hear," he went on, "that rations of grain are available in Egypt. Go down there and buy some for us, that we may stay alive rather than die of hunger." 3 So ten of Joseph's brothers went down to buy an emergency supply of grain from Egypt. 4 It was only Joseph's full brother Benjamin that Jacob did not send with the rest, for he thought some disaster might befall him. 5 Thus, since there was famine in the land of Canaan also, the sons of Israel were among those who came to procure rations.

6 It was Joseph, as governor of the country, who dispensed the rations to all the people. When Joseph's brothers came and knelt down before him with their faces to the ground, 7 he recognized them as soon as he saw them. But he concealed his own identity from them and spoke sternly to them. "Where do you come from?" he asked them. They answered, "From the land of Canaan, to procure food."

8 When Joseph recognized his brothers, although they did not recognize him, 9 he was reminded of the dreams he had about them. He said to them: "You are spies. You have come to see the nakedness of the land." 10 "No, my lord," they replied. "On the contrary, your servants have come to procure food. 11 All of us are sons of the same man. We are honest men; your servants have never been spies." 12 But he answered them: "Not so! You have come to see the nakedness of the land." 13 "We your servants," they said, "were twelve brothers, sons of a certain man in Canaan; but the youngest one is at present with our father, and the other one is gone." 14 "It is just as I said," Joseph persisted; "you are spies. 15 This is how you shall be tested: unless your youngest brother comes here, I swear by the life of Pharaoh that you shall not leave here. 16 So send one of your number to get your brother, while the rest of you stay here under arrest. Thus shall your words be tested for their truth; if they are untrue, as Pharaoh lives, you are spies!" 17 With that, he locked them up in the guardhouse for three days.

18 On the third day Joseph said to them: "Do this, and you shall live; for I am a God-fearing man. 19 If you have been honest, only one of your brothers need be confined in this prison, while the rest of you may go and take home provisions for your starving families. 20 But you must come back to me with your youngest brother. Your words will thus be verified, and you will not die." To this they agreed. 21 To one another, however, they said: "Alas, we are being punished because of our brother. We saw the anguish of his heart when he pleaded with us, yet we paid no heed; that is why this anguish has now come upon us." 22 "Didn't I tell you," broke in Reuben, "not to do wrong to the boy? But you wouldn't listen! Now comes the reckoning for his blood." 23 They did not know, of course, that Joseph understood what they said, since he spoke with them through an interpreter. 24 But turning away from them, he wept. When

Ephraim, 'Because', he said, 'God has made me fruitful in the country of my misfortune.'

53 Then the seven years of plenty that there had been in Egypt came to an end, 54 and the seven years of famine set in, as Joseph had predicted. There was famine in every country, but throughout Egypt there was food. 55 But when all Egypt too began to feel the famine and the people appealed to Pharaoh for food, Pharaoh told all the Egyptians, 'Go to Joseph and do whatever he tells you.' 56 There was famine all over the world. Then Joseph opened all the granaries and rationed out grain to the Egyptians, as the famine grew even worse in Egypt. 57 People came to Egypt from all over the world to get supplies from Joseph, for the famine had grown severe throughout the world.

42 Jacob, seeing that there were supplies to be had in Egypt, said to his sons, 'Why do you keep staring at one another? 2 I hear', he said, 'that there are supplies in Egypt. Go down and procure some for us there, so that we may survive and not die.' 3 So ten of Joseph's brothers went down to procure grain in Egypt. 4 But Jacob did not send Joseph's brother Benjamin with his brothers. 'Nothing must happen to him,' he thought.

5 Thus the sons of Israel were among the other people who came to get supplies, there being famine in Canaan. 6 It was Joseph, as the man in authority over the country, who allocated the rations to the entire population. So Joseph's brothers went and bowed down before him, their faces touching the ground. 7 As soon as Joseph saw his brothers he recognised them. But he did not make himself known to them, and he spoke harshly to them. 'Where have you come from?' he asked. 'From Canaan to get food,' they replied.

8 Now when Joseph recognised his brothers, but they did not recognise him, 9 Joseph remembered the dreams he had had about them, and said to them, 'You are spies. You have come to discover the country's weak points.' 10 'No, my lord,' they said, 'your servants have come to get food. 11 We are all sons of the same man. We are honest men, your servants are not spies.' 12 'Oh no,' he replied, 'you have come to discover the country's weak points.' 13 'Your servants were twelve brothers,' they said, 'sons of the same man in Canaan, but the youngest is at present with our father, and the other one is no more.' 14 To which Joseph retorted, 'It is as I said, you are spies. 15 This is the test you are to undergo: as sure as Pharaoh lives you shall not leave unless your youngest brother comes here. 16 Send one of your number to fetch your brother; you others will remain under arrest, so that your statements can be tested to see whether or not you are honest. If not, then as sure as Pharaoh lives you are spies.' 17 Whereupon, he put them all into custody for three days.

18 On the third day Joseph said to them, 'Do this and you will live, for I am a man who fears God. 19 If you are honest men, let one of your brothers be detained where you are imprisoned; the rest of you, go and take supplies home for your starving families. 20 But you must bring your youngest brother back to me; in this way, what you have said will be verified, and you will not have to die!' And this is what they did. 21 And they said to one another, 'Clearly, we are being punished for what we did to our brother. We saw his deep misery when he pleaded with us, but we would not listen, and now this misery has come home to us.' 22 Reuben retorted to them, 'Did I not tell you not to wrong the boy? But you would not listen. Now comes the accounting.' 23 They did not know that Joseph understood, because there was an interpreter between them. 24 He turned away from them and

NEW REVISED STANDARD VERSION

and wept; then he returned and spoke to them. And he picked out Simeon and had him bound before their eyes. 25 Joseph then gave orders to fill their bags with grain, to return every man's money to his sack, and to give them provisions for their journey. This was done for them.

26 They loaded their donkeys with their grain, and departed. 27 When one of them opened his sack to give his donkey fodder at the lodging place, he saw his money at the top of the sack. 28 He said to his brothers, "My money has been put back; here it is in my sack!" At this they lost heart and turned trembling to one another, saying, "What is this that God has done to us?"

29 When they came to their father Jacob in the land of Canaan, they told him all that had happened to them, saying, 30 "The man, the lord of the land, spoke harshly to us, and charged us with spying on the land. 31 But we said to him, 'We are honest men, we are not spies. 32 We are twelve brothers, sons of our father; one is no more, and the youngest is now with our father in the land of Canaan.' 33 Then the man, the lord of the land, said to us, 'By this I shall know that you are honest men: leave one of your brothers with me, take grain for the famine of your households, and go your way. 34 Bring your youngest brother to me, and I shall know that you are not spies but honest men. Then I will release your brother to you, and you may trade in the land.' "

35 As they were emptying their sacks, there in each one's sack was his bag of money. When they and their father saw their bundles of money, they were dismayed. 36 And their father Jacob said to them, "I am the one you have bereaved of children: Joseph is no more, and Simeon is no more, and now you would take Benjamin. All this has happened to me!" 37 Then Reuben said to his father, "You may kill my two sons if I do not bring him back to you. Put him in my hands, and I will bring him back to you." 38 But he said, "My son shall not go down with you, for his brother is dead, and he alone is left. If harm should come to him on the journey that you are to make, you would bring down my gray hairs with sorrow to Sheol."

43 Now the famine was severe in the land. 2 And when they had eaten up the grain that they had brought from Egypt, their father said to them, "Go again, buy us a little more food." 3 But Judah said to him, "The man solemnly warned us, saying, 'You shall not see my face unless your brother is with you.' 4 If you will send our brother with us, we will go down and buy you food; 5 but if you will not send him, we will not go down, for the man said to us, 'You shall not see my face, unless your brother is with you.' " 6 Israel said, "Why did you treat me so badly as to tell the man that you had another brother?" 7 They replied, "The man questioned us carefully about ourselves and our kindred, saying, 'Is your father still alive? Have you another brother?' What we told him was in answer to these questions. Could we in any way know that he would say, 'Bring your brother down'?" 8 Then Judah said to his father Israel, "Send the boy with me, and let us be on our way, so that we may live and not die—you and we and also our little ones. 9 I myself will be surety for him; you can hold me accountable for him. If I do not bring him back to you and set him before you, then let me bear the blame forever. 10 If we had not delayed, we would now have returned twice."

11 Then their father Israel said to them, "If it must be so, then do this: take some of the choice fruits of the land in your bags, and carry them down as a present to the man—a little balm and a little honey, gum, resin, pistachio nuts, and almonds. 12 Take double the money with you.

REVISED ENGLISH BIBLE

away from them and wept. Then he went back to speak to them, and took Simeon from among them and had him bound before their eyes. 25 He gave orders to fill their bags with grain, to put each man's silver back into his sack again, and to give them provisions for the journey. After this had been done, 26 they loaded their grain on their donkeys and set off. 27 When they stopped for the night, one of them opened his sack to give feed to his donkey, and there at the top was the silver. 28 He said to his brothers, 'My silver has been returned; here it is in my pack.' Bewildered and trembling, they asked one another, 'What is this that God has done to us?'

29 When they came to their father Jacob in Canaan, they gave him an account of all that had happened to them. They said: 30 'The man who is lord of the country spoke harshly to us and made out that we were spies. 31 But we said to him, "We are honest men, we are not spies. 32 There were twelve of us, all brothers, sons of the same father. One has disappeared, and the youngest is with our father in Canaan." 33 Then the man, the lord of the country, said to us, "This is how I shall discover if you are honest men: leave one of your brothers with me, take food for your starving households and go; 34 bring your youngest brother to me, and I shall know that you are honest men and not spies. Then I shall restore your brother to you, and you can move around the country freely." ' 35 But on emptying their sacks, each of them found his silver inside, and when they and their father saw the bundles of silver, they were afraid. 36 Their father Jacob said to them, 'You have robbed me of my children. Joseph is lost; Simeon is lost; and now you would take Benjamin. Everything is against me.' 37 Reuben said to his father, 'You may put both my sons to death if I do not bring him back to you. Entrust him to me, and I shall bring him back.' 38 But Jacob said, 'My son must not go with you, for his brother is dead and he alone is left. Should he come to any harm on the journey, you will bring down my grey hairs in sorrow to the grave.'

43 The famine was still severe in the land. 2 When the grain they had brought from Egypt was all used up, their father said to them, 'Go again and buy some more grain for us to eat.' 3 Judah replied, 'But the man warned us that we must not go into his presence unless our brother was with us. 4 If you let our brother go with us, we will go down and buy you food. 5 But if you will not let him go, we cannot go, for the man declared, "You shall not come into my presence unless your brother is with you." ' 6 Israel said, 'Why have you treated me so badly by telling the man that you had another brother?' 7 They answered, 'The man questioned us closely about ourselves and our family: "Is your father still alive?" he asked, "Have you a brother?" and we answered his questions. How were we to know he would tell us to bring our brother down?' 8 Judah said to Israel his father, 'Send the boy with me; then we can start at once, and save everyone's life, ours, yours, and those of our children. 9 I shall go surety for him, and you may hold me responsible. If I do not bring him back and restore him to you, you can blame me for it all my life. 10 If we had not wasted all this time, we could have made the journey twice by now.'

11 Their father Israel said to them, 'If it must be so, then do this: in your baggage take, as a gift for the man, some of the produce for which our country is famous: a little balm and honey, with gum tragacanth, myrrh, pistachio nuts, and almonds. 12 Take double the amount of silver with you and

42:33 food: so Gk; Heb. omits.   42:38 the grave: Heb. Sheol.

NEW AMERICAN BIBLE

he was able to speak to them again, he had Simeon taken from them and bound before their eyes. 25 Then Joseph gave orders to have their containers filled with grain, their money replaced in each one's sack, and provisions given them for their journey. After this had been done for them, 26 they loaded their donkeys with the rations and departed.

27 At the night encampment, when one of them opened his bag to give his donkey some fodder, he was surprised to see his money in the mouth of his bag. 28 "My money has been returned!" he cried out to his brothers. "Here it is in my bag!" At that their hearts sank. Trembling, they asked one another, "What is this that God has done to us?"

29 When they got back to their father Jacob in the land of Canaan, they told him all that had happened to them. 30 "The man who is lord of the country," they said, "spoke to us sternly and put us in custody as if we were spying on the land. 31 But we said to him: 'We are honest men; we have never been spies. 32 There were twelve of us brothers, sons of the same father; but one is gone, and the youngest one is at present with our father in the land of Canaan.' 33 Then the man who is lord of the country said to us: 'This is how I shall know if you are honest men: leave one of your brothers with me, while the rest of you go home with rations for your starving families. 34 When you come back to me with your youngest brother, and I know that you are honest men and not spies, I will restore your brother to you, and you may move about freely in the land.' "

35 When they were emptying their sacks, there in each one's sack was his moneybag! At the sight of their money-bags, they and their father were dismayed. 36 Their father Jacob said to them: "Must you make me childless? Joseph is gone, and Simeon is gone, and now you would take away Benjamin! Why must such things always happen to me!" 37 Then Reuben told his father: "Put him in my care, and I will bring him back to you. You may kill my own two sons if I do not return him to you." 38 But Jacob replied: "My son shall not go down with you. Now that his full brother is dead, he is the only one left. If some disaster should befall him on the journey you must make, you would send my white head down to the nether world in grief."

43 Now the famine in the land grew more severe. 2 So when they had used up all the rations they had brought from Egypt, their father said to them, "Go back and procure us a little more food." 3 But Judah replied: "The man strictly warned us, 'You shall not appear in my presence unless your brother is with you.' 4 If you are willing to let our brother go with us, we will go down to procure food for you. 5 But if you are not willing, we will not go down, because the man told us, 'You shall not appear in my presence unless your brother is with you.' " 6 Israel demanded, "Why did you bring this trouble on me by telling the man that you had another brother?" 7 They answered: "The man kept asking about ourselves and our family: 'Is your father still living? Do you have another brother?' We had to answer his questions. How could we know that he would say, 'Bring your brother down here'?"

8 Then Judah urged his father Israel: "Let the boy go with me, that we may be off and on our way if you and we and our children are to keep from starving to death. 9 I myself will stand surety for him. You can hold me responsible for him. If I fail to bring him back, to set him in your presence, you can hold it against me forever. 10 Had we not dilly-dallied, we could have been there and back twice by now!"

11 Their father Israel then told them: "If it must be so, then do this: Put some of the land's best products in your baggage and take them down to the man as gifts: some balm and honey, gum and resin, and pistachios and almonds. 12 Also take extra money along, for you must return the

NEW JERUSALEM BIBLE

wept. When he was able to speak to them again, he chose Simeon out of their number and had him bound while they looked on.

25 Joseph gave the order to fill their panniers with grain, to put back each man's money in his sack, and to give them provisions for the journey. This was done for them. 26 Then they loaded their supplies on their donkeys and went away. 27 But when they camped for the night, one of them opened his sack to give his donkey some fodder and saw his money —there it was in the mouth of his sack. 28 He said to his brothers, 'My money has been put back; here it is, in my sack!' Their hearts sank, and they looked at one another in panic, saying, 'What is this that God has done to us?'

29 Returning to their father Jacob in Canaan, they gave him a full report of what had happened to them, 30 'The man who is lord of the country spoke harshly to us, accusing us of spying on the country. 31 We told him, "We are honest men, we are not spies. 32 We were twelve brothers, sons of the same father. One of us is no more, and the youngest is at present with our father in Canaan." 33 But the man who is lord of the country said to us, "This is how I shall know whether you are honest: leave one of your brothers with me. Take supplies for your starving families and be gone, 34 but bring me back your youngest brother and then I shall know that you are not spies but honest men. Then I shall give your brother back to you and you will be free to move about the country." '

35 As they emptied their sacks, each discovered his bag of money in his sack. On seeing their bags of money they were afraid, and so was their father. 36 Then their father Jacob said to them, 'You are robbing me of my children; Joseph is no more; Simeon is no more; and now you want to take Benjamin. I bear the brunt of all this!' 37 Then Reuben said to his father, 'You may put my two sons to death if I do not bring him back to you. Put him in my care and I will bring him back to you.' 38 But he replied, 'My son is not going down with you, for now his brother is dead he is the only one left. If any harm came to him on the journey you are undertaking, you would send my white head down to Sheol with grief!'

43 But the famine in the country grew worse, 2 and when they had finished eating the supplies which they had brought from Egypt their father said to them, 'Go back and get us a little food.' 3 'But', Judah replied, 'the man expressly warned us, "You will not be admitted to my presence unless your brother is with you." 4 If you are ready to send our brother with us, we will go down and get food for you. 5 But if you are not ready to send him, we will not go down, in view of the man's warning, "You will not be admitted to my presence unless your brother is with you." ' 6 Then Israel said, 'Why did you bring this misery on me by telling the man you had another brother?' 7 They replied, 'He kept questioning us about ourselves and our family, asking, "Is your father still alive?" and, "Have you another brother?" That is why we told him. How could we know he was going to say, "Bring your brother down here"?' 8 Judah then said to his father Israel, 'Send the boy with me, and let us be off and go, if we are to survive and not die, we, you, and our dependants. 9 I will go surety for him, and you can hold me responsible for him. If I do not bring him back to you and produce him before you, let me bear the blame all my life. 10 Indeed, if we had not wasted so much time we should have been there and back twice by now!'

11 Then their father Israel said to them, 'If it must be so, then do this: take some of the country's best products in your baggage and take them to the man as a gift: some balsam, some honey, gum tragacanth, resin, pistachio nuts and almonds. 12 Take double the amount of money with you

NEW REVISED STANDARD VERSION

Carry back with you the money that was returned in the top of your sacks; perhaps it was an oversight. 13 Take your brother also, and be on your way again to the man; 14 may God Almighty*p* grant you mercy before the man, so that he may send back your other brother and Benjamin. As for me, if I am bereaved of my children, I am bereaved." 15 So the men took the gift, and they took double the money with them, as well as Benjamin. Then they went on their way down to Egypt, and stood before Joseph.

16   When Joseph saw Benjamin with them, he said to the steward of his house, "Bring the men into the house, and slaughter an animal and make ready, for the men are to dine with me at noon." 17 The man did as Joseph said, and brought the men to Joseph's house. 18 Now the men were afraid because they were brought to Joseph's house, and they said, "It is because of the money, replaced in our sacks the first time, that we have been brought in, so that he may have an opportunity to fall upon us, to make slaves of us and take our donkeys." 19 So they went up to the steward of Joseph's house and spoke with him at the entrance to the house. 20 They said, "Oh, my lord, we came down the first time to buy food; 21 and when we came to the lodging place we opened our sacks, and there was each one's money in the top of his sack, our money in full weight. So we have brought it back with us. 22 Moreover we have brought down with us additional money to buy food. We do not know who put our money in our sacks." 23 He replied, "Rest assured, do not be afraid; your God and the God of your father must have put treasure in your sacks for you; I received your money." Then he brought Simeon out to them. 24 When the steward*q* had brought the men into Joseph's house, and given them water, and they had washed their feet, and when he had given their donkeys fodder, 25 they made the present ready for Joseph's coming at noon, for they had heard that they would dine there.

26   When Joseph came home, they brought him the present that they had carried into the house, and bowed to the ground before him. 27 He inquired about their welfare, and said, "Is your father well, the old man of whom you spoke? Is he still alive?" 28 They said, "Your servant our father is well; he is still alive." And they bowed their heads and did obeisance. 29 Then he looked up and saw his brother Benjamin, his mother's son, and said, "Is this your youngest brother, of whom you spoke to me? God be gracious to you, my son!" 30 With that, Joseph hurried out, because he was overcome with affection for his brother, and he was about to weep. So he went into a private room and wept there. 31 Then he washed his face and came out; and controlling himself he said, "Serve the meal." 32 They served him by himself, and them by themselves, and the Egyptians who ate with him by themselves, because the Egyptians could not eat with the Hebrews, for that is an abomination to the Egyptians. 33 When they were seated before him, the firstborn according to his birthright and the youngest according to his youth, the men looked at one another in amazement. 34 Portions were taken to them from Joseph's table, but Benjamin's portion was five times as much as any of theirs. So they drank and were merry with him.

44   Then he commanded the steward of his house, "Fill the men's sacks with food, as much as they can carry, and put each man's money in the top of his sack. 2 Put my cup, the silver cup, in the top of the sack of the youngest, with his money for the grain." And he did as Joseph told him. 3 As soon as the morning was light, the men were sent away with their donkeys. 4 When they had gone only a

REVISED ENGLISH BIBLE

give back what was returned to you in your packs; perhaps there was some mistake. 13 Take your brother with you and go straight back to the man. 14 May God Almighty make him kindly disposed to you, and may he send back the one whom you left behind, and Benjamin too. As for me, if I am bereaved, I am bereaved.' 15 So they took the gift and double the amount of silver, and accompanied by Benjamin they started at once for Egypt, where they presented themselves to Joseph.

16 When Joseph saw Benjamin with them, he said to his steward, 'Bring these men indoors; then kill a beast and prepare a meal, for they are to eat with me at midday.' 17 He brought the men into Joseph's house as he had been ordered. 18 They were afraid because they had been brought there; they thought, 'We have been brought in here because of that affair of the silver which was replaced in our packs the first time. He means to make some charge against us, to inflict punishment on us, seize our donkeys, and make us his slaves.' 19 So they approached Joseph's steward and spoke to him at the door of the house. 20 'Please listen, my lord,' they said. 'After our first visit to buy food, 21 when we reached the place where we were to spend the night, we opened our packs and each of us found his silver, the full amount of it, at the top of his pack. We have brought it back with us, 22 and we have more silver to buy food. We do not know who put the silver in our packs.' 23 He answered, 'Calm yourselves; do not be afraid. It must have been your God, the God of your father, who hid treasure for you in your packs. I did receive the silver.' Then he brought Simeon out to them.

24 The steward conducted them into Joseph's house and gave them water to bathe their feet, and provided feed for their donkeys. 25 They had their gifts ready against Joseph's arrival at midday, for they had heard that they were to eat there. 26 When he came into the house, they presented him with the gifts which they had brought, bowing to the ground before him. 27 He asked them how they were and said, 'Is your father well, the old man of whom you spoke? Is he still alive?' 28 'Yes, my lord, our father is still alive and well,' they answered, bowing low in obeisance. 29 When Joseph looked around he saw his own mother's son, his brother Benjamin, and asked, 'Is this your youngest brother, of whom you told me?' and to Benjamin he said, 'May God be gracious to you, my son!' 30 Joseph, suddenly overcome by his feelings for his brother, was almost in tears, and he went into the inner room and wept. 31 Then, having bathed his face, he came out and, with his feelings now under control, he ordered the meal to be served. 32 He was served by himself, and the brothers by themselves; the Egyptians who were at the meal were also served separately, for to Egyptians it is abhorrent to eat with Hebrews. 33 When at his direction the brothers were seated, the eldest first and so on down to the youngest, they looked at one another in astonishment. 34 Joseph sent them each a portion from what was before him, but Benjamin's portion was five times larger than any of the others. So they feasted and drank with him.

44   Joseph gave the steward these instructions: 'Fill the men's packs with food, as much as they can carry, and put each man's silver at the top of his pack. 2 And put my goblet, the silver one, at the top of the youngest brother's pack along with the silver for the grain.' He did as Joseph had told him. 3 At first light the brothers were allowed to take their donkeys and set off; 4 but before they had

43:14 **the one:** *so Samar.; Heb.* the other.   43:23 **father:** *or, with Samar.,* fathers.

p Traditional rendering of Heb *El Shaddai*   *q* Heb *the man*

amount that was put back in the mouths of your bags; it may have been a mistake. 13 Take your brother, too, and be off on your way back to the man. 14 May God Almighty dispose the man to be merciful toward you, so that he may let your other brother go, as well as Benjamin. As for me, if I am to suffer bereavement, I shall suffer it."

15 So the men got the gifts, took double the amount of money with them, and, accompanied by Benjamin, were off on their way down to Egypt to present themselves to Joseph. 16 When Joseph saw Benjamin with them, he told his head steward, "Take these men into the house, and have an animal slaughtered and prepared, for they are to dine with me at noon." 17 Doing as Joseph had ordered, the steward conducted the men to Joseph's house. 18 But on being led to his house, they became apprehensive. "It must be," they thought, "on account of the money put back in our bags the first time, that we are taken inside; they want to use it as a pretext to attack us and take our donkeys and seize us as slaves." 19 So they went up to Joseph's head steward and talked to him at the entrance of the house. 20 "If you please, sir," they said, "we came down here once before to procure food. 21 But when we arrived at a night's encampment and opened our bags, there was each man's money in the mouth of his bag—our money in the full amount! We have now brought it back. 22 We have brought other money to procure food with. We do not know who put the first money in our bags." 23 "Be at ease," he replied; "you have no need to fear. Your God and the God of your father must have put treasures in your bags for you. As for your money, I received it." With that, he led Simeon out to them.

24 The steward then brought the men inside Joseph's house. He gave them water to bathe their feet, and got fodder for their donkeys. 25 Then they set out their gifts to await Joseph's arrival at noon, for they had heard that they were to dine there. 26 When Joseph came home, they presented him with the gifts they had brought inside, while they bowed down before him to the ground. 27 After inquiring how they were, he asked them, "And how is your aged father, of whom you spoke? Is he still in good health?" 28 "Your servant our father is thriving and still in good health," they said, as they bowed respectfully. 29 When Joseph's eye fell on his full brother Benjamin, he asked, "Is this your youngest brother, of whom you told me?" Then he said to him, "May God be gracious to you, my boy!" 30 With that, Joseph had to hurry out, for he was so overcome with affection for his brother that he was on the verge of tears. He went into a private room and wept there.

31 After washing his face, he reappeared and, now in control of himself, gave the order, "Serve the meal." 32 It was served separately to him, to the brothers, and to the Egyptians who partook of his board. (Egyptians may not eat with Hebrews; that is abhorrent to them.) 33 When they were seated by his directions according to their age, from the oldest to the youngest, they looked at one another in amazement; 34 and as portions were brought to them from Joseph's table, Benjamin's portion was five times as large as anyone else's. So they drank freely and made merry with him.

44 Then Joseph gave his head steward these instructions: "Fill the men's bags with as much food as they can carry, and put each man's money in the mouth of his bag. 2 In the mouth of the youngest one's bag put also my silver goblet, together with the money for his rations." The steward carried out Joseph's instructions. 3 At daybreak the men and their donkeys were sent off. 4 They had not

and return the money put back in the mouths of your sacks; it may have been a mistake. 13 Take your brother, and go back to the man. 14 May El Shaddai move the man to be kind to you, and allow you to bring back your other brother and Benjamin. As for me, if I must be bereaved, bereaved I must be.'

15 The men took this gift; they took double the amount of money with them, and Benjamin. They set off, went down to Egypt and presented themselves before Joseph. 16 When Joseph saw Benjamin with them he said to his chamberlain, 'Take these men into the house. Slaughter a beast and prepare it, for these men are to eat with me at midday.' 17 The man did as Joseph had ordered, and took the men to Joseph's house.

18 The men were afraid at being taken to Joseph's house and said, 'We are being taken there because of the money replaced in our sacks the first time. They will set on us; they will fall on us and make slaves of us, and take our donkeys too.' 19 So they went up to Joseph's chamberlain and spoke to him at the entrance to the house. 20 'By your leave, sir,' they said, 'we came down once before to get supplies, 21 and when we reached camp and opened our sacks, there was each man's money in the mouth of his sack, to the full. But we have brought it back with us, 22 and we have brought more money with us for the supplies. We do not know who put our money in our sacks.' 23 'Set your minds at ease,' he replied, 'do not be afraid. Your God and the God of your father put treasure in your sacks for you. I received your money.' And he brought Simeon out to them.

24 The man then took the men into Joseph's house. He offered them water to wash their feet, and gave their donkeys fodder. 25 They arranged their gift while they waited for Joseph to come at midday, for they had heard they were to dine there.

26 When Joseph arrived at the house they offered him the gift they had with them, bowing low before him. 27 He greeted them pleasantly, asking, 'Is your father well, the old man you told me of? Is he still alive?' 28 'Your servant our father is well,' they replied, 'he is still alive,' and they bowed respectfully. 29 Looking about, he saw his brother Benjamin, his mother's son. 'Is this your youngest brother', he asked, 'of whom you told me?' And he added, 'God be good to you, my son.' 30 Joseph hurried out; so strong was the affection he felt for his brother that he wanted to cry. He went into his room and there he wept. 31 After washing his face he returned and, controlling himself, gave the order: 'Serve the meal.' 32 He was served separately; so were they, and so were the Egyptians who ate in his household, for the Egyptians could not take food with Hebrews; Egyptians have a horror of doing so. 33 They were placed facing him in order of seniority, from the eldest to the youngest, and the men looked at one another in amazement. 34 He had portions carried to them from his own dish, the portion for Benjamin being five times larger than any of the others. And they feasted with him and drank freely.

44 Then Joseph instructed his chamberlain as follows: 'Fill these men's sacks with as much food as they can carry, and put each man's money in the mouth of his sack. 2 And put my cup, the silver one, in the mouth of the youngest one's sack as well as the money for his rations.' He did as Joseph had instructed.

3 At daybreak, the men were sent off with their donkeys.

NEW REVISED STANDARD VERSION	REVISED ENGLISH BIBLE

short distance from the city, Joseph said to his steward, "Go, follow after the men; and when you overtake them, say to them, 'Why have you returned evil for good? Why have you stolen my silver cup?[r] 5 Is it not from this that my lord drinks? Does he not indeed use it for divination? You have done wrong in doing this.' "

6 When he overtook them, he repeated these words to them. 7 They said to him, "Why does my lord speak such words as these? Far be it from your servants that they should do such a thing! 8 Look, the money that we found at the top of our sacks, we brought back to you from the land of Canaan; why then would we steal silver or gold from your lord's house? 9 Should it be found with any one of your servants, let him die; moreover the rest of us will become my lord's slaves." 10 He said, "Even so; in accordance with your words, let it be: he with whom it is found shall become my slave, but the rest of you shall go free." 11 Then each one quickly lowered his sack to the ground, and each opened his sack. 12 He searched, beginning with the eldest and ending with the youngest; and the cup was found in Benjamin's sack. 13 At this they tore their clothes. Then each one loaded his donkey, and they returned to the city.

14 Judah and his brothers came to Joseph's house while he was still there; and they fell to the ground before him. 15 Joseph said to them, "What deed is this that you have done? Do you not know that one such as I can practice divination?" 16 And Judah said, "What can we say to my lord? What can we speak? How can we clear ourselves? God has found out the guilt of your servants; here we are then, my lord's slaves, both we and also the one in whose possession the cup has been found." 17 But he said, "Far be it from me that I should do so! Only the one in whose possession the cup was found shall be my slave; but as for you, go up in peace to your father."

18 Then Judah stepped up to him and said, "O my lord, let your servant please speak a word in my lord's ears, and do not be angry with your servant; for you are like Pharaoh himself. 19 My lord asked his servants, saying, 'Have you a father or a brother?' 20 And we said to my lord, 'We have a father, an old man, and a young brother, the child of his old age. His brother is dead; he alone is left of his mother's children, and his father loves him.' 21 Then you said to your servants, 'Bring him down to me, so that I may set my eyes on him.' 22 We said to my lord, 'The boy cannot leave his father, for if he should leave his father, his father would die.' 23 Then you said to your servants, 'Unless your youngest brother comes down with you, you shall see my face no more.' 24 When we went back to your servant my father we told him the words of my lord. 25 And when our father said, 'Go again, buy us a little food,' 26 we said, 'We cannot go down. Only if our youngest brother goes with us, will we go down; for we cannot see the man's face unless our youngest brother is with us.' 27 Then your servant my father said to us, 'You know that my wife bore me two sons; 28 one left me, and I said, Surely he has been torn to pieces; and I have never seen him since. 29 If you take this one also from me, and harm comes to him, you will bring down my gray hairs in sorrow to Sheol.' 30 Now therefore, when I come to your servant my father and the boy is not with us, then, as his life is bound up in the boy's life, 31 when he sees that the boy is not with us, he will die; and your servants will bring down the gray hairs of your servant our father with sorrow to Sheol. 32 For your servant became surety for the boy to

gone very far from the city, Joseph said to his steward, 'Go after those men at once, and when you catch up with them, say, "Why have you repaid good with evil? 5 Why have you stolen the silver goblet? It is the one my lord drinks from, and which he uses for divination. This is a wicked thing you have done." ' 6 When the steward overtook them, he reported his master's words. 7 But they replied, 'My lord, how can you say such things? Heaven forbid that we should do such a thing! 8 Look! The silver we found at the top of our packs we brought back to you from Canaan. Why, then, should we steal silver or gold from your master's house? 9 If any one of us is found with the goblet, he shall die; and, what is more, my lord, the rest of us shall become your slaves.' 10 He said, 'Very well; I accept what you say. Only the one in whose possession it is found will become my slave; the rest will go free.' 11 Each quickly lowered his pack to the ground and opened it, 12 and when the steward searched, beginning with the eldest and finishing with the youngest, the goblet was found in Benjamin's pack. 13 At this they tore their clothes; then one and all they loaded their donkeys and returned to the city.

14 Joseph was still in the house when Judah and his brothers arrived, and they threw themselves on the ground before him. 15 Joseph said, 'What is this you have done? You might have known that a man such as I am uses divination.' 16 Judah said, 'What can we say, my lord? What can we plead, or how can we clear ourselves? God has uncovered our crime. Here we are, my lord, ready to be made your slaves, we ourselves as well as the one who was found with the goblet.' 17 'Heaven forbid that I should do such a thing!' answered Joseph. 'Only the one who was found with the goblet shall become my slave; the rest of you can go home to your father safe and sound.'

18 Then Judah went up to him and said, 'Please listen, my lord, and let your servant speak a word, I beg. Do not be angry with me, for you are as great as Pharaoh himself. 19 My lord, you asked us whether we had a father or a brother. 20 We answered, "We have an aged father, and he has a young son born in his old age; this boy's full brother is dead, and since he alone is left of his mother's children, his father loves him." 21 You said to us, your servants, "Bring him down to me so that I may set eyes on him." 22 We told you, my lord, that the boy could not leave his father; his father would die if he left him. 23 But you said, "Unless your youngest brother comes down with you, you shall not enter my presence again." 24 We went back to your servant my father, and reported to him what your lordship had said, 25 so when our father told us to go again and buy food, 26 we answered, "We cannot go down; for without our youngest brother we cannot enter the man's presence; but if our brother is with us, we will go." 27 Then your servant my father said to us, "You know that my wife bore me two sons. 28 One left me, and I said, 'He must have been torn to pieces.' I have not seen him since. 29 If you take this one from me as well, and he comes to any harm, then you will bring down my grey hairs in misery to the grave." 30 Now, my lord, if I return to my father without the boy—and remember, his life is bound up with the boy's—31 what will happen is this: he will see that the boy is not with us and he will die, and your servants will have brought down our father's grey hairs in sorrow to the grave. 32 Indeed, my

gone far out of the city when Joseph said to his head steward: "Go at once after the men! When you overtake them, say to them, 'Why did you repay good with evil? Why did you steal the silver goblet from me? 5 It is the very one from which my master drinks and which he uses for divination. What you have done is wrong.' "

6 When the steward overtook them and repeated these words to them, 7 they remonstrated with him: "How can my lord say such things? Far be it from your servants to do such a thing! 8 We even brought back to you from the land of Canaan the money that we found in the mouths of our bags. Why, then, would we steal silver or gold from your master's house? 9 If any of your servants is found to have the goblet, he shall die, and as for the rest of us, we shall become my lord's slaves." 10 But he replied, "Even though it ought to be as you propose, only the one who is found to have it shall become my slave, and the rest of you shall be exonerated." 11 Then each of them eagerly lowered his bag to the ground and opened it; 12 and when a search was made, starting with the oldest and ending with the youngest, the goblet turned up in Benjamin's bag. 13 At this, they tore their clothes. Then, when each man had reloaded his donkey, they returned to the city.

14 As Judah and his brothers reentered Joseph's house, he was still there; so they flung themselves on the ground before him. 15 "How could you do such a thing?" Joseph asked them. "You should have known that such a man as I could discover by divination what happened." 16 Judah replied: "What can we say to my lord? How can we plead or how try to prove our innocence? God has uncovered your servant's guilt. Here we are, then, the slaves of my lord — the rest of us no less than the one in whose possession the goblet was found." 17 "Far be it from me to act thus!" said Joseph. "Only the one in whose possession the goblet was found shall become my slave; the rest of you may go back safe and sound to your father."

18 Judah then stepped up to him and said: "I beg you, my lord, let your servant speak earnestly to my lord, and do not become angry with your servant, for you are the equal of Pharaoh. 19 My lord asked your servants, 'Have you a father, or another brother?' 20 So we said to my lord, 'We have an aged father, and a young brother, the child of his old age. This one's full brother is dead, and since he is the only one by that mother who is left, his father dotes on him.' 21 Then you told your servants, 'Bring him down to me that my eyes may look on him.' 22 We replied to my lord, 'The boy cannot leave his father; his father would die if he were to leave him.' 23 But you told your servants, 'Unless your youngest brother comes back with you, you shall not come into my presence again.' 24 When we returned to your servant our father, we reported to him the words of my lord.

25 "Later, our father told us to come back and buy some food for the family. 26 So we reminded him, 'We cannot go down there; only if our youngest brother is with us can we go, for we may not see the man if our youngest brother is not with us.' 27 Then your servant our father said to us, 'As you know, my wife bore me two sons. 28 One of them, however, disappeared, and I had to conclude that he must have been torn to pieces by wild beasts; I have not seen him since. 29 If you now take this one away from me, too, and some disaster befalls him, you will send my white head down to the nether world in grief.'

30 "If then the boy is not with us when I go back to your servant my father, whose very life is bound up with his, he will die as soon as he sees that the boy is missing; 31 and your servants will thus send the white head of our father down to the nether world in grief. 32 Besides, I, your ser-

4 They had gone only a little way from the city, when Joseph said to his chamberlain, 'Away now and follow those men. When you catch up with them, say to them, "Why have you repaid good with evil? 5 Is this not what my lord uses for drinking and also for reading omens? What you have done is wrong." '

6 So when he caught up with them he repeated these words. 7 They asked him, 'What does my lord mean? Your servants would never think of doing such a thing. 8 Look, we brought you back the money we found in the mouths of our sacks, all the way from Canaan. Are we likely to have stolen silver or gold from your master's house? 9 Whichever of your servants is found to have it shall die, and the rest of us shall be slaves of my lord.' 10 'Very well, then, it shall be as you say,' he replied, 'the one on whom it is found shall become my slave, but the rest of you can go free.' 11 Each of them quickly lowered his sack to the ground, and each opened his own. 12 He searched, beginning with the eldest and ending with the youngest, and found the cup in Benjamin's sack. 13 Then they tore their clothes, and when each man had reloaded his donkey they returned to the city.

14 When Judah and his brothers arrived at Joseph's house he was still there, so they fell on the ground in front of him. 15 'What do you mean by doing this?' Joseph asked them. 'Did you not know that a man such as I am is a reader of omens?' 16 'What can we answer my lord?' Judah replied. 'What can we say? How can we clear ourselves? God himself has uncovered your servants' guilt. Here we are then, my lord's slaves, we no less than the one in whose possession the cup was found.' 17 'I could not think of doing such a thing,' he replied. 'The man in whose possession the cup was found shall be my slave, but you can go back unhindered to your father.'

18 At this, Judah went up to him and said, 'May it please my lord, let your servant have a word privately with my lord. Do not be angry with your servant, for you are like Pharaoh himself. 19 My lord questioned his servants, "Have you father or brother?" 20 And we said to my lord, "We have an old father, and a younger brother born of his old age. His brother is dead, so he is the only one by that mother now left, and his father loves him." 21 Then you said to your servants, "Bring him down to me, so that I can set eyes on him." 22 We replied to my lord, "The boy cannot leave his father. If he leaves him, his father will die." 23 But you said to your servants, "If your youngest brother does not come down with you, you will not be admitted to my presence again." 24 When we went back to your servant my father, we repeated to him what my lord had said. 25 So when our father said, "Go back and get us a little food," 26 we said, "We cannot go down. We shall go only if our youngest brother is with us for, unless our youngest brother is with us, we shall not be admitted to the man's presence." 27 So your servant our father said to us, "You know that my wife bore me two children. 28 When one of them left me, I supposed that he must have been torn to pieces, and I have never seen him since. 29 If you take this one from me too and any harm comes to him, you will send my white head down to Sheol with grief." 30 If I go to your servant my father now, and we do not have the boy with us, he will die as soon as he sees that the boy is not with us, for his heart is bound up with him; 31 and your servants will have sent your servant our father's white head down to Sheol with grief. 32 Now your servant went surety to my father for the

my father, saying, 'If I do not bring him back to you, then I will bear the blame in the sight of my father all my life.' 33 Now therefore, please let your servant remain as a slave to my lord in place of the boy; and let the boy go back with his brothers. 34 For how can I go back to my father if the boy is not with me? I fear to see the suffering that would come upon my father."

45 Then Joseph could no longer control himself before all those who stood by him, and he cried out, "Send everyone away from me." So no one stayed with him when Joseph made himself known to his brothers. 2 And he wept so loudly that the Egyptians heard it, and the household of Pharaoh heard it. 3 Joseph said to his brothers, "I am Joseph. Is my father still alive?" But his brothers could not answer him, so dismayed were they at his presence.

4 Then Joseph said to his brothers, "Come closer to me." And they came closer. He said, "I am your brother, Joseph, whom you sold into Egypt. 5 And now do not be distressed, or angry with yourselves, because you sold me here; for God sent me before you to preserve life. 6 For the famine has been in the land these two years; and there are five more years in which there will be neither plowing nor harvest. 7 God sent me before you to preserve for you a remnant on earth, and to keep alive for you many survivors. 8 So it was not you who sent me here, but God; he has made me a father to Pharaoh, and lord of all his house and ruler over all the land of Egypt. 9 Hurry and go up to my father and say to him, 'Thus says your son Joseph, God has made me lord of all Egypt; come down to me, do not delay. 10 You shall settle in the land of Goshen, and you shall be near me, you and your children and your children's children, as well as your flocks, your herds, and all that you have. 11 I will provide for you there — since there are five more years of famine to come — so that you and your household, and all that you have, will not come to poverty.' 12 And now your eyes and the eyes of my brother Benjamin see that it is my own mouth that speaks to you. 13 You must tell my father how greatly I am honored in Egypt, and all that you have seen. Hurry and bring my father down here." 14 Then he fell upon his brother Benjamin's neck and wept, while Benjamin wept upon his neck. 15 And he kissed all his brothers and wept upon them; and after that his brothers talked with him.

16 When the report was heard in Pharaoh's house, "Joseph's brothers have come," Pharaoh and his servants were pleased. 17 Pharaoh said to Joseph, "Say to your brothers, 'Do this: load your animals and go back to the land of Canaan. 18 Take your father and your households and come to me, so that I may give you the best of the land of Egypt, and you may enjoy the fat of the land.' 19 You are further charged to say, 'Do this: take wagons from the land of Egypt for your little ones and for your wives, and bring your father, and come. 20 Give no thought to your possessions, for the best of all the land of Egypt is yours.' "

21 The sons of Israel did so. Joseph gave them wagons according to the instruction of Pharaoh, and he gave them provisions for the journey. 22 To each one of them he gave a set of garments; but to Benjamin he gave three hundred pieces of silver and five sets of garments. 23 To his father he sent the following: ten donkeys loaded with the good things of Egypt, and ten female donkeys loaded with grain, bread, and provision for his father on the journey. 24 Then he sent his brothers on their way, and as they were leaving he said to them, "Do not quarrel s along the way."

25 So they went up out of Egypt and came to their father Jacob in the land of Canaan. 26 And they told him, "Joseph

lord, it was I who went surety for the boy to my father. I said, "If I do not bring him back to you, then you can blame me for it all my life." 33 Now, my lord, let me remain in place of the boy as my lord's slave, and let him go with his brothers. 34 How can I return to my father without the boy? I could not bear to see the misery which my father would suffer.'

45 Joseph was no longer able to control his feelings in front of all his attendants, and he called, 'Let everyone leave my presence!' There was nobody present when Joseph made himself known to his brothers, 2 but he wept so loudly that the Egyptians heard him, and news of it got to Pharaoh's household. 3 Joseph said to his brothers, 'I am Joseph! Can my father be still alive?' They were so dumbfounded at finding themselves face to face with Joseph that they could not answer. 4 Joseph said to them, 'Come closer to me,' and when they did so, he said, 'I am your brother Joseph, whom you sold into Egypt. 5 Now do not be distressed or blame yourselves for selling me into slavery here; it was to save lives that God sent me ahead of you. 6 For there have now been two years of famine in the land, and there will be another five years with neither ploughing nor harvest. 7 God sent me on ahead of you to ensure that you will have descendants on earth, and to preserve for you a host of survivors. 8 It is clear that it was not you who sent me here, but God, and he has made me Pharaoh's chief counsellor, lord over his whole household and ruler of all Egypt. 9 Hurry back to my father and give him this message from his son Joseph: "God has made me lord of all Egypt. Come down to me without delay. 10 You will live in the land of Goshen and be near me, you, your children and grandchildren, your flocks and herds, and all that you have. 11 I shall provide for you there and see that you and your household and all that you have are not reduced to want; for there are still five years of famine to come." 12 You can see for yourselves, and so can my brother Benjamin, that it is really Joseph himself who is speaking to you. 13 Tell my father of all the honour which I enjoy in Egypt, tell him all you have seen, and bring him down here with all speed.' 14 He threw his arms round his brother Benjamin and wept, and Benjamin too embraced him weeping. 15 He then kissed each of his brothers and wept over them; after that his brothers were able to talk with him.

16 When the report reached the royal palace that Joseph's brothers had come, Pharaoh and his officials were pleased. 17 Pharaoh told Joseph to say to his brothers: 'This is what you must do. Load your beasts and go straight back to Canaan. 18 Fetch your father and your households and come to me. I shall give you the best region there is in Egypt, and you will enjoy the fat of the land.' 19 He was also to tell them: 'Take wagons from Egypt for your dependants and your wives and fetch your father back here. 20 Have no regrets at leaving your possessions, for all the best there is in the whole of Egypt is yours.'

21 Israel's sons followed these instructions, and Joseph supplied them with wagons, as Pharaoh had ordered, and provisions for the journey. 22 To each of them he gave new clothes, but to Benjamin he gave three hundred pieces of silver and five sets of clothes. 23 Moreover he sent his father ten donkeys carrying the finest products of Egypt, and ten she-donkeys laden with grain, bread, and other provisions for the journey. 24 He sent his brothers on their way, warning them not to quarrel among themselves on the road. 25 They set off, and went up from Egypt to their father Jacob in Canaan. 26 When they told him that Joseph was still alive

---

s Or be agitated

45:8 chief counsellor: lit. father.

vant, got the boy from his father by going surety for him, saying, 'If I fail to bring him back to you, father, you can hold it against me forever.' 33 Let me, your servant, therefore, remain in place of the boy as the slave of my lord, and let the boy go back with his brothers. 34 How could I go back to my father if the boy were not with me? I could not bear to see the anguish that would overcome my father."

45 Joseph could no longer control himself in the presence of all his attendants, so he cried out, "Have everyone withdraw from me!" Thus no one else was about when he made himself known to his brothers. 2 But his sobs were so loud that the Egyptians heard him, and so the news reached Pharaoh's palace. 3 "I am Joseph," he said to his brothers. "Is my father still in good health?" But his brothers could give him no answer, so dumbfounded were they at him.

4 "Come closer to me," he told his brothers. When they had done so, he said: "I am your brother Joseph, whom you once sold into Egypt. 5 But now do not be distressed, and do not reproach yourselves for having sold me here. It was really for the sake of saving lives that God sent me here ahead of you. 6 For two years now the famine has been in the land, and for five more years tillage will yield no harvest. 7 God, therefore, sent me on ahead of you to ensure for you a remnant on earth and to save your lives in an extraordinary deliverance. 8 So it was not really you but God who had me come here; and he has made of me a father to Pharaoh, lord of all his household, and ruler over the whole land of Egypt.

9 "Hurry back, then, to my father and tell him: 'Thus says your son Joseph: God has made me lord of all Egypt; come to me without delay. 10 You will settle in the region of Goshen, where you will be near me — you and your children and grandchildren, your flocks and herds, and everything that you own. 11 Since five years of famine still lie ahead, I will provide for you there, so that you and your family and all that are yours may not suffer want.' 12 Surely, you can see for yourselves, and Benjamin can see for himself, that it is I, Joseph, who am speaking to you. 13 Tell my father all about my high position in Egypt and what you have seen. But hurry and bring my father down here." 14 Thereupon he flung himself on the neck of his brother Benjamin and wept, and Benjamin wept in his arms. 15 Joseph then kissed all his brothers, crying over each of them; and only then were his brothers able to talk with him.

16 When the news reached Pharaoh's palace that Joseph's brothers had come, Pharaoh and his courtiers were pleased. 17 So Pharaoh told Joseph: "Say to your brothers: 'This is what you shall do: Load up your animals and go without delay to the land of Canaan. 18 There get your father and your families, and then come back here to me; I will assign you the best land in Egypt, where you will live off the fat of the land.' 19 Instruct them further: 'Do this. Take wagons from the land of Egypt for your children and your wives and to transport your father on your way back here. 20 Do not be concerned about your belongings, for the best in the whole land of Egypt shall be yours.' "

21 The sons of Israel acted accordingly. Joseph gave them the wagons, as Pharaoh had ordered, and he supplied them with provisions for the journey. 22 He also gave to each of them fresh clothing, but to Benjamin he gave three hundred shekels of silver and five sets of garments. 23 Moreover, what he sent to his father was ten jackasses loaded with the finest products of Egypt and ten jennies loaded with grain and bread and other provisions for his journey. 24 As he sent his brothers on their way, he told them, "Let there be no recriminations on the way."

25 So they left Egypt and made their way to their father Jacob in the land of Canaan. 26 When they told him, "Joseph

boy. I said: "If I do not bring him back to you, let me bear the blame before my father all my life." 33 Let your servant stay, then, as my lord's slave in place of the boy, I implore you, and let the boy go back with his brothers. 34 How indeed could I go back to my father and not have the boy with me? I could not bear to see the misery that would overwhelm my father.'

45 Then Joseph could not control his feelings in front of all his retainers, and he exclaimed, 'Let everyone leave me.' No one therefore was present with him while Joseph made himself known to his brothers, 2 but he wept so loudly that all the Egyptians heard, and the news reached Pharaoh's palace.

3 Joseph said to his brothers, 'I am Joseph. Is my father really still alive?' His brothers could not answer him, they were so dumbfounded at seeing him. 4 Then Joseph said to his brothers, 'Come closer to me.' When they had come closer to him he said, 'I am your brother Joseph whom you sold into Egypt. 5 But now, do not grieve, do not reproach yourselves for having sold me here, since God sent me before you to preserve your lives. 6 For this is the second year there has been famine in the country, and there are still five years to come without ploughing or harvest. 7 God sent me before you to assure the survival of your race on earth and to save your lives by a great deliverance. 8 So it was not you who sent me here but God, and he has set me up as a father to Pharaoh, as lord of all his household and governor of the whole of Egypt.

9 'Return quickly to your father and tell him, "Your son Joseph says this: 'God has made me lord of all Egypt. Come down to me without delay. 10 You will live in the region of Goshen where you will be near me, you, your children and your grandchildren, your flocks, your cattle and all your possessions. 11 There I shall provide for you — for there are five years of famine still to come — so that you, your household and all yours are not reduced to penury.' " 12 You can see with your own eyes, and my brother Benjamin can see too, that I am who I say I am. 13 Give my father a full report of all the honour I enjoy in Egypt, and of all you have seen; and quickly bring my father down here.'

14 Then throwing his arms round the neck of his brother Benjamin he wept; and Benjamin wept on his shoulder. 15 He kissed all his brothers, weeping on each one. Only then were his brothers able to talk to him.

16 News reached Pharaoh's palace that Joseph's brothers had come, and Pharaoh was pleased to hear it, as were his servants. 17 Pharaoh told Joseph, 'Say to your brothers, "Do this: load your beasts and hurry away to Canaan. 18 Fetch your father and your families, and come back to me. I will give you the best territory in Egypt, where you will live off the fat of the land." 19 And you, for your part, give them this order: "Do this: take waggons from Egypt, for your little ones and your wives. Get your father and come. 20 Never mind about your property, for the best of all Egypt will be yours." '

21 Israel's sons did as they were told. Joseph gave them waggons as Pharaoh had ordered, and he gave them provisions for the journey. 22 To each and every one he gave new clothes, and to Benjamin three hundred shekels of silver and five changes of clothes. 23 And to his father he sent ten donkeys laden with the best that Egypt offered, and ten she-donkeys laden with grain, bread and food for his father's journey. 24 And so he sent his brothers on their way. His final words to them were, 'And let there be no upsets on the way!'

25 And so they left Egypt. When they reached their father Jacob in Canaan, 26 they gave him this report, 'Joseph is

is still alive! He is even ruler over all the land of Egypt." He was stunned; he could not believe them. 27 But when they told him all the words of Joseph that he had said to them, and when he saw the wagons that Joseph had sent to carry him, the spirit of their father Jacob revived. 28 Israel said, "Enough! My son Joseph is still alive. I must go and see him before I die."

46 When Israel set out on his journey with all that he had and came to Beer-sheba, he offered sacrifices to the God of his father Isaac. 2 God spoke to Israel in visions of the night, and said, "Jacob, Jacob." And he said, "Here I am." 3 Then he said, "I am God,*t* the God of your father; do not be afraid to go down to Egypt, for I will make of you a great nation there. 4 I myself will go down with you to Egypt, and I will also bring you up again; and Joseph's own hand shall close your eyes."

5 Then Jacob set out from Beer-sheba; and the sons of Israel carried their father Jacob, their little ones, and their wives, in the wagons that Pharaoh had sent to carry him. 6 They also took their livestock and the goods that they had acquired in the land of Canaan, and they came into Egypt, Jacob and all his offspring with him, 7 his sons, and his sons' sons with him, his daughters, and his sons' daughters; all his offspring he brought with him into Egypt.

8 Now these are the names of the Israelites, Jacob and his offspring, who came to Egypt. Reuben, Jacob's firstborn, 9 and the children of Reuben: Hanoch, Pallu, Hezron, and Carmi. 10 The children of Simeon: Jemuel, Jamin, Ohad, Jachin, Zohar, and Shaul,*u* the son of a Canaanite woman. 11 The children of Levi: Gershon, Kohath, and Merari. 12 The children of Judah: Er, Onan, Shelah, Perez, and Zerah (but Er and Onan died in the land of Canaan); and the children of Perez were Hezron and Hamul. 13 The children of Issachar: Tola, Puvah, Jashub,*v* and Shimron. 14 The children of Zebulun: Sered, Elon, and Jahleel 15 (these are the sons of Leah, whom she bore to Jacob in Paddan-aram, together with his daughter Dinah; in all his sons and his daughters numbered thirty-three). 16 The children of Gad: Ziphion, Haggi, Shuni, Ezbon, Eri, Arodi, and Areli. 17 The children of Asher: Imnah, Ishvah, Ishvi, Beriah, and their sister Serah. The children of Beriah: Heber and Malchiel 18 (these are the children of Zilpah, whom Laban gave to his daughter Leah; and these she bore to Jacob — sixteen persons). 19 The children of Jacob's wife Rachel: Joseph and Benjamin. 20 To Joseph in the land of Egypt were born Manasseh and Ephraim, whom Asenath daughter of Potiphera, priest of On, bore to him. 21 The children of Benjamin: Bela, Becher, Ashbel, Gera, Naaman, Ehi, Rosh, Muppim, Huppim, and Ard 22 (these are the children of Rachel, who were born to Jacob — fourteen persons in all). 23 The children of Dan: Hashum.*w* 24 The children of Naphtali: Jahzeel, Guni, Jezer, and Shillem 25 (these are the children of Bilhah, whom Laban gave to his daughter Rachel, and these she bore to Jacob — seven persons in all). 26 All the persons belonging to Jacob who came into Egypt, who were his own offspring, not including the wives of his sons, were sixty-six persons in all. 27 The children of Joseph, who were born to him in Egypt, were two; all the persons of the house of Jacob who came into Egypt were seventy.

28 Israel*x* sent Judah ahead to Joseph to lead the way before him into Goshen. When they came to the land of Goshen, 29 Joseph made ready his chariot and went up to meet his father Israel in Goshen. He presented himself to him, fell on his neck, and wept on his neck a good while. 30 Israel said to Joseph, "I can die now, having seen for myself that you are still alive." 31 Joseph said to his brothers

and was ruler of the whole of Egypt, he was stunned at the news and did not believe them. 27 However when they reported to him all that Joseph had said to them, and when he saw the wagons which Joseph had provided to fetch him, his spirit revived. 28 Israel said, 'It is enough! Joseph my son is still alive; I shall go and see him before I die.'

46 ISRAEL set out with all that he had and came to Beersheba, where he offered sacrifices to the God of his father Isaac. 2 God called to Israel in a vision by night, 'Jacob! Jacob!' and he answered, 'I am here.' 3 God said, 'I am God, the God of your father. Do not be afraid to go down to Egypt, for there I shall make you a great nation. 4 I shall go down to Egypt with you, and I myself shall bring you back again without fail; and Joseph's will be the hands that close your eyes.' 5 So Jacob set out from Beersheba. Israel's sons conveyed their father Jacob along with their wives and children in the wagons which Pharaoh had sent to bring him. 6 They took their herds and the goods they had acquired in Canaan and came to Egypt, Jacob and all his family with him; 7 his sons and their sons, his daughters and his sons' daughters, he brought them all to Egypt.

8 These are the names of the Israelites, Jacob and his sons, who entered Egypt: Reuben, Jacob's eldest son, 9 and the sons of Reuben: Enoch, Pallu, Hezron, and Carmi. 10 The sons of Simeon: Jemuel, Jamin, Ohad, Jachin, Zohar, and Saul, who was the son of a Canaanite woman. 11 The sons of Levi: Gershon, Kohath, and Merari. 12 The sons of Judah: Er, Onan, Shelah, Perez, and Zerah; of these Er and Onan died in Canaan. The sons of Perez were Hezron and Hamul. 13 The sons of Issachar: Tola, Pua, Iob, and Shimron. 14 The sons of Zebulun: Sered, Elon, and Jahleel. 15 These are the sons of Leah whom she bore to Jacob in Paddan-aram, and there was also his daughter Dinah. His sons and daughters numbered thirty-three in all.

16 The sons of Gad: Ziphion, Haggi, Shuni, Ezbon, Eri, Arodi, and Areli. 17 The sons of Asher: Imnah, Ishvah, Ishvi, Beriah, and their sister Serah. The sons of Beriah: Heber and Malchiel. 18 These are the descendants of Zilpah whom Laban gave to his daughter Leah, sixteen in all, born to Jacob.

19 The sons of Jacob's wife Rachel: Joseph and Benjamin. 20 Manasseh and Ephraim were born to Joseph in Egypt; Asenath daughter of Potiphera priest of On bore them to him. 21 The sons of Benjamin: Bela, Becher, and Ashbel; and the sons of Bela: Gera, Naaman, Ehi, Rosh, Muppim, Huppim, and Ard. 22 These are the descendants of Rachel, fourteen in all, born to Jacob.

23 The son of Dan: Hushim. 24 The sons of Naphtali: Jahzeel, Guni, Jezer, and Shillem. 25 These are the descendants of Bilhah whom Laban had given to his daughter Rachel, seven in all, born to Jacob.

26 All the persons who came to Egypt with Jacob, his direct descendants, not including the wives of his sons, were sixty-six in all. 27 Two sons were born to Joseph in Egypt. Thus the whole house of Jacob numbered seventy when it entered Egypt.

28 Jacob sent Judah ahead to Joseph to advise him that he was on his way to Goshen. They entered Goshen, 29 and Joseph had his chariot yoked to go up there to meet Israel his father. When they met, Joseph threw his arms round him and wept on his shoulder for a long time. 30 Israel said to Joseph, 'I have seen for myself that you are still alive. Now I am ready to die.' 31 Joseph said to his brothers and to his

---

t Heb *the God*   *u* Or *Saul*   *v* Compare Sam Gk Num 26.24; 1 Chr 7.1: MT *Iob*   *w* Gk: Heb *Hushim*   *x* Heb *He*

46:21 **and the sons of Bela:** *so Gk; Heb. omits.*

is still alive — in fact, it is he who is ruler of all the land of Egypt," he was dumbfounded; he could not believe them. 27 But when they recounted to him all that Joseph had told them, and when he saw the wagons that Joseph had sent for his transport, the spirit of their father Jacob revived. 28 "It is enough," said Israel. "My son Joseph is still alive! I must go and see him before I die."

46 Israel set out with all that was his. When he arrived at Beer-sheba, he offered sacrifices to the God of his father Isaac. 2 There God, speaking to Israel in a vision by night, called, "Jacob! Jacob!" "Here I am," he answered. 3 Then he said: "I am God, the God of your father. Do not be afraid to go down to Egypt, for there I will make you a great nation. 4 Not only will I go down to Egypt with you; I will also bring you back here, after Joseph has closed your eyes."

5 So Jacob departed from Beer-sheba, and the sons of Israel put their father and their wives and children on the wagons that Pharaoh had sent for his transport. 6 They took with them their livestock and the possessions they had acquired in the land of Canaan. Thus Jacob and all his descendants migrated to Egypt. 7 His sons and his grandsons, his daughters and his granddaughters — all his descendants — he took with him to Egypt.

8 These are the names of the Israelites, Jacob and his descendants, who migrated to Egypt. Reuben, Jacob's first-born, 9 and the sons of Reuben: Hanoch, Pallu, Hezron and Carmi. 10 The sons of Simeon: Nemuel, Jamin, Ohad, Jachin, Zohar, and Shaul, son of a Canaanite woman. 11 The sons of Levi: Gershon, Kohath and Merari. 12 The sons of Judah: Er, Onan, Shelah, Perez and Zerah — but Er and Onan had died in the land of Canaan; and the sons of Perez were Hezron and Hamul. 13 The sons of Issachar: Tola Puah, Jashub and Shimron. 14 The sons of Zebulun: Sered, Elon and Jahleel. 15 These were the sons whom Leah bore to Jacob in Paddan-aram, along with his daughter Dinah — thirty-three persons in all, male and female.

16 The sons of Gad: Zephon, Haggi, Shuni, Ezbon, Eri, Arod and Areli. 17 The sons of Asher: Imnah, Ishvah, Ishvi and Beriah, with their sister Serah; and the sons of Beriah: Heber and Malchiel. 18 These were the descendants of Zilpah, whom Laban had given to his daughter Leah; these she bore to Jacob — sixteen persons in all.

19 The sons of Jacob's wife Rachel: Joseph and Benjamin. 20 In the land of Egypt Joseph became the father of Manasseh and Ephraim, whom Asenath, daughter of Potiphera, priest of Heliopolis, bore to him. 21 The sons of Benjamin: Bela, Becher, Ashbel, Gera, Naaman, Ahiram, Shupham, Hupham and Ard. 22 These were the sons whom Rachel bore to Jacob — fourteen persons in all.

23 The sons of Dan: Hushim. 24 The sons of Naphtali: Jahzeel, Guni, Jezer and Shillem. 25 These were the sons of Bilhah, whom Laban had given to his daughter Rachel; these she bore to Jacob — seven persons in all.

26 Jacob's people who migrated to Egypt — his direct descendants, not counting the wives of Jacob's sons — numbered sixty-six persons in all. 27 Together with Joseph's sons who were born to him in Egypt — two persons — all the people comprising Jacob's family who had come to Egypt amounted to seventy persons in all.

28 Israel had sent Judah ahead to Joseph, so that he might meet him in Goshen. On his arrival in the region of Goshen, 29 Joseph hitched the horses to his chariot and rode to meet his father Israel in Goshen. As soon as he saw him, he flung himself on his neck and wept a long time in his arms. 30 And Israel said to Joseph, "At last I can die, now that I have seen for myself that Joseph is still alive."

still alive. He is at this moment governor of all Egypt!' But he was as one stunned, for he did not believe them. 27 However, when they told him all Joseph had said to them, and when he saw the waggons that Joseph had sent to fetch him, the spirit of their father Jacob revived, 28 and Israel said, 'That is enough! My son Joseph is still alive. I must go and see him before I die.'

46 So Israel set out with all his possessions. Arriving at Beersheba, he offered sacrifices to the God of his father Isaac. 2 God spoke to Israel in a vision at night, 'Jacob, Jacob,' he said. 'Here I am,' he replied. 3 'I am El, God of your father,' he said. 'Do not be afraid of going down to Egypt, for I will make you into a great nation there. 4 I shall go down to Egypt with you and I myself shall bring you back again, and Joseph's hand will close your eyes.'

5 So Jacob left Beersheba. Israel's sons conveyed their father Jacob, their little children and their wives in the waggons Pharaoh had sent to fetch him.

6 Taking their livestock and all that they had acquired in Canaan, they arrived in Egypt — Jacob and all his offspring. 7 With him to Egypt, he brought his sons and grandsons, his daughters and granddaughters — all his offspring.

8 ' These were the names of the Israelites, Jacob and his descendants, who arrived in Egypt:

Reuben, Jacob's first-born, 9 and the sons of Reuben: Hanoch, Pallu, Hezron and Carmi. 10 The sons of Simeon: Jemuel, Jamin, Ohad, Jachin, Zohar, and Shaul the son of the Canaanite woman. 11 The sons of Levi: Gershon, Kohath and Merari. 12 The sons of Judah: Er, Onan, Shelah, Perez, and Zerah (Er and Onan had died in Canaan), and Hezron and Hamul sons of Perez. 13 The sons of Issachar: Tola, Puvah, Jashub and Shimron. 14 The sons of Zebulun: Sered, Elon and Jahleel. 15 These were the sons that Leah had borne to Jacob in Paddan-Aram, besides his daughter Dinah; in all, his sons and daughters numbered thirty-three.

16 The sons of Gad: Ziphion, Haggi, Shuni, Ezbon, Eri, Arodi and Areli. 17 The sons of Asher: Jimnah, Jishvah, Jishvi, Beriah, with their sister Serah; the sons of Beriah: Heber and Malchiel. 18 These were the sons of Zilpah whom Laban gave to his daughter Leah; she bore these to Jacob — sixteen persons.

19 The sons of Rachel wife of Jacob: Joseph and Benjamin. 20 Born to Joseph in Egypt were: Manasseh and Ephraim sons of Asenath, daughter of Potiphera priest of On. 21 The sons of Benjamin: Bela, Becher, Ashbel, Gera, Naaman, Ehi, Rosh, Muppim, Huppim and Ard. 22 These were the sons that Rachel bore to Jacob — fourteen persons in all.

23 The sons of Dan: Hushim. 24 The sons of Naphtali: Jahzeel, Guni, Jezer and Shillem. 25 These were the sons of Bilhah whom Laban gave to his daughter Rachel; she bore these to Jacob — seven persons in all.

26 Altogether, the members of Jacob's family who arrived with him in Egypt — his own issue, not counting the wives of Jacob's sons — numbered sixty-six all told. 27 With Joseph's sons born to him in Egypt — two persons — the members of Jacob's family who went to Egypt totalled seventy.

28 Israel sent Judah ahead to Joseph, so that Judah might present himself to Joseph in Goshen. When they arrived in Goshen, 29 Joseph had his chariot made ready and went up to Goshen to meet his father Israel. As soon as he appeared he threw his arms round his neck and for a long time wept on his shoulder. 30 Israel said to Joseph, 'Now I can die, now that I have seen you in person and seen you still alive.'

and to his father's household, "I will go up and tell Pharaoh, and will say to him, 'My brothers and my father's household, who were in the land of Canaan, have come to me. 32 The men are shepherds, for they have been keepers of livestock; and they have brought their flocks, and their herds, and all that they have.' 33 When Pharaoh calls you, and says, 'What is your occupation?' 34 you shall say, 'Your servants have been keepers of livestock from our youth even until now, both we and our ancestors' — in order that you may settle in the land of Goshen, because all shepherds are abhorrent to the Egyptians."

47 So Joseph went and told Pharaoh, "My father and my brothers, with their flocks and herds and all that they possess, have come from the land of Canaan; they are now in the land of Goshen." 2 From among his brothers he took five men and presented them to Pharaoh. 3 Pharaoh said to his brothers, "What is your occupation?" And they said to Pharaoh, "Your servants are shepherds, as our ancestors were." 4 They said to Pharaoh, "We have come to reside as aliens in the land; for there is no pasture for your servants' flocks because the famine is severe in the land of Canaan. Now, we ask you, let your servants settle in the land of Goshen." 5 Then Pharaoh said to Joseph, "Your father and your brothers have come to you. 6 The land of Egypt is before you; settle your father and your brothers in the best part of the land; let them live in the land of Goshen; and if you know that there are capable men among them, put them in charge of my livestock."

7 Then Joseph brought in his father Jacob, and presented him before Pharaoh, and Jacob blessed Pharaoh. 8 Pharaoh said to Jacob, "How many are the years of your life?" 9 Jacob said to Pharaoh, "The years of my earthly sojourn are one hundred thirty; few and hard have been the years of my life. They do not compare with the years of the life of my ancestors during their long sojourn." 10 Then Jacob blessed Pharaoh, and went out from the presence of Pharaoh. 11 Joseph settled his father and his brothers, and granted them a holding in the land of Egypt, in the best part of the land, in the land of Rameses, as Pharaoh had instructed. 12 And Joseph provided his father, his brothers, and all his father's household with food, according to the number of their dependents.

13 Now there was no food in all the land, for the famine was very severe. The land of Egypt and the land of Canaan languished because of the famine. 14 Joseph collected all the money to be found in the land of Egypt and in the land of Canaan, in exchange for the grain that they bought; and Joseph brought the money into Pharaoh's house. 15 When the money from the land of Egypt and from the land of Canaan was spent, all the Egyptians came to Joseph, and said, "Give us food! Why should we die before your eyes? For our money is gone." 16 And Joseph answered, "Give me your livestock, and I will give you food in exchange for your livestock, if your money is gone." 17 So they brought their livestock to Joseph; and Joseph gave them food in exchange for the horses, the flocks, the herds, and the donkeys. That year he supplied them with food in exchange for all their livestock. 18 When that year was ended, they came to him the following year, and said to him, "We can not hide from my lord that our money is all spent; and the herds of cattle are my lord's. There is nothing left in the sight of my lord but our bodies and our lands. 19 Shall we die before your eyes, both we and our land? Buy us and our land in exchange for food. We with our land will become slaves to Pharaoh; just give us seed, so that we may live and not die, and that the land may not become desolate."

father's household, 'I shall go up and inform Pharaoh; I shall tell him, "My brothers and my father's household who were in Canaan have come to me. 32 The men are shepherds with their own flocks and herds, and they have brought with them these flocks and herds and everything they possess." 33 So when Pharaoh summons you and asks what your occupation is, 34 you must answer, "My lord, we have herded flocks all our lives, as our fathers did before us." You must say this if you are to settle in Goshen, because shepherds are regarded as unclean by Egyptians.'

47 Joseph came and reported to Pharaoh, 'My father and my brothers have arrived from Canaan, with their flocks and herds and everything they possess, and they are now in Goshen.' 2 He had chosen five of his brothers, and he brought them into Pharaoh's presence. 3 When he asked them what their occupation was, they answered, 'We are shepherds like our fathers before us, 4 and we have come to stay in this country, because owing to the severe famine in Canaan there is no pasture there for our flocks. We ask your majesty's leave to settle now in Goshen.' 5 Pharaoh said to Joseph, 'As to your father and your brothers who have come to you, 6 the land of Egypt is at your disposal; settle them in the best part of it. Let them live in Goshen, and if you know of any among them with the skill, make them chief herdsmen in charge of my cattle.'

7 Then Joseph brought his father in and presented him to Pharaoh. Jacob blessed Pharaoh, 8 who asked him his age, 9 and he answered, 'The years of my life on earth are one hundred and thirty; few and hard have they been — fewer than the years my fathers lived.' 10 Jacob then blessed Pharaoh and withdrew from his presence. 11 As Pharaoh had ordered, Joseph settled his father and his brothers, and allotted land to them in Egypt, in the best part of the country, the district of Rameses. 12 He supported his father, his brothers, and his father's whole household with the food they needed.

13 There was no food anywhere, so very severe was the famine; Egypt and Canaan were laid low by it. 14 Joseph gathered in all the money in Egypt and Canaan in exchange for the grain which the people bought, and put it in Pharaoh's treasury. 15 When the money in Egypt and Canaan had come to an end, the Egyptians all came to Joseph. 'Give us food,' they said, 'or we shall perish before your very eyes. Our money is all gone.' 16 Joseph replied, 'If your money is all gone, hand over your livestock and I shall give you food in return.' 17 So they brought their livestock to Joseph, who gave them food in exchange for their horses, their flocks of sheep, their herds of cattle, and their donkeys. He supported them that year with food in exchange for all their herds. 18 The year came to an end, and in the following year they came to him and said, 'My lord, we cannot conceal from you that with our money finished and our herds of cattle made over to you, there is nothing left for your lordship but our bodies and our lands. 19 Why should we perish before your eyes, we and our land as well? Take us and our land in payment for food, and we and our land alike will be in bondage to Pharaoh. Give us seed-corn to keep us alive, or we shall die and our land will become desert.'

|

31 Joseph then said to his brothers and his father's household: "I will go and inform Pharaoh, telling him: 'My brothers and my father's household, whose home is in the land of Canaan, have come to me. 32 The men are shepherds, having long been keepers of livestock; and they have brought with them their flocks and herds, as well as everything else they own.' 33 So when Pharaoh summons you and asks what your occupation is, 34 you must answer. 'We your servants, like our ancestors, have been keepers of livestock from the beginning until now,' in order that you may stay in the region of Goshen, since all shepherds are abhorrent to the Egyptians."

47 Joseph went and told Pharaoh, "My father and my brothers have come from the land of Canaan, with their flocks and herds and everything else they own; and they are now in the region of Goshen." 2 He then presented to Pharaoh five of his brothers whom he had selected from their full number. 3 When Pharaoh asked them what their occupation was, they answered, "We, your servants, like our ancestors, are shepherds. 4 We have come," they continued, "in order to stay in this country, for there is no pasture for your servants' flocks in the land of Canaan, so severe has the famine been there. Please, therefore, let your servants settle in the region of Goshen." 5 Pharaoh said to Joseph, "They may settle in the region of Goshen; and if you know any of them to be qualified, you may put them in charge of my own livestock."

Thus, when Jacob and his sons came to Joseph in Egypt, and Pharaoh, king of Egypt, heard about it, Pharaoh said to Joseph, "Now that your father and brothers have come to you, 6 the land of Egypt is at your disposal; settle your father and brothers in the pick of the land." 7 Then Joseph brought his father Jacob and presented him to Pharaoh. After Jacob had paid his respects to Pharaoh, 8 Pharaoh asked him, "How many years have you lived?" 9 Jacob replied: "The years I have lived as a wayfarer amount to a hundred and thirty. Few and hard have been these years of my life, and they do not compare with the years that my ancestors lived as wayfarers." 10 Then Jacob bade Pharaoh farewell and withdrew from his presence.

11 As Pharaoh had ordered, Joseph settled his father and brothers and gave them holdings in Egypt on the pick of the land, in the region of Rameses. 12 And Joseph sustained his father and brothers and his father's whole household, down to the youngest, with food.

13 Since there was no food in any country because of the extreme severity of the famine, and the lands of Egypt and Canaan were languishing from hunger, 14 Joseph gathered in, as payment for the rations that were being dispensed, all the money that was to be found in Egypt and Canaan, and he put it in Pharaoh's palace. 15 When all the money in Egypt and Canaan was spent, all the Egyptians came to Joseph, pleading; "Give us food or we shall perish under your eyes; for our money is gone." 16 "Since your money is gone," replied Joseph, "give me your livestock, and I will sell you bread in return for your livestock." 17 So they brought their livestock to Joseph, and he sold them food in return for their horses, their flocks of sheep and herds of cattle, and their donkeys. Thus he got them through that year with bread in exchange for all their livestock. 18 When that year ended, they came to him in the following one and said: "We cannot hide from my lord that, with our money spent and our livestock made over to my lord, there is nothing left to put at my lord's disposal except our bodies and our farm land. 19 Why should we and our land perish before your very eyes? Take us and our land in exchange for food, and we will become Pharaoh's slaves and our land his property; only give us seed, that we may survive and not perish, and that our land may not turn into a waste."

31 Then Joseph said to his brothers and his father's family, 'I shall go back and break the news to Pharaoh. I shall tell him, "My brothers and my father's family who were in Canaan have come to me. 32 The men are shepherds and look after livestock, and they have brought their flocks and cattle and all their possessions." Thus, when Pharaoh summons you and asks, "What is your occupation?", 34 you are to say, "Ever since our boyhood your servants have looked after livestock, we and our fathers before us," so that you can stay in the Goshen region — for the Egyptians have a horror of all shepherds.'

47 So Joseph went and told Pharaoh, 'My father and brothers have arrived from Canaan with their flocks and cattle and all their possessions. Here they are, in the region of Goshen.' 2 He had taken five of his brothers, and he now presented them to Pharaoh. 3 Pharaoh asked his brothers, 'What is your occupation?' and they gave Pharaoh the answer, 'Your servants are shepherds, like our fathers before us.' 4 They went on to tell Pharaoh, 'We have come to stay in this country for the time being, since there is no pasturage for your servants' flocks, Canaan being stricken with famine. So now please allow your servants to settle in the region of Goshen.' 5a Then Pharaoh said to Joseph, 6b 'They may stay in the region of Goshen, and if you know of any capable men among them, put them in charge of my own livestock.'

5b Jacob and his sons went to Egypt where Joseph was. Pharaoh king of Egypt heard about this and said to Joseph, 'Your father and brothers have come to you. 6a The country of Egypt is open to you: settle your father and brothers in the best region.' 7 Joseph brought his father and presented him to Pharaoh. Jacob paid his respects to Pharaoh. 8 Pharaoh asked Jacob, 'How many years have you lived?' 9 Jacob said to Pharaoh, 'The years of my stay on earth add up to one hundred and thirty years. Few and unhappy my years have been, falling short of my ancestors' years in their stay on earth.' 10 Jacob then took leave of Pharaoh and withdrew from his presence. 11 Joseph then settled his father and brothers, giving them land holdings in Egypt, in the best part of the country, the region of Rameses, as Pharaoh had ordered.

12 Joseph provided his father, brothers and all his father's family with food, down to the least of them.

13 And on all the earth around there was now no food anywhere, for the famine had grown very severe, and Egypt and Canaan were both weak with hunger. 14 Joseph accumulated all the money to be found in Egypt and Canaan, in exchange for the supplies being handed out, and put the money in Pharaoh's palace. 15 When all the money in Egypt and Canaan was exhausted, all the Egyptians came to Joseph, pleading, 'Give us food, unless you want us to die before your eyes! For our money has come to an end.' 16 Joseph replied, 'Hand over your livestock and I shall issue you food in exchange for your livestock, if your money has come to an end.' 17 So they brought their livestock to Joseph, and Joseph gave them food in exchange for horses and livestock, whether sheep or cattle, and for donkeys. Thus he saw them through that year with food in exchange for all their livestock.

18 When that year was over, they came to him the next year, and said to him, 'We cannot hide it from my lord: the truth is, our money has run out and the livestock is in my lord's possession. There is nothing left for my lord except our bodies and our land. 19 If we and our land are not to perish, take us and our land in exchange for food, and we with our land will become Pharaoh's serfs; only give us seed, so that we can survive and not die and the land not revert to desert!'

NEW REVISED STANDARD VERSION

20 So Joseph bought all the land of Egypt for Pharaoh. All the Egyptians sold their fields, because the famine was severe upon them; and the land became Pharaoh's. 21 As for the people, he made slaves of them y from one end of Egypt to the other. 22 Only the land of the priests he did not buy; for the priests had a fixed allowance from Pharaoh, and lived on the allowance that Pharaoh gave them; therefore they did not sell their land. 23 Then Joseph said to the people, "Now that I have this day bought you and your land for Pharaoh, here is seed for you; sow the land. 24 And at the harvests you shall give one-fifth to Pharaoh, and four-fifths shall be your own, as seed for the field and as food for yourselves and your households, and as food for your little ones." 25 They said, "You have saved our lives; may it please my lord, we will be slaves to Pharaoh." 26 So Joseph made it a statute concerning the land of Egypt, and it stands to this day, that Pharaoh should have the fifth. The land of the priests alone did not become Pharaoh's.

27 Thus Israel settled in the land of Egypt, in the region of Goshen; and they gained possessions in it, and were fruitful and multiplied exceedingly. 28 Jacob lived in the land of Egypt seventeen years; so the days of Jacob, the years of his life, were one hundred forty-seven years.

29 When the time of Israel's death drew near, he called his son Joseph and said to him, "If I have found favor with you, put your hand under my thigh and promise to deal loyally and truly with me. Do not bury me in Egypt. 30 When I lie down with my ancestors, carry me out of Egypt and bury me in their burial place." He answered, "I will do as you have said." 31 And he said, "Swear to me"; and he swore to him. Then Israel bowed himself on the head of his bed.

48 After this Joseph was told, "Your father is ill." So he took with him his two sons, Manasseh and Ephraim. 2 When Jacob was told, "Your son Joseph has come to you," he z summoned his strength and sat up in bed. 3 And Jacob said to Joseph, "God Almighty a appeared to me at Luz in the land of Canaan, and he blessed me, 4 and said to me, 'I am going to make you fruitful and increase your numbers; I will make of you a company of peoples, and will give this land to your offspring after you for a perpetual holding.' 5 Therefore your two sons, who were born to you in the land of Egypt before I came to you in Egypt, are now mine; Ephraim and Manasseh shall be mine, just as Reuben and Simeon are. 6 As for the offspring born to you after them, they shall be yours. They shall be recorded under the names of their brothers with regard to their inheritance. 7 For when I came from Paddan, Rachel, alas, died in the land of Canaan on the way, while there was still some distance to go to Ephrath; and I buried her there on the way to Ephrath" (that is, Bethlehem).

8 When Israel saw Joseph's sons, he said, "Who are these?" 9 Joseph said to his father, "They are my sons, whom God has given me here." And he said, "Bring them to me, please, that I may bless them." 10 Now the eyes of Israel were dim with age, and he could not see well. So Joseph brought them near him; and he kissed them and embraced them. 11 Israel said to Joseph, "I did not expect to see your face; and here God has let me see your children also." 12 Then Joseph removed them from his father's knees, b and he bowed himself with his face to the earth. 13 Joseph took them both, Ephraim in his right hand toward Israel's left, and Manasseh in his left hand toward Israel's right, and brought them near him. 14 But Israel stretched out

REVISED ENGLISH BIBLE

20 So Joseph acquired for Pharaoh all the land in Egypt: because the Egyptians, hard-pressed by the famine, sold all their fields, and the land became Pharaoh's. 21 Joseph moved the people into the towns throughout the whole territory of Egypt. 22 Only the land which belonged to the priests Joseph did not buy; they had a fixed allowance from Pharaoh and lived on this, so that they did not have to sell their land.

23 Joseph said to the people, 'Listen; I have now bought you and your land for Pharaoh. Here is seed-corn for you. Sow the land, 24 but at harvest give one fifth of the crop to Pharaoh. Four fifths shall be yours to provide seed for your fields and food for yourselves, your households, and your dependants.' 25 'You have saved our lives,' the people said. 'If it please your lordship, we shall be Pharaoh's slaves.' 26 Joseph established it as a law in Egypt that one fifth of the produce should belong to Pharaoh, and so it has been from that day to this. It was only the priests' land that did not pass into Pharaoh's hands.

27 Thus Israel settled in Egypt, in Goshen, where they acquired land, and were fruitful, and increased greatly. 28 Jacob lived in Egypt for seventeen years and died at the age of a hundred and forty-seven. 29 When the hour of his death drew near, he summoned his son Joseph and said to him, 'I have a favour to ask: give me your solemn oath that you will deal loyally and faithfully with me; do not bury me in Egypt. 30 So that I may lie with my forefathers, you are to take me up from Egypt and bury me in their grave.' He answered, 'I shall do as you say.' 31 'Swear that you will,' said Jacob. So he gave him his oath, and Israel bowed in worship by the head of his bed.

48 Some time later Joseph was informed that his father was ill, so he took his two sons, Manasseh and Ephraim, with him and came to Jacob. 2 When Jacob heard that his son Joseph had come to him, he gathered his strength and sat up in bed. 3 Jacob said to Joseph, 'God Almighty appeared to me at Luz in Canaan and blessed me; 4 he said to me, "I shall make you fruitful and increase your descendants until they become a host of nations. I shall give this land to them after you as a possession for all time." 5 Now,' Jacob went on, 'your two sons, who were born in Egypt before I came to join you here, will be counted as my sons; Ephraim and Manasseh will be mine as Reuben and Simeon are. 6 But the children born to you after them will be counted as yours; in respect of their tribal territory they will be reckoned under their elder brothers' names. 7 In Canaan on my return from Paddan-aram and while we were still some distance from Ephrath, your mother Rachel died on the way, and I buried her there by the road to Ephrath' (that is Bethlehem).

8 When Israel saw Joseph's sons, he said, 'Who are these?' 9 'They are my sons', replied Joseph, 'whom God has given me here.' Israel said, 'Then bring them to me, that I may bless them.' 10 Now Israel's eyes were dim with age, and he could hardly see. Joseph brought the boys close to his father, and he kissed them and embraced them. 11 He said to Joseph, 'I had not expected to see your face again, and now God has let me see your sons as well.' 12 Joseph removed them from his father's knees and bowed to the ground. 13 Then he took the two of them and brought them close to Israel: Ephraim on the right, that is Israel's left; and Manasseh on the left, that is Israel's right. 14 But Israel,

y Sam Gk Compare Vg: MT *He removed them to the cities*
z Heb *Israel*   a Traditional rendering of Heb *El Shaddai*
b Heb *from his knees*

47:29 **give . . . oath:** *lit.* put your hand under my thigh.
47:31 **head of his bed:** *or, with Gk,* top of his staff (*cp. Hebrews 11:21*).   48:7 **Paddan-aram:** *so Samar.; Heb.* Paddan. **your mother:** *so Samar.; Heb.* omits.   48:9 **bless them:** *or* take them on my knees.

20 Thus Joseph acquired all the farm land of Egypt for Pharaoh, since with the famine too much for them to bear, every Egyptian sold his field; so the land passed over to Pharaoh, 21 and the people were reduced to slavery, from one end of Egypt's territory to the other. 22 Only the priests' lands Joseph did not take over. Since the priests had a fixed allowance from Pharaoh and lived off the allowance Pharaoh had granted them, they did not have to sell their land.

23 Joseph told the people: "Now that I have acquired you and your land for Pharaoh, here is your seed for sowing the land. 24 But when the harvest is in, you must give a fifth of it to Pharaoh, while you keep four-fifths as seed for your fields, and as food for yourselves and your families [and as food for your children]." 25 "You have saved our lives!" they answered. "We are grateful to my lord that we can be Pharaoh's slaves." 26 Thus Joseph made it a law for the land in Egypt, which is still in force, that a fifth of its produce should go to Pharaoh. Only the land of the priests did not pass over to Pharaoh.

27 Thus Israel settled in the land of Egypt, in the region of Goshen. There they acquired property, were fertile, and increased greatly. 28 Jacob lived in the land of Egypt for seventeen years; the span of his life came to a hundred and forty-seven years. 29 When the time approached for Israel to die, he called his son Joseph and said to him: "If you really wish to please me, put your hand under my thigh as a sign of your constant loyalty to me; do not let me be buried in Egypt. 30 When I lie down with my ancestors, have me taken out of Egypt and buried in their burial place." 31 "I will do as you say," he replied. But his father demanded, "Swear it to me!" So Joseph swore to him. Then Israel bowed at the head of the bed.

48 Some time afterward, Joseph was informed, "Your father is failing." So he took along with him his two sons, Manasseh and Ephraim. 2 When Jacob was told, "Your son Joseph has come to you," he rallied his strength and sat up in bed.

3 Jacob then said to Joseph: "God Almighty appeared to me at Luz in the land of Canaan, and blessing me, 4 he said, 'I will make you fertile and numerous and raise you into an assembly of tribes, and I will give this land to your descendants after you as a permanent possession.' 5 Your two sons, therefore, who were born to you in the land of Egypt before I joined you here, shall be mine; Ephraim and Manasseh shall be mine as much as Reuben and Simeon are mine. 6 Progeny born to you after them shall remain yours; but their heritage shall be recorded in the names of their two brothers. 7 I do this because, when I was returning from Paddan, your mother Rachel died, to my sorrow, during the journey in Canaan, while we were still a short distance from Ephrath; and I buried her there on the way to Ephrath [that is, Bethlehem]."

8 When Israel saw Joseph's sons, he asked, "Who are these?" 9 "They are my sons," Joseph answered his father, "whom God has given me here." "Bring them to me," said his father, "that I may bless them." 10 (Now Israel's eyes were dim from age, and he could not see well.) When Joseph brought his sons close to him, he kissed and embraced them. 11 Then Israel said to Joseph, "I never expected to see your face again, and now God has allowed me to see your descendants as well!"

12 Joseph removed them from his father's knees and bowed down before him with his face to the ground. 13 Then Joseph took the two, Ephraim with his right hand, to Israel's left, and Manasseh with his left hand, to Israel's right, and led them to him. 14 But Israel, crossing his hands,

20 Thus Joseph acquired all the land in Egypt for Pharaoh, since one by one the Egyptians sold their fields, so hard pressed were they by the famine; and the whole country passed into Pharaoh's possession, 21 while the people he reduced to serfdom from one end of Egypt to the other. 22 The only land he did not acquire belonged to the priests, for the priests received an allowance from Pharaoh and lived on the allowance that Pharaoh gave them. Hence they had no need to sell their land.

23 Then Joseph said to the people, 'This is how we stand: I have bought you out, with your land, on Pharaoh's behalf. Here is seed for you to sow the land. 24 But of the harvest you must give a fifth to Pharaoh. The other four-fifths you can have for sowing your fields, to provide food for yourselves and your households, and food for your children.' 25 'You have saved our lives!' they replied. 'If it please my lord, we will become serfs to Pharaoh.' 26 So Joseph made a law, still in force today, as regards the soil of Egypt, that one-fifth should go to Pharaoh. Only the land of the priests did not go to Pharaoh.

27 Thus Israel settled in Egypt, in the region of Goshen. They acquired property there; they were fruitful and grew very numerous. 28 Jacob lived seventeen years in Egypt; thus Jacob's total age came to a hundred and forty-seven years. 29 When Israel's time to die drew near he sent for his son Joseph and said to him,[u] 'If you really love me, place your hand under my thigh as pledge that you will act with faithful love towards me: do not bury me in Egypt! 30 When I lie down with my ancestors, carry me out of Egypt and bury me in their tomb.' 'I shall do as you say,' he replied. 31 'Swear to me,' he insisted. So he swore to him, and Israel sank back on the pillow.

48 Some time later, Joseph was informed, 'Your father has been taken ill.' So he took with him his two sons Manasseh and Ephraim. 2 When Jacob was told, 'Look, your son Joseph has come to you,' Israel, summoning his strength, sat up in bed. 3 'El Shaddai appeared to me at Luz in Canaan,' Jacob told Joseph, 'and he blessed me, 4 saying to me, "I shall make you fruitful and numerous, and shall make you into an assembly of peoples and give this country to your descendants after you, to own in perpetuity." 5 Now your two sons, born to you in Egypt before I came to you in Egypt, shall be mine; Ephraim and Manasseh shall be as much mine as Reuben and Simeon. 6 But with regard to the children you have had since them, they shall be yours, and they shall be known by their brothers' names for the purpose of their inheritance.

7 'When I was on my way from Paddan, to my sorrow death took your mother Rachel from me in Canaan, on the journey while only a short distance from Ephrath. I buried her there on the road to Ephrath — now Bethlehem.'

8 When Israel saw Joseph's two sons, he asked, 'Who are these?' 9 'They are my sons, whom God has given me here,' Joseph told his father. 'Then bring them to me', he said, 'so that I may bless them.' 10 Now, Israel's eyes were dim with age, and he could not see. So Joseph made them come closer to him and he kissed and embraced them. 11 Then Israel said to Joseph, 'I did not think I should ever see you again, and now God has let me see your children as well!' 12 Then Joseph took them from his lap and bowed to the ground.

13 Then Joseph took the two of them, Ephraim with his right hand so that he should be on Israel's left, and Manasseh with his left hand, so that he should be on Israel's right, and brought them close to him. 14 But Israel held out his

u 47 = 49:29–32; = 50:6.

NEW REVISED STANDARD VERSION

his right hand and laid it on the head of Ephraim, who was the younger, and his left hand on the head of Manasseh, crossing his hands, for Manasseh was the firstborn. 15 He blessed Joseph, and said,

"The God before whom my ancestors Abraham
and Isaac walked,
the God who has been my shepherd all my life to
this day,
16 the angel who has redeemed me from all harm,
bless the boys;
and in them let my name be perpetuated, and the
name of my ancestors Abraham and Isaac;
and let them grow into a multitude on the earth."

17 When Joseph saw that his father laid his right hand on the head of Ephraim, it displeased him; so he took his father's hand, to remove it from Ephraim's head to Manasseh's head. 18 Joseph said to his father, "Not so, my father! Since this one is the firstborn, put your right hand on his head." 19 But his father refused, and said, "I know, my son, I know; he also shall become a people, and he also shall be great. Nevertheless his younger brother shall be greater than he, and his offspring shall become a multitude of nations." 20 So he blessed them that day, saying,

"By you*c* Israel will invoke blessings, saying,
'God make you*c* like Ephraim and like
Manasseh.'"

So he put Ephraim ahead of Manasseh. 21 Then Israel said to Joseph, "I am about to die, but God will be with you and will bring you again to the land of your ancestors. 22 I now give to you one portion*d* more than to your brothers, the portion*d* that I took from the hand of the Amorites with my sword and with my bow."

49 Then Jacob called his sons, and said: "Gather around, that I may tell you what will happen to you in days to come.

2 Assemble and hear, O sons of Jacob;
listen to Israel your father.

3 Reuben, you are my firstborn,
my might and the first fruits of my vigor,
excelling in rank and excelling in power.
4 Unstable as water, you shall no longer excel
because you went up onto your father's bed;
then you defiled it — you*e* went up onto my
couch!

5 Simeon and Levi are brothers;
weapons of violence are their swords.
6 May I never come into their council;
may I not be joined to their company —
for in their anger they killed men,
and at their whim they hamstrung oxen.
7 Cursed be their anger, for it is fierce,
and their wrath, for it is cruel!
I will divide them in Jacob,
and scatter them in Israel.

8 Judah, your brothers shall praise you;
your hand shall be on the neck of your
enemies;
your father's sons shall bow down before you.
9 Judah is a lion's whelp;
from the prey, my son, you have gone up.
He crouches down, he stretches out like a lion,
like a lioness — who dares rouse him up?

REVISED ENGLISH BIBLE

crossing his hands, stretched out his right hand and laid it on Ephraim's head, although he was the younger, and laid his left hand on Manasseh's head, even though he was the firstborn. 15 He blessed Joseph and said:

'The God in whose presence my forefathers lived,
my forefathers Abraham and Isaac,
the God who has been my shepherd all my life to
this day,
16 the angel who rescued me from all misfortune,
may he bless these boys;
they will be called by my name,
and by the names of my forefathers, Abraham and
Isaac;
may they grow into a great people on earth.'

17 When Joseph saw his father laying his right hand on Ephraim's head, he was displeased and took hold of his father's hand to move it from Ephraim's head to Manasseh's. 18 He said, 'That is not right, father. This is the firstborn; lay your right hand on his head.' 19 But his father refused; he said, 'I know, my son, I know. He too will become a people, and he too will become great. Yet his younger brother will be greater than he, and his descendants will be a whole nation in themselves.' 20 So he blessed them that day and said:

'When a blessing is pronounced in Israel,
men shall use your names and say,
"May God make you like Ephraim and
Manasseh."'

So he set Ephraim before Manasseh. 21 Then Israel said to Joseph, 'I am about to die, but God will be with you and bring you back to the land of your fathers, 22 where I assign you one ridge of land more than your brothers; I took it from the Amorites with sword and bow.'

49 JACOB summoned his sons. 'Come near,' he said, 'and I shall tell you what is to happen to you in days to come.

2 'Gather round me and listen, you sons of Jacob;
listen to Israel your father.

3 'Reuben, you are my firstborn,
my strength and the first fruit of my vigour,
excelling in pride, excelling in might.
4 Uncontrollable as a flood, you will excel no more,
because you climbed into your father's bed,
and defiled his concubine's couch.

5 'Simeon and Levi are brothers,
weapons of violence are their counsels.
6 My soul will not enter their council,
my heart will not join their assembly;
for in anger they killed men,
wantonly they hamstrung oxen.
7 A curse be on their anger, for it was fierce;
a curse on their wrath, for it was ruthless!
I shall scatter them in Jacob,
I shall disperse them in Israel.

8 'Judah, your brothers will praise you;
your hand will be on the neck of your enemies.
Your father's sons will bow to you in homage.
9 Judah, a lion's whelp,
you have returned from the kill, my son;
you crouch and stretch like a lion,
like a lion no one dares rouse.

---

c you here is singular in Heb   *d* Or *mountain slope* (Heb *shekem*, a play on the name of the town and district of Shechem)   *e* Gk Syr Tg: Heb *he*

48:22 **ridge of land:** Heb. shechem, *meaning* shoulder.
49:5 **counsels:** Heb. *word of uncertain meaning.*

put out his right hand and laid it on the head of Ephraim, although he was the younger, and his left hand on the head of Manasseh, although he was the first-born. 15 Then he blessed them with these words:

"May the God in whose ways
   my fathers Abraham and Isaac walked,
The God who has been my shepherd
   from my birth to this day,
16 The Angel who has delivered me from all harm,
   bless these boys
That in them my name be recalled,
   and the names of my fathers, Abraham
      and Isaac,
And they may become teeming multitudes
   upon the earth!"

17 When Joseph saw that his father had laid his right hand on Ephraim's head, this seemed wrong to him; so he took hold of his father's hand, to remove it from Ephraim's head to Manasseh's, 18 saying, "That is not right, father; the other one is the first-born; lay your right hand on his head!" 19 But his father resisted. "I know it, son," he said, "I know. That one too shall become a tribe, and he too shall be great. Nevertheless, his younger brother shall surpass him, and his descendants shall become a multitude of nations." 20 So when he blessed them that day and said, "By you shall the people of Israel pronounce blessings; may they say, 'God make you like Ephraim and Manasseh,'" he placed Ephraim before Manasseh.

21 Then Israel said to Joseph: "I am about to die. But God will be with you and will restore you to the land of your fathers. 22 As for me, I give to you, as to the one above his brothers, Shechem, which I captured from the Amorites with my sword and bow."

49

Jacob called his sons and said: "Gather around, that I may tell you what is to happen to you in days to come.

2 "Assemble and listen, sons of Jacob,
   listen to Israel, your father.

3 "You, Reuben, my first-born,
   my strength and the first fruit of my manhood,
   excelling in rank and excelling in power!
4 Unruly as water, you shall no longer excel,
   for you climbed into your father's bed
   and defiled my couch to my sorrow.

5 "Simeon and Levi, brothers indeed,
   weapons of violence are their knives.
6 Let not my soul enter their council,
   or my spirit be joined with their company;
For in their fury they slew men,
   in their willfulness they maimed oxen.
7 Cursed be their fury so fierce,
   and their rage so cruel!
I will scatter them in Jacob,
   disperse them throughout Israel.

8 "You, Judah, shall your brothers praise
   — your hand on the neck of your enemies;
   the sons of your father shall bow down to you.
9 Judah, like a lion's whelp,
   you have grown up on prey, my son.
He crouches like a lion recumbent,
   the king of beasts — who would dare rouse him?

right hand and laid it on the head of Ephraim, the younger, and his left on the head of Manasseh, crossing his hands — Manasseh was, in fact, the elder. 15 Then he blessed Joseph saying:

May the God in whose presence my fathers
   Abraham and Isaac walked,
the God who has been my shepherd from my birth
   until this day,
16 the Angel who has saved me from all harm, bless
   these boys,
so that my name may live on in them, and the
   names of my ancestors Abraham and Isaac,
   and they grow into teeming multitudes on earth!

17 Joseph saw that his father was laying his right hand on the head of Ephraim, and this he thought was wrong, so he took his father's hand and tried to shift it from the head of Ephraim to the head of Manasseh. 18 Joseph protested to his father, 'Not like that, father! This one is the elder; put your right hand on his head.' 19 But his father refused. 'I know, my son, I know,' he said. 'He too shall become a people; he too will be great. But his younger brother will be greater, his offspring will be sufficient to constitute nations.'

20 So he blessed them that day, saying:

By you shall Israel bless itself, saying,
   'God make you like Ephraim and Manasseh!'
putting Ephraim before Manasseh.

21 Then Israel said to Joseph, 'Now I am about to die. But God will be with you and take you back to the land of your ancestors. 22 As for me, I give you a Shechem[v] more than your brothers, the one I took from the Amorites with my sword and bow.'

49

Jacob called his sons and said, 'Gather round, so that I can tell you what is in store for you in the final days.

2 Gather round, sons of Jacob, and listen;
   listen to Israel your father.

3 Reuben, you are my first-born,
   my vigour, and the first-fruit of my manhood,
   foremost in pride, foremost in strength,
4 uncontrolled as water: you will not be foremost,
   for you climbed into your father's bed,
   and so defiled my couch, to my sorrow.

5 Simeon and Levi are brothers
   in carrying out their malicious plans.
6 May my soul not enter their council
   nor my heart join their company,
for in their rage they have killed men
   and hamstrung oxen at their whim.
7 Accursed be their rage for its ruthlessness,
   their wrath for its ferocity.
I shall disperse them in Jacob,
   I shall scatter them through Israel.

8 Judah, your brothers will praise you:
   you grip your enemies by the neck,
   your father's sons will do you homage.
9 Judah is a lion's whelp;
   You stand over your prey, my son.
Like a lion he crouches and lies down,
   a mighty lion: who dare rouse him?

---

[v] **48** *Shekem* = shoulder, but it is also the name of Joseph's burial-town.

NEW REVISED STANDARD VERSION	REVISED ENGLISH BIBLE

10 The scepter shall not depart from Judah,
  nor the ruler's staff from between his feet,
until tribute comes to him;*f*
  and the obedience of the peoples is his.
	10 The sceptre will not pass from Judah,
	  nor the staff from between his feet,
	until he receives what is his due
	  and the obedience of the nations is his.

11 Binding his foal to the vine
  and his donkey's colt to the choice vine,
he washes his garments in wine
  and his robe in the blood of grapes;
	11 He tethers his donkey to the vine,
	  and its colt to the red vine;
	he washes his cloak in wine,
	  his robe in the blood of grapes.

12 his eyes are darker than wine,
  and his teeth whiter than milk.
	12 Darker than wine are his eyes,
	  whiter than milk his teeth.

13 Zebulun shall settle at the shore of the sea;
  he shall be a haven for ships,
  and his border shall be at Sidon.
	13 'Zebulun lives by the seashore;
	  his coast is a haven for ships,
	  and his frontier touches Sidon.

14 Issachar is a strong donkey,
  lying down between the sheepfolds;
	14 'Issachar, a gelded donkey
	  lying down in the cattle pens,

15 he saw that a resting place was good,
  and that the land was pleasant;
so he bowed his shoulder to the burden,
  and became a slave at forced labor.
	15 saw that a settled home was good
	  and that the land was pleasant,
	so he bent his back to the burden
	  and submitted to forced labour.

16 Dan shall judge his people
  as one of the tribes of Israel.
	16 'Dan—his people will be strong
	  as any tribe in Israel!

17 Dan shall be a snake by the roadside,
  a viper along the path,
that bites the horse's heels
  so that its rider falls backward.
	17 Let Dan be a viper on the road,
	  a horned snake on the path,
	that bites the horse's fetlock
	  so that the rider is thrown off backwards.

18 I wait for your salvation, O LORD.	18 'I wait in hope for salvation from you, LORD.

19 Gad shall be raided by raiders,
  but he shall raid at their heels.
	19 'Gad is raided by raiders,
	  and he will raid them from the rear.

20 Asher's*g* food shall be rich,
  and he shall provide royal delicacies.
	20 'Asher will feast every day,
	  and provide dishes fit for a king.

21 Naphtali is a doe let loose
  that bears lovely fawns.*h*
	21 'Naphtali is a spreading terebinth
	  putting forth lovely boughs.

22 Joseph is a fruitful bough,
  a fruitful bough by a spring;
  his branches run over the wall.*i*
	22 'Joseph is a fruitful tree by a spring,
	  whose branches climb over the wall.

23 The archers fiercely attacked him;
  they shot at him and pressed him hard.
	23 The archers savagely attacked him,
	  shooting and assailing him fiercely,

24 Yet his bow remained taut,
  and his arms*j* were made agile
by the hands of the Mighty One of Jacob,
  by the name of the Shepherd, the Rock of
    Israel,
	24 but Joseph's bow remained unfailing
	  and his arms were tireless
	by the power of the Strong One of Jacob,
	  by the name of the Shepherd of Israel,

25 by the God of your father, who will help you,
  by the Almighty*k* who will bless you
with blessings of heaven above,
  blessings of the deep that lies beneath,
  blessings of the breasts and of the womb.
	25 by the God of your father—so may he help you!
	  By God Almighty—so may he bless you
	with the blessings of heaven above,
	  and the blessings of the deep that lies below!
	  The blessings of breast and womb

26 The blessings of your father
  are stronger than the blessings of the eternal
    mountains,
  the bounties*l* of the everlasting hills;
may they be on the head of Joseph,
  on the brow of him who was set apart from his
    brothers.
	26 and the blessings of your father are stronger
	  than the blessings of the eternal mountains
	  and the bounty of the everlasting hills.
	May they rest on the head of Joseph,
	  on the brow of him who was prince among his
	    brothers.

27 Benjamin is a ravenous wolf,
  in the morning devouring the prey,
  and at evening dividing the spoil."
	27 'Benjamin is a ravening wolf:
	  in the morning he devours the prey,
	  in the evening he snatches a share of the spoil.'

f Or *until Shiloh comes* or *until he comes to Shiloh* or (with Syr) *until he comes to whom it belongs*   *g* Gk Vg Syr: Heb *From Asher*
h Or *that gives beautiful words*   *i* Meaning of Heb uncertain
j Heb *the arms of his hands*   *k* Traditional rendering of Heb *Shaddai*
l Cn Compare Gk: Heb *of my progenitors to the boundaries*

49:10 **he receives . . . his due:** *or, as otherwise read,* Shiloh comes.
49:14 **gelded:** *so* Samar.; *or* Heb. bony.   49:16 **Dan . . . Israel:**
or Dan will govern his people as one of the tribes of Israel.
49:24 **Shepherd:** *prob. rdg; Heb.* adds stone.

NEW AMERICAN BIBLE

NEW JERUSALEM BIBLE

10 The scepter shall never depart from Judah,
    or the mace from between his legs,
While tribute is brought to him,
    and he receives the people's homage.
11 He tethers his donkey to the vine,
    his purebred ass to the choicest stem.
In wine he washes his garments,
    his robe in the blood of grapes.
12 His eyes are darker than wine,
    and his teeth are whiter than milk.
13 "Zebulun shall dwell by the seashore
    [This means a shore for ships],
    and his flank shall be based on Sidon.

14 "Issachar is a rawboned ass,
    crouching between the saddlebags.
15 When he saw how good a settled life was,
    and how pleasant the country,
He bent his shoulder to the burden
    and became a toiling serf.

16 "Dan shall achieve justice for his kindred
    like any other tribe of Israel.
17 Let Dan be a serpent by the roadside,
    a horned viper by the path,
That bites the horse's heel,
    so that the rider tumbles backward.

18 "[I long for your deliverance, O LORD!]

19 "Gad shall be raided by raiders,
    but he shall raid at their heels.

20 "Asher's produce is rich,
    and he shall furnish dainties for kings.

21 "Naphtali is a hind let loose,
    which brings forth lovely fawns.

22 "Joseph is a wild colt,
    a wild colt by a spring,
    a wild ass on a hillside.
23 Harrying and attacking,
    the archers opposed him;
24 But each one's bow remained stiff,
    as their arms were unsteady,
By the power of the Mighty One of Jacob,
    because of the Shepherd, the Rock of Israel,
25 The God of your father, who helps you,
    God Almighty, who blesses you,
With the blessings of the heavens above,
    the blessings of the abyss that crouches below,
The blessings of breasts and womb,
26   the blessings of fresh grain and blossoms,
The blessings of the everlasting mountains,
    the delights of the eternal hills.
May they rest on the head of Joseph,
    on the brow of the prince among his brothers.

27 "Benjamin is a ravenous wolf;
    mornings he devours the prey,
    and evenings he distributes the spoils."

10 The sceptre shall not pass from Judah,
    nor the ruler's staff from between his feet,
until tribute be brought him
    and the peoples render him obedience.
11 He tethers his donkey to the vine,
    to its stock the foal of his she-donkey.
He washes his clothes in wine,
    his robes in the blood of the grape.
12 His eyes are darkened with wine
    and his teeth are white with milk.
13 Zebulun will live by the seashore
    and be a sailor on board the ships,
    with Sidon on his flank.

14 Issachar is a strong donkey
    lying down among sheepfolds.
15 When he saw how good the resting-place
    and how pleasant the country,
he bowed his shoulder to the load
    and became a slave to forced labour.

16 Dan will govern his people
    like any other of the tribes of Israel.
17 May Dan be a snake on the road,
    a viper on the path,
who bites the horse on the hock
    so that its rider falls off backwards!

18 I long for your deliverance, Yahweh!

19 Gad will be raided by raiders,
    and he will raid at their heels.

20 Rich the food produced by Asher:
    he will furnish food fit for kings.

21 Naphtali is a swift hind
    bearing lovely fawns.

22 Joseph is a fruitful plant near a spring
    whose tendrils reach over the wall.
23 Archers in their hostility
    drew their bows and attacked him.
24 But their bows were broken by a mighty One,
    the sinews of their arms were snapped
by the power of the Mighty One of Jacob,
    by the Name of the Stone of Israel,
25 the God of your father who assists you,
    El Shaddai who blesses you:
blessings of heaven above,
    blessings of the deep lying below,
    blessings of the breasts and womb,
26 blessings of the grain and flowers,
    blessings of the eternal mountains,
bounty of the everlasting hills —
    may they descend on Joseph's head,
on the crown of the one dedicated from among his
    brothers!

27 Benjamin is a ravening wolf,
    in the morning he devours the prey,
    in the evening he is still sharing out the spoil.'

NEW REVISED STANDARD VERSION

28 All these are the twelve tribes of Israel, and this is what their father said to them when he blessed them, blessing each one of them with a suitable blessing.

29 Then he charged them, saying to them, "I am about to be gathered to my people. Bury me with my ancestors — in the cave in the field of Ephron the Hittite, 30 in the cave in the field at Machpelah, near Mamre, in the land of Canaan, in the field that Abraham bought from Ephron the Hittite as a burial site. 31 There Abraham and his wife Sarah were buried; there Isaac and his wife Rebekah were buried; and there I buried Leah— 32 the field and the cave that is in it were purchased from the Hittites." 33 When Jacob ended his charge to his sons, he drew up his feet into the bed, breathed his last, and was gathered to his people.

50 Then Joseph threw himself on his father's face and wept over him and kissed him. 2 Joseph commanded the physicians in his service to embalm his father. So the physicians embalmed Israel; 3 they spent forty days in doing this, for that is the time required for embalming. And the Egyptians wept for him seventy days.

4 When the days of weeping for him were past, Joseph addressed the household of Pharaoh, "If now I have found favor with you, please speak to Pharaoh as follows: 5 My father made me swear an oath; he said, 'I am about to die. In the tomb that I hewed out for myself in the land of Canaan, there you shall bury me.' Now therefore let me go up, so that I may bury my father; then I will return." 6 Pharaoh answered, "Go up, and bury your father, as he made you swear to do."

7 So Joseph went up to bury his father. With him went up all the servants of Pharaoh, the elders of his household, and all the elders of the land of Egypt, 8 as well as all the household of Joseph, his brothers, and his father's household. Only their children, their flocks, and their herds were left in the land of Goshen. 9 Both chariots and charioteers went up with him. It was a very great company. 10 When they came to the threshing floor of Atad, which is beyond the Jordan, they held there a very great and sorrowful lamentation; and he observed a time of mourning for his father seven days. 11 When the Canaanite inhabitants of the land saw the mourning on the threshing floor of Atad, they said, "This is a grievous mourning on the part of the Egyptians." Therefore the place was named Abel-mizraim;*m* it is beyond the Jordan. 12 Thus his sons did for him as he had instructed them. 13 They carried him to the land of Canaan and buried him in the cave of the field at Machpelah, the field near Mamre, which Abraham bought as a burial site from Ephron the Hittite. 14 After he had buried his father, Joseph returned to Egypt with his brothers and all who had gone up with him to bury his father.

15 Realizing that their father was dead, Joseph's brothers said, "What if Joseph still bears a grudge against us and pays us back in full for all the wrong that we did to him?" 16 So they approached*n* Joseph, saying, "Your father gave this instruction before he died, 17 'Say to Joseph: I beg you, forgive the crime of your brothers and the wrong they did in harming you.' Now therefore please forgive the crime of the servants of the God of your father." Joseph wept when they spoke to him. 18 Then his brothers also wept,*o* fell down before him, and said, "We are here as your slaves." 19 But Joseph said to them, "Do not be afraid! Am I in the place of God? 20 Even though you intended to do harm to me, God intended it for good, in order to preserve a numerous people, as he is doing today. 21 So have no fear; I myself will provide for you and your little ones." In this way he reassured them, speaking kindly to them.

REVISED ENGLISH BIBLE

28 These are the tribes of Israel, twelve in all, and this was what their father said to them, when he blessed them each in turn. 29 Then he gave them his last charge and said, 'I am about to be gathered to my ancestors; bury me with my forefathers in the cave on the plot of land which belonged to Ephron the Hittite, 30 that is the cave on the plot of land at Machpelah east of Mamre in Canaan, the field which Abraham bought from Ephron the Hittite for a burial-place. 31 There Abraham was buried with his wife Sarah; there Isaac and his wife Rebecca were buried; and that is where I buried Leah. 32 The land and the cave there were bought from the Hittites.' 33 When Jacob had finished giving these instructions to his sons, he drew up his feet on to the bed, breathed his last, and was gathered to his ancestors.

50 Then Joseph threw himself upon his father, weeping over him and kissing him. 2 He gave orders to the physicians in his service to embalm his father, and they did so, 3 finishing the task in forty days, the usual time required for embalming. 4 The Egyptians mourned Israel for seventy days. 5 When the period of mourning was over, Joseph spoke to members of Pharaoh's household: 'May I ask a favour—please speak for me to Pharaoh. Tell him that my father on his deathbed made me swear that I would bury him in the grave that he had bought for himself in Canaan. Ask Pharaoh to let me go up and bury my father; and afterwards I shall return.' 6 Pharaoh's reply was: 'Go and bury your father in accordance with your oath.' 7 So Joseph went up to bury his father, and with him went all Pharaoh's officials, the elders of his household, and all the elders of Egypt, 8 as well as all Joseph's own household, his brothers, and his father's household; only their children, with the flocks and herds, were left in Goshen. 9 Chariots as well as horsemen went up with him, a very great company.

10 When they came to the threshing-floor of Atad beside the river Jordan, they raised a loud and bitter lamentation; and Joseph observed seven days' mourning for his father. 11 When the Canaanites who lived there saw this mourning at the threshing-floor of Atad, they said, 'How bitterly the Egyptians are mourning!' So they named the place beside the Jordan Abel-mizraim.

12 Thus Jacob's sons did to him as he had instructed them: 13 they took him to Canaan and buried him in the cave on the plot of land at Machpelah, the land which Abraham had bought as a burial-place from Ephron the Hittite, to the east of Mamre. 14 After burying his father, Joseph returned to Egypt with his brothers and all who had gone up with him for the burial.

15 Now that their father was dead, Joseph's brothers were afraid, for they said, 'What if Joseph should bear a grudge against us and pay us back for all the harm we did to him?' 16 They therefore sent a messenger to Joseph to say, 'In his last words to us before he died, your father gave us this message: 17 "Say this to Joseph: I ask you to forgive your brothers' crime and wickedness; I know they did you harm." So now we beg you: forgive our crime, for we are servants of your father's God.' Joseph was moved to tears by their words. 18 His brothers approached and bowed to the ground before him. 'We are your slaves,' they said. 19 But Joseph replied, 'Do not be afraid. Am I in the place of God? 20 You meant to do me harm; but God meant to bring good out of it by preserving the lives of many people, as we see today. 21 Do not be afraid. I shall provide for you and your dependants.' Thus he comforted them and set their minds at rest.

---

m That is *mourning* (or *meadow*) *of Egypt*   *n* Gk Syr: Heb *they commanded*   *o* Cn: Heb *also came*

50:5 **bought:** *or* dug.   50:11 **Abel-mizraim:** *that is* Mourning of Egypt.

NEW AMERICAN BIBLE

28 All these are the twelve tribes of Israel, and this is what their father said about them, as he bade them farewell and gave to each of them an appropriate message. 29 Then he gave them this charge: "Since I am about to be taken to my kindred, bury me with my fathers in the cave that lies in the field of Ephron the Hittite, 30 the cave in the field of Machpelah, facing on Mamre, in the land of Canaan, the field that Abraham bought from Ephron the Hittite for a burial ground. 31 There Abraham and his wife Sarah are buried, and so are Isaac and his wife Rebekah, and there, too, I buried Leah— 32 the field and the cave in it that had been purchased from the Hittites."

33 When Jacob had finished giving these instructions to his sons, he drew his feet into the bed, breathed his last, and was taken to his kindred.

50 Joseph threw himself on his father's face and wept over him as he kissed him. 2 Then he ordered the physicians in his service to embalm his father. When they embalmed Israel, 3 they spent forty days at it, for that is the full period of embalming; and the Egyptians mourned him for seventy days. 4 When that period of mourning was over, Joseph spoke to Pharaoh's courtiers. "Please do me this favor," he said, "and convey to Pharaoh this request of mine. 5 Since my father, at the point of death, made me promise on oath to bury him in the tomb that he had prepared for himself in the land of Canaan, may I go up there to bury my father and then come back?" 6 Pharaoh replied, "Go and bury your father, as he made you promise on oath."

7 So Joseph left to bury his father; and with him went all of Pharaoh's officials who were senior members of his court and all the other dignitaries of Egypt, 8 as well as Joseph's whole household, his brothers, and his father's household; only their children and their flocks and herds were left in the region of Goshen. 9 Chariots, too, and charioteers went up with him; it was a very large retinue.

10 When they arrived at Goren-ha-atad, which is beyond the Jordan, they held there a very great and solemn memorial service; and Joseph observed seven days of mourning for his father. 11 When the Canaanites who inhabited the land saw the mourning at Goren-ha-atad, they said, "This is a solemn funeral the Egyptians are having." That is why the place was named Abel-mizraim. It is beyond the Jordan.

12 Thus Jacob's sons did for him as he had instructed them. 13 They carried him to the land of Canaan and buried him in the cave in the field of Machpelah, facing on Mamre, the field that Abraham had bought for a burial ground from Ephron the Hittite.

14 After Joseph had buried his father he returned to Egypt, together with his brothers and all who had gone up with him for the burial of his father.

15 Now that their father was dead, Joseph's brothers became fearful and thought, "Suppose Joseph has been nursing a grudge against us and now plans to pay us back in full for all the wrong we did him!" 16 So they approached Joseph and said: "Before your father died, he gave us these instructions: 17 'You shall say to Joseph, Jacob begs you to forgive the criminal wrongdoing of your brothers, who treated you so cruelly.' Please, therefore, forgive the crime that we, the servants of your father's God, committed." When they spoke these words to him, Joseph broke into tears. 18 Then his brothers proceeded to fling themselves down before him and said, "Let us be your slaves!" 19 But Joseph replied to them: "Have no fear. Can I take the place of God? 20 Even though you meant harm to me, God meant it for good, to achieve his present end, the survival of many people. 21 Therefore have no fear. I will provide for you and for your children." By thus speaking kindly to them, he reassured them.

NEW JERUSALEM BIBLE

28 All these make up the tribes of Israel, twelve in number, and this is what their father said to them as he bade them farewell, giving each an appropriate blessing.

29 w Then he gave them these instructions, 'I am about to be gathered to my people. Bury me with my ancestors, in the cave that is in the field of Ephron the Hittite, 30 in the cave in the field at Machpelah, facing Mamre, in Canaan, which Abraham bought from Ephron the Hittite as a burial site of his own. 31 There Abraham and his wife Sarah were buried. There Isaac and his wife Rebekah were buried; and there I buried Leah— 32 the field and the cave in it which were bought from the Hittites.'

33 When Jacob had finished giving his instructions to his sons, he drew his feet up into the bed, and breathing his last was gathered to his people.

50 At this Joseph threw himself on his father's face, covering it with tears and kisses. 2 Then Joseph ordered the doctors in his service to embalm his father. The doctors embalmed Israel, 3 and it took them forty days, for embalming takes forty days to complete.

The Egyptians mourned him for seventy days. 4 When the period of mourning for him was over, Joseph said to Pharaoh's household, 'If you have any affection for me, see that this message reaches Pharaoh's ears, 5 "My father put me under oath, saying: I am about to die. In the tomb which I dug for myself in Canaan, that is where you are to bury me. So may I have leave to go up and bury my father, and then come back?" ' 6 Pharaoh replied, 'Go up and bury your father, as he made you swear to do.' x

7 Joseph went up to bury his father, and with him went all Pharaoh's officials, the dignitaries of his palace and all the dignitaries of Egypt, 8 as well as all Joseph's family, his brothers and his father's family. The only people they left behind in Goshen were those unfit to travel, and their flocks and cattle. 9 Chariots and horsemen went up with him too; it was a very large retinue.

10 On arriving at Goren-ha-Atad, which is across the Jordan, they there held a long and solemn lamentation, and Joseph observed seven days' mourning for his father. 11 When the Canaanites, the local inhabitants, witnessed the mourning at Goren-ha-Atad, they said, 'This is a solemn act of mourning by the Egyptians,' which is why the place was given the name Abel-Mizraim—it is across the Jordan.

12 His sons did what he had ordered them to do for him. 13 His sons carried him to Canaan and buried him in the cave in the field at Machpelah, facing Mamre, which Abraham had bought from Ephron the Hittite as a burial site of his own.

14 Then Joseph returned to Egypt with his brothers and all those who had come up with him to bury his father.

15 Seeing that their father was dead, Joseph's brothers said, 'What if Joseph intends to treat us as enemies and pay us back for all the wrong we did him?' 16 So they sent this message to Joseph: 'Before your father died, he gave us this order: 17 "You are to say to Joseph: Now please forgive the crime and faults of your brothers and all the wrong they did you." So now please forgive the crime of the servants of your father's God.' Joseph wept at the message they sent to him.

18 Then his brothers went to him themselves and, throwing themselves at his feet, said, 'Take us as your slaves!' 19 But Joseph replied, 'Do not be afraid; is it for me to put myself in God's place? 20 The evil you planned to do me has by God's design been turned to good, to bring about the present result: the survival of a numerous people. 21 So there is no need to be afraid; I shall provide for you and your dependants.' In this way he reassured them by speaking affectionately to them.

w 49 49:29seq. = 47:29–31; = 50:6.   x 50 = 47:29–31; = 49:29–32.

NEW REVISED STANDARD VERSION

22 So Joseph remained in Egypt, he and his father's household; and Joseph lived one hundred ten years. 23 Joseph saw Ephraim's children of the third generation; the children of Machir son of Manasseh were also born on Joseph's knees.

24 Then Joseph said to his brothers, "I am about to die; but God will surely come to you, and bring you up out of this land to the land that he swore to Abraham, to Isaac, and to Jacob." 25 So Joseph made the Israelites swear, saying, "When God comes to you, you shall carry up my bones from here." 26 And Joseph died, being one hundred ten years old; he was embalmed and placed in a coffin in Egypt.

REVISED ENGLISH BIBLE

22 Joseph remained in Egypt, he and his father's household. He lived to be a hundred and ten years old, 23 and saw Ephraim's children to the third generation; he also recognized as his the children of Manasseh's son Machir. 24 He said to his brothers, 'I am about to die; but God will not fail to come to your aid and take you from here to the land which he promised on oath to Abraham, Isaac, and Jacob.' 25 He made the sons of Israel solemnly swear that when God came to their aid, they would carry his bones up with them from there. 26 So Joseph died in Egypt at the age of a hundred and ten, and he was embalmed and laid in a coffin.

22 Joseph remained in Egypt, together with his father's family. He lived a hundred and ten years. 23 He saw Ephraim's children to the third generation, and the children of Manasseh's son Machir were also born on Joseph's knees.

24 Joseph said to his brothers: "I am about to die. God will surely take care of you and lead you out of this land to the land that he promised on oath to Abraham, Isaac and Jacob." 25 Then, putting the sons of Israel under oath, he continued, "When God thus takes care of you, you must bring my bones up with you from this place." 26 Joseph died at the age of a hundred and ten. He was embalmed and laid to rest in a coffin in Egypt.

22 So Joseph stayed in Egypt with his father's family; and Joseph lived a hundred and ten years. 23 Joseph saw the third generation of Ephraim's line, as also the children of Machir son of Manasseh, who were born on Joseph's lap. 24 At length Joseph said to his brothers, 'I am about to die; but God will be sure to remember you kindly and take you out of this country to the country which he promised on oath to Abraham, Isaac and Jacob.' 25 And Joseph put Israel's sons on oath, saying, 'When God remembers you with kindness, be sure to take my bones away from here.'

26 Joseph died at the age of a hundred and ten; he was embalmed and laid in a coffin in Egypt.

Exodus

1 These are the names of the sons of Israel who came to Egypt with Jacob, each with his household: 2 Reuben, Simeon, Levi, and Judah, 3 Issachar, Zebulun, and Benjamin, 4 Dan and Naphtali, Gad and Asher. 5 The total number of people born to Jacob was seventy. Joseph was already in Egypt. 6 Then Joseph died, and all his brothers, and that whole generation. 7 But the Israelites were fruitful and prolific; they multiplied and grew exceedingly strong, so that the land was filled with them.

8 Now a new king arose over Egypt, who did not know Joseph. 9 He said to his people, "Look, the Israelite people are more numerous and more powerful than we. 10 Come, let us deal shrewdly with them, or they will increase and, in the event of war, join our enemies and fight against us and escape from the land." 11 Therefore they set taskmasters over them to oppress them with forced labor. They built supply cities, Pithom and Rameses, for Pharaoh. 12 But the more they were oppressed, the more they multiplied and spread, so that the Egyptians came to dread the Israelites. 13 The Egyptians became ruthless in imposing tasks on the Israelites, 14 and made their lives bitter with hard service in mortar and brick and in every kind of field labor. They were ruthless in all the tasks that they imposed on them.

15 The king of Egypt said to the Hebrew midwives, one of whom was named Shiphrah and the other Puah, 16 "When you act as midwives to the Hebrew women, and see them on the birthstool, if it is a boy, kill him; but if it is a girl, she shall live." 17 But the midwives feared God; they did not do as the king of Egypt commanded them, but they let the boys live. 18 So the king of Egypt summoned the midwives and said to them, "Why have you done this, and allowed the boys to live?" 19 The midwives said to Pharaoh, "Because the Hebrew women are not like the Egyptian women; for they are vigorous and give birth before the midwife comes to them." 20 So God dealt well with the midwives; and the people multiplied and became very strong. 21 And because the midwives feared God, he gave them families. 22 Then Pharaoh commanded all his people, "Every boy that is born to the Hebrews*a* you shall throw into the Nile, but you shall let every girl live."

2 Now a man from the house of Levi went and married a Levite woman. 2 The woman conceived and bore a son; and when she saw that he was a fine baby, she hid him three months. 3 When she could hide him no longer she got a papyrus basket for him, and plastered it with bitumen and pitch; she put the child in it and placed it among the reeds on the bank of the river. 4 His sister stood at a distance, to see what would happen to him.

5 The daughter of Pharaoh came down to bathe at the river, while her attendants walked beside the river. She saw the basket among the reeds and sent her maid to bring it. 6 When she opened it, she saw the child. He was crying, and she took pity on him, "This must be one of the Hebrews' children," she said. 7 Then his sister said to Pharaoh's daughter, "Shall I go and get you a nurse from the Hebrew women to nurse the child for you?" 8 Pharaoh's daughter said to her, "Yes." So the girl went and called the child's mother. 9 Pharaoh's daughter said to her, "Take this child

Exodus

1 THESE are the names of the sons of Israel who, along with their households, accompanied Jacob to Egypt: 2 Reuben, Simeon, Levi, and Judah; 3 Issachar, Zebulun, and Benjamin; 4 Dan and Naphtali, Gad and Asher. 5 All told there were seventy direct descendants of Jacob. Joseph was already in Egypt.

6 In course of time Joseph and all his brothers and that entire generation died. 7 The Israelites were prolific and increased greatly, becoming so numerous and strong that the land was full of them. 8 When a new king ascended the throne of Egypt, one who did not know about Joseph, 9 he said to his people, 'These Israelites have become too many and too strong for us. 10 We must take steps to ensure that they increase no further; otherwise we shall find that, if war comes, they will side with our enemies, fight against us, and become masters of the country.' 11 So taskmasters were appointed over them to oppress them with forced labour. This is how Pharaoh's store cities, Pithom and Rameses, were built. 12 But the more oppressive the treatment of the Israelites, the more they increased and spread, until the Egyptians came to loathe them. 13 They ground down their Israelite slaves, 14 and made life bitter for them with their harsh demands, setting them to make mortar and bricks and to do all sorts of tasks in the fields. In every kind of labour they made ruthless use of them.

15 The king of Egypt issued instructions to the Hebrew midwives, of whom one was called Shiphrah, the other Puah. 16 'When you are attending the Hebrew women in childbirth,' he told them, 'check as the child is delivered: if it is a boy, kill him; if it is a girl, however, let her live.' 17 But the midwives were godfearing women, and did not heed the king's words; they let the male children live. 18 Pharaoh summoned the midwives and, when he asked them why they had done this and let the male children live, 19 they answered, 'Hebrew women are not like Egyptian women; they go into labour and give birth before the midwife arrives.' 20 God made the midwives prosper, and the people increased in numbers and strength; 21 and because the midwives feared God he gave them families of their own. 22 Pharaoh then issued an order to all the Egyptians that every new-born Hebrew boy was to be thrown into the Nile, but all the girls were to be allowed to live.

2 A CERTAIN man, a descendant of Levi, married a Levite woman. 2 She conceived and bore a son, and when she saw what a fine child he was, she kept him hidden for three months. 3 Unable to conceal him any longer, she got a rush basket for him, made it watertight with pitch and tar, laid him in it, and placed it among the reeds by the bank of the Nile. 4 The child's sister stood some distance away to see what would happen to him.

5 Pharaoh's daughter came down to bathe in the river, while her ladies-in-waiting walked on the bank. She noticed the basket among the reeds and sent her slave-girl to bring it. 6 When she opened it, there was the baby; it was crying, and she was moved with pity for it. 'This must be one of the Hebrew children,' she said. 7 At this the sister approached Pharaoh's daughter: 'Shall I go and fetch you one of the Hebrew women to act as a wet-nurse for the child?' 8 When Pharaoh's daughter told her to do so, she went and called the baby's mother. 9 Pharaoh's daughter said to her, 'Take

---

a Sam Gk Tg: Heb lacks *to the Hebrews*

1:10 **become . . . country:** *or* escape from the country.

THE BOOK OF
Exodus

Exodus

1 These are the names of the sons of Israel who, accompanied by their households, migrated with Jacob into Egypt: 2 Reuben, Simeon, Levi and Judah; 3 Issachar, Zebulun and Benjamin; 4 Dan and Naphtali; Gad and Asher. 5 The total number of the direct descendants of Jacob was seventy. Joseph was already in Egypt.

6 Now Joseph and all his brothers and that whole generation died. 7 But the Israelites were fruitful and prolific. They became so numerous and strong that the land was filled with them.

8 Then a new king, who knew nothing of Joseph, came to power in Egypt. 9 He said to his subjects, "Look how numerous and powerful the Israelite people are growing, more so than we ourselves! 10 Come, let us deal shrewdly with them to stop their increase; otherwise, in time of war they too may join our enemies to fight against us, and so leave our country."

11 Accordingly, taskmasters were set over the Israelites to oppress them with forced labor. Thus they had to build for Pharaoh the supply cities of Pithom and Raamses. 12 Yet the more they were oppressed, the more they multiplied and spread. The Egyptians, then, dreaded the Israelites 13 and reduced them to cruel slavery, 14 making life bitter for them with hard work in mortar and brick and all kinds of field work — the whole cruel fate of slaves.

15 The king of Egypt told the Hebrew midwives, one of whom was called Shiphrah and the other Puah, 16 "When you act as midwives for the Hebrew women and see them giving birth, if it is a boy, kill him; but if it is a girl, she may live." 17 The midwives, however, feared God; they did not do as the king of Egypt had ordered them, but let the boys live. 18 So the king summoned the midwives and asked them, "Why have you acted thus, allowing the boys to live?" 19 The midwives answered Pharaoh, "The Hebrew women are not like the Egyptian women. They are robust and give birth before the midwife arrives." 20 Therefore God dealt well with the midwives. The people, too, increased and grew strong. 21 And because the midwives feared God, he built up families for them. 22 Pharaoh then commanded all his subjects, "Throw into the river every boy that is born to the Hebrews, but you may let all the girls live."

2 Now a certain man of the house of Levi married a Levite woman, 2 who conceived and bore a son. Seeing that he was a goodly child, she hid him for three months. 3 When she could hide him no longer, she took a papyrus basket, daubed it with bitumen and pitch, and putting the child in it, placed it among the reeds on the river bank. 4 His sister stationed herself at a distance to find out what would happen to him.

5 Pharaoh's daughter came down to the river to bathe, while her maids walked along the river bank. Noticing the basket among the reeds, she sent her handmaid to fetch it. 6 On opening it, she looked, and lo, there was a baby boy, crying! She was moved with pity for him and said, "It is one of the Hebrews' children." 7 Then his sister asked Pharaoh's daughter, "Shall I go and call one of the Hebrew women to nurse the child for you?" 8 "Yes, do so," she answered. So the maiden went and called the child's own mother. 9 Phar-

1 These are the names of the Israelites who went with Jacob to Egypt, each of them went with his family: 2 Reuben, Simeon, Levi and Judah, 3 Issachar, Zebulun and Benjamin, 4 Dan and Naphtali, Gad and Asher. 5 In all, the descendants of Jacob numbered seventy persons. Joseph was in Egypt already. 6 Then Joseph died, and his brothers, and all that generation. 7 But the Israelites were fruitful and prolific; they became so numerous and powerful that eventually the whole land was full of them.

8 Then there came to power in Egypt a new king who had never heard of Joseph. 9 'Look,' he said to his people, 'the Israelites are now more numerous and stronger than we are. 10 We must take precautions to stop them from increasing any further, or if war should break out, they might join the ranks of our enemies. They might take arms against us and then escape from the country.' 11 Accordingly they put taskmasters over the Israelites to wear them down by forced labour. In this way they built the store-cities of Pithom and Rameses for Pharaoh. 12 But the harder their lives were made, the more they increased and spread, until people came to fear the Israelites. 13 So the Egyptians gave them no mercy in the demands they made, 14 making their lives miserable with hard labour: with digging clay, making bricks, doing various kinds of field-work — all sorts of labour that they imposed on them without mercy.

15 The king of Egypt then spoke to the Hebrew midwives, one of whom was called Shiphrah, and the other Puah. 16 'When you attend Hebrew women in childbirth,' he said, 'look at the two stones. If it is a boy, kill him; if a girl, let her live.' 17 But the midwives were God-fearing women and did not obey the orders of the king of Egypt, but allowed the boys to live. 18 So the king of Egypt summoned the midwives and said to them, 'What do you mean by allowing the boys to live?' 19 The midwives said to Pharaoh, 'Hebrew women are not like Egyptian women, they are hardy and give birth before the midwife can get to them.' 20 For this, God was good to the midwives, and the people went on increasing and growing more powerful; 21 and since the midwives feared God, he gave them families of their own.

22 Pharaoh then gave all his people this command: 'Throw every new-born boy into the river, but let all the girls live.'

2 There was a man descended from Levi who had taken a woman of Levi as his wife. 2 She conceived and gave birth to a son and, seeing what a fine child he was, she kept him hidden for three months. 3 When she could hide him no longer, she got a papyrus basket for him; coating it with bitumen and pitch, she put the child inside and laid it among the reeds at the River's edge. 4 His sister took up position some distance away to see what would happen to him.

5 Now Pharaoh's daughter went down to bathe in the river, while her maids walked along the riverside. Among the reeds she noticed the basket, and she sent her maid to fetch it. 6 She opened it and saw the child: the baby was crying. Feeling sorry for it, she said, 'This is one of the little Hebrews.' 7 The child's sister then said to Pharaoh's daughter, 'Shall I go and find you a nurse among the Hebrew women to nurse the child for you?' 8 'Yes,' said Pharaoh's daughter, and the girl went and called the child's own mother. 9 Pharaoh's daughter said to her, 'Take this child

and nurse it for me, and I will give you your wages." So the woman took the child and nursed it. 10 When the child grew up, she brought him to Pharaoh's daughter, and she took him as her son. She named him Moses,*b* "because," she said, "I drew him out*c* of the water."

11 One day, after Moses had grown up, he went out to his people and saw their forced labor. He saw an Egyptian beating a Hebrew, one of his kinsfolk. 12 He looked this way and that, and seeing no one he killed the Egyptian and hid him in the sand. 13 When he went out the next day, he saw two Hebrews fighting; and he said to the one who was in the wrong, "Why do you strike your fellow Hebrew?" 14 He answered, "Who made you a ruler and judge over us? Do you mean to kill me as you killed the Egyptian?" Then Moses was afraid and thought, "Surely the thing is known." 15 When Pharaoh heard of it, he sought to kill Moses.

But Moses fled from Pharaoh. He settled in the land of Midian, and sat down by a well. 16 The priest of Midian had seven daughters. They came to draw water, and filled the troughs to water their father's flock. 17 But some shepherds came and drove them away. Moses got up and came to their defense and watered their flock. 18 When they returned to their father Reuel, he said, "How is it that you have come back so soon today?" 19 They said, "An Egyptian helped us against the shepherds; he even drew water for us and watered the flock." 20 He said to his daughters, "Where is he? Why did you leave the man? Invite him to break bread." 21 Moses agreed to stay with the man, and he gave Moses his daughter Zipporah in marriage. 22 She bore a son, and he named him Gershom; for he said, "I have been an alien*d* residing in a foreign land."

23 After a long time the king of Egypt died. The Israelites groaned under their slavery, and cried out. Out of the slavery their cry for help rose up to God. 24 God heard their groaning, and God remembered his covenant with Abraham, Isaac, and Jacob. 25 God looked upon the Israelites, and God took notice of them.

3 Moses was keeping the flock of his father-in-law Jethro, the priest of Midian; he led his flock beyond the wilderness, and came to Horeb, the mountain of God. 2 There the angel of the Lord appeared to him in a flame of fire out of a bush; he looked, and the bush was blazing, yet it was not consumed. 3 Then Moses said, "I must turn aside and look at this great sight, and see why the bush is not burned up." 4 When the Lord saw that he had turned aside to see, God called to him out of the bush, "Moses, Moses!" And he said, "Here I am." 5 Then he said, "Come no closer! Remove the sandals from your feet, for the place on which you are standing is holy ground." 6 He said further, "I am the God of your father, the God of Abraham, the God of Isaac, and the God of Jacob." And Moses hid his face, for he was afraid to look at God.

7 Then the Lord said, "I have observed the misery of my people who are in Egypt; I have heard their cry on account of their taskmasters. Indeed, I know their sufferings, 8 and I have come down to deliver them from the Egyptians, and to bring them up out of that land to a good and broad land, a land flowing with milk and honey, to the country of the Canaanites, the Hittites, the Amorites, the Perizzites, the Hivites, and the Jebusites. 9 The cry of the Israelites has now come to me; I have also seen how the Egyptians oppress them. 10 So come, I will send you to

the child, nurse him for me, and I shall pay you for it.' She took the child and nursed him at her breast. 10 Then, when he was old enough, she brought him to Pharaoh's daughter, who adopted him and called him Moses, 'because', said she, 'I drew him out of the water'.

11 One day after Moses was grown up, he went out to his own kinsmen and observed their labours. When he saw an Egyptian strike one of his fellow-Hebrews, 12 he looked this way and that, and, seeing no one about, he struck the Egyptian down and hid his body in the sand. 13 Next day when he went out, he came across two Hebrews fighting. He asked the one who was in the wrong, 'Why are you striking your fellow-countryman?' 14 The man replied, 'Who set you up as an official and judge over us? Do you mean to murder me as you murdered the Egyptian?' Moses was alarmed and said to himself, 'The affair must have become known.' 15 When it came to Pharaoh's ears, he tried to have Moses put to death, but Moses fled from his presence and went and settled in Midian.

As Moses sat by a well one day, 16 the seven daughters of a priest of Midian came to draw water, and when they had filled the troughs to water their father's sheep, 17 some shepherds came and drove them away. But Moses came to the help of the girls and watered the sheep. 18 When they returned to Reuel, their father, he said, 'How is it that you are back so quickly today?' 19 'An Egyptian rescued us from the shepherds,' they answered; 'he even drew water for us and watered the sheep.' 20 'Then where is he?' their father asked. 'Why did you leave him there? Go and invite him to eat with us.' 21 So it came about that Moses agreed to stay with the man, and he gave Moses his daughter Zipporah in marriage. 22 She bore him a son, and Moses called him Gershom, 'because', he said, 'I have become an alien in a foreign land.'

23 Years passed, during which time the king of Egypt died, but the Israelites still groaned in slavery. They cried out, and their plea for rescue from slavery ascended to God. 24 He heard their groaning and called to mind his covenant with Abraham, Isaac, and Jacob; 25 he observed the plight of Israel and took heed of it.

3 While tending the sheep of his father-in-law Jethro, priest of Midian, Moses led the flock along the west side of the wilderness and came to Horeb, the mountain of God. 2 There an angel of the Lord appeared to him as a fire blazing out from a bush. Although the bush was on fire, it was not being burnt up, 3 and Moses said to himself, 'I must go across and see this remarkable sight. Why ever does the bush not burn away?' 4 When the Lord saw that Moses had turned aside to look, he called to him out of the bush, 'Moses, Moses!' He answered, 'Here I am!' 5 God said, 'Do not come near! Take off your sandals, for the place where you are standing is holy ground.' 6 Then he said, 'I am the God of your father, the God of Abraham, Isaac, and Jacob.' Moses hid his face, for he was afraid to look at God.

7 The Lord said, 'I have witnessed the misery of my people in Egypt and have heard them crying out because of their oppressors. I know what they are suffering 8 and have come down to rescue them from the power of the Egyptians and to bring them up out of that country into a fine, broad land, a land flowing with milk and honey, the territory of Canaanites, Amorites, Perizzites, Hivites, and Jebusites. 9 Now the Israelites' cry has reached me, and I have also seen how hard the Egyptians oppress them. 10 Come, I

---

b Heb *Mosheh*   *c* Heb *mashah*   *d* Heb *ger*

2:10 **Moses:** *Heb*. Mosheh. **drew:** *Heb. verb* mashah.
2:22 **alien:** *Heb*. ger.   3:2 **as a fire:** *or* in a fire.

aoh's daughter said to her, "Take this child and nurse it for me, and I will repay you." The woman therefore took the child and nursed it. 10 When the child grew, she brought him to Pharaoh's daughter, who adopted him as her son and called him Moses; for she said, "I drew him out of the water."

11 On one occasion, after Moses had grown up, when he visited his kinsmen and witnessed their forced labor, he saw an Egyptian striking a Hebrew, one of his own kinsmen. 12 Looking about and seeing no one, he slew the Egyptian and hid him in the sand. 13 The next day he went out again, and now two Hebrews were fighting! So he asked the culprit, "Why are you striking your fellow Hebrew?" 14 But he replied, "Who has appointed you ruler and judge over us? Are you thinking of killing me as you killed the Egyptian?" Then Moses became afraid and thought, "The affair must certainly be known."

15 Pharaoh, too, heard of the affair and sought to put him to death. But Moses fled from him and stayed in the land of Midian. As he was seated there by a well, 16 seven daughters of a priest of Midian came to draw water and fill the troughs to water their father's flock. 17 But some shepherds came and drove them away. Then Moses got up and defended them and watered their flock. 18 When they returned to their father Reuel, he said to them, "How is it you have returned so soon today?" 19 They answered, "An Egyptian saved us from the interference of the shepherds. He even drew water for us and watered the flock!" 20 "Where is the man?" he asked his daughters. "Why did you leave him there? Invite him to have something to eat." 21 Moses agreed to live with him, and the man gave him his daughter Zipporah in marriage. 22 She bore him a son, whom he named Gershom; for he said, "I am a stranger in a foreign land."

23 A long time passed, during which the king of Egypt died. Still the Israelites groaned and cried out because of their slavery. As their cry for release went up to God, 24 he heard their groaning and was mindful of his covenant with Abraham, Isaac and Jacob. 25 He saw the Israelites and knew. . . .

3 Meanwhile Moses was tending the flock of his father-in-law Jethro, the priest of Midian. Leading the flock across the desert, he came to Horeb, the mountain of God. 2 There an angel of the LORD appeared to him in fire flaming out of a bush. As he looked on, he was surprised to see that the bush, though on fire, was not consumed. 3 So Moses decided, "I must go over to look at this remarkable sight, and see why the bush is not burned."

4 When the LORD saw him coming over to look at it more closely, God called out to him from the bush, "Moses! Moses!" He answered, "Here I am." 5 God said, "Come no nearer! Remove the sandals from your feet, for the place where you stand is holy ground. 6 I am the God of your father," he continued, "the God of Abraham, the God of Isaac, the God of Jacob." Moses hid his face, for he was afraid to look at God. 7 But the LORD said, "I have witnessed the affliction of my people in Egypt and have heard their cry of complaint against their slave drivers, so I know well what they are suffering. 8 Therefore I have come down to rescue them from the hands of the Egyptians and lead them out of that land into a good and spacious land, a land flowing with milk and honey, the country of the Canaanites, Hittites, Amorites, Perizzites, Hivites and Jebusites. 9 So indeed the cry of the Israelites has reached me, and I have truly noted that the Egyptians are oppressing them.

away and nurse it for me. I shall pay you myself for doing so.' So the woman took the child away and nursed it. 10 When the child grew up, she brought him to Pharaoh's daughter who treated him like a son; she named him Moses 'because', she said, 'I drew him out of the water.'[a]

11 It happened one day, when Moses was grown up, that he went to see his kinsmen. While he was watching their forced labour he also saw an Egyptian striking a Hebrew, one of his kinsmen. 12 Looking this way and that and seeing no one in sight, he killed the Egyptian and hid him in the sand. 13 On the following day he came back, and there were two Hebrews, fighting. He said to the man who was in the wrong, 'What do you mean by hitting your kinsman?' 14 'And who appointed you', the man retorted, 'to be prince over us and judge? Do you intend to kill me as you killed the Egyptian?' Moses was frightened. 'Clearly that business has come to light,' he thought. 15 When Pharaoh heard of the matter, he tried to put Moses to death, but Moses fled from Pharaoh. He went into Midianite territory and sat down beside a well.

16 Now there was a priest of Midian with seven daughters. They used to come to draw water and fill the troughs to water their father's flock. 17 Some shepherds came and drove them away, but Moses sprang to their help and watered their flock. 18 When they returned to their father Reuel, he said to them, 'Why are you back so early today?' 19 'An Egyptian protected us from the shepherds,' they said, 'and he even drew water for us and watered the flock.' 20 'And where is he?' he asked his daughters. 'Why did you leave the man there? Ask him to eat with us.' 21 Moses agreed to stay on there with the man, who gave him his daughter Zipporah in marriage. 22 She gave birth to a son, whom he named Gershom 'because', he said, 'I am an alien in a foreign land.'

23 During this long period the king of Egypt died. The Israelites, groaning in their slavery, cried out for help and from the depths of their slavery their cry came up to God. 24 God heard their groaning; God remembered his covenant with Abraham, Isaac and Jacob. 25 God saw the Israelites and took note.

3 [b] Moses was looking after the flock of his father-in-law Jethro, the priest of Midian; he led it to the far side of the desert and came to Horeb, the mountain of God. 2 The angel of Yahweh appeared to him in a flame blazing from the middle of a bush. Moses looked; there was the bush blazing, but the bush was not being burnt up. 3 Moses said, 'I must go across and see this strange sight, and why the bush is not being burnt up.' 4 When Yahweh saw him going across to look, God called to him from the middle of the bush. 'Moses, Moses!' he said. 'Here I am,' he answered. 5 'Come no nearer,' he said. 'Take off your sandals, for the place where you are standing is holy ground. 6 I am the God of your ancestors,' he said, 'the God of Abraham, the God of Isaac and the God of Jacob.' At this Moses covered his face, for he was afraid to look at God.

7 Yahweh then said, 'I have indeed seen the misery of my people in Egypt. I have heard them crying for help on account of their taskmasters. Yes, I am well aware of their sufferings. 8 And I have come down to rescue them from the clutches of the Egyptians and bring them up out of that country, to a country rich and broad, to a country flowing with milk and honey, to the home of the Canaanites, the Hittites, the Amorites, the Perizzites, the Hivites and the Jebusites. 9 Yes indeed, the Israelites' cry for help has reached me, and I have also seen the cruel way in which the Egyptians are oppressing them. 10 So now I am sending you

a 2 Popular Hebr. explanation of an Egyptian name.
b 3 3:1seq. = 6:2–13.

Pharaoh to bring my people, the Israelites, out of Egypt." 11 But Moses said to God, "Who am I that I should go to Pharaoh, and bring the Israelites out of Egypt?" 12 He said, "I will be with you; and this shall be the sign for you that it is I who sent you: when you have brought the people out of Egypt, you shall worship God on this mountain."

13 But Moses said to God, "If I come to the Israelites and say to them, 'The God of your ancestors has sent me to you,' and they ask me, 'What is his name?' what shall I say to them?" 14 God said to Moses, "I AM WHO I AM."*e* He said further, "Thus you shall say to the Israelites, 'I AM has sent me to you.'" 15 God also said to Moses, "Thus you shall say to the Israelites, 'The LORD,*f* the God of your ancestors, the God of Abraham, the God of Isaac, and the God of Jacob, has sent me to you':

This is my name forever,
and this my title for all generations.

16 Go and assemble the elders of Israel, and say to them, 'The LORD, the God of your ancestors, the God of Abraham, of Isaac, and of Jacob, has appeared to me, saying: I have given heed to you and to what has been done to you in Egypt. 17 I declare that I will bring you up out of the misery of Egypt, to the land of the Canaanites, the Hittites, the Amorites, the Perizzites, the Hivites, and the Jebusites, a land flowing with milk and honey.' 18 They will listen to your voice; and you and the elders of Israel shall go to the king of Egypt and say to him, 'The LORD, the God of the Hebrews, has met with us; let us now go a three days' journey into the wilderness, so that we may sacrifice to the LORD our God.' 19 I know, however, that the king of Egypt will not let you go unless compelled by a mighty hand.*g* 20 So I will stretch out my hand and strike Egypt with all my wonders that I will perform in it; after that he will let you go. 21 I will bring this people into such favor with the Egyptians that, when you go, you will not go empty-handed; 22 each woman shall ask her neighbor and any woman living in the neighbor's house for jewelry of silver and of gold, and clothing, and you shall put them on your sons and on your daughters; and so you shall plunder the Egyptians."

4 Then Moses answered, "But suppose they do not believe me or listen to me, but say, 'The LORD did not appear to you.'" 2 The LORD said to him, "What is that in your hand?" He said, "A staff." 3 And he said, "Throw it on the ground." So he threw the staff on the ground, and it became a snake; and Moses drew back from it. 4 Then the LORD said to Moses, "Reach out your hand, and seize it by the tail"—so he reached out his hand and grasped it, and it became a staff in his hand— 5 "so that they may believe that the LORD, the God of their ancestors, the God of Abraham, the God of Isaac, and the God of Jacob, has appeared to you."

6 Again, the LORD said to him, "Put your hand inside your cloak." He put his hand into his cloak; and when he took it out, his hand was leprous,*h* as white as snow. 7 Then God said, "Put your hand back into your cloak"—so he put his hand back into his cloak, and when he took it out, it was restored like the rest of his body— 8 "If they will not believe you or heed the first sign, they may believe the second sign. 9 If they will not believe even these two signs or heed you, you shall take some water from the Nile and pour it on the dry ground; and the water that you shall take from the Nile will become blood on the dry ground."

shall send you to Pharaoh, and you are to bring my people Israel out of Egypt." 11 'But who am I', Moses said to God, 'that I should approach Pharaoh and that I should bring the Israelites out of Egypt?' 12 God answered, 'I am with you. This will be your proof that it is I who have sent you: when you have brought the people out of Egypt, you will all worship God here at this mountain.'

13 Moses said to God, 'If I come to the Israelites and tell them that the God of their forefathers has sent me to them, and they ask me his name, what am I to say to them?' 14 God answered, 'I AM that I am. Tell them that I AM has sent you to them.' 15 He continued, 'You are to tell the Israelites that it is the LORD, the God of their forefathers, the God of Abraham, Isaac, and Jacob, who has sent you to them. This is my name for ever; this is my title in every generation.

16 'Go and assemble the elders of Israel; tell them that the LORD, the God of their forefathers, the God of Abraham, Isaac, and Jacob, has appeared to you and said, "I have watched over you and have seen what has been done to you in Egypt, 17 and I have resolved to bring you up out of the misery of Egypt into the country of the Canaanites, Hittites, Amorites, Perizzites, Hivites, and Jebusites, a land flowing with milk and honey." 18 The elders will attend to what you say, and then you must go along with them to the king of Egypt and say to him, "The LORD the God of the Hebrews has encountered us. Now, we request you to give us leave to go a three days' journey into the wilderness to offer sacrifice to the LORD our God." 19 I know well that the king of Egypt will not allow you to go unless he is compelled. 20 I shall then stretch out my hand and assail the Egyptians with all the miracles I shall work among them. After that he will send you away. 21 What is more, I shall bring this people into such favour with the Egyptians that, when you go, you will not go empty-handed. 22 Every woman must ask her neighbour or any woman living in her house for silver and gold jewellery and for clothing; put them on your sons and daughters, and plunder the Egyptians.'

4 'But they will never believe me or listen to what I say,' Moses protested; 'they will say that it is untrue that the LORD appeared to me.' 2 The LORD said, 'What is that in your hand?' 'A staff,' replied Moses. 3 The LORD said, 'Throw it on the ground.' He did so, and it turned into a snake. Moses drew back hastily, 4 but the LORD said, 'Put your hand out and seize it by the tail.' When he took hold of it, it turned back into a staff in his hand. 5 'This', said the LORD, 'is to convince the people that the LORD the God of their forefathers, the God of Abraham, of Isaac, and of Jacob, did appear to you.'

6 Then the LORD said to him, 'Put your hand inside the fold of your cloak.' He did so, and when he drew his hand out the skin was white as snow with disease. 7 The LORD said, 'Put your hand in again'; he did so, and when he drew it out this time it was as healthy as the rest of his body. 8 'Now,' said the LORD, 'if they do not believe you and do not accept the evidence of the first sign, they may be persuaded by the second. 9 But if they are not convinced even by these two signs and will not accept what you say, then fetch some water from the Nile and pour it out on the dry land, and the water from the Nile will turn to blood on the ground.'

---

e Or *I AM WHAT I AM* or *I WILL BE WHAT I WILL BE*   *f* The word "LORD" when spelled with capital letters stands for the divine name, *YHWH*, which is here connected with the verb *hayah*, "to be"   *g* Gk Vg: Heb *no, not by a mighty hand*   *h* A term for several skin diseases; precise meaning uncertain

3:12 **I am:** *or* I shall be.   3:14 **I AM . . . I am:** *or* I will be what I will be.   3:15 **the LORD:** *the Hebrew consonants are* YHWH, *probably pronounced* Yahweh, *but traditionally read* Jehovah.

10 Come, now! I will send you to Pharaoh to lead my people, the Israelites, out of Egypt."

11 But Moses said to God, "Who am I that I should go to Pharaoh and lead the Israelites out of Egypt?" 12 He answered, "I will be with you; and this shall be your proof that it is I who have sent you: when you bring my people out of Egypt, you will worship God on this very mountain." 13 "But," said Moses to God, "when I go to the Israelites and say to them, 'The God of your fathers has sent me to you,' if they ask me, 'What is his name?' what am I to tell them?" 14 God replied, "I am who am." Then he added, "This is what you shall tell the Israelites: I AM sent me to you."

15 God spoke further to Moses, "Thus shall you say to the Israelites: The LORD, the God of your fathers, the God of Abraham, the God of Isaac, the God of Jacob, has sent me to you.

"This is my name forever;
    this is my title for all generations.

16 "Go and assemble the elders of the Israelites, and tell them: The LORD, the God of your fathers, the God of Abraham, Isaac and Jacob, has appeared to me and said: I am concerned about you and about the way you are being treated in Egypt; 17 so I have decided to lead you up out of the misery of Egypt into the land of the Canaanites, Hittites, Amorites, Perizzites, Hivites and Jebusites, a land flowing with milk and honey.

18 "Thus they will heed your message. Then you and the elders of Israel shall go to the king of Egypt and say to him: The LORD, the God of the Hebrews, has sent us word. Permit us, then, to go a three-days' journey in the desert, that we may offer sacrifice to the LORD, our God.

19 "Yet I know that the king of Egypt will not allow you to go unless he is forced. 20 I will stretch out my hand, therefore, and smite Egypt by doing all kinds of wondrous deeds there. After that he will send you away. 21 I will even make the Egyptians so well-disposed toward this people that, when you leave, you will not go empty-handed. 22 Every woman shall ask her neighbor and her house guest for silver and gold articles and for clothing to put on your sons and daughters. Thus you will despoil the Egyptians."

4 "But," objected Moses, "suppose they will not believe me, nor listen to my plea? For they may say, 'The LORD did not appear to you.' " 2 The LORD therefore asked him, "What is that in your hand?" "A staff," he answered. 3 The LORD then said, "Throw it on the ground." When he threw it on the ground it was changed into a serpent, and Moses shied away from it. 4 "Now, put out your hand," the LORD said to him, "and take hold of its tail." So he put out his hand and laid hold of it, and it became a staff in his hand. 5 "This will take place so that they may believe," he continued, "that the LORD, the God of their fathers, the God of Abraham, the God of Isaac, the God of Jacob, did appear to you."

6 Again the LORD said to him, "Put your hand in your bosom." He put it in his bosom, and when he withdrew it, to his surprise his hand was leprous, like snow. 7 The LORD then said, "Now, put your hand back in your bosom." Moses put his hand back in his bosom, and when he withdrew it, to his surprise it was again like the rest of his body. 8 "If they will not believe you, nor heed the message of the first sign, they should believe the message of the second. 9 And if they will not believe even these two signs, nor heed your plea, take some water from the river and pour it on the dry land. The water you take from the river will become blood on the dry land."

to Pharaoh, for you to bring my people the Israelites out of Egypt.'

11 Moses said to God, 'Who am I to go to Pharaoh and bring the Israelites out of Egypt?' 12 'I shall be with you,' God said, 'and this is the sign by which you will know that I was the one who sent you. After you have led the people out of Egypt, you will worship God on this mountain.'

13 Moses then said to God, 'Look, if I go to the Israelites and say to them, "The God of your ancestors has sent me to you," and they say to me, "What is his name?" what am I to tell them?' 14 God said to Moses, 'I am he who is.' And he said, 'This is what you are to say to the Israelites, "I am has sent me to you." ' 15 God further said to Moses, 'You are to tell the Israelites, "Yahweh,c the God of your ancestors, the God of Abraham, the God of Isaac and the God of Jacob, has sent me to you." This is my name for all time, and thus I am to be invoked for all generations to come.

16 'Go, gather the elders of Israel together and tell them, "Yahweh, the God of your ancestors, has appeared to me — the God of Abraham, of Isaac and of Jacob — and has indeed visited you and seen what is being done to you in Egypt, 17 and has said: I shall bring you out of the misery of Egypt to the country of the Canaanites, the Hittites, the Amorites, the Perizzites, the Hivites and the Jebusites, to a country flowing with milk and honey." 18 They will listen to your words, and you and the elders of Israel are to go to the king of Egypt and say to him, "Yahweh, the God of the Hebrews, has encountered us. So now please allow us to make a three-days' journey into the desert and sacrifice to Yahweh our God." 19 I am well aware that the king of Egypt will not let you go unless he is compelled by a mighty hand; 20 he will not let you go until I have stretched out my arm and struck Egypt with all the wonders I intend to work there.

21 'I shall ensure that the Egyptians are so much impressed with this people that when you go, you will not go empty-handed. 22 Every woman will ask her neighbour and the woman staying in her house for silver and golden jewellery, and clothing. In these you will dress your own sons and daughters, despoiling the Egyptians of them.'

4 Moses replied as follows, 'But suppose they will not believe me or listen to my words, and say to me, "Yahweh has not appeared to you"?' 2 Yahweh then said, 'What is that in your hand?' 'A staff,' he said. 3 'Throw it on the ground,' said Yahweh. Moses threw it on the ground; the staff turned into a snake and Moses recoiled from it. 4 Yahweh then said to Moses, 'Reach out your hand and catch it by the tail.' He reached out his hand, caught it, and in his hand it turned back into a staff. 5 'Thus they may believe that Yahweh, the God of their ancestors, the God of Abraham, the God of Isaac and the God of Jacob, has appeared to you.'

6 Next, Yahweh said to him, 'Put your hand inside your tunic.' He put his hand inside his tunic, then drew it out again: and his hand was diseased, white as snow. 7 Yahweh then said, 'Put your hand back inside your tunic.' He put his hand back inside his tunic and when he drew it out, there it was restored, just like the rest of his flesh. 8 'Even so: should they not believe you nor be convinced by the first sign, the second sign will convince them; 9 but should they not be convinced by either of these two signs and refuse to listen to what you say, you are to take some water from the River and pour it on the ground, and the water you have taken from the River will turn to blood on the dry land.'

c 3 'Yahweh' may be some form of the verb 'to be'. God either refuses to give a name or reveals that he is the key to existence. The Gk understands it as a statement that God is Being itself.

NEW REVISED STANDARD VERSION

10 But Moses said to the LORD, "O my Lord, I have never been eloquent, neither in the past nor even now that you have spoken to your servant; but I am slow of speech and slow of tongue." 11 Then the LORD said to him, "Who gives speech to mortals? Who makes them mute or deaf, seeing or blind? Is it not I, the LORD? 12 Now go, and I will be with your mouth and teach you what you are to speak." 13 But he said, "O my Lord, please send someone else." 14 Then the anger of the LORD was kindled against Moses and he said, "What of your brother Aaron, the Levite? I know that he can speak fluently; even now he is coming out to meet you, and when he sees you his heart will be glad. 15 You shall speak to him and put the words in his mouth; and I will be with your mouth and with his mouth, and will teach you what you shall do. 16 He indeed shall speak for you to the people; he shall serve as a mouth for you, and you shall serve as God for him. 17 Take in your hand this staff, with which you shall perform the signs."

18 Moses went back to his father-in-law Jethro and said to him, "Please let me go back to my kindred in Egypt and see whether they are still living." And Jethro said to Moses, "Go in peace." 19 The LORD said to Moses in Midian, "Go back to Egypt; for all those who were seeking your life are dead." 20 So Moses took his wife and his sons, put them on a donkey and went back to the land of Egypt; and Moses carried the staff of God in his hand.

21 And the LORD said to Moses, "When you go back to Egypt, see that you perform before Pharaoh all the wonders that I have put in your power; but I will harden his heart, so that he will not let the people go. 22 Then you shall say to Pharaoh, 'Thus says the LORD: Israel is my firstborn son. 23 I said to you, "Let my son go that he may worship me." But you refused to let him go; now I will kill your firstborn son.' "

24 On the way, at a place where they spent the night, the LORD met him and tried to kill him. 25 But Zipporah took a flint and cut off her son's foreskin, and touched Moses'[i] feet with it, and said, "Truly you are a bridegroom of blood to me!" 26 So he let him alone. It was then she said, "A bridegroom of blood by circumcision."

27 The LORD said to Aaron, "Go into the wilderness to meet Moses." So he went; and he met him at the mountain of God and kissed him. 28 Moses told Aaron all the words of the LORD with which he had sent him, and all the signs with which he had charged him. 29 Then Moses and Aaron went and assembled all the elders of the Israelites. 30 Aaron spoke all the words that the LORD had spoken to Moses, and performed the signs in the sight of the people. 31 The people believed; and when they heard that the LORD had given heed to the Israelites and that he had seen their misery, they bowed down and worshiped.

5 Afterward Moses and Aaron went to Pharaoh and said, "Thus says the LORD, the God of Israel, 'Let my people go, so that they may celebrate a festival to me in the wilderness.' " 2 But Pharaoh said, "Who is the LORD, that I should heed him and let Israel go? I do not know the LORD, and I will not let Israel go." 3 Then they said, "The God of the Hebrews has revealed himself to us; let us go a three days' journey into the wilderness to sacrifice to the LORD our God, or he will fall upon us with pestilence or sword." 4 But the king of Egypt said to them, "Moses and Aaron, why are you taking the people away from their work? Get to your labors!" 5 Pharaoh continued, "Now they are more numerous than the people of the land[j] and yet you want them to stop working!" 6 That same day Pharaoh com-

REVISED ENGLISH BIBLE

10 'But, LORD,' Moses protested, 'I have never been a man of ready speech, never in my life, not even now that you have spoken to me; I am slow and hesitant.' 11 The LORD said to him, 'Who is it that gives man speech? Who makes him dumb or deaf? Who makes him keen-sighted or blind? Is it not I, the LORD? 12 Go now; I shall help you to speak and show you what to say.' 13 Moses said, 'Lord, send anyone else you like.' 14 At this the LORD became angry with Moses: 'Do you not have a brother, Aaron the Levite? He, I know, will do all the speaking. He is already on his way out to meet you, and he will be overjoyed when he sees you. 15 You are to speak to him and put the words in his mouth; I shall help both of you to speak and tell you both what to do. 16 He will do all the speaking to the people for you; he will be the mouthpiece, and you will be the god he speaks for. 17 And take this staff in your hand; with it you are to work the signs.'

18 Moses then went back to Jethro his father-in-law and said, 'Let me return to Egypt and see whether my kinsfolk are still alive.' Jethro said, 'Go, and may you have a safe journey.'

19 THE LORD spoke to Moses in Midian. 'Go back to Egypt,' he said, 'for all those who wanted to kill you are now dead.' 20 Moses took his wife and children, mounted them on a donkey, and set out for Egypt with the staff of God in his hand. 21 The LORD said to Moses, 'While you are on your way back to Egypt, keep in mind all the portents I have given you power to show. You are to display these before Pharaoh, but I shall make him obstinate and he will not let the people go. 22 Then tell Pharaoh that these are the words of the LORD: Israel is my firstborn son. 23 I tell you, let my son go to worship me. Should you refuse to let him go, I shall kill your firstborn son.'

24 On the journey, while they were encamped for the night, the LORD met Moses and would have killed him, 25 but Zipporah picked up a sharp flint, cut off her son's foreskin, and touched Moses' genitals with it, saying, 'You are my blood-bridegroom.' 26 So the LORD let Moses alone. It was on that occasion she said, 'Blood-bridegroom by circumcision.'

27 Meanwhile the LORD had ordered Aaron to go and meet Moses in the wilderness. Aaron did so; he met him at the mountain of God and kissed him. 28 Moses told Aaron everything, the words the LORD had sent him to say and the signs he had commanded him to perform. 29 Moses and Aaron then went and assembled all the elders of Israel. 30 Aaron repeated to them everything that the LORD had said to Moses; he performed the signs before the people, 31 and they were convinced. When they heard that the LORD had shown his concern for the Israelites and seen their misery, they bowed to the ground in worship.

5 After this, Moses and Aaron came to Pharaoh and told him, 'These are the words of the LORD the God of Israel: Let my people go so that they may keep a pilgrim-feast in my honour in the wilderness.' 2 'Who is the LORD,' said Pharaoh, 'that I should listen to him and let Israel go? I do not acknowledge the LORD: and I tell you I will not let Israel go.' 3 They replied, 'The God of the Hebrews confronted us. Now we request leave to go three days' journey into the wilderness to offer sacrifice to the LORD our God, or else he may attack us with pestilence or sword.' 4 But the Egyptian king answered, 'What do you mean, Moses and Aaron, by distracting the people from their work? Back to your labours! 5 Your people already outnumber the native Egyptians; yet you would have them stop working!'

4:20 **children:** *or, possibly,* son (cp. 2:22; 4:25). 4:25 **Moses' genitals:** *lit.* his feet. 4:26 **It was . . . said:** *or* Therefore women say. 5:5 **Your people . . . Egyptians:** *prob. rdg, cp. Samar.; Heb.* The people of the land are already many.

[i] Heb *his*   [j] Sam: Heb *The people of the land are now many*

|

10 Moses, however, said to the LORD, "If you please, Lord, I have never been eloquent, neither in the past, nor recently, nor now that you have spoken to your servant; but I am slow of speech and tongue." 11 The LORD said to him, "Who gives one man speech and makes another deaf and dumb? Or who gives sight to one and makes another blind? Is it not I, the LORD? 12 Go, then! It is I who will assist you in speaking and will teach you what you are to say." 13 Yet he insisted, "If you please, Lord, send someone else!" 14 Then the LORD became angry with Moses and said, "Have you not your brother, Aaron the Levite? I know that he is an eloquent speaker. Besides, he is now on his way to meet you. 15 When he sees you, his heart will be glad. You are to speak to him, then, and put the words in his mouth. I will assist both you and him in speaking and will teach the two of you what you are to do. 16 He shall speak to the people for you: he shall be your spokesman, and you shall be as God to him. 17 Take this staff in your hand; with it you are to perform the signs."

18 After this Moses returned to his father-in-law Jethro and said to him, "Let me go back, please, to my kinsmen in Egypt, to see whether they are still living." Jethro replied, "Go in peace." 19 In Midian the LORD said to Moses, "Go back to Egypt, for all the men who sought your life are dead." 20 So Moses took his wife and his sons, and started back to the land of Egypt, with them riding the ass. The staff of God he carried with him. 21 The LORD said to him, "On your return to Egypt, see that you perform before Pharaoh all the wonders I have put in your power. I will make him obstinate, however, so that he will not let the people go. 22 So you shall say to Pharaoh: Thus says the LORD: Israel is my son, my first-born. 23 Hence I tell you: Let my son go, that he may serve me. If you refuse to let him go, I warn you, I will kill your son, your first-born."

24 On the journey, at a place where they spent the night, the Lord came upon Moses and would have killed him. 25 But Zipporah took a piece of flint and cut off her son's foreskin and, touching his person, she said, "You are a spouse of blood to me." 26 Then God let Moses go. At that time she said, "A spouse of blood," in regard to the circumcision.

27 The LORD said to Aaron, "Go into the desert to meet Moses." So he went, and when they met at the mountain of God, Aaron kissed him. 28 Moses informed him of all the LORD had said in sending him, and of the various signs he had enjoined upon him. 29 Then Moses and Aaron went and assembled all the elders of the Israelites. 30 Aaron told them everything the LORD had said to Moses, and he performed the signs before the people. 31 The people believed, and when they heard that the LORD was concerned about them and had seen their affliction, they bowed down in worship.

5 After that, Moses and Aaron went to Pharaoh and said, "Thus says the LORD, the God of Israel: Let my people go, that they may celebrate a feast to me in the desert." 2 Pharaoh answered, "Who is the LORD, that I should heed his plea to let Israel go? I do not know the LORD; even if I did, I would not let Israel go." 3 They replied, "The God of the Hebrews has sent us word. Let us go a three days' journey in the desert, that we may offer sacrifice to the LORD, our God; otherwise he will punish us with pestilence or the sword."

4 The king of Egypt answered them, "What do you mean, Moses and Aaron, by taking the people away from their work? Off to your labor! 5 Look how numerous the people of the land are already," continued Pharaoh, "and yet you would give them rest from their labor!"

10 Moses said to Yahweh, 'Please, my Lord, I have never been eloquent, even since you have spoken to your servant, for I am slow and hesitant of speech.' 11 'Who gave a person a mouth?' Yahweh said to him. 'Who makes a person dumb or deaf, gives sight or makes blind? Is it not I, Yahweh? 12 Now go, I shall help you speak and instruct you what to say.'

13 'Please, my Lord,' Moses replied, 'send anyone you decide to send!' 14 At this, Yahweh's anger kindled against Moses, and he said to him, 'There is your brother Aaron the Levite, is there not? I know that he is a good speaker. Here he comes to meet you. When he sees you, his heart will be full of joy. 15 You will speak to him and tell him what message to give. I shall help you speak, and him too, and instruct you what to do. 16 He will speak to the people in your place; he will be your mouthpiece, and you will be as the god inspiring him. 17 And take this staff in your hand; with this you will perform the signs.'

18 Moses went back to his father-in-law Jethro and said to him, 'Give me leave to return to my kinsmen in Egypt and see if they are still alive.' And Jethro said to Moses, 'Go in peace.'

19 Yahweh said to Moses in Midian, 'Go, return to Egypt, for all those who wanted to kill you are dead.' 20 So Moses took his wife and his son and, putting them on a donkey, started back for Egypt; and Moses took the staff of God in his hand. 21 Yahweh said to Moses, 'Think of the wonders I have given you power to perform, once you are back in Egypt! You are to perform them before Pharaoh, but I myself shall make him obstinate, and he will not let the people go. 22 You will then say to Pharaoh, "This is what Yahweh says: Israel is my first-born son. 23 I told you: Let my son go and worship me; but since you refuse to let him go, well then! I shall put your first-born son to death." '

24 On the journey, when he had halted for the night, Yahweh encountered him and tried to kill him. 25 Then Zipporah, taking up a flint, cut off her son's foreskin and with it touched his feet and said, 'You are my blood-bridegroom!' 26 So he let him go. She said, 'Blood-bridegroom' then, with reference to the circumcision.

27 Yahweh said to Aaron, 'Go into the desert to meet Moses.' So he went, and met him at the mountain of God and kissed him. 28 Moses then told Aaron all that Yahweh had said when sending him and all the signs he had ordered him to perform. 29 Moses and Aaron then went and gathered all the elders of the Israelites together, 30 and Aaron repeated everything that Yahweh had said to Moses, and in the sight of the people performed the signs. 31 The people were convinced, and they rejoiced that Yahweh had visited the Israelites and seen their misery, and they bowed to the ground in worship.

5 After this, Moses and Aaron went to Pharaoh and said to him, 'This is what Yahweh, God of Israel, says, "Let my people go, so that they can hold a feast in my honour in the desert." ' 2 'Who is Yahweh,' Pharaoh replied, 'for me to obey when he says and let Israel go? I know nothing of Yahweh, and I will not let Israel go.' 3 'The God of the Hebrews has encountered us,' they replied. 'Give us leave to make a three-days' journey into the desert and sacrifice to Yahweh our God, or he will strike us with a plague or with the sword.' 4 The king of Egypt said to them, 'Moses and Aaron, what do you mean by distracting the people from their work? Get back to your forced labour.' 5 And Pharaoh said, 'Now that the people have grown to such numbers in the country, what do you mean by interrupting their forced labour?'

NEW REVISED STANDARD VERSION

manded the taskmasters of the people, as well as their supervisors, 7 "You shall no longer give the people straw to make bricks, as before; let them go and gather straw for themselves. 8 But you shall require of them the same quantity of bricks as they have made previously; do not diminish it, for they are lazy; that is why they cry, 'Let us go and offer sacrifice to our God.' 9 Let heavier work be laid on them; then they will labor at it and pay no attention to deceptive words."

10 So the taskmasters and the supervisors of the people went out and said to the people, "Thus says Pharaoh, 'I will not give you straw. 11 Go and get straw yourselves, wherever you can find it; but your work will not be lessened in the least.' " 12 So the people scattered throughout the land of Egypt, to gather stubble for straw. 13 The taskmasters were urgent, saying, "Complete your work, the same daily assignment as when you were given straw." 14 And the supervisors of the Israelites, whom Pharaoh's taskmasters had set over them, were beaten, and were asked, "Why did you not finish the required quantity of bricks yesterday and today, as you did before?"

15 Then the Israelite supervisors came to Pharaoh and cried, "Why do you treat your servants like this? 16 No straw is given to your servants, yet they say to us, 'Make bricks!' Look how your servants are beaten! You are unjust to your own people."k 17 He said, "You are lazy, lazy; that is why you say, 'Let us go and sacrifice to the LORD.' 18 Go now, and work; for no straw shall be given you, but you shall still deliver the same number of bricks." 19 The Israelite supervisors saw that they were in trouble when they were told, "You shall not lessen your daily number of bricks." 20 As they left Pharaoh, they came upon Moses and Aaron who were waiting to meet them. 21 They said to them, "The LORD look upon you and judge! You have brought us into bad odor with Pharaoh and his officials, and have put a sword in their hand to kill us."

22 Then Moses turned again to the LORD and said, "O LORD, why have you mistreated this people? Why did you ever send me? 23 Since I first came to Pharaoh to speak in your name, he has mistreated this people, and you have done nothing at all to deliver your people."

6 Then the LORD said to Moses, "Now you shall see what I will do to Pharaoh: Indeed, by a mighty hand he will let them go; by a mighty hand he will drive them out of his land."

2 God also spoke to Moses and said to him: "I am the LORD. 3 I appeared to Abraham, Isaac, and Jacob as God Almighty,l but by my name 'The LORD'm I did not make myself known to them. 4 I also established my covenant with them, to give them the land of Canaan, the land in which they resided as aliens. 5 I have also heard the groaning of the Israelites whom the Egyptians are holding as slaves, and I have remembered my covenant. 6 Say therefore to the Israelites, 'I am the LORD, and I will free you from the burdens of the Egyptians and deliver you from slavery to them. I will redeem you with an outstretched arm and with mighty acts of judgment. 7 I will take you as my people, and I will be your God. You shall know that I am the LORD your God, who has freed you from the burdens of the Egyptians. 8 I will bring you into the land that I swore to give to Abraham, Isaac, and Jacob; I will give it to you for a possession. I am the LORD.' " 9 Moses told this to the Israelites; but they would not listen to Moses, because of their broken spirit and their cruel slavery.

10 Then the LORD spoke to Moses, 11 "Go and tell Phar-

REVISED ENGLISH BIBLE

6 Pharaoh issued orders that same day to the people's slave-masters and their foremen 7 not to supply the people with the straw used in making bricks, as they had done hitherto. 'Let them go and collect their own straw, 8 but see that they produce the same tally of bricks as before; on no account reduce it. They are lazy, and that is why they are clamouring to go and offer sacrifice to their God. 9 Keep these men hard at work; let them attend to that. Take no notice of their lies.' 10 The slave-masters and foremen went out and said to the people, 'Pharaoh's orders are that no more straw is to be supplied. 11 Go and get it for yourselves wherever you can find it; but there is to be no reduction in your daily task.' 12 So the people scattered all over Egypt to gather stubble for the straw they needed, 13 while the slave-masters kept urging them on, demanding that they should complete, day after day, the same quantity as when straw had been supplied. 14 The Israelite foremen were flogged because they were held responsible by Pharaoh's slave-masters, who demanded, 'Why did you not complete the usual number of bricks yesterday or today?'

15 The foremen came and appealed to Pharaoh: 'Why does your majesty treat us like this?' they said. 16 'We are given no straw, yet they keep telling us to make bricks. Here are we being flogged, but the fault lies with your people.' 17 The king replied, 'You are lazy, bone lazy! That is why you keep on about going to offer sacrifice to the LORD. 18 Now get on with your work. You will not be given straw, but you must produce the full tally of bricks.' 19 When they were told that they must not let the daily number of bricks fall short, the Israelite foremen realized the trouble they were in. 20 As they came from Pharaoh's presence they found Moses and Aaron waiting to meet them, 21 and said, 'May this bring the LORD's judgement down on you! You have made us stink in the nostrils of Pharaoh and his subjects; you have put a sword in their hands to slay us.'

22 Moses went back to the LORD and said, 'Lord, why have you brought trouble on this people? And why did you ever send me? 23 Since I first went to Pharaoh to speak in your name he has treated your people cruelly, and you have done nothing at all to rescue them.' 1 The LORD answered, 'Now you will see what I shall do to Pharaoh: he will be compelled to let them go, he will be forced to drive them from his country.'

6 2 God said to Moses, 'I am the LORD. 3 I appeared to Abraham, Isaac, and Jacob as God Almighty; but I did not let myself be known to them by my name, the LORD. 4 I also established my covenant with them to give them Canaan, the land where for a time they settled as foreigners. 5 And now I have heard the groaning of the Israelites, enslaved by the Egyptians, and I am mindful of my covenant. 6 Therefore say to the Israelites, "I am the LORD. I shall free you from your labours in Egypt and deliver you from slavery. I shall rescue you with outstretched arm and with mighty acts of judgement. 7 I shall adopt you as my people, and I shall be your God. You will know that I, the LORD, am your God, the God who frees you from your labours in Egypt. 8 I shall lead you to the land which I swore with uplifted hand to give to Abraham, to Isaac, and to Jacob. I shall give it you for your possession. I am the LORD." ' 9 But when Moses repeated those words to the Israelites, they would not listen to him; because of their cruel slavery, they had reached the depths of despair.

10 Then the LORD said to Moses, 11 'Go and bid Pharaoh

k Gk Compare Syr Vg: Heb *beaten, and the sin of your people*
l Traditional rendering of Heb *El Shaddai*   m Heb *YHWH*; see note at 3.15

6:3 the LORD: see note on 3:15.

NEW AMERICAN BIBLE

6 That very day Pharaoh gave the taskmasters and foremen of the people this order: 7 "You shall no longer supply the people with straw for their brickmaking as you have previously done. Let them go and gather straw themselves! 8 Yet you shall levy upon them the same quota of bricks as they have previously made. Do not reduce it. They are lazy; that is why they are crying, 'Let us go to offer sacrifice to our God.' 9 Increase the work for the men, so that they keep their mind on it and pay no attention to lying words."

10 So the taskmasters and foremen of the people went out and told them, "Thus says Pharaoh: I will not provide you with straw. 11 Go and gather the straw yourselves, wherever you can find it. Yet there must not be the slightest reduction in your work." 12 The people, then, scattered throughout the land of Egypt to gather stubble for straw, 13 while the taskmasters kept driving them on, saying, "Finish your work, the same daily amount as when your straw was supplied."

14 The foremen of the Israelites, whom the taskmasters of Pharaoh had placed over them, were beaten, and were asked, "Why have you not completed your prescribed amount of bricks yesterday and today, as before?"

15 Then the Israelite foremen came and made this appeal to Pharaoh: "Why do you treat your servants in this manner? 16 No straw is supplied to your servants, and still we are told to make bricks. Look how your servants are beaten! It is you who are at fault." 17 Pharaoh answered, "It is just because you are lazy that you keep saying, 'Let us go and offer sacrifice to the LORD.' 18 Off to work, then! Straw shall not be provided for you, but you must still deliver your quota of bricks."

19 The Israelite foremen knew they were in a sorry plight, having been told not to reduce the daily amount of bricks. 20 When, therefore, they left Pharaoh and came upon Moses and Aaron, who were waiting to meet them, 21 they said to them, "The LORD look upon you and judge! You have brought us into bad odor with Pharaoh and his servants and have put a sword in their hands to slay us."

22 Moses again had recourse to the LORD and said, "Lord, why do you treat this people so badly? And why did you send me on such a mission? 23 Ever since I went to Pharaoh to speak in your name, he has maltreated this people of yours, and you have done nothing to rescue them."

6 Then the LORD answered Moses, "Now you shall see what I will do to Pharaoh. Forced by my mighty hand, he will send them away; compelled by my outstretched arm, he will drive them from his land."

2 God also said to Moses, "I am the LORD. 3 As God the Almighty I appeared to Abraham, Isaac and Jacob, but my name, LORD, I did not make known to them. 4 I also established my covenant with them, to give them the land of Canaan, the land in which they were living as aliens. 5 And now that I have heard the groaning of the Israelites, whom the Egyptians are treating as slaves, I am mindful of my covenant. 6 Therefore, say to the Israelites: I am the LORD. I will free you from the forced labor of the Egyptians and will deliver you from their slavery. I will rescue you by my outstretched arm and with mighty acts of judgment. 7 I will take you as my own people, and you shall have me as your God. You will know that I, the LORD, am your God when I free you from the labor of the Egyptians 8 and bring you into the land which I swore to give to Abraham, Isaac and Jacob. I will give it to you as your own possession—I, the LORD!" 9 But when Moses told this to the Israelites, they would not listen to him because of their dejection and hard slavery.

10 Then the LORD said to Moses, 11 "Go and tell Pharaoh,

NEW JERUSALEM BIBLE

6 That very day, Pharaoh gave the order to the people's taskmasters and their scribes, 7 'Do not go on providing the people with straw for brickmaking as before; let them go and gather straw for themselves. 8 But you will exact the same quantity of bricks from them as before, not reducing it at all, since they are lazy, and that is why their cry is, "Let us go and sacrifice to our God." 9 Give these people more work to do, and see they do it instead of listening to lying speeches.'

10 The people's taskmasters and scribes went out to speak to the people and said, 'Pharaoh says this, "I shall not provide you with any more straw. 11 Go and collect straw for yourselves where you can find it. But your output is not to be any less."' 12 So the people scattered all over Egypt to gather stubble for their straw. 13 The taskmasters harassed them. 'You must complete your daily quota,' they said, 'just as when the straw was there.' 14 And the Israelites' foremen whom Pharaoh's taskmasters had put in charge of them, were flogged and asked, 'Why have you not fulfilled your quota of bricks made today as before?'

15 The Israelites' foremen went and appealed to Pharaoh. 'Why do you treat your servants like this?' they said. 16 'No straw is provided for your servants, yet still the cry is, "Make bricks!" And now your servants are being flogged!...' 17 'You are lazy, lazy,' he retorted. 'That is why you say, "Let us go and sacrifice to Yahweh." 18 Get back to your work at once. You will not be provided with straw; all the same, you will deliver the quota of bricks.'

19 The Israelites' foremen saw they were in a difficult position on being told, 'You will not reduce your daily production of bricks.' 20 As they left Pharaoh's presence, they met Moses and Aaron who were standing in their way. 21 'May Yahweh look down at you and judge!' they said to them. 'You have brought us into bad odour with Pharaoh and his officials; you have put a sword into their hand to kill us.' 22 Moses went back to Yahweh and said, 'Lord, why do you treat this people so harshly? Why did you send me? 23 Ever since I came to Pharaoh and spoke to him in your name, he has ill-treated this people, and you have done nothing at all about rescuing your people.'

6 Yahweh then said to Moses, 'Now you will see what I am going to do to Pharaoh. A mighty hand will force him to let them go, a mighty hand will force him to expel them from his country.'

2 d God spoke to Moses and said to him, 'I am Yahweh. 3 To Abraham, Isaac and Jacob I appeared as El Shaddai, but I did not make my name Yahweh known to them. 4 I also made my covenant with them to give them the land of Canaan, the country in which they were living as aliens. 5 Furthermore, I have heard the groaning of the Israelites, enslaved by the Egyptians, and have remembered my covenant. 6 So say to the Israelites, "I am Yahweh. I shall free you from the forced labour of the Egyptians; I shall rescue you from their slavery and I shall redeem you with outstretched arm and mighty acts of judgement. 7 I shall take you as my people and I shall be your God. And you will know that I am Yahweh your God, who have freed you from the forced labour of the Egyptians. 8 Then I shall lead you into the country which I swore I would give to Abraham, Isaac and Jacob, and shall give it to you as your heritage, I, Yahweh."' 9 And Moses repeated this to the Israelites, but they would not listen to Moses, so crushed was their spirit and so cruel their slavery.

10 Yahweh then said to Moses, 11 'Go to Pharaoh, king of

d 6 6:2seq. = 3:1—4:23.

aoh king of Egypt to let the Israelites go out of his land." 12 But Moses spoke to the LORD, "The Israelites have not listened to me; how then shall Pharaoh listen to me, poor speaker that I am?"*n* 13 Thus the LORD spoke to Moses and Aaron, and gave them orders regarding the Israelites and Pharaoh king of Egypt, charging them to free the Israelites from the land of Egypt.

14 The following are the heads of their ancestral houses: the sons of Reuben, the firstborn of Israel: Hanoch, Pallu, Hezron, and Carmi; these are the families of Reuben. 15 The sons of Simeon: Jemuel, Jamin, Ohad, Jachin, Zohar, and Shaul,*o* the son of a Canaanite woman; these are the families of Simeon. 16 The following are the names of the sons of Levi according to their genealogies: Gershon,*p* Kohath, and Merari, and the length of Levi's life was one hundred thirty-seven years. 17 The sons of Gershon:*p* Libni and Shimei, by their families. 18 The sons of Kohath: Amram, Izhar, Hebron, and Uzziel, and the length of Kohath's life was one hundred thirty-three years. 19 The sons of Merari: Mahli and Mushi. These are the families of the Levites according to their genealogies. 20 Amram married Jochebed his father's sister and she bore him Aaron and Moses, and the length of Amram's life was one hundred thirty-seven years. 21 The sons of Izhar: Korah, Nepheg, and Zichri. 22 The sons of Uzziel: Mishael, Elzaphan, and Sithri. 23 Aaron married Elisheba, daughter of Amminadab and sister of Nahshon, and she bore him Nadab, Abihu, Eleazar, and Ithamar. 24 The sons of Korah: Assir, Elkanah, and Abiasaph; these are the families of the Korahites. 25 Aaron's son Eleazar married one of the daughters of Putiel, and she bore him Phinehas. These are the heads of the ancestral houses of the Levites by their families.

26 It was this same Aaron and Moses to whom the LORD said, "Bring the Israelites out of the land of Egypt, company by company." 27 It was they who spoke to Pharaoh king of Egypt to bring the Israelites out of Egypt, the same Moses and Aaron.

28 On the day when the LORD spoke to Moses in the land of Egypt, 29 he said to him, "I am the LORD; tell Pharaoh king of Egypt all that I am speaking to you." 30 But Moses said in the LORD's presence, "Since I am a poor speaker,*q* why would Pharaoh listen to me?"

7 The LORD said to Moses, "See, I have made you like God to Pharaoh, and your brother Aaron shall be your prophet. 2 You shall speak all that I command you, and your brother Aaron shall tell Pharaoh to let the Israelites go out of his land. 3 But I will harden Pharaoh's heart, and I will multiply my signs and wonders in the land of Egypt. 4 When Pharaoh does not listen to you, I will lay my hand upon Egypt and bring my people the Israelites, company by company, out of the land of Egypt by great acts of judgment. 5 The Egyptians shall know that I am the LORD, when I stretch out my hand against Egypt and bring the Israelites out from among them." 6 Moses and Aaron did so; they did just as the LORD commanded them. 7 Moses was eighty years old and Aaron eighty-three when they spoke to Pharaoh.

8 The LORD said to Moses and Aaron, 9 "When Pharaoh says to you, 'Perform a wonder,' then you shall say to Aaron, 'Take your staff and throw it down before Pharaoh, and it will become a snake.'" 10 So Moses and Aaron went to Pharaoh and did as the LORD had commanded; Aaron threw down his staff before Pharaoh and his officials, and it became a snake. 11 Then Pharaoh summoned the wise

---

king of Egypt let the Israelites leave his country.' 12 Moses protested to the LORD, 'If the Israelites do not listen to me, how will Pharaoh listen to such a halting speaker as me?' 13 The LORD then spoke to both Moses and Aaron and gave them their commission concerning the Israelites and Pharaoh, which was that they should bring the Israelites out of Egypt.

14 THESE were the heads of families.

Sons of Reuben, Israel's eldest son: Enoch, Pallu, Hezron, and Carmi; these were the families of Reuben.

15 Sons of Simeon: Jemuel, Jamin, Ohad, Jachin, Zohar, and Saul, who was the son of a Canaanite woman; these were the families of Simeon.

16 These were the names of the sons of Levi in order of seniority: Gershon, Kohath, and Merari. Levi lived to be a hundred and thirty-seven.

17 Sons of Gershon, family by family: Libni and Shimei.

18 Sons of Kohath: Amram, Izhar, Hebron, and Uzziel. Kohath lived to be a hundred and thirty-three.

19 Sons of Merari: Mahli and Mushi.

These were the families of Levi in order of seniority. 20 Amram married his father's sister Jochebed, and she bore him Aaron and Moses. Amram lived to be a hundred and thirty-seven.

21 Sons of Izhar: Korah, Nepheg, and Zichri.

22 Sons of Uzziel: Mishael, Elzaphan, and Sithri.

23 Aaron married Elisheba, who was the daughter of Amminadab and the sister of Nahshon, and she bore him Nadab, Abihu, Eleazar, and Ithamar.

24 Sons of Korah: Assir, Elkanah, and Abiasaph; these were the Korahite families.

25 Eleazar son of Aaron married one of the daughters of Putiel, and she bore him Phinehas. These were the heads of the Levite families, family by family.

26 It was this Aaron, together with Moses, to whom the LORD said, 'Bring the Israelites out of Egypt, mustered in their tribal hosts.' 27 These were the men, this same Moses and Aaron, who told Pharaoh king of Egypt to let the Israelites leave Egypt.

28 WHEN the LORD spoke to Moses in Egypt he said, 29 'I am the LORD. Report to Pharaoh king of Egypt all that I say to you.' 30 Moses protested to the LORD, 'I am a halting speaker; how will Pharaoh listen to me?' 1 The LORD answered, 'See now, I have made you like a god for Pharaoh, with your brother Aaron as your spokesman. 2 Tell Aaron all I command you to say, and he will tell Pharaoh to let the Israelites leave his country. 3 But I shall make him stubborn, and though I show sign after sign and portent after portent in the land of Egypt, 4 Pharaoh will not listen to you. Then I shall assert my power in Egypt, and with mighty acts of judgement I shall bring my people, the Israelites, out of Egypt in their tribal hosts. 5 When I exert my power against Egypt and bring the Israelites out from there, then the Egyptians will know that I am the LORD.' 6 Moses and Aaron did exactly as the LORD had commanded. 7 At the time when they spoke to Pharaoh, Moses was eighty years old and Aaron eighty-three.

8 The LORD said to Moses and Aaron, 9 'If Pharaoh demands some portent from you, then you, Moses, must say to Aaron, "Take your staff and throw it down in front of Pharaoh," and it will turn into a serpent.' 10 When Moses and Aaron came to Pharaoh, they did as the LORD had told them; Aaron threw down his staff in front of Pharaoh and his courtiers, and it turned into a serpent. 11 At this, Pharaoh

---

n Heb *me? I am uncircumcised of lips*   *o* Or *Saul*   *p* Also spelled *Gershom*; see 2.22   *q* Heb *am uncircumcised of lips*; see 6.12

6:12 **to such . . . me:** lit. to me, seeing I am uncircumcised of lips. 6:14–16 Cp. Gen. 46:8–11; Num. 26:5,6,12,13.   7:1 **spokesman:** lit. prophet.

king of Egypt, to let the Israelites leave his land." 12 But Moses protested to the LORD, "If the Israelites would not listen to me, how can it be that Pharaoh will listen to me, poor speaker that I am!" 13 Still, the LORD, to bring the Israelites out of Egypt, spoke to Moses and Aaron and gave them his orders regarding both the Israelites and Pharaoh, king of Egypt.

14 These are the heads of the ancestral houses. The sons of Reuben, the first-born of Israel, were Hanoch, Pallu, Hezron and Carmi; these are the clans of Reuben. 15 The sons of Simeon were Jemuel, Jamin, Ohad, Jachin, Zohar and Shaul, who was the son of a Canaanite woman; these are the clans of Simeon. 16 The names of the sons of Levi, in their genealogical order, are Gershon, Kohath and Merari. Levi lived one hundred and thirty-seven years.

17 The sons of Gershon, as heads of clans, were Libni and Shimei. 18 The sons of Kohath were Amram, Izhar, Hebron and Uzziel. Kohath lived one hundred and thirty-three years. 19 The sons of Merari were Mahli and Mushi. These are the clans of Levi in their genealogical order.

20 Amram married his aunt Jochebed, who bore him Aaron, Moses and Miriam. Amram lived one hundred and thirty-seven years. 21 The sons of Izhar were Korah, Nepheg and Zichri. 22 The sons of Uzziel were Mishael, Elzaphan and Sithri. 23 Aaron married Amminadab's daughter, Elisheba, the sister of Nahshon; she bore him Nadab, Abihu, Eleazar and Ithamar. 24 The sons of Korah were Assir, Elkanah and Abiasaph. These are the clans of the Korahites. 25 Aaron's son, Eleazar, married one of Putiel's daughters, who bore him Phinehas. These are the heads of the ancestral clans of the Levites. 26 This is the Aaron and this the Moses to whom the LORD said, "Lead the Israelites from the land of Egypt, company by company." 27 These are the ones who spoke to Pharaoh, king of Egypt, to bring the Israelites out of Egypt — the same Moses and Aaron.

28 On the day the LORD spoke to Moses in Egypt 29 he said, "I am the LORD. Repeat to Pharaoh, king of Egypt, all that I tell you." 30 But Moses protested to the LORD, "Since I am a poor speaker, how can it be that Pharaoh will listen to me?"

7 The LORD answered him, "See! I have made you as God to Pharaoh, and Aaron your brother shall act as your prophet. 2 You shall tell him all that I command you. In turn, your brother Aaron shall tell Pharaoh to let the Israelites leave his land. 3 Yet I will make Pharaoh so obstinate that, despite the many signs and wonders that I will work in the land of Egypt, 4 he will not listen to you. Therefore I will lay my hand on Egypt and by great acts of judgment I will bring the hosts of my people, the Israelites, out of the land of Egypt, 5 so that the Egyptians may learn that I am the LORD, as I stretch out my hand against Egypt and lead the Israelites out of their midst."

6 Moses and Aaron did as the LORD had commanded them. 7 Moses was eighty years old and Aaron eighty-three when they spoke to Pharaoh.

8 The LORD told Moses and Aaron, 9 "If Pharaoh demands that you work a sign or wonder, you shall say to Aaron: Take your staff and throw it down before Pharaoh, and it will be changed into a snake." 10 Then Moses and Aaron went to Pharaoh and did as the LORD had commanded. Aaron threw his staff down before Pharaoh and his servants, and it was changed into a snake. 11 Pharaoh, in turn, sum-

Egypt, and tell him to let the Israelites leave his country.' 12 But Moses spoke out in Yahweh's presence and said, 'The Israelites have not listened to me, so why should Pharaoh take any notice of a poor speaker like me?' 13 Yahweh spoke to Moses and Aaron and sent them to Pharaoh king of Egypt, to lead the Israelites out of Egypt.

14 These were their heads of families:

The sons of Reuben, Israel's first-born: Hanoch, Pallu, Hezron and Carmi: these are the clans of Reuben.

15 The sons of Simeon: Jemuel, Jamin, Ohad, Jachin, Zohar, and Shaul son of the Canaanite woman: these are the clans of Simeon.

16 These were the names of the sons of Levi with their descendants: Gershon, Kohath and Merari. Levi lived for a hundred and thirty-seven years.

17 The sons of Gershon: Libni and Shimei, with their clans.

18 The sons of Kohath: Amram, Izhar, Hebron and Uzziel. Kohath lived for a hundred and thirty-three years.

19 The sons of Merari: Mahli and Mushi. These are the clans of Levi with their descendants.

20 Amram married Jochebed, his aunt, who bore him Aaron and Moses. Amram lived for a hundred and thirty-seven years.

21 The sons of Izhar were: Korah, Nepheg and Zichri.

22 And the sons of Uzziel: Mishael, Elzaphan and Sithri.

23 Aaron married Elisheba daughter of Amminadab and sister of Nahshon, and she bore him Nadab, Abihu, Eleazar and Ithamar.

24 The sons of Korah: Assir, Elkanah and Abiasaph. These are the clans of the Korahites.

25 Eleazar, son of Aaron, married one of Putiel's daughters who bore him Phinehas.

These were the Levitical heads of families, according to clan.

26 It was to this Aaron and Moses that Yahweh said, 'Lead the Israelites out of Egypt in their armies.' 27 It was they who spoke to Pharaoh, king of Egypt, to lead the Israelites out of Egypt — namely Moses and Aaron.

28 Now the day when Yahweh spoke to Moses in Egypt, 29 Yahweh said to Moses, 'Tell Pharaoh king of Egypt everything that I am going to say to you.' 30 But Moses said to Yahweh's face, 'I am a poor speaker, so why should Pharaoh take any notice of me?'

7 Yahweh then said to Moses, 'Look, I have made you as a god for Pharaoh, and your brother Aaron is to be your prophet. 2 You must say whatever I command you, and your brother Aaron will repeat to Pharaoh that he is to let the Israelites leave his country. 3 But I myself shall make Pharaoh stubborn and shall perform many a sign and wonder in Egypt. 4 Since Pharaoh will not listen to you, I shall lay my hand on Egypt and with great acts of judgement lead my armies, my people, the Israelites, out of Egypt. 5 And the Egyptians will know that I am Yahweh when I stretch out my hand against the Egyptians and lead the Israelites out of their country.'

6 Moses and Aaron did exactly as Yahweh had ordered. 7 Moses was eighty years old and Aaron eighty-three, when they spoke to Pharaoh.

8 Yahweh said to Moses and Aaron, 9 'If Pharaoh says to you, "Display some marvel," you must say to Aaron, "Take your staff and throw it down in front of Pharaoh, and let it turn into a serpent!" ' 10 Moses and Aaron went to Pharaoh and did as Yahweh had ordered. Aaron threw down his staff in front of Pharaoh and his officials, and it turned into a serpent. 11 Then Pharaoh in his turn called for the sages and

men and the sorcerers; and they also, the magicians of Egypt, did the same by their secret arts. 12 Each one threw down his staff, and they became snakes; but Aaron's staff swallowed up theirs. 13 Still Pharaoh's heart was hardened, and he would not listen to them, as the LORD had said.

14 Then the LORD said to Moses, "Pharaoh's heart is hardened; he refuses to let the people go. 15 Go to Pharaoh in the morning, as he is going out to the water; stand by at the river bank to meet him, and take in your hand the staff that was turned into a snake. 16 Say to him, 'The LORD, the God of the Hebrews, sent me to you to say, "Let my people go, so that they may worship me in the wilderness." But until now you have not listened.' 17 Thus says the LORD, "By this you shall know that I am the LORD." See, with the staff that is in my hand I will strike the water that is in the Nile, and it shall be turned to blood. 18 The fish in the river shall die, the river itself shall stink, and the Egyptians shall be unable to drink water from the Nile.' " 19 The LORD said to Moses, "Say to Aaron, 'Take your staff and stretch out your hand over the waters of Egypt — over its rivers, its canals, and its ponds, and all its pools of water — so that they may become blood; and there shall be blood throughout the whole land of Egypt, even in vessels of wood and in vessels of stone.' "

20 Moses and Aaron did just as the LORD commanded. In the sight of Pharaoh and of his officials he lifted up the staff and struck the water in the river, and all the water in the river was turned into blood, 21 and the fish in the river died. The river stank so that the Egyptians could not drink its water, and there was blood throughout the whole land of Egypt. 22 But the magicians of Egypt did the same by their secret arts; so Pharaoh's heart remained hardened, and he would not listen to them; as the LORD had said. 23 Pharaoh turned and went into his house, and he did not take even this to heart. 24 And all the Egyptians had to dig along the Nile for water to drink, for they could not drink the water of the river.

25 Seven days passed after the LORD had struck the Nile.

8 r Then the LORD said to Moses, "Go to Pharaoh and say to him, 'Thus says the LORD: Let my people go, so that they may worship me. 2 If you refuse to let them go, I will plague your whole country with frogs. 3 The river shall swarm with frogs; they shall come up into your palace, into your bedchamber and your bed, and into the houses of your officials and of your people, s and into your ovens and your kneading bowls. 4 The frogs shall come up on you and on your people and on all your officials.' " 5 t And the LORD said to Moses, "Say to Aaron, 'Stretch out your hand with your staff over the rivers, the canals, and the pools, and make frogs come up on the land of Egypt.' " 6 So Aaron stretched out his hand over the waters of Egypt; and the frogs came up and covered the land of Egypt. 7 But the magicians did the same by their secret arts, and brought frogs up on the land of Egypt.

8 Then Pharaoh called Moses and Aaron, and said, "Pray to the LORD to take away the frogs from me and my people, and I will let the people go to sacrifice to the LORD." 9 Moses said to Pharaoh, "Kindly tell me when I am to pray for you and for your officials and for your people, that the frogs may be removed from you and your houses and be left only in the Nile." 10 And he said, "Tomorrow." Moses said, "As you say! So that you may know that there is no one like the LORD our God, 11 the frogs shall leave you and your houses and your officials and your people; they shall be left only in the Nile." 12 Then Moses and Aaron

summoned the wise men and the sorcerers, and the Egyptian magicians did the same thing by their spells: 12 every man threw his staff down, and each staff turned into a serpent. But Aaron's staff swallowed up theirs. 13 Pharaoh, however, was obstinate; as the LORD had foretold, he would not listen to Moses and Aaron.

14 The LORD said to Moses, 'Pharaoh has been obdurate: he has refused to let the people go. 15 In the morning go to him on his way out to the river. Stand on the bank of the Nile to meet him, and take with you the staff that turned into a snake. 16 Say to him: "The LORD the God of the Hebrews sent me with this message for you: Let my people go in order to worship me in the wilderness. So far you have not listened. 17 Now the LORD says: By this you will know that I am the LORD. With this rod I hold in my hand, I shall strike the water of the Nile and it will be changed into blood. 18 The fish will die and the river will stink, and the Egyptians will be unable to drink water from the Nile." '

19 The LORD told Moses to say to Aaron, 'Take your staff and stretch your hand out over the waters of Egypt, its rivers and its canals, and over every pool and cistern, to turn them into blood. There will be blood throughout the whole of Egypt, blood even in their wooden bowls and stone jars.' 20 Moses and Aaron did as the LORD had commanded. In the sight of Pharaoh and his courtiers Aaron lifted his staff and struck the water of the Nile, and all the water was changed to blood. 21 The fish died and the river stank, so that the Egyptians could not drink water from the Nile. There was blood everywhere in Egypt. 22 But the Egyptian magicians did the same thing by their spells. So Pharaoh still remained obstinate, as the LORD had foretold, and he did not listen to Moses and Aaron. 23 He turned and went into his palace, dismissing the matter from his mind. 24 The Egyptians all dug for drinking water round about the river, because they could not drink from the waters of the Nile itself. 25 This lasted for seven days from the time when the LORD struck the Nile.

8 The LORD then told Moses to go to Pharaoh and say, 'These are the words of the LORD: Let my people go in order to worship me. 2 If you refuse, I shall bring a plague of frogs over the whole of your territory. 3 The Nile will swarm with them. They will come up from the river into your palace, into your bedroom and onto your bed, into the houses of your courtiers and your people, into your ovens and your kneading troughs. 4 The frogs will clamber over you, your people, and all your courtiers.'

5 The LORD told Moses to say to Aaron, 'Take your staff in your hand and stretch it out over the rivers, canals, and pools, to bring up frogs on the land of Egypt.' 6 When Aaron stretched his hand over the waters of Egypt, the frogs came up and covered the land. 7 But the magicians did the same thing by their spells: they too brought up frogs on the land of Egypt.

8 Pharaoh summoned Moses and Aaron. 'Pray to the LORD', he said, 'to remove the frogs from me and my people, and I shall let the people go to sacrifice to the LORD.' 9 Moses said, 'I give your majesty the choice of a time for me to intercede for you, your courtiers, and your people, to rid you and your houses of the frogs; none will be left except in the Nile.' 10 'Tomorrow,' said Pharaoh. 'It will be as you say,' replied Moses, 'so that you may know there is no one like our God, the LORD. 11 The frogs will leave you, your houses, courtiers, and people: none will be left except in the Nile.' 12 Moses and Aaron left Pharaoh's

---

r Ch 7.26 in Heb   s Gk: Heb upon your people   t Ch 8.1 in Heb   8:1 In Heb. 7:26.   8:5 In Heb. 8:1.

moned wise men and sorcerers, and they also, the magicians of Egypt, did likewise by their magic arts. 12 Each one threw down his staff, and it was changed into a snake. But Aaron's staff swallowed their staffs. 13 Pharaoh, however, was obstinate and would not listen to them, just as the LORD had foretold.

14 Then the LORD said to Moses, "Pharaoh is obdurate in refusing to let the people go. 15 Tomorrow morning, when he sets out for the water, go and present yourself by the river bank, holding in your hand the staff that turned into a serpent. 16 Say to him: The LORD, the God of the Hebrews, sent me to you with the message: Let my people go to worship me in the desert. But as yet you have not listened. 17 The LORD now says: This is how you shall know that I am the LORD. I will strike the water of the river with the staff I hold, and it shall be changed into blood. 18 The fish in the river shall die, and the river itself shall become so polluted that the Egyptians will be unable to drink its water."

19 The LORD then said to Moses, "Say to Aaron: Take your staff and stretch out your hand over the waters of Egypt—their streams and canals and pools, all their supplies of water—that they may become blood. Throughout the land of Egypt there shall be blood, even in the wooden pails and stone jars."

20 Moses and Aaron did as the LORD had commanded. Aaron raised his staff and struck the waters of the river in full view of Pharaoh and his servants, and all the water of the river was changed into blood. 21 The fish in the river died, and the river itself became so polluted that the Egyptians could not drink its water. There was blood throughout the land of Egypt. 22 But the Egyptian magicians did the same by their magic arts. So Pharaoh remained obstinate and would not listen to Moses and Aaron, just as the LORD had foretold. 23 He turned away and went into his house, with no concern even for this. 24 All the Egyptians had to dig in the neighborhood of the river for drinking water, since they could not drink the river water.

25 Seven days passed after the LORD had struck the river. 26 Then the LORD said to Moses, "Go to Pharaoh and tell him: Thus says the LORD: Let my people go to worship me. 27 If you refuse to let them go, I warn you, I will send a plague of frogs over all your territory. 28 The river will teem with frogs. They will come up into your palace and into your bedroom and onto your bed, into the houses of your servants, too, and your subjects, even into your ovens and your kneading bowls. 29 The frogs will swarm all over you and your subjects and your servants."

8 The LORD then told Moses, "Say to Aaron: Stretch out your hand and your staff over the streams and canals and pools, to make frogs overrun the land of Egypt." 2 Aaron stretched out his hand over the waters of Egypt, and the frogs came up and covered the land of Egypt. 3 But the magicians did the same by their magic arts. They, too, made frogs overrun the land of Egypt.

4 Then Pharaoh summoned Moses and Aaron and said, "Pray the LORD to remove the frogs from me and my subjects, and I will let the people go to offer sacrifice to the LORD." 5 Moses answered Pharaoh, "Do me the favor of appointing the time when I am to pray for you and your servants and your subjects, that the frogs may be taken away from you and your houses and be left only in the river." 6 "Tomorrow," said Pharaoh. Then Moses replied, "It shall be as you have said, so that you may learn that there is none like the LORD, our God. 7 The frogs shall leave you and your houses, your servants and your subjects; only in the river shall they be left."

sorcerers, and by their spells the magicians of Egypt did the same. 12 Each threw his staff down and these turned into serpents. But Aaron's staff swallowed up theirs. 13 Pharaoh, however, remained obstinate and, as Yahweh had foretold, refused to listen to Moses and Aaron.

14 Yahweh then said to Moses, 'Pharaoh is adamant. He refuses to let the people go. 15 Go to Pharaoh tomorrow morning as he makes his way to the water, confront him on the river bank and in your hand take the staff that turned into a snake. 16 Say to him, "Yahweh, God of the Hebrews, sent me to say: Let my people go and worship me in the desert. Up till now, you have refused to listen. 17 This is what Yahweh says: You will know that I am Yahweh by this: with the staff that is in my hand I shall strike the waters of the River and they will turn to blood. 18 The fish in the river will die, and the River will stink, and the Egyptians will not be able to drink the river water." '

19 Yahweh said to Moses, 'Say to Aaron, "Take your staff and stretch out your hand over the waters of Egypt—over their rivers and canals, their marshland, and all their reservoirs—and they will turn to blood. There will be blood throughout the whole of Egypt, even in sticks and stones." ' 20 Moses and Aaron did as Yahweh ordered. He raised his staff and struck the waters of the River, with Pharaoh and his officials looking on, and all the water in the River turned to blood. 21 The fish in the River died, and the River stank; and the Egyptians could no longer drink the River water. Throughout the whole of Egypt there was blood. 22 But by their spells the magicians of Egypt did the same; Pharaoh remained obstinate and, as Yahweh had foretold, refused to listen to Moses and Aaron. 23 Pharaoh turned away and went back into his palace, taking no notice even of this. 24 And the Egyptians all dug holes along the river-bank in search of drinking water, since they could not drink the River water. 25 After Yahweh struck the River, seven days went by.

26 Then Yahweh said to Moses, 'Go to Pharaoh and say to him, "Yahweh says this: Let my people go and worship me. 27 If you refuse to let them go, I shall strike your whole territory with frogs. 28 The River will swarm with frogs; they will make their way into your palace, into your bedroom, onto your bed, into the houses of your officials and subjects, into your ovens, into your kneading bowls. 29 The frogs will actually clamber onto you, onto your subjects and onto all your officials." '

8 Yahweh then said to Moses, 'Say to Aaron, "Stretch out your hand with your staff, over the rivers, the canals and the marshland, and bring the frogs up over the land of Egypt." ' 2 So Aaron stretched out his hand over the waters of Egypt, and the frogs came up and covered the land of Egypt. 3 But by their spells the magicians did the same, bringing frogs over the land of Egypt.

4 Pharaoh then summoned Moses and Aaron and said, 'Entreat Yahweh to take the frogs away from me and my subjects, and I promise to let the people go and sacrifice to Yahweh.' 5 Moses said to Pharaoh, 'You are the one to gain by it: when would you like me to pray for you, your officials and your subjects, so as to rid you and your houses of the frogs so that they will be left only in the River?' 6 'Tomorrow,' he said. Moses said, 'It shall be as you say, so that you will know that there is no one like Yahweh our God. 7 The frogs will leave you, your houses, your officials and your subjects and will be left only in the River.' 8 Moses

7, 26—8, 28: This is Ex 8, 1-32 in the verse enumeration of the Vulgate.

went out from Pharaoh; and Moses cried out to the LORD concerning the frogs that he had brought upon Pharaoh. *u* 13 And the LORD did as Moses requested: the frogs died in the houses, the courtyards, and the fields. 14 And they gathered them together in heaps, and the land stank. 15 But when Pharaoh saw that there was a respite, he hardened his heart, and would not listen to them, just as the LORD had said.

16 Then the LORD said to Moses, "Say to Aaron, 'Stretch out your staff and strike the dust of the earth, so that it may become gnats throughout the whole land of Egypt.'" 17 And they did so; Aaron stretched out his hand with his staff and struck the dust of the earth, and gnats came on humans and animals alike; all the dust of the earth turned into gnats throughout the whole land of Egypt. 18 The magicians tried to produce gnats by their secret arts, but they could not. There were gnats on both humans and animals. 19 And the magicians said to Pharaoh, "This is the finger of God!" But Pharaoh's heart was hardened, and he would not listen to them, just as the LORD had said.

20 Then the LORD said to Moses, "Rise early in the morning and present yourself before Pharaoh, as he goes out to the water, and say to him, 'Thus says the LORD: Let my people go, so that they may worship me. 21 For if you will not let my people go, I will send swarms of flies on you, your officials, and your people, and into your houses; and the houses of the Egyptians shall be filled with swarms of flies; so also the land where they live. 22 But on that day I will set apart the land of Goshen, where my people live, so that no swarms of flies shall be there, that you may know that I the LORD am in this land. 23 Thus I will make a distinction*v* between my people and your people. This sign shall appear tomorrow.'" 24 The LORD did so, and great swarms of flies came into the house of Pharaoh and into his officials' houses; in all of Egypt the land was ruined because of the flies.

25 Then Pharaoh summoned Moses and Aaron, and said, "Go, sacrifice to your God within the land." 26 But Moses said, "It would not be right to do so; for the sacrifices that we offer to the LORD our God are offensive to the Egyptians. If we offer in the sight of the Egyptians sacrifices that are offensive to them, will they not stone us? 27 We must go a three days' journey into the wilderness and sacrifice to the LORD our God as he commands us." 28 So Pharaoh said, "I will let you go to sacrifice to the LORD your God in the wilderness, provided you do not go very far away. Pray for me." 29 Then Moses said, "As soon as I leave you, I will pray to the LORD that the swarms of flies may depart tomorrow from Pharaoh, from his officials, and from his people; only do not let Pharaoh again deal falsely by not letting the people go to sacrifice to the LORD."

30 So Moses went out from Pharaoh and prayed to the LORD. 31 And the LORD did as Moses asked: he removed the swarms of flies from Pharaoh, from his officials, and from his people; not one remained. 32 But Pharaoh hardened his heart this time also, and would not let the people go.

9 Then the LORD said to Moses, "Go to Pharaoh, and say to him, 'Thus says the LORD, the God of the Hebrews: Let my people go, so that they may worship me. 2 For if you refuse to let them go and still hold them, 3 the hand of the LORD will strike with a deadly pestilence on your livestock in the field: the horses, the donkeys, the camels, the herds, and the flocks. 4 But the LORD will make a distinction between the livestock of Israel and the livestock of Egypt, so that nothing shall die of all that belongs to the Israelites.'" 5 The LORD set a time, saying, "Tomorrow the LORD will do this thing in the land." 6 And on the next day the LORD did

presence, and Moses asked the LORD to remove the frogs which he had brought on Pharaoh. 13 The LORD granted the request, and in house, farmyard, and field all the frogs perished. 14 They were piled into countless heaps and the land stank. 15 But when Pharaoh found that he was given relief he became obdurate; as the LORD had foretold, he would not listen to Moses and Aaron.

16 The LORD told Moses to say to Aaron, 'Stretch out your staff and strike the dust on the ground, and it will turn into maggots throughout the whole of Egypt.' 17 They obeyed, and when Aaron stretched out his hand with his staff in it and struck the dust, it turned into maggots on man and beast. Throughout Egypt all the dust turned into maggots. 18 The magicians tried to produce maggots in the same way by their spells, but they failed. The maggots were everywhere, on man and beast. 19 'It is the hand of God,' said the magicians to Pharaoh, but Pharaoh remained obstinate; as the LORD had foretold, he would not listen.

20 The LORD told Moses to rise early in the morning and stand in Pharaoh's path as he went out to the river, and to say to him, 'These are the words of the LORD: Let my people go in order to worship me. 21 If you refuse, I shall send swarms of flies on you, your courtiers, your people, and your houses; the houses of the Egyptians will be filled with the swarms and so will all the land they live in. 22 But on that day I shall make an exception of Goshen, the land where my people live: there will be no swarms there. Thus you will know that I, the LORD, am here in the land. 23 I shall make a distinction between my people and yours. Tomorrow this sign will appear.' 24 The LORD did this; dense swarms of flies infested Pharaoh's palace and the houses of his courtiers; throughout Egypt the land was threatened with ruin by the swarms. 25 Pharaoh summoned Moses and Aaron and said to them, 'Go and sacrifice to your God, but in this country.' 26 'That is impossible,' replied Moses, 'because the victim we are to sacrifice to the LORD our God is an abomination to the Egyptians. If the Egyptians see us offer such an animal, they will surely stone us to death. 27 We must go a three days' journey into the wilderness to sacrifice to the LORD our God, as he commands us.' 28 'I shall let you go,' said Pharaoh, 'and you may sacrifice to your God in the wilderness; only do not go far. Now intercede for me.' 29 Moses answered, 'As soon as I leave you I shall intercede with the LORD. Tomorrow swarms will depart from Pharaoh, his courtiers, and his people. Only your majesty must not trifle any more with the people by preventing them from going to sacrifice to the LORD.'

30 Then Moses left Pharaoh and interceded with the LORD. 31 The LORD did as Moses had promised; he removed the swarms from Pharaoh, his courtiers, and his people; not one was left. 32 But once again Pharaoh became obdurate and would not let the people go.

9 The LORD said to Moses, 'Go in to Pharaoh and tell him, "The LORD the God of the Hebrews says: Let my people go in order to worship me. 2 If you refuse to let them go, if you still keep them in subjection, 3 the LORD will strike your livestock out in the country, the horses and donkeys, camels, cattle, and sheep with a devastating pestilence. 4 But the LORD will make a distinction between Israel's livestock and the livestock of the Egyptians. Of all that belong to Israel not a single one will die." ' 5 The LORD fixed a time and said, 'Tomorrow I shall do this throughout the land.' 6 The next day the LORD struck. All the livestock

---

u Or *frogs, as he had agreed with Pharaoh*   *v* Gk Vg: Heb *will set redemption*

8:23 **distinction:** *so Gk; Heb.* redemption.

NEW AMERICAN BIBLE

8 After Moses and Aaron left Pharaoh's presence, Moses implored the LORD to fulfill the promise he had made to Pharaoh about the frogs; 9 and the LORD did as Moses had asked. The frogs in the houses and courtyards and fields died off. 10 Heaps and heaps of them were gathered up, and there was a stench in the land. 11 But when Pharaoh saw that there was a respite, he became obdurate and would not listen to them, just as the LORD had foretold.

12 Thereupon the LORD said to Moses, "Tell Aaron to stretch out his staff and strike the dust of the earth, that it may be turned into gnats throughout the land of Egypt." 13 They did so. Aaron stretched out his hand, and with his staff he struck the dust of the earth, and gnats came upon man and beast. The dust of the earth was turned into gnats throughout the land of Egypt. 14 Though the magicians tried to bring forth gnats by their magic arts, they could not do so. As the gnats infested man and beast, 15 the magicians said to Pharaoh, "This is the finger of God." Yet Pharaoh remained obstinate and would not listen to them, just as the LORD had foretold.

16 Again the LORD told Moses, "Early tomorrow morning present yourself to Pharaoh when he goes forth to the water, and say to him: Thus says the LORD: Let my people go to worship me. 17 If you will not let my people go, I warn you, I will loose swarms of flies upon you and your servants and your subjects and your houses. The houses of the Egyptians and the very ground on which they stand shall be filled with swarms of flies. 18 But on that day I will make an exception of the land of Goshen: there shall be no flies where my people dwell, that you may know that I am the LORD in the midst of the earth. 19 I will make this distinction between my people and your people. This sign shall take place tomorrow." 20 This the LORD did. Thick swarms of flies entered the house of Pharaoh and houses of his servants; throughout Egypt the land was infested with flies.

21 Then Pharaoh summoned Moses and Aaron and said to them, "Go and offer sacrifice to your God in this land." 22 But Moses replied, "It is not right to do so, for the sacrifices we offer to the LORD, our God, are an abomination to the Egyptians. If before their very eyes we offer sacrifices which are an abomination to them, will not the Egyptians stone us? 23 We must go a three days' journey in the desert to offer sacrifice to the LORD, our God, as he commands us." 24 "Well, then," said Pharaoh, "I will let you go to offer sacrifice to the LORD, your God, in the desert, provided that you do not go too far away and that you pray for me." 25 Moses answered, "As soon as I leave your presence I will pray to the LORD that the flies may depart tomorrow from Pharaoh and his servants and his subjects. Pharaoh, however, must not play false again by refusing to let the people go to offer sacrifice to the LORD." 26 When Moses left Pharaoh's presence, he prayed to the LORD; 27 and the LORD did as Moses had asked. He removed the flies from Pharaoh and his servants and subjects. Not one remained. 28 But once more Pharaoh became obdurate and would not let the people go.

9 Then the LORD said to Moses, "Go to Pharaoh and tell him: Thus says the LORD, the God of the Hebrews: Let my people go to worship me. 2 If you refuse to let them go and persist in holding them, 3 I warn you, the LORD will afflict all your livestock in the field—your horses, asses, camels, herds and flocks—with a very severe pestilence. 4 But the LORD will distinguish between the livestock of Israel and that of Egypt, so that none belonging to the Israelites will die." 5 And setting a definite time, the LORD added, "Tomorrow the LORD shall do this in the land."

NEW JERUSALEM BIBLE

and Aaron left Pharaoh's presence, and Moses pleaded with Yahweh about the frogs which he had inflicted on Pharaoh. 9 Yahweh did as Moses asked, and in house and courtyard and field the frogs died. 10 They piled them up in heaps and the country stank. 11 But once Pharaoh saw that there had been a respite, he became obstinate and, as Yahweh had foretold, refused to listen to them.

12 Yahweh then said to Moses, 'Say to Aaron, " Stretch out your staff and strike the dust of the earth, and it will turn into mosquitoes throughout the whole of Egypt." ' 13 Aaron stretched out his hand, with his staff, and struck the dust of the earth, and there were mosquitoes on man and beast; all the dust of the earth turned into mosquitoes throughout the whole of Egypt. 14 By their spells the magicians tried to produce mosquitoes in the same way but failed, and there were mosquitoes on man and beast. 15 So the magicians said to Pharaoh, 'This is the finger of God.' But Pharaoh was obstinate and, as Yahweh had foretold, refused to listen to them.

16 Yahweh then said to Moses, 'Get up early in the morning and confront Pharaoh as he makes his way to the water. Say to him, "Yahweh says this: Let my people go and worship me. 17 But if you will not let my people go, I shall send horseflies on you, on your officials, your subjects and your houses. The Egyptians' houses will swarm with horseflies, and so will the very ground they stand on. 18 But I shall exempt the region of Goshen, where my people are living, that day; there will be no horseflies there, so that you will know that I am Yahweh, here in this country. 19 I shall make a distinction between my people and your people. This sign will take place tomorrow." ' 20 Yahweh did this, and great swarms of horseflies found their way into Pharaoh's palace, into his officials' houses and all over Egypt; the country was ruined by the horseflies.

21 Pharaoh then summoned Moses and Aaron and said, 'Go and sacrifice to your God, inside the country.' 22 'That would never do,' Moses said, 'since what we sacrifice to Yahweh our God is outrageous to the Egyptians. If the Egyptians see us offering sacrifices which outrage them, won't they stone us? 23 We shall make a three-days' journey into the desert to sacrifice to Yahweh our God, as he has ordered us.' 24 Pharaoh said, 'I will let you go and sacrifice to Yahweh your God in the desert, provided you do not go very far. Pray for me.' 25 'The moment I leave you,' Moses said, 'I shall pray to Yahweh. Tomorrow morning the horseflies will leave Pharaoh, his officials and his subjects. But Pharaoh must stop trifling with us by not allowing the people to go and sacrifice to Yahweh.' 26 Moses then left Pharaoh's presence and prayed to Yahweh, 27 and Yahweh did as Moses asked; the horseflies left Pharaoh, his officials and his subjects; not one remained. 28 But Pharaoh became obstinate this time too and did not let the people go.

9 Yahweh then said to Moses, 'Go to Pharaoh and say to him, "Yahweh, God of the Hebrews, says this: Let my people go and worship me. 2 If you refuse to let them go and detain them any longer, 3 look, the hand of Yahweh will strike your livestock in the fields, horses, donkeys, camels, oxen and flocks with a deadly plague. 4 Yahweh will discriminate between the livestock of Israel and the livestock of Egypt: nothing of what belongs to the Israelites will die. 5 Yahweh has fixed the time. Tomorrow, he has said, Yahweh will do this in the country." ' 6 Next day Yahweh did

NEW REVISED STANDARD VERSION

REVISED ENGLISH BIBLE

so; all the livestock of the Egyptians died, but of the livestock of the Israelites not one died. 7 Pharaoh inquired and found that not one of the livestock of the Israelites was dead. But the heart of Pharaoh was hardened, and he would not let the people go.

8 Then the LORD said to Moses and Aaron, "Take handfuls of soot from the kiln, and let Moses throw it in the air in the sight of Pharaoh. 9 It shall become fine dust all over the land of Egypt, and shall cause festering boils on humans and animals throughout the whole land of Egypt." 10 So they took soot from the kiln, and stood before Pharaoh, and Moses threw it in the air, and it caused festering boils on humans and animals. 11 The magicians could not stand before Moses because of the boils, for the boils afflicted the magicians as well as all the Egyptians. 12 But the LORD hardened the heart of Pharaoh, and he would not listen to them, just as the LORD had spoken to Moses.

13 Then the LORD said to Moses, "Rise up early in the morning and present yourself before Pharaoh, and say to him, 'Thus says the LORD, the God of the Hebrews: Let my people go, so that they may worship me. 14 For this time I will send all my plagues upon you yourself, and upon your officials, and upon your people, so that you may know that there is no one like me in all the earth. 15 For by now I could have stretched out my hand and struck you and your people with pestilence, and you would have been cut off from the earth. 16 But this is why I have let you live: to show you my power, and to make my name resound through all the earth. 17 You are still exalting yourself against my people, and will not let them go. 18 Tomorrow at this time I will cause the heaviest hail to fall that has ever fallen in Egypt from the day it was founded until now. 19 Send, therefore, and have your livestock and everything that you have in the open field brought to a secure place; every human or animal that is in the open field and is not brought under shelter will die when the hail comes down upon them.' " 20 Those officials of Pharaoh who feared the word of the LORD hurried their slaves and livestock off to a secure place. 21 Those who did not regard the word of the LORD left their slaves and livestock in the open field.

22 The LORD said to Moses, "Stretch out your hand toward heaven so that hail may fall on the whole land of Egypt, on humans and animals and all the plants of the field in the land of Egypt." 23 Then Moses stretched out his staff toward heaven, and the LORD sent thunder and hail, and fire came down on the earth. And the LORD rained hail on the land of Egypt; 24 there was hail with fire flashing continually in the midst of it, such heavy hail as had never fallen in all the land of Egypt since it became a nation. 25 The hail struck down everything that was in the open field throughout all the land of Egypt, both human and animal; the hail also struck down all the plants of the field, and shattered every tree in the field. 26 Only in the land of Goshen, where the Israelites were, there was no hail.

27 Then Pharaoh summoned Moses and Aaron, and said to them, "This time I have sinned; the LORD is in the right, and I and my people are in the wrong. 28 Pray to the LORD! Enough of God's thunder and hail! I will let you go; you need stay no longer." 29 Moses said to him, "As soon as I have gone out of the city, I will stretch out my hands to the LORD; the thunder will cease, and there will be no more hail, so that you may know that the earth is the LORD's. 30 But as for you and your officials, I know that you do not yet fear the LORD God." 31 (Now the flax and the barley were ruined, for the barley was in the ear and the flax was in bud. 32 But the wheat and the spelt were not ruined, for they are late in coming up.) 33 So Moses left Pharaoh, went

of Egypt died, but from Israel's livestock not one single beast died. 7 Pharaoh made enquiries and was told that from Israel's livestock not an animal had died; and yet he remained obdurate and would not let the people go.

8 The LORD said to Moses and Aaron, 'Take handfuls of soot from a kiln, and when Moses tosses it into the air in Pharaoh's sight, 9 it will turn into a fine dust over the whole of Egypt. Throughout the land it will produce festering boils on man and beast.' 10 They took the soot from the kiln and when they stood before Pharaoh, Moses tossed it into the air, and it produced festering boils on man and beast. 11 The magicians were no match for Moses because of the boils, which attacked them and all the Egyptians. 12 But the LORD made Pharaoh obstinate; as the LORD had foretold to Moses, he would not listen to Moses and Aaron.

13 The LORD then told Moses to rise early and confront Pharaoh, saying to him, 'The LORD the God of the Hebrews has said: Let my people go in order to worship me. 14 This time I shall strike home with all my plagues against you yourself, your courtiers, and your people, so that you may know that there is none like me in all the world. 15 By now I could have stretched out my hand, and struck you and your people with pestilence, and you would have vanished from the earth. 16 I have let you live only to show you my power and to spread my fame all over the world. 17 Since you still obstruct my people and will not let them go, 18 tomorrow at this time I shall cause a violent hailstorm to come, such as has never been in Egypt from its first beginnings until now. 19 Send now and bring your herds under cover, and everything you have out in the open field. Anything which happens to be left out in the open, whether man or beast, will die when the hail falls on it.' 20 Those of Pharaoh's subjects who feared the warning of the LORD hurried their slaves and livestock into shelter; 21 but those who did not take it to heart left them in the open.

22 The LORD said to Moses, 'Stretch your hand towards the sky to bring down hail on the whole land of Egypt, on man and beast and every growing thing throughout the land.' 23 As Moses stretched his staff towards the sky, the LORD sent thunder and hail, with fire flashing to the ground. The LORD rained down hail on the land of Egypt, 24 hail and fiery flashes through the hail, so heavy that there had been nothing like it in all Egypt from the time that Egypt became a nation. 25 Throughout Egypt the hail struck down everything in the fields, both man and beast; it beat down every growing thing and shattered every tree. 26 Only in the land of Goshen, where the Israelites lived, was there no hail.

27 Pharaoh summoned Moses and Aaron. 'This time I have sinned,' he said; 'the LORD is in the right; I and my people are in the wrong. 28 Intercede with the LORD, for we can bear no more of this thunder and hail. I shall let you go; you need stay no longer.' 29 Moses said, 'As soon as I leave the city I shall spread out my hands in prayer to the LORD. The thunder will cease, and there will be no more hail, so that you may know that the earth is the LORD's. 30 But you and your subjects, I know, do not yet fear the LORD God.' 31 (The flax and barley were destroyed because the barley was in the ear and the flax in bud, 32 but the wheat and vetches were not destroyed because they come later.) 33 Mo-

6 And on the next day the LORD did so. All the livestock of the Egyptians died, but not one beast belonging to the Israelites. 7 But though Pharaoh's messengers informed him that not even one beast belonging to the Israelites had died, he still remained obdurate and would not let the people go.

8 Then the LORD said to Moses and Aaron, "Take a double handful of soot from a furnace, and in the presence of Pharaoh let Moses scatter it toward the sky. 9 It will then turn into fine dust over the whole land of Egypt and cause festering boils on man and beast throughout the land."

10 So they took soot from a furnace and stood in the presence of Pharaoh. Moses scattered it toward the sky, and it caused festering boils on man and beast. 11 The magicians could not stand in Moses' presence, for there were boils on the magicians no less than on the rest of the Egyptians. 12 But the LORD made Pharaoh obstinate, and he would not listen to them, just as the LORD had foretold to Moses.

13 Then the LORD told Moses, "Early tomorrow morning present yourself to Pharaoh and say to him: Thus says the LORD, the God of the Hebrews: Let my people go to worship me, 14 or this time I will hurl all my blows upon you and your servants and your subjects, that you may know that there is none like me anywhere on earth. 15 For by now I would have stretched out my hand and struck you and your subjects with such pestilence as would wipe you from the earth. 16 But this is why I have spared you: to show you my power and to make my name resound throughout the earth! 17 Will you still block the way for my people by refusing to let them go? 18 I warn you, then, tomorrow at this hour I will rain down such fierce hail as there has never been in Egypt from the day the nation was founded up to the present. 19 Therefore, order all your livestock and whatever else you have in the open fields to be brought to a place of safety. Whatever man or beast remains in the fields and is not brought to shelter shall die when the hail comes upon them." 20 Some of Pharaoh's servants feared the warning of the LORD and hurried their servants and livestock off to shelter. 21 Others, however, did not take the warning of the LORD to heart and left their servants and livestock in the fields.

22 The LORD then said to Moses, "Stretch out your hand toward the sky, that hail may fall upon the entire land of Egypt, on man and beast and every growing thing in the land of Egypt." 23 When Moses stretched out his staff toward the sky, the LORD sent forth hail and peals of thunder. Lightning flashed toward the earth, and the LORD rained down hail upon the land of Egypt; 24 and lightning constantly flashed through the hail, such fierce hail as had never been seen in the land since Egypt became a nation. 25 It struck down every man and beast that was in the open throughout the land of Egypt; it beat down every growing thing and splintered every tree in the fields. 26 Only in the land of Goshen, where the Israelites dwelt, was there no hail.

27 Then Pharaoh summoned Moses and Aaron and said to them, "I have sinned again! The LORD is just; it is I and my subjects who are at fault. 28 Pray to the LORD, for we have had enough of God's thunder and hail. Then I will let you go; you need stay no longer." 29 Moses replied, "As soon as I leave the city I will extend my hands to the LORD; the thunder will cease, and there will be no more hail. Thus you shall learn that the earth is the LORD's. 30 But you and your servants, I know, do not yet fear the LORD God."

31 Now the flax and the barley were ruined, because the barley was in ear and the flax in bud. 32 But the wheat and the spelt were not ruined, for they grow later.

this: all the Egyptians' livestock died, but nothing of the livestock owned by the Israelites died. 7 Pharaoh had enquiries made, and found that of the livestock owned by the Israelites not a single beast had died. But Pharaoh was obstinate and did not let the people go.

8 Yahweh then said to Moses and Aaron, 'Take handfuls of soot from the kiln, and before Pharaoh's eyes let Moses throw it in the air. 9 It will turn into fine dust over the whole of Egypt and produce boils breaking into sores on man and beast throughout the whole of Egypt.' 10 So they took soot from the kiln and stood in front of Pharaoh, and Moses threw it in the air, and on man and beast it brought out boils breaking into sores. 11 And the magicians could not compete with Moses in the matter of the boils, for the magicians were covered with boils like all the other Egyptians. 12 But Yahweh made Pharaoh stubborn and, as Yahweh had foretold to Moses, he did not listen to them.

13 Yahweh then said to Moses, 'Get up early in the morning and confront Pharaoh. Say to him, "Yahweh, God of the Hebrews, says this: Let my people go and worship me. 14 For this time I am going to inflict all my plagues on you, on your officials and on your subjects, so that you will know that there is no one like me in the whole world. 15 Had I stretched out my hand to strike you and your subjects with pestilence, you would have been swept from the earth. 16 But I have let you survive for this reason: to display my power to you and to have my name talked of throughout the world. 17 Since you take a high hand with my people, refusing to let them go, 18 very well, at about this time tomorrow, I shall cause so severe a hail to fall as was never known in Egypt from the day of its foundation until now. 19 So now send word to have your livestock and everything else you own in the fields put under cover. On man or beast, all that happen to be in the fields and are not brought indoors, the hail will fall and they will die." ' 20 Those of Pharaoh's officials who respected what Yahweh said, brought their slaves and livestock indoors, 21 but those who did not take to heart what Yahweh said left their slaves and livestock in the fields.

22 Yahweh then said to Moses, 'Stretch out your hand towards heaven so that it hails throughout the whole of Egypt, on man and beast and on everything growing anywhere in Egypt.' 23 Moses stretched out his staff towards heaven, and Yahweh thundered and rained down hail. Lightning struck the earth and Yahweh rained down hail on Egypt. 24 And so there was hail, and lightning accompanied the hail, very severe, such as had never been known anywhere in Egypt since it first became a nation. 25 All over Egypt the hail struck down everything in the fields, man and beast, and the hail beat down everything growing in the fields and shattered all the trees in the fields. 26 The only place where there was no hail was in the Goshen region, where the Israelites lived.

27 Pharaoh then sent for Moses and Aaron and said, 'This time, I have sinned. Yahweh is in the right; I and my subjects are in the wrong. 28 Pray to Yahweh, for we cannot bear any more of this thunder and hail. I promise to let you go. You need stay no longer.' 29 Moses said to him, 'The moment I leave the city I shall stretch out my hands to Yahweh. The thunder will stop, and there will be no more hail, so that you may know that the earth belongs to Yahweh. 30 But as for you and your officials, I know very well that you still have no respect for Yahweh God.' 31 The flax and the barley were ruined, since the barley was in the ear and the flax in bud, 32 but the wheat and spelt were not destroyed, being late crops.

| NEW REVISED STANDARD VERSION | REVISED ENGLISH BIBLE |

out of the city, and stretched out his hands to the LORD; then the thunder and the hail ceased, and the rain no longer poured down on the earth. 34 But when Pharaoh saw that the rain and the hail and the thunder had ceased, he sinned once more and hardened his heart, he and his officials. 35 So the heart of Pharaoh was hardened, and he would not let the Israelites go, just as the LORD had spoken through Moses.

10 Then the LORD said to Moses, "Go to Pharaoh; for I have hardened his heart and the heart of his officials, in order that I may show these signs of mine among them, 2 and that you may tell your children and grandchildren how I have made fools of the Egyptians and what signs I have done among them — so that you may know that I am the LORD."

3 So Moses and Aaron went to Pharaoh, and said to him, "Thus says the LORD, the God of the Hebrews, 'How long will you refuse to humble yourself before me? Let my people go, so that they may worship me. 4 For if you refuse to let my people go, tomorrow I will bring locusts into your country. 5 They shall cover the surface of the land, so that no one will be able to see the land. They shall devour the last remnant left you after the hail, and they shall devour every tree of yours that grows in the field. 6 They shall fill your houses, and the houses of all your officials and of all the Egyptians — something that neither your parents nor your grandparents have seen, from the day they came on earth to this day.'" Then he turned and went out from Pharaoh.

7 Pharaoh's officials said to him, "How long shall this fellow be a snare to us? Let the people go, so that they may worship the LORD their God; do you not yet understand that Egypt is ruined?" 8 So Moses and Aaron were brought back to Pharaoh, and he said to them, "Go, worship the LORD your God! But which ones are to go?" 9 Moses said, "We will go with our young and our old; we will go with our sons and daughters and with our flocks and herds, because we have the LORD's festival to celebrate." 10 He said to them, "The LORD indeed will be with you, if ever I let your little ones go with you! Plainly, you have some evil purpose in mind. 11 No, never! Your men may go and worship the LORD, for that is what you are asking." And they were driven out from Pharaoh's presence.

12 Then the LORD said to Moses, "Stretch out your hand over the land of Egypt, so that the locusts may come upon it and eat every plant in the land, all that the hail has left." 13 So Moses stretched out his staff over the land of Egypt, and the LORD brought an east wind upon the land all that day and all that night; when morning came, the east wind had brought the locusts. 14 The locusts came upon all the land of Egypt and settled on the whole country of Egypt, such a dense swarm of locusts as had never been before, nor ever shall be again. 15 They covered the surface of the whole land, so that the land was black; and they ate all the plants in the land and all the fruit of the trees that the hail had left; nothing green was left, no tree, no plant in the field, in all the land of Egypt. 16 Pharaoh hurriedly summoned Moses and Aaron and said, "I have sinned against the LORD your God, and against you. 17 Do forgive my sin just this once, and pray to the LORD your God that at the least he remove this deadly thing from me." 18 So he went out from Pharaoh and prayed to the LORD. 19 The LORD changed the wind into a very strong west wind, which lifted the locusts and drove them into the Red Sea;[w] not a single locust was left in all the country of Egypt. 20 But the LORD hardened Pharaoh's heart, and he would not let the Israelites go.

ses left Pharaoh's presence and went out of the city, where he lifted up his hands to the LORD in prayer: the thunder and hail ceased, and no more rain fell. 34 When Pharaoh saw that the downpour, the hail, and the thunder had ceased, he went back to his sinful obduracy, he and his courtiers. 35 Pharaoh remained obstinate; as the LORD had foretold through Moses, he would not let the people go.

10 The LORD said to Moses, 'Go in to Pharaoh. I have made him and his courtiers obdurate, so that I may show these signs among them, 2 and so that you can tell your children and grandchildren the story: how I toyed with the Egyptians, and what signs I showed among them. Thus you will know that I am the LORD.'

3 Moses and Aaron went to Pharaoh and said to him, 'The LORD the God of the Hebrews has said: How long will you refuse to humble yourself before me? Let my people go in order to worship me. 4 If you refuse to let them go, tomorrow I am going to bring locusts into your country. 5 They will cover the face of the land so that it cannot be seen. They will eat up the last remnant left you by the hail. They will devour every tree that grows in your countryside. 6 Your houses and your courtiers' houses, every house in Egypt, will be full of them; your fathers never saw the like, nor their fathers before them; such a thing has not happened from their time until now.' With that he turned and left Pharaoh's presence.

7 Pharaoh's courtiers said to him, 'How long must we be caught in this man's toils? Let their menfolk go and worship the LORD their God. Do you not know by now that Egypt is ruined?' 8 So Moses and Aaron were brought back to Pharaoh, and he said to them, 'Go, worship the LORD your God; but who exactly is to go?' 9 'Everyone,' said Moses, 'young and old, boys and girls, sheep and cattle; for we have to keep the LORD's pilgrim-feast.' 10 Pharaoh replied, 'The LORD be with you if I let you and your dependants go! You have some sinister purpose in mind. 11 No, your menfolk may go and worship the LORD, for that is what you were asking for.' And they were driven from Pharaoh's presence.

12 The LORD said to Moses, 'Stretch out your hand over Egypt so that locusts may come and invade the land and devour all the vegetation in it, whatever the hail has left.' 13 When Moses stretched out his staff over the land of Egypt, the LORD sent a wind roaring in from the east all that day and all that night; and when morning came the east wind had brought the locusts. 14 They invaded the whole land of Egypt, and settled on all its territory in swarms so dense that the like of them had never been seen before, nor ever will be again. 15 They covered the surface of the whole land till it was black with them; they devoured all the vegetation and all the fruit of the trees that the hail had spared; there was no green left on tree or plant throughout all Egypt.

16 Pharaoh hastily summoned Moses and Aaron. 'I have sinned against the LORD your God and against you,' he said. 17 'Forgive my sin, I pray, just this once, and intercede with the LORD your God to remove this deadly plague from me.' 18 When Moses left Pharaoh and interceded with the LORD, 19 the wind was changed by the LORD into a westerly gale, which carried the locusts away and swept them into the Red Sea. Not one locust was left within the borders of Egypt. 20 But the LORD made Pharaoh obstinate, and he would not let the Israelites go.

10:12 **so that . . . come:** *so Gk; Heb.* with the locusts.
10:19 **Red Sea:** *or* sea of Reeds.

[w] Or *Sea of Reeds*

132

33 When Moses had left Pharaoh's presence and had gone out of the city, he extended his hands to the LORD. Then the thunder and the hail ceased, and the rain no longer poured down upon the earth. 34 But Pharaoh, seeing that the rain and hail and thunder had ceased, sinned again: he with his servants became obdurate, 35 and in his obstinacy he would not let the Israelites go, as the LORD had foretold through Moses.

10 Then the LORD said to Moses, "Go to Pharaoh, for I have made him and his servants obdurate in order that I may perform these signs of mine among them 2 and that you may recount to your son and grandson how ruthlessly I dealt with the Egyptians and what signs I wrought among them, so that you may know that I am the LORD."

3 So Moses and Aaron went to Pharaoh and told him, "Thus says the LORD, the God of the Hebrews: How long will you refuse to submit to me? Let my people go to worship me. 4 If you refuse to let my people go, I warn you, tomorrow I will bring locusts into your country. 5 They shall cover the ground, so that the ground itself will not be visible. They shall eat up the remnant you saved unhurt from the hail, as well as all the foliage that has since sprouted in your fields. 6 They shall fill your houses and the houses of your servants and of all the Egyptians; such a sight your fathers or grandfathers have not seen from the day they first settled on this soil up to the present day." With that he turned and left Pharaoh.

7 But Pharaoh's servants said to him, "How long must he be a menace to us? Let the men go to worship the LORD, their God. Do you not yet realize that Egypt is being destroyed?" 8 So Moses and Aaron were brought back to Pharaoh, who said to them, "You may go and worship the LORD, your God. But how many of you will go?" 9 "Young and old must go with us," Moses answered, "our sons and daughters as well as our flocks and herds must accompany us. That is what a feast of the LORD means to us." 10 "The LORD help you," Pharaoh replied, "if I ever let your little ones go with you! Clearly, you have some evil in mind. 11 No, no! Just you men can go and worship the LORD. After all, that is what you want." With that they were driven from Pharaoh's presence.

12 The LORD then said to Moses, "Stretch out your hand over the land of Egypt, that locusts may swarm over it and eat up all the vegetation and whatever the hail has left." 13 So Moses stretched out his staff over the land of Egypt, and the LORD sent an east wind blowing over the land all that day and all that night. At dawn the east wind brought the locusts. 14 They swarmed over the whole land of Egypt and settled down on every part of it. Never before had there been such a fierce swarm of locusts, nor will there ever be. 15 They covered the surface of the whole land, till it was black with them. They ate up all the vegetation in the land and the fruit of whatever trees the hail had spared. Nothing green was left on any tree or plant throughout the land of Egypt.

16 Hastily Pharaoh summoned Moses and Aaron and said, "I have sinned against the LORD, your God, and against you. 17 But now, do forgive me my sin once more, and pray the LORD, your God, to take at least this deadly pest from me." 18 When Moses left the presence of Pharaoh, he prayed to the LORD, 19 and the LORD changed the wind to a very strong west wind, which took up the locusts and hurled them into the Red Sea. But though not a single locust remained within the confines of Egypt, 20 the LORD made Pharaoh obstinate, and he would not let the Israelites go.

33 Moses left Pharaoh and went out of the city. He stretched out his hands to Yahweh and the thunder and hail ceased and the rain stopped pouring down on the earth. 34 When Pharaoh saw that rain and hail and thunder had stopped, he relapsed into sin, 35 and he and his officials became obstinate again. Pharaoh was stubborn and, as Yahweh had foretold through Moses, refused to let the Israelites go.

10 Yahweh then said to Moses, 'Go to Pharaoh, for I have made him and his officials stubborn, to display these signs of mine among them; 2 so that you can tell your sons and your grandsons how I made fools of the Egyptians and what signs I performed among them, so that you would know that I am Yahweh.' 3 Moses and Aaron then went to Pharaoh and said to him, 'Yahweh, God of the Hebrews, says this, "How much longer will you refuse to submit to me? Let my people go and worship me. 4 Or, if you refuse to let my people go, tomorrow I shall send locusts into your country. 5 They will cover the surface of the soil so that the soil cannot be seen. They will devour the remainder of what has escaped, of what you have been left after the hail; they will devour all your trees growing in the fields; 6 they will fill your houses, all your officials' houses and all the Egyptians' houses — something your ancestors and your ancestors' ancestors have never seen from the day they first appeared on earth until now." ' Then he turned on his heel and left Pharaoh's presence. 7 At which, Pharaoh's officials said to him, 'How much longer are we to be tricked by this fellow? Let the people go and worship Yahweh their God. Do you not finally realise that Egypt is on the brink of ruin?'

8 So Moses and Aaron were brought back to Pharaoh who said to them, 'Go and worship Yahweh your God. But who are to go?' 9 Moses replied, 'We shall take our young men and our old men, we shall take our sons and daughters, our flocks and our herds, since we are going to hold a feast in Yahweh's honour.' 10 Pharaoh said, 'So I must let you go with your wives and children! May Yahweh preserve you! Plainly, you are up to no good! 11 Oh no! You men may go and worship Yahweh, since that was your original request.' With that, they were driven from Pharaoh's presence.

12 Yahweh then said to Moses, 'Stretch out your hand over Egypt for the locusts. Let them invade Egypt and devour whatever is growing in the country, whatever the hail has left!' 13 Moses stretched his staff over Egypt, and over the country Yahweh sent an east wind which blew all that day and night. By morning, the east wind had brought the locusts. 14 The locusts invaded the whole of Egypt and settled all over Egypt, in great swarms; never had there been so many locusts before, nor would there be again. 15 They covered the surface of the ground till the land was devastated. They devoured whatever was growing in the fields and all the fruit on the trees that the hail had left. No green was left on tree or plant in the fields anywhere in Egypt.

16 Pharaoh sent urgently for Moses and Aaron and said, 'I have sinned against Yahweh your God and against you. 17 Now forgive my sin, I implore you, just this once, and entreat Yahweh your God to turn this deadly thing away from me.' 18 When Moses left Pharaoh's presence he prayed to Yahweh, 19 and Yahweh changed the wind into a west wind, very strong, which carried the locusts away and swept them into the Sea of Reeds. There was not one locust left in the whole of Egypt. 20 But Yahweh made Pharaoh stubborn, and he did not let the Israelites go.

NEW REVISED STANDARD VERSION	REVISED ENGLISH BIBLE

21 Then the LORD said to Moses, "Stretch out your hand toward heaven so that there may be darkness over the land of Egypt, a darkness that can be felt." 22 So Moses stretched out his hand toward heaven, and there was dense darkness in all the land of Egypt for three days. 23 People could not see one another, and for three days they could not move from where they were; but all the Israelites had light where they lived. 24 Then Pharaoh summoned Moses, and said, "Go, worship the LORD. Only your flocks and your herds shall remain behind. Even your children may go with you." 25 But Moses said, "You must also let us have sacrifices and burnt offerings to sacrifice to the LORD our God. 26 Our livestock also must go with us; not a hoof shall be left behind, for we must choose some of them for the worship of the LORD our God, and we will not know what to use to worship the LORD until we arrive there." 27 But the LORD hardened Pharaoh's heart, and he was unwilling to let them go. 28 Then Pharaoh said to him, "Get away from me! Take care that you do not see my face again, for on the day you see my face you shall die." 29 Moses said, "Just as you say! I will never see your face again."

11 The LORD said to Moses, "I will bring one more plague upon Pharaoh and upon Egypt; afterwards he will let you go from here; indeed, when he lets you go, he will drive you away. 2 Tell the people that every man is to ask his neighbor and every woman is to ask her neighbor for objects of silver and gold." 3 The LORD gave the people favor in the sight of the Egyptians. Moreover, Moses himself was a man of great importance in the land of Egypt, in the sight of Pharaoh's officials and in the sight of the people.

4 Moses said, "Thus says the LORD: About midnight I will go out through Egypt. 5 Every firstborn in the land of Egypt shall die, from the firstborn of Pharaoh who sits on his throne to the firstborn of the female slave who is behind the handmill, and all the firstborn of the livestock. 6 Then there will be a loud cry throughout the whole land of Egypt, such as has never been or will ever be again. 7 But not a dog shall growl at any of the Israelites—not at people, not at animals—so that you may know that the LORD makes a distinction between Egypt and Israel. 8 Then all these officials of yours shall come down to me, and bow low to me, saying, 'Leave us, you and all the people who follow you.' After that I will leave." And in hot anger he left Pharaoh.

9 The LORD said to Moses, "Pharaoh will not listen to you, in order that my wonders may be multiplied in the land of Egypt." 10 Moses and Aaron performed all these wonders before Pharaoh; but the LORD hardened Pharaoh's heart, and he did not let the people of Israel go out of his land.

12 The LORD said to Moses and Aaron in the land of Egypt: 2 This month shall mark for you the beginning of months; it shall be the first month of the year for you. 3 Tell the whole congregation of Israel that on the tenth of this month they are to take a lamb for each family, a lamb for each household. 4 If a household is too small for a whole lamb, it shall join its closest neighbor in obtaining one; the lamb shall be divided in proportion to the number of people who eat of it. 5 Your lamb shall be without blemish, a year-old male; you may take it from the sheep or from the goats. 6 You shall keep it until the fourteenth day of this month; then the whole assembled congregation of Israel shall slaughter it at twilight. 7 They shall take some of the blood and put it on the two doorposts and the lintel of the houses in which they eat it. 8 They shall eat the lamb that

21 Then the LORD said to Moses, 'Stretch out your hand towards the sky so that over the land of Egypt there may be a darkness so dense that it can be felt.' 22 Moses stretched out his hand towards the sky, and for three days pitch darkness covered the whole land of Egypt. 23 People could not see one another, and for three days no one stirred from where he was. But where the Israelites were living there was no darkness.

24 Pharaoh summoned Moses. 'Go, worship the LORD,' he said. 'Your dependants may go with you; but your flocks and herds must remain here.' 25 But Moses said, 'No, you yourself must supply us with animals for sacrifice and whole-offering to the LORD our God; 26 and our own livestock must go with us too—not a hoof must be left behind. We may need animals from our own flocks to worship the LORD our God; we ourselves cannot tell until we are there how we are to worship the LORD.' 27 The LORD made Pharaoh obstinate, and he refused to let them go. 28 'Be off! Leave me!' he said to Moses. 'Mind you do not see my face again, for on the day you do, you die.' 29 'You are right,' said Moses; 'I shall not see your face again.'

11 The LORD said to Moses, 'One last plague I shall bring on Pharaoh and Egypt. When he finally lets you go, he will drive you out forcibly as a man might dismiss a rejected bride. 2 Tell the people that everyone, men and women, should ask their neighbours for silver and gold jewellery.' 3 The LORD made the Egyptians well disposed towards them and, moreover, in Egypt Moses was a very great man in the eyes of Pharaoh's courtiers and of the people.

4 Moses said, 'The LORD said: At midnight I shall go out among the Egyptians. 5 All the firstborn in Egypt shall die, from the firstborn of Pharaoh on his throne to the firstborn of the slave-girl at the handmill, besides the firstborn of the cattle. 6 From all over Egypt there will go up a great cry, the like of which has never been heard before, nor ever will be again. 7 But throughout all Israel no sound will be heard from man or beast, not even a dog's bark. Thus you will know that the LORD distinguishes between Egypt and Israel. 8 All these courtiers of yours will come down to me, prostrate themselves, and cry, "Go away, you and all the people who follow at your heels." When that time comes I shall go.' In hot anger, Moses left Pharaoh's presence.

9 The LORD said to Moses, 'Pharaoh will not listen to you; I shall therefore show still more portents in the land of Egypt.' 10 Moses and Aaron had shown all these portents in the presence of Pharaoh, and yet the LORD made him obstinate, and he would not let the Israelites leave his country.

12 THE LORD said to Moses and Aaron in Egypt: 2 'This month is to be for you the first of the months; you are to make it the first month of the year. 3 Say to the whole community of Israel: On the tenth day of this month let each man procure a lamb or kid for his family, one for each household, 4 but if a household is too small for one lamb or kid, then, taking into account the number of persons, the man and his nearest neighbour may take one between them. They are to share the cost according to the amount each person eats. 5 Your animal, taken either from the sheep or the goats, must be without blemish, a yearling male. 6 Have it in safe keeping until the fourteenth day of this month, and then let all the assembled community of Israel must slaughter the victims between dusk and dark. 7 They must take some of the blood and smear it on the two doorposts and on the lintel of the houses in which they eat the victims. 8 On that night they must eat the flesh roasted on

12:6 **between . . . dark:** *lit.* between the two evenings.

21 Then the LORD said to Moses, "Stretch out your hand toward the sky, that over the land of Egypt there may be such intense darkness that one can feel it." 22 So Moses stretched out his hand toward the sky, and there was dense darkness throughout the land of Egypt for three days. 23 Men could not see one another, nor could they move from where they were, for three days. But all the Israelites had light where they dwelt.

24 Pharaoh then summoned Moses and Aaron and said, "Go and worship the LORD. Your little ones, too, may go with you. But your flocks and herds must remain." 25 Moses replied, "You must also grant us sacrifices and holocausts to offer up to the LORD, our God. 26 Hence, our livestock also must go with us. Not an animal must be left behind. Some of them we must sacrifice to the LORD, our God, but we ourselves shall not know which ones we must sacrifice to him until we arrive at the place itself." 27 But the LORD made Pharaoh obstinate, and he would not let them go. 28 "Leave my presence," Pharaoh said to him, "and see to it that you do not appear before me again! The day you appear before me you shall die!" 29 Moses replied, "Well said! I will never appear before you again."

11 Then the LORD told Moses, "One more plague will I bring upon Pharaoh and upon Egypt. After that he will let you depart. In fact, he will not merely let you go; he will drive you away. 2 Instruct your people that every man is to ask his neighbor, and every woman her neighbor, for silver and gold articles and for clothing." 3 The LORD indeed made the Egyptians well-disposed toward the people; Moses himself was very highly regarded by Pharaoh's servants and the people in the land of Egypt.

4 Moses then said, "Thus says the LORD: At midnight I will go forth through Egypt. 5 Every first-born in this land shall die, from the first-born of Pharaoh on the throne to the first-born of the slave-girl at the handmill, as well as all the first-born of the animals. 6 Then there shall be loud wailing throughout the land of Egypt, such as has never been, nor will ever be again. 7 But among the Israelites and their animals not even a dog shall growl, so that you may know how the LORD distinguishes between the Egyptians and the Israelites. 8 All these servants of yours shall then come down to me, and prostrate before me, they shall beg me, 'Leave us, you and all your followers!' Only then will I depart." With that he left Pharaoh's presence in hot anger.

9 The LORD said to Moses, "Pharaoh refuses to listen to you that my wonders may be multiplied in the land of Egypt." 10 Thus, although Moses and Aaron performed these various wonders in Pharaoh's presence, the LORD made Pharaoh obstinate, and he would not let the Israelites leave his land.

12 The LORD said to Moses and Aaron in the land of Egypt, 2 "This month shall stand at the head of your calendar; you shall reckon it the first month of the year. 3 Tell the whole community of Israel: On the tenth of this month every one of your families must procure for itself a lamb, a apiece for each household. 4 If a family is too small for a whole lamb, it shall join the nearest household in procuring one and shall share in the lamb in proportion to the number of persons who partake of it. 5 The lamb must be a year-old male and without blemish. You may take it from either the sheep or the goats. 6 You shall keep it until the fourteenth day of this month, and then, with the whole assembly of Israel present, it shall be slaughtered during the evening twilight. 7 They shall take some of its blood and apply it to the two doorposts and the lintel of every house in which they partake of the lamb. 8 That same night they

21 Yahweh then said to Moses, 'Stretch out your hand towards heaven, and let darkness, darkness so thick that it can be felt, cover Egypt.' 22 So Moses stretched out his hand towards heaven, and for three days there was thick darkness over the whole of Egypt. 23 No one could see anyone else or move about for three days, but all the Israelites did have light where they were living.

24 Pharaoh summoned Moses and said, 'Go and worship Yahweh, but your flocks and herds are to stay here. Your wives and children can go with you too.' 25 Moses said, 'But now you must give us sacrifices and burnt offerings to offer to Yahweh our God. 26 And our livestock will go with us too; not a hoof will be left behind; for we may need animals from these to worship Yahweh our God; for until we get there we ourselves cannot tell how we are to worship Yahweh.'

27 But Yahweh made Pharaoh stubborn, and he refused to let them go. 28 Pharaoh said to Moses, 'Out of my sight! Be sure you never see my face again, for the next time you see my face you die!' 29 Moses then said, 'You yourself have said it. I shall never see your face again.'

11 Yahweh then said to Moses, 'I shall inflict one more plague on Pharaoh and Egypt, after which he will let you go away. When he lets you go, he will actually drive you out! 2 Now instruct the people that every man is to ask his neighbour, and every woman hers, for silver and golden jewellery.' 3 And Yahweh made the Egyptians impressed with the people, while Moses himself was a man of great importance in Egypt in the opinion of Pharaoh's officials and the people.

4 Moses then said, 'Yahweh says this, "At midnight I shall pass through Egypt, 5 and all the first-born in Egypt will die, from the first-born of Pharaoh, heir to his throne, to the first-born of the slave-girl at the mill, and all the first-born of the livestock. 6 And throughout Egypt there will be great wailing, such as never was before, nor will be again. 7 But against the Israelites, whether man or beast, never a dog shall bark, so that you may know that Yahweh discriminates between Egypt and Israel. 8 Then all these officials of yours will come down to me and, bowing low before me, say: Go away, you and all the people who follow you! After which, I shall go." ' And, hot with anger, he left Pharaoh's presence.

9 Yahweh then said to Moses, 'Pharaoh will not listen to you, so that more of my wonders may be displayed in Egypt.' 10 Moses and Aaron worked all these wonders in Pharaoh's presence, but Yahweh made Pharaoh stubborn, and he did not let the Israelites leave his country.

12 Yahweh said to Moses and Aaron in Egypt, 2 'This month must be the first of all the months for you, the first month of your year. 3 Speak to the whole community of Israel and say, "On the tenth day of this month each man must take an animal from the flock for his family: one animal for each household. 4 If the household is too small for the animal, he must join with his neighbour nearest to his house, depending on the number of persons. When you choose the animal, you will take into account what each can eat. 5 It must be an animal without blemish, a male one year old; you may choose it either from the sheep or from the goats. 6 You must keep it till the fourteenth day of the month when the whole assembly of the community of Israel will slaughter it at twilight. 7 Some of the blood must then be taken and put on both door-posts and the lintel of the houses where it is eaten. 8 That night, the flesh must be eaten,

NEW REVISED STANDARD VERSION

same night; they shall eat it roasted over the fire with unleavened bread and bitter herbs. 9 Do not eat any of it raw or boiled in water, but roasted over the fire, with its head, legs, and inner organs. 10 You shall let none of it remain until the morning; anything that remains until the morning you shall burn. 11 This is how you shall eat it: your loins girded, your sandals on your feet, and your staff in your hand; and you shall eat it hurriedly. It is the passover of the LORD. 12 For I will pass through the land of Egypt that night, and I will strike down every firstborn in the land of Egypt, both human beings and animals; on all the gods of Egypt I will execute judgments: I am the LORD. 13 The blood shall be a sign for you on the houses where you live: when I see the blood, I will pass over you, and no plague shall destroy you when I strike the land of Egypt.

14 This day shall be a day of remembrance for you. You shall celebrate it as a festival to the LORD; throughout your generations you shall observe it as a perpetual ordinance. 15 Seven days you shall eat unleavened bread; on the first day you shall remove leaven from your houses, for whoever eats leavened bread from the first day until the seventh day shall be cut off from Israel. 16 On the first day you shall hold a solemn assembly, and on the seventh day a solemn assembly; no work shall be done on those days; only what everyone must eat, that alone may be prepared by you. 17 You shall observe the festival of unleavened bread, for on this very day I brought your companies out of the land of Egypt: you shall observe this day throughout your generations as a perpetual ordinance. 18 In the first month, from the evening of the fourteenth day until the evening of the twenty-first day, you shall eat unleavened bread. 19 For seven days no leaven shall be found in your houses; for whoever eats what is leavened shall be cut off from the congregation of Israel, whether an alien or a native of the land. 20 You shall eat nothing leavened; in all your settlements you shall eat unleavened bread.

21 Then Moses called all the elders of Israel and said to them, "Go, select lambs for your families, and slaughter the passover lamb. 22 Take a bunch of hyssop, dip it in the blood that is in the basin, and touch the lintel and the two doorposts with the blood in the basin. None of you shall go outside the door of your house until morning. 23 For the LORD will pass through to strike down the Egyptians; when he sees the blood on the lintel and on the two doorposts, the LORD will pass over that door and will not allow the destroyer to enter your houses to strike you down. 24 You shall observe this rite as a perpetual ordinance for you and your children. 25 When you come to the land that the LORD will give you, as he has promised, you shall keep this observance. 26 And when your children ask you, 'What do you mean by this observance?' 27 you shall say, 'It is the passover sacrifice to the LORD, for he passed over the houses of the Israelites in Egypt, when he struck down the Egyptians but spared our houses.' " And the people bowed down and worshiped.

28 The Israelites went and did just as the LORD had commanded Moses and Aaron.

29 At midnight the LORD struck down all the firstborn in the land of Egypt, from the firstborn of Pharaoh who sat on his throne to the firstborn of the prisoner who was in the dungeon, and all the firstborn of the livestock. 30 Pharaoh arose in the night, he and all his officials and all the Egyptians; and there was a loud cry in Egypt, for there was not a house without someone dead. 31 Then he summoned Moses and Aaron in the night, and said, "Rise up, go away from my people, both you and the Israelites! Go, worship the LORD, as you said. 32 Take your flocks and your herds, as you said, and be gone. And bring a blessing on me too!"

REVISED ENGLISH BIBLE

the fire; they must eat it with unleavened bread and bitter herbs. 9 You are not to eat any of it raw or even boiled in water, but roasted: head, shins, and entrails. 10 You are not to leave any of it till morning; anything left over until morning must be destroyed by fire.

11 'This is the way in which you are to eat it: have your belt fastened, sandals on your feet, and your staff in your hand, and you must eat in urgent haste. It is the LORD's Passover. 12 On that night I shall pass through the land of Egypt and kill every firstborn of man and beast. Thus I shall execute judgement, I the LORD, against all the gods of Egypt. 13 As for you, the blood will be a sign on the houses in which you are: when I see the blood I shall pass over you; when I strike Egypt, the mortal blow will not touch you.

14 'You are to keep this day as a day of remembrance, and make it a pilgrim-feast, a festival of the LORD; generation after generation you are to observe it as a statute for all time. 15 For seven days you are to eat unleavened bread. On the very first day you must rid your houses of leaven; from the first day to the seventh anyone who eats leavened bread is to be expelled from Israel. 16 On the first day there is to be a sacred assembly and on the seventh day a sacred assembly: on these days no work is to be done, except what must be done to provide food for everyone; only that will be allowed. 17 You are to observe the feast of Unleavened Bread because it was on this very day that I brought you out of Egypt in your tribal hosts. Observe this day from generation to generation as a statute for all time.

18 'You are to eat unleavened bread in the first month from the evening which begins the fourteenth day until the evening which begins the twenty-first day. 19 For seven days no leaven must be found in your houses; anyone who eats anything fermented is to be expelled from the community of Israel, be he foreigner or native. 20 You must eat nothing fermented; wherever you live, you must eat unleavened bread.'

21 Moses summoned all the elders of Israel and said, 'Go at once, procure lambs for your families, and slaughter the Passover. 22 Then take a bunch of marjoram, dip it in the blood in the basin, and smear some blood from the basin on the lintel and the two doorposts. Nobody may go out through the door of his house till morning. 23 The LORD will go throughout Egypt and strike it, but when he sees the blood on the lintel and the two doorposts, he will pass over that door and not let the destroyer enter to strike you. 24 You are to observe this as a statute for you and your children for all time; 25 when you enter the land which the LORD will give you as he promised, you are to observe this rite. 26 When your children ask you, "What is the meaning of this rite?" 27 you must say, "It is the LORD's Passover, for he passed over the houses of the Israelites in Egypt when he struck the Egyptians and spared our houses." ' The people bowed low in worship.

28 The Israelites went and did exactly as the LORD had commanded Moses and Aaron; 29 and by midnight the LORD had struck down all the firstborn in Egypt, from the firstborn of Pharaoh on his throne to the firstborn of the prisoner in the dungeon, besides the firstborn of cattle. 30 Before night was over Pharaoh rose, he and all his courtiers and all the Egyptians, and there was great wailing, for not a house in Egypt was without its dead.

31 Pharaoh summoned Moses and Aaron while it was still night and said, 'Up with you! Be off, and leave my people, you and the Israelites. Go and worship the LORD, as you request; 32 take your sheep and cattle, and go; and ask God's blessing on me also.' 33 The Egyptians urged on the people

12:11 **belt fastened:** *lit.* loins girt.   12:13 **pass over:** *or* stand guard over.   12:22 **marjoram:** *or* hyssop. **in the basin:** *or* on the threshold. **from the basin:** *or* from the threshold.

shall eat its roasted flesh with unleavened bread and bitter herbs. 9 It shall not be eaten raw or boiled, but roasted whole, with its head and shanks and inner organs. 10 None of it must be kept beyond the next morning; whatever is left over in the morning shall be burned up.

11 "This is how you are to eat it: with your loins girt, sandals on your feet and your staff in hand, you shall eat like those who are in flight. It is the Passover of the LORD. 12 For on this same night I will go through Egypt, striking down every first-born of the land, both man and beast, and executing judgment on all the gods of Egypt—I, the LORD! 13 But the blood will mark the houses where you are. Seeing the blood, I will pass over you; thus, when I strike the land of Egypt, no destructive blow will come upon you.

14 "This day shall be a memorial feast for you, which all your generations shall celebrate with pilgrimage to the LORD, as a perpetual institution. 15 For seven days you must eat unleavened bread. From the very first day you shall have your houses clear of all leaven. Whoever eats leavened bread from the first day to the seventh shall be cut off from Israel. 16 On the first day you shall hold a sacred assembly, and likewise on the seventh. On these days you shall not do any sort of work, except to prepare the food that everyone needs.

17 "Keep, then, this custom of the unleavened bread. Since it was on this very day that I brought your ranks out of the land of Egypt, you must celebrate this day throughout your generations as a perpetual institution. 18 From the evening of the fourteenth day of the first month until the evening of the twenty-first day of this month you shall eat unleavened bread. 19 For seven days no leaven may be found in your houses. Anyone, be he a resident alien or a native, who eats leavened food shall be cut off from the community of Israel. 20 Nothing leavened may you eat; wherever you dwell you may eat only unleavened bread."

21 Moses called all the elders of Israel and said to them, "Go and procure lambs for your families, and slaughter them as Passover victims. 22 Then take a bunch of hyssop, and dipping it in the blood that is in the basin, sprinkle the lintel and the two doorposts with this blood. But none of you shall go outdoors until morning. 23 For the LORD will go by, striking down the Egyptians. Seeing the blood on the lintel and the two doorposts, the LORD will pass over that door and not let the destroyer come into your houses to strike you down.

24 "You shall observe this as a perpetual ordinance for yourselves and your descendants. 25 Thus, you must also observe this rite when you have entered the land which the LORD will give you as he promised. 26 When your children ask you, 'What does this rite of yours mean?' 27 you shall reply, 'This is the Passover sacrifice of the LORD, who passed over the houses of the Israelites in Egypt; when he struck down the Egyptians, he spared our houses.'"

Then the people bowed down in worship, 28 and the Israelites went and did as the LORD had commanded Moses and Aaron.

29 At midnight the LORD slew every first-born in the land of Egypt, from the first-born of Pharaoh on the throne to the first-born of the prisoner in the dungeon, as well as all the first-born of the animals. 30 Pharaoh arose in the night, he and all his servants and all the Egyptians; and there was loud wailing throughout Egypt, for there was not a house without its dead.

31 During the night Pharaoh summoned Moses and Aaron and said, "Leave my people at once, you and the Israelites with you! Go and worship the LORD as you said. 32 Take your flocks, too, and your herds, as you demanded, and begone; and you will be doing me a favor."

roasted over the fire; it must be eaten with unleavened bread and bitter herbs. 9 Do not eat any of it raw or boiled in water, but roasted over the fire, with the head, feet and entrails. 10 You must not leave any of it over till the morning: whatever is left till morning you must burn. 11 This is how you must eat it: with a belt round your waist, your sandals on your feet and your staff in your hand. You must eat it hurriedly: it is a Passover[e] in Yahweh's honour. 12 That night, I shall go through Egypt and strike down all the first-born in Egypt, man and beast alike, and shall execute justice on all the gods of Egypt, I, Yahweh! 13 The blood will be a sign for you on the houses where you are. When I see the blood I shall pass over you, and you will escape the destructive plague when I strike Egypt. 14 This day must be commemorated by you, and you must keep it as a feast in Yahweh's honour. You must keep it as a feast-day for all generations; this is a decree for all time.

15 "For seven days you must eat unleavened bread. On the first day you must clean the leaven out of your houses, for anyone who eats leavened bread from the first to the seventh day must be outlawed from Israel. 16 On the first day you must hold a sacred assembly, and on the seventh day a sacred assembly. On those days no work may be done; you will prepare only what each requires to eat. 17 You must keep the feast of Unleavened Bread because it was on that same day that I brought your armies out of Egypt. You will keep that day, generation after generation; this is a decree for all time. 18 In the first month, from the evening of the fourteenth day until the evening of the twenty-first day, you must eat unleavened bread. 19 For seven days there may be no leaven in your houses, since anyone, either stranger or citizen of the country, who eats leavened bread will be outlawed from the community of Israel. 20 You will eat nothing with leaven in it; wherever you live, you will eat unleavened bread." '

21 Moses summoned all the elders of Israel and said to them, 'Go and choose a lamb or kid for your families, and kill the Passover victim. 22 Then take a bunch of hyssop, dip it in the blood that is in the basin, and with the blood from the basin touch the lintel and both door-posts; then let none of you venture out of the house till morning. 23 Then, when Yahweh goes through Egypt to strike it, and sees the blood on the lintel and on both door-posts, he will pass over the door and not allow the Destroyer to enter your homes and strike. 24 You will observe this as a decree binding you and your children for all time, 25 and when you have entered the country which Yahweh will give you, as he has promised, you will observe this ritual. 26 And when your children ask you, "What does this ritual mean?" 27 you will tell them, "It is the Passover sacrifice in honour of Yahweh who passed over the houses of the Israelites in Egypt, and struck Egypt but spared our houses." ' And the people bowed in worship. 28 The Israelites then went away and did as Yahweh had ordered Moses and Aaron.

29 And at midnight Yahweh struck down all the first-born in Egypt from the first-born of Pharaoh, heir to his throne, to the first-born of the prisoner in the dungeon, and the first-born of all the livestock. 30 Pharaoh and all his officials and all the Egyptians got up in the night, and there was great wailing in Egypt, for there was not a house without its dead. 31 It was still dark when Pharaoh summoned Moses and Aaron and said, 'Up, leave my subjects, you and the Israelites! Go and worship Yahweh as you have asked! 32 And take your flocks and herds as you have asked, and go! And bless me too!' 33 The Egyptians urged the people on and

e 12 Once a herdsmen's new year festival, the Passover receives a new meaning as the memorial of the exodus. The Feast of Unleavened Bread, an agricultural feast, is of separate origin.

33 The Egyptians urged the people to hasten their departure from the land, for they said, "We shall all be dead." 34 So the people took their dough before it was leavened, with their kneading bowls wrapped up in their cloaks on their shoulders. 35 The Israelites had done as Moses told them; they had asked the Egyptians for jewelry of silver and gold, and for clothing, 36 and the LORD had given the people favor in the sight of the Egyptians, so that they let them have what they asked. And so they plundered the Egyptians.

37 The Israelites journeyed from Rameses to Succoth, about six hundred thousand men on foot, besides children. 38 A mixed crowd also went up with them, and livestock in great numbers, both flocks and herds. 39 They baked unleavened cakes of the dough that they had brought out of Egypt; it was not leavened, because they were driven out of Egypt and could not wait, nor had they prepared any provisions for themselves.

40 The time that the Israelites had lived in Egypt was four hundred thirty years. 41 At the end of four hundred thirty years, on that very day, all the companies of the LORD went out from the land of Egypt. 42 That was for the LORD a night of vigil, to bring them out of the land of Egypt. That same night is a vigil to be kept for the LORD by all the Israelites throughout their generations.

43 The LORD said to Moses and Aaron: This is the ordinance for the passover: no foreigner shall eat of it, 44 but any slave who has been purchased may eat of it after he has been circumcised; 45 no bound or hired servant may eat of it. 46 It shall be eaten in one house; you shall not take any of the animal outside the house, and you shall not break any of its bones. 47 The whole congregation of Israel shall celebrate it. 48 If an alien who resides with you wants to celebrate the passover to the LORD, all his males shall be circumcised; then he may draw near to celebrate it; he shall be regarded as a native of the land. But no uncircumcised person shall eat of it; 49 there shall be one law for the native and for the alien who resides among you.

50 All the Israelites did just as the LORD had commanded Moses and Aaron. 51 That very day the LORD brought the Israelites out of the land of Egypt, company by company.

13 The LORD said to Moses: 2 Consecrate to me all the firstborn; whatever is the first to open the womb among the Israelites, of human beings and animals, is mine.

3 Moses said to the people, "Remember this day on which you came out of Egypt, out of the house of slavery, because the LORD brought you out from there by strength of hand; no leavened bread shall be eaten. 4 Today, in the month of Abib, you are going out. 5 When the LORD brings you into the land of the Canaanites, the Hittites, the Amorites, the Hivites, and the Jebusites, which he swore to your ancestors to give you, a land flowing with milk and honey, you shall keep this observance in this month. 6 Seven days you shall eat unleavened bread, and on the seventh day there shall be a festival to the LORD. 7 Unleavened bread shall be eaten for seven days; no leavened bread shall be seen in your possession, and no leaven shall be seen among you in all your territory. 8 You shall tell your child on that day, 'It is because of what the LORD did for me when I came out of Egypt.' 9 It shall serve for you as a sign on your hand and as a reminder on your forehead, so that the teaching of the LORD may be on your lips; for with a strong hand the LORD brought you out of Egypt. 10 You shall keep this ordinance at its proper time from year to year.

and hurried them out of the country, 'or else', they said, 'we shall all be dead'. 34 The people picked up their dough before it was leavened, wrapped their kneading troughs in their cloaks, and slung them on their shoulders. 35 Meanwhile, as Moses had told them, the Israelites had asked the Egyptians for silver and gold jewellery and for clothing. 36 Because the LORD had made the Egyptians well disposed towards them, they let the Israelites have whatever they asked; in this way the Egyptians were plundered.

37 THE Israelites set out from Rameses on the way to Succoth, about six hundred thousand men on foot, as well as women and children. 38 With them too went a large company of others, and animals in great numbers, both flocks and herds. 39 The dough they had brought from Egypt they baked into unleavened loaves of bread, because there was no leaven; for they had been driven out of Egypt and had no time even to get food ready for themselves.

40 The Israelites had been settled in Egypt for four hundred and thirty years. 41 At the end of the four hundred and thirty years to the very day, all the tribes of the LORD came out of Egypt. 42 This was the night when the LORD kept vigil to bring them out of Egypt. It is the LORD's night, a vigil for all Israelites generation after generation.

43 The LORD said to Moses and Aaron: 'This is the statute for the Passover: No foreigner may partake of it; 44 any bought slave may partake provided you have circumcised him; 45 no visitor or hired man may partake of it. 46 Each Passover victim must be eaten inside one house, and you must not take any of the flesh outside. You must not break any of its bones. 47 The whole community of Israel is to keep this feast.

48 'If aliens settled among you keep the Passover to the LORD, every male among them must first be circumcised, and then he can take part; he will rank as native-born. No male who is uncircumcised may eat of it. 49 The same law will apply both to the native-born and to the alien who is living among you.'

50 All the Israelites did exactly as the LORD had commanded Moses and Aaron; 51 and on that very day the LORD brought the Israelites out of Egypt mustered in their tribal hosts.

13 The LORD spoke to Moses. He said, 2 'Every firstborn, the first birth of every womb among the Israelites, you must dedicate to me, both man and beast; it belongs to me.'

3 Then Moses said to the people, 'Remember this day, the day on which you have come out of Egypt, the land of slavery, because the LORD by the strength of his hand has brought you out. Nothing leavened may be eaten this day, 4 for today, in the month of Abib, is the day of your exodus. 5 When the LORD has brought you into the land of the Canaanites, Hittites, Amorites, Hivites, and Jebusites, the land which he swore to your forefathers to give you, a land flowing with milk and honey, then in this same month you must observe this rite: 6 for seven days you are to eat unleavened bread, and on the seventh day there is to be a pilgrim-feast of the LORD. 7 Only unleavened bread is to be eaten during the seven days; nothing fermented or leavened must be seen throughout your territory. 8 On that day you are to tell your son, 'This is because of what the LORD did for me when I came out of Egypt.' 9 You must have the record of it as a sign upon your hand, and as a reminder on your forehead to make sure that the law of the LORD is always on your lips, because the LORD with a strong hand brought you out of Egypt. 10 This is a statute to be kept by you at the appointed time from year to year.

NEW AMERICAN BIBLE

33 The Egyptians likewise urged the people on, to hasten their departure from the land; they thought that otherwise they would all die. 34 The people, therefore, took their dough before it was leavened, in their kneading bowls wrapped in their cloaks on their shoulders. 35 The Israelites did as Moses had commanded: they asked the Egyptians for articles of silver and gold and for clothing. 36 The LORD indeed had made the Egyptians so well-disposed toward the people that they let them have whatever they asked for. Thus did they despoil the Egyptians.

37 The Israelites set out from Rameses for Succoth, about six hundred thousand men on foot, not counting the children. 38 A crowd of mixed ancestry also went up with them, besides their livestock, very numerous flocks and herds. 39 Since the dough they had brought out of Egypt was not leavened, they baked it into unleavened loaves. They had been rushed out of Egypt and had no opportunity even to prepare food for the journey.

40 The time the Israelites had stayed in Egypt was four hundred and thirty years. 41 At the end of four hundred and thirty years, all the hosts of the LORD left the land of Egypt on this very date. 42 This was a night of vigil for the LORD, as he led them out of the land of Egypt; so on this same night all the Israelites must keep a vigil for the LORD throughout their generations.

43 The LORD said to Moses and Aaron, "These are the regulations for the Passover. No foreigner may partake of it. 44 However, any slave who has been bought for money may partake of it, provided you have first circumcised him. 45 But no transient alien or hired servant may partake of it. 46 It must be eaten in one and the same house; you may not take any of its flesh outside the house. You shall not break any of its bones. 47 The whole community of Israel must keep this feast. 48 If any aliens living among you wish to celebrate the Passover of the LORD, all the males among them must first be circumcised, and then they may join in its observance just like the natives. But no man who is uncircumcised may partake of it. 49 The law shall be the same for the resident alien as for the native."

50 All the Israelites did just as the LORD had commanded Moses and Aaron. 51 On that same day the LORD brought the Israelites out of Egypt company by company.

13 The LORD spoke to Moses and said, 2 "Consecrate to me every first-born that opens the womb among the Israelites, both of man and of beast, for it belongs to me."

3 Moses said to the people, "Remember this day on which you came out of Egypt, that place of slavery. It was with a strong hand that the LORD brought you away. Nothing made with leaven must be eaten. 4 This day of your departure is in the month of Abib. 5 Therefore, it is in this month that you must celebrate this rite, after the LORD, your God, has brought you into the land of the Canaanites, Hittites, Amorites, Hivites and Jebusites, which he swore to your fathers he would give you, a land flowing with milk and honey. 6 For seven days you shall eat unleavened bread, and the seventh day shall also be a festival to the LORD. 7 Only unleavened bread may be eaten during the seven days; no leaven and nothing leavened may be found in all your territory. 8 On this day you shall explain to your son, 'This is because of what the LORD did for me when I came out of Egypt.' 9 It shall be as a sign on your hand and as a reminder on your forehead; thus the law of the LORD will ever be on your lips, because with a strong hand the LORD brought you out of Egypt. 10 Therefore, you shall keep this prescribed rite at its appointed time from year to year.

NEW JERUSALEM BIBLE

hurried them out of the country because, they said, 'Otherwise we shall all be dead.' 34 So the people carried off their dough still unleavened, their bowls wrapped in their cloaks, on their shoulders.

35 The Israelites did as Moses had told them and asked the Egyptians for silver and golden jewellery, and clothing. 36 Yahweh made the Egyptians so much impressed with the people that they gave them what they asked. So they despoiled the Egyptians.

37 The Israelites left Rameses for Succoth, about six hundred thousand on the march — men, that is, not counting their families. 38 A mixed crowd of people went with them, and flocks and herds, quantities of livestock. 39 And with the dough which they had brought from Egypt they baked unleavened cakes, because the dough had not risen, since they had been driven out of Egypt without time to linger or to prepare food for themselves. 40 The time that the Israelites spent in Egypt was four hundred and thirty years. 41 And on the very day the four hundred and thirty years ended, all Yahweh's armies left Egypt. 42 The night when Yahweh kept vigil to bring them out of Egypt must be kept as a vigil in honour of Yahweh by all Israelites, for all generations.

43 Yahweh said to Moses and Aaron, 'This is the ritual for the Passover: no alien may eat it, 44 but any slave bought for money may eat it, once you have circumcised him. 45 No stranger and no hired servant may eat it. 46 It must be eaten in one house alone; you will not take any of the meat out of the house; nor may you break any of its bones. 47 'The whole community of Israel must keep it. 48 Should a stranger residing with you wish to keep the Passover in honour of Yahweh, all the males of his household must be circumcised: he will then be allowed to keep it and will count as a citizen of the country. But no uncircumcised person may eat it. 49 The same law will apply to the citizen and the stranger resident among you.' 50 The Israelites all did as Yahweh had ordered Moses and Aaron, 51 and that same day Yahweh brought the Israelites out of Egypt in their armies.

13 Yahweh spoke to Moses and said, 2 'Consecrate all the first-born to me, the first birth from every womb, among the Israelites. Whether man or beast, it is mine.'

3 Moses said to the people, 'Remember this day, on which you came out of Egypt, from the place of slave-labour, for by the strength of his hand Yahweh brought you out of it; no leavened bread may be eaten. 4 On this day, in the month of Abib, you are leaving, 5 and when Yahweh has brought you into the country of the Canaanites, the Hittites, the Amorites, the Hivites and the Jebusites, flowing with milk and honey, which he swore to your ancestors that he would give you, then you must observe this rite in the same month. 6 For seven days you will eat unleavened bread, and on the seventh day there must be a feast in Yahweh's honour. 7 During these seven days unleavened bread may be eaten; no leavened bread may be seen among you, no leaven among you throughout your territory. 8 And on that day you will explain to your son, "This is because of what Yahweh did for me when I came out of Egypt." 9 This will serve as a sign on your hand would serve, or a reminder on your forehead, and in that way the law of Yahweh will be ever on your lips: for with a mighty hand Yahweh brought you out of Egypt. 10 You shall observe this law at its appointed time, year by year.

NEW REVISED STANDARD VERSION	REVISED ENGLISH BIBLE

NEW REVISED STANDARD VERSION

11 "When the LORD has brought you into the land of the Canaanites, as he swore to you and your ancestors, and has given it to you, 12 you shall set apart to the LORD all that first opens the womb. All the firstborn of your livestock that are males shall be the LORD's. 13 But every firstborn donkey you shall redeem with a sheep; if you do not redeem it, you must break its neck. Every firstborn male among your children you shall redeem. 14 When in the future your child asks you, 'What does this mean?' you shall answer, 'By strength of hand the LORD brought us out of Egypt, from the house of slavery. 15 When Pharaoh stubbornly refused to let us go, the LORD killed all the firstborn in the land of Egypt, from human firstborn to the firstborn of animals. Therefore I sacrifice to the LORD every male that first opens the womb, but every firstborn of my sons I redeem.' 16 It shall serve as a sign on your hand and as an emblem*x* on your forehead that by strength of hand the LORD brought us out of Egypt."

17 When Pharaoh let the people go, God did not lead them by way of the land of the Philistines, although that was nearer; for God thought, "If the people face war, they may change their minds and return to Egypt." 18 So God led the people by the roundabout way of the wilderness toward the Red Sea.*y* The Israelites went up out of the land of Egypt prepared for battle. 19 And Moses took with him the bones of Joseph who had required a solemn oath of the Israelites, saying, "God will surely take notice of you, and then you must carry my bones with you from here." 20 They set out from Succoth, and camped at Etham, on the edge of the wilderness. 21 The LORD went in front of them in a pillar of cloud by day, to lead them along the way, and in a pillar of fire by night, to give them light, so that they might travel by day and by night. 22 Neither the pillar of cloud by day nor the pillar of fire by night left its place in front of the people.

14 Then the LORD said to Moses: 2 Tell the Israelites to turn back and camp in front of Pi-hahiroth, between Migdol and the sea, in front of Baal-zephon; you shall camp opposite it, by the sea. 3 Pharaoh will say of the Israelites, 'They are wandering aimlessly in the land; the wilderness has closed in on them.' 4 I will harden Pharaoh's heart, and he will pursue them, so that I will gain glory for myself over Pharaoh and all his army; and the Egyptians shall know that I am the LORD. And they did so.

5 When the king of Egypt was told that the people had fled, the minds of Pharaoh and his officials were changed toward the people, and they said, "What have we done, letting Israel leave our service?" 6 So he had his chariot made ready, and took his army with him; 7 he took six hundred picked chariots and all the other chariots of Egypt with officers over all of them. 8 The LORD hardened the heart of Pharaoh king of Egypt and he pursued the Israelites, who were going out boldly. 9 The Egyptians pursued them, all Pharaoh's horses and chariots, his chariot drivers and his army; they overtook them camped by the sea, by Pi-hahiroth, in front of Baal-zephon.

10 As Pharaoh drew near, the Israelites looked back, and there were the Egyptians advancing on them. In great fear the Israelites cried out to the LORD. 11 They said to Moses, "Was it because there were no graves in Egypt that you have taken us away to die in the wilderness? What have you done to us, bringing us out of Egypt? 12 Is this not the very thing we told you in Egypt, 'Let us alone and let us serve the Egyptians'? For it would have been better for us to serve the Egyptians than to die in the wilderness." 13 But

REVISED ENGLISH BIBLE

11 'After the LORD has brought you into the land of the Canaanites and given it to you, as he swore to you and to your forefathers, 12 you are to make over to the LORD the first birth of every womb; and of all firstborn offspring of your animals the males belong to the LORD. 13 Every firstborn male donkey you may redeem with a kid or lamb, but if you do not redeem it, you must break its neck. Every firstborn among your sons you must redeem.

14 'When in time to come your son asks you what this means, say to him, "By the strength of his hand the LORD brought us out of Egypt, out of the land of slavery. 15 Pharaoh stubbornly refused to let us go, and the LORD killed all the firstborn in Egypt, both man and beast. That is why I sacrifice to the LORD the first birth of every womb if it is a male, and why I redeem every firstborn of my sons. 16 You must have the record of it as a sign on your hand, and as a phylactery on your forehead, because by the strength of his hand the LORD brought us out of Egypt." '

17 WHEN Pharaoh let the people go, God did not guide them by the road leading towards the Philistines, although that was the shortest way; for he said, 'The people may change their minds when war confronts them, and they may turn back to Egypt.' 18 So God made them go round by way of the wilderness towards the Red Sea. Thus the fifth generation of Israelites departed from Egypt.

19 Moses took the bones of Joseph with him, because Joseph had exacted an oath from the Israelites: 'Some day', he said, 'God will show his care for you, and then, as you leave, you must take my bones with you.'

20 They set out from Succoth and encamped at Etham on the edge of the wilderness. 21 And all the time the LORD went before them, by day a pillar of cloud to guide them on their journey, by night a pillar of fire to give them light; so they could travel both by day and by night. 22 The pillar of cloud never left its place in front of the people by day, nor did the pillar of fire by night.

14 The LORD spoke to Moses. 2 'Tell the Israelites', he said, 'they are to turn back and encamp to the east of Baal-zephon; your camp shall be opposite, by the sea. 3 Pharaoh will then think that the Israelites are finding themselves in difficult country, and are hemmed in by the wilderness. 4 I shall make Pharaoh obstinate, and he will pursue them, so that I may win glory for myself at the expense of Pharaoh and all his army; and the Egyptians will know that I am the LORD.' The Israelites did as they were ordered.

5 When it was reported to the Egyptian king that the Israelites had gone, he and his courtiers had a change of heart and said, 'What is this we have done? We have let our Israelite slaves go free!' 6 Pharaoh had his chariot yoked, and took his troops with him, 7 six hundred picked chariots and all the other chariots of Egypt, with a commander in each. 8 Then, made obstinate by the LORD, Pharaoh king of Egypt pursued the Israelites as they marched defiantly away. 9 The Egyptians, all Pharaoh's chariots and horses, cavalry and infantry, went in pursuit, and overtook them encamped beside the sea by Pi-hahiroth to the east of Baal-zephon.

10 Pharaoh was almost upon them when the Israelites looked up and saw the Egyptians close behind, and in terror they clamoured to the LORD for help. 11 They said to Moses, 'Were there no graves in Egypt, that you have brought us here to perish in the wilderness? See what you have done to us by bringing us out of Egypt! 12 Is this not just what we meant when we said in Egypt, "Leave us alone; let us be slaves to the Egyptians"? Better for us to serve as slaves to the Egyptians than to perish in the wilderness.' 13 But Mo-

---

x Or *as a frontlet*; Meaning of Heb uncertain   *y* Or *Sea of Reeds*   14:2 **before Pi-hahiroth:** *or* where the desert tracks begin.

NEW AMERICAN BIBLE

11 "When the LORD, your God, has brought you into the land of the Canaanites, which he swore to you and your fathers he would give you, 12 you shall dedicate to the LORD every son that opens the womb; and all the male firstlings of your animals shall belong to the LORD. 13 Every first-born of an ass you shall redeem with a sheep. If you do not redeem it, you shall break its neck. Every first-born son you must redeem. 14 If your son should ask you later on, 'What does this mean?' you shall tell him, 'With a strong hand the LORD brought us out of Egypt, that place of slavery. 15 When Pharaoh stubbornly refused to let us go, the LORD killed every first-born in the land of Egypt, every first-born of man and of beast. That is why I sacrifice to the LORD everything of the male sex that opens the womb, and why I redeem every first-born of my sons.' 16 Let this, then, be as a sign on your hand and as a pendant on your forehead: with a strong hand the LORD brought us out of Egypt."

17 Now, when Pharaoh let the people go, God did not lead them by way of the Philistines' land, though this was the nearest; for he thought, should the people see that they would have to fight, they might change their minds and return to Egypt. 18 Instead, he rerouted them toward the Red Sea by way of the desert road. In battle array the Israelites marched out of Egypt. 19 Moses also took Joseph's bones along, for Joseph had made the Israelites swear solemnly that, when God should come to them, they would carry his bones away with them.

20 Setting out from Succoth, they camped at Etham near the edge of the desert.

21 The Lord preceded them, in the daytime by means of a column of cloud to show them the way, and at night by means of a column of fire to give them light. Thus they could travel both day and night. 22 Neither the column of cloud by day nor the column of fire by night ever left its place in front of the people.

14 Then the LORD said to Moses, 2 "Tell the Israelites to turn about and camp before Pi-hahiroth, between Migdol and the sea. You shall camp in front of Baal-zephon, just opposite, by the sea. 3 Pharaoh will then say, 'The Israelites are wandering about aimlessly in the land. The desert has closed in on them.' 4 Thus will I make Pharaoh so obstinate that he will pursue them. Then I will receive glory through Pharaoh and all his army, and the Egyptians will know that I am the LORD."

This the Israelites did. 5 When it was reported to the king of Egypt that the people had fled, Pharaoh and his servants changed their minds about them. "What have we done!" they exclaimed. "Why, we have released Israel from our service!" 6 So Pharaoh made his chariots ready and mustered his soldiers — 7 six hundred first-class chariots and all the other chariots of Egypt, with warriors on them all. 8 So obstinate had the LORD made Pharaoh that he pursued the Israelites even while they were marching away in triumph. 9 The Egyptians, then, pursued them; Pharaoh's whole army, his horses, chariots and charioteers, caught up with them as they lay encamped by the sea, at Pi-hahiroth, in front of Baal-zephon.

10 Pharaoh was already near when the Israelites looked up and saw that the Egyptians were on the march in pursuit of them. In great fright they cried out to the LORD. 11 And they complained to Moses, "Were there no burial places in Egypt that you had to bring us out here to die in the desert? Why did you do this to us? Why did you bring us out of Egypt? 12 Did we not tell you this in Egypt, when we said, 'Leave us alone. Let us serve the Egyptians'? Far better for us to be the slaves of the Egyptians than to die in the desert."

NEW JERUSALEM BIBLE

11 'When Yahweh has brought you into the Canaanites' country, as he swore to you and your ancestors that he would, and given it to you, 12 to Yahweh you must make over whatever first issues from the womb, and every first-born cast by animals belonging to you: these males belong to Yahweh. 13 But every first-born donkey you will redeem with a lamb or kid; if you do not redeem it, you must break its neck. All the human first-born, however, among your sons, you will redeem. 14 And when your son asks you in days to come, "What does this mean?" you will tell him, "By the strength of his hand Yahweh brought us out of Egypt, out of the place of slave-labour. 15 When Pharaoh stubbornly refused to let us go, Yahweh killed all the first-born in Egypt, of man and beast alike. This is why I sacrifice every male first issuing from the womb to Yahweh and redeem every first-born of my sons." 16 This will serve as a sign on your hand would serve, or a headband on your forehead, for by the strength of his hand Yahweh brought us out of Egypt.'

17 When Pharaoh had let the people go, God did not let them take the road to the Philistines' territory, although that was the shortest, 'in case', God thought, 'the prospect of fighting makes the people change their minds and turn back to Egypt.' 18 Instead, God led the people a roundabout way through the desert of the Sea of Reeds. The Israelites left Egypt fully armed. 19 Moses took with him the bones of Joseph, since Joseph had put the Israelites on solemn oath with the words, 'It is sure that God will visit you,' he had said, 'and when that day comes you must take my bones away from here with you.'

20 They set out from Succoth and encamped at Etham, on the edge of the desert.

21 Yahweh preceded them, by day in a pillar of cloud to show them the way, and by night in a pillar of fire to give them light, so that they could march by day and by night. 22 The pillar of cloud never left its place ahead of the people during the day, nor the pillar of fire during the night.

14 Yahweh spoke to Moses and said, 2 'Tell the Israelites to turn back and pitch camp in front of Pi-Hahiroth, between Migdol and the sea, facing Baal-Zephon. You must pitch your camp opposite this place, beside the sea, 3 and then Pharaoh will think, "The Israelites are wandering to and fro in the countryside; the desert has closed in on them." 4 I shall then make Pharaoh stubborn and he will set out in pursuit of them; and I shall win glory for myself at the expense of Pharaoh and his whole army, and then the Egyptians will know that I am Yahweh.' And the Israelites did this.

5 When Pharaoh king of Egypt was told that the people had fled, he and his officials changed their attitude towards the people. 'What have we done,' they said, 'allowing Israel to leave our service?' 6 So Pharaoh had his chariot harnessed and set out with his troops, 7 taking six hundred of the best chariots and all the other chariots in Egypt, with officers in each. 8 Yahweh made Pharaoh king of Egypt stubborn, and he gave chase to the Israelites. The Israelites marched confidently away, 9 but the Egyptians, all Pharaoh's horses, his chariots, his horsemen and his army, gave chase and caught up with them where they lay encamped beside the sea near Pi-Hahiroth, facing Baal-Zephon. 10 As Pharaoh approached, the Israelites looked up — and there were the Egyptians in pursuit of them! The Israelites were terrified and cried out to Yahweh for help. 11 To Moses they said, 'Was it for lack of graves in Egypt, that you had to lead us out to die in the desert? What was the point of bringing us out of Egypt? 12 Did we not tell you as much in Egypt? Leave us alone, we said, we would rather work for the Egyptians! We prefer to work for the Egyptians than to

Moses said to the people, "Do not be afraid, stand firm, and see the deliverance that the LORD will accomplish for you today; for the Egyptians whom you see today you shall never see again. 14 The LORD will fight for you, and you have only to keep still."

15 Then the LORD said to Moses, "Why do you cry out to me? Tell the Israelites to go forward. 16 But you lift up your staff, and stretch out your hand over the sea and divide it, that the Israelites may go into the sea on dry ground. 17 Then I will harden the hearts of the Egyptians so that they will go in after them; and so I will gain glory for myself over Pharaoh and all his army, his chariots, and his chariot drivers. 18 And the Egyptians shall know that I am the LORD, when I have gained glory for myself over Pharaoh, his chariots, and his chariot drivers."

19 The angel of God who was going before the Israelite army moved and went behind them; and the pillar of cloud moved from in front of them and took its place behind them. 20 It came between the army of Egypt and the army of Israel. And so the cloud was there with the darkness, and it lit up the night; one did not come near the other all night.

21 Then Moses stretched out his hand over the sea. The LORD drove the sea back by a strong east wind all night, and turned the sea into dry land; and the waters were divided. 22 The Israelites went into the sea on dry ground, the waters forming a wall for them on their right and on their left. 23 The Egyptians pursued, and went into the sea after them, all of Pharaoh's horses, chariots, and chariot drivers. 24 At the morning watch the LORD in the pillar of fire and cloud looked down upon the Egyptian army, and threw the Egyptian army into panic. 25 He clogged*z* their chariot wheels so that they turned with difficulty. The Egyptians said, "Let us flee from the Israelites, for the LORD is fighting for them against Egypt."

26 Then the LORD said to Moses, "Stretch out your hand over the sea, so that the water may come back upon the Egyptians, upon their chariots and chariot drivers." 27 So Moses stretched out his hand over the sea, and at dawn the sea returned to its normal depth. As the Egyptians fled before it, the LORD tossed the Egyptians into the sea. 28 The waters returned and covered the chariots and the chariot drivers, the entire army of Pharaoh that had followed them into the sea; not one of them remained. 29 But the Israelites walked on dry ground through the sea, the waters forming a wall for them on their right and on their left.

30 Thus the LORD saved Israel that day from the Egyptians; and Israel saw the Egyptians dead on the seashore. 31 Israel saw the great work that the LORD did against the Egyptians. So the people feared the LORD and believed in the LORD and in his servant Moses.

15 Then Moses and the Israelites sang this song to the LORD:

"I will sing to the LORD, for he has triumphed gloriously;
    horse and rider he has thrown into the sea.
2 The LORD is my strength and my might,*a*
    and he has become my salvation;
this is my God, and I will praise him,
    my father's God, and I will exalt him.
3 The LORD is a warrior;
    the LORD is his name.

4 "Pharaoh's chariots and his army he cast into the sea;
    his picked officers were sunk in the Red Sea.*b*

z Sam Gk Syr: MT *removed*   *a* Or *song*   *b* Or *Sea of Reeds*

ses answered, 'Have no fear; stand firm and see the deliverance that the LORD will bring you this day; for as sure as you see the Egyptians now, you will never see them again. 14 The LORD will fight for you; so say no more.'

15 The LORD said to Moses, 'What is the meaning of this clamour? Tell the Israelites to strike camp, 16 and you are to raise high your staff and hold your hand out over the sea to divide it asunder, so that the Israelites can pass through the sea on dry ground. 17 For my part I shall make the Egyptians obstinate and they will come after you; thus I shall win glory for myself at the expense of Pharaoh and his army, chariots and cavalry all together. 18 The Egyptians will know that I am the LORD when I win glory for myself at the expense of their Pharaoh, his chariots and horsemen.'

19 The angel of God, who had travelled in front of the Israelites, now moved away to the rear. The pillar of cloud moved from the front and took up its position behind them, 20 thus coming between the Egyptians and the Israelites. The cloud brought on darkness and early nightfall, so that contact was lost throughout the night.

21 Then Moses held out his hand over the sea, and the LORD drove the sea away with a strong east wind all night long, and turned the seabed into dry land. The waters were divided asunder, 22 and the Israelites went through the sea on the dry ground, while the waters formed a wall to right and left of them. 23 The Egyptians, all Pharaoh's horse, his chariots and cavalry, followed in pursuit into the sea. 24 In the morning watch the LORD looked down on the Egyptian army through the pillar of fire and cloud, and he threw them into a panic. 25 He clogged their chariot wheels and made them drag along heavily, so that the Egyptians said, 'It is the LORD fighting for Israel against Egypt; let us flee.'

26 Then the LORD said to Moses, 'Hold your hand out over the sea, so that the water may flow back on the Egyptians, their chariots and horsemen.' 27 Moses held his hand out over the sea, and at daybreak the water returned to its usual place and the Egyptians fled before its advance, but the LORD swept them into the sea. 28 As the water came back it covered all Pharaoh's army, the chariots and cavalry, which had pressed the pursuit into the sea. Not one survived. 29 Meanwhile the Israelites had passed along the dry ground through the sea, with the water forming a wall for them to right and to left. 30 That day the LORD saved Israel from the power of Egypt. When the Israelites saw the Egyptians lying dead on the seashore, 31 and saw the great power which the LORD had put forth against Egypt, the people were in awe of the LORD and put their faith in him and in Moses his servant.

15 Then Moses and the Israelites sang this song to the LORD:

'I shall sing to the LORD, for he has risen up in triumph;
    horse and rider he has hurled into the sea.
2 The LORD is my refuge and my defence;
    he has shown himself my deliverer.
He is my God, and I shall glorify him;
    my father's God, and I shall exalt him.
3 The LORD is a warrior; the LORD is his name.
4 Pharaoh's chariots and his army
    he has cast into the sea;
the flower of his officers
    are engulfed in the Red Sea.

14:25 **clogged:** *so Samar.; Heb.* removed.   15:2 **defence:** *or* song.

13 But Moses answered the people, "Fear not! Stand your ground, and you will see the victory the LORD will win for you today. These Egyptians whom you see today you will never see again. 14 The LORD himself will fight for you; you have only to keep still."

15 Then the LORD said to Moses, "Why are you crying out to me? Tell the Israelites to go forward. 16 And you, lift up your staff and, with hand outstretched over the sea, split the sea in two, that the Israelites may pass through it on dry land. 17 But I will make the Egyptians so obstinate that they will go in after them. Then I will receive glory through Pharaoh and all his army, his chariots and charioteers. 18 The Egyptians shall know that I am the LORD, when I receive glory through Pharaoh and his chariots and charioteers."

19 The angel of God, who had been leading Israel's camp, now moved and went around behind them. The column of cloud also, leaving the front, took up its place behind them, 20 so that it came between the camp of the Egyptians and that of Israel. But the cloud now became dark, and thus the night passed without the rival camps coming any closer together all night long. 21 Then Moses stretched out his hand over the sea, and the LORD swept the sea with a strong east wind throughout the night and so turned it into dry land. When the water was thus divided, 22 the Israelites marched into the midst of the sea on dry land, with the water like a wall to their right and to their left.

23 The Egyptians followed in pursuit; all Pharaoh's horses and chariots and charioteers went after them right into the midst of the sea. 24 In the night watch just before dawn the LORD cast through the column of the fiery cloud upon the Egyptian force a glance that threw it into a panic; 25 and he so clogged their chariot wheels that they could hardly drive. With that the Egyptians sounded the retreat before Israel, because the LORD was fighting for them against the Egyptians.

26 Then the LORD told Moses, "Stretch out your hand over the sea, that the water may flow back upon the Egyptians, upon their chariots and their charioteers." 27 So Moses stretched out his hand over the sea, and at dawn the sea flowed back to its normal depth. The Egyptians were fleeing head on toward the sea, when the LORD hurled them into its midst. 28 As the water flowed back, it covered the chariots and the charioteers of Pharaoh's whole army which had followed the Israelites into the sea. Not a single one of them escaped. 29 But the Israelites had marched on dry land through the midst of the sea, with the water like a wall to their right and to their left. 30 Thus the LORD saved Israel on that day from the power of the Egyptians. When Israel saw the Egyptians lying dead on the seashore 31 and beheld the great power that the LORD had shown against the Egyptians, they feared the LORD and believed in him and in his servant Moses.

15 Then Moses and the Israelites sang this song to the LORD:

> I will sing to the LORD, for he is
>   gloriously triumphant;
>   horse and chariot he has cast into the sea.
> 2 My strength and my courage is the LORD,
>   and he has been my savior.
> He is my God, I praise him;
>   the God of my father, I extol him.
> 3 The LORD is a warrior,
>   LORD is his name!
> 4 Pharaoh's chariots and army he hurled into the sea;
>   the elite of his officers were submerged in the
>   Red Sea.

die in the desert!' 13 Moses said to the people, 'Do not be afraid! Stand firm, and you will see what Yahweh will do to rescue you today: the Egyptians you see today you will never see again. 14 Yahweh will do the fighting for you; all you need to do is to keep calm.'

15 Yahweh then said to Moses, 'Why cry out to me? Tell the Israelites to march on. 16 Your part is to raise your staff and stretch out your hand over the sea and divide it, so that the Israelites can walk through the sea on dry ground, 17 while I, for my part, shall make the Egyptians so stubborn that they will follow them, and I shall win glory for myself at the expense of Pharaoh and all his army, chariots and horsemen. 18 And when I have won glory for myself at the expense of Pharaoh and his chariots and horsemen, the Egyptians will know that I am Yahweh.'

19 Then the angel of God, who preceded the army of Israel, changed station and followed behind them. The pillar of cloud moved from their front and took position behind them. 20 It came between the army of the Egyptians and the army of Israel. The cloud was dark, and the night passed without the one drawing any closer to the other the whole night long. 21 Then Moses stretched out his hand over the sea, and Yahweh drove the sea back with a strong easterly wind all night and made the sea into dry land. The waters were divided 22 and the Israelites went on dry ground right through the sea, with walls of water to right and left of them. 23 The Egyptians gave chase, and all Pharaoh's horses, chariots and horsemen went into the sea after them. 24 In the morning watch, Yahweh looked down on the army of the Egyptians from the pillar of fire and cloud and threw the Egyptian army into confusion. 25 He so clogged their chariot wheels that they drove on only with difficulty, which made the Egyptians say, 'Let us flee from Israel, for Yahweh is fighting on their side against the Egyptians!' 26 Then Yahweh said to Moses, 'Stretch out your hand over the sea and let the waters flow back on the Egyptians and on their chariots and their horsemen.' 27 Moses stretched out his hand over the sea and, as day broke, the sea returned to its bed. The fleeing Egyptians ran straight into it, and Yahweh overthrew the Egyptians in the middle of the sea. 28 The returning waters washed right over the chariots and horsemen of Pharaoh's entire army, which had followed the Israelites into the sea; not a single one of them was left. 29 The Israelites, however, had marched through the sea on dry ground, with walls of water to right and left of them. 30 That day, Yahweh rescued Israel from the clutches of the Egyptians, and Israel saw the Egyptians lying dead on the sea-shore. 31 When Israel saw the mighty deed that Yahweh had performed against the Egyptians, the people revered Yahweh and put their faith in Yahweh and in Moses, his servant.

15 It was then that Moses and the Israelites sang this song in Yahweh's honour:

> I shall sing to Yahweh, for he has covered himself
>   in glory,
>   horse and rider he has thrown into the sea.
> 2 Yah is my strength and my song,
>   to him I owe my deliverance.
> He is my God and I shall praise him,
>   my father's God and I shall extol him.
> 3 Yahweh is a warrior;
>   Yahweh is his name.
>
> 4 Pharaoh's chariots and army he has hurled into the
>   sea
>   the pick of his officers have been drowned in the
>   Sea of Reeds.

5 The floods covered them;
    they went down into the depths like a stone.
6 Your right hand, O LORD, glorious in power—
    your right hand, O LORD, shattered the enemy.
7 In the greatness of your majesty you overthrew
        your adversaries;
    you sent out your fury, it consumed them like
        stubble.
8 At the blast of your nostrils the waters piled up,
    the floods stood up in a heap;
    the deeps congealed in the heart of the sea.
9 The enemy said, 'I will pursue, I will overtake,
    I will divide the spoil, my desire shall have its
        fill of them.
    I will draw my sword, my hand shall destroy
        them.'
10 You blew with your wind, the sea covered them;
    they sank like lead in the mighty waters.

11 "Who is like you, O LORD, among the gods?
    Who is like you, majestic in holiness,
    awesome in splendor, doing wonders?
12 You stretched out your right hand,
    the earth swallowed them.

13 "In your steadfast love you led the people whom
        you redeemed;
    you guided them by your strength to your holy
        abode.
14 The peoples heard, they trembled;
    pangs seized the inhabitants of Philistia.
15 Then the chiefs of Edom were dismayed;
    trembling seized the leaders of Moab;
    all the inhabitants of Canaan melted away.
16 Terror and dread fell upon them;
    by the might of your arm, they became still as
        a stone
    until your people, O LORD, passed by,
    until the people whom you acquired passed by.
17 You brought them in and planted them on the
        mountain of your own possession,
    the place, O LORD, that you made your abode,
    the sanctuary, O LORD, that your hands have
        established.
18 The LORD will reign forever and ever."

19 When the horses of Pharaoh with his chariots and his
chariot drivers went into the sea, the LORD brought back the
waters of the sea upon them; but the Israelites walked
through the sea on dry ground.

20 Then the prophet Miriam, Aaron's sister, took a tambourine in her hand; and all the women went out after her
with tambourines and with dancing. 21 And Miriam sang to
them:
    "Sing to the LORD, for he has triumphed
        gloriously;
    horse and rider he has thrown into the sea."

22 Then Moses ordered Israel to set out from the Red
Sea,c and they went into the wilderness of Shur. They went
three days in the wilderness and found no water. 23 When
they came to Marah, they could not drink the water of
Marah because it was bitter. That is why it was called
Marah.d 24 And the people complained against Moses, saying, "What shall we drink?" 25 He cried out to the LORD; and
the LORD showed him a piece of wood;e he threw it into the
water, and the water became sweet.
    There the LORDf made for them a statute and an ordi-
nance and there he put them to the test. 26 He said, "If you

5 The watery abyss has covered them;
    they sank to the depths like a stone.
6 Your right hand, LORD, is majestic in strength;
    your right hand, LORD, shattered the enemy.
7 In the fullness of your triumph
    you overthrew those who opposed you:
    you let loose your fury;
    it consumed them like stubble.
8 At the blast of your anger the sea piled up;
    the water stood up like a bank;
    out at sea the great deep congealed.
9 'The enemy boasted, "I shall pursue, I shall
        overtake;
    I shall divide the spoil,
    I shall glut my appetite on them;
    I shall draw my sword,
    I shall rid myself of them."
10 You blew with your blast; the sea covered them;
    they sank like lead in the swelling waves.

11 'LORD, who is like you among the gods?
    Who is like you, majestic in holiness,
    worthy of awe and praise, worker of wonders?
12 You stretched out your right hand;
    the earth engulfed them.

13 'In your constant love you led the people
    whom you had redeemed:
    you guided them by your strength
    to your holy dwelling-place.
14 Nations heard and trembled;
    anguish seized the dwellers in Philistia.
15 The chieftains of Edom were then dismayed,
    trembling seized the leaders of Moab,
    the inhabitants of Canaan were all panic-stricken;
16 terror and dread fell upon them:
    through the might of your arm
    they stayed stone-still
    while your people passed, LORD,
    while the people whom you made your own passed
        by.
17 You will bring them in and plant them
    in the mount that is your possession,
    the dwelling-place, LORD, of your own making,
    the sanctuary, LORD, which your own hands
        established.
18 The LORD will reign for ever and for ever.'

19 When Pharaoh's horse, both chariots and cavalry, went
into the sea, the LORD brought back the waters over them;
but Israel had passed through the sea on dry ground. 20 The
prophetess Miriam, Aaron's sister, took up her tambourine,
and all the women followed her, dancing to the sound of
tambourines; 21 and Miriam sang them this refrain:
    'Sing to the LORD, for he has risen up in triumph:
    horse and rider he has hurled into the sea.'

22 Moses led Israel from the Red Sea out into the wilderness of Shur, where for three days they travelled through the
wilderness without finding water. 23 When they came to
Marah, they could not drink the water there because it was
bitter; that is why the place was called Marah. 24 The people
complained to Moses, asking, 'What are we to drink?'
25 Moses cried to the LORD, who showed him a log which,
when thrown into the water, made the water sweet.
    It was there that the LORD laid down a statute and rule of
life; there he put the people to the test. 26 He said, 'If only

---

c Or Sea of Reeds   d That is Bitterness   e Or a tree   f Heb he

15:11 **among the gods:** or in might.   15:16 **made your own:** or
created.

NEW AMERICAN BIBLE

5 The flood waters covered them,
  they sank into the depths like a stone.

6 Your right hand, O LORD, magnificent in power,
  your right hand, O LORD, has shattered
    the enemy.
7 In your great majesty you overthrew
    your adversaries;
  you loosed your wrath to consume them
    like stubble.
8 At a breath of your anger the waters piled up,
  the flowing waters stood like a mound,
  the flood waters congealed in the midst of
    the sea.
9 The enemy boasted, "I will pursue and
    overtake them;
  I will divide the spoils and have my fill of them;
  I will draw my sword; my hand shall
    despoil them!"
10 When your wind blew, the sea covered them;
  like lead they sank in the mighty waters.

11 Who is like to you among the gods, O LORD?
  Who is like to you, magnificent in holiness?
  O terrible in renown, worker of wonders,
12   when you stretched out your right hand, the
    earth swallowed them!
13 In your mercy you led the people you redeemed;
  in your strength you guided them to your
    holy dwelling.
14 The nations heard and quaked:
  anguish gripped the dwellers in Philistia.
15 Then were the princes of Edom dismayed;
  trembling seized the chieftains of Moab;
  All the dwellers in Canaan melted away;
16   terror and dread fell upon them.
  By the might of your arm they were frozen
    like stone,
  while your people, O LORD, passed over,
  while the people you had made your own
    passed over.

17 And you brought them in and planted them on the
    mountain of your inheritance —
  the place where you made your seat, O LORD,
  the sanctuary, O LORD, which your
    hands established.

18 The LORD shall reign forever and ever.

19 They sang thus because Pharaoh's horses and chariots
and charioteers had gone into the sea, and the LORD made
the waters of the sea flow back upon them, though the
Israelites had marched on dry land through the midst of the
sea. 20 The prophetess Miriam, Aaron's sister, took a tambourine in her hand, while all the women went out after her
with tambourines, dancing; 21 and she led them in the refrain:
  Sing to the LORD, for he is gloriously triumphant;
    horse and chariot he has cast into the sea.
22 Then Moses led Israel forward from the Red Sea, and
they marched out to the desert of Shur. After traveling for
three days through the desert without finding water, 23 they
arrived at Marah, where they could not drink the water,
because it was too bitter. Hence this place was called Marah. 24 As the people grumbled against Moses, saying,
"What are we to drink?" 25 he appealed to the LORD, who
pointed out to him a certain piece of wood. When he threw
this into the water, the water became fresh.
  It was here that the LORD, in making rules and regulations
for them, put them to the test. 26 "If you really listen to the

NEW JERUSALEM BIBLE

5 The ocean has closed over them;
  they have sunk to the bottom like a stone.
6 Your right hand, Yahweh, wins glory by its
    strength,
  your right hand, Yahweh, shatters your foes,
7 and by your great majesty you fell your assailants;
  you unleash your fury, it consumes them like
    chaff.
8 A blast from your nostrils and the waters piled
    high;
  the waves stood firm as a dyke;
  the bed of the sea became firm ground.

9 The enemy said, 'I shall give chase and overtake,
  'I shall share out the spoil and glut myself on
    them,
  'I shall draw my sword, my hand will destroy
    them.'
10 You blew with your breath, the sea closed over
    them;
  they sank like lead in the terrible waters.
11 Yahweh, who is like you, majestic in sanctity,
  who like you among the holy ones,
  fearsome of deed, worker of wonders?
12 You stretched your right hand out, the earth
    swallowed them!
13 In your faithful love you led out the people you
    had redeemed,
  in your strength you have guided them to your
    holy dwelling.
14 Hearing of this, the peoples tremble;
  pangs seize on the people of Philistia;
15 the chieftains of Edom are dismayed,
  Moab's princes — panic has seized them,
  all the inhabitants of Canaan have melted away.
16 On them fall terror and dread;
  through the power of your arm they are still as
    stone
  while your people are passing, Yahweh,
  while the people you have purchased are passing.
17 You will bring them in and plant them
  on the mountain which is your heritage,
  the place which you, Yahweh, have made your
    dwelling,
  the sanctuary, Yahweh, prepared by your own
    hands.
18   Yahweh will be king for ever and ever.

19 For when Pharaoh's cavalry, with his chariots and
horsemen, had gone into the sea, Yahweh brought the waters of the sea back over them, though the Israelites went on
dry ground right through the sea.
20 The prophetess Miriam, Aaron's sister, took a tambourine, and all the women followed her with tambourines,
dancing, 21 while Miriam took up from them the refrain:
  Sing to Yahweh, for he has covered himself in
    glory,
  horse and rider he has thrown into the sea.
22 Moses led Israel away from the Sea of Reeds, and they
entered the desert of Shur. They then travelled through the
desert for three days without finding water. 23 When they
reached Marah, they could not drink the Marah water because it was bitter; this is why the place was named Marah.
24 The people complained to Moses saying, 'What are we to
drink?' 25 Moses appealed to Yahweh for help, and Yahweh
showed him a piece of wood. When Moses threw it into the
water, the water became sweet.
  There he laid down a statute and law for them
    and there he put them to the test.
  Then he said, 26 'If you listen carefully to the voice of

will listen carefully to the voice of the Lord your God, and do what is right in his sight, and give heed to his commandments and keep all his statutes, I will not bring upon you any of the diseases that I brought upon the Egyptians; for I am the Lord who heals you."

27 Then they came to Elim, where there were twelve springs of water and seventy palm trees; and they camped there by the water.

16 The whole congregation of the Israelites set out from Elim; and Israel came to the wilderness of Sin, which is between Elim and Sinai, on the fifteenth day of the second month after they had departed from the land of Egypt. 2 The whole congregation of the Israelites complained against Moses and Aaron in the wilderness. 3 The Israelites said to them, "If only we had died by the hand of the Lord in the land of Egypt, when we sat by the fleshpots and ate our fill of bread; for you have brought us out into this wilderness to kill this whole assembly with hunger."

4 Then the Lord said to Moses, "I am going to rain bread from heaven for you, and each day the people shall go out and gather enough for that day. In that way I will test them, whether they will follow my instruction or not. 5 On the sixth day, when they prepare what they bring in, it will be twice as much as they gather on other days." 6 So Moses and Aaron said to all the Israelites, "In the evening you shall know that it was the Lord who brought you out of the land of Egypt, 7 and in the morning you shall see the glory of the Lord, because he has heard your complaining against the Lord. For what are we, that you complain against us?" 8 And Moses said, "When the Lord gives you meat to eat in the evening and your fill of bread in the morning, because the Lord has heard the complaining that you utter against him — what are we? Your complaining is not against us but against the Lord."

9 Then Moses said to Aaron, "Say to the whole congregation of the Israelites, 'Draw near to the Lord, for he has heard your complaining.' " 10 And as Aaron spoke to the whole congregation of the Israelites, they looked toward the wilderness, and the glory of the Lord appeared in the cloud. 11 The Lord spoke to Moses and said, 12 "I have heard the complaining of the Israelites; say to them, 'At twilight you shall eat meat, and in the morning you shall have your fill of bread; then you shall know that I am the Lord your God.' "

13 In the evening quails came up and covered the camp; and in the morning there was a layer of dew around the camp. 14 When the layer of dew lifted, there on the surface of the wilderness was a fine flaky substance, as fine as frost on the ground. 15 When the Israelites saw it, they said to one another, "What is it?" [g] For they did not know what it was. Moses said to them, "It is the bread that the Lord has given you to eat. 16 This is what the Lord has commanded: 'Gather as much of it as each of you needs, an omer to a person according to the number of persons, all providing for those in their own tents.' " 17 The Israelites did so, some gathering more, some less. 18 But when they measured it with an omer, those who gathered much had nothing over, and those who gathered little had no shortage; they gathered as much as each of them needed. 19 And Moses said to them, "Let no one leave any of it over until morning." 20 But they did not listen to Moses; some left part of it until morning, and it bred worms and became foul. And Moses was angry with them. 21 Morning by morning they gathered it, as much as each needed; but when the sun grew hot, it melted.

you will obey the Lord your God, if you will do what is right in his eyes, if you will listen to his commands and keep all his statutes, then I shall never bring on you any of the sufferings which I brought on the Egyptians; for I the Lord am your healer.'

27 They came to Elim, where there were twelve springs and seventy palm trees, and there they encamped beside the water.

16 The whole Israelite community, setting out from Elim, arrived at the wilderness of Sin, which lies between Elim and Sinai. This was on the fifteenth day of the second month after they left Egypt.

2 The Israelites all complained to Moses and Aaron in the wilderness. 3 They said, 'If only we had died at the Lord's hand in Egypt, where we sat by the fleshpots and had plenty of bread! But you have brought us out into this wilderness to let this whole assembly starve to death.' 4 The Lord said to Moses, 'I shall rain down bread from heaven for you. Each day the people are to go out and gather a day's supply, so that I can put them to the test and see whether they follow my instructions or not. 5 But on the sixth day, when they prepare what they bring in, it should be twice as much as they gather on other days.' 6 Moses and Aaron said to all the Israelites, 'In the evening you will know that it was the Lord who brought you out of Egypt, 7 and in the morning you will see the glory of the Lord, because he has listened to your complaints against him. Who are we that you should bring complaints against us?' 8 'You will know this', Moses said, 'when in answer to your complaints the Lord gives you flesh to eat in the evening, and in the morning bread in plenty. What are we? It is against the Lord that you bring your complaints, not against us.'

9 Moses told Aaron to say to the whole community of Israel, 'Come into the presence of the Lord, for he has listened to your complaints.' 10 While Aaron was addressing the whole Israelite community, they looked towards the wilderness, and there was the glory of the Lord appearing in the cloud. 11 The Lord spoke to Moses: 12 'I have heard the complaints of the Israelites. Say to them: Between dusk and dark you will have flesh to eat and in the morning bread in plenty. You will know that I the Lord am your God.'

13 That evening a flock of quails flew in and settled over the whole camp; in the morning a fall of dew lay all around it. 14 When the dew was gone, there over the surface of the wilderness fine flakes appeared, fine as hoar-frost on the ground. 15 When the Israelites saw it, they said one to another, 'What is that?' because they did not know what it was. Moses said to them, 'That is the bread which the Lord has given you to eat. 16 Here is the command the Lord has given: Each of you is to gather as much as he can eat: let every man take an omer apiece for every person in his tent.' 17 The Israelites did this, and they gathered, some more, some less, 18 but when they measured it by the omer, those who had gathered more had not too much, and those who had gathered less had not too little. Each had just as much as he could eat. 19 Moses said, 'No one is to keep any of it till morning.' 20 Some, however, did not listen to him; they kept part of it till morning, and it became full of maggots and stank, and Moses was angry with them.

21 Each morning every man gathered as much as he needed; it melted away when the sun grew hot. 22 On the sixth

---

[g] Or "It is manna" (Heb man hu, see verse 31)

16:15 **What is that:** Heb. man-hu (cp. verse 31).

NEW AMERICAN BIBLE

NEW JERUSALEM BIBLE

voice of the LORD, your God," he told them, "and do what is right in his eyes: if you heed his commandments and keep all his precepts, I will not afflict you with any of the diseases with which I afflicted the Egyptians; for I, the LORD, am your healer."

27 Then they came to Elim, where there were twelve springs of water and seventy palm trees, and they camped there near the water.

16 Having set out from Elim, the whole Israelite community came into the desert of Sin, which is between Elim and Sinai, on the fifteenth day of the second month after their departure from the land of Egypt. 2 Here in the desert the whole Israelite community grumbled against Moses and Aaron. 3 The Israelites said to them, "Would that we had died at the LORD's hand in the land of Egypt, as we sat by our fleshpots and ate our fill of bread! But you had to lead us into this desert to make the whole community die of famine!"

4 Then the LORD said to Moses, "I will now rain down bread from heaven for you. Each day the people are to go out and gather their daily portion; thus will I test them, to see whether they follow my instructions or not. 5 On the sixth day, however, when they prepare what they bring in, let it be twice as much as they gather on the other days."

6 So Moses and Aaron told all the Israelites, "At evening you will know that it was the LORD who brought you out of the land of Egypt; 7 and in the morning you will see the glory of the LORD, as he heeds your grumbling against him. But what are we that you should grumble against us? 8 When the LORD gives you flesh to eat in the evening," continued Moses, "and in the morning your fill of bread, as he heeds the grumbling you utter against him, what then are we? Your grumbling is not against us, but against the LORD."

9 Then Moses said to Aaron, "Tell the whole Israelite community: Present yourselves before the LORD, for he has heard your grumbling." 10 When Aaron announced this to the whole Israelite community, they turned toward the desert, and lo, the glory of the LORD appeared in the cloud! 11 The LORD spoke to Moses and said, 12 "I have heard the grumbling of the Israelites. Tell them: In the evening twilight you shall eat flesh, and in the morning you shall have your fill of bread, so that you may know that I, the LORD, am your God."

13 In the evening quail came up and covered the camp. In the morning a dew lay all about the camp, 14 and when the dew evaporated, there on the surface of the desert were fine flakes like hoarfrost on the ground. 15 On seeing it, the Israelites asked one another, "What is this?" for they did not know what it was. But Moses told them, "This is the bread which the LORD has given you to eat.

16 "Now, this is what the LORD has commanded. So gather it that everyone has enough to eat, an omer for each person, as many of you as there are, each man providing for those of his own tent." 17 The Israelites did so. Some gathered a large and some a small amount. 18 But when they measured it out by the omer, he who had gathered a large amount did not have too much, and he who had gathered a small amount did not have too little. They so gathered that everyone had enough to eat. 19 Moses also told them, "Let no one keep any of it over until tomorrow morning." 20 But they would not listen to him. When some kept a part of it over until the following morning, it became wormy and rotten. Therefore Moses was displeased with them.

21 Morning after morning they gathered it, till each had enough to eat; but when the sun grew hot, the manna melted

Yahweh your God and do what he regards as right, if you pay attention to his commandments and keep all his laws, I shall never inflict on you any of the diseases that I inflicted on the Egyptians, for I am Yahweh your Healer.'

27 So they came to Elim where there were twelve springs and seventy palm trees; and there they pitched camp beside the water.

16 f Setting out from Elim, the whole community of Israelites entered the desert of Sin, lying between Elim and Sinai — on the fifteenth day of the second month after they had left Egypt. 2 And the whole community of Israelites began complaining about Moses and Aaron in the desert 3 and said to them, 'Why did we not die at Yahweh's hand in Egypt, where we used to sit round the flesh pots and could eat to our heart's content! As it is, you have led us into this desert to starve this entire assembly to death!'

4 Yahweh then said to Moses, 'Look, I shall rain down bread for you from the heavens. Each day the people must go out and collect their ration for the day; I propose to test them in this way to see whether they will follow my law or not. 5 On the sixth day, however, when they prepare what they have brought in, this must be twice as much as they collect on ordinary days.'

6 Moses and Aaron then said to the whole community of Israelites, 'This evening you will know that it was Yahweh who brought you out of Egypt, 7 and tomorrow morning you will see the glory of Yahweh, for Yahweh has heard your complaints about him. What are we, that your complaint should be against us?' 8 Moses then said, 'This evening Yahweh will give you meat to eat, and tomorrow morning bread to your heart's content, for Yahweh has heard your complaints about him. What do we count for? Your complaints are not against us, but against Yahweh.'

9 Moses then said to Aaron, 'Say to the whole community of Israelites, "Approach Yahweh's presence, for he has heard your complaints." ' 10 As Aaron was speaking to the whole community of Israelites, they turned towards the desert, and there the glory of Yahweh appeared in the cloud. 11 Yahweh then spoke to Moses and said, 12 'I have heard the Israelites' complaints. Speak to them as follows, "At twilight you will eat meat, and in the morning you will have bread to your heart's content, and then you will know that I am Yahweh your God." '

13 That evening, quails flew in and covered the camp, and next morning there was a layer of dew all round the camp. 14 When the layer of dew lifted, there on the surface of the desert was something fine and granular, as fine as hoarfrost on the ground. 15 As soon as the Israelites saw this, they said to one another, 'What is that g?' not knowing what it was. 'That', Moses told them, 'is the food which Yahweh has given you to eat. 16 These are Yahweh's orders: Each of you must collect as much as he needs to eat — a homer per head for each person in his tent.'

17 The Israelites did this. They collected it, some more, some less. 18 When they measured out what they had collected by the homer, no one who had collected more had too much, no one who had collected less had too little. Each had collected as much as he needed to eat.

19 Moses then said, 'No one may keep any of it for tomorrow.' 20 But some of them took no notice of Moses and kept part of it for the following day, and it bred maggots and smelt foul; and Moses was angry with them. 21 Morning by morning they collected it, each man as much as he needed to eat, and once the sun grew hot, it melted away.

f 16 // Nb 11.   g 16 Hebr. Man hu. Popular explanation of the name. Manna is an insect secretion found on tamarisks.

NEW REVISED STANDARD VERSION

22 On the sixth day they gathered twice as much food, two omers apiece. When all the leaders of the congregation came and told Moses, 23 he said to them, "This is what the LORD has commanded: 'Tomorrow is a day of solemn rest, a holy sabbath to the LORD; bake what you want to bake and boil what you want to boil, and all that is left over put aside to be kept until morning.' " 24 So they put it aside until morning, as Moses commanded them; and it did not become foul, and there were no worms in it. 25 Moses said, "Eat it today, for today is a sabbath to the LORD; today you will not find it in the field. 26 Six days you shall gather it; but on the seventh day, which is a sabbath, there will be none."

27 On the seventh day some of the people went out to gather, and they found none. 28 The LORD said to Moses, "How long will you refuse to keep my commandments and instructions? 29 See! The LORD has given you the sabbath, therefore on the sixth day he gives you food for two days; each of you stay where you are; do not leave your place on the seventh day." 30 So the people rested on the seventh day.

31 The house of Israel called it manna; it was like coriander seed, white, and the taste of it was like wafers made with honey. 32 Moses said, "This is what the LORD has commanded: 'Let an omer of it be kept throughout your generations, in order that they may see the food with which I fed you in the wilderness, when I brought you out of the land of Egypt.' " 33 And Moses said to Aaron, "Take a jar, and put an omer of manna in it, and place it before the LORD, to be kept throughout your generations." 34 As the LORD commanded Moses, so Aaron placed it before the covenant, *h* for safekeeping. 35 The Israelites ate manna forty years, until they came to a habitable land; they ate manna, until they came to the border of the land of Canaan. 36 An omer is a tenth of an ephah.

17 From the wilderness of Sin the whole congregation of the Israelites journeyed by stages, as the LORD commanded. They camped at Rephidim, but there was no water for the people to drink. 2 The people quarreled with Moses, and said, "Give us water to drink." Moses said to them, "Why do you quarrel with me? Why do you test the LORD?" 3 But the people thirsted there for water; and the people complained against Moses and said, "Why did you bring us out of Egypt, to kill us and our children and livestock with thirst?" 4 So Moses cried out to the LORD, "What shall I do with this people? They are almost ready to stone me." 5 The LORD said to Moses, "Go on ahead of the people, and take some of the elders of Israel with you; take in your hand the staff with which you struck the Nile, and go. 6 I will be standing there in front of you on the rock at Horeb. Strike the rock, and water will come out of it, so that the people may drink." Moses did so, in the sight of the elders of Israel. 7 He called the place Massah*i* and Meribah, *j* because the Israelites quarreled and tested the LORD, saying, "Is the LORD among us or not?"

8 Then Amalek came and fought with Israel at Rephidim. 9 Moses said to Joshua, "Choose some men for us and go out, fight with Amalek. Tomorrow I will stand on the top of the hill with the staff of God in my hand." 10 So Joshua did as Moses told him, and fought with Amalek, while Moses, Aaron, and Hur went up to the top of the hill. 11 Whenever Moses held up his hand, Israel prevailed; and whenever he lowered his hand, Amalek prevailed. 12 But Moses' hands grew weary; so they took a stone and put it under him, and he sat on it. Aaron and Hur held up his hands, one on one side, and the other on the other side; so his hands were steady until the sun set. 13 And Joshua defeated Amalek and his people with the sword.

REVISED ENGLISH BIBLE

day they gathered twice as much food, two omers each, and when the chiefs of the community all came and told Moses, 23 'This', he answered, 'is what the LORD has said: Tomorrow is a day of sacred rest, a sabbath holy to the LORD. So bake what you want to bake now, and boil what you want to boil; what remains over put aside to be kept till morning.' 24 So they put it aside till morning as Moses had commanded, and it neither stank nor became infested with maggots. 25 'Eat it today,' said Moses, 'because today is a sabbath of the LORD. Today you will find none outside. 26 For six days you may gather it, but on the seventh day, the sabbath, there will be none.'

27 Some of the people did go out to gather it on the seventh day, but they found nothing. 28 The LORD said to Moses, 'How long will you Israelites refuse to obey my commands and instructions? 29 You are aware the LORD has given you the sabbath, and so he gives you two days' food every sixth day. Let everyone stay where he is; no one may stir from his home on the seventh.' 30 So the people kept the sabbath on the seventh day.

31 Israel called the food manna; it was like coriander seed, but white, and it tasted like a wafer made with honey. 32 'This', said Moses, 'is the command which the LORD has given: Take a full omer of it to be kept for future generations, so that they may see the bread with which I fed you in the wilderness when I brought you out of Egypt.' 33 Moses said to Aaron, 'Take a jar and fill it with an omer of manna, and store it in the presence of the LORD to be kept for future generations.' 34 Aaron did as the LORD had commanded Moses, and stored it before the Testimony for safe keeping. 35 The Israelites ate the manna for forty years until they came to a land where they could settle; they ate it until they came to the border of Canaan. 36 (An omer is one tenth of an ephah.)

17 The whole community of Israel set out from the wilderness of Sin and travelled by stages as the LORD directed. They encamped at Rephidim, but there was no water for the people to drink, 2 and a dispute arose between them and Moses. When they said, 'Give us water to drink,' Moses said, 'Why do you dispute with me? Why do you challenge the LORD?' 3 The people became so thirsty there that they raised an outcry against Moses: 'Why have you brought us out of Egypt with our children and our herds to let us die of thirst?' 4 Moses appealed to the LORD, 'What shall I do with these people? In a moment they will be stoning me.' 5 The LORD answered, 'Go forward ahead of the people; take with you some of the elders of Israel and bring along the staff with which you struck the Nile. Go, 6 you will find me waiting for you there, by a rock in Horeb. Strike the rock; water will pour out of it for the people to drink.' Moses did this in the sight of the elders of Israel. 7 He named the place Massah and Meribah, because the Israelites had disputed with him and put the LORD to the test with their question, 'Is the LORD in our midst or not?'

8 The Amalekites came and attacked Israel at Rephidim. 9 Moses said to Joshua, 'Pick men for us, and march out tomorrow to fight against Amalek; and I shall stand on the hilltop with the staff of God in my hand.' 10 Joshua did as Moses commanded and fought against Amalek, while Moses, Aaron, and Hur climbed to the top of the hill. 11 Whenever Moses raised his hands Israel had the advantage, and when he lowered his hands the advantage passed to Amalek. 12 When his arms grew heavy they took a stone and put it under him and, as he sat, Aaron and Hur held up his hands, one on each side, so that his hands remained steady till sunset. 13 Thus Joshua defeated Amalek and put its people to the sword.

---

h Or *treaty* or *testimony*; Heb *eduth*   *i* That is *Test*   *j* That is *Quarrel*

17:7 **Massah:** *that is* Test. **Meribah:** *that is* Dispute.

NEW AMERICAN BIBLE

away. 22 On the sixth day they gathered twice as much food, two omers for each person. When all the leaders of the community came and reported this to Moses, 23 he told them, "That is what the LORD prescribed. Tomorrow is a day of complete rest, the sabbath, sacred to the LORD. You may either bake or boil the manna, as you please; but whatever is left put away and keep for the morrow." 24 When they put it away for the morrow, as Moses commanded, it did not become rotten or wormy. 25 Moses then said, "Eat it today, for today is the sabbath of the LORD. On this day you will not find any of it on the ground. 26 On the other six days you can gather it, but on the seventh day, the sabbath, none of it will be there." 27 Still, on the seventh day some of the people went out to gather it, although they did not find any. 28 Then the LORD said to Moses, "How long will you refuse to keep my commandments and laws? 29 Take note! The LORD has given you the sabbath. That is why on the sixth day he gives you food for two days. On the seventh day everyone is to stay home and no one is to go out." 30 After that the people rested on the seventh day.

31 The Israelites called this food manna. It was like coriander seed, but white, and it tasted like wafers made with honey.

32 Moses said, "This is what the LORD has commanded. Keep an omerful of manna for your descendants, that they may see what food I gave you to eat in the desert when I brought you out of the land of Egypt." 33 Moses then told Aaron, "Take an urn and put an omer of manna in it. Then place it before the LORD in safekeeping for your descendants." 34 So Aaron placed it in front of the commandments for safekeeping, as the LORD had commanded Moses.

35 The Israelites ate this manna for forty years, until they came to settled land; they ate manna until they reached the borders of Canaan. 36 [An omer is one tenth of an ephah.]

17 From the desert of Sin the whole Israelite community journeyed by stages, as the LORD directed, and encamped at Rephidim.

Here there was no water for the people to drink. 2 They quarreled, therefore, with Moses and said, "Give us water to drink." Moses replied, "Why do you quarrel with me? Why do you put the LORD to a test?" 3 Here, then, in their thirst for water, the people grumbled against Moses, saying, "Why did you ever make us leave Egypt? Was it just to have us die here of thirst with our children and our livestock?" 4 So Moses cried out to the LORD, "What shall I do with this people? A little more and they will stone me!" 5 The LORD answered Moses, "Go over there in front of the people, along with some of the elders of Israel, holding in your hand, as you go, the staff with which you struck the river. 6 I will be standing there in front of you on the rock in Horeb. Strike the rock, and the water will flow from it for the people to drink." This Moses did, in the presence of the elders of Israel. 7 The place was called Massah and Meribah, because the Israelites quarreled there and tested the LORD, saying, "Is the LORD in our midst or not?"

8 At Rephidim, Amalek came and waged war against Israel. 9 Moses, therefore, said to Joshua, "Pick out certain men, and tomorrow go out and engage Amalek in battle. I will be standing on top of the hill with the staff of God in my hand." 10 So Joshua did as Moses told him: he engaged Amalek in battle after Moses had climbed to the top of the hill with Aaron and Hur. 11 As long as Moses kept his hands raised up, Israel had the better of the fight, but when he let his hands rest, Amalek had the better of the fight. 12 Moses' hands, however, grew tired; so they put a rock in place for him to sit on. Meanwhile Aaron and Hur supported his hands, one on one side and one on the other, so that his hands remained steady till sunset. 13 And Joshua mowed down Amalek and his people with the edge of the sword.

NEW JERUSALEM BIBLE

22 Now, on the sixth day they collected twice the amount of food: two *homer* per person, and all the leaders of the community came and told Moses this. 23 Moses replied, 'This is what Yahweh said, "Tomorrow is a day of complete rest, a Sabbath sacred to Yahweh. Bake what you want to bake, boil what you want to boil; put aside what is left over, to be kept for tomorrow." 24 So, as Moses ordered, they put it aside for the following day, and its smell was not foul nor were there maggots in it. 25 'Eat it today,' Moses said, 'for today is a Sabbath for Yahweh; you will find none in the fields today. 26 For six days you will collect it, but on the seventh day, the Sabbath, there will be none.' 27 On the seventh day some of the people went out to collect it, but they found none. 28 Yahweh then said to Moses, 'How much longer will you refuse to obey my commandments and laws? 29 Look, Yahweh has given you the Sabbath; this is why he gives you two days' food on the sixth day; each of you must stay in his place; on the seventh day no one may leave his home.' 30 So on the seventh day the people rested.

31 The House of Israel named it 'manna'. It was like coriander seed; it was white and its taste was like that of wafers made with honey.

32 Moses then said, 'These are Yahweh's orders: Fill a *homer* with it and preserve it for your descendants, so that they can see the bread on which I fed you in the desert when I brought you out of Egypt.' 33 Moses then said to Aaron, 'Take a jar and in it put a full *homer* of manna and store it in Yahweh's presence, to be kept for your descendants.' 34 Accordingly, Aaron stored it in front of the Testimony, to be preserved, as Yahweh had ordered Moses.

35 The Israelites ate manna for forty years, up to the time they reached inhabited country: they ate manna up to the time they reached the frontiers of Canaan. 36 A *homer* is one-tenth of an *ephah*.

17 h The whole community of Israelites left the desert of Sin, travelling by stages as Yahweh ordered. They pitched camp at Rephidim where there was no water for the people to drink. 2 The people took issue with Moses for this and said, 'Give us water to drink.' Moses replied, 'Why take issue with me? Why do you put Yahweh to the test?' 3 But tormented by thirst, the people complained to Moses. 'Why did you bring us out of Egypt,' they said, 'only to make us, our children and our livestock, die of thirst?' 4 Moses appealed to Yahweh for help. 'How am I to deal with this people?' he said. 'Any moment now they will stone me!' 5 Yahweh then said to Moses, 'Go on ahead of the people, taking some of the elders of Israel with you; in your hand take the staff with which you struck the River, and go. 6 I shall be waiting for you there on the rock (at Horeb). Strike the rock, and water will come out for the people to drink.' This was what Moses did, with the elders of Israel looking on. 7 He gave the place the names Massah and Meribah because of the Israelites' contentiousness and because they put Yahweh to the test by saying, 'Is Yahweh with us, or not?'

8 The Amalekites then came and attacked Israel at Rephidim. 9 Moses said to Joshua, 'Pick some men and tomorrow morning go out and engage Amalek. I, for my part, shall take my stand on the hilltop with the staff of God in my hand.' 10 Joshua did as Moses had told him and went out to engage Amalek, while Moses, Aaron and Hur went up to the top of the hill. 11 As long as Moses kept his arms raised, Israel had the advantage; when he let his arms fall, the advantage went to Amalek. 12 But Moses' arms grew heavy, so they took a stone and put it under him and on this he sat, with Aaron and Hur supporting his arms on each side.

Thus his arms remained unwavering till sunset, 13 and Joshua defeated Amalek, putting their people to the sword.

h 17 17:1seq. // Nb 20:1–13.

NEW REVISED STANDARD VERSION

14 Then the LORD said to Moses, "Write this as a reminder in a book and recite it in the hearing of Joshua: I will utterly blot out the remembrance of Amalek from under heaven." 15 And Moses built an altar and called it, The LORD is my banner. 16 He said, "A hand upon the banner of the LORD! k The LORD will have war with Amalek from generation to generation."

18 Jethro, the priest of Midian, Moses' father-in-law, heard of all that God had done for Moses and for his people Israel, how the LORD had brought Israel out of Egypt. 2 After Moses had sent away his wife Zipporah, his father-in-law Jethro took her back, 3 along with her two sons. The name of the one was Gershom (for he said, "I have been an alien l in a foreign land"), 4 and the name of the other, Eliezer m (for he said, "The God of my father was my help, and delivered me from the sword of Pharaoh"). 5 Jethro, Moses' father-in-law, came into the wilderness where Moses was encamped at the mountain of God, bringing Moses' sons and wife to him. 6 He sent word to Moses, "I, your father-in-law Jethro, am coming to you, with your wife and her two sons." 7 Moses went out to meet his father-in-law; he bowed down and kissed him; each asked after the other's welfare, and they went into the tent. 8 Then Moses told his father-in-law all that the LORD had done to Pharaoh and to the Egyptians for Israel's sake, all the hardship that had beset them on the way, and how the LORD had delivered them. 9 Jethro rejoiced for all the good that the LORD had done to Israel, in delivering them from the Egyptians.

10 Jethro said, "Blessed be the LORD, who has delivered you from the Egyptians and from Pharaoh. 11 Now I know that the LORD is greater than all gods, because he delivered the people from the Egyptians, n when they dealt arrogantly with them." 12 And Jethro, Moses' father-in-law, brought a burnt offering and sacrifices to God; and Aaron came with all the elders of Israel to eat bread with Moses' father-in-law in the presence of God.

13 The next day Moses sat as judge for the people, while the people stood around him from morning until evening. 14 When Moses' father-in-law saw all that he was doing for the people, he said, "What is this that you are doing for the people? Why do you sit alone, while all the people stand around you from morning until evening?" 15 Moses said to his father-in-law, "Because the people come to me to inquire of God. 16 When they have a dispute, they come to me and I decide between one person and another, and I make known to them the statutes and instructions of God." 17 Moses' father-in-law said to him, "What you are doing is not good. 18 You will surely wear yourself out, both you and these people with you. For the task is too heavy for you; you cannot do it alone. 19 Now listen to me. I will give you counsel, and God be with you! You should represent the people before God, and you should bring their cases before God; 20 teach them the statutes and instructions and make known to them the way they are to go and the things they are to do. 21 You should also look for able men among all the people, men who fear God, are trustworthy, and hate dishonest gain; set such men over them as officers over thousands, hundreds, fifties and tens. 22 Let them sit as judges for the people at all times; let them bring every important case to you, but decide every minor case themselves. So it will be easier for you, and they will bear the burden with you. 23 If you do this, and God so commands you, then you will be able to endure, and all these people will go to their home in peace."

24 So Moses listened to his father-in-law and did all that he had said. 25 Moses chose able men from all Israel and

REVISED ENGLISH BIBLE

14 The LORD said to Moses, 'Record this in writing, and tell it to Joshua in these words: I am resolved to blot out all memory of Amalek from under heaven.' 15 Moses built an altar, and named it 'The LORD is my Banner' and said, 16 'My oath upon it: the LORD is at war with Amalek generation after generation.'

18 JETHRO priest of Midian, father-in-law of Moses, heard all that God had done for Moses and for Israel his people, and how the LORD had brought Israel out of Egypt. 2 When Moses had sent away his wife Zipporah, Jethro his father-in-law had received her 3 and her two sons. The name of the one was Gershom, 'for', said Moses, 'I have become an alien living in a foreign land'; 4 the other's name was Eliezer, 'for', he said, 'the God of my father was my help and saved me from Pharaoh's sword.' 5 Jethro, Moses' father-in-law, now came to him with his sons and his wife, to the wilderness where he was encamped at the mountain of God. 6 Moses was told, 'Here is Jethro, your father-in-law, coming to you with your wife and her two sons.' 7 Moses went out to meet his father-in-law, bowed low to him, and kissed him. After they had greeted one another and come into the tent, 8 Moses told him all that the LORD had done to Pharaoh and to Egypt for Israel's sake, and about all their hardships on the journey, and how the LORD had saved them. 9 Jethro rejoiced at all the good the LORD had done for Israel in saving them from the power of Egypt.

10-11 He said, 'Blessed be the LORD who has delivered you from the power of Egypt and of Pharaoh. Now I know that the LORD is the greatest of all gods, because he has delivered the people from the Egyptians who dealt so arrogantly with them.' 12 Jethro, Moses' father-in-law, brought a whole-offering and sacrifices for God; and Aaron and all the elders of Israel came and shared the meal with Jethro in the presence of God.

13 The next day Moses took his seat to settle disputes among the people, and he was surrounded from morning till evening. 14 At the sight of all that he was doing for the people, Jethro asked, 'What is this you are doing for the people? Why do you sit alone with all of them standing round you from morning till evening?' 15 'The people come to me to seek God's guidance,' Moses answered. 16 'Whenever there is a dispute among them, they come to me, and I decide between one party and the other. I make known the statutes and laws of God.' 17 His father-in-law said to him, 'This is not the best way to do it. 18 You will only wear yourself out and wear out the people who are here. The task is too heavy for you; you cannot do it alone. 19 Now listen to me: take my advice, and God be with you. It is for you to be the people's representative before God, and bring their disputes to him, 20 to instruct them in the statutes and laws, and teach them how they must behave and what they must do. 21 But you should search for capable, godfearing men among all the people, honest and incorruptible men, and appoint them over the people as officers over units of a thousand, of a hundred, of fifty, or of ten. 22 They can act as judges for the people at all times; difficult cases they should refer to you, but decide simple cases themselves. In this way your burden will be lightened, as they will be sharing it with you. 23 If you do this, then God will direct you and you will be able to go on. And, moreover, this whole people will arrive at its destination in harmony.'

24 Moses heeded his father-in-law and did all he had suggested. 25 He chose capable men from all Israel and appoint-

---

k Cn: Meaning of Heb uncertain   l Heb ger   m Heb Eli, my God; ezer, help   n The clause because . . . Egyptians has been transposed from verse 10

17:16 **My oath upon it:** so Samar.; lit. Hand upon buttock; Heb. unintelligible.   18:3 **an alien:** cp. 2:22.   18:4 **Eliezer:** that is God is help.   18:6 **Here is:** so Gk; Heb. I am.

14 Then the LORD said to Moses, "Write this down in a document as something to be remembered, and recite it in the ears of Joshua. I will completely blot out the memory of Amalek from under the heavens." 15 Moses also built an altar there, which he called Yahweh-nissi; 16 for he said, "The LORD takes in hand his banner; the LORD will war against Amalek through the centuries."

18 Now Moses' father-in-law Jethro, the priest of Midian, heard of all that God had done for Moses and for his people Israel: how the LORD had brought Israel out of Egypt. 2 So his father-in-law Jethro took along Zipporah, Moses' wife, whom Moses had sent back to him, 3 and her two sons. One of these was called Gershom; for he said, "I am a stranger in a foreign land." 4 The other was called Eliezer; for he said, "My father's God is my helper; he has rescued me from Pharaoh's sword." 5 Together with Moses' wife and sons, then, his father-in-law Jethro came to him in the desert where he was encamped near the mountain of God, 6 and he sent word to Moses, "I, Jethro, your father-in-law, am coming to you, along with your wife and her two sons."

7 Moses went out to meet his father-in-law, bowed down before him, and kissed him. Having greeted each other, they went into the tent. 8 Moses then told his father-in-law of all that the LORD had done to Pharaoh and the Egyptians for the sake of Israel, and of all the hardships they had had to endure on their journey, and how the LORD had come to their rescue. 9 Jethro rejoiced over all the goodness that the LORD had shown Israel in rescuing them from the hands of the Egyptians. 10 "Blessed be the LORD," he said, "who has rescued his people from the hands of Pharaoh and the Egyptians. 11 Now I know that the LORD is a deity great beyond any other; for he took occasion of their being dealt with insolently to deliver the people from the power of the Egyptians." 12 Then Jethro, the father-in-law of Moses, brought a holocaust and other sacrifices to God, and Aaron came with all the elders of Israel to participate with Moses' father-in-law in the meal before God.

13 The next day Moses sat in judgment for the people, who waited about him from morning until evening. 14 When his father-in-law saw all that he was doing for the people, he inquired, "What sort of thing is this that you are doing for the people? Why do you sit alone while all the people have to stand about you from morning till evening?" 15 Moses answered his father-in-law, "The people come to me to consult God. 16 Whenever they have a disagreement, they come to me to have me settle the matter between them and make known to them God's decisions and regulations."

17 "You are not acting wisely," his father-in-law replied. 18 "You will surely wear yourself out, and not only yourself but also these people with you. The task is too heavy for you; you cannot do it alone. 19 Now, listen to me, and I will give you some advice, that God may be with you. Act as the people's representative before God, bringing to him whatever they have to say. 20 Enlighten them in regard to the decisions and regulations, showing them how they are to live and what they are to do. 21 But you should also look among all the people for able and God-fearing men, trustworthy men who hate dishonest gain, and set them as officers over groups of thousands, of hundreds, of fifties, and of tens. 22 Let these men render decisions for the people in all ordinary cases. More important cases they should refer to you, but all the lesser cases they can settle themselves. Thus, your burden will be lightened, since they will bear it with you. 23 If you do this, when God gives you orders you will be able to stand the strain, and all these people will go home satisfied."

24 Moses followed the advice of his father-in-law and did all that he had suggested. 25 He picked out able men from

14 Yahweh then said to Moses, 'Write this down in a book to commemorate it, and repeat it over to Joshua, for I shall blot out all memory of Amalek under heaven.' 15 Moses then built an altar and named it Yahweh-Nissi 16 meaning, 'Lay hold of Yahweh's banner! Yahweh will be at war with Amalek generation after generation.'

18 Jethro, priest of Midian, Moses' father-in-law, had heard all about what God had done for Moses and for Israel his people: how Yahweh had brought Israel out of Egypt. 2 Jethro, Moses' father-in-law, then took back Zipporah, Moses' wife, whom Moses had sent home, 3 with her two sons; one of them was called Gershom because, he had said, 'I am an alien in a foreign land,' 4 and the other called Eliezer because 'My father's God is my help and has delivered me from Pharaoh's sword.'

5 Then Jethro, Moses' father-in-law, with Moses' sons and wife, came to Moses in the desert where he was encamped, at the mountain of God. 6 'Here is your father-in-law Jethro approaching', Moses was told, 'with your wife and her two sons.' 7 So Moses went out to greet his father-in-law, bowed low to him and kissed him; and when each had asked how the other was they went into the tent. 8 Moses then told his father-in-law all about what Yahweh had done to Pharaoh and the Egyptians for Israel's sake, and about all the hardships that they had encountered on the way, and how Yahweh had rescued them. 9 And Jethro was delighted at all Yahweh's goodness to Israel in having rescued them from the clutches of the Egyptians. 10 'Blessed be Yahweh', Jethro exclaimed, 'for having rescued you from the clutches of the Egyptians and the clutches of Pharaoh, for having rescued the people from the grasp of the Egyptians! 11 Now I know that Yahweh is greater than all other gods. . .'

12 Jethro, Moses' father-in-law, then offered a burnt offering and other sacrifices to God; and Aaron and all the elders of Israel came and ate with Moses' father-in-law in the presence of God.

13 *i*On the following day, Moses took his seat to administer justice for the people, and the people were standing round him from morning till evening. 14 Seeing all he did for the people, Moses' father-in-law said to him, 'Why do you do this for the people, why sit here alone with the people standing round you from morning till evening?' 15 Moses replied to his father-in-law, 'Because the people come to me to consult God. 16 When they have a problem they come to me, and I give a ruling between the one and the other and make God's statutes and laws known to them.' 17 Moses' father-in-law then said to him, 'What you are doing is not right. 18 You will only tire yourself out, and the people with you too, for the work is too heavy for you. You cannot do it all yourself. 19 Now listen to the advice I am going to give you, and God be with you! Your task is to represent the people to God, to lay their cases before God, 20 and to teach them the statutes and laws, and show them the way they ought to follow and how they ought to behave. 21 At the same time, from the people at large choose capable and God-fearing men, men who are trustworthy and incorruptible, and put them in charge of them as heads of thousands, hundreds, fifties and tens, 22 and make them the people's permanent judges. They will refer all important matters to you, but all minor matters they will decide themselves, so making things easier for you by sharing the burden with you. 23 If you do this — and may God so command you — you will be able to stand the strain, and all these people will go home satisfied.'

24 Moses took his father-in-law's advice and did just as he said. 25 Moses chose capable men from all Israel and put

i **18** 18:13seq. // Dt 1:9–18.

| NEW REVISED STANDARD VERSION | REVISED ENGLISH BIBLE |

appointed them as heads over the people, as officers over thousands, hundreds, fifties, and tens. 26 And they judged the people at all times; hard cases they brought to Moses, but any minor case they decided themselves. 27 Then Moses let his father-in-law depart, and he went off to his own country.

19 On the third new moon after the Israelites had gone out of the land of Egypt, on that very day, they came into the wilderness of Sinai. 2 They had journeyed from Rephidim, entered the wilderness of Sinai, and camped in the wilderness; Israel camped there in front of the mountain. 3 Then Moses went up to God; the LORD called to him from the mountain, saying, "Thus you shall say to the house of Jacob, and tell the Israelites: 4 You have seen what I did to the Egyptians, and how I bore you on eagles' wings and brought you to myself. 5 Now therefore, if you obey my voice and keep my covenant, you shall be my treasured possession out of all the peoples. Indeed, the whole earth is mine, 6 but you shall be for me a priestly kingdom and a holy nation. These are the words that you shall speak to the Israelites."

7 So Moses came, summoned the elders of the people, and set before them all these words that the LORD had commanded him. 8 The people all answered as one: "Everything that the LORD has spoken we will do." Moses reported the words of the people to the LORD. 9 Then the LORD said to Moses, "I am going to come to you in a dense cloud, in order that the people may hear when I speak with you and so trust you ever after."

When Moses had told the words of the people to the LORD, 10 the LORD said to Moses: "Go to the people and consecrate them today and tomorrow. Have them wash their clothes 11 and prepare for the third day, because on the third day the LORD will come down upon Mount Sinai in the sight of all the people. 12 You shall set limits for the people all around, saying, 'Be careful not to go up the mountain or to touch the edge of it. Any who touch the mountain shall be put to death. 13 No hand shall touch them, but they shall be stoned or shot with arrows;*o* whether animal or human being, they shall not live.' When the trumpet sounds a long blast, they may go up on the mountain." 14 So Moses went down from the mountain to the people. He consecrated the people, and they washed their clothes. 15 And he said to the people, "Prepare for the third day; do not go near a woman."

16 On the morning of the third day there was thunder and lightning, as well as a thick cloud on the mountain, and a blast of a trumpet so loud that all the people who were in the camp trembled. 17 Moses brought the people out of the camp to meet God. They took their stand at the foot of the mountain. 18 Now Mount Sinai was wrapped in smoke, because the LORD had descended upon it in fire; the smoke went up like the smoke of a kiln, while the whole mountain shook violently. 19 As the blast of the trumpet grew louder and louder, Moses would speak and God would answer him in thunder. 20 When the LORD descended upon Mount Sinai, to the top of the mountain, the LORD summoned Moses to the top of the mountain, and Moses went up. 21 Then the LORD said to Moses, "Go down and warn the people not to break through to the LORD to look; otherwise many of them will perish. 22 Even the priests who approach the LORD must consecrate themselves or the LORD will break out against them." 23 Moses said to the LORD, "The people are not permitted to come up to Mount Sinai; for you yourself warned us, saying, 'Set limits around the mountain and keep it holy.'" 24 The LORD said to him, "Go down, and

o Heb lacks *with arrows*

19 IN the third month after Israel had left Egypt, they came to the wilderness of Sinai. 2 They set out from Rephidim and, entering the wilderness of Sinai, they encamped there, pitching their tents in front of the mountain. 3 Moses went up to God, and the LORD called to him from the mountain and said, 'This is what you are to say to the house of Jacob and tell the sons of Israel: 4 You yourselves have seen what I did to Egypt, and how I have carried you on eagles' wings and brought you here to me. 5 If only you will now listen to me and keep my covenant, then out of all peoples you will become my special possession; for the whole earth is mine. 6 You will be to me a kingdom of priests, my holy nation. Those are the words you are to speak to the Israelites.'

7 Moses went down, and summoning the elders of the people he set before them all these commands which the LORD had laid on him. 8 As one the people answered, 'Whatever the LORD has said we shall do.' When Moses brought this answer back to the LORD, 9 the LORD said to him, 'I am coming to you in a thick cloud, so that I may speak to you in the hearing of the people, and so their faith in you may never fail.'

When Moses reported to the LORD the pledge given by the people, 10 the LORD said to him, 'Go to the people and hallow them today and tomorrow and have them wash their clothes. 11 They must be ready by the third day, because on that day the LORD will descend on Mount Sinai in the sight of all the people. 12 You must set bounds for the people, saying, "Take care not to go up the mountain or even to touch its base." Anyone who touches the mountain shall be put to death. 13 No hand may touch him; he is to be stoned to death or shot: neither man nor beast may live. But when the ram's horn sounds, they may go up the mountain.' 14 Moses came down from the mountain to the people. He hallowed them and they washed their clothes. 15 He said, 'Be ready by the third day; do not go near a woman.' 16 At dawn on the third day there were peals of thunder and flashes of lightning, dense cloud on the mountain, and a loud trumpet-blast; all the people in the camp trembled.

17 Moses brought the people out from the camp to meet God, and they took their stand at the foot of the mountain. 18 Mount Sinai was enveloped in smoke because the LORD had come down on it in fire; the smoke rose like the smoke from a kiln; all the people trembled violently, 19 and the sound of the trumpet grew ever louder. Whenever Moses spoke, God answered him in a peal of thunder. 20 The LORD came down on the top of Mount Sinai and summoned Moses up to the mountaintop. 21 The LORD said to him, 'Go down; warn the people solemnly that they must not force their way through to the LORD to see him, or many of them will perish. 22 Even the priests, who may approach the LORD, must hallow themselves, for fear that the LORD may break out against them.' 23 Moses answered the LORD, 'The people cannot come up Mount Sinai, because you solemnly warned us to set bounds to the mountain and keep it holy.'

19:1 **after . . . Egypt:** *prob. rdg; Heb.* adds on this day. 19:13 **shot:** *or* hurled to his death. 19:18 **the people:** *so some MSS; others* the mountain. 19:19 **in . . . thunder:** *or* by voice.

|

all Israel and put them in charge of the people as officers over groups of thousands, of hundreds, of fifties, and of tens. 26 They rendered decisions for the people in all ordinary cases. The more difficult cases they referred to Moses, but all the lesser cases they settled themselves. 27 Then Moses bade farewell to his father-in-law, who went off to his own country.

19 In the third month after their departure from the land of Egypt, on its first day, the Israelites came to the desert of Sinai. 2 After the journey from Rephidim to the desert of Sinai, they pitched camp.

While Israel was encamped here in front of the mountain, 3 Moses went up the mountain to God. Then the LORD called to him and said, "Thus shall you say to the house of Jacob; 4 tell the Israelites: You have seen for yourselves how I treated the Egyptians and how I bore you up on eagle wings and brought you here to myself. 5 Therefore, if you hearken to my voice and keep my covenant, you shall be my special possession, dearer to me than all other people, though all the earth is mine. 6 You shall be to me a kingdom of priests, a holy nation. That is what you must tell the Israelites." 7 So Moses went and summoned the elders of the people. When he set before them all that the LORD had ordered him to tell them, 8 the people all answered together, "Everything the LORD has said, we will do." Then Moses brought back to the LORD the response of the people.

9 The LORD also told him, "I am coming to you in a dense cloud, so that when the people hear me speaking with you, they may always have faith in you also." When Moses, then, had reported to the LORD the response of the people, 10 the LORD added, "Go to the people and have them sanctify themselves today and tomorrow. Make them wash their garments 11 and be ready for the third day; for on the third day the LORD will come down on Mount Sinai before the eyes of all the people. 12 Set limits for the people all around the mountain, and tell them: Take care not to go up the mountain, or even to touch its base. If anyone touches the mountain he must be put to death. 13 No hand shall touch him; he must be stoned to death or killed with arrows. Such a one, man or beast, must not be allowed to live. Only when the ram's horn resounds may they go up to the mountain." 14 Then Moses came down from the mountain to the people and had them sanctify themselves and wash their garments. 15 He warned them, "Be ready for the third day. Have no intercourse with any woman."

16 On the morning of the third day there were peals of thunder and lightning, and a heavy cloud over the mountain, and a very loud trumpet blast, so that all the people in the camp trembled. 17 But Moses led the people out of the camp to meet God, and they stationed themselves at the foot of the mountain. 18 Mount Sinai was all wrapped in smoke, for the LORD came down upon it in fire. The smoke rose from it as though from a furnace, and the whole mountain trembled violently. 19 The trumpet blast grew louder and louder, while Moses was speaking and God answering him with thunder.

20 When the LORD came down to the top of Mount Sinai, he summoned Moses to the top of the mountain, and Moses went up to him. 21 Then the LORD told Moses, "Go down and warn the people not to break through toward the LORD in order to see him; otherwise many of them will be struck down. 22 The priests, too, who approach the LORD must sanctify themselves; else he will vent his anger upon them." 23 Moses said to the LORD, "The people cannot go up to Mount Sinai, for you yourself warned us to set limits around the mountain to make it sacred." 24 The LORD repeated, "Go

them in charge of the people as heads of thousands, hundreds, fifties and tens. 26 These acted as the people's permanent judges. They referred hard cases to Moses but decided minor matters themselves.

27 Moses then set his father-in-law on his way, and he travelled back to his own country.

19 Three months to the day after leaving Egypt, the Israelites reached the desert of Sinai. 2 Setting out from Rephidim, they reached the desert of Sinai and pitched camp in the desert; there, facing the mountain, Israel pitched camp.

3 Moses then went up to God, and Yahweh called to him from the mountain, saying, 'Say this to the House of Jacob! Tell the Israelites, 4 "You have seen for yourselves what I did to the Egyptians and how I carried you away on eagle's wings and brought you to me. 5 So now, if you are really prepared to obey me and keep my covenant, you, out of all peoples, shall be my personal possession, for the whole world is mine. 6 For me you shall be a kingdom of priests, a holy nation." Those are the words you are to say to the Israelites.' 7 So Moses went and summoned the people's elders and acquainted them with everything that Yahweh had bidden him, 8 and the people all replied with one accord, 'Whatever Yahweh has said, we will do.' Moses then reported to Yahweh what the people had said.

9 Yahweh then said to Moses, 'Look, I shall come to you in a dense cloud so that the people will hear when I speak to you and believe you ever after.' Moses then told Yahweh what the people had said.

10 Yahweh then said to Moses, 'Go to the people and tell them to sanctify themselves today and tomorrow. They must wash their clothes 11 and be ready for the day after tomorrow; for the day after tomorrow, in the sight of all the people, Yahweh will descend on Mount Sinai. 12 You will mark out the limits of the mountain and say, "Take care not to go up the mountain or to touch the edge of it. Anyone who touches the mountain will be put to death. 13 No one may lay a hand on him: he must be stoned or shot by arrow; whether man or beast, he shall not live." When the ram's horn sounds a long blast, they must go up the mountain.'

14 So Moses came down from the mountain to the people; he made the people sanctify themselves and they washed their clothes. 15 He then said to the people, 'Be ready for the day after tomorrow; do not touch a woman.'

16 Now at daybreak two days later, there were peals of thunder and flashes of lightning, dense cloud on the mountain and a very loud trumpet blast; and, in the camp, all the people trembled. 17 Then Moses led the people out of the camp to meet God; and they took their stand at the bottom of the mountain. 18 Mount Sinai was entirely wrapped in smoke, because Yahweh had descended on it in the form of fire. The smoke rose like smoke from a furnace and the whole mountain shook violently. 19 Louder and louder grew the trumpeting. Moses spoke, and God answered him in the thunder. 20 Yahweh descended on Mount Sinai, on the top of the mountain, and Yahweh called Moses to the top of the mountain; and Moses went up. 21 Yahweh then said to Moses, 'Go down and warn the people not to break through to look at Yahweh, or many of them will perish. 22 Even the priests, who do have access to Yahweh, must sanctify themselves, or Yahweh may burst out against them.' 23 Moses said to Yahweh, 'The people cannot come up Mount Sinai, since you yourself warned us to mark out the limits of the mountain and declare it sacred.' 24 Yahweh said, 'Away

NEW REVISED STANDARD VERSION

come up bringing Aaron with you; but do not let either the priests or the people break through to come up to the LORD; otherwise he will break out against them." 25 So Moses went down to the people and told them.

20 Then God spoke all these words:
2 I am the LORD your God, who brought you out of the land of Egypt, out of the house of slavery; 3 you shall have no other gods before*p* me.

4 You shall not make for yourself an idol, whether in the form of anything that is in heaven above, or that is on the earth beneath, or that is in the water under the earth. 5 You shall not bow down to them or worship them; for I the LORD your God am a jealous God, punishing children for the iniquity of parents, to the third and the fourth generation of those who reject me, 6 but showing steadfast love to the thousandth generation*q* of those who love me and keep my commandments.

7 You shall not make wrongful use of the name of the LORD your God, for the LORD will not acquit anyone who misuses his name.

8 Remember the sabbath day, and keep it holy. 9 Six days you shall labor and do all your work. 10 But the seventh day is a sabbath to the LORD your God; you shall not do any work—you, your son or your daughter, your male or female slave, your livestock, or the alien resident in your towns. 11 For in six days the LORD made heaven and earth, the sea, and all that is in them, but rested the seventh day; therefore the LORD blessed the sabbath day and consecrated it.

12 Honor your father and your mother, so that your days may be long in the land that the LORD your God is giving you.

13 You shall not murder.*r*

14 You shall not commit adultery.

15 You shall not steal.

16 You shall not bear false witness against your neighbor.

17 You shall not covet your neighbor's house; you shall not covet your neighbor's wife, or male or female slave, or ox, or donkey, or anything that belongs to your neighbor.

18 When all the people witnessed the thunder and lightning, the sound of the trumpet, and the mountain smoking, they were afraid*s* and trembled and stood at a distance, 19 and said to Moses, "You speak to us, and we will listen; but do not let God speak to us, or we will die." 20 Moses said to the people, "Do not be afraid; for God has come only to test you and to put the fear of him upon you so that you do not sin." 21 Then the people stood at a distance, while Moses drew near to the thick darkness where God was.

22 The LORD said to Moses: Thus you shall say to the Israelites: "You have seen for yourselves that I spoke with you from heaven. 23 You shall not make gods of silver alongside me, nor shall you make for yourselves gods of gold. 24 You need make for me only an altar of earth and sacrifice on it your burnt offerings and your offerings of well-being, your sheep and your oxen; in every place where I cause my name to be remembered I will come to you and bless you. 25 But if you make for me an altar of stone, do not build it of hewn stones; for if you use a chisel upon it you profane it. 26 You shall not go up by steps to my altar, so that your nakedness may not be exposed on it."

REVISED ENGLISH BIBLE

24 The LORD said, 'Go down; then come back, bringing Aaron with you, but let neither priests nor people force their way up to the LORD, for fear that he may break out against them.' 25 So Moses went down to the people and spoke to them.

20 God spoke all these words:
2 I am the LORD your God who brought you out of Egypt, out of the land of slavery.

3 You must have no other god besides me.

4 You must not make a carved image for yourself, nor the likeness of anything in the heavens above, or on the earth below, or in the waters under the earth. 5 You must not bow down to them in worship; for I, the LORD your God, am a jealous God, punishing the children for the sins of the parents to the third and fourth generation of those who reject me. 6 But I keep faith with thousands, those who love me and keep my commandments.

7 You must not make wrong use of the name of the LORD your God; the LORD will not leave unpunished anyone who misuses his name.

8 Remember to keep the sabbath day holy. 9 You have six days to labour and do all your work; 10 but the seventh day is a sabbath of the LORD your God; that day you must not do any work, neither you, nor your son or your daughter, your slave or your slave-girl, your cattle, or the alien residing among you; 11 for in six days the LORD made the heavens and the earth, the sea, and all that is in them, and on the seventh day he rested. Therefore the LORD blessed the sabbath day and declared it holy.

12 Honour your father and your mother, so that you may enjoy long life in the land which the LORD your God is giving you.

13 Do not commit murder.

14 Do not commit adultery.

15 Do not steal.

16 Do not give false evidence against your neighbour.

17 Do not covet your neighbour's household: you must not covet your neighbour's wife, his slave, his slave-girl, his ox, his donkey, or anything that belongs to him.

18 WHEN all the people saw how it thundered and the lightning flashed, when they heard the trumpet sound and saw the mountain in smoke, they were afraid and trembled. They stood at a distance 19 and said to Moses, 'Speak to us yourself and we will listen; but do not let God speak to us or we shall die.' 20 Moses answered, 'Do not be afraid. God has come only to test you, so that the fear of him may remain with you and preserve you from sinning.' 21 So the people kept their distance, while Moses approached the dark cloud where God was.

22 THE LORD said to Moses, Say this to the Israelites: You know now that I have spoken from heaven to you. 23 You must not make gods of silver to be worshipped besides me, nor may you make yourselves gods of gold. 24 The altar you make for me is to be of earth, and you are to sacrifice on it both your whole-offerings and your shared-offerings, your sheep and goats and your cattle. Wherever I cause my name to be invoked, I will come to you and bless you. 25 If you make an altar of stones for me, you must not build it of hewn stones, for if you use a tool on them, you profane them. 26 You must not mount up to my altar by steps, in case your private parts are exposed over against it.

---

p Or *besides*   *q* Or *to thousands*   *r* Or *kill*   *s* Sam Gk Syr Vg: MT *they saw*

20:3 **god:** *or* gods.   20:6 **with thousands:** *or* for a thousand generations with.   20:24 **shared-offerings:** *exact meaning of Heb. uncertain.*

down now! Then come up again along with Aaron. But the priests and the people must not break through to come up to the LORD; else he will vent his anger upon them." 25 So Moses went down to the people and told them this.

20 Then God delivered all these commandments: 2 "I, the LORD, am your God, who brought you out of the land of Egypt, that place of slavery. 3 You shall not have other gods besides me. 4 You shall not carve idols for yourselves in the shape of anything in the sky above or on the earth below or in the waters beneath the earth; 5 you shall not bow down before them or worship them. For I, the LORD, your God, am a jealous God, inflicting punishment for their fathers' wickedness on the children of those who hate me, down to the third and fourth generation; 6 but bestowing mercy down to the thousandth generation, on the children of those who love me and keep my commandments.

7 "You shall not take the name of the LORD, your God, in vain. For the LORD will not leave unpunished him who takes his name in vain.

8 "Remember to keep holy the sabbath day. 9 Six days you may labor and do all your work, 10 but the seventh day is the sabbath of the LORD, your God. No work may be done then either by you, or your son or daughter, or your male or female slave, or your beast, or by the alien who lives with you. 11 In six days the LORD made the heavens and the earth, the sea and all that is in them; but on the seventh day he rested. That is why the LORD has blessed the sabbath day and made it holy.

12 "Honor your father and your mother, that you may have a long life in the land which the Lord, your God, is giving you.

13 "You shall not kill.

14 "You shall not commit adultery.

15 "You shall not steal.

16 "You shall not bear false witness against your neighbor.

17 "You shall not covet your neighbor's house. You shall not covet your neighbor's wife, nor his male or female slave, nor his ox or ass, nor anything else that belongs to him."

18 When the people witnessed the thunder and lightning, the trumpet blast and the mountain smoking, they all feared and trembled. So they took up a position much farther away 19 and said to Moses, "You speak to us, and we will listen; but let not God speak to us, or we shall die." 20 Moses answered the people, "Do not be afraid, for God has come to you only to test you and put his fear upon you, lest you should sin." 21 Still the people remained at a distance, while Moses approached the cloud where God was.

22 The LORD told Moses, "Thus shall you speak to the Israelites: You have seen for yourselves that I have spoken to you from heaven. 23 Do not make anything to rank with me; neither gods of silver nor gods of gold shall you make for yourselves.

24 "An altar of earth you shall make for me, and upon it you shall sacrifice your holocausts and peace offerings, your sheep and your oxen. In whatever place I choose for the remembrance of my name I will come to you and bless you. 25 If you make an altar of stone for me, do not build it of cut stone, for by putting a tool to it you desecrate it. 26 You shall not go up by steps to my altar, on which you must not be indecently uncovered.

with you! Go down! Then come back bringing Aaron with you. But do not allow the priests and people to break through to come up to Yahweh, or he may burst out against them.' 25 So Moses went down to the people and spoke to them.

20 *j*Then God spoke all these words. He said, 2 'I am Yahweh your God who brought you out of Egypt, where you lived as slaves.

3 'You shall have no other gods to rival me.

4 'You shall not make yourself a carved image or any likeness of anything in heaven above or on earth beneath or in the waters under the earth.

5 'You shall not bow down to them or serve them. For I, Yahweh your God, am a jealous God and I punish a parent's fault in the children, the grandchildren, and the great-grandchildren among those who hate me; 6 but I act with faithful love towards thousands of those who love me and keep my commandments.

7 'You shall not misuse the name of Yahweh your God, for Yahweh will not leave unpunished anyone who misuses his name.

8 'Remember the Sabbath day and keep it holy. 9 For six days you shall labour and do all your work, 10 but the seventh day is a Sabbath for Yahweh your God. You shall do no work that day, neither you nor your son nor your daughter nor your servants, men or women, nor your animals nor the alien living with you. 11 For in six days Yahweh made the heavens, earth and sea and all that these contain, but on the seventh day he rested; that is why Yahweh has blessed the Sabbath day and made it sacred.

12 'Honour your father and your mother so that you may live long in the land that Yahweh your God is giving you.

13 'You shall not kill.

14 'You shall not commit adultery.

15 'You shall not steal.

16 'You shall not give false evidence against your neighbour.

17 'You shall not set your heart on your neighbour's house. You shall not set your heart on your neighbour's spouse, or servant, man or woman, or ox, or donkey, or any of your neighbour's possessions.'

18 Seeing the thunder pealing, the lightning flashing, the trumpet blasting and the mountain smoking, the people were all terrified and kept their distance. 19 'Speak to us yourself,' they said to Moses, 'and we will obey; but do not let God speak to us, or we shall die.' 20 Moses said to the people, 'Do not be afraid; God has come to test you, so that your fear of him, being always in your mind, may keep you from sinning.' 21 So the people kept their distance while Moses approached the dark cloud where God was.

22 Yahweh said to Moses, 'Tell the Israelites this, "You have seen for yourselves how I have spoken to you from heaven. 23 You must not make gods of silver to rival me, nor must you make yourselves gods of gold.

24 "You must make me an altar of earth on which to sacrifice your burnt offerings and communion sacrifices, your sheep and cattle. Wherever I choose to have my name remembered, I shall come to you and bless you. 25 If you make me an altar of stone, do not build it of dressed stones; for if you use a chisel on it, you will profane it. 26 You must not go up to my altar by steps, in case you expose your nakedness on them." '

j **20** 20:1seq. // Dt 5:6–22.

NEW REVISED STANDARD VERSION

21 These are the ordinances that you shall set before them:

2 When you buy a male Hebrew slave, he shall serve six years, but in the seventh he shall go out a free person, without debt. 3 If he comes in single, he shall go out single; if he comes in married, then his wife shall go out with him. 4 If his master gives him a wife and she bears him sons or daughters, the wife and her children shall be her master's and he shall go out alone. 5 But if the slave declares, "I love my master, my wife, and my children; I will not go out a free person," 6 then his master shall bring him before God.[t] He shall be brought to the door or the doorpost; and his master shall pierce his ear with an awl; and he shall serve him for life.

7 When a man sells his daughter as a slave, she shall not go out as the male slaves do. 8 If she does not please her master, who designated her for himself, then he shall let her be redeemed; he shall have no right to sell her to a foreign people, since he has dealt unfairly with her. 9 If he designates her for his son, he shall deal with her as with a daughter. 10 If he takes another wife to himself, he shall not diminish the food, clothing, or marital rights of the first wife.[u] 11 And if he does not do these three things for her, she shall go out without debt, without payment of money.

12 Whoever strikes a person mortally shall be put to death. 13 If it was not premeditated, but came about by an act of God, then I will appoint for you a place to which the killer may flee. 14 But if someone willfully attacks and kills another by treachery, you shall take the killer from my altar for execution.

15 Whoever strikes father or mother shall be put to death.

16 Whoever kidnaps a person, whether that person has been sold or is still held in possession, shall be put to death.

17 Whoever curses father or mother shall be put to death.

18 When individuals quarrel and one strikes the other with a stone or fist so that the injured party, though not dead, is confined to bed, 19 but recovers and walks around outside with the help of a staff, then the assailant shall be free of liability, except to pay for the loss of time, and to arrange for full recovery.

20 When a slaveowner strikes a male or female slave with a rod and the slave dies immediately, the owner shall be punished. 21 But if the slave survives a day or two, there is no punishment; for the slave is the owner's property.

22 When people who are fighting injure a pregnant woman so that there is a miscarriage, and yet no further harm follows, the one responsible shall be fined what the woman's husband demands, paying as much as the judges determine. 23 If any harm follows, then you shall give life for life, 24 eye for eye, tooth for tooth, hand for hand, foot for foot, 25 burn for burn, wound for wound, stripe for stripe.

26 When a slaveowner strikes the eye of a male or female slave, destroying it, the owner shall let the slave go, a free person, to compensate for the eye. 27 If the owner knocks out a tooth of a male or female slave, the slave shall be let go, a free person, to compensate for the tooth.

28 When an ox gores a man or a woman to death, the ox shall be stoned, and its flesh shall not be eaten; but the owner of the ox shall not be liable. 29 If the ox has been accustomed to gore in the past, and its owner has been warned but has not restrained it, and it kills a man or a woman, the ox shall be stoned, and its owner also shall be put to death. 30 If a ransom is imposed on the owner, then

REVISED ENGLISH BIBLE

21 These are the laws you are to set before them:

2 When you purchase a Hebrew as a slave, he will be your slave for six years; in the seventh year he is to go free without paying anything.

3 If he comes to you alone, he is to go away alone; but if he is already a married man, his wife is to go away with him. 4 If his master gives him a wife, and she bears him sons or daughters, the woman with her children belongs to her master, and the man must go away alone. 5 But if the slave should say, 'I am devoted to my master and my wife and children; I do not wish to go free,' 6 then his master must bring him to God: he is to be brought to the door or the doorpost, and his master will pierce his ear with an awl; the man will then be his slave for life.

7 When a man sells his daughter into slavery, she is not to go free as male slaves may. 8 If she proves unpleasing to her master who had designated her for himself, he must let her be redeemed; he has treated her unfairly, and therefore he has no right to sell her to foreigners. 9 If he assigns her to his son, he must allow her the rights of a daughter. 10 If he takes another woman, he must not deprive the first of meat, clothes, and conjugal rights; 11 if he does not provide her with these three things, she is to go free without payment.

12 Whoever strikes another man and kills him must be put to death. 13 But if he did not act with intent, but it came about by act of God, the slayer may flee to a place which I shall appoint for you. 14 But if a man wilfully kills another by treachery, you are to take him even from my altar to be put to death.

15 Whoever strikes his father or mother must be put to death.

16 Whoever kidnaps an Israelite must be put to death, whether he has sold him, or the man is found in his possession.

17 Whoever reviles his father or mother must be put to death.

18 When men quarrel and one hits another with a stone or with his fist, and the man is not killed but takes to his bed, 19 and if he recovers so as to walk about outside with his staff, then the one who struck him has no liability, except that he must pay compensation for the other's loss of time and see that his recovery is complete.

20 When a man strikes his slave or his slave-girl with a stick and the slave dies on the spot, he must be punished. 21 But he is not to be punished if the slave survives for one day or two, because the slave is his property.

22 When, in the course of a brawl, a man knocks against a pregnant woman so that she has a miscarriage but suffers no further injury, then the offender must pay whatever fine the woman's husband demands after assessment. 23 But where injury ensues, you are to give life for life, 24 eye for eye, tooth for tooth, hand for hand, foot for foot, 25 burn for burn, bruise for bruise, wound for wound.

26 When a man strikes his slave or slave-girl in the eye and destroys it, he must let the slave go free in compensation for the eye. 27 When he knocks out the tooth of a slave or a slave-girl, he must let the slave go free in compensation for the tooth.

28 When an ox gores a man or a woman to death, the ox must be put to death by stoning, and its flesh is not to be eaten; the owner of the ox will be free from liability. 29 If, however, the ox has for some time past been a vicious animal, and the owner has been duly warned but has not kept it under control, and the ox kills a man or a woman, then the ox must be stoned to death, and the owner put to death as well. 30 If, however, the penalty is commuted for

---

[t]Or *to the judges*   [u]Heb *of her*

21:6 **God:** *or* the gods *or* the judges.   21:18 **fist:** *or* hoe.

NEW AMERICAN BIBLE

21 "These are the rules you shall lay before them. 2 When you purchase a Hebrew slave, he is to serve you for six years, but in the seventh year he shall be given his freedom without cost. 3 If he comes into service alone, he shall leave alone; if he comes with a wife, his wife shall leave with him. 4 But if his master gives him a wife and she bears him sons or daughters, the woman and her children shall remain the master's property and the man shall leave alone. 5 If, however, the slave declares, 'I am devoted to my master and my wife and children; I will not go free,' 6 his master shall bring him to God and there, at the door or doorpost, he shall pierce his ear with an awl, thus keeping him as his slave forever.

7 "When a man sells his daughter as a slave, she shall not go free as male slaves do. 8 But if her master, who had destined her for himself, dislikes her, he shall let her be redeemed. He has no right to sell her to a foreigner, since he has broken faith with her. 9 If he destines her for his son, he shall treat her like a daughter. 10 If he takes another wife, he shall not withhold her food, her clothing, or her conjugal rights. 11 If he does not grant her these three things, she shall be given her freedom absolutely, without cost to her.

12 "Whoever strikes a man a mortal blow must be put to death. 13 He, however, who did not hunt a man down, but caused his death by an act of God, may flee to a place which I will set apart for this purpose. 14 But when a man kills another after maliciously scheming to do so, you must take him even from my altar and put him to death. 15 Whoever strikes his father or mother shall be put to death.

16 "A kidnaper, whether he sells his victim or still has him when caught, shall be put to death.

17 "Whoever curses his father or mother shall be put to death.

18 "When men quarrel and one strikes the other with a stone or with his fist, not mortally, but enough to put him in bed, 19 the one who struck the blow shall be acquitted, provided the other can get up and walk around with the help of his staff. Still, he must compensate him for his enforced idleness and provide for his complete cure.

20 "When a man strikes his male or female slave with a rod so hard that the slave dies under his hand, he shall be punished. 21 If, however, the slave survives for a day or two, he is not to be punished, since the slave is his own property.

22 "When men have a fight and hurt a pregnant woman, so that she suffers a miscarriage, but no further injury, the guilty one shall be fined as much as the woman's husband demands of him, and he shall pay in the presence of the judges. 23 But if injury ensues, you shall give life for life, 24 eye for eye, tooth for tooth, hand for hand, foot for foot, 25 burn for burn, wound for wound, stripe for stripe.

26 "When a man strikes his male or female slave in the eye and destroys the use of it, he shall let the slave go free in compensation for the eye. 27 If he knocks out a tooth of his male or female slave, he shall let the slave go free in compensation for the tooth.

28 "When an ox gores a man or a woman to death, the ox must be stoned; its flesh may not be eaten. The owner of the ox, however, shall go unpunished. 29 But if an ox was previously in the habit of goring people and its owner, though warned, would not keep it in; should it then kill a man or a woman, not only must the ox be stoned, but its owner also must be put to death. 30 If, however, a fine is imposed on

NEW JERUSALEM BIBLE

21 'These are the laws you must give them: 2 'When you buy a Hebrew slave, his service will last for six years. In the seventh year he will leave a free man without paying compensation. 3 If he came single, he will depart single; if he came married, his wife will depart with him. 4 If his master gives him a wife and she bears him sons or daughters, the wife and her children will belong to her master, and he will depart alone. 5 But if the slave says, "I love my master and my wife and children; I do not wish to be freed," 6 then his master will bring him before God and then, leading him to the door or the doorpost, his master will pierce his ear with an awl, and the slave will be permanently his. 7 If a man sells his daughter as a slave, she will not leave as male slaves do. 8 If she does not please her master who intended her for himself, he must let her be bought back: he has not the right to sell her to foreigners, for this would be a breach of faith with her. 9 If he intends her for his son, he must treat her as custom requires daughters to be treated. 10 If he takes another wife, he must not reduce the food, clothing or conjugal rights of the first one. 11 Should he deprive her of these three things she will leave a free woman, without paying compensation.

12 'Anyone who by violence causes a death must be put to death. 13 If, however, he has not planned to do it but it comes from God by his hand, he can take refuge in a place which I shall appoint for you. 14 But should any person dare to kill another with deliberate planning, you will take that person even from my altar to be put to death.

15 'Anyone who strikes father or mother will be put to death. 16 Anyone who abducts a person — whether that person has since been sold or is still held — will be put to death. 17 Anyone who curses father or mother will be put to death.

18 'If people quarrel and one strikes the other a blow with stone or fist so that the injured party, though not dead, is confined to bed, 19 but later recovers and can go about, even with a stick, the one who struck the blow will have no liability, other than to compensate the injured party for the enforced inactivity and to take care of the injured party until the cure is complete.

20 'If someone beats his slave, male or female, and the slave dies at his hands, he must pay the penalty. 21 But should the slave survive for one or two days, he will pay no penalty because the slave is his by right of purchase.

22 'If people, when brawling, hurt a pregnant woman and she suffers a miscarriage but no further harm is done, the person responsible will pay compensation as fixed by the woman's master, paying as much as the judges decide. 23 If further harm is done, however, you will award life for life, 24 eye for eye, tooth for tooth, hand for hand, foot for foot, 25 burn for burn, wound for wound, stroke for stroke.

26 'If anyone strikes the eye of his slave, male or female, and destroys the use of it, he will give the slave his freedom to compensate for the eye. 27 If he knocks out the tooth of his slave, male or female, he will give the slave his freedom to compensate for the tooth.

28 'If an ox gores a man or a woman to death, the ox will be stoned and its meat will not be eaten, but the owner of the ox will not be liable. 29 But if the ox has been in the habit of goring before, and if its owner has been warned but has not kept it under control, then should this ox kill a man or woman, it will be stoned and its owner put to death. 30 If

NEW REVISED STANDARD VERSION	REVISED ENGLISH BIBLE

the owner shall pay whatever is imposed for the redemption of the victim's life. 31 If it gores a boy or a girl, the owner shall be dealt with according to this same rule. 32 If the ox gores a male or female slave, the owner shall pay to the slaveowner thirty shekels of silver, and the ox shall be stoned.

33 If someone leaves a pit open, or digs a pit and does not cover it, and an ox or a donkey falls into it, 34 the owner of the pit shall make restitution, giving money to its owner, but keeping the dead animal.

35 If someone's ox hurts the ox of another, so that it dies, then they shall sell the live ox and divide the price of it; and the dead animal they shall also divide. 36 But if it was known that the ox was accustomed to gore in the past, and its owner has not restrained it, the owner shall restore ox for ox, but keep the dead animal.

22 *v* When someone steals an ox or a sheep, and slaughters it or sells it, the thief shall pay five oxen for an ox, and four sheep for a sheep. *w* The thief shall make restitution, but if unable to do so, shall be sold for the theft. 4 When the animal, whether ox or donkey or sheep, is found alive in the thief's possession, the thief shall pay double.

2 *x* If a thief is found breaking in, and is beaten to death, no bloodguilt is incurred; 3 but if it happens after sunrise, bloodguilt is incurred.

5 When someone causes a field or vineyard to be grazed over, or lets livestock loose to graze in someone else's field, restitution shall be made from the best in the owner's field or vineyard.

6 When fire breaks out and catches in thorns so that the stacked grain or the standing grain or the field is consumed, the one who started the fire shall make full restitution.

7 When someone delivers to a neighbor money or goods for safekeeping, and they are stolen from the neighbor's house, then the thief, if caught, shall pay double. 8 If the thief is not caught, the owner of the house shall be brought before God, *y* to determine whether or not the owner had laid hands on the neighbor's goods.

9 In any case of disputed ownership involving ox, donkey, sheep, clothing, or any other loss, of which one party says, "This is mine," the case of both parties shall come before God; *y* the one whom God condemns *z* shall pay double to the other.

10 When someone delivers to another a donkey, ox, sheep, or any other animal for safekeeping, and it dies or is injured or is carried off, without anyone seeing it, 11 an oath before the LORD shall decide between the two of them that the one has not laid hands on the property of the other; the owner shall accept the oath, and no restitution shall be made. 12 But if it was stolen, restitution shall be made to its owner. 13 If it was mangled by beasts, let it be brought as evidence; restitution shall not be made for the mangled remains.

14 When someone borrows an animal from another and it is injured or dies, the owner not being present, full restitution shall be made. 15 If the owner was present, there shall be no restitution; if it was hired, only the hiring fee is due.

a money payment, he must pay in redemption of his life whatever is imposed upon him. 31 If the ox gores a son or a daughter, the same ruling applies. 32 If the ox gores a slave or slave-girl, its owner must pay thirty shekels of silver to their master, and the ox must be stoned to death.

33 When a man removes the cover of a cistern or digs a cistern and leaves it uncovered, then if an ox or a donkey falls into it, 34 the owner of the cistern must make good the loss; he must pay the owner the price of the animal, and the dead beast will be his.

35 When one man's ox butts another's and kills it, they must sell the live ox, share the price, and also share the dead beast. 36 But if it is known that the ox has for some time past been vicious and the owner has not kept it under control, he must make good the loss, ox for ox, but the dead beast is his.

22 When a man steals an ox or a sheep and slaughters or sells it, he must repay five beasts for the ox and four sheep for the sheep. 2–4 He must pay in full; if he has no means, he is to be sold to pay for the theft. But if the animal is found alive in his possession, be it ox, donkey, or sheep, he must repay two for each one stolen.

If a burglar is caught in the act and receives a fatal injury, it is not murder; but if he breaks in after sunrise and receives a fatal injury, then it is murder.

5 When a man burns off a field or a vineyard and lets the fire spread so that it burns another man's field, he must make restitution from his own field according to the yield expected; and if the whole field is laid waste, he must make restitution from the best part of his own field or vineyard.

6 When a fire starts and spreads to a thorn hedge, so that sheaves, or standing grain, or a whole field is destroyed, whoever started the fire must make full restitution.

7 When someone gives another silver or chattels for safe keeping, and they are stolen from that person's house, the thief, if apprehended, must restore twofold. 8 But if the thief is not apprehended, the owner of the house will have to appear before God for it to be ascertained whether or not he has laid hands on his neighbour's property. 9 In every case of misappropriation involving an ox, a donkey, or a sheep, a cloak, or any lost property which may be claimed, each party must bring his case before God; the one whom God declares to be in the wrong will have to restore double to his neighbour.

10 When someone gives a donkey, an ox, a sheep, or any beast into a neighbour's keeping, and it dies or is injured or is carried off, there being no witness, 11 then by swearing by the LORD it will have to be settled between them whether or not the neighbour has laid hands on the other's property. If not, no restitution is to be made and the owner must accept this. 12 If it has been stolen from the neighbour, he must make restitution to its owner. 13 If it has been mauled by a wild beast, he must bring it in as evidence; he will not have to make restitution for what has been mauled.

14 When a man borrows a beast from his neighbour and it is injured or dies while its owner is not present, the borrower must make full restitution. 15 but if the owner is with it, the borrower does not have to make restitution. If it was hired, only the hire is due.

21:33 **cistern:** *or* pit.   22:1 *In Heb. 21:37.*   22:2–4 *Verses rearranged thus: 3b,4,2,3a.*   22:2–4 **If a burglar:** *in Heb. the beginning of 22:1.*   22:5 **When . . . man's field:** *or* When a man uses his field or vineyard for grazing, and lets his beast loose, and it feeds in another man's field. **he must . . . waste:** *so Samar.; Heb. omits.*   22:8,9 **God:** *or* the judges.   22:14 **a beast:** *so Scroll; Heb. omits.*

v Ch 21.37 in Heb   *w* Verses 2, 3, and 4 rearranged thus: 3b, 4, 2, 3a   *x* Ch 22.1 in Heb   *y* Or *before the judges*   *z* Or *the judges condemn*

NEW AMERICAN BIBLE

him, he must pay in ransom for his life whatever amount is imposed on him. 31 This law applies if it is a boy or a girl that the ox gores. 32 But if it is a male or a female slave that it gores, he must pay the owner of the slave thirty shekels of silver, and the ox must be stoned.

33 "When a man uncovers or digs a cistern and does not cover it over again, should an ox or an ass fall into it, 34 the owner of the cistern must make good by restoring the value of the animal to its owner; the dead animal, however, he may keep.

35 "When one man's ox hurts another's ox so badly that it dies, they shall sell the live ox and divide this money as well as the dead animal equally between them. 36 But if it was known that the ox was previously in the habit of goring and its owner would not keep it in, he must make full restitution, an ox for an ox; but the dead animal he may keep.

37 "When a man steals an ox or a sheep and slaughters or sells it, he shall restore five oxen for the one ox, and four sheep for the one sheep.

22 "[If a thief is caught in the act of housebreaking and beaten to death, there is no bloodguilt involved. 2 But if after sunrise he is thus beaten, there is bloodguilt.] He must make full restitution. If he has nothing, he shall be sold to pay for his theft. 3 If what he stole is found alive in his possession, be it an ox, an ass or a sheep, he shall restore two animals for each one stolen.

4 "When a man is burning over a field or a vineyard, if he lets the fires spread so that it burns in another's field, he must make restitution with the best produce of his own field or vineyard. 5 If the fire spreads further, and catches on to thorn bushes, so that shocked grain or standing grain or the field itself is burned up, the one who started the fire must make full restitution.

6 "When a man gives money or any article to another for safekeeping and it is stolen from the latter's house, the thief, if caught, must make twofold restitution. 7 If the thief is not caught, the owner of the house must be brought to God, to swear that he himself did not lay hands on his neighbor's property. 8 In every question of dishonest appropriation, whether it be about an ox, or an ass, or a sheep, or a garment, or anything else that has disappeared, where another claims that the thing is his, both parties shall present their case before God; the one whom God convicts must make two-fold restitution to the other.

9 "When a man gives an ass, or an ox, or a sheep, or any other animal to another for safekeeping, if it dies, or is maimed or snatched away, without anyone witnessing the fact, 10 the custodian shall swear by the LORD that he did not lay hands on his neighbor's property; the owner must accept the oath, and no restitution is to be made. 11 But if the custodian is really guilty of theft, he must make restitution to the owner. 12 If it has been killed by a wild beast, let him bring it as evidence, and he need not make restitution for the mangled animal.

13 "When a man borrows an animal from his neighbor, if it is maimed or dies while the owner is not present, the man must make restitution. 14 But if the owner is present, he need not make restitution. If it was hired, this was covered by the price of its hire.

NEW JERUSALEM BIBLE

a ransom is imposed on the owner, he will pay whatever is imposed, to redeem his life. 31 If the ox gores a boy or a girl, it will be treated in accordance with this same rule. 32 If the ox gores a slave, male or female, its owner will pay the price — thirty shekels — to their master, and the ox will be stoned.

33 'If anyone leaves a pit uncovered, or digs a pit and does not cover it, and an ox, or donkey falls into it, 34 then the owner of the pit will make good the loss by compensating its owner, and the dead animal will be his. 35 If anyone's ox injures anyone else's ox causing its death, the owners will sell and share the money for it; they will also share the dead animal. 36 But if it is common knowledge that the ox has been in the habit of goring before, and its owner has not kept it under control, the owner will repay ox for ox, and will keep the dead animal.

37 'If anyone steals an ox or a sheep and slaughters or sells it, he will pay back five beasts from the herd for the ox, and four animals from the flock for the sheep.'

22 'If a thief is caught breaking in and is struck a mortal blow, his blood may not be avenged, 2 but if it happens after sunrise, his blood may be avenged. He will make full restitution; if he has not the means, he will be sold to pay for what he has stolen. 3 If the stolen animal is found alive in his possession, be it ox, donkey or animal from the flock, he will pay back double.

4 'If anyone puts his animals out to graze in a field or vineyard and lets them graze in someone else's field, he will make restitution for the part of the field that has been grazed on the basis of its yield. But if he has let the whole field be grazed, he will make restitution in proportion to the best crop of the field or vineyard.

5 'If a fire breaks out, setting light to thorn bushes and burning stacks, standing corn or the field as a result, the person who started the fire will make full restitution.

6 'If anyone entrusts money or goods to someone else's keeping and these are stolen from that person's house, the thief, if he can be discovered, will repay double. 7 Should the thief not be discovered, the owner of the house will come into the presence of God, to declare that he has not laid hands on the other person's property. 8 'In every case of law-breaking involving an ox, donkey, animal from the flock, clothing or lost property of any sort, the ownership of which is disputed, both parties will lay their case before God. The party whom God pronounces guilty will pay back double to the other.

9 'If anyone entrusts a donkey, ox, animal from the flock or any other animal to someone else's keeping, and it dies or breaks a limb or is carried off without anyone seeing, 10 an oath by Yahweh will decide between the two parties whether the keeper has laid hands on the other's property or not. The owner will take what remains, the keeper will not have to make good the loss. 11 Only if the animal has been stolen from him, will he make restitution to the owner. 12 If it has been savaged by a wild animal, he must bring the savaged remains of the animal as evidence, and will then not have to make restitution.

13 'If anyone borrows an animal from someone else, and it breaks a limb or dies in the owner's absence, he will make full restitution. 14 But if the animal's owner has been present, he will not have to make good the loss. If the owner has hired it out, he will get the cost of its hire.

21, 37—22, 30: In the Vulgate, 22, 1-31. **22, 1f:** If a thief is caught: this seems to be a fragment of what was once a longer law on housebreaking, which has been inserted here into the middle of a law on stealing animals. He must make full restitution: this stood originally immediately after 21, 37.

NEW REVISED STANDARD VERSION

16 When a man seduces a virgin who is not engaged to be married, and lies with her, he shall give the bride-price for her and make her his wife. 17 But if her father refuses to give her to him, he shall pay an amount equal to the bride-price for virgins.

18 You shall not permit a female sorcerer to live.

19 Whoever lies with an animal shall be put to death.

20 Whoever sacrifices to any god, other than the LORD alone, shall be devoted to destruction.

21 You shall not wrong or oppress a resident alien, for you were aliens in the land of Egypt. 22 You shall not abuse any widow or orphan. 23 If you do abuse them, when they cry out to me, I will surely heed their cry; 24 my wrath will burn, and I will kill you with the sword, and your wives shall become widows and your children orphans.

25 If you lend money to my people, to the poor among you, you shall not deal with them as a creditor; you shall not exact interest from them. 26 If you take your neighbor's cloak in pawn, you shall restore it before the sun goes down; 27 for it may be your neighbor's only clothing to use as cover; in what else shall that person sleep? And if your neighbor cries out to me, I will listen, for I am compassionate.

28 You shall not revile God, or curse a leader of your people.

29 You shall not delay to make offerings from the fullness of your harvest and from the outflow of your presses. a

The firstborn of your sons you shall give to me. 30 You shall do the same with your oxen and with your sheep: seven days it shall remain with its mother; on the eighth day you shall give it to me.

31 You shall be people consecrated to me; therefore you shall not eat any meat that is mangled by beasts in the field; you shall throw it to the dogs.

23 You shall not spread a false report. You shall not join hands with the wicked to act as a malicious witness. 2 You shall not follow a majority in wrongdoing; when you bear witness in a lawsuit, you shall not side with the majority so as to pervert justice; 3 nor shall you be partial to the poor in a lawsuit.

4 When you come upon your enemy's ox or donkey going astray, you shall bring it back.

5 When you see the donkey of one who hates you lying under its burden and you would hold back from setting it free, you must help to set it free. a

6 You shall not pervert the justice due to your poor in their lawsuits. 7 Keep far from a false charge, and do not kill the innocent and those in the right, for I will not acquit the guilty. 8 You shall take no bribe, for a bribe blinds the officials, and subverts the cause of those who are in the right.

9 You shall not oppress a resident alien; you know the heart of an alien, for you were aliens in the land of Egypt.

10 For six years you shall sow your land and gather in its yield; 11 but the seventh year you shall let it rest and lie fallow, so that the poor of your people may eat; and what they leave the wild animals may eat. You shall do the same with your vineyard, and with your olive orchard.

12 Six days you shall do your work, but on the seventh day you shall rest, so that your ox and your donkey may have relief, and your homeborn slave and the resident alien may be refreshed. 13 Be attentive to all that I have said to you. Do not invoke the names of other gods; do not let them be heard on your lips.

REVISED ENGLISH BIBLE

16 When a man seduces a virgin who is not yet betrothed, he must pay the bride-price for her to be his wife. 17 If her father refuses to give her to him, the seducer must pay in silver a sum equal to the bride-price for virgins.

18 You must not allow a witch to live.

19 Whoever has sexual intercourse with a beast must be put to death.

20 Whoever sacrifices to any god but the LORD must be put to death under solemn ban.

21 You must not wrong or oppress an alien; you were yourselves aliens in Egypt.

22 You must not wrong a widow or a fatherless child. 23 If you do, and they appeal to me, be sure that I shall listen; 24 my anger will be roused and I shall kill you with the sword; your own wives will become widows and your children fatherless.

25 If you advance money to any poor man amongst my people, you are not to act like a moneylender; you must not exact interest from him.

26 If you take your neighbour's cloak in pawn, return it to him by sunset, 27 because it is his only covering. It is the cloak in which he wraps his body; in what else can he sleep? If he appeals to me, I shall listen, for I am full of compassion.

28 You must not revile God, nor curse a chief of your own people.

29 You must not hold back the first of your harvest, whether grain or wine. You must give me your firstborn sons. 30 You must do the same with your oxen and your sheep. They should stay with the mother for seven days; on the eighth day you are to give them to me.

31 You must be holy to me: you are not to eat the flesh of anything killed by beasts in the open country; you are to throw it to the dogs.

23 You must not spread a baseless rumour, nor make common cause with a wicked man by giving malicious evidence.

2 You must not be led into wrongdoing by the majority, nor, when you give evidence in a lawsuit, should you side with the majority to pervert justice; 3 nor should you show favouritism to a poor person in his lawsuit.

4 Should you come upon your enemy's ox or donkey straying, you must take it back to him. 5 Should you see the donkey of someone who hates you lying helpless under its load, however unwilling you may be to help, you must lend a hand with it.

6 You must not deprive the poor man of justice in his lawsuit. 7 Avoid all lies, and do not cause the death of the innocent and guiltless; for I the LORD will never acquit the guilty. 8 Do not accept a bribe, for bribery makes the discerning person blind and the just person give a crooked answer.

9 Do not oppress the alien, for you know how it feels to be an alien; you yourselves were aliens in Egypt.

10 For six years you may sow your land and gather its produce; 11 but in the seventh year you must let it lie fallow and leave it alone. Let it provide food for the poor of your people, and what they leave the wild animals may eat. You are to do likewise with your vineyard and your olive grove.

12 For six days you may do your work, but on the seventh day abstain from work, so that your ox and your donkey may rest, and your home-born slave and the alien may refresh themselves.

13 Be attentive to every word of mine. You must not invoke other gods: their names are not to cross your lips.

a Meaning of Heb uncertain

NEW AMERICAN BIBLE

15 "When a man seduces a virgin who is not betrothed, and lies with her, he shall pay her marriage price and marry her. 16 If her father refuses to give her to him, he must still pay him the customary marriage price for virgins.

17 "You shall not let a sorceress live.

18 "Anyone who lies with an animal shall be put to death.

19 "Whoever sacrifices to any god, except to the LORD alone, shall be doomed.

20 "You shall not molest or oppress an alien, for you were once aliens yourselves in the land of Egypt. 21 You shall not wrong any widow or orphan. 22 If ever you wrong them and they cry out to me, I will surely hear their cry. 23 My wrath will flare up, and I will kill you with the sword; then your own wives will be widows, and your children orphans.

24 "If you lend money to one of your poor neighbors among my people, you shall not act like an extortioner toward him by demanding interest from him. 25 If you take your neighbor's cloak as a pledge, you shall return it to him before sunset; 26 for this cloak of his is the only covering he has for his body. What else has he to sleep in? If he cries out to me, I will hear him; for I am compassionate.

27 "You shall not revile God, nor curse a prince of your people.

28 "You shall not delay the offering of your harvest and your press. You shall give me the first-born of your sons. 29 You must do the same with your oxen and your sheep; for seven days the firstling may stay with its mother, but on the eighth day you must give it to me.

30 "You shall be men sacred to me. Flesh torn to pieces in the field you shall not eat; throw it to the dogs.

23 "You shall not repeat a false report. Do not join the wicked in putting your hand, as an unjust witness, upon anyone. 2 Neither shall you allege the example of the many as an excuse for doing wrong, nor shall you, when testifying in a lawsuit, side with the many in perverting justice. 3 You shall not favor a poor man in his lawsuit.

4 "When you come upon your enemy's ox or ass going astray, see to it that it is returned to him. 5 When you notice the ass of one who hates you lying prostrate under its burden, by no means desert him; help him, rather, to raise it up.

6 "You shall not deny one of your needy fellow men his rights in his lawsuit. 7 You shall keep away from anything dishonest. The innocent and the just you shall not put to death, nor shall you acquit the guilty. 8 Never take a bribe, for a bribe blinds even the most clear-sighted and twists the words even of the just. 9 You shall not oppress an alien; you well know how it feels to be an alien, since you were once aliens yourselves in the land of Egypt.

10 "For six years you may sow your land and gather in its produce. 11 But the seventh year you shall let the land lie untilled and unharvested, that the poor among you may eat of it and the beasts of the field may eat what the poor leave. So also shall you do in regard to your vineyard and your olive grove.

12 "For six days you may do your work, but on the seventh day you must rest, that your ox and your ass may also have rest, and that the son of your maidservant and the alien may be refreshed. 13 Give heed to all that I have told you.

"Never mention the name of any other god; it shall not be heard from your lips.

NEW JERUSALEM BIBLE

15 'If a man seduces a virgin who is not engaged to be married, he will pay her bride-price and make her his wife. 16 If her father absolutely refuses to let him have her, he will pay a sum equivalent to the bride-price of a virgin.

17 'You will not allow a sorceress to live.

18 'Anyone who has intercourse with an animal will be put to death.

19 'Anyone who sacrifices to other gods will be put under the curse of destruction.

20 'You will not molest or oppress aliens, for you yourselves were once aliens in Egypt. 21 You will not ill-treat widows or orphans; 22 if you ill-treat them in any way and they make an appeal to me for help, I shall certainly hear their appeal, 23 my anger will be roused and I shall put you to the sword; then your own wives will be widows and your own children orphans.

24 'If you lend money to any of my people, to anyone poor among you, you will not play the usurer with him: you will not demand interest from him.

25 'If you take someone's cloak in pledge, you will return it to him at sunset. 26 It is all the covering he has; it is the cloak he wraps his body in; what else will he sleep in? If he appeals to me, I shall listen. At least with me he will find compassion!

27 'You will not revile God, nor curse your people's leader.

28 'Do not be slow about making offerings from your abundance and your surplus. You will give me the first-born of your children; 29 you will do the same with your flocks and herds. For the first seven days the first-born will stay with its mother; on the eighth day you will give it to me.

30 'You must be people consecrated to me. You will not eat the meat of anything in the countryside savaged by wild animals; you will throw it to the dogs.'

23 'You will not spread false rumours. You will not lend support to the wicked by giving untrue evidence. 2 You will not be led into wrong-doing by the majority nor, when giving evidence in a lawsuit, side with the majority to pervert the course of justice; 3 nor will you show partiality to the poor in a lawsuit.

4 'If you come on your enemy's ox or donkey straying, you will take it back to him. 5 If you see the donkey of someone who hates you fallen under its load, do not stand back; you must go and help him with it.

6 'You will not cheat the poor among you of their rights at law. 7 Keep clear of fraud. Do not cause the death of the innocent or upright, and do not acquit the guilty. 8 You will accept no bribes, for a bribe blinds the clear-sighted and is the ruin of the cause of the upright.

9 'You will not oppress the alien; you know how an alien feels, for you yourselves were once aliens in Egypt.

10 'For six years you will sow your land and gather its produce, 11 but in the seventh year you will let it lie fallow and forgo all produce from it, so that those of your people who are poor can take food from it and the wild animals eat what they have left. You will do the same with your vineyard and your olive grove.

12 'For six days you will do your work, and on the seventh you will rest, so that your ox and your donkey may rest and the child of your slave-girl and the alien too.

13 'Take notice of everything I have told you and do not mention the name of any other god: let none ever be heard from your lips.

14 Three times in the year you shall hold a festival for me. 15 You shall observe the festival of unleavened bread; as I commanded you, you shall eat unleavened bread for seven days at the appointed time in the month of Abib, for in it you came out of Egypt.

No one shall appear before me empty-handed.

16 You shall observe the festival of harvest, of the first fruits of your labor, of what you sow in the field. You shall observe the festival of ingathering at the end of the year, when you gather in from the field the fruit of your labor. 17 Three times in the year all your males shall appear before the Lord GOD.

18 You shall not offer the blood of my sacrifice with anything leavened, or let the fat of my festival remain until the morning.

19 The choicest of the first fruits of your ground you shall bring into the house of the LORD your God.

You shall not boil a kid in its mother's milk.

20 I am going to send an angel in front of you, to guard you on the way and to bring you to the place that I have prepared. 21 Be attentive to him and listen to his voice; do not rebel against him, for he will not pardon your transgression; for my name is in him. 22 But if you listen attentively to his voice and do all that I say, then I will be an enemy to your enemies and a foe to your foes.

23 When my angel goes in front of you, and brings you to the Amorites, the Hittites, the Perizzites, the Canaanites, the Hivites, and the Jebusites, and I blot them out, 24 you shall not bow down to their gods, or worship them, or follow their practices, but you shall utterly demolish them and break their pillars in pieces. 25 You shall worship the LORD your God, and I[b] will bless your bread and your water; and I will take sickness away from among you. 26 No one shall miscarry or be barren in your land; I will fulfill the number of your days. 27 I will send my terror in front of you, and will throw into confusion all the people against whom you shall come, and I will make all your enemies turn their backs to you. 28 And I will send the pestilence[c] in front of you, which shall drive out the Hivites, the Canaanites, and the Hittites from before you. 29 I will not drive them out from before you in one year, or the land would become desolate and the wild animals would multiply against you. 30 Little by little I will drive them out from before you, until you have increased and possess the land. 31 I will set your borders from the Red Sea[d] to the sea of the Philistines, and from the wilderness to the Euphrates; for I will hand over to you the inhabitants of the land, and you shall drive them out before you. 32 You shall make no covenant with them and their gods. 33 They shall not live in your land, or they will make you sin against me; for if you worship their gods, it will surely be a snare to you.

24 Then he said to Moses, "Come up to the LORD, you and Aaron, Nadab, and Abihu, and seventy of the elders of Israel, and worship at a distance. 2 Moses alone shall come near the LORD; but the others shall not come near, and the people shall not come up with him."

3 Moses came and told the people all the words of the LORD and all the ordinances; and all the people answered with one voice, and said, "All the words that the LORD has spoken we will do." 4 And Moses wrote down all the words of the LORD. He rose early in the morning, and built an altar at the foot of the mountain, and set up twelve pillars, corresponding to the twelve tribes of Israel. 5 He sent young men of the people of Israel, who offered burnt offerings and sacrificed oxen as offerings of well-being to the LORD.

14 Three times a year you are to keep a pilgrim-feast to me. 15 You are to celebrate the pilgrim-feast of Unleavened Bread: for seven days, as I have commanded you, you are to eat unleavened bread at the appointed time in the month of Abib, for in that month you came out of Egypt; and no one is to come into my presence without an offering. 16 You are to celebrate the pilgrim-feast of Harvest, with the first-fruits of your work in sowing the land, and the pilgrim-feast of Ingathering at the end of the year, when you gather the fruits of your work in from the land. 17 Those three times a year all your males are to come into the presence of the Lord GOD.

18 Do not offer the blood of my sacrifice at the same time as anything leavened.

The fat of my festal offering is not to remain overnight till morning.

19 You must bring the choicest firstfruits of your soil to the house of the LORD your God.

Do not boil a kid in its mother's milk.

20 And now I am sending an angel before you to guard you on your way and to bring you to the place I have prepared. 21 Heed him and listen to his voice. Do not defy him; he will not pardon your rebelliousness, for my authority rests in him. 22 If you will only listen to his voice and do all I tell you, then I shall be an enemy to your enemies, and I shall harass those who harass you. 23 My angel will go before you and bring you to the Amorites, the Hittites, the Perizzites, the Canaanites, the Hivites, and the Jebusites, and I will make an end of them. 24 You are not to bow down to their gods; you are not to worship them or observe their rites. Rather, you must tear down all their images and smash their sacred pillars. 25 You are to worship the LORD your God, and he will bless your bread and your water. I shall take away all sickness out of your midst. 26 No woman will miscarry or be barren in your land. I shall grant you a full span of life.

27 I shall send terror of me ahead of you and throw into panic every people you find in your path. I shall make all your enemies turn their backs towards you. 28 I shall spread panic before you to drive out the Hivites, the Canaanites, and the Hittites in front of you. 29 I shall not drive them out all in one year, or the land would become waste and the wild beasts too many for you, 30 but I shall drive them out little by little until you have grown numerous enough to take possession of the country. 31 I shall establish your frontiers from the Red Sea to the sea of the Philistines, and from the wilderness to the river Euphrates. I shall give the inhabitants of the land into your power, and you will drive them out before you. 32 You are not to make any alliance with them and their gods. 33 They must not stay in your land, for fear they make you sin against me by ensnaring you into the worship of their gods.

24 THE LORD said to Moses, 'Come up to the LORD, you and Aaron, Nadab and Abihu, and seventy of the Israelite elders. While you are still at a distance, you are to bow down; 2 then Moses is to approach the LORD by himself, but not the others. The people must not go up with him.'

3 Moses went and repeated to the people all the words of the LORD, all his laws. With one voice the whole people answered, 'We will do everything the LORD has told us.' 4 Moses wrote down all the words of the LORD. Early in the morning he built an altar at the foot of the mountain, and erected twelve sacred pillars for the twelve tribes of Israel. 5 He sent the young men of Israel and they sacrificed bulls to the LORD as whole-offerings and shared-offerings. 6 Mo-

---

[b] Gk Vg: Heb he   [c] Or hornets: Meaning of Heb uncertain
[d] Or Sea of Reeds

23:15 come . . . presence: lit. see my face.   23:16 end: or beginning; lit. going out.   23:17 come . . . of: lit. see the face of.

14 "Three times a year you shall celebrate a pilgrim feast to me. 15 You shall keep the feast of Unleavened Bread. As I have commanded you, you must eat unleavened bread for seven days at the prescribed time in the month of Abib, for it was then that you came out of Egypt. No one shall appear before me empty-handed. 16 You shall also keep the feast of the grain harvest with the first of the crop that you have sown in the field; and finally, the feast at the fruit harvest at the end of the year, when you gather in the produce from the fields. 17 Thrice a year shall all your men appear before the LORD God.

18 "You shall not offer the blood of my sacrifice with leavened bread; nor shall the fat of my feast be kept overnight till the next day. 19 The choicest first fruits of your soil you shall bring to the house of the LORD, your God.

"You shall not boil a kid in its mother's milk.

20 "See, I am sending an angel before you, to guard you on the way and bring you to the place I have prepared. 21 Be attentive to him and heed his voice. Do not rebel against him, for he will not forgive your sin. My authority resides in him. 22 If you heed his voice and carry out all I tell you, I will be an enemy to your enemies and a foe to your foes.

23 "My angel will go before you and bring you to the Amorites, Hittites, Perizzites, Canaanites, Hivites and Jebusites; and I will wipe them out. 24 Therefore, you shall not bow down in worship before their gods, nor shall you make anything like them; rather, you must demolish them and smash their sacred pillars. 25 The LORD, your God, you shall worship; then I will bless your food and drink, and I will remove all sickness from your midst; 26 no woman in your land will be barren or miscarry; and I will give you a full span of life.

27 "I will have the fear of me precede you, so that I will throw into panic every nation you reach. I will make all your enemies turn from you in flight, 28 and ahead of you I will send hornets to drive the Hivites, Canaanites and Hittites out of your way. 29 But not in one year will I drive them all out before you; else the land will become so desolate that the wild beasts will multiply against you. 30 Instead, I will drive them out little by little before you, until you have grown numerous enough to take possession of the land. 31 I will set your boundaries from the Red Sea to the sea of the Philistines, and from the desert to the River; all who dwell in this land I will hand over to you to be driven out of your way. 32 You shall not make a covenant with them or their gods. 33 They must not abide in your land, lest they make you sin against me by ensnaring you into worshiping their gods."

24 Moses himself was told, "Come up to the LORD, you and Aaron, with Nadab, Abihu, and seventy of the elders of Israel. You shall all worship at some distance, 2 but Moses alone is to come close to the LORD; the others shall not come too near, and the people shall not come up at all with Moses."

3 When Moses came to the people and related all the words and ordinances of the LORD, they all answered with one voice, "We will do everything that the LORD has told us." 4 Moses then wrote down all the words of the LORD and, rising early the next day, he erected at the foot of the mountain an altar and twelve pillars for the twelve tribes of Israel. 5 Then, having sent certain young men of the Israelites to offer holocausts and sacrifice young bulls as peace offerings to the LORD, 6 Moses took half of the blood and

14 'Three times a year you will hold a festival in my honour. 15 You will observe the feast of Unleavened Bread. For seven days you will eat unleavened bread, as I have commanded you, at the appointed time in the month of Abib, for in that month you came out of Egypt. No one will appear before me empty-handed. 16 You will also observe the feast of Harvest, of the first-fruits of your labours in sowing the fields, and the feast of Ingathering, at the end of the year, once you have brought the fruits of your labours in from the fields. 17 Three times a year all your menfolk will appear before Lord Yahweh.

18 'You will not offer the blood of my victim with leavened bread, nor will the fat of my feast be kept till the following day.

19 'You will bring the best of the first-fruits of your soil to the house of Yahweh your God.

'You will not boil a kid in its mother's milk.

20 'Look, I am sending an angel to precede you, to guard you as you go and bring you to the place that I have prepared. 21 Revere him and obey what he says. Do not defy him: he will not forgive any wrong-doing on your part, for my name is in him. 22 If, however, you obey what he says and do whatever I order, I shall be an enemy to your enemies and a foe to your foes. 23 My angel will precede you and lead you to the home of the Amorites, the Hittites, the Perizzites, the Canaanites, the Hivites and the Jebusites, whom I shall exterminate. 24 You will not bow down to their gods or worship them or observe their rites, but throw them down and smash their cultic stones. 25 You will worship Yahweh your God, and then I shall bless your food and water, and keep you free of sickness. 26 In your country no woman will miscarry, none be sterile, and I shall give you your full term of life.

27 'I shall send terror of myself ahead of you; I shall throw all the peoples you encounter into confusion, and make all your enemies take to their heels. 28 I shall send hornets ahead of you to drive Hivite, Canaanite and Hittite out before you. 29 I shall not drive them out ahead of you in a single year, or the land might become a desert where wild animals would multiply to your cost. 30 I shall drive them out little by little before you, until your numbers grow sufficient for you to take possession of the land. 31 And your frontiers I shall fix from the Sea of Reeds to the Sea of the Philistines, and from the desert to the River, for I shall put the inhabitants of the territory at your mercy, and you will drive them out before you. 32 You will make no pact with them or with their gods. 33 They may not stay in your country or they might make you sin against me, for you would serve their gods, and that would be a snare for you!'

24 He then said to Moses, 'Come up to Yahweh, you and Aaron, Nadab and Abihu, and seventy of the elders of Israel and bow down at a distance. 2 Moses alone will approach Yahweh; the others will not approach, nor will the people come up with him.'

3 Moses went and told the people all Yahweh's words and all the laws, and all the people answered with one voice, 'All the words Yahweh has spoken we will carry out!' 4 Moses put all Yahweh's words into writing, and early next morning he built an altar at the foot of the mountain, with twelve standing-stones for the twelve tribes of Israel. 5 Then he sent certain young Israelites to offer burnt offerings and sacrifice bullocks to Yahweh as communion sacrifices.

NEW REVISED STANDARD VERSION

REVISED ENGLISH BIBLE

6 Moses took half of the blood and put it in basins, and half of the blood he dashed against the altar. 7 Then he took the book of the covenant, and read it in the hearing of the people; and they said, "All that the LORD has spoken we will do, and we will be obedient." 8 Moses took the blood and dashed it on the people, and said, "See the blood of the covenant that the LORD has made with you in accordance with all these words."

9 Then Moses and Aaron, Nadab, and Abihu, and seventy of the elders of Israel went up, 10 and they saw the God of Israel. Under his feet there was something like a pavement of sapphire stone, like the very heaven for clearness. 11 God^e did not lay his hand on the chief men of the people of Israel; also they beheld God, and they ate and drank.

12 The LORD said to Moses, "Come up to me on the mountain, and wait there; and I will give you the tablets of stone, with the law and the commandment, which I have written for their instruction." 13 So Moses set out with his assistant Joshua, and Moses went up into the mountain of God. 14 To the elders he had said, "Wait here for us, until we come to you again; for Aaron and Hur are with you; whoever has a dispute may go to them."

15 Then Moses went up on the mountain, and the cloud covered the mountain. 16 The glory of the LORD settled on Mount Sinai, and the cloud covered it for six days; on the seventh day he called to Moses out of the cloud. 17 Now the appearance of the glory of the LORD was like a devouring fire on the top of the mountain in the sight of the people of Israel. 18 Moses entered the cloud, and went up on the mountain. Moses was on the mountain for forty days and forty nights.

25 The LORD said to Moses: 2 Tell the Israelites to take for me an offering; from all whose hearts prompt them to give you shall receive the offering for me. 3 This is the offering that you shall receive from them: gold, silver, and bronze, 4 blue, purple, and crimson yarns and fine linen, goats' hair, 5 tanned rams' skins, fine leather,^{f} acacia wood, 6 oil for the lamps, spices for the anointing oil and for the fragrant incense, 7 onyx stones and gems to be set in the ephod and for the breastpiece. 8 And have them make me a sanctuary, so that I may dwell among them. 9 In accordance with all that I show you concerning the pattern of the tabernacle and of all its furniture, so you shall make it.

10 They shall make an ark of acacia wood; it shall be two and a half cubits long, a cubit and a half wide, and a cubit and a half high. 11 You shall overlay it with pure gold, inside and outside you shall overlay it, and you shall make a molding of gold upon it all around. 12 You shall cast four rings of gold for it and put them on its four feet, two rings on the one side of it, and two rings on the other side. 13 You shall make poles of acacia wood, and overlay them with gold. 14 And you shall put the poles into the rings on the sides of the ark, by which to carry the ark. 15 The poles shall remain in the rings of the ark; they shall not be taken from it. 16 You shall put into the ark the covenant^g that I shall give you.

17 Then you shall make a mercy seat^h of pure gold; two cubits and a half shall be its length, and a cubit and a half its width. 18 You shall make two cherubim of gold; you shall make them of hammered work, at the two ends of the mercy seat.^{i} 19 Make one cherub at the one end, and one cherub at the other; of one piece with the mercy seat^i you shall make the cherubim at its two ends. 20 The cherubim

ses took half the blood and put it in basins, and the other half he flung against the altar. 7 Then he took the Book of the Covenant and read it aloud for the people to hear. They said, 'We shall obey, and do all that the LORD has said.' 8 Moses then took the blood and flung it over the people, saying, 'This is the blood of the covenant which the LORD has made with you on the terms of this book.'

9 Moses went up with Aaron, Nadab, and Abihu, and seventy of the elders of Israel, 10 and they saw the God of Israel. Under his feet there was, as it were, a pavement of sapphire, clear blue as the very heavens; 11 but the LORD did not stretch out his hand against the leaders of Israel. They saw God; they ate and they drank. 12 The LORD said to Moses, 'Come up to me on the mountain, stay there, and let me give you the stone tablets with the law and commandment I have written down for their instruction.' 13 Moses with Joshua his assistant set off up the mountain of God; 14 he said to the elders, 'Wait for us here until we come back to you. You have Aaron and Hur; if anyone has a dispute, let him go to them.'

15 So Moses went up the mountain and a cloud covered it. 16 The glory of the LORD rested on Mount Sinai, and the cloud covered the mountain for six days; on the seventh day he called to Moses out of the cloud. 17 To the Israelites the glory of the LORD looked like a devouring fire on the mountaintop. 18 Moses entered the cloud and went up the mountain; there he stayed forty days and forty nights.

25 THE LORD spoke to Moses and said: 2 Tell the Israelites to set aside a contribution for me; you are to accept whatever contribution each man freely offers. 3 You may accept any of the following: gold, silver, copper; 4 violet, purple, and scarlet yarn; fine linen and goats' hair; 5 tanned rams' skins and dugong-hides; acacia-wood; 6 oil for the lamp, spices for the anointing oil and for the fragrant incense; 7 cornelians and other stones ready for setting on the ephod and the breastpiece.

8 Make me a sanctuary, and I shall dwell among the Israelites. 9 Make it exactly according to the design I show you, the design for the Tabernacle and for all its furniture. This is how you must make it: 10 Make an Ark, a chest of acacia-wood two and a half cubits long, one and a half cubits wide, and one and a half cubits high. 11 Overlay it with pure gold both inside and out, and put a band of gold all round it. 12 Cast four gold rings for it, and fasten them to its four feet, two rings on each side. 13 Make poles of acacia-wood and overlay them with gold, 14 and insert the poles in the rings at the sides of the Ark to lift it. 15 The poles are to remain in the rings of the Ark and never be removed. 16 Put into the Ark the Testimony which I shall give you.

17 Make a cover of pure gold two and a half cubits long and one and a half cubits wide. 18 Make two gold cherubim of beaten work at the ends of the cover, 19 one at each end; make each cherub of one piece with the cover. 20 They are

---

^{e} Heb *He* ^{f} Meaning of Heb uncertain ^{g} Or *treaty*, or *testimony*; Heb *eduth* ^{h} Or *a cover* ^{i} Or *the cover*

24:6 **against:** or upon.   24:10 **they saw:** or they were afraid of. **sapphire:** or lapis lazuli.   24:11 **They saw:** or They stayed before. 25:7 **breastpiece:** or pouch.

put it in large bowls; the other half he splashed on the altar. 7 Taking the book of the covenant, he read it aloud to the people, who answered, "All that the LORD has said, we will heed and do." 8 Then he took the blood and sprinkled it on the people, saying, "This is the blood of the covenant which the LORD has made with you in accordance with all these words of his."

9 Moses then went up with Aaron, Nadab, Abihu, and seventy elders of Israel, 10 and they beheld the God of Israel. Under his feet there appeared to be sapphire tilework, as clear as the sky itself. 11 Yet he did not smite these chosen Israelites. After gazing on God, they could still eat and drink.

12 The LORD said to Moses, "Come up to me on the mountain and, while you are there, I will give you the stone tablets on which I have written the commandments intended for their instruction." 13 So Moses set out with Joshua, his aide, and went up to the mountain of God. 14 The elders, however, had been told by him, "Wait here for us until we return to you. Aaron and Hur are staying with you. If anyone has a complaint, let him refer the matter to them." 15 After Moses had gone up, a cloud covered the mountain. 16 The glory of the LORD settled upon Mount Sinai. The cloud covered it for six days, and on the seventh day he called to Moses from the midst of the cloud. 17 To the Israelites the glory of the LORD was seen as a consuming fire on the mountaintop. 18 But Moses passed into the midst of the cloud as he went up on the mountain; and there he stayed for forty days and forty nights.

25 This is what the LORD then said to Moses: 2 "Tell the Israelites to take up a collection for me. From every man you shall accept the contribution that his heart prompts him to give me. 3 These are the contributions you shall accept from them: gold, silver and bronze; 4 violet, purple and scarlet yarn; fine linen and goat hair; 5 rams' skins dyed red, and tahash skins; acacia wood; 6 oil for the light; spices for the anointing oil and for the fragrant incense; 7 onyx stones and other gems for mounting on the ephod and the breastpiece.

8 "They shall make a sanctuary for me, that I may dwell in their midst. 9 This Dwelling and all its furnishings you shall make exactly according to the pattern that I will now show you.

10 "You shall make an ark of acacia wood, two and a half cubits long, one and a half cubits wide, and one and a half cubits high. 11 Plate it inside and outside with pure gold, and put a molding of gold around the top of it. 12 Cast four gold rings and fasten them on the four supports of the ark, two rings on one side and two on the opposite side. 13 Then make poles of acacia wood and plate them with gold. 14 These poles you are to put through the rings on the sides of the ark, for carrying it; 15 they must remain in the rings of the ark and never be withdrawn. 16 In the ark you are to put the commandments which I will give you.

17 "You shall then make a propitiatory of pure gold, two cubits and a half long, and one and a half cubits wide. 18 Make two cherubim of beaten gold for the two ends of the propitiatory, 19 fastening them so that one cherub springs direct from each end. 20 The cherubim shall have their

6 Moses then took half the blood and put it into basins, and the other half he sprinkled on the altar. 7 Then, taking the Book of the Covenant, he read it to the listening people, who then said, 'We shall do everything that Yahweh has said; we shall obey.' 8 Moses then took the blood and sprinkled it over the people, saying, 'This is the blood of the covenant which Yahweh has made with you, entailing all these stipulations.'

9 Moses, Aaron, Nadab, Abihu and seventy elders of Israel then went up, 10 and they saw the God of Israel beneath whose feet there was what looked like a sapphire pavement pure as the heavens themselves, 11 but he did no harm to the Israelite notables; they actually gazed on God and then ate and drank.

12 Yahweh said to Moses, 'Come up to me on the mountain. Stay there, and I will give you the stone tablets — the law and the commandment — which I have written for their instruction.' 13 Moses made ready, with Joshua his assistant, and they went up the mountain of God. 14 He said to the elders, 'Wait here for us until we come back to you. You have Aaron and Hur with you; if anyone has any matter to settle, let him go to them.' 15 Moses then went up the mountain.

Cloud covered the mountain. 16 The glory of Yahweh rested on Mount Sinai and the cloud covered it for six days. On the seventh day Yahweh called to Moses from inside the cloud. 17 To the watching Israelites, the glory of Yahweh looked like a devouring fire on the mountain top. 18 Moses went right into the cloud and went on up the mountain. Moses stayed on the mountain for forty days and forty nights.

25 k Yahweh spoke to Moses and said, 2 'Tell the Israelites to set aside a contribution for me; you will accept a contribution from everyone whose heart prompts him to give it. 3 And this is what you will accept from them: gold, silver and bronze; 4 materials dyed violet-purple, red-purple and crimson, fine linen, goats' hair; 5 rams' skins dyed red, fine leather, acacia wood; 6 oil for the light, spices for the anointing oil and fragrant incense; 7 cornelian and other stones to be set in the *ephod* and breastplate. 8 Make me a sanctuary so that I can reside among them. 9 You will make it all according to the design for the Dwelling and the design for its furnishings which I shall now show you.

10 'You must make me an ark l of acacia wood, two and a half cubits long, one and a half cubits wide and one and a half cubits high. 11 You will overlay it, inside and out, with pure gold and make a gold moulding all round it. 12 You will cast four gold rings for it and fix them to its four supports: two rings on one side and two on the other. 13 You will also make shafts of acacia wood and overlay them with gold 14 and pass the shafts through the rings on the sides of the ark, by which to carry it. 15 The shafts will stay in the rings of the ark and not be withdrawn. 16 Inside the ark you will put the Testimony which I am about to give you.

17 'You will also make a mercy-seat m of pure gold, two and a half cubits long and one and a half cubits wide, 18 and you will model two great winged creatures of beaten gold, you will make them at the two ends of the mercy-seat. 19 Model one of the winged creatures at one end and the other winged creature at the other end; you will model the winged creatures of a piece with the mercy-seat at either end. 20 The winged creatures must have their wings spread

k 25 25:1seq. = 35–40.   l 25 A wooden chest, symbol of God's presence, finally housed in the Temple. It disappeared in the destruction of 586 BC.   m 25 This covering of the ark is the place of God's appearing to Moses. The winged creatures correspond to Babylonian *karibu*, half-animal, half-human guards of the temples.

| NEW REVISED STANDARD VERSION | REVISED ENGLISH BIBLE |

shall spread out their wings above, overshadowing the mercy seat*j* with their wings. They shall face one to another; the faces of the cherubim shall be turned toward the mercy seat.*j* 21 You shall put the mercy seat*j* on the top of the ark; and in the ark you shall put the covenant*k* that I shall give you. 22 There I will meet with you, and from above the mercy seat,*j* from between the two cherubim that are on the ark of the covenant,*k* I will deliver to you all my commands for the Israelites.

23 You shall make a table of acacia wood, two cubits long, one cubit wide, and a cubit and a half high. 24 You shall overlay it with pure gold, and make a molding of gold around it. 25 You shall make around it a rim a handbreadth wide, and a molding of gold around the rim. 26 You shall make for it four rings of gold, and fasten the rings to the four corners at its four legs. 27 The rings that hold the poles used for carrying the table shall be close to the rim. 28 You shall make the poles of acacia wood, and overlay them with gold, and the table shall be carried with these. 29 You shall make its plates and dishes for incense, and its flagons and bowls with which to pour drink offerings; you shall make them of pure gold. 30 And you shall set the bread of the Presence on the table before me always.

31 You shall make a lampstand of pure gold. The base and the shaft of the lampstand shall be made of hammered work; its cups, its calyxes, and its petals shall be of one piece with it; 32 and there shall be six branches going out of its sides, three branches of the lampstand out of one side of it and three branches of the lampstand out of the other side of it; 33 three cups shaped like almond blossoms, each with calyx and petals, on one branch, and three cups shaped like almond blossoms, each with calyx and petals, on the other branch — so for the six branches going out of the lampstand. 34 On the lampstand itself there shall be four cups shaped like almond blossoms, each with its calyxes and petals. 35 There shall be a calyx of one piece with it under the first pair of branches, a calyx of one piece with it under the next pair of branches, and a calyx of one piece with it under the last pair of branches — so for the six branches that go out of the lampstand. 36 Their calyxes and their branches shall be of one piece with it, the whole of it one hammered piece of pure gold. 37 You shall make the seven lamps for it; and the lamps shall be set up so as to give light on the space in front of it. 38 Its snuffers and trays shall be of pure gold. 39 It, and all these utensils, shall be made from a talent of pure gold. 40 And see that you make them according to the pattern for them, which is being shown you on the mountain.

26 Moreover you shall make the tabernacle with ten curtains of fine twisted linen, and blue, purple, and crimson yarns; you shall make them with cherubim skillfully worked into them. 2 The length of each curtain shall be twenty-eight cubits, and the width of each curtain four cubits; all the curtains shall be of the same size. 3 Five curtains shall be joined to one another; and the other five curtains shall be joined to one another. 4 You shall make loops of blue on the edge of the outermost curtain in the first set; and likewise you shall make loops on the edge of the outermost curtain in the second set. 5 You shall make fifty loops on the one curtain, and you shall make fifty loops on the edge of the curtain that is in the second set; the loops shall be opposite one another. 6 You shall make fifty clasps of gold, and join the curtains to one another with the clasps, so that the tabernacle may be one whole.

7 You shall also make curtains of goats' hair for a tent over the tabernacle; you shall make eleven curtains. 8 The length of each curtain shall be thirty cubits, and the width of each curtain four cubits; the eleven curtains shall be of the same size. 9 You shall join five curtains by themselves,

to be made with wings spread out and pointing upwards to screen the cover with their wings. They will be face to face, looking inwards over the cover. 21 Place the cover on the Ark, and put into the Ark the Testimony that I shall give you. 22 It is there that I shall meet you; from above the cover, between the two cherubim over the Ark of the Testimony, I shall deliver to you all my commands for the Israelites.

23 Make a table of acacia-wood two cubits long, one cubit wide, and one and a half cubits high. 24 Overlay it with pure gold, and put a band of gold all round it. 25 Make a rim round it a hand's breadth wide, and a gold band round the rim. 26 Make four gold rings for the table, and put the rings at the four corners by the four legs. 27 The rings, which are to receive the poles for carrying the table, must be adjacent to the rim. 28 Make the poles of acacia-wood and overlay them with gold; they are to be used for carrying the table. 29 Make dishes and saucers for it, and flagons and bowls from which drink-offerings may be poured; make them of pure gold. 30 Put the Bread of the Presence on the table, to be always before me.

31 Make a lampstand of pure gold. The lampstand, stem and branches, shall be of beaten work: its cups, both calyxes and petals, shall be of one piece with it. 32 There are to be six branches springing from the sides of the lampstand, three branches from one side and three branches from the other. 33 There shall be three cups shaped like almond blossoms with calyx and petals on the first branch, three cups shaped like almond blossoms with calyx and petals on the next branch, and similarly for all six branches springing from the lampstand. 34 On the main stem of the lampstand there are to be four cups shaped like almond blossoms with calyx and petals, 35 and there shall be calyxes of one piece with it under the six branches which spring from the lampstand, a single calyx under each pair of branches. 36 The calyxes and the branches are to be of one piece with it, all a single piece of beaten work of pure gold. 37 Make seven lamps for this and mount them to shed light over the space in front of the lampstand. 38 Its tongs and firepans are to be of pure gold. 39 The lampstand and all these fittings are to be made from one talent of pure gold. 40 See that you work to the design shown to you on the mountain.

26 Make the Tabernacle itself of ten hangings of finely woven linen, and violet, purple, and scarlet yarn, with cherubim worked on them, all made by a seamster. 2 The length of each hanging is to be twenty-eight cubits and the breadth four cubits; all are to be of the same size. 3 Five of the hangings are to be joined together, and similarly the other five. 4 Make violet loops along the outer edge of the last hanging in each set, 5 fifty for each set; they must be opposite one another. 6 Make fifty gold fasteners, join the hangings one to another with them, and the Tabernacle will form a single whole.

7 Make hangings of goats' hair, eleven in all, to form a tent over the Tabernacle; 8 each hanging is to be thirty cubits long and four cubits wide; all eleven are to be of the same size. 9 Join five of the hangings together, and similarly the

---

j Or the cover *k Or treaty*, or *testimony*; Heb *eduth* 25:30 **Bread of the Presence:** or Shewbread.

wings spread out above, covering the propitiatory with them; they shall be turned toward each other, but with their faces looking toward the propitiatory. 21 This propitiatory you shall then place on top of the ark. In the ark itself you are to put the commandments which I will give you. 22 There I will meet you and there, from above the propitiatory, between the two cherubim on the ark of the commandments, I will tell you all the commands that I wish to give the Israelites.

23 "You shall also make a table of acacia wood, two cubits long, a cubit wide, and a cubit and a half high. 24 Plate it with pure gold and make a molding of gold around it. 25 Surround it with a frame, a handsbreadth high, with a molding of gold around the frame. 26 You shall also make four rings of gold for it and fasten them at the four corners, one at each leg, 27 on two opposite sides of the frame as holders for the poles to carry the table. 28 These poles for carrying the table you shall make of acacia wood and plate with gold. 29 Of pure gold you shall make its plates and cups, as well as its pitchers and bowls for pouring libations. 30 On the table you shall always keep showbread set before me.

31 "You shall make a lampstand of pure beaten gold — its shaft and branches — with its cups and knobs and petals springing directly from it. 32 Six branches are to extend from the sides of the lampstand, three branches on one side, and three on the other. 33 On one branch there are to be three cups, shaped like almond blossoms, each with its knob and petals; on the opposite branch there are to be three cups, shaped like almond blossoms, each with its knob and petals; and so for the six branches that extend from the lampstand. 34 On the shaft there are to be four cups, shaped like almond blossoms, with their knobs and petals, 35 including a knob below each of the three pairs of branches that extend from the lampstand. 36 Their knobs and branches shall so spring from it that the whole will form but a single piece of pure beaten gold. 37 You shall then make seven lamps for it and so set up the lamps that they shed their light on the space in front of the lampstand. 38 These, as well as the trimming shears and trays, must be of pure gold. 39 Use a talent of pure gold for the lampstand and all its appurtenances. 40 See that you make them according to the pattern shown you on the mountain.

26 "The Dwelling itself you shall make out of sheets woven of fine linen twined and of violet, purple and scarlet yarn, with cherubim embroidered on them. 2 The length of each shall be twenty-eight cubits, and the width four cubits; all the sheets shall be of the same size. 3 Five of the sheets are to be sewed together, edge to edge; and the same for the other five. 4 Make loops of violet yarn along the edge of the end sheet in one set, and the same along the edge of the end sheet in the other set. 5 There are to be fifty loops along the edge of the end sheet in the first set, and fifty loops along the edge of the corresponding sheet in the second set, and so placed that the loops are directly opposite each other. 6 Then make fifty clasps of gold, with which to join the two sets of sheets, so that the Dwelling forms one whole.

7 "Also make sheets woven of goat hair, to be used as a tent covering over the Dwelling. 8 Eleven such sheets are to be made; the length of each shall be thirty cubits, and the width four cubits: all eleven sheets shall be of the same size.

upwards, protecting the mercy-seat with their wings and facing each other, their faces being towards the mercy-seat. 21 You will put the mercy-seat on the top of the ark, and inside the ark you will put the Testimony which I am about to give you. 22 There I shall come to meet you; from above the mercy-seat, from between the two winged creatures which are on the ark of the Testimony, I shall give you all my orders for the Israelites.

23 'You must also make a table of acacia wood, two cubits long, one cubit wide and one and a half cubits high. 24 You will overlay it with pure gold, and make a gold moulding all round it. 25 You will fit it with struts of a hand's breadth and make a gold moulding round the struts. 26 You will make four gold rings for it and fix the four rings at the four corners where the four legs are. 27 The rings must lie close to the struts to hold the shafts for carrying the table. 28 You must make the shafts of acacia wood and overlay them with gold. The table must be carried by these. 29 You must make dishes, cups, jars and libation bowls for it; you must make these of pure gold, 30 and on the table, in my presence, you will always put the loaves of permanent offering.

31 'You will also make a lamp-stand of pure gold; the lamp-stand must be of beaten gold, base and stem. Its cups, calyxes and petals, must be of a piece with it. 32 Six branches must spring from its sides: three of the lamp-stand's branches from one side, three of the lamp-stand's branches from the other. 33 The first branch must carry three cups shaped like almond blossoms, each with its calyx and petals; the second branch, too, must carry three cups shaped like almond blossoms, each with its calyx and bud, and similarly for all six branches springing from the lamp-stand. 34 The lamp-stand itself must carry four cups shaped like almond blossoms, each with its calyx and bud: 35 one calyx under the first two branches springing from the lamp-stand, one calyx under the next pair of branches and one calyx under the last pair of branches — thus for all six branches springing from the lamp-stand. 36 The calyxes and the branches will be of a piece with the lamp-stand, and the whole made from a single piece of pure gold, beaten out. 37 You will also make seven lamps for it and mount the lamps in such a way that they light up the space in front of it. 38 The snuffers and trays must be of pure gold. 39 You will use a talent of pure gold for the lamp-stand and all its accessories; 40 and see that you work to the design which was shown you on the mountain.'

26 'The Dwelling itself you will make with ten sheets of finely woven linen dyed violet-purple, red-purple and crimson. You will have them embroidered with great winged creatures. 2 The length of a single sheet is to be twenty-eight cubits, its width four cubits, all the sheets to be of the same size. 3 Five of the sheets are to be joined to one another, and the other five sheets are to be joined to one another. 4 You will make violet loops along the edge of the first sheet, at the end of the set, and do the same along the edge of the last sheet in the other set. 5 You will make fifty loops on the first sheet and fifty loops along the outer edge of the sheet of the second set, the loops corresponding to one another. 6 You will also make fifty gold clasps, and join the sheets together with the clasps. In this way the Dwelling will be a unified whole.

7 'You will make sheets of goats' hair to form a tent over the Dwelling; you will make eleven of these. 8 The length of a single sheet must be thirty cubits and its width four cubits, the eleven sheets to be all of the same size. 9 You will join

NEW REVISED STANDARD VERSION

and six curtains by themselves, and the sixth curtain you shall double over at the front of the tent. 10 You shall make fifty loops on the edge of the curtain that is outermost in one set, and fifty loops on the edge of the curtain that is outermost in the second set.

11 You shall make fifty clasps of bronze, and put the clasps into the loops, and join the tent together, so that it may be one whole. 12 The part that remains of the curtains of the tent, the half curtain that remains, shall hang over the back of the tabernacle. 13 The cubit on the one side, and the cubit on the other side, of what remains in the length of the curtains of the tent, shall hang over the sides of the tabernacle, on this side and that side, to cover it. 14 You shall make for the tent a covering of tanned rams' skins and an outer covering of fine leather.[l]

15 You shall make upright frames of acacia wood for the tabernacle. 16 Ten cubits shall be the length of a frame, and a cubit and a half the width of each frame. 17 There shall be two pegs in each frame to fit the frames together; you shall make these for all the frames of the tabernacle. 18 You shall make the frames for the tabernacle: twenty frames for the south side; 19 and you shall make forty bases of silver under the twenty frames, two bases under the first frame for its two pegs, and two bases under the next frame for its two pegs; 20 and for the second side of the tabernacle, on the north side twenty frames, 21 and their forty bases of silver, two bases under the first frame, and two bases under the next frame; 22 and for the rear of the tabernacle westward you shall make six frames. 23 You shall make two frames for corners of the tabernacle in the rear; 24 they shall be separate beneath, but joined at the top, at the first ring; it shall be the same with both of them; they shall form the two corners. 25 And so there shall be eight frames, with their bases of silver, sixteen bases; two bases under the first frame, and two bases under the next frame.

26 You shall make bars of acacia wood, five for the frames of the one side of the tabernacle, 27 and five bars for the frames of the other side of the tabernacle, and five bars for the frames of the side of the tabernacle at the rear westward. 28 The middle bar, halfway up the frames, shall pass through from end to end. 29 You shall overlay the frames with gold, and shall make their rings of gold to hold the bars; and you shall overlay the bars with gold. 30 Then you shall erect the tabernacle according to the plan for it that you were shown on the mountain.

31 You shall make a curtain of blue, purple, and crimson yarns, and of fine twisted linen; it shall be made with cherubim skillfully worked into it. 32 You shall hang it on four pillars of acacia overlaid with gold, which have hooks of gold and rest on four bases of silver. 33 You shall hang the curtain under the clasps, and bring the ark of the covenant[m] in there, within the curtain; and the curtain shall separate for you the holy place from the most holy. 34 You shall put the mercy seat[n] on the ark of the covenant[m] in the most holy place. 35 You shall set the table outside the curtain, and the lampstand on the south side of the tabernacle opposite the table; and you shall put the table on the north side.

36 You shall make a screen for the entrance of the tent, of blue, purple, and crimson yarns, and of fine twisted linen, embroidered with needlework. 37 You shall make for the screen five pillars of acacia, and overlay them with gold; their hooks shall be of gold, and you shall cast five bases of bronze for them.

REVISED ENGLISH BIBLE

other six; then fold the sixth hanging double at the front of the tent. 10 Make fifty loops on the edge of the last hanging in the first set and make fifty loops on the joining edge of the second set. 11 Make fifty bronze fasteners, insert them into the loops, and join up the tent to make it a single whole. 12 The additional length of the tent hanging is to fall over the back of the Tabernacle. 13 On each side there will be an additional cubit in the length of the tent hangings; this must fall over the two sides of the Tabernacle to cover it. 14 Make for the tent a cover of tanned rams' skins and an outer covering of dugong-hides.

15 Make for the Tabernacle frames of acacia-wood as uprights, 16 each frame ten cubits long and one and a half cubits wide, 17 and two tenons for each frame joined to each other. Do the same for all the frames of the Tabernacle. 18 Arrange the frames thus: twenty frames for the south side, facing southwards, 19 with forty silver sockets under them, two sockets under each frame for its two tenons; 20 and for the second or northern side of the Tabernacle twenty frames 21 with forty silver sockets, two under each frame. 22 Make six frames for the far end of the Tabernacle on the west. 23 Make two frames for the corners of the Tabernacle at the far end; 24 at the bottom they are to be alike, and at the top, both alike, they are to fit into a single ring. Do the same for both of them; they will be for the two corners. 25 There will be eight frames with their silver sockets, sixteen sockets in all, two sockets under each frame.

26 Make bars of acacia-wood: five for the frames on one side of the Tabernacle, 27 five for the frames on the other side, and five for the frames on the far side of the Tabernacle on the west. 28 The middle bar is to run along from end to end half-way up the frames. 29 Overlay the frames with gold, make rings of gold on them to hold the bars, and overlay the bars with gold. 30 Set up the Tabernacle according to the design you were shown on the mountain.

31 Make a curtain of finely woven linen and violet, purple, and scarlet yarn, with cherubim worked on it, all made by a seamster. 32 Fasten it with hooks of gold to four posts of acacia-wood overlaid with gold, standing in four silver sockets. 33 Hang the curtain below the fasteners and bring the Ark of the Testimony inside the curtain. Thus the curtain will make a clear separation for you between the Holy Place and the Holy of Holies. 34 Place the cover over the Ark of the Testimony in the Holy of Holies. 35 Put the table outside the curtain and the lampstand at the south side of the Tabernacle, opposite the table which you are to put at the north side.

36 For the entrance of the tent make a screen of finely woven linen, embroidered with violet, purple, and scarlet. 37 Make five posts of acacia-wood for the screen and overlay them with gold; make golden hooks for them and cast five bronze sockets for them.

26:11 **bronze:** *or* copper *and so throughout the descriptions of the Tabernacle.*   26:12 **The additional . . . hanging:** *prob. rdg; Heb. adds* half the hanging which remains over.   26:24 **both alike:** *so Samar.; Heb.* both perfect.

---

[l] Meaning of Heb uncertain   [m] Or *treaty,* or *testimony;* Heb *eduth*
[n] Or *the cover*

NEW AMERICAN BIBLE

9 Sew five of the sheets, edge to edge, into one set, and the other six sheets into another set. Use the sixth sheet double at the front of the tent. 10 Make fifty loops along the edge of the end sheet in one set, and fifty loops along the edge of the end sheet in the second set. 11 Also make fifty bronze clasps and put them into the loops, to join the tent into one whole. 12 There will be an extra half sheet of tent covering, which shall be allowed to hang down over the rear of the Dwelling. 13 Likewise, the sheets of the tent will have an extra cubit's length to be left hanging down on either side of the Dwelling to protect it. 14 Over the tent itself you shall make a covering of rams' skins dyed red, and above that, a covering of tahash skins.

15 "You shall make boards of acacia wood as walls for the Dwelling. 16 The length of each board is to be ten cubits, and its width one and a half cubits. 17 Each board shall have two arms that shall serve to fasten the boards in line. In this way all the boards of the Dwelling are to be made. 18 Set up the boards of the Dwelling as follows: twenty boards on the south side, 19 with forty silver pedestals under the twenty boards, so that there are two pedestals under each board, at its two arms; 20 twenty boards on the other side of the Dwelling, the north side, 21 with their forty silver pedestals, two under each board; 22 six boards for the rear of the Dwelling, to the west; 23 and two boards for the corners at the rear of the Dwelling. 24 These two shall be double at the bottom, and likewise double at the top, to the first ring. That is how both boards in the corners are to be made. 25 Thus, there shall be in the rear eight boards, with their sixteen silver pedestals, two pedestals under each board. 26 Also make bars of acacia wood: five for the boards on one side of the Dwelling, 27 five for those on the other side, and five for those at the rear, toward the west. 28 The center bar, at the middle of the boards, shall reach across from end to end. 29 Plate the boards with gold, and make gold rings on them as holders for the bars, which are also to be plated with gold. 30 You shall erect the Dwelling according to the pattern shown you on the mountain.

31 "You shall have a veil woven of violet, purple and scarlet yarn, and of fine linen twined, with cherubim embroidered on it. 32 It is to be hung on four gold-plated columns of acacia wood, which shall have hooks of gold and shall rest on four silver pedestals. 33 Hang the veil from clasps. The ark of the commandments you shall bring inside, behind this veil which divides the holy place from the holy of holies. 34 Set the propitiatory on the ark of the commandments in the holy of holies.

35 "Outside the veil you shall place the table and the lampstand, the latter on the south side of the Dwelling, opposite the table, which is to be put on the north side. 36 For the entrance of the tent make a variegated curtain of violet, purple and scarlet yarn and of fine linen twined. 37 Make five columns of acacia wood for this curtain; have them plated with gold, with their hooks of gold; and cast five bronze pedestals for them.

NEW JERUSALEM BIBLE

five sheets together into one set, and six sheets into another; the sixth you will fold double over the front of the tent. 10 You will make fifty loops along the edge of the first sheet, at the end of the first set, and fifty loops along the edge of the sheet of the second set. 11 You will make fifty bronze clasps and insert the clasps into the loops, to draw the tent together and to make it a unified whole.

12 'Of the extra part of the sheets that overlap, half is to hang down the back of the Dwelling. 13 The extra cubit on either side along the length of the tent sheets must hang down the sides of the Dwelling on either side to cover it.

14 'And for the tent you will make a cover of rams' skins dyed red and a cover of fine leather over that.

15 'For the Dwelling you will make vertical frames of acacia wood. 16 Each frame must be ten cubits long and one and a half cubits wide. 17 Each frame must have twin tenons; that is how all the frames for the Dwelling must be made. 18 You will make frames for the Dwelling: twenty frames for the south side, to the south, 19 and make forty silver sockets under the twenty frames, two sockets under one frame for its two tenons, two sockets under the next frame for its two tenons; 20 and for the other side of the Dwelling, the north side, twenty frames 21 and forty silver sockets, two sockets under one frame, two sockets under the next frame. 22 For the back of the Dwelling, on the west, you will make six frames, 23 and make two frames for the corners at the back of the Dwelling; 24 these must be coupled together at the bottom, and right up to the top, to the level of the first ring; this for the two frames that must form the two corners. 25 Thus there will be eight frames with their silver sockets: sixteen sockets; two sockets under one frame and two sockets under the next frame.

26 'You will make crossbars of acacia wood: five for the frames of the first side of the Dwelling, 27 five crossbars for the frames of the opposite side of the Dwelling, and five crossbars for the frames which form the back of the Dwelling, to the west. 28 The middle bar must join the frames from one end to the other, halfway up. 29 You will overlay the frames with gold, make gold rings for them, through which to place the crossbars, and overlay the crossbars with gold. 30 This is how you must erect the Dwelling, following the design shown you on the mountain.

31 'You will make a curtain of finely woven linen, dyed violet-purple, red-purple and crimson, and embroidered with great winged creatures, 32 and put it on four poles of acacia wood overlaid with gold, with golden hooks for them, set in four sockets of silver. 33 You will put the curtain below the clasps, so that inside behind the curtain, you can place the ark of the Testimony, and the curtain will mark the division for you between the Holy Place and the Holy of Holies. 34 You will put the mercy-seat on the ark of the Testimony in the Holy of Holies. 35 You will place the table outside the curtain, and the lamp-stand on the south side of the Dwelling, opposite the table; you will put the table on the north side. 36 For the entrance to the tent you will make a screen of finely woven linen embroidered with violet-purple, red-purple and crimson, 37 and for the screen you will make five poles of acacia wood and overlay them with gold, with golden hooks, and for them you will cast five sockets of bronze.'

27 You shall make the altar of acacia wood, five cubits long and five cubits wide; the altar shall be square, and it shall be three cubits high. 2 You shall make horns for it on its four corners; its horns shall be of one piece with it, and you shall overlay it with bronze. 3 You shall make pots for it to receive its ashes, and shovels and basins and forks and firepans; you shall make all its utensils of bronze. 4 You shall also make for it a grating, a network of bronze; and on the net you shall make four bronze rings at its four corners. 5 You shall set it under the ledge of the altar so that the net shall extend halfway down the altar. 6 You shall make poles for the altar, poles of acacia wood, and overlay them with bronze; 7 the poles shall be put through the rings, so that the poles shall be on the two sides of the altar when it is carried. 8 You shall make it hollow, with boards. They shall be made just as you were shown on the mountain.

9 You shall make the court of the tabernacle. On the south side the court shall have hangings of fine twisted linen one hundred cubits long for that side; 10 its twenty pillars and their twenty bases shall be of bronze, but the hooks of the pillars and their bands shall be of silver. 11 Likewise for its length on the north side there shall be hangings one hundred cubits long, their pillars twenty and their bases twenty, of bronze, but the hooks of the pillars and their bands shall be of silver. 12 For the width of the court on the west side there shall be fifty cubits of hangings, with ten pillars and ten bases. 13 The width of the court on the front to the east shall be fifty cubits. 14 There shall be fifteen cubits of hangings on the one side, with three pillars and three bases. 15 There shall be fifteen cubits of hangings on the other side, with three pillars and three bases. 16 For the gate of the court there shall be a screen twenty cubits long, of blue, purple, and crimson yarns, and of fine twisted linen, embroidered with needlework; it shall have four pillars and with them four bases. 17 All the pillars around the court shall be banded with silver; their hooks shall be of silver, and their bases of bronze. 18 The length of the court shall be one hundred cubits, the width fifty, and the height five cubits, with hangings of fine twisted linen and bases of bronze. 19 All the utensils of the tabernacle for every use, and all its pegs and all the pegs of the court, shall be of bronze.

20 You shall further command the Israelites to bring you pure oil of beaten olives for the light, so that a lamp may be set up to burn regularly. 21 In the tent of meeting, outside the curtain that is before the covenant,*o* Aaron and his sons shall tend it from evening to morning before the LORD. It shall be a perpetual ordinance to be observed throughout their generations by the Israelites.

28 Then bring near to you your brother Aaron, and his sons with him, from among the Israelites, to serve me as priests — Aaron and Aaron's sons, Nadab and Abihu, Eleazar and Ithamar. 2 You shall make sacred vestments for the glorious adornment of your brother Aaron. 3 And you shall speak to all who have ability, whom I have endowed with skill, that they make Aaron's vestments to consecrate him for my priesthood. 4 These are the vestments that they shall make: a breastpiece, an ephod, a robe, a checkered tunic, a turban, and a sash. When they make these sacred vestments for your brother Aaron and his sons to serve me as priests, 5 they shall use gold, blue, purple, and crimson yarns, and fine linen.

6 They shall make the ephod of gold, of blue, purple, and crimson yarns, and of fine twisted linen, skillfully worked. 7 It shall have two shoulder-pieces attached to its two edges, so that it may be joined together. 8 The decorated

27 Make the altar of acacia-wood; it is to be square, five cubits long by five cubits broad, and its height is to be three cubits. 2 Make horns at the four corners and let them be of one piece with it; then overlay it with bronze. 3 Make for it pots to take away the fat and the ashes, with shovels, tossing-bowls, forks, and firepans, all of bronze. 4 Make a grating for it of bronze network, and fit bronze rings on the network, one at each of its four corners. 5 Put it below the ledge of the altar, so that the network comes half-way up the altar. 6 Make poles of acacia-wood for the altar and overlay them with bronze. 7 They are to be inserted in the rings at either side of the altar to carry it. 8 Leave the altar hollow inside its boards. As you were shown on the mountain, so must it be made.

9 Make the court of the Tabernacle. On the south side facing southwards, the court is to have hangings of finely woven linen a hundred cubits long, 10 with twenty posts and twenty bronze sockets; the hooks and bands on the posts will be of silver. 11 Similarly along the north side there will be hangings of a hundred cubits, with twenty posts and twenty bronze sockets; the hooks and bands on the posts will be of silver. 12 For the breadth of the court, on the west side, there are to be hangings fifty cubits long, with ten posts and ten sockets. 13 On the east side, towards the sunrise, which will be fifty cubits, 14 hangings will extend fifteen cubits from one corner, with three posts and three sockets, 15 and hangings will extend fifteen cubits from the other corner, with three posts and three sockets. 16 At the gateway of the court, there will be a screen twenty cubits long of finely woven linen embroidered with violet, purple, and scarlet, with four posts and four sockets. 17 The posts all round the court are to have bands of silver, with silver hooks and bronze sockets. 18 The length of the court is to be a hundred cubits, and the breadth fifty, and the height five cubits, with hangings of finely woven linen and with bronze sockets throughout. 19 All the equipment needed for serving the Tabernacle, all its pegs and those of the court, will be of bronze.

20 You are to order the Israelites to bring you pure oil of pounded olives ready for the regular mounting of the lamp. 21 In the Tent of Meeting outside the curtain that conceals the Testimony, Aaron and his sons must keep the lamp in trim from dusk to dawn before the LORD. This is a rule binding on their descendants among the Israelites for all time.

28 Out of all the Israelites you are to summon to your presence your brother Aaron and his sons to serve as my priests: Aaron and his sons Nadab and Abihu, Eleazar and Ithamar. 2 For your brother Aaron make sacred vestments, to give him dignity and grandeur. 3 To all the craftsmen whom I have endowed with skill give instructions for making the vestments for the consecration of Aaron as my priest. 4 These are the vestments they are to make: a breastpiece, an ephod, a mantle, a chequered tunic, a turban, and a sash. For Aaron your brother and his sons to wear when they serve as my priests they are to make sacred vestments, 5 using gold, violet, purple, and scarlet yarn, and fine linen.

6 The ephod will be made of gold, and with violet, purple, and scarlet yarn, and with finely woven linen worked by a seamster. 7 It will have two shoulder-pieces joined back and front. 8 The waistband on it will be of the same work-

---

o Or *treaty*, or *testimony*; Heb *eduth*

27:18 **the breadth fifty:** *so Samar.; Heb. adds by fifty.*

170

27 "You shall make an altar of acacia wood, on a square, five cubits long and five cubits wide; it shall be three cubits high. 2 At the four corners there are to be horns, so made that they spring directly from the altar. You shall then plate it with bronze. 3 Make pots for removing the ashes, as well as shovels, basins, forks and fire pans, all of which shall be of bronze. 4 Make a grating of bronze network for it; this to have four bronze rings, one at each of its four corners. 5 Put it down around the altar, on the ground. This network is to be half as high as the altar. 6 You shall also make poles of acacia wood for the altar, and plate them with bronze. 7 These poles are to be put through the rings, so that they are on either side of the altar when it is carried. 8 Make the altar itself in the form of a hollow box, just as it was shown you on the mountain.

9 "You shall also make a court for the Dwelling. On the south side the court shall have hangings a hundred cubits long, woven of fine linen twined, 10 with twenty columns and twenty pedestals of bronze; the hooks and bands on the columns shall be of silver. 11 On the north side there shall be similar hangings, a hundred cubits long, with twenty columns and twenty pedestals of bronze; the hooks and bands on the columns shall be of silver. 12 On the west side, across the width of the court, there shall be hangings, fifty cubits long, with ten columns and ten pedestals. 13 The width of the court on the east side shall be fifty cubits. 14 On one side there shall be hangings to the extent of fifteen cubits, with three columns and three pedestals; 15 on the other side there shall be hangings to the extent of fifteen cubits, with three columns and three pedestals.

16 "At the entrance of the court there shall be a variegated curtain, twenty cubits long, woven of violet, purple and scarlet yarn and of fine linen twined. It shall have four columns and four pedestals.

17 "All the columns around the court shall have bands and hooks of silver, and pedestals of bronze. 18 The enclosure of the court is to be one hundred cubits long, fifty cubits wide, and five cubits high. Fine linen twined must be used, and the pedestals must be of bronze. 19 All the fittings of the Dwelling, whatever be their use, as well as all its tent pegs and all the tent pegs of the court, must be of bronze.

20 "You shall order the Israelites to bring you clear oil of crushed olives, to be used for the light, so that you may keep lamps burning regularly. 21 From evening to morning Aaron and his sons shall maintain them before the LORD in the meeting tent, outside the veil which hangs in front of the commandments. This shall be a perpetual ordinance for the Israelites throughout their generations.

28 "From among the Israelites have your brother Aaron, together with his sons Nadab, Abihu, Eleazar and Ithamar, brought to you, that they may be my priests. 2 For the glorious adornment of your brother Aaron you shall have sacred vestments made. 3 Therefore, to the various expert workmen whom I have endowed with skill, you shall give instructions to make such vestments for Aaron as will set him apart for his sacred service as my priest. 4 These are the vestments they shall make: a breastpiece, an ephod, a robe, a brocaded tunic, a miter and a sash. In making these sacred vestments which your brother Aaron and his sons are to wear in serving as my priests, 5 they shall use gold, violet, purple and scarlet yarn and fine linen.

6 "The ephod they shall make of gold thread and of violet, purple and scarlet yarn, embroidered on cloth of fine linen twined. 7 It shall have a pair of shoulder straps joined to its two upper ends. 8 The embroidered belt on the ephod shall

27 'You will make the altar of acacia wood, five cubits long and five cubits wide; the altar will be square and three cubits high. 2 At its four corners you will make horns, the horns must be of a piece with it, and you will overlay it with bronze. 3 And for it you will make pans for taking away the fatty ashes, and shovels, sprinkling basins, hooks and fire pans; you will make all the altar accessories of bronze. 4 You will also make a grating for it of bronze network, and on the four corners of the grating you will make four bronze rings. 5 You will put it below the ledge of the altar, underneath, so that it comes halfway up the altar. 6 You will make shafts for the altar, shafts of acacia wood and overlay them with bronze. 7 The shafts will be passed through the rings in such a way that the shafts are on either side of the altar, for carrying it. 8 You will make the altar hollow, out of boards; you will make it as you were shown on the mountain.

9 'Then you will make the court of the Dwelling. On the south side, the curtaining of the court must be of finely woven linen, one hundred cubits long (for the first side), 10 its twenty poles and their twenty sockets being of bronze, and the poles' hooks and rods of silver. 11 So too for the north side, there must be a hundred cubits of curtaining, its twenty poles and their twenty sockets being of bronze, and the poles' hooks and rods of silver. 12 Across the width of the court, on the west side, there must be fifty cubits of curtaining, with its ten poles and their ten sockets. 13 The width of the court on the east side, facing the sunrise, must be fifty cubits, 14 with fifteen cubits of curtaining on one side of the entrance, with its three poles and their three sockets, 15 and on the other side of the entrance, fifteen cubits of curtaining, with its three poles and their three sockets; 16 and for the gateway to the court there must be a twenty-cubit screen of finely woven linen embroidered with violet-purple, red-purple and crimson, with its four poles and their four sockets. 17 All the poles round the court must be connected by silver rods; their hooks must be of silver and their sockets of bronze. 18 The length of the court must be one hundred cubits, its width fifty cubits and its height five cubits. All the curtaining must be made of finely woven linen, and their sockets of bronze. 19 All the accessories for general use in the Dwelling, all its pegs and all the pegs of the court, must be of bronze.

20 'You will order the Israelites to bring you pure pounded olive oil for the light, and to keep a lamp burning all the time. 21 Aaron and his sons will tend it in the Tent of Meeting, outside the curtain hanging in front of the Testimony, from dusk to dawn, before Yahweh. This is a perpetual decree for all generations of Israelites.'

28 'From among the Israelites, summon your brother Aaron and his sons to be priests in my service: Aaron and Aaron's sons Nadab, Abihu, Eleazar and Ithamar. 2 For your brother Aaron you will make sacred vestments to give dignity and magnificence. 3 You will instruct all the skilled men, whom I have endowed with skill, to make Aaron's vestments for his consecration to my priesthood. 4 These are the vestments which they must make: a pectoral, an *ephod*,[n] a robe, an embroidered tunic, a turban and a belt. They must make sacred vestments for your brother Aaron and his sons, for them to be priests in my service. 5 They will use gold and violet material, red-purple and crimson, and finely woven linen.

6 'They will make the *ephod* of finely woven linen embroidered with gold, violet-purple, red-purple and crimson. 7 It will have two shoulder-straps joined to it; it will be joined to them by its two edges. 8 The waistband on the

n **28** This can mean **1** a sort of pouch, **2** a priest's loin-cloth, **3** the high priest's breastplate.

NEW REVISED STANDARD VERSION	REVISED ENGLISH BIBLE

band on it shall be of the same workmanship and materials, of gold, of blue, purple, and crimson yarns, and of fine twisted linen. 9 You shall take two onyx stones, and engrave on them the names of the sons of Israel, 10 six of their names on the one stone, and the names of the remaining six on the other stone, in the order of their birth. 11 As a gem-cutter engraves signets, so you shall engrave the two stones with the names of the sons of Israel; you shall mount them in settings of gold filigree. 12 You shall set the two stones on the shoulder-pieces of the ephod, as stones of remembrance for the sons of Israel; and Aaron shall bear their names before the LORD on his two shoulders for remembrance. 13 You shall make settings of gold filigree, 14 and two chains of pure gold, twisted like cords; and you shall attach the corded chains to the settings.

15 You shall make a breastpiece of judgment, in skilled work; you shall make it in the style of the ephod; of gold, of blue and purple and crimson yarns, and of fine twisted linen you shall make it. 16 It shall be square and doubled, a span in length and a span in width. 17 You shall set in it four rows of stones. A row of carnelian,*p* chrysolite, and emerald shall be the first row; 18 and the second row a turquoise, a sapphire*q* and a moonstone; 19 and the third row a jacinth, an agate, and an amethyst; 20 and the fourth row a beryl, an onyx, and a jasper; they shall be set in gold filigree. 21 There shall be twelve stones with names corresponding to the names of the sons of Israel; they shall be like signets, each engraved with its name, for the twelve tribes. 22 You shall make for the breastpiece chains of pure gold, twisted like cords; 23 and you shall make for the breastpiece two rings of gold, and put the two rings on the two edges of the breastpiece. 24 You shall put the two cords of gold in the two rings at the edges of the breastpiece; 25 the two ends of the two cords you shall attach to the two settings, and so attach it in front to the shoulder-pieces of the ephod. 26 You shall make two rings of gold, and put them at the two ends of the breastpiece, on its inside edge next to the ephod. 27 You shall make two rings of gold, and attach them in front to the lower part of the two shoulder-pieces of the ephod, at its joining above the decorated band of the ephod. 28 The breastpiece shall be bound by its rings to the rings of the ephod with a blue cord, so that it may lie on the decorated band of the ephod, and so that the breastpiece shall not come loose from the ephod. 29 So Aaron shall bear the names of the sons of Israel in the breastpiece of judgment on his heart when he goes into the holy place, for a continual remembrance before the LORD. 30 In the breastpiece of judgment you shall put the Urim and the Thummim, and they shall be on Aaron's heart when he goes in before the LORD; thus Aaron shall bear the judgment of the Israelites on his heart before the LORD continually.

31 You shall make the robe of the ephod all of blue. 32 It shall have an opening for the head in the middle of it, with a woven binding around the opening, like the opening in a coat of mail,*r* so that it may not be torn. 33 On its lower hem you shall make pomegranates of blue, purple, and crimson yarns, all around the lower hem, with bells of gold between them all around — 34 a golden bell and a pomegranate alternating all around the lower hem of the robe. 35 Aaron shall wear it when he ministers, and its sound shall be heard when he goes into the holy place before the LORD, and when he comes out, so that he may not die.

36 You shall make a rosette of pure gold, and engrave on it, like the engraving of a signet, "Holy to the LORD." 37 You shall fasten it on the turban with a blue cord; it shall be on the front of the turban. 38 It shall be on Aaron's

manship and material as the fabric of the ephod, and will be of gold, with violet, purple, and scarlet yarn, and finely woven linen. 9 You are to take two cornelians and engrave on them the names of the sons of Israel: 10 six of their names on one stone, and the six other names on the second, all in order of seniority. 11 With the skill of a craftsman, a seal-cutter, you are to engrave the two stones with the names of the sons of Israel; set them in gold rosettes, 12 and fasten them on the shoulder-pieces of the ephod, as reminders of the sons of Israel. Aaron will bear their names on his shoulders as a reminder before the LORD. 13 Make gold rosettes 14 and two chains of pure gold worked into the form of cords, which you will fix on the rosettes.

15 Make the breastpiece of judgement; it is to be made in gold, like the ephod, by a seamster, with violet, purple, and scarlet yarn, and finely woven linen. 16 It will form a square when folded double, a span long and a span wide. 17 Arrange on it four rows of precious stones: the first row, sardin, chrysolite, and green feldspar; 18 the second row, purple garnet, sapphire, and jade; 19 the third row, turquoise, agate, and jasper; 20 the fourth row, topaz, cornelian, and green jasper, all set in gold rosettes. 21 The stones will correspond to the twelve sons of Israel name by name, each stone bearing the name of one of the twelve tribes engraved as on a seal.

22 Make for the breastpiece chains of pure gold worked into a cord. 23 Make two gold rings, and fix them on the two upper corners of the breastpiece. 24 Fasten the two gold cords to the two rings at those corners of the breastpiece, 25 and the other ends of the ropes to the two rosettes, thus binding the breastpiece to the shoulder-pieces on the front of the ephod. 26 Make two gold rings and put them at the two lower corners of the breastpiece on the inner side next to the ephod. 27 Make two gold rings and fix them on the two shoulder-pieces of the ephod, low down in front, along its seam above the waistband of the ephod. 28 Then the breastpiece is to be bound by its rings to the rings of the ephod with violet braid, just above the waistband of the ephod, so that the breastpiece does not become loosened from the ephod. 29 So, when Aaron enters the Holy Place, he will bear over his heart in the breastpiece of judgement the names of the sons of Israel, as a constant reminder before the LORD.

30 Finally, put the Urim and the Thummim into the breastpiece of judgement, and they will be over Aaron's heart when he enters the presence of the LORD. So Aaron will bear these symbols of judgement upon the sons of Israel over his heart constantly before the LORD.

31 Make the mantle of the ephod a single piece of violet stuff. 32 Make an opening for the head in the middle of it. All round the opening there will be a hem of woven work, with an oversewn edge, to prevent it tearing. 33 On its hem make pomegranates of violet, purple, and scarlet stuff, with golden bells between them, 34 a golden bell and a pomegranate alternately the whole way round the hem of the mantle. 35 Aaron is to wear it when he ministers, and the sound of it will be heard when he enters the Holy Place before the LORD and when he comes out; and so he will not die.

36 Make a medallion of pure gold and engrave on it as on a seal: 'Holy to the LORD'. 37 Fasten it on a violet braid and set it on the front of the turban. 38 It is to be on Aaron's

---

p The identity of several of these stones is uncertain   *q* Or *lapis lazuli*   *r* Meaning of Heb uncertain

28:32 **with . . . edge:** *lit.* like the opening of a womb.   28:36 **as . . . LORD:** or 'YHWH' as on a seal in sacred characters.

extend out from it and, like it, be made of gold thread, of violet, purple and scarlet yarn, and of fine linen twined.

9 "Get two onyx stones and engrave on them the names of the sons of Israel: 10 six of their names on one stone, and the other six on the other stone, in the order of their birth. 11 As a gem-cutter engraves a seal, so shall you have the two stones engraved with the names of the sons of Israel and then mounted in gold filigree work. 12 Set these two stones on the shoulder straps of the ephod as memorial stones of the sons of Israel. Thus Aaron shall bear their names on his shoulders as a reminder before the LORD. 13 Make filigree rosettes of gold, 14 as well as two chains of pure gold, twisted like cords, and fasten the cordlike chains to the filigree rosettes.

15 "The breastpiece of decision you shall also have made, embroidered like the ephod with gold thread and violet, purple and scarlet yarn on cloth of fine linen twined. 16 It is to be square when folded double, a span high and a span wide. 17 On it you shall mount four rows of precious stones: in the first row, a carnelian, a topaz and an emerald; 18 in the second row, a garnet, a sapphire and a beryl; 19 in the third row, a jacinth, an agate and an amethyst; 20 in the fourth row, a chrysolite, an onyx and a jasper. These stones are to be mounted in gold filigree work, 21 twelve of them to match the names of the sons of Israel, each stone engraved like a seal with the name of one of the twelve tribes.

22 "When the chains of pure gold, twisted like cords, have been made for the breastpiece, 23 you shall then make two rings of gold for it and fasten them to the two upper ends of the breastpiece. 24 The gold cords are then to be fastened to the two rings at the upper ends of the breastpiece, 25 the other two ends of the cords being fastened in front to the two filigree rosettes which are attached to the shoulder straps of the ephod. 26 Make two other rings of gold and put them on the two lower ends of the breastpiece, on its edge that faces the ephod. 27 Then make two more rings of gold and fasten them to the bottom of the shoulder straps next to where they join the ephod in front, just above its embroidered belt. 28 Violet ribbons shall bind the rings of the breastpiece to the rings of the ephod, so that the breastpiece will stay right above the embroidered belt of the ephod and not swing loose from it.

29 "Whenever Aaron enters the sanctuary, he will thus bear the names of the sons of Israel on the breastpiece of decision over his heart as a constant reminder before the LORD. 30 In this breastpiece of decision you shall put the Urim and Thummim, that they may be over Aaron's heart whenever he enters the presence of the LORD. Thus he shall always bear the decisions for the Israelites over his heart in the LORD's presence.

31 "The robe of the ephod you shall make entirely of violet material. 32 It shall have an opening for the head in the center, and around this opening there shall be a selvage, woven as at the opening of a shirt, to keep it from being torn. 33 All around the hem at the bottom you shall make pomegranates, woven of violet, purple and scarlet yarn and fine linen twined, with gold bells between them; 34 first a gold bell, then a pomegranate, and thus alternating all around the hem of the robe. 35 Aaron shall wear it when ministering, that its tinkling may be heard as he enters and leaves the LORD's presence in the sanctuary; else he will die.

36 "You shall also make a plate of pure gold and engrave on it, as on a seal engraving, "Sacred to the LORD." 37 This plate is to be tied over the miter with a violet ribbon in such a way that it rests on the front of the miter, 38 over Aaron's

ephod to hold it in position must be of the same workmanship and be of a piece with it: of gold, violet-purple, red-purple and crimson materials and finely woven linen. 9 You will then take two cornelians and engrave them with the names of the sons of Israel, 10 six of their names on one stone, the remaining six names on the other, in the order of their birth. 11 By the stone-carver's art — seal engraving — you will engrave the two stones with the names of the sons of Israel. You will have them mounted in gold settings 12 and will put the two stones on the shoulder-straps of the ephod, to commemorate the sons of Israel. In this way Aaron will bear their names on his two shoulders, before Yahweh, as a reminder. 13 You will also make golden rosettes, 14 and two chains of pure gold twisted like cord, and will attach the cord-like chains to the rosettes.

15 'You will make the breastplate of judgement of the same embroidered work as the ephod; you will make it of gold, violet-purple, red-purple and crimson materials and finely woven linen. 16 It must be square and doubled over, a span in length and a span in width. 17 In it you will set four rows of stones: a sard, topaz and emerald for the first row; 18 for the second row, a garnet, sapphire and diamond; 19 for the third row, a hyacinth, a ruby and an amethyst; 20 and for the fourth row, a beryl, a cornelian and a jasper. These must be mounted in gold settings. 21 The stones will correspond to the names of the sons of Israel, twelve like their names, engraved like seals, each with the name of one of the twelve tribes. 22 For the breastplate you will make chains of pure gold twisted like cords, 23 and on the breastplate you will make two gold rings, putting the two rings on the two outside edges of the breastplate 24 and fastening the two gold cords to the two rings on the outside edges of the breastplate. 25 The other two ends of the cords you will fasten to the two rosettes, putting these on the shoulder-straps of the ephod, on the front. 26 You will also make two gold rings and put them on the two edges of the breastplate, on the inner side, against the ephod; 27 and you will make two gold rings and put them low down on the front of the two shoulder-pieces of the ephod, close to the join, above the waistband of the ephod. 28 The breastplate will be secured by a violet-purple cord passed through its rings and those of the ephod, so that the breastplate will sit above the waistband and not come apart from the ephod. 29 Thus Aaron will bear the names of the sons of Israel on the breastplate of judgement, on his heart, when he enters the sanctuary, as a reminder, before Yahweh, always. 30 To the breastplate of judgement you will add the urim and the thummim, and these will be on Aaron's heart when he goes into Yahweh's presence, and Aaron will bear the Israelites' judgement on his heart, in Yahweh's presence, always.

31 'You will make the robe of the ephod entirely of violet-purple. 32 In the centre it will have an opening for the head, the opening to have round it a border woven like the neck of a coat of mail, so that it will not get torn. 33 On its lower hem, you will make pomegranates of violet-purple, red-purple and crimson, and finely woven linen all round the hem, with golden bells between them all round: 34 a golden bell and then a pomegranate, alternately, all round the lower hem of the robe. 35 Aaron must wear it when he officiates, and the tinkling will be heard when he goes into the sanctuary into Yahweh's presence, or leaves it, and so he will not incur death.

36 'You will make a flower of pure gold and on it, as you would engrave a seal, you will engrave, "Consecrated to Yahweh". 37 You will put it on a violet-purple cord; it will go on the turban; the front of the turban is the place where it must go. 38 This will go on Aaron's brow, and Aaron will

| NEW REVISED STANDARD VERSION | REVISED ENGLISH BIBLE |

forehead, and Aaron shall take on himself any guilt incurred in the holy offering that the Israelites consecrate as their sacred donations; it shall always be on his forehead, in order that they may find favor before the LORD.

39 You shall make the checkered tunic of fine linen, and you shall make a turban of fine linen, and you shall make a sash embroidered with needlework.

40 For Aaron's sons you shall make tunics and sashes and headdresses; you shall make them for their glorious adornment. 41 You shall put them on your brother Aaron, and on his sons with him, and shall anoint them and ordain them and consecrate them, so that they may serve me as priests. 42 You shall make for them linen undergarments to cover their naked flesh; they shall reach from the hips to the thighs; 43 Aaron and his sons shall wear them when they go into the tent of meeting, or when they come near the altar to minister in the holy place; or they will bring guilt on themselves and die. This shall be a perpetual ordinance for him and for his descendants after him.

29 Now this is what you shall do to them to consecrate them, so that they may serve me as priests. Take one young bull and two rams without blemish, 2 and unleavened bread, unleavened cakes mixed with oil, and unleavened wafers spread with oil. You shall make them of choice wheat flour. 3 You shall put them in one basket and bring them in the basket, and bring the bull and the two rams. 4 You shall bring Aaron and his sons to the entrance of the tent of meeting, and wash them with water. 5 Then you shall take the vestments, and put on Aaron the tunic and the robe of the ephod, and the ephod, and the breastpiece, and gird him with the decorated band of the ephod; 6 and you shall set the turban on his head, and put the holy diadem on the turban. 7 You shall take the anointing oil, and pour it on his head and anoint him. 8 Then you shall bring his sons, and put tunics on them, 9 and you shall gird them with sashes*s* and tie the headdresses on them; and the priesthood shall be theirs by a perpetual ordinance. You shall then ordain Aaron and his sons.

10 You shall bring the bull in front of the tent of meeting. Aaron and his sons shall lay their hands on the head of the bull, 11 and you shall slaughter the bull before the LORD, at the entrance of the tent of meeting, 12 and shall take some of the blood of the bull and put it on the horns of the altar with your finger, and all the rest of the blood you shall pour out at the base of the altar. 13 You shall take all the fat that covers the entrails, and the appendage of the liver, and the two kidneys with the fat that is on them, and turn them into smoke on the altar. 14 But the flesh of the bull, and its skin, and its dung, you shall burn with fire outside the camp; it is a sin offering.

15 Then you shall take one of the rams, and Aaron and his sons shall lay their hands on the head of the ram, 16 and you shall slaughter the ram, and shall take its blood and dash it against all sides of the altar. 17 Then you shall cut the ram into its parts, and wash its entrails and its legs, and put them with its parts and its head, 18 and turn the whole ram into smoke on the altar; it is a burnt offering to the LORD; it is a pleasing odor, an offering by fire to the LORD.

19 You shall take the other ram; and Aaron and his sons shall lay their hands on the head of the ram, 20 and you shall slaughter the ram, and take some of its blood and put it on the lobe of Aaron's right ear and on the lobes of the right ears of his sons, and on the thumbs of their right hands, and on the big toes of their right feet, and dash the rest of the blood against all sides of the altar. 21 Then you shall take

forehead; he has to bear the blame for defects in the rites with which the Israelites offer their sacred gifts, and the medallion will be always on his forehead so that they may be acceptable to the LORD.

39 Make the chequered tunic and the turban of fine linen, but the sash of embroidered work. 40 For Aaron's sons make tunics and sashes; and make tall headdresses to give them dignity and grandeur. 41 With these invest your brother Aaron and his sons, anoint them, install them, and consecrate them; so they will serve me as priests. 42 Make for them linen shorts reaching to the thighs to cover their private parts; 43 and Aaron and his sons must wear them when they enter the Tent of Meeting or approach the altar to minister in the sanctuary. Thus they will not incur guilt and die. This is a statute binding on him and his descendants for all time.

29 In their consecration to be my priests this is the rite to be observed. Take a young bull and two rams without blemish. 2 Take unleavened bread, unleavened loaves mixed with oil, and unleavened wafers smeared with oil, all made of wheaten flour; 3 put them in a basket and bring them in it. Bring also the bull and the two rams. 4 When you have brought Aaron and his sons to the entrance of the Tent of Meeting, wash them with water. 5 Take the vestments and dress Aaron in the tunic, the mantle of the ephod, the ephod itself, and the breastpiece, and fasten the ephod to him with its waistband. 6 Set the turban on his head, and attach the symbol of holy dedication to the turban. 7 Take the anointing oil, pour it on his head, and anoint him. 8 Then bring his sons forward, dress them in tunics, 9 gird them with the sashes, and tie their tall headdresses on them. They will hold the priesthood by a statute binding for all time.

Next install Aaron and his sons. 10 Bring the bull to the front of the Tent of Meeting, where they must lay their hands on its head. 11 Slaughter the bull before the LORD at the entrance to the Tent. 12 Take some of its blood, and smear it with your finger on the horns of the altar. Pour the rest of it at the base of the altar. 13 Then take all the fat covering the entrails, the long lobe of the liver, and the two kidneys with the fat upon them, and burn them on the altar; 14 but the flesh of the bull, and its skin and offal, you must destroy by fire outside the camp. It is a purification-offering.

15 Take one of the rams and, after Aaron and his sons have laid their hands on its head, 16 slaughter it; take its blood, and fling it against the sides of the altar. 17 Cut up the ram; wash its entrails and its shins, lay them with the pieces and the head, 18 and burn the whole ram on the altar: it is a whole-offering to the LORD; it is a soothing odour, a food-offering to the LORD.

19 Take the second ram and, after Aaron and his sons have laid their hands on its head, 20 slaughter it; take some of its blood, and put it on the lobes of the right ears of Aaron and his sons, and on their right thumbs and the big toes of their right feet. Fling the rest of the blood against the sides of the altar. 21 Take some of the blood which is on the altar

28:41 **install them:** *lit.* fill their hands.   29:9 **gird them:** *so Gk; Heb. adds* Aaron and his sons.   29:12 **the rest:** *so Gk; Heb. omits.*

s Gk: Heb *sashes, Aaron and his sons*

forehead. Since Aaron bears whatever guilt the Israelites may incur in consecrating any of their sacred gifts, this plate must always be over his forehead, so that they may find favor with the LORD. 39 "The tunic of fine linen shall be brocaded. The miter shall be made of fine linen. The sash shall be of variegated work.

40 "Likewise, for the glorious adornment of Aaron's sons you shall have tunics and sashes and turbans made. 41 With these you shall clothe your brother Aaron and his sons. Anoint and ordain them, consecrating them as my priests. 42 You must also make linen drawers for them, to cover their naked flesh from their loins to their thighs. 43 Aaron and his sons shall wear them whenever they go into the meeting tent or approach the altar to minister in the sanctuary, lest they incur guilt and die. This shall be a perpetual ordinance for him and for his descendants.

29

"This is the rite you shall perform in consecrating them as my priests. Procure a young bull and two unblemished rams. 2 With fine wheat flour make unleavened cakes mixed with oil, and unleavened wafers spread with oil, 3 and put them in a basket. Take the basket of them along with the bullock and the two rams. 4 Aaron and his sons you shall also bring to the entrance of the meeting tent, and there wash them with water. 5 Take the vestments and clothe Aaron with the tunic, the robe of the ephod, the ephod itself, and the breastpiece, fastening the embroidered belt of the ephod around him. 6 Put the miter on his head, the sacred diadem on the miter. 7 Then take the anointing oil and anoint him with it, pouring it on his head. 8 Bring forward his sons also and clothe them with the tunics, 9 gird them with the sashes, and tie the turbans on them. Thus shall the priesthood be theirs by perpetual law, and thus shall you ordain Aaron and his sons.

10 "Now bring forward the bullock in front of the meeting tent. There Aaron and his sons shall lay their hands on its head. 11 Then slaughter the bullock before the LORD, at the entrance of the meeting tent. 12 Take some of its blood and with your finger put it on the horns of the altar. All the rest of the blood you shall pour out at the base of the altar. 13 All the fat that covers its inner organs, as well as the lobe of its liver and its two kidneys, together with the fat that is on them, you shall take and burn on the altar. 14 But the flesh and hide and offal of the bullock you must burn up outside the camp, since this is a sin offering.

15 "Then take one of the rams, and after Aaron and his sons have laid their hands on its head, 16 slaughter it. The blood you shall take and splash on all the sides of the altar. 17 Cut the ram into pieces; its inner organs and shanks you shall first wash, and then put them with the pieces and with the head. 18 The entire ram shall then be burned on the altar, since it is a holocaust, a sweet-smelling oblation to the LORD.

19 "After this take the other ram, and when Aaron and his sons have laid their hands on its head, 20 slaughter it. Some of its blood you shall take and put on the tip of Aaron's right ear and on the tips of his sons' right ears and on the thumbs of their right hands and the great toes of their right feet. Splash the rest of the blood on all the sides of the altar.

thus take on himself the short-comings in the holy things consecrated by the Israelites, in all their holy offerings. It will be on his brow permanently, to make them acceptable to Yahweh. 39 The tunic you will weave of fine linen, and make a turban of fine linen, and an embroidered waistband.

40 'For the sons of Aaron you will make tunics and waistbands. You will also make them head-dresses to give dignity and magnificence. 41 You will dress your brother Aaron and his sons in these; you will then anoint them, invest them and consecrate them to serve me in the priesthood. 42 You will also make them linen breeches reaching from waist to thigh, to cover their bare flesh. 43 Aaron and his sons will wear these when they go into the Tent of Meeting and when they approach the altar to serve in the sanctuary, as a precaution against incurring mortal guilt. This is a perpetual decree for Aaron and for his descendants after him.'

29

'This is what you will do to them, to consecrate them to my priesthood. Take one young bull and two rams without blemish; 2 also unleavened bread, unleavened cakes mixed with oil, and unleavened wafers spread with oil, made from fine wheat flour, 3 and put these into a basket and present them in the basket, at the same time as the bull and the two rams.

4 'You will bring Aaron and his sons to the entrance of the Tent of Meeting and bathe them. 5 You will then take the vestments and dress Aaron in the tunic, the robe of the *ephod*, the *ephod*, and the breastplate, and tie the waistband of the *ephod* round his waist. 6 Then you will place the turban on his head, and on it put the symbol of holy consecration. 7 You will then take the anointing oil and pour it on his head and so anoint him.

8 'Next, you will bring his sons and dress them in tunics, 9 and fasten waistbands round their waists and put the head-dresses on their heads. By perpetual decree the priesthood will be theirs. Then you will invest Aaron and his sons.

10 'You will bring the bull in front of the Tent of Meeting, and Aaron and his sons will lay their hands on the bull's head. 11 You will then slaughter the bull before Yahweh at the entrance to the Tent of Meeting. 12 You will then take some of the bull's blood and with your finger put it on the horns of the altar. Next, pour out the rest of the blood at the foot of the altar. 13 And then take all the fat covering the entrails, the fatty mass over the liver, the two kidneys with their covering fat, and burn them on the altar. 14 But the young bull's flesh, its skin and its offal, you will burn outside the camp, for this is a sin offering.

15 'Next, you will take one of the rams, and Aaron and his sons will lay their hands on the ram's head. 16 You will then slaughter the ram, take its blood and pour it against the altar, all round. 17 Next, cut the ram into quarters, wash the entrails and legs and put them on the quarters and head. 18 Then burn the whole ram on the altar. This will be a burnt offering for Yahweh, a pleasing smell, a food offering burnt for Yahweh.

19 'Next, you will take the other ram, and Aaron and his sons will lay their hands on the ram's head. 20 You will then slaughter the ram, take some of its blood and put it on the lobe of Aaron's right ear, on the lobes of his sons' right ears, the thumbs of their right hands, and the big toes of their right feet, and pour the rest of the blood against the altar, all round. 21 You will then take some of the blood on

some of the blood that is on the altar, and some of the anointing oil, and sprinkle it on Aaron and his vestments and on his sons and his sons' vestments with him; then he and his vestments shall be holy, as well as his sons and his sons' vestments.

22 You shall also take the fat of the ram, the fat tail, the fat that covers the entrails, the appendage of the liver, the two kidneys with the fat that is on them, and the right thigh (for it is a ram of ordination), 23 and one loaf of bread, one cake of bread made with oil, and one wafer, out of the basket of unleavened bread that is before the LORD; 24 and you shall place all these on the palms of Aaron and on the palms of his sons, and raise them as an elevation offering before the LORD. 25 Then you shall take them from their hands, and turn them into smoke on the altar on top of the burnt offering of pleasing odor before the LORD; it is an offering by fire to the LORD.

26 You shall take the breast of the ram of Aaron's ordination and raise it as an elevation offering before the LORD; and it shall be your portion. 27 You shall consecrate the breast that was raised as an elevation offering and the thigh that was raised as an elevation offering from the ram of ordination, from that which belonged to Aaron and his sons. 28 These things shall be a perpetual ordinance for Aaron and his sons from the Israelites, for this is an offering; and it shall be an offering by the Israelites from their sacrifice of offerings of well-being, their offering to the LORD.

29 The sacred vestments of Aaron shall be passed on to his sons after him; they shall be anointed in them and ordained in them. 30 The son who is priest in his place shall wear them seven days, when he comes into the tent of meeting to minister in the holy place.

31 You shall take the ram of ordination, and boil its flesh in a holy place; 32 and Aaron and his sons shall eat the flesh of the ram and the bread that is in the basket, at the entrance of the tent of meeting. 33 They themselves shall eat the food by which atonement is made, to ordain and consecrate them, but no one else shall eat of them, because they are holy. 34 If any of the flesh for the ordination, or of the bread, remains until the morning, then you shall burn the remainder with fire; it shall not be eaten, because it is holy.

35 Thus you shall do to Aaron and to his sons, just as I have commanded you; through seven days you shall ordain them. 36 Also every day you shall offer a bull as a sin offering for atonement. Also you shall offer a sin offering for the altar, when you make atonement for it, and shall anoint it, to consecrate it. 37 Seven days you shall make atonement for the altar, and consecrate it, and the altar shall be most holy; whatever touches the altar shall become holy.

38 Now this is what you shall offer on the altar: two lambs a year old regularly each day. 39 One lamb you shall offer in the morning, and the other lamb you shall offer in the evening; 40 and with the first lamb one-tenth of a measure of choice flour mixed with one-fourth of a hin of beaten oil, and one-fourth of a hin of wine for a drink offering. 41 And the other lamb you shall offer in the evening, and shall offer with it a grain offering and its drink offering, as in the morning, for a pleasing odor, an offering by fire to the LORD. 42 It shall be a regular burnt offering throughout your generations at the entrance of the tent of meeting before the LORD, where I will meet with you, to speak to you there. 43 I will meet with the Israelites there, and it shall be sanctified by my glory; 44 I will consecrate the tent of meeting and the altar; Aaron also and his sons I will consecrate, to serve me as priests. 45 I will dwell among the Israelites, and I will be their God. 46 And they shall know that I am the LORD their God, who brought them out of the land of Egypt that I might dwell among them; I am the LORD their God.

and some of the anointing oil, and sprinkle it on Aaron and his vestments, and on his sons and their vestments. So he, his sons, and the vestments will become sacred.

22 Take the fat from the ram, the fat-tail, the fat covering the entrails, the long lobe of the liver, the two kidneys with the fat upon them, and the right leg: for it is a ram of installation. 23 Take also one round loaf of bread, one cake cooked with oil, and one wafer from the basket of unleavened bread that is before the LORD. 24 Place all these on the hands of Aaron and of his sons and present them as a special gift before the LORD. 25 Then receive them back from their hands, and burn them on the altar with the whole-offering for a soothing odour to the LORD: it is a food-offering to the LORD.

26 Take the breast of Aaron's ram of installation and present it as a special gift before the LORD; it is to be your perquisite. 27 Hallow the breast of the special gift and the leg of the contribution, that which is presented and that which is set aside from the ram of installation, that which is for Aaron and that which is for his sons; 28 they are to belong to Aaron and his sons, by a statute binding for all time, as a gift from the Israelites, for it is a contribution set aside from their shared-offerings, their contribution to the LORD.

29 Aaron's sacred vestments must be kept for the anointing and installation of his sons after him. 30 The priest appointed in his stead from among his sons, the one who enters the Tent of Meeting to minister in the Holy Place, is to wear them for seven days.

31 Take the ram of installation and boil its flesh in a sacred place; 32 Aaron and his sons are to eat the ram's flesh and the bread left in the basket, at the entrance to the Tent of Meeting. 33 They are to eat the things with which expiation was made at their installation and their consecration. No lay person may eat them, for they are holy. 34 If any of the flesh of the installation, or any of the bread, is left over till morning, you must destroy it by fire; it is not to be eaten, for it is holy.

35 Do this with Aaron and his sons as I have commanded you, spending seven days over their installation.

36 Offer a bull each day, a purification-offering as expiation for sin; offer the purification-offering on the altar when you make expiation for it, and consecrate it by anointing. 37 For seven days you are to purify the altar and consecrate it; it will be most holy. Whoever touches the altar must be treated as holy.

38 This is what you have to offer on the altar: two yearling rams regularly every day. 39 Offer one ram at dawn, and the second between dusk and dark. 40 With the first lamb offer a tenth of an ephah of flour mixed with a quarter of a hin of pure oil of pounded olives, and a drink-offering of a quarter of a hin of wine. 41 Offer the second ram between dusk and dark, and with it the same grain-offering and drink-offering as at dawn, for a soothing odour: it is a food-offering to the LORD, 42 a regular whole-offering generation after generation for all time; you are to make the offering at the entrance of the Tent of Meeting before the LORD, where I meet you and speak to you. 43 I shall meet the Israelites there, and the place will be hallowed by my glory. 44 I shall consecrate the Tent of Meeting and the altar; and Aaron and his sons I shall consecrate to serve me as priests. 45 I shall dwell in the midst of the Israelites, I shall become their God, 46 and by my dwelling among them they will know that I am the LORD their God who brought them out of Egypt. I am the LORD their God.

29:30 **the one who enters:** or when he enters.   29:37 **Whoever:** or Whatever.

|

21 Then take some of the blood that is on the altar, together with some of the anointing oil, and sprinkle this on Aaron and his vestments, as well as on his sons and their vestments, that his sons and their vestments may be sacred.

22 "Now, from this ram you shall take its fat: its fatty tail, the fat that covers its inner organs, the lobe of its liver, its two kidneys with the fat that is on them, and its right thigh, since this is the ordination ram; 23 then, out of the basket of unleavened food that you have set before the LORD, you shall take one of the loaves of bread, one of the cakes made with oil, and one of the wafers. 24 All these things you shall put into the hands of Aaron and his sons, so that they may wave them as a wave offering before the LORD. 25 After you have received them back from their hands, you shall burn them on top of the holocaust on the altar as a sweet-smelling oblation to the LORD. 26 Finally, take the breast of Aaron's ordination ram and wave it as a wave offering before the LORD; this is to be your own portion.

27 "Thus shall you set aside the breast of whatever wave offering is waved, as well as the thigh of whatever raised offering is raised up, whether this be the ordination ram or anything else belonging to Aaron or to his sons. 28 Such things are due to Aaron and his sons from the Israelites by a perpetual ordinance as a contribution. From their peace offerings, too, the Israelites shall make a contribution, their contribution to the LORD.

29 "The sacred vestments of Aaron shall be passed down to his descendants, that in them they may be anointed and ordained. 30 The descendant who succeeds him as priest and who is to enter the meeting tent to minister in the sanctuary shall be clothed with them for seven days.

31 "You shall take the flesh of the ordination ram and boil it in a holy place. 32 At the entrance of the meeting tent Aaron and his sons shall eat the flesh of the ram and the bread that is in the basket. 33 They themselves are to eat of these things by which atonement was made at their ordination and consecration; but no layman may eat of them, since they are sacred. 34 If some of the flesh of the ordination sacrifice or some of the bread remains over on the next day, this remnant must be burned up; it is not to be eaten, since it is sacred. 35 Carry out all these orders in regard to Aaron and his sons just as I have given them to you.

"Seven days you shall spend in ordaining them, 36 sacrificing a bullock each day as a sin offering, to make atonement. Thus also shall you purge the altar in making atonement for it; you shall anoint it in order to consecrate it. 37 Seven days you shall spend in making atonement for the altar and in consecrating it. Then the altar will be most sacred, and whatever touches it will become sacred.

38 "Now, this is what you shall offer on the altar: two yearling lambs as the sacrifice established for each day; 39 one lamb in the morning and the other lamb at the evening twilight. 40 With the first lamb there shall be a tenth of an ephah of fine flour mixed with a fourth of a hin of oil of crushed olives and, as its libation, a fourth of a hin of wine. 41 The other lamb you shall offer at the evening twilight, with the same cereal offering and libation as in the morning. You shall offer this as a sweet-smelling oblation to the LORD. 42 Throughout your generations this established holocaust shall be offered before the LORD at the entrance of the meeting tent, where I will meet you and speak to you.

43 "There, at the altar, I will meet the Israelites; hence, it will be made sacred by my glory. 44 Thus I will consecrate the meeting tent and the altar, just as I also consecrate Aaron and his sons to be my priests. 45 I will dwell in the midst of the Israelites and will be their God. 46 They shall know that I, the LORD, am their God who brought them out of the land of Egypt, so that I, the LORD, their God, might dwell among them.

the altar and some of the anointing oil, and sprinkle it on Aaron and his vestments and on his sons and on his sons' vestments: so that he and his vestments will be consecrated and his sons too, and his sons' vestments.

22 'You will then take the fatty parts of the ram: the tail, the fat covering the entrails, the fatty mass over the liver, the two kidneys with their covering fat and also the right thigh — for this is a ram of investiture — 23 and a loaf of bread, a cake of bread made with oil, and a wafer, from the basket of unleavened bread before Yahweh, 24 and put it all on the palms of Aaron and his sons, and make the gesture of offering before Yahweh. 25 Then you will take them back and burn them on the altar, on top of the burnt offering, as a smell pleasing before Yahweh, a food offering burnt for Yahweh.

26 'You will then take the forequarters of the ram of Aaron's investiture and with it make the gesture of offering before Yahweh; this will be your portion. 27 You will consecrate the forequarters that have been thus offered, as also the thigh that is set aside — what has been offered and what has been set aside from the ram of investiture of Aaron and his sons. 28 This, by perpetual decree, will be the portion that Aaron and his sons will receive from the Israelites, since it is the portion set aside, the portion set aside for Yahweh by the Israelites from their communion sacrifices: a portion set aside for Yahweh.

29 'Aaron's sacred vestments must pass to his sons after him, and they will wear them for their anointing and investiture. 30 Whichever of the sons of Aaron succeeds him in the priesthood and enters the Tent of Meeting to serve in the sanctuary, will wear them for seven days.

31 'You will take the ram of investiture and cook its meat in a holy place. 32 Aaron and his sons will eat the meat of the ram and the bread which is in the basket, at the entrance to the Tent of Meeting. 33 They will eat what was used in making expiation for them at their investiture and consecration. No unauthorised person may eat these; they are holy things. 34 If any of the meat from the investiture sacrifice, or the bread, should be left till morning, you will burn what is left. It may not be eaten; it is a holy thing. 35 This is what you will do for Aaron and his sons, implementing all the orders I have given you. You will take seven days over their investiture.

36 'On each of the days you will also offer a young bull as a sacrifice for sin, in expiation. You will offer a sin sacrifice for the altar when you make expiation for it; then you will consecrate it by anointing it. 37 For seven days you will make expiation for the altar, then you will consecrate it; it will then be especially holy, and whatever touches the altar will become holy.

38 'This is what you must offer on the altar: two yearling male lambs each day in perpetuity. 39 The first lamb you will offer at dawn, and the second at twilight, 40 and with the first lamb, one-tenth of a measure of fine flour mixed with one-quarter of a hin of pounded olive oil and, for a libation, one-quarter of a hin of wine. 41 The second lamb you will offer at twilight, and do it with a similar cereal offering and libation as at dawn, as a pleasing smell, as an offering burnt for Yahweh, 42 a perpetual burnt offering for all your generations to come, at the entrance to the Tent of Meeting before Yahweh, where I shall meet you and speak to you.

43 'There I shall meet the Israelites in the place consecrated by my glory. 44 I shall consecrate the Tent of Meeting and the altar; I shall also consecrate Aaron and his sons, to be priests in my service. 45 And I shall live with the Israelites and be their God, 46 and they will know that I am Yahweh their God, who brought them out of Egypt to live among them: I, Yahweh their God.'

NEW REVISED STANDARD VERSION

REVISED ENGLISH BIBLE

30 You shall make an altar on which to offer incense; you shall make it of acacia wood. 2 It shall be one cubit long, and one cubit wide; it shall be square, and shall be two cubits high; its horns shall be of one piece with it. 3 You shall overlay it with pure gold, its top, and its sides all around and its horns; and you shall make for it a molding of gold all around. 4 And you shall make two golden rings for it; under its molding on two opposite sides of it you shall make them, and they shall hold the poles with which to carry it. 5 You shall make the poles of acacia wood, and overlay them with gold. 6 You shall place it in front of the curtain that is above the ark of the covenant,[t] in front of the mercy seat[u] that is over the covenant,[t] where I will meet with you. 7 Aaron shall offer fragrant incense on it; every morning when he dresses the lamps he shall offer it, 8 and when Aaron sets up the lamps in the evening, he shall offer it, a regular incense offering before the LORD throughout your generations. 9 You shall not offer unholy incense on it, or a burnt offering, or a grain offering; and you shall not pour a drink offering on it. 10 Once a year Aaron shall perform the rite of atonement on its horns. Throughout your generations he shall perform the atonement for it once a year with the blood of the atoning sin offering. It is most holy to the LORD.

11 The LORD spoke to Moses: 12 When you take a census of the Israelites to register them, at registration all of them shall give a ransom for their lives to the LORD, so that no plague may come upon them for being registered. 13 This is what each one who is registered shall give: half a shekel according to the shekel of the sanctuary (the shekel is twenty gerahs), half a shekel as an offering to the LORD. 14 Each one who is registered, from twenty years old and upward, shall give the LORD's offering. 15 The rich shall not give more, and the poor shall not give less, than the half shekel, when you bring this offering to the LORD to make atonement for your lives. 16 You shall take the atonement money from the Israelites and shall designate it for the service of the tent of meeting; before the LORD it will be a reminder to the Israelites of the ransom given for your lives.

17 The LORD spoke to Moses: 18 You shall make a bronze basin with a bronze stand for washing. You shall put it between the tent of meeting and the altar, and you shall put water in it; 19 with the water[v] Aaron and his sons shall wash their hands and their feet. 20 When they go into the tent of meeting, or when they come near the altar to minister, to make an offering by fire to the LORD, they shall wash with water, so that they may not die. 21 They shall wash their hands and their feet, so that they may not die: it shall be a perpetual ordinance for them, for him and for his descendants throughout their generations.

22 The LORD spoke to Moses: 23 Take the finest spices: of liquid myrrh five hundred shekels, and of sweet-smelling cinnamon half as much, that is, two hundred fifty, and two hundred fifty of aromatic cane, 24 and five hundred of cassia —measured by the sanctuary shekel—and a hin of olive oil; 25 and you shall make of these a sacred anointing oil blended as by the perfumer; it shall be a holy anointing oil. 26 With it you shall anoint the tent of meeting and the ark of the covenant,[t] 27 and the table and all its utensils, and the lampstand and its utensils, and the altar of incense, 28 and the altar of burnt offering with all its utensils, and the basin with its stand; 29 you shall consecrate them, so that they may be most holy; whatever touches them will become holy. 30 You shall anoint Aaron and his sons, and consecrate them, in order that they may serve me as priests. 31 You shall say to the Israelites, "This shall be my holy anointing oil throughout your generations. 32 It shall not be used in

30 Make an altar on which to burn incense; make it of acacia-wood. 2 It is to be square, a cubit long by a cubit broad, and stand two cubits high; its horns are to be of one piece with it. 3 Overlay it with pure gold, the top, all the sides, and the horns; and put round it a band of gold. 4 Make pairs of gold rings for it; put them under the gold band at the two corners on both sides to receive the poles by which it is to be carried. 5 The poles are to be of acacia-wood overlaid with gold. 6 Put the altar before the curtain which is in front of the Ark of the Testimony where I shall meet you. 7 On it Aaron must burn fragrant incense; every morning when he trims the lamps he is to burn the incense, 8 and when he tends the lamps between dusk and dark he is to burn the incense; so let there be a regular burning of incense before the LORD for all time. 9 You must not offer on it any unauthorized incense, nor any whole-offering or grain-offering; and you must not pour a drink-offering over it. 10 Once a year Aaron is to make expiation with blood on its horns; this must be done for all time with blood from the purification-offering of the yearly expiation for it. It is most holy to the LORD.

11 The LORD said to Moses: 12 When you take a census of the Israelites, each man is to give a ransom for his life to the LORD, to avert plague among them during the registration. 13 As each man crosses over to those already counted he must give half a shekel by the sacred standard at the rate of twenty gerahs to the shekel, as a contribution levied for the LORD. 14 Everyone aged twenty or more who has crossed over to those already counted will give a contribution for the LORD. 15 The rich man will give no more than the half-shekel, and the poor man no less, when you give the contribution for the LORD to make expiation for your lives. 16 The money received from the Israelites for expiation you are to apply to the service of the Tent of Meeting. The expiation for your lives is to be a reminder of the Israelites before the LORD.

17 The LORD said to Moses: 18 Make a bronze basin for ablution with its stand of bronze; place it between the Tent of Meeting and the altar, and fill it with water 19 with which Aaron and his sons are to wash their hands and feet. 20 When they enter the Tent of Meeting they must wash with water, lest they die. Likewise when they approach the altar to minister, to burn a food-offering to the LORD, 21 they must wash their hands and feet, lest they die. It is to be a statute for all time binding on him and his descendants in every generation.

22 The LORD said to Moses: 23 Take spices as follows: five hundred shekels of sticks of myrrh, half that amount, that is two hundred and fifty shekels, of fragrant cinnamon, two hundred and fifty shekels of aromatic cane, 24 five hundred shekels of cassia by the sacred standard, and a hin of olive oil. 25 From these prepare sacred anointing oil, a perfume compounded by the perfumer's art. This will be the sacred anointing oil. 26 Anoint with it the Tent of Meeting and the Ark of the Testimony, 27 the table and all its vessels, the lampstand and its fittings, the altar of incense, 28 the altar of whole-offering and all its vessels, the basin and its stand. 29 Consecrate them, and they will be most holy; whoever touches them will be treated as holy. 30 Anoint Aaron and his sons, and consecrate them to be my priests. 31 Speak to the Israelites and say: This will be the holy anointing oil for my service in every generation. 32 It must not be used for

---

30:6 **Put . . . Testimony:** so Samar.; Heb. adds before the cover over the Testimony.   30:10 **expiation:** or atonement.   30:12 **to the LORD:** so Gk; Heb. adds because of the registration.
30:29 **whoever:** or whatever.

[t] Or treaty, or testimony; Heb eduth   [u] Or the cover   [v] Heb it

30 "For burning incense you shall make an altar of acacia wood, 2 with a square surface, a cubit long, a cubit wide, and two cubits high, with horns that spring directly from it. 3 Its grate on top, its walls on all four sides, and its horns you shall plate with pure gold. Put a gold molding around it. 4 Underneath the molding you shall put gold rings, two on one side and two on the opposite side, as holders for the poles used in carrying it. 5 Make the poles, too, of acacia wood and plate them with gold. 6 This altar you are to place in front of the veil that hangs before the ark of the commandments where I will meet you.

7 "On it Aaron shall burn fragrant incense. Morning after morning, when he prepares the lamps, 8 and again in the evening twilight, when he lights the lamps, he shall burn incense. Throughout your generations this shall be the established incense offering before the LORD. 9 On this altar you shall not offer up any profane incense, or any holocaust or cereal offering; nor shall you pour out a libation upon it. 10 Once a year Aaron shall perform the atonement rite on its horns. Throughout your generations this atonement is to be made once a year with the blood of the atoning sin offering. This altar is most sacred to the LORD."

11 The LORD also said to Moses, 12 "When you take a census of the Israelites who are to be registered, each one, as he is enrolled, shall give the LORD a forfeit for his life, so that no plague may come upon them for being registered. 13 Everyone who enters the registered group must pay a half-shekel, according to the standard of the sanctuary shekel, twenty gerahs to the shekel. This payment of a half-shekel is a contribution to the LORD. 14 Everyone of twenty years or more who enters the registered group must give this contribution to the LORD. 15 The rich need not give more, nor shall the poor give less, than a half-shekel in this contribution to the LORD to pay the forfeit for their lives. 16 When you receive this forfeit money from the Israelites, you shall donate it to the service of the meeting tent, that there it may be the Israelites' reminder, before the LORD, of the forfeit paid for their lives."

17 The LORD said to Moses, 18 "For ablutions you shall make a bronze laver with a bronze base. Place it between the meeting tent and the altar, and put water in it. 19 Aaron and his sons shall use it in washing their hands and feet. 20 When they are about to enter the meeting tent, they must wash with water, lest they die. Likewise when they approach the altar in their ministry, to offer an oblation to the LORD, 21 they must wash their hands and feet, lest they die. This shall be a perpetual ordinance for him and his descendants throughout their generations."

22 The LORD said to Moses, 23 "Take the finest spices: five hundred shekels of free-flowing myrrh; half that amount, that is, two hundred and fifty shekels, of fragrant cinnamon; two hundred and fifty shekels of fragrant cane; 24 five hundred shekels of cassia — all according to the standard of the sanctuary shekel; together with a hin of olive oil; 25 and blend them into sacred anointing oil, perfumed ointment expertly prepared. 26 With this sacred anointing oil you shall anoint the meeting tent and the ark of the commandments, 27 the table and all its appurtenances, the lamp-stand and its appurtenances, the altar of incense 28 and the altar of holocausts with all its appurtenances, and the laver with its base. 29 When you have consecrated them, they shall be most sacred; whatever touches them shall be sacred. 30 Aaron and his sons you shall also anoint and consecrate as my priests. 31 To the Israelites you shall say: As sacred anointing oil this shall belong to me throughout your generations. 32 It may not be used in any ordinary anointing

30 'You will make an altar on which to burn incense; you will make it of acacia wood, 2 one cubit long, and one cubit wide — it must be square — and two cubits high; its horns must be of a piece with it. 3 You will overlay its top, its sides all round and its horns with pure gold and make a gold moulding to go all round. 4 You will make two gold rings for it below the moulding on its two opposite sides, to take the shafts used for carrying it. 5 You will make the shafts of acacia wood and overlay them with gold.

6 'You will put it in front of the curtain by the ark of Testimony, in front of the mercy-seat which is on the Testimony, where I shall meet you. 7 On it Aaron will burn fragrant incense each morning; when he trims the lamps, he will burn incense on it; 8 and when Aaron puts back the lamps at twilight, he will burn incense on it, incense perpetually before Yahweh for all your generations to come. 9 You will not offer unauthorised incense, or burnt offering, or cereal offering on it, and you will not pour any libation over it. 10 Once a year, Aaron will perform the rite of expiation on the horns of the altar; once a year, on the Day of Expiation, with the blood of the sacrifice for sin, he will make expiation for himself, for all your generations to come. It is especially holy for Yahweh.'

11 Yahweh then spoke to Moses and said, 12 'When you count the Israelites by census, each one of them must pay Yahweh a ransom for his life, to avoid any incidence of plague among them while you are holding the census. 13 Everyone subject to the census will pay half a shekel, reckoning by the sanctuary shekel: twenty *gerah* to the shekel. This half-shekel will be set aside for Yahweh. 14 Everyone subject to the census, that is to say of twenty years and over, will pay the sum set aside for Yahweh. 15 The rich man must not give more, nor the poor man less, than half a shekel when he pays the sum set aside for Yahweh in ransom for your lives. 16 You will take the ransom money of the Israelites and apply it to the service of the Tent of Meeting, for it to be a reminder of the Israelites before Yahweh, as the ransom for your lives.'

17 Yahweh then spoke to Moses and said, 18 'You will also make a bronze basin on its bronze stand, for washing. You will put it between the Tent of Meeting and the altar and put water in it, 19 in which Aaron and his sons will wash their hands and feet. 20 Whenever they are to enter the Tent of Meeting, they will wash, to avoid incurring death; and whenever they approach the altar for their service, to burn an offering for Yahweh, 21 they will wash their hands and feet, to avoid incurring death. This is a perpetual decree for him and his descendants for all their generations to come.'

22 Yahweh spoke further to Moses and said, 23 'Take the finest spices: five hundred shekels of fresh myrrh, half as much (two hundred and fifty shekels) of fragrant cinnamon, two hundred and fifty shekels of scented reed, 24 five hundred shekels (reckoning by the sanctuary shekel) of cassia, and one *hin* of olive oil. 25 You will make this into a holy anointing oil, such a blend as the perfumer might make; this will be a holy anointing oil. 26 With it you will anoint the Tent of Meeting and the ark of the Testimony, 27 the table and all its accessories, the lamp-stand and its accessories, the altar of burnt offerings and all its accessories, and the basin with its stand, 29 consecrating them, so that they will be especially holy and whatever touches them will become holy. 30 You will also anoint Aaron and his sons and consecrate them to be priests in my service. 31 You will then speak to the Israelites and say, "This anointing oil will be holy for you for all your generations to come. 32 It must not be used for anointing the hu-

any ordinary anointing of the body, and you shall make no other like it in composition; it is holy, and it shall be holy to you. 33 Whoever compounds any like it or whoever puts any of it on an unqualified person shall be cut off from the people."

34 The LORD said to Moses: Take sweet spices, stacte, and onycha, and galbanum, sweet spices with pure frankincense (an equal part of each), 35 and make an incense blended as by the perfumer, seasoned with salt, pure and holy; 36 and you shall beat some of it into powder, and put part of it before the covenant*w* in the tent of meeting where I shall meet with you; it shall be for you most holy. 37 When you make incense according to this composition, you shall not make it for yourselves; it shall be regarded by you as holy to the LORD. 38 Whoever makes any like it to use as perfume shall be cut off from the people.

31 The LORD spoke to Moses: 2 See, I have called by name Bezalel son of Uri son of Hur, of the tribe of Judah: 3 and I have filled him with divine spirit,*x* with ability, intelligence, and knowledge in every kind of craft, 4 to devise artistic designs, to work in gold, silver, and bronze, 5 in cutting stones for setting, and in carving wood, in every kind of craft. 6 Moreover, I have appointed with him Oholiab son of Ahisamach, of the tribe of Dan; and I have given skill to all the skillful, so that they may make all that I have commanded you: 7 the tent of meeting, and the ark of the covenant,*w* and the mercy seat*y* that is on it, and all the furnishings of the tent, 8 the table and its utensils, and the pure lampstand with all its utensils, and the altar of incense, 9 and the altar of burnt offering with all its utensils, and the basin with its stand, 10 and the finely worked vestments, the holy vestments for the priest Aaron and the vestments of his sons, for their service as priests, 11 and the anointing oil and the fragrant incense for the holy place. They shall do just as I have commanded you.

12 The LORD said to Moses: 13 You yourself are to speak to the Israelites: "You shall keep my sabbaths, for this is a sign between me and you throughout your generations, given in order that you may know that I, the LORD, sanctify you. 14 You shall keep the sabbath, because it is holy for you; everyone who profanes it shall be put to death; whoever does any work on it shall be cut off from among the people. 15 Six days shall work be done, but the seventh day is a sabbath of solemn rest, holy to the LORD; whoever does any work on the sabbath day shall be put to death. 16 Therefore the Israelites shall keep the sabbath, observing the sabbath throughout their generations, as a perpetual covenant. 17 It is a sign forever between me and the people of Israel that in six days the LORD made heaven and earth, and on the seventh day he rested, and was refreshed."

18 When God*z* finished speaking with Moses on Mount Sinai, he gave him the two tablets of the covenant,*w* tablets of stone, written with the finger of God.

32 When the people saw that Moses delayed to come down from the mountain, the people gathered around Aaron, and said to him, "Come, make gods for us, who shall go before us; as for this Moses, the man who brought us up out of the land of Egypt, we do not know what has become of him." 2 Aaron said to them, "Take off the gold rings that are on the ears of your wives, your sons, and your daughters, and bring them to me." 3 So all the people took off the gold rings from their ears, and brought them to Aaron. 4 He took the gold from them, formed it in

anointing the human body, and you must not prepare any oil like it after the same prescription. It is holy, and you are to treat it as holy. 33 The man who compounds perfume like it, or who puts any of it on any lay person, will be cut off from his father's kin.

34 The LORD said to Moses, Take fragrant spices: gum resin, aromatic shell, galbanum; add clear frankincense to the spices in equal proportions. 35 Make it into incense, perfume made by the perfumer's craft, salted and pure, a holy thing. 36 Pound some of it into fine powder, and put it in front of the Testimony in the Tent of Meeting, where I shall meet you; you are to treat it as most holy. 37 The incense prepared according to this prescription you must not make for your personal use; you are to treat it as holy to the LORD. 38 The man who makes any like it for his own enjoyment will be cut off from his father's kin.

31 THE LORD said to Moses, 2 Take note that I have specially chosen Bezalel son of Uri, son of Hur, of the tribe of Judah. 3 I have filled him with the spirit of God, making him skilful and ingenious, expert in every craft, 4 and a master of design, whether in gold, silver, copper, 5 or cutting precious stones for setting, or carving wood, for workmanship of every kind. 6 Further, I have appointed Aholiab son of Ahisamach of the tribe of Dan to be his assistant, and I have endowed every skilled craftsman with the skill which he has. They are to make everything that I have commanded you: 7 the Tent of Meeting, the Ark for the Testimony, the cover over it, and all the furnishings of the tent; 8 the table and its vessels, the pure lampstand and all its fittings, the altar of incense, 9 the altar of whole-offering and all its vessels, the basin and its stand; 10 the stitched vestments, that is the sacred vestments for Aaron the priest and the vestments for his sons when they minister as priests, 11 the anointing oil, and the fragrant incense for the Holy Place. They are to carry it all out as I commanded you.

12 The LORD said to Moses, 13 Say to the Israelites: Above all you must keep my sabbaths, for the sabbath is a sign between me and you in every generation that you may know that I am the LORD who hallows you. 14 You are to keep the sabbath, because for you it is a holy day. If anyone profanes it he must be put to death. Anyone who does work on it is to be cut off from his father's kin. 15 Work may be done for six days, but on the seventh day there is a sabbath of solemn abstinence from work, holy to the LORD. Whoever does any work on the sabbath day shall be put to death. 16 The Israelites must keep the sabbath, observing it in every generation as a covenant for ever. 17 It is a sign for ever between me and the Israelites, for in six days the LORD made the heavens and the earth, but on the seventh day he ceased work and refreshed himself.

18 When he had finished speaking with Moses on Mount Sinai, the LORD gave him the two tablets of the Testimony, stone tablets written with the finger of God.

32 WHEN the people saw that Moses was so long in coming down from the mountain, they congregated before Aaron and said, 'Come, make us gods to go before us. As for this Moses, who brought us up from Egypt, we do not know what has become of him.' 2 Aaron answered, 'Take the gold rings from the ears of your wives and daughters, and bring them to me.' 3 So all the people stripped themselves of their gold ear-rings and brought them to Aaron. 4 He received them from their hands, cast the metal in

---

w Or *treaty,* or *testimony;* Heb *eduth*   *x* Or *with the spirit of God*
y Or *the cover*   *z* Heb *he*

30:34 **gum resin:** *or* mastic.   31:6 **Aholiab:** *or* Oholiab.
32:2 **wives:** *so Gk; Heb. adds* and sons.

of the body, nor may you make any other oil of a like mixture. It is sacred, and shall be treated as sacred by you. 33 Whoever prepares a perfume like this, or whoever puts any of this on a layman, shall be cut off from his kinsmen."

34 The LORD told Moses, "Take these aromatic substances: storax and onycha and galbanum, these and pure frankincense in equal parts; 35 and blend them into incense. This fragrant powder, expertly prepared, is to be salted and so kept pure and sacred. 36 Grind some of it into fine dust and put this before the commandments in the meeting tent where I will meet you. This incense shall be treated as most sacred by you. 37 You may not make incense of a like mixture for yourselves; you must treat it as sacred to the LORD. 38 Whoever makes an incense like this for his own enjoyment of its fragrance, shall be cut off from his kinsmen."

31 The LORD said to Moses, 2 "See, I have chosen Bezalel, son of Uri, son of Hur, of the tribe of Judah, 3 and I have filled him with a divine spirit of skill and understanding and knowledge in every craft: 4 in the production of embroidery, in making things of gold, silver or bronze, 5 in cutting and mounting precious stones, in carving wood, and in every other craft. 6 As his assistant I have appointed Oholiab, son of Ahisamach, of the tribe of Dan. I have also endowed all the experts with the necessary skill to make all the things I have ordered you to make: 7 the meeting tent, the ark of the commandments with the propitiatory on top of it, all the furnishings of the tent, 8 the table with its appurtenances, the pure gold lampstand with all its appurtenances, the altar of incense, 9 the altar of holocausts with all its appurtenances, the laver with its base, 10 the service cloths, the sacred vestments for Aaron the priest, the vestments for his sons in their ministry, 11 the anointing oil, and the fragrant incense for the sanctuary. All these things they shall make just as I have commanded you."

12 The LORD said to Moses, 13 "You must also tell the Israelites: Take care to keep my sabbaths, for that is to be the token between you and me throughout the generations, to show that it is I, the LORD, who make you holy. 14 Therefore, you must keep the sabbath as something sacred. Whoever desecrates it shall be put to death. If anyone does work on that day, he must be rooted out of his people. 15 Six days there are for doing work, but the seventh day is the sabbath of complete rest, sacred to the LORD. Anyone who does work on the sabbath day shall be put to death. 16 So shall the Israelites observe the sabbath, keeping it throughout their generations as a perpetual covenant. 17 Between me and the Israelites it is to be an everlasting token; for in six days the LORD made the heavens and the earth, but on the seventh day he rested at his ease."

18 When the LORD had finished speaking to Moses on Mount Sinai, he gave him the two tablets of the commandments, the stone tablets inscribed by God's own finger.

32 When the people became aware of Moses' delay in coming down from the mountain, they gathered around Aaron and said to him, "Come, make us a god who will be our leader; as for the man Moses who brought us out of the land of Egypt, we do not know what has happened to him." 2 Aaron replied, "Have your wives and sons and daughters take off the golden earrings they are wearing, and bring them to me." 3 So all the people took off their earrings and brought them to Aaron, 4 who accepted their offering,

man body, nor may you make any of the same mixture. It is a holy thing; you will regard it as holy. 33 Anyone who makes up the same oil or uses it on an unauthorised person will be outlawed from his people." '

34 Yahweh then said to Moses, 'Take sweet spices: storax, onycha, galbanum, sweet spices and pure frankincense in equal parts, 35 and compound an incense, such a blend as the perfumer might make, salted, pure, and holy. 36 You will grind some of this up very fine and put it in front of the Testimony in the Tent of Meeting, where I shall meet you. You will regard it as especially holy. 37 You may not make any incense of similar composition for your own use. You will regard it as holy, reserved for Yahweh. Anyone who makes up the same thing to use as perfume will be outlawed from his people.'

31 Yahweh then spoke to Moses and said, 2 'Look, I have singled out Bezalel son of Uri, son of Hur, of the tribe of Judah, 3 and have filled him with the spirit of God in wisdom, knowledge and skill in every kind of craft: 4 in designing and carrying out work in gold and silver and bronze, 5 in cutting stones to be set, in wood carving and in executing every kind of work. 6 And to help him I have given him Oholiab son of Ahisamach, of the tribe of Dan, and have endowed the hearts of all the skilled men with the skill to make everything I have ordered you: 7 the Tent of Meeting; the ark of the Testimony; the mercy-seat above it; and all the furniture of the tent; 8 the table and all its accessories; the pure lamp-stand and all its equipment; the altar of incense; 9 the altar of burnt offerings and all its accessories; the basin and its stand; 10 the liturgical vestments, sacred vestments for Aaron the priest, and the vestments for his sons, for their priestly functions; 11 the anointing oil and the fragrant incense for the sanctuary. They will do everything as I have ordered you.'

12 Yahweh then said to Moses, 13 'Speak to the Israelites and say, "You will keep my Sabbaths properly, for this is a sign between myself and you for all your generations to come, so that you will know that it is I, Yahweh, who sanctify you. 14 You will keep the Sabbath, then; you will regard it as holy. Anyone who profanes it will be put to death; anyone who does any work on that day will be outlawed from his people. 15 Work must be done for six days, but the seventh day will be a day of complete rest, consecrated to Yahweh. Anyone who works on the Sabbath day will be put to death. 16 The Israelites will keep the Sabbath, observing the Sabbath for all their generations to come: this is an eternal covenant. 17 Between myself and the Israelites, this is a sign for ever, for in six days Yahweh made heaven and earth, but on the seventh day he rested and drew breath." '

18 When he had finished speaking to Moses on Mount Sinai, he gave him the two tablets of the Testimony, tablets of stone inscribed by the finger of God.

32 o When the people saw that Moses was a long time before coming down the mountain, they gathered round Aaron and said to him, 'Get to work, make us a god to go at our head; for that Moses, the man who brought us here from Egypt — we do not know what has become of him.' 2 Aaron replied, 'Strip off the gold rings in the ears of your wives and your sons and daughters, and bring them to me.' 3 The people all stripped off the gold rings from their ears and brought them to Aaron. 4 He received what they

NEW REVISED STANDARD VERSION

a mold,ᵃ and cast an image of a calf; and they said, "These are your gods, O Israel, who brought you up out of the land of Egypt!" ⁵When Aaron saw this, he built an altar before it; and Aaron made proclamation and said, "Tomorrow shall be a festival to the LORD." ⁶They rose early the next day, and offered burnt offerings and brought sacrifices of well-being; and the people sat down to eat and drink, and rose up to revel.

7 The LORD said to Moses, "Go down at once! Your people, whom you brought up out of the land of Egypt, have acted perversely; ⁸they have been quick to turn aside from the way that I commanded them; they have cast for themselves an image of a calf, and have worshiped it and sacrificed to it, and said, 'These are your gods, O Israel, who brought you up out of the land of Egypt!'" ⁹The LORD said to Moses, "I have seen this people, how stiff-necked they are. ¹⁰Now let me alone, so that my wrath may burn hot against them and I may consume them; and of you I will make a great nation."

11 But Moses implored the LORD his God, and said, "O LORD, why does your wrath burn hot against your people, whom you brought out of the land of Egypt with great power and with a mighty hand? ¹²Why should the Egyptians say, 'It was with evil intent that he brought them out to kill them in the mountains, and to consume them from the face of the earth'? Turn from your fierce wrath; change your mind and do not bring disaster on your people. ¹³Remember Abraham, Isaac, and Israel, your servants, how you swore to them by your own self, saying to them, 'I will multiply your descendants like the stars of heaven, and all this land that I have promised I will give to your descendants, and they shall inherit it forever.'" ¹⁴And the LORD changed his mind about the disaster that he planned to bring on his people.

15 Then Moses turned and went down from the mountain, carrying the two tablets of the covenantᵇ in his hands, tablets that were written on both sides, written on the front and on the back. ¹⁶The tablets were the work of God, and the writing was the writing of God, engraved on the tablets. ¹⁷When Joshua heard the noise of the people as they shouted, he said to Moses, "There is a noise of war in the camp." ¹⁸But he said,

"It is not the sound made by victors,
    or the sound made by losers;
it is the sound of revelers that I hear."

¹⁹As soon as he came near the camp and saw the calf and the dancing, Moses' anger burned hot, and he threw the tablets from his hands and broke them at the foot of the mountain. ²⁰He took the calf that they had made, burned it with fire, ground it to powder, scattered it on the water, and made the Israelites drink it.

21 Moses said to Aaron, "What did this people do to you that you have brought so great a sin upon them?" ²²And Aaron said, "Do not let the anger of my lord burn hot; you know the people, that they are bent on evil. ²³They said to me, 'Make us gods, who shall go before us; as for this Moses, the man who brought us up out of the land of Egypt, we do not know what has become of him.' ²⁴So I said to them, 'Whoever has gold, take it off'; so they gave it to me, and I threw it into the fire, and out came this calf!"

25 When Moses saw that the people were running wild (for Aaron had let them run wild, to the derision of their enemies), ²⁶then Moses stood in the gate of the camp, and said, "Who is on the LORD's side? Come to me!" And all the sons of Levi gathered around him. ²⁷He said to them, "Thus

REVISED ENGLISH BIBLE

a mould, and made it into the image of a bull-calf; then they said, 'Israel, these are your gods that brought you up from Egypt.' ⁵Seeing this, Aaron built an altar in front of it and announced, 'Tomorrow there is to be a feast to the LORD.' ⁶Next day the people rose early, offered whole-offerings, and brought shared-offerings. After this they sat down to eat and drink and then gave themselves up to revelry.

⁷The LORD said to Moses, 'Go down at once, for your people, the people you brought up from Egypt, have committed a monstrous act. ⁸They have lost no time in turning aside from the way which I commanded them to follow, and cast for themselves a metal image of a bull-calf; they have prostrated themselves before it, sacrificed to it, and said, "Israel, these are your gods that brought you up from Egypt."' ⁹The LORD said to Moses, 'I have considered this people, and I see their stubbornness. ¹⁰Now, let me alone to pour out my anger on them, so that I may put an end to them and make a great nation spring from you.'

¹¹Moses set himself to placate the LORD his God: 'LORD,' he said, 'why pour out your anger on your people, whom you brought out of Egypt with great power and a strong hand? ¹²Why let the Egyptians say, "He meant evil when he took them out, to kill them in the mountains and wipe them off the face of the earth"? Turn from your anger, and think better of the evil you intend against your people. ¹³Remember Abraham, Isaac, and Israel, your servants, to whom you swore by your own self: "I shall make your descendants countless as the stars in the heavens, and all this land, of which I have spoken, I shall give to them, and they will possess it for ever."' ¹⁴So the LORD thought better of the evil with which he had threatened his people.

¹⁵Moses went back down the mountain holding the two tablets of the Testimony, inscribed on both sides, on the front and on the back. ¹⁶The tablets were the handiwork of God, and the writing was God's writing, engraved on the tablets. ¹⁷Joshua, hearing the uproar the people were making, said to Moses, 'Listen! There is fighting in the camp.' ¹⁸Moses replied,

    'This is not the sound of warriors,
    nor the sound of a defeated people;
    it is the sound of singing that I hear.'

¹⁹As he approached the camp, Moses saw the bull-calf and the dancing, and in a burst of anger he flung down the tablets and shattered them at the foot of the mountain. ²⁰He took the calf they had made and burnt it; he ground it to powder, sprinkled it on water, and made the Israelites drink it.

²¹He demanded of Aaron, 'What did this people do to you that you should have brought such great guilt upon them?' ²²Aaron replied, 'Please do not be angry, my lord. You know how wicked the people are. ²³They said to me, "Make us gods to go ahead of us, because, as for this Moses, who brought us up from Egypt, we do not know what has become of him." ²⁴So I said to them, "Those of you who have any gold, take it off." They gave it to me, I threw it in the fire, and out came this bull-calf.'

²⁵Moses saw that the people were out of control and that Aaron had laid them open to the secret malice of their enemies. ²⁶He took his place at the gate of the camp and said, 'Who is on the LORD's side? Come here to me'; and the Levites all rallied to him. ²⁷He said to them, 'The LORD

ᵃ Or fashioned it with a graving tool; Meaning of Heb uncertain
ᵇ Or treaty, or testimony; Heb eduth

and fashioning this gold with a graving tool, made a molten calf. Then they cried out, "This is your God, O Israel, who brought you out of the land of Egypt." 5 On seeing this, Aaron built an altar before the calf and proclaimed, "Tomorrow is a feast of the LORD." 6 Early the next day the people offered holocausts and brought peace offerings. Then they sat down to eat and drink, and rose up to revel.

7 With that, the LORD said to Moses, "Go down at once to your people, whom you brought out of the land of Egypt, for they have become depraved. 8 They have soon turned aside from the way I pointed out to them, making for themselves a molten calf and worshiping it, sacrificing to it and crying out, 'This is your God, O Israel, who brought you out of the land of Egypt!' 9 I see how stiff-necked this people is," continued the LORD to Moses. 10 "Let me alone, then, that my wrath may blaze up against them to consume them. Then I will make of you a great nation."

11 But Moses implored the LORD, his God, saying, "Why, O LORD, should your wrath blaze up against your own people, whom you brought out of the land of Egypt with such great power and with so strong a hand? 12 Why should the Egyptians say, 'With evil intent he brought them out, that he might kill them in the mountains and exterminate them from the face of the earth'? Let your blazing wrath die down; relent in punishing your people. 13 Remember your servants Abraham, Isaac and Israel, and how you swore to them by your own self, saying, 'I will make your descendants as numerous as the stars in the sky; and all this land that I promised, I will give your descendants as their perpetual heritage.' " 14 So the LORD relented in the punishment he had threatened to inflict on his people.

15 Moses then turned and came down the mountain with the two tablets of the commandments in his hands, tablets that were written on both sides, front and back; 16 tablets that were made by God, having inscriptions on them that were engraved by God himself. 17 Now, when Joshua heard the noise of the people shouting, he said to Moses, "That sounds like a battle in the camp." 18 But Moses answered, "It does not sound like cries of victory, nor does it sound like cries of defeat; the sounds that I hear are cries of revelry." 19 As he drew near the camp, he saw the calf and the dancing. With that, Moses' wrath flared up, so that he threw the tablets down and broke them on the base of the mountain. 20 Taking the calf they had made, he fused it in the fire and then ground it down to powder, which he scattered on the water and made the Israelites drink.

21 Moses asked Aaron, "What did this people ever do to you that you should lead them into so grave a sin?" Aaron replied, "Let not my lord be angry. 22 You know well enough how prone the people are to evil. 23 They said to me, 'Make us a god to be our leader; as for the man Moses who brought us out of the land of Egypt, we do not know what has happened to him.' 24 So I told them, 'Let anyone who has gold jewelry take it off.' They gave it to me, and I threw it into the fire, and this calf came out."

25 When Moses realized that, to the scornful joy of their foes, Aaron had let the people run wild, 26 he stood at the gate of the camp and cried, "Whoever is for the LORD, let him come to me!" All the Levites then rallied to him, 27 and

gave him, melted it down in a mould and with it made the statue of a calf. 'Israel,' the people shouted, 'here is your God who brought you here from Egypt!' 5 Observing this, Aaron built an altar before the statue and made this proclamation, 'Tomorrow will be a feast in Yahweh's honour.'

6 Early next morning they sacrificed burnt offerings and brought communion sacrifices. The people then sat down to eat and drink, and afterwards got up to amuse themselves.

7 Yahweh then said to Moses, 'Go down at once, for your people whom you brought here from Egypt have become corrupt. 8 They have quickly left the way which I ordered them to follow. They have cast themselves a metal calf, worshipped it and offered sacrifice to it, shouting, "Israel, here is your God who brought you here from Egypt!" ' 9 Yahweh then said to Moses, 'I know these people; I know how obstinate they are! 10 So leave me now, so that my anger can blaze at them and I can put an end to them! I shall make a great nation out of you instead.'

11 Moses tried to pacify Yahweh his God. 'Yahweh,' he said, 'why should your anger blaze at your people, whom you have brought out of Egypt by your great power and mighty hand? 12 Why should the Egyptians say, "He brought them out with evil intention, to slaughter them in the mountains and wipe them off the face of the earth?" Give up your burning wrath; relent over this disaster intended for your people. 13 Remember your servants Abraham, Isaac and Jacob, to whom you swore by your very self and made this promise: "I shall make your offspring as numerous as the stars of heaven, and this whole country of which I have spoken, I shall give to your descendants, and it will be their heritage for ever." ' 14 Yahweh then relented over the disaster which he had intended to inflict on his people.

15 Moses turned and came down the mountain with the two tablets of the Testimony in his hands, tablets inscribed on both sides, inscribed on the front and on the back. 16 The tablets were the work of God, and the writing on them was God's writing, engraved on the tablets.

17 When Joshua heard the noise of the people shouting, he said to Moses, 'There is the sound of battle in the camp!' 18 But he replied:

No song of victory is this sound,
no lament for defeat this sound;
but answering choruses I hear!

19 And there, as he approached the camp, he saw the calf and the groups dancing. Moses blazed with anger. He threw down the tablets he was holding, shattering them at the foot of the mountain. 20 He seized the calf they had made and burned it, grinding it into powder which he scattered on the water, and made the Israelites drink it. 21 Moses then said to Aaron, 'What have these people done to you for you to have brought so great a sin on them?' 22 Aaron replied, 'My lord should not be so angry. You yourself know what a bad state these people are in! 23 They said to me, "Make us a god to go at our head; for that Moses, the man who brought us here from Egypt — we do not know what has become of him." 24 I then said to them, "Anyone with gold, strip it off!" They gave it to me. I threw it into the fire and out came this calf!'

25 When Moses saw that the people were out of hand — for Aaron had let them get out of hand to the derision of their enemies all round them — 26 Moses then stood at the gate of the camp and shouted, 'Who is for Yahweh? To me!' And all the Levites rallied round him. 27 He said to

says the LORD, the God of Israel, 'Put your sword on your side, each of you! Go back and forth from gate to gate throughout the camp, and each of you kill your brother, your friend, and your neighbor.' " 28 The sons of Levi did as Moses commanded, and about three thousand of the people fell on that day. 29 Moses said, "Today you have ordained yourselves[c] for the service of the LORD, each one at the cost of a son or a brother, and so have brought a blessing on yourselves this day."

30 On the next day Moses said to the people, "You have sinned a great sin. But now I will go up to the LORD; perhaps I can make atonement for your sin." 31 So Moses returned to the LORD and said, "Alas, this people has sinned a great sin; they have made for themselves gods of gold. 32 But now, if you will only forgive their sin — but if not, blot me out of the book that you have written." 33 But the LORD said to Moses, "Whoever has sinned against me I will blot out of my book. 34 But now go, lead the people to the place about which I have spoken to you; see, my angel shall go in front of you. Nevertheless, when the day comes for punishment, I will punish them for their sin."

35 Then the LORD sent a plague on the people, because they made the calf — the one that Aaron made.

33 The LORD said to Moses, "Go, leave this place, you and the people whom you have brought up out of the land of Egypt, and go to the land of which I swore to Abraham, Isaac, and Jacob, saying, 'To your descendants I will give it.' 2 I will send an angel before you, and I will drive out the Canaanites, the Amorites, the Hittites, the Perizzites, the Hivites, and the Jebusites. 3 Go up to a land flowing with milk and honey; but I will not go up among you, or I would consume you on the way, for you are a stiff-necked people."

4 When the people heard these harsh words, they mourned, and no one put on ornaments. 5 For the LORD had said to Moses, "Say to the Israelites, 'You are a stiff-necked people; if for a single moment I should go up among you, I would consume you. So now take off your ornaments, and I will decide what to do to you.' " 6 Therefore the Israelites stripped themselves of their ornaments, from Mount Horeb onward.

7 Now Moses used to take the tent and pitch it outside the camp, far off from the camp; he called it the tent of meeting. And everyone who sought the LORD would go out to the tent of meeting, which was outside the camp. 8 Whenever Moses went out to the tent, all the people would rise and stand, each of them, at the entrance of their tents and watch Moses until he had gone into the tent. 9 When Moses entered the tent, the pillar of cloud would descend and stand at the entrance of the tent, and the LORD would speak with Moses. 10 When all the people saw the pillar of cloud standing at the entrance of the tent, all the people would rise and bow down, all of them, at the entrance of their tent. 11 Thus the LORD used to speak to Moses face to face, as one speaks to a friend. Then he would return to the camp; but his young assistant, Joshua son of Nun, would not leave the tent.

12 Moses said to the LORD, "See, you have said to me, 'Bring up this people'; but you have not let me know whom you will send with me. Yet you have said, 'I know you by name, and you have also found favor in my sight.' 13 Now if I have found favor in your sight, show me your ways, so that I may know you and find favor in your sight. Consider too that this nation is your people." 14 He said, "My presence will go with you, and I will give you rest." 15 And he said to him, "If your presence will not go, do not carry us up from here. 16 For how shall it be known that I have found

the God of Israel has said: Arm yourselves, each of you, with his sword. Go through the camp from gate to gate and back again. Each of you kill brother, friend, neighbour.' 28 The Levites obeyed, and about three thousand of the people died that day. 29 Moses said, 'You have been installed as priests to the LORD today, because you have turned each against his own son and his own brother and so have brought a blessing this day upon yourselves.'

30 The next day Moses said to the people, 'You have committed a great sin. Now I shall go up to the LORD; perhaps I may be able to secure pardon for your sin.' 31 When he went back to the LORD he said, 'Oh, what a great sin this people has committed: they have made themselves gods of gold. 32 Now if you will forgive them, forgive; but if not, blot out my name, I pray, from your book which you have written.' 33 The LORD answered Moses, 'Whoever has sinned against me, him I shall blot out from my book. 34 Now go, lead the people to the place of which I have told you. My angel will go ahead of you, but a day will come when I shall punish them for their sin.' 35 Then the LORD punished the people who through Aaron made the bull-calf.

33 The LORD spoke to Moses: 'Set out, you and the people you have brought up from Egypt, go from here to the land which I swore to Abraham, Isaac, and Jacob that I would give to their descendants. 2 I shall send an angel ahead of you, and drive out the Canaanites, the Amorites and the Hittites and the Perizzites, the Hivites and the Jebusites. 3 I shall bring you to a land flowing with milk and honey, but I shall not journey in your company, for fear that I should destroy you on the way, for you are a stubborn people.' 4 When the people heard this harsh sentence they went about like mourners, and no one put on his ornaments. 5 The LORD said to Moses, 'Tell the Israelites: You are a stubborn people; at any moment, if I journeyed in your company, I might destroy you. Put away your ornaments now, and I shall determine what to do to you.' 6 So the Israelites stripped off their ornaments, and wore them no more from Mount Horeb onwards.

7 Moses used to take the Tent and set it up outside the camp some distance away. He called it the Tent of Meeting, and everyone who sought the LORD would go outside the camp to the Tent of Meeting. 8 Whenever Moses went out to the Tent, all the people would rise and stand, each at the door of his tent, and follow Moses with their eyes until he had entered the Tent. 9 When Moses entered it, the pillar of cloud came down, and stayed at the entrance to the Tent while the LORD spoke with Moses. 10 As soon as the people saw the pillar of cloud standing at the entrance to the Tent, they would all prostrate themselves, each at the door of his tent. 11 The LORD used to speak with Moses face to face, as one man speaks to another, but his attendant, Joshua son of Nun, never moved from inside the Tent.

12 Moses said to the LORD, 'You tell me to lead up this people without letting me know whom you will send with me, even though you have said to me, "I know you by name, and, what is more, you have found favour with me." 13 If I have indeed won your favour, then teach me to know your ways, so that I can know you and continue in favour with you, for this nation is your own people.' 14 The LORD answered, 'I shall go myself and set your mind at rest.' 15 Moses said to him, 'Indeed if you do not go yourself, do not send us up from here; 16 for how can it ever be known

---

c Gk Vg Compare Tg: Heb *Today ordain yourselves*

33:3 **I shall bring you:** *so Gk; Heb. omits.*

he told them, "Thus says the LORD, the God of Israel: Put your sword on your hip, every one of you! Now go up and down the camp, from gate to gate, and slay your own kinsmen, your friends and neighbors!" 28 The Levites carried out the command of Moses, and that day there fell about three thousand of the people. 29 Then Moses said, "Today you have been dedicated to the LORD, for you were against your own sons and kinsmen, to bring a blessing upon yourselves this day."

30 On the next day Moses said to the people, "You have committed a grave sin. I will go up to the LORD, then; perhaps I may be able to make atonement for your sin." 31 So Moses went back to the LORD and said, "Ah, this people has indeed committed a grave sin in making a god of gold for themselves! 32 If you would only forgive their sin! If you will not, then strike me out of the book that you have written." 33 The LORD answered, "Him only who has sinned against me will I strike out of my book. 34 Now, go and lead the people whither I have told you. My angel will go before you. When it is time for me to punish, I will punish them for their sin."

35 Thus the LORD smote the people for having had Aaron make the calf for them.

33 The LORD told Moses, "You and the people whom you have brought up from the land of Egypt, are to go up from here to the land which I swore to Abraham, Isaac and Jacob I would give to their descendants. 2 Driving out the Canaanites, Amorites, Hittites, Perizzites, Hivites and Jebusites, I will send an angel before you 3 to the land flowing with milk and honey. But I myself will not go up in your company, because you are a stiff-necked people; otherwise I might exterminate you on the way." 4 When the people heard this bad news, they went into mourning, and no one wore his ornaments.

5 The LORD said to Moses, "Tell the Israelites: You are a stiff-necked people. Were I to go up in your company even for a moment, I would exterminate you. Take off your ornaments, therefore; I will then see what I am to do with you." 6 So, from Mount Horeb onward, the Israelites laid aside their ornaments.

7 The tent, which was called the meeting tent, Moses used to pitch at some distance away, outside the camp. Anyone who wished to consult the LORD would go to this meeting tent outside the camp. 8 Whenever Moses went out to the tent, the people would all rise and stand at the entrance of their own tents, watching Moses until he entered the tent. 9 As Moses entered the tent, the column of cloud would come down and stand at its entrance while the LORD spoke with Moses. 10 On seeing the column of cloud stand at the entrance of the tent, all the people would rise and worship at the entrance of their own tents. 11 The LORD used to speak to Moses face to face, as one man speaks to another. Moses would then return to the camp, but his young assistant, Joshua, son of Nun, would not move out of the tent.

12 Moses said to the LORD, "You, indeed, are telling me to lead this people on; but you have not let me know whom you will send with me. Yet you have said, 'You are my intimate friend,' and also, 'You have found favor with me.' 13 Now if I have found favor with you, do let me know your ways so that, in knowing you, I may continue to find favor with you. Then, too, this nation is, after all, your own people." 14 "I myself," the LORD answered, "will go along, to give you rest." 15 Moses replied, "If you are not going yourself, do not make us go up from here. 16 For how can

them, 'Yahweh, God of Israel, says this, "Buckle on your sword, each of you, and go up and down the camp from gate to gate, every man of you slaughtering brother, friend and neighbour." ' 28 The Levites did as Moses said, and of the people about three thousand men perished that day. 29 'Today', Moses said, 'you have consecrated yourselves to Yahweh, one at the cost of his son, another of his brother; and so he bestows a blessing on you today.'

30 On the following day Moses said to the people, 'You have committed a great sin. But now I shall go up to Yahweh: perhaps I can secure expiation for your sin.' 31 Moses then went back to Yahweh and said, 'Oh, this people has committed a great sin by making themselves a god of gold. 32 And yet, if it pleased you to forgive their sin . . .! If not, please blot me out of the book you have written!' 33 Yahweh said to Moses, 'Those who have sinned against me are the ones I shall blot out of my book. 34 So now go and lead the people to the place I promised to you. My angel will indeed go at your head but, on the day of punishment, I shall punish them for their sin.' 35 And Yahweh punished the people for having made the calf, the one Aaron had made.

33 Yahweh then said to Moses, 'Leave, move on from here, you and the people whom you have brought here from Egypt, to the country that I swore to Abraham, Isaac and Jacob that I would give to their descendants. 2 I shall send an angel in front of you and drive out the Canaanites, the Amorites, the Hittites, the Perizzites, the Hivites and the Jebusites. 3 Move on towards a country flowing with milk and honey, but I myself shall not be going with you or I might annihilate you on the way, for you are an obstinate people.' 4 On hearing these stern words the people went into mourning and no one wore his ornaments.

5 Yahweh then said to Moses, 'Say to the Israelites, "You are an obstinate people. If I were to go with you even for a moment, I should annihilate you. So now take off your ornaments, and then I shall decide how to deal with you!" ' 6 So, from Mount Horeb onwards, the Israelites stripped themselves of their ornaments.

7 Moses used to take the Tent and pitch it outside the camp, far away from the camp. He called it the Tent of Meeting. Anyone who wanted to consult Yahweh would go out to the Tent of Meeting, outside the camp. 8 Whenever Moses went out to the Tent, the people would all stand up and every man would stand at the door of his tent and watch Moses until he went into the Tent. 9 And whenever Moses went into the Tent, the pillar of cloud would come down and station itself at the entrance to the Tent, while Yahweh spoke with Moses. 10 The people could all see the pillar of cloud stationed at the entrance to the Tent and the people would all stand up and bow low, each at the door of his tent. 11 Yahweh would talk to Moses face to face, as a man talks to his friend, and afterwards he would come back to the camp, but the young man who was his servant, Joshua son of Nun, never left the inside of the Tent.

12 Moses said to Yahweh, 'Look, you say to me, "Make the people move on," but you have not told me whom you are going to send with me, although you have said, "I know you by name and you enjoy my favour." 13 If indeed I enjoy your favour, please show me your ways, so that I understand you and continue to enjoy your favour; consider too that this nation is your people.' 14 Yahweh then said, 'I myself shall go with you and I shall give you rest.' 15 To which he said, 'If you do not come yourself, do not make us move on from here, 16 for how can it be known that I and

NEW REVISED STANDARD VERSION

favor in your sight, I and your people, unless you go with us? In this way, we shall be distinct, I and your people, from every people on the face of the earth."

17 The LORD said to Moses, "I will do the very thing that you have asked; for you have found favor in my sight, and I know you by name." 18 Moses said, "Show me your glory, I pray." 19 And he said, "I will make all my goodness pass before you, and will proclaim before you the name, 'The LORD';d and I will be gracious to whom I will be gracious, and will show mercy on whom I will show mercy. 20 But," he said, "you cannot see my face; for no one shall see me and live." 21 And the LORD continued, "See, there is a place by me where you shall stand on the rock; 22 and while my glory passes by I will put you in a cleft of the rock, and I will cover you with my hand until I have passed by; 23 then I will take away my hand, and you shall see my back; but my face shall not be seen."

34 The LORD said to Moses, "Cut two tablets of stone like the former ones, and I will write on the tablets the words that were on the former tablets, which you broke. 2 Be ready in the morning, and come up in the morning to Mount Sinai and present yourself there to me, on the top of the mountain. 3 No one shall come up with you, and do not let anyone be seen throughout all the mountain; and do not let flocks or herds graze in front of that mountain." 4 So Moses cut two tablets of stone like the former ones; and he rose early in the morning and went up on Mount Sinai, as the LORD had commanded him, and took in his hand the two tablets of stone. 5 The LORD descended in the cloud and stood with him there, and proclaimed the name, "The LORD."d 6 The LORD passed before him, and proclaimed,

"The LORD, the LORD,
a God merciful and gracious,
slow to anger,
and abounding in steadfast love and faithfulness,
7 keeping steadfast love for the thousandth
generation,e
forgiving iniquity and transgression and sin,
yet by no means clearing the guilty,
but visiting the iniquity of the parents
upon the children
and the children's children,
to the third and the fourth generation."

8 And Moses quickly bowed his head toward the earth, and worshiped. 9 He said, "If now I have found favor in your sight, O Lord, I pray, let the Lord go with us. Although this is a stiff-necked people, pardon our iniquity and our sin, and take us for your inheritance."

10 He said: I hereby make a covenant. Before all your people I will perform marvels, such as have not been performed in all the earth or in any nation; and all the people among whom you live shall see the work of the LORD; for it is an awesome thing that I will do with you.

11 Observe what I command you today. See, I will drive out before you the Amorites, the Canaanites, the Hittites, the Perizzites, the Hivites, and the Jebusites. 12 Take care not to make a covenant with the inhabitants of the land to which you are going, or it will become a snare among you. 13 You shall tear down their altars, break their pillars, and cut down their sacred polesf 14 (for you shall worship no other god, because the LORD, whose name is Jealous, is a jealous God). 15 You shall not make a covenant with the inhabitants of the land, for when they prostitute themselves to their gods and sacrifice to their gods, someone among them will invite you, and you will eat of the sacrifice.

REVISED ENGLISH BIBLE

that I and your people have found favour with you, except by your going with us? So we shall be distinct, I and your people, from all the peoples on earth.' 17 The LORD said to Moses, 'I shall do what you have asked, because you have found favour with me, and I know you by name.'

18 But Moses prayed, 'Show me your glory.' 19 The LORD answered, 'I shall make all my goodness pass before you, and I shall pronounce in your hearing the name "LORD". I shall be gracious to whom I shall be gracious, and I shall have compassion on whom I shall have compassion.' 20 But he added, 'My face you cannot see, for no mortal may see me and live.' 21 The LORD said, 'Here is a place beside me. Take your stand on the rock 22 and, when my glory passes by, I shall put you in a crevice of the rock and cover you with my hand until I have passed by. 23 Then I shall take away my hand, and you will see my back, but my face must not be seen.'

34 The LORD said to Moses, 'Cut for yourself two stone tablets like the former ones, and I shall write on them the words which were on the first tablets which you broke. 2 Be ready by morning, and then go up Mount Sinai, and present yourself to me there on the top. 3 No one is to go up with you, no one must even be seen anywhere on the mountain, nor must flocks or herds graze within sight of that mountain.' 4 So Moses cut two stone tablets like the first, and early in the morning he went up Mount Sinai as the LORD had commanded him, taking the two stone tablets in his hands. 5 The LORD came down in the cloud, and, as Moses stood there in his presence, he pronounced the name 'LORD'. 6 He passed in front of Moses and proclaimed: 'The LORD, the LORD, a God compassionate and gracious, long-suffering, ever faithful and true, 7 remaining faithful to thousands, forgiving iniquity, rebellion, and sin but without acquitting the guilty, one who punishes children and grandchildren to the third and fourth generation for the iniquity of their fathers!' 8 At once Moses bowed to the ground in worship. 9 He said, 'If I have indeed won your favour, Lord, then please go in our company. However stubborn a people they are, forgive our iniquity and our sin, and take us as your own possession.'

10 The LORD said: Here and now I am making a covenant. In full view of all your people I shall do such miracles as have never been performed in all the world or in any nation. All the peoples among whom you live shall see the work of the LORD, for it is an awesome thing that I shall do for you. 11 Observe all I command you this day; and I for my part shall drive out before you the Amorites, Canaanites, Hittites, Perizzites, Hivites, and Jebusites. 12 Beware of making an alliance with the inhabitants of the land against which you are going, or they will prove a snare in your midst. 13 You must demolish their altars, smash their sacred pillars, and cut down their sacred poles. 14 You are not to bow in worship to any other god, for the LORD's name is the Jealous God, and a jealous God he is. 15 Avoid any alliance with the inhabitants of the land, or, when they go wantonly after their gods and sacrifice to them, you, any one of you, may be invited to partake of their sacrifices, 16 and marry

---

d Heb YHWH; see note at 3.15   e Or for thousands
f Heb Asherim

33:16 peoples: so Gk; Heb. people.   33:19 goodness: or character.
LORD: see note on 3:15.   34:13 sacred poles: Heb. asherim.

it be known that we, your people and I, have found favor with you, except by your going with us? Then we, your people and I, will be singled out from every other people on the earth." 17 The LORD said to Moses, "This request, too, which you have just made, I will carry out, because you have found favor with me and you are my intimate friend."

18 Then Moses said, "Do let me see your glory!" 19 He answered, "I will make all my beauty pass before you, and in your presence I will pronounce my name, 'LORD'; I who show favors to whom I will, I who grant mercy to whom I will. 20 But my face you cannot see, for no man sees me and still lives. 21 Here," continued the LORD, "is a place near me where you shall station yourself on the rock. 22 When my glory passes I will set you in the hollow of the rock and will cover you with my hand until I have passed by. 23 Then I will remove my hand, so that you may see my back; but my face is not to be seen."

34 The LORD said to Moses, "Cut two stone tablets like the former, that I may write on them the commandments which were on the former tablets that you broke. 2 Get ready for tomorrow morning, when you are to go up Mount Sinai and there present yourself to me on the top of the mountain. 3 No one shall come up with you, and no one is even to be seen on any part of the mountain; even the flocks and the herds are not to go grazing toward this mountain." 4 Moses then cut two stone tablets like the former, and early the next morning he went up Mount Sinai as the LORD had commanded him, taking along the two stone tablets.

5 Having come down in a cloud, the LORD stood with him there and proclaimed his name, "LORD." 6 Thus the LORD passed before him and cried out, "The LORD, the LORD, a merciful and gracious God, slow to anger and rich in kindness and fidelity, 7 continuing his kindness for a thousand generations, and forgiving wickedness and crime and sin; yet not declaring the guilty guiltless, but punishing children and grandchildren to the third and fourth generation for their fathers' wickedness!" 8 Moses at once bowed down to the ground in worship. 9 Then he said, "If I find favor with you, O LORD, do come along in our company. This is indeed a stiff-necked people; yet pardon our wickedness and sins, and receive us as your own."

10 "Here, then," said the LORD, "is the covenant I will make. Before the eyes of all your people I will work such marvels as have never been wrought in any nation anywhere on earth, so that this people among whom you live may see how awe-inspiring are the deeds which I, the LORD, will do at your side. 11 But you, on your part, must keep the commandments I am giving you today.

"I will drive out before you the Amorites, Canaanites, Hittites, Perizzites, Hivites, and Jebusites. 12 Take care, therefore, not to make a covenant with these inhabitants of the land that you are to enter; else they will become a snare among you. 13 Tear down their altars; smash their sacred pillars, and cut down their sacred poles. 14 You shall not worship any other god, for the LORD is 'the Jealous One'; a jealous God is he. 15 Do not make a covenant with the inhabitants of that land; else, when they render their wanton worship to their gods and sacrifice to them, one of them may invite you and you may partake of his sacrifice. 16 Nei-

my people enjoy your favour, if not by your coming with us? By this we shall be marked out, I and your people, from all the peoples on the face of the earth.' 17 Yahweh then said to Moses, 'Again I shall do what you have asked, because you enjoy my favour and because I know you by name.'

18 He then said, 'Please show me your glory.' 19 Yahweh said, 'I shall make all my goodness pass before you, and before you I shall pronounce the name Yahweh; and I am gracious to those to whom I am gracious and I take pity on those on whom I take pity. 20 But my face', he said, 'you cannot see, for no human being can see me and survive.' 21 Then Yahweh said, 'Here is a place near me. You will stand on the rock, 22 and when my glory passes by, I shall put you in a cleft of the rock and shield you with my hand until I have gone past. 23 Then I shall take my hand away and you will see my back; but my face will not be seen.'

34 Yahweh said to Moses, 'Cut two tablets of stone like the first ones and come up to me on the mountain, and I will write on the tablets the words that were on the first tablets, which you broke. 2 Be ready at dawn; at dawn come up Mount Sinai and wait for me there at the top of the mountain. 3 No one may come up with you, no one may be seen anywhere on the mountain; the flocks and herds may not even graze in front of this mountain.' 4 So he cut two tablets of stone like the first and, with the two tablets of stone in his hands, Moses went up Mount Sinai in the early morning as Yahweh had ordered. 5 And Yahweh descended in a cloud and stood with him there and pronounced the name Yahweh.

6 Then Yahweh passed before him and called out, 'Yahweh, Yahweh, God of tenderness and compassion, slow to anger, rich in faithful love and constancy, 7 maintaining his faithful love to thousands, forgiving fault, crime and sin, yet letting nothing go unchecked, and punishing the parent's fault in the children and in the grandchildren to the third and fourth generation!' 8 Moses immediately bowed to the ground in worship, 9 then he said, 'If indeed I do enjoy your favour, please, my Lord, come with us, although they are an obstinate people; and forgive our faults and sins, and adopt us as your heritage.'

10 He then said, 'Look, I am now making a covenant: I shall work such wonders at the head of your whole people as have never been worked in any other country or nation, and all the people round you will see what Yahweh can do, for what I shall do through you will be awe-inspiring. 11 Mark, then, what I command you today. I am going to drive out the Amorites, the Canaanites, the Hittites, the Perizzites, the Hivites and the Jebusites before you. 12 Take care you make no pact with the inhabitants of the country which you are about to enter, or they will prove a snare in your community. 13 You will tear down their altars, smash their cultic stones and cut down their sacred poles, 14 for you will worship no other god, since Yahweh's name is the Jealous One; he is a jealous God. 15 Make no pact with the inhabitants of the country or, when they prostitute themselves to their own gods and sacrifice to them, they will invite you and you will partake of their sacrifice, 16 and then

16 And you will take wives from among their daughters for your sons, and their daughters who prostitute themselves to their gods will make your sons also prostitute themselves to their gods.

17 You shall not make cast idols.

18 You shall keep the festival of unleavened bread. Seven days you shall eat unleavened bread, as I commanded you, at the time appointed in the month of Abib; for in the month of Abib you came out from Egypt.

19 All that first opens the womb is mine, all your male*g* livestock, the firstborn of cow and sheep. 20 The firstborn of a donkey you shall redeem with a lamb, or if you will not redeem it you shall break its neck. All the firstborn of your sons you shall redeem.

No one shall appear before me empty-handed.

21 Six days you shall work, but on the seventh day you shall rest; even in plowing time and in harvest time you shall rest. 22 You shall observe the festival of weeks, the first fruits of wheat harvest, and the festival of ingathering at the turn of the year. 23 Three times in the year all your males shall appear before the LORD God, the God of Israel. 24 For I will cast out nations before you, and enlarge your borders; no one shall covet your land when you go up to appear before the LORD your God three times in the year.

25 You shall not offer the blood of my sacrifice with leaven, and the sacrifice of the festival of the passover shall not be left until the morning.

26 The best of the first fruits of your ground you shall bring to the house of the LORD your God.

You shall not boil a kid in its mother's milk.

27 The LORD said to Moses: Write these words; in accordance with these words I have made a covenant with you and with Israel. 28 He was there with the LORD forty days and forty nights; he neither ate bread nor drank water. And he wrote on the tablets the words of the covenant, the ten commandments.*h*

29 Moses came down from Mount Sinai. As he came down from the mountain with the two tablets of the covenant*i* in his hand, Moses did not know that the skin of his face shone because he had been talking with God. 30 When Aaron and all the Israelites saw Moses, the skin of his face was shining, and they were afraid to come near him. 31 But Moses called to them; and Aaron and all the leaders of the congregation returned to him, and Moses spoke with them. 32 Afterward all the Israelites came near, and he gave them in commandment all that the LORD had spoken with him on Mount Sinai. 33 When Moses had finished speaking with them, he put a veil on his face; 34 but whenever Moses went in before the LORD to speak with him, he would take the veil off, until he came out; and when he came out, and told the Israelites what he had been commanded, 35 the Israelites would see the face of Moses, that the skin of his face was shining; and Moses would put the veil on his face again, until he went in to speak with him.

35 Moses assembled all the congregation of the Israelites and said to them: These are the things that the LORD has commanded you to do:

2 Six days shall work be done, but on the seventh day you shall have a holy sabbath of solemn rest to the LORD; whoever does any work on it shall be put to death. 3 You shall kindle no fire in all your dwellings on the sabbath day.

4 Moses said to all the congregation of the Israelites: This is the thing that the LORD has commanded: 5 Take from

your sons to their daughters, and when their daughters go wantonly after their gods, they may lead your sons astray too.

17 Do not make yourselves gods of cast metal.

18 You are to celebrate the pilgrim-feast of Unleavened Bread: for seven days, as I have commanded you, you are to eat unleavened bread at the appointed time in the month of Abib, because it was in Abib that you came out from Egypt.

19 The first birth of every womb belongs to me, the males of all your herds, both cattle and sheep. 20 The first birth of a donkey you may redeem with a lamb, but if you do not redeem it, you must break its neck. Every firstborn among your sons you must redeem, and no one is to come into my presence without an offering.

21 For six days you may work, but on the seventh abstain from work; even at ploughing time and harvest you must cease work.

22 You are to observe the pilgrim-feast of Weeks, the firstfruits of the wheat harvest, and the pilgrim-feast of Ingathering at the turn of the year. 23 Those three times a year all your males are to come into the presence of the Lord, the LORD the God of Israel; 24 for after I have dispossessed the nations before you and extended your frontiers, there will be no danger from covetous neighbours when you go up those three times to enter the presence of the LORD your God.

25 Do not offer the blood of my sacrifice at the same time as anything leavened; nor is any portion of the victim of the pilgrim-feast of Passover to remain overnight till morning.

26 You must bring the choicest firstfruits of your soil to the house of the LORD your God.

Do not boil a kid in its mother's milk.

27 The LORD said to Moses, 'Write these words down, because the covenant I make with you and with Israel is on those terms.' 28 So Moses remained there with the LORD forty days and forty nights without food or drink. The LORD wrote down the words of the covenant, the Ten Commandments, on the tablets.

29 At length Moses came down from Mount Sinai with the two stone tablets of the Testimony in his hands, and when he came down, he did not know that the skin of his face shone because he had been talking with the LORD. 30 When Aaron and the Israelites saw how the skin of Moses' face shone, they were afraid to approach him. 31 He called out to them, and Aaron and all the chiefs in the community turned towards him. Moses spoke to them, 32 and after that all the Israelites drew near. He gave them all the commands with which the LORD had charged him on Mount Sinai.

33 When Moses finished what he had to say, he put a veil over his face. 34 But whenever he went in before the LORD to speak with him, he left the veil off until he came out. Then he would go out and tell the Israelites all the commands he had received. 35 The Israelites would see how the skin of Moses' face shone, and he would put the veil back over his face until he went in again to speak with the LORD.

35 MOSES called the whole community of Israelites together: 'These', he said, 'are the LORD's commands to you: 2 Work may be done for six days, but the seventh you are to keep as a sabbath of solemn abstinence from work, holy to the LORD. Whoever does any work on that day is to be put to death. 3 Wherever you live, you are not even to light your fire on the sabbath day.'

4 Moses said to the whole Israelite community: 'This is the command the LORD has given: 5 Each of you is to set

g Gk Theodotion Vg Tg: Meaning of Heb uncertain   *h* Heb words
i Or treaty, or testimony; Heb eduth

34:19 **the males:** *so* Gk; *Heb. unintelligible.*   34:20 **come . . .
presence:** *lit.* see my face.   34:28 **Ten Commandments:** *lit.* Ten
Words.

ther shall you take their daughters as wives for your sons; otherwise, when their daughters render their wanton worship to their gods, they will make your sons do the same.

17 "You shall not make for yourselves molten gods.

18 "You shall keep the feast of Unleavened Bread. For seven days at the prescribed time in the month of Abib you are to eat unleavened bread, as I commanded you; for in the month of Abib you came out of Egypt.

19 "To me belongs every first-born male that opens the womb among all your livestock, whether in the herd or in the flock. 20 The firstling of an ass you shall redeem with one of the flock; if you do not redeem it, you must break its neck. The first-born among your sons you shall redeem.

"No one shall appear before me empty-handed.

21 "For six days you may work, but on the seventh day you shall rest; on that day you must rest even during the seasons of plowing and harvesting.

22 "You shall keep the feast of Weeks with the first of the wheat harvest; likewise, the feast at the fruit harvest at the close of the year. 23 Three times a year all your men shall appear before the Lord, the LORD God of Israel. 24 Since I will drive out the nations before you to give you a large territory, there will be no one to covet your land when you go up three times a year to appear before the LORD, your God.

25 "You shall not offer me the blood of sacrifice with leavened bread, nor shall the sacrifice of the Passover feast be kept overnight for the next day.

26 "The choicest first fruits of your soil you shall bring to the house of the LORD, your God.

"You shall not boil a kid in its mother's milk."

27 Then the LORD said to Moses, "Write down these words, for in accordance with them I have made a covenant with you and with Israel." 28 So Moses stayed there with the LORD for forty days and forty nights, without eating any food or drinking any water, and he wrote on the tablets the words of the covenant, the ten commandments.

29 As Moses came down from Mount Sinai with the two tablets of the commandments in his hands, he did not know that the skin of his face had become radiant while he conversed with the LORD. 30 When Aaron, then, and the other Israelites saw Moses and noticed how radiant the skin of his face had become, they were afraid to come near him. 31 Only after Moses called to them did Aaron and all the rulers of the community come back to him. Moses then spoke to them. 32 Later on, all the Israelites came up to him, and he enjoined on them all that the LORD had told him on Mount Sinai. 33 When he finished speaking with them, he put a veil over his face. 34 Whenever Moses entered the presence of the LORD to converse with him, he removed the veil until he came out again. On coming out, he would tell the Israelites all that had been commanded. 35 Then the Israelites would see that the skin of Moses' face was radiant; so he would again put the veil over his face until he went in to converse with the LORD.

35 Moses assembled the whole Israelite community and said to them, "This is what the LORD has commanded to be done. 2 On six days work may be done, but the seventh day shall be sacred to you as the sabbath of complete rest to the LORD. Anyone who does work on that day shall be put to death. 3 You shall not even light a fire in any of your dwellings on the sabbath day."

4 Moses told the whole Israelite community, "This is what the LORD has commanded: 5 Take up among you a

you will choose wives for your sons from among their daughters, and their daughters, prostituting themselves to their own gods, will induce your sons to prostitute themselves to their gods.

17 'You will not cast metal gods for yourself.

18 'You will observe the feast of Unleavened Bread. For seven days you will eat unleavened bread, as I have commanded you, at the appointed time in the month of Abib, for in the month of Abib you came out of Egypt.

19 'All that first issues from the womb belongs to me: every male, every first-born of flock or herd. 20 But the first-born donkey you will redeem with an animal from the flock; if you do not redeem it, you must break its neck. All the first-born of your sons you will redeem, and no one will appear before me empty-handed.

21 'For six days you will labour, but on the seventh day you will rest; you will stop work even during ploughing and harvesting.

22 'You will observe the feast of Weeks, of the first-fruits of the wheat harvest, and the feast of Ingathering at the close of the year.

23 'Three times a year all your menfolk will appear before Lord Yahweh, God of Israel, 24 for I shall dispossess the nations before you and extend your frontiers, and no one will set his heart on your territory when you go away to appear before Yahweh your God three times a year.

25 'You will not offer the blood of my sacrificial victim with leavened bread, nor is the victim offered at the feast of Passover to be left until the following day.

26 'You will bring the best of the first-fruits of your soil to the house of Yahweh your God.

'You will not boil a kid in its mother's milk.'

27 Yahweh then said to Moses, 'Put these words in writing, for they are the terms of the covenant which I have made with you and with Israel.'

28 He stayed there with Yahweh for forty days and forty nights, eating and drinking nothing, and on the tablets he wrote the words of the covenant — the Ten Words.

29 When Moses came down from Mount Sinai with the two tablets of the Testimony in his hands, as he was coming down the mountain, Moses did not know that the skin of his face was radiant because he had been talking to him. 30 And when Aaron and all the Israelites saw Moses, the skin on his face was so radiant that they were afraid to go near him. 31 But Moses called to them, and Aaron and all the leaders of the community rejoined him, and Moses talked to them, 32 after which all the Israelites came closer, and he passed on to them all the orders that Yahweh had given to him on Mount Sinai. 33 Once Moses had finished speaking to them, he put a veil over his face. 34 Whenever Moses went into Yahweh's presence to speak with him, he took the veil off until he came out. And when he came out, he would tell the Israelites what orders he had been given, 35 and the Israelites would see Moses' face radiant. Then Moses would put the veil back over his face until he went in to speak to him next time.

35 Moses assembled the whole community of Israelites and said, 'These are the things Yahweh has ordered to be done: 2 Work must be done for six days, but the seventh must be a holy day for you, a day of complete rest, in honour of Yahweh. Anyone who does any work on that day will be put to death. 3 You will not light a fire on the Sabbath day in any of your homes.'

4 Moses spoke to the whole community of Israelites. 'This', he said, 'is what Yahweh has ordered: 5 Set aside a

among you an offering to the LORD; let whoever is of a generous heart bring the LORD's offering: gold, silver, and bronze; 6 blue, purple, and crimson yarns, and fine linen; goats' hair, 7 tanned rams' skins, and fine leather; *j* acacia wood, 8 oil for the light, spices for the anointing oil and for the fragrant incense, 9 and onyx stones and gems to be set in the ephod and the breastpiece.

10 All who are skillful among you shall come and make all that the LORD has commanded: the tabernacle, 11 its tent and its covering, its clasps and its frames, its bars, its pillars, and its bases; 12 the ark with its poles, the mercy seat, *k* and the curtain for the screen; 13 the table with its poles and all its utensils, and the bread of the Presence; 14 the lampstand also for the light, with its utensils and its lamps, and the oil for the light; 15 and the altar of incense, with its poles, and the anointing oil and the fragrant incense, and the screen for the entrance, the entrance of the tabernacle; 16 the altar of burnt offering, with its grating of bronze, its poles, and all its utensils, the basin with its stand; 17 the hangings of the court, its pillars and its bases, and the screen for the gate of the court; 18 the pegs of the tabernacle and the pegs of the court, and their cords; 19 the finely worked vestments for ministering in the holy place, the holy vestments for the priest Aaron, and the vestments of his sons, for their service as priests.

20 Then all the congregation of the Israelites withdrew from the presence of Moses. 21 And they came, everyone whose heart was stirred, and everyone whose spirit was willing, and brought the LORD's offering to be used for the tent of meeting, and for all its service, and for the sacred vestments. 22 So they came, both men and women; all who were of a willing heart brought brooches and earrings and signet rings and pendants, all sorts of gold objects, everyone bringing an offering of gold to the LORD. 23 And everyone who possessed blue or purple or crimson yarn or fine linen or goats' hair or tanned rams' skins or fine leather, *j* brought them. 24 Everyone who could make an offering of silver or bronze brought it as the LORD's offering; and everyone who possessed acacia wood of any use in the work, brought it. 25 All the skillful women spun with their hands, and brought what they had spun in blue and purple and crimson yarns and fine linen; 26 all the women whose hearts moved them to use their skill spun the goats' hair. 27 And the leaders brought onyx stones and gems to be set in the ephod and the breastpiece, 28 and spices and oil for the light, and for the anointing oil, and for the fragrant incense. 29 All the Israelite men and women whose hearts made them willing to bring anything for the work that the LORD had commanded by Moses to be done, brought it as a freewill offering to the LORD.

30 Then Moses said to the Israelites: See, the LORD has called by name Bezalel son of Uri son of Hur, of the tribe of Judah; 31 he has filled him with divine spirit, *l* with skill, intelligence, and knowledge in every kind of craft, 32 to devise artistic designs, to work in gold, silver, and bronze, 33 in cutting stones for setting, and in carving wood, in every kind of craft. 34 And he has inspired him to teach, both him and Oholiab son of Ahisamach, of the tribe of Dan. 35 He has filled them with skill to do every kind of work done by an artisan or by a designer or by an embroiderer in blue, purple, and crimson yarns, and in fine linen, or by a weaver — by any sort of artisan or skilled designer.

aside a contribution to the LORD. Let all who wish bring a contribution to the LORD: gold, silver, copper; 6 violet, purple, and scarlet yarn; fine linen and goats' hair; 7 tanned rams' skins and dugong-hides; and acacia-wood; 8 oil for the lamp, spices for the anointing oil and for the fragrant incense; 9 cornelians and other stones ready for setting on the ephod and the breastpiece.

10 'Let all the skilled craftsmen among you come and make everything the LORD has commanded: 11 the Tabernacle, its tent and covering, fasteners, planks, bars, posts, and sockets, 12 the Ark and its poles, the cover and the curtain of the screen, 13 the table, its poles and all its vessels, and the Bread of the Presence; 14 the lampstand for the light, its fittings, lamps, and the lamp oil; 15 the altar of incense and its poles, the anointing oil, the fragrant incense, and the screen for the entrance of the Tabernacle, 16 the altar of whole-offering, its bronze grating, poles, and all appurtenances, the basin and its stand; 17 the hangings of the court, its posts and sockets, and the screen for the gateway of the court; 18 the pegs of the Tabernacle and court and their cords, 19 the stitched vestments for ministering in the Holy Place, that is the sacred vestments for Aaron the priest and the vestments for his sons when they minister as priests.'

20 The whole community of the Israelites went out from Moses' presence, 21 and everyone who was so minded brought of his own free will a contribution to the LORD for the making of the Tent of Meeting and for all its service, and for the sacred vestments. 22 Men and women alike came and freely brought clasps, ear-rings, finger-rings, and pendants, gold ornaments of every kind, every one of them presenting a special gift of gold to the LORD. 23 Every man brought what he possessed of violet, purple, and scarlet yarn, fine linen and goats' hair, tanned rams' skins, and dugong-hides. 24 Every man, setting aside a contribution of silver or copper, brought it as a contribution to the LORD, and all who had acacia-wood suitable for any part of the work brought it. 25 Every woman with the skill spun and brought the violet, purple, and scarlet yarn, and fine linen. 26 The women, all whose skill moved them, spun the goats' hair. 27 The chiefs brought cornelians and other stones ready for setting in the ephod and the breastpiece, 28 the spices and oil for the lamp, for the anointing oil, and for the fragrant incense. 29 Every Israelite man and woman who was minded to bring offerings to the LORD for all the work which he had commanded through Moses did so freely.

30 Moses said to the Israelites, 'Take note that the LORD has specially chosen Bezalel son of Uri, son of Hur, of the tribe of Judah. 31 He has filled him with the spirit of God, making him skilful and ingenious, expert in every craft, 32 and a master of design, whether in gold, silver, and copper, 33 or cutting precious stones for setting, or carving wood, in every kind of design. 34 He has inspired both him and Aholiab son of Ahisamach of the tribe of Dan to instruct 35 workers and designers of every kind, engravers, seamsters, embroiderers in violet, purple, and scarlet yarn and fine linen, and weavers, fully endowing them with skill to execute all kinds of work.

j Meaning of Heb uncertain   *k* Or *the cover*   *l* Or *the spirit of God*

35:22 **pendants:** *Heb. word of uncertain meaning.*

NEW AMERICAN BIBLE

collection for the LORD. Everyone, as his heart prompts him, shall bring, as a contribution to the LORD, gold, silver and bronze; 6 violet, purple and scarlet yarn; fine linen and goat hair; 7 rams' skins dyed red, and tahash skins; acacia wood; 8 oil for the light; spices for the anointing oil and for the fragrant incense; 9 onyx stones and other gems for mounting on the ephod and on the breastpiece.

10 "Let every expert among you come and make all that the LORD has commanded: 11 the Dwelling, with its tent, its covering, its clasps, its boards, its bars, its columns and its pedestals; 12 the ark, with its poles, the propitiatory, and the curtain veil; 13 the table, with its poles and all its appurtenances, and the showbread; 14 the lampstand, with its appurtenances, the lamps, and the oil for the light; 15 the altar of incense, with its poles; the anointing oil, and the fragrant incense; the entrance curtain for the entrance of the Dwelling; 16 the altar of holocausts, with its bronze grating, its poles, and all its appurtenances; the laver, with its base; 17 the hangings of the court, with their columns and pedestals; the curtain for the entrance of the court; 18 the tent pegs for the Dwelling and for the court, with their ropes; 19 the service cloths for use in the sanctuary; the sacred vestments for Aaron, the priest, and the vestments worn by his sons in their ministry."

20 When the whole Israelite community left Moses' presence, 21 everyone, as his heart suggested and his spirit prompted, brought a contribution to the LORD for the construction of the meeting tent, for all its services, and for the sacred vestments. 22 Both the men and the women, all as their hearts prompted them, brought brooches, earrings, rings, necklaces and various other gold articles. Everyone who could presented an offering of gold to the LORD. 23 Everyone who happened to have violet, purple or scarlet yarn, fine linen or goat hair, rams' skins dyed red or tahash skins, brought them. 24 Whoever could make a contribution of silver or bronze offered it to the LORD; and everyone who happened to have acacia wood for any part of the work, brought it. 25 All the women who were expert spinners brought hand-spun violet, purple and scarlet yarn and fine linen thread. 26 All the women who possessed the skill, spun goat hair. 27 The princes brought onyx stones and other gems for mounting on the ephod and on the breastpiece; 28 as well as spices, and oil for the light, anointing oil, and fragrant incense. 29 Every Israelite man and woman brought to the LORD such voluntary offerings as they thought best, for the various kinds of work which the LORD had commanded Moses to have done.

30 Moses said to the Israelites, "See, the LORD has chosen Bezalel, son of Uri, son of Hur, of the tribe of Judah, 31 and has filled him with a divine spirit of skill and understanding and knowledge in every craft: 32 in the production of embroidery, in making things of gold, silver or bronze, 33 in cutting and mounting precious stones, in carving wood, and in every other craft. 34 He has also given both him and Oholiab, son of Ahisamach, of the tribe of Dan, the ability to teach others. 35 He has endowed them with skill to execute all types of work: engraving, embroidering, the making of variegated cloth of violet, purple and scarlet yarn and fine linen thread, weaving, and all other arts and crafts.

NEW JERUSALEM BIBLE

contribution for Yahweh out of your possessions. Everyone whose heart prompts him to do so should bring a contribution for Yahweh: gold, silver and bronze; 6 materials dyed violet-purple, red-purple and crimson, finely woven linen, goats' hair, 7 rams' skins dyed red, fine leather, acacia wood, 8 oil for the light, spices for the anointing oil and for the fragrant incense; 9 cornelian and other stones to be set in the *ephod* and breastplate. 10 And all those of you who have the skill must come and make everything that Yahweh has ordered: 11 the Dwelling, its tent and its covering, its clasps and its frames, its crossbars, its pillars and its sockets; 12 the ark, its shafts and all its accessories, the mercy-seat and the screening curtain; 13 the table, its shafts and all its accessories, and the loaves of permanent offering; 14 the lamp-stand for the light, its accessories, its lamps, and the oil for the light; 15 the altar of incense and its shafts, the anointing oil, the fragrant incense, and the screen for the entrance, for the entrance of the tent; 16 the altar of burnt offerings and its bronze grating, its shafts, and all its accessories; the basin and its stand; 17 the curtaining for the court, its poles, its sockets, and the screen for the entrance to the court; 18 the pegs for the Dwelling and the pegs for the court, and their cords; 19 the liturgical vestments for service in the sanctuary — the sacred vestments for Aaron the priest, and the vestments for his sons, for their priestly functions.'

20 The whole community of Israelites then withdrew from Moses' presence. 21 And all those whose heart stirred them and all those whose spirit prompted them brought a contribution for Yahweh, for the work on the Tent of Meeting, for its general service and for the sacred vestments. 22 Men and women, they came, all those whose heart prompted them, bringing brooches, rings, bracelets, necklaces, golden objects of every kind — all those who had vowed gold to Yahweh, 23 while all those who happened to own violet-purple, red-purple or crimson materials, finely woven linen, goats' hair, rams' skins dyed red, or fine leather, brought that. 24 All those offering a contribution of silver or bronze brought their contribution for Yahweh and all who happened to own acacia wood, suitable for any of the work to be done, brought that. 25 All the skilled women set their hands to spinning, and brought what they had spun: violet-purple, red-purple or crimson materials, and fine linen, 26 while all those women whose heart stirred them by virtue of their skill, spun goats' hair. 27 The leaders brought cornelians and other stones to be set in the *ephod* and breastplate, 28 and the spices and oil for the light, for the anointing oil and for the fragrant incense. 29 All those Israelites, men and women, whose heart prompted them to contribute to the entire work that Yahweh had ordered through Moses to be done, brought a contribution to Yahweh.

30 Moses then said to the Israelites, 'Look, Yahweh has singled out Bezalel son of Uri, son of Hur, of the tribe of Judah, 31 and has filled him with the spirit of God in wisdom, knowledge and skill in every kind of craft: 32 in designing and carrying out work in gold and silver and bronze, 33 in cutting stones to be set, in wood carving and in executing every kind of work. 34 And on him and on Oholiab son of Ahisamach, of the tribe of Dan, he has bestowed the gift of teaching, 35 and filled them with the skill to carry out every kind of work, that of the engraver, that of the embroiderer, that of the needleworker in violet-purple, red-purple and crimson materials and fine linen, that of the weaver, and indeed that of every kind of craftsman and designer.'

36 Bezalel and Oholiab and every skillful one to whom the LORD has given skill and understanding to know how to do any work in the construction of the sanctuary shall work in accordance with all that the LORD has commanded.

2 Moses then called Bezalel and Oholiab and every skillful one to whom the LORD had given skill, everyone whose heart was stirred to come to do the work; 3 and they received from Moses all the freewill offerings that the Israelites had brought for doing the work on the sanctuary. They still kept bringing him freewill offerings every morning, 4 so that all the artisans who were doing every sort of task on the sanctuary came, each from the task being performed, 5 and said to Moses, "The people are bringing much more than enough for doing the work that the LORD has commanded us to do." 6 So Moses gave command, and word was proclaimed throughout the camp: "No man or woman is to make anything else as an offering for the sanctuary." So the people were restrained from bringing; 7 for what they had already brought was more than enough to do all the work.

8 All those with skill among the workers made the tabernacle with ten curtains; they were made of fine twisted linen, and blue, purple, and crimson yarns, with cherubim skillfully worked into them. 9 The length of each curtain was twenty-eight cubits, and the width of each curtain four cubits; all the curtains were of the same size.

10 He joined five curtains to one another, and the other five curtains he joined to one another. 11 He made loops of blue on the edge of the outermost curtain of the first set; likewise he made them on the edge of the outermost curtain of the second set; 12 he made fifty loops on the one curtain, and he made fifty loops on the edge of the curtain that was in the second set; the loops were opposite one another. 13 And he made fifty clasps of gold, and joined the curtains one to the other with clasps; so the tabernacle was one whole.

14 He also made curtains of goats' hair for a tent over the tabernacle; he made eleven curtains. 15 The length of each curtain was thirty cubits, and the width of each curtain four cubits; the eleven curtains were of the same size. 16 He joined five curtains by themselves, and six curtains by themselves. 17 He made fifty loops on the edge of the outermost curtain of the one set, and fifty loops on the edge of the other connecting curtain. 18 He made fifty clasps of bronze to join the tent together so that it might be one whole. 19 And he made for the tent a covering of tanned rams' skins and an outer covering of fine leather. *m*

20 Then he made the upright frames for the tabernacle of acacia wood. 21 Ten cubits was the length of a frame, and a cubit and a half the width of each frame. 22 Each frame had two pegs for fitting together; he did this for all the frames of the tabernacle. 23 The frames for the tabernacle he made in this way: twenty frames for the south side; 24 and he made forty bases of silver under the twenty frames, two bases under the first frame for its two pegs, and two bases under the next frame for its two pegs. 25 For the second side of the tabernacle, on the north side, he made twenty frames 26 and their forty bases of silver, two bases under the first frame and two bases under the next frame. 27 For the rear of the tabernacle westward he made six frames. 28 He made two frames for corners of the tabernacle in the rear. 29 They were separate beneath, but joined at the top, at the first ring; he made two of them in this way, for the two corners. 30 There were eight frames with their bases of silver: sixteen bases, under every frame two bases.

31 He made bars of acacia wood, five for the frames of the one side of the tabernacle, 32 and five bars for the frames

36 1 Bezalel and Aholiab are to work exactly as the LORD has commanded, and so also is every craftsman whom the LORD has made skilful and ingenious in these matters so that they may know how to execute every kind of work for the service of the sanctuary.'

2 Moses summoned Bezalel, Aholiab, and every other craftsman to whom the LORD had given skill and who was willing, to come forward and set to work. 3 They took from before Moses all the contributions which the Israelites had brought for the work of the service of the sanctuary, but the people still brought freewill-offerings morning after morning. 4 The craftsmen at work on the sanctuary therefore left what they were doing, every one of them, 5 and came to Moses and said, 'The people are bringing much more than we need for doing the work which the LORD has commanded.' 6 So Moses sent word round the camp that no man or woman should prepare anything more as a contribution for the sanctuary. The people stopped bringing gifts; 7 what was there already was more than enough for all the work they had to do.

8 So all the skilled craftsmen among the workers made the Tabernacle of ten hangings of finely woven linen, and violet, purple, and scarlet yarn, with cherubim worked on them, all made by a seamster. 9 The length of each hanging was twenty-eight cubits and the breadth four cubits, all of the same size. 10 They joined five of the hangings together, and similarly the other five. 11 They made violet loops along the outer edge of one set of hangings and they did the same for the outer edge of the other set of hangings. 12 They made fifty loops for each hanging; they made also fifty loops for the end hanging in the second set, the loops being opposite each other. 13 They made fifty gold fasteners, with which they joined the hangings one to another, and the Tabernacle became a single whole.

14 They made hangings of goats' hair, eleven in all, to form a tent over the Tabernacle; 15 each hanging was thirty cubits long and four cubits wide, all eleven of the same size. 16 They joined five of the hangings together, and similarly the other six. 17 They made fifty loops on the edge of the last hanging in the first set and fifty loops on the joining edge of the second set, 18 and fifty bronze fasteners to join up the tent and make it a single whole. 19 They made for the tent a cover of tanned rams' skins and an outer covering of dugong-hides.

20 They made for the Tabernacle frames of acacia-wood as uprights, 21 each frame ten cubits long and one and a half cubits wide, 22 and two tenons for each frame joined to each other. They did the same for all the frames of the Tabernacle. 23 They arranged the frames thus: twenty frames for the south side facing southwards, 24 with forty silver sockets under them, two sockets under each frame for its two tenons; 25 and for the second or northern side of the Tabernacle twenty frames 26 with forty silver sockets, two under each frame. 27 They made six frames for the far end of the Tabernacle on the west. 28 They made two frames for the corners of the Tabernacle at the far end; 29 at the bottom they were alike, and at the top, both alike, they fitted into a single ring. They did the same for both of them at the two corners. 30 There were eight frames with their silver sockets, sixteen sockets in all, two sockets under each frame.

31 They made bars of acacia-wood: five for the frames on one side of the Tabernacle, 32 five bars for the frames on the

---

m Meaning of Heb uncertain

36:29 **both alike:** *so Samar.; Heb.* both perfect.

NEW AMERICAN BIBLE

36 "Bezalel, therefore, will set to work with Oholiab and with all the experts whom the LORD has endowed with skill and understanding in knowing how to execute all the work for the service of the sanctuary, just as the LORD has commanded."

2 Moses then called Bezalel and Oholiab and all the other experts whom the LORD had endowed with skill, men whose hearts moved them to come and take part in the work. 3 They received from Moses all the contributions which the Israelites had brought for establishing the service of the sanctuary. Still, morning after morning the people continued to bring their voluntary offerings to Moses. 4 Thereupon the experts who were executing the various kinds of work for the sanctuary, all left the work they were doing, 5 and told Moses, "The people are bringing much more than is needed to carry out the work which the LORD has commanded us to do." 6 Moses, therefore, ordered a proclamation to be made throughout the camp: "Let neither man nor woman make any more contributions for the sanctuary." So the people stopped bringing their offerings; 7 there was already enough at hand, in fact, more than enough, to complete the work to be done.

8 The various experts who were executing the work, made the Dwelling with its ten sheets woven of fine linen twined, having cherubim embroidered on them with violet, purple and scarlet yarn. 9 The length of each sheet was twenty-eight cubits, and the width four cubits; all the sheets were of the same size. 10 Five of the sheets were sewed together, edge to edge; and the same for the other five. 11 Loops of violet yarn were made along the edge of the end sheet in the first set, and the same along the edge of the end sheet in the second set. 12 Fifty loops were thus put on one inner sheet, and fifty loops on the inner sheet in the other set, with the loops directly opposite each other. 13 Then fifty clasps of gold were made, with which the sheets were joined so that the Dwelling formed one whole.

14 Sheets of goat hair were also woven as a tent over the Dwelling. Eleven such sheets were made. 15 The length of each sheet was thirty cubits and the width four cubits; all eleven sheets were of the same size. 16 Five of these sheets were sewed edge to edge into one set; and the other six sheets into another set. 17 Fifty loops were made along the edge of the end sheet in one set, and fifty loops along the edge of the corresponding sheet in the other set. 18 Fifty bronze clasps were made with which the tent was joined so that it formed one whole. 19 A covering for the tent was made of rams' skins dyed red, and above that, a covering of tahash skins.

20 Boards of acacia wood were made as walls for the Dwelling. 21 The length of each board was ten cubits, and the width one and a half cubits. 22 Each board had two arms, fastening them in line. In this way all the boards of the Dwelling were made. 23 They were set up as follows: twenty boards on the south side, 24 with forty silver pedestals under the twenty boards, so that there were two pedestals under each board, at its two arms; 25 twenty boards on the other side of the Dwelling, the north side, 26 with their forty silver pedestals, two under each board; 27 six boards at the rear of the Dwelling, to the west; 28 and two boards at the corners in the rear of the Dwelling. 29 These were double at the bottom, and likewise double at the top, to the first ring. That is how both boards in the corners were made. 30 Thus, there were in the rear eight boards, with their sixteen silver pedestals, two pedestals under each board. 31 Bars of acacia wood were also made, five for the boards on one side of the Dwelling, 32 five for those on the other side, and five for

NEW JERUSALEM BIBLE

36 'Bezalel, Oholiab and all the men whom Yahweh has endowed with the skill and knowledge to know how to carry out all the work to be done on the sanctuary, will do exactly as Yahweh has ordered.'

2 Moses then summoned Bezalel, Oholiab and all the skilled men whose hearts Yahweh had endowed with skill, all whose heart stirred them to come forward and do the work. 3 From Moses they received everything that the Israelites had brought as contributions for carrying out the work of building the sanctuary, and, as they went on bringing their offerings every morning, 4 the skilled men who were doing all the work for the sanctuary, all left their particular work 5 and said to Moses, 'The people are bringing more than is needed for the work Yahweh has ordered to be done.' 6 Moses then gave the order and proclamation was made throughout the camp, 'No one, whether man or woman, must do anything more towards contributing for the sanctuary.' So the people were prevented from bringing any more, 7 for the material to hand was enough, and more than enough, to complete all the work.

8 All the most skilled of the men doing the work made the Dwelling. Moses made it with ten sheets of finely woven linen, dyed violet-purple, red-purple and crimson and embroidered with great winged creatures. 9 The length of a single sheet was twenty-eight cubits, its width four cubits, all the sheets being of the same size. 10 He joined five of the sheets to one another, and the other five sheets to one another. 11 He made violet loops along the edge of the first sheet, at the end of the set, and did the same along the edge of the last sheet in the other set. 12 He made fifty loops on the first sheet and fifty loops along the outer edge of the sheet of the second set, the loops corresponding to one another. 13 He made fifty gold clasps and joined the sheets together with the clasps. In this way the Dwelling was a unified whole.

14 Next he made sheets of goats' hair for the tent over the Dwelling; he made eleven of these. 15 The length of a single sheet was thirty cubits and its width four cubits; the eleven sheets were all of the same size. 16 He joined five sheets together into one set and six sheets into another. 17 He made fifty loops along the edge of the last sheet of the first set, and fifty loops along the edge of the sheet of the second set. 18 He made fifty bronze clasps, to draw the tent together and make it a unified whole. 19 And for the tent he made a cover of rams' skins dyed red, and a cover of fine leather over that.

20 For the Dwelling he made vertical frames of acacia wood. 21 Each frame was ten cubits long and one and a half cubits wide. 22 Each frame had twin tenons; this was how he made all the frames for the Dwelling. He made frames for the Dwelling: twenty frames for the south side, to the south, 24 and made forty silver sockets under the twenty frames, two sockets under one frame for its two tenons, two sockets under the next frame for its two tenons; 25 and for the other side of the Dwelling, the north side, twenty frames 26 and forty silver sockets, two sockets under one frame, two sockets under the next frame. 27 For the back of the Dwelling, on the west, he made six frames. 28 He also made two frames for the corners at the back of the Dwelling; 29 these were coupled together at the bottom, staying so up to the top, to the level of the first ring; this he did with the two frames forming the two corners. 30 Thus there were eight frames with their sixteen silver sockets; two sockets under each frame. 31 He made crossbars of acacia wood: five for the frames of the first side of the Dwelling, 32 five crossbars

of the other side of the tabernacle, and five bars for the frames of the tabernacle at the rear westward. 33 He made the middle bar to pass through from end to end halfway up the frames. 34 And he overlaid the frames with gold, and made rings of gold for them to hold the bars, and overlaid the bars with gold.

35 He made the curtain of blue, purple, and crimson yarns, and fine twisted linen, with cherubim skillfully worked into it. 36 For it he made four pillars of acacia, overlaid them with gold; their hooks were of gold, and he cast for them four bases of silver. 37 He also made a screen for the entrance to the tent, of blue, purple, and crimson yarns, and fine twisted linen, embroidered with needlework; 38 and its five pillars with their hooks. He overlaid their capitals and their bases with gold, but their five bases were of bronze.

37 Bezalel made the ark of acacia wood; it was two and a half cubits long, a cubit and a half wide, and a cubit and a half high. 2 He overlaid it with pure gold inside and outside, and made a molding of gold around it. 3 He cast for it four rings of gold for its four feet, two rings on its one side and two rings on its other side. 4 He made poles of acacia wood, and overlaid them with gold, 5 and put the poles into the rings on the sides of the ark, to carry the ark. 6 He made a mercy seat[n] of pure gold; two cubits and a half was its length, and a cubit and a half its width. 7 He made two cherubim of hammered gold; at the two ends of the mercy seat[o] he made them, 8 one cherub at the one end, and one cherub at the other end; of one piece with the mercy seat[o] he made the cherubim at its two ends. 9 The cherubim spread out their wings above, overshadowing the mercy seat[o] with their wings. They faced one another; the faces of the cherubim were turned toward the mercy seat.[o]

10 He also made the table of acacia wood, two cubits long, one cubit wide, and a cubit and a half high. 11 He overlaid it with pure gold, and made a molding of gold around it. 12 He made around it a rim a handbreadth wide, and made a molding of gold around the rim. 13 He cast for it four rings of gold, and fastened the rings to the four corners at its four legs. 14 The rings that held the poles used for carrying the table were close to the rim. 15 He made the poles of acacia wood to carry the table, and overlaid them with gold. 16 And he made the vessels of pure gold that were to be on the table, its plates and dishes for incense, and its bowls and flagons with which to pour drink offerings.

17 He also made the lampstand of pure gold. The base and the shaft of the lampstand were made of hammered work; its cups, its calyxes, and its petals were of one piece with it. 18 There were six branches going out of its sides, three branches of the lampstand out of one side of it and three branches of the lampstand out of the other side of it; 19 three cups shaped like almond blossoms, each with calyx and petals, on one branch, and three cups shaped like almond blossoms, each with calyx and petals, on the other branch — so for the six branches going out of the lampstand. 20 On the lampstand itself there were four cups shaped like almond blossoms, each with its calyxes and petals. 21 There was a calyx of one piece with it under the first pair of branches, a calyx of one piece with it under the next pair of branches, and a calyx of one piece with it under the last pair of branches. 22 Their calyxes and their branches were of one piece with it, the whole of it one hammered piece of pure gold. 23 He made its seven lamps and its snuffers and its trays of pure gold. 24 He made it and all its utensils of a talent of pure gold.

second side of the Tabernacle, and five bars for the frames on the far end of the Tabernacle on the west. 33 They made the middle bar to run along from end to end half-way up the frames. 34 They overlaid the frames with gold and made rings of gold on them to hold the bars, which were also overlaid with gold.

35 They made the curtain of finely woven linen and violet, purple, and scarlet yarn, with cherubim worked on it, all made by a seamster. 36 They made for it four posts of acacia-wood overlaid with gold, with gold hooks, and cast four silver sockets for them. 37 For the entrance of the tent a screen of finely woven linen was made, embroidered with violet, purple, and scarlet, 38 and five posts of acacia-wood with their hooks. They overlaid the tops of the posts and the bands round them with gold; the five sockets for them were of bronze.

37 Bezalel then made the Ark, a chest of acacia-wood two and a half cubits long, one and a half cubits wide, and one and a half cubits high. 2 He overlaid it with pure gold both inside and out, and put a band of gold all round it. 3 He cast four gold rings to be on its four feet, two rings on each side. 4 He made poles of acacia-wood and overlaid them with gold, 5 and inserted the poles in the rings at the sides of the Ark to lift it. 6 He made a cover of pure gold two and a half cubits long and one and a half cubits wide. 7 He made two gold cherubim of beaten work at the ends of the cover, 8 one at each end; he made each cherub of one piece with the cover. 9 They had wings spread out and pointing upwards, screening the cover with their wings; they stood face to face, looking inwards over the cover.

10 He made the table of acacia-wood two cubits long, one cubit wide, and one and a half cubits high. 11 He overlaid it with pure gold and put a band of gold all round it. 12 He made a rim round it a hand's breadth wide, and a gold band round the rim. 13 He cast four gold rings for it, and put the rings at the four corners by the four legs. 14 The rings, which were to receive the poles for carrying the table, were adjacent to the rim. 15 These poles he made of acacia-wood and overlaid them with gold. 16 He made the vessels for the table, its dishes and saucers, and its flagons and bowls from which drink-offerings were to be poured; he made them of pure gold.

17 He made the lampstand of pure gold. The lampstand, stem and branches, was of beaten work, its cups, both calyxes and petals, being of one piece with it. 18 There were six branches springing from the sides of the lampstand, three branches from one side and three branches from the other. 19 There were three cups shaped like almond blossoms with calyx and petals on the first branch, three cups shaped like almond blossoms with calyx and petals on the next branch, and similarly for all six branches springing from the lampstand. 20 On the main stem of the lampstand there were four cups shaped like almond blossoms with calyx and petals, 21 and there were calyxes of one piece with it under the six branches which sprang from the lampstand, a single calyx under each pair of branches. 22 The calyxes and the branches were of one piece with it, all a single piece of beaten work of pure gold. 23 He made its seven lamps, its tongs, and firepans of pure gold. 24 The lampstand and all these fittings were made from one talent of pure gold.

---

n Or a cover   o Or the cover

those at the rear, to the west. 33 The center bar, at the middle of the boards, was made to reach across from end to end. 34 The boards were plated with gold, and gold rings were made on them as holders for the bars, which were also plated with gold.

35 The veil was woven of violet, purple and scarlet yarn, and of fine linen twined, with cherubim embroidered on it. 36 Four gold-plated columns of acacia wood, with gold hooks, were made for it, and four silver pedestals were cast for them.

37 The curtain for the entrance of the tent was made of violet, purple and scarlet yarn, and of fine linen twined, woven in a variegated manner. 38 Its five columns, with their hooks as well as their capitals and bands, were plated with gold; their five pedestals were of bronze.

37 Bezalel made the ark of acacia wood, two and a half cubits long, one and a half cubits wide, and one and a half cubits high. 2 The inside and outside were plated with gold, and a molding of gold was put around it. 3 Four gold rings were cast and put on its four supports, two rings for one side and two for the opposite side. 4 Poles of acacia wood were made and plated with gold; 5 these were put through the rings on the sides of the ark, for carrying it.

6 The propitiatory was made of pure gold, two and a half cubits long and one and a half cubits wide. 7 Two cherubim of beaten gold were made for the two ends of the propitiatory, 8 one cherub fastened at one end, the other at the other end, springing directly from the propitiatory at its two ends. 9 The cherubim had their wings spread out above, covering the propitiatory with them. They were turned toward each other, but with their faces looking toward the propitiatory.

10 The table was made of acacia wood, two cubits long, one cubit wide, and one and a half cubits high. 11 It was plated with pure gold, and a molding of gold was put around it. 12 A frame a handbreadth high was also put around it, with a molding of gold around the frame. 13 Four rings of gold were cast for it and fastened, one at each of the four corners. 14 The rings were alongside the frame as holders for the poles to carry the table. 15 These poles were made of acacia wood and plated with gold. 16 The vessels that were set on the table, its plates and cups, as well as its pitchers and bowls for pouring libations, were of pure gold.

17 The lampstand was made of pure beaten gold — its shaft and branches as well as its cups and knobs and petals springing directly from it. 18 Six branches extended from its sides, three branches on one side and three on the other. 19 On one branch there were three cups, shaped like almond blossoms, each with its knob and petals; on the opposite branch there were three cups, shaped like almond blossoms, each with its knob and petals; and so for the six branches that extended from the lampstand. 20 On the shaft there were four cups, shaped like almond blossoms, with their knobs and petals, 21 including a knob below each of the three pairs of branches that extended from the lampstand. 22 The knobs and branches sprang so directly from it that the whole formed but a single piece of pure beaten gold. 23 Its seven lamps, as well as its trimming shears and trays, were made of pure gold. 24 A talent of pure gold was used for the lampstand and its various appurtenances.

for the frames of the other side of the Dwelling and five crossbars for the frames which formed the back of the Dwelling, to the west. 33 He made the middle bar, to join the frames from one end to the other, halfway up. 34 He overlaid the frames with gold, made gold rings for them, through which to place the crossbars, and overlaid the crossbars with gold.

35 He made a curtain of finely woven linen, dyed violet-purple, red-purple and crimson and embroidered with great winged creatures, 36 and for it he made four poles of acacia wood, overlaying them with gold, with golden hooks for them, for which he cast four sockets of silver. 37 For the entrance to the tent he made a screen of finely woven linen embroidered with violet-purple, red-purple and crimson, 38 as also the five columns for it and their hooks; he overlaid their capitals and rods with gold, but their five sockets were of bronze.

37 Bezalel made the ark of acacia wood, two and a half cubits long, one and a half cubits wide and one and a half cubits high. 2 He overlaid it, inside and out, with pure gold, and made a gold moulding all round it. 3 He cast four gold rings for it at its four supports: two rings on one side and two rings on the other. 4 He also made shafts of acacia wood and overlaid them with gold, 5 and passed the shafts through the rings on the sides of the ark, by which to carry it. 6 He also made a mercy-seat of pure gold, two and a half cubits long and one and a half cubits wide, 7 and modelled two great winged creatures of beaten gold, putting them at the two ends of the mercy-seat, 8 one winged creature at one end and the other winged creature at the other end, making the winged creatures of a piece with the mercy-seat at either end. 9 The winged creatures had their wings spread upwards, protecting the ark with their wings and facing each other, their faces being towards the mercy-seat.

10 He made the table of acacia wood, two cubits long, one cubit wide and one and a half cubits high, 11 and made a gold moulding all round it. 12 He fitted it with struts a hand's breadth wide and made a gold moulding round the struts. 13 He cast four gold rings for it and fixed the rings at the four corners where the four legs were. 14 The rings lay close to the struts to hold the shafts for carrying the table. 15 He made the shafts of acacia wood and overlaid them with gold; these were for carrying the table. 16 He made the accessories which were to go on the table: its dishes, cups, jars and libation bowls, of pure gold.

17 He also made the lamp-stand of pure gold, making the lamp-stand, base and stem, of beaten gold, its cups, calyxes and bud being of a piece with it. 18 Six branches sprang from its sides: three of the lamp-stand's branches from one side, three of the lamp-stand's branches from the other. 19 The first branch carried three cups shaped like almond blossoms, each with its calyx and bud; the second branch, too, carried three cups shaped like almond blossoms, each with its calyx and bud, and similarly all six branches springing from the lamp-stand. 20 The lamp-stand itself carried four cups shaped like almond blossoms, each with its calyx and bud: 21 one calyx under the first two branches springing from the lamp-stand, one calyx under the next pair of branches and one calyx under the last pair of branches — thus for all six branches springing from the lamp-stand. 22 The calyxes and the branches were of a piece with the lamp-stand, and the whole was made from a single piece of pure gold, beaten out. 23 He also made its seven lamps, its snuffers and trays of pure gold. 24 He made the lamp-stand and all its accessories from a talent of pure gold.

25 He made the altar of incense of acacia wood, one cubit long, and one cubit wide; it was square, and was two cubits high; its horns were of one piece with it. 26 He overlaid it with pure gold, its top, and its sides all around, and its horns; and he made for it a molding of gold all around, 27 and made two golden rings for it under its molding, on two opposite sides of it, to hold the poles with which to carry it. 28 And he made the poles of acacia wood, and overlaid them with gold.

29 He made the holy anointing oil also, and the pure fragrant incense, blended as by the perfumer.

38 He made the altar of burnt offering also of acacia wood; it was five cubits long, and five cubits wide; it was square, and three cubits high. 2 He made horns for it on its four corners; its horns were of one piece with it, and he overlaid it with bronze. 3 He made all the utensils of the altar, the pots, the shovels, the basins, the forks, and the firepans: all its utensils he made of bronze. 4 He made for the altar a grating, a network of bronze, under its ledge, extending halfway down. 5 He cast four rings on the four corners of the bronze grating to hold the poles; 6 he made the poles of acacia wood, and overlaid them with bronze. 7 And he put the poles through the rings on the sides of the altar, to carry it with them; he made it hollow, with boards.

8 He made the basin of bronze with its stand of bronze, from the mirrors of the women who served at the entrance to the tent of meeting.

9 He made the court; for the south side the hangings of the court were of fine twisted linen, one hundred cubits long; 10 its twenty pillars and their twenty bases were of bronze, but the hooks of the pillars and their bands were of silver. 11 For the north side there were hangings one hundred cubits long; its twenty pillars and their twenty bases were of bronze, but the hooks of the pillars and their bands were of silver. 12 For the west side there were hangings fifty cubits long, with ten pillars and ten bases; the hooks of the pillars and their bands were of silver. 13 And for the front to the east, fifty cubits. 14 The hangings for one side of the gate were fifteen cubits, with three pillars and three bases. 15 And so for the other side; on each side of the gate of the court were hangings of fifteen cubits, with three pillars and three bases. 16 All the hangings around the court were of fine twisted linen. 17 The bases for the pillars were of bronze, but the hooks of the pillars and their bands were of silver; the overlaying of their capitals was also of silver, and all the pillars of the court were banded with silver. 18 The screen for the entrance to the court was embroidered with needlework in blue, purple, and crimson yarns and fine twisted linen. It was twenty cubits long and, along the width of it, five cubits high, corresponding to the hangings of the court. 19 There were four pillars; their four bases were of bronze, their hooks of silver, and the overlaying of their capitals and their bands of silver. 20 All the pegs for the tabernacle and for the court all around were of bronze.

21 These are the records of the tabernacle, the tabernacle of the covenant,*p* which were drawn up at the commandment of Moses, the work of the Levites being under the direction of Ithamar son of the priest Aaron. 22 Bezalel son of Uri son of Hur, of the tribe of Judah, made all that the LORD commanded Moses; 23 and with him was Oholiab son of Ahisamach, of the tribe of Dan, engraver, designer, and embroiderer in blue, purple, and crimson yarns, and in fine linen.

24 All the gold that was used for the work, in all the construction of the sanctuary, the gold from the offering, was twenty-nine talents and seven hundred thirty shekels, measured by the sanctuary shekel. 25 The silver from those

25 He made the altar of incense of acacia-wood; it was square, a cubit long by a cubit broad, and it stood two cubits high, its horns of one piece with it. 26 He overlaid it with pure gold, the top, all the sides, and the horns, and he put round it a band of gold. 27 He made pairs of gold rings for it; he put them under the gold band at the two corners on both sides to receive the poles by which it was to be carried. 28 He made the poles of acacia-wood and overlaid them with gold.

29 He prepared the sacred anointing oil and the fragrant incense, pure, compounded by the perfumer's art.

38 He made the altar of whole offering from acacia-wood; it was square, five cubits long by five cubits broad, and its height was three cubits. 2 Its horns at the four corners were of one piece with it, and he overlaid it with bronze. 3 He made all the vessels for the altar, its pots, shovels, tossing-bowls, forks, and firepans, all of bronze. 4 He made for the altar a grating of bronze network under the ledge, coming half-way up. 5 He cast four rings for the four corners of the bronze grating to receive the poles, 6 and he made the poles of acacia-wood and overlaid them with bronze. 7 He inserted the poles in the rings at the sides of the altar to carry it. The altar was made of boards and left hollow.

8 The basin and its stand of bronze he made out of the bronze mirrors of the women waiting at the entrance to the Tent of Meeting.

9 He made the court. On the south side facing southwards the hangings of the court were of finely woven linen a hundred cubits long, 10 with twenty posts and twenty bronze sockets; the hooks and bands on the posts were of silver. 11 Along the north side there were hangings of a hundred cubits, with twenty posts and twenty bronze sockets; the hooks and bands on the posts were of silver. 12 On the west side there were hangings fifty cubits long, with ten posts and ten sockets; the hooks and bands on the posts were of silver. 13 On the east side, towards the sunrise, fifty cubits; 14–15 there were hangings on either side of the gateway of the court; they extended fifteen cubits to one corner, with their three posts and three sockets, and fifteen cubits to the second corner, with their three posts and three sockets. 16 The hangings of the court all round were of finely woven linen. 17 The sockets for the posts were of bronze; the hooks were of silver as were the bands on the posts, the tops of them overlaid with silver, and all the posts of the court were bound with silver. 18 The screen at the gateway of the court was of finely woven linen, embroidered with violet, purple, and scarlet, twenty cubits long and five cubits high to correspond to the hangings of the court, 19 with four posts and four sockets of bronze, their hooks of silver, and the tops of them and their bands overlaid with silver. 20 All the pegs for the Tabernacle and those for the court were of bronze.

21 These were the appointments of the Tabernacle, that is the Tabernacle of the Testimony which was assigned by Moses to the charge of the Levites under Ithamar son of Aaron the priest. 22 Bezalel son of Uri, son of Hur, of the tribe of Judah, made everything the LORD had commanded Moses. 23 He was assisted by Aholiab son of Ahisamach of the tribe of Dan, an engraver, a seamster, and an embroiderer in fine linen with violet, purple, and scarlet yarn.

24 The gold of the special gift used for the work of the sanctuary amounted in all to twenty-nine talents seven hundred and thirty shekels by the sacred standard. 25 The silver

---

p Or *treaty*, or *testimony*; Heb *eduth*

NEW AMERICAN BIBLE

25 The altar of incense was made of acacia wood, on a square, a cubit long, a cubit wide, and two cubits high, having horns that sprang directly from it. 26 Its grate on top, its walls on all four sides, and its horns were plated with pure gold; and a molding of gold was put around it. 27 Underneath the molding gold rings were placed, two on one side and two on the opposite side, as holders for the poles to carry it. 28 The poles, too, were made of acacia wood and plated with gold.

29 The sacred anointing oil and the fragrant incense were prepared in their pure form by a perfumer.

38 The altar of holocausts was made of acacia wood, on a square, five cubits long and five cubits wide; its height was three cubits. 2 At the four corners horns were made that sprang directly from the altar. The whole was plated with bronze. 3 All the utensils of the altar, the pots, shovels, basins, forks and fire pans, were likewise made of bronze. 4 A grating of bronze network was made for the altar and placed round it, on the ground, half as high as the altar itself. 5 Four rings were cast for the four corners of the bronze grating, as holders for the poles, 6 which were made of acacia wood and plated with bronze. 7 The poles were put through the rings on the sides of the altar for carrying it. The altar was made in the form of a hollow box.

8 The bronze laver, with its bronze base, was made from the mirrors of the women who served at the entrance of the meeting tent.

9 The court was made as follows. On the south side of the court there were hangings, woven of fine linen twined, a hundred cubits long, 10 with twenty columns and twenty pedestals of bronze, the hooks and bands of the columns being of silver. 11 On the north side there were similar hangings, one hundred cubits long, with twenty columns and twenty pedestals of bronze, the hooks and bands of the columns being of silver. 12 On the west side there were hangings, fifty cubits long, with ten columns and ten pedestals, the hooks and bands of the columns being of silver. 13 On the east side the court was fifty cubits long. 14 Toward one side there were hangings to the extent of fifteen cubits, with three columns and three pedestals; 15 toward the other side, beyond the entrance of the court, there were likewise hangings to the extent of fifteen cubits, with three columns and three pedestals. 16 The hangings on all sides of the court were woven of fine linen twined. 17 The pedestals of the columns were of bronze, while the hooks and bands of the columns were of silver; the capitals were silver-plated, and all the columns of the court were banded with silver.

18 At the entrance of the court there was a variegated curtain, woven of violet, purple and scarlet yarn and of fine linen twined, twenty cubits long and five cubits wide, in keeping with the hangings of the court. 19 There were four columns and four pedestals of bronze for it, while their hooks were of silver. 20 All the tent pegs for the Dwelling and for the court around it were of bronze.

21 The following is an account of the various amounts used on the Dwelling, the Dwelling of the commandments, drawn up at the command of Moses by the Levites under the direction of Ithamar, son of Aaron the priest. 22 However, it was Bezalel, son of Uri, son of Hur, of the tribe of Judah, who made all that the Lord commanded Moses, 23 and he was assisted by Oholiab, son of Ahisamach, of the tribe of Dan, who was an engraver, an embroiderer, and a weaver of variegated cloth of violet, purple and scarlet yarn and of fine linen.

24 All the gold used in the entire construction of the sanctuary, having previously been given as an offering, amounted to twenty-nine talents and seven hundred and thirty shekel, according to the standard of the sanctuary shekel. 25 The amount of the silver received from the com-

NEW JERUSALEM BIBLE

25 He made the altar of incense of acacia wood, one cubit long, and one cubit wide — it was square — and two cubits high, its horns were of a piece with it. 26 He overlaid its top, its sides all round and its horns with pure gold and made a moulding to go all round. 27 He made two gold rings for it below the moulding on its two opposite sides, to take the shafts used for carrying it. 28 He made the shafts of acacia wood and overlaid them with gold. 29 He also made the holy anointing oil and the fragrant incense, blending it as a perfumer would.

38 He made the altar of burnt offerings of acacia wood, five cubits long and five cubits wide; it was square and three cubits high. 2 At its four corners he made horns, the horns being of a piece with it, and overlaid it with bronze. 3 He made all the altar accessories: the ash pans, shovels, sprinkling basins, hooks and fire pans; he made all the altar accessories of bronze. 4 He also made a grating for the altar of bronze network, below its ledge, underneath, coming halfway up. 5 He cast four rings for the four corners of the bronze grating to take the shafts. 6 He made the shafts of acacia wood and overlaid them with bronze. 7 He passed the shafts through the rings on the sides of the altar for carrying it. He made the altar hollow, out of boards.

8 He made the bronze basin and its bronze stand from the mirrors of the women who served at the entrance to the Tent of Meeting.

9 He made the court. On the south side, on the south, the curtaining of the court was of finely woven linen a hundred cubits long. 10 Its twenty poles and their sockets being of bronze, and their hooks and rods of silver; 11 and on the north side, a hundred cubits of curtaining, its twenty poles and their twenty sockets being of bronze, and their hooks and rods of silver. 12 On the west side there were fifty cubits of curtaining, with its ten poles and their ten sockets, the poles' hooks and rods being of silver; 13 and on the east side on the east, there were fifty cubits. 14 On the one side there were fifteen cubits of curtaining, with its three poles and their three sockets, 15 and on the other side — either side of the gateway to the court — there were fifteen cubits of curtaining with its three poles and their three sockets. 16 All the curtaining round the court was of finely woven linen, 17 the sockets for the poles were of bronze, the poles' hooks and rods of silver, their capitals were overlaid with silver and all the poles of the court had silver rods. 18 The screen for the gateway to the court was of finely woven linen embroidered with violet-purple, red-purple and crimson, twenty cubits long and five cubits high (all the way along) like the curtaining of the court, 19 its four poles and their four sockets being of bronze, their hooks of silver, their capitals overlaid with silver, and their rods of silver. 20 All the pegs round the Dwelling and the court were of bronze.

21 These are the accounts for the Dwelling — the Dwelling of the Testimony — drawn up by order of Moses, the work of Levites, produced by Ithamar son of Aaron, the priest. 22 Bezalel son of Uri, son of Hur, of the tribe of Judah, made everything that Yahweh ordered Moses to make, 23 his assistant being Oholiab son of Ahisamach, of the tribe of Dan, an engraver, embroiderer and needleworker in violet-purple, red-purple and crimson materials and fine linen.

24 The amount of gold used for the work, for the entire work for the sanctuary (the gold consecrated for the purpose) was twenty-nine talents and seven hundred and thirty shekels, reckoned by the sanctuary shekel. 25 The silver

of the congregation who were counted was one hundred talents and one thousand seven hundred seventy-five shekels, measured by the sanctuary shekel; 26 a beka a head (that is, half a shekel, measured by the sanctuary shekel), for everyone who was counted in the census, from twenty years old and upward, for six hundred three thousand, five hundred fifty men. 27 The hundred talents of silver were for casting the bases of the sanctuary, and the bases of the curtain; one hundred bases for the hundred talents, a talent for a base. 28 Of the thousand seven hundred seventy-five shekels he made hooks for the pillars, and overlaid their capitals and made bands for them. 29 The bronze that was contributed was seventy talents, and two thousand four hundred shekels; 30 with it he made the bases for the entrance of the tent of meeting, the bronze altar and the bronze grating for it and all the utensils of the altar, 31 the bases all around the court, and the bases of the gate of the court, all the pegs of the tabernacle, and all the pegs around the court.

39 Of the blue, purple, and crimson yarns they made finely worked vestments, for ministering in the holy place; they made the sacred vestments for Aaron; as the LORD had commanded Moses.

2 He made the ephod of gold, of blue, purple, and crimson yarns, and of fine twisted linen. 3 Gold leaf was hammered out and cut into threads to work into the blue, purple, and crimson yarns and into the fine twisted linen, in skilled design. 4 They made for the ephod shoulder-pieces, joined to it at its two edges. 5 The decorated band on it was of the same materials and workmanship, of gold, of blue, purple, and crimson yarns, and of fine twisted linen; as the LORD had commanded Moses.

6 The onyx stones were prepared, enclosed in settings of gold filigree and engraved like the engravings of a signet, according to the names of the sons of Israel; 7 He set them on the shoulder-pieces of the ephod, to be stones of remembrance for the sons of Israel; as the LORD had commanded Moses.

8 He made the breastpiece, in skilled work, like the work of the ephod, of gold, of blue, purple, and crimson yarns, and of fine twisted linen. 9 It was square; the breastpiece was made double, a span in length and a span in width when doubled. 10 They set in it four rows of stones. A row of carnelian,*q* chrysolite, and emerald was the first row; 11 and the second row, a turquoise, a sapphire,*r* and a moonstone; 12 and the third row, a jacinth, an agate, and an amethyst; 13 and the fourth row, a beryl, an onyx, and a jasper; they were enclosed in settings of gold filigree. 14 There were twelve stones with names corresponding to the names of the sons of Israel; they were like signets, each engraved with its name, for the twelve tribes. 15 They made on the breastpiece chains of pure gold, twisted like cords; 16 and they made two settings of gold filigree and two gold rings, and put the two rings on the two edges of the breastpiece; 17 and they put the two cords of gold in the two rings at the edges of the breastpiece. 18 Two ends of the two cords they had attached to the two settings of filigree; in this way they attached it in front to the shoulder-pieces of the ephod. 19 Then they made two rings of gold, and put them at the two ends of the breastpiece, on its inside edge next to the ephod. 20 They made two rings of gold, and attached them in front to the lower part of the two shoulder-pieces of the ephod, at its joining above the decorated band of the ephod.

contributed by the community when registered was one hundred talents one thousand seven hundred and seventy-five shekels by the sacred standard.

26 This amounted to a beka a head, that is half a shekel by the sacred standard, for every man aged twenty years or more, who had been registered, a total of six hundred and three thousand five hundred and fifty men. 27 The hundred talents of silver were for casting the sockets for the sanctuary and those for the curtain, a hundred sockets to a hundred talents, a talent to a socket. 28 With the one thousand seven hundred and seventy-five shekels he made hooks for the posts, overlaid the tops of the posts, and put bands round them. 29 The bronze of the special gift came to seventy talents two thousand four hundred shekels; 30 with this he made sockets for the entrance to the Tent of Meeting, the bronze altar and its bronze grating, all the vessels for the altar, 31 the sockets all round the court, the sockets for the posts at the gateway of the court, all the pegs for the Tabernacle, and the pegs all round the court.

39 They used violet, purple, and scarlet yarn in making the stitched vestments for ministering in the sanctuary and in making the sacred vestments for Aaron, as the LORD had commanded Moses.

2 They made the ephod of gold, with violet, purple, and scarlet yarn, and finely woven linen. 3 The gold was beaten into thin plates, cut and twisted into braid to be worked in by a seamster with the violet, purple, and scarlet yarn, and fine linen. 4 They made shoulder-pieces for it, joined back and front. 5 The waistband on it was of the same workmanship and material as the fabric of the ephod; it was gold, with violet, purple, and scarlet yarn, and finely woven linen, as the LORD had commanded Moses.

6 They prepared the cornelians, fixed in gold rosettes, engraved by the art of a seal-cutter with the names of the sons of Israel, and fastened them on the shoulder-pieces of the ephod as reminders of the sons of Israel, as the LORD had commanded Moses.

8 They made the breastpiece; it was worked in gold like the ephod by a seamster, with violet, purple, and scarlet yarn, and finely woven linen. 9 They made the breastpiece square when folded double, a span long and a span wide. 10 They set in it four rows of precious stones: the first row, sardin, chrysolite, and green feldspar; 11 the second row, purple garnet, sapphire, and jade; 12 the third row, turquoise, agate, and jasper; 13 the fourth row, topaz, cornelian, and green jasper, all set in gold rosettes. 14 The stones corresponded to the twelve sons of Israel, name by name, each stone bearing the name of one of the twelve tribes engraved as on a seal.

15 They made for the breastpiece chains of pure gold worked into a cord. 16 They made two gold rosettes and two gold rings, and they fixed the two rings on the two corners of the breastpiece. 17 They fastened the two gold cords to the two rings at those corners of the breastpiece, 18 and the other ends of the two cords to the two rosettes, thus binding them to the shoulder-pieces on the front of the ephod. 19 They made two gold rings and put them at the two corners of the breastpiece on the inner side next to the ephod. 20 They made two gold rings and fixed them on the two shoulder-pieces of the ephod, low down and in front, close to its seam above the waistband of the ephod. 21 They bound

q The identification of several of these stones is uncertain
r Or lapis lazuli

39:8 **They:** *so Gk; Heb.* He.

munity was one hundred talents and one thousand seven hundred and seventy-five shekels, according to the standard of the sanctuary shekel; 26 one bekah apiece, that is, a half-shekel apiece, according to the standard of the sanctuary shekel, was received from every man of twenty years or more who entered the registered group; the number of these was six hundred and three thousand five hundred and fifty men. 27 One hundred talents of silver were used for casting the pedestals of the sanctuary and the pedestals of the veil, one talent for each pedestal, or one hundred talents for the one hundred pedestals. 28 The remaining one thousand seven hundred and seventy-five shekels were used for making the hooks on the columns, for plating the capitals, and for banding them with silver. 29 The bronze, given as an offering, amounted to seventy talents and two thousand four hundred shekels. 30 With this were made the pedestals at the entrance of the meeting tent, the bronze altar with its bronze gratings and all the appurtenances of the altar, 31 the pedestals around the court, the pedestals at the entrance of the court, and all the tent pegs for the Dwelling and for the court around it.

39 With violet, purple and scarlet yarn were woven the service cloths for use in the sanctuary, as well as the sacred vestments for Aaron, as the LORD had commanded Moses.

2 The ephod was woven of gold thread and of violet, purple and scarlet yarn and of fine linen twined. 3 Gold was first hammered into gold leaf and then cut up into threads, which were woven with the violet, purple and scarlet yarn into an embroidered pattern on the fine linen. 4 Shoulder straps were made for it and joined to its two upper ends. 5 The embroidered belt on the ephod extended out from it, and like it, was made of gold thread, of violet, purple and scarlet yarn, and of fine linen twined, as the LORD had commanded Moses. 6 The onyx stones were prepared and mounted in gold filigree work; they were engraved like seal engravings with the names of the sons of Israel. 7 These stones were set on the shoulder straps of the ephod as memorial stones of the sons of Israel, just as the LORD had commanded Moses.

8 The breastpiece was embroidered like the ephod, with gold thread and violet, purple and scarlet yarn on cloth of fine linen twined. 9 It was square and folded double, a span high and a span wide in its folded form. 10 Four rows of precious stones were mounted on it: in the first row a carnelian, a topaz and an emerald; 11 in the second row, a garnet, a sapphire and a beryl; 12 in the third row a jacinth, an agate and an amethyst; 13 in the fourth row a chrysolite, an onyx and a jasper. They were mounted in gold filigree work. 14 These stones were twelve, to match the names of the sons of Israel, and each stone was engraved like a seal with the name of one of the twelve tribes.

15 Chains of pure gold, twisted like cords, were made for the breastpiece, 16 together with two gold filigree rosettes and two gold rings. The two rings were fastened to the two upper ends of the breastpiece. 17 The two gold chains were then fastened to the two rings at the ends of the breastpiece. 18 The other two ends of the two chains were fastened in front to the two filigree rosettes, which were attached to the shoulder straps of the ephod. 19 Two other gold rings were made and put on the two lower ends of the breastpiece, on the edge facing the ephod. 20 Two more gold rings were made and fastened to the bottom of the two shoulder straps next to where they joined the ephod in front, just above its embroidered belt. 21 Violet ribbons bound the rings of the

from the census of the community was one hundred talents and one thousand seven hundred and seventy-five shekels, reckoned by the sanctuary shekel, 26 one *beqa* per head, half a shekel reckoned by the sanctuary shekel, for everyone of twenty years and over included in the census, for six hundred and three thousand five hundred and fifty persons. 27 A hundred talents of silver were used for casting the sockets for the sanctuary and the sockets for the curtain: a hundred sockets from a hundred talents, one talent per socket. 28 From the one thousand seven hundred and seventy-five shekels he made the hooks for the poles, overlaid their capitals and made the rods for them. 29 The bronze consecrated for the purpose amounted to seventy talents and two thousand four hundred shekels, 30 and from it he made the sockets for the entrance of the Tent of Meeting, the bronze altar, its bronze grating and all the altar accessories, 31 the sockets all round the court, the sockets for the gateway to the court, all the pegs for the Dwelling and all the pegs round the court.

39 From the violet-purple, red-purple and crimson materials, they made the liturgical vestments for service in the sanctuary. They made the sacred vestments for Aaron, as Yahweh had ordered Moses.

2 They made the *ephod* of gold, of violet-purple, red-purple and crimson materials and finely woven linen. 3 They beat gold into thin plates and cut these into threads to work into the violet-purple, red-purple and crimson materials and the fine linen by needlework. 4 For the *ephod* they made shoulder-straps which were joined to it at its two edges. 5 The waistband on the *ephod* to hold it in position, was of a piece with it and of the same workmanship: of gold, violet-purple, red-purple and finely woven linen, as Yahweh had ordered Moses. 6 They worked the cornelians, mounted in gold setting, and engraved, like an engraved seal, with the names of the sons of Israel, 7 and put the stones on the shoulder-straps of the *ephod*, to commemorate the sons of Israel, as Yahweh had ordered Moses.

8 They made the breastplate of the same embroidered work as the *ephod*: of gold, violet-purple, red-purple and crimson materials and finely woven linen. 9 It was square and doubled over, a span in length and a span in width. 10 In it they set four rows of stones: a sard, a topaz and an emerald, for the first row; 11 for the second row, a garnet, a sapphire and a diamond; 12 for the third row, a hyacinth, a ruby and an amethyst; 13 and for the fourth row, a beryl, a cornelian and a jasper: mounted in gold settings, 14 the stones corresponding to the names of the sons of Israel, twelve like their names, engraved like seals, each with the name of one of the twelve tribes. 15 For the breastplate they made chains of pure gold twisted like cords, 16 and they made two gold rosettes and two gold rings, putting the two rings on the two outside edges of the breastplate 17 and fastening the two gold cords to the two rings on the outside edges of the breastplate. 18 The other two ends of the cords they fastened to the two rosettes, putting these on the shoulder-straps of the *ephod*, on the front. 19 They also made two gold rings and put them on the two outside edges of the breastplate, on the inner side, against the *ephod*; 20 and they made two more gold rings and put them low down on the front of the two shoulder-straps of the *ephod*, close to the join, above the waistband of the *ephod*. 21 They

NEW REVISED STANDARD VERSION

21 They bound the breastpiece by its rings to the rings of the ephod with a blue cord, so that it should lie on the decorated band of the ephod, and that the breastpiece should not come loose from the ephod; as the LORD had commanded Moses.

22 He also made the robe of the ephod woven all of blue yarn; 23 and the opening of the robe in the middle of it was like the opening in a coat of mail,s with a binding around the opening, so that it might not be torn. 24 On the lower hem of the robe they made pomegranates of blue, purple, and crimson yarns, and of fine twisted linen. 25 They also made bells of pure gold, and put the bells between the pomegranates on the lower hem of the robe all around, between the pomegranates; 26 a bell and a pomegranate, a bell and a pomegranate all around on the lower hem of the robe for ministering; as the LORD had commanded Moses.

27 They also made the tunics, woven of fine linen, for Aaron and his sons, 28 and the turban of fine linen, and the headdresses of fine linen, and the linen undergarments of fine twisted linen, 29 and the sash of fine twisted linen, and of blue, purple, and crimson yarns, embroidered with needlework; as the LORD had commanded Moses.

30 They made the rosette of the holy diadem of pure gold, and wrote on it an inscription, like the engraving of a signet, "Holy to the LORD." 31 They tied to it a blue cord, to fasten it on the turban above; as the LORD had commanded Moses.

32 In this way all the work of the tabernacle of the tent of meeting was finished; the Israelites had done everything just as the LORD had commanded Moses. 33 Then they brought the tabernacle to Moses, the tent and all its utensils, its hooks, its frames, its bars, its pillars, and its bases; 34 the covering of tanned rams' skins and the covering of fine leather,s and the curtain for the screen; 35 the ark of the covenantt with its poles and the mercy seat;u 36 the table with all its utensils, and the bread of the Presence; 37 the pure lampstand with its lamps set on it and all its utensils, and the oil for the light; 38 the golden altar, the anointing oil and the fragrant incense, and the screen for the entrance of the tent; 39 the bronze altar, and its grating of bronze, its poles, and all its utensils; the basin with its stand; 40 the hangings of the court, its pillars, and its bases, and the screen for the gate of the court, its cords, and its pegs; and all the utensils for the service of the tabernacle, for the tent of meeting; 41 the finely worked vestments for ministering in the holy place, the sacred vestments for the priest Aaron, and the vestments of his sons to serve as priests. 42 The Israelites had done all of the work just as the LORD had commanded Moses. 43 When Moses saw that they had done all the work just as the LORD had commanded, he blessed them.

40 The LORD spoke to Moses: 2 On the first day of the first month you shall set up the tabernacle of the tent of meeting. 3 You shall put in it the ark of the covenant,t and you shall screen the ark with the curtain. 4 You shall bring in the table, and arrange its setting; and you shall bring in the lampstand, and set up its lamps. 5 You shall put the golden altar for incense before the ark of the covenant,t and set up the screen for the entrance of the tabernacle. 6 You shall set the altar of burnt offering before the entrance of the tabernacle of the tent of meeting, 7 and place the basin between the tent of meeting and the altar, and put water in it. 8 You shall set up the court all around, and hang up the screen for the gate of the court. 9 Then you shall take the anointing oil, and anoint the tabernacle and all that is in it, and consecrate it and all its furniture, so that it shall become holy. 10 You shall also anoint the altar of burnt offering and

REVISED ENGLISH BIBLE

the breastpiece by its rings to the rings of the ephod with a violet braid, just above the waistband on the ephod, so that the breastpiece would not become loosened from the ephod; so the LORD had commanded Moses.

22 They made the mantle of the ephod a single piece of woven violet stuff, 23 with an opening in the middle of it which had a hem round it, with an oversewn edge to prevent it from tearing. 24 On its hem they made pomegranates of violet, purple, and scarlet stuff, and finely woven linen. 25 They made bells of pure gold and put them all round the hem of the mantle between the pomegranates, 26 a bell and a pomegranate alternately the whole way round the hem of the mantle, to be worn when ministering, as the LORD had commanded Moses.

27 They made the tunics of fine linen, woven work, for Aaron and his sons, 28 the turban of fine linen, the tall headdresses and their bands all of fine linen, the shorts of finely woven linen, 29 and the sashes of finely woven linen, embroidered in violet, purple, and scarlet, as the LORD had commanded Moses.

30 They made a medallion of pure gold as the symbol of their holy dedication and inscribed on it as the engraving on a seal, 'Holy to the LORD', 31 and they fastened on it a violet braid to fix it on the turban at the top, as the LORD had commanded Moses.

32 Thus all the work of the Tabernacle of the Tent of Meeting was completed, and the Israelites did everything exactly as the LORD had commanded Moses. 33 They brought the Tabernacle to Moses, the tent and all its furnishings, its fasteners, frames, bars, posts, and sockets, 34 the covering of tanned rams' skins and the outer covering of dugong-hides, the curtain of the screen, 35 the Ark of the Testimony and its poles, the cover, 36 the table and its vessels, and the Bread of the Presence, 37 the pure lampstand with its lamps in a row and all its fittings, and the lamp oil, 38 the gold altar, the anointing oil, the fragrant incense, and the screen at the entrance of the tent, 39 the bronze altar, the bronze grating attached to it, its poles and all its furnishings, the basin and its stand, 40 the hangings of the court, its posts and sockets, the screen for the gateway of the court, its cords and pegs, and all the equipment for the service of the Tabernacle for the Tent of Meeting, 41 the stitched vestments for ministering in the sanctuary, that is the sacred vestments for Aaron the priest and the vestments for his sons when ministering as priests. 42 As the LORD had commanded Moses, so the Israelites carried out the whole work. 43 Moses inspected all the work, and saw that they had carried it out according to the command of the LORD; and he blessed them.

40 THE LORD said to Moses: 2 On the first day of the first month you are to set up the Tabernacle of the Tent of Meeting. 3 Put the Ark of the Testimony in it and screen the Ark with the curtain. 4 Bring in the table and lay it; then bring in the lampstand and mount its lamps. 5 Then set the gold altar of incense in front of the Ark of the Testimony and put the screen of the entrance of the Tabernacle in place. 6 Place the altar of whole-offering in front of the entrance of the Tabernacle of the Tent of Meeting, 7 and the basin between the Tent of Meeting and the altar, and put water in it. 8 Set up the court all round, and put in place the screen at the entrance of the court.

9 With the anointing oil anoint the Tabernacle and everything in it, thus consecrating it and all its furnishings; it will then be holy. 10 Anoint the altar of whole-offering and all its

---

s Meaning of Heb uncertain   t Or treaty, or testimony; Heb eduth
u Or the cover

39:23 oversewn edge: see 28:32.   39:24 linen: so Samar.; Heb. omits.   39:30 on it . . . LORD: or 'YHWH' on it in sacred characters as engraved on a seal.

breastpiece to the rings of the ephod, so that the breastpiece stayed right above the embroidered belt of the ephod and did not swing loose from it. All this was just as the LORD had commanded Moses.

22 The robe of the ephod was woven entirely of violet yarn, 23 with an opening in its center like the opening of a shirt, with selvage around the opening to keep it from being torn. 24 At the hem of the robe pomegranates were made of violet, purple and scarlet yarn and of fine linen twined; 25 bells of pure gold were also made and put between the pomegranates all around the hem of the robe: 26 first a bell, then a pomegranate, and thus alternating all around the hem of the robe which was to be worn in performing the ministry — all this, just as the LORD had commanded Moses.

27 For Aaron and his sons there were also woven tunics of fine linen; 28 the miter of fine linen; the ornate turbans of fine linen; drawers of linen [of fine linen twined]; 29 and sashes of variegated work made of fine linen twined and of violet, purple and scarlet yarn, as the LORD had commanded Moses. 30 The plate of the sacred diadem was made of pure gold and inscribed, as on a seal engraving: "Sacred to the LORD." 31 It was tied over the miter with a violet ribbon, as the LORD had commanded Moses.

32 Thus the entire work of the Dwelling of the meeting tent was completed. The Israelites did the work just as the LORD had commanded Moses. 33 They then brought to Moses the Dwelling, the tent with all its appurtenances, the clasps, the boards, the bars, the columns, the pedestals, 34 the covering of rams' skins dyed red, the covering of tahash skins, the curtain veil; 35 the ark of the commandments with its poles, the propitiatory, 36 the table with all its appurtenances and the showbread, 37 the pure gold lampstand with its lamps set up on it and with all its appurtenances, the oil for the light, 38 the golden altar, the anointing oil, the fragrant incense; the curtain for the entrance of the tent, 39 the altar of bronze with its bronze grating, its poles and all its appurtenances, the laver with its base, 40 the hangings of the court with their columns and pedestals, the curtain for the entrance of the court with its ropes and tent pegs, all the equipment for the service of the Dwelling of the meeting tent; 41 the service cloths for use in the sanctuary, the sacred vestments for Aaron the priest, and the vestments to be worn by his sons in their ministry. 42 The Israelites had carried out all the work just as the LORD had commanded Moses. 43 So when Moses saw that all the work was done just as the LORD had commanded, he blessed them.

40 Then the LORD said to Moses, 2 "On the first day of the first month you shall erect the Dwelling of the meeting tent. 3 Put the ark of the commandments in it, and screen off the ark with the veil. 4 Bring in the table and set it. Then bring in the lampstand and set up the lamps on it. 5 Put the golden altar of incense in front of the ark of the commandments, and hang the curtain at the entrance of the Dwelling. 6 Put the altar of holocausts in front of the entrance of the Dwelling of the meeting tent. 7 Place the laver between the meeting tent and the altar, and put water in it. 8 Set up the court round about, and put the curtain at the entrance of the court.

9 "Take the anointing oil and anoint the Dwelling and everything in it, consecrating it and all its furnishings, so that it will be sacred. 10 Anoint the altar of holocausts and

secured the pectoral by a violet-purple cord passed through its rings and those of the *ephod*, so that the pectoral would sit above the waistband and not come apart from the *ephod*, as Yahweh had ordered Moses.

22 They made the robe of the *ephod* woven entirely of violet-purple. 23 The opening in the centre of the robe was like the neck of a coat of mail; round the opening was a border, so that it would not get torn. 24 On the lower hem of the robe, they made pomegranates of violet-purple, red-purple and crimson and finely woven linen, 25 and made bells of pure gold, putting the bells between the pomegranates all round the lower hem of the robe: 26 alternately, a bell and then a pomegranate, all round the lower hem of the robe of office, as Yahweh had ordered Moses.

27 They made the tunics of finely woven linen for Aaron and his sons, 28 the turban of fine linen, the head-dresses of fine linen, the breeches of finely woven linen, 29 the waistbands of finely woven linen embroidered with violet-purple, red-purple and crimson, as Yahweh had ordered Moses.

30 They also made the flower — the symbol of holy consecration — of pure gold and on it, like an engraved seal, they engraved, 'Consecrated to Yahweh'. 31 They put it on a violet-purple cord, to fasten it high up on the turban, as Yahweh had ordered Moses.

32 So all the work for the Dwelling, for the Tent of Meeting, was completed. They had done everything exactly as Yahweh had ordered Moses.

33 They then brought Moses the Dwelling, the Tent and all its accessories: its clasps, frames, crossbars, poles and sockets; 34 the cover of rams' skins dyed red, the cover of fine leather and the screening curtain; 35 the ark of the Testimony and its shafts, and the mercy-seat; 36 the table, all its accessories and the loaves of permanent offering; 37 the lamp-stand of pure gold, its lamps — the array of lamps — and all its accessories, and the oil for the light; 38 the golden altar, the anointing oil, the fragrant incense and the screen for the entrance to the tent; 39 the bronze altar and its bronze grating, its shafts and all its accessories; the basin and its stand; 40 the curtaining for the court, its poles, its sockets, and the screen for the gateway to the court, its cords, its pegs and all the accessories for the service of the Dwelling, for the Tent of Meeting; 41 the liturgical vestments for officiating in the sanctuary — the sacred vestments for Aaron the priest, and the vestments for his sons — for the priestly functions. 42 The Israelites had done all the work exactly as Yahweh had ordered Moses.

43 Moses inspected all the work: they had indeed done it as Yahweh had ordered; and Moses blessed them.

40 Yahweh then spoke to Moses and said, 2 'On the first day of the first month, you will erect the Dwelling, the Tent of Meeting, 3 and place the ark of the Testimony in it and screen the ark with the curtain. 4 You will then bring in the table and arrange what has to be arranged on it. You will then bring in the lamp-stand and set up its lamps. 5 You will place the golden altar of incense in front of the ark of the Testimony, and place the screen at the entrance to the Dwelling. 6 You will place the altar of burnt offerings in front of the entrance to the Dwelling, the Tent of Meeting, 7 and you will place the basin between the Tent of Meeting and the altar, and fill it with water. 8 You will then set up the surrounding court and hang the screen at the gateway of the court. 9 Then, taking the anointing oil, you will anoint the Dwelling and everything inside, consecrating it and all its accessories; it will then be holy. 10 You will

NEW REVISED STANDARD VERSION	REVISED ENGLISH BIBLE

all its utensils, and consecrate the altar, so that the altar shall be most holy. 11 You shall also anoint the basin with its stand, and consecrate it. 12 Then you shall bring Aaron and his sons to the entrance of the tent of meeting, and shall wash them with water, 13 and put on Aaron the sacred vestments, and you shall anoint him and consecrate him, so that he may serve me as priest. 14 You shall bring his sons also and put tunics on them, 15 and anoint them, as you anointed their father, that they may serve me as priests: and their anointing shall admit them to a perpetual priesthood throughout all generations to come.

16 Moses did everything just as the LORD had commanded him. 17 In the first month in the second year, on the first day of the month, the tabernacle was set up. 18 Moses set up the tabernacle; he laid its bases, and set up its frames, and put in its poles, and raised up its pillars; 19 and he spread the tent over the tabernacle, and put the covering of the tent over it; as the LORD had commanded Moses. 20 He took the covenant*v* and put it into the ark, and put the poles on the ark, and set the mercy seat*w* above the ark; 21 and he brought the ark into the tabernacle, and set up the curtain for screening, and screened the ark of the covenant;*v* as the LORD had commanded Moses. 22 He put the table in the tent of meeting, on the north side of the tabernacle, outside the curtain, 23 and set the bread in order on it before the LORD; as the LORD had commanded Moses. 24 He put the lampstand in the tent of meeting, opposite the table on the south side of the tabernacle, 25 and set up the lamps before the LORD; as the LORD had commanded Moses. 26 He put the golden altar in the tent of meeting before the curtain, 27 and offered fragrant incense on it; as the LORD had commanded Moses. 28 He also put in place the screen for the entrance of the tabernacle. 29 He set the altar of burnt offering at the entrance of the tabernacle of the tent of meeting, and offered on it the burnt offering and the grain offering as the LORD had commanded Moses. 30 He set the basin between the tent of meeting and the altar, and put water in it for washing, 31 with which Moses and Aaron and his sons washed their hands and their feet. 32 When they went into the tent of meeting, and when they approached the altar, they washed; as the LORD had commanded Moses. 33 He set up the court around the tabernacle and the altar, and put up the screen at the gate of the court. So Moses finished the work.

34 Then the cloud covered the tent of meeting, and the glory of the LORD filled the tabernacle. 35 Moses was not able to enter the tent of meeting because the cloud settled upon it, and the glory of the LORD filled the tabernacle. 36 Whenever the cloud was taken up from the tabernacle, the Israelites would set out on each stage of their journey; 37 but if the cloud was not taken up, then they did not set out until the day that it was taken up. 38 For the cloud of the LORD was on the tabernacle by day, and fire was in the cloud*x* by night, before the eyes of all the house of Israel at each stage of their journey.

*v*Or *treaty*, or *testimony*; Heb *eduth*   *w*Or *the cover*   *x*Heb *it*

vessels, thus consecrating it; it will be most holy. 11 Anoint the basin and its stand and consecrate it.

12 Bring Aaron and his sons to the entrance of the Tent of Meeting and wash them with the water. 13 Then clothe Aaron with the sacred vestments, anoint him, and consecrate him to be my priest. 14 Then bring forward his sons, clothe them in tunics, 15 and anoint them as you anointed their father; and they will be my priests. Their anointing inaugurates a hereditary priesthood for all time.

16 Moses did everything exactly as the LORD had commanded him. 17 In the first month of the second year, on the first day of that month, the Tabernacle was set up. 18 Moses erected the Tabernacle: he put the sockets in place, inserted the frames, fixed the crossbars, and set up the posts. 19 He spread the tent over the Tabernacle and fixed the covering of the tent on top of that, as the LORD had commanded him.

20 He took the Testimony and put it into the Ark, inserted the poles in the Ark, and put the cover over the top of the Ark. 21 He brought the Ark into the Tabernacle, set up the curtain of the screen, and so screened the Ark of the Testimony, as the LORD had commanded him.

22 He put the table in the Tent of Meeting on the north side of the Tabernacle outside the curtain 23 and arranged bread on it before the LORD, as the LORD had commanded him. 24 He set the lampstand in the Tent of Meeting opposite the table at the south side of the Tabernacle 25 and mounted the lamps before the LORD, as the LORD had commanded him. 26 He set up the gold altar in the Tent of Meeting in front of the curtain 27 and burnt fragrant incense on it, as the LORD had commanded him.

28 He set up the screen at the entrance of the Tabernacle, 29 fixed the altar of whole-offering at the entrance of the Tabernacle of the Tent of Meeting, and offered on it whole-offerings and grain-offerings, as the LORD had commanded him. 30 He set up the basin between the Tent of Meeting and the altar and put water there for washing. 31 Moses and Aaron and Aaron's sons used to wash their hands and feet 32 when they entered the Tent of Meeting or approached the altar, as the LORD had commanded Moses. 33 He set up the court all round the Tabernacle and the altar, and put the screen at the entrance of the court.

Moses completed the work, 34 and the cloud covered the Tent of Meeting, and the glory of the LORD filled the Tabernacle. 35 Moses was unable to enter the Tent of Meeting, because the cloud had settled on it and the glory of the LORD filled the Tabernacle. 36 At every stage of their journey, when the cloud lifted from the Tabernacle, the Israelites used to break camp; 37 but if the cloud did not lift from the Tabernacle, they used not to break camp until such time as it did lift. 38 For the cloud of the LORD was over the Tabernacle by day, and there was fire in the cloud by night, and all the Israelites could see it at every stage of their journey.

all its appurtenances, consecrating it, so that it will be most sacred. 11 Likewise, anoint the laver with its base, and thus consecrate it.

12 "Then bring Aaron and his sons to the entrance of the meeting tent, and there wash them with water. 13 Clothe Aaron with the sacred vestments and anoint him, thus consecrating him as my priest. 14 Bring forward his sons also, and clothe them with the tunics. 15 As you have anointed their father, anoint them also as my priests. Thus, by being anointed, they shall receive a perpetual priesthood throughout all future generations."

16 Moses did exactly as the LORD had commanded him. 17 On the first day of the first month of the second year the Dwelling was erected. 18 It was Moses who erected the Dwelling. He placed its pedestals, set up its boards, put in its bars, and set up its columns. 19 He spread the tent over the Dwelling and put the covering on top of the tent, as the LORD had commanded him. 20 He took the commandments and put them in the ark; he placed poles alongside the ark and set the propitiatory upon it. 21 He brought the ark into the Dwelling and hung the curtain veil, thus screening off the ark of the commandments, as the LORD had commanded him. 22 He put the table in the meeting tent, on the north side of the Dwelling, outside the veil, 23 and arranged the bread on it before the LORD, as the LORD had commanded him. 24 He placed the lampstand in the meeting tent, opposite the table, on the south side of the Dwelling, 25 and he set up the lamps before the LORD, as the LORD had commanded him. 26 He placed the golden altar in the meeting tent, in front of the veil, 27 and on it he burned fragrant incense, as the LORD had commanded him. 28 He hung the curtain at the entrance of the Dwelling. 29 He put the altar of holocausts in front of the entrance of the Dwelling of meeting tent, and offered holocausts and cereal offerings on it, as the LORD had commanded him. 30 He placed the laver between the meeting tent and the altar, and put water in it for washing. 31 Moses and Aaron and his sons used to wash their hands and feet there, 32 for they washed themselves whenever they went into the meeting tent or approached the altar, as the LORD commanded Moses. 33 Finally, he set up the court around the Dwelling and the altar and hung the curtain at the entrance of the court. Thus Moses finished all the work.

34 Then the cloud covered the meeting tent, and the glory of the LORD filled the Dwelling. 35 Moses could not enter the meeting tent, because the cloud settled down upon it and the glory of the LORD filled the Dwelling. 36 Whenever the cloud rose from the Dwelling, the Israelites would set out on their journey. 37 But if the cloud did not lift, they would not go forward; only when it lifted did they go forward. 38 In the daytime the cloud of the LORD was seen over the Dwelling; whereas at night, fire was seen in the cloud by the whole house of Israel in all the stages of their journey.

then anoint the altar of burnt offerings and all its accessories, consecrating the altar; the altar will then be especially holy. 11 You will then anoint the basin and its stand, and consecrate it. 12 You will then bring Aaron and his sons to the entrance of the Tent of Meeting, bathe them thoroughly 13 and then dress Aaron in the sacred vestments, and anoint and consecrate him, to serve me in the priesthood. 14 You will then bring his sons, dress them in tunics 15 and anoint them as you anointed their father, to serve me in the priesthood. Their anointing will confer an everlasting priesthood on them for all their generations to come.'

16 Moses did this; he did exactly as Yahweh had ordered him. 17 On the first day of the first month in the second year the Dwelling was erected. 18 Moses erected the Dwelling. He fixed its sockets, set up its frames, put its crossbars in position and set up its poles. 19 He spread the tent over the Dwelling and the covering for the tent over that, as Yahweh had ordered Moses. 20 He took the Testimony and put it in the ark, positioned the shafts on the ark and put the mercy-seat on top of the ark. 21 He brought the ark into the Dwelling and put the screening curtain in place, screening the ark of the Testimony, as Yahweh had ordered Moses. 22 He put the table inside the Tent of Meeting, against the side of the Dwelling, on the north, outside the curtain, 23 and on it arranged the loaves before Yahweh, as Yahweh had ordered Moses. 24 He put the lamp-stand inside the Tent of Meeting, opposite the table, on the south side of the Dwelling, 25 and set up the lamps before Yahweh, as Yahweh had ordered Moses. 26 He put the golden altar inside the Tent of Meeting, in front of the curtain, 27 and on it burnt fragrant incense, as Yahweh had ordered Moses. 28 He then put the screen at the entrance to the Dwelling. 29 He put the altar of burnt offerings at the entrance to the Dwelling, to the Tent of Meeting, and on it offered the burnt offering and cereal offering, as Yahweh had ordered Moses. 30 He put the basin between the Tent of Meeting and the altar and put water in it for the ablutions, 31 where Moses, Aaron and his sons washed their hands and feet, 32 whenever they entered the Tent of Meeting or approached the altar they washed, as Yahweh had ordered Moses. 33 He then set up the court round the Dwelling and the altar and set up the screen at the gate-way to the court. Thus Moses completed the work.

34 The cloud then covered the Tent of Meeting and the glory of Yahweh filled the Dwelling. 35 Moses could not enter the Tent of Meeting, since the cloud stayed over it and the glory of Yahweh filled the Dwelling. 36 At every stage of their journey, whenever the cloud rose from the Dwelling, the Israelites would resume their march. 37 If the cloud did not rise, they would not resume their march until the day it did rise. 38 For Yahweh's cloud stayed over the Dwelling during the daytime and there was fire inside the cloud at night, for the whole House of Israel to see, at every stage of their journey.

Leviticus

1 The LORD summoned Moses and spoke to him from the tent of meeting, saying: 2 Speak to the people of Israel and say to them: When any of you bring an offering of livestock to the LORD, you shall bring your offering from the herd or from the flock.

3 If the offering is a burnt offering from the herd, you shall offer a male without blemish; you shall bring it to the entrance of the tent of meeting, for acceptance in your behalf before the LORD. 4 You shall lay your hand on the head of the burnt offering, and it shall be acceptable in your behalf as atonement for you. 5 The bull shall be slaughtered before the LORD; and Aaron's sons the priests shall offer the blood, dashing the blood against all sides of the altar that is at the entrance of the tent of meeting. 6 The burnt offering shall be flayed and cut up into its parts. 7 The sons of the priest Aaron shall put fire on the altar and arrange wood on the fire. 8 Aaron's sons the priests shall arrange the parts, with the head and the suet, on the wood that is on the fire on the altar; 9 but its entrails and its legs shall be washed with water. Then the priest shall turn the whole into smoke on the altar as a burnt offering, an offering by fire of pleasing odor to the LORD.

10 If your gift for a burnt offering is from the flock, from the sheep or goats, your offering shall be a male without blemish. 11 It shall be slaughtered on the north side of the altar before the LORD, and Aaron's sons the priests shall dash its blood against all sides of the altar. 12 It shall be cut up into its parts, with its head and its suet, and the priest shall arrange them on the wood that is on the fire on the altar; 13 but the entrails and the legs shall be washed with water. Then the priest shall offer the whole and turn it into smoke on the altar; it is a burnt offering, an offering by fire of pleasing odor to the LORD.

14 If your offering to the LORD is a burnt offering of birds, you shall choose your offering from turtledoves or pigeons. 15 The priest shall bring it to the altar and wring off its head, and turn it into smoke on the altar; and its blood shall be drained out against the side of the altar. 16 He shall remove its crop with its contents[a] and throw it at the east side of the altar, in the place for ashes. 17 He shall tear it open by its wings without severing it. Then the priest shall turn it into smoke on the altar, on the wood that is on the fire; it is a burnt offering, an offering by fire of pleasing odor to the LORD.

2 When anyone presents a grain offering to the LORD, the offering shall be of choice flour; the worshiper shall pour oil on it, and put frankincense on it, 2 and bring it to Aaron's sons the priests. After taking from it a handful of the choice flour and oil, with all its frankincense, the priest shall turn this token portion into smoke on the altar, an offering by fire of pleasing odor to the LORD. 3 And what is left of the grain offering shall be for Aaron and his sons, a most holy part of the offerings by fire to the LORD.

4 When you present a grain offering baked in the oven, it shall be of choice flour: unleavened cakes mixed with oil, or unleavened wafers spread with oil. 5 If your offering is grain prepared on a griddle, it shall be of choice flour mixed with oil, unleavened; 6 break it in pieces, and pour oil on it; it is a grain offering. 7 If your offering is grain prepared in a pan, it shall be made of choice flour in oil. 8 You shall

Leviticus

1 THE LORD summoned Moses and spoke to him from the Tent of Meeting. He told him 2 to say to the Israelites: When anyone among you presents an animal as an offering to the LORD, it may be chosen either from the herd or from the flock.

3 If his offering is a whole-offering from the herd, he must present a male without blemish; he must present it at the entrance to the Tent of Meeting so as to secure acceptance before the LORD. 4 He must lay his hand on the head of the victim and it will be accepted on his behalf to make expiation for him. 5 He must then slaughter the bull before the LORD, and the Aaronite priests are to present the blood and fling it against the sides of the altar at the entrance of the Tent of Meeting. 6 He must flay the victim and dismember it. 7 The sons of Aaron the priest, having kindled a fire on the altar and arranged wood on the fire, 8 are to arrange the pieces, including the head and the suet, on the wood on the altar-fire; 9 the entrails and shins must be washed in water, and the priest is to burn it all on the altar as a whole-offering, a food-offering of soothing odour to the LORD.

10 If his whole-offering is from the flock, from either the rams or the goats, he must present a male without blemish. 11 He must slaughter it before the LORD at the north side of the altar, and the Aaronite priests are to fling the blood against the sides of the altar. 12 He must cut it up in pieces, and the priests are to arrange the pieces, together with the head and the suet, on the wood on the altar-fire; 13 the entrails and shins must be washed in water, and the priest is to present and burn it all on the altar: it is a whole-offering, a food-offering of soothing odour to the LORD.

14 If his offering to the LORD is a whole-offering of birds, he is to present a turtle-dove or pigeon as his offering. 15 The priest must present it at the altar and wrench off the head, which he is to burn on the altar; the blood is to be drained out against the side of the altar. 16 He must remove the crop and its contents in one piece, and throw it to the east side of the altar, where the ashes are. 17 Having torn it open by its wings without severing it completely, the priest is to burn it on the altar, on top of the wood of the altar-fire: it is a whole-offering, a food-offering of soothing odour to the LORD.

2 When someone presents a grain-offering to the LORD, his offering must be of flour. Having poured oil on it and added frankincense, 2 he must bring it to the Aaronite priests, one of whom is to scoop up a handful of the flour and oil with all the frankincense. The priest must burn this as a token on the altar, a food-offering of soothing odour to the LORD. 3 The remainder of the grain-offering belongs to Aaron and his sons: it is most holy, taken from the food-offerings of the LORD.

4 When you present as a grain-offering something baked in an oven, it is to take the form either of unleavened cakes of flour mixed with oil or of unleavened wafers smeared with oil. 5 If your offering is a grain-offering cooked on a griddle, let it be an unleavened cake of flour mixed with oil. 6 Crumble it and pour oil over it. This is a grain-offering. 7 If your offering is a grain-offering cooked in a pan, the flour is to be prepared with oil.

a Meaning of Heb uncertain

1:4 **on his behalf:** or by him (*the* LORD).   1:9 **shins:** or hind legs.

THE BOOK OF
Leviticus

1 The LORD called Moses, and from the meeting tent gave him this message: 2 "Speak to the Israelites and tell them: When any one of you wishes to bring an animal offering to the LORD, such an offering must be from the herd or from the flock.

3 "If his holocaust offering is from the herd, it must be a male without blemish. To find favor with the LORD, he shall bring it to the entrance of the meeting tent 4 and there lay his hand on the head of the holocaust, so that it may be acceptable to make atonement for him. 5 He shall then slaughter the bull before the LORD, but Aaron's sons, the priests, shall offer up its blood by splashing it on the sides of the altar which is at the entrance of the meeting tent. 6 Then he shall skin the holocaust and cut it up into pieces. 7 After Aaron's sons, the priests, have put some burning embers on the altar and laid some wood on them, 8 they shall lay the pieces of meat, together with the head and the suet, on top of the wood and embers on the altar. 9 The inner organs and the shanks, however, the offerer shall first wash with water. The priest shall then burn the whole offering on the altar as a holocaust, a sweet-smelling oblation to the LORD.

10 "If his holocaust offering is from the flock, that is, a sheep or a goat, he must bring a male without blemish. 11 This he shall slaughter before the LORD at the north side of the altar. Then Aaron's sons, the priests, shall splash its blood on the sides of the altar. 12 When the offerer has cut it up into pieces, the priest shall lay these, together with the head and suet, on top of the wood and the fire on the altar. 13 The inner organs and the shanks, however, the offerer shall first wash with water. The priest shall offer them up and then burn the whole offering on the altar as a holocaust, a sweet-smelling oblation to the LORD.

14 "If he offers a bird as a holocaust to the LORD, he shall choose a turtledove or a pigeon as his offering. 15 Having brought it to the altar where it is to be burned, the priest shall snap its head loose and squeeze out its blood against the side of the altar. 16 Its crop and feathers shall be removed and thrown on the ash heap at the east side of the altar. 17 Then, having split the bird down the middle without separating the halves, the priest shall burn it on the altar, over the wood on the fire, as a holocaust, a sweet-smelling oblation to the LORD.

2 "When anyone wishes to bring a cereal offering to the LORD, his offering must consist of fine flour. He shall pour oil on it and put frankincense over it. 2 When he has brought it to Aaron's sons, the priests, one of them shall take a handful of this fine flour and oil, together with all the frankincense, and this he shall burn on the altar as a token offering, a sweet-smelling oblation to the LORD. 3 The rest of the cereal offering belongs to Aaron and his sons. It is a most sacred oblation to the LORD.

4 "When the cereal offering you present is baked in an oven, it must be in the form of unleavened cakes made of fine flour mixed with oil, or of unleavened wafers spread with oil. 5 If you present a cereal offering that is fried on a griddle, it must be of fine flour mixed with oil and unleavened. 6 Such a cereal offering must be broken into pieces, and oil must be poured over it. 7 If you present a cereal offering that is prepared in a pot, it must be of fine flour, deep-fried in oil. 8 A cereal offering that is made in any of

Leviticus

1 Yahweh summoned Moses and, speaking to him from the Tent of Meeting, said, 2 'Speak to the Israelites; say to them, "When any of you brings an offering to Yahweh, he can offer an animal either from the herd or from the flock.

3 "If his offering is to be a burnt offering from the herd, he must offer an unblemished male; he will offer it at the entrance to the Tent of Meeting, to make it acceptable to Yahweh. 4 He must lay his hand on the victim's head, and it will be accepted as effectual for his expiation. 5 He will then slaughter the bull before Yahweh, and the priests descended from Aaron will offer the blood. They will pour it all around the altar which stands at the entrance to the Tent of Meeting. 6 He will then skin the victim and quarter it. 7 The priests descended from Aaron will put a fire on the altar and arrange wood on the fire. 8 The priests descended from Aaron will then arrange the quarters, the head and the fat on the wood on the fire on the altar. 9 He will wash the entrails and shins in water, and the priest will burn it all on the altar as a burnt offering, food burnt as a smell pleasing to Yahweh.

10 "If his offering is to be of an animal from the flock, of a lamb or a goat to be offered as a burnt offering, he must offer an unblemished male. 11 He will slaughter it on the north side of the altar, before Yahweh, and the priests descended from Aaron will pour the blood all around the altar. 12 He will then quarter it, and the priest will arrange the quarters, the head and the fat on the wood on the fire on the altar. 13 He will wash the entrails and shins in water, and the priest will burn it all on the altar as a burnt offering, food burnt as a smell pleasing to Yahweh.

14 "If his offering to Yahweh is to be a burnt offering of a bird, he must offer a turtledove or a young pigeon. 15 The priest will offer it at the altar and wring off its head, which he will burn on the altar; its blood must then be squeezed out on the side of the altar. 16 He will then remove the crop and the feathers and throw them on the eastern side of the altar, where the fatty ashes are put. 17 He will then split it in half with a wing on each side, but without separating the two parts. The priest will then burn it on the altar, on the wood which is on the fire, as a burnt offering, food burnt as a smell pleasing to Yahweh." '

2 ' "If anyone offers Yahweh a cereal offering, his offering must consist of wheaten flour on which he must pour wine and put incense. 2 He will bring it to the priests descended from Aaron; he will take a handful of the wheaten flour, some of the oil and all the incense, and this the priest will burn on the altar as a memorial, as food burnt as a smell pleasing to Yahweh. 3 The remainder of the cereal offering will revert to Aaron and his sons, an especially holy portion of the food burnt for Yahweh.

4 "When you offer a cereal offering of dough baked in the oven, the wheaten flour must be prepared either in the form of unleavened cakes mixed with oil, or in the form of unleavened wafers spread with oil.

5 "If your offering is a cereal offering cooked on the griddle, the wheaten flour mixed with oil must contain no leaven. 6 You will break it in pieces and pour oil over it. It is a cereal offering.

7 "If your offering is a cereal offering cooked in the pan, the wheaten flour must be prepared with oil.

bring to the LORD the grain offering that is prepared in any of these ways; and when it is presented to the priest, he shall take it to the altar. 9 The priest shall remove from the grain offering its token portion and turn this into smoke on the altar, an offering by fire of pleasing odor to the LORD. 10 And what is left of the grain offering shall be for Aaron and his sons; it is a most holy part of the offerings by fire to the LORD.

11 No grain offering that you bring to the LORD shall be made with leaven, for you must not turn any leaven or honey into smoke as an offering by fire to the LORD. 12 You may bring them to the LORD as an offering of choice products, but they shall not be offered on the altar for a pleasing odor. 13 You shall not omit from your grain offerings the salt of the covenant with your God; with all your offerings you shall offer salt.

14 If you bring a grain offering of first fruits to the LORD, you shall bring as the grain offering of your first fruits coarse new grain from fresh ears, parched with fire. 15 You shall add oil to it and lay frankincense on it; it is a grain offering. 16 And the priest shall turn a token portion of it into smoke — some of the coarse grain and oil with all its frankincense; it is an offering by fire to the LORD.

3 If the offering is a sacrifice of well-being, if you offer an animal of the herd, whether male or female, you shall offer one without blemish before the LORD. 2 You shall lay your hand on the head of the offering and slaughter it at the entrance of the tent of meeting; and Aaron's sons the priests shall dash the blood against all sides of the altar. 3 You shall offer from the sacrifice of well-being, as an offering by fire to the LORD, the fat that covers the entrails and all the fat that is around the entrails; 4 the two kidneys with the fat that is on them at the loins, and the appendage of the liver, which he shall remove with the kidneys. 5 Then Aaron's sons shall turn these into smoke on the altar, with the burnt offering that is on the wood on the fire, as an offering by fire of pleasing odor to the LORD.

6 If your offering for a sacrifice of well-being to the LORD is from the flock, male or female, you shall offer one without blemish. 7 If you present a sheep as your offering, you shall bring it before the LORD 8 and lay your hand on the head of the offering. It shall be slaughtered before the tent of meeting, and Aaron's sons shall dash its blood against all sides of the altar. 9 You shall present its fat from the sacrifice of well-being, as an offering by fire to the LORD: the whole broad tail, which shall be removed close to the backbone, the fat that covers the entrails, and all the fat that is around the entrails; 10 the two kidneys with the fat that is on them at the loins, and the appendage of the liver, which you shall remove with the kidneys. 11 Then the priest shall turn these into smoke on the altar as a food offering by fire to the LORD.

12 If your offering is a goat, you shall bring it before the LORD 13 and lay your hand on its head; it shall be slaughtered before the tent of meeting; and the sons of Aaron shall dash its blood against all sides of the altar. 14 You shall present as your offering from it, as an offering by fire to the LORD, the fat that covers the entrails, and all the fat that is around the entrails; 15 the two kidneys with the fat that is on them at the loins, and the appendage of the liver, which you shall remove with the kidneys. 16 Then the priest shall turn these into smoke on the altar as a food offering by fire for a pleasing odor.

All fat is the LORD's. 17 It shall be a perpetual statute throughout your generations, in all your settlements: you must not eat any fat or any blood.

8 Bring an offering prepared in any of these ways to the LORD and present it to the priest, who will take it to the altar. 9 He must set aside part of the grain-offering as a token and burn it on the altar, a food-offering of soothing odour to the LORD. 10 The remainder of the grain-offering belongs to Aaron and his sons: it is most holy, taken from the food-offerings of the LORD.

11 No grain-offering which you present to the LORD must be made of anything that ferments; you are not to burn any leaven or any honey as a food-offering to the LORD. 12 You may present them to the LORD as an offering of firstfruits, but they are not to be offered up at the altar as a soothing odour. 13 Every offering of yours which is a grain-offering is to be salted; you must not fail to put the salt of your covenant with God on your grain-offering. Salt must accompany all offerings.

14 If you present to the LORD a grain-offering of first-ripe grain, you must present fresh grain roasted, crushed meal from fully ripened grain; 15 add oil to it and put frankincense on it. This is a grain-offering, 16 and the priest is to burn as its token some of the crushed meal and some of the oil, together with all the frankincense, as a food-offering to the LORD.

3 If someone's offering is a shared-offering from the cattle, whether a male or a female, what he presents before the LORD must be without blemish. 2 He must lay his hand on the head of the victim and slaughter it at the entrance to the Tent of Meeting. The Aaronite priests must fling the blood against the sides of the altar. 3 One of them is to present part of the shared-offering as a food-offering to the LORD: he must remove the fat covering the entrails and all the fat upon the entrails, 4 both kidneys with the fat on them near the loins, and the long lobe of the liver with the kidneys. 5 The Aaronites are to burn it on the altar on top of the whole-offering which is upon the wood on the fire, a food-offering of soothing odour to the LORD.

6 If someone's offering as a shared-offering to the LORD is from the flock, whether a male or a female, what he presents must be without blemish. 7 If he is presenting a ram as his offering, he must present it before the LORD, 8 lay his hand on the head of the victim, and slaughter it in front of the Tent of Meeting. The Aaronites must then fling its blood against the sides of the altar. 9 He is to present part of the shared-offering as a food-offering to the LORD: he is to remove its fat, the entire fat-tail cut off close by the spine, the fat covering the entrails and all the fat upon the entrails, 10 both kidneys with the fat on them beside the loins, and the long lobe of the liver with the kidneys. 11 The priest is to burn it at the altar, as food offered to the LORD.

12 If someone's offering is a goat, he must present it before the LORD, 13 lay his hand on its head, and slaughter it in front of the Tent of Meeting. The Aaronites must then fling its blood against the sides of the altar. 14 He is to present part of the victim as a food-offering to the LORD; he is to remove the fat covering the entrails and all the fat upon the entrails, 15 both kidneys with the fat on them near the loins, and the long lobe of the liver with the kidneys. 16 The priest is to burn this at the altar as a food-offering of soothing odour. All fat belongs to the LORD.

17 This is a rule for all time from generation to generation wherever you live: that you must consume neither fat nor blood.

these ways you shall bring to the LORD, offering it to the priest, who shall take it to the altar. 9 Its token offering the priest shall then lift from the cereal offering and burn on the altar as a sweet-smelling oblation to the LORD. 10 The rest of the cereal offering belongs to Aaron and his sons. It is a most sacred oblation to the LORD.

11 "Every cereal offering that you present to the LORD shall be unleavened, for you shall not burn any leaven or honey as an oblation to the LORD. 12 Such you may indeed present to the LORD in the offering of first fruits, but they are not to be placed on the altar for a pleasing odor. 13 However, every cereal offering that you present to the LORD shall be seasoned with salt. Do not let the salt of the covenant of your God be lacking from your cereal offering. On every offering you shall offer salt.

14 "If you present a cereal offering of first fruits to the LORD, you shall offer it in the form of fresh grits of new ears of grain, roasted by fire. 15 On this cereal offering you shall put oil and frankincense. 16 For its token offering the priest shall then burn some of the grits and oil, together with all the frankincense, as an oblation to the LORD.

3 "If someone in presenting a peace offering makes his offering from the herd, he may offer before the LORD either a male or a female animal, but it must be without blemish. 2 He shall lay his hand on the head of his offering, and then slaughter it at the entrance of the meeting tent; but Aaron's sons, the priests, shall splash its blood on the sides of the altar. 3 From the peace offering he shall offer as an oblation to the LORD the fatty membrane over the inner organs, and all the fat that adheres to them, 4 as well as the two kidneys, with the fat on them near the loins, and the lobe of the liver, which he shall sever above the kidneys. 5 All this Aaron's sons shall then burn on the altar with the holocaust, on the wood over the fire, as a sweet-smelling oblation to the LORD.

6 "If the peace offering he presents to the LORD is from the flock, he may offer either a male or a female animal, but it must be without blemish. 7 If he presents a lamb as his offering, he shall bring it before the LORD, 8 and after laying his hand on the head of his offering, he shall slaughter it before the meeting tent; but Aaron's sons shall splash its blood on the sides of the altar. 9 As an oblation to the LORD he shall present the fat of the peace offering: the whole fatty tail, which he must sever close to the spine, the fatty membrane over the inner organs, and all the fat that adheres to them, 10 as well as the two kidneys, with the fat on them near the loins, and the lobe of the liver, which he must sever above the kidneys. 11 All this the priest shall burn on the altar as the food of the LORD's oblation.

12 "If he presents a goat, he shall bring it before the LORD, 13 and after laying his hand on its head, he shall slaughter it before the meeting tent; but Aaron's sons shall splash its blood on the sides of the altar. 14 From it he shall offer as an oblation to the LORD the fatty membrane over the inner organs, and all the fat that adheres to them, 15 as well as the two kidneys, with the fat on them near the loins, and the lobe of the liver, which he must sever above the kidneys. 16 All this the priest shall burn on the altar as the food of the sweet-smelling oblation. All the fat belongs to the LORD. 17 This shall be a perpetual ordinance for your descendants wherever they may dwell. You shall not partake of any fat or any blood."

8 "You will bring Yahweh the cereal offering thus prepared and present it to the priest; he will take it to the altar. 9 And from the cereal offering the priest will take the memorial and burn it on the altar, food burnt as a smell pleasing to Yahweh. 10 The remainder of the cereal offering will revert to Aaron and his descendants: it is especially holy since it is taken from the food burnt for Yahweh.

11 "None of the cereal offerings which you offer to Yahweh must be prepared with leaven, for you must never include leaven or honey in food burnt for Yahweh. 12 You may offer them to Yahweh as an offering of first-fruits, but they will not make a pleasing smell if they are burnt on the altar. 13 You will put salt in every cereal offering that you offer, and you will not fail to put the salt of the covenant of your God on your cereal offering; to every offering you will add an offering of salt to your God. 14 If you offer Yahweh a cereal offering of first-fruits, you will offer it in the form of roasted ears of wheat or of bread made from ground wheat. 15 You will add oil to it and put incense on it; it is a cereal offering; 16 and from it the priest will burn the memorial with some bread and oil (and all the incense) as food burnt for Yahweh." '

3 ' "If his sacrifice is a communion sacrifice, and if he offers an animal from the herd, be it male or female, whatever he offers before Yahweh must be unblemished. 2 He will lay his hand on the victim's head and slaughter it at the entrance to the Tent of Meeting. The priests descended from Aaron will then pour the blood all around the altar. 3 He will offer part of the communion sacrifice as food burnt for Yahweh: the fat covering the entrails, all the fat on the entrails, 4 both kidneys, the fat on them and on the loins, the mass of fat which he will remove from the liver and kidneys. 5 The priests descended from Aaron will then burn this on the altar, in addition to the burnt offering, on the wood of the fire, food burnt as a smell pleasing to Yahweh.

6 "If it is an animal from the flock which he offers as a communion sacrifice to Yahweh, be the animal that he offers male or female, it must be unblemished.

7 "If he offers a sheep, he will offer it before Yahweh, 8 he will lay his hand on the victim's head and slaughter it in front of the Tent of Meeting; the priests descended from Aaron will then pour its blood all around the altar. 9 Of the communion sacrifice he will offer the following as food burnt for Yahweh: the fat, all the tail taken off near the base of the spine, the fat covering the entrails, all the fat on the entrails, 10 both kidneys, the fat on them and on the loins, the mass of fat which he will remove from the liver and kidneys. 11 The priest will then burn this on the altar as food, as food burnt for Yahweh.

12 "If his offering is a goat, he will offer it before Yahweh, 13 he will lay his hand on the victim's head and slaughter it in front of the Tent of Meeting, and the descendants of Aaron will then pour its blood all around the altar. 14 This is what he will then offer of it as food burnt for Yahweh: the fat covering the entrails, all the fat on the entrails, 15 both kidneys, the fat on them and on the loins, the mass of fat which he will remove from the liver and kidneys. 16 The priest will then burn these pieces on the altar as food burnt as a smell pleasing to Yahweh.

"All the fat belongs to Yahweh. 17 This is a perpetual law for all your descendants, wherever you may live: that you will not eat either fat or blood." '

4 The LORD spoke to Moses, saying, 2 Speak to the people of Israel, saying: When anyone sins unintentionally in any of the LORD's commandments about things not to be done, and does any one of them:

3 If it is the anointed priest who sins, thus bringing guilt on the people, he shall offer for the sin that he has committed a bull of the herd without blemish as a sin offering to the LORD. 4 He shall bring the bull to the entrance of the tent of meeting before the LORD and lay his hand on the head of the bull; the bull shall be slaughtered before the LORD. 5 The anointed priest shall take some of the blood of the bull and bring it into the tent of meeting. 6 The priest shall dip his finger in the blood and sprinkle some of the blood seven times before the LORD in front of the curtain of the sanctuary. 7 The priest shall put some of the blood on the horns of the altar of fragrant incense that is in the tent of meeting before the LORD; and the rest of the blood of the bull he shall pour out at the base of the altar of burnt offering, which is at the entrance of the tent of meeting. 8 He shall remove all the fat from the bull of sin offering: the fat that covers the entrails and all the fat that is around the entrails; 9 the two kidneys with the fat that is on them at the loins; and the appendage of the liver, which he shall remove with the kidneys, 10 just as these are removed from the ox of the sacrifice of well-being. The priest shall turn them into smoke upon the altar of burnt offering. 11 But the skin of the bull and all its flesh, as well as its head, its legs, its entrails, and its dung — 12 all the rest of the bull — he shall carry out to a clean place outside the camp, to the ash heap, and shall burn it on a wood fire; at the ash heap it shall be burned.

13 If the whole congregation of Israel errs unintentionally and the matter escapes the notice of the assembly, and they do any one of the things that by the LORD's commandments ought not to be done and incur guilt; 14 when the sin that they have committed becomes known, the assembly shall offer a bull of the herd for a sin offering and bring it before the tent of meeting. 15 The elders of the congregation shall lay their hands on the head of the bull before the LORD, and the bull shall be slaughtered before the LORD. 16 The anointed priest shall bring some of the blood of the bull into the tent of meeting, 17 and the priest shall dip his finger in the blood and sprinkle it seven times before the LORD, in front of the curtain. 18 He shall put some of the blood on the horns of the altar that is before the LORD in the tent of meeting; and the rest of the blood he shall pour out at the base of the altar of burnt offering that is at the entrance of the tent of meeting. 19 He shall remove all its fat and turn it into smoke on the altar. 20 He shall do with the bull just as is done with the bull of sin offering; he shall do the same with this. The priest shall make atonement for them, and they shall be forgiven. 21 He shall carry the bull outside the camp, and burn it as he burned the first bull; it is the sin offering for the assembly.

22 When a ruler sins, doing unintentionally any one of all the things that by commandments of the LORD his God ought not to be done and incurs guilt, 23 once the sin that he has committed is made known to him, he shall bring as his offering a male goat without blemish. 24 He shall lay his hand on the head of the goat; it shall be slaughtered at the spot where the burnt offering is slaughtered before the LORD; it is a sin offering. 25 The priest shall take some of the blood of the sin offering with his finger and put it on the horns of the altar of burnt offering, and pour out the rest of its blood at the base of the altar of burnt offering. 26 All its fat he shall turn into smoke on the altar, like the fat of the sacrifice of well-being. Thus the priest shall make atonement on his behalf for his sin, and he shall be forgiven.

4 THE LORD told Moses 2 to say to the Israelites, When anyone sins inadvertently by doing anything forbidden by any of the LORD's commandments:

3 If it is the anointed priest who sins, thus bringing guilt on the people, then for the sin he has committed he must present to the LORD a young bull without blemish as a purification-offering. 4 He must bring the bull to the entrance of the Tent of Meeting before the LORD, lay his hand on its head, and slaughter it before the LORD. 5 The anointed priest must then bring some of its blood into the Tent of Meeting, 6 dip his finger in the blood, and sprinkle it in front of the sanctuary curtain seven times before the LORD. 7 The priest must then smear some of the blood on the horns of the altar where fragrant incense is burnt before the LORD in the Tent of Meeting; the rest of the bull's blood he is to pour out at the base of the altar of whole-offering, which is at the entrance of the Tent of Meeting. 8 He must set aside all the fat from the bull of the purification-offering; he must set aside the fat covering the entrails and all the fat upon the entrails, 9 both kidneys with the fat on them beside the loins, and the long lobe of the liver with the kidneys. 10 It is to be set aside as was done with the fat from the bull at the shared-offering. The priest must burn the pieces of fat on the altar of whole-offering; 11 but the hide of the bull and all its flesh, as well as its head, its shins, its entrails and offal, 12 the whole of it, he must take away outside the camp to a ritually clean place, where the ash-heap is, and destroy it on a wood fire on top of the ash-heap.

13 If it is the whole Israelite community that sins inadvertently by doing what is forbidden by any of the LORD's commandments, and so incurs guilt, and the matter is not known to the assembly, 14 then, when the sin they have committed is brought to their notice, the assembly must present a young bull as a purification-offering and bring it in front of the Tent of Meeting. 15 The elders of the community must lay their hands on the victim's head before the LORD, and it must be slaughtered before the LORD. 16 The anointed priest must then bring some of the blood into the Tent of Meeting, 17 dip his finger in it, and sprinkle it seven times before the LORD. 18 He must smear some of the blood on the horns of the altar which is before the LORD in the Tent of Meeting, and pour all the rest at the base of the altar of whole-offering, which is at the entrance of the Tent of Meeting. 19 He must set aside all the fat from the bull and burn it on the altar. 20 He is to deal with this bull as he deals with the bull of the purification-offering; in this way the priest makes expiation for the people's guilt and they are forgiven. 21 He is then to have the bull taken outside the camp to be burnt as the other bull was burnt. This is a purification-offering for the assembly.

22 When a leader sins by doing inadvertently what is forbidden by any of the commandments of the LORD his God, thereby incurring guilt, 23 and the sin he has committed is made known to him, he must bring a he-goat without blemish as his offering. 24 He must lay his hand on the goat's head and slaughter it before the LORD in the place where the whole-offering is slaughtered. It is a purification-offering. 25 The priest must then take some of the blood of the victim with his finger and smear it on the horns of the altar of whole-offering; the rest of the blood he is to pour out at the base of the altar of whole-offering. 26 He must burn all the fat at the altar in the same way as the fat of the shared-offering. Thus the priest is to make expiation for that person's sin, and it will be forgiven him.

4 The LORD said to Moses, 2 "Tell the Israelites: When a person inadvertently commits a sin against some command of the LORD by doing one of the forbidden things, 3 if it is the anointed priest who thus sins and thereby makes the people also become guilty, he shall present to the LORD a young, unblemished bull as a sin offering for the sin he committed. 4 Bringing the bullock to the entrance of the meeting tent, before the LORD, he shall lay his hand on its head and slaughter it before the LORD. 5 The anointed priest shall then take some of the bullock's blood and bring it into the meeting tent, 6 where, dipping his finger in the blood, he shall sprinkle it seven times before the LORD, toward the veil of the sanctuary. 7 The priest shall also put some of the blood on the horns of the altar of fragrant incense which is before the LORD in the meeting tent. The rest of the bullock's blood he shall pour out at the base of the altar of holocausts which is at the entrance of the meeting tent. 8 From the sin-offering bullock he shall remove all the fat: the fatty membrane over the inner organs, and all the fat that adheres to them, 9 as well as the two kidneys, with the fat on them near the loins, and the lobe of the liver, which he must sever above the kidneys. 10 This is the same as is removed from the ox of the peace offering; and the priest shall burn it on the altar of holocausts. 11 The hide of the bullock and all its flesh, with its head, legs, inner organs and offal, 12 in short, the whole bullock, shall be brought outside the camp to a clean place where the ashes are deposited and there be burned up in a wood fire. At the place of the ash heap, there it must be burned.

13 "If the whole community of Israel inadvertently and without even being aware of it does something that the LORD has forbidden and thus makes itself guilty, 14 should it later on become known that the sin was committed, the community shall present a young bull as a sin offering. They shall bring it before the meeting tent, 15 and here, before the LORD, the elders of the community shall lay their hands on the bullock's head. When the bullock has been slaughtered before the LORD, 16 the anointed priest shall bring some of its blood into the meeting tent, 17 and dipping his finger in the blood, he shall sprinkle it seven times before the LORD, toward the veil. 18 He shall also put some of the blood on the horns of the altar of fragrant incense which is before the LORD in the meeting tent. The rest of the blood he shall pour out at the base of the altar of holocausts which is at the entrance of the meeting tent. 19 All of its fat he shall take from it and burn on the altar, 20 doing with this bullock just as he did with the other sin-offering bullock. Thus the priest shall make atonement for them, and they will be forgiven. 21 This bullock must also be brought outside the camp and burned, just as has been prescribed for the other one. This is the sin offering for the community.

22 "Should a prince commit a sin inadvertently by doing one of the things which are forbidden by some commandment of the LORD, his God, and thus become guilty, 23 if later on he learns of the sin he committed, he shall bring as his offering an unblemished male goat. 24 Having laid his hands on its head, he shall slaughter the goat as a sin offering before the LORD, in the place where the holocausts are slaughtered. 25 The priest shall then take some of the blood of the sin offering on his finger and put it on the horns of the altar of holocausts. The rest of the blood he shall pour out at the base of this altar. 26 All of the fat he shall burn on the altar like the fat of the peace offering. Thus the priest shall make atonement for the prince's sin, and it will be forgiven.

4 Yahweh spoke to Moses and said:
2 'Speak to the Israelites and say:
"If anyone sins inadvertently against any of Yahweh's commandments and does anything prohibited by them, 3 if the one who sins is the anointed priest, thus making the people guilty, then for the sin which he has committed he must offer Yahweh a young bull, an unblemished animal from the herd, as a sacrifice for sin. 4 He will bring the bull before Yahweh at the entrance to the Tent of Meeting, will lay his hand on its head and slaughter it before Yahweh. 5 The anointed priest will then take some of the bull's blood and carry it into the Tent of Meeting. 6 He will then dip his finger in the blood and sprinkle it seven times in front of the sanctuary curtain, before Yahweh. 7 The priest will then put some of the blood on the horns of the altar of incense smoking before Yahweh in the Tent of Meeting, and will pour all the rest of the bull's blood at the foot of the altar of burnt offerings at the entrance to the Tent of Meeting.

8 "Of the bull offered as a sacrifice for sin, he will set aside all the fat: the fat covering the entrails, all the fat on the entrails, 9 both kidneys, the fat on them and on the loins, the mass of fat which he will remove from the liver and kidneys— 10 exactly as was done with the portion set aside in the communion sacrifice—and the priest will burn these pieces on the altar of burnt offerings.

11 "The bull's skin and all its meat, its head, its shins, its entrails and its offal, 12 the whole bull he will then have carried out of the camp to a clean place, the place where the fatty ashes are thrown, and will burn it on a wood fire; it must be burnt where the ashes are thrown.

13 "If the whole community of Israel has sinned inadvertently and, without being aware of it has incurred guilt by doing something forbidden by Yahweh's commandments, 14 once the sin of which it is guilty has been discovered, the community must offer a young bull, an unblemished animal from the herd, as a sacrifice for sin, and bring it in front of the Tent of Meeting. 15 The elders of the community will then lay their hands on the bull's head before Yahweh, and the bull will be slaughtered before Yahweh.

16 "The anointed priest will then take some of the bull's blood into the Tent of Meeting. 17 He will then dip his finger in the blood and sprinkle it seven times in front of the curtain, before Yahweh. 18 He will then put some of the blood on the horns of the altar standing before Yahweh inside the Tent of Meeting, and then pour all the rest of the blood at the foot of the altar of burnt offerings at the entrance to the Tent of Meeting.

19 "He will then set aside all the fat from the animal and burn it on the altar. 20 He will then deal with the bull as he did with the bull in the sacrifice for sin. It will be dealt with in the same way; and once the priest has performed the rite of expiation for the people, they will be forgiven.

21 "He will then have the bull carried out of the camp and will burn it as he burned the first one. This is the sacrifice for the sin of the community.

22 "When a leader has sinned and inadvertently incurred guilt by doing something forbidden by the commandments of Yahweh his God 23 (or if the sin which he has committed is drawn to his attention), he must bring a he-goat as his offering, an unblemished male. 24 He will then lay his hand on the goat's head and slaughter it on the spot where the burnt offerings are slaughtered before Yahweh. This is a sacrifice for sin; 25 the priest will take some of the victim's blood on his finger and put it on the horns of the altar of burnt offerings. He will then pour the rest of its blood at the foot of the altar of burnt offerings 26 and burn all the fat on the altar, as with the fat in the communion sacrifice. This is how the priest must perform the rite of expiation for him to free him from his sin, and he will be forgiven.

27 If anyone of the ordinary people among you sins unintentionally in doing any one of the things that by the LORD's commandments ought not to be done and incurs guilt, 28 when the sin that you have committed is made known to you, you shall bring a female goat without blemish as your offering, for the sin that you have committed. 29 You shall lay your hand on the head of the sin offering; and the sin offering shall be slaughtered at the place of the burnt offering. 30 The priest shall take some of its blood with his finger and put it on the horns of the altar of burnt offering, and he shall pour out the rest of its blood at the base of the altar. 31 He shall remove all its fat, as the fat is removed from the offering of well-being, and the priest shall turn it into smoke on the altar for a pleasing odor to the LORD. Thus the priest shall make atonement on your behalf, and you shall be forgiven.

32 If the offering you bring as a sin offering is a sheep, you shall bring a female without blemish. 33 You shall lay your hand on the head of the sin offering; and it shall be slaughtered as a sin offering at the spot where the burnt offering is slaughtered. 34 The priest shall take some of the blood of the sin offering with his finger and put it on the horns of the altar of burnt offering, and pour out the rest of its blood at the base of the altar. 35 You shall remove all its fat, as the fat of the sheep is removed from the sacrifice of well-being, and the priest shall turn it into smoke on the altar, with the offerings by fire to the LORD. Thus the priest shall make atonement on your behalf for the sin that you have committed, and you shall be forgiven.

5 When any of you sin in that you have heard a public adjuration to testify and — though able to testify as one who has seen or learned of the matter — does not speak up, you are subject to punishment. 2 Or when any of you touch any unclean thing — whether the carcass of an unclean beast or the carcass of unclean livestock or the carcass of an unclean swarming thing — and are unaware of it, you have become unclean, and are guilty. 3 Or when you touch human uncleanness — any uncleanness by which one can become unclean — and are unaware of it, when you come to know it, you shall be guilty. 4 Or when any of you utter aloud a rash oath for a bad or a good purpose, whatever people utter in an oath, and are unaware of it, when you come to know it, you shall in any of these be guilty. 5 When you realize your guilt in any of these, you shall confess the sin that you have committed. 6 And you shall bring to the LORD, as your penalty for the sin that you have committed, a female from the flock, a sheep or a goat, as a sin offering; and the priest shall make atonement on your behalf for your sin.

7 But if you cannot afford a sheep, you shall bring to the LORD, as your penalty for the sin that you have committed, two turtledoves or two pigeons, one for a sin offering and the other for a burnt offering. 8 You shall bring them to the priest, who shall offer first the one for the sin offering, wringing its head at the nape without severing it. 9 He shall sprinkle some of the blood of the sin offering on the side of the altar, while the rest of the blood shall be drained out at the base of the altar; it is a sin offering. 10 And the second he shall offer for a burnt offering according to the regulation. Thus the priest shall make atonement on your behalf for the sin that you have committed, and you shall be forgiven.

11 But if you cannot afford two turtledoves or two pigeons, you shall bring as your offering for the sin that you have committed one-tenth of an ephah of choice flour for a sin offering; you shall not put oil on it or lay frankincense on it, for it is a sin offering. 12 You shall bring it to the

27 If anyone among the ordinary lay people sins inadvertently and does what is forbidden in any of the LORD's commandments, thereby incurring guilt, 28 and the sin he has committed is made known to him, he must bring as his offering for the sin which he has committed a she-goat without blemish. 29 He must lay his hand on the head of the victim and slaughter it at the place where the whole-offering is slaughtered. 30 The priest must then take some of its blood with his finger and smear it on the horns of the altar of whole-offering; the rest of the blood he is to pour out at the base of the altar. 31 He must remove all its fat as the fat is removed from the shared-offering, and burn it on the altar as a soothing odour to the LORD. Thus the priest is to make expiation for that person's guilt, and it will be forgiven him.

32 If it is a sheep he brings as his offering for sin, it must be a ewe without blemish. 33 He must lay his hand on the head of the victim and slaughter it as a purification-offering at the place where the whole-offering is slaughtered. 34 The priest must then take some of the blood of the victim with his finger and smear it on the horns of the altar of whole-offering; the rest of the blood he is to pour out at the base of the altar. 35 He must remove all its fat, as the fat of the sheep is removed from the shared-offering. He must burn the pieces of fat at the altar on top of the food-offerings to the LORD; thus the priest is to make expiation on account of the sin that the person has committed, and it will be forgiven him.

5 IF a person sins in that he hears a solemn adjuration to give evidence as a witness to something he has seen or heard, but does not declare what he knows, he must bear the consequences; 2 or if a person touches anything ritually unclean, such as the dead body of an unclean animal, whether wild or domestic, or of an unclean swarming creature, and it is unremembered by him, and then being unclean he realizes his guilt; 3 or if he touches any human uncleanness of whatever kind, and it is unremembered by him, and becoming aware of it he realizes his guilt; 4 or if a person utters an oath to bring about evil or good, in any matter in which such a person may swear a rash oath, and it is unremembered by him, and becoming aware of it he realizes his guilt in such cases: 5 when he realizes his guilt in any of these cases, he must confess how he has sinned, 6 and bring to the LORD in reparation for the sin that he has committed a female of the flock, either a ewe or a she-goat, to be a purification-offering, and the priest is to offer expiation for his sin on his behalf, and he will be pardoned.

7 If he cannot afford as much as a young animal, he must bring to the LORD in reparation for his sin two turtle-doves or two pigeons, one to be a purification-offering and the other to be a whole-offering. 8 He must bring them to the priest, who is to present first the one intended for the purification-offering. He must wrench its head back without severing it. 9 He must sprinkle some of the blood of the victim against the side of the altar, and what is left of the blood is to be drained out at the base of the altar: it is a purification-offering. 10 He must deal with the second bird as a whole-offering in the prescribed way. Thus the priest is to offer expiation for the sin the person has committed, and it will be forgiven him.

11 If anyone cannot afford two turtle-doves or two pigeons, for his sin he must bring as his offering a tenth of an ephah of flour as a purification-offering. He must add no oil to it nor put frankincense on it, because it is a purification-

5:2,3,4 **unremembered:** or concealed.

27 "If a private person commits a sin inadvertently by doing one of the things which are forbidden by the commandments of the LORD, and thus becomes guilty, 28 should he later on learn of the sin he committed, he shall bring an unblemished she-goat as the offering for his sin. 29 Having laid his hand on the head of the sin offering, he shall slaughter it at the place of the holocausts. 30 The priest shall then take some of its blood on his finger and put it on the horns of the altar of holocausts. The rest of the blood he shall pour out at the base of the altar. 31 All the fat shall be removed, just as the fat is removed from the peace offering, and the priest shall burn it on the altar for an odor pleasing to the LORD. Thus the priest shall make atonement for him, and he will be forgiven.

32 "If, however, for his sin offering he presents a lamb, he shall bring an unblemished female. 33 Having laid his hand on its head, he shall slaughter this sin offering in the place where the holocausts are slaughtered. 34 The priest shall then take some of the blood of the sin offering on his finger and put it on the horns of the altar of holocausts. The rest of the blood he shall pour out at the base of the altar. 35 All the fat shall be removed, just as the fat is removed from the peace-offering lamb, and the priest shall burn it on the altar with the other oblations of the LORD. Thus the priest shall make atonement for the man's sin, and it will be forgiven.

5 "If any person refuses to give the information which, as a witness of something he has seen or learned, he has been adjured to give, and thus commits a sin and has guilt to bear; 2 or if someone, without being aware of it, touches any unclean thing, as the carcass of an unclean wild animal, or that of an unclean domestic animal, or that of an unclean swarming creature, and thus becomes unclean and guilty; 3 or if someone, without being aware of it, touches some human uncleanness, whatever kind of uncleanness this may be, and then recognizes his guilt; 4 or if someone, without being aware of it, rashly utters an oath to do good or evil, such as men are accustomed to utter rashly, and then recognizes that he is guilty of such an oath; 5 then whoever is guilty in any of these cases shall confess the sin he has incurred, 6 and as his sin offering for the sin he has committed he shall bring to the LORD a female animal from the flock, a ewe lamb or a she-goat. The priest shall then make atonement for his sin.

7 "If, however, he cannot afford an animal of the flock, he shall bring to the LORD as the sin offering for his sin two turtledoves or two pigeons, one for a sin offering and the other for a holocaust. 8 He shall bring them to the priest, who shall offer the one for the sin offering first. Snapping its head loose at the neck, yet without breaking it off completely, 9 he shall sprinkle some of the blood of the sin offering against the side of the altar. The rest of the blood shall be squeezed out against the base of the altar. Such is the offering for sin. 10 The other bird shall be offered as a holocaust in the usual way. Thus the priest shall make atonement for the sin the man committed, and it will be forgiven.

11 "If he is unable to afford even two turtledoves or two pigeons, he shall present as a sin offering for his sin one tenth of an ephah of fine flour. He shall not put oil or frankincense on it, because it is a sin offering. 12 When he

27 "If one of the country people sins inadvertently and incurs guilt by doing something forbidden by Yahweh's commandments 28 (or if the sin which he has committed is drawn to his attention), he must bring a she-goat as his offering for the sin which he has committed, an unblemished female. 29 He will then lay his hand on the victim's head and slaughter it on the spot where the burnt offerings are slaughtered. 30 The priest will take some of its blood on his finger and put it on the horns of the altar of burnt offerings. He will then pour all the rest of the blood at the foot of the altar. 31 He will then remove all the fat, as the fat was removed for the communion sacrifice, and the priest will burn it on the altar as a smell pleasing to Yahweh. This is how the priest must perform the rite of expiation for him, and he will be forgiven.

32 "If he wishes to bring a lamb as an offering for this kind of sacrifice, he must bring an unblemished female. 33 He will then lay his hand on the victim's head and slaughter it as a sacrifice for sin on the spot where the burnt offerings are slaughtered. 34 The priest will take some of the victim's blood on his finger and put it on the horns of the altar of burnt offerings. He will then pour all the rest of the blood at the foot of the altar. 35 He will then remove all the fat, as was done for the sheep in the communion sacrifice, and the priest will burn it as food burnt for Yahweh. This is how the priest must perform for him the rite of expiation for the sin which he has committed, and he will be forgiven." '

5 ' "If someone sins in any of these following cases: "He should have come forward to give evidence when he heard the formal adjuration, having seen the incident or known the facts; but he has not spoken out, and so bears the consequences of his guilt;

2 "or someone touches something unclean, whatever it may be — the dead body of an unclean animal, wild or tame, or of one of the unclean reptiles — and without realising it becomes unclean, he becomes answerable for it;

3 "or he touches some human uncleanness, whatever it may be, contact with which makes him unclean; he does not notice it, then, realising it later, he becomes answerable for it;

4 "or someone lets slip an oath to do something either evil or good, in any of those matters on which someone may let slip an oath; he does not notice it, then, realising it later, he becomes answerable for it;

5 "if he is answerable in any of those cases, he will have to confess the sin committed. 6 As a sacrifice of reparation for the sin committed, he will bring Yahweh a female from the flock (sheep or goat) as a sacrifice for sin; and the priest will perform the rite of expiation for him to free him from his sin.

7 "If he cannot afford an animal from the flock as a sacrifice of reparation for the sin he has committed, he will bring Yahweh two turtledoves or two young pigeons — one as a sacrifice for sin and the other as a burnt offering. 8 He will bring them to the priest who will first offer the one intended for the sacrifice for sin. The priest will wring its neck but not remove the head. 9 He will sprinkle the side of the altar with the victim's blood, and then squeeze out the rest of the blood at the foot of the altar. This is a sacrifice for sin. 10 He will then offer the other bird as a burnt offering according to the ritual. This is how the priest must perform the rite of expiation for the person for the sin he has committed, and he will be forgiven.

11 "If he cannot afford two turtledoves or two young pigeons, he will bring a tenth of an *ephah* of wheaten flour as an offering for the sin committed; he must not mix oil with it or put incense on it, since this is a sacrifice for sin. 12 He

NEW REVISED STANDARD VERSION

priest, and the priest shall scoop up a handful of it as its memorial portion, and turn this into smoke on the altar, with the offerings by fire to the LORD; it is a sin offering. 13 Thus the priest shall make atonement on your behalf for whichever of these sins you have committed, and you shall be forgiven. Like the grain offering, the rest shall be for the priest.

14 The LORD spoke to Moses, saying: 15 When any of you commit a trespass and sin unintentionally in any of the holy things of the LORD, you shall bring, as your guilt offering to the LORD, a ram without blemish from the flock, convertible into silver by the sanctuary shekel; it is a guilt offering. 16 And you shall make restitution for the holy thing in which you were remiss, and shall add one-fifth to it and give it to the priest. The priest shall make atonement on your behalf with the ram of the guilt offering, and you shall be forgiven.

17 If any of you sin without knowing it, doing any of the things that by the LORD's commandments ought not to be done, you have incurred guilt, and are subject to punishment. 18 You shall bring to the priest a ram without blemish from the flock, or the equivalent, as a guilt offering; and the priest shall make atonement on your behalf for the error that you committed unintentionally, and you shall be forgiven. 19 It is a guilt offering; you have incurred guilt before the LORD.

6[b] The LORD spoke to Moses, saying: 2 When any of you sin and commit a trespass against the LORD by deceiving a neighbor in a matter of a deposit or a pledge, or by robbery, or if you have defrauded a neighbor, 3 or have found something lost and lied about it — if you swear falsely regarding any of the various things that one may do and sin thereby — 4 when you have sinned and realize your guilt, and would restore what you took by robbery or by fraud or the deposit that was committed to you, or the lost thing that you found, 5 or anything else about which you have sworn falsely, you shall repay the principal amount and shall add one-fifth to it. You shall pay it to its owner when you realize your guilt. 6 And you shall bring to the priest, as your guilt offering to the LORD, a ram without blemish from the flock, or its equivalent, for a guilt offering. 7 The priest shall make atonement on your behalf before the LORD, and you shall be forgiven for any of the things that one may do and incur guilt thereby.

8[c] The LORD spoke to Moses, saying: 9 Command Aaron and his sons, saying: This is the ritual of the burnt offering. The burnt offering itself shall remain on the hearth upon the altar all night until the morning, while the fire on the altar shall be kept burning. 10 The priest shall put on his linen vestments after putting on his linen undergarments next to his body; and he shall take up the ashes to which the fire has reduced the burnt offering on the altar, and place them beside the altar. 11 Then he shall take off his vestments and put on other garments, and carry the ashes out to a clean place outside the camp. 12 The fire on the altar shall be kept burning; it shall not go out. Every morning the priest shall add wood to it, lay out the burnt offering on it, and turn into smoke the fat pieces of the offerings of well-being. 13 A perpetual fire shall be kept burning on the altar; it shall not go out.

14 This is the ritual of the grain offering: The sons of Aaron shall offer it before the LORD, in front of the altar. 15 They shall take from it a handful of the choice flour and oil of the grain offering, with all the frankincense that is on the offering, and they shall turn its memorial portion into smoke on the altar as a pleasing odor to the LORD. 16 Aaron

[b] Ch 5.20 in Heb   [c] Ch 6.1 in Heb

REVISED ENGLISH BIBLE

offering. 12 He must bring it to the priest, who is to scoop up a handful from it as a token and burn it on the altar on the food-offerings to the LORD: it is a purification-offering. 13 The priest is to offer expiation for the sin the person has committed in any one of these cases, and it will be forgiven him. As with the grain-offering, the remainder belongs to the priest.

14 The LORD spoke to Moses and said: 15 When any person commits an offence by inadvertently defaulting in dues sacred to the LORD, he must bring to the LORD as his reparation-offering a ram without blemish from the flock; the value is to be determined by you in silver shekels by the sacred standard, for a reparation-offering; 16 he must make good his default in sacred dues, adding one fifth of the value. He must give it to the priest, who is to offer expiation for his sin with the ram of the reparation-offering, and it will be forgiven him.

17 If and when any person sins unwittingly and does what is forbidden by any commandment of the LORD, thereby incurring guilt, he must bear the consequences. 18 He must bring to the priest as a reparation-offering a ram without blemish from the flock, valued by you, and the priest is to offer expiation for the error into which he has unwittingly fallen, and it will be forgiven him. 19 It is a reparation-offering; he has been guilty of an offence against the LORD.

6 When the LORD spoke to Moses he said: 2 When any person sins by false use of the LORD's name, whether the person lies to a fellow-countryman about a deposit or contract, or a theft, or wrongs him by extortion, 3 or finds lost property and then lies about it, and swears a false oath in regard to any sin of this sort that he commits — 4 if he does this and realizes his guilt, he must restore what he has stolen or gained by extortion, or the deposit entrusted to him, or the lost property which he found, 5 or anything at all concerning which he swore a false oath. He must make full restitution, adding one fifth of the value to it, and give it back to the aggrieved party on the day when he realizes his guilt. 6 He must bring to the priest as his reparation-offering to the LORD a ram without blemish from the flock, valued by you, as a reparation-offering. 7 When the priest makes expiation for his guilt before the LORD, he will be forgiven for any act for which he has realized his guilt.

8 THE LORD told Moses 9 to give these commands to Aaron and his sons: This is the law of the whole-offering. The whole-offering is to remain on the altar-hearth overnight till morning, and the altar-fire is to be kept burning there. 10 The priest, having donned his linen robe and put on linen shorts to cover himself, must remove the ashes to which the fire reduces the whole-offering on the altar and put them beside the altar. 11 Then having changed into other garments he is to take the ashes outside the camp to a place which is ritually clean.

12 The fire on the altar is to be kept burning; it must never go out. Every morning the priest must add fresh wood, arrange the whole-offering on it, and on top burn the fat from the shared-offerings. 13 Fire must always be kept burning on the altar; it must not go out.

14 This is the law of the grain-offering. The Aaronites must present it before the LORD in front of the altar. 15 The priest must set aside a handful of the flour from it, with the oil of the grain-offering, and all the frankincense on it, and burn this token of it on the altar as a soothing odour to the LORD. 16 Aaron and his sons are to eat the rest; it is to be

5:13 the remainder: so Gk; Heb. omits.   6:1 In Heb. 5:20.
6:8 In Heb. 6:1.

has brought it to the priest, the latter shall take a handful of this flour as a token offering, and this he shall burn as a sin offering on the altar with the other oblations of the LORD. 13 Thus the priest shall make atonement for the sin that the man committed in any of the above cases, and it will be forgiven. The rest of the flour, like the cereal offerings, shall belong to the priest."

14 The LORD said to Moses, 15 "If someone commits a sin by inadvertently cheating in the LORD's sacred dues, he shall bring to the LORD as his guilt offering an unblemished ram from the flock, valued at two silver shekels according to the standard of the sanctuary shekel. 16 He shall also restore what he has sinfully withheld from the sanctuary, adding to it a fifth of its value. This is to be given to the priest, who shall then make atonement for him with the guilt-offering ram, and he will be forgiven.

17 "If someone, without being aware of it, commits such a sin by doing one of the things which are forbidden by some commandment of the LORD, that he incurs guilt for which he must answer, 18 he shall bring as a guilt offering to the priest an unblemished ram of the flock of the established value. The priest shall then make atonement for the fault which was unwittingly committed, and it will be forgiven. 19 Such is the offering for guilt; the penalty of the guilt must be paid to the LORD."

20 The LORD said to Moses, 21 "If someone commits a sin of dishonesty against the LORD by denying his neighbor a deposit or a pledge for a stolen article, or by otherwise retaining his neighbor's goods unjustly, 22 or if, having found a lost article, he denies the fact and swears falsely about it with any of the sinful oaths that men make in such cases, 23 he shall therefore, since he has incurred guilt by his sin, restore the thing that was stolen or unjustly retained by him or the deposit left with him or the lost article he found 24 or whatever else he swore falsely about; on the day of his guilt offering he shall make full restitution of the thing itself, and in addition, give the owner one fifth of its value. 25 As his guilt offering he shall bring to the LORD an unblemished ram of the flock of the established value. When he has presented this as his guilt offering to the priest, 26 the latter shall make atonement for him before the LORD, and he will be forgiven whatever guilt he may have incurred."

6 The LORD said to Moses, 2 "Give Aaron and his sons the following command: This is the ritual for holocausts. The holocaust is to remain on the hearth of the altar all night until the next morning, and the fire is to be kept burning on the altar. 3 The priest, clothed in his linen robe and wearing linen drawers on his body, shall take away the ashes to which the fire has reduced the holocaust on the altar, and lay them at the side of the altar. 4 Then, having taken off these garments and put on other garments, he shall carry the ashes to a clean place outside the camp. 5 The fire on the altar is to be kept burning; it must not go out. Every morning the priest shall put firewood on it. On this he shall lay out the holocaust and burn the fat of the peace offerings. 6 The fire is to be kept burning continuously on the altar; it must not go out.

7 "This is the ritual of the cereal offering. One of Aaron's sons shall first present it before the LORD, in front of the altar. 8 Then he shall take from it a handful of its fine flour and oil, together with all the frankincense that is on it, and this he shall burn on the altar as its token offering, a sweet-smelling oblation to the LORD. 9 The rest of it Aaron and his

will bring it to the priest, who will take a handful of it as a memorial, and burn this on the altar in addition to the offerings of food burnt for Yahweh. This is a sacrifice for sin. 13 This is how the priest must perform the rite of expiation for the person for the sin he has committed in any of those cases, and he will be forgiven. In this case, the priest has the same rights as in the case of a cereal offering." '

14 Yahweh spoke to Moses and said:

15 'If someone is unfaithful and sins inadvertently by infringing Yahweh's sacred rights, as a sacrifice of reparation he must bring Yahweh an unblemished ram from his flock, the value of which will be decided by you in silver shekels according to the rate of the sanctuary-shekel. 16 He will make amends for what his sin subtracted from the sacred rights, adding one-fifth to the value, and give it to the priest. The priest will then perform the rite of expiation for him with the ram for the sacrifice of reparation and he will be forgiven.

17 'If someone sins and without realising it does one of the things forbidden by Yahweh's commandments, he will answer for it and bear the consequences of his guilt. 18 As a sacrifice of reparation he must bring the priest an unblemished ram from his flock to the value which you decide, and the priest will perform the rite of expiation for him for the oversight unwittingly committed, and he will be forgiven. 19 This is a sacrifice of reparation; the man was certainly answerable to Yahweh.'

20 Yahweh spoke to Moses and said:

21 'If someone sins and is unfaithful against Yahweh by deceiving his fellow-countryman over a deposit or a security, or by withholding something due to him or by exploiting him;

22 'or if he finds lost property and denies it;

'or if he perjures himself about anything that a human being may do criminally in such matters;

23 'if he sins and so becomes answerable, he must restore what he has taken or demanded in excess: the deposit confided to him, the lost property that he has found, 24 or any object about which he has perjured himself. He will add one-fifth to the principal and pay the whole to the person who held the property rights on the day when he incurred the guilt. 25 He will then bring Yahweh an unblemished ram from his flock to the value which you decide, to the priest as a sacrifice of reparation, 26 and the priest will perform the rite of expiation for him before Yahweh and he will be forgiven, whatever the act by which he incurred guilt.'

6 Yahweh spoke to Moses and said:

2 'Give these orders to Aaron and his sons:

"This is the ritual for the burnt offering (that is, the burnt offering that stays on the altar brazier all night until morning and is consumed by the altar fire).

3 "The priest will put on his linen tunic and put his linen drawers on to cover himself. He will then remove the fatty ashes of the burnt offering consumed by the altar fire and put them at the side of the altar. 4 He will then take off his clothes, put on others and carry the ashes to a clean place outside the camp.

5 "The fire on the altar that consumes the burnt offering must not be allowed to go out. Every morning the priest will make it up with wood, arranging the burnt offering on it and burning the fat from the communion sacrifices. 6 The fire must always be burning on the altar; it must never go out.

7 'This is the ritual for the cereal offering:

"One of the descendants of Aaron will bring it into Yahweh's presence in front of the altar, 8 will take a handful of the wheaten flour (with the oil and all the incense which have been added to it) and burn the memorial on the altar as a smell pleasing to Yahweh; 9 and Aaron and his sons will

and his sons shall eat what is left of it; it shall be eaten as unleavened cakes in a holy place; in the court of the tent of meeting they shall eat it. 17 It shall not be baked with leaven. I have given it as their portion of my offerings by fire; it is most holy, like the sin offering and the guilt offering. 18 Every male among the descendants of Aaron shall eat of it, as their perpetual due throughout your generations, from the LORD's offerings by fire; anything that touches them shall become holy.

19 The LORD spoke to Moses, saying: 20 This is the offering that Aaron and his sons shall offer to the LORD on the day when he is anointed: one-tenth of an ephah of choice flour as a regular offering, half of it in the morning and half in the evening. 21 It shall be made with oil on a griddle; you shall bring it well soaked, as a grain offering of baked*d* pieces, and you shall present it as a pleasing odor to the LORD. 22 And so the priest, anointed from among Aaron's descendants as a successor, shall prepare it; it is the LORD's — a perpetual due — to be turned entirely into smoke. 23 Every grain offering of a priest shall be wholly burned; it shall not be eaten.

24 The LORD spoke to Moses, saying: 25 Speak to Aaron and his sons, saying: This is the ritual of the sin offering. The sin offering shall be slaughtered before the LORD at the spot where the burnt offering is slaughtered; it is most holy. 26 The priest who offers it as a sin offering shall eat of it; it shall be eaten in a holy place, in the court of the tent of meeting. 27 Whatever touches its flesh shall become holy; and when any of its blood is spattered on a garment, you shall wash the bespattered part in a holy place. 28 An earthen vessel in which it was boiled shall be broken; but if it is boiled in a bronze vessel, that shall be scoured and rinsed in water. 29 Every male among the priests shall eat of it; it is most holy. 30 But no sin offering shall be eaten from which any blood is brought into the tent of meeting for atonement in the holy place; it shall be burned with fire.

7 This is the ritual of the guilt offering. It is most holy; 2 at the spot where the burnt offering is slaughtered, they shall slaughter the guilt offering, and its blood shall be dashed against all sides of the altar. 3 All its fat shall be offered: the broad tail, the fat that covers the entrails, 4 the two kidneys with the fat that is on them at the loins, and the appendage of the liver, which shall be removed with the kidneys. 5 The priest shall turn them into smoke on the altar as an offering by fire to the LORD; it is a guilt offering. 6 Every male among the priests shall eat of it; it shall be eaten in a holy place; it is most holy.

7 The guilt offering is like the sin offering, there is the same ritual for them; the priest who makes atonement with it shall have it. 8 So, too, the priest who offers anyone's burnt offering shall keep the skin of the burnt offering that he has offered. 9 And every grain offering baked in the oven, and all that is prepared in a pan or on a griddle, shall belong to the priest who offers it. 10 But every other grain offering, mixed with oil or dry, shall belong to all the sons of Aaron equally.

11 This is the ritual of the sacrifice of the offering of well-being that one may offer to the LORD. 12 If you offer it for thanksgiving, you shall offer with the thank offering unleavened cakes mixed with oil, unleavened wafers spread with oil, and cakes of choice flour well soaked in oil.

eaten in the form of unleavened cakes and in a holy place, the court of the Tent of Meeting. 17 It must not be baked with leaven. I have allotted this to them as their share of my food-offerings. Like the purification and the reparation-offerings, it is most holy. 18 Only Aaron's descendants may eat it, as a due from the food-offerings to the LORD, for generation after generation for all time. Whoever touches it is to be treated as holy.

19 When the LORD spoke to Moses he said: 20 This is the offering which Aaron and his sons are to present to the LORD: one tenth of an ephah of flour, the usual grain-offering, half of it in the morning and half in the evening. 21 It is to be cooked with oil on a griddle. Bring it well-mixed, and present it crumbled in small pieces as a grain-offering, a soothing odour to the LORD. 22 The priest in the line of Aaron anointed to succeed him is to offer it. This is a rule binding for all time; it must be burnt in sacrifice to the LORD as a complete offering. 23 Every grain-offering of a priest shall be a complete offering; it must not be eaten.

24 The LORD told Moses 25 to say to Aaron and his sons: This is the law of the purification-offering. This offering is to be slaughtered before the LORD in the place where the whole-offering is slaughtered; it is most holy. 26 The priest who officiates is to eat of the flesh; it must be eaten in a sacred place, in the court of the Tent of Meeting. 27 Whoever touches its flesh is to be treated as holy, and if any of the blood is splashed on clothing, it must be washed in a sacred place. 28 Any earthenware vessel in which the purification-offering is boiled must be broken; if it has been boiled in a copper vessel, that must be scoured and rinsed with water. 29 Any male of priestly family may eat of this offering; it is most holy. 30 If, however, part of the blood is brought to the Tent of Meeting to make expiation in the holy place, the offering must not be eaten; it must be destroyed by fire.

7 This is the law of the reparation-offering. It is most holy; 2 the reparation victim must be slaughtered in the place where the whole-offering is slaughtered, and its blood flung against the sides of the altar. 3 The priest must present all the fat from it: the fat-tail and the fat covering the entrails, 4 both kidneys with the fat on them beside the loins, and the long lobe of the liver with the kidneys. 5 The priest must burn those pieces on the altar as a food-offering to the LORD: it is a reparation-offering. 6 Only males belonging to the priestly family may eat it. It is to be eaten in a sacred place; it is most holy. 7 There is one law for both purification-offering and reparation-offering: they belong to the priest who performs the rite of expiation. 8 The hide of anyone's whole-offering belongs to the priest who presents it. 9 Every grain-offering baked in an oven and everything that is cooked in a pan or on a griddle belong to the priest who presents them. 10 Every grain-offering, whether mixed with oil or dry, is to be shared equally among all the Aaronites.

11 This is the law of the shared-offering presented to the LORD. 12 If someone presents it as a thank-offering, then, in addition to the thank-offering, he must present unleavened bread mixed with oil, wafers of unleavened flour smeared with oil, and flat bread-cakes of well-mixed flour moistened with oil. 13 He must present flat cakes of leavened bread in

d Meaning of Heb uncertain

6:18 **Whoever:** or Whatever.   6:20 **This . . . LORD:** prob. rdg; Heb. adds on the day when he is anointed.   6:21 **crumbled:** Heb. word of uncertain meaning.   6:27 **Whoever:** or Whatever. **must be washed:** so Gk; Heb. you must wash.

sons may eat; but it must be eaten in the form of unleavened cakes and in a sacred place: in the court of the meeting tent they shall eat it. 10 It shall not be baked with leaven. I have given it to them as their portion from the oblations of the LORD; it is most sacred, like the sin offering and the guilt offering. 11 All the male descendants of Aaron may partake of it as their rightful share in the oblations of the LORD perpetually throughout your generations. Whatever touches the oblations becomes sacred."

12 The LORD said to Moses, 13 "This is the offering that Aaron and his sons shall present to the LORD [on the day he is anointed]: one tenth of an ephah of fine flour for the established cereal offering, half in the morning and half in the evening. 14 It shall be well kneaded and fried in oil on a griddle when you bring it in. Having broken the offering into pieces, you shall present it as a sweet-smelling oblation to the LORD. 15 Aaron's descendant who succeeds him as the anointed priest shall do likewise. This is a perpetual ordinance: for the Lord the whole offering shall be burned. 16 Every cereal offering of a priest shall be a whole burnt offering; it may not be eaten."

17 The LORD said to Moses, 18 "Tell Aaron and his sons: This is the ritual for sin offerings. At the place where holocausts are slaughtered, there also, before the LORD, shall the sin offering be slaughtered. It is most sacred. 19 The priest who presents the sin offering may partake of it; but it must be eaten in a sacred place, in the court of the meeting tent. 20 Whatever touches its flesh shall become sacred. If any of its blood is spilled on a garment, the stained part must be washed in a sacred place. 21 A clay vessel in which it has been cooked shall thereafter be broken; if it is cooked in a bronze vessel, this shall be scoured afterward and rinsed with water. 22 All the males of the priestly line may partake of the sin offering, since it is most sacred. 23 But no one may partake of any sin offering of which some blood has been brought into the meeting tent to make atonement in the sanctuary; such an offering must be burned up in the fire.

7 "This is the ritual for guilt offerings, which are most sacred. 2 At the place where the holocausts are slaughtered, there also shall the guilt offering be slaughtered. Its blood shall be splashed on the sides of the altar. 3 All of its fat shall be taken from it and offered up: the fatty tail, the fatty membrane over the inner organs, 4 as well as the two kidneys with the fat on them near the loins, and the lobe of the liver, which must be severed above the kidneys. 5 All this the priest shall burn on the altar as an oblation to the LORD. This is the guilt offering. 6 All the males of the priestly line may partake of it; but it must be eaten in a sacred place, since it is most sacred.

7 "Because the sin offering and the guilt offering are alike, both having the same ritual, the guilt offering likewise belongs to the priest who makes atonement with it. 8 Similarly, the priest who offers a holocaust for someone may keep for himself the hide of the holocaust that he has offered. 9 Also, every cereal offering that is baked in an oven or deep-fried in a pot or fried on a griddle shall belong to the priest who offers it, 10 whereas all cereal offerings that are offered up dry or mixed with oil shall belong to all of Aaron's sons without distinction.

11 "This is the ritual for the peace offerings that are presented to the LORD. 12 When anyone makes a peace offering in thanksgiving, together with his thanksgiving sacrifice he shall offer unleavened cakes mixed with oil, unleavened wafers spread with oil, and cakes made of fine flour mixed with oil and well kneaded. 13 His offering shall also include

eat the remainder in the form of unleavened loaves. They will eat it inside the holy place, in the court of the Tent of Meeting. 10 The portion I give them of the food burnt for me must not be baked with leaven; it is especially holy, like the sacrifice for sin and the sacrifice of reparation. 11 All male descendants of Aaron are entitled to eat this portion of the food burnt for Yahweh (this is a perpetual law for all your descendants) and anyone who touches it will become holy." '

12 Yahweh spoke to Moses and said:

13 'This is the offering that Aaron and his sons must make to Yahweh on the day they are anointed: one-tenth of an ephah of wheaten flour as a perpetual cereal offering, half in the morning and half in the evening. 14 It will be prepared on the griddle and mixed with oil; you will bring the paste as a cereal offering in several pieces, offering them as a smell pleasing to Yahweh. 15 When one of his sons is anointed priest to succeed him, he will do the same. This is a perpetual law.

'The entire cereal offering will be burnt for Yahweh. 16 Every cereal offering made by a priest will be a total sacrifice; none of it will be eaten.'

17 Yahweh spoke to Moses and said, 18 'Speak to Aaron and his sons and say:

"This is the ritual for the sacrifice for sin:

"The victim must be slaughtered before Yahweh on the spot where the burnt offerings are slaughtered. It is especially holy. 19 The priest who offers this sacrifice will eat it. It will be eaten inside the holy place, in the court of the Tent of Meeting. 20 Everything touching the victim's meat will become holy, and if any of the blood splashes on clothing, the stain will be washed off inside the holy place. 21 The earthenware vessel in which the meat is cooked must be broken; if a bronze vessel has been used for the cooking, it must be scrubbed and thoroughly rinsed with water. 22 Any male who is a priest may eat the sacrifice. It is especially holy. 23 But no one may eat any of the victims offered for sin, the blood of which has been taken into the Tent of Meeting to make expiation inside the sanctuary. These must be burnt." '

7 ' "This is the ritual for the sacrifice of reparation:

"It is especially holy. 2 The victim must be slaughtered where the burnt offerings are slaughtered, and the priest will pour the blood all around the altar. 3 He will then offer all the fat: the tail, the fat covering the entrails, 4 both kidneys, the fat on them and on the loins, the mass of fat which he will remove from the liver and kidneys. 5 The priest will burn these pieces on the altar as food burnt for Yahweh. This is a sacrifice of reparation. 6 Every male who is a priest may eat it. It will be eaten inside the holy place; it is especially holy.

7 "As with the sacrifice for sin, so with the sacrifice of reparation—the ritual is the same for both. The offering with which the priest performs the rite of expiation will revert to the priest. 8 The hide of the victim presented by someone to the priest to be offered as a burnt offering will revert to the priest. 9 Every cereal offering baked in the oven, every cereal offering cooked in the pan or on the griddle will revert to the priest who offers it. 10 Every cereal offering, mixed with oil or dry, will revert to all the descendants of Aaron without distinction.

11 "This is the ritual for the communion sacrifice to be offered to Yahweh:

12 "If this is offered as a sacrifice with praise, to the latter must be added an offering of unleavened cakes mixed with oil, unleavened wafers spread with oil, and wheaten flour in the form of cakes mixed with oil. 13 This offering, then,

NEW REVISED STANDARD VERSION

REVISED ENGLISH BIBLE

13 With your thanksgiving sacrifice of well-being you shall bring your offering with cakes of leavened bread. 14 From this you shall offer one cake from each offering, as a gift to the LORD; it shall belong to the priest who dashes the blood of the offering of well-being. 15 And the flesh of your thanksgiving sacrifice of well-being shall be eaten on the day it is offered; you shall not leave any of it until morning. 16 But if the sacrifice you offer is a votive offering or a freewill offering, it shall be eaten on the day that you offer your sacrifice, and what is left of it shall be eaten the next day; 17 but what is left of the flesh of the sacrifice shall be burned up on the third day. 18 If any of the flesh of your sacrifice of well-being is eaten on the third day, it shall not be acceptable, nor shall it be credited to the one who offers it; it shall be an abomination, and the one who eats of it shall incur guilt.

19 Flesh that touches any unclean thing shall not be eaten; it shall be burned up. As for other flesh, all who are clean may eat such flesh. 20 But those who eat flesh from the LORD's sacrifice of well-being while in a state of uncleanness shall be cut off from their kin. 21 When any one of you touches any unclean thing—human uncleanness or an unclean animal or any unclean creature—and then eats flesh from the LORD's sacrifice of well-being, you shall be cut off from your kin.

22 The LORD spoke to Moses, saying: 23 Speak to the people of Israel, saying: You shall eat no fat of ox or sheep or goat. 24 The fat of an animal that died or was torn by wild animals may be put to any use, but you must not eat it. 25 If any one of you eats the fat from an animal of which an offering by fire may be made to the LORD, you who eat it shall be cut off from your kin. 26 You must not eat any blood whatever, either of bird or of animal, in any of your settlements. 27 Any one of you who eats any blood shall be cut off from your kin.

28 The LORD spoke to Moses, saying: 29 Speak to the people of Israel, saying: Any one of you who would offer to the LORD your sacrifice of well-being must yourself bring to the LORD your offering from your sacrifice of well-being. 30 Your own hands shall bring the LORD's offering by fire; you shall bring the fat with the breast, so that the breast may be raised as an elevation offering before the LORD. 31 The priest shall turn the fat into smoke on the altar, but the breast shall belong to Aaron and his sons. 32 And the right thigh from your sacrifices of well-being you shall give to the priest as an offering; 33 the one among the sons of Aaron who offers the blood and fat of the offering of well-being shall have the right thigh for a portion. 34 For I have taken the breast of the elevation offering, and the thigh that is offered, from the people of Israel, from their sacrifices of well-being, and have given them to Aaron the priest and to his sons, as a perpetual due from the people of Israel. 35 This is the portion allotted to Aaron and to his sons from the offerings made by fire to the LORD, once they have been brought forward to serve the LORD as priests; 36 these the LORD commanded to be given them, when he anointed them, as a perpetual due from the people of Israel throughout their generations.

37 This is the ritual of the burnt offering, the grain offering, the sin offering, the guilt offering, the offering of ordination, and the sacrifice of well-being, 38 which the LORD commanded Moses on Mount Sinai, when he commanded the people of Israel to bring their offerings to the LORD, in the wilderness of Sinai.

addition to his shared thank-offering. 14 One part of every offering he is to present as a contribution for the LORD: it is to belong to the priest who flings the blood of the shared-offering against the altar. 15 The flesh must be eaten on the day it is presented; none of it may be put aside till morning.

16 If, however, anyone's sacrifice is a votive offering or a freewill-offering, it may be eaten on the day it is presented or on the next day; 17 but any flesh left over on the third day must be destroyed by fire. 18 If any flesh of his shared-offering is eaten on the third day, the one who has presented it will not be accepted. It will not be counted to his credit, but will be reckoned as tainted, and the person who eats any of it must accept responsibility.

19 If the flesh comes into contact with anything unclean it must not be eaten; it must be destroyed by fire. Flesh may be eaten by anyone who is clean, 20 but the person who, while unclean, eats flesh from a shared-offering presented to the LORD is to be cut off from his father's kin. 21 When any person is contaminated by contact with anything unclean, be it man, beast, or swarming creature, and then eats any of the flesh from the shared-offerings presented to the LORD, that person is to be cut off from his father's kin.

22 The LORD told Moses 23 to say to the Israelites: You must not eat the fat of any ox, sheep, or goat. 24 The fat of an animal that has died a natural death or has been mauled by wild beasts may be put to any other use, but you are not to eat it. 25 Everyone who eats fat from a beast from which food-offerings are presented to the LORD is to be cut off from his father's kin.

26 You are not to consume any of the blood, whether of bird or of beast, wherever you may live. 27 Anyone consuming any of the blood is to be cut off from his father's kin.

28 The LORD told Moses 29 to say to the Israelites: Whoever comes to present a shared-offering must set aside part of it as an offering to the LORD. 30 With his own hands he is to bring the food-offerings to the LORD. He must also bring the fat together with the breast which is to be presented as a dedicated portion before the LORD. 31 The priest must burn the fat on the altar, but the breast is to belong to Aaron and his descendants. 32 Give the right hind leg of your shared-offerings as a contribution for the priest; 33 it will be the perquisite of the Aaronite who presents the blood and the fat of the shared-offering. 34 I have taken from the Israelites the breast of the dedicated portion and the leg of the contribution made out of the shared-offerings, and have given them as a due from the Israelites to Aaron the priest and his descendants for all time. 35 This is the portion allotted to Aaron and his descendants out of the LORD's food-offerings, appointed on the day when they were presented as priests to the LORD; 36 and on the day when they were anointed, the LORD commanded that these prescribed portions should be given to them by the Israelites. This is a rule binding on their descendants for all time.

37 Such, then, is the law concerning the whole-offering, the grain-offering, the purification-offering, the reparation-offering, the ordination-offering, and the shared-offering, 38 with which the LORD charged Moses on Mount Sinai on the day when he commanded the Israelites to present their offerings to the LORD in the wilderness of Sinai.

7:16 **next day:** so Gk; Heb. adds and the rest of it must be eaten.
7:21 **swarming creature:** so some MSS; others noxious thing.

|

loaves of leavened bread along with the victim of his peace offering for thanksgiving. 14 From each of his offerings he shall present one portion as a contribution to the LORD; this shall belong to the priest who splashes the blood of the peace offering.

15 "The flesh of the thanksgiving sacrifice shall be eaten on the day it is offered; none of it may be kept till the next day. 16 However, if the sacrifice is a votive or a free-will offering, it should indeed be eaten on the day the sacrifice is offered, but what is left over may be eaten on the next day. 17 Should any flesh from the sacrifice be left over on the third day, it must be burned up in the fire. 18 If, therefore, any of the flesh of the peace offering is eaten on the third day, it shall not win favor for him nor shall it be reckoned to his credit; rather, it shall be considered as refuse, and anyone who eats of it shall have his guilt to bear. 19 Should the flesh touch anything unclean, it may not be eaten, but shall be burned up in the fire.

"All who are clean may partake of this flesh. 20 If, however, someone while in a state of uncleanness eats any of the flesh of a peace offering belonging to the LORD, that person shall be cut off from his people. 21 Likewise, if someone touches anything unclean, whether the uncleanness be of human or of animal origin or from some loathsome crawling creature, and then eats of a peace offering belonging to the LORD, that person, too, shall be cut off from his people."

22 The LORD said to Moses, 23 "Tell the Israelites: You shall not eat the fat of any ox or sheep or goat. 24 Although the fat of an animal that has died a natural death or has been killed by wild beasts may be put to any other use, you may not eat it. 25 If anyone eats the fat of an animal from which an oblation is made to the LORD, such a one shall be cut off from his people. 26 Wherever you dwell, you shall not partake of any blood, be it of bird or of animal. 27 Every person who partakes of any blood shall be cut off from his people."

28 The LORD said to Moses, 29 "Tell the Israelites: He who presents a peace offering to the LORD shall bring a part of it as his special offering to him, 30 carrying in with his own hands the oblations to the LORD. The fat is to be brought in, together with the breast, which is to be waved as a wave offering before the LORD. 31 The priest shall burn the fat on the altar, but the breast belongs to Aaron and his sons. 32 Moreover, from your peace offering you shall give to the priest the right leg as a raised offering. 33 The descendant of Aaron who offers up the blood and fat of the peace offering shall have the right leg as his portion, 34 for from the peace offerings of the Israelites I have taken the breast that is waved and the leg that is raised up, and I have given them to Aaron, the priest, and to his sons by a perpetual ordinance as a contribution from the Israelites."

35 This is the priestly share from the oblations of the LORD, allotted to Aaron and his sons on the day he called them to be the priests of the LORD; 36 on the day he anointed them the LORD ordered the Israelites to give them this share by a perpetual ordinance throughout their generations.

37 This is the ritual for holocausts, cereal offerings, sin offerings, guilt offerings, [ordination offerings] and peace offerings, 38 which the LORD enjoined on Moses at Mount Sinai at the time when he commanded the Israelites in the wilderness of Sinai to bring their offerings to the LORD.

must be added to the cakes of leavened bread and to the communion sacrifice with praise. 14 One of the cakes of this offering must be presented as an offering to Yahweh; it will revert to the priest who pours out the blood of the communion sacrifice. 15 The meat of the victim will be eaten on the day the offering is made; nothing may be left until next morning.

16 "If the victim is offered as a votive or a voluntary sacrifice, it must be eaten on the day it is offered, and the remainder may be eaten on the following day; 17 but on the third day whatever is left of the meat of the victim must be burnt.

18 "If any of the meat of a victim offered as a communion sacrifice is eaten on the third day, the person who has offered it will not be acceptable and will receive no credit for it. It will count as rotten meat, and the person who eats it will bear the consequences of the guilt.

19 "Meat that has touched anything unclean cannot be eaten; it must be burnt.

"Anyone clean may eat the meat, 20 but anyone unclean who eats the meat of a communion sacrifice offered to Yahweh will be outlawed from his people. 21 Furthermore, if anyone touches anything unclean, human or animal, or any foul thing, and then eats the meat of a communion sacrifice offered to Yahweh, that individual will be outlawed from his people." '

22 Yahweh spoke to Moses and said, 23 'Speak to the Israelites and say:

"You may not eat the fat of ox, sheep or goat. 24 The fat of an animal that has died a natural death or been savaged by beasts may be used for any other purpose, but you are not to eat it. 25 Anyone who eats the fat of an animal offered as food burnt for Yahweh will be outlawed from his people.

26 "Wherever you live, you will never eat blood, whether it be of bird or or of beast. 27 Anyone who eats any blood will be outlawed from his people." '

28 Yahweh spoke to Moses and said, 29 'Speak to the Israelites and say:

"Anyone who offers Yahweh a communion sacrifice must bring him part of his sacrifice as an offering. 30 He must bring the food to be burnt for Yahweh, that is to say, the fat adhering to the forequarters, with his own hands. He will bring it, and also the forequarters, with which he will make the gesture of offering before Yahweh. 31 The priest will then burn the fat on the altar, and the forequarters will revert to Aaron and his descendants. 32 You will set aside the right thigh from your communion sacrifice and give it to the priest. 33 The right thigh will be the portion of the descendant of Aaron who offers the blood and fat of the communion sacrifice. 34 For I have deprived the Israelites of the forequarter offered and the thigh presented in their communion sacrifices, and given them to the priest Aaron and his descendants; this is a perpetual law for the Israelites." '

35 Such was the portion of Aaron and his descendants in the food burnt for Yahweh, the day he presented them to Yahweh for them to become his priests. 36 This was what Yahweh ordered the Israelites to give them on the day they were anointed: a perpetual law for all their descendants.

37 Such was the ritual for burnt offering, cereal offering, sacrifice for sin, sacrifice of reparation, investiture sacrifice and communion sacrifice, 38 which Yahweh laid down for Moses on Mount Sinai, the day he ordered the Israelites to make their offerings to Yahweh in the desert of Sinai.

NEW REVISED STANDARD VERSION

8 The LORD spoke to Moses, saying: 2 Take Aaron and his sons with him, the vestments, the anointing oil, the bull of sin offering, the two rams, and the basket of unleavened bread; 3 and assemble the whole congregation at the entrance of the tent of meeting. 4 And Moses did as the LORD commanded him. When the congregation was assembled at the entrance of the tent of meeting, 5 Moses said to the congregation, "This is what the LORD has commanded to be done."

6 Then Moses brought Aaron and his sons forward, and washed them with water. 7 He put the tunic on him, fastened the sash around him, clothed him with the robe, and put the ephod on him. He then put the decorated band of the ephod around him, tying the ephod to him with it. 8 He placed the breastpiece on him, and in the breastpiece he put the Urim and the Thummim. 9 And he set the turban on his head, and on the turban, in front, he set the golden ornament, the holy crown, as the LORD commanded Moses.

10 Then Moses took the anointing oil and anointed the tabernacle and all that was in it, and consecrated them. 11 He sprinkled some of it on the altar seven times, and anointed the altar and all its utensils, and the basin and its base, to consecrate them. 12 He poured some of the anointing oil on Aaron's head and anointed him, to consecrate him. 13 And Moses brought forward Aaron's sons, and clothed them with tunics, and fastened sashes around them, and tied headdresses on them, as the LORD commanded Moses.

14 He led forward the bull of sin offering; and Aaron and his sons laid their hands upon the head of the bull of sin offering, 15 and it was slaughtered. Moses took the blood and with his finger put some on each of the horns of the altar, purifying the altar; then he poured out the blood at the base of the altar. Thus he consecrated it, to make atonement for it. 16 Moses took all the fat that was around the entrails, and the appendage of the liver, and the two kidneys with their fat, and turned them into smoke on the altar. 17 But the bull itself, its skin and flesh and its dung, he burned with fire outside the camp, as the LORD commanded Moses.

18 Then he brought forward the ram of burnt offering. Aaron and his sons laid their hands on the head of the ram, 19 and it was slaughtered. Moses dashed the blood against all sides of the altar. 20 The ram was cut into its parts, and Moses turned into smoke the head and the parts and the suet. 21 And after the entrails and the legs were washed with water, Moses turned into smoke the whole ram on the altar; it was a burnt offering for a pleasing odor, an offering by fire to the LORD, as the LORD commanded Moses.

22 Then he brought forward the second ram, the ram of ordination. Aaron and his sons laid their hands on the head of the ram, 23 and it was slaughtered. Moses took some of its blood and put it on the lobe of Aaron's right ear and on the thumb of his right hand and on the big toe of his right foot. 24 After Aaron's sons were brought forward, Moses put some of the blood on the lobes of their right ears and on the thumbs of their right hands and on the big toes of their right feet; and Moses dashed the rest of the blood against all sides of the altar. 25 He took the fat — the broad tail, all the fat that was around the entrails, the appendage of the liver, and the two kidneys with their fat — and the right thigh. 26 From the basket of unleavened bread that was before the LORD, he took one cake of unleavened bread, one cake of bread with oil, and one wafer, and placed them on the fat and on the right thigh. 27 He placed all these on the palms of Aaron and on the palms of his sons, and raised them as an elevation offering before the LORD. 28 Then Moses took them from their hands and turned them into smoke on the altar with the burnt offering. This was an ordination offering for a pleasing odor, an offering by fire to the LORD.

REVISED ENGLISH BIBLE

8 WHEN the LORD spoke to Moses he said: 2 Bring Aaron and his sons, along with the vestments, the anointing oil, the bull for a purification-offering, the two rams, and the basket of unleavened bread, 3 and assemble all the community at the entrance to the Tent of Meeting. 4 Moses did as the LORD commanded him, and when the community assembled at the entrance to the Tent of Meeting, 5 he told them that this was what the LORD had ordered to be done.

6 Moses brought forward Aaron and his sons and washed them with water. 7 He invested Aaron with the tunic, girded him with the sash, robed him with the mantle, put the ephod on him, tied it with its waistband, and fastened the ephod to him with the band. 8 He put the breastpiece on him and set the Urim and Thummim in it. 9 He placed the turban on his head, with the gold medallion as a symbol of holy dedication on the front of the turban, as the LORD had commanded him.

10 Moses then took the anointing oil, and anointed the Tabernacle and all that was in it, so consecrating them. 11 With some of the oil he sprinkled the altar seven times, anointing it and all its vessels, along with the basin with its stand, to consecrate them, 12 and poured some of the anointing oil on Aaron's head to consecrate him. 13 Moses brought Aaron's sons forward and, as the LORD had commanded him, he invested them with tunics, girded them with sashes, and tied their headdresses.

14 Moses had the bull for the purification-offering brought, and Aaron and his sons laid their hands on its head. 15 Moses slaughtered it, and taking some of the blood he smeared it with his finger on the horns at the corners of the altar to purify it. He poured out the remaining blood at the base of the altar, which he consecrated by purifying it. 16 He took all the fat on the entrails, the long lobe of the liver, and both kidneys with their fat, and burnt them on the altar, 17 but the rest of the bull with its hide, flesh, and offal he destroyed by fire outside the camp, as commanded by the LORD.

18 Moses then had the ram of the whole-offering brought, and Aaron and his sons laid their hands on the ram's head. 19 Moses slaughtered it, and flung its blood against the sides of the altar. 20 He cut the ram into pieces and burnt the head, the pieces, and the suet. 21 He washed the entrails and the shins in water and burnt the whole on the altar. This was a whole-offering, to be a food-offering of soothing odour to the LORD, as the LORD had commanded Moses.

22 Moses had the second ram brought forward, the ram for the ordination of priests, and Aaron and his sons laid their hands on its head. 23 Moses slaughtered it, and taking some of its blood he put it on the lobe of Aaron's right ear, on his right thumb, and on the big toe of his right foot. 24 He then brought forward the sons of Aaron and put some of the blood on the lobes of their right ears, on their right thumbs, and on the big toes of their right feet. The rest of the blood he flung against the sides of the altar. 25 He took the fat, the fat-tail, the fat covering the entrails, the long lobe of the liver, both kidneys with their fat, and the right leg. 26 From the basket of unleavened bread before the LORD he took one unleavened cake, one cake of bread made with oil, and one wafer, and laid them on the fatty parts and the right leg. 27 He put it all on the hands of Aaron and of his sons, presenting it as a dedicated portion before the LORD. 28 Moses then took it from their hands and burnt it on the altar on top of the whole-offering. This was an ordination-offering, a food-offering of soothing odour to the LORD. 29 He took

8:8 **breastpiece:** *or* pouch.   8:13 **sashes:** *so Samar.; Heb.* sash.   8:15 **some of:** *so Gk; Heb. omits.*   8:18 **Moses:** *so Gk; Heb. omits.*   8:27 **presenting:** *or, with Lat.,* who presented.

8 The LORD said to Moses, ²"Take Aaron and his sons, together with the vestments, the anointing oil, the bullock for a sin offering, the two rams, and the basket of unleavened food. ³Then assemble the whole community at the entrance of the meeting tent." ⁴And Moses did as the LORD had commanded. When the community had assembled at the entrance of the meeting tent, ⁵Moses told them what the LORD had ordered to be done. ⁶Bringing forward Aaron and his sons, he first washed them with water. ⁷Then he put the tunic on Aaron, girded him with the sash, clothed him with the robe, placed the ephod on him, and girded him with the embroidered belt of the ephod, fastening it around him. ⁸He then set the breastpiece on him, with the Urim and Thummim in it, ⁹and put the miter on his head, attaching the gold plate, the sacred diadem, over the front of the miter, at his forehead, as the LORD had commanded him to do.

¹⁰Taking the anointing oil, Moses anointed and consecrated the Dwelling, with all that was in it. ¹¹Then he sprinkled some of this oil seven times on the altar, and anointed the altar, with all its appurtenances, and the laver, with its base, thus consecrating them. ¹²He also poured some of the anointing oil on Aaron's head, thus consecrating him. ¹³Moses likewise brought forward Aaron's sons, clothed them with tunics, girded them with sashes, and put turbans on them, as the LORD had commanded him to do.

¹⁴When he had brought forward the bullock for a sin offering, Aaron and his sons laid their hands on its head. ¹⁵Then Moses slaughtered it, and taking some of its blood, with his finger he put it on the horns around the altar, thus purifying the altar. He also made atonement for the altar by pouring out the blood at its base when he consecrated it. ¹⁶Taking all the fat that was over the inner organs, as well as the lobe of the liver and the two kidneys with their fat, Moses burned them on the altar. ¹⁷The bullock, however, with its hide and flesh and offal he burned in the fire outside the camp, as the LORD had commanded him to do.

¹⁸He next brought forward the holocaust ram, and Aaron and his sons laid their hands on its head. ¹⁹When he had slaughtered it, Moses splashed its blood on all sides of the altar. ²⁰After cutting up the ram into pieces, he burned the head, the cut-up pieces and the suet; ²¹then, having washed the inner organs and the shanks with water, he also burned these remaining parts of the ram on the altar as a holocaust, a sweet-smelling oblation to the LORD, as the LORD had commanded him to do.

²²Then he brought forward the second ram, the ordination ram, and Aaron and his sons laid their hands on its head. ²³When he had slaughtered it, Moses took some of its blood and put it on the tip of Aaron's right ear, on the thumb of his right hand, and on the big toe of his right foot. ²⁴Moses had the sons of Aaron also come forward, and he put some of the blood on the tips of their right ears, on the thumbs of their right hands, and on the big toes of their right feet. The rest of the blood he splashed on the sides of the altar. ²⁵He then took the fat: the fatty tail and all the fat over the inner organs, the lobe of the liver and the two kidneys with their fat, and likewise the right leg; ²⁶from the basket of unleavened food that was set before the LORD he took one unleavened cake, one loaf of bread made with oil, and one wafer; these he placed on top of the portions of fat and the right leg. ²⁷He then put all these things into the hands of Aaron and his sons, whom he had wave them as a wave offering before the LORD. ²⁸When he had received them back, Moses burned them with the holocaust on the altar as the ordination offering, a sweet-smelling oblation to the LORD. ²⁹He then took the breast and waved it as a wave

8 ᵃYahweh spoke to Moses and said: ²'Take Aaron and with him his sons, the vestments, the anointing oil, the bull for the sacrifice for sin, the two rams and the basket of unleavened bread. ³Then call the whole community together at the entrance to the Tent of Meeting.'

⁴Moses did as Yahweh ordered; the community gathered at the entrance to the Tent of Meeting, ⁵and Moses said to them, 'This is what Yahweh has ordered to be done.'

⁶He made Aaron and his sons come forward and washed them with water.

⁷He then dressed him in the tunic, passed the waistband round his waist, vested him in the robe and put the *ephod* on him. He then put the waistband of the *ephod* round his waist, fastening it to him. ⁸He put the breastplate on him, and placed the *urim* and *thummim* in it. ⁹He put the turban on his head, and on the front of the turban, the golden flower; this was the symbol of holy consecration, which Yahweh had prescribed to Moses.

¹⁰Moses then took the anointing oil and anointed the Dwelling and everything inside it, to consecrate them. ¹¹He sprinkled the altar seven times and anointed the altar and its accessories, the basin and its stand, to consecrate them. ¹²He then poured some of the anointing oil on Aaron's head and anointed him to consecrate him.

¹³Moses then made Aaron's sons come forward; he dressed them in tunics, passed the waistbands round their waists and put on their head-dresses, as Yahweh had ordered him.

¹⁴He then had the bull for the sacrifice for sin brought forward. Aaron and his sons laid their hands on the victim's head ¹⁵and Moses slaughtered it. He then took the blood and with his finger put some of it on the horns on the corners of the altar to purify the altar. He then poured the rest of the blood at the foot of the altar, which he consecrated by performing the rite of expiation over it. ¹⁶He then took all the fat covering the entrails, the mass of fat over the liver, both kidneys and their fat; and he burnt this on the altar, ¹⁷but the bull's skin, its meat and its offal he burnt outside the camp, as Yahweh had ordered Moses.

¹⁸He then had the ram for the burnt offering brought forward. Aaron and his sons laid their hands on the ram's head ¹⁹and Moses slaughtered it. He poured its blood all around the altar. ²⁰He then quartered the ram and burned the head, the quarters and the fat. ²¹He then washed the entrails and shins, and burnt the whole ram on the altar, as a burnt offering, offered to be a pleasing smell, as food burnt for Yahweh, as Yahweh had ordered Moses.

²²He then had the other ram brought forward, the ram for the investiture sacrifice. Aaron and his sons laid their hands on its head ²³and Moses slaughtered it. He took some of its blood and put it on the lobe of Aaron's right ear, on the thumb of his right hand, and on the big toe of his right foot. ²⁴He then made Aaron's sons come forward and he put some of the blood on the lobes of their right ears, on the thumbs of their right hands and on the big toes of their right feet. Next, Moses poured the rest of the blood all around the altar. ²⁵He then took the fat: the tail, all the fat covering the entrails, the mass of fat over the liver, both kidneys and their fat, and the right thigh. ²⁶From the basket of unleavened bread placed before Yahweh, he took an unleavened cake, a cake of bread made with oil, and a wafer; he placed these on the fat and the right thigh, ²⁷and put it all into Aaron's hands and those of his sons, and made the gesture of offering before Yahweh. ²⁸Moses then took them away from them and burned them on the altar, with the burnt offering. This was the investiture sacrifice, offered to be a pleasing smell, as food burnt for Yahweh. ²⁹Moses then

ᵃ8 // Ex 28:1—29:35.

29 Moses took the breast and raised it as an elevation offering before the LORD; it was Moses' portion of the ram of ordination, as the LORD commanded Moses.

30 Then Moses took some of the anointing oil and some of the blood that was on the altar and sprinkled them on Aaron and his vestments, and also on his sons and their vestments. Thus he consecrated Aaron and his vestments, and also his sons and their vestments.

31 And Moses said to Aaron and his sons, "Boil the flesh at the entrance of the tent of meeting, and eat it there with the bread that is in the basket of ordination offerings, as I was commanded, 'Aaron and his sons shall eat it'; 32 and what remains of the flesh and the bread you shall burn with fire. 33 You shall not go outside the entrance of the tent of meeting for seven days, until the day when your period of ordination is completed. For it will take seven days to ordain you; 34 as has been done today, the LORD has commanded to be done to make atonement for you. 35 You shall remain at the entrance of the tent of meeting day and night for seven days, keeping the LORD's charge so that you do not die; for so I am commanded." 36 Aaron and his sons did all the things that the LORD commanded through Moses.

9 On the eighth day Moses summoned Aaron and his sons and the elders of Israel. 2 He said to Aaron, "Take a bull calf for a sin offering and a ram for a burnt offering, without blemish, and offer them before the LORD. 3 And say to the people of Israel, 'Take a male goat for a sin offering; a calf and a lamb, yearlings without blemish, for a burnt offering; 4 and an ox and a ram for an offering of well-being to sacrifice before the LORD; and a grain offering mixed with oil. For today the LORD will appear to you.'" 5 They brought what Moses commanded to the front of the tent of meeting; and the whole congregation drew near and stood before the LORD. 6 And Moses said, "This is the thing that the LORD commanded you to do, so that the glory of the LORD may appear to you." 7 Then Moses said to Aaron, "Draw near to the altar and sacrifice your sin offering and your burnt offering, and make atonement for yourself and for the people; and sacrifice the offering of the people, and make atonement for them; as the LORD has commanded."

8 Aaron drew near to the altar, and slaughtered the calf of the sin offering, which was for himself. 9 The sons of Aaron presented the blood to him, and he dipped his finger in the blood and put it on the horns of the altar; and the rest of the blood he poured out at the base of the altar. 10 But the fat, the kidneys, and the appendage of the liver from the sin offering he turned into smoke on the altar, as the LORD commanded Moses; 11 and the flesh and the skin he burned with fire outside the camp.

12 Then he slaughtered the burnt offering. Aaron's sons brought him the blood, and he dashed it against all sides of the altar. 13 And they brought him the burnt offering piece by piece, and the head, which he turned into smoke on the altar. 14 He washed the entrails and the legs and, with the burnt offering, turned them into smoke on the altar.

15 Next he presented the people's offering. He took the goat of the sin offering that was for the people, and slaughtered it, and presented it as a sin offering like the first one. 16 He presented the burnt offering, and sacrificed it according to regulation. 17 He presented the grain offering, and, taking a handful of it, he turned it into smoke on the altar, in addition to the burnt offering of the morning.

the breast and presented it as a dedicated portion before the LORD; it was his portion of the ram of ordination, as the LORD had commanded him.

30 Moses took some of the anointing oil and some of the blood on the altar and sprinkled it on Aaron and his vestments, and also on his sons and their vestments. Thus he consecrated Aaron and his vestments, along with his sons and their vestments.

31 Moses said to Aaron and his sons, 'Boil the flesh of the ram at the entrance to the Tent of Meeting, and eat it there, together with the bread that is in the ordination-basket, in accordance with the command: "Aaron and his sons are to eat it." 32 What remains of the flesh and bread you are to destroy by fire. 33 You are not to go outside the entrance to the Tent of Meeting for seven days, until the day which completes the period of your ordination, for it lasts seven days. 34 What was done this day followed the LORD's command to make expiation for you. 35 Stay by the entrance to the Tent of Meeting day and night for seven days, keeping vigil to the LORD, so that you do not die, for so I was commanded.'

36 Aaron and his sons did everything that the LORD had commanded through Moses.

9 On the eighth day, when Moses had summoned Aaron and his sons and the Israelite elders, 2 he said to Aaron, 'Take for yourself a bull-calf for a purification-offering and a ram for a whole-offering, both without blemish, and present them before the LORD. 3 Then bid the Israelites take a he-goat for a purification-offering, a calf and a lamb, both yearlings without blemish, for a whole-offering, 4 and a bull and a ram for shared-offerings to be sacrificed before the LORD, together with a grain-offering mixed with oil. For today the LORD will appear to you.'

5 They brought what Moses had commanded to the front of the Tent of Meeting, and the whole community approached and stood before the LORD. 6 Moses said, 'This is what the LORD has commanded you to do, so that the glory of the LORD may appear to you.' 7 Moses said to Aaron, 'Approach the altar; sacrifice your purification-offering and your whole-offering, making expiation for yourself and for your household. Then sacrifice the offering of the people and make expiation for them, as the LORD has commanded.'

8 So Aaron approached the altar and slaughtered the calf, which was his purification-offering. 9 His sons presented the blood to him, and he dipped his finger in the blood and smeared it on the horns of the altar; the rest of the blood he poured out at the base of the altar. 10 Part of the purification-offering, namely the fat, the kidneys, and the long lobe of the liver, he burnt on the altar as the LORD had commanded Moses; 11 the flesh and the hide he destroyed by fire outside the camp. 12 Then Aaron slaughtered the whole-offering. His sons handed him the blood, and he flung it against the sides of the altar; 13 they handed him the pieces of the whole-offering and the head, and he burnt them on the altar. 14 He washed the entrails and the shins and burnt them on the altar, on top of the whole-offering.

15 Next he brought forward the offering of the people. He took the he-goat, the people's purification-offering, slaughtered it, and performed the rite of the purification-offering as he had previously done for himself. 16 He presented the whole-offering and sacrificed it in the manner prescribed. 17 He brought forward the grain-offering, took a handful of it, and burnt it on the altar, in addition to the morning whole-offering.

9:7 for your household: so Gk; Heb. for the people.

offering before the LORD; this was Moses' own portion of the ordination ram. All this was in keeping with the LORD's command to Moses. 30 Taking some of the anointing oil and some of the blood that was on the altar, Moses sprinkled with it Aaron and his vestments, as well as his sons and their vestments, thus consecrating both Aaron and his vestments and his sons and their vestments.

31 Finally, Moses said to Aaron and his sons, "Boil the flesh at the entrance of the meeting tent, and there eat it with the bread that is in the basket of the ordination offering, in keeping with the command I have received: 'Aaron and his sons shall eat of it.' 32 What is left over of the flesh and the bread you shall burn up in the fire. 33 Moreover, you are not to depart from the entrance of the meeting tent for seven days, until the days of your ordination are completed; for your ordination is to last for seven days. 34 The LORD has commanded that what has been done today be done to make atonement for you. 35 Hence you must remain at the entrance of the meeting tent day and night for seven days, carrying out the prescriptions of the LORD; otherwise you shall die; for this is the command I have received." 36 So Aaron and his sons did all that the LORD had commanded through Moses.

9 On the eighth day Moses summoned Aaron and his sons, together with the elders of Israel, 2 and said to Aaron, "Take a calf for a sin offering and a ram for a holocaust, both without blemish, and offer them before the LORD. 3 Tell the elders of Israel, too: Take a he-goat for a sin offering, a calf and a lamb, both unblemished yearlings, for a holocaust, 4 and an ox and a ram for a peace offering, to sacrifice them before the LORD, along with a cereal offering mixed with oil; for today the LORD will reveal himself to you." 5 So they brought what Moses had ordered. When the whole community had come forward and stood before the LORD, 6 Moses said, "This is what the LORD orders you to do, that the glory of the LORD may be revealed to you." 7 Come up to the altar," Moses then told Aaron, "and offer your sin offering and your holocaust in atonement for yourself and for your family; then present the offering of the people in atonement for them, as the LORD has commanded."

8 Going up to the altar, Aaron first slaughtered the calf that was his own sin offering. 9 When his sons presented the blood to him, he dipped his finger in the blood and put it on the horns of the altar. The rest of the blood he poured out at the base of the altar. 10 He then burned on the altar the fat, the kidneys and the lobe of the liver that were taken from the sin offering, as the LORD had commanded Moses; 11 but the flesh and the hide he burned up in the fire outside the camp. 12 Then Aaron slaughtered his holocaust. When his sons brought him the blood, he splashed it on all sides of the altar. 13 They then brought him the pieces and the head of the holocaust, and he burned them on the altar. 14 Having washed the inner organs and the shanks, he burned these also with the holocaust on the altar.

15 Thereupon he had the people's offering brought up. Taking the goat that was for the people's sin offering, he slaughtered it and offered it up for sin as before. 16 Then he brought forward the holocaust, other than the morning holocaust, and offered it in the usual manner. 17 He then presented the cereal offering; taking a handful of it, he burned

took the forequarter and made the gesture of offering before Yahweh. This was the portion of the ram of investiture that reverted to Moses, as Yahweh had ordered Moses.

30 Moses then took some of the anointing oil and some of the blood that was on the altar and sprinkled Aaron and his vestments, and his sons and their vestments, with it. In this way he consecrated Aaron and his vestments and his sons and their vestments.

31 Moses then said to Aaron and his sons, 'Cook the meat at the entrance to the Tent of Meeting, and eat it there, as also the bread of the investiture sacrifice still in the basket of the investiture offerings, as I ordered, when I said, "Aaron and his sons must eat it." 32 What remains of the meat and bread you will burn. 33 For seven days you will not leave the entrance to the Tent of Meeting, until the time of your investiture is complete; for your investiture will require seven days. 34 Yahweh has ordered us to do as we have done today to perform the rite of expiation for you; 35 hence, for seven days, day and night, you will remain at the entrance to the Tent of Meeting observing Yahweh's ritual; do this, and you will not incur death. For this was the order I received.' 36 So Aaron and his sons did everything that Yahweh had ordered through Moses.

9 On the eighth day Moses summoned Aaron and his sons and the elders of Israel; 2 he said to Aaron, 'Take a calf to offer a sacrifice for sin, and a ram for a burnt offering, both without blemish, and bring them before Yahweh. 3 Then say to the Israelites, "Take a goat to be offered as a sacrifice for sin, a calf and a lamb one year old (both without blemish) for a burnt offering, 4 a bull and a ram for communion sacrifices to be slaughtered before Yahweh, and a cereal offering mixed with oil. For Yahweh will appear to you today." '

5 They brought what Moses had ordered in front of the Tent of Meeting; then the whole community approached and stood before Yahweh. 6 Moses then said, 'This is what Yahweh has ordered you to do, so that his glory may be visible to you.' 7 Moses then addressed Aaron, 'Go to the altar and offer your sacrifice for sin and your burnt offering, and so perform the rite of expiation for yourself and your family. Then present the people's offering and perform the rite of expiation for them, as Yahweh has ordered.'

8 Aaron went to the altar and slaughtered the calf as a sacrifice for his own sin. 9 Aaron's sons then presented the blood to him; he dipped his finger in it and put some on the horns of the altar, and then poured the rest of the blood at the foot of the altar. 10 The fat of the sacrifice for sin and the kidneys and the mass of fat over the liver he burned on the altar, as Yahweh had ordered Moses, 11 and the meat and the skin he burned outside the camp.

12 He then slaughtered the burnt offering; Aaron's sons then handed him the blood, which he poured all around the altar. 13 They then handed him the quartered victim and the head, and he burned these on the altar. 14 He then washed the entrails and shins and burned them with the burnt offering on the altar.

15 He then presented the people's offering. He took the goat for the people's sacrifice for sin, slaughtered it, and made a sacrifice for sin with it in the same way as with the first. 16 He then had the burnt offering brought forward and proceeded according to the ritual. 17 He then had the cereal offering brought forward, took a handful of it and burned it on the altar in addition to the morning burnt offering.

NEW REVISED STANDARD VERSION

18 He slaughtered the ox and the ram as a sacrifice of well-being for the people. Aaron's sons brought him the blood, which he dashed against all sides of the altar, 19 and the fat of the ox and of the ram — the broad tail, the fat that covers the entrails, the two kidneys and the fat on them,*e* and the appendage of the liver. 20 They first laid the fat on the breasts, and the fat was turned into smoke on the altar; 21 and the breasts and the right thigh Aaron raised as an elevation offering before the LORD, as Moses had commanded. 22 Aaron lifted his hands toward the people and blessed them; and he came down after sacrificing the sin offering, the burnt offering, and the offering of well-being. 23 Moses and Aaron entered the tent of meeting, and then came out and blessed the people; and the glory of the LORD appeared to all the people. 24 Fire came out from the LORD and consumed the burnt offering and the fat on the altar; and when all the people saw it, they shouted and fell on their faces.

10 Now Aaron's sons, Nadab and Abihu, each took his censer, put fire in it, and laid incense on it; and they offered unholy fire before the LORD, such as he had not commanded them. 2 And fire came out from the presence of the LORD and consumed them, and they died before the LORD. 3 Then Moses said to Aaron, "This is what the LORD meant when he said,

'Through those who are near me
   I will show myself holy,
and before all the people
   I will be glorified.' "

And Aaron was silent.

4 Moses summoned Mishael and Elzaphan, sons of Uzziel the uncle of Aaron, and said to them, "Come forward, and carry your kinsmen away from the front of the sanctuary to a place outside the camp." 5 They came forward and carried them by their tunics out of the camp, as Moses had ordered. 6 And Moses said to Aaron and to his sons Eleazar and Ithamar, "Do not dishevel your hair, and do not tear your vestments, or you will die and wrath will strike all the congregation; but your kindred, the whole house of Israel, may mourn the burning that the LORD has sent. 7 You shall not go outside the entrance of the tent of meeting, or you will die; for the anointing oil of the LORD is on you." And they did as Moses had ordered.

8 And the LORD spoke to Aaron: 9 Drink no wine or strong drink, neither you nor your sons, when you enter the tent of meeting, that you may not die; it is a statute forever throughout your generations. 10 You are to distinguish between the holy and the common, and between the unclean and the clean; 11 and you are to teach the people of Israel all the statutes that the LORD has spoken to them through Moses.

12 Moses spoke to Aaron and to his remaining sons, Eleazar and Ithamar: Take the grain offering that is left from the LORD's offerings by fire, and eat it unleavened beside the altar, for it is most holy; 13 you shall eat it in a holy place, because it is your due and your sons' due, from the offerings by fire to the LORD; for so I am commanded. 14 But the breast that is elevated and the thigh that is raised, you and your sons and daughters as well may eat in any clean place; for they have been assigned to you and your children from the sacrifices of the offerings of well-being of the people of Israel. 15 The thigh that is raised and the breast that is elevated they shall bring, together with the offerings by fire of the fat, to raise for an elevation offering before the LORD; they are to be your due and that of your children forever, as the LORD has commanded.

e Gk: Heb *the broad tail, and that which covers, and the kidneys*

REVISED ENGLISH BIBLE

18 He slaughtered the bull and the ram, the shared-offerings of the people. His sons handed him the blood, and he flung it against the sides of the altar. 19 But the portions of fat from the bull, the fat-tail of the ram, the fat covering the entrails, and both kidneys with the fat upon them, and the long lobe of the liver, 20 all this fat they first put on the breasts of the animals and then Aaron burnt it on the altar. 21 He presented the breasts and the right leg as a dedicated portion before the LORD, as Moses had been commanded. 22 Aaron lifted up his hands towards the people and pronounced the blessing over them. After performing the rites of the purification-offering, the whole-offering, and the shared-offerings, he came down, 23 and Moses and Aaron entered the Tent of Meeting. When they came out, they blessed the people, and the glory of the LORD appeared to all the people. 24 Fire came out from before the LORD and consumed the whole-offering and the portions of fat on the altar. At the sight, all the people shouted joyfully and prostrated themselves.

10 AARON's sons Nadab and Abihu took their censers, put fire in them, threw incense on the fire, and presented before the LORD illicit fire, such as he had not commanded them to present. 2 Fire came out from before the LORD and destroyed them; so they died in the presence of the LORD. 3 Moses said to Aaron, 'This is what the LORD meant when he said:

Among those who approach me I must be treated
   as holy;
in the presence of all the people I must be given
   honour.'

Aaron kept silent.

4 Moses sent for Mishael and Elzaphan, the sons of Aaron's uncle Uzziel, and said to them, 'Come and carry your cousins outside the camp away from the sanctuary.' 5 They came and carried them away in their tunics out of the camp, as Moses had told them. 6 Moses said to Aaron and to his sons Eleazar and Ithamar, 'You are not to let your hair hang loose or tear your clothes in mourning, or you may die and the LORD be angry with the whole community. Your kinsmen, all the house of Israel, shall weep for the destruction by fire which the LORD has kindled. 7 You must not leave the entrance to the Tent of Meeting; otherwise you may die, because the LORD's anointing oil is on you.' They did as Moses had said.

8 WHEN the LORD spoke to Aaron he said: 9 You and your sons with you must not drink wine or strong drink when you are to enter the Tent of Meeting, that you may not die. This is a rule binding on your descendants for all time, 10 to make a distinction between sacred and profane, between clean and unclean, 11 and to teach the Israelites all the decrees which the LORD has spoken to them through Moses.

12 Moses said to Aaron and his surviving sons, Eleazar and Ithamar, 'Take what is left over of the grain-offering out of the food-offerings of the LORD, and eat it unleavened beside the altar; it is most holy. 13 Eat it in a sacred place; it is your due and that of your sons out of the LORD's food-offerings, for so I was commanded. 14 You and your sons and daughters must eat in a clean place the breast of the dedicated portion and the leg which is a contribution for the priests, for they have been given to you and your children as your due out of the shared-offerings of the Israelites. 15 The leg of the contribution and the breast of the dedicated portion must be brought, along with the food-offerings of fat, to be presented as a dedicated portion before the LORD; it will belong to you and your children as a due for all time; for so the LORD has commanded.'

9:19 **the fat covering . . . upon them:** *so Gk; Heb.* and the covering and the kidneys. 10:1 **illicit:** *or* alien.

it on the altar. 18 Finally he slaughtered the ox and the ram, the peace offering of the people. When his sons brought him the blood, Aaron splashed it on all sides of the altar. 19 The portions of fat from the ox and from the ram, the fatty tail, the fatty membrane over the inner organs, the two kidneys, with the fat that is on them, and the lobe of the liver, 20 he placed on top of the breasts and burned them on the altar, 21 having first waved the breasts and the right legs as a wave offering before the LORD, in keeping with the LORD's command to Moses.

22 Aaron then raised his hands over the people and blessed them. When he came down from offering the sin offering and holocaust and peace offering, 23 Moses and Aaron went into the meeting tent. On coming out they again blessed the people. Then the glory of the LORD was revealed to all the people. 24 Fire came forth from the LORD's presence and consumed the holocaust and the remnants of the fat on the altar. Seeing this, all the people cried out and fell prostrate.

10 During this time Aaron's sons Nadab and Abihu took their censers and, strewing incense on the fire they had put in them, they offered up before the LORD profane fire, such as he had not authorized. 2 Fire therefore came forth from the LORD's presence and consumed them, so that they died in his presence. 3 Moses then said to Aaron, "This is as the LORD said:

Through those who approach me I will manifest
my sacredness;
In the sight of all the people I will reveal
my glory."

But Aaron said nothing. 4 Then Moses summoned Mishael and Elzaphan, the sons of Aaron's uncle Uzziel, with the order, "Come, remove your kinsmen from the sanctuary and carry them to a place outside the camp." 5 So they went in and took them, in their tunics, outside the camp, as Moses had commanded.

6 Moses said to Aaron and his sons Eleazar and Ithamar, "Do not bare your heads or tear your garments, lest you bring not only death on yourselves but God's wrath also on the whole community. Your kinsmen, the rest of the house of Israel, shall mourn for those whom the LORD's fire has smitten; 7 but do not you go beyond the entry of the meeting tent, else you shall die; for the anointing oil of the LORD is upon you." So they did as Moses told them.

8 The LORD said to Aaron, 9 "When you are to go to the meeting tent, you and your sons are forbidden under pain of death, by a perpetual ordinance throughout your generations, to drink any wine or strong drink. 10 You must be able to distinguish between what is sacred and what is profane, between what is clean and what is unclean; 11 you must teach the Israelites all the laws that the LORD has given them through Moses."

12 Moses said to Aaron and his surviving sons, Eleazar and Ithamar, "Take the cereal offering left over from the oblations of the LORD, and eat it beside the altar in the form of unleavened cakes. Since it is most sacred, 13 you must eat it in a sacred place. This is your due from the oblations of the LORD, and that of your sons; such is the command I have received. 14 With your sons and daughters you shall also eat the breast of the wave offering and the leg of the raised offering, in a clean place; for these have been assigned to you and your children as your due from the peace offerings of the Israelites. 15 The leg of the raised offering and the breast of the wave offering shall first be brought in with the oblations, the fatty portions, that are to be waved as a wave offering before the LORD. Then they shall belong to you and your children by a perpetual ordinance, as the LORD has commanded."

18 Then he slaughtered the bull and the ram as a communion sacrifice for the people. Aaron's sons handed him the blood and he poured it all around the altar. 19 The fat of the bull and the ram, the tail, the covering fat, the kidneys, the mass of fat over the liver, 20 he placed on the ribs and then burned on the altar. 21 With the ribs and the right thigh Aaron made the gesture of offering as Yahweh had ordered Moses.

22 Aaron then raised his hands towards the people and blessed them. Having thus performed the sacrifice for sin, the burnt offering and the communion sacrifice, he came down 23 and entered the Tent of Meeting with Moses. Then they came out together to bless the people and the glory of Yahweh appeared to the entire people: 24 a flame leapt out from Yahweh's presence and consumed the burnt offering and fat on the altar. At this sight the entire people shouted for joy and fell on their faces.

10 Aaron's sons Nadab and Abihu each took his censer, put fire in it and incense on the fire, and presented unauthorised fire before Yahweh, which was not in accordance with his orders. 2 At this a flame leapt out from Yahweh's presence and swallowed them up, and they perished before Yahweh. 3 Moses then said to Aaron, 'That is what Yahweh meant when he said:

In those who are close to me I show my holiness,
and before all the people I show my glory.'

Aaron remained silent.

4 Moses summoned Mishael and Elzaphan, sons of Aaron's uncle Uzziel, and said to them, 'Come here and take your brothers away from the sanctuary, out of the camp.' 5 They came and carried them away, still in their tunics, out of the camp, as Moses had said.

6 Moses said to Aaron and his sons Eleazar and Ithamar, 'Do not disorder your hair or tear your clothes; or you may incur death and his retribution may overtake the whole community. No, it is for the entire House of Israel to lament your brothers who have been the victims of Yahweh's fire. 7 To avoid incurring death, do not leave the entrance to the Tent of Meeting, for Yahweh's anointing oil is on you.' And they did as Moses said.

8 Yahweh spoke to Aaron and said:

9 'When you come to the Tent of Meeting, you and your sons with you, to avoid incurring death you may not drink wine or any other fermented liquor. This is a perpetual law for all your descendants. 10 And so shall it be also when you separate the sacred from the profane, the unclean from the clean, 11 and when you teach the Israelites any of the decrees that Yahweh has pronounced for them through Moses.'

12 Moses said to Aaron and his surviving sons, Eleazar and Ithamar, 'Take the cereal offering left over from the food burnt for Yahweh. Eat the unleavened part of it beside the altar, since it is especially holy. 13 Eat it in the holy place, since it is the portion of the food burnt for Yahweh that is prescribed for you and your sons; this is the order I have received.

14 'You, your sons and daughters with you, will eat in a clean place the forequarter offered and the thigh presented, for these have been given to you and your children as your due from the Israelites' communion sacrifices. 15 The thigh presented and the forequarter offered, once the fat has been burnt, revert to you and your sons with you, after they have been presented before Yahweh with the gesture of offering, in virtue of a perpetual law as Yahweh has ordered.'

NEW REVISED STANDARD VERSION

16 Then Moses made inquiry about the goat of the sin offering, and — it had already been burned! He was angry with Eleazar and Ithamar, Aaron's remaining sons, and said, 17"Why did you not eat the sin offering in the sacred area? For it is most holy, and God*f* has given it to you that you may remove the guilt of the congregation, to make atonement on their behalf before the LORD. 18Its blood was not brought into the inner part of the sanctuary. You should certainly have eaten it in the sanctuary, as I commanded." 19And Aaron spoke to Moses, "See, today they offered their sin offering and their burnt offering before the LORD; and yet such things as these have befallen me! If I had eaten the sin offering today, would it have been agreeable to the LORD?" 20And when Moses heard that, he agreed.

11 The LORD spoke to Moses and Aaron, saying to them: 2Speak to the people of Israel, saying:
From among all the land animals, these are the creatures that you may eat. 3Any animal that has divided hoofs and is cleft-footed and chews the cud — such you may eat. 4But among those that chew the cud or have divided hoofs, you shall not eat the following: the camel, for even though it chews the cud, it does not have divided hoofs; it is unclean for you. 5The rock badger, for even though it chews the cud, it does not have divided hoofs; it is unclean for you. 6The hare, for even though it chews the cud, it does not have divided hoofs; it is unclean for you. 7The pig, for even though it has divided hoofs and is cleft-footed, it does not chew the cud; it is unclean for you. 8Of their flesh you shall not eat, and their carcasses you shall not touch; they are unclean for you.
9 These you may eat, of all that are in the waters. Everything in the waters that has fins and scales, whether in the seas or in the streams — such you may eat. 10But anything in the seas or the streams that does not have fins and scales, of the swarming creatures in the waters and among all the other living creatures that are in the waters — they are detestable to you 11and detestable they shall remain. Of their flesh you shall not eat, and their carcasses you shall regard as detestable. 12Everything in the waters that does not have fins and scales is detestable to you.
13 These you shall regard as detestable among the birds. They shall not be eaten; they are an abomination: the eagle, the vulture, the osprey, 14the buzzard, the kite of any kind; 15every raven of any kind; 16the ostrich, the nighthawk, the sea gull, the hawk of any kind; 17the little owl, the cormorant, the great owl, 18the water hen, the desert owl,*g* the carrion vulture, 19the stork, the heron of any kind, the hoopoe, and the bat.*h*
20 All winged insects that walk upon all fours are detestable to you. 21But among the winged insects that walk on all fours you may eat those that have jointed legs above their feet, with which to leap on the ground. 22Of them you may eat: the locust according to its kind, the bald locust according to its kind, the cricket according to its kind, and the grasshopper according to its kind. 23But all other winged insects that have four feet are detestable to you.
24 By these you shall become unclean; whoever touches the carcass of any of them shall be unclean until the evening, 25and whoever carries any part of the carcass of any of them shall wash his clothes and be unclean until the evening. 26Every animal that has divided hoofs but is not cleft-footed or does not chew the cud is unclean for you; everyone who touches one of them shall be unclean. 27All that walk on their paws, among the animals that walk on all fours, are unclean for you; whoever touches the carcass of any of them shall be unclean until the evening, 28and the

REVISED ENGLISH BIBLE

16When Moses made searching enquiry about the goat of the purification-offering and found it had been burnt, he was angry with Eleazar and Ithamar, Aaron's surviving sons, and said, 17'Why did you not eat the purification-offering in the sacred place? It is most holy. It was given to you to take away the guilt of the community by making expiation for them before the LORD. 18Since the blood was not brought within the sacred precincts, you should have eaten the purification-offering there as I was commanded.' 19But Aaron replied to Moses, 'See, they have today presented their purification-offering and their whole-offering before the LORD, and this is what has happened to me! If I had eaten a purification-offering today, would the LORD have considered it right?' 20When Moses heard this, he considered Aaron was right.

11 THE LORD told Moses and Aaron 2to say to the Israelites: These are the creatures you may eat: Of all the larger land animals 3you may eat any hoofed animal which has cloven hoofs and also chews the cud; 4those which only have cloven hoofs or only chew the cud you must not eat. These are: the camel, because though it chews the cud it does not have cloven hoofs, and is unclean for you; 5the rock-badger, because though it chews the cud it does not have cloven hoofs, and is unclean for you; 6the hare, because though it chews the cud it does not have a parted foot; it is unclean for you; 7the pig, because although it is a hoofed animal with cloven hoofs it does not chew the cud, and is unclean for you. 8You are not to eat the flesh of these or even touch their dead carcasses; they are unclean for you.
9Of creatures that live in water these may be eaten: all, whether in salt water or fresh, that have fins and scales; 10but all, whether in salt or fresh water, that have neither fins nor scales, including both small creatures in shoals and larger creatures, you are to regard as prohibited. 11They are prohibited to you; you must not eat their flesh, and their dead bodies you are to treat as prohibited. 12Every creature in the water that has neither fins nor scales is prohibited to you.
13These are the birds you are to regard as prohibited, and for that reason they must not be eaten: the griffon-vulture, the black vulture, and the bearded vulture; 14the kite and every kind of falcon; 15every kind of crow, 16the desert-owl, the short-eared owl, the long-eared owl, and every kind of hawk; 17the tawny owl, the fisher-owl, and the screech-owl; 18the little owl, the horned owl, the osprey, 19the stork, the various kinds of cormorant, the hoopoe, and the bat.
20All winged creatures that swarm and go on all fours are prohibited to you, 21except those which have legs jointed above their feet for leaping on the ground. 22Of these you may eat every kind of great locust, every kind of long-headed locust, every kind of green locust, and every kind of desert locust. 23Every other swarming winged creature that has four legs is prohibited to you.
24These are the creatures that will make you unclean: whoever touches their dead bodies will be unclean till evening, 25and whoever picks up the dead body of any of them must wash his clothes and remain unclean till evening. 26Every animal which has hoofs but not cloven hoofs and does not chew the cud is to be unclean to you: whoever touches them will be unclean. 27You are to regard as unclean all four-footed wild animals that walk on flat paws; whatever touches their dead bodies will be unclean till evening, 28and whoever takes up their dead bodies must wash

---

f Heb he   *g* Or *pelican*   *h* Identification of several of the birds in verses 13-19 is uncertain

11:5 **rock-badger:** *or* rock-rabbit.   11:13 **griffon-vulture:** *or* eagle. **bearded vulture:** *or* ossifrage.   11:15 **crow:** *or* raven.
11:19 **stork:** *or* heron.   11:24,26 **whoever:** *or* whatever.

16 When Moses inquired about the goat of the sin offering, he discovered that it had all been burned. So he was angry with the surviving sons of Aaron, Eleazar and Ithamar, and said, 17 "Why did you not eat the sin offering in the sacred place, since it is most sacred? It has been given to you that you might bear the guilt of the community and make atonement for them before the LORD. 18 If its blood was not brought into the inmost part of the sanctuary, you should certainly have eaten the offering in the sanctuary, in keeping with the command I had received." 19 Aaron answered Moses, "Even though they presented their sin offering and holocaust before the LORD today, yet this misfortune has befallen me. Had I then eaten of the sin offering today, would it have been pleasing to the LORD?" 20 On hearing this, Moses was satisfied.

11 The LORD said to Moses and Aaron, 2 "Speak to the Israelites and tell them: Of all land animals these are the ones you may eat: 3 any animal that has hoofs you may eat, provided it is cloven-footed and chews the cud. 4 But you shall not eat any of the following that only chew the cud or only have hoofs: the camel, which indeed chews the cud, but does not have hoofs and is therefore unclean for you; 5 the rock badger, which indeed chews the cud, but does not have hoofs and is therefore unclean for you; 6 the hare, which indeed chews the cud, but does not have hoofs and is therefore unclean for you; and the pig, 7 which does indeed have hoofs and is cloven-footed, but does not chew the cud and is therefore unclean for you. 8 Their flesh you shall not eat, and their dead bodies you shall not touch; they are unclean for you.

9 "Of the various creatures that live in the water, you may eat the following: whatever in the seas or in river waters has both fins and scales you may eat. 10 But of the various creatures that crawl or swim in the water, whether in the sea or in the rivers, all those that lack either fins or scales are loathsome for you, 11 and you shall treat them as loathsome. Their flesh you shall not eat, and their dead bodies you shall loathe. 12 Every water creature that lacks fins or scales is loathsome for you.

13 "Of the birds, these you shall loathe and, as loathsome, they shall not be eaten: the eagle, the vulture, the osprey, 14 the kite, the various species of falcons, 15 the various species of crows, 16 the ostrich, the nightjar, the gull, the various species of hawks, 17 the owl, the cormorant, the screech owl, 18 the barn owl, the desert owl, the buzzard, 19 the stork, the various species of herons, the hoopoe, and the bat.

20 "The various winged insects that walk on all fours are loathsome for you. 21 But of the various winged insects that walk on all fours you may eat those that have jointed legs for leaping on the ground; 22 hence of these you may eat the following: the various kinds of locusts, the various kinds of grasshoppers, the various kinds of katydids, and the various kinds of crickets. 23 All other winged insects that have four legs are loathsome for you.

24 "Such is the uncleanness that you contract, that everyone who touches their dead bodies shall be unclean until evening, 25 and everyone who picks up any part of their dead bodies shall wash his garments and be unclean until evening. 26 All hoofed animals that are not cloven-footed or do not chew the cud are unclean for you; everyone who touches them becomes unclean. 27 Of the various quadrupeds, all those that walk on paws are unclean for you; everyone who touches their dead bodies shall be unclean until evening, 28 and everyone who picks up their dead bod-

16 Moses then enquired carefully about the goat offered as a sacrifice for sin, and found that they had burnt it. He was angry with Eleazar and Ithamar, Aaron's surviving sons, and said, 17 'Why did you not eat this victim for sin in the holy place, since it is especially holy and was given to you to take away the community's guilt, by performing the rite of expiation for them before Yahweh? 18 Since its blood was not taken inside the sanctuary, you should have eaten its meat there, as I ordered you.' 19 Aaron said to Moses, 'Look, today they offered their sacrifice for sin and their burnt offering before Yahweh, and these disasters have befallen me. If I had eaten the sin offering today, would this have met with Yahweh's approval?' 20 And when Moses heard this, he was satisfied.

11 b Yahweh spoke to Moses and Aaron and said to them, 2 'Speak to the Israelites and say:
"Of all animals living on land these are the creatures you may eat:
3 "You may eat any animal that has a cloven hoof, divided into two parts, and that is a ruminant. 4 The following, which either chew the cud or have a cloven hoof, are the ones that you may not eat: you will regard the camel as unclean, because though it is ruminant, it does not have a cloven hoof; 5 you will regard the coney as unclean, because though it is ruminant, it does not have a cloven hoof; 6 you will regard the hare as unclean, because though it is ruminant, it does not have a cloven hoof; 7 you will regard the pig as unclean, because though it has a cloven hoof, divided into two parts, it is not a ruminant. 8 You will not eat the meat of these or touch their dead bodies; you will regard them as unclean.

9 "Of all that lives in water, these you may eat:
"Anything that has fins and scales, and lives in the water, whether in sea or river, you may eat. 10 But anything in sea or river that does not have fins and scales, of all the small water-creatures and all the living things found there, you will regard as detestable. 11 You will regard them as detestable; you must not eat their meat and you will regard their carcases as detestable. 12 Anything that lives in water, but not having fins and scales, you will regard as detestable.

13 "Of the birds these are the ones that you will regard as detestable; they may not be eaten, they are detestable for eating:
"The tawny vulture, the griffon, the osprey, 14 the kite, the various kinds of buzzard, 15 all kinds of raven, 16 the ostrich, the screech owl, the seagull, the various kinds of hawk, 17 horned owl, night owl, cormorant, barn owl, 18 ibis, pelican, white vulture, 19 stork, the various kinds of heron, the hoopoe and the bat.

20 "All winged insects moving on four feet you will regard as detestable for eating. 21 Of all these winged insects you may eat only the following: those with the sort of legs above their feet which enable them to leap over the ground. 22 These are the ones you may eat: the various kinds of migratory locust, the various kinds of *solham* locust, *hargol* locust and *hagab* locust. 23 But all other winged insects on four feet you will regard as detestable for eating.

24 "By the following you will be made unclean. Anyone who touches the carcase of one will be unclean until evening. 25 Anyone who picks up their carcases must wash his clothing and will be unclean until evening. 26 Animals that have hoofs, but not cloven, and that are not ruminant, you will regard as unclean; anyone who touches them will be unclean. 27 Those four-footed animals which walk on the flat of their paws you will regard as unclean; anyone who touches their carcases will be unclean until evening, 28 and

one who carries the carcass shall wash his clothes and be unclean until the evening; they are unclean for you.

29 These are unclean for you among the creatures that swarm upon the earth: the weasel, the mouse, the great lizard according to its kind, 30 the gecko, the land crocodile, the lizard, the sand lizard, and the chameleon. 31 These are unclean for you among all that swarm; whoever touches one of them when they are dead shall be unclean until the evening. 32 And anything upon which any of them falls when they are dead shall be unclean, whether an article of wood or cloth or skin or sacking, any article that is used for any purpose; it shall be dipped into water, and it shall be unclean until the evening, and then it shall be clean. 33 And if any of them falls into any earthen vessel, all that is in it shall be unclean, and you shall break the vessel. 34 Any food that could be eaten shall be unclean if water from any such vessel comes upon it; and any liquid that could be drunk shall be unclean if it was in any such vessel. 35 Everything on which any part of the carcass falls shall be unclean; whether an oven or stove, it shall be broken in pieces; they are unclean, and shall remain unclean for you. 36 But a spring or a cistern holding water shall be clean, while whatever touches the carcass in it shall be unclean. 37 If any part of their carcass falls upon any seed set aside for sowing, it is clean; 38 but if water is put on the seed and any part of their carcass falls on it, it is unclean for you.

39 If an animal of which you may eat dies, anyone who touches its carcass shall be unclean until the evening. 40 Those who eat of its carcass shall wash their clothes and be unclean until the evening; and those who carry the carcass shall wash their clothes and be unclean until the evening.

41 All creatures that swarm upon the earth are detestable; they shall not be eaten. 42 Whatever moves on its belly, and whatever moves on all fours, or whatever has many feet, all the creatures that swarm upon the earth, you shall not eat; for they are detestable. 43 You shall not make yourselves detestable with any creature that swarms; you shall not defile yourselves with them, and so become unclean. 44 For I am the Lord your God; sanctify yourselves therefore, and be holy, for I am holy. You shall not defile yourselves with any swarming creature that moves on the earth. 45 For I am the Lord who brought you up from the land of Egypt, to be your God; you shall be holy, for I am holy.

46 This is the law pertaining to land animal and bird and every living creature that moves through the waters and every creature that swarms upon the earth, 47 to make a distinction between the unclean and the clean, and between the living creature that may be eaten and the living creature that may not be eaten.

12 The Lord spoke to Moses, saying: 2 Speak to the people of Israel, saying:

If a woman conceives and bears a male child, she shall be ceremonially unclean seven days; as at the time of her menstruation, she shall be unclean. 3 On the eighth day the flesh of his foreskin shall be circumcised. 4 Her time of blood purification shall be thirty-three days; she shall not touch any holy thing, or come into the sanctuary, until the days of her purification are completed. 5 If she bears a female child, she shall be unclean two weeks, as in her menstruation; her time of blood purification shall be sixty-six days.

6 When the days of her purification are completed, whether for a son or for a daughter, she shall bring to the priest at the entrance of the tent of meeting a lamb in its first year for a burnt offering, and a pigeon or a turtledove for a sin offering. 7 He shall offer it before the Lord, and make

his clothes and remain unclean till evening. They are to be unclean to you.

29 The following creatures that swarm on the ground are to be unclean to you: the mole-rat, the jerboa, and every kind of thorn-tailed lizard; 30 the gecko, the sand-gecko, the wall-gecko, the great lizard, and the chameleon. 31 Those among swarming creatures are to be unclean to you; whoever touches them when they are dead will be unclean till evening. 32 Anything on which any of them falls when dead will be unclean, any article of wood, any garment or hide or sacking, any article which may be put to use; it must be immersed in water and remain unclean till evening, when it will be clean. 33 If any of the creatures falls into an earthenware vessel, its contents will be unclean, and you must break the vessel. 34 Any food which is fit for eating and then comes in contact with water from such a vessel will be unclean, and any drink in such a vessel will be unclean. 35 Anything on which the dead body of such a creature falls will be unclean; a clay oven or pot must be broken, for they are unclean and you must treat them as such; 36 but a spring or a cistern where water collects will remain clean, though whoever touches the dead body will be unclean. 37 When any of their dead bodies falls on seed intended for sowing, the seed remains clean; 38 but if the seed has been soaked in water and any dead body falls on it, it will be unclean for you.

39 When any animal allowed as food dies, anyone who touches the carcass will be unclean till evening. 40 Whoever eats any of the carcass must wash his clothes and remain unclean till evening, and whoever takes up the carcass must wash his clothes and be unclean till evening.

41 All creatures that swarm on the ground are prohibited; they must not be eaten. 42 All creatures that swarm on the ground, whether they crawl on their bellies or go on all fours or have many legs, you must not eat, because they are prohibited. 43 You must not contaminate yourselves through any creatures that swarm; you must not defile yourselves with them and make yourselves unclean by them. 44 For I am the Lord your God; you are to make yourselves holy and keep yourselves holy, because I am holy. You must not defile yourselves with any creatures that swarm and creep on the ground. 45 I am the Lord who brought you up from Egypt to become your God. You are to keep yourselves holy, because I am holy.

46 Such, then, is the law concerning beast and bird, every living creature that moves in the water, and all living creatures that swarm on the land, 47 the purpose of the law being to make a distinction between the unclean and the clean, between living creatures that may be eaten and those that may not be eaten.

12 The Lord told Moses 2 to say to the Israelites: When a woman becomes pregnant and gives birth to a male child, she will be unclean for seven days, as in the period of her impurity through menstruation. 3 On the eighth day, the child is to have the flesh of his foreskin circumcised. 4 The woman must then wait for thirty-three days because her blood requires purification; she must touch nothing that is holy, and must not enter the sanctuary till her days of purification are completed. 5 If she bears a female child, she will be unclean as in menstruation for fourteen days and must wait for sixty-six days because her blood requires purification.

6 When her days of purification are completed for either son or daughter, she must bring a yearling ram for a whole-offering and a pigeon or a turtle-dove for a purification-offering to the priest at the entrance to the Tent of Meeting.

11:29 mole-rat: or weasel.   11:31 whoever: or whatever.
11:36 whoever: or whatever.

NEW AMERICAN BIBLE

NEW JERUSALEM BIBLE

ies shall wash his garments and be unclean until evening. Such is their uncleanness for you.

29 "Of the creatures that swarm on the ground, the following are unclean for you: the rat, the mouse, the various kinds of lizards, 30 the gecko, the chameleon, the agama, the skink, and the mole. 31 Among the various swarming creatures, these are unclean for you. Everyone who touches them when they are dead shall be unclean until evening. 32 Everything on which one of them falls when dead becomes unclean. Any such article that men use, whether it be an article of wood, cloth, leather or goat hair, must be put in water and remain unclean until evening, when it again becomes clean. 33 Should any of these creatures fall into a clay vessel, everything in it becomes unclean, and the vessel itself you must break. 34 Any solid food that was in contact with water, and any liquid that men drink, in any such vessel become unclean. 35 Any object on which one of their dead bodies falls, becomes unclean; if it is an oven or a jar-stand, this must be broken to pieces; they are unclean and shall be treated as unclean by you. 36 However, a spring or a cistern for collecting water remains clean; but whoever touches the dead body becomes unclean. 37 Any sort of cultivated grain remains clean even though one of their dead bodies falls on it; 38 but if the grain has become moistened, it becomes unclean when one of these falls on it.

39 "When one of the animals that you could otherwise eat, dies of itself, anyone who touches its dead body shall be unclean until evening; 40 and anyone who eats of its dead body shall wash his garments and be unclean until evening; so also, anyone who removes its dead body shall wash his garments and be unclean until evening.

41 "All the creatures that swarm on the ground are loathsome and shall not be eaten. 42 Whether it crawls on its belly, goes on all fours, or has many legs, you shall eat no swarming creature: they are loathsome. 43 Do not make yourselves loathsome or unclean with any swarming creature through being contaminated by them. 44 For I, the LORD, am your God; and you shall make and keep yourselves holy, because I am holy. You shall not make yourselves unclean, then, by any swarming creature that crawls on the ground. 45 Since I, the LORD, brought you up from the land of Egypt that I might be your God, you shall be holy, because I am holy.

46 "This is the law for animals and birds and for all the creatures that move about in the water or swarm on the ground, 47 that you may distinguish between the clean and the unclean, between creatures that may be eaten and those that may not be eaten."

12 The LORD said to Moses, 2 "Tell the Israelites: When a woman has conceived and gives birth to a boy, she shall be unclean for seven days, with the same uncleanness as at her menstrual period. 3 On the eighth day, the flesh of the boy's foreskin shall be circumcised, 4 and then she shall spend thirty-three days more in becoming purified of her blood; she shall not touch anything sacred nor enter the sanctuary till the days of her purification are fulfilled. 5 If she gives birth to a girl, for fourteen days she shall be as unclean as at her menstruation, after which she shall spend sixty-six days in becoming purified of her blood.

6 "When the days of her purification for a son or for a daughter are fulfilled, she shall bring to the priest at the entrance of the meeting tent a yearling lamb for a holocaust and a pigeon or a turtledove for a sin offering. 7 The priest

anyone who picks up their carcases must wash his clothing and will be unclean until evening. You will regard them as unclean.

29 "Of the small creatures which crawl along the ground, these are the ones which you will regard as unclean: the mole, the rat, the various kinds of lizard: 30 gecko, *koah*, *letaah*, chameleon and *tinshamet*.

31 "Of all the small creatures, these are the animals which you must regard as disgusting. Anyone who touches them when they are dead will be unclean until evening.

32 "Any object on which one of these creatures falls when it is dead becomes unclean: wooden utensil, clothing, skin, sacking, any utensil whatever. It must be immersed in water and will remain unclean until evening: then it will be clean. 33 If the creature falls into an earthenware vessel, the vessel must be broken; whatever the vessel contains is unclean. 34 Any edible food will be unclean if the water touches it; any drinkable liquid will be unclean, no matter what its container. 35 Anything on which the carcase of such a creature may fall will be unclean: be it oven or stove, it must be destroyed; for they are unclean and you will regard them as unclean 36 (although springs, wells and stretches of water will remain clean); anyone who touches one of their carcases will be unclean. 37 If one of their carcases falls on any kind of seed, the seed will remain clean; 38 but if the seed has been moistened and one of their carcases falls on it, you will regard it as unclean.

39 "If one of the animals that you use as food dies, anyone who touches the carcase will be unclean until evening; 40 anyone who eats any of the carcase must wash his clothing and will remain unclean until evening; anyone who picks up the carcase must wash his clothing and will remain unclean until evening.

41 "Any creature that swarms on the ground is detestable for eating; it must not be eaten. 42 Anything that moves on its belly, anything that moves on four legs or more — in short all the creatures that swarm on the ground — you will not eat, since they are detestable. 43 Do not make yourselves detestable with all these swarming creatures; do not defile yourselves with them, do not be defiled by them. 44 For it is I, Yahweh, who am your God. You have been sanctified and have become holy because I am holy: do not defile yourselves with all these creatures that swarm on the ground. 45 Yes, it is I, Yahweh, who brought you out of Egypt to be your God: you must therefore be holy because I am holy." '

46 Such is the law concerning animals, birds, all living creatures that move in water and all creatures that swarm on the ground. 47 Its purpose is to distinguish the clean from the unclean, the creatures that may be eaten from those that may not be eaten.

12 Yahweh spoke to Moses and said, 2 'Speak to the Israelites and say:

"If a woman becomes pregnant and gives birth to a boy, she will be unclean for seven days as when in a state of pollution due to menstruation. 3 On the eighth day the child's foreskin must be circumcised, 4 and she will wait another thirty-three days for her blood to be purified. She will not touch anything consecrated nor go to the sanctuary until the time of her purification is over.

5 "If she gives birth to a girl, she will be unclean for two weeks, as during her monthly periods; and will wait another sixty-six days for her blood to be purified. 6 "When the period of her purification is over, for either boy or girl, she will bring the priest at the entrance to the Tent of Meeting a lamb one year old for a burnt offering, and a young pigeon or turtledove as a sacrifice for sin. 7 The

227

NEW REVISED STANDARD VERSION	REVISED ENGLISH BIBLE

atonement on her behalf; then she shall be clean from her flow of blood. This is the law for her who bears a child, male or female. 8 If she cannot afford a sheep, she shall take two turtledoves or two pigeons, one for a burnt offering and the other for a sin offering; and the priest shall make atonement on her behalf, and she shall be clean.

13 The LORD spoke to Moses and Aaron, saying: 2 When a person has on the skin of his body a swelling or an eruption or a spot, and it turns into a leprous[i] disease on the skin of his body, he shall be brought to Aaron the priest or to one of his sons the priests. 3 The priest shall examine the disease on the skin of his body, and if the hair in the diseased area has turned white and the disease appears to be deeper than the skin of his body, it is a leprous[i] disease; after the priest has examined him he shall pronounce him ceremonially unclean. 4 But if the spot is white in the skin of his body, and appears no deeper than the skin, and the hair in it has not turned white, the priest shall confine the diseased person for seven days. 5 The priest shall examine him on the seventh day, and if he sees that the disease is checked and the disease has not spread in the skin, then the priest shall confine him seven days more. 6 The priest shall examine him again on the seventh day, and if the disease has abated and the disease has not spread in the skin, the priest shall pronounce him clean; it is only an eruption; and he shall wash his clothes, and be clean. 7 But if the eruption spreads in the skin after he has shown himself to the priest for his cleansing, he shall appear again before the priest. 8 The priest shall make an examination, and if the eruption has spread in the skin, the priest shall pronounce him unclean; it is a leprous[i] disease.

9 When a person contracts a leprous[i] disease, he shall be brought to the priest. 10 The priest shall make an examination, and if there is a white swelling in the skin that has turned the hair white, and there is quick raw flesh in the swelling, 11 it is a chronic leprous[i] disease in the skin of his body. The priest shall pronounce him unclean; he shall not confine him, for he is unclean. 12 But if the disease breaks out in the skin, so that it covers all the skin of the diseased person from head to foot, so far as the priest can see, 13 then the priest shall make an examination, and if the disease has covered all his body, he shall pronounce him clean of the disease; since it has all turned white, he is clean. 14 But if raw flesh ever appears on him, he shall be unclean; 15 the priest shall examine the raw flesh and pronounce him unclean. Raw flesh is unclean, for it is a leprous[i] disease. 16 But if the raw flesh again turns white, he shall come to the priest; 17 the priest shall examine him, and if the disease has turned white, the priest shall pronounce the diseased person clean. He is clean.

18 When there is on the skin of one's body a boil that has healed, 19 and in the place of the boil there appears a white swelling or a reddish-white spot, it shall be shown to the priest. 20 The priest shall make an examination, and if it appears deeper than the skin and its hair has turned white, the priest shall pronounce him unclean; this is a leprous[i] disease, broken out in the boil. 21 But if the priest examines it and the hair on it is not white, nor is it deeper than the skin but has abated, the priest shall confine him seven days. 22 If it spreads in the skin, the priest shall pronounce him unclean; it is diseased. 23 But if the spot remains in one place and does not spread, it is the scar of the boil; the priest shall pronounce him clean.

7 He will present it before the LORD and offer expiation for her, and she will be clean from her issue of blood. This is the law for the woman who gives birth to a child, whether male or female. 8 If she cannot afford a ram, she is to bring two turtle-doves or two pigeons, one for a whole-offering and the other for a purification-offering. The priest then offers expiation for her, and she will be clean.

13 When the LORD spoke to Moses and Aaron he said: 2 When anyone has a discoloration on the skin of his body, a pustule or inflammation, and it may develop into the sores of a virulent skin disease, that person is to be brought to the priest, either to Aaron or to one of his sons. 3 The priest is to examine the sore on the skin; if the hairs on the affected part have turned white and it appears to be more than skin deep, it must be considered the sore of a virulent skin disease, and, after examination, the priest will pronounce the person ritually unclean. 4 But if the inflammation on his skin is white and seems no deeper than the skin, and not a single hair has turned white, the priest must isolate the affected person for seven days. 5 If, when he examines him on the seventh day, the sore remains as it was and has not spread in the skin, he is to keep him in isolation for a further seven days. 6 When on the seventh day the priest examines him again, if he finds that the sore has faded and has not spread on the skin, the priest will pronounce him ritually clean. It is only a scab; after washing his clothes, he will be clean. 7 But if the scab spreads on the skin after he has been to the priest to be pronounced ritually clean, he must show himself a second time to the priest, 8 who must examine him again. If it continues to spread, the priest will pronounce him ritually unclean; it is a virulent skin disease.

9 When anyone has the sores of a virulent skin disease, he is to be brought to the priest, 10 who then examines him. If there is a white mark on the skin, turning hairs white, and an ulceration appears in the mark, 11 it is a chronic skin disease on the body, and the priest must pronounce him ritually unclean; there is no need for isolation because he is unclean already. 12 If the skin disease spreads and covers the affected person from head to foot as far as the priest can see, 13 the priest is to examine him, and if he finds the condition covers the whole body, he must pronounce him ritually clean. It has all gone white; he is clean. 14 But as soon as raw flesh appears, he must be considered unclean. 15 The priest, when he sees it, must pronounce him unclean. Raw flesh is to be considered unclean; it is a virulent skin disease. 16 On the other hand, when the raw flesh heals and turns white, he is to go to the priest, 17 who will examine him, and if the sores have gone white, he will pronounce him clean. He is ritually clean.

18 When a fester appears on the skin and heals up, 19 but is followed by a white mark or reddish-white inflammation on the site of the fester, the person affected must show himself to the priest. 20 The priest will examine him, and if it seems to be beneath the skin and the hairs have turned white, the priest must pronounce him ritually unclean; it is a virulent skin disease which has broken out on the site of the fester. 21 But if the priest on examination finds that it has no white hairs, is not beneath the skin, and has faded, he must isolate him for seven days. 22 If the affection has spread at all in the skin, then the priest must pronounce him unclean; for it is a virulent skin disease. 23 But if the inflammation is no worse and has not spread, it is only the scar of the fester, and the priest will pronounce him ritually clean.

---

[i] A term for several skin diseases; precise meaning uncertain

13:22 **virulent skin disease:** so one MS; others sore.

shall offer them up before the LORD to make atonement for her, and thus she will be clean again after her flow of blood. Such is the law for the woman who gives birth to a boy or a girl child. 8 If, however, she cannot afford a lamb, she may take two turtledoves or two pigeons, the one for a holocaust and the other for a sin offering. The priest shall make atonement for her, and thus she will again be clean."

13 The LORD said to Moses and Aaron, 2 "If someone has on his skin a scab or pustule or blotch which appears to be the sore of leprosy, he shall be brought to Aaron, the priest, or to one of the priests among his descendants, 3 who shall examine the sore on his skin. If the hair on the sore has turned white and the sore itself shows that it has penetrated below the skin, it is indeed the sore of leprosy; the priest, on seeing this, shall declare the man unclean. 4 If, however, the blotch on the skin is white, but does not seem to have penetrated below the skin, nor has the hair turned white, the priest shall quarantine the stricken man for seven days. 5 On the seventh day the priest shall again examine him. If he judges that the sore has remained unchanged and has not spread on the skin, the priest shall quarantine him for another seven days, 6 and once more examine him on the seventh day. If the sore is now dying out and has not spread on the skin, the priest shall declare the man clean; it was merely eczema. The man shall wash his garments and so become clean. 7 But if, after he has shown himself to the priest to be declared clean, the eczema spreads at all on his skin, he shall once more show himself to the priest. 8 Should the priest, on examining it, find that the eczema has indeed spread on the skin, he shall declare the man unclean; it is leprosy.

9 "When someone is stricken with leprosy, he shall be brought to the priest. 10 Should the priest, on examining him, find that there is a white scab on the skin which has turned the hair white and that there is raw flesh in it, 11 it is skin leprosy that has long developed. The priest shall declare the man unclean without first quarantining him, since he is certainly unclean. 12 If leprosy breaks out on the skin and, as far as the priest can see, covers all the skin of the stricken man from head to foot, 13 should the priest then, on examining him, find that the leprosy does cover his whole body, he shall declare the stricken man clean; since it has all turned white, the man is clean. 14 But as soon as raw flesh appears on him, he is unclean; 15 on observing the raw flesh, the priest shall declare him unclean, because raw flesh is unclean; it is leprosy. 16 If, however, the raw flesh again turns white, he shall return to the priest; 17 should the latter, on examining him, find that the sore has indeed turned white, he shall declare the stricken man clean, and thus he will be clean.

18 "If a man who had a boil on his skin which later healed, 19 should now in the place of the boil have a white scab or a pink blotch, he shall show himself to the priest. 20 If the latter, on examination, sees that it is deeper than the skin and that the hair has turned white, he shall declare the man unclean: it is the sore of leprosy that has broken out in the boil. 21 But if the priest, on examining him, finds that there is no white hair in it and that it is not deeper than the skin and is already dying out, the priest shall quarantine him for seven days. 22 If it has then spread on the skin, the priest shall declare him unclean; the man is stricken. 23 But if the blotch remains in its place without spreading, it is merely the scar of the boil; the priest shall therefore declare him clean.

priest must offer this before Yahweh, perform the rite of expiation for her, and she will be purified from her discharge of blood.

"Such is the law concerning a woman who gives birth to either a boy or a girl. 8 If she cannot afford a lamb, she must take two turtledoves or two young pigeons, one for the burnt offering and the other for the sacrifice for sin: the priest will perform the rite of expiation for her and she will be purified." '

13 Yahweh said to Moses and Aaron, 2 'If a swelling or scab or spot appears on someone's skin, which could develop into a contagious skin-disease, that person must then be taken to the priest, either Aaron or one of his sons. 3 The priest will examine the disease on the skin. If the hair on the diseased part has turned white, or if the disease bites into the skin, the skin-disease is contagious, and after examination the priest will declare the person unclean. 4 But if there is a white spot on the skin without any visible depression of the skin or whitening of the hair, the priest will isolate the sick person for seven days. 5 On the seventh day he will examine the person, and if he observes that the disease persists though without spreading over the skin, he will isolate the person for a further seven days 6 and examine him again on the seventh. If he finds that the disease has faded and has not spread over the skin, the priest will declare the person clean. This was merely a scab. Once he has washed his clothing he will be clean.

7 'But if the scab spreads over the skin after the sick person has been examined by the priest and declared clean, then he will let himself be examined again by the priest. 8 After examining him and certifying the spread of the scab over the skin, the priest will declare him unclean: it is a contagious skin-disease.

9 'Someone who has a contagious skin-disease must be taken to the priest. 10 The priest will examine the sick person, and if he finds a whitish swelling with whitening of the hair and an ulcer forming on the skin, 11 this is a dormant skin-disease, and the priest will declare the person unclean. He will not isolate him; he is obviously unclean.

12 'But if the disease spreads all through the skin, if it covers the person entirely from head to foot so far as the priest can see, 13 the priest will then examine the sick person and, if he finds that the skin-disease covers his whole body, declare the sick person clean. Since it has all become white, he is clean. 14 But as soon as an ulcer appears on him, he will be unclean. 15 After examining the ulcer, the priest will declare him unclean: the ulcer is unclean, it is contagious. 16 But if the ulcer becomes white again, the sick person will go to the priest; 17 the priest will examine him and if he finds that the disease has turned white, he will declare the sick person clean: he is clean.

18 'When an ulcer appears on someone's skin, and then gets better, 19 and if then a white swelling or a reddish-white spot forms on the same place, the sick person will show himself to the priest. 20 The priest will examine him, and if he finds a visible depression in the skin and a whitening of the hair, he will declare the person unclean: this is a case of contagious skin-disease breaking out in an ulcer. 21 But if on examination the priest finds neither white hair nor depression of the skin, but a fading of the affected part, he will isolate the sick person for seven days. 22 If the disease has then spread over the skin, he will declare the person unclean: this is a case of contagious skin-disease. 23 But if the spot has stayed where it was and has not spread, it is the scar of the ulcer and the priest will declare the person clean.

24 Or, when the body has a burn on the skin and the raw flesh of the burn becomes a spot, reddish-white or white, 25 the priest shall examine it. If the hair in the spot has turned white and it appears deeper than the skin, it is a leprous*j* disease; it has broken out in the burn, and the priest shall pronounce him unclean. This is a leprous*j* disease. 26 But if the priest examines it and the hair in the spot is not white, and it is no deeper than the skin but has abated, the priest shall confine him seven days. 27 The priest shall examine him the seventh day; if it is spreading in the skin, the priest shall pronounce him unclean. This is a leprous*j* disease. 28 But if the spot remains in one place and does not spread in the skin but has abated, it is a swelling from the burn, and the priest shall pronounce him clean; for it is the scar of the burn.

29 When a man or woman has a disease on the head or in the beard, 30 the priest shall examine the disease. If it appears deeper than the skin and the hair in it is yellow and thin, the priest shall pronounce him unclean; it is an itch, a leprous*j* disease of the head or the beard. 31 If the priest examines the itching disease, and it appears no deeper than the skin and there is no black hair in it, the priest shall confine the person with the itching disease for seven days. 32 On the seventh day the priest shall examine the itch; if the itch has not spread, and there is no yellow hair in it, and the itch appears to be no deeper than the skin, 33 he shall shave, but the itch he shall not shave. The priest shall confine the person with the itch for seven days more. 34 On the seventh day the priest shall examine the itch; if the itch has not spread in the skin and it appears to be no deeper than the skin, the priest shall pronounce him clean. He shall wash his clothes and be clean. 35 But if the itch spreads in the skin after he was pronounced clean, 36 the priest shall examine him. If the itch has spread in the skin, the priest need not seek for the yellow hair; he is unclean. 37 But if in his eyes the itch is checked, and black hair has grown in it, the itch is healed, he is clean; and the priest shall pronounce him clean.

38 When a man or a woman has spots on the skin of the body, white spots, 39 the priest shall make an examination, and if the spots on the skin of the body are of a dull white, it is a rash that has broken out on the skin; he is clean.

40 If anyone loses the hair from his head, he is bald but he is clean. 41 If he loses the hair from his forehead and temples, he has baldness of the forehead but he is clean. 42 But if there is on the bald head or the bald forehead a reddish-white diseased spot, it is a leprous*j* disease breaking out on his bald head or his bald forehead. 43 The priest shall examine him; if the diseased swelling is reddish-white on his bald head or on his bald forehead, which resembles a leprous*j* disease in the skin of the body, 44 he is leprous, *j* he is unclean. The priest shall pronounce him unclean; the disease is on his head.

45 The person who has the leprous*j* disease shall wear torn clothes and let the hair of his head be disheveled; and he shall cover his upper lip and cry out, "Unclean, unclean." 46 He shall remain unclean as long as he has the disease; he is unclean. He shall live alone; his dwelling shall be outside the camp.

47 Concerning clothing: when a leprous*j* disease appears in it, in woolen or linen cloth, 48 in warp or woof of linen or wool, or in a skin or in anything made of skin, 49 if the disease shows greenish or reddish in the garment, whether in warp or woof or in skin or in anything made of skin, it is a leprous*j* disease and shall be shown to the priest. 50 The priest shall examine the disease, and put the

24 Again, in the case of a burn on the skin, if the raw spot left by the burn becomes a reddish-white or white inflammation, 25 the priest is to examine it. If hair on the inflammation has turned white and it is deeper than the skin, it is a virulent skin disease which has broken out at the site of the burn. The priest must pronounce the person ritually unclean; it is a virulent skin disease. 26 But if the priest on examination finds that there are no white hairs on the inflammation and it is not beneath the skin and has faded, he must keep him in isolation for seven days. 27 When the priest examines him on the seventh day, if the inflammation has spread at all in the skin, the priest must pronounce him unclean; it is a virulent skin disease. 28 But if the inflammation is no worse, has not spread, and has faded, it is only a mark from the burn. The priest will pronounce him ritually clean because it is the scar of the burn.

29 When a man, or woman, has a sore on the head or chin, 30 the priest is to examine it, and if it seems deeper than the skin and the hair is yellow and sparse, the priest must pronounce the person ritually unclean; it is a scale, a virulent skin disease of the head or chin. 31 But when the priest sees the sore, if it appears to be no deeper than the skin and yet there are no yellow hairs on the place, the priest must isolate the affected person for seven days. 32 When the priest examines the sore on the seventh day, if the scale has not spread and there are no yellow hairs on it and it seems no deeper than the skin, 33 the person must be shaved except for the scurfy part, and be kept in isolation for another seven days. 34 When the priest examines it again on the seventh day, if the scale has not spread on the skin and appears to be no deeper than the skin, the priest will pronounce the person clean. After washing his clothes the person will be ritually clean. 35 But if the scale spreads at all in the skin after the person has been pronounced clean, 36 the priest must make a further examination. If it has spread in the skin, the priest need not even look for yellow hairs; the person is unclean. 37 If, however, the scale remains as it was but black hair has begun to grow on it, it has healed. The person is ritually clean and the priest will pronounce this.

38 When a man, or woman, has inflamed patches on the skin and they are white, 39 the priest is to examine them. If they are white and fading, it is vitiligo that has broken out on the skin. The person is ritually clean.

40 When someone's hair falls out from his head, he is bald but not ritually unclean. 41 If the hair falls out from the front of the scalp, he is bald on the forehead but clean. 42 But if on the bald patch on his head or forehead there is a reddish-white sore, it is a virulent skin disease breaking out on those parts. 43 The priest must examine him, and if the discoloured sore on the bald patch on his head or forehead is reddish-white, similar in appearance to a virulent skin disease on the body, 44 the person is suffering from such a disease; he is ritually unclean and the priest must not fail to pronounce him so. The symptoms are in this case on his head.

45 Anyone who suffers from a virulent skin disease must wear torn clothes and have his hair all dishevelled; he must conceal his upper lip, and call out, 'Unclean, unclean.' 46 So long as the sore persists, he is to be considered ritually unclean, and live alone, staying outside the camp.

47 When there is a stain of mould, whether on a garment of wool or linen, 48 or on the threads or woven piece of linen or wool, or on a hide or anything made of hide; 49 if the stain is greenish or reddish in colour on the garment or hide, or on the threads or woven piece of cloth, or on anything made of hide, it is a stain of mould which must be shown to the priest. 50 The priest must examine it and put the stained

---

j A term for several skin diseases; precise meaning uncertain

13:31 **yellow:** *so Gk; Heb.* black.   13:39 **vitiligo:** *or* dull-white leprosy.

24 "If a man had a burn on his skin, and the proud flesh of the burn now becomes a pink or a white blotch, 25 the priest shall examine it. If the hair has turned white on the blotch and this seems to have penetrated below the skin, it is leprosy that has broken out in the burn; the priest shall therefore declare him unclean and stricken with leprosy. 26 But if the priest, on examining it, finds that there is no white hair on the blotch and that this is not deeper than the skin and is already dying out, the priest shall quarantine him for seven days. 27 Should the priest, when examining it on the seventh day, find that it has spread at all on the skin, he shall declare the man unclean and stricken with leprosy. 28 But if the blotch remains in its place without spreading on the skin and is already dying out, it is merely the scab of the burn; the priest shall therefore declare the man clean, since it is only the scar of the burn.

29 "When a man or a woman has a sore on the head or cheek, 30 should the priest, on examining it, find that the sore has penetrated below the skin and that there is fine yellow hair on it, the priest shall declare the person unclean, for this is scall, a leprous disease of the head or cheek. 31 But if the priest, on examining the scall sore, finds that it has not penetrated below the skin, though the hair on it may not be black, the priest shall quarantine the person with scall sore for seven days, 32 and on the seventh day again examine the sore. If the scall has not spread and has no yellow hair on it and does not seem to have penetrated below the skin, 33 the man shall shave himself, but not on the diseased spot. Then the priest shall quarantine him for another seven days. 34 If the priest, when examining the scall on the seventh day, finds that it has not spread on the skin and that it has not penetrated below the skin, he shall declare the man clean; the latter shall wash his garments, and thus he will be clean. 35 But if the scall spreads at all on his skin after he has been declared clean, 36 the priest shall again examine it. If the scall has indeed spread on the skin, he need not look for yellow hair; the man is surely unclean. 37 If, however, he judges that the scall has remained in its place and that black hair has grown on it, the disease has been healed; the man is clean, and the priest shall declare him clean.

38 "When the skin of a man or a woman is spotted with white blotches, 39 the priest shall make an examination. If the blotches on the skin are white and already dying out, it is only tetter that has broken out on the skin, and the person therefore is clean.

40 "When a man loses the hair of his head, he is not unclean merely because of his bald crown. 41 So too, if he loses the hair on the front of his head, he is not unclean merely because of his bald forehead. 42 But when there is a pink sore on his bald crown or bald forehead, it is leprosy that is breaking out there. 43 The priest shall examine him; and if the scab on the sore of the bald spot has the same pink appearance as that of skin leprosy of the fleshy part of the body, 44 the man is leprous and unclean, and the priest shall declare him unclean by reason of the sore on his head.

45 "The one who bears the sore of leprosy shall keep his garments rent and his head bare, and shall muffle his beard; he shall cry out, 'Unclean, unclean!' 46 As long as the sore is on him he shall declare himself unclean, since he is in fact unclean. He shall dwell apart, making his abode outside the camp.

47 "When a leprous infection is on a garment of wool or of linen, 48 or on woven or knitted material of linen or wool, or on a hide or anything made of leather, 49 if the infection on the garment or hide, or on the woven or knitted material, or on any leather article is greenish or reddish, the thing is indeed infected with leprosy and must be shown to the priest. 50 Having examined the infection, the priest shall

24 'If someone has a burn on the skin and an abscess, a reddish-white or white spot, forms on the burn, 25 the priest will then examine it. If he finds a whitening of the hair or a visible depression of the mark on the skin, a contagious disease has broken out in the burn. The priest will declare the sick person unclean: this is a contagious skin-disease. 26 If on the other hand the priest on examination does not find white hair on the mark or depression of the skin, but a fading of the mark, the priest will isolate the person for seven days. 27 He will examine the person on the seventh day and, if the disease has spread over the skin, he will declare the sick person unclean: this is a case of contagious skin-disease. 28 If the mark has stayed where it was and has not spread over the skin, but has faded instead, it was only a swelling due to the burn. The priest will declare the person clean: it is merely a burn scar.

29 'If a man or a woman has a sore on the head or chin, 30 the priest will examine the sore; and if he finds a depression visible in the skin, with the hair on it yellow and thin, he will declare the sick person unclean: this is tinea, that is to say, a contagious skin-disease of the head or chin. 31 If on examining this case of tinea the priest finds no visible depression in the skin and no yellow hair, he will isolate the person so affected for seven days. 32 He will examine the infected part on the seventh day, and if he finds that the tinea has not spread, that the hair on it is not yellow, and that there is no visible depression in the skin, 33 the sick person will shave his hair off, all except the part affected with tinea, and the priest will again isolate him for seven days. 34 He will examine the infected part on the seventh day, and if he finds that it has not spread over the skin, and that there is no visible depression of the skin, the priest will declare the sick person clean. After washing his clothes the person will be clean. 35 But if after this purification the tinea does spread over the skin, 36 the priest will examine the person; if he finds that the tinea has indeed spread over the skin, the sick person is unclean, and there is no need to verify whether the hair is yellow. 37 Whereas if, so far as he can see, the tinea is arrested and dark hair is beginning to grow on it, the sick person is cured. He is clean, and the priest will declare him clean.

38 'If spots break out on the skin of a man or woman, and if these spots are white, 39 the priest will examine them. If he finds that the spots are of a dull white, this is a rash that has broken out on the skin: the sick person is clean.

40 'If someone loses the hair of the scalp, this is baldness of the scalp but the person is clean. 41 If he loses hair off the front of the head, this is baldness of the forehead but the person is clean. 42 If, however, a reddish-white sore appears on scalp or forehead, a contagious skin-disease has broken out on the scalp or forehead. 43 The priest will examine it, and if he finds a reddish-white swelling on scalp or forehead, looking like a contagious skin-disease, 44 the person has such a disease: he is unclean. The priest will declare him unclean; he has a contagious skin-disease of the head.

45 'Anyone with a contagious skin-disease will wear torn clothing and disordered hair; and will cover the upper lip and shout, "Unclean, unclean." 46 As long as the disease lasts, such a person will be unclean and, being unclean, will live alone and live outside the camp.

47 'When a piece of clothing is infected with mould, be it woollen or linen clothing, 48 linen or woollen fabric or covering, or leather or anything made of leather, 49 if the spot on the clothing, leather, fabric, covering or object made of leather is a greenish or reddish colour, it is a disease to be shown to the priest. 50 The priest will examine the infection

| NEW REVISED STANDARD VERSION | REVISED ENGLISH BIBLE |

diseased article aside for seven days. 51 He shall examine the disease on the seventh day. If the disease has spread in the cloth, in warp or woof, or in the skin, whatever be the use of the skin, this is a spreading leprous*k* disease; it is unclean. 52 He shall burn the clothing, whether diseased in warp or woof, woolen or linen, or anything of skin, for it is a spreading leprous*k* disease; it shall be burned in fire.

53 If the priest makes an examination, and the disease has not spread in the clothing, in warp or woof or in anything of skin, 54 the priest shall command them to wash the article in which the disease appears, and he shall put it aside seven days more. 55 The priest shall examine the diseased article after it has been washed. If the diseased spot has not changed color, though the disease has not spread, it is unclean; you shall burn it in fire, whether the leprous*k* spot is on the inside or on the outside.

56 If the priest makes an examination, and the disease has abated after it is washed, he shall tear the spot out of the cloth, in warp or woof, or out of skin. 57 If it appears again in the garment, in warp or woof, or in anything of skin, it is spreading; you shall burn with fire that in which the disease appears. 58 But the cloth, warp or woof, or anything of skin from which the disease disappears when you have washed it, shall then be washed a second time, and it shall be clean.

59 This is the ritual for a leprous*k* disease in a cloth of wool or linen, either in warp or woof, or in anything of skin, to decide whether it is clean or unclean.

14 The LORD spoke to Moses, saying: 2 This shall be the ritual for the leprous*k* person at the time of his cleansing:

He shall be brought to the priest; 3 the priest shall go out of the camp, and the priest shall make an examination. If the disease is healed in the leprous*k* person, 4 the priest shall command that two living clean birds and cedarwood and crimson yarn and hyssop be brought for the one who is to be cleansed. 5 The priest shall command that one of the birds be slaughtered over fresh water in an earthen vessel. 6 He shall take the living bird with the cedarwood and the crimson yarn and the hyssop, and dip them and the living bird in the blood of the bird that was slaughtered over the fresh water. 7 He shall sprinkle it seven times upon the one who is to be cleansed of the leprous*k* disease; then he shall pronounce him clean, and he shall let the living bird go into the open field. 8 The one who is to be cleansed shall wash his clothes, and shave off all his hair, and bathe himself in water, and he shall be clean. After that he shall come into the camp, but shall live outside his tent seven days. 9 On the seventh day he shall shave all his hair: of head, beard, eyebrows; he shall shave all his hair. Then he shall wash his clothes, and bathe his body in water, and he shall be clean.

10 On the eighth day he shall take two male lambs without blemish, and one ewe lamb in its first year without blemish, and a grain offering of three-tenths of an ephah of choice flour mixed with oil, and one log*l* of oil. 11 The priest who cleanses shall set the person to be cleansed, along with these things, before the LORD, at the entrance of the tent of meeting. 12 The priest shall take one of the lambs, and offer it as a guilt offering, along with the log*l* of oil, and raise them as an elevation offering before the LORD. 13 He shall slaughter the lamb in the place where the sin offering and the burnt offering are slaughtered in the holy place; for the guilt offering, like the sin offering, belongs to the priest: it is most holy. 14 The priest shall take some of

material aside by itself for seven days. 51 On the seventh day he must examine it again. If the stain has spread on the garment, threads, piece of cloth, or hide, whatever the use of the hide, the stain is a rotting mould: it is ritually unclean. 52 He must burn the garment or the threads or woven piece, whether wool or linen, or anything of hide which is stained; because it is a rotting mould, it must be destroyed by fire. 53 But if the priest sees that the stain has not spread on the garment, threads, or piece of woven cloth, or anything made of hide, 54 he is to give orders for the stained material to be washed, and then put it aside for another seven days. 55 After it has been washed the priest must examine the stain; if it has not changed its appearance, even though it has not spread, it is unclean and you must destroy it by fire, whether the rot is on the right side or the wrong. 56 If the priest examines it and finds the stain faded after being washed, he is to tear it out of the garment, or the hide, or the threads, or woven piece. 57 If, however, the stain reappears in the garment, threads, or woven piece, or in anything made of hide, it is breaking out afresh and you must destroy by fire whatever is stained. 58 If you wash the garment, threads, piece of woven cloth, or the article made of hide and the stain disappears, it must be washed a second time and then it will be ritually clean.

59 Such is the law concerning stain of mould on a garment of wool or linen, on threads or a piece of woven cloth, or on anything made of hide; by it they will be pronounced ritually clean or unclean.

14 WHEN the LORD spoke to Moses he said: 2 This is the law concerning anyone suffering from a virulent skin disease. On the day when he is to be cleansed he is to be brought to the priest; 3 who will go outside the camp and examine him. If the person has recovered from his disease, 4 then the priest is to order two ritually clean small birds to be brought alive for the person who is to be cleansed, together with cedar-wood, scarlet thread, and marjoram. 5 He must order one of the birds to be killed over an earthenware bowl containing fresh water. 6 He will then take the live bird together with the cedar-wood, scarlet thread, and marjoram and dip them all in the blood of the bird that has been killed over the fresh water. 7 He must sprinkle the blood seven times on the one who is to be cleansed from the skin disease and so cleanse him; the live bird he will release to fly away over the open country. 8 The person to be cleansed must wash his clothes, shave off all his hair, bathe in water, and so be ritually clean. He may then enter the camp, but must stay outside his tent for seven days. 9 On the seventh day he must shave off all the hair on his head, his beard, and his eyebrows, and then shave the rest of his hair, wash his clothes, and bathe in water; then he will be ritually clean.

10 On the eighth day he must bring two yearling rams and one yearling ewe, all three without blemish, a grain-offering of three tenths of an ephah of flour mixed with oil, and one log measure of oil. 11 The officiating priest must place the person to be cleansed and his offerings before the LORD at the entrance to the Tent of Meeting.

12 The priest must take one of the rams and offer it with the log of oil as a reparation-offering, presenting them as a dedicated portion before the LORD. 13 The ram must be slaughtered where the purification-offerings and the whole-offerings are slaughtered, within the sacred precincts, because the reparation-offering, like the purification-offering, belongs to the priest. It is most holy. 14 The priest must then

---

k A term for several skin diseases; precise meaning uncertain   *l* A liquid measure

14:4 **marjoram:** or hyssop.   14:10 **yearling rams:** so Samar.; Heb. omits yearling.

quarantine the infected article for seven days.
51 "On the seventh day the priest shall again examine the infection. If it has spread on the garment, or on the woven or knitted material, or on the leather, whatever be its use, the infection is malignant leprosy, and the article is unclean. 52 He shall therefore burn up the garment, or the woven or knitted material of wool or linen, or the leather article, whatever it may be, which is infected; since it has malignant leprosy, it must be destroyed by fire. 53 But if the priest, on examining the infection, finds that it has not spread on the garment, or on the woven or knitted material, or on the leather article, 54 he shall give orders to have the infected article washed and then quarantined for another seven days. 55 "Then the priest shall again examine the infected article after it has been washed. If the infection has not changed its appearance, even though it may not have spread, the article is unclean and shall be destroyed by fire. 56 But if the priest, on examining the infection, finds that it is dying out after the washing, he shall tear the infected part out of the garment, or the leather, or the woven or knitted material. 57 If, however, the infection again appears on the garment, or on the woven or knitted material, or on the leather article, it is still virulent and the thing infected shall be destroyed by fire. 58 But if, after the washing, the infection has left the garment, or the woven or knitted material, or the leather article, the thing shall be washed a second time, and thus it will be clean. 59 This is the law for leprous infection on a garment of wool or linen, or on woven or knitted material, or on any leather article, to determine whether it is clean or unclean."

14 The LORD said to Moses, 2 "This is the law for the victim of leprosy at the time of his purification. He shall be brought to the priest, 3 who is to go outside the camp to examine him. If the priest finds that the sore of leprosy has healed in the leper, 4 he shall order the man who is to be purified, to get two live, clean birds, as well as some cedar wood, scarlet yarn, and hyssop. 5 The priest shall then order him to slay one of the birds over an earthen vessel with spring water in it. 6 Taking the living bird with the cedar wood, the scarlet yarn and the hyssop, the priest shall dip them all in the blood of the bird that was slain over the spring water, 7 and then sprinkle seven times the man to be purified from his leprosy. When he has thus purified him, he shall let the living bird fly away over the countryside. 8 The man being purified shall then wash his garments and shave off all his hair and bathe in water; only when he is thus made clean may he come inside the camp; but he shall still remain outside his tent for seven days. 9 On the seventh day he shall again shave off all the hair of his head, his beard, his eyebrows, and any other hair he may have, and also wash his garments and bathe his body in water; and so he will be clean.

10 "On the eighth day he shall take two unblemished male lambs, one unblemished yearling ewe lamb, three tenths of an ephah of fine flour mixed with oil for a cereal offering, and one log of oil. 11 The priest who performs the purification ceremony shall place the man who is being purified, as well as all these offerings, before the LORD at the entrance of the meeting tent. 12 Taking one of the male lambs, the priest shall present it as a guilt offering, along with the log of oil, waving them as a wave offering before the LORD. 13 (This lamb he shall slaughter in the sacred place where the sin offering and the holocaust are slaughtered; because, like the sin offering, the guilt offering belongs to the priest and is most sacred.) 14 Then the priest shall take some of the

and isolate the object for seven days. 51 If on the seventh day he observes that the infection has spread on the clothing, fabric, covering, leather or object made of leather, whatever it may be, this is a contagious disease and the object is unclean. 52 He will burn this clothing, fabric, linen or woollen covering or leather object whatever it may be, on which the infection has appeared; for this is a contagious disease which must be destroyed by fire.

53 'But if on examination the priest finds that the infection has not spread on the clothing, fabric, covering, or leather object whatever it may be, 54 he will order the infected object to be washed and will isolate it again for a period of seven days. 55 After the washing, he will examine the infection and if he finds that there is no change in its appearance, even though it has not spread, the article is unclean. You will burn it; it is infected through and through.

56 'But if on examination the priest finds that the infection has diminished after washing, he will tear it out of the clothing, leather, fabric or covering. 57 But if the infection reappears on the same clothing, fabric, covering or leather object whatever it may be, this means that the infection is active; you will burn whatever is infected. 58 The clothing, fabric, covering or leather object whatever it may be, from which the infection disappears after being washed, will be clean after it has been washed a second time.

59 'Such is the law governing disease in a linen or woollen garment, a fabric or covering or leather object whatever it may be,' when it is a question of declaring them clean or unclean.'

14 Yahweh spoke to Moses and said:
2 'This is the law to be applied on the day of the purification of someone who has suffered from a contagious skin-disease. Such a person will be taken to the priest, 3 and the priest will go outside the camp. If he finds on examination that the person has recovered from the disease, 4 he will order the following to be brought for his purification: two live birds that are clean, some cedar wood, scarlet material and hyssop. 5 He will then order one of the birds to be slaughtered in an earthenware pot over running water. 6 He will then take the live bird, the cedar wood, the scarlet material and the hyssop and dip all this (including the live bird) into the blood of the bird slaughtered over running water. 7 He will then sprinkle the person to be purified of the skin-disease seven times, and having declared the person clean, will set the live bird free to fly off into the countryside. 8 The person who is being purified will then wash all clothing, shave off all hair, and wash, and will then be clean. After this he will return to the camp, although he will remain outside his tent for seven days. 9 On the seventh day he will shave off all his hair — head, beard and eyebrows; he will shave off all his hair. After washing his clothing and his body he will be clean.

10 'On the eighth day he will take two unblemished lambs, an unblemished ewe one year old, three-tenths of wheaten flour mixed with oil for the cereal offering, and one log of oil. 11 The priest who is performing the purification will place the person who is being purified, with all his offerings, at the entrance to the Tent of Meeting, before Yahweh. 12 He will then take one of the lambs and offer it as a sacrifice of reparation, as also the log of oil. With these he will make the gesture of offering before Yahweh. 13 He will then slaughter the lamb on that spot inside the holy place where the victims for the sacrifice for sin and for the burnt offering are slaughtered. This reparatory offering, like the sacrifice for sin, will revert to the priest: it is especially holy. 14 The priest will then take some blood of this sacrifice

NEW REVISED STANDARD VERSION | REVISED ENGLISH BIBLE

the blood of the guilt offering and put it on the lobe of the right ear of the one to be cleansed, and on the thumb of the right hand, and on the big toe of the right foot. 15 The priest shall take some of the log[m] of oil and pour it into the palm of his own left hand, 16 and dip his right finger in the oil that is in his left hand and sprinkle some oil with his finger seven times before the LORD. 17 Some of the oil that remains in his hand the priest shall put on the lobe of the right ear of the one to be cleansed, and on the thumb of the right hand, and on the big toe of the right foot, on top of the blood of the guilt offering. 18 The rest of the oil that is in the priest's hand he shall put on the head of the one to be cleansed. Then the priest shall make atonement on his behalf before the LORD: 19 the priest shall offer the sin offering, to make atonement for the one to be cleansed from his uncleanness. Afterward he shall slaughter the burnt offering; 20 and the priest shall offer the burnt offering and the grain offering on the altar. Thus the priest shall make atonement on his behalf and he shall be clean.

21 But if he is poor and cannot afford so much, he shall take one male lamb for a guilt offering to be elevated, to make atonement on his behalf, and one-tenth of an ephah of choice flour mixed with oil for a grain offering and a log[m] of oil; 22 also two turtledoves or two pigeons, such as he can afford, one for a sin offering and the other for a burnt offering. 23 On the eighth day he shall bring them for his cleansing to the priest, to the entrance of the tent of meeting, before the LORD; 24 and the priest shall take the lamb of the guilt offering and the log[m] of oil, and the priest shall raise them as an elevation offering before the LORD. 25 The priest shall slaughter the lamb of the guilt offering and shall take some of the blood of the guilt offering, and put it on the lobe of the right ear of the one to be cleansed, and on the thumb of the right hand, and on the big toe of the right foot. 26 The priest shall pour some of the oil into the palm of his own left hand, 27 and shall sprinkle with his right finger some of the oil that is in his left hand seven times before the LORD. 28 The priest shall put some of the oil that is in his hand on the lobe of the right ear of the one to be cleansed, and on the thumb of the right hand, and the big toe of the right foot, where the blood of the guilt offering was placed. 29 The rest of the oil that is in the priest's hand he shall put on the head of the one to be cleansed, to make atonement on his behalf before the LORD. 30 And he shall offer, of the turtledoves or pigeons such as he can afford, 31 one[n] for a sin offering and the other for a burnt offering, along with a grain offering; and the priest shall make atonement before the LORD on behalf of the one being cleansed. 32 This is the ritual for the one who has a leprous[o] disease, who cannot afford the offerings for his cleansing.

33 The LORD spoke to Moses and Aaron, saying:

34 When you come into the land of Canaan, which I give you for a possession, and I put a leprous[o] disease in a house in the land of your possession, 35 the owner of the house shall come and tell the priest, saying, "There seems to me to be some sort of disease in my house." 36 The priest shall command that they empty the house before the priest goes to examine the disease, or all that is in the house will become unclean; and afterward the priest shall go in to inspect the house. 37 He shall examine the disease; if the disease is in the walls of the house with greenish or reddish spots, and if it appears to be deeper than the surface, 38 the priest shall go outside to the door of the house and shut up the house seven days. 39 The priest shall come again on the seventh day and make an inspection; if the disease has spread in the walls of the house, 40 the priest shall command

take some of the blood of the reparation-offering and put it on the lobe of the right ear of the person to be cleansed, and on his right thumb and the big toe of his right foot. 15 He must next take the log of oil and pour some of it on the palm of his own left hand, 16 dip his right forefinger into the oil on his left palm, and sprinkle some of it with his finger seven times before the LORD. 17 He must then put some of the oil remaining on his palm on the lobe of the right ear of the person to be cleansed, on his right thumb, and on the big toe of his right foot, on top of the blood of the reparation-offering. 18 The remainder of the oil on the priest's palm is to be put upon the head of the person to be cleansed, and thus the priest makes expiation for him before the LORD. 19 The priest will then offer the purification-offering and make expiation for the uncleanness of the person who is to be cleansed. After this he must slaughter the whole-offering 20 and offer it and the grain-offering on the altar. Thus the priest makes expiation for him, and he will be clean.

21 If the person is poor and cannot afford these offerings, he must bring one young ram as a reparation-offering to be a dedicated portion making expiation for him, and a grain-offering of a tenth of an ephah of flour mixed with oil, and a log measure of oil, 22 also two turtle-doves or two pigeons, whichever he can afford, one for a purification-offering and the other for a whole-offering. 23 He must bring them on the eighth day to the priest for his cleansing, at the entrance to the Tent of Meeting before the LORD. 24 The priest will take the ram for the reparation-offering and the log of oil, and present them as a dedicated portion before the LORD. 25 The ram for the reparation-offering must then be slaughtered, and the priest must take some of the blood of the reparation-offering, and put it on the lobe of the right ear of the man to be cleansed and on his right thumb and on the big toe of his right foot. 26 The priest must pour some of the oil on the palm of his own left hand 27 and sprinkle some of it with his right forefinger seven times before the LORD. 28 He will then put some of the oil remaining on his palm on the lobe of the right ear of the man to be cleansed, and on his right thumb and on the big toe of his right foot exactly where the blood of the reparation-offering was put. 29 The remainder of the oil on the priest's palm is to be put upon the head of the person to be cleansed to make expiation for him before the LORD. 30–31 Of the birds which the person has been able to afford, turtle-doves or pigeons, whichever it may be, the priest must deal with one as a purification-offering and with the other as a whole-offering and make the grain-offering with them. Thus the priest makes expiation before the LORD for the person who is to be cleansed. 32 Such is the law for anyone with a virulent skin disease who cannot afford the regular offering for his cleansing.

33 When the LORD spoke to Moses and Aaron he said: 34 When you have entered Canaan, which I am giving you to occupy, if I inflict a fungous infection upon a house in the land you have occupied, 35 the owner must come and report to the priest that there appears to him to be a patch of infection in his house. 36 The priest must order the house to be emptied before he goes in to examine the infection, or everything in it will become unclean. After this the priest must go in to inspect the house. 37 If on inspection he finds the patch on the walls consists of greenish or reddish depressions, apparently going deeper than the surface, 38 he is to go out of the house, and at the entrance put it in quarantine for seven days. 39 On the seventh day he must return and inspect the house, and if the patch has spread in the walls, 40 he must order the infected stones to be pulled out

---

[m] A liquid measure   [n] Gk Syr: Heb afford, 31 such as he can afford, one   [o] A term for several skin diseases; precise meaning uncertain

blood of the guilt offering and put it on the tip of the man's right ear, the thumb of his right hand, and the big toe of his right foot. 15 The priest shall also take the log of oil and pour some of it into the palm of his own left hand; 16 then, dipping his right forefinger in it, he shall sprinkle it seven times before the LORD. 17 Of the oil left in his hand the priest shall put some on the tip of the man's right ear, the thumb of his right hand, and the big toe of his right foot, over the blood of the guilt offering. 18 The rest of the oil in his hand the priest shall put on the head of the man being purified. Thus shall the priest make atonement for him before the LORD. 19 Only after he has offered the sin offering in atonement for the man's uncleanness shall the priest slaughter the holocaust 20 and offer it, together with the cereal offering, on the altar before the LORD. When the priest has thus made atonement for him, the man will be clean.

21 "If a man is poor and cannot afford so much, he shall take one male lamb for a guilt offering, to be used as a wave offering in atonement for himself, one tenth of an ephah of fine flour mixed with oil for a cereal offering, a log of oil, 22 and two turtledoves or pigeons, which he can more easily afford, the one as a sin offering and the other as a holocaust. 23 On the eighth day of his purification he shall bring them to the priest, at the entrance of the meeting tent before the LORD. 24 Taking the guilt-offering lamb, along with the log of oil, the priest shall wave them as a wave offering before the LORD. 25 When he has slaughtered the guilt-offering lamb, he shall take some of its blood, and put it on the tip of the right ear of the man being purified, on the thumb of his right hand, and on the big toe of his right foot. 26 The priest shall then pour some of the oil into the palm of his own left hand 27 and with his right forefinger sprinkle it seven times before the LORD. 28 Some of the oil in his hand the priest shall also put on the tip of the man's right ear, the thumb of his right hand, and the big toe of his right foot, over the blood of the guilt offering. 29 The rest of the oil in his hand the priest shall put on the man's head. Thus shall he make atonement for him before the LORD. 30 Then, of the turtledoves or pigeons, such as the man can afford, 31 the priest shall offer up one as a sin offering and the other as a holocaust, along with the cereal offering. Thus shall the priest make atonement before the LORD for the man who is to be purified. 32 This is the law for one afflicted with leprosy who has insufficient means for his purification."

33 The LORD said to Moses and Aaron, 34 "When you come into the land of Canaan, which I am giving you to possess, if I put a leprous infection on any house of the land you occupy, 35 the owner of the house shall come and report to the priest, 'It looks to me as if my house were infected.' 36 The priest shall then order the house to be cleared out before he goes in to examine the infection, lest everything in the house become unclean. Only after this is he to go in to examine the house. 37 If the priest, on examining it, finds that the infection on the walls of the house consists of greenish or reddish depressions which seem to go deeper than the surface of the wall, 38 he shall close the door of the house behind him and quarantine the house for seven days. 39 On the seventh day the priest shall return to examine the house again. If he finds that the infection has spread on the walls, 40 he shall order the infected stones to be pulled out

and put it on the lobe of the right ear, the thumb of the right hand, and the big toe of the right foot of the person who is being purified. 15 He will then take the *log* of oil and pour a little into the hollow of his left hand. 16 He will dip a finger of his right hand into the oil in the hollow of his left hand, and sprinkle the oil with his finger seven times before Yahweh. 17 He will then take some of the oil left in the hollow of his hand and put it on the lobe of the right ear, the thumb of the right hand, and the big toe of the right foot of the person being purified, in addition to the blood of the sacrifice of reparation. 18 The rest of the oil in the hollow of his hand he will put on the head of the person who is being purified. This is how the priest will perform the rite of expiation for such a person before Yahweh.

19 'The priest will then offer the sacrifice for sin, and perform the rite of expiation for uncleanness for the person who is being purified. After this, he will slaughter the burnt offering 20 and offer this and the cereal offering on the altar. So, when the priest has performed the rite of expiation for him the person will be clean.

21 'If he is poor and cannot afford all this, he need take only one lamb, the one for the sacrifice of reparation, and this will be presented with the gesture of offering to perform the rite of expiation for him. And for the cereal offering he will only take one-tenth of wheaten flour mixed with oil, and the *log* of oil, 22 and two turtledoves or two young pigeons, whichever he can afford, one for a sacrifice for sin and the other for the burnt offering. 23 He will bring these on the eighth day to the priest at the entrance to the Tent of Meeting before Yahweh, for his purification. 24 The priest will take the lamb for the sacrifice of reparation and the *log* of oil, and present them before Yahweh with the gesture of offering. 25 He will then slaughter the lamb for the sacrifice of reparation, take some of its blood and put it on the lobe of the right ear, the thumb of the right hand and the big toe of the right foot of the person who is being purified. 26 He will pour the oil into the hollow of his left hand, 27 and with his finger sprinkle the oil in the hollow of his left hand seven times before Yahweh. 28 He will then put some of the oil on the lobe of the right ear, the thumb of the right hand and the big toe of the right foot of the person who is being purified, as he did with the blood of the sacrifice of reparation. 29 The remainder of the oil in the hollow of his hand he will put on the head of the person who is being purified, thus performing the rite of expiation for him before Yahweh. 30 Of the two turtledoves or two young pigeons — whatever he has been able to afford — he will offer 31 a sacrifice for sin with one, and with the other a burnt offering with a cereal offering — whatever he has been able to afford. This is how the priest will perform before Yahweh the rite of expiation for the person who is being purified.

32 'Such is the law concerning someone with a contagious skin-disease who cannot afford the means of purification.'

33 Yahweh spoke to Moses and Aaron and said:

34 'When you reach Canaan, which I am giving you as your possession, if I infect a house with a disease in the country which you are to possess, 35 the owner will come and inform the priest and say, "I have seen something like a skin-disease in the house." 36 The priest will order the house to be emptied before he goes to examine the infection, or everything in the house will become unclean; after which, the priest will go inside and examine the house; 37 and if on examination he finds the walls of the house pitted with reddish or greenish depressions which appear to be eating away the wall, 38 the priest will then go out of the house, to the door, and shut it up for seven days. 39 On the seventh day, the priest will come back and if on examination he finds that the infection has spread over the walls of the house, 40 he will order the infected stones to be removed

that the stones in which the disease appears be taken out and thrown into an unclean place outside the city. 41 He shall have the inside of the house scraped thoroughly, and the plaster that is scraped off shall be dumped in an unclean place outside the city. 42 They shall take other stones and put them in the place of those stones, and take other plaster and plaster the house.

43 If the disease breaks out again in the house, after he has taken out the stones and scraped the house and plastered it, 44 the priest shall go and make inspection; if the disease has spread in the house, it is a spreading leprous *p* disease in the house; it is unclean. 45 He shall have the house torn down, its stones and timber and all the plaster of the house, and taken outside the city to an unclean place. 46 All who enter the house while it is shut up shall be unclean until the evening; 47 and all who sleep in the house shall wash their clothes; and all who eat in the house shall wash their clothes.

48 If the priest comes and makes an inspection, and the disease has not spread in the house after the house was plastered, the priest shall pronounce the house clean; the disease is healed. 49 For the cleansing of the house he shall take two birds, with cedarwood and crimson yarn and hyssop, 50 and shall slaughter one of the birds over fresh water in an earthen vessel, 51 and shall take the cedarwood and the hyssop and the crimson yarn, along with the living bird, and dip them in the blood of the slaughtered bird and the fresh water, and sprinkle the house seven times. 52 Thus he shall cleanse the house with the blood of the bird, and with the fresh water, and with the living bird, and with the cedarwood and hyssop and crimson yarn; 53 and he shall let the living bird go out of the city into the open field; so he shall make atonement for the house, and it shall be clean.

54 This is the ritual for any leprous *p* disease: for an itch, 55 for leprous *p* diseases in clothing and houses, 56 and for a swelling or an eruption or a spot, 57 to determine when it is unclean and when it is clean. This is the ritual for leprous *p* diseases.

15 The LORD spoke to Moses and Aaron, saying: 2 Speak to the people of Israel and say to them: When any man has a discharge from his member,*q* his discharge makes him ceremonially unclean. 3 The uncleanness of his discharge is this: whether his member*q* flows with his discharge, or his member*q* is stopped from discharging, it is uncleanness for him. 4 Every bed on which the one with the discharge lies shall be unclean; and everything on which he sits shall be unclean. 5 Anyone who touches his bed shall wash his clothes, and bathe in water, and be unclean until the evening. 6 All who sit on anything on which the one with the discharge has sat shall wash their clothes, and bathe in water, and be unclean until the evening. 7 All who touch the body of the one with the discharge shall wash their clothes, and bathe in water, and be unclean until the evening. 8 If the one with the discharge spits on persons who are clean, then they shall wash their clothes, and bathe in water, and be unclean until the evening. 9 Any saddle on which the one with the discharge rides shall be unclean. 10 All who touch anything that was under him shall be unclean until the evening, and all who carry such a thing shall wash their clothes, and bathe in water, and be unclean until the evening. 11 All those whom the one with the discharge touches without his having rinsed his hands in water shall wash their clothes, and bathe in water, and be unclean until the evening. 12 Any earthen vessel that the one with the discharge touches shall be broken; and every vessel of wood shall be rinsed in water.

and thrown away outside the town in an unclean place. 41 He must then have the house scraped inside throughout, and all the daub they have scraped off is to be tipped outside the town in an unclean place. 42 They must take fresh stones to replace the others and replaster the house with fresh daub.

43 If the infection reappears in the house and spreads after the stones have been pulled out and the house scraped and redaubed, 44 the priest must come and inspect it. If the infection has spread in the house, it is a corrosive growth; the house is unclean. 45 The house must be demolished, stones, timber, and daub, and everything must be taken away outside the town to an unclean place. 46 Anyone who has entered the house during the time it has been in quarantine will be unclean till evening. 47 Anyone who has slept or eaten a meal in the house must wash his clothes.

48 If, when the priest goes into the house and inspects it, he finds that the infection has not spread after the redaubing, then he must pronounce the house ritually clean, because the infection has been cured. 49 In order to rid the house of impurity, the priest must take two small birds along with cedar-wood, scarlet thread, and marjoram. 50 He must kill one of the birds over an earthenware bowl containing fresh water. 51 He must then take the cedar-wood, marjoram, and scarlet thread, together with the live bird, dip them in the blood of the bird that has been killed and in the fresh water, and sprinkle the house seven times. 52 Thus he must purify the house, using the blood of the bird, the fresh water, the live bird, the cedar-wood, the marjoram, and the scarlet thread. 53 He is to set the live bird free outside the town to fly away over the open country. So he will purify the house, and it will be clean.

54 Such is the law for all virulent skin diseases, and for scale, 55 for mould in clothes and fungus in houses, 56 for a discoloration of the skin, scab, and inflammation, 57 in deciding when these are pronounced unclean and when clean. It is the law for skin disease, mould, and fungus.

15 The LORD told Moses and Aaron 2 to say to the Israelites: When anyone has a discharge from his private parts, the discharge is ritually unclean. 3 This is the law concerning the uncleanness due to his discharge whether it continues or has been stopped; in either case he is unclean.

4 All bedding on which anyone with such a discharge lies will be ritually unclean, and everything on which he sits will be unclean. 5 Anyone who touches the bedding must wash his clothes, bathe in water, and remain unclean till evening. 6 Whoever sits on anything on which the person with this discharge has sat must wash his clothes, bathe in water, and remain unclean till evening. 7 Whoever touches the body of a person with the discharge must wash his clothes, bathe in water, and remain unclean till evening. 8 If the person with such a discharge spits on one who is ritually clean, the latter must wash his clothes, bathe in water, and remain unclean till evening. 9 Everything on which this person sits when riding will be unclean. 10 Whoever touches anything that has been under him will be unclean till evening, and whoever handles such things must wash his clothes, bathe in water, and remain unclean till evening. 11 Anyone whom the person with the discharge touches without having rinsed his hands in water must wash his clothes, bathe in water, and remain unclean till evening. 12 Every earthenware bowl touched by the person must be broken, and every wooden bowl be rinsed with water.

---

p A term for several skin diseases; precise meaning uncertain
q Heb *flesh*

14:41 **daub:** *or* mud. **have scraped off:** *so Syriac; Heb.* have brought to an end.   14:43 **scraped:** *so Gk; Heb.* brought to an end.   15:3 **the law concerning:** *so Gk; Heb. omits.*

and cast in an unclean place outside the city. 41 The whole inside of the house shall then be scraped, and the mortar that has been scraped off shall be dumped in an unclean place outside the city. 42 Then new stones shall be brought and put in the place of the old stones, and new mortar shall be made and plastered on the house.

43 "If the infection breaks out once more after the stones have been pulled out and the house has been scraped and replastered, 44 the priest shall come again; and if he finds that the infection has spread in the house, it is corrosive leprosy, and the house is unclean. 45 It shall be pulled down, and all its stones, beams and mortar shall be hauled away to an unclean place outside the city. 46 Whoever enters a house while it is quarantined shall be unclean until evening. 47 Whoever sleeps or eats in such a house shall also wash his garments. 48 If the priest finds, when he comes to examine the house, that the infection has in fact not spread after the plastering, he shall declare the house clean, since the infection has been healed. 49 To purify the house, he shall take two birds, as well as cedar wood, scarlet yarn, and hyssop. 50 One of the birds he shall slay over an earthen vessel with spring water in it. 51 Then, taking the cedar wood, the hyssop and the scarlet yarn, together with the living bird, he shall dip them all in the blood of the slain bird and the spring water, and sprinkle the house seven times. 52 Thus shall he purify the house with the bird's blood and the spring water, along with the living bird, the cedar wood, the hyssop, and the scarlet yarn. 53 He shall then let the living bird fly away over the countryside outside the city. When he has thus made atonement for it, the house will be clean.

54 "This is the law for every kind of human leprosy and scall, 55 for leprosy of garments and houses, 56 as well as for scabs, pustules and blotches, 57 so that it may be manifest when there is a state of uncleanness and when a state of cleanness. This is the law for leprosy."

15 The LORD said to Moses and Aaron, 2 "Speak to the Israelites and tell them: Every man who is afflicted with a chronic flow from his private parts is thereby unclean. 3 Such is his uncleanness from this flow that it makes no difference whether the flow drains off or is blocked up; his uncleanness remains. 4 Any bed on which the man afflicted with the flow lies, is unclean, and any piece of furniture on which he sits, is unclean. 5 Anyone who touches his bed shall wash his garments, bathe in water, and be unclean until evening. 6 Whoever sits on a piece of furniture on which the afflicted man was sitting, shall wash his garments, bathe in water, and be unclean until evening. 7 Whoever touches the body of the afflicted man shall wash his garments, bathe in water, and be unclean until evening. 8 If the afflicted man spits on a clean man, the latter shall wash his garments, bathe in water, and be unclean until evening. 9 Any saddle on which the afflicted man rides, is unclean. 10 Whoever touches anything that was under him shall be unclean until evening; whoever lifts up any such thing shall wash his garments, bathe in water, and be unclean until evening. 11 Anyone whom the afflicted man touches with unrinsed hands shall wash his garments, bathe in water, and be unclean until evening. 12 Earthenware touched by the afflicted man shall be broken; and every wooden article shall be rinsed with water.

and thrown into some unclean place outside the town. 41 He will then have all the inside of the house scraped, and the plaster that comes off will be emptied in an unclean place outside the town. 42 The stones will then be replaced with new ones and the house given a new coat of plaster.

43 'If the infection spreads again after the stones have been removed and the house scraped and replastered, 44 the priest will come and examine it. If he finds that the infection has spread, this means that there is a contagious disease in the house: it is unclean. 45 It must be pulled down and the stones, woodwork and all the plaster be taken to an unclean place outside the town.

46 'Anyone who enters the house while it is closed will be unclean until evening. 47 Anyone who sleeps there will wash his clothes. Anyone who eats there will wash his clothes. 48 But if the priest finds, when he comes to examine the infection, that it has not spread in the house since it was plastered, he will declare the house clean, for the infection is cured.

49 'As a sacrifice for the defilement of the house, he will take two birds, some cedar wood, scarlet material and hyssop. 50 He will slaughter one of the birds in an earthenware pot over running water. 51 He will then take the cedar wood, the hyssop, the scarlet material and the live bird, dip them into the blood of the slaughtered bird and into the running water and sprinkle the house seven times; 52 and after offering the sacrifice for the defilement of the house with the blood of the bird, the running water, the live bird, the cedar wood, the hyssop and the scarlet material, 53 he will set the live bird free to fly out of the town into the countryside. Once the rite of expiation has been performed for the house in this way it will be clean.

54 'Such is the law governing all kinds of skin-disease and tinea, 55 diseases of clothing and houses, 56 swellings, scabs and spots. It defines the occasions when things are unclean and when clean. 57 Such is the law on skin-diseases.'

15 Yahweh spoke to Moses and Aaron and said: 2 'Speak to the Israelites and say to them:

"When a man has a discharge from his body, that discharge is unclean. 3 While the discharge continues, the nature of his uncleanness is as follows:

"Whether his body allows the discharge to flow or whether it retains it, he is unclean.

4 "Any bed the man lies on and anything he sits on will be unclean.

5 "Anyone who touches his bed must wash clothing and body and will be unclean until evening.

6 "Anyone who sits where the man has sat must wash clothing and body and will be unclean until evening.

7 "Anyone who touches the body of the man with the discharge must wash clothing and body and will be unclean until evening.

8 "If the man with the discharge spits on someone who is clean, that person must wash clothing and body and will be unclean until evening.

9 "Any saddle the man has ridden on will be unclean.

10 "All those who touch any object that has been under him will be unclean until evening.

"Anyone who picks up such an object must wash clothing and body and will be unclean until evening.

11 "All those whom the man with the discharge touches without having washed his hands must wash clothing and body and will be unclean until evening.

12 "The earthenware vessel he touches must be broken and any wooden utensil must be rinsed.

13 When the one with a discharge is cleansed of his discharge, he shall count seven days for his cleansing; he shall wash his clothes and bathe his body in fresh water, and he shall be clean. 14 On the eighth day he shall take two turtledoves or two pigeons and come before the LORD to the entrance of the tent of meeting and give them to the priest. 15 The priest shall offer them, one for a sin offering and the other for a burnt offering; and the priest shall make atonement on his behalf before the LORD for his discharge.

16 If a man has an emission of semen, he shall bathe his whole body in water, and be unclean until the evening. 17 Everything made of cloth or of skin on which the semen falls shall be washed with water, and be unclean until the evening. 18 If a man lies with a woman and has an emission of semen, both of them shall bathe in water, and be unclean until the evening.

19 When a woman has a discharge of blood that is her regular discharge from her body, she shall be in her impurity for seven days, and whoever touches her shall be unclean until the evening. 20 Everything upon which she lies during her impurity shall be unclean; everything also upon which she sits shall be unclean. 21 Whoever touches her bed shall wash his clothes, and bathe in water, and be unclean until the evening. 22 Whoever touches anything upon which she sits shall wash his clothes, and bathe in water, and be unclean until the evening; 23 whether it is the bed or anything upon which she sits, when he touches it he shall be unclean until the evening. 24 If any man lies with her, and her impurity falls on him, he shall be unclean seven days; and every bed on which he lies shall be unclean.

25 If a woman has a discharge of blood for many days, not at the time of her impurity, or if she has a discharge beyond the time of her impurity, all the days of the discharge she shall continue in uncleanness; as in the days of her impurity, she shall be unclean. 26 Every bed on which she lies during all the days of her discharge shall be treated as the bed of her impurity; and everything on which she sits shall be unclean, as in the uncleanness of her impurity. 27 Whoever touches these things shall be unclean, and shall wash his clothes, and bathe in water, and be unclean until the evening. 28 If she is cleansed of her discharge, she shall count seven days, and after that she shall be clean. 29 On the eighth day she shall take two turtledoves or two pigeons and bring them to the priest to the entrance of the tent of meeting. 30 The priest shall offer one for a sin offering and the other for a burnt offering; and the priest shall make atonement on her behalf before the LORD for her unclean discharge.

31 Thus you shall keep the people of Israel separate from their uncleanness, so that they do not die in their uncleanness by defiling my tabernacle that is in their midst.

32 This is the ritual for those who have a discharge: for him who has an emission of semen, becoming unclean thereby, 33 for her who is in the infirmity of her period, for anyone, male or female, who has a discharge, and for the man who lies with a woman who is unclean.

16 The LORD spoke to Moses after the death of the two sons of Aaron, when they drew near before the LORD and died. 2 The LORD said to Moses:

Tell your brother Aaron not to come just at any time into the sanctuary inside the curtain before the mercy seat*r* that is upon the ark, or he will die; for I appear in the cloud upon the mercy seat.*r* 3 Thus shall Aaron come into the holy place: with a young bull for a sin offering and a ram for a burnt offering. 4 He shall put on the holy linen tunic, and

13 When such a person is cleansed from his discharge, he must reckon seven days to his cleansing; then wash his clothes, bathe his body in fresh water, and be ritually clean. 14 On the eighth day he must obtain two turtle-doves or two pigeons, come before the LORD at the entrance to the Tent of Meeting, and give them to the priest. 15 The priest must deal with one as a purification-offering and with the other as a whole-offering, and offer for him before the LORD the expiation on account of the discharge.

16 When a man has emitted semen, he must bathe his whole body in water and be unclean till evening. 17 Every piece of clothing or leather on which there is any semen is to be washed and remain unclean till evening. 18 This applies also to the woman with whom a man has had intercourse; both must bathe in water and remain unclean till evening.

19 When a woman has her discharge of blood, her impurity will last for seven days; anyone who touches her will be unclean till evening. 20 Everything on which she lies or sits during her impurity will be unclean, 21 and whoever touches her bedding must wash his clothes, bathe in water, and remain unclean till evening. 22 Whoever touches anything on which she sits must wash his clothes, bathe in water, and remain unclean till evening. 23 If it is the bed or seat where she is sitting, by touching it he will become unclean till evening. 24 If a man goes so far as to have intercourse with her and any of her discharge gets on to him, then he will be unclean for seven days, and any bedding on which he lies down will be unclean.

25 If a woman has a prolonged discharge of blood not at the time of her menstruation, or if her discharge continues beyond the period of menstruation, her impurity will last all the time of her discharge; she will be unclean as during the period of her menstruation. 26 Any bedding on which she lies during the time of her discharge will be like that which she used during menstruation, and everything on which she sits will be unclean as in her menstrual uncleanness. 27 Anyone who touches them will be unclean; he must wash his clothes, bathe in water, and remain unclean till evening. 28 If she becomes cleansed from her discharge, she must reckon seven days and after that she will be ritually clean. 29 On the eighth day she is to obtain two turtle-doves or two pigeons and bring them to the priest at the entrance to the Tent of Meeting. 30 The priest must deal with one as a purification-offering and with the other as a whole-offering, and offer for her before the LORD the expiation on account of her unclean discharge.

31 In this way you must warn the Israelites against uncleanness, in order that they may not die by bringing uncleanness upon the Tabernacle where I dwell among them.

32 Such is the law for the man who has a discharge, for him who has an emission of semen and is thereby unclean, 33 and for the woman who is suffering her menstruation— for everyone, male or female, who has a discharge, and for the man who has intercourse with a woman who is unclean.

16 THE LORD spoke to Moses after the death of Aaron's two sons, who died when they offered illicit fire before the LORD. 2 He said to him: Tell your brother Aaron that on pain of death he must not enter the sanctuary behind the curtain, which is in front of the cover over the Ark, except at the appointed time; for I appear in the cloud above the cover. 3 When Aaron enters the sanctuary, this is what he must do. He must bring a young bull for a purification-offering and a ram for a whole-offering; 4 he is to wear

16:1 **when . . . LORD:** *so Gk; Heb.* when they came near before the LORD.

r Or the cover

13 "When a man who has been afflicted with a flow becomes free of his affliction, he shall wait seven days for his purification. Then he shall wash his garments and bathe his body in fresh water, and so he will be clean. 14 On the eighth day he shall take two turtledoves or two pigeons, and going before the LORD, to the entrance of the meeting tent, he shall give them to the priest, 15 who shall offer them up, the one as a sin offering and the other as a holocaust. Thus shall the priest make atonement before the LORD for the man's flow.

16 "When a man has an emission of seed, he shall bathe his whole body in water and be unclean until evening. 17 Any piece of cloth or leather with seed on it shall be washed with water and be unclean until evening.

18 "If a man lies carnally with a woman, they shall both bathe in water and be unclean until evening.

19 "When a woman has her menstrual flow, she shall be in a state of impurity for seven days. Anyone who touches her shall be unclean until evening. 20 Anything on which she lies or sits during her impurity shall be unclean. 21 Anyone who touches her bed shall wash his garments, bathe in water, and be unclean until evening. 22 Whoever touches any article of furniture on which she was sitting, shall wash his garments, bathe in water, and be unclean until evening. 23 But if she is on the bed or on the seat when he touches it, he shall be unclean until evening. 24 If a man dares to lie with her, he contracts her impurity and shall be unclean for seven days; every bed on which he then lies also becomes unclean.

25 "When a woman is afflicted with a flow of blood for several days outside her menstrual period, or when her flow continues beyond the ordinary period, as long as she suffers this unclean flow she shall be unclean, just as during her menstrual period. 26 Any bed on which she lies during such a flow becomes unclean, as it would during her menstruation, and any article of furniture on which she sits becomes unclean just as during her menstruation. 27 Anyone who touches them becomes unclean; he shall wash his garments, bathe in water, and be unclean until evening.

28 "If she becomes freed from her affliction, she shall wait seven days, and only then is she to be purified. 29 On the eighth day she shall take two turtledoves or two pigeons and bring them to the priest at the entrance of the meeting tent. 30 The priest shall offer up one of them as a sin offering and the other as a holocaust. Thus shall the priest make atonement before the LORD for her unclean flow.

31 "You shall warn the Israelites of their uncleanness, lest by defiling my Dwelling, which is in their midst, their uncleanness be the cause of their death.

32 "This is the law for the man who is afflicted with a chronic flow, or who has an emission of seed, and thereby becomes unclean; 33 as well as for the woman who has her menstrual period, or who is afflicted with a chronic flow; the law for male and female; and also for the man who lies with an unclean woman."

16 After the death of Aaron's two sons, who died when they approached the LORD's presence, the LORD spoke to Moses 2 and said to him, "Tell your brother Aaron that he is not to come whenever he pleases into the sanctuary, inside the veil, in front of the propitiatory on the ark; otherwise, when I reveal myself in a cloud above the propitiatory, he will die. 3 Only in this way may Aaron enter the sanctuary. He shall bring a young bullock for a sin offering and a ram for a holocaust. 4 He shall wear the

13 "Once the man with the discharge is cured, he will allow seven days for his purification. He will wash his clothes and wash his body in running water and he will be clean. 14 On the eighth day he will take two turtledoves or two young pigeons and come before Yahweh at the entrance to the Tent of Meeting and give them to the priest. 15 The priest will offer one of them as a sacrifice for sin and the other as a burnt offering. And in this way the priest will perform the rite of expiation for him before Yahweh for his discharge.

16 "When a man has a seminal discharge, he must wash his whole body with water and will be unclean until evening. 17 Any clothing or leather touched by the seminal discharge must be washed and will be unclean until evening. 18 When a woman has had intercourse with a man, both of them must wash and will be unclean until evening.

19 "Whenever a woman has a discharge and the discharge from her body is of blood, she will remain in a state of menstrual pollution for seven days.

"Anyone who touches her will be unclean until evening. 20 "Anything she lies on in this polluted state will be unclean; anything she sits on will be unclean.

21 "Anyone who touches her bed must wash clothing and body and will be unclean until evening.

22 "Anyone who touches anything she has sat on must wash clothing and body and will be unclean until evening. 23 If there is anything on the bed or where she is sitting, anyone who touches it will be unclean until evening.

24 "If a man goes so far as to sleep with her, he will contract her menstrual pollution and will be unclean for seven days. Any bed he lies on will be unclean.

25 "If a woman has a prolonged discharge of blood outside the period, or if the period is prolonged, during the time this discharge lasts she will be in the same state of uncleanness as during her monthly periods. 26 Any bed she lies on during the time this discharge lasts will be polluted in the same way as the bed she lies on during her monthly periods. Anything she sits on will be unclean as during her monthly periods. 27 Anyone who touches it will be unclean and must wash clothing and body and will be unclean until evening.

28 "Once she is cured of her discharge, she will allow seven days to go by; after that she will be clean. 29 On the eighth day she will take two turtledoves or two young pigeons and bring them to the priest at the entrance to the Tent of Meeting. 30 The priest will offer one of them as a sacrifice for sin and the other as a burnt offering. And in this way the priest will perform the rite of expiation for her before Yahweh for the discharge which made her unclean.

31 "Hence you will warn the Israelites against contracting a state of uncleanness, rather than incurring death by defiling my Dwelling which is among them.

32 "Such is the law governing a man with a discharge or who is made unclean by a seminal discharge, 33 a woman in a state of pollution due to menstruation, a man or a woman with a discharge, or a man who sleeps with a woman when she is unclean." '

16 c Yahweh spoke to Moses after the death of the two sons of Aaron who died when offering unauthorised fire. 2 Yahweh spoke to Moses and said:

'Tell Aaron your brother that he may not enter the sanctuary inside the curtain in front of the mercy-seat on the ark whenever he chooses, in case he incurs death, for I appear in a cloud on the mercy-seat.

3 'This is how he must enter the sanctuary: with a young bull for a sacrifice for sin and a ram for a burnt offering.

c 16 The Day of Expiation: An important annual festival combining 1 a sacrifice of expiation by blood and 2 a primitive ritual of driving the bearer of sin away from the community.

shall have the linen undergarments next to his body, fasten the linen sash, and wear the linen turban; these are the holy vestments. He shall bathe his body in water, and then put them on. 5 He shall take from the congregation of the people of Israel two male goats for a sin offering, and one ram for a burnt offering.

6 Aaron shall offer the bull as a sin offering for himself, and shall make atonement for himself and for his house. 7 He shall take the two goats and set them before the LORD at the entrance of the tent of meeting; 8 and Aaron shall cast lots on the two goats, one lot for the LORD and the other lot for Azazel.s 9 Aaron shall present the goat on which the lot fell for the LORD, and offer it as a sin offering; 10 but the goat on which the lot fell for Azazels shall be presented alive before the LORD to make atonement over it, that it may be sent away into the wilderness to Azazel.s

11 Aaron shall present the bull as a sin offering for himself, and shall make atonement for himself and for his house; he shall slaughter the bull as a sin offering for himself. 12 He shall take a censer full of coals of fire from the altar before the LORD, and two handfuls of crushed sweet incense, and he shall bring it inside the curtain 13 and put the incense on the fire before the LORD, that the cloud of the incense may cover the mercy seatt that is upon the covenant,u or he will die. 14 He shall take some of the blood of the bull, and sprinkle it with his finger on the front of the mercy seat,t and before the mercy seatt he shall sprinkle the blood with his finger seven times.

15 He shall slaughter the goat of the sin offering that is for the people and bring its blood inside the curtain, and do with its blood as he did with the blood of the bull, sprinkling it upon the mercy seatt and before the mercy seat.t 16 Thus he shall make atonement for the sanctuary, because of the uncleannesses of the people of Israel, and because of their transgressions, all their sins; and so he shall do for the tent of meeting, which remains with them in the midst of their uncleannesses. 17 No one shall be in the tent of meeting from the time he enters to make atonement in the sanctuary until he comes out and has made atonement for himself and for his house and for all the assembly of Israel. 18 Then he shall go out to the altar that is before the LORD and make atonement on its behalf, and shall take some of the blood of the bull and of the blood of the goat, and put it on each of the horns of the altar. 19 He shall sprinkle some of the blood on it with his finger seven times, and cleanse it and hallow it from the uncleannesses of the people of Israel.

20 When he has finished atoning for the holy place and the tent of meeting and the altar, he shall present the live goat. 21 Then Aaron shall lay both his hands on the head of the live goat, and confess over it all the iniquities of the people of Israel, and all their transgressions, all their sins, putting them on the head of the goat, and sending it away into the wilderness by means of someone designated for the task.v 22 The goat shall bear on itself all their iniquities to a barren region; and the goat shall be set free in the wilderness.

23 Then Aaron shall enter the tent of meeting, and shall take off the linen vestments that he put on when he went into the holy place, and shall leave them there. 24 He shall bathe his body in water in a holy place, and put on his vestments; then he shall come out and offer his burnt offering and the burnt offering of the people, making atonement for himself and for the people. 25 The fat of the sin offering he shall turn into smoke on the altar. 26 The one who sets the goat free for Azazels shall wash his clothes and bathe his body in water, and afterward may come into the camp.

a sacred linen tunic and linen shorts to cover himself, and he is to put a linen sash round his waist and wind a linen turban round his head; all these are sacred vestments, and he must bathe in water before putting them on. 5 He is to receive from the community of the Israelites two he-goats for a purification-offering and a ram for a whole-offering.

6 He must offer the bull reserved for his purification-offering and make expiation for himself and his household. 7 Then he must take the two he-goats and set them before the LORD at the entrance to the Tent of Meeting. 8 He must cast lots over the two goats, one to be for the LORD and the other for Azazel. 9 He must present the goat on which the lot for the LORD has fallen and deal with it as a purification-offering; 10 but the goat on which the lot for Azazel has fallen is to be made to stand alive before the LORD, for expiation to be made over it, before it is driven away into the wilderness to Azazel.

11 Aaron must present his bull as a purification-offering, making expiation for himself and his household. He is to slaughter the bull as a purification-offering, 12 and then take a censer full of glowing embers from the altar before the LORD, and a double handful of powdered fragrant incense, and bring them behind the curtain. 13 He is to put the incense on the fire before the LORD, and the cloud of incense will hide the cover over the Tokens so that he may not die. 14 He must take some of the bull's blood and sprinkle it with his finger both on the surface of the cover, eastwards, and seven times in front of the cover.

15 He must then slaughter the goat for the people's purification-offering, bring its blood behind the curtain, and do with its blood as he did with the bull's blood, sprinkling it on the cover and in front of it. 16 So is he to purge the sanctuary of the ritual uncleanness of the Israelites and their acts of rebellion, that is, of all their sins; and he must do the same for the Tent of Meeting, which is present among them in the midst of their uncleanness. 17 No one else must be within the Tent of Meeting from the time when he goes in to effect cleansing in the sanctuary until he comes out. So is he to make expiation for himself, his household, and the whole assembly of Israel.

18 Then he is to come out to the altar which is before the LORD and purify it, take some of the bull's blood and some of the goat's blood, and smear them over each of the horns of the altar; 19 he is to sprinkle some of the blood on the altar with his finger seven times. So he will purify it from all the uncleanness of the Israelites and hallow it.

20 When Aaron has finished the purification of the sanctuary, the Tent of Meeting, and the altar, he is to bring forward the live goat. 21 Laying both his hands on its head he must confess over it all the iniquities of the Israelites and all their acts of rebellion, that is all their sins; he is to lay his hands on the head of the goat and send it away into the wilderness in the charge of a man who is waiting ready. 22 The goat will carry all their iniquities upon itself into some barren waste, where the man will release it, there in the wilderness.

23 Aaron is then to enter the Tent of Meeting, take off the linen clothes which he had put on when he entered the sanctuary, and leave them there. 24 He must bathe in water in a consecrated place and, after putting on his vestments, he is to go out and perform his own whole-offering and that of the people, thus making expiation for himself and for the people. 25 He must burn the fat of the purification-offering upon the altar.

26 The man who drove the goat away to Azazel must wash his clothes and bathe in water, and not till then may he enter the camp. 27 The two purification-offerings, the bull and the

---

NEW AMERICAN BIBLE	NEW JERUSALEM BIBLE

NEW AMERICAN BIBLE

sacred linen tunic, with the linen drawers next his flesh, gird himself with the linen sash and put on the linen miter. But since these vestments are sacred, he shall not put them on until he has first bathed his body in water. 5 From the Israelite community he shall receive two male goats for a sin offering and one ram for a holocaust.

6 "Aaron shall bring in the bullock, his sin offering to atone for himself and for his household. 7 Taking the two male goats, and setting them before the LORD at the entrance of the meeting tent, 8 he shall cast lots to determine which one is for the LORD and which for Azazel. 9 The goat that is determined by lot for the LORD, Aaron shall bring in and offer up as a sin offering. 10 But the goat determined by lot for Azazel he shall set alive before the LORD, so that with it he may make atonement by sending it off to Azazel in the desert.

11 "Thus shall Aaron offer up the bullock, his sin offering, to atone for himself and for his family. When he has slaughtered it, 12 he shall take a censer full of glowing embers from the altar before the LORD, as well as a double handfull of finely ground fragrant incense, and bringing them inside the veil, 13 there before the LORD he shall put incense on the fire, so that a cloud of incense may cover the propitiatory over the commandments; else he will die. 14 Taking some of the bullock's blood, he shall sprinkle it with his finger on the fore part of the propitiatory and likewise sprinkle some of the blood with his finger seven times in front of the propitiatory.

15 "Then he shall slaughter the people's sin-offering goat, and bringing its blood inside the veil, he shall do with it as he did with the bullock's blood, sprinkling it on the propitiatory and before it. 16 Thus he shall make atonement for the sanctuary because of all the sinful defilements and faults of the Israelites. He shall do the same for the meeting tent, which is set up among them in the midst of their uncleanness. 17 No one else may be in the meeting tent from the time he enters the sanctuary to make atonement until he departs. When he has made atonement for himself and his household, as well as for the whole Israelite community, 18 he shall come out to the altar before the LORD and make atonement for it also. Taking some of the bullock's and the goat's blood, he shall put it on the horns around the altar, 19 and with his finger sprinkle some of the blood on it seven times. Thus he shall render it clean and holy, purged of the defilements of the Israelites.

20 "When he has completed the atonement rite for the sanctuary, the meeting tent and the altar, Aaron shall bring forward the live goat. 21 Laying both hands on its head, he shall confess over it all the sinful faults and transgressions of the Israelites, and so put them on the goat's head. He shall then have it led into the desert by an attendant. 22 Since the goat is to carry off their iniquities to an isolated region, it must be sent away into the desert.

23 "After Aaron has again gone into the meeting tent, he shall strip off and leave in the sanctuary the linen vestments he had put on when he entered there. 24 After bathing his body with water in a sacred place, he shall put on his vestments, and then come out and offer his own and the people's holocaust, in atonement for himself and for the people, 25 and also burn the fat of the sin offering on the altar.

26 "The man who has led away the goat for Azazel shall wash his garments and bathe his body in water; only then may he enter the camp. 27 The sin-offering bullock and goat

NEW JERUSALEM BIBLE

4 He will put on a tunic of consecrated linen, wear linen drawers on his body, a linen waistband round his waist, and a linen turban on his head. These are the sacred vestments he will put on after washing himself.

5 'From the community of Israelites he will receive two he-goats for a sacrifice for sin and a ram for a burnt offering. 6 After offering the bull as a sacrifice for his own sin and performing the rite of expiation for himself and his family, 7 he will take the two he-goats and place them before Yahweh at the entrance to the Tent of Meeting. 8 Aaron will then draw lots over the two goats, one lot to be for Yahweh and the other lot for Azazel. 9 Aaron will then take the goat on which the lot "For Yahweh" has fallen, and offer it as a sacrifice for sin. 10 But the goat on which the lot "For Azazel" has fallen, will be placed alive before Yahweh, for the rite of expiation to be performed with it, and for it then to be sent to Azazel in the desert.

11 'Having offered the bull as a sacrifice for his own sin and performed the rite of expiation for himself and for his family, and slaughtered the bull as a sacrifice for sin, 12 Aaron will then fill a censer with live coals from the altar before Yahweh, take two handfuls of finely ground aromatic incense and bring this inside the curtain. 13 He will then put the incense on the fire before Yahweh, so that the cloud of incense hides the mercy-seat which is on the Testimony and he does not incur death. 14 He will then take some of the bull's blood and sprinkle it with his finger on the eastern side of the mercy-seat. He will sprinkle some of the blood seven times with his finger in front of the mercy-seat.

15 'He will then slaughter the goat for the sacrifice for the sin of the people, and take its blood inside the curtain, and with this blood do as he did with the blood of the bull, sprinkling it on the mercy-seat and in front of it. 16 This is how he must perform the rite of expiation for the sanctuary for the uncleanness of the Israelites, for their acts of rebellion and all their sins.

'And this is what he must do for the Tent of Meeting which remains with them, surrounded by their uncleanness. 17 No one must be inside the Tent of Meeting, from the moment he enters to make expiation in the sanctuary until the time he comes out.

'When he has made expiation for himself, for his family, and for the whole community of Israel, 18 he must come outside, go to the altar before Yahweh and perform the rite of expiation for it. He will take some of the bull's blood and some of the goat's blood and put it on the horns at the corners of the altar all around it, 19 and sprinkle some of the blood on it seven times with his finger, thus purifying it and setting it apart from the uncleanness of the Israelites.

20 'Once expiation for the sanctuary, the Tent of Meeting and the altar is complete, he will bring the goat which is still alive. 21 Aaron will then lay both his hands on its head and over it confess all the guilt of the Israelites, all their acts of rebellion and all their sins. Having thus laid them on the goat's head, he will send it out into the desert under the charge of a man waiting ready, 22 and the goat will bear all their guilt away into some desolate place.

'When he has sent the goat into the desert, 23 Aaron will go back into the Tent of Meeting and take off the linen vestments which he wore to enter the sanctuary and leave them there. 24 He will then wash his body inside the holy place, put on his vestments and come outside to offer his own and the people's burnt offering. He will perform the rite of expiation for himself and for the people, 25 and burn the fat of the sacrifice for sin on the altar.

26 'The man who led the goat away to Azazel will wash his clothes and body before entering the camp. 27 The bull

NEW REVISED STANDARD VERSION

27 The bull of the sin offering and the goat of the sin offering, whose blood was brought in to make atonement in the holy place, shall be taken outside the camp; their skin and their flesh and their dung shall be consumed in fire. 28 The one who burns them shall wash his clothes and bathe his body in water, and afterward may come into the camp.

29 This shall be a statute to you forever: In the seventh month, on the tenth day of the month, you shall deny yourselves,*w* and shall do no work, neither the citizen nor the alien who resides among you. 30 For on this day atonement shall be made for you, to cleanse you; from all your sins you shall be clean before the LORD. 31 It is a sabbath of complete rest to you, and you shall deny yourselves;*w* it is a statute forever. 32 The priest who is anointed and consecrated as priest in his father's place shall make atonement, wearing the linen vestments, the holy vestments. 33 He shall make atonement for the sanctuary, and he shall make atonement for the tent of meeting and for the altar, and he shall make atonement for the priests and for all the people of the assembly. 34 This shall be an everlasting statute for you, to make atonement for the people of Israel once in the year for all their sins. And Moses did as the LORD had commanded him.

17 The LORD spoke to Moses: 2 Speak to Aaron and his sons and to all the people of Israel and say to them: This is what the LORD has commanded. 3 If anyone of the house of Israel slaughters an ox or a lamb or a goat in the camp, or slaughters it outside the camp, 4 and does not bring it to the entrance of the tent of meeting, to present it as an offering to the LORD before the tabernacle of the LORD, he shall be held guilty of bloodshed; he has shed blood, and he shall be cut off from the people. 5 This is in order that the people of Israel may bring their sacrifices that they offer in the open field, that they may bring them to the LORD, to the priest at the entrance of the tent of meeting, and offer them as sacrifices of wellbeing to the LORD. 6 The priest shall dash the blood against the altar of the LORD at the entrance of the tent of meeting, and turn the fat into smoke as a pleasing odor to the LORD, 7 so that they may no longer offer their sacrifices for goatdemons, to whom they prostitute themselves. This shall be a statute forever to them throughout their generations.

8 And say to them further: Anyone of the house of Israel or of the aliens who reside among them who offers a burnt offering or sacrifice, 9 and does not bring it to the entrance of the tent of meeting, to sacrifice it to the LORD, shall be cut off from the people.

10 If anyone of the house of Israel or of the aliens who reside among them eats any blood, I will set my face against that person who eats blood, and will cut that person off from the people. 11 For the life of the flesh is in the blood; and I have given it to you for making atonement for your lives on the altar; for, as life, it is the blood that makes atonement. 12 Therefore I have said to the people of Israel: No person among you shall eat blood, nor shall any alien who resides among you eat blood. 13 And anyone of the people of Israel, or of the aliens who reside among them, who hunts down an animal or bird that may be eaten shall pour out its blood and cover it with earth.

14 For the life of every creature — its blood is its life; therefore I have said to the people of Israel: You shall not eat the blood of any creature, for the life of every creature is its blood; whoever eats it shall be cut off. 15 All persons, citizens or aliens, who eat what dies of itself or what has been torn by wild animals, shall wash their clothes, and bathe themselves in water, and be unclean until the evening; then they shall be clean. 16 But if they do not wash themselves or bathe their body, they shall bear their guilt.

REVISED ENGLISH BIBLE

goat, the blood of which was brought behind the curtain to purge the sanctuary of ritual uncleanness, must be taken outside the camp and destroyed by fire — hide, flesh, and offal. 28 The man who burns them must wash his clothes and bathe in water, and not till then may he enter the camp.

29 This is to be a rule binding on you for all time: on the tenth day of the seventh month you must fast; you, whether native Israelite or alien settler among you, must do no work, 30 because on this day expiation will be made on your behalf to cleanse you, and so make you clean before the LORD from all your sins. 31 This is a sabbath of solemn abstinence from work for you, and you must mortify yourselves; it is a rule binding for all time. 32 Expiation is to be made by the priest duly anointed and ordained to serve in succession to his father; he is to put on the sacred linen clothes 33 and purify of ritual uncleanness the holy sanctuary, the Tent of Meeting, and the altar, on behalf of the priests and the whole assembly of the people. 34 This is to become a rule binding on you for all time, to offer for the Israelites once a year the expiation required by all their sins.

It was carried out as the LORD commanded Moses.

17 THE LORD told Moses 2 to say to Aaron, his sons, and all the Israelites: This is what the LORD has commanded. 3 Any Israelite who slaughters an ox, a sheep, or a goat, either inside or outside the camp, 4 and has not brought it to the entrance of the Tent of Meeting to present it as an offering to the LORD before his Tabernacle is to be held guilty of bloodshed: he has shed blood and will be cut off from his people. 5 The purpose is that the Israelites should bring to the LORD the animals which they have been slaughtering in the open country; they must bring them to the priest at the entrance to the Tent of Meeting and offer them as shared-offerings to the LORD. 6 The priest will fling the blood against the altar of the LORD at the entrance to the Tent of Meeting, and burn the fat as a soothing odour to the LORD. 7 No longer are they to offer their slaughtered beasts to the demons whom they wantonly follow. This is to be a rule binding on them and their descendants for all time.

8 You must warn them: Any Israelite or alien settled in Israel who offers a whole-offering or a sacrifice 9 and does not bring it to the entrance of the Tent of Meeting to offer it to the LORD is to be cut off from his father's kin.

10 If any Israelite or alien settled in Israel consumes any blood, I shall set my face against him and cut him off from his people, 11 because the life of a creature is the blood, and I appoint it to make expiation on the altar for yourselves: it is the blood, which is the life, that makes expiation. 12 Therefore I have told you Israelites that neither you, nor any alien settled among you, is to consume blood.

13 Any Israelite or alien settled in Israel who hunts beasts or birds that may lawfully be eaten must drain out the blood and cover it with earth, 14 because the life of every living creature is its blood, and I have forbidden the Israelites to consume the blood of any creature, because the life of every creature is its blood: whoever eats it is to be cut off.

15 Every person, native or alien, who eats something which has died a natural death or has been mauled by wild beasts must wash his clothes and bathe in water, and remain ritually unclean till evening; then he will be clean. 16 But if he does not wash his clothes and bathe his body, he must accept responsibility.

---

w Or *shall fast*   16:29 **This:** *so Gk; Heb. omits.*   17:7 **demons:** *or satyrs.*

NEW AMERICAN BIBLE

whose blood was brought into the sanctuary to make atonement, shall be taken outside the camp, where their hides and flesh and offal shall be burned up in the fire. 28 The one who burns them shall wash his garments and bathe his body in water; only then may he enter the camp.

29 "This shall be an everlasting ordinance for you: on the tenth day of the seventh month every one of you, whether a native or a resident alien, shall mortify himself and shall do no work. 30 Since on this day atonement is made for you to make you clean, so that you may be cleansed of all your sins before the LORD, 31 by everlasting ordinance it shall be a most solemn sabbath for you, on which you must mortify yourselves.

32 "This atonement is to be made by the priest who has been anointed and ordained to the priesthood in succession to his father. He shall wear the linen garments, the sacred vestments, 33 and make atonement for the sacred sanctuary, the meeting tent and the altar, as well as for the priests and all the people of the community. 34 This, then, shall be an everlasting ordinance for you: once a year atonement shall be made for all the sins of the Israelites."

Thus was it done, as the LORD had commanded Moses.

17 The LORD said to Moses, 2 "Speak to Aaron and his sons, as well as to all the Israelites, and tell them: This is what the LORD has commanded. 3 Any Israelite who slaughters an ox or a sheep or a goat, whether in the camp or outside of it, 4 without first bringing it to the entrance of the meeting tent to present it as an offering to the LORD in front of his Dwelling, shall be judged guilty of bloodshed; and for this, such a man shall be cut off from among his people. 5 Therefore, such sacrifices as they used to offer up in the open field the Israelites shall henceforth offer to the LORD, bringing them to the priest at the entrance of the meeting tent and sacrificing them there as peace offerings to the LORD. 6 The priest shall splash the blood on the altar of the LORD at the entrance of the meeting tent and there burn the fat for an odor pleasing to the LORD. 7 No longer shall they offer their sacrifices to the satyrs to whom they used to render their wanton worship. This shall be an everlasting ordinance for them and their descendants.

8 "Tell them, therefore: Anyone, whether of the house of Israel or of the aliens residing among them, who offers a holocaust or sacrifice 9 without bringing it to the entrance of the meeting tent to offer it to the LORD, shall be cut off from his kinsmen. 10 And if anyone, whether of the house of Israel or of the aliens residing among them, partakes of any blood, I will set myself against that one who partakes of blood and will cut him off from among his people. 11 Since the life of a living body is in its blood, I have made you put it on the altar, so that atonement may thereby be made for your own lives, because it is the blood, as the seat of life, that makes atonement. 12 That is why I have told the Israelites: No one among you, not even a resident alien, may partake of blood.

13 "Anyone hunting, whether of the Israelites or of the aliens residing among them, who catches an animal or a bird that may be eaten, shall pour out its blood and cover it with earth. 14 Since the life of every living body is its blood, I have told the Israelites: You shall not partake of the blood of any meat. Since the life of every living body is its blood, anyone who partakes of it shall be cut off.

15 "Everyone, whether a native or an alien, who eats of an animal that died of itself or was killed by a wild beast, shall wash his garments, bathe in water, and be unclean until evening, and then he will be clean. 16 If he does not wash or does not bathe his body, he shall have the guilt to bear."

NEW JERUSALEM BIBLE

and the goat offered as a sacrifice for sin, the blood of which was taken into the sanctuary for the rite of expiation, must be taken outside the camp, where their skin, meat and offal are to be burnt. 28 The man who burns them will wash his clothes and body before entering the camp.

29 'This will be a perpetual law for you.

'On the tenth day of the seventh month you will fast and refrain from work, both citizen and resident alien; 30 for this is the day on which the rite of expiation will be performed for you to purify you, to purify you before Yahweh from all your sins. 31 It will be a sabbatical rest for you and you will fast. This is a perpetual law.

32 'The rite of expiation will be performed by the priest who has been anointed and installed to officiate in succession to his father. He will put on the linen vestments, the sacred vestments, 33 and perform the rite of expiation for the holy sanctuary, the Tent of Meeting and the altar, and will then perform the rite of expiation for the priests and all the people of the community. 34 This will be a perpetual law for you; once a year the rite of expiation will be made for the Israelites for all their sins.'

And as Yahweh ordered Moses, so it was done.

17 Yahweh spoke to Moses and said: 2 'Speak to Aaron and his sons and all the Israelites and say:

"This is the order that Yahweh has given:

3 "Any man of the House of Israel who slaughters a bull, lamb or goat, whether inside the camp or outside it, 4 without bringing it to the entrance of the Tent of Meeting to make an offering of it to Yahweh in front of his Dwelling, that man will be answerable for bloodshed; he has shed blood, and that man will be outlawed from his people. 5 The purpose of this is that the Israelites should instead bring their sacrifices, which they would otherwise offer in the countryside, to Yahweh at the entrance to the Tent of Meeting, to the priest, and offer them as communion sacrifices to Yahweh; 6 and the priest will sprinkle the blood on Yahweh's altar at the entrance to the Tent of Meeting and will burn the fat as a smell pleasing to Yahweh. 7 No longer may they offer their sacrifices to the satyrs in whose service they used to prostitute themselves. This is a perpetual law for them and for their descendants."

8 'You will also say to them, "Any member of the House of Israel or any resident alien who offers a burnt offering or sacrifice 9 without bringing it to the entrance to the Tent of Meeting to offer it to Yahweh, will be outlawed from his people.

10 "If any member of the House of Israel or any resident alien consumes blood of any kind, I shall set my face against that individual who consumes blood and shall outlaw him from his people. 11 For the life of the creature is in the blood, and I have given it to you for performing the rite of expiation on the altar for your lives, for blood is what expiates for a life. 12 That is why I told the Israelites: None of you will consume blood, nor will any resident alien consume blood.

13 "Anyone, whether Israelite or resident alien, who hunts and catches game, whether animal or bird, which it is lawful to eat, must pour out its blood and cover it with earth. 14 For the life of every creature is its blood, and I have told the Israelites: You will not consume the blood of any creature, for the life of every creature is its blood, and anyone who consumes it will be outlawed.

15 "Anyone, citizen or alien, who eats an animal that has died a natural death or been savaged, must wash clothing and body, and will be unclean until evening, but will then be clean. 16 But anyone who does not wash clothing and body will bear the consequences of his guilt." '

18 The LORD spoke to Moses, saying: 2 Speak to the people of Israel and say to them: I am the LORD your God. 3 You shall not do as they do in the land of Egypt, where you lived, and you shall not do as they do in the land of Canaan, to which I am bringing you. You shall not follow their statutes. 4 My ordinances you shall observe and my statutes you shall keep, following them: I am the LORD your God. 5 You shall keep my statutes and my ordinances; by doing so one shall live: I am the LORD.

6 None of you shall approach anyone near of kin to uncover nakedness: I am the LORD. 7 You shall not uncover the nakedness of your father, which is the nakedness of your mother; she is your mother, you shall not uncover her nakedness. 8 You shall not uncover the nakedness of your father's wife; it is the nakedness of your father. 9 You shall not uncover the nakedness of your sister, your father's daughter or your mother's daughter, whether born at home or born abroad. 10 You shall not uncover the nakedness of your son's daughter or of your daughter's daughter, for their nakedness is your own nakedness. 11 You shall not uncover the nakedness of your father's wife's daughter, begotten by your father, since she is your sister. 12 You shall not uncover the nakedness of your father's sister; she is your father's flesh. 13 You shall not uncover the nakedness of your mother's sister, for she is your mother's flesh. 14 You shall not uncover the nakedness of your father's brother, that is, you shall not approach his wife; she is your aunt. 15 You shall not uncover the nakedness of your daughter-in-law: she is your son's wife; you shall not uncover her nakedness. 16 You shall not uncover the nakedness of your brother's wife; it is your brother's nakedness. 17 You shall not uncover the nakedness of a woman and her daughter, and you shall not take[x] her son's daughter or her daughter's daughter to uncover her nakedness; they are your[y] flesh; it is depravity. 18 And you shall not take[x] a woman as a rival to her sister, uncovering her nakedness while her sister is still alive.

19 You shall not approach a woman to uncover her nakedness while she is in her menstrual uncleanness. 20 You shall not have sexual relations with your kinsman's wife, and defile yourself with her. 21 You shall not give any of your offspring to sacrifice them[z] to Molech, and so profane the name of your God: I am the LORD. 22 You shall not lie with a male as with a woman; it is an abomination. 23 You shall not have sexual relations with any animal and defile yourself with it, nor shall any woman give herself to an animal to have sexual relations with it: it is perversion.

24 Do not defile yourselves in any of these ways, for by all these practices the nations I am casting out before you have defiled themselves. 25 Thus the land became defiled; and I punished it for its iniquity, and the land vomited out its inhabitants. 26 But you shall keep my statutes and my

18 THE LORD told Moses 2 to say to the Israelites: I am the LORD your God. 3 You must not do as they do in Egypt where once you dwelt, nor may you do as they do in Canaan to which I am bringing you; you must not conform to their customs. 4 You must keep my laws and conform faithfully to my statutes: I am the LORD your God. 5 Observe my statutes and my laws: whoever keeps them will have life through them. I am the LORD.

6 No man may approach a blood relation for intercourse. I am the LORD. 7 You must not bring shame on your father by intercourse with your mother: she is your mother; do not bring shame on her. 8 You must not have intercourse with a wife of your father: that is to bring shame upon your father. 9 You must not have intercourse with your sister, either your father's daughter or your mother's daughter, whether brought up in the family or in another home; you must not bring shame on them. 10 You must not have intercourse with your son's daughter or your daughter's daughter: that is to bring shame on yourself. 11 You must not have intercourse with a daughter of a wife of your father, begotten by your father, because she is your sister; do not bring shame on her. 12 You must not have intercourse with your father's sister; she is a blood relation of your father. 13 You must not have intercourse with your mother's sister: she is a blood relation of your mother. 14 You must not bring shame on your father's brother by approaching his wife, because she is your aunt. 15 You must not have intercourse with your daughter-in-law, because she is your son's wife; you must not bring shame on her. 16 You must not have intercourse with your brother's wife: that is to bring shame on him. 17 You must not have intercourse with both a woman and her daughter, nor may you take her son's daughter or her daughter's daughter to have intercourse with them: they are blood relations, and such conduct is lewdness. 18 You must not take a woman who is your wife's sister to make her a rival wife, and to have intercourse with her during her sister's lifetime.

19 You must not approach a woman to have intercourse with her during her period of menstruation. 20 Do not have sexual intercourse with the wife of your fellow-countryman and so make yourself unclean with her. 21 You must not surrender any of your children to Molech and thus profane the name of your God: I am the LORD. 22 You must not lie with a man as with a woman: that is an abomination. 23 You must not have sexual intercourse with any animal to make yourself unclean with it, nor may a woman submit herself to intercourse with an animal: that is a violation of nature.

24 You must not make yourselves unclean in any of those ways; for in such ways the nations, whom I am driving out before you, made themselves unclean. 25 That is how the land became unclean, and I punished it for its iniquity so that it spewed out its inhabitants. 26 You, unlike them, must

18 The LORD said to Moses, 2 "Speak to the Israelites and tell them: I, the LORD, am your God. 3 You shall not do as they do in the land of Egypt, where you once lived, nor shall you do as they do in the land of Canaan, where I am bringing you; do not conform to their customs. 4 My decrees you shall carry out, and my statutes you shall take care to follow. I, the LORD, am your God. 5 Keep, then, my statutes and decrees, for the man who carries them out will find life through them. I am the LORD.

6 "None of you shall approach a close relative to have sexual intercourse with her. I am the LORD. 7 You shall not disgrace your father by having intercourse with your mother. Besides, since she is your own mother, you shall not have intercourse with her. 8 You shall not have intercourse with your father's wife, for that would be a disgrace to your father. 9 You shall not have intercourse with your sister, your father's daughter or your mother's daughter, whether she was born in your own household or born elsewhere. 10 You shall not have intercourse with your son's daughter or with your daughter's daughter, for that would be a disgrace to your own family. 11 You shall not have intercourse with the daughter whom your father's wife bore to him, since she, too, is your sister. 12 You shall not have intercourse with your father's sister, since she is your father's relative. 13 You shall not have intercourse with your mother's sister, since she is your mother's relative. 14 You shall not disgrace your father's brother by being intimate with his wife, since she, too, is your aunt. 15 You shall not have intercourse with your daughter-in-law; she is your son's wife, and therefore you shall not disgrace her. 16 You shall not have intercourse with your brother's wife, for that would be a disgrace to your brother. 17 You shall not have intercourse with a woman and also with her daughter, nor shall you marry and have intercourse with her son's daughter or her daughter's daughter; this would be shameful, because they are related to her. 18 While your wife is still living you shall not marry her sister as her rival; for thus you would disgrace your first wife.

19 "You shall not approach a woman to have intercourse with her while she is unclean from menstruation. 20 You shall not have carnal relations with your neighbor's wife, defiling yourself with her. 21 You shall not offer any of your offspring to be immolated to Molech, thus profaning the name of your God. I am the LORD. 22 You shall not lie with a male as with a woman; such a thing is an abomination. 23 You shall not have carnal relations with an animal, defiling yourself with it; nor shall a woman set herself in front of an animal to mate with it; such things are abhorrent.

24 "Do not defile yourselves by any of these things by which the nations whom I am driving out of your way have defiled themselves. 25 Because their land has become defiled, I am punishing it for its wickedness, by making it vomit out its inhabitants. 26 You, however, whether natives

18 Yahweh spoke to Moses and said: 2 'Speak to the Israelites and say:

"I am Yahweh your God: 3 You must not behave as they do in Egypt where you used to live; you must not behave as they do in Canaan where I am taking you, nor must you follow their laws. 4 You must observe my customs and keep my laws, following them.

"I, Yahweh, am your God: 5 hence you will keep my laws and my customs. Whoever complies with them will find life in them.

"I am Yahweh.

6 "None of you will approach a woman who is closely related to him, to have intercourse with her. I am Yahweh. 7 You will not have intercourse with your father or your mother. She is your mother — you will not have intercourse with her.

8 "You will not have intercourse with your father's wife; it is your father's sexual prerogative.

9 "You will not have intercourse with your sister, whether she is your father's or your mother's daughter. Whether she was born in the same house or elsewhere, you will not have intercourse with her.

10 "You will not have intercourse with your son's or your daughter's daughter; for their sexual privacy is your own.

11 "You will not have intercourse with the daughter of your father's wife, born to your father. She is your sister; you will not have intercourse with her.

12 "You will not have intercourse with your father's sister; for she is your father's own flesh and blood.

13 "You will not have intercourse with your mother's sister; for she is your mother's own flesh and blood.

14 "You will not have intercourse with your father's brother; you will not approach his wife. She is your aunt.

15 "You will not have intercourse with your daughter-in-law. She is your son's wife; you will not have intercourse with her.

16 "You will not have intercourse with your brother's wife; it is your brother's sexual prerogative.

17 "You will not have intercourse with a woman and her daughter; nor will you take her son's or her daughter's daughter, to have intercourse with them. They are your own flesh and blood; it would be incest.

18 "You will not take a woman and her sister into your harem at the same time, to have intercourse with the latter while the former is still alive.

19 "You will not approach and have intercourse with a woman who is in a state of menstrual pollution.

20 "Furthermore, you will not have intercourse with your fellow-citizen's wife; you would become unclean by doing so.

21 "You will not allow any of your children to be sacrificed to Molech, d thus profaning the name of your God. I am Yahweh.

22 "You will not have intercourse with a man as you would with a woman. This is a hateful thing.

23 "You will not have intercourse with any kind of animal; you would become unclean by doing so. Nor will a woman offer herself to an animal, to have intercourse with it. This would be a violation of nature.

24 "Do not make yourselves unclean by any of these practices, for it was by such things that the nations that I am driving out before you made themselves unclean. 25 The country has become unclean; hence I am about to punish it for its guilt, and the country itself will vomit out its inhabitants.

d 18 A sacrifice by fire, Phoenician in origin, practised in Jerusalem right up to the Exile.

ordinances and commit none of these abominations, either the citizen or the alien who resides among you 27 (for the inhabitants of the land, who were before you, committed all of these abominations, and the land became defiled); 28 otherwise the land will vomit you out for defiling it, as it vomited out the nation that was before you. 29 For whoever commits any of these abominations shall be cut off from their people. 30 So keep my charge not to commit any of these abominations that were done before you, and not to defile yourselves by them: I am the LORD your God.

19 The LORD spoke to Moses, saying: 2 Speak to all the congregation of the people of Israel and say to them: You shall be holy, for I the LORD your God am holy. 3 You shall each revere your mother and father, and you shall keep my sabbaths: I am the LORD your God. 4 Do not turn to idols or make cast images for yourselves: I am the LORD your God.

5 When you offer a sacrifice of well-being to the LORD, offer it in such a way that it is acceptable on your behalf. 6 It shall be eaten on the same day you offer it, or on the next day; and anything left over until the third day shall be consumed in fire. 7 If it is eaten at all on the third day, it is an abomination; it will not be acceptable. 8 All who eat it shall be subject to punishment, because they have profaned what is holy to the LORD; and any such person shall be cut off from the people.

9 When you reap the harvest of your land, you shall not reap to the very edges of your field, or gather the gleanings of your harvest. 10 You shall not strip your vineyard bare, or gather the fallen grapes of your vineyard; you shall leave them for the poor and the alien: I am the LORD your God.

11 You shall not steal; you shall not deal falsely; and you shall not lie to one another. 12 And you shall not swear falsely by my name, profaning the name of your God: I am the LORD.

13 You shall not defraud your neighbor; you shall not steal; and you shall not keep for yourself the wages of a laborer until morning. 14 You shall not revile the deaf or put a stumbling block before the blind; you shall fear your God: I am the LORD.

15 You shall not render an unjust judgment; you shall not be partial to the poor or defer to the great: with justice you shall judge your neighbor. 16 You shall not go around as a slandererᵃ among your people, and you shall not profit by the bloodᵇ of your neighbor: I am the LORD.

17 You shall not hate in your heart anyone of your kin; you shall reprove your neighbor, or you will incur guilt yourself. 18 You shall not take vengeance or bear a grudge against any of your people, but you shall love your neighbor as yourself: I am the LORD.

19 You shall keep my statutes. You shall not let your animals breed with a different kind; you shall not sow your field with two kinds of seed; nor shall you put on a garment made of two different materials.

20 If a man has sexual relations with a woman who is a slave, designated for another man but not ransomed or given her freedom, an inquiry shall be held. They shall not be put to death, since she has not been freed; 21 but he shall bring a guilt offering for himself to the LORD, at the entrance of the tent of meeting, a ram as guilt offering. 22 And the priest shall make atonement for him with the ram of guilt offering before the LORD for his sin that he committed; and the sin he committed shall be forgiven him.

observe my statutes and my laws: none of you, whether natives or aliens settled among you, may do any of those abominable things. 27 The people who were there before you did those abominable things and the land became unclean. 28 So do not let the land spew you out for making it unclean as it spewed them out; 29 for anyone who does any of those abominable things will be cut off from his people. 30 Observe my charge, therefore, and follow none of the abominable institutions customary before your time; do not make yourselves unclean with them. I am the LORD your God.

19 THE LORD told Moses 2 to say to the whole Israelite community: You must be holy, because I, the LORD your God, am holy. 3 Each one of you must revere his mother and father. You must keep my sabbaths. I am the LORD your God. 4 Do not resort to idols or make for yourselves gods of cast metal. I am the LORD your God.

5 When you sacrifice a shared-offering to the LORD, you are to slaughter it so as to win acceptance for yourselves. 6 It must be eaten on the day of your sacrifice or on the next day. Anything left over till the third day must be destroyed by fire; 7 it is tainted, and if any of it is eaten on the third day, it will not be acceptable. 8 He who eats it must accept responsibility, because he has profaned the holy-gift to the LORD: that person will be cut off from his father's kin.

9 When you reap the harvest in your land, do not reap right up to the edges of your field, or gather the gleanings of your crop. 10 Do not completely strip your vineyard, or pick up the fallen grapes; leave them for the poor and for the alien. I am the LORD your God.

11 You must not steal; you must not cheat or deceive a fellow-countryman. 12 You must not swear in my name with intent to deceive and thus profane the name of your God. I am the LORD. 13 You are not to oppress your neighbour or rob him. Do not keep back a hired man's wages till next morning. 14 Do not treat the deaf with contempt, or put an obstacle in the way of the blind; you are to fear your God. I am the LORD.

15 You are not to pervert justice, either by favouring the poor or by subservience to the great. You are to administer justice to your fellow-countryman with strict fairness. 16 Do not go about spreading slander among your father's kin; do not take sides against your neighbour on a capital charge. I am the LORD. 17 You are not to nurse hatred towards your brother. Reprove your fellow-countryman frankly, and so you will have no share in his guilt. 18 Never seek revenge or cherish a grudge towards your kinsfolk; you must love your neighbour as yourself. I am the LORD.

19 You must observe my statutes. You may not allow two different kinds of animal to mate together. You are not to plant your field with two kinds of seed, nor to wear a garment woven with two kinds of yarn.

20 When a man has intercourse with a slave-girl who has been assigned to another but has been neither redeemed nor given her freedom, enquiry should be made. They are not to be put to death, because she has not been freed. 21 The man is to bring his reparation-offering, a ram, to the LORD to the entrance of the Tent of Meeting, 22 and with it the priest will make expiation for him before the LORD for his sin, and he will be forgiven the sin he has committed.

ᵃ Meaning of Heb uncertain   ᵇ Heb *stand against the blood*   19:17 **and . . . guilt:** *or* and for that you will incur no blame.

or resident aliens, must keep my statutes and decrees forbidding all such abominations 27 by which the previous inhabitants defiled the land; 28 otherwise the land will vomit you out also for having defiled it, just as it vomited out the nations before you. 29 Everyone who does any of these abominations shall be cut off from among his people. 30 Heed my charge, then, not to defile yourselves by observing the abominable customs that have been observed before you. I, the LORD, am your God."

19 The LORD said to Moses, 2 "Speak to the whole Israelite community and tell them: Be holy, for I, the LORD, your God, am holy. 3 Revere your mother and father, and keep my sabbaths. I, the LORD, am your God. 4 "Do not turn aside to idols, nor make molten gods for yourselves. I, the LORD, am your God.

5 "When you sacrifice your peace offering to the LORD, if you wish it to be acceptable, 6 it must be eaten on the very day of your sacrifice or on the following day. Whatever is left over until the third day shall be burned up in the fire. 7 If any of it is eaten on the third day, the sacrifice will be unacceptable as refuse; 8 whoever eats of it then shall pay the penalty for having profaned what is sacred to the LORD. Such a one shall be cut off from his people.

9 "When you reap the harvest of your land, you shall not be so thorough that you reap the field to its very edge, nor shall you glean the stray ears of grain. 10 Likewise, you shall not pick your vineyard bare, nor gather up the grapes that have fallen. These things you shall leave for the poor and the alien. I, the LORD, am your God.

11 "You shall not steal. You shall not lie or speak falsely to one another. 12 You shall not swear falsely by my name, thus profaning the name of your God. I am the LORD. 13 "You shall not defraud or rob your neighbor. You shall not withhold overnight the wages of your day laborer. 14 You shall not curse the deaf, or put a stumbling block in front of the blind, but you shall fear your God. I am the LORD.

15 "You shall not act dishonestly in rendering judgment. Show neither partiality to the weak nor deference to the mighty, but judge your fellow men justly. 16 You shall not go about spreading slander among your kinsmen; nor shall you stand by idly when your neighbor's life is at stake. I am the LORD.

17 "You shall not bear hatred for your brother in your heart. Though you may have to reprove your fellow man, do not incur sin because of him. 18 Take no revenge and cherish no grudge against your fellow countrymen. You shall love your neighbor as yourself. I am the LORD.

19 "Keep my statutes: do not breed any of your domestic animals with others of a different species; do not sow a field of yours with two different kinds of seed; and do not put on a garment woven with two different kinds of thread.

20 "If a man has carnal relations with a female slave who has already been living with another man but has not yet been redeemed or given her freedom, they shall be punished but not put to death, because she is not free. 21 The man, moreover, shall bring to the entrance of the meeting tent a ram as his guilt offering to the LORD. 22 With this ram the priest shall make atonement before the LORD for the sin he has committed, and it will be forgiven him.

26 "You, however, must keep my laws and customs and not do any of these hateful things: none of your citizens, none of your resident aliens. 27 For all these hateful things were done by the people who lived in the country before you, and the country became unclean. 28 If you make it unclean, will it not vomit you out as it vomited out the nations there before you? 29 Yes, anyone who does any of these hateful things, whatever it may be, any person doing so, will be outlawed from his people; 30 so keep my rules and do not observe any of the hateful laws which were in force before you came; then you will not be made unclean by them. I am Yahweh your God." '

19 Yahweh spoke to Moses and said: 2 'Speak to the whole community of Israelites and say:

"Be holy, for I, Yahweh your God, am holy. 3 "Each of you will respect father and mother. "And you will keep my Sabbaths; I am Yahweh your God. 4 "Do not turn to idols and do not cast metal gods for yourselves. I am Yahweh your God.

5 "If you offer a communion sacrifice to Yahweh, make it in such a way as to be acceptable. 6 It must be eaten the same day or the day after; whatever is left on the third day must be burnt. 7 If eaten on the third day it would be rotten food and not be acceptable. 8 Anyone who eats it must bear the consequences of this guilt, having profaned Yahweh's holiness; that person will be outlawed from his people.

9 "When you reap the harvest of your land, you will not reap to the very edges of the field, nor will you gather the gleanings of the harvest; 10 nor will you strip your vineyard bare, nor pick up the fallen grapes. You will leave them for the poor and the stranger. I am Yahweh your God.

11 "You will not steal, nor deal deceitfully or fraudulently with your fellow-citizen. 12 You will not swear by my name with intent to deceive and thus profane the name of your God. I am Yahweh. 13 You will not exploit or rob your fellow. You will not keep back the labourer's wage until next morning. 14 You will not curse the dumb or put an obstacle in the way of the blind, but will fear your God. I am Yahweh.

15 "You will not be unjust in administering justice. You will neither be partial to the poor nor overawed by the great, but will administer justice to your fellow-citizen justly. 16 You will not go about slandering your own family, nor will you put your neighbour's life in jeopardy. I am Yahweh. 17 You will not harbour hatred for your brother. You will reprove your fellow-countryman firmly and thus avoid burdening yourself with a sin. 18 You will not exact vengeance on, or bear any sort of grudge against, the members of your race, but will love your neighbour as yourself. I am Yahweh.

19 "You will keep my laws.

"You will not mate your cattle with those of another kind; you will not sow two kinds of grain in your field; you will not wear a garment made from two kinds of fabric.

20 "If someone has intercourse with a woman who is the concubine slave of a man from whom she has not been redeemed and she has not been given her freedom, he will be liable for a fine, but they will not incur death, since she was not a free woman. 21 He will bring a sacrifice of reparation for Yahweh to the entrance of the Tent of Meeting. This will be a ram of reparation, 22 and with the ram of reparation the priest will perform the rite of expiation for him before Yahweh for the sin committed; and the sin he has committed will be forgiven.

NEW REVISED STANDARD VERSION

23 When you come into the land and plant all kinds of trees for food, then you shall regard their fruit as forbidden;*c* three years it shall be forbidden*d* to you, it must not be eaten. 24 In the fourth year all their fruit shall be set apart for rejoicing in the LORD. 25 But in the fifth year you may eat of their fruit, that their yield may be increased for you: I am the LORD your God.

26 You shall not eat anything with its blood. You shall not practice augury or witchcraft. 27 You shall not round off the hair on your temples or mar the edges of your beard. 28 You shall not make any gashes in your flesh for the dead or tattoo any marks upon you: I am the LORD.

29 Do not profane your daughter by making her a prostitute, that the land not become prostituted and full of depravity. 30 You shall keep my sabbaths and reverence my sanctuary: I am the LORD.

31 Do not turn to mediums or wizards; do not seek them out, to be defiled by them: I am the LORD your God.

32 You shall rise before the aged, and defer to the old; and you shall fear your God: I am the LORD.

33 When an alien resides with you in your land, you shall not oppress the alien. 34 The alien who resides with you shall be to you as the citizen among you; you shall love the alien as yourself, for you were aliens in the land of Egypt: I am the LORD your God.

35 You shall not cheat in measuring length, weight, or quantity. 36 You shall have honest balances, honest weights, an honest ephah, and an honest hin: I am the LORD your God, who brought you out of the land of Egypt. 37 You shall keep all my statutes and all my ordinances, and observe them: I am the LORD.

20 The LORD spoke to Moses, saying: 2 Say further to the people of Israel:

Any of the people of Israel, or of the aliens who reside in Israel, who give any of their offspring to Molech shall be put to death; the people of the land shall stone them to death. 3 I myself will set my face against them, and will cut them off from the people, because they have given of their offspring to Molech, defiling my sanctuary and profaning my holy name. 4 And if the people of the land should ever close their eyes to them, when they give of their offspring to Molech, and do not put them to death, 5 I myself will set my face against them and against their family, and will cut them off from among their people, them and all who follow them in prostituting themselves to Molech.

6 If any turn to mediums and wizards, prostituting themselves to them, I will set my face against them, and will cut them off from the people. 7 Consecrate yourselves therefore, and be holy; for I am the LORD your God. 8 Keep my statutes, and observe them; I am the LORD; I sanctify you. 9 All who curse father or mother shall be put to death; having cursed father or mother, their blood is upon them.

10 If a man commits adultery with the wife of*e* his neighbor, both the adulterer and the adulteress shall be put to death. 11 The man who lies with his father's wife has uncovered his father's nakedness; both of them shall be put to death; their blood is upon them. 12 If a man lies with his daughter-in-law, both of them shall be put to death; they have committed perversion, their blood is upon them. 13 If

REVISED ENGLISH BIBLE

23 When you enter the land, and plant any kind of tree for food, you are to treat it as bearing forbidden fruit. For three years it is forbidden and may not be eaten. 24 In the fourth year all its fruit is to be holy for a praise-offering to the LORD, a festal jubilation. 25 In the fifth year you may eat its fruit. Thus the yield it gives you will be increased. I am the LORD your God.

26 Never eat meat with the blood in it. You must not practise divination or soothsaying. 27 You are not to cut off your hair from your temples or shave the edge of your beards. 28 You must not gash yourselves in mourning for the dead or tattoo yourselves. I am the LORD.

29 Do not debase your daughter by making her become a prostitute. The land is not to play the prostitute and be full of lewdness. 30 You must keep my sabbaths and revere my sanctuary. I am the LORD.

31 Do not resort to ghosts and spirits or make yourselves unclean by seeking them out. I am the LORD your God.

32 Rise in the presence of grey hairs, give honour to the aged, and fear your God. I am the LORD.

33 When an alien resides with you in your land, you must not oppress him. 34 He is to be treated as a native born among you. Love him as yourself, because you were aliens in Egypt. I am the LORD your God.

35 You are not to falsify measures of length, weight, or quantity. 36 You must use true scales and weights, true dry and liquid measures. I am the LORD your God who brought you out of Egypt. 37 You must observe all my statutes and all my laws and carry them out. I am the LORD.

20 The LORD told Moses 2 to say to the Israelites: Anyone, whether Israelite or alien settled in Israel, who gives any of his children to Molech must be put to death: the people are to stone him. 3 I for my part shall set my face against that man and cut him off from his people, for by giving a child of his to Molech he has made my sanctuary unclean and profaned my holy name. 4 If the people connive at it when a man has given a child of his to Molech and do not put him to death, 5 I shall set my face against that man and his family, and cut him off from their people both him and all who follow him in his wanton worship of Molech.

6 I shall set my face against anyone who wantonly resorts to ghosts and spirits, and I shall cut that person off from his people. 7 Hallow yourselves and be holy, because I am the LORD your God. 8 Observe my statutes and obey them: I am the LORD who hallows you.

9 When anyone reviles his father and his mother, he must be put to death. Since he has reviled his father and his mother, let his blood be on his own head. 10 If a man commits adultery with another's wife, that is with the wife of a fellow-countryman, both adulterer and adulteress must be put to death. 11 The man who has intercourse with his father's wife has brought shame on his father. Both must be put to death; their blood be on their own heads! 12 If a man has intercourse with his daughter-in-law, both must be put to death. Their deed is a violation of nature; their blood be on their own heads! 13 If a man has intercourse with a man

---

c Heb *as their uncircumcision*   *d* Heb *uncircumcision*
e Heb repeats *if a man commits adultery with the wife of*

19:23 **forbidden:** *lit.* uncircumcised.

| NEW AMERICAN BIBLE | NEW JERUSALEM BIBLE |

23 "When you come into the land and plant any fruit tree there, first look upon its fruit as if it were uncircumcised. For three years, while its fruit remains uncircumcised, it may not be eaten. 24 In the fourth year, however, all of its fruit shall be sacred to the LORD as a thanksgiving feast to him. 25 Not until the fifth year may you eat its fruit. Thus it will continue its yield for you. I, the LORD, am your God.

26 "Do not eat meat with the blood still in it. Do not practice divination or soothsaying. 27 Do not clip your hair at the temples, nor trim the edges of your beard. 28 Do not lacerate your bodies for the dead, and do not tattoo yourselves. I am the LORD.

29 "You shall not degrade your daughter by making her a prostitute of her; else the land will become corrupt and full of lewdness. 30 Keep my sabbaths, and reverence my sanctuary. I am the LORD.

31 "Do not go to mediums or consult fortune-tellers, for you will be defiled by them. I, the LORD, am your God.

32 "Stand up in the presence of the aged, and show respect for the old; thus shall you fear your God. I am the LORD.

33 "When an alien resides with you in your land, do not molest him. 34 You shall treat the alien who resides with you no differently than the natives born among you; have the same love for him as for yourself; for you too were once aliens in the land of Egypt. I, the LORD, am your God.

35 "Do not act dishonestly in using measures of length or weight or capacity. 36 You shall have a true scale and true weights, an honest ephah and an honest hin. I, the LORD, am your God, who brought you out of the land of Egypt. 37 Be careful, then, to observe all my statutes and decrees. I am the LORD."

20 The LORD said to Moses, 2 "Tell the Israelites: Anyone, whether an Israelite or an alien residing in Israel, who gives any of his offspring to Molech shall be put to death. Let his fellow citizens stone him. 3 I myself will turn against such a man and cut him off from the body of his people; for in giving his offspring to Molech, he has defiled my sanctuary and profaned my holy name. 4 Even if his fellow citizens connive at such a man's crime of giving his offspring to Molech, and fail to put him to death, 5 I myself will set my face against that man and his family and will cut off from their people both him and all who join him in his wanton worship of Molech. 6 Should anyone turn to mediums and fortune-tellers and follow their wanton ways, I will turn against such a one and cut him off from his people. 7 Sanctify yourselves, then, and be holy; for I, the LORD, your God, am holy. 8 Be careful, therefore, to observe what I, the LORD, who make you holy, have prescribed.

9 "Anyone who curses his father or mother shall be put to death; since he has cursed his father or mother, he has forfeited his life. 10 If a man commits adultery with his neighbor's wife, both the adulterer and the adulteress shall be put to death. 11 If a man disgraces his father by lying with his father's wife, both the man and his stepmother shall be put to death; they have forfeited their lives. 12 If a man lies with his daughter-in-law, both of them shall be put to death; since they have committed an abhorrent deed, they have forfeited their lives. 13 If a man lies with a male as with a

23 "Once you have entered the country and planted any kind of fruit tree, you will regard its fruit as uncircumcised. For three years you will count it as uncircumcised and it will not be eaten; 24 in the fourth year, all its fruit will be consecrated to Yahweh in a feast of praise; 25 and in the fifth year you may eat its fruit, so that it may yield you even more. I am Yahweh your God.

26 "You will eat nothing with blood in it. You will not practise divination or magic.

27 "You will not round off your hair at the edges or trim the edges of your beard. 28 You will not gash your bodies when someone dies, and you will not tattoo yourselves. I am Yahweh.

29 "Do not profane your daughter by making her a prostitute, or the country itself will become prostituted and filled with incest.

30 "You will keep my Sabbaths and revere my sanctuary. I am Yahweh.

31 "Do not have recourse to the spirits of the dead or to magicians; they will defile you. I, Yahweh, am your God.

32 "You will stand up in the presence of grey hair, you will honour the person of the aged and fear your God. I am Yahweh.

33 "If you have resident aliens in your country, you will not molest them. 34 You will treat resident aliens as though they were native-born and love them as yourself — for you yourselves were once aliens in Egypt. I am Yahweh your God.

35 "You will not be unjust in administering justice as regards measures of length, weight or capacity. 36 You will have just scales, just weights, a just *ephah* and a just *hin*. I am Yahweh your God who brought you out of Egypt; 37 hence you are to keep all my laws and all my customs and put them into practice. I am Yahweh." '

20 Yahweh spoke to Moses and said: 2 'Say to the Israelites: "Anyone, be he Israelite or alien resident in Israel, who gives any of his children to Molech, will be put to death. The people of the country must stone him, 3 and I shall set my face against that man and outlaw him from his people; for by giving a child of his to Molech he has defiled my sanctuary and profaned my holy name. 4 If the people of the country choose to close their eyes to the man's action when he gives a child of his to Molech, and do not put him to death, 5 I myself shall turn my face against that man and his clan. I shall outlaw them from their people, both him and all those after him who prostitute themselves by following Molech.

6 "If anyone has recourse to the spirits of the dead or to magicians, to prostitute himself by following them, I shall set my face against him and outlaw him from his people.

7 "Sanctify yourselves and be holy, for I am Yahweh your God.

8 "You will keep my laws and put them into practice, for it is I, Yahweh, who make you holy. 9 Hence:

"Anyone who curses father or mother will be put to death. Having cursed father or mother, the blood will be on that person's own head.

10 "The man who commits adultery with his neighbour's wife will be put to death, he and the woman.

11 "The man who has intercourse with his father's wife has infringed his father's sexual prerogative. Both of them will be put to death; their blood will be on their own heads.

12 "The man who has intercourse with his daughter-in-law: both of them will be put to death; they have violated nature, their blood will be on their own heads.

NEW REVISED STANDARD VERSION

a man lies with a male as with a woman, both of them have committed an abomination; they shall be put to death; their blood is upon them. 14 If a man takes a wife and her mother also, it is depravity; they shall be burned to death, both he and they, that there may be no depravity among you. 15 If a man has sexual relations with an animal, he shall be put to death; and you shall kill the animal. 16 If a woman approaches any animal and has sexual relations with it, you shall kill the woman and the animal; they shall be put to death, their blood is upon them.

17 If a man takes his sister, a daughter of his father or a daughter of his mother, and sees her nakedness, and she sees his nakedness, it is a disgrace, and they shall be cut off in the sight of their people; he has uncovered his sister's nakedness, he shall be subject to punishment. 18 If a man lies with a woman having her sickness and uncovers her nakedness, he has laid bare her flow and she has laid bare her flow of blood; both of them shall be cut off from their people. 19 You shall not uncover the nakedness of your mother's sister or of your father's sister, for that is to lay bare one's own flesh; they shall be subject to punishment. 20 If a man lies with his uncle's wife, he has uncovered his uncle's nakedness; they shall be subject to punishment; they shall die childless. 21 If a man takes his brother's wife, it is impurity; he has uncovered his brother's nakedness; they shall be childless.

22 You shall keep all my statutes and all my ordinances, and observe them, so that the land to which I bring you to settle in may not vomit you out. 23 You shall not follow the practices of the nation that I am driving out before you. Because they did all these things, I abhorred them. 24 But I have said to you: You shall inherit their land, and I will give it to you to possess, a land flowing with milk and honey. I am the LORD your God; I have separated you from the peoples. 25 You shall therefore make a distinction between the clean animal and the unclean, and between the unclean bird and the clean; you shall not bring abomination on yourselves by animal or by bird or by anything with which the ground teems, which I have set apart for you to hold unclean. 26 You shall be holy to me; for I the LORD am holy, and I have separated you from the other peoples to be mine.

27 A man or a woman who is a medium or a wizard shall be put to death; they shall be stoned to death, their blood is upon them.

21 The LORD said to Moses: Speak to the priests, the sons of Aaron, and say to them:

No one shall defile himself for a dead person among his relatives, 2 except for his nearest kin: his mother, his father, his son, his daughter, his brother; 3 likewise, for a virgin sister, close to him because she has had no husband, he may defile himself for her. 4 But he shall not defile himself as a husband among his people and so profane himself. 5 They shall not make bald spots upon their heads, or shave off the edges of their beards, or make any gashes in their flesh. 6 They shall be holy to their God, and not profane the name of their God; for they offer the LORD's offerings by fire, the food of their God; therefore they shall be holy. 7 They shall

REVISED ENGLISH BIBLE

as with a woman, both commit an abomination. They must be put to death; their blood be on their own heads! 14 If a man takes both a woman and her mother, that is lewdness. Both he and they must be burnt, so that there may be no lewdness in your midst. 15 A man who has sexual intercourse with an animal must be put to death, and you are to kill the beast. 16 If a woman approaches an animal to mate with it, you must kill both woman and beast. They must be put to death; their blood be on their own heads! 17 If a man takes his sister, whether his father's daughter or his mother's daughter, and they see one another naked, it is an infamous disgrace. They are to be cut off in the presence of their people. The man has had intercourse with his sister and he must be held responsible. 18 If a man lies with a woman during her monthly period, uncovering her body, he has exposed her discharge and she has uncovered the source of her discharge; they are both to be cut off from their people. 19 You must not have intercourse with your mother's sister or your father's sister: it is the exposure of a blood relation. Both must accept responsibility. 20 A man who has intercourse with his uncle's wife has brought shame on his uncle. They must accept responsibility for their sin and be proscribed and put to death. 21 If a man takes his brother's wife, it is impurity. He has brought shame on his brother; they are to be proscribed.

22 You are to observe my statutes and my laws and carry them out, so that the land into which I am bringing you to live may not spew you out. 23 You must not conform to the institutions of the nations whom I am driving out before you: they did all these things and I abhorred them, 24 and I told you that you should occupy their land, and I would give you possession of it, a land flowing with milk and honey. I am the LORD your God: I have made a clear separation between you and the nations, 25 and you are to make a clear separation between clean beasts and unclean beasts and between unclean and clean birds. You must not contaminate yourselves through beast or bird or anything that creeps on the ground, for I have made a clear separation between them and you, declaring them unclean. 26 You must be holy to me, because I the LORD am holy. I have made a clear separation between you and the heathen, that you may belong to me. 27 Any man or woman among you who calls up ghosts or spirits must be put to death. The people are to stone them; their blood be on their own heads!

21 THE LORD told Moses to say to the priests, the sons of Aaron: A priest is not to render himself unclean for the death of any of his kin 2 except for a near blood relation, that is for mother, father, son, daughter, brother, 3 or full sister who is unmarried and a virgin; 4 nor is he to make himself unclean for any married woman among his father's kin, and so profane himself.

5 Priests are not to make bald patches on their heads as a sign of mourning, or cut the edges of their beards, or gash their bodies. 6 They must be holy to their God, and must not profane the name of their God, because they present the food-offerings of the LORD, the food of their God, and they must be holy. 7 A priest must not marry a prostitute or a girl

---

21:4 **for any married woman:** *prob. rdg; Heb.* husband.

NEW AMERICAN BIBLE

NEW JERUSALEM BIBLE

woman, both of them shall be put to death for their abominable deed; they have forfeited their lives. 14 If a man marries a woman and her mother also, the man and the two women as well shall be burned to death for their shameful conduct, so that such shamefulness may not be found among you. 15 If a man has carnal relations with an animal, the man shall be put to death, and the animal shall be slain. 16 If a woman goes up to any animal to mate with it, the woman and the animal shall be slain; let them both be put to death; their lives are forfeit. 17 If a man consummates marriage with his sister or his half-sister, they shall be publicly cut off from their people for this shameful deed; the man shall pay the penalty of having had intercourse with his own sister. 18 If a man lies in sexual intercourse with a woman during her menstrual period, both of them shall be cut off from their people, because they have laid bare the flowing fountain of her blood. 19 You shall not have intercourse with your mother's sister or your father's sister; whoever does so shall pay the penalty of incest. 20 If a man disgraces his uncle by having intercourse with his uncle's wife, the man and his aunt shall pay the penalty by dying childless. 21 If a man marries his brother's wife and thus disgraces his brother, they shall be childless because of this incest.

22 "Be careful to observe all my statutes and all my decrees; otherwise the land where I am bringing you to dwell will vomit you out. 23 Do not conform, therefore, to the customs of the nations whom I am driving out of your way, because all these things that they have done have filled me with disgust for them. 24 But to you I have said: Their land shall be your possession, a land flowing with milk and honey. I am giving it to you as your own, I, the LORD, your God, who have set you apart from the other nations. 25 You, too, must set apart, then, the clean animals from the unclean, and the clean birds from the unclean, so that you may not be contaminated with the uncleanness of any beast or bird or of any swarming creature in the land that I have set apart for you. 26 To me, therefore, you shall be sacred; for I, the LORD, am sacred, I, who have set you apart from the other nations to be my own.

27 "A man or a woman who acts as a medium or fortune-teller shall be put to death by stoning; they have no one but themselves to blame for their death."

13 "The man who has intercourse with a man in the same way as with a woman: they have done a hateful thing together; they will be put to death; their blood will be on their own heads.

14 "The man who marries a woman and her mother: this is incest. They will be burnt alive, he and they; you will not tolerate incest.

15 "The man who has intercourse with an animal will be put to death; you will kill the animal too.

16 "The woman who approaches any animal to have intercourse with it: you will kill the woman and the animal. They will be put to death; their blood will be on their own heads.

17 "The man who marries his father's or his mother's daughter: if they have intercourse together, this is an outrage. They will be executed in public, for the man has had intercourse with his sister; he will bear the consequences of his guilt.

18 "The man who has intercourse with a woman during her monthly periods and exposes her nakedness: he has laid bare the source of her blood, and she has exposed the source of her blood, and both of them will be outlawed from their people.

19 "You will not have intercourse with your mother's sister or your father's sister. Whoever does so, has had intercourse with a close relation; they will bear the consequences of their guilt.

20 "The man who has intercourse with the wife of his paternal uncle has infringed his uncle's sexual prerogative; they will bear the consequences of their guilt and die childless.

21 "The man who marries his brother's wife: this is pollution; he has infringed his brother's sexual prerogative; they will die childless.

22 "You will keep all my laws, all my decisions, and put them into practice, so that the country where I am taking you to live will not vomit you out. 23 You will not follow the laws of the nations whom I am driving out before you; they practised all these things, which is why I detested them. 24 As I have already told you, you will take possession of their soil, I myself shall give you possession of it, a country flowing with milk and honey.

"Since I, Yahweh your God, have set you apart from these peoples, 25 you for your part will make a distinction between clean animals and unclean ones and between unclean birds and clean ones, and will not make yourselves detestable with any animal or bird or reptile, which I have set apart from you as unclean.

26 "Be consecrated to me, for I, Yahweh, am holy, and I shall set you apart from all these peoples, for you to be mine.

27 "Any man or woman of yours who is a necromancer or magician will be put to death; they will be stoned to death; their blood will be on their own heads." '

21 The LORD said to Moses, "Speak to Aaron's sons, the priests, and tell them: None of you shall make himself unclean for any dead person among his people, 2 except for his nearest relatives, his mother or father, his son or daughter, his brother 3 or his maiden sister, who is of his own family while she remains unmarried; for these he may make himself unclean. 4 But for a sister who has married out of his family he shall not make himself unclean; this would be a profanation.

5 "The priests shall not make bare the crown of the head, nor shave the edges of the beard, nor lacerate the body. 6 To their God they shall be sacred, and not profane his name; since they offer up the oblations of the LORD, the food of their God, they must be holy.

21 Yahweh said to Moses:
'Speak to the priests descended from Aaron and say:
"None of them must make himself unclean by touching the corpse of one of his people, 2 unless it be of one of his closest relations — father, mother, son, daughter, brother, 3 or virgin sister, since she being unmarried is still his close relation: he can make himself unclean for her; 4 but for a close female relation who is married he will not make himself unclean; he would profane himself.

5 "They will not make tonsures on their heads, shave the edges of their beards, or gash their bodies. 6 They will be consecrated to their God and will not profane the name of their God. For their function is to offer the food burnt for Yahweh, the food of their God, and so they must be holy.

not marry a prostitute or a woman who has been defiled; neither shall they marry a woman divorced from her husband. For they are holy to their God, 8 and you shall treat them as holy, since they offer the food of your God; they shall be holy to you, for I the LORD, I who sanctify you, am holy. 9 When the daughter of a priest profanes herself through prostitution, she profanes her father; she shall be burned to death.

10 The priest who is exalted above his fellows, on whose head the anointing oil has been poured and who has been consecrated to wear the vestments, shall not dishevel his hair, nor tear his vestments. 11 He shall not go where there is a dead body; he shall not defile himself even for his father or mother. 12 He shall not go outside the sanctuary and thus profane the sanctuary of his God; for the consecration of the anointing oil of his God is upon him: I am the LORD. 13 He shall marry only a woman who is a virgin. 14 A widow, or a divorced woman, or a woman who has been defiled, a prostitute, these he shall not marry. He shall marry a virgin of his own kin, 15 that he may not profane his offspring among his kin; for I am the LORD; I sanctify him.

16 The LORD spoke to Moses, saying: 17 Speak to Aaron and say: No one of your offspring throughout their generations who has a blemish may approach to offer the food of his God. 18 For no one who has a blemish shall draw near, one who is blind or lame, or one who has a mutilated face or a limb too long, 19 or one who has a broken foot or a broken hand, 20 or a hunchback, or a dwarf, or a man with a blemish in his eyes or an itching disease or scabs or crushed testicles. 21 No descendant of Aaron the priest who has a blemish shall come near to offer the LORD's offerings by fire; since he has a blemish, he shall not come near to offer the food of his God. 22 He may eat the food of his God, of the most holy as well as of the holy. 23 But he shall not come near the curtain or approach the altar, because he has a blemish, that he may not profane my sanctuaries; for I am the LORD; I sanctify them. 24 Thus Moses spoke to Aaron and to his sons and to all the people of Israel.

22

The LORD spoke to Moses, saying: 2 Direct Aaron and his sons to deal carefully with the sacred donations of the people of Israel, which they dedicate to me, so that they may not profane my holy name; I am the LORD. 3 Say to them: If anyone among all your offspring throughout your generations comes near the sacred donations, which the people of Israel dedicate to the LORD, while he is in a state of uncleanness, that person shall be cut off from my presence: I am the LORD. 4 No one of Aaron's offspring who has a leprous *f* disease or suffers a discharge may eat of the sacred donations until he is clean. Whoever touches anything made unclean by a corpse or a man who has had an emission of semen, 5 and whoever touches any swarming thing by which he may be made unclean or any human being by whom he may be made unclean — whatever his uncleanness may be — 6 the person who touches any such shall be unclean until evening and shall not eat of the sacred donations unless he has washed his body in water. 7 When the sun sets he shall be clean; and afterward he may eat of the sacred donations, for they are his food. 8 That which died or was torn by wild animals he shall not eat, becoming unclean by it: I am the LORD. 9 They shall keep my charge, so that they may not incur guilt and die in the sanctuary *g* for having profaned it: I am the LORD; I sanctify them.

who has lost her virginity, or marry a woman divorced from her husband; for he is holy to his God. 8 You must keep him holy because he presents the food of your God; you are to regard him as holy, because I the LORD, I who hallow them, am holy. 9 When a priest's daughter makes herself profane by becoming a prostitute, she profanes her father. She must be burnt.

10 The high priest, the one among his fellows who has had the anointing oil poured on his head and has been ordained to wear the priestly vestments, must neither let his hair hang loose nor tear his clothes. 11 He must not enter the place where any dead body lies; not even for his father or his mother may he render himself unclean. 12 He must not go out of the sanctuary, for fear that he dishonour the sanctuary of his God, because the consecration of the anointing oil of his God is on him. I am the LORD. 13 He is to marry a woman who is still a virgin. 14 He is not to marry a widow, a divorced woman, a woman who has lost her virginity, or a prostitute, but only a virgin from his father's kin; 15 he must not dishonour his descendants among his father's kin, for I am the LORD who hallows them.

16 The LORD told Moses 17 to say to Aaron: No man among your descendants for all time who has any physical defect is to come and present the food of his God. 18 No man with a defect is to come, whether a blind man, a lame man, a man stunted or overgrown, 19 a man deformed in foot or hand, 20 or with misshapen brows or a film over his eye or a discharge from it, a man who has a scab or eruption or has had a testicle ruptured. 21 No descendant of Aaron the priest who has any defect in his body may approach the altar to present the food-offerings of the LORD; because he has a defect he must not approach the altar to present the food of his God. 22 He may eat the bread of God both from the holy-gifts and from the holiest of holy-gifts, 23 but not come up to the curtain or approach the altar, because he has a defect in his body; he is not to profane my sanctuaries, for I am the LORD who hallows them.

24 Thus Moses spoke to Aaron and his sons and to all the Israelites.

22

The LORD told Moses 2 to say to Aaron and his sons: You must be scrupulous in your handling of the holy-gifts of the Israelites which you hallow to me, so that you do not profane my holy name. I am the LORD. 3 Say to them: Any man of your descent for all time who in a state of uncleanness approaches the holy-gifts which the Israelites hallow to the LORD is to be cut off from my presence. I am the LORD. 4 No man descended from Aaron who suffers from a virulent skin disease, or has a bodily discharge, may eat of the holy-gifts until he is cleansed. A man who touches anything which makes him unclean, or who has an emission of semen, 5 a man who touches any creature which makes him unclean or any human being who makes him unclean: 6 any person who touches such a thing is unclean till sunset and unless he has washed his body he must not eat of the holy-gifts. 7 When the sun goes down, he will be clean, and after that he may eat from the holy-gifts, because they are his food. 8 He must not eat an animal that has died a natural death or has been mauled by wild beasts, thereby making himself unclean. I am the LORD. 9 The priests must observe my charge, lest they make themselves guilty and die for profaning my name. I am the LORD who hallows them.

---

f A term for several skin diseases; precise meaning uncertain
g Vg: Heb *incur guilt for it and die in it*

21:8 **them:** *so Samar.* (cp. verse 23); *Heb.* you.   21:20 **film . . . discharge:** *the Heb. words are of uncertain meaning.*

7 "A priest shall not marry a woman who has been a prostitute or has lost her honor, nor a woman who has been divorced by her husband; for the priest is sacred to his God. 8 Honor him as sacred who offers up the food of your God; treat him as sacred, because I, the LORD, who have consecrated him, am sacred.

9 "A priest's daughter who loses her honor by committing fornication and thereby dishonors her father also, shall be burned to death.

10 "The most exalted of the priests, upon whose head the anointing oil has been poured and who has been ordained to wear the special vestments, shall not bare his head or rend his garments, 11 nor shall he go near any dead person. Not even for his father or mother may he thus become unclean 12 or leave the sanctuary; otherwise he will profane the sanctuary of his God, for with the anointing oil upon him, he is dedicated to his God, to me, the LORD.

13 "The priest shall marry a virgin. 14 Not a widow or a woman who has been divorced or a woman who has lost her honor as a prostitute, but a virgin, taken from his own people, shall he marry; 15 otherwise he will have base offspring among his people. I, the LORD, have made him sacred."

16 The LORD said to Moses, 17 "Speak to Aaron and tell him: None of your descendants, of whatever generation, who has any defect shall come forward to offer up the food of his God. 18 Therefore, he who has any of the following defects may not come forward: he who is blind, or lame, or who has any disfigurement or malformation, 19 or a crippled foot or hand, 20 or who is humpbacked or weakly or wall-eyed, or who is afflicted with eczema, ringworm or hernia. 21 No descendant of Aaron the priest who has any such defect may draw near to offer up the oblations of the LORD; on account of his defect he may not draw near to offer up the food of his God. 22 He may, however, partake of the food of his God: of what is most sacred as well as of what is sacred. 23 Only, he may not approach the veil nor go up to the altar on account of his defect; he shall not profane these things that are sacred to me, for it is I, the LORD, who make them sacred."

24 Moses, therefore, told this to Aaron and his sons and to all the Israelites.

22 The LORD said to Moses, 2 "Tell Aaron and his sons to respect the sacred offerings which the Israelites consecrate to me; else they will profane my holy name. I am the LORD.

3 "Tell them: If any one of you, or of your descendants in any future generation, dares, while he is in a state of uncleanness, to draw near the sacred offerings which the Israelites consecrate to the LORD, such a one shall be cut off from my presence. I am the LORD.

4 "No descendant of Aaron who is stricken with leprosy, or who suffers from a flow, may eat of these sacred offerings, unless he again becomes clean. Moreover, if anyone touches a person who has become unclean by contact with a corpse, or if anyone has had an emission of seed, 5 or if anyone touches any swarming creature or any man whose uncleanness, of whatever kind it may be, is contagious, 6 the one who touches such as these shall be unclean until evening and may not eat of the sacred portions until he has first bathed his body in water; 7 then, when the sun sets, he again becomes clean. Only then may he eat of the sacred offerings, which are his food. 8 He shall not make himself unclean by eating of any animal that has died of itself or has been killed by wild beasts. I am the LORD.

9 "They shall keep my charge and not do wrong in this matter; else they will die for their profanation. I am the LORD who have consecrated them.

7 "They will not marry a woman profaned by prostitution, or one divorced by her husband, for the priest is consecrated to his God. 8 "You will treat him as holy, for he offers the food of your God. For you, he will be a holy person, for I, Yahweh, who sanctify you, am holy.

9 "If a priest's daughter profanes herself by prostitution, she profanes her father and will be burnt alive.

10 "The priest who is pre-eminent over his brothers, on whose head the anointing oil has been poured, and who, robed in the sacred vestments, has received investiture, will not disorder his hair or tear his clothes; 11 he will not go near any corpse or make himself unclean even for his father or mother. 12 He will not leave the holy place in such a way as to profane the sanctuary of his God; for he bears the consecration of the anointing oil of his God. I am Yahweh.

13 "He will marry a woman who is still a virgin. 14 He will not marry a woman who has been widowed or divorced or profaned by prostitution, but will marry a virgin from his own people: 15 he must not make his own children profane, for I, Yahweh, have sanctified him.'"

16 Yahweh spoke to Moses and said:

17 'Speak to Aaron and say:

"None of your descendants, for all time, may come forward to offer the food of his God if he has any infirmity, 18 for none may come forward if he has an infirmity, be he blind or lame, disfigured or deformed, 19 or with an injured foot or arm, 20 a hunchback, someone with rickets or ophthalmia or the scab or running sores, or a eunuch. 21 No descendant of the priest Aaron may come forward to offer the food burnt for Yahweh if he has any infirmity; if he has an infirmity, he will not come forward to offer the food of his God.

22 "He may eat the food of his God, things especially holy and things holy, 23 but he will not go near the curtain or approach the altar, since he has an infirmity and must not profane my holy things; for I, Yahweh, have sanctified them."'

24 And Moses promulgated this to Aaron, to his sons and to all the Israelites.

22 Yahweh spoke to Moses and said:

2 'Speak to Aaron and his sons. They must be consecrated by the holy offerings of the Israelites and must not profane my holy name; for my sake they must sanctify it; I am Yahweh. 3 Say to them:

"Any one of your descendants, for all time, who in a state of uncleanness approaches the holy offerings consecrated to Yahweh by the Israelites, will be outlawed from my presence. I am Yahweh.

4 "Anyone of Aaron's line who is afflicted with a contagious skin-disease or a discharge will not eat holy things until he is clean. Anyone who touches anything made unclean by a dead body, or who has a seminal discharge, 5 or who is made unclean by touching any kind of reptile or any one who has contaminated him with his own uncleanness, be it what it may, 6 in short, anyone who has had any such contact will be unclean until evening, and must not eat holy things until he has washed his body. 7 At sunset he will be clean and may then eat holy things, for these are his food.

8 "He must not eat an animal that has died a natural death or been savaged; he would contract uncleanness from it. I am Yahweh.

9 "They must keep my rules and not burden themselves with sin. If they profane them, they will incur death; I, Yahweh, have sanctified them.

10 No lay person shall eat of the sacred donations. No bound or hired servant of the priest shall eat of the sacred donations; 11 but if a priest acquires anyone by purchase, the person may eat of them; and those that are born in his house may eat of his food. 12 If a priest's daughter marries a layman, she shall not eat of the offering of the sacred donations; 13 but if a priest's daughter is widowed or divorced, without offspring, and returns to her father's house, as in her youth, she may eat of her father's food. No lay person shall eat of it. 14 If a man eats of the sacred donation unintentionally, he shall add one-fifth of its value to it, and give the sacred donation to the priest. 15 No one shall profane the sacred donations of the people of Israel, which they offer to the LORD, 16 causing them to bear guilt requiring a guilt offering, by eating their sacred donations: for I am the LORD; I sanctify them.

17 The LORD spoke to Moses, saying: 18 Speak to Aaron and his sons and all the people of Israel and say to them: When anyone of the house of Israel or of the aliens residing in Israel presents an offering, whether in payment of a vow or as a freewill offering that is offered to the LORD as a burnt offering, 19 to be acceptable in your behalf it shall be a male without blemish, of the cattle or the sheep or the goats. 20 You shall not offer anything that has a blemish, for it will not be acceptable in your behalf.

21 When anyone offers a sacrifice of well-being to the LORD, in fulfillment of a vow or as a freewill offering, from the herd or from the flock, to be acceptable it must be perfect; there shall be no blemish in it. 22 Anything blind, or injured, or maimed, or having a discharge or an itch or scabs — these you shall not offer to the LORD or put any of them on the altar as offerings by fire to the LORD. 23 An ox or a lamb that has a limb too long or too short you may present for a freewill offering; but it will not be accepted for a vow. 24 Any animal that has its testicles bruised or crushed or torn or cut, you shall not offer to the LORD; such you shall not do within your land, 25 nor shall you accept any such animals from a foreigner to offer as food to your God; since they are mutilated, with a blemish in them, they shall not be accepted in your behalf.

26 The LORD spoke to Moses, saying: 27 When an ox or a sheep or a goat is born, it shall remain seven days with its mother, and from the eighth day on it shall be acceptable as the LORD's offering by fire. 28 But you shall not slaughter, from the herd or the flock, an animal with its young on the same day. 29 When you sacrifice a thanksgiving offering to the LORD, you shall sacrifice it so that it may be acceptable in your behalf. 30 It shall be eaten on the same day; you shall not leave any of it until morning: I am the LORD.

31 Thus you shall keep my commandments and observe them: I am the LORD. 32 You shall not profane my holy name, that I may be sanctified among the people of Israel: I am the LORD; I sanctify you, 33 I who brought you out of the land of Egypt to be your God: I am the LORD.

23 The LORD spoke to Moses, saying: 2 Speak to the people of Israel and say to them: These are the appointed festivals of the LORD that you shall proclaim as holy convocations, my appointed festivals.

3 Six days shall work be done; but the seventh day is a sabbath of complete rest, a holy convocation; you shall do no work: it is a sabbath to the LORD throughout your settlements.

4 These are the appointed festivals of the LORD, the holy convocations, which you shall celebrate at the time appointed for them. 5 In the first month, on the fourteenth day

10 No lay person may eat a holy-gift; neither a stranger who is a priest's guest nor a priest's hired man may eat it. 11 A slave bought by a priest with his own money may do so, and slaves born in his household may also share his food. 12 When a priest's daughter marries a layman, she may not eat any of the contributions of holy-gifts; 13 but if she is widowed or divorced and is childless and returns to live in her father's house as in her youth, she may share her father's food. No lay person may eat any of it.

14 When anyone inadvertently eats a holy-gift, he must make good the holy-gift to the priest, adding one fifth to its value. 15 The priests must not profane the holy-gifts of the Israelites which they set aside for the LORD; 16 they are not to let anyone eat their holy-gifts and so incur guilt and its penalty, for I am the LORD who hallows them.

17 The LORD said to Moses: 18 Tell Aaron, his sons, and all the Israelites that whenever anyone belonging to the Israelite community or any alien settled in Israel presents, whether as a votive offering or as a freewill-offering, an offering such as is presented to the LORD for a whole-offering 19 so as to win acceptance for yourselves, it must be a male without defect from the cattle, sheep, or goats. 20 You are not to present anything which has a defect, because it will not be acceptable on your behalf. 21 When a man presents a shared-offering to the LORD, whether cattle or sheep, to fulfil a special vow or as a freewill-offering, if it is to be acceptable it must be perfect; there must be no defect in it. 22 You are to present to the LORD nothing blind, disabled, mutilated, with a running sore, scab, or eruption, nor are you to set any such creature on the altar as a food-offering to the LORD. 23 If a bull or a sheep is overgrown or stunted, you may make of it a freewill-offering, but it will not be acceptable in fulfilment of a vow. 24 If its testicles have been crushed or bruised, torn or cut, do not present it to the LORD; this is forbidden in your own land, 25 and you must not procure any such creature from a foreigner and present it as food for your God. Their deformity is inherent in them, a permanent defect, and they will not be acceptable on your behalf.

26 When the LORD spoke to Moses he said: 27 When a calf, a lamb, or a kid is born, it must not be taken from its mother for seven days. From the eighth day onwards it will be acceptable when offered as a food-offering to the LORD. 28 You must not slaughter a cow or a sheep at the same time as its young. 29 When you make a thank-offering to the LORD, you must sacrifice it so as to win acceptance for yourselves; 30 it is to be eaten that same day, and none must be left over till morning. I am the LORD.

31 Observe my commandments and perform them. I am the LORD. 32 You must not profane my holy name; I am to be hallowed among the Israelites. I am the LORD who hallows you, 33 who brought you out of Egypt to become your God. I am the LORD.

23 THE LORD told Moses 2 to say to the Israelites: These are the appointed seasons of the LORD, and you are to proclaim them as sacred assemblies; these are my appointed seasons. 3 On six days work may be done, but every seventh day is a day of solemn abstinence from work, a day of sacred assembly, on which you must do no work. Wherever you live, it is the LORD's sabbath.

4 These are the appointed seasons of the LORD, the sacred assemblies which you are to proclaim in their appointed order. 5 In the first month on the fourteenth day between

---

22:21 **fulfil a special:** *or* discharge a.

10 "Neither a lay person nor a priest's tenant or hired servant may eat of any sacred offering. 11 But a slave whom a priest acquires by purchase or who is born in his house may eat of his food. 12 A priest's daughter who is married to a layman may not eat of the sacred contributions. 13 But if a priest's daughter is widowed or divorced and, having no children, returns to her father's house, she may then eat of her father's food as in her youth. No layman, however, may eat of it. 14 If such a one eats of a sacred offering through inadvertence, he shall make restitution to the priest for the sacred offering, with an increment of one fifth of the amount. 15 The sacred offerings which the Israelites contribute to the LORD the priests shall not allow to be profaned 16 nor in the eating of the sacred offering shall they bring down guilt that must be punished; it is I, the LORD, who make them sacred."

17 The LORD said to Moses, 18 "Speak to Aaron and his sons and to all the Israelites, and tell them: When anyone of the house of Israel, or any alien residing in Israel, who wishes to offer a sacrifice, brings a holocaust as a votive offering or as a free-will offering to the LORD, 19 if it is to be acceptable, the ox or sheep or goat that he offers must be an unblemished male. 20 You shall not offer one that has any defect, for such a one would not be acceptable for you. 21 When anyone presents a peace offering to the LORD from the herd or the flock in fulfillment of a vow, or as a free-will offering, if it is to find acceptance, it must be unblemished; it shall not have any defect. 22 One that is blind or crippled or maimed, or one that has a running sore or mange or ringworm, you shall not offer to the LORD; do not put such an animal on the altar as an oblation to the LORD. 23 An ox or a sheep that is in any way ill-proportioned or stunted you may indeed present as a free-will offering, but it will not be acceptable as a votive offering. 24 One that has its testicles bruised or crushed or torn out or cut off you shall not offer to the LORD. You shall neither do this in your own land 25 nor receive from a foreigner any such animals to offer up as the food of your God; since they are deformed or defective, they will not be acceptable for you."

26 The LORD said to Moses, 27 "When an ox or a lamb or a goat is born, it shall remain with its mother for seven days; only from the eighth day onward will it be acceptable, to be offered as an oblation to the LORD. 28 You shall not slaughter an ox or a sheep on one and the same day with its young. 29 Whenever you offer a thanksgiving sacrifice to the LORD, so offer it that it may be acceptable for you; 30 it must, therefore, be eaten on the same day; none of it shall be left over until the next day. I am the LORD.

31 "Be careful to observe the commandments which I, the LORD, give you, 32 and do not profane my holy name; in the midst of the Israelites I, the LORD, must be held as sacred. It is I who made you sacred 33 and led you out of the land of Egypt, that I, the LORD, might be your God."

23 The LORD said to Moses, 2 "Speak to the Israelites and tell them: The following are the festivals of the LORD, my feast days, which you shall celebrate with a sacred assembly.

3 "For six days work may be done; but the seventh day is the sabbath rest, a day for sacred assembly, on which you shall do no work. The sabbath shall belong to the LORD wherever you dwell.

4 "These, then, are the festivals of the LORD which you shall celebrate at their proper time with a sacred assembly.

10 "No lay person may eat anything holy; no guest or employee of a priest may eat anything holy. 11 But if the priest has acquired a slave by purchase, the slave may eat it like anyone born in his household; they will share his food.

12 "If a priest's daughter marries a layman, she will have no share in the holy things set aside, 13 but if she is widowed or divorced and, being childless, has had to return to her father's house as when she was young, she may share her father's food. No lay person may share it; 14 anyone who does eat a holy thing by inadvertence, will restore it to the priest with one-fifth added.

15 "They may not profane the holy offerings which the Israelites have set aside for Yahweh. 16 By eating these, they would burden them with guilt requiring a sacrifice of reparation; for I, Yahweh, have sanctified these offerings." '

17 Yahweh spoke to Moses and said:

18 'Speak to Aaron, to his sons, and to all the Israelites and say:

"Any member of the House of Israel or any alien resident in Israel who brings an offering either in payment of a vow or as a voluntary gift, and offers it as a burnt offering to Yahweh, 19 must, if he is to be acceptable, offer an unblemished male, be it bull or sheep or goat. 20 You will not offer anything with a blemish, for it would not make you acceptable.

21 "If anyone offers Yahweh a communion sacrifice, either to fulfil a vow or as a voluntary offering, the animal, be it from the herd or flock, must be perfect, if he is to be acceptable; it must be unblemished. 22 You will not offer Yahweh any animal which is blind, lame, mutilated, ulcerous, scabby or covered in sores. No part of such an animal will be offered on the altar as food burnt for Yahweh. 23 As a voluntary offering, you may offer a bull or a lamb that is underdeveloped or deformed; but such will not be acceptable in payment of a vow. 24 You will not offer Yahweh an animal if its testicles have been bruised, crushed, torn or cut off. You may not do that in your country, 25 and you may not accept any such from the hands of a stranger, to be offered as food for your God. Their deformity is a blemish, and they would not make you acceptable." '

26 Yahweh spoke to Moses and said:

27 'A calf, lamb, or kid will stay with its dam for seven days after being born. From the eighth day onwards, it will be acceptable as food burnt for Yahweh. 28 But no animal, whether cow or ewe, will be slaughtered on the same day as its young.

29 'If you offer Yahweh a sacrifice with praise, do it in the acceptable manner; 30 it must be eaten the same day; you will leave nothing over till next morning. I am Yahweh.

31 'You will keep my commands and put them into practice. I am Yahweh. 32 You will not profane my holy name — so that I may be honoured as holy among the Israelites, I, Yahweh, who make you holy, 33 I who brought you out of Egypt, to be your God, I, Yahweh.'

23 Yahweh spoke to Moses and said:

2 'Speak to the Israelites and say:

(The solemn festivals of Yahweh to which you will summon them are my sacred assemblies.)

"These are my solemn festivals:

3 "You will work for six days, but the seventh will be a day of complete rest, a day for the sacred assembly on which you do no work at all. Wherever you live, this is a Sabbath for Yahweh.

4 "These are Yahweh's solemn festivals, the sacred assemblies to which you will summon the Israelites on the appointed day:

NEW REVISED STANDARD VERSION

of the month, at twilight,ʰ there shall be a passover offering to the LORD, 6 and on the fifteenth day of the same month is the festival of unleavened bread to the LORD; seven days you shall eat unleavened bread. 7 On the first day you shall have a holy convocation; you shall not work at your occupations. 8 For seven days you shall present the LORD's offerings by fire; on the seventh day there shall be a holy convocation: you shall not work at your occupations.

9 The LORD spoke to Moses: 10 Speak to the people of Israel and say to them: When you enter the land that I am giving you and you reap its harvest, you shall bring the sheaf of the first fruits of your harvest to the priest. 11 He shall raise the sheaf before the LORD, that you may find acceptance; on the day after the sabbath the priest shall raise it. 12 On the day when you raise the sheaf, you shall offer a lamb a year old, without blemish, as a burnt offering to the LORD. 13 And the grain offering with it shall be two-tenths of an ephah of choice flour mixed with oil, an offering by fire of pleasing odor to the LORD; and the drink offering with it shall be of wine, one-fourth of a hin. 14 You shall eat no bread or parched grain or fresh ears until that very day, until you have brought the offering of your God: it is a statute forever throughout your generations in all your settlements.

15 And from the day after the sabbath, from the day on which you bring the sheaf of the elevation offering, you shall count off seven weeks; they shall be complete. 16 You shall count until the day after the seventh sabbath, fifty days; then you shall present an offering of new grain to the LORD. 17 You shall bring from your settlements two loaves of bread as an elevation offering, each made of two-tenths of an ephah; they shall be of choice flour, baked with leaven, as first fruits to the LORD. 18 You shall present with the bread seven lambs a year old without blemish, one young bull, and two rams; they shall be a burnt offering to the LORD, along with their grain offering and their drink offerings, an offering by fire of pleasing odor to the LORD. 19 You shall also offer one male goat for a sin offering, and two male lambs a year old as a sacrifice of well-being. 20 The priest shall raise them with the bread of the first fruits as an elevation offering before the LORD, together with the two lambs; they shall be holy to the LORD for the priest. 21 On that same day you shall make proclamation; you shall hold a holy convocation; you shall not work at your occupations. This is a statute forever in all your settlements throughout your generations.

22 When you reap the harvest of your land, you shall not reap to the very edges of your field, or gather the gleanings of your harvest; you shall leave them for the poor and for the alien: I am the LORD your God.

23 The LORD spoke to Moses, saying: 24 Speak to the people of Israel, saying: In the seventh month, on the first day of the month, you shall observe a day of complete rest, a holy convocation commemorated with trumpet blasts. 25 You shall not work at your occupations; and you shall present the LORD's offering by fire.

26 The LORD spoke to Moses, saying: 27 Now, the tenth day of this seventh month is the day of atonement; it shall be a holy convocation for you: you shall deny yourselvesⁱ and present the LORD's offering by fire; 28 and you shall do no work during that entire day; for it is a day of atonement, to make atonement on your behalf before the LORD your God. 29 For anyone who does not practice self-denialʲ during that entire day shall be cut off from the people. 30 And anyone who does any work during that entire day, such a one I will destroy from the midst of the people. 31 You shall

REVISED ENGLISH BIBLE

dusk and dark is the LORD's Passover. 6 On the fifteenth day of the same month begins the LORD's pilgrim-feast of Unleavened Bread; for seven days you are to eat unleavened bread. 7 On the first day there will be a sacred assembly; you are not to do your daily work. 8 For seven days you must present your food-offerings to the LORD. On the seventh day also there will be a sacred assembly; you are not to do your daily work.

9 The LORD told Moses 10 to say to the Israelites: When you enter the land which I am giving you, and you reap its harvest, you are to bring the first sheaf of your harvest to the priest. 11 He will present the sheaf as a dedicated portion before the LORD on the day after the sabbath, so as to gain acceptance for you. 12 On the day you present the sheaf, you are to prepare a perfect yearling ram for a whole-offering to the LORD, 13 together with the proper grain-offering, two tenths of an ephah of flour mixed with oil, as a food-offering to the LORD, of soothing odour, and also with the proper drink-offering, a quarter of a hin of wine. 14 You are to eat neither bread nor roasted or fully ripened grain until that day, the day on which you bring your God his offering; this is a rule binding on your descendants for all time wherever you live.

15 From the day after the sabbath, the day on which you bring your sheaf as a dedicated portion, you are to count off seven full weeks. 16 The day after the seventh sabbath will make fifty days, and then you will present to the LORD a grain-offering from the new crop. 17 Bring from your homes two loaves as a dedicated portion; they are to contain two tenths of an ephah of flour and be baked with leaven. They are the LORD's firstfruits. 18 In addition to the bread you are to present seven perfect yearling sheep, one young bull and two rams. They will be a whole-offering to the LORD with the proper grain-offering and the proper drink-offering, a food-offering of soothing odour to the LORD. 19 You must also prepare one he-goat as a purification-offering and two yearling sheep as a shared-offering, 20 and the priest will present the two sheep in addition to the bread of the firstfruits as a dedicated portion before the LORD. They are a holy-gift to the LORD for the priest. 21 On that same day you are to proclaim a sacred assembly for yourselves; you must not do your daily work. This is a rule binding on your descendants for all time wherever you live.

22 When you reap the harvest in your land, do not reap right up to the edges of your field or gather the gleanings of your crop. Leave them for the poor and for the alien. I am the LORD your God.

23 When the LORD spoke to Moses he said: 24 Tell the Israelites that in the seventh month they are to keep the first day as a day of solemn abstinence from work, a day of remembrance and acclamation, of sacred assembly. 25 They must not do their daily work, but are to present a food-offering to the LORD.

26 When the LORD spoke to Moses he said: 27 Further, the tenth day of this seventh month is the Day of Atonement. There is to be a sacred assembly; you yourselves must fast and present a food-offering to the LORD. 28 On that day you are to do no work because it is a day of expiation, on which expiation is made for you before the LORD your God. 29 Everyone who does not fast on that day must be cut off from his father's kin, 30 and everyone who does any work on that day I shall root out from among them. 31 Do no work what-

---

ʰ Heb *between the two evenings*   ⁱ Or *shall fast*   ʲ Or *does not fast*

23:11 **on the day:** *or* from the day.   23:20 **before the LORD:** *so Lat.; Heb.* adds in addition to the two sheep.   23:27 **Atonement:** *or* Expiation.

5 The Passover of the LORD falls on the fourteenth day of the first month, at the evening twilight. 6 The fifteenth day of this month is the LORD's feast of Unleavened Bread. For seven days you shall eat unleavened bread. 7 On the first of these days you shall hold a sacred assembly and do no sort of work. 8 On each of the seven days you shall offer an oblation to the LORD. Then on the seventh day you shall again hold a sacred assembly and do no sort of work."

9 The LORD said to Moses, 10 "Speak to the Israelites and tell them: When you come into the land which I am giving you, and reap your harvest, you shall bring a sheaf of the first fruits of your harvest to the priest, 11 who shall wave the sheaf before the LORD that it may be acceptable for you. On the day after the sabbath the priest shall do this. 12 On this day, when your sheaf is waved, you shall offer to the LORD for a holocaust an unblemished yearling lamb. 13 Its cereal offering shall be two tenths of an ephah of fine flour mixed with oil, as a sweet-smelling oblation to the LORD; and its libation shall be a fourth of a hin of wine. 14 Until this day, when you bring your God this offering, you shall not eat any bread or roasted grain or fresh kernels. This shall be a perpetual statute for you and your descendants wherever you dwell.

15 "Beginning with the day after the sabbath, the day on which you bring the wave-offering sheaf, you shall count seven full weeks, 16 and then on the day after the seventh week, the fiftieth day, you shall present the new cereal offering to the LORD. 17 For the wave offering of your first fruits to the LORD, you shall bring with you from wherever you live two loaves of bread made of two tenths of an ephah of fine flour and baked with leaven. 18 Besides the bread, you shall offer to the LORD a holocaust of seven unblemished yearling lambs, one young bull, and two rams, along with their cereal offering and libations, as a sweet-smelling oblation to the LORD. 19 One male goat shall be sacrificed as a sin offering, and two yearling lambs as a peace offering. 20 The priest shall wave the bread of the first fruits and the two lambs as a wave offering before the LORD; these shall be sacred to the LORD and belong to the priest. 21 On this same day you shall by proclamation have a sacred assembly, and no sort of work may be done. This shall be a perpetual statute for you and your descendants wherever you dwell.

22 "When you reap the harvest of your land, you shall not be so thorough that you reap the field to its very edge, nor shall you glean the stray ears of your grain. These things you shall leave for the poor and the alien. I, the LORD, am your God."

23 The LORD said to Moses, 24 "Tell the Israelites: On the first day of the seventh month you shall keep a sabbath rest, with a sacred assembly and with the trumpet blasts as a reminder; 25 you shall then do no sort of work, and you shall offer an oblation to the LORD."

26 The LORD said to Moses, 27 "The tenth of this seventh month is the Day of Atonement, when you shall hold a sacred assembly and mortify yourselves and offer an oblation to the LORD. 28 On this day you shall not do any work, because it is the Day of Atonement, when atonement is made for you before the LORD, your God. 29 Anyone who does not mortify himself on this day shall be cut off from his people; 30 and if anyone does any work on this day, I will remove him from the midst of his people. 31 This is a

5 "The fourteenth day of the first month, at twilight, is the Passover of Yahweh; 6 and the fifteenth day of the same month is the feast of Unleavened Bread for Yahweh. For seven days you will eat unleavened bread. 7 On the first day you will hold a sacred assembly; you will do no heavy work. 8 For seven days you will offer food burnt for Yahweh. On the seventh day there will be a sacred assembly; you will do no heavy work." '

9 Yahweh spoke to Moses and said:

10 'Speak to the Israelites and say:

"When you enter the country which I am giving you and reap the harvest there, you will bring the priest the first sheaf of your harvest, 11 and he will present it to Yahweh with the gesture of offering, for you to be acceptable. The priest will make this offering on the day after the Sabbath, 12 and on the same day as you make this offering, you will offer Yahweh an unblemished lamb one year old as a burnt offering. 13 The cereal offering for that day will be two-tenths of wheaten flour mixed with oil, as food burnt as a smell pleasing to Yahweh. The libation will be a quarter of a hin of wine. 14 You will eat no bread, roasted ears of wheat or fresh produce before this day, before making the offering to your God. This is a perpetual law for all your descendants, wherever you live.

15 "From the day after the Sabbath, the day on which you bring the sheaf of offering, you will count seven full weeks. 16 You will count fifty days, to the day after the seventh Sabbath, and then you will offer Yahweh a new cereal offering. 17 You will bring bread from your homes to present with the gesture of offering — two loaves, made of two-tenths of wheaten flour baked with leaven; these are first-fruits for Yahweh. 18 In addition to the bread, you will offer seven unblemished lambs a year old, a young bull and two rams, as a burnt offering to Yahweh with a cereal offering and a libation, as food burnt as a smell pleasing to Yahweh. 19 You will also offer a goat as a sacrifice for sin, and two lambs a year old as communion sacrifice. 20 The priest will present them before Yahweh with the gesture of offering, in addition to the bread of the first-fruits. These, and the two lambs, are holy things for Yahweh, and will revert to the priest.

21 "On the same day, you will hold an assembly; for you this will be a sacred assembly; you will do no heavy work. This is a perpetual law for your descendants, wherever you live.

22 "When you reap the harvest in your country, you will not reap to the very edges of your field, nor will you gather the gleanings of the harvest. You will leave them for the poor and the stranger. I am Yahweh your God." '

23 Yahweh spoke to Moses and said:

24 'Speak to the Israelites and say:

"The first day of the seventh month[e] will be a day of rest for you, of remembrance and acclamation, a sacred assembly. 25 You will do no heavy work and you will offer food burnt for Yahweh." '

26 Yahweh spoke to Moses and said:

27 'But the tenth day of this seventh month will be the Day of Expiation. You will hold a sacred assembly. You will fast and offer food burnt for Yahweh. 28 You will do no work that day, for it is the Day of Expiation, on which the rite of expiation will be performed for you before Yahweh your God. 29 Anyone who fails to fast that day will be outlawed from his people; 30 anyone who works that day I shall eliminate from his people. 31 No work will be done —

e 23 A Canaanite new-moon festival, but held now in one month only, the first of autumn.

NEW REVISED STANDARD VERSION	REVISED ENGLISH BIBLE

NEW REVISED STANDARD VERSION

do no work: it is a statute forever throughout your generations in all your settlements. 32 It shall be to you a sabbath of complete rest, and you shall deny yourselves;k on the ninth day of the month at evening, from evening to evening you shall keep your sabbath.

33 The LORD spoke to Moses, saying: 34 Speak to the people of Israel, saying: On the fifteenth day of this seventh month, and lasting seven days, there shall be the festival of boothsl to the LORD. 35 The first day shall be a holy convocation; you shall not work at your occupations. 36 Seven days you shall present the LORD's offerings by fire; on the eighth day you shall observe a holy convocation and present the LORD's offerings by fire; it is a solemn assembly; you shall not work at your occupations.

37 These are the appointed festivals of the LORD, which you shall celebrate as times of holy convocation, for presenting to the LORD offerings by fire — burnt offerings and grain offerings, sacrifices and drink offerings, each on its proper day — 38 apart from the sabbaths of the LORD, and apart from your gifts, and apart from all your votive offerings, and apart from all your freewill offerings, which you give to the LORD.

39 Now, the fifteenth day of the seventh month, when you have gathered in the produce of the land, you shall keep the festival of the LORD, lasting seven days; a complete rest on the first day, and a complete rest on the eighth day. 40 On the first day you shall take the fruit of majesticm trees, branches of palm trees, boughs of leafy trees, and willows of the brook; and you shall rejoice before the LORD your God for seven days. 41 You shall keep it as a festival to the LORD seven days in the year; you shall keep it in the seventh month as a statute forever throughout your generations. 42 You shall live in booths for seven days; all that are citizens in Israel shall live in booths, 43 so that your generations may know that I made the people of Israel live in booths when I brought them out of the land of Egypt: I am the LORD your God.

44 Thus Moses declared to the people of Israel the appointed festivals of the LORD.

24 The LORD spoke to Moses, saying: 2 Command the people of Israel to bring you pure oil of beaten olives for the lamp, that a light may be kept burning regularly. 3 Aaron shall set it up in the tent of meeting, outside the curtain of the covenant,n to burn from evening to morning before the LORD regularly; it shall be a statute forever throughout your generations. 4 He shall set up the lamps on the lampstand of pure goldo before the LORD regularly.

5 You shall take choice flour, and bake twelve loaves of it; two-tenths of an ephah shall be in each loaf. 6 You shall place them in two rows, six in a row, on the table of pure gold.p 7 You shall put pure frankincense with each row, to be a token offering for the bread, as an offering by fire to the LORD. 8 Every sabbath day Aaron shall set them in order before the LORD regularly as a commitment of the people of Israel, as a covenant forever. 9 They shall be for Aaron and his descendants, who shall eat them in a holy place, for they are most holy portions for him from the offerings by fire to the LORD, a perpetual due.

10 A man whose mother was an Israelite and whose father was an Egyptian came out among the people of Israel; and the Israelite woman's son and a certain Israelite began fighting in the camp. 11 The Israelite woman's son blasphemed the Name in a curse. And they brought him to Moses — now his mother's name was Shelomith, daughter of Dibri, of the tribe of Dan — 12 and they put him in cus-

REVISED ENGLISH BIBLE

soever; it is a rule binding on your descendants for all time wherever you live. 32 It is for you a day of solemn abstinence from work, and you must fast. From the evening of the ninth day to the following evening you are to keep your sabbath rest.

33 The LORD told Moses 34 to say to the Israelites: On the fifteenth day of this seventh month the LORD's pilgrim-feast of Booths begins, and it lasts for seven days. 35 On the first day there is to be a sacred assembly; you are not to do your daily work. 36 For seven days present a food-offering to the LORD; on the eighth day there will be a sacred assembly, and you are to present a food-offering to the LORD. It is the closing ceremony; you must not do your daily work.

37 These are the appointed seasons of the LORD which you are to proclaim as sacred assemblies for presenting food-offerings to the LORD, whole-offerings and grain-offerings, shared-offerings and drink-offerings, each on its day, 38 besides the LORD's sabbaths and all your gifts, your votive offerings and your freewill-offerings to the LORD.

39 Further, from the fifteenth day of the seventh month, when the harvest has been gathered, you are to keep the LORD's pilgrim-feast for seven days. The first day is a day of solemn abstinence from work and so is the eighth day. 40 On the first day take the fruit of citrus trees, palm-fronds, and leafy branches, and willows from the riverside, and rejoice before the LORD your God for seven days. 41 You are to keep this as a pilgrim-feast in the LORD's honour for seven days every year. It is a rule binding for all time on your descendants; in the seventh month you are to hold this pilgrim-feast. 42 You are to live in booths for seven days, all who are native Israelites, 43 so that your descendants may be reminded how I made the Israelites live in booths when I brought them out of Egypt. I am the LORD your God.

44 Thus Moses announced to the Israelites the appointed seasons of the LORD.

24 WHEN the LORD spoke to Moses he said: 2 Order the Israelites to bring pure oil of pounded olives ready for the regular mounting of the lamp 3 outside the curtain of the Testimony in the Tent of Meeting. Aaron must keep the lamp in trim regularly from dusk to dawn before the LORD: this is a rule binding on your descendants for all time. 4 The lamps on the lampstand, ritually clean, must be regularly kept trimmed by him before the LORD.

5 You are to take flour and bake it into twelve loaves, two tenths of an ephah to each. 6 Arrange them in two rows, six to a row on the table, ritually clean, before the LORD. 7 Sprinkle pure frankincense on the rows, and this will be a token of the bread, offered to the LORD as a food-offering. 8 Regularly, sabbath after sabbath, it is to be arranged before the LORD as a gift from the Israelites. This is a covenant for ever; 9 it is the privilege of Aaron and his sons, and they are to eat the bread in a holy place, because it is the holiest of holy-gifts. It is his due out of the food-offerings of the LORD for all time.

10-11 IN the Israelite camp there was a certain man whose mother was an Israelite and his father an Egyptian; his mother's name was Shelomith daughter of Dibri of the tribe of Dan. He went out and, becoming involved in a brawl with an Israelite of pure descent, he uttered the holy name in blasphemy. He was brought to Moses, 12 and put in cus-

---

k Or *shall fast* l Or *tabernacles*: Heb *succoth* m Meaning of Heb uncertain n Or *treaty*, or *testament*; Heb *eduth* o Heb *pure lampstand* p Heb *pure table*

23:34 **Booths:** *or* Tabernacles. 23:40 **willows:** *or* poplars.

perpetual statute for you and your descendants wherever you dwell: you shall do no work, 32 but shall keep a sabbath of complete rest and mortify yourselves. Beginning on the evening of the ninth of the month, you shall keep this sabbath of yours from evening to evening."

33 The LORD said to Moses, 34 "Tell the Israelites: The fifteenth day of this seventh month is the LORD's feast of Booths, which shall continue for seven days. 35 On the first day there shall be a sacred assembly, and you shall do no sort of work. 36 For seven days you shall offer an oblation to the LORD, and on the eighth day you shall again hold a sacred assembly and offer an oblation to the LORD. On that solemn closing you shall do no sort of work.

37 "These, therefore, are the festivals of the LORD on which you shall proclaim a sacred assembly, and offer as an oblation to the LORD holocausts and cereal offerings, sacrifices and libations, as prescribed for each day, 38 in addition to those of the LORD's sabbaths, your donations, your various votive offerings and the free-will offerings that you present to the LORD.

39 "On the fifteenth day, then, of the seventh month, when you have gathered in the produce of the land, you shall celebrate a pilgrim feast of the LORD for a whole week. The first and the eighth day shall be days of complete rest. 40 On the first day you shall gather foliage from majestic trees, branches of palms and boughs of myrtles and of valley poplars, and then for a week you shall make merry before the LORD, your God. 41 By perpetual statute for you and your descendants you shall keep this pilgrim feast of the LORD for one whole week in the seventh month of the year. 42 During this week every native Israelite among you shall dwell in booths, 43 that your descendants may realize that, when I led the Israelites out of the land of Egypt, I made them dwell in booths. I, the LORD, am your God."

44 Thus did Moses announce to the Israelites the festivals of the LORD.

24 The LORD said to Moses, 2 "Order the Israelites to bring you clear oil of crushed olives for the light, so that you may keep lamps burning regularly. 3 In the meeting tent, outside the veil that hangs in front of the commandments, Aaron shall set up the lamps to burn before the LORD regularly, from evening till morning. Thus, by a perpetual statute for you and your descendants, 4 the lamps shall be set up on the pure gold lampstand, to burn regularly before the LORD.

5 "You shall take fine flour and bake it into twelve cakes, using two tenths of an ephah of flour for each cake. 6 These you shall place in two piles, six in each pile, on the pure gold table before the LORD. 7 On each pile put some pure frankincense, which shall serve as an oblation to the LORD, a token offering for the bread. 8 Regularly on each sabbath day this bread shall be set out afresh before the LORD, offered on the part of the Israelites by an everlasting agreement. 9 It shall belong to Aaron and his sons, who must eat it in a sacred place, since, as something most sacred among the various oblations to the LORD, it is his by perpetual right."

10 Among the Israelites there was a man born of an Israelite mother (Shelomith, daughter of Dibri, of the tribe of Dan) and an Egyptian father. 11 This man quarreled publicly with another Israelite and cursed and blasphemed the LORD's name. So the people brought him to Moses, 12 who

this is a perpetual law for your descendants wherever you live. 32 It must be a day of complete rest for you. You will fast; on the evening of the ninth day of the month, from this evening till the following evening, you will rest completely.'

33 Yahweh spoke to Moses and said:
34 'Speak to the Israelites and say:
"On the fifteenth day of this seventh month there will be the feast of Shelters for Yahweh, lasting for seven days. 35 The first day will be a day of sacred assembly; you will do no heavy work. 36 For seven days you will offer food burnt for Yahweh. On the eighth day you will hold a sacred assembly and you will offer food burnt for Yahweh. It is a day of solemn meeting; you will do no heavy work.

37 "These are Yahweh's solemn festivals to which you will summon the Israelites, the sacred assemblies for the purpose of offering food burnt for Yahweh, consisting of burnt offerings, cereal offerings, sacrifices and libations, each on its appropriate day, 38 besides Yahweh's Sabbaths, and your presents and all your votive and voluntary gifts that you make to Yahweh.

39 "But on the fifteenth day of the seventh month, when you have gathered in the produce of the land, you will celebrate the feast of Yahweh for seven days. The first and eighth days will be days of rest. 40 On the first day you will take choice fruit, palm branches, boughs of leafy trees and flowering shrubs from the river bank, and for seven days enjoy yourselves before Yahweh your God. 41 You will celebrate a feast for Yahweh in this way for seven days every year. This is a perpetual law for your descendants.

"You will keep this feast in the seventh month. 42 For seven days you will live in shelters: all the citizens of Israel will live in shelters, 43 so that your descendants may know that I made the Israelites live in shelters when I brought them out of Egypt, I, Yahweh your God." '

44 Moses then promulgated Yahweh's solemn festivals to the Israelites.

24 Yahweh spoke to Moses and said:
2 'Order the Israelites to bring you crushed-olive oil for the lamp-stand, and keep a flame burning there continually. 3 Aaron will keep it permanently in trim from evening to morning, outside the curtain of the Testimony in the Tent of Meeting, before Yahweh. This is a perpetual decree for your descendants: 4 Aaron will keep the lamps permanently trimmed on the pure lamp-stand before Yahweh.

5 'You will take wheaten flour and with it bake twelve loaves, each of two-tenths of an ephah. 6 You will then place them in two rows of six on the pure table before Yahweh 7 and put pure incense on each row, to make it food offered as a memorial, food burnt for Yahweh. 8 Every Sabbath they will be arranged before Yahweh. The Israelites will provide them as a permanent covenant. 9 They will belong to Aaron and his sons, who will eat them inside the holy place since, for him, they are an especially holy part of the food burnt for Yahweh. This is a permanent law.'

10 There was a man whose mother was an Israelite woman and whose father was an Egyptian. He came out of his house and, in the camp, surrounded by the Israelites, he began to quarrel with a man who was an Israelite. 11 Now the son of the Israelite woman blasphemed the Name and cursed it. He was then taken to Moses (his mother's name was Shelomith daughter of Dibri, of the tribe of Dan). 12 He

NEW REVISED STANDARD VERSION

REVISED ENGLISH BIBLE

tody, until the decision of the LORD should be made clear to them.

13 The LORD said to Moses, saying: 14 Take the blasphemer outside the camp; and let all who were within hearing lay their hands on his head, and let the whole congregation stone him. 15 And speak to the people of Israel, saying: Anyone who curses God shall bear the sin. 16 One who blasphemes the name of the LORD shall be put to death; the whole congregation shall stone the blasphemer. Aliens as well as citizens, when they blaspheme the Name, shall be put to death. 17 Anyone who kills a human being shall be put to death. 18 Anyone who kills an animal shall make restitution for it, life for life. 19 Anyone who maims another shall suffer the same injury in return: 20 fracture for fracture, eye for eye, tooth for tooth; the injury inflicted is the injury to be suffered. 21 One who kills an animal shall make restitution for it; but one who kills a human being shall be put to death. 22 You shall have one law for the alien and for the citizen: for I am the LORD your God. 23 Moses spoke thus to the people of Israel; and they took the blasphemer outside the camp, and stoned him to death. The people of Israel did as the LORD had commanded Moses.

tody until the LORD's will should be made clear to them.

13 When the LORD spoke to Moses he said: 14 The man who blasphemed is to be taken outside the camp, and let everyone who heard him lay a hand on his head, and let the whole community stone him to death. 15 Say to the Israelites: When anyone, whoever he is, blasphemes his God, he must accept responsibility for his sin. 16 Whoever utters the name of the LORD must be put to death. The whole community must stone him; whether alien or native, if he utters the name, he must be put to death.

17 If one person strikes another and kills him, he must be put to death. 18 Whoever strikes an animal and kills it is to make restitution, life for life. 19 If anyone injures and disfigures a fellow-countryman, it must be done to him as he has done: 20 fracture for fracture, eye for eye, tooth for tooth; the injury and disfigurement that he has inflicted on another must in turn be inflicted on him.

21 Whoever strikes and kills an animal is to make restitution, but whoever strikes a man and kills him must be put to death. 22 You must have one and the same law for resident alien and native Israelite. For I am the LORD your God. 23 Moses spoke thus to the Israelites, and they took the man who had blasphemed out of the camp and stoned him to death. The Israelites did as the LORD had commanded Moses.

25 The LORD spoke to Moses on Mount Sinai, saying: 2 Speak to the people of Israel and say to them: When you enter the land that I am giving you, the land shall observe a sabbath for the LORD. 3 Six years you shall sow your field, and six years you shall prune your vineyard, and gather in their yield; 4 but in the seventh year there shall be a sabbath of complete rest for the land, a sabbath for the LORD: you shall not sow your field or prune your vineyard. 5 You shall not reap the aftergrowth of your harvest or gather the grapes of your unpruned vine: it shall be a year of complete rest for the land. 6 You may eat what the land yields during its sabbath—you, your male and female slaves, your hired and your bound laborers who live with you; 7 for your livestock also, and for the wild animals in your land all its yield shall be for food.

8 You shall count off seven weeks*q* of years, seven times seven years, so that the period of seven weeks of years gives forty-nine years. 9 Then you shall have the trumpet sounded loud; on the tenth day of the seventh month—on the day of atonement—you shall have the trumpet sounded throughout all your land. 10 And you shall hallow the fiftieth year and you shall proclaim liberty throughout the land to all its inhabitants. It shall be a jubilee for you: you shall return, every one of you, to your property and every one of you to your family. 11 That fiftieth year shall be a jubilee for you: you shall not sow, or reap the aftergrowth, or harvest the unpruned vines. 12 For it is a jubilee; it shall be holy to you: you shall eat only what the field itself produces.

13 In this year of jubilee you shall return, every one of you, to your property. 14 When you make a sale to your neighbor or buy from your neighbor, you shall not cheat one another. 15 When you buy from your neighbor, you shall pay only for the number of years since the jubilee; the seller shall charge you only for the remaining crop years. 16 If the years are more, you shall increase the price, and if the years are fewer, you shall diminish the price; for it is a certain number of harvests that are being sold to you. 17 You shall not cheat one another, but you shall fear your God; for I am the LORD your God.

25 WHEN the LORD spoke to Moses on Mount Sinai he told him 2 to say to the Israelites: When you enter the land which I am giving you, the land must keep sabbaths to the LORD. 3 For six years you may sow your fields and prune your vineyards and gather the harvest, 4 but in the seventh year the land is to have a sabbatical rest, a sabbath to the LORD. You are not to sow your field or prune your vineyard; 5 you are not to harvest the crop that grows from fallen grain, or gather in the grapes from the unpruned vines. It is to be a year of rest for the land. 6 Yet what the land itself produces in the sabbath year will be food for you, for your male and female slaves, for your hired man, and for the stranger lodging under your roof, 7 for your cattle and for the wild animals in your country. Everything it produces may be used for food.

8 You are to count off seven sabbaths of years, that is seven times seven years, forty-nine years, 9 and in the seventh month on the tenth day of the month, on the Day of Atonement, you are to send the ram's horn throughout your land to sound a blast. 10 Hallow the fiftieth year and proclaim liberation in the land for all its inhabitants. It is to be a jubilee year for you: each of you is to return to his holding, everyone to his family. 11 The fiftieth year is to be a jubilee for you: you are not to sow, and you are not to harvest the self-sown crop, or gather in the grapes from the unpruned vines, 12 for it is a jubilee, to be kept holy by you. You are to eat the produce direct from the land.

13 In this year of jubilee every one of you is to return to his holding. 14 When you sell or buy land amongst yourselves, neither party must exploit the other. 15 You must pay your fellow-countryman according to the number of years since the jubilee, and he must sell to you according to the remaining number of annual crops. 16 The more years there are to run, the higher the price; the fewer the years, the lower, because what he is selling you is a series of crops. 17 You must not victimize one another, but fear your God, because I am the LORD your God. 18 Observe my statutes,

---

q Or sabbaths

25:9 **Atonement:** *or* Expiation.

kept him in custody till a decision from the LORD should settle the case for them. 13 The LORD then said to Moses, 14 "Take the blasphemer outside the camp, and when all who heard him have laid their hands on his head, let the whole community stone him. 15 Tell the Israelites: Anyone who curses his God shall bear the penalty of his sin; 16 whoever blasphemes the name of the LORD shall be put to death. The whole community shall stone him; alien and native alike must be put to death for blaspheming the LORD'S name.

17 "Whoever takes the life of any human being shall be put to death; 18 whoever takes the life of an animal shall make restitution of another animal. A life for a life! 19 Anyone who inflicts an injury on his neighbor shall receive the same in return. 20 Limb for limb, eye for eye, tooth for tooth! The same injury that a man gives another shall be inflicted on him in return. 21 Whoever slays an animal shall make restitution, but whoever slays a man shall be put to death. 22 You shall have but one rule, for alien and native alike. I, the LORD, am your God."

23 When Moses told this to the Israelites, they took the blasphemer outside the camp and stoned him; they carried out the command that the LORD had given Moses.

25 The LORD said to Moses on Mount Sinai, 2 "Speak to the Israelites and tell them: When you enter the land that I am giving you, let the land, too, keep a sabbath for the LORD. 3 For six years you may sow your field, and for six years prune your vineyard, gathering in their produce. 4 But during the seventh year the land shall have a complete rest, a sabbath for the LORD, when you may neither sow your field nor prune your vineyard. 5 The aftergrowth of your harvest you shall not reap, nor shall you pick the grapes of your untrimmed vines in this year of sabbath rest for the land. 6 While the land has its sabbath, all its produce will be food equally for you yourself and for your male and female slaves, for your hired help and the tenants who live with you, 7 and likewise for your livestock and for the wild animals on your land.

8 "Seven weeks of years shall you count — seven times seven years — so that the seven cycles amount to forty-nine years. 9 Then, on the tenth day of the seventh month let the trumpet resound; on this, the Day of Atonement, the trumpet blast shall re-echo throughout your land. 10 This fiftieth year you shall make sacred by proclaiming liberty in the land for all its inhabitants. It shall be a jubilee for you, when every one of you shall return to his own property, every one to his own family estate. 11 In this fiftieth year, your year of jubilee, you shall not sow, nor shall you reap the aftergrowth or pick the grapes from the untrimmed vines. 12 Since this is the jubilee, which shall be sacred for you, you may not eat of its produce, except as taken directly from the field.

13 "In this year of jubilee, then, every one of you shall return to his own property. 14 Therefore, when you sell any land to your neighbor or buy any from him, do not deal unfairly. 15 On the basis of the number of years since the last jubilee shall you purchase the land from him; and so also, on the basis of the number of years for crops, shall he sell it to you. 16 When the years are many, the price shall be so much the more; when the years are few, the price shall be so much the less. For it is really the number of crops that he sells you. 17 Do not deal unfairly, then; but stand in fear of your god. I, the LORD, am your God.

was then put under guard until Yahweh's will should be made clear to them.

13 Yahweh spoke to Moses and said:

14 'Take the man who pronounced the curse outside the camp. All those who heard him must then lay their hands on his head, and the whole community must then stone him. 15 Then say to the Israelites:

"Anyone who curses his God will bear the consequences of his sin, 16 and anyone who blasphemes the name of Yahweh will be put to death; the whole community will stone him; be he alien or native-born, if he blasphemes the Name, he will be put to death.

17 "Anyone who strikes down any other human being will be put to death.

18 "Anyone who strikes down an animal will make restitution for it: a life for a life.

19 "Anyone who injures a neighbour shall receive the same in return, 20 broken limb for broken limb, eye for eye, tooth for tooth. As the injury inflicted, so will be the injury suffered. 21 Whoever strikes down an animal will make restitution for it, and whoever strikes down a human being will be put to death. 22 The sentence you pass will be the same, whether on native-born or on alien; for I am Yahweh your God." '

23 Moses having told the Israelites this, they took the man who had pronounced the curse out of the camp and stoned him. And so the Israelites carried out Yahweh's order to Moses.

25 Yahweh spoke to Moses on Mount Sinai and said: 2 'Speak to the Israelites and say to them:

"When you enter the country which I am giving you, the land must keep a Sabbath's rest for Yahweh. 3 For six years you will sow your field, for six years you will prune your vineyard and gather its produce. 4 But in the seventh year the land will have a sabbatical rest, a Sabbath for Yahweh. You will neither sow your field, nor prune your vineyard, 5 nor reap any grain which has grown of its own accord, nor gather the grapes from your untrimmed vine. It will be a year of rest for the land. 6 But what the land produces in its Sabbath will serve to feed you, your slave, male or female, your employee and your guest residing with you; 7 for your cattle too, and the wild animals of your country, whatever it produces will serve as food.

8 "You will count seven weeks of years — seven times seven years, that is to say a period of seven weeks of years, forty-nine years. 9 And on the tenth day of the seventh month you will sound the trumpet; on the Day of Expiation you will sound the trumpet throughout the land. 10 You will declare this fiftieth year to be sacred and proclaim the liberation of all the country's inhabitants. You will keep this as a jubilee: each of you will return to his ancestral property, each to his own clan. 11 This fiftieth year will be a jubilee year for you; in it you will not sow, you will not harvest the grain that has come up on its own or in it gather grapes from your untrimmed vine. 12 The jubilee will be a holy thing for you; during it you will eat whatever the fields produce.

13 "In this year of jubilee, each of you will return to his ancestral property. 14 If you buy land from, or sell land to, your fellow-countryman, neither of you may exploit the other. 15 In buying from your fellow-countryman, you will take account of the number of years since the jubilee; the sale-price he fixes for you will depend on the number of productive years still to run. 16 The greater the number of years, the higher the price you will ask for it; the fewer the number of years, the greater the reduction; for what he is selling you is a certain number of harvests. 17 So you will not exploit one another, but fear your God, for I am Yahweh your God.

18 You shall observe my statutes and faithfully keep my ordinances, so that you may live on the land securely. 19 The land will yield its fruit, and you will eat your fill and live on it securely. 20 Should you ask, What shall we eat in the seventh year, if we may not sow or gather in our crop? 21 I will order my blessing for you in the sixth year, so that it will yield a crop for three years. 22 When you sow in the eighth year, you will be eating from the old crop; until the ninth year, when its produce comes in, you shall eat the old. 23 The land shall not be sold in perpetuity, for the land is mine; with me you are but aliens and tenants. 24 Throughout the land that you hold, you shall provide for the redemption of the land.

25 If anyone of your kin falls into difficulty and sells a piece of property, then the next of kin shall come and redeem what the relative has sold. 26 If the person has no one to redeem it, but then prospers and finds sufficient means to do so, 27 the years since its sale shall be computed and the difference shall be refunded to the person to whom it was sold, and the property shall be returned. 28 But if there is not sufficient means to recover it, what was sold shall remain with the purchaser until the year of jubilee; in the jubilee it shall be released, and the property shall be returned.

29 If anyone sells a dwelling house in a walled city, it may be redeemed until a year has elapsed since its sale; the right of redemption shall be one year. 30 If it is not redeemed before a full year has elapsed, a house that is in a walled city shall pass in perpetuity to the purchaser, throughout the generations; it shall not be released in the jubilee. 31 But houses in villages that have no walls around them shall be classed as open country; they may be redeemed, and they shall be released in the jubilee. 32 As for the cities of the Levites, the Levites shall forever have the right of redemption of the houses in the cities belonging to them. 33 Such property as may be redeemed from the Levites—houses sold in a city belonging to them—shall be released in the jubilee; because the houses in the cities of the Levites are their possession among the people of Israel. 34 But the open land around their cities may not be sold; for that is their possession for all time.

35 If any of your kin fall into difficulty and become dependent on you, *r* you shall support them; they shall live with you as though resident aliens. 36 Do not take interest in advance or otherwise make a profit from them, but fear your God; let them live with you. 37 You shall not lend them your money at interest taken in advance, or provide them food at a profit. 38 I am the Lord your God, who brought you out of the land of Egypt, to give you the land of Canaan, to be your God.

39 If any who are dependent on you become so impoverished that they sell themselves to you, you shall not make them serve as slaves. 40 They shall remain with you as hired or bound laborers. They shall serve with you until the year of the jubilee. 41 Then they and their children shall be free from your authority; they shall go back to their own family and return to their ancestral property. 42 For they are my servants, whom I brought out of the land of Egypt; they shall not be sold as slaves are sold. 43 You shall not rule over them with harshness, but shall fear your God. 44 As for the male and female slaves whom you may have, it is from the nations around you that you may acquire male and female slaves. 45 You may also acquire them from

keep my judgements, and carry them out; and you will live without any fear in the land. 19 The land will yield its harvest; you will eat your fill and live there secure. 20 If you ask what you are to eat during the seventh year, seeing that you will neither sow nor gather the harvest, 21 I shall ordain my blessing for you in the sixth year and the land will produce a crop sufficient for three years. 22 When you sow in the eighth year, you will still be eating from the earlier crop; you will eat the old until the new crop is gathered in the ninth year.

23 No land may be sold outright, because the land is mine, and you come to it as aliens and tenants of mine. 24 Throughout the whole land you hold, you must allow a right of redemption over land which has been sold.

25 If one of you is reduced to poverty and sells part of his holding, his next-of-kin who has the duty of redemption may come and redeem what his kinsman has sold. 26 When a man has no such next-of-kin and himself becomes able to afford its redemption, 27 he must take into account the years since the sale and repay the purchaser the balance up to the jubilee. Then he may return to his holding. 28 But if the man cannot afford to buy back the property, it remains in the hands of the purchaser till the jubilee year. It then reverts to the original owner, and he can return to his holding.

29 When a man sells a dwelling-house in a walled town, he must retain the right of redemption till a full year has elapsed after the sale; for that time he has the right of redemption. 30 If it is not redeemed before a full year is out, the house in the walled town will belong for ever to the buyer and his descendants; it does not revert to its former owner at the jubilee. 31 But houses in unwalled hamlets are to be treated as property in the open country: the right of redemption will hold good, and in any case the house reverts at the jubilee.

32 Levites are to have the perpetual right to redeem houses which they hold in towns belonging to them. 33 If one of the Levites does not redeem his house in such a town, then it will still revert to him at the jubilee, because the houses in Levite towns are their holding in Israel. 34 The common land surrounding their towns cannot be sold, because it is their property in perpetuity.

35 If your brother-Israelite is reduced to poverty and cannot support himself in the community, you must assist him as you would an alien or a stranger, and he will live with you. 36 You must not charge him interest on a loan, either by deducting it in advance from the capital sum, or by adding it on repayment. Fear your God, and let your brother live with you; 37 do not deduct interest when advancing him money, or add interest to the payment due for food supplied on credit. 38 I am the Lord your God who brought you out of Egypt to give you Canaan and to become your God.

39 If your fellow-countryman is reduced to poverty and sells himself to you, you must not use him to work for you as a slave. 40 His status will be that of a hired man or a stranger lodging with you; he will work for you only until the jubilee year. 41 He will then leave your service, with his children, and go back to his family and to his ancestral property: 42 because they are my slaves whom I brought out of Egypt, they must not be sold as slaves are sold. 43 You must not work him ruthlessly, but you are to fear your God. 44 Such slaves as you have, male or female, should come from the nations round about you; from them you may buy slaves. 45 You may also buy the children of those who have

25:30 **walled:** *so Gk; Heb.* unwalled.   25:33 **does not redeem:** *so Lat.; Heb.* redeems. **in such a town:** *so Gk; Heb.* and such a town. 25:35 **as you would:** *Gk* as; *Heb.* omits.

r Meaning of Heb uncertain

18 "Observe my precepts and be careful to keep my regulations, for then you will dwell securely in the land. 19 The land will yield its fruit and you will have food in abundance, so that you may live there without worry. 20 Therefore, do not say, 'What shall we eat in the seventh year, if we do not then sow or reap our crop?' 21 I will bestow such blessings on you in the sixth year that there will then be crop enough for three years. 22 When you sow in the eighth year, you will continue to eat from the old crop; and even into the ninth year, when the crop comes in, you will still have the old to eat from.

23 "The land shall not be sold in perpetuity; for the land is mine, and you are but aliens who have become my tenants. 24 Therefore, in every part of the country that you occupy, you must permit the land to be redeemed. 25 When one of your countrymen is reduced to poverty and has to sell some of his property, his closest relative, who has the right to redeem it, may go and buy back what his kinsman has sold. 26 If, however, the man has no relative to redeem his land, but later on acquires sufficient means to buy it back in his own name, 27 he shall make a deduction from the price in proportion to the number of years since the sale, and then pay back the balance to the one to whom he sold it, so that he may thus regain his own property. 28 But if he does not acquire sufficient means to buy back his land, what he has sold shall remain in the possession of the purchaser until the jubilee, when it must be released and returned to its original owner.

29 "When someone sells a dwelling in a walled town, he has the right to buy it back during the time of one full year from its sale. 30 But if such a house in a walled town has not been redeemed at the end of a full year, it shall belong in perpetuity to the purchaser and his descendants; nor shall it be released in the jubilee. 31 However, houses in villages that are not encircled by walls shall be considered as belonging to the surrounding farm land; they may be redeemed at any time, and in the jubilee they must be released.

32 "In levitical cities the Levites shall always have the right to redeem the town houses that are their property. 33 Any town house of the Levites in their cities that had been sold and not redeemed, shall be released in the jubilee; for the town houses of the Levites are their hereditary property in the midst of the Israelites. 34 Moreover, the pasture land belonging to their cities shall not be sold at all; it must always remain their hereditary property.

35 "When one of your fellow countrymen is reduced to poverty and is unable to hold out beside you, extend to him the privileges of an alien or a tenant, so that he may continue to live with you. 36 Do not exact interest from your countryman either in money or in kind, but out of fear of God let him live with you. 37 You are to lend him neither money at interest nor food at a profit. 38 I, the LORD, am your God, who brought you out of the land of Egypt to give you the land of Canaan and to be your God.

39 "When, then, your countryman becomes so impoverished beside you that he sells you his services, do not make him work as a slave. 40 Rather, let him be like a hired servant or like your tenant, working with you until the jubilee year, 41 when he, together with his children, shall be released from your service and return to his kindred and to the property of his ancestors. 42 Since those whom I brought out of the land of Egypt are servants of mine, they shall not be sold as slaves to any man. 43 Do not lord it over them harshly, but stand in fear of your God.

44 "Slaves, male and female, you may indeed possess, provided you buy them from among the neighboring nations. 45 You may also buy them from among the aliens who

18 "Hence, you will put my laws and customs into practice; you will keep them and put them into practice, and you will live securely in the country. 19 The land will give its fruit, and you will eat your fill and live in security.

20 "In case you should ask: What shall we eat in this seventh year if we do not sow or harvest our produce? 21 I shall order my blessing to be on you in the sixth year, which will yield you enough produce for three years. 22 You will have the old produce to eat while you are sowing in the eighth year, and even in the ninth year, you will be eating the old produce, while waiting for the harvest of that year.

23 "Land will not be sold absolutely, for the land belongs to me, and you are only strangers and guests of mine. 24 You will allow a right of redemption over any ancestral property. 25 If your brother becomes impoverished and sells off part of his ancestral property, his nearest male relative will come and exercise his family rights over what his brother has sold. 26 The man who has no one to exercise this right may, once he has found the means to effect the redemption, 27 calculate the number of years that the alienation would have lasted, repay to the purchaser the sum due for the time still to run, and so recover his ancestral property. 28 If he cannot find the sum in compensation, the property sold will remain in the possession of the purchaser until the jubilee year. In the jubilee year, the latter will vacate it and return to his own ancestral property.

29 "If anyone sells a dwelling house inside a walled town, he will have the right of redemption until the expiry of the year following the sale. His right of redemption is limited to the year; 30 and if the redemption has not been effected by the end of the year, the house in the walled town will become the property of the purchaser and his descendants in perpetuity; he need not vacate it at the jubilee. 31 But houses in villages not enclosed by walls will be considered as situated in the open country; they carry the right of redemption, and the purchaser will vacate them at the jubilee.

32 "As regards the towns of the Levites, town houses forming part of their ancestral property will carry a perpetual right of redemption in their favour. 33 If a Levite is the one to be affected by the right of redemption, at the jubilee he will vacate the purchased property and return to his own home, to the town in which he has a title to property. The houses in the Levites' towns represent their ancestral property in Israel, 34 and the arable land depending on these towns cannot be sold, being their ancestral property for ever.

35 "If your brother becomes impoverished and cannot support himself in the community, you will assist him as you would a stranger or guest, so that he can go on living with you. 36 Do not charge him interest on a loan, but fear your God, and let your brother live with you. 37 You will not lend him money on interest or give him food to make a profit out of it. 38 I am Yahweh your God who brought you out of Egypt to give you the land of Canaan and be your God.

39 "If your brother becomes impoverished while with you and sells himself to you, you will not make him do the work of a slave; 40 you will treat him like an employee or guest, and he will work for you until the jubilee year. 41 He will then leave you, both he and his children, and return to his clan and regain possession of his ancestral property. 42 For they are my servants whom I have brought out of Egypt, and they may not be bought and sold as slaves. 43 You will not oppress your brother-Israelites harshly but will fear your God.

44 "The male and female slaves you have will come from the nations round you; from these you may purchase male and female slaves. 45 As slaves, you may also purchase the

NEW REVISED STANDARD VERSION

among the aliens residing with you, and from their families that are with you, who have been born in your land; and they may be your property. 46 You may keep them as a possession for your children after you, for them to inherit as property. These you may treat as slaves, but as for your fellow Israelites, no one shall rule over the other with harshness.

47 If resident aliens among you prosper, and if any of your kin fall into difficulty with one of them and sell themselves to an alien, or to a branch of the alien's family, 48 after they have sold themselves they shall have the right of redemption; one of their brothers may redeem them, 49 or their uncle or their uncle's son may redeem them, or anyone of their family who is of their own flesh may redeem them; or if they prosper they may redeem themselves. 50 They shall compute with the purchaser the total from the year when they sold themselves to the alien until the jubilee year; the price of the sale shall be applied to the number of years: the time they were with the owner shall be rated as the time of a hired laborer. 51 If many years remain, they shall pay for their redemption in proportion to the purchase price; 52 and if few years remain until the jubilee year, they shall compute thus: according to the years involved they shall make payment for their redemption. 53 As a laborer hired by the year they shall be under the alien's authority, who shall not, however, rule with harshness over them in your sight. 54 And if they have not been redeemed in any of these ways, they and their children with them shall go free in the jubilee year. 55 For to me the people of Israel are servants; they are my servants whom I brought out from the land of Egypt: I am the Lord your God.

26 You shall make for yourselves no idols and erect no carved images or pillars, and you shall not place figured stones in your land, to worship at them; for I am the Lord your God. 2 You shall keep my sabbaths and reverence my sanctuary: I am the Lord.

3 If you follow my statutes and keep my commandments and observe them faithfully, 4 I will give you your rains in their season, and the land shall yield its produce, and the trees of the field shall yield their fruit. 5 Your threshing shall overtake the vintage, and the vintage shall overtake the sowing; you shall eat your bread to the full, and live securely in your land. 6 And I will grant peace in the land, and you shall lie down, and no one shall make you afraid; I will remove dangerous animals from the land, and no sword shall go through your land. 7 You shall give chase to your enemies, and they shall fall before you by the sword. 8 Five of you shall give chase to a hundred, and a hundred of you shall give chase to ten thousand; your enemies shall fall before you by the sword. 9 I will look with favor upon you and make you fruitful and multiply you; and I will maintain my covenant with you. 10 You shall eat old grain long stored, and you shall have to clear out the old to make way for the new. 11 I will place my dwelling in your midst, and I shall not abhor you. 12 And I will walk among you, and will be your God, and you shall be my people. 13 I am the Lord your God who brought you out of the land of Egypt, to be their slaves no more; I have broken the bars of your yoke and made you walk erect.

14 But if you will not obey me, and do not observe all these commandments, 15 if you spurn my statutes, and abhor my ordinances, so that you will not observe all my commandments, and you break my covenant, 16 I in turn will do this to you: I will bring terror on you; consumption and fever that waste the eyes and cause life to pine away. You shall sow your seed in vain, for your enemies shall eat it. 17 I will set my face against you, and you shall be struck

REVISED ENGLISH BIBLE

settled and lodge with you and such of their family as are born in your land. These may become your property, 46 and you may leave them to your sons after you; you may use them as slaves permanently. But your fellow-Israelites you must not work ruthlessly.

47 If an alien or a stranger living among you becomes rich, and one of your fellow-countrymen becomes poor and sells himself to the alien or stranger or to a member of some alien family, 48 he is to keep the right of redemption after he has sold himself. One of his brothers may redeem him, 49 or his uncle, his cousin, or any blood relation of his family, or, if he has the means, he may redeem himself. 50 He and his purchaser together must reckon from the year when he sold himself to the year of jubilee, and the price will be adjusted to the number of years. His period of service with his owner will be reckoned at the rate of a hired man. 51 If there are still many years to run to the year of jubilee, he must pay for his redemption a proportionate amount of the sum for which he sold himself; 52 if there are only a few, he is to reckon and repay accordingly. 53 He will have the status of a labourer hired from year to year, and you must not let him be worked ruthlessly by his owner. 54 If the man is not redeemed in the intervening years, he and his children must be released in the year of jubilee; 55 for it is to me that the Israelites are slaves, my slaves whom I brought out of Egypt. I am the Lord your God.

26 You must not make idols for yourselves or erect carved images or sacred pillars; you must not put a stone carved figure on your land to worship, because I am the Lord your God. 2 You must keep my sabbaths and revere my sanctuary. I am the Lord.

3 If you conform to my statutes, if you observe and carry out my commandments, 4 I shall give you rain at the proper season; the land will yield its produce and the trees of the countryside their fruit. 5 Threshing will last till vintage, and vintage till sowing; you will eat your fill and live secure in your land.

6 I shall give peace in the land, and you will lie down to sleep with none to terrify you. I shall rid the land of beasts of prey and it will not be ravaged by the sword. 7 You will put your enemies to flight and they will fall in battle before you. 8 Five of you will give chase to a hundred and a hundred of you chase ten thousand; so will the enemy fall by your sword. 9 I shall look upon you with favour, making you fruitful and increasing your numbers; I shall give full effect to my covenant with you. 10 Your harvest will last you in store until you have to clear out the old to make room for the new. 11 I shall establish my Tabernacle among you and never spurn you. 12 I shall be ever present among you; I shall become your God and you will become my people. 13 I am the Lord your God who brought you out of Egypt to be slaves there no longer; I broke the bars of your yoke and enabled you to walk erect.

14 But if you do not listen to me, if you fail to keep all these commandments, 15 if you reject my statutes, spurn my judgements, and fail to obey all my commandments, and if you break my covenant, 16 then assuredly this is what I shall do to you: I shall bring upon you sudden terror, wasting disease, recurrent fever, and plagues that dim the sight and cause the appetite to fail. You will sow your seed to no purpose, for your enemies will eat the crop. 17 I shall set my

reside with you and from their children who are born and reared in your land. Such slaves you may own as chattels, 46 and leave to your sons as their hereditary property, making them perpetual slaves. But you shall not lord it harshly over any of the Israelites, your kinsmen.

47 "When one of your countrymen is reduced to such poverty that he sells himself to a wealthy alien who has a permanent or a temporary residence among you, or to one of the descendants of an immigrant family, 48 even after he has thus sold his services he still has the right of redemption; he may be redeemed by one of his own brothers, 49 or by his uncle or cousin, or by some other relative or fellow clansman; or, if he acquires the means, he may redeem himself. 50 With his purchaser he shall compute the years from the sale to the jubilee, distributing the sale price over these years as though he had been hired as a day laborer. 51 The more such years there are, the more of the sale price he shall pay back as ransom; 52 the fewer years there are left before the jubilee year, the more he has to his credit; in proportion to his years of service shall he pay his ransom. 53 The alien shall treat him as a servant hired on an annual basis, and he shall not lord it over him harshly under your very eyes. 54 If he is not thus redeemed, he shall nevertheless be released, together with his children, in the jubilee year. 55 For to me the Israelites belong as servants; they are servants of mine, because I brought them out of the land of Egypt, I, the LORD, your God.

26 "Do not make false gods for yourselves. You shall not erect an idol or a sacred pillar for yourselves, nor shall you set up a stone figure for worship in your land; for I, the LORD, am your God. 2 Keep my sabbaths, and reverence my sanctuary. I am the LORD.

3 "If you live in accordance with my precepts and are careful to observe my commandments, 4 I will give you rain in due season, so that the land will bear its crops, and the trees their fruit; 5 your threshing will last till vintage time, and your vintage till the time for sowing, and you will have food to eat in abundance, so that you may dwell securely in your land. 6 I will establish peace in the land, that you may lie down to rest without anxiety. I will rid the country of ravenous beasts, and keep the sword of war from sweeping across your land. 7 You will rout your enemies and lay them low with your sword. 8 Five of you will put a hundred of your foes to flight, and a hundred of you will chase ten thousand of them, till they are cut down by your sword. 9 I will look with favor upon you, and make you fruitful and numerous, as I carry out my covenant with you. 10 So much of the old crops will you have stored up for food that you will have to discard them to make room for the new. 11 I will set my Dwelling among you, and will not disdain you. 12 Ever present in your midst, I will be your God, and you will be my people; 13 for it is I, the LORD, your God, who brought you out of the land of the Egyptians and freed you from their slavery, breaking the yoke they had laid upon you and letting you walk erect.

14 "But if you do not heed me and do not keep all these commandments, 15 if you reject my precepts and spurn my decrees, refusing to obey all my commandments and breaking my covenant, 16 then I, in turn, will give you your deserts. I will punish you with terrible woes — with wasting and fever to dim the eyes and sap the life. You will sow your seed in vain, for your enemies will consume the crop.

children of aliens resident among you, and also members of their families living with you who have been born on your soil; and they will become your property, 46 and you may leave them as a legacy to your sons after you as their perpetual possession. These you may have for slaves; but you will not oppress your brother-Israelites.

47 "If a stranger or guest living with you gets rich and your brother, in the course of dealings with him, becomes impoverished and sells himself to this stranger or guest, or to the descendant of a stranger's family, 48 he will enjoy the right of redemption after being sold, and one of his brothers may redeem him. 49 His paternal uncle, his uncle's son, or a member of his own family may redeem him; if he has the means, he may redeem himself. 50 By agreement with his purchaser, he will count the number of years between the year of sale and the jubilee year; his sale-price will be proportionate to the number of years, his time being valued as that of an employee. 51 If there are still many years to run, in proportion to their number he will refund part of his sale-price as payment for his redemption. 52 And if there are only a few years still to run before the jubilee year, he will calculate with him what should be refunded for his redemption, in proportion to their number, 53 as though he were hired by the year. You will see to it that he is not harshly oppressed.

54 "If he has not been redeemed in any of these ways, he will go free in the jubilee year, both he and his children; 55 for the Israelites are my servants; they are my servants whom I brought out of Egypt. I am Yahweh your God." '

26 ' "You will not make idols for yourselves; you will not erect statues or cultic stones, or erect carved stones in your country, for you to worship: for I, Yahweh, am your God. 2 You will keep my Sabbaths and revere my sanctuary. I am Yahweh.

3 "If you live according to my laws, if you keep my commandments and put them into practice, 4 I shall give you the rain you need at the right time; the soil will yield its produce and the trees of the countryside their fruit; 5 you will thresh until vintage time and gather grapes until sowing time. You will eat your fill of bread and live secure in your land.

6 "I shall give peace in the land, and you will go to sleep with no one to frighten you. I shall rid the land of beasts of prey. The sword will not pass through your land. 7 You will pursue your enemies and they will fall before your sword; 8 five of you pursuing a hundred of them, one hundred pursuing ten thousand; and your enemies will fall before your sword.

9 "I shall turn towards you, I shall make you fertile and make your numbers grow, and I shall uphold my covenant with you.

10 "Having eaten all you need of last year's harvest, you will throw out the old to make room for the new.

11 "I shall fix my home among you and never reject you. 12 I shall live among you; I shall be your God and you will be my people, 13 I, Yahweh your God, who brought you out of Egypt so that you should be their slaves no longer, and who broke the bonds of your yoke and made you walk with head held high.

14 "But if you will not listen to me and do not put all these commandments into practice, 15 if you reject my laws and detest my customs, and you break my covenant by not putting all my commandments into practice, 16 this is how I shall treat you:

"I shall subject you to terror, consumption and fever, making you dim of sight and short of breath. You will sow your seed in vain, for your enemies will eat it. 17 I shall turn

NEW REVISED STANDARD VERSION

down by your enemies; your foes shall rule over you, and you shall flee though no one pursues you. 18 And if in spite of this you will not obey me, I will continue to punish you sevenfold for your sins. 19 I will break your proud glory, and I will make your sky like iron and your earth like copper. 20 Your strength shall be spent to no purpose: your land shall not yield its produce, and the trees of the land shall not yield their fruit.

21 If you continue hostile to me, and will not obey me, I will continue to plague you sevenfold for your sins. 22 I will let loose wild animals against you, and they shall bereave you of your children and destroy your livestock; they shall make you few in number, and your roads shall be deserted.

23 If in spite of these punishments you have not turned back to me, but continue hostile to me, 24 then I too will continue hostile to you: I myself will strike you sevenfold for your sins. 25 I will bring the sword against you, executing vengeance for the covenant; and if you withdraw within your cities, I will send pestilence among you, and you shall be delivered into enemy hands. 26 When I break your staff of bread, ten women shall bake your bread in a single oven, and they shall dole out your bread by weight; and though you eat, you shall not be satisfied.

27 But if, despite this, you disobey me, and continue hostile to me, 28 I will continue hostile to you in fury; I in turn will punish you myself sevenfold for your sins. 29 You shall eat the flesh of your sons, and you shall eat the flesh of your daughters. 30 I will destroy your high places and cut down your incense altars; I will heap your carcasses on the carcasses of your idols. I will abhor you. 31 I will lay your cities waste, will make your sanctuaries desolate, and I will not smell your pleasing odors. 32 I will devastate the land, so that your enemies who come to settle in it shall be appalled at it. 33 And you I will scatter among the nations, and I will unsheathe the sword against you; your land shall be a desolation, and your cities a waste.

34 Then the land shall enjoy*s* its sabbath years as long as it lies desolate, while you are in the land of your enemies; then the land shall rest, and enjoy*s* its sabbath years. 35 As long as it lies desolate, it shall have the rest it did not have on your sabbaths when you were living on it. 36 And as for those of you who survive, I will send faintness into their hearts in the lands of their enemies; the sound of a driven leaf shall put them to flight, and they shall flee as one flees from the sword, and they shall fall though no one pursues. 37 They shall stumble over one another, as if to escape a sword, though no one pursues; and you shall have no power to stand against your enemies. 38 You shall perish among the nations, and the land of your enemies shall devour you. 39 And those of you who survive shall languish in the land of your enemies because of their iniquities; also they shall languish because of the iniquities of their ancestors.

40 But if they confess their iniquity and the iniquity of their ancestors, in that they committed treachery against me and, moreover, that they continued hostile to me— 41 so that I, in turn, continued hostile to them and brought them into the land of their enemies; if then their uncircumcised heart is humbled and they make amends for their iniquity, 42 then will I remember my covenant with Jacob; I will remember also my covenant with Isaac and also my covenant with Abraham, and I will remember the land. 43 For the land shall be deserted by them, and enjoy*s* its sabbath years by lying desolate without them, while they shall make amends for their iniquity, because they dared to spurn my ordinances, and they abhorred my statutes. 44 Yet for all

s Or make up for

REVISED ENGLISH BIBLE

face against you, and you will be routed by your enemies. Those that hate you will hound you, and you will run when there is no one pursuing.

18 If after all this you will not listen to me, I shall go on to punish you seven times over for your sins. 19 I shall break down your stubborn pride. I shall make the sky above you like iron, and the earth beneath you like bronze. 20 Your strength will be spent in vain; your land will not yield its produce, nor the trees in it their fruit.

21 If you still defy me and refuse to listen, I shall increase your calamities seven times, as your sins deserve. 22 I shall send wild beasts in among you; they will tear your children from you, destroy your cattle, and bring your numbers low, until your roads are deserted. 23 If after all this you have not learnt discipline but still defy me, 24 I in turn shall show hostility to you and scourge you seven times over for your sins. 25 I shall bring the sword against you to avenge the covenant; you will be herded into your cities, where I shall send pestilence among you, and you will be given into the clutches of the enemy. 26 I shall cut short your daily bread until ten women can bake your bread in a single oven; they will dole it out by weight, and though you eat, you will not be satisfied.

27 If in spite of this you do not listen to me and still oppose me, 28 I shall oppose you in anger, and I myself shall punish you seven times over for your sins. 29 Instead of meat you will eat your sons and your daughters. 30 I shall destroy your shrines and demolish your incense-altars. I shall pile your corpses on your lifeless idols, and I shall spurn you. 31 I shall make your cities desolate and lay waste your sanctuaries; I shall not accept the soothing odour of your offerings. 32 I shall destroy your land, and the enemies who occupy it will be appalled. 33 I shall scatter you among the heathen, pursue you with drawn sword; your land will be desert and your cities heaps of rubble. 34 Then, all the time that it lies desolate, while you are in exile among your enemies, your land will enjoy its sabbaths to the full. 35 All the time of its desolation it will have the sabbath rest which it did not have while you were living there. 36 And I shall make those of you who are left in the land of your enemies so fearful that, when a leaf rustles behind them in the wind, they will run as if it were a sword after them; they will fall with no one in pursuit. 37 Though no one pursues them they will stumble over one another, as if a sword were after them, and you will be helpless to make a stand against the enemy. 38 You will meet your end among the heathen, and your enemies' land will swallow you up. 39 Those who survive will pine away in an enemy land because of their iniquities, and also because of their forefathers' iniquities they will pine away just as they did.

40 But though they confess their iniquity, their own and that of their forefathers, their treachery and their opposition to me, 41 I in my turn shall oppose them and carry them off into their enemies' land. If then their stubborn spirit is broken and they accept their punishment in full, 42 I shall remember my covenant with Jacob, my covenant also with Isaac, and my covenant with Abraham, and I shall remember the land. 43 The land, deserted by its people, will enjoy in full its sabbaths while it lies desolate; they will pay the penalty in full because they rejected my judgements and spurned my statutes. 44 Yet even then while they are in their

26:26 **I . . . daily bread**: *lit.* I shall break your stick of bread.
26:41 **stubborn**: *lit.* uncircumcised.

NEW AMERICAN BIBLE

17 I will turn against you, till you are beaten down before your enemies and lorded over by your foes. You will take to flight though no one pursues you.

18 "If even after this you do not obey me, I will increase the chastisement for your sins sevenfold, 19 to break your haughty confidence. I will make the sky above you as hard as iron, and your soil as hard as bronze, 20 so that your strength will be spent in vain; your land will bear no crops, and its trees no fruit.

21 "If then you become defiant in your unwillingness to obey me, I will multiply my blows another sevenfold, as your sins deserve. 22 I will unleash the wild beasts against you, to rob you of your children and wipe out your livestock, till your population dwindles away and your roads become deserted.

23 "If, with all this, you still refuse to be chastened by me and continue to defy me, 24 I, too, will defy you and will smite you for your sins seven times harder than before. 25 I will make the sword, the avenger of my covenant, sweep over you. Though you then huddle together in your walled cities, I will send in pestilence among you, till you are forced to surrender to the enemy. 26 And as I cut off your supply of bread, ten women will need but one oven for baking all the bread they dole out to you in rations — not enough food to still your hunger.

27 "If, despite all this, you still persist in disobeying and defying me, 28 I, also, will meet you with fiery defiance and will chastise you with sevenfold fiercer punishment for your sins, 29 till you begin to eat the flesh of your own sons and daughters. 30 I will demolish your high places, overthrow your incense stands, and cast your corpses on those of your idols. In my abhorrence of you, 31 I will lay waste your cities and devastate your sanctuaries, refusing to accept your sweet-smelling offerings. 32 So devastated will I leave the land that your very enemies who come to live there will stand aghast at the sight of it. 33 You yourselves I will scatter among the nations at the point of my drawn sword, leaving your countryside desolate and your cities deserted. 34 Then shall the land retrieve its lost sabbaths during all the time it lies waste, while you are in the land of your enemies; then shall the land have rest and make up for its sabbaths 35 during all the time that it lies desolate, enjoying the rest that you would not let it have on the sabbaths when you lived there.

36 "Those of you who survive in the lands of their enemies I will make so fainthearted that, if leaves rustle behind them, they will flee headlong, as if from the sword, though no one pursues them; 37 stumbling over one another as if to escape a weapon, while no one is after them — so helpless will you be to take a stand against your foes! 38 You will be lost among the Gentiles, swallowed up in your enemies' country. 39 Those of you who survive in the lands of their enemies will waste away for their own and their fathers' guilt.

40 "Thus they will have to confess that they and their fathers were guilty of having rebelled against me and of having defied me, 41 so that I, too, had to defy them and bring them into their enemies' land. Then, when their uncircumcised hearts are humbled and they make amends for their guilt, 42 I will remember my covenant with Jacob, my covenant with Isaac, and my covenant with Abraham; and of the land, too, I will be mindful. 43 But the land must first be rid of them, that in its desolation it may make up its lost sabbaths, and that they, too, may make good the debt of their guilt for having spurned my precepts and abhorred my statutes. 44 Yet even so, even while they are in their ene-

NEW JERUSALEM BIBLE

against you and you will be defeated by your enemies. Your foes will have the mastery over you, and you will flee when no one is pursuing you.

18 "And if, in spite of this, you will not listen to me, I shall punish you seven times over for your sins. 19 I shall break your proud strength. I shall make the sky like iron for you, and your soil like bronze. 20 You will wear out your strength in vain, your land will not yield its produce, nor the trees of the country their fruit.

21 "And if you go against me and will not listen to me, I shall heap seven times more plagues on you for your sins. 22 I shall send wild animals to attack you and rob you of your children, destroy your cattle and reduce your numbers until your roads are deserted.

23 "And if that does not reform you, and you still go against me, 24 then I shall go against you and punish you another seven times over for your sins. 25 I shall bring the sword on you, which will avenge the covenant, and when you huddle inside your towns, I shall send pestilence among you, and you will fall into the enemy's clutches. 26 When I take away the bread which supports you, ten women will be able to bake your bread in one oven and will then dole your bread out by weight; you will eat but not be satisfied.

27 "And if, in spite of this, you will not listen to me but go against me, 28 I shall go against you in fury and punish you seven times over for your sins. 29 You will eat the flesh of your own sons, you will eat the flesh of your own daughters. 30 I shall destroy your high places and smash your incense-altars; I shall pile your corpses on the corpses of your foul idols and shall reject you. 31 I shall reduce your cities to ruins; I shall lay waste your sanctuary and refuse to inhale from you smells intended to please. 32 I shall make such a desolation of the country that your enemies who come to live there will be appalled by it. 33 And I shall scatter you among the nations. I shall unsheathe the sword against you, reducing your country to desert and your towns to ruins. 34 Then the country will indeed observe its Sabbaths, all the while it lies deserted, while you are in the country of your enemies. Then indeed the country will rest and observe its Sabbaths. 35 And as it lies deserted it will rest, as it never did on your Sabbaths when you were living there. 36 I shall strike such fear into the hearts of those of you who survive in the countries of their enemies that the sound of a falling leaf will set them fleeing; they will flee as though fleeing from the sword, and fall when no one is pursuing. 37 They will stumble over one another as though fleeing before the sword, when no one is pursuing. You will be powerless to stand up to your enemies; 38 you will perish among the nations, and the land of your enemies will swallow you up. 39 Those of you who survive will pine away in their guilt in the countries of their enemies and, bearing the guilt of their ancestors too, will pine away like them.

40 "Then they shall admit their guilt and that of their ancestors and their infidelities against me, and further, their setting themselves against me.

41 "I in my turn will go against them and bring them into the land of their enemies. Then their uncircumcised hearts will grow humble and then they will accept the punishment for their guilt. 42 I shall remember my covenant with Jacob, I shall remember my covenant with Isaac and my covenant with Abraham; and I shall remember the country too.

43 "Abandoned, the country will keep its Sabbaths, as it lies deserted in their absence, and they will have to accept the punishment for their guilt, since they detested my customs and rejected my laws.

that, when they are in the land of their enemies, I will not spurn them, or abhor them so as to destroy them utterly and break my covenant with them; for I am the LORD their God; 45 but I will remember in their favor the covenant with their ancestors whom I brought out of the land of Egypt in the sight of the nations, to be their God: I am the LORD.

46 These are the statutes and ordinances and laws that the LORD established between himself and the people of Israel on Mount Sinai through Moses.

27 The LORD spoke to Moses, saying: 2 Speak to the people of Israel and say to them: When a person makes an explicit vow to the LORD concerning the equivalent for a human being, 3 the equivalent for a male shall be: from twenty to sixty years of age the equivalent shall be fifty shekels of silver by the sanctuary shekel. 4 If the person is a female, the equivalent is thirty shekels. 5 If the age is from five to twenty years of age, the equivalent is twenty shekels for a male and ten shekels for a female. 6 If the age is from one month to five years, the equivalent for a male is five shekels of silver, and for a female the equivalent is three shekels of silver. 7 And if the person is sixty years old or over, then the equivalent for a male is fifteen shekels, and for a female ten shekels. 8 If any cannot afford the equivalent, they shall be brought before the priest and the priest shall assess them; the priest shall assess them according to what each one making a vow can afford.

9 If it concerns an animal that may be brought as an offering to the LORD, any such that may be given to the LORD shall be holy. 10 Another shall not be exchanged or substituted for it, either good for bad or bad for good; and if one animal is substituted for another, both that one and its substitute shall be holy. 11 If it concerns any unclean animal that may not be brought as an offering to the LORD, the animal shall be presented before the priest. 12 The priest shall assess it: whether good or bad, according to the assessment of the priest, so it shall be. 13 But if it is to be redeemed, one-fifth must be added to the assessment.

14 If a person consecrates a house to the LORD, the priest shall assess it: whether good or bad, as the priest assesses it, so it shall stand. 15 And if the one who consecrates the house wishes to redeem it, one-fifth shall be added to its assessed value, and it shall revert to the original owner.

16 If a person consecrates to the LORD any inherited landholding, its assessment shall be in accordance with its seed requirements: fifty shekels of silver to a homer of barley seed. 17 If the person consecrates the field as of the year of jubilee, that assessment shall stand; 18 but if the field is consecrated after the jubilee, the priest shall compute the price for it according to the years that remain until the year of jubilee, and the assessment shall be reduced. 19 And if the one who consecrates the field wishes to redeem it, then one-fifth shall be added to its assessed value, and it shall revert to the original owner; 20 but if the field is not redeemed, or if it has been sold to someone else, it shall no longer be redeemable. 21 But when the field is released in the jubilee, it shall be holy to the LORD as a devoted field; it becomes the priest's holding. 22 If someone consecrates to the LORD a field that has been purchased, which is not a part of the inherited landholding, 23 the priest shall compute for it the proportionate assessment up to the year of jubilee, and the assessment shall be paid as of that day, a sacred donation to the LORD. 24 In the year of jubilee the field shall return to the one from whom it was bought, whose holding the land is. 25 All assessments shall be by the sanctuary

enemies' land, I shall not have so rejected and spurned them as to bring them to an end and break my covenant with them, because I am the LORD their God. 45 I shall remember on their behalf the covenant with the former generation whom I brought out of Egypt in full sight of the nations, that I might be their God. I am the LORD.

46 These are the statutes, the judgements, and the laws which the LORD established between himself and the Israelites through Moses on Mount Sinai.

27 WHEN the LORD spoke to Moses he said, 2 Speak to the Israelites and tell them: When anyone makes a special vow to the LORD which requires your valuation of living persons, 3 a male between twenty and sixty years old is to be valued at fifty silver shekels by the sacred standard. 4 If it is a female, she is to be valued at thirty shekels. 5 If it is someone between five years old and twenty, the valuation will be twenty shekels for a male and ten for a female. 6 If it is someone between a month and five years old, the valuation will be five silver shekels for a male and three for a female. 7 If it is someone over sixty and a male, the valuation will be fifteen shekels, but if a female, ten shekels. 8 If the person who is making the vow is too poor to pay the amount of your valuation, the person to be valued must be set before the priest, who will then set the value according to what the person who makes the vow can afford: the priest will make the valuation.

9 If the vow concerns an animal acceptable as an offering to the LORD, then such a gift is holy to the LORD. 10 It must not be exchanged or substituted for another, whether good for bad or bad for good. But if a substitution is in fact made of one animal for another, then both the original animal and its substitute are holy. 11 If the vow concerns an unclean animal unacceptable as an offering to the LORD, then the animal is to be brought before the priest, 12 and he must value it whether good or bad. The priest's valuation is decisive; 13 in case of redemption the payment must be increased by one fifth.

14 When a man dedicates his house as holy to the LORD, the priest is to judge whether it is good or bad, and the priest's valuation must be decisive. 15 If the donor redeems his house, he must pay the amount of the valuation increased by one fifth, and the house then reverts to him. 16 If someone dedicates to the LORD part of his ancestral land, you are to value it according to the amount of seed-corn it can carry, at the rate of fifty shekels of silver for a homer of barley seed. 17 If he dedicates his land from the year of jubilee, it stands at your valuation; 18 but if he dedicates it after the year of jubilee, the priest must estimate the price in silver according to the number of years remaining until the next year of jubilee, and this will be deducted from your valuation. 19 If the one who dedicates his field should redeem it, he has to pay the amount of your valuation in silver, increased by one fifth, and it then reverts to him. 20 If he does not redeem it but sells the land to another, it is no longer redeemable; 21 when the land reverts at the year of jubilee, it will be like land that has been dedicated, holy to the LORD. It will belong to the priest as his holding.

22 If someone dedicates to the LORD land which he has bought, land which is not part of his ancestral land, 23 the priest must estimate the amount of the value for the period until the year of jubilee, and the person must give the amount fixed as at that day; it is holy to the LORD. 24 At the year of jubilee the land reverts to the person from whom it was bought, whose holding it is. 25 Every valuation you

---

27:2 **makes a special:** *or* discharges a.

mies' land, I will not reject or spurn them, lest, by wiping them out, I make void my covenant with them; for I, the LORD, am their God. 45 I will remember them because of the covenant I made with their forefathers, whom I brought out of the land of Egypt under the very eyes of the Gentiles, that I, the LORD, might be their God."

46 These are the precepts, decrees and laws which the LORD had Moses promulgate on Mount Sinai in the pact between himself and the Israelites.

27 The LORD said to Moses, 2 "Speak to the Israelites and tell them: When anyone fulfills a vow of offering one or more persons to the LORD, who are to be ransomed at a fixed sum of money, 3 for persons between the ages of twenty and sixty, the fixed sum, in sanctuary shekels, shall be fifty silver shekels for a man, 4 and thirty shekels for a woman; 5 for persons between the ages of five and twenty, the fixed sum shall be twenty shekels for a youth, and ten for a maiden; 6 for persons between the ages of one month and five years, the fixed sum shall be five silver shekels for a boy, and three for a girl; 7 for persons of sixty or more, the fixed sum shall be fifteen shekels for a man, and ten for a woman. 8 However, if the one who took the vow is too poor to meet the fixed sum, the person must be set before the priest, who shall determine the sum for his ransom in keeping with the means of the one who made the vow.

9 "If the offering vowed to the LORD is an animal that may be sacrificed, every such animal, when vowed to the LORD, becomes sacred. 10 The offerer shall not present a substitute for it by exchanging either a better for a worse one or a worse for a better one. If he attempts to offer one animal in place of another, both the original and its substitute shall be treated as sacred. 11 If the animal vowed to the LORD is unclean and therefore unfit for sacrifice, it must be set before the priest, 12 who shall determine its value in keeping with its good or bad qualities, and the value set by the priest shall stand. 13 If the offerer wishes to redeem the animal, he shall pay one fifth more than this valuation.

14 "When someone dedicates his house as sacred to the LORD, the priest shall determine its value in keeping with its good or bad points, and the value set by the priest shall stand. 15 If the one who dedicated his house wishes to redeem it, he shall pay one fifth more than the price thus established, and then it will again be his.

16 "If the object which someone dedicates to the LORD is a piece of his hereditary land, its valuation shall be made according to the amount of seed required to sow it, the acreage sown with a homer of barley seed being valued at fifty silver shekels. 17 If the dedication of a field is made at the beginning of a jubilee period, the full valuation shall hold; 18 but if it is some time after this, the priest shall estimate its money value according to the number of years left until the next jubilee year, with a corresponding rebate on the valuation. 19 If the one who dedicated his field wishes to redeem it, he shall pay one fifth more than the price thus established, and so reclaim it. 20 If, instead of redeeming such a field, he sells it to someone else, it may no longer be redeemed; 21 but at the jubilee it shall be released as sacred to the LORD; like a field that is doomed, it shall become priestly property.

22 "If the field that some man dedicates to the LORD is one he had purchased and not a part of his hereditary property, 23 the priest shall compute its value in proportion to the number of years until the next jubilee, and on the same day the price thus established shall be given as sacred to the LORD; 24 at the jubilee, however, the field shall revert to the hereditary owner of this land from whom it had been purchased.

44 "Yet, in spite of all this, when they are in the land of their enemies, I shall not so utterly reject or detest them as to destroy them completely and break my covenant with them; for I am Yahweh their God. 45 For their sake I shall remember the covenant I made with those first generations that I brought out of Egypt while other nations watched, so that I should be their God, I, Yahweh." '

46 Such were the decrees, customs and laws which Yahweh established between himself and the Israelites on Mount Sinai through Moses.

27 Yahweh spoke to Moses and said: 2 'Speak to the Israelites and say:

"If anyone vows the value of a person to Yahweh and wishes to discharge the vow:

3 "a man between twenty and sixty years of age will be valued at fifty silver shekels — the sanctuary shekel; 4 a woman will be valued at thirty shekels;

5 "between five and twenty years, a boy will be valued at twenty shekels, a girl at ten shekels;

6 "between one month and five years, a boy will be valued at five silver shekels, a girl at three silver shekels;

7 "at sixty years and over, a man will be valued at fifteen shekels and a woman at ten shekels.

8 "If the person who made the vow cannot meet this valuation, he will present the person concerned to the priest, and the priest will set a value proportionate to the resources of the person who made the vow.

9 "In the case of an animal suitable for offering to Yahweh, any such animal given to Yahweh will be holy. 10 It cannot be exchanged or replaced, a good one instead of a bad one, or a bad one instead of a good one. If one animal is substituted for another, both of them will become holy. 11 In the case of an unclean animal unsuitable for offering to Yahweh, whatever it may be, it will be presented to the priest 12 and he will set a value on it, in relation to its worth. His valuation will be decisive; 13 but if the person wishes to redeem it, he will add one-fifth to the valuation.

14 "If a man consecrates his house to Yahweh, the priest will set a value on it, in relation to its worth. His valuation will be decisive. 15 If the man who has vowed his house wishes to redeem it, he will add one-fifth to the valuation, and it will revert to him.

16 "If a man consecrates one of the fields of his ancestral property to Yahweh, its value will be calculated in terms of its yield, at the rate of fifty silver shekels to one *homer* of barley.

17 "If he consecrates the field during the jubilee year, he will abide by this valuation. 18 But if he consecrates it after the jubilee, the priest will calculate the price in terms of the number of years still to run until the next jubilee and the valuation will be reduced accordingly.

19 "If he wishes to redeem the field, he will add one-fifth to the valuation, and the field will revert to him. 20 If he does not redeem it but sells it to someone else, the right of redemption ceases; 21 when the purchaser has to vacate it at the jubilee year, it becomes consecrated to Yahweh, like a field vowed unconditionally; ownership of it passes to the priest.

22 "If he consecrates to Yahweh a field which he has bought, but which is not part of his ancestral property, 23 the priest will calculate the valuation in terms of the number of years still to run before the jubilee year; and the man will pay this sum the same day since it is consecrated to Yahweh. 24 In the jubilee year the field will revert to the vendor, the man to whose ancestral property the land belongs. 25 All

NEW REVISED STANDARD VERSION

shekel: twenty gerahs shall make a shekel.

26 A firstling of animals, however, which as a firstling belongs to the LORD, cannot be consecrated by anyone; whether ox or sheep, it is the LORD's. 27 If it is an unclean animal, it shall be ransomed at its assessment, with one-fifth added; if it is not redeemed, it shall be sold at its assessment.

28 Nothing that a person owns that has been devoted to destruction for the LORD, be it human or animal, or inherited landholding, may be sold or redeemed; every devoted thing is most holy to the LORD. 29 No human beings who have been devoted to destruction can be ransomed; they shall be put to death.

30 All tithes from the land, whether the seed from the ground or the fruit from the tree, are the LORD's; they are holy to the LORD. 31 If persons wish to redeem any of their tithes, they must add one-fifth to them. 32 All tithes of herd and flock, every tenth one that passes under the shepherd's staff, shall be holy to the LORD. 33 Let no one inquire whether it is good or bad, or make substitution for it; if one makes substitution for it, then both it and the substitute shall be holy and cannot be redeemed.

34 These are the commandments that the LORD gave to Moses for the people of Israel on Mount Sinai.

REVISED ENGLISH BIBLE

make is to be made by the sacred standard at the rate of twenty gerahs to the shekel.

26 No one may dedicate to the LORD the firstborn of an animal which in any case has to be offered as a firstborn, whether from the herd or the flock. It is the LORD's. 27 If it is an unclean animal, he may redeem it at your valuation and add one fifth; but if it is not redeemed, it is to be sold at your valuation. 28 Nothing, however, which anyone devotes to the LORD irredeemably from his own property, whether a human being, an animal, or ancestral land, may be sold or redeemed. Everything so devoted is most holy to the LORD. 29 No human being thus devoted may be redeemed; he must be put to death.

30 Every tithe on land, whether from grain or from the fruit of a tree, belongs to the LORD; it is holy to the LORD. 31 If anyone wishes to redeem any of his tithe, he must pay its value increased by one fifth. 32 Every tenth creature that passes under the counting rod is holy to the LORD; this applies to all tithes of cattle and sheep. 33 There is to be no enquiry whether it is good or bad, and no substitution. If any substitution is made, then the tithe-animal and its substitute are both forfeit as holy; they cannot be redeemed.

34 These are the commandments which the LORD gave to Moses on Mount Sinai for the Israelites.

25 "Every valuation shall be made according to the standard of the sanctuary shekel. There are twenty gerahs to the shekel.

26 "Note that a first-born animal, which as such already belongs to the LORD, may not be dedicated by vow to him. If it is an ox or a sheep, it shall be ceded to the LORD; 27 but if it is an unclean animal, it may be redeemed by paying one fifth more than its fixed value. If it is not redeemed, it shall be sold at its fixed value.

28 "Note, also, that any one of his possessions which a man vows as doomed to the LORD, whether it is a human being or an animal or a hereditary field, shall be neither sold nor ransomed; everything that is thus doomed becomes most sacred to the LORD. 29 All human beings that are doomed lose the right to be redeemed; they must be put to death.

30 "All tithes of the land, whether in grain from the fields or in fruit from the trees, belong to the LORD, as sacred to him. 31 If someone wishes to buy back any of his tithes, he shall pay one fifth more than their value. 32 The tithes of the herd and the flock shall be determined by ceding to the LORD as sacred every tenth animal as they are counted by the herdsman's rod. 33 It shall not matter whether good ones or bad ones are thus chosen, and no exchange may be made. If any exchange is attempted, both the original animal and its substitute shall be treated as sacred, without the right of being bought back."

34 These are the commandments which the LORD gave Moses on Mount Sinai for the Israelites.

your valuations will be made in sanctuary shekels, at the rate of twenty *gerah* to the shekel.

26 "The first-born of livestock is born to Yahweh; no one may consecrate it, whether it be cattle or sheep, for it belongs to Yahweh anyway. 27 But if it is an unclean animal, it may be redeemed at the valuation price with one-fifth added; if the animal is not redeemed, it will be sold at the valuation price.

28 "Nothing, however, that someone vows unconditionally to Yahweh may be redeemed, nothing he possesses, be it a human being or animal or field of his ancestral property. What is vowed unconditionally is especially holy and belongs to Yahweh. 29 A human being vowed unconditionally cannot be redeemed but will be put to death.

30 "All tithes on land, levied on the produce of the soil or on the fruit of trees, belong to Yahweh; they are consecrated to Yahweh. 31 If anyone wishes to redeem part of his tithe, he will add one-fifth to its value.

32 "In all tithes on herds or flocks, the tenth animal of all that pass under the herdsman's staff will be consecrated to Yahweh; 33 there will be no examining whether it is good or bad, and no substitution. If substitution takes place, the animal and its substitute will both become holy without possibility of redemption." '

34 Such were the orders which Yahweh gave Moses on Mount Sinai for the Israelites.

Numbers

1 The LORD spoke to Moses in the wilderness of Sinai, in the tent of meeting, on the first day of the second month, in the second year after they had come out of the land of Egypt, saying: 2 Take a census of the whole congregation of Israelites, in their clans, by ancestral houses, according to the number of names, every male individually; 3 from twenty years old and upward, everyone in Israel able to go to war. You and Aaron shall enroll them, company by company. 4 A man from each tribe shall be with you, each man the head of his ancestral house. 5 These are the names of the men who shall assist you:

From Reuben, Elizur son of Shedeur.
6 From Simeon, Shelumiel son of Zurishaddai.
7 From Judah, Nahshon son of Amminadab.
8 From Issachar, Nethanel son of Zuar.
9 From Zebulun, Eliab son of Helon.
10 From the sons of Joseph:
from Ephraim, Elishama son of Ammihud;
from Manasseh, Gamaliel son of Pedahzur.
11 From Benjamin, Abidan son of Gideoni.
12 From Dan, Ahiezer son of Ammishaddai.
13 From Asher, Pagiel son of Ochran.
14 From Gad, Eliasaph son of Deuel.
15 From Naphtali, Ahira son of Enan.

16 These were the ones chosen from the congregation, the leaders of their ancestral tribes, the heads of the divisions of Israel.

17 Moses and Aaron took these men who had been designated by name, 18 and on the first day of the second month they assembled the whole congregation together. They registered themselves in their clans, by their ancestral houses, according to the number of names from twenty years old and upward, individually, 19 as the LORD commanded Moses. So he enrolled them in the wilderness of Sinai.

20 The descendants of Reuben, Israel's firstborn, their lineage, in their clans, by their ancestral houses, according to the number of names, individually, every male from twenty years old and upward, everyone able to go to war: 21 those enrolled of the tribe of Reuben were forty-six thousand five hundred.

22 The descendants of Simeon, their lineage, in their clans, by their ancestral houses, those of them that were numbered, according to the number of names, individually, every male from twenty years old and upward, everyone able to go to war: 23 those enrolled of the tribe of Simeon were fifty-nine thousand three hundred.

24 The descendants of Gad, their lineage, in their clans, by their ancestral houses, according to the number of names, from twenty years old and upward, everyone able to go to war: 25 those enrolled of the tribe of Gad were forty-five thousand six hundred fifty.

26 The descendants of Judah, their lineage, in their clans, by their ancestral houses, according to the number of names, from twenty years old and upward, everyone able to go to war: 27 those enrolled of the tribe of Judah were seventy-four thousand six hundred.

28 The descendants of Issachar, their lineage, in their clans, by their ancestral houses, according to the number of names, from twenty years old and upward, everyone able to go to war: 29 those enrolled of the tribe of Issachar were fifty-four thousand four hundred.

Numbers

1 ON the first day of the second month in the second year after the Israelites came out of Egypt, the LORD spoke to Moses in the Tent of Meeting in the wilderness of Sinai. He said: 2 'Make a census of the whole community of Israel by families in the father's line, recording the name of every male person 3 aged twenty years and upwards fit for military service. You and Aaron are to make a list of them by their tribal hosts, 4 and to assist you you will have one head of family from each tribe. 5 These are their names:

from Reuben, Elizur son of Shedeur;
6 from Simeon, Shelumiel son of Zurishaddai;
7 from Judah, Nahshon son of Amminadab;
8 from Issachar, Nethanel son of Zuar;
9 from Zebulun, Eliab son of Helon;
10 from Joseph: of Ephraim, Elishama son of Ammihud;
of Manasseh, Gamaliel son of Pedahzur;
11 from Benjamin, Abidan son of Gideoni;
12 from Dan, Ahiezer son of Ammishaddai;
13 from Asher, Pagiel son of Ochran;
14 from Gad, Eliasaph son of Reuel;
15 from Naphtali, Ahira son of Enan.'

16 These were the representatives of the community, chiefs of their fathers' tribes and heads of Israelite clans. 17 Moses and Aaron took those men who had been indicated by name, 18 and on the first day of the second month they summoned the whole community, and recorded every male person aged twenty years and upwards, registering their descent by families in the father's line, 19 as the LORD had commanded Moses. He drew up the lists as follows in the wilderness of Sinai.

20 The tribal list of Reuben, Israel's eldest son, by families in the father's line, with the name of every male person aged twenty years and upwards for service, 21 the number in the list of the tribe of Reuben being forty-six thousand five hundred.

22 The tribal list of Simeon, by families in the father's line, with the name of every male person aged twenty years and upwards fit for service, 23 the number in the list of the tribe of Simeon being fifty-nine thousand three hundred.

24 The tribal list of Gad, by families in the father's line, with the names of all men aged twenty years and upwards fit for service, 25 the number in the list of the tribe of Gad being forty-five thousand six hundred and fifty.

26 The tribal list of Judah, by families in the father's line, with the names of all men aged twenty years and upwards fit for service, 27 the number in the list of the tribe of Judah being seventy-four thousand six hundred.

28 The tribal list of Issachar, by families in the father's line, with the names of all men aged twenty years and upwards fit for service, 29 the number in the list of the tribe of Issachar being fifty-four thousand four hundred.

1:14 **Reuel:** *so Gk (cp. 2:14); Heb.* Deuel *(so also 7:42,47).*

THE BOOK OF
Numbers

1 In the year following that of the Israelites' departure from the land of Egypt, on the first day of the second month, the Lord said to Moses in the meeting tent in the desert of Sinai: 2 "Take a census of the whole community of the Israelites, by clans and ancestral houses, registering each male individually. 3 You and Aaron shall enroll in companies all the men in Israel of twenty years or more who are fit for military service.

4 "To assist you there shall be a man from each tribe, the head of his ancestral house. 5 These are the names of those who are to assist you:

from Reuben: Elizur, son of Shedeur;
6 from Simeon: Shelumiel, son of Zurishaddai;
7 from Judah: Nahshon, son of Amminadab;
8 from Issachar: Nethanel, son of Zuar;
9 from Zebulun: Eliab, son of Helon;
10 from Ephraim: Elishama, son of Ammihud,
and from Manasseh: Gamaliel, son of Pedahzur,
for the descendants of Joseph;
11 from Benjamin: Abidan, son of Gideoni;
12 from Dan: Ahiezer, son of Ammishaddai;
13 from Asher: Pagiel, son of Ochran;
14 from Gad: Eliasaph, son of Reuel;
15 from Naphtali: Ahira, son of Enan."

16 These were councilors of the community, princes of their ancestral tribes, chiefs of the troops of Israel. 17 So Moses and Aaron took these men who had been designated, 18 and assembled the whole community on the first day of the second month. Every man of twenty years or more then declared his name and lineage according to clan and ancestral house, 19 as the Lord had commanded Moses.

This is their census as taken in the desert of Sinai. 20 Of the descendants of Reuben, the first-born of Israel, registered by lineage in clans and ancestral houses: when all the males of twenty years or more who were fit for military service were polled, 21 forty-six thousand five hundred were enrolled in the tribe of Reuben.

22 Of the descendants of Simeon, registered by lineage in clans and ancestral houses: when all the males of twenty years or more who were fit for military service were polled, 23 fifty-nine thousand three hundred were enrolled in tribe of Simeon.

24 Of the descendants of Gad, registered by lineage in clans and ancestral houses: when all the males of twenty years or more who were fit for military service were polled, 25 forty-five thousand six hundred and fifty were enrolled in the tribe of Gad.

26 Of the descendants of Judah, registered by lineage in clans and ancestral houses: when all the males of twenty years or more who were fit for military service were polled, 27 seventy-four thousand six hundred were enrolled in tribe of Judah.

28 Of the descendants of Issachar, registered by lineage in clans and ancestral houses: when all the males of twenty years or more who were fit for military service were polled, 29 fifty-four thousand four hundred were enrolled in the tribe of Issachar.

Numbers

1 Yahweh spoke to Moses, in the desert of Sinai, in the Tent of Meeting, on the first day of the second month, in the second year after the exodus from Egypt, and said: 2 'Take a census*a* of the whole community of Israelites by clans and families, taking a count of the names of all the males, head by head. 3 You and Aaron will register all those in Israel, twenty years of age and over, fit to bear arms, company by company; 4 you will have one man from each tribe, the head of his family, to help you.

5 'These are the names of those who must help you:
For Reuben, Elizur son of Shedeur.
6 For Simeon, Shelumiel son of Zurishaddai.
7 For Judah, Nahshon son of Amminadab.
8 For Issachar, Nethanel son of Zuar.
9 For Zebulun, Eliab son of Helon.
10 Of the sons of Joseph: for Ephraim, Elishama son of Ammihud; for Manasseh, Gamaliel son of Pedahzur.
11 For Benjamin, Abidan son of Gideoni.
12 For Dan, Ahiezer son of Ammishaddai.
13 For Asher, Pagiel son of Ochran.
14 For Gad, Eliasaph son of Reuel.
15 For Naphtali, Ahira son of Enan.'

16 These were men of repute in the community; they were the leaders of their ancestral tribes, the heads of Israel's thousands.

17 Moses and Aaron took these men who had been named 18 and on the first day of the second month they mustered the whole community. The Israelites established their pedigrees by clans and families, and one by one the names of all men of twenty years and over were recorded. 19 As Yahweh had ordered, Moses registered them in the desert of Sinai.

20 Once the pedigrees of the descendants of Reuben, Israel's first-born, had been established by clans and families, the names of all the males of twenty years and over, fit to bear arms, were recorded one by one. 21 The total of these for the tribe of Reuben was forty-six thousand five hundred.

22 Once the pedigrees of Simeon's descendants had been established by clans and families, the names of all the males of twenty years and over, fit to bear arms, were recorded one by one. 23 The total of these for the tribe of Simeon was fifty-nine thousand three hundred.

24 Once the pedigrees of Gad's descendants had been established by clans and families, the names of all the males of twenty years and over, fit to bear arms, were recorded one by one. 25 The total of these for the tribe of Gad was forty-five thousand six hundred and fifty.

26 Once the pedigrees of Judah's descendants had been established by clans and families, the names of all the males of twenty years and over, fit to bear arms, were recorded one by one. 27 The total of these for the tribe of Judah was seventy-four thousand six hundred.

28 Once the pedigrees of Issachar's descendants had been established by clans and families, the names of all the males of twenty years and over, fit to bear arms, were recorded one by one. 29 The total of these for the tribe of Issachar was fifty-four thousand four hundred.

---

a **1** Israel is shown as a settled community, centred on the Levites. The numbers fit that period.

| NEW REVISED STANDARD VERSION | REVISED ENGLISH BIBLE |

30 The descendants of Zebulun, their lineage, in their clans, by their ancestral houses, according to the number of names, from twenty years old and upward, everyone able to go to war: 31 those enrolled of the tribe of Zebulun were fifty-seven thousand four hundred.

32 The descendants of Joseph, namely, the descendants of Ephraim, their lineage, in their clans, by their ancestral houses, according to the number of names, from twenty years old and upward, everyone able to go to war: 33 those enrolled of the tribe of Ephraim were forty thousand five hundred.

34 The descendants of Manasseh, their lineage, in their clans, by their ancestral houses, according to the number of names, from twenty years old and upward, everyone able to go to war: 35 those enrolled of the tribe of Manasseh were thirty-two thousand two hundred.

36 The descendants of Benjamin, their lineage, in their clans, by their ancestral houses, according to the number of names, from twenty years old and upward, everyone able to go to war: 37 those enrolled of the tribe of Benjamin were thirty-five thousand four hundred.

38 The descendants of Dan, their lineage, in their clans, by their ancestral houses, according to the number of names, from twenty years old and upward, everyone able to go to war: 39 those enrolled of the tribe of Dan were sixty-two thousand seven hundred.

40 The descendants of Asher, their lineage, in their clans, by their ancestral houses, according to the number of names, from twenty years old and upward, everyone able to go to war: 41 those enrolled of the tribe of Asher were forty-one thousand five hundred.

42 The descendants of Naphtali, their lineage, in their clans, by their ancestral houses, according to the number of names, from twenty years old and upward, everyone able to go to war: 43 those enrolled of the tribe of Naphtali were fifty-three thousand four hundred.

44 These are those who were enrolled, whom Moses and Aaron enrolled with the help of the leaders of Israel, twelve men, each representing his ancestral house. 45 So the whole number of the Israelites, by their ancestral houses, from twenty years old and upward, everyone able to go to war in Israel — 46 their whole number was six hundred three thousand five hundred fifty. 47 The Levites, however, were not numbered by their ancestral tribe along with them.

48 The LORD had said to Moses: 49 Only the tribe of Levi you shall not enroll, and you shall not take a census of them with the other Israelites. 50 Rather you shall appoint the Levites over the tabernacle of the covenant,a and over all its equipment, and over all that belongs to it; they are to carry the tabernacle and all its equipment, and they shall tend it, and shall camp around the tabernacle. 51 When the tabernacle is to set out, the Levites shall take it down; and when the tabernacle is to be pitched, the Levites shall set it up. And any outsider who comes near it shall be put to death. 52 The other Israelites shall camp in their respective regimental camps, by companies; 53 but the Levites shall camp around the tabernacle of the covenant,a that there may be no wrath on the congregation of the Israelites; and the Levites shall perform the guard duty of the tabernacle of the covenant.a 54 The Israelites did so; they did just as the LORD commanded Moses.

2 The LORD spoke to Moses and Aaron, saying: 2 The Israelites shall camp each in their respective regiments, under ensigns by their ancestral houses; they shall camp facing the tent of meeting on every side. 3 Those to camp on

30 The tribal list of Zebulun, by families in the father's line, with the names of all men aged twenty years and upwards fit for service, 31 the number in the list of the tribe of Zebulun being fifty-seven thousand four hundred.

32 The tribal lists of Joseph: that of Ephraim, by families in the father's line, with the names of all men aged twenty years and upwards fit for service, 33 the number in the list of the tribe of Ephraim being forty thousand five hundred; 34 that of Manasseh, by families in the father's line, with the names of all men aged twenty years and upwards fit for service, 35 the number in the list of the tribe of Manasseh being thirty-two thousand two hundred.

36 The tribal list of Benjamin, by families in the father's line, with the names of all men aged twenty years and upwards fit for service, 37 the number in the list of the tribe of Benjamin being thirty-five thousand four hundred.

38 The tribal list of Dan, by families in the father's line, with the names of all men aged twenty years and upwards fit for service, 39 the number in the list of the tribe of Dan being sixty-two thousand seven hundred.

40 The tribal list of Asher, by families in the father's line, with the names of all men aged twenty years and upwards fit for service, 41 the number in the list of the tribe of Asher being forty-one thousand five hundred.

42 The tribal list of Naphtali, by families in the father's line, with the names of all men aged twenty years and upwards fit for service, 43 the number in the list of the tribe of Naphtali being fifty-three thousand four hundred.

44 These were the numbers recorded in the lists by Moses, Aaron, and the twelve chiefs of Israel, each representing one tribe and being the head of a family. 45 The total number of Israelites aged twenty years and upwards fit for service, recorded in the lists of fathers' families, 46 was six hundred and three thousand five hundred and fifty.

47 A list of the Levites by their fathers' families was not made. 48 The LORD said to Moses, 49 'You are not to record the total number of the Levites or make a census of them among the Israelites. 50 You are to put the Levites in charge of the Tabernacle of the Testimony with all its equipment and everything in it. They will carry the Tabernacle and all its equipment; they alone will be its attendants and pitch their tents round it. 51 The Levites will take the Tabernacle down when it is due to move and put it up when it halts; any lay person who comes near it must be put to death. 52 The other Israelites will pitch their tents, each tribal host in its proper camp and under its own standard. 53 But the Levites are to encamp round the Tabernacle of the Testimony, so that divine wrath may not come on the community of Israel; the Tabernacle of the Testimony will be in their charge.'

54 The Israelites did everything exactly as the LORD had commanded Moses.

2 The LORD said to Moses and Aaron, 2 'The Israelites are to encamp each under his own standard by the emblems of his father's family; they are to pitch their tents round the Tent of Meeting, facing it.

1:44 each . . . family: prob. rdg (cp. Samar. and Gk); Heb. each representing a family.

a Or treaty, or testimony; Heb eduth

30 Of the descendants of Zebulun, registered by lineage in clans and ancestral houses: when all the males of twenty years or more who were fit for military service were polled, 31 fifty-seven thousand four hundred were enrolled in the tribe of Zebulun.

32 Of the descendants of Joseph —

Of the descendants of Ephraim, registered by lineage in clans and ancestral houses: when all the males of twenty years or more who were fit for military service were polled, 33 forty thousand five hundred were enrolled in the tribe of Ephraim.

34 Of the descendants of Manasseh, registered by lineage in clans and ancestral houses: when all the males of twenty years or more who were fit for military service were polled, 35 thirty-two thousand two hundred were enrolled in the tribe of Manasseh.

36 Of the descendants of Benjamin, registered by lineage in clans and ancestral houses: when all the males of twenty years or more who were fit for military service were polled, 37 thirty-five thousand four hundred were enrolled in the tribe of Benjamin.

38 Of the descendants of Dan, registered by lineage in clans and ancestral houses: when all the males of twenty years or more who were fit for military service were polled, 39 sixty-two thousand seven hundred were enrolled in the tribe of Dan.

40 Of the descendants of Asher, registered by lineage in clans and ancestral houses: when all the males of twenty years or more who were fit for military service were polled, 41 forty-one thousand five hundred were enrolled in the tribe of Asher.

42 Of the descendants of Naphtali, registered by lineage in clans and ancestral houses: when all the males of twenty years or more who were fit for military service were polled, 43 fifty-three thousand four hundred were enrolled in the tribe of Naphtali.

44 It was these who were registered, each according to his ancestral house, in the census taken by Moses and Aaron and the twelve princes of Israel. 45 The total number of the Israelites of twenty years or more who were fit for military service, registered by ancestral houses, 46 was six hundred and three thousand five hundred and fifty.

47 The Levites, however, were not registered by ancestral tribe with the others. 48 For the Lord had told Moses, 49 "The tribe of Levi alone you shall not enroll nor include in the census along with the other Israelites. 50 You are to give the Levites charge of the Dwelling of the commandments with all its equipment and all that belongs to it. It is they who shall carry the Dwelling with all its equipment and who shall be its ministers. They shall therefore camp around the Dwelling. 51 When the Dwelling is to move on, the Levites shall take it down; when the Dwelling is to be pitched, it is the Levites who shall set it up. Any layman who comes near it shall be put to death. 52 While the other Israelites shall camp by companies, each in his own division of the camp, 53 the Levites shall camp around the Dwelling of the commandments. Otherwise God's wrath will strike the Israelite community. The Levites, then, shall have charge of the Dwelling of the commandments." 54 All this the Israelites fulfilled as the Lord had commanded Moses.

2 The Lord said to Moses and Aaron: 2 "The Israelites shall camp, each in his own division, under the ensigns of their ancestral houses. They shall camp around the meeting tent, but at some distance from it.

30 Once the pedigrees of Zebulun's descendants had been established by clans and families, the names of all the males of twenty years and over, fit to bear arms, were recorded one by one. 31 The total of these for the tribe of Zebulun was fifty-seven thousand four hundred.

32 As regards the descendants of Joseph: once the pedigrees of Ephraim's descendants had been established by clans and families, the names of all the males of twenty years and over, fit to bear arms, were recorded one by one. 33 The total of these for the tribe of Ephraim was forty thousand five hundred.

34 Once the pedigrees of Manasseh's descendants had been established by clans and families, the names of all the males of twenty years and over, fit to bear arms, were recorded one by one. 35 The total of these for the tribe of Manasseh was thirty-two thousand two hundred.

36 Once the pedigrees of Benjamin's descendants had been established by clans and families, the names of all the males of twenty years and over, fit to bear arms, were recorded one by one. 37 The total of these for the tribe of Benjamin was thirty-five thousand four hundred.

38 Once the pedigrees of Dan's descendants had been established by clans and families, the names of all the males of twenty years and over, fit to bear arms, were recorded one by one. 39 The total of these for the tribe of Dan was sixty-two thousand seven hundred.

40 Once the pedigrees of Asher's descendants had been established by clans and families, the names of all the males of twenty years and over, fit to bear arms, were recorded one by one. 41 The total of these for the tribe of Asher was forty-one thousand five hundred.

42 Once the pedigrees of Naphtali's descendants had been established by clans and families, the names of all the males of twenty years and over, fit to bear arms, were recorded one by one. 43 The total of these for the tribe of Naphtali was fifty-three thousand four hundred.

44 Such were the men registered by Moses, Aaron and the leaders of Israel, of whom there were twelve, each representing his family. 45 All the Israelites of twenty years and over, fit to bear arms, were counted by families. 46 Altogether, the total came to six hundred and three thousand five hundred and fifty.

47 But the Levites and their tribes were not included in the count.

48 Yahweh spoke to Moses and said:

49 'Do not, however, take a census of the Levites, or register them with the other Israelites, 50 but enrol the Levites to take charge of the Dwelling where the Testimony is and of all its furnishings and belongings. They must carry the Dwelling and all its furnishings; they must look after the Dwelling and pitch their camp round it. 51 Whenever the Dwelling is moved, the Levites will dismantle it; whenever the Dwelling stops for the night, the Levites will erect it. Any unauthorised person coming near it will be put to death. 52 The Israelites will pitch their tents, each in their own encampment and by their own standard, company by company, 53 but the Levites will pitch their tents round the Dwelling where the Testimony is. In this way Retribution will be kept from falling on the whole community of Israelites, and the Levites will keep charge of the Dwelling of the Testimony.'

54 The Israelites did exactly as Yahweh had ordered Moses. They did as he said.

2 Yahweh spoke to Moses and to Aaron and said:

2 'The Israelites must pitch their tents, each man by his own standard, under his family emblems. They must pitch their tents round the Dwelling where the Testimony is, some distance away.

the east side toward the sunrise shall be of the regimental encampment of Judah by companies. The leader of the people of Judah shall be Nahshon son of Amminadab, 4 with a company as enrolled of seventy-four thousand six hundred. 5 Those to camp next to him shall be the tribe of Issachar. The leader of the Issacharites shall be Nethanel son of Zuar, 6 with a company as enrolled of fifty-four thousand four hundred. 7 Then the tribe of Zebulun: The leader of the Zebulunites shall be Eliab son of Helon, 8 with a company as enrolled of fifty-seven thousand four hundred. 9 The total enrollment of the camp of Judah, by companies, is one hundred eighty-six thousand four hundred. They shall set out first on the march.

10 On the south side shall be the regimental encampment of Reuben by companies. The leader of the Reubenites shall be Elizur son of Shedeur, 11 with a company as enrolled of forty-six thousand five hundred. 12 And those to camp next to him shall be the tribe of Simeon. The leader of the Simeonites shall be Shelumiel son of Zurishaddai, 13 with a company as enrolled of fifty-nine thousand three hundred. 14 Then the tribe of Gad: The leader of the Gadites shall be Eliasaph son of Reuel, 15 with a company as enrolled of forty-five thousand six hundred fifty. 16 The total enrollment of the camp of Reuben, by companies, is one hundred fifty-one thousand four hundred fifty. They shall set out second.

17 The tent of meeting, with the camp of the Levites, shall set out in the center of the camps; they shall set out just as they camp, each in position, by their regiments.

18 On the west side shall be the regimental encampment of Ephraim by companies. The leader of the people of Ephraim shall be Elishama son of Ammihud, 19 with a company as enrolled of forty thousand five hundred. 20 Next to him shall be the tribe of Manasseh. The leader of the people of Manasseh shall be Gamaliel son of Pedahzur, 21 with a company as enrolled of thirty-two thousand two hundred. 22 Then the tribe of Benjamin: The leader of the Benjaminites shall be Abidan son of Gideoni, 23 with a company as enrolled of thirty-five thousand four hundred. 24 The total enrollment of the camp of Ephraim, by companies, is one hundred eight thousand one hundred. They shall set out third on the march.

25 On the north side shall be the regimental encampment of Dan by companies. The leader of the Danites shall be Ahiezer son of Ammishaddai, 26 with a company as enrolled of sixty-two thousand seven hundred. 27 Those to camp next to him shall be the tribe of Asher. The leader of the Asherites shall be Pagiel son of Ochran, 28 with a company as enrolled of forty-one thousand five hundred. 29 Then the tribe of Naphtali: The leader of the Naphtalites shall be Ahira son of Enan, 30 with a company as enrolled of fifty-three thousand four hundred. 31 The total enrollment of the camp of Dan is one hundred fifty-seven thousand six hundred. They shall set out last, by companies.*b*

32 This was the enrollment of the Israelites by their ancestral houses; the total enrollment in the camps by their companies was six hundred three thousand five hundred fifty. 33 Just as the LORD had commanded Moses, the Levites were not enrolled among the other Israelites.

3 'In front of it, on the east, the division of Judah is to be stationed under the standard of its camp by tribal hosts. The chief of Judah will be Nahshon son of Amminadab. 4 His host, with its members as listed, numbers seventy-four thousand six hundred men. 5 Next to Judah the tribe of Issachar is to be stationed. Its chief will be Nethanel son of Zuar; 6 his host, with its members as listed, numbers fifty-four thousand four hundred. 7 Then the tribe of Zebulun; its chief will be Eliab son of Helon; 8 his host, with its members as listed, numbers fifty-seven thousand four hundred. 9 The number listed in the camp of Judah, by hosts, is one hundred and eighty-six thousand four hundred. They will be the first to march.

10 'To the south the division of Reuben is to be stationed under the standard of its camp by tribal hosts. The chief of Reuben will be Elizur son of Shedeur; 11 his host, with its members as listed, numbers forty-six thousand five hundred. 12 Next to him the tribe of Simeon is to be stationed. Its chief will be Shelumiel son of Zurishaddai; 13 his host, with its members as listed, numbers fifty-nine thousand three hundred. 14 Then the tribe of Gad: its chief will be Eliasaph son of Reuel; 15 his host, with its members as listed, numbers forty-five thousand six hundred and fifty. 16 The number listed in the camp of Reuben, by hosts, is one hundred and fifty-one thousand four hundred and fifty. They will be the second to march.

17 'When the Tent of Meeting moves, the camp of the Levites must keep its station in the centre of the other camps; let them move in the order of their encamping, each man in his proper place under his standard.

18 'To the west the division of Ephraim is to be stationed under the standard of its camp by tribal hosts. The chief of Ephraim will be Elishama son of Ammihud; 19 his host, with its members as listed, numbers forty thousand five hundred. 20 Next to him the tribe of Manasseh is to be stationed. Its chief will be Gamaliel son of Pedahzur; 21 his host, with its members as listed, numbers thirty-two thousand two hundred. 22 Then the tribe of Benjamin: its chief will be Abidan son of Gideoni; 23 his host, with its members as listed, numbers thirty-five thousand four hundred. 24 The number listed in the camp of Ephraim, by hosts, is one hundred and eight thousand one hundred. They will be the third to march.

25 'To the north the division of Dan is to be stationed under the standard of its camp by tribal hosts. The chief of Dan will be Ahiezer son of Ammishaddai; 26 his host, with its members as listed, numbers sixty-two thousand seven hundred. 27 Next to him the tribe of Asher is to be stationed. Its chief will be Pagiel son of Ochran; 28 his host, with its members as listed, numbers forty-one thousand five hundred. 29 Then the tribe of Naphtali: its chief will be Ahira son of Enan; 30 his host, with its members as listed, numbers fifty-three thousand four hundred. 31 The number listed in the camp of Dan is one hundred and fifty-seven thousand six hundred. They will march last, under their standards.'

32 Those were the Israelites listed by their fathers' families. The total number in the camp, recorded by tribal hosts, was six hundred and three thousand five hundred and fifty. 33 The Levites were not included in the lists with their fellow-Israelites, for so the LORD had commanded Moses.

b Compare verses 9, 16, 24: Heb *by their regiments*

3 "Encamped on the east side, toward the sunrise, shall be the divisional camp of Judah, arranged in companies. [The prince of the Judahites was Nahshon, son of Amminadab, 4 and his soldiers amounted in the census to seventy-four thousand six hundred.] 5 With Judah shall camp the tribe of Issachar [their prince was Nethanel, son of Zuar, 6 and his soldiers amounted in the census to fifty-four thousand four hundred] 7 and the tribe of Zebulun. [Their prince was Eliab, son of Helon, 8 and his soldiers amounted in the census to fifty-seven thousand four hundred. 9 The total number of those registered by companies in the camp of Judah was one hundred and eighty-six thousand four hundred.] These shall be first on the march.

10 "On the south side shall be the divisional camp of Reuben, arranged in companies. [Their prince was Elizur, son of Shedeur, 11 and his soldiers amounted in the census to forty-six thousand five hundred.] 12 Beside them shall camp the tribe of Simeon [their prince was Shelumiel, son of Zurishaddai, 13 and his soldiers amounted in the census to fifty-nine thousand three hundred] 14 and next the tribe of Gad. [Their prince was Eliasaph, son of Reuel, 15 and his soldiers amounted in the census to forty-five thousand six hundred and fifty. 16 The total number of those registered by companies in the camp of Reuben was one hundred and fifty-one thousand four hundred and fifty.] These shall be second on the march.

17 "Then the meeting tent and the camp of the Levites shall set out in the middle of the line. As in camp, so also on the march, every man shall be in his proper place, with his own division.

18 "On the west side shall be the divisional camp of Ephraim, arranged in companies. [Their prince was Elishama, son of Ammihud, 19 and his soldiers amounted in the census to forty thousand five hundred.] 20 Beside them shall camp the tribe of Manasseh [their prince was Gamaliel, son of Pedahzur, 21 and his soldiers amounted in the census to thirty-two thousand two hundred] 22 and the tribe of Benjamin. [Their prince was Abidan, son of Gideoni, 23 and his soldiers amounted in the census to thirty-five thousand four hundred. 24 The total number of those registered by companies in the camp of Ephraim was one hundred and eight thousand one hundred.] These shall be third on the march.

25 "On the north side shall be the divisional camp of Dan, arranged in companies. [Their prince was Ahiezer, son of Ammishaddai, 26 and his soldiers amounted in the census to sixty-two thousand seven hundred.] 27 Beside them shall camp the tribe of Asher [their prince was Pagiel, son of Ochran, 28 and his soldiers amounted in the census to forty-one thousand five hundred] 29 and next the tribe of Naphtali. [Their prince was Ahira, son of Enan, 30 and his soldiers amounted in the census to fifty-three thousand four hundred. 31 The total number of those registered by companies in the camp of Dan was one hundred and fifty-seven thousand six hundred.] These shall be the last of the divisions on the march."

32 This was the census of the Israelites taken by ancestral houses. The total number of those registered by companies in the camps was six hundred and three thousand five hundred and fifty. 33 The Levites, however, were not registered with the other Israelites, for so the LORD had commanded

3 'Encamped on the east side:
'Furthest towards the east, the standard of the camp of Judah, unit by unit. Leader of the Judahites: Nahshon son of Amminadab. 4 His company: seventy-four thousand six hundred men.
5 'Next to him:
'The tribe of Issachar. Leader of the Issacharites: Nethanel son of Zuar. 6 His company: fifty-four thousand four hundred men.
7 'The tribe of Zebulun. Leader of the Zebulunites: Eliab son of Helon. 8 His company: fifty-seven thousand four hundred men.
9 'The tribal forces in the camp of Judah number in all a hundred and eighty-six thousand four hundred. These will be the first to break camp.
10 'On the south side, the standard of the camp of Reuben, unit by unit. Leader of the Reubenites: Elizur son of Shedeur. 11 His company: forty-six thousand five hundred men.
12 'Next to him:
'The tribe of Simeon. Leader of the Simeonites: Shelumiel son of Zurishaddai. 13 His company: fifty-nine thousand three hundred men.
14 'The tribe of Gad. Leader of the Gadites: Eliasaph son of Reuel. 15 His company: forty-five thousand six hundred and fifty men.
16 'The tribal forces in the camp of Reuben number in all a hundred and fifty-one thousand four hundred and fifty. They will be second to break camp.
17 'Next, the Tent of Meeting will move, since the camp of the Levites is situated in the middle of the other camps. The order of movement will be the order of encampment, each man under his own standard.
18 'On the west side, the standard of the camp of Ephraim, unit by unit. Leader of the Ephraimites: Elishama son of Ammihud. 19 His company: forty thousand five hundred men.
20 'Next to him:
'The tribe of Manasseh. Leader of the Manassehites: Gamaliel son of Pedahzur. 21 His company: thirty-two thousand two hundred men.
22 'The tribe of Benjamin. Leader of the Benjaminites: Abidan son of Gideoni. 23 His company: thirty-five thousand four hundred men.
24 'The tribal forces in the camp of Ephraim number in all a hundred and eight thousand one hundred. They will be third to break camp.
25 'On the north side, the standard of the camp of Dan, unit by unit. Leader of the Danites: Ahiezer son of Ammishaddai. 26 His company: sixty-two thousand seven hundred men.
27 'Next to him:
'The tribe of Asher. Leader of the Asherites: Pagiel son of Ochran. 28 His company: forty-one thousand five hundred men.
29 'The tribe of Naphtali. Leader of the Naphtalites: Ahira son of Enan. 30 His company: fifty-three thousand four hundred men.
31 'The tribal forces in the camp of Dan number in all a hundred and fifty-seven thousand six hundred. They will be the last to break camp.
'All under their appropriate standards.'
32 Such was the tally of the Israelites when the census was taken by families. The full count of the entire camp, unit by unit, came to six hundred and three thousand five hundred and fifty. 33 But, as Yahweh had ordered Moses, the Levites were not included in the census of the Israelites.

NEW REVISED STANDARD VERSION	REVISED ENGLISH BIBLE

NEW REVISED STANDARD VERSION

34 The Israelites did just as the LORD had commanded Moses: They camped by regiments, and they set out the same way, everyone by clans, according to ancestral houses.

3 This is the lineage of Aaron and Moses at the time when the LORD spoke with Moses on Mount Sinai. 2 These are the names of the sons of Aaron: Nadab the firstborn, and Abihu, Eleazar, and Ithamar; 3 these are the names of the sons of Aaron, the anointed priests, whom he ordained to minister as priests. 4 Nadab and Abihu died before the LORD when they offered illicit fire before the LORD in the wilderness of Sinai, and they had no children. Eleazar and Ithamar served as priests in the lifetime of their father Aaron.

5 Then the LORD spoke to Moses, saying: 6 Bring the tribe of Levi near, and set them before Aaron the priest, so that they may assist him. 7 They shall perform duties for him and for the whole congregation in front of the tent of meeting, doing service at the tabernacle; 8 they shall be in charge of all the furnishings of the tent of meeting, and attend to the duties for the Israelites as they do service at the tabernacle. 9 You shall give the Levites to Aaron and his descendants; they are unreservedly given to him from among the Israelites. 10 But you shall make a register of Aaron and his descendants; it is they who shall attend to the priesthood, and any outsider who comes near shall be put to death.

11 Then the LORD spoke to Moses, saying: 12 I hereby accept the Levites from among the Israelites as substitutes for all the firstborn that open the womb among the Israelites. The Levites shall be mine, 13 for all the firstborn are mine; when I killed all the firstborn in the land of Egypt, I consecrated for my own all the firstborn in Israel, both human and animal; they shall be mine. I am the LORD.

14 Then the LORD spoke to Moses in the wilderness of Sinai, saying: 15 Enroll the Levites by ancestral houses and by clans. You shall enroll every male from a month old and upward. 16 So Moses enrolled them according to the word of the LORD, as he was commanded. 17 The following were the sons of Levi, by their names: Gershon, Kohath, and Merari. 18 These are the names of the sons of Gershon by their clans: Libni and Shimei. 19 The sons of Kohath by their clans: Amram, Izhar, Hebron, and Uzziel. 20 The sons of Merari by their clans: Mahli and Mushi. These are the clans of the Levites, by their ancestral houses.

21 To Gershon belonged the clan of the Libnites and the clan of the Shimeites; these were the clans of the Gershonites. 22 Their enrollment, counting all the males from a month old and upward, was seven thousand five hundred. 23 The clans of the Gershonites were to camp behind the tabernacle on the west, 24 with Eliasaph son of Lael as head of the ancestral house of the Gershonites. 25 The responsibility of the sons of Gershon in the tent of meeting was to be the tabernacle, the tent with its covering, the screen for the entrance of the tent of meeting, 26 the hangings of the court, the screen for the entrance of the court that is around the tabernacle and the altar, and its cords — all the service pertaining to these.

27 To Kohath belonged the clan of the Amramites, the clan of the Izharites, the clan of the Hebronites, and the clan of the Uzzielites; these are the clans of the Kohathites. 28 Counting all the males, from a month old and upward, there were eight thousand six hundred, attending to the duties of the sanctuary. 29 The clans of the Kohathites were to camp on the south side of tabernacle, 30 with Elizaphan son of Uzziel as head of the ancestral house of the clans of the Kohathites. 31 Their responsibility was to be the

REVISED ENGLISH BIBLE

34 The Israelites did everything just as the LORD had commanded Moses, pitching and breaking camp standard by standard, each man according to his family in his father's line.

3 THESE were the descendants of Aaron and Moses at the time when the LORD spoke to Moses on Mount Sinai. 2 The names of the sons of Aaron were Nadab the eldest, Abihu, Eleazar, and Ithamar. 3 These were the names of Aaron's sons, the anointed priests who had been installed in the priestly office. 4 Nadab and Abihu fell dead before the LORD because they had presented illicit fire before the LORD in the wilderness of Sinai; they left no sons. Eleazar and Ithamar continued to perform the priestly office during their father's lifetime.

5 The LORD said to Moses, 6 'Bring forward the tribe of Levi and appoint them to serve Aaron the priest and to minister to him. 7 They are to be in attendance on him and on the whole community before the Tent of Meeting, undertaking the service of the Tabernacle. 8 They are to be in charge of all the equipment in the Tent of Meeting, and be in attendance on the Israelites, undertaking the service of the Tabernacle. 9 You are to assign the Levites to Aaron and his sons as especially dedicated to him out of all the Israelites. 10 Commit the priestly office to Aaron and his line, and they are to perform its duties; any lay person who encroaches on it must be put to death.'

11 The LORD said to Moses, 12 'I take for myself, out of all the Israelites, the Levites as a substitute for the eldest male child of every woman; the Levites are to be mine. 13 For every eldest child, if a boy, became mine when I destroyed all the eldest sons in Egypt. So I have consecrated to myself all the firstborn in Israel, both man and beast. They are to be mine. I am the LORD.'

14 The LORD said to Moses in the wilderness of Sinai, 15 'Make a list of all the Levites by their families in the father's line, every male aged one month or more.' 16 Moses made a list of them in accordance with the command given him by the LORD. 17 Now these were the names of the sons of Levi.

Gershon, Kohath, and Merari.

18 Descendants of Gershon, by families: Libni and Shimei.

19 Descendants of Kohath, by families: Amram, Izhar, Hebron, and Uzziel.

20 Descendants of Merari, by families: Mahli and Mushi. These were the families of Levi, by fathers' families.

21 Gershon: the family of Libni and the family of Shimei. These were the families of Gershon, 22 and the number of males in their list as drawn up, aged one month or more, was seven thousand five hundred. 23 The families of Gershon were stationed on the west, behind the Tabernacle. 24 Their chief was Eliasaph son of Lael, 25 and in the service of the Tent of Meeting they were in charge of the Tabernacle and the Tent, its covering, and the screen at the entrance to the Tent of Meeting, 26 the hangings of the court, the screen at the entrance to the court all round the Tabernacle and the altar, and of all else needed for its maintenance.

27 Kohath: the family of Amram, the family of Izhar, the family of Hebron, the family of Uzziel. These were the families of Kohath, 28 and the number of males aged one month or more was eight thousand six hundred. They were the guardians of the holy things. 29 The families of Kohath were stationed on the south, at the side of the Tabernacle. 30 Their chief was Elizaphan son of Uzziel; 31 they were in

Moses. 34 The Israelites did just as the LORD had commanded Moses; both in camp and on the march they were in their own divisions, every man according to his clan and his ancestral house.

3 The following were the descendants of Aaron and Moses at the time that the LORD spoke to Moses on Mount Sinai. 2 The sons of Aaron were Nadab his first-born, Abihu, Eleazar, and Ithamar. 3 These are the names of the sons of Aaron, the anointed priests who were ordained to exercise the priesthood. 4 But when Nadab and Abihu offered profane fire before the LORD in the desert of Sinai, they met death in the presence of the LORD, and left no sons. Thereafter only Eleazar and Ithamar performed the priestly functions under the direction of their father Aaron. 5 Now the LORD said to Moses: 6 "Summon the tribe of Levi and present them to Aaron the priest, as his assistants. 7 They shall discharge his obligations and those of the whole community before the meeting tent by serving at the Dwelling. 8 They shall have custody of all the furnishings of the meeting tent and discharge the duties of the Israelites in the service of the Dwelling. 9 You shall give the Levites to Aaron and his sons; they have been set aside from among the Israelites as dedicated to me. 10 But only Aaron and his descendants shall you appoint to have charge of the priestly functions. Any layman who comes near shall be put to death."

11 The LORD said to Moses, 12 "It is I who have chosen the Levites from the Israelites in place of every first-born that opens the womb among the Israelites. The Levites, therefore, are mine, 13 because every first-born is mine. When I slew all the first-born in the land of Egypt, I made all the first-born in Israel sacred to me, both of man and of beast. They belong to me; I am the LORD."

14 The LORD said to Moses in the desert of Sinai, 15 "Take a census of the Levites by ancestral houses and clans, registering every male of a month or more." 16 Moses, therefore, took their census in accordance with the command the LORD had given him.

17 The sons of Levi were named Gershon, Kohath and Merari. 18 The descendants of Gershon, by clans, were named Libni and Shimei. 19 The descendants of Kohath, by clans, were Amram, Izhar, Hebron and Uzziel. 20 The descendants of Merari, by clans, were Mahli and Mushi. These were the clans of the Levites by ancestral houses.

21 To Gershon belonged the clan of the Libnites and the clan of the Shimeites; these were the clans of the Gershonites. 22 When all their males of a month or more were registered, they numbered seven thousand five hundred. 23 The clans of the Gershonites camped behind the Dwelling, to the west. 24 The prince of their ancestral house was Eliasaph, son of Lael. 25 At the meeting tent they had charge of whatever pertained to the Dwelling, the tent and its covering, the curtain at the entrance of the meeting tent, 26 the hangings of the court, the curtain at the entrance of the court enclosing both the Dwelling and the altar, and the ropes.

27 To Kohath belonged the clans of the Amramites, the Izharites, the Hebronites, and the Uzzielites; these were the clans of the Kohathites. 28 When all their males of a month or more were registered, they numbered eight thousand three hundred. They had charge of the sanctuary. 29 The clans of the Kohathites camped at the south side of the Dwelling. 30 The prince of their ancestral house was Elizaphan, son of Uzziel. 31 They had charge of whatever per-

34 The Israelites did exactly as Yahweh had ordered Moses. This was how they pitched camp, grouped by standards. This was how they broke camp, each man in his own clan, each man with his own family.

3 These were the descendants of Aaron and Moses, at the time when Yahweh spoke to Moses on Mount Sinai. 2 These were the names of Aaron's sons: Nadab the eldest, then Abihu, Eleazar and Ithamar. 3 Such were the names of Aaron's sons, priests anointed and invested with the powers of the priesthood. 4 Nadab and Abihu died in Yahweh's presence, in the desert of Sinai, when they offered unauthorised fire before Yahweh. They left no children and so it fell to Eleazar and Ithamar to exercise the priesthood under their father Aaron.

5 Yahweh spoke to Moses and said: 6 'Muster the tribe of Levi and put it at the disposal of the priest Aaron: they must be at his service. 7 They will undertake the duties incumbent on him and the whole community before the Tent of Meeting, in serving the Dwelling, 8 and they will be in charge of all the furnishings of the Tent of Meeting and undertake the duties incumbent on the Israelites in serving the Dwelling. 9 You will present the Levites to Aaron and his sons as men dedicated; they will be given to him by the Israelites.

10 'You will register Aaron and his sons, who will carry out their priestly duty. But any unauthorised person who comes near must be put to death.'

11 Yahweh spoke to Moses and said: 12 'Look, I myself have chosen the Levites from the Israelites instead of all the first-born, those who emerge first from the womb in Israel; the Levites therefore belong to me. 13 For every first-born belongs to me. On the day when I struck down all the first-born in Egypt, I consecrated all the first-born in Israel, human and animal, to be my own. They are mine, Yahweh's.'

14 Yahweh spoke to Moses in the desert of Sinai and said: 15 'You must take a census of Levi's descendants by families and clans; all the males of the age of one month and over will be counted.'

16 At Yahweh's word Moses took a census of them, as Yahweh had ordered. 17 These were the names of Levi's sons: Gershon, Kohath and Merari.

18 These were the names of Gershon's sons by their clans: Libni and Shimei; 19 Kohath's sons by their clans: Amram, Izhar, Hebron and Uzziel; 20 Merari's sons by their clans: Mahli and Mushi. These were the clans of Levi, grouped by families.

21 From Gershon were descended the Libnite and Shimeite clans; these were the Gershonite clans. 22 Their full number, counting the males of one month and over, came to seven thousand five hundred. 23 The Gershonite clans pitched their camp behind the Dwelling, on the west side. 24 The leader of the House of Gershon was Eliasaph son of Lael. 25 As regards the Tent of Meeting, the Gershonites had charge of the Dwelling, the Tent and its covering, the screen for the entrance to the Tent of Meeting, 26 the curtaining of the court, the screen for the entrance to the court surrounding the Dwelling and the altar, and the cords required in dealing with all this.

27 From Kohath were descended the Amramite, Izharite, Hebronite and Uzzielite clans; these were the Kohathite clans. 28 Their full number, counting the males of one month and over, came to eight thousand three hundred. They were in charge of the sanctuary. 29 The Kohathite clans pitched their camp on the south side of the Dwelling. 30 The leader of the house of the Kohathite clans was Elizaphan son of Uzziel. 31 They were in charge of the ark, the

ark, the table, the lampstand, the altars, the vessels of the sanctuary with which the priests minister, and the screen — all the service pertaining to these. ³²Eleazar son of Aaron the priest was to be chief over the leaders of the Levites, and to have oversight of those who had charge of the sanctuary.

33 To Merari belonged the clan of the Mahlites and the clan of the Mushites: these are the clans of Merari. ³⁴Their enrollment, counting all the males from a month old and upward, was six thousand two hundred. ³⁵The head of the ancestral house of the clans of Merari was Zuriel son of Abihail; they were to camp on the north side of the tabernacle. ³⁶The responsibility assigned to the sons of Merari was to be the frames of the tabernacle, the bars, the pillars, the bases, and all their accessories — all the service pertaining to these; ³⁷also the pillars of the court all around, with their bases and pegs and cords.

38 Those who were to camp in front of the tabernacle on the east — in front of the tent of meeting toward the east — were Moses and Aaron and Aaron's sons, having charge of the rites within the sanctuary, whatever had to be done for the Israelites; and any outsider who came near was to be put to death. ³⁹The total enrollment of the Levites whom Moses and Aaron enrolled at the commandment of the Lord, by their clans, all the males from a month old and upward, was twenty-two thousand.

40 Then the Lord said to Moses: Enroll all the firstborn males of the Israelites, from a month old and upward, and count their names. ⁴¹But you shall accept the Levites for me — I am the Lord — as substitutes for all the firstborn among the Israelites, and the livestock of the Levites as substitutes for all the firstborn among the livestock of the Israelites. ⁴²So Moses enrolled all the firstborn among the Israelites, as the Lord commanded him. ⁴³The total enrollment, all the firstborn males from a month old and upward, counting the number of names, was twenty-two thousand two hundred seventy-three.

44 Then the Lord spoke to Moses, saying: ⁴⁵Accept the Levites as substitutes for all the firstborn among the Israelites, and the livestock of the Levites as substitutes for their livestock; and the Levites shall be mine. I am the Lord. ⁴⁶As the price of redemption of the two hundred seventy-three of the firstborn of the Israelites, over and above the number of the Levites, ⁴⁷you shall accept five shekels apiece, reckoning by the shekel of the sanctuary, a shekel of twenty gerahs. ⁴⁸Give to Aaron and his sons the money by which the excess number of them is redeemed. ⁴⁹So Moses took the redemption money from those who were over and above those redeemed by the Levites; ⁵⁰from the firstborn of the Israelites he took the money, one thousand three hundred sixty-five shekels, reckoned by the shekel of the sanctuary; ⁵¹and Moses gave the redemption money to Aaron and his sons, according to the word of the Lord, as the Lord had commanded Moses.

4 The Lord spoke to Moses and Aaron, saying: ²Take a census of the Kohathites separate from the other Levites, by their clans and their ancestral houses, ³from thirty years old up to fifty years old, all who qualify to do work relating to the tent of meeting. ⁴The service of the Kohathites relating to the tent of meeting concerns the most holy things.

5 When the camp is to set out, Aaron and his sons shall go in and take down the screening curtain, and cover the ark of the covenantᶜ with it; ⁶then they shall put on it a covering of fine leather,ᵈ and spread over that a cloth all of blue, and shall put its poles in place. ⁷Over the table of the bread of the Presence they shall spread a blue cloth, and put on it the plates, the dishes for incense, the bowls, and the flagons for the drink offering; the regular bread also shall be on it;

charge of the Ark, the table, the lampstands and the altars, together with the sacred vessels used in their service, and the screen with everything needed for its maintenance. ³²The chief over all the chiefs of the Levites was Eleazar son of Aaron the priest, who was appointed overseer of those in charge of the sanctuary.

33 Merari: the family of Mahli, the family of Mushi. These were the families of Merari, ³⁴and the number of males in their list as drawn up, aged one month or more, was six thousand two hundred. ³⁵Their chief was Zuriel son of Abihail; they were stationed on the north, at the side of the Tabernacle. ³⁶The Merarites were in charge of the planks, bars, posts, and sockets of the Tabernacle, together with its vessels and all the equipment needed for its maintenance, ³⁷the posts, sockets, pegs, and cords of the surrounding court.

38 In front of the Tabernacle on the east, Moses was stationed, with Aaron and his sons, in front of the Tent of Meeting eastwards. They were in charge of the sanctuary on behalf of the Israelites; any lay person who came near would be put to death. ³⁹The number of Levites recorded by Moses on the list by families at the command of the Lord was twenty-two thousand males aged one month or more.

40 The Lord said to Moses, 'Make a list of all the male firstborn in Israel aged one month or more, and count the number of persons. ⁴¹You are to reserve the Levites for me — I am the Lord — in substitution for the eldest sons of the Israelites, and in the same way the Levites' cattle in substitution for the firstborn cattle of the Israelites.' ⁴²As the Lord had commanded him, Moses made a list of all the eldest sons of the Israelites, ⁴³and the total number of firstborn males recorded by name in the register, aged one month or more, was twenty-two thousand two hundred and seventy-three.

44 The Lord said to Moses, ⁴⁵'Take the Levites as a substitute for all the eldest sons in Israel and the cattle of the Levites as a substitute for their cattle. The Levites are to be mine. I am the Lord. ⁴⁶The eldest sons in Israel will outnumber the Levites by two hundred and seventy-three. ⁴⁷This remainder must be redeemed, and for each of them you are to accept five shekels by the sacred standard, at the rate of twenty gerahs to the shekel; ⁴⁸give the money with which they are redeemed to Aaron and his sons.'

49 Moses took the money paid to redeem those who remained over when the substitution of Levites was complete. ⁵⁰The amount received was one thousand three hundred and sixty-five shekels of silver by the sacred standard. ⁵¹In accordance with what the Lord had said, he gave the money to Aaron and his sons, doing what the Lord had commanded him.

4 The Lord said to Moses and Aaron, ²⁻³'Among the Levites, make a count of the descendants of Kohath between the ages of thirty and fifty, by families in the father's line, comprising everyone who comes to take duty in the service of the Tent of Meeting.

4 'This is the service to be rendered by the Kohathites in the Tent of Meeting; it is most holy. ⁵When the camp is due to move, let Aaron and his sons come and take down the curtain of the screen, and cover the Ark of the Testimony with it; ⁶over this they are to put a covering of dugong-hide and over that again a violet cloth all of one piece; they will then put its poles in place. ⁷Over the table of the Bread of the Presence they are to spread a violet cloth and lay on it the dishes, saucers, and flagons, and the bowls for drink-offerings; the Bread regularly presented will also lie on it;

ᶜOr treaty, or testimony; Heb eduth   ᵈMeaning of Heb uncertain   3:39 Moses: so some MSS; others add and Aaron.

NEW AMERICAN BIBLE

tained to the ark, the table, the lampstand, the altars, the utensils with which the ministry of the sanctuary was exercised, and the veil. 32 The chief prince of the Levites, however, was Eleazar, son of Aaron the priest; he was supervisor over those who had charge of the sanctuary.

33 To Merari belonged the clans of the Mahlites and the Mushites; these were the clans of Merari. 34 When all their males of a month or more were registered, they numbered six thousand two hundred. 35 The prince of the ancestral house of the clans of Merari was Zuriel, son of Abihail. They camped at the north side of the Dwelling. 36 The Merarites were charged with the care of whatever pertained to the boards of the Dwelling, its bars, columns, pedestals, and all its fittings, 37 as well as the columns of the surrounding court with their pedestals, pegs and ropes.

38 East of the Dwelling, that is, in front of the meeting tent, toward the sunrise, were camped Moses and Aaron and the latter's sons. They discharged the obligations of the sanctuary for the Israelites. Any layman who came near was to be put to death.

39 The total number of male Levites a month old or more whom Moses had registered by clans in keeping with the LORD's command, was twenty-two thousand.

40 The LORD then said to Moses, "Take a census of all the first-born males of the Israelites a month old or more, and compute their total number. 41 Then assign the Levites to me, the LORD, in place of all the first-born of the Israelites, as well as their cattle in place of all the first-born among the cattle of the Israelites." 42 So Moses took a census of all the first-born of the Israelites, as the LORD had commanded him. 43 When all the first-born males of a month or more were registered, they numbered twenty-two thousand two hundred and seventy-three.

44 The LORD said to Moses: 45 "Take the Levites in place of all the first-born of the Israelites, and the Levites' cattle in place of their cattle, that the Levites may belong to me. I am the LORD. 46 As ransom for the two hundred and seventy-three first-born of the Israelites who outnumber the Levites, 47 you shall take five shekels for each individual, according to the standard of the sanctuary shekel, twenty gerahs to the shekel. 48 Give this silver to Aaron and his sons as ransom for the extra number." 49 So Moses took the silver as ransom from those who were left when the rest had been redeemed by the Levites. 50 From the first-born of the Israelites he received in silver one thousand three hundred and sixty-five shekels according to the sanctuary standard. 51 He then gave this ransom silver to Aaron and his sons, as the LORD had commanded him.

4 The LORD said to Moses and Aaron: 2 "Among the Levites take a total of the Kohathites, by clans and ancestral houses, all the men of the Kohathites 3 between thirty and fifty years of age; these are to undertake obligatory tasks in the meeting tent.

4 "The service of the Kohathites in the meeting tent concerns the most sacred objects. 5 In breaking camp, Aaron and his sons shall go in and take down the screening curtain and cover the ark of the commandments with it. 6 Over these they shall put a cover of tahash skin, and on top of this spread an all-violet cloth. They shall then put the poles in place. 7 On the table of the Presence they shall spread a violet cloth and put on it the plates and cups, as well as the bowls and pitchers for libations; the established bread offering shall remain on the table. 8 Over these they shall spread

NEW JERUSALEM BIBLE

table, the lamp-stand, the altars, the sacred vessels used in the liturgy, and the curtain with all its fittings.

32 The chief of the Levite leaders was Eleazar, son of Aaron the priest. He supervised the people responsible for the sanctuary.

33 From Merari were descended the Mahlite and Mushite clans; these were the Merarite clans. 34 Their full number, counting the males of one month and over, came to six thousand two hundred. 35 The leader of the House of the Merarite clans was Zuriel, son of Abihail. They pitched their camp on the north side of the Dwelling. 36 The Merarites were in charge of the framework of the Dwelling, with its crossbars, poles, sockets and all its accessories and fittings, 37 and also the poles round the court, with their sockets, pegs and cords.

38 Finally, on the east side, in front of the Dwelling, in front of the Tent of Meeting, towards the east, was the camp of Moses and Aaron and his sons, who had charge of the sanctuary on behalf of the Israelites. Any unauthorised person coming near was to be put to death.

39 The total number of male Levites of the age of one month and over, whom Moses counted by clans as Yahweh had ordered, came to twenty-two thousand.

40 Yahweh said to Moses:

'Take a census of all the first-born of the Israelites, all the males from the age of one month and over; take a census of them by name. 41 You will then present the Levites to me, Yahweh, instead of Israel, and similarly the Levites' cattle instead of the first-born cattle of the Israelites.'

42 As Yahweh ordered, Moses took a census of all the first-born of the Israelites. 43 The total count, by name, of the first-born from the age of one month and over came to twenty-two thousand two hundred and seventy-three.

44 Yahweh then spoke to Moses and said:

45 'Take the Levites instead of all the first-born of the Israelites, and the Levites' cattle instead of their cattle; the Levites will be mine, Yahweh's. 46 For the ransom of the two hundred and seventy-three first-born of the Israelites in excess of the number of Levites, 47 you will take five shekels for each, by the sanctuary shekel, at twenty gerah to the shekel; 48 you will then give this money to Aaron and his sons as the ransom for the extra number.'

49 Moses took the ransom money for the extra ones unransomed by the Levites; 50 he took the money for the first-born of the Israelites: one thousand three hundred and sixty-five shekels, by the sanctuary shekel; 51 and Moses then handed over their ransom money to Aaron and his sons, at Yahweh's bidding, as Yahweh had ordered Moses.

4 Yahweh spoke to Moses and said: 2 'Take a census by clans and families of the Levites descended from Kohath: 3 all the men between thirty and fifty years of age and eligible for military service, who will have their duties in the Tent of Meeting.

4 'These are the duties of the Kohathites: looking after those things that are especially holy.

5 'When camp is broken, Aaron and his sons must come and take down the screening curtain, and cover the ark of the Testimony with it. 6 Over this, they will put a covering of fine leather, over which they will spread a cloth entirely of violet-purple. They will then fix the poles to the ark.

7 'Over the offertory table they will spread a violet cloth, and on it put the dishes, cups, bowls and libation jars; the bread of permanent offering will also be on it. 8 Over these

8 then they shall spread over them a crimson cloth, and cover it with a covering of fine leather,*e* and shall put its poles in place. 9 They shall take a blue cloth, and cover the lampstand for the light, with its lamps, its snuffers, its trays, and all the vessels for oil with which it is supplied; 10 and they shall put it with all its utensils in a covering of fine leather,*e* and put it on the carrying frame. 11 Over the golden altar they shall spread a blue cloth, and cover it with a covering of fine leather,*e* and shall put its poles in place; 12 and they shall take all the utensils of the service that are used in the sanctuary, and put them in a blue cloth, and cover them with a covering of fine leather,*e* and put them on the carrying frame. 13 They shall take away the ashes from the altar, and spread a purple cloth over it; 14 and they shall put on it all the utensils of the altar, which are used for the service there, the firepans, the forks, the shovels, and the basins, all the utensils of the altar; and they shall spread on it a covering of fine leather,*e* and shall put its poles in place. 15 When Aaron and his sons have finished covering the sanctuary and all the furnishings of the sanctuary, as the camp sets out, after that the Kohathites shall come to carry these, but they must not touch the holy things, or they will die. These are the things of the tent of meeting that the Kohathites are to carry.

16 Eleazar son of Aaron the priest shall have charge of the oil for the light, the fragrant incense, the regular grain offering, and the anointing oil, the oversight of all the tabernacle and all that is in it, in the sanctuary and in its utensils.

17 Then the LORD spoke to Moses and Aaron, saying: 18 You must not let the tribe of the clans of the Kohathites be destroyed from among the Levites. 19 This is how you must deal with them in order that they may live and not die when they come near to the most holy things: Aaron and his sons shall go in and assign each to a particular task or burden. 20 But the Kohathites *f* must not go in to look on the holy things even for a moment; otherwise they will die.

21 Then the LORD spoke to Moses, saying: 22 Take a census of the Gershonites also, by their ancestral houses and by their clans; 23 from thirty years old up to fifty years old you shall enroll them, all who qualify to do work in the tent of meeting. 24 This is the service of the clans of the Gershonites, in serving and bearing burdens: 25 They shall carry the curtains of the tabernacle, and the tent of meeting with its covering, and the outer covering of fine leather*e* that is on top of it, and the screen for the entrance of the tent of meeting, 26 and the hangings of the court, and the screen for the entrance of the gate of the court that is around the tabernacle and the altar, and their cords, and all the equipment for their service; and they shall do all that needs to be done with regard to them. 27 All the service of the Gershonites shall be at the command of Aaron and his sons, in all that they are to carry, and in all that they have to do; and you shall assign to their charge all that they are to carry. 28 This is the service of the clans of the Gershonites relating to the tent of meeting, and their responsibilities are to be under the oversight of Ithamar son of Aaron the priest.

29 As for the Merarites, you shall enroll them by their clans and their ancestral houses; 30 from thirty years old up to fifty years old you shall enroll them, everyone who qualifies to do the work of the tent of meeting. 31 This is what they are charged to carry, as the whole of their service in the tent of meeting: the frames of the tabernacle, with its bars, pillars, and bases, 32 and the pillars of the court all around with their bases, pegs, and cords, with all their equipment and all their related service; and you shall assign by name the objects that they are required to carry. 33 This is the

8 then they are to spread over them a scarlet cloth and over that a covering of dugong-hide, and put the poles in place. 9 They are to take a violet cloth and cover the lampstand, its lamps, tongs, firepans, and all the containers for the oil used in its service; 10 they are to put it with all its equipment in a sheet of dugong-hide slung from a pole. 11 Over the gold altar let them spread a violet cloth, cover it with a dugong-hide covering, and put its poles in place. 12 They are to take all the articles used for the service of the sanctuary, put them on a violet cloth, cover them with a dugong-hide covering, and sling them from a pole. 13 They are to clear the altar of the fat and ashes, spread a purple cloth over it, 14 and then lay on it all the equipment used in its service, the firepans, forks, shovels, tossing-bowls, and all the equipment of the altar, spread a covering of dugong-hide over it, and put the poles in place. 15 Once Aaron and his sons have finished covering the sanctuary and all the sacred equipment, when the camp is due to move, the Kohathites are to do the carrying; they must not touch the sacred objects, on pain of death. Those things are the load to be carried by the Kohathites, the things connected with the Tent of Meeting.

16 'Eleazar son of Aaron the priest is to have charge of the lamp oil, the fragrant incense, the regular grain-offering, and the anointing oil, with the general oversight of the whole Tabernacle and its contents, the sanctuary and its equipment.'

17 The LORD said to Moses and Aaron, 18 'You must not let the families of Kohath be wiped out and lost to the tribe of Levi. 19 If they are to live and not die when they approach the most holy things, this is what you must do: let Aaron and his sons come and set each man to his appointed task and to his load, 20 but the Kohathites themselves must not enter to cast even a passing glance at the sanctuary, on pain of death.'

21 The LORD said to Moses, 22 'Number the Gershonites by families in the father's line. 23 Make a list of all those between the ages of thirty and fifty who come on duty to perform service in the Tent of Meeting. 24 'This is the service to be rendered by the Gershonite families, comprising their general duty and their loads. 25 They are to transport the hangings of the Tabernacle, the Tent of Meeting, its covering, that is the covering of dugong-hide which is over it, the screen at the entrance to the Tent of Meeting, 26 the hangings of the court, the screen at the entrance to the court surrounding the Tabernacle and the altar, their cords, and all the equipment for their service; and they are to perform all the tasks connected with them. These are the acts of service they have to render. 27 All the service of the Gershonites, their loads and their other duties, will be directed by Aaron and his sons; you will assign them the loads for which they will be responsible. 28 That is the service assigned to the Gershonite families in connection with the Tent of Meeting; Ithamar son of Aaron the priest is to be in charge of them.

29 'Make a list of the Merarites by families in the father's line, 30 all those between the ages of thirty and fifty, who come on duty to perform service in the Tent of Meeting. 31 'These are the loads for which they are to be responsible in virtue of their service in the Tent of Meeting: the planks of the Tabernacle with its bars, posts, and sockets, 32 the posts of the surrounding court with their sockets, pegs, and cords, and all that is needed for the maintenance of them; you should assign to each man by name the load for which he is responsible. 33 Those are the duties of the

---

e Meaning of Heb uncertain   *f* Heb *they*

4:20 **to cast . . . glance:** *lit.* to look as they swallow.

a scarlet cloth and cover all this with tahash skin. They shall then put the poles in place. 9 They shall use a violet cloth to cover the lampstand with its lamps, trimming shears, and trays, as well as the various containers of oil from which it is supplied. 10 The lampstand with all its utensils they shall then enclose in a covering of tahash skin, and place on a litter. 11 Over the golden altar they shall spread a violet cloth, and cover this also with a covering of tahash skin. They shall then put the poles in place. 12 Taking the utensils of the sanctuary service, they shall wrap them all in violet cloth and cover them with tahash skin. They shall then place them on a litter. 13 After cleansing the altar of its ashes, they shall spread a purple cloth over it. 14 On this they shall put all the utensils with which it is served: the fire pans, forks, shovels, basins, and all the utensils of the altar. They shall then spread a covering of tahash skin over this, and put the poles in place.

15 "Only after Aaron and his sons have finished covering the sacred objects and all their utensils on breaking camp, shall the Kohathites enter to carry them. But they shall not touch the sacred objects; if they do they will die. These, then, are the objects in the meeting tent that the Kohathites shall carry.

16 "Eleazar, son of Aaron the priest, shall be in charge of the oil for the light, the fragrant incense, the established cereal offering, and the anointing oil. He shall be in charge of the whole Dwelling with all the sacred objects and utensils that are in it."

17 The LORD said to Moses and Aaron: 18 "Do not let the group of Kohathite clans perish from the body of the Levites. 19 That they may live and not die when they approach the most sacred objects, this is what you shall do for them: Aaron and his sons shall go in and assign to each of them his task and what he must carry; 20 but the Kohathites shall not go in to look upon the sacred objects, even for an instant; if they do, they will die."

21 The LORD said to Moses, 22 "Take a total among the Gershonites also, by ancestral houses and clans, 23 of all the men between thirty and fifty years of age; these are to undertake obligatory tasks in the meeting tent. 24 This is the task of the clans of the Gershonites, what they must do and what they must carry: 25 they shall carry the sheets of the Dwelling, the meeting tent with its covering and the outer wrapping of tahash skin, the curtain at the entrance of the meeting tent, 26 the hangings of the court, the curtain at the entrance of the court that encloses both the Dwelling and the altar, together with their ropes and all other objects necessary in their use. Whatever is to be done with these things shall be their task. 27 The service of the Gershonites shall be entirely under the direction of Aaron and his sons, with regard to what they must do and what they must carry; you shall make each man of them responsible for what he is to carry. 28 This, then, is the task of the Gershonites in the meeting tent; and they shall be under the supervision of Ithamar, son of Aaron the priest.

29 "Among the Merarites, too, you shall enroll by clans and ancestral houses 30 all their men between thirty and fifty years of age; these are to undertake obligatory tasks in the meeting tent. 31 This is what they shall be responsible for carrying, all the years of their service in the meeting tent: the boards of the Dwelling with its bars, columns and pedestals, 32 and the columns of the surrounding court with their pedestals, pegs and ropes. You shall designate for each man of them all the objects connected with his service, which he shall be responsible for carrying. 33 This, then, is

they will spread a scarlet cloth and cover the whole with a covering of fine leather. They will then fix the poles to the table.

9 'They will then take a violet cloth and cover the lampstand, its lamps, snuffers, trays and all the oil jars used for it, 10 and will lay it and all its accessories in a covering of fine leather and put it on the litter.

11 'Over the golden altar they will spread a violet cloth, and cover that with a covering of fine leather. They will then fix the poles to it.

12 'They will then take all the other objects used in the service of the sanctuary, put them in a violet cloth, with a covering of fine leather, and put it all on the litter.

13 'When they have removed the ashes from the altar, they will spread a scarlet cloth over it, 14 and on this place all the objects used in the liturgy, the fire pans, hooks, scoops, sprinkling basins and all the altar accessories. Over this they will spread a covering of fine leather. They will then fix the poles to it.

15 'Once Aaron and his sons have finished covering the holy things and all their accessories at the breaking of camp, then the Kohathites will come and carry them, but without touching any of the holy things on pain of death. Such is the load for the Kohathites in the Tent of Meeting. 16 But Eleazar, son of Aaron the priest, is responsible for looking after the oil for the light, the fragrant incense, the daily cereal offering and the anointing oil, and for supervising the entire Dwelling and everything in it, the holy things and their accessories.'

17 Yahweh spoke to Moses and said:

18 'You must not let the group of Kohathite clans be lost to the rest of the Levites. 19 But deal with them in this way, so that they may survive and not incur death by approaching those things that are especially holy. Aaron and his sons will go in and assign to each of them his task and load, 20 in such a way that they have no need to incur the death penalty by going in and setting eyes on the holy things, even for an instant.'

21 Yahweh spoke to Moses and said:

22 'Take a census of the Gershonites by families and clans, too: 23 all the men between thirty and fifty years of age, eligible for military service, who will have their duties in the Tent of Meeting.

24 'These are the duties of the Gershonite clans, their functions and their loads. 25 They will carry the curtaining of the Dwelling, the Tent of Meeting with its covering and the covering of fine leather that goes over it, the screen for the entrance to the Tent of Meeting, 26 the curtaining of the court, the screen for the entrance to the court surrounding the Dwelling and the altar, the cords, all the accessories for worship, and all the necessary equipment.

'They will be responsible for these things. 27 All the duties of the Gershonites, their functions and their loads, will be carried out under the direction of Aaron and his sons: you will see that they fulfil their charge. 28 Such are the duties of the Gershonite clans in the Tent of Meeting. Their work will be supervised by Ithamar, son of Aaron the priest.

29 'You will take a census of the Merarites by clans and families. 30 You will take a census of all the men between thirty and fifty years of age, eligible for military service, who will have their duties in the Tent of Meeting.

31 'The load they carry and the duties incumbent on them in the Tent of Meeting will be as follows: the framework of the Dwelling, its cross-bars, poles and sockets, 32 the poles round the court with their sockets, pegs, cords and all their tackle. You will draw up a list of their names with the loads for which each is responsible.

service of the clans of the Merarites, the whole of their service relating to the tent of meeting, under the hand of Ithamar son of Aaron the priest.

34 So Moses and Aaron and the leaders of the congregation enrolled the Kohathites, by their clans and their ancestral houses, 35 from thirty years old up to fifty years old, everyone who qualified for work relating to the tent of meeting; 36 and their enrollment by clans was two thousand seven hundred fifty. 37 This was the enrollment of the clans of the Kohathites, all who served at the tent of meeting, whom Moses and Aaron enrolled according to the commandment of the LORD by Moses.

38 The enrollment of the Gershonites, by their clans and their ancestral houses, 39 from thirty years old up to fifty years old, everyone who qualified for work relating to the tent of meeting — 40 their enrollment by their clans and their ancestral houses was two thousand six hundred thirty. 41 This was the enrollment of the clans of the Gershonites, all who served at the tent of meeting, whom Moses and Aaron enrolled according to the commandment of the LORD.

42 The enrollment of the clans of the Merarites, by their clans and their ancestral houses, 43 from thirty years old up to fifty years old, everyone who qualified for work relating to the tent of meeting — 44 their enrollment by their clans was three thousand two hundred. 45 This is the enrollment of the clans of the Merarites, whom Moses and Aaron enrolled according to the commandment of the LORD by Moses.

46 All those who were enrolled of the Levites, whom Moses and Aaron and the leaders of Israel enrolled, by their clans and their ancestral houses, 47 from thirty years old up to fifty years old, everyone who qualified to do the work of service and the work of bearing burdens relating to the tent of meeting, 48 their enrollment was eight thousand five hundred eighty. 49 According to the commandment of the LORD through Moses they were appointed to their several tasks of serving or carrying; thus they were enrolled by him, as the LORD commanded Moses.

5 The LORD spoke to Moses, saying: 2 Command the Israelites to put out of the camp everyone who is leprous,g or has a discharge, and everyone who is unclean through contact with a corpse; 3 you shall put out both male and female, putting them outside the camp; they must not defile their camp, where I dwell among them. 4 The Israelites did so, putting them outside the camp; as the LORD had spoken to Moses, so the Israelites did.

5 The LORD spoke to Moses, saying: 6 Speak to the Israelites: When a man or a woman wrongs another, breaking faith with the LORD, that person incurs guilt 7 and shall confess the sin that has been committed. The person shall make full restitution for the wrong, adding one fifth to it, and giving it to the one who was wronged. 8 If the injured party has no next of kin to whom restitution may be made for the wrong, the restitution for wrong shall go to the LORD for the priest, in addition to the ram of atonement with which atonement is made for the guilty party. 9 Among all the sacred donations of the Israelites, every gift that they bring to the priest shall be his. 10 The sacred donations of all are their own; whatever anyone gives to the priest shall be his.

11 The LORD spoke to Moses, saying: 12 Speak to the Israelites and say to them: If any man's wife goes astray and is unfaithful to him, 13 if a man has had intercourse with her

Merarite families in virtue of their service in the Tent of Meeting. Ithamar son of Aaron the priest shall be in charge of them.'

34 Moses and Aaron and the chiefs of the community made a list of the Kohathites by families in the father's line, 35 taking all between the ages of thirty and fifty who came on duty to perform service in the Tent of Meeting. 36 The number recorded by families in the lists was two thousand seven hundred and fifty. 37 This was the total number in the lists of the Kohathite families who did duty in the Tent of Meeting; they were recorded by Moses and Aaron as the LORD had commanded them through Moses.

38-39 The Gershonites between the ages of thirty and fifty, who came on duty for service in the Tent of Meeting, were recorded in lists by families in the father's line. 40 Their number, by families in the father's line, was two thousand six hundred and thirty. 41 This was the total recorded in the lists of the Gershonite families who came on duty in the Tent of Meeting and were recorded by Moses and Aaron as the LORD had commanded them.

42-43 The families of Merari, between the ages of thirty and fifty, who came on duty to perform service in the Tent of Meeting, were recorded in lists by families in the father's line. 44 Their number by families was three thousand two hundred. 45 These were recorded in the Merarite families by Moses and Aaron as the LORD had commanded them through Moses.

46 Thus Moses and Aaron and the chiefs of Israel made a list of all the Levites by families in the father's line, 47 between the ages of thirty and fifty years; these were all who came to perform their various duties and carry their loads in the service of the Tent of Meeting. 48 Their number was eight thousand five hundred and eighty. 49 They were recorded one by one by Moses at the command of the LORD, according to their general duty and the loads they carried. For so the LORD had commanded Moses.

5 THE LORD said to Moses: 2 'Command the Israelites to expel from the camp everyone who suffers from a ritually unclean skin disease or a discharge, and everyone ritually unclean through contact with a corpse. 3 Put them outside the camp, both male and female, so that they do not defile your camps in which I dwell among you.' 4 The Israelites did this: they expelled them from the camp, doing exactly as the LORD had said when he spoke to Moses.

5 The LORD told Moses 6 to say to the Israelites: 'When anyone, man or woman, wrongs another and thereby breaks faith with the LORD, that person has incurred guilt which demands reparation. 7 He must confess the sin he has committed, make restitution in full with the addition of one fifth, and give it to the one to whom compensation is due. 8 If there is no next-of-kin to whom compensation can be paid, the compensation payable in that case is to be the LORD's, for the use of the priest, in addition to the ram of expiation with which the priest makes expiation for him.

9 'Every contribution made by way of holy-gift which the Israelites bring to the priest is to be the priest's. 10 The priest is to have the holy-gifts which a man gives; whatever is given to him is to be his.'

11 The LORD told Moses 12 to say to the Israelites: 'When a married woman goes astray and is unfaithful to her husband 13 by having sexual intercourse with another man, and

---

g A term for several skin diseases; precise meaning uncertain

4:49 **according . . . carried:** *prob. rdg; Heb. adds* and his registered ones.   5:3 **your camps . . . you:** *so Syriac; Heb.* their camps . . . among them.

NEW AMERICAN BIBLE

the task of the clans of the Merarites during all their service in the meeting tent under the supervision of Ithamar, son of Aaron the priest."

³⁴ So Moses and Aaron and the princes of the community made a registration among the Kohathites, by clans and ancestral houses, ³⁵ of all the men between thirty and fifty years of age. These were to undertake obligatory tasks in the meeting tent; ³⁶ as registered by clans, they numbered two thousand seven hundred and fifty. ³⁷ Such was the census of all the men of the Kohathite clans who were to serve in the meeting tent, which Moses took, together with Aaron, as the LORD bade him.

³⁸ The registration was then made among the Gershonites, by clans and ancestral houses, ³⁹ of all the men between thirty and fifty years of age. These were to undertake obligatory tasks in the meeting tent; ⁴⁰ as registered by clans and ancestral houses, they numbered two thousand six hundred and thirty. ⁴¹ Such was the census of all the men of the Gershonite clans who were to serve in the meeting tent, which Moses took, together with Aaron, at the LORD's bidding.

⁴² Then the registration was made among the Merarites, by clans and ancestral houses, ⁴³ of all the men from thirty up to fifty years of age. These were to undertake obligatory tasks in the meeting tent; ⁴⁴ as registered by clans, they numbered three thousand two hundred. ⁴⁵ Such was the census of the men of the Merarite clans which Moses took, together with Aaron, as the LORD bade him.

⁴⁶ Therefore, when Moses and Aaron and the Israelite princes had completed the registration among the Levites, by clans and ancestral houses, ⁴⁷ of all the men between thirty and fifty years of age who were to undertake tasks of service or transport of the meeting tent, ⁴⁸ the total number registered was eight thousand five hundred and eighty. ⁴⁹ According to the LORD's bidding to Moses, they gave them their individual assignments for service and for transport; so the LORD had commanded Moses.

5 The LORD said to Moses: ² "Order the Israelites to expel from camp every leper, and everyone suffering from a discharge, and everyone who has become unclean by contact with a corpse. ³ Male and female alike, you shall compel them to go out of the camp; they are not to defile the camp in which I dwell." ⁴ The Israelites obeyed the command that the LORD had given Moses; they expelled them from the camp.

⁵ The LORD said to Moses, ⁶ "Tell the Israelites: If a man (or woman) commits a fault against his fellow man and wrongs him, thus breaking faith with the LORD, ⁷ he shall confess the wrong he has done, restore his ill-gotten goods in full, and in addition give one fifth of their value to the one he has wronged. ⁸ However, if the latter has no next of kin to whom restoration of the ill-gotten goods can be made, the goods to be restored shall be the LORD's and shall fall to the priest; this is apart from the atonement ram with which the priest makes amends for the guilty man. ⁹ Likewise, every sacred contribution that the Israelites are bound to make shall fall to the priest. ¹⁰ Each Israelite man may dispose of his own sacred contributions; they become the property of the priest to whom he gives them."

¹¹ The LORD said to Moses, ¹² "Speak to the Israelites and tell them: If a man's wife goes astray and becomes unfaithful to him ¹³ by having intercourse with another man,

NEW JERUSALEM BIBLE

³³ 'Such are the duties of the Merarite clans. All their duties in the Tent of Meeting will be supervised by Ithamar, son of Aaron the priest.'

³⁴ Moses, Aaron and the leaders of the community took a census of the Kohathites by clans and families: ³⁵ all the men between thirty and fifty years of age, eligible for military service, for duties in the Tent of Meeting. ³⁶ The number of men counted in their clans came to two thousand seven hundred and fifty. ³⁷ Such was the total number of men in the Kohathite clans who were eligible for duties in the Tent of Meeting and whom Moses and Aaron counted at Yahweh's bidding through Moses.

³⁸ A census was taken of the Gershonites by clans and families: ³⁹ all the men between thirty and fifty years of age, eligible for military service, for duties in the Tent of Meeting. ⁴⁰ The number of men counted in their clans and families came to two thousand six hundred and thirty. ⁴¹ Such was the total number of men in the Gershonite clans who were eligible for duties in the Tent of Meeting, and whom Moses and Aaron counted at Yahweh's bidding.

⁴² A census was taken of the Merarite clans by clans and families: ⁴³ all the men between thirty and fifty years of age, eligible for military service, for duties in the Tent of Meeting. ⁴⁴ The number of men counted in their clans came to three thousand two hundred. ⁴⁵ Such was the total number of men in the Merarite clans, whom Moses and Aaron counted at Yahweh's bidding through Moses.

⁴⁶ The total number of Levites whom Moses, Aaron and the leaders of Israel counted in their clans and families, ⁴⁷ all the men between thirty and fifty years of age, eligible for religious duties and for those of transporting the Tent of Meeting ⁴⁸ came to eight thousand five hundred and eighty. ⁴⁹ At Yahweh's bidding through Moses, a census was taken of them and each man was assigned his duty and load. And so the census was conducted by Moses as Yahweh had ordered him.

5 Yahweh spoke to Moses and said: ² 'Order the Israelites to expel from the camp all those suffering from a contagious skin-disease or from a discharge, or who have become unclean by touching a corpse. ³ Whether man or woman, you will expel them; you will expel them from the camp, so that they do not pollute their encampments, in the heart of which I dwell.'

⁴ The Israelites did so: they expelled them from the camp. The Israelites did as Yahweh had told Moses.

⁵ Yahweh spoke to Moses and said, ⁶ 'Speak to the Israelites:

"If a man or woman commits any of the sins by which people break faith with Yahweh, that person incurs guilt. ⁷ The person must confess the sin committed and restore in full the amount owed, with one-fifth added. Payment is to be made to the person wronged. ⁸ If, however, the latter has no relation to whom restitution can be made, the restitution due to Yahweh reverts to the priest, apart from the ram of expiation with which the priest makes expiation for the guilty party. ⁹ For of everything the Israelites consecrate and bring to the priest he has a right to the portion set aside. ¹⁰ Whatever anyone consecrates is his own; whatever is given to the priest belongs to the priest." '

¹¹ Yahweh spoke to Moses and said, ¹² 'Speak to the Israelites and say:

"If anyone has a wife who goes astray and is unfaithful to him, ¹³ if some other man sleeps with the woman without

NEW REVISED STANDARD VERSION

but it is hidden from her husband, so that she is undetected though she has defiled herself, and there is no witness against her since she was not caught in the act; 14 if a spirit of jealousy comes on him, and he is jealous of his wife who has defiled herself; or if a spirit of jealousy comes on him, and he is jealous of his wife, though she has not defiled herself; 15 then the man shall bring his wife to the priest. And he shall bring the offering required for her, one-tenth of an ephah of barley flour. He shall pour no oil on it and put no frankincense on it, for it is a grain offering of jealousy, a grain offering of remembrance, bringing iniquity to remembrance.

16 Then the priest shall bring her near, and set her before the LORD; 17 the priest shall take holy water in an earthen vessel, and take some of the dust that is on the floor of the tabernacle and put it into the water. 18 The priest shall set the woman before the LORD, dishevel the woman's hair, and place in her hands the grain offering of remembrance, which is the grain offering of jealousy. In his own hand the priest shall have the water of bitterness that brings the curse. 19 Then the priest shall make her take an oath, saying, "If no man has lain with you, if you have not turned aside to uncleanness while under your husband's authority, be immune to this water of bitterness that brings the curse. 20 But if you have gone astray while under your husband's authority, if you have defiled yourself and some man other than your husband has had intercourse with you," 21 — let the priest make the woman take the oath of the curse and say to the woman — "the LORD make you an execration and an oath among your people, when the LORD makes your uterus drop, your womb discharge; 22 now may this water that brings the curse enter your bowels and make your womb discharge, your uterus drop!" And the woman shall say, "Amen. Amen."

23 Then the priest shall put these curses in writing, and wash them off into the water of bitterness. 24 He shall make the woman drink the water of bitterness that brings the curse, and the water that brings the curse shall enter her and cause bitter pain. 25 The priest shall take the grain offering of jealousy out of the woman's hand, and shall elevate the grain offering before the LORD and bring it to the altar; 26 and the priest shall take a handful of the grain offering, as its memorial portion, and turn it into smoke on the altar, and afterward shall make the woman drink the water. 27 When he has made her drink the water, then, if she has defiled herself and has been unfaithful to her husband, the water that brings the curse shall enter into her and cause bitter pain, and her womb shall discharge, her uterus drop, and the woman shall become an execration among her people. 28 But if the woman has not defiled herself and is clean, then she shall be immune and be able to conceive children.

29 This is the law in cases of jealousy, when a wife, while under her husband's authority, goes astray and defiles herself, 30 or when a spirit of jealousy comes on a man and he is jealous of his wife; then he shall set the woman before the LORD, and the priest shall apply this entire law to her. 31 The man shall be free from iniquity, but the woman shall bear her iniquity.

6 The LORD spoke to Moses, saying: 2 Speak to the Israelites and say to them: When either men or women make a special vow, the vow of a nazirite, _h_ to separate themselves to the LORD, 3 they shall separate themselves

REVISED ENGLISH BIBLE

this happens without the husband's knowledge, and without the woman being detected because, though she has been defiled, there is no direct evidence against her and she was not caught in the act, 14 and when in such a case a fit of jealousy comes over the husband which makes him suspect his wife, whether she is defiled or not; 15 then the husband must bring his wife to the priest together with the prescribed offering for her, a tenth of an ephah of barley-meal. He must not pour oil on it or put frankincense on it, because it is a grain-offering for jealousy, a grain-offering of protestation conveying an imputation of guilt.

16 'The priest must bring her forward and set her before the LORD. 17 He is to take holy water in an earthenware vessel, and take dust from the floor of the Tabernacle and add it to the water. 18 He must set the woman before the LORD, uncover her head, and place the grain-offering of protestation in her hands; it is a grain-offering for jealousy. Holding in his own hand the ordeal-water which tests under pain of curse, 19 the priest must put the woman on oath and say to her, "If no man has had intercourse with you, if you have not gone astray and let yourself become defiled while owing obedience to your husband, may your innocence be established by the ordeal-water. 20 But if, while owing him obedience, you have gone astray and let yourself become defiled, if any man other than your husband has had intercourse with you," 21 (the priest shall here put the woman on oath with an adjuration, and shall continue) "may the LORD make an example of you among your people in adjurations and in swearing of oaths by bringing upon you miscarriage and untimely birth; 22 and let this ordeal-water that tests under pain of curse enter your body, bringing upon you miscarriage and untimely birth." The woman must respond, "Amen, Amen."

23 'The priest is to write these curses on a scroll, wash them off into the ordeal-water, 24 and make the woman drink the ordeal-water; it will enter her body to test her. 25 The priest is to take the grain-offering for jealousy from the woman's hand, present it as a special gift before the LORD, and offer it at the altar. 26 He is to take a handful from the grain-offering by way of token, and burn it at the altar. Finally he must make the woman drink the water. 27 If she has let herself become defiled and has been unfaithful to her husband, then, when the priest makes her drink the ordeal-water and it enters her body to test her, she will suffer a miscarriage or untimely birth, and her name will become an example in adjuration among her kin. 28 But if the woman has not let herself become defiled and is pure, then her innocence is established and she will bear her child.

29 'Such is the law for cases of jealousy, where a woman, owing obedience to her husband, goes astray and lets herself become defiled, 30 or where a fit of jealousy comes over a man which causes him to suspect his wife. When he sets her before the LORD, the priest must deal with her as this law prescribes. 31 No guilt will attach to the husband, but the woman must bear the penalty of her guilt.'

6 The LORD told Moses 2 to say to the Israelites: 'When anyone, man or woman, makes a special vow dedicating himself to the LORD as a Nazirite, 3 he is to abstain from

---

_h_ That is _one separated_ or _one consecrated_

5:21 **by bringing ... birth:** _lit._ by making your thigh to fall and your belly to melt away; _similarly in verses 22 and 27._
6:2 **Nazirite:** _that is_ separated one _or_ dedicated one.

though her husband has not sufficient evidence of the fact, so that her impurity remains unproved for lack of a witness who might have caught her in the act; 14 or if a man is overcome by a feeling of jealousy that makes him suspect his wife, whether she was actually impure or not: 15 he shall bring his wife to the priest and shall take along as an offering for her a tenth of an ephah of barley meal. However, he shall not pour oil on it nor put frankincense over it, since it is a cereal offering of jealousy, a cereal offering for an appeal in a question of guilt.

16 "The priest shall first have the woman come forward and stand before the LORD. 17 In an earthen vessel he shall meanwhile put some holy water, as well as some dust that he has taken from the floor of the Dwelling. 18 Then, as the woman stands before the LORD, the priest shall uncover her head and place in her hands the cereal offering of her appeal, that is, the cereal offering of jealousy, while he himself shall hold the bitter water that brings a curse. 19 Then he shall adjure the woman, saying to her, 'If no other man has had intercourse with you, and you have not gone astray by impurity while under the authority of your husband, be immune to the curse brought by this bitter water. 20 But if you have gone astray while under the authority of your husband and have acted impurely by letting a man other than your husband have intercourse with you' — 21 so shall the priest adjure the woman with this oath of imprecation — 'may the LORD make you an example of malediction and imprecation among your people by causing your thighs to waste away and your belly to swell! 22 May this water, then, that brings a curse, enter your body to make your belly swell and your thighs waste away!' And the woman shall say, 'Amen, amen!' 23 The priest shall put these imprecations in writing and shall then wash them off into the bitter water, 24 which he is to have the woman drink, so that it may go into her with all its bitter curse. 25 But first he shall take the cereal offering of jealousy from the woman's hand, and having waved this offering before the LORD, shall put it near the altar, 26 where he shall take a handful of the cereal offering as its token offering and burn it on the altar. Only then shall he have the woman drink the water. 27 Once she has done so, if she has been impure and unfaithful to her husband, this bitter water that brings a curse will go into her, and her belly will swell and her thighs will waste away, so that she will become an example of imprecation among her people. 28 If, however, the woman has not defiled herself, but is still pure, she will be immune and will still be able to bear children.

29 "This, then, is the law for jealousy: When a woman goes astray while under the authority of her husband and acts impurely, 30 or when such a feeling of jealousy comes over a man that he becomes suspicious of his wife, he shall have her stand before the LORD, and the priest shall apply this law in full to her. 31 The man shall be free from guilt, but the woman shall bear such guilt as she may have."

6 The LORD said to Moses: 2 "Speak to the Israelites and tell them: When a man (or a woman) solemnly takes the nazirite vow to dedicate himself to the LORD, 3 he shall

the husband's knowledge, and she secretly makes herself unclean, without any witness against her, and without anyone catching her in the act; 14 if, then, a spirit of suspicion comes over the husband and makes him suspicious of the wife who has disgraced herself, or again if this spirit of suspicion comes over him and makes him suspicious of his wife even when she is innocent, 15 the man will bring his wife before the priest, and on her behalf make an offering of one-tenth of an ephah of barley meal. He will not pour oil over it or put incense on it, because this is a cereal offering for a case of suspicion, a memorial offering to recall guilt to mind.

16 "The priest will then bring the woman forward and place her before Yahweh. 17 The priest will then take fresh water in an earthen jar, and on the water throw dust that he has taken from the floor of the Dwelling. 18 After he has placed the woman before Yahweh, he will unbind her hair and put the commemorative cereal offering (that is, the cereal offering for a case of suspicion) into her hands. In his own hands the priest will hold the water of bitterness and cursing.

19 "The priest will then put the woman on oath. He will say to her: If it is not true that a man has slept with you, that you have gone astray and made yourself unclean while under your husband's authority, may this water of bitterness and cursing do you no harm. 20 But if it is true that you have gone astray while under your husband's authority, that you have made yourself unclean and that a man other than your husband has slept with you . . . 21 Here the priest will impose an imprecatory oath on the woman. He will say to her: . . . May Yahweh make you the object of your people's execration and curses, by making your sexual organs shrivel and your belly swell! 22 May this water of cursing entering your bowels, make your belly swell and your sexual organs shrivel! To which the woman will reply: Amen! Amen!

23 "Having written these curses on a scroll and washed them off in the water of bitterness, 24 the priest will make the woman drink the water of bitterness and cursing; when the water of cursing enters into her, it will become bitter. 25 "The priest will then take the cereal offering for a case of suspicion from the woman's hands, and hold it up before Yahweh with a gesture of offering, and so carry it up to the altar. 26 He will take a handful of it as a memorial and burn it on the altar.

"After this, he will make the woman drink the water. 27 After he has made her drink it, if it is true that she has made herself unclean and been unfaithful to her husband, the water of cursing entering into her will indeed be bitter: her belly will swell and her sexual organs shrivel, and she will be an object of execration to her people. 28 But if she has not made herself unclean, but is clean, then she will go unscathed and will bear children.

29 "Such is the ritual in cases of suspicion, when a woman has gone astray and made herself unclean while under her husband's authority, 30 or when a spirit of suspicion has come over a man and made him suspicious of his wife. When a husband brings such a woman before Yahweh, the priest will apply this ritual to her in full. 31 The husband will be guiltless, but the woman will bear the consequences of her guilt." '

6 Yahweh spoke to Moses and said, 2 'Speak to the Israelites and say:

"If a man or a woman wishes to make a vow, the nazirite vow, to vow himself to Yahweh, 3 he will abstain from wine

from wine and strong drink; they shall drink no wine vinegar or other vinegar, and shall not drink any grape juice or eat grapes, fresh or dried. 4 All their days as nazirites[i] they shall eat nothing that is produced by the grapevine, not even the seeds or the skins.

5 All the days of their nazirite vow no razor shall come upon the head; until the time is completed for which they separate themselves to the LORD, they shall be holy; they shall let the locks of the head grow long.

6 All the days that they separate themselves to the LORD they shall not go near a corpse. 7 Even if their father or mother, brother or sister, should die, they may not defile themselves; because their consecration to God is upon the head. 8 All their days as nazirites[i] they are holy to the LORD.

9 If someone dies very suddenly nearby, defiling the consecrated head, then they shall shave the head on the day of their cleansing; on the seventh day they shall shave it. 10 On the eighth day they shall bring two turtledoves or two young pigeons to the priest at the entrance of the tent of meeting, 11 and the priest shall offer one as a sin offering and the other as a burnt offering, and make atonement for them, because they incurred guilt by reason of the corpse. They shall sanctify the head that same day, 12 and separate themselves to the LORD for their days as nazirites,[i] and bring a male lamb a year old as a guilt offering. The former time shall be void, because the consecrated head was defiled.

13 This is the law for the nazirites[i] when the time of their consecration has been completed: they shall be brought to the entrance of the tent of meeting, 14 and they shall offer their gift to the LORD, one male lamb a year old without blemish as a burnt offering, one ewe lamb a year old without blemish as a sin offering, one ram without blemish as an offering of well-being, 15 and a basket of unleavened bread, cakes of choice flour mixed with oil and unleavened wafers spread with oil, with their grain offering and their drink offerings. 16 The priest shall present them before the LORD and offer their sin offering and burnt offering, 17 and shall offer the ram as a sacrifice of well-being to the LORD, with the basket of unleavened bread; the priest also shall make the accompanying grain offering and drink offering. 18 Then the nazirites[i] shall shave the consecrated head at the entrance of the tent of meeting, and shall take the hair from the consecrated head and put it on the fire under the sacrifice of well-being. 19 The priest shall take the shoulder of the ram, when it is boiled, and one unleavened cake out of the basket, and one unleavened wafer, and shall put them in the palms of the nazirites,[i] after they have shaved the consecrated head. 20 Then the priest shall elevate them as an elevation offering before the LORD; they are a holy portion for the priest, together with the breast that is elevated and the thigh that is offered. After that the nazirites[i] may drink wine.

21 This is the law for the nazirites[i] who take a vow. Their offering to the LORD must be in accordance with the nazirite[j] vow, apart from what else they can afford. In accordance with whatever vow they take, so they shall do, following the law for their consecration.

22 The LORD spoke to Moses, saying: 23 Speak to Aaron and his sons, saying, Thus you shall bless the Israelites: You shall say to them,

24 The LORD bless you and keep you;
25 the LORD make his face to shine upon you, and be gracious to you;
26 the LORD lift up his countenance upon you, and give you peace.

wine and strong drink. These he must not drink, nor anything made from the juice of grapes; nor is he to eat grapes, fresh or dried. 4 During the whole term of his vow he must eat nothing that comes from the vine, nothing whatever, skin or seed. 5 During the whole term of his vow no razor is to touch his head; he must let his hair grow in long locks until he has completed the term of his dedication: he is to keep himself holy to the LORD. 6 During the whole term of his vow to the LORD he must not go near a dead person, 7 not even when it is his father or mother, brother or sister who has died; he must not make himself ritually unclean for them, because the Nazirite vow to his God is on his head. 8 He must keep himself holy to the LORD during the whole term of his Nazirite vow.

9 'If someone suddenly falls dead by his side, touching him and thereby making his hair, which has been dedicated, ritually unclean, he must shave his head on the day when he becomes clean; he shall shave it on the seventh day. 10 On the eighth day he must bring two turtle-doves or two pigeons to the priest at the entrance to the Tent of Meeting. 11 The priest will offer one as a purification-offering and the other as a whole-offering and so make expiation for him for the sin he has incurred through contact with the dead body; he must consecrate his head afresh on that day. 12 The man must rededicate himself to the LORD for the full term of his vow and bring a yearling ram as a guilt-offering. The previous period is not to be included, because the hair which he dedicated became unclean.

13 'The law for the Nazirite, when the term of his dedication is complete, is this. He is to be brought to the entrance to the Tent of Meeting 14 and present his offering to the LORD: one yearling ram without blemish as a whole-offering, one yearling ewe without blemish as a purification-offering, one ram without blemish as a shared-offering, 15 and a basket of bread made of flour mixed with oil, and of wafers smeared with oil, both unleavened, together with the proper grain-offerings and drink-offerings. 16 The priest will present all these before the LORD and offer the man's purification-offering and whole-offering; 17 the ram he offers is a shared-offering to the LORD, together with the basket of unleavened bread and the proper grain-offering and drink-offering. 18 The Nazirite will shave his head at the entrance to the Tent of Meeting, take the hair which had been dedicated, and put it on the fire where the shared-offering is burning. 19 The priest will take the shoulder of the ram, after boiling it, and take also one unleavened loaf from the basket and one unleavened wafer, and put them on the palms of the Nazirite's hands, his hair which had been dedicated having been shaved. 20 The priest will then present them as a dedicated portion before the LORD; these, together with the breast of the dedicated portion and the leg of the contribution, are holy and belong to the priest. When this has been done, the Nazirite is again free to drink wine.

21 'Such is the law for the Nazirite who has made his vow. Such is the offering he must make to the LORD for his dedication, apart from anything else that he can afford. He must carry out his vow in full according to the law governing his dedication.'

22 The LORD said to Moses, 23 'Say this to Aaron and his sons: These are the words with which you are to bless the Israelites:

24 May the LORD bless you and guard you;
25 may the LORD make his face shine on you and be gracious to you;
26 may the LORD look kindly on you and give you peace.

---

[i]That is *those separated* or *those consecrated*   [j]That is *one separated* or *one consecrated*

6:4 **skin or seed:** *the two Heb. words are of uncertain meaning.*

abstain from wine and strong drink; he may neither drink wine vinegar, other vinegar, or any kind of grape juice, nor eat either fresh or dried grapes. 4 As long as he is a nazirite he shall not eat anything of the produce of the vine; not even unripe grapes or grapeskins. 5 While he is under the nazirite vow, no razor shall touch his hair. Until the period of his dedication to the LORD is over, he shall be sacred, and shall let the hair of his head grow freely. 6 As long as he is dedicated to the LORD, he shall not enter where a dead person is. 7 Not even for his father or mother, his sister or brother, should they die, may he become unclean, since his head bears his dedication to God. 8 As long as he is a nazirite he is sacred to the LORD.

9 "If someone dies very suddenly in his presence, so that his dedicated head becomes unclean, he shall shave his head on the day of his purification, that is, on the seventh day. 10 On the eighth day he shall bring two turtledoves or two pigeons to the priest at the entrance of the meeting tent. 11 The priest shall offer up the one as a sin offering and the other as a holocaust, thus making atonement for him for the sin he has committed by reason of the dead person. On the same day he shall reconsecrate his head 12 and begin anew the period of his dedication to the LORD as a nazirite, bringing a yearling lamb as a guilt offering. The previous period is not valid, because his dedicated head became unclean.

13 "This is the ritual for the nazirite: On the day he completes the period of his dedication he shall go to the entrance of the meeting tent, 14 bringing as his offering to the LORD one unblemished yearling lamb for a holocaust, one unblemished yearling ewe lamb for a sin offering, one unblemished ram as a peace offering, along with their cereal offerings and libations, 15 and a basket of unleavened cakes of fine flour mixed with oil and of unleavened wafers spread with oil. 16 The priest shall present them before the LORD, and shall offer up the sin offering and the holocaust for him. 17 He shall then offer up the ram as a peace offering to the LORD, with its cereal offering and libation, and the basket of unleavened cakes. 18 Then at the entrance of the meeting tent the nazirite shall shave his dedicated head, collect the hair, and put it in the fire that is under the peace offering. 19 After the nazirite has shaved off his dedicated hair, the priest shall take a boiled shoulder of the ram, as well as one unleavened cake and one unleavened wafer from the basket, and shall place them in the hands of the nazirite. 20 The priest shall then wave them as a wave offering before the LORD. They become sacred and shall belong to the priest, along with the breast of the wave offering and the leg of the raised offering. Only after this may the nazirite drink wine.

21 "This, then, is the law for the nazirite; this is the offering to the LORD which is included in his vow of dedication apart from anything else which his means may allow. Thus shall he carry out the law of his dedication in keeping with the vow he has taken."

22 The LORD said to Moses: 23 "Speak to Aaron and his sons and tell them: This is how you shall bless the Israelites. Say to them:

24 The LORD bless you and keep you!
25 The LORD let his face shine upon you, and be
gracious to you!
26 The LORD look upon you kindly and give
you peace!

and fermented liquor, he will not drink vinegar derived from one or the other, he will not drink grape-juice or eat grapes, be they fresh or dried. 4 For the duration of his vow he will eat nothing that comes from the vine, not even juice of unripe grapes or skins of grapes. 5 As long as he is bound by his vow, no razor will touch his head; until the time for which he has vowed himself to Yahweh is completed, he remains consecrated and will let his hair grow freely. 6 For the entire period of his vow to Yahweh, he will not go near a corpse, 7 he will not make himself unclean for his father or his mother, or his brother or his sister, should they die, since on his head he carries his vow to his God. 8 Throughout the whole of his vow he is a person consecrated to Yahweh.

9 "If anyone suddenly dies near him, making his vowed hair unclean, he will shave his head on the day he is purified, he will shave his head on the seventh day. 10 On the eighth day, he will bring two turtledoves or two young pigeons to the priest, at the entrance to the Tent of Meeting. 11 The priest will offer one as a sacrifice for sin, and the other as a burnt offering and will then perform for the person the rite of expiation for the pollution which he has contracted from the corpse. He will consecrate his head that same day; 12 he will vow himself to Yahweh for the period of his nazirate, and will bring a male yearling lamb as a sacrifice of reparation. The time already spent will not count, since his hair had become unclean.

13 "This is the ritual for the nazirite on the day when the period of his vow is completed. He will be led to the entrance of the Tent of Meeting, 14 bringing his offering to Yahweh: an unblemished male yearling lamb as a burnt offering, an unblemished yearling ewe lamb as a sacrifice for sin, an unblemished ram as a peace offering, 15 and a basket of unleavened loaves made of fine flour mixed with oil, and of unleavened wafers spread with oil, with the cereal offerings and libations appropriate to them. 16 The priest, having brought all this before Yahweh, will offer the nazirite's sin sacrifice and burnt offering. 17 The latter will then offer the ram as a communion sacrifice with the basket of unleavened bread, and the priest will offer the accompanying cereal offering and libation. 18 The nazirite will then shave off his vowed hair at the entrance to the Tent of Meeting and, taking the locks of his vowed head, he will put them in the fire of the communion sacrifice. 19 The priest will take the shoulder of the ram, as soon as it is cooked, with an unleavened cake from the basket, and an unleavened wafer, and put them into the hands of the nazirite once he has shaved off his hair. 20 With these he will make the gesture of offering before Yahweh; as it is a holy thing, it reverts to the priest, in addition to the forequarter that has been presented and the thigh that has been set aside. After this, the nazirite may drink wine.

21 "Such is the ritual for the nazirite. If, besides his hair, he has also vowed a personal offering to Yahweh, he will (apart from anything else that his means allow) fulfil the vow that he has made, in addition to what the ritual prescribes for his hair." '

22 Yahweh spoke to Moses and said, 23 'Speak to Aaron and his sons and say:

"This is how you must bless the Israelites. You will say:
24 May Yahweh bless you and keep you.
25 May Yahweh let his face shine on you and be
gracious to you.
26 May Yahweh show you his face and bring you
peace."

27 So they shall put my name on the Israelites, and I will bless them.

7 On the day when Moses had finished setting up the tabernacle, and had anointed and consecrated it with all its furnishings, and had anointed and consecrated the altar with all its utensils, 2 the leaders of Israel, heads of their ancestral houses, the leaders of the tribes, who were over those who were enrolled, made offerings. 3 They brought their offerings before the LORD, six covered wagons and twelve oxen, a wagon for every two of the leaders, and for each one an ox; they presented them before the tabernacle. 4 Then the LORD said to Moses: 5 Accept these from them, that they may be used in doing the service of the tent of meeting, and give them to the Levites, to each according to his service. 6 So Moses took the wagons and the oxen, and gave them to the Levites. 7 Two wagons and four oxen he gave to the Gershonites, according to their service; 8 and four wagons and eight oxen he gave to the Merarites, according to their service, under the direction of Ithamar son of Aaron the priest. 9 But to the Kohathites he gave none, because they were charged with the care of the holy things that had to be carried on the shoulders.

10 The leaders also presented offerings for the dedication of the altar at the time when it was anointed; the leaders presented their offering before the altar. 11 The LORD said to Moses: They shall present their offerings, one leader each day, for the dedication of the altar.

12 The one who presented his offering the first day was Nahshon son of Amminadab, of the tribe of Judah; 13 his offering was one silver plate weighing one hundred thirty shekels, one silver basin weighing seventy shekels, according to the shekel of the sanctuary, both of them full of choice flour mixed with oil for a grain offering; 14 one golden dish weighing ten shekels, full of incense; 15 one young bull, one ram, one male lamb a year old, for a burnt offering; 16 one male goat for a sin offering; 17 and for the sacrifice of well-being, two oxen, five rams, five male goats, and five male lambs a year old. This was the offering of Nahshon son of Amminadab.

18 On the second day Nethanel son of Zuar, the leader of Issachar, presented an offering; 19 he presented for his offering one silver plate weighing one hundred thirty shekels, one silver basin weighing seventy shekels, according to the shekel of the sanctuary, both of them full of choice flour mixed with oil for a grain offering; 20 one golden dish weighing ten shekels, full of incense; 21 one young bull, one ram, one male lamb a year old, as a burnt offering; 22 one male goat as a sin offering; 23 and for the sacrifice of well-being, two oxen, five rams, five male goats, and five male lambs a year old. This was the offering of Nethanel son of Zuar.

24 On the third day Eliab son of Helon, the leader of the Zebulunites: 25 his offering was one silver plate weighing one hundred thirty shekels, one silver basin weighing seventy shekels, according to the shekel of the sanctuary, both of them full of choice flour mixed with oil for a grain offering; 26 one golden dish weighing ten shekels, full of incense; 27 one young bull, one ram, one male lamb a year old, for a burnt offering; 28 one male goat for a sin offering; 29 and for the sacrifice of well-being, two oxen, five rams, five male goats, and five male lambs a year old. This was the offering of Eliab son of Helon.

30 On the fourth day Elizur son of Shedeur, the leader of the Reubenites: 31 his offering was one silver plate weighing one hundred thirty shekels, one silver basin weighing seventy shekels, according to the shekel of the sanctuary, both of them full of choice flour mixed with oil for a grain offering; 32 one golden dish weighing ten shekels, full of incense; 33 one young bull, one ram, one male lamb a year

27 'So they are to invoke my name on the Israelites, and I shall bless them.'

7 On the day that Moses completed the setting up of the Tabernacle, he anointed and consecrated it and all its equipment, along with the altar and all its vessels. 2 The chief men of Israel, heads of families — that is the tribal chiefs in charge of the enrolled men — came forward 3 and brought their offering before the LORD, six covered wagons and twelve oxen, one wagon from every two chiefs and from every chief one ox. These they brought forward before the Tabernacle; 4 and the LORD said to Moses, 5 'Accept these from them: they are for use in the service of the Tent of Meeting. Assign them to the Levites as their several duties require.'

6 So Moses accepted the wagons and oxen and assigned them to the Levites. 7 He gave two wagons and four oxen to the Gershonites as required for their service; 8 four wagons and eight oxen to the Merarites as required for their service, in charge of Ithamar the son of Aaron the priest. 9 He gave none to the Kohathites because the service laid upon them was that of the holy things: these they had to carry on their shoulders.

10 When the altar was anointed, the chiefs brought their gift for its dedication and presented their offering before it. 11 The LORD said to Moses, 'Let the chiefs present their offering for the dedication of the altar one by one, on consecutive days.'

12 The chief who presented his offering on the first day was Nahshon son of Amminadab of the tribe of Judah. 13 His offering was one silver dish weighing a hundred and thirty shekels by the sacred standard, and one silver tossing-bowl weighing seventy, both full of flour mixed with oil as a grain-offering; 14 one gold saucer weighing ten shekels, filled with incense; 15 one young bull, one full-grown ram, and one yearling ram, as a whole-offering; 16 one he-goat as a purification-offering; 17 and two bulls, five full-grown rams, five he-goats, and five yearling rams, as a shared-offering. This was the offering of Nahshon son of Amminadab.

18 On the second day Nethanel son of Zuar, chief of Issachar, brought his offering. 19 He brought one silver dish weighing a hundred and thirty shekels by the sacred standard, and one silver tossing-bowl weighing seventy, both full of flour mixed with oil as a grain-offering; 20 one gold saucer weighing ten shekels, filled with incense; 21 one young bull, one full-grown ram, and one yearling ram, as a whole-offering; 22 one he-goat as a purification-offering; 23 and two bulls, five full-grown rams, five he-goats, and five yearling rams, as a shared-offering. This was the offering of Nethanel son of Zuar.

24 On the third day the chief of the Zebulunites, Eliab son of Helon, came. 25 His offering was one silver dish weighing a hundred and thirty shekels by the sacred standard, and one silver tossing-bowl weighing seventy, both full of flour mixed with oil as a grain-offering; 26 one gold saucer weighing ten shekels, filled with incense; 27 one young bull, one full-grown ram, and one yearling ram, as a whole-offering; 28 one he-goat as a purification-offering; 29 and two bulls, five full-grown rams, five he-goats, and five yearling rams, as a shared-offering. This was the offering of Eliab son of Helon.

30 On the fourth day the chief of the Reubenites, Elizur son of Shedeur, came. 31 His offering was one silver dish weighing a hundred and thirty shekels by the sacred standard, and one silver tossing-bowl weighing seventy, both full of flour mixed with oil as a grain-offering; 32 one gold saucer weighing ten shekels, filled with incense; 33 one young

27 So shall they invoke my name upon the Israelites, and I will bless them."

7 Now, when Moses had completed the erection of the Dwelling and had anointed and consecrated it with all its equipment (as well as the altar with all its equipment), 2 an offering was made by the princes of Israel, who were heads of ancestral houses; the same princes of the tribes who supervised the census. 3 The offering they brought before the LORD consisted of six baggage wagons and twelve oxen, that is, a wagon for every two princes, and an ox for every prince. These they presented as their offering before the Dwelling.

4 The LORD then said to Moses, 5 "Accept their offering, that these things may be put to use in the service of the meeting tent. Assign them to the Levites, to each group in proportion to its duties." 6 So Moses accepted the wagons and oxen, and assigned them to the Levites. 7 He gave two wagons and four oxen to the Gershonites in proportion to their duties, 8 and four wagons and eight oxen to the Merarites in proportion to their duties, under the supervision of Ithamar, son of Aaron the priest. 9 He gave none to the Kohathites, because they had to carry on their shoulders the sacred objects which were their charge.

10 For the dedication of the altar also, the princes brought offerings before the altar on the day it was anointed. 11 But the LORD said to Moses, "Let one prince a day present his offering for the dedication of the altar."

12 The one who presented his offering on the first day was Nahshon, son of Amminadab, prince of the tribe of Judah. 13 His offering consisted of one silver plate weighing a hundred and thirty shekels according to the sanctuary standard and one silver basin weighing seventy shekels, both filled with fine flour mixed with oil for a cereal offering; 14 one gold cup of ten shekels' weight filled with incense; 15 one young bull, one ram, and one yearling lamb for a holocaust; 16 one goat for a sin offering; 17 and two oxen, five rams, five goats, and five yearling lambs for a peace offering. This was the offering of Nahshon, son of Amminadab.

18 On the second day Nethanel, son of Zuar, prince of Issachar, made his offering. 19 He presented as his offering one silver plate weighing a hundred and thirty shekels according to the sanctuary standard and one silver basin weighing seventy shekels, both filled with fine flour mixed with oil for a cereal offering; 20 one gold cup of ten shekels' weight filled with incense; 21 one young bull, one ram, and one yearling lamb for a holocaust; 22 one goat for a sin offering; 23 and two oxen, five rams, five goats, and five yearling lambs for a peace offering. This was the offering of Nethanel, son of Zuar.

24 On the third day it was the turn of Eliab, son of Helon, prince of the Zebulunites. 25 His offering consisted of one silver plate weighing a hundred and thirty shekels according to the sanctuary standard and one silver basin weighing seventy shekels, both filled with fine flour mixed with oil for a cereal offering; 26 one gold cup of ten shekels' weight filled with incense; 27 one young bull, one ram, and one yearling lamb for a holocaust; 28 one goat for a sin offering; 29 and two oxen, five rams, five goats, and five yearling lambs for a peace offering. This was the offering of Eliab, son of Helon.

30 On the fourth day it was the turn of Elizur, son of Shedeur, prince of the Reubenites. 31 His offering consisted of one silver plate weighing a hundred and thirty shekels according to the sanctuary standard and one silver basin weighing seventy shekels, both filled with fine flour mixed with oil for a cereal offering; 32 one gold cup of ten shekels' weight filled with incense; 33 one young bull, one ram, and

27 This is how they must call down my name on the Israelites, and then I shall bless them.'

7 On the day Moses finished erecting the Dwelling, he anointed and consecrated it and all its furniture, as well as the altar and all its equipment. When he had anointed and consecrated it all, 2 the leaders of Israel made an offering; they were the heads of their families, the tribal leaders who had presided over the census. 3 They brought their offering before Yahweh: six covered wagons and twelve oxen, one wagon for every two leaders and one ox each. They brought them in front of the Dwelling. 4 Yahweh spoke to Moses and said, 5 'Accept these from them, and let them be set apart for the service of the Tent of Meeting. You will give them to the Levites, to each as his duties require.' 6 Moses took the wagons and oxen, and gave them to the Levites. 7 To the Gershonites he gave two wagons and four oxen for the duties they had to perform. 8 To the Merarites he gave four wagons and eight oxen for the duties they had to perform under the direction of Ithamar, son of Aaron the priest. 9 But to the Kohathites he gave none at all, because the sacred charge entrusted to them had to be carried on their shoulders.

10 The leaders then made an offering for the dedication of the altar, on the day it was anointed. They brought their offering before the altar, 11 and Yahweh said to Moses, 'Each day one of the leaders must bring his offering for the dedication of the altar.'

12 On the first day an offering was brought by Nahshon son of Amminadab, of the tribe of Judah. 13 His offering consisted of: one silver bowl weighing a hundred and thirty shekels, one silver sprinkling bowl weighing seventy shekels (sanctuary shekels), both of them full of fine flour mixed with oil as a cereal offering, 14 one golden bowl weighing ten shekels, full of incense, 15 one young bull, one ram and one male yearling lamb as a burnt offering, 16 one he-goat as a sacrifice for sin, 17 and two bulls, five rams, five he-goats and five male yearling lambs as a communion sacrifice. Such was the offering of Nahshon son of Amminadab.

18 On the second day an offering was brought by Nethanel son of Zuar, leader of Issachar. 19 His offering consisted of: one silver bowl weighing a hundred and thirty shekels, one silver sprinkling bowl weighing seventy shekels (sanctuary shekels), both of them full of fine flour mixed with oil as a cereal offering, 20 one golden bowl weighing ten shekels, full of incense, 21 one young bull, one ram and one male yearling lamb as a burnt offering, 22 one he-goat as a sacrifice for sin, 23 and two bulls, five rams, five he-goats and five male yearling lambs as a communion sacrifice. Such was the offering of Nethanel son of Zuar.

24 On the third day an offering was brought by Eliab son of Helon, leader of the Zebulunites. 25 His offering consisted of: one silver bowl weighing a hundred and thirty shekels, one silver sprinkling bowl weighing seventy shekels (sanctuary shekels), both of them full of fine flour mixed with oil as a cereal offering, 26 one golden bowl weighing ten shekels, full of incense, 27 one young bull, one ram and one male yearling lamb as a burnt offering, 28 one he-goat as a sacrifice for sin, 29 and two bulls, five rams, five he-goats and five male yearling lambs as a communion sacrifice. Such was the offering of Eliab son of Helon.

30 On the fourth day an offering was brought by Elizur son of Shedeur, leader of the Reubenites. 31 His offering consisted of: one silver bowl weighing a hundred and thirty shekels, one silver sprinkling bowl weighing seventy shekels (sanctuary shekels), both of them full of fine flour mixed with oil as a cereal offering, 32 one golden bowl weighing ten shekels, full of incense, 33 one young bull, one ram and

old, for a burnt offering; 34 one male goat for a sin offering; 35 and for the sacrifice of well-being, two oxen, five rams, five male goats, and five male lambs a year old. This was the offering of Elizur son of Shedeur.

36 On the fifth day Shelumiel son of Zurishaddai, the leader of the Simeonites: 37 his offering was one silver plate weighing one hundred thirty shekels, one silver basin weighing seventy shekels, according to the shekel of the sanctuary, both of them full of choice flour mixed with oil for a grain offering; 38 one golden dish weighing ten shekels, full of incense; 39 one young bull, one ram, one male lamb a year old, for a burnt offering; 40 one male goat for a sin offering; 41 and for the sacrifice of well-being, two oxen, five rams, five male goats, and five male lambs a year old. This was the offering of Shelumiel son of Zurishaddai.

42 On the sixth day Eliasaph son of Deuel, the leader of the Gadites: 43 his offering was one silver plate weighing one hundred thirty shekels, one silver basin weighing seventy shekels, according to the shekel of the sanctuary, both of them full of choice flour mixed with oil for a grain offering; 44 one golden dish weighing ten shekels, full of incense; 45 one young bull, one ram, one male lamb a year old, for a burnt offering; 46 one male goat for a sin offering; 47 and for the sacrifice of well-being, two oxen, five rams, five male goats, and five male lambs a year old. This was the offering of Eliasaph son of Deuel.

48 On the seventh day Elishama son of Ammihud, the leader of the Ephraimites: 49 his offering was one silver plate weighing one hundred thirty shekels, one silver basin weighing seventy shekels, according to the shekel of the sanctuary, both of them full of choice flour mixed with oil for a grain offering; 50 one golden dish weighing ten shekels, full of incense; 51 one young bull, one ram, one male lamb a year old, for a burnt offering; 52 one male goat for a sin offering; 53 and for the sacrifice of well-being, two oxen, five rams, five male goats, and five male lambs a year old. This was the offering of Elishama son of Ammihud.

54 On the eighth day Gamaliel son of Pedahzur, the leader of the Manassites: 55 his offering was one silver plate weighing one hundred thirty shekels, one silver basin weighing seventy shekels, according to the shekel of the sanctuary, both of them full of choice flour mixed with oil for a grain offering; 56 one golden dish weighing ten shekels, full of incense; 57 one young bull, one ram, one male lamb a year old, for a burnt offering; 58 one male goat for a sin offering; 59 and for the sacrifice of well-being, two oxen, five rams, five male goats, and five male lambs a year old. This was the offering of Gamaliel son of Pedahzur.

60 On the ninth day Abidan son of Gideoni, the leader of the Benjaminites: 61 his offering was one silver plate weighing one hundred thirty shekels, one silver basin weighing seventy shekels, according to the shekel of the sanctuary, both of them full of choice flour mixed with oil for a grain offering; 62 one golden dish weighing ten shekels, full of incense; 63 one young bull, one ram, one male lamb a year old, for a burnt offering; 64 one male goat for a sin offering; 65 and for the sacrifice of well-being, two oxen, five rams, five male goats, and five male lambs a year old. This was the offering of Abidan son of Gideoni.

66 On the tenth day Ahiezer son of Ammishaddai, the leader of the Danites: 67 his offering was one silver plate weighing one hundred thirty shekels, one silver basin weighing seventy shekels, according to the shekel of the sanctuary, both of them full of choice flour mixed with oil for a grain offering; 68 one golden dish weighing ten shekels, full of incense; 69 one young bull, one ram, one male lamb a year old, for a burnt offering; 70 one male goat for

bull, one full-grown ram, and one yearling ram, as a whole-offering; 34 one he-goat as a purification-offering; 35 and two bulls, five full-grown rams, five he-goats, and five yearling rams, as a shared-offering. This was the offering of Elizur son of Shedeur.

36 On the fifth day the chief of the Simeonites, Shelumiel son of Zurishaddai, came. 37 His offering was one silver dish weighing a hundred and thirty shekels by the sacred standard, and one silver tossing-bowl weighing seventy, both full of flour mixed with oil as a grain-offering; 38 one gold saucer weighing ten shekels, filled with incense; 39 one young bull, one full-grown ram, and one yearling ram, as a whole-offering; 40 one he-goat as a purification-offering; 41 and two bulls, five full-grown rams, five he-goats, and five yearling rams, as a shared-offering. This was the offering of Shelumiel son of Zurishaddai.

42 On the sixth day the chief of the Gadites, Eliasaph son of Reuel, came. 43 His offering was one silver dish weighing a hundred and thirty shekels by the sacred standard, and one silver tossing-bowl weighing seventy, both full of flour mixed with oil as a grain-offering; 44 one gold saucer weighing ten shekels, filled with incense; 45 one young bull, one full-grown ram, and one yearling ram, as a whole-offering; 46 one he-goat as a purification-offering; 47 and two bulls, five full-grown rams, five he-goats, and five yearling rams, as a shared-offering. This was the offering of Eliasaph son of Reuel.

48 On the seventh day the chief of the Ephraimites, Elishama son of Ammihud, came. 49 His offering was one silver dish weighing a hundred and thirty shekels by the sacred standard, and one silver tossing-bowl weighing seventy, both full of flour mixed with oil as a grain-offering; 50 one gold saucer weighing ten shekels, filled with incense; 51 one young bull, one full-grown ram, and one yearling ram, as a whole-offering; 52 one he-goat as a purification-offering; 53 and two bulls, five full-grown rams, five he-goats, and five yearling rams, as a shared-offering. This was the offering of Elishama son of Ammihud.

54 On the eighth day the chief of the Manassites, Gamaliel son of Pedahzur, came. 55 His offering was one silver dish weighing a hundred and thirty shekels by the sacred standard, and one silver tossing-bowl weighing seventy, both full of flour mixed with oil as a grain-offering; 56 one gold saucer weighing ten shekels, filled with incense; 57 one young bull, one full-grown ram, and one yearling ram, as a whole-offering; 58 one he-goat as a purification-offering; 59 and two bulls, five full-grown rams, five he-goats, and five yearling rams, as a shared-offering. This was the offering of Gamaliel son of Pedahzur.

60 On the ninth day the chief of the Benjamites, Abidan son of Gideoni, came. 61 His offering was one silver dish weighing a hundred and thirty shekels by the sacred standard, and one silver tossing-bowl weighing seventy, both full of flour mixed with oil as a grain-offering; 62 one gold saucer weighing ten shekels, filled with incense; 63 one young bull, one full-grown ram, and one yearling ram, as a whole-offering; 64 one he-goat as a purification-offering; 65 and two bulls, five full-grown rams, five he-goats, and five yearling rams, as a shared-offering. This was the offering of Abidan son of Gideoni.

66 On the tenth day the chief of the Danites, Ahiezer son of Ammishaddai, came. 67 His offering was one silver dish weighing a hundred and thirty shekels by the sacred standard, and one silver tossing-bowl weighing seventy, both full of flour mixed with oil as a grain-offering; 68 one gold saucer weighing ten shekels, filled with incense; 69 one young bull, one full-grown ram, and one yearling ram, as a whole-offering; 70 one he-goat as a purification-offering; 71 and two

one yearling lamb for a holocaust; 34 one goat for a sin offering; 35 and two oxen, five rams, five goats, and five yearling lambs for a peace offering. This was the offering of Elizur, son of Shedeur.

36 On the fifth day it was the turn of Shelumiel, son of Zurishaddai, prince of the Simeonites. 37 His offering consisted of one silver plate weighing a hundred and thirty shekels according to the sanctuary standard and one silver basin weighing seventy shekels, both filled with fine flour mixed with oil for a cereal offering; 38 one gold cup of ten shekels' weight filled with incense; 39 one young bull, one ram, and one yearling lamb for a holocaust; 40 one goat for a sin offering; 41 and two oxen, five rams, five goats, and five yearling lambs for a peace offering. This was the offering of Shelumiel, son of Zurishaddai.

42 On the sixth day it was the turn of Eliasaph, son of Reuel, prince of the Gadites. 43 His offering consisted of one silver plate weighing a hundred and thirty shekels according to the sanctuary standard and one silver basin weighing seventy shekels, both filled with fine flour mixed with oil for a cereal offering; 44 one gold cup of ten shekels' weight filled with incense; 45 one young bull, one ram, and one yearling lamb for a holocaust; 46 one goat for a sin offering; 47 and two oxen, five rams, five goats, and five yearling lambs for a peace offering. This was the offering of Eliasaph, son of Reuel.

48 On the seventh day it was the turn of Elishama, son of Ammihud, prince of the Ephraimites. 49 His offering consisted of one silver plate weighing a hundred and thirty shekels according to the sanctuary standard and one silver basin weighing seventy shekels, both filled with fine flour mixed with oil for a cereal offering; 50 one gold cup of ten shekels' weight filled with incense; 51 one young bull, one ram, and one yearling lamb for a holocaust; 52 one goat for a sin offering; 53 and two oxen, five rams, five goats, and five yearling lambs for a peace offering. This was the offering of Elishama, son of Ammihud.

54 On the eighth day it was the turn of Gamaliel, son of Pedahzur, prince of the Manassehites. 55 His offering consisted of one silver plate weighing a hundred and thirty shekels according to the sanctuary standard and one silver basin weighing seventy shekels, both filled with fine flour mixed with oil for a cereal offering; 56 one gold cup of ten shekels' weight filled with incense; 57 one young bull, one ram, and one yearling lamb for a holocaust; 58 one goat for a sin offering; 59 and two oxen, five rams, five goats, and five yearling lambs for a peace offering. This was the offering of Gamaliel, son of Pedahzur.

60 On the ninth day it was the turn of Abidan, son of Gideoni, prince of the Benjaminites. 61 His offering consisted of one silver plate weighing a hundred and thirty shekels according to the sanctuary standard and one silver basin weighing seventy shekels, both filled with fine flour mixed with oil for a cereal offering; 62 one gold cup of ten shekels' weight filled with incense; 63 one young bull, one ram, and one yearling lamb for a holocaust; 64 one goat for a sin offering; 65 and two oxen, five rams, five goats, and five yearling lambs for a peace offering. This was the offering of Abidan, son of Gideoni.

66 On the tenth day it was the turn of Ahiezer, son of Ammishaddai, prince of the Danites. 67 His offering consisted of one silver plate weighing a hundred and thirty shekels according to the sanctuary standard and one silver basin weighing seventy shekels, both filled with fine flour mixed with oil for a cereal offering; 68 one gold cup of ten shekels' weight filled with incense; 69 one young bull, one ram, and one yearling lamb for a holocaust; 70 one goat for

one male yearling lamb as a burnt offering, 34 one he-goat as a sacrifice for sin, 35 and two bulls, five rams, five he-goats and five male yearling lambs as a communion sacrifice. Such was the offering of Elizur son of Shedeur.

36 On the fifth day an offering was brought by Shelumiel son of Zurishaddai, leader of the Simeonites. 37 His offering consisted of: one silver bowl weighing a hundred and thirty shekels, one silver sprinkling bowl weighing seventy shekels (sanctuary shekels), both of them full of fine flour mixed with oil as a cereal offering, 38 one golden bowl weighing ten shekels, full of incense, 39 one young bull, one ram and one male yearling lamb as a burnt offering, 40 one he-goat as a sacrifice for sin, 41 and two bulls, five rams, five he-goats and five male yearling lambs as a communion sacrifice. Such was the offering of Shelumiel son of Zurishaddai.

42 On the sixth day an offering was brought by Eliasaph son of Reuel, leader of the Gadites. 43 His offering consisted of: one silver bowl weighing a hundred and thirty shekels, one silver sprinkling bowl weighing seventy shekels (sanctuary shekels), both of them full of fine flour mixed with oil as a cereal offering, 44 one golden bowl weighing ten shekels, full of incense, 45 one young bull, one ram and one male yearling lamb as a burnt offering, 46 one he-goat as a sacrifice for sin, 47 and two bulls, five rams, five he-goats and five male yearling lambs as a communion sacrifice. Such was the offering of Eliasaph son of Reuel.

48 On the seventh day an offering was brought by Elishama son of Ammihud, leader of the Ephraimites. 49 His offering consisted of: one silver bowl weighing a hundred and thirty shekels, one silver sprinkling bowl weighing seventy shekels (sanctuary shekels), both of them full of fine flour mixed with oil as a cereal offering, 50 one golden bowl weighing ten shekels, full of incense, 51 one young bull, one ram and one male yearling lamb as a burnt offering, 52 one he-goat as a sacrifice for sin, 53 and two bulls, five rams, five he-goats and five male yearling lambs as a communion sacrifice. Such was the offering of Elishama son of Ammihud.

54 On the eighth day an offering was brought by Gamaliel son of Pedahzur, leader of the Manassehites. 55 His offering consisted of: one silver bowl weighing a hundred and thirty shekels, one silver sprinkling bowl weighing seventy shekels (sanctuary shekels), both of them full of fine flour mixed with oil as a cereal offering, 56 one golden bowl weighing ten shekels, full of incense, 57 one young bull, one ram and one male yearling lamb as a burnt offering, 58 one he-goat as a sacrifice for sin, 59 and two bulls, five rams, five he-goats and five male yearling lambs as a communion sacrifice. Such was the offering of Gamaliel son of Pedahzur.

60 On the ninth day an offering was brought by Abidan son of Gideoni, leader of the Benjaminites. 61 His offering consisted of: one silver bowl weighing a hundred and thirty shekels, one sprinkling bowl weighing seventy shekels (sanctuary shekels), both of them full of fine flour mixed with oil as a cereal offering, 62 one golden bowl weighing ten shekels, full of incense, 63 one young bull, one ram and one male yearling lamb as a burnt offering, 64 one he-goat as a sacrifice for sin, 65 and two bulls, five rams, five he-goats and five male yearling lambs as a communion sacrifice. Such was the offering of Abidan son of Gideoni.

66 On the tenth day an offering was brought by Ahiezer son of Ammishaddai, leader of the Danites. 67 His offering consisted of: one silver bowl weighing a hundred and thirty shekels, one silver sprinkling bowl weighing seventy shekels (sanctuary shekels), both of them full of fine flour mixed with oil as a cereal offering, 68 one golden bowl weighing ten shekels, full of incense, 69 one young bull, one ram and one male yearling lamb as a burnt offering, 70 one he-goat

a sin offering; 71 and for the sacrifice of well-being, two oxen, five rams, five male goats, and five male lambs a year old. This was the offering of Ahiezer son of Ammishaddai.

72 On the eleventh day Pagiel son of Ochran, the leader of the Asherites: 73 his offering was one silver plate weighing one hundred thirty shekels, one silver basin weighing seventy shekels, according to the shekel of the sanctuary, both of them full of choice flour mixed with oil for a grain offering; 74 one golden dish weighing ten shekels, full of incense; 75 one young bull, one ram, one male lamb a year old, for a burnt offering; 76 one male goat for a sin offering; 77 and for the sacrifice of well-being, two oxen, five rams, five male goats, and five male lambs a year old. This was the offering of Pagiel son of Ochran.

78 On the twelfth day Ahira son of Enan, the leader of the Naphtalites: 79 his offering was one silver plate weighing one hundred thirty shekels, one silver basin weighing seventy shekels, according to the shekel of the sanctuary, both of them full of choice flour mixed with oil for a grain offering; 80 one golden dish weighing ten shekels, full of incense; 81 one young bull, one ram, one male lamb a year old, for a burnt offering; 82 one male goat for a sin offering; 83 and for the sacrifice of well-being, two oxen, five rams, five male goats, and five male lambs a year old. This was the offering of Ahira son of Enan.

84 This was the dedication offering for the altar, at the time when it was anointed, from the leaders of Israel: twelve silver plates, twelve silver basins, twelve golden dishes, 85 each silver plate weighing one hundred thirty shekels and each basin seventy, all the silver of the vessels two thousand four hundred shekels according to the shekel of the sanctuary, 86 the twelve golden dishes, full of incense, weighing ten shekels apiece according to the shekel of the sanctuary, all the gold of the dishes being one hundred twenty shekels; 87 all the livestock for the burnt offering twelve bulls, twelve rams, twelve male lambs a year old, with their grain offering; and twelve male goats for a sin offering; 88 and all the livestock for the sacrifice of well-being twenty-four bulls, the rams sixty, the male goats sixty, the male lambs a year old sixty. This was the dedication offering for the altar, after it was anointed.

89 When Moses went into the tent of meeting to speak with the Lord,k he would hear the voice speaking to him from above the mercy seatl that was on the ark of the covenantm from between the two cherubim; thus it spoke to him.

8 The Lord spoke to Moses, saying: 2 Speak to Aaron and say to him: When you set up the lamps, the seven lamps shall give light in front of the lampstand. 3 Aaron did so; he set up its lamps to give light in front of the lampstand, as the Lord had commanded Moses. 4 Now this was how the lampstand was made, out of hammered work of gold. From its base to its flowers, it was hammered work; according to the pattern that the Lord had shown Moses, so he made the lampstand.

5 The Lord spoke to Moses, saying: 6 Take the Levites from among the Israelites and cleanse them. 7 Thus you shall do to them, to cleanse them: sprinkle the water of purification on them, have them shave their whole body with a razor and wash their clothes, and so cleanse themselves. 8 Then let them take a young bull and its grain offering of choice flour mixed with oil, and you shall take another young bull for a sin offering. 9 You shall bring the Levites before the tent of meeting, and assemble the whole congregation of the Israelites. 10 When you bring the Levites before the Lord, the Israelites shall lay their hands on the Levites, 11 and Aaron shall present the Levites before

bulls, five full-grown rams, five he-goats, and five yearling rams, as a shared-offering. This was the offering of Ahiezer son of Ammishaddai.

72 On the eleventh day the chief of the Asherites, Pagiel son of Ochran, came. 73 His offering was one silver dish weighing a hundred and thirty shekels by the sacred standard, and one silver tossing-bowl weighing seventy, both full of flour mixed with oil as a grain-offering; 74 one gold saucer weighing ten shekels, filled with incense; 75 one young bull, one full-grown ram, and one yearling ram, as a whole-offering; 76 one he-goat as a purification-offering; 77 and two bulls, five full-grown rams, five he-goats, and five yearling rams, as a shared-offering. This was the offering of Pagiel son of Ochran.

78 On the twelfth day the chief of the Naphtalites, Ahira son of Enan, came. 79 His offering was one silver dish weighing a hundred and thirty shekels by the sacred standard, and one silver tossing-bowl weighing seventy, both full of flour mixed with oil as a grain-offering; 80 one gold saucer weighing ten shekels, filled with incense; 81 one young bull, one full-grown ram, and one yearling ram, as a whole-offering; 82 one he-goat as a purification-offering; 83 and two bulls, five full-grown rams, five he-goats, and five yearling rams, as a shared-offering. This was the offering of Ahira son of Enan.

84 This was the gift from the chiefs of Israel for the dedication of the altar when it was anointed: twelve silver dishes, twelve silver tossing-bowls, and twelve gold saucers; 85 each silver dish weighed a hundred and thirty shekels, each silver tossing-bowl seventy shekels. The total weight of the silver vessels was two thousand four hundred shekels by the sacred standard. 86 There were twelve gold saucers full of incense, ten shekels each by the sacred standard: the total weight of the gold of the saucers was a hundred and twenty shekels. 87 The number of beasts for the whole-offering was twelve bulls, twelve full-grown rams, and twelve yearling rams, with the prescribed grain-offerings, and twelve he-goats for the purification-offering. 88 The number of beasts for the shared-offering was twenty-four bulls, sixty full-grown rams, sixty he-goats, and sixty yearling rams. This was the gift for the dedication of the altar when it was anointed. 89 When Moses entered the Tent of Meeting to speak with the Lord, he heard the voice speaking from above the cover over the Ark of the Testimony from between the two cherubim: the voice spoke to him.

8 The Lord told Moses 2 to say to Aaron: 'When you put the seven lamps in position, see that they shed their light forwards in front of the lampstand.' 3 Aaron did this: he positioned the lamps so as to shed light forwards in front of the lampstand, as the Lord had instructed Moses. 4 The lampstand was made of beaten work in gold from stem to petals, made to match the pattern the Lord had shown Moses.

5 The Lord said to Moses: 6 'Separate the Levites from the rest of the Israelites and cleanse them ritually. 7 This is how the cleansing is to be done. Sprinkle lustral water over them; they are then to shave their whole bodies, wash their clothes, and so be cleansed. 8 Next, they must take a young bull as a whole-offering with its prescribed grain-offering, flour mixed with oil, while you take a second young bull as a purification-offering. 9 Bring the Levites before the Tent of Meeting and, when you have called the whole community of Israelites together, 10 bring the Levites before the Lord, and let the Israelites lay their hands on the Levites' heads. 11 Aaron must present the Levites before the Lord as

---

k Heb him　　l Or the cover　　m Or treaty, or testimony; Heb eduth　　　8:8 as a whole-offering: prob. rdg; Heb. omits.

294

a sin offering; 71 and two oxen, five rams, five goats, and five yearling lambs for a peace offering. This was the offering of Ahiezer, son of Ammishaddai.

72 On the eleventh day it was the turn of Pagiel, son of Ochran, prince of the Asherites. 73 His offering consisted of one silver plate weighing a hundred and thirty shekels according to the sanctuary standard and one silver basin weighing seventy shekels, both filled with fine flour mixed with oil for a cereal offering; 74 one gold cup of ten shekels' weight filled with incense; 75 one young bull, one ram, and one yearling lamb for a holocaust; 76 one goat for a sin offering; 77 and two oxen, five rams, five goats, and five yearling lambs for a peace offering. This was the offering of Pagiel, son of Ochran.

78 On the twelfth day it was the turn of Ahira, son of Enan, prince of the Naphtalites. 79 His offering consisted of one silver plate weighing a hundred and thirty shekels according to the sanctuary standard and one silver basin weighing seventy shekels, both filled with fine flour mixed with oil for a cereal offering; 80 one gold cup of ten shekels' weight filled with incense; 81 one young bull, one ram, and one yearling lamb for a sin offering; 82 one goat for a sin offering; 83 and two oxen, five rams, five goats, and five yearling lambs for a peace offering. This was the offering of Ahira, son of Enan.

84 These were the offerings for the dedication of the altar, given by the princes of Israel on the occasion of its anointing: twelve silver plates, twelve silver basins, and twelve gold cups. 85 Each silver plate weighed a hundred and thirty shekels, and each silver basin seventy, so that all the silver of these vessels amounted to two thousand four hundred shekels, according to the sanctuary standard. 86 The twelve gold cups that were filled with incense weighed ten shekels apiece, according to the sanctuary standard, so that all the gold of the cups amounted to one hundred and twenty shekels. 87 The animals for the holocausts were, in all, twelve young bulls, twelve rams, and twelve yearling lambs, with their cereal offerings; those for the sin offerings were twelve goats. 88 The animals for the peace offerings were, in all, twenty-four oxen, sixty rams, sixty goats, and sixty yearling lambs. These, then, were the offerings for the dedication of the altar after it was anointed.

89 When Moses entered the meeting tent to speak with him, he heard the voice addressing him from above the propitiatory on the ark of the commandments, from between the two cherubim; and it spoke to him. . . .

8 The LORD spoke to Moses, and said, 2 "Give Aaron this command: When you set up the seven lamps, have them throw their light toward the front of the lampstand." 3 Aaron did so, setting up the lamps to face toward the front of the lampstand, just as the LORD had commanded Moses. 4 The lampstand was made of beaten gold in both its shaft and its branches, according to the pattern which the LORD had shown Moses.

5 The LORD said to Moses: 6 "Take the Levites from among the Israelites and purify them. 7 This is what you shall do to them to purify them. Sprinkle them with the water of remission; then have them shave their whole bodies and wash their clothes, and so purify themselves. 8 They shall take a young bull, along with its cereal offering of fine flour mixed with oil; you shall take another young bull for a sin offering. 9 Then have the Levites come forward in front of the meeting tent, where you shall assemble also the whole community of the Israelites. 10 While the Levites are present before the LORD, the Israelites shall lay their hands upon them. 11 Let Aaron then offer the Levites before the

as a sacrifice for sin, 71 and two bulls, five rams, five he-goats and five male yearling lambs as a communion sacrifice. Such was the offering of Ahiezer son of Ammishaddai.

72 On the eleventh day an offering was brought by Pagiel son of Ochran, leader of the Asherites. 73 His offering consisted of: one silver bowl weighing a hundred and thirty shekels, one silver sprinkling bowl weighing seventy shekels (sanctuary shekels), both of them full of fine flour mixed with oil as a cereal offering, 74 one golden bowl weighing ten shekels, full of incense, 75 one young bull, one ram and one male yearling lamb as a burnt offering, 76 one he-goat as a sacrifice for sin, 77 and two bulls, five rams, five he-goats and five male yearling lambs as a communion sacrifice. Such was the offering of Pagiel son of Ochran.

78 On the twelfth day an offering was brought by Ahira son of Enan, leader of the Naphtalites. 79 His offering consisted of: one silver bowl weighing a hundred and thirty shekels, one silver sprinkling bowl weighing seventy shekels (sanctuary shekels), both of them full of fine flour mixed with oil as a cereal offering, 80 one golden bowl weighing ten shekels, full of incense, 81 one young bull, one ram and one male yearling lamb as a burnt offering, 82 one he-goat as a sacrifice for sin, 83 and two bulls, five rams, five he-goats and five male yearling lambs as a communion sacrifice. Such was the offering of Ahira son of Enan.

84 Such were the offerings made by the leaders of Israel for the dedication of the altar on the day it was anointed: twelve silver bowls, twelve silver sprinkling bowls, and twelve golden bowls. 85 Each silver bowl weighed a hundred and thirty shekels, and each sprinkling bowl seventy, the silver of these objects weighing in all two thousand four hundred sanctuary shekels. 86 The twelve golden bowls full of incense each weighed ten shekels (sanctuary shekels), the gold of these bowls weighing in all a hundred and twenty shekels.

87 The sum total of animals for the burnt offering: twelve bulls, twelve rams, twelve male yearling lambs, with their cereal offerings. For the sacrifice for sin, twelve he-goats. 88 The sum total of animals for the communion sacrifice: twenty-four bulls, sixty rams, sixty he-goats and sixty male yearling lambs.

Such were the offerings for the dedication of the altar, after it had been anointed.

89 When Moses went into the Tent of Meeting to speak with him, he heard the voice speaking to him from above the mercy-seat on the ark of the Testimony, from between the two great winged creatures. He then spoke to him.

8 Yahweh spoke to Moses and said: 2 'Speak to Aaron and say, "When you set up the lamps, the seven lamps must throw their light towards the front of the lamp-stand." ' 3 Aaron did this. He set up the lamps to the front of the lamp-stand, as Yahweh had ordered Moses. 4 This lamp-stand was worked in beaten gold, including its stem and its petals, which were also of beaten gold. This lamp-stand had been made according to the pattern Yahweh had shown to Moses.

5 Yahweh spoke to Moses and said, 6 'Separate the Levites from the Israelites and purify them. 7 This is how you must purify them: you will sprinkle them with purifying water, and they will shave their bodies all over and wash their clothes. They will then be clean. 8 They will then take a young bull, with the accompanying cereal offering of fine flour mixed with oil, and you will take a second young bull for a sacrifice for sin. 9 You will then bring the Levites in front of the Tent of Meeting, and assemble the whole community of Israelites. 10 Once you have brought the Levites before Yahweh, the Israelites will lay their hands on them.

the LORD as an elevation offering from the Israelites, that they may do the service of the LORD. 12 The Levites shall lay their hands on the heads of the bulls, and he shall offer the one for a sin offering and the other for a burnt offering to the LORD, to make atonement for the Levites. 13 Then you shall have the Levites stand before Aaron and his sons, and you shall present them as an elevation offering to the LORD.

14 Thus you shall separate the Levites from among the other Israelites, and the Levites shall be mine. 15 Thereafter the Levites may go in to do service at the tent of meeting, once you have cleansed them and presented them as an elevation offering. 16 For they are unreservedly given to me from among the Israelites; I have taken them for myself, in place of all that open the womb, the firstborn of all the Israelites. 17 For all the firstborn among the Israelites are mine, both human and animal. On the day that I struck down all the firstborn in the land of Egypt I consecrated them for myself, 18 but I have taken the Levites in place of all the firstborn among the Israelites. 19 Moreover, I have given the Levites as a gift to Aaron and his sons from among the Israelites, to do the service for the Israelites at the tent of meeting, and to make atonement for the Israelites, in order that there may be no plague among the Israelites for coming too close to the sanctuary.

20 Moses and Aaron and the whole congregation of the Israelites did with the Levites accordingly; the Israelites did with the Levites just as the LORD had commanded Moses concerning them. 21 The Levites purified themselves from sin and washed their clothes; then Aaron presented them as an elevation offering before the LORD, and Aaron made atonement for them to cleanse them. 22 Thereafter the Levites went in to do their service in the tent of meeting in attendance on Aaron and his sons. As the LORD had commanded Moses concerning the Levites, so they did with them.

23 The LORD spoke to Moses, saying: 24 This applies to the Levites: from twenty-five years old and upward they shall begin to do duty in the service of the tent of meeting; 25 and from the age of fifty years they shall retire from the duty of the service and serve no more. 26 They may assist their brothers in the tent of meeting in carrying out their duties, but they shall perform no service. Thus you shall do with the Levites in assigning their duties.

9 The LORD spoke to Moses in the wilderness of Sinai, in the first month of the second year after they had come out of the land of Egypt, saying: 2 Let the Israelites keep the passover at its appointed time. 3 On the fourteenth day of this month, at twilight,[n] you shall keep it at its appointed time; according to all its statutes and all its regulations you shall keep it. 4 So Moses told the Israelites that they should keep the passover. 5 They kept the passover in the first month, on the fourteenth day of the month, at twilight,[n] in the wilderness of Sinai. Just as the LORD had commanded Moses, so the Israelites did. 6 Now there were certain people who were unclean through touching a corpse, so that they could not keep the passover on that day. They came before Moses and Aaron on that day, 7 and said to him, "Although we are unclean through touching a corpse, why must we be kept from presenting the LORD's offering at its appointed time among the Israelites?" 8 Moses spoke to them, "Wait, so that I may hear what the LORD will command concerning you."

9 The LORD spoke to Moses, saying: 10 Speak to the Israelites, saying: Anyone of you or your descendants who is unclean through touching a corpse, or is away on a journey, shall still keep the passover to the LORD. 11 In the

[n] Heb between the two evenings

a special gift from the Israelites, and they will be dedicated to the service of the LORD. 12 The Levites must lay their hands on the heads of the bulls, one bull to be offered as a purification-offering and the other as a whole-offering to the LORD, to make expiation for the Levites. 13 Then stand the Levites before Aaron and his sons, presenting them to the LORD as a special gift. 14 You thus separate the Levites from the rest of the Israelites, and they are to be mine.

15 'After this, the Levites may enter the Tent of Meeting to serve in it, ritually cleansed and presented as a special gift; 16 for out of all the Israelites they are assigned and dedicated to me. I have accepted them as mine in place of all that comes first from the womb, every first child among the Israelites; 17 for every firstborn male creature, man or beast, among the Israelites is mine. On the day when I struck down every firstborn creature in Egypt, I consecrated all the firstborn of the Israelites to myself, 18 and I have accepted the Levites in their place. 19 I have assigned the Levites to Aaron and his sons, dedicated among the Israelites to perform the service of the Israelites in the Tent of Meeting and to make expiation for them; then no calamity will befall the Israelites should they come close to the sanctuary.'

20 Moses and Aaron and the whole community of Israelites carried out all the commands the LORD had given to Moses for the dedication of the Levites. 21 The Levites purified themselves of sin and washed their clothes, and Aaron presented them as a dedicated gift before the LORD and made expiation for them, to cleanse them. 22 Then at last they went in to perform their service in the Tent of Meeting, before Aaron and his sons. Thus the commands the LORD had given to Moses concerning the Levites were all carried out.

23 The LORD said to Moses, 24 'As regards the Levites, they are to begin their active work in the service of the Tent of Meeting at the age of twenty-five. 25 At the age of fifty a Levite must retire from regular service and serve no longer. 26 He may continue to assist his fellow-Levites in attendance in the Tent of Meeting, but no longer perform regular service. That is how you are to arrange the duties of the Levites.'

9 In the first month of the second year after they came out of Egypt, the LORD spoke to Moses in the wilderness of Sinai. He said, 2 'Let the Israelites prepare the Passover at the time appointed for it. 3 This is to be between dusk and dark on the fourteenth day of this month; keep it at this appointed time, observing every rule and custom proper to it.' 4 So Moses told the Israelites to prepare the Passover, 5 and they prepared it on the fourteenth day of the first month, between dusk and dark, in the wilderness of Sinai. The Israelites did everything exactly as the LORD had instructed Moses.

6 It happened that some men were ritually unclean through contact with a dead body and so could not keep the Passover on the right day. They came that day before Moses and Aaron 7 and said, 'We are unclean through contact with a dead body. Must we therefore be debarred from presenting the LORD's offering at its appointed time with the rest of the Israelites?' 8 Moses answered, 'Wait, and let me hear what command the LORD has for you.'

9 The LORD told Moses 10 to say to the Israelites: 'If any one of you or of your descendants is ritually unclean through contact with a dead body, or if he is far away on a journey, he must keep a Passover to the LORD none the less.

LORD as a wave offering from the Israelites, thus devoting them to the service of the LORD. 12 The Levites in turn shall lay their hands on the heads of the bullocks, which shall then be immolated, the one as a sin offering and the other as a holocaust to the LORD, in atonement for the Levites. 13 Thus, then, shall you have the Levites stand before Aaron and his sons, to be offered as a wave offering to the LORD; 14 and thus shall you set aside the Levites from the rest of the Israelites, that they may be mine.

15 "Only then shall the Levites enter upon their service in the meeting tent. You shall purify them and offer them as a wave offering; 16 because they, among the Israelites, are strictly dedicated to me; I have taken them for myself in place of every first-born that opens the womb among the Israelites. 17 Indeed, all the first-born among the Israelites, both of man and of beast, belong to me; I consecrated them to myself on the day I slew all the first-born in the land of Egypt. 18 But in place of all the first-born Israelites I have taken the Levites; 19 and I have given these dedicated Israelites to Aaron and his sons to discharge the duties of the Israelites in the meeting tent and to make atonement for them, so that no plague may strike among the Israelites should they come near the sanctuary."

20 Thus, then, did Moses and Aaron and the whole community of the Israelites deal with the Levites, carrying out exactly the command which the LORD had given Moses concerning them. 21 When the Levites had cleansed themselves of sin and washed their clothes, Aaron offered them as a wave offering before the LORD, and made atonement for them to purify them. 22 Only then did they enter upon their service in the meeting tent under the supervision of Aaron and his sons. The command which the LORD had given Moses concerning the Levites was carried out.

23 The LORD said to Moses: 24 "This is the rule for the Levites. Each from his twenty-fifth year onward shall perform the required service in the meeting tent. 25 When he is fifty years old, he shall retire from the required service and work no longer. 26 His service with his fellow Levites shall consist in sharing their responsibilities in the meeting tent, but he shall not do the work. This, then, is how you are to regulate the duties of the Levites."

9 In the first month of the year following their departure from the land of Egypt, the LORD said to Moses in the desert of Sinai, 2 "Tell the Israelites to celebrate the Passover at the prescribed time. 3 The evening twilight of the fourteenth day of this month is the prescribed time when you shall celebrate it, observing all its rules and regulations." 4 Moses, therefore, told the Israelites to celebrate the Passover. 5 And they did so, celebrating the Passover in the desert of Sinai during the evening twilight of the fourteenth day of the first month, just as the LORD had commanded Moses.

6 There were some, however, who were unclean because of a human corpse and so could not keep the Passover that day. These men came up to Moses and Aaron that same day 7 and said, "Although we are unclean because of a corpse, why should we be deprived of presenting the LORD's offering at its proper time along with the other Israelites?" 8 Moses answered them, "Wait until I learn what the LORD will command in your regard."

9 The LORD then said to Moses: 10 "Speak to the Israelites and say: If any one of you or of your descendants is unclean because of a corpse, or if he is absent on a journey, he may still keep the LORD's Passover. 11 But he shall keep it in the

11 Aaron will then offer the Levites, making the gesture of offering before Yahweh on behalf of the Israelites, admitting them to Yahweh's service.

12 'The Levites will then lay their hands on the heads of the bulls, one of which you will offer as a sacrifice for sin, and the other as a burnt offering to Yahweh, to perform the rite of expiation for the Levites. 13 Having brought the Levites before Aaron and his sons, you will present them to Yahweh with the gesture of offering. 14 That is how you will set the Levites apart from the Israelites, for them to be mine. 15 The Levites will then begin their ministry in the Tent of Meeting.

'You will purify them and offer them with the gesture of offering 16 because, of the Israelites, they have been dedicated to me in place of all those who first emerge from the womb, instead of the first-born; of all the Israelites, I have taken them for my own. 17 For all the first-born of the Israelites, whether human or animal, do indeed belong to me: the day I struck down all the first-born in Egypt, I consecrated them to myself, 18 and now, in place of all the first-born of the Israelites, I have taken the Levites. 19 Of the Israelites, I give the Levites to Aaron and his sons, as dedicated men, to minister in the Tent of Meeting on behalf of the Israelites and perform the rite of expiation for them, so that no disaster befalls the Israelites when the Israelites come close to the sanctuary.'

20 Moses, Aaron and the whole community of Israelites dealt with the Levites exactly as Yahweh had ordered Moses concerning them; this is what the Israelites did with them. 21 The Levites purified themselves and washed their clothes, and Aaron presented them with the gesture of offering before Yahweh. He then performed the rite of expiation for them to purify them. 22 The Levites were then allowed to perform their ministry in the Tent of Meeting in the presence of Aaron and his sons. As Yahweh had ordered Moses concerning the Levites, so it was done with them.

23 Yahweh spoke to Moses and said:

24 'This concerns the Levites. From the age of twenty-five onwards, the Levite will exercise his ministry and do duty in the Tent of Meeting. 25 After the age of fifty, he is no longer bound to the ministry; he will have no further duties; 26 but he will still help his brothers to assure the services in the Tent of Meeting, though he himself will no longer have any ministry. That is how you will act as regards the ministry of the Levites.'

9 Yahweh spoke to Moses, in the desert of Sinai, in the second year after the exodus from Egypt, in the first month, and said:

2 'The Israelites must keep the Passover at its appointed time. 3 The fourteenth day of this month, at twilight, is the time appointed for you to keep it. You will keep it with all the laws and customs proper to it.'

4 Moses told the Israelites to keep the Passover. 5 They kept it, in the desert of Sinai, in the first month, on the fourteenth day of the month, at twilight. The Israelites did everything as Yahweh had ordered Moses.

6 It happened that some men had become unclean by touching a dead body; they could not keep the Passover that day. They came the same day to Moses and Aaron, 7 and said, 'We have become unclean by touching a dead body. Why should we be excluded from bringing an offering to Yahweh at the proper time with the rest of the Israelites?' 8 Moses replied, 'Wait here until I hear what order Yahweh gives about you.'

9 Yahweh spoke to Moses and said, 10 'Speak to the Israelites and say:

"Any of you or your descendants who becomes unclean by touching a dead body, or is away on a long journey, can still keep a Passover for Yahweh. 11 Such persons will keep

NEW REVISED STANDARD VERSION

REVISED ENGLISH BIBLE

second month on the fourteenth day, at twilight,*o* they shall keep it; they shall eat it with unleavened bread and bitter herbs. 12 They shall leave none of it until morning, nor break a bone of it; according to all the statute for the passover they shall keep it. 13 But anyone who is clean and is not on a journey, and yet refrains from keeping the passover, shall be cut off from the people for not presenting the Lord's offering at its appointed time; such a one shall bear the consequences for the sin. 14 Any alien residing among you who wishes to keep the passover to the Lord shall do so according to the statute of the passover and according to its regulation; you shall have one statute for both the resident alien and the native.

15 On the day the tabernacle was set up, the cloud covered the tabernacle, the tent of the covenant;*p* and from evening until morning it was over the tabernacle, having the appearance of fire. 16 It was always so: the cloud covered it by day*q* and the appearance of fire by night. 17 Whenever the cloud lifted from over the tent, then the Israelites would set out; and in the place where the cloud settled down, there the Israelites would camp. 18 At the command of the Lord the Israelites would set out, and at the command of the Lord they would camp. As long as the cloud rested over the tabernacle, they would remain in camp. 19 Even when the cloud continued over the tabernacle many days, the Israelites would keep the charge of the Lord, and would not set out. 20 Sometimes the cloud would remain a few days over the tabernacle, and according to the command of the Lord they would remain in camp; then according to the command of the Lord they would set out. 21 Sometimes the cloud would remain from evening until morning; and when the cloud lifted in the morning, they would set out, or if it continued for a day and a night, when the cloud lifted they would set out. 22 Whether it was two days, or a month, or a longer time, that the cloud continued over the tabernacle, resting upon it, the Israelites would remain in camp and would not set out; but when it lifted they would set out. 23 At the command of the Lord they would camp, and at the command of the Lord they would set out. They kept the charge of the Lord, at the command of the Lord by Moses.

10 The Lord spoke to Moses, saying: 2 Make two silver trumpets; you shall make them of hammered work; and you shall use them for summoning the congregation, and for breaking camp. 3 When both are blown, the whole congregation shall assemble before you at the entrance of the tent of meeting. 4 But if only one is blown, then the leaders, the heads of the tribes of Israel, shall assemble before you. 5 When you blow an alarm, the camps on the east side shall set out; 6 when you blow a second alarm, the camps on the south side shall set out. An alarm is to be blown whenever they are to set out. 7 But when the assembly is to be gathered, you shall blow, but you shall not sound an alarm. 8 The sons of Aaron, the priests, shall blow the trumpets; this shall be a perpetual institution for you throughout your generations. 9 When you go to war in your land against the adversary who oppresses you, you shall sound an alarm with the trumpets, so that you may be remembered before the Lord your God and be saved from your enemies. 10 Also on your days of rejoicing, at your appointed festivals, and at the beginnings of your months, you shall blow the trumpets over your burnt offerings and over your sacrifices of well-being; they shall serve as a reminder on your behalf before the Lord your God: I am the Lord your God.

11 But in that case he is to prepare the victim in the second month, between dusk and dark on the fourteenth day. It must be eaten with unleavened bread and bitter herbs; 12 let nothing be left over till morning, and let no bone of it be broken. The Passover is to be kept exactly as the law prescribes. 13 The man who, being ritually clean and not absent on a journey, neglects to keep the Passover, will be cut off from his father's kin, because he has not presented the Lord's offering at its appointed time. That man must accept responsibility for his sin.

14 'When an alien is settled among you, he also is to keep the Passover to the Lord, observing every rule and custom proper to it. The same statute applies to you all, to alien and native-born alike.'

15 On the day when they set up the Tabernacle, that is the Tent of the Testimony, cloud covered it, and in the evening a brightness like fire appeared over it till morning. 16 So it was always: the cloud covered it by day and a brightness like fire by night. 17 Whenever the cloud lifted from the tent, the Israelites struck camp, and at the place where the cloud settled, there they pitched their camp. 18 At the command of the Lord they struck camp, and at his command they encamped again, and continued in camp as long as the cloud rested over the Tabernacle. 19 When the cloud stayed long over the Tabernacle, the Israelites kept the Lord's injunction and did not move; 20 and it was the same when the cloud continued over the Tabernacle only a few days: at the command of the Lord they remained in camp, and at his command they struck camp. 21 There were also times when the cloud continued only from evening till morning, and in the morning, when the cloud lifted, they moved on. Whether by day or by night, they moved as soon as the cloud lifted. 22 Whether it was for a day or two, for a month or longer, whenever the cloud stayed long over the Tabernacle, the Israelites remained where they were and did not move on; they did so only when the cloud lifted. 23 At the command of the Lord they encamped, and at his command they struck camp. They kept the Lord's injunction at the Lord's command, given through Moses.

10 The Lord said to Moses: 2 'Make two trumpets of beaten silver and use them for summoning the community and for breaking camp. 3 When both are sounded, the whole community is to muster before you at the entrance to the Tent of Meeting. 4 If a single trumpet is sounded, the chiefs who are heads of the Israelite clans will muster. 5 When a fanfare is sounded, those encamped on the east side are to move off. 6 When a second fanfare is sounded, those encamped on the south are to move off. A fanfare is the signal to move off. 7 When you convene the assembly, a trumpet-call must be sounded, not a fanfare. 8 This sounding of the trumpets is the duty of the Aaronite priests; let it be a rule binding for all time on your descendants.

9 'When you go into battle against an invader and are hard pressed by him, sound a fanfare on the trumpets, and this will serve as a reminder of you before the Lord your God and you will be delivered from your enemies. 10 On your festal days and at your appointed seasons and on the first day of every month, sound the trumpets over your whole-offerings and your shared-offerings; the trumpets will be a reminder on your behalf before your God. I am the Lord your God.'

---

o Heb *between the two evenings*   *p* Or *treaty,* or *testimony;* Heb *eduth*   *q* Gk Syr Vg: Heb lacks *by day*

9:16 **by day:** *so* Gk; Heb. *omits.*

NEW AMERICAN BIBLE

NEW JERUSALEM BIBLE

second month, during the evening twilight of the fourteenth day of that month, eating it with unleavened bread and bitter herbs, 12 and not leaving any of it over till morning, nor breaking any of its bones, but observing all the rules of the Passover. 13 However, anyone who is clean and not away on a journey, who yet fails to keep the Passover, shall be cut off from his people, because he did not present the LORD's offering at the prescribed time. That man shall bear the consequences of his sin.

14 "If an alien who lives among you wishes to keep the LORD's Passover, he too shall observe the rules and regulations for the Passover. You shall have the same law for the resident alien as for the native of the land."

15 On the day when the Dwelling was erected, the cloud covered the Dwelling, the tent of the commandments; but from evening until morning it took on the appearance of fire over the Dwelling. 16 It was always so: during the day the Dwelling was covered by the cloud, which at night had the appearance of fire. 17 Whenever the cloud rose from the tent, the Israelites would break camp; wherever the cloud came to rest, they would pitch camp. 18 At the bidding of the LORD the Israelites moved on, and at his bidding they encamped. As long as the cloud stayed over the Dwelling, they remained in camp.

19 Even when the cloud tarried many days over the Dwelling, the Israelites obeyed the LORD and would not move on; 20 yet sometimes the cloud was over the Dwelling only for a few days. It was at the bidding of the LORD that they stayed in camp, and it was at his bidding that they departed. 21 Sometimes the cloud remained there only from evening until morning; and when it rose in the morning, they would depart. Or if the cloud lifted during the day, or even at night, they would then set out. 22 Whether the cloud tarried over the Dwelling for two days or for a month or longer, the Israelites remained in camp and did not depart; but when it lifted, they moved on. 23 Thus, it was always at the bidding of the LORD that they encamped, and at his bidding that they set out; ever heeding the charge of the LORD, as he had bidden them through Moses.

10 The LORD said to Moses: 2 "Make two trumpets of beaten silver, which you shall use in assembling the community and in breaking camp. 3 When both are blown, the whole community shall gather round you at the entrance of the meeting tent; 4 but when one of them is blown, only the princes, the chiefs of the troops of Israel, shall gather round you. 5 When you sound the first alarm, those encamped on the east side shall set out; 6 when you sound the second alarm, those encamped on the south side shall set out; when you sound the third alarm, those encamped on the west side shall set out; when you sound the fourth alarm, those encamped on the north side shall set out. Thus shall the alarm be sounded for them to depart. 7 But in calling forth an assembly you are to blow an ordinary blast, without sounding the alarm.

8 "It is the sons of Aaron, the priests, who shall blow the trumpets; and the use of them is prescribed by perpetual statute for you and your descendants. 9 When in your own land you go to war against an enemy that is attacking you, you shall sound the alarm on the trumpets, and the LORD, your God, will remember you and save you from your foes. 10 On your days of celebration, your festivals, and your new-moon feasts, you shall blow the trumpets over your holocausts and your peace offerings; this will serve as a reminder of you before your God. I, the LORD, am your God."

it in the second month, on the fourteenth day, at twilight. They will eat it with unleavened bread and bitter herbs; 12 nothing of it must be left over until morning, nor will they break any of its bones. They will keep it, following the entire Passover ritual. 13 But anyone who is clean, or who is not on a journey, but fails to keep the Passover, such a person will be outlawed from his people. For not having brought the offering to Yahweh at its appointed time, the person will bear the consequences of the sin.

14 "A resident alien who keeps a Passover for Yahweh, will keep it in accordance with the ritual and customs of the Passover. You will have one law for alien and citizen alike." '

15 On the day the Dwelling was erected, the cloud covered the Dwelling, the Tent of the Testimony. From nightfall until morning it remained over the Dwelling looking like fire. 16 So the cloud covered it all the time, and at night it looked like fire.

17 Whenever the cloud rose from the Tent, the Israelites broke camp, and wherever the cloud halted, there the Israelites pitched camp. 18 At Yahweh's order, the Israelites set out and, at Yahweh's order, the Israelites pitched camp. They remained in camp for as long as the cloud rested on the Dwelling. 19 If the cloud stayed for many days on the Dwelling, the Israelites performed their duty to Yahweh and did not set out. 20 But if the cloud happened to stay for only a few days on the Dwelling, just as they had pitched camp at Yahweh's order, at Yahweh's order they set out. 21 If the cloud happened to remain only from evening to morning, they set out when it lifted the next morning. Or, if it stayed for a whole day and night, they set out only when it lifted. 22 Sometimes it stayed there for two days, a month, or a longer time; however long the cloud rested on the Dwelling, the Israelites remained in camp, and when it lifted they set out. 23 At Yahweh's order they pitched camp, and at Yahweh's order they set out. They performed their duty to Yahweh, as Yahweh had ordered through Moses.

10 Yahweh spoke to Moses and said: 2 'Make yourself two trumpets; make them of beaten silver, so that you can use them for summoning the community, and for sounding the order to break camp. 3 Whenever they are sounded, the whole community must gather round you, at the entrance to the Tent of Meeting. 4 But if only one trumpet is sounded, then only the leaders, the heads of Israel's thousands, must gather round you.

5 'When the trumpet blast is accompanied by a battle cry,b the encampments pitched to the east will set out. 6 At the second blast accompanied by a battle cry, the encampments pitched to the south will set out. For breaking camp, the trumpet blast will be accompanied by a battle cry, 7 but for assembling the community the trumpets will be sounded without battle cry. 8 The Aaronite priests will sound the trumpets; this is a perpetual decree for you and your descendants.

9 'When in your country you go to war against an enemy who is oppressing you, you will sound trumpets with a battle cry, and Yahweh your God will remember you, and you will be delivered from your enemies. 10 At your festivals, solemnities and new-moon feasts, you will sound the trumpets over your burnt offerings and communion sacrifices, so that they recall you to the remembrance of your God. I am Yahweh your God.'

---

b 10 Battle cry or cry of acclamation used also on royal occasions and in worship.

NEW REVISED STANDARD VERSION	REVISED ENGLISH BIBLE

NEW REVISED STANDARD VERSION

11 In the second year, in the second month, on the twentieth day of the month, the cloud lifted from over the tabernacle of the covenant.*r* 12 Then the Israelites set out by stages from the wilderness of Sinai, and the cloud settled down in the wilderness of Paran. 13 They set out for the first time at the command of the LORD by Moses. 14 The standard of the camp of Judah set out first, company by company, and over the whole company was Nahshon son of Amminadab. 15 Over the company of the tribe of Issachar was Nethanel son of Zuar; 16 and over the company of the tribe of Zebulun was Eliab son of Helon.

17 Then the tabernacle was taken down, and the Gershonites and the Merarites, who carried the tabernacle, set out. 18 Next the standard of the camp of Reuben set out, company by company; and over the whole company was Elizur son of Shedeur. 19 Over the company of the tribe of Simeon was Shelumiel son of Zurishaddai, 20 and over the company of the tribe of Gad was Eliasaph son of Deuel.

21 Then the Kohathites, who carried the holy things, set out; and the tabernacle was set up before their arrival. 22 Next the standard of the Ephraimite camp set out, company by company, and over the whole company was Elishama son of Ammihud. 23 Over the company of the tribe of Manasseh was Gamaliel son of Pedahzur, 24 and over the company of the tribe of Benjamin was Abidan son of Gideoni.

25 Then the standard of the camp of Dan, acting as the rear guard of all the camps, set out, company by company, and over the whole company was Ahiezer son of Ammishaddai. 26 Over the company of the tribe of Asher was Pagiel son of Ochran, 27 and over the company of the tribe of Naphtali was Ahira son of Enan. 28 This was the order of march of the Israelites, company by company, when they set out.

29 Moses said to Hobab son of Reuel the Midianite, Moses' father-in-law, "We are setting out for the place of which the LORD said, 'I will give it to you'; come with us, and we will treat you well; for the LORD has promised good to Israel." 30 But he said to him, "I will not go, but I will go back to my own land and to my kindred." 31 He said, "Do not leave us, for you know where we should camp in the wilderness, and you will serve as eyes for us. 32 Moreover, if you go with us, whatever good the LORD does for us, the same we will do for you."

33 So they set out from the mount of the LORD three days' journey with the ark of the covenant of the LORD going before them three days' journey, to seek out a resting place for them, 34 the cloud of the LORD being over them by day when they set out from the camp.

35 Whenever the ark set out, Moses would say,
"Arise, O LORD, let your enemies be scattered,
and your foes flee before you."
36 And whenever it came to rest, he would say,
"Return, O LORD of the ten thousand thousands
of Israel."*s*

11 Now when the people complained in the hearing of the LORD about their misfortunes, the LORD heard it and his anger was kindled. Then the fire of the LORD burned against them, and consumed some outlying parts of the camp. 2 But the people cried out to Moses; and Moses prayed to the LORD, and the fire abated. 3 So that place was called Taberah,*t* because the fire of the LORD burned against them.

REVISED ENGLISH BIBLE

11 In the second year, on the twentieth day of the second month, the cloud lifted from the Tabernacle of the Testimony, 12 and the Israelites moved by stages from the wilderness of Sinai, until the cloud came to rest in the wilderness of Paran. 13 The first time that they broke camp at the command of the LORD given through Moses, 14 the standard of the division of Judah moved off in the lead with its tribal hosts: the host of Judah under Nahshon son of Amminadab, 15 the host of Issachar under Nethanel son of Zuar, 16 and the host of Zebulun under Eliab son of Helon. 17 Then the Tabernacle was taken down, and its bearers, the sons of Gershon and Merari, moved off.

18 Secondly, the standard of the division of Reuben moved off with its tribal hosts: the host of Reuben under Elizur son of Shedeur, 19 the host of Simeon under Shelumiel son of Zurishaddai, 20 and the host of Gad under Eliasaph son of Reuel. 21 The Kohathites, the bearers of the holy objects, moved off next, and on their arrival found the Tabernacle set up.

22 Thirdly, the standard of the division of Ephraim moved off with its tribal hosts: the host of Ephraim under Elishama son of Ammihud, 23 the host of Manasseh under Gamaliel son of Pedahzur, 24 and the host of Benjamin under Abidan son of Gideoni.

25 Lastly, the standard of the division of Dan, the rearguard of all the divisions, moved off with its tribal hosts: the host of Dan under Ahiezer son of Ammishaddai, 26 the host of Asher under Pagiel son of Ochran, 27 and the host of Naphtali under Ahira son of Enan. 28 This was the order of march for the Israelites, mustered in their hosts, and in this order they broke camp.

29 Moses said to Hobab his brother-in-law, son of Reuel the Midianite, 'We are setting out for the place which the LORD promised to give us. Come with us, and we shall deal generously with you, for the LORD has given an assurance of prosperity for Israel.' 30 But he replied, 'No, I would rather go to my own country and my own people.' 31 Moses said, 'Do not leave us, I beg you; for you know where we ought to camp in the wilderness, and you will be our guide. 32 If you will go with us, then all the prosperity with which the LORD favours us we shall share with you.'

33 Then they moved off from the mountain of the LORD and journeyed for three days, and the Ark of the Covenant of the LORD kept three days' journey ahead of them to find them a place to rest. 34 The cloud of the LORD was over them by day when they moved camp. 35 Whenever the Ark set out, Moses said,
'Arise, LORD, and may your enemies be scattered;
may those hostile to you flee at your approach.'
36 Whenever it halted, he said,
'Rest, LORD of the countless thousands of Israel.'

11 THE people began complaining loudly to the LORD about their hardships, and when he heard he became angry. Fire from the LORD broke out among them, and raged on the outskirts of the camp. 2 Moses, when appealed to by the people, interceded with the LORD, and the fire died down. 3 They named that place Taberah, because fire from the LORD had burned among them.

---

r Or *treaty*, or *testimony*; Heb *eduth*   *s* Meaning of Heb uncertain   *t* That is *Burning*

10:20 **Reuel:** *so Gk (cp. 2:14); Heb.* Deuel.   10:21 **holy objects:** *so Gk; Heb.* sanctuary.   11:3 **Taberah:** *that is* Burning.

11 In the second year, on the twentieth day of the second month, the cloud rose from the Dwelling of the commandments. 12 The Israelites moved on from the desert of Sinai by stages, until the cloud came to rest in the desert of Paran.

13 The first time that they broke camp at the bidding of the LORD through Moses, 14 the camp of the Judahites, under its own standard and arranged in companies, was the first to set out. Nahshon, son of Amminadab, was over their host, 15 and Nethanel, son of Zuar, over the host of the tribe of Issachar, 16 and Eliab, son of Helon, over the host of the tribe of Zebulun. 17 Then, after the Dwelling was dismantled, the clans of Gershon and Merari set out, carrying the Dwelling. 18 The camp of the Reubenites, under its own standard and arranged in companies, was the next to set out, with Elizur, son of Shedeur, over their host, 19 and Shelumiel, son of Zurishaddai, over the host of the tribe of Simeon, 20 and Eliasaph, son of Reuel, over the host of the tribe of Gad. 21 The clan of Kohath then set out, carrying the sacred objects for the Dwelling, which was to be erected before their arrival. 22 The camp of the Ephraimites next set out, under its own standard and arranged in companies, with Elishama, son of Ammihud, over their host, 23 and Gamaliel, son of Pedahzur, over the host of the tribe of Manasseh, 24 and Abidan, son of Gideoni, over the host of the tribe of Benjamin. 25 Finally, as rear guard for all the camps, the camp of the Danites set out, under its own standard and arranged in companies, with Ahiezer, son of Amishaddai, over their host, 26 and Pagiel, son of Ochran, over the host of the tribe of Asher, 27 and Ahira, son of Enan, over the host of the tribe of Naphtali. 28 This was the order of departure for the Israelites, company by company.

As they were setting out, 29 Moses said to his brother-in-law Hobab, son of Reuel the Midianite, "We are setting out for the place which the LORD has promised to give us. Come with us, and we will be generous toward you, for the LORD has promised prosperity to Israel." 30 But he answered, "No, I will not come. I am going instead to my own country and to my own kindred." 31 Moses said, "Please, do not leave us; you know where we can camp in the desert, and you will serve as eyes for us. 32 If you come with us, we will share with you the prosperity the LORD will bestow on us."

33 They moved on from the mountain of the LORD, a three days' journey, and the ark of the covenant of the LORD which was to seek out their resting place went the three days' journey with them. 34 And when they set out from camp, the cloud of the LORD was over them by day. 35 Whenever the ark set out, Moses would say,

"Arise, O LORD, that your enemies may
    be scattered,
    and those who hate you may flee before you."
36 And when it came to rest, he would say,

"Return, O LORD, you who ride upon the clouds,
    to the troops of Israel."

11 Now the people complained in the hearing of the LORD; and when he heard it his wrath flared up so that the fire of the LORD burned among them and consumed the outskirts of the camp. 2 But when the people cried out to Moses, he prayed to the LORD and the fire died out. 3 Hence that place was called Taberah, because there the fire of the LORD burned among them.

11 In the second year, in the second month, on the twentieth day of the month, the cloud rose from where the Dwelling of the Testimony was, 12 and the Israelites set out, in marching order, from the desert of Sinai. The cloud came to rest in the desert of Paran.

13 These were the men who set out in the vanguard, at Yahweh's order through Moses: 14 first went the standard of the camp of the Judahites and their units, with Nahshon son of Amminadab commanding that contingent; 15 Nethanel son of Zuar commanding the tribal contingent of the Issacharites; 16 and Eliab son of Helon commanding the tribal contingent of the Zebulunites.

17 The Dwelling was then dismantled and the Gershonites and Merarites set out, carrying the Dwelling.

18 Then came the standard of the camp of the Reubenites and their units, with Elizur son of Shedeur commanding that contingent; 19 Shelumiel son of Zurishaddai commanding the tribal contingent of the Simeonites; 20 and Eliasaph son of Reuel commanding the tribal contingent of the Gadites.

21 Then came the Kohathites carrying the sanctuary (the Dwelling was erected before they arrived).

22 Then came the standard of the camp of the Ephraimites and their units, with Elishama son of Ammihud commanding that contingent; 23 Gamaliel son of Pedahzur commanding the tribal contingent of the Manassehites; 24 and Abidan son of Gideoni commanding the tribal contingent of the Benjaminites.

25 Last of all, the rearguard of all the camps, came the standard of the camp of the Danites and their units, with Ahiezer son of Ammishaddai commanding that contingent; 26 Pagiel son of Ochran commanding the tribal contingent of the Asherites; 27 and Ahira son of Enan commanding the tribal contingent of the Naphtalites.

28 Such was the order of march for the Israelites, unit by unit. So they set out.

29 Moses said to Hobab son of Reuel the Midianite, his father-in-law, 'We are setting out for the country of which Yahweh has said: I shall give it to you. Come with us, and we will treat you well, for Yahweh has promised good things for Israel.' 30 'I will not come with you,' he replied, 'but shall go to my own country and kin.' 31 'Do not leave us,' Moses said, 'for you know where we can camp in the desert, and so you will be our eyes. 32 If you come with us, we shall share with you whatever blessings Yahweh gives us.'

33 They set out from Yahweh's mountain and travelled for three days, while the ark of the covenant of Yahweh preceded them on the three-day journey, searching out a place for them to halt.

34 In the daytime, Yahweh's cloud was over them, once they had broken camp. 35 Whenever the ark set out, Moses would say:

Rise, Yahweh, may your enemies be scattered
    and those who hate you flee at your approach!
36 And when it halted, he would say:

Come back, Yahweh,
    to the countless thousands of Israel!

11 Now the people began to complain, which was offensive to Yahweh's ears. When Yahweh heard, his anger was aroused and the fire of Yahweh broke out among them; it devoured one end of the camp. 2 The people appealed to Moses who interceded with Yahweh and the fire died down. 3 So the place was called Taberah, because the fire of Yahweh had broken out among them.

4 The rabble among them had a strong craving; and the Israelites also wept again, and said, "If only we had meat to eat! 5 We remember the fish we used to eat in Egypt for nothing, the cucumbers, the melons, the leeks, the onions, and the garlic; 6 but now our strength is dried up, and there is nothing at all but this manna to look at."

7 Now the manna was like coriander seed, and its color was like the color of gum resin. 8 The people went around and gathered it, ground it in mills or beat it in mortars, then boiled it in pots and made cakes of it; and the taste of it was like the taste of cakes baked with oil. 9 When the dew fell on the camp in the night, the manna would fall with it.

10 Moses heard the people weeping throughout their families, all at the entrances of their tents. Then the LORD became very angry, and Moses was displeased. 11 So Moses said to the LORD, "Why have you treated your servant so badly? Why have I not found favor in your sight, that you lay the burden of all this people on me? 12 Did I conceive all this people? Did I give birth to them, that you should say to me, 'Carry them in your bosom, as a nurse carries a sucking child,' to the land that you promised on oath to their ancestors? 13 Where am I to get meat to give to all this people? For they come weeping to me and say, 'Give us meat to eat!' 14 I am not able to carry all this people alone, for they are too heavy for me. 15 If this is the way you are going to treat me, put me to death at once — if I have found favor in your sight — and do not let me see my misery."

16 So the LORD said to Moses, "Gather for me seventy of the elders of Israel, whom you know to be the elders of the people and officers over them; bring them to the tent of meeting, and have them take their place there with you. 17 I will come down and talk with you there; and I will take some of the spirit that is on you and put it on them; and they shall bear the burden of the people along with you so that you will not bear it all by yourself. 18 And say to the people: Consecrate yourselves for tomorrow, and you shall eat meat; for you have wailed in the hearing of the LORD, saying, 'If only we had meat to eat! Surely it was better for us in Egypt.' Therefore the LORD will give you meat, and you shall eat. 19 You shall eat not only one day, or two days, or five days, or ten days, or twenty days, 20 but for a whole month — until it comes out of your nostrils and becomes loathsome to you — because you have rejected the LORD who is among you, and have wailed before him, saying, 'Why did we ever leave Egypt?' " 21 But Moses said, "The people I am with number six hundred thousand on foot; and you say, 'I will give them meat, that they may eat for a whole month'! 22 Are there enough flocks and herds to slaughter for them? Are there enough fish in the sea to catch for them?" 23 The LORD said to Moses, "Is the LORD's power limited?u Now you shall see whether my word will come true for you or not."

24 So Moses went out and told the people the words of the LORD; and he gathered seventy elders of the people, and placed them all around the tent. 25 Then the LORD came down in the cloud and spoke to him, and took some of the spirit that was on him and put it on the seventy elders; and when the spirit rested upon them, they prophesied. But they did not do so again.

26 Two men remained in the camp, one named Eldad, and the other named Medad, and the spirit rested on them; they were among those registered, but they had not gone out to the tent, and so they prophesied in the camp. 27 And a young man ran and told Moses, "Eldad and Medad are prophesying in the camp." 28 And Joshua son of Nun, the assistant of Moses, one of his chosen men,v said, "My lord Moses, stop them!" 29 But Moses said to him, "Are you

4 A mixed company of strangers had joined the Israelites, and these people began to be greedy for better things. Even the Israelites themselves with renewed weeping cried out, 'If only we had meat! 5 Remember how in Egypt we had fish for the asking, cucumbers and water-melons, leeks and onions and garlic. 6 Now our appetite is gone; wherever we look there is nothing except this manna.' 7 (The manna looked like coriander seed, the colour of bdellium. 8 The people went about collecting it to grind in handmills or pound in mortars; they cooked it in a pot and made it into cakes, which tasted like butter-cakes. 9 When dew fell on the camp at night, the manna would fall with it.) 10 Moses heard all the people lamenting in their families at the opening of their tents. The LORD became very angry, and Moses was troubled, 11 and said to the LORD, 'Why have you brought trouble on your servant? How have I displeased the LORD that I am burdened with all this people? 12 Am I their mother? Have I brought them into the world, and am I called on to carry them in my arms, like a nurse with a baby, to the land promised by you on oath to their fathers? 13 Where am I to find meat to give them all? They pester me with their wailing and their "Give us meat to eat." 14 This whole people is a burden too heavy for me; I cannot carry it alone. 15 If that is your purpose for me, then kill me outright: if I have found favour with you, spare me this trouble afflicting me.'

16 The LORD answered Moses, 'Assemble for me seventy of Israel's elders, men known to you as elders and officers in the community; bring them to the Tent of Meeting, and there let them take their place with you. 17 I shall come down and speak with you there. I shall withdraw part of the spirit which is conferred on you and bestow it on them, and they will share with you the burden of the people; then you will not have to bear it alone. 18 And say to the people: Sanctify yourselves in readiness for tomorrow; you will have meat to eat. You wailed in the LORD's hearing; you said, "If only we had meat! In Egypt we lived well." The LORD will give you meat and you will eat it. 19 Not for one day only, nor for two days, nor five, nor ten, nor twenty, 20 but for a whole month you will eat it until it comes out at your nostrils and makes you sick; because you have rejected the LORD who is in your midst, wailing in his presence and saying, "Why did we ever come out of Egypt?" '

21 Moses said, 'Here am I with six hundred thousand men on the march around me, and you promise them meat to eat for a whole month! 22 How can the sheep and oxen be slaughtered that would be enough for them? If all the fish in the sea could be caught, would they be enough?' 23 The LORD replied, 'Is there a limit to the power of the LORD? You will now see whether or not my words come true.'

24 Moses went out and told the people what the LORD had said. He assembled seventy men from the elders of the people and stationed them round the Tent. 25 Then the LORD descended in the cloud and spoke to him. He withdrew part of the spirit which had been conferred on Moses and bestowed it on the seventy elders; as the spirit alighted on them, they were seized by a prophetic ecstasy, for the first and only time.

26 Two men, one named Eldad and the other Medad, who had been enrolled with the seventy, were left behind in the camp. Though they had not gone out to the Tent, the spirit alighted on them none the less, and they were seized by prophetic ecstasy there in the camp. 27 A young man ran and told Moses that Eldad and Medad were in an ecstasy in the camp, 28 whereupon Joshua son of Nun, who had served since boyhood with Moses, broke in, 'Moses my lord, stop them!' 29 But Moses said to him, 'Are you jealous on my

---

u Heb LORD's hand too short?   v Or of Moses from his youth

11:7 **bdellium:** or gum resin.

4 The foreign elements among them were so greedy for meat that even the Israelites lamented again, "Would that we had meat for food! 5 We remember the fish we used to eat without cost in Egypt, and the cucumbers, the melons, the leeks, the onions, and the garlic. 6 But now we are famished; we see nothing before us but this manna."

7 Manna was like coriander seed and had the appearance of bdellium. 8 When they had gone about and gathered it up, the people would grind it between millstones or pound it in a mortar, then cook it in a pot and make it into loaves, which tasted like cakes made with oil. 9 At night, when the dew fell upon the camp, the manna also fell.

10 When Moses heard the people, family after family, crying at the entrance of their tents, so that the LORD became very angry, he was grieved. 11 "Why do you treat your servant so badly?" Moses asked the LORD. "Why are you so displeased with me that you burden me with all this people? 12 Was it I who conceived all this people? or was it I who gave them birth, that you tell me to carry them at my bosom, like a foster father carrying an infant, to the land you have promised under oath to their fathers? 13 Where can I get meat to give to all this people? For they are crying to me, 'Give us meat for our food.' 14 I cannot carry all this people by myself, for they are too heavy for me. 15 If this is the way you will deal with me, then please do me the favor of killing me at once, so that I need no longer face this distress."

16 Then the LORD said to Moses, "Assemble for me seventy of the elders of Israel, men you know for true elders and authorities among the people, and bring them to the meeting tent. When they are in place beside you, 17 I will come down and speak with you there. I will also take some of the spirit that is on you and will bestow it on them, that they may share the burden of the people with you. You will then not have to bear it by yourself.

18 "To the people, however, you shall say: Sanctify yourselves for tomorrow, when you shall have meat to eat. For in the hearing of the LORD you have cried, 'Would that we had meat for food! Oh, how well off we were in Egypt!' Therefore the LORD will give you meat for food, 19 and you will eat it, not for one day, or two days, or five, or ten, or twenty days, 20 but for a whole month — until it comes out of your very nostrils and becomes loathsome to you. For you have spurned the LORD who is in your midst, and in his presence you have wailed, 'Why did we ever leave Egypt?' "

21 But Moses said, "The people around me include six hundred thousand soldiers; yet you say, 'I will give them meat to eat for a whole month.' 22 Can enough sheep and cattle be slaughtered for them? If all the fish of the sea were caught for them, would they have enough?" 23 The LORD answered Moses, "Is this beyond the LORD's reach? You shall see now whether or not what I have promised you takes place."

24 So Moses went out and told the people what the LORD had said. Gathering seventy elders of the people, he had them stand around the tent. 25 The LORD then came down in the cloud and spoke to him. Taking some of the spirit that was on Moses, he bestowed it on the seventy elders; and as the spirit came to rest on them, they prophesied.

26 Now two men, one named Eldad and the other Medad, were not in the gathering but had been left in the camp. They too had been on the list, but had not gone out to the tent; yet the spirit came to rest on them also, and they prophesied in the camp. 27 So, when a young man quickly told Moses, "Eldad and Medad are prophesying in the camp," 28 Joshua, son of Nun, who from his youth had been Moses' aide, said, "Moses, my lord, stop them." 29 But Moses answered him, "Are you jealous for my sake? Would

4 c The rabble who had joined the people were feeling the pangs of hunger, and the Israelites began to weep again. 'Who will give us meat to eat?' they said. 5 'Think of the fish we used to eat free in Egypt, the cucumbers, melons, leeks, onions and garlic! 6 But now we are withering away; there is nothing wherever we look except this manna!'

7 The manna was like coriander seed and had the appearance of bdellium. 8 The people went round gathering it, and ground it in a mill or crushed it with a pestle; it was then cooked in a pot and made into pancakes. It tasted like cake made with oil. 9 When the dew fell on the camp at nighttime, the manna fell with it.

10 Moses heard the people weeping, each family at the door of its tent. Yahweh's anger was greatly aroused; Moses too found it disgraceful, 11 and he said to Yahweh:

'Why do you treat your servant so badly? In what respect have I failed to win your favour, for you to lay the burden of all these people on me? 12 Was it I who conceived all these people, was I their father, for you to say to me, "Carry them in your arms, like a foster-father carrying an unweaned child, to the country which I swore to give their fathers"? 13 Where am I to find meat to give all these people, pestering me with their tears and saying, "Give us meat to eat"? 14 I cannot carry all these people on my own; the weight is too much for me. 15 If this is how you mean to treat me, please kill me outright! If only I could win your favour and be spared the sight of my misery!'

16 Yahweh said to Moses, 'Collect me seventy of the elders of Israel, men you know to be the people's elders and scribes. Bring them to the Tent of Meeting, and let them stand beside you there. 17 I shall come down and talk to you there and shall take some of the spirit which is on you and put it on them. Then they will bear the burden of the people with you, and you will no longer have to bear it on your own.

18 'And say to the people, "Purify yourselves for tomorrow and you will have meat to eat, since you have wept in Yahweh's hearing, saying: Who will give us meat to eat? How happy we were in Egypt! Very well, Yahweh will give you meat to eat. 19 You will eat it not for one day, or two, or five, or ten or twenty, 20 but for a whole month, until it comes out of your nostrils and sickens you, since you have rejected Yahweh who is among you, and have wept before him saying: Why did we ever leave Egypt?" '

21 Moses said, 'The people round me number six hundred thousand foot soldiers, and you say, "I shall give them meat to eat for a whole month"! 22 If all the flocks and herds were slaughtered, would that be enough for them? If all the fish in the seas were collected, would that be enough for them?' 23 Yahweh said to Moses, 'Is the arm of Yahweh so short? You shall see whether the promise I have made to you comes true or not.'

24 Moses went out and told the people what Yahweh had said. Then he collected seventy of the people's elders and stationed them round the Tent. 25 Yahweh descended in the cloud. He spoke to him and took some of the spirit that was on him and put it on the seventy elders. When the spirit came on them they prophesied — but only once.

26 Two men had stayed back in the camp; one was called Eldad and the other Medad. The spirit came down on them; though they had not gone to the Tent, their names were enrolled among the rest. These began to prophesy in the camp. 27 A young man ran to tell Moses this. 'Look,' he said, 'Eldad and Medad are prophesying in the camp.' 28 Joshua son of Nun, who had served Moses since he was a boy, spoke up and said, 'My lord Moses, stop them!' 29 Moses replied, 'Are you jealous on my account? If only

c 11 11:4seq. // Ex 16.

jealous for my sake? Would that all the LORD's people were prophets, and that the LORD would put his spirit on them!" 30 And Moses and the elders of Israel returned to the camp.

31 Then a wind went out from the LORD, and it brought quails from the sea and let them fall beside the camp, about a day's journey on this side and a day's journey on the other side, all around the camp, about two cubits deep on the ground. 32 So the people worked all that day and night and all the next day, gathering the quails; the least anyone gathered was ten homers; and they spread them out for themselves all around the camp. 33 But while the meat was still between their teeth, before it was consumed, the anger of the LORD was kindled against the people, and the LORD struck the people with a very great plague. 34 So that place was called Kibroth-hattaavah, *w* because there they buried the people who had the craving. 35 From Kibroth-hattaavah the people journeyed to Hazeroth.

12 While they were at Hazeroth, Miriam and Aaron spoke against Moses because of the Cushite woman whom he had married (for he had indeed married a Cushite woman); 2 and they said, "Has the LORD spoken only through Moses? Has he not spoken through us also?" And the LORD heard it. 3 Now the man Moses was very humble,*x* more so than anyone else on the face of the earth. 4 Suddenly the LORD said to Moses, Aaron, and Miriam, "Come out, you three, to the tent of meeting." So the three of them came out. 5 Then the LORD came down in a pillar of cloud, and stood at the entrance of the tent, and called Aaron and Miriam; and they both came forward. 6 And he said, "Hear my words:

When there are prophets among you,
    I the LORD make myself known to them in
        visions;
    I speak to them in dreams.
7 Not so with my servant Moses;
    he is entrusted with all my house.
8   With him I speak face to face — clearly, not in
        riddles;
    and he beholds the form of the LORD.

Why then were you not afraid to speak against my servant Moses?" 9 And the anger of the LORD was kindled against them, and he departed.

10 When the cloud went away from over the tent, Miriam had become leprous,*y* as white as snow. And Aaron turned towards Miriam and saw that she was leprous. 11 Then Aaron said to Moses, "Oh, my lord, do not punish us*z* for a sin that we have so foolishly committed. 12 Do not let her be like one stillborn, whose flesh is half consumed when it comes out of its mother's womb." 13 And Moses cried to the LORD, "O God, please heal her." 14 But the LORD said to Moses, "If her father had but spit in her face, would she not bear her shame for seven days? Let her be shut out of the camp for seven days, and after that she may be brought in again." 15 So Miriam was shut out of the camp for seven days; and the people did not set out on the march until Miriam had been brought in again. 16 After that the people set out from Hazeroth, and camped in the wilderness of Paran.

13 The LORD said to Moses, 2 "Send men to spy out the land of Canaan, which I am giving to the Israelites; from each of their ancestral tribes you shall send a man, every one a leader among them." 3 So Moses sent them from

account? I wish that all the LORD's people were prophets and that the LORD would bestow his spirit on them all!' 30 Moses then rejoined the camp with the elders of Israel.

31 There sprang up a wind from the LORD, which drove quails in from the west, and they were flying all round the camp for the distance of a day's journey, three feet above the ground. 32 The people were busy gathering quails all that day and night, and all next day, and even those who got least gathered ten homers of them. They spread them out to dry all about the camp. 33 But the meat was scarcely between their teeth, and they had not so much as bitten it, when the LORD's anger flared up against the people and he struck them with a severe plague. 34 That place came to be called Kibroth-hattaavah, because there they buried the people who had been greedy for meat.

35 From Kibroth-hattaavah the Israelites went on to Hazeroth, and while they were there, 1 Miriam and **12** Aaron began to find fault with Moses. They criticized him for his Cushite wife (for he had married a Cushite woman), 2–3 and they complained, 'Is Moses the only one by whom the LORD has spoken? Has he not spoken by us as well?' — though Moses was a man of great humility, the most humble man on earth. But the LORD heard them 4 and at once said to Moses, Aaron, and Miriam, 'Go out all three of you to the Tent of Meeting.' When they went out, 5 the LORD descended in a pillar of cloud and, standing at the entrance to the tent, he summoned Aaron and Miriam. The two of them came forward, 6 and the LORD said,

'Listen to my words.
    If he were your prophet and nothing more,
    I would make myself known to him in a vision,
    I would speak with him in a dream.
7 But my servant Moses is not such a prophet;
    of all my household he alone is faithful.
8 With him I speak face to face,
    openly and not in riddles.
    He sees the very form of the LORD.
    How dare you speak against my servant Moses?'

9 With his anger still hot against them, the LORD left them; 10 and as the cloud moved from the tent, there was Miriam, her skin diseased and white as snow. When Aaron, turning towards her, saw her skin diseased, 11 he said to Moses, 'My lord, do not make us pay the penalty of sin, foolish and wicked though we have been. 12 Let her not be like something stillborn, whose flesh is half eaten away when it comes from the womb.' 13 So Moses cried, 'LORD, not this! Heal her, I pray.' 14 The LORD answered, 'Suppose her father had spat in her face, would she not have to remain in disgrace for seven days? Let her be confined outside the camp for seven days and then be brought back.' 15 So Miriam was shut outside for seven days, and the people did not strike camp until she was brought back. 16 After that they moved on from Hazeroth and pitched camp in the wilderness of Paran.

13 THE LORD said to Moses, 2 'Send men out to explore Canaan, the land which I am going to give to the Israelites; from each ancestral tribe send one man, a man of high rank.' 3 So at the LORD's command Moses sent them

---

w That is *Graves of craving*   *x* Or *devout*   *y* A term for several skin diseases; precise meaning uncertain   *z* Heb *do not lay sin upon us*

11:31 **three feet:** *lit.* two cubits.   11:34 **Kibroth-hattaavah:** *that is the Graves of Greed.*   12:2–3 **by:** *or* with.   12:6 **If he were:** *prob. rdg; Heb.* If the LORD were.

that all the people of the LORD were prophets! Would that the LORD might bestow his spirit on them all!" 30 Then Moses retired to the camp, along with the elders of Israel.

31 There arose a wind sent by the LORD, that drove in quail from the sea and brought them down over the camp site at a height of two cubits from the ground for the distance of a day's journey all around the camp. 32 All that day, all night, and all the next day the people gathered in the quail. Even the one who got the least gathered ten homers of them. Then they spread them out all around the camp. 33 But while the meat was still between their teeth, before it could be consumed, the LORD's wrath flared up against the people, and he struck them with a very great plague. 34 So that place was named Kibroth-hattaavah, because it was there that the greedy people were buried.

35 From Kibroth-hattaavah the people set out for Hazeroth.

12 While they were in Hazeroth, 1 Miriam and Aaron spoke against Moses on the pretext of the marriage he had contracted with a Cushite woman. 2 They complained, "Is it through Moses alone that the LORD speaks? Does he not speak through us also?" And the LORD heard this. 3 Now, Moses himself was by far the meekest man on the face of the earth. 4 So at once the LORD said to Moses and Aaron and Miriam, "Come out, you three, to the meeting tent." And the three of them went. 5 Then the LORD came down in the column of cloud, and standing at the entrance of the tent, called Aaron and Miriam. When both came forward, 6 he said, "Now listen to the words of the LORD:

Should there be a prophet among you,
in visions will I reveal myself to him,
in dreams will I speak to him;
7 Not so with my servant Moses!
Throughout my house he bears my trust:
8 face to face I speak to him,
plainly and not in riddles.
The presence of the LORD he beholds.

Why, then, did you not fear to speak against my servant Moses?"

9 So angry was the Lord against them that when he departed, 10 and the cloud withdrew from the tent, there was Miriam, a snow-white leper! When Aaron turned and saw her a leper, 11 "Ah, my lord!" he said to Moses, "please do not charge us with the sin that we have foolishly committed! 12 Let her not thus be like the stillborn babe that comes forth from its mother's womb with its flesh half consumed." 13 Then Moses cried to the LORD, "Please, not this! Pray, heal her!" 14 But the LORD answered Moses, "Suppose her father had spit in her face, would she not hide in shame for seven days? Let her be confined outside the camp for seven days; only then may she be brought back." 15 So Miriam was confined outside the camp for seven days, and the people did not start out again until she was brought back. 16 After that the people set out from Hazeroth and encamped in the desert of Paran.

13 The LORD said to Moses, 2 "Send men to reconnoiter the land of Canaan, which I am giving the Israelites. You shall send one man from each ancestral tribe, all of them princes." 3 So Moses dispatched them

all Yahweh's people were prophets, and Yahweh had given them his spirit!" 30 Moses then went back to the camp with the elders of Israel.

31 A wind, sent by Yahweh, started blowing from the sea bringing quails which it deposited on the camp. They lay for a distance of a day's march either side of the camp, two cubits thick on the ground. 32 The people were up all that day and night and all the next day collecting quails: the least gathered by anyone was ten *homer*; then they spread them out round the camp. 33 The meat was still between their teeth, not even chewed, when Yahweh's anger was aroused by the people. Yahweh struck them with a very great plague.

34 The name given to this place was Kibroth-ha-Taavah, because it was there that they buried the people who had indulged their greed.

35 From Kibroth-ha-Taavah the people set out for Hazeroth, and at Hazeroth they pitched camp.

12 Miriam, and Aaron too, criticised Moses over the Cushite woman he had married. He had indeed married a Cushite woman. 2 They said, 'Is Moses the only one through whom Yahweh has spoken? Has he not spoken through us too?' Yahweh heard this. 3 Now Moses was extremely humble, the humblest man on earth.

4 Suddenly Yahweh said to Moses, Aaron and Miriam, 'Come out, all three of you, to the Tent of Meeting.' They went, all three of them, 5 and Yahweh descended in a pillar of cloud and stood at the entrance of the Tent. He called Aaron and Miriam and they both came forward. 6 Yahweh said:

Listen to my words!
if there is a prophet among you,
I reveal myself to him in a vision,
I speak to him in a dream.
7 Not so with my servant Moses;
to him my whole household is entrusted;
8 to him I speak face to face,
plainly and not in riddles,
and he sees Yahweh's form.

How, then, could you dare
to criticise my servant Moses?

9 Yahweh's anger was aroused by them. He went away, 10 and as soon as the cloud left the Tent, there was Miriam covered with a virulent skin-disease, white as snow! Aaron turned to look at her and saw that she had contracted a virulent skin-disease.

11 Aaron said to Moses:
'Oh, my Lord, please do not punish us for the sin we have been foolish enough to commit. 12 Do not let her be like some monster with its flesh half eaten away when it leaves its mother's womb!'

13 Moses pleaded with Yahweh. 'O God,' he said, 'I beg you, please heal her!'

14 Yahweh then said to Moses, 'If her father had done no more than spit in her face, would she not be unclean for seven days? Have her shut out of the camp for seven days, and then have her brought in again.'

15 Miriam was shut out of the camp for seven days. The people did not set out until she returned. 16 Then the people moved on from Hazeroth and pitched camp in the desert of Paran.

13 d Yahweh spoke to Moses and said, 2 'Send out men, one from each tribe, to reconnoitre the land of Canaan which I am giving the Israelites. Each of them is to be a leading man of the tribe.'

d **13** 13:1seq. // Dt 1:20–29.

the wilderness of Paran, according to the command of the LORD, all of them leading men among the Israelites. 4 These were their names: From the tribe of Reuben, Shammua son of Zaccur; 5 from the tribe of Simeon, Shaphat son of Hori; 6 from the tribe of Judah, Caleb son of Jephunneh; 7 from the tribe of Issachar, Igal son of Joseph; 8 from the tribe of Ephraim, Hoshea son of Nun; 9 from the tribe of Benjamin, Palti son of Raphu; 10 from the tribe of Zebulun, Gaddiel son of Sodi; 11 from the tribe of Joseph (that is, from the tribe of Manasseh), Gaddi son of Susi; 12 from the tribe of Dan, Ammiel son of Gemalli; 13 from the tribe of Asher, Sethur son of Michael; 14 from the tribe of Naphtali, Nahbi son of Vophsi; 15 from the tribe of Gad, Geuel son of Machi. 16 These were the names of the men whom Moses sent to spy out the land. And Moses changed the name of Hoshea son of Nun to Joshua.

17 Moses sent them to spy out the land of Canaan, and said to them, "Go up there into the Negeb, and go up into the hill country, 18 and see what the land is like, and whether the people who live in it are strong or weak, whether they are few or many, 19 and whether the land they live in is good or bad, and whether the towns that they live in are unwalled or fortified, 20 and whether the land is rich or poor, and whether there are trees in it or not. Be bold, and bring some of the fruit of the land." Now it was the season of the first ripe grapes.

21 So they went up and spied out the land from the wilderness of Zin to Rehob, near Lebo-hamath. 22 They went up into the Negeb, and came to Hebron; and Ahiman, Sheshai, and Talmai, the Anakites, were there. (Hebron was built seven years before Zoan in Egypt.) 23 And they came to the Wadi Eshcol, and cut down from there a branch with a single cluster of grapes, and they carried it on a pole between two of them. They also brought some pomegranates and figs. 24 That place was called the Wadi Eshcol,ᵃ because of the cluster that the Israelites cut down from there.

25 At the end of forty days they returned from spying out the land. 26 And they came to Moses and Aaron and to all the congregation of the Israelites in the wilderness of Paran, at Kadesh; they brought back word to them and to all the congregation, and showed them the fruit of the land. 27 And they told him, "We came to the land to which you sent us; it flows with milk and honey, and this is its fruit. 28 Yet the people who live in the land are strong, and the towns are fortified and very large; and besides, we saw the descendants of Anak there. 29 The Amalekites live in the land of the Negeb; the Hittites, the Jebusites, and the Amorites live in the hill country; and the Canaanites live by the sea, and along the Jordan."

30 But Caleb quieted the people before Moses, and said, "Let us go up at once and occupy it, for we are well able to overcome it." 31 Then the men who had gone up with him said, "We are not able to go up against this people, for they are stronger than we." 32 So they brought to the Israelites an unfavorable report of the land that they had spied out, saying, "The land that we have gone through as spies is a land that devours its inhabitants; and all the people that we saw in it are of great size. 33 There we saw the Nephilim (the Anakites come from the Nephilim); and to ourselves we seemed like grasshoppers, and so we seemed to them."

14 Then all the congregation raised a loud cry, and the people wept that night. 2 And all the Israelites com-

out from the wilderness of Paran, all of them leading men among the Israelites. 4 These were their names:

from the tribe of Reuben, Shammua son of Zaccur;
5 from the tribe of Simeon, Shaphat son of Hori;
6 from the tribe of Judah, Caleb son of Jephunneh;
7 from the tribe of Issachar, Igal son of Joseph;
8 from the tribe of Ephraim, Hoshea son of Nun;
9 from the tribe of Benjamin, Palti son of Raphu;
10 from the tribe of Zebulun, Gaddiel son of Sodi;
11 from the tribe of Joseph (that is from the tribe of Manasseh), Gaddi son of Susi;
12 from the tribe of Dan, Ammiel son of Gemalli;
13 from the tribe of Asher, Sethur son of Michael;
14 from the tribe of Naphtali, Nahbi son of Vophsi;
15 from the tribe of Gad, Geuel son of Machi.

16 Those are the names of the men whom Moses sent to explore the land. But Moses named the son of Nun Joshua, instead of Hoshea.

17 When Moses sent them to explore Canaan, he said, 'Make your way up by the Negeb, up into the hill-country, 18 and see what the land is like, and whether the people who live there are strong or weak, few or many. 19 See whether the country in which they live is easy or difficult, and whether their towns are open or fortified. 20 Is the land fertile or barren, and is it wooded or not? Go boldly in and bring some of its fruit.' It was the season when the first grapes were ripe.

21 They went up and explored the country from the wilderness of Zin as far as Rehob by Lebo-hamath. 22 Going up by the Negeb they came to Hebron, where Ahiman, Sheshai, and Talmai, the descendants of Anak, were living. (Hebron was built seven years before Zoan in Egypt.) 23 They came to the wadi Eshcol, and there they cut a branch with a single bunch of grapes, which they carried on a pole between two of them; they also picked pomegranates and figs. 24 That place was named the wadi Eshcol from the bunch of grapes the Israelites cut there.

25 After forty days they returned from exploring the country 26 and, coming back to Moses and Aaron and the whole community of Israelites at Kadesh in the wilderness of Paran, they made their report, and showed them the fruit of the country. 27 They gave Moses this account: 'We made our way into the land to which you sent us. It is flowing with milk and honey, and here is the fruit it grows; 28 but its inhabitants are formidable, and the towns are fortified and very large; indeed, we saw there the descendants of Anak. 29 We also saw the Amalekites who live in the Negeb, Hittites, Jebusites, and Amorites who live in the hill-country, and the Canaanites who live by the sea and along the Jordan.'

30 Caleb silenced the people for Moses. 'Let us go up at once and occupy the country,' he said; 'we are well able to conquer it.' 31 But the men who had gone with him said, 'No, we cannot attack these people; they are too strong for us.' 32 Their report to the Israelites about the land which they had explored was discouraging: 'The country we explored', they said, 'will swallow up any who go to live in it. All the people we saw there are men of gigantic stature. 33 When we set eyes on the Nephilim (the sons of Anak belong to the Nephilim) we felt no bigger than grasshoppers; and that is how we must have been in their eyes.'

14 At this the whole Israelite community cried out in dismay and the people wept all night long. 2 Every-

13:19 **are . . . fortified:** *prob. rdg; cp. Samar. MSS; Heb.* are in camps or in walled towns.   13:22 **descendants of Anak:** *or* tall men.   13:23 **Eshcol:** *that is* Bunch of Grapes.   13:29 **Hittites:** *or, with Samar.,* Hivites.   13:33 **Nephilim:** *or* giants. **sons of Anak:** *or* tall men.

ᵃ That is *Cluster*

from the desert of Paran, as the Lord had ordered. All of them were leaders among the Israelites; 4by name they were:

Shammua, son of Zaccur, of the tribe of Reuben;
5Shaphat, son of Hori, of the tribe of Simeon;
6Caleb, son of Jephunneh, of the tribe of Judah;
7Igal [son of Joseph] of the tribe of Issachar;
10Gaddiel, son of Sodi, of the tribe of Zebulun;
11Gaddi, son of Susi, of the tribe of Manasseh, for
    the Josephites, with
8Hoshea, son of Nun, of the tribe of Ephraim;
9Palti, son of Raphu, of the tribe of Benjamin;
12Ammiel, son of Gemalli, of the tribe of Dan;
13Sethur, son of Michael, of the tribe of Asher;
14Nahbi, son of Vophsi, of the tribe of Naphtali;
15Geuel, son of Machi, of the tribe of Gad.

16These are the names of the men whom Moses sent out to reconnoiter the land. But Hoshea, son of Nun, Moses called Joshua.

17In sending them to reconnoiter the land of Canaan, Moses said to them, "Go up here in the Negeb, up into the highlands, 18and see what kind of land it is. Are the people living there strong or weak, few or many? 19Is the country in which they live good or bad? Are the towns in which they dwell open or fortified? 20Is the soil fertile or barren, wooded or clear? And do your best to get some of the fruit of the land." It was then the season for early grapes.

21So they went up and reconnoitered the land from the desert of Zin as far as where Rehob adjoins Labo of Hamath. 22Going up by way of the Negeb, they reached Hebron, where Ahiman, Sheshai and Talmai, descendants of the Anakim, were living. [Hebron had been built seven years before Zoan in Egypt.] 23They also reached the Wadi Eshcol, where they cut down a branch with a single cluster of grapes on it, which two of them carried on a pole, as well as some pomegranates and figs. 24It was because of the cluster the Israelites cut there that they called the place Wadi Eshcol.

25After reconnoitering the land for forty days they returned, 26met Moses and Aaron and the whole community of the Israelites in the desert of Paran at Kadesh, made a report to them all, and showed them the fruit of the country. 27They told Moses: "We went into the land to which you sent us. It does indeed flow with milk and honey, and here is its fruit. 28However, the people who are living in the land are fierce, and the towns are fortified and very strong. Besides, we saw descendants of the Anakim there. 29Amalekites live in the region of the Negeb; Hittites, Jebusites and Amorites dwell in the highlands, and Canaanites along the seacoast and the banks of the Jordan."

30Caleb, however, to quiet the people toward Moses, said, "We ought to go up and seize the land, for we can certainly do so." 31But the men who had gone up with him said, "We cannot attack these people; they are too strong for us." 32So they spread discouraging reports among the Israelites about the land they had scouted, saying, "The land that we explored is a country that consumes its inhabitants. And all the people we saw there are huge men, 33veritable giants [the Anakim were a race of giants]; we felt like mere grasshoppers, and so we must have seemed to them."

14 At this, the whole community broke out with loud cries, and even in the night the people wailed. 2All

3At Yahweh's order, Moses sent them from the desert of Paran. All of them were leading men of Israel. 4These were their names:

For the tribe of Reuben, Shammua son of Zaccur:
5for the tribe of Simeon, Shaphat son of Hori;
6for the tribe of Judah, Caleb son of Jephunneh;
7for the tribe of Issachar, Igal son of Joseph;
8for the tribe of Ephraim, Hoshea son of Nun;
9for the tribe of Benjamin, Palti son of Raphu;
10for the tribe of Zebulun, Gaddiel son of Sodi;
11for the tribe of Joseph, for the tribe of Manasseh, Gaddi son of Susi;
12for the tribe of Dan, Ammiel son of Gemalli;
13for the tribe of Asher, Sethur son of Michael;
14for the tribe of Naphtali, Nahbi son of Vophsi;
15for the tribe of Gad, Geuel son of Machi.

16Such were the names of the men whom Moses sent to reconnoitre the country. Moses then gave Hoshea son of Nun the name Joshua.

17Moses sent them to reconnoitre the land of Canaan, 'Go up into the Negeb,' he said, 'then go up into the highlands. 18See what sort of country it is, and what sort of people the inhabitants are, whether they are strong or weak, few or many, 19what sort of land they live on, whether it is good or poor; what sort of towns they live in, whether they are open or fortified; 20what sort of land it is, fertile or barren, wooded or open. Be bold, and bring back some of the country's produce.'

It was the season for early grapes. 21They went up and reconnoitred the country from the desert of Zin to Rehob, the Pass of Hamath. 22They went up by way of the Negeb as far as Hebron, where Ahiman, Sheshai and Talmai, the Anakim, lived. (Hebron was founded seven years before Tanis in Egypt.) 23Reaching the Vale of Eshcol, there they lopped off a vine branch with a cluster of grapes, which two of them carried away on a pole, as well as pomegranates and figs. 24This place was called the Vale of Eshcol after the cluster which the Israelites cut there.

25After forty days they returned from reconnoitring the country. 26Making their way to Moses, Aaron and the whole community of Israel, in the desert of Paran, at Kadesh, they made their report to them and the whole community, and displayed the country's produce.

27This was the report they gave: 'We made our way into the country where you sent us. It does indeed flow with milk and honey; here is what it produces. 28At the same time, its inhabitants are a powerful people; the towns are fortified and very big; yes, and we saw the Anakim there. 29The Amalekites occupy the Negeb area, the Hittites, Jebusites and Amorites the highlands, and the Canaanites the sea coast and the banks of the Jordan.'

30Caleb called the people round Moses to silence and then said, 'We must march in immediately and take it; we are certainly able to conquer it.' 31But the men who had been with him said, 'We cannot attack these people; they are stronger than we are.' 32And they began disparaging to the Israelites the country they had reconnoitred, saying, 'The country we have been to reconnoitre is a country that devours its inhabitants. All the people we saw there were of enormous size. 33We saw giants there too (the Anakim, descended from the Giants). We felt like grasshoppers, and so we seemed to them.'

14 eThe whole community then cried out in dismay, and the people wept all that night. 2All the Israel-

---

e14 14:1seq. // Dt 1:26–32.

plained against Moses and Aaron; the whole congregation said to them, "Would that we had died in the land of Egypt! Or would that we had died in this wilderness! 3 Why is the LORD bringing us into this land to fall by the sword? Our wives and our little ones will become booty; would it not be better for us to go back to Egypt?" 4 So they said to one another, "Let us choose a captain, and go back to Egypt."

5 Then Moses and Aaron fell on their faces before all the assembly of the congregation of the Israelites. 6 And Joshua son of Nun and Caleb son of Jephunneh, who were among those who had spied out the land, tore their clothes 7 and said to all the congregation of the Israelites, "The land that we went through as spies is an exceedingly good land. 8 If the LORD is pleased with us, he will bring us into this land and give it to us, a land that flows with milk and honey. 9 Only, do not rebel against the LORD; and do not fear the people of the land, for they are no more than bread for us; their protection is removed from them, and the LORD is with us; do not fear them." 10 But the whole congregation threatened to stone them.

Then the glory of the LORD appeared at the tent of meeting to all the Israelites. 11 And the LORD said to Moses, "How long will this people despise me? And how long will they refuse to believe in me, in spite of all the signs that I have done among them? 12 I will strike them with pestilence and disinherit them, and I will make of you a nation greater and mightier than they."

13 But Moses said to the LORD, "Then the Egyptians will hear of it, for in your might you brought up this people from among them, 14 and they will tell the inhabitants of this land. They have heard that you, O LORD, are in the midst of this people; for you, O LORD, are seen face to face, and your cloud stands over them and you go in front of them, in a pillar of cloud by day and in a pillar of fire by night. 15 Now if you kill this people all at one time, then the nations who have heard about you will say, 16 'It is because the LORD was not able to bring this people into the land he swore to give them that he has slaughtered them in the wilderness.' 17 And now, therefore, let the power of the LORD be great in the way that you promised when you spoke, saying,

18 'The LORD is slow to anger,
   and abounding in steadfast love,
   forgiving iniquity and transgression,
   but by no means clearing the guilty,
   visiting the iniquity of the parents
   upon the children
   to the third and the fourth generation.'

19 Forgive the iniquity of this people according to the greatness of your steadfast love, just as you have pardoned this people, from Egypt even until now."

20 Then the LORD said, "I do forgive, just as you have asked; 21 nevertheless — as I live, and as all the earth shall be filled with the glory of the LORD — 22 none of the people who have seen my glory and the signs that I did in Egypt and in the wilderness, and yet have tested me these ten times and have not obeyed my voice, 23 shall see the land that I swore to give to their ancestors; none of those who despised me shall see it. 24 But my servant Caleb, because he has a different spirit and has followed me wholeheartedly, I will bring into the land into which he went, and his descendants shall possess it. 25 Now, since the Amalekites and the Canaanites live in the valleys, turn tomorrow and set out for the wilderness by the way to the Red Sea."[b]

26 And the LORD spoke to Moses and to Aaron, saying: 27 How long shall this wicked congregation complain against me? I have heard the complaints of the Israelites, which they complain against me. 28 Say to them, "As I

[b] Or Sea of Reeds

one complained against Moses and Aaron: 'If only we had died in Egypt or in the wilderness!' they said. 3 'Why should the LORD bring us to this land, to die in battle and leave our wives and our dependants to become the spoils of war? It would be better for us to go back to Egypt.' 4 And they spoke of choosing someone to lead them back there.

5 Then Moses and Aaron flung themselves on the ground before the assembled community of the Israelites, 6 and two of those who had explored the land, Joshua son of Nun and Caleb son of Jephunneh, tore their clothes, 7 and encouraged the whole community: 'The country we travelled through and explored', they said, 'is a very good land indeed. 8 If the LORD is pleased with us, he will bring us into this land, a land flowing with milk and honey, and give it to us. 9 But you must not act in defiance of the LORD. You need not fear the people of the country, for we shall devour them. They have lost the protection that they had: the LORD is with us. You have nothing to fear from them.' 10 As the whole assembly threatened to stone them, the glory of the LORD appeared in the Tent of Meeting to all the Israelites.

11 The LORD said to Moses, 'How much longer will this people set me at naught? How much longer will they refuse to trust me in spite of all the signs I have shown among them? 12 I shall strike them with pestilence. I shall deny them their heritage, and you and your descendants I shall make into a nation greater and more numerous than they.'

13 But Moses answered the LORD, 'What if the Egyptians hear of it? You brought this people out of Egypt by your might. 14 What if they tell the inhabitants of this land? They too have heard of you, LORD, that you are with this people and are seen face to face, that your cloud stays over them, and that you go before them in a pillar of cloud by day and in a pillar of fire by night. 15 If then you do put them all to death at one blow, the nations who have heard these reports about you will say, 16 "The LORD could not bring this people into the land which he promised them by oath; and so he destroyed them in the wilderness."

17 'Now let the LORD's might be shown in its greatness, true to your proclamation of yourself — 18 "The LORD, long-suffering, ever faithful, who forgives iniquity and rebellion, and punishes children to the third and fourth generation for the iniquity of their fathers, though he does not sweep them clean away." 19 You have borne with this people from Egypt all the way here; forgive their iniquity, I beseech you, as befits your great and constant love.'

20 The LORD said, 'Your prayer is answered, and I pardon them. 21 But as I live, and as the glory of the LORD fills the whole earth, 22–23 not one of all those who have seen my glory and the signs which I wrought in Egypt and in the wilderness shall see the country which I promised on oath to their fathers. Ten times they have challenged me and not obeyed my voice. None of those who have set me at naught shall see this land. 24–25 But my servant Caleb showed a different spirit and remained loyal to me. Because of this, I shall bring him into the land in which he has already set foot, the territory of the Amalekites and the Canaanites who dwell in the Vale, and I shall put his descendants in possession of it. Tomorrow you must turn back and set out for the wilderness by way of the Red Sea.'

26 The LORD said to Moses and Aaron, 27 'How long must I tolerate the complaints of this wicked community? I have heard the Israelites making complaints against me. 28 Tell

14:24–25 **Red Sea:** or sea of Reeds.   14:27 **must I tolerate:** prob. rdg; Heb. for.

the Israelites grumbled against Moses and Aaron, the whole community saying to them, "Would that we had died in the land of Egypt, or that here in the desert we were dead! ³ Why is the LORD bringing us into this land only to have us fall by the sword? Our wives and little ones will be taken as booty. Would it not be better for us to return to Egypt?" ⁴ So they said to one another, "Let us appoint a leader and go back to Egypt."

⁵ But Moses and Aaron fell prostrate before the whole assembled community of the Israelites; ⁶ while Joshua, son of Nun, and Caleb, son of Jephunneh; who had been in the party that scouted the land, tore their garments ⁷ and said to the whole community of the Israelites, "The country which we went through and explored is a fine, rich land. ⁸ If the LORD is pleased with us, he will bring us in and give us that land, a land flowing with milk and honey. ⁹ But do not rebel against the LORD! You need not be afraid of the people of that land; they are but food for us! Their defense has left them, but the LORD is with us. Therefore, do not be afraid of them." ¹⁰ In answer, the whole community threatened to stone them.

But then the glory of the LORD appeared at the meeting tent to all the Israelites. ¹¹ And the LORD said to Moses, "How long will this people spurn me? How long will they refuse to believe in me, despite all the signs I have performed among them? ¹² I will strike them with pestilence and wipe them out. Then I will make of you a nation greater and mightier than they."

¹³ But Moses said to the LORD: "Are the Egyptians to hear of this? For by your power you brought out this people from among them. ¹⁴ And are they to tell of it to the inhabitants of this land? It has been heard that you, O LORD, are in the midst of this people; you, LORD, who plainly reveal yourself! Your cloud stands over them, and you go before them by day in a column of cloud and by night in a column of fire. ¹⁵ If now you slay this whole people, the nations who have heard such reports of you will say, ¹⁶ 'The LORD was not able to bring this people into the land he swore to give them; that is why he slaughtered them in the desert.' ¹⁷ Now then, let the power of my Lord be displayed in its greatness, even as you have said, ¹⁸ 'The LORD is slow to anger and rich in kindness, forgiving wickedness and crime; yet not declaring the guilty guiltless, but punishing children to the third and fourth generation for their fathers' wickedness.' ¹⁹ Pardon, then, the wickedness of this people in keeping with your great kindness, even as you have forgiven them from Egypt until now."

²⁰ The LORD answered: "I pardon them as you have asked. ²¹ Yet, by my life and the LORD's glory that fills the whole earth, ²² of all the men who have seen my glory and the signs I worked in Egypt and in the desert, and who nevertheless have put me to the test ten times already and have failed to heed my voice, ²³ not one shall see the land which I promised on oath to their fathers. None of these who have spurned me shall see it. ²⁴ But because my servant Caleb has a different spirit and follows me unreservedly, I will bring him into the land where he has just been, and his descendants shall possess it. ²⁵ But now, since the Amalekites and Canaanites are living in the valleys, turn away tomorrow and set out in the desert on the Red Sea road."

²⁶ The LORD also said to Moses and Aaron: ²⁷ "How long will this wicked community grumble against me? I have heard the grumblings of the Israelites against me. ²⁸ Tell

ites muttered at Moses and Aaron, and the whole community said to them, 'Would to God we had died in Egypt, or even that we had died in this desert! ³ Why has Yahweh brought us to this country, for us to perish by the sword and our wives and children to be seized as booty? Should we not do better to go back to Egypt?' ⁴ And they said to one another, 'Let us appoint a leader and go back to Egypt.'

⁵ At this, Moses and Aaron threw themselves on their faces in front of the whole assembled community of Israelites, ⁶ while Joshua son of Nun and Caleb son of Jephunneh, two of the men who had reconnoitred the country, tore their clothes ⁷ and addressed the whole community of Israelites as follows, 'The country we went to reconnoitre is a good country, an excellent country. ⁸ If Yahweh is pleased with us, he will lead us into this country and give it to us. It is a country flowing with milk and honey. ⁹ But do not rebel against Yahweh or be afraid of the people of the country, for we shall gobble them up. Their protecting shade has deserted them, while we have Yahweh on our side. Do not be afraid of them.'

¹⁰ ᶠ The whole community was talking of stoning them, when the glory of Yahweh appeared to all the Israelites, inside the Tent of Meeting, ¹¹ and Yahweh said to Moses:

'How much longer will these people treat me with contempt? How much longer will they refuse to trust me, in spite of all the signs I have displayed among them? ¹² I shall strike them with pestilence and disown them. And of you I shall make a new nation, greater and mightier than they are.'

¹³ Moses said to Yahweh:

'Suppose the Egyptians hear about this—for by your power you brought these people out of their country— ¹⁴ and tell the people living in this country. They have heard that you, Yahweh, are with this people, and that you, Yahweh, show yourself to them face to face; that your cloud stands over them and that you go before them in a pillar of cloud by day and a pillar of fire by night. ¹⁵ If you kill this people now as though it were one man, then the nations who have heard about you will say, ¹⁶ "Yahweh was not able to bring this people into the country which he had sworn to give them, and so he has slaughtered them in the desert." ¹⁷ No, my Lord! Now is the time to assert your power as you promised when you said, earlier, ¹⁸ "Yahweh, slow to anger and rich in faithful love, forgiving faults and transgressions, and yet letting nothing go unchecked, punishing the parents' guilt in the children to the third and fourth generation." ¹⁹ In your most faithful love, please forgive this people's guilt, as you have done from Egypt until now.'

²⁰ ᵍ Yahweh said, 'I forgive them as you ask. ²¹ But—as I live, and as the glory of Yahweh fills the whole world— ²² of all these people who have seen my glory and the signs that I worked in Egypt and in the desert, who have put me to the test ten times already and not obeyed my voice, ²³ not one shall see the country which I promised to give their ancestors. Not one of those who have treated me contemptuously will see it. ²⁴ However, since my servant Caleb is of another spirit and since he has obeyed me completely, I shall bring him into the country where he has been, and his descendants will own it ²⁵ (the Amalekites and Canaanites occupy the plain). Tomorrow you will turn about and go back into the desert, in the direction of the Sea of Suph.'

²⁶ Yahweh then spoke to Moses and Aaron and said:

²⁷ 'How much longer am I to endure this perverse community muttering against me? I have heard what the Israelites mutter against me. ²⁸ Say to them, "As I live, Yahweh

ᶠ14 14:10seq. // Ex 32:7–14; 34:6–7.   ᵍ14 14:20seq. // Dt 1:34–40.

309

live," says the LORD, "I will do to you the very things I heard you say: 29 your dead bodies shall fall in this very wilderness; and of all your number, included in the census, from twenty years old and upward, who have complained against me, 30 not one of you shall come into the land in which I swore to settle you, except Caleb son of Jephunneh and Joshua son of Nun. 31 But your little ones, who you said would become booty, I will bring in, and they shall know the land that you have despised. 32 But as for you, your dead bodies shall fall in this wilderness. 33 And your children shall be shepherds in the wilderness for forty years, and shall suffer for your faithlessness, until the last of your dead bodies lies in the wilderness. 34 According to the number of the days in which you spied out the land, forty days, for every day a year, you shall bear your iniquity, forty years, and you shall know my displeasure." 35 I the LORD have spoken; surely I will do thus to all this wicked congregation gathered together against me: in this wilderness they shall come to a full end, and there they shall die.

36 And the men whom Moses sent to spy out the land, who returned and made all the congregation complain against him by bringing a bad report about the land — 37 the men who brought an unfavorable report about the land died by a plague before the LORD. 38 But Joshua son of Nun and Caleb son of Jephunneh alone remained alive, of those men who went to spy out the land.

39 When Moses told these words to all the Israelites, the people mourned greatly. 40 They rose early in the morning and went up to the heights of the hill country, saying, "Here we are. We will go up to the place that the LORD has promised, for we have sinned." 41 But Moses said, "Why do you continue to transgress the command of the LORD? That will not succeed. 42 Do not go up, for the LORD is not with you; do not let yourselves be struck down before your enemies. 43 For the Amalekites and the Canaanites will confront you there, and you shall fall by the sword; because you have turned back from following the LORD, the LORD will not be with you." 44 But they presumed to go up to the heights of the hill country, even though the ark of the covenant of the LORD, and Moses, had not left the camp. 45 Then the Amalekites and the Canaanites who lived in that hill country came down and defeated them, pursuing them as far as Hormah.

15 The LORD spoke to Moses, saying: 2 Speak to the Israelites and say to them: When you come into the land you are to inhabit, which I am giving you, 3 and you make an offering by fire to the LORD from the herd or from the flock — whether a burnt offering or a sacrifice, to fulfill a vow or as a freewill offering or at your appointed festivals — to make a pleasing odor for the LORD, 4 then whoever presents such an offering to the LORD shall present also a grain offering, one-tenth of an ephah of choice flour, mixed with one-fourth of a hin of oil. 5 Moreover, you shall offer one-fourth of a hin of wine as a drink offering with the burnt offering or the sacrifice, for each lamb. 6 For a ram, you shall offer a grain offering, two-tenths of an ephah of choice flour mixed with one-third of a hin of oil; 7 and as a drink offering you shall offer one-third of a hin of wine, a pleasing odor to the LORD. 8 When you offer a bull as a burnt offering or a sacrifice, to fulfill a vow or as an offering of well-being to the LORD, 9 then you shall present with the bull a grain offering, three-tenths of an ephah of choice flour, mixed with half a hin of oil, 10 and you shall present as a drink offering half a hin of wine, as an offering by fire, a pleasing odor to the LORD.

11 Thus it shall be done for each ox or ram, or for each of the male lambs or the kids. 12 According to the number that you offer, so you shall do with each and every one.

them that this is the word of the LORD: As I live, I shall do to you the very things I have heard you say. 29 Here in this wilderness your bones will lie, every one of you on the register aged twenty or more, because you have made these complaints against me. 30 Not one of you will enter the land which I swore with uplifted hand should be your own, except only Caleb son of Jephunneh and Joshua son of Nun. 31 Your dependants, who, you said, would become the spoils of war, those dependants I shall bring into the land you have rejected, and they will enjoy it. 32 But as for the rest of you, your bones will lie in this wilderness; 33 your children will be wanderers in the wilderness forty years, paying the penalty of your wanton faithlessness till the last one of you dies there. 34 Forty days you spent exploring the country, and forty years, a year for each day, you will spend paying the penalty of your iniquities. You will know what it means to have me against you. 35 I, the LORD, have spoken. This I swear to do to all this wicked community who have combined against me. There will be an end of them here in this wilderness; here they will die.'

36 The men whom Moses had sent to explore the land, and who came back and by their report set all the community complaining against him, 37 died of a plague before the LORD; they died of plague because they had made a bad report. 38 Of those who went to explore the land, Joshua son of Nun and Caleb son of Jephunneh alone survived.

39 When Moses reported the LORD's words to all the Israelites, there was great lamentation. 40 Early next morning they set out and made for the heights of the hill-country, saying, 'Look, we are on our way up to the place the LORD spoke of. We admit that we have been wrong.' 41 But Moses replied, 'Must you persist in disobeying the LORD's command? No good will come of this. 42 Go no farther; you will not have the LORD with you, and your enemies will defeat you. 43 For in front of you are the Amalekites and Canaanites, and you will fall by the sword, because you have ceased to follow the LORD, and he will no longer be with you.' 44 But they went on recklessly towards the heights of the hill-country, though neither the Ark of the Covenant of the LORD nor Moses moved from the camp; 45 and the Amalekites and Canaanites who lived in those hills came down to the attack and inflicted a crushing defeat on them at Hormah.

15 THE LORD told Moses 2 to say to the Israelites: 'When you enter the land which I am giving you to live in, 3 make food-offerings to the LORD; they may be whole-offerings or any sacrifice made in fulfilment of a special vow or by way of freewill-offering or at one of the appointed seasons. When you thus make an offering of soothing odour from herd or flock to the LORD, 4 whoever presents the offering should add a grain-offering consisting of a tenth of an ephah of flour mixed with a quarter of a hin of oil. 5 Add to the whole-offering or shared-offering a quarter of a hin of wine as a drink-offering with each lamb sacrificed.

6 'If the animal is a ram, the grain-offering should consist of two tenths of an ephah of flour mixed with a third of a hin of oil, 7 and the wine for the drink-offering a third of a hin; in this way you will make an offering of soothing odour to the LORD.

8 'When you offer to the LORD a young bull, whether as a whole-offering or as a sacrifice to fulfil a special vow, or as a shared-offering, 9 add a grain-offering of three tenths of an ephah of flour mixed with half a hin of oil, 10 and for the drink-offering, half a hin of wine; the whole will thus be a food-offering of soothing odour to the LORD. 11 This is what must be done in each case, for every bull or ram, lamb or kid, 12 whatever the number of each that you offer. 13 Every

14:34 **to have . . . you:** *or* to thwart me.

them: By my life, says the LORD, I will do to you just what I have heard you say. 29 Here in the desert shall your dead bodies fall. Of all your men of twenty years or more, registered in the census, who grumbled against me, 30 not one shall enter the land where I solemnly swore to settle you, except Caleb, son of Jephunneh, and Joshua, son of Nun. 31 Your little ones, however, who you said would be taken as booty, I will bring in, and they shall appreciate the land you spurned. 32 But as for you, your bodies shall fall here in the desert, 33 here where your children must wander for forty years, suffering for your faithlessness, till the last of you lies dead in the desert. 34 Forty days you spent in scouting the land; forty years shall you suffer for your crimes: one year for each day. Thus you will realize what it means to oppose me. 35 I, the LORD, have sworn to do this to all this wicked community that conspired against me: here in the desert they shall die to the last man."

36 And so it happened to the men whom Moses had sent to reconnoiter the land and who on returning had set the whole community grumbling against him by spreading discouraging reports about the land; 37 these men who had given out the bad report about the land were struck down by the LORD and died. 38 Of all the men who had gone to reconnoiter the land, only Joshua, son of Nun, and Caleb, son of Jephunneh, survived.

39 When Moses repeated these words to all the Israelites, the people felt great remorse. 40 Early the next morning they started up into the foothills, saying, "Here we are, ready to go up to the place that the LORD spoke of: for we were indeed doing wrong." 41 But Moses said, "Why are you again disobeying the LORD's orders? This cannot succeed. 42 Do not go up, because the LORD is not in your midst; if you go, you will be beaten down before your enemies. 43 For there the Amalekites and Canaanites face you, and you will fall by the sword. You have turned back from following the LORD; therefore the LORD will not be with you."

44 Yet they dared to go up into the foothills, even though neither the ark of the covenant of the LORD nor Moses left the camp. 45 And the Amalekites and Canaanites who dwelt in that hill country came down and defeated them, beating them back as far as Hormah.

15 The LORD said to Moses, 2 "Give the Israelites these instructions: When you have entered the land that I will give you for your homesteads, 3 if you make to the LORD a sweet-smelling oblation from the herd or from the flock, in holocaust, in fulfillment of a vow, or as a freewill offering, or for one of your festivals, 4 whoever does so shall also present to the LORD a cereal offering consisting of a tenth of an ephah of fine flour mixed with a fourth of a hin of oil, 5 as well as a libation of a fourth of a hin of wine, with each lamb sacrificed in holocaust or otherwise. 6 With each sacrifice of a ram you shall present a cereal offering of two tenths of an ephah of fine flour mixed with a third of a hin of oil, 7 and a libation of a third of a hin of wine, thus making a sweet-smelling offering to the LORD. 8 When you sacrifice an ox as a holocaust, or in fulfillment of a vow, or as a peace offering to the LORD, 9 with it you shall present a cereal offering of three tenths of an ephah of fine flour mixed with half a hin of oil, 10 and a libation of half a hin of wine, as a sweet-smelling oblation to the LORD. 11 The same is to be done for each ox, ram, lamb or goat. 12 Whatever the number you offer, do the same for each of them.

declares, I shall do to you what I have heard you saying. 29 In this desert your dead bodies will fall, all you who were counted in the census, from the age of twenty years and over who have muttered against me. 30 I swear none of you will enter the country where I swore most solemnly to settle you, except Caleb son of Jephunneh, and Joshua son of Nun. 31 Your children, who you said would be seized as booty, will be the ones whom I shall bring in so that they get to know the country you disdained, 32 but, as for you, your dead bodies will fall in this desert 33 and your children will be nomads in the desert for forty years, bearing the consequences of your faithlessness, until the last one of you lies dead in the desert. 34 For forty days you reconnoitred the country. Each day will count as a year: for forty years you will bear the consequences of your guilt and learn what it means to reject me." 35 I, Yahweh, have spoken: this is how I swear to treat this entire perverse community united against me. In this desert, to the last man, they shall die.'

36 The men whom Moses had sent to reconnoitre the country and who on their return had incited the whole community of Israel to mutter about him by disparaging it, 37 these men who had disparaged the country were all struck dead before Yahweh. 38 Of the men who had gone to reconnoitre the country, only Joshua son of Nun and Caleb son of Jephunneh were left alive.

39 When Moses told all the Israelites what had been said, the people set up a great outcry. 40 Early next morning they set out for the heights of the hill country saying, 'Look, we will set out for the place about which Yahweh said that we have sinned.' 41 To which, Moses said, 'Why disobey Yahweh's order? No success will come of doing so. 42 Do not go, for Yahweh is not among you, and you will be defeated by your enemies. 43 For the Amalekites and the Canaanites are ahead of you, and you will be put to the sword, since you have turned away from Yahweh, and Yahweh is not with you.' 44 All the same, they presumptuously set off for the heights of the hill country. Neither the ark of the covenant of Yahweh nor Moses left the camp. 45 The Amalekites and Canaanites living in those highlands then came down, defeated them and harried them all the way to Hormah.

15 Yahweh spoke to Moses and said, 2 'Speak to the Israelites and say:

"When you have arrived in the country where you are to live and which I am giving to you, 3 and you burn food as an offering to Yahweh either as a burnt offering or as a sacrifice, whether in payment of a vow, or as a voluntary gift, or on the occasion of one of your solemn feasts, from your herds and flocks as a smell pleasing to Yahweh: 4 the offerer will, as his personal gift to Yahweh, bring a cereal offering of one-tenth of an *ephah* of fine flour mixed with one-quarter of a *hin* of oil. 5 You will also make a libation of wine, one-quarter of a *hin* to each lamb, in addition to the burnt offering or sacrifice. 6 For a ram, you will make a cereal offering of two-tenths of an *ephah* of fine flour mixed with one-third of a *hin* of oil, 7 and a libation of one-third of a *hin* of wine as a smell pleasing to Yahweh. 8 If you offer a bull as a burnt offering or sacrifice, in payment of a vow or as a communion sacrifice for Yahweh, 9 in addition to the animal you will offer a cereal offering of three-tenths of an *ephah* of fine flour mixed with half a *hin* of oil, 10 and you will offer a libation of half a *hin* of wine, as food burnt as a smell pleasing to Yahweh. 11 This will be done for every bull, every ram, every lamb or kid. 12 Whatever the number of victims you intend to offer, you will do the same for each of them, however many there are.

NEW REVISED STANDARD VERSION

13 Every native Israelite shall do these things in this way, in presenting an offering by fire, a pleasing odor to the LORD. 14 An alien who lives with you, or who takes up permanent residence among you, and wishes to offer an offering by fire, a pleasing odor to the LORD, shall do as you do. 15 As for the assembly, there shall be for both you and the resident alien a single statute, a perpetual statute throughout your generations; you and the alien shall be alike before the LORD. 16 You and the alien who resides with you shall have the same law and the same ordinance.

17 The LORD spoke to Moses, saying: 18 Speak to the Israelites and say to them: After you come into the land to which I am bringing you, 19 whenever you eat of the bread of the land, you shall present a donation to the LORD. 20 From your first batch of dough you shall present a loaf as a donation; you shall present it just as you present a donation from the threshing floor. 21 Throughout your generations you shall give to the LORD a donation from the first of your batch of dough.

22 But if you unintentionally fail to observe all these commandments that the LORD has spoken to Moses — 23 everything that the LORD has commanded you by Moses, from the day the LORD gave commandment and thereafter, throughout your generations — 24 then if it was done unintentionally without the knowledge of the congregation, the whole congregation shall offer one young bull for a burnt offering, a pleasing odor to the LORD, together with its grain offering and its drink offering, according to the ordinance, and one male goat for a sin offering. 25 The priest shall make atonement for all the congregation of the Israelites, and they shall be forgiven; it was unintentional, and they have brought their offering, an offering by fire to the LORD, and their sin offering before the LORD, for their error. 26 All the congregation of the Israelites shall be forgiven, as well as the aliens residing among them, because the whole people was involved in the error.

27 An individual who sins unintentionally shall present a female goat a year old for a sin offering. 28 And the priest shall make atonement before the LORD for the one who commits an error, when it is unintentional, to make atonement for the person, who then shall be forgiven. 29 For both the native among the Israelites and the alien residing among them — you shall have the same law for anyone who acts in error. 30 But whoever acts high-handedly, whether a native or an alien, affronts the LORD, and shall be cut off from among the people. 31 Because of having despised the word of the LORD and broken his commandment, such a person shall be utterly cut off and bear the guilt.

32 When the Israelites were in the wilderness, they found a man gathering sticks on the sabbath day. 33 Those who found him gathering sticks brought him to Moses, Aaron, and to the whole congregation. 34 They put him in custody, because it was not clear what should be done to him. 35 Then the LORD said to Moses, "The man shall be put to death; all the congregation shall stone him outside the camp." 36 The whole congregation brought him outside the camp and stoned him to death, just as the LORD had commanded Moses.

37 The LORD said to Moses: 38 Speak to the Israelites, and tell them to make fringes on the corners of their garments throughout their generations and to put a blue cord on the fringe at each corner. 39 You have the fringe so that, when you see it, you will remember all the commandments of the LORD and do them, and not follow the lust of your own heart and your own eyes. 40 So you shall remember and do all my commandments, and you shall be holy to your

REVISED ENGLISH BIBLE

native Israelite must observe these rules whenever he offers a food-offering of soothing odour to the LORD.

14 'When an alien residing with you or permanently settled among you offers a food-offering of soothing odour to the LORD, he should do as you do. 15 There is one and the same statute for you and for the resident alien, a rule binding for all time on your descendants; before the LORD you and the alien are alike. 16 There must be one law and one custom for you and for the alien residing among you.'

17 The LORD told Moses 18 to say to the Israelites: 'After you have entered the land into which I am bringing you, 19 whenever you eat the bread of the country, set aside a contribution for the LORD. 20 Set aside a loaf made of your first kneading of dough, as you set aside the contribution from the threshing-floor. 21 You must give a contribution to the LORD from your first kneading of dough; this rule is binding on your descendants.

22 'When through inadvertence you omit to carry out any of these commands which the LORD gave to Moses — 23 any command whatever that the LORD gave you through Moses on that first day and thereafter and made binding on your descendants — 24 if it be done inadvertently, unnoticed by the community, then the whole community must offer one young bull as a whole-offering, a soothing odour to the LORD, with its proper grain-offering and drink-offering according to custom; and they are to add one he-goat as a purification-offering. 25 The priest must make expiation for the whole Israelite community, and they will be forgiven. The omission was inadvertent; and they have brought their offering, a food-offering to the LORD; they have made their purification-offering before the LORD for their inadvertence; 26 the whole community of Israelites and the aliens residing among you will be forgiven. The inadvertence was shared by the whole people.

27 'If it is an individual who sins inadvertently, he should present a yearling she-goat as a purification-offering, 28 and the priest will make expiation before the LORD for that person, who will then be forgiven. 29 For anyone who sins inadvertently, there must be one law for all, whether native Israelite or resident alien.

30 'But the person, be he native or alien, who sins presumptuously, insults the LORD; that person is to be cut off from the people. 31 For he has brought the word of the LORD into contempt and violated his command, that person will be cut off completely; the guilt will be on his head alone.'

32 During the time that the Israelites were in the wilderness, a man was found gathering sticks on the sabbath day. 33 Those who had caught him in the act brought him to Moses and Aaron and all the community, 34 and they kept him in custody, because it was not clearly known what was to be done with him. 35 The LORD said to Moses, 'The man must be put to death; he must be stoned by the whole community outside the camp.' 36 So the whole community took him outside the camp, where he was stoned to death, as the LORD had commanded Moses.

37 The LORD told Moses 38 to say to the Israelites: 'Make tassels on the corners of your garments, you and your children's children. Into this tassel you are to work a violet thread, 39 and whenever you see this in the tassel, you will remember all the LORD's commands and obey them, and not go your own wanton ways, led astray by your own hearts and eyes. 40 This token is to ensure that you remember and obey all my commands, and keep yourselves holy, consecrated to your God.

15:14 **as you do:** *so Syriac; Heb. adds* the assembly.

13 "All the native-born shall make these offerings in the same way, whenever they present a sweet-smelling oblation to the LORD. 14 Likewise, in any future generation, any alien residing with you permanently or for a time, who presents a sweet-smelling oblation to the LORD, shall do as you do. 15 There is but one rule for you and for the resident alien, a perpetual rule for all your descendants. Before the LORD you and the alien are alike, 16 with the same law and the same application of it for the alien residing among you as for yourselves."

17 The LORD said to Moses, 18 "Speak to the Israelites and tell them: When you enter the land into which I will bring you 19 and begin to eat of the food of that land, you shall offer the LORD a contribution 20 consisting of a cake of your first batch of dough. You shall offer it just as you offer a contribution from the threshing floor. 21 Throughout your generations you shall give a contribution to the LORD from your first batch of dough.

22 "When through inadvertence you fail to carry out any of these commandments which the LORD gives to Moses, 23 and through Moses to you, from the time the LORD first issues the commandment down through your generations: 24 if the community itself unwittingly becomes guilty of the fault of inadvertence, the whole community shall offer the holocaust of one young bull as a sweet-smelling oblation pleasing to the LORD, along with its prescribed cereal offering and libation, as well as one he-goat as a sin offering. 25 Then the priest shall make atonement for the whole Israelite community; thus they will be forgiven the inadvertence for which they have brought their holocaust as an oblation to the LORD. 26 Not only the whole Israelite community, but also the aliens residing among you, shall be forgiven, since the fault of inadvertence affects all the people.

27 "However, if it is an individual who sins inadvertently, he shall bring a yearling she-goat as a sin offering, 28 and the priest shall make atonement before the LORD for him who sinned inadvertently; when atonement has been made for him, he will be forgiven. 29 You shall have but one law for him who sins inadvertently, whether he be a native Israelite or an alien residing with you.

30 "But anyone who sins defiantly, whether he be a native or an alien, insults the LORD, and shall be cut off from among his people. 31 Since he has despised the word of the LORD and has broken his commandment, he must be cut off. He has only himself to blame."

32 While the Israelites were in the desert, a man was discovered gathering wood on the sabbath day. 33 Those who caught him at it brought him to Moses and Aaron and the whole assembly. 34 But they kept him in custody, for there was no clear decision as to what should be done with him. 35 Then the LORD said to Moses, "This man shall be put to death; let the whole community stone him outside the camp." 36 So the whole community led him outside the camp and stoned him to death, as the LORD had commanded Moses.

37 The LORD said to Moses, 38 "Speak to the Israelites and tell them that they and their descendants must put tassels on the corners of their garments, fastening each corner tassel with a violet cord. 39 When you use these tassels, let the sight of them remind you to keep all the commandments of the LORD, without going wantonly astray after the desires of your hearts and eyes. 40 Thus you will remember to keep all my commandments and be holy to your God. 41 I, the LORD,

13 "Every citizen of the country will act in this way whenever he offers food burnt as a smell pleasing to Yahweh; 14 and if an alien residing with you or with your descendants intends to offer food burnt as a smell pleasing to Yahweh, he will do as you do. 15 There will be one law for you, members of the community, and the resident alien alike, a law binding your descendants for ever: before Yahweh you and the resident alien are no different.' 16 One law, one statute, will apply for you and the resident alien." '

17 Yahweh spoke to Moses and said, 18 'Speak to the Israelites and say:

"When you have entered the country to which I am bringing you, 19 you will set a portion aside for Yahweh when you eat that country's bread. 20 You will set one cake aside as the first-fruits of your dough; you will set this offering aside like the one set aside from your threshing. 21 For all future generations you will set a portion of your dough aside for Yahweh.

22 "If through inadvertence you fail in any of these orders which Yahweh has given to Moses 23 (whatever orders Yahweh has given you or your descendants through Moses, from the day when Yahweh gave his orders), 24 this is what must be done:

"If it is an inadvertence on the part of the community, the community as a whole will offer a young bull as a burnt offering, as a smell pleasing to Yahweh, with the prescribed accompanying cereal offering and libation, and a he-goat as a sacrifice for sin. 25 The priest will perform the rite of expiation for the entire community of Israelites, and they will be forgiven, since it was an inadvertence. Once they have brought their offering as food burnt for Yahweh, and have presented their sacrifice for sin before Yahweh to make amends for their inadvertence, 26 the whole community of Israelites will be forgiven, as also the alien residing with them, since the entire people acted by inadvertence.

27 "If it is an individual who has sinned by inadvertence, he will offer a yearling kid as a sacrifice for sin. 28 The priest will perform the rite of expiation before Yahweh for the person who has gone astray owing to this sin of inadvertence and, expiation having been made for him, he will be forgiven; 29 whether he is an Israelite citizen or a resident alien, you will have one law for anyone who sins by inadvertence.

30 "But the individual who acts deliberately, be he citizen or alien, commits an outrage against Yahweh, and such a man will be outlawed from his people. 31 Since he has treated Yahweh's word with contempt and has disobeyed his order, such a man will be outlawed absolutely and will bear the consequences of his guilt." '

32 While the Israelites were in the desert, a man was caught gathering wood on the Sabbath day. 33 Those who caught him gathering wood brought him before Moses, Aaron and the whole community. 34 He was kept in custody, because the penalty he should undergo had not yet been fixed. 35 Yahweh said to Moses, 'This man must be put to death. The whole community will stone him outside the camp.' 36 The whole community took him outside the camp and stoned him till he was dead, as Yahweh had ordered Moses.

37 Yahweh spoke to Moses and said, 38 'Speak to the Israelites and tell them, for all generations to come, to put tassels on the hems of their clothes and work a violet thread into the tassel at the hem. 39 You will thus have a tassel, and the sight of it will remind you of all Yahweh's orders and how you are to put them into practice, and not follow the dictates of your own heart and eyes, which have led you to be unfaithful.

40 'This will remind you of all my orders; put them into practice, and you will be consecrated to your God. 41 I,

NEW REVISED STANDARD VERSION	REVISED ENGLISH BIBLE

God. 41 I am the LORD your God, who brought you out of the land of Egypt, to be your God: I am the LORD your God.

16 Now Korah son of Izhar son of Kohath son of Levi, along with Dathan and Abiram sons of Eliab, and On son of Peleth — descendants of Reuben — took 2 two hundred fifty Israelite men, leaders of the congregation, chosen from the assembly, well-known men,c and they confronted Moses. 3 They assembled against Moses and against Aaron, and said to them, "You have gone too far! All the congregation are holy, every one of them, and the LORD is among them. So why then do you exalt yourselves above the assembly of the LORD?" 4 When Moses heard it, he fell on his face. 5 Then he said to Korah and all his company, "In the morning the LORD will make known who is his, and who is holy, and who will be allowed to approach him; the one whom he will choose he will allow to approach him. 6 Do this: take censers, Korah and all yourd company, 7 and tomorrow put fire in them, and lay incense on them before the LORD; and the man whom the LORD chooses shall be the holy one. You Levites have gone too far!" 8 Then Moses said to Korah, "Hear now, you Levites! 9 Is it too little for you that the God of Israel has separated you from the congregation of Israel, to allow you to approach him in order to perform the duties of the LORD's tabernacle, and to stand before the congregation and serve them? 10 He has allowed you to approach him, and all your brother Levites with you; yet you seek the priesthood as well! 11 Therefore you and all your company have gathered together against the LORD. What is Aaron that you rail against him?"

12 Moses sent for Dathan and Abiram sons of Eliab; but they said, "We will not come! 13 Is it too little that you have brought us up out of a land flowing with milk and honey to kill us in the wilderness, that you must also lord it over us? 14 It is clear you have not brought us into a land flowing with milk and honey, or given us an inheritance of fields and vineyards. Would you put out the eyes of these men? We will not come!"

15 Moses was very angry and said to the LORD, "Pay no attention to their offering. I have not taken one donkey from them, and I have not harmed any one of them." 16 And Moses said to Korah, "As for you and all your company, be present tomorrow before the LORD, you and they and Aaron; 17 and let each one of you take his censer, and put incense on it, and each one of you present his censer before the LORD, two hundred fifty censers; you also, and Aaron, each his censer." 18 So each man took his censer, and they put fire in the censers and laid incense on them, and they stood at the entrance of the tent of meeting with Moses and Aaron. 19 Then Korah assembled the whole congregation against them at the entrance of the tent of meeting. And the glory of the LORD appeared to the whole congregation.

20 Then the LORD spoke to Moses and to Aaron, saying: 21 Separate yourselves from this congregation, so that I may consume them in a moment. 22 They fell on their faces, and said, "O God, the God of the spirits of all flesh, shall one person sin and you become angry with the whole congregation?"

23 And the LORD spoke to Moses, saying: 24 Say to the congregation: Get away from the dwellings of Korah, Da-

41 'I am the LORD your God who brought you out of Egypt to become your God. I am the LORD your God.'

16 KORAH son of Izhar, son of Kohath, son of Levi, along with the Reubenites Dathan and Abiram sons of Eliab and On son of Peleth, challenged the authority of Moses. 2 Siding with them in their revolt were two hundred and fifty Israelites, all chiefs of the community, conveners of assembly and men of good standing. 3 They confronted Moses and Aaron and said, 'You take too much on yourselves. Each and every member of the community is holy and the LORD is among them. Why do you set yourselves up above the assembly of the LORD?' 4 When Moses heard this, he prostrated himself, 5 and he said to Korah and all his company, 'Tomorrow morning the LORD will declare who is his, who is holy and who may present offerings to him. The man whom the LORD chooses may present them. 6 This is what you must do, you, Korah, and all your company: you must take censers, 7 and put fire in them and place incense on them before the LORD tomorrow. The man whom the LORD then chooses is the man who is holy. You take too much on yourselves, you Levites.'

8 Moses said to Korah, 'Listen, you Levites. 9 Is it not enough for you that the God of Israel has set you apart from the community of Israel, bringing you near him to maintain the service of the Tabernacle of the LORD and to stand before the community as their ministers? 10 He has had you come near him, and all your brother Levites with you; now do you seek the priesthood as well? 11 That is why you and all your company have combined together against the LORD. What is Aaron that you should make these complaints against him?'

12 Moses sent to fetch Dathan and Abiram sons of Eliab, but they answered, 'We will not come. 13 Is it not enough that you have brought us away from a land flowing with milk and honey to let us die in the wilderness? Must you also set yourself up as prince over us? 14 What is more, you have not brought us into a land flowing with milk and honey, nor have you given us fields and vineyards to inherit. Do you think you can hoodwink men like us? We are not coming.' 15 Moses became very angry, and said to the LORD, 'Take no notice of their murmuring. I have not taken from them so much as a single donkey; I have not wronged any of them.'

16 Moses said to Korah, 'Present yourselves before the LORD tomorrow, you and all your company, you and they and Aaron. 17 Each man of you is to take his censer and put incense on it. Then you shall present them before the LORD with their two hundred and fifty censers, and you and Aaron shall also bring your censers.' 18 So each man took his censer, put fire in it, and placed incense on it. Moses and Aaron took their stand at the entrance to the Tent of Meeting, 19 and Korah gathered his whole company together and faced them at the entrance to the Tent of Meeting.

Then the glory of the LORD appeared to the whole community, 20 and the LORD said to Moses and Aaron, 21 'Stand apart from them, so that I may make an end of them in a single moment.' 22 But Moses and Aaron prostrated themselves and said, 'God, you God of the spirits of all mankind, if one man sins, will you be angry with the whole community?' 23 But the LORD said to Moses, 24 'Tell them all to stand back from the dwellings of Korah, Dathan, and Abiram.'

---

c Cn: Heb *and they confronted Moses, and two hundred fifty men . . . well-known men*   d Heb *his*

16:14 **hoodwink:** *lit.* gouge out the eyes of.   16:18 **Moses . . . Meeting:** *so some MSS; others* They stood at the entrance to the Tent of Meeting, and Moses and Aaron.   16:19 **his:** *so Gk; Heb.* the.

NEW AMERICAN BIBLE

NEW JERUSALEM BIBLE

am your God who, as God, brought you out of Egypt that I, the LORD, may be your God."

16 Korah, son of Izhar, son of Kohath, son of Levi, [and Dathan and Abiram, sons of Eliab, son of Pallu, son of Reuben] took 2 two hundred and fifty Israelites who were leaders in the community, members of the council and men of note. They stood before Moses, 3 and held an assembly against Moses and Aaron, to whom they said, "Enough from you! The whole community, all of them, are holy; the LORD is in their midst. Why then should you set yourselves over the LORD's congregation?"

4 When Moses heard this, he fell prostrate. 5 Then he said to Korah and to all his band, "May the LORD make known tomorrow morning who belongs to him and who is the holy one and whom he will have draw near to him! Whom he chooses, he will have draw near him. 6 Do this: take your censers [Korah and all his band] 7 and put fire in them and place incense in them before the LORD tomorrow. He whom the LORD then chooses is the holy one. Enough from you Levites!"

8 Moses also said to Korah, "Listen to me, you Levites! 9 Is it too little for you that the God of Israel has singled you out from the community of Isreal, to have you draw near him for the service of the LORD's Dwelling and to stand before the community to minister for them? 10 He has allowed you and your kinsmen, the descendants of Levi, to approach him, and yet you now seek the priesthood too. 11 It is therefore against the LORD that you and all your band are conspiring. For what has Aaron done that you should grumble against him?"

12 Moses summoned Dathan and Abiram, sons of Eliab, but they answered, "We will not go. 13 Are you not satisfied with having led us here away from a land flowing with milk and honey, to make us perish in the desert, that you must now lord it over us? 14 Far from bringing us to a land flowing with milk and honey, or giving us fields and vineyards for our inheritance, will you also gouge out our eyes? No, we will not go."

15 Then Moses became very angry and said to the LORD, "Pay no heed to their offering. I have never taken a single ass from them, nor have I wronged any one of them."

16 Moses said to Korah, "You and all your band shall appear before the LORD tomorrow — you and they and Aaron too. 17 Then each of your two hundred and fifty followers shall take his own censer, put incense in it, and offer it to the LORD; and you and Aaron, each with his own censer, shall do the same." 18 So they all took their censers, and laying incense on the fire they had put in them, they took their stand by the entrance of the meeting tent along with Moses and Aaron. 19 Then, when Korah had assembled all his band against them at the entrance of the meeting tent, the glory of the LORD appeared to the entire community, 20 and the LORD said to Moses and Aaron, 21 "Stand apart from this band, that I may consume them at once." 22 But they fell prostrate and cried out, "O God, God of the spirits of all mankind, will one man's sin make you angry with the whole community?" 23 The LORD answered Moses, 24 "Speak to the community and tell them: Withdraw from the space around the Dwelling" [of Korah, Dathan and Abiram].

16, 1ff: The evidence seems to show that there were two distinct rebellions: one of Korah and his band (Nm 27, 3) and the other of Dathan and Abiram (Dt 11, 6); cf Ps 106. The present account combines both events into one narrative; but even here it is rather easy to separate the two, once certain proper names (vv 1. 6. 24. 32. 35) have been identified as glosses. The parts of the present section which refer to the rebellion of Dathan and Abiram are vv 12-15 and vv 25-34 of chapter 16; the rest of chapter 16 and all of chapter 17 concern the rebellion of Korah.

Yahweh your God, have brought you out of Egypt, to be your God, I, Yahweh your God.'

16 Now Korah son of Izhar, son of Kohath the Levite, and the Reubenites Dathan and Abiram sons of Eliab, and On son of Peleth were proud 2 and rebelled against Moses with two hundred and fifty Israelites who were leaders of the community, prominent at the solemn feasts, men of repute. 3 These banded together against Moses and Aaron and said to them, 'You take too much on yourselves! The whole community, all its members, are consecrated, and Yahweh lives among them. Why set yourselves higher than Yahweh's community?'

4 On hearing this, Moses threw himself on his face. 5 Then he said to Korah and all in his party, 'Tomorrow morning Yahweh will reveal who is his, who the consecrated man whom he will allow to approach him. The one he allows to approach is the one whom he has chosen. 6 This is what you must do: take the censers of Korah and all in his party, 7 put fire in them and put incense in them before Yahweh tomorrow, and the one whom Yahweh chooses will be the consecrated man. Levites, you take too much on yourselves!'

8 Moses then said to Korah, 'Now listen, you Levites! 9 Is it not enough for you that the God of Israel has singled you out of the community of Israel, and called you to be near him, to serve in Yahweh's Dwelling and to represent the community by officiating on its behalf? 10 He has called you to be near him, you and all your brother Levites with you, and now you want to be priests as well! 11 For which reason, you and all in your party have banded together against Yahweh himself: for what is Aaron, that you should mutter against him?'

12 Moses then summoned Dathan and Abiram sons of Eliab. They replied, 'We will not come. 13 Is it not enough for you to have brought us away from a country flowing with milk and honey to kill us in the desert, without your making yourself our absolute ruler? 14 What is more, you have not brought us to a country flowing with milk and honey and you have not given us fields and vineyards for our heritage. Do you think you can hoodwink these people? We will not come.' 15 Moses flew into a rage and said to Yahweh, 'Disregard their cereal offering! I have not taken so much as a donkey from them, nor have I wronged any of them.'

16 Moses said to Korah, 'You and all your party, come before Yahweh tomorrow, you and they, and Aaron too. 17 Each will take his censer, put incense in it, and bring his censer before Yahweh — two hundred and fifty censers. You and Aaron too will each bring his censer.' 18 Each of them took his censer, put fire in it and placed incense on it, and stood at the entrance to the Tent of Meeting with Moses and Aaron. 19 Then, Korah having assembled the whole community to confront them at the entrance to the Tent of Meeting, the glory of Yahweh appeared to the whole community.

20 Yahweh then spoke to Moses and Aaron. He said, 21 'Get away from this community. I am going to destroy them here and now.' 22 They threw themselves on their faces and cried out, 'O God, God of the spirits that give life to every living thing, will you be angry with the whole community because one man has sinned?' 23 Yahweh then said to Moses, 24 'Speak to the community and say, "Stand well clear of Korah's tent." '

NEW REVISED STANDARD VERSION	REVISED ENGLISH BIBLE

than, and Abiram. 25 So Moses got up and went to Dathan and Abiram; the elders of Israel followed him. 26 He said to the congregation, "Turn away from the tents of these wicked men, and touch nothing of theirs, or you will be swept away for all their sins." 27 So they got away from the dwellings of Korah, Dathan, and Abiram; and Dathan and Abiram came out and stood at the entrance of their tents, together with their wives, their children, and their little ones. 28 And Moses said, "This is how you shall know that the LORD has sent me to do all these works; it has not been of my own accord: 29 If these people die a natural death, or if a natural fate comes on them, then the LORD has not sent me. 30 But if the LORD creates something new, and the ground opens its mouth and swallows them up, with all that belongs to them, and they go down alive into Sheol, then you shall know that these men have despised the LORD."

31 As soon as he finished speaking all these words, the ground under them was split apart. 32 The earth opened its mouth and swallowed them up, along with their households — everyone who belonged to Korah and all their goods. 33 So they with all that belonged to them went down alive into Sheol; the earth closed over them, and they perished from the midst of the assembly. 34 All Israel around them fled at their outcry, for they said, "The earth will swallow us too!" 35 And fire came out from the LORD and consumed the two hundred fifty men offering the incense.

36 *e* Then the LORD spoke to Moses, saying: 37 Tell Eleazar son of Aaron the priest to take the censers out of the blaze; then scatter the fire far and wide. 38 For the censers of these sinners have become holy at the cost of their lives. Make them into hammered plates as a covering for the altar, for they presented them before the LORD and they became holy. Thus they shall be a sign to the Israelites. 39 So Eleazar the priest took the bronze censers that had been presented by those who were burned; and they were hammered out as a covering for the altar — 40 a reminder to the Israelites that no outsider, who is not of the descendants of Aaron, shall approach to offer incense before the LORD, so as not to become like Korah and his company — just as the LORD had said to him through Moses.

41 On the next day, however, the whole congregation of the Israelites rebelled against Moses and against Aaron, saying, "You have killed the people of the LORD." 42 And when the congregation had assembled against them, Moses and Aaron turned toward the tent of meeting; the cloud had covered it and the glory of the LORD appeared. 43 Then Moses and Aaron came to the front of the tent of meeting, 44 and the LORD spoke to Moses, saying, 45 "Get away from this congregation, so that I may consume them in a moment." And they fell on their faces. 46 Moses said to Aaron, "Take your censer, put fire on it from the altar and lay incense on it, and carry it quickly to the congregation and make atonement for them. For wrath has gone out from the LORD; the plague has begun." 47 So Aaron took it as Moses had ordered, and ran into the middle of the assembly, where the plague had already begun among the people. He put on the incense, and made atonement for the people. 48 He stood between the dead and the living; and the plague was stopped. 49 Those who died by the plague were fourteen thousand seven hundred, besides those who died in the affair of Korah. 50 When the plague was stopped, Aaron returned to Moses at the entrance of the tent of meeting.

25 Moses rose and went to Dathan and Abiram, and the elders of Israel followed him. 26 He said to the whole community, 'Stand well away from the tents of these wicked men; touch nothing of theirs, or you will be swept away because of all their sins.' 27 So they moved away from the dwellings of Korah, Dathan, and Abiram. Dathan and Abiram had come out and were standing at the entrance of their tents with their wives, their children, and their dependants. 28 Moses said, 'By this you shall know that it is the LORD who sent me to do all I have done, and it was not my own heart that prompted me. 29 If these men die a natural death, merely sharing the common fate of man, then the LORD has not sent me; 30 but if the LORD works a miracle, and the ground opens its mouth and swallows them and all that is theirs, and they go down alive to Sheol, then you will know that these men have set the LORD at naught.'

31 Hardly had Moses spoken when the ground beneath them split apart; 32 the earth opened its mouth and swallowed them and their homes — all the followers of Korah and all their property. 33 They went down alive into Sheol with all that they had; the earth closed over them, and they vanished from the assembly. 34 At their cries all the Israelites around them fled. 'Look out!' they shouted. 'The earth might swallow us.' 35 Fire came out from the LORD and consumed the two hundred and fifty men presenting the incense.

36 Then the LORD said to Moses, 37 'Order Eleazar son of Aaron the priest to set aside the censers from the burnt remains, and scatter the fire from them a long way off, because they are holy. 38 The censers of these men who sinned at the cost of their lives you shall make into beaten plates to overlay the altar; they are holy, because they have been presented before the LORD. Let them be a sign to the Israelites.' 39 Eleazar the priest took the bronze censers which the victims of the fire had presented, and they were beaten into plates to cover the altar, 40 to be a reminder to the Israelites that no lay person, no one not descended from Aaron, should come forward to burn incense before the LORD, or his fate would be that of Korah and his company. All this was done as the LORD commanded Eleazar through Moses.

41 Next day the whole Israelite community raised complaints against Moses and Aaron and taxed them with causing the death of some of the LORD's people. 42 As they gathered against Moses and Aaron, they turned towards the Tent of Meeting and saw that the cloud covered it, and the glory of the LORD appeared. 43 When Moses and Aaron came to the front of the Tent of Meeting, 44 the LORD said to them, 45 'Stand well clear of this community, so that in a single moment I may make an end of them.' They prostrated themselves, 46 and then Moses said to Aaron, 'Take your censer, put fire from the altar in it, set incense on it, and go with it quickly to the assembled community to make expiation for them. Wrath has gone forth already from the presence of the LORD; the plague has begun.' 47 As Moses had directed him, Aaron took his censer, ran into the midst of the assembly, and found that the plague had indeed begun among the people. He put incense on the censer and made expiation for the people, 48 standing between the dead and the living, and the plague was stopped. 49 Fourteen thousand seven hundred died of it, in addition to those who had died for Korah's offence. 50 When Aaron came back to Moses at the entrance to the Tent of Meeting, the plague had stopped.

16:30 **works a miracle:** *lit.* creates a creation.   16:30,33 **Sheol:** *or* the underworld.   16:36 *In Heb. 17:1.*   16:39 **bronze:** *or* copper.

e Ch 17.1 in Heb

25 Moses, followed by the elders of Israel, arose and went to Dathan and Abiram. 26 Then he warned the community, "Keep away from the tents of these wicked men and do not touch anything that is theirs: otherwise you too will be swept away because of all their sins." 27 When Dathan and Abiram had come out and were standing at the entrances of their tents with their wives and sons and little ones, 28 Moses said, "This is how you shall know that it was the LORD who sent me to do all I have done, and that it was not I who planned it: 29 if these men die an ordinary death, merely suffering the fate common to all mankind, then it was not the LORD who sent me. 30 But if the LORD does something entirely new, and the ground opens its mouth and swallows them alive down into the nether world, with all belonging to them, then you will know that these men have defied the LORD." 31 No sooner had he finished saying all this than the ground beneath them split open, 32 and the earth opened its mouth and swallowed them and their families [and all of Korah's men] and all their possessions. 33 They went down alive to the nether world with all belonging to them; the earth closed over them, and they perished from the community. 34 But all the Israelites near them fled at their shrieks, saying, "The earth might swallow us too!"

35 So they withdrew from the space around the Dwelling [of Korah, Dathan and Abiram]. And fire from the LORD came forth which consumed the two hundred and fifty men who were offering the incense.

17 The LORD said to Moses, 2 "Tell Eleazar, son of Aaron the priest, to remove the censers from the embers; and scatter the fire some distance away, 3 for these sinners have consecrated the censers at the cost of their lives. Have them hammered into plates to cover the altar, because in being presented before the LORD they have become sacred. In this way they shall serve as a sign to the Israelites." 4 So Eleazar the priest had the bronze censers of those burned during the offering hammered into a covering for the altar, 5 in keeping with the orders which the LORD had given him through Moses. This cover was to be a reminder to the Israelites that no layman, no one who was not a descendant of Aaron, should approach the altar to offer incense before the LORD, lest he meet the fate of Korah and his band.

6 The next day the whole Israelite community grumbled against Moses and Aaron, saying, "It is you who have slain the LORD's people." 7 But while the community was deliberating against them, Moses and Aaron turned toward the meeting tent, and the cloud now covered it and the glory of the LORD appeared. 8 Then Moses and Aaron came to the front of the meeting tent, 9 and the LORD said to Moses and Aaron, 10 "Depart from this community, that I may consume them at once." But they fell prostrate. 11 Then Moses said to Aaron, "Take your censer, put fire from the altar in it, lay incense on it, and bring it quickly to the community to make atonement for them; for wrath has come forth from the LORD and the blow is falling." 12 Obeying the orders of Moses, Aaron took his censer and ran in among the community, where the blow was already falling on the people. Then, as he offered the incense and made atonement for the people, 13 standing there between the living and the dead, the scourge was checked. 14 Yet fourteen thousand seven hundred died from the scourge, in addition to those who died because of Korah. 15 When the scourge had been checked, Aaron returned to Moses at the entrance of the meeting tent.

25 Moses stood up and went to Dathan and Abiram; the elders of Israel followed him. 26 He spoke to the community and said, 'Stand away, I tell you, from the tents of these sinners, and touch nothing that belongs to them, for fear that with all their sins you too will be swept away.' 27 So they moved away from Korah's tent.

Dathan and Abiram had come out and were standing at their tent doors, with their wives, their sons and their little ones. 28 Moses said, 'This is how you will know that Yahweh himself has sent me to perform all these tasks and that I am not doing them of my own accord. 29 If these people die a natural death such as people commonly die, then Yahweh has not sent me. 30 But if Yahweh does something utterly new, if the earth should open its mouth and swallow them and all their belongings, so that they go down alive to Sheol, then you will know that they held Yahweh in contempt.'

31 The moment he finished saying all this, the ground split apart under their feet, 32 the earth opened its mouth and swallowed them, their families, all Korah's people and all their property.

33 They went down alive to Sheol with all their belongings. The earth closed over them and they disappeared in the middle of the community. 34 At their cries, all the Israelites round them took to their heels, saying, 'We do not want the earth to swallow us too!'

35 Fire then shot out from Yahweh and consumed the two hundred and fifty men offering incense.

17 Yahweh then spoke to Moses and said, 2 'Tell Eleazar son of Aaron the priest to pick the censers out of the smouldering remains and scatter the fire from them away from here, 3 for these sinful censers have become sanctified at the price of human lives. Since they were brought before Yahweh and thus became consecrated, they must be hammered into sheets to cover the altar. They will be an object-lesson to the Israelites.'

4 The priest Eleazar took the bronze censers which had been carried by the men destroyed by the fire. They were hammered into sheets to cover the altar. 5 They are a reminder to the Israelites that no unauthorised person, no one not of Aaron's line, may approach and offer incense before Yahweh, on pain of suffering the fate of Korah and his party, as Yahweh had said through Moses.

6 On the following day, the whole community of Israelites were muttering against Moses and Aaron and saying, 'You are responsible for killing Yahweh's people!' 7 Now, as the community was banding together against Moses and Aaron, they turned towards the Tent of Meeting, and there was the cloud covering it, and the glory of Yahweh appeared. 8 Moses and Aaron then went to the front of the Tent of Meeting.

9 Yahweh spoke to Moses and said, 10 'Get away from this community. I am going to destroy them here and now.' They threw themselves on their faces. 11 Moses then said to Aaron, 'Take a censer, put fire in it from the altar, place incense on it and hurry to the community to perform the rite of expiation for them: for retribution has come from Yahweh, plague has broken out.' 12 Aaron took it as Moses said and ran into the middle of the community, but plague had already broken out among the people. He put in the incense and performed the rite of expiation for the people. 13 Then he stood between the living and the dead, and the plague stopped. 14 There were fourteen thousand seven hundred victims of the plague, apart from those who died because of Korah. 15 Aaron then went back to Moses at the entrance to the Tent of Meeting; the plague had been halted.

16, 35: This verse continues v 24; the first sentence is transposed from v 27.

17 f The LORD spoke to Moses, saying: 2 Speak to the Israelites, and get twelve staffs from them, one for each ancestral house, from all the leaders of their ancestral houses. Write each man's name on his staff, 3 and write Aaron's name on the staff of Levi. For there shall be one staff for the head of each ancestral house. 4 Place them in the tent of meeting before the covenant,g where I meet with you. 5 And the staff of the man whom I choose shall sprout; thus I will put a stop to the complaints of the Israelites that they continually make against you. 6 Moses spoke to the Israelites; and all their leaders gave him staffs, one for each leader, according to their ancestral houses, twelve staffs; and the staff of Aaron was among theirs. 7 So Moses placed the staffs before the LORD in the tent of the covenant.g

8 When Moses went into the tent of the covenantg on the next day, the staff of Aaron for the house of Levi had sprouted. It put forth buds, produced blossoms, and bore ripe almonds. 9 Then Moses brought out all the staffs from before the LORD to all the Israelites; and they looked, and each man took his staff. 10 And the LORD said to Moses, "Put back the staff of Aaron before the covenant,g to be kept as a warning to rebels, so that you may make an end of their complaints against me, or else they will die." 11 Moses did so; just as the LORD commanded him, so he did.

12 The Israelites said to Moses, "We are perishing; we are lost, all of us are lost! 13 Everyone who approaches the tabernacle of the LORD will die. Are we all to perish?"

18 The LORD said to Aaron: You and your sons and your ancestral house with you shall bear responsibility for offenses connected with the sanctuary, while you and your sons alone shall bear responsibility for offenses connected with the priesthood. 2 So bring with you also your brothers of the tribe of Levi, your ancestral house, in order that they may be joined to you, and serve you while you and your sons with you are in front of the tent of the covenant.g 3 They shall perform duties for you and for the whole tent. But they must not approach either the utensils of the sanctuary or the altar, otherwise both they and you will die. 4 They are attached to you in order to perform the duties of the tent of meeting, for all the service of the tent; no outsider shall approach you. 5 You yourselves shall perform the duties of the sanctuary and the duties of the altar, so that wrath may never again come upon the Israelites. 6 It is I who now take your brother Levites from among the Israelites; they are now yours as a gift, dedicated to the LORD, to perform the service of the tent of meeting. 7 But you and your sons with you shall diligently perform your priestly duties in all that concerns the altar and the area behind the curtain. I give your priesthood as a gift; h any outsider who approaches shall be put to death.

8 The LORD spoke to Aaron: I have given you charge of the offerings made to me, all the holy gifts of the Israelites; I have given them to you and your sons as a priestly portion due you in perpetuity. 9 This shall be yours from the most holy things, reserved from the fire: every offering of theirs that they render to me as a most holy thing, whether grain offering, sin offering, or guilt offering, shall belong to you and your sons. 10 As a most holy thing you shall eat it; every male may eat it; it shall be holy to you. 11 This also is yours: I have given to you, together with your sons and daughters, as a perpetual due, whatever is set aside from the gifts of all the elevation offerings of the Israelites; everyone who is clean in your house may eat them. 12 All the best of the oil

17 The LORD said to Moses, 2 'Speak to the Israelites and get from them a staff for each tribe, one from every tribal chief, twelve in all, and write each man's name on his staff. 3 On Levi's staff write Aaron's name, for there must be one staff for each head of a tribe. 4 Put them all in the Tent of Meeting before the Testimony, where I meet you, 5 and the staff of the man whom I choose will put forth buds. I shall rid myself of the complaints of these Israelites, who keep on complaining against you.'

6 Moses gave those instructions to the Israelites, and each of their chiefs handed him a staff for his tribe, twelve in all, and Aaron's staff among them. 7 Moses laid them before the LORD in the Tent of the Testimony, 8 and next day when he entered the tent, he found that Aaron's staff, the staff for the tribe of Levi, had budded. Indeed, it had put forth buds, blossomed, and produced ripe almonds. 9 Moses then brought out the staffs from before the LORD and showed them to all the Israelites; they saw for themselves, and each man took his own staff. 10 The LORD said to Moses, 'Put back Aaron's staff in front of the Testimony to be kept as a warning to rebels, so that you may rid me of their complaints, and then they will not die.' 11 Moses did this, doing exactly as the LORD had commanded him.

12 THE Israelites said to Moses, 'This is the end of us! We must perish, one and all! 13 Everyone who goes near the Tabernacle of the LORD will die. Is this to be our final end?'

18 The LORD said to Aaron: 'You and your sons, together with the members of your father's tribe, are to be fully answerable for the sanctuary. You and your sons alone will be answerable for your priestly office; 2 but admit your kinsmen of Levi, your father's tribe, to be attached to you and assist you while you and your sons are before the Tent of the Testimony. 3 Let them be in attendance on you and fulfil all the duties of the Tent, but they must not go near the sacred vessels or the altar, otherwise they will die and you with them. 4 They will be attached to you and be responsible for the maintenance of the Tent of Meeting in every detail. No lay person is to come near you, 5 for you by yourselves will be responsible for the duties of the sanctuary and the altar, so that wrath may not fall again on the Israelites. 6 It is I who have selected the Levites your kinsmen out of all the Israelites as a gift for you, made over to the LORD for the maintenance of the Tent of Meeting. 7 But only you and your sons may fulfil the duties of your priestly office that concern the altar or lie within the curtain. This duty is yours; I bestow on you this gift of priestly service. Any person who is not a priest and who usurps it must be put to death.'

8 The LORD said to Aaron: 'I, the LORD, commit to your control the contributions made to me, that is all the holy-gifts of the Israelites. I give them to you and to your sons for your allotted portion due to you for all time. 9 Out of the most holy gifts kept back from the altar-fire this part is to belong to you: every offering, whether grain-offering, purification-offering, or reparation-offering, rendered to me as a most holy gift, belongs to you and to your sons. 10 You must eat it in a most holy place; every male may eat it. You are to regard it as holy.

11 'This also is yours: the contribution from all such of their gifts as are presented as offerings dedicated by the Israelites. I give it to you and to your sons and daughters with you as a due for all time. Every person in your household who is ritually clean may eat it.

---

f Ch 17.16 in Heb   g Or treaty, or testimony; Heb eduth
h Heb as a service of gift

17:1 In Heb. 17:16.

NEW AMERICAN BIBLE

16 The LORD now said to Moses, 17 "Speak to the Israelites and get one staff from them for each ancestral house, twelve staffs in all, one from each of their tribal princes. Mark each man's name on his staff; 18 and mark Aaron's name on Levi's staff, for the head of Levi's ancestral house shall also have a staff. 19 Then lay them down in the meeting tent, in front of the commandments, where I meet you. 20 There the staff of the man of my choice shall sprout. Thus will I suppress from my presence the Israelites' grumbling against you."

21 So Moses spoke to the Israelites, and their princes gave him staffs, twelve in all, one from each tribal prince; and Aaron's staff was with them. 22 Then Moses laid the staffs down before the LORD in the tent of the commandments. 23 The next day, when Moses entered the tent, Aaron's staff, representing the house of Levi, had sprouted and put forth not only shoots, but blossoms as well, and even bore ripe almonds! 24 Moses thereupon brought out all the staffs from the LORD's presence to the Israelites. After each prince identified his own staff and took it, 25 the LORD said to Moses, "Put back Aaron's staff in front of the commandments, to be kept there as a warning to the rebellious, so that their grumbling may cease before me; if it does not, they will die." 26 And Moses did as the LORD had commanded him.

27 Then the Israelites cried out to Moses, "We are perishing; we are lost, we are all lost! 28 Every time anyone approaches the Dwelling of the LORD, he dies! Are we to perish to the last man?"

18 The LORD said to Aaron, "You and your sons as well as the other members of your ancestral house shall be responsible for the sanctuary; but the responsibility of the priesthood shall rest on you and your sons alone. 2 Bring with you also your other kinsmen of the tribe of Levi, your ancestral tribe, as your associates and assistants, while you and your sons are in front of the tent of the commandments. 3 They shall look after your persons and the whole tent; however, they shall not come near the sacred vessels or the altar, lest both they and you die. 4 As your associates they shall have charge of all the work connected with the meeting tent. But no layman shall come near you. 5 You shall have charge of the sanctuary and of the altar, that wrath may not fall again upon the Israelites.

6 "Remember, it is I who have taken your kinsmen, the Levites, from the body of the Israelites; they are a gift to you, dedicated to the LORD for the service of the meeting tent. 7 But only you and your sons are to have charge of performing the priestly functions in whatever concerns the altar and the room within the veil. I give you the priesthood as a gift. Any layman who draws near shall be put to death."

8 The LORD said to Aaron, "I myself have given you charge of the contributions made to me in the various sacred offerings of the Israelites; by perpetual ordinance I have assigned them to you and to your sons as your priestly share. 9 You shall have the right to share in the oblations that are most sacred, in whatever they offer me as cereal offerings or sin offerings or guilt offerings; these shares shall accrue to you and to your sons. 10 In eating them you shall treat them as most sacred; every male among you may partake of them. As sacred, they belong to you.

11 "You shall also have what is removed from the gift in every wave offering of the Israelites; by perpetual ordinance I have assigned it to you and to your sons and daughters. All in your family who are clean may partake of it. 12 I have

NEW JERUSALEM BIBLE

16 Yahweh spoke to Moses and said, 17 'Tell the Israelites to give you a branch for each of their families, one for each leader of each family: twelve branches. Write the name of each on his branch; 18 and on the branch of Levi write Aaron's name, since the head of the Levite families must have a branch too. 19 You will then put them inside the Tent of Meeting in front of the Testimony, where I make myself known to you. 20 The man whose branch sprouts will be the one I have chosen; this is how I shall put an end to the mutterings of the Israelites about you.'

21 Moses spoke to the Israelites, and all their leaders gave him one branch each, twelve branches in all for their families; Aaron's branch was among them. 22 Moses placed them before Yahweh in the Tent of the Testimony. 23 On the following day Moses went to the Tent of the Testimony and there, already sprouting, was Aaron's branch, representing the House of Levi: buds had formed, flowers had bloomed and almonds had already ripened. 24 Moses then brought out all the branches from before Yahweh to all the Israelites; they examined them and each one took back his own branch.

25 Yahweh then said to Moses, 'Put Aaron's branch back in front of the Testimony, where it will have its ritual place as a warning to the rebellious; thus you will rid me of their muttering for good, without their incurring death.' 26 Moses did as Yahweh had ordered. That is what he did.

27 The Israelites then said to Moses, 'We are lost! We are dead men! We are all dead men! 28 Anyone who approaches Yahweh's Dwelling with an offering will die. Are we to be doomed to the last man?'

18 Yahweh then said to Aaron:
'You, your sons and your ancestor's line with you will be answerable for offences against the sanctuary. You and your sons with you will be answerable for the offences of your priesthood. 2 You will admit your brothers of the branch of Levi, your ancestor's tribe, to join you and serve you, yourself and your sons, before the Tent of the Testimony. 3 They must be at your service and the service of the whole Tent. Provided they do not come near the sacred vessels or the altar, they will be in no more danger of death than you. 4 They must join you, they must take charge of the Tent of Meeting for the entire ministry of the Tent, and no unauthorised person will come near you. 5 You will take charge of the sanctuary and charge of the altar, and retribution will never again befall the Israelites. 6 Of the Israelites, I myself have chosen your brothers the Levites as a gift to you. As men dedicated, they will belong to Yahweh, to serve at the Tent of Meeting. 7 You and your sons will undertake the priestly duties in all that concerns the altar and all that lies behind the curtain. You will perform the liturgy, the duties of which I entrust to your priesthood. But an unauthorised person approaching will incur death.'

8 Yahweh said to Aaron:
'I myself have put you in charge of everything set aside for me. Everything consecrated by the Israelites I give to you and your sons as your portion by perpetual decree. 9 Of the things especially holy, of the food offered, this is what will revert to you: every offering that the Israelites give back to me, whether it be a cereal offering, a sacrifice for sin or a sacrifice of reparation, is a thing especially holy and will revert to you and your sons. 10 You will eat the things especially holy. Every male may eat them. You will regard them as sacred.

11 'To you will revert also whatever is set aside from the offerings of the Israelites, whatever is held out with the gesture of offering; this I give to you and your sons and daughters, by perpetual decree. All members of your household may eat it unless they are unclean. 12 All the best of the

and all the best of the wine and of the grain, the choice produce that they give to the LORD, I have given to you. 13 The first fruits of all that is in their land, which they bring to the LORD, shall be yours; everyone who is clean in your house may eat of it. 14 Every devoted thing in Israel shall be yours. 15 The first issue of the womb of all creatures, human and animal, which is offered to the LORD, shall be yours; but the firstborn of human beings you shall redeem, and the firstborn of unclean animals you shall redeem. 16 Their redemption price, reckoned from one month of age, you shall fix at five shekels of silver, according to the shekel of the sanctuary (that is, twenty gerahs). 17 But the firstborn of a cow, or the firstborn of a sheep, or the firstborn of a goat, you shall not redeem; they are holy. You shall dash their blood on the altar, and shall turn their fat into smoke as an offering by fire for a pleasing odor to the LORD; 18 but their flesh shall be yours, just as the breast that is elevated and as the right thigh are yours. 19 All the holy offerings that the Israelites present to the LORD I have given to you, together with your sons and daughters, as a perpetual due; it is a covenant of salt forever before the LORD for you and your descendants as well. 20 Then the LORD said to Aaron: You shall have no allotment in their land, nor shall you have any share among them; I am your share and your possession among the Israelites.

21 To the Levites I have given every tithe in Israel for a possession in return for the service that they perform, the service in the tent of meeting. 22 From now on the Israelites shall no longer approach the tent of meeting, or else they will incur guilt and die. 23 But the Levites shall perform the service of the tent of meeting, and they shall bear responsibility for their own offenses; it shall be a perpetual statute throughout your generations. But among the Israelites they shall have no allotment, 24 because I have given to the Levites as their portion the tithe of the Israelites, which they set apart as an offering to the LORD. Therefore I have said of them that they shall have no allotment among the Israelites.

25 Then the LORD spoke to Moses, saying: 26 You shall speak to the Levites, saying: When you receive from the Israelites the tithe that I have given you from them for your portion, you shall set apart an offering from it to the LORD, a tithe of the tithe. 27 It shall be reckoned to you as your gift, the same as the grain of the threshing floor and the fullness of the wine press. 28 Thus you also shall set apart an offering to the LORD from all the tithes that you receive from the Israelites; and from them you shall give the LORD's offering to the priest Aaron. 29 Out of all the gifts to you, you shall set apart every offering due to the LORD; the best of all of them is the part to be consecrated. 30 Say also to them: When you have set apart the best of it, then the rest shall be reckoned to the Levites as produce of the threshing floor, and as produce of the wine press. 31 You may eat it in any place, you and your households; for it is your payment for your service in the tent of meeting. 32 You shall incur no guilt by reason of it, when you have offered the best of it. But you shall not profane the holy gifts of the Israelites, on pain of death.

19 The LORD spoke to Moses and Aaron, saying: 2 This is a statute of the law that the LORD has commanded: Tell the Israelites to bring you a red heifer without defect, in which there is no blemish and on which no yoke has been laid. 3 You shall give it to the priest Eleazar, and it shall be taken outside the camp and slaughtered in his presence. 4 The priest Eleazar shall take some of its blood with his finger and sprinkle it seven times towards the front of the tent of meeting. 5 Then the heifer shall be burned in

12 'I give you all the choicest of the oil, the choicest of the new wine and the corn, the firstfruits which are given to the LORD. 13 The first-ripe fruits of all produce in the land which are brought to the LORD are to be yours. Everyone in your household who is ritually clean may eat them.

14 'Everything in Israel which has been devoted to God is to be yours.

15 'All the firstborn of man or animal which are brought to the LORD are to be yours. Notwithstanding, you must accept payment in redemption of every firstborn of man and of unclean beasts: 16 at the end of one month you may redeem it at the fixed price of five shekels of silver by the sacred standard, at the rate of twenty gerahs to the shekel. 17 You must not, however, allow the redemption of the firstborn of a cow, sheep, or goat; they are holy. You must fling their blood against the altar and burn their fat in sacrifice as a food-offering of soothing odour to the LORD; 18 their flesh is yours, as are the breast of the dedicated portion and the right leg.

19 'All the dedicated portions, which the Israelites set aside for the LORD, I give to you and to your sons and daughters with you as a due for all time. This is a perpetual covenant of salt before the LORD with you and your descendants also.'

20 The LORD said to Aaron: 'You are to have no holding in Israel, no share of land among them; I am your holding in Israel, I am your share.

21 'To the Levites I give every tithe in Israel to be their share, in return for the service they render in maintaining the Tent of Meeting. 22 In order that the Israelites may not henceforth approach the Tent and thus incur the penalty of death, 23 the Levites alone are to perform the service of the Tent and accept full responsibility for it. This rule is binding on your descendants for all time. They are to have no share of land among the Israelites, 24 because as their holding I give them the tithe which the Israelites set aside as a contribution to the LORD. Therefore I say concerning them: They are to have no holding among the Israelites.'

25 The LORD told Moses 26 to say to the Levites: 'When you receive from the Israelites the tithe which I give you from them as your share, you are to set aside from it the contribution to the LORD, a tithe of the tithe. 27 Your contribution will count for you as if it were corn from the threshing-floor and juice from the wine vat. 28 In this way you too will set aside the contribution due to the LORD out of all tithes which you receive from the Israelites, and you will give the LORD's contribution to Aaron the priest. 29 Out of all the gifts you receive you are to set aside the contribution due to the LORD; and the gift which you consecrate must be taken from the choicest of them.

30 'Say to them also: When you have set aside the choicest part of your portion, what remains will count for you as the produce of the threshing-floor and the wine vat, 31 and you may eat it anywhere, you and your households. It is your payment for service in the Tent of Meeting. 32 When you have set aside its choicest part, you will incur no penalty in respect of it, and you will not be profaning the holy gifts of the Israelites; so you will escape death.'

19 THE LORD said to Moses and Aaron: 2 'This is a statute of the law which the LORD has ordained. Tell the Israelites to bring you a red cow without blemish or defect, one which has never borne a yoke. 3 Give it to Eleazar the priest, to be taken outside the camp and slaughtered to the east of it. 4 Eleazar the priest is to take some of the blood on his finger and sprinkle it seven times towards the front of the Tent of Meeting. 5 The cow must be burnt

also assigned to you all the best of the new oil and of the new wine and grain that they give to the LORD as their first fruits; 13 and likewise, of whatever grows on their land, the first products that they bring in to the LORD shall be yours; all of your family who are clean may partake of them. 14 Whatever is doomed in Israel shall be yours. 15 Every living thing that opens the womb, whether of man or of beast, such as are to be offered to the LORD, shall be yours; but you must let the first-born of man, as well as of unclean animals, be redeemed. 16 The ransom for a boy is to be paid when he is a month old; it is fixed at five silver shekels according to the sanctuary standard, twenty gerahs to the shekel. 17 But the first-born of cattle, sheep or goats shall not be redeemed; they are sacred. Their blood you must splash on the altar and their fat you must burn as a sweet-smelling oblation to the LORD. 18 Their meat, however, shall be yours, just as the breast and the right leg of the wave offering belong to you. 19 By perpetual ordinance I have assigned to you and to your sons and daughters all the contributions from the sacred gifts which the Israelites make to the LORD; this is an inviolable covenant to last forever before the LORD, for you and for your descendants." 20 Then the LORD said to Aaron, "You shall not have any heritage in the land of the Israelites nor hold any portion among them; I will be your portion and your heritage among them. 21 "To the Levites, however, I hereby assign all tithes in Israel as their heritage in recompense for the service they perform in the meeting tent. 22 The Israelites may no longer approach the meeting tent; else they will incur guilt deserving death. 23 Only the Levites are to perform the service of the meeting tent, and they alone shall be held responsible; this is a perpetual ordinance for all your generations. The Levites, therefore, shall not have any heritage among the Israelites, 24 for I have assigned to them as their heritage the tithes which the Israelites give as a contribution to the LORD. That is why I have ordered that they are not to have any heritage among the Israelites."

25 The LORD said to Moses, 26 "Give the Levites these instructions: When you receive from the Israelites the tithes I have assigned you from them as your heritage, you are to make a contribution from them to the LORD, a tithe of the tithes; 27 and your contribution will be credited to you as if it were grain from the threshing floor or new wine from the press. 28 Thus you too shall make a contribution from all the tithes you receive from the Israelites, handing over to Aaron the priest the part to be contributed to the LORD. 29 From all the gifts that you receive, and from the best parts, you are to consecrate to the LORD your own full contribution. 30 "Tell them also: Once you have made your contribution from the best part, the rest of the tithes will be credited to you Levites as if it were produce of the threshing floor or of the wine press. 31 Your families, as well as you, may eat them anywhere, since they are your recompense for service at the meeting tent. 32 You will incur no guilt so long as you make a contribution of the best part. Do not profane the sacred gifts of the Israelites and so bring death on yourselves."

19 The LORD said to Moses and Aaron: 2 "This is the regulation which the law of the LORD prescribes. Tell the Israelites to procure for you a red heifer that is free from every blemish and defect and on which no yoke has ever been laid. 3 This is to be given to Eleazar the priest, to be led outside the camp and slaughtered in his presence. 4 Eleazar the priest shall take some of its blood on his finger and sprinkle it seven times toward the front of the meeting tent. 5 Then the heifer shall be burned in his sight, with its

oil, all the best of the new wine and wheat, these first-fruits offered by them to Yahweh I give to you. 13 All the first produce of the country brought by them to Yahweh will revert to you. All members of your household may eat it unless they are unclean. 14 Everything in Israel put under the curse of destruction will revert to you. 15 Every first-born of all creatures brought to Yahweh, human or animal, will revert to you, but you will have to redeem the first-born of man; you will also redeem the first-born of an unclean animal. 16 You will redeem it in the month in which it is born, valuing it at five shekels, at the sanctuary shekel, which is twenty *gerah*. 17 But you will not redeem the first-born of cow, sheep and goat. They are holy: you will sprinkle their blood on the altar and burn the fat as food burnt to be a smell pleasing to Yahweh; 18 the meat will revert to you, as will the forequarter that has been presented with the gesture of offering, and the right thigh. 19 Everything the Israelites set aside for Yahweh from the holy things, I give to you and your sons and daughters, by perpetual decree. This is a covenant of salt for ever before Yahweh, for you and your descendants too.'

20 Yahweh said to Aaron:
'You will have no heritage in their country, you will not have a portion like them; I shall be your portion and your heritage among the Israelites.
21 'Look, as heritage I give the Levites all the tithes collected in Israel, in return for their services, for the ministry they render in the Tent of Meeting. 22 The Israelites will no longer approach the Tent of Meeting, on pain of committing a deadly sin. 23 Levi will discharge the duties of the Tent of Meeting, and the Levites will bear the consequences of their own guilt. This is a perpetual decree binding all your descendants: the Levites will have no heritage among the Israelites, 24 for the tithe which the Israelites set aside for Yahweh is the heritage I have given the Levites. This is why I have told them that they will have no heritage among the Israelites.'

25 Yahweh spoke to Moses and said, 26 'Speak to the Levites and say:
"When from the Israelites you receive the tithe which I have given you from them as your heritage, you will set a portion of this aside for Yahweh: a tithe of the tithe. 27 It will take the place of the portion set aside that is due from you, like the wheat from the threshing-floor and new wine from the press. 28 Thus you too will set a portion aside for Yahweh out of all the tithes you receive from the Israelites. You will give what you have set aside for Yahweh to the priest Aaron. 29 Out of all the gifts you receive, you will set a portion aside for Yahweh. Out of all these things, you will set aside the best, the sacred portion."
30 'You will say to them, "After you have set the best aside, the remainder will take the place, in the Levites' case, of the produce of the threshing-floor and wine-press. 31 You may consume this anywhere, you and the members of your households; this is your recompense for serving in the Tent of Meeting, 32 and you will not incur sin by doing so, once you have set aside the best; you will not be profaning the things consecrated by the Israelites and will not incur death." '

19 Yahweh spoke to Moses and Aaron and said:
2 'This is a decree of the Law which Yahweh has prescribed. Tell the Israelites, they are to bring you a red heifer without fault or blemish that has never borne the yoke. 3 You will give it to the priest Eleazar. It will then be taken outside the camp and slaughtered in his presence. 4 The priest Eleazar will then take some of the victim's blood on his finger, and sprinkle this blood seven times towards the entrance to the Tent of Meeting. 5 The heifer

his sight; its skin, its flesh, and its blood, with its dung, shall be burned. 6 The priest shall take cedarwood, hyssop, and crimson material, and throw them into the fire in which the heifer is burning. 7 Then the priest shall wash his clothes and bathe his body in water, and afterwards he may come into the camp; but the priest shall remain unclean until evening. 8 The one who burns the heifer*i* shall wash his clothes in water and bathe his body in water; he shall remain unclean until evening. 9 Then someone who is clean shall gather up the ashes of the heifer, and deposit them outside the camp in a clean place; and they shall be kept for the congregation of the Israelites for the water for cleansing. It is a purification offering. 10 The one who gathers the ashes of the heifer shall wash his clothes and be unclean until evening.

This shall be a perpetual statute for the Israelites and for the alien residing among them. 11 Those who touch the dead body of any human being shall be unclean seven days. 12 They shall purify themselves with the water on the third day and on the seventh day, and so be clean; but if they do not purify themselves on the third day and on the seventh day, they will not become clean. 13 All who touch a corpse, the body of a human being who has died, and do not purify themselves, defile the tabernacle of the LORD; such persons shall be cut off from Israel. Since water for cleansing was not dashed on them, they remain unclean; their uncleanness is still on them.

14 This is the law when someone dies in a tent: everyone who comes into the tent, and everyone who is in the tent, shall be unclean seven days. 15 And every open vessel with no cover fastened on it is unclean. 16 Whoever in the open field touches one who has been killed by a sword, or who has died naturally,*j* or a human bone, or a grave, shall be unclean seven days. 17 For the unclean they shall take some ashes of the burnt purification offering, and running water shall be added in a vessel; 18 then a clean person shall take hyssop, dip it in the water, and sprinkle it on the tent, on all the furnishings, on the persons who were there, and on whoever touched the bone, the slain, the corpse, or the grave. 19 The clean person shall sprinkle the unclean ones on the third day and on the seventh day, thus purifying them on the seventh day. Then they shall wash their clothes and bathe themselves in water, and at evening they shall be clean. 20 Any who are unclean but do not purify themselves, those persons shall be cut off from the assembly, for they have defiled the sanctuary of the LORD. Since the water for cleansing has not been dashed on them, they are unclean.

21 It shall be a perpetual statute for them. The one who sprinkles the water for cleansing shall wash his clothes, and whoever touches the water for cleansing shall be unclean until evening. 22 Whatever the unclean person touches shall be unclean, and anyone who touches it shall be unclean until evening.

20 The Israelites, the whole congregation, came into the wilderness of Zin in the first month, and the people stayed in Kadesh. Miriam died there, and was buried there.

2 Now there was no water for the congregation; so they gathered together against Moses and against Aaron. 3 The people quarreled with Moses and said, "Would that we had died when our kindred died before the LORD! 4 Why have you brought the assembly of the LORD into this wilderness for us and our livestock to die here? 5 Why have you brought us up out of Egypt, to bring us to this wretched place? It is no place for grain, or figs, or vines, or pomegranates; and there is no water to drink." 6 Then Moses and Aaron went

in his sight, skin, flesh, and blood, together with the offal. 6 The priest must then take cedar-wood, marjoram, and scarlet thread, and throw them into the heart of the fire in which the cow is burning. 7 He must wash his clothes and bathe his body in water; after which he may enter the camp, but he remains ritually unclean till sunset. 8 The man who burnt the cow must wash his clothes and bathe his body in water; he also remains unclean till sunset. 9 Then a man who is clean is to collect the ashes of the cow and deposit them outside the camp in a clean place. They shall be reserved for use by the Israelite community in the water of ritual purification; for the cow is a purification-offering. 10 The man who collected the ashes of the cow must wash his clothes, and he remains unclean till sunset. This statute is to be binding for all time on the Israelites and on the alien living among them.

11 'Whoever touches a dead body is ritually unclean for seven days. 12 He must get himself purified with the water of ritual purification on the third day and on the seventh day, and then he is clean. If he is not purified both on the third day and on the seventh, he is not clean. 13 Anyone who touches a dead person, that is the body of a person who has died, and does not purify himself, defiles the Tabernacle of the LORD; he is to be cut off from Israel. The water of purification has not been flung over him; he remains unclean, and his impurity is still upon him.

14 'When someone dies in a tent, this is the law: everyone who enters the tent and everyone already in it is ritually unclean for seven days, 15 and every open vessel which has no covering tied over it is unclean. 16 In the open, anyone who touches someone killed with a weapon or someone who has died naturally, or anyone who touches a human bone or a grave, is unclean for seven days. 17 For such uncleanness, they must take some of the ash from the burnt mass of the purification-offering and add fresh water to it in a vessel. 18 Then a person who is clean should take marjoram, dip it in the water, and sprinkle the tent and all the vessels in it and all the people who were there, or anyone who has touched a human bone, a corpse (whether the person was killed or died naturally), or a grave. 19 The one who is clean must sprinkle the one who is unclean on the third day and on the seventh; on the seventh day he is to purify him; then the one who is unclean must wash his clothes and bathe in water, and at sunset he will be clean. 20 If anyone who is unclean does not get himself purified, that person is to be cut off from the assembly, because he has defiled the sanctuary of the LORD. As long as the water of purification has not been flung over him, he is unclean. 21 This rule is to be binding on you for all time. The man who sprinkles the water of purification must also wash his clothes, and whoever touches the water is unclean till sunset. 22 Whatever the unclean man touches is unclean, and anyone who touches it will be unclean till sunset.'

20 IN the first month the whole community of Israel arrived in the wilderness of Zin and stayed some time at Kadesh. Miriam died and was buried there.

2 As the community was without water, the people gathered against Moses and Aaron. 3 They disputed with Moses. 'If only we had perished when our brothers perished before the LORD!' they said. 4 'Why have you brought the LORD's assembly into this wilderness for us and our livestock to die here? 5 Why did you make us come up from Egypt to land us in this terrible place, where nothing will grow, neither grain nor figs nor vines nor pomegranates? There is not even water to drink.'

---

i Heb *it* *j* Heb lacks *naturally*

19:21 **you:** *so some MSS; others* them.

hide and flesh, its blood and offal; 6 and the priest shall take some cedar wood, hyssop and scarlet yarn and throw them into the fire in which the heifer is being burned. 7 The priest shall then wash his garments and bathe his body in water. He remains unclean until the evening, and only afterward may he return to the camp. 8 Likewise, he who burned the heifer shall wash his garments, bathe his body in water, and be unclean until evening. 9 Finally, a man who is clean shall gather up the ashes of the heifer and deposit them in a clean place outside the camp. There they are to be kept for preparing lustral water for the Israelite community. The heifer is a sin offering. 10 He who has gathered up the ashes of the heifer shall also wash his garments and be unclean until evening. This is a perpetual ordinance, both for the Israelites and for the aliens residing among them.

11 "Whoever touches the dead body of any human being shall be unclean for seven days; 12 he shall purify himself with the water on the third and on the seventh day, and then he will be clean again. But if he fails to purify himself on the third and on the seventh day, he will not become clean. 13 Everyone who fails to purify himself after touching the body of any deceased person, defiles the Dwelling of the LORD and shall be cut off from Israel. Since the lustral water has not been splashed over him, he remains unclean: his uncleanness still clings to him.

14 "This is the law: When a man dies in a tent, everyone who enters the tent, as well as everyone already in it, shall be unclean for seven days; 15 likewise, every vessel that is open, or with its lid unfastened, shall be unclean. 16 Moreover, everyone who in the open country touches a dead person, whether he was slain by the sword or died naturally, or who touches a human bone or a grave, shall be unclean for seven days. 17 For anyone who is thus unclean, ashes from the sin offering shall be put in a vessel, and spring water shall be poured on them. 18 Then a man who is clean shall take some hyssop, dip it in this water, and sprinkle it on the tent and on all the vessels and persons that were in it, or on him who touched a bone, a slain person or other dead body, or a grave. 19 The clean man shall sprinkle the unclean on the third and on the seventh day; thus purified on the seventh day, he shall wash his garments and bathe his body in water, and in the evening he will be clean again. 20 Any unclean man who fails to have himself purified shall be cut off from the community, because he defiles the sanctuary of the LORD. As long as the lustral water has not been splashed over him, he remains unclean. 21 This shall be a perpetual ordinance for you.

"One who sprinkles the lustral water shall wash his garments, and anyone who comes in contact with this water shall be unclean until evening. 22 Moreover, whatever the unclean person touches becomes unclean itself, and anyone who touches it becomes unclean until evening."

20 The whole Israelite community arrived in the desert of Zin in the first month, and the people settled at Kadesh. It was here that Miriam died, and here that she was buried.

2 As the community had no water, they held a council against Moses and Aaron. 3 The people contended with Moses, exclaiming, "Would that we too had perished with our kinsmen in the LORD's presence! 4 Why have you brought the LORD's community into this desert where we and our livestock are dying? 5 Why did you lead us out of Egypt, only to bring us to this wretched place which has neither grain nor figs nor vines nor pomegranates? Here there is not even water to drink!" 6 But Moses and Aaron went away

will then be burnt while he looks on; its hide, flesh, blood and offal will be burnt. 6 The priest will then take some cedar wood, hyssop and scarlet material and throw them on the fire where the heifer is burning. 7 He will then wash his clothes and bathe himself; after which he will go back to the camp, though he will remain unclean until evening. 8 The man who has burnt the heifer will wash his clothes and bathe himself and will remain unclean until evening. 9 The man who gathers up the ashes of the heifer must be ritually clean; he will deposit them outside the camp, in a clean place. They will be kept for the ritual use of the Israelite community for making water for purification; it is a sacrifice for sin. 10 The man who has gathered up the ashes of the heifer will wash his clothes and remain unclean until evening. For the Israelites as for the resident alien, this will be a perpetual decree.

11 'Anyone who touches the corpse of anyone whatever will be unclean for seven days. 12 Such a person must be purified with these waters on the third and seventh day and will then be clean; otherwise he will not be clean. 13 Anyone who touches the corpse of anyone who has died and is not purified, defiles Yahweh's Dwelling; such a person will be outlawed from Israel, since the water for purification has not been sprinkled over him; he is unclean, and his uncleanness remains in him.

14 'This is the law when someone dies in a tent. Anyone who goes into the tent, or anyone who is already in it, will be unclean for seven days, 15 and every open vessel with no cover tied over it will also be unclean.

16 'Anyone in the open country who touches a murder victim, a corpse, human bones or a grave will be unclean for seven days.

17 'For someone thus unclean, some of the ashes of the victim burnt as a sacrifice for sin will be taken and spring water must be poured over them, in a vessel. 18 Someone who is ritually clean will then take some hyssop and dip it in the water. This person will then sprinkle the tent, all the vessels and people who were there, and similarly anyone who has touched human bones, a murder victim, a corpse or a grave. 19 On the third and the seventh day the clean one will sprinkle the unclean, who on the seventh day will be clean. The latter will then wash his clothes and bathe in water, and in the evening he will be clean. 20 Anyone who fails to be purified in this way will be outlawed from the community, and would defile Yahweh's sanctuary. Such a person is unclean, not having been sprinkled with the water for purification.

21 'This will be a perpetual decree for them. The person who sprinkles the water for purification will wash his clothes, and anyone who touches the water for purification will be unclean until evening. 22 Anything that an unclean person touches will be unclean, and anyone who touches it will be unclean until evening.'

20 h The Israelites, the whole community, arrived in the first month at the desert of Zin. The people settled at Kadesh. There Miriam died and was buried.

2 There was no water for the community, so they banded together against Moses and Aaron. 3 The people laid the blame on Moses. 'We would rather have died', they said, 'as our brothers died before Yahweh! 4 Why have you brought Yahweh's community into this desert, for us and our livestock to die here? 5 Why did you lead us out of Egypt, only to bring us to this wretched place? It is a place unfit for sowing, it has no figs, no vines, no pomegranates, and there is not even water to drink!'

h 20 20:1seq. // Ex 17:1–7.

NEW REVISED STANDARD VERSION

away from the assembly to the entrance of the tent of meeting; they fell on their faces, and the glory of the LORD appeared to them. 7 The LORD spoke to Moses, saying: 8 Take the staff, and assemble the congregation, you and your brother Aaron, and command the rock before their eyes to yield its water. Thus you shall bring water out of the rock for them; thus you shall provide drink for the congregation and their livestock.

9 So Moses took the staff from before the LORD, as he had commanded him. 10 Moses and Aaron gathered the assembly together before the rock, and he said to them, "Listen, you rebels, shall we bring water for you out of this rock?" 11 Then Moses lifted up his hand and struck the rock twice with his staff; water came out abundantly, and the congregation and their livestock drank. 12 But the LORD said to Moses and Aaron, "Because you did not trust in me, to show my holiness before the eyes of the Israelites, therefore you shall not bring this assembly into the land that I have given them." 13 These are the waters of Meribah, *k* where the people of Israel quarreled with the LORD, and by which he showed his holiness.

14 Moses sent messengers from Kadesh to the king of Edom, "Thus says your brother Israel: You know all the adversity that has befallen us: 15 how our ancestors went down to Egypt, and we lived in Egypt a long time; and the Egyptians oppressed us and our ancestors; 16 and when we cried to the LORD, he heard our voice, and sent an angel and brought us out of Egypt; and here we are in Kadesh, a town on the edge of your territory. 17 Now let us pass through your land. We will not pass through field or vineyard, or drink water from any well; we will go along the King's Highway, not turning aside to the right hand or to the left until we have passed through your territory."

18 But Edom said to him, "You shall not pass through, or we will come out with the sword against you." 19 The Israelites said to him, "We will stay on the highway; and if we drink of your water, we and our livestock, then we will pay for it. It is only a small matter; just let us pass through on foot." 20 But he said, "You shall not pass through." And Edom came out against them with a large force, heavily armed. 21 Thus Edom refused to give Israel passage through their territory; so Israel turned away from them.

22 They set out from Kadesh, and the Israelites, the whole congregation, came to Mount Hor. 23 Then the LORD said to Moses and Aaron at Mount Hor, on the border of the land of Edom, 24 "Let Aaron be gathered to his people. For he shall not enter the land that I have given to the Israelites, because you rebelled against my command at the waters of Meribah. 25 Take Aaron and his son Eleazar, and bring them up Mount Hor; 26 strip Aaron of his vestments, and put them on his son Eleazar. But Aaron shall be gathered to his people, *l* and shall die there." 27 Moses did as the LORD had commanded; they went up Mount Hor in the sight of the whole congregation. 28 Moses stripped Aaron of his vestments, and put them on his son Eleazar; and Aaron died there on the top of the mountain. Moses and Eleazar came down from the mountain. 29 When all the congregation saw that Aaron had died, all the house of Israel mourned for Aaron thirty days.

21 When the Canaanite, the king of Arad, who lived in the Negeb, heard that Israel was coming by the way of Atharim, he fought against Israel and took some of them captive. 2 Then Israel made a vow to the LORD and said, "If you will indeed give this people into our hands, then we will utterly destroy their towns." 3 The LORD listened to the

REVISED ENGLISH BIBLE

6 Moses and Aaron went from the assembly to the entrance of the Tent of Meeting, where they prostrated themselves, and the glory of the LORD appeared to them. 7 The LORD said to Moses, 8 'Take your staff, and then with Aaron your brother assemble the community, and in front of them all command the rock to yield its waters. Thus you will produce water for the community out of the rock, for them and their livestock to drink.' 9 Moses took his staff from before the LORD, as he had been ordered. 10 He with Aaron assembled the people in front of the rock, and said to them, 'Listen, you rebels. Must we get water for you out of this rock?' 11 Moses raised his hand and struck the rock twice with his staff. Water gushed out in abundance and they all drank, men and animals. 12 But the LORD said to Moses and Aaron, 'You did not trust me so far as to uphold my holiness in the sight of the Israelites; therefore you will not lead this assembly into the land I am giving them.' 13 Such were the waters of Meribah, where the people disputed with the LORD and through which his holiness was upheld.

14 FROM Kadesh Moses sent envoys to the king of Edom: 'This message is from your brother Israel. You know all the hardships we have encountered, 15 how our ancestors went down to Egypt, and we lived there for many years. The Egyptians ill-treated us and our fathers before us, 16 and we cried to the LORD for help. He listened to us, sent an angel, and brought us out of Egypt.

'Now we are here at Kadesh, a town on your frontier. 17 Grant us, we ask, passage through your country. We shall not trespass on field or vineyard, nor drink from your wells. We shall keep to the king's highway, not turning off to right or left until we have crossed your territory.' 18 But the Edomites answered, 'You shall not cross our land. If you do, we shall march out and attack you.' 19 The Israelites said, 'But we shall keep to the main road. If we and our flocks drink your water, we shall pay you for it. Ours is a trifling request: we would simply cross your land on foot.' 20 But the Edomites refused, and marched out to oppose them with a large army in full strength. 21 Since the Edomites would not allow Israel to cross their frontier, Israel turned and went a different way.

22 The whole community of Israel set out from Kadesh and came to Mount Hor. 23 There, near the frontier of Edom, the LORD said to Moses and Aaron, 24 'Aaron is now to be gathered to his father's kin. He will not enter the land which I am giving to the Israelites, because over the waters of Meribah you both rebelled against my command. 25 Take Aaron and his son Eleazar, and go up Mount Hor. 26 Strip Aaron of his robes and invest Eleazar his son with them, for Aaron is to be taken from you: he will die there.' 27 Moses did as the LORD had commanded: in full view of the whole community they went up Mount Hor, 28 where Moses stripped Aaron of his robes and invested his son Eleazar with them. Aaron died there on the mountaintop. When Moses and Eleazar came down from the mountain, 29 the whole Israelite community saw that Aaron had died, and all the people mourned for thirty days.

21 When the Canaanite king of Arad, who lived in the Negeb, heard that the Israelites were coming by way of Atharim, he gave battle and took some of the Israelites prisoner. 2 Israel made this vow to the LORD, 'If you deliver this people into our power, we will utterly destroy their towns.' 3 The LORD listened to Israel and delivered up

---

k That is *Quarrel*   *l* Heb lacks *to his people*   20:13 **Meribah:** *that is* Dispute.

from the assembly to the entrance of the meeting tent, where they fell prostrate.

Then the glory of the LORD appeared to them, 7 and the LORD said to Moses, 8 "Take the staff and assemble the community, you and your brother Aaron, and in their presence order the rock to yield its waters. From the rock you shall bring forth water for the community and their livestock to drink." 9 So Moses took the staff from its place before the LORD, as he was ordered. 10 He and Aaron assembled the community in front of the rock, where he said to them, "Listen to me, you rebels! Are we to bring water for you out of this rock?" 11 Then, raising his hand, Moses struck the rock twice with his staff, and water gushed out in abundance for the community and their livestock to drink. 12 But the LORD said to Moses and Aaron, "Because you were not faithful to me in showing forth my sanctity before the Israelites, you shall not lead this community into the land I will give them."

13 These are the waters of Meribah, where the Israelites contended against the LORD, and where he revealed his sanctity among them.

14 From Kadesh Moses sent men to the king of Edom with the message: "Your brother Israel has this to say: You know of all the hardships that have befallen us, 15 how our fathers went down to Egypt, where we stayed a long time, how the Egyptians maltreated us and our fathers, 16 and how, when we cried to the LORD, he heard our cry and sent an angel who led us out of Egypt. Now here we are at the town of Kadesh at the edge of your territory. 17 Kindly let us pass through your country. We will not cross any fields or vineyards, nor drink any well water, but we will go straight along the royal road without turning to the right or to the left, until we have passed through your territory."

18 But Edom answered him, "You shall not pass through here; if you do, I will advance against you with the sword." 19 The Israelites insisted, "We want only to go up along the highway. If we or our livestock drink any of your water, we will pay for it. Surely there is no harm in merely letting us march through." 20 But Edom still said, "No, you shall not pass through," and advanced against them with a large and heavily armed force. 21 Therefore, since Edom refused to let them pass through their territory, Israel detoured around them.

22 Setting out from Kadesh, the whole Israelite community came to Mount Hor. 23 There at Mount Hor, on the border of the land of Edom, the LORD said to Moses and Aaron, 24 "Aaron is about to be taken to his people; he shall not enter the land I am giving to the Israelites, because you both rebelled against my commandment at the waters of Meribah. 25 Take Aaron and his son Eleazar and bring them up on Mount Hor. 26 Then strip Aaron of his garments and put them on his son Eleazar; for there Aaron shall be taken in death."

27 Moses did as the LORD commanded. When they had climbed Mount Hor in view of the whole community, 28 Moses stripped Aaron of his garments and put them on his son Eleazar. Then Aaron died there on top of the mountain. When Moses and Eleazar came down from the mountain, 29 all the community understood that Aaron had passed away; and for thirty days the whole house of Israel mourned him.

21 When the Canaanite king of Arad, who lived in the Negeb, heard that the Israelites were coming along the way of Atharim, he engaged them in battle and took some of them captive. 2 Israel then made this vow to the LORD: "If you deliver this people into my hand, I will doom their cities." 3 Later, when the LORD heeded Israel's prayer

6 Leaving the assembly, Moses and Aaron went to the entrance of the Tent of Meeting. They threw themselves on their faces, and the glory of Yahweh appeared to them. 7 Yahweh then spoke to Moses and said, 8 'Take the branch and call the community together, you and your brother Aaron. Then, in full view of them, order this rock to release its water. You will release water from the rock for them and provide drink for the community and their livestock.'

9 Moses took up the branch from before Yahweh, as he had directed him. 10 Moses and Aaron then called the assembly together in front of the rock. He then said to them, 'Listen now, you rebels. Shall we make water gush from this rock for you?' 11 Moses then raised his hand and struck the rock twice with the branch; water gushed out in abundance, and the community and their livestock drank.

12 Yahweh then said to Moses and Aaron, 'Because you did not believe that I could assert my holiness before the Israelites' eyes, you will not lead this assembly into the country which I am giving them.'

13 These were the Waters of Meribah, where the Israelites laid the blame on Yahweh and where, by their means, he asserted his holiness.

14 Moses sent messengers from Kadesh: 'To the king of Edom. Your brother Israel says this: You are aware of the great hardships we have encountered. 15 Our ancestors went down to Egypt and there we stayed for a long time. But the Egyptians treated us badly, as they had our ancestors. 16 When we appealed to Yahweh, he heard our cry and, sending an angel, brought us out of Egypt, and here we are, now, at Kadesh, a town on the borders of your territory. 17 We ask permission to pass through your country. We shall not go through the fields or vineyards; we shall not drink the water from the wells; we shall keep to the king's highway without turning to right or left until we have passed through your territory.' 18 To which, Edom replied, 'You will not pass through my country; if you do, I shall oppose you by force of arms.' 19 To which the Israelites replied, 'We shall keep to the high road; if I and my flocks drink any of your water, I am willing to pay for it. All I am asking is to pass through on foot.' 20 Edom replied: 'You shall not pass,' and Edom opposed them in great numbers and great force. 21 At Edom's refusal to grant Israel passage through his territory, Israel turned away.

22 They set out from Kadesh, and the Israelites, the whole community, came to Mount Hor. 23 Yahweh spoke to Moses and Aaron at Mount Hor, on the frontier of Edom, and said, 24 'Aaron is to be gathered to his people; he will not enter the country which I have given to the Israelites, since you both disobeyed my order at the Waters of Meribah. 25 Take Aaron and his son Eleazar and bring them up Mount Hor. 26 Then take Aaron's robes off him and dress his son Eleazar in them. Aaron will then be gathered to his people; that is where he will die.'

27 Moses did as Yahweh ordered. With the whole community watching, they went up Mount Hor. 28 Moses took Aaron's robes off him and dressed his son Eleazar in them, and there Aaron died, on the mountain-top. Moses and Eleazar then came back down the mountain. 29 The whole community saw that Aaron had died, and for thirty days the whole House of Israel mourned for Aaron.

21 The king of Arad, the Canaanite living in the Negeb, learned that Israel was coming by way of Atharim. He attacked Israel and took some prisoners. 2 Israel then made this vow to Yahweh, 'If you deliver this people into my power, I shall curse their towns with destruction.' 3 Yahweh heard Israel's words and delivered the

NEW REVISED STANDARD VERSION

voice of Israel, and handed over the Canaanites; and they utterly destroyed them and their towns; so the place was called Hormah.*m*

4 From Mount Hor they set out by the way to the Red Sea,*n* to go around the land of Edom; but the people became impatient on the way. 5 The people spoke against God and against Moses, "Why have you brought us up out of Egypt to die in the wilderness? For there is no food and no water, and we detest this miserable food." 6 Then the LORD sent poisonous*o* serpents among the people, and they bit the people, so that many Israelites died. 7 The people came to Moses and said, "We have sinned by speaking against the LORD and against you; pray to the LORD to take away the serpents from us." So Moses prayed for the people. 8 And the LORD said to Moses, "Make a poisonous*p* serpent, and set it on a pole; and everyone who is bitten shall look at it and live." 9 So Moses made a serpent of bronze, and put it upon a pole; and whenever a serpent bit someone, that person would look at the serpent of bronze and live.

10 The Israelites set out, and camped in Oboth. 11 They set out from Oboth, and camped at Iye-abarim, in the wilderness bordering Moab toward the sunrise. 12 From there they set out, and camped in the Wadi Zered. 13 From there they set out, and camped on the other side of the Arnon, in*q* the wilderness that extends from the boundary of the Amorites; for the Arnon is the boundary of Moab, between Moab and the Amorites. 14 Wherefore it is said in the Book of the Wars of the LORD,

"Waheb in Suphah and the wadis.
The Arnon 15 and the slopes of the wadis
that extend to the seat of Ar,
and lie along the border of Moab."*r*

16 From there they continued to Beer;*s* that is the well of which the LORD said to Moses, "Gather the people together, and I will give them water." 17 Then Israel sang this song:

"Spring up, O well! — Sing to it! —
18 the well that the leaders sank,
that the nobles of the people dug,
with the scepter, with the staff."

From the wilderness to Mattanah, 19 from Mattanah to Nahaliel, from Nahaliel to Bamoth, 20 and from Bamoth to the valley lying in the region of Moab by the top of Pisgah that overlooks the wasteland.*t*

21 Then Israel sent messengers to King Sihon of the Amorites, saying, 22 "Let me pass through your land; we will not turn aside into field or vineyard; we will not drink the water of any well; we will go by the King's Highway until we have passed through your territory." 23 But Sihon would not allow Israel to pass through his territory. Sihon gathered all his people together, and went out against Israel to the wilderness; he came to Jahaz, and fought against Israel. 24 Israel put him to the sword, and took possession of his land from the Arnon to the Jabbok, as far as to the Ammonites; for the boundary of the Ammonites was strong. 25 Israel took all these towns, and Israel settled in all the towns of the Amorites, in Heshbon, and in all its villages. 26 For Heshbon was the city of King Sihon of the Amorites, who had fought against the former king of Moab and captured all his land as far as the Arnon. 27 Therefore the ballad singers say,

"Come to Heshbon, let it be built;
let the city of Sihon be established.

m Heb *Destruction*   *n* Or *Sea of Reeds*   *o* Or *fiery*; Heb *seraphim*
p Or *fiery*; Heb *seraph*   *q* Gk: Heb *which is in*   *r* Meaning of Heb
uncertain   *s* That is *Well*   *t* Or *Jeshimon*

REVISED ENGLISH BIBLE

the Canaanites to them. Israel destroyed them and their towns, and the place became known as Hormah.

4 From Mount Hor they left by way of the Red Sea to march round the flank of Edom. But on the way the people grew impatient 5 and spoke against God and Moses. 'Why have you brought us up from Egypt', they said, 'to die in the desert where there is neither food nor water? We are heartily sick of this miserable fare.' 6 Then the LORD sent venomous snakes among them, and they bit the Israelites so that many of them died. 7 The people came to Moses and said, 'We sinned when we spoke against the LORD and you. Plead with the LORD to rid us of the snakes.' Moses interceded for the people, 8 and the LORD told him to make a serpent and erect it as a standard, so that anyone who had been bitten could look at it and recover. 9 So Moses made a bronze serpent and erected it as a standard, in order that anyone bitten by a snake could look at the bronze serpent and recover.

10 The Israelites continued their journey and encamped at Oboth. 11 From there they moved on and encamped at Iye-abarim in the wilderness on the eastern frontier of Moab. 12 When they moved from there they encamped by the wadi Zared. 13 From the Zared they moved on and encamped by the farther side of the Arnon in the wilderness which extends into Amorite territory, for the Arnon was the Moabite frontier, the frontier between Moab and the Amorites. 14 That is why the Book of the Wars of the LORD speaks of Waheb in Suphah and the wadis:

Arnon 15 and the watershed of the wadis
that falls away towards the dwellings at Ar
and slopes towards the frontier of Moab.

16 From there they went on to Be-er: this is the well where the LORD said to Moses, 'Gather the people together and I shall give them water.' 17 It was then that Israel sang this song:

Spring up, O well! Greet it with song,
18 the well dug by the princes,
laid open by the leaders of the people
with sceptre and staff,
a gift from the wilderness.

19 From Be-er they proceeded to Nahaliel, and from Nahaliel to Bamoth; 20 then from Bamoth to the valley in the Moabite country below the summit of Pisgah overlooking Jeshimon.

21 Israel sent envoys to Sihon the Amorite king with this request: 22 'Grant us passage through your country. We shall not trespass on field or vineyard, nor drink from your wells. We shall keep to the king's highway until we have crossed your territory.' 23 But Sihon refused Israel passage through his territory; he mustered his whole army and marched out to oppose Israel in the wilderness. He advanced as far as Jahaz and gave battle, 24 but Israel put them to the sword, and occupied their land from the Arnon to the Jabbok, the territory of the Ammonites, where the country became difficult. 25 Israel seized all those Amorite towns and settled in them, that is in Heshbon and all its dependent villages. 26 Heshbon was the capital of the Amorite king Sihon, who had fought against the former king of Moab, and stripped him of all his territory as far as the Arnon. 27 Therefore the bards say:

Come to Heshbon! Let it be rebuilt!
Let Sihon's capital be restored!

21:3 **to them:** *so Samar.; Heb.* omits. **Hormah:** *that is* Destruction.
21:6 **venomous:** *lit.* burning.   21:8 **a serpent:** *lit.* a burning
thing.   21:14 **Waheb:** *name meaning* Watershed.   21:16 **Be-er:**
name meaning Water-hole.   21:18 **a gift from:** *so Samar.; Heb.*
and from.   21:19 **From Be-er:** *prob. rdg; Heb.* From a gift.

and delivered up the Canaanites, they doomed them and their cities. Hence that place was named Hormah.

4 From Mount Hor they set out on the Red Sea road, to bypass the land of Edom. But with their patience worn out by the journey, 5 the people complained against God and Moses, "Why have you brought us up from Egypt to die in this desert, where there is no food or water? We are disgusted with this wretched food!"

6 In punishment the LORD sent among the people saraph serpents, which bit the people so that many of them died. 7 Then the people came to Moses and said, "We have sinned in complaining against the LORD and you. Pray the LORD to take the serpents from us." So Moses prayed for the people, 8 and the LORD said to Moses, "Make a saraph and mount it on a pole, and if anyone who has been bitten looks at it, he will recover." 9 Moses accordingly made a bronze serpent and mounted it on a pole, and whenever anyone who had been bitten by a serpent looked at the bronze serpent, he recovered.

10 The Israelites moved on and encamped in Oboth. 11 Setting out from Oboth, they encamped in Iye-abarim in the desert fronting Moab on the east. 12 Setting out from there, they encamped in the Wadi Zered. 13 Setting out from there, they encamped on the other side of the Arnon, in the desert that extends from the territory of the Amorites; for the Arnon forms Moab's boundary with the Amorites. 14 Hence it is said in the "Book of the Wars of the LORD" :

"Waheb in Suphah and the wadies,
15   Arnon and the wadi gorges
     That reach back toward the site of Ar
        and slant to the border of Moab."

16 From there they went to Beer, where there was the well of which the LORD said to Moses, "Bring the people together, and I will give them water." 17 Then it was that Israel sang this song:

"Spring up, O well! — so sing to it —
18 The well that the princes sank,
     that the nobles of the people dug,
     with their scepters and their staffs."

From Beer they went to Mattanah, 19 from Mattanah to Nahaliel, from Nahaliel to Bamoth, 20 from Bamoth to the cleft in the plateau of Moab at the headland of Pisgah that overlooks Jeshimon.

21 Now Israel sent men to Sihon, king of the Amorites, with the message, 22 "Let us pass through your country. We will not turn aside into any field or vineyard, nor will we drink any well water, but we will go straight along the royal road until we have passed through your territory." 23 Sihon, however, would not let Israel pass through his territory, but mustered all his forces and advanced into the desert against Israel. When he reached Jahaz, he engaged Israel in battle. 24 But Israel defeated him at the point of the sword, and took possession of his land from the Arnon to the Jabbok and as far as the country of the Ammonites, whose boundary was at Jazer. 25 Israel seized all the towns here and settled in these towns of the Amorites, in Heshbon and all its dependencies. 26 Now Heshbon was the capital of Sihon, king of the Amorites, who had fought against the former king of Moab and had seized all his land from Jazer to the Arnon. 27 That is why the poets say:

"Come to Heshbon, let it be rebuilt,
     let Sihon's capital be firmly constructed.

Canaanites into their power, and they destroyed them in accordance with their curse. Hence the place was given the name Hormah.

4 They left Mount Hor by the road to the Sea of Suph, to skirt round Edom. On the way the people lost patience. 5 They spoke against God and against Moses, 'Why did you bring us out of Egypt to die in the desert? For here is neither food nor water here; we are sick of this meagre diet.'

6 At this, God sent fiery serpents among the people; their bite brought death to many in Israel. 7 The people came and said to Moses, 'We have sinned by speaking against Yahweh and against you. Intercede for us with Yahweh to save us from these serpents.' Moses interceded for the people, 8 and Yahweh replied, 'Make a fiery serpent and raise it as a standard. Anyone who is bitten and looks at it will survive.' 9 Moses then made a serpent out of bronze and raised it as a standard, and anyone who was bitten by a serpent and looked at the bronze serpent survived.

10 The Israelites set out and camped at Oboth. 11 Then they left Oboth and camped at Iye-Abarim, in the desert on the eastern border of Moab. 12 They set out from there and camped in the gorge of the Zered. 13 They set out from there and camped on the other side of the Arnon.

This gorge in the desert begins in the territory of the Amorites. For the Arnon is the frontier of Moab, between the Moabites and the Amorites. 14 That is why it says in the Book of the Wars of Yahweh:

'. . .Waheb near Suphah and the gorges of the Arnon
15 and the slope of the ravine running down to the site of Ar
     and over against the frontier of Moab.'

16 And from there they went to Beer, that being the well in connection with which Yahweh had said to Moses, 'Call the people together and I will give them water.' 17 Then it was that Israel sang this song:

Spring up, well!
Sing out for the well,
18 sunk by the princes,
     dug by the people's leaders
     with the sceptre, with their staves!

— and from the desert to Mattanah, 19 and from Mattanah to Nahaliel, and from Nahaliel to Bamoth, 20 and from Bamoth to the valley that opens into the country of Moab, towards the heights of Pisgah overlooking the desert.

21 *i*Israel sent messengers to say to Sihon king of the Amorites, 22 'I wish to pass through your country. We shall not stray into the fields or vineyards; we shall not drink the water from the wells; we shall keep to the king's highway until we have passed through your territory.'

23 But Sihon would not give Israel leave to pass through his country. He assembled all his people, marched into the desert to meet Israel, and reached Jahaz, where he gave battle to Israel. 24 Israel defeated him by force of arms and conquered his country from the Arnon to the Jabbok, as far as the Ammonites, for Jazer marked the Ammonite frontier. 25 Israel took all these towns. Israel occupied all the Amorite towns, Heshbon and all its dependencies, 26 Heshbon being the capital of Sihon king of the Amorites, who had made war on the first king of Moab and captured all his territory as far as the Arnon. 27 Hence the poets say:

Come to Heshbon!
Let the city of Sihon
be rebuilt on firm foundations!

i 21 21:21seq. // Dt 2:26–36.

28 For fire came out from Heshbon,
    flame from the city of Sihon.
It devoured Ar of Moab,
    and swallowed up[u] the heights of the Arnon.
29 Woe to you, O Moab!
    You are undone, O people of Chemosh!
He has made his sons fugitives,
    and his daughters captives,
    to an Amorite king, Sihon.
30 So their posterity perished
    from Heshbon[v] to Dibon,
and we laid waste until fire spread to
    Medeba."[w]

31 Thus Israel settled in the land of the Amorites. 32 Moses sent to spy out Jazer; and they captured its villages, and dispossessed the Amorites who were there.

33 Then they turned and went up the road to Bashan; and King Og of Bashan came out against them, he and all his people, to battle at Edrei. 34 But the LORD said to Moses, "Do not be afraid of him; for I have given him into your hand, with all his people, and all his land. You shall do to him as you did to King Sihon of the Amorites, who ruled in Heshbon." 35 So they killed him, his sons, and all his people, until there was no survivor left; and they took possession of his land.

22 The Israelites set out, and camped in the plains of Moab across the Jordan from Jericho. 2 Now Balak son of Zippor saw all that Israel had done to the Amorites. 3 Moab was in great dread of the people, because they were so numerous; Moab was overcome with fear of the people of Israel. 4 And Moab said to the elders of Midian, "This horde will now lick up all that is around us, as an ox licks up the grass of the field." Now Balak son of Zippor was king of Moab at that time. 5 He sent messengers to Balaam son of Beor at Pethor, which is on the Euphrates, in the land of Amaw,[x] to summon him, saying, "A people has come out of Egypt; they have spread over the face of the earth, and they have settled next to me. 6 Come now, curse this people for me, since they are stronger than I; perhaps I shall be able to defeat them and drive them from the land; for I know that whomever you bless is blessed, and whomever you curse is cursed."

7 So the elders of Moab and the elders of Midian departed with the fees for divination in their hand; and they came to Balaam, and gave him Balak's message. 8 He said to them, "Stay here tonight, and I will bring back word to you, just as the LORD speaks to me"; so the officials of Moab stayed with Balaam. 9 God came to Balaam and said, "Who are these men with you?" 10 Balaam said to God, "King Balak son of Zippor of Moab, has sent me this message: 11 'A people has come out of Egypt and has spread over the face of the earth; now come, curse them for me; perhaps I shall be able to fight against them and drive them out.' " 12 God said to Balaam, "You shall not go with them; you shall not curse the people, for they are blessed." 13 So Balaam rose in the morning, and said to the officials of Balak, "Go to your own land, for the LORD has refused to let me go with you." 14 So the officials of Moab rose and went to Balak, and said, "Balaam refuses to come with us."

15 Once again Balak sent officials, more numerous and more distinguished than these. 16 They came to Balaam and said to him, "Thus says Balak son of Zippor: 'Do not let anything hinder you from coming to me; 17 for I will surely

28 For fire blazed out from Heshbon
and flames from Sihon's city.
It devoured Ar of Moab,
and swept the heights of Arnon.
29 Woe betide you, Moab;
people of Kemosh, it is the end of you.
He has made his sons fugitives
and his daughters captives
of Sihon the Amorite king.
30 From Heshbon to Dibon
their very embers are burnt out
and they are extinct,
while the fire spreads onward to Medeba.

31 Thus Israel occupied the territory of the Amorites. 32 After Moses had sent men to reconnoitre Jazer, the Israelites captured it together with its dependent villages and drove out the Amorites there.

33 They then turned and advanced along the road to Bashan. King Og of Bashan, with his whole army, took the field against them at Edrei, 34 but the LORD said to Moses, 'Do not be afraid of him. I have delivered him into your hands, with all his people and his land. Deal with him as you dealt with Sihon the Amorite king living in Heshbon.' 35 So they put him to the sword with his sons and all his people, until there was no survivor left, and they took possession of his land.

22 THE Israelites moved on and encamped in the lowlands of Moab on the farther side of the Jordan opposite Jericho.

2 Balak son of Zippor saw all that Israel had done to the Amorites, 3 and Moab was in terror of the people because there were so many of them. The Moabites were overcome with fear at the sight of them; 4 and they said to the elders of Midian, 'This horde will soon eat up everything round us as an ox eats up the new grass in the field.' Balak son of Zippor, who was at that time king of Moab, 5 sent a deputation to summon Balaam son of Beor, who was at Pethor by the Euphrates in the land of the Amavites, with this message, 'A whole nation has just arrived from Egypt: they cover the face of the country and are settling at my very door. 6 Come at once and lay a curse on them, because they are too many for me. I may then be able to defeat them and drive them out of the country. I know that those whom you bless are blessed, and those whom you curse are cursed.'

7 The elders of Moab and Midian took the fees for augury with them, and coming to Balaam they gave him Balak's message. 8 'Spend this night here,' he replied, 'and I shall give you whatever answer the LORD gives me.' So the Moabite chiefs stayed with Balaam. 9 God came to Balaam and asked him, 'Who are these men with you?' 10 Balaam replied, 'Balak son of Zippor king of Moab has sent them to me and he says, 11 "A people which has just come out of Egypt is covering the face of the country. Come at once and put a curse on them for me; then I may be able to give battle and drive them away." ' 12 God said to Balaam, 'You are not to go with them or curse the people, because they are to be blessed.' 13 So when Balaam rose in the morning he said to Balak's chiefs, 'Go back to your own country; the LORD has refused to let me go with you.' 14 The Moabite chiefs took their leave and went back to Balak, and reported to him that Balaam had refused to come with them.

15 Balak sent a second embassy, larger and more high-powered than the first. 16 When they came to Balaam they said, 'This is the message from Balak son of Zippor: "Let nothing stand in the way of your coming to me. 17 I shall

[u] Gk: Heb *and the lords of* [v] Gk: Heb *we have shot at them; Heshbon has perished* [w] Compare Sam Gk: Meaning of MT uncertain [x] Or *land of his kinsfolk*

21:30 **while the fire:** so *Samar.*; *Heb.* which. 21:32 **captured . . . villages:** so *Gk; Heb.* captured its dependent villages.
22:12 **are to be blessed:** *or* are blessed.

28 For fire went forth from Heshbon
  and a blaze from the city of Sihon;
It consumed the cities of Moab
  and swallowed up the high places of the Arnon.
29 Woe to you, O Moab!
  You are ruined, O people of Chemosh!
He let his sons become fugitives
  and his daughters be taken captive
by the Amorite king Sihon.
30 Their plowland is ruined from Heshbon to Dibon;
  Ar is laid waste; fires blaze as far as Medeba."

31 When Israel had settled in the land of the Amorites, 32 Moses sent spies to Jazer; Israel then captured it with its dependencies and dispossessed the Amorites who were there.

33 Then they turned and went up along the road to Bashan. But Og, king of Bashan, advanced against them with all his people to give battle at Edrei. 34 The LORD, however, said to Moses, "Do not be afraid of him; for into your hand I will deliver him with all his people and his land. Do to him as you did to Sihon, king of the Amorites, who lived in Heshbon." 35 So they struck him down with his sons and all his people, until not a survivor was left to him, and they took possession of his land.

22 Then the Israelites moved on and encamped in the plains of Moab on the other side of the Jericho stretch of the Jordan.

2 Now Balak, son of Zippor, saw all that Israel did to the Amorites. 3 Indeed, Moab feared the Israelites greatly because of their numbers, and detested them. 4 So Moab said to the elders of Midian, "Soon this horde will devour all the country around us as an ox devours the grass of the field." And Balak, Zippor's son, who was king of Moab at that time, 5 sent messengers to Balaam, son of Beor, at Pethor on the Euphrates, in the land of the Amawites, summoning him with these words, "A people has come here from Egypt who now cover the face of the earth and are settling down opposite us! 6 Please come and curse this people for us; they are stronger than we are. We may then be able to defeat them and drive them out of the country. For I know that whoever you bless is blessed and whoever you curse is cursed." 7 Then the elders of Moab and of Midian left with the divination fee in hand and went to Balaam. When they had given him Balak's message, 8 he said to them in reply, "Stay here overnight, and I will give you whatever answer the LORD gives me." So the princes of Moab lodged with Balaam.

9 Then God came to Balaam and said, "Who are these men visiting you?" 10 Balaam answered God, "Balak, son of Zippor, king of Moab, sent me the message: 11 'This people that came here from Egypt now cover the face of the earth. Please come and lay a curse on them for us; we may then be able to give them battle and drive them out.'" 12 But God said to Balaam, "Do not go with them and do not curse this people, for they are blessed." 13 The next morning Balaam arose and told the princes of Balak, "Go back to your own country, for the LORD has refused to let me go with you." 14 So the princes of Moab went back to Balak with the report, "Balaam refused to come with us."

15 Balak again sent princes, who were more numerous and more distinguished than the others. 16 On coming to Balaam they told him, "This is what Balak, son of Zippor, has to say: Please do not refuse to come to me. 17 I will

28 For fire has burst from Heshbon, *j*
  a flame from the city of Sihon,
devouring Ar of Moab,
  engulfing the heights of the Arnon.
29 Oh, unhappy Moab!
  People of Chemosh, you are lost!
He has resigned his sons as fugitives,
  and his daughters as prisoners
to Sihon king of the Amorites.
30 Their posterity has been destroyed
  from Heshbon all the way to Dibon,
  and we have lit a fire
  all the way from Nophah to Medeba.

31 Thus Israel occupied the Amorites' territory. 32 Moses then sent men to reconnoitre Jazer, and Israel took it and its dependencies, evicting the Amorites who lived there.

33 They then turned and marched on Bashan. Og king of Bashan and all his people marched to meet them and give battle at Edrei. 34 Yahweh said to Moses, 'Do not be afraid of him, for I have put him, all his people and his country at your mercy. Treat him as you treated Sihon king of the Amorites, who lived in Heshbon.' 35 So they pressed their attack against him, his sons and all his people until there was no one left alive. And they took possession of his country.

22 The Israelites then set out and pitched their camp in the Plains of Moab, beyond the Jordan opposite Jericho.

2 Balak son of Zippor saw all that Israel had done to the Amorites, 3 and Moab was terrified of the people, because there were so many of them.

Moab was afraid of the Israelites; 4 he said to the elders of Midian, 'This horde will soon have cropped everything round us as closely as an ox crops grass in the countryside.' Now Balak son of Zippor was king of Moab at the time. 5 He sent messengers to summon Balaam son of Beor, at Pethor on the River, in the territory of the Amawites, saying, 'Look, a people coming from Egypt has overrun the whole countryside; they have halted at my very door. 6 I beg you come and curse this people for me, for they are stronger than I am. We may then be able to defeat them and drive them out of the country. For this I know: anyone you bless is blessed, anyone you curse is accursed.'

7 The elders of Moab and the elders of Midian set out, taking the fee for the divination with them. They found Balaam and gave him Balak's message. 8 He said to them, 'Stay the night here, and I will answer as Yahweh directs me.' So the chiefs of Moab stayed with Balaam. 9 God came to Balaam and said, 'Who are these men staying with you?' 10 Balaam said to God, 'Balak son of Zippor, king of Moab, has sent me this message, 11 "Look, a people coming from Egypt has overrun the whole countryside. Come now and curse them for me; I may then be able to defeat them and drive them out."' 12 God said to Balaam, 'You are not to go with them. You are not to curse the people, for they are blessed.' 13 In the morning Balaam got up and said to the chiefs sent by Balak, 'Go back to your country, for Yahweh will not let me go with you.' 14 So the chiefs of Moab got up, went back to Balak and said, 'Balaam refuses to come with us.'

15 And again Balak sent chiefs, more numerous and more renowned than the first. 16 They came to Balaam and said, 'A message from Balak son of Zippor, "Now do not refuse to come to me. 17 I will load you with honours and do

do you great honor, and whatever you say to me I will do; come, curse this people for me.'" 18 But Balaam replied to the servants of Balak, "Although Balak were to give me his house full of silver and gold, I could not go beyond the command of the LORD my God, to do less or more. 19 You remain here, as the others did, so that I may learn what more the LORD may say to me." 20 That night God came to Balaam and said to him, "If the men have come to summon you, get up and go with them; but do only what I tell you to do." 21 So Balaam got up in the morning, saddled his donkey, and went with the officials of Moab.

22 God's anger was kindled because he was going, and the angel of the LORD took his stand in the road as his adversary. Now he was riding on the donkey, and his two servants were with him. 23 The donkey saw the angel of the LORD standing in the road, with a drawn sword in his hand; so the donkey turned off the road, and went into the field; and Balaam struck the donkey, to turn it back onto the road. 24 Then the angel of the LORD stood in a narrow path between the vineyards, with a wall on either side. 25 When the donkey saw the angel of the LORD, it scraped against the wall, and scraped Balaam's foot against the wall; so he struck it again. 26 Then the angel of the LORD went ahead, and stood in a narrow place, where there was no way to turn either to the right or to the left. 27 When the donkey saw the angel of the LORD, it lay down under Balaam; and Balaam's anger was kindled, and he struck the donkey with his staff. 28 Then the LORD opened the mouth of the donkey, and it said to Balaam, "What have I done to you, that you have struck me these three times?" 29 Balaam said to the donkey, "Because you have made a fool of me! I wish I had a sword in my hand! I would kill you right now!" 30 But the donkey said to Balaam, "Am I not your donkey, which you have ridden all your life to this day? Have I been in the habit of treating you this way?" And he said, "No."

31 Then the LORD opened the eyes of Balaam, and he saw the angel of the LORD standing in the road, with his drawn sword in his hand; and he bowed down, falling on his face. 32 The angel of the LORD said to him, "Why have you struck your donkey these three times? I have come out as an adversary, because your way is perverse y before me. 33 The donkey saw me, and turned away from me these three times. If it had not turned away from me, surely just now I would have killed you and let it live." 34 Then Balaam said to the angel of the LORD, "I have sinned, for I did not know that you were standing in the road to oppose me. Now therefore, if it is displeasing to you, I will return home." 35 The angel of the LORD said to Balaam, "Go with the men; but speak only what I tell you to speak." So Balaam went on with the officials of Balak.

36 When Balak heard that Balaam had come, he went out to meet him at Ir-moab, on the boundary formed by the Arnon, at the farthest point of the boundary. 37 Balak said to Balaam, "Did I not send to summon you? Why did you not come to me? Am I not able to honor you?" 38 Balaam said to Balak, "I have come to you now, but do I have power to say just anything? The word God puts in my mouth, that is what I must say." 39 Then Balaam went with Balak, and they came to Kiriath-huzoth. 40 Balak sacrificed oxen and sheep, and sent them to Balaam and to the officials who were with him.

41 On the next day Balak took Balaam and brought him up to Bamoth-baal; and from there he could see part of the people of Israel. z

confer great honour upon you and do whatever you ask me. But you must come and put a curse on this people for me.' 18 Balaam gave this answer to Balak's messengers: 'Even if Balak were to give me all the silver and gold in his palace, I could not disobey the command of the LORD my God in anything, small or great. 19 But stay here for this night, as the others did, that I may learn what more the LORD may have to say to me.' 20 During the night God came to Balaam and said to him, 'If these men have come to summon you, then rise and go with them, but do only what I tell you.' 21 When morning came Balaam rose, saddled his donkey, and went with the Moabite chiefs.

22 But God was angry because Balaam was going, and as he came riding on his donkey, accompanied by his two servants, the angel of the LORD took his stand in the road to bar his way. 23 When the donkey saw the angel standing in the road with his sword drawn, she turned off the road into the fields, and Balaam beat her to bring her back on to the road. 24 The angel of the LORD then stood where the road ran through a hollow, with enclosed vineyards on either side. 25 The donkey saw the angel and, squeezing herself against the wall, she crushed Balaam's foot against it, and again he beat her. 26 The angel of the LORD moved on farther and stood in a narrow place where there was no room to turn to either right or left. 27 When the donkey saw the angel, she lay down under Balaam. At that Balaam lost his temper and beat the donkey with his staff. 28 The LORD then made the donkey speak, and she said to Balaam, 'What have I done? This is the third time you have beaten me.' 29 Balaam answered, 'You have been making a fool of me. If I had had a sword with me, I should have killed you on the spot.' 30 But the donkey answered, 'Am I not still the donkey which you have ridden all your life? Have I ever taken such a liberty with you before?' He said, 'No.' 31 Then the LORD opened Balaam's eyes: he saw the angel of the LORD standing in the road with his sword drawn, and he bowed down and prostrated himself. 32 The angel said to him, 'What do you mean by beating your donkey three times like this? I came out to bar your way, but you made straight for me, 33 and three times your donkey saw me and turned aside. If she had not turned aside, I should by now have killed you, while sparing her.' 34 'I have done wrong,' Balaam replied to the angel of the LORD. 'I did not know that you stood confronting me in the road. But now, if my journey displeases you, I shall turn back.' 35 The angel of the LORD said to Balaam, 'Go with the men; but say only what I tell you.' So Balaam went on with Balak's chiefs.

36 When Balak heard that Balaam was coming, he went out to meet him as far as Ar of Moab by the Arnon on his frontier. 37 Balak said to Balaam, 'Did I not send time and again to summon you? Why did you not come? Did you think that I could not do you honour?' 38 Balaam replied, 'I have come, as you see. But now that I am here, what power have I of myself to say anything? It is only whatever word God puts into my mouth that I can speak.' 39 So Balaam went with Balak till they came to Kiriath-huzoth, 40 and Balak slaughtered cattle and sheep and sent portions to Balaam and to the chiefs who were with him.

41 In the morning Balak took Balaam and led him up to Bamoth-baal, from where he could see the full extent of the Israelite host.

---

y Meaning of Heb uncertain   z Heb lacks of Israel   22:33 If she had not: so Gk; Heb. Perhaps she had.

reward you very handsomely and will do anything you ask of me. Please come and lay a curse on this people for me." 18 But Balaam replied to Balak's officials, "Even if Balak gave me his house full of silver and gold, I could not do anything, small or great, contrary to the command of the LORD, my God. 19 But, you too shall stay here overnight, till I learn what else the LORD may tell me."

20 That night God came to Balaam and said to him, "If these men have come to summon you, you may go with them; yet only on the condition that you do exactly as I tell you." 21 So the next morning when Balaam arose, he saddled his ass, and went off with the princes of Moab.

22 But now the anger of God flared up at him for going, and the angel of the LORD stationed himself on the road to hinder him as he was riding along on his ass, accompanied by two of his servants. 23 When the ass saw the angel of the LORD standing on the road with sword drawn, she turned off the road and went into the field, and Balaam had to beat her to bring her back on the road. 24 Then the angel of the LORD took his stand in a narrow lane between vineyards with a stone wall on each side. 25 When the ass saw the angel of the LORD there, she shrank against the wall; and since she squeezed Balaam's leg against it, he beat her again. 26 The angel of the LORD then went ahead, and stopped next in a passage so narrow that there was no room to move either to the right or to the left. 27 When the ass saw the angel of the LORD there, she cowered under Balaam. So, in anger, he again beat the ass with his stick.

28 But now the LORD opened the mouth of the ass, and she asked Balaam, "What have I done to you that you should beat me these three times?" 29 "You have acted so willfully against me," said Balaam to the ass, "that if I but had a sword at hand, I would kill you here and now." 30 But the ass said to Balaam, "Am I not your own beast, and have you not always ridden upon me until now? Have I been in the habit of treating you this way before?" "No," replied Balaam.

31 Then the LORD removed the veil from Balaam's eyes, so that he too saw the angel of the LORD standing on the road with sword drawn; and he fell on his knees and bowed to the ground. 32 But the angel of the LORD said to him, "Why have you beaten your ass these three times? It is I who have come armed to hinder you because this rash journey of yours is directly opposed to me. 33 When the ass saw me, she turned away from me these three times. If she had not turned away from me, I would have killed you; her I would have spared." 34 Then Balaam said to the angel of the LORD, "I have sinned. Yet I did not know that you stood against me to oppose my journey. Since it has displeased you, I will go back home." 35 But the angel of the LORD said to Balaam, "Go with the men; but you may say only what I tell you." So Balaam went on with the princes of Balak.

36 When Balak heard that Balaam was coming, he went out to meet him at the boundary city Ir-Moab on the Arnon at the end of the Moabite territory. 37 And he said to Balaam, "I sent an urgent summons to you! Why did you not come to me? Did you think I could not reward you?" 38 Balaam answered him, "Well, I have come to you after all. But what power have I to say anything? I can speak only what God puts in my mouth." 39 Then Balaam went with Balak, and they came to Kiriath-huzoth. 40 Here Balak slaughtered oxen and sheep, and sent portions to Balaam and to the princes who were with him.

41 The next morning Balak took Balaam up on Bamoth-baal, and from there he saw some of the clans.

whatever you say. I beg you come and curse this people for me.' " 18 In reply, Balaam said to Balak's envoys, 'Even if Balak gave me his house full of silver and gold, I could not go against the order of Yahweh my God in anything, great or small. 19 Now please stay the night here yourselves, and I will learn what else Yahweh has to tell me.' 20 God came to Balaam during the night and said to him, 'Have not these men come to summon you? Get up, go with them, but do only what I tell you to do.' 21 Balaam got up and saddled his donkey and set out with the chiefs of Moab.

22 His going kindled Yahweh's anger, and the angel of Yahweh took his stand on the road to bar his way. Balaam was riding his donkey and his two servants were with him. 23 Now the donkey saw the angel of Yahweh standing in the road with a drawn sword in his hand, and she turned off the road into the open country. Balaam then struck the donkey to turn her back onto the road.

24 The angel of Yahweh then went and stood on a narrow path among the vineyards, with a wall to the right and a wall to the left. 25 The donkey saw the angel of Yahweh and scraped against the wall, scraping Balaam's foot against it, so he struck her again.

26 The angel of Yahweh then moved and stood in a place so narrow that there was no room to pass either to right or left. 27 When the donkey saw the angel of Yahweh, she lay down under Balaam. Balaam flew into a rage and struck the donkey with his stick.

28 Yahweh then gave the donkey the power to talk, and she said to Balaam, 'What harm have I done you, for you to strike me three times like this?' 29 Balaam answered the donkey, 'Because you have been making a fool of me! If I had been carrying a sword, I should have killed you by now.' 30 The donkey said to Balaam, 'Am I not your donkey, and have I not been your mount all your life? Have I ever behaved like this with you before?' 'No,' he replied.

31 Yahweh then opened Balaam's eyes and he saw the angel of Yahweh standing in the road with a drawn sword in his hand; and he bowed his head and threw himself on his face. 32 And the angel of Yahweh said to him, 'Why did you strike your donkey three times like that? I myself had come to bar your way; while I am here your road is blocked. 33 The donkey saw me and turned aside because of me three times. You are lucky she did turn aside, or I should have killed you by now, though I would have spared her.' 34 Balaam said to the angel of Yahweh, 'I have sinned. I did not know you were standing in the road to stop me. But if what I am doing displeases you, I will go home again.' 35 The angel of Yahweh said to Balaam, 'Go with these men, but say only what I tell you to say.' So Balaam went on with the chiefs sent by Balak.

36 Balak learned that Balaam was coming and went out to meet him, in the direction of Ar in Moab, at the Arnon frontier on the country's furthest boundary. 37 Balak said to Balaam, 'Did I not send messengers to summon you? Why did you not come to me? Did you think, perhaps, I could confer no honours on you?' 38 Balaam said to Balak, 'I have come to you after all. I suppose you know I cannot say anything on my own? The words God puts into my mouth are what I shall say.'

39 Balaam set out with Balak. They came to Kiriath-Huzoth. 40 Balak sacrificed oxen and sheep, and offered portions to Balaam and the chiefs who were with him. 41 Next morning Balak took Balaam and brought him up to Bamoth-Baal, from where he could see the edge of the camp.

NEW REVISED STANDARD VERSION

23 [1] Then Balaam said to Balak, "Build me seven altars here, and prepare seven rams for me." [2] Balak did as Balaam had said; and Balak and Balaam offered a bull and a ram on each altar. [3] Then Balaam said to Balak, "Stay here beside your burnt offerings while I go aside. Perhaps the LORD will come to meet me. Whatever he shows me I will tell you." And he went to a bare height.

[4] Then God met Balaam; and Balaam said to him, "I have arranged the seven altars, and have offered a bull and a ram on each altar." [5] The LORD put a word in Balaam's mouth, and said, "Return to Balak, and this is what you must say." [6] So he returned to Balak,[a] who was standing beside his burnt offerings with all the officials of Moab. [7] Then Balaam[b] uttered his oracle, saying:

"Balak has brought me from Aram,
    the king of Moab from the eastern mountains:
'Come, curse Jacob for me;
    Come, denounce Israel!'
[8] How can I curse whom God has not cursed?
    How can I denounce those whom the LORD has
      not denounced?
[9] For from the top of the crags I see him,
    from the hills I behold him;
Here is a people living alone,
    and not reckoning itself among the nations!
[10] Who can count the dust of Jacob,
    or number the dust-cloud[c] of Israel?
Let me die the death of the upright,
    and let my end be like his!"

[11] Then Balak said to Balaam, "What have you done to me? I brought you to curse my enemies, but now you have done nothing but bless them." [12] He answered, "Must I not take care to say what the LORD puts into my mouth?"

[13] So Balak said to him, "Come with me to another place from which you may see them; you shall see only part of them, and shall not see them all; then curse them for me from there." [14] So he took him to the field of Zophim, to the top of Pisgah. He built seven altars, and offered a bull and a ram on each altar. [15] Balaam said to Balak, "Stand here beside your burnt offerings, while I meet the LORD over there." [16] The LORD met Balaam, put a word in his mouth, and said, "Return to Balak, and this is what you shall say." [17] When he came to him, he was standing beside his burnt offerings with the officials of Moab. Balak said to him, "What has the LORD said?" [18] Then Balaam uttered his oracle, saying:

"Rise, Balak, and hear;
    listen to me, O son of Zippor:
[19] God is not a human being, that he should lie,
    or a mortal, that he should change his mind.
Has he promised, and will he not do it?
    Has he spoken, and will he not fulfill it?
[20] See, I received a command to bless;
    he has blessed, and I cannot revoke it.
[21] He has not beheld misfortune in Jacob;
    nor has he seen trouble in Israel.
The LORD their God is with them,
    acclaimed as a king among them.
[22] God, who brings them out of Egypt,
    is like the horns of a wild ox for them.
[23] Surely there is no enchantment against Jacob,
    no divination against Israel;
now it shall be said of Jacob and Israel,
    'See what God has done!'

REVISED ENGLISH BIBLE

23 [1] Then Balaam said to Balak, 'Build me here seven altars and prepare for me seven bulls and seven rams.' [2] Balak followed Balaam's instructions; after offering a bull and a ram on each altar, [3-4] he said to him, 'I have prepared the seven altars, and I have offered the bull and the ram on each altar.' Balaam answered, 'You stand here beside your sacrifice, and let me go off by myself. It may be that the LORD will meet me. Whatever he reveals to me, I shall tell you.' He went off to a height, where God met him. [5] The LORD put words into Balaam's mouth and said, 'Go back to Balak, and speak as I tell you.' [6] He went back, and found Balak standing by his sacrifice, and with him all the Moabite chiefs. [7] Then Balaam uttered his oracle:

'From Aram, from the mountains of the east,
    Balak king of Moab has brought me:
"Come, lay a curse on Jacob for me," he said.
    "Come, denounce Israel."
[8] How can I curse someone God has not cursed,
    how denounce someone the LORD has not
      denounced?
[9] From the rocky heights I see them,
    I watch them from the rounded hills.
I see a people that dwells apart,
    that has not made itself one with the nations.
[10] Who can count the host of Jacob
    or number the myriads of Israel?
Let me die as those who are righteous die;
    grant that my end may be as theirs!'

[11] Balak said, 'What is this you have done? I sent for you to put a curse on my enemies, and what you have done is to bless them.' [12] Balaam replied, 'I can but keep to the words which the LORD puts into my mouth.'

[13] Balak then said to him, 'Come with me now to another place from which you will see them, though not the full extent of them; you will not see them all. Curse them for me from there.' [14] So he took him to the Field of the Watchers on the summit of Pisgah, where he built seven altars and offered a bull and a ram on each altar. [15] Balaam said to Balak, 'You stand beside your sacrifice; I shall meet the LORD over there.' [16] The LORD met Balaam and put words into his mouth, and said, 'Go back to Balak, and speak as I tell you.' [17] He went, and found him standing beside his sacrifice with the Moabite chiefs. Balak asked what the LORD had said, [18] and Balaam uttered his oracle:

'Up, Balak, and listen:
    hear what I am charged to say, son of Zippor.
[19] God is not a mortal that he should lie,
    not a man that he should change his mind.
Would he speak, and not make it good?
    What he proclaims, will he not fulfil?
[20] I have received a command to bless;
    I shall bless, and I cannot gainsay it.
[21] He has discovered no iniquity in Jacob
    and has seen no mischief in Israel.
The LORD their God is with them,
    acclaimed among them as King.
[22] What its curving horns are to the wild ox,
    God is to them, who brought them out of Egypt.
[23] Surely there is no divination in Jacob,
    and no augury in Israel;
now it is said to Jacob
    and to Israel, "See what God has wrought!"

23:2 **after offering:** so some MSS; others and Balak and Balaam offered.   23:7 **Aram:** or Syria.   23:14 **Field of the Watchers:** or Field of Zophim.   23:19 **change his mind:** or feel regret.   23:20 **I shall bless:** so Samar.; Heb. he blessed.

---

[a] Heb *him*   [b] Heb *he*   [c] Or *fourth part*

23 Then Balaam said to Balak, "Build me seven altars, and prepare seven bullocks and seven rams for me here." ²So he did as Balaam had ordered, offering a bullock and a ram on each altar. And Balak said to him, "I have erected the seven altars, and have offered a bullock and a ram on each." ³Balaam then said to him, "Stand here by your holocaust while I go over there. Perhaps the LORD will meet me, and then I will tell you whatever he lets me see." He went out on the barren height, ⁴and God met him. ⁵When he had put an utterance in Balaam's mouth, the LORD said to him, "Go back to Balak, and speak accordingly." ⁶So he went back to Balak, who was still standing by his holocaust together with all the princes of Moab. ⁷Then Balaam gave voice to his oracle:

From Aram has Balak brought me here,
  Moab's king, from the Eastern Mountains:
"Come and lay a curse for me on Jacob,
  come and denounce Israel."
⁸How can I curse whom God has not cursed?
  How denounce whom the LORD has
    not denounced?
⁹For from the top of the crags I see him,
  from the heights I behold him.
Here is a people that lives apart
  and does not reckon itself among the nations.
¹⁰Who has ever counted the dust of Jacob,
  or numbered Israel's wind-borne particles?
May I die the death of the just,
  may my descendants be as many as theirs!

¹¹"What have you done to me?" cried Balak to Balaam. "It was to curse my foes that I brought you here; instead, you have even blessed them." ¹²Balaam replied, "Is it not what the LORD puts in my mouth that I must repeat with care?"

¹³Then Balak said to him, "Please come with me to another place from which you can see only some and not all of them, and from there curse them for me." ¹⁴So he brought him to the lookout field on the top of Pisgah, where he built seven altars and offered a bullock and a ram on each of them. ¹⁵Balaam then said to Balak, "Stand here by your holocaust, while I seek a meeting over there." ¹⁶Then the LORD met Balaam, and having put an utterance in his mouth, he said to him, "Go back to Balak, and speak accordingly." ¹⁷So he went back to Balak, who was still standing by his holocaust together with the princes of Moab. When Balak asked him, "What did the LORD say?" ¹⁸Balaam gave voice to his oracle:

Be aroused, O Balak, and hearken;
  give ear to my testimony, O son of Zippor!
¹⁹God is not man that he should speak falsely,
  nor human, that he should change his mind.
Is he one to speak and not act,
  to decree and not fulfill?
²⁰It is a blessing I have been given to pronounce;
  a blessing which I cannot restrain.
²¹Misfortune is not observed in Jacob,
  nor misery seen in Israel.
The LORD, his God, is with him;
  with him is the triumph of his King.
²²It is God who brought him out of Egypt,
  a wild bull of towering might.
²³No, there is no sorcery against Jacob,
  nor omen against Israel.
It shall yet be said of Jacob,
  and of Israel, "Behold what God has wrought!"

23 Balaam said to Balak, 'Build me seven altars here and prepare me seven bulls and seven rams.' ²Balak did as Balaam said and offered a burnt offering of one bull and one ram on each altar. ³Balaam then said to Balak, 'Stand beside your burnt offerings while I go away. Perhaps Yahweh will come and meet me. If he does, I shall tell you whatever he reveals to me.' And he withdrew to a bare hill.

⁴God came to meet Balaam, who said to him, 'I have prepared the seven altars and offered a burnt offering of one bull and one ram on each altar.' ⁵Yahweh put a prophecy into his mouth and said to him, 'Go back to Balak, and that is what you must say to him.' ⁶So Balaam went back to him, and found him still standing beside his burnt offering, with all the chiefs of Moab. ⁷He then declaimed his poem as follows:

Balak has brought me from Aram,
  the king of Moab from the hills of Kedem:
'Come and curse Jacob for me,
  come and denounce Israel!'
⁸How shall I curse someone whom God has not
    cursed,
  how denounce someone God has not denounced?
⁹Yes, from the top of the crags I see him,
  from the hills I descry him:
a people that dwells on its own,
  not to be reckoned among other nations!
¹⁰Who can count the dust of Jacob?
  Who can number the cloud of Israel?
May I die the death of the just,
  and may my future be like theirs!

¹¹Balak said to Balaam, 'What have you done to me? I brought you to curse my enemies, and you have heaped blessings on them!' ¹²Balaam replied, 'Am I to depart from what Yahweh puts into my mouth?' ¹³Balak then said, 'Please come somewhere else. From here you can see only the fringe of them, you cannot see them all. Curse them for me over there.' ¹⁴He led him to the Lookouts' Field on the top of Pisgah. There he built seven altars and offered a burnt offering of one bull and one ram on each altar. ¹⁵Balaam said to Balak, 'Stand here beside your burnt offerings while I wait over there.' ¹⁶God came to meet Balaam, he put a prophecy into his mouth and said to him, 'Go back to Balak, and that is what you must say to him.' ¹⁷So Balaam went to him and found him still standing beside his burnt offering and all the chiefs of Moab with him. 'What did Yahweh say?' Balak said to him. ¹⁸Balaam then declaimed his poem, as follows:

Stand up, Balak, and listen,
  give ear to me, son of Zippor.
¹⁹God is no human being that he should lie,
  no child of Adam to change his mind.
Is it his to say and not to do,
  is it his to speak and not fulfil?
²⁰The charge laid on me is to bless,
  I shall bless, and I cannot reverse it.
²¹I have perceived no guilt in Jacob,
  have seen no perversity in Israel.
Yahweh his God is with him,
  and a royal acclamation to greet him.
²²God has brought him out of Egypt,
  is like the wild ox's horns to him.
²³There is no omen whatever against Jacob,
  no augury at all against Israel.
Well may people say of Jacob,
  of Israel, 'What has God achieved?'

NEW REVISED STANDARD VERSION

24 Look, a people rising up like a lioness,
  and rousing itself like a lion!
It does not lie down until it has eaten the prey
  and drunk the blood of the slain."

25 Then Balak said to Balaam, "Do not curse them at all, and do not bless them at all." 26 But Balaam answered Balak, "Did I not tell you, 'Whatever the LORD says, that is what I must do'?"

27 So Balak said to Balaam, "Come now, I will take you to another place; perhaps it will please God that you may curse them for me from there." 28 So Balak took Balaam to the top of Peor, which overlooks the wasteland.d 29 Balaam said to Balak, "Build me seven altars here, and prepare seven bulls and seven rams for me." 30 So Balak did as Balaam had said, and offered a bull and a ram on each altar.

24 Now Balaam saw that it pleased the LORD to bless Israel, so he did not go, as at other times, to look for omens, but set his face toward the wilderness. 2 Balaam looked up and saw Israel camping tribe by tribe. Then the spirit of God came upon him, 3 and he uttered his oracle, saying:
  "The oracle of Balaam son of Beor,
    the oracle of the man whose eye is clear,e
4 the oracle of one who hears the words of God,
    who sees the vision of the Almighty,f
    who falls down, but with eyes uncovered:
5 how fair are your tents, O Jacob,
    your encampments, O Israel!
6 Like palm groves that stretch far away,
    like gardens beside a river,
  like aloes that the LORD has planted,
    like cedar trees beside the waters.
7 Water shall flow from his buckets,
    and his seed shall have abundant water,
  his king shall be higher than Agag,
    and his kingdom shall be exalted.
8 God who brings him out of Egypt,
    is like the horns of a wild ox for him;
  he shall devour the nations that are his foes
    and break their bones.
  He shall strike with his arrows.g
9 He crouched, he lay down like a lion,
    and like a lioness; who will rouse him up?
  Blessed is everyone who blesses you,
    and cursed is everyone who curses you."

10 Then Balak's anger was kindled against Balaam, and he struck his hands together. Balak said to Balaam, "I summoned you to curse my enemies, but instead you have blessed them these three times. 11 Now be off with you! Go home! I said, 'I will reward you richly,' but the LORD has denied you any reward." 12 And Balaam said to Balak, "Did I not tell your messengers whom you sent to me, 13 'If Balak should give me his house full of silver and gold, I would not be able to go beyond the word of the LORD, to do either good or bad of my own will; what the LORD says, that is what I will say'? 14 So now, I am going to my people; let me advise you what this people will do to your people in days to come."

15 So he uttered his oracle, saying:
  "The oracle of Balaam son of Beor,
    the oracle of the man whose eye is clear,e
16 the oracle of one who hears the words of God,
    and knows the knowledge of the Most High,h
  who sees the vision of the Almighty,f
    who falls down, but with his eyes uncovered:

REVISED ENGLISH BIBLE

24 Behold a people rearing up like a lioness,
  rampant like a lion;
he will not couch till he has devoured the prey
  and drunk the blood of the slain.'

25 Then Balak said to Balaam, 'You will not put a curse on them; then at least do not bless them.' 26 He answered, 'Did I not warn you that I must do whatever the LORD tells me?'

27 Balak said, 'Come, let me take you to another place; perhaps God will be pleased to let you curse them for me there.' 28 So he took Balaam to the summit of Peor overlooking Jeshimon, 29 and Balaam told him to build seven altars for him there and prepare seven bulls and seven rams. 30 Balak did as Balaam had said, and he offered a bull and a ram on each altar.

24 But now that Balaam knew that the LORD wished him to bless Israel, he did not go and resort to divination as before. He turned towards the desert, 2 and before his eyes he saw Israel encamped tribe by tribe; and, the spirit of God coming on him, 3 he uttered his oracle:
  'The word of Balaam son of Beor,
    the word of the man whose sight is clear,
4 the word of him who hears the words of God,
    who with opened eyes sees in a trance
    the vision from the Almighty:
5 Jacob, how fair are your tents,
    Israel, your encampments,
6 like long palm groves,
    like gardens by a river,
  like aloe trees planted by the LORD,
    like cedars beside the waters!
7 The water in his vessels shall overflow,
    and his seed shall be like great waters
  so that his king may be taller than Agag,
    and his kingdom lifted high.
8 What its curving horns are to the wild ox,
    God is to him, who brought him out of Egypt;
  he will devour hostile nations,
    crunch their bones, and break their backs.
9 When he reclines he couches like a lion
    or like a lioness; who dares to rouse him?
  Blessed be those who bless you,
    and let them who curse you be accursed!'

10 At that Balak's anger was aroused against Balaam; beating his hands together, he cried, 'It was to curse my enemies that I summoned you, and three times you have persisted in blessing them. 11 Off with you at once to your own place! I promised to confer great honour upon you, but now the LORD has kept this honour from you.' 12 Balaam answered, 'But I said to your messengers: 13 "Were Balak to give me all the silver and gold in his palace, I could not disobey the command of the LORD by doing anything of my own will, good or bad. What the LORD says to me, that is what I must say." 14 Now I am going to my own people; but first, let me warn you what this people will do to yours in the days to come.' 15 Then he uttered his oracle:
  'The word of Balaam son of Beor,
    the word of the man whose sight is clear,
16 the word of him who hears the words of God,
    who shares the knowledge of the Most High,
  who with opened eyes sees in a trance
    the vision from the Almighty:

---

d Or overlooks Jeshimon   e Or closed or open   f Traditional
rendering of Heb Shaddai   g Meaning of Heb uncertain   h Or of
Elyon

24:8 backs: prob. meaning; Heb. arrows.

24 Here is a people that springs up like a lioness,
and stalks forth like a lion;
It rests not till it has devoured its prey
and has drunk the blood of the slain.
25 "Even though you cannot curse them," said Balak to
Balaam, "at least do not bless them." 26 But Balaam answered Balak, "Did I not warn you that I must do all that
the LORD tells me?"
27 Then Balak said to Balaam, "Come, let me bring you
to another place; perhaps God will approve of your cursing
them for me from there." 28 So he took Balaam to the top of
Peor, that overlooks Jeshimon. 29 Balaam then said to him,
"Here build me seven altars; and here prepare for me seven
bullocks and seven rams." 30 And Balak did as Balaam had
ordered, offering a bullock and a ram on each altar.

24 Balaam, however, perceiving that the LORD was
pleased to bless Israel, did not go aside as before to
seek omens, but turned his gaze toward the desert. 2 When
he raised his eyes and saw Israel encamped, tribe by tribe,
the spirit of God came upon him, 3 and he gave voice to his
oracle:
The utterance of Balaam, son of Beor,
the utterance of the man whose eye is true,
4 The utterance of one who hears what God says,
and knows what the Most High knows,
Of one who sees what the Almighty sees,
enraptured, and with eyes unveiled:
5 How goodly are your tents, O Jacob;
your encampments, O Israel!
6 They are like gardens beside a stream,
like the cedars planted by the LORD.
7 His wells shall yield free-flowing waters,
he shall have the sea within reach;
His king shall rise higher than. . . .
and his royalty shall be exalted.
8 It is God who brought him out of Egypt,
a wild bull of towering might.
He shall devour the nations like grass,
their bones he shall strip bare.
9 He lies crouching like a lion,
or like a lioness; who shall arouse him?
Blessed is he who blesses you,
and cursed is he who curses you!
10 Balak beat his palms together in a blaze of anger at
Balaam and said to him, "It was to curse my foes that I
summoned you; yet three times now you have even
blessed them instead! 11 Be off at once, then, to your home.
I promised to reward you richly, but the LORD has withheld
the reward from you!" 12 Balaam replied to Balak, "Did I
not warn the very messengers whom you sent to me,
13 'Even if Balak gave me his house full of silver and gold,
I could not of my own accord do anything, good or evil,
contrary to the command of the LORD'? Whatever the LORD
says I must repeat.
14 "But now that I am about to go to my own people, let
me first warn you what this people will do to your people
in the days to come." 15 Then Balaam gave voice to his
oracle:
The utterance of Balaam, son of Beor,
the utterance of the man whose eye is true,
16 The utterance of one who hears what God says,
and knows what the Most High knows,
Of one who sees what the Almighty sees,
enraptured and with eyes unveiled.

24 for here is a people like a lioness rising,
poised like a lion to spring;
nor will he lie down till he has devoured his prey
and drunk the blood of his slain.
25 Balak said to Balaam, 'Very well! Do not curse them. But
at least do not bless them!' 26 Balaam retorted to Balak,
'Did I not tell you? Whatever Yahweh says, I must do.'
27 Balak then said to Balaam, 'Come with me now and I
shall take you somewhere else. From there perhaps it will
please God to curse them for me.' 28 So Balak led Balaam
to the summit of Peor, overlooking the wastelands. 29 Balaam then said to Balak, 'Build me seven altars here and
prepare me seven bulls and seven rams.' 30 Balak did as
Balaam said and offered a burnt offering of one bull and one
ram on each altar.

24 Balaam then saw that it pleased Yahweh to bless
Israel. He did not go as before to seek omens but
turned towards the desert. 2 Raising his eyes Balaam saw
Israel settled tribe by tribe; the spirit of God came on him
3 and he declaimed his poem, as follows:
The prophecy of Balaam son of Beor,
the prophecy of the man with far-seeing eyes,
4 the prophecy of one who hears the words of
God.
He sees what Shaddai makes him see,
receives the divine answer, and his eyes are
opened.
5 How fair your tents are, Jacob,
how fair your dwellings, Israel,
6 like valleys that stretch afar,
like gardens by the banks of a river,
like aloes planted by Yahweh,
like cedars beside the waters!
7 A hero arises from their stock,
he reigns over countless peoples.
His king is greater than Agag,
and his kingship held in honour.
8 God has brought him out of Egypt,
is like the wild ox's horns to him.
He devours the corpses of his enemies,
breaking their bones,
piercing them with his arrows.
9 He has crouched, he has lain down,
like a lion, like a lioness;
who dare rouse him?
Blessed be those who bless you,
and accursed be those who curse you!
10 Balak flew into a rage with Balaam. He struck his
hands together and said to Balaam, 'I brought you to curse
my enemies, and you have insisted on blessing them three
times over! 11 So now go home as fast as your legs can carry
you. I promised to load you with honours. Yahweh himself
has deprived you of them.' 12 Balaam retorted to Balak,
'Did I not tell the messengers you sent me, 13 'Even if Balak
gave me his house full of gold and silver I could not go
against Yahweh's order and do anything of my own accord,
whether for good or ill; whatever Yahweh says is what I
shall say"? 14 Now that I am going back to my own folk, let
me warn you what this people will do to your people, in
days to come.' 15 He then declaimed his poem, as follows:
The prophecy of Balaam son of Beor,
the prophecy of the man with far-seeing eyes,
16 the prophecy of one who hears the words of God,
of one who knows the knowledge of the Most
High.
He sees what Shaddai makes him see,
receives the divine answer, and his eyes are
opened.

| NEW REVISED STANDARD VERSION | REVISED ENGLISH BIBLE |

NEW REVISED STANDARD VERSION

17 I see him, but not now;
    I behold him, but not near —
a star shall come out of Jacob,
    and a scepter shall rise out of Israel;
    it shall crush the borderlands*i* of Moab,
    and the territory*j* of all the Shethites.
18 Edom will become a possession,
    Seir a possession of its enemies,*k*
    while Israel does valiantly.
19 One out of Jacob shall rule,
    and destroy the survivors of Ir."

20 Then he looked on Amalek, and uttered his oracle, saying:
    "First among the nations was Amalek,
    but its end is to perish forever."
21 Then he looked on the Kenite, and uttered his oracle, saying:
    "Enduring is your dwelling place,
    and your nest is set in the rock;
22   yet Kain is destined for burning.
    How long shall Asshur take you away captive?"
23 Again he uttered his oracle, saying:
    "Alas, who shall live when God does this?
24   But ships shall come from Kittim
    and shall afflict Asshur and Eber;
    and he also shall perish forever."

25 Then Balaam got up and went back to his place, and Balak also went his way.

25 While Israel was staying at Shittim, the people began to have sexual relations with the women of Moab. 2 These invited the people to the sacrifices of their gods, and the people ate and bowed down to their gods. 3 Thus Israel yoked itself to the Baal of Peor, and the LORD's anger was kindled against Israel. 4 The LORD said to Moses, "Take all the chiefs of the people, and impale them in the sun before the LORD, in order that the fierce anger of the LORD may turn away from Israel." 5 And Moses said to the judges of Israel, "Each of you shall kill any of your people who have yoked themselves to the Baal of Peor."

6 Just then one of the Israelites came and brought a Midianite woman into his family, in the sight of Moses and in the sight of the whole congregation of the Israelites, while they were weeping at the entrance of the tent of meeting. 7 When Phinehas son of Eleazar, son of Aaron the priest, saw it, he got up and left the congregation. Taking a spear in his hand, 8 he went after the Israelite man into the tent, and pierced the two of them, the Israelite and the woman, through the belly. So the plague was stopped among the people of Israel. 9 Nevertheless those that died by the plague were twenty-four thousand.

10 The LORD spoke to Moses, saying: 11 "Phinehas son of Eleazar, son of Aaron the priest, has turned back my wrath from the Israelites by manifesting such zeal among them on my behalf that in my jealousy I did not consume the Israelites. 12 Therefore say, 'I hereby grant him my covenant of peace. 13 It shall be for him and for his descendants after him a covenant of perpetual priesthood, because he was zealous for his God, and made atonement for the Israelites.' "

14 The name of the slain Israelite man, who was killed with the Midianite woman, was Zimri son of Salu, head of an ancestral house belonging to the Simeonites. 15 The name of the Midianite woman who was killed was Cozbi daughter of Zur, who was the head of a clan, an ancestral house in Midian.

16 The LORD said to Moses, 17 "Harass the Midianites,

REVISED ENGLISH BIBLE

17 I see him, but not now;
    I behold him, but not near:
a star will come forth out of Jacob,
    a comet will arise from Israel.
He will smite the warriors of Moab,
    and beat down all the sons of Sheth.
18 Edom will be his by conquest
    and Seir, his enemy, will become his.
Israel will do valiant deeds;
19 Jacob will trample them down,
    the last survivor from Ar will he destroy.'

20 He saw Amalek and uttered his oracle:
    'First of all the nations was Amalek,
    but his end will be utter destruction.'
21 He saw the Kenites and uttered his oracle:
    'Your refuge, though it seems secure,
    your nest, though set on the mountain crag,
22 is doomed, Cain, to be burnt,
    when Asshur takes you captive.'
23 He uttered his oracle:
    'Alas, who are these assembling in the north,
24 invaders from the region of Kittim?
They will lay waste Asshur; they will lay Eber waste:
    he too will perish utterly.'

25 Then Balaam arose and returned home, and Balak also went on his way.

25 WHEN the Israelites were in Shittim, the men began to intercourse with Moabite women, 2 who invited them to the sacrifices offered to their gods. The Israelites ate the sacrificial food and prostrated themselves before the gods of Moab; 3 they joined in the worship of the Baal of Peor. This aroused the anger of the LORD, 4 who said to Moses, 'Take all the leaders of the people and hurl them down to their death before the LORD in the full light of day, that the fury of my anger may turn away from Israel.' 5 Moses gave this order to the judges of Israel: 'Each of you put to death those of his tribe who have joined in the worship of the Baal of Peor.'

6 One of the Israelites brought a Midianite woman into his family in open defiance of Moses and all the community of Israel, while they were weeping by the entrance of the Tent of Meeting. 7 When Phinehas son of Eleazar, son of Aaron the priest, saw him, he got up from the assembly and took a spear, 8 and went into the nuptial tent after the Israelite, where he transfixed the two of them, the Israelite and the woman, pinning them together. Then the plague which had attacked the Israelites was brought to a stop; 9 but twenty-four thousand had already died.

10 The LORD said to Moses, 11 'Phinehas son of Eleazar, son of Aaron the priest, has turned my wrath away from the Israelites; he displayed among them the same jealous anger that moved me, and therefore I did not exterminate the Israelites in my jealous anger. 12 Make known that I hereby grant him my covenant pledge of prosperity: 13 he and his descendants after him shall enjoy the priesthood under a covenant for all time, because he showed his zeal for his God and made expiation for the Israelites.' 14 The name of the Israelite struck down with the Midianite woman was Zimri son of Salu, a chief in a Simeonite family, 15 and the Midianite woman's name was Cozbi daughter of Zur, who was the tribal head of an ancestral house in Midian.

16 The LORD said to Moses, 17–18 'Make the Midianites

---

i Or *forehead*   *j* Some Mss read *skull*   *k* Heb *Seir, its enemies, a possession*

24:24 **invaders:** *so Gk; Heb. obscure.*   25:8 **together:** *lit.* into her belly.

NEW AMERICAN BIBLE

17 I see him, though not now;
    I behold him, though not near:
A star shall advance from Jacob,
    and a staff shall rise from Israel,
That shall smite the brows of Moab,
    and the skulls of all the Shuthites,
18 Till Edom is dispossessed,
    and no fugitive is left in Seir.
Israel shall do valiantly,
19   and Jacob shall overcome his foes.
20 Upon seeing Amalek, Balaam gave voice to his oracle:
    First of the peoples was Amalek,
    but his end is to perish forever.
21 Upon seeing the Kenites, he gave voice to his oracle:
    Your abode is enduring, O smith,
    and your nest is set on a cliff;
22 Yet destined for burning —
    even as I watch — are your inhabitants.
23 Upon seeing . . . he gave voice to his oracle:
    Alas, who shall survive of Ishmael,
24   to deliver his people from the hands of
    the Kittim?
When they have conquered Asshur and
    conquered Eber,
He too shall perish forever.
25 Then Balaam set out on his journey home; and Balak also went his way.

25 While Israel was living at Shittim, the people degraded themselves by having illicit relations with the Moabite women. 2 These then invited the people to the sacrifices of their god, and the people ate of the sacrifices and worshiped their god. 3 When Israel thus submitted to the rites of Baal of Peor, the LORD's anger flared up against Israel, 4 and he said to Moses, "Gather all the leaders of the people, and hold a public execution of the guilty ones before the LORD, that his blazing wrath may be turned away from Israel." 5 So Moses told the Israelite judges, "Each of you shall kill those of his men who have submitted to the rites of Baal of Peor."

6 Yet a certain Israelite came and brought in a Midianite woman to his clansmen in the view of Moses and of the whole Israelite community, while they were weeping at the entrance of the meeting tent. 7 When Phinehas, son of Eleazar, son of Aaron the priest, saw this, he left the assembly, and taking a lance in hand, 8 followed the Israelite into his retreat where he pierced the pair of them, the Israelite and the woman. Thus the slaughter of Israelites was checked; 9 but only after twenty-four thousand had died.

10 Then the LORD said to Moses, 11 "Phinehas, son of Eleazar, son of Aaron the priest, has turned my anger from the Israelites by his zeal for my honor among them; that is why I did not put an end to the Israelites for the offense to my honor. 12 Announce, therefore, that I hereby give him my pledge of friendship, 13 which shall be for him and for his descendants after him the pledge of an everlasting priesthood, because he was zealous on behalf of his God and thus made amends for the Israelites."

14 The Israelite slain with the Midianite woman was Zimri, son of Salu, prince of an ancestral house of the Simeonites. 15 The slain Midianite woman was Cozbi, daughter of Zur, who was head of a clan, an ancestral house, in Midian.

16 The LORD then said to Moses, 17 "Treat the Midianites

NEW JERUSALEM BIBLE

17 I see him — but not in the present.
    I perceive him — but not close at hand:
a star is emerging from Jacob,
    a sceptre is rising from Israel,
to strike the brow of Moab,
    the skulls of all the children of Seth. k
18 Edom too will be a conquered land,
    Seir too will be a conquered land,
    when Israel exerts his strength,
19   when Jacob tramples on his enemies
    and destroys the last survivors of Ar.
20 Balaam then looked at Amalek and declaimed his poem, as follows:
    Amalek, the earliest of nations!
    But his posterity will perish forever.
21 He then looked at the Kenites and declaimed his poem, as follows:
    Your dwelling was firm, Kain,
    your nest perched high in the rock.
22 But the nest belongs to Beor;
    how long will you be Asshur's captive?
23 He then declaimed his poem, as follows:
    The Sea-people are gathering in the north,
24   the vessels from the coasts of Kittim.
    They will bear down on Asshur, bear down on
    Eber;
    he too will perish forever.
25 Balaam then got up, left and went home, and Balak too went his way.

25 Israel settled at Shittim. The people gave themselves over to prostitution with Moabite women. 2 These invited them to the sacrifices of their gods, and the people ate and bowed down before their gods. 3 With Israel thus committed to the Baal of Peor, Yahweh's anger was aroused against them.

4 Yahweh said to Moses, 'Take all the leaders of the people. Impale them facing the sun, for Yahweh, to deflect his burning anger from Israel.' 5 Moses said to the judges of Israel, 'Each of you will put to death those of his people who have committed themselves to the Baal of Peor.'

6 One of the Israelites came along, bringing the Midianite woman into his family, under the very eyes of Moses and the whole community of Israelites as they were weeping at the entrance to the Tent of Meeting. 7 The priest Phinehas son of Eleazar, son of Aaron, on seeing this, stood up, left the assembly, seized a lance, 8 followed the Israelite into the alcove, and there ran them both through, the Israelite and the woman, through the stomach. Thus the plague which had struck the Israelites was arrested. 9 In the plague twenty-four thousand of them had died.

10 Yahweh then spoke and said, 11 'The priest Phinehas son of Eleazar, son of Aaron has deflected my wrath from the Israelites, he being the only one of them to have the same zeal as I have; for which reason, I did not make an end of the Israelites in my zeal. 12 For this reason I say: To him I grant my covenant of peace. 13 To him and his descendants after him, this covenant will assure the priesthood for ever. In reward for his zeal for his God, he will have the right to perform the ritual of expiation for the Israelites.'

14 The Israelite who had been killed (the one who was killed with the Midianite woman) was called Zimri son of Salu, leader of one of the Simeonite families. 15 The woman, the Midianite who was killed, was called Cozbi, daughter of Zur, chief of a clan, of a family, in Midian.

16 Yahweh then spoke to Moses and said, 17 'Harass the

k 24 The peoples mentioned will in fact be conquered by David.

and defeat them; 18 for they have harassed you by the trickery with which they deceived you in the affair of Peor, and in the affair of Cozbi, the daughter of a leader of Midian, their sister; she was killed on the day of the plague that resulted from Peor."

26 After the plague the LORD said to Moses and to Eleazar son of Aaron the priest, 2 "Take a census of the whole congregation of the Israelites, from twenty years old and upward, by their ancestral houses, everyone in Israel able to go to war." 3 Moses and Eleazar the priest spoke with them in the plains of Moab by the Jordan opposite Jericho, saying, 4 "Take a census of the people,ʲ from twenty years old and upward," as the LORD commanded Moses.

The Israelites, who came out of the land of Egypt, were: 5 Reuben, the firstborn of Israel. The descendants of Reuben: of Hanoch, the clan of the Hanochites; of Pallu, the clan of the Palluites; 6 of Hezron, the clan of the Hezronites; of Carmi, the clan of the Carmites. 7 These are the clans of the Reubenites; the number of those enrolled was forty-three thousand seven hundred thirty. 8 And the descendants of Pallu: Eliab. 9 The descendants of Eliab: Nemuel, Dathan, and Abiram. These are the same Dathan and Abiram, chosen from the congregation, who rebelled against Moses and Aaron in the company of Korah, when they rebelled against the LORD, 10 and the earth opened its mouth and swallowed them up along with Korah, when that company died, when the fire devoured two hundred fifty men; and they became a warning. 11 Notwithstanding, the sons of Korah did not die.

12 The descendants of Simeon by their clans: of Nemuel, the clan of the Nemuelites; of Jamin, the clan of the Jaminites; of Jachin, the clan of the Jachinites; 13 of Zerah, the clan of the Zerahites; of Shaul, the clan of the Shaulites.ᵐ 14 These are the clans of the Simeonites, twenty-two thousand two hundred.

15 The children of Gad by their clans: of Zephon, the clan of the Zephonites; of Haggi, the clan of the Haggites; of Shuni, the clan of the Shunites; 16 of Ozni, the clan of the Oznites; of Eri, the clan of the Erites; 17 of Arod, the clan of the Arodites; of Areli, the clan of the Arelites. 18 These are the clans of the Gadites: the number of those enrolled was forty thousand five hundred.

19 The sons of Judah: Er and Onan; Er and Onan died in the land of Canaan. 20 The descendants of Judah by their clans were: of Shelah, the clan of the Shelanites; of Perez, the clan of the Perezites; of Zerah, the clan of the Zerahites. 21 The descendants of Perez were: of Hezron, the clan of the Hezronites; of Hamul, the clan of the Hamulites. 22 These are the clans of Judah: the number of those enrolled was seventy-six thousand five hundred.

23 The descendants of Issachar by their clans: of Tola, the clan of the Tolaites; of Puvah, the clan of the Punites; 24 of Jashub, the clan of the Jashubites; of Shimron, the clan of the Shimronites. 25 These are the clans of Issachar: sixty-four thousand three hundred enrolled.

26 The descendants of Zebulun by their clans: of Sered, the clan of the Seredites; of Elon, the clan of the Elonites; of Jahleel, the clan of the Jahleelites. 27 These are the clans of the Zebulunites; the number of those enrolled was sixty thousand five hundred.

28 The sons of Joseph by their clans: Manasseh and Ephraim. 29 The descendants of Manasseh: of Machir, the clan of the Machirites; and Machir was the father of Gilead; of Gilead, the clan of the Gileadites. 30 These are the de-

suffer as they made you suffer with their wiles, and strike them down; their wiles were your undoing at Peor and in the affair of Cozbi their sister, the daughter of a Midianite chief, who was struck down at the time of the plague that resulted from Peor.'

26 AFTER the plague the LORD said to Moses and Eleazar the priest, son of Aaron, 2 'Make a census of the whole community of Israel by fathers' families, recording everyone in Israel aged twenty years and upwards fit for military service.' 3 Moses and Eleazar the priest collected them all in the lowlands of Moab by the Jordan near Jericho, 4 all who were twenty years of age and upwards, as the LORD had commanded Moses.

These were the Israelites who came out of Egypt.

5 Reubenites (Reuben was Israel's eldest son): Enoch, the Enochite family; Pallu, the Palluite family; 6 Hezron, the Hezronite family; Carmi, the Carmite family. 7 These were the Reubenite families: the number in their list was forty-three thousand seven hundred and thirty. 8 Son of Pallu: Eliab. 9 Sons of Eliab: Nemuel, Dathan, and Abiram. These were the same Dathan and Abiram, conveners of the community, who defied Moses and Aaron and joined the company of Korah in defying the LORD. 10 Then the earth opened its mouth and swallowed them up with Korah, and so their company died, while fire burnt up the two hundred and fifty men, and they became a warning. 11 The Korahites, however, did not die.

12 Simeonites, by their families: Nemuel, the Nemuelite family; Jamin, the Jaminite family; Jachin, the Jachinite family; 13 Zerah, the Zarhite family; Saul, the Saulite family. 14 These were the Simeonite families; the number in their list was twenty-two thousand two hundred.

15 Gadites, by their families: Zephon, the Zephonite family; Haggi, the Haggite family; Shuni, the Shunite family; 16 Ozni, the Oznite family; Eri, the Erite family; 17 Arod, the Arodite family; Areli, the Arelite family. 18 These were the Gadite families; the number in their list was forty thousand five hundred.

19 The sons of Judah were Er, Onan, Shelah, Perez, and Zerah; Er and Onan died in Canaan. 20 Judahites, by their families: Shelah, the Shelanite family; Perez, the Perezite family; Zerah, the Zarhite family. 21 Perezites: Hezron, the Hezronite family; Hamul, the Hamulite family. 22 These were the families of Judah; the number in their list was seventy-six thousand five hundred.

23 Issacharites, by their families: Tola, the Tolaite family; Pua, the Puite family; 24 Jashub, the Jashubite family; Shimron, the Shimronite family. 25 These were the families of Issachar; the number in their list was sixty-four thousand three hundred.

26 Zebulunites, by their families: Sered, the Sardite family; Elon, the Elonite family; Jahleel, the Jahleelite family. 27 These were the Zebulunite families; the number in their list was sixty thousand five hundred.

28 Josephites, by their families: Manasseh and Ephraim. 29 Manassites: Machir, the Machirite family. Machir was the father of Gilead: Gilead, the Gileadite family. 30 Gilead-

---

ʲHeb lacks *take a census of the people*: Compare verse 2   *m Or Saul . . . Saulites*

26:3 **Jericho:** *prob. rdg; Heb.* adds saying.   26:14 **in their list:** *so Gk; Heb.* omits.   26:19 **Er . . . Zerah:** *so some Gk MSS (cp. Gen. 46:12); Heb.* Er and Onan.   26:23 **Puite:** *so Samar.; Heb.* Punite.

NEW AMERICAN BIBLE

as enemies and crush them, 18 for they have been your enemies by their wily dealings with you as regards Peor and as regards their kinswoman Cozbi, the daughter of the Midianite prince, who was killed at the time of the slaughter because of Peor."

26 19 After the slaughter 1 the LORD said to Moses and Eleazar, son of Aaron the priest, 2 "Take a census, by ancestral houses, throughout the community of the Israelites of all those of twenty years or more who are fit for military service in Israel." 3 So on the plains of Moab along the Jericho stretch of the Jordan, Moses and the priest Eleazar registered 4 those of twenty years or more, as the LORD had commanded Moses.

The Israelites who came out of the land of Egypt were as follows:

5 Of Reuben, the first-born of Israel, the Reubenites by clans were: through Hanoch the clan of the Hanochites, through Pallu the clan of the Palluites, 6 through Hezron the clan of the Hezronites, through Carmi the clan of the Carmites. 7 These were the clans of the Reubenites, of whom forty-three thousand seven hundred and thirty men were registered.

8 From Pallu descended Eliab, 9 and the descendants of Eliab were Dathan and Abiram — the same Dathan and Abiram, councilors of the community, who revolted against Moses and Aaron [like Korah's band when it rebelled against the LORD]. 10 The earth opened its mouth and swallowed them as a warning [Korah too and the band that died when the fire consumed two hundred and fifty men. 11 The descendants of Korah, however, did not die out].

12 The Simeonites by clans were: through Nemuel the clan of the Nemuelites, through Jamin the clan of the Jaminites, through Jachin the clan of the Jachinites, 13 through Sohar the clan of the Soharites, through Shaul the clan of the Shaulites. 14 These were the clans of the Simeonites, of whom twenty-two thousand two hundred men were registered.

15 The Gadites by clans were: through Zephon the clan of the Zephonites, through Haggi the clan of the Haggites, through Shuni the clan of the Shunites, 16 through Ozni the clan of the Oznites, through Eri the clan of the Erites, 17 through Arod the clan of the Arodites, through Areli the clan of the Arelites. 18 These were the clans of the Gadites, of whom forty thousand five hundred men were registered.

19 The sons of Judah who died in the land of Canaan were Er and Onan. 20 The Judahites by clans were: through Shelah the clan of the Shelahites, through Perez the clan of the Perezites, through Zerah the clan of the Zerahites. 21 The Perezites were: through Hezron the clan of the Hezronites, through Hamul the clan of the Hamulites. 22 These were the clans of Judah, of whom seventy-six thousand five hundred men were registered.

23 The Issacharites by clans were: through Tola the clan of the Tolaites, through Puvah the clan of the Puvahites, 24 through Jashub the clan of the Jashubites, through Shimron the clan of the Shimronites. 25 These were the clans of Issachar, of whom sixty-four thousand three hundred men were registered.

26 The Zebulunites by clans were: through Sered the clan of the Seredites, through Elon the clan of the Elonites, through Jahleel the clan of the Jahleelites. 27 These were the clans of the Zebulunites, of whom sixty thousand five hundred men were registered.

28 The sons of Joseph were Manasseh, and Ephraim. 29 The Manassehites by clans were: through Machir the clan of the Machirites, through Gilead, a descendant of Machir, the clan of the Gileadites. 30 The Gileadites were: through

26, 19: This is the last verse of Ch 25.

NEW JERUSALEM BIBLE

Midianites, strike them down, 18 for harassing you with their guile in the Peor affair and in the affair of their sister Cozbi, the daughter of a prince of Midian, the woman who was killed the day the plague came on account of the business of Peor.'

26 After this plague, Yahweh spoke to Moses and to the priest Eleazar son of Aaron and said:
2 'Take a census of the whole community of Israelites, by families: all those of twenty years and over, fit to bear arms in Israel.'

3 So Moses and the priest Eleazar took a census of them on the Plains of Moab, near the Jordan by Jericho. They counted 4 (as Yahweh had ordered Moses and the Israelites after leaving Egypt) men of twenty years and over:

5 Reuben, the first-born of Israel. The sons of Reuben: for Hanoch, the Hanochite clan; for Pallu, the Palluite clan; 6 for Hezron, the Hezronite clan; for Carmi, the Carmite clan. 7 These were the Reubenite clans. They numbered forty-three thousand seven hundred and thirty men.

8 The sons of Pallu: Eliab. 9 The sons of Eliab: Nemuel, Dathan and Abiram. These two, Dathan and Abiram, men of repute in the community, were the ones who revolted against Moses and Aaron; they belonged to Korah's group when it revolted against Yahweh. 10 The earth opened its mouth and swallowed them (with Korah when that group perished), when fire consumed the two hundred and fifty men. They were a sign. 11 Korah's sons, however, did not perish.

12 The sons of Simeon by clans: for Nemuel, the Nemuelite clan; for Jamin, the Jaminite clan; for Jachin, the Jachinite clan; 13 for Zerah, the Zerahite clan; for Shaul, the Shaulite clan. 14 These were the Simeonite clans. They numbered twenty-two thousand two hundred men.

15 The sons of Gad by clans: for Zephon, the Zephonite clan; for Haggi, the Haggite clan; for Shuni, the Shunite clan; 16 for Ozni, the Oznite clan; for Eri, the Erite clan; 17 for Arod, the Arodite clan; for Areli, the Arelite clan. 18 These were the clans of the sons of Gad. They numbered forty thousand five hundred men.

19 The sons of Judah: Er and Onan. Er and Onan died in the land of Canaan. 20 The other sons of Judah became clans: for Shelah, the Shelahite clan; for Perez, the Perezite clan; for Zerah, the Zerahite clan. 21 The sons of Perez were: for Hezron, the Hezronite clan; for Hamul, the Hamulite clan. 22 These were the clans of Judah. They numbered seventy-six thousand five hundred men.

23 The sons of Issachar by clans: for Tola, the Tolaite clan; for Puvah, the Puvahite clan; 24 for Jashub, the Jashubite clan; for Shimron, the Shimronite clan. 25 These were the clans of Issachar. They numbered sixty-four thousand three hundred men.

26 The sons of Zebulun by clans: for Sered, the Seredite clan; for Elon, the Elonite clan; for Jahleel, the Jahleelite clan. 27 These were the clans of Zebulun. They numbered sixty thousand five hundred men.

28 The sons of Joseph by clans: Manasseh and Ephraim. 29 The sons of Manasseh: for Machir, the Machirite clan; Machir fathered Gilead: for Gilead, the Gileadite clan.

scendants of Gilead: of Iezer, the clan of the Iezerites; of Helek, the clan of the Helekites; 31 and of Asriel, the clan of the Asrielites; and of Shechem, the clan of the Shechemites; 32 and of Shemida, the clan of the Shemidaites; and of Hepher, the clan of the Hepherites. 33 Now Zelophehad son of Hepher had no sons, but daughters: and the names of the daughters of Zelophehad were Mahlah, Noah, Hoglah, Milcah, and Tirzah. 34 These are the clans of Manasseh; the number of those enrolled was fifty-two thousand seven hundred.

35 These are the descendants of Ephraim according to their clans: of Shuthelah, the clan of the Shuthelahites; of Becher, the clan of the Becherites; of Tahan, the clan of the Tahanites. 36 And these are the descendants of Shuthelah: of Eran, the clan of the Eranites. 37 These are the clans of the Ephraimites: the number of those enrolled was thirty-two thousand five hundred. These are the descendants of Joseph by their clans.

38 The descendants of Benjamin by their clans: of Bela, the clan of the Belaites; of Ashbel, the clan of the Ashbelites; of Ahiram, the clan of the Ahiramites; 39 of Shephupham, the clan of the Shuphamites; of Hupham, the clan of the Huphamites. 40 And the sons of Bela were Ard and Naaman: of Ard, the clan of the Ardites; of Naaman, the clan of the Naamites. 41 These are the descendants of Benjamin by their clans; the number of those enrolled was forty-five thousand six hundred.

42 These are the descendants of Dan by their clans: of Shuham, the clan of the Shuhamites. These are the clans of Dan by their clans. 43 All the clans of the Shuhamites: sixty-four thousand four hundred enrolled.

44 The descendants of Asher by their families: of Imnah, the clan of the Imnites; of Ishvi, the clan of the Ishvites; of Beriah, the clan of the Beriites. 45 Of the descendants of Beriah: of Heber, the clan of the Heberites; of Malchiel, the clan of the Malchielites. 46 And the name of the daughter of Asher was Serah. 47 These are the clans of the Asherites: the number of those enrolled was fifty-three thousand four hundred.

48 The descendants of Naphtali by their clans: of Jahzeel, the clan of the Jahzeelites; of Guni, the clan of the Gunites; 49 of Jezer, the clan of the Jezerites; of Shillem, the clan of the Shillemites. 50 These are the Naphtalites[n] by their clans: the number of those enrolled was forty-five thousand four hundred.

51 This was the number of the Israelites enrolled: six hundred and one thousand seven hundred thirty.

52 The LORD spoke to Moses, saying: 53 To these the land shall be apportioned for inheritance according to the number of names. 54 To a large tribe you shall give a large inheritance, and to a small tribe you shall give a small inheritance; every tribe shall be given its inheritance according to its enrollment. 55 But the land shall be apportioned by lot; according to the names of their ancestral tribes they shall inherit. 56 Their inheritance shall be apportioned according to lot between the larger and the smaller.

57 This is the enrollment of the Levites by their clans: of Gershon, the clan of the Gershonites; of Kohath, the clan of the Kohathites; of Merari, the clan of the Merarites. 58 These are the clans of Levi: the clan of the Libnites, the clan of the Hebronites, the clan of the Mahlites, the clan of the Mushites, the clan of the Korahites. Now Kohath was the father of Amram. 59 The name of Amram's wife was Jochebed daughter of Levi, who was born to Levi in Egypt; and she bore to Amram: Aaron, Moses, and their sister Miriam. 60 To Aaron were born Nadab, Abihu, Eleazar, and Ithamar. 61 But Nadab and Abihu died when they offered

ites: Jeezer, the Jeezerite family; Helek, the Helekite family; 31 Asriel, the Asrielite family; Shechem, the Shechemite family; 32 Shemida, the Shemidaite family; Hepher, the Hepherite family. 33 Zelophehad son of Hepher had no sons, only daughters; their names were Mahlah, Noah, Hoglah, Milcah, and Tirzah. 34 These were the families of Manasseh; the number in their list was fifty-two thousand seven hundred.

35 Ephraimites, by their families: Shuthelah, the Shuthalhite family; Becher, the Bachrite family; Tahan, the Tahanite family. 36 Shuthalhites: Eran, the Eranite family. 37 These were the Ephraimite families; the number in their list was thirty-two thousand five hundred. These were the Josephites, by families.

38 Benjamites, by their families: Bela, the Belaite family; Ashbel, the Ashbelite family; Ahiram, the Ahiramite family; 39 Shupham, the Shuphamite family; Hupham, the Huphamite family. 40 Belaites: Ard and Naaman. Ard, the Ardite family; Naaman, the Naamite family. 41 These were the Benjamite families; the number in their list was forty-five thousand six hundred.

42 Danites, by their families: Shuham, the Shuhamite family. These were the families of Dan by their families; 43 the number in the list of the Shuhamite family was sixty-four thousand four hundred.

44 Asherites, by their families: Imna, the Imnite family; Ishvi, the Ishvite family; Beriah, the Beriite family; 45 Beriite families: Heber, the Heberite family; Malchiel, the Malchielite family. 46 The daughter of Asher was named Serah. 47 These were the Asherite families; the number in their list was fifty-three thousand four hundred.

48 Naphtalites, by their families: Jahzeel, the Jahzeelite family; Guni, the Gunite family; 49 Jezer, the Jezerite family; Shillem, the Shillemite family. 50 These were the Naphtalite families by their families; the number in their list was forty-five thousand four hundred.

51 The total in the Israelite lists was six hundred and one thousand seven hundred and thirty.

52 The LORD said to Moses, 53 'The land is to be apportioned among these tribes according to the number of names recorded. 54 To the larger group give a larger share of territory and to the smaller a smaller; a share will be given to each in proportion to its size as shown in the census. 55 The land, however, is to be apportioned by lot, the lots being cast for the territory by families in the father's line, 56 and shares apportioned by lot between the larger families and the smaller.'

57 The lists of Levi, by families: Gershon, the Gershonite family; Kohath, the Kohathite family; Merari, the Merarite family. 58 These were the families of Levi: the Libnite, Hebronite, Mahlite, Mushite, and Korahite families. Kohath was the father of Amram; 59 Amram's wife was named Jochebed daughter of Levi, born to him in Egypt. She bore to Amram Aaron, Moses, and their sister Miriam. 60 Aaron's sons were Nadab, Abihu, Eleazar, and Ithamar. 61 Nadab and Abihu died because they had presented illicit fire before the LORD.

---

[n] Heb clans of Naphtali

26:39 **Shupham:** so some MSS; others Shephupham.   26:40 **Ard, the:** so Samar.; Heb. omits Ard.

Abiezer the clan of the Abiezrites, through Helek the clan of the Helekites, 31 through Asriel the clan of the Asrielites, through Shechem the clan of the Shechemites, 32 through Shemida the clan of the Shemidaites, through Hepher the clan of the Hepherites. 33 Zelophehad, son of Hepher, had no sons, but only daughters, whose names were Mahlah, Noah, Hoglah, Milcah and Tirzah. 34 These were the clans of Manasseh, of whom fifty-two thousand seven hundred men were registered.

35 The Ephraimites by clans were: through Shuthelah the clan of the Shuthelahites, through Becher the clan of the Bechrites, through Tahan the clan of the Tahanites. 36 The Shuthelahites were: through Eran the clan of the Eranites. 37 These were the clans of the Ephraimites, of whom thirty-two thousand five hundred men were registered.

These were the descendants of Joseph by clans.

38 The Benjaminites by clans were: through Bela the clan of the Belaites, through Ashbel the clan of the Ashbelites, through Ahiram the clan of the Ahiramites, 39 through Shupham the clan of the Shuphamites, through Hupham the clan of the Huphamites. 40 The descendants of Bela were Arad and Naaman: through Arad the clan of the Aradites, through Naaman the clan of the Naamanites. 41 These were the Benjaminites by clans, of whom forty-five thousand six hundred men were registered.

42 The Danites by clans were: through Shuham the clan of the Shuhamites. These were the clans of Dan, 43 of whom sixty-four thousand four hundred men were registered.

44 The Asherites by clans were: through Imnah the clan of the Imnites, through Ishvi the clan of the Ishvites, through Beriah the clan of the Beriites, 45 through Heber the clan of the Heberites, through Malchiel the clan of the Malchielites. 46 The name of Asher's daughter was Serah. 47 These were the clans of Asher, of whom fifty-three thousand four hundred men were registered.

48 The Naphtalites by clans were: through Jahzeel the clan of the Jahzeelites, through Guni the clan of the Gunites, 49 through Jezer the clan of the Jezerites, through Shillem the clan of the Shillemites. 50 These were the clans of Naphtali, of whom forty-five thousand four hundred men were registered.

51 These six hundred and one thousand seven hundred and thirty were the Israelites who were registered.

52 The LORD said to Moses, 53 "Among these groups the land shall be divided as their heritage in keeping with the number of individuals in each group. 54 To a large group you shall assign a large heritage, to a small group a small heritage, each group receiving its heritage in proportion to the number of men registered in it. 55 But the land shall be divided by lot, as the heritage of the various ancestral tribes. 56 As the lot falls shall each group, large or small, be assigned its heritage."

57 The Levites registered by clans were: through Gershon the clan of the Gershonites, through Kohath the clan of the Kohathites, through Merari the clan of the Merarites. 58 These also were clans of Levi: the clan of the Libnites, the clan of the Hebronites, the clan of the Mahlites, the clan of the Mushites, the clan of the Korahites.

Among the descendants of Kohath was Amram, 59 whose wife was named Jochebed. She also was of the tribe of Levi, born to the tribe in Egypt. To Amram she bore Aaron and Moses and their sister Miriam. 60 To Aaron were born Nadab and Abihu, Eleazar and Ithamar. 61 But Nadab and Abihu died when they offered profane fire before the LORD.

30 These were the sons of Gilead: for Iezer, the Iezerite clan; for Helek, the Helekite clan; 31 Asriel, the Asrielite clan; Shechem, the Shechemite clan; 32 Shemida, the Shemidaite clan; Hepher, the Hepherite clan. 33 Zelophehad son of Hepher had no sons, only daughters; the names of Zelophehad's daughters were Mahlah, Noah, Hoglah, Milcah and Tirzah. 34 These were the clans of Manasseh. They numbered fifty-two thousand seven hundred men.

35 These were the sons of Ephraim by clans: for Shuthelah, the Shuthelahite clan; for Becher, the Becherite clan; for Tahan, the Tahanite clan. 36 These were the sons of Shuthelah: for Eran, the Eranite clan. 37 These were the clans of Ephraim. They numbered thirty-two thousand five hundred men.

These were the sons of Joseph by clans.

38 The sons of Benjamin by clans: for Bela, the Belaite clan; for Ashbel, the Ashbelite clan; for Ahiram, the Ahiramite clan; 39 for Shephupham, the Shephuphamite clan; for Hupham, the Huphamite clan. 40 Bela's sons were Ard and Naaman; for Ard, the Ardite clan; for Naaman, the Naamanite clan. 41 These were the sons of Benjamin by clans. They numbered forty-five thousand six hundred men.

42 These were the sons of Dan by clans: for Shuham, the Shuhamite clan. These were the sons of Dan by clans. 43 All the Shuhamite clans numbered sixty-four thousand four hundred men.

44 The sons of Asher by clans: for Imnah, the Imnahite clan; for Ishvi, the Ishvihite clan; for Beriah, the Beriahite clan. 45 For the sons of Beriah: for Heber, the Heberite clan; for Malchiel, the Malchielite clan. 46 The daughter of Asher was called Serah. 47 These were the clans of Asher. They numbered fifty-three thousand four hundred men.

48 The sons of Naphtali by clans: for Jahzeel, the Jahzeelite clan; for Guni, the Gunite clan; 49 for Jezer, the Jezerite clan; for Shillem, the Shillemite clan. 50 These were the clans of Naphtali as divided into clans. The sons of Naphtali numbered forty-five thousand four hundred men.

51 Of the Israelites thus numbered, there were six hundred and one thousand seven hundred and thirty men.

52 Yahweh then spoke to Moses and said, 53 'The country must be shared out among these as a heritage, proportionately to the number of those inscribed. 54 To the large in number you will give a large area of land, to the small in number a small area; to each the heritage will be in proportion to the number registered. 55 The sharing out of the country must, however, be done by lot. Each will receive a heritage proportionate to the number of names in their patriarchal tribes; 56 the heritage of each tribe will be shared out by lot, depending on its larger or smaller numbers.'

57 These, by clans, are the Levites that were registered: for Gershon, the Gershonite clan; for Kohath, the Kohathite clan; for Merari, the Merarite clan.

58 These are the Levite clans: the Libnite clan, the Hebronite clan, the Mahlite clan, the Mushite clan, the Korahite clan.

Kohath fathered Amram. 59 Amram's wife was called Jokebed daughter of Levi, born to him in Egypt. To Amram she bore Aaron, Moses and Miriam their sister. 60 Aaron fathered Nadab and Abihu, Eleazar and Ithamar. 61 Nadab and Abihu died when they brought unauthorised fire before Yahweh.

NEW REVISED STANDARD VERSION

illict fire before the LORD. 62 The number of those enrolled was twenty-three thousand, every male one month old and up; for they were not enrolled among the Israelites because there was no allotment given to them among the Israelites.

63 These were those enrolled by Moses and Eleazar the priest, who enrolled the Israelites in the plains of Moab by the Jordan opposite Jericho. 64 Among these there was not one of those enrolled by Moses and Aaron the priest, who had enrolled the Israelites in the wilderness of Sinai. 65 For the LORD had said of them, "They shall die in the wilderness." Not one of them was left, except Caleb son of Jephunneh and Joshua son of Nun.

27 Then the daughters of Zelophehad came forward. Zelophehad was son of Hepher son of Gilead son of Machir son of Manasseh son of Joseph, a member of the Manassite clans. The names of his daughters were: Mahlah, Noah, Hoglah, Milcah, and Tirzah. 2 They stood before Moses, Eleazar the priest, the leaders, and all the congregation, at the entrance of the tent of meeting, and they said, 3 "Our father died in the wilderness; he was not among the company of those who gathered themselves together against the LORD in the company of Korah, but died for his own sin; and he had no sons. 4 Why should the name of our father be taken away from his clan because he had no son? Give to us a possession among our father's brothers."

5 Moses brought their case before the LORD. 6 And the LORD spoke to Moses, saying: 7 The daughters of Zelophehad are right in what they are saying; you shall indeed let them possess an inheritance among their father's brothers and pass the inheritance of their father on to them. 8 You shall also say to the Israelites, "If a man dies, and has no son, then you shall pass his inheritance on to his daughter. 9 If he has no daughter, then you shall give his inheritance to his brothers. 10 If he has no brothers, then you shall give his inheritance to his father's brothers. 11 And if his father has no brothers, then you shall give his inheritance to the nearest kinsman of his clan, and he shall possess it. It shall be for the Israelites a statute and ordinance, as the LORD commanded Moses."

12 The LORD said to Moses, "Go up this mountain of the Abarim range, and see the land that I have given to the Israelites. 13 When you have seen it, you also shall be gathered to your people, as your brother Aaron was, 14 because you rebelled against my word in the wilderness of Zin when the congregation quarreled with me. *o* You did not show my holiness before their eyes at the waters." (These are the waters of Meribath-kadesh in the wilderness of Zin.) 15 Moses spoke to the LORD, saying, 16 "Let the LORD, the God of the spirits of all flesh, appoint someone over the congregation 17 who shall go out before them and come in before them, who shall lead them out and bring them in, so that the congregation of the LORD may not be like sheep without a shepherd." 18 So the LORD said to Moses, "Take Joshua son of Nun, a man in whom is the spirit, and lay your hand upon him; 19 have him stand before Eleazar the priest and all the congregation, and commission him in their sight. 20 You shall give him some of your authority, so that all the congregation of the Israelites may obey. 21 But he shall stand before Eleazar the priest, who shall inquire for him by the decision of the Urim before the LORD; at his word they shall go out, and at his word they shall come in, both he and all the Israelites with him, the whole congregation." 22 So Moses did as the LORD commanded him. He took Joshua and had him stand before Eleazar the priest and the whole congregation; 23 he laid his hands on him and commissioned him—as the LORD had directed through Moses.

o Heb lacks *with me*

REVISED ENGLISH BIBLE

62 In the lists of Levi the number of males, aged one month and upwards, was twenty-three thousand. They were recorded separately from the other Israelites because no holding was allotted to them among the Israelites.

63 These were the lists prepared by Moses and Eleazar the priest when they made a census of the Israelites in the lowlands of Moab by the Jordan near Jericho. 64 Among them there was not a single one of the Israelites whom Moses and Aaron the priest had recorded in the wilderness of Sinai; 65 for the LORD had said they should all die in the wilderness. None of them was still living except Caleb son of Jephunneh and Joshua son of Nun.

27 A claim was presented by the daughters of Zelophehad son of Hepher, son of Gilead, son of Machir, son of Manasseh, son of Joseph. Their names were Mahlah, Noah, Hoglah, Milcah, and Tirzah. 2 They appeared before Moses, Eleazar the priest, the chiefs, and all the community at the entrance of the Tent of Meeting, and spoke as follows: 3 'Our father died in the wilderness. But he was not among the company of Korah which combined together against the LORD; he died for his own sin and left no sons. 4 Is it right that, because he had no son, our father's name should disappear from his family? Give us our holding on the same footing as our father's brothers.'

5 Moses brought their case before the LORD, 6 who said to him, 7 'The claim of the daughters of Zelophehad is good: you must allow them to inherit on the same footing as their father's brothers, and let their father's holding pass to them. 8 Intimate this to the Israelites: When a man dies leaving no son, his holding is to pass to his daughter. 9 If he has no daughter, give it to his brothers. 10 If he has no brothers, give it to his father's brothers. 11 If his father had no brothers, then give possession to the nearest survivor in his family, and he will inherit. This is to be a legal precedent for the Israelites, as the LORD has commanded Moses.'

12 The LORD said to Moses, 'Go up this mountain, Mount Abarim, and view the land which I have given to the Israelites. 13 Then, when you have seen it, you too will be gathered to your father's kin as was your brother Aaron; 14 for you and Aaron disobeyed my command when the community disputed with me in the wilderness of Zin: you did not uphold my holiness before them at the waters.' These were the waters of Meribah-by-Kadesh in the wilderness of Zin.

15 Then Moses said to the LORD, 16 'Let the LORD, the God of the spirits of all mankind, appoint a man over the community 17 to go out and come in at their head, to lead them out and bring them home, so that the community of the LORD may not be like sheep without a shepherd.' 18 The LORD answered, 'Take Joshua son of Nun, a man powerful in spirit; lay your hand on him 19 and have him stand before Eleazar the priest and all the community. Give him his commission in their presence, 20 and delegate some of your authority to him, so that the entire Israelite community will obey him. 21 He must present himself before Eleazar the priest, who will obtain a decision for him by consulting the Urim before the LORD; at his word they are to go out and come home, both Joshua and the whole community of the Israelites.'

22 Moses did as the LORD had commanded him. He took Joshua, presented him to Eleazar the priest and the whole community, 23 laid his hands on him, and gave him his commission, as instructed by the LORD.

27:1 **Manasseh:** *so Lat.; Heb. adds* of the families of Manasseh.

NEW AMERICAN BIBLE

NEW JERUSALEM BIBLE

62 The total number of male Levites one month or more of age, who were registered, was twenty-three thousand. They were not registered with the other Israelites, however, for no heritage was given them among the Israelites.

63 These, then, were the men registered by Moses and the priest Eleazar in the census of the Israelites taken on the plains of Moab along the Jericho stretch of the Jordan. 64 Among them there was not a man of those who had been registered by Moses and the priest Aaron in the census of the Israelites taken in the desert of Sinai; 65 For the LORD had told them that they would surely die in the desert, and not one of them was left except Caleb, son of Jephunneh, and Joshua, son of Nun.

27 Zelophehad, son of Hepher, son of Gilead, son of Machir, son of Manasseh, son of Joseph, had daughters named Mahlah, Noah, Hoglah, Milcah and Tirzah. They came forward, 2 and standing in the presence of Moses, the priest Eleazar, the princes, and the whole community at the entrance of the meeting tent, said: 3 "Our father died in the desert. Although he did not join those who banded together against the LORD [in Korah's band], he died for his own sin without leaving any sons. 4 But why should our father's name be withdrawn from his clan merely because he had no son? Let us, therefore, have property among our father's kinsmen."

5 When Moses laid their case before the LORD, 6 the LORD said to him, 7 "The plea of Zelophehad's daughters is just; you shall give them hereditary property among their father's kinsmen, letting their father's heritage pass on to them. 8 Therefore, tell the Israelites: If a man dies without leaving a son, you shall let his heritage pass on to his daughter; 9 if he has no daughter, you shall give his heritage to his brothers; 10 if he has no brothers, you shall give his heritage to his father's brothers; 11 if his father had no brothers, you shall give his heritage to his nearest relative in his clan, who shall then take possession of it." This is the legal norm for the Israelites, as the LORD commanded Moses.

12 The LORD said to Moses, "Go up here into the Abarim Mountains and view the land that I am giving to the Israelites. 13 When you have viewed it, you too shall be taken to your people, as was your brother Aaron, 14 because in the rebellion of the community in the desert of Zin you both rebelled against my order to manifest my sanctity to them by means of the water." [This is the water of Meribah of Kadesh in the desert of Zin.]

15 Then Moses said to the LORD, 16 "May the LORD, the God of the spirits of all mankind, set over the community a man 17 who shall act as their leader in all things, to guide them in all their actions; that the LORD's community may not be like sheep without a shepherd." 18 And the LORD replied to Moses, "Take Joshua, son of Nun, a man of spirit, and lay your hand upon him. 19 Have him stand in the presence of the priest Eleazar and of the whole community, and commission him before their eyes. 20 Invest him with some of your own dignity, that the whole Israelite community may obey him. 21 He shall present himself to the priest Eleazar, to have him seek out for him the decisions of the Urim in the LORD's presence; and as he directs, Joshua, all the Israelites with him, and the community as a whole shall perform all their actions."

22 Moses did as the LORD had commanded him. Taking Joshua and having him stand in the presence of the priest Eleazar and of the whole community, 23 he laid his hands on him and gave him his commission, as the LORD had directed through Moses.

62 Altogether twenty-three thousand males of one month and over were registered. They were not registered with the Israelites, since they were given no heritage with the Israelites.

63 Such were the men registered by Moses and the priest Eleazar who took a census of the Israelites on the Plains of Moab near the Jordan by Jericho. 64 Not one of them was among those whom Moses and the priest Aaron had registered when they counted the Israelites in the desert of Sinai; 65 for Yahweh had told them that these were to die in the desert and that none of them would be left except Caleb son of Jephunneh and Joshua son of Nun.

27 There then came forward the daughters of Zelophehad son of Hepher, son of Gilead, son of Machir, son of Manasseh; he belonged to the clans of Manasseh son of Joseph. His daughters' names were Mahlah, Noah, Hoglah, Milcah and Tirzah. 2 They appeared before Moses, the priest Eleazar, the leaders and the whole community, at the entrance to the Tent of Meeting, and said, 'Our father died in the desert. He was not a member of the party who banded together against Yahweh, Korah's party; it was for his own sin that he died without sons. 4 Why should our father's name be lost to his clan? Since he had no son, give us some property like our father's kinsmen.'

5 Moses took their case before Yahweh, 6 and Yahweh spoke to Moses and said, 'Zelophehad's daughters are right in what they say. You will indeed give them a property to be their heritage among their father's kinsmen; see that their father's heritage is passed on to them. 8 Then speak to the Israelites and say, "If a man dies without sons, his heritage will pass to his daughter. 9 If he has no daughter, the heritage will go to his brothers. 10 If he has no brothers, his heritage will go to his father's brothers. 11 If his father has no brothers, his heritage will go to the member of his clan who is most nearly related; it will become his property. This will be a legal rule for the Israelites, as Yahweh has ordered Moses." '

12 Yahweh said to Moses, 'Climb this mountain of the Abarim range, and look at the country which I have given to the Israelites. 13 After you have seen it, you will be gathered to your people, as Aaron your brother was. 14 For you both rebelled in the desert of Zin when the community disputed with me and when I ordered you to assert my holiness before their eyes by means of the water.' (These were the Waters of Meribah of Kadesh, in the desert of Zin.)

15 Moses then said to Yahweh, 16 'May it please Yahweh, God of the spirits that give life to all living creatures, to appoint a leader for this community, 17 to be at their head in all their undertakings, a man who will lead them out and bring them in, so that Yahweh's community will not be like sheep without a shepherd.' 18 Yahweh then said to Moses, 'Take Joshua son of Nun, a man in whom the spirit dwells, and lay your hand on him. 19 Bring him before the priest Eleazar and the whole community and give him your orders in their presence, 20 conferring some of your own authority on him, so that the whole community of Israelites will obey him. 21 He will present himself to the priest Eleazar who will consult Yahweh on his behalf by means of the rite of the *urim*; at his command, they will go out and, at his command, they will come in, he and all the Israelites with him, the whole community.'

22 Moses did as Yahweh had ordered. He took Joshua, brought him before the priest Eleazar and the whole community, 23 laid his hands on him and gave him his orders, as Yahweh had directed through Moses.

28 The LORD spoke to Moses, saying: 2 Command the Israelites, and say to them: My offering, the food for my offerings by fire, my pleasing odor, you shall take care to offer to me at its appointed time. 3 And you shall say to them, This is the offering by fire that you shall offer to the LORD: two male lambs a year old without blemish, daily, as a regular offering. 4 One lamb you shall offer in the morning, and the other lamb you shall offer at twilight*p* 5 also one-tenth of an ephah of choice flour for a grain offering, mixed with one-fourth of a hin of beaten oil. 6 It is a regular burnt offering, ordained at Mount Sinai for a pleasing odor, an offering by fire to the LORD. 7 Its drink offering shall be one-fourth of a hin for each lamb; in the sanctuary you shall pour out a drink offering of strong drink to the LORD. 8 The other lamb you shall offer at twilight*p* with a grain offering and a drink offering like the one in the morning; you shall offer it as an offering by fire, a pleasing odor to the LORD.

9 On the sabbath day: two male lambs a year old without blemish, and two-tenths of an ephah of choice flour for a grain offering, mixed with oil, and its drink offering — 10 this is the burnt offering for every sabbath, in addition to the regular burnt offering and its drink offering.

11 At the beginnings of your months you shall offer a burnt offering to the LORD: two young bulls, one ram, seven male lambs a year old without blemish; 12 also three-tenths of an ephah of choice flour for a grain offering, mixed with oil, for each bull; and two-tenths of choice flour for a grain offering, mixed with oil, for the one ram; 13 and one-tenth of choice flour mixed with oil as a grain offering for every lamb — a burnt offering of pleasing odor, an offering by fire to the LORD. 14 Their drink offerings shall be half a hin of wine for a bull, one-third of a hin for a ram, and one-fourth of a hin for a lamb. This is the burnt offering of every month throughout the months of the year. 15 And there shall be one male goat for a sin offering to the LORD; it shall be offered in addition to the regular burnt offering and its drink offering.

16 On the fourteenth day of the first month there shall be a passover offering to the LORD. 17 And on the fifteenth day of this month is a festival; seven days shall unleavened bread be eaten. 18 On the first day there shall be a holy convocation. You shall not work at your occupations. 19 You shall offer an offering by fire, a burnt offering to the LORD: two young bulls, one ram, and seven male lambs a year old; see that they are without blemish. 20 Their grain offering shall be of choice flour mixed with oil: three-tenths of an ephah shall you offer for a bull, and two-tenths for a ram; 21 one-tenth shall you offer for each of the seven lambs; 22 also one male goat for a sin offering, to make atonement for you. 23 You shall offer these in addition to the burnt offering of the morning, which belongs to the regular burnt offering. 24 In the same way you shall offer daily, for seven days, the food of an offering by fire, a pleasing odor to the LORD; it shall be offered in addition to the regular burnt offering and its drink offering. 25 And on the seventh day you shall have a holy convocation; you shall not work at your occupations.

26 On the day of the first fruits, when you offer a grain offering of new grain to the LORD at your festival of weeks, you shall have a holy convocation; you shall not work at your occupations. 27 You shall offer a burnt offering, a pleasing odor to the LORD: two young bulls, one ram, seven male lambs a year old. 28 Their grain offering shall be of choice flour mixed with oil, three-tenths of an ephah for each bull, two-tenths for one ram, 29 one-tenth for each of the seven lambs; 30 with one male goat, to make atonement for you. 31 In addition to the regular burnt offering with its

p Heb *between the two evenings*

28 THE LORD told Moses 2 to say to the Israelites: See that my offerings, the food for the food-offering of soothing odour, are presented to me at the appointed time. 3 Tell them: This is the food-offering which you are to present to the LORD: the regular daily whole-offering of two yearling rams without blemish; 4 one you must sacrifice in the morning and the second between dusk and dark. 5 The grain-offering is to be a tenth of an ephah of flour mixed with a quarter of a hin of oil of pounded olives. 6 (This was the regular whole-offering instituted at Mount Sinai, a soothing odour, a food-offering to the LORD.) 7 The wine for the proper drink-offering is to be a quarter of a hin to each ram; you are to pour out this strong drink in the holy place as an offering to the LORD. 8 You are to sacrifice the second ram between dusk and dark, with the same grain-offering as at the morning sacrifice and with the proper drink-offering; it is a food-offering of soothing odour to the LORD.

9 For the sabbath day: two yearling rams without blemish, a grain-offering of two tenths of an ephah of flour mixed with oil, and the proper drink-offering. 10 This whole-offering, presented every sabbath, is in addition to the regular whole-offering and the proper drink-offering.

11 On the first day of every month present a whole-offering to the LORD, consisting of two young bulls, one ram, and seven yearling rams without blemish. 12 The grain-offering is to be three tenths of flour mixed with oil for each bull, two tenths of flour mixed with oil for the full-grown ram, 13 and one tenth of flour mixed with oil for each young ram. This is a whole-offering, a food-offering of soothing odour to the LORD. 14 The proper drink-offering is half a hin of wine for each bull, a third for the full-grown ram, and a quarter for each young ram. This is the whole-offering to be made, month by month, throughout the year. 15 Further, one he-goat is to be sacrificed as a purification-offering to the LORD, in addition to the regular whole-offering and the proper drink-offering.

16 The Passover of the LORD is to be held on the fourteenth day of the first month, 17 and on the fifteenth day there is to be a pilgrim-feast; for seven days you must eat only unleavened bread. 18 On the first day there must be a sacred assembly; you must not do your daily work. 19 As a food-offering, a whole-offering to the LORD, you will present two young bulls, one ram, and seven yearling rams, all without blemish. 20 Offer the proper grain-offerings of flour mixed with oil, three tenths for each bull, two tenths for the ram, 21 and one tenth for each of the seven rams; 22 and as a purification-offering, one he-goat to make expiation for you. 23 All these you must offer in addition to the morning whole-offering, which is the regular sacrifice. 24 Repeat this daily till the seventh day, presenting food as a food-offering of soothing odour to the LORD, in addition to the regular whole-offering and the proper drink-offering. 25 On the seventh day there will be a sacred assembly; you must not do your daily work.

26 On the day of Firstfruits, when you bring to the LORD your grain-offering from the new crop at your feast of Weeks, there is to be a sacred assembly; you must not do your daily work. 27 Bring a whole-offering as a soothing odour to the LORD: two young bulls, one full-grown ram, and seven yearling rams. 28 The proper grain-offering will be of flour mixed with oil, three tenths for each bull, two tenths for the one ram, 29 and a tenth for each of the seven young rams, 30 and there must be one he-goat as a purification-offering to make expiation for you; 31 they must all be

28:7 **The wine:** *so Gk; Heb. omits.* 28:30 **as a purification-offering:** *so Samar.; Heb. omits.*

28 The LORD said to Moses, 2 "Give the Israelites this commandment: At the times I have appointed, you shall be careful to present me the food offerings that are offered to me as sweet-smelling oblations.

3 "You shall tell them therefore: This is the oblation which you shall offer to the LORD: two unblemished yearling lambs each day as the established holocaust, 4 offering one lamb in the morning and the other during the evening twilight, 5 each with a cereal offering of one tenth of an ephah of fine flour mixed with a fourth of a hin of oil of crushed olives. 6 This is the established holocaust that was offered at Mount Sinai as a sweet-smelling oblation to the LORD. 7 And as the libation for the first lamb, you shall pour out to the LORD in the sanctuary a fourth of a hin of wine. 8 The other lamb, to be offered during the evening twilight, you shall offer with the same cereal offering and the same libation as in the morning, as a sweet-smelling oblation to the LORD.

9 "On the sabbath day you shall offer two unblemished yearling lambs, with their cereal offering, two tenths of an ephah of fine flour mixed with oil, and with their libations. 10 Each sabbath there shall be the sabbath holocaust in addition to the established holocaust and its libation.

11 "On the first of each month you shall offer as a holocaust to the LORD two bullocks, one ram, and seven unblemished yearling lambs, 12 with three tenths of an ephah of fine flour mixed with oil as the cereal offering for each bullock, two tenths of an ephah of fine flour mixed with oil as the cereal offering for the ram, 13 and one tenth of an ephah of fine flour mixed with oil as the cereal offering for each lamb, that the holocaust may be a sweet-smelling oblation to the LORD. 14 Their libations shall be half a hin of wine for each bullock, a third of a hin for the ram, and a fourth of a hin for each lamb. This is the new moon holocaust for every new moon of the year. 15 Moreover, one goat shall be sacrificed as a sin offering to the LORD. These are to be offered in addition to the established holocaust and its libation.

16 "On the fourteenth day of the first month falls the Passover of the LORD, 17 and the fifteenth day of this month is the pilgrimage feast. For seven days unleavened bread is to be eaten. 18 On the first of these days you shall hold a sacred assembly, and do no sort of work. 19 As an oblation you shall offer a holocaust to the LORD, which shall consist of two bullocks, one ram, and seven yearling lambs that you are sure are unblemished, 20 with their cereal offerings of fine flour mixed with oil, offering three tenths of an ephah for each bullock, two tenths for the ram, 21 and one tenth for each of the seven lambs; 22 and offer one goat as a sin offering in atonement for yourselves. 23 These offerings you shall make in addition to the established morning holocaust: 24 you shall make exactly the same offerings each day for seven days as food offerings, in addition to the established holocaust with its libation, for a sweet-smelling oblation to the LORD. 25 On the seventh day you shall hold a sacred assembly, and do no sort of work.

26 "On the day of first fruits, on your feast of Weeks, when you present to the LORD the new cereal offering, you shall hold a sacred assembly, and do no sort of work. 27 You shall offer as a sweet-smelling holocaust to the LORD two bullocks, one ram, and seven yearling lambs that you are sure are unblemished, 28 with their cereal offerings of fine flour mixed with oil; offering three tenths of an ephah for each bullock, two tenths for the ram, 29 and one tenth for each of the seven lambs. 30 Moreover, one goat shall be offered as a sin offering in atonement for yourselves. 31 You

28 Yahweh spoke to Moses and said, 2 'Give the Israelites this order:

"Take care to bring me my offering, my sustenance in the form of food burnt as a smell pleasing to me, at the proper time."

3 'You will then say to them: "This is the food which you will burn in offering to Yahweh:

"Every day, two unblemished yearling lambs as a perpetual burnt offering. 4 You will offer the first lamb in the morning and the second lamb at twilight, 5 with a cereal offering of one-tenth of an *ephah* of fine flour mixed with one-quarter of a *hin* of crushed-olive oil. 6 Such was the perpetual burnt offering made on Mount Sinai as a pleasing smell, as food burnt for Yahweh. 7 The accompanying libation will be of one-quarter of a *hin* for each lamb; the libation of fermented liquor for Yahweh will be poured inside the sanctuary. 8 The second lamb you will offer at twilight, offering it with the same cereal offering and the same libation as in the morning, as food burnt as a smell pleasing to Yahweh.

9 "On the Sabbath day, you will offer two unblemished yearling lambs and two-tenths of an *ephah* of fine flour as a cereal offering, mixed with oil, as well as the accompanying libation. 10 The Sabbath burnt offering will be offered every Sabbath in addition to the perpetual burnt offering, and the accompanying libation similarly.

11 "At the beginning of each of your months you will offer a burnt offering to Yahweh: two young bulls, one ram and seven yearling lambs, without blemish; 12 for each bull a cereal offering of three-tenths of an *ephah* of fine flour mixed with oil; for each ram, a cereal offering of two-tenths of fine flour mixed with oil; 13 for each lamb, a cereal offering of one-tenth of fine flour mixed with oil: as a burnt offering, as a pleasing smell, as food burnt for Yahweh. 14 The accompanying libations will be of half a *hin* of wine for a bull, one-third of a *hin* for a ram and one-quarter of a *hin* for a lamb. This will be the monthly burnt offering, month after month, every month of the year. 15 In addition to the perpetual burnt offering, a goat will be offered to Yahweh, as a sacrifice for sin, with its accompanying libation.

16 "The fourteenth day of the first month is the Passover of Yahweh, 17 and the fifteenth day of this month is a feast day. For seven days unleavened bread will be eaten. 18 On the first day there will be a sacred assembly; you will do no heavy work. 19 As food burnt as a burnt offering you will offer Yahweh two young bulls, a ram and seven yearling lambs, without blemish. 20 The accompanying cereal offering of fine flour mixed with oil will be three-tenths of an *ephah* for a bull, two-tenths for a ram, 21 and one-tenth for each of the seven lambs. 22 There will also be a goat as a sacrifice for sin, for performing the rite of expiation for you. 23 You will offer these in addition to the morning burnt offering, which is a perpetual burnt offering. 24 You will do this every day for seven days. It is sustenance, food burnt as a smell pleasing to Yahweh, to be offered in addition to the perpetual burnt offering and its accompanying libation. 25 On the seventh day you will hold a sacred assembly; you will do no heavy work.

26 "On the day of the first-fruits, when you make your offering of new fruits to Yahweh at your feast of Weeks, you will hold a sacred assembly; you will do no heavy work. 27 As a burnt offering as a smell pleasing to Yahweh, you will offer two young bulls, one ram and seven yearling lambs. 28 The accompanying cereal offering of fine flour mixed with oil will be three-tenths of an *ephah* for each bull, two-tenths for the ram, 29 and one-tenth for each of the seven lambs. 30 There will also be a goat as a sacrifice for sin, for performing the rite of expiation for you. 31 You will

NEW REVISED STANDARD VERSION	REVISED ENGLISH BIBLE

NEW REVISED STANDARD VERSION

grain offering, you shall offer them and their drink offering. They shall be without blemish.

29 On the first day of the seventh month you shall have a holy convocation; you shall not work at your occupations. It is a day for you to blow the trumpets, 2 and you shall offer a burnt offering, a pleasing odor to the LORD: one young bull, one ram, seven male lambs a year old without blemish. 3 Their grain offering shall be of choice flour mixed with oil, three-tenths of one ephah for the bull, two-tenths for the ram, 4 and one-tenth for each of the seven lambs; 5 with one male goat for a sin offering, to make atonement for you. 6 These are in addition to the burnt offering of the new moon and its grain offering, and the regular burnt offering and its grain offering, and their drink offerings, according to the ordinance for them, a pleasing odor, an offering by fire to the LORD.

7 On the tenth day of this seventh month you shall have a holy convocation, and deny yourselves;q you shall do no work. 8 You shall offer a burnt offering to the LORD, a pleasing odor: one young bull, one ram, seven male lambs a year old. They shall be without blemish. 9 Their grain offering shall be of choice flour mixed with oil, three-tenths of an ephah for the bull, two-tenths for the one ram, 10 one-tenth for each of the seven lambs; 11 with one male goat for a sin offering, in addition to the sin offering of atonement, and the regular burnt offering and its grain offering, and their drink offerings.

12 On the fifteenth day of the seventh month you shall have a holy convocation; you shall not work at your occupations. You shall celebrate a festival to the LORD seven days. 13 You shall offer a burnt offering, an offering by fire, a pleasing odor to the LORD: thirteen young bulls, two rams, fourteen male lambs a year old. They shall be without blemish. 14 Their grain offering shall be of choice flour mixed with oil, three-tenths of an ephah for each of the thirteen bulls, two-tenths for each of the two rams, 15 and one-tenth for each of the fourteen lambs; 16 also one male goat for a sin offering, in addition to the regular burnt offering, its grain offering and its drink offering.

17 On the second day: twelve young bulls, two rams, fourteen male lambs a year old without blemish, 18 with the grain offering and the drink offerings for the bulls, for the rams, and for the lambs, as prescribed in accordance with their number; 19 also one male goat for a sin offering, in addition to the regular burnt offering and its grain offering, and their drink offerings.

20 On the third day: eleven bulls, two rams, fourteen male lambs a year old without blemish, 21 with the grain offering and the drink offerings for the bulls, for the rams, and for the lambs, as prescribed in accordance with their number; 22 also one male goat for a sin offering, in addition to the regular burnt offering and its grain offering and its drink offering.

23 On the fourth day: ten bulls, two rams, fourteen male lambs a year old without blemish, 24 with the grain offering and the drink offerings for the bulls, for the rams, and for the lambs, as prescribed in accordance with their number; 25 also one male goat for a sin offering, in addition to the regular burnt offering, its grain offering and its drink offering.

26 On the fifth day: nine bulls, two rams, fourteen male lambs a year old without blemish, 27 with the grain offering and the drink offerings for the bulls, for the rams, and for the lambs, as prescribed in accordance with their number; 28 also one male goat for a sin offering, in addition to the regular burnt offering and its grain offering and its drink offering.

REVISED ENGLISH BIBLE

without blemish. All these are to be offered in addition to the regular whole-offering with the proper grain-offering and drink-offering.

29 On the first day of the seventh month hold a sacred assembly; you must not do your daily work. It is to be a day of acclamation. 2 You are to sacrifice a whole-offering as a soothing odour to the LORD: one young bull, one full-grown ram, and seven yearling rams, without blemish. 3 Their proper grain-offering is flour mixed with oil, three tenths for the bull, two tenths for the one ram, 4 and one tenth for each of the seven young rams, 5 and there will be one he-goat as a purification-offering to make expiation for you. 6 This is in addition to the monthly whole-offering and the regular whole-offering with their proper grain-offerings and drink-offerings according to custom; it is a food-offering of soothing odour to the LORD.

7 On the tenth day of this seventh month hold a sacred assembly, when you are to mortify yourselves. You must do no work. 8 You are to bring a whole-offering to the LORD as a soothing odour: one young bull, one full-grown ram, and seven yearling rams, everything without blemish. 9 The proper grain-offering is flour mixed with oil, three tenths for the bull, two tenths for the one ram, 10 and one tenth for each of the seven young rams, 11 and there will be one he-goat as a purification-offering, in addition to the expiatory sin-offering and the regular whole-offering, with the proper grain-offering and drink-offering.

12 On the fifteenth day of the seventh month hold a sacred assembly. You must not do your daily work, but for seven days keep a pilgrim-feast to the LORD. 13 As a whole-offering, a food-offering of soothing odour to the LORD, you are to bring thirteen young bulls, two full-grown rams, and fourteen yearling rams, everything without blemish. 14 The proper grain-offering is flour mixed with oil, three tenths for each of the thirteen bulls, two tenths for each of the two rams, 15 and one tenth for each of the fourteen young rams, 16 and there will be one he-goat as a purification-offering, in addition to the regular whole-offering with the proper grain-offering and drink-offering.

17 On the second day: twelve young bulls, two full-grown rams, and fourteen yearling rams, without blemish, 18 together with the proper grain-offerings and drink-offerings for bulls, full-grown rams, and young rams, as prescribed according to their number, 19 and there will be one he-goat as a purification-offering, in addition to the regular whole-offering with the proper grain-offering and drink-offering.

20 On the third day: eleven bulls, two full-grown rams, and fourteen yearling rams, without blemish, 21 together with the proper grain-offerings and drink-offerings for bulls, full-grown rams, and young rams, as prescribed according to their number, 22 and there will be one he-goat as a purification-offering, in addition to the regular whole-offering with the proper grain-offering and drink-offering.

23 On the fourth day: ten bulls, two full-grown rams, and fourteen yearling rams, without blemish, 24 together with the proper grain-offerings and drink-offerings for bulls, full-grown rams, and young rams, as prescribed according to their number, 25 and there will be one he-goat as a purification-offering, in addition to the regular whole-offering with the proper grain-offering and drink-offering.

26 On the fifth day: nine bulls, two full-grown rams, and fourteen yearling rams, without blemish, 27 together with the proper grain-offerings and drink-offerings for bulls, full-grown rams, and young rams, as prescribed according to their number, 28 and there will be one he-goat as a purification-offering, in addition to the regular whole-offering with the proper grain-offering and drink-offering.

29:11 **drink-offering:** *so Gk; Heb.* drink-offerings.
29:19 **drink-offering:** *so some MSS; others* drink-offerings.

q Or *and fast*

shall make these offerings, together with their libations, in addition to the established holocaust with its cereal offering.

29 "On the first day of the seventh month you shall hold a sacred assembly, and do no sort of work; it shall be a day on which you sound the trumpet. 2 You shall offer as a sweet-smelling holocaust to the LORD one bullock, one ram, and seven unblemished yearling lambs, 3 with their cereal offerings of fine flour mixed with oil; offering three tenths of an ephah for the bullock, two tenths for the ram, 4 and one tenth for each of the seven lambs. 5 Moreover, one goat shall be offered as a sin offering in atonement for yourselves. 6 These are to be offered in addition to the ordinary new moon holocaust with its cereal offering, and in addition to the established holocaust with its cereal offering, together with the libations prescribed for them, as a sweet-smelling oblation to the LORD.

7 "On the tenth day of this seventh month you shall hold a sacred assembly, and mortify yourselves, and do no sort of work. 8 You shall offer as a sweet-smelling holocaust to the LORD one bullock, one ram, and seven yearling lambs that you are sure are unblemished, 9 with their cereal offerings of fine flour mixed with oil; offering three tenths of an ephah for the bullock, two tenths for the ram, 10 and one tenth for each of the seven lambs. 11 Moreover, one goat shall be sacrificed as a sin offering. These are to be offered in addition to the atonement sin offering, the established holocaust with its cereal offering, and their libations.

12 "On the fifteenth day of the seventh month you shall hold a sacred assembly, and do no sort of work; then, for seven days following, you shall celebrate a pilgrimage feast to the LORD. 13 You shall offer as a sweet-smelling holocaust to the LORD thirteen bullocks, two rams, and fourteen yearling lambs that are unblemished, 14 with their cereal offerings of fine flour mixed with oil; offering three tenths of an ephah for each of the thirteen bullocks, two tenths for each of the two rams, 15 and one tenth for each of the fourteen lambs. 16 Moreover, one goat shall be sacrificed as a sin offering. These are to be offered in addition to the established holocaust with its cereal offering and libation.

17 "On the second day you shall offer twelve bullocks, two rams, and fourteen unblemished yearling lambs, 18 with their cereal offerings and libations as prescribed for the bullocks, rams and lambs in proportion to their number, 19 as well as one goat for a sin offering, besides the established holocaust with its cereal offering and libation.

20 "On the third day you shall offer eleven bullocks, two rams, and fourteen unblemished yearling lambs, 21 with their cereal offerings and libations as prescribed for the bullocks, rams and lambs in proportion to their number, 22 as well as one goat for a sin offering, besides the established holocaust with its cereal offering and libation.

23 "On the fourth day you shall offer ten bullocks, two rams, and fourteen unblemished yearling lambs, 24 with their cereal offerings and libations as prescribed for the bullocks, rams and lambs in proportion to their number, 25 as well as one goat for a sin offering, besides the established holocaust with its cereal offering and libation.

26 "On the fifth day you shall offer nine bullocks, two rams, and fourteen unblemished yearling lambs, 27 with their cereal offerings and libations as prescribed for the bullocks, rams and lambs in proportion to their number, 28 as well as one goat for a sin offering, besides the established holocaust with its cereal offering and libation.

offer these in addition to the perpetual burnt offering and its accompanying cereal offering and libations." '

29 ' "In the seventh month, on the first day of the month, you will hold a sacred assembly; you will do no heavy work. For you this will be a day of Acclamations. 2 As a burnt offering, as a smell pleasing to Yahweh, you will offer one young bull, one ram and seven yearling lambs, without blemish. 3 The accompanying cereal offering of fine flour mixed with oil will be three-tenths of an ephah for the bull, two-tenths for the ram, 4 and one-tenth for each of the seven lambs. 5 There will also be a goat as a sacrifice for sin, for performing the rite of expiation for you. 6 This is in addition to the monthly burnt offering and its cereal offering, the perpetual burnt offering and its cereal offering, and the accompanying libations enjoined by law, as a pleasing smell, as food burnt for Yahweh.

7 "On the tenth day of this seventh month, you will hold a sacred assembly; you will fast and do no work. 8 As a burnt offering for Yahweh, as a pleasing smell, you will offer one young bull, one ram and seven yearling lambs, which you will choose as being without blemish. 9 The accompanying cereal offering of fine flour mixed with oil will be three-tenths of an ephah for the bull, two-tenths for the ram, 10 and one-tenth for each of the seven lambs. 11 And a goat will be offered as a sacrifice for sin. This is in addition to the victim for sin at the feast of Expiation, to the perpetual burnt offering and its cereal offering, and their accompanying libations.

12 "On the fifteenth day of the seventh month you will hold a sacred assembly; you will do no heavy work, and for seven days you will celebrate a feast for Yahweh. 13 As a burnt offering, as food burnt as a smell pleasing to Yahweh, you will offer thirteen young bulls, two rams and fourteen yearling lambs, without blemish. 14 The accompanying cereal offering of fine flour mixed with oil will be three-tenths of an ephah for each of the thirteen bulls, two-tenths for each of the two rams, 15 and one-tenth for each of the fourteen lambs; 16 also one goat as a sacrifice for sin. This is in addition to the perpetual burnt offering and its cereal offering and libation.

17 "On the second day: twelve young bulls, two rams and fourteen yearling lambs, without blemish; 18 the accompanying cereal offering and libations, as prescribed, in proportion to the number of bulls, rams and lambs; 19 also one goat as a sacrifice for sin. This is in addition to the perpetual burnt offering and its cereal offering and libations.

20 "On the third day: eleven bulls, two rams and fourteen yearling lambs, without blemish; 21 the accompanying cereal offering and libations, as prescribed, in proportion to the number of bulls, rams and lambs; 22 also one goat as a sacrifice for sin. This is in addition to the perpetual burnt offering and its cereal offering and libations.

23 "On the fourth day: ten bulls, two rams and fourteen yearling lambs, without blemish; 24 the accompanying cereal offering and libations, as prescribed, in proportion to the number of bulls, rams and lambs; 25 also one goat as a sacrifice for sin. This is in addition to the perpetual burnt offering and its cereal offering and libation.

26 "On the fifth day: nine bulls, two rams and fourteen yearling lambs, without blemish; 27 the accompanying cereal offering and libations, as prescribed, in proportion to the number of bulls, rams and lambs; 28 also one goat as a sacrifice for sin. This is in addition to the perpetual burnt offering and its cereal offering and libation.

NEW REVISED STANDARD VERSION

29 On the sixth day: eight bulls, two rams, fourteen male lambs a year old without blemish, 30 with the grain offering and the drink offerings for the bulls, for the rams, and for the lambs, as prescribed in accordance with their number; 31 also one male goat for a sin offering, in addition to the regular burnt offering, its grain offering, and its drink offerings.

32 On the seventh day: seven bulls, two rams, fourteen male lambs a year old without blemish, 33 with the grain offering and the drink offerings for the bulls, for the rams, and for the lambs, as prescribed in accordance with their number; 34 also one male goat for a sin offering, besides the regular burnt offering, its grain offering, and its drink offering.

35 On the eighth day you shall have a solemn assembly; you shall not work at your occupations. 36 You shall offer a burnt offering, an offering by fire, a pleasing odor to the LORD: one bull, one ram, seven male lambs a year old without blemish, 37 and the grain offering and the drink offerings for the bull, for the ram, and for the lambs, as prescribed in accordance with their number; 38 also one male goat for a sin offering, in addition to the regular burnt offering and its grain offering and its drink offering.

39 These you shall offer to the LORD at your appointed festivals, in addition to your votive offerings and your freewill offerings, as your burnt offerings, your grain offerings, your drink offerings, and your offerings of well-being.

40r So Moses told the Israelites everything just as the LORD had commanded Moses.

30 Then Moses said to the heads of the tribes of the Israelites: This is what the LORD has commanded. 2 When a man makes a vow to the LORD, or swears an oath to bind himself by a pledge, he shall not break his word; he shall do according to all that proceeds out of his mouth.

3 When a woman makes a vow to the LORD, or binds herself by a pledge, while within her father's house, in her youth, 4 and her father hears of her vow or her pledge by which she has bound herself, and says nothing to her; then all her vows shall stand, and any pledge by which she has bound herself shall stand. 5 But if her father expresses disapproval to her at the time that he hears of it, no vow of hers, and no pledge by which she has bound herself, shall stand; and the LORD will forgive her, because her father had expressed to her his disapproval.

6 If she marries, while obligated by her vows or any thoughtless utterance of her lips by which she has bound herself, 7 and her husband hears of it and says nothing to her at the time that he hears, then her vows shall stand, and her pledges by which she has bound herself shall stand. 8 But if, at the time that her husband hears of it, he expresses disapproval to her, then he shall nullify the vow by which she was obligated, or the thoughtless utterance of her lips, by which she bound herself; and the LORD will forgive her. 9 (But every vow of a widow or of a divorced woman, by which she has bound herself, shall be binding upon her.) 10 And if she made a vow in her husband's house, or bound herself by a pledge with an oath, 11 and her husband heard it and said nothing to her, and did not express disapproval to her, then all her vows shall stand, and any pledge by which she bound herself shall stand. 12 But if her husband nullifies them at the time that he hears them, then whatever proceeds out of her lips concerning her vows, or concerning her pledge of herself, shall not stand. Her husband has nullified them, and the LORD will forgive her. 13 Any vow

REVISED ENGLISH BIBLE

29 On the sixth day: eight bulls, two full-grown rams, and fourteen yearling rams, without blemish, 30 together with the proper grain-offerings and drink-offerings for bulls, full-grown rams, and young rams, as prescribed according to their number, 31 and there will be one he-goat as a purification-offering, in addition to the regular whole-offering with the proper grain-offering and drink-offering.

32 On the seventh day: seven bulls, two full-grown rams, and fourteen yearling rams, without blemish, 33 together with the proper grain-offerings and drink-offerings for bulls, full-grown rams, and young rams, as prescribed according to their number, 34 and there will be one he-goat as a purification-offering, in addition to the regular whole-offering with the proper grain-offering and drink-offering.

35 The eighth day keep as a closing ceremony; you must not do your daily work. 36 As a whole-offering, a food-offering of soothing odour to the LORD, you must bring one bull, one full-grown ram, and seven yearling rams, without blemish, 37 together with the proper grain-offerings and drink-offerings for bulls, full-grown rams, and young rams, as prescribed according to their number, 38 and there will be one he-goat as a purification-offering, in addition to the regular whole-offering with the proper grain-offering and drink-offering.

39 These are the sacrifices which you are to offer to the LORD at the appointed seasons, in addition to the votive offerings, the freewill-offerings, the whole-offerings, the grain-offerings, the drink-offerings, and the shared-offerings.

40 Moses passed everything on to the Israelites exactly as the LORD had commanded him.

30 MOSES spoke to the heads of the Israelite tribes and said: 'This is the LORD's command: 2 When a man makes a vow to the LORD or by an oath puts himself under a binding obligation, he must not break his word. Every word he has spoken, he must make good. 3 When a woman, still young and living in her father's house, makes a vow to the LORD or puts herself under a binding obligation, 4 if her father hears of it and keeps silence, then any such vow or obligation is valid. 5 But if her father disallows it when he hears of it, none of her vows or her obligations is valid; the LORD will absolve her, because her father has disallowed it. 6 If the woman is married when she is under a vow or a binding obligation rashly uttered, 7 then if her husband hears of it and keeps silence when he hears, her vow or her obligation by which she has bound herself is valid. 8 If, however, her husband disallows it when he hears of it and repudiates the vow which she has taken upon herself or the rash utterance with which she has bound herself, then the LORD will absolve her. 9 Every vow by which a widow or a divorced woman has bound herself is valid. 10 But if it is in her husband's house that a woman makes a vow or puts herself under a binding obligation by an oath, 11 and her husband, hearing of it, keeps silence and does not disallow it, then every vow and every obligation under which she has put herself is valid; 12 but if her husband clearly repudiates them when he hears of them, then nothing that she has uttered, whether it is a vow or an obligation, is valid. Her husband has repudiated them, and the LORD will absolve her.

29:31 drink-offering: so some MSS; others drink-offerings.
29:40 In Heb. 30:1.

r Ch 30.1 in Heb

NEW AMERICAN BIBLE

29 "On the sixth day you shall offer eight bullocks, two rams, and fourteen unblemished yearling lambs, 30 with their cereal offerings and libations as prescribed for the bullocks, rams and lambs in proportion to their number, 31 as well as one goat for a sin offering, besides the established holocaust with its cereal offering and libation.

32 "On the seventh day you shall offer seven bullocks, two rams, and fourteen unblemished yearling lambs, 33 with their cereal offerings and libations as prescribed for the bullocks, rams and lambs in proportion to their number, 34 as well as one goat for a sin offering, besides the established holocaust with its cereal offering and libation.

35 "On the eighth day you shall hold a solemn meeting, and do no sort of work. 36 You shall offer up in holocaust as a sweet-smelling oblation to the LORD one bullock, one ram, and seven unblemished yearling lambs, 37 with their cereal offerings and libations as prescribed for the bullocks, rams and lambs in proportion to their number, 38 as well as one goat for a sin offering, besides the established holocaust with its cereal offering and libation.

39 "These are the offerings you shall make to the LORD on your festivals, besides whatever holocausts, cereal offerings, libations, and peace offerings you present as your votive or free-will offerings."

30 Moses then gave the Israelites these instructions, just as the LORD had ordered him.

2 Moses said to the heads of the Israelite tribes, "This is what the LORD has commanded: 3 When a man makes a vow to the LORD or binds himself under oath to a pledge of abstinence, he shall not violate his word, but must fulfill exactly the promise he has uttered.

4 "When a woman, while still a maiden in her father's house, makes a vow to the LORD, or binds herself to a pledge, 5 if her father learns of her vow or the pledge to which she bound herself and says nothing to her about it, then any vow or any pledge she has made remains valid. 6 But if on the day he learns of it her father expresses to her his disapproval, then any vow or any pledge she has made becomes null and void; and the LORD releases her from it, since her father has expressed to her his disapproval.

7 "If she marries while under a vow or under a rash pledge to which she bound herself, 8 and her husband learns of it, yet says nothing to her that day about it, then the vow or pledge she had made remains valid. 9 But if on the day he learns of it her husband expresses to her his disapproval, he thereby annuls the vow she had made or the rash pledge to which she had bound herself, and the LORD releases her from it. 10 The vow of a widow or of a divorced woman, or any pledge to which such a woman binds herself, is valid.

11 "If it is in her husband's house that she makes a vow or binds herself under oath to a pledge, 12 and her husband learns of it yet says nothing to express to her his disapproval, then any vow or any pledge she has made remains valid. 13 But if on the day he learns of them her husband annuls them, then whatever she has expressly promised in her vow or in her pledge becomes null and void; since her husband has annulled them, the LORD releases her from them.

NEW JERUSALEM BIBLE

29 "On the sixth day: eight bulls, two rams and fourteen yearling lambs, without blemish; 30 the accompanying cereal offering and libations, as prescribed, in proportion to the number of bulls, rams and lambs; 31 also one goat as a sacrifice for sin. This is in addition to the perpetual burnt offering and its cereal offering and libations.

32 "On the seventh day: seven bulls, two rams and fourteen yearling lambs, without blemish; 33 the accompanying cereal offering and libations, as prescribed, in proportion to the number of bulls, rams and lambs; 34 also one goat as a sacrifice for sin. This is in addition to the perpetual burnt offering and its cereal offering and libation.

35 "On the eighth day you will hold an assembly; you will do no heavy work. 36 As a burnt offering, as food burnt as a smell pleasing to Yahweh, you will offer one bull, one ram and seven yearling lambs, without blemish; 37 the accompanying cereal offering and libations, as prescribed, in proportion to the number of bulls, rams and lambs; 38 also one goat as a sacrifice for sin. This is in addition to the perpetual burnt offering and its cereal offering and libation.

39 "This is what you are to do for Yahweh at your solemn feasts, over and above your votive offerings and your voluntary offerings, your burnt offerings, cereal offerings and libations, and your peace offerings." '

30 Moses told the Israelites exactly what Yahweh had ordered him.

2 Moses spoke to the tribal leaders of the Israelites and said, 'This is what Yahweh has ordered:

3 "If a man makes a vow to Yahweh or a formal pledge under oath, he must not break his word: whatever he promises by word of mouth he must do.

4 "If a woman makes a vow to Yahweh or a formal pledge during her youth, while she is still in her father's house, 5 and if her father hears about this vow or pledge made by her and says nothing to her, her vow, whatever it may be, will be binding, and the pledge she has taken, whatever it may be, will be binding. 6 But if her father on the day he learns of it expresses his disapproval of it, then none of the vows or pledges she has taken will be binding. Yahweh will not hold her to it, since her father has expressed his disapproval.

7 "If, being bound by vows or by a pledge voiced without due reflection, she then marries, 8 and if her husband hears of it but says nothing on the day he learns of it, her vows will be binding and the pledges she has taken will be binding. 9 But if on the day he learns of it he expresses his disapproval to her, this will annul the vow that she has made or the pledge that binds her, voiced without due reflection. Yahweh will not hold her to it.

10 "The vow of a widow or a divorced woman and all pledges taken by her are binding on her.

11 "If she has made a vow or taken a pledge under oath while in her husband's house, 12 and if when the husband learns of it he says nothing to her and does not express disapproval to her, then the vow, whatever it is, will be binding, and the pledge, whatever it is, will be binding. 13 But if the husband when he hears of it annuls it on the day he learns of it, no undertaking of hers, be it vow or pledge, will be binding. Since the husband has annulled it, Yahweh will not hold her to it.

NEW REVISED STANDARD VERSION

or any binding oath to deny herself,[s] her husband may allow to stand, or her husband may nullify. 14 But if her husband says nothing to her from day to day,[t] then he validates all her vows, or all her pledges, by which she is obligated; he has validated them, because he said nothing to her at the time that he heard of them. 15 But if he nullifies them some time after he has heard of them, then he shall bear her guilt.

16 These are the statutes that the LORD commanded Moses concerning a husband and his wife, and a father and his daughter while she is still young and in her father's house.

31 The LORD spoke to Moses, saying, 2 "Avenge the Israelites on the Midianites; afterward you shall be gathered to your people." 3 So Moses said to the people, "Arm some of your number for the war, so that they may go against Midian, to execute the LORD's vengeance on Midian. 4 You shall send a thousand from each of the tribes of Israel to the war." 5 So out of the thousands of Israel, a thousand from each tribe were conscripted, twelve thousand armed for battle. 6 Moses sent them to the war, a thousand from each tribe, along with Phinehas son of Eleazar the priest,[u] with the vessels of the sanctuary and the trumpets for sounding the alarm in his hand. 7 They did battle against Midian, as the LORD had commanded Moses, and killed every male. 8 They killed the kings of Midian: Evi, Rekem, Zur, Hur, and Reba, the five kings of Midian, in addition to others who were slain by them; and they also killed Balaam son of Beor with the sword. 9 The Israelites took the women of Midian and their little ones captive; and they took all their cattle, their flocks, and all their goods as booty. 10 All their towns where they had settled, and all their encampments, they burned, 11 but they took all the spoil and all the booty, both people and animals. 12 Then they brought the captives and the booty and the spoil to Moses, to Eleazar the priest, and to the congregation of the Israelites, at the camp on the plains of Moab by the Jordan at Jericho.

13 Moses, Eleazar the priest, and all the leaders of the congregation went to meet them outside the camp. 14 Moses became angry with the officers of the army, the commanders of thousands and the commanders of hundreds, who had come from service in the war. 15 Moses said to them, "Have you allowed all the women to live? 16 These women here, on Balaam's advice, made the Israelites act treacherously against the LORD in the affair of Peor, so that the plague came among the congregation of the LORD. 17 Now therefore, kill every male among the little ones, and kill every woman who has known a man by sleeping with him. 18 But all the young girls who have not known a man by sleeping with him, keep alive for yourselves. 19 Camp outside the camp seven days; whoever of you has killed any person or touched a corpse, purify yourselves and your captives on the third and on the seventh day. 20 You shall purify every garment, every article of skin, everything made of goats' hair, and every article of wood."

21 Eleazar the priest said to the troops who had gone to battle: "This is the statute of the law that the LORD has commanded Moses: 22 gold, silver, bronze, iron, tin, and lead— 23 everything that can withstand fire, shall be passed through fire, and it shall be clean. Nevertheless it shall also be purified with the water for purification; and whatever cannot withstand fire, shall be passed through the water. 24 You must wash your clothes on the seventh day, and you shall be clean; afterward you may come into the camp."

25 The LORD spoke to Moses, saying, 26 "You and Elea-

REVISED ENGLISH BIBLE

13 'The husband can confirm or repudiate any vow or any oath by which a woman binds herself to mortification. 14 If he maintains silence day after day, he thereby confirms any vow or any obligation under which she has put herself: he confirms them, because he kept silence at the time when he heard them. 15 If he repudiates them some time after he has heard them, he is to be held responsible for her default.'

16 Such are the decrees which the LORD gave to Moses concerning a husband and his wife, and a father and his daughter still young and living in her father's house.

31 THE LORD said to Moses, 2 'You are to exact vengeance for Israel on the Midianites. After that you will be gathered to your father's kin.'

3 Moses addressed the people: 'Let men among you be drafted for active service; they are to fall on Midian and exact vengeance in the LORD's name. 4 Send out a thousand men from each of the tribes of Israel.' 5 So men were called up from the clans of Israel, a thousand from each tribe, twelve thousand in all, drafted for active service. 6 Moses sent out this force, a thousand from each tribe, with Phinehas son of Eleazar the priest, who was in charge of the sacred equipment and of the trumpets to give the signal for the battle cry. 7 They made war on Midian as the LORD had commanded Moses, and slew every male. 8 In addition to those slain in battle they killed the five kings of Midian— Evi, Rekem, Zur, Hur, and Reba—and they put to death also Balaam son of Beor. 9 The Israelites took the Midianites' women and dependants captive, and carried off all their herds, flocks, and property. 10 They set fire to all the towns in which they lived, and all their encampments. 11 They collected the spoil and plunder, both man and beast, 12 and brought it all—captives, plunder, and spoil—to Moses and Eleazar the priest and to the whole Israelite community at the camp in the lowlands of Moab by the Jordan over against Jericho.

13 Moses and Eleazar the priest and all the chiefs of the community went to meet them outside the camp. 14 Moses spoke angrily to the officers of the army, the commanders of units of a thousand and of a hundred, who were returning from the campaign: 15 'Have you spared all the women?' he said. 16 'Remember, it was they who, on Balaam's departure, set about seducing the Israelites into disloyalty to the LORD in the affair at Peor, so that the plague struck the community of the LORD. 17 Now kill every male child, and kill every woman who has had intercourse with a man, 18 but you may spare for yourselves every woman among them who has not had intercourse. 19 You yourselves, every one of you who has taken life and every one who has touched the dead, must remain outside the camp for seven days. Purify yourselves and your captives on the third day and on the seventh day, 20 and purify also every piece of clothing, every article made of hide, everything woven of goats' hair, and everything made of wood.'

21 Eleazar the priest said to the soldiers returning from battle, 'This is a statute of the law which the LORD has ordained through Moses. 22-23 Anything which will stand fire, whether gold, silver, copper, iron, tin, or lead, you must pass through fire and then it will be clean. Other things must be purified by the water of ritual purification; whatever cannot stand fire is to be passed through the water. 24 On the seventh day wash your clothes and be clean; after that you may re-enter the camp.'

25 The LORD said to Moses, 26 'You and Eleazar the priest

---

[s] Or to fast   [t] Or from that day to the next   [u] Gk: Heb adds to the war

NEW AMERICAN BIBLE

14 "Any vow or any pledge that she makes under oath to mortify herself, her husband can either allow to remain valid or render null and void. 15 But if her husband, day after day, says nothing at all to her about them, he thereby allows as valid any vow or any pledge she has made; he has allowed them to remain valid, because on the day he learned of them he said nothing to her about them. 16 If, however, he countermands them some time after he first learned of them, he is responsible for her guilt."

17 These are the statutes which the LORD prescribed through Moses concerning the relationship between a husband and his wife, as well as between a father and his daughter while she is still a maiden in her father's house.

31 The LORD said to Moses, 2 "Avenge the Israelites on the Midianites, and then you shall be taken to your people." 3 So Moses told the people, "Select men from your midst and arm them for war, to attack the Midianites and execute the LORD's vengeance on them. 4 From each of the tribes of Israel you shall send a band of one thousand men to war." 5 From the clans of Israel, therefore, a thousand men of each tribe were levied, so that there were twelve thousand men armed for war. 6 Moses sent them out on the campaign, a thousand from each tribe, with Phinehas, son of Eleazar, the priest for the campaign, who had with him the sacred vessels and the trumpets for sounding the alarm. 7 They waged war against the Midianites, as the LORD had commanded Moses, and killed every male among them. 8 Besides those slain in battle, they killed the five Midianite kings: Evi, Rekem, Zur, Hur and Reba; and they also executed Balaam, son of Beor, with the sword. 9 But the Israelites kept the women of the Midianites with their little ones as captives, and all their herds and flocks and wealth as spoil, 10 while they set on fire all the towns where they had settled and all their encampments. 11 Then they took all the booty, with the people and beasts they had captured, and brought the captives, together with the spoils and booty, 12 to Moses and the priest Eleazar and to the Israelite community at their camp on the plains of Moab, along the Jericho stretch of the Jordan.

13 When Moses and the priest Eleazar, with all the princes of the community, went outside the camp to meet them, 14 Moses became angry with the officers of the army, the clan and company commanders, who were returning from combat. 15 "So you have spared all the women!" he exclaimed. 16 "Why, they are the very ones who on Balaam's advice prompted the unfaithfulness of the Israelites toward the LORD in the Peor affair, which began the slaughter of the LORD's community. 17 Slay, therefore, every male child and every woman who has had intercourse with a man. 18 But you may spare and keep for yourselves all girls who had no intercourse with a man.

19 "Moreover, you shall stay outside the camp for seven days, and those of you who have slain anyone or touched anyone slain in battle shall purify yourselves on the third and on the seventh day. This applies both to you and to your captives. 20 You shall also purify every article of cloth, leather, goats' hair, or wood."

21 Eleazar the priest told the soldiers who had returned from combat: "This is what the law, as prescribed by the LORD to Moses, ordains: 22 Whatever can stand fire, such as gold, silver, bronze, iron, tin and lead, 23 you shall put into the fire, that it may become clean; however, it must also be purified with lustral water. But whatever cannot stand fire you shall put into the water. 24 On the seventh day you shall wash your clothes, and then you will again be clean. After that you may enter the camp."

25 The LORD said to Moses: 26 "With the help of the priest

NEW JERUSALEM BIBLE

14 "Every vow or oath that is binding on the wife may be endorsed or annulled by the husband.

15 "If by the following day the husband has said nothing to her, it means that he endorses her vow, whatever it may be, or her pledge, whatever it may be. He endorses them if he says nothing on the day he learns of them. 16 But if, having learnt of them, he annuls them later, he will bear the consequences for his wife's guilt." '

17 Such were the laws which Yahweh prescribed to Moses, concerning the relationship between a man and his wife, and between a father and his daughter while still young and living in her father's home.

31 Yahweh spoke to Moses and said, 2 'Exact the full vengeance for the Israelites on the Midianites. Afterwards you will be gathered to your people.'

3 Moses said to the people, 'Some of you are to take up arms for Yahweh's campaign against Midian, to carry out the vengeance of Yahweh on Midian. 4 You will put a thousand men in the field from each of the tribes of Israel.'

5 In this way Israel's thousands provided twelve thousand men equipped for war, one thousand from each tribe: 6 Moses put them in the field, one thousand from each tribe, with Phinehas, son of the priest Eleazar, to go with them carrying the sacred objects and the trumpets for the battle cry.

7 They made war on Midian, as Yahweh had ordered Moses, and put every male to death. 8 What is more, they killed the kings of Midian, Evi, Rekem, Zur, Hur and Reba, the five Midianite kings; they also put Balaam son of Beor to the sword. 9 The Israelites took the Midianite women and their little ones captive and carried off all their cattle, all their flocks and all their goods as booty. 10 They set fire to the towns where they lived and to all their encampments. 11 Then, taking all their booty, everything they had captured, human and animal, 12 they brought the captives, spoil and booty to Moses, the priest Eleazar and the whole community of Israelites at the camp on the Plains of Moab, near the Jordan by Jericho.

13 Moses, the priest Eleazar and all the leaders of the community went out of the camp to meet them. 14 Moses was enraged with the officers of the army, the commanders of the thousands and commanders of the hundreds, who had come back from this military expedition. 15 He said, 'Why have you spared the life of all the women? 16 They were the very ones who, on Balaam's advice, caused the Israelites to be unfaithful to Yahweh in the affair at Peor: hence the plague which struck Yahweh's community. 17 So kill all the male children and kill all the women who have ever slept with a man; 18 but spare the lives of the young girls who have never slept with a man, and keep them for yourselves.

19 As for you, bivouac outside the camp for seven days, everyone who has killed anyone or touched a corpse. Purify yourselves and your prisoners on the third and seventh days, 20 and purify all clothing, everything made of skin, everything woven of goat's hair and everything made of wood.'

21 The priest Eleazar said to the soldiers who had come back from the campaign, 'This is an article of the Law which Yahweh prescribed to Moses: 22 although gold, silver, bronze, iron, tin and lead, 23 everything that can withstand fire can be cleaned by being passed through fire, it must still be purified with water for purification. Whatever cannot resist fire you must pass through water.

24 'Wash your clothes on the seventh day and you will then be clean. You may then re-enter the camp.'

25 Yahweh spoke to Moses and said:

26 'With the priest Eleazar and the heads of families in the

NEW REVISED STANDARD VERSION	REVISED ENGLISH BIBLE

zar the priest and the heads of the ancestral houses of the congregation make an inventory of the booty captured, both human and animal. 27 Divide the booty into two parts, between the warriors who went out to battle and all the congregation. 28 From the share of the warriors who went out to battle, set aside as tribute for the LORD, one item out of every five hundred, whether persons, oxen, donkeys, sheep, or goats. 29 Take it from their half and give it to Eleazar the priest as an offering to the LORD. 30 But from the Israelites' half you shall take one out of every fifty, whether persons, oxen, donkeys, sheep, or goats — all the animals — and give them to the Levites who have charge of the tabernacle of the LORD."

31 Then Moses and Eleazar the priest did as the LORD had commanded Moses:

32 The booty remaining from the spoil that the troops had taken totaled six hundred seventy-five thousand sheep, 33 seventy-two thousand oxen, 34 sixty-one thousand donkeys, 35 and thirty-two thousand persons in all, women who had not known a man by sleeping with him.

36 The half-share, the portion of those who had gone out to war, was in number three hundred thirty-seven thousand five hundred sheep and goats, 37 and the LORD's tribute of sheep and goats was six hundred seventy-five. 38 The oxen were thirty-six thousand, of which the LORD's tribute was seventy-two. 39 The donkeys were thirty thousand five hundred, of which the LORD's tribute was sixty-one. 40 The persons were sixteen thousand, of which the LORD's tribute was thirty-two persons. 41 Moses gave the tribute, the offering for the LORD, to Eleazar the priest, as the LORD had commanded Moses.

42 As for the Israelites' half, which Moses separated from that of the troops, 43 the congregation's half was three hundred thirty-seven thousand five hundred sheep and goats, 44 thirty-six thousand oxen, 45 thirty thousand five hundred donkeys, 46 and sixteen thousand persons. 47 From the Israelites' half Moses took one of every fifty, both of persons and of animals, and gave them to the Levites who had charge of the tabernacle of the LORD; as the LORD had commanded Moses.

48 Then the officers who were over the thousands of the army, the commanders of thousands and the commanders of hundreds, approached Moses, 49 and said to Moses, "Your servants have counted the warriors who are under our command, and not one of us is missing. 50 And we have brought the LORD's offering, what each of us found, articles of gold, armlets and bracelets, signet rings, earrings, and pendants, to make atonement for ourselves before the LORD." 51 Moses and Eleazar the priest received the gold from them, all in the form of crafted articles. 52 And all the gold of the offering that they offered to the LORD, from the commanders of thousands and the commanders of hundreds, was sixteen thousand seven hundred fifty shekels. 53 (The troops had all taken plunder for themselves.) 54 So Moses and Eleazar the priest received the gold from the commanders of thousands and of hundreds, and brought it into the tent of meeting as a memorial for the Israelites before the LORD.

32 Now the Reubenites and the Gadites owned a very great number of cattle. When they saw that the land of Jazer and the land of Gilead was a good place for cattle, 2 the Gadites and the Reubenites came and spoke to Moses, to Eleazar the priest, and to the leaders of the congregation, saying, 3 "Ataroth, Dibon, Jazer, Nimrah, Heshbon, Elealeh, Sebam, Nebo, and Beon — 4 the land that the LORD subdued before the congregation of Israel — is a land for cattle; and your servants have cattle." 5 They continued, "If

and the heads of families in the community must count everything that has been captured, whether human beings or animals, 27 and divide them equally between the fighting men who went on the campaign and the rest of the community. 28 Levy a tribute for the LORD: from the combatants it is to be one out of every five hundred, whether human beings, cattle, donkeys, or sheep, 29 to be taken out of their share and given to Eleazar the priest as a contribution for the LORD. 30 Out of the Israelites' share it is to be one out of every fifty given, whether human beings or cattle, donkeys, or sheep, all the animals, to be given to the Levites who are in charge of the LORD's Tabernacle.' 31 Moses and Eleazar the priest did as the LORD had commanded Moses.

32 These were the spoils which remained of the plunder taken by the fighting men: six hundred and seventy-five thousand sheep, 33 seventy-two thousand cattle, 34 sixty-one thousand donkeys; 35 and of persons, thirty-two thousand young women who had had no intercourse with a man.

36 The half share of those who took part in the campaign was thus three hundred and thirty-seven thousand five hundred sheep, 37 the tribute for the LORD from these being six hundred and seventy-five; 38 thirty-six thousand cattle, the tribute being seventy-two; 39 thirty thousand five hundred donkeys, the tribute being sixty-one; 40 and sixteen thousand persons, the tribute being thirty-two. 41 Moses gave to Eleazar the priest the tribute levied for the LORD, as the LORD had commanded him.

42-43 The share of the community, being the half share for the Israelites which Moses separated from that of the combatants, was three hundred and thirty-seven thousand five hundred sheep, 44 thirty-six thousand cattle, 45 thirty thousand five hundred donkeys, 46 and sixteen thousand persons. 47 Moses took one out of every fifty, whether man or animal, from the half share of the Israelites, and gave it to the Levites who were in charge of the LORD's Tabernacle, as the LORD had commanded him.

48 Then the officers who had commanded the forces on the campaign, the commanders of units of a thousand and of a hundred, came to Moses 49 and said to him, 'Sir, we have checked the roll of the fighting men who were under our command, and not one of them is missing. 50 So we have brought the gold ornaments, the armlets, bracelets, signet rings, ear-rings, and pendants that each man has found, to offer them before the LORD as expiation for our lives.'

51 Moses and Eleazar the priest received this gold from the commanders of units of a thousand and of a hundred, all of it craftsman's work, 52 and the gold thus given as a contribution to the LORD weighed sixteen thousand seven hundred and fifty shekels; 53 for every man in the army had taken plunder. 54 Moses and Eleazar the priest received the gold from the commanders of units of a thousand and of a hundred, and brought it to the Tent of Meeting that the LORD might remember Israel.

32 The Reubenites and the Gadites owned a very large amount of livestock, and when they saw that the land of Jazer and Gilead was good grazing country, 2 they came to Moses and Eleazar the priest and to the chiefs of the community and said, 3 'Ataroth, Dibon, Jazer, Nimrah, Heshbon, Elealeh, Sebam, Nebo, and Beon, 4 the region which the LORD has subdued before the advance of the Israelite community, is grazing country, and livestock is our main possession. 5 If we have found favour with you, sir,

---

31:50 **pendants:** *Heb. word of uncertain meaning.*   32:3 **Sebam:** Sibmah *in verse 38.*

NEW AMERICAN BIBLE

Eleazar and of the heads of the ancestral houses, count up all the human captives and the beasts that have been taken; 27 then divide them evenly, giving half to those who took active part in the war by going out to combat, and half to the rest of the community. 28 You shall levy a tax for the LORD on the warriors who went out to combat: one out of every five hundred persons, oxen, asses and sheep 29 in their half of the spoil you shall turn over to the priest Eleazar as a contribution to the LORD. 30 From the Israelites' half you shall take one out of every fifty persons, and the same from the different beasts, oxen, asses and sheep, and give them to the Levites, who have charge of the LORD's Dwelling." 31 So Moses and the priest Eleazar did this, as the LORD had commanded Moses.

32 This booty, what was left of the loot which the soldiers had taken, amounted to six hundred and seventy-five thousand sheep, 33 seventy-two thousand oxen, 34 sixty-one thousand asses, 35 and thirty-two thousand girls who were still virgins.

36 The half that fell to those who had gone out to combat was: three hundred and thirty-seven thousand five hundred sheep, 37 of which six hundred and seventy-five fell as tax to the LORD; 38 thirty-six thousand oxen, of which seventy-two fell as tax to the LORD; 39 thirty thousand five hundred asses, of which sixty-one fell as tax to the LORD; 40 and sixteen thousand persons, of whom thirty-two fell as tax to the LORD. 41 The taxes contributed to the LORD, Moses gave to the priest Eleazar, as the LORD had commanded him.

42 The half for the other Israelites, which fell to the community when Moses had taken it from the soldiers, was: 43 three hundred and thirty-seven thousand five hundred sheep, 44 thirty-six thousand oxen, 45 thirty thousand five hundred asses, 46 and sixteen thousand persons. 47 From this, the Israelites' share, Moses, as the LORD had ordered, took one out of every fifty, both of persons and of beasts, and gave them to the Levites, who had charge of the LORD's Dwelling.

48 Then the officers who had been clan and company commanders of the army came up to Moses 49 and said to him, "Your servants have counted up the soldiers under our command, and not one is missing. 50 So, to make atonement for ourselves before the LORD, each of us will bring as an offering to the LORD some gold article he has picked up, such as an anklet, a bracelet, a ring, an earring, or a necklace." 51 Moses and the priest Eleazar accepted this gold from them, all of it in well-wrought articles. 52 The gold that they gave as a contribution to the LORD amounted in all to sixteen thousand seven hundred and fifty shekels. This was from the clan and company commanders; 53 what the common soldiers had looted each one kept for himself. 54 Moses, then, and the priest Eleazar accepted the gold from the clan and company commanders, and put it in the meeting tent as a memorial for the Israelites before the LORD.

32 Now the Reubenites and Gadites had a very large number of livestock. Noticing that the land of Jazer and of Gilead was grazing country, 2 they came to Moses and the priest Eleazar and to the princes of the community and said, 3 "The region of Ataroth, Dibon, Jazer, Nimrah, Heshbon, Elealeh, Sebam, Nebo and Baal-meon, 4 which the LORD has laid low before the community of Israel, is grazing country. Now, since your servants have livestock,"

NEW JERUSALEM BIBLE

community, take a count of the spoils and captives, human and animal. 27 You will then share out the spoil, half and half, between those who fought the campaign and the rest of the community. 28 From the share of the combatants who took part in the campaign, you will set aside one out of every five hundred persons, oxen, donkeys and sheep as Yahweh's portion. 29 You will take this from the half share coming to them and give it to the priest Eleazar as the portion set aside for Yahweh. 30 From the half coming to the Israelites, you will take one out of every fifty persons, oxen, donkeys, sheep, and all other animals, and give them to the Levites who are responsible for Yahweh's Dwelling.'

31 Moses and the priest Eleazar did as Yahweh had ordered Moses. 32 The spoils, the remainder of the booty captured by the soldiers, came to six hundred and seventy-five thousand sheep and goats, 33 seventy-two thousand head of cattle, 34 sixty-one thousand donkeys, 35 and in persons, women who had never slept with a man, thirty-two thousand in all. 36 Half was assigned to those who had taken part in the war, namely three hundred and thirty-seven thousand five hundred sheep and goats, 37 of which Yahweh's portion was six hundred and seventy-five, 38 thirty-six thousand head of cattle, of which Yahweh's portion was seventy-two, 39 thirty thousand five hundred donkeys, of which Yahweh's portion was sixty-one, 40 and sixteen thousand persons, of which Yahweh's portion was thirty-two. 41 Moses gave the priest Eleazar the portion set aside for Yahweh, as Yahweh had ordered Moses.

42 As for the half coming to the Israelites which Moses had separated from that of the combatants, 43 this half, the community's share, came to three hundred and thirty-seven thousand five hundred sheep and goats, 44 thirty-six thousand head of cattle, 45 thirty thousand five hundred donkeys 46 and sixteen thousand persons. 47 From this half, the Israelites' share, Moses took one out of every fifty, human and animal, and gave them to the Levites who were responsible for Yahweh's Dwelling, as Yahweh had ordered Moses.

48 The officers of the thousands who had fought the campaign, the commanders of the thousands and commanders of the hundreds, came to Moses 49 and said, 'Your servants have numbered the soldiers under their command: none of our men is missing. 50 So, as an offering for Yahweh, we have brought what each of us has found in the way of gold ornaments, armlets and bracelets, rings, earrings and breastplates, to make expiation for ourselves before Yahweh.' 51 Moses and the priest Eleazar accepted this gold from them, all this jewellery. 52 This portion of gold given to Yahweh by the commanders of the thousands and commanders of the hundreds amounted to sixteen thousand seven hundred and fifty shekels.

53 Each of the soldiers took his own booty. 54 But Moses and the priest Eleazar, having accepted the gold from the commanders of the thousands and commanders of the hundreds, brought it into the Tent of Meeting, to be a reminder of the Israelites before Yahweh.

32 ¹Now, the Reubenites and Gadites owned very large herds of cattle. Having seen that the territories of Jazer and Gilead formed an ideal region for raising stock, 2 the Gadites and Reubenites went to Moses, the priest Eleazar and the leaders of the community, and said to them, 3 'The territory of Ataroth, Dibon, Jazer, Nimrah, Heshbon, Elealeh, Sebam, Nebo and Beon, 4 which Yahweh has conquered before the advancing community of Israel, is ideal land for raising stock, and your servants are cattle breeders.

132 // Dt 3:12–20.

we have found favor in your sight, let this land be given to your servants for a possession; do not make us cross the Jordan."

6 But Moses said to the Gadites and to the Reubenites, "Shall your brothers go to war while you sit here? 7 Why will you discourage the hearts of the Israelites from going over into the land that the LORD has given them? 8 Your fathers did this, when I sent them from Kadesh-barnea to see the land. 9 When they went up to the Wadi Eshcol and saw the land, they discouraged the hearts of the Israelites from going into the land that the LORD had given them. 10 The LORD's anger was kindled on that day and he swore, saying, 11 'Surely none of the people who came up out of Egypt, from twenty years old and upward, shall see the land that I swore to give to Abraham, to Isaac, and to Jacob, because they have not unreservedly followed me — 12 none except Caleb son of Jephunneh the Kenizzite and Joshua son of Nun, for they have unreservedly followed the LORD.' 13 And the LORD's anger was kindled against Israel, and he made them wander in the wilderness for forty years, until all the generation that had done evil in the sight of the LORD had disappeared. 14 And now you, a brood of sinners, have risen in place of your fathers, to increase the LORD's fierce anger against Israel! 15 If you turn away from following him, he will again abandon them in the wilderness; and you will destroy all this people."

16 Then they came up to him and said, "We will build sheepfolds here for our flocks, and towns for our little ones, 17 but we will take up arms as a vanguardᵛ before the Israelites, until we have brought them to their place. Meanwhile our little ones will stay in the fortified towns because of the inhabitants of the land. 18 We will not return to our homes until all the Israelites have obtained their inheritance. 19 We will not inherit with them on the other side of the Jordan and beyond, because our inheritance has come to us on this side of the Jordan to the east."

20 So Moses said to them, "If you do this — if you take up arms to go before the LORD for the war, 21 and all those of you who bear arms cross the Jordan before the LORD, until he has driven out his enemies from before him 22 and the land is subdued before the LORD — then after that you may return and be free of obligation to the LORD and to Israel, and this land shall be your possession before the LORD. 23 But if you do not do this, you have sinned against the LORD; and be sure your sin will find you out. 24 Build towns for your little ones, and folds for your flocks; but do what you have promised."

25 Then the Gadites and the Reubenites said to Moses, "Your servants will do as my lord commands. 26 Our little ones, our wives, our flocks, and all our livestock shall remain there in the towns of Gilead; 27 but your servants will cross over, everyone armed for war, to do battle for the LORD, just as my lord orders."

28 So Moses gave command concerning them to Eleazar the priest, to Joshua son of Nun, and to the heads of the ancestral houses of the Israelite tribes. 29 And Moses said to them, "If the Gadites and the Reubenites, everyone armed for battle before the LORD, will cross over the Jordan with you and the land shall be subdued before you, then you shall give them the land of Gilead for a possession; 30 but if they will not cross over with you armed, they shall have possessions among you in the land of Canaan." 31 The Gadites and the Reubenites answered, "As the LORD has spoken to your servants, so we will do. 32 We will cross over armed before the LORD into the land of Canaan, but the possession of our inheritance shall remain with us on this side ofʷ the Jordan."

then let this country be given to us as our possession, and do not make us cross the Jordan.' 6 Moses demanded, 'Are your kinsmen to go into battle while you Gadites and Reubenites stay here? 7 How dare you discourage the Israelites from crossing over to the land which the LORD has given them? 8 This is what your fathers did when I sent them out from Kadesh-barnea to view the land. 9 They went up as far as the wadi Eshcol and viewed the land, and on their return so discouraged the Israelites that they would not enter the land which the LORD had given them. 10 The LORD's anger was aroused that day, and he solemnly swore: 11 "Because they have not loyally followed me, none of the men aged twenty or more who came up out of Egypt will see the land which I promised on oath to Abraham, Isaac, and Jacob." 12 This meant all except Caleb son of Jephunneh the Kenizzite and Joshua son of Nun; they followed the LORD with their whole heart. 13 In his anger the LORD made Israel wander in the wilderness for forty years until that whole generation was gone which had done what was wrong in his eyes. 14 You are now following in your fathers' footsteps, a fresh brood of sinful men to fire the LORD's anger once more against Israel. 15 If you refuse to follow him, he will again abandon this whole people in the wilderness and you will be the cause of their destruction.'

16 Presently they came forward with this offer: 'We shall build pens for our livestock here and towns for our dependants. 17 Then we can be drafted as a fighting force to go at the head of the Israelites until we have brought them to their destination. Meanwhile our dependants can live in the fortified towns, safe from the natives of the land. 18 We shall not return to our homes until every Israelite is settled in possession of his own holding; 19 we shall not claim any share of the land with them over the Jordan and beyond, because our holding has already been allotted to us on this side, east of Jordan.' 20 Moses answered, 'If you stand by your promise, if in the presence of the LORD you are drafted for battle, 21 and the whole draft crosses the Jordan in front of the LORD and remains there until the LORD has driven out his enemies, 22 and the land has been subdued before him, then you may come back and be quit of your obligation to the LORD and to Israel; and this land will be your holding in the sight of the LORD. 23 But I warn you, if you fail to do all this, you will have sinned against the LORD, and your sin will find you out. 24 Build towns for your dependants and folds for your sheep; but carry out your promise.'

25 The Gadites and Reubenites answered Moses, 'Sir, we are your servants and shall do as you command. 26 Our dependants and wives, our flocks and all our animals will remain here in the towns of Gilead; 27 but we, all who have been drafted for active service with the LORD, shall cross the river and fight, according to your command.'

28 Moses gave instructions to Eleazar the priest and Joshua son of Nun and to the heads of the families in the Israelite tribes. 29 He said, 'If the Gadites and Reubenites, all who have been drafted for battle before the LORD, cross the Jordan with you, then when the land falls into your hands, you are to give them Gilead for their holding. 30 But if they fail to cross as drafted troops with you, then they will have to acquire land alongside you in Canaan.' 31 The Gadites and Reubenites said in response, 'Sir, the LORD has spoken, and we shall obey. 32 Once we have been drafted, we shall cross over before the LORD into Canaan; but we shall have our holding here on this side of Jordan.'

ᵛ Cn: Heb hurrying   ʷ Heb beyond

32:17 as . . . force: so Gk; Heb. obscure.

5 they continued, "if we find favor with you, let this land be given to your servants as their property. Do not make us cross the Jordan."

6 But Moses answered the Gadites and Reubenites: "Are your kinsmen, then, to engage in war, while you remain here? 7 Why do you wish to discourage the Israelites from crossing to the land the LORD has given them? 8 That is just what your fathers did when I sent them from Kadesh-barnea to reconnoiter the land. 9 They went up to the Wadi Eshcol and reconnoitered the land, then so discouraged the Israelites that they would not enter the land the LORD had given them. 10 At that time the wrath of the LORD flared up, and he swore, 11 'Because they have not followed me unreservedly, none of these men of twenty years or more who have come up from Egypt shall ever see this country I promised under oath to Abraham and Isaac and Jacob, 12 except the Kenizzite Caleb, son of Jephunneh, and Joshua, son of Nun, who have followed the LORD unreservedly.' 13 So in his anger with the Israelites the LORD made them wander in the desert forty years, until the whole generation that had done evil in the sight of the LORD had died out. 14 And now here you are, a brood of sinners, rising up in your fathers' place to add still more to the LORD's blazing wrath against the Israelites. 15 If you turn away from following him, he will make them stay still longer in the desert, and so you will bring about the ruin of this whole nation."

16 But they were insistent with him: "We wish only to build sheepfolds here for our flocks, and towns for our families; 17 but we ourselves will march as troops in the van of the Israelites, until we have led them to their destination. Meanwhile our families can remain here in the fortified towns, safe from attack by the natives. 18 We will not return to our homes until every one of the Israelites has taken possession of his heritage, 19 and will not claim any heritage with them once we cross the Jordan, so long as we receive a heritage for ourselves on this eastern side of the Jordan."

20 Moses said to them in reply: "If you keep your word to march as troops in the LORD's vanguard 21 and to cross the Jordan in full force before the LORD until he has driven his enemies out of his way 22 and the land is subdued before him, then you may return here, quit of every obligation to the LORD and to Israel, and this region shall be your possession before the LORD. 23 But if you do not do this, you will sin against the LORD, and you can be sure that you will not escape the consequences of your sin. 24 Build the towns, then, for your families, and the folds for your flocks, but also fulfill your express promise."

25 The Gadites and Reubenites answered Moses, "Your servants will do as you command, my lord. 26 While our wives and children, our herds and other livestock remain in the towns of Gilead, 27 all your servants will go across as armed troops to battle before the LORD, just as your lordship says."

28 Moses, therefore, gave this order in their regard to the priest Eleazar, to Joshua, son of Nun, and to the heads of the ancestral tribes of the Israelites: 29 "If all the Gadites and Reubenites cross the Jordan with you as combat troops before the LORD, you shall give them Gilead as their property when the land has been subdued before you. 30 But if they will not go across with you as combat troops before the LORD, you shall bring their wives and children and livestock across before you into Canaan, and they shall have their property with you in the land of Canaan."

31 To this the Gadites and Reubenites replied, "We will do what the LORD has commanded us, your servants. 32 We ourselves will go across into the land of Canaan as troops before the LORD, but we will retain our hereditary property on this side of the Jordan." 33 So Moses gave them [the

5 So', they said, 'if you approve, give your servants this land for us to own; do not make us cross the Jordan.'

6 Moses said to the Gadites and Reubenites, 'Do you intend your brothers to go into battle while you stay here? 7 Why are you discouraging the Israelites from crossing to the country which Yahweh has given them? 8 Your fathers behaved in the same way when I sent them from Kadesh-Barnea to see the country, 9 for, having gone as far as the Valley of Eshcol and seen the country, they discouraged the Israelites from entering the country which Yahweh had given them. 10 Hence Yahweh's anger was aroused that day and he swore this oath, 11 "No man of twenty years and over, who left Egypt, shall set eyes on the country which I promised on oath to Abraham, Isaac and Jacob . . . , for they have not followed me absolutely, 12 except for Caleb son of Jephunneh the Kenizzite, and Joshua son of Nun: these indeed have followed Yahweh absolutely." 13 Yahweh's anger being aroused by Israel, he made them wander in the desert for forty years, until the generation that offended Yahweh had all disappeared. 14 And now you rise up in your father's place, offshoot of sinful stock, to increase Yahweh's burning anger with Israel even more! 15 If you turn away from him, he will prolong the time spent in the desert, and you will bring about this entire people's ruin.'

16 They came to Moses and said, 'We should like to build sheepfolds here for our flocks and towns for our little ones. 17 We ourselves will take up arms and lead the Israelites until we have brought them to the place appointed for them, while our little ones stay in the fortified towns to be safe from the local inhabitants. 18 We will not return to our homes until every one of the Israelites has taken possession of his heritage. 19 For we shall have no heritage with them on the other bank of the Jordan or beyond, since our heritage has fallen to us here, east of the Jordan.'

20 Moses said to them, 'If you do as you have said, if you are prepared to fight before Yahweh, 21 and if all those of you who bear arms cross the Jordan before Yahweh, until he has driven all his enemies out before him, 22 then, once the country has become subject to Yahweh, you may go back, and will have discharged your obligation to Yahweh and Israel, and Yahweh will consider this territory yours. 23 But if you do not, you will sin against Yahweh, and be sure your sin will find you out. 24 Build towns, then, for your little ones and folds for your flocks; but do what you have promised.'

25 The Gadites and Reubenites said to Moses, 'Your servants will do as my lord directs. 26 Our little ones, our wives, our flocks and all our livestock will stay in the towns of Gilead, 27 but your servants, each armed for war, will cross in Yahweh's name and fight, as my lord says.'

28 So Moses gave orders about them to the priest Eleazar, Joshua son of Nun, and the heads of families in the Israelite tribes. 29 Moses said to them, 'If the Gadites and Reubenites, all those under arms, cross the Jordan with you to fight in Yahweh's name, then, once the country has become subject to you, you will give them the territory of Gilead as theirs. 30 But if they will not cross with you under arms, they will receive their domains in Canaan with the rest of you.'

31 To this, the Gadites and Reubenites replied, 'What Yahweh has said to your servants, we shall do. 32 Under arms, we shall cross in Yahweh's name into Canaan, so that ownership of our heritage on this side of the Jordan will be ours.' 33 Moses then gave them — the Gadites, the Reuben-

NEW REVISED STANDARD VERSION	REVISED ENGLISH BIBLE

33 Moses gave to them — to the Gadites and to the Reubenites and to the half-tribe of Manasseh son of Joseph — the kingdom of King Sihon of the Amorites and the kingdom of King Og of Bashan, the land and its towns, with the territories of the surrounding towns. 34 And the Gadites rebuilt Dibon, Ataroth, Aroer, 35 Atroth-shophan, Jazer, Jogbehah, 36 Beth-nimrah, and Beth-haran, fortified cities, and folds for sheep. 37 And the Reubenites rebuilt Heshbon, Elealeh, Kiriathaim, 38 Nebo, and Baal-meon (some names being changed), and Sibmah; and they gave names to the towns that they rebuilt. 39 The descendants of Machir son of Manasseh went to Gilead, captured it, and dispossessed the Amorites who were there; 40 so Moses gave Gilead to Machir son of Manasseh, and he settled there. 41 Jair son of Manasseh went and captured their villages, and renamed them Havvoth-jair.x 42 And Nobah went and captured Kenath and its villages, and renamed it Nobah after himself.

33 These are the stages by which the Israelites went out of the land of Egypt in military formation under the leadership of Moses and Aaron. 2 Moses wrote down their starting points, stage by stage, by command of the LORD; and these are their stages according to their starting places. 3 They set out from Rameses in the first month, on the fifteenth day of the first month; on the day after the passover the Israelites went out boldly in the sight of all the Egyptians, 4 while the Egyptians were burying all their firstborn, whom the LORD had struck down among them. The LORD executed judgments even against their gods.
5 So the Israelites set out from Rameses, and camped at Succoth. 6 They set out from Succoth, and camped at Etham, which is on the edge of the wilderness. 7 They set out from Etham, and turned back to Pi-hahiroth, which faces Baal-zephon; and they camped before Migdol. 8 They set out from Pi-hahiroth, passed through the sea into the wilderness, went a three days' journey in the wilderness of Etham, and camped at Marah. 9 They set out from Marah and came to Elim; at Elim there were twelve springs of water and seventy palm trees, and they camped there. 10 They set out from Elim and camped by the Red Sea.y 11 They set out from the Red Seay and camped in the wilderness of Sin. 12 They set out from the wilderness of Sin and camped at Dophkah. 13 They set out from Dophkah and camped at Alush. 14 They set out from Alush and camped at Rephidim, where there was no water for the people to drink. 15 They set out from Rephidim and camped in the wilderness of Sinai. 16 They set out from the wilderness of Sinai and camped at Kibroth-hattaavah. 17 They set out from Kibroth-hattaavah and camped at Hazeroth. 18 They set out from Hazeroth and camped at Rithmah. 19 They set out from Rithmah and camped at Rimmon-perez. 20 They set out from Rimmon-perez and camped at Libnah. 21 They set out from Libnah and camped at Rissah. 22 They set out from Rissah and camped at Kehelathah. 23 They set out from Kehelathah and camped at Mount Shepher. 24 They set out from Mount Shepher and camped at Haradah. 25 They set out from Haradah and camped at Makheloth. 26 They set out from Makheloth and camped at Tahath. 27 They set out from Tahath and camped at Terah. 28 They set out from Terah and camped at Mithkah. 29 They set out from Mithkah and

33 So Moses assigned to the Gadites, the Reubenites, and half the tribe of Manasseh son of Joseph the kingdoms of Sihon king of the Amorites and King Og of Bashan, the whole land with its towns and the country round them. 34 The Gadites rebuilt Dibon, Ataroth, Aroer, 35 Atroth-shophan, Jazer, Jogbehah, 36 Beth-nimrah, and Beth-haran, all of them fortified towns with folds for their sheep. 37 The Reubenites rebuilt Heshbon, Elealeh, Kiriathaim, 38 Nebo, Baal-meon (whose names were changed), and Sibmah; these were the names they gave to the towns they restored.
39 The sons of Machir son of Manasseh invaded Gilead, took it, and drove out the Amorite inhabitants; 40 Moses then assigned Gilead to Machir son of Manasseh, and he made his home there. 41 Jair son of Manasseh attacked and took the tent-villages of Ham and called them Havvoth-jair. 42 Nobah attacked and took Kenath and its villages, and gave it his own name, Nobah.

33 THESE are the stages in the journey of the Israelites, when they were led by Moses and Aaron in their tribal hosts out of Egypt. 2 Moses recorded their starting-points stage by stage as the LORD commanded him. These are their stages from one starting-point to the next.
3 The Israelites left Rameses on the fifteenth day of the first month, the day after the Passover; they marched out defiantly in full view of all the Egyptians, 4 while the Egyptians were burying all the firstborn struck down by the LORD as a judgement on their gods.
5 The Israelites left Rameses and encamped at Succoth.
6 They left Succoth and encamped at Etham on the edge of the wilderness.
7 They left Etham, turned back near Pi-hahiroth on the east of Baal-zephon, and encamped before Migdol.
8 They left Pi-hahiroth, and passed through the Sea into the wilderness; they marched for three days through the wilderness of Etham, and encamped at Marah.
9 They left Marah and came to Elim; in Elim there were twelve springs of water and seventy palm trees, so they encamped there.
10 They left Elim and encamped by the Red Sea.
11 They left the Red Sea and encamped in the wilderness of Sin.
12 They left the wilderness of Sin and encamped at Dophkah.
13 They left Dophkah and encamped at Alush.
14 They left Alush and encamped at Rephidim, where there was no water for the people to drink.
15 They left Rephidim and encamped in the wilderness of Sinai.
16 They left the wilderness of Sinai and encamped at Kibroth-hattaavah.
17 They left Kibroth-hattaavah and encamped at Hazeroth.
18 They left Hazeroth and encamped at Rithmah.
19 They left Rithmah and encamped at Rimmon-parez.
20 They left Rimmon-parez and encamped at Libnah.
21 They left Libnah and encamped at Rissah.
22 They left Rissah and encamped at Kehelathah.
23 They left Kehelathah and encamped at Mount Shapher.
24 They left Mount Shapher and encamped at Haradah.
25 They left Haradah and encamped at Makheloth.
26 They left Makheloth and encamped at Tahath.
27 They left Tahath and encamped at Tarah.
28 They left Tarah and encamped at Mithcah.

32:37,38 Cp. verse 3. 32:41 the tent-villages of Ham: prob. rdg; Heb. their tent-villages. Havvoth-jair: that is Tent-villages of Jair. 33:7 Pi-hahiroth: see Exod. 14:2. 33:8 They left Pi-hahiroth: so Samar.; Heb. They left from before Hahiroth. 33:12,13 Dophkah: or, with Gk, Rophkah.

x That is the villages of Jair y Or Sea of Reeds

Gadites and Reubenites, as well as half the tribe of Manasseh, son of Joseph, the kingdom of Sihon, king of the Amorites, and the kingdom of Og, king of Bashan,] the land with its towns and the districts that surrounded them.

34 The Gadites rebuilt the fortified towns of Dibon, Ataroth, Aroer, 35 Atroth-shophan, Jazer, Jogbehah, 36 Bethnimrah and Beth-haran, and they built sheepfolds. 37 The Reubenites rebuilt Heshbon, Elealeh, Kiriathaim, 38 Nebo, Baal-meon [names to be changed!], and Sibmah. These towns, which they rebuilt, they called by their old names.

39 The descendants of Machir, son of Manasseh, invaded Gilead and captured it, driving out the Amorites who were there. 40 [Moses gave Gilead to Machir, son of Manasseh, and he settled there.] 41 Jair, a Manassehite clan, campaigned against the tent villages, captured them and called them Havvoth-jair. 42 Nobah also campaigned against Kenath, captured it with its dependencies and called it Nobah after his own name.

33 The following are the stages by which the Israelites journeyed up by companies from the land of Egypt under the guidance of Moses and Aaron. 2 By the LORD's command Moses recorded the starting places of the various stages. The starting places of the successive stages were:
3 They set out from Rameses in the first month,
 on the fifteenth day of the first month.
 On the Passover morrow the Israelites went forth
 in triumph, in view of all Egypt,
4 While the Egyptians buried their first-born
 all of whom the LORD had struck down;
 on their gods, too, the LORD
 executed judgments.

5 Setting out from Rameses, the Israelites camped at Succoth. 6 Setting out from Succoth, they camped at Etham near the edge of the desert. 7 Setting out from Etham, they turned back to Pi-hahiroth, which is opposite Baal-zephon, and they camped opposite Migdol. 8 Setting out from Pi-hahiroth, they crossed over through the sea into the desert, and after a three days' journey in the desert of Etham, they camped at Marah. 9 Setting out from Marah, they came to Elim, where there were twelve springs of water and seventy palm trees, and they camped there. 10 Setting out from Elim, they camped beside the Red Sea. 11 Setting out from the Red Sea, they camped in the desert of Sin. 12 Setting out from the desert of Sin, they camped at Dophkah. 13 Setting out from Dophkah, they camped at Alush. 14 Setting out from Alush, they camped at Rephidim, where there was no water for the people to drink. 15 Setting out from Rephidim, they camped in the desert of Sinai.

16 Setting out from the desert of Sinai, they camped at Kibroth-hattaavah. 17 Setting out from Kibroth-hattaavah, they camped at Rithmah. 18 Setting out from Hazeroth, they camped at Rithmah. 19 Setting out from Rithmah, they camped at Rimmon-perez. 20 Setting out from Rimmon-perez, they camped at Libnah. 21 Setting out from Libnah, they camped at Rissah. 22 Setting out from Rissah, they camped at Kehelathah. 23 Setting out from Kehelathah, they camped at Mount Shepher. 24 Setting out from Mount Shepher, they camped at Haradah. 25 Setting out from Haradah, they camped at Makheloth. 26 Setting out from Makheloth, they camped at Tahath. 27 Setting out from Tahath, they camped at Terah. 28 Setting out from Terah, they camped at Mithkah. 29 Setting out from Mithkah, they camped at

ites and the half-tribe of Manasseh son of Joseph—the kingdom of Sihon king of the Amorites and the kingdom of Og king of Bashan, the country and the towns within its territory, and the country's frontier-towns.

34 The Gadites rebuilt Dibon, Ataroth, Aroer, 35 Atroth-Shophan, Jazer, Jogbehah, 36 Beth-Nimrah and Beth-Haran as fortified towns with folds for the flocks.
37 The Reubenites rebuilt Heshbon, Elealeh, Kiriathaim, 38 Nebo and Baal-Meon (the names of which were altered), and Sibmah, giving new names to the towns which they rebuilt.

39 The descendants of Machir son of Manasseh went to Gilead. They conquered it and drove out the Amorites who were there. 40 Moses gave Gilead to Machir son of Manasseh, and he settled there. 41 Jair son of Manasseh went and seized their encampments, renaming them the Encampments of Jair. 42 Nobah went and seized Kenat with its dependent townships, and called it Nobah after himself.

33 These were the stages of the journey made by the Israelites when they left Egypt in their companies under the leadership of Moses and Aaron. 2 Moses recorded their starting-points in writing whenever they moved on at Yahweh's order. The stages, from one starting-point to another, were as follows:
3 They left Rameses in the first month. It was the fifteenth day of the first month, the day following the Passover, when the Israelites confidently set out, under the eyes of all Egypt. 4 The Egyptians were burying those of their own people whom Yahweh had struck down, all the first-born; Yahweh had carried out his judgement on their gods.

5 The Israelites left Rameses and camped at Succoth. 6 Then they left Succoth and encamped at Etham which is on the edge of the desert. 7 They left Etham, turned back to Pi-Hahiroth, opposite Baal-Zephon, and encamped before Migdol. 8 They left Pi-Hahiroth, crossed the sea into the desert, and after marching for three days in the desert of Etham they encamped at Marah. 9 They left Marah and reached Elim. At Elim there were twelve springs of water and seventy palm trees; they encamped there. 10 They left Elim and encamped by the Sea of Reeds. 11 They left the Sea of Reeds and encamped in the desert of Sin. 12 They left the desert of Sin and encamped at Dophkah. 13 They left Dophkah and encamped at Alush. 14 They left Alush and encamped at Rephidim; the people found no drinking water there. 15 They left Rephidim and encamped in the desert of Sinai. 16 They left the desert of Sinai and encamped at Kibroth-ha-Taavah. 17 They left Kibroth-ha-Taavah and encamped at Hazeroth. 18 They left Hazeroth and encamped at Rithmah. 19 They left Rithmah and encamped at Rimmon-Perez. 20 They left Rimmon-Perez and encamped at Libnah. 21 They left Libnah and encamped at Rissah. 22 They left Rissah and encamped at Kehelathah. 23 They left Kehelathah and encamped at Mount Shepher. 24 They left Mount Shepher and encamped at Haradah. 25 They left Haradah and encamped at Makheloth. 26 They left Makheloth and encamped at Tahath. 27 They left Tahath and encamped at Terah. 28 They left Terah and encamped at Mithkah. 29 They

---

32, 38: The phrase in brackets is a gloss, warning the reader either to change the order of the preceding names, or, more probably, to read some other word, such as bosheth, "shame," for Baal.

NEW REVISED STANDARD VERSION

camped at Hashmonah. 30 They set out from Hashmonah and camped at Moseroth. 31 They set out from Moseroth and camped at Bene-jaakan. 32 They set out from Bene-jaakan and camped at Hor-haggidgad. 33 They set out from Hor-haggidgad and camped at Jotbathah. 34 They set out from Jotbathah and camped at Abronah. 35 They set out from Abronah and camped at Ezion-geber. 36 They set out from Ezion-geber and camped in the wilderness of Zin (that is, Kadesh). 37 They set out from Kadesh and camped at Mount Hor, on the edge of the land of Edom.

38 Aaron the priest went up Mount Hor at the command of the LORD and died there in the fortieth year after the Israelites had come out of the land of Egypt, on the first day of the fifth month. 39 Aaron was one hundred twenty-three years old when he died on Mount Hor.

40 The Canaanite, the king of Arad, who lived in the Negeb in the land of Canaan, heard of the coming of the Israelites.

41 They set out from Mount Hor and camped at Zalmonah. 42 They set out from Zalmonah and camped at Punon. 43 They set out from Punon and camped at Oboth. 44 They set out from Oboth and camped at Iye-abarim, in the territory of Moab. 45 They set out from Iyim and camped at Dibon-gad. 46 They set out from Dibon-gad and camped at Almon-diblathaim. 47 They set out from Almon-diblathaim and camped in the mountains of Abarim, before Nebo. 48 They set out from the mountains of Abarim and camped in the plains of Moab by the Jordan at Jericho; 49 they camped by the Jordan from Beth-jeshimoth as far as Abel-shittim in the plains of Moab.

50 In the plains of Moab by the Jordan at Jericho, the LORD spoke to Moses, saying: 51 Speak to the Israelites, and say to them: When you cross over the Jordan into the land of Canaan, 52 you shall drive out all the inhabitants of the land from before you, destroy all their figured stones, destroy all their cast images, and demolish all their high places. 53 You shall take possession of the land and settle in it, for I have given you the land to possess. 54 You shall apportion the land by lot according to your clans; to a large one you shall give a large inheritance, and to a small one you shall give a small inheritance; the inheritance shall belong to the person on whom the lot falls; according to your ancestral tribes you shall inherit. 55 But if you do not drive out the inhabitants of the land from before you, then those whom you let remain shall be as barbs in your eyes and thorns in your sides; they shall trouble you in the land where you are settling. 56 And I will do to you as I thought to do to them.

34 The LORD spoke to Moses, saying: 2 Command the Israelites, and say to them: When you enter the land of Canaan (this is the land that shall fall to you for an inheritance, the land of Canaan, defined by its boundaries), 3 your south sector shall extend from the wilderness of Zin along the side of Edom. Your southern boundary shall begin from the end of the Dead Sea[z] on the east; 4 your boundary shall turn south of the ascent of Akrabbim, and cross to Zin, and its outer limit shall be south of Kadesh-barnea; then it shall go on to Hazar-addar, and cross to Azmon; 5 the boundary shall turn from Azmon to the Wadi of Egypt, and its termination shall be at the Sea.

6 For the western boundary, you shall have the Great Sea and its[a] coast; this shall be your western boundary.

7 This shall be your northern boundary: from the Great Sea you shall mark out your line to Mount Hor; 8 from

REVISED ENGLISH BIBLE

29 They left Mithcah and encamped at Hashmonah. 30 They left Hashmonah and encamped at Moseroth. 31 They left Moseroth and encamped at Bene-jaakan. 32 They left Bene-jaakan and encamped at Hor-haggidgad. 33 They left Hor-haggidgad and encamped at Jotbathah. 34 They left Jotbathah and encamped at Ebronah. 35 They left Ebronah and encamped at Ezion-geber. 36 They left Ezion-geber and encamped in the wilderness of Zin, that is Kadesh. 37 They left Kadesh and encamped on Mount Hor on the frontier of Edom.

38 Aaron the priest went up Mount Hor at the command of the LORD and there he died, on the first day of the fifth month in the fortieth year after the Israelites came out of Egypt; 39 when he died there he was a hundred and twenty-three years old.

40 The Canaanite king of Arad, who lived in the Canaanite Negeb, heard that the Israelites were coming.

41 They left Mount Hor and encamped at Zalmonah. 42 They left Zalmonah and encamped at Punon. 43 They left Punon and encamped at Oboth. 44 They left Oboth and encamped at Iye-abarim on the frontier of Moab. 45 They left Iyim and encamped at Dibon-gad. 46 They left Dibon-gad and encamped at Almon-diblathaim. 47 They left Almon-diblathaim and encamped in the mountains of Abarim east of Nebo. 48 They left the mountains of Abarim and encamped in the lowlands of Moab by the Jordan near Jericho. 49 Their camp beside the Jordan extended from Beth-jeshimoth to Abel-shittim in the lowlands of Moab.

50 In the lowlands of Moab by the Jordan opposite Jericho the LORD told Moses 51 to say this to the Israelites: 'You will soon be crossing the Jordan to enter Canaan. 52 You must drive out all its inhabitants as you advance, destroy all their stone carved figures and their images of cast metal, and lay their shrines in ruins. 53 You are to take possession of the land and settle there, for I have given the land for you to occupy. 54 You must divide it by lot among your families, each taking its own share of territory, the larger family a larger share and the small family a smaller. It will be assigned to them according to the fall of the lot, each tribe and family taking its own territory. 55 But if you do not drive out the inhabitants of the land as you advance, any whom you leave in possession will become like a barbed hook in your eye and a thorn in your side. They will continually dispute your possession of the land, 56 and what I meant to do to them I shall do to you.'

34 The LORD said to Moses, 2 'Give these instructions to the Israelites: Soon you will be entering Canaan. This is the land assigned to you as your portion, the land of Canaan thus defined by its frontiers. 3 Your southern border will start from the wilderness of Zin, where it marches with Edom, and run southwards from the end of the Dead Sea on its eastern side. 4 It will then turn from the south up the ascent of Akrabbim and pass by Zin, and its southern limit will be Kadesh-barnea. It will proceed by Hazar-addar to Azmon 5 and from Azmon turn towards the wadi of Egypt, and its limit will be the sea. 6 Your western frontier will be the Great Sea and the seaboard; this will be your frontier to the west. 7 This will be your northern frontier: you will draw a line from the Great Sea to Mount Hor 8 and from Mount

z Heb *Salt Sea*   *a* Syr: Heb lacks *its*

Hashmonah. 30 Setting out from Hashmonah, —
They camped at Moseroth. 31 Setting out from Moseroth, they camped at Bene-jaakan. 32 Setting out from Bene-jaakan, they camped at Mount Gidgad. 33 Setting out from Mount Gidgad, they camped at Jotbathah. 34 Setting out from Jotbathah, they camped at Abronah. 35 Setting out from Abronah, they camped at Ezion-geber. 36 Setting out from Ezion-geber, —
They camped in the desert of Zin, at Kadesh. 37 Setting out from Kadesh, they camped at Mount Hor on the border of the land of Edom. 38 [Aaron the priest ascended Mount Hor at the LORD's command, and there he died in the fortieth year from the departure of the Israelites from the land of Egypt, on the first day of the fifth month. 39 Aaron was a hundred and twenty-three years old when he died on Mount Hor. 40 Now, when the Canaanite king of Arad, who lived in the Negeb in the land of Canaan, heard that the Israelites were coming. . . .] 41 Setting out from Mount Hor, —
They camped at Zalmonah. 42 Setting out from Zalmonah, they camped at Punon. 43 Setting out from Punon, they camped at Oboth. 44 Setting out from Oboth, they camped at Iye-abarim on the border of Moab. 45 Setting out from Iye-abarim, they camped at Dibon-gad. 46 Setting out from Dibon-gad, they camped at Almon-diblathaim. 47 Setting out from Almon-diblathaim, they camped in the Abarim Mountains opposite Nebo. 48 Setting out from the Abarim Mountains, they camped on the plains of Moab along the Jericho stretch of the Jordan. 49 Their camp along the Jordan on the plains of Moab extended from Beth-jeshimoth to Abel-shittim.
50 The LORD spoke to Moses on the plains of Moab beside the Jericho stretch of the Jordan and said to him: 51 "Tell the Israelites: When you go across the Jordan into the land of Canaan, 52 drive out all the inhabitants of the land before you; destroy all their stone figures and molten images, and demolish all their high places.
53 "You shall take possession of the land and settle in it, for I have given you the land as your property. 54 You shall apportion the land among yourselves by lot, clan by clan, assigning a large heritage to a large group and a small heritage to a small group. Wherever anyone's lot falls, there shall his property be within the heritage of his ancestral tribe.
55 "But if you do not drive out the inhabitants of the land before you, those whom you allow to remain will become as barbs in your eyes and thorns in your sides, and they will harass you in the country where you live, 56 and I will treat you as I had intended to treat them."

34 The LORD said to Moses, 2 "Give the Israelites this order: When you enter the land of Canaan, this is the territory that shall fall to you as your heritage — the land of Canaan with its boundaries:
3 "Your southern boundary shall be at the desert of Zin along the border of Edom; on the east it shall begin at the end of the Salt Sea, 4 and turning south of the Akrabbim Pass, it shall cross Zin, and extend south of Kadesh-barnea to Hazar-addar; thence it shall cross to Azmon, 5 and turning from Azmon to the Wadi of Egypt, shall terminate at the Sea.
6 "For your western boundary you shall have the Great Sea with its coast; this shall be your western boundary.
7 "The following shall be your boundary on the north: from the Great Sea you shall draw a line to Mount Hor,

left Mithkah and encamped at Hashmonah. 30 They left Hashmonah and encamped at Moseroth. 31 They left Moseroth and encamped at Bene-Jaakan. 32 They left Bene-Jaakan and encamped at Hor-Gidgad. 33 They left Hor-Gidgad and encamped at Jotbathah. 34 They left Jotbathah and encamped at Abronah. 35 They left Abronah and encamped at Ezion-Geber. 36 They left Ezion-Geber and encamped in the desert of Zin, that is, at Kadesh. 37 They left Kadesh and encamped at Mount Hor, on the borders of the land of Edom. 38 The priest Aaron went up Mount Hor on Yahweh's orders and died there in the fortieth year of the exodus of the Israelites from Egypt, in the fifth month, on the first day of the month. 39 Aaron was a hundred and twenty-three years old when he died on Mount Hor. 40 The king of Arad, the Canaanite who lived in the Negeb of Canaan, heard of the Israelites' arrival. 41 They left Mount Hor and encamped at Zalmonah. 42 They left Zalmonah and encamped at Punon. 43 They left Punon and encamped at Oboth. 44 They left Oboth and encamped in Moabite territory at Iye-Abarim. 45 They left Iyim and encamped at Dibon-Gad. 46 They left Dibon-Gad and encamped at Almon-Diblathaim. 47 They left Almon-Diblathaim and encamped in the Abarim mountains facing Nebo. 48 They left the Abarim mountains and encamped on the Plains of Moab, near the Jordan opposite Jericho. 49 They encamped near the Jordan between Beth-ha-Jeshimoth and Abel-ha-Shittim, on the Plains of Moab.
50 Yahweh spoke to Moses on the Plains of Moab, near the Jordan by Jericho, and said:
51 'Speak to the Israelites and say:
"When you have crossed the Jordan into Canaan, 52 you will drive out all the local inhabitants before you. You will destroy all their painted images, you will destroy all their metal statues and you will demolish all their high places. 53 You will take possession of the country and settle in it, for I have given you the country as your property. 54 You will share it out by lot among your clans. To a large clan you will give a larger heritage, and to a smaller clan you will give a smaller heritage. Where the lot falls for each, that will be his. Your heritage will depend on the size of your tribe. 55 If, however, you do not drive out the local inhabitants before you, the ones you allow to remain will be thorns in your eyes and thistles in your sides and will harass you in the country where you are living, 56 and I shall treat you as I intended to treat them." '

34 Yahweh spoke to Moses and said, 2 'Give the Israelites this order. Say: "When you enter the country (Canaan), this will be the country which forms your heritage. This is Canaan as defined by its boundaries:
3 "The southern part of your country will start from the desert of Zin, on the borders of Edom. Your southern boundary will start on the east at the end of the Salt Sea. 4 It will then turn south towards the Ascent of the Scorpions and go by Zin to end in the south at Kadesh-Barnea. It will then run towards Hazar-Addar and pass through Azmon. 5 From Azmon the boundary will turn towards the Torrent of Egypt and end at the Sea.
6 "Your seaboard will be on the Great Sea; this will be your western boundary.
7 "Your northern boundary will be as follows: you will draw a line from the Great Sea to Mount Hor, 8 then from

33, 36b–41a It seems very probable that this section stood originally immediately after v 30a.
33, 41b–49 It seems that this section stood originally immediately after v 36a.

Mount Hor you shall mark it out to Lebo-hamath, and the outer limit of the boundary shall be at Zedad; 9 then the boundary shall extend to Ziphron, and its end shall be at Hazar-enan; this shall be your northern boundary.

10 You shall mark out your eastern boundary from Hazar-enan to Shepham; 11 and the boundary shall continue down from Shepham to Riblah on the east side of Ain; and the boundary shall go down, and reach the eastern slope of the sea of Chinnereth; 12 and the boundary shall go down to the Jordan, and its end shall be at the Dead Sea.*b* This shall be your land with its boundaries all around.

13 Moses commanded the Israelites, saying: This is the land that you shall inherit by lot, which the LORD has commanded to give to the nine tribes and to the half-tribe; 14 for the tribe of the Reubenites by their ancestral houses and the tribe of the Gadites by their ancestral houses have taken their inheritance, and also the half-tribe of Manasseh; 15 the two tribes and the half-tribe have taken their inheritance beyond the Jordan at Jericho eastward, toward the sunrise.

16 The LORD spoke to Moses, saying: 17 These are the names of the men who shall apportion the land to you for inheritance: the priest Eleazar and Joshua son of Nun. 18 You shall take one leader of every tribe to apportion the land for inheritance. 19 These are the names of the men: Of the tribe of Judah, Caleb son of Jephunneh. 20 Of the tribe of the Simeonites, Shemuel son of Ammihud. 21 Of the tribe of Benjamin, Elidad son of Chislon. 22 Of the tribe of the Danites a leader, Bukki son of Jogli. 23 Of the Josephites: of the tribe of the Manassites a leader, Hanniel son of Ephod, 24 and of the tribe of the Ephraimites a leader, Kemuel son of Shiphtan. 25 Of the tribe of the Zebulunites a leader, Eli-zaphan son of Parnach. 26 Of the tribe of the Issacharites a leader, Paltiel son of Azzan. 27 And of the tribe of the Asherites a leader, Ahihud son of Shelomi. 28 Of the tribe of the Naphtalites a leader, Pedahel son of Ammihud. 29 These were the ones whom the LORD commanded to apportion the inheritance for the Israelites in the land of Canaan.

35

In the plains of Moab by the Jordan at Jericho, the LORD spoke to Moses, saying: 2 Command the Israelites to give, from the inheritance that they possess, towns for the Levites to live in; you shall also give to the Levites pasture lands surrounding the towns. 3 The towns shall be theirs to live in, and their pasture lands shall be for their cattle, for their livestock, and for all their animals. 4 The pasture lands of the towns, which you shall give to the Levites, shall reach from the wall of the town outward a thousand cubits all around. 5 You shall measure, outside the town, for the east side two thousand cubits, for the south side two thousand cubits, for the west side two thousand cubits, and for the north side two thousand cubits, with the town in the middle; this shall belong to them as pasture land for their towns.

6 The towns that you give to the Levites shall include the six cities of refuge, where you shall permit a slayer to flee, and in addition to them you shall give forty-two towns. 7 The towns that you give to the Levites shall total forty-eight, with their pasture lands. 8 And as for the towns that

Hor to Lebo-hamath, and the limit of the frontier will be Zedad. 9 From there it will run to Ziphron, and its limit will be Hazar-enan; this will be your frontier to the north. 10 To the east you will draw a line from Hazar-enan to Shepham; 11 it will run down from Shepham to Riblah east of Ain, continuing until it strikes the ridge east of the sea of Kinnereth. 12 The frontier will then run down to the Jordan and its limit will be the Dead Sea. The land defined by these frontiers will be your land.'

13 Moses gave these instructions to the Israelites: 'This is the land which you are to assign by lot as holdings; it is the land which the LORD has commanded to be given to nine tribes and a half tribe. 14 For the Reubenites, the Gadites, and the half tribe of Manasseh have already taken possession of their holdings, family by family. 15 These two and a half tribes have received their holding here beyond the Jordan, east of Jericho, towards the sunrise.'

16 The LORD said to Moses, 17 'These are the men who are to assign the land for you: Eleazar the priest and Joshua son of Nun. 18 You must also take one chief from each tribe to assign the land. 19 These are their names:

from the tribe of Judah: Caleb son of Jephunneh;
20 from the tribe of Simeon: Samuel son of Ammihud;
21 from the tribe of Benjamin: Elidad son of Kislon;
22 from the tribe of Dan: the chief Bukki son of Jogli;
23 from the Josephites: from Manasseh, the chief Hanniel son of Ephod;
24 and from Ephraim, the chief Kemuel son of Shiphtan;
25 from Zebulun: the chief Elizaphan son of Parnach;
26 from Issachar: the chief Paltiel son of Azzan;
27 from Asher: the chief Ahihud son of Shelomi;
28 from Naphtali: the chief Pedahel son of Ammihud.'
29 These were the men whom the LORD appointed to assign the holdings in the land of Canaan.

35

THE LORD spoke to Moses in the lowlands of Moab by the Jordan near Jericho. He said: 2 'Tell the Israelites to set aside towns in their holdings as homes for the Levites, and give them also the common land surrounding the towns. 3 They are to live in the towns, and keep their animals, their herds, and all their livestock on the common land. 4 The land of the towns which you give the Levites will extend from the centre of the town outwards for a thousand cubits in each direction. 5 Starting from the town the eastern boundary will measure two thousand cubits, the southern two thousand, the western two thousand, and the northern two thousand, with the town in the centre. They will have this as the common land adjoining their towns.

6 'When you give the Levites their towns, six of them are to be cities of refuge, in which the homicide may take sanctuary; and you are to give them forty-two other towns. 7 The total number of towns to be given to the Levites, each with its common land, is forty-eight. 8 When you set aside

b Heb *Salt Sea*

35:4 **centre:** *meaning of Heb. uncertain in context.*

NEW AMERICAN BIBLE

NEW JERUSALEM BIBLE

8 and shall continue it from Mount Hor to Labo in the land of Hamath, with the boundary extending through Zedad. 9 Thence the boundary shall reach to Ziphron and terminate at Hazar-enan. This shall be your northern boundary.

10 "For your eastern boundary you shall draw a line from Hazar-enan to Shepham. 11 From Shepham the boundary shall go down to Ar-Baal, east of Ain, and descending further, shall strike the ridge on the east side of the Sea of Chinnereth; 12 thence the boundary shall continue along the Jordan and terminate with the Salt Sea.

"This is the land that shall be yours, with the boundaries that surround it."

13 Moses also gave this order to the Israelites: "This is the land, to be apportioned among you by lot, which the LORD has commanded to be given to the nine and one half tribes. 14 For all the ancestral houses of the tribe of Reuben, and the ancestral houses of the tribe of Gad, as well as half of the tribe of Manasseh, have already received their heritage; 15 these two and one half tribes have received their heritage on the eastern side of the Jericho stretch of the Jordan, toward the sunrise."

16 The LORD said to Moses, 17 "These are the names of the men who shall apportion the land among you: Eleazar the priest, and Joshua, son of Nun, 18 and one prince from each of the tribes whom you shall designate for this task. 19 These shall be as follows:

from the tribe of Judah: Caleb, son of Jephunneh;
20 from the tribe of Simeon: Samuel, son of Ammihud;
21 from the tribe of Benjamin: Elidad, son of Chislon;
22 from the tribe of Dan: Bukki, son of Jogli;
23 from the tribe of Manasseh: Hanniel, son of Ephod; and
24 from the tribe of Ephraim: Kemuel, son of Shiphtan, for the descendants of Joseph;
25 from the tribe of Zebulun: Elizaphan, son of Parnach;
26 from the tribe of Issachar: Paltiel, son of Azzan;
27 from the tribe of Asher: Ahihud, son of Shelomi;
28 from the tribe of Naphtali: Pedahel, son of Ammihud."
29 These are they whom the LORD commanded to assign the Israelites their heritage in the land of Canaan.

35 The LORD gave these instructions to Moses on the plains of Moab beside the Jericho stretch of the Jordan: 2 "Tell the Israelites that out of their hereditary property they shall give the Levites cities for homes, as well as pasture lands around the cities. 3 The cities shall serve them to dwell in, and the pasture lands shall serve their herds and flocks and other animals. 4 The pasture lands of the cities to be assigned the Levites shall extend a thousand cubits from the city walls in each direction. 5 Thus you shall measure out two thousand cubits outside the city along each side — east, south, west and north — with the city lying in the center. This shall serve them as the pasture lands of their cities.

6 "Now these are the cities you shall give to the Levites: the six cities of asylum which you must establish as places where a homicide can take refuge, and in addition forty-two other cities — 7 a total of forty-eight cities with their pasture lands to be assigned the Levites. 8 In assigning the cities

Mount Hor you will draw a line to the Pass of Hamath, and the boundary will end at Zedad. 9 From there it will run on to Ziphron and end at Hazar-Enan. This will be your northern boundary.

10 "You will then draw your eastern boundary from Hazar-Enan to Shepham. 11 The boundary will run down from Shepham towards Riblah on the east side of Ain. Further down it will keep to the eastern shore of the Sea of Chinnereth. 12 The frontier will then follow the Jordan and end at the Salt Sea.

"Such will be your country with the boundaries surrounding it." '

13 Moses then gave the Israelites this order:

'This is the country, where your heritages will be assigned by lot, and which Yahweh has ordered to be given to the nine tribes and the half-tribe, 14 for the tribe of the Reubenites with their families and the tribe of the Gadites with their families have already received their heritage; the half-tribe of Manasseh has also received its heritage. 15 These two tribes and the half-tribe have received their heritage on the other side of the Jordan by Jericho, to the east, towards the sunrise.'

16 Yahweh spoke to Moses and said:

17 'Here are the names of the men who will divide the country up for you: the priest Eleazar and Joshua son of Nun, 18 and you will take one leader from each tribe to divide the country up into heritages. 19 Here are the names of these men:

'For the tribe of Judah, Caleb son of Jephunneh;
20 'for the tribe of the Simeonites, Shemuel son of Ammihud;
21 'for the tribe of Benjamin, Elidad son of Chislon;
22 'for the tribe of the Danites, the leader Bukki son of Jogli;
23 'for the sons of Joseph: for the tribe of Manasseh, the leader Hanniel son of Ephod;
24 'for the tribe of the Ephraimites, the leader Kemuel son of Shiphtan;
25 'for the tribe of the Zebulunites, the leader Elizaphan son of Parnach;
26 'for the tribe of the Issacharites, the leader Paltiel son of Azzan;
27 'for the tribe of the Asherites, the leader Ahihud son of Shelomi;
28 'for the tribe of the Naphtalites, the leader Pedahel son of Ammihud.'
29 These were the men whom Yahweh ordered to divide Canaan into heritages for the Israelites.

35 Yahweh spoke to Moses on the Plains of Moab, near the Jordan by Jericho, and said:

2 'Order the Israelites, from the heritage they possess, to give the Levites towns in which to live and pasture land round the towns. You will give these to the Levites. 3 The towns must be their homes and the surrounding pasture land must be for their cattle, their possessions and all their animals. 4 The pasture land surrounding the towns which you give to the Levites will extend, from the walls of the towns, for a thousand cubits all round.

5 'Outside the town, measure two thousand cubits to the east, two thousand cubits to the south, two thousand cubits to the west and two thousand cubits to the north, the town lying in the centre; such will be the pasture lands of these towns. 6 The towns you give to the Levites will be six cities of refuge, ceded by you as sanctuary for those who commit manslaughter; and you will give forty-two towns in addition. 7 Altogether you will give the Levites forty-eight towns,' with their pasture lands. 8 Of the towns which you

you shall give from the possession of the Israelites, from the larger tribes you shall take many, and from the smaller tribes you shall take few; each, in proportion to the inheritance that it obtains, shall give of its towns to the Levites.

9 The LORD spoke to Moses, saying: 10 Speak to the Israelites, and say to them: When you cross the Jordan into the land of Canaan, 11 then you shall select cities to be cities of refuge for you, so that a slayer who kills a person without intent may flee there. 12 The cities shall be for you a refuge from the avenger, so that the slayer may not die until there is a trial before the congregation.

13 The cities that you designate shall be six cities of refuge for you: 14 you shall designate three cities beyond the Jordan, and three cities in the land of Canaan, to be cities of refuge. 15 These six cities shall serve as refuge for the Israelites, for the resident or transient alien among them, so that anyone who kills a person without intent may flee there.

16 But anyone who strikes another with an iron object, and death ensues, is a murderer; the murderer shall be put to death. 17 Or anyone who strikes another with a stone in hand that could cause death, and death ensues, is a murderer; the murderer shall be put to death. 18 Or anyone who strikes another with a weapon of wood in hand that could cause death, and death ensues, is a murderer; the murderer shall be put to death. 19 The avenger of blood is the one who shall put the murderer to death; when they meet, the avenger of blood shall execute the sentence. 20 Likewise, if someone pushes another from hatred, or hurls something at another, lying in wait, and death ensues, 21 or in enmity strikes another with the hand, and death ensues, then the one who struck the blow shall be put to death; that person is a murderer; the avenger of blood shall put the murderer to death, when they meet.

22 But if someone pushes another suddenly without enmity, or hurls any object without lying in wait, 23 or, while handling any stone that could cause death, unintentionally[c] drops it on another and death ensues, though they were not enemies, and no harm was intended, 24 then the congregation shall judge between the slayer and the avenger of blood, in accordance with these ordinances; 25 and the congregation shall rescue the slayer from the avenger of blood. Then the congregation shall send the slayer back to the original city of refuge. The slayer shall live in it until the death of the high priest who was anointed with the holy oil. 26 But if the slayer shall at any time go outside the bounds of the original city of refuge, 27 and is found by the avenger of blood outside the bounds of the city of refuge, and is killed by the avenger, no bloodguilt shall be incurred. 28 For the slayer must remain in the city of refuge until the death of the high priest; but after the death of the high priest the slayer may return home.

29 These things shall be a statute and ordinance for you throughout your generations wherever you live.

30 If anyone kills another, the murderer shall be put to death on the evidence of witnesses; but no one shall be put to death on the testimony of a single witness. 31 Moreover you shall accept no ransom for the life of a murderer who is subject to the death penalty; a murderer must be put to death. 32 Nor shall you accept ransom for one who has fled to a city of refuge, enabling the fugitive to return to live in the land before the death of the high priest. 33 You shall not pollute the land in which you live; for blood pollutes the land, and no expiation can be made for the land, for the blood that is shed in it, except by the blood of the one who shed it. 34 You shall not defile the land in which you live, in which I also dwell; for I the LORD dwell among the Israelites.

these towns out of the territory of the Israelites, you should allot more from a larger tribe and less from a smaller; each tribe must give towns to the Levites in proportion to the portion assigned to it.'

9 The LORD told Moses 10 to say to the Israelites: 'When you cross the Jordan into Canaan, 11 you are to designate certain cities to be places of refuge, in which the homicide who has inadvertently killed a man may take sanctuary. 12 These cities will be places of refuge from the dead man's next-of-kin, so that the homicide is not put to death without a trial before the community. 13 The cities appointed as places of refuge are to be six in number, 14 three east of the Jordan and three in Canaan. 15 These six cities will be places of refuge, so that any man who has taken life inadvertently, whether he be Israelite, resident alien, or temporary settler, may take sanctuary in one of them.

16 'If anyone strikes his victim with anything made of iron, and he dies, then he is a murderer: the murderer must be put to death. 17 If a man has a stone in his hand capable of causing death and strikes another man and he dies, he is a murderer: the murderer must be put to death. 18 If a man has a wooden thing in his hand capable of causing death, and strikes another man and he dies, he is a murderer: the murderer must be put to death. 19 The dead man's next-of-kin is to put the murderer to death; he is to put him to death because he attacked his victim. 20 If the homicide sets upon a man openly and deliberately or aims a missile at him of set purpose and he dies, 21 or if in enmity he falls upon him with his bare hands and he dies, then the assailant must be put to death; he is a murderer. The next-of-kin is to put the murderer to death because he attacked his victim.

22 'If the homicide has attacked anyone on the spur of the moment, not being his enemy, 23 or has hurled a missile at him not of set purpose, or if without looking he has thrown a stone capable of causing death and it hits someone, then if that person dies, provided the attacker was not his enemy and was not harming him of set purpose, 24 the community is to judge between the attacker and the next-of-kin according to these rules. 25 The community must protect the homicide from the vengeance of the kinsman and take him back to the city of refuge where he had taken sanctuary. He must stay there till the death of the duly anointed high priest. 26 If the homicide ever goes beyond the boundaries of the city where he has taken sanctuary, 27 and the next-of-kin finds him outside and kills him, then the next-of-kin is not guilty of murder. 28 The homicide must remain in the city of refuge till the death of the high priest; after the death of the high priest he may go back to his own holding. 29 These will be for you legal precedents for all time wherever you live.

30 'The homicide may be put to death as a murderer only on the testimony of witnesses; the testimony of a single witness is not enough to bring him to his death. 31 You should not accept payment for the life of a homicide guilty of a capital offence; he must be put to death. 32 You should not accept a payment from a man who has taken sanctuary in a city of refuge, allowing him to go back before the death of the high priest and live at large. 33 You must not defile your land by bloodshed. Blood defiles the land; no expiation can be made on behalf of the land for blood shed on it, except by the blood of him who shed it. 34 You must not make the land which you inhabit unclean, the land in which I dwell; for I, the LORD, dwell among the Israelites.'

[c] Heb without seeing

from the property of the Israelites, take more from a larger group and fewer from a smaller one, so that each group will cede cities to the Levites in proportion to its own heritage."

9 The LORD said to Moses, 10 "Tell the Israelites: When you go across the Jordan into the land of Canaan, 11 select for yourselves cities to serve as cities of asylum, where a homicide who has killed someone unintentionally may take refuge. 12 These cities shall serve you as places of asylum from the avenger of blood, so that a homicide shall not be put to death unless he is first tried before the community. 13 Six cities of asylum shall you assign: 14 three beyond the Jordan, and three in the land of Canaan. 15 These six cities of asylum shall serve not only the Israelites but all the resident or transient aliens among them, so that anyone who has killed another unintentionally may take refuge there.

16 "If a man strikes another with an iron instrument and causes his death, he is a murderer and shall be put to death. 17 If a man strikes another with a death-dealing stone in his hand and causes his death, he is a murderer and shall be put to death. 18 If a man strikes another with a death-dealing club in his hand and causes his death, he is a murderer and shall be put to death. 19 The avenger of blood may execute the murderer, putting him to death on sight.

20 "If a man pushes another out of hatred, or after lying in wait for him throws something at him, and causes his death, 21 or if he strikes another out of enmity and causes his death, he shall be put to death as a murderer. The avenger of blood may execute the murderer on sight.

22 "However, if a man pushes another accidentally and not out of enmity, or if without lying in wait for him he throws some object at him, 23 or without seeing him throws a death-dealing stone which strikes him and causes his death, although he was not his enemy nor seeking to harm him: 24 then the community, deciding the case between the slayer and the avenger of blood in accordance with these norms, 25 shall free the homicide from the avenger of blood and shall remand him to the city of asylum where he took refuge; and he shall stay there until the death of the high priest who has been anointed with sacred oil. 26 If the homicide of his own accord leaves the bounds of the city of asylum where he has taken refuge, 27 and the avenger of blood finds him beyond these bounds and kills him, the avenger incurs no blood-guilt; 28 the homicide was bound to stay in his city of asylum until the death of the high priest. Only after the death of the high priest may the homicide return to his own district.

29 "These shall be norms for you and all your descendants, wherever you live, for rendering judgment.

30 "Whenever someone kills another, the evidence of witnesses is required for the execution of the murderer. The evidence of a single witness is not sufficient for putting a person to death.

31 "You shall not accept indemnity in place of the life of a murderer who deserves the death penalty; he must be put to death. 32 Nor shall you accept indemnity to allow a refugee to leave his city of asylum and again dwell elsewhere in the land before the death of the high priest. 33 You shall not desecrate the land where you live. Since bloodshed desecrates the land, the land can have no atonement for the blood shed on it except through the blood of him who shed it. 34 Do not defile the land in which you live and in the midst of which I dwell; for I am the LORD who dwells in the midst of the Israelites."

give from the Israelites' possessions, you will give more from those who have more, and less from those who have less. Each will give some of his towns to the Levites, in proportion to the heritage he himself has received.'

9 Yahweh spoke to Moses and said:

10 'Speak to the Israelites and say:

"Once you have crossed the Jordan into Canaan, 11 you will find towns, some of which you will make into cities of refuge where those who have accidentally committed manslaughter can take sanctuary. 12 These towns will afford you refuge from the avenger of blood, so that the killer will not be put to death before standing trial before the community. 13 Of the towns you give, six will serve you as cities of refuge: 14 as cities of refuge, you will give three towns on the other side of the Jordan and will give three towns in Canaan. 15 These six towns will serve as refuge for the Israelites, for the foreigner and for the resident alien, where anyone who has accidentally killed someone can take sanctuary.

16 "But if he has struck the person with an iron object so as to cause death, he is a murderer. The murderer will be put to death. 17 If he has struck him with a stone meant for killing, and has killed him, he is a murderer. The murderer will be put to death. 18 Or if he has struck him with a wooden instrument meant for killing, and has killed him, he is a murderer. The murderer will be put to death. 19 The avenger of blood will put the murderer to death. Whenever he finds him, he will put him to death.

20 "If the killer has maliciously manhandled his victim, or thrown some lethal missile to strike him down, 21 or out of enmity dealt him the death-blow with his fist, then he who struck the blow will be put to death; he is a murderer; the avenger of blood will put him to death whenever he finds him. 22 If, however, he has manhandled his victim by chance, without malice, or thrown some missile at him not meaning to hit him 23 or, without seeing him, dropped on him a stone meant for killing and so killed him, so long as he bore him no malice and wished him no harm, 24 then the community will decide in accordance with these rules between the one who struck the blow and the avenger of blood, 25 and will save the killer from the clutches of the avenger of blood. They will send him back to the city of refuge where he had taken sanctuary, and there he will stay until the death of the high priest who has been anointed with the holy oil. 26 Should the killer leave the bounds of the city of refuge in which he has taken sanctuary 27 and the avenger of blood encounter him outside the bounds of his city of refuge, the avenger of blood may kill him without fear of reprisal; 28 since the killer should stay in his city of refuge until the death of the high priest; only after the death of the high priest is he free to go back to his own piece of property. 29 Such will be the legal rule for you and your descendants, wherever you may live.

30 "In any case of homicide, the evidence of witnesses will determine whether the killer must be put to death; but a single witness is not enough to sustain a capital charge. 31 You will not accept a ransom for the life of a murderer condemned to death; he must die. 32 Nor will you accept a ransom for anyone who, having taken sanctuary in his city or refuge, wishes to come back and live at home before the death of the high priest. 33 Do not profane the country you live in. Blood profanes the country and, for the country, the only expiation for the blood shed in it is the blood of the man who shed it. 34 So do not defile the country which you live in and where I live; for I, Yahweh, live among the Israelites." '

36 The heads of the ancestral houses of the clans of the descendants of Gilead son of Machir son of Manasseh, of the Josephite clans, came forward and spoke in the presence of Moses and the leaders, the heads of the ancestral houses of the Israelites; 2 they said, "The LORD commanded my lord to give the land for inheritance by lot to the Israelites; and my lord was commanded by the LORD to give the inheritance of our brother Zelophehad to his daughters. 3 But if they are married into another Israelite tribe, then their inheritance will be taken from the inheritance of our ancestors and added to the inheritance of the tribe into which they marry; so it will be taken away from the allotted portion of our inheritance. 4 And when the jubilee of the Israelites comes, then their inheritance will be added to the inheritance of the tribe into which they have married; and their inheritance will be taken from the inheritance of our ancestral tribe."

5 Then Moses commanded the Israelites according to the word of the LORD, saying, "The descendants of the tribe of Joseph are right in what they are saying. 6 This is what the LORD commands concerning the daughters of Zelophehad, 'Let them marry whom they think best; only it must be into a clan of their father's tribe that they are married, 7 so that no inheritance of the Israelites shall be transferred from one tribe to another; for all Israelites shall retain the inheritance of their ancestral tribes. 8 Every daughter who possesses an inheritance in any tribe of the Israelites shall marry one from the clan of her father's tribe, so that all Israelites may continue to possess their ancestral inheritance. 9 No inheritance shall be transferred from one tribe to another; for each of the tribes of the Israelites shall retain its own inheritance.' "

10 The daughters of Zelophehad did as the LORD had commanded Moses. 11 Mahlah, Tirzah, Hoglah, Milcah, and Noah, the daughters of Zelophehad, married sons of their father's brothers. 12 They were married into the clans of the descendants of Manasseh son of Joseph, and their inheritance remained in the tribe of their father's clan.

13 These are the commandments and the ordinances that the LORD commanded through Moses to the Israelites in the plains of Moab by the Jordan at Jericho.

36 THE heads of the fathers' families of Gilead son of Machir, son of Manasseh, one of the families of the sons of Joseph, approached Moses and the chiefs, heads of families in Israel, and addressed them. 2 'The LORD commanded you, sir,' they said, 'to distribute the land by lot to the Israelites, and you were also commanded to give the portion of our brother Zelophehad to his daughters. 3 Now if any of them should be married to a husband from another Israelite tribe, her share would be lost to the portion of our fathers and be added to that of the tribe into which she marries, and so part of our allotted portion would be lost. 4 When the jubilee year comes round in Israel, her share would be added to the share of the tribe into which she marries, and it would be permanently lost to the portion of our fathers' tribe.'

5 Instructed by the LORD, Moses gave the Israelites this ruling: 'The tribe of the sons of Joseph is right. 6 This is the LORD's command for the daughters of Zelophehad: They may marry whom they please, but only within a family of their father's tribe. 7 No portion in Israel shall pass from one tribe to another, but every Israelite shall retain his father's portion. 8 Any woman of an Israelite tribe who is an heiress may marry a man from any family in her father's tribe. Thus each of the Israelites shall retain the portion of his forefathers. 9 No portion shall pass from one tribe to another, but every tribe in Israel shall retain its own share.'

10 The daughters of Zelophehad acted in accordance with the LORD's command to Moses; 11 Mahlah, Tirzah, Hoglah, Milcah, and Noah, the daughters of Zelophehad, married sons of their father's brothers. 12 They married within the families of the sons of Manasseh son of Joseph, and their portion remained with the tribe of their father's family.

13 These are the commandments and the decrees which the LORD issued to the Israelites through Moses in the lowlands of Moab by the Jordan near Jericho.

NEW AMERICAN BIBLE

36 The heads of the ancestral houses in the clan of descendants of Gilead, son of Machir, son of Manasseh—one of the Josephite clans—came up and laid this plea before Moses and the priest Eleazar and before the princes who were the heads of the ancestral houses of the other Israelites. 2 They said: "The LORD commanded you, my lord, to apportion the land by lot among the Israelites; and you, my lord, were also commanded by the LORD to give the heritage of our kinsman Zelophehad to his daughters. 3 But if they marry into one of the other Israelite tribes, their heritage will be withdrawn from our ancestral heritage and will be added to that of the tribe into which they marry; thus the heritage that fell to us by lot will be diminished. 4 When the Israelites celebrate the jubilee year, the heritage of these women will be permanently added to that of the tribe into which they marry and will be withdrawn from that of our ancestral tribe."

5 So Moses gave this regulation to the Israelites according to the instructions of the LORD: "The tribe of the Josephites are right in what they say. 6 This is what the LORD commands with regard to the daughters of Zelophehad: They may marry anyone they please, provided they marry into a clan of their ancestral tribe, 7 so that no heritage of the Israelites will pass from one tribe to another, but all the Israelites will retain their own ancestral heritage. 8 Therefore, every daughter who inherits property in any of the Israelite tribes shall marry someone belonging to a clan of her own ancestral tribe, in order that all the Israelites may remain in possession of their own ancestral heritage. 9 Thus, no heritage can pass from one tribe to another, but all the Israelite tribes will retain their own ancestral heritage."

10 The daughters of Zelophehad obeyed the command which the LORD had given to Moses. 11 Mahlah, Tirzah, Hoglah, Milcah and Noah, Zelophehad's daughters, married relatives on their father's side 12 within the clans of the descendants of Manasseh, son of Joseph; hence their heritage remained in the tribe of their father's clan.

13 These are the commandments and decisions which the LORD prescribed for the Israelites through Moses, on the plains of Moab beside the Jericho stretch of the Jordan.

NEW JERUSALEM BIBLE

36 Then the heads of families of the clan descended from Gilead, son of Machir, son of Manasseh, one of the clans descended from Joseph, came forward and, addressing Moses and the leaders, the Israelite heads of families, 2 they said:

'Yahweh has ordered my lord to apportion the Israelites' heritages in the country by lot and my lord has been ordered by Yahweh to give the heritage of our brother Zelophehad to his daughters. 3 Now, if they marry someone from another Israelite tribe, their heritage will be alienated from our ancestral heritage. The heritage of the tribe to which they will then belong will be increased, and the heritage allotted to us will be diminished. 4 And when the jubilee for the Israelites comes round, these women's heritage will become part of the heritage of the tribe to which they then belong, and be alienated from the heritage of our ancestral tribe.'

5 At Yahweh's bidding, Moses gave the Israelites this order. He said:

'What the Josephite tribe says is true. 6 This is Yahweh's ruling for Zelophehad's daughters: "They may marry whom they please, providing they marry into a clan of their father's tribe. 7 But the heritages of Israelites are not to be transferred from tribe to tribe; each Israelite will stick to the heritage of his own tribe. 8 Any daughter who owns a heritage in an Israelite tribe will marry into a clan of her own paternal tribe, so that the Israelites may each preserve the heritage of his father. 9 No heritage may be transferred from one tribe to another; each Israelite tribe will stick to its own heritage." '

10 Zelophehad's daughters did as Yahweh had ordered Moses. 11 Mahlah, Tirzah, Hoglah, Milcah and Noah, daughters of Zelophehad, married the sons of their father's brothers. 12 Since they married into clans descended from Manasseh son of Joseph, their heritage reverted to the tribe of their father's clan.

13 Such were the commandments and laws that Yahweh prescribed for the Israelites through Moses on the Plains of Moab near the Jordan by Jericho.

Deuteronomy

Deuteronomy

1 These are the words that Moses spoke to all Israel beyond the Jordan—in the wilderness, on the plain opposite Suph, between Paran and Tophel, Laban, Hazeroth, and Di-zahab. 2(By the way of Mount Seir it takes eleven days to reach Kadesh-barnea from Horeb.) 3In the fortieth year, on the first day of the eleventh month, Moses spoke to the Israelites just as the LORD had commanded him to speak to them. 4This was after he had defeated King Sihon of the Amorites, who reigned in Heshbon, and King Og of Bashan, who reigned in Ashtaroth and*a* in Edrei. 5Beyond the Jordan in the land of Moab, Moses undertook to expound this law as follows:

6 The LORD our God spoke to us at Horeb, saying, "You have stayed long enough at this mountain. 7Resume your journey, and go into the hill country of the Amorites as well as into the neighboring regions—the Arabah, the hill country, the Shephelah, the Negeb, and the seacoast—the land of the Canaanites and the Lebanon, as far as the great river, the river Euphrates. 8See, I have set the land before you; go in and take possession of the land that I*b* swore to your ancestors, to Abraham, to Isaac, and to Jacob, to give to them and to their descendants after them."

9 At that time I said to you, "I am unable by myself to bear you. 10The LORD your God has multiplied you, so that today you are as numerous as the stars of heaven. 11May the LORD, the God of your ancestors, increase you a thousand times more and bless you, as he has promised you! 12But how can I bear the heavy burden of your disputes all by myself? 13Choose for each of your tribes individuals who are wise, discerning, and reputable to be your leaders." 14You answered me, "The plan you have proposed is a good one." 15So I took the leaders of your tribes, wise and reputable individuals, and installed them as leaders over you, commanders of thousands, commanders of hundreds, commanders of fifties, commanders of tens, and officials, throughout your tribes. 16I charged your judges at that time: "Give the members of your community a fair hearing, and judge rightly between one person and another, whether citizen or resident alien. 17You must not be partial in judging: hear out the small and the great alike; you shall not be intimidated by anyone, for the judgment is God's. Any case that is too hard for you, bring to me, and I will hear it." 18So I charged you at that time with all the things that you should do.

19 Then, just as the LORD our God had ordered us, we set out from Horeb and went through all that great and terrible wilderness that you saw, on the way to the hill country of the Amorites, until we reached Kadesh-barnea. 20I said to you, "You have reached the hill country of the Amorites, which the LORD our God is giving us. 21See, the LORD your God has given the land to you; go up, take possession, as the LORD, the God of your ancestors, has promised you; do not fear or be dismayed."

22 All of you came to me and said, "Let us send men ahead of us to explore the land for us and bring back a report to us regarding the route by which we should go up and the cities we will come to." 23The plan seemed good to me, and I selected twelve of you, one from each tribe. 24They set out and went up into the hill country, and when they reached the Valley of Eshcol they spied it out 25and gath-

1 THESE are the words that Moses addressed to all Israel in the wilderness beyond the Jordan, that is to say, in the Arabah opposite Suph, between Paran on the one side and Tophel, Laban, Hazeroth, and Dizahab on the other. 2(The journey from Horeb through the hill-country of Seir to Kadesh-barnea takes eleven days.)

3On the first day of the eleventh month of the fortieth year, Moses repeated to the Israelites all the commands that the LORD had given him for them. 4This was after the defeat of Sihon king of the Amorites who ruled in Heshbon, and the defeat at Edrei of King Og of Bashan who ruled in Ashtaroth, 5and it was beyond the Jordan, in Moab, that Moses resolved to expound this law.

These were his words.

6The LORD our God speaking to us at Horeb said, 'You have stayed at this mountain long enough; 7up, break camp, and make for the hill-country of the Amorites, and pass on to all their neighbours in the Arabah, in the hill-country, in the Shephelah, in the Negeb, and on the coast: in short, all Canaan and the Lebanon as far as the Great River, the Euphrates. 8I have laid the land open before you; go in and occupy it, the land which the LORD swore to give to your forefathers Abraham, Isaac, and Jacob, and to their descendants after them.'

9At that time I said to you, 'You are too heavy a burden for me to bear unaided. 10The LORD your God has so increased you that today you are as numerous as the stars in the heavens. 11May the LORD, the God of your forefathers, increase your numbers a thousand times and bless you as he promised! 12How can I bear unaided the heavy burden you are to me, and put up with your complaints? 13Choose men of wisdom, understanding, and repute for each of your tribes, and I shall set them in authority over you.' 14Your answer was, 'What you propose to do is good.' 15So I took leading men of your tribes, men of wisdom and repute, and set them in authority over you, some as commanders over units of a thousand, of a hundred, of fifty, or of ten, and others as officers, for each of your tribes. 16At that time also I gave your judges this command: 'Hear the cases that arise among your kinsmen and judge fairly between one person and another, whether fellow-countryman or resident alien. 17You must be impartial and listen to high and low alike: have no fear of your fellows, for judgement belongs to God. But should any case be too difficult for you, refer it to me and I shall hear it.' 18At the same time I instructed you in all your duties.

19We set out from Horeb, in obedience to the orders of the LORD our God, and made our way through that vast and terrible wilderness, as you found it to be, on the way to the hill-country of the Amorites. When we came to Kadesh-barnea, 20I said to you, 'You have reached the hill-country of the Amorites which the LORD our God is giving us. 21The LORD your God has now laid the land open before you. Go forward and occupy it in fulfilment of the promise which the LORD the God of your forefathers made you; do not be afraid or discouraged.' 22But you all came to me and said, 'Let us send men ahead to explore the country and report back to us about the route we should take and the towns we shall find.' 23I approved of the plan and picked twelve of your number, one from each tribe. 24They set out and made their way up into the hill-country which they reconnoitred as far as the wadi of Eshcol. 25They collected samples of

---

a Gk Syr Vg Compare Josh 12.4: Heb lacks *and*   *b* Sam Gk: MT *the* LORD

THE BOOK OF

Deuteronomy

Deuteronomy

1 These are the words which Moses spoke to all Israel beyond the Jordan [in the desert, in the Arabah, opposite Suph, between Paran and Tophel, Laban, Hazeroth and Dizahab; ² it is a journey of eleven days from Horeb to Kadesh-barnea by way of the highlands of Seir].

³ In the fortieth year, on the first day of the eleventh month, Moses spoke to the Israelites all the commands that the LORD had given him in their regard. ⁴ After he had defeated Sihon, king of the Amorites, who lived in Heshbon, and Og, king of Bashan, who lived in Ashtaroth and in Edrei, ⁵ Moses began to explain the law in the land of Moab beyond the Jordan, as follows:

⁶ "The LORD, our God, said to us at Horeb, 'You have stayed long enough at this mountain. ⁷ Leave here and go to the hill country of the Amorites and to all the surrounding regions, the land of the Canaanites in the Arabah, the mountains, the foothills, the Negeb and the seacoast; to Lebanon, and as far as the Great River [the Euphrates]. ⁸ I have given that land over to you. Go now and occupy the land I swore to your fathers, Abraham, Isaac and Jacob, I would give to them and to their descendants.'

⁹ "At that time I said to you, 'Alone, I am unable to carry you. ¹⁰ The LORD, your God, has so multiplied you that you are now as numerous as the stars in the sky. ¹¹ May the LORD, the God of your fathers, increase you a thousand times over, and bless you as he promised! ¹² But how can I alone bear the crushing burden that you are, along with your bickering? ¹³ Choose wise, intelligent and experienced men from each of your tribes, that I may appoint them as your leaders.' ¹⁴ You answered me, 'We agree to do as you have proposed.' ¹⁵ So I took outstanding men of your tribes, wise and experienced, and made them your leaders as officials over thousands, over hundreds, over fifties and over tens, and other tribal officers. ¹⁶ I charged your judges at that time, 'Listen to complaints among your kinsmen, and administer true justice to both parties even if one of them is an alien. ¹⁷ In rendering judgment, do not consider who a person is; give ear to the lowly and to the great alike, fearing no man, for judgment is God's. Refer to me any case that is too hard for you and I will hear it.' ¹⁸ Thereupon I gave you all the commands you were to fulfill.

¹⁹ "Then, in obedience to the command of the LORD, our God, we set out from Horeb and journeyed through the whole desert, vast and fearful as you have seen, in the direction of the hill country of the Amorites. We had reached Kadesh-barnea ²⁰ when I said to you, 'You have come to the hill country of the Amorites, which the LORD, our God, is giving us. ²¹ The LORD, your God, has given this land over to you. Go up and occupy it, as the LORD, the God of your fathers, commands you. Do not fear or lose heart.' ²² Then all of you came up to me and said, 'Let us send men ahead to reconnoiter the land for us and report to us on the road we must follow and the cities we must take.' ²³ Agreeing with the proposal, I chose twelve men from your number, one from each tribe. ²⁴ They set out into the hill country as far as the Wadi Eshcol, and explored it.

1 These are the words which Moses addressed to all Israel beyond the Jordan, in the desert, in the Arabah facing Suph, between Paran and Tophel, Laban, Hazeroth and Dizahab. ² It is eleven days' journey from Horeb by way of Mount Seir to Kadesh-Barnea. ³ It was in the fortieth year, on the first day of the eleventh month, that Moses told the Israelites everything that Yahweh had ordered him to tell them.

⁴ He had defeated Sihon king of the Amorites, who lived at Heshbon, and Og king of Bashan, who lived at Ashtaroth and Edrei. ⁵ There, in Moab beyond the Jordan, Moses resolved to expound this Law. He said:

⁶ 'Yahweh our God said to us at Horeb, "You have stayed long enough at this mountain. ⁷ Move on, continue your journey, go to the highlands of the Amorites, to all those who live in the Arabah, in the highlands, in the lowlands, in the Negeb and in the coastland; go into Canaan and to Lebanon as far as the great River Euphrates. ⁸ Look, that is the country I have given you; go and take possession of the country that Yahweh promised on oath to give to your ancestors, Abraham, Isaac and Jacob, and to their descendants after them."

⁹ 'At the same time, I told you,ᵃ "I cannot be responsible for you by myself. ¹⁰ Yahweh your God has increased your numbers, until you are now as numerous as the stars of heaven. ¹¹ And Yahweh your God is going to increase you a thousand times more, and bless you as he has promised you. ¹² So how can I cope by myself with the bitter burden that you are, and with your bickering? ¹³ From each of your tribes pick wise, shrewd and experienced men for me to make your leaders." ¹⁴ You replied, "Your plan is good." ¹⁵ So I took your tribal leaders, wise, experienced men, and appointed them to lead you, as captains of thousands, hundreds, fifties, tens, and as scribes for your tribes. ¹⁶ At that same time I told your judges, "You must give your brothers a fair hearing and see justice done between one person and his brother or the foreigner living with him. ¹⁷ You must be impartial in judgement and give an equal hearing to small and great alike. Do not be afraid of any human person, for the verdict is God's. Should a case be too difficult, bring it for me to hear. ¹⁸ And on that occasion I gave you instructions about everything you were to do."

¹⁹ ᵇ 'So, as Yahweh our God had ordered, we left Horeb and made our way through that vast and terrible desert, which you saw on the way to the Amorite highlands, and arrived at Kadesh-Barnea. ²⁰ I then said, "You have now reached the Amorite highlands, which Yahweh our God has given us. ²¹ Look, Yahweh your God has given you this country. March up, take possession of it as Yahweh, the God of your ancestors, has said; do not be afraid or discouraged." ²² Then you all came to me and said, "Let us send men ahead of us to explore the country; they shall report to us which way we ought to take and what towns we shall come to." ²³ This seemed good advice to me and I selected twelve men from among you, one from each tribe. ²⁴ These men made towards the highlands and went up into them; they reached the Valley of Eshcol and reconnoitred it.

a **1** // Ex 18:13—26.   *b* **1** 1:19seq. // Nb 13:1—14:9.

367

ered some of the land's produce, which they brought down to us. They brought back a report to us, and said, "It is a good land that the LORD our God is giving us."

26 But you were unwilling to go up. You rebelled against the command of the LORD your God; 27 you grumbled in your tents and said, "It is because the LORD hates us that he has brought us out of the land of Egypt, to hand us over to the Amorites to destroy us. 28 Where are we headed? Our kindred have made our hearts melt by reporting, 'The people are stronger and taller than we; the cities are large and fortified up to heaven! We actually saw there the offspring of the Anakim!' " 29 I said to you, "Have no dread or fear of them. 30 The LORD your God, who goes before you, is the one who will fight for you, just as he did for you in Egypt before your very eyes, 31 and in the wilderness, where you saw how the LORD your God carried you, just as one carries a child, all the way that you traveled until you reached this place. 32 But in spite of this, you have no trust in the LORD your God, 33 who goes before you on the way to seek out a place for you to camp, in fire by night, and in the cloud by day, to show you the route you should take."

34 When the LORD heard your words, he was wrathful and swore: 35 "Not one of these — not one of this evil generation — shall see the good land that I swore to give to your ancestors, 36 except Caleb son of Jephunneh. He shall see it, and to him and to his descendants I will give the land on which he set foot, because of his complete fidelity to the LORD." 37 Even with me the LORD was angry on your account, saying, "You also shall not enter there. 38 Joshua son of Nun, your assistant, shall enter there; encourage him, for he is the one who will secure Israel's possession of it. 39 And as for your little ones, who you thought would become booty, your children, who today do not yet know right from wrong, they shall enter there; to them I will give it, and they shall take possession of it. 40 But as for you, journey back into the wilderness, in the direction of the Red Sea."c

41 You answered me, "We have sinned against the LORD! We are ready to go up and fight, just as the LORD our God commanded us." So all of you strapped on your battle gear, and thought it easy to go up into the hill country. 42 The LORD said to me, "Say to them, 'Do not go up and do not fight, for I am not in the midst of you; otherwise you will be defeated by your enemies.' " 43 Although I told you, you would not listen. You rebelled against the command of the LORD and presumptuously went up into the hill country. 44 The Amorites who lived in that hill country then came out against you and chased you as bees do. They beat you down in Seir as far as Hormah. 45 When you returned and wept before the LORD, the LORD would neither heed your voice nor pay you any attention.

46 After you had stayed at Kadesh as many days as you
2 did, 1 we journeyed back into the wilderness, in the direction of the Red Sea,c as the LORD had told me and skirted Mount Seir for many days. 2 Then the LORD said to me: 3 "You have been skirting this hill country long enough. Head north, 4 and charge the people as follows: You are about to pass through the territory of your kindred, the descendants of Esau, who live in Seir. They will be afraid of you, so, be very careful 5 not to engage in battle with them, for I will not give you even so much as a foot's length of their land, since I have given Mount Seir to Esau as a possession. 6 You shall purchase food from them for money, so that you may eat; and you shall also buy water from them for money, so that you may drink. 7 Surely the

the fruit of the country to bring back to us, and in their report they said: 'It is a rich land that the LORD our God is giving us.'

26 However, you refused to go up, rebelling against the command of the LORD your God, 27 muttering treason in your tents and saying, 'It was because the LORD hated us that he brought us out of Egypt to hand us over to the Amorites to be wiped out. 28 What shall we find up there? Our kinsmen have discouraged us by their report of a people bigger and taller than we are, and of great cities with fortifications towering to the sky. Besides, they saw the descendants of the Anakim there.'

29 I said to you, 'You must not dread them or be afraid. 30 The LORD your God, who goes at your head, will fight for you; he will do again what you saw him do for you in Egypt 31 and in the wilderness. You saw there how the LORD your God carried you all the way to this place, as a father carries his son.' 32 In spite of this you persisted in not trusting the LORD your God, 33 who went ahead on the journey to find a place for your camp. He went in fire by night and in a cloud by day to show you the route you should take.

34 When the LORD heard your complaints, he was angry and solemnly swore: 35 'Not one of these men, this wicked generation, will see the good land which I swore to give your forefathers, 36 none except Caleb son of Jephunneh; he will see it, and to him and his descendants I shall give the land on which he has set foot, because he followed the LORD loyally.'

37 On your account the LORD was angry with me also and said, 'Neither will you yourself go in there; 38 only Joshua son of Nun, who is in attendance on you, will go. Support him, for he will put Israel in possession of that land. 39 Your dependants who, you thought, would become spoils of war, and your children who do not yet know good from evil, they will enter; I shall give it to them, and they are to occupy it. 40 You yourselves must turn and set out for the wilderness making towards the Red Sea.'

41 You answered me, 'We have sinned against the LORD; we ourselves shall go up and make the attack just as the LORD our God commanded us.' Every man of you, thinking it an easy thing to invade the hill-country, fastened on his weapons. 42 But the LORD said to me, 'Warn them not to go up and fight, for I shall not be with them, and the enemy will defeat them.' 43 I told you this, but you would not listen; you rebelled against the LORD's command and defiantly went up to the hill-country. 44 Then the Amorites living there came out against you and swarmed after you like bees; they crushed you at Hormah in Seir. 45 When you came back you wept before the LORD, but he would not hear you or listen to you. 46 That is why you remained in Kadesh as long as you did.

2 When we turned and set out for the wilderness, making towards the Red Sea as the LORD had instructed me, we spent many days marching round the hill-country of Seir. 2 Then the LORD said to me, 3 'You have been marching round these hills long enough; turn northwards. 4 Give the people this charge: You are about to pass through the territory of your kinsmen, the descendants of Esau, who live in Seir. Although they are afraid of you, be very careful 5 not to quarrel with them; for I shall not give you any of their land, not so much as a foot's breadth: I have given the hill-country of Seir to Esau as a possession. 6 You may purchase food from them to eat and buy water to drink.'

---

c Or Sea of Reeds

1:28 **descendants . . . Anakim:** or giants.   1:40 **Red Sea:** or sea of Reeds.   2:6 **buy:** or dig for.

25 Then, taking along some of the fruit of the land, they brought it down to us and reported, 'The land which the LORD, our God, gives us is good.'

26 "But you refused to go up, and after defying the command of the LORD, your God, 27 you set to murmuring in your tents, 'Out of hatred for us the LORD has brought us up out of the land of Egypt, to deliver us into the hands of the Amorites and destroy us. 28 What shall we meet with up there? Our kinsmen have made us fainthearted by reporting that the people are stronger and taller than we, and their cities are large and fortified to the sky; besides, they saw the Anakim there.'

29 "But I said to you, 'Have no dread or fear of them. 30 The LORD, your God, who goes before you, will himself fight for you, just as he took your part before your very eyes in Egypt, 31 as well as in the desert, where you saw how the LORD, your God, carried you, as a man carries his child, all along your journey until you arrived at this place.' 32 Despite this, you would not trust the LORD, your God, 33 who journeys before you to find you a resting place — by day in the cloud, and by night in the fire, to show the way you must go. 34 When the LORD heard your words, he was angry; 35 and he swore, 'Not one man of this evil generation shall look upon the good land I swore to give to your fathers, 36 except Caleb, son of Jephunneh; he shall see it. For to him and to his sons I will give the land he trod upon, because he has followed the LORD unreservedly.'

37 "The LORD was angered against me also on your account, and said, 'Not even you shall enter there, 38 but your aide Joshua, son of Nun, shall enter. Encourage him, for he is to give Israel its heritage. 39 Your little ones, who you said would become booty, and your children, who as yet do not know good from bad — they shall enter; to them I will give it, and they shall occupy it. 40 But as for yourselves; turn about and proceed into the desert on the Red Sea road.'

41 "In reply you said to me, 'We have sinned against the LORD. We will go up ourselves and fight, just as the LORD, our God, commanded us.' And each of you girded on his weapons, making light of going up into the hill country. 42 But the LORD said to me, 'Warn them: Do not go up and fight, lest you be beaten down before your enemies, for I will not be in your midst.' 43 I gave you this warning but you would not listen. In defiance of the LORD's command you arrogantly marched off into the hill country. 44 Then the Amorites living there came out against you and, like bees, chased you, cutting you down in Seir as far as Hormah. 45 On your return you wept before the LORD, but he did not listen to your cry or give ear to you. 46 That is why you had to stay as long as you did at Kadesh.

2 "When we did turn and proceed into the desert on the Red Sea road, as the LORD had commanded me, we circled around the highlands of Seir for a long time. 2 Finally the LORD said to me, 3 'You have wandered round these highlands long enough; turn and go north. 4 Give this order to the people: You are now about to pass through the territory of your kinsmen, the descendants of Esau, who live in Seir. Though they are afraid of you, be very careful 5 not to come in conflict with them, for I will not give you so much as a foot of their land, since I have already given Esau possession of the highlands of Seir. 6 You shall purchase from them with silver the food you eat and the well water you drink. 7 The LORD, your God, has blessed you in

25 They collected some of the produce of the country and brought it down to us; and they made us this report, "Yahweh our God has given us a fine country." 26 You, however, refused to go up there and rebelled against the voice of Yahweh your God. 27 You muttered in your tents, saying, "Yahweh hates us, and that is why he has brought us out of Egypt, to put us into the Amorites' power and so destroy us. 28 What kind of place are we making for? Our brothers have discouraged us by saying that the people are stronger and taller than we are, the cities immense, with walls reaching to the sky. And we have seen Anakimᶜ there too."

29 'And I said to you, "Do not take fright, do not be afraid of them. 30 Yahweh your God goes ahead of you and will be fighting on your side, just as you saw him act in Egypt. 31 You have seen him in the desert too: Yahweh your God continued to support you, as a man supports his son, all along the road you followed until you arrived here." 32 But for all this, you put no faith in Yahweh your God, 33 going ahead of you on the journey to find you a camping ground, by night in the fire to light your path, and in the cloud by day.

34 ᵈ'Yahweh heard what you were saying and in his anger swore this oath, 35 "Not one of these people, this perverse generation, will see the fine country I swore to give your ancestors, 36 except Caleb son of Jephunneh. He will see it. To him and to his children I shall give the land he has set foot on, for he has been perfectly obedient to Yahweh." 37 Yahweh was angry with me too, because of you. "You will not go in either," he said. 38 "Your assistant, Joshua son of Nun, will be the one to enter. Encourage him, since he is to bring Israel into possession of the country. 39 And your little ones too, who, you said, would be seized as booty, these children of yours who do not yet know good from evil, they will go in; I shall give it to them and they will own it. 40 But, as regards yourselves, turn round, go back into the desert, towards the Sea of Suph."

41 'In reply, you then said to me, "We have sinned against Yahweh our God. We shall go up and fight just as Yahweh our God has ordered us." And each one of you buckled on his arms and equipped himself to march up into the highlands. 42 But Yahweh said to me, "Tell them this: Do not go up and fight. I am not with you. Do not let yourselves be defeated by your enemies." 43 So I told you, but you would not listen, and you rebelled against the voice of Yahweh; presumptuously you marched into the highlands. 44 The Amorites, who live in that country of hills, came swarming out against you like bees, pursued you and beat you from Seir to Hormah. 45 On your return, you wept in Yahweh's presence, but he would not listen to your cries or pay attention. 46 That was why you had to stay at Kadesh as long as you did.'

2 'We then turned round and made for the desert, in the direction of the Sea of Suph, as Yahweh had ordered me. For many days we skirted Mount Seir. 2 Yahweh then said to me, 3 "You have gone far enough round this mountain; now turn north. 4 And give the people this order: You are about to pass through the territory of your kinsmen, the sons of Esau who live in Seir. They are afraid of you, and you will be well protected. 5 Do not provoke them, for I shall give you none of their land, no, not so much as a foot's length of it. I have given the highlands of Seir to Esau as his domain. 6 Pay them in money for what food you eat; and pay them in money for the water you drink. 7 Yahweh your

ᶜ 1 According to legend, the Anakim and Rephaim are the original dwellers in Palestine, pictured as giants.
ᵈ 1 1:34seq. // Nb 14:21–35.

NEW REVISED STANDARD VERSION

LORD your God has blessed you in all your undertakings; he knows your going through this great wilderness. These forty years the LORD your God has been with you; you have lacked nothing." 8 So we passed by our kin, the descendants of Esau who live in Seir, leaving behind the route of the Arabah, and leaving behind Elath and Ezion-geber.

When we had headed out along the route of the wilderness of Moab, 9 the LORD said to me: "Do not harass Moab or engage them in battle, for I will not give you any of its land as a possession, since I have given Ar as a possession to the descendants of Lot." 10 (The Emim — a large and numerous people, as tall as the Anakim — had formerly inhabited it. 11 Like the Anakim, they are usually reckoned as Rephaim, though the Moabites call them Emim. 12 Moreover, the Horim had formerly inhabited Seir, but the descendants of Esau dispossessed them, destroying them and settling in their place, as Israel has done in the land that the LORD gave them as a possession.) 13 "Now then, proceed to cross over the Wadi Zered."

So we crossed over the Wadi Zered. 14 And the length of time we had traveled from Kadesh-barnea until we crossed the Wadi Zered was thirty-eight years, until the entire generation of warriors had perished from the camp, as the LORD had sworn concerning them. 15 Indeed, the LORD's own hand was against them, to root them out from the camp, until all had perished.

16 Just as soon as all the warriors had died off from among the people, 17 the LORD spoke to me, saying, 18 "Today you are going to cross the boundary of Moab at Ar. 19 When you approach the frontier of the Ammonites, do not harass them or engage them in battle, for I will not give the land of the Ammonites to you as a possession, because I have given it to the descendants of Lot." 20 (It also is usually reckoned as a land of Rephaim. Rephaim formerly inhabited it, though the Ammonites call them Zamzummim, 21 a strong and numerous people, as tall as the Anakim. But the LORD destroyed them from before the Ammonites so that they could dispossess them and settle in their place. 22 He did the same for the descendants of Esau, who live in Seir, by destroying the Horim before them so that they could dispossess them and settle in their place even to this day. 23 As for the Avvim, who had lived in settlements in the vicinity of Gaza, the Caphtorim, who came from Caphtor, destroyed them and settled in their place.) 24 "Proceed on your journey and cross the Wadi Arnon. See, I have handed over to you King Sihon the Amorite of Heshbon, and his land. Begin to take possession by engaging him in battle. 25 This day I will begin to put the dread and fear of you upon the peoples everywhere under heaven; when they hear report of you, they will tremble and be in anguish because of you."

26 So I sent messengers from the wilderness of Kedemoth to King Sihon of Heshbon with the following terms of peace: 27 "If you let me pass through your land, I will travel only along the road; I will turn aside neither to the right nor to the left. 28 You shall sell me food for money, so that I may eat, and supply me water for money, so that I may drink. Only allow me to pass through on foot — 29 just as the descendants of Esau who live in Seir have done for me and likewise the Moabites who live in Ar — until I cross the Jordan into the land that the LORD our God is giving us." 30 But King Sihon of Heshbon was not willing to let us pass through, for the LORD your God had hardened his spirit and made his heart defiant in order to hand him over to you, as he has now done.

31 The LORD said to me, "See, I have begun to give Sihon and his land over to you. Begin now to take possession of his land." 32 So when Sihon came out against us, he and all his people for battle at Jahaz, 33 the LORD our God

REVISED ENGLISH BIBLE

7 The LORD your God has blessed you in everything you have undertaken. He has watched over your journey through this great wilderness; these forty years the LORD your God has been with you, and you have gone short of nothing.

8 So we went on past our kinsmen, the descendants of Esau who live in Seir, and along the road of the Arabah which comes from Elath and Ezion-geber, and we turned and went in the direction of the wilderness of Moab. 9 There the LORD warned me, 'Do not harass the Moabites or provoke them to battle, for I shall not give you any of their land as a possession. I have given Ar to the descendants of Lot as a possession.' 10 (Formerly the Emim lived there — 11 a great and numerous people, as tall as the Anakim. The Rephaim also were reckoned as Anakim, but the Moabites called them Emim. 12 The Horites lived in Seir at one time, but the descendants of Esau occupied their territory: they exterminated them as they advanced and settled in their place, just as Israel did in the territory which the LORD gave them.) 13 'Come, cross the wadi of the Zared,' said the LORD. So we went across. 14 The journey from Kadesh-barnea to the crossing of the Zared lasted thirty-eight years, until the entire generation of fighting men had passed away, as the LORD had sworn that they would. 15 The LORD's hand was against them, and he rooted them out of the camp to the last man.

16 When the last of the fighting men among the people had died, 17 the LORD spoke to me. 18 'Today', he said, 'you are to cross by Ar which lies on the frontier of Moab, 19 and when you reach the territory of the Ammonites, you must not harass them or provoke them to battle, for I shall not give you any Ammonite land as a possession; I have assigned it to the descendants of Lot.' 20 (This also is reckoned as the territory of the Rephaim, who lived there at one time; but the Ammonites called them Zamzummim. 21 They were a great and numerous people, as tall as the Anakim, but the LORD destroyed them as the Ammonites advanced and occupied their territory, 22 just as he had done for Esau's descendants who lived in Seir. As they advanced, he destroyed the Horites so that they occupied their territory and took possession instead of them: so it is to this day. 23 It was Caphtorites from Caphtor who destroyed the Avvim who lived in the hamlets near Gaza, and settled in the land instead of them.) 24 'Come, move on and cross the wadi of the Arnon, for I have delivered Sihon the Amorite, king of Heshbon, and his territory into your hands. Begin the conquest; engage him in battle. 25 Today I shall start to put the fear and dread of you into all the peoples under heaven; if they so much as hear a rumour of you, they will quake and tremble before you.'

26 From the wilderness of Kedemoth I sent envoys to King Sihon of Heshbon with the following overtures: 27 'Grant us passage through your country: we shall keep to the highway, trespassing neither to right nor to left, 28 and we shall pay you the full price for the food we eat and the water we drink. 29 The descendants of Esau who live in Seir granted us passage, and so did the Moabites in Ar. We shall simply pass through your land on foot, until we cross the Jordan to the land which the LORD our God is giving us.' 30 But King Sihon of Heshbon refused to grant us passage; for the LORD your God had made him stubborn and obstinate, in order that he and his land might become subject to you, as it is to this day.

31 The LORD said to me, 'Come, I have begun to deliver Sihon and his territory into your hands. Begin the conquest; occupy his land.' 32 When Sihon with all his people marched out to oppose us in battle at Jahaz, 33 the LORD our

2:8 **along**; *so Gk; Heb.* past.

all your undertakings; he has been concerned about your journey through this vast desert. It is now forty years that he has been with you, and you have never been in want.'

8 "Then we left behind us the Arabah route, Elath, Ezion-geber, and Seir, where our kinsmen, the descendants of Esau, live; and we went on toward the desert of Moab. 9 And the LORD said to me, 'Do not show hostility to the Moabites or engage them in battle, for I will not give you possession of any of their land, since I have given Ar to the descendants of Lot as their own. 10 [Formerly the Emim lived there, a people strong and numerous and tall like the Anakim; 11 like them they were considered Rephaim. It was the Moabites who called them Emim. 12 In Seir, however, the former inhabitants were the Horites; the descendants of Esau dispossessed them, clearing them out of the way and taking their place, just as the Israelites have done in the land of their heritage which the LORD has given them.] 13 Get ready, then, to cross the Wadi Zered.' So we crossed it. 14 Thirty-eight years had elapsed between our departure from Kadesh-barnea and that crossing; in the meantime the whole generation of soldiers had perished from the camp, as the LORD had sworn they should. 15 For it was the LORD's hand that was against them, till he wiped them out of the camp completely.

16 "When at length death had put an end to all the soldiers among the people, 17 the LORD said to me, 18 'You are now about to leave Ar and the territory of Moab behind. 19 As you come opposite the Ammonites, do not show hostility or come in conflict with them, for I will not give you possession of any land of the Ammonites, since I have given it to the descendants of Lot as their own. 20 [This also was considered a country of the Rephaim from its former inhabitants, whom the Ammonites called Zamzummim, 21 a people strong and numerous and tall like the Anakim. But these, too, the LORD cleared out of the way for the Ammonites, who ousted them and took their place. 22 He had done the same for the descendants of Esau, who dwell in Seir, by clearing the Horites out of their way, so that the descendants of Esau have taken their place down to the present. 23 So also the Caphtorim, migrating from Caphtor, cleared away the Avvim, who once dwelt in villages as far as Gaza, and took their place.]

24 " 'Advance now across the Wadi Arnon. I now deliver into your hands Sihon, the Amorite king of Heshbon, and his land. Begin the occupation; engage him in battle. 25 This day I will begin to put a fear and dread of you into every nation under the heavens, so that at the mention of your name they will quake and tremble before you.'

26 "So I sent messengers from the desert of Kedemoth to Sihon, king of Heshbon, with this offer of peace: 27 'Let me pass through your country by the highway; I will go along it without turning aside to the right or to the left. 28 For the food I eat which you will supply, and for the water you give me to drink, you shall be paid in silver. Only let me march through, 29 as the descendants of Esau who dwell in Seir and the Moabites who dwell in Ar have done, until I cross the Jordan into the land which the LORD, our God, is about to give us.' 30 But Sihon, king of Heshbon, refused to let us pass through his land, because the LORD, your God, made him stubborn in mind and obstinate in heart that he might deliver him up to you, as indeed he has now done.

31 "Then the LORD said to me, 'Now that I have already begun to hand over to you Sihon and his land, begin the actual occupation.' 32 So Sihon and all his people advanced against us to join battle at Jahaz; 33 but since the LORD, our

God has blessed you in all you do; he has watched over your journeying through this vast desert. Yahweh your God has been with you these forty years and you have never been in want."

8 'So we passed beyond those relatives of ours, the children of Esau who live in Seir, by the road through the Arabah, Elath and Ezion-Geber; then, changing direction, we took the road towards the Plains of Moab. 9 Yahweh then said to me, "Do not attack Moab, do not provoke him to fight, for I shall give you none of his land, since I have given Ar to the children of Lot as their domain." 10 (At one time the Emim lived there, a great and numerous people, tall as the Anakim; 11 and, like the Anakim, they were considered to be Rephaim, though the Moabites call them Emim. 12 The Horites, too, lived in Seir at one time; these, however, were dispossessed and exterminated by the children of Esau who settled there in place of them, just as Israel has done in the country given to it by Yahweh as a heritage.) 13 "On your way, then! Cross the Wadi Zered!"

'And so we crossed the Wadi Zered. 14 From Kadesh-Barnea to the crossing of the Wadi Zered our wanderings had taken thirty-eight years; as a result of which, the entire generation of those of age to bear arms had been eliminated, as Yahweh had sworn to them. 15 Yahweh's hand had been against them, to eliminate them completely from the camp.

16 'When death had carried off from the people those of age to bear arms, to the last man, 17 Yahweh said this to me, 18 "You are now crossing Ar, the country of Moab, 19 and soon you will encounter the children of Ammon. Do not attack them, do not provoke them, for I shall give you none of the land belonging to the children of Ammon as your domain. I have given it to the children of Lot as theirs." 20 (This used also to be considered as Rephaim territory; at one time the Rephaim lived there, though the Ammonites call them Zamzummim, 21 a great and numerous people, and tall like the Anakim. Yahweh exterminated them for the Ammonites who dispossessed them and settled there in place of them, 22 just as he had done for the children of Esau who live in Seir, so that they dispossessed the Horites and settled there instead of them and are still there now. 23 It was the same with the Avvites who occupied encampments as far as Gaza: the Caphtorim, coming from Caphtor, exterminated them and settled there instead.) 24 "On your way! Break camp and cross the Wadi Arnon. See, I am putting Sihon the Amorite, king of Heshbon, at your mercy, and his country too. Set about the conquest; engage him in battle. 25 Today and henceforth, I shall fill the peoples under all heaven with fear and terror of you; whoever hears word of your approach will tremble and writhe in anguish because of you."

26 'So, from the desert of Kedemoth I sent envoys to Sihon king of Heshbon with this peaceful message, 27 "I intend to cross your country. I shall go my way, straying neither to right nor to left. 28 I shall eat and pay for the food you choose to sell me, and I shall drink and pay for the water you let me have. I only want to march through, 29 just as the children of Esau who live in Seir permitted, as well as the Moabites who live in Ar, until I cross the Jordan into the country that Yahweh our God is giving us.'

30 'But Sihon king of Heshbon would not give us leave to pass through his territory; Yahweh our God had made his spirit obstinate and his heart stubborn, to put him at your mercy, as he still is. 31 Yahweh said to me, "You see, I am starting to give you Sihon and his country. Begin the conquest by seizing his country." 32 Sihon marched out against us, he and all his people, to give battle at Jahaz. 33 And

NEW REVISED STANDARD VERSION

REVISED ENGLISH BIBLE

gave him over to us; and we struck him down, along with his offspring and all his people. 34 At that time we captured all his towns, and in each town we utterly destroyed men, women, and children. We left not a single survivor. 35 Only the livestock we kept as spoil for ourselves, as well as the plunder of the towns that we had captured. 36 From Aroer on the edge of the Wadi Arnon (including the town that is in the wadi itself) as far as Gilead, there was no citadel too high for us. The LORD our God gave everything to us. 37 You did not encroach, however, on the land of the Ammonites, avoiding the whole upper region of the Wadi Jabbok as well as the towns of the hill country, just as*d* the LORD our God had charged.

3 When we headed up the road to Bashan, King Og of Bashan came out against us, he and all his people, for battle at Edrei. 2 The LORD said to me, "Do not fear him, for I have handed him over to you, along with his people and his land. Do to him as you did to King Sihon of the Amorites, who reigned in Heshbon." 3 So the LORD our God also handed over to us King Og of Bashan and all his people. We struck him down until not a single survivor was left. 4 At that time we captured all his towns; there was no citadel that we did not take from them — sixty towns, the whole region of Argob, the kingdom of Og in Bashan. 5 All these were fortress towns with high walls, double gates, and bars, besides a great many villages. 6 And we utterly destroyed them, as we had done to King Sihon of Heshbon, in each city utterly destroying men, women, and children. 7 But all the livestock and the plunder of the towns we kept as spoil for ourselves.

8 So at that time we took from the two kings of the Amorites the land beyond the Jordan, from the Wadi Arnon to Mount Hermon 9 (the Sidonians call Hermon Sirion, while the Amorites call it Senir), 10 all the towns of the tableland, the whole of Gilead, and all of Bashan, as far as Salecah and Edrei, towns of Og's kingdom in Bashan. 11 (Now only King Og of Bashan was left of the remnant of the Rephaim. In fact his bed, an iron bed, can still be seen in Rabbah of the Ammonites. By the common cubit it is nine cubits long and four cubits wide.) 12 As for the land that we took possession of at that time, I gave to the Reubenites and Gadites the territory north of Aroer,*e* that is on the edge of the Wadi Arnon, as well as half the hill country of Gilead with its towns, 13 and I gave to the half-tribe of Manasseh the rest of Gilead and all of Bashan, Og's kingdom. (The whole region of Argob: all that portion of Bashan used to be called a land of Rephaim; 14 Jair the Manassite acquired the whole region of Argob as far as the border of the Geshurites and the Maacathites, and he named them — that is, Bashan — after himself, Havvoth-jair,*f* as it is to this day.) 15 To Machir I gave Gilead. 16 And to the Reubenites and the Gadites I gave the territory from Gilead as far as the Wadi Arnon, with the middle of the wadi as a boundary, and up to the Jabbok, the wadi being boundary of the Ammonites; 17 the Arabah also, with the Jordan and its banks, from Chinnereth down to the sea of the Arabah, the Dead Sea,*g* with the lower slopes of Pisgah on the east.

18 At that time, I charged you as follows: "Although the LORD your God has given you this land to occupy, all your troops shall cross over armed as the vanguard of your Israelite kin. 19 Only your wives, your children, and your

God delivered him into our hands; we killed him along with his sons and all his army. 34 We captured all his towns at that time and put to death under solemn ban everyone in them, men, women, and dependants; we left no survivors. 35 We carried off the cattle as spoil and plundered the towns we captured. 36 From Aroer on the edge of the wadi of the Arnon and the town in the wadi, as far as Gilead, no town had walls too lofty for us; the LORD our God laid everything open to us. 37 But you avoided the territory of the Ammonites, both the parts along the wadi of the Jabbok and their towns in the hills, thus fulfilling all that the LORD our God had commanded.

3 Next we turned and advanced along the road to Bashan. King Og of Bashan came out with his whole army to give battle at Edrei. 2 The LORD assured me, 'Do not be afraid of him, for I have delivered him into your hands, with all his people and his land. Deal with him as you dealt with King Sihon of the Amorites who lived in Heshbon.' 3 So the LORD our God also delivered King Og of Bashan into our hands, with all his people. We slaughtered them and left him no survivor, 4 and at the same time we captured all his towns; there was not one town that we did not take from them. In all we captured sixty towns, the whole region of Argob, the kingdom of Og in Bashan; 5 all these were fortified towns with high walls and barred gates; in addition we took a great many open settlements. 6 In every town we put to death under solemn ban all the men, women, and dependants, as we did to King Sihon of Heshbon. 7 All the cattle and the spoil from the towns we carried off for ourselves.

8 At that time we seized from the two Amorite kings beyond the Jordan the territory that runs from the wadi of the Arnon to Mount Hermon 9 (the mountain that the Sidonians call Sirion and the Amorites Senir), 10 all the towns of the tableland, and the whole of Gilead and Bashan as far as Salcah and Edrei, towns in the kingdom of Og in Bashan. 11 (Only King Og of Bashan remained, as the sole survivor of the Rephaim. His sarcophagus of basalt was over thirteen feet long and six feet wide, and it may still be seen in the Ammonite town of Rabbah.)

12 When at that time we occupied this territory, I assigned to the Reubenites and Gadites the land beyond Aroer on the wadi of the Arnon and half the hill-country of Gilead with its towns, 13 while the rest of Gilead and the whole of Bashan the kingdom of Og, all the region of Argob, I assigned to half the tribe of Manasseh. (All Bashan used to be called the land of the Rephaim. 14 Jair son of Manasseh captured all the region of Argob as far as the Geshurite and Maacathite border. There are tent-villages in Bashan still bearing his name, Havvoth-jair.) 15 To Machir I assigned Gilead, 16 and to the Reubenites and the Gadites I assigned land from Gilead to the wadi of the Arnon, that is to the middle of the wadi; its territory ran to the wadi of the Jabbok, the Ammonite frontier, 17 and included the Arabah, with the Jordan and land adjacent, from Kinnereth to the sea of the Arabah, that is the Dead Sea, below the watershed of Pisgah on the east.

18 At that time I gave you this command: 'Since the LORD your God has given you this land to occupy, let all your fighting men be drafted and cross at the head of their fellow-Israelites. 19 Only your wives and dependants and your

2:37 **thus . . . all:** *so Gk; Heb.* and all. 3:11 **basalt:** *or iron.* **over . . . wide:** *lit.* nine cubits long and four cubits wide by the common standard. 3:14 **Havvoth-jair:** *that is* Tent-villages of Jair. 3:16 **that is . . . ran:** *or* including the bed of the wadi and the adjacent strip of land. **its territory ran:** *prob. rdg; Heb.* and territory and.

d Gk Tg: Heb *and all*   *e* Heb *territory from Aroer*   *f* That is *Settlement of Jair*   *g* Heb *Salt Sea*

NEW AMERICAN BIBLE

God, had delivered him to us, we defeated him and his sons and all his people. 34 At that time we seized all his cities and doomed them all, with their men, women and children; we left no survivor. 35 Our only booty was the livestock and the loot of the captured cities. 36 From Aroer on the edge of the Wadi Arnon and from the city in the wadi itself, as far as Gilead, no city was too well fortified for us to whom the LORD had delivered them up. 37 However, in obedience to the command of the LORD, our God, you did not encroach upon any of the Ammonite land, neither the region bordering on the Wadi Jabbok, nor the cities of the highlands.

3 "Then we turned and proceeded toward Bashan. But Og, king of Bashan, advanced against us with all his people to give battle at Edrei. 2 The LORD, however, said to me, 'Do not be afraid of him, for I have delivered him into your hand with all his people and his land. Do to him as you did to Sihon, king of the Amorites, who lived in Heshbon.' 3 And thus the LORD, our God, delivered into our hands Og, king of Bashan, with all his people. We defeated him so completely that we left him no survivor. 4 At that time we captured all his cities, none of them eluding our grasp, the whole region of Argob, the kingdom of Og in Bashan: sixty cities in all, 5 to say nothing of the great number of unwalled towns. All the cities were fortified with high walls and gates and bars. 6 As we had done to Sihon, king of Heshbon, so also here we doomed all the cities, with their men, women and children; 7 but all the livestock and the loot of each city we took as booty for ourselves.

8 "And so at that time we took from the two kings of the Amorites beyond the Jordan the territory from the Wadi Arnon to Mount Hermon 9 [which is called Sirion by the Sidonians and Senir by the Amorites], 10 comprising all the cities of the plateau and all Gilead and all the cities of the kingdom of Og in Bashan including Salecah and Edrei. 11 [Og, king of Bashan, was the last remaining survivor of the Rephaim. He had a bed of iron, nine regular cubits long and four wide, which is still preserved in Rabbah of the Ammonites.]

12 "When we occupied the land at that time, I gave Reuben and Gad the territory from Aroer, on the edge of the Wadi Arnon, halfway up into the highlands of Gilead, with the cities therein. 13 The rest of Gilead and all of Bashan, the kingdom of Og, the whole Argob region, I gave to the half-tribe of Manasseh. [All this region of Bashan was once called a land of the Rephaim. 14 Jair, a Manassehite clan, took all the region of Argob as far as the border of the Geshurites and Maacathites, and called it after his own name Bashan Havvoth-jair, the name it bears today.] 15 To Machir I gave Gilead, 16 and to Reuben and Gad the territory from Gilead to the Wadi Arnon — including the wadi bed and its banks — and to the Wadi Jabbok, which is the border of the Ammonites, 17 as well as the Arabah with the Jordan and its eastern banks from Chinnereth to the Salt Sea of the Arabah, under the slopes of Pisgah.

18 "At that time I charged them as follows: 'The LORD, your God, has given you this land as your own. But all you troops equipped for battle must cross over in the vanguard of your brother Israelites. 19 Only your wives and children,

NEW JERUSALEM BIBLE

Yahweh our God handed him over to us: we defeated him and his sons and all his people. 34 We captured all his towns and laid all these towns under the curse of destruction: men, women and children, we left no survivors 35 except the livestock which we took as our booty, and the spoils of the captured towns. 36 From Aroer on the edge of the Arnon valley and from the town down in the valley, as far as Gilead, not one town was beyond our reach; Yahweh our God delivered them all to us. 37 You did not, however, go near the country of the Ammonites, or the region of the River Jabbok, or the towns in the highlands, or anywhere forbidden us by Yahweh our God.'

3 f 'We then turned on Bashan and invaded that. And Og king of Bashan marched out against us, he and all his people, to give battle at Edrei. 2 Yahweh said to me, "Do not be afraid of him, for I have put him at your mercy, him, all his people and his country. You will treat him as you treated Sihon king of the Amorites who lived in Heshbon." 3 So, Yahweh our God put Og king of Bashan at our mercy too, with all his people. We beat him so thoroughly that nobody was left. 4 That was when we captured all his towns; there was not a town of theirs we did not take: sixty towns, the whole confederation of Argob, Og's kingdom in Bashan, 5 all of them fortresses defended by high walls and fortified with gates and bars, not to mention the Perizzite towns, which were very numerous. 6 We laid them under the curse of destruction as we had done Sihon king of Heshbon, laying all these towns under the curse of destruction: men, women and children — 7 but we seized the livestock and spoils of the towns as booty for ourselves.

8 'Thus, by then we had taken the country of the two Amorite kings beyond the Jordan, stretching from the Wadi Arnon to Mount Hermon 9 (the Sidonians call Hermon 'Sirion' and the Amorites call it 'Senir'): 10 all the towns of the tableland, all Gilead, and all Bashan as far as Salecah and Edrei, the capital cities of Og in Bashan. 11 (Og king of Bashan was the last survivor of the Rephaim; his bed was the iron bed that can be seen at Rabbah-of-the-Ammonites, nine cubits long and four wide, according to the human cubit.)

12 g 'Then we took possession of this country, from Aroer on the Wadi Arnon. To the Reubenites and Gadites I gave half the highlands of Gilead with its towns. 13 To the half-tribe of Manasseh I gave the rest of Gilead and the whole of Bashan, Og's kingdom. (The whole confederation of Argob and the whole of Bashan is called the country of the Rephaim. 14 Since Jair son of Manasseh occupied the whole confederation of Argob as far as the frontiers of the Geshurites and Maacathites, after him Bashan is called the Encampments of Jair even today.) 15 To Machir I gave Gilead. 16 To the Reubenites and the Gadites I gave the region from Gilead to the Wadi Arnon, the middle of the ravine marking the boundary, and up as far as the Jabbok, the ravine marking the frontier of the Ammonites. 17 The Arabah and the Jordan serve as frontiers from Chinnereth down to the Sea of the Arabah (the Salt Sea), at the foot of the slopes of Pisgah on the east.

18 'I then gave you this order: "Yahweh your God has given you this country to be yours. Armed, every one of you fit to fight must go ahead of your brothers the Israelites.

---

f 3 3:1seq. // Nb 21:33–35.   g 3 3:12seq. // Nb 32.

livestock — I know that you have much livestock — shall stay behind in the towns that I have given to you. 20 When the LORD gives rest to your kindred, as to you, and they too have occupied the land that the LORD your God is giving them beyond the Jordan, then each of you may return to the property that I have given to you." 21 And I charged Joshua as well at that time, saying: "Your own eyes have seen everything that the LORD your God has done to these two kings; so the LORD will do to all the kingdoms into which you are about to cross. 22 Do not fear them, for it is the LORD your God who fights for you."

23 At that time, too, I entreated the LORD, saying: 24 "O Lord GOD, you have only begun to show your servant your greatness and your might; what god in heaven or on earth can perform deeds and mighty acts like yours! 25 Let me cross over to see the good land beyond the Jordan, that good hill country and the Lebanon." 26 But the LORD was angry with me on your account and would not heed me. The LORD said to me, "Enough from you! Never speak to me of this matter again! 27 Go up to the top of Pisgah and look around you to the west, to the north, to the south, and to the east. Look well, for you shall not cross over this Jordan. 28 But charge Joshua, and encourage and strengthen him, because it is he who shall cross over at the head of this people and who shall secure their possession of the land that you will see." 29 So we remained in the valley opposite Beth-peor.

4 So now, Israel, give heed to the statutes and ordinances that I am teaching you to observe, so that you may live to enter and occupy the land that the LORD, the God of your ancestors, is giving you. 2 You must neither add anything to what I command you nor take away anything from it, but keep the commandments of the LORD your God with which I am charging you. 3 You have seen for yourselves what the LORD did with regard to the Baal of Peor — how the LORD your God destroyed from among you everyone who followed the Baal of Peor, 4 while those of you who held fast to the LORD your God are all alive today.

5 See, just as the LORD my God has charged me, I now teach you statutes and ordinances for you to observe in the land that you are about to enter and occupy. 6 You must observe them diligently, for this will show your wisdom and discernment to the peoples, who, when they hear all these statutes, will say, "Surely this great nation is a wise and discerning people!" 7 For what other great nation has a god so near to it as the LORD our God is whenever we call to him? 8 And what other great nation has statutes and ordinances as just as this entire law that I am setting before you today?

9 But take care and watch yourselves closely, so as neither to forget the things that your eyes have seen nor to let them slip from your mind all the days of your life; make them known to your children and your children's children — 10 how you once stood before the LORD your God at Horeb, when the LORD said to me, "Assemble the people for me, and I will let them hear my words, so that they may learn to fear me as long as they live on the earth, and may teach their children so"; 11 you approached and stood at the foot of the mountain while the mountain was blazing up to the very heavens, shrouded in dark clouds. 12 Then the LORD spoke to you out of the fire. You heard the sound of words but saw no form; there was only a voice. 13 He declared to you his covenant, which he charged you to observe, that is, the ten commandments;h and he wrote them on two stone tablets. 14 And the LORD charged me at that time to teach you statutes and ordinances for you to observe in the land that you are about to cross into and occupy.

livestock — I know you have much livestock — may remain in the towns I have given you. 20 This you are to do until the LORD gives your kinsfolk security as he has given it to you, and until they too occupy the land which the LORD your God is giving them on the other side of the Jordan; then you may each return to the possession I have given you.'

21 Also at that time I gave Joshua this charge: 'You have seen for yourself all that the LORD your God has done to these two kings; he will do the same to all the kingdoms into which you are about to cross. 22 Do not be afraid of them, for the LORD your God himself will fight for you.'

23 It was then I made this plea to the LORD: 24 'LORD God,' I said, 'you have begun to show to your servant your great power and your strong hand: what god is there in heaven or on earth who can match your works and mighty deeds? 25 Let me cross over, I beg, and see that good land which lies on the other side of the Jordan, and the fine hill-country and the Lebanon.' 26 But because of you the LORD angrily brushed me aside and would not listen. 'Enough!' he answered. 'Say no more about this. 27 Go to the top of Pisgah and look west and north, south and east; look well at what you see, for you will not cross this river Jordan. 28 Give Joshua his commission, support and strengthen him, for he will lead this people across, and he will put them in possession of the land you see before you.'

29 So we remained in the glen opposite Beth-peor.

4 AND now, Israel, listen to the statutes and laws which I am about to teach you; obey them, so that you may live and go in to occupy the land which the LORD the God of your forefathers is giving you. 2 You must not add anything to the charge I decree or take anything away from it; you must carry out the commandments of the LORD your God which I lay upon you.

3 You saw for yourselves what the LORD did at Baal-peor; the LORD your God destroyed from among you everyone who went over to the Baal of Peor, 4 but you who held fast to the LORD your God are all alive today. 5 I have taught you statutes and laws, as the LORD my God commanded me; see that you keep them when you go into and occupy the land. 6 Observe them carefully, for thereby you will display your wisdom and understanding to other peoples. When they hear about all these statutes, they will say, 'What a wise and understanding people this great nation is!' 7 What great nation has a god close at hand as the LORD our God is close to us whenever we call to him? 8 What great nation is there whose statutes and laws are so just, as is all this code of laws which I am setting before you today?

9 But take care: keep careful watch on yourselves so that you do not forget the things that you have seen with your own eyes; do not let them pass from your minds as long as you live, but teach them to your children and to your children's children. 10 You must never forget the day when you stood before the LORD your God at Horeb, and the LORD said to me, 'Assemble the people for me; I shall make them hear my words and they will learn to fear me all their lives in the land, and they will teach their children to do so.' 11 Then you came near and stood at the foot of the mountain, which was ablaze with fire to the very skies, and there was dark cloud and thick mist. 12 When the LORD spoke to you from the heart of the fire you heard a voice speaking, but you saw no form; there was only a voice. 13 He announced to you the terms of his covenant, which he wrote on two stone tablets. 14 At the same time the LORD charged me to teach you statutes and laws which you should observe in the land into which you are about to cross to occupy it.

---

h Heb the ten words

4:13 **Commandments:** lit. Words.

as well as your livestock, of which I know you have a large number, shall remain behind in the towns I have given you, 20 until the LORD has settled your kinsmen as well, and they too possess the land which the LORD, your God, will give them on the other side of the Jordan. Then you may all return to the possessions I have given you.'

21 "It was then that I instructed Joshua, 'Your eyes have seen all that the LORD, your God, has done to both these kings; so, too, will the LORD do to all the kingdoms which you will encounter over there. 22 Fear them not, for the LORD, your God, will fight for you.'

23 "And it was then that I besought the LORD, 24 'O Lord GOD, you have begun to show to your servant your greatness and might. For what god in heaven or on earth can perform deeds as mighty as yours? 25 Ah, let me cross over and see this good land beyond the Jordan, this fine hill country, and the Lebanon!' 26 But the LORD was angry with me on your account and would not hear me. 'Enough!' the LORD said to me. 'Speak to me no more of this. 27 Go up to the top of Pisgah and look out to the west, and to the north, and to the south, and to the east. Look well, for you shall not cross this Jordan. 28 Commission Joshua, and encourage and strengthen him, for he shall cross at the head of this people and shall put them in possession of the land you are to see.' 29 This was while we were in the ravine opposite Beth-peor.

4 "Now, Israel, hear the statutes and decrees which I am teaching you to observe, that you may live, and may enter in and take possession of the land which the LORD, the God of your fathers, is giving you. 2 In your observance of the commandments of the LORD, your God, which I enjoin upon you, you shall not add to what I command you nor subtract from it. 3 You have seen with your own eyes what the LORD did at Baal-peor: the LORD, your God, destroyed from your midst everyone that followed the Baal of Peor; 4 but you, who clung to the LORD, your God, are all alive today. 5 Therefore, I teach you the statutes and decrees as the LORD, my God, has commanded me, that you may observe them in the land you are entering to occupy. 6 Observe them carefully, for thus will you give evidence of your wisdom and intelligence to the nations, who will hear of all these statutes and say, 'This great nation is truly a wise and intelligent people.' 7 For what great nation is there that has gods so close to it as the LORD, our God, is to us whenever we call upon him? 8 Or what great nation has statutes and decrees that are as just as this whole law which I am setting before you today?

9 "However, take care and be earnestly on your guard not to forget the things which your own eyes have seen, nor let them slip from your memory as long as you live, but teach them to your children and to your children's children: 10 There was the day on which you stood before the LORD, your God, at Horeb, and he said to me, 'Assemble the people for me; I will have them hear my words, that they may learn to fear me as long as they live in the land and may so teach their children.' 11 You came near and stood at the foot of the mountain, which blazed to the very sky with fire and was enveloped in a dense black cloud. 12 Then the LORD spoke to you from the midst of the fire. You heard the sound of the words, but saw no form; there was only a voice. 13 He proclaimed to you his covenant, which he commanded you to keep: the ten commandments, which he wrote on two tablets of stone. 14 The LORD charged me at that time to teach you the statutes and decrees which you are to observe over in the land you will occupy.

19 Only your wives, your children and your flocks (you have many flocks, I know) must stay behind in the towns which I have given you, 20 until Yahweh has brought your brothers to rest as he has already brought you, and they too possess the territory which Yahweh your God is giving them on the other side of the Jordan; after that, you can go home, each to the domain I have given you." 21 I then gave Joshua this order, "You can see for yourself everything that Yahweh our God has done to these two kings; Yahweh will do the same to all the kingdoms through which you pass. 22 Do not be afraid of them: Yahweh your God himself is fighting for you."

23 'I then pleaded with Yahweh. 24 "My Lord Yahweh," I said, "now that you have begun to reveal your greatness and your power to your servant with works and mighty deeds no God in heaven or on earth can rival, 25 may I not go across and see this fine country on the other side of the Jordan, that fine upland country and the Lebanon?" 26 But, because of you, Yahweh was angry with me and would not listen. "Enough!" he said, "Do not mention this subject again! 27 Climb to the top of Pisgah; turn your eyes to the west, the north, the south, the east. Look well, for across this Jordan you shall not go. 28 Give Joshua your instructions; encourage him, strengthen him; for he will be the one to cross at the head of this people; he will be the one to bring them into possession of the country which you will see."

29 'We then stayed in the valley, close to Beth-Peor.'

4 'And now, Israel, listen to the laws and customs which I am teaching you today, so that, by observing them, you may survive to enter and take possession of the country which Yahweh, God of your ancestors, is giving you. 2 You must add nothing to what I command you, and take nothing from it, but keep the commandments of Yahweh your God just as I lay them down for you. 3 You can see for yourselves what Yahweh has done about the Baal of Peor; Yahweh your God has destroyed all those of you who followed the Baal of Peor; 4 but those of you who stayed faithful to Yahweh your God are all alive today. 5 Look: as Yahweh my God commanded me, I have taught you laws and customs, for you to observe in the country of which you are going to take possession. 6 Keep them, put them into practice, and other peoples will admire your wisdom and prudence. Once they know what all these laws are, they will exclaim, "No other people is as wise and prudent as this great nation!" 7 And indeed, what great nation has its gods as near as Yahweh our God is to us whenever we call to him? 8 And what great nation has laws and customs as upright as the entirety of this Law which I am laying down for you today?

9 'But take care, as you value your lives! Do not forget the things which you yourselves have seen, or let them slip from your heart as long as you live; teach them, rather, to your children and to your children's children. 10 The day you stood at Horeb in the presence of Yahweh your God, Yahweh said to me, "Summon the people to me; I want them to hear me speaking, so that they will learn to fear me all the days they live on earth, and teach this to their children." 11 So you came and stood at the foot of the mountain, and the mountain flamed to the very sky, a sky darkened by cloud, murky and thunderous. 12 Yahweh then spoke to you from the heart of the fire; you heard the sound of words but saw no shape; there was only a voice. 13 He revealed his covenant to you and commanded you to observe it, the Ten Words which he inscribed on two tablets of stone. 14 Yahweh then ordered me to teach you the laws and customs that you were to observe in the country into which you are about to cross, to take possession of it.

15 Since you saw no form when the LORD spoke to you at Horeb out of the fire, take care and watch yourselves closely, 16 so that you do not act corruptly by making an idol for yourselves, in the form of any figure—the likeness of male or female, 17 the likeness of any animal that is on the earth, the likeness of any winged bird that flies in the air, 18 the likeness of anything that creeps on the ground, the likeness of any fish that is in the water under the earth. 19 And when you look up to the heavens and see the sun, the moon, and the stars, all the host of heaven, do not be led astray and bow down to them and serve them, things that the LORD your God has allotted to all the peoples everywhere under heaven. 20 But the LORD has taken you and brought you out of the iron-smelter, out of Egypt, to become a people of his very own possession, as you are now.

21 The LORD was angry with me because of you, and he vowed that I should not cross the Jordan and that I should not enter the good land that the LORD your God is giving for your possession. 22 For I am going to die in this land without crossing over the Jordan, but you are going to cross over to take possession of that good land. 23 So be careful not to forget the covenant that the LORD your God made with you, and not to make for yourselves an idol in the form of anything that the LORD your God has forbidden you. 24 For the LORD your God is a devouring fire, a jealous God.

25 When you have had children and children's children, and become complacent in the land, if you act corruptly by making an idol in the form of anything, thus doing what is evil in the sight of the LORD your God, and provoking him to anger, 26 I call heaven and earth to witness against you today that you will soon utterly perish from the land that you are crossing the Jordan to occupy; you will not live long on it, but will be utterly destroyed. 27 The LORD will scatter you among the peoples; only a few of you will be left among the nations where the LORD will lead you. 28 There you will serve other gods made by human hands, objects of wood and stone that neither see, nor hear, nor eat, nor smell. 29 From there you will seek the LORD your God, and you will find him if you search after him with all your heart and soul. 30 In your distress, when all these things have happened to you in time to come, you will return to the LORD your God and heed him. 31 Because the LORD your God is a merciful God, he will neither abandon you nor destroy you; he will not forget the covenant with your ancestors that he swore to them.

32 For ask now about former ages, long before your own, ever since the day that God created human beings on the earth; ask from one end of heaven to the other: has anything so great as this ever happened or has its like ever been heard of? 33 Has any people ever heard the voice of a god speaking out of a fire, as you have heard, and lived? 34 Or has any god ever attempted to go and take a nation for himself from the midst of another nation, by trials, by signs and wonders, by war, by a mighty hand and an outstretched arm, and by terrifying displays of power, as the LORD your God did for you in Egypt before your very eyes? 35 To you it was shown so that you would acknowledge that the LORD is God; there is no other besides him. 36 From heaven he made you hear his voice to discipline you. On earth he showed you his great fire, while you heard his words coming out of the fire. 37 And because he loved your ancestors, he chose their descendants after them. He brought you out of Egypt with his own presence, by his great power, 38 driving out before you nations greater and mightier than yourselves, to bring you in, giving you their land for a possession, as it is still today. 39 So acknowledge today and take to heart that the LORD is God in heaven above and on the earth beneath; there is no other. 40 Keep his statutes and his

15 On the day when the LORD spoke to you from the heart of the fire at Horeb, you saw no form of any kind; so take good care 16 not to fall into the infamous practice of making for yourselves carved images in the form of any statue of a man or woman, 17 or of any animal on earth or bird that flies in the air, 18 or of anything that creeps on the ground or of any fish in the waters under the earth. 19 Nor must you raise your eyes to the heavens and look up to the sun, the moon, and the stars, all the host of heaven, and be led astray to bow down to them in worship; the LORD your God assigned these for all the peoples everywhere under heaven. 20 But you are the people whom the LORD brought out of Egypt, from the smelting furnace, and took for his own possession, as you are to this day.

21 The LORD was angry with me on your account and solemnly swore that I should not cross the Jordan or enter the good land which the LORD your God is about to give you as your holding. 22 I myself am to die in this country; I shall not cross the Jordan, but you are about to cross and occupy that good land. 23 Take care that you do not forget the covenant which the LORD your God made with you; do not make for yourselves a carved image in any form; the LORD your God has forbidden it. 24 For the LORD your God is a devouring fire, a jealous God.

25 When you have children and grandchildren and have grown old in the land, if you then fall into the infamous practice of making carved images in any form, doing what is wrong in the eyes of the LORD your God and provoking him to anger, 26 I summon heaven and earth to witness against you this day: you will soon perish from upon the land which you are to occupy after crossing the Jordan. You will not enjoy long life in it; you will be swept away. 27 The LORD will scatter you among the peoples, and you will be left few in number among the nations to which the LORD will lead you. 28 There you will serve gods made by human hands out of wood and stone, gods that can neither see nor hear, eat nor smell. 29 But should you from there seek the LORD your God, you will find him, if it is with all your heart and soul that you search. 30 When you are in distress and all those things happen to you, you will in time to come turn back to the LORD your God and obey him. 31 The LORD your God is a merciful God; he will never fail you or destroy you; he will not forget the covenant with your forefathers which he guaranteed by oath.

32 Search into days gone by, long before your time, beginning at the day when God created man on earth; search from one end of heaven to the other, and ask if any deed as mighty as this has been seen or heard. 33 Did any people ever hear the voice of a god speaking from the heart of the fire, as you heard it, and remain alive? 34 Or did a god ever attempt to come and take a nation for himself away from another nation, with a challenge, and with signs, portents, and wars, with a strong hand and an outstretched arm, and with great deeds of terror, like all you saw the LORD your God do for you in Egypt? 35 You have had sure proof that the LORD is God; there is none other. 36 From heaven he let you hear his voice for your instruction, and on earth he let you see his great fire, and from the heart of the fire you heard his words. 37 Because he loved your fathers and chose their children after them, he in his own person brought you out of Egypt by his great strength, 38 so that he might drive out before you nations greater and more powerful than you and bring you in to give you their land in possession, as it is to this day.

39 Be sure to bear in mind this day that the LORD is God in heaven above and on earth below; there is none other.

15 "You saw no form at all on the day the LORD spoke to you at Horeb from the midst of the fire. Be strictly on your guard, therefore, 16 not to degrade yourselves by fashioning an idol to represent any figure, whether it be the form of a man or of a woman, 17 of any animal on the earth or of any bird that flies in the sky, 18 of anything that crawls on the ground or of any fish in the waters under the earth. 19 And when you look up to the heavens and behold the sun or the moon or any star among the heavenly hosts, do not be led astray into adoring them and serving them. These the LORD, your God, has let fall to the lot of all other nations under the heavens; 20 but you he has taken and led out of that iron foundry, Egypt, that you might be his very own people, as you are today. 21 Since the LORD was angered against me on your account and swore that I should not cross the Jordan nor enter the good land which he is giving you as a heritage, 22 I myself shall die in this country without crossing the Jordan; but you will cross over and take possession of that good land. 23 Take heed, therefore, lest, forgetting the covenant which the LORD, your God, has made with you, you fashion for yourselves against his command an idol in any form whatsoever. 24 For the LORD, your God, is a consuming fire, a jealous God.

25 "When you have children and grandchildren, and have grown old in the land, should you then degrade yourselves by fashioning an idol in any form and by this evil done in his sight provoke the LORD, your God, 26 I call heaven and earth this day to witness against you, that you shall all quickly perish from the land which you will occupy when you cross the Jordan. You shall not live in it for any length of time but shall be promptly wiped out. 27 The LORD will scatter you among the nations, and there shall remain but a handful of you among the nations to which the LORD will lead you. 28 There you shall serve gods fashioned by the hands of man out of wood and stone, gods which can neither see nor hear, neither eat nor smell. 29 Yet there too you shall seek the LORD, your God; and you shall indeed find him when you search after him with your whole heart and your whole soul. 30 In your distress, when all these things shall have come upon you, you shall finally return to the LORD, your God, and heed his voice. 31 Since the LORD, your God, is a merciful God, he will not abandon and destroy you, nor forget the covenant which under oath he made with your fathers.

32 "Ask now of the days of old, before your time, ever since God created man upon the earth; ask from one end of the sky to the other: Did anything so great ever happen before? Was it ever heard of? 33 Did a people ever hear the voice of God speaking from the midst of fire, as you did, and live? 34 Or did any god venture to go and take a nation for himself from the midst of another nation, by testings, by signs and wonders, by war, with his strong hand and outstretched arm, and by great terrors, all of which the LORD, your God, did for you in Egypt before your very eyes? 35 All this you were allowed to see that you might know the LORD is God and there is no other. 36 Out of the heavens he let you hear his voice to discipline you; on earth he let you see his great fire, and you heard him speaking out of the fire. 37 For love of your fathers he chose their descendants and personally led you out of Egypt by his great power, 38 driving out of your way nations greater and mightier than you, so as to bring you in and to make their land your heritage, as it is today. 39 This is why you must now know, and fix in your heart, that the LORD is God in the heavens above and on earth below, and that there is no other. 40 You must keep his

15 'Hence, be very careful what you do. Since you saw no shape that day at Horeb when Yahweh spoke to you from the heart of the fire, 16 see that you do not corrupt yourselves by making an image in the shape of anything whatever: be it statue of man or of woman, 17 or of any animal on the earth, or of any bird that flies in the heavens, 18 or of any reptile that crawls on the ground, or of any fish in the waters under the earth. 19 When you raise your eyes to heaven, when you see the sun, the moon, the stars — the entire array of heaven — do not be tempted to worship them and serve them. Yahweh your God has allotted these to all the other peoples under heaven, 20 but Yahweh has chosen you, bringing you out of the iron-foundry, Egypt, to be his own people, his own people as you still are today. 21 'Yahweh is angry with me because of you; he has sworn that I shall not cross the Jordan or enter the fine country which Yahweh your God is giving you as your heritage. 22 Yes, I am to die in this country; I shall not cross this Jordan; you will go over and take possession of that rich land. 23 Be careful not to forget the covenant which Yahweh your God has made with you, by sculpting an image or making a statue of anything, since Yahweh your God has forbidden this; 24 for Yahweh your God is a consuming fire, a jealous God.

25 'When you have fathered children and grandchildren and have grown old in the country, when you have grown corrupt and made some image, doing what Yahweh regards as wrong and so provoking his anger — 26 today I call heaven and earth to witness against you — you will quickly vanish from the country which you are crossing the Jordan to possess. Your days will not be prolonged there, for you will be utterly destroyed. 27 Yahweh will scatter you among the peoples, and only a small number of you will remain among the nations where Yahweh will have driven you. 28 There you will serve gods made by human hand, of wood and of stone, that cannot see or hear, eat or smell. 29 'If, however, from there you start searching once more for Yahweh your God, and if you search for him honestly and sincerely, you will find him. 30 You will suffer; everything I have said will befall you, but in the final days you will return to Yahweh your God and listen to his voice. 31 For Yahweh your God is a merciful God and will not desert or destroy you or forget the covenant which he made on oath with your ancestors.

32 'Put this question, then, to the ages that are past, that have gone before you, from when God created the human race on earth: Was there ever a word so majestic, from one end of heaven to the other? Was anything like it ever heard? 33 Did ever a people hear the voice of the living God speaking from the heart of the fire, as you have heard it, and remain alive? 34 Has it ever been known before that any god took action himself to bring one nation out of another one, by ordeals, signs, wonders, war with mighty hand and outstretched arm, by fearsome terrors — all of which things Yahweh your God has done for you before your eyes in Egypt? 35 'This he showed you, so that you might know that Yahweh is the true God and that there is no other. 36 To instruct you, he made you hear his voice from heaven, and on earth he let you see his great fire, and from the heart of the fire you heard his words. 37 Because he loved your ancestors and, after them, chose their descendants, he has brought you out of Egypt, displaying his presence and mighty power, 38 dispossessing for you nations who were larger and stronger than you, to make way for you and to give you your country as your heritage, as it still is today. 39 'Hence, grasp this today and meditate on it carefully: Yahweh is the true God, in heaven above as on earth beneath, he and no other. 40 Keep his laws and command-

NEW REVISED STANDARD VERSION

commandments, which I am commanding you today for your own well-being and that of your descendants after you, so that you may long remain in the land that the LORD your God is giving you for all time.

41 Then Moses set apart on the east side of the Jordan three cities 42 to which a homicide could flee, someone who unintentionally kills another person, the two not having been at enmity before; the homicide could flee to one of these cities and live: 43 Bezer in the wilderness on the tableland belonging to the Reubenites, Ramoth in Gilead belonging to the Gadites, and Golan in Bashan belonging to the Manassites.

44 This is the law that Moses set before the Israelites. 45 These are the decrees and the statutes and ordinances that Moses spoke to the Israelites when they had come out of Egypt, 46 beyond the Jordan in the valley opposite Beth-peor, in the land of King Sihon of the Amorites, who reigned at Heshbon, whom Moses and the Israelites defeated when they came out of Egypt. 47 They occupied his land and the land of King Og of Bashan, the two kings of the Amorites on the eastern side of the Jordan: 48 from Aroer, which is on the edge of the Wadi Arnon, as far as Mount Sirion[i] (that is, Hermon), 49 together with all the Arabah on the east side of the Jordan as far as the Sea of the Arabah, under the slopes of Pisgah.

5 Moses convened all Israel, and said to them:
Hear, O Israel, the statutes and ordinances that I am addressing to you today; you shall learn them and observe them diligently. 2 The LORD our God made a covenant with us at Horeb. 3 Not with our ancestors did the LORD make this covenant, but with us, who are all of us here alive today. 4 The LORD spoke with you face to face at the mountain, out of the fire. 5 (At that time I was standing between the LORD and you to declare to you the words[j] of the LORD; for you were afraid because of the fire and did not go up the mountain.) And he said:

6 I am the LORD your God, who brought you out of the land of Egypt, out of the house of slavery; 7 you shall have no other gods before[k] me.

8 You shall not make for yourself an idol, whether in the form of anything that is in heaven above, or that is on the earth beneath, or that is in the water under the earth. 9 You shall not bow down to them or worship them; for I the LORD your God am a jealous God, punishing children for the iniquity of parents, to the third and fourth generation of those who reject me, 10 but showing steadfast love to the thousandth generation[l] of those who love me and keep my commandments.

11 You shall not make wrongful use of the name of the LORD your God, for the LORD will not acquit anyone who misuses his name.

12 Observe the sabbath day and keep it holy, as the LORD your God commanded you. 13 Six days you shall labor and do all your work. 14 But the seventh day is a sabbath to the LORD your God; you shall not do any work — you, or your son or your daughter, or your male or female slave, or your ox or your donkey, or any of your livestock, or the resident alien in your towns, so that your male and female slave may rest as well as you. 15 Remember that you were a slave in the land of Egypt, and the LORD your God brought you out from there with a mighty hand and an outstretched arm; therefore the LORD your God commanded you to keep the sabbath day.

REVISED ENGLISH BIBLE

40 You must keep his statutes and his commands which I give you today; so all will be well with you and with your children after you, and you will enjoy long life in the land which the LORD your God is giving you for all time.

41 Then Moses set apart three cities in the east beyond the Jordan 42 to be places of refuge for the homicide who kills someone without malice aforethought. If he took sanctuary in one of these cities his life would be safe. 43 The cities were: Bezer-in-the-wilderness on the tableland for the Reubenites, Ramoth in Gilead for the Gadites, and Golan in Bashan for the Manassites.

44 This is the code of laws which Moses laid down for the Israelites. 45 These are the precepts, the statutes, and the laws which Moses proclaimed to the Israelites, when they had come out of Egypt 46 and were beyond the Jordan in the valley opposite Beth-peor in the land of Sihon king of the Amorites who lived in Heshbon. Moses and the Israelites had defeated him when they came out of Egypt 47 and had occupied his territory and the territory of King Og of Bashan, the two Amorite kings east of the Jordan. 48 The territory ran from Aroer on the wadi of the Arnon to Mount Sirion, that is Hermon; 49 it included all the Arabah beyond the Jordan, as far as the sea of the Arabah below the watershed of Pisgah.

5 Moses summoned all Israel and said to them: Israel,
listen to the statutes and the laws which I proclaim to you this day. Learn them, and be careful to observe them. 2 The LORD our God made a covenant with us at Horeb. 3 It was not with our forefathers that the LORD made this covenant, but with us, all of us who are alive and are here this day. 4 The LORD spoke with you face to face on the mountain out of the heart of the fire. 5 I stood between the LORD and you at that time to report the words of the LORD; for you were afraid of the fire and did not go up the mountain. The LORD said:

6 I am the LORD your God who brought you out of Egypt, out of that land where you lived as slaves.

7 You must have no other gods beside me.

8 You are not to make a carved image for yourself, nor the likeness of anything in the heavens above, or on the earth below, or in the waters under the earth. 9 You must not worship or serve them; for I am the LORD your God, a jealous God, punishing children for the sins of their parents to the third and fourth generations of those who reject me. 10 But I keep faith with thousands, those who love me and keep my commandments.

11 You shall not make wrong use of the name of the LORD your God; the LORD will not leave unpunished anyone who misuses his name.

12 Observe the sabbath day and keep it holy as the LORD your God commanded you. 13 You have six days to labour and do all your work; 14 but the seventh day there is a sabbath of the LORD your God; that day you must not do any work, neither you, nor your son or your daughter, your slave or your slave-girl, your ox, your donkey, or any of your cattle, or the alien residing among you, so that your slaves and slave-girls may rest as you do. 15 Bear in mind that you were slaves in Egypt, and the LORD your God brought you out with a strong hand and an outstretched arm, and for that reason the LORD your God has commanded you to keep the sabbath day.

---

[i]Syr: Heb Sion   [j]Q Mss Sam Gk Syr Vg Tg: MT word   [k]Or besides   [l]Or to thousands

4:48 **Sirion:** so Syriac, cp. 3:9; Heb. Sion.   5:5 **words:** so Samar.; Heb. word.   5:7 **gods:** or god.   5:8 **nor:** so many MSS; others omit.   5:10 **with thousands:** or for a thousand generations with.

NEW AMERICAN BIBLE

statutes and commandments which I enjoin on you today, that you and your children after you may prosper, and that you may have long life on the land which the LORD, your God, is giving you forever."

41 Then Moses set apart three cities in the region east of the Jordan, 42 that a homicide might take refuge there if he unwittingly killed his neighbor to whom he had previously borne no malice, and that he might save his life by fleeing to one of these cities: 43 Bezer in the desert, in the region of the plateau, for the Reubenites; Ramoth in Gilead for the Gadites; and Golan in Bashan for the Manassehites.

44 This is the law which Moses set before the Israelites. 45 These are the ordinances, statutes and decrees which he proclaimed to them when they had come out of Egypt 46 and were beyond the Jordan in the ravine opposite Beth-peor, in the land of Sihon, king of the Amorites, who dwelt in Heshbon and whom Moses and the Israelites defeated after coming out of Egypt. 47 They occupied his land and the land of Og, king of Bashan, as well — the land of these two kings of the Amorites in the region east of the Jordan: 48 from Aroer on the edge of the Wadi Arnon to Mount Sion (that is, Hermon) 49 and all the Arabah east of the Jordan, as far as the Arabah Sea under the slopes of Pisgah.

5 Moses summoned all Israel and said to them, "Hear, O Israel, the statutes and decrees which I proclaim in your hearing this day, that you may learn them and take care to observe them. 2 The LORD, our God, made a covenant with us at Horeb; 3 not with our fathers did he make this covenant, but with us, all of us who are alive here this day. 4 The LORD spoke with you face to face on the mountain from the midst of the fire. 5 Since you were afraid of the fire and would not go up the mountain, I stood between the LORD and you at that time, to announce to you these words of the LORD:

6 'I, the LORD, am your God, who brought you out of the land of Egypt, that place of slavery. 7 You shall not have other gods besides me. 8 You shall not carve idols for yourselves in the shape of anything in the sky above or on the earth below or in the waters beneath the earth; 9 you shall not bow down before them or worship them. For I, the LORD, your God, am a jealous God, inflicting punishments for their fathers' wickedness on the children of those who hate me, down to the third and fourth generation 10 but bestowing mercy, down to the thousandth generation, on the children of those who love me and keep my commandments.

11 'You shall not take the name of the LORD, your God, in vain. For the LORD will not leave unpunished him who takes his name in vain.

12 'Take care to keep holy the sabbath day as the LORD, your God, commanded you. 13 Six days you may labor and do all your work; 14 but the seventh day is the sabbath of the LORD, your God. No work may be done then, whether by you, or your son or daughter, or your male or female slave, or your ox or ass or any of your beasts, or the alien who lives with you. Your male and female slave should rest as you do. 15 For remember that you too were once slaves in Egypt, and the LORD, your God, brought you from there with his strong hand and outstretched arm. That is why the LORD, your God, has commanded you to observe the sabbath day.

NEW JERUSALEM BIBLE

ments as I give them to you today, so that you and your children after you may prosper and live long in the country that Yahweh your God is giving you for ever.'

41 Moses then set aside three towns in the east, beyond the Jordan, 42 to which any killer might flee who had accidentally, without any previous feud, killed his fellow; by taking refuge in one of these towns he could save his life. 43 These were, for the Reubenites, Bezer in the desert on the tableland; for the Gadites, Ramoth in Gilead; for the Manassehites, Golan in Bashan.

44 This is the Law which Moses presented to the Israelites. 45 These are the stipulations, the laws and the customs which Moses gave the Israelites after they had left Egypt, 46 beyond the Jordan in the valley near Beth-Peor, in the country of Sihon the Amorite king who had lived at Heshbon. Moses and the Israelites had defeated him when they left Egypt, 47 and had taken possession of his country, as well as that of Og king of Bashan — two Amorite kings to the east beyond the Jordan, 48 from Aroer on the edge of the Arnon Valley, all the way to Mount Sion (that is, Hermon) — 49 and of the whole Arabah east of the Jordan as far as the Sea of the Arabah, at the foot of the slopes of Pisgah.

5 Moses called all Israel together and said to them, 'Listen, Israel, to the laws and customs that I proclaim to you today. Learn them and take care to observe them.

2 'Yahweh our God made a covenant with us at Horeb. 3 Yahweh made this covenant not with our ancestors, but with us, with all of us alive here today. 4 On the mountain, from the heart of the fire, Yahweh spoke to you face to face, 5 while I stood between you and Yahweh to let you know what Yahweh was saying, since you were afraid of the fire and had not gone up the mountain. He said:

6 ' "I am Yahweh your God who brought you out of Egypt, out of the place of slave-labour.

7 ' "You will have no gods other than me.

8 ' "You must not make yourselves any image or any likeness of anything in heaven above or on earth beneath or in the waters under the earth; 9 you must not bow down to these gods or serve them. For I, Yahweh your God, am a jealous God and I punish the parents' fault in the children, the grandchildren and the great-grandchildren, among those who hate me; 10 but I show faithful love to thousands, to those who love me and keep my commandments.

11 ' "You must not misuse the name of Yahweh your God, for Yahweh will not leave unpunished anyone who uses his name for what is false.

12 ' "Observe the Sabbath day and keep it holy, as Yahweh your God has commanded you. 13 Labour for six days, doing all your work, 14 but the seventh day is a Sabbath for Yahweh your God. You must not do any work that day, neither you, nor your son, nor your daughter, nor your servants — male or female — nor your ox, nor your donkey, nor any of your animals, nor the foreigner who has made his home with you; 15 so that your servants, male and female, may rest, as you do. Remember that you were once a slave in Egypt, and that Yahweh your God brought you out of there with mighty hand and outstretched arm; this is why Yahweh your God has commanded you to keep the Sabbath day.

h 5 // Ex 20:1–17.

16 Honor your father and your mother, as the LORD your God commanded you, so that your days may be long and that it may go well with you in the land that the LORD your God is giving you.

17 You shall not murder. *m*

18 Neither shall you commit adultery.

19 Neither shall you steal.

20 Neither shall you bear false witness against your neighbor.

21 Neither shall you covet your neighbor's wife.

Neither shall you desire your neighbor's house, or field, or male or female slave, or ox, or donkey, or anything that belongs to your neighbor.

22 These words the LORD spoke with a loud voice to your whole assembly at the mountain, out of the fire, the cloud, and the thick darkness, and he added no more. He wrote them on two stone tablets, and gave them to me. 23 When you heard the voice out of the darkness, while the mountain was burning with fire, you approached me, all the heads of your tribes and your elders; 24 and you said, "Look, the LORD our God has shown us his glory and greatness, and we have heard his voice out of the fire. Today we have seen that God may speak to someone and the person may still live. 25 So now why should we die? For this great fire will consume us; if we hear the voice of the LORD our God any longer, we shall die. 26 For who is there of all flesh that has heard the voice of the living God speaking out of fire, as we have, and remained alive? 27 Go near, you yourself, and hear all that the LORD our God will say. Then tell us everything that the LORD our God tells you, and we will listen and do it."

28 The LORD heard your words when you spoke to me, and the LORD said to me: "I have heard the words of this people, which they have spoken to you; they are right in all that they have spoken. 29 If only they had such a mind as this, to fear me and to keep all my commandments always, so that it might go well with them and with their children forever! 30 Go say to them, 'Return to your tents.' 31 But you, stand here by me, and I will tell you all the commandments, the statutes and the ordinances, that you shall teach them, so that they may do them in the land that I am giving them to possess." 32 You must therefore be careful to do as the LORD your God has commanded you; you shall not turn to the right or to the left. 33 You must follow exactly the path that the LORD your God has commanded you, so that you may live, and that it may go well with you, and that you may live long in the land that you are to possess.

6 Now this is the commandment—the statutes and the ordinances—that the LORD your God charged me to teach you to observe in the land that you are about to cross into and occupy, 2 so that you and your children and your children's children may fear the LORD your God all the days of your life, and keep all his decrees and his commandments that I am commanding you, so that your days may be long. 3 Hear therefore, O Israel, and observe them diligently, so that it may go well with you, and so that you may multiply greatly in a land flowing with milk and honey, as the LORD, the God of your ancestors, has promised you.

4 Hear, O Israel: The LORD is our God, the LORD alone. *n* 5 You shall love the LORD your God with all your heart, and with all your soul, and with all your might. 6 Keep these words that I am commanding you today in your heart. 7 Recite them to your children and talk about them when you are at home and when you are away, when you lie down and when you rise. 8 Bind them as a sign on your

16 Honour your father and your mother, as the LORD your God commanded you, so that you may enjoy long life, and it will be well with you in the land which the LORD your God is giving you.

17 Do not commit murder.

18 Do not commit adultery.

19 Do not steal.

20 Do not give baseless evidence against your neighbour.

21 Do not lust after your neighbour's wife; do not covet your neighbour's household, his land, his slave, his slave-girl, his ox, his donkey, or anything that belongs to him.

22 These commandments the LORD spoke in a loud voice to your whole assembly on the mountain out of the fire, the cloud, and the thick mist; then he said no more. He wrote them on two stone tablets, which he gave to me.

23 When you heard the voice out of the darkness, while the mountain was ablaze with fire, all the heads of your tribes and the elders came to me 24 and said, 'The LORD our God has indeed shown us his glory and his great power, and we have heard his voice from the midst of the fire: today we have seen that people may still live after God has spoken with them. 25 But why should we now risk death, for this great fire will devour us? If we hear the voice of the LORD our God again, we shall die. 26 Is there any creature like us who has heard the voice of the living God speaking out of the fire and remained alive? 27 Go near and listen to all that the LORD our God says to you, and report to us whatever the LORD our God says; we shall listen and obey.'

28 When the LORD heard these words which you spoke to me, he said, 'I have heard what this people has said to you; every word they have spoken is right. 29 Would that they may always be of a mind to fear me and observe my commandments, so that all will be well with them and their children for ever! 30 Go, and tell them to return to their tents, 31 but you yourself stand here beside me; I will set forth to you all the commandments, statutes, and laws which you are to teach them to observe in the land which I am about to give them to occupy.'

32 You must be careful to do as the LORD your God has commanded you; do not deviate from it to right or to left. 33 You must conform to all the LORD your God commands you, if you would live and prosper and remain long in the land you are to occupy.

6 These are the commandments, statutes, and laws which the LORD your God commanded me to teach you to observe in the land into which you are crossing to occupy it, a land flowing with milk and honey, 2 so that you may fear the LORD your God and keep all his statutes and commandments which I am giving you, both you, your children, and your descendants all your days, that you may enjoy long life. 3 If you listen, Israel, and are careful to observe them, you will prosper and increase greatly as the LORD the God of your forefathers promised you.

4 Hear, Israel: the LORD is our God, the LORD our one God; 5 and you must love the LORD your God with all your heart and with all your soul and with all your strength. 6 These commandments which I give you this day are to be remembered and taken to heart; 7 repeat them to your children, and speak of them both indoors and out of doors, when you lie down and when you get up. 8 Bind them as a

---

m Or kill *n* Or *The LORD our God is one LORD*, or *The LORD our God, the LORD is one*, or *The LORD is our God, the LORD is one*

6:1 **a land . . . honey:** *transposed from verse 3.* 6:4 **LORD:** *see note on Exod. 3:15.*

NEW AMERICAN BIBLE

16 'Honor your father and your mother, as the LORD, your God, has commanded you, that you may have a long life and prosperity in the land which the LORD, your God, is giving you.

17 'You shall not kill.

18 'You shall not commit adultery.

19 'You shall not steal.

20 'You shall not bear dishonest witness against your neighbor.

21 'You shall not covet your neighbor's wife.

'You shall not desire your neighbor's house or field, nor his male or female slave, nor his ox or ass, nor anything that belongs to him.'

22 "These words, and nothing more, the LORD spoke with a loud voice to your entire assembly on the mountain from the midst of the fire and the dense cloud. He wrote them upon two tablets of stone and gave them to me. 23 But when you heard the voice from the midst of the darkness, while the mountain was ablaze with fire, you came to me in the person of all your tribal heads and elders, 24 and said, 'The LORD, our God, has indeed let us see his glory and his majesty! We have heard his voice from the midst of the fire and have found out today that a man can still live after God has spoken with him. 25 But why should we die now? Surely this great fire will consume us. If we hear the voice of the LORD, our God, any more, we shall die. 26 For what mortal has heard, as we have, the voice of the living God speaking from the midst of fire, and survived? 27 Go closer, you, and hear all that the LORD, our God, will say, and then tell us what the LORD, our God, tells you; we will listen and obey.'

28 "The LORD heard your words as you were speaking to me and said to me, 'I have heard the words these people have spoken to you, which are all well said. 29 Would that they might always be of such a mind, to fear me and to keep all my commandments! Then they and their descendants would prosper forever. 30 Go, tell them to return to their tents. 31 Then you wait here near me and I will give you all the commandments, the statutes and decrees you must teach them, that they may observe them in the land which I am giving them to possess.'

32 "Be careful, therefore, to do as the LORD, your God, has commanded you, not turning aside to the right or to the left, 33 but following exactly the way prescribed for you by the LORD, your God, that you may live and prosper, and may have long life in the land which you are to occupy.

6 "These then are the commandments, the statutes and decrees which the LORD, your God, has ordered that you be taught to observe in the land into which you are crossing for conquest, 2 so that you and your son and your grandson may fear the LORD, your God, and keep, throughout the days of your lives, all his statutes and commandments which I enjoin on you, and thus have long life. 3 Hear then, Israel, and be careful to observe them, that you may grow and prosper the more, in keeping with the promise of the LORD, the God of your fathers, to give you a land flowing with milk and honey.

4 "Hear, O Israel! The LORD is our God, the LORD alone! 5 Therefore, you shall love the LORD, your God, with all your heart, and with all your soul, and with all your strength. 6 Take to heart these words which I enjoin on you today. 7 Drill them into your children. Speak of them at home and abroad, whether you are busy or at rest. 8 Bind

NEW JERUSALEM BIBLE

16 ' "Honour your father and your mother, as Yahweh your God has commanded you, so that you may have long life and may prosper in the country which Yahweh your God is giving you.

17 ' "You must not kill.

18 ' "You must not commit adultery.

19 ' "You must not steal.

20 ' "You must not give false evidence against your fellow.

21 ' "You must not set your heart on your neighbour's spouse, you must not set your heart on your neighbour's house, or field, or servant — man or woman — or ox, or donkey or any of your neighbour's possessions."

22 'These were the words Yahweh spoke to you when you were all assembled on the mountain. Thunderously, he spoke to you from the heart of the fire, in cloud and thick darkness. He added nothing, but wrote them on two tablets of stone which he gave to me.

23 'Now, having heard this voice coming out of the darkness, while the mountain was all on fire, you came to me, all of you, heads of tribes and elders, 24 and said, "Yahweh our God has shown us his glory and his greatness, and we have heard his voice from the heart of the fire. Today we have seen that God can speak with a human being and that person still live. 25 So why should we expose ourselves to death again? For this great fire might devour us if we go on listening to the voice of Yahweh our God, and then we should die. 26 For what creature of flesh could possibly live after hearing, as we have heard, the voice of the living God speaking from the heart of the fire? 27 Go nearer yourself and listen to everything that Yahweh our God may say, and then tell us everything that Yahweh our God has told you; we shall listen and put it into practice!"

28 'Yahweh heard what you were saying to me, and he then said to me, "I have heard what these people are saying. Everything they have said is well said. 29 If only their heart were always so, set on fearing me and on keeping my commandments, so that they and their children might prosper for ever! 30 Go and tell them to go back to their tents. 31 But you yourself stay here with me, and I shall tell you all the commandments, the laws and the customs which you are to teach them and which they are to observe in the country which I am giving them as their possession."

32 'Keep them and put them into practice: such is Yahweh's command to you. Stray neither to right nor to left. 33 Follow the whole way that Yahweh has marked for you, and you will survive to prosper and live long in the country which you are going to possess.'

6 'Such, then, are the commandments, the laws and the customs which Yahweh your God has instructed me to teach you, for you to observe in the country which you are on your way to possess. 2 And hence, if, throughout your lives, you fear Yahweh your God and keep all his laws and commandments, which I am laying down for you today, you will live long, you and your child and your grandchild. 3 Listen then, Israel, keep and observe what will make you prosperous and numerous, as Yahweh, God of your ancestors, has promised you, in giving you a country flowing with milk and honey.

4 'Listen, Israel: Yahweh our God is the one, the only Yahweh. 5 You must love Yahweh your God with all your heart, with all your soul, with all your strength. 6 Let the words I enjoin on you today stay in your heart. 7 You shall tell them to your children, and keep on telling them, when you are sitting at home, when you are out and about, when you are lying down and when you are standing up; 8 you

hand, fix them as an emblem^o on your forehead, 9 and write them on the doorposts of your house and on your gates.

10 When the LORD your God has brought you into the land that he swore to your ancestors, to Abraham, to Isaac, and to Jacob, to give you — a land with fine, large cities that you did not build, 11 houses filled with all sorts of goods that you did not fill, hewn cisterns that you did not hew, vineyards and olive groves that you did not plant — and when you have eaten your fill, 12 take care that you do not forget the LORD, who brought you out of the land of Egypt, out of the house of slavery. 13 The LORD your God you shall fear; him you shall serve, and by his name alone you shall swear. 14 Do not follow other gods, any of the gods of the peoples who are all around you, 15 because the LORD your God, who is present with you, is a jealous God. The anger of the LORD your God would be kindled against you and he would destroy you from the face of the earth.

16 Do not put the LORD your God to the test, as you tested him at Massah. 17 You must diligently keep the commandments of the LORD your God, and his decrees, and his statutes that he has commanded you. 18 Do what is right and good in the sight of the LORD, so that it may go well with you, and so that you may go in and occupy the good land that the LORD swore to your ancestors to give you, 19 thrusting out all your enemies from before you, as the LORD has promised.

20 When your children ask you in time to come, "What is the meaning of the decrees and the statutes and the ordinances that the LORD our God has commanded you?" 21 then you shall say to your children, "We were Pharaoh's slaves in Egypt, but the LORD brought us out of Egypt with a mighty hand. 22 The LORD displayed before our eyes great and awesome signs and wonders against Egypt, against Pharaoh and all his household. 23 He brought us out from there in order to bring us in, to give us the land that he promised on oath to our ancestors. 24 Then the LORD commanded us to observe all these statutes, to fear the LORD our God, for our lasting good, so as to keep us alive, as is now the case. 25 If we diligently observe this entire commandment before the LORD our God, as he has commanded us, we will be in the right."

7 When the LORD your God brings you into the land that you are about to enter and occupy, and he clears away many nations before you — the Hittites, the Girgashites, the Amorites, the Canaanites, the Perizzites, the Hivites, and the Jebusites, seven nations mightier and more numerous than you — 2 and when the LORD your God gives them over to you and you defeat them, then you must utterly destroy them. Make no covenant with them and show them no mercy. 3 Do not intermarry with them, giving your daughters to their sons or taking their daughters for your sons, 4 for that would turn away your children from following me, to serve other gods. Then the anger of the LORD would be kindled against you, and he would destroy you quickly. 5 But this is how you must deal with them: break down their altars, smash their pillars, hew down their sacred poles,^p and burn their idols with fire. 6 For you are a people holy to the LORD your God; the LORD your God has chosen you out of all the peoples on earth to be his people, his treasured possession.

7 It was not because you were more numerous than any other people that the LORD set his heart on you and chose you — for you were the fewest of all peoples. 8 It was because the LORD loved you and kept the oath that he swore to your ancestors, that the LORD has brought you out with a mighty hand, and redeemed you from the house of slavery, from the hand of Pharaoh king of Egypt. 9 Know there-

sign on your hand and wear them as a pendant on your forehead; 9 write them on the doorposts of your houses and on your gates.

10 The LORD your God will bring you into the land which he swore to your forefathers Abraham, Isaac, and Jacob that he would give you, a land of large, fine towns which you did not build, 11 houses full of good things which you did not provide, cisterns hewn from the rock but not by you, and vineyards and olive groves which you did not plant. When he brings you in and you have all you want to eat, 12 see that you do not forget the LORD who brought you out of Egypt, out of that land of slavery. 13 You are to fear the LORD your God; serve him alone, and take your oaths in his name. 14 You must not go after other gods, gods of the nations around you; 15 if you do, the anger of the LORD your God who is among you will be roused against you, and he will sweep you off the face of the earth, for the LORD your God is a jealous God.

16 You must not put the LORD your God to the test as you did at Massah. 17 You must diligently keep the commandments of the LORD your God and the precepts and statutes which he gave you. 18 You must do what is right and good in the eyes of the LORD, so that all may go well with you, and you may enter and occupy the good land which the LORD promised on oath to your forefathers; 19 then, as the LORD promised, you will drive out all your enemies before you.

20 When in time to come your son asks you, 'What is the meaning of the precepts, statutes, and laws which the LORD our God gave you?' 21 say to him, 'We were Pharaoh's slaves in Egypt, and the LORD brought us out of Egypt with his strong hand. 22 He harrowed the Egyptians including Pharaoh and all his court with mighty signs and portents, as we saw for ourselves. 23 But he led us out from there to bring us into the land and give it to us as he had promised to our forefathers. 24 The LORD commanded us to observe all these statutes and to fear the LORD our God; it will be for our own good at all times, and he will continue to preserve our lives. 25 For us to be in the right we should keep all these commandments before the LORD our God, as he has commanded us to do.'

7 WHEN the LORD your God brings you into the land which you are about to enter to occupy it, when he drives out many nations before you — Hittites, Girgashites, Amorites, Canaanites, Perizzites, Hivites, and Jebusites, seven nations more numerous and powerful than you — 2 and when the LORD your God delivers them into your power for you to defeat, you must exterminate them. You must not make an alliance with them or spare them. 3 You must not intermarry with them, giving your daughters to their sons or taking their daughters for your sons, 4 because if you do, they will draw your children away from the LORD to serve other gods. Then the anger of the LORD will be roused against you and he will soon destroy you. 5 But this is what you must do to them: pull down their altars, break their sacred pillars, hack down their sacred poles, and burn their idols, 6 for you are a people holy to the LORD your God, and he has chosen you out of all peoples on earth to be his special possession.

7 It was not because you were more numerous than any other nation that the LORD cared for you and chose you, for you were the smallest of all nations; 8 it was because the LORD loved you and stood by his oath to your forefathers, that he brought you out with his strong hand and redeemed you from the place of slavery, from the power of Pharaoh king of Egypt. 9 Know then that the LORD your God is God,

^o Or *as a frontlet*   ^p Heb *Asherim*

NEW AMERICAN BIBLE

NEW JERUSALEM BIBLE

them at your wrist as a sign and let them be as a pendant on your forehead. 9 Write them on the doorposts of your houses and on your gates.

10 "When the LORD, your God, brings you into the land which he swore to your fathers, Abraham, Isaac and Jacob, that he would give you, a land with fine, large cities that you did not build, 11 with houses full of goods of all sorts that you did not garner, with cisterns that you did not dig, with vineyards and olive groves that you did not plant; and when, therefore, you eat your fill, 12 take care not to forget the LORD, who brought you out of the land of Egypt, that place of slavery. 13 The LORD, your God, shall you fear; him shall you serve, and by his name shall you swear. 14 You shall not follow other gods, such as those of the surrounding nations, 15 lest the wrath of the LORD, your God, flare up against you and he destroy you from the face of the land; for the LORD, your God, who is in your midst, is a jealous God.

16 "You shall not put the LORD, your God, to the test, as you did at Massah. 17 But keep the commandments of the LORD, your God, and the ordinances and statutes he has enjoined on you. 18 Do what is right and good in the sight of the LORD, that you may, according to his word, prosper, and may enter in and possess the good land which the LORD promised on oath to your fathers, 19 thrusting all your enemies out of your way.

20 "Later on, when your son asks you what these ordinances, statutes and decrees mean which the LORD, our God, has enjoined on you, 21 you shall say to your son, 'We were once slaves of Pharaoh in Egypt, but the LORD brought us out of Egypt with his strong hand 22 and wrought before our eyes signs and wonders, great and dire, against Egypt and against Pharaoh and his whole house. 23 He brought us from there to lead us into the land he promised on oath to our fathers, and to give it to us. 24 Therefore, the LORD commanded us to observe all these statutes in fear of the LORD, our God, that we may always have as prosperous and happy a life as we have today; 25 and our justice before the LORD, our God, is to consist in carefully observing all these commandments he has enjoined on us.'

7 "When the LORD, your God, brings you into the land which you are to enter and occupy, and dislodges great nations before you — the Hittites, Girgashites, Amorites, Canaanites, Perizzites, Hivites and Jebusites: seven nations more numerous and powerful than you — 2 and when the LORD, your God, delivers them up to you and you defeat them, you shall doom them. Make no covenant with them and show them no mercy. 3 You shall not intermarry with them, neither giving your daughters to their sons nor taking their daughters for your sons. 4 For they would turn your sons from following me to serving other gods, and then the wrath of the LORD would flare up against you and quickly destroy you.

5 "But this is how you must deal with them: Tear down their altars, smash their sacred pillars, chop down their sacred poles, and destroy their idols by fire. 6 For you are a people sacred to the LORD, your God; he has chosen you from all the nations on the face of the earth to be a people peculiarly his own. 7 It was not because you are the largest of all nations that the LORD set his heart on you and chose you, for you are really the smallest of all nations. 8 It was because the LORD loved you and because of his fidelity to the oath he had sworn to your fathers, that he brought you out with his strong hand from the place of slavery, and ransomed you from the hand of Pharaoh, king of Egypt.

must fasten them on your hand as a sign and on your forehead as a headband; 9 you must write them on the doorposts of your house and on your gates.

10 'When Yahweh has brought you into the country which he swore to your ancestors Abraham, Isaac and Jacob that he would give you, with great and prosperous cities you have not built, 11 with houses full of good things you have not provided, with wells you have not dug, with vineyards and olive trees you have not planted, and then, when you have eaten as much as you want, 12 be careful you do not forget Yahweh who has brought you out of Egypt, out of the place of slave-labour. 13 Yahweh your God is the one you must fear, him alone you must serve, his is the name by which you must swear.

14 'Do not follow other gods, gods of the peoples round you, 15 for Yahweh your God among you is a jealous God; the wrath of Yahweh your God would blaze out against you, and he would wipe you off the face of the earth. 16 Do not put Yahweh your God to the test as you tested him at Massah. 17 Keep the commandments of Yahweh your God, and his instructions and laws which he has laid down for you, 18 and do what Yahweh regards as right and good, so that you may prosper and take possession of the fine country which Yahweh swore to give your ancestors, 19 driving out your enemies before you; such was Yahweh's promise.

20 'In times to come, when your child asks you, "What is the meaning of these instructions, laws and customs which Yahweh our God has laid down for you?" 21 you are to tell your child, "Once we were Pharaoh's slaves in Egypt, and Yahweh brought us out of Egypt by his mighty hand. 22 Before our eyes, Yahweh worked great and terrible signs and wonders against Egypt, against Pharaoh and his entire household. 23 And he brought us out of there, to lead us into the country which he had sworn to our ancestors that he would give us. 24 And Yahweh has commanded us to observe all these laws and to fear Yahweh our God, so as to be happy for ever and to survive, as we do to this day. 25 For us, right living will mean this: to keep and observe all these commandments in obedience to Yahweh our God, as he has commanded us." '

7 'When Yahweh your God has brought you into the country which you are going to make your own, many nations will fall before you: Hittites, Girgashites, Amorites, Canaanites, Perizzites, Hivites and Jebusites, seven nations greater and stronger than yourselves. 2 Yahweh your God will put them at your mercy and you will conquer them. You must put them under the curse of destruction. You must not make any treaty with them or show them any pity. 3 You must not intermarry with them; you must not give a daughter of yours to a son of theirs, or take a daughter of theirs for a son of yours, 4 for your son would be seduced from following me into serving other gods; the wrath of Yahweh would blaze out against you and he would instantly destroy you. 5 Instead, treat them like this: tear down their altars, smash their standing-stones, cut down their sacred poles and burn their idols. 6 For you are a people consecrated to Yahweh your God; of all the peoples on earth, you have been chosen by Yahweh your God to be his own people.

7 'Yahweh set his heart on you and chose you not because you were the most numerous of all peoples — for indeed you were the smallest of all — 8 but because he loved you and meant to keep the oath which he swore to your ancestors: that was why Yahweh brought you out with his mighty hand and redeemed you from the place of slave-labour, from the power of Pharaoh king of Egypt. 9 From this you can see

fore that the LORD your God is God, the faithful God who maintains covenant loyalty with those who love him and keep his commandments, to a thousand generations, 10 and who repays in their own person those who reject him. He does not delay but repays in their own person those who reject him. 11 Therefore, observe diligently the commandment — the statutes, and the ordinances — that I am commanding you today.

12 If you heed these ordinances, by diligently observing them, the LORD your God will maintain with you the covenant loyalty that he swore to your ancestors; 13 he will love you, bless you, and multiply you; he will bless the fruit of your womb and the fruit of your ground, your grain and your wine and your oil, the increase of your cattle and the issue of your flock, in the land that he swore to your ancestors to give you. 14 You shall be the most blessed of peoples, with neither sterility nor barrenness among you or your livestock. 15 The LORD will turn away from you every illness; all the dread diseases of Egypt that you experienced, he will not inflict on you, but he will lay them on all who hate you. 16 You shall devour all the peoples that the LORD your God is giving over to you, showing them no pity; you shall not serve their gods, for that would be a snare to you.

17 If you say to yourself, "These nations are more numerous than I; how can I dispossess them?" 18 do not be afraid of them. Just remember what the LORD your God did to Pharaoh and to all Egypt, 19 the great trials that your eyes saw, the signs and wonders, the mighty hand and the outstretched arm by which the LORD your God brought you out. The LORD your God will do the same to all the peoples of whom you are afraid. 20 Moreover, the LORD your God will send the pestilence*q* against them, until even the survivors and the fugitives are destroyed. 21 Have no dread of them, for the LORD your God, who is present with you, is a great and awesome God. 22 The LORD your God will clear away these nations before you little by little; you will not be able to make a quick end of them, otherwise the wild animals would become too numerous for you. 23 But the LORD your God will give them over to you, and throw them into great panic, until they are destroyed. 24 He will hand their kings over to you and you shall blot out their name from under heaven; no one will be able to stand against you, until you have destroyed them. 25 The images of their gods you shall burn with fire. Do not covet the silver or the gold that is on them and take it for yourself, because you could be ensnared by it; for it is abhorrent to the LORD your God. 26 Do not bring an abhorrent thing into your house, or you will be set apart for destruction like it. You must utterly detest and abhor it, for it is set apart for destruction.

8 This entire commandment that I command you today you must diligently observe, so that you may live and increase, and go in and occupy the land that the LORD promised on oath to your ancestors. 2 Remember the long way that the LORD your God has led you these forty years in the wilderness, in order to humble you, testing you to know what was in your heart, whether or not you would keep his commandments. 3 He humbled you by letting you hunger, then by feeding you with manna, with which neither you nor your ancestors were acquainted, in order to make you understand that one does not live by bread alone, but by every word that comes from the mouth of the LORD.*r* 4 The clothes on your back did not wear out and your feet did not swell these forty years. 5 Know then in

the faithful God; with those who love him and keep his commandments he keeps covenant and faith for a thousand generations, 10 but those who defy and reject him he repays with destruction: he will not be slow to requite any who reject him.

11 You are to observe these commandments, statutes, and laws which I give you this day, and keep them.

12 Because you listen to these laws and are careful to observe them, the LORD your God will observe the sworn covenant he made with your forefathers and will keep faith with you. 13 He will love you, bless you, and increase your numbers. He will bless the fruit of your body and the fruit of your soil, your grain and new wine and oil, the young of your herds and lambing flocks, in the land which he swore to your forefathers he would give you. 14 You will be blessed above every other nation; neither among your people nor among your cattle will there be an impotent male or a barren female. 15 The LORD will keep you free from all sickness; he will not bring on you any of the foul diseases of Egypt which you have experienced; but he will bring them on all who are hostile to you. 16 You are to devour all the nations which the LORD your God is giving over to you. Show none of them mercy, so that you do not serve their gods; that is the snare which awaits you.

17 You may say to yourselves, 'These nations outnumber us; how can we drive them out?' 18 You need have no fear of them; only bear in mind what the LORD your God did to Pharaoh and the whole of Egypt, 19 the great challenge which you yourselves witnessed, the signs and portents, the strong hand and the outstretched arm by which the LORD your God brought you out. So will he deal with all the nations of whom you are afraid. 20 Moreover the LORD will spread panic among them until all who are left and are in hiding will perish before you.

21 Feel no dread of them, for the LORD your God is among you, a great and terrible God. 22 Little by little he will drive out these nations before you. You cannot exterminate them quickly, for fear the wild beasts become too numerous for you. 23 The LORD your God will deliver these nations over to you and throw them into utter confusion until they are wiped out. 24 He will put their kings into your hands, and you must wipe out their name from under heaven. No one will be able to withstand you; you will destroy them. 25 Their idols you must destroy by fire; you are not to covet the silver and gold on them and take it for yourselves; you might be ensnared by it, and these things are an abomination to the LORD your God. 26 You must not introduce any abominable idol into your houses and thus bring yourselves under solemn ban along with it. You shall hold it loathsome and abominable, for it is proscribed under the ban.

8 You must carefully observe every command I give you this day so that you may live and increase in numbers and enter and occupy the land which the LORD promised on oath to your forefathers. 2 Remember the whole way by which the LORD your God has led you these forty years in the wilderness to humble and test you, and to discover whether or not it was in your heart to keep his commandments. 3 So he afflicted you with hunger and then fed you on manna which neither you nor your fathers had known before, to teach you that people cannot live on bread alone, but that they live on every word that comes from the mouth of the LORD. 4 The clothes on your backs did not wear out, nor did your feet blister, all these forty years. 5 Take to heart

q Or *hornets*: Meaning of Heb uncertain   *r* Or *by anything that the* LORD *decrees*

9 Understand, then, that the LORD, your God, is God indeed, the faithful God who keeps his merciful covenant down to the thousandth generation toward those who love him and keep his commandments, 10 but who repays with destruction the person who hates him; he does not dally with such a one, but makes him personally pay for it. 11 You shall therefore carefully observe the commandments, the statutes and the decrees which I enjoin on you today.

12 "As your reward for heeding these decrees and observing them carefully, the LORD, your God, will keep with you the merciful covenant which he promised on oath to your fathers. 13 He will love and bless and multiply you; he will bless the fruit of your womb and the produce of your soil, your grain and wine and oil, the issue of your herds and the young of your flocks, in the land which he swore to your fathers he would give you. 14 You will be blessed above all peoples; no man or woman among you shall be childless nor shall your livestock be barren. 15 The LORD will remove all sickness from you; he will not afflict you with any of the malignant diseases that you know from Egypt, but will leave them with all your enemies.

16 "You shall consume all the nations which the LORD, your God, will deliver up to you. You are not to look on them with pity, lest you be ensnared into serving their gods. 17 Perhaps you will say to yourselves, 'These nations are greater than we. How can we dispossess them?' 18 But do not be afraid of them. Rather, call to mind what the LORD, your God, did to Pharaoh and to all Egypt: 19 the great testings which your own eyes have seen, the signs and wonders, his strong hand and outstretched arm with which the LORD, your God, brought you out. The same also will he do to all the nations of whom you are now afraid. 20 Moreover, the LORD, your God, will send hornets among them, until the survivors who have hidden from you are destroyed. 21 Therefore, do not be terrified by them, for the LORD, your God, who is in your midst, is a great and awesome God. 22 He will dislodge these nations before you little by little. You cannot exterminate them all at once, lest the wild beasts become too numerous for you. 23 The LORD, your God, will deliver them up to you and will rout them utterly until they are annihilated. 24 He will deliver their kings into your hand, that you may make their names perish from under the heavens. No man will be able to stand up against you, till you have put an end to them. 25 The images of their gods you shall destroy by fire. Do not covet the silver or gold on them, nor take it for yourselves, lest you be ensnared by it; for it is an abomination to the LORD, your God. 26 You shall not bring any abominable thing into your house, lest you be doomed with it; loathe and abhor it utterly as a thing that is doomed.

8 "Be careful to observe all the commandments I enjoin on you today, that you may live and increase, and may enter in and possess the land which the LORD promised on oath to your fathers. 2 Remember how for forty years now the LORD, your God, has directed all your journeying in the desert, so as to test you by affliction and find out whether or not it was your intention to keep his commandments. 3 He therefore let you be afflicted with hunger, and then fed you with manna, a food unknown to you and your fathers, in order to show you that not by bread alone does man live, but by every word that comes forth from the mouth of the LORD. 4 The clothing did not fall from you in tatters, nor did your feet swell these forty years. 5 So you must realize that

that Yahweh your God is the true God, the faithful God who, though he is true to his covenant and his faithful love for a thousand generations as regards those who love him and keep his commandments, 10 punishes in their own persons those that hate him. He destroys anyone who hates him, without delay; and it is in their own persons that he punishes them. 11 Hence, you must keep and observe the commandments, laws and customs which I am laying down for you today.

12 'Listen to these ordinances, be true to them and observe them, and in return Yahweh your God will be true to the covenant and love which he promised on oath to your ancestors. 13 He will love you and bless you and increase your numbers; he will bless the fruit of your body and the produce of your soil, your corn, your new wine, your oil, the issue of your cattle, the young of your flock, in the country which he swore to your ancestors that he would give you. 14 You will be the most blessed of all peoples. None of you, man or woman, will be sterile, no male or female of your beasts infertile. 15 Yahweh will deflect all illness from you; he will not afflict you with those evil plagues of Egypt which you have known, but will inflict them on all who hate you.

16 'So, devour all the peoples whom Yahweh your God puts at your mercy, show them no pity, do not serve their gods: or you will be ensnared.

17 'You may say in your heart, "These nations outnumber me; how shall I be able to dispossess them?" 18 Do not be afraid of them: remember how Yahweh your God treated Pharaoh and all Egypt, 19 the great ordeals that you yourselves have seen, the signs and wonders, the mighty hand and outstretched arm with which Yahweh your God brought you out. This is how Yahweh your God will treat all the peoples whom you fear to face. 20 And what is more, Yahweh your God will send hornets to destroy those who are left and who hide from you.

21 'Do not be afraid of them, for Yahweh your God is among you, a great and terrible God. 22 Little by little, Yahweh your God will clear away these nations before you; you cannot destroy them all at once, or wild animals will breed and be disastrous for you. 23 But Yahweh your God will put them at your mercy, and disaster after disaster will overtake them until they are finally destroyed. 24 He will put their kings at your mercy and you will blot out their names under heaven; no one will be able to resist you — until you have destroyed them all.

25 'You must burn the statues of their gods, not coveting the gold and silver that covers them; take it and you will be caught in a snare: it is detestable to Yahweh your God. 26 You must not bring any detestable thing into your house: or you, like it, will come under the curse of destruction. You must regard them as unclean and loathsome, for they are under the curse of destruction.'

8 'You must keep and put into practice all the commandments which I enjoin on you today, so that you may survive and increase in numbers and enter the country which Yahweh promised on oath to your ancestors, and make it your own. 2 Remember the long road by which Yahweh your God led you for forty years in the desert, to humble you, to test you and know your inmost heart — whether you would keep his commandments or not. 3 He humbled you, he made you feel hunger, he fed you with manna which neither you nor your ancestors had ever known, to make you understand that human beings live not on bread alone but on every word that comes from the mouth of Yahweh. 4 The clothes on your back did not wear out and your feet were not swollen, all those forty years.

| NEW REVISED STANDARD VERSION | REVISED ENGLISH BIBLE |

your heart that as a parent disciplines a child so the LORD your God disciplines you. 6 Therefore keep the commandments of the LORD your God, by walking in his ways and by fearing him. 7 For the LORD your God is bringing you into a good land, a land with flowing streams, with springs and underground waters welling up in valleys and hills, 8 a land of wheat and barley, of vines and fig trees and pomegranates, a land of olive trees and honey, 9 a land where you may eat bread without scarcity, where you will lack nothing, a land whose stones are iron and from whose hills you may mine copper. 10 You shall eat your fill and bless the LORD your God for the good land that he has given you.

11 Take care that you do not forget the LORD your God, by failing to keep his commandments, his ordinances, and his statutes, which I am commanding you today. 12 When you have eaten your fill and have built fine houses and live in them, 13 and when your herds and flocks have multiplied, and your silver and gold is multiplied, and all that you have is multiplied, 14 then do not exalt yourself, forgetting the LORD your God, who brought you out of the land of Egypt, out of the house of slavery, 15 who led you through the great and terrible wilderness, an arid wasteland with poisonous⁵ snakes and scorpions. He made water flow for you from flint rock, 16 and fed you in the wilderness with manna that your ancestors did not know, to humble you and to test you, and in the end to do you good. 17 Do not say to yourself, "My power and the might of my own hand have gotten me this wealth." 18 But remember the LORD your God, for it is he who gives you power to get wealth, so that he may confirm his covenant that he swore to your ancestors, as he is doing today. 19 If you do forget the LORD your God and follow other gods to serve and worship them, I solemnly warn you today that you shall surely perish. 20 Like the nations that the LORD is destroying before you, so shall you perish, because you would not obey the voice of the LORD your God.

9 Hear, O Israel! You are about to cross the Jordan today, to go in and dispossess nations larger and mightier than you, great cities, fortified to the heavens, 2 a strong and tall people, the offspring of the Anakim, whom you know. You have heard it said of them, "Who can stand up to the Anakim?" 3 Know then today that the LORD your God is the one who crosses over before you as a devouring fire; he will defeat them and subdue them before you, so that you may dispossess and destroy them quickly, as the LORD has promised you.

4 When the LORD your God thrusts them out before you, do not say to yourself, "It is because of my righteousness that the LORD has brought me in to occupy this land"; it is rather because of the wickedness of these nations that the LORD is dispossessing them before you. 5 It is not because of your righteousness or the uprightness of your heart that you are going in to occupy their land; but because of the wickedness of these nations the LORD your God is dispossessing them before you, in order to fulfill the promise that the LORD made on oath to your ancestors, to Abraham, to Isaac, and to Jacob.

6 Know, then, that the LORD your God is not giving you this good land to occupy because of your righteousness; for you are a stubborn people. 7 Remember and do not forget how you provoked the LORD your God to wrath in the wilderness; you have been rebellious against the LORD from the day you came out of the land of Egypt until you came to this place.

this lesson: that the LORD your God was disciplining you as a father disciplines his son. 6 Keep the commandments of the LORD your God, conforming to his ways and fearing him.

7 The LORD your God is bringing you to a good land, a land with streams, springs, and underground waters gushing out in valley and hill, 8 a land with wheat and barley, vines, fig trees, and pomegranates, a land with olive oil and honey. 9 It is a land where you will never suffer any scarcity of food to eat, nor want for anything, a land whose stones are iron ore and from whose hills you will mine copper. 10 When you have plenty to eat, bless the LORD your God for the good land he has given you.

11 See that you do not forget the LORD your God by failing to keep his commandments, laws, and statutes which I give you this day. 12 When you have plenty to eat and live in fine houses of your own building, 13 when your herds and flocks, your silver and gold, and all your possessions increase, 14 do not become proud and forget the LORD your God who brought you out of Egypt, out of that land of slavery; 15 he led you through the vast and terrible wilderness infested with venomous snakes and scorpions, a thirsty, waterless land where he caused water to flow for you from the flinty rock; 16 he fed you in the wilderness with manna which your fathers had never known, to humble and test you, and in the end to make you prosper. 17 Nor must you say to yourselves, 'My own strength and energy have gained me this wealth.' 18 Remember the LORD your God; it is he who gives you strength to become prosperous, so fulfilling the covenant guaranteed by oath with your forefathers, as he does to this day.

19 If you forget the LORD your God and go after other gods, serving them and bowing down to them, I give you a solemn warning this day that you will certainly be destroyed. 20 Because of your disobedience to the LORD your God, you will be destroyed as surely as were the nations whom the LORD destroyed at your coming.

9 Hear, Israel; this day you will be crossing the Jordan to go in and occupy the territory of nations greater and more powerful than you, and great cities with fortifications towering to the sky. 2 They are a great and tall people, the descendants of the Anakim, of whom you know, for you have heard it said, 'Who can withstand the sons of Anak?' 3 Know then this day that it is the LORD your God himself who crosses at your head as a devouring fire; it is he who will subdue them and destroy them as you advance; you will drive them out and soon overwhelm them, as he promised you.

4 When the LORD your God drives them out before you, do not say to yourselves, 'It is because of our merits that the LORD has brought us in to occupy this land.' 5 It is not because of your merit or your integrity that you are entering their land to occupy it; it is because of the wickedness of these nations that the LORD your God is driving them out before you, and to fulfil the promise which the LORD made on oath to your forefathers, Abraham, Isaac, and Jacob.

6 Know that it is not because of any merit of yours that the LORD your God is giving you this good land to occupy; indeed, you are a stubborn people. 7 Remember, and never forget, how you angered the LORD your God in the wilderness: from the day you left Egypt until you came to this

9:4 this land: so Gk; Heb. adds and because of the wickedness of these nations the LORD is driving them out before you.

⁵ Or fiery; Heb seraph

NEW AMERICAN BIBLE

NEW JERUSALEM BIBLE

the LORD, your God, disciplines you even as a man disciplines his son.

6 "Therefore, keep the commandments of the LORD, your God, by walking in his ways and fearing him. 7 For the LORD, your God, is bringing you into a good country, a land with streams of water, with springs and fountains welling up in the hills and valleys, 8 a land of wheat and barley, of vines and fig trees and pomegranates, of olive trees and of honey, 9 a land where you can eat bread without stint and where you will lack nothing, a land whose stones contain iron and in whose hills you can mine copper. 10 But when you have eaten your fill, you must bless the LORD, your God, for the good country he has given you. 11 Be careful not to forget the LORD, your God, by neglecting his commandments and decrees and statutes which I enjoin on you today: 12 lest, when you have eaten your fill, and have built fine houses and lived in them, 13 and have increased your herds and flocks, your silver and gold, and all your property, 14 you then become haughty of heart and unmindful of the LORD, your God, who brought you out of the land of Egypt, that place of slavery; 15 who guided you through the vast and terrible desert with its saraph serpents and scorpions, its parched and waterless ground; who brought forth water for you from the flinty rock 16 and fed you in the desert with manna, a food unknown to your fathers, that he might afflict you and test you, but also make you prosperous in the end. 17 Otherwise, you might say to yourselves, 'It is my own power and the strength of my own hand that has obtained for me this wealth.' 18 Remember then, it is the LORD, your God, who gives you the power to acquire wealth, by fulfilling, as he has now done, the covenant which he swore to your fathers. 19 But if you forget the LORD, your God, and follow other gods, serving and worshiping them, I forewarn you this day that you will perish utterly. 20 Like the nations which the LORD destroys before you, so shall you too perish for not heeding the voice of the LORD, your God.

9 "Hear, O Israel! You are now about to cross the Jordan to enter in and dispossess nations greater and stronger than yourselves, having large cities fortified to the sky, 2 the Anakim, a people great and tall. You know of them and have heard it said of them, 'Who can stand up against the Anakim?' 3 Understand, then, today that it is the LORD, your God, who will cross over before you as a consuming fire; he it is who will reduce them to nothing and subdue them before you, so that you can drive them out and destroy them quickly, as the LORD promised you. 4 After the LORD, your God, has thrust them out of your way, do not say to yourselves, 'It is because of my merits that the LORD has brought me in to possess this land'; for it is really because of the wickedness of these nations that the LORD is driving them out before you. 5 No, it is not because of your merits or the integrity of your heart that you are going in to take possession of their land; but the LORD, your God, is driving these nations out before you on account of their wickedness and in order to keep the promise which he made on oath to your fathers, Abraham, Isaac and Jacob. 6 Understand this, therefore: it is not because of your merits that the LORD, your God, is giving you this good land to possess, for you are a stiff-necked people.

7 "Bear in mind and do not forget how you angered the LORD, your God, in the desert. From the day you left the land of Egypt until you arrived in this place, you have been

5 'Learn from this that Yahweh your God was training you as a man trains his child, 6 and keep the commandments of Yahweh your God, and so follow his ways and fear him. 7 'But Yahweh your God is bringing you into a fine country, a land of streams and springs, of waters that well up from the deep in valleys and hills, 8 a land of wheat and barley, of vines, of figs, of pomegranates, a land of olives, of oil, of honey, 9 a land where you will eat bread without stint, where you will want nothing, a land where the stones are iron and where the hills may be quarried for copper. 10 You will eat and have all you want and you will bless Yahweh your God in the fine country which he has given you.

11 'Be careful not to forget Yahweh your God, by neglecting his commandments, customs and laws which I am laying down for you today. 12 When you have eaten all you want, when you have built fine houses to live in, 13 when you have seen your flocks and herds increase, your silver and gold abound and all your possessions grow great, 14 do not become proud of heart. Do not then forget Yahweh your God who brought you out of Egypt, out of the place of slave-labour, 15 who guided you through this vast and dreadful desert, a land of fiery snakes, scorpions, thirst; 16 who in this waterless place brought you water out of the flinty rock; who in this desert fed you with manna unknown to your ancestors, to humble you and test you and so make your future the happier. 17 'Beware of thinking to yourself, "My own strength and the might of my own hand have given me the power to act like this." 18 Remember Yahweh your God; he was the one who gave you the strength to act effectively like this, thus keeping then, as today, the covenant which he swore to your ancestors. 19 Be sure: if you forget Yahweh your God, if you follow other gods, if you serve them and bow down to them—I testify to you today—you will perish. 20 Like the nations Yahweh is to destroy before you, so you yourselves will perish, for not having listened to the voice of Yahweh your God.'

9 'Listen, Israel; today you are about to cross the Jordan, to go and dispossess nations greater and stronger than yourself, and cities immense, with walls reaching to the sky. 2 A people great and tall, these Anakim, as you know; you have heard the saying: Who can stand up to the sons of Anak? 3 Know then today that Yahweh your God himself will go ahead of you, destroying them like a devouring fire, and that he himself will subdue them before you so that you can dispossess and quickly make an end of them, as Yahweh has already said. 4 Do not think to yourself, once Yahweh your God has driven them before you, "Yahweh has brought me into possession of this country because I am upright," when Yahweh is dispossessing these nations for you, because they do wrong. 5 You are not going into their country to take possession because of any right behaviour or uprightness on your part; rather, it is because of their wickedness that Yahweh is dispossessing these nations for you, and also to keep the pact which he swore to your ancestors, Abraham, Isaac and Jacob. 6 Be clear about this: Yahweh is not giving you possession of this fine country because of any right conduct on your part, for you are an obstinate people.

7 i 'Remember; never forget how you provoked Yahweh your God in the desert. From the very day that you left Egypt until you arrived here, you have been rebels against

NEW REVISED STANDARD VERSION

8 Even at Horeb you provoked the LORD to wrath, and the LORD was so angry with you that he was ready to destroy you. 9 When I went up the mountain to receive the stone tablets, the tablets of the covenant that the LORD made with you, I remained on the mountain forty days and forty nights; I neither ate bread nor drank water. 10 And the LORD gave me the two stone tablets written with the finger of God; on them were all the words that the LORD had spoken to you at the mountain out of the fire on the day of the assembly. 11 At the end of forty days and forty nights the LORD gave me the two stone tablets, the tablets of the covenant. 12 Then the LORD said to me, "Get up, go down quickly from here, for your people whom you have brought from Egypt have acted corruptly. They have been quick to turn from the way that I commanded them; they have cast an image for themselves." 13 Furthermore the LORD said to me, "I have seen that this people is indeed a stubborn people. 14 Let me alone that I may destroy them and blot out their name from under heaven; and I will make of you a nation mightier and more numerous than they."

15 So I turned and went down from the mountain, while the mountain was ablaze; the two tablets of the covenant were in my two hands. 16 Then I saw that you had indeed sinned against the LORD your God, by casting for yourselves an image of a calf; you had been quick to turn from the way that the LORD had commanded you. 17 So I took hold of the two tablets and flung them from my two hands, smashing them before your eyes. 18 Then I lay prostrate before the LORD as before, forty days and forty nights; I neither ate bread nor drank water, because of all the sin you had committed, provoking the LORD by doing what was evil in his sight. 19 For I was afraid that the anger that the LORD bore against you was so fierce that he would destroy you. But the LORD listened to me that time also. 20 The LORD was so angry with Aaron that he was ready to destroy him, but I interceded also on behalf of Aaron at that same time. 21 Then I took the sinful thing you had made, the calf, and burned it with fire and crushed it, grinding it thoroughly, until it was reduced to dust; and I threw the dust of it into the stream that runs down the mountain.

22 At Taberah also, and at Massah, and at Kibroth-hattaavah, you provoked the LORD to wrath. 23 And when the LORD sent you from Kadesh-barnea, saying, "Go up and occupy the land that I have given you," you rebelled against the command of the LORD your God, neither trusting him nor obeying him. 24 You have been rebellious against the LORD as long as he has[i] known you.

25 Throughout the forty days and forty nights that I lay prostrate before the LORD when the LORD intended to destroy you, 26 I prayed to the LORD and said, "Lord GOD, do not destroy the people who are your very own possession, whom you redeemed in your greatness, whom you brought out of Egypt with a mighty hand. 27 Remember your servants, Abraham, Isaac, and Jacob; pay no attention to the stubbornness of this people, their wickedness and their sin, 28 otherwise the land from which you have brought us might say, 'Because the LORD was not able to bring them into the land that he promised them, and because he hated them, he has brought them out to let them die in the wilderness.' 29 For they are the people of your very own possession, whom you brought out by your great power and by your outstretched arm."

10 At that time the LORD said to me, "Carve out two tablets of stone like the former ones, and come up to me on the mountain, and make an ark of wood. 2 I will

REVISED ENGLISH BIBLE

place you have defied the LORD. 8 Even at Horeb you roused the LORD's anger, and the LORD in his wrath was ready to destroy you. 9 When I went up the mountain to receive the stone tablets, the tablets of the covenant which the LORD made with you, I remained on the mountain forty days and forty nights without food or drink. 10 Then the LORD gave me the two stone tablets written with the finger of God, and on them were all the words the LORD had spoken to you from the heart of the fire, on the mountain during the day of the assembly. 11 At the end of forty days and forty nights the LORD gave me the two stone tablets, the tablets of the covenant, 12 and said to me, 'Go down from the mountain at once, because your people whom you brought out of Egypt have committed a monstrous act: they have lost no time in turning from the way which I commanded them to follow, and have cast for themselves a metal image.'

13 The LORD said to me, 'I have observed this people and I find them a stubborn people. 14 Let me be, and I shall destroy them and blot out their name from under heaven; and I shall make you a nation more powerful and numerous than they.'

15 I went back down the mountain; it was ablaze, and I had the two tablets of the covenant in my hands. 16 When I saw how you had sinned against the LORD your God and had made for yourselves a cast image of a bull-calf, losing no time in turning from the way the LORD had told you to follow, 17 I flung down the two tablets which I held and shattered them in the sight of you all. 18 Then, as before, I lay prostrate before the LORD, forty days and forty nights without food or drink, on account of all the sin that you had committed, and because, in doing what was wrong in the eyes of the LORD, you had provoked him to anger. 19 I was in dread of the LORD's anger and the wrath with which he threatened to destroy you; but once again the LORD listened to me. 20 The LORD was greatly incensed with Aaron also and would have killed him; so I interceded for him at that time. 21 I took the calf, that sinful object you had made, and burnt it and pounded it, grinding it until it was as fine as dust; then I flung its dust into the torrent that flowed down from the mountain.

22 At Taberah also you roused the LORD's anger, and at Massah, and at Kibroth-hattaavah. 23 Again, when the LORD sent you from Kadesh-barnea with orders to advance and occupy the land which he was giving you, you defied the LORD your God and did not trust him or obey him. 24 You were defiant from the day that the LORD first knew you. 25 Forty days and forty nights I lay prostrate before the LORD because he had threatened to destroy you; 26 I prayed to the LORD and said, 'Lord God, do not destroy your people, your own possession, whom you redeemed by your great power and brought out of Egypt by your strong hand. 27 Remember your servants, Abraham, Isaac, and Jacob, and overlook the stubbornness of this people, their wickedness, and their sin; 28 otherwise the people in the land from which you led us will say, "It is because the LORD was not able to bring them into the land which he promised them and because he hated them, that he has led them out to let them die in the wilderness." 29 But they are your people, your own possession, whom you brought out by your great strength, by your outstretched arm.'

10 AT that time the LORD said to me, 'Cut for yourself two stone tablets like the former ones, and make also a wooden chest, an ark. Come up to me on the mountain, 2 and I shall write on the tablets the words that were on

9:24 the LORD: so Samar.; Heb. I.   9:28 the people in: so Samar.; Heb. omits.

[i] Sam Gk: MT I have

NEW AMERICAN BIBLE

NEW JERUSALEM BIBLE

rebellious toward the LORD. 8 At Horeb you so provoked the LORD that he was angry enough to destroy you, 9 when I had gone up the mountain to receive the stone tablets of the covenant which the LORD made with you. Meanwhile I stayed on the mountain forty days and forty nights without eating or drinking, 10 till the LORD gave me the two tablets of stone inscribed, by God's own finger, with a copy of all the words that the LORD spoke to you on the mountain from the midst of the fire on the day of the assembly. 11 Then, at the end of the forty days and forty nights, when the LORD had given me the two stone tablets of the covenant, 12 he said to me, 'Go down from here now, quickly, for your people whom you have brought out of Egypt have become depraved; they have already turned aside from the way I pointed out to them and have made for themselves a molten idol. 13 I have seen now how stiff-necked this people is,' the LORD said to me. 14 'Let me be, that I may destroy them and blot out their name from under the heavens. I will then make of you a nation mightier and greater than they.'

15 "When I had come down again from the blazing, fiery mountain, with the two tablets of the covenant in both my hands, 16 I saw how you had sinned against the LORD, your God: you had already turned aside from the way which the LORD had pointed out to you by making for yourselves a molten calf! 17 Raising the two tablets with both hands I threw them from me and broke them before your eyes. 18 Then, as before, I lay prostrate before the LORD for forty days and forty nights without eating or drinking, because of all the sin you had committed in the sight of the LORD and the evil you had done to provoke him. 19 For I dreaded the fierce anger of the LORD against you: his wrath would destroy you. Yet once again the LORD listened to me. 20 With Aaron, too, the LORD was deeply angry, and would have killed him had I not prayed for him also at that time. 21 Then, taking the calf, the sinful object you had made, and fusing it with fire, I ground it down to powder as fine as dust, which I threw into the wadi that went down the mountainside.

22 "At Taberah, at Massah, and at Kibroth-hattaavah likewise, you provoked the LORD to anger. 23 And when he sent you up from Kadesh-barnea to take possession of the land he was giving you, you rebelled against this command of the LORD, your God, and would not trust or obey him. 24 Ever since I have known you, you have been rebels against the LORD.

25 "Those forty days, then, and forty nights, I lay prostrate before the LORD, because he had threatened to destroy you. 26 This was my prayer to him: O Lord GOD, destroy not your people, the heritage which your majesty has ransomed and brought out of Egypt with your strong hand. 27 Remember your servants, Abraham, Isaac and Jacob. Look not upon the stubbornness of this people nor upon their wickedness and sin, 28 lest the people from whose land you have brought us say, 'The LORD was not able to bring them into the land he promised them'; or 'Out of hatred for them he brought them out to slay them in the desert,' 29 They are, after all, your people and your heritage, whom you have brought out by your great power and with your outstretched arm.

10 "At that time the LORD said to me, 'Cut two tablets of stone like the former; then come up the mountain to me. Also make an ark of wood. 2 I will write upon the

Yahweh. 8 At Horeb, you provoked Yahweh, and Yahweh was so angry with you that he was ready to destroy you. 9 I had gone up the mountain to receive the stone tablets, the tablets of the covenant that Yahweh was making with you. I stayed forty days and forty nights on the mountain, with nothing to eat or drink. 10 Yahweh gave me the two stone tablets inscribed by the finger of God, exactly corresponding to what Yahweh had said to you on the mountain, from the heart of the fire, on the day of the Assembly. 11 After forty days and forty nights, having given me the two stone tablets, the tablets of the covenant, 12 Yahweh said to me, "Get up, go down quickly, for your people, whom you have brought out of Egypt, are corrupting one another. They have been quick to leave the way I marked out for them; they have cast themselves a metal idol." 13 Yahweh then said to me, "I have seen this people, and what an obstinate people they are! 14 Leave me, I am going to destroy them and wipe out their name under heaven; and I shall make you into a mightier and more numerous nation than they are!"

15 'I went back down the mountain, which was blazing with fire, and in my hands were the two tablets of the covenant. 16 When I looked, I saw that you had been sinning against Yahweh your God. You had cast yourselves a metal calf; you had been quick to leave the way marked out for you by Yahweh. 17 I seized the two tablets and with my two hands threw them down and broke them before your eyes. 18 Then I fell prostrate before Yahweh; as before, I spent forty days and forty nights with nothing to eat or drink, on account of all the sins which you had committed, by doing what was displeasing to Yahweh and thus arousing his anger. 19 For I was afraid of this anger, of the fury which so roused Yahweh against you that he was ready to destroy you. And, once again, Yahweh heard my prayer. 20 Yahweh was enraged with Aaron and was ready to destroy him too; I also pleaded for Aaron on that occasion. 21 That work of sin, the calf you had made, I took and burned and broke to pieces; having ground it to the finest dust, I threw its dust into the stream that comes down from the mountain.

22 'At Taberah too and at Massah and Kibroth-ha-Taavah, you provoked Yahweh. 23 And when Yahweh, meaning you to leave Kadesh-Barnea, said, "Go up and take possession of the country which I have given you," you rebelled against the command of Yahweh your God and would not believe him or listen to his voice. 24 You have been rebels against Yahweh from the day he first knew you.

25 'So I fell prostrate before Yahweh and lay there those forty days and forty nights, Yahweh having said that he was going to destroy you. 26 And I pleaded with Yahweh. "My Lord Yahweh," I said, "do not destroy your people, your heritage whom in your greatness you have redeemed, whom you have brought out of Egypt with your mighty hand. 27 Remember your servants, Abraham, Isaac, and Jacob; take no notice of this people's stubbornness, their wickedness, and their sin, 28 so that, in the country from which you have brought us, it may not be said, 'Yahweh was not able to bring them to the country which he had promised them. He hated them; that was why he brought them out — to slaughter them in the desert.' 29 But these are your people, your heritage, whom you yourself have brought out by your great power and your outstretched arm." '

10 'Yahweh then said to me, "Cut two stone tablets like the first ones, and come up to me on the mountain. Make an ark of wood; 2 on the tablets I shall inscribe

write on the tablets the words that were on the former tablets, which you smashed, and you shall put them in the ark." 3 So I made an ark of acacia wood, cut two tablets of stone like the former ones, and went up the mountain with the two tablets in my hand. 4 Then he wrote on the tablets the same words as before, the ten commandments u that the LORD had spoken to you on the mountain out of the fire on the day of the assembly; and the LORD gave them to me. 5 So I turned and came down from the mountain, and put the tablets in the ark that I had made; and there they are, as the LORD commanded me.

6 (The Israelites journeyed from Beeroth-bene-jaakan v to Moserah. There Aaron died, and there he was buried; his son Eleazar succeeded him as priest. 7 From there they journeyed to Gudgodah, and from Gudgodah to Jotbathah, a land with flowing streams. 8 At that time the LORD set apart the tribe of Levi to carry the ark of the covenant of the LORD, to stand before the LORD to minister to him, and to bless in his name, to this day. 9 Therefore Levi has no allotment or inheritance with his kindred; the LORD is his inheritance, as the LORD your God promised him.)

10 I stayed on the mountain forty days and forty nights, as I had done the first time. And once again the LORD listened to me. The LORD was unwilling to destroy you. 11 The LORD said to me, "Get up, go on your journey at the head of the people, that they may go in and occupy the land that I swore to their ancestors to give them."

12 So now, O Israel, what does the LORD your God require of you? Only to fear the LORD your God, to walk in all his ways, to love him, to serve the LORD your God with all your heart and with all your soul, 13 and to keep the commandments of the LORD your God w and his decrees that I am commanding today, for your own well-being. 14 Although heaven and the heaven of heavens belong to the LORD your God, the earth with all that is in it, 15 yet the LORD set his heart in love on your ancestors alone and chose you, their descendants after them, out of all the peoples, as it is today. 16 Circumcise, then, the foreskin of your heart, and do not be stubborn any longer. 17 For the LORD your God is God of gods and Lord of lords, the great God, mighty and awesome, who is not partial and takes no bribe, 18 who executes justice for the orphan and the widow, and who loves the strangers, providing them food and clothing. 19 You shall also love the stranger, for you were strangers in the land of Egypt. 20 You shall fear the LORD your God; him alone you shall worship; to him you shall hold fast, and by his name you shall swear. 21 He is your praise; he is your God, who has done for you these great and awesome things that your own eyes have seen. 22 Your ancestors went down to Egypt seventy persons; and now the LORD your God has made you as numerous as the stars in heaven.

11 You shall love the LORD your God, therefore, and keep his charge, his decrees, his ordinances, and his commandments always. 2 Remember today that it was not your children (who have not known or seen the discipline of the LORD your God), but it is you who must acknowledge his greatness, his mighty hand and his outstretched arm, 3 his signs and his deeds that he did in Egypt to Pharaoh, the king of Egypt, and to all his land; 4 what he did to the Egyptian army, to their horses and chariots, how he made the water of the Red Sea x flow over them as they pursued you, so that the LORD has destroyed them to this day; 5 what he did to you in the wilderness, until you came to this place; 6 and what he did to Dathan and Abiram, sons

the first tablets, which you broke; you are to put them into the ark.' 3 When I had made an ark of acacia-wood and cut two stone tablets like the first, I went up the mountain taking the tablets in my hands. 4 Then in the same writing as before, the LORD wrote down the Ten Commandments which he had spoken to you from the heart of the fire, at the mountain on the day of the assembly, and the LORD gave them to me. 5 I came back down the mountain, and as the LORD had commanded I put the tablets in the ark I had made, and there they have remained ever since.

6 (The Israelites journeyed by stages from Beeroth-bene-jaakan to Moserah. Aaron died and was buried there; and his son Eleazar succeeded him as priest. 7 From there they travelled to Gudgodah and from Gudgodah to Jotbathah, a land of many wadis. 8 At that time the LORD set apart the tribe of Levi to carry the Ark of the Covenant of the LORD, to be in attendance on the LORD and minister to him, and to bless in his name, as they have done to this day. 9 That is why the Levites have no holding of ancestral land like their kinsmen; the LORD is their holding, as he promised them.)

10 I remained on the mountain forty days and forty nights, as I did before, and once again the LORD listened to me; he consented not to destroy you. 11 The LORD said to me, 'Set out now at the head of the people so that they may enter and occupy the land which I swore to give to their forefathers.'

12 What then, Israel, does the LORD your God ask of you? Only this: to fear the LORD your God, to conform to all his ways, to love him, and to serve him with all your heart and soul. 13 This you will do by observing the commandments of the LORD and his statutes which I give you this day for your good. 14 To the LORD your God belong heaven itself, the highest heaven, the earth and everything in it; 15 yet the LORD was attached to your forefathers by his love for them, and he chose their descendants after them. Out of all nations you were his chosen people, as you are this day. 16 So now you must circumcise your hearts and not be stubborn any more, 17 for the LORD your God is God of gods and Lord of lords, the great, mighty, and terrible God. He is no respecter of persons; he is not to be bribed; 18 he secures justice for the fatherless and the widow, and he shows love towards the alien who lives among you, giving him food and clothing. 19 You too must show love towards the alien, for you once lived as aliens in Egypt. 20 You are to fear the LORD your God, serve him, hold fast to him, and take your oaths in his name. 21 He is your proud boast, your God who has done for you these great and terrible things which you saw for yourselves. 22 When your forefathers went down into Egypt they were only seventy strong, but now the LORD your God has made you as countless as the stars in the heavens.

11 Love the LORD your God and keep for all time the charge he laid upon you, his statutes, laws, and commandments. 2 This day you know the discipline of the LORD, though your children who have neither known nor experienced it do not; you know his great power, his strong hand and outstretched arm, 3 the signs he worked and his deeds in Egypt against Pharaoh the king and his whole country, 4 and what he did to the Egyptian army, its horses and chariots, when he caused the waters of the Red Sea to engulf them as they pursued you. In this way the LORD completely destroyed them, and so things remain to this day. 5 You know what he did for you in the wilderness as you journeyed to this place, 6 and what he did to Dathan and

u Heb the ten words   v Or the wells of the Bene-jaakan   w Q Ms
Gk Syr: MT lacks your God   x Or Sea of Reeds

10:4 **Commandments:** lit. Words.

tablets the commandments that were on the former tablets that you broke, and you shall place them in the ark.' 3 So I made an ark of acacia wood, and cut two tablets of stone like the former, and went up the mountain carrying the two tablets. 4 The LORD then wrote on them, as he had written before, the ten commandments which he spoke to you on the mountain from the midst of the fire on the day of the assembly. After the LORD had given them to me, 5 I turned and came down the mountain, and placed the tablets in the ark I had made. There they have remained, in keeping with the command the LORD gave me.

6 [The Israelites set out from Beeroth Bene-jaakan for Moserah, where Aaron died and was buried, his son Eleazar succeeding him in the priestly office. 7 From there they set out for Gudgodah, and from Gudgodah for Jotbathah, a region where there is water in the wadies.]

8 "At that time the LORD set apart the tribe of Levi to carry the ark of the covenant of the LORD, to be in attendance before the LORD and minister to him, and to give blessings in his name, as they have done to this day. 9 For this reason, Levi has no share in the heritage with his brothers; the LORD himself is his heritage, as the LORD, your God, has told him.

10 "After I had spent these other forty days and forty nights on the mountain, and the LORD had once again heard me and decided not to destroy you, 11 he said to me, 'Go now and set out at the head of your people, that they may enter in and occupy the land which I swore to their fathers I would give them.'

12 "And now, Israel, what does the LORD, your God, ask of you but to fear the LORD, your God, and follow his ways exactly, to love and serve the LORD, your God, with all your heart and all your soul, 13 to keep the commandments and statutes of the LORD which I enjoin on you today for your own good? 14 Think! The heavens, even the highest heavens, belong to the LORD, your God, as well as the earth and everything on it. 15 Yet in his love for your fathers the LORD was so attached to them as to choose you, their descendants, in preference to all other peoples, as indeed he has now done. 16 Circumcise your hearts, therefore, and be no longer stiff-necked. 17 For the LORD, your God, is the God of gods, the LORD of lords, the great God, mighty and awesome, who has no favorites, accepts no bribes; 18 who executes justice for the orphan and the widow, and befriends the alien, feeding and clothing him. 19 So you too must befriend the alien, for you were once aliens yourselves in the land of Egypt. 20 The LORD, your God, shall you fear, and him shall you serve; hold fast to him and swear by his name. 21 He is your glory, he, your God, who has done for you those great and terrible things which your own eyes have seen. 22 Your ancestors went down to Egypt seventy strong, and now the LORD, your God, has made you as numerous as the stars of the sky.

11 "Love the LORD, your God, therefore, and always heed his charge: his statutes, decrees and commandments. 2 It is not your children, who have not known it from experience, but you yourselves who must now understand the discipline of the LORD, your God; his majesty, his strong hand and outstretched arm; 3 the signs and deeds he wrought among the Egyptians, on Pharaoh, king of Egypt, and on all his land; 4 what he did to the Egyptian army and to their horses and chariots, engulfing them in the water of the Red Sea as they pursued you, and bringing ruin upon them even to this day; 5 what he did for you in the desert until you arrived in this place; 6 and what he did to the

the words that were on the first tablets, which you broke; put them in the ark." 3 So I made an ark of acacia wood, cut two stone tablets like the first and went up the mountain with the two tablets in my hand. 4 And he inscribed the tablets, as he had inscribed them before, with the Ten Words which Yahweh had said to you on the mountain, from the heart of the fire, on the day of the Assembly. Yahweh then gave them to me. 5 I turned and came down from the mountain and put the tablets in the ark I had made, and there they stayed, as Yahweh had commanded me.

6 'The Israelites left the wells of the Bene-Jaakan for Moserah, where Aaron died; he was buried there, and his son Eleazar succeeded him in the priesthood. 7 From there, they set out for Gudgodah, and from Gudgodah for Jotbathah, an area rich in streams. 8 Yahweh then set apart the tribe of Levi to carry the ark of Yahweh's covenant, to stand in the presence of Yahweh, to serve him and to bless in his name, as they still do today. 9 This is why Levi has no share or heritage with his brothers: Yahweh is his heritage, as Yahweh your God then told him.

10 'And, as before, I stayed on the mountain for forty days and forty nights. And again Yahweh heard my prayer and agreed not to destroy you. 11 And Yahweh said to me, "Be on your way at the head of this people, so that they can go and take possession of the country which I swore to their ancestors that I would give them."

12 'And now, Israel, what does Yahweh your God ask of you? Only this: to fear Yahweh your God, to follow all his ways, to love him, to serve Yahweh your God with all your heart and all your soul, 13 to keep the commandments and laws of Yahweh, which I am laying down for you today for your own good.

14 'Look, to Yahweh your God belong heaven and the heaven of heavens, the earth and everything on it; 15 yet it was on your ancestors, for love of them, that Yahweh set his heart to love them, and he chose their descendants after them, you yourselves, out of all nations, up to the present day. 16 Circumcise your heart then and be obstinate no longer; 17 for Yahweh your God is God of gods and Lord of lords, the great God, triumphant and terrible, free of favouritism, never to be bribed. 18 It is he who sees justice done for the orphan and the widow, who loves the stranger and gives him food and clothing. 19 (Love the stranger then, for you were once strangers in Egypt.) 20 Yahweh your God is the one whom you must fear and serve; to him you must hold firm; in his name take your oaths. 21 Him you must praise, he is your God: for you he has done these great and terrible things which you have seen for yourselves; 22 and, although your ancestors numbered only seventy persons when they went down to Egypt, Yahweh your God has now made you as many as the stars of heaven.'

11 'You must love Yahweh your God and always keep his observances, his laws, his customs, his commandments. 2 You are the ones who have had the experience, not your children. They have not had the experience, they have not witnessed the lessons of Yahweh your God, his greatness, his mighty hand and his outstretched arm, 3 the signs and the deeds which he performed in the heart of Egypt, against Pharaoh king of Egypt and his entire country, 4 what he did to the armies of Egypt, to their horses and their chariots, by overwhelming them with the waters of the Sea of Reeds when they were pursuing you, and leaving no trace of them to this day; 5 what he did for you in the desert, until you arrived here; 6 what he did to Dathan and Abiram

of Eliab son of Reuben, how in the midst of all Israel the earth opened its mouth and swallowed them up, along with their households, their tents, and every living being in their company; 7 for it is your own eyes that have seen every great deed that the LORD did.

8 Keep, then, this entire commandment that I am commanding you today, so that you may have strength to go in and occupy the land that you are crossing over to occupy, 9 and so that you may live long in the land that the LORD swore to your ancestors to give them and to their descendants, a land flowing with milk and honey. 10 For the land that you are about to enter to occupy is not like the land of Egypt, from which you have come, where you sow your seed and irrigate by foot like a vegetable garden. 11 But the land that you are crossing over to occupy is a land of hills and valleys, watered by rain from the sky, 12 a land that the LORD your God looks after. The eyes of the LORD your God are always on it, from the beginning of the year to the end of the year.

13 If you will only heed his every commandment*y* that I am commanding you today — loving the LORD your God, and serving him with all your heart and with all your soul — 14 then he*z* will give the rain for your land in its season, the early rain and the later rain, and you will gather in your grain, your wine, and your oil; 15 and he*z* will give grass in your fields for your livestock, and you will eat your fill. 16 Take care, or you will be seduced into turning away, serving other gods and worshiping them, 17 for then the anger of the LORD will be kindled against you and he will shut up the heavens, so that there will be no rain and the land will yield no fruit; then you will perish quickly off the good land that the LORD is giving you.

18 You shall put these words of mine in your heart and soul, and you shall bind them as a sign on your hand, and fix them as an emblem*a* on your forehead. 19 Teach them to your children, talking about them when you are at home and when you are away, when you lie down and when you rise. 20 Write them on the doorposts of your house and on your gates, 21 so that your days and the days of your children may be multiplied in the land that the LORD swore to your ancestors to give them, as long as the heavens are above the earth.

22 If you will diligently observe this entire commandment that I am commanding you, loving the LORD your God, walking in all his ways, and holding fast to him, 23 then the LORD will drive out all these nations before you, and you will dispossess nations larger and mightier than yourselves. 24 Every place on which you set foot shall be yours; your territory shall extend from the wilderness to the Lebanon and from the River, the river Euphrates, to the Western Sea. 25 No one will be able to stand against you; the LORD your God will put the fear and dread of you on all the land on which you set foot, as he promised you.

26 See, I am setting before you today a blessing and a curse: 27 the blessing, if you obey the commandments of the LORD your God that I am commanding you today; 28 and the curse, if you do not obey the commandments of the LORD your God, but turn from the way that I am commanding you today, to follow other gods that you have not known.

29 When the LORD your God has brought you into the land that you are entering to occupy, you shall set the blessing on Mount Gerizim and the curse on Mount Ebal. 30 As you know, they are beyond the Jordan, some distance to the west, in the land of the Canaanites who live in the Arabah, opposite Gilgal, beside the oak*b* of Moreh.

Abiram, sons of Eliab the Reubenite, when the earth opened its mouth and swallowed them in the midst of all Israel, together with their households, their tents, and every living thing in their company. 7 It was you who saw for yourselves all the great work which the LORD did.

8 Observe all the commands I give you this day, so that you may have the strength to enter and occupy the land into which you are about to cross, 9 and so that you may enjoy long life in the land which the LORD swore to your forefathers to give them and their descendants, a land flowing with milk and honey. 10 The land which you are about to enter and occupy is not like the land of Egypt from which you have come, where, after sowing your seed, you regulated the water by means of your foot as in a vegetable garden. 11 But the land into which you are about to cross to occupy it is a land of mountains and valleys watered by the rain of heaven. 12 It is a land which the LORD your God tends and on which his eye rests from one year's end to the next. 13 If you pay heed to the commandments which I give you this day, to love the LORD your God and serve him with all your heart and soul, 14 then I shall send rain for your land in season, both autumn and spring rains, and you will gather in your corn and new wine and oil, 15 and I shall provide pasture in the fields for your cattle: you will have all you want to eat. 16 Take care not to be led astray in your hearts, and serve and worship other gods, 17 or the LORD's anger will be roused against you: he will shut up the heavens and there will be no rain, your soil will not yield its harvest, and you will quickly perish from upon the good land which the LORD is giving you.

18 Take these commandments of mine to heart and keep them in mind. Bind them as a sign on your hands and wear them as a pendant on your foreheads. 19 Teach them to your children, and speak of them indoors and out of doors, when you lie down and when you get up. 20 Write them on the doorposts of your houses and on your gates. 21 Then you will live long, you and your children, in the land which the LORD swore to your forefathers to give them, for as long as the heavens are above the earth.

22 If you diligently keep all these commandments that I now charge you to observe, loving the LORD your God, conforming to his ways, and holding fast to him, 23 the LORD will drive out all these nations before you and you will occupy the territory of nations greater and more powerful than you are. 24 Every place where you set foot will be yours. Your borders will run from the wilderness to the Lebanon, and from the river, the Euphrates, to the western sea. 25 No one will be able to withstand you; the LORD your God will put the fear and dread of you on the whole land on which you set foot, as he promised you.

26 See, this day I offer you the choice of a blessing or a curse: 27 the blessing if you obey the commandments of the LORD your God which I give you this day; 28 the curse if you do not obey the commandments of the LORD your God, but turn from the way that I command you this day and go after other gods of whom you have had no experience.

29 When the LORD your God brings you into the land which you are entering to occupy, there on Mount Gerizim you shall pronounce the blessing and on Mount Ebal the curse. 30 (These mountains are on the other side of the Jordan, close to Gilgal beside the terebinth of Moreh, beyond the road to the west which lies in the territory of the Canaanites of the Arabah.) 31 You are about to cross the Jordan to

---

y Compare Gk: Heb *my commandments*   *z* Sam Gk Vg: MT *I*   *a* Or *as a frontlet*   *b* Gk Syr: Compare Gen 12.6; Heb *oaks or terebinths*

11:12 **which . . . tends:** *or* whose soil the LORD your God has made firm.   11:24 **to the Lebanon:** *prob. rdg; Heb.* and the Lebanon.   11:30 **terebinth:** *so Gk; Heb.* terebinths.

Reubenites Dathan and Abiram, sons of Eliab, when the ground opened its mouth and swallowed them up out of the midst of Israel, with their families and tents and every living thing that belonged to them. 7 With your own eyes you have seen all these great deeds that the LORD has done. 8 Keep all the commandments, then, which I enjoin on you today, that you may be strong enough to enter in and take possession of the land into which you are crossing, 9 and that you may have long life on the land which the LORD swore to your fathers he would give to them and their descendants, a land flowing with milk and honey.

10 "For the land which you are to enter and occupy is not like the land of Egypt from which you have come, where you would sow your seed and then water it by hand, as in a vegetable garden. 11 No, the land into which you are crossing for conquest is a land of hills and valleys that drinks in rain from the heavens, 12 a land which the LORD, your God, looks after; his eyes are upon it continually from the beginning of the year to the end. 13 If, then, you truly heed my commandments which I enjoin on you today, loving and serving the LORD, your God, with all your heart and all your soul, 14 I will give the seasonal rain to your land, the early rain and the late rain, that you may have your grain, wine and oil to gather in; 15 and I will bring forth grass in your fields for your animals. Thus you may eat your fill. 16 But be careful lest your heart be so lured away that you serve other gods and worship them. 17 For then the wrath of the LORD will flare up against you and he will close up the heavens, so that no rain will fall, and the soil will not yield its crops, and you will soon perish from the good land he is giving you.

18 "Therefore, take these words of mine into your heart and soul. Bind them at your wrist as a sign, and let them be a pendant on your forehead. 19 Teach them to your children, speaking of them at home and abroad, whether you are busy or at rest. 20 And write them on the doorposts of your houses and on your gates, 21 so that, as long as the heavens are above the earth, you and your children may live on in the land which the LORD swore to your fathers he would give them.

22 "For if you are careful to observe all these commandments I enjoin on you, loving the LORD, your God, and following his ways exactly, and holding fast to him, 23 the LORD will drive all these nations out of your way, and you will dispossess nations greater and mightier than yourselves. 24 Every place where you set foot shall be yours: from the desert and from Lebanon, from the Euphrates River to the Western Sea, shall be your territory. 25 None shall stand up against you; the LORD, your God, will spread the fear and dread of you through any land where you set foot, as he promised you.

26 "I set before you here, this day, a blessing and a curse: 27 a blessing for obeying the commandments of the LORD, your God, which I enjoin on you today; 28 a curse if you do not obey the commandments of the LORD, your God, but turn aside from the way I ordain for you today, to follow other gods, whom you have not known. 29 When the LORD, your God, brings you into the land which you are to enter and occupy, then you shall pronounce the blessing on Mount Gerizim, the curse on Mount Ebal. 30 [Are they not beyond the Jordan, on the other side of the western road in the country of the Canaanites who live in the Arabah, opposite the Gilgal beside the terebinth of Moreh?] 31 For you are

the sons of Eliab the Reubenite, when, with all Israel standing round, the earth opened its mouth and swallowed them, with their families, their tents and all their supporters. 7 All these great deeds of Yahweh you have seen with your own eyes.

8 'You must keep all the commandments which I enjoin on you today, so that you may have the strength to conquer the country into which you are about to cross, to take possession of it, 9 and so that you may live long in the country which Yahweh promised on oath to bestow on your ancestors and their descendants, a country flowing with milk and honey.

10 'For the country which you are about to enter and make your own is not like the country of Egypt from which you have come, where, having done your sowing, you had to water the seed by foot, as though in a vegetable garden. 11 No, the country which you are about to enter and make your own, is a country of hills and valleys watered by the rain of heaven. 12 Yahweh your God looks after this country, the eyes of Yahweh your God are always on it, from the beginning of the year to the end. 13 Depend on it: if you faithfully obey the commandments I enjoin on you today, loving Yahweh your God and serving him with all your heart and all your soul, 14 I shall give your country rain at the right time, rain in autumn, rain in spring, so that you can harvest your wheat, your new wine and your oil, 15 I shall provide grass in the fields for your cattle, and you will eat to your heart's content. 16 Beware of letting your heart be seduced: if you go astray, serve other gods and bow down to them, 17 Yahweh's anger will be kindled against you, he will shut the heavens, there will be no more rain, the soil will not yield its produce and, in the fine country given you by Yahweh, you will quickly perish.

18 'Let these words of mine remain in your heart and in your soul; fasten them on your hand as a sign and on your forehead as a headband. 19 Teach them to your children, and keep on telling them, when you are sitting at home, when you are out and about, when you are lying down and when you are standing up. 20 Write them on the doorposts of your house and on your gates, 21 so that you and your children may live long in the country which Yahweh swore to your ancestors that he would give them for as long as there is a sky above the earth.

22 'For if you faithfully keep and observe all these commandments that I enjoin on you today, loving Yahweh your God, following all his ways and holding fast to him, 23 Yahweh will dispossess all these nations before you, and you will dispossess nations greater and more powerful than yourselves. 24 Wherever the sole of your foot treads will be yours; your territory will run from the desert all the way to the Lebanon; and from the River, from the River Euphrates, as far as the Western Sea, will be your territory. 25 No one will be able to resist you; Yahweh your God will make you feared and dreaded throughout the territory you tread, as he has promised you.

26 'Today, look, I am offering you a blessing and a curse: 27 a blessing, if you obey the commandments of Yahweh your God which I enjoin on you today; 28 a curse, if you disobey the commandments of Yahweh your God and leave the way which today I have marked out for you, by following other gods hitherto unknown to you. 29 And when Yahweh your God has brought you into the country which you are about to enter and make your own, you must set the blessing on Mount Gerizim and the curse on Mount Ebal. 30 (These mountains, as everyone knows, are on the other side of the Jordan on the westward road, in the territory of the Canaanites who live in the Arabah, opposite Gilgal, near the Oak of Moreh.) 31 For you are about to cross the

NEW REVISED STANDARD VERSION	REVISED ENGLISH BIBLE

31 When you cross the Jordan to go in to occupy the land that the LORD your God is giving you, and when you occupy it and live in it, 32 you must diligently observe all the statutes and ordinances that I am setting before you today.

12 These are the statutes and ordinances that you must diligently observe in the land that the LORD, the God of your ancestors, has given you to occupy all the days that you live on the earth. 2 You must demolish completely all the places where the nations whom you are about to dispossess served their gods, on the mountain heights, on the hills, and under every leafy tree. 3 Break down their altars, smash their pillars, burn their sacred poles[c] with fire, and hew down the idols of their gods, and thus blot out their name from their places. 4 You shall not worship the LORD your God in such ways. 5 But you shall seek the place that the LORD your God will choose out of all your tribes as his habitation to put his name there. You shall go there, 6 bringing there your burnt offerings and your sacrifices, your tithes and your donations, your votive gifts, your freewill offerings, and the firstlings of your herds and flocks. 7 And you shall eat there in the presence of the LORD your God, you and your households together, rejoicing in all the undertakings in which the LORD your God has blessed you.

8 You shall not act as we are acting here today, all of us according to our own desires, 9 for you have not yet come into the rest and the possession that the LORD your God is giving you. 10 When you cross over the Jordan and live in the land that the LORD your God is allotting to you, and when he gives you rest from your enemies all around so that you live in safety, 11 then you shall bring everything that I command you to the place that the LORD your God will choose as a dwelling for his name: your burnt offerings and your sacrifices, your tithes and your donations, and all your choice votive gifts that you vow to the LORD. 12 And you shall rejoice before the LORD your God, you together with your sons and your daughters, your male and female slaves, and the Levites who reside in your towns (since they have no allotment or inheritance with you).

13 Take care that you do not offer your burnt offerings at any place you happen to see. 14 But only at the place that the LORD will choose in one of your tribes — there you shall offer your burnt offerings and there you shall do everything I command you.

15 Yet whenever you desire you may slaughter and eat meat within any of your towns, according to the blessing that the LORD your God has given you; the unclean and the clean may eat of it, as they would of gazelle or deer. 16 The blood, however, you must not eat; you shall pour it out on the ground like water. 17 Nor may you eat within your towns the tithe of your grain, your wine, and your oil, the first-lings of your herds and your flocks, any of your votive gifts that you vow, your freewill offerings, or your donations; 18 these you shall eat in the presence of the LORD your God at the place that the LORD your God will choose, you to-gether with your son and your daughter, your male and female slaves, and the Levites resident in your towns, re-joicing in the presence of the LORD your God in all your undertakings. 19 Take care that you do not neglect the Levite as long as you live in your land.

20 When the LORD your God enlarges your territory, as he has promised you, and you say, "I am going to eat some meat," because you wish to eat meat, you may eat meat whenever you have the desire. 21 If the place where the

enter and occupy the land which the LORD your God is giving you. Occupy it and settle in it, 32 and be careful to observe all the statutes and laws which I have set before you this day.

12 THESE are the statutes and laws which you must be careful to observe in the land which the LORD the God of your forefathers is giving you to occupy all your earthly life. 2 You are to demolish completely all the sanctuaries where the nations whom you are dispossessing worship their gods, whether on high mountains or on hills or under every spreading tree. 3 Pull down their altars, break their sacred pillars, burn their sacred poles, and hack down the idols of their gods, and thus blot out the name of them from the place. 4 You must not adopt such practices in the worship of the LORD your God; 5 instead you are to resort to the place which the LORD your God will choose out of all your tribes to receive his name that it may dwell there. Come there 6 and bring your whole-offerings and sacrifices, your tithes and contributions, your vows and freewill-offerings, and the firstborn of your herds and flocks. 7 You are to eat there before the LORD your God; so you will find joy in whatever you undertake, you and your families, because the LORD your God has blessed you.

8 You are not to act as we act here today, everyone doing as he pleases, 9 for till now you have not reached the rest-ing-place, the territory which the LORD your God is giving you. 10 When you cross the Jordan and settle in the land which the LORD your God allots you as your holding, when he grants you peace from all your enemies on every side, and you live in security, 11 then you must bring everything that I command you to the place which the LORD your God chooses as a dwelling for his name — your whole-offerings and sacrifices, your tithes and contributions, and all the choice gifts that you have vowed to the LORD. 12 You will rejoice in the presence of the LORD your God with your sons and daughters, your male and female slaves, and the Levites who live in your settlements because they have no holding, no ancestral portion among you.

13 See that you do not offer your whole-offerings in any sanctuary at random, 14 but offer them only at the place which the LORD will choose in one of your tribes, and there you must do all I command you. 15 On the other hand, you may freely slaughter for food in any of your settlements, as the LORD your God blesses you. Clean and unclean alike may eat it, as they would eat the meat of gazelle or deer. 16 But on no account may you partake of the blood; you are to pour it out on the ground like water.

17 In your settlements you may not eat the tithe of your grain and new wine and oil, any of the firstborn of your cattle and sheep, any of the gifts that you vow, or any of your freewill-offerings and contributions; 18 these you must eat in the presence of the LORD your God in the place that the LORD your God will choose—you, your sons and daughters, your male and female slaves, and the Levites living in your settlements; so you will find joy before the LORD your God in all that you undertake. 19 Be careful not to neglect the Levites as long as you live in your land.

20 When the LORD your God enlarges your territory, as he has promised, and you say to yourselves, 'I should like to eat meat,' because you have a craving for it, then you may freely eat it. 21 If the place where the LORD your God will

---

about to cross the Jordan to enter and occupy the land which the LORD, your God, is giving you. When therefore, you take possession of it and settle there, 32 be careful to observe all the statutes and decrees that I set before you today.

12 "These are the statutes and decrees which you must be careful to observe in the land which the LORD, the God of your fathers, has given you to occupy, as long as you live on its soil. 2 Destroy without fail every place on the high mountains, on the hills, and under every leafy tree where the nations you are to dispossess worship their gods. 3 Tear down their altars, smash their sacred pillars, destroy by fire their sacred poles, and shatter the idols of their gods, that you may stamp out the remembrance of them in any such place.

4 "That is not how you are to worship the LORD, your God. 5 Instead, you shall resort to the place which the LORD, your God, chooses out of all your tribes and designates as his dwelling 6 and there you shall bring your holocausts and sacrifices, your tithes and personal contributions, your votive and freewill offerings, and the firstlings of your herds and flocks. 7 There, too, before the LORD, your God, you and your families shall eat and make merry over all your undertakings, because the LORD, your God, has blessed you. 8 You shall not do as we are now doing; here, everyone does what seems right to himself, 9 since you have not yet reached your resting place, the heritage which the LORD, your God, will give you. 10 But after you have crossed the Jordan and dwell in the land which the LORD, your God, is giving you as a heritage, when he has given you rest from all your enemies round about and you live there in security, 11 then to the place which the LORD, your God, chooses as the dwelling place for his name you shall bring all the offerings I command you: your holocausts and sacrifices, your tithes and personal contributions, and every special offering you have vowed to the LORD. 12 You shall make merry before the LORD, your God, with your sons and daughters, your male and female slaves, as well as with the Levite who belongs to your community but has no share of his own in your heritage. 13 Take care not to offer up your holocausts in any place you fancy, 14 but offer them up in the place which the LORD chooses from among your tribes; there you shall make whatever offerings I enjoin upon you.

15 "However, in any of your communities you may slaughter and eat to your heart's desire as much meat as the LORD, your God, has blessed you with; and the unclean as well as the clean may eat it, as they do the gazelle or the deer. 16 Only, you shall not partake of the blood, but must pour it out on the ground like water. 17 Moreover, you shall not, in your own communities, partake of your tithe of grain or wine or oil, of the first-born of your herd or flock, of any offering you have vowed, of your freewill offerings, or of your personal contributions. 18 These you must eat before the LORD, your God, in the place he chooses, along with your son and daughter, your male and female slave, and the Levite who belongs to your community; and there, before the LORD, you shall make merry over all your undertakings. 19 Take care, also, that you do not neglect the Levite as long as you live in the land.

20 "After the LORD, your God, has enlarged your territory, as he promised you, when you wish meat for food, you may eat it at will, to your heart's desire; 21 and if the

Jordan, to enter and take possession of the country given you by Yahweh your God. You will possess it, you will live in it, 32 and you must keep and observe all the laws and customs promulgated by me to you today.'

12 'Now, these are the laws and customs which you must keep in the country which Yahweh, God of your ancestors, is giving you as yours, and which you must observe every day that you live in that country.

2 'You must completely destroy all the places where the nations you dispossess have served their gods, on high mountains, on hills, under any spreading tree; 3 you must tear down their altars, smash their sacred stones, burn their sacred poles, hack to bits the statues of their gods and obliterate their name from that place.

4 'Not so must you behave towards Yahweh your God. 5 You must seek Yahweh your God in the place which he will choose from all your tribes, there to set his name and give it a home: that is where you must go. 6 That is where you must bring your burnt offerings and your sacrifices, your tithes and offerings held high, your votive offerings and your voluntary offerings, and the first-born of your herd and flock; 7 and that is where you must eat in the presence of Yahweh your God, rejoicing over your labours, you and your households, because Yahweh your God has blessed you.

8 'You must not behave as we are behaving here today, each of you doing what he himself sees fit, 9 since you have not yet come to the resting place and the heritage that Yahweh your God is going to give you. 10 You are about to cross the Jordan and live in the country given you by Yahweh your God as your heritage; he will grant you peace from all the enemies surrounding you, and you will live in safety. 11 To the place chosen by Yahweh your God as a home for his name, to that place you must bring all the things that I am laying down for you: your burnt offerings and your sacrifices, your tithes and offerings held high, and all the best of your possessions dedicated by you to Yahweh. 12 That is where you will rejoice in the presence of Yahweh your God, you and your sons and daughters, your serving men and women, and the Levite living in your community since he has no share or heritage of his own among you.

13 'Take care you do not offer your burnt offerings in all the sacred places you see; 14 only in the place that Yahweh chooses in one of your tribes may you offer your burnt offerings and do all the things which I have commanded you.

15 'This notwithstanding, and whenever you wish, you may slaughter and eat meat wherever you live — as much as the blessing of Yahweh affords you. Clean or unclean may eat it, as though it were gazelle or deer. 16 You will not, however, eat the blood, but will pour that like water on the ground.

17 'You must not eat the tithe of your wheat, of your new wine or of your oil, or the first-born of your herd or flock, or any of your votive offerings or voluntary offerings, or your offerings held high to Yahweh, at home. 18 You must eat these in the presence of Yahweh your God in the place Yahweh your God chooses and there alone, you, your son and your daughter, your serving man and serving woman, and the Levite living in your community, expressing your joy in all your labours in the presence of Yahweh your God. 19 As long as you live on your soil, be careful not to neglect the Levite.

20 'When Yahweh your God enlarges your territory as he has promised you, and you say, "I should like to eat meat," if you want to eat meat you may eat as much as you like.

NEW REVISED STANDARD VERSION

LORD your God will choose to put his name is too far from you, and you slaughter as I have commanded you any of your herd or flock that the LORD has given you, then you may eat within your towns whenever you desire. 22 Indeed, just as gazelle or deer is eaten, so you may eat it; the unclean and the clean alike may eat it. 23 Only be sure that you do not eat the blood; for the blood is the life, and you shall not eat the life with the meat. 24 Do not eat it; you shall pour it out on the ground like water. 25 Do not eat it, so that all may go well with you and your children after you, because you do what is right in the sight of the LORD. 26 But the sacred donations that are due from you, and your votive gifts, you shall bring to the place that the LORD will choose. 27 You shall present your burnt offerings, both the meat and the blood, on the altar of the LORD your God; the blood of your other sacrifices shall be poured out beside*d* the altar of the LORD your God, but the meat you may eat.

28 Be careful to obey all these words that I command you today,*e* so that it may go well with you and with your children after you forever, because you will be doing what is good and right in the sight of the LORD your God.

29 When the LORD your God has cut off before you the nations whom you are about to enter to dispossess them, when you have dispossessed them and live in their land, 30 take care that you are not snared into imitating them, after they have been destroyed before you: do not inquire concerning their gods, saying, "How did these nations worship their gods? I also want to do the same." 31 You must not do the same for the LORD your God, because every abhorrent thing that the LORD hates they have done for their gods. They would even burn their sons and their daughters in the fire to their gods. 32 *f* You must diligently observe everything that I command you; do not add to it or take anything from it.

13 *g* If prophets or those who divine by dreams appear among you and promise you omens or portents, 2 and the omens or the portents declared by them take place, and they say, "Let us follow other gods" (whom you have not known) "and let us serve them," 3 you must not heed the words of those prophets or those who divine by dreams; for the LORD your God is testing you, to know whether you indeed love the LORD your God with all your heart and soul. 4 The LORD your God you shall follow, him alone you shall fear, his commandments you shall keep, his voice you shall obey, him you shall serve, and to him you shall hold fast. 5 But those prophets or those who divine by dreams shall be put to death for having spoken treason against the LORD your God — who brought you out of the land of Egypt and redeemed you from the house of slavery — to turn you from the way in which the LORD your God commanded you to walk. So you shall purge the evil from your midst.

6 If anyone secretly entices you — even if it is your brother, your father's son or*h* your mother's son, or your own son or daughter, or the wife you embrace, or your most intimate friend — saying, "Let us go worship other gods," whom neither you nor your ancestors have known, 7 any of the gods of the peoples that are around you, whether near you or far away from you, from one end of the earth to the other, 8 you must not yield to or heed any such persons. Show them no pity or compassion and do not shield them. 9 But you shall surely kill them; your own hand shall be first against them to execute them, and afterwards the hand of all the people. 10 Stone them to death for trying to turn you away from the LORD your God, who brought you out of the land of Egypt, out of the house of slavery. 11 Then all Israel

REVISED ENGLISH BIBLE

choose to set his name is too far away, then you may slaughter a beast from the herds or flocks which the LORD has given you and freely eat it in your settlements as I command you. 22 You may eat it as you would the meat of gazelle or deer; both clean and unclean alike may eat it. 23 But you must strictly refrain from partaking of the blood, because the blood is the life; you must not eat the life with the flesh. 24 You must not consume it; you must pour it out on the ground like water. 25 If you abstain from it, all will be well with you and your children after you; for you will be doing what is right in the eyes of the LORD.

26 But such holy-gifts as you may have and the gifts you have vowed you must bring to the place which the LORD will choose. 27 You must present your whole-offerings, both the flesh and the blood, on the altar of the LORD your God; but of your shared-offerings you are to eat the flesh, while the blood is to be poured on the altar of the LORD your God.

28 See that you listen, and do all that I command you, and then it will go well with you and your children after you for ever; for you will be doing what is good and right in the eyes of the LORD your God.

29 When, as you advance, the LORD your God exterminates the nations whose country you are entering to occupy, you will take their place and settle in their land. 30 After they have been destroyed, take care that you are not ensnared into their ways. Do not enquire about their gods, saying, 'How used these nations to serve their gods? I too shall do the same.' 31 You must not do for the LORD your God what they do, for all that they do for their gods is hateful and abominable to the LORD. Even their sons and their daughters they burn in honour of their gods.

32 See that you carry out exactly what I command you: you must not add anything to it or take anything away from it.

13 Should a prophet or a pedlar of dreams appear among you and offer you a sign or a portent, 2 and call on you to go after other gods whom you have not known and to worship them, even if the sign or portent should come true 3 do not heed the words of that prophet or dreamer. The LORD your God is testing you to discover whether you love him with all your heart and soul. 4 It is the LORD your God you must follow and him you must fear; you must keep his commandments and obey him, serve him and hold fast to him. 5 As for that prophet or dreamer, he must be put to death for preaching rebellion against the LORD your God who brought you out of Egypt and redeemed you from that land of slavery; he has tried to lead you astray from the path which the LORD your God commanded you to take. You must get rid of this wickedness from your midst.

6 If your brother, your father's son or your mother's son, or your son or daughter, or your beloved wife, or your dearest friend should entice you secretly to go and serve other gods — gods of whom neither you nor your fathers have had experience, 7 gods of the people round about you, near or far, at one end of the land or the other — 8 then you must not consent or listen. Show none of them mercy, neither spare nor shield them; 9 you are to put them to death, your own hand being the first to be raised against them, and then all the people are to follow. 10 Stone them to death, because they tried to lead you astray from the LORD your God who brought you out of Egypt, out of that land where you were slaves. 11 All Israel when they hear of it will be afraid; never

---

d Or *on*   *e* Gk Sam Syr: MT lacks *today*   *f* Ch 13.1 in Heb
g Ch 13.2 in Heb   *h* Sam Gk Compare Tg: MT lacks *your father's son or*

12:28 **and do:** *so Samar.; Heb. omits.*   12:32 *In Heb. 13:1.*
13:6 **your father's son or:** *so Samar.; Heb. omits.*

place which the LORD, your God, chooses for the abode of his name is too far, you may slaughter in the manner I have told you any of your herd or flock that the LORD has given you, and eat it to your heart's desire in your own community. 22 You may eat it as you would the gazelle or the deer: the unclean and the clean eating it alike. 23 But make sure that you do not partake of the blood; for blood is life, and you shall not consume this seat of life with the flesh. 24 Do not partake of the blood, therefore, but pour it out on the ground like water. 25 Abstain from it, that you and your children after you may prosper for doing what is right in the sight of the LORD. 26 However, any sacred gifts or votive offerings that you may have, you shall bring with you to the place which the LORD chooses, 27 and there you must offer both the flesh and the blood of your holocausts on the altar of the LORD, your God; of your other sacrifices the blood indeed must be poured out against the altar of the LORD, your God, but their flesh may be eaten. 28 Be careful to heed all these commandments I enjoin on you, that you and your descendants may always prosper for doing what is good and right in the sight of the LORD, your God.

29 "When the LORD, your God, removes the nations from your way as you advance to dispossess them, be on your guard! Otherwise, once they have been wiped out before you and you have replaced them and are settled in their land, 30 you will be lured into following them. Do not inquire regarding their gods, 'How did these nations worship their gods? I, too, would do the same.' 31 You shall not thus worship the LORD, your God, because they offered to their gods every abomination that the LORD detests, even burning their sons and daughters to their gods.

13 "Every command that I enjoin on you, you shall be careful to observe, neither adding to it nor subtracting from it.

2 "If there arises among you a prophet or a dreamer who promises you a sign or wonder, 3 urging you to follow other gods, whom you have not known, and to serve them: even though the sign or wonder he has foretold you comes to pass, 4 pay no attention to the words of that prophet or that dreamer; for the LORD, your God, is testing you to learn whether you really love him with all your heart and with all your soul. 5 The LORD, your God, shall you follow, and him shall you fear; his commandment shall you observe, and his voice shall you heed, serving him and holding fast to him alone. 6 But that prophet or that dreamer shall be put to death, because, in order to lead you astray from the way which the LORD, your God, has directed you to take, he has preached apostasy from the LORD, your God, who brought you out of the land of Egypt and ransomed you from that place of slavery. Thus shall you purge the evil from your midst.

7 "If your own full brother, or your son or daughter, or your beloved wife, or your intimate friend, entices you secretly to serve other gods, whom you and your fathers have not known, 8 gods of any other nation, near at hand or far away, from one end of the earth to the other: 9 do not yield to him or listen to him, nor look with pity upon him, to spare or shield him, 10 but kill him. Your hand shall be the first raised to slay him; the rest of the people shall join in with you. 11 You shall stone him to death, because he sought to lead you astray from the LORD, your God, who brought you out of the land of Egypt, that place of slavery.

21 If the place in which Yahweh your God chooses to set his name is too far away, you may slaughter any of your herd or flock that Yahweh has given you, as I have prescribed for you; you may eat as much of it as you please at home. 22 But you must eat it as you would gazelle or deer; clean and unclean may eat it together. 23 Take care, however, not to eat the blood, since blood is life, and you must not eat the life with the meat. 24 You must not eat it, but must pour it like water on the ground. 25 You must not eat it — so that you, and your children after you, may prosper, doing what is right in Yahweh's eyes. 26 But the holy things of yours and the things which you have dedicated, you must go and take to the place chosen by Yahweh. 27 The burnt offerings of meat and blood must be presented on the altar of Yahweh your God; whereas, in your sacrifices, the blood must be poured on the altar of Yahweh your God; the meat you yourselves may eat. 28 Faithfully keep and obey all these orders which I am giving you, so that you and your children after you may prosper for ever, doing what is good and right in the eyes of Yahweh your God.

29 'When Yahweh your God has annihilated the nations confronting you, whom you are going to dispossess, and when you have dispossessed them and made your home in their country, 30 beware of being entrapped into copying them, after they have been destroyed to make way for you, and do not enquire about their gods, saying, "How did these nations worship their gods? I am going to do the same too." 31 This is not the way to treat Yahweh your God. For in honour of their gods they have done everything detestable that Yahweh hates; yes, in honour of their gods, they even burn their own sons and daughters as sacrifices!'

13 'Whatever I am now commanding you, you must keep and observe, adding nothing to it, taking nothing away.

2 'If a prophet or a dreamer of dreams arises among you, offering you some sign or wonder, 3 and the sign or wonder comes about; and if he then says to you, "Let us follow other gods (hitherto unknown to you) and serve them," 4 you must not listen to that prophet's words or to that dreamer's dreams. Yahweh your God is testing you to know if you love Yahweh your God with all your heart and all your soul. 5 Yahweh your God is the one whom you must follow, him you must fear, his commandments you must keep, his voice you must obey, him you must serve, to him you must hold fast. 6 That prophet or that dreamer of dreams must be put to death, since he has preached apostasy from Yahweh your God who brought you out of Egypt and redeemed you from the place of slave-labour; and he would have diverted you from the way in which Yahweh your God has commanded you to walk. You must banish this evil from among you.

7 'If your brother, the son of your father or of your mother, or your son or daughter, or the spouse whom you embrace, or your most intimate friend, tries secretly to seduce you, saying, "Let us go and serve other gods," unknown to you or your ancestors before you, 8 gods of the peoples surrounding you, whether near you or far away, anywhere throughout the world, 9 you must not consent, you must not listen to him; you must show him no pity, you must not spare him or conceal his guilt. 10 No, you must kill him, your hand must strike the first blow in putting him to death and the hands of the rest of the people following. 11 You must stone him to death, since he has tried to divert you from Yahweh your God who brought you out of Egypt, from the place of slave-labour. 12 All Israel, hearing of this,

NEW REVISED STANDARD VERSION

shall hear and be afraid, and never again do any such wickedness.

12 If you hear it said about one of the towns that the LORD your God is giving you to live in, 13 that scoundrels from among you have gone out and led the inhabitants of the town astray, saying, "Let us go and worship other gods," whom you have not known, 14 then you shall inquire and make a thorough investigation. If the charge is established that such an abhorrent thing has been done among you, 15 you shall put the inhabitants of that town to the sword, utterly destroying it and everything in it — even putting its livestock to the sword. 16 All of its spoil you shall gather into its public square; then burn the town and all its spoil with fire, as a whole burnt offering to the LORD your God. It shall remain a perpetual ruin, never to be rebuilt. 17 Do not let anything devoted to destruction stick to your hand, so that the LORD may turn from his fierce anger and show you compassion, and in his compassion multiply you, as he swore to your ancestors, 18 if you obey the voice of the LORD your God by keeping all his commandments that I am commanding you today, doing what is right in the sight of the LORD your God.

14 You are children of the LORD your God. You must not lacerate yourselves or shave your forelocks for the dead. 2 For you are a people holy to the LORD your God; it is you the LORD has chosen out of all the peoples on earth to be his people, his treasured possession.

3 You shall not eat any abhorrent thing. 4 These are the animals you may eat: the ox, the sheep, the goat, 5 the deer, the gazelle, the roebuck, the wild goat, the ibex, the antelope, and the mountain-sheep. 6 Any animal that divides the hoof and has the hoof cleft in two, and chews the cud, among the animals, you may eat. 7 Yet of those that chew the cud or have the hoof cleft you shall not eat these: the camel, the hare, and the rock badger, because they chew the cud but do not divide the hoof; they are unclean for you. 8 And the pig, because it divides the hoof but does not chew the cud, is unclean for you. You shall not eat their meat, and you shall not touch their carcasses.

9 Of all that live in water you may eat these: whatever has fins and scales you may eat. 10 And whatever does not have fins and scales you shall not eat; it is unclean for you. 11 You may eat any clean birds. 12 But these are the ones that you shall not eat: the eagle, the vulture, the osprey, 13 the buzzard, the kite, of any kind; 14 every raven of any kind; 15 the ostrich, the nighthawk, the sea gull, the hawk, of any kind; 16 the little owl and the great owl, the water hen 17 and the desert owl,*i* the carrion vulture and the cormorant, 18 the stork, the heron, of any kind; the hoopoe and the bat.*j* 19 And all winged insects are unclean for you; they shall not be eaten. 20 You may eat any clean winged creature.

21 You shall not eat anything that dies of itself; you may give it to aliens residing in your towns for them to eat, or you may sell it to a foreigner. For you are a people holy to the LORD your God.

You shall not boil a kid in its mother's milk.

REVISED ENGLISH BIBLE

again will anything as wicked as this be done among you.

12-13 When you hear that miscreants have appeared in any of the towns which the LORD your God is giving you to occupy, and have led its inhabitants astray by calling on them to serve other gods whom you have not known, 14 then you are to investigate the matter carefully. If, after diligent examination, the report proves to be true and it is confirmed that this abominable thing has been done among you, 15 you must put the inhabitants of that town to the sword, and lay the town under solemn ban together with everything in it. 16 Gather all its goods into the public square and burn both town and goods as a complete offering to the LORD your God; and let it remain a mound of ruins and never be rebuilt. 17 Nothing out of all that has been laid under the ban must be found in your possession; in this way the LORD may turn from his fierce anger and show you compassion; and in his compassion he will make you grow as he swore to your forefathers, 18 provided that you obey the LORD your God and keep all his commandments which I give you this day, doing only what is right in the eyes of the LORD your God.

14 YOU ARE the children of the LORD your God: you must not gash yourselves or shave your forelocks in mourning for the dead. 2 You are a people holy to the LORD your God, and he has chosen you out of all peoples on earth to be his special possession.

3 You must not eat any abominable thing. 4 These are the animals you may eat: ox, sheep, goat, 5 buck, gazelle, roebuck, ibex, white-rumped deer, long-horned antelope, and rock-goat. 6 You may eat any hoofed animal which has cloven hoofs and also chews the cud; 7 those which only chew the cud or only have cloven hoofs you must not eat. These are: the camel, the hare, and the rock-badger, because they chew the cud but do not have cloven hoofs; they are unclean for you; 8 and the pig, because it has cloven hoofs but does not chew the cud, it is unclean for you. You are not to eat their flesh or even touch their dead carcasses. 9 Of creatures that live in water these may be eaten: all that have fins and scales; 10 but you may not eat any that have neither fins nor scales; they are unclean for you. 11 You may eat any clean bird. 12 These are the birds you may not eat: the griffon-vulture, the black vulture, the bearded vulture, 13 the kite, every kind of falcon, 14 every kind of crow, 15 the desert-owl, the short-eared owl, the long-eared owl, every kind of hawk, 16 the tawny owl, the screech-owl, the little owl, 17 the horned owl, the osprey, the fisher-owl, 18 the stork, the various kinds of cormorant, the hoopoe, and the bat.

19 All swarming winged creatures are unclean for you; they may not be eaten. 20 You may eat any clean winged creature.

21 You must not eat anything that has died a natural death. You may give it to aliens residing among you, and they may eat it, or you may sell it to a foreigner; but you are a people holy to the LORD your God.

Do not boil a kid in its mother's milk.

13:12–13 **miscreants:** *lit.* sons of Belial. 13:15 **in it:** *so Gk; Heb. adds* and the cattle to the sword. 14:1 **your forelocks:** *lit.* between your eyes. 14:7 **rock-badger:** *or* rock-rabbit.
14:12 **griffon-vulture:** *or* eagle. **bearded vulture:** *or* ossifrage.
14:13 **kite:** *so Samar., cp. Lev. 11:14; Heb. has an unknown word.*
falcon: *so some MSS; others add* kite. 14:14 **crow:** *or* raven.
14:18 **stork:** *or* heron.

---

i Or *pelican* *j* Identification of several of the birds in verses 12-18 is uncertain

12 And all Israel, hearing of it, shall fear and never again do such evil as this in your midst.

13 "If, in any of the cities which the LORD, your God, gives you to dwell in, you hear it said 14 that certain scoundrels have sprung up among you and have led astray the inhabitants of their city to serve other gods whom you have not known, 15 you must inquire carefully into the matter and investigate it thoroughly. If you find that it is true and an established fact that this abomination has been committed in your midst, 16 you shall put the inhabitants of that city to the sword, dooming the city and all life that is in it, even its cattle, to the sword. 17 Having heaped up all its spoils in the middle of its square, you shall burn the city with all its spoils as a whole burnt offering to the LORD, your God. Let it be a heap of ruins forever, never to be rebuilt. 18 You shall not retain anything that is doomed, that the blazing wrath of the LORD may die down and he may show you mercy and in his mercy for you may multiply you as he promised your fathers on oath; 19 because you have heeded the voice of the LORD, your God, keeping all his commandments which I enjoin on you today, doing what is right in his sight.

14 "You are children of the LORD, your God. You shall not gash yourselves nor shave the hair above your foreheads for the dead. 2 For you are a people sacred to the LORD, your God, who has chosen you from all the nations on the face of the earth to be a people peculiarly his own.

3 "You shall not eat any abominable thing. 4 These are the animals you may eat: the ox, the sheep, the goat, 5 the red deer, the gazelle, the roe deer, the ibex, the addax, the oryx, and the mountain sheep. 6 Any animal that has hoofs you may eat, provided it is cloven-footed and chews the cud. 7 But you shall not eat any of the following that only chew the cud or only have cloven hoofs: the camel, the hare and the rock badger, which indeed chew the cud, but do not have hoofs and are therefore unclean for you; 8 and the pig, which indeed has hoofs and is cloven-footed, but does not chew the cud and is therefore unclean for you. Their flesh you shall not eat, and their dead bodies you shall not touch.

9 "Of the various creatures that live in the water, whatever has both fins and scales you may eat, 10 but all those that lack either fins or scales you shall not eat; they are unclean for you.

11 "You may eat all clean birds. 12 But you shall not eat any of the following: the eagle, the vulture, the osprey, 13 the various kites and falcons, 14 all the various species of crows, 15 the ostrich, the nightjar, the gull, the various species of hawks, 16 the owl, the screech owl, the ibis, 17 the desert owl, the buzzard, the cormorant, 18 the stork, the various species of herons, the hoopoe, and the bat. 19 All winged insects, too, are unclean for you and shall not be eaten. 20 But you may eat any clean winged creatures.

21 "You must not eat any animal that has died of itself, for you are a people sacred to the LORD, your God. But you may give it to an alien who belongs to your community, and he may eat it, or you may sell it to a foreigner.

"You shall not boil a kid in its mother's milk.

will be afraid, and none of you will do such a wicked thing again.

13 'If you hear that in one of the towns which Yahweh your God has given you for a home, 14 there are men, scoundrels from your own stock, who have led their fellow-citizens astray, saying, "Let us go and serve other gods," hitherto unknown to you, 15 it is your duty to look into the matter, examine it, and enquire most carefully. If it is proved and confirmed that such a hateful thing has taken place among you, 16 you must put the inhabitants of that town to the sword; you must lay it under the curse of destruction — the town and everything in it. 17 You must pile up all its loot in the public square and burn the town and all its loot, offering it all to Yahweh your God. It is to be a ruin for all time, and never rebuilt. 18 From what is thus put under the curse of destruction you must keep nothing back, so that Yahweh may turn from the ferocity of his anger and show you mercy, and have pity on you and increase your numbers, as he swore he would to your ancestors, 19 on condition that you listen to the voice of Yahweh your God by keeping all his commandments which I am enjoining on you today, and by doing what is right in the eyes of Yahweh your God.'

14 'You are children of Yahweh your God. You must not gash yourselves or shave your foreheads for the dead. 2 For you are a people consecrated to Yahweh your God, and Yahweh has chosen you to be his own people from all the peoples on the earth.

3 j 'You must not eat anything disgusting. 4 These are the animals you may eat: ox, sheep, goat, 5 deer, gazelle, roebuck, ibex, antelope, oryx, mountain sheep. 6 You may eat any animal that has a divided and cloven hoof and that is a ruminant. 7 Of those, however, that are ruminants and of those that have a divided and cloven hoof you may not eat the following: the camel, the hare and the coney, which are ruminants but have no cloven hoof; you must class them as unclean. 8 So also the pig, which though it has a cloven hoof is not a ruminant; you must class it as unclean. You must neither eat the meat of such animals nor touch their dead bodies.

9 'Of whatever lives in water you may eat the following: you may eat anything that has fins and scales. 10 But you must not eat anything without fins and scales: you must class it as unclean.

11 'You may eat all clean birds, 12 but the following birds you must not eat: the tawny vulture, the griffon, the osprey, 13 the kite and the several kinds of buzzard, 14 all kinds of raven, 15 the ostrich, the screech owl, the seagull, the several kinds of hawk, 16 owl, barn owl, ibis, 17 pelican, white vulture, cormorant, 18 stork, the several kinds of heron, hoopoe and bat. 19 You are to class all winged insects as unclean and must not eat them. 20 You may eat any clean fowl.

21 'You must not eat any animal that has died a natural death. You may give it to a resident foreigner to eat, or sell it to a foreigner. For you are a people consecrated to Yahweh your God.

'You must not boil a kid in its mother's milk.

---

j 14 14:3seq. // Lv 11:1.

NEW REVISED STANDARD VERSION

22 Set apart a tithe of all the yield of your seed that is brought in yearly from the field. 23 In the presence of the LORD your God, in the place that he will choose as a dwelling for his name, you shall eat the tithe of your grain, your wine, and your oil, as well as the firstlings of your herd and flock, so that you may learn to fear the LORD your God always. 24 But if, when the LORD your God has blessed you, the distance is so great that you are unable to transport it, because the place where the LORD your God will choose to set his name is too far away from you, 25 then you may turn it into money. With the money secure in hand, go to the place that the LORD your God will choose; 26 spend the money for whatever you wish — oxen, sheep, wine, strong drink, or whatever you desire. And you shall eat there in the presence of the LORD your God, you and your household rejoicing together. 27 As for the Levites resident in your towns, do not neglect them, because they have no allotment or inheritance with you.

28 Every third year you shall bring out the full tithe of your produce for that year, and store it within your towns; 29 the Levites, because they have no allotment or inheritance with you, as well as the resident aliens, the orphans, and the widows in your towns, may come and eat their fill so that the LORD your God may bless you in all the work that you undertake.

15 Every seventh year you shall grant a remission of debts. 2 And this is the manner of the remission: every creditor shall remit the claim that is held against a neighbor, not exacting it of a neighbor who is a member of the community, because the LORD's remission has been proclaimed. 3 Of a foreigner you may exact it, but you must remit your claim on whatever any member of your community owes you. 4 There will, however, be no one in need among you, because the LORD is sure to bless you in the land that the LORD your God is giving you as a possession to occupy, 5 if only you will obey the LORD your God by diligently observing this entire commandment that I command you today. 6 When the LORD your God has blessed you, as he promised, you will lend to many nations, but you will not borrow; you will rule over many nations, but they will not rule over you.

7 If there is among you anyone in need, a member of your community in any of your towns within the land that the LORD your God is giving you, do not be hard-hearted or tight-fisted toward your needy neighbor. 8 You should rather open your hand, willingly lending enough to meet the need, whatever it may be. 9 Be careful that you do not entertain a mean thought, thinking, "The seventh year, the year of remission, is near," and therefore view your needy neighbor with hostility and give nothing; your neighbor might cry to the LORD against you, and you would incur guilt. 10 Give liberally and be ungrudging when you do so, for on this account the LORD your God will bless you in all your work and in all that you undertake. 11 Since there will never cease to be some in need on the earth, I therefore command you, "Open your hand to the poor and needy neighbor in your land."

12 If a member of your community, whether a Hebrew man or a Hebrew woman, is sold^k to you and works for you six years, in the seventh year you shall set that person free. 13 And when you send a male slave^l out from you a free person, you shall not send him out empty-handed.

REVISED ENGLISH BIBLE

22 Year by year you are to set aside a tithe of all the produce of your sowing, of everything that grows on the land. 23 You must eat it in the presence of the LORD your God in the place which he will choose as a dwelling for his name — the tithe of your grain and new wine and oil, and the firstborn of your cattle and sheep, so that for all time you may learn to fear the LORD your God. 24 When the LORD your God has blessed you with prosperity, and the place where he will choose to set his name is too far away and the journey too great for you to carry your tithe, 25 then you may convert it into money. Tie up the money and take it with you to the place which the LORD your God will choose. 26 There you may spend it as you choose on cattle or sheep, wine or strong drink, or anything else you please, and there feast with rejoicing, both you and your family, in the presence of the LORD your God.

27 Also, the Levites who live in your settlements must not suffer neglect at your hands, for they have no holding of ancestral land among you. 28 At the end of every third year you are to bring out all the tithe of your produce for that year and leave it in your settlements 29 so that the Levites, who have no holding of ancestral land among you, and the aliens, orphans, and widows in your settlements may come and have plenty to eat. If you do this the LORD your God will bless you in everything to which you set your hand.

15 At the end of every seventh year you must make a remission of debts. 2 This is how it is to be made: everyone who holds a pledge shall return the pledge of the person indebted to him. He must not press a fellow-countryman for repayment, for the LORD's year of remission has been declared. 3 You may press foreigners; but if it is a fellow-countryman that holds anything of yours, you must renounce all claim on it.

4-5 There will never be any poor among you if only you obey the LORD your God by carefully keeping these commandments which I lay upon you this day; for the LORD your God will bless you with great prosperity in the land which he is giving you to occupy as your holding. 6 When the LORD your God blesses you, as he promised, you will lend to people of many nations, but you yourselves will borrow from none; you will rule many nations, but none will rule you.

7 When in any of your settlements in the land which the LORD your God is giving you one of your fellow-countrymen becomes poor, do not be hard-hearted or close-fisted towards him in his need. 8 Be open-handed towards him and lend him on pledge as much as he needs. 9 See that you do not harbour the villainous thought that the seventh year, the year of remission, is near, and look askance at your needy countryman and give him nothing. If you do, he will appeal to the LORD against you, and you will be found guilty of sin. 10 Give freely to him and do not begrudge him your bounty, because it is for this very bounty that the LORD your God will bless you in everything that you do or undertake. 11 The poor will always be with you in your land, and that is why I command you to be open-handed towards any of your countrymen there who are in poverty and need.

12 Should a fellow-Hebrew, be it a man or a woman, sell himself to you as a slave, he is to serve you for six years. In the seventh year you must set him free, 13 and when you set him free, do not let him go empty-handed. 14 Give to

---

^kOr *sells himself or herself*   ^lHeb *him*

15:2 **has been declared:** *or* has come.   15:9 **villainous thought:** *lit.* thought of Belial.

22 "Each year you shall tithe all the produce that grows in the field you have sown; 23 then in the place which the LORD, your God, chooses as the dwelling place of his name you shall eat in his presence your tithe of the grain, wine and oil, as well as the firstlings of your herd and flock, that you may learn always to fear the LORD, your God. 24 If, however, the journey is too much for you and you are not able to bring your tithe, because the place which the LORD, your God, chooses for the abode of his name is too far for you, considering how the LORD has blessed you, 25 you may exchange the tithe for money and, with the purse of money in hand, go to the place which the LORD, your God, chooses. 26 You may then exchange the money for whatever you desire, oxen or sheep, wine or strong drink, or anything else you would enjoy, and there before the LORD, your God, you shall partake of it and make merry with your family. 27 But do not neglect the Levite who belongs to your community, for he has no share in the heritage with you.

28 "At the end of every third year you shall bring out all the tithes of your produce for that year and deposit them in community stores, 29 that the Levite who has no share in the heritage with you, and also the alien, the orphan and the widow who belong to your community, may come and eat their fill; so that the LORD, your God, may bless you in all that you undertake.

15 "At the end of every seven-year period you shall have a relaxation of debts, 2 which shall be observed as follows. Every creditor shall relax his claim on what he has loaned his neighbor; he must not press his neighbor, his kinsman, because a relaxation in honor of the LORD has been proclaimed. 3 You may press a foreigner, but you shall relax the claim on your kinsman for what is yours. 4 Nay, more! since the LORD, your God, will bless you abundantly in the land he will give you to occupy as your heritage, there should be no one of you in need. 5 If you but heed the voice of the LORD, your God, and carefully observe all these commandments which I enjoin on you today, 6 you will lend to many nations, and borrow from none; you will rule over many nations, and none will rule over you, since the LORD, your God, will bless you as he promised. 7 If one of your kinsmen in any community is in need in the land which the LORD, your God, is giving you, you shall not harden your heart nor close your hand to him in his need. 8 Instead, you shall open your hand to him and freely lend him enough to meet his need. 9 Be on your guard lest, entertaining the mean thought that the seventh year, the year of relaxation, is near, you grudge help to your needy kinsman and give him nothing; else he will cry to the LORD against you and you will be held guilty. 10 When you give to him, give freely and not with ill will; for the LORD, your God, will bless you for this in all your works and undertakings. 11 The needy will never be lacking in the land; that is why I command you to open your hand to your poor and needy kinsman in your country.

12 "If your kinsman, a Hebrew man or woman, sells himself to you, he is to serve you for six years, but in the seventh year you shall dismiss him from your service, a free man. 13 When you do so, you shall not send him away empty-handed, 14 but shall weight him down with gifts from

22 'Every year, you must take a tithe of what your fields produce from what you have sown 23 and, in the presence of Yahweh your God, in the place where he chooses to give his name a home, you must eat the tithe of your wheat, of your new wine and of your oil, and the first-born of your herd and flock; and by so doing, you will learn always to fear Yahweh your God.

24 'If the road is too long for you, if you cannot bring your tithe because the place in which Yahweh chooses to make a home for his name is too far away, when Yahweh your God has blessed you, 25 you must convert it into money and, with the money clasped in your hand, you must go to the place chosen by Yahweh your God; 26 there you may spend the money on whatever you like, oxen, sheep, wine, fermented liquor, anything you please. There you must eat in the presence of Yahweh your God and rejoice, you and your household. 27 Do not neglect the Levite living in your community, since he has no share or heritage of his own among you.

28 'At the end of every three years, you must take all the tithes of your harvests for that year and collect them in community. 29 Then the Levite — since he has no share or heritage of his own among you — the foreigner, the orphan and the widow living in your community, will come and eat all they want. And so Yahweh your God will bless you in all the labours that you undertake.'

15 'At the end of every seven years, you must grant remission. 2 The nature of the remission is as follows: any creditor holding a personal pledge obtained from his fellow must release him from it; he must not exploit his fellow or his brother once the latter has appealed to Yahweh for remission. 3 A foreigner you may exploit, but you must remit whatever claim you have on your brother. 4 There must, then, be no poor among you. For Yahweh will grant you his blessing in the country which Yahweh your God is giving you to possess as your heritage, 5 only if you pay careful attention to the voice of Yahweh your God, by keeping and practising all these commandments which I am enjoining on you today. 6 If Yahweh your God blesses you as he has promised, you will be creditors to many nations but debtors to none; you will rule over many nations, and be ruled by none.

7 'Is there anyone poor among you, one of your brothers, in any town of yours in the country which Yahweh your God is giving you? Do not harden your heart or close your hand against that poor brother of yours, 8 but be open handed with him and lend him enough for his needs. 9 Do not allow this mean thought in your heart, "The seventh year, the year of remission, is near," and scowl at your poor brother and give him nothing; he could appeal against you to Yahweh, and you would incur guilt! 10 When you give to him, you must give with an open heart; for this, Yahweh your God will bless you in all your actions and in all your undertakings. 11 Of course, there will never cease to be poor people in the country, and that is why I am giving you this command: Always be open handed with your brother, and with anyone in your country who is in need and poor.

12 'If your fellow Hebrew, man or woman, sells himself to you, he can serve you for six years. In the seventh year you must set him free, 13 and in setting him free you must not let him go empty handed. 14 By way of present, you will

NEW REVISED STANDARD VERSION

14 Provide liberally out of your flock, your threshing floor, and your wine press, thus giving to him some of the bounty with which the LORD your God has blessed you. 15 Remember that you were a slave in the land of Egypt, and the LORD your God redeemed you; for this reason I lay this command upon you today. 16 But if he says to you, "I will not go out from you," because he loves you and your household, since he is well off with you, 17 then you shall take an awl and thrust it through his earlobe into the door, and he shall be your slave[m] forever.

You shall do the same with regard to your female slave.[n]

18 Do not consider it a hardship when you send them out from you free persons, because for six years they have given you services worth the wages of hired laborers; and the LORD your God will bless you in all that you do.

19 Every firstling male born of your herd and flock you shall consecrate to the LORD your God; you shall not do work with your firstling ox nor shear the firstling of your flock. 20 You shall eat it, you together with your household, in the presence of the LORD your God year by year at the place that the LORD will choose. 21 But if it has any defect—any serious defect, such as lameness or blindness—you shall not sacrifice it to the LORD your God; 22 within your towns you may eat it, the unclean and the clean alike, as you would a gazelle or deer. 23 Its blood, however, you must not eat; you shall pour it out on the ground like water.

16 Observe the month[o] of Abib by keeping the passover for the LORD your God, for in the month of Abib the LORD your God brought you out of Egypt by night. 2 You shall offer the passover sacrifice for the LORD your God, from the flock and the herd, at the place that the LORD will choose as a dwelling for his name. 3 You must not eat with it anything leavened. For seven days you shall eat unleavened bread with it—the bread of affliction—because you came out of the land of Egypt in great haste, so that all the days of your life you may remember the day of your departure from the land of Egypt. 4 No leaven shall be seen with you in all your territory for seven days; and none of the meat of what you slaughter on the evening of the first day shall remain until morning. 5 You are not permitted to offer the passover sacrifice within any of your towns that the LORD your God is giving you. 6 But at the place that the LORD your God will choose as a dwelling for his name, only there shall you offer the passover sacrifice, in the evening at sunset, the time of day when you departed from Egypt. 7 You shall cook it and eat it at the place that the LORD your God will choose; the next morning you may go back to your tents. 8 For six days you shall continue to eat unleavened bread, and on the seventh day there shall be a solemn assembly for the LORD your God, when you shall do no work.

9 You shall count seven weeks; begin to count the seven weeks from the time the sickle is first put to the standing grain. 10 Then you shall keep the festival of weeks for the LORD your God, contributing a freewill offering in proportion to the blessing that you have received from the LORD your God. 11 Rejoice before the LORD your God—you and your sons and your daughters, your male and female slaves, the Levites resident in your towns, as well as the strangers, the orphans, and the widows who are among you—at the place that the LORD your God will choose as a dwelling for his name. 12 Remember that you were a slave in Egypt, and diligently observe these statutes.

13 You shall keep the festival of booths[p] for seven days, when you have gathered in the produce from your threshing floor and your wine press. 14 Rejoice during your

REVISED ENGLISH BIBLE

him lavishly from your flock, from your threshing-floor and your winepress. Be generous to him, as the LORD your God has blessed you. 18 Do not resent it when you have to set him free, for his six years' service to you has been worth twice the wage of a hired man. Then the LORD your God will bless you in everything you do. 15 Bear in mind that you were slaves in Egypt and the LORD your God redeemed you; that is why I am giving you this command today.

16 If, however, a slave is content to be with you and says, 'I shall not leave you; I love you and your family,' 17 then take an awl and pierce through his ear to the door, and he will be your slave for life. Treat a slave-girl in the same way. ‡15.18: see above‡

19 You must dedicate to the LORD your God every male firstborn of your herds and flocks. You must not plough with the firstborn of your cattle or shear the firstborn of your sheep. 20 Year by year you and your household must eat them in the presence of the LORD your God, in the place which the LORD will choose. 21 If any animal has a defect, if it is lame or blind or has any other serious defect, you may not sacrifice it to the LORD your God. 22 Eat it in your settlements; both clean and unclean alike may eat it as they would the meat of gazelle or deer. 23 But on no account may you partake of its blood; you must pour it out on the ground like water.

16 OBSERVE the month of Abib and celebrate the Passover to the LORD your God, for it was in that month that the LORD your God brought you out of Egypt by night. 2 Slaughter an animal from flock or herd as a Passover victim to the LORD your God in the place which he will choose as a dwelling for his name. 3 You must eat nothing leavened with it; for seven days you must eat unleavened bread, the bread of affliction, because you came out of Egypt in urgent haste. Thus as long as you live you are to commemorate the day of your coming out of Egypt. 4 No leaven must be seen in all your territory for seven days, nor must any of the flesh which you have slaughtered in the evening of the first day remain overnight till morning.

5 You may not slaughter the Passover victim in any of the settlements which the LORD your God is giving you, 6 but only in the place which he will choose as a dwelling for his name; there you are to slaughter the Passover victim in the evening as the sun goes down, the time of your coming out of Egypt. 7 Cook it and eat it in the place which the LORD your God will choose, and then next morning set off back to your tents. 8 For six days you must eat unleavened loaves, and on the seventh day hold a closing ceremony in honour of the LORD your God; you must do no work.

9 Seven weeks should be counted off: start counting them from the time when the sickle is put to the standing grain; 10 then celebrate the pilgrim-feast of Weeks to the LORD your God and offer a freewill-offering in proportion to the blessing that the LORD your God has given you. 11 Rejoice before the LORD your God, with your sons and daughters, your male and female slaves, the Levites who live in your settlements, and the aliens, fatherless, and widows among you. Rejoice in the place which the LORD your God will choose as a dwelling for his name 12 and keep in mind that you were slaves in Egypt. You are to be careful to observe all these statutes.

13 After you bring in the produce from your threshing-floor and winepress, you are to celebrate the pilgrim-feast of Booths for seven days. 14 Rejoice at your feast with your

---

your flock and threshing floor and wine press, in proportion to the blessing the LORD, your God, has bestowed on you. 15 For remember that you too were once slaves in the land of Egypt, and the LORD, your God, ransomed you. That is why I am giving you this command today. 16 If, however, he tells you that he does not wish to leave you, because he is devoted to you and your household, since he fares well with you, 17 you shall take an awl and thrust it through his ear into the door, and he shall then be your slave forever. Your female slave, also, you shall treat in the same way. 18 You must not be reluctant to let your slave go free, since the service he has given you for six years was worth twice a hired man's salary; then also the LORD, your God, will bless you in everything you do.

19 "You shall consecreate to the LORD, your God, all the male firstlings of your herd and of your flock. You shall not work the firstlings of your cattle, nor shear the firstlings of your flock. 20 Year after year you and your family shall eat them before the LORD, your God, in the place he chooses. 21 If, however, a firstling is lame or blind or has any other serious defect, you shall not sacrifice it to the LORD, your God, 22 but in your own communities you may eat it, the unclean and the clean eating it alike, as you would a gazelle or a deer. 23 Only, you shall not partake of its blood, which must be poured out on the ground like water.

16 "Observe the month of Abib by keeping the Passover of the LORD, your God, since it was in the month of Abib that he brought you by night out of Egypt. 2 You shall offer the Passover sacrifice from your flock or your herd to the LORD, your God, in the place which he chooses as the dwelling place of his name. 3 You shall not eat leavened bread with it. For seven days you shall eat with it only unleavened bread, the bread of affliction, that you may remember as long as you live the day of your departure from the land of Egypt; for in frightened haste you left the land of Egypt. 4 Nothing leavened may be found in all your territory for seven days, and none of the meat which you sacrificed on the evening of the first day shall be kept overnight for the next day.

5 "You may not sacrifice the Passover in any of the communities which the LORD, your God, gives you; 6 only at the place which he chooses as the dwelling place of his name, and in the evening at sunset, on the anniversary of your departure from Egypt, shall you sacrifice the Passover. 7 You shall cook and eat it at the place the LORD, your God, chooses; then in the morning you may return to your tents. 8 For six days you shall eat unleavened bread, and on the seventh there shall be a solemn meeting in honor of the LORD, your God; on that day you shall not do any sort of work.

9 "You shall count off seven weeks, computing them from the day when the sickle is first put to the standing grain. 10 You shall then keep the feast of Weeks in honor of the LORD, your God, and the measure of your own freewill offering shall be in proportion to the blessing the LORD, your God, has bestowed on you. 11 In the place which the LORD, your God, chooses as the dwelling place of his name, you shall make merry in his presence together with your son and daughter, your male and female slave, and the Levite who belongs to your community, as well as the alien, the orphan and the widow among you. 12 Remember that you too were once slaves in Egypt, and carry out these statutes carefully.

13 "You shall celebrate the feast of Booths for seven days, when you have gathered in the produce from your threshing floor and wine press. 14 You shall make merry at your feast,

load his shoulders with things from your flock, from your threshing-floor and from your winepress; as Yahweh your God has blessed you, so you must give to him. 15 Remember that you were once a slave in Egypt and that Yahweh your God redeemed you; that is why I am giving you this order today.

16 'But if he says to you, "I do not want to leave you," because he loves you and your household and is happy with you, 17 you must take an awl and drive it through his ear into the door and he will be your servant for ever. You must do the same to a female slave.

18 'Do not think it hard on you to have to give him his freedom; he is worth twice what a paid servant would cost you, and has served you for six years. And Yahweh your God will bless you in everything you do.

19 'You must consecrate every first-born male from your herd and flock to Yahweh your God. You must not put the first-born of your herd to work, or shear the first-born of your flock. 20 You must eat it, you and your household, each year, in the presence of Yahweh your God, in the place which Yahweh chooses. 21 If it has any defect, if it is lame or blind — any serious defect — you must not sacrifice it to Yahweh your God. 22 You will eat it at home, unclean and clean together, as you would gazelle or deer; 23 only, you will not eat its blood, but pour that like water on the ground.'

16 'Observe the month of Abib and celebrate the Passover for Yahweh your God, because it was in the month of Abib that Yahweh your God brought you out of Egypt by night. 2 You must sacrifice a Passover from your flock or herd for Yahweh your God in the place where Yahweh chooses to give his name a home. 3 You must not eat leavened bread with this; for seven days you must eat it with unleavened bread — the bread of affliction — since you left Egypt in great haste; this is so that, as long as you live, you will remember the day you came out of Egypt. 4 For seven days no leaven must be found in any house throughout your territory, nor must any of the meat that you sacrifice in the evening of the first day be kept overnight until the next day. 5 You must sacrifice the Passover not in any of the towns given you by Yahweh your God, 6 but in the place where Yahweh your God chooses to give his name a home; there you must sacrifice the Passover, in the evening at sunset, at the hour when you came out of Egypt. 7 You will cook it and eat it in the place chosen by Yahweh your God, and in the morning you must return and go to your tents. 8 For six days you will eat unleavened bread; on the seventh day there will be an assembly for Yahweh your God; and you must do no work.

9 'You must count seven weeks, counting these seven weeks from the time you begin to put your sickle into the standing corn. 10 You will then celebrate the feast of Weeks for Yahweh your God with the gift of a voluntary offering proportionate to the degree in which Yahweh your God has blessed you. 11 You must rejoice in the presence of Yahweh your God, in the place where Yahweh your God chooses to give his name a home, you, your son and your daughter, your serving men and women, the Levite living in your community, the foreigner, the orphan and the widow living among you. 12 Remember that you were once a slave in Egypt, and carefully observe these laws.

13 'You must celebrate the feast of Shelters for seven days, at the time when you gather in the produce of your threshing-floor and winepress. 14 You must rejoice at your

festival, you and your sons and your daughters, your male and female slaves, as well as the Levites, the strangers, the orphans, and the widows resident in your towns. 15 Seven days you shall keep the festival for the LORD your God at the place that the LORD will choose; for the LORD your God will bless you in all your produce and in all your undertakings, and you shall surely celebrate.

16 Three times a year all your males shall appear before the LORD your God at the place that he will choose: at the festival of unleavened bread, at the festival of weeks, and at the festival of booths. q They shall not appear before the LORD empty-handed; 17 all shall give as they are able, according to the blessing of the LORD your God that he has given you.

18 You shall appoint judges and officials throughout your tribes, in all your towns that the LORD your God is giving you, and they shall render just decisions for the people. 19 You must not distort justice; you must not show partiality; and you must not accept bribes, for a bribe blinds the eyes of the wise and subverts the cause of those who are in the right. 20 Justice, and only justice, you shall pursue, so that you may live and occupy the land that the LORD your God is giving you.

21 You shall not plant any tree as a sacred pole r beside the altar that you make for the LORD your God; 22 nor shall you set up a stone pillar—things that the LORD your God hates.

17 You must not sacrifice to the LORD your God an ox or a sheep that has a defect, anything seriously wrong; for that is abhorrent to the LORD your God.
2 If there is found among you, in one of your towns that the LORD your God is giving you, a man or woman who does what is evil in the sight of the LORD your God, and transgresses his covenant 3 by going to serve other gods and worshiping them—whether the sun or the moon or any of the host of heaven, which I have forbidden— 4 and if it is reported to you or you hear of it, and you make a thorough inquiry, and the charge is proved true that such an abhorrent thing has occurred in Israel, 5 then you shall bring out to your gates that man or that woman who has committed this crime and you shall stone the man or woman to death. 6 On the evidence of two or three witnesses the death sentence shall be executed; a person must not be put to death on the evidence of only one witness. 7 The hands of the witnesses shall be the first raised against the person to execute the death penalty, and afterward the hands of all the people. So you shall purge the evil from your midst.

8 If a judicial decision is too difficult for you to make between one kind of bloodshed and another, one kind of legal right and another, or one kind of assault and another—any such matters of dispute in your towns—then you shall immediately go up to the place that the LORD your God will choose, 9 where you shall consult with the levitical priests and the judge who is in office in those days; and they shall announce to you the decision in the case. 10 Carry out exactly the decision that they announce to you from the place that the LORD will choose, diligently observing everything they instruct you. 11 You must carry out fully the law that they interpret for you or the ruling that they announce to you; do not turn aside from the decision that they announce to you, either to the right or to the left. 12 As for anyone who presumes to disobey the priest appointed to minister there to the LORD your God, or the judge, that person shall die. So you shall purge the evil from Israel. 13 All the people will hear and be afraid, and will not act presumptuously again.

sons and daughters, your male and female slaves, the Levites, aliens, fatherless, and widows living in your settlements. 15 For seven days you are to celebrate this feast to the LORD your God in the place which he will choose, when the LORD your God gives you his blessing in all your harvest and in all your work; you shall keep the feast with joy.

16 Three times a year all your males must come into the presence of the LORD your God in the place which he will choose: at the pilgrim-feasts of Unleavened Bread, of Weeks, and of Booths. No one may come into the presence of the LORD without an offering; 17 each of you is to bring such a gift as he can in proportion to the blessing which the LORD your God has given you.

18 In every settlement which the LORD your God is giving you, you must appoint for yourselves judges and officers, tribe by tribe, and they will dispense true justice to the people. 19 You must not pervert the course of justice or show favour or accept a bribe; for bribery makes the wise person blind and the just person give a crooked answer. 20 Justice, and justice alone, must be your aim, so that you may live and occupy the land which the LORD your God is giving you.

21 Do not plant any kind of tree as a sacred pole beside the altar of the LORD your God which you will build, 22 nor erect a sacred pillar; for all such are hateful to the LORD your God.

17 You must not sacrifice to the LORD your God a bull or sheep that has any defect or serious blemish, for that would be abominable to the LORD your God.
2 Should there be found among you, in any of the settlements which the LORD your God is giving you, a man or woman who does what is wrong in the eyes of the LORD your God, by violating his covenant 3 and going to serve other gods, prostrating himself before them or before the sun and moon and all the host of heaven—a thing that I have forbidden— 4 then, if it is reported to you or you hear of it, make careful enquiry. If the report proves to be true, and it is confirmed that this abominable thing has been done in Israel, 5 then bring the man or woman who has done this wicked deed to the gate of the town to be stoned to death. 6 Sentence of death is to be carried out on the testimony of two or of three witnesses: no one must be put to death on the testimony of a single witness. 7 The first stones are to be thrown by the witnesses and then all the people must follow; so you will get rid of the wickedness in your midst.

8 When the issue in any lawsuit that is disputed in your courts is beyond your competence, whether it be a case of accidental or premeditated homicide, civil rights, or personal injury, then resort without delay to the place which the LORD your God will choose. 9 Appear before the levitical priests or the judge then in office and seek guidance; they will give you the verdict. 10 Act on the pronouncement which they make from the place chosen by the LORD, and see that you carry out all their instructions. 11 Act on the instruction they give you, or on the precedent they cite; do not deviate from the decision they hand down to you, either to right or to left. 12 Anyone who presumes to reject the decision either of the priest ministering there to the LORD your God, or of the judge, is to be put to death; thus you will purge Israel of wickedness. 13 Then all the people when they hear of it will be afraid, and never again show such presumption.

---

q Or tabernacles; Heb succoth   r Heb Asherah

16:21 **sacred pole:** *Heb.* asherah.   17:5 **town:** *so Gk; Heb. adds* the man or the woman.   17:8 **in your courts:** *lit.* in your gates.

404

NEW AMERICAN BIBLE

NEW JERUSALEM BIBLE

together with your son and daughter, your male and female slave, and also the Levite, the alien, the orphan and the widow who belong to your community. 15 For seven days you shall celebrate this pilgrim feast in honor of the LORD, your God, in the place which he chooses; since the LORD, your God, has blessed you in all your crops and in all your undertakings, you shall do naught but make merry.

16 "Three times a year, then, every male among you shall appear before the LORD, your God, in the place which he chooses: at the feast of Unleavened Bread, at the feast of Weeks, and at the feast of Booths. No one shall appear before the LORD empty-handed, 17 but each of you with as much as he can give, in proportion to the blessings which the LORD, your God, has bestowed on you.

18 "You shall appoint judges and officials throughout your tribes to administer true justice for the people in all the communities which the LORD, your God, is giving you. 19 You shall not distort justice; you must be impartial. You shall not take a bribe; for a bribe blinds the eyes even of the wise and twists the words even of the just. 20 Justice and justice alone shall be your aim, that you may have life and may possess the land which the LORD, your God, is giving you.

21 "You shall not plant a sacred pole of any kind of wood beside the altar of the LORD, your God, which you will build; 22 nor shall you erect a sacred pillar, such as the LORD, your God, detests.

17 "You shall not sacrifice to the LORD, your God, from the herd or from the flock an animal with any serious defect; that would be an abomination to the LORD, your God.

2 "If there is found among you, in any one of the communities which the LORD, your God, gives you, a man or a woman who does evil in the sight of the LORD, your God, and transgresses his covenant, 3 by serving other gods, or by worshiping the sun or the moon or any of the host of the sky, against my command; 4 and if, on being informed of it, you find by careful investigation that it is true and an established fact that this abomination has been committed in Israel; 5 you shall bring the man (or woman) who had done the evil deed out to your city gates and stone him to death. 6 The testimony of two or three witnesses is required for putting a person to death; no one shall be put to death on the testimony of only one witness. 7 At the execution, the witnesses are to be the first to raise their hands against him; afterward all the people are to join in. Thus shall you purge the evil from your midst.

8 "If in your own community there is a case at issue which proves too complicated for you to decide, in a matter of bloodshed or of civil rights or of personal injury, you shall then go up to the place which the LORD, your God, chooses, 9 to the levitical priests or to the judge who is in office at that time. They shall study the case and then hand down to you their decision. 10 According to this decision that they give you in the place which the LORD chooses, you shall act, being careful to do exactly as they direct. 11 You shall carry out the directions they give you and the verdict they pronounce for you, without turning aside to the right or to the left from the decision they hand down to you. 12 Any man who has the insolence to refuse to listen to the priest who officiates there in the ministry of the LORD, your God, or to the judge, shall die. Thus shall you purge the evil from your midst. 13 And all the people, on hearing of it, shall fear, and never again be so insolent.

feast, you, your son and your daughter, your serving men and women, the Levite, the foreigner, the orphan and the widow living in your community. 15 For seven days, you must celebrate the feast for Yahweh your God in the place chosen by Yahweh; for Yahweh your God will bless you in all your produce and in all your undertakings, so that you will have good reason to rejoice.

16 'Three times a year all your menfolk must appear before Yahweh your God in the place chosen by him: at the feast of Unleavened Bread, at the feast of Weeks, at the feast of Shelters. No one must appear empty-handed before Yahweh, 17 but each must give what he can, in proportion to the blessing which Yahweh your God has bestowed on you.

18 'You must appoint judges and scribes in each of the towns that Yahweh your God is giving you, for all your tribes; these are to mete out proper justice to the people. 19 You must not pervert the law; you must be impartial; you will take no bribes, for a bribe blinds the eyes of the wise and ruins the cause of the upright. 20 Strict justice must be your ideal, so that you may live long in possession of the country given you by Yahweh your God.

21 'You must not plant a sacred pole of any wood whatsoever beside the altar which you erect for Yahweh your God; 22 nor will you set up a standing-stone, a thing Yahweh your God would abhor.'

17 'To Yahweh your God you must sacrifice nothing from herd or flock that has any blemish or defect whatsoever, for Yahweh your God holds this detestable.

2 'If there is anyone, man or woman, among you in any of the towns given you by Yahweh your God, who does what is wrong in the eyes of Yahweh your God by violating his covenant, 3 who goes and serves other gods and worships them, or the sun or the moon or any of heaven's array — a thing I have forbidden — 4 and this person is denounced to you: if after careful enquiry it is found true and confirmed that this hateful thing has been done in Israel, 5 you must take the man or woman guilty of this evil deed outside your city gates, and there you must stone that man or woman to death. 6 A death sentence may be passed only on the word of two witnesses or three; and no one must be put to death on the word of one witness alone. 7 The witnesses' hands must strike the first blow in putting the condemned to death, the rest of the people following. You must banish this evil from among you.

8 'If a case comes before you which is too difficult for you, a case of murder, conflicting claims, damage to property — any kind of dispute — in your towns, you must make your way to the place chosen by Yahweh your God, 9 and approach the levitical priests and the judge then in office. They will hold an enquiry and let you know their sentence. 10 You must abide by the verdict which they give you in this place chosen by Yahweh, and you will take care to carry out all their instructions. 11 You will abide by the decision which they give you and by the sentence which they pronounce, not deviating to right or to left from the verdict which they have given you. 12 If anyone presumes to disobey either the priest who is there in the service of Yahweh your God, or the judge, that person must die. You must banish this evil from Israel. 13 And when the people hear of this they will be afraid and not act presumptuously any more.

NEW REVISED STANDARD VERSION

14 When you have come into the land that the LORD your God is giving you, and have taken possession of it and settled in it, and you say, "I will set a king over me, like all the nations that are around me," 15 you may indeed set over you a king whom the LORD your God will choose. One of your own community you may set as king over you; you are not permitted to put a foreigner over you, who is not of your own community. 16 Even so, he must not acquire many horses for himself, or return the people to Egypt in order to acquire more horses, since the LORD has said to you, "You must never return that way again." 17 And he must not acquire many wives for himself, or else his heart will turn away; also silver and gold he must not acquire in great quantity for himself. 18 When he has taken the throne of his kingdom, he shall have a copy of this law written for him in the presence of the levitical priests. 19 It shall remain with him and he shall read in it all the days of his life, so that he may learn to fear the LORD his God, diligently observing all the words of this law and these statutes, 20 neither exalting himself above other members of the community nor turning aside from the commandment, either to the right or to the left, so that he and his descendants may reign long over his kingdom in Israel.

18 The levitical priests, the whole tribe of Levi, shall have no allotment or inheritance within Israel. They may eat the sacrifices that are the LORD's portion[s] 2 but they shall have no inheritance among the other members of the community; the LORD is their inheritance, as he promised them. 3 This shall be the priests' due from the people, from those offering a sacrifice, whether an ox or a sheep: they shall give to the priest the shoulder, the two jowls, and the stomach. 4 The first fruits of your grain, your wine, and your oil, as well as the first of the fleece of your sheep, you shall give him. 5 For the LORD your God has chosen Levi[t] out of all your tribes, to stand and minister in the name of the LORD, him and his sons for all time. 6 If a Levite leaves any of your towns, from wherever he has been residing in Israel, and comes to the place that the LORD will choose (and he may come whenever he wishes), 7 then he may minister in the name of the LORD his God, like all his fellow-Levites who stand to minister there before the LORD. 8 They shall have equal portions to eat, even though they have income from the sale of family possessions.[s]

9 When you come into the land that the LORD your God is giving you, you must not learn to imitate the abhorrent practices of those nations. 10 No one shall be found among you who makes a son or daughter pass through fire, or who practices divination, or is a soothsayer, or an augur, or a sorcerer, 11 or one who casts spells, or who consults ghosts or spirits, or who seeks oracles from the dead. 12 For whoever does these things is abhorrent to the LORD; it is because of such abhorrent practices that the LORD your God is driving them out before you. 13 You must remain completely loyal to the LORD your God. 14 Although these nations that you are about to dispossess do give heed to soothsayers and diviners, as for you, the LORD your God does not permit you to do so.

15 The LORD your God will raise up for you a prophet[u] like me from among your own people; you shall heed such a prophet.[v] 16 This is what you requested of the LORD your God at Horeb on the day of the assembly when you said: "If I hear the voice of the LORD my God any more, or ever again see this great fire, I will die." 17 Then the LORD replied to me: "They are right in what they have said. 18 I will

REVISED ENGLISH BIBLE

14 After you come into the land which the LORD your God is giving you, and have occupied it and settled there, if you then say, 'Let us appoint a king over us, as all the surrounding nations do,' 15 you must appoint as king the man whom the LORD your God will choose. You must appoint over you a man of your own people; you must not appoint a foreigner, one who is not of your own people. 16 He must not acquire numerous horses, or send men to Egypt to obtain more horses, for the LORD said to you: 'You are never to go back that way.' 17 Your king must not acquire numerous wives and so be led astray, or amass for himself silver and gold in great quantities.

18 When he has ascended the throne of the kingdom, he is to make a copy of this law in a book at the dictation of the levitical priests. 19 He is to have it by him and read from it all his life, so that he may learn to fear the LORD his God and keep all the words of this law and observe these statutes. 20 Thus he will avoid alienation from his fellow-countrymen through pride, and not deviate from these commandments to right or to left; then he and his sons will reign long in Israel.

18 The levitical priests, the whole tribe of Levi, are to have no holding of ancestral land in Israel; they are to eat the food-offerings of the LORD as their share. 2 They will have no holding among their fellow-countrymen; the LORD is their holding, as he promised them. 3 This is to be the customary due of the priests from those of the people who offer sacrifice, whether a bull or a sheep: the shoulder, the cheeks, and the stomach are to be given to the priests. 4 Give them also the firstfruits of your grain and new wine and oil, and the first fleece at the shearing of your flock. 5 For it was they whom the LORD your God chose from all your tribes to attend on the LORD and to minister in the name of the LORD, both they and their sons for all time. 6 When a Levite from any settlement in Israel where he may be resident comes to the place which the LORD will choose, if he comes in the eagerness of his heart 7 and ministers in the name of the LORD his God, like all his fellow-Levites who attend on the LORD there, 8 he is to have an equal share of food with them, besides what he may inherit from his father's family.

9 After you come into the land which the LORD your God is giving you, do not learn to imitate the abominable practices of those other nations. 10 Let no one be found among you who makes his son or daughter pass through fire, no augur or soothsayer or diviner or sorcerer, 11 no one who casts spells or traffics with ghosts and spirits, and no necromancer. 12 Those who do such things are abominable to the LORD, and it is on account of these abominable practices that the LORD your God is driving them out before you. 13 You must be undivided in your service of the LORD your God. 14 These nations whose place you are taking listen to soothsayers and augurs, but the LORD your God does not permit you to do this.

15 The LORD your God will raise up for you a prophet like me from among your own people; it is to him you must listen. 16 All this follows from your request to the LORD your God at Horeb on the day of the assembly. There you said, 'Let us not hear again the voice of the LORD our God, nor see this great fire again, or we shall die.' 17 Then the LORD said to me, 'What they have said is right. 18 I shall

---

14 "When you have come into the land which the LORD, your God, is giving you, and have occupied it and settled in it, should you then decide to have a king over you like all the surrounding nations, 15 you shall set that man over you as your king whom the LORD, your God, chooses. He whom you set over you as king must be your kinsman; a foreigner, who is no kin of yours, you may not set over you. 16 But he shall not have a great number of horses; nor shall he make his people go back again to Egypt to acquire them, against the LORD's warning that you must never go back that way again. 17 Neither shall he have a great number of wives, lest his heart be estranged, nor shall he accumulate a vast amount of silver and gold. 18 When he is enthroned in his kingdom, he shall have a copy of this law made from the scroll that is in the custody of the levitical priests. 19 He shall keep it with him and read it all the days of his life that he may learn to fear the LORD, his God, and to heed and fulfill all the words of this law and these statutes. 20 Let him not become estranged from his countrymen through pride, nor turn aside to the right or to the left from these commandments. Then he and his descendants will enjoy a long reign in Israel.

18 "The whole priestly tribe of Levi shall have no share in the heritage with Israel; they shall live on the oblations of the LORD and the portions due to him. 2 Levi shall have no heritage among his brothers; the LORD himself is his heritage, as he has told him. 3 The priests shall have a right to the following things from the people: from those who are offering a sacrifice, whether the victim is from the herd or from the flock, the priest shall receive the shoulder, the jowls and the stomach. 4 You shall also give him the first fruits of your grain and wine and oil, as well as the first fruits of the shearing of your flock; 5 for the LORD, your God, has chosen him and his sons out of all your tribes to be always in attendance to minister in the name of the LORD.

6 "When a Levite goes from one of your communities anywhere in Israel in which he ordinarily resides, to visit, as his heart may desire, the place which the LORD chooses, 7 he may minister there in the name of the LORD, his God, like all his fellow Levites who are in attendance there before the LORD. 8 He shall then receive the same portions to eat as the rest, along with his monetary offerings and heirlooms.

9 "When you come into the land which the LORD, your God, is giving you, you shall not learn to imitate the abominations of the peoples there. 10 Let there not be found among you anyone who immolates his son or daughter in the fire, nor a fortune-teller, soothsayer, charmer, diviner, 11 or caster of spells, nor one who consults ghosts and spirits or seeks oracles from the dead. 12 Anyone who does such things is an abomination to the LORD, and because of such abominations the LORD, your God, is driving these nations out of your way. 13 You, however, must be altogether sincere toward the LORD, your God. 14 Though these nations whom you are to dispossess listen to their soothsayers and fortune-tellers, the LORD, your God, will not permit you to do so.

15 "A prophet like me will the LORD, your God, raise up for you from among your own kinsmen; to him you shall listen. 16 This is exactly what you requested of the LORD, your God, at Horeb on the day of the assembly, when you said, 'Let us not again hear the voice of the LORD, our God, nor see this great fire any more, lest we die.' 17 And the LORD said to me, 'This was well said. 18 I will raise up for

14 'If, having reached the country given by Yahweh your God and having taken possession of it and, while living there, you think, "I should like to appoint a king to rule me — like all the surrounding nations," 15 the king whom you appoint to rule you must be chosen by Yahweh your God; the appointment of a king must be made from your own brothers; on no account must you appoint as king some foreigner who is not a brother of yours.

16 'He must not, however, acquire more and more horses, or send the people back to Egypt with a view to increasing his cavalry, since Yahweh has told you, "You must never go back that way again." 17 Nor must he keep on acquiring more and more wives, for that could lead his heart astray. Nor must he acquire vast quantities of silver and gold. 18 Once seated on his royal throne, and for his own use, he must write a copy of this Law on a scroll, at the dictation of the levitical priests. 19 It must never leave him, and he must read it every day of his life and learn to fear Yahweh his God by keeping all the words of this Law and observing these rules, 20 so that he will not think himself superior to his brothers, and not deviate from these commandments either to right or to left. So doing, long will he occupy his throne, he and his sons, in Israel.'

18 'The levitical priests, the whole tribe of Levi will be without share or heritage of their own in Israel; they will live on the foods offered to Yahweh and on his heritage. 2 Levi will have no heritage of his own among his brothers; Yahweh will be his heritage, as he has promised him.

3 'This is what is due to the priests from the people, from those who offer an ox or a sheep in sacrifice: the priest must be given the shoulder, the cheeks and the stomach. 4 You must give him the first-fruits of your wheat, of your new wine and of your oil, as well as the first-fruits of your sheep-shearing. 5 For Yahweh your God has chosen him from all your tribes to stand before Yahweh your God, to do the duties of the sacred ministry, and to bless in Yahweh's name — him and his sons for all time.

6 'If a Levite living in one of your towns anywhere in Israel decides to move to the place chosen by Yahweh, 7 he shall minister there in the name of Yahweh his God like all his fellow Levites who stand ministering there in the presence of Yahweh, 8 eating equal shares with them — what he has from the sale of his patrimony notwithstanding.

9 'When you have entered the country given you by Yahweh your God, you must not learn to imitate the detestable practices of the nations there already. 10 There must never be anyone among you who makes his son or daughter pass through the fire of sacrifice, who practises divination, who is soothsayer, augur or sorcerer, 11 weaver of spells, consulter of ghosts or mediums, or necromancer. 12 For anyone who does these things is detestable to Yahweh your God; it is because of these detestable practices that Yahweh your God is driving out these nations before you.

13 'You must be faultless in your relationship with Yahweh your God. 14 For these nations whom you are going to dispossess have listened to soothsayers and mediums, but Yahweh your God does not permit you to do this. From among yourselves, from among your own brothers, 15 Yahweh your God will raise up a prophet like me; you will listen to him. 16 This is exactly what you asked Yahweh your God to do — at Horeb, on the day of the Assembly, when you said, "Never let me hear the voice of Yahweh my God or see this great fire again, or I shall die." 17 Then Yahweh said to me, 18 "What they have said is well said.

raise up for them a prophet[w] like you from among their own people; I will put my words in the mouth of the prophet,[x] who shall speak to them everything that I command. 19 Anyone who does not heed the words that the prophet[y] shall speak in my name, I myself will hold accountable. 20 But any prophet who speaks in the name of other gods, or who presumes to speak in my name a word that I have not commanded the prophet to speak — that prophet shall die." 21 You may say to yourself, "How can we recognize a word that the LORD has not spoken?" 22 If a prophet speaks in the name of the LORD but the thing does not take place or prove true, it is a word that the LORD has not spoken. The prophet has spoken it presumptuously; do not be frightened by it.

19 When the LORD your God has cut off the nations whose land the LORD your God is giving you, and you have dispossessed them and settled in their towns and in their houses, 2 you shall set apart three cities in the land that the LORD your God is giving you to possess. 3 You shall calculate the distances[z] and divide into three regions the land that the LORD your God gives you as a possession, so that any homicide can flee to one of them.

4 Now this is the case of a homicide who might flee there and live, that is, someone who has killed another person unintentionally when the two had not been at enmity before: 5 Suppose someone goes into the forest with another to cut wood, and when one of them swings the ax to cut down a tree, the head slips from the handle and strikes the other person who then dies; the killer may flee to one of these cities and live. 6 But if the distance is too great, the avenger of blood in hot anger might pursue and overtake and put the killer to death, although a death sentence was not deserved, since the two had not been at enmity before. 7 Therefore I command you: You shall set apart three cities.

8 If the LORD your God enlarges your territory, as he swore to your ancestors — and he will give you all the land that he promised your ancestors to give you, 9 provided you diligently observe this entire commandment that I command you today, by loving the LORD your God and walking always in his ways — then you shall add three more cities to these three, 10 so that the blood of an innocent person may not be shed in the land that the LORD your God is giving you as an inheritance, thereby bringing bloodguilt upon you.

11 But if someone at enmity with another lies in wait and attacks and takes the life of that person, and flees into one of these cities, 12 then the elders of the killer's city shall send to have the culprit taken from there and handed over to the avenger of blood to be put to death. 13 Show no pity; you shall purge the guilt of innocent blood from Israel, so that it may go well with you.

14 You must not move your neighbor's boundary marker, set up by former generations, on the property that will be allotted to you in the land that the LORD your God is giving you to possess.

15 A single witness shall not suffice to convict a person of any crime or wrongdoing in connection with any offense that may be committed. Only on the evidence of two or three witnesses shall a charge be sustained. 16 If a malicious witness comes forward to accuse someone of wrongdoing, 17 then both parties to the dispute shall appear before the LORD, before the priests and the judges who are in office in those days, 18 and the judges shall make a thorough inquiry. If the witness is a false witness, having testified falsely against another, 19 then you shall do to the false witness just

raise up for them a prophet like you, one of their own people, and I shall put my words into his mouth. He will declare to them whatever I command him; 19 if anyone refuses to listen to the words which he will speak in my name I shall call that person to account. 20 But the prophet who presumes to utter in my name what I have not commanded him, or who speaks in the name of other gods — that prophet must be put to death.'

21 If you wonder, 'How are we to recognize a word that the LORD has not uttered?' 22 here is the answer: When a word spoken by a prophet in the name of the LORD is not fulfilled and does not come true, it is not a word spoken by the LORD. The prophet has spoken presumptuously; have no fear of him.

19 WHEN the LORD your God exterminates the nations whose land he is giving you, and you take their place and settle in their towns and houses, 2 you are to set apart three cities in the land which he is giving you to occupy. 3 Divide into three districts the territory which the LORD your God is giving you as a holding, and determine where each city shall lie. These are to be places in which homicides may take sanctuary.

4 This is the kind of homicide who may take sanctuary there and save his life: one who strikes another accidentally and with no malice aforethought; 5 for instance, the man who goes into a wood with another to fell trees, and as he swings the axe to cut a tree the head glances off the tree, hits the other man, and kills him. The homicide may take sanctuary in any one of these cities, and his life is to be safe. 6 Otherwise, when the dead man's next-of-kin on whom lies the duty of vengeance pursued him in the heat of temper, he might overtake him if the distance were great, and take his life, although the homicide was not liable to the death penalty because there had been no previous enmity on his part. 7 That is why I command you to set apart three cities.

8 If the LORD your God enlarges your territory, as he promised on oath to your forefathers, and gives you the whole land which he promised to them, 9 because you keep all the commandments that I am laying down today and carry them out by loving the LORD your God and by conforming to his ways for all time, then you shall add three more cities of refuge to these three. 10 Let no innocent blood be shed in the land which the LORD your God is allotting to you, or blood-guilt will fall on you.

11 When one person has a feud with another, and lies in wait for him, attacks him, and strikes him a fatal blow, and then takes sanctuary in one of these cities, 12 the elders of his own town must send to fetch him and hand him over to the next-of-kin to be put to death. 13 You are to show him no mercy, but rid Israel of the guilt of innocent blood; then all will be well with you.

14 Do not move your neighbour's boundary stone, fixed by the men of former times in the holding which you will occupy in the land the LORD your God is giving you for your possession.

15 A single witness may not give evidence against anyone in the matter of any crime or sin which he may have committed: a charge must be established on the evidence of two or of three witnesses.

16 When a malicious witness comes forward to accuse a person of a crime, 17 the two parties to the dispute must appear in the presence of the LORD, before the priests or the judges then in office; 18 if, after careful examination by the judges, he is proved to be a false witness giving false evidence against his fellow, 19 treat him as he intended to treat

18:22 **fear of him:** or fear of it.

them a prophet like you from among their kinsmen, and will put my words into his mouth; he shall tell them all that I command him. ¹⁹If any man will not listen to my words which he speaks in my name, I myself will make him answer for it. ²⁰But if a prophet presumes to speak in my name an oracle that I have not commanded him to speak, or speaks in the name of other gods, he shall die.'

²¹"If you say to yourselves, 'How can we recognize an oracle which the LORD has spoken?', ²²know that, even though a prophet speaks in the name of the LORD, if his oracle is not fulfilled or verified, it is an oracle which the LORD did not speak. The prophet has spoken it presumptuously, and you shall have no fear of him.

19 "When the LORD, your God, removes the nations whose land he is giving you, and you have taken their place and are settled in their cities and houses, ²you shall set apart three cities in the land which the LORD, your God, is giving you to occupy. ³You shall thereby divide into three regions the land which the LORD, your God, will give you as a heritage, and so arrange the routes that every homicide will be able to find a refuge.

⁴"It is in the following case that a homicide may take refuge in such a place to save his life: when someone unwittingly kills his neighbor to whom he had previously borne no malice. ⁵For example, if he goes with his neighbor to a forest to cut wood, and as he swings his ax to fell a tree, its head flies off the handle and hits his neighbor a mortal blow, he may take refuge in one of these cities to save his life. ⁶Should the distance be too great, the avenger of blood may in the heat of his anger pursue the homicide and overtake him and strike him dead, even though he does not merit death since he had previously borne the slain man no malice. ⁷That is why I order you to set apart three cities.

⁸"But if the LORD, your God, enlarges your territory, as he swore to your fathers, and gives you all the land he promised your fathers he would give ⁹in the event that you carefully observe all these commandments which I enjoin on you today, loving the LORD, your God, and ever walking in his ways: then add three cities to these three. ¹⁰Thus, in the land which the LORD, your God, is giving you as a heritage, innocent blood will not be shed and you will not become guilty of bloodshed.

¹¹"However, if someone lies in wait for his neighbor out of hatred for him, and rising up against him, strikes him mortally, and then takes refuge in one of these cities, ¹²the elders of his own city shall send for him and have him taken from there, and shall hand him over to be slain by the avenger of blood. ¹³Do not look on him with pity, but purge from Israel the stain of shedding innocent blood, that you may prosper.

¹⁴"You shall not move your neighbor's landmarks erected by your forefathers in the heritage you receive in the land which the LORD, your God, is giving you to occupy.

¹⁵"One witness alone shall not take the stand against a man in regard to any crime or any offense of which he may be guilty; a judicial fact shall be established only on the testimony of two or three witnesses.

¹⁶"If an unjust witness takes the stand against a man to accuse him of a defection from the law, ¹⁷the two parties in the dispute shall appear before the LORD in the presence of the priests or judges in office at that time; ¹⁸and if after a thorough investigation the judges find that the witness is a false witness and has accused his kinsman falsely, ¹⁹you

From their own brothers I shall raise up a prophet like yourself; ¹⁹I shall put my words into his mouth and he will tell them everything I command him. Anyone who refuses to listen to my words, spoken by him in my name, will have to render an account to me. ²⁰But the prophet who presumes to say something in my name which I have not commanded him to say, or who speaks in the name of other gods, that prophet must die."

²¹'You may be privately wondering, "How are we to tell that a prophecy does not come from Yahweh?" ²²When a prophet speaks in the name of Yahweh and the thing does not happen and the word is not fulfilled, then it has not been said by Yahweh. The prophet has spoken presumptuously. You have nothing to fear from him.'

19 'When Yahweh your God has annihilated the nations whose country Yahweh your God is going to give you, and you have dispossessed them and are living in their towns and in their houses, ²you must set aside three towns, centrally placed in the country which Yahweh your God is giving you for your own. ³You will keep the approaches to them in good order, dividing the area of the country which Yahweh your God is giving you as your heritage, into three parts, so that any killer can flee to these towns. ⁴Here is an example of how someone may save his life by fleeing to them.

'If anyone has struck his fellow accidentally, without any previous feud with him ⁵(for example, he goes with his fellow into the forest to cut wood; his arm swings the axe to fell a tree; the head slips off the handle and strikes his companion dead), that man may take refuge in one of these towns and save his life. ⁶It must not be allowed that the avenger of blood, in the heat of his anger, should pursue the killer and that the length of the road should help him to overtake and wound him fatally; for the man has not deserved to die, having had no previous feud with his victim.

⁷'Hence I am giving you this order: You must set aside three towns, ⁸and if Yahweh your God enlarges your territory, as he swore to your ancestors that he would, and gives you the whole country which he promised to give to your ancestors— ⁹provided that you keep and observe all the commandments which I am enjoining on you today, loving Yahweh your God and always following his ways—then, to those three towns you will add three more. ¹⁰In this way, innocent blood will not be shed in the country which Yahweh your God is going to give you as your heritage; otherwise you would incur blood-guilt.

¹¹'But if it happens that a man has a feud with his fellow and lies in wait for him and attacks him and fatally wounds him and he dies, and the man takes refuge in one of these towns, ¹²the elders of his own town must send there and have him taken and handed over to the avenger of blood, to be put to death. ¹³You must show him no pity. You must banish the shedding of innocent blood from Israel, and then you will prosper.

¹⁴'You must not displace your neighbour's boundary mark, positioned by men of old in the heritage soon to be yours, in the country which Yahweh your God is about to give you.

¹⁵'A single witness will not suffice to convict anyone of a crime or offence of any kind; whatever the misdemeanour, the evidence of two witnesses or three is required to sustain the charge.

¹⁶'If someone gives false evidence against anyone, laying a charge of apostasy, ¹⁷both parties to this dispute before Yahweh must appear before the priests and judges then in office. ¹⁸The judges will make a careful enquiry, and if it turns out that the witness is a liar and has made a false accusation against his brother, ¹⁹you must treat the witness

as the false witness had meant to do to the other. So you shall purge the evil from your midst. 20 The rest shall hear and be afraid, and a crime such as this shall never again be committed among you. 21 Show no pity: life for life, eye for eye, tooth for tooth, hand for hand, foot for foot.

20 When you go out to war against your enemies, and see horses and chariots, an army larger than your own, you shall not be afraid of them; for the LORD your God is with you, who brought you up from the land of Egypt. 2 Before you engage in battle, the priest shall come forward and speak to the troops, 3 and shall say to them: "Hear, O Israel! Today you are drawing near to do battle against your enemies. Do not lose heart, or be afraid, or panic, or be in dread of them; 4 for it is the LORD your God who goes with you, to fight for you against your enemies, to give you victory." 5 Then the officials shall address the troops, saying, "Has anyone built a new house but not dedicated it? He should go back to his house, or he might die in the battle and another dedicate it. 6 Has anyone planted a vineyard but not yet enjoyed its fruit? He should go back to his house, or he might die in the battle and another be first to enjoy its fruit. 7 Has anyone become engaged to a woman but not yet married her? He should go back to his house, or he might die in the battle and another marry her." 8 The officials shall continue to address the troops, saying, "Is anyone afraid or disheartened? He should go back to his house, or he might cause the heart of his comrades to melt like his own." 9 When the officials have finished addressing the troops, then the commanders shall take charge of them.

10 When you draw near to a town to fight against it, offer it terms of peace. 11 If it accepts your terms of peace and surrenders to you, then all the people in it shall serve you at forced labor. 12 If it does not submit to you peacefully, but makes war against you, then you shall besiege it; 13 and when the LORD your God gives it into your hand, you shall put all its males to the sword. 14 You may, however, take as your booty the women, the children, livestock, and everything else in the town, all its spoil. You may enjoy the spoil of your enemies, which the LORD your God has given you. 15 Thus you shall treat all the towns that are very far from you, which are not towns of the nations here. 16 But as for the towns of these peoples that the LORD your God is giving you as an inheritance, you must not let anything that breathes remain alive. 17 You shall annihilate them—the Hittites and the Amorites, the Canaanites and the Perizzites, the Hivites and the Jebusites—just as the LORD your God has commanded, 18 so that they may not teach you to do all the abhorrent things that they do for their gods, and you thus sin against the LORD your God.

19 If you besiege a town for a long time, making war against it in order to take it, you must not destroy its trees by wielding an ax against them. Although you may take food from them, you must not cut them down. Are trees in the field human beings that they should come under siege from you? 20 You may destroy only the trees that you know do not produce food; you may cut them down for use in building siegeworks against the town that makes war with you, until it falls.

21 If, in the land that the LORD your God is giving you to possess, a body is found lying in open country, and it is not known who struck the person down, 2 then your elders and your judges shall come out to measure the distances to the towns that are near the body. 3 The elders of the town nearest the body shall take a heifer that has never been worked, one that has not pulled in the yoke; 4 the

his fellow. You must rid yourselves of this wickedness. 20 The rest of the people when they hear of it will be afraid, and never again will anything as wicked as this be done among you. 21 You must show no mercy: life for life, eye for eye, tooth for tooth, hand for hand, foot for foot!

20 WHEN you take the field against your enemies and are faced by horses and chariots, a force greater than yours, you need have no fear of them, for the LORD your God, who brought you up from Egypt, will be with you. 2 Then when fighting impends, the priest must come forward and address the army in these words: 3 'Hear, Israel! Now that you are about to join battle with your enemy, do not lose heart or be afraid; do not let alarm affect you, and do not give way to panic in face of them. 4 The LORD your God accompanies you to fight for you against your enemy and give you the victory.' 5 The officers are to say to the army: 'Any man who has built a new house and has not dedicated it should go back to his house; otherwise he may die in battle and another man dedicate it. 6 Any man who has planted a vineyard and has not begun to use it should go back home; otherwise he may die in battle and another man get the use of it. 7 Any man who has pledged himself to take a woman in marriage and has not taken her should go back home; otherwise he may die in battle and another man take her.' 8 The officers must also say to the army: 'Let anyone who is afraid and has lost heart go back home; or his faint-heartedness may affect his comrades.' 9 When the officers have finished addressing the army, commanders will assume command.

10 When you advance on a town to attack it, make an offer of peace. 11 If the offer is accepted and the town opens its gates to you, then all the people who live there are to be put to forced labour and work for you. 12 If the town does not make peace with you but gives battle, you are to lay siege to it 13 and, when the LORD your God delivers it into your hands, put every male in it to the sword; 14 but you may take the women, the dependants, and the livestock for yourselves, and plunder everything else in the town. You may enjoy the use of the spoil from your enemies which the LORD your God gives you.

15 That is how you are to deal with towns at a great distance, as opposed to those which belong to nations near at hand. 16 In the towns of these nations whose land the LORD your God is giving you as your holding, you must not leave a soul alive. 17 As the LORD your God commanded you, you must destroy them under solemn ban—Hittites, Amorites, Canaanites, Perizzites, Hivites, Jebusites—18 so that they may not teach you to imitate the abominable practices they have carried on for their gods, and so cause you to sin against the LORD your God.

19 When in the course of war you lay siege to a town for a long time in order to take it, do not destroy its trees by taking an axe to them, for they provide you with food; you must not cut them down. The trees of the field are not people, that you should besiege them. 20 But you may destroy or cut down any trees that you know do not yield food, and use them in siege-works against the town that is at war with you, until it falls.

21 When a murder victim is found lying in open country, in the land which the LORD your God is giving you to occupy, and it is not known who struck the blow, 2 your elders and your judges are to come out and measure the distance to the surrounding towns to establish which is nearest. 3 The elders of that town are to take a heifer that has never been put to work or worn a yoke, 4 and bring it down

shall do to him as he planned to do to his kinsman. Thus shall you purge the evil from your midst. 20 The rest, on hearing of it, shall fear, and never again do a thing so evil among you. 21 Do not look on such a man with pity. Life for life, eye for eye, tooth for tooth, hand for hand, and foot for foot!

20 "When you go out to war against your enemies and you see horses and chariots and an army greater than your own, do not be afraid of them, for the LORD, your God, who brought you up from the land of Egypt, will be with you.

2 "When you are about to go into battle, the priest shall come forward and say to the soldiers: 3 'Hear, O Israel! Today you are going into battle against your enemies. Be not weakhearted or afraid; be neither alarmed nor frightened by them. 4 For it is the LORD, your God, who goes with you to fight for you against your enemies and give you victory.'

5 "Then the officials shall say to the soldiers, 'Is there anyone who has built a new house and not yet had the housewarming? Let him return home, lest he die in battle and another dedicate it. 6 Is there anyone who has planted a vineyard and never yet enjoyed its fruits? Let him return home, lest he die in battle and another enjoy its fruits in his stead. 7 Is there anyone who has betrothed a woman and not yet taken her as his wife? Let him return home, lest he die in battle and another take her to wife.' 8 In fine, the officials shall say to the soldiers, 'Is there anyone who is afraid and weakhearted? Let him return home, lest he make his fellows as fainthearted as himself.'

9 "When the officials have finished speaking to the soldiers, military officers shall be appointed over the army.

10 "When you march up to attack a city, first offer it terms of peace. 11 If it agrees to your terms of peace and opens its gates to you, all the people to be found in it shall serve you in forced labor. 12 But if it refuses to make peace with you and instead offers you battle, lay siege to it, 13 and when the LORD, your God, delivers it into your hand, put every male in it to the sword; 14 but the women and children and livestock and all else in it that is worth plundering you may take as your booty, and you may use this plunder of your enemies which the LORD, your God, has given you.

15 "That is how you shall deal with any city at a considerable distance from you, which does not belong to the peoples of this land. 16 But in the cities of those nations which the LORD, your God, is giving you as your heritage, you shall not leave a single soul alive. 17 You must doom them all — the Hittites, Amorites, Canaanites, Perizzites, Hivites and Jebusites — as the LORD, your God, has commanded you, 18 lest they teach you to make any such abominable offerings as they make to their gods, and you thus sin against the LORD, your God.

19 "When you are at war with a city and have to lay siege to it for a long time before you capture it, you shall not destroy its trees by putting an ax to them. You may eat their fruit, but you must not cut down the trees. After all, are the trees of the field men, that they should be included in your siege? 20 However, those trees which you know are not fruit trees you may destroy, cutting them down to build siege-works with which to reduce the city that is resisting you.

21 "If the corpse of a slain man is found lying in the open on the land which the LORD, your God, is giving you to occupy, and it is not known who killed him, 2 your elders and judges shall go out and measure the distances to the cities that are in the neighborhood of the corpse. 3 When it is established which city is nearest the corpse, the elders of that city shall take a heifer that has never been put to work as a draft animal under a yoke, 4 and

as he would have treated his brother. You must banish this evil from among you. 20 The rest, hearing of this, will be afraid and never again do such an evil thing among you. 21 You must show no pity.

'Life for life, eye for eye, tooth for tooth, hand for hand, foot for foot.'

20 'When you go to war against your enemies and see horses and chariots and an army greater than your own, you must not be afraid of them; Yahweh your God is with you, he who brought you out of Egypt. 2 When you are about to join battle, the priest must come forward and address the people. 3 He must say to them, "Listen, Israel: today you are about to join battle with your enemies. Do not be faint hearted. Let there be no fear or trembling or alarm as you face them. 4 Yahweh your God is marching with you, to fight your enemies for you and make you victorious."

5 'The scribes will then address the people, as follows: "Has anyone built a new house and not yet dedicated it? Let him go home, in case he dies in battle and someone else performs the dedication.

6 "Has anyone planted a vineyard and not yet enjoyed its fruit? Let him go home, in case he dies in battle and someone else enjoys its fruit.

7 "Has anyone contracted to marry a girl and not yet married her? Let him go home, in case he dies in battle and someone else marries her."

8 'Finally, the scribes will say to the people: "Is anyone frightened or faint hearted? Let him go home, in case he makes his brothers faint hearted too!"

9 'Then, when the scribes have finished speaking to the people, commanders will be appointed to lead them.

10 'When you advance on a town to attack it, first offer it peace-terms. 11 If it accepts these and opens its gates to you, all the people inside will owe you forced labour and work for you. 12 But if it refuses peace and gives battle, you must besiege it. 13 Yahweh your God having handed it over to you, you will put the whole male population to the sword. 14 But the women, children, livestock and whatever the town contains by way of spoil, you may take for yourselves as booty. You will feed on the spoils of the enemies whom Yahweh your God has handed over to you.

15 'That is how you will treat towns far away and not belonging to the nations near you. 16 But as regards the towns of those peoples whom Yahweh your God is giving you as your heritage, you must not spare the life of any living thing. 17 Instead, you must lay them under the curse of destruction: Hittites, Amorites, Canaanites, Perizzites, Hivites and Jebusites, as Yahweh your God has commanded, 18 so that they may not teach you to do all the detestable things which they do to honour their gods: in doing these, you would sin against Yahweh your God.

19 'If, when attacking a town, you have to besiege it for a long time before you capture it, you must not destroy its trees by taking the axe to them: eat their fruit but do not cut them down. Is the tree in the fields human, that you should besiege it too? 20 Any trees, however, which you know are not fruit trees, you may destroy and cut down and use to build siege-works against the hostile town until it falls.'

21 'If, in the country which Yahweh your God gives you as your possession, a victim of murder is found lying in the open country and it is not known who has killed that person, 2 your elders and scribes must measure the distance between the victim and the surrounding towns, 3 and establish which town is the nearest to the victim. The elders of that town must then take a heifer that has not yet been put to work or used as a draught animal under the yoke. 4 The

| NEW REVISED STANDARD VERSION | REVISED ENGLISH BIBLE |

elders of that town shall bring the heifer down to a wadi with running water, which is neither plowed nor sown, and shall break the heifer's neck there in the wadi. 5 Then the priests, the sons of Levi, shall come forward, for the LORD your God has chosen them to minister to him and to pronounce blessings in the name of the LORD, and by their decision all cases of dispute and assault shall be settled. 6 All the elders of that town nearest the body shall wash their hands over the heifer whose neck was broken in the wadi, 7 and they shall declare: "Our hands did not shed this blood, nor were we witnesses to it. 8 Absolve, O LORD, your people Israel, whom you redeemed; do not let the guilt of innocent blood remain in the midst of your people Israel." Then they will be absolved of bloodguilt. 9 So you shall purge the guilt of innocent blood from your midst, because you must do what is right in the sight of the LORD.

10 When you go out to war against your enemies, and the LORD your God hands them over to you and you take them captive, 11 suppose you see among the captives a beautiful woman whom you desire and want to marry, 12 and so you bring her home to your house: she shall shave her head, pare her nails, 13 discard her captive's garb, and shall remain in your house a full month, mourning for her father and mother; after that you may go in to her and be her husband, and she shall be your wife. 14 But if you are not satisfied with her, you shall let her go free and not sell her for money. You must not treat her as a slave, since you have dishonored her.

15 If a man has two wives, one of them loved and the other disliked, and if both the loved and the disliked have borne him sons, the firstborn being the son of the one who is disliked, 16 then on the day when he wills his possessions to his sons, he is not permitted to treat the son of the loved as the firstborn in preference to the son of the disliked, who is the firstborn. 17 He must acknowledge as firstborn the son of the one who is disliked, giving him a double portion[a] of all that he has; since he is the first issue of his virility, the right of the firstborn is his.

18 If someone has a stubborn and rebellious son who will not obey his father and mother, who does not heed them when they discipline him, 19 then his father and his mother shall take hold of him and bring him out to the elders of his town at the gate of that place. 20 They shall say to the elders of his town, "This son of ours is stubborn and rebellious. He will not obey us. He is a glutton and a drunkard." 21 Then all the men of the town shall stone him to death. So you shall purge the evil from your midst; and all Israel will hear, and be afraid.

22 When someone is convicted of a crime punishable by death and is executed, and you hang him on a tree, 23 his corpse must not remain all night upon the tree; you shall bury him that same day, for anyone hung on a tree is under God's curse. You must not defile the land that the LORD your God is giving you for possession.

22 You shall not watch your neighbor's ox or sheep straying away and ignore them; you shall take them back to their owner. 2 If the owner does not reside near you or you do not know who the owner is, you shall bring it to your own house, and it shall remain with you until the owner claims it; then you shall return it. 3 You shall do the same with a neighbor's donkey; you shall do the same with a neighbor's garment; and you shall do the same with anything else that your neighbor loses and you find. You may not withhold your help.

4 You shall not see your neighbor's donkey or ox fallen on the road and ignore it; you shall help to lift it up.

---

to a wadi where there is a stream that never runs dry and the ground is never tilled or sown, and there in the wadi they are to break its neck. 5 The priests, the sons of Levi, are then to come forward; for the LORD your God has chosen them to minister to him and to bless in the name of the LORD, and their voice shall be decisive in all cases of dispute and assault. 6 All the elders of the town nearest to the dead body will then wash their hands over the heifer whose neck has been broken in the wadi, 7 and solemnly declare: 'Our hands did not shed this blood, nor did we witness the bloodshed. 8 Accept expiation, O LORD, for your people Israel whom you redeemed, and do not let the guilt of innocent blood rest upon your people Israel: let this bloodshed be expiated on their behalf.' 9 Thus, by doing what is right in the eyes of the LORD, you will rid yourselves of the guilt of innocent blood.

10 When you go to battle against your enemies and the LORD your God delivers them into your hands and you take some of them captive, 11 then if you see a comely woman among the prisoners and are attracted to her, you may take her as your wife. 12 Bring her into your house; there she must shave her head, pare her nails, 13 and discard the clothes which she had when captured. For a full month she is to stay in your house mourning for her father and mother. After that you may have intercourse with her, and be man and wife. 14 But if you no longer find her pleasing, let her go free. You must not sell her or treat her harshly, since you have had your will with her.

15 When a man has two wives, one loved and the other unloved, if they both bear him sons, and the son of the unloved wife is the elder, 16 then, when the day comes for him to divide his property among his sons, he must not treat the son of the loved wife as his firstborn in preference to his true firstborn, the son of the unloved wife. 17 He must recognize the rights of his firstborn, the son of the unloved wife, and give him a double share of all that he possesses; for he was the firstfruits of his manhood, and the right of the firstborn is his.

18 When a man has a son who is rebellious and out of control, who does not obey his father and mother, or take heed when they punish him, 19 then his father and mother are to lay hold of him and bring him out to the elders of the town at the town gate, 20 and say, 'This son of ours is rebellious and out of control; he will not obey us, he is a wastrel and a drunkard.' 21 Then all the men of the town must stone him to death, and you will thereby rid yourselves of this wickedness. All Israel when they hear of it will be afraid.

22 When someone is convicted of a capital offence and is put to death, and you hang him on a gibbet, 23 his body must not remain there overnight; it must be buried on the same day. Anyone hanged is accursed in the sight of God, and the land which the LORD your God is giving you as your holding must not be polluted.

22 SHOULD you see a fellow-countryman's ox or sheep straying, do not ignore it; you must take it back to him. 2 If the owner is not a near neighbour and you do not know who he is, bring the animal to your own house and keep it with you until he claims it; then give it back to him. 3 Do the same with his donkey or his cloak or anything else that your fellow-countryman loses. You may not ignore it.

4 Should you see your fellow-countryman's donkey or ox lying on the road, do not ignore it; you must help him to raise it to its feet.

---

[a] Heb two-thirds

NEW AMERICAN BIBLE

NEW JERUSALEM BIBLE

bringing it down to a wadi with an ever-flowing stream at a place that has not been plowed or sown, they shall cut the heifer's throat there in the wadi. 5 The priests, the descendants of Levi, shall also be present, for the LORD, your God, has chosen them to minister to him and to give blessings in his name, and every case of dispute or violence must be settled by their decision. 6 Then all the elders of that city nearest the corpse shall wash their hands over the heifer whose throat was cut in the wadi, 7 and shall declare, 'Our hands did not shed this blood, and our eyes did not see the deed. 8 Absolve, O LORD, your people Israel, whom you have ransomed, and let not the guilt of shedding innocent blood remain in the midst of your people Israel.' Thus they shall be absolved from the guilt of bloodshed, 9 and you shall purge from your midst the guilt of innocent blood, that you may prosper for doing what is right in the sight of the LORD.

10 "When you go out to war against your enemies and the LORD, your God, delivers them into your hand, so that you take captives, 11 if you see a comely woman among the captives and become so enamored of her that you wish to have her as wife, 12 you may take her home to your house. But before she may live there, she must shave her head and pare her nails 13 and lay aside her captive's garb. After she has mourned her father and mother for a full month, you may have relations with her, and you shall be her husband and she shall be your wife. 14 However, if later on you lose your liking for her, you shall give her her freedom, if she wishes it; but you shall not sell her or enslave her, since she was married to you under compulsion.

15 "If a man with two wives loves one and dislikes the other; and if both bear him sons, but the first-born is of her whom he dislikes: 16 when he comes to bequeath his property to his sons he may not consider as his first-born the son of the wife he loves, in preference to his true first-born, the son of the wife whom he dislikes. 17 On the contrary, he shall recognize as his first-born the son of her whom he dislikes, giving him a double share of whatever he happens to own, since he is the first fruits of his manhood, and to him belong the rights of the first-born.

18 "If a man has a stubborn and unruly son who will not listen to his father or mother, and will not obey them even though they chastise him, 19 his father and mother shall have him apprehended and brought out to the elders at the gate of his home city, 20 where they shall say to those city elders, 'This son of ours is a stubborn and unruly fellow who will not listen to us; he is a glutton and a drunkard.' 21 Then all his fellow citizens shall stone him to death. Thus you shall purge the evil from your midst, and all Israel, on hearing of it, shall fear.

22 "If a man guilty of a capital offense is put to death and his corpse hung on a tree, 23 it shall not remain on the tree overnight. You shall bury it the same day; otherwise, since God's curse rests on him who hangs on a tree, you will defile the land which the LORD, your God, is giving you as an inheritance.

22 "You shall not see your kinsman's ox or sheep driven astray without showing concern about it; see to it that it is returned to your kinsman. 2 If this kinsman does not live near you, or you do not know who he may be, take it to your own place and keep it with you until he claims it; then give it back to him. 3 You shall do the same with his ass, or his garment, or anything else which your kinsman loses and you happen to find; you may not be unconcerned about them. 4 You shall not see your kinsman's ass or ox foundering on the road without showing concern; see to it that you help him lift it up.

elders of that town must bring the heifer down to a permanently flowing river, to a spot that has been neither ploughed nor sown, and there by the river they must break the heifer's neck. 5 The priests, the sons of Levi, will then step forward, these being the men whom Yahweh your God has chosen to serve him and to bless in Yahweh's name, and it being their business to settle all cases of dispute or of violence. 6 All the elders of the town nearest to the victim of murder must then wash their hands in the stream, over the slaughtered heifer. 7 They must pronounce these words, "Our hands have not shed this blood and our eyes have seen nothing. 8 O Yahweh, forgive your people Israel whom you have redeemed, and let no innocent blood be shed among your people Israel. May this bloodshed be forgiven them!" 9 You must banish all shedding of innocent blood from among you, if you mean to do what is right in the eyes of Yahweh.

10 'When you go to war against your enemies and Yahweh your God delivers them into your power and you take prisoners, 11 and among the prisoners you see a beautiful woman, and you fall in love with her, and you take her to be your wife 12 and bring her home; she must shave her head and cut her nails, 13 and take off her prisoner's garb; she must stay inside your house and mourn her father and mother for a full month. You may then go to her and be a husband to her, and she will be your wife. 14 Should she cease to please you, you will let her go where she wishes, not selling her for money: you must not make any profit out of her, since you have exploited her.

15 'If a man has two wives, one loved and the other unloved, and the loved one and the unloved both bear him children, and if the first-born son is of the unloved wife, 16 when the man comes to bequeath his goods to his sons, he may not treat the son of the wife whom he loves as the first-born, at the expense of the son of the wife whom he does not love, the true first-born. 17 As his first-born he must acknowledge the son of the wife whom he does not love, giving him a double share of his estate; this son being the first-fruit of his vigour, the right of the first-born is his.

18 'If a man has a stubborn and rebellious son who will not listen to the voice either of his father or of his mother and, even when they punish him, still will not pay attention to them, 19 his father and mother must take hold of him and bring him out to the elders of his town at the gate of that place. 20 To the elders of his town, they will say, "This son of ours is stubborn and rebellious and will not listen to us; he is a wastrel and a drunkard." 21 All his fellow-citizens must then stone him to death. You must banish this evil from among you. All Israel, hearing of this, will be afraid.

22 'If a man guilty of a capital offence is to be put to death, and you hang him from a tree, 23 his body must not remain on the tree overnight; you must bury him the same day, since anyone hanged is a curse of God, and you must not bring pollution on the soil which Yahweh your God is giving you as your heritage.'

22 'If you see your brother's ox or one of his sheep straying, you must not disregard it: you must take it back to your brother. 2 And if he is not close at hand or you do not know who he is, you must take it home with you and keep it by you until your brother comes to look for it; you will then return it to him.

3 'You must do the same with his donkey, the same with his cloak, the same with anything that your brother loses and that you find; you must not disregard it.

4 'If you see your brother's donkey or ox fall over on the road, you must not disregard it, but must help your brother get it on its feet again.

NEW REVISED STANDARD VERSION

5 A woman shall not wear a man's apparel, nor shall a man put on a woman's garment; for whoever does such things is abhorrent to the LORD your God.

6 If you come on a bird's nest, in any tree or on the ground, with fledglings or eggs, with the mother sitting on the fledglings or on the eggs, you shall not take the mother with the young. 7 Let the mother go, taking only the young for yourself, in order that it may go well with you and you may live long.

8 When you build a new house, you shall make a parapet for your roof; otherwise you might have bloodguilt on your house, if anyone should fall from it.

9 You shall not sow your vineyard with a second kind of seed, or the whole yield will have to be forfeited, both the crop that you have sown and the yield of the vineyard itself.

10 You shall not plow with an ox and a donkey yoked together.

11 You shall not wear clothes made of wool and linen woven together.

12 You shall make tassels on the four corners of the cloak with which you cover yourself.

13 Suppose a man marries a woman, but after going in to her, he dislikes her 14 and makes up charges against her, slandering her by saying, "I married this woman; but when I lay with her, I did not find evidence of her virginity." 15 The father of the young woman and her mother shall then submit the evidence of the young woman's virginity to the elders of the city at the gate. 16 The father of the young woman shall say to the elders: "I gave my daughter in marriage to this man but he dislikes her; 17 now he has made up charges against her, saying, 'I did not find evidence of your daughter's virginity.' But here is the evidence of my daughter's virginity." Then they shall spread out the cloth before the elders of the town. 18 The elders of that town shall take the man and punish him; 19 they shall fine him one hundred shekels of silver (which they shall give to the young woman's father) because he has slandered a virgin of Israel. She shall remain his wife; he shall not be permitted to divorce her as long as he lives.

20 If, however, this charge is true, that evidence of the young woman's virginity was not found, 21 then they shall bring the young woman out to the entrance of her father's house and the men of her town shall stone her to death, because she committed a disgraceful act in Israel by prostituting herself in her father's house. So you shall purge the evil from your midst.

22 If a man is caught lying with the wife of another man, both of them shall die, the man who lay with the woman as well as the woman. So you shall purge the evil from Israel.

23 If there is a young woman, a virgin already engaged to be married, and a man meets her in the town and lies with her, 24 you shall bring both of them to the gate of that town and stone them to death, the young woman because she did not cry for help in the town and the man because he violated his neighbor's wife. So you shall purge the evil from your midst.

25 But if the man meets the engaged woman in the open country, and the man seizes her and lies with her, then only the man who lay with her shall die. 26 You shall do nothing to the young woman; the young woman has not committed an offense punishable by death, because this case is like that of someone who attacks and murders a neighbor. 27 Since he found her in the open country, the engaged woman may have cried for help, but there was no one to rescue her.

28 If a man meets a virgin who is not engaged, and seizes her and lies with her, and they are caught in the act,

REVISED ENGLISH BIBLE

5 No woman may wear an article of man's clothing, nor may a man put on woman's dress; for those who do these things are abominable to the LORD your God.

6 When you come upon a bird's nest by the road, in a tree or on the ground, with fledgelings or eggs in it and the mother bird on the nest, do not take both mother and young. 7 Let the mother bird go free, and take only the young; then you will prosper and enjoy long life.

8 When you build a new house, put a parapet along the roof, or you will bring the guilt of bloodshed on your house if anyone should fall from it.

9 You are not to sow two kinds of seed between your vine rows, or the full yield will be forfeit, both the yield of the seeds you sow and the fruit of the vineyard. 10 You are not to plough with an ox and a donkey yoked together. 11 You are not to wear clothes woven with two kinds of yarn, wool and flax together.

12 Make twisted tassels on the four corners of the garment which you wrap round you.

13 When a man takes a wife and, after intercourse, turns against her 14 and brings trumped-up charges against her, giving her a bad name and saying, 'I took this woman and slept with her and did not find proof of virginity in her,' 15 then the girl's father and mother should take the proof of her virginity to the elders of the town at the town gate. 16 The girl's father will say to the elders, 'I gave my daughter in marriage to this man, and he has turned against her. 17 He has trumped up a charge and said, "I have not found proofs of virginity in your daughter." Here are the proofs.' They must then spread the cloth before the elders of the town. 18 The elders must take the man and punish him: 19 they are to fine him a hundred pieces of silver because he has given a bad name to a virgin of Israel, and the money is to be handed over to the girl's father. She will remain his wife: he will not be free to divorce her all his days.

20 If, on the other hand, the accusation turns out to be true, no proof of the girl's virginity being found, 21 then they must bring her out to the door of her father's house and the men of her town will stone her to death. She has committed an outrage in Israel by playing the prostitute in her father's house: you must rid yourselves of this wickedness.

22 When a man is discovered lying with a married woman, both are to be put to death, the woman as well as the man who lay with her: you must purge Israel of this wickedness.

23 When a virgin is pledged in marriage to a man, and another man encounters her in the town and lies with her, 24 bring both of them out to the gate of that town and stone them to death; the girl because, although she was in the town, she did not cry for help, and the man because he violated another man's wife: you must rid yourselves of this wickedness.

25 But if it is out in the country that the man encounters and rapes such a girl, then the man alone is to be put to death because he lay with her. 26 Do nothing to the girl; no guilt deserving of death attaches to her: this case is like that of a man who attacks another and murders him: 27 the man came upon her in the country and, though the girl may have cried for help, there was no one to come to her rescue.

28 When a man encounters a virgin who is not yet betrothed and forces her to lie with him, and they are discov-

5 "A woman shall not wear an article proper to a man, nor shall a man put on a woman's dress; for anyone who does such things is an abomination to the LORD, your God.

6 "If, while walking along, you chance upon a bird's nest with young birds or eggs in it, in any tree or on the ground, and the mother bird is sitting on them, you shall not take away the mother bird along with her brood; 7 you shall let her go, although you may take her brood away. It is thus that you shall have prosperity and a long life.

8 "When you build a new house, put a parapet around the roof; otherwise, if someone falls off, you will bring blood-guilt upon your house.

9 "You shall not sow your vineyard with two different kinds of seed; if you do, its produce shall become forfeit, both the crop you have sown and the yield of the vineyard. 10 You shall not plow with an ox and an ass harnessed together. 11 You shall not wear cloth of two different kinds of thread, wool and linen, woven together.

12 "You shall put twisted cords on the four corners of the cloak that you wrap around you.

13 "If a man, after marrying a woman and having relations with her, comes to dislike her, 14 and makes monstrous charges against her and defames her by saying, 'I married this woman, but when I first had relations with her I did not find her a virgin,' 15 the father and mother of the girl shall take the evidence of her virginity and bring it to the elders at the city gate. 16 There the father of the girl shall say to the elders, 'I gave my daughter to this man in marriage, but he has come to dislike her, 17 and now brings monstrous charges against her, saying: I did not find your daughter a virgin. But here is the evidence of my daughter's virginity!' And they shall spread out the cloth before the elders of the city. 18 Then these city elders shall take the man and chastise him, 19 besides fining him one hundred silver shekels, which they shall give to the girl's father, because the man defamed a virgin in Israel. Moreover, she shall remain his wife, and he may not divorce her as long as he lives.

20 "But if this charge is true, and evidence of the girl's virginity is not found, 21 they shall bring the girl to the entrance of her father's house and there her townsmen shall stone her to death, because she committed a crime against Israel by her unchasteness in her father's house. Thus shall you purge the evil from your midst.

22 "If a man is discovered having relations with a woman who is married to another, both the man and the woman with whom he has had relations shall die. Thus shall you purge the evil from your midst.

23 "If within the city a man comes upon a maiden who is betrothed, and has relations with her, 24 you shall bring them both out to the gate of the city and there stone them to death: the girl because she did not cry out for help though she was in the city, and the man because he violated his neighbor's wife. Thus shall you purge the evil from your midst.

25 "If, however, it is in the open fields that a man comes upon such a betrothed maiden, seizes her and has relations with her, the man alone shall die. 26 You shall do nothing to the maiden, since she is not guilty of a capital offense. This case is like that of a man who rises up against his neighbor and murders him: 27 it was in the open fields that he came upon her, and though the betrothed maiden may have cried out for help, there was no one to come to her aid.

28 "If a man comes upon a maiden that is not betrothed, takes her and has relations with her, and their deed is dis-

5 'A woman must not dress like a man, nor a man like a woman; anyone who does this is detestable to Yahweh your God.

6 'If, when out walking, you come across a bird's nest, in a tree or on the ground, with chicks or eggs and the mother bird sitting on the chicks or the eggs, you must not take the mother as well as the chicks. 7 Let the mother go; the young you may take for yourself. Thus will you have prosperity and long life.

8 'When you build a new house, you must give your roof a parapet; then your house will not incur blood-vengeance, should anyone fall off the top.

9 'You must not sow any other crop in your vineyard, or the whole yield may become forfeit, both the crop you have sown and the yield of your vines.

10 'You must not plough with ox and donkey together.

11 'You must not wear clothing woven part of wool, part of linen.

12 'You must make tassels for the four corners of the cloak in which you wrap yourself.

13 'If a man marries a woman, has sexual intercourse with her and then, turning against her, 14 taxes her with misconduct and publicly defames her by saying, "I married this woman and when I had sexual intercourse with her I did not find evidence of her virginity," 15 the girl's father and mother must take the evidence of her virginity and produce it before the elders of the town, at the gate. 16 To the elders, the girl's father will say, "I gave this man my daughter for a wife and he has turned against her, 17 and now he taxes her with misconduct, saying, 'I have found no evidence of virginity in your daughter. Here is the evidence of my daughter's virginity!'" 18 They must then display the cloth to the elders of the town. 19 The elders of the town in question will have the man arrested and flogged, and fine him a hundred silver shekels for publicly defaming a virgin of Israel, and give this money to the girl's father. She will remain his wife; as long as he lives, he may not divorce her.

20 'But if the accusation that the girl cannot show evidence of virginity is substantiated, 21 she must be taken out, and at the door of her father's house her fellow-citizens must stone her to death for having committed an infamy in Israel by bringing disgrace on her father's family. You must banish this evil from among you.

22 'If a man is caught having sexual intercourse with another man's wife, both must be put to death: the man who has slept with her and the woman herself. You must banish this evil from Israel.

23 'If a virgin is engaged to a man, and another man encounters her in the town and has sexual intercourse with her, 24 you will take them both to the gate of the town in question and stone them to death: the girl, for not having called for help in the town; the man, for having exploited his fellow-citizen's wife. You must banish this evil from among you. 25 But if the man ran into the betrothed girl in the open country and slept with her, having taken her by force, her ravisher alone must die; 26 you must do nothing to the girl, she has not committed a capital offence. The case is like that of a man who attacks and kills his fellow: 27 since he came across her in the open country, the betrothed girl may have called out, without anyone's coming to her rescue.

28 'If a man meets a young virgin who is not betrothed and seizes her, sleeps with her and is caught in the act,

NEW REVISED STANDARD VERSION	REVISED ENGLISH BIBLE

NEW REVISED STANDARD VERSION

29 the man who lay with her shall give fifty shekels of silver to the young woman's father, and she shall become his wife. Because he violated her he shall not be permitted to divorce her as long as he lives.

30 *b* A man shall not marry his father's wife, thereby violating his father's rights. *c*

23 No one whose testicles are crushed or whose penis is cut off shall be admitted to the assembly of the LORD.

2 Those born of an illicit union shall not be admitted to the assembly of the LORD. Even to the tenth generation, none of their descendants shall be admitted to the assembly of the LORD.

3 No Ammonite or Moabite shall be admitted to the assembly of the LORD. Even to the tenth generation, none of their descendants shall be admitted to the assembly of the LORD, 4 because they did not meet you with food and water on your journey out of Egypt, and because they hired against you Balaam son of Beor, from Pethor of Mesopotamia, to curse you. 5 (Yet the LORD your God refused to heed Balaam; the LORD your God turned the curse into a blessing for you, because the LORD your God loved you.) 6 You shall never promote their welfare or their prosperity as long as you live.

7 You shall not abhor any of the Edomites, for they are your kin. You shall not abhor any of the Egyptians, because you were an alien residing in their land. 8 The children of the third generation that are born to them may be admitted to the assembly of the LORD.

9 When you are encamped against your enemies you shall guard against any impropriety.

10 If one of you becomes unclean because of a nocturnal emission, then he shall go outside the camp; he must not come within the camp. 11 When evening comes, he shall wash himself with water, and when the sun has set, he may come back into the camp.

12 You shall have a designated area outside the camp to which you shall go. 13 With your utensils you shall have a trowel; when you relieve yourself outside, you shall dig a hole with it and then cover up your excrement. 14 Because the LORD your God travels along with your camp, to save you and to hand over your enemies to you, therefore your camp must be holy, so that he may not see anything indecent among you and turn away from you.

15 Slaves who have escaped to you from their owners shall not be given back to them. 16 They shall reside with you, in your midst, in any place they choose in any one of your towns, wherever they please; you shall not oppress them.

17 None of the daughters of Israel shall be a temple prostitute; none of the sons of Israel shall be a temple prostitute. 18 You shall not bring the fee of a prostitute or the wages of a male prostitute *d* into the house of the LORD your God in payment for any vow, for both of these are abhorrent to the LORD your God.

19 You shall not charge interest on loans to another Israelite, interest on money, interest on provisions, interest on anything that is lent. 20 On loans to a foreigner you may charge interest, but on loans to another Israelite you may not charge interest, so that the LORD your God may bless you in all your undertakings in the land that you are about to enter and possess.

21 If you make a vow to the LORD your God, do not postpone fulfilling it; for the LORD your God will surely require it of you, and you would incur guilt. 22 But if you refrain from vowing, you will not incur guilt. 23 Whatever

REVISED ENGLISH BIBLE

ered, 29 then the man who lies with her must give the girl's father fifty pieces of silver, and she will be his wife because he has violated her. He is not free to divorce her all his days.

30 A man must not take his father's wife: he must not bring shame on his father.

23 No man whose testicles have been crushed or whose organ has been cut off may become a member of the assembly of the LORD.

2 No descendant of an irregular union, even down to the tenth generation, may become a member of the assembly of the LORD.

3 No Ammonite or Moabite, even down to the tenth generation, may become a member of the assembly of the LORD. They must never become members of the assembly of the LORD 4 because they did not meet you with food and water on your journey from Egypt, and because they hired Balaam son of Beor from Pethor in Aram-naharaim to curse you. 5 The LORD your God refused to listen to Balaam and turned the curse into a blessing for you, because the LORD your God loved you. 6 As long as you live you are not to seek their welfare or their good.

7 Do not regard an Edomite as an abomination, for he is your own kin; nor an Egyptian, for you were aliens in his land. 8 The third generation of children born to them may become members of the assembly of the LORD.

9 When you are encamped against an enemy, you must be careful to avoid any foulness. 10 When one of your number is unclean because of an emission of seed at night, he must go outside the camp; he may not come into it. 11 Towards evening he is to wash himself in water, and at sunset he may re-enter the camp. 12 You must have a sign outside the camp showing where you can withdraw to relieve yourself. 13 As part of your equipment you are to have a trowel, and when you squat outside, you are to scrape a hole with it and then turn and cover your excrement. 14 For the LORD your God moves with your camp, to keep you safe and to hand over your enemies to you as you advance, and your camp must be kept holy for fear that he should see something offensive and go with you no farther.

15 You must not surrender to his master a slave who has taken refuge with you. 16 Let him stay with you anywhere he chooses in any one of your settlements, wherever suits him best; you must not force him.

17 No Israelite woman may become a temple-prostitute, nor may an Israelite man.

18 You must not allow a common prostitute's fee, or the pay of a male prostitute, to be brought into the house of the LORD your God in fulfilment of any vow, for both of them are abominable to the LORD your God.

19 You are not to exact interest on anything you lend to a fellow-countryman, whether money or food or anything else on which interest can be charged. 20 You may exact interest on a loan to a foreigner but not on a loan to a fellow-countryman, and then the LORD your God will bless you in all you undertake in the land which you are entering to occupy.

21 When you make a vow to the LORD your God, do not put off its fulfilment; otherwise the LORD your God will require satisfaction from you and you will be guilty of sin. 22 If you choose not to make a vow, you will not be guilty of sin; 23 but if you voluntarily make a vow to the LORD your

---

b Ch 23.1 in Heb   *c* Heb *uncovering his father's skirt*   *d* Heb *a dog*

22:30 *In Heb. 23:1.*   23:4 **Aram-naharaim:** *that is* Aram of Two Rivers.

covered, 29 the man who had relations with her shall pay the girl's father fifty silver shekels and take her as his wife, because he has deflowered her. Moreover, he may not divorce her as long as he lives.

23 "A man shall not marry his father's wife, nor shall he dishonor his father's bed.

2 "No one whose testicles have been crushed or whose penis has been cut off, may be admitted into the community of the Lord. 3 No child of an incestuous union may be admitted into the community of the LORD, nor any descendant of his even to the tenth generation. 4 No Ammonite or Moabite may ever be admitted into the community of the LORD, nor any descendants of theirs even to the tenth generation, 5 because they would not succor you with food and water on your journey after you left Egypt, and because Moab hired Balaam, son of Beor, from Pethor in Aram Naharaim, to curse you; 6 though the LORD, your God, would not listen to Balaam and turned his curse into a blessing for you, because he loves you. 7 Never promote their peace and prosperity as long as you live. 8 But do not abhor the Edomite, since he is your brother, nor the Egyptian, since you were an alien in his country. 9 Children born to them may in the third generation be admitted into the community of the LORD.

10 "When you are in camp during an expedition against your enemies, you shall keep yourselves from everything offensive. 11 If one of you becomes unclean because of a nocturnal emission, he shall go outside the camp, and not return until, 12 toward evening, he has bathed in water; then, when the sun has set, he may come back into the camp. 13 Outside the camp you shall have a place set aside to be used as a latrine. 14 You shall also keep a trowel in your equipment and with it, when you go outside to ease nature, you shall first dig a hole and afterward cover up your excrement. 15 Since the LORD, your God, journeys along within your camp to defend you and to put your enemies at your mercy, your camp must be holy; otherwise, if he sees anything indecent in your midst, he will leave your company.

16 "You shall not hand over to his master a slave who has taken refuge from him with you. 17 Let him live with you wherever he chooses, in any one of your communities that pleases him. Do not molest him.

18 "There shall be no temple harlot among the Israelite women, nor a temple prostitute among the Israelite men. 19 You shall not offer a harlot's fee or a dog's price as any kind of votive offering in the house of the LORD, your God; both these things are an abomination to the LORD, your God.

20 "You shall not demand interest from your countrymen on a loan of money or of food or of anything else on which interest is usually demanded. 21 You may demand interest from a foreigner, but not from your countryman, so that the LORD, your God, may bless you in all your undertakings on the land you are to enter and occupy.

22 "When you make a vow to the LORD, your God, you shall not delay in fulfilling it; otherwise you will be held guilty, for the LORD, your God, is strict in requiring it of you. 23 Should you refrain from making a vow, you will not be held guilty. 24 But you must keep your solemn word and

29 her ravisher must give the girl's father fifty silver shekels; since he has exploited her, she must be his wife and, as long as he lives, he may not divorce her.'

23 'A man must not take his father's wife; he must not withdraw the skirt of his father's cloak from her.

2 'A man whose testicles have been crushed or whose male member has been cut off must not be admitted to the assembly of Yahweh. 3 No half-breed may be admitted to the assembly of Yahweh; not even his descendants to the tenth generation may be admitted to the assembly of Yahweh. 4 No Ammonite or Moabite may be admitted to the assembly of Yahweh; not even his descendants to the tenth generation may be admitted to the assembly of Yahweh, and this is for all time; 5 since they did not come to meet you with food and drink when you were on your way out of Egypt, and even hired Balaam son of Beor to oppose you by cursing you, from Pethor in Aram Naharaim. 6 But Yahweh your God refused to listen to Balaam, and Yahweh your God turned the curse on you into a blessing, because Yahweh your God loved you. 7 Never, as long as you live, must you seek their welfare or their prosperity.

8 'You must not regard the Edomite as detestable, for he is your brother; you must not regard the Egyptian as detestable, since you were once a foreigner in his country. 9 The third generation of children born to these may be admitted to the assembly of Yahweh.

10 'When you are in camp, at war with your enemies, you must avoid anything bad. 11 If any one of you is unclean by reason of a nocturnal emission, he must leave and not come back into camp, 12 but towards evening wash himself, and return to camp at sunset.

13 'You must have a latrine outside the camp, and go out to this; 14 you must have a trowel in your equipment and, when you squat outside, you must scrape a hole with it, then turn round and cover up your excrement. 15 For Yahweh your God goes about the inside of your camp to guard you and put your enemies at your mercy. Your camp must therefore be a holy place; Yahweh must not see anything indecent there or he will desert you.

16 'You must not allow a master to imprison a slave who has escaped from him and come to you. 17 Let him make his home with you and yours, wherever he pleases in whichever of your towns he prefers; you must not molest him.

18 'There must be no sacred prostitute among the women of Israel, and no sacred prostitute among the men of Israel. 19 You must not bring the wages of a prostitute or the earnings of a 'dog' k to the house of Yahweh your God, whatever vow you may have made: both are detestable to Yahweh your God.

20 'You must not lend on interest to your brother, whether the loan be of money, of food, or of anything else that may earn interest. 21 You may demand interest on a loan to a foreigner, but you must not demand interest from your brother; so that Yahweh your God may bless you in all your labours, in the country which you are about to enter and make your own.

22 'If you make a vow to Yahweh your God, you must not be slack about fulfilling it: Yahweh your God will certainly hold you answerable for it and you will incur guilt. 23 If, however, you make no vow, you do not incur guilt. 24 Whatever passes your lips you must keep to, and the vow

---

k **23** Contemptuous term for a male prostitute.

NEW REVISED STANDARD VERSION

your lips utter you must diligently perform, just as you have freely vowed to the LORD your God with your own mouth.

24 If you go into your neighbor's vineyard, you may eat your fill of grapes, as many as you wish, but you shall not put any in a container.

25 If you go into your neighbor's standing grain, you may pluck the ears with your hand, but you shall not put a sickle to your neighbor's standing grain.

24 Suppose a man enters into marriage with a woman, but she does not please him because he finds something objectionable about her, and so he writes her a certificate of divorce, puts it in her hand, and sends her out of his house; she then leaves his house 2 and goes off to become another man's wife. 3 Then suppose the second man dislikes her, writes her a bill of divorce, puts it in her hand, and sends her out of his house (or the second man who married her dies); 4 her first husband, who sent her away, is not permitted to take her again to be his wife after she has been defiled; for that would be abhorrent to the LORD, and you shall not bring guilt on the land that the LORD your God is giving you as a possession.

5 When a man is newly married, he shall not go out with the army or be charged with any related duty. He shall be free at home one year, to be happy with the wife whom he has married.

6 No one shall take a mill or an upper millstone in pledge, for that would be taking a life in pledge.

7 If someone is caught kidnaping another Israelite, enslaving or selling the Israelite, then that kidnaper shall die. So you shall purge the evil from your midst.

8 Guard against an outbreak of a leprous[e] skin disease by being very careful; you shall carefully observe whatever the levitical priests instruct you, just as I have commanded them. 9 Remember what the LORD your God did to Miriam on your journey out of Egypt.

10 When you make your neighbor a loan of any kind, you shall not go into the house to take the pledge. 11 You shall wait outside, while the person to whom you are making the loan brings the pledge out to you. 12 If the person is poor, you shall not sleep in the garment given you as[f] the pledge. 13 You shall give the pledge back by sunset, so that your neighbor may sleep in the cloak and bless you; and it will be to your credit before the LORD your God.

14 You shall not withhold the wages of poor and needy laborers, whether other Israelites or aliens who reside in your land in one of your towns. 15 You shall pay them their wages daily before sunset, because they are poor and their livelihood depends on them; otherwise they might cry to the LORD against you, and you would incur guilt.

16 Parents shall not be put to death for their children, nor shall children be put to death for their parents; only for their own crimes may persons be put to death.

17 You shall not deprive a resident alien or an orphan of justice; you shall not take a widow's garment in pledge. 18 Remember that you were a slave in Egypt and the LORD your God redeemed you from there; therefore I command you to do this.

19 When you reap your harvest in your field and forget a sheaf in the field, you shall not go back to get it; it shall be left for the alien, the orphan, and the widow, so that the LORD your God may bless you in all your undertakings. 20 When you beat your olive trees, do not strip what is left; it shall be for the alien, the orphan, and the widow.

REVISED ENGLISH BIBLE

God, mind what you say and do what you have promised.

24 When you go into another man's vineyard, you may eat as many grapes as you wish to satisfy your hunger, but you may not put any into your basket.

25 When you go into another man's standing grain, you may pluck ears to rub in your hands, but you may not put a sickle to the standing crop.

24 If a man has taken a woman in marriage, but she does not win his favour because he finds something offensive in her, and he writes her a certificate of divorce, gives it to her, and dismisses her, 2 and if after leaving his house she goes off to become the wife of another man, 3 and this second husband turns against her and writes her a certificate of divorce, gives it to her, and dismisses her, or dies after making her his wife, 4 then her first husband who had dismissed her is not free to take her to be his wife again; for him she has become unclean. This would be abominable to the LORD, and you must not bring sin upon the land which the LORD your God is giving you as your holding.

5 When a man is newly married, he is not to be liable for military service or any other public duty. He must remain at home exempt from service for one year and be happy with the wife he has taken.

6 No one may take millstones, or even the upper millstone alone, in pledge; that would be taking a life in pledge.

7 When a man is found to have kidnapped a fellow-countryman, an Israelite, and to have treated him harshly or sold him, he must suffer the death penalty, and so you will rid yourselves of this wickedness.

8 Be careful how you act in all cases of virulent skin disease; be careful to observe all that the levitical priests tell you; you must obey the instructions I gave them. 9 Keep in mind what the LORD your God did to Miriam as you journeyed from Egypt.

10 When you make any loan to anyone, do not enter his house to take a pledge from him. 11 Wait outside, and the person whose creditor you are must bring the pledge out to you. 12 If he is a poor man, do not sleep in the cloak he has pledged. 13 Return it to him at sunset so that he may sleep in it and bless you; then it will be counted to your credit in the sight of the LORD your God.

14 You must not keep back the wages of a man who is poor and needy, whether a fellow-countryman or an alien living in your country in one of your settlements. 15 Pay him his wages on the same day before sunset, for he is poor and he relies on them: otherwise he may appeal to the LORD against you, and you will be guilty of sin.

16 Parents are not to be put to death for their children, nor children for their parents; each one may be put to death only for his own sin.

17 You must not deprive aliens and the fatherless of justice or take a widow's cloak in pledge. 18 Bear in mind that you were slaves in Egypt and the LORD your God redeemed you from there; that is why I command you to do this.

19 When you reap the harvest in your field and overlook a sheaf, do not go back to pick it up; it is to be left for the alien, the fatherless, and the widow, so that the LORD your God may bless you in all that you undertake.

20 When you beat your olive trees, do not strip them afterwards; what is left is for the alien, the fatherless, and the widow.

---

[e] A term for several skin diseases; precise meaning uncertain
[f] Heb lacks the garment given you as

24:14 **keep . . . man:** so Scroll; Heb. oppress a hired man.
24:17 **and:** so Gk; Heb. omits.

fulfill the votive offering you have freely promised to the LORD.

25 "When you go through your neighbor's vineyard, you may eat as many of his grapes as you wish, but do not put them in your basket. 26 When you go through your neighbor's grainfield, you may pluck some of the ears with your hand, but do not put a sickle to your neighbor's grain.

24 "When a man, after marrying a woman and having relations with her, is later displeased with her because he finds in her something indecent, and therefore he writes out a bill of divorce and hands it to her, thus dismissing her from his house: 2 if on leaving his house she goes and becomes the wife of another man, 3 and the second husband, too, comes to dislike her and dismisses her from his house by handing her a written bill of divorce; 4 or if this second man who has married her, dies; then her former husband, who dismissed her, may not again take her as his wife after she has become defiled. That would be an abomination before the LORD, and you shall not bring such guilt upon the land which the LORD, your God, is giving you as a heritage.

5 "When a man is newly wed, he need not go out on a military expedition, nor shall any public duty be imposed on him. He shall be exempt for one year for the sake of his family, to bring joy to the wife he has married.

6 "No one shall take a hand mill or even its upper stone as a pledge for debt, for he would be taking the debtor's sustenance as a pledge.

7 "If any man is caught kidnaping a fellow Israelite in order to enslave him and sell him, the kidnaper shall be put to death. Thus shall you purge the evil from your midst.

8 "In an attack of leprosy you shall be careful to observe exactly and to carry out all the directions of the levitical priests. Take care to act in accordance with the instructions I have given them. 9 Remember what the LORD, your God, did to Miriam on the journey after you left Egypt.

10 "When you make a loan of any kind to your neighbor, you shall not enter his house to receive a pledge from him, 11 but shall wait outside until the man to whom you are making the loan brings his pledge outside to you. 12 If he is a poor man, you shall not sleep in the mantle he gives as a pledge, 13 but shall return it to him at sunset that he himself may sleep in it. Then he will bless you, and it will be a good deed of yours before the LORD, your God.

14 "You shall not defraud a poor and needy hired servant, whether he be one of your own countrymen or one of the aliens who live in your communities. 15 You shall pay him each day's wages before sundown on the day itself, since he is poor and looks forward to them. Otherwise he will cry to the LORD against you, and you will be held guilty.

16 "Fathers shall not be put to death for their children, nor children for their fathers; only for his own guilt shall a man be put to death.

17 "You shall not violate the rights of the alien or of the orphan, nor take the clothing of a widow as a pledge. 18 For, remember, you were once slaves in Egypt, and the LORD, your God, ransomed you from there; that is why I command you to observe this rule.

19 "When you reap the harvest in your field and overlook a sheaf there, you shall not go back to get it; let it be for the alien, the orphan or the widow, that the LORD, your God, may bless you in all your undertakings. 20 When you knock down the fruit of your olive trees, you shall not go over the branches a second time; let what remains be for the alien, the orphan and the widow. 21 When you pick your grapes,

that you have made to Yahweh, your generous God, you must fulfil.

25 'If you go into your neighbour's vineyard, you may eat as many grapes as you please, but you must not put any in your basket. 26 If you go into your neighbour's standing corn, you may pick ears by hand, but you must not put a sickle into your neighbour's corn.'

24 'Suppose a man has taken a wife and consummated the marriage; but she has not pleased him and he has found some impropriety of which to accuse her; he has therefore made out a writ of divorce for her and handed it to her and then dismissed her from his house; 2 she leaves his home and goes away to become the wife of another man. 3 Then suppose this second man who has married her takes a dislike to her and makes out a writ of divorce for her and hands it to her and dismisses her from his house or if this other man who took her as his wife dies, 4 her first husband, who has repudiated her, may not take her back as his wife now that she has been made unclean in this way. For that is detestable in Yahweh's eyes and you must not bring guilt on the country which Yahweh your God is giving you as your heritage.

5 'If a man is newly married, he must not join the army, nor must he be pestered at home; he must be left at home, free of all obligations for one year, to make his new wife happy.

6 'No one may take a mill or a millstone in pledge; that would be to take life itself in pledge.

7 'If anyone is caught, having kidnapped one of his brother-Israelites, whether he makes him his slave or sells him, that thief must die. You must banish this evil from among you.

8 'In a case of a virulent skin-disease, take care you faithfully observe and exactly carry out everything that the levitical priests direct you to do. You must keep and observe everything that I have commanded them. 9 Remember what Yahweh your God did to Miriam when you were on your way out of Egypt.

10 'If you are making your brother a loan on pledge, you must not go into his house and seize the pledge, whatever it may be. 11 You must stay outside, and the man to whom you are making the loan must bring the pledge out to you. 12 And if the man is poor, you must not go to bed with his pledge in your possession; 13 you must return it to him at sunset so that he can sleep in his cloak and bless you; and it will be an upright action on your part in God's view.

14 'You must not exploit a poor and needy wage-earner, be he one of your brothers or a foreigner resident in your community. 15 You must pay him his wages each day, not allowing the sun to set before you do, since he, being poor, needs them badly; otherwise he may appeal to Yahweh against you, and you would incur guilt.

16 'Parents may not be put to death for their children, nor children for parents, but each must be put to death for his own crime.

17 'You must not infringe the rights of the foreigner or orphan; you must not take a widow's clothes in pledge. 18 Remember that you were once a slave in Egypt and that Yahweh your God redeemed you from that. That is why I am giving you this order.

19 'If, when reaping the harvest in your field, you overlook a sheaf in that field, do not go back for it. The foreigner, the orphan and the widow shall have it, so that Yahweh your God may bless you in all your undertakings.

20 'When you beat your olive tree, you must not go over the branches twice. The foreigner, the orphan and the widow shall have the rest.

21 When you gather the grapes of your vineyard, do not glean what is left; it shall be for the alien, the orphan, and the widow. 22 Remember that you were a slave in the land of Egypt; therefore I am commanding you to do this.

25 Suppose two persons have a dispute and enter into litigation, and the judges decide between them, declaring one to be in the right and the other to be in the wrong. 2 If the one in the wrong deserves to be flogged, the judge shall make that person lie down and be beaten in his presence with the number of lashes proportionate to the offense. 3 Forty lashes may be given but not more; if more lashes than these are given, your neighbor will be degraded in your sight.

4 You shall not muzzle an ox while it is treading out the grain.

5 When brothers reside together, and one of them dies and has no son, the wife of the deceased shall not be married outside the family to a stranger. Her husband's brother shall go in to her, taking her in marriage, and performing the duty of a husband's brother to her, 6 and the firstborn whom she bears shall succeed to the name of the deceased brother, so that his name may not be blotted out of Israel. 7 But if the man has no desire to marry his brother's widow, then his brother's widow shall go up to the elders at the gate and say, "My husband's brother refuses to perpetuate his brother's name in Israel; he will not perform the duty of a husband's brother to me." 8 Then the elders of his town shall summon him and speak to him. If he persists, saying, "I have no desire to marry her," 9 then his brother's wife shall go up to him in the presence of the elders, pull his sandal off his foot, spit in his face, and declare, "This is what is done to the man who does not build up his brother's house." 10 Throughout Israel his family shall be known as "the house of him whose sandal was pulled off."

11 If men get into a fight with one another, and the wife of one intervenes to rescue her husband from the grip of his opponent by reaching out and seizing his genitals, 12 you shall cut off her hand; show no pity.

13 You shall not have in your bag two kinds of weights, large and small. 14 You shall not have in your house two kinds of measures, large and small. 15 You shall have only a full and honest weight; you shall have only a full and honest measure, so that your days may be long in the land that the LORD your God is giving you. 16 For all who do such things, all who act dishonestly, are abhorrent to the LORD your God.

17 Remember what Amalek did to you on your journey out of Egypt, 18 how he attacked you on the way, when you were faint and weary, and struck down all who lagged behind you; he did not fear God. 19 Therefore when the LORD your God has given you rest from all your enemies on every hand, in the land that the LORD your God is giving you as an inheritance to possess, you shall blot out the remembrance of Amalek from under heaven; do not forget.

26 When you have come into the land that the LORD your God is giving you as an inheritance to possess, and you possess it, and settle in it, 2 you shall take some of the first of all the fruit of the ground, which you harvest from the land that the LORD your God is giving you, and you shall put it in a basket and go to the place that the LORD your God will choose as a dwelling for his name. 3 You shall go to the priest who is in office at that time, and say to him, "Today I declare to the LORD your God that I have come into the land that the LORD swore to our ancestors to give us." 4 When the priest takes the basket from your hand and sets it down before the altar of the LORD your God, 5 you shall make this response before the LORD your God:

21 When you gather the grapes from your vineyard, do not glean afterwards; what is left is for the alien, the fatherless, and the widow. 22 Keep in mind that you were slaves in Egypt; that is why I command you to do this.

25 When two go to law and present themselves for judgement, the judges are to try the case; they must acquit the innocent and condemn the guilty. 2 If the guilty party is sentenced to be flogged, the judge is to have him lie down and be beaten in his presence; the number of lashes will correspond to the gravity of the offence. 3 They may give him forty strokes, but not more; otherwise, if they go farther and exceed this number, your fellow-countryman will have been publicly degraded.

4 You are not to muzzle an ox while it is treading out the grain.

5 When brothers live together and one of them dies without leaving a son, his widow is not to marry outside the family. Her husband's brother is to have intercourse with her; he should take her in marriage and do his duty by her as her husband's brother. 6 The first son she bears will perpetuate the dead brother's name so that it may not be blotted out from Israel. 7 But if the man is unwilling to take his brother's wife, she must go to the elders at the town gate and say, 'My husband's brother refuses to perpetuate his brother's name in Israel; he will not do his duty by me.' 8 At this the elders of the town should summon him and reason with him. If he still stands his ground and says, 'I refuse to take her,' 9 his brother's widow must go up to him in the presence of the elders, pull his sandal off his foot, spit in his face, and declare: 'Thus shall be done to the man who will not build up his brother's family.' 10 His family will be known in Israel as the house of the unsandalled man.

11 When two men are fighting and the wife of one of them intervenes to drag her husband clear of his opponent, if she puts out her hand and catches hold of the man by the genitals, 12 you must cut off her hand and show her no mercy.

13 You must not have unequal weights in your bag, one heavy, the other light. 14 You must not have unequal measures in your house, one large, the other small. 15 You must have true and correct weights and true and correct measures, so that you may enjoy long life in the land which the LORD your God is giving you. 16 All who do such things, all who deal dishonestly, are abominable to the LORD your God.

17 Bear in mind what the Amalekites did to you on your journey from Egypt, 18 how they fell on you on the road when you were faint and weary and cut off those at the rear, all who were lagging behind exhausted: they showed no fear of God. 19 When the LORD your God gives you peace from your enemies on every side, in the land which he is giving you to occupy as your holding, you must without fail blot out all memory of Amalek from under heaven.

26 AFTER you come into the land which the LORD your God is giving you to occupy as your holding and settle in it, 2 you are to take some of the firstfruits of all the produce of the soil, which you harvest from the land which the LORD your God is giving you, and, having put them in a basket, go to the place which the LORD your God will choose as a dwelling for his name. 3 When you come to the priest, whoever he is at that time, say to him, 'I acknowledge this day to the LORD your God that I have entered the land which the LORD swore to our forefathers to give us.' 4 The priest will receive the basket from your hand and set it down before the altar of the LORD your God. 5 Then you must solemnly recite before the LORD your God: 'My father

25:14,15 **measures:** *Heb.* ephahs.

NEW AMERICAN BIBLE

NEW JERUSALEM BIBLE

you shall not go over the vineyard a second time; let what remains be for the alien, the orphan, and the widow. 22 For remember that you were once slaves in Egypt; that is why I command you to observe this rule.

25 "When men have a dispute and bring it to court, and a decision is handed down to them acquitting the innocent party and condemning the guilty party, 2 if the latter deserves stripes, the judge shall have him lie down and in his presence receive the number of stripes his guilt deserves. 3 Forty stripes may be given him, but no more; lest, if he were beaten with more stripes than these, your kinsman should be looked upon as disgraced because of the severity of the beating.

4 "You shall not muzzle an ox when it is treading out grain.

5 "When brothers live together and one of them dies without a son, the widow of the deceased shall not marry anyone outside the family; but her husband's brother shall go to her and perform the duty of a brother-in-law by marrying her. 6 The first-born son she bears shall continue the line of the deceased brother, that his name may not be blotted out from Israel. 7 If, however, a man does not care to marry his brother's wife, she shall go up to the elders at the gate and declare, 'My brother-in-law does not intend to perform his duty toward me and refuses to perpetuate his brother's name in Israel.' 8 Thereupon the elders of his city shall summon him and admonish him. If he persists in saying, 'I am not willing to marry her,' 9 his sister-in-law, in the presence of the elders, shall go up to him and strip his sandal from his foot and spit in his face, saying publicly, 'This is how one should be treated who will not build up his brother's family!' 10 And his lineage shall be spoken of in Israel as 'the family of the man stripped of his sandal.'

11 "When two men are fighting and the wife of one intervenes to save her husband from the blows of his opponent, if she stretches out her hand and seizes the latter by his private parts, 12 you shall chop off her hand without pity.

13 "You shall not keep two differing weights in your bag, one large and the other small; 14 nor shall you keep two different measures in your house, one large and the other small. 15 But use a true and just weight, and a true and just measure, that you may have a long life on the land which the LORD, your God, is giving you. 16 Everyone who is dishonest in any of these matters is an abomination to the LORD, your God.

17 "Bear in mind what Amalek did to you on the journey after you left Egypt, 18 how without fear of any god he harassed you along the way, weak and weary as you were, and cut off at the rear all those who lagged behind. 19 Therefore, when the LORD, your God, gives you rest from all your enemies round about in the land which he is giving you to occupy as your heritage, you shall blot out the memory of Amalek from under the heavens. Do not forget!

26 "When you have come into the land which the LORD, your God, is giving you as a heritage, and have occupied it and settled in it, 2 you shall take some first fruits of the various products of the soil which you harvest from the land which the LORD, your God, gives you, and, putting them in a basket, you shall go to the place which the LORD, your God, chooses for the dwelling place of his name. 3 There you shall go to the priest in office at that time and say to him, 'Today I acknowledge to the LORD, my God, that I have indeed come into the land which he swore to our fathers he would give us.' 4 The priest shall then receive the basket from you and shall set it in front of the altar of the LORD, your God. 5 Then you shall declare before

21 'When you harvest your vineyard, you must not pick it over a second time. The foreigner, the orphan and the widow shall have the rest.

22 'Remember that you were once a slave in Egypt. That is why I am giving you this order.'

25 'If people fall out, they must go to court for judgement; the judges must declare the one who is right to be in the right, the one who is wrong to be in the wrong. 2 If the one who is in the wrong deserves a flogging, the judge must have him laid on the ground and flogged in his presence, the number of strokes proportionate to his offence. 3 He may impose forty strokes but no more; otherwise, by the infliction of more, serious injury may be caused and your brother be humiliated before you.

4 'You must not muzzle an ox when it is treading out the corn.

5 'If brothers live together and one of them dies childless, the dead man's wife may not marry a stranger outside the family. Her husband's brother must come to her and, exercising his duty as brother, make her his wife, 6 and the first son she bears must assume the dead brother's name; by this means his name will not be obliterated from Israel. 7 But if the man declines to take his brother's wife, she must go to the elders at the gate and say, "I have no brother-in-law willing to perpetuate his brother's name in Israel; he declines to exercise his duty as brother in my favour." 8 The elders of the town must summon the man and talk to him. If, on appearing before them, he says, "I refuse to take her," 9 then the woman to whom he owes duty as brother must go up to him in the presence of the elders, take the sandal off his foot, spit in his face, and pronounce the following words, "This is what is done to the man who refuses to restore his brother's house," 10 and his family must henceforth be known in Israel as House of the Unshod.'

11 'If, when two men are fighting, the wife of one intervenes to protect her husband from the other's blows by reaching out and seizing the other by his private parts, 12 you must cut off her hand and show no pity.

13 'You must not keep two different weights in your bag, one heavy, one light. 14 You must not keep two different measures in your house, one large, one small. 15 You must keep one weight, full and accurate, so that you may have long life in the country given you by Yahweh your God. 16 For anyone who does things of this kind and acts dishonestly is detestable to Yahweh your God.

17 'Remember how Amalek treated you when you were on your way out of Egypt. 18 He met you on your way and, after you had gone by, he fell on you from the rear and cut off the stragglers; when you were faint and weary, he had no fear of God. 19 When Yahweh your God has granted you peace from all the enemies surrounding you, in the country given you by Yahweh your God to own as your heritage, you must blot out the memory of Amalek under heaven. Do not forget.'

26 'When you have entered the country which Yahweh your God is giving you as heritage, when you have taken possession of it and are living in it, 2 you must set aside the first-fruits of all the produce of the soil raised by you in your country, given you by Yahweh your God. You must put these in a basket and go to the place where Yahweh your God chooses to give his name a home. 3 You will go to the priest then in office and say to him, "Today I declare to Yahweh my God that I have reached the country which Yahweh swore to our ancestors that he would give us."

4 'The priest will then take the basket from your hand and lay it before the altar of Yahweh your God. 5 In the presence of Yahweh your God, you will then pronounce these words:

| NEW REVISED STANDARD VERSION | REVISED ENGLISH BIBLE |

"A wandering Aramean was my ancestor; he went down into Egypt and lived there as an alien, few in number, and there he became a great nation, mighty and populous. 6 When the Egyptians treated us harshly and afflicted us, by imposing hard labor on us, 7 we cried to the LORD, the God of our ancestors; the LORD heard our voice and saw our affliction, our toil, and our oppression. 8 The LORD brought us out of Egypt with a mighty hand and an outstretched arm, with a terrifying display of power, and with signs and wonders; 9 and he brought us into this place and gave us this land, a land flowing with milk and honey. 10 So now I bring the first of the fruit of the ground that you, O LORD, have given me." You shall set it down before the LORD your God and bow down before the LORD your God. 11 Then you, together with the Levites and the aliens who reside among you, shall celebrate with all the bounty that the LORD your God has given to you and to your house.

12 When you have finished paying all the tithe of your produce in the third year (which is the year of the tithe), giving it to the Levites, the aliens, the orphans, and the widows, so that they may eat their fill within your towns, 13 then you shall say before the LORD your God: "I have removed the sacred portion from the house, and I have given it to the Levites, the resident aliens, the orphans, and the widows, in accordance with your entire commandment that you commanded me; I have neither transgressed nor forgotten any of your commandments: 14 I have not eaten of it while in mourning; I have not removed any of it while I was unclean; and I have not offered any of it to the dead. I have obeyed the LORD my God, doing just as you commanded me. 15 Look down from your holy habitation, from heaven, and bless your people Israel and the ground that you have given us, as you swore to our ancestors — a land flowing with milk and honey."

16 This very day the LORD your God is commanding you to observe these statutes and ordinances; so observe them diligently with all your heart and with all your soul. 17 Today you have obtained the LORD's agreement: to be your God; and for you to walk in his ways, to keep his statutes, his commandments, and his ordinances, and to obey him. 18 Today the LORD has obtained your agreement: to be his treasured people, as he promised you, and to keep his commandments; 19 for him to set you high above all nations that he has made, in praise and in fame and in honor; and for you to be a people holy to the LORD your God, as he promised.

27 Then Moses and the elders of Israel charged all the people as follows: Keep the entire commandment that I am commanding you today. 2 On the day that you cross over the Jordan into the land that the LORD your God is giving you, you shall set up large stones and cover them with plaster. 3 You shall write on them all the words of this law when you have crossed over, to enter the land that the LORD your God is giving you, a land flowing with milk and honey, as the LORD, the God of your ancestors, promised you. 4 So when you have crossed over the Jordan, you shall set up these stones, about which I am commanding you today, on Mount Ebal, and you shall cover them with plaster. 5 And you shall build an altar there to the LORD your God, an altar of stones on which you have not used an iron tool. 6 You must build the altar of the LORD your God of unhewn[g] stones. Then offer up burnt offerings on it to the LORD your God, 7 make sacrifices of well-being, and eat them there, rejoicing before the LORD your God. 8 You shall write on the stones all the words of this law very clearly.

was a homeless Aramaean who went down to Egypt and lived there with a small band of people, but there it became a great, powerful, and large nation. 6 The Egyptians treated us harshly and humiliated us; they imposed cruel slavery on us. 7 We cried to the LORD the God of our fathers for help, and he listened to us, and, when he saw our misery and hardship and oppression, 8 the LORD led us out of Egypt with a strong hand and outstretched arm, with terrifying deeds, and with signs and portents. 9 He brought us to this place and gave us this land, a land flowing with milk and honey. 10 Now I have brought here the firstfruits of the soil which you, LORD, have given me.' You are then to set the basket before the LORD your God and bow in worship before him. 11 You are to rejoice, you and the Levites and the aliens living among you, in all the good things which the LORD your God has bestowed on you and your household.

12 In the third year, the tithe-year, when you have finished taking the tithe of your produce and have given it to the Levites and to the aliens, the fatherless, and the widows, so that they may eat it in your settlements and be well fed, 13 then declare before the LORD your God: 'I have rid my house of the tithe that was holy to you and given it to the Levites, to the aliens, the fatherless, and the widows, according to all the commandments which you laid on me. I have not infringed or forgotten any of your commandments. 14 I have not eaten any of the tithe while in mourning, nor have I got rid of any of it while unclean, nor offered any to the dead. I have obeyed the LORD my God, doing all that you commanded me. 15 Look down from heaven, your holy dwelling-place, and bless your people Israel and the soil which you have given to us as you promised on oath to our forefathers, a land flowing with milk and honey.'

16 This day the LORD your God commands you to keep these statutes and laws: be careful to observe them with all your heart and soul. 17 You have recognized the LORD this day as your God; you are to conform to his ways, to keep his statutes, his commandments, and his laws, and to obey him. 18 The LORD has recognized you this day as his special possession, as he promised you, and you are to keep all his commandments; 19 high above all the nations which he has made he will raise you, to bring him praise and fame and glory, and to be a people holy to the LORD your God, according to his promise.

27 MOSES, with the elders of Israel, gave the people this charge: Keep all the commandments that I now lay upon you. 2 On the day you cross the Jordan to the land which the LORD your God is giving you, you are to set up great stones. Coat them with plaster, 3 and inscribe on them all the words of this law, when you have crossed over to enter the land which the LORD your God is giving you, a land flowing with milk and honey, as the LORD the God of your forefathers promised you.

4 When you have crossed the Jordan you are to set up these stones on Mount Ebal, as I instruct you this day, and coat them with plaster. 5 Build an altar there to the LORD your God, an altar of stones on which no iron tool is to be used. 6 Build the altar of the LORD your God with blocks of undressed stone, and offer whole-offerings on it to the LORD your God. 7 Slaughter shared-offerings and eat them there, and rejoice before the LORD your God. 8 Inscribe on the stones all the words of this law, engraving them clearly and carefully.

26:5 **homeless**: or wandering.   26:14 **nor have . . . unclean**: mng of Heb. obscure. **to the dead**: or for the dead.   27:4 **Ebal**: Gerizim in Samar.

g Heb whole

| NEW AMERICAN BIBLE | NEW JERUSALEM BIBLE |

NEW AMERICAN BIBLE

the LORD, your God, 'My father was a wandering Aramean who went down to Egypt with a small household and lived there as an alien. But there he became a nation great, strong and numerous. 6 When the Egyptians maltreated and oppressed us, imposing hard labor upon us, 7 we cried to the LORD, the God of our fathers, and he heard our cry and saw our affliction, our toil and our oppression. 8 He brought us out of Egypt with his strong hand and outstretched arm, with terrifying power, with signs and wonders; 9 and bringing us into this country, he gave us this land flowing with milk and honey. 10 Therefore, I have now brought you the first fruits of the products of the soil which you, O LORD, have given me.' And having set them before the LORD, your God, you shall bow down in his presence. 11 Then you and your family, together with the Levite and the aliens who live among you, shall make merry over all these good things which the LORD, your God, has given you.

12 "When you have finished setting aside all the tithes of your produce in the third year, the year of the tithes, and you have given them to the Levite, the alien, the orphan and the widow, that they may eat their fill in your own community, 13 you shall declare before the LORD, your God, 'I have purged my house of the sacred portion and I have given it to the Levite, the alien, the orphan and the widow, just as you have commanded me. In this I have not broken or forgotten any of your commandments: 14 I have not eaten any of the tithe as a mourner; I have not brought any of it out as one unclean; I have not offered any of it to the dead. I have thus hearkened to the voice of the LORD, my God, doing just as you have commanded me. 15 Look down, then, from heaven, your holy abode, and bless your people Israel and the soil you have given us in the land flowing with milk and honey which you promised on oath to our fathers.'

16 "This day the LORD, your god, commands you to observe these statutes and decrees. Be careful, then, to observe them with all your heart and with all your soul. 17 Today you are making this agreement with the LORD: he is to be your God and you are to walk in his ways and observe his statutes, commandments and decrees, and to hearken to his voice. 18 And today the LORD is making this agreement with you: you are to be a people peculiarly his own, as he promised you; and provided you keep all his commandments, 19 he will then raise you high in praise and renown and glory above all other nations he has made, and you will be a people sacred to the LORD, your God, as he promised."

27 Then Moses, with the elders of Israel, gave the people this order: "Keep all these commandments which I enjoin on you today. 2 On the day you cross the Jordan into the land which the LORD, your God, is giving you, set up some large stones and coat them with plaster. 3 Also write on them, at the time you cross, all the words of this law, that you may thus enter into the land flowing with milk and honey, which the LORD, your God, and the God of your fathers, is giving you as he promised you. 4 When, moreover, you have crossed the Jordan, besides setting up on Mount Ebal these stones concerning which I command you today, and coating them with plaster, 5 you shall also build to the LORD, your God, an altar made of stones that no iron tool has touched. 6 You shall make this altar of the LORD, your God, with undressed stones, and shall offer on it holocausts to the LORD, your God. 7 You shall also sacrifice peace offerings and eat them there, making merry before the LORD, your God. 8 On the stones you shall inscribe all the words of this law very clearly."

NEW JERUSALEM BIBLE

"My father was a wandering Aramaean, who went down to Egypt with a small group of men, and stayed there, until he there became a great, powerful and numerous nation. 6 The Egyptians ill-treated us, they oppressed us and inflicted harsh slavery on us. 7 But we called on Yahweh, God of our ancestors. Yahweh heard our voice and saw our misery, our toil and our oppression; 8 and Yahweh brought us out of Egypt with mighty hand and outstretched arm, with great terror, and with signs and wonders. 9 He brought us here and has given us this country, a country flowing with milk and honey. 10 Hence, I now bring the first-fruits of the soil that you, Yahweh, have given me."

'You will then lay them before Yahweh your God, and prostrate yourself in the presence of Yahweh your God. 11 You must then rejoice in all the good things that Yahweh your God has bestowed on you and your family — you, the Levite and the foreigner living with you.

12 'In the third year, the tithing year, when you have finished taking the tithe of your whole income and have given it to the Levite, the foreigner, the orphan and the widow so that, in your towns, they may eat to their heart's content, 13 in the presence of Yahweh your God, you must say:

"I have cleared my house of what was consecrated. Yes, I have given it to the Levite, the foreigner, the orphan and the widow, in accordance with all the commandments you have imposed on me, neither going beyond your commandments nor neglecting them. 14 When in mourning, I have not eaten any of it; when unclean, I have taken none of it away; I have given none of it for the dead. I have obeyed the voice of Yahweh my God and I have behaved in every way as you have commanded me. 15 Look down from your holy dwelling, from heaven, and bless your people Israel and the country which you have given us, as you swore to our ancestors, a country flowing with milk and honey." '

16 'Yahweh your God commands you today to observe these laws and customs; you must keep and observe them with all your heart and with all your soul.

17 'Today you have obtained this declaration from Yahweh: that he will be your God, but only if you follow his ways, keep his statutes, his commandments, his customs, and listen to his voice. 18 And today Yahweh has obtained this declaration from you: that you will be his own people — as he has said — but only if you keep all his commandments; 19 then for praise and renown and honour, he will raise you higher than every other nation he has made, and you will be a people consecrated to Yahweh, as he has promised.'

27 Moses and the elders of Israel gave the people this command: 'Keep all the commandments which I am laying down for you today. 2 After you have crossed the Jordan into the country which Yahweh your God is giving you, you must set up tall stones, coat them with lime 3 and on them write all the words of this Law, when you have crossed and entered the country which Yahweh your God is giving you, a country flowing with milk and honey, as Yahweh, God of your ancestors, has promised you.

4 'When you have crossed the Jordan, you must erect these stones on Mount Ebal, as I command you today, and coat them with lime. 5 There, for Yahweh your God, you must build an altar of stones, on which no iron has been used. 6 You must build the altar of Yahweh your God of rough stones, and on this altar you will present burnt offerings to Yahweh your God, 7 and immolate communion sacrifices and eat them there, rejoicing in the presence of Yahweh your God. 8 On these stones you must write all the words of this Law; cut them carefully.'

423

NEW REVISED STANDARD VERSION

9 Then Moses and the levitical priests spoke to all Israel, saying: Keep silence and hear, O Israel! This very day you have become the people of the LORD your God. 10 Therefore obey the LORD your God, observing his commandments and his statutes that I am commanding you today.

11 The same day Moses charged the people as follows: 12 When you have crossed over the Jordan, these shall stand on Mount Gerizim for the blessing of the people: Simeon, Levi, Judah, Issachar, Joseph, and Benjamin. 13 And these shall stand on Mount Ebal for the curse: Reuben, Gad, Asher, Zebulun, Dan, and Naphtali. 14 Then the Levites shall declare in a loud voice to all the Israelites:

15 "Cursed be anyone who makes an idol or casts an image, anything abhorrent to the LORD, the work of an artisan, and sets it up in secret." All the people shall respond, saying, "Amen!"

16 "Cursed be anyone who dishonors father or mother." All the people shall say, "Amen!"

17 "Cursed be anyone who moves a neighbor's boundary marker." All the people shall say, "Amen!"

18 "Cursed be anyone who misleads a blind person on the road." All the people shall say, "Amen!"

19 "Cursed be anyone who deprives the alien, the orphan, and the widow of justice." All the people shall say, "Amen!"

20 "Cursed be anyone who lies with his father's wife, because he has violated his father's rights." *h* All the people shall say, "Amen!"

21 "Cursed be anyone who lies with any animal." All the people shall say, "Amen!"

22 "Cursed be anyone who lies with his sister, whether the daughter of his father or the daughter of his mother." All the people shall say, "Amen!"

23 "Cursed be anyone who lies with his mother-in-law." All the people shall say, "Amen!"

24 "Cursed be anyone who strikes down a neighbor in secret." All the people shall say, "Amen!"

25 "Cursed be anyone who takes a bribe to shed innocent blood." All the people shall say, "Amen!"

26 "Cursed be anyone who does not uphold the words of this law by observing them." All the people shall say, "Amen!"

28 If you will only obey the LORD your God, by diligently observing all his commandments that I am commanding you today, the LORD your God will set you high above all the nations of the earth; 2 all these blessings shall come upon you and overtake you, if you obey the LORD your God:

3 Blessed shall you be in the city, and blessed shall you be in the field.

4 Blessed shall be the fruit of your womb, the fruit of your ground, and the fruit of your livestock, both the increase of your cattle and the issue of your flock.

5 Blessed shall be your basket and your kneading bowl.

6 Blessed shall you be when you come in, and blessed shall you be when you go out.

7 The LORD will cause your enemies who rise against you to be defeated before you; they shall come out against you one way, and flee before you seven ways. 8 The LORD will command the blessing upon you in your barns, and in all that you undertake; he will bless you in the land that the LORD your God is giving you. 9 The LORD will establish you

REVISED ENGLISH BIBLE

9 Moses and the levitical priests said to all Israel: Be silent, Israel, and listen; this day you have become a people belonging to the LORD your God. 10 Obey the LORD your God, and observe his commandments and statutes that I now lay upon you.

11 That day Moses gave the people this command: 12 When you have crossed the Jordan those who are to stand on Mount Gerizim to bless the people are: Simeon, Levi, Judah, Issachar, Joseph, and Benjamin. 13 Those who are to stand on Mount Ebal to pronounce the curse are: Reuben, Gad, Asher, Zebulun, Dan, and Naphtali.

14 The Levites, in the hearing of all Israel, are to intone these words: 15 'A curse on anyone who carves an image or casts an idol, anything abominable to the LORD, a craftsman's handiwork, and sets it up in secret': the people must all respond, 'Amen.'

16 'A curse on anyone who slights his father or his mother': the people must all say, 'Amen.'

17 'A curse on anyone who moves his neighbour's boundary stone': the people must all say, 'Amen.'

18 'A curse on anyone who misdirects a blind man': the people must all say, 'Amen.'

19 'A curse on anyone who withholds justice from the alien, the fatherless, and the widow': the people must all say, 'Amen.'

20 'A curse on anyone who lies with his father's wife, for he brings shame upon his father': the people must all say, 'Amen.'

21 'A curse on anyone who lies with any animal': the people must all say, 'Amen.'

22 'A curse on anyone who lies with his sister, whether his father's daughter or his mother's daughter': the people must all say, 'Amen.'

23 'A curse on anyone who lies with his wife's mother': the people must all say, 'Amen.'

24 'A curse on anyone who strikes another in secret': the people must all say, 'Amen.'

25 'A curse on anyone who accepts payment for killing an innocent person': the people must all say, 'Amen.'

26 'A curse on anyone who does not fulfil this law by doing all that it prescribes': the people must all say, 'Amen.'

28 IF you faithfully obey the LORD your God by diligently observing all his commandments which I lay on you this day, then the LORD your God will raise you high above all nations of the earth, 2 and the following blessings will all come and light on you, because you obey the LORD your God.

3 A blessing on you in the town; a blessing on you in the country.

4 A blessing on the fruit of your body, the fruit of your land and cattle, the offspring of your herds and lambing flocks.

5 A blessing on your basket and your kneading trough.

6 A blessing on you as you come in, and a blessing on you as you go out.

7 May the LORD deliver up to you the enemies who attack you, and let them be put to rout before you. Though they come out against you by one way, they will flee before you by seven.

8 May the LORD grant you a blessing in your granaries and on all your labours; may the LORD your God bless you in the land which he is giving you.

---

h Heb *uncovered his father's skirt*

27:14 **intone:** *lit.* recite in a high-pitched voice.

NEW AMERICAN BIBLE

NEW JERUSALEM BIBLE

9 Moses, with the levitical priests, then said to all Israel: "Be silent, O Israel, and listen! This day you have become the people of the LORD, your God. 10 You shall therefore hearken to the voice of the LORD, your God, and keep his commandments and statutes which I enjoin on you today."

11 That same day Moses gave the people this order: 12 "When you cross the Jordan, Simeon, Levi, Judah, Issachar, Joseph and Benjamin shall stand on Mount Gerizim to pronounce blessings over the people, 13 while Reuben, Gad, Asher, Zebulun, Dan and Naphtali shall stand on Mount Ebal to pronounce curses.

14 "The Levites shall proclaim aloud to all the men of Israel: 15 'Cursed be the man who makes a carved or molten idol — an abomination to the LORD, the product of a craftsman's hands — and sets it up in secret!' And all the people shall answer, 'Amen!'

16 'Cursed be he who dishonors his father or his mother!' And all the people shall answer, 'Amen!'

17 'Cursed be he who moves his neighbor's landmarks!' And all the people shall answer, 'Amen!'

18 'Cursed be he who misleads a blind man on his way!' And all the people shall answer, 'Amen!'

19 'Cursed be he who violates the rights of the alien, the orphan or the widow!' And all the people shall answer, 'Amen!'

20 'Cursed be he who has relations with his father's wife, for he dishonors his father's bed!' And all the people shall answer, 'Amen!'

21 'Cursed be he who has relations with any animal!' And all the people shall answer, 'Amen!'

22 'Cursed be he who has relations with his sister or his half-sister!' And all the people shall answer, 'Amen!'

23 'Cursed be he who has relations with his mother-in-law!' And all the people shall answer, 'Amen!'

24 'Cursed be he who slays his neighbor in secret!' And all the people shall answer, 'Amen!'

25 'Cursed be he who accepts payment for slaying an innocent man!' And all the people shall answer, 'Amen!'

26 'Cursed be he who fails to fulfill any of the provisions of this law!' And all the people shall answer, 'Amen!'

28 "Thus, then, shall it be: if you continue to heed the voice of the LORD, your God, and are careful to observe all his commandments which I enjoin on you today, the LORD, your God, will raise you high above all the nations of the earth. 2 When you hearken to the voice of the LORD, your God, all these blessings will come upon you and overwhelm you:

3 "May you be blessed in the city,
and blessed in the country!

4 "Blessed be the fruit of your womb,
the produce of your soil and the offspring of
your livestock,
the issue of your herds and the young of
your flocks!

5 "Blessed be your grain bin and your
kneading bowl!

6 "May you be blessed in your coming in,
and blessed in your going out!

7 "The LORD will beat down before you the enemies that rise up against you; though they come out against you from but one direction, they will flee before you in seven. 8 The LORD will affirm his blessing upon you, on your barns and on all your undertakings, blessing you in the land that the LORD, your God, gives you. 9 Provided that you keep the

9 Moses and the levitical priests then said to all Israel: 'Be silent, Israel, and listen. Today you have become a people for Yahweh your God. 10 You must listen to the voice of Yahweh your God and observe the commandments and laws which I am laying down for you today.'

11 That day Moses gave the people this order: 12 'When you have crossed the Jordan, the following will stand on Mount Gerizim to bless the people: Simeon and Levi, Judah and Issachar, Joseph and Benjamin. 13 And the following will stand on Mount Ebal for the curse: Reuben, Gad and Asher, Zebulun, Dan and Naphtali. 14 The Levites will then speak, proclaiming loudly to all the Israelites:

15 "Accursed be anyone who makes a carved or cast idol, a thing detestable to Yahweh, a workman's artefact, and sets it up in secret." And the people are all to respond by saying, Amen.

16 "Accursed be anyone who treats father or mother dishonourably." And the people must all say, Amen.

17 "Accursed be anyone who displaces a neighbour's boundary mark." And the people must all say, Amen.

18 "Accursed be anyone who leads the blind astray on the road." And the people must all say, Amen.

19 "Accursed be anyone who violates the rights of the foreigner, the orphan and the widow." And the people must all say, Amen.

20 "Accursed be anyone who has sexual intercourse with his father's wife and withdraws the skirt of his father's cloak from her." And the people must all say, Amen.

21 "Accursed be anyone who has sexual intercourse with any kind of animal." And the people must all say, Amen.

22 "Accursed be anyone who has sexual intercourse with his sister, the daughter of his father or of his mother." And the people must all say, Amen.

23 "Accursed be anyone who has sexual intercourse with his mother-in-law." And the people must all say, Amen.

24 "Accursed be anyone who secretly strikes down his neighbour." And the people must all say, Amen.

25 "Accursed be anyone who accepts a bribe to take an innocent life." And the people must all say, Amen.

26 "Accursed be anyone who does not make the words of this Law effective by putting them into practice." And the people must all say, Amen.'

28 'But if you faithfully obey the voice of Yahweh your God, by keeping and observing all his commandments, which I am laying down for you today, Yahweh your God will raise you higher than every other nation in the world. 2 and all these blessings will befall and overtake you, for having obeyed the voice of Yahweh your God.

3 'You will be blessed in the town and blessed in the countryside; 4 blessed, the offspring of your body, the yield of your soil, the yield of your livestock, the young of your cattle and the increase of your flocks; 5 blessed, your basket and your kneading trough. 6 You will be blessed in coming home, and blessed in going out. 7 The enemies who attack you, Yahweh will defeat before your eyes; they will advance on you from one direction and flee from you in seven. 8 Yahweh will command blessedness to be with you, on your barns and on all your undertakings, and he will bless you in the country given you by Yahweh your God.

NEW REVISED STANDARD VERSION

as his holy people, as he has sworn to you, if you keep the commandments of the LORD your God and walk in his ways. 10 All the peoples of the earth shall see that you are called by the name of the LORD, and they shall be afraid of you. 11 The LORD will make you abound in prosperity, in the fruit of your womb, in the fruit of your livestock, and in the fruit of your ground in the land that the LORD swore to your ancestors to give you. 12 The LORD will open for you his rich storehouse, the heavens, to give the rain of your land in its season and to bless all your undertakings. You will lend to many nations, but you will not borrow. 13 The LORD will make you the head, and not the tail; you shall be only at the top, and not at the bottom — if you obey the commandments of the LORD your God, which I am commanding you today, by diligently observing them, 14 and if you do not turn aside from any of the words that I am commanding you today, either to the right or to the left, following other gods to serve them.

15 But if you will not obey the LORD your God by diligently observing all his commandments and decrees, which I am commanding you today, then all these curses shall come upon you and overtake you:

16 Cursed shall you be in the city, and cursed shall you be in the field.

17 Cursed shall be your basket and your kneading bowl.

18 Cursed shall be the fruit of your womb, the fruit of your ground, the increase of your cattle and the issue of your flock.

19 Cursed shall you be when you come in, and cursed shall you be when you go out.

20 The LORD will send upon you disaster, panic, and frustration in everything you attempt to do, until you are destroyed and perish quickly, on account of the evil of your deeds, because you have forsaken me. 21 The LORD will make the pestilence cling to you until it has consumed you off the land that you are entering to possess. 22 The LORD will afflict you with consumption, fever, inflammation, with fiery heat and drought, and with blight and mildew; they shall pursue you until you perish. 23 The sky over your head shall be bronze, and the earth under you iron. 24 The LORD will change the rain of your land into powder, and only dust shall come down upon you from the sky until you are destroyed.

25 The LORD will cause you to be defeated before your enemies; you shall go out against them one way and flee before them seven ways. You shall become an object of horror to all the kingdoms of the earth. 26 Your corpses shall be food for every bird of the air and animal of the earth, and there shall be no one to frighten them away. 27 The LORD will afflict you with the boils of Egypt, with ulcers, scurvy, and itch, of which you cannot be healed. 28 The LORD will afflict you with madness, blindness, and confusion of mind; 29 you shall grope about at noon as blind people grope in darkness, but you shall be unable to find your way; and you shall be continually abused and robbed, without anyone to help. 30 You shall become engaged to a woman, but another man shall lie with her. You shall build a house, but not live in it. You shall plant a vineyard, but not enjoy its fruit. 31 Your ox shall be butchered before your eyes, but you shall not eat of it. Your donkey shall be stolen in front of you, and shall not be restored to you. Your sheep shall be given to your enemies, without anyone to help you. 32 Your sons and daughters shall be given to another people, while you look on; you will strain your eyes looking for them all day but be powerless to do anything. 33 A people whom you

REVISED ENGLISH BIBLE

9 The LORD will establish you as his own holy people, as he swore to you, provided you keep the commandments of the LORD your God and conform to his ways. 10 All people on earth seeing that the LORD has named you as his very own will go in fear of you. 11 The LORD will make you prosper greatly in the fruit of your body and of your cattle, and in the fruit of the soil in the land which he swore to your forefathers to give you. 12 May the LORD open the heavens for you, his rich storehouse, to give your land rain at the proper time and bless everything to which you turn your hand. You may lend to many nations, but borrow from none; 13 the LORD will make you the head and not the tail: you will always be at the top and never at the bottom, if you listen to the commandments of the LORD your God, which I give you this day to keep and to fulfil. 14 Deviate neither to right nor to left from all the things which I command you this day, and do not go after other gods to serve them.

15 BUT if you will not obey the LORD your God by diligently observing all his commandments and statutes which I lay upon you this day, then all the following curses will come and light upon you.

16 A curse on you in the town, a curse in the country.

17 A curse on your basket and your kneading trough.

18 A curse on the fruit of your body, the fruit of your land, the offspring of your herds and your lambing flocks.

19 A curse on you as you come in, and a curse on you as you go out.

20 May the LORD send on you cursing, confusion, and rebuke in whatever you are doing, until you are destroyed and soon perish for the evil you have done in forsaking him. 21 May the LORD cause pestilence to haunt you until he has exterminated you out of the land which you are entering to occupy; 22 may the LORD afflict you with wasting disease and recurrent fever, ague, and eruptions; with drought, and black blight and red; and may these plague you until you perish. 23 May the skies above you be brazen, and the earth beneath you iron. 24 May the LORD turn the rain in your country to fine sand, and may dust descend on you from the sky until you are blotted out.

25 May the LORD put you to rout before your enemies. Though you go out against them by one way, you will flee before them by seven. May you be repugnant to all the kingdoms on earth. 26 May your bodies become food for all the birds of the air and all the wild beasts, with no one to scare them off. 27 May the LORD strike you with Egyptian boils and with tumours, scabs, and itch, for which you will find no cure. 28 May the LORD strike you with madness, blindness, and stupefaction; 29 so that you will grope about in broad daylight, just as a blind man gropes in darkness, and you will fail to find your way. You will be oppressed and robbed, day in, day out, with no one to save you. 30 A woman will be betrothed to you, but someone will ravish her; you will build a house but not live in it; you will plant a vineyard but not enjoy its fruit. 31 Your ox will be slaughtered before your eyes, but you will not eat of it; and while you watch your donkey will be stolen and will not come back to you; your sheep will be given to the enemy, and there will be no one to recover them. 32 Your sons and daughters will be given to another people with you looking on; your eyes will strain after them all day long, but you will be powerless. 33 A nation which you do not know will eat the prod-

28:20 **cursing . . . rebuke:** or starvation, burning thirst, and dysentery. **him:** prob. rdg.; Heb. me. 28:27 **tumours:** or, as otherwise read, haemorrhoids.

commandments of the LORD, your God, and walk in his ways, he will establish you as a people sacred to himself, as he swore to you; 10 so that, when all the nations of the earth see you bearing the name of the LORD, they will stand in awe of you. 11 The LORD will increase in more than goodly measure the fruit of your womb, the offspring of your livestock, and the produce of your soil, in the land which he swore to your fathers he would give you. 12 The LORD will open up for you his rich treasure house of the heavens, to give your land rain in due season, blessing all your undertakings, so that you will lend to many nations and borrow from none. 13 The LORD will make you the head, not the tail, and you will always mount higher and not decline, as long as you obey the commandments of the LORD, your God, which I order you today to observe carefully; 14 not turning aside to the right or to the left from any of the commandments which I now give you, in order to follow other gods and serve them.

15 "But if you do not hearken to the voice of the LORD, your God, and are not careful to observe all his commandments which I enjoin on you today, all these curses shall come upon you and overwhelm you:

16 "May you be cursed in the city,
and cursed in the country!

17 "Cursed be your grain bin and your kneading bowl!

18 "Cursed be the fruit of your womb,
the produce of your soil and the offspring of
your livestock,
the issue of your herds and the young of
your flocks!

19 "May you be cursed in your coming in,
and cursed in your going out!

20 "The LORD will put a curse on you, defeat and frustration in every enterprise you undertake, until your are speedily destroyed and perish for the evil you have done in forsaking me. 21 The LORD will bring a pestilence upon you that will persist until he has exterminated you from the land you are entering to occupy. 22 The LORD will strike you with wasting and fever, with scorching, fiery drought, with blight and searing wind, that will plague you until you perish. 23 The sky over your heads will be like bronze and the earth under your feet like iron. 24 For rain the LORD will give your land powdery dust, which will come down upon you from the sky until you are destroyed. 25 The LORD will let you be beaten down before your enemies; though you advance against them from one direction, you will flee before them in seven, so that you will become a terrifying example to all the kingdoms of the earth. 26 Your carcasses will become food for all the birds of the air and for the beasts of the field, with no one to frighten them off. 27 The LORD will strike you with Egyptian boils and with tumors, eczema and the itch, until you cannot be cured. 28 And the LORD will strike you with madness, blindness and panic, 29 so that even at midday you will grope like a blind man in the dark, unable to find your way.

"You will be oppressed and robbed continually, with no one to come to your aid. 30 Though you betroth a wife, another man will have her. Though you build a house, you will not live in it. Though you plant a vineyard, you will not enjoy its fruits. 31 Your ox will be slaughtered before your eyes, and you will not eat of its flesh. Your ass will be stolen in your presence, but you will not recover it. Your flocks will be given to your enemies, with no one to come to your aid. 32 Your sons and daughters will be given to a foreign nation while you look on and grieve for them in constant helplessness. 33 A people whom you do not know

9 'From you Yahweh will make a people consecrated to himself, as he has sworn to you, if you keep the commandments of Yahweh your God and follow his ways. 10 The peoples of the world, seeing that you bear Yahweh's name, will all be afraid of you. 11 Yahweh will make you abound in possessions: in the offspring of your body, in the yield of your cattle and in the yield of your soil, in the country which he swore to your ancestors that he would give you. 12 For you Yahweh will open his treasury of rain, the heavens, to give your country its rain at the right time, and to bless all your labours. You will make many nations your subjects, yet you will be subject to none. 13 Yahweh will put you at the head, not at the tail; you will always be on top and never underneath, if you listen to the commandments of Yahweh your God, which I am laying down for you today, and then keep them and put them into practice, 14 not deviating to right or to left from any of the words which I am laying down for you today, by following other gods and serving them.

15 'But if you do not obey the voice of Yahweh your God, and do not keep and observe all his commandments and laws which I am laying down for you today then all these curses will befall and overtake you.

16 'You will be accursed in the town and accursed in the countryside; 17 accursed, your basket and your kneading trough; 18 accursed, the offspring of your body, the yield of your soil, the young of your cattle and the increase of your flock. 19 You will be accursed in coming home, and accursed in going out.

20 'Yahweh will send a curse on you, a spell, an imprecation on all your labours until you have been destroyed and quickly perish, because of your perverse behaviour, for having deserted me. 21 Yahweh will fasten the plague on you, until it has exterminated you from the country which you are about to enter and make your own. 22 Yahweh will strike you down with consumption, fever, inflammation, burning fever, drought, wind-blast, mildew, and these will pursue you to your ruin. 23 The heavens above you will be brass, the earth beneath you iron. 24 Your country's rain Yahweh will turn into dust and sand; it will fall on you from the heavens until you perish. 25 Yahweh will have you defeated by your enemies; you will advance on them from one direction and flee from them in seven; and you will be a terrifying object-lesson to all the kingdoms of the world. 26 Your carcase will be carrion for all wild birds and all wild animals, with no one to scare them away.

27 'Yahweh will strike you down with Egyptian ulcers, with swellings in the groin, with scurvy and the itch, for which you will find no cure. 28 Yahweh will strike you down with madness, blindness, distraction of mind, 29 until you grope your way at noon like a blind man groping in the dark, and your steps will lead you nowhere.

'You will never be anything but exploited and plundered, with no one to save you. 30 Get engaged to a woman, another man will have her; build a house, you will not live in it; plant a vineyard, you will not gather its first-fruits. 31 Your ox will be slaughtered before your eyes and you will eat none of it; your donkey will be carried off in front of you and not be returned to you; your sheep will be given to your enemies, and no one will come to your help. 32 Your sons and daughters will be handed over to another people, and every day you will wear your eyes out watching for them, while your hands are powerless. 33 A nation hitherto un-

do not know shall eat up the fruit of your ground and of all your labors; you shall be continually abused and crushed, 34 and driven mad by the sight that your eyes shall see. 35 The LORD will strike you on the knees and on the legs with grievous boils of which you cannot be healed, from the sole of your foot to the crown of your head. 36 The LORD will bring you, and the king whom you set over you, to a nation that neither you nor your ancestors have known, where you shall serve other gods, of wood and stone. 37 You shall become an object of horror, a proverb, and a byword among all the peoples where the LORD will lead you.

38 You shall carry much seed into the field but shall gather little in, for the locust shall consume it. 39 You shall plant vineyards and dress them, but you shall neither drink the wine nor gather the grapes, for the worm shall eat them. 40 You shall have olive trees throughout all your territory, but you shall not anoint yourself with the oil, for your olives shall drop off. 41 You shall have sons and daughters, but they shall not remain yours, for they shall go into captivity. 42 All your trees and the fruit of your ground the cicada shall take over. 43 Aliens residing among you shall ascend above you higher and higher, while you shall descend lower and lower. 44 They shall lend to you but you shall not lend to them; they shall be the head and you shall be the tail.

45 All these curses shall come upon you, pursuing and overtaking you until you are destroyed, because you did not obey the LORD your God, by observing the commandments and the decrees that he commanded you. 46 They shall be among you and your descendants as a sign and a portent forever.

47 Because you did not serve the LORD your God joyfully and with gladness of heart for the abundance of everything, 48 therefore you shall serve your enemies whom the LORD will send against you, in hunger and thirst, in nakedness and lack of everything. He will put an iron yoke on your neck until he has destroyed you. 49 The LORD will bring a nation from far away, from the end of the earth, to swoop down on you like an eagle, a nation whose language you do not understand, 50 a grim-faced nation showing no respect to the old or favor to the young. 51 It shall consume the fruit of your livestock and the fruit of your ground until you are destroyed, leaving you neither grain, wine, and oil, nor the increase of your cattle and the issue of your flock, until it has made you perish. 52 It shall besiege you in all your towns until your high and fortified walls, in which you trusted, come down throughout your land; it shall besiege you in all your towns throughout the land that the LORD your God has given you. 53 In the desperate straits to which the enemy siege reduces you, you will eat the fruit of your womb, the flesh of your own sons and daughters whom the LORD your God has given you. 54 Even the most refined and gentle of men among you will begrudge food to his own brother, to the wife whom he embraces, and to the last of his remaining children, 55 giving to none of them any of the flesh of his children whom he is eating, because nothing else remains to him, in the desperate straits to which the enemy siege will reduce you in all your towns. 56 She who is the most refined and gentle among you, so gentle and refined that she does not venture to set the sole of her foot on the ground, will begrudge food to the husband whom she embraces, to her own son, and to her own daughter, 57 begrudging even the afterbirth that comes out from between her thighs, and the children that she bears, because she is eating them in secret for lack of anything else, in the desperate straits to which the enemy siege will reduce you in your towns.

ucts of your land and of all your toil, and your lot will be nothing but grievous oppression. 34 The sights you see will drive you mad. 35 May the LORD strike you on knee and leg with severe boils for which you will find no cure; they will spread from the sole of your foot to the crown of your head.

36 May the LORD give you up, and the king whom you have appointed, to a nation which neither you nor your fathers have known, and there you will serve other gods, gods of wood and stone. 37 You will become a horror, a byword, and an object-lesson to all the peoples amongst whom the LORD disperses you.

38 You will carry plentiful seed to your fields, but you will harvest little, for locusts will devour it. 39 You will plant vineyards and cultivate them, but you will not drink the wine or gather the grapes, for the grub will eat them. 40 You will have olive trees everywhere in your territory, but you will not anoint yourselves with the oil, for your olives will drop off. 41 You will have sons and daughters, but they will not remain yours, for they will go into captivity. 42 All your trees and the fruit of the ground will be infested with the mole-cricket. 43 The alien who lives with you will raise himself higher and higher, and you will sink lower and lower. 44 He will lend to you but you will not lend to him: he will be the head and you the tail. 45 All these curses will come on you; they will pursue and overtake you until you are destroyed, because you did not obey the LORD your God by keeping the commandments and statutes which he gave you. 46 They will be a sign and a portent to you and your descendants for ever.

47 You have not served the LORD your God, rejoicing in gladness of heart over all your blessings; 48 therefore in hunger and thirst, in nakedness and extreme want, you will have to serve the enemies whom the LORD will send against you. He will put a yoke of iron on your neck until you are subdued.

49 May the LORD bring against you from afar, from the end of the earth, a nation which will swoop upon you like a vulture, a nation whose language you will not understand, 50 a nation of grim aspect with no regard for the old, no pity for the young. 51 When you have been subdued, they will devour the offspring of your cattle and the fruit of your land. They will leave you neither grain nor new wine nor oil, neither calves from your herds nor lambs from your flocks, until you are brought to ruin. 52 They will besiege you in all your towns until they overthrow your high fortifications, those walls throughout your land in which you trust. They will besiege you within all your towns, throughout the land which the LORD your God has given you. 53 Then, because of the dire straits to which you will be reduced when your enemy besieges you, you will eat the flesh of your sons and daughters whom the LORD your God has given you. 54 The most delicately bred and sensitive man will not share with his brother, or with the wife he loves, or with his own remaining children 55 any of the meat which he is eating, the flesh of his own children. He is left with nothing else because of the dire straits to which you will be reduced within all your towns when the enemy besieges you. 56 The most delicately bred and sensitive woman, so delicate and sensitive that she would never venture to put a foot to the ground, will not share with her own husband or her son or her daughter 57 the afterbirth which she expels, or any boy or girl that she may bear. During the siege she herself will eat them secretly in her extreme want, in the dire straits to which the enemy will reduce you in your towns.

28:52 **towns:** *lit.* gates.

will consume the fruit of your soil and of all your labor, and you will be oppressed and crushed at all times without surcease, 34 until you are driven mad by what your eyes must look upon. 35 The LORD will strike you with malignant boils of which you cannot be cured, on your knees and legs, and from the soles of your feet to the crown of your head.

36 "The LORD will bring you, and your king whom you have set over you, to a nation which you and your fathers have not known, and there you will serve strange gods of wood and stone, 37 and will call forth amazement, reproach and barbed scorn from all the nations to which the LORD will lead you.

38 "Though you spend much seed on your field, you will harvest but little, for the locusts will devour the crop. 39 Though you plant and cultivate vineyards, you will not drink or store up the wine, for the grubs will eat the vines clean. 40 Though you have olive trees throughout your country, you will have no oil for ointment, for your olives will drop off unripe. 41 Though you beget sons and daughters, they will not remain with you, but will go into captivity. 42 Buzzing insects will infest all your trees and the crops of your soil. 43 The alien residing among you will rise higher and higher above you, while you sink lower and lower. 44 He will lend to you, not you to him. He will become the head, you the tail.

45 "All these curses will come upon you, pursuing you and overwhelming you, until you are destroyed, because you would not hearken to the voice of the LORD, your God, nor keep the commandments and statutes he gave you. 46 They will light on you and your descendants as a sign and a wonder for all time. 47 Since you would not serve the LORD, your God, with joy and gratitude for abundance of every kind, 48 therefore in hunger and thirst, in nakedness and utter poverty, you will serve the enemies whom the LORD will send against you. He will put an iron yoke on your neck, until he destroys you.

49 "The LORD will raise up against you a nation from afar, from the end of the earth, that swoops down like an eagle, a nation whose tongue you do not understand, 50 a nation of stern visage, that shows neither respect for the aged nor pity for the young. 51 They will consume the offspring of your livestock and the produce of your soil, until you are destroyed; they will leave you no grain or wine or oil, no issue of your herds or young of your flocks, until they have brought about your ruin. 52 They will besiege you in each of your communities, until the great, unscalable walls you trust in come tumbling down all over your land. They will so besiege you in every community throughout the land which the LORD, your God, has given you, 53 that in the distress of the siege to which your enemy subjects you, you will eat the fruit of your womb, the flesh of your own sons and daughters whom the LORD, your God, has given you. 54 The most refined and fastidious man among you will begrudge his brother and his beloved wife and his surviving children 55 any share in the flesh of his children that he himself is using for food when nothing else is left him in the straits of the siege to which your enemy will subject you in all your communities. 56 The most refined and delicate woman among you, so delicate and refined that she would not venture to set the sole of her foot on the ground, will begrudge her beloved husband and her son and daughter 57 the afterbirth that issues from her womb and the infant she brings forth when she secretly uses them for food for want of anything else, in the straits of the siege to which your enemy will subject you in your communities.

known to you will eat the yield of your soil and of all your hard work. You will never be anything but exploited and crushed. 34 You will be driven mad by the sights you will see. 35 Yahweh will strike you down with foul ulcers on knee and leg, for which you will find no cure — from the sole of your foot to the top of your head.

36 'Yahweh will send away both you and the king whom you have appointed to rule you to a nation unknown either to you or to your ancestors, and there you will serve other gods, made of wood and stone. 37 And you will be the astonishment, the byword, the laughing-stock of all the peoples where Yahweh is taking you.

38 'You will cast seed in plenty on the fields but harvest little, since the locust will devour it. 39 You will plant and till your vineyards but not drink the wine or gather the grapes, since the grub will eat them up. 40 You will grow olive trees throughout your territory but not anoint yourself with the oil, since your olive trees will be cut down. 41 You will father sons and daughters but they will not belong to you, since they will go into captivity. 42 All your trees and the whole yield of your soil will be the prey of insects.

43 'The foreigners living with you will rise higher and higher at your expense, while you yourself sink lower and lower. 44 You will be subject to them, not they to you; they will be the ones at the head, and you the one at the tail.

45 'All these curses will befall you, pursue you and overtake you until you have been destroyed, for not having obeyed the voice of Yahweh your God by keeping his commandments and laws which he has laid down for you. 46 They will be a sign and a wonder over you and your descendants for ever.

47 'For not having joyfully and with happy heart served Yahweh your God, despite the abundance of everything, 48 you will have to serve the enemy whom Yahweh will send against you, in hunger, thirst, lack of clothing and total privation. He will put an iron yoke on your neck, until he has destroyed you.

49 'Against you Yahweh will raise a distant nation from the ends of the earth like an eagle taking wing: a nation whose language you do not understand, 50 a nation grim of face, with neither respect for the old, nor pity for the young. 51 He will eat the yield of your cattle and the yield of your soil until you have been destroyed; he will leave you neither wheat, nor wine, nor oil, nor the young of your cattle, nor increase of your flock, until he has made an end of you. 52 He will besiege you inside all your towns until your loftiest and most strongly fortified walls collapse, on which, throughout your country, you have relied. He will besiege you inside all the towns throughout your country, given you by Yahweh your God. 53 During the siege and in the distress to which your enemy will reduce you, you will eat the offspring of your own body, the flesh of the sons and daughters given you by Yahweh your God. 54 The gentlest and tenderest of your men will scowl at his brother, and at the wife whom he embraces, and at his remaining children, 55 not willing to give any of them any of his own children's flesh, which he is eating; because of the siege and the distress to which your enemy will reduce you in all your towns, he will have nothing left. 56 The most refined and fastidious of your women, so refined, so fastidious that she has never ventured to set the sole of her foot to the ground, will scowl at the husband whom she embraces, and at her son and daughter, and at the after-birth when it leaves her womb, and at the child to which she has given birth — 57 she will hide away and eat them, so complete will be the starvation resulting from the siege and the distress to which your enemy will reduce you in all your towns.

NEW REVISED STANDARD VERSION

58 If you do not diligently observe all the words of this law that are written in this book, fearing this glorious and awesome name, the LORD your God, 59 then the LORD will overwhelm both you and your offspring with severe and lasting afflictions and grievous and lasting maladies. 60 He will bring back upon you all the diseases of Egypt, of which you were in dread, and they shall cling to you. 61 Every other malady and affliction, even though not recorded in the book of this law, the LORD will inflict on you until you are destroyed. 62 Although once you were as numerous as the stars in heaven, you shall be left few in number, because you did not obey the LORD your God. 63 And just as the LORD took delight in making you prosperous and numerous, so the LORD will take delight in bringing you to ruin and destruction; you shall be plucked off the land that you are entering to possess. 64 The LORD will scatter you among all peoples, from one end of the earth to the other; and there you shall serve other gods, of wood and stone, which neither you nor your ancestors have known. 65 Among those nations you shall find no ease, no resting place for the sole of your foot. There the LORD will give you a trembling heart, failing eyes, and a languishing spirit. 66 Your life shall hang in doubt before you; night and day you shall be in dread, with no assurance of your life. 67 In the morning you shall say, "If only it were evening!" and at evening you shall say, "If only it were morning!" — because of the dread that your heart shall feel and the sights that your eyes shall see. 68 The LORD will bring you back in ships to Egypt, by a route that I promised you would never see again; and there you shall offer yourselves for sale to your enemies as male and female slaves, but there will be no buyer.

29 _i_ These are the words of the covenant that the LORD commanded Moses to make with the Israelites in the land of Moab, in addition to the covenant that he had made with them at Horeb.

2 _j_ Moses summoned all Israel and said to them: You have seen all that the LORD did before your eyes in the land of Egypt, to Pharaoh and to all his servants and to all his land, 3 the great trials that your eyes saw, the signs, and those great wonders. 4 But to this day the LORD has not given you a mind to understand, or eyes to see, or ears to hear. 5 I have led you forty years in the wilderness. The clothes on your back have not worn out, and the sandals on your feet have not worn out; 6 you have not eaten bread, and you have not drunk wine or strong drink — so that you may know that I am the LORD your God. 7 When you came to this place, King Sihon of Heshbon and King Og of Bashan came out against us for battle, but we defeated them. 8 We took their land and gave it as an inheritance to the Reubenites, the Gadites, and the half-tribe of Manasseh. 9 Therefore diligently observe the words of this covenant, in order that you may succeed _k_ in everything that you do.

10 You stand assembled today, all of you, before the LORD your God — the leaders of your tribes, _l_ your elders, and your officials, all the men of Israel, 11 your children, your women, and the aliens who are in your camp, both those who cut your wood and those who draw your water — 12 to enter into the covenant of the LORD your God, sworn by an oath, which the LORD your God is making with you today; 13 in order that he may establish you today as his people, and that he may be your God, as he promised you and as he swore to your ancestors, to Abraham, to Isaac, and to Jacob. 14 I am making this covenant, sworn by an

REVISED ENGLISH BIBLE

58 If you do not observe and fulfil all the law written down in this book, if you do not revere this honoured and dreaded name, this name 'the LORD your God', 59 then the LORD will strike you and your descendants with unimaginable plagues, virulent and chronic, and with lingering and severe sickness. 60 He will bring on you once again all the diseases of Egypt which you dreaded, and they will cling to you. 61 The LORD will bring upon you sickness and plague of every kind, even those not recorded in this book of the law, until you are destroyed. 62 Then you who were countless as the stars in the heavens will be left few in number, because you did not obey the LORD your God. 63 Just as the LORD took delight in you, prospering you and increasing your numbers, so now it will be his delight to ruin and exterminate you, and you will be uprooted from the land which you are entering to occupy.

64 The LORD will disperse you among all peoples from one end of the earth to the other, and there you will serve other gods of whom neither you nor your forefathers have had experience, gods of wood and stone. 65 Among those nations you will find no peace, no resting-place for the sole of your foot. Then the LORD will give you an unquiet mind, dim eyes, and failing appetite. 66 Your life will hang continually in suspense, fear will beset you night and day, and you will find no security all your life long. 67 Every morning you will say, 'Would God it were evening!' and every evening, 'Would God it were morning!' because of the terror that fills your heart and because of the sights you see. 68 The LORD will bring you back sorrowing to Egypt by that very road of which I said to you, 'You shall not see that road again'; there you will offer yourselves for sale as slaves to your enemies, but there will be no buyer.

29 These are the terms of the covenant which the LORD commanded Moses to make with the Israelites in Moab, in addition to the covenant which he made with them on Horeb.

2 MOSES summoned all the Israelites and addressed them: You have seen for yourselves all that the LORD did in Egypt to Pharaoh, to all his courtiers, and to his whole land, 3 the great challenge which you yourselves witnessed, those great signs and portents, 4 but to this day the LORD has not given you a mind to understand or eyes to see or ears to hear. 5 I led you for forty years in the wilderness; the clothes on your back did not wear out, nor did your sandals become worn and fall off your feet; 6 you ate no bread and drank no wine or strong drink, in order that you might learn that I am the LORD your God. 7 When you reached this place King Sihon of Heshbon and King Og of Bashan launched an attack on us. We defeated them, 8 took their land, and gave it as a holding to the Reubenites, the Gadites, and half the tribe of Manasseh. 9 Observe the provisions of this covenant and keep them so that you may be successful in all you do.

10 You are standing here today before the LORD your God, all of you leaders of tribes, elders, and officers, all the men of Israel, 11 with your dependants, your wives, the aliens who live in your camp — all of them, from those who cut wood for you to those who draw water — 12 and you are ready to accept the oath and enter into the covenant which the LORD your God is making with you now. 13 The covenant is to constitute you his people this day, and he will be your God, as he promised you and as he swore to your forefathers, Abraham, Isaac, and Jacob. 14 It is not with you

---

_i_ Ch 28.69 in Heb   _j_ Ch 29.1 in Heb   _k_ Or _deal wisely_
_l_ Gk Syr: Heb _your leaders, your tribes_

28:58 LORD: _see note on Exod. 3:15._   29:1 _In Heb._ 28:69.
29:2 _In Heb._ 29:1.

58 "If you are not careful to observe every word of the law which is written in this book, and to revere the glorious and awesome name of the LORD, your God, 59 he will smite you and your descendants with severe and constant blows, malignant and lasting maladies. 60 He will again afflict you with all the diseases of Egypt which you dread, and they will persist among you. 61 Should there be any kind of sickness or calamity not mentioned in this book of the law, that too the LORD will bring upon you until you are destroyed. 62 Of you who were numerous as the stars in the sky, only a few will be left, because you would not hearken to the voice of the LORD, your God.

63 "Just as the LORD once took delight in making you grow and prosper, so will he now take delight in ruining and destroying you, and you will be plucked out of the land you are now entering to occupy. 64 The LORD will scatter you among all the nations from one end of the earth to the other, and there you will serve strange gods of wood and stone, such as you and your fathers have not known. 65 Among these nations you will find no repose, not a foot of ground to stand upon, for there the LORD will give you an anguished heart and wasted eyes and a dismayed spirit. 66 You will live in constant suspense and stand in dread both day and night, never sure of your existence. 67 In the morning you will say, 'Would that it were evening!' and in the evening you will say, 'Would that it were morning!' for the dread that your heart must feel and the sight that your eyes must see. 68 The LORD will send you back in galleys to Egypt, to the region I told you that you were never to see again; and there you will offer yourselves for sale to your enemies as male and female slaves, but there will be no buyer."

69 These are the words of the covenant which the LORD ordered Moses to make with the Israelites in the land of Moab, in addition to the covenant which he made with them at Horeb.

29 Moses summoned all Israel and said to them, "You have seen all that the LORD did in the land of Egypt before your very eyes to Pharaoh and all his servants and to all his land; 2 the great testings your own eyes have seen, and those great signs and wonders. 3 But not even at the present day has the LORD yet given you a mind to understand, or eyes to see, or ears to hear. 4 'I led you for forty years in the desert. Your clothes did not fall from you in tatters nor your sandals from your feet; 5 bread was not your food, nor wine or beer your drink. Thus you should know that I, the LORD, am your God.' 6 When we came to this place, Sihon, king of Heshbon, and Og, king of Bashan, came out to engage us in battle, but we defeated them 7 and took over their land, which we then gave as a heritage to the Reubenites, Gadites, and half the tribe of Manasseh. 8 Keep the terms of this covenant, therefore, and fulfill them, that you may succeed in whatever you do.

9 "You are all now standing before the LORD, your God — your chiefs and judges, your elders and officials, and all of the men of Israel, 10 together with your wives and children and the aliens who live in your camp, down to those who hew wood and draw water for you — 11 that you may enter into the covenant of the LORD, your God, which he concluded with you today under this sanction of a curse; 12 so that he may now establish you as his people and he may be your God, as he promised you and as he swore to your fathers Abraham, Isaac and Jacob. 13 But it is not with you

58 'If you do not keep and observe all the words of this Law, which are written in this book, in the fear of this glorious and awe-inspiring name: Yahweh your God, 59 Yahweh will strike you down with monstrous plagues, you and your descendants: with plagues grievous and lasting, diseases pernicious and enduring. 60 He will afflict you with all the maladies of Egypt which you used to dread, and they will fasten on you. 61 What is more, Yahweh will afflict you with all the plagues and all the diseases not mentioned in the book of this Law, until you have been destroyed. 62 There will only be a small group of you left, you who were once as numerous as the stars of heaven.

'For not having obeyed the voice of Yahweh your God, 63 just as Yahweh used to delight in making you happy and in making your numbers grow, so will he take delight in ruining and destroying you. You will be torn from the country which you are about to enter and make your own. 64 Yahweh will scatter you throughout every people, from one end of the earth to the other; there you will serve other gods made of wood and stone, hitherto unknown either to you or to your ancestors. 65 Among these nations there will be no repose for you, no rest for the sole of your foot; there Yahweh will give you a quaking heart, weary eyes, halting breath. 66 Your life ahead of you will hang in doubt; you will be afraid day and night, uncertain of your life. 67 In the morning you will say, "How I wish it were evening!", and in the evening you will say, "How I wish it were morning!", such terror will grip your heart and such sights you will see! 68 Yahweh will send you back to Egypt, either by ship or by a road which I promised you would never see again. And there you will want to offer yourselves for sale to your enemies as serving men and women, but no one will buy you.'

69 These are the words of the covenant which Yahweh ordered Moses to make with the Israelites in Moab, in addition to the covenant which he had made with them at Horeb.

29 Moses called all Israel together and said to them: 'You have seen everything that Yahweh did before your eyes in Egypt, to Pharaoh, to his servants and to his whole country — 2 the great ordeals which you yourselves witnessed, those signs and the great wonders. 3 But until today Yahweh has not given you a heart to understand, eyes to see, or ears to hear.

4 'I have been leading you for forty years in the desert, yet the clothes which you have been wearing have not worn out, nor have the sandals on your feet. 5 You have had no bread to eat, you have had no wine or fermented liquor to drink, so that you would learn that I, Yahweh, am your God.

6 'When you reached this place, Sihon king of Heshbon and Og king of Bashan came out to do battle against us; we defeated them. 7 We conquered their country and gave it as heritage to Reuben, Gad and the half-tribe of Manasseh.

8 'Keep the words of this covenant, put them into practice, and you will thrive in everything you do.

9 'All of you are standing here today in the presence of Yahweh your God: your tribal leaders, your elders, your scribes, all the men of Israel, 10 with your children and your wives (and the foreigner too who is in your camp, be he your wood-cutter or your water-carrier), 11 and you are about to pass into the covenant of Yahweh your God, sworn with imprecation, which he has made with you today, 12 and by which, today, he makes you a nation for himself and he himself becomes a God to you, as he has promised you, and as he swore to your ancestors Abraham, Isaac and Jacob.

NEW REVISED STANDARD VERSION

oath, not only with you who stand here with us today before the LORD our God, 15 but also with those who are not here with us today. 16 You know how we lived in the land of Egypt, and how we came through the midst of the nations through which you passed. 17 You have seen their detestable things, the filthy idols of wood and stone, of silver and gold, that were among them. 18 It may be that there is among you a man or woman, or a family or tribe, whose heart is already turning away from the LORD our God to serve the gods of those nations. It may be that there is among you a root sprouting poisonous and bitter growth. 19 All who hear the words of this oath and bless themselves, thinking in their hearts, "We are safe even though we go our own stubborn ways" (thus bringing disaster on moist and dry alike)^m — 20 the LORD will be unwilling to pardon them, for the LORD's anger and passion will smoke against them. All the curses written in this book will descend on them, and the LORD will blot out their names from under heaven. 21 The LORD will single them out from all the tribes of Israel for calamity, in accordance with all the curses of the covenant written in this book of the law. 22 The next generation, your children who rise up after you, as well as the foreigner who comes from a distant country, will see the devastation of that land and the afflictions with which the LORD has afflicted it — 23 all its soil burned out by sulfur and salt, nothing planted, nothing sprouting, unable to support any vegetation, like the destruction of Sodom and Gomorrah, Admah and Zeboiim, which the LORD destroyed in his fierce anger — 24 they and indeed all the nations will wonder, "Why has the LORD done thus to this land? What caused this great display of anger?" 25 They will conclude, "It is because they abandoned the covenant of the LORD, the God of their ancestors, which he made with them when he brought them out of the land of Egypt. 26 They turned and served other gods, worshiping them, gods whom they had not known and whom he had not allotted to them; 27 so the anger of the LORD was kindled against that land, bringing on it every curse written in this book. 28 The LORD uprooted them from their land in anger, fury, and great wrath, and cast them into another land, as is now the case." 29 The secret things belong to the LORD our God, but the revealed things belong to us and to our children forever, to observe all the words of this law.

30 When all these things have happened to you, the blessings and the curses that I have set before you, if you call them to mind among all the nations where the LORD your God has driven you, 2 and return to the LORD your God, and you and your children obey him with all your heart and with all your soul, just as I am commanding you today, 3 then the LORD your God will restore your fortunes and have compassion on you, gathering you again from all the peoples among whom the LORD your God has scattered you. 4 Even if you are exiled to the ends of the world,^{n} from there the LORD your God will gather you, and from there he will bring you back. 5 The LORD your God will bring you into the land that your ancestors possessed, and you will possess it; he will make you more prosperous and numerous than your ancestors.

6 Moreover, the LORD your God will circumcise your heart and the heart of your descendants, so that you will love the LORD your God with all your heart and with all your soul, in order that you may live. 7 The LORD your God

REVISED ENGLISH BIBLE

alone that I am making this covenant and this oath, 15 but with all those who stand here with us today before the LORD our God and also with those who are not here with us today.

16 You know how we lived in Egypt and how we and you, as we passed through the nations, 17 saw their loathsome idols and the false gods they had, gods made of wood and stone, of silver and gold. 18 If there should be among you a man or woman, family or tribe, who is moved today to turn from the LORD our God and to go and serve the gods of those nations — if there is among you such a root from which springs gall and wormwood, 19 then any such person on hearing the terms of this oath may inwardly flatter himself and think, 'All will be well with me even if I follow the promptings of my stubborn heart'; but this will bring sweeping disaster. 20 The LORD will not be willing to forgive him; but his anger and resentment will overwhelm this person, and the curses described in this book will fall heavily on him, and the LORD will blot out his name from under heaven. 21 The LORD will single him out from all the tribes of Israel for disaster to fall on him, according to the oath required by the covenant and prescribed in this book of the law.

22 The next generation, your children who follow you, and the foreigners who come from distant countries, will see the plagues of this land and the diseases which the LORD has brought upon its people, 23 the whole land burnt up with brimstone and salt, nothing sown, nothing growing, not a plant in sight. It will be as desolate as Sodom and Gomorrah, Admah and Zeboyim, when the LORD overthrew them in raging anger. 24 Then they, and all the nations with them, will ask, 'Why has the LORD so afflicted this land? Why this great outburst of anger?' 25 The answer will be: 'Because they forsook the covenant of the LORD the God of their forefathers which he made with them when he brought them out of Egypt. 26 They began to serve other gods and to bow down to them, gods of whom they had no experience and whom the LORD had not assigned to them. 27 The anger of the LORD was roused against that land, so that he brought on it all the curses described in this book. 28 The LORD uprooted them from their soil in anger, in rage and great fury, and banished them to another land, where they are to this day.'

29 There are things hidden, and they belong to the LORD our God, but what is revealed belongs to us and our children for ever; it is for us to observe all that is prescribed in this law.

30 When all these things have happened to you, the blessing and the curse of which I have offered you the choice, if you take them to heart there among all the nations to which the LORD your God has banished you, 2 if you and your children turn back to him and obey him heart and soul in all that I command you this day, 3 then the LORD your God will restore your fortunes. In compassion for you he will gather you again from all the peoples to which he has dispersed you. 4 Even though he has banished you to the ends of the earth, the LORD your God will gather you from there, and from there he will fetch you home. 5 The LORD your God will bring you into the land which your forefathers occupied, and you will occupy it again; then he will bring you prosperity and make you more numerous than your forefathers were.

6 The LORD your God will circumcise your hearts and the hearts of your descendants, so that you will love him with all your heart and soul and you will live. 7 The LORD your

^{m} Meaning of Heb uncertain ^{n} Heb of heaven

29:19 **but . . . disaster:** *lit.* to the sweeping away of moist and dry.
29:22 **diseases:** *or* ulcers.

NEW AMERICAN BIBLE

alone that I am making this covenant, under this sanction of a curse; 14 it is just as much with those who are not here among us today as it is with those of us who are now here present before the LORD, our God.

15 "You know in what surroundings we lived in the land of Egypt and what we passed by in the nations we traversed, 16 and you saw the loathsome idols of wood and stone, of gold and silver, that they possess. 17 Let there be, then, no man or woman, no clan or tribe among you, who would now turn away their hearts from the LORD, our God, to go and serve these pagan gods! Let there be no root that would bear such poison and wormwood among you! 18 If any such person, upon hearing the words of this curse, should beguile himself into thinking that he can safely persist in his stubbornness of heart, as though to sweep away both the watered soil and the parched ground, 19 the LORD will never consent to pardon him. Instead, the LORD's wrath and jealousy will flare up against that man, and every curse mentioned in this book will alight on him. The LORD will blot out his name from under the heavens 20 and will single him out from all the tribes of Israel for doom, in keeping with all the curses of the covenant inscribed in this book of the law.

21 "Future generations, your own descendants who will rise up after you, as well as the foreigners who will come here from far-off lands, when they see the calamities of this land and the ills with which the LORD has smitten it — 22 all its soil being nothing but sulphur and salt, a burnt-out waste, unsown and unfruitful, without a blade of grass, destroyed like Sodom and Gomorrah, Admah and Zeboiim, which the LORD overthrew in his furious wrath — 23 they and all the nations will ask, 'Why has the LORD dealt thus with this land? Why this fierce outburst of wrath?' 24 And the answer will be, 'Because they forsook the covenant which the LORD, the God of their fathers, had made with them when he brought them out of the land of Egypt, 25 and they went and served other gods and adored them, gods whom they did not know and whom he had not let fall to their lot: 26 that is why the LORD was angry with this land and brought on it all the imprecations listed in this book; 27 in his furious wrath and tremendous anger the LORD uprooted them from their soil and cast them out into a strange land, where they are today.' 28 [Both what is still hidden and what has already been revealed concern us and our descendants forever, that we may carry out all the words of this law.]

30 "When all these things which I have set before you, the blessings and the curses, are fulfilled in you, and from among whatever nations the LORD, your God, may have dispersed you, you ponder them in your heart: 2 then, provided that you and your children return to the LORD, your God, and heed his voice with all your heart and all your soul, just as I now command you, 3 the LORD, your God, will change your lot; and taking pity on you, he will again gather you from all the nations wherein he has scattered you. 4 Though you may have been driven to the farthest corner of the world, even from there will the LORD, your God, gather you; even from there will he bring you back. 5 The LORD, your God, will then bring you into the land which your fathers once occupied, that you too may occupy it, and he will make you more prosperous and numerous than your fathers. 6 The LORD, your God, will circumcise your hearts and the hearts of your descendants, that you may love the LORD, your God, with all your heart and all your soul, and so may live. 7 But all those curses the

13 Not only on your behalf am I today making this covenant and pronouncing this solemn curse, 14 not only on behalf of those standing here with us in the presence of Yahweh our God today, but also on behalf of those not here with us today.

15 'Yes, you know the people with whom we used to live in Egypt, and those through whose countries we have travelled — the nations through whom we have passed. 16 You have seen their abominations and their idols made of wood and stone, silver and gold, which were there. 17 'Let there be no man or woman of you, no clan or tribe, whose heart turns away from Yahweh your God today, to go and serve the gods of these nations. Among you let there be no root which bears poison or wormwood. 18 If, after hearing this imprecation, anyone, blessing himself, should say in his heart, "I shall do well enough if I follow the dictates of my heart; much water drives away thirst," 19 Yahweh will not pardon him. The wrath and jealousy of Yahweh will blaze against such a person; every curse written in this book will fall on him, and Yahweh will blot his name out under heaven. 20 Yahweh will single him out of all the tribes of Israel for misfortune, in accordance with all the curses of the covenant written in the book of this Law.

21 'The future generation, that of your children coming after you, and the foreigner arriving from some far-away land, on seeing the plagues and diseases inflicted on this country by Yahweh, will exclaim, 22 "Sulphur! Salt! — The whole country is burning! No one will sow, nothing grow, no vegetation spring ever again! Devastation like that of Sodom and Gomorrah, Admah and Zeboiim, devastated by Yahweh in his furious wrath!" 23 And all the nations will exclaim, "Why has Yahweh treated this country like this? Why this great blaze of anger?" 24 'And people will say, "Because they deserted the covenant of Yahweh, God of their ancestors, the covenant which he made with them when he brought them out of Egypt; 25 because they went and served other gods and worshipped them, gods hitherto unknown to them, gods that were no part of their heritage from him: 26 this is why Yahweh's anger has blazed against this country, afflicting it with all the curses written in this book. 27 In anger, in fury, in fierce wrath, Yahweh has torn them from their own country and flung them into another country, where they are today." 28 Things hidden belong to Yahweh our God, but things revealed are ours and our children's for ever, so that we can put all the words of this Law into practice.'

30 'And when all these words have come true for you — the blessing and the curse, which I have offered you — if you meditate on them in your heart wherever among the nations Yahweh your God has driven you, 2 if you return to Yahweh your God, if with all your heart and with all your soul you obey his voice, you and your children, in everything that I am laying down for you today, 3 then Yahweh your God will bring back your captives, he will have pity on you and gather you back from all the peoples among whom Yahweh your God has scattered you. 4 Should you have been banished to the very sky's end, Yahweh your God will gather you again even from there, will come there to reclaim you 5 and bring you back to the country which belonged to your ancestors, so that you may possess it in your turn, and be made prosperous there and more numerous than your ancestors.

6 'Yahweh your God will circumcise your heart and the heart of your descendants, so that you will love Yahweh your God with all your heart and soul, and so will live.

will put all these curses on your enemies and on the adversaries who took advantage of you. 8 Then you shall again obey the LORD, observing all his commandments that I am commanding you today, 9 and the LORD your God will make you abundantly prosperous in all your undertakings, in the fruit of your body, in the fruit of your livestock, and in the fruit of your soil. For the LORD will again take delight in prospering you, just as he delighted in prospering your ancestors, 10 when you obey the LORD your God by observing his commandments and decrees that are written in this book of the law, because you turn to the LORD your God with all your heart and with all your soul.

11 Surely, this commandment that I am commanding you today is not too hard for you, nor is it too far away. 12 It is not in heaven, that you should say, "Who will go up to heaven for us, and get it for us so that we may hear it and observe it?" 13 Neither is it beyond the sea, that you should say, "Who will cross to the other side of the sea for us, and get it for us so that we may hear it and observe it?" 14 No, the word is very near to you; it is in your mouth and in your heart for you to observe.

15 See, I have set before you today life and prosperity, death and adversity. 16 If you obey the commandments of the LORD your God*o* that I am commanding you today, by loving the LORD your God, walking in his ways, and observing his commandments, decrees, and ordinances, then you shall live and become numerous, and the LORD your God will bless you in the land that you are entering to possess. 17 But if your heart turns away and you do not hear, but are led astray to bow down to other gods and serve them, 18 I declare to you today that you shall perish; you shall not live long in the land that you are crossing the Jordan to enter and possess. 19 I call heaven and earth to witness against you today that I have set before you life and death, blessings and curses. Choose life so that you and your descendants may live, 20 loving the LORD your God, obeying him, and holding fast to him; for that means life to you and length of days, so that you may live in the land that the LORD swore to give to your ancestors, to Abraham, to Isaac, and to Jacob.

31 When Moses had finished speaking all*p* these words to all Israel, 2 he said to them: "I am now one hundred twenty years old. I am no longer able to get about, and the LORD has told me, 'You shall not cross over this Jordan.' 3 The LORD your God himself will cross over before you. He will destroy these nations before you, and you shall dispossess them. Joshua also will cross over before you, as the LORD promised. 4 The LORD will do to them as he did to Sihon and Og, the kings of the Amorites, and to their land, when he destroyed them. 5 The LORD will give them over to you and you shall deal with them in full accord with the command that I have given to you. 6 Be strong and bold; have no fear or dread of them, because it is the LORD your God who goes with you; he will not fail you or forsake you."

7 Then Moses summoned Joshua and said to him in the sight of all Israel: "Be strong and bold, for you are the one who will go with this people into the land that the LORD has sworn to their ancestors to give them; and you will put them in possession of it. 8 It is the LORD who goes before you. He will be with you; he will not fail you or forsake you. Do not fear or be dismayed."

9 Then Moses wrote down this law, and gave it to the priests, the sons of Levi, who carried the ark of the covenant of the LORD, and to all the elders of Israel. 10 Moses

God will turn all these curses against your enemies and the foes who persecute you. 8 Then you will obey the LORD once more and keep all his commandments which I give you this day. 9–10 The LORD your God will make you more than prosperous in all that you do, in the fruit of your body and of your cattle and in the fruits of your soil; for, when you obey the LORD your God by keeping his commandments and statutes, as they are written in this book of the law, and when you turn back to the LORD your God with all your heart and soul, he will again rejoice over you and be good to you, as he rejoiced over your forefathers.

11 This commandment that I lay on you today is not too difficult for you or beyond your reach. 12 It is not in the heavens, that you should say, 'Who will go up to the heavens for us to fetch it and tell it to us, so that we can keep it?' 13 Nor is it beyond the sea, that you should say, 'Who will cross the sea for us to fetch it and tell it to us, so that we can keep it?' 14 It is a thing very near to you, on your lips and in your heart ready to be kept.

15 Today I offer you the choice of life and good, or death and evil. 16 If you obey the commandments of the LORD your God which I give you this day, by loving the LORD your God, conforming to his ways, and keeping his commandments, statutes, and laws, then you will live and increase, and the LORD your God will bless you in the land which you are about to enter to occupy. 17 But if in your heart you turn away and do not listen, and you are led astray to worship other gods and serve them, 18 I tell you here and now that you will perish, and not enjoy long life in the land which you will enter to occupy after crossing the Jordan. 19 I summon heaven and earth to witness against you this day: I offer you the choice of life or death, blessing or curse. Choose life and you and your descendants will live; 20 love the LORD your God, obey him, and hold fast to him: that is life for you and length of days on the soil which the LORD swore to give to your forefathers, Abraham, Isaac, and Jacob.

31 Moses, finishing this address to all Israel, 2 went on to say: At a hundred and twenty years old, I am no longer able to lead the campaign; and the LORD has told me that I shall not cross the Jordan. 3 It is the LORD your God who will cross over at your head and destroy these nations before your advance, and you will occupy their lands; and, as he directed, Joshua will lead you across. 4 The LORD will do to these nations as he did to Sihon and Og, kings of the Amorites, and to their lands, when he destroyed them. 5 The LORD will deliver them into your power, and you are to do to them as I have commanded you. 6 Be strong and resolute; you must not dread them or be afraid, for the LORD your God himself accompanies you; he will not let you down or forsake you.

7 Moses summoned Joshua and in the sight of all Israel said to him: Be strong and resolute, for it is you who will lead this people into the land which the LORD swore to give their forefathers; you are to bring them into possession of it. 8 The LORD himself goes at your head; he will be with you; he will not let you down or forsake you. Do not be afraid or discouraged.

9 Moses wrote down this law and gave it to the priests, the sons of Levi, who carried the Ark of the Covenant of the LORD, and to all the elders of Israel. 10 Moses gave them

*o*Gk: Heb lacks *If you obey the commandments of the* LORD *your God*
*p*Q Ms Gk: MT *Moses went and spoke*

30:16 **If you . . . of the** LORD **your God:** *so Gk; Heb. omits.*
31:1 **finishing this address:** *so Scroll; Heb.* went and spoke.

LORD, your God, will assign to your enemies and the foes who persecuted you. 8 You, however, must again heed the LORD's voice and carry out all his commandments which I now enjoin on you. 9 Then the LORD, your God, will increase in more than goodly measure the returns from all your labors, the fruit of your womb, the offspring of your livestock, and the produce of your soil; for the LORD, your God, will again take delight in your prosperity, even as he took delight in your fathers', 10 if only you heed the voice of the LORD, your God, and keep his commandments and statutes that are written in this book of the law, when you return to the LORD, your God, with all your heart and all your soul.

11 "For this command which I enjoin on you today is not too mysterious and remote for you. 12 It is not up in the sky, that you should say, 'Who will go up in the sky to get it for us and tell us of it, that we may carry it out?' 13 Nor is it across the sea, that you should say, 'Who will cross the sea to get it for us and tell us of it, that we may carry it out?' 14 No, it is something very near to you, already in your mouths and in your hearts; you have only to carry it out.

15 "Here, then, I have today set before you life and prosperity, death and doom. 16 If you obey the commandments of the LORD, your God, which I enjoin on you today, loving him, and walking in his ways, and keeping his commandments, statutes and decrees, you will live and grow numerous, and the LORD, your God, will bless you in the land you are entering to occupy. 17 If, however, you turn away your hearts and will not listen, but are led astray and adore and serve other gods, 18 I tell you now that you will certainly perish; you will not have a long life on the land which you are crossing the Jordan to enter and occupy. 19 I call heaven and earth today to witness against you: I have set before you life and death, the blessing and the curse. Choose life, then, that you and your descendants may live, 20 by loving the LORD, your God, heeding his voice, and holding fast to him. For that will mean life for you, a long life for you to live on the land which the LORD swore he would give to your fathers Abraham, Isaac and Jacob."

31 When Moses had finished speaking these words to all Israel, 2 he said to them, "I am now one hundred and twenty years old and am no longer able to move about freely; besides, the LORD has told me that I shall not cross this Jordan. 3 It is the LORD your God, who will cross before you; he will destroy these nations before you, that you may supplant them. [It is Joshua who will cross before you, as the LORD promised.] 4 The LORD will deal with them just as he dealt with Sihon and Og, the kings of the Amorites whom he destroyed, and with their country. 5 When, therefore, the LORD delivers them up to you, you must deal with them exactly as I have ordered you. 6 Be brave and steadfast; have no fear or dread of them, for it is the LORD, your God, who marches with you; he will never fail you or forsake you."

7 Then Moses summoned Joshua and in the presence of all Israel said to him, "Be brave and steadfast, for you must bring this people into the land which the LORD swore to their fathers he would give them; you must put them in possession of their heritage. 8 It is the LORD who marches before you; he will be with you and will never fail you or forsake you. So do not fear or be dismayed."

9 When Moses had written down this law, he entrusted it to the levitical priests who carry the ark of the covenant of the LORD, and to all the elders of Israel, 10 giving them this

7 Yahweh your God will make all these curses recoil on your foes and on your enemies who have persecuted you. 8 And once again you will obey the voice of Yahweh your God and you will put all his commandments into practice, which I am laying down for you today. 9 Yahweh your God will make you prosper in all your labours, in the offspring of your body, in the yield of your cattle and in the yield of your soil. For once again Yahweh will delight in your prosperity as he used to take delight in the prosperity of your ancestors, 10 if you obey the voice of Yahweh your God, by keeping his commandments and decrees written in the book of this Law, and if you return to Yahweh your God with all your heart and soul.

11 'For this Law which I am laying down for you today is neither obscure for you nor beyond your reach. 12 It is not in heaven, so that you need to wonder, "Who will go up to heaven for us and bring it down to us, so that we can hear and practise it?" 13 Nor is it beyond the seas, so that you need to wonder, "Who will cross the seas for us and bring it back to us, so that we can hear and practise it?" 14 No, the word is very near to you, it is in your mouth and in your heart for you to put into practice.

15 'Look, today I am offering you life and prosperity, death and disaster. 16 If you obey the commandments of Yahweh your God, which I am laying down for you today, if you love Yahweh your God and follow his ways, if you keep his commandments, his laws and his customs, you will live and grow numerous, and Yahweh your God will bless you in the country which you are about to enter and make your own. 17 But if your heart turns away, if you refuse to listen, if you let yourself be drawn into worshipping other gods and serving them, 18 I tell you today, you will most certainly perish; you will not live for long in the country which you are crossing the Jordan to enter and possess. 19 Today, I call heaven and earth to witness against you: I am offering you life or death, blessing or curse. Choose life, then, so that you and your descendants may live, 20 in the love of Yahweh your God, obeying his voice, holding fast to him; for in this your life consists, and on this depends the length of time that you stay in the country which Yahweh swore to your ancestors Abraham, Isaac and Jacob that he would give them.'

31 Moses went and spoke to all Israel as follows, 2 'Today, I am one hundred and twenty years old, and can no longer act as leader. Yahweh has told me, "You shall not cross this Jordan." 3 Yahweh your God himself will lead you across, he himself will destroy and dispossess these nations confronting you; Joshua too will lead you across, as Yahweh has said. 4 Yahweh will treat them as he has treated Sihon and Og the Amorite kings and their country — he destroyed them. 5 Yahweh will put them at your mercy, and you will deal with them exactly as prescribed by the commandments which I have laid down for you. 6 Be strong, stand firm, have no fear, do not be afraid of them, for Yahweh your God is going with you; he will not fail you or desert you.'

7 Moses then summoned Joshua and, in the presence of all Israel, said to him, 'Be strong, stand firm; you will be the one to go with this people into the country which Yahweh has sworn to their ancestors that he would give them; you are to be the one who puts them into possession of it. 8 Yahweh himself will lead you; he will be with you; he will not fail you or desert you. Have no fear, do not be alarmed.'

9 Moses committed this Law to writing and gave it to the priests, the sons of Levi, who carried the ark of Yahweh's covenant, and to all the elders of Israel. 10 And Moses gave

commanded them: "Every seventh year, in the scheduled year of remission, during the festival of booths,*q* 11 when all Israel comes to appear before the LORD your God at the place that he will choose, you shall read this law before all Israel in their hearing. 12 Assemble the people — men, women, and children, as well as the aliens residing in your towns — so that they may hear and learn to fear the LORD your God and to observe diligently all the words of this law, 13 and so that their children, who have not known it, may hear and learn to fear the LORD your God, as long as you live in the land that you are crossing over the Jordan to possess."

14 The LORD said to Moses, "Your time to die is near; call Joshua and present yourselves in the tent of meeting, so that I may commission him." So Moses and Joshua went and presented themselves in the tent of meeting, 15 and the LORD appeared at the tent in a pillar of cloud; the pillar of cloud stood at the entrance to the tent.

16 The LORD said to Moses, "Soon you will lie down with your ancestors. Then this people will begin to prostitute themselves to the foreign gods in their midst, the gods of the land into which they are going; they will forsake me, breaking my covenant that I have made with them. 17 My anger will be kindled against them in that day. I will forsake them and hide my face from them; they will become easy prey, and many terrible troubles will come upon them. In that day they will say, 'Have not these troubles come upon us because our God is not in our midst?' 18 On that day I will surely hide my face on account of all the evil they have done by turning to other gods. 19 Now therefore write this song, and teach it to the Israelites; put it in their mouths, in order that this song may be a witness for me against the Israelites. 20 For when I have brought them into the land flowing with milk and honey, which I promised on oath to their ancestors, and they have eaten their fill and grown fat, they will turn to other gods and serve them, despising me and breaking my covenant. 21 And when many terrible troubles come upon them, this song will confront them as a witness, because it will not be lost from the mouths of their descendants. For I know what they are inclined to do even now, before I have brought them into the land that I promised them on oath." 22 That very day Moses wrote this song and taught it to the Israelites.

23 Then the LORD commissioned Joshua son of Nun and said, "Be strong and bold, for you shall bring the Israelites into the land that I promised them; I will be with you."

24 When Moses had finished writing down in a book the words of this law to the very end, 25 Moses commanded the Levites who carried the ark of the covenant of the LORD, saying, 26 "Take this book of the law and put it beside the ark of the covenant of the LORD your God; let it remain there as a witness against you. 27 For I know well how rebellious and stubborn you are. If you already have been so rebellious toward the LORD while I am still alive among you, how much more after my death! 28 Assemble to me all the elders of your tribes and your officials, so that I may recite these words in their hearing and call heaven and earth to witness against them. 29 For I know that after my death you will surely act corruptly, turning aside from the way that I have commanded you. In time to come trouble will befall you, because you will do what is evil in the sight of the LORD, provoking him to anger through the work of your hands."

30 Then Moses recited the words of this song, to the very end, in the hearing of the whole assembly of Israel:

this command: At the end of every seven years, at the appointed time for the year of remission, at the pilgrim-feast of Booths, 11 when all Israel comes to appear before the LORD your God in the place which he will choose, this law is to be read in the hearing of all Israel. 12 Assemble the people, men, women, and dependants, together with the aliens residing in your settlements, so that they may listen, and learn to fear the LORD your God and observe all these laws with care. 13 Their children, too, who do not know the laws, will hear them, and learn to fear the LORD your God all their lives in the land which you will occupy after crossing the Jordan.

14 THE LORD said to Moses, 'The time of your death is drawing near. Summon Joshua, and present yourselves in the Tent of Meeting so that I may give him his commission.' When Moses and Joshua went and presented themselves in the Tent of Meeting, 15 the LORD appeared in a pillar of cloud, which stood over the entrance of the Tent.

16 The LORD said to Moses, 'You are about to die and join your forefathers, and then this people, when they come into the land and live among foreigners, will wantonly worship their gods; they will abandon me and break the covenant which I have made with them. 17 My anger will be roused against them on that day, and I shall abandon them and hide my face from them. They will be an easy prey, and many terrible disasters will come upon them. On that day they will say, "These disasters have come because our God is not among us." 18 On that day I shall hide my face because of all the evil they have done in turning to other gods.

19 'Now write down this song and teach it to the Israelites; make them repeat it, so that it may be a witness for me against them. 20 When I have brought them into the land which I swore to give to their forefathers, a land flowing with milk and honey, and they have plenty to eat and are thriving, then they will turn to other gods and serve them, spurning me and breaking my covenant; 21 and many terrible disasters will follow. Then this song will confront them as a witness, for it will not be forgotten by their descendants. For even before I bring them into the land which I swore to give them, I already know which way their thoughts incline.'

22 That day Moses wrote down this song and taught it to the Israelites. 23 The LORD gave Joshua son of Nun his commission in these words: 'Be strong and resolute; for you are to lead the Israelites into the land which I swore to give them, and I shall be with you.'

24 When Moses had finished writing down these laws from beginning to end in a book, 25 he gave this command to the Levites who carried the Ark of the Covenant of the LORD: 26 Take this book of the law and put it beside the Ark of the Covenant of the LORD your God, and let it be there as a witness against you. 27 For I know how defiant and stubborn you are; even during my lifetime you have defied the LORD; how much more, then, will you do so after my death! 28 Assemble for me all the elders of your tribes and your officers; I shall say all these words in their hearing and summon heaven and earth to witness against them. 29 For I know that, when I am dead, you will take to infamous practices and turn aside from the way which I told you to follow. In days to come disaster will befall you, for in doing what is wrong in the eyes of the LORD you provoked him to anger.

30 MOSES recited this song from beginning to end in the hearing of the whole assembly of Israel:

---

q Or *tabernacles*; Heb *succoth*

31:11 **appear before:** *lit.* see the face of.   31:13 **their lives:** *so Samar.; Heb.* your lives.   31:19 **song:** *or* rule of life.
31:23 **The LORD:** *prob. rdg; Heb.* He.

order: "On the feast of Booths, at the prescribed time in the year of relaxation which comes at the end of every seven-year period, 11 when all Israel goes to appear before the LORD, your God, in the place which he chooses, you shall read this law aloud in the presence of all Israel. 12 Assemble the people — men, women and children, as well as the aliens who live in your communities — that they may hear it and learn it, and so fear the LORD, your God, and carefully observe all the words of this law. 13 Their children also, who do not know it yet, must hear it and learn it, that they too may fear the LORD, your God, as long as you live on the land which you will cross the Jordan to occupy."

14 The LORD said to Moses, "The time is now approaching for you to die. Summon Joshua, and present yourselves at the meeting tent that I may give him his commission." So Moses and Joshua went and presented themselves at the meeting tent. 15 And the LORD appeared at the tent in a column of cloud, which stood still at the entrance of the tent.

16 The LORD said to Moses, "Soon you will be at rest with your fathers, and then this people will take to rendering wanton worship to the strange gods among whom they will live in the land they are about to enter. They will forsake me and break the covenant which I have made with them. 17 At that time my anger will flare up against them; I will forsake them and hide my face from them, so that they will become a prey to be devoured, and many evils and troubles will befall them. At that time they will indeed say, 'Is it not because our God is not among us that these evils have befallen us?' 18 Yet I will be hiding my face from them at that time only because of all the evil they have done in turning to other gods. 19 Write out this song, then, for yourselves. Teach it to the Israelites and have them recite it, so that this song may be a witness for me against the Israelites. 20 For when I have brought them into the land flowing with milk and honey which I promised on oath to their fathers, and they have eaten their fill and grown fat, if they turn to other gods and serve them, despising me and breaking my covenant; 21 then, when many evils and troubles befall them, this song, which their descendants will not have forgotten to recite, will bear witness against them. For I know what they are inclined to do even at the present time, before I have brought them into the land which I promised on oath to their fathers." 22 So Moses wrote this song that same day, and he taught it to the Israelites.

23 Then the LORD commissioned Joshua, son of Nun, and said to him, "Be brave and steadfast, for it is you who must bring the Israelites into the land which I promised them on oath. I myself will be with you."

24 When Moses had finished writing out on a scroll the words of the law in their entirety, 25 he gave the Levites who carry the ark of the covenant of the LORD this order: 26 "Take this scroll of the law and put it beside the ark of the covenant of the LORD, your God, that there it may be a witness against you. 27 For I already know how rebellious and stiff-necked you will be. Why, even now, while I am alive among you, you have been rebels against the LORD! How much more, then, after I am dead! 28 Therefore, assemble all your tribal elders and your officials before me, that I may speak these words for them to hear, and so may call heaven and earth to witness against them. 29 For I know that after my death you are sure to become corrupt and to turn aside from the way along which I directed you, so that evil will befall you in some future age because you have done evil in the LORD's sight, and provoked him by your deeds."

30 Then Moses recited the words of this song from beginning to end, for the whole assembly of Israel to hear:

them this command, 'At the end of every seven years, at the time fixed for the year of remission, at the feast of Shelters, 11 when all Israel assembles in the presence of Yahweh your God in the place chosen by him, you must proclaim this Law in the hearing of all Israel. 12 Call the people together, men, women, children, and the foreigner residing with you, so that, hearing it, they may learn to fear Yahweh your God and keep and observe all the words of this Law. 13 Their children, who as yet do not know it, will hear it and learn to fear Yahweh your God, all the time you live in the country which you are crossing the Jordan to possess.'

14 Yahweh said to Moses, 'And now the time is near when you must die. Summon Joshua and take your places at the Tent of Meeting, so that I can give him his orders.' Moses and Joshua went and took their places at the Tent of Meeting, 15 and Yahweh showed himself at the Tent in a pillar of cloud; the pillar of cloud stood at the door of the Tent.

16 Yahweh said to Moses, 'You will soon be sleeping with your ancestors, and this people is about to play the harlot by following the gods of the foreigners of the country, among whom they are going to live. They will desert me and break my covenant, which I have made with them. 17 That very day, my anger will blaze against them; I shall desert them and hide my face from them. A host of disasters and misfortunes will overtake them to devour them, and when that day comes they will say, "If such disasters overtake me, surely Yahweh my God cannot be with me?" 18 Yes indeed, I shall hide my face that day, on account of all the evil which they will have done by turning to other gods.

19 'Now write down this song for you to use; teach it to the Israelites, put it into their mouths, for it to be a witness on my behalf against the Israelites: 20 against Israel, whom I am bringing into the country which I swore to his ancestors that I would give him, a country flowing with milk and honey: against Israel, who will eat to his heart's content and grow fat, and will then turn to other gods and serve them, despising me and breaking my covenant. 21 When a host of disasters and misfortunes overtakes him, this song, like a witness, will give evidence against him, since his descendants will not have forgotten it. Yes, even today, before I have brought him to the country which I have promised him on oath, I know what plans he has in mind.' 22 So, that day, Moses wrote out this song and taught it to the Israelites.

23 To Joshua son of Nun, Yahweh gave this order, 'Be strong and stand firm, for you are to be the one to bring the Israelites into the country which I have promised them on oath, and I myself shall be with you.'

24 When Moses had completely finished writing the words of this Law in a book, 25 he gave this command to the Levites who carried the ark of Yahweh's covenant: 26 'Take the book of this Law and put it beside the ark of the covenant of Yahweh your God. Let it lie there as evidence against you. 27 For I know how rebellious and stiff-necked you are. If today, while I am still alive and with you, you rebel against Yahweh, how much more will you rebel against him after my death!

28 'Gather all your tribal elders and scribes round me, so that I may be sure that they hear these words, as I call heaven and earth to witness against them. 29 For I know that after my death you are certain to grow corrupt; you will leave the way which I have marked out for you; in the final days disaster will befall you for having done what is evil in Yahweh's eyes, for having provoked his anger by your behaviour.'

30 In the hearing of the whole assembly of Israel, Moses then recited the words of this song to the end:

32 Give ear, O heavens, and I will speak;
    let the earth hear the words of my mouth.
2 May my teaching drop like the rain,
    my speech condense like the dew;
    like gentle rain on grass,
    like showers on new growth.
3 For I will proclaim the name of the LORD;
    ascribe greatness to our God!

4 The Rock, his work is perfect,
    and all his ways are just.
A faithful God, without deceit,
    just and upright is he;
5 yet his degenerate children have dealt falsely with
    him,*r*
    a perverse and crooked generation.
6 Do you thus repay the LORD,
    O foolish and senseless people?
Is not he your father, who created you,
    who made you and established you?
7 Remember the days of old,
    consider the years long past;
ask your father, and he will inform you;
    your elders, and they will tell you.
8 When the Most High*s* apportioned the nations,
    when he divided humankind,
he fixed the boundaries of the peoples
    according to the number of the gods;*t*
9 the LORD's own portion was his people,
    Jacob his allotted share.

10 He sustained*u* him in a desert land,
    in a howling wilderness waste;
he shielded him, cared for him,
    guarded him as the apple of his eye.
11 As an eagle stirs up its nest,
    and hovers over its young;
as it spreads its wings, takes them up,
    and bears them aloft on its pinions,
12 the LORD alone guided him;
    no foreign god was with him.
13 He set him atop the heights of the land,
    and fed him with*v* produce of the field;
he nursed him with honey from the crags,
    with oil from flinty rock;
14 curds from the herd, and milk from the flock,
    with fat of lambs and rams;
Bashan bulls and goats,
    together with the choicest wheat —
    you drank fine wine from the blood of grapes.
15 Jacob ate his fill;*w*
    Jeshurun grew fat, and kicked.
    You grew fat, bloated, and gorged!
He abandoned God who made him,
    and scoffed at the Rock of his salvation.
16 They made him jealous with strange gods,
    with abhorrent things they provoked him.
17 They sacrificed to demons, not God,
    to deities they had never known,
to new ones recently arrived,
    whom your ancestors had not feared.

32 Give ear, you heavens, to what I say;
    listen, earth, to the words I speak.
2 May my teaching fall like raindrops,
    my words distil like dew,
    like fine rain on tender grass,
    like lavish showers on growing plants.
3 When I proclaim the name of the LORD,
    you will respond: 'Great is our God,
4 the Creator, whose work is perfect,
    for all his ways are just,
    a faithful God who does no wrong;
    how righteous and true is he!'

5 Perverted and crooked generation
    whose faults have proved you no children of his,
6 is this how you repay the LORD,
    you senseless, stupid people?
Is he not your father who formed you?
    Did he not make you and establish you?
7 Remember the days of old,
    think of the years, age upon age;
ask your father to inform you,
    the elders to tell you.
8 When the Most High gave each nation its heritage,
    when he divided all mankind,
he laid down the boundaries for peoples
    according to the number of the sons of God;
9 but the LORD's share was his own people,
    Jacob was his allotted portion.

10 He found his people in a desert land,
    in a barren, howling waste.
He protected and trained them,
    he guarded them as the apple of his eye.
11 As an eagle watches over its nest,
    hovers above its young,
    spreads its pinions and takes them up,
    and bears them on its wings,
12 the LORD alone led his people,
    no alien god at his side.

13 He made them ride over the heights of the earth
    and fed them on the harvest of the fields;
he satisfied them with honey from the crags
    and oil from the flinty rock,
14 curds from the cattle, milk from the herd,
    the fat of lambs' kidneys,
of Bashan rams, and of goats,
    with the finest flour of wheat;
and you, his people, drank red wine from the juice
    of the grape.

15 Jacob ate and was well fed,
    Jeshurun grew fat and unruly,
    they grew fat and bloated and sleek.
They forsook God their Maker
    and dishonoured the Rock of their salvation.
16 They roused his jealousy with alien gods
    and provoked him to anger with abominable
    practices.
17 They sacrificed to demons that are no gods,
    to gods who were strangers to them;
they consorted with upstart gods from their
    neighbours,
gods whom your fathers did not acknowledge.

---

r Meaning of Heb uncertain   *s* Traditional rendering of Heb *Elyon*
t Q Ms Compare Gk Tg: MT *the Israelites*   *u* Sam Gk Compare Tg:
MT *found*   *v* Sam Gk Syr Tg: MT *he ate*   *w* Q Mss Sam Gk: MT
lacks *Jacob ate his fill*

32:4 **Creator:** *or* Rock.   32:8 **sons of God:** *so Scroll; Heb.* sons
of Israel.   32:14 **kidneys:** *transposed from fourth line.*
32:15 **Jacob . . . fed:** *so Samar.; Heb.* omits. **unruly:** *or* kicked.

32

A

Give ear, O heavens, while I speak;
  let the earth hearken to the words of my mouth!
2 May my instruction soak in like the rain,
  and my discourse permeate like the dew,
Like a downpour upon the grass,
  like a shower upon the crops:
3 For I will sing the LORD's renown.
  Oh, proclaim the greatness of our God!
4 The Rock — how faultless are his deeds,
  how right all his ways!
A faithful God, without deceit,
  how just and upright he is!
5 Yet basely has he been treated by his
    degenerate children,
  a perverse and crooked race!
6 Is the LORD to be thus repaid by you,
  O stupid and foolish people?
Is he not your father who created you?
  Has he not made you and established you?

7 Think back on the days of old,
  reflect on the years of age upon age.
Ask your father and he will inform you,
  ask your elders and they will tell you:
8 When the Most High assigned the nations
    their heritage,
  when he parceled out the descendants of Adam,
He set up the boundaries of the peoples
  after the number of the sons of God;
9 While the LORD's own portion was Jacob,
  his hereditary share was Israel.

10 He found them in a wilderness,
  a wasteland of howling desert.
He shielded them and cared for them,
  guarding them as the apple of his eye.
11 As an eagle incites its nestlings forth
  by hovering over its brood,
So he spread his wings to receive them
  and bore them up on his pinions.
12 The LORD alone was their leader,
  no strange god was with him.
13 He had them ride triumphant over the summits of
    the land
  and live off the products of its fields,
Giving them honey to suck from its rocks
  and olive oil from its hard, stony ground;
14 Butter from its cows and milk from its sheep,
  with the fat of its lambs and rams;
Its Bashan bulls and its goats,
  with the cream of its finest wheat;
  and the foaming blood of its grapes you drank.

B

15 [So Jacob ate his fill,]
  the darling grew fat and frisky;
  you became fat and gross and gorged.
They spurned the God who made them
  and scorned their saving Rock.
16 They provoked him with strange gods
  and angered him with abominable idols.

17 They offered sacrifice to demons, to "no-gods,"
  to gods whom they had not known before,
To newcomers just arrived,
  of whom their fathers had never stood in awe.

32

Listen, heavens, while I speak;
  hear, earth, the words that I shall say!
2 May my teaching fall like the rain,
  may my word drop down like the dew,
like showers on the grass,
  like light rain on the turf!
3 For I shall proclaim the name of Yahweh.
  Oh, tell the greatness of our God!

4 He is the Rock, his work is perfect,
  for all his ways are equitable.
A trustworthy God who does no wrong,
  he is the Honest, the Upright One!
5 They have acted perversely, those he fathered
    without blemish,
  a deceitful and underhand brood.
6 Is this the return you make to Yahweh?
  O people brainless and unwise!
Is this not your father, who gave you being,
  who made you, by whom you subsist?
7 Think back on the days of old,
  think over the years, down the ages.
Question your father, let him explain to you,
  your elders, and let them tell you!
8 When the Most High gave the nations each their
    heritage,
  when he partitioned out the human race,
he assigned the boundaries of nations
  according to the number of the children of God,
9 but Yahweh's portion was his people,
  Jacob was to be the measure of his inheritance.

10 In the desert he finds him,
  in the howling expanses of the wastelands.
He protects him, rears him, guards him
  as the pupil of his eye.
11 Like an eagle watching its nest,
  hovering over its young,
he spreads out his wings to hold him,
  he supports him on his pinions.
12 Yahweh alone is his guide;
  no alien god for him!
13 He gives him the heights of the land to ride,
  he feeds him on the yield of the mountains,
he gives him honey from the rock to taste,
  and oil from the flinty crag;
14 curds from the cattle, milk from the flock,
  and the richness of the pasture,
rams of Bashan's breed, and goats,
  the richness of the wheat kernel;
  the fermented blood of the grape for drink.

15 Jacob has eaten to his heart's content,
  Jeshurun,¹ grown fat, has now lashed out.
(You have grown fat, gross, bloated.)
He has disowned the God who made him,
  and dishonoured the Rock, his salvation,
16 whose jealousy they aroused with foreigners —
  with things detestable they angered him.
17 They sacrificed to demons who are not God,
  to gods hitherto unknown to them,
to newcomers of yesterday
  whom their ancestors had never respected.

---

¹**32** A name for Israel (also in 33:5) of uncertain sense and origin.

18 You were unmindful of the Rock that bore you;*x*
      you forgot the God who gave you birth.

19 The LORD saw it, and was jealous*y*
      he spurned*z* his sons and daughters.

20 He said: I will hide my face from them,
      I will see what their end will be;
    for they are a perverse generation,
      children in whom there is no faithfulness.

21 They made me jealous with what is no god,
      provoked me with their idols.
    So I will make them jealous with what is no
        people,
      provoke them with a foolish nation.

22 For a fire is kindled by my anger,
      and burns to the depths of Sheol;
    it devours the earth and its increase,
      and sets on fire the foundations of the
        mountains.

23 I will heap disasters upon them,
      spend my arrows against them:

24 wasting hunger,
      burning consumption,
      bitter pestilence.
    The teeth of beasts I will send against them,
      with venom of things crawling in the dust.

25 In the street the sword shall bereave,
      and in the chambers terror,
    for young man and woman alike,
      nursing child and old gray head.

26 I thought to scatter them*a*
      and blot out the memory of them from
        humankind;

27 but I feared provocation by the enemy,
      for their adversaries might misunderstand
    and say, "Our hand is triumphant;
      it was not the LORD who did all this."

28 They are a nation void of sense;
      there is no understanding in them.

29 If they were wise, they would understand this;
      they would discern what the end would be.

30 How could one have routed a thousand,
      and two put a myriad to flight,
    unless their Rock had sold them,
      the LORD had given them up?

31 Indeed their rock is not like our Rock;
      our enemies are fools. *a*

32 Their vine comes from the vinestock of Sodom,
      from the vineyards of Gomorrah;
    their grapes are grapes of poison,
      their clusters are bitter;

33 their wine is the poison of serpents,
      the cruel venom of asps.

34 Is not this laid up in store with me,
      sealed up in my treasuries?

35 Vengeance is mine, and recompense,
      for the time when their foot shall slip;
    because the day of their calamity is at hand,
      their doom comes swiftly.

36 Indeed the LORD will vindicate his people,
      have compassion on his servants,
    when he sees that their power is gone,
      neither bond nor free remaining.

18 You forsook the Creator who begot you
      and ceased to care for God who brought you to
        birth.

19 The LORD saw and spurned them;
      his own sons and daughters provoked his anger.

20 'I shall hide my face from them,' he said;
      'let me see what their end will be,
    for they are a subversive generation,
      children not to be trusted.

21 They roused my jealousy with a god of no account,
      with their worthless idols they provoked me to
        anger;
    so I shall rouse their jealousy with a people of no
        account,
      with a foolish nation I shall provoke them.

22 For fire is set ablaze by my anger,
      it burns to the depths of Sheol;
    it devours earth and its harvest
      and the flames reach the very roots of the
        mountains.

23 'I shall heap on them one disaster after another,
      and expend my arrows on them:

24 pangs of hunger, ravages of plague,
      and bitter pestilence.
    I shall harry them with the fangs of wild beasts
      and the poison of creatures that crawl in the dust.

25 The sword will make orphans in the streets,
      make widows in their homes;
    it will take toll of young men and girls,
      of babes in arms as well as of the aged.

26 I had resolved to strike them down
      and to destroy all memory of them,

27 but I feared that I should be provoked by their
        foes,
    that their enemies would take the credit,
      saying, "It was not the LORD,
      but we who got the upper hand." '

28 They are a nation devoid of good counsel,
      that lacks all understanding.

29 If only they had the wisdom to discern this
      and understand what their end is to be!

30 How could one man rout a thousand of them,
      how could two put ten thousand to flight,
    if their Rock had not sold them to their enemies,
      if the LORD had not handed them over?

31 For the enemy have no Rock like ours;
      in themselves they are mere fools.

32 Their vines are from the vines of Sodom,
      grown on the terraces of Gomorrah;
    their grapes are poisonous,
      the clusters bitter to the taste.

33 Their wine is the venom of serpents,
      the cruel poison of asps;

34 all this I have in reserve,
      sealed up in my storehouses

35 till the day of punishment and vengeance,
      till the moment when their foot slips;
    for the day of their downfall is near,
      their doom is fast approaching.

36 The LORD will judge his people
      and have compassion on his servants;
    for he will see that their strength is gone:
      no one, either fettered or free, is left.

---

*x*Or *that begot you*   *y*Q Mss Gk: MT lacks *was jealous*
*z*Cn: Heb *he spurned because of provocation*   *a*Gk: Meaning of
Heb uncertain

32:18 **Creator:** *or* Rock.   32:22 **Sheol:** *or* the underworld.
32:31 **fools:** *so* Gk; *Heb.* judges.   32:35 **till the day of:** *so*
Samar.; *Heb.* for me.

18 You were unmindful of the Rock that begot you,
You forgot the God who gave you birth.
19 When the LORD saw this, he was filled
with loathing
and anger toward his sons and daughters.
20 "I will hide my face from them," he said,
"and see what will then become of them.
What a fickle race they are,
sons with no loyalty in them!
21 "Since they have provoked me with their 'no god'
and angered me with their vain idols,
I will provoke them with a 'no-people';
with a foolish nation I will anger them.

22 "For by my wrath a fire is enkindled
that shall rage to the depths of the netherworld,
Consuming the earth with its yield,
and licking with flames the roots of
the mountains.
23 I will spend on them woe upon woe
and exhaust all my arrows against them:

24 "Emaciating hunger and consuming fever
and bitter pestilence,
And the teeth of wild beasts I will send
among them,
with the venom of reptiles gliding in the dust.

25 "Snatched away by the sword in the street
and by sheer terror at home
Shall be the youth and the maiden alike,
the nursing babe as well as the hoary old man.

26 "I would have said, 'I will make an end of them
and blot out their name from men's memories,'
27 Had I not feared the insolence of their enemies,
feared that these foes would mistakenly boast,
'Our own hand won the victory;
the LORD had nothing to do with it.'"

28 For they are a people devoid of reason,
having no understanding.
29 If they had insight they would realize
what happened,
they would understand their future and say,
C
30 "How could one man rout a thousand,
or two men put ten thousand to flight,
Unless it was because their Rock sold them
and the LORD delivered them up?"
31 Indeed, their "rock" is not like our Rock,
and our foes are under condemnation.

32 They are a branch of Sodom's vine-stock,
from the vineyards of Gomorrah.
Poisonous are their grapes and bitter their clusters.
33 Their wine is the venom of dragons
and the cruel poison of cobras.

34 "Is not this preserved in my treasury,
sealed up in my storehouse,
35 Against the day of vengeance and requital,
against the time they lose their footing?"
Close at hand is the day of their disaster,
and their doom is rushing upon them!

36 Surely, the LORD shall do justice for his people;
on his servants he shall have pity.
When he sees their strength failing,
and their protected and unprotected alike
disappearing,

18 (You forget the Rock who fathered you,
the God who made you, you no longer remember.)
19 Yahweh saw it and, in anger,
he spurned his sons and daughters.
20 'I shall hide my face from them,' he said,
'and see what will become of them.
For they are a deceitful brood,
children with no loyalty in them.
21 They have roused me to jealousy with a non-god,
they have exasperated me with their idols.
In my turn I shall rouse them to jealousy with a
non-people,
I shall exasperate them with a stupid nation.

22 Yes, a fire has blazed from my anger,
it will burn right down to the depths of Sheol;
it will devour the earth and all its produce,
it will set fire to the footings of the mountains.
23 I shall hurl disasters on them,
on them I shall use up all my arrows.
24 They will be weakened by hunger,
eaten away by plague and the bitter scourge.
Against them I shall send the fang of wild animals
and the poison of snakes that glide in the dust.
25 Outside, the sword bereaves,
while inside terror will reign.
Young man and girl alike will perish,
suckling and greybeard both together.
26 I should crush them to dust, I said,
I should wipe out all memory of them,
27 did I not fear the boasting of the enemy.'
But do not let their foes be mistaken!
Do not let them say, 'We have got the upper hand
and Yahweh plays no part in this.'
28 What a short-sighted nation this is,
how thoroughly imperceptive!
29 Were they wise, they would succeed,
they would be able to read their destiny.
30 How else could one man rout a thousand,
how could two put ten thousand to flight,
were it not that their Rock has sold them,
that Yahweh has delivered them up?
31 But their rock is not like our Rock;
our enemies cannot pray for us!
32 For their vine springs from the stock of Sodom
and from the groves of Gomorrah:
their grapes are poisonous grapes,
their clusters are bitter;
33 their wine is snakes' poison,
the vipers' cruel venom.
34 But he, is he not safe with me,
sealed inside my treasury?
35 Vengeance is mine, I will pay them back,
for the time when they make a false step.
For the day of their ruin is close,
doom is rushing towards them,
for he will see to it that their power fails,
that neither serf nor free man remains.
36 (For Yahweh will see his people righted,
he will take pity on his servants.)

37 Then he will say: Where are their gods,
    the rock in which they took refuge,
38 who ate the fat of their sacrifices,
    and drank the wine of their libations?
Let them rise up and help you,
    let them be your protection!

39 See now that I, even I, am he;
    there is no god besides me.
I kill and I make alive;
    I wound and I heal;
    and no one can deliver from my hand.
40 For I lift up my hand to heaven,
    and swear: As I live forever,
41 when I whet my flashing sword,
    and my hand takes hold on judgment;
I will take vengeance on my adversaries,
    and will repay those who hate me.
42 I will make my arrows drunk with blood,
    and my sword shall devour flesh—
with the blood of the slain and the captives,
    from the long-haired enemy.

43 Praise, O heavens,*b* his people,
    worship him, all you gods!*c*
For he will avenge the blood of his children,*d*
    and take vengeance on his adversaries;
he will repay those who hate him,*c*
    and cleanse the land for his people.*e*

44 Moses came and recited all the words of this song in the hearing of the people, he and Joshua*f* son of Nun. 45 When Moses had finished reciting all these words to all Israel, 46 he said to them: "Take to heart all the words that I am giving in witness against you today; give them as a command to your children, so that they may diligently observe all the words of this law. 47 This is no trifling matter for you, but rather your very life; through it you may live long in the land that you are crossing over the Jordan to possess."

48 On that very day the LORD addressed Moses as follows: 49 "Ascend this mountain of the Abarim, Mount Nebo, which is in the land of Moab, across from Jericho, and view the land of Canaan, which I am giving to the Israelites for a possession; 50 you shall die there on the mountain that you ascend and shall be gathered to your kin, as your brother Aaron died on Mount Hor and was gathered to his kin; 51 because both of you broke faith with me among the Israelites at the waters of Meribath-kadesh in the wilderness of Zin, by failing to maintain my holiness among the Israelites. 52 Although you may view the land from a distance, you shall not enter it—the land that I am giving to the Israelites."

33 This is the blessing with which Moses, the man of God, blessed the Israelites before his death. 2 He said:

    The LORD came from Sinai,
        and dawned from Seir upon us;*g*
    he shone forth from Mount Paran.
    With him were myriads of holy ones;*h*
        at his right, a host of his own.*i*
3 Indeed, O favorite among*j* peoples,
    all his holy ones were in your charge;
    they marched at your heels,
        accepted direction from you.

37 He will ask, 'Where are your gods,
    the rock in which you sought refuge,
38 the gods who ate the fat of your sacrifices
    and drank the wine of your drink-offerings?
Let them rise to help you!
    Let them be your protection!
39 See now that I, I am He,
    and besides me there is no god:
I put to death and I keep alive,
    I inflict wounds and I heal;
    there is no rescue from my grasp.
40 I raise my hand towards heaven
    and swear: As I live for ever,
41 when I have whetted my flashing sword,
    when I have set my hand to judgement,
then I shall punish my adversaries
    and wreak vengeance on my foes.
42 I shall make my arrows drunk with blood,
    my sword will devour flesh,
blood of slain and captives,
    the heads of the enemy princes.'

43 Rejoice with him, you heavens,
    bow down, all you gods, before him;
for he will avenge the blood of his sons
    and take vengeance on his adversaries;
he will punish those who hate him
    and cleanse his people's land.

44 These are the words of the song that Moses, when he came with Joshua son of Nun, recited in full in the hearing of the people.

45 When Moses had finished reciting all these words to Israel 46 he said: Take to heart all the warnings which I give you this day: command your children to be careful to observe all the words of this law. 47 For you they are no empty words; they are your very life, and by them you will enjoy long life in the land which you are to occupy after crossing the Jordan.

48 That same day the LORD said to Moses, 49 'Go up the mountain of the Abarim, Mount Nebo in Moab, to the east of Jericho, and view the land of Canaan that I am giving to the Israelites for their possession. 50 On this mountain you will die and be gathered to your father's kin, just as Aaron your brother died on Mount Hor and was gathered to his father's kin. 51 This is because both of you broke faith with me at the waters of Meribath-kadesh in the wilderness of Zin, when you did not uphold my holiness among the Israelites. 52 You may see the land from a distance, but you may not enter the land I am giving to the Israelites.'

33 THIS is the blessing that Moses, the man of God, pronounced on the Israelites before his death:

2 The LORD came from Sinai
    and shone forth from Seir.
He appeared from Mount Paran,
    and with him were myriads of holy ones
    streaming along at his right hand.
3 Truly he loves his people
    and blesses his holy ones.
They sit at his feet
    and receive his instruction,

---

b Q Ms Gk: MT *nations*   *c* Q Ms Gk: MT lacks this line   *d* Q Ms Gk: MT *his servants*   *e* Q Ms Sam Gk Vg: MT *his land his people*   *f* Sam Gk Syr Vg: MT *Hoshea*   *g* Gk Syr Vg Compare Tg: Heb *upon them*   *h* Cn Compare Gk Sam Syr Vg: MT *He came from Ribeboth-kadesh,*   *i* Cn Compare Gk: meaning of Heb uncertain   *j* Or *O lover of the*

32:43 **Rejoice . . . before him:** so *Scroll,* cp. *Gk; Heb.* Cause his people to rejoice, you nations. **sons:** so *Scroll; Heb.* servants. **he will punish . . . land:** so *Scroll; Heb.* and make expiation for his land, his people.   32:44 **Joshua:** Heb. Hoshea (*cp. Num. 13:16*).   33:2 **and with . . . ones:** *prob. rdg; Heb.* and he came from myriads of holiness.   33:3 **his people:** so *Gk; Heb.* peoples. **blesses:** so *Syriac; Heb.* in your hand. **his feet . . . his instruction:** so *Lat.; Heb.* your feet . . . your instruction.

NEW AMERICAN BIBLE

37 He will say, "Where are their gods
  whom they relied on as their 'rock'?
38 Let those who ate the fat of your sacrifices
  and drank the wine of your libations
Rise up now and help you!
  Let them be your protection!

39 "Learn then that I, I alone, am God,
  and there is no god besides me.
It is I who bring both death and life,
  I who inflict wounds and heal them,
  and from my hand there is no rescue.

40 "To the heavens I raise my hand and swear:
  As surely as I live forever,
41 I will sharpen my flashing sword,
  and my hand shall lay hold of my quiver.

"With vengeance I will repay my foes
  and requite those who hate me.
42 I will make my arrows drunk with blood,
  and my sword shall gorge itself with flesh—
With the blood of the slain and the captured,
  Flesh from the heads of the enemy leaders."

43 Exult with him, you heavens,
  glorify him, all you angels of God;
For he avenges the blood of his servants
  and purges his people's land.

44 So Moses, together with Joshua, son of Nun, went and recited all the words of this song for the people to hear. 45 When Moses had finished speaking all these words to all Israel, 46 he said, "Take to heart all the warning which I have now given you and which you must impress on your children, that you may carry out carefully every word of this law. 47 For this is no trivial matter for you; rather, it means your very life, since it is by this means that you are to enjoy a long life on the land which you will cross the Jordan to occupy."

48 On that very day the LORD said to Moses, 49 "Go up on Mount Nebo, here in the Abarim Mountains [it is in the land of Moab facing Jericho], and view the land of Canaan, which I am giving to the Israelites as their possession. 50 Then you shall die on the mountain you have climbed, and shall be taken to your people, just as your brother Aaron died on Mount Hor and there was taken to his people; 51 because both of you broke faith with me among the Israelites at the waters of Meribath-kadesh in the desert of Zin by failing to manifest my sanctity among the Israelites. 52 You may indeed view the land at a distance, but you shall not enter that land which I am giving to the Israelites."

33 This is the blessing which Moses, the man of God, pronounced upon the Israelites before he died. 2 He said:

"The LORD came from Sinai
  and dawned on his people from Seir;
He shone forth from Mount Paran
  and advanced from Meribath-kadesh,
While at his right hand a fire blazed forth
  and his wrath devastated the nations.
3 But all his holy ones were in his hand;
  they followed at his feet
  and he bore them up on his pinions.

NEW JERUSALEM BIBLE

37 'Where are their gods then?' he will ask,
  'the rock where they sought refuge,
38 who ate the fat of their sacrifices
  and drank the wine of their libations?'
Let these arise and help you,
  let these be the shelter above you!
39 See now that I, I am he,
  and beside me there is no other god.
It is I who deal death and life;
  when I have struck, it is I who heal
  (no one can rescue anyone from me).

40 Yes, I raise my hand to heaven,
  and I say, 'As surely as I live for ever,
41 When I have whetted my flashing sword,
  I shall enforce justice,
  I shall return vengeance to my foes,
  I shall take vengeance on my foes.
42 I shall make my arrows drunk with blood,
  and my sword will feed on flesh:
  the blood of the wounded and the prisoners,
  the dishevelled heads of the enemy!'

43 Heavens, rejoice with him,
  let all the children of God pay him homage!
Nations, rejoice with his people,
  let God's envoys tell of his power!
For he will avenge the blood of his servants,
  he will return vengeance to my foes,
  he will repay those who hate him
  and purify his people's country.

44 Moses came with Joshua son of Nun and recited all the words of this song in the people's hearing. 45 When Moses had finished reciting these words to all Israel, 46 he said to them, 'Take all these words to heart; I intend them today to be evidence against you. You must order your children to keep and observe all the words of this Law. 47 You must not think of this as empty words, for the Law is your life, and by its means you will live long in the country which you are crossing the Jordan to possess.'

48 Yahweh spoke to Moses that same day and said to him, 49 'Climb this mountain of the Abarim, Mount Nebo, in the country of Moab, opposite Jericho, and view the Canaan which I am giving to the Israelites as their domain. 50 Die on the mountain you have climbed, and be gathered to your people, as your brother Aaron died on Mount Hor and was gathered to his people. 51 Because, with the other Israelites, you broke faith with me at the Waters of Meribah-Kadesh in the desert of Zin, because you did not make my holiness clear to the Israelites; 52 you may only see the country from outside; you cannot enter it—the country which I am giving to the Israelites.'

33 This is the blessing that Moses, man of God, pronounced over the Israelites before he died. 2 He said:

Yahweh came from Sinai,
  from Seir he dawned on us,
  from Mount Paran blazed forth,
For them he came, after the mustering at Kadesh,
  from his zenith as far as the foothills.

3 You who love the ancestors!
  Your holy ones are all at your command.
At your feet they fell,
  under your guidance went swiftly on.

4 Moses charged us with the law,
  as a possession for the assembly of Jacob.
5 There arose a king in Jeshurun,
  when the leaders of the people assembled—
  the united tribes of Israel.

6 May Reuben live, and not die out,
  even though his numbers are few.

7 And this he said of Judah:
  O LORD, give heed to Judah,
  and bring him to his people;
  strengthen his hands for him,^{k}
  and be a help against his adversaries.

8 And of Levi he said:
  Give to Levi^l your Thummim,
  and your Urim to your loyal one,
  whom you tested at Massah,
  with whom you contended at the waters of
  Meribah;
9 who said of his father and mother,
  "I regard them not";
  he ignored his kin,
  and did not acknowledge his children.
  For they observed your word,
  and kept your covenant.
10 They teach Jacob your ordinances,
  and Israel your law;
  they place incense before you,
  and whole burnt offerings on your altar.
11 Bless, O LORD, his substance,
  and accept the work of his hands;
  crush the loins of his adversaries,
  of those that hate him, so that they do not rise
  again.

12 Of Benjamin he said:
  The beloved of the LORD rests in safety—
  the High God^m surrounds him all day long—
  the beloved^n rests between his shoulders.

13 And of Joseph he said:
  Blessed by the LORD be his land,
  with the choice gifts of heaven above,
  and of the deep that lies beneath;
14 with the choice fruits of the sun,
  and the rich yield of the months;
15 with the finest produce of the ancient mountains,
  and the abundance of the everlasting hills;
16 with the choice gifts of the earth and its fullness,
  and the favor of the one who dwells on
  Sinai.^{o}
  Let these come on the head of Joseph,
  on the brow of the prince among his brothers.
17 A firstborn^p bull—majesty is his!
  His horns are the horns of a wild ox;
  with them he gores the peoples,
  driving them to^q the ends of the earth;
  such are the myriads of Ephraim,
  such the thousands of Manasseh.

18 And of Zebulun he said:
  Rejoice, Zebulun, in your going out;
  and Issachar, in your tents.

4 the law which Moses laid upon us,
  as a possession for the assembly of Jacob.
5 Then a king arose in Jeshurun,
  when the chiefs of the people were assembled
  together with all the tribes of Israel.

6 Of Reuben he said:
  May Reuben live and not die out,
  but may he be few in number.

7 And of Judah he said this:
  Hear, LORD, the cry of Judah
  and join him to his people;
  strengthen his hands for him,
  be his helper against his adversaries.

8 Of Levi he said:
  Give your Thummim to Levi,
  your Urim to your loyal servant
  whom you tested at Massah,
  for whom you pleaded at the waters of Meribah,
9 who said of his parents, 'I do not know them,'
  who did not acknowledge his brothers,
  who disowned his children.
  But they observe your word
  and keep your covenant;
10 they teach your precepts to Jacob,
  your law to Israel.
  They furnish you with the smoke of sacrifice
  and offerings on your altar.
11 Bless his powers, LORD,
  and accept the work of his hands.
  Strike his adversaries hip and thigh,
  and may those hostile to him rise no more.

12 Of Benjamin he said:
  The LORD's beloved dwells securely,
  the High God shields him all the day long,
  and he dwells under his protection.

13 Of Joseph he said:
  May the LORD's blessing be on his land
  with choice fruit watered from heaven above
  and from the deep that lies below,
14 with choice fruit ripened by the sun,
  choice fruit, the produce of the months,
15 with all good things from the ancient mountains,
  the choice fruit of the everlasting hills,
16 the choice fruits of earth and its fullness,
  by the favour of him who dwells in the burning
  bush.
  May this rest on the head of Joseph,
  on the brow of him who was prince among his
  brothers.
17 In majesty he shall be like a firstborn bull,
  his horns those of a wild ox
  with which he will gore nations
  and drive them to the ends of the earth.
  Such will be the myriads of Ephraim,
  and such the thousands of Manasseh.

18 Of Zebulun he said:
  Rejoice, Zebulun, when you set forth,
  rejoice in your tents, Issachar.

33:5 **a king arose:** or there was a king.   33:6 **Of Reuben he
said:** prob. rdg; Heb. omits.   33:8 **Give . . . servant:** so Gk;
Heb. Your Thummim and Urim belong to your loyal servant.
33:11 **powers:** or skill.   33:12 **the High God:** prob. rdg; Heb.
upon him. **under his protection:** lit. between his shoulders.
33:13 **above:** so some MSS; others with dew.   33:16 **May this
rest:** prob. rdg, cp. Gen. 49:26; Heb. has an unintelligible form.
33:17 **and drive:** prob. rdg; Heb. together.

^{k}Cn: Heb with his hands he contended ^{l}Q Ms Gk: MT lacks Give
to Levi ^{m}Heb above him ^{n}Heb he ^{o}Cn: Heb in the bush
^{p}Q Ms Gk Syr Vg: MT His firstborn ^{q}Cn: Heb the peoples,
together

NEW AMERICAN BIBLE

4 A law he gave to us;
 he made the community of Jacob his domain,
5   and he became king of his darling,
 When the chiefs of the people assembled
   and the tribes of Israel came together.
6 "May Reuben live and not die out,
   but let his men be few."

7 The following is for Judah. He said:
 "The LORD hears the cry of Judah;
   you will bring him to his people.
 His own hands defend his cause
   and you will be his help against his foes."

8 Of Levi he said:
 "To Levi belong your Thummim,
   to the man of your favor your Urim;
 For you put him to the test at Massah
   and you contended with him at the waters
     of Meribah.
9 He said of his father, 'I regard him not';
   his brothers he would not acknowledge,
   and his own children he refused to recognize.
 Thus the Levites keep your words,
   and your covenant they uphold.
10 They promulgate your decisions to Jacob
   and your law to Israel.
 They bring the smoke of sacrifice to your nostrils,
   and burnt offerings to your altar.
11 Bless, O LORD, his possessions
   and accept the ministry of his hands.
 Break the backs of his adversaries
   and of his foes, that they may not rise."

12 Of Benjamin he said:
 "Benjamin is the beloved of the LORD,
   who shelters him all the day,
   while he abides securely at his breast."

13 Of Joseph he said:
 "Blessed by the LORD is his land
   with the best of the skies above
   and of the abyss crouching beneath;
14 With the best of the produce of the year,
   and the choicest sheaves of the months;
15 With the finest gifts of the age-old mountains
   and the best from the timeless hills;
16 With the best of the earth and its fullness,
   and the favor of him who dwells in the bush.
 These shall come upon the head of Joseph
   and upon the brow of the prince among
     his brothers,
17 The majestic bull, his father's first-born,
   whose horns are those of the wild ox
 With which to gore the nations,
   even those at the ends of the earth."
 [These are the myriads of Ephraim,
   and these the thousands of Manasseh.]

18 Of Zebulun he said:
 "Rejoice, O Zebulun, in your pursuits,
   and you, Issachar, in your tents!

NEW JERUSALEM BIBLE

4 (Moses enjoined a law on us.)
 The assembly of Jacob comes into its inheritance;
5 there was a king in Jeshurun
   when the heads of the people foregathered
   and the tribes of Israel were all assembled!

6 May Reuben survive and not die out,
   survive though his men be few!

7 Of Judah he said this:
 Listen, Yahweh, to the voice of Judah,
   and bring him back to his people.
 That his hands may defend his rights,
   come to his help against his foes!

8 Of Levi he said:
 To Levi, give your *urim*,
   to your faithful one, your *thummim*,
   having tested him at Massah,
   having striven with him at the Waters of Meribah.
9 Of his father and mother, he says,
   'I have not seen them.'
 He does not acknowledge his brothers,
   nor does he know his own children.
 Yes, they have kept your word,
   they hold firmly to your covenant.
10 They will teach your customs to Jacob,
   and your Law to Israel.
 They will put incense before you
   and burnt offerings on your altar.
11 Yahweh, bless his worthiness,
   and accept the actions he performs.
 Crush the loins of those who rise against him
   and of his foes, so that they rise no more!

12 Of Benjamin he said:
 Beloved of Yahweh, he rests trustfully near him.
 The Most High protects him day after day
   and dwells between his hillsides.

13 Of Joseph he said:
 His land is blessed by Yahweh.
 For him the best of heaven's dew
   and of the deep that lies below,
14 the best of what the sun makes grow,
   of what springs with every month,
15 the first-fruits of the ancient mountains,
   the best from the hills of old
16 the best of the land and all it holds,
   the favour of him who dwells in the Bush.
 May the hair grow thick on the head of Joseph,
   on the brow of the consecrated one among his
     brothers!
17 First-born of the Bull, his glory.
 His horns are the wild ox's horns,
   with which he gores the peoples
   to the very ends of the earth.
 Such are the myriads of Ephraim,
   such are the thousands of Manasseh.

18 Of Zebulun he said:
 Prosper, Zebulun, in your expeditions,
   and you, Issachar, in your tents!

19 They call peoples to the mountain;
   there they offer the right sacrifices;
   for they suck the affluence of the seas
   and the hidden treasures of the sand.

20 And of Gad he said:
   Blessed be the enlargement of Gad!
   Gad lives like a lion;
   he tears at arm and scalp.
21 He chose the best for himself,
   for there a commander's allotment was
      reserved;
   he came at the head of the people,
   he executed the justice of the LORD,
   and his ordinances for Israel.

22 And of Dan he said:
   Dan is a lion's whelp
   that leaps forth from Bashan.

23 And of Naphtali he said:
   O Naphtali, sated with favor,
   full of the blessing of the LORD,
   possess the west and the south.

24 And of Asher he said:
   Most blessed of sons be Asher;
   may he be the favorite of his brothers,
   and may he dip his foot in oil.
25 Your bars are iron and bronze;
   and as your days, so is your strength.

26 There is none like God, O Jeshurun,
   who rides through the heavens to your help,
   majestic through the skies.
27 He subdues the ancient gods,[r]
   shatters[s] the forces of old;[t]
   he drove out the enemy before you,
   and said, "Destroy!"
28 So Israel lives in safety,
   untroubled is Jacob's abode[u]
   in a land of grain and wine,
   where the heavens drop down dew.
29 Happy are you, O Israel! Who is like you,
   a people saved by the LORD,
   the shield of your help,
   and the sword of your triumph!
   Your enemies shall come fawning to you,
   and you shall tread on their backs.

34 Then Moses went up from the plains of Moab to Mount Nebo, to the top of Pisgah, which is opposite Jericho, and the LORD showed him the whole land: Gilead as far as Dan, 2 all Naphtali, the land of Ephraim and Manasseh, all the land of Judah as far as the Western Sea, 3 the Negeb, and the Plain—that is, the valley of Jericho, the city of palm trees—as far as Zoar. 4 The LORD said to him, "This is the land of which I swore to Abraham, to Isaac, and to Jacob, saying, 'I will give it to your descendants'; I have let you see it with your eyes, but you shall not cross over there." 5 Then Moses, the servant of the LORD, died there in the land of Moab, at the LORD's command. 6 He was buried in a valley in the land of Moab, opposite Beth-peor, but no one knows his burial place to this day. 7 Moses was one hundred twenty years old when he died; his sight was unimpaired and his vigor had not abated. 8 The Israelites wept for Moses in the plains of Moab thirty days; then the period of mourning for Moses was ended.

19 They will summon peoples to the mountain;
   there they will offer true sacrifices,
   for they will draw from the abundance of the sea,
   from the hidden wealth of the sand.

20 Of Gad he said:
   Blessed be Gad, in his wide domain;
   he couches like a lion
   tearing an arm or a scalp.
21 He chose the best for himself,
   for to him was allotted a ruler's portion,
   when the chiefs of the people were assembled
      together.
   He did what the LORD deemed right,
   observing his ordinances for Israel.

22 Of Dan he said:
   Dan is a lion's cub
   springing out from Bashan.

23 Of Naphtali he said:
   Naphtali is richly favoured
   and full of the blessings of the LORD;
   his domain stretches to the sea and southward.

24 Of Asher he said:
   Asher is the most blest of sons;
   may he be the favourite among his brothers
   and bathe his feet in oil!
25 May your bolts be of iron and bronze,
   and your strength last as long as you live.

26 There is none like the God of Jeshurun
   who rides on the heavens to your aid,
   on the clouds in his glory,
27 who humbled the gods of old
   and subdued the ancient powers;
   who drove out the enemy before you
   and gave the command to destroy.
28 Israel lives in security,
   and Jacob dwells alone
   in a land of grain and wine
   where the skies drip with dew.
29 Happy are you, Israel, peerless, set free!
   The LORD is the shield that guards you,
   the Blessed One is your glorious sword.
   When your enemies come cringing to you,
   you will trample their backs underfoot.

34 Moses went up from the lowlands of Moab to Mount Nebo, to the top of Pisgah eastwards from Jericho, and the LORD showed him the whole land, from Gilead to Dan; 2 the whole of Naphtali; the territory of Ephraim and Manasseh, and all Judah as far as the western sea; 3 the Negeb and the plain; the valley of Jericho, city of palm trees, as far as Zoar. 4 The LORD said to him, 'This is the land which I swore to Abraham, Isaac, and Jacob that I would give to their descendants. I have let you see it with your own eyes, but you will not cross over into it.' 5 There in the Moabite country Moses the servant of the LORD died, as the LORD had said. 6 He was buried in a valley in Moab opposite Beth-peor; but to this day no one knows his burial-place. 7 Moses was a hundred and twenty years old when he died; his sight undimmed, his vigour unimpaired. 8 The Israelites wept for Moses in the lowlands of Moab for thirty days.

The time of mourning for Moses came to an end. 9 Joshua

33:21 **were assembled together:** so Gk; Heb. obscure.
33:24 **among:** or of. 33:27 **subdued:** prob. rdg; Heb. under.
33:28 **dwells:** prob. rdg; Heb. fountain. **wine:** or new wine.
33:29 **the Blessed One:** Heb. Asher.

---

[r] Or The eternal God is a dwelling place   [s] Cn: Heb from
underneath   [t] Or the everlasting arms   [u] Or fountain

NEW AMERICAN BIBLE	NEW JERUSALEM BIBLE

19 You who invite the tribes to the mountains
  where feasts are duly held,
Because you suck up the abundance of the seas
  and the hidden treasures of the sand."

20 Of Gad he said:
"Blessed be he who has made Gad so vast!
He lies there like a lion
  that has seized the arm and head of the prey.
21 He saw that the best should be his
  when the princely portion was assigned,
  while the heads of the people were gathered.
He carried out the justice of the LORD
  and his decrees respecting Israel."

22 Of Dan he said:
"Dan is a lion's whelp,
  that springs forth from Bashan!"

23 Of Naphtali he said:
"Naphtali is enriched with favors
  and filled with the blessings of the LORD;
The lake and south of it are his possession!"

24 Of Asher he said:
"More blessed than the other sons be Asher!
May he be the favorite among his brothers,
  as the oil of his olive trees runs over his feet!
25 May your bolts be of iron and bronze;
  may your strength endure through all
    your days!"

26 "There is no god like the God of the darling,
  who rides the heavens in his power,
  and rides the skies in his majesty;
27 He spread out the primeval tent;
  he extended the ancient canopy.
He drove the enemy out of your way
  and the Amorite he destroyed.
28 Israel has dwelt securely,
  and the fountain of Jacob has been undisturbed.
In a land of grain and wine,
  where the heavens drip with dew.
29 How fortunate you are, O Israel!
  Where else is a nation victorious in the LORD?
The LORD is your saving shield,
  and his sword is your glory.
Your enemies fawn upon you,
  as you stride upon their heights."

34 Then Moses went up from the plains of Moab to Mount Nebo, the headland of Pisgah which faces Jericho, and the LORD showed him all the land — Gilead, and as far as Dan, 2 all Naphtali, the land of Ephraim and Manasseh, all the land of Judah as far as the Western Sea, 3 the Negeb, the circuit of the Jordan with the lowlands at Jericho, city of palms, and as far as Zoar. 4 The LORD then said to him, "This is the land which I swore to Abraham, Isaac and Jacob that I would give to their descendants. I have let you feast your eyes upon it, but you shall not cross over." 5 So there, in the land of Moab, Moses, the servant of the LORD, died as the LORD had said; 6 and he was buried in the ravine opposite Beth-peor in the land of Moab, but to this day no one day no one knows the place of his burial. 7 Moses was one hundred and twenty years old when he died, yet his eyes were undimmed and his vigor unabated. 8 For thirty days the Israelites wept for Moses in the plains of Moab, till they had completed the period of grief and mourning for Moses.

19 On the mountain where the people come to pray
they offer upright sacrifices,
  for they taste the riches of the seas
  and the treasures hidden in the sands.

20 Of Gad he said:
Blessed be he who gives Gad space enough!
He lies there like a lioness;
  he has savaged arm and face and head.
21 Then he took the first portion for himself,
  saw that there was stored up for him a leader's
    share.
He has come at the head of the people,
  has carried out the saving justice of Yahweh
  and his judgements on Israel.

22 Of Dan he said:
Dan is a lion cub
  leaping from Bashan.

23 Of Naphtali he said:
Naphtali, sated with favours,
  filled with the blessings of Yahweh:
  the west and south are to be his domain.

24 Of Asher he said:
Most blessed of the sons let Asher be!
Let him be the most privileged of his brothers
  and let him bathe his feet in oil!
25 Be your bolts of iron and of bronze
  and your security as lasting as your days!

26 No one is like the God of Jeshurun:
  he rides the heavens to your rescue,
  rides the clouds in his majesty!
27 The God of old is your refuge,
  his the eternal arm which here below
  drives the enemy before you;
  he it is who says, 'Destroy!'
28 Israel rests trustfully.
The well-spring of Jacob is chosen out
  for a land of corn and wine;
  there heaven itself rains down dew.
29 Blessed are you, O Israel!
Who is like you, O victorious people?
Yahweh is the shield that protects you
  and the sword that leads you to triumph.
Your enemies will try to corrupt you,
  but you yourself will trample on their backs.

34 Then, leaving the Plains of Moab, Moses went up Mount Nebo, the peak of Pisgah opposite Jericho, and Yahweh showed him the whole country: Gilead as far as Dan, 2 the whole of Naphtali, the country of Ephraim and Manasseh, the whole country of Judah as far as the Western Sea, 3 the Negeb, and the region of the Valley of Jericho, city of palm trees, as far as Zoar. 4 Yahweh said to him, 'This is the country which I promised on oath to give to Abraham, Isaac and Jacob, saying: I shall give it to your descendants. I have allowed you to see it for yourself, but you will not cross into it.' 5 There in the country of Moab, Moses, servant of Yahweh, died as Yahweh decreed; 6 he[m] buried him in the valley, in the country of Moab, opposite Beth-Peor; but to this day no one has ever found his grave. 7 Moses was a hundred and twenty years old when he died, his eye undimmed, his vigour unimpaired. 8 The Israelites wept for Moses on the Plains of Moab for thirty days. The days of weeping for the mourning rites of Moses came to an end.

m 34 i.e. Yahweh, but Sam. and some Greek texts read 'they'.

NEW REVISED STANDARD VERSION

9 Joshua son of Nun was full of the spirit of wisdom, because Moses had laid his hands on him; and the Israelites obeyed him, doing as the LORD had commanded Moses.

10 Never since has there arisen a prophet in Israel like Moses, whom the LORD knew face to face. 11 He was unequaled for all the signs and wonders that the LORD sent him to perform in the land of Egypt, against Pharaoh and all his servants and his entire land, 12 and for all the mighty deeds and all the terrifying displays of power that Moses performed in the sight of all Israel.

REVISED ENGLISH BIBLE

son of Nun was filled with the spirit of wisdom, for Moses had laid his hands on him. The Israelites listened to him and did what the LORD had commanded Moses.

10 There has never yet risen in Israel a prophet like Moses, whom the LORD knew face to face: 11 remember all the signs and portents which the LORD sent him to show in Egypt to Pharaoh and all his servants and the whole land; 12 remember the strong hand of Moses and the awesome deeds which he did in the sight of all Israel.

9 Now Joshua, son of Nun, was filled with the spirit of wisdom, since Moses had laid his hands upon him; and so the Israelites gave him their obedience, thus carrying out the LORD's command to Moses.

10 Since then no prophet has arisen in Israel like Moses, whom the LORD knew face to face. 11 He had no equal in all the signs and wonders the LORD sent him to perform in the land of Egypt against Pharaoh and all his servants and against all his land, 12 and for the might and the terrifying power that Moses exhibited in the sight of all Israel.

9 Joshua son of Nun was filled with the spirit of wisdom, for Moses had laid his hands on him, and him the Israelites obeyed, carrying out the order which Yahweh had given to Moses.

10 Since then, there has never been such a prophet in Israel as Moses, the man whom Yahweh knew face to face. 11 What signs and wonders Yahweh caused him to perform in Egypt against Pharaoh, all his servants and his whole country! 12 How mighty the hand and great the fear that Moses wielded in the eyes of all Israel!

THE BOOK OF

Joshua

Joshua

1 After the death of Moses the servant of the LORD, the LORD spoke to Joshua son of Nun, Moses' assistant, saying, 2 "My servant Moses is dead. Now proceed to cross the Jordan, you and all this people, into the land that I am giving to them, to the Israelites. 3 Every place that the sole of your foot will tread upon I have given to you, as I promised to Moses. 4 From the wilderness and the Lebanon as far as the great river, the river Euphrates, all the land of the Hittites, to the Great Sea in the west shall be your territory. 5 No one shall be able to stand against you all the days of your life. As I was with Moses, so I will be with you; I will not fail you or forsake you. 6 Be strong and courageous; for you shall put this people in possession of the land that I swore to their ancestors to give them. 7 Only be strong and very courageous, being careful to act in accordance with all the law that my servant Moses commanded you; do not turn from it to the right hand or to the left, so that you may be successful wherever you go. 8 This book of the law shall not depart out of your mouth; you shall meditate on it day and night, so that you may be careful to act in accordance with all that is written in it. For then you shall make your way prosperous, and then you shall be successful. 9 I hereby command you: Be strong and courageous; do not be frightened or dismayed, for the LORD your God is with you wherever you go."

10 Then Joshua commanded the officers of the people, 11 "Pass through the camp, and command the people: 'Prepare your provisions; for in three days you are to cross over the Jordan, to go in to take possession of the land that the LORD your God gives you to possess.' "

12 To the Reubenites, the Gadites, and the half-tribe of Manasseh Joshua said, 13 "Remember the word that Moses the servant of the LORD commanded you, saying, 'The LORD your God is providing you a place of rest, and will give you this land.' 14 Your wives, your little ones, and your livestock shall remain in the land that Moses gave you beyond the Jordan. But all the warriors among you shall cross over armed before your kindred and shall help them, 15 until the LORD gives rest to your kindred as well as to you, and they too take possession of the land that the LORD your God is giving them. Then you shall return to your own land and take possession of it, the land that Moses the servant of the LORD gave you beyond the Jordan to the east."

16 They answered Joshua: "All that you have commanded us we will do, and wherever you send us we will go. 17 Just as we obeyed Moses in all things, so we will obey you. Only may the LORD your God be with you, as he was with Moses! 18 Whoever rebels against your orders and disobeys your words, whatever you command, shall be put to death. Only be strong and courageous."

2 Then Joshua son of Nun sent two men secretly from Shittim as spies, saying, "Go, view the land, especially Jericho." So they went, and entered the house of a prostitute whose name was Rahab, and spent the night there. 2 The king of Jericho was told, "Some Israelites have come here tonight to search out the land." 3 Then the king of Jericho sent orders to Rahab, "Bring out the men who have come to you, who entered your house, for they have come only to search out the whole land." 4 But the woman

1 AFTER the death of Moses the LORD's servant, the LORD said to Joshua son of Nun, Moses' assistant, 2 'Now that my servant Moses is dead, get ready to cross the Jordan, you and all this people, to the land which I am giving to the Israelites. 3 Every place where you set foot is yours: I have given it to you, as I promised Moses. 4 From the desert and this Lebanon to the great river, the Euphrates, and across all the Hittite country westwards to the Great Sea, all of it is to be your territory. 5 As long as you live no one will be able to stand against you: as I was with Moses, so shall I be with you; I shall not fail you or forsake you. 6 Be strong, be resolute; it is you who are to put this people in possession of the land which I swore to their forefathers I would give them. 7 Only be very strong and resolute. Observe diligently all the law which my servant Moses has given you; if you would succeed wherever you go, you must not swerve from it either to right or to left. 8 This book of the law must never be off your lips; you must keep it in mind day and night so that you may diligently observe everything that is written in it. Then you will prosper and be successful in everything you do. 9 This is my command: be strong, be resolute; do not be fearful or discouraged, for wherever you go the LORD your God is with you.'

10 Then Joshua instructed the officers 11 to pass through the camp and give this order to the people: 'Get food ready to take with you, for within three days you will be crossing this Jordan to occupy the country which the LORD your God is giving you to possess.'

12 To the Reubenites, the Gadites, and the half tribe of Manasseh, Joshua said, 13 'Remember what Moses the servant of the LORD commanded when he said, "The LORD your God will grant you security here and will give you this territory." 14 Your wives and dependants and your livestock may stay east of the Jordan in the territory which Moses has assigned you; but as for yourselves, all the warriors among you must cross over as a fighting force at the head of your kinsmen. You are to assist them, 15 until the LORD grants them security like you have, and they too take possession of the land which the LORD your God is giving them. You may then return and occupy the land which is your possession, the territory which Moses the servant of the LORD has assigned you east of the Jordan.' 16 They answered Joshua, 'Whatever you tell us, we shall do; wherever you send us, we shall go. 17 As we obeyed Moses in all things, so shall we obey you; and may the LORD your God be with you as he was with Moses! 18 Anyone who rebels against your command, and fails to carry out all your orders, is to be put to death. Only be strong and resolute.'

2 JOSHUA son of Nun sent out two spies secretly from Shittim with orders to reconnoitre the land and especially Jericho. The two men set off and came to the house of a prostitute named Rahab to spend the night there. 2 When it was reported to the king of Jericho that some Israelites had arrived that night to explore the country, 3 he sent word to Rahab: 'Bring out the men who have come to you and are now in your house, for they have come to spy out the whole country.' 4 The woman, who had taken the

---

1:4 **Great Sea:** or Mediterranean Sea.

THE BOOK OF
Joshua

1 After Moses, the servant of the LORD, had died, the LORD said to Moses' aid Joshua, son of Nun: 2 "My servant Moses is dead. So prepare to cross the Jordan here, with all the people, into the land I will give the Israelites. 3 As I promised Moses, I will deliver to you every place where you set foot. 4 Your domain is to be all the land of the Hittites, from the desert and from Lebanon east to the great river Euphrates and west to the Great Sea. 5 No one can withstand you while you live. I will be with you as I was with Moses: I will not leave you nor forsake you. 6 Be firm and steadfast, so that you may give this people possession of the land which I swore to their fathers I would give them. 7 Above all, be firm and steadfast, taking care to observe the entire law which my servant Moses enjoined on you. Do not swerve from it either to the right or to the left, that you may succeed wherever you go. 8 Keep this book of the law on your lips. Recite it by day and by night, that you may observe carefully all that is written in it; then you will successfully attain your goal. 9 I command you: be firm and steadfast! Do not fear nor be dismayed, for the LORD, your God, is with you wherever you go."

10 So Joshua commanded the officers of the people: 11 "Go through the camp and instruct the people, 'Prepare your provisions, for three days from now you shall cross the Jordan here, to march in and take possession of the land which the LORD, your God, is giving you.'"

12 Joshua reminded the Reubenites, the Gadites, and the half-tribe of Manasseh: 13 "Remember what Moses, the servant of the LORD, commanded you when he said, 'The LORD, your God, will permit you to settle in this land.' 14 Your wives, your children, and your livestock shall remain in the land Moses gave you here beyond the Jordan. But all the warriors among you must cross over armed ahead of your kinsmen and you must help them 15 until the LORD has settled your kinsmen, and they like you possess the land which the LORD, your God, is giving them. Afterward you may return and occupy your own land, which Moses, the servant of the LORD, has given you east of the Jordan." 16 "We will do all you have commanded us," they answered Joshua, "and we will go wherever you send us. We will obey you as completely as we obeyed Moses. 17 But may the LORD, your God, be with you as he was with Moses. 18 If anyone rebels against your orders and does not obey every command you give him, he shall be put to death. But be firm and steadfast."

2 Then Joshua, son of Nun, secretly sent out two spies from Shittim, saying, "Go, reconnoiter the land and Jericho." When the two reached Jericho, they went into the house of a harlot named Rahab, where they lodged. 2 But a report was brought to the king of Jericho that some Israelites had come there that night to spy out the land. 3 So the king of Jericho sent Rahab the order, "Put out the visitors who have entered your house, for they have come to spy out the entire land." 4 The woman had taken the two men and hid-

THE BOOK OF
Joshua

1 When Moses, servant of Yahweh, was dead, Yahweh spoke to Joshua son of Nun, Moses' adjutant. He said, 2 'Moses my servant is dead; go now and cross this Jordan, you and this whole people, into the country which I am giving to them (the Israelites). 3 Every place you tread with the soles of your feet I shall give you, as I declared to Moses that I would. 4 From the desert and the Lebanon, to the Great River, the Euphrates (the entire country of the Hittites), and as far as the Great Sea to westward, is to be your territory. 5 As long as you live, no one will be able to resist you; I shall be with you as I was with Moses; I shall not fail you or desert you.

6 'Be strong and stand firm, for you are the man to give this people possession of the land which I swore to their ancestors that I would give them. 7 Only be strong and stand very firm and be careful to keep the whole Law which my servant Moses laid down for you. Do not swerve from this either to right or to left, and then you will succeed wherever you go. 8 Have the book of this Law always on your lips; meditate on it day and night, so that you may carefully keep everything that is written in it. Then your undertakings will prosper, then you will have success. 9 Have I not told you: Be strong and stand firm? Be fearless and undaunted, for go where you may, Yahweh your God is with you.'

10 Joshua then gave the people's officials this instruction: 11 'Go through the camp and give the people this order, "Make provisions ready, for in three days' time you will cross this Jordan and go on to take possession of the land which Yahweh your God is giving you as your own."' 12 Joshua then said to the Reubenites and Gadites and the half-tribe of Manasseh, 13 'Remember the order given you by Moses, servant of Yahweh: Yahweh your God, in bringing you to rest, has given you the land where we are. 14 Your wives, your little ones and your cattle must stay in the country given you by Moses beyond the Jordan. But all you fighting men must cross in battle formation at the head of your brothers and help them, 15 until they too have taken possession of the land which Yahweh your God is giving to them. Then you may go back and take possession of the land which belongs to you and which Moses, servant of Yahweh, has given you on the eastern side of the Jordan.' 16 They answered Joshua, 'We will do whatever you order us, and wherever you send us we will go. 17 We obeyed Moses in everything, and now we will obey you. Only may Yahweh your God be with you as he was with Moses! 18 If anyone rebels against your orders or will not listen to your commands, let him be put to death. Only be strong and stand firm.'

2 From Shittim, Joshua son of Nun secretly sent two men to reconnoitre. He said, 'Go and explore the country and Jericho.' They left; they went into the house of a prostitute called Rahab, to spend the night there. 2 The king of Jericho was told, 'Some men have come here tonight from the Israelites, to reconnoitre the country.' 3 The king of Jericho then sent a message to Rahab, 'Send out the men who came to you and are lodging in your house, for they have come to reconnoitre the whole country.' 4 But the

NEW REVISED STANDARD VERSION

took the two men and hid them. Then she said, "True, the men came to me, but I did not know where they came from. 5 And when it was time to close the gate at dark, the men went out. Where the men went I do not know. Pursue them quickly, for you can overtake them." 6 She had, however, brought them up to the roof and hidden them with the stalks of flax that she had laid out on the roof. 7 So the men pursued them on the way to the Jordan as far as the fords. As soon as the pursuers had gone out, the gate was shut.

8 Before they went to sleep, she came up to them on the roof 9 and said to the men: "I know that the LORD has given you the land, and that dread of you has fallen on us, and that all the inhabitants of the land melt in fear before you. 10 For we have heard how the LORD dried up the water of the Red Sea*a* before you when you came out of Egypt, and what you did to the two kings of the Amorites that were beyond the Jordan, to Sihon and Og, whom you utterly destroyed. 11 As soon as we heard it, our hearts melted, and there was no courage left in any of us because of you. The LORD your God is indeed God in heaven above and on earth below. 12 Now then, since I have dealt kindly with you, swear to me by the LORD that you in turn will deal kindly with my family. Give me a sign of good faith 13 that you will spare my father and mother, my brothers and sisters, and all who belong to them, and deliver our lives from death." 14 The men said to her, "Our life for yours! If you do not tell this business of ours, then we will deal kindly and faithfully with you when the LORD gives us the land."

15 Then she let them down by a rope through the window, for her house was on the outer side of the city wall and she resided within the wall itself. 16 She said to them, "Go toward the hill country, so that the pursuers may not come upon you. Hide yourselves there three days, until the pursuers have returned; then afterward you may go your way." 17 The men said to her, "We will be released from this oath that you have made us swear to you 18 if we invade the land and you do not tie this crimson cord in the window through which you let us down, and you do not gather into your house your father and mother, your brothers, and all your family. 19 If any of you go out of the doors of your house into the street, they shall be responsible for their own death, and we shall be innocent; but if a hand is laid upon any who are with you in the house, we shall bear the responsibility for their death. 20 But if you tell this business of ours, then we shall be released from this oath that you made us swear to you." 21 She said, "According to your words, so be it." She sent them away and they departed. Then she tied the crimson cord in the window.

22 They departed and went into the hill country and stayed there three days, until the pursuers returned. The pursuers had searched all along the way and found nothing. 23 Then the two men came down again from the hill country. They crossed over, came to Joshua son of Nun, and told him all that had happened to them. 24 They said to Joshua, "Truly the LORD has given all the land into our hands; moreover all the inhabitants of the land melt in fear before us."

3 Early in the morning Joshua rose and set out from Shittim with all the Israelites, and they came to the Jordan. They camped there before crossing over. 2 At the end of three days the officers went through the camp 3 and commanded the people, "When you see the ark of the covenant of the LORD your God being carried by the levitical priests, then you shall set out from your place. Follow it,

REVISED ENGLISH BIBLE

two men and hidden them, replied, 'True, the men did come to me, but I did not know where they came from; 5 and at nightfall when it was time to shut the gate, they had gone. I do not know where they were going, but if you hurry after them you may overtake them.' 6 In fact, she had brought them up on to the roof and concealed them among the stalks of flax which she had laid out there in rows. 7 The messengers went in pursuit of them in the direction of the fords of the Jordan, and as soon as they had gone out the gate was closed.

8 The men had not yet settled down, when Rahab came up to them on the roof, 9 and said, 'I know that the LORD has given the land to you; terror of you has fallen upon you, and the whole country is panic-stricken. 10 We have heard how the LORD dried up the waters of the Red Sea before you when you came out of Egypt, and what you did to Sihon and Og, the two Amorite kings beyond the Jordan, for you destroyed them. 11 When we heard this, our courage failed; your coming has left no spirit in any of us; for the LORD your God is God in heaven above and on earth below. 12 Swear to me by the LORD that you will keep faith with my family, as I have kept faith with you. Give me a token of good faith; 13 promise that you will spare the lives of my father and mother, my brothers and sisters, and all who belong to them, and preserve us from death.' 14 The men replied, 'Our lives for yours, so long as you do not betray our business. When the LORD gives us the country, we shall deal loyally and faithfully by you.'

15 She then let them down through a window by a rope; for the house where she lived was on an angle of the wall. 16 'Make for the hills,' she said, 'or the pursuers will come upon you. Hide there for three days until they return; then go on your way.' 17 The men warned her that, unless she did what they told her, they would be free from the oath she had made them take. 18 'When we invade the land,' they said, 'you must fasten this strand of scarlet cord in the window through which you have lowered us, and get everybody together here inside the house, your father and mother, your brothers, and all your family. 19 Should anybody go out of doors into the street, his blood will be on his own head; we shall be free of the oath. But if a hand is laid on anyone who stays indoors with you, his blood be on our heads! 20 Remember too that, if you betray our business, then we shall be free of the oath you have made us take.' 21 'It shall be as you say,' she replied, and sent them on their way. When they had gone, she fastened the strand of scarlet cord in the window.

22 The men made their way into the hills and stayed there for three days until the pursuers returned. They had searched all along the road, but had not found them. 23 The two men then came down from the hills and crossed the river. When they joined up with Joshua son of Nun, they reported all that had happened to them. 24 'The LORD has delivered the whole country into our hands,' they said; 'the inhabitants are all panic-stricken at our approach.'

3 Early in the morning Joshua and all the Israelites set out from Shittim and came to the Jordan, where they encamped before crossing. 2 At the end of three days the officers passed through the camp, 3 giving the people these instructions: 'When you see the Ark of the Covenant of the LORD your God being carried forward by the levitical priests, then you too must leave your positions and set out.

2:4 **them:** *prob. rdg; Heb.* him.   2:10 **Red Sea:** *or* sea of Reeds.
2:22 **three days . . . found them:** *or* three days while the pursuers scoured the land and searched all along the road, but did not find them.

a Or Sea of Reeds

den them, so she said, "True, the men you speak of came to me, but I did not know where they came from. 5 At dark, when it was time for the gate to be shut, they left, and I do not know where they went. You will have to pursue them immediately to overtake them." 6 Now, she had led them to the roof, and hidden them among her stalks of flax spread out there. 7 But the pursuers set out along the way to the fords of the Jordan, and once they had left, the gate was shut.

8 Before the spies fell asleep, Rahab came to them on the roof 9 and said: "I know that the LORD has given you the land, that a dread of you has come upon us, and that all the inhabitants of the land are overcome with fear of you. 10 For we have heard how the LORD dried up the waters of the Red Sea before you when you came out of Egypt, and how you dealt with Sihon and Og, the two kings of the Amorites beyond the Jordan, whom you doomed to destruction. 11 At these reports, we are disheartened; everyone is discouraged because of you, since the LORD, your God, is God in heaven above and on earth below. 12 Now then, swear to me by the LORD that, since I am showing kindness to you, you in turn will show kindness to my family; and give me an unmistakable token 13 that you are to spare my father and mother, brothers and sisters, and all their kin, and save us from death." 14 "We pledge our lives for yours," the men answered her. "If you do not betray this errand of ours, we will be faithful in showing kindness to you when the LORD gives us the land."

15 Then she let them down through the window with a rope; for she lived in a house built into the city wall. 16 "Go up into the hill country," she suggested to them, "that your pursuers may not find you. Hide there for three days, until they return; then you may proceed on your way." 17 The men answered her, "This is how we will fulfill the oath you made us take: 18 When we come into the land, tie this scarlet cord in the window through which you are letting us down; and gather your father and mother, your brothers and all your family into your house. 19 Should any of them pass outside the doors of your house, he will be responsible for his own death, and we shall be guiltless. But we shall be responsible if anyone in the house with you is harmed. 20 If, however, you betray this errand of ours, we shall be quit of the oath you have made us take." 21 "Let it be as you say," she replied, and bade them farewell. When they were gone, she tied the scarlet cord in the window.

22 They went up into the hills, where they stayed three days until their pursuers, who had sought them all along the road without finding them, returned. 23 Then the two came back down from the hills, crossed the Jordan to Joshua, son of Nun, and reported all that had befallen them. 24 They assured Joshua, "The LORD has delivered all this land into our power; indeed, all the inhabitants of the land are overcome with fear of us."

3 Early the next morning, Joshua moved with all the Israelites from Shittim to the Jordan, where they lodged before crossing over. 2 Three days later the officers went through the camp 3 and issued these instructions to the people: "When you see the ark of the covenant of the LORD, your God, which the levitical priests will carry, you must also break camp and follow it, 4 that you may know the way

woman took the two men and hid them. 'It is true,' she said, 'the men did come to me, but I did not know where they came from. 5 When the city gate was about to be closed at nightfall, the men went out and I cannot say where they have gone. Follow them quickly and you will overtake them.'

6 She had taken them up to the roof and hidden them under some stalks of flax which she had laid out there. 7 The men hurried in pursuit of them towards the Jordan, as far as the fords, and the gate was shut once the pursuers had gone through.

8 The two men had not yet settled down for the night when Rahab came up to them on the roof. 9 She said to them, 'I know that Yahweh has given you this country, that we are afraid of you and that everyone living in this country has been seized with terror at your approach; 10 for we have heard how Yahweh dried up the Sea of Reeds before you when you came out of Egypt and what you did to the two Amorite kings across the Jordan, Sihon and Og, whom you put under the curse of destruction. 11 When we heard this, our hearts failed us, and now no one has any courage left to resist you, since Yahweh your God is God both in heaven above and on earth beneath. 12 So, swear to me now by Yahweh, since I have been kind to you, 13 that you in your turn will be kind to my father's family; and give me a sure sign of this: that you will spare the lives of my father and mother, my brothers and sisters and all who belong to them, and will preserve us from death.'

14 The men replied, 'We pledge you our lives, provided that you say nothing about our mission. When Yahweh has given us the country, we shall treat you kindly and faithfully.' 15 She then let them down from the window on a rope, as her house was against the city wall and she actually lived in the wall. 16 'Make for the hills,' she said, 'or you may run into your pursuers. Hide there for three days, until your pursuers have come back, and then go on your way.' 17 The men said, 'This is how we shall fulfil the oath which you have made us swear: 18 when we invade the country, you must tie this scarlet cord to the window from which you let us down, and collect your father, mother, brothers and entire family inside your house. 19 If anyone goes out of the doors of your house into the street, his blood will be on his own head and we shall not be to blame; but the blood of all staying inside the house with you will be on our heads if a hand is laid on any of them. 20 But if you divulge our mission in the meanwhile, we shall be free of the oath which you have made us swear.' 21 She replied, 'Let it be as you say.' She let them go, and they left. She then tied the scarlet cord to the window.

22 They left and made for the hills. They stayed there for three days, until their pursuers had gone home, having scoured the countryside without finding them. 23 The two men then came down again from the hills, crossed over and, going to Joshua son of Nun, told him everything that had happened to them. 24 To Joshua they said, 'Yahweh has put the whole country at our mercy, and its inhabitants are all panic-stricken at our approach.'

3 Early in the morning, Joshua struck camp and set out from Shittim with all the Israelites. They went as far as the Jordan and there they camped before they crossed. 2 Three days later, the officials went through the camp 3 and gave the people these instructions, 'When you see the ark of the covenant of Yahweh your God being carried by the levitical priests, you will leave your position and follow it,

4 so that you may know the way you should go, for you have not passed this way before. Yet there shall be a space between you and it, a distance of about two thousand cubits; do not come any nearer to it." 5 Then Joshua said to the people, "Sanctify yourselves; for tomorrow the LORD will do wonders among you." 6 To the priests Joshua said, "Take up the ark of the covenant, and pass on in front of the people." So they took up the ark of the covenant and went in front of the people.

7 The LORD said to Joshua, "This day I will begin to exalt you in the sight of all Israel, so that they may know that I will be with you as I was with Moses. 8 You are the one who shall command the priests who bear the ark of the covenant, 'When you come to the edge of the waters of the Jordan, you shall stand still in the Jordan.' " 9 Joshua then said to the Israelites, "Draw near and hear the words of the LORD your God." 10 Joshua said, "By this you shall know that among us is the living God who without fail will drive out from before you the Canaanites, Hittites, Hivites, Perizzites, Girgashites, Amorites, and Jebusites: 11 the ark of the covenant of the Lord of all the earth is going to pass before you into the Jordan. 12 So now select twelve men from the tribes of Israel, one from each tribe. 13 When the soles of the feet of the priests who bear the ark of the LORD, the Lord of all the earth, rest in the waters of the Jordan, the waters of the Jordan flowing from above shall be cut off; they shall stand in a single heap."

14 When the people set out from their tents to cross over the Jordan, the priests bearing the ark of the covenant were in front of the people. 15 Now the Jordan overflows all its banks throughout the time of harvest. So when those who bore the ark had come to the Jordan, and the feet of the priests bearing the ark were dipped in the edge of the water, 16 the waters flowing from above stood still, rising up in a single heap far off at Adam, the city that is beside Zarethan, while those flowing toward the sea of the Arabah, the Dead Sea,b were wholly cut off. Then the people crossed over opposite Jericho. 17 While all Israel were crossing over on dry ground, the priests who bore the ark of the covenant of the LORD stood on dry ground in the middle of the Jordan, until the entire nation finished crossing over the Jordan.

4 When the entire nation had finished crossing over the Jordan, the LORD said to Joshua: 2 "Select twelve men from the people, one from each tribe, 3 and command them, 'Take twelve stones from here out of the middle of the Jordan, from the place where the priests' feet stood, carry them over with you, and lay them down in the place where you camp tonight.' " 4 Then Joshua summoned the twelve men from the Israelites, whom he had appointed, one from each tribe. 5 Joshua said to them, "Pass on before the ark of the LORD your God into the middle of the Jordan, and each of you take up a stone on his shoulder, one for each of the tribes of the Israelites, 6 so that this may be a sign among you. When your children ask in time to come, 'What do those stones mean to you?' 7 then you shall tell them that the waters of the Jordan were cut off in front of the ark of the covenant of the LORD. When it crossed over the Jordan, the waters of the Jordan were cut off. So these stones shall be to the Israelites a memorial forever."

8 The Israelites did as Joshua commanded. They took up twelve stones out of the middle of the Jordan, according to the number of the tribes of the Israelites, as the LORD told Joshua, carried them over with them to the place where they camped, and laid them down there. 9 (Joshua set up twelve stones in the middle of the Jordan, in the place where the feet of the priests bearing the ark of the covenant had stood; and they are there to this day.)

b Heb Salt Sea

Follow it, 4 but do not go close to it; keep some distance behind, about two thousand cubits. It will show you the route you are to follow, for you have not travelled this way before.' 5 Joshua said to the people, 'Consecrate yourselves, for tomorrow the LORD will perform a great miracle among you.' 6 To the priests he said, 'Lift the Ark of the Covenant and move ahead of the people.' So they lifted it up and went at the head of the people.

7 The LORD said to Joshua, 'Today I shall begin to exalt you in the eyes of all Israel, and they will know that I shall be with you as I was with Moses. 8 Give this order to the priests who carry the Ark of the Covenant: When you come to the edge of the waters of the Jordan, you are to take your stand in the river.'

9 Joshua said to the Israelites, 'Draw near and listen to the words of the LORD your God.' 10 He went on, 'By this you will know that the living God is among you and that he will without fail drive out before you the Canaanites, Hittites, Hivites, Perizzites, Girgashites, Amorites, and Jebusites: 11 the Ark of the Covenant of the Lord of all the earth is to cross the Jordan at your head. 12 Choose now twelve men from the tribes of Israel, one from each tribe. 13 As soon as the priests carrying the Ark of the LORD, the Lord of all the earth, set foot in the waters of the Jordan, then the waters of the Jordan will be cut off; the water coming down from upstream will stand piled up like a bank.'

14 The people set out from their encampment to cross the Jordan, with the priests in front carrying the Ark of the Covenant. 15 Now the Jordan is in full flood in all its reaches throughout the time of harvest, but as soon as the priests reached the Jordan and their feet touched the water at the edge, 16 the water flowing down from upstream was brought to a standstill; it piled up like a bank for a long way back, as far as Adam, a town near Zarethan. The water coming down to the sea of the Arabah, the Dead Sea, was completely cut off, and the people crossed over opposite Jericho. 17 The priests carrying the Ark of the Covenant of the LORD stood firmly on the dry bed in the middle of the river, and all Israel passed over on dry ground, until the whole nation had completed the crossing of the Jordan.

4 WHEN the whole nation had completed the crossing of the Jordan, the LORD said to Joshua, 2 'Choose twelve men from the people, one from each tribe, 3 and order them to take up twelve stones from this place in the middle of the Jordan, where the priests have taken their stand. They are to carry the stones across and place them in the camp where you spend the night.' 4 Joshua summoned the twelve Israelites whom he had appointed, one man from each tribe, 5 and said to them, 'Go over in front of the Ark of the LORD your God as far as the middle of the Jordan, and let each of you take up a stone on his shoulder, one for each of the tribes of Israel. 6 These stones are to stand as a memorial among you: in days to come, when your children ask what these stones mean, 7 you will tell them how the waters of the Jordan were cut off before the Ark of the Covenant of the LORD; when it crossed the Jordan the waters of the Jordan were cut off. These stones will always be a reminder to the Israelites.' 8 The Israelites did as Joshua had commanded: they took up twelve stones from the middle of the Jordan, as the LORD had instructed Joshua, one for each of the tribes of Israel, carried them across to the camp, and placed them there.

9 Joshua also erected twelve stones in the middle of the Jordan at the place where the priests who carried the Ark of the Covenant had stood; they are there to this day. 10 The

3:16 Dead Sea: lit. Salt Sea.   4:10 fulfilled: so Gk; Heb. adds according to all that Moses commanded Joshua.

|

NEW AMERICAN BIBLE

to take, for you have not gone over this road before. But let there be a space of two thousand cubits between you and the ark. Do not come nearer to it." 5 Joshua also said to the people, "Sanctify yourselves, for tomorrow the LORD will perform wonders among you." 6 And he directed the priests to take up the ark of the covenant and go on ahead of the people; and they did so.

7 Then the LORD said to Joshua, "Today I will begin to exalt you in the sight of all Israel, that they may know I am with you, as I was with Moses. 8 Now command the priests carrying the ark of the covenant to come to a halt in the Jordan when they reach the edge of the waters."

9 So Joshua said to the Israelites, "Come here and listen to the words of the LORD, your God." 10 He continued: "This is how you will know that there is a living God in your midst, who at your approach will dispossess the Canaanites, Hittites, Hivites, Perizzites, Girgashites, Amorites and Jebusites. 11 The ark of the covenant of the LORD of the whole earth will precede you into the Jordan. 12 [Now choose twelve men, one from each of the tribes of Israel.] 13 When the soles of the feet of the priests carrying the ark of the LORD, the Lord of the whole earth, touch the water of the Jordan, it will cease to flow; for the water flowing down from upstream will halt in a solid bank."

14 The people struck their tents to cross the Jordan, with the priests carrying the ark of the covenant ahead of them. 15 No sooner had these priestly bearers of the ark waded into the waters at the edge of the Jordan, which overflows all its banks during the entire season of the harvest, 16 than the waters flowing from upstream halted, backing up in a solid mass for a very great distance indeed, from Adam, a city in the direction of Zarethan; while those flowing downstream toward the Salt Sea of the Arabah disappeared entirely. Thus the people crossed over opposite Jericho. 17 While all Israel crossed over on dry ground, the priests carrying the ark of the covenant of the LORD remained motionless on dry ground in the bed of the Jordan until the whole nation had completed the passage.

4 After the entire nation had crossed the Jordan, the LORD said to Joshua, 2 "Choose twelve men from the people, one from each tribe, 3 and instruct them to take up twelve stones from this spot in the bed of the Jordan where the priests have been standing motionless. Carry them over with you, and place them where you are to stay tonight."

4 Summoning the twelve men whom he had selected from among the Israelites, one from each tribe, 5 Joshua said to them: "Go to the bed of the Jordan in front of the ark of the LORD, your God; lift to your shoulders one stone apiece, so that they will equal in number the tribes of the Israelites. 6 In the future, these are to be a sign among you. When your children ask you what these stones mean to you, 7 you shall answer them, 'The waters of the Jordan ceased to flow before the ark of the covenant of the LORD when it crossed the Jordan.' Thus these stones are to serve as a perpetual memorial to the Israelites." 8 The twelve Israelites did as Joshua had commanded: they took up as many stones from the bed of the Jordan as there were tribes of the Israelites, and carried them along to the camp site, where they placed them, according to the LORD's direction. 9 Joshua also had twelve stones set up in the bed of the Jordan on the spot where the priests stood who were carrying the ark of the covenant. They are there to this day.

NEW JERUSALEM BIBLE

4b so that you may know which way to take, since you have never gone this way before. 4a Between you and the ark, however, keep a distance of about two thousand cubits: do not go near it.' 5 Joshua said to the people, 'Sanctify yourselves, since tomorrow Yahweh will work wonders among you.' 6 Joshua then said to the priests, 'Take up the ark of the covenant and cross at the head of the people.' They took up the ark of the covenant and moved to the head of the people.

7 Yahweh said to Joshua, 'This very day, I shall begin to make you great in the eyes of all Israel so that they will know that, as I was with Moses, so I shall be with you. 8 Now, give this order to the priests carrying the ark of the covenant, "When you have reached the brink of the waters of the Jordan, you must halt in the Jordan itself." ' 9 To the Israelites, Joshua then said, 'Come closer and hear the words of Yahweh your God.' 10 Joshua said, 'By this, you are to know that the living God is with you and without a doubt will expel the Canaanites, the Hittites, the Hivites, Perizzites, Girgashites, Amorites and Jebusites before you. 11 Look, the ark of the covenant of the Lord of the whole earth is about to move into the Jordan at your head. 12 Now choose twelve men from the tribes of Israel, one man from each tribe. 13 As soon as the priests carrying the ark of Yahweh, Lord of the whole earth, have set the soles of their feet in the waters of the Jordan, the waters of the Jordan will be cut off; the upper waters flowing down will stop as a single mass.'

14 Accordingly, when the people left their tents to cross the Jordan, the priests carried the ark of the covenant ahead of the people. 15 As soon as the bearers of the ark reached the Jordan and the feet of the priests carrying the ark touched the waters—the Jordan is in spate throughout the harvest season— 16 the upper waters stood still and formed a single mass over a great distance, at Adam, the town near Zarethan, while those flowing down to the Sea of the Arabah, the Salt Sea, were completely separated. The people crossed opposite Jericho. 17 The priests carrying the ark of the covenant of Yahweh stood firm on dry ground in mid-Jordan, while all Israel crossed on dry ground, until the whole nation had completed its crossing of the Jordan.

4 When the whole nation had finished crossing the Jordan, Yahweh spoke to Joshua and said, 2 'Choose twelve men from the people, one man from each tribe, and give them this order, 3 "Here, from mid-Jordan, from the place where the priests' feet were standing, take twelve stones; carry them with you and set them down in the camp where you pass the night." ' 4 Joshua called the twelve men whom he had selected from the Israelites, one man from each tribe, 5 and Joshua said to them, 'Go on ahead of the ark of Yahweh your God into mid-Jordan, and each of you take one stone on his shoulder, corresponding to the number of the tribes of Israel, 6 to make this a sign among you; and when, in the future, your children ask you, "What do these stones mean for you?" 7 you will then tell them, "The waters of the Jordan separated before the ark of the covenant of Yahweh; when it crossed the Jordan, the waters of the river separated. These stones are an everlasting reminder of this to the Israelites." ' 8 The Israelites did as Joshua ordered; they took twelve stones from mid-Jordan corresponding to the number of the tribes of Israel, as Yahweh had told Joshua; they carried them over to the camp and set them down there. 9 Joshua then erected twelve stones in mid-Jordan, on the spot where the feet of the priests carrying the ark of the covenant had stood; and they are still there today.

NEW REVISED STANDARD VERSION	REVISED ENGLISH BIBLE

10 The priests who bore the ark remained standing in the middle of the Jordan, until everything was finished that the LORD commanded Joshua to tell the people, according to all that Moses had commanded Joshua. The people crossed over in haste. 11 As soon as all the people had finished crossing over, the ark of the LORD, and the priests, crossed over in front of the people. 12 The Reubenites, the Gadites, and the half-tribe of Manasseh crossed over armed before the Israelites, as Moses had ordered them. 13 About forty thousand armed for war crossed over before the LORD to the plains of Jericho for battle.

14 On that day the LORD exalted Joshua in the sight of all Israel; and they stood in awe of him, as they had stood in awe of Moses, all the days of his life.

15 The LORD said to Joshua, 16 "Command the priests who bear the ark of the covenant,c to come up out of the Jordan." 17 Joshua therefore commanded the priests, "Come up out of the Jordan." 18 When the priests bearing the ark of the covenant of the LORD came up from the middle of the Jordan, and the soles of the priests' feet touched dry ground, the waters of the Jordan returned to their place and overflowed all its banks, as before.

19 The people came up out of the Jordan on the tenth day of the first month, and they camped in Gilgal on the east border of Jericho. 20 Those twelve stones, which they had taken out of the Jordan, Joshua set up in Gilgal, 21 saying to the Israelites, "When your children ask their parents in time to come, 'What do these stones mean?' 22 then you shall let your children know, 'Israel crossed over the Jordan here on dry ground.' 23 For the LORD your God dried up the waters of the Jordan for you until you crossed over, as the LORD your God did to the Red Sea,d which he dried up for us until we crossed over, 24 so that all the peoples of the earth may know that the hand of the LORD is mighty, and so that you may fear the LORD your God forever."

5 When all the kings of the Amorites beyond the Jordan to the west, and all the kings of the Canaanites by the sea, heard that the LORD had dried up the waters of the Jordan for the Israelites until they had crossed over, their hearts melted, and there was no longer any spirit in them, because of the Israelites.

2 At that time the LORD said to Joshua, "Make flint knives and circumcise the Israelites a second time." 3 So Joshua made flint knives, and circumcised the Israelites at Gibeath-haaraloth.e 4 This is the reason why Joshua circumcised them: all the males of the people who came out of Egypt, all the warriors, had died during the journey through the wilderness after they had come out of Egypt. 5 Although all the people who came out had been circumcised, yet all the people born on the journey through the wilderness after they had come out of Egypt had not been circumcised. 6 For the Israelites traveled forty years in the wilderness, until all the nation, the warriors who came out of Egypt, perished, not having listened to the voice of the LORD. To them the LORD swore that he would not let them see the land that he had sworn to their ancestors to give us, a land flowing with milk and honey. 7 So it was their children, whom he raised up in their place, that Joshua circumcised; for they were uncircumcised, because they had not been circumcised on the way.

8 When the circumcising of all the nation was done, they remained in their places in the camp until they were healed. 9 The LORD said to Joshua, "Today I have rolled away from you the disgrace of Egypt." And so that place is called Gilgalf to this day.

priests carrying the Ark remained standing in the middle of the Jordan until every command which the LORD had told Joshua to give the people was fulfilled. The people crossed hurriedly, 11 and when they had all got across, then the Ark of the LORD crossed, and the priests with it to lead the people. 12 At the head of the Israelites, there crossed over the Reubenites, the Gadites, and the half tribe of Manasseh, as a fighting force, as Moses had told them to do; 13 forty thousand strong, drafted for active service, they crossed over to the lowlands of Jericho in the presence of the LORD to do battle.

14 That day the LORD exalted Joshua in the eyes of all Israel, and the people revered him, as they had revered Moses all his life.

15 The LORD said to Joshua, 16 'Command the priests carrying the Ark of the Testimony to come up from the Jordan.' 17 Joshua passed the command to the priests; 18 and no sooner had the priests carrying the Ark of the Covenant of the LORD come up from the river bed, and set foot on dry land, than the waters of the Jordan returned to their course and filled up all its reaches as before.

19 On the tenth day of the first month the people went up from the Jordan and encamped in Gilgal in the district east of Jericho, 20 and there Joshua set up these twelve stones they had taken from the Jordan. 21 He said to the Israelites, 'In days to come, when your descendants ask their fathers what these stones mean, 22 you are to explain to them that Israel crossed this Jordan on dry land, 23 for the LORD your God dried up the waters of the Jordan in front of you until you had gone across, just as the LORD your God did at the Red Sea when he dried it up for us until we had crossed. 24 Thus all people on earth will know how strong is the hand of the LORD; and thus you will always stand in awe of the LORD your God.'

5 When all the Amorite kings to the west of the Jordan and all the Canaanite kings by the sea-coast heard how the LORD had dried up the waters of the Jordan before the advance of the Israelites until they had crossed, their courage failed them; there was no more spirit left in them because of the Israelites.

2 At that time the LORD said to Joshua, 'Fashion knives out of flint, and make Israel a circumcised people again.' 3 So Joshua made knives of flint, and the Israelites were circumcised at Gibeath-haaraloth. 4 This is why he had them circumcised: all the males who came out of Egypt, all the fighting men, had died in the wilderness on the journey from Egypt. 5 The people who came out of Egypt had all been circumcised, but not those who had been born in the wilderness during the journey. 6 The Israelites had travelled in the wilderness for forty years, until the whole generation, all the fighting men in the nation, died, who came out of Egypt and had disobeyed the LORD. The LORD swore that he would not allow any of these to see the land which he had sworn to their fathers to give us, a land flowing with milk and honey. 7 So it was their sons, whom the LORD raised up in their place, that Joshua circumcised; they were uncircumcised because they had not been circumcised on the journey. 8 When the circumcision of the whole nation was complete, they stayed where they were in camp until they had recovered. 9 The LORD then said to Joshua, 'Today I have rolled away from you the reproaches of the Egyptians.' Therefore the place is called Gilgal to this day.

---

c Or treaty, or testimony; Heb eduth   d Or Sea of Reeds   e That is the Hill of the Foreskins   f Related to Heb galal to roll

5:3 Gibeath-haaraloth: that is the Hill of Foreskins.   5:9 Gilgal: that is Rolling Stones.

NEW AMERICAN BIBLE

10 The priests carrying the ark remained in the bed of the Jordan until everything had been done that the LORD had commanded Joshua to tell the people. The people crossed over quickly, 11 and when all had reached the other side, the ark of the LORD, borne by the priests, also crossed to its place in front of them. 12 The Reubenites, Gadites, and half-tribe of Manasseh, armed, marched in the vanguard of the Israelites, as Moses had ordered. 13 About forty thousand troops equipped for battle passed over before the LORD to the plains of Jericho.

14 That day the LORD exalted Joshua in the sight of all Israel, and thenceforth during his whole life they respected him as they had respected Moses.

15 Then the LORD said to Joshua, 16 "Command the priests carrying the ark of the commandments to come up from the Jordan." 17 Joshua did so, 18 and when the priests carrying the ark of the covenant of the LORD had come up from the bed of the Jordan, as the soles of their feet regained the dry ground, the waters of the Jordan resumed their course and as before overflowed all its banks.

19 The people came up from the Jordan on the tenth day of the first month, and camped in Gilgal on the eastern limits of Jericho. 20 At Gilgal Joshua set up the twelve stones which had been taken from the Jordan, 21 saying to the Israelites, "In the future, when the children among you ask their fathers what these stones mean, 22 you shall inform them, 'Israel crossed the Jordan here on dry ground.' 23 For the LORD, your God, dried up the waters of the Jordan in front of you until you crossed over, just as the LORD, your God, had done at the Red Sea, which he dried up in front of us until we crossed over; 24 in order that all the peoples of the earth may learn that the hand of the LORD is mighty, and that you may fear the LORD, your God, forever."

5 When all the kings of Amorites to the west of the Jordan and all the kings of the Canaanites by the sea heard that the LORD had dried up the waters of the Jordan before the Israelites until they crossed over, they were disheartened and lost courage at their approach.

2 On this occasion the LORD said to Joshua, "Make flint knives and circumcise the Israelite nation for the second time." 3 So Joshua made flint knives and circumcised the Israelites at Gibeath-haaraloth, 4 under these circumstances: Of all the people who came out of Egypt, every man of military age had died in the desert during the journey after they left Egypt. 5 Though all the men who came out were circumcised, none of those born in the desert during the journey after the departure from Egypt were circumcised. 6 Now the Israelites had wandered forty years in the desert, until all the warriors among the people that came forth from Egypt died off because they had not obeyed the command of the LORD. For the LORD swore that he would not let them see the land flowing with milk and honey which he had promised their fathers he would give us. 7 It was the children whom he raised up in their stead whom Joshua circumcised, for these were yet with foreskins, not having been circumcised on the journey. 8 When the rite had been performed, the whole nation remained in camp where they were, until they recovered. 9 Then the LORD said to Joshua, "Today I have removed the reproach of Egypt from you." Therefore the place is called Gilgal to the present day.

NEW JERUSALEM BIBLE

10 The priests carrying the ark stood still in mid-Jordan, until everything had been done that Yahweh had ordered Joshua to tell the people (in accordance with everything that Moses had ordered Joshua); and the people hurried across. 11 When the people had finished crossing, the ark of Yahweh then crossed, with the priests, to the head of the people. 12 The sons of Reuben, the sons of Gad and the half-tribe of Manasseh crossed in battle formation at the head of the Israelites, as Moses had told them. 13 Some forty thousand warriors in arms, they crossed in Yahweh's presence, ready for battle, towards the plain of Jericho. 14 That day, Yahweh made Joshua great in the eyes of all Israel, who respected him as they had respected Moses, as long as he lived. 15 Yahweh said to Joshua, 16 'Order the priests carrying the ark of the Testimony to come up out of the Jordan.' 17 And Joshua gave the order to the priests, 'Come up, out of the Jordan!' 18 Now, when the priests carrying the ark of the covenant of Yahweh came up out of mid-Jordan, no sooner had the soles of the priests' feet touched solid ground, than the waters of the Jordan returned to their bed and ran on, in spate as before.

19 It was the tenth day of the first month when the people came up from the Jordan and made their camp at Gilgal, on the eastern border of Jericho. 20 As regards those twelve stones, which they had taken from the Jordan, Joshua set them up at Gilgal. 21 He then said to the Israelites, 'When, in the future, your children ask their fathers, "What are these stones?" 22 you will explain to your children, "Israel crossed this Jordan dry-shod. 23 For Yahweh your God dried up the waters of the Jordan in front of you until you had crossed, just as Yahweh your God did to the Sea of Reeds, which he dried up before us until we had crossed it; 24 so that all the peoples of the earth may know how mighty the hand of Yahweh is, and always stand in awe of Yahweh your God." '

5 When all the kings of the Amorites living to westward across the Jordan, and all the kings of the Canaanites living on the seaboard, heard that Yahweh had dried up the waters of the Jordan before the Israelites until they had crossed, their hearts failed and they lost all courage to resist the Israelites.

2 At this time Yahweh said to Joshua, 'Make flint knives and circumcise the Israelites again (a second time). 3 Joshua made flint knives and circumcised the Israelites on the Hill of Foreskins.

4 The reason why Joshua circumcised them was this. All the males of the people who had come out of Egypt of age to bear arms had died in the desert on their journey after leaving Egypt. 5 Now, all the people who came out had been circumcised; but none of those born in the desert, during the journey, after leaving Egypt, had been circumcised; 6 for the Israelites walked the desert for forty years, until the whole nation had died out, that is, the men who had come out of Egypt of age to bear arms; they had not obeyed the voice of Yahweh, and Yahweh had sworn to them never to let them see the land which he had sworn to their ancestors that he would give us, a land flowing with milk and honey. 7 But in place of these he set their sons, and these were the ones whom Joshua circumcised; they were uncircumcised because they had not been circumcised during the journey. 8 When the circumcising of the whole nation was finished, they stayed resting in the camp till they were well again. 9 Yahweh then said to Joshua, 'Today I have taken the shame of Egypt away from you.' Hence, the place has been called Gilgal[a] ever since.

---

a 5 Word-play with galloti (= I have taken away). In fact Gilgal = circle, cf. 4:20.

NEW REVISED STANDARD VERSION	REVISED ENGLISH BIBLE

NEW REVISED STANDARD VERSION

10 While the Israelites were camped in Gilgal they kept the passover in the evening on the fourteenth day of the month in the plains of Jericho. 11 On the day after the passover, on that very day, they ate the produce of the land, unleavened cakes and parched grain. 12 The manna ceased on the day they ate the produce of the land, and the Israelites no longer had manna; they ate the crops of the land of Canaan that year.

13 Once when Joshua was by Jericho, he looked up and saw a man standing before him with a drawn sword in his hand. Joshua went to him and said to him, "Are you one of us, or one of our adversaries?" 14 He replied, "Neither; but as commander of the army of the LORD I have now come." And Joshua fell on his face to the earth and worshiped, and he said to him, "What do you command your servant, my lord?" 15 The commander of the army of the LORD said to Joshua, "Remove the sandals from your feet, for the place where you stand is holy." And Joshua did so.

6 Now Jericho was shut up inside and out because of the Israelites; no one came out and no one went in. 2 The LORD said to Joshua, "See, I have handed Jericho over to you, along with its king and soldiers. 3 You shall march around the city, all the warriors circling the city once. Thus you shall do for six days, 4 with seven priests bearing seven trumpets of rams' horns before the ark. On the seventh day you shall march around the city seven times, the priests blowing the trumpets. 5 When they make a long blast with the ram's horn, as soon as you hear the sound of the trumpet, then all the people shall shout with a great shout; and the wall of the city will fall down flat, and all the people shall charge straight ahead." 6 So Joshua son of Nun summoned the priests and said to them, "Take up the ark of the covenant, and have seven priests carry seven trumpets of rams' horns in front of the ark of the LORD." 7 To the people he said, "Go forward and march around the city; have the armed men pass on before the ark of the LORD."

8 As Joshua had commanded the people, the seven priests carrying the seven trumpets of rams' horns before the LORD went forward, blowing the trumpets, with the ark of the covenant of the LORD following them. 9 And the armed men went before the priests who blew the trumpets; the rear guard came after the ark, while the trumpets blew continually. 10 To the people Joshua gave this command: "You shall not shout or let your voice be heard, nor shall you utter a word, until the day I tell you to shout. Then you shall shout." 11 So the ark of the LORD went around the city, circling it once; and they came into the camp, and spent the night in the camp.

12 Then Joshua rose early in the morning, and the priests took up the ark of the LORD. 13 The seven priests carrying the seven trumpets of rams' horns before the ark of the LORD passed on, blowing the trumpets continually. The armed men went before them, and the rear guard came after the ark of the LORD, while the trumpets blew continually. 14 On the second day they marched around the city once and then returned to the camp. They did this for six days.

15 On the seventh day they rose early, at dawn, and marched around the city in the same manner seven times. It was only on that day that they marched around the city seven times. 16 And at the seventh time, when the priests had blown the trumpets, Joshua said to the people, "Shout! For the LORD has given you the city. 17 The city and all that

REVISED ENGLISH BIBLE

10 While the Israelites were encamped in Gilgal, at sunset on the fourteenth day of the month they kept the Passover in the lowlands of Jericho. 11 On the day after the Passover they ate of the produce of the country, roasted grain and loaves made without leaven. 12 It was from that day, when they first ate the produce of the country, that the manna ceased. The Israelites got no more manna; that year they ate what had grown in the land of Canaan.

13 When Joshua was near Jericho he looked up and saw a man standing in front of him with a drawn sword in his hand. Joshua approached him and asked, 'Are you for us or for our enemies?' 14 The man replied, 'Neither! I am here as captain of the army of the LORD.' Joshua prostrated himself in homage, and said, 'What have you to say to your servant, my lord?' 15 The captain of the LORD's army answered, 'Remove your sandals, for the place where you are standing is holy'; and Joshua did so.

6 JERICHO was bolted and barred against the Israelites; no one could go out or in. 2 The LORD said to Joshua, 'See, I am delivering Jericho, its king, and his warriors into your hands. 3 You are to march round the city with all your fighting men, making the circuit of it once a day for six days. 4 Seven priests carrying seven trumpets made from rams' horns are to go ahead of the Ark. On the seventh day you are to march round the city seven times with the priests blowing their trumpets. 5 At the blast of the rams' horns, when you hear the trumpet sound, the whole army must raise a great shout; the city wall will collapse and the army will advance, every man straight ahead.'

6 Joshua son of Nun summoned the priests and gave them instructions: 'Take up the Ark of the Covenant; let seven priests with seven trumpets of ram's horn go ahead of the Ark of the LORD.' 7 Then he gave orders to the army: 'Move on, march round the city, and let the men who have been drafted go in front of the Ark of the LORD.'

8 After Joshua had issued this command to the army, the seven priests carrying the seven trumpets of ram's horn before the LORD moved on and blew the trumpets; the Ark of the Covenant of the LORD followed them. 9 The drafted men marched in front of the priests who blew the trumpets, and the rearguard came behind the Ark, the trumpets sounding as they marched. 10 But Joshua commanded the army not to shout, or to raise their voices or even utter a word, till the day when he would tell them to shout; then they were to give a mighty shout. 11 Thus he made the Ark of the LORD go round the city, making the circuit of it once, and then they returned to the camp and spent the night there. 12 Joshua rose early next morning, and the priests took up the Ark of the LORD. 13 The seven priests carrying the seven trumpets of ram's horn marched in front of the Ark of the LORD, blowing the trumpets as they went, with the drafted men in front of them and the rearguard following the Ark, the trumpets sounding as they marched. 14 They marched round the city once on the second day and returned to the camp; this they did for six days.

15 On the seventh day they rose at dawn and marched seven times round the city in the same way; that was the only day on which they marched round seven times. 16 The seventh time, as the priests blew the trumpets, Joshua said to the army, 'Shout! The LORD has given you the city.

5:14 **The man . . . I:** *so some MSS; others* The man said, 'No, I.

10 While the Israelites were encamped at Gilgal on the plains of Jericho, they celebrated the Passover on the evening of the fourteenth of the month. 11 On the day after the Passover they ate of the produce of the land in the form of unleavened cakes and parched grain. On that same day 12 after the Passover on which they ate of the produce of the land, the manna ceased. No longer was there manna for the Israelites, who that year ate of the yield of the land of Canaan.

13 While Joshua was near Jericho, he raised his eyes and saw one who stood facing him, drawn sword in hand. Joshua went up to him and asked, "Are you one of us or of our enemies?" 14 He replied, "Neither. I am the captain of the host of the LORD and I have just arrived." Then Joshua fell prostrate to the ground in worship, and said to him, "What has my lord to say to his servant?" 15 The captain of the host of the LORD replied to Joshua, "Remove your sandals from your feet, for the place on which you are standing is holy." And Joshua obeyed.

6 Now Jericho was in a state of siege because of the presence of the Israelites, so that no one left or entered. 2 And to Joshua the LORD said, "I have delivered Jericho and its king into your power. 3 Have all the soldiers circle the city, marching once around it. Do this for six days, 4 with seven priests carrying ram's horns ahead of the ark. On the seventh day march around the city seven times, and have the priests blow the horns. 5 When they give a long blast on the ram's horns and you hear that signal, all the people shall shout aloud. The wall of the city will collapse, and they will be able to make a frontal attack."

6 Summoning the priests, Joshua, son of Nun, then ordered them to take up the ark of the covenant with seven of the priests carrying ram's horns in front of the ark of the LORD. 7 And he ordered the people to proceed in a circle around the city, with the picked troops marching ahead of the ark of the LORD. 8 At this order they proceeded, with the seven priests who carried the ram's horns before the LORD blowing their horns, and the ark of the covenant of the LORD following them. 9 In front of the priests with the horns marched the picked troops; the rear guard followed the ark, and the blowing of horns was kept up continually as they marched. 10 But the people had been commanded by Joshua not to shout or make any noise or outcry until he gave the word: only then were they to shout. 11 So he had the ark of the LORD circle the city, going once around it, after which they returned to camp for the night.

12 Early the next morning, Joshua had the priests take up the ark of the LORD. 13 The seven priests bearing the ram's horns marched in front of the ark of the LORD, blowing their horns. Ahead of these marched the picked troops, while the rear guard followed the ark of the LORD, and the blowing of horns was kept up continually. 14 On this second day they again marched around the city once before returning to camp; and for six days in all they did the same.

15 On the seventh day, beginning at daybreak, they marched around the city seven times in the same manner; on that day only did they march around the city seven times. 16 The seventh time around, the priests blew the horns and Joshua said to the people, "Now shout, for the LORD has given you the city 17 and everything in it. It is under the

10 The Israelites pitched their camp at Gilgal and kept the Passover there on the fourteenth day of the month, at evening, in the plain of Jericho. 11 On the very next day after the Passover, they ate what the land produced, unleavened bread and roasted ears of corn. 12 The manna stopped the day after they had eaten the produce of the land. The Israelites from that year onwards ate the produce of Canaan and had no more manna.

13 Now when Joshua was near Jericho, he looked up and saw a man standing in front of him, grasping a naked sword. Joshua walked towards him and said to him, 'Are you on our side or on that of our enemies?' 14 He replied, 'On neither side. I have come now as the captain of the army of Yahweh.' Joshua fell on his face to the ground, worshipping him, and said, 'What has my Lord to say to his servant?' 15 The captain of the army of Yahweh answered Joshua, 'Take your sandals off your feet, for the place where you are standing is holy.' And Joshua did so.

6 b Now, Jericho had shut and barricaded its gates (against the Israelites): no one came out and no one went in. 2 Yahweh then said to Joshua, 'Look, I am putting Jericho, its picked troops and its king, at your mercy. 3 All you warriors must march round the city (go right round the city once, doing the same on six successive days. 4 Seven priests must carry seven ram's-horn trumpets in front of the ark. On the seventh day, you will go seven times round the city and the priests will blow their trumpets). 5 When the ram's horn sounds (when you hear the sound of the trumpet), the entire people must utter a mighty war cry and the city wall will collapse then and there; the people will then go into the assault, each man straight ahead.'

6 Joshua son of Nun summoned the priests and said to them, 'Take up the ark of the covenant, and let seven priests carry seven ram's-horn trumpets ahead of the ark of Yahweh.' 7 To the people he then said, 'Forward! March round the city, and let the vanguard march ahead of the ark of Yahweh!' 8 (Everything was done as Joshua had given orders to the people.) Seven priests, carrying seven ram's-horn trumpets ahead of Yahweh, moved forward blowing their trumpets; the ark of the covenant of Yahweh came behind them, 9 the vanguard marched ahead of the priests, who blew their trumpets, the rearguard followed behind the ark; the men marched, the trumpets sounded.

10 Joshua had given the people the following orders, 'Do not raise a war cry, do not let your voice be heard (not a word must pass your lips), until the day when I say, "Raise the war cry." That is when you must raise the war cry.' 11 He made the ark go round the city (going round it once), then they went back to camp, where they spent the night. 12 Joshua got up early, and the priests took up the ark of Yahweh. 13 Carrying the seven ram's-horn trumpets, the seven priests walked ahead of the ark of Yahweh, blowing their trumpets as they went, while the vanguard marched ahead of them and the rearguard behind the ark of Yahweh, and the march went on to the sound of the trumpet.

14 They marched once round the city (on the second day) and went back to camp; and so on for six days. 15 On the seventh day, they got up at dawn and marched (in the same manner) round the city seven times. (This was the only day when they marched round the city seven times.) 16 At the seventh time, the priests blew their trumpets and Joshua said to the people, 'Raise the war cry, for Yahweh has given you the city!

b 6 The Hebr. text is longer than the Gk, which omits passages given here in brackets.

NEW REVISED STANDARD VERSION

is in it shall be devoted to the LORD for destruction. Only Rahab the prostitute and all who are with her in her house shall live because she hid the messengers we sent. 18 As for you, keep away from the things devoted to destruction, so as not to covet*g* and take any of the devoted things and make the camp of Israel an object for destruction, bringing trouble upon it. 19 But all silver and gold, and vessels of bronze and iron, are sacred to the LORD; they shall go into the treasury of the LORD." 20 So the people shouted, and the trumpets were blown. As soon as the people heard the sound of the trumpets, they raised a great shout, and the wall fell down flat; so the people charged straight ahead into the city and captured it. 21 Then they devoted to destruction by the edge of the sword all in the city, both men and women, young and old, oxen, sheep, and donkeys.

22 Joshua said to the two men who had spied out the land, "Go into the prostitute's house, and bring the woman out of it and all who belong to her, as you swore to her." 23 So the young men who had been spies went in and brought Rahab out, along with her father, her mother, her brothers, and all who belonged to her—they brought all her kindred out—and set them outside the camp of Israel. 24 They burned down the city, and everything in it; only the silver and gold, and the vessels of bronze and iron, they put into the treasury of the house of the LORD. 25 But Rahab the prostitute, with her family and all who belonged to her, Joshua spared. Her family*h* has lived in Israel ever since. For she hid the messengers whom Joshua sent to spy out Jericho.

26 Joshua then pronounced this oath, saying,
"Cursed before the LORD be anyone who tries
   to build this city—this Jericho!
At the cost of his firstborn he shall lay its
   foundation,
   and at the cost of his youngest he shall set up
      its gates!"
27 So the LORD was with Joshua; and his fame was in all the land.

7 But the Israelites broke faith in regard to the devoted things: Achan son of Carmi son of Zabdi son of Zerah, of the tribe of Judah, took some of the devoted things; and the anger of the LORD burned against the Israelites.

2 Joshua sent men from Jericho to Ai, which is near Beth-aven, east of Bethel, and said to them, "Go up and spy out the land." And the men went up and spied out Ai. 3 Then they returned to Joshua and said to him, "Not all the people need go up; about two or three thousand men should go up and attack Ai. Since they are so few, do not make the whole people toil up there." 4 So about three thousand of the people went up there; and they fled before the men of Ai. 5 The men of Ai killed about thirty-six of them, chasing them from outside the gate as far as Shebarim and killing them on the slope. The hearts of the people melted and turned to water.

6 Then Joshua tore his clothes, and fell to the ground on his face before the ark of the LORD until the evening, he and the elders of Israel; and they put dust on their heads. 7 Joshua said, "Ah, Lord GOD! Why have you brought this people across the Jordan at all, to hand us over to the Amorites so as to destroy us? Would that we had been content to settle beyond the Jordan! 8 O Lord, what can I say, now that Israel has turned their backs to their enemies!

REVISED ENGLISH BIBLE

17 The city is to be under solemn ban: everything in it belongs to the LORD. No one is to be spared except the prostitute Rahab and everyone who is with her in the house, because she hid the men we sent. 18 And you must beware of coveting anything that is forbidden under the ban; you must take none of it for yourselves, or else you will put the Israelite camp itself under the ban and bring disaster on it. 19 All silver and gold, all the vessels of copper and iron, are to be holy; they belong to the LORD and must go into his treasury.'

20 So the trumpets were blown, and when the army heard the trumpets sound, they raised a great shout, and the wall collapsed. The army advanced on the city, every man straight ahead, and they captured it. 21 Under the ban they destroyed everything there; they put everyone to the sword, men and women, young and old, as well as the cattle, the sheep, and the donkeys.

22 The two men who had been sent out to reconnoitre the land were told by Joshua to go to the prostitute's house and bring out the woman and all who belonged to her, as they had sworn to do. 23 The young men went and brought out Rahab, her father and mother, her brothers, and all who belonged to her; they brought the whole family and placed them outside the Israelite camp. 24 The city and everything in it were then set on fire, except that the silver and gold and the vessels of copper and iron were deposited in the treasury of the LORD's house. 25 Thus Joshua spared the lives of Rahab the prostitute, her household, and all who belonged to her, because she had hidden the men whom Joshua had sent to reconnoitre Jericho; she and her family settled permanently among the Israelites.

26 At that time Joshua pronounced this curse:
'May the LORD's curse light on anyone who comes
   forward to rebuild this city of Jericho:
   the laying of its foundations shall cost him his
      eldest son,
   the setting up of its gates shall cost him his
      youngest.'

27 THE LORD was with Joshua, and his fame spread throughout the country.

7 In a perfidious act, however, Israelites violated the ban: Achan son of Carmi, son of Zabdi, son of Zerah, of the tribe of Judah, took some of the forbidden things, and the LORD's anger blazed out against Israel.

2 Joshua sent men from Jericho with orders to go up to Ai, near Beth-aven, east of Bethel, and reconnoitre the land. The men went and explored Ai, 3 and on their return reported to Joshua that there was no need for the whole army to move: 'Let some two or three thousand men advance to attack Ai. Do not have the whole army toil up there; the population is small.' 4 About three thousand troops went up, but they were routed by the men of Ai, 5 who killed some thirty-six of them; they chased the rest all the way from the gate to the Quarries and killed them on the pass. At this the courage of the people melted and flowed away like water.

6 Joshua and the elders of Israel tore their clothes and flung themselves face downwards on the ground; throwing dust on their heads, they lay in front of the Ark of the LORD till evening. 7 Joshua cried, 'Alas, Lord GOD, why did you bring this people across the Jordan just to hand us over to the Amorites to be destroyed? If only we had been content to settle on the other side of the Jordan! 8 I beseech you, Lord; what can I say, now that Israel has been routed by the enemy? 9 When the Canaanites and all the other natives of

---

6:18 **coveting:** *so Gk; Heb.* putting under the ban.   6:20 **So:** *so Gk; Heb. adds* the people shouted and.   7:5 **the Quarries:** *or* Shebarim.

---

g Gk: Heb *devote to destruction* Compare 7.21   *h* Heb *She*

LORD's ban. Only the harlot Rahab and all who are in the house with her are to be spared, because she hid the messengers we sent. 18 But be careful not to take, in your greed, anything that is under the ban; else you will bring upon the camp of Israel this ban and the misery of it. 19 All silver and gold, and the articles of bronze or iron, are sacred to the LORD. They shall be put in the treasury of the LORD."

20 As the horns blew, the people began to shout. When they heard the signal horn, they raised a tremendous shout. The wall collapsed, and the people stormed the city in a frontal attack and took it. 21 They observed the ban by putting to the sword all living creatures in the city: men and women, young and old, as well as oxen, sheep and asses.

22 Joshua directed the two men who had spied out the land, "Go into the harlot's house and bring out the woman with all her kin, as you swore to her you would do." 23 The spies entered and brought out Rahab, with her father, mother, brothers, and all her kin. Her entire family they led forth and placed them outside the camp of Israel. 24 The city itself they burned with all that was in it, except the silver, gold, and articles of bronze and iron, which were placed in the treasury of the house of the LORD. 25 Because Rahab the harlot had hidden the messengers whom Joshua had sent to reconnoiter Jericho, Joshua spared her with her family and all her kin, who continue in the midst of Israel to this day.

26 On that occasion Joshua imposed the oath: Cursed before the LORD be the man who attempts to rebuild this city, Jericho. He shall lose his first-born when he lays its foundation, and he shall lose his youngest son when he sets up its gates.

27 Thus the LORD was with Joshua so that his fame spread throughout the land.

7 But the Israelites violated the ban; Achan, son of Carmi, son of Zerah, son of Zara of the tribe of Judah, took goods that were under the ban, and the anger of the LORD flared up against the Israelites.

2 Joshua next sent men from Jericho to Ai, which is near Bethel on its eastern side, with instructions to go up and reconnoiter the land. When they had explored Ai, 3 they returned to Joshua and advised, "Do not send all the people up; if only about two or three thousand go up, they can overcome Ai. The enemy there are few; you need not call for an effort from all the people." 4 About three thousand of the people made the attack, but they were defeated by those at Ai, 5 who killed some thirty-six of them. They pressed them back across the clearing in front of the city gate till they broke ranks, and defeated them finally on the descent, so that the confidence of the people melted away like water.

6 Joshua, together with the elders of Israel, rent his garments and lay prostrate before the ark of the LORD until evening; and they threw dust on their heads. 7 "Alas, O Lord GOD," Joshua prayed, "why did you ever allow this people to pass over the Jordan, delivering us into the power of the Amorites, that they might destroy us? Would that we had been content to dwell on the other side of the Jordan. 8 Pray, Lord, what can I say, now that Israel has turned its back to its enemies? 9 When the Canaanites and the other

17 'The city and everyone in it must be devoted to Yahweh under the curse of destruction; the life of Rahab the prostitute alone must be spared, with all those with her in her house, since she hid the messengers we sent. 18 But beware of the curse of destruction, yourselves, for fear that, moved by greed, you take something lying under the curse; that would put the camp of Israel under the same curse and bring disaster on it. 19 All the silver and all the gold, everything made of bronze or iron, will be consecrated to Yahweh and put in his treasury.'

20 The people raised the war cry, the trumpets sounded. When the people heard the sound of the trumpet, they raised a mighty war cry and the wall collapsed then and there. At once the people stormed the city, each man going straight forward; and they captured the city. 21 They enforced the curse of destruction on everyone in the city: men and women, young and old, including the oxen, the sheep and the donkeys, slaughtering them all.

22 Joshua said to the two men who had reconnoitred the country, 'Go into the prostitute's house, and bring the woman out with all who belong to her, as you swore to her that you would.' 23 The young men who had been spies went and brought Rahab out, with her father and mother and brothers and all who belonged to her. They brought out all her clansmen too, and put them in a place of safety outside the camp of Israel.

24 They burned the city and everything inside it, except the silver, the gold and the things of bronze or iron; these they put into the treasury of Yahweh's house. 25 But Rahab the prostitute, her father's family and all who belonged to her, these Joshua spared. She is still living in Israel even today, for having hidden the messengers whom Joshua sent to reconnoitre Jericho.

26 At that time Joshua made them take this oath before Yahweh:

Accursed before Yahweh be the man who rises up
and rebuilds this city (Jericho)!
On his first-born will he lay its foundations,
on his youngest son set up its gates!

27 So Yahweh was with Joshua, whose fame spread throughout the country.

7 But the Israelites were unfaithful to the curse of destruction. Achan son of Carmi, son of Zabdi, son of Zerah, of the tribe of Judah, took something that fell under the curse of destruction, and the anger of Yahweh was aroused against the Israelites.

2 Now Joshua sent men from Jericho to Aic (which is near Beth-Aven), to the east of Bethel, having said to them, 'Go up and reconnoitre the country.' They went up and reconnoitred Ai. 3 Coming back to Joshua, they said, 'There is no need for the whole people to go up; let some two or three thousand go and attack Ai. Spare the whole people such an effort; there are only a few of them!' 4 Of the people, some three thousand marched up, but these broke before the people of Ai, 5 who killed some thirty-six of them and pursued them from the town gate as far as Shebarim, and on the slope cut them to pieces. The hearts of the people melted away and turned to water.

6 Joshua then tore his clothes and prostrated himself before the ark of Yahweh till nightfall; the elders of Israel did the same, and all poured dust on their heads. 7 And Joshua said, 'Alas, Lord Yahweh, why did you bother to bring this nation across the Jordan, if it was only to put us at the mercy of the Amorites and destroy us? If only we could have settled down on the other side of the Jordan! 8 Forgive me, Lord, but what can I say, now that Israel has turned tail on the enemy? 9 The Canaanites, all the inhabitants of the land,

c 7 The word *ai* = ruin, and the site is a spectacular ruin.

9 The Canaanites and all the inhabitants of the land will hear of it, and surround us, and cut off our name from the earth. Then what will you do for your great name?"

10 The LORD said to Joshua, "Stand up! Why have you fallen upon your face? 11 Israel has sinned; they have transgressed my covenant that I imposed on them. They have taken some of the devoted things; they have stolen, they have acted deceitfully, and they have put them among their own belongings. 12 Therefore the Israelites are unable to stand before their enemies; they turn their backs to their enemies, because they have become a thing devoted to destruction themselves. I will be with you no more, unless you destroy the devoted things from among you. 13 Proceed to sanctify the people, and say, 'Sanctify yourselves for tomorrow; for thus says the LORD, the God of Israel, "There are devoted things among you, O Israel; you will be unable to stand before your enemies until you take away the devoted things from among you." 14 In the morning therefore you shall come forward tribe by tribe. The tribe that the LORD takes shall come near by clans, the clan that the LORD takes shall come near by households, and the household that the LORD takes shall come near one by one. 15 And the one who is taken as having the devoted things shall be burned with fire, together with all that he has, for having transgressed the covenant of the LORD, and for having done an outrageous thing in Israel.' "

16 So Joshua rose early in the morning, and brought Israel near tribe by tribe, and the tribe of Judah was taken. 17 He brought near the clans of Judah, and the clan of the Zerahites was taken; and he brought near the clan of the Zerahites, family by family,*i* and Zabdi was taken. 18 And he brought near his household one by one, and Achan son of Carmi son of Zabdi son of Zerah, of the tribe of Judah, was taken. 19 Then Joshua said to Achan, "My son, give glory to the LORD God of Israel and make confession to him. Tell me now what you have done; do not hide it from me." 20 And Achan answered Joshua, "It is true; I am the one who sinned against the LORD God of Israel. This is what I did: 21 when I saw among the spoil a beautiful mantle from Shinar, and two hundred shekels of silver, and a bar of gold weighing fifty shekels, then I coveted them and took them. They now lie hidden in the ground inside my tent, with the silver underneath."

22 So Joshua sent messengers, and they ran to the tent; and there it was, hidden in his tent with the silver underneath. 23 They took them out of the tent and brought them to Joshua and all the Israelites; and they spread them out before the LORD. 24 Then Joshua and all Israel with him took Achan son of Zerah, with the silver, the mantle, and the bar of gold, with his sons and daughters, with his oxen, donkeys, and sheep, and his tent and all that he had; and they brought them up to the Valley of Achor. 25 Joshua said, "Why did you bring trouble on us? The LORD is bringing trouble on you today." And all Israel stoned him to death; they burned them with fire, cast stones on them, 26 and raised over him a great heap of stones that remains to this day. Then the LORD turned from his burning anger. Therefore that place to this day is called the Valley of Achor.*j*

the country hear of this, they will close in upon us and wipe us off the face of the earth. What will you do then for the honour of your great name?'

10 The LORD answered, 'Stand up; why lie prostrate on your face? 11 Israel has sinned: they have violated the covenant which I laid upon them; they have taken things forbidden under the ban; they have stolen them; they have concealed them by putting them among their own possessions. 12 That is why the Israelites cannot stand against their enemies: they are defeated because they have brought themselves under the ban. Unless you Israelites destroy every single thing among you that is forbidden under the ban, I shall be with you no longer.

13 'Get up and consecrate the people; tell them they must consecrate themselves for tomorrow. Say to them that these are the words of the LORD the God of Israel: You have among you forbidden things, Israel, and you will not be able to stand against your enemies until you have rid yourselves of these things. 14 In the morning come forward tribe by tribe, and the tribe which the LORD takes must come forward clan by clan; the clan which the LORD takes must come forward family by family, and the family which the LORD takes must come forward man by man. 15 The man who is taken as the harbourer of forbidden things must be burnt, he and all that is his, because he has violated the covenant of the LORD and committed an outrage in Israel.'

16 Early next morning Joshua rose and had Israel come forward tribe by tribe, and the tribe of Judah was taken; 17 he brought forward the clans of Judah, and the clan of Zerah was taken; then the clan of Zerah family by family, and the family of Zabdi was taken. 18 He had that family brought forward man by man, and Achan son of Carmi, son of Zabdi, son of Zerah, of the tribe of Judah, was taken. 19 Then Joshua said to Achan, 'My son, give honour to the LORD the God of Israel and make your confession to him. Tell me what you have done; hide nothing from me.' 20 Achan answered, 'It is true, I have sinned against the LORD the God of Israel. This is what I did: 21 among the booty I saw a fine mantle from Shinar, two hundred shekels of silver, and a bar of gold weighing fifty shekels; I coveted them and I took them. You will find them hidden in the ground inside my tent, with the silver underneath.' 22 Joshua sent messengers, who went straight to the tent, and there it was hidden in the tent with the silver underneath. 23 They took the things from the tent, brought them to Joshua and all the Israelites, and laid them out before the LORD.

24 Then Joshua and all Israel with him took Achan son of Zerah, with the silver, the mantle, and the bar of gold, together with his sons and daughters, his oxen, his donkeys, and his sheep, his tent, and everything he had, and they brought them up to the vale of Achor. 25 Joshua said, 'What trouble you have brought on us! Now the LORD will bring trouble on you.' Then all the Israelites stoned him to death; 26 and they raised over him a great cairn of stones which is there to this day. So the LORD's anger was abated. That is why to this day the place is called the vale of Achor.

---

i Mss Syr: MT *man by man*   *j* That is *Trouble*

7:17 **family by family:** *so some MSS; others* man by man. **the family of:** *so Gk; Heb. omits.*   7:24 **Achor:** *that is* Trouble. 7:25 **to death:** *so Gk; Heb. adds* and they burnt them with fire and pelted them with stones.

inhabitants of the land hear of it, they will close in around us and efface our name from the earth. What will you do for your great name?"

10 The LORD replied to Joshua: "Stand up. Why are you lying prostrate? 11 Israel has sinned: they have violated the covenant which I enjoined on them. They have stealthily taken goods subject to the ban, and have deceitfully put them in their baggage. 12 If the Israelites cannot stand up to their enemies, but must turn their back to them, it is because they are under the ban. I will not remain with you unless you remove from among you whoever has incurred the ban. 13 Rise, sanctify the people. Tell them to sanctify themselves before tomorrow, for the LORD, the God of Israel, says: You are under the ban, O Israel. You cannot stand up to your enemies until you remove from among you whoever has incurred the ban. 14 In the morning you must present yourselves by tribes. The tribe which the LORD designates shall come forward by clans; the clan which the LORD designates shall come forward by families; the family which the LORD designates shall come forward one by one. 15 He who is designated as having incurred the ban shall be destroyed by fire, with all that is his, because he has violated the covenant of the LORD and has committed a shameful crime in Israel."

16 Early the next morning Joshua had Israel come forward by tribes, and the tribe of Judah was designated. 17 Then he had the clans of Judah come forward, and the clan of Zerah was designated. He had the clan of Zerah come forward by families, and Zabdi was designated. 18 Finally he had that family come forward one by one, and Achan, son of Carmi, son of Zabdi, son of Zerah of the tribe of Judah, was designated. 19 Joshua said to Achan, "My son, give to the LORD, the God of Israel, glory and honor by telling me what you have done; do not hide it from me." 20 Achan answered Joshua, "I have indeed sinned against the LORD, the God of Israel. This is what I have done: 21 Among the spoils, I saw a beautiful Babylonian mantle, two hundred shekels of silver, and a bar of gold fifty shekels in weight; in my greed I took them. They are now hidden in the ground inside my tent, with the silver underneath." 22 The messengers whom Joshua sent hastened to the tent and found them hidden there, with the silver underneath. 23 They took them from the tent, brought them to Joshua and all the Israelites, and spread them out before the LORD.

24 Then Joshua and all Israel took Achan, son of Zerah, with the silver, the mantle, and the bar of gold, and with his sons and daughters, his ox, his ass and his sheep, his tent, and all his possessions, and led them off to the Valley of Achor. 25 Joshua said, "The LORD bring upon you today the misery with which you have afflicted us!" And all Israel stoned him to death 26 and piled a great heap of stones over him, which remains to the present day. Then the anger of the LORD relented. That is why the place is called the Valley of Achor to this day.

will hear of it; they will unite against us to wipe our name from the earth. And what will you do about your great Name then?'

10 Yahweh said to Joshua, 'Stand up! Why are you lying prostrate like this? 11 Israel has sinned; they have violated the covenant which I imposed on them. They have gone so far as to take what was under the curse of destruction, they have even stolen it; they have actually hidden it; they have put it in their baggage. 12 That is why the Israelites cannot stand up to their foes, why they have turned tail on their enemies: because they have come under the curse of destruction themselves. Unless you get rid of the object among you which has been put under the curse of destruction, I shall be with you no longer.'

13 'Get up, sanctify the people and say, "Sanctify yourselves for tomorrow, since Yahweh, the God of Israel, declares: The curse of destruction has now fallen on you, Israel; you will not be able to stand up to your enemies, until you have rid yourselves of that object which has been put under the curse of destruction. 14 Tomorrow morning, therefore, you will come forward tribe by tribe, and then the tribe which Yahweh selects by lot will come forward clan by clan, and the clan which Yahweh selects by lot will come forward family by family, and the family which Yahweh selects by lot will come forward man by man. 15 And the man indicated by lot as regards the object which has been put under the curse of destruction will be delivered to the flames, he and all his possessions, for having violated the covenant with Yahweh and for having committed an infamy in Israel." '

16 Joshua got up early; he made Israel come forward tribe by tribe, and the lot indicated the tribe of Judah. 17 He summoned the clans of Judah, and the lot indicated the clan of Zerah. He summoned the clan of Zerah, family by family, and the lot indicated Zabdi. 18 Joshua then summoned the family of Zabdi, man by man, and the lot indicated Achan son of Carmi, son of Zabdi, son of Zerah, of the tribe of Judah.

19 Joshua then said to Achan, 'My son, give glory to Yahweh, God of Israel, and confess; tell me what you have done and hide nothing from me.' 20 Achan replied to Joshua, 'Yes, I am the man who has sinned against Yahweh, God of Israel, and this is what I have done. 21 In the loot, I saw a fine robe from Shinar and two hundred shekels of silver and an ingot of gold weighing fifty shekels, I set my heart on them and I took them. They are hidden in the ground inside my tent, with the silver underneath.'

22 Joshua sent messengers; they ran to the tent, and the robe was indeed hidden in the tent, with the silver underneath. 23 They took the things out of the tent and, bringing them to Joshua and all the Israelites, laid them out before Yahweh.

24 Joshua then took Achan son of Zerah and led him up to the Vale of Achor, with the silver and the robe and the ingot of gold, his sons, his daughters, his oxen, his donkeys, his sheep, his goats, his tent and all his belongings. All Israel went with him.

25 Joshua said, 'Why have you brought misfortune on us? Today may Yahweh bring misfortune on you!' And all Israel stoned him to death (and they burned them and threw stones at them).

26 Over him, they raised a great mound of stones, which is still there today. Yahweh then relented from his fierce anger. That was why the place was called the Vale of Achor,[d] as it still is today.

d 7 Word-play with 'akar (= bring bad luck).

8 Then the LORD said to Joshua, "Do not fear or be dismayed; take all the fighting men with you, and go up now to Ai. See, I have handed over to you the king of Ai with his people, his city, and his land. 2 You shall do to Ai and its king as you did to Jericho and its king; only its spoil and its livestock you may take as booty for yourselves. Set an ambush against the city, behind it."

3 So Joshua and all the fighting men set out to go up against Ai. Joshua chose thirty thousand warriors and sent them out by night 4 with the command, "You shall lie in ambush against the city, behind it; do not go very far from the city, but all of you stay alert. 5 I and all the people who are with me will approach the city. When they come out against us, as before, we shall flee from them. 6 They will come out after us until we have drawn them away from the city; for they will say, 'They are fleeing from us, as before.' While we flee from them, 7 you shall rise up from the ambush and seize the city; for the LORD your God will give it into your hand. 8 And when you have taken the city, you shall set the city on fire, doing as the LORD has ordered; see, I have commanded you." 9 So Joshua sent them out; and they went to the place of ambush, and lay between Bethel and Ai, to the west of Ai; but Joshua spent that night in the camp. *k*

10 In the morning Joshua rose early and mustered the people, and went up, with the elders of Israel, before the people to Ai. 11 All the fighting men who were with him went up, and drew near before the city, and camped on the north side of Ai, with a ravine between them and Ai. 12 Taking about five thousand men, he set them in ambush between Bethel and Ai, to the west of the city. 13 So they stationed the forces, the main encampment that was north of the city and its rear guard west of the city. But Joshua spent that night in the valley. 14 When the king of Ai saw this, he and all his people, the inhabitants of the city, hurried out early in the morning to the meeting place facing the Arabah to meet Israel in battle; but he did not know that there was an ambush against him behind the city. 15 And Joshua and all Israel made a pretense of being beaten before them, and fled in the direction of the wilderness. 16 So all the people who were in the city were called together to pursue them, and as they pursued Joshua they were drawn away from the city. 17 There was not a man left in Ai or Bethel who did not go out after Israel; they left the city open, and pursued Israel.

18 Then the LORD said to Joshua, "Stretch out the sword that is in your hand toward Ai; for I will give it into your hand." And Joshua stretched out the sword that was in his hand toward the city. 19 As soon as he stretched out his hand, the troops in ambush rose quickly out of their place and rushed forward. They entered the city, took it, and at once set the city on fire. 20 So when the men of Ai looked back, the smoke of the city was rising to the sky. They had no power to flee this way or that, for the people who fled to the wilderness turned back against the pursuers. 21 When Joshua and all Israel saw that the ambush had taken the city and that the smoke of the city was rising, then they turned back and struck down the men of Ai. 22 And the others came out from the city against them; so they were surrounded by Israelites, some on one side, and some on the other; and Israel struck them down until no one was left who survived or escaped. 23 But the king of Ai was taken alive and brought to Joshua.

24 When Israel had finished slaughtering all the inhabitants of Ai in the open wilderness where they pursued them, and when all of them to the very last had fallen by the edge of the sword, all Israel returned to Ai, and attacked it with the edge of the sword. 25 The total of those who fell that

k Heb *among the people*

8 THE LORD said to Joshua, 'Do not be afraid or discouraged; take the whole army with you and go and attack Ai. I am delivering the king of Ai into your hands, along with his people, his city, and his territory. 2 Deal with Ai and its king as you dealt with Jericho and its king, except that you may keep for yourselves the cattle and any other spoil you take. Set an ambush for the city to the west of it.'

3 Joshua and the army prepared for the assault on Ai. He chose thirty thousand warriors and dispatched them by night, 4 with these orders: 'Lie in ambush to the west of the city, not far distant from it, and hold yourselves in readiness, all of you. 5 I myself will advance on the city with the rest of the army, and when the enemy come out to meet us as they did last time, we shall turn and flee before them. 6 They will come in pursuit until we have drawn them away from the city, for they will think we are in flight as before. While we are retreating, 7 rise from your ambush and occupy the city; the LORD your God will deliver it into your hands. 8 When you have taken it, set it on fire. Thus you will do what the LORD commands; these are my orders to you.' 9 After Joshua sent them off, they went to the place of ambush and lay in wait between Bethel and Ai to the west of Ai, while Joshua spent the night with the army.

10 Early in the morning Joshua mustered the army and, with Joshua himself and the elders of Israel at its head, they marched against Ai. 11 All the armed forces with him marched on until they came within sight of the city, where they encamped north of Ai, with the valley between them and the city. 12 Joshua took some five thousand men and set them in ambush between Bethel and Ai to the west of the city. 14 When the king of Ai saw them, he and the citizens set off hurriedly and marched out to do battle against Israel, being unaware that an ambush had been prepared for him to the west of the city. 15 Joshua and the Israelites made as if they were worsted by them and fled towards the wilderness, 16 while all the people of the city were called out in pursuit. In pursuing Joshua they were drawn away from the city, 17 until not a man was left in Ai; they had all gone out in pursuit of the Israelites and thus had left the place wide open.

18 The LORD then said to Joshua, 'Point towards Ai with the dagger you are holding, for I will deliver the city into your hands.' Joshua pointed with his dagger towards Ai 19 and, at his signal, the men in ambush rose quickly from their position; dashing into the city, they captured it and at once set it on fire. 20 The men of Ai looked back and saw the smoke from the city already going up to the sky; they were powerless to make their escape in any direction.

The Israelites who had feigned flight towards the wilderness now turned on their pursuers, 21 for when Joshua and all the Israelites with him saw that the men in ambush had seized the city and that smoke from it was already going up, they faced about and attacked the men of Ai. 22 Those who had come out to contend with the Israelites were now hemmed in by Israelites on both sides of them, and the Israelites cut them down until there was not a single survivor; no one escaped. 23 Only the king of Ai was taken alive and brought to Joshua.

24 When the Israelites had slain all the inhabitants of Ai in the open country and the wilderness where they had pursued them, and the massacre was complete, they all went back to Ai and put it to the sword. 25 The number who

8:12 **the city:** *so Gk; Heb. adds* 13 So the army pitched camp to the north of the city, and the rearguard to the west, while Joshua went that night into the valley.   8:14 **Israel:** *so Gk; Heb. adds* for the appointed time, before the Arabah.   8:17 **Ai:** *so Gk; Heb. adds* or Bethel.

8 The LORD then said to Joshua, "Do not be afraid or dismayed. Take all the army with you and prepare to attack Ai. I have delivered the king of Ai into your power, with his people, city, and land. 2 Do to Ai and its king what you did to Jericho and its king; except that you may take its spoil and livestock as booty. Set an ambush behind the city." 3 So Joshua and all the soldiers prepared to attack Ai. Picking out thirty thousand warriors, Joshua sent them off by night 4 with these orders: "See that you ambush the city from the rear, at no great distance; then all of you be on the watch. 5 The rest of the people and I will come up to the city, and when they make a sortie against us as they did the last time, we will flee from them. 6 They will keep coming out after us until we have drawn them away from the city, for they will think we are fleeing from them as we did the last time. When this occurs, 7 rise from ambush and take possession of the city, which the LORD, your God, will deliver into your power. 8 When you have taken the city, set it afire in obedience to the LORD's command. These are my orders to you." 9 Then Joshua sent them away. They went to the place of ambush, taking up their position to the west of Ai, toward Bethel. Joshua, however, spent that night in the plain.

10 Early the next morning Joshua mustered the army and went up to Ai at its head, with the elders of Israel. 11 When all the troops he led were drawn up in position before the city, they pitched camp north of Ai, on the other side of the ravine. 12 [He took about five thousand men and set them in ambush between Bethel and Ai, west of the city.] 13 Thus the people took up their stations, with the main body north of the city and the ambush west of it, and Joshua waited overnight among his troops. 14 The king of Ai saw this, and he and all his army came out very early in the morning to engage Israel in battle at the descent toward the Arabah, not knowing that there was an ambush behind the city. 15 Joshua and the main body of the Israelites fled in seeming defeat toward the desert, 16 till the last of the soldiers in the city had been called out to pursue them. 17 Since they were drawn away from the city, with every man engaged in this pursuit of Joshua and the Israelites, not a soldier remained in Ai [or Bethel], and the city was open and unprotected.

18 Then the LORD directed Joshua, "Stretch out the javelin in your hand toward Ai, for I will deliver it into your power." Joshua stretched out the javelin in his hand toward the city, 19 and as soon as he did so, the men in ambush rose from their post, rushed in, captured the city, and immediately set it on fire. 20 By the time the men of Ai looked back, the smoke from the city was already sky-high. Escape in any direction was impossible, because the Israelites retreating toward the desert now turned on their pursuers; 21 for when Joshua and the main body of Israelites saw that the city had been taken from ambush and was going up in smoke, they struck back at the men of Ai. 22 Since those in the city came out to intercept them, the men of Ai were hemmed in by Israelites on either side, who cut them down without any fugitives or survivors 23 except the king, whom they took alive and brought to Joshua.

24 All the inhabitants of Ai who had pursued the Israelites into the desert were slain by the sword there in the open, down to the last man. Then all Israel returned and put to the sword those inside the city. 25 There fell that day a total of

8 Yahweh then said to Joshua, 'Be fearless and undaunted. Take all your fighting men with you. Up! March against Ai. Look, I have put the king of Ai, his people, his town and his territory at your mercy. 2 You must treat Ai and its king as you treated Jericho and its king. The only booty you will take are the spoils and the cattle. Take up a concealed position by the town, to the rear of it.'

3 Joshua set out to march against Ai with all the fighting men. Joshua chose thirty thousand of the bravest and sent them out under cover of dark, 4 having given them these orders, 'Pay attention! You must take up a concealed position by the town, at the rear, not very far from the town, and be sure you all keep alert! 5 I, and the whole people with me, shall advance on the town, and when the people of Ai come out to engage us as they did the first time, we shall run away from them. 6 They will then give chase, and we shall draw them away from the town, since they will think, "They are running away from us as they did the first time." 7 You will then burst out of your concealed position and seize the town; Yahweh your God will put it at your mercy. 8 When you have captured the town, set fire to it, in obedience to Yahweh's command. Well then, these are my orders.'

9 Joshua sent them off, and they made their way to the place of ambush and took up position between Bethel and Ai, to the west of Ai. Joshua spent the night with the people, 10 then, getting up early next morning, reviewed the people and, with the elders of Israel, marched on Ai at their head. 11 All the warriors marching with him advanced on the front of the town and pitched camp north of Ai, with the valley between them and the town. 12 Joshua took about five thousand men and concealed these between Bethel and Ai, to the west of the town. 13 The people pitched the main camp to the north of the town and set up its ambush to the west of the town. Joshua went that night into the middle of the plain.

14 The king of Ai had seen this; the people of the town got up early and hurried out, so that he and all his people could engage Israel in battle on the slope facing the Arabah; but he did not know that an ambush had been laid for him to the rear of the town. 15 Joshua and all Israel pretended to be beaten by them and took to their heels along the road to the desert. 16 All the people in the town joined in the pursuit and, in pursuing Joshua, were drawn away from the town. 17 Not a man was left in Ai (nor in Bethel), who had not gone in pursuit of Israel; and in pursuing Israel they left the town undefended.

18 Yahweh then said to Joshua, 'Point the sabre in your hand at Ai; for I am about to put the town at your mercy.' Joshua pointed the sabre in his hand towards the town. 19 No sooner had he stretched out his hand than the men in ambush burst from their position, ran forward, entered the town, captured it and quickly set it on fire.

20 When the men of Ai looked back, they saw smoke rising from the town into the sky. None of them had the courage to run in any direction, for the people fleeing towards the desert turned back on their pursuers. 21 For, once Joshua and all Israel saw that the town had been seized by the men in ambush, and that smoke was rising from the town, they turned about and attacked the men of Ai. 22 The others came out from the town to engage them too, and the men of Ai were thus surrounded by Israelites, some on this side and some on that. The Israelites struck them down until not one was left alive and none to flee; 23 but the king of Ai was taken alive, and brought to Joshua. 24 When Israel had finished killing all the inhabitants of Ai in the open ground, and in the desert where they had pursued them, and when every single one had fallen to the sword, all Israel returned to Ai and slaughtered its remaining population. 25 The num-

NEW REVISED STANDARD VERSION

day, both men and women, was twelve thousand — all the people of Ai. 26 For Joshua did not draw back his hand, with which he stretched out the sword, until he had utterly destroyed all the inhabitants of Ai. 27 Only the livestock and the spoil of that city Israel took as their booty, according to the word of the LORD that he had issued to Joshua. 28 So Joshua burned Ai, and made it forever a heap of ruins, as it is to this day. 29 And he hanged the king of Ai on a tree until evening; and at sunset Joshua commanded, and they took his body down from the tree, threw it down at the entrance of the gate of the city, and raised over it a great heap of stones, which stands there to this day.

30 Then Joshua built on Mount Ebal an altar to the LORD, the God of Israel, 31 just as Moses the servant of the LORD had commanded the Israelites, as it is written in the book of the law of Moses, "an altar of unhewn[l] stones, on which no iron tool has been used"; and they offered on it burnt offerings to the LORD, and sacrificed offerings of well-being. 32 And there, in the presence of the Israelites, Joshua[m] wrote on the stones a copy of the law of Moses, which he had written. 33 All Israel, alien as well as citizen, with their elders and officers and their judges, stood on opposite sides of the ark in front of the levitical priests who carried the ark of the covenant of the LORD, half of them in front of Mount Gerizim and half of them in front of Mount Ebal, as Moses the servant of the LORD had commanded at the first, that they should bless the people of Israel. 34 And afterward he read all the words of the law, blessings and curses, according to all that is written in the book of the law. 35 There was not a word of all that Moses commanded that Joshua did not read before all the assembly of Israel, and the women, and the little ones, and the aliens who resided among them.

9 Now when all the kings who were beyond the Jordan in the hill country and in the lowland all along the coast of the Great Sea toward Lebanon — the Hittites, the Amorites, the Canaanites, the Perizzites, the Hivites, and the Jebusites — heard of this, 2 they gathered together with one accord to fight Joshua and Israel.

3 But when the inhabitants of Gibeon heard what Joshua had done to Jericho and to Ai, 4 they on their part acted with cunning: they went and prepared provisions,[n] and took worn-out sacks for their donkeys, and wineskins, worn-out and torn and mended, 5 with worn-out, patched sandals on their feet, and worn-out clothes; and all their provisions were dry and moldy. 6 They went to Joshua in the camp at Gilgal, and said to him and to the Israelites, "We have come from a far country; so now make a treaty with us." 7 But the Israelites said to the Hivites, "Perhaps you live among us; then how can we make a treaty with you?" 8 They said to Joshua, "We are your servants." And Joshua said to them, "Who are you? And where do you come from?" 9 They said to him, "Your servants have come from a very far country, because of the name of the LORD your God; for we have heard a report of him, of all that he did in Egypt, 10 and of all that he did to the two kings of the Amorites who were beyond the Jordan, King Sihon of Heshbon, and King Og of Bashan who lived in Ashtaroth. 11 So our elders and all the inhabitants of our country said to us, 'Take provisions in your hand for the journey; go to meet them, and say to them, "We are your servants; come now, make a treaty with us." ' 12 Here is our bread; it was still warm when we took it from our houses as our food for the journey, on the day we set out to come to you, but now, see, it is dry and moldy;

REVISED ENGLISH BIBLE

fell that day, men and women, was twelve thousand, the whole population of Ai. 26 Joshua held out his dagger and did not draw back his hand until all who lived in Ai had been destroyed; 27 but the Israelites kept for themselves the cattle and any other spoil that they took, following the LORD's instructions given to Joshua.

28 So Joshua burnt Ai to the ground, and left it the desolate ruined mound it remains to this day. 29 He hanged the king of Ai on a gibbet and left him there till evening. At sunset they cut down the body on Joshua's orders and flung it on the ground at the entrance of the city gate. Over it they raised a great cairn of stones, which is there to this day.

30 At that time Joshua built an altar to the LORD the God of Israel on Mount Ebal. 31 The altar was of blocks of undressed stone on which no iron tool had been used; this followed the commands given to the Israelites by Moses the servant of the LORD, as is described in the book of the law of Moses. On the altar they offered whole-offerings to the LORD, and slaughtered shared-offerings. 32 There in the presence of the Israelites Joshua engraved on blocks of stone a copy of the law of Moses. 33 All Israel, native-born and resident alien alike, with the elders, officers, and judges, took their stand on either side of the Ark, facing the levitical priests who carried the Ark of the Covenant of the LORD. Half of them stood facing Mount Gerizim and half facing Mount Ebal, to fulfil the command of Moses the servant of the LORD that the blessing should be pronounced first. 34 Then Joshua recited the whole of the blessing and the cursing word by word, as they are written in the book of the law; 35 there was not a single word of all that Moses had commanded which Joshua did not read aloud in the presence of the whole congregation of Israel, including the women and dependants and the aliens resident among them.

9 News of these happenings reached all the kings west of the Jordan, in the hill-country, in the Shephelah, and in all the coast of the Great Sea running up to the Lebanon, and the kings of the Hittites, Amorites, Canaanites, Perizzites, Hivites, and Jebusites 2 agreed to join forces and fight against Joshua and Israel.

3 When the inhabitants of Gibeon heard how Joshua had dealt with Jericho and Ai, 4 they resorted to a ruse: they set out after disguising themselves, with old sacks on their donkeys, old wineskins split and mended, 5 old and patched sandals for their feet, old clothing to wear, and by way of provisions nothing but dry and crumbling bread. 6 They came to Joshua in the camp at Gilgal, where they said to him and the Israelites, 'We have come from a distant country to ask you now to grant us a treaty.' 7 The Israelites said to these Hivites, 'But it may be that you live in our neighbourhood: if so, how can we grant you a treaty?' 8 They said to Joshua, 'We are your slaves.'

Joshua asked them who they were and where they came from. 9 'Sir,' they replied, 'our country is very far away, and we have come because of the renown of the LORD your God. We have heard the report of all that he did to Egypt 10 and to the two Amorite kings east of the Jordan, King Sihon of Heshbon and King Og of Bashan who lived at Ashtaroth. 11 Our elders and all the people of our country told us to take provisions for the journey and come to meet you, and say, "We are your slaves; please grant us a treaty." 12 Look at our bread; it was hot from the oven when we packed it at home on the day we came away. Now, as you see, it is dry and crumbling. 13 Here are our wineskins; they

8:32 **on blocks:** *or* on the blocks. **Moses:** *so Gk; Heb. adds* which he had engraved.

---

[l] Heb *whole*   [m] Heb *he*   [n] Cn: Meaning of Heb uncertain

twelve thousand men and women, the entire population of Ai. 26 Joshua kept the javelin in his hand stretched out until he had fulfilled the doom on all the inhabitants of Ai. 27 However, the Israelites took for themselves as booty the livestock and the spoil of that city, according to the command of the LORD issued to Joshua. 28 Then Joshua destroyed the place by fire, reducing it to an everlasting mound of ruins, as it remains today. 29 He had the king of Ai hanged on a tree until evening; then at sunset Joshua ordered the body removed from the tree and cast at the entrance of the city gate, where a great heap of stones was piled up over it, which remains to the present day.

30 Later Joshua built an altar to the LORD, the God of Israel, on Mount Ebal, 31 of unhewn stones on which no iron tool had been used, in keeping with the command to the Israelites of Moses, the servant of the LORD, as recorded in the book of the law. On this altar they offered holocausts and peace offerings to the LORD. 32 There, in the presence of the Israelites, Joshua inscribed upon the stones a copy of the law written by Moses. 33 And all Israel, stranger and native alike, with their elders, officers and judges, stood on either side of the ark facing the levitical priests who were carrying the ark of the covenant of the LORD. Half of them were facing Mount Gerizim and half Mount Ebal, thus carrying out the instructions of Moses, the servant of the LORD, for the blessing of the people of Israel on this first occasion. 34 Then were read aloud all the words of the law, the blessings and the curses, exactly as written in the book of the law. 35 Every single word that Moses had commanded, Joshua read aloud to the entire community, including the women and children, and the strangers who had accompanied Israel.

9 When the news reached the kings west of the Jordan, in the mountain regions and in the foothills, and all along the coast of the Great Sea as far as Lebanon: Hittites, Amorites, Canaanites, Perizzites, Hivites and Jebusites, 2 they all formed an alliance to launch a common attack against Joshua and Israel.

3 On learning what Joshua had done to Jericho and Ai, the inhabitants of Gibeon 4 put into effect a device of their own. They chose provisions for a journey, making use of old sacks for their asses, and old wineskins, torn and mended. 5 They wore old, patched sandals and shabby garments; and all the bread they took was dry and crumbly. 6 Thus they journeyed to Joshua in the camp at Gilgal, where they said to him and to the men of Israel, "We have come from a distant land to propose that you make an alliance with us." 7 But the men of Israel replied to the Hivites, "You may be living in land that is ours. How, then, can we make an alliance with you?" 8 But they answered Joshua, "We are your servants." Then Joshua asked them, "Who are you? Where do you come from?" 9 They answered him, "Your servants have come from a far-off land, because of the fame of the LORD, your God. For we have heard reports of all that he did in Egypt 10 and all that he did to the two kings of the Amorites beyond the Jordan, Sihon, king of Heshbon, and Og, king of Bashan, who lived in Ashtaroth. 11 So our elders and all the inhabitants of our country said to us, 'Take along provisions for the journey and go to meet them. Say to them: We are your servants; we propose that you make an alliance with us.' 12 This bread of ours was still warm when we brought it from home as provisions the day we left to come to you, but now it is dry and crumbled. 13 Here are our

ber of those who fell that day, men and women together, was twelve thousand, all people of Ai. 26 Joshua did not draw back the hand with which he had pointed the sabre until he had subjected all the inhabitants of Ai to the curse of destruction. 27 For booty, Israel took only the cattle and the spoils of this town, in accordance with the order that Yahweh had given to Joshua. 28 Joshua then burned Ai, making it a ruin for evermore, a desolate place even today. 29 He hanged the king of Ai from a tree till evening; but at sunset Joshua ordered his body to be taken down from the tree. It was then thrown down at the entrance to the town gate and on top of it was raised a great mound of stones, which is still there today.

30 Joshua then built an altar to Yahweh, God of Israel, on Mount Ebal, 31 as Moses, servant of Yahweh, had ordered the Israelites, as is written in the law of Moses: an altar of undressed stones, on which no iron has been used. On this they presented burnt offerings to Yahweh and communion sacrifices as well.

32 There, Joshua wrote on the stones a copy of the Law of Moses, which Moses had written in the presence of the Israelites. 33 All Israel, with their elders, their officials and their judges, stood on either side of the ark, facing the levitical priests who were carrying the ark of the covenant of Yahweh, foreigners with the native-born, half of them on the upper slopes of Mount Gerizim, and half of them on the upper slopes of Mount Ebal, as Moses, servant of Yahweh, had originally ordered for the blessing of the people of Israel. 34 After this, Joshua read all the words of the Law — the blessing and the cursing — exactly as it stands written in the Book of the Law. 35 Of every word laid down by Moses, not one was left unread by Joshua in the presence of the whole assembly of Israel, including the women and children, and the foreigners living with them.

9 Hearing these things, all the kings on this side of the Jordan, in the highlands and in the lowlands, all along the coast of the Great Sea towards the Lebanon, Hittites, Amorites, Canaanites, Perizzites, Hivites and Jebusites, with one consent 2 formed a fighting alliance against Joshua and Israel.

3 When the inhabitants of Gibeon learned how Joshua had treated Jericho and Ai, for their part, 4 they had recourse to a ruse. They provided themselves with supplies, and loaded their donkeys with old sacks and with old wineskins which had burst and been sewn up again. 5 They put on patched old sandals and worn-out clothes. The only bread they took with them to eat was dried up and crumbling. 6 They came to Joshua in the camp at Gilgal, and to him and the men of Israel they said, 'We come from a distant country, so make a treaty with us.' 7 The Israelites answered these Hivites, 'For all we know, you may live right among us. How then could we make a treaty with you?' 8 They said to Joshua, 'We are your servants.' 'But who are you?' Joshua asked them, 'and where do you come from?' 9 They said, 'Your servants have come from a country very far away, because of the fame of Yahweh your God; for we have heard of him and of all that he did in Egypt, 10 and of all that he did to the two Amorite kings who used to live on the other side of the Jordan: Sihon king of Heshbon, and Og king of Bashan, who used to live at Ashtaroth. 11 Because of which, our elders and all the people of our country said to us, "Take provisions with you for the journey; go and meet them and say to them: We are your servants; so make a treaty with us." 12 Here is our bread; it was warm when we took it from home to provide for our journey the day we set out to come to you, and now, you can see, it is dried up and crumbling. 13 These wineskins were new when we filled

13 these wineskins were new when we filled them, and see, they are burst; and these garments and sandals of ours are worn out from the very long journey." 14 So the leaders*o* partook of their provisions, and did not ask direction from the LORD. 15 And Joshua made peace with them, guaranteeing their lives by a treaty; and the leaders of the congregation swore an oath to them.

16 But when three days had passed after they had made a treaty with them, they heard that they were their neighbors and were living among them. 17 So the Israelites set out and reached their cities on the third day. Now their cities were Gibeon, Chephirah, Beeroth, and Kiriath-jearim. 18 But the Israelites did not attack them, because the leaders of the congregation had sworn to them by the LORD, the God of Israel. Then all the congregation murmured against the leaders. 19 But all the leaders said to all the congregation, "We have sworn to them by the LORD, the God of Israel, and now we must not touch them. 20 This is what we will do to them: We will let them live, so that wrath may not come upon us, because of the oath that we swore to them." 21 The leaders said to them, "Let them live." So they became hewers of wood and drawers of water for all the congregation, as the leaders had decided concerning them.

22 Joshua summoned them, and said to them, "Why did you deceive us, saying, 'We are very far from you,' while in fact you are living among us? 23 Now therefore you are cursed, and some of you shall always be slaves, hewers of wood and drawers of water for the house of my God." 24 They answered Joshua, "Because it was told to your servants for a certainty that the LORD your God had commanded his servant Moses to give you all the land, and to destroy all the inhabitants of the land before you; so we were in great fear for our lives because of you, and did this thing. 25 And now we are in your hand: do as it seems good and right in your sight to do to us." 26 This is what he did for them: he saved them from the Israelites; and they did not kill them. 27 But on that day Joshua made them hewers of wood and drawers of water for the congregation and for the altar of the LORD, to continue to this day, in the place that he should choose.

10 When King Adoni-zedek of Jerusalem heard how Joshua had taken Ai, and had utterly destroyed it, doing to Ai and its king as he had done to Jericho and its king, and how the inhabitants of Gibeon had made peace with Israel and were among them, 2 he*p* became greatly frightened, because Gibeon was a large city, like one of the royal cities, and was larger than Ai, and all its men were warriors. 3 So King Adoni-zedek of Jerusalem sent a message to King Hoham of Hebron, to King Piram of Jarmuth, to King Japhia of Lachish, and to King Debir of Eglon, saying, 4 "Come up and help me, and let us attack Gibeon; for it has made peace with Joshua and with the Israelites." 5 Then the five kings of the Amorites — the king of Jerusalem, the king of Hebron, the king of Jarmuth, the king of Lachish, and the king of Eglon — gathered their forces, and went up with all their armies and camped against Gibeon, and made war against it.

6 And the Gibeonites sent to Joshua at the camp in Gilgal, saying, "Do not abandon your servants; come up to us quickly, and save us, and help us; for all the kings of the Amorites who live in the hill country are gathered against us." 7 So Joshua went up from Gilgal, he and all the fighting force with him, all the mighty warriors. 8 The LORD said to Joshua, "Do not fear them, for I have handed them over to you; not one of them shall stand before you." 9 So Joshua came upon them suddenly, having marched up all night from Gilgal. 10 And the LORD threw them into a panic be-

o Gk: Heb *men*   *p* Heb *they*

were new when we filled them, and now they are all split; look at our clothes and our sandals, worn out by the very long journey.' 14 Without seeking guidance from the LORD, the leaders of the community accepted some of their provisions. 15 Joshua received them peaceably and granted them a treaty, promising to spare their lives, and the leaders ratified it on oath.

16 However, within three days of granting them the treaty the Israelites learnt that these people were in fact neighbours, living nearby. 17 The Israelites then set out and on the third day they reached their towns, Gibeon, Kephirah, Beeroth, and Kiriath-jearim. 18 The Israelites did not attack them, because of the oath which the chief men of the community had sworn to them by the LORD the God of Israel. When the whole community was indignant with the leaders, 19 they all made this reply: 'We swore an oath to them by the LORD the God of Israel; so now we cannot touch them. 20 What we shall do is this: we shall spare their lives so that the oath which we swore to them may bring down no wrath on us. 21 But though their lives must be spared, they will be set to cut wood and draw water for the community.' The people agreed to do as their chiefs had said.

22 Joshua summoned the Gibeonites and said to them, 'Why did you play this trick on us? You told us that you live a long way off, when in fact you are near neighbours. 23 From now there is a curse on you: for all time you shall provide us with slaves, to cut wood and draw water for the house of my God.' 24 They answered Joshua, 'We were told, sir, that the LORD your God had commanded his servant Moses to give you the whole country and to wipe out its inhabitants; so because of you we were in terror of our lives, and that is why we did this. 25 We are in your hands: do with us whatever you think right and proper.' 26 What he did was this: he saved them from death at the hands of the Israelites, and they did not kill them; 27 but from that day he assigned them to cut wood and draw water for the community and for the altar of the LORD. And to this day they do so at the place which the LORD chose.

10 WHEN King Adoni-zedek of Jerusalem heard that Joshua had captured and destroyed Ai, dealing with Ai and its king as he had dealt with Jericho and its king, and also that the inhabitants of Gibeon had come to terms with Israel and were living among them, 2 he was greatly alarmed; for Gibeon was a large place, like a royal city: it was larger than Ai, and its men were all good fighters. 3 So King Adoni-zedek of Jerusalem sent this message to King Hoham of Hebron, King Piram of Jarmuth, King Japhia of Lachish, and King Debir of Eglon: 4 'Come up and assist me to attack Gibeon, because it has come to terms with Joshua and the Israelites.' 5 The five Amorite kings, the kings of Jerusalem, Hebron, Jarmuth, Lachish, and Eglon, advanced with their united forces to take up position for the attack on Gibeon. 6 The Gibeonites sent word to Joshua in the camp at Gilgal: 'Do not abandon your slaves; come quickly to our relief. Come and help us, for all the Amorite kings in the hill-country have joined forces against us.' 7 When Joshua went up from Gilgal followed by his whole force, all his warriors, 8 the LORD said to him, 'Do not be afraid; I have delivered these kings into your hands, and not one of them will be able to withstand you.' 9 After a night march from Gilgal, Joshua launched a surprise assault on the five kings,

9:14 **the leaders:** *so Gk; Heb.* the men.   9:21 **But though:** *so Gk; Heb. prefixes* And the chiefs said to them. **will be:** *so Gk; Heb.* were. **The people ... do:** *so some Gk MSS; Heb.* omits.   10:2 **he was:** *so Syriac; Heb.* they were.

wineskins, which were new when we filled them, but now they are torn. Look at our garments and sandals, which are worn out from the very long journey." 14 Then the Israelite princes partook of their provisions, without seeking the advice of the LORD. 15 So Joshua made an alliance with them and entered into an agreement to spare them, which the princes of the community sealed with an oath.

16 Three days after the agreement was entered into, the Israelites learned that these people were from nearby, and would be living in Israel. 17 The third day on the road, the Israelites came to their cities of Gibeon, Chephirah, Beeroth and Kiriath-jearim, 18 but did not attack them, because the princes of the community had sworn to them by the LORD, the God of Israel. When the entire community grumbled against the princes, 19 these all remonstrated with the people, "We have sworn to them by the LORD, the God of Israel, and so we cannot harm them. 20 Let us therefore spare their lives and so deal with them that we shall not be punished for the oath we have sworn to them." 21 Thus the princes recommended that they be let live, as hewers of wood and drawers of water for the entire community; and the community did as the princes advised them.

22 Joshua summoned the Gibeonites and said to them, "Why did you lie to us and say that you lived at a great distance from us, when you will be living in our very midst? 23 For this are you accursed: every one of you shall always be a slave [hewers of wood and drawers of water] for the house of my God." 24 They answered Joshua, "Your servants were fully informed of how the LORD, your God, commanded his servant Moses that you be given the entire land and that all its inhabitants be destroyed before you. Since, therefore, at your advance, we were in great fear for our lives, we acted as we did. 25 And now that we are in your power, do with us what you think fit and right." 26 Joshua did what he had decided: while he saved them from being killed by the Israelites, 27 at the same time he made them, as they still are, hewers of wood and drawers of water for the community and for the altar of the LORD, in the place of the LORD'S choice.

10 Now Adonizedek, king of Jerusalem, heard that, in the capture and destruction of Ai, Joshua had done to that city and its king as he had done to Jericho and its king. He heard also that the inhabitants of Gibeon had made their peace with Israel, remaining among them, 2 and that there was great fear abroad, because Gibeon was large enough for a royal city, larger even than the city of Ai, and all its men were brave. 3 So Adonizedek, king of Jerusalem, sent for Hoham, king of Hebron, Piram, king of Jarmuth, Japhia, king of Lachish, and Debir, king of Eglon, 4 to come to his aid for an attack on Gibeon, since it had concluded peace with Joshua and the Israelites. 5 The five Amorite kings, of Jerusalem, Hebron, Jarmuth, Lachish and Eglon, united all their forces and marched against Gibeon, where they took up siege positions. 6 Thereupon, the men of Gibeon sent an appeal to Joshua in his camp at Gilgal: "Do not abandon your servants. Come up here quickly and save us. Help us, because all the Amorite kings of the mountain country have joined forces against us."

7 So Joshua marched up from Gilgal with his picked troops and the rest of his soldiers. 8 Meanwhile the LORD said to Joshua, "Do not fear them, for I have delivered them into your power. Not one of them will be able to withstand you." 9 And when Joshua made his surprise attack upon them after an all-night march from Gilgal, 10 the LORD

them; you can see, they have burst; and these clothes and sandals of ours are worn out from travelling such a long way.'

14 The leaders sampled some of the food they offered, but they did not ask Yahweh's orders. 15 Joshua made peace with them, and struck a treaty with them guaranteeing their lives, and the leaders of the community ratified it by oath.

16 Now it so happened that three days after the treaty had been made, it became known that they were a neighbouring people, living in Israel's region. 17 The Israelites set out from camp, arriving in their towns three days later. Their towns were Gibeon, Chephirah, Beeroth and Kiriath-Jearim. 18 The Israelites did not attack them, since the leaders of the community had sworn to them by Yahweh, God of Israel, but the whole community muttered against the leaders.

19 The leaders, however, all said to the whole community, 'Since we have sworn an oath to them by Yahweh, God of Israel, we cannot touch them now. 20 This is what we shall do with them: let them live, rather than bring retribution down on ourselves on account of the oath which we have sworn to them.' 21 And the leaders went on, 'Let them live, but let them be wood-cutters and water-carriers for the whole community.' Thus spoke the leaders. 22 Joshua sent for the Gibeonites and asked them, 'Why did you deceive us by saying, "We live very far away," when in fact you live right among us? 23 From now on, you are accursed and will for ever be serfs, as wood-cutters and water-carriers in the house of my God.' 24 Their answer to Joshua was, 'We did it because your servants had been rightly told that Yahweh your God had ordered his servant Moses to give you the whole of this country and destroy all its inhabitants before you; also because, as you advanced on us, we feared very greatly for our lives. That was why we did this. 25 Now, as you see, we are at your mercy; do to us whatever you think good and right.' 26 What he did with them was this: he saved them from the hand of the Israelites, who did not kill them. 27 But that very day Joshua made them wood-cutters and water-carriers for the community and for the altar of Yahweh, at the place which he would eventually choose; and so they are today.

10 Now, it happened that Adoni-Zedek king of Jerusalem, learned that Joshua had conquered Ai and put the town under the curse of destruction, treating Ai and its king as he had already treated Jericho and its king; and also that the inhabitants of Gibeon had made peace with Israel and were living with them. 2 There was consternation at this, since Gibeon was as important a town as any of the royal towns themselves (it was larger than Ai), while all its citizens were fighting men. 3 Consequently, Adoni-Zedek king of Jerusalem sent word to Hoham king of Hebron, Piram king of Jarmuth, Japhia king of Lachish, and Debir king of Eglon, 4 'Join me up here and help me to conquer Gibeon, since it has made peace with Joshua and the Israelites.' 5 The five Amorite kings joined forces and went up there, that is, the king of Jerusalem, the king of Hebron, the king of Jarmuth, the king of Lachish and the king of Eglon, they and all their armies; laying siege to Gibeon, they attacked it.

6 The men of Gibeon sent word to Joshua in the camp at Gilgal, 'Do not desert your servants; come up here quickly to save us and help us, since all the Amorite kings living in the highlands have allied themselves against us.' 7 Joshua came up from Gilgal, he, all the fighting men and all the bravest of his army. 8 Yahweh said to Joshua, 'Do not be afraid of these people; I have put them at your mercy; not one of them will put up any resistance.' 9 Having marched from Gilgal throughout the night, Joshua caught them unawares.

fore Israel, who inflicted a great slaughter on them at Gibeon, chased them by the way of the ascent of Beth-horon, and struck them down as far as Azekah and Makkedah. 11 As they fled before Israel, while they were going down the slope of Beth-horon, the LORD threw down huge stones from heaven on them as far as Azekah, and they died; there were more who died because of the hailstones than the Israelites killed with the sword.

12 On the day when the LORD gave the Amorites over to the Israelites, Joshua spoke to the LORD; and he said in the sight of Israel,

"Sun, stand still at Gibeon,
and Moon, in the valley of Aijalon."
13 And the sun stood still, and the moon stopped,
until the nation took vengeance on their
enemies.

Is this not written in the Book of Jashar? The sun stopped in midheaven, and did not hurry to set for about a whole day. 14 There has been no day like it before or since, when the LORD heeded a human voice; for the LORD fought for Israel.

15 Then Joshua returned, and all Israel with him, to the camp at Gilgal.

16 Meanwhile, these five kings fled and hid themselves in the cave at Makkedah. 17 And it was told Joshua, "The five kings have been found, hidden in the cave at Makkedah." 18 Joshua said, "Roll large stones against the mouth of the cave, and set men by it to guard them; 19 but do not stay there yourselves; pursue your enemies, and attack them from the rear. Do not let them enter their towns, for the LORD your God has given them into your hand." 20 When Joshua and the Israelites had finished inflicting a very great slaughter on them, until they were wiped out, and when the survivors had entered into the fortified towns, 21 all the people returned safe to Joshua in the camp at Makkedah; no one dared to speak*q* against any of the Israelites.

22 Then Joshua said, "Open the mouth of the cave, and bring those five kings out to me from the cave." 23 They did so, and brought the five kings out to him from the cave, the king of Jerusalem, the king of Hebron, the king of Jarmuth, the king of Lachish, and the king of Eglon. 24 When they brought the kings out to Joshua, Joshua summoned all the Israelites, and said to the chiefs of the warriors who had gone with him, "Come near, put your feet on the necks of these kings." Then they came near and put their feet on their necks. 25 And Joshua said to them, "Do not be afraid or dismayed; be strong and courageous; for thus the LORD will do to all the enemies against whom you fight." 26 Afterward Joshua struck them down and put them to death, and he hung them on five trees. And they hung on the trees until evening. 27 At sunset Joshua commanded, and they took them down from the trees and threw them into the cave where they had hidden themselves; they set large stones against the mouth of the cave, which remain to this very day.

28 Joshua took Makkedah on that day, and struck it and its king with the edge of the sword; he utterly destroyed every person in it; he left no one remaining. And he did to the king of Makkedah as he had done to the king of Jericho.

29 Then Joshua passed on from Makkedah, and all Israel with him, to Libnah, and fought against Libnah. 30 The LORD gave it also and its king into the hand of Israel; and he struck it with the edge of the sword, and every person in it; he left no one remaining in it; and he did to its king as he had done to the king of Jericho.

31 Next Joshua passed on from Libnah, and all Israel with him, to Lachish, and laid siege to it, and assaulted it.

q Heb *moved his tongue*

10 and the LORD threw them into confusion before the Israelites. Joshua utterly defeated them at Gibeon; he pursued them down the pass of Beth-horon and kept up the attack as far as Azekah and Makkedah. 11 As they fled from Israel down the pass, the LORD hurled great hailstones at them out of the sky all the way to Azekah, and they perished: more died from the hailstones than were slain by the swords of the Israelites.

12 On that day when the LORD delivered up the Amorites into the hands of Israel, Joshua spoke with the LORD, and in the presence of Israel said:

'Stand still, you sun, at Gibeon;
you moon, at the vale of Aijalon.'
13 The sun stood still and the moon halted until the nation had taken vengeance on its enemies, as indeed is written in the Book of Jashar. The sun stayed in mid-heaven and made no haste to set for almost a whole day. 14 Never before or since has there been such a day as that on which the LORD listened to the voice of a mortal. Surely the LORD fought for Israel! 15 Then Joshua returned with all the Israelites to the camp at Gilgal.

16 The five kings fled and hid in a cave at Makkedah, 17 and Joshua was told that they had been found hiding there. 18 Joshua replied, 'Roll large stones against the mouth of the cave, and post men there to keep watch over the kings. 19 But you yourselves must not stay. Keep up the pursuit, attack your enemies from the rear and do not let them reach their towns; the LORD your God has delivered them into your hands.'

20 When Joshua and the Israelites had completed the work of slaughter and everyone had been put to the sword—all except a few survivors who escaped into the fortified towns—21 the whole army returned safely to Joshua at Makkedah; not one of the Israelites suffered so much as a scratch.

22 Joshua gave the order: 'Open up the mouth of the cave, and bring out those five kings to me.' 23 This was done; the five kings, the kings of Jerusalem, Hebron, Jarmuth, Lachish, and Eglon, were taken from the cave 24 and brought to Joshua. When he had summoned all the Israelites he said to the commanders of the troops who had served with him, 'Come forward and put your feet on the necks of these kings.' They did so, 25 and Joshua said to them, 'Do not be afraid or discouraged; be strong and resolute; for the LORD will do this to every enemy whom you fight.' 26 He fell on the kings and slew them; then he hung their bodies on five gibbets, where they remained hanging till evening. 27 At sunset they were taken down on Joshua's orders and thrown into the cave in which they had hidden; large stones were piled against its mouth, where they remain to this very day.

28 On that same day Joshua captured Makkedah and put both king and people to the sword, destroying under the ban both them and every living thing in the city. He left no survivor, and he dealt with the king of Makkedah as he had dealt with the king of Jericho. 29 Then Joshua with all the Israelites marched on from Makkedah to Libnah and attacked it. 30 The LORD delivered the city and its king to the Israelites, and they put its people and every living thing in it to the sword; they left no survivor there, and dealt with its king as they had dealt with the king of Jericho. 31 From Libnah Joshua and all the Israelites marched on to Lachish, where they took up their positions against it and attacked it.

10:13 **Book of Jashar:** *or* Book of the Upright.   10:21 **returned:** *so Gk; Heb. adds* to the camp. **not one . . . scratch:** *Heb. adds* on his tongue; *or* no one raised his voice against the Israelites.

threw them into disorder before him. The Israelites inflicted a great slaughter on them at Gibeon and pursued them down the Beth-horon slope, harassing them as far as Azekah and Makkedah. 11 While they fled before Israel along the descent from Beth-horon, the LORD hurled great stones from the sky above them all the way to Azekah, killing many. More died from these hailstones than the Israelites slew with the sword. 12 On this day, when the LORD delivered up the Amorites to the Israelites,

Joshua prayed to the LORD,
and said in the presence of Israel:
Stand still, O sun, at Gibeon,
O moon, in the valley of Aijalon!
13 And the sun stood still,
and the moon stayed,
while the nation took vengeance on its foes.

Is this not recorded in the Book of Jashar? The sun halted in the middle of the sky; not for a whole day did it resume its swift course. 14 Never before or since was there a day like this, when the LORD obeyed the voice of a man; for the LORD fought for Israel. 15 [Then Joshua and all Israel returned to the camp at Gilgal.]

16 Meanwhile the five kings who had fled, hid in a cave at Makkedah. 17 When Joshua was told that the five kings had been discovered hiding in a cave at Makkedah, 18 he said, "Roll large stones to the mouth of the cave and post men over it to guard them. 19 But do not remain there yourselves. Pursue your enemies, and harry them in the rear. Do not allow them to escape to their cities, for the LORD, your God, has delivered them into your power."

20 Once Joshua and the Israelites had finally inflicted the last blows in this very great slaughter, and the survivors had escaped from them into the fortified cities, 21 all the army returned safely to Joshua and the camp at Makkedah, no man uttering a sound against the Israelites. 22 Then Joshua said, "Open the mouth of the cave and bring out those five kings to me." 23 Obediently, they brought out to him from the cave the five kings, of Jerusalem, Hebron, Jarmuth, Lachish and Eglon. 24 When they had done so, Joshua summoned all the men of Israel and said to the commanders of the soldiers who had marched with him, "Come forward and put your feet on the necks of these kings." They came forward and put their feet upon their necks. 25 Then Joshua said to them, "Do not be afraid or dismayed, be firm and steadfast. This is what the LORD will do to all the enemies against whom you fight." 26 Thereupon Joshua struck and killed them, and hanged them on five trees, where they remained hanging until evening. 27 At sunset they were removed from the trees at the command of Joshua and cast into the cave where they had hidden; over the mouth of the cave large stones were placed, which remain until this very day.

28 Makkedah, too, Joshua captured and put to the sword at that time. He fulfilled the doom on the city, on its king, and on every person in it, leaving no survivors. Thus he did to the king of Makkedah what he had done to the king of Jericho. 29 Joshua then passed on with all Israel from Makkedah to Libnah, which he attacked. 30 Libnah also, with its king, the LORD delivered into the power of Israel. He put it to the sword with every person there, leaving no survivors. Thus he did to its king what he had done to the king of Jericho. 31 Joshua next passed on with all Israel from Libnah to Lachish, where they set up a camp during the attack.

10 Yahweh threw them into disorder at the sight of Israel, defeating them completely at Gibeon; furthermore, he pursued them by way of the Descent of Beth-Horon and harassed them as far as Azekah (and as far as Makkedah). 11 And as they fled from Israel down the Descent of Beth-Horon, Yahweh hurled huge hailstones from heaven on them all the way to Azekah, and they died. More of them died under the hailstones than under the swords of the Israelites. 12 Joshua then spoke to Yahweh, the day Yahweh delivered the Amorites to the Israelites. In the presence of Israel, Joshua said:

Sun, stand still over Gibeon,
and, moon, you too, over the Vale of Aijalon!

13 And the sun stood still, and the moon halted, until the people had taken vengeance on their enemies.

Is this not written in the Book of the Just? The sun stood still in the middle of the sky and delayed its setting for almost a whole day. 14 There was never a day like that before or since, when Yahweh obeyed the voice of a man — for Yahweh was fighting for Israel. 15 Joshua, and all Israel with him, then went back to the camp at Gilgal.

16 As regards the five kings, these had fled and hidden in the cave of Makkedah, 17 and news of this was brought to Joshua. 'The five kings have been found hiding in the cave at Makkedah.' 18 Joshua said, 'Roll great stones over the mouth of the cave and post men there to keep guard. 19 You yourselves, do not stay there doing nothing; pursue the enemy, cut off their line of retreat and do not let them enter their towns, for Yahweh your God has put them at your mercy.'

20 When Joshua and the Israelites had finished inflicting a very great defeat on them, to the point of destroying them, those who had escaped alive took refuge in their fortresses. 21 The people came back to Joshua's camp at Makkedah; they were all safe and sound, and no one dared to attempt anything against the Israelites. 22 Joshua then said, 'Clear the mouth of the cave and bring the five kings out to me.' 23 They did so, and brought the five kings out of the cave to take them to him: the king of Jerusalem, the king of Hebron, the king of Jarmuth, the king of Lachish and the king of Eglon. 24 When these kings had been brought out, Joshua assembled all the men of Israel and said to the chiefs of the warriors who had fought with him, 'Come forward and put your feet on the necks of these kings!' They came forward and put their feet on their necks. 25 'Be fearless and undaunted,' Joshua went on, 'be strong and stand firm, for this is how Yahweh will deal with all the enemies you fight.' 26 With this, Joshua struck and killed them and had them hanged on five trees; they hung there till evening.

27 At the hour of sunset, on Joshua's orders, they were taken down from the trees and thrown into the cave where they had been hiding. Great stones were laid over the mouth of the cave, and these are still there to this very day.

28 The same day Joshua captured Makkedah, putting it and its king to the sword; he delivered them over to the curse of destruction, with every living creature there, and let no one escape, and he treated the king of Makkedah as he had treated the king of Jericho.

29 Joshua, and all Israel with him, went on from Makkedah to Libnah and attacked it 30 and Yahweh put this, too, and its king at Israel's mercy; and Israel put every living creature there to the sword, and left none alive, and treated its king like the king of Jericho.

31 Joshua, and all Israel with him, went on from Libnah to Lachish and besieged it and attacked it. 32 Yahweh put

| NEW REVISED STANDARD VERSION | REVISED ENGLISH BIBLE |

NEW REVISED STANDARD VERSION

32 The LORD gave Lachish into the hand of Israel, and he took it on the second day, and struck it with the edge of the sword, and every person in it, as he had done to Libnah.

33 Then King Horam of Gezer came up to help Lachish; and Joshua struck him and his people, leaving him no survivors.

34 From Lachish Joshua passed on with all Israel to Eglon; and they laid siege to it, and assaulted it; 35 and they took it that day, and struck it with the edge of the sword; and every person in it he utterly destroyed that day, as he had done to Lachish.

36 Then Joshua went up with all Israel from Eglon to Hebron; they assaulted it, 37 and took it, and struck it with the edge of the sword, and its king and its towns, and every person in it; he left no one remaining, just as he had done to Eglon, and utterly destroyed it with every person in it.

38 Then Joshua, with all Israel, turned back to Debir and assaulted it, 39 and he took it with its king and all its towns; they struck them with the edge of the sword, and utterly destroyed every person in it; he left no one remaining; just as he had done to Hebron, and, as he had done to Libnah and its king, so he did to Debir and its king.

40 So Joshua defeated the whole land, the hill country and the Negeb and the lowland and the slopes, and all their kings; he left no one remaining, but utterly destroyed all that breathed, as the LORD God of Israel commanded. 41 And Joshua defeated them from Kadesh-barnea to Gaza, and all the country of Goshen, as far as Gibeon. 42 Joshua took all these kings and their land at one time, because the LORD God of Israel fought for Israel. 43 Then Joshua returned, and all Israel with him, to the camp at Gilgal.

11 When King Jabin of Hazor heard of this, he sent to King Jobab of Madon, to the king of Shimron, to the king of Achshaph, 2 and to the kings who were in the northern hill country, and in the Arabah south of Chinneroth, and in the lowland, and in Naphoth-dor on the west, 3 to the Canaanites in the east and the west, the Amorites, the Hittites, the Perizzites, and the Jebusites in the hill country, and the Hivites under Hermon in the land of Mizpah. 4 They came out, with all their troops, a great army, in number like the sand on the seashore, with very many horses and chariots. 5 All these kings joined their forces, and came and camped together at the waters of Merom, to fight with Israel.

6 And the LORD said to Joshua, "Do not be afraid of them, for tomorrow at this time I will hand over all of them, slain, to Israel; you shall hamstring their horses, and burn their chariots with fire." 7 So Joshua came suddenly upon them with all his fighting force, by the waters of Merom, and fell upon them. 8 And the LORD handed them over to Israel, who attacked them and chased them as far as Great Sidon and Misrephoth-maim, and eastward as far as the valley of Mizpeh. They struck them down, until they had left no one remaining. 9 And Joshua did to them as the LORD commanded him; he hamstrung their horses, and burned their chariots with fire.

10 Joshua turned back at that time, and took Hazor, and struck its king down with the sword. Before that time Hazor was the head of all those kingdoms. 11 And they put to the sword all who were in it, utterly destroying them; there was no one left who breathed, and he burned Hazor with fire. 12 And all the towns of those kings, and all their kings, Joshua took, and struck them with the edge of the sword, utterly destroying them, as Moses the servant of the LORD had commanded. 13 But Israel burned none of the towns that stood on mounds except Hazor, which Joshua did burn.

REVISED ENGLISH BIBLE

32 The LORD delivered Lachish into their hands; they took it on the second day and put every living thing in it to the sword, as they had done at Libnah.

33 Meanwhile King Horam of Gezer had advanced to the relief of Lachish; but Joshua attacked him and his army until not a survivor was left to him. 34 From Lachish Joshua and all the Israelites marched on to Eglon, took up their positions against it, and attacked it; 35 that same day they captured it and put its inhabitants to the sword, destroying every living thing in it as they had done at Lachish. 36 From Eglon Joshua and all the Israelites advanced to Hebron and attacked it. 37 They captured it and put its king to the sword together with every living thing in it and in all its villages; as at Eglon, he left no survivor, destroying it and every living thing in it. 38 Then Joshua and all the Israelites wheeled round towards Debir and attacked it. 39 They captured the king, the city, and all its villages, put them to the sword, and destroyed every living thing; they left no survivor. They dealt with Debir and its king as they had dealt with Hebron and with Libnah and its king.

40 So Joshua conquered the whole region — the hill-country, the Negeb, the Shephelah, the watersheds — and all its kings. He left no survivor, destroying everything that drew breath, as the LORD the God of Israel had commanded. 41 Joshua's conquests extended from Kadesh-barnea to Gaza, over the whole land of Goshen, and as far as Gibeon. 42 All these kings he captured at the same time, and their country with them, for the LORD the God of Israel fought for Israel. 43 Then Joshua returned with all the Israelites to the camp at Gilgal.

11 When King Jabin of Hazor heard of these events, he sent to King Jobab of Madon, to the kings of Shimron and Akshaph, 2 to the northern kings in the hill-country, in the Arabah opposite Kinnereth, in the Shephelah, and in the district of Dor on the west, 3 the Canaanites to the east and the west, the Amorites, Hittites, Perizzites, and Jebusites in the hill-country, and the Hivites below Hermon in the land of Mizpah. 4 They took the field with all their forces, a great host countless as the grains of sand on the seashore, among them a very large number of horses and chariots. 5 All these kings, making common cause, came and encamped at the waters of Merom to fight against Israel.

6 The LORD said to Joshua, 'Do not be afraid of them, for at this time tomorrow I shall deliver them to Israel all dead men; you are to hamstring their horses and burn their chariots.' 7 Joshua with his whole army launched a surprise attack on them by the waters of Merom, 8 and the LORD delivered them into the hands of Israel, who defeated them, cutting down the fugitives the whole way to Greater Sidon, Misrephoth on the west, and the vale of Mizpah on the east. They cut them down until they had left not a single survivor. 9 Joshua dealt with them as the LORD had commanded: he hamstrung their horses and burnt their chariots.

10 At this point, Joshua turned his forces against Hazor, formerly the leader among all these kingdoms. He captured the city and put its king to death with the sword. 11 They put under the ban and killed every living thing in it; they spared nothing that drew breath, and Hazor itself was destroyed by fire.

12 So Joshua captured these kings and their cities and put them to the sword, destroying them all, as Moses the servant of the LORD had commanded. 13 The cities whose ruined mounds are still standing were not burnt by the Israelites; it was Hazor alone that Joshua burnt. 14 The Israelites

11:2 **opposite:** *so Gk; Heb.* south of.

32 The LORD delivered Lachish into the power of Israel, so that on the second day Joshua captured it and put it to the sword with every person in it, just as he had done to Libnah. 33 At that time Horam, king of Gezer, came up to help Lachish, but Joshua defeated him and his people, leaving him no survivors. 34 From Lachish, Joshua passed on with all Israel to Eglon; encamping near it, they attacked it 35 and captured it the same day, putting it to the sword. He fulfilled the doom that day on every person in it, just as he had done at Lachish. 36 From Eglon, Joshua went up with all Israel to Hebron, which they attacked 37 and captured. They put it to the sword with its king, all its towns, and every person there, leaving no survivors, just as Joshua had done to Eglon. He fulfilled the doom on it and on every person there. 38 Then Joshua and all Israel turned back to Debir and attacked it, 39 capturing it with its king and all its towns. They put them to the sword and fulfilled the doom on every person there, leaving no survivors. Thus was done to Debir and its king what had been done to Hebron, as well as to Libnah and its king.

40 Joshua conquered the entire country; the mountain regions, the Negeb, the foothills, and the mountain slopes, with all their kings. He left no survivors, but fulfilled the doom on all who lived there, just as the LORD, the God of Israel, had commanded. 41 Joshua conquered from Kadesh-barnea to Gaza, and all the land of Goshen to Gibeon. 42 All these kings and their lands Joshua captured in a single campaign, for the LORD, the God of Israel, fought for Israel. 43 Thereupon Joshua with all Israel returned to the camp at Gilgal.

11 When Jabin, king of Hazor, learned of this, he sent a message to Jobab, king of Madon, to the king of Shimron, to the king of Achshaph, 2 and to the northern kings in the mountain regions and in the Arabah near Chinneroth, in the foothills, and in Naphath-dor to the west. 3 These were Canaanites to the east and west, Amorites, Hittites, Perizzites and Jebusites in the mountain regions, and Hivites at the foot of Hermon in the land of Mizpah. 4 They came out with all their troops, an army numerous as the sands on the seashore, and with a multitude of horses and chariots. 5 All these kings joined forces and marched to the waters of Merom, where they encamped together to fight against Israel.

6 The LORD said to Joshua, "Do not fear them, for by this time tomorrow I will stretch them slain before Israel. You must hamstring their horses and burn their chariots." 7 Joshua with his whole army came upon them at the waters of Merom in a surprise attack. 8 The LORD delivered them into the power of the Israelites, who defeated them and pursued them to Greater Sidon, to Misrephoth-maim, and eastward to the valley of Mizpah. They struck them all down, leaving no survivors. 9 Joshua did to them as the LORD had commanded: he hamstrung their horses and burned their chariots.

10 At that time Joshua, turning back, captured Hazor and slew its king with the sword; for Hazor formerly was the chief of all those kingdoms. 11 He also fulfilled the doom by putting every person there to the sword, till none was left alive. Hazor itself he burned. 12 Joshua thus captured all those kings with their cities and put them to the sword, fulfilling the doom on them, as Moses, the servant of the LORD, had commanded. 13 However, Israel did not destroy by fire any of the cities built on raised sites, except Hazor,

Lachish at Israel's mercy, and Israel took it on the second day and put it and every living creature in it to the sword, as they had treated Libnah. 33 Horam king of Gezer then marched up to help Lachish, but Joshua beat him and his people until not one was left alive.

34 Joshua, and all Israel with him, went on from Lachish to Eglon. They besieged it and attacked it. 35 The same day they took it and put it to the sword. That day he delivered over to the curse of destruction every living creature there, treating it as he had treated Lachish.

36 Joshua, and all Israel with him, went on up from Eglon to Hebron. They attacked it, 37 took it and put it to the sword, with its king, its dependencies and every living creature in it. As he had treated Eglon, so here, he left no one alive. He delivered it over to the curse of destruction, with every living creature in it.

38 Joshua, and all Israel with him, then turned back on Debir and attacked it. 39 He took it and its king and all the places belonging to it; they put them to the sword, and every living creature there they delivered over to the curse of destruction. He left no one alive. As he had treated Hebron, as he had treated Libnah and its king, so he treated Debir and its king.

40 Thus Joshua subjugated the whole country: the highlands, the Negeb, the lowlands and watered foothills, and all their kings. He left not one survivor and put every living thing under the curse of destruction, as Yahweh, God of Israel, had commanded. 41 Joshua conquered them from Kadesh-Barnea to Gaza, and the whole region of Goshen as far as Gibeon. 42 All these kings and their territory Joshua captured in a single campaign, because Yahweh, God of Israel, fought for Israel. 43 And then Joshua, and all Israel with him, went back to the camp at Gilgal.

11 When Jabin king of Hazor heard about this, he sent word to Jobab king of Merom, to the king of Shimron, to the king of Achshaph 2 and to the kings in the northern highlands, in the plain south of Chinneroth, and those in the lowlands and on the slopes of Dor to the west. 3 To eastward and to westward lived the Canaanites: in the highlands, the Amorites, Hittites, Perizzites and Jebusites; the Hivites, at the foot of Hermon in the area of Mizpah. 4 They set out with all their troops, a people as numerous as the sands of the sea, with a huge number of horses and chariots.

5 These kings, having all agreed on a meeting place, came and set up camp together at the Waters of Merom, to fight Israel. 6 Yahweh then said to Joshua, 'Do not be afraid of them, for by this time tomorrow I shall hand them all over, cut to pieces, to Israel; you will hamstring their horses and burn their chariots.' 7 With all his warriors Joshua caught them unawares near the Waters of Merom and fell on them. 8 Yahweh put them at Israel's mercy they defeated them and pursued them as far as Sidon the Great, and as far as Misrephoth to the west, and as far as the Vale of Mizpah to the east; they harried them until not one of them was left alive. 9 Joshua treated them as Yahweh had told him; he hamstrung their horses and burned their chariots.

10 Joshua then turned back and captured Hazor, putting its king to the sword. Hazor in olden days was the capital of all these kingdoms. 11 In compliance with the curse of destruction, they put every living creature there to the sword. Not a living soul was left, and Hazor was burnt to the ground. 12 All these royal cities and all their kings Joshua put to the sword in compliance with the curse of destruction, as Moses, servant of Yahweh, had ordered.

13 Yet of all these towns standing on their mounds, Israel burned none, apart from Hazor, burnt by Joshua. 14 All the

| NEW REVISED STANDARD VERSION | REVISED ENGLISH BIBLE |

14 All the spoil of these towns, and the livestock, the Israelites took for their booty; but all the people they struck down with the edge of the sword, until they had destroyed them, and they did not leave any who breathed. 15 As the LORD had commanded his servant Moses, so Moses commanded Joshua, and so Joshua did; he left nothing undone of all that the LORD had commanded Moses.

16 So Joshua took all that land: the hill country and all the Negeb and all the land of Goshen and the lowland and the Arabah and the hill country of Israel and its lowland, 17 from Mount Halak, which rises toward Seir, as far as Baal-gad in the valley of Lebanon below Mount Hermon. He took all their kings, struck them down, and put them to death. 18 Joshua made war a long time with all those kings. 19 There was not a town that made peace with the Israelites, except the Hivites, the inhabitants of Gibeon; all were taken in battle. 20 For it was the LORD's doing to harden their hearts so that they would come against Israel in battle, in order that they might be utterly destroyed, and might receive no mercy, but be exterminated, just as the LORD had commanded Moses.

21 At that time Joshua came and wiped out the Anakim from the hill country, from Hebron, from Debir, from Anab, and from all the hill country of Judah, and from all the hill country of Israel; Joshua utterly destroyed them with their towns. 22 None of the Anakim was left in the land of the Israelites; some remained only in Gaza, in Gath, and in Ashdod. 23 So Joshua took the whole land, according to all that the LORD had spoken to Moses; and Joshua gave it for an inheritance to Israel according to their tribal allotments. And the land had rest from war.

12 Now these are the kings of the land, whom the Israelites defeated, whose land they occupied beyond the Jordan toward the east, from the Wadi Arnon to Mount Hermon, with all the Arabah eastward: 2 King Sihon of the Amorites who lived at Heshbon, and ruled from Aroer, which is on the edge of the Wadi Arnon, and from the middle of the valley as far as the river Jabbok, the boundary of the Ammonites, that is, half of Gilead, 3 and the Arabah to the Sea of Chinneroth eastward, and in the direction of Beth-jeshimoth, to the sea of the Arabah, the Dead Sea,r southward to the foot of the slopes of Pisgah; 4 and King Ogs of Bashan, one of the last of the Rephaim, who lived at Ashtaroth and at Edrei 5 and ruled over Mount Hermon and Salecah and all Bashan to the boundary of the Geshurites and the Maacathites, and over half of Gilead to the boundary of King Sihon of Heshbon. 6 Moses, the servant of the LORD, and the Israelites defeated them; and Moses the servant of the LORD gave their land for a possession to the Reubenites and the Gadites and the half-tribe of Manasseh.

7 The following are the kings of the land whom Joshua and the Israelites defeated on the west side of the Jordan, from Baal-gad in the valley of Lebanon to Mount Halak, that rises toward Seir (and Joshua gave their land to the tribes of Israel as a possession according to their allotments, 8 in the hill country, in the lowland, in the Arabah, in the slopes, in the wilderness, and in the Negeb, the land of the Hittites, Amorites, Canaanites, Perizzites, Hivites, and Jebusites):

	9	the king of Jericho	one
		the king of Ai, which is next to Bethel	one
	10	the king of Jerusalem	one
		the king of Hebron	one
	11	the king of Jarmuth	one
		the king of Lachish	one

plundered all these cities and kept for themselves the cattle and any other spoil they took; but they put every living soul to the sword until they had destroyed everyone; they did not leave alive anyone that drew breath. 15 The LORD had laid his commands on his servant Moses, and Moses laid these same commands on Joshua, and Joshua carried them out. Not one of the commands laid on Moses by the LORD was left unfulfilled.

16 Thus Joshua took the whole land, the hill-country, all the Negeb, all the land of Goshen, the Shephelah, the Arabah, and the Israelite hill-country with the adjoining lowlands. 17 His conquests extended from the bare mountain which leads up to Seir as far as Baal-gad in the vale of Lebanon under Mount Hermon. He captured all their kings, struck them down, and put them to death. 18 It was a lengthy campaign he waged against all those kingdoms; 19 except for the Hivites who lived in Gibeon, not one of their towns or cities came to terms with the Israelites; all had to be taken by storm. 20 It was the LORD's purpose that they should offer stubborn resistance to the Israelites, and thus be annihilated and utterly destroyed without mercy, as the LORD had commanded Moses.

21 It was then that Joshua proceeded to wipe out the Anakim from the hill-country, from Hebron, Debir, Anab, all the hill-country of Judah, and all the hill-country of Israel, destroying both them and their towns. 22 No Anakim were left in the land taken by the Israelites; they survived only in Gaza, Gath, and Ashdod.

23 Joshua took the whole land, fulfilling all the commands that the LORD had laid on Moses; he assigned it to Israel, allotting to each tribe its share. Then the land was at peace.

12 These are the names of the kings of the land whom the Israelites slew, and whose territory they occupied beyond the Jordan towards the sunrise from the wadi of the Arnon as far as Mount Hermon and all the Arabah on the east. 2 Sihon the Amorite king who lived in Heshbon: his rule extended from Aroer, which is on the edge of the wadi of the Arnon, along the middle of the wadi and over half Gilead as far as the wadi of the Jabbok, the Ammonite frontier; 3 along the Arabah as far as the eastern side of the sea of Kinnereth and as far as the eastern side of the sea of the Arabah, the Dead Sea, by the road to Beth-jeshimoth and from Teman under the watershed of Pisgah. 4 King Og of Bashan, one of the survivors of the Rephaim, who lived in Ashtaroth and Edrei: 5 he ruled over Mount Hermon, Salcah, all Bashan as far as the Geshurite and Maacathite borders, and half Gilead as far as the boundary of King Sihon of Heshbon. 6 Moses the servant of the LORD put them to death, he and the Israelites, and he assigned their land to the Reubenites, the Gadites, and half the tribe of Manasseh.

7 These are the kings whom Joshua and the Israelites put to death on the west side of Jordan, from Baal-gad in the vale of Lebanon as far as the bare mountain that leads up to Seir; Joshua assigned their land to the Israelite tribes according to their allotted shares, 8 in the hill-country, the Shephelah, the Arabah, the watersheds, the wilderness, and the Negeb; lands of the Hittites, Amorites, Canaanites, Perizzites, Hivites, and Jebusites: 9 the king of Jericho; the king of Ai which is beside Bethel; 10 the king of Jerusalem; the king of Hebron; 11 the king of Jarmuth; the king of Lachish;

---

r Heb Salt Sea   s Gk: Heb the boundary of King Og

12:3 **Dead Sea:** lit. Salt Sea.   12:4 **King Og:** so Gk; Heb. The boundary of King Og.   12:5 **Gilead as far as:** so Gk (Luc.); Heb. omits as far as.

which Joshua burned. 14 The Israelites took all the spoil and livestock of these cities as their booty; but the people they put to the sword, until they had exterminated the last of them, leaving none alive. 15 As the LORD had commanded his servant Moses, so Moses commanded Joshua, and Joshua acted accordingly. He left nothing undone that the LORD had commanded Moses should be done.

16 So Joshua captured all this land: the mountain regions, the entire Negeb, all the land of Goshen, the foothills, the Arabah, as well as the mountain regions and foothills of Israel, 17 from Mount Halak that rises toward Seir as far as Baal-gad in the Lebanon valley at the foot of Mount Hermon. All their kings he captured and put to death. 18 Joshua waged war against all these kings for a long time. 19 With the exception of the Hivites who lived in Gibeon, no city made peace with the Israelites; all were taken in battle. 20 For it was the design of the LORD to encourage them to wage war against Israel, that they might be doomed to destruction and thus receive no mercy, but be exterminated, as the LORD had commanded Moses.

21 At that time Joshua penetrated the mountain regions and exterminated the Anakim in Hebron, Debir, Anab, the entire mountain region of Judah, and the entire mountain region of Israel. Joshua fulfilled the doom on them and on their cities, 22 so that no Anakim were left in the land of the Israelites. However, some survived in Gaza, in Gath, and in Ashdod. 23 Thus Joshua captured the whole country, just as the LORD had foretold to Moses. Joshua gave it to Israel as their heritage, apportioning it among the tribes. And the land enjoyed peace.

12 The kings of the land east of the Jordan, from the River Arnon to Mount Hermon, including all the eastern section of the Arabah, whom the Israelites conquered and whose lands they occupied: 2 First, Sihon, king of the Amorites, who lived in Heshbon. His domain extended from Aroer, which is on the bank of the Wadi Arnon, to include the wadi itself, and the land northward through half of Gilead to the Wadi Jabbok, 3 as well as the Arabah from the eastern side of the Sea of Chinnereth, as far south as the eastern side of the Salt Sea of the Arabah in the direction of Beth-jeshimoth, to a point under the slopes of Pisgah. 4 Secondly, Og, king of Bashan, a survivor of the Rephaim, who lived at Ashtaroth and Edrei. 5 He ruled over Mount Hermon, Salecah, and all Bashan as far as the boundary of the Geshurites and Maacathites, and over half of Gilead as far as the territory of Sihon, king of Heshbon. 6 After Moses, the servant of the LORD, and the Israelites conquered them, he assigned their land to the Reubenites, the Gadites, and the half-tribe of Manasseh, as their property.

7 This is a list of the kings whom Joshua and the Israelites conquered west of the Jordan and whose land, from Baal-gad in the Lebanon valley to Mount Halak which rises toward Seir, Joshua apportioned to the tribes of Israel. 8 It included the mountain regions and foothills, the Arabah, the slopes, the desert, and the Negeb, belonging to the Hittites, Amorites, Canaanites, Perizzites, Hivites and Jebusites. 9 They were the kings of Jericho, Ai (which is near Bethel), 10 Jerusalem, Hebron, 11 Jarmuth, Lachish, 12 Eglon, Gezer,

spoils of these towns, including the livestock, the Israelites took as booty for themselves. But they put all the human beings to the sword till they had destroyed them completely; they did not leave a living soul.

15 What Yahweh had ordered his servant Moses, Moses in turn had ordered Joshua, and Joshua carried it out, leaving nothing undone of what Yahweh had ordered Moses. 16 In consequence, Joshua captured this entire country: the highlands, the whole Negeb and the whole of Goshen, the lowlands, the Arabah, the highlands and lowlands of Israel.

17 From Mount Halak, which rises towards Seir, to Baal-Gad in the Vale of Lebanon at the foot of Mount Hermon, he captured all their kings, struck them down and put them to death. 18 For many a day Joshua made war on all these kings; 19 no city had made peace with the Israelites except the Hivites who lived at Gibeon; all the rest had been captured in battle. 20 For Yahweh had decided to harden the hearts of these men, so that they would engage Israel in battle and thus come under the curse of destruction and so receive no quarter but be exterminated, as Yahweh had ordered Moses.

21 Joshua then went and wiped out the Anakim of the highlands, of Hebron, of Debir, of Anab, of all the highlands of Judah and of all the highlands of Israel; he delivered them and their towns over to the curse of destruction. 22 No Anakim were left in the territory of the Israelites, except at Gaza, Gath and Ashdod. 23 Joshua captured the entire country, just as Yahweh had told Moses, and he gave it as heritage to Israel, to be shared out between their tribes.

And the country had rest from warfare.

12 The kings of the country, whom the Israelites conquered and whose territory they took, on the further, eastern side of the Jordan, from the Wadi Arnon to Mount Hermon, with the entire Arabah to the east, were as follows:

2 Sihon king of the Amorites, who lived at Heshbon, ruled from Aroer which is on the edge of the Arnon Valley, including the bottom of the valley, half Gilead and as far as the Jabbok, the river forming the frontier with the Ammonites; 3 the eastern Arabah up to the Sea of Chinneroth, and as far as the Sea of the Arabah, or Salt Sea, on the eastern side, in the direction of Beth-Jeshimoth, and, in the south, the watered foothills of Mount Pisgah.

4 Og king of Bashan, one of the last of the Rephaim, who lived at Ashtaroth and Edrei, 5 ruled over Mount Hermon and Salecah, the whole of Bashan to the frontier of the Geshurites and Maacathites, and half Gilead to the frontier of Sihon king of Heshbon.

6 Moses, servant of Yahweh, and the Israelites conquered these, and Moses, servant of Yahweh, conferred their territory on the Reubenites, the Gadites and the half-tribe of Manasseh.

7 The kings of the country whom Joshua and the Israelites conquered on the nearer, western side of the Jordan, from Baal-Gad in the Vale of Lebanon to Mount Halak rising towards Seir, and whose heritage Joshua distributed to the tribes of Israel, dividing it up between them, were as follows:

8 In the highlands and the lowlands, in the Arabah and in the watered foothills, in the desert and in the Negeb, belonging to the Hittites, the Amorites, the Canaanites, the Perizzites, the Hivites and the Jebusites:

9 the king of Jericho,	one;
the king of Ai near Bethel,	one;
10 the king of Jerusalem,	one;
the king of Hebron,	one;
11 the king of Jarmuth,	one;
the king of Lachish,	one;

NEW REVISED STANDARD VERSION		REVISED ENGLISH BIBLE

12	the king of Eglon	one
	the king of Gezer	one
13	the king of Debir	one
	the king of Geder	one
14	the king of Hormah	one
	the king of Arad	one
15	the king of Libnah	one
	the king of Adullam	one
16	the king of Makkedah	one
	the king of Bethel	one
17	the king of Tappuah	one
	the king of Hepher	one
18	the king of Aphek	one
	the king of Lasharon	one
19	the king of Madon	one
	the king of Hazor	one
20	the king of Shimron-meron	one
	the king of Achshaph	one
21	the king of Taanach	one
	the king of Megiddo	one
22	the king of Kedesh	one
	the king of Jokneam in Carmel	one
23	the king of Dor in Naphath-dor	one
	the king of Goiim in Galilee,[t]	one
24	the king of Tirzah	one

thirty-one kings in all.

12 the king of Eglon; the king of Gezer; 13 the king of Debir; the king of Geder; 14 the king of Hormah; the king of Arad; 15 the king of Libnah; the king of Adullam; 16 the king of Makkedah; the king of Bethel; 17 the king of Tappuah; the king of Hepher; 18 the king of Aphek; the king of Aphek-in-Sharon; 19 the king of Madon; the king of Hazor; 20 the king of Shimron-meron; the king of Akshaph; 21 the king of Taanach; the king of Megiddo; 22 the king of Kedesh; the king of Jokneam-in-Carmel; 23 the king of Dor in the district of Dor; the king of Gaiam-in-Galilee; 24 the king of Tirzah: thirty-one kings in all, one of each town.

13 Now Joshua was old and advanced in years; and the LORD said to him, "You are old and advanced in years, and very much of the land still remains to be possessed. 2 This is the land that still remains: all the regions of the Philistines, and all those of the Geshurites 3 (from the Shihor, which is east of Egypt, northward to the boundary of Ekron, it is reckoned as Canaanite; there are five rulers of the Philistines, those of Gaza, Ashdod, Ashkelon, Gath, and Ekron), and those of the Avvim, 4 in the south, all the land of the Canaanites, and Mearah that belongs to the Sidonians, to Aphek, to the boundary of the Amorites, 5 and the land of the Gebalites, and all Lebanon, toward the east, from Baal-gad below Mount Hermon to Lebo-hamath, 6 all the inhabitants of the hill country from Lebanon to Misrephoth-maim, even all the Sidonians. I will myself drive them out from before the Israelites; only allot the land to Israel for an inheritance, as I have commanded you. 7 Now therefore divide this land for an inheritance to the nine tribes and the half-tribe of Manasseh."

8 With the other half-tribe of Manasseh[u] the Reubenites and the Gadites received their inheritance, which Moses gave them, beyond the Jordan eastward, as Moses the servant of the LORD gave them: 9 from Aroer, which is on the edge of the Wadi Arnon, and the town that is in the middle of the valley, and all the tableland from[v] Medeba as far as Dibon; 10 and all the cities of King Sihon of the Amorites, who reigned in Heshbon, as far as the boundary of the Ammonites; 11 and Gilead, and the region of the Geshurites and Maacathites, and all Mount Hermon, and all Bashan to Salecah; 12 all the kingdom of Og in Bashan, who reigned in Ashtaroth and in Edrei (he alone was left of the survivors of the Rephaim); these Moses had defeated and driven out. 13 Yet the Israelites did not drive out the Geshurites or the Maacathites; but Geshur and Maacath live within Israel to this day.

14 To the tribe of Levi alone Moses gave no inheritance;

13 BY this time Joshua had become very old, and the LORD said to him, 'You are now a very old man, and much of the country still remains to be occupied. 2 The remaining territory is this: all the districts of the Philistines and all the Geshurite country 3 (this is reckoned as Canaanite territory from Shihor to the east of Egypt as far north as Ekron; and it belongs to the five lords of the Philistines, those of Gaza, Ashdod, Ashkelon, Gath, and Ekron); all the districts of the Avvim 4 on the south; all the Canaanite country from Mearah which belongs to the Sidonians as far as Aphek, the Amorite frontier; 5 the land of the Gebalites and all the Lebanon to the east from Baal-gad under Mount Hermon as far as Lebo-hamath. 6 I shall drive out in favour of the Israelites all the inhabitants of the hill-country from the Lebanon as far as Misrephoth on the west, and all the Sidonians. In the mean time, following my command, you are to allot all this to the Israelites as their holding. 7 Distribute this country now to the nine tribes and the half tribe of Manasseh as their holding.'

8 HALF the tribe of Manasseh, and with them the Reubenites and the Gadites, had taken the holding which Moses gave them east of the Jordan, as Moses the servant of the LORD had ordained. 9 It started from Aroer which is on the edge of the wadi of the Arnon, and the level land half-way along the wadi, and included all the tableland from Medeba as far as Dibon, 10 all the towns of Sihon, the Amorite king who ruled in Heshbon, as far as the Ammonite frontier; 11 and it also included Gilead and the Geshurite and Maacathite territory, and all Mount Hermon and the whole of Bashan as far as Salcah, 12 all the kingdom of Og which he ruled from both Ashtaroth and Edrei in Bashan. He was a survivor from the remnant of the Rephaim, but Moses put both kings to death and occupied their lands. 13 But the Israelites failed to drive out the Geshurites and the Maacathites, and they live among Israel to this day. 14 The tribe of Levi, however,

---

[t] Gk: Heb Gilgal
[u] Cn: Heb With it
[v] Compare Gk: Heb lacks from

12:18 **of Aphek-in-Sharon:** prob. rdg; Heb. omits Aphek.
12:20 **Shimron-meron:** in 11:1 Shimron.
12:23 **Gaiam-in-Galilee:** prob. rdg, cp. Gk; Heb. nations to Gilgal.
13:8 **Half . . . Manasseh, and:** prob. rdg; Heb. omits.

13 Debir, Geder, 14 Hormah, Arad, 15 Libnah, Adullam, 16 Makkedah, Bethel, 17 Tappuah, Hepher, 18 Aphek, Lasharon, 19 Madon, Hazor, 20 Shimron, Achshaph, 21 Taanach, Megiddo, 22 Kedesh, Jokneam (at Carmel), 23 and Dor (in Naphath-dor), the foreign king at Gilgal, 24 and the king of Tirzah, thirty-one kings in all.

12 the king of Eglon,   one;
    the king of Gezer,   one;
13 the king of Debir,   one;
    the king of Geder,   one;
14 the king of Hormah,   one;
    the king of Arad,   one;
15 the king of Libnah,   one;
    the king of Adullam,   one;
16 the king of Makkedah,   one;
    the king of Bethel,   one;
17 the king of Tappuah,   one;
    the king of Hepher,   one;
18 the king of Aphek,   one;
    the king of Sharon,   one;
19 the king of Merom,   one;
    the king of Hazor,   one;
20 the king of Shimron Meron,   one;
    the king of Achshaph,   one;
21 the king of Taanach,   one;
    the king of Megiddo,   one;
22 the king of Kedesh,   one;
    the king of Jokneam in Carmel,   one;
23 the king of Dor, on the Slopes of Dor,   one;
    the king of the nations in Galilee,   one;
24 the king of Tirzah,   one.
Total number of all these kings: thirty-one.

13 When Joshua was old and advanced in years, the LORD said to him: "Though now you are old and advanced in years, a very large part of the land still remains to be conquered. 2 This additional land includes all Geshur and all the districts of the Philistines 3 (from the stream adjoining Egypt to the boundary of Ekron in the north is reckoned Canaanite territory, though held by the five lords of the Philistines in Gaza, Ashdod, Ashkelon, Gath and Ekron); also where the Avvim are in the south; 4 all the land of the Canaanites from Mearah of the Sidonians to Aphek, and the boundaries of the Amorites; 5 and the Gebalite territory; and all the Lebanon to the east, from Baal-gad at the foot of Mount Hermon to Labo in the land of Hamath. 6 At the advance of the Israelites I will drive out all the Sidonian inhabitants of the mountain regions between Lebanon and Misrephoth-maim; at least include these areas in the division of the Israelite heritage, just as I have commanded you. 7 Now, therefore, apportion among the nine tribes and the half-tribe of Manasseh the land which is to be their heritage."

8 Now the other half of the tribe of Manasseh, as well as the Reubenites and Gadites, had received their heritage which Moses, the servant of the LORD, had given them east of the Jordan: 9 from Aroer on the bank of the Wadi Arnon and the city in the wadi itself, through the tableland of Medeba and Dibon, 10 with the rest of the cities of Sihon, king of the Amorites, who reigned in Heshbon, to the boundary of the Ammonites; 11 also Gilead and the territory of the Geshurites and Maacathites, all Mount Hermon, and all Bashan as far as Salecah, 12 the entire kingdom in Bashan of Og, a survivor of the Rephaim, who reigned in Ashtaroth and Edrei. Though Moses conquered and occupied these territories, 13 the Israelites did not dislodge the Geshurites and Maacathites, so that Geshur and Maacath survive in the midst of Israel to this day. 14 However, to the

13 Now Joshua had grown old and advanced in years. Yahweh said to him, 'You are now old and advanced in years, yet there is still a great deal of territory left to be taken possession of. 2 This is all the territory left: 'All the districts of the Philistines and the whole country of the Geshurites; 3 from the Shihor, facing Egypt, to the frontier of Ekron in the north, is reckoned as Canaanite territory. The five rulers of the Philistines have their seats at Gaza, Ashdod, Ashkelon, Gath and Ekron, respectively; the Avvites are in 4 the south. The entire territory of the Canaanites, and Mearah which belongs to the Sidonians, as far as Aphekah and as far as the frontier of the Amorites; 5 and then the country of the Gebalites with the entire Lebanon eastwards from Baal-Gad at the foot of Mount Hermon to the Pass of Hamath.

6 'All who live in the highlands from the Lebanon to Misrephoth in the west — all the Sidonians — I myself shall dispossess before the Israelites. All you have to do is to distribute the territory as a heritage for the Israelites as I have ordered you. 7 The time has come to divide this territory as a heritage between the nine tribes and the half-tribe of Manasseh: from the Jordan as far as the Great Sea in the west, you must give it them; the Great Sea will be their limit.'

8 As regards the other half-tribe of Manasseh, this and the Reubenites and Gadites had already received their heritage, given them by Moses on the further, eastern side of the Jordan, the one which Moses, servant of Yahweh, had already given them: 9 The country onwards from Aroer on the edge of the Arnon Valley, with the town in the bottom of the valley and the entire tableland from Medeba to Dibon; 10 all the towns of Sihon king of the Amorites, who had reigned in Heshbon, to the frontier of the Ammonites; 11 then Gilead and the territory of the Geshurites and Maacathites with the whole Hermon range and the whole of Bashan as far as Salecah; 12 and in Bashan, the whole kingdom of Og, who had reigned in Ashtaroth and Edrei, and was the last of the survivors of the Rephaim. Moses had conquered and dispossessed these two kings. 13 The Israelites did not, however, dispossess either the Geshurites or the Maacathites, hence Geshur and Maacah survive inside Israel even today.

14 To the tribe of Levi alone no heritage was given;

NEW REVISED STANDARD VERSION

REVISED ENGLISH BIBLE

the offerings by fire to the LORD God of Israel are their inheritance, as he said to them.

15 Moses gave an inheritance to the tribe of the Reubenites according to their clans. 16 Their territory was from Aroer, which is on the edge of the Wadi Arnon, and the town that is in the middle of the valley, and all the tableland by Medeba; 17 with Heshbon, and all its towns that are in the tableland; Dibon, and Bamoth-baal, and Beth-baal-meon, 18 and Jahaz, and Kedemoth, and Mephaath, 19 and Kiriathaim, and Sibmah, and Zereth-shahar on the hill of the valley, 20 and Beth-peor, and the slopes of Pisgah, and Beth-jeshimoth, 21 that is, all the towns of the tableland, and all the kingdom of King Sihon of the Amorites, who reigned in Heshbon, whom Moses defeated with the leaders of Midian, Evi and Rekem and Zur and Hur and Reba, as princes of Sihon, who lived in the land. 22 Along with the rest of those they put to death, the Israelites also put to the sword Balaam son of Beor, who practiced divination. 23 And the border of the Reubenites was the Jordan and its banks. This was the inheritance of the Reubenites, according to their families with their towns and villages.

24 Moses gave an inheritance also to the tribe of the Gadites, according to their families. 25 Their territory was Jazer, and all the towns of Gilead, and half the land of the Ammonites, to Aroer, which is east of Rabbah, 26 and from Heshbon to Ramath-mizpeh and Betonim, and from Mahanaim to the territory of Debir,*w* 27 and in the valley Beth-haram, Beth-nimrah, Succoth, and Zaphon, the rest of the kingdom of King Sihon of Heshbon, the Jordan and its banks, as far as the lower end of the Sea of Chinnereth, eastward beyond the Jordan. 28 This is the inheritance of the Gadites according to their clans, with their towns and villages.

29 Moses gave an inheritance to the half-tribe of Manasseh; it was allotted to the half-tribe of the Manassites according to their families. 30 Their territory extended from Mahanaim, through all Bashan, the whole kingdom of King Og of Bashan, and all the settlements of Jair, which are in Bashan, sixty towns, 31 and half of Gilead, and Ashtaroth, and Edrei, the towns of the kingdom of Og in Bashan; these were allotted to the people of Machir son of Manasseh according to their clans — for half the Machirites.

32 These are the inheritances that Moses distributed in the plains of Moab, beyond the Jordan east of Jericho. 33 But to the tribe of Levi Moses gave no inheritance; the LORD God of Israel is their inheritance, as he said to them.

14 These are the inheritances that the Israelites received in the land of Canaan, which the priest Eleazar, and Joshua son of Nun, and the heads of the families of the tribes of the Israelites distributed to them. 2 Their inheritance was by lot, as the LORD had commanded Moses for the nine and one-half tribes. 3 For Moses had given an inheritance to the two and one-half tribes beyond the Jordan; but to the Levites he gave no inheritance among them. 4 For the people of Joseph were two tribes, Manasseh and Ephraim; and no portion was given to the Levites in the land, but only towns to live in, with their pasture lands for their flocks and herds. 5 The Israelites did as the LORD commanded Moses; they allotted the land.

6 Then the people of Judah came to Joshua at Gilgal; and Caleb son of Jephunneh the Kenizzite said to him, "You know what the LORD said to Moses the man of God in Kadesh-barnea concerning you and me. 7 I was forty years old when Moses the servant of the LORD sent me from Kadesh-barnea to spy out the land; and I brought him an honest report. 8 But my companions who went up with me

received no holding; the LORD the God of Israel is their portion, as he promised them.

15 So Moses allotted territory to the tribe of the Reubenites family by family. 16 Their territory started from Aroer which is on the edge of the wadi of the Arnon, and the level land half-way along the wadi, and included all the tableland as far as Medeba; 17 Heshbon and all its towns on the tableland, Dibon, Bamoth-baal, Beth-baal-meon, 18 Jahaz, Kedemoth, Mephaath, 19 Kiriathaim, Sibmah, Zereth-shahar on the hill in the valley, 20 Beth-peor, the watershed of Pisgah, and Beth-jeshimoth, 21 all the towns of the tableland, all the kingdom of Sihon the Amorite king who ruled in Heshbon, whom Moses put to death together with the princes of Midian: Evi, Rekem, Zur, Hur, and Reba, the vassals of Sihon who dwelt in the country. 22 Balaam son of Beor, who practised augury, was among those whom the Israelites put to the sword. 23 The boundary of the Reubenites was the Jordan and the land adjacent: this is the holding of the Reubenites family by family, both the towns and their hamlets.

24 Moses allotted territory to the Gadites family by family. 25 Their territory was Jazer, all the towns of Gilead, and half the Ammonite country as far as Aroer which is east of Rabbah. 26 It reached from Heshbon as far as Ramath-mizpeh and Betonim, and from Mahanaim as far as the boundary of Lo-debar; 27 it included, in the valley, Beth-haram, Beth-nimrah, Succoth, and Zaphon, the rest of the kingdom of King Sihon of Heshbon. The boundary was the Jordan and the adjacent land as far as the end of the sea of Kinnereth east of the Jordan. 28 This is the holding of the Gadites family by family, both the towns and their hamlets.

29 Moses allotted territory to the half tribe of Manasseh: it was for half the tribe of the Manassites family by family. 30 Their territory ran from Mahanaim and included all Bashan, all the kingdom of King Og of Bashan, and all Havvoth-jair in Bashan — sixty towns. 31 Half Gilead, and Ashtaroth and Edrei, the royal cities of Og in Bashan, belong to the sons of Machir son of Manasseh on behalf of half the Machirites family by family.

32 These are the territories which Moses allotted to the tribes as their holdings in the lowlands of Moab east of the Jordan. 33 But to the tribe of Levi he gave no holding: the LORD the God of Israel is their portion, as he promised them.

14 THE following are the possessions which the Israelites acquired in the land of Canaan, as Eleazar the priest, Joshua son of Nun, and the heads of the families of the Israelite tribes allotted them. 2 They were assigned by lot, following the LORD's command given through Moses, to the nine and a half tribes. 3 To two and a half tribes Moses had given holdings beyond the Jordan; but he gave none to the Levites as he did to the other tribes. 4 The tribe of Joseph formed the two tribes of Manasseh and Ephraim. The Levites were given no share in the land, only towns to live in, with their common land for flocks and herds. 5 So the Israelites assigned the land according to the LORD's command given to Moses.

6 The tribe of Judah had come to Joshua at Gilgal, and Caleb son of Jephunneh the Kenizzite said to him, 'You remember what the LORD said to Moses the man of God concerning you and me at Kadesh-barnea. 7 I was forty years old when Moses the servant of the LORD sent me from there to reconnoitre the land, and I brought back an honest report. 8 The others who went up with me discouraged the

---

w Gk Syr Vg: Heb *Lidebir*

13:14 **holding:** *so Gk; Heb. adds* the food-offerings of.
13:24 **allotted:** *so Gk; Heb. adds* to the tribe of Gad.
13:32 **Jordan:** *so Syriac; Heb. adds* Jericho.

tribe of Levi Moses assigned no heritage since, as the LORD had promised them, the LORD, the God of Israel, is their heritage.

15 What Moses gave to the Reubenite clans: 16 Their territory reached from Aroer, on the bank of the Wadi Arnon, and the city in the wadi itself, through the tableland about Medeba, 17 to include Heshbon and all its towns which are on the tableland, Dibon, Bamoth-baal, Beth-baal-meon, 18 Jahaz, Kedemoth, Mephaath, 19 Kiriathaim, Sibmah, Zereth-shahar on the knoll within the valley, 20 Beth-peor, the slopes of Pisgah, Beth-jeshimoth, 21 and the other cities of the tableland and, generally, of the kingdom of Sihon. This Amorite king, who reigned in Heshbon, Moses had killed, with his vassals, the princes of Midian, who were settled in the land: Evi, Rekem, Zur, Hur and Reba; 22 and among their slain followers the Israelites put to the sword also the soothsayer Balaam, son of Beor. 23 The boundary of the Reubenites was the bank of the Jordan. These cities and their villages were the heritage of the clans of the Reubenites.

24 What Moses gave to the Gadite clans: 25 Their territory included Jazer, all the cities of Gilead, and half the land of the Ammonites as far as Aroer, toward Rabbah 26 (that is, from Heshbon to Ramath-mizpeh and Betonim, and from Mahanaim to the boundary of Lodebar); 27 and in the Jordan valley: Beth-haram, Beth-nimrah, Succoth, Zaphon, the other part of the kingdom of Sihon, king of Heshbon, with the bank of the Jordan to the southeastern tip of the Sea of Chinnereth. 28 These cities and their villages were the heritage of the clans of the Gadites.

29 What Moses gave to the clans of the half-tribe of Manasseh: 30 Their territory included Mahanaim, all of Bashan, the entire kingdom of Og, king of Bashan, and all the villages of Jair, which are sixty cities in Bashan. 31 Half of Gilead, with Ashtaroth and Edrei, once the royal cities of Og in Bashan, fell to the descendants of Machir, son of Manasseh, for half the clans descended from Machir.

32 These are the portions which Moses gave when he was in the plains of Moab, beyond the Jordan east of Jericho. 33 However, Moses gave no heritage to the tribe of Levi, since the LORD himself, the God of Israel, is their heritage, as he promised.

14 Here follow the portions which the Israelites received in the land of Canaan. Eleazar the priest, Joshua, son of Nun, and the heads of families in the tribes of the Israelites determined 2 their heritage by lot, in accordance with the instructions the LORD had given through Moses concerning the remaining nine and a half tribes. 3 For to two and a half tribes Moses had already given a heritage beyond the Jordan; and though the Levites were given no heritage among the tribes, 4 the descendants of Joseph formed two tribes, Manasseh and Ephraim. The Levites themselves received no share of the land except cities to live in, with their pasture lands for the cattle and flocks.

5 Thus, in apportioning the land, did the Israelites carry out the instructions of the LORD to Moses.

6 When the Judahites came up to Joshua in Gilgal, the Kenizzite Caleb, son of Jephunneh, said to him: "You know what the LORD said to the man of God, Moses, about you and me in Kadesh-barnea. 7 I was forty years old when the servant of the LORD, Moses, sent me from Kadesh-barnea to reconnoiter the land; and I brought back to him a conscientious report. 8 My fellow scouts who went up with me

Yahweh, God of Israel, was his heritage, as he had told him.

15 Moses had given the tribe of the sons of Reuben a share by clans. 16 Thus, their territory was the entire tableland from Aroer on the edge of the Arnon Valley, with the town in the bottom of the valley, as far as Medeba, 17 Heshbon with all the towns on the tableland: Dibon, Bamoth-Baal, Beth-Baal-Meon, 18 Jahaz, Kedemoth, Mephaath, 19 Kiriathaim, Sibmah and, in the highlands of the Arabah, Zereth-Shahar; 20 Beth-Peor, the watered foothills of Mount Pisgah, Beth-ha-Jeshimoth, 21 all the towns on the tableland and the entire kingdom of Sihon king of the Amorites, who had reigned in Heshbon; he had been defeated by Moses, and with him the princes of Midian, Evi, Rekem, Zur, Hur and Reba, vassals of Sihon, formerly living in the country.

22 As regards Balaam son of Beor, the soothsayer, the Israelites had put him to the sword with those whom they had killed.

23 The boundary of the Reubenites was the Jordan and its territory.

Such was the heritage of the sons of Reuben, by clans, with the towns and villages belonging to them.

24 Moses had given the tribe of Gad, the sons of Gad, a share by clans. 25 Their territory was Jazer, all the towns of Gilead, half the country of the Ammonites as far as Aroer facing Rabbah, 26 and from Heshbon to Ramath-Mizpeh and Betonim; from Mahanaim as far as the territory of Lo-Debar, 27 and in the valley: Beth-Haram, Beth-Nimrah, Succoth, and Zaphon — the rest of the kingdom of Sihon king of Heshbon — the Jordan and the territory running to the tip of the Sea of Chinneroth, on the further, eastern side of the Jordan.

28 Such was the heritage of the sons of Gad, by clans, with their towns and villages belonging to them.

29 Moses had given the half-tribe of Manasseh a share by clans. 30 Their territory, starting from Mahanaim, was the whole of Bashan, the entire kingdom of Og king of Bashan, all the Encampments of Jair in Bashan: sixty towns. 31 Half of Gilead, with Ashtaroth, and Edrei, the royal cities of Og in Bashan, were allotted to the sons of Machir son of Manasseh, to half of the sons of Machir, by clans.

32 This was what Moses had conferred in heritage on the Plains of Moab on the further, eastern side of the Jordan opposite Jericho. 33 To the tribe of Levi, however, Moses gave no heritage; Yahweh, God of Israel, was his heritage, as he had told him.

14 This was what the Israelites received as their heritage in Canaan, which was given them as their heritage by the priest, Eleazar, and by Joshua son of Nun, with the heads of families of the tribes of Israel. 2 They received their heritage by lot, as Yahweh had ordered through Moses, as regards the nine tribes and the half-tribe. 3 For Moses himself had given the two-and-a-half tribes their heritage on the further side of the Jordan, although to the Levites he had given no heritage with them. 4 Since the sons of Joseph formed two tribes, Manasseh and Ephraim, no share in the country was given to the Levites, apart from some towns to live in, with their pasture lands for their livestock and their possessions. 5 The Israelites did as Yahweh had ordered Moses, and shared out the country.

6 Some sons of Judah came to Joshua at Gilgal, and Caleb son of Jephunneh the Kenizzite said to him, 'You know what Yahweh said to Moses, man of God, at Kadesh-Barnea concerning you and me. 7 I was forty years old when Moses, servant of Yahweh, sent me from Kadesh-Barnea to reconnoitre this country, and I made him a completely honest report. 8 The brothers, however, who had gone up with

NEW REVISED STANDARD VERSION

made the heart of the people melt; yet I wholeheartedly followed the LORD my God. 9 And Moses swore on that day, saying, 'Surely the land on which your foot has trodden shall be an inheritance for you and your children forever, because you have wholeheartedly followed the LORD my God.' 10 And now, as you see, the LORD has kept me alive, as he said, these forty-five years since the time that the LORD spoke this word to Moses, while Israel was journeying through the wilderness; and here I am today, eighty-five years old. 11 I am still as strong today as I was on the day that Moses sent me; my strength now is as my strength was then, for war, and for going and coming. 12 So now give me this hill country of which the LORD spoke on that day; for you heard on that day how the Anakim were there, with great fortified cities; it may be that the LORD will be with me, and I shall drive them out, as the LORD said."

13 Then Joshua blessed him, and gave Hebron to Caleb son of Jephunneh for an inheritance. 14 So Hebron became the inheritance of Caleb son of Jephunneh the Kenizzite to this day, because he wholeheartedly followed the LORD, the God of Israel. 15 Now the name of Hebron formerly was Kiriath-arba;ˣ this Arba wasʸ the greatest man among the Anakim. And the land had rest from war.

15 The lot for the tribe of the people of Judah according to their families reached southward to the boundary of Edom, to the wilderness of Zin at the farthest south. 2 And their south boundary ran from the end of the Dead Sea,ᶻ from the bay that faces southward; 3 it goes out southward of the ascent of Akrabbim, passes along to Zin, and goes up south of Kadesh-barnea, along by Hezron, up to Addar, makes a turn to Karka, 4 passes along to Azmon, goes out by the Wadi of Egypt, and comes to its end at the sea. This shall be your south boundary. 5 And the east boundary is the Dead Sea,ᶻ to the mouth of the Jordan. And the boundary on the north side runs from the bay of the sea at the mouth of the Jordan; 6 and the boundary goes up to Beth-hoglah, and passes along north of Beth-arabah; and the boundary goes up to the Stone of Bohan, Reuben's son; 7 and the boundary goes up to Debir from the Valley of Achor, and so northward, turning toward Gilgal, which is opposite the ascent of Adummim, which is on the south side of the valley; and the boundary passes along to the waters of En-shemesh, and ends at En-rogel; 8 then the boundary goes up by the valley of the son of Hinnom at the southern slope of the Jebusites (that is, Jerusalem); and the boundary goes up to the top of the mountain that lies over against the valley of Hinnom, on the west, at the northern end of the valley of Rephaim; 9 then the boundary extends from the top of the mountain to the spring of the Waters of Nephtoah, and from there to the towns of Mount Ephron; then the boundary bends around to Baalah (that is, Kiriath-jearim); 10 and the boundary circles west of Baalah to Mount Seir, passes along to the northern slope of Mount Jearim (that is, Chesalon), and goes down to Beth-shemesh, and passes along by Timnah; 11 the boundary goes out to the slope of the hill north of Ekron, then the boundary bends around to Shikkeron, and passes along to Mount Baalah, and goes out to Jabneel; then the boundary comes to an end at the sea. 12 And the west boundary was the Mediterranean with its coast. This is the boundary surrounding the people of Judah according to their families.

13 According to the commandment of the LORD to Joshua, he gave to Caleb son of Jephunneh a portion among the people of Judah, Kiriath-arba,ˣ that is, Hebron (Arba was the father of Anak). 14 And Caleb drove out from there the three sons of Anak: Sheshai, Ahiman, and Talmai, the descendants of Anak. 15 From there he went up against the

REVISED ENGLISH BIBLE

people, but I loyally carried out the purpose of the LORD my God. 9 Moses swore an oath that day: "The land on which you have set foot", he said, "is to be your holding and your sons' after you as a possession for ever; for you have loyally carried out the purpose of the LORD my God." 10 Well, the LORD has spared my life as he promised; it is forty-five years since he made this promise to Moses, at the time when Israel was journeying in the wilderness. Now here I am at eighty-five, 11 still as strong as I was on the day when Moses sent me out; I am as fit now for war as I was then and am ready to take the field again. 12 Give me today this hill-country which the LORD then promised me. You yourself heard on that day that the Anakim were there and their towns were large and fortified. Perhaps the LORD will be with me, and I shall drive them out as he promised.'

13 Joshua blessed Caleb and gave him Hebron for his holding, 14 and that is why Hebron remains to this day in the possession of Caleb son of Jephunneh the Kenizzite. It is because he loyally carried out the purpose of the LORD the God of Israel. 15 Formerly the name of Hebron was Kiriath-arba; this Arba was the chief man of the Anakim.

The land was now at peace.

15 This is the territory allotted to the tribe of the sons of Judah family by family. It started from the Edomite frontier at the wilderness of Zin and ran as far as the Negeb at its southern end, 2 and it had a common border with the Negeb at the end of the Dead Sea, where an inlet of water bends towards the Negeb. 3 It continued from the south by the ascent of Akrabbim, passed by Zin, went up from the south of Kadesh-barnea, passed by Hezron, went on to Addar, and turned round to Karka. 4 It then passed along to Azmon, reached the wadi of Egypt, and its limit was the sea. This was their southern boundary.

5 The eastern boundary is the Dead Sea as far as the mouth of the Jordan and the adjacent land northwards from the inlet of the sea, at the mouth of the Jordan. 6 The boundary goes up to Beth-hoglah; it passes north of Beth-arabah and thence to the stone of Bohan son of Reuben, 7 thence to Debir from the vale of Achor, and then turns north to the districts in front of the ascent of Adummim south of the wadi. The boundary then passes the waters of En-shemesh and the limit there is En-rogel. 8 It then goes up by the valley of Ben-hinnom to the southern slope of the Jebusites (that is Jerusalem). Thence it goes up to the top of the hill which faces the valley of Hinnom on the west; this is at the northern end of the vale of Rephaim. 9 The boundary then bends round from the top of the hill to the spring of the waters of Nephtoah and runs round to the cities of Mount Ephron and to Baalah, that is Kiriath-jearim. 10 It then continues westwards from Baalah to Mount Seir, passes on to the north side of the slope of Mount Jearim, that is Kesalon, down to Beth-shemesh and on to Timnah. 11 The boundary then goes north to the slope of Ekron, bends round to Shikkeron, crosses to Mount Baalah, and reaches Jebneel; its limit is the sea. 12 The western boundary is the Great Sea and the land adjacent. This is the whole circuit of the boundary of the tribe of Judah family by family.

13 Caleb son of Jephunneh received his share of the land within the tribe of Judah as the LORD had told Joshua. It was Kiriath-arba, that is Hebron; this Arba was the ancestor of the Anakim. 14 Caleb drove out the three Anakim, Sheshai, Ahiman, and Talmai, descendants of Anak. 15 From there

---

ˣ That is *the city of Arba*   ʸ Heb lacks *this Arba was*   ᶻ Heb *Salt Sea*

15:4 **their:** *so Gk; Heb.* your.   15:7 **to the districts:** *prob. rdg, cp. 18:17; Heb.* to Gilgal.

discouraged the people, but I was completely loyal to the LORD, my God. 9 On that occasion Moses swore this oath, 'The land where you have set foot shall become your heritage and that of your descendants forever, because you have been completely loyal to the LORD, my God.' 10 Now, as he promised, the LORD has preserved me while Israel was journeying through the desert, for the forty-five years since the LORD spoke thus to Moses; and although I am now eighty-five years old, 11 I am still as strong today as I was the day Moses sent me forth, with no less vigor whether for war or for ordinary tasks. 12 Give me, therefore, this mountain region which the LORD promised me that day, as you yourself heard. True, the Anakim are there, with large fortified cities, but if the LORD is with me I shall be able to drive them out, as the LORD promised." 13 Joshua blessed Caleb, son of Jephunneh, and gave him Hebron as his heritage. 14 Therefore Hebron remains the heritage of the Kenizzite Caleb, son of Jephunneh, to the present day, because he was completely loyal to the LORD, the God of Israel. 15 Hebron was formerly called Kiriath-arba, for Arba, the greatest among the Anakim. And the land enjoyed peace.

15 The lot for the clans of the Judahite tribe fell in the extreme south toward the boundary of Edom, the desert of Zin in the Negeb. 2 The boundary there ran from the bay that forms the southern end of the Salt Sea, 3 southward below the pass of Akrabbim, across through Zin, up to a point south of Kadesh-barnea, across to Hezron, and up to Addar; from there, looping around Karka, 4 it crossed to Azmon and then joined the Wadi of Egypt before coming out at the sea. [This is your southern boundary.] 5 The eastern boundary was the Salt Sea as far as the mouth of the Jordan.

6 The northern boundary climbed from the bay where the Jordan meets the sea, up to Beth-hoglah, and ran north of Beth-arabah, up to Eben-Bohan-ben-Reuben. 7 Thence it climbed to Debir, north of the vale of Achor, in the direction of the Gilgal that faces the pass of Adummim, on the south side of the wadi; from there it crossed to the waters of En-shemesh and emerged at En-rogel. 8 Climbing again to the Valley of Ben-Hinnom on the southern flank of the Jebusites [that is, Jerusalem], the boundary rose to the top of the mountain at the northern end of the Valley of Rephaim, which bounds the Valley of Hinnom on the west. 9 From the top of the mountain it ran to the fountain of waters of Nephtoah, extended to the cities of Mount Ephron, and continued to Baalah, or Kiriath-jearim. 10 From Baalah the boundary curved westward to Mount Seir and passed north of the ridge of Mount Jearim (that is, Chesalon); thence it descended to Beth-shemesh, and ran across to Timnah. 11 It then extended along the northern flank of Ekron, continued through Shikkeron, and across to Mount Baalah, thence to include Jabneel, before it came out at the sea. 12 The western boundary was the Great Sea and its coast. This was the complete boundary of the clans of the Judahites.

13 As the LORD had commanded, Joshua gave Caleb, son of Jephunneh, a portion among the Judahites, namely, Kiriath-arba (Arba was the father of Anak), that is, Hebron. 14 And Caleb drove out from there the three Anakim, the descendants of Anak: Sheshai, Ahiman and Talmai. 15 From

me discouraged the people, whereas I myself scrupulously obeyed Yahweh my God. 9 That day Moses swore this oath, "Be sure of this, that the country your foot has trodden will be a heritage for you and your children for ever, since you have scrupulously obeyed Yahweh my God." 10 From then till now, Yahweh has kept me alive in observance of his promise. It is forty-five years since Yahweh said this to Moses — Israel was then going through the desert — and now I am eighty-five years old. 11 Today I am still as strong as the day when Moses sent me out on that errand; for fighting, for going and coming, I am as strong now as then. 12 It is time you gave me the highlands, of which Yahweh spoke to me that day. You heard that day that there were Anakim and large, fortified towns there; but if Yahweh is with me, I shall drive them out, as Yahweh has said.'

13 Joshua blessed Caleb son of Jephunneh and gave him Hebron as heritage. 14 And hence Hebron down to the present day has remained the heritage of Caleb son of Jephunneh the Kenizzite, since he had scrupulously obeyed Yahweh, God of Israel. 15 Hebron in olden days was called Kiriath-Arba. Arba had been the greatest of the Anakim. And the country had rest from warfare.

15 The portion falling to the tribe of the sons of Judah, by clans, was near the frontier of Edom, from the desert of Zin southwards to Kadesh in the south. 2 Their southern frontier began at the tip of the Salt Sea, at the southerly bay; 3 it proceeded south of the Ascent of Scorpions, crossed Zin and came up to Kadesh-Barnea from the south; past Hezron, it went on to Addar and turned towards Karka; 4 the frontier then went on to Azmon, came out at the Torrent of Egypt and reached as far as the sea. This is to be your southern frontier.

5 The eastern frontier was the Salt Sea as far as the mouth of the Jordan.

6 The northern frontier began at the bay at the mouth of the Jordan. The boundary went up to Beth-Hoglah, passed north of Beth-ha-Arabah and went on to the Stone of Bohan son of Reuben. 7 The boundary then went on to Debir from the Vale of Achor and turned north towards the stone circle opposite the Ascent of Adummim, which is south of the Torrent; the boundary went on to the Waters of En-Shemesh and came out at En-Rogel. 8 It then went back up the Valley of Hinnom, coming from the south to the flank of the Jebusite — that is, Jerusalem — and climbed to the crest of the mountain barring the Valley of Hinnom to the west, at the northern end of the Valley of the Rephaim. 9 From the mountain top, the boundary curved round to the spring of the Waters of Nephtoah, went on to the towns of Mount Ephron and then turned towards Baalah — that is, Kiriath-Jearim. 10 From Baalah, the boundary curved westwards to the highlands of Seir, skirted the northern slope of Mount Jearim — that is, Chesalon — went down to Beth-Shemesh and through Timnah, 11 came out on the northern flank of Ekron, turned towards Shikkeron and, passing through the highlands of Baalah, came out at Jabneel, and reached as far as the sea.

12 The western boundary was the Great Sea itself. Such was the frontier surrounding the sons of Judah, by clans.

13 Caleb son of Jephunneh was given a share within that of the sons of Judah, in accordance with Yahweh's order to Joshua: Kiriath-Arba, the town of the father of Anak — that is, Hebron. 14 Caleb drove out the three sons of Anak: Sheshai, Ahiman and Talmai, descended from Anak. 15 From

inhabitants of Debir; now the name of Debir formerly was Kiriath-sepher. 16 And Caleb said, "Whoever attacks Kiriath-sepher and takes it, to him I will give my daughter Achsah as wife." 17 Othniel son of Kenaz, the brother of Caleb, took it; and he gave to him his daughter Achsah as wife. 18 When she came to him, she urged him to ask her father for a field. As she dismounted from her donkey, Caleb said to her, "What do you wish?" 19 She said to him, "Give me a present; since you have set me in the land of the Negeb, give me springs of water as well." So Caleb gave her the upper springs and the lower springs.

20 This is the inheritance of the tribe of the people of Judah according to their families. 21 The towns belonging to the tribe of the people of Judah in the extreme South, toward the boundary of Edom, were Kabzeel, Eder, Jagur, 22 Kinah, Dimonah, Adadah, 23 Kedesh, Hazor, Ithnan, 24 Ziph, Telem, Bealoth, 25 Hazor-hadattah, Kerioth-hezron (that is, Hazor), 26 Amam, Shema, Moladah, 27 Hazar-gaddah, Heshmon, Beth-pelet, 28 Hazar-shual, Beer-sheba, Biziothiah, 29 Baalah, Iim, Ezem, 30 Eltolad, Chesil, Hormah, 31 Ziklag, Madmannah, Sansannah, 32 Lebaoth, Shilhim, Ain, and Rimmon: in all, twenty-nine towns, with their villages.

33 And in the Lowland, Eshtaol, Zorah, Ashnah, 34 Zanoah, En-gannim, Tappuah, Enam, 35 Jarmuth, Adullam, Socoh, Azekah, 36 Shaaraim, Adithaim, Gederah, Gederothaim: fourteen towns with their villages.

37 Zenan, Hadashah, Migdal-gad, 38 Dilan, Mizpeh, Joktheel, 39 Lachish, Bozkath, Eglon, 40 Cabbon, Lahmam, Chitlish, 41 Gederoth, Beth-dagon, Naamah, and Makkedah: sixteen towns with their villages.

42 Libnah, Ether, Ashan, 43 Iphtah, Ashnah, Nezib, 44 Keilah, Achzib, and Mareshah: nine towns with their villages.

45 Ekron, with its dependencies and its villages; 46 from Ekron to the sea, all that were near Ashdod, with their villages.

47 Ashdod, its towns and its villages; Gaza, its towns and its villages; to the Wadi of Egypt, and the Great Sea with its coast.

48 And in the hill country, Shamir, Jattir, Socoh, 49 Dannah, Kiriath-sannah (that is, Debir), 50 Anab, Eshtemoh, Anim, 51 Goshen, Holon, and Giloh: eleven towns with their villages.

52 Arab, Dumah, Eshan, 53 Janim, Beth-tappuah, Aphekah, 54 Humtah, Kiriath-arba (that is, Hebron), and Zior: nine towns with their villages.

55 Maon, Carmel, Ziph, Juttah, 56 Jezreel, Jokdeam, Zanoah, 57 Kain, Gibeah, and Timnah: ten towns with their villages.

58 Halhul, Beth-zur, Gedor, 59 Maarath, Beth-anoth, and Eltekon: six towns with their villages.

60 Kiriath-baal (that is, Kiriath-jearim), and Rabbah: two towns with their villages.

61 In the wilderness, Beth-arabah, Middin, Secacah, 62 Nibshan, the City of Salt, and En-gedi: six towns with their villages.

63 But the people of Judah could not drive out the Jebusites, the inhabitants of Jerusalem; so the Jebusites live with the people of Judah in Jerusalem to this day.

he attacked the inhabitants of Debir, formerly called Kiriath-sepher. 16 Caleb announced that whoever should attack and capture Kiriath-sepher would receive his daughter Achsah in marriage. 17 It was captured by Othniel, son of Caleb's brother Kenaz, and Caleb gave him his daughter Achsah. 18 When she became his wife, he induced her to ask her father for a piece of land. She dismounted from her donkey, and Caleb asked her, 'What do you want?' 19 She replied, 'Grant me this favour: you have put me in this arid Negeb; you must give me pools of water as well.' So Caleb gave her the upper pool and the lower pool.

20 This is the holding of the tribe of the sons of Judah family by family. 21 These are the towns belonging to the tribe of Judah, the full count. By the Edomite frontier in the Negeb: Kabzeel, Eder, Jagur, 22 Kinah, Dimonah, Ararah, 23 Kedesh, Hazor, Ithnan, 24 Ziph, Telem, Bealoth, 25 Hazor-hadattah, Kerioth-hezron, 26 Amam, Shema, Moladah, 27 Hazar-gaddah, Heshmon, Beth-pelet, 28 Hazar-shual, Beersheba and its villages, 29 Baalah, Iyim, Ezem, 30 Eltolad, Kesil, Hormah, 31 Ziklag, Madmannah, Sansannah, 32 Lebaoth, Shilhim, Ain, and Rimmon: in all, twenty-nine towns with their hamlets.

33 In the Shephelah: Eshtaol, Zorah, Ashnah, 34 Zanoah, En-gannim, Tappuah, Enam, 35 Jarmuth, Adullam, Socoh, Azekah, 36 Shaaraim, Adithaim, Gederah, namely both parts of Gederah: fourteen towns with their hamlets. 37 Zenan, Hadashah, Migdal-gad, 38 Dilan, Mizpeh, Joktheel, 39 Lachish, Bozkath, Eglon, 40 Cabbon, Lahmas, Kithlish, 41 Gederoth, Beth-dagon, Naamah, and Makkedah: sixteen towns with their hamlets. 42 Libnah, Ether, Ashan, 43 Jiphtah, Ashnah, Nezib, 44 Keilah, Achzib, and Mareshah: nine towns with their hamlets. 45 Ekron, with its villages and hamlets, 46 and from Ekron westwards, all the towns near Ashdod and their hamlets. 47 Ashdod with its villages and hamlets, Gaza with its villages and hamlets as far as the wadi of Egypt and the Great Sea and the land beyond.

48 In the hill-country: Shamir, Jattir, Socoh, 49 Dannah, Kiriath-sannah, that is Debir, 50 Anab, Eshtemoh, Anim, 51 Goshen, Holon, and Giloh: eleven towns in all with their hamlets. 52 Arab, Dumah, Eshan, 53 Janim, Beth-tappuah, Aphek, 54 Humtah, Kiriath-arba, that is Hebron, and Zior: nine towns in all with their hamlets. 55 Maon, Carmel, Ziph, Juttah, 56 Jezreel, Jokdeam, Zanoah, 57 Kain, Gibeah, and Timnah: ten towns in all with their hamlets. 58 Halhul, Beth-zur, Gedor, 59 Maarath, Beth-anoth, and Eltekon: six towns in all with their hamlets. Tekoa, Ephrathah, that is Bethlehem, Peor, Etam, Culom, Tatam, Sores, Carem, Gallim, Baither, and Manach: eleven towns in all with their hamlets. 60 Kiriath-baal, that is Kiriath-jearim, and Rabbah: two towns with their hamlets.

61 In the wilderness: Beth-arabah, Middin, Secacah, 62 Nibshan, Irmelach, and En-gedi: six towns with their hamlets.

63 At Jerusalem, the men of Judah failed to drive out the Jebusites living there, and to this day Jebusites and men of Judah live together in Jerusalem.

15:18 **he induced her:** *so some Gk MSS; Heb.* she induced him. 15:22 **Ararah:** *prob. rdg; Heb.* Adadah. 15:23, 24 **Hazor and Ziph** *omitted by Gk.* 15:25 **Hazor-hadattah:** *omitted by Gk.* **Kerioth-hezron:** *so Syriac; Heb. adds* that is, Hazor. 15:27 **Heshmon:** *omitted by Gk.* 15:28 **its villages:** *so Gk; Heb.* Biziothiah. 15:29 **Iyim:** *omitted in 19:3 (cp. 1 Chr. 4:29).* 15:42 **Ether:** *or, with 1 Sam. 30:30,* Athak. 15:53 **Aphek:** *or* Aphekah. 15:59 **Tekoa . . . hamlets:** *so Gk; Heb. omits.*

there he marched up against the inhabitants of Debir, which was formerly called Kiriath-sepher. 16 Caleb said, "I will give my daughter Achsah in marriage to the one who attacks Kiriath-sepher and captures it." 17 Othniel, son of Caleb's brother Kenaz, captured it, and so Caleb gave him his daughter Achsah in marriage. 18 On the day of her marriage to Othniel, she induced him to ask her father for some land. Then, as she alighted from the ass, Caleb asked her, "What is troubling you?" 19 She answered, "Give me an additional gift! Since you have assigned to me land in the Negeb, give me also pools of water." So he gave her the upper and the lower pools.

20 This is the heritage of the clans of the tribe of Judahites: 21 The cities of the tribe of the Judahites in the extreme southern district toward Edom were: Kabzeel, Eder, Jagur, 22 Kinah, Dimonah, Adadah, 23 Kedesh, Hazor and Ithnan; 24 Ziph, Telem, Bealoth, 25 Hazor-hadattah, and Kerioth-hezron (that is, Hazor); 26 Amam, Shema, Moladah, 27 Hazar-gaddah, Heshmon, Beth-pelet, 28 Hazar-shual, Beer-sheba, and Biziothiah, 29 Baalah, Iim, Ezem, 30 Eltolad, Chesil, Hormah, 31 Ziklag, Madmannah, Sansannah, 32 Lebaoth, Shilhim and En-rimmon; a total of twenty-nine cities with their villages.

33 In the foothills: Eshtaol, Zorah, Ashnah, 34 Zanoah, Engannim, Tappuah, Enam, 35 Jarmuth, Adullam, Socoh, Azekah, 36 Shaaraim, Adithaim, Gederah, and Gederothaim; fourteen cities and their villages. 37 Zenan, Hadashah, Migdal-gad, 38 Dilean, Mizpeh, Joktheel, 39 Lachish, Bozkath, Eglon, 40 Cabbon, Lahmam, Chitlish, 41 Gederoth, Beth-dagon, Naamah and Makkedah; sixteen cities and their villages. 42 Libnah, Ether, Ashan, 43 Iphtah, Ashnah, Nezib, 44 Keilah, Achzib and Mareshah; nine cities and their villages. 45 Ekron and its towns and villages; 46 from Ekron to the sea, all the towns that lie alongside Ashdod and their villages; 47 Ashdod and its towns and villages; Gaza and its towns and villages, as far as the Wadi of Egypt and the coast of the Great Sea.

48 In the mountain regions: Shamir, Jattir, Socoh, 49 Dannah, Kiriath-sannah (that is, Debir), 50 Anab, Eshtemoh, Anim, 51 Goshen, Holon and Giloh; eleven cities and their villages. 52 Arab, Dumah, Eshan, 53 Janim, Beth-tappuah, Aphekah, 54 Humtah, Kiriath-arba (that is, Hebron), and Zior; nine cities and their villages. 55 Maon, Carmel, Ziph, Juttah, 56 Jezreel, Jokdeam, Zanoah, 57 Kain, Gibbeah and Timnah; ten cities and their villages. 58 Halhul, Beth-zur, Gedor, 59 Maarath, Beth-anoth and Eltekon; six cities and their villages. Tekoa, Ephrathah (that is, Bethlehem), Peor, Etam, Kulom, Tatam, Zores, Karim, Gallim, Bether and Manoko; eleven cities and their villages. 60 Kiriath-baal (that is, Kiriath-jearim) and Rabbah: two cities and their villages.

61 In the desert: Beth-arabah, Middin, Secacah, 62 Nibshan, Ir-hamelah and En-gedi; six cities and their villages. 63 [But the Jebusites who lived in Jerusalem the Judahites could not drive out; so the Jebusites dwell in Jerusalem beside the Judahites to the present day.]

there he marched on the inhabitants of Debir; Debir in olden days was called Kiriath-Sepher. 16 Caleb then said, 'To the man who attacks and takes Kiriath-Sepher, I shall give my daughter Achsah as wife.' 17 The man who captured it was Othniel son of Kenaz, brother of Caleb, who gave him his daughter Achsah as wife. 18 When she arrived, he urged her to ask her father for arable land, but when she alighted from the donkey and Caleb asked her, 'What is the matter?' 19 she said to him, 'Grant me a blessing! As the land you have given me is the Negeb, give me springs of water too!' So Caleb gave her what she wanted, the upper springs and the lower springs.

20 Such was the heritage of the tribe of the sons of Judah, by clans.

21 Towns at the extremity of the tribe of the sons of Judah, near the frontier of Edom in the Negeb:

Kabzeel, Arad, Jagur, 22 Kinah, Dimon, Aroer, 23 Kedesh, Hazor-Ithnan, 24 Ziph, Telem, Bealoth, 25 Hazor-Hadattah, Kiriath-Hezron — that is, Hazor — 26 Amam, Shema, Moladah, 27 Hazar-Gaddah, Heshmon, Beth-Pelet, 28 Hazar-Shual, Beersheba and its dependencies, 29 Baalah, Iim, Ezem, 30 Eltolad, Chesil, Hormah, 31 Ziklag, Madmannah, Sansannah, 32 Lebaoth, Shilhim, Ain and Rimmon: in all, twenty-nine towns with their villages.

33 In the lowlands:

Eshtaol, Zorah, Ashnah, 34 Zanoah, En-Gannim, Tappuah, Enam, 35 Jarmuth, Adullam, Socoh, Azekah, 36 Shaaraim, Aditaim, Ha-Gederah and Gederothaim: fourteen towns with their villages.

37 Zenan, Hadashah, Migdal-Gad, 38 Dilean, Ha-Mizpeh, Jokteel, 39 Lachish, Bozkath, Eglon, 40 Cabbon, Lahmas, Chitlish, 41 Gederoth, Beth-Dagon, Naamah and Makkedah: sixteen towns with their villages.

42 Libna, Ether, Asham, 43 Iphtah, Ashnah, Nezib, 44 Keilah, Achzib and Mareshah: nine towns with their villages.

45 Ekron with its dependencies and its villages. 46 From Ekron to the sea, everything to the side of Ashdod, with its villages. 47 Ashdod with its dependencies and its villages; Gaza with its dependencies and its villages as far as the Torrent of Egypt, the Great Sea forming the boundary.

48 In the highlands:

Shamir, Jattir, Socoh, 49 Dannah, Kiriath-Sepher, now Debir, 50 Anab, Eshtemoh, Anim, 51 Goshen, Holon and Giloh: eleven towns with their villages.

52 Arab, Dumah, Eshan, 53 Janum, Beth-Tappuah, Aphekah, 54 Humtah, Kiriath-Arba, now Hebron, and Zior: nine towns with their villages.

55 Maon, Carmel, Ziph, Juttah, 56 Jezreel, Jokdeam, Zanoah, 57 Ha-Kain, Gibeah and Timnah: ten towns with their villages.

58 Halhul, Beth-Zur, Gedor, 59 Maarath, Beth-Anoth and Eltekon: six towns with their villages.

Tekoa, Ephrathah, now Bethlehem, Peor, Etam, Kulon, Tatam, Sores, Carem, Gallim, Bether and Manach: eleven towns with their villages.

60 Kiriath-Baal, that is Kiriath-Jearim, and Rabbah: two towns with their villages.

61 In the desert:

Beth-Arabah, Middin, Secacah, 62 Nibshan, Salt Town and En-Gedi: six towns with their villages.

63 The Jebusites, however, who lived in Jerusalem, the sons of Judah were unable to dispossess, and the Jebusites still live in Jerusalem today, side by side with the sons of Judah.

NEW REVISED STANDARD VERSION

16 The allotment of the Josephites went from the Jordan by Jericho, east of the waters of Jericho, into the wilderness, going up from Jericho into the hill country to Bethel; 2 then going from Bethel to Luz, it passes along to Ataroth, the territory of the Archites; 3 then it goes down westward to the territory of the Japhletites, as far as the territory of Lower Beth-horon, then to Gezer, and it ends at the sea.

4 The Josephites — Manasseh and Ephraim — received their inheritance.

5 The territory of the Ephraimites by their families was as follows: the boundary of their inheritance on the east was Ataroth-addar as far as Upper Beth-horon, 6 and the boundary goes from there to the sea; on the north is Michmethath; then on the east the boundary makes a turn toward Taanath-shiloh, and passes along beyond it on the east to Janoah, 7 then it goes down from Janoah to Ataroth and to Naarah, and touches Jericho, ending at the Jordan. 8 From Tappuah the boundary goes westward to the Wadi Kanah, and ends at the sea. Such is the inheritance of the tribe of the Ephraimites by their families, 9 together with the towns that were set apart for the Ephraimites within the inheritance of the Manassites, all those towns with their villages. 10 They did not, however, drive out the Canaanites who lived in Gezer: so the Canaanites have lived within Ephraim to this day but have been made to do forced labor.

17 Then allotment was made to the tribe of Manasseh, for he was the firstborn of Joseph. To Machir the firstborn of Manasseh, the father of Gilead, were allotted Gilead and Bashan, because he was a warrior. 2 And allotments were made to the rest of the tribe of Manasseh, by their families, Abiezer, Helek, Asriel, Shechem, Hepher, and Shemida; these were the male descendants of Manasseh son of Joseph, by their families.

3 Now Zelophehad son of Hepher son of Gilead son of Machir son of Manasseh had no sons, but only daughters; and these are the names of his daughters: Mahlah, Noah, Hoglah, Milcah, and Tirzah. 4 They came before the priest Eleazar and Joshua son of Nun and the leaders, and said, "The LORD commanded Moses to give us an inheritance along with our male kin." So according to the commandment of the LORD he gave them an inheritance among the kinsmen of their father. 5 Thus there fell to Manasseh ten portions, besides the land of Gilead and Bashan, which is on the other side of the Jordan, 6 because the daughters of Manasseh received an inheritance along with his sons. The land of Gilead was allotted to the rest of the Manassites.

7 The territory of Manasseh reached from Asher to Michmethath, which is east of Shechem; then the boundary goes along southward to the inhabitants of En-tappuah. 8 The land of Tappuah belonged to Manasseh, but the town of Tappuah on the boundary of Manasseh belonged to the Ephraimites. 9 Then the boundary went down to the Wadi Kanah. The towns here, to the south of the wadi, among the towns of Manasseh, belong to Ephraim. Then the boundary of Manasseh goes along the north side of the wadi and ends at the sea. 10 The land to the south is Ephraim's and that to the north is Manasseh's, with the sea forming its boundary; on the north Asher is reached, and on the east Issachar.

REVISED ENGLISH BIBLE

16 This is the lot that fell to the sons of Joseph: the boundary runs from the Jordan at Jericho, east of the waters of Jericho by the wilderness, and goes up from Jericho into the hill-country to Bethel. 2 It runs on from Bethel to Luz and crosses the Archite border at Ataroth. 3 Westwards it descends to the boundary of the Japhletites as far as the boundary of Lower Beth-horon and Gezer; its limit is the sea. 4 Here Manasseh and Ephraim the sons of Joseph received their holding.

5 This was the boundary of the Ephraimites family by family: their eastern boundary ran from Ataroth-addar up to Upper Beth-horon. 6 It continued westwards to Michmethath on the north, going round by the east of Taanath-shiloh and passing by it on the east of Janoah. 7 It descends from Janoah to Ataroth and Naarath, touches Jericho and continues to the Jordan, 8 and from Tappuah it goes westwards by the wadi of Kanah; and its limit is the sea. This is the holding of the tribe of Ephraim family by family. 9 There were also towns reserved for the Ephraimites within the holding of the Manassites, each of these towns with its hamlets. 10 They did not however drive out the Canaanites who lived in Gezer; the Canaanites have lived among the Ephraimites to the present day but have been subject to forced labour.

17 This is the territory allotted to the tribe of Manasseh, Joseph's eldest son. Machir was Manasseh's eldest son and father of Gilead, a fighting man; Gilead and Bashan were allotted to him.

2 The rest of the Manassites family by family were the sons of Abiezer, the sons of Helek, the sons of Asriel, the sons of Shechem, the sons of Hepher, and the sons of Shemida; these were the male offspring of Manasseh son of Joseph family by family.

3 Zelophehad son of Hepher, son of Gilead, son of Machir, son of Manasseh, had no sons but only daughters: their names were Mahlah, Noah, Hoglah, Milcah, and Tirzah. 4 They presented themselves before Eleazar the priest and Joshua son of Nun, and before the leaders, and said, 'The LORD commanded Moses to allow us to inherit on the same footing as our kinsmen.' They were therefore given a holding on the same footing as their father's brothers according to the commandment of the LORD.

5 There fell to Manasseh's lot ten shares, apart from the country of Gilead and Bashan beyond the Jordan, 6 because Manasseh's daughters had received a holding on the same footing as his sons. The country of Gilead belonged to the rest of Manasseh's sons.

7 The boundary of Manasseh reached from Asher as far as Michmethath, which is to the east of Shechem, and thence southwards towards Jashub by Entappuah. 8 The territory of Tappuah belonged to Manasseh, but Tappuah itself was on the border of Manasseh and belonged to Ephraim. 9 The boundary then followed the wadi of Kanah to the south of the wadi (these towns belong to Ephraim, although they lie among the towns of Manasseh), the boundary of Manasseh being on the north of the wadi; its limit was the sea. 10 The southern side belonged to Ephraim and the northern to Manasseh, and their boundary was the sea. They marched with Asher on the north and Issachar on the east. 11 But in Issa-

---

17:7 **Jashub by:** *prob. rdg; Heb.* the inhabitants of. 17:9 **these towns:** *prob. reading.* 17:10 **their:** *so Gk; Heb.* his. 17:11 **The third . . . Dor:** *prob. rdg; Heb.* The three districts.

16 The lot that fell to the Josephites extended from the Jordan at Jericho to the waters of Jericho east of the desert; then the boundary went up from Jericho to the heights at Bethel. 2 Leaving Bethel for Luz, it crossed the ridge to the border of the Archites at Ataroth, 3 and descended westward to the border of the Japhletites, to that of Lower Beth-horon, and to Gezer, ending thence at the sea.

4 Within the heritage of Manasseh and Ephraim, sons of Joseph, 5 the dividing line for the heritage of the clans of the Ephraimites ran from east of Ataroth-addar to Upper Beth-horon 6 and thence to the sea. From Michmethath on the north, their boundary curved eastward around Taanath-shiloh, and continued east of it to Janoah; 7 from there it descended to Ataroth and Naarah, and skirting Jericho, it ended at the Jordan. 8 From Tappuah the boundary ran westward to the Wadi Kanah and ended at the sea. This was the heritage of the clans of the Ephraimites, 9 including the villages that belonged to each city set aside for the Ephraimites within the territory of the Manassehites. 10 But they did not drive out the Canaanites living in Gezer, who live on within Ephraim to the present day, though they have been impressed as laborers.

17 Now as for the lot that fell to the tribe of Manasseh as the first-born of Joseph: since his eldest son, Machir, the father of Gilead, was a warrior, who had already obtained Gilead and Bashan, 2 the allotment was now made to the other descendants of Manasseh, the clans of Abiezer, Helek, Asriel, Shechem, Hepher and Shemida, the other male children of Manasseh, son of Joseph.

3 Furthermore, Zelophehad, son of Hepher, son of Gilead, son of Machir, son of Manasseh, had had no sons, but only daughters, whose names were Mahlah, Noah, Hoglah, Milcah, and Tirzah. 4 These presented themselves to Eleazar the priest, to Joshua, son of Nun, and to the princes, saying, "The LORD commanded Moses to give us a heritage among our kinsmen." So in obedience to the command of the LORD a heritage was given to each of them among their father's kinsmen. 5 Thus ten shares fell to Manasseh apart from the land of Gilead and Bashan beyond the Jordan, 6 since these female descendants of Manasseh received each a portion among his sons. The land of Gilead fell to the rest of the Manassehites.

7 Manasseh bordered on Asher. From Michmethath, near Shechem, another boundary ran southward to include the natives of En-Tappuah, 8 because the district of Tappuah belonged to Manasseh, although Tappuah itself was an Ephraimite city on the border of Manasseh. 9 This same boundary continued down to the Wadi Kanah. The cities that belonged to Ephraim from among the cities of Manasseh were those to the south of the wadi; thus the territory of Manasseh ran north of the wadi and ended at the sea. 10 The land on the south belonged to Ephraim and that on the north to Manasseh; with the sea as their common boundary, they reached Asher on the north and Issachar on the east.

16 The portion of the sons of Joseph started on the east at the Jordan opposite Jericho (the Waters of Jericho) through the desert rising from Jericho into the highlands of Bethel; 2 from Bethel it went to Luz, and on towards the frontier of the Archites at Ataroth; 3 then passed downwards and westwards to the frontier of the Japhletites as far as the border of Lower Beth-Horon and on to Gezer, and reached as far as the sea.

4 Such was the heritage of the sons of Joseph, Manasseh and Ephraim.

5 As regards the territory of the sons of Ephraim, by clans, the frontier of their heritage ran from Ataroth-Arach to Upper Beth-Horon; 6 the frontier then reached as far as the sea . . . the Michmethath in the north, and the frontier turned east to Tanaath-Shiloh which it crossed in an easterly direction to Janoah; 7 it ran down to Ataroth and Naarah, touched Jericho and ended at the Jordan. 8 From Tappuah, the frontier ran westwards to the Torrent of Kanah and reached as far as the sea.

Such was the heritage of the tribe of the sons of Ephraim, by clans, 9 apart from the towns reserved for the sons of Ephraim inside the heritage of the sons of Manasseh, all these towns and their villages. 10 The Canaanites living in Gezer were not driven out; they have remained in Ephraim to the present day but are obliged to do forced labour.

17 The portion of the tribe of Manasseh, who was in fact Joseph's first-born — went to Machir, Manasseh's first-born, father of Gilead, for he was a warrior; he had Gilead and Bashan. 2 The other sons of Manasseh had theirs, by clans: for the sons of Abiezer, for the sons of Helek, for the sons of Asriel, for the sons of Shechem, for the sons of Hepher, and for the sons of Shemida: these were the male children of Manasseh son of Joseph, by clans. 3 Zelophehad son of Hepher, son of Gilead, son of Machir, son of Manasseh, had no sons but only daughters, whose names were these: Mahlah, Noah, Hoglah, Milcah and Tirzah. 4 These approached the priest Eleazar, Joshua son of Nun and the leaders, and said, 'Yahweh ordered Moses to give us a heritage among our brothers.' In compliance with Yahweh's order, therefore, they were given a heritage among their father's brothers. 5 In this way ten portions fell to Manasseh, apart from Gilead and Bashan lying on the further side of the Jordan, 6 since Manasseh's daughters received a heritage as well as his sons. Gilead itself belonged to Manasseh's other sons.

7 On the side of Asher, the frontier of Manasseh was the Michmethath, which is opposite Shechem, and thence continued to the right to Jashib, which is at the spring of Tappuah. 8 The territory of Tappuah belonged to Manasseh, but Tappuah on Manasseh's border belonged to the sons of Ephraim. 9 The boundary went down to the Torrent of Kanah; south of the Torrent were the towns of Ephraim, excluding those owned by Ephraim among the towns of Manasseh; the boundary of Manasseh was north of the Torrent and reached as far as the sea. 10 The south belonged to Ephraim and the north to Manasseh and reached as far as the sea; they touched Asher to the north and Issachar to the east.

| NEW REVISED STANDARD VERSION | REVISED ENGLISH BIBLE |

11 Within Issachar and Asher, Manasseh had Beth-shean and its villages, Ibleam and its villages, the inhabitants of Dor and its villages, the inhabitants of En-dor and its villages, the inhabitants of Taanach and its villages, and the inhabitants of Megiddo and its villages (the third is Naphath).*a* 12 Yet the Manassites could not take possession of those towns; but the Canaanites continued to live in that land. 13 But when the Israelites grew strong, they put the Canaanites to forced labor, but did not utterly drive them out.

14 The tribe of Joseph spoke to Joshua, saying, "Why have you given me but one lot and one portion as an inheritance, since we are a numerous people, whom all along the LORD has blessed?" 15 And Joshua said to them, "If you are a numerous people, go up to the forest, and clear ground there for yourselves in the land of the Perizzites and the Rephaim, since the hill country of Ephraim is too narrow for you." 16 The tribe of Joseph said, "The hill country is not enough for us; yet all the Canaanites who live in the plain have chariots of iron, both those in Beth-shean and its villages and those in the Valley of Jezreel." 17 Then Joshua said to the house of Joseph, to Ephraim and Manasseh, "You are indeed a numerous people, and have great power; you shall not have one lot only, 18 but the hill country shall be yours, for though it is a forest, you shall clear it and possess it to its farthest borders; for you shall drive out the Canaanites, though they have chariots of iron, and though they are strong."

18 Then the whole congregation of the Israelites assembled at Shiloh, and set up the tent of meeting there. The land lay subdued before them.

2 There remained among the Israelites seven tribes whose inheritance had not yet been apportioned. 3 So Joshua said to the Israelites, "How long will you be slack about going in and taking possession of the land that the LORD, the God of your ancestors, has given you? 4 Provide three men from each tribe, and I will send them out that they may begin to go throughout the land, writing a description of it with a view to their inheritances. Then come back to me. 5 They shall divide it into seven portions, Judah continuing in its territory on the south, and the house of Joseph in their territory on the north. 6 You shall describe the land in seven divisions and bring the description here to me; and I will cast lots for you here before the LORD our God. 7 The Levites have no portion among you, for the priesthood of the LORD is their heritage; and Gad and Reuben and the half-tribe of Manasseh have received their inheritance beyond the Jordan eastward, which Moses the servant of the LORD gave them."

8 So the men started on their way; and Joshua charged those who went to write the description of the land, saying, "Go throughout the land and write a description of it, and come back to me; and I will cast lots for you here before the LORD in Shiloh." 9 So the men went and traversed the land and set down in a book a description of it by towns in seven divisions; then they came back to Joshua in the camp at Shiloh, 10 and Joshua cast lots for them in Shiloh before the LORD; and there Joshua apportioned the land to the Israelites, to each a portion.

11 The lot of the tribe of Benjamin according to its families came up, and the territory allotted to it fell between the tribe of Judah and the tribe of Joseph. 12 On the north side their boundary began at the Jordan; then the boundary goes up to the slope of Jericho on the north, then up through the hill country westward; and it ends at the wilderness of Beth-aven. 13 From there the boundary passes along south-

char and Asher, Manasseh possessed Beth-shean and its villages, Ibleam and its villages, the inhabitants of Dor and its villages, the inhabitants of En-dor and its villages, the inhabitants of Taanach and its villages, and the inhabitants of Megiddo and its villages. (The third is the district of Dor.) 12 The Manassites were unable to occupy these towns; the Canaanites maintained their hold on that part of the country. 13 When the Israelites grew stronger, they put the Canaanites to forced labour, but did not drive them out.

14 The sons of Joseph appealed to Joshua: 'Why have you given us only one lot and one share as our holding? We are a numerous people; so far the LORD has blessed us.' 15 Joshua replied, 'If you are so numerous, go up into the forest in the territory of the Perizzites and the Rephaim and clear it for yourselves. You are their near neighbours in the hill-country of Ephraim.' 16 The sons of Joseph contended, 'The hill-country is not enough for us; besides, all the Canaanites have iron-clad chariots, both those who inhabit the valley beside Beth-shean and its villages and also those in the valley of Jezreel.' 17 Joshua said to the house of Joseph, that is Ephraim and Manasseh: 'You are a numerous people of great vigour. You shall not have one lot only. 18 The hill-country is to be yours. It is forest land; clear it and it will be yours to its farthest limits. The Canaanites may be powerful and equipped with iron-clad chariots, but you will be able to drive them out.'

18 THE whole Israelite community assembled at Shiloh and established the Tent of Meeting there. The country now lay subdued at their feet; 2 but there remained seven tribes among the Israelites who had not yet taken possession of the holdings which would fall to them. 3 Joshua therefore said to them, 'How much longer will you neglect to take possession of the land which the LORD the God of your fathers has assigned to you? 4 Appoint three men from each tribe, and I shall send them out to travel throughout the country. They are to make a survey of it showing the holding suitable for each tribe, and come back to me, 5 and then it can be shared out among you in seven portions. Judah will retain his boundary in the south, and the house of Joseph their boundary in the north. 6 Survey the land in seven portions, and bring your findings to me, and I shall cast lots for you in the presence of the LORD our God. 7 Levi has no share among you, because his share is the priesthood of the LORD; and Gad, Reuben, and the half tribe of Manasseh have each taken possession of their holding east of the Jordan, which Moses the servant of the LORD assigned to them.'

8 The men set out on their journey. Joshua ordered the emissaries to survey the country: 'Go through the whole country,' he said, 'survey it, and return to me, and I shall cast lots for you here before the LORD in Shiloh.' 9 So the men went and passed through the country; they recorded the survey on a scroll, town by town, in seven portions. Then they came to Joshua in the camp at Shiloh; 10 he cast lots for them in Shiloh before the LORD, and apportioned the land there to the Israelites in their proper shares.

11 This is the lot which fell to the tribe of the Benjamites family by family. The territory allotted to them lay between the territories of Judah and Joseph. 12 Their boundary at its northern corner starts from the Jordan; it goes up the slope on the north side of Jericho, continuing westwards into the hill-country, and its limit there is the wilderness of Beth-aven. 13 From there it runs on to Luz, to the southern slope

---

a Meaning of Heb uncertain

17:15 **You are . . . neighbours:** *prob. rdg; Heb. obscure.*

NEW AMERICAN BIBLE

NEW JERUSALEM BIBLE

11 Moreover, in Issachar and in Asher Manasseh was awarded Beth-shean and its towns, Ibleam and its towns, Dor and its towns and the natives there, Endor and its towns and natives, Taanach and its towns and natives, and Megiddo and its towns and natives [the third is Naphath-dor]. 12 Since the Manassehites could not conquer these cities, the Canaanites persisted in this region. 13 When the Israelites grew stronger they impressed the Canaanites as laborers, but they did not drive them out.

14 The descendants of Joseph said to Joshua, "Why have you given us only one lot and one share as our heritage? Our people are too many, because of the extent to which the LORD has blessed us." 15 Joshua answered them, "If you are too many, go up to the forest and clear out a place for yourselves there in the land of the Perizzites and Rephaim, since the mountain regions of Ephraim are so narrow." 16 For the Josephites said, "Our mountain regions are not enough for us; on the other hand, the Canaanites living in the valley region all have iron chariots, in particular those in Beth-shean and its towns, and those in the valley of Jezreel." 17 Joshua therefore said to Ephraim and Manasseh, the house of Joseph, "You are a numerous people and very strong. You shall have not merely one share, 18 for the mountain region which is now forest shall be yours when you clear it. Its adjacent land shall also be yours if, despite their strength and iron chariots, you drive out the Canaanites."

18 After they had subdued the land, the whole community of the Israelites assembled at Shiloh, where they set up the meeting tent.

2 Seven tribes among the Israelites had not yet received their heritage. 3 Joshua therefore said to the Israelites, "How much longer will you put off taking steps to possess the land which the LORD, the God of your fathers, has given you? 4 Choose three men from each of your tribes; I will commission them to begin a survey of the land, which they shall describe for purposes of inheritance. When they return to me, 5 you shall divide it into seven parts. Judah is to retain its territory in the south, and the house of Joseph its territory in the north. 6 You shall bring here to me the description of the land in seven sections. I will then cast lots for you here before the LORD, our God. 7 For the Levites have no share among you, because the priesthood of the LORD is their heritage; while Gad, Reuben, and the half-tribe of Manasseh have already received the heritage east of the Jordan which Moses, the servant of the LORD, gave them."

8 When those who were to map out the land were ready for the journey, Joshua instructed them to survey the land, prepare a description of it, and return to him; then he would cast lots for them there before the LORD in Shiloh. 9 So they went through the land, listed its cities in writing in seven sections, and returned to Joshua in the camp at Shiloh. 10 Joshua then divided up the land for the Israelites into their separate shares, casting lots for them before the LORD in Shiloh.

11 One lot fell to the clans of the tribe of Benjaminites. The territory allotted them lay between the descendants of Judah and those of Joseph. 12 Their northern boundary began at the Jordan and went over the northern flank of Jericho, up westward into the mountains, till it reached the desert of Beth-aven. 13 From there it crossed over to the

11 With Issachar and Asher, Manasseh shared Beth-Shean and its dependent towns, Ibleam and its dependent towns, the inhabitants of Dor and of its dependent towns, the inhabitants of Taanach and Megiddo and of their dependent towns: the Three of the Slopes. 12 But because the sons of Manasseh could not take possession of these towns, the Canaanites managed to live on in that territory. 13 When, however, the Israelites became stronger, they subjected the Canaanites to forced labour, though they never dispossessed them.

14 The sons of Joseph spoke as follows to Joshua, 'Why have you given me only one share, only one portion, as heritage, when I am a numerous people, since Yahweh has so blessed me?' 15 Joshua replied, 'If your people are so many, go up to the wooded area and clear space for yourselves in the area belonging to the Perizzites and Rephaim, since the highlands of Ephraim are too small for you.' 16 The sons of Joseph replied, 'The highlands are not enough for us, and what is more, all the Canaanites living on the land of the plain have iron chariots, so do those in Beth-Shean and its dependent towns, and those in the plain of Jezreel.' 17 Joshua said to the House of Joseph, to Ephraim and to Manasseh, 'You are a numerous people and your strength is great; you will not only have one share, 18 but a mountain will be yours as well; even if it is a forest, you can clear it and its territories will be yours. And you will dispossess the Canaanites, although they have iron chariots and although they are strong.'

18 The whole community of the Israelites assembled at Shiloh, and the Tent of Meeting was set up there; the whole country had been subdued for them. 2 But among the Israelites there were still seven tribes left who had not received their heritage. 3 Joshua then said to the Israelites, 'How much more time are you going to waste before you go and take possession of the country which Yahweh, God of your ancestors, has given to you? 4 Choose three men from each tribe for me to send all over the country so that they can make a survey with a view to their inheritances and then come back to me. 5 They will divide the country into seven portions. Judah will remain in his territory in the south, and those of the House of Joseph will remain in their territory in the north. 6 You must survey the country in seven sections and bring your findings to me here, so that I can cast lots for you here, in the presence of Yahweh our God. 7 The Levites, however, will have no portion with the rest of you; the priesthood of Yahweh will be their heritage. As regards Gad and Reuben and the half-tribe of Manasseh, they have received their heritage on the further, eastern side of the Jordan, the one given them by Moses, servant of Yahweh.'

8 The men stood up and set off. To those who were to survey the country Joshua gave this order, 'Start out, then, go all over the country, survey it, and then come back to me; and I shall cast lots for you here, in the presence of Yahweh, at Shiloh.' 9 The men left, went all over the country and surveyed it by towns, in seven sections, writing down their findings in a book, and then went back to Joshua in the camp at Shiloh.

10 Joshua cast lots for them in Yahweh's presence at Shiloh, and there Joshua divided the country between the Israelites, share by share.

11 A portion fell first to the tribe of the sons of Benjamin, by clans: the territory of their portion lay between the sons of Judah and the sons of Joseph. 12 Their northern frontier began at the Jordan, went up the flank of Jericho to the north, climbed westwards through the highlands and came out at the desert of Beth-Aven. 13 Thence, the frontier went

ward in the direction of Luz, to the slope of Luz (that is, Bethel), then the boundary goes down to Ataroth-addar, on the mountain that lies south of Lower Beth-horon. 14 Then the boundary goes in another direction, turning on the western side southward from the mountain that lies to the south, opposite Beth-horon, and it ends at Kiriath-baal (that is, Kiriath-jearim), a town belonging to the tribe of Judah. This forms the western side. 15 The southern side begins at the outskirts of Kiriath-jearim; and the boundary goes from there to Ephron,b to the spring of the Waters of Nephtoah; 16 then the boundary goes down to the border of the mountain that overlooks the valley of the son of Hinnom, which is at the north end of the valley of Rephaim; and it then goes down the valley of Hinnom, south of the slope of the Jebusites, and downward to En-rogel; 17 then it bends in a northerly direction going on to En-shemesh, and from there goes to Geliloth, which is opposite the ascent of Adummim; then it goes down to the Stone of Bohan, Reuben's son; 18 and passing on to the north of the slope of Beth-arabahc it goes down to the Arabah; 19 then the boundary passes on to the north of the slope of Beth-hoglah; and the boundary ends at the northern bay of the Dead Sea,d at the south end of the Jordan: this is the southern border. 20 The Jordan forms its boundary on the eastern side. This is the inheritance of the tribe of Benjamin, according to its families, boundary by boundary all around.

21 Now the towns of the tribe of Benjamin according to their families were Jericho, Beth-hoglah, Emek-keziz, 22 Beth-arabah, Zemaraim, Bethel, 23 Avvim, Parah, Ophrah, 24 Chephar-ammoni, Ophni, and Geba — twelve towns with their villages. 25 Gibeon, Ramah, Beeroth, 26 Mizpeh, Chephirah, Mozah, 27 Rekem, Irpeel, Taralah, 28 Zela, Haeleph, Jebuse (that is, Jerusalem), Gibeahf and Kiriath-jearimg — fourteen towns with their villages. This is the inheritance of the tribe of Benjamin according to its families.

19 The second lot came out for Simeon, for the tribe of Simeon, according to its families; its inheritance lay within the inheritance of the tribe of Judah. 2 It had for its inheritance Beer-sheba, Sheba, Moladah, 3 Hazar-shual, Balah, Ezem, 4 Eltolad, Bethul, Hormah, 5 Ziklag, Beth-marcaboth, Hazar-susah, 6 Beth-lebaoth, and Sharuhen — thirteen towns with their villages; 7 Ain, Rimmon, Ether, and Ashan — four towns with their villages; 8 together with all the villages all around these towns as far as Baalath-beer, Ramah of the Negeb. This was the inheritance of the tribe of Simeon according to its families. 9 The inheritance of the tribe of Simeon formed part of the territory of Judah; because the portion of the tribe of Judah was too large for them, the tribe of Simeon obtained an inheritance within their inheritance.

10 The third lot came up for the tribe of Zebulun, according to its families. The boundary of its inheritance reached as far as Sarid; 11 then its boundary goes up westward, and on to Maralah, and touches Dabbesheth, then the wadi that is east of Jokneam; 12 from Sarid it goes in the other direction eastward toward the sunrise to the boundary of Chisloth-tabor; from there it goes to Daberath, then up to Japhia; 13 from there it passes along on the east toward the sunrise to Gath-hepher, to Eth-kazin, and going on to Rimmon it bends toward Neah; 14 then on the north the boundary makes a turn to Hannathon, and it ends at the valley of Iphtah-el; 15 and Kattath, Nahalal, Shimron, Idalah, and Bethlehem — twelve towns with their villages. 16 This is the inheritance of the tribe of Zebulun, according to its families — these towns with their villages.

of Luz, that is Bethel, and down to Ataroth-addar over the hill-country south of Lower Beth-horon. 14 The boundary then bends round at the west corner southwards from the hill-country above Beth-horon, and its limit is Kiriath-baal, that is Kiriath-jearim, which belongs to Judah. This is the western side. 15 The southern side starts from the edge of Kiriath-jearim and ends at the spring of the waters of Nephtoah. 16 It goes down to the edge of the hill to the east of the valley of Ben-hinnom, north of the vale of Rephaim, down the valley of Hinnom, to the southern slope of the Jebusites and so to En-rogel. 17 It then bends round north and comes out at En-shemesh, goes on to the districts in front of the ascent of Adummim and thence down to the stone of Bohan son of Reuben. 18 It passes to the northern side of the slope facing the Arabah and goes down to the Arabah, 19 passing the northern slope of Beth-hoglah, and its limit is the northern inlet of the Dead Sea, at the southern mouth of the Jordan. This forms the southern boundary. 20 The Jordan is the boundary on the east side. This is the holding of the Benjamites, the complete circuit of their boundaries family by family.

21 The towns belonging to the tribe of the Benjamites family by family are: Jericho, Beth-hoglah, Emek-keziz, 22 Beth-arabah, Zemaraim, Bethel, 23 Avvim, Parah, Ophrah, 24 Kephar-ammoni, Ophni, and Geba: twelve towns in all with their hamlets. 25 Gibeon, Ramah, Beeroth, 26 Mizpah, Kephirah, Mozah, 27 Rekem, Irpeel, Taralah, 28 Zela, Eleph, Jebus, that is Jerusalem, Gibeah, and Kiriath-jearim: fourteen towns in all with their hamlets. This is the holding of the Benjamites family by family.

19 The second lot cast was for Simeon, the tribe of the Simeonites family by family. Their holding was included in that of Judah. 2 For their holding they had Beer-sheba, Moladah, 3 Hazar-shual, Balah, Ezem, 4 Eltolad, Bethul, Hormah, 5 Ziklag, Beth-marcaboth, Hazar-susah, 6 Beth-lebaoth, and Sharuhen: in all, thirteen towns and their hamlets. 7 They had Ain, Rimmon, Ether, and Ashan: four towns and their hamlets, 8 all the hamlets round these towns as far as Baalath-beer and Ramath-negeb. This was the holding of the tribe of Simeon family by family. 9 The holding of the Simeonites was part of the land allotted to the men of Judah, because their share was larger than they needed. The Simeonites therefore had their holding within the territory of Judah.

10 The third lot fell to the Zebulunites family by family. The boundary of their holding extended to Shadud. 11 Their boundary went up westwards as far as Maralah and touched Dabbesheth and the wadi east of Jokneam. 12 It turned back from Shadud eastwards towards the sunrise up to the border of Kisloth-tabor, on to Daberath and up to Japhia. 13 From there it crossed eastwards towards the sunrise to Gath-hepher, to Ittah-kazin, out to Rimmon, and bent round to Neah. 14 The northern boundary went round to Hannathon, and its limits were the valley of Jiphtah-el, 15 Kattath, Nahalal, Shimron, Idalah, and Bethlehem: twelve towns in all with their hamlets. 16 These towns and their hamlets were the holding of Zebulun family by family.

18:15 **ends:** *prob. rdg; Heb.* adds westwards and ends.
18:28 **Jebus:** *so Gk; Heb.* the Jebusite. **Kiriath-jearim:** *so Gk; Heb.* Kiriath. 19:2 **Beersheba:** *prob. rdg, cp. 1 Chr. 4:28; Heb.* adds and Sheba. 19:10 **Shadud:** *prob. rdg; Heb.* Sarid (*similarly in verse 12*). 19:13 **and bent round:** *prob. rdg; Heb.* which stretched.

---

b Cn See 15.9. Heb *westward*   c Gk: Heb *to the slope over against the Arabah*   d Heb *Salt Sea*   e Gk Syr Vg: Heb *the Jebusite*   f Heb *Gibeath*   g Gk: Heb *Kiriath*

southern flank of Luz (that is, Bethel). Then it ran down to Ataroth-addar, on the mountaintop south of Lower Beth-horon. 14 For the western border, the boundary line swung south from the mountaintop opposite Beth-horon till it reached Kiriath-baal (that is, Kiriath-jearim), which city belonged to the Judahites. This was the western boundary. 15 The southern boundary began at the limits of Kiriath-jearim and projected to the spring at Nephtoah. 16 It went down to the edge of the mountain on the north of the Valley of Rephaim, where it faces the Valley of Ben-hinnom; and continuing down the Valley of Hinnom along the southern flank of the Jebusites, reached En-rogel. 17 Inclining to the north, it extended to En-shemesh, and thence to Geliloth, opposite the pass of Adummim. Then it dropped to Eben-Bohan-ben-Reuben, 18 across the northern flank of the Arabah overlook, down into the Arabah. 19 From there the boundary continued across the northern flank of Beth-hoglah and extended to the northern tip of the Salt Sea, at the southern end of the Jordan. This was the southern boundary. 20 The Jordan bounded it on the east. This was how the heritage of the clans of the Benjaminites was bounded on all sides.

21 Now the cities belonging to the clans of the tribe of the Benjaminites were: Jericho, Beth-hoglah, Emek-keziz, 22 Beth-arabah, Zemaraim, Bethel, 23 Avvim, Parah, Ophra, 24 Chephar-ammoni, Ophni and Geba; twelve cities and their villages. 25 Also Gibeon, Ramah, Beeroth, 26 Miz-peh, Chephirah, Mozah, 27 Rekem, Irpeel, Taralah, 28 Zela, Haeleph, the Jebusite city (that is, Jerusalem), Gibeah and Kiriath; fourteen cities and their villages. This was the heritage of the clans of Benjaminites.

19

The second lot fell to Simeon. The heritage of the clans of the tribe of Simeonites lay within that of the Judahites. 2 For their heritage they received Beer-sheba, Shema, Moladah, 3 Hazar-shual, Balah, Ezem, 4 Eltolad, Bethul, Hormah, 5 Ziklag, Bethmar-caboth, Hazar-susah, 6 Beth-lebaoth and Sharuhen; thirteen cities and their villages. 7 Also En-rimmon, Ether and Ashan; four cities and their villages, 8 besides all the villages around these cities as far as Baalath-beer (that is, Ramoth-negeb). This was the heritage of the clans of the tribe of the Simeonites. 9 This heritage of the Simeonites was within the confines of the Judahites; for since the portion of the latter was too large for them, the Simeonites obtained their heritage within it.

10 The third lot fell to the clans of the Zebulunites. The limit of their heritage was at Sarid. 11 Their boundary went up west . . . and through Mareal, reaching Dabbesheth and the wadi that is near Jokneam. 12 From Sarid eastward it ran to the district of Chisloth-tabor, on to Daberath, and up to Japhia. 13 From there it continued eastward to Gath-hepher and to Eth-kazin, extended to Rimmon, and turned to Neah. 14 Skirting north of Hannathon, the boundary ended at the valley of Iphtahel. 15 Thus, with Kattath, Nahalal, Shimron, Idalah and Bethlehem, there were twelve cities and their villages 16 to comprise the heritage of the clans of the Zebulunites.

on to Luz, on the southern flank of Luz — now Bethel — and then down to Ataroth-Arach, on the mountain south of Lower Beth-Horon. 14 At this westerly point, the frontier curved round and turned south, from the mountain facing Beth-Horon from the south and came out at Kiriath-Baal, now Kiriath-Jearim, a town of the sons of Judah. That was the western side.

15 This was the south side: from the tip of Kiriath-Jearim, the frontier went to Gasin and came out near the spring of the Waters of Nephtoah, 16 it then went down to the edge of the mountain facing the Valley of Hinnom, in the Valley of the Rephaim to the north; it then went down into the Valley of Hinnom, past the southerly flank of the Jebusite, and went down to En-Rogel. 17 It then curved northwards, coming out at En-Shemesh, and came out at the stone circle opposite the Ascent of Adummim, then went down to the Stone of Bohan son of Reuben. 18 It then went on to Che-teph on the flank of Beth-ha-Arabah northwards, and went down into the Arabah; 19 the frontier then passed round the northern flank of Beth-Hoglah, and the frontier came out at the northern bay of the Salt Sea, at the southern end of the Jordan. Such was the southern frontier. 20 The Jordan itself formed the frontier on the east.

Such was the heritage of the sons of Benjamin as defined by their frontier, by clans.

21 The towns of the tribe of the sons of Benjamin, by clans, were: 22 Jericho, Beth-Hoglah, Emek-Keziz; 23 Beth-Arabah, Zemaraim, Bethel; Avvim, Parah, Ophrah; 24 Chephar-Ammoni, Ophni, Geba: twelve towns and their villages. 25 Gibeon, Ramah, Beeroth; 26 Mizpeh, Chephirah, Mo-zah; 27 Rekem, Irpeel, Taralah; 28 Zela-ha-Eleph, the Jebusite — that is, Jerusalem — Gibeah and Kiriath: fourteen towns with their villages.

Such was the heritage of the sons of Benjamin, by clans.

19

The second lot to come out was for Simeon, for the tribe of the sons of Simeon, by clans; their heritage was within the heritage of the sons of Judah. 2 As heritage, they received:

3 Beersheba, Shema, Moladah, 4 Hazar-Shual, Balah, Ezem, Eltolad, Bethul, Hormah, 5 Ziklag, Beth-ha-Marcaboth, Hazar-Susa, 6 Beth-Lebaoth and Sharuhen: thirteen towns and their villages.

7 Ain, Rimmon, Ether and Ashan: four towns and their villages, 8 with all the villages situated near these towns as far as Baalath-Beer and Ramah of the Negeb.

Such was the heritage of the tribe of the sons of Simeon, by clans. 9 The heritage of the sons of Simeon was taken out of the portion of the sons of Judah, because the share of the sons of Judah was too large for them; hence, the sons of Simeon received their heritage within the heritage of the sons of Judah.

10 The third lot fell to the sons of Zebulun, by clans; the territory of their heritage stretched as far as Sadud; 11 their frontier climbed westwards to Maraalah, touching Dabbe-sheth and the torrent facing Jokneam. 12 From Sadud, the frontier turned east, towards the rising sun, as far as the frontier of Chisloth-Tabor; it came out at Dobrath and went up to Japhia. 13 Thence, it went east, towards the sunrise, to Gath-Hepher and Ittah-Kazin, came out at Rimmon and turned towards Neah. 14 The northern frontier turned to-wards Hannathon and came to an end in the Valley of Iphtah-El; 15 with Kattath, Nahalal, Shimron, Iralah and Bethlehem: twelve towns with their villages.

16 Such was the heritage of the sons of Zebulun, by clans: these towns with their villages.

NEW REVISED STANDARD VERSION

17 The fourth lot came out for Issachar, for the tribe of Issachar, according to its families. 18 Its territory included Jezreel, Chesulloth, Shunem, 19 Hapharaim, Shion, Anaharath, 20 Rabbith, Kishion, Ebez, 21 Remeth, En-gannim, En-haddah, Beth-pazzez; 22 the boundary also touches Tabor, Shahazumah, and Beth-shemesh, and its boundary ends at the Jordan — sixteen towns with their villages. 23 This is the inheritance of the tribe of Issachar, according to its families — the towns with their villages.

24 The fifth lot came out for the tribe of Asher according to its families. 25 Its boundary included Helkath, Hali, Beten, Achshaph, 26 Allammelech, Amad, and Mishal; on the west it touches Carmel and Shihor-libnath, 27 then it turns eastward, goes to Beth-dagon, and touches Zebulun and the valley of Iphtah-el northward to Beth-emek and Neiel; then it continues in the north to Cabul, 28 Ebron, Rehob, Hammon, Kanah, as far as Great Sidon; 29 then the boundary turns to Ramah, reaching to the fortified city of Tyre; then the boundary turns to Hosah, and it ends at the sea; Mahalab,ʰ Achzib, 30 Ummah, Aphek, and Rehob — twenty-two towns with their villages. 31 This is the inheritance of the tribe of Asher according to its families — these towns with their villages.

32 The sixth lot came out for the tribe of Naphtali, for the tribe of Naphtali, according to its families. 33 And its boundary ran from Heleph, from the oak in Zaanannim, and Adami-nekeb, and Jabneel, as far as Lakkum; and it ended at the Jordan; 34 then the boundary turns westward to Aznoth-tabor, and goes from there to Hukkok, touching Zebulun at the south, and Asher on the west, and Judah on the east at the Jordan. 35 The fortified towns are Ziddim, Zer, Hammath, Rakkath, Chinnereth, 36 Adamah, Ramah, Hazor, 37 Kedesh, Edrei, En-hazor, 38 Iron, Migdal-el, Horem, Beth-anath, and Beth-shemesh — nineteen towns with their villages. 39 This is the inheritance of the tribe of Naphtali according to its families — the towns with their villages.

40 The seventh lot came out for the tribe of Dan, according to its families. 41 The territory of its inheritance included Zorah, Eshtaol, Ir-shemesh, 42 Shaalabbin, Aijalon, Ithlah, 43 Elon, Timnah, Ekron, 44 Eltekeh, Gibbethon, Baalath, 45 Jehud, Bene-berak, Gath-rimmon, 46 Me-jarkon, and Rakkon at the border opposite Joppa. 47 When the territory of the Danites was lost to them, the Danites went up and fought against Leshem, and after capturing it and putting it to the sword, they took possession of it and settled in it, calling Leshem, Dan, after their ancestor Dan. 48 This is the inheritance of the tribe of Dan, according to their families — these towns with their villages.

49 When they had finished distributing the several territories of the land as inheritances, the Israelites gave an inheritance among them to Joshua son of Nun. 50 By command of the LORD they gave him the town that he asked for, Timnath-serah in the hill country of Ephraim; he rebuilt the town, and settled in it.

51 These are the inheritances that the priest Eleazar and Joshua son of Nun and the heads of the families of the tribes of the Israelites distributed by lot at Shiloh before the LORD, at the entrance of the tent of meeting. So they finished dividing the land.

REVISED ENGLISH BIBLE

17 The fourth lot cast was for the sons of Issachar family by family. 18 Their boundary included Jezreel, Kesulloth, Shunem, 19 Hapharaim, Shion, Anaharath, 20 Rabbith, Kishon, Ebez, 21 Remeth, En-gannim, En-haddah, and Beth-pazzez. 22 The boundary touched Tabor, Shahazumah, and Beth-shemesh, and its limit was the Jordan: sixteen towns with their hamlets. 23 This was the holding of the tribe of the sons of Issachar family by family, both towns and hamlets.

24 The fifth lot cast was for the tribe of the Asherites family by family. 25 Their boundary included Helkath, Hali, Beten, Akshaph, 26 Alammelech, Amad, and Mishal; it touched Carmel on the west and the swamp of Libnath. 27 It then turned back towards the east to Beth-dagon, touched Zebulun and the valley of Jiphtah-el on the north at Beth-emek and Neiel, and reached Cabul on its northern side, 28 and Abdon, Rehob, Hammon, and Kanah as far as Greater Sidon. 29 The boundary turned at Ramah, going as far as the fortress city of Tyre, and then back again to Hosah, and its limits to the west were Mehalbeh, Achzib, 30 Acco, Aphek, and Rehob: twenty-two towns in all with their hamlets. 31 This was the holding of the tribe of Asher family by family, these towns and their hamlets.

32 The sixth lot cast was for the sons of Naphtali family by family. 33 Their boundary started from Heleph and from Elon-bezaanannim and ran past Adami-nekeb and Jabneel as far as Lakkum, and its limit was the Jordan. 34 The boundary turned back westwards to Aznoth-tabor and from there on to Hukok. It touched Zebulun on the south, Asher on the west, and the low-lying land by the Jordan on the east. 35 Their fortified towns were Ziddim, Zer, Hamath, Rakkath, Kinnereth, 36 Adamah, Ramah, Hazor, 37 Kedesh, Edrei, En-hazor, 38 Iron, Migdal-el, Horem, Beth-anath, and Beth-shemesh: nineteen towns with their hamlets. 39 This was the holding of the tribe of Naphtali family by family, both towns and hamlets.

40 The seventh lot cast was for the tribe of the sons of Dan family by family. 41 The boundary of their holding was Zorah, Eshtaol, Ir-shemesh, 42 Shaalabbin, Aijalon, Jithlah, 43 Elon, Timnah, Ekron, 44 Eltekeh, Gibbethon, Baalath, 45 Jehud, Bene-berak, and Gath-rimmon; 46 and on the west, Jarkon was the boundary opposite Joppa. 47 But the Danites, when they lost this territory, marched against Leshem, which they attacked and captured. They put its people to the sword, occupied it, and settled there; and they renamed the place Dan after their ancestor Dan. 48 This was the holding of the tribe of the sons of Dan family by family, these towns and their hamlets.

49 So the Israelites finished allocating the land and marking out its frontiers; and they gave Joshua son of Nun a holding within their territory. 50 They followed the commands of the LORD and gave him the town for which he asked, Timnath-serah in the hill-country of Ephraim; he rebuilt it and settled there.

51 These are the holdings which Eleazar the priest and Joshua son of Nun and the heads of families assigned by lot to the Israelite tribes at Shiloh before the LORD at the entrance of the Tent of Meeting. Thus they completed the distribution of the land.

19:28 **Abdon:** *so some MSS, cp. 21:30, 1 Chr. 6:74; others* Ebron.
19:29 **Mehalbeh:** *in Judg. 1:31* Ahlab. 19:29–30 **Mehalbeh . . .**
Acco: *prob. rdg; Heb.* from the district of Achzib and Ummah.
19:33 **from Heleph and:** *prob. rdg, cp. Gk; Heb.* omits.
19:46 **and on . . . boundary:** *so Gk; Heb.* Me-jarkon and Rakkon
were on the boundary. 19:50 **Timnath-serah:** *in Judg. 2:9*
Timnath-heres.

ʰCn Compare Gk: Heb *Mehebel*

NEW AMERICAN BIBLE

17 The fourth lot fell to Issachar. The territory of the clans of the Issacharites 18 included Jezreel, Chesulloth, Shunem, 19 Hapharaim, Shion, Anaharath, 20 Rabbith, Kishion, Ebez, 21 Remeth, En-gannim, En-haddah and Beth-pazzez. 22 The boundary reached Tabor, Shahazumah and Beth-shemesh, ending at the Jordan. These sixteen cities and their villages 23 were the heritage of the clans of the Issacharites.

24 The fifth lot fell to the clans of the tribe of the Asherites. 25 Their territory include Helkath, Hali, Beten, Achshaph, 26 Allammelech, Amad and Mishal, and reached Carmel on the west, and Shihor-libnath. 27 In the other direction, it ran eastward of Beth-dagon, reached Zebulun and the valley of Iphtahel; then north of Beth-emek and Neiel, it extended to Cabul, 28 Mishal, Abdon, Rehob, Hammon and Kanah, near Greater Sidon. 29 Then the boundary turned back to Ramah and to the fortress city of Tyre; thence it cut back to Hosah and ended at the sea. Thus, with Mahalab, Achzib, 30 Ummah, Amad, Acco, Aphek and Rehob, there were twenty-two cities and their villages 31 to comprise the heritage of the clans of the tribe of the Asherites.

32 The sixth lot fell to the Naphtalites. The boundary of the clans of the Naphtalites 33 extended from Heleph, from the oak at Zaanannim to Lakkum, including Adami-nekeb and Jabneel, and ended at the Jordan. 34 In the opposite direction, westerly, it ran through Aznoth-tabor and from there extended to Hukkok; it touched Zebulun on the south, Asher on the west, and the Jordan on the east. 35 The fortified cities were Ziddim, Zer, Hammath, Rakkath, Chinnereth, 36 Adamah, Ramah, Hazor, 37 Kedesh, Edrei, Enhazor, 38 Yiron, Migdal-el, Horem, Beth-anath and Beth-shemesh; nineteen cities and their villages, 39 to comprise the heritage of the clans of the tribe of the Naphtalites.

40 The seventh lot fell to the clans of the tribe of Danites. 41 Their heritage was the territory of Zorah, Eshtaol, Irshemesh, 42 Shaalabbin, Aijalon, Ithlah, 43 Elon, Timnah, Ekron, 44 Eltekoh, Gibbethon, Baalath, 45 Jehud, Beneberak, Gath-rimmon, 46 Me-jarkon and Rakkon, with the coast at Joppa. 47 But the territory of the Danites was too small for them; so the Danites marched up and attacked Leshem, which they captured and put to the sword. Once they had taken possession of Leshem, they renamed the settlement after their ancestor Dan. 48 These cities and their villages were the heritage of the clans of the tribe of the Danites.

49 When the last of them had received the portions of the land they were to inherit, the Israelites assigned a heritage in their midst to Joshua, son of Nun. 50 In obedience to the command of the LORD, they gave him the city which he requested, Timnah-serah in the mountain region of Ephraim. He rebuilt the city and made it his home.

51 These are the final portions into which Eleazar the priest, Joshua, son of Nun, and the heads of families in the tribes of the Israelites divided the land by lot in the presence of the LORD, at the door of the meeting tent in Shiloh.

NEW JERUSALEM BIBLE

17 The fourth lot came out for Issachar, for the sons of Issachar, by clans. 18 Their territory stretched towards Jezreel and included Chesulloth, Shunem, 19 Hapharaim, Shion, Anaharath, 20 Dobrath, Kishion, Ebez, 21 Remeth, En-Gannim, En-Haddah and Beth-Pazzez. 22 Their frontier touched Tabor, Shahazimah and Beth-Shemesh, and the frontier came to an end at the Jordan: sixteen towns with their villages.

23 Such was the heritage of the tribe of the sons of Issachar, by clans: the towns and their villages.

24 The fifth lot came out for the tribe of Asher, by clans. 25 Their territory included Helkath, Hali, Beten, Achshaph, 26 Alammelech, Amad and Mishal. 27 On the west, it touched Carmel and the course of the Libnath. On the side of the rising sun, it went as far as Beth-Dagon, touched Zebulun, the Valley of Iphtah-El on the north side, Beth-ha-Emek and Neiel, coming out with Cabul on the left, 28 with Abdon, Rehob, Hammon and Kanah as far as Sidon the Great. The frontier then turned towards Ramah, as far as the fortress-town of Tyre; 29 the frontier then went to Hosah and reached as far as the sea at Mahalab and Achzib, 30 with Acco, Aphek and Rehob: twenty-two towns with their villages.

31 Such was the heritage of the tribe of the sons of Asher, by clans; these towns and their villages.

32 To the sons of Naphtali fell the sixth portion, to the sons of Naphtali, by clans. 33 Their frontier went from Heleph and the Oak of Zanaannim, with Adami-ha-Negeb and Jabneel, as far as Lakkum, and ended at the Jordan. 34 The westward boundary ran to Aznoth-Tabor and thence came out at Hukkok, marching with Zebulun in the south, Asher in the west and the Jordan in the east. 35 The fortified towns were Ziddim, Zer, Hammath, Rakkath, Chinnereth, 36 Adamah, Ramah, Hazor, 37 Kedesh, Edrei, En-Hazor, 38 Jiron, Migdal-El, Horem, Beth-Anath and Beth-Shemesh: nineteen towns and their villages.

39 Such was the heritage of the sons of Naphtali, by clans: the towns and their villages.

40 To the tribe of the sons of Dan, by clans, fell the seventh portion. 41 The territory of their heritage comprised: Zorah, Eshtaol, Ir-Shemesh, 42 Shaalbim, Aijalon, Silatha, 43 Elon, Timnah, Ekron, 44 Eltekeh, Gibbethon, 45 Baalath, Azor, Bene-Berak and Gath-Rimmon; 46 and, by the sea, Jerakon with the territory facing Jaffa.

47 The territory of the sons of Dan eluded them, however, and the sons of Dan consequently went up and attacked Leshem, captured it and put it to the sword. Having gained possession of it, they settled there and called Leshem, Dan, after Dan their ancestor.

48 Such was the heritage of the tribe of the sons of Dan, by clans: these towns and their villages.

49 Having finished dividing the country, frontier by frontier, the Israelites gave Joshua son of Nun a heritage among themselves; 50 at Yahweh's command, they gave him the town which he had asked for, Timnath-Serah in the highlands of Ephraim; he rebuilt the town and settled there.

51 Such are the heritages which the priest Eleazar, Joshua son of Nun, and the heads of each family apportioned by lot between the tribes of Israel at Shiloh, in Yahweh's presence, at the door of the Tent of Meeting; and thus the apportioning of the country was completed.

20 Then the LORD spoke to Joshua, saying, 2 "Say to the Israelites, 'Appoint the cities of refuge, of which I spoke to you through Moses, 3 so that anyone who kills a person without intent or by mistake may flee there; they shall be for you a refuge from the avenger of blood. 4 The slayer shall flee to one of these cities and shall stand at the entrance of the gate of the city, and explain the case to the elders of that city; then the fugitive shall be taken into the city, and given a place, and shall remain with them. 5 And if the avenger of blood is in pursuit, they shall not give up the slayer, because the neighbor was killed by mistake, there having been no enmity between them before. 6 The slayer shall remain in that city until there is a trial before the congregation, until the death of the one who is high priest at the time: then the slayer may return home, to the town in which the deed was done.' "

7 So they set apart Kedesh in Galilee in the hill country of Naphtali, and Shechem in the hill country of Ephraim, and Kiriath-arba (that is, Hebron) in the hill country of Judah. 8 And beyond the Jordan east of Jericho, they appointed Bezer in the wilderness on the tableland, from the tribe of Reuben, and Ramoth in Gilead, from the tribe of Gad, and Golan in Bashan, from the tribe of Manasseh. 9 These were the cities designated for all the Israelites, and for the aliens residing among them, that anyone who killed a person without intent could flee there, so as not to die by the hand of the avenger of blood, until there was a trial before the congregation.

21 Then the heads of the families of the Levites came to the priest Eleazar and to Joshua son of Nun and to the heads of the families of the tribes of the Israelites; 2 they said to them at Shiloh in the land of Canaan, "The LORD commanded through Moses that we be given towns to live in, along with their pasture lands for our livestock." 3 So by command of the LORD the Israelites gave to the Levites the following towns and pasture lands out of their inheritance.

4 The lot came out for the families of the Kohathites. So those Levites who were descendants of Aaron the priest received by lot thirteen towns from the tribes of Judah, Simeon, and Benjamin.

5 The rest of the Kohathites received by lot ten towns from the families of the tribe of Ephraim, from the tribe of Dan, and the half-tribe of Manasseh.

6 The Gershonites received by lot thirteen towns from the families of the tribe of Issachar, from the tribe of Asher, from the tribe of Naphtali, and from the half-tribe of Manasseh in Bashan.

7 The Merarites according to their families received twelve towns from the tribe of Reuben, the tribe of Gad, and the tribe of Zebulun.

8 These towns and their pasture lands the Israelites gave by lot to the Levites, as the LORD had commanded through Moses.

9 Out of the tribe of Judah and the tribe of Simeon they gave the following towns mentioned by name, 10 which went to the descendants of Aaron, one of the families of the Kohathites who belonged to the Levites, since the lot fell to them first. 11 They gave them Kiriath-arba (Arba being the father of Anak), that is Hebron, in the hill country of Judah, along with the pasture lands around it. 12 But the fields of the town and its villages had been given to Caleb son of Jephunneh as his holding.

13 To the descendants of Aaron the priest they gave Hebron, the city of refuge for the slayer, with its pasture lands, Libnah with its pasture lands, 14 Jattir with its pasture lands, Eshtemoa with its pasture lands, 15 Holon with its pasture lands, Debir with its pasture lands, 16 Ain with its

20 THE LORD spoke to Joshua 2 and commanded him to say this to the Israelites: 'You must now appoint your cities of refuge, of which I spoke to you through Moses. 3 They are to be places where the homicide, the man who kills another inadvertently and without intent, may take sanctuary. Single them out as cities of refuge from the vengeance of the dead man's next-of-kin. 4 When a man takes sanctuary in one of them, he must stop at the entrance of the city gate and present his case in the hearing of the elders of that city; if they admit him into the city, they will grant him a place where he may live as one of themselves. 5 When the next-of-kin comes in pursuit, they are not to surrender him: he struck down his fellow without intent and had not previously been at enmity with him. 6 The homicide may stay in that city until he stands trial before the community. On the death of the ruling high priest, he may return to the town and home from which he has fled.' 7 They dedicated Kedesh in Galilee in the hill-country of Naphtali, Shechem in the hill-country of Ephraim, and Kiriath-arba, that is Hebron, in the hill-country of Judah. 8 Across the Jordan eastwards from Jericho they appointed these cities: from the tribe of Reuben, Bezer-in-the-wilderness on the tableland, from the tribe of Gad, Ramoth in Gilead, and from the tribe of Manasseh, Golan in Bashan. 9 These were the appointed cities where any Israelite or any alien residing among them might take sanctuary. They were intended for any man who killed another inadvertently, to ensure that no one should die at the hand of the next-of-kin until he had stood trial before the community.

21 The heads of the Levite families approached Eleazar the priest and Joshua son of Nun and the heads of the families of the tribes of Israel. 2 They came before them at Shiloh in Canaan and said, 'The LORD gave his command through Moses that we were to receive towns to live in, together with the common land belonging to them for our cattle.' 3 The Israelites, therefore, in obedience to the LORD's command, assigned to the Levites out of their own holdings the following towns with their common land.

4 When lots were cast the first fell to the Kohathite family. Those Levites who were descended from Aaron the priest received thirteen towns chosen by lot from the tribes of Judah, Simeon, and Benjamin; 5 the rest of the Kohathites were allotted family by family ten towns from the tribes of Ephraim, Dan, and half Manasseh.

6 The Gershonites were allotted family by family thirteen towns from the tribes of Issachar, Asher, Naphtali, and the half tribe of Manasseh in Bashan.

7 The Merarites were allotted family by family twelve towns from the tribes of Reuben, Gad, and Zebulun.

8 So the Israelites gave the Levites these towns with their common land, allocating them by lot as the LORD had commanded through Moses.

9 The Israelites designated the following towns out of the tribes of Judah and Simeon 10 for those sons of Aaron who were of the Kohathite families of the Levites, because their lot came out first. 11 They gave them Kiriath-arba (Arba was the father of Anak), that is Hebron, in the hill-country of Judah, and the common land round it, 12 but they gave the open country near the town, and its hamlets, to Caleb son of Jephunneh as his holding.

13 To the sons of Aaron the priest they gave Hebron, a city of refuge for the homicide, Libnah, 14 Jattir, Eshtemoa, 15 Holon, Debir, 16 Ashan, Juttah, and Beth-shemesh, each

21:5 **family by family:** *prob. rdg;* Heb. from the families (*similarly in verse* 6). 21:7 **were allotted:** *so Gk; Heb. omits.* 21:13–39 *Cp. 1 Chr. 6:57–81.* 21:16 **Ashan:** *prob. rdg, cp. 1 Chr. 6:59; Heb. Ain.*

20 The LORD said to Joshua: 2"Tell the Israelites to designate the cities of which I spoke to them through Moses, 3 to which one guilty of accidental and unintended homicide may flee for asylum from the avenger of blood. 4 To one of these cities the killer shall flee, and standing at the entrance of the city gate, he shall plead his case before the elders, who must receive him and assign him a place in which to live among them. 5 Though the avenger of blood pursues him, they are not to deliver up the homicide who slew his fellow man unintentionally and not out of previous hatred. 6 Once he has stood judgment before the community, he shall live on in that city till the death of the high priest who is in office at the time. Then the killer may go back home to his own city from which he fled."

7 So they set apart Kedesh in Galilee in the mountain region of Naphtali, Shechem in the mountain region of Ephraim, and Kiriath-arba (that is, Hebron) in the mountain region of Judah. 8 And beyond the Jordan east of Jericho they designated Bezer on the open tableland in the tribe of Reuben, Ramoth in Gilead in the tribe of Gad, and Golan in Bashan in the tribe of Manasseh. 9 These were the designated cities to which any Israelite or stranger living among them who had killed a person accidentally might flee to escape death at the hand of the avenger of blood, until he could appear before the community.

21 The heads of the Levite families came up to Eleazar the priest, to Joshua, son of Nun, and to the heads of families of the other tribes of the Israelites 2 at Shiloh in the land of Canaan, and said to them, "The LORD commanded, through Moses, that cities be given us to dwell in, with pasture lands for our livestock." 3 Out of their own heritage, in obedience to this command of the LORD, the Israelites gave the Levites the following cities with their pasture lands.

4 When the first lot among the Levites fell to the clans of the Kohathites, the descendants of Aaron the priest obtained thirteen cities by lot from the tribes of Judah, Simeon and Benjamin. 5 The rest of the Kohathites obtained ten cities by lot from the clans of the tribe of Ephraim, from the tribe of Dan, and from the half-tribe of Manasseh. 6 The Gershonites obtained thirteen cities by lot from the clans of the tribe of Issachar, from the tribe of Asher, from the tribe of Naphtali, and from the half-tribe of Manasseh. 7 The clans of the Merarites obtained twelve cities from the tribes of Reuben, Gad and Zebulun. 8 These cities with their pasture lands the Israelites allotted to the Levites in obedience to the LORD's command through Moses.

9 From the tribes of the Judahites and Simeonites they designated the following cities, 10 and assigned them to the descendants of Aaron in the Kohathite clan of the Levites, since the first lot fell to them: 11 first, Kiriath-arba (Arba was the father of Anak), that is, Hebron, in the mountain region of Judah, with the adjacent pasture lands, 12 although the open country and villages belonging to the city had been given to Caleb, son of Jephunneh, as his property. 13 Thus to the descendants of Aaron the priest were given the city of asylum for homicides at Hebron, with its pasture lands; also, Libnah with its pasture lands, 14 Jattir with its pasture lands, Eshtemoa with its pasture lands, 15 Holon with its pasture lands, Debir with its pasture lands, 16 Ashan with its

20 Yahweh said to Joshua, 2 'Speak to the Israelites and say to them, "Choose yourselves the cities of refuge of which I spoke to you through Moses, 3 to which anyone who has accidentally (unintentionally) killed someone else may flee, and which will serve you as refuge from the avenger of blood. 4 (The killer must flee to one of these towns. He will stop at the entrance to the town gate and explain his case to the town elders. These will admit him to their town and assign him a place to live among them. 5 If the avenger of blood pursues him, they must not hand the killer over to him, since he has killed his fellow unintentionally and was not motivated by long-standing hatred for him. 6 He must stay in this town) until he is brought to trial before the community (until the death of the high priest then in office. Only then may the killer go back to his own town and to his own house in the town from which he has fled)." '

7 For this purpose they designated Kedesh in Galilee, in the highlands of Naphtali, Shechem in the highlands of Ephraim, and Kiriath-Arba — now Hebron — in the highlands of Judah. 8 On the other, eastern, side of the Jordan opposite Jericho, in the desert of the tableland, they chose Bezer of the tribe of Reuben, Ramoth in Gilead of the tribe of Gad, and Golan in Bashan of the tribe of Manasseh. 9 Such were the towns designated for all the Israelites and for foreigners living among them, so that anyone who had accidentally killed someone could flee there and might escape the hand of the avenger of blood, until brought to trial before the community.

21 The heads of families of the Levites then came to the priest, Eleazar, Joshua son of Nun and the heads of families of the tribes of Israel — 2 they were then at Shiloh in Canaan. They said to them, 'Through Moses, Yahweh ordered us to be given towns to live in, with their pasture lands for our livestock.' 3 In compliance with Yahweh's order, the Israelites consequently and from their own heritage gave the Levites the following towns with their pasture lands:

4 Lots were cast for the clans of the Kohathites: to those Levites who were sons of Aaron the priest, fell thirteen towns from the tribes of Judah, Simeon and Benjamin; 5 to the other sons of Kohath, by clans, 6 fell ten towns from the tribes of Ephraim, Dan, and the half-tribe of Manasseh. To the sons of Gershon, by clans, fell thirteen towns from the tribes of Issachar, Asher, Naphtali and the half-tribe of Manasseh in Bashan. 7 To the sons of Merari, by clans, fell twelve towns from the tribes of Reuben, Gad and Zebulun.

8 The Israelites assigned these towns and their pasture lands to the Levites by lot, as Yahweh had ordered through Moses.

9 From the tribe of Judah and the tribe of Simeon, they gave the towns named below. 10 The first portion was for the sons of Aaron, belonging to the clans of the Kohathites, to the sons of Levi, since the first lot was theirs. 11 They gave them Kiriath-Arba, Anak's father's town — now Hebron — in the highlands of Judah, with its surrounding pasture lands. 12 The fields and villages of this town, however, they gave to Caleb son of Jephunneh as his property. 13 To the sons of Aaron the priest they gave Hebron, a city of refuge for those who had killed, with its pasture lands, as well as Libnah with its pasture lands, 14 Jattir with its pasture lands, Eshtemoa with its pasture lands, 15 Holon with its pasture lands, Debir with its pasture lands, 16 Ashan

pasture lands, Juttah with its pasture lands, and Beth-shemesh with its pasture lands — nine towns out of these two tribes. 17 Out of the tribe of Benjamin: Gibeon with its pasture lands, Geba with its pasture lands, 18 Anathoth with its pasture lands, and Almon with its pasture lands — four towns. 19 The towns of the descendants of Aaron — the priests — were thirteen in all, with their pasture lands.

20 As to the rest of the Kohathites belonging to the Kohathite families of the Levites, the towns allotted to them were out of the tribe of Ephraim. 21 To them were given Shechem, the city of refuge for the slayer, with its pasture lands in the hill country of Ephraim, Gezer with its pasture lands, 22 Kibzaim with its pasture lands, and Beth-horon with its pasture lands — four towns. 23 Out of the tribe of Dan: Elteke with its pasture lands, Gibbethon with its pasture lands, 24 Aijalon with its pasture lands, Gath-rimmon with its pasture lands — four towns. 25 Out of the half-tribe of Manasseh: Taanach with its pasture lands, and Gath-rimmon with its pasture lands — two towns. 26 The towns of the families of the rest of the Kohathites were ten in all, with their pasture lands.

27 To the Gershonites, one of the families of the Levites, were given out of the half-tribe of Manasseh, Golan in Bashan with its pasture lands, the city of refuge for the slayer, and Beeshterah with its pasture lands — two towns. 28 Out of the tribe of Issachar: Kishion with its pasture lands, Daberath with its pasture lands, 29 Jarmuth with its pasture lands, En-gannim with its pasture lands — four towns; 30 Out of the tribe of Asher: Mishal with its pasture lands, Abdon with its pasture lands, 31 Helkath with its pasture lands, and Rehob with its pasture lands — four towns. 32 Out of the tribe of Naphtali: Kedesh in Galilee with its pasture lands, the city of refuge for the slayer, Hammoth-dor with its pasture lands, and Kartan with its pasture lands — three towns. 33 The towns of the several families of the Gershonites were in all thirteen, with their pasture lands.

34 To the rest of the Levites — the Merarite families — were given out of the tribe of Zebulun: Jokneam with its pasture lands, Kartah with its pasture lands, 35 Dimnah with its pasture lands, Nahalal with its pasture lands — four towns. 36 Out of the tribe of Reuben: Bezer with its pasture lands, Jahzah with its pasture lands, 37 Kedemoth with its pasture lands, and Mephaath with its pasture lands — four towns. 38 Out of the tribe of Gad: Ramoth in Gilead with its pasture lands, the city of refuge for the slayer, Mahanaim with its pasture lands, 39 Heshbon with its pasture lands, Jazer with its pasture lands — four towns in all. 40 As for the towns of the several Merarite families, that is, the remainder of the families of the Levites, those allotted to them were twelve in all.

41 The towns of the Levites within the holdings of the Israelites were in all forty-eight towns with their pasture lands. 42 Each of these towns had its pasture lands around it; so it was with all these towns.

43 Thus the LORD gave to Israel all the land that he swore to their ancestors that he would give them; and having taken possession of it, they settled there. 44 And the LORD gave them rest on every side just as he had sworn to their ancestors; not one of all their enemies had withstood them, for the LORD had given all their enemies into their hands. 45 Not one of all the good promises that the LORD had made to the house of Israel had failed; all came to pass.

with its common land: nine towns from these two tribes. 17 They also gave towns from the tribe of Benjamin, Gibeon, Geba, 18 Anathoth, and Almon, each with its common land: four towns. 19 The number of the towns with their common land given to the sons of Aaron, the priests, was thirteen.

20 The towns which the rest of the Kohathite families of the Levites received by lot were from the tribe of Ephraim. 21 They gave them Shechem, a city of refuge for the homicide in the hill-country of Ephraim, Gezer, 22 Kibzaim, and Beth-horon, each with its common land: four towns. 23 From the tribe of Dan, they gave them Elteheh, Gibbethon, 24 Aijalon, and Gath-rimmon, each with its common land: four towns. 25 From the half tribe of Manasseh, they gave them Taanach and Gath-rimmon, each with its common land: two towns. 26 The number of the towns belonging to the rest of the Kohathite families with their common land was ten.

27 The Gershonite families of the Levites received, out of the share of the half tribe of Manasseh, Golan in Bashan, a city of refuge for the homicide, and Be-ashtaroth, each with its common land: two towns. 28 From the tribe of Issachar they received Kishon, Daberath, 29 Jarmuth, and En-gannim, each with its common land: four towns. 30 From the tribe of Asher they received Mishal, Abdon, 31 Helkath, and Rehob, each with its common land: four towns. 32 From the tribe of Naphtali they received Kedesh in Galilee, a city of refuge for the homicide, Hammoth-dor, and Kartan, each with its common land: three towns. 33 The number of the towns of the Gershonite families with their common land was thirteen.

34 From the tribe of Zebulun the rest of the Merarite families of the Levites received Jokneam, Kartah, 35 Rimmon, and Nahalal, each with its common land: four towns. 36 East of the Jordan at Jericho, from the tribe of Reuben they were given Bezer-in-the-wilderness on the tableland, a city of refuge for the homicide, Jahaz, 37 Kedemoth, and Mephaath, each with its common land: four towns. 38 From the tribe of Gad they received Ramoth in Gilead, a city of refuge for the homicide, Mahanaim, 39 Heshbon, and Jazer, each with its common land: four towns in all. 40 Twelve towns in all fell by lot to the rest of the Merarite families of the Levites.

41 The towns of the Levites within the Israelite holdings numbered forty-eight in all, with their common land. 42 Each town had its common land round it, and it was the same for all of them.

43 Thus the LORD gave Israel all the land which he had sworn to give to their forefathers; they occupied it and settled in it. 44 The LORD gave them security on every side as he had sworn to their forefathers. Of all their enemies not a man could withstand them; the LORD delivered all their enemies into their hands. 45 Not a word of the LORD's promises to the house of Israel went unfulfilled; they all came true.

21:27 **Be-ashtaroth:** *prob. rdg; Heb.* Be-eshterah.
21:29 **Jarmuth:** *or, with Gk,* Remeth, *cp. 19:21.*
21:35 **Rimmon:** *prob. rdg, cp. 19:13, 1 Chr. 6:77; Heb.* Dimnah.
21:36–37 *Some important Heb. MSS omit these verses.*

pasture lands, Juttah with its pasture lands, and Beth-shemesh with its pasture lands: nine cities from the two tribes mentioned. 17 From the tribe of Benjamin they obtained the four cities of Gibeon with its pasture lands, Geba with its pasture lands, 18 Anathoth with its pasture lands, and Almon with its pasture lands. 19 These cities which with their pasture lands belonged to the priestly descendants of Aaron, were thirteen in all.

20 The rest of the Kohathite clans among the Levites obtained by lot, from the tribe of Ephraim, four cities. 21 They were assigned, with its pasture lands, the city of asylum for homicides at Shechem in the mountain region of Ephraim; also Gezer with its pasture lands, 22 Kibzaim with its pasture lands, and Beth-horon with its pasture lands. 23 From the tribe of Dan they obtained the four cities of Elteke with its pasture lands, Gibbethon with its pasture lands, 24 Aijalon with its pasture lands, and Gath-rimmon with its pasture lands; 25 and from the half-tribe of Manasseh the two cities of Taanach with its pasture lands and Ibleam with its pasture lands. 26 These cities which with their pasture lands belonged to the rest of the Kohathite clans were ten in all.

27 The Gershonite clan of the Levites received from the half-tribe of Manasseh two cities: the city of asylum for homicides at Golan with its pasture lands; and also Beth-Astharoth with its pasture lands. 28 From the tribe of Issachar they obtained the four cities of Kishion with its pasture lands, Daberath with its pasture lands, 29 Jarmuth with its pasture lands, and En-gannim with its pasture lands; 30 from the tribe of Asher, the four cities of Mishal with its pasture lands, Abdon with its pasture lands, 31 Helkath with its pasture lands, and Rehob with its pasture lands; 32 and from the tribe of Naphtali, three cities: the city of asylum for homicides at Kedesh in Galilee, with its pasture lands; also Hammath with its pasture lands, and Rakkath with its pasture lands. 33 These cities which with their pasture lands belonged to the Gershonite clans were thirteen in all.

34 The Merarite clans, the last of the Levites, received from the tribe of Zebulun the four cities of Jokneam with its pasture lands, Kartah with its pasture lands, 35 Rimmon with its pasture lands, and Nahalal with its pasture lands; 36 also, across the Jordan, from the tribe of Reuben, four cities: the city of asylum for homicides at Bezer with its pasture lands, Jahaz with its pasture lands, 37 Kedemoth with its pasture lands, and Mephaath with its pasture lands; 38 and from the tribe of Gad a total of four cities: the city of asylum for homicides at Ramoth in Gilead with its pasture lands, also Mahanaim with its pasture lands, 39 Heshbon with its pasture lands, and Jazer with its pasture lands. 40 The cities which were allotted to the Merarite clans, the last of the Levites, were therefore twelve in all.

41 Thus the total number of cities within the territory of the Israelites which, with their pasture lands, belonged to the Levites, was forty-eight. 42 With each and every one of these cities went the pasture lands round about it.

43 And so the LORD gave Israel all the land he had sworn to their fathers he would give them. Once they had conquered and occupied it, 44 the LORD gave them peace on every side, just as he had promised their fathers. Not one of their enemies could withstand them; the LORD brought all their enemies under their power. 45 Not a single promise that the LORD made to the house of Israel was broken; every one was fulfilled.

with its pasture lands, Juttah with its pasture lands, and Beth-Shemesh with its pasture lands: nine towns taken from these two tribes; 17 and, from the tribe of Benjamin, Gibeon with its pasture lands, Geba with its pasture lands, 18 Anathoth with its pasture lands and Almon with its pasture lands: four towns.

19 Total number of towns for the priests, the sons of Aaron: thirteen towns with their pasture lands.

20 As regards the clans of the sons of Kohath, those Levites still left of the sons of Kohath, the towns of their lot were taken from the tribe of Ephraim. 21 They were given Shechem, a city of refuge for those who had killed, with its pasture lands, in the highlands of Ephraim, as well as Gezer with its pasture lands, 22 Kibzaim with its pasture lands, and Beth-Horon with its pasture lands: four towns; 23 from the tribe of Dan, Elteke with its pasture lands, Gibbethon with its pasture lands, 24 Aijalon with its pasture lands and Gath-Rimmon with its pasture lands: four towns; 25 and, from the half-tribe of Manasseh, Taanach with its pasture lands and Jibleam with its pasture lands: two towns.

26 In all: ten towns with their pasture lands for the remaining clans of the sons of Kohath.

27 To the sons of Gershon, of the levitical clans, were given: from the half-tribe of Manasseh, Golan in Bashan, a city of refuge for those who had killed, with its pasture lands, and Ashtaroth with its pasture lands — two towns; 28 from the tribe of Issachar, Kishion with its pasture lands, Dobrath with its pasture lands, 29 Jarmuth with its pasture lands and En-Gannim with its pasture lands — four towns; 30 from the tribe of Asher, Mishal with its pasture lands, Abdon with its pasture lands, 31 Helkath with its pasture lands and Rehob with its pasture lands — four towns; 32 and, from the tribe of Naphtali, Kedesh in Galilee, a city of refuge for those who had killed, with its pasture lands, Hammoth-Dor with its pasture lands and Kartan with its pasture lands — three towns.

33 Total number of towns of the Gershonites, by clans: thirteen towns with their pasture lands.

34 To the clans of the sons of Merari, the remainder of the Levites, fell: from the tribe of Zebulun, Jokneam with its pasture lands, Kartah with its pasture lands, 35 Rimmon with its pasture lands and Nahalal with its pasture lands — four towns; 36 on the other side of the Jordan opposite Jericho, from the tribe of Reuben, Bezer in the desert, on the tableland, a city of refuge for those who had killed, with its pasture lands, Jahaz with its pasture lands, 37 Kedemoth with its pasture lands and Mephaath with its pasture lands — four towns; 38 and, from the tribe of Gad, Ramoth in Gilead, a city of refuge for those who had killed, with its pasture lands, Mahanaim with its pasture lands, 39 Heshbon with its pasture lands and Jazer with its pasture lands — four towns.

40 Total number of towns forming the lot of the sons of Merari by clans, of the remaining levitical clans: twelve towns.

41 The total number of towns for the Levites in Israelite territory was forty-eight towns with their pasture lands. 42 These towns consisted in each case of the town itself and the pasture land round it. This was the case with all the towns.

43 This was how Yahweh gave the Israelites the entire country which he had sworn to give to their ancestors. They took possession of it and settled in it. 44 Yahweh granted them tranquillity on all their frontiers just as he had sworn to their ancestors and, of all their enemies, not one succeeded in resisting them. Yahweh put all their enemies at their mercy. 45 Of all the promises that Yahweh had made to the House of Israel, not one failed; all were fulfilled.

NEW REVISED STANDARD VERSION

22 Then Joshua summoned the Reubenites, the Gadites, and the half-tribe of Manasseh, 2 and said to them, "You have observed all that Moses the servant of the LORD commanded you, and have obeyed me in all that I have commanded you; 3 you have not forsaken your kindred these many days, down to this day, but have been careful to keep the charge of the LORD your God. 4 And now the LORD your God has given rest to your kindred, as he promised them; therefore turn and go to your tents in the land where your possession lies, which Moses the servant of the LORD gave you on the other side of the Jordan. 5 Take good care to observe the commandment and instruction that Moses the servant of the LORD commanded you, to love the LORD your God, to walk in all his ways, to keep his commandments, and to hold fast to him, and to serve him with all your heart and with all your soul." 6 So Joshua blessed them and sent them away, and they went to their tents.

7 Now to the one half of the tribe of Manasseh Moses had given a possession in Bashan; but to the other half Joshua had given a possession beside their fellow Israelites in the land west of the Jordan. And when Joshua sent them away to their tents and blessed them, 8 he said to them, "Go back to your tents with much wealth, and with very much livestock, with silver, gold, bronze, and iron, and with a great quantity of clothing; divide the spoil of your enemies with your kindred." 9 So the Reubenites and the Gadites and the half-tribe of Manasseh returned home, parting from the Israelites at Shiloh, which is in the land of Canaan, to go to the land of Gilead, their own land of which they had taken possession by command of the LORD through Moses.

10 When they came to the region[i] near the Jordan that lies in the land of Canaan, the Reubenites and the Gadites and the half-tribe of Manasseh built there an altar by the Jordan, an altar of great size. 11 The Israelites heard that the Reubenites and the Gadites and the half-tribe of Manasseh had built an altar at the frontier of the land of Canaan, in the region[j] near the Jordan, on the side that belongs to the Israelites. 12 And when the people of Israel heard of it, the whole assembly of the Israelites gathered at Shiloh, to make war against them.

13 Then the Israelites sent the priest Phinehas son of Eleazar to the Reubenites and the Gadites and the half-tribe of Manasseh, in the land of Gilead, 14 and with him ten chiefs, one from each of the tribal families of Israel, every one of them the head of a family among the clans of Israel. 15 They came to the Reubenites, the Gadites, and the half-tribe of Manasseh, in the land of Gilead, and they said to them, 16 "Thus says the whole congregation of the LORD, 'What is this treachery that you have committed against the God of Israel in turning away today from following the LORD, by building yourselves an altar today in rebellion against the LORD? 17 Have we not had enough of the sin at Peor from which even yet we have not cleansed ourselves, and for which a plague came upon the congregation of the LORD, 18 that you must turn away today from following the LORD! If you rebel against the LORD today, he will be angry with the whole congregation of Israel tomorrow. 19 But now, if your land is unclean, cross over into the LORD's land where the LORD's tabernacle now stands, and take for yourselves a possession among us; only do not rebel against the LORD, or rebel against us[k] by building yourselves an altar other than the altar of the LORD our God. 20 Did not Achan son of Zerah break faith in the matter of the devoted things, and wrath fell upon all the congregation of Israel? And he did not perish alone for his iniquity!' "

REVISED ENGLISH BIBLE

22 AT that time Joshua summoned the Reubenites, the Gadites, and the half tribe of Manasseh, 2 and said to them, 'You have observed all the commands of Moses the servant of the LORD, and you have obeyed me in every command I laid on you. 3 All this time you have not deserted your kinsmen; right up to the present day you have faithfully observed the charge laid on you by the LORD your God. 4 The LORD your God has now given your kinsmen security as he promised them. Now you may return to your homes, to your own land which Moses the servant of the LORD assigned to you east of the Jordan. 5 But be very careful to keep the commands and the law which Moses the servant of the LORD gave you: to love the LORD your God; to conform to all his ways; to observe his commandments; to hold fast to him; to serve him with your whole heart and soul.' 6 Joshua blessed them and dismissed them, and they went to their homes. 7-8 When he sent them away with his blessing, he said: 'Go to your homes richly laden, with great herds, with silver and gold, copper and iron, and with large stores of clothing. See that you share with your kinsmen the spoil you have taken from your enemies.'

To one half of the tribe of Manasseh Moses had given territory in Bashan; to the other half Joshua gave territory west of the Jordan among their kinsmen.

9 So at Shiloh in Canaan the Reubenites, the Gadites, and the half tribe of Manasseh parted from the rest of the Israelites to go into Gilead, the land which belonged to them according to the decree of the LORD given through Moses. 10 When these tribes came to Geliloth by the Jordan, they built there by the river a great altar for all to see. 11 The Israelites heard that the Reubenites, the Gadites, and the half tribe of Manasseh had built the altar facing the land of Canaan, at Geliloth by the Jordan opposite the Israelite side, 12 and, at the news, the whole Israelite community assembled at Shiloh to march against them.

13 At the same time the Israelites sent Phinehas son of Eleazar the priest into the land of Gilead, to the Reubenites, the Gadites, and the half tribe of Manasseh; 14 he was accompanied by ten leading men, one from each of the tribes of Israel, all of them heads of households among the clans of Israel. 15 They came to the Reubenites, the Gadites, and the half tribe of Manasseh in the land of Gilead, and remonstrated with them: 16 'We speak for the whole community of the LORD,' they declared. 'What is this treachery you have committed against the God of Israel? Are you ceasing to follow the LORD, and are you building your own altar this day in defiance of the LORD? 17 Remember our offence at Peor, for which a plague struck the community of the LORD; to this day we have not been purified from it. Was that offence so slight 18 that you dare cease to follow the LORD today? If today you defy the LORD, tomorrow he will be angry with the whole community of Israel. 19 If the land you have taken is unclean, then cross over to the LORD's own land, where the Tabernacle of the LORD now rests, and take a share of it with us. But do not defy the LORD and involve us in your defiance by building an altar of your own besides the altar of the LORD our God. 20 Remember the treachery of Achan son of Zerah, who defied the ban, and the whole community of Israel suffered for it; he was not the only one who paid with his life for that sin.'

22:10 **Geliloth . . . Jordan:** *prob. rdg; Heb. adds* which was in Canaan.

---

[i] Or to Geliloth [j] Or at Geliloth [k] Or make rebels of us

496

NEW AMERICAN BIBLE

22 At that time Joshua summoned the Reubenites, the Gadites, and the half-tribe of Manasseh 2 and said to them: "You have done all that Moses, the servant of the LORD, commanded you, and have obeyed every command I gave you. 3 For many years now you have not once abandoned your kinsmen, but have faithfully carried out the commands of the LORD, your God. 4 Since, therefore, the LORD, your God, has settled your kinsmen as he promised them, you may now return to your tents beyond the Jordan; to your own land, which Moses, the servant of the LORD, gave you. 5 But be very careful to observe the precept and law which Moses, the servant of the LORD, enjoined upon you: love the LORD, your God; follow him faithfully; keep his commandments; remain loyal to him; and serve him with your whole heart and soul." 6 Joshua then blessed them and sent them away to their own tents.

7 (For, to half the tribe of Manasseh Moses had assigned land in Bashan; and to the other half Joshua had given a portion along with their kinsmen west of the Jordan.) What Joshua said to them when he sent them off to their tents with his blessing was, 8 "Now that you are returning to your own tents with great wealth, with very numerous livestock, with silver, gold, bronze and iron, and with a very large supply of clothing, divide these spoils of your enemies with your kinsmen there." 9 So the Reubenites, the Gadites, and the half-tribe of Manasseh left the other Israelites at Shiloh in the land of Canaan and returned to the land of Gilead, their own property, which they had received according to the LORD's command through Moses.

10 When the Reubenites, the Gadites, and the half-tribe of Manasseh came to the region of the Jordan in the land of Canaan, they built there at the Jordan a conspicuously large altar. 11 The other Israelites heard the report that the Reubenites, the Gadites, and the half-tribe of Manasseh had built an altar in the region of the Jordan facing the land of Canaan, across from them, 12 and therefore they assembled their whole community at Shiloh to declare war on them.

13 First, however, they sent to the Reubenites, the Gadites, and the half-tribe of Manasseh in the land of Gilead an embassy consisting of Phinehas, son of Eleazar the priest, 14 and ten princes, one from every tribe of Israel, each one being both prince and military leader of his ancestral house. 15 When these came to the Reubenites, the Gadites, and the half-tribe of Manasseh in the land of Gilead, they said to them: 16 "The whole community of the LORD sends this message: What act of treachery is this you have committed against the God of Israel? You have seceded from the LORD this day, and rebelled against him by building an altar of your own! 17 For the sin of Peor, a plague came upon the community of the LORD. 18 We are still not free of that; must you now add to it? You are rebelling against the LORD today and by tomorrow he will be angry with the whole community of Israel! 19 If you consider the land you now possess unclean, cross over to the land the LORD possesses, where the Dwelling of the LORD stands, and share that with us. But do not rebel against the LORD, nor involve us in rebellion, by building an altar of your own in addition to the altar of the LORD, our God. 20 When Achan, son of Zerah, violated the ban, did not wrath fall upon the entire community of Israel? Though he was but a single man, he did not perish alone for his guilt!"

NEW JERUSALEM BIBLE

22 Joshua then summoned the Reubenites, the Gadites and the half-tribe of Manasseh 2 and said to them, 'You have observed everything that Moses, servant of Yahweh, ordered you, and whenever I have given you an order you have listened to me. 3 You have not deserted your brothers, from long ago until today, keeping the observance of the commandment of Yahweh your God. 4 Now that Yahweh your God has granted your brothers the rest that he promised them, go back to your tents, to the country belonging to you which Moses, servant of Yahweh, gave you on the other side of the Jordan. 5 But take great care to practise the commandments and the Law which Moses, servant of Yahweh, has given you: to love Yahweh your God, always to follow his paths, to keep his commandments, to be loyal to him and to serve him with all your heart and with all your soul.'

6 Joshua blessed them and sent them away, and they went home to their tents.

7 To one half of the tribe of Manasseh, Moses had given a territory in Bashan; to the other half, Joshua gave another among their brothers on the west bank of the Jordan. As Joshua sent them home to their tents, he blessed them 8 and said to them, 'You are going back to your tents with great wealth, with a great deal of livestock, with silver and gold, bronze and iron and great quantities of clothing; share the spoils of your enemies with your brothers.'

9 The Reubenites, the Gadites and the half-tribe of Manasseh returned home, leaving the Israelites at Shiloh in Canaan, and made for Gilead, the territory which belonged to them as a result of Yahweh's order given through Moses. 10 When they came to the stone circle by the Jordan, in Canaanite territory, the Reubenites, the Gadites and the half-tribe of Manasseh built an altar there beside the Jordan, a large, imposing altar.

11 This came to the ears of the Israelites. 'Look,' the word went round, 'the Reubenites, the Gadites and the half-tribe of Manasseh have built this altar on the Canaanite side, near the stone circle by the Jordan, on the Israelites' bank.' 12 At this news, the whole community of the Israelites mustered at Shiloh, to march against them and make war on them.

13 The Israelites sent the priest Phinehas son of Eleazar to the Reubenites, the Gadites and the half-tribe of Manasseh, in Gilead, 14 and with him ten leading men, one man from a leading family from each of the tribes of Israel, each of them being head of his family in the clans of Israel. 15 Having reached the Reubenites, the Gadites and the half-tribe of Manasseh in Gilead, they said this: 16 'The whole community of Israel says as follows, "What do you mean by this infidelity, which you have committed against the God of Israel by now repudiating your allegiance to Yahweh, and by building yourselves an altar with the intention now of rebelling against Yahweh? 17 "Was the crime which we committed at Peor so slight — although we have not managed to purify ourselves from that even now, in spite of the plague which has ravaged the community of Yahweh — 18 that you must now repudiate your allegiance to Yahweh? For since you are in rebellion against him today, tomorrow his anger will be aroused against the whole community of Israel. 19 "Is the country in which you have settled unclean? Then cross over into the country where Yahweh has settled, there where Yahweh's Dwelling now stands, and settle among us. But do not rebel against Yahweh or involve us in your rebellion by building a rival altar to the altar of Yahweh our God. 20 When Achan son of Zerah was unfaithful to the curse of destruction, did not the retribution come down on the whole community of Israel, although he was only one man? Did he not have to die for his crime?" '

NEW REVISED STANDARD VERSION

21 Then the Reubenites, the Gadites, and the half-tribe of Manasseh said in answer to the heads of the families of Israel, 22 "The LORD, God of gods! The LORD, God of gods! He knows; and let Israel itself know! If it was in rebellion or in breach of faith toward the LORD, do not spare us today 23 for building an altar to turn away from following the LORD; or if we did so to offer burnt offerings or grain offerings or offerings of well-being on it, may the LORD himself take vengeance. 24 No! We did it from fear that in time to come your children might say to our children, 'What have you to do with the LORD, the God of Israel? 25 For the LORD has made the Jordan a boundary between us and you, you Reubenites and Gadites; you have no portion in the LORD.' So your children might make our children cease to worship the LORD. 26 Therefore we said, 'Let us now build an altar, not for burnt offering, nor for sacrifice, 27 but to be a witness between us and you, and between the generations after us, that we do perform the service of the LORD in his presence with our burnt offerings and sacrifices and offerings of well-being; so that your children may never say to our children in time to come, "You have no portion in the LORD." ' 28 And we thought, If this should be said to us or to our descendants in time to come, we could say, 'Look at this copy of the altar of the LORD, which our ancestors made, not for burnt offerings, nor for sacrifice, but to be a witness between us and you.' 29 Far be it from us that we should rebel against the LORD, and turn away this day from following the LORD by building an altar for burnt offering, grain offering, or sacrifice, other than the altar of the LORD our God that stands before his tabernacle!"

30 When the priest Phinehas and the chiefs of the congregation, the heads of the families of Israel who were with him, heard the words that the Reubenites and the Gadites and the Manassites spoke, they were satisfied. 31 The priest Phinehas son of Eleazar said to the Reubenites and the Gadites and the Manassites, "Today we know that the LORD is among us, because you have not committed this treachery against the LORD; now you have saved the Israelites from the hand of the LORD."

32 Then the priest Phinehas son of Eleazar and the chiefs returned from the Reubenites and the Gadites in the land of Gilead to the land of Canaan, to the Israelites, and brought back word to them. 33 The report pleased the Israelites; and the Israelites blessed God and spoke no more of making war against them, to destroy the land where the Reubenites and the Gadites were settled. 34 The Reubenites and the Gadites called the altar Witness;/ "For," said they, "it is a witness between us that the LORD is God."

23 A long time afterward, when the LORD had given rest to Israel from all their enemies all around, and Joshua was old and well advanced in years, 2 Joshua summoned all Israel, their elders and heads, their judges and officers, and said to them, "I am now old and well advanced in years; 3 and you have seen all that the LORD your God has done to all these nations for your sake, for it is the LORD your God who has fought for you. 4 I have allotted to you as an inheritance for your tribes those nations that remain, along with all the nations that I have already cut off, from the Jordan to the Great Sea in the west. 5 The LORD your

REVISED ENGLISH BIBLE

21 In reply the Reubenites, the Gadites, and the half tribe of Manasseh said to the heads of the clans of Israel: 22 'The LORD the God of gods, the LORD the God of gods, he knows, and Israel must know: if this had been an act of defiance or treachery against the LORD, you could not save us today. 23 If we had built ourselves an altar and meant to forsake the LORD, or had offered whole-offerings and grain-offerings on it, or had presented shared-offerings, the LORD himself would exact punishment. 24 The truth is that we have done this for fear that the day may come when your children will say to ours, "What have you to do with the LORD, the God of Israel? 25 The LORD put the Jordan as a boundary between us and you. You have no share in the LORD, you Reubenites and Gadites." So your children would prevent ours from worshipping the LORD.

26 'We resolved to build an altar, not for whole-offerings and sacrifices, 27 but as a witness between us and you, and between the generations to come. Thus we shall be able to perform service before the LORD, as we do now, with our whole-offerings, our sacrifices, and our shared-offerings; and your children will never be able to say to our children in time to come, "You have no share in the LORD." 28 And we thought, if ever they do say this to us and to our descendants, we will point to this copy of the altar of the LORD which we have made, not for whole-offerings and not for sacrifices, but as a witness between us and you. 29 God forbid that we should defy the LORD and forsake him now by building another altar for whole-offerings, grain-offerings, and sacrifices, in addition to the altar of the LORD our God which stands in front of his tabernacle.'

30 When Phinehas the priest and the leaders of the community, the heads of the Israelite clans, who were with him, heard what the Reubenites, Gadites, and Manassites had to say, they were satisfied. 31 Phinehas son of Eleazar the priest said to the Reubenites, Gadites, and Manassites, 'Now we know that the LORD is in our midst; you have not acted treacherously against the LORD, but have preserved all Israel from punishment at his hand.'

32 Phinehas son of Eleazar the priest and the leaders left the Reubenites and the Gadites in Gilead and made their report to the Israelites in Canaan. 33 The Israelites were satisfied, and they blessed God and thought no more of attacking and ravaging the land where Reuben and Gad had settled. 34 The Reubenites and Gadites declared, 'The altar is a witness between us that the LORD is God,' and they named it 'Witness'.

23 A LONG time had passed since the LORD had given Israel security from all their enemies around them, and Joshua was now very old. 2 He summoned all Israel, their elders and heads of families, their judges and officers, and said to them, 'I am now an old man, far advanced in years. 3 You have seen for yourselves everything the LORD your God has done to all these peoples for your sake; it was the LORD God himself who fought for you. 4 I have allotted to you tribe by tribe your holdings, the land of all the peoples that I have wiped out and of all these that remain between the Jordan and the Great Sea which lies towards the setting sun. 5 The LORD your God himself drove them out at

22:24 **for fear:** so Syriac; Heb. adds from a word.
22:34 **'Witness':** so some MSS; others omit.

/ Cn Compare Syr: Heb lacks Witness

21 The Reubenites, the Gadites, and the half-tribe of Manasseh replied to the military leaders of the Israelites: "The LORD is the God of gods. 22 The LORD, the God of gods, knows and Israel shall know. If now we have acted out of rebellion or treachery against the LORD, our God, 23 and if we have built an altar of our own to secede from the LORD, or to offer holocausts, grain offerings or peace offerings upon it, the LORD himself will exact the penalty. 24 We did it rather out of our anxious concern lest in the future your children should say to our children: 'What have you to do with the LORD, the God of Israel? 25 For the LORD has placed the Jordan as a boundary between you and us. You descendants of Reuben and Gad have no share in the LORD.' Thus your children would prevent ours from revering the LORD. 26 So we decided to guard our interests by building this altar of our own: not for holocausts or for sacrifices, 27 but as evidence for you on behalf of ourselves and our descendants, that we have the right to worship the LORD in his presence with our holocausts, sacrifices, and peace offerings. Now in the future your children cannot say to our children, 'You have no share in the LORD.' 28 Our thought was, that if in the future they should speak thus to us or to our descendants, we could answer: 'Look at the model of the altar of the LORD which our fathers made, not for holocausts or for sacrifices, but to witness between you and us.' 29 Far be it from us to rebel against the LORD or to secede now from the LORD by building an altar for holocaust, grain offering, or sacrifice in addition to the altar of the LORD, our God, which stands before his Dwelling."

30 When Phinehas the priest and the princes of the community, the military leaders of the Israelites, heard what the Reubenites, the Gadites and the Manassehites had to say, they were satisfied. 31 Phinehas, son of Eleazar the priest, said to the Reubenites, the Gadites and the Manassehites, "Now we know that the LORD is with us. Since you have not committed this act of treachery against the LORD, you have kept the Israelites free from punishment by the LORD."

32 Phinehas, son of Eleazar the priest, and the princes returned from the Reubenites and the Gadites in the land of Gilead to the Israelites in the land of Canaan, and reported the matter to them. 33 The report satisfied the Israelites, who blessed God and decided against declaring war on the Reubenites and Gadites or ravaging the land they occupied.

34 The Reubenites and the Gadites gave the altar its name as a witness among them that the LORD is God.

23 Many years later, after the LORD had given the Israelites rest from all their enemies round about them, and when Joshua was old and advanced in years, 2 he summoned all Israel (including their elders, leaders, judges and officers) and said to them: "I am old and advanced in years. 3 You have seen all that the LORD, your God, has done for you against all these nations; for it has been the LORD, your God, himself who fought for you. 4 Bear in mind that I have apportioned among your tribes as their heritage the nations that survive [as well as those I destroyed] between the Jordan and the Great Sea in the west. 5 The LORD, your God,

21 The Reubenites, the Gadites and the half-tribe of Manasseh spoke in their turn and answered the heads of the clans of Israel:

22 'The God of gods, Yahweh, the God of gods, Yahweh well knows, and let Israel know it too: if there has been rebellion or infidelity to Yahweh on our part, may he refuse to save us today! 23 And if we have built ourselves an altar with the intention of repudiating our allegiance to Yahweh and of presenting burnt offering and oblation or of offering communion sacrifices on it, may Yahweh himself call us to account for it! 24 The truth is, we have done this as a precaution: in the future, your descendants might say to ours, "What connection do you have with Yahweh, God of Israel? 25 Has not Yahweh set the frontier of the Jordan between us and you, you Reubenites and Gadites? You have no share in Yahweh." Thus, your descendants would be the cause of stopping ours from fearing Yahweh.

26 'So we said to each other, "Let us build this altar, not for burnt offerings or other sacrifices 27 but as a witness between us and you and between our descendants after us, attesting that we too have the right to worship Yahweh, in his presence, with our burnt offerings, our victims and our communion sacrifices. And so, in the future your descendants will not be able to say to ours: You have no share in Yahweh." 28 And we furthermore said, "If ever it were to happen that they did say this either to us or to our descendants in the future, we should reply: Look at this structure, Yahweh's altar, made by our ancestors not for burnt offerings or other sacrifices but as a witness between us and you." 29 Far be it from us to rebel against Yahweh or now to repudiate our allegiance to Yahweh by building an altar for burnt offerings or oblations or sacrifices, in rivalry with the altar of Yahweh our God that stands before his Dwelling!'

30 When the priest Phinehas, the leaders of the community and the heads of the clans of Israel who were with him, heard the words spoken by the Gadites, the Reubenites and the Manassehites, they approved of them. 31 The priest Phinehas son of Eleazar then said to the Reubenites, the Gadites and the Manassehites, 'Today, we can see that Yahweh is among us, since you have not been unfaithful to Yahweh in this matter; this means that you have spared the Israelites from Yahweh's avenging hand.'

32 The priest Phinehas son of Eleazar and the leaders left the Reubenites and the Gadites and went back from Gilead to Canaan and the Israelites, to whom they reported the answer. 33 The Israelites were pleased to hear this; the Israelites gave thanks to God and spoke no more of marching against them to make war on them and to ravage the country inhabited by the Reubenites and the Gadites. 34 The Reubenites and the Gadites called the altar . . . , 'Because', they said, 'it will be a witness between us that Yahweh is God.'

23 Now long after Yahweh had given Israel rest from all the enemies surrounding them — Joshua was old now, far advanced in years — 2 Joshua summoned all Israel, their elders, leaders, judges and officials, and said to them, 'I myself am old, far advanced in years; 3 you for your part have witnessed all that Yahweh your God has done to all these nations for your sake; Yahweh your God himself has fought for you. 4 Look, these nations still remaining, and all the nations which I have exterminated from the Jordan all the way to the Great Sea in the west, I have allotted to you as the heritage for your tribes. 5 Yahweh your God will

NEW REVISED STANDARD VERSION	REVISED ENGLISH BIBLE

God will push them back before you, and drive them out of your sight; and you shall possess their land, as the Lord your God promised you. 6 Therefore be very steadfast to observe and do all that is written in the book of the law of Moses, turning aside from it neither to the right nor to the left, 7 so that you may not be mixed with these nations left here among you, or make mention of the names of their gods, or swear by them, or serve them, or bow yourselves down to them, 8 but hold fast to the Lord your God, as you have done to this day. 9 For the Lord has driven out before you great and strong nations; and as for you, no one has been able to withstand you to this day. 10 One of you puts to flight a thousand, since it is the Lord your God who fights for you, as he promised you. 11 Be very careful, therefore, to love the Lord your God. 12 For if you turn back, and join the survivors of these nations left here among you, and intermarry with them, so that you marry their women and they yours, 13 know assuredly that the Lord your God will not continue to drive out these nations before you; but they shall be a snare and a trap for you, a scourge on your sides, and thorns in your eyes, until you perish from this good land that the Lord your God has given you.

14 "And now I am about to go the way of all the earth, and you know in your hearts and souls, all of you, that not one thing has failed of all the good things that the Lord your God promised concerning you; all have come to pass for you, not one of them has failed. 15 But just as all the good things that the Lord your God promised concerning you have been fulfilled for you, so the Lord will bring upon you all the bad things, until he has destroyed you from this good land that the Lord your God has given you. 16 If you transgress the covenant of the Lord your God, which he enjoined on you, and go and serve other gods and bow down to them, then the anger of the Lord will be kindled against you, and you shall perish quickly from the good land that he has given to you."

24 Then Joshua gathered all the tribes of Israel to Shechem, and summoned the elders, the heads, the judges, and the officers of Israel; and they presented themselves before God. 2 And Joshua said to all the people, "Thus says the Lord, the God of Israel: Long ago your ancestors—Terah and his sons Abraham and Nahor—lived beyond the Euphrates and served other gods. 3 Then I took your father Abraham from beyond the River and led him through all the land of Canaan and made his offspring many. I gave him Isaac; 4 and to Isaac I gave Jacob and Esau. I gave Esau the hill country of Seir to possess, but Jacob and his children went down to Egypt. 5 Then I sent Moses and Aaron, and I plagued Egypt with what I did in its midst; and afterwards I brought you out. 6 When I brought your ancestors out of Egypt, you came to the sea; and the Egyptians pursued your ancestors with chariots and horsemen to the Red Sea.m 7 When they cried out to the Lord, he put darkness between you and the Egyptians, and made the sea come upon them and cover them; and your eyes saw what I did to Egypt. Afterwards you lived in the wilderness a long time. 8 Then I brought you to the land of the Amorites, who lived on the other side of the Jordan; they fought with you, and I handed them over to you, and you took possession of their land, and I destroyed them before you. 9 Then King Balak son of Zippor of Moab, set out to fight against Israel. He sent and invited Balaam son of Beor to curse you, 10 but I would not listen to Balaam;

your approach; he dispossessed them to make way for you, and you occupied their land, as the Lord your God had promised you.

6 'Be very resolute therefore to observe and perform everything written in the book of the law of Moses, without swerving either to the right or to the left. 7 You must not associate with these peoples that are still here among you; you must not invoke their gods or swear by them or bow down to them in worship. 8 You must hold fast to the Lord your God as you have done up to this day.

9 'The Lord has driven out great and powerful nations before you; to this day not a man of them has withstood you. 10 One of you can rout a thousand, because the Lord your God fights for you, as he promised. 11 For your own sakes be very careful to love the Lord your God. 12 But if you do turn away and attach yourselves to the peoples still remaining among you, and intermarry with them and associate with them and they with you, 13 then be sure that the Lord will not continue to drive out those peoples from before you. They will be snares to entrap you, whips for your backs, and barbed hooks in your eyes, until you perish from this good land which the Lord your God has given you.

14 'Now, as you see, I am going the way of all mortals. You know in your heart of hearts, all of you, that nothing the Lord your God promised you has failed to come true, not one word of it. 15 But the same Lord God who has kept his word to you to such good effect can equally bring every kind of evil on you, until he has rooted you out from this good land which he has given you. 16 If you violate the covenant which the Lord your God has laid upon you and go and serve other gods and worship them, then the Lord's anger will be roused against you and the good land he has given you will soon see you no more.'

24 Joshua assembled all the tribes of Israel at Shechem. He summoned the elders of Israel, the heads of families, the judges and officers. When they presented themselves before God, 2 Joshua said to all the people: 'This is the word of the Lord the God of Israel: Long ago your forefathers, including Terah the father of Abraham and Nahor, lived beyond the Euphrates and served other gods. 3 I took your ancestor Abraham from beside the Euphrates and led him through the length and breadth of Canaan. I gave him many descendants: I gave him Isaac, 4 and to Isaac I gave Jacob and Esau. I assigned the hill-country of Seir to Esau as his possession; Jacob and his sons went down to Egypt.

5 'Later I sent Moses and Aaron, and I struck the Egyptians with plagues—you know well what I did among them—and after that I brought you out; 6 I brought your forefathers out of Egypt, but at the Red Sea the Egyptians sent their chariots and cavalry to pursue them. 7 When they appealed to the Lord, he put a screen of darkness between you and the Egyptians, and brought the sea down on them to engulf them; you saw for yourselves what I did to Egypt.

'For a long time you lived in the wilderness, 8 and then I brought you into the land of the Amorites who lived east of the Jordan. They fought against you, but I delivered them into your power; you took possession of their country, when I destroyed them before you. 9 The king of Moab, Balak son of Zippor, took the field against Israel. He sent for Balaam son of Beor to lay a curse on you, 10 but I would not listen

---

m Or Sea of Reeds

24:6 **Red Sea:** or sea of Reeds.

NEW AMERICAN BIBLE

NEW JERUSALEM BIBLE

will drive them out and dislodge them at your approach, so that you will take possession of their land as the LORD, your God, promised you. 6 Therefore strive hard to observe and carry out all that is written in the book of the law of Moses, not straying from it in any way, 7 or mingling with these nations while they survive among you. You must not invoke their gods, or swear by them, or serve them, or worship them, 8 but you must remain loyal to the LORD, your God, as you have been to this day. 9 At your approach the LORD has driven out large and strong nations, and to this day no one has withstood you. 10 One of you puts to flight a thousand, because it is the LORD, your God, himself who fights for you, as he promised you. 11 Take great care, however, to love the LORD, your God. 12 For if you ever abandon him and ally yourselves with the remnant of these nations while they survive among you, by intermarrying and intermingling with them, 13 know for certain that the LORD, your God, will no longer drive these nations out of your way. Instead they will be a snare and a trap for you, a scourge for your sides and thorns for your eyes, until you perish from this good land which the LORD, your God, has given you.

14 "Today, as you see, I am going the way of all men. So now acknowledge with your whole heart and soul that not one of all the promises the LORD, your God, made to you has remained unfulfilled. Every promise has been fulfilled for you, with not one single exception. 15 But just as every promise the LORD, your God, made to you has been fulfilled for you, so will he fulfill every threat, even so far as to exterminate you from this good land which the LORD, your God, has given you. 16 If you transgress the covenant of the LORD, your God, which he enjoined on you, serve other gods and worship them, the anger of the LORD will flare up against you and you will quickly perish from the good land which he has given you."

24 Joshua gathered together all the tribes of Israel at Shechem, summoning their elders, their leaders, their judges and their officers. When they stood in ranks before God, 2 Joshua addressed all the people: "Thus says the LORD, the God of Israel: In times past your fathers, down to Terah, father of Abraham and Nahor, dwelt beyond the River and served other gods. 3 But I brought your father Abraham from the region beyond the River and led him through the entire land of Canaan. I made his descendants numerous, and gave him Isaac. 4 To Isaac I gave Jacob and Esau. To Esau I assigned the mountain region of Seir in which to settle, while Jacob and his children went down to Egypt.

5 "Then I sent Moses and Aaron, and smote Egypt with the prodigies which I wrought in her midst. 6 Afterward I led you out of Egypt, and when you reached the sea, the Egyptians pursued your fathers to the Red Sea with chariots and horsemen. 7 Because they cried out to the LORD, he put darkness between your people and the Egyptians, upon whom he brought the sea so that it engulfed them. After you witnessed what I did to Egypt, and dwelt a long time in the desert, 8 I brought you into the land of the Amorites who lived east of the Jordan. They fought against you, but I delivered them into your power. You took possession of their land, and I destroyed them [the two kings of the Amorites] before you. 9 Then Balak, son of Zippor, king of Moab, prepared to war against Israel. He summoned Balaam, son of Beor, to curse you; 10 but I would not listen to Balaam.

himself drive them out before you; he will dispossess them before you and you will take possession of their country, as Yahweh your God has promised you.

6 'So be very firm about keeping and doing everything written in the Book of the Law of Moses, not swerving from that either to right or to left. 7 Never mix with the peoples who are still left beside you. Do not utter the names of their gods, do not swear by them, do not serve them and do not bow down to them. 8 On the contrary, you must be loyal to Yahweh your God as you have been till now. 9 Yahweh has dispossessed great and powerful nations before you, and no one so far has been able to resist you. 10 One man of you was able to rout a thousand of them, since Yahweh your God was himself fighting for you, as he had promised you. 11 Be very careful, as you value your life, to love Yahweh your God.

12 'But should you in any way relapse, if you make friends with the remnant of these nations still living beside you, if you intermarry with them, if you mix with them and they with you, 13 then know for certain that Yahweh your God will stop dispossessing these nations before you, and for you they will be a snare, a pitfall, thorns in your sides and thistles in your eyes, until you vanish from this fine country given you by Yahweh your God.

14 'Today, you see, I am going the way of all the earth. Acknowledge with all your heart and soul that of all the promises made to you by Yahweh your God, not one has failed: all have been fulfilled — not one has failed.

15 'As every promise made to you by Yahweh your God has been fulfilled for you, by the same token Yahweh will fulfil all his threats against you, even to exterminating you from this fine country given you by Yahweh your God. 16 'For if you violate the covenant which Yahweh your God has imposed on you, if you go and serve other gods and bow down to them, then Yahweh's anger will be roused against you and you will quickly vanish from the fine country which he has given you.'

24 Joshua gathered all the tribes of Israel together at Shechem; he then summoned all the elders of Israel, its leaders, judges and officials, and they presented themselves in God's presence. 2 Joshua then said to all the people:

'Yahweh, the God of Israel, says this, "From time immemorial, your ancestors, Terah, father of Abraham and Nahor, lived beyond the River, and served other gods. 3 I then brought your ancestor Abraham from beyond the River and led him through the length and breadth of Canaan. I increased his descendants and I gave him Isaac. 4 To Isaac I gave Jacob and Esau. To Esau I gave possession of the mountainous country of Seir. Jacob and his sons went down into Egypt. 5 I then sent Moses and Aaron, and plagued Egypt with the wonders that I worked there; finally I brought you out. 6 I brought your ancestors out of Egypt, and you came to the Sea; the Egyptians pursued your ancestors with chariots and horsemen, to the Sea of Reeds. 7 They then called to Yahweh, and he spread a thick fog between you and the Egyptians, and made the sea go back on them and cover them. You saw with your own eyes what I did in Egypt. Then, for a long while, you lived in the desert. 8 I then brought you into the country of the Amorites, who used to live on the further side of the Jordan; they made war on you and I put them at your mercy; after which, you took possession of their country, since I destroyed them before you. 9 Next, Balak son of Zippor, king of Moab, rose to make war on Israel, and sent for Balaam son of Beor to come and curse you. 10 But I would not listen to Balaam;

| NEW REVISED STANDARD VERSION | REVISED ENGLISH BIBLE |

therefore he blessed you; so I rescued you out of his hand. 11 When you went over the Jordan and came to Jericho, the citizens of Jericho fought against you, and also the Amorites, the Perizzites, the Canaanites, the Hittites, the Girgashites, the Hivites, and the Jebusites; and I handed them over to you. 12 I sent the hornet[n] ahead of you, which drove out before you the two kings of the Amorites; it was not by your sword or by your bow. 13 I gave you a land on which you had not labored, and towns that you had not built, and you live in them; you eat the fruit of vineyards and olive-yards that you did not plant.

14 "Now therefore revere the LORD, and serve him in sincerity and in faithfulness; put away the gods that your ancestors served beyond the River and in Egypt, and serve the LORD. 15 Now if you are unwilling to serve the LORD, choose this day whom you will serve, whether the gods your ancestors served in the region beyond the River or the gods of the Amorites in whose land you are living; but as for me and my household, we will serve the LORD."

16 Then the people answered, "Far be it from us that we should forsake the LORD to serve other gods; 17 for it is the LORD our God who brought us and our ancestors up from the land of Egypt, out of the house of slavery, and who did those great signs in our sight. He protected us along all the way that we went, and among all the peoples through whom we passed; 18 and the LORD drove out before us all the peoples, the Amorites who lived in the land. Therefore we also will serve the LORD, for he is our God."

19 But Joshua said to the people, "You cannot serve the LORD, for he is a holy God. He is a jealous God; he will not forgive your transgressions or your sins. 20 If you forsake the LORD and serve foreign gods, then he will turn and do you harm, and consume you, after having done you good." 21 And the people said to Joshua, "No, we will serve the LORD!" 22 Then Joshua said to the people, "You are witnesses against yourselves that you have chosen the LORD, to serve him." And they said, "We are witnesses." 23 He said, "Then put away the foreign gods that are among you, and incline your hearts to the LORD, the God of Israel." 24 The people said to Joshua, "The LORD our God we will serve, and him we will obey." 25 So Joshua made a covenant with the people that day, and made statutes and ordinances for them at Shechem. 26 Joshua wrote these words in the book of the law of God; and he took a large stone, and set it up there under the oak in the sanctuary of the LORD. 27 Joshua said to all the people, "See, this stone shall be a witness against us; for it has heard all the words of the LORD that he spoke to us; therefore it shall be a witness against you, if you deal falsely with your God." 28 So Joshua sent the people away to their inheritances.

29 After these things Joshua son of Nun, the servant of the LORD, died, being one hundred ten years old. 30 They buried him in his own inheritance at Timnath-serah, which is in the hill country of Ephraim, north of Mount Gaash.

31 Israel served the LORD all the days of Joshua, and all the days of the elders who outlived Joshua and had known all the work that the LORD did for Israel.

32 The bones of Joseph, which the Israelites had brought up from Egypt, were buried at Shechem, in the portion of ground that Jacob had bought from the children of Hamor, the father of Shechem, for one hundred pieces of money;[o] it became an inheritance of the descendants of Joseph.

33 Eleazar son of Aaron died; and they buried him at Gibeah, the town of his son Phinehas, which had been given him in the hill country of Ephraim.

to Balaam. Instead of that he was constrained to bless you, and so I saved you from Balak's clutches. 11 Then you crossed the Jordan and came to Jericho. Its people fought against you, but I delivered them into your hands. 12 I spread panic before your advance, and it was this, not your sword or your bow, that drove out the two kings of the Amorites. 13 I gave you land on which you had not laboured, towns which you had not built; you have settled in those towns and you eat the produce of vineyards and olive groves which you did not plant.

14 'Now hold the LORD in awe, and serve him in loyalty and truth. Put away the gods your fathers served beyond the Euphrates and in Egypt, and serve the LORD. 15 But if it does not please you to serve the LORD, choose here and now whom you will serve: the gods whom your forefathers served beyond the Euphrates, or the gods of the Amorites in whose land you are living. But I and my family, we shall serve the LORD.'

16 The people answered, 'God forbid that we should forsake the LORD to serve other gods!' They declared: 17 'The LORD our God it was who brought us and our forefathers up from Egypt, that land of slavery; it was he who displayed those great signs before our eyes, who guarded us on all our wanderings among the many peoples through whose lands we passed. 18 The LORD drove out before us the Amorites and all the peoples who lived in that country. We too shall serve the LORD; he is our God.'

19 Joshua said to the people, 'You may not be able to serve the LORD. He is a holy God, a jealous God, and he will not forgive your rebellion and your sins. 20 If you forsake the LORD and serve foreign deities, he will turn and bring disaster on you and make an end of you, even though he once brought you prosperity.' 21 The people answered, 'No; we shall serve the LORD.' 22 He said to them, 'You are witnesses against yourselves that you have chosen the LORD and will serve him.' 'Yes,' they answered, 'we are witnesses.' 23 'Then here and now banish the foreign gods that are among you,' he said to them, 'and turn your hearts to the LORD the God of Israel.' 24 The people replied, 'We shall serve the LORD our God and his voice we shall obey.'

25 So Joshua made a covenant for the people that day; he drew up a statute and an ordinance for them in Shechem 26 and recorded its terms in the book of the law of God. He took a great stone and set it up there under the terebinth in the sanctuary of the LORD. 27 He said to all the people, 'You see this stone — it will be a witness against us; for it has heard all the words which the LORD has spoken to us. If you renounce your God, it will be a witness against you.' 28 Then Joshua dismissed the people, each man to his allotted holding.

29 After these events, Joshua son of Nun, the servant of the LORD, died at the age of a hundred and ten. 30 They buried him within his own holding in Timnath-serah to the north of Mount Gaash in the hill-country of Ephraim. 31 Israel served the LORD throughout the lifetime of Joshua and of the elders who outlived him and who knew all that the LORD had done for Israel.

32 The bones of Joseph, which the Israelites had brought up from Egypt, were buried in Shechem, in the plot of land which Jacob had bought from the sons of Hamor father of Shechem for a hundred sheep; and they passed into the ancestral holding of the house of Joseph.

33 Eleazar son of Aaron died and was buried in the hill which had been assigned to Phinehas his son in the hill-country of Ephraim.

24:11 **against you:** prob. rdg; Heb. adds Amorites, Perizzites, Canaanites, Hittites, Girgashites, Hivites, and Jebusites.
24:32 **sheep:** or pieces of money.

[n] Meaning of Heb uncertain   [o] Heb one hundred qesitah

NEW AMERICAN BIBLE

On the contrary, he had to bless you, and I saved you from him. ¹¹ Once you crossed the Jordan and came to Jericho, the men of Jericho fought against you, but I delivered them also into your power. ¹² And I sent the hornets ahead of you which drove them [the Amorites, Perizzites, Canaanites, Hittites, Girgashites, Hivites and Jebusites] out of your way; it was not your sword or your bow.

¹³ "I gave you a land which you had not tilled and cities which you had not built, to dwell in; you have eaten of vineyards and olive groves which you did not plant.

¹⁴ "Now, therefore, fear the LORD and serve him completely and sincerely. Cast out the gods your fathers served beyond the River and in Egypt, and serve the LORD. ¹⁵ If it does not please you to serve the LORD, decide today whom you will serve, the gods your fathers served beyond the River or the gods of the Amorites in whose country you are dwelling. As for me and my household, we will serve the LORD."

¹⁶ But the people answered, "Far be it from us to forsake the LORD for the service of other gods. ¹⁷ For it was the LORD, our God, who brought us and our fathers up out of the land of Egypt, out of a state of slavery. He performed those great miracles before our very eyes and protected us along our entire journey and among all the peoples through whom we passed. ¹⁸ At our approach the LORD drove out [all the peoples, including] the Amorites who dwelt in the land. Therefore we also will serve the LORD, for he is our God."

¹⁹ Joshua in turn said to the people, "You may not be able to serve the LORD, for he is a holy God; he is a jealous God who will not forgive your transgressions or your sins. ²⁰ If, after the good he has done for you, you forsake the LORD and serve strange gods, he will do evil to you and destroy you."

²¹ But the people answered Joshua, "We will still serve the LORD." ²² Joshua therefore said to the people, "You are your own witnesses that you have chosen to serve the LORD." They replied, "We are, indeed!" ²³ "Now, therefore, put away the strange gods that are among you and turn your hearts to the LORD, the God of Israel." ²⁴ Then the people promised Joshua, "We will serve the LORD, our God, and obey his voice."

²⁵ So Joshua made a covenant with the people that day and made statutes and ordinances for them at Shechem, ²⁶ which he recorded in the book of the law of God. Then he took a large stone and set it up there under the oak that was in the sanctuary of the LORD. ²⁷ And Joshua said to all the people, "This stone shall be our witness, for it has heard all the words which the LORD spoke to us. It shall be a witness against you, should you wish to deny your God." ²⁸ Then Joshua dismissed the people, each to his own heritage.

²⁹ After these events, Joshua, son of Nun, servant of the LORD, died at the age of a hundred and ten. ³⁰ He was buried within the limits of his heritage at Timnath-serah in the mountain region of Ephraim north of Mount Gaash. ³¹ Israel served the LORD during the entire lifetime of Joshua and that of the elders who outlived Joshua and knew all that the LORD had done for Israel. ³² The bones of Joseph, which the Israelites had brought up from Egypt, were buried in Shechem in the plot of ground Jacob had bought from the sons of Hamor, father of Shechem, for a hundred pieces of money. This was a heritage of the descendants of Joseph. ³³ When Eleazar, son of Aaron, also died, he was buried on the hill which had been given to his son Phinehas in the mountain region of Ephraim.

NEW JERUSALEM BIBLE

instead, he had to bless you, and I saved you from his power.

¹¹ "You then crossed the Jordan and came to Jericho, but the inhabitants of Jericho made war on you: Amorites, Perizzites, Canaanites, Hittites, Girgashites, Hivites and Jebusites, and I put them all at your mercy. ¹² I sent hornets ahead of you, which drove out the two Amorite kings before you; this was not the work of your sword or of your bow. ¹³ And now I have given you a country for which you have not toiled, towns you have not built, although you live in them, vineyards and olive groves you have not planted, although you eat their fruit.'

¹⁴ 'So now, fear Yahweh and serve him truly and sincerely; banish the gods whom your ancestors served beyond the River and in Egypt, and serve Yahweh. ¹⁵ But if serving Yahweh seems a bad thing to you, today you must make up your minds whom you do mean to serve, whether the gods whom your ancestors served beyond the River, or the gods of the Amorites in whose country you are now living. As regards my family and me, we shall serve Yahweh.'

¹⁶ The people replied, 'Far be it from us to desert Yahweh and to serve other gods! ¹⁷ Yahweh our God was the one who brought us and our ancestors here from Egypt, from the place of slave-labour, who worked those great wonders before our eyes and who kept us safe all along the way we travelled and among all the peoples through whom we passed. ¹⁸ And Yahweh has driven all the nations out for us, including the Amorites who used to live in the country. We too shall serve Yahweh, for he is our God.'

¹⁹ Joshua then said to the people, 'You will not be able to serve Yahweh, since he is a holy God, he is a jealous God who will not tolerate either your misdeeds or your sins. ²⁰ If you desert Yahweh and serve the foreigners' gods, he will turn and maltreat you anew and, in spite of having been good to you in the past, will destroy you.' ²¹ The people replied to Joshua, 'No! Yahweh is the one we mean to serve.' ²² Joshua then said to the people, 'You are witnesses to yourselves that you have chosen Yahweh, to serve him.' They replied, 'Witnesses we are!' ²³ 'Then banish the foreign gods which you have with you and give your allegiance to Yahweh, God of Israel!' ²⁴ The people replied to Joshua, 'Yahweh our God is the one whom we shall serve; his voice we shall obey!'

²⁵ That day Joshua made a covenant for the people; he laid down a statute and ordinance for them at Shechem. ²⁶ Joshua wrote these words in the Book of the Law of God. He then took a large stone and set it up there, under the oak tree in Yahweh's sanctuary. ²⁷ Joshua then said to all the people, 'Look, this stone will be a witness to us, since it has heard all the words that Yahweh has spoken to us: it will be a witness against you, in case you should deny your God.' ²⁸ Joshua then dismissed the people, every one to his own heritage.

²⁹ After this, Joshua son of Nun, servant of Yahweh, died; he was a hundred and ten years old. ³⁰ He was buried on the estate which he had received as his heritage, at Timnath-Serah which lies in the highlands of Ephraim, north of Mount Gaash. ³¹ Israel served Yahweh throughout the lifetime of Joshua and throughout the lifetime of those elders who outlived Joshua and had known all the deeds which Yahweh had done for the sake of Israel.

³² As regards the bones of Joseph, which the Israelites had brought from Egypt, these were buried at Shechem in the plot of ground which Jacob had bought for a hundred pieces of silver from the sons of Hamor father of Shechem, and which had become the heritage of the sons of Joseph. ³³ Eleazar son of Aaron then died and was buried at Gibeah, the town of his son Phinehas, which had been given to him in the highlands of Ephraim.

Judges

THE BOOK OF
Judges

1 After the death of Joshua, the Israelites inquired of the LORD, "Who shall go up first for us against the Canaanites, to fight against them?" 2 The LORD said, "Judah shall go up. I hereby give the land into his hand." 3 Judah said to his brother Simeon, "Come up with me into the territory allotted to me, that we may fight against the Canaanites; then I too will go with you into the territory allotted to you." So Simeon went with him. 4 Then Judah went up and the LORD gave the Canaanites and the Perizzites into their hand; and they defeated ten thousand of them at Bezek. 5 They came upon Adoni-bezek at Bezek, and fought against him, and defeated the Canaanites and the Perizzites. 6 Adoni-bezek fled; but they pursued him, and caught him, and cut off his thumbs and big toes. 7 Adoni-bezek said, "Seventy kings with their thumbs and big toes cut off used to pick up scraps under my table; as I have done, so God has paid me back." They brought him to Jerusalem, and he died there.

8 Then the people of Judah fought against Jerusalem and took it. They put it to the sword and set the city on fire. 9 Afterward the people of Judah went down to fight against the Canaanites who lived in the hill country, in the Negeb, and in the lowland. 10 Judah went against the Canaanites who lived in Hebron (the name of Hebron was formerly Kiriath-arba); and they defeated Sheshai and Ahiman and Talmai.

11 From there they went against the inhabitants of Debir (the name of Debir was formerly Kiriath-sepher). 12 Then Caleb said, "Whoever attacks Kiriath-sepher and takes it, I will give him my daughter Achsah as wife." 13 And Othniel son of Kenaz, Caleb's younger brother, took it; and he gave him his daughter Achsah as wife. 14 When she came to him, she urged him to ask her father for a field. As she dismounted from her donkey, Caleb said to her, "What do you wish?" 15 She said to him, "Give me a present; since you have set me in the land of the Negeb, give me also Gulloth-mayim."a So Caleb gave her Upper Gulloth and Lower Gulloth.

16 The descendants of Hobabb the Kenite, Moses' father-in-law, went up with the people of Judah from the city of palms into the wilderness of Judah, which lies in the Negeb near Arad. Then they went and settled with the Amalekites.c 17 Judah went with his brother Simeon, and they defeated the Canaanites who inhabited Zephath, and devoted it to destruction. So the city was called Hormah. 18 Judah took Gaza with its territory, Ashkelon with its territory, and Ekron with its territory. 19 The LORD was with Judah, and he took possession of the hill country, but could not drive out the inhabitants of the plain, because they had chariots of iron. 20 Hebron was given to Caleb, as Moses had said; and he drove out from it the three sons of Anak. 21 But the Benjaminites did not drive out the Jebusites who lived in Jerusalem; so the Jebusites have lived in Jerusalem among the Benjaminites to this day.

22 The house of Joseph also went up against Bethel; and the LORD was with them. 23 The house of Joseph sent out spies to Bethel (the name of the city was formerly Luz). 24 When the spies saw a man coming out of the city, they said to him, "Show us the way into the city, and we will deal kindly with you." 25 So he showed them the way into

1 AFTER the death of Joshua the Israelites enquired of the LORD which tribe should go up first to attack the Canaanites. 2 The LORD answered, 'Judah is to go up; I have delivered the country into their power.' 3 The Judahites said to their kinsmen, the Simeonites, 'Go up with us into the territory allotted to us, and let us do battle with the Canaanites, and we in turn shall go with you into your territory.' So the Simeonites went with them.

4 Judah advanced to the attack, and the LORD delivered the Canaanites and the Perizzites into their hands, so that they slaughtered ten thousand of them at Bezek. 5 At Bezek they came upon Adoni-bezek, engaged him in battle, and defeated the Canaanites and Perizzites. 6 Adoni-bezek fled, but they pursued him, and having taken him prisoner cut off his thumbs and his big toes. 7 Adoni-bezek said, 'I once had seventy kings with their thumbs and big toes cut off who were picking up the scraps under my table. What I have done, God has done to me.' He was brought to Jerusalem, and he died there.

8 The men of Judah made an assault on Jerusalem and captured it; they put its people to the sword, and set fire to the city. 9 Then they turned south to fight the Canaanites living in the hill-country, the Negeb, and the Shephelah. 10 Judah attacked the Canaanites in Hebron, formerly called Kiriath-arba, and defeated Sheshai, Ahiman, and Talmai. 11 From there they marched against the inhabitants of Debir, formerly called Kiriath-sepher.

12 Caleb said, 'I shall give my daughter Achsah in marriage to the man who attacks and captures Kiriath-sepher.' 13 Othniel, son of Caleb's younger brother Kenaz, captured it, and Caleb gave him his daughter Achsah. 14 When she became his wife, Othniel induced her to ask her father for a piece of land. She dismounted from her donkey, and Caleb asked her, 'What do you want?' 15 She replied, 'Grant me this favour: you have put me in this arid Negeb; you must give me pools of water as well.' So Caleb gave her the upper pool and the lower pool.

16 The descendants of the Kenite, Moses' father-in-law, went up with the Judahites from the city of palm trees to the wilderness of Judah which is in the Negeb of Arad, and they settled among the Amalekites. 17 The Judahites then set out with their kinsmen the Simeonites, attacked the Canaanites in Zephath, and utterly destroyed it; hence the town was given the name Hormah. 18 Judah took Gaza, Ashkelon, and Ekron, along with the territory of each. 19 As the LORD was with the Judahites, they occupied the hill-country; but they failed to drive out the inhabitants of the plain because they had iron-clad chariots. 20 As Moses had directed, Hebron was given to Caleb, who drove out the three Anakim. 21 But the Benjamites failed to drive out the Jebusite inhabitants of Jerusalem, and the Jebusites have lived on in Jerusalem alongside the Benjamites to this day.

22 The men of Joseph also attacked Bethel, and the LORD was with them. 23 They reconnoitred Bethel, formerly called Luz, 24 and when the spies saw a man coming out of the town they said to him, 'Show us a way into the town, and we will see that you come to no harm.' 25 When he

---

a That is Basins of Water   b Gk: Heb lacks Hobab
c See 1 Sam 15.6: Heb people

1:14 **Othniel induced her:** so Gk; Heb. she induced him.
dismounted: or made a noise.   1:16 **Amalekites:** so some Gk
MSS; Heb. people.   1:17 **Hormah:** that is Destruction.

THE BOOK OF
Judges

1 After the death of Joshua the Israelites consulted the
LORD, asking, "Who shall be first among us to attack
the Canaanites and to do battle with them?" 2 The LORD
answered, "Judah shall attack: I have delivered the land into
his power." 3 Judah then said to his brother Simeon, "Come
up with me into the territory allotted to me, and let us
engage the Canaanites in battle. I will likewise accompany
you into the territory allotted to you." So Simeon went with
him.

4 When the forces of Judah attacked, the LORD delivered
the Canaanites and Perizzites into their power, and they
slew ten thousand of them in Bezek. 5 It was in Bezek that
they came upon Adonibezek and fought against him. When
they defeated the Canaanites and Perizzites, 6 Adonibezek
fled. They set out in pursuit, and when they caught him, cut
off his thumbs and his big toes. 7 At this Adonibezek said,
"Seventy kings, with their thumbs and big toes cut off, used
to pick up scraps under my table. As I have done, so has
God repaid me." He was brought to Jerusalem, and there he
died. 8 [The Judahites fought against Jerusalem and captured it, putting it to the sword; then they destroyed the city
by fire.]

9 Afterward the Judahites went down to fight against the
Canaanites who lived in the mountain region, in the Negeb,
and in the foothills, 10 Judah also marched against the Canaanites who dwelt in Hebron, which was formerly called
Kiriath-Arba, and defeated Sheshai, Ahiman and Talmai.
11 From there they marched against the inhabitants of Debir,
which was formerly called Kiriath-sepher. 12 And Caleb
said, "I will give my daughter Achsah in marriage to the one
who attacks Kiriath-sepher and captures it." 13 Othniel, son
of Caleb's younger brother Kenaz, captured it; so Caleb
gave him his daughter Achsah in marriage. 14 On the day of
her marriage to Othniel she induced him to ask her father for
some land. Then, as she alighted from the ass, Caleb asked
her, "What is troubling you?" 15 "Give me an additional
gift," she answered. "Since you have assigned land in the
Negeb to me, give me also pools of water." So Caleb gave
her the upper and the lower pool. 16 The descendants of the
Kenite, Moses' father-in-law, came up with the Judahites
from the city of palms to the desert at Arad [which is in the
Negeb]. But they later left and settled among the Amalekites.

17 Judah then went with his brother Simeon, and they
defeated the Canaanites who dwelt in Zephath. After having
doomed the city to destruction, they renamed it Hormah.
18 Judah, however, did not occupy Gaza with its territory,
Ashkelon with its territory, or Ekron with its territory.
19 Since the LORD was with Judah, he gained possession of
the mountain region. Yet he could not dislodge those who
lived on the plain, because they had iron chariots. 20 As
Moses had commanded, Hebron was given to Caleb, who
then drove from it the three sons of Anak.

21 The Benjaminites did not dislodge the Jebusites who
dwelt in Jerusalem, with the result that the Jebusites live in
Jerusalem beside the Benjaminites to the present day.

22 The house of Joseph, too, marched up against Bethel,
and the LORD was with them. 23 The house of Joseph had a
reconnaissance made of Bethel, which formerly was called
Luz. 24 The scouts saw a man coming out of the city and
said to him, "Show us a way into the city, and we will spare
you." 25 He showed them a way into the city, which they

THE BOOK OF
Judges

1 Now after Joshua's death, the Israelites consulted Yahweh, asking, 'Which of us is to march on the Canaanites first, to make war on them?' 2 And Yahweh replied,
'Judah is to march on them first; I am delivering the country
into his hands.' 3 Judah then said to his brother Simeon,
'March with me into the territory allotted to me; we shall
make war on the Canaanites, and then I in my turn shall
march into your territory with you.' And Simeon marched
with him. 4 So Judah marched on them, and Yahweh delivered the Canaanites and Perizzites into their hands, and they
defeated them at Bezek — ten thousand of them! 5 At Bezek
they came upon Adoni-Bezek; they joined battle with him
and defeated the Canaanites and Perizzites. 6 Adoni-Bezek
took to flight, but they chased and captured him and cut off
his thumbs and big toes. 7 Adoni-Bezek said, 'Seventy
kings with their thumbs and big toes cut off used to pick up
the crumbs under my table. As I did, God does to me.' He
was taken to Jerusalem, and there he died. 8 (The sons of
Judah attacked Jerusalem and took it: they put its people to
the sword and set fire to the city.)

9 After this the sons of Judah went down to make war on
the Canaanites who were living in the highlands, the Negeb
and the lowlands. 10 Judah next marched on the Canaanites
living in Hebron — the name of Hebron in olden days was
Kiriath-Arba — and beat Sheshai, Ahiman and Talmai.
11 From there, he marched on the inhabitants of Debir — the
name of Debir in olden days was Kiriath-Sepher. 12 Caleb
said, 'To the man who conquers and captures Kiriath-
Sepher, I shall give my daughter Achsah as wife.' 13 The
man who captured it was Othniel son of Kenaz, younger
brother of Caleb, who gave him his daughter Achsah as
wife. 14 When she arrived, he urged her to ask her father for
arable land, but when she alighted from the donkey and
Caleb asked her, 'What is the matter?' 15 she said to him,
'Grant me a blessing! As the land you have given me is the
Negeb, give me springs of water, too!' So Caleb gave her
what she wanted: the upper springs and the lower springs.

16 The sons of Hobab the Kenite, father-in-law of Moses,
marched up with the sons of Judah from the City of Palm
Trees into the desert of Judah lying in the Negeb of Arad,
where they went and settled among the people.

17 Judah then set out with his brother Simeon. They beat
the Canaanites who lived in Zephath and delivered it over
to the curse of destruction; hence the town was given the
name of Hormah. 18 Judah then captured Gaza and its territory, Ashkelon and its territory, Ekron and its territory.
19b And Yahweh was with Judah, who made himself master
of the highlands; 19a he could not, however, dispossess the
inhabitants of the plain, since they had iron chariots.

20 As Moses had directed, Hebron was given to Caleb,
and he drove the three sons of Anak out of it. 21 As regards
the Jebusites living in Jerusalem, the sons of Benjamin did
not dispossess them, and the Jebusites have been living in
Jerusalem with the sons of Benjamin ever since.

22 Similarly, the House of Joseph marched on Bethel, and
Yahweh was with them. 23 The House of Joseph made a
reconnaissance of Bethel. (In olden days, the name of the
town was Luz.) 24 The scouts saw a man coming out of the
town and said to him, 'Show us how to get into the town
and we shall show you faithful love.' 25 And when he had

NEW REVISED STANDARD VERSION

the city; and they put the city to the sword, but they let the man and all his family go. 26 So the man went to the land of the Hittites and built a city, and named it Luz; that is its name to this day.

27 Manasseh did not drive out the inhabitants of Beth-shean and its villages, or Taanach and its villages, or the inhabitants of Dor and its villages, or the inhabitants of Ibleam and its villages, or the inhabitants of Megiddo and its villages; but the Canaanites continued to live in that land. 28 When Israel grew strong, they put the Canaanites to forced labor, but did not in fact drive them out.

29 And Ephraim did not drive out the Canaanites who lived in Gezer; but the Canaanites lived among them in Gezer.

30 Zebulun did not drive out the inhabitants of Kitron, or the inhabitants of Nahalol; but the Canaanites lived among them, and became subject to forced labor.

31 Asher did not drive out the inhabitants of Acco, or the inhabitants of Sidon, or of Ahlab, or of Achzib, or of Helbah, or of Aphik, or of Rehob; 32 but the Asherites lived among the Canaanites, the inhabitants of the land; for they did not drive them out.

33 Naphtali did not drive out the inhabitants of Beth-shemesh, or the inhabitants of Beth-anath, but lived among the Canaanites, the inhabitants of the land; nevertheless the inhabitants of Beth-shemesh and of Beth-anath became subject to forced labor for them.

34 The Amorites pressed the Danites back into the hill country; they did not allow them to come down to the plain. 35 The Amorites continued to live in Har-heres, in Aijalon, and in Shaalbim, but the hand of the house of Joseph rested heavily on them, and they became subject to forced labor. 36 The border of the Amorites ran from the ascent of Akrabbim, from Sela and upward.

2 Now the angel of the LORD went up from Gilgal to Bochim, and said, "I brought you up from Egypt, and brought you into the land that I had promised to your ancestors. I said, 'I will never break my covenant with you. 2 For your part, do not make a covenant with the inhabitants of this land; tear down their altars.' But you have not obeyed my command. See what you have done! 3 So now I say, I will not drive them out before you; but they shall become adversaries[d] to you, and their gods shall be a snare to you." 4 When the angel of the LORD spoke these words to all the Israelites, the people lifted up their voices and wept. 5 So they named that place Bochim,[e] and there they sacrificed to the LORD.

6 When Joshua dismissed the people, the Israelites all went to their own inheritances to take possession of the land. 7 The people worshiped the LORD all the days of Joshua, and all the days of the elders who outlived Joshua, who had seen all the great work that the LORD had done for Israel. 8 Joshua son of Nun, the servant of the LORD, died at the age of one hundred ten years. 9 So they buried him within the bounds of his inheritance in Timnath-heres, in the hill country of Ephraim, north of Mount Gaash. 10 Moreover, that whole generation was gathered to their ancestors, and another generation grew up after them, who did not know the LORD or the work that he had done for Israel.

11 Then the Israelites did what was evil in the sight of the LORD and worshiped the Baals; 12 and they abandoned

REVISED ENGLISH BIBLE

showed them how to enter, they put the town to the sword, but let the man and his family go unscathed. 26 The man went into Hittite country, where he built a town, which he called Luz, the name it bears to this day.

27 Manasseh failed to drive out the inhabitants of Beth-shean, Taanach, Dor, Ibleam, and Megiddo and their villages; the Canaanites maintained their hold on that region. 28 Later, when Israel became strong, they put them to forced labour, but never completely drove them out.

29 Ephraim failed to drive out the Canaanites who lived in Gezer; the Canaanites lived among them there.

30 Zebulun failed to drive out the inhabitants of Kitron and Nahalol; the Canaanites lived among them and were put to forced labour.

31 Asher failed to drive out the inhabitants of Acco and Sidon, of Ahlab, Achzib, Helbah, Aphik, and Rehob; 32 thus the Asherites lived among the Canaanite inhabitants and did not drive them out.

33 Naphtali failed to drive out the inhabitants of Beth-shemesh and of Beth-anath, and lived among the Canaanite inhabitants, putting the inhabitants of Beth-shemesh and Beth-anath to forced labour.

34 The Amorites pressed the Danites back into the hill-country and did not allow them to come down into the plain. 35 The Amorites maintained their hold on Mount Heres and on Aijalon and Shaalbim, but the Joseph tribes increased their pressure on them until they reduced them to forced labour.

36 The boundary of the Edomites ran from the ascent of Akrabbim, upwards from Sela.

2 THE angel of the LORD went up from Gilgal to Bokim, and said, 'I brought you up out of Egypt and into the country which I promised on oath I would give to your forefathers. I said: I shall never annul my covenant with you, 2 and you in turn must make no covenant with the inhabitants of this country; you must pull down their altars. But you did not obey me, and look what you have done! 3 So I said, I shall not drive them out before you; they will entice you astray, and their gods will become a snare for you.' 4 When the angel of the LORD said this to the Israelites, they all broke into loud lamentation. 5 They called the place Bokim and offered sacrifices there to the LORD.

6 JOSHUA dismissed the people, and the Israelites went off to occupy the country, each to his allotted holding. 7 The people served the LORD as long as Joshua and the elders who outlived him were alive—everyone, that is, who had witnessed all the great deeds the LORD had done for Israel. 8 At the age of a hundred and ten Joshua son of Nun, the servant of the LORD, died, 9 and was buried within his own holding in Timnath-heres to the north of Mount Gaash in the hill-country of Ephraim.

10 When that whole generation was gathered to its forefathers, and was succeeded by another generation, who did not acknowledge the LORD and did not know what he had done for Israel, 11 then the Israelites did what was wrong in the eyes of the LORD by serving the baalim. 12 They forsook

---

1:31 **Ahlab:** Mehalbeh *in Josh.* 19:29.   1:36 **Edomites:** *so one form of Gk; Heb.* Amorites.   2:1 **I brought:** *prob. rdg; Heb.* I will bring.   2:5 **Bokim:** *that is* Weepers.

d OL Vg Compare Gk: Heb *sides*   *e* That is *Weepers*

then put to the sword; but they let the man and his whole clan go free. 26 He then went to the land of the Hittites, where he built a city and called it Luz, as it is still called.

27 Manasseh did not take possession of Beth-shean with its towns or of Taanach with its towns. Neither did he dislodge the inhabitants of Dor and its towns, those of Ibleam and its towns, or those of Megiddo and its towns. The Canaanites kept their hold in this district. 28 When the Israelites grew stronger, they impressed the Canaanites as laborers, but did not drive them out. 29 Similarly, the Ephraimites did not drive out the Canaanites living in Gezer, and so the Canaanites live in Gezer in their midst.

30 Zebulun did not dislodge the inhabitants of Kitron or those of Nahalol; the Canaanites live among them, but have become forced laborers.

31 Nor did Asher drive out the inhabitants of Acco or those of Sidon, or take possession of Mahaleb, Achzib, Helbah, Aphik or Rehob. 32 The Asherites live among the Canaanite natives of the land, whom they have not dislodged.

33 Naphtali did not drive out the inhabitants of Beth-shemesh or those of Beth-anath, and so they live among the Canaanite natives of the land. However, the inhabitants of Beth-shemesh and Beth-anath have become forced laborers for them.

34 The Amorites hemmed in the Danites in the mountain region, not permitting them to go down into the plain. 35 The Amorites had a firm hold in Harheres, Aijalon and Shaalbim, but as the house of Joseph gained the upper hand, they were impressed as laborers.

36 The territory of the Amorites extended from the Akrabbim pass to Sela and beyond.

2 An angel of the LORD went up from Gilgal to Bochim and said, "It was I who brought you up from Egypt and led you into the land which I promised on oath to your fathers. I said that I would never break my covenant with you, 2 but that you were not to make a pact with the inhabitants of this land, and you were to pull down their altars. Yet you have not obeyed me. What did you mean by this? 3 For now I tell you, I will not clear them out of your way; they shall oppose you and their gods shall become a snare for you."

4 When the angel of the LORD had made these threats to all the Israelites, the people wept aloud; 5 and so that place came to be called Bochim. They offered sacrifice there to the LORD.

6 When Joshua dismissed the people, each Israelite went to take possession of his own hereditary land. 7 The people served the LORD during the entire lifetime of Joshua, and of those elders who outlived Joshua and who had seen all the great work which the LORD had done for Israel. 8 Joshua, son of Nun, the servant of the LORD, was a hundred and ten years old when he died; 9 and they buried him within the borders of his heritage at Timnath-heres in the mountain region of Ephraim north of Mount Gaash.

10 But once the rest of that generation were gathered to their fathers, and a later generation arose that did not know the LORD, or what he had done for Israel, 11 the Israelites offended the LORD by serving the Baals. 12 Abandoning the

shown them a way into the town, they put the town to the sword but let the man and his whole clan go. 26 The man went off to the country of the Hittites and built a town which he called Luz; and that has been its name ever since.

27 Manasseh did not dispossess Beth-Shean and its dependencies, nor Taanach and its dependencies, nor the inhabitants of Dor and its dependencies, nor the inhabitants of Ibleam and its dependencies, nor the inhabitants of Megiddo and its dependencies; in those parts the Canaanites held their ground. 28 But when the Israelites became stronger, they subjected the Canaanites to forced labour, although they did not dispossess them. 29 Nor did Ephraim dispossess the Canaanites living in Gezer; thus, the Canaanites went on living in Gezer with him. 30 Zebulun did not dispossess the inhabitants of Kitron or of Nahalol. The Canaanites lived on with Zebulun but were subjected to forced labour. 31 Asher did not dispossess the inhabitants of Acco, nor those of Sidon, of Mahalab, of Achzib, of Helbah, of Aphek or of Rehob. 32 So the Asherites lived among the Canaanite inhabitants of the country, not having dispossessed them. 33 Naphtali did not dispossess the inhabitants of Beth-Shemesh or of Beth-Anath; they settled among the Canaanite inhabitants of the country, but the inhabitants of Beth-Shemesh and of Beth-Anath were subjected to forced labour for them. 34 The Amorites drove the Danites back into the highlands and would not let them come down into the plain. 35 The Amorites held their ground at Har-Heres and Shaalbim, but when the hand of the House of Joseph grew heavier, they were subjected to forced labour.

(36 The territory of the Edomites begins at the Ascent of Scorpions, runs to the Rock and continues on upwards.)

2 The Angel of Yahweh[a] went up from Gilgal to Bethel and said, 'I have brought you out of Egypt and led you into this country, which I promised on oath to your ancestors. I said, "I shall never break my covenant with you. 2 You for your part must make no covenant with the inhabitants of this country; you will destroy their altars." But you have not listened to my voice. What is the reason for this? 3 Very well, I now say this, "I am not going to drive these nations out before you. They will become your oppressors, and their gods will be a snare for you." ' 4 When the angel of Yahweh had spoken these words to all the Israelites, the people began to wail at the top of their voices. 5 And they called the place Bochim, and offered sacrifices to Yahweh there.

6 Joshua having dismissed the people, the Israelites then went away, each one to his own heritage, to occupy the country.[b] 7 The people served Yahweh throughout the lifetime of Joshua and throughout the lifetime of those elders who outlived Joshua and had known all the great deeds which Yahweh had done for the sake of Israel. 8 Joshua son of Nun, servant of Yahweh, was a hundred and ten years old when he died. 9 He was buried on the estate which he had received as his heritage at Timnath-Heres in the highlands of Ephraim, north of Mount Gaash. 10 And when that whole generation had been gathered to its ancestors, another generation followed it which knew neither Yahweh nor the deeds which he had done for the sake of Israel.

11 The Israelites then did what is evil in Yahweh's eyes and served the Baals. 12 They deserted Yahweh, God of

a 2 An expression for Yahweh himself in visible form.
b 2 // Jos 24:29–31.

the LORD, the God of their ancestors, who had brought them out of the land of Egypt; they followed other gods, from among the gods of the peoples who were all around them, and bowed down to them; and they provoked the LORD to anger. 13 They abandoned the LORD, and worshiped Baal and the Astartes. 14 So the anger of the LORD was kindled against Israel, and he gave them over to plunderers who plundered them, and he sold them into the power of their enemies all around, so that they could no longer withstand their enemies. 15 Whenever they marched out, the hand of the LORD was against them to bring misfortune, as the LORD had warned them and sworn to them; and they were in great distress.

16 Then the LORD raised up judges, who delivered them out of the power of those who plundered them. 17 Yet they did not listen even to their judges; for they lusted after other gods and bowed down to them. They soon turned aside from the way in which their ancestors had walked, who had obeyed the commandments of the LORD; they did not follow their example. 18 Whenever the LORD raised up judges for them, the LORD was with the judge, and he delivered them from the hand of their enemies all the days of the judge; for the LORD would be moved to pity by their groaning because of those who persecuted and oppressed them. 19 But whenever the judge died, they would relapse and behave worse than their ancestors, following other gods, worshiping them and bowing down to them. They would not drop any of their practices or their stubborn ways. 20 So the anger of the LORD was kindled against Israel; and he said, "Because this people have transgressed my covenant that I commanded their ancestors, and have not obeyed my voice, 21 I will no longer drive out before them any of the nations that Joshua left when he died." 22 In order to test Israel, whether or not they would take care to walk in the way of the LORD as their ancestors did, 23 the LORD had left those nations, not driving them out at once, and had not handed them over to Joshua.

3 Now these are the nations that the LORD left to test all those in Israel who had no experience of any war in Canaan 2 (it was only that successive generations of Israelites might know war, to teach those who had no experience of it before): 3 the five lords of the Philistines, and all the Canaanites, and the Sidonians, and the Hivites who lived on Mount Lebanon, from Mount Baal-hermon as far as Lebohamath. 4 They were for the testing of Israel, to know whether Israel would obey the commandments of the LORD, which he commanded their ancestors by Moses. 5 So the Israelites lived among the Canaanites, the Hittites, the Amorites, the Perizzites, the Hivites, and the Jebusites; 6 and they took their daughters as wives for themselves, and their own daughters they gave to their sons; and they worshiped their gods.

7 The Israelites did what was evil in the sight of the LORD, forgetting the LORD their God, and worshiping the Baals and the Asherahs. 8 Therefore the anger of the LORD was kindled against Israel, and he sold them into the hand of King Cushan-rishathaim of Aram-naharaim; and the Israelites served Cushan-rishathaim eight years. 9 But when the Israelites cried out to the LORD, the LORD raised up a deliverer for the Israelites, who delivered them, Othniel son of Kenaz, Caleb's younger brother. 10 The spirit of the LORD came upon him, and he judged Israel; he went out to war, and the LORD gave King Cushan-rishathaim of Aram into his hand; and his hand prevailed over Cushan-rishathaim. 11 So the land had rest forty years. Then Othniel son of Kenaz died.

the LORD, their fathers' God who had brought them out of Egypt, and went after other gods, the gods of the peoples among whom they lived; by bowing down before them they provoked the LORD to anger; 13 they forsook the LORD and served the baalim and the ashtaroth. 14 In his anger the LORD made them the prey of bands of raiders and plunderers; he sold them into the power of their enemies around them, so that they could no longer stand against them. 15 Every time they went out to do battle the LORD brought disaster on them, as he had said when he gave them his solemn warning; and they were in dire straits.

16 THEN the LORD raised up judges to rescue them from the marauding bands, 17 yet even to their judges they did not listen. They prostituted themselves by worshipping other gods and bowed down before them; all too soon they abandoned the path of obedience to the LORD's commands which their forefathers had followed. They did not obey the LORD. 18 Whenever the LORD set up a judge over them, he was with that judge, and kept them safe from their enemies so long as the judge lived. The LORD would relent when he heard them groaning under oppression and tyranny. 19 But on the death of the judge they would relapse into corruption deeper than that of their predecessors and go after other gods; serving them and bowing before them, they would give up none of their evil practices and wilful ways. 20 So the LORD's anger was roused against Israel and he said, 'Because this nation has violated the covenant which I laid upon their forefathers, and has not obeyed me, 21 I for my part shall not drive out before them one individual of all the nations which Joshua left at his death. 22 Through them I shall test Israel, to see whether or not they will keep strictly to the way of the LORD as their forefathers did.' 23 So the LORD left those nations alone and made no haste to drive them out or give them into Joshua's hands.

3 As a means of testing all the Israelites who had not taken part in the battles for Canaan, the LORD left these nations, 2 his purpose being to train succeeding generations of Israel in the art of warfare, or those at least who had not learnt it in former times. 3 They were: the five lords of the Philistines, all the Canaanites, the Sidonians, and the Hivites who lived in Mount Lebanon and from Mount Baalhermon as far as Lebo-hamath. 4 His purpose also was to test whether the Israelites would obey the commandments which the LORD had given to their forefathers through Moses. 5 Thus the Israelites lived among the Canaanites, the Hittites, the Amorites, the Perizzites, the Hivites, and the Jebusites; 6 they took their daughters in marriage and gave their own daughters to their sons; and they served their gods.

7 The Israelites did what was wrong in the eyes of the LORD: forgetting the LORD their God, they served the baalim and the asheroth. 8 The anger of the LORD was roused against Israel and he sold them into the power of King Cushan-rishathaim of Aram-naharaim, who kept them in subjection for eight years. 9 Then the Israelites cried to the LORD for help, and to deliver them he raised up Othniel son of Caleb's younger brother Kenaz, and he set them free. 10 The spirit of the LORD came upon him and he became judge over Israel. He took the field, and the LORD delivered King Cushan-rishathaim of Aram into his hands; Othniel was too strong for him. 11 Thus the land was at peace for forty years until Othniel son of Kenaz died.

LORD, the God of their fathers, who had led them out of the land of Egypt, they followed the other gods of the various nations around them, and by their worship of these gods provoked the LORD. 13 Because they had thus abandoned him and served Baal and the Ashtaroth, 14 the anger of the LORD flared up against Israel, and he delivered them over to plunderers who despoiled them. He allowed them to fall into the power of their enemies round about whom they were no longer able to withstand. 15 Whatever they undertook, the LORD turned into disaster for them, as in his warning he had sworn he would do, till they were in great distress. 16 Even when the LORD raised up judges to deliver them from the power of their despoilers, 17 they did not listen to their judges, but abandoned themselves to the worship of other gods. They were quick to stray from the way their fathers had taken, and did not follow their example of obedience to the commandments of the LORD. 18 Whenever the LORD raised up judges for them, he would be with the judge and save them from the power of their enemies as long as the judge lived; it was thus the LORD took pity on their distressful cries of affliction under their oppressors. 19 But when the judge died, they would relapse and do worse than their fathers, following other gods in service and worship, relinquishing none of their evil practices or stubborn conduct.

20 In his anger toward Israel the LORD said, "Inasmuch as this nation has violated my covenant which I enjoined on their fathers, and has disobeyed me, 21 I for my part will not clear away for them any more of the nations which Joshua left when he died." 22 Through these nations the Israelites were to be made to prove whether or not they would keep to the way of the LORD and continue in it as their fathers had done; 23 therefore the LORD allowed them to remain instead of expelling them immediately, or delivering them into the power of Israel.

3 The following are the nations which the LORD allowed to remain, so that through them he might try all those Israelites who had no experience of the battles with Canaan 2 [just to instruct, by training them in battle, those generations only of the Israelites who would not have had that previous experience]: 3 the five lords of the Philistines, and all the Canaanites, the Sidonians, and the Hivites who dwell in the mountain region of Lebanon between Baal-hermon and the entrance to Hamath. 4 These served to put Israel to the test, to determine whether they would obey the commandments the LORD had enjoined on their fathers through Moses. 5 Besides, the Israelites were living among the Canaanites, Hittites, Amorites, Perizzites, Hivites and Jebusites. 6 In fact, they took their daughters in marriage, and gave their own daughters to their sons in marriage, and served their gods.

7 Because the Israelites had offended the LORD by forgetting the LORD, their God, and serving the Baals and the Asherahs, 8 the anger of the LORD flared up against them, and he allowed them to fall into the power of Cushan-rishathaim, king of Aram Naharaim, whom they served for eight years. 9 But when the Israelites cried out to the LORD, he raised up for them a savior, Othniel, son of Caleb's younger brother Kenaz, who rescued them. 10 The spirit of the LORD came upon him, and he judged Israel. When he went out to war, the LORD delivered Cushan-rishathaim, king of Aram, into his power, so that he made him subject. 11 The land then was at rest for forty years, until Othniel, son of Kenaz, died.

their ancestors, who had brought them out of Egypt, and they followed other gods, from those of the surrounding peoples. They bowed down to these; they provoked Yahweh; 13 they deserted Yahweh to serve Baal and Astartes. c 14 Then Yahweh's anger grew hot against Israel. He handed them over to pillagers who plundered them; he delivered them to the enemies surrounding them, and they were no longer able to resist their enemies. 15 Whenever they mounted an expedition, Yahweh's hand was there to foil them, as Yahweh had told them and as Yahweh had sworn to them, so that they were in dire distress.

16 Yahweh then appointed them judges, who rescued them from the hands of their plunderers. 17 But even to their judges they refused to listen. They prostituted themselves to other gods and bowed down before these. Very quickly they left the path which their ancestors had trodden in obedience to the orders of Yahweh; they did not follow their example. 18 When Yahweh appointed judges for them, Yahweh was with the judge and rescued them from the hands of their enemies as long as the judge lived, since Yahweh relented at their groans under their persecutors and oppressors. 19 But once the judge was dead, they relapsed into even worse corruption than their ancestors. They followed other gods; they served them and bowed before them and would not give up the practices and stubborn ways of their ancestors at all.

20 Yahweh's anger then blazed out against Israel, and he said, 'Since this people has broken the covenant which I laid down for their ancestors, since they have not listened to my voice, 21 in future I shall not drive before them any one of those nations which Joshua left when he died, 22 in order, by means of them, to put Israel to the test, to see whether or not they would tread the paths of Yahweh as once their ancestors had trodden them.' 23 Hence, Yahweh allowed these nations to remain; he did not hurry to drive them out, and did not deliver them into the hands of Joshua.

3 These are the nations which Yahweh allowed to remain, by their means to put all those Israelites to the test who had not experienced any of the Canaanite wars 2 (this was only to instruct the Israelites' descendants, to teach them the art of war, those at least who had not experienced it previously): 3 the five chiefs of the Philistines, all the Canaanites, the Sidonians, and the Hittites who lived in the range of the Lebanon, from the uplands of Baal-Hermon to the Pass of Hamath. 4 They were used to put Israel to the test and see if they would keep the orders which Yahweh had given their ancestors through Moses. 5 The Israelites lived among the Canaanites, Hittites and Amorites, the Perizzites, Hivites and Jebusites; 6 they married their daughters, they gave their own sons to their daughters and served their gods.

7 The Israelites did what is evil in Yahweh's eyes. They forgot Yahweh their God and served Baals and Asherahs. 8 Then Yahweh's anger blazed out against Israel: he handed them over to Cushan-Rishathaim king of Edom, and the Israelites were enslaved to Cushan-Rishathaim for eight years. 9 The Israelites then cried to Yahweh and Yahweh raised for the Israelites a deliverer who rescued them, Othniel son of Kenaz, Caleb's younger brother. 10 The spirit of Yahweh was on him; he became judge in Israel and set out for war. Yahweh delivered Cushan-Rishathaim king of Edom into his hands, and he triumphed over Cushan-Rishathaim. 11 The country then had peace for forty years. Othniel son of Kenaz then died.

c 2 Canaanite deities, the male and female fertility gods. Astarte is also called Asherah.

NEW REVISED STANDARD VERSION

12 The Israelites again did what was evil in the sight of the LORD; and the LORD strengthened King Eglon of Moab against Israel, because they had done what was evil in the sight of the LORD. 13 In alliance with the Ammonites and the Amalekites, he went and defeated Israel; and they took possession of the city of palms. 14 So the Israelites served King Eglon of Moab eighteen years.

15 But when the Israelites cried out to the LORD, the LORD raised up for them a deliverer, Ehud son of Gera, the Benjaminite, a left-handed man. The Israelites sent tribute by him to King Eglon of Moab. 16 Ehud made for himself a sword with two edges, a cubit in length; and he fastened it on his right thigh under his clothes. 17 Then he presented the tribute to King Eglon of Moab. Now Eglon was a very fat man. 18 When Ehud had finished presenting the tribute, he sent the people who carried the tribute on their way. 19 But he himself turned back at the sculptured stones near Gilgal, and said, "I have a secret message for you, O king." So the king said,f "Silence!" and all his attendants went out from his presence. 20 Ehud came to him, while he was sitting alone in his cool roof chamber, and said, "I have a message from God for you." So he rose from his seat. 21 Then Ehud reached with his left hand, took the sword from his right thigh, and thrust it into Eglon'sg belly; 22 the hilt also went in after the blade, and the fat closed over the blade, for he did not draw the sword out of his belly; and the dirt came out.h 23 Then Ehud went out into the vestibule,i and closed the doors of the roof chamber on him, and locked them.

24 After he had gone, the servants came. When they saw that the doors of the roof chamber were locked, they thought, "He must be relieving himselfj in the cool chamber." 25 So they waited until they were embarrassed. When he still did not open the doors of the roof chamber, they took the key and opened them. There was their lord lying dead on the floor.

26 Ehud escaped while they delayed, and passed beyond the sculptured stones, and escaped to Seirah. 27 When he arrived, he sounded the trumpet in the hill country of Ephraim; and the Israelites went down with him from the hill country, having him at their head. 28 He said to them, "Follow after me; for the LORD has given your enemies the Moabites into your hand." So they went down after him, and seized the fords of the Jordan against the Moabites, and allowed no one to cross over. 29 At that time they killed about ten thousand of the Moabites, all strong, able-bodied men; no one escaped. 30 So Moab was subdued that day under the hand of Israel. And the land had rest eighty years.

31 After him came Shamgar son of Anath, who killed six hundred of the Philistines with an oxgoad. He too delivered Israel.

4 The Israelites again did what was evil in the sight of the LORD, after Ehud died. 2 So the LORD sold them into the hand of King Jabin of Canaan, who reigned in Hazor; the commander of his army was Sisera, who lived in Harosheth-ha-goiim. 3 Then the Israelites cried out to the LORD for help; for he had nine hundred chariots of iron, and had oppressed the Israelites cruelly twenty years.

4 At that time Deborah, a prophetess, wife of Lappidoth, was judging Israel. 5 She used to sit under the palm of Deborah between Ramah and Bethel in the hill country of Ephraim; and the Israelites came up to her for judgment.

REVISED ENGLISH BIBLE

12 Once again the Israelites did what was wrong in the eyes of the LORD, and because of this he roused King Eglon of Moab against Israel. 13 Eglon mustered the Ammonites and the Amalekites, attacked Israel, and took possession of the city of palm trees. 14 The Israelites were subject to King Eglon of Moab for eighteen years.

15 Then they cried to the LORD for help, and to deliver them he raised up Ehud son of Gera the Benjamite; he was left-handed. The Israelites sent him to hand over their tribute to King Eglon. 16 Ehud had made himself a two-edged sword, about eighteen inches long, which he fastened on his right side under his clothes 17 when he brought the tribute to King Eglon. Eglon was a very fat man. 18 After Ehud had finished presenting the tribute, he sent on the men who had carried it, 19 while he himself turned back from the Carved Stones at Gilgal. 'My lord king,' he said, 'I have a message for you in private.' Eglon called for silence and dismissed all his attendants. 20 Ehud then approached him as he sat in the roof-chamber of his summer palace. He said, 'Your majesty, I have a message from God for you.' As Eglon rose from his seat, 21 Ehud reached with his left hand, drew the sword from his right side, and drove it into Eglon's belly. 22 The hilt went in after the blade and the fat closed over the blade, for he did not draw the sword out but left it protruding behind. 23 Ehud then went out to the porch, where he shut the door on him and fastened it.

24 After he had gone, Eglon's servants came and, finding the doors fastened, they said, 'He must be relieving himself in the closet of his summer palace.' 25 They waited until they became alarmed and, when he still did not open the door of the roof-chamber, they took the key and opened the door; and there was their master lying dead on the floor.

26 While they had been waiting, Ehud had made good his escape; he passed the Carved Stones and escaped to Seirah. 27 Once there, he sounded the trumpet in the hill-country of Ephraim, and the Israelites went down from the hills with him at their head. 28 He said to them, 'Follow me, for the LORD has delivered your enemies, the Moabites, into your hands.' They went down after him, and held the fords of the Jordan against the Moabites, allowing no one to cross. 29 They killed at that time some ten thousand Moabites, all of them stalwart and valiant fighters; not one escaped. 30 Moab became subject to Israel on that day, and the land was at peace for eighty years.

31 After Ehud there was Shamgar son of Anath. He killed six hundred Philistines with an ox-goad, and he too delivered Israel.

4 AFTER Ehud's death the Israelites once again did what was wrong in the eyes of the LORD, 2 and he sold them into the power of Jabin, the Canaanite king who ruled in Hazor. The commander of his forces was Sisera, who lived in Harosheth-of-the-Gentiles. 3 The Israelites cried to the LORD for help, because Sisera with his nine hundred ironclad chariots had oppressed Israel harshly for twenty years.

4 At that time Deborah wife of Lappidoth, a prophetess, was judge in Israel. 5 It was her custom to sit under the Palm Tree of Deborah between Ramah and Bethel in the hill-country of Ephraim, and Israelites seeking a judgement

---

f Heb he said   g Heb his   h With Tg Vg: Meaning of Heb uncertain   i Meaning of Heb uncertain   j Heb covering his feet

3:16 **about . . . long:** lit. a short cubit in length.   3:22 **behind:** Heb. word of uncertain meaning.   3:23 **porch:** Heb. word of uncertain meaning.

NEW AMERICAN BIBLE

12 Again the Israelites offended the LORD, who because of this offense strengthened Eglon, king of Moab, against Israel. 13 In alliance with the Ammonites and Amalekites, he attacked and defeated Israel, taking possession of the city of palms. 14 The Israelites then served Eglon, king of Moab, for eighteen years.

15 But when the Israelites cried out to the LORD, he raised up for them a savior, the Benjaminite Ehud, son of Gera, who was left-handed. It was by him that the Israelites sent their tribute to Eglon, king of Moab. 16 Ehud made himself a two-edged dagger a foot long, and wore it under his clothes over his right thigh. 17 He presented the tribute to Eglon, king of Moab, who was very fat, 18 and after the presentation went off with the tribute bearers. 19 He returned, however, from where the idols are, near Gilgal, and said, "I have a private message for you, O king." And the king said, "Silence!" Then when all his attendants had left his presence, 20 and Ehud went in to him where he sat alone in his cool upper room, Ehud said, "I have a message from God for you." So the king rose from his chair, 21 and then Ehud with his left hand drew the dagger from his right thigh, and thrust it into Eglon's belly. 22 The hilt also went in after the blade, and the fat closed over the blade because he did not withdraw the dagger from his body.

23 Then Ehud went out into the hall, shutting the doors of the upper room on him and locking them. 24 When Ehud had left and the servants came, they saw that the doors of the upper room were locked, and thought, "He must be easing himself in the cool chamber." 25 They waited until they finally grew suspicious. Since he did not open the doors of the upper room, they took the key and opened them. There on the floor, dead, lay their lord!

26 During their delay Ehud made good his escape and, passing the idols, took refuge in Seirah. 27 On his arrival he sounded the horn in the mountain region of Ephraim, and the Israelites went down from the mountains with him as their leader. 28 "Follow me," he said to them, "for the LORD has delivered your enemies the Moabites into your power." So they followed him down and seized the fords of the Jordan leading to Moab, permitting no one to cross. 29 On that occasion they slew about ten thousand Moabites, all of them strong and valiant men. Not a man escaped. 30 Thus was Moab brought under the power of Israel at that time; and the land had rest for eighty years.

31 After him there was Shamgar, son of Anath, who slew six hundred Philistines with an oxgoad. He, too, rescued Israel.

4 After Ehud's death, however, the Israelites again offended the LORD. 2 So the LORD allowed them to fall into the power of the Canaanite king, Jabin, who reigned in Hazor. The general of his army was Sisera, who dwelt in Harosheth-ha-goiim. 3 But the Israelites cried out to the LORD; for with his nine hundred iron chariots he sorely oppressed the Israelites for twenty years.

4 At this time the prophetess Deborah, wife of Lappidoth, was judging Israel. 5 She used to sit under Deborah's palm tree, situated between Ramah and Bethel in the mountain region of Ephraim, and there the Israelites came up to her for judgment. 6 She sent and summoned Barak, son of Abin-

NEW JERUSALEM BIBLE

12 Again the Israelites began doing what is evil in Yahweh's eyes, and Yahweh strengthened Eglon king of Moab against Israel, since they were doing what is evil in Yahweh's eyes. 13 Eglon in conjunction with the sons of Ammon and Amalek marched on Israel, beat them and captured the City of Palm Trees. d 14 The Israelites were enslaved to Eglon king of Moab for eighteen years.

15 The Israelites then cried to Yahweh, and Yahweh raised a deliverer for them, Ehud son of Gera, a Benjaminite; he was left-handed. The Israelites appointed him to take their tribute to Eglon king of Moab. 16 Ehud made himself a dagger — it was double-edged and a foot long — and strapped it under his clothes on his right thigh. 17 He presented the tribute to Eglon king of Moab. This Eglon was a very fat man. 18 Having presented the tribute, Ehud sent away the men who had been carrying it; 19 but he himself, on reaching the Idols which are near Gilgal, went back and said, 'I have a secret message for you, O king.' The king commanded silence, and all his attendants withdrew. 20 Ehud went up to him; he was sitting in his private room upstairs, where it was cool. Ehud said to him, 'I have a message from God for you, O king.' The latter immediately rose from his seat. 21 Then Ehud, reaching with his left hand, drew the dagger he was carrying on his right thigh and thrust it into the king's belly. 22 The hilt too went in after the blade, and the fat closed over the blade, since Ehud did not pull the dagger out of his belly again. 23 Ehud went out through the privies, having shut and bolted the doors of the upstairs room behind him.

24 When he had gone, the servants came back and looked; the doors of the upstairs room were bolted. They thought, 'He is probably covering his feet in the inner part of the cool room.' 25 They waited until they became embarrassed, but still he did not open the doors of the upstairs room. Eventually, they took the key and opened the door; and there lay their master, dead, on the ground.

26 Meanwhile, Ehud had got away, passed the Idols and made good his escape to safety in Seirah. 27 Once there, he sounded the horn in the highlands of Ephraim, and the Israelites came down from the hills with him at their head. 28 And he said to them, 'Follow me, because Yahweh has delivered your enemy Moab into your hands.' So they followed him, seized the fords of the Jordan against Moab and allowed no one to cross. 29 On that occasion they beat the Moabites, some ten thousand men, all tough and seasoned fighters, and not one escaped. 30 That day Moab was humbled under the hand of Israel, and the country had peace for eighty years.

31 After him came Shamgar son of Anath. He routed six hundred of the Philistines with an ox-goad; he too was a deliverer of Israel.

4 Once Ehud was dead, the Israelites again began doing what is evil in Yahweh's eyes, 2 and Yahweh handed them over to Jabin king of Canaan, who reigned at Hazor. The commander of his army was Sisera, who lived in Haroshet-ha-Goiim.

3 The Israelites then cried to Yahweh; for Jabin had nine hundred iron chariots and had cruelly oppressed the Israelites for twenty years.

4 Deborah, a prophetess, wife of Lappidoth, was judging Israel at the time. 5 She used to sit under Deborah's Palm between Ramah and Bethel in the highlands of Ephraim, and the Israelites would come to her for justice. 6 She sent

d 3 Jericho, well within the territory of Benjamin.

6 She sent and summoned Barak son of Abinoam from Kedesh in Naphtali, and said to him, "The LORD, the God of Israel, commands you, 'Go, take position at Mount Tabor, bringing ten thousand from the tribe of Naphtali and the tribe of Zebulun. 7 I will draw out Sisera, the general of Jabin's army, to meet you by the Wadi Kishon with his chariots and his troops; and I will give him into your hand.'" 8 Barak said to her, "If you will go with me, I will go; but if you will not go with me, I will not go." 9 And she said, "I will surely go with you; nevertheless, the road on which you are going will not lead to your glory, for the LORD will sell Sisera into the hand of a woman." Then Deborah got up and went with Barak to Kedesh. 10 Barak summoned Zebulun and Naphtali to Kedesh; and ten thousand warriors went up behind him; and Deborah went up with him.

11 Now Heber the Kenite had separated from the other Kenites,^{k} that is, the descendants of Hobab the father-in-law of Moses, and had encamped as far away as Elon-bezaanannim, which is near Kedesh.

12 When Sisera was told that Barak son of Abinoam had gone up to Mount Tabor, 13 Sisera called out all his chariots, nine hundred chariots of iron, and all the troops who were with him, from Harosheth-ha-goiim to the Wadi Kishon. 14 Then Deborah said to Barak, "Up! For this is the day on which the LORD has given Sisera into your hand. The LORD is indeed going out before you." So Barak went down from Mount Tabor with ten thousand warriors following him. 15 And the LORD threw Sisera and all his chariots and all his army into a panic^l before Barak; Sisera got down from his chariot and fled away on foot, 16 while Barak pursued the chariots and the army to Harosheth-ha-goiim. All the army of Sisera fell by the sword; no one was left.

17 Now Sisera had fled away on foot to the tent of Jael wife of Heber the Kenite; for there was peace between King Jabin of Hazor and the clan of Heber the Kenite. 18 Jael came out to meet Sisera, and said to him, "Turn aside, my lord, turn aside to me; have no fear." So he turned aside to her into the tent, and she covered him with a rug. 19 Then he said to her, "Please give me a little water to drink; for I am thirsty." So she opened a skin of milk and gave him a drink and covered him. 20 He said to her, "Stand at the entrance of the tent, and if anybody comes and asks you, 'Is anyone here?' say, 'No.'" 21 But Jael wife of Heber took a tent peg, and took a hammer in her hand, and went softly to him and drove the peg into his temple, until it went down into the ground—he was lying fast asleep from weariness—and he died. 22 Then, as Barak came in pursuit of Sisera, Jael went out to meet him, and said to him, "Come, and I will show you the man whom you are seeking." So he went into her tent; and there was Sisera lying dead, with the tent peg in his temple.

23 So on that day God subdued King Jabin of Canaan before the Israelites. 24 Then the hand of the Israelites bore harder and harder on King Jabin of Canaan, until they destroyed King Jabin of Canaan.

5 Then Deborah and Barak son of Abinoam sang on that day, saying:

2 "When locks are long in Israel,
    when the people offer themselves willingly—
    bless^m the LORD!

3 "Hear, O kings; give ear, O princes;
    to the LORD I will sing,
    I will make melody to the LORD, the God of Israel.

went up to her. 6 She sent for Barak son of Abinoam from Kedesh in Naphtali and said to him, 'This is the command of the LORD the God of Israel: Go and lead out ten thousand men from Naphtali and bring them with you to Mount Tabor. 7 I shall draw out to you at the wadi Kishon Jabin's commander Sisera, along with his chariots and troops, and deliver him into your power.' 8 Barak answered, 'If you go with me, I shall go, but if you will not go, neither shall I.' 9 'Certainly I shall go with you,' she said, 'but this venture will bring you no glory, because the LORD will leave Sisera to fall into the hands of a woman.' Deborah set off with Barak and went to Kedesh. 10 Barak mustered Zebulun and Naphtali to Kedesh and marched up with ten thousand followers; Deborah went up with him.

11 Now Heber the Kenite had parted company with the Kenites, the descendants of Hobab, Moses' brother-in-law, and he had pitched his tent at Elon-bezaanannim near Kedesh.

12 When it was reported to Sisera that Barak son of Abinoam had gone up to Mount Tabor, 13 he mustered all nine hundred of his iron-clad chariots, along with all the troops he had, and marched from Harosheth-of-the-Gentiles to the wadi Kishon. 14 Deborah said to Barak, 'Up! This day the LORD is to give Sisera into your hands. See, the LORD has marched out at your head!' Barak came down from Mount Tabor with ten thousand men at his back, 15 and the LORD threw Sisera and all his chariots and army into panic-stricken rout before Barak's onslaught; Sisera himself dismounted from his chariot and fled on foot. 16 Barak pursued the chariots and the troops as far as Harosheth, and the whole army was put to the sword; not a man was left alive.

17 Meanwhile Sisera fled on foot to the tent of Jael wife of Heber the Kenite, because King Jabin of Hazor and the household of Heber the Kenite were on friendly terms. 18 Jael came out to greet Sisera and said, 'Come in, my lord, come in here; do not be afraid.' He went into the tent, and she covered him with a rug. 19 He said to her, 'Give me some water to drink, for I am thirsty.' She opened a skin of milk, gave him a drink, and covered him again. 20 He said to her, 'Stand at the tent door, and if anyone comes and asks if there is a man here, say "No."' 21 But as Sisera lay fast asleep through exhaustion Jael took a tent-peg, picked up a mallet, and, creeping up to him, drove the peg into his temple, so that it went down into the ground, and Sisera died. 22 When Barak came by in pursuit of Sisera, Jael went out to meet him. 'Come,' she said, 'I shall show you the man you are looking for.' He went in with her, and there was Sisera lying dead with the tent-peg in his temple. 23 That day God gave victory to the Israelites over King Jabin of Canaan, 24 and they pressed home their attacks upon him until he was destroyed.

5 On that day Deborah and Barak son of Abinoam sang this song:

2 'For the leaders, the leaders in Israel,
    for the people who answered the call,
    bless the LORD.
3 Hear, you kings; princes, give ear!
    I shall sing, I shall sing to the LORD,
    making music to the LORD, the God of Israel.

---

^{k} Heb from the Kain ^{l} Heb adds to the sword; compare verse 16
^{m} Or You who offer yourselves willingly among the people, bless

4:21 it went down: prob. mng; Heb. obscure.   5:2 For . . .
Israel: or For those who had flowing locks in Israel.

oam, from Kedesh of Naphtali. "This is what the LORD, the God of Israel, commands," she said to him; "go, march on Mount Tabor, and take with you ten thousand Naphtalites and Zebulunites. 7 I will lead Sisera, the general of Jabin's army, out to you at the Wadi Kishon, together with his chariots and troops, and will deliver them into your power." 8 But Barak answered her, "If you come with me, I will go; if you do not come with me, I will not go." 9 "I will certainly go with you," she replied, "but you shall not gain the glory in the expedition on which you are setting out, for the LORD will have Sisera fall into the power of a woman." So Deborah joined Barak and journeyed with him to Kedesh.

10 Barak summoned Zebulun and Naphtali to Kedesh, and ten thousand men followed him. Deborah also went up with him. 11 Now the Kenite Heber had detached himself from his own people, the descendants of Hobab, Moses' brother-in-law, and had pitched his tent by the terebinth of Zaanannim, which was near Kedesh.

12 It was reported to Sisera that Barak, son of Abinoam, had gone up to Mount Tabor. 13 So Sisera assembled from Harosheth-ha-goiim at the Wadi Kishon all nine hundred of his iron chariots and all his forces. 14 Deborah then said to Barak, "Be off, for this is the day on which the LORD has delivered Sisera into your power. The LORD marches before you." So Barak went down Mount Tabor, followed by his ten thousand men. 15 And the LORD put Sisera and all his chariots and all his forces to rout before Barak. Sisera himself dismounted from his chariot and fled on foot. 16 Barak, however, pursued the chariots and the army as far as Harosheth-ha-goiim. The entire army of Sisera fell beneath the sword, not even one man surviving.

17 Sisera, in the meantime, had fled on foot to the tent of Jael, wife of the Kenite Heber, since Jabin, king of Hazor, and the family of the Kenite Heber were at peace with one another. 18 Jael went out to meet Sisera and said to him, "Come in, my lord, come in with me; do not be afraid." So he went into her tent, and she covered him with a rug. 19 He said to her, "Please give me a little water to drink. I am thirsty." But she opened a jug of milk for him to drink, and then covered him over. 20 "Stand at the entrance of the tent," he said to her. "If anyone comes and asks, 'Is there someone here?' say, 'No!'" 21 Instead Jael, wife of Heber, got a tent peg and took a mallet in her hand. While Sisera was sound asleep, she stealthily approached him and drove the peg through his temple down into the ground, so that he perished in death. 22 Then when Barak came in pursuit of Sisera, Jael went out to meet him and said to him, "Come, I will show you the man you seek." So he went in with her, and there lay Sisera dead, with the tent peg through his temple.

23 Thus on that day God humbled the Canaanite king, Jabin, before the Israelites; 24 their power weighed ever heavier upon him, till at length they destroyed the Canaanite king, Jabin.

5 On that day Deborah [and Barak, son of Abinoam] sang this song:

2 Of chiefs who took the lead in Israel,
    of noble deeds by the people who bless
        the LORD,
3 Hear, O kings! Give ear, O princes!
    I to the LORD will sing my song,
    my hymn to the LORD, the God of Israel.

for Barak son of Abinoam from Kedesh in Naphtali, and said to him, 'Has not Yahweh, God of Israel, commanded, "Go! March to Mount Tabor and with you take ten thousand of the sons of Naphtali and the sons of Zebulun. 7 I shall entice Sisera, the commander of Jabin's army, to encounter you at the Torrent of Kishon with his chariots and troops; and I shall put him into your power"? ' 8 Barak replied, 'If you come with me, I shall go; if you will not come, I shall not go, for I do not know how to choose the day when the angel of Yahweh will grant me success.' 9 'I shall go with you then,' she said, 'but, the way you are going about it, the glory will not be yours; for Yahweh will deliver Sisera into the hands of a woman.' Deborah then stood up and went with Barak to Kedesh. 10 Barak summoned Zebulun and Naphtali. Ten thousand men marched behind him, and Deborah went with him.

11 Heber the Kenite had parted company with the tribe of Kain and with the sons of Hobab, father-in-law of Moses; he had pitched his tent near the Oak of Zaanannim, not far from Kedesh.

12 Sisera was informed that Barak son of Abinoam had encamped on Mount Tabor. 13 Sisera summoned all his chariots — nine hundred iron chariots — and all the troops he had, from Harosheth-ha-Goiim to the Torrent of Kishon. 14 Deborah said to Barak, 'Up! For today is the day when Yahweh has put Sisera into your power. Is not Yahweh marching at your head?' And Barak charged down from Mount Tabor with ten thousand men behind him. 15 At Barak's advance, Yahweh struck terror into Sisera, all his chariots and his entire army. Sisera leapt down from his chariot and fled on foot. 16 Barak pursued the chariots and the army as far as Harosheth-ha-Goiim. Sisera's whole army fell by the edge of the sword; not one man was spared.

17 Sisera meanwhile fled on foot towards the tent of Jael, the wife of Heber the Kenite. For there was peace between Jabin king of Hazor and the family of Heber the Kenite. 18 Jael came out to meet Sisera and said to him, 'Stay here, my lord, with me; do not be afraid!' He stayed with her in her tent, and she covered him with a rug. 19 He said to her, 'Please give me a little water to drink, for I am thirsty.' She opened the skin of milk, gave him some to drink and covered him up again. 20 Then he said to her, 'Stand at the tent door, and if anyone comes and questions you — if he asks, "Is there a man here?" say, "No." ' 21 But Jael the wife of Heber took a tent-peg and picked up a mallet; she crept up softly to him and drove the peg into his temple right through to the ground. He was lying fast asleep, worn out; and so he died. 22 And now Barak came up in pursuit of Sisera. Jael went out to meet him and said, 'Come in, and I will show you the man you are looking for.' He went into her tent; and there was Sisera dead, with the tent-peg through his temple.

23 Thus God that day humbled Jabin king of Canaan before the Israelites. 24 And the Israelites bore down more and more heavily on that king of Canaan, Jabin, until he was utterly destroyed.

5 They sang a song that day, Deborah and Barak son of Abinoam, and the words were:

2 That the warriors in Israel unbound their hair,
    that the people came forward with a will,
        bless Yahweh!
3 Listen, you kings! Give ear, you princes!
    From me, from me comes a song for Yahweh.
    I shall glorify Yahweh, God of Israel.

4 "LORD, when you went out from Seir,
    when you marched from the region of Edom,
    the earth trembled,
    and the heavens poured,
    the clouds indeed poured water.
5 The mountains quaked before the LORD, the One
        of Sinai,
    before the LORD, the God of Israel.

6 "In the days of Shamgar son of Anath,
    in the days of Jael, caravans ceased
    and travelers kept to the byways.
7 The peasantry prospered in Israel,
    they grew fat on plunder,
    because you arose, Deborah,
    arose as a mother in Israel.
8 When new gods were chosen,
    then war was in the gates.
    Was shield or spear to be seen
    among forty thousand in Israel?
9 My heart goes out to the commanders of Israel
    who offered themselves willingly among the
        people.
    Bless the LORD.

10 "Tell of it, you who ride on white donkeys,
    you who sit on rich carpets[n]
    and you who walk by the way.
11 To the sound of musicians[n] at the watering
        places,
    there they repeat the triumphs of the LORD,
    the triumphs of his peasantry in Israel.

    "Then down to the gates marched the people of
        the LORD.

12 "Awake, awake, Deborah!
    Awake, awake, utter a song!
    Arise, Barak, lead away your captives,
    O son of Abinoam.
13 Then down marched the remnant of the noble;
    the people of the LORD marched down for
        him[o] against the mighty.
14 From Ephraim they set out[p] into the valley,[q]
    following you, Benjamin, with your kin;
    from Machir marched down the commanders,
    and from Zebulun those who bear the marshal's
        staff;
15 the chiefs of Issachar came with Deborah,
    and Issachar faithful to Barak;
    into the valley they rushed out at his heels.
    Among the clans of Reuben
    there were great searchings of heart.
16 Why did you tarry among the sheepfolds,
    to hear the piping for the flocks?
    Among the clans of Reuben
    there were great searchings of heart.
17 Gilead stayed beyond the Jordan;
    and Dan, why did he abide with the ships?
    Asher sat still at the coast of the sea,
    settling down by his landings.
18 Zebulun is a people that scorned death;
    Naphtali too, on the heights of the field.

4 'LORD, when you set forth from Seir,
    when you marched from the land of Edom,
    earth trembled; heaven quaked;
    the clouds streamed down in torrents.
5 Mountains shook in fear before the LORD, the Lord
        of Sinai,
    before the LORD, the God of Israel.

6 'In the days of Shamgar son of Anath,
    in the days of Jael, caravans plied no longer;
    travellers who had followed the high roads
    went round by devious paths.
7 Champions there were none,
    none left in Israel,
    until you, Deborah, arose,
    arose as a mother in Israel.
8 They chose new gods,
    they consorted with demons.
    Not a shield was to be seen, not a lance
    among forty thousand Israelites.

9 'My heart goes out to you, the marshals of Israel;
    you among the people that answered the call,
    bless the LORD.
10 You that sit on saddle-cloths
    riding your tawny she-donkeys,
    and you that take the road on foot,
    ponder on this.
11 Hark, the sound of the merrymakers
    at the places where they draw water!
    There they commemorate the victories of the
        LORD,
    his triumphs as the champion of Israel.

    'Down to the gates came the LORD's people:
12 'Rouse yourself, rouse yourself, Deborah,
    rouse yourself, break into song.
    Up, Barak! Take prisoners in plenty,
    you son of Abinoam.'
13 'Then down marched the column and its chieftains,
    the people of the LORD marching down like
        warriors.
14 The men of Ephraim rallied in the vale,
    crying, "We are with you, Benjamin! Your
        clansmen are here!"
    Down came the marshals from Machir,
    from Zebulun the bearers of the musterer's staff.
15 The princes of Issachar were with Deborah,
    Issachar with Barak;
    down into the valley they rushed in pursuit.

    'Reuben however was split into factions;
    great were their heart-searchings.
16 Why did you linger by the sheepfolds
    to listen to the shrill calling of the shepherds?
17 Gilead stayed beyond Jordan;
    and Dan, why did he tarry by the ships?
    Asher remained by the seashore,
    by its creeks he stayed.
18 The people of Zebulun risked their lives;
    so did Naphtali on the heights of the battlefield.

5:7 you: or I.   5:11 merrymakers: prob. rdg; Heb. obscure.
5:13 column: prob. rdg; Heb. survivor. marching down: prob. rdg;
Heb. adds to me.   5:14 rallied: prob. rdg; Heb. their root. the
vale: so Gk; Heb. Amalek.   5:15 heart-searchings: so some
MSS; others have an unknown word.   5:16 shepherds: prob. rdg;
Heb. adds Reuben was split into factions; great were their
heart-searchings.

[n] Meaning of Heb uncertain   [o] Gk: Heb me   [p] Cn: Heb From
Ephraim their root   [q] Gk: Heb in Amalek

4 O LORD, when you went out from Seir,
  when you marched from the land of Edom,
The earth quaked and the heavens were shaken,
  while the clouds sent down showers.
5 Mountains trembled
  in the presence of the LORD, the One of Sinai,
  in the presence of the LORD, the God of Israel.

6 In the days of Shamgar, son of Anath,
  in the days of slavery caravans ceased;
Those who traveled the roads
  went by roundabout paths.
7 Gone was freedom beyond the walls
  gone indeed from Israel.

  When I, Deborah, rose,
  when I rose, a mother in Israel,
8 New gods were their choice;
  then the war was at their gates.
Not a shield could be seen, nor a lance,
  among forty thousand in Israel!

9 My heart is with the leaders of Israel,
  nobles of the people who bless the LORD;
10 They who ride on white asses,
  seated on saddlecloths as they go their way;
11 Sing of them to the strains of the harpers at
  the wells,
  where men recount the just deeds of the LORD,
  his just deeds that brought freedom to Israel.

12 Awake, awake, Deborah!
  awake, awake, strike up a song.
Strength! arise, Barak,
  make despoilers your spoil, son of Abinoam.
13 Then down came the fugitives with the mighty,
  the people of the LORD came down for me
  as warriors.

14 From Ephraim, princes were in the valley;
  behind you was Benjamin, among your troops.
From Machir came down commanders,
  from Zebulun wielders of the marshal's staff.

15 With Deborah were the princes of Issachar;
  Barak, too, was in the valley, his
  course unchecked.

  Among the clans of Reuben
  great were the searchings of heart.
16 Why do you stay beside your hearths
  listening to the lowing of the herds?
Among the clans of Reuben
  great were the searchings of heart!

17 Gilead, beyond the Jordan, rests;
  why does Dan spend his time in ships?
Asher, who dwells along the shore,
  is resting in his coves.
18 Zebulun is the people defying death;
  Naphtali, too, on the open heights!

4 Yahweh, when you set out from Seir,
  when you marched from the field of Edom,
  the earth shook,
  the heavens pelted,
  the clouds pelted down water.
5 The mountains melted before Yahweh of Sinai,
  before Yahweh, God of Israel.

6 In the days of Shamgar son of Anath,
  in the days of Jael,
  there were no more caravans;
  those who went forth on their travels
  took their way along by-paths.

7 The villages in Israel were no more,
  they were no more
  until you arose, O Deborah,
  until you arose, mother of Israel!

8 They were choosing new gods
  when war was at the gates.
  Was there one shield, one spear to be found
  among the forty thousand men in Israel?

9 My heart is with the leaders of Israel,
  with the people who came forward with a will!
  Bless Yahweh!

10 You who ride white donkeys
  and sit on saddle-blankets as you ride,
  and you who go on foot,
11 sing — to the sound of the shepherds
  at the watering places!
  There they extol Yahweh's blessings,
  his saving acts for his villages in Israel!
  (Then Yahweh's people marched down to the
  gates.)

12 Awake, awake, Deborah!
  Awake, awake, declaim a song!
  Take heart, to your feet, Barak,
  capture your captors, son of Abinoam!

13 Then Israel marched down to the gates;
  like champions, Yahweh's people marched down to
  fight for him!

14 The princes of Ephraim are in the valley.
  Behind you, Benjamin is in your ranks.

  Captains have come down from Machir,
  those who wield the commander's staff, from
  Zebulun.

15 The princes of Issachar are with Deborah;
  Naphtali, with Barak, in the valley follows in hot
  pursuit.

  In the clans of Reuben
  there was much searching of heart.
16 Why did you stay among the sheepfolds,
  listening for the whistle, with the flocks?
  (In the clans of Reuben,
  there was much searching of heart.)

17 Gilead stayed on the other side of the Jordan,
  and why should Dan have stayed aboard ship?
  Asher remained beside the sea,
  peacefully living within his ports.

18 Zebulun is a people who have braved death,
  Naphtali too, on the high ground of the country.

19 "The kings came, they fought;
   then fought the kings of Canaan,
at Taanach, by the waters of Megiddo;
   they got no spoils of silver.
20 The stars fought from heaven,
   from their courses they fought against Sisera.
21 The torrent Kishon swept them away,
   the onrushing torrent, the torrent Kishon.
March on, my soul, with might!
22 "Then loud beat the horses' hoofs
   with the galloping, galloping of his steeds.

23 "Curse Meroz, says the angel of the LORD,
   curse bitterly its inhabitants,
because they did not come to the help of the
   LORD,
   to the help of the LORD against the mighty.

24 "Most blessed of women be Jael,
   the wife of Heber the Kenite,
of tent-dwelling women most blessed.
25 He asked water and she gave him milk,
   she brought him curds in a lordly bowl.
26 She put her hand to the tent peg
   and her right hand to the workmen's mallet;
she struck Sisera a blow,
   she crushed his head,
   she shattered and pierced his temple.
27 He sank, he fell,
   he lay still at her feet;
at her feet he sank, he fell;
   where he sank, there he fell dead.

28 "Out of the window she peered,
   the mother of Sisera gazed^r through the
     lattice:
'Why is his chariot so long in coming?
   Why tarry the hoofbeats of his chariots?'
29 Her wisest ladies make answer,
   indeed, she answers the question herself:
30 'Are they not finding and dividing the spoil?—
   A girl or two for every man;
spoil of dyed stuffs for Sisera,
   spoil of dyed stuffs embroidered,
   two pieces of dyed work embroidered for my
     neck as spoil?'

31 "So perish all your enemies, O LORD!
   But may your friends be like the sun as it rises
     in its might."

And the land had rest forty years.

6 The Israelites did what was evil in the sight of the
LORD, and the LORD gave them into the hand of Midian
seven years. 2 The hand of Midian prevailed over Israel; and
because of Midian the Israelites provided for themselves
hiding places in the mountains, caves and strongholds. 3 For
whenever the Israelites put in seed, the Midianites and the
Amalekites and the people of the east would come up
against them. 4 They would encamp against them and destroy the produce of the land, as far as the neighborhood of
Gaza, and leave no sustenance in Israel, and no sheep or ox
or donkey. 5 For they and their livestock would come up,
and they would even bring their tents, as thick as locusts;
neither they nor their camels could be counted; so they
wasted the land as they came in. 6 Thus Israel was greatly
impoverished because of Midian; and the Israelites cried out
to the LORD for help.

7 When the Israelites cried to the LORD on account of
the Midianites, 8 the LORD sent a prophet to the Israelites;

19 'Kings came, they fought;
   then fought the kings of Canaan
at Taanach, by the waters of Megiddo;
   no plunder of silver did they take.
20 The stars fought from heaven,
   the stars in their courses fought against Sisera.
21 The torrent of Kishon swept him away,
   the torrent barred his flight, the torrent of Kishon.
March on in might, my soul!
22 Then hammered the hoofs of his horses,
   his chargers galloped, galloped away.

23 'A curse on Meroz, said the angel of the LORD;
a curse, a curse on its inhabitants,
because they did not come to the help of the LORD,
to the help of the LORD and the fighting men.

24 'Blest above women be Jael
   wife of Heber the Kenite;
blest above all women in the tents.
25 He asked for water: she gave him milk,
   she offered him curds in a bowl fit for a chieftain.
26 She reached out her hand for the tent-peg,
   her right hand for the workman's hammer.
With the hammer she struck Sisera, crushing his
     head;
   with a shattering blow she pierced his temple.
27 At her feet he sank, he fell, he lay prone;
   at her feet he sank down and fell.
Where he sank down, there he fell, done to death.

28 'The mother of Sisera peered through the lattice,
   through the window she peered and cried,
"Why is his chariot so long in coming?
   Why is the clatter of his chariots so delayed?"
29 The wisest of her ladies answered her,
   yes, she found her own answer:
30 "They must be finding spoil, taking their shares,
   a damsel for each man, two damsels,
booty of dyed stuffs for Sisera,
booty of dyed stuffs,
dyed stuff and brocade, two lengths of brocade
to grace the victor's neck."

31 'So perish all your enemies, LORD;
   but let those who love you be like the sun rising in
     strength.'

The land was at peace for forty years.

6 The Israelites did what was wrong in the eyes of the
LORD and he delivered them into the hands of Midian
for seven years. 2 The Midianites were too strong for the
Israelites, who were forced to find themselves hollow
places in the mountains, in caves and fastnesses. 3 If the
Israelites had sown seed, the Midianites and the Amalekites
and other eastern tribes would come up and attack Israel,
4 pitching their camps in the country and destroying the
crops as far as the outskirts of Gaza. They left nothing to
support life in Israel, neither sheep nor ox nor donkey.
5 They came up with their herds and their tents, swarming
like locusts; they and their camels were past counting. They
would come into the land and lay it waste. 6 The Israelites,
brought to destitution by the Midianites, cried to the LORD
for help.

7 When the Israelites cried to the LORD because of what
they were suffering from the Midianites, 8 he sent them a

---

^r Gk Compare Tg: Heb *exclaimed*

5:31 **you**: *so Syriac; Heb.* him.

19 The kings came and fought;
  then they fought, those kings of Canaan,
At Taanach by the waters of Megiddo;
  no silver booty did they take.
20 From the heavens the stars, too, fought;
  from their courses they fought against Sisera.
21 The Wadi Kishon swept them away;
  a wadi . . . , the Kishon.
22 Then the hoofs of the horses pounded,
  with the dashing, dashing of his steeds.

23 "Curse Meroz," says the LORD,
  "hurl a curse at its inhabitants!
For they came not to my help,
  as warriors to the help of the LORD."

24 Blessed among women be Jael,
  blessed among tent-dwelling women.
25 He asked for water, she gave him milk;
  in a princely bowl she offered curds.
26 With her left hand she reached for the peg,
  with her right, for the workman's mallet.

She hammered Sisera, crushed his head;
  she smashed, stove in his temple.
27 At her feet he sank down, fell, lay still;
  down at her feet he sank and fell;
  where he sank down, there he fell, slain.

28 From the window peered down and wailed
  the mother of Sisera, from the lattice:
"Why is his chariot so long in coming?
  why are the hoofbeats of his chariots delayed?"
29 The wisest of her princesses answers her,
  and she, too, keeps answering herself:
30 "They must be dividing the spoil they took:
  there must be a damsel or two for each man,
Spoils of dyed cloth as Sisera's spoil,
  an ornate shawl or two for me in the spoil."
31 May all your enemies perish thus, O LORD!
  but your friends be as the sun rising in its might!

And the land was at rest for forty years.

6 The Israelites offended the LORD, who therefore delivered them into the power of Midian for seven years, 2 so that Midian held Israel subject. For fear of Midian the Israelites established the fire signals on the mountains, the caves for refuge, and the strongholds. 3 And it used to be that when the Israelites had completed their sowing, Midian, Amalek and the Kedemites would come up, 4 encamp opposite them, and destroy the produce of the land as far as the outskirts of Gaza, leaving no sustenance in Israel, nor sheep, oxen or asses. 5 For they would come up with their livestock, and their tents would become as numerous as locusts; and neither they nor their camels could be numbered, when they came into the land to lay it waste. 6 Thus was Israel reduced to misery by Midian, and so the Israelites cried out to the LORD.

7 When Israel cried out to the LORD because of Midian, 8 he sent a prophet to the Israelites who said to them, "The

19 The kings came and they fought,
  how they fought, those kings of Canaan,
at Taanach, near the Waters of Megiddo,
  but no booty of silver did they take!
20 The stars fought from heaven,
  from their orbits they fought against Sisera.
21 The torrent of Kishon swept them away,
  the torrent of old, the torrent of Kishon.
  — March on, be strong my soul!

22 The horses' hooves then hammer the ground:
  galloping, galloping go his steeds.
23 'Curse Meroz,' said the Angel of Yahweh,
  'curse, curse the people living there
for not having come to Yahweh's help,
  to Yahweh's help as warriors!'

24 Most blessed of women be Jael
  (the wife of Heber the Kenite);
  of tent-dwelling women, may she be most blessed!
25 He asked for water; she gave him milk;
  she offered him curds in a lordly dish.
26 She reached her hand out to seize the peg,
  her right hand to seize the workman's mallet.

She hammered Sisera, she crushed his head,
  she pierced his temple and shattered it.
27 Between her feet, he crumpled, he fell, he lay;
  at her feet, he crumpled, he fell.
  Where he crumpled, there he fell, destroyed.

28 At the window, she leans and watches,
  Sisera's mother, through the lattice,
'Why is his chariot so long coming?
  Why so delayed the hoof-beats from his chariot?'
29 The wisest of her ladies answers,
  and she to herself repeats,
30 'Are they not collecting and sharing out the spoil:
  a girl, two girls for each warrior;
a booty of coloured and embroidered stuff for
  Sisera,
one scarf, two embroidered scarves for me!'
31 So perish all your enemies, Yahweh!
  And let those who love you be like the sun
  when he emerges in all his strength!

And the country had peace for forty years.

6 The Israelites did what is evil in Yahweh's eyes, and for seven years Yahweh handed them over to Midian; 2 and Midian bore down heavily on Israel. To escape from the Midianites[e] the Israelites used the mountain clefts and the caves and shelters. 3 Whenever Israel sowed seed the Midianites would march up with Amalek and the sons of the East. They would march on Israel. 4 They would pitch camp on their territory and destroy the produce of the country as far as Gaza. They left Israel nothing to live on, not a sheep or an ox or a donkey, 5 for they came up as thick as locusts with their cattle and their tents; they and their camels were innumerable, they invaded the country to pillage it. 6 Thus, Midian brought Israel to great distress, and the Israelites cried to Yahweh.

7 When the Israelites cried to Yahweh because of Midian, 8 Yahweh sent a prophet to the Israelites. He said to them,

NEW REVISED STANDARD VERSION

and he said to them, "Thus says the LORD, the God of Israel: I led you up from Egypt, and brought you out of the house of slavery; 9 and I delivered you from the hand of the Egyptians, and from the hand of all who oppressed you, and drove them out before you, and gave you their land; 10 and I said to you, 'I am the LORD your God; you shall not pay reverence to the gods of the Amorites, in whose land you live.' But you have not given heed to my voice."

11 Now the angel of the LORD came and sat under the oak at Ophrah, which belonged to Joash the Abiezrite, as his son Gideon was beating out wheat in the wine press, to hide it from the Midianites. 12 The angel of the LORD appeared to him and said, "The LORD is with you, you mighty warrior." 13 Gideon answered him, "But sir, if the LORD is with us, why then has all this happened to us? And where are all his wonderful deeds that our ancestors recounted to us, saying, 'Did not the LORD bring us up from Egypt?' But now the LORD has cast us off, and given us into the hand of Midian." 14 Then the LORD turned to him and said, "Go in might of yours and deliver Israel from the hand of Midian; I hereby commission you." 15 He responded, "But sir, how can I deliver Israel? My clan is the weakest in Manasseh, and I am the least in my family." 16 The LORD said to him, "But I will be with you, and you shall strike down the Midianites, every one of them." 17 Then he said to him, "If now I have found favor with you, then show me a sign that it is you who speak with me. 18 Do not depart from here until I come to you, and bring out my present, and set it before you." And he said, "I will stay until you return."

19 So Gideon went into his house and prepared a kid, and unleavened cakes from an ephah of flour; the meat he put in a basket, and the broth he put in a pot, and brought them to him under the oak and presented them. 20 The angel of God said to him, "Take the meat and the unleavened cakes, and put them on this rock, and pour out the broth." And he did so. 21 Then the angel of the LORD reached out the tip of the staff that was in his hand, and touched the meat and the unleavened cakes; and fire sprang up from the rock and consumed the meat and the unleavened cakes; and the angel of the LORD vanished from his sight. 22 Then Gideon perceived that it was the angel of the LORD; and Gideon said, "Help me, Lord GOD! For I have seen the angel of the LORD face to face." 23 But the LORD said to him, "Peace be to you; do not fear, you shall not die." 24 Then Gideon built an altar there to the LORD, and called it, The LORD is peace. To this day it still stands at Ophrah, which belongs to the Abiezrites.

25 That night the LORD said to him, "Take your father's bull, the second bull seven years old, and pull down the altar of Baal that belongs to your father, and cut down the sacred poles that is beside it; 26 and build an altar to the LORD your God on the top of the stronghold here, in proper order; then take the second bull, and offer it as a burnt offering with the wood of the sacred poles that you shall cut down." 27 So Gideon took ten of his servants, and did as the LORD had told him; but because he was too afraid of his family and the townspeople to do it by day, he did it by night.

28 When the townspeople rose early in the morning, the altar of Baal was broken down, and the sacred poles beside it was cut down, and the second bull was offered on the altar that had been built. 29 So they said to one another, "Who has done this?" After searching and inquiring, they were told, "Gideon son of Joash did it." 30 Then the townspeople said to Joash, "Bring out your son, so that he may die, for he has pulled down the altar of Baal and cut down the sacred poles beside it." 31 But Joash said to all who were arrayed against

s Heb Asherah

REVISED ENGLISH BIBLE

prophet who said to them, 'These are the words of the LORD the God of Israel: I brought you up from Egypt, that land of slavery. 9 I rescued you from the Egyptians and from all your oppressors, whom I drove out before you to give you their lands. 10 I said to you, "I am the LORD your God: do not worship the gods of the Amorites in whose country you are settling." But you did not listen to me.'

11 The angel of the LORD came to Ophrah and sat under the terebinth which belonged to Joash the Abiezrite. While Gideon son of Joash was threshing wheat in the winepress, so that he might keep it out of sight of the Midianites, 12 the angel of the LORD appeared to him and said, 'You are a brave man, and the LORD is with you.' 13 'Pray, my lord,' said Gideon, 'if the LORD really is with us, why has all this happened to us? What has become of all those wonderful deeds of his, of which we have heard from our forefathers, when they told us how the LORD brought us up from Egypt? But now the LORD has cast us off and delivered us into the power of the Midianites.'

14 The LORD turned to him and said, 'Go and use this strength of yours to free Israel from the Midianites. It is I who send you.' 15 Gideon said, 'Pray, my lord, how can I save Israel? Look at my clan: it is the weakest in Manasseh, and I am the least in my father's family.' 16 The LORD answered, 'I shall be with you, and you will lay low all Midian as one man.' 17 He replied, 'If I stand so well with you, give me a sign that it is you who speak to me. 18 Do not leave this place, I beg you, until I come with my gift and lay it before you.' He answered, 'I shall stay until you return.'

19 So Gideon went in, and prepared a young goat and made an ephah of flour into unleavened bread. He put the meat in a basket, poured the broth into a pot, and brought it out to the angel under the terebinth. As he approached, 20 the angel of God said to him, 'Take the meat and the bread, and put them here on the rock and pour out the broth.' When he did so, 21 the angel of the LORD reached out the staff in his hand and touched the meat and bread with the tip of it. Fire sprang up from the rock and consumed the meat and the bread. Then the angel of the LORD vanished from his sight. 22 Gideon realized it was the angel of the LORD and said, 'Alas, Lord GOD! Then it is true: I have seen the angel of the LORD face to face.' 23 But the LORD said to him, 'Peace be with you! Do not be afraid; you shall not die.' 24 Gideon built an altar there to the LORD and named it The LORD is Peace. It stands to this day at Ophrah-of-the-Abiezrites.

25 That night the LORD said to Gideon, 'Take a young bull of your father's, the yearling bull; tear down the altar of Baal belonging to your father, and cut down the sacred pole which stands beside it. 26 Then build an altar of the proper pattern to the LORD your God on the top of this earthwork; take the yearling bull and offer it as a whole-offering with the wood of the sacred pole that you cut down.' 27 Gideon took ten of his servants and did as the LORD had told him; but because he was afraid of his father's family and the people of the town, he did it by night and not by day. 28 When the people rose early next morning, they found the altar of Baal overturned, the sacred pole which had stood beside it cut down, and the yearling bull offered up as a whole-offering on an altar which had been built. 29 They asked among themselves who had done it, and, after searching enquiries, they declared it was Gideon son of Joash. 30 The townspeople said to Joash, 'Bring out your son. He has overturned the altar of Baal and cut down the sacred pole beside it; he must die.' 31 But as they crowded round

6:25 **the yearling bull:** *prob. rdg; Heb.* the second bull seven years old. **beside:** *or* on. 6:26 **of . . . pattern:** *or* with the stones in rows. **earthwork:** *or* stronghold *or* refuge.

LORD, the God of Israel, says: I led you up from Egypt; I brought you out of the place of slavery. 9 I rescued you from the power of Egypt and of all your other oppressors. I drove them out before you and gave you their land. 10 And I said to you: I, the LORD, am your God; you shall not venerate the gods of the Amorites in whose land you are dwelling. But you did not obey me."

11 Then the angel of the LORD came and sat under the terebinth in Ophrah that belonged to Joash the Abiezrite. While his son Gideon was beating out wheat in the wine press to save it from the Midianites, 12 the angel of the LORD appeared to him and said, "The LORD is with you, O champion!" 13 "My LORD," Gideon said to him, "if the LORD is with us, why has all this happened to us? Where are his wondrous deeds of which our fathers told us when they said, 'Did not the LORD bring us up from Egypt?' For now the LORD has abandoned us and has delivered us into the power of Midian." 14 The LORD turned to him and said, "Go with the strength you have and save Israel from the power of Midian. It is I who send you." 15 But he answered him, "Please, my lord, how can I save Israel? My family is the meanest in Manasseh, and I am the most insignificant in my father's house." 16 "I shall be with you," the LORD said to him, "and you will cut down Midian to the last man." 17 He answered him, "If I find favor with you, give me a sign that you are speaking with me. 18 Do not depart from here, I pray you, until I come back to you and bring out my offering and set it before you." He answered, "I will await your return."

19 So Gideon went off and prepared a kid and an ephah of flour in the form of unleavened cakes. Putting the meat in a basket and the broth in a pot, he brought them out to him under the terebinth and presented them. 20 The angel of God said to him, "Take the meat and unleavened cakes and lay them on this rock; then pour out the broth." When he had done so, 21 the angel of the LORD stretched out the tip of the staff he held, and touched the meat and unleavened cakes. Thereupon a fire came up from the rock which consumed the meat and unleavened cakes, and the angel of the LORD disappeared from sight. 22 Gideon, now aware that it had been the angel of the LORD, said, "Alas, Lord, GOD, that I have seen the angel of the LORD face to face!" 23 The LORD answered him, "Be calm, do not fear. You shall not die." 24 So Gideon built there an altar to the LORD and called it Yahweh-shalom. To this day it is still in Ophrah of the Abiezrites.

25 That same night the LORD said to him, "Take the seven-year-old spare bullock and destroy your father's altar to Baal and cut down the sacred pole that is by it. 26 You shall build, instead, the proper kind of altar to the LORD, your God, on top of this stronghold. Then take the spare bullock and offer it as a holocaust on the wood from the sacred pole you have cut down." 27 So Gideon took ten of his servants and did as the LORD had commanded him. But through fear of his family and of the townspeople, he would not do it by day, but did it at night. 28 Early the next morning the townspeople found that the altar of Baal had been destroyed, the sacred pole near it cut down, and the spare bullock offered on the altar that was built. 29 They asked one another, "Who did this?" Their inquiry led them to the conclusion that Gideon, son of Joash, had done it. 30 So the townspeople said to Joash, "Bring out your son that he may die, for he has destroyed the altar of Baal and has cut down the sacred pole that was near it." 31 But Joash replied to all

'This is what Yahweh, God of Israel, says, "It was I who brought you out of Egypt, and led you out of the place of slave-labour. 9 I rescued you from the power of the Egyptians and from the power of all who oppressed you. I drove them out before you and gave you their country to yours. 10 And I said to you: I am Yahweh your God. You are not to fear the gods of the Amorites in whose country you are now living. But you have not listened to my voice." '

11 The Angel of Yahweh came and sat under the terebinth at Ophrah which belonged to Joash of Abiezer. Gideon his son was threshing wheat inside the wine-press, to keep it hidden from Midian, 12 and the Angel of Yahweh appeared to him and said, 'Yahweh is with you, valiant warrior!' 13 Gideon replied, 'Excuse me, my lord, but if Yahweh is with us, why is all this happening to us? And where are all his miracles which our ancestors used to tell us about when they said, "Did not Yahweh bring us out of Egypt?" But now Yahweh has deserted us; he has abandoned us to Midian.'

14 At this, Yahweh turned to him and said, 'Go in this strength of yours, and you will rescue Israel from the power of Midian. Am I not sending you myself?' 15 Gideon replied, 'Forgive me, my lord, but how can I deliver Israel? My clan is the weakest in Manasseh and I am the least important of my father's family.' 16 Yahweh replied, 'I shall be with you and you will crush Midian as though it were one man.' 17 Gideon said, 'If I have found favour in your sight, give me a sign that you are speaking to me. 18 Please do not go away from here until I come back to you, bringing you my offering and laying it before you.' And he replied, 'I shall stay until you come back.'

19 Gideon went away, he prepared a young goat and from an *ephah* of flour he made unleavened cakes. He put the meat into a basket and the broth into a pot, then brought it all to him under the terebinth. As he approached, 20 the Angel of Yahweh said to him, 'Take the meat and unleavened cakes, put them on this rock and pour the broth over them.' Gideon did so. 21 The Angel of Yahweh then stretched out the tip of the staff which he was carrying, and touched the meat and unleavened cakes. Fire sprang from the rock and consumed the meat and unleavened cakes, and the Angel of Yahweh vanished before his eyes. 22 Gideon then knew that this was the Angel of Yahweh, and he said, 'Alas, my Lord Yahweh! Now I have seen the Angel of Yahweh face to face!' 23 Yahweh answered, 'Peace be with you; have no fear; you will not die.' 24 Gideon built an altar there to Yahweh and called it Yahweh-Peace. This altar stands in our own day at Ophrah of Abiezer.

25 Now that night, Yahweh said to Gideon, 'Take your father's bull, the seven-year-old bull, and pull down the altar to Baal belonging to your father and cut down the sacred pole beside it. 26 Then, on top of this strong-point, build a proper altar to Yahweh your God. Then take the bull and burn it as a burnt offering on the wood of the sacred pole which you have cut down.' 27 Gideon then took ten of his servants and did as Yahweh had ordered him. But, being too frightened of his family and of the townspeople to do it in daylight, he did it at night. 28 Next morning, when the townspeople got up, they found that the altar to Baal had been destroyed, the sacred pole standing beside it had been cut down and the bull had been sacrificed as a burnt offering on the newly built altar. 29 'Who has done this?' they asked one another. They searched, made enquiries and declared, 'Gideon son of Joash has done it.' 30 The townspeople then said to Joash, 'Bring out your son; he must die for having destroyed Baal's altar and cut down the sacred pole which stood beside it.' 31 To the people all crowding round him,

NEW REVISED STANDARD VERSION

him, "Will you contend for Baal? Or will you defend his cause? Whoever contends for him shall be put to death by morning. If he is a god, let him contend for himself, because his altar has been pulled down." 32 Therefore on that day Gideon[t] was called Jerubbaal, that is to say, "Let Baal contend against him," because he pulled down his altar.

33 Then all the Midianites and the Amalekites and the people of the east came together, and crossing the Jordan they encamped in the Valley of Jezreel. 34 But the spirit of the LORD took possession of Gideon; and he sounded the trumpet, and the Abiezrites were called out to follow him. 35 He sent messengers throughout all Manasseh, and they too were called out to follow him. He also sent messengers to Asher, Zebulun, and Naphtali, and they went up to meet them.

36 Then Gideon said to God, "In order to see whether you will deliver Israel by my hand, as you have said, 37 I am going to lay a fleece of wool on the threshing floor; if there is dew on the fleece alone, and it is dry on all the ground, then I shall know that you will deliver Israel by my hand, as you have said." 38 And it was so. When he rose early next morning and squeezed the fleece, he wrung enough dew from the fleece to fill a bowl with water. 39 Then Gideon said to God, "Do not let your anger burn against me, let me speak one more time; let me, please, make trial with the fleece just once more; let it be dry only on the fleece, and on all the ground let there be dew." 40 And God did so that night. It was dry on the fleece only, and on all the ground there was dew.

7 Then Jerubbaal (that is, Gideon) and all the troops that were with him rose early and encamped beside the spring of Harod; and the camp of Midian was north of them, below[u] the hill of Moreh, in the valley.

2 The LORD said to Gideon, "The troops with you are too many for me to give the Midianites into their hand. Israel would only take the credit away from me, saying, 'My own hand has delivered me.' 3 Now therefore proclaim this in the hearing of the troops, 'Whoever is fearful and trembling, let him return home.' " Thus Gideon sifted them out;[v] twenty-two thousand returned, and ten thousand remained.

4 Then the LORD said to Gideon, "The troops are still too many; take them down to the water and I will sift them out for you there. When I say, 'This one shall go with you,' he shall go with you; and when I say, 'This one shall not go with you,' he shall not go." 5 So he brought the troops down to the water; and the LORD said to Gideon, "All those who lap the water with their tongues, as a dog laps, you shall put to one side; all those who kneel down to drink, putting their hands to their mouths,[w] you shall put to the other side." 6 The number of those that lapped was three hundred; but all the rest of the troops knelt down to drink water. 7 Then the LORD said to Gideon, "With the three hundred that lapped I will deliver you, and give the Midianites into your hand. Let all the others go to their homes." 8 So he took the jars of the troops from their hands,[x] and their trumpets; and he sent all the rest of Israel back to their own tents, but retained the three hundred. The camp of Midian was below him in the valley.

9 That same night the LORD said to him, "Get up, attack the camp; for I have given it into your hand. 10 But if you fear to attack, go down to the camp with your servant Purah;

REVISED ENGLISH BIBLE

him Joash retorted, 'Are you pleading Baal's cause then? Do you think it is for you to save him? Whoever pleads his cause shall be put to death at dawn. If Baal is a god, and someone has torn down his altar, let him take up his own cause.' 32 That day Joash named Gideon Jerubbaal, saying, 'Let Baal plead his own cause against this man, for he has torn down his altar.'

33 When all the Midianites, the Amalekites, and the eastern tribes joined forces, crossed the river, and encamped in the valley of Jezreel, 34 the spirit of the LORD took possession of Gideon. He sounded the trumpet to call out the Abiezrites to follow him, 35 and sent messengers all through Manasseh; and they too rallied to him. He sent messengers to Asher, Zebulun, and Naphtali, and they advanced to meet the others.

36 Gideon said to God, 'If indeed you are going to deliver Israel through me as you promised, 37 I shall put a fleece of wool on the threshing-floor, and if there is dew on the fleece while all the ground is dry, then I shall be sure that it is through me you will deliver Israel as you promised.' 38 And that is what happened. When he rose early next day and wrung out the fleece, he squeezed enough dew from it to fill a bowl with water. 39 Gideon then said to God, 'Do not be angry with me, but give me leave to speak once again. Allow me, I pray, to make one more test with the fleece. This time let the fleece be dry, and all the ground be covered with dew.' 40 God let it be so that night: the fleece alone was dry, and all over the ground there was dew.

7 Early next morning Jerubbaal, that is Gideon, with all his troops pitched camp at En-harod; the Midianite encampment was in the valley to the north of his by the hill at Moreh. 2 The LORD said to Gideon, 'Those with you are more than I need to deliver Midian into their hands: Israel might claim the glory for themselves and say that it is their own strength that has given them the victory. 3 Make a proclamation now to the army to say that anyone who is afraid or anxious is to leave Mount Galud at once and go home.' Twenty-two thousand of them went, and ten thousand remained.

4 'There are still too many,' said the LORD to Gideon. 'Bring them down to the water, and I shall separate them for you there. If I say to you, "This man shall go with you," he shall go; and if I say, "This man shall not go," he shall not go.' 5 When Gideon brought the men down to the water, the LORD said to him, 'Make every man who laps the water with his tongue like a dog stand on one side, and on the other every man who kneels down and drinks.' 6 The number of those who lapped, putting their hands to their mouths, was three hundred; all the rest had gone down on their knees to drink. 7 The LORD said, 'By means of the three hundred men who lapped I shall save you and give Midian into your power; the rest may go home.' 8 Gideon sent all these Israelites home, but he kept the three hundred, and they took with them the jars and the trumpets which the people had.

The Midianite camp was below him in the valley, 9 and that night the LORD said to Gideon, 'Go down at once and attack the camp, for I have delivered it into your hands. 10 If you are afraid to do so, then go down first with your servant

---

[t] Heb he   [u] Heb from   [v] Cn: Heb home, and depart from Mount Gilead'"   [w] Heb places the words putting their hands to their mouths after the word lapped in verse 6   [x] Cn: Heb So the people took provisions in their hands

6:32 Jerubbaal: that is Let Baal plead.   6:34 took possession of: lit. clothed itself with.   7:1 En-harod: that is Spring of Fright.
7:3 Mount Galud: prob. rdg; Heb. Mount Gilead.   7:5 on the other: so Gk; Heb. omits.   7:8 jars: prob. rdg; Heb. provisions.

who were standing around him, "Do you intend to act in Baal's stead, or be his champion? If anyone acts for him, he shall be put to death by morning. If he whose altar has been destroyed is a god, let him act for himself!" 32 So on that day Gideon was called Jerubbaal, because of the words, "Let Baal take action against him, since he destroyed his altar."

33 Then all Midian and Amalek and the Kedemites mustered and crossed over into the valley of Jezreel, where they encamped. 34 The spirit of the LORD enveloped Gideon; he blew the horn that summoned Abiezer to follow him. 35 He sent messengers, too, throughout Manasseh, which also obeyed his summons; through Asher, Zebulun and Naphtali, likewise, he sent messengers and these tribes advanced to meet the others. 36 Gideon said to God, "If indeed you are going to save Israel through me, as you promised, 37 I am putting this woolen fleece on the threshing floor. If dew comes on the fleece alone, while all the ground is dry, I shall know that you will save Israel through me, as you promised." 38 That is what took place. Early the next morning he wrung the dew from the fleece, squeezing out of it a bowlful of water. 39 Gideon then said to God, "Do not be angry with me if I speak once more. Let me make just one more test with the fleece. Let the fleece alone be dry, but let there be dew on all the ground." 40 That night God did so; the fleece alone was dry, but there was dew on all the ground.

7 Early the next morning Jerubbaal (that is, Gideon) encamped by En-harod with all his soldiers. The camp of Midian was in the valley north of Gibeath-hammoreh. 2 The LORD said to Gideon, "You have too many soldiers with you for me to deliver Midian into their power, lest Israel vaunt itself against me and say, 'My own power brought me the victory.' 3 Now proclaim to all the soldiers, 'If anyone is afraid or fearful, let him leave.' " When Gideon put them to this test on the mountain, twenty-two thousand of the soldiers left, but ten thousand remained. 4 The LORD said to Gideon, "There are still too many soldiers. Lead them down to the water and I will test them for you there. If I tell you that a certain man is to go with you, he must go with you. But no one is to go if I tell you he must not." 5 When Gideon led the soldiers down to the water, the LORD said to him, "You shall set to one side everyone who laps up the water as a dog does with its tongue; to the other, everyone who kneels down to drink." 6 Those who lapped up the water raised to their mouths by hand numbered three hundred, but all the rest of the soldiers knelt down to drink the water. 7 The LORD said to Gideon, "By means of the three hundred who lapped up the water I will save you and will deliver Midian into your power. So let all the other soldiers go home." 8 Their horns, and such supplies as the soldiers had with them, were taken up, and Gideon ordered the rest of the Israelites to their tents, but kept the three hundred men. Now the camp of Midian was beneath him in the valley.

9 That night the LORD said to Gideon, "Go, descend on the camp, for I have delivered it up to you. 10 If you are afraid to attack, go down to the camp with your aide Purah.

Joash replied, 'Is it your job to plead for Baal? Is it your job to champion his cause? (Anyone who pleads for Baal must be put to death before dawn.) If he is a god, let him plead for himself, now that Gideon has destroyed his altar.' 32 That day, Gideon was given the name Jerubbaal, because, they said, 'Baal must plead against him, because he has destroyed his altar!'

33 All Midian and Amalek and the sons of the East joined forces and, having crossed the Jordan, pitched camp in the plain of Jezreel. 34 And the spirit of Yahweh clothed Gideon around; he sounded the horn and Abiezer rallied behind him. 35 He sent messengers throughout Manasseh, and Manasseh too rallied behind him; he sent messengers to Asher, Zebulun and Naphtali, and they marched out to meet him. 36 Gideon said to God, 'If it is really you delivering Israel by means of me, as you have said, 37 look, I am going to put a woollen fleece on the threshing-floor; if there is dew only on the fleece and all the ground stays dry, then I shall know that you will deliver Israel by means of me, as you have said.' 38 And so it happened. Early next morning, Gideon got up, squeezed the fleece and wrung enough dew out of the fleece to fill a cup. 39 Gideon then said to God, 'Do not be angry with me if I speak just once more. Allow me to make the fleece-test just once more: let the fleece alone be dry and there be dew all over the ground!' 40 And God did so that night. The fleece alone stayed dry, and there was dew all over the ground.

7 Jerubbaal (that is, Gideon) got up very early, as did all the people who were with him; he pitched camp at En-Harod; the camp of Midian was north of his, under the Hill of Moreh in the valley. 2 Yahweh then said to Gideon, 'There are too many people with you for me to put Midian into their power; Israel might claim the credit for themselves at my expense: they might say, "My own hand has rescued me." 3 So now make this proclamation to the people, "Anyone trembling with fear is to go back and watch from Mount Gilboa." ' Twenty-two thousand of the people went back, and ten thousand remained. 4 Yahweh said to Gideon, 'There are still too many people. Take them down to the waterside and I shall sort them out for you there. If I say of someone, "He is to go with you," that man is to go with you. And if I say of anyone, "He is not to go with you," that man is not to go.' 5 So Gideon took the people down to the waterside, and Yahweh said to him, 'All those who lap the water with their tongues, as a dog laps, put these on one side. And all those who kneel down to drink, put these on the other side.' 6 The number of those who lapped with their hands to their mouth was three hundred; all the rest of the people had knelt to drink. 7 Yahweh then said to Gideon, 'With the three hundred who lapped the water, I shall rescue you and put Midian into your power. Let the people as a whole disperse to their homes.' 8 So they took the people's provisions and their horns, and then Gideon sent all the Israelites back to their tents, keeping only the three hundred. The camp of Midian was below his in the valley.

9 Now it happened, that same night, that Yahweh said to him, 'Get up and go down to the camp. I am putting it into your power. 10 If, however, you are nervous about going down, go down to the camp with your servant Purah; 11 lis

NEW REVISED STANDARD VERSION

11 and you shall hear what they say, and afterward your hands shall be strengthened to attack the camp." Then he went down with his servant Purah to the outposts of the armed men that were in the camp. 12 The Midianites and the Amalekites and all the people of the east lay along the valley as thick as locusts; and their camels were without number, countless as the sand on the seashore. 13 When Gideon arrived, there was a man telling a dream to his comrade; and he said, "I had a dream, and in it a cake of barley bread tumbled into the camp of Midian, and came to the tent, and struck it so that it fell; it turned upside down, and the tent collapsed." 14 And his comrade answered, "This is no other than the sword of Gideon son of Joash, a man of Israel; into his hand God has given Midian and all the army."

15 When Gideon heard the telling of the dream and its interpretation, he worshiped; and he returned to the camp of Israel, and said, "Get up; for the LORD has given the army of Midian into your hand." 16 After he divided the three hundred men into three companies, and put trumpets into the hands of all of them, and empty jars, with torches inside the jars, 17 he said to them, "Look at me, and do the same; when I come to the outskirts of the camp, do as I do. 18 When I blow the trumpet, I and all who are with me, then you also blow the trumpets around the whole camp, and shout, 'For the LORD and for Gideon!'"

19 So Gideon and the hundred who were with him came to the outskirts of the camp at the beginning of the middle watch, when they had just set the watch; and they blew trumpets and smashed the jars that were in their hands. 20 So the three companies blew the trumpets and broke the jars, holding in their left hands the torches, and in their right hands the trumpets to blow; and they cried, "A sword for the LORD and for Gideon!" 21 Every man stood in his place all around the camp, and all the men in camp ran; they cried out and fled. 22 When they blew the three hundred trumpets, the LORD set every man's sword against his fellow and against all the army; and the army fled as far as Beth-shittah toward Zererah,*y* as far as the border of Abel-meholah, by Tabbath. 23 And the men of Israel were called out from Naphtali and from Asher and from all Manasseh, and they pursued after the Midianites.

24 Then Gideon sent messengers throughout all the hill country of Ephraim, saying, "Come down against the Midianites and seize the waters against them, as far as Beth-barah, and also the Jordan." So all the men of Ephraim were called out, and they seized the waters as far as Beth-barah, and also the Jordan. 25 They captured the two captains of Midian, Oreb and Zeeb; they killed Oreb at the rock of Oreb, and Zeeb they killed at the wine press of Zeeb, as they pursued the Midianites. They brought the heads of Oreb and Zeeb to Gideon beyond the Jordan.

8 Then the Ephraimites said to him, "What have you done to us, not to call us when you went to fight against the Midianites?" And they upbraided him violently. 2 So he said to them, "What have I done now in comparison with you? Is not the gleaning of the grapes of Ephraim better than the vintage of Abiezer? 3 God has given into your hands the captains of Midian, Oreb and Zeeb; what have I been able to do in comparison with you?" When he said this, their anger against him subsided.

4 Then Gideon came to the Jordan and crossed over, he and the three hundred who were with him, exhausted and famished.*z* 5 So he said to the people of Succoth, "Please give some loaves of bread to my followers, for they are exhausted, and I am pursuing Zebah and Zalmunna, the kings of Midian." 6 But the officials of Succoth said, "Do

REVISED ENGLISH BIBLE

Purah, 11 and when you hear what they are saying, that will give you courage to attack the camp.' So he and his servant Purah went down to the outposts of the camp where the fighting men were stationed. 12 The Midianites, the Amalekites, and all the eastern tribes were so many that they lay there in the valley like a swarm of locusts; there was no counting their camels, which in number were like grains of sand on the seashore. 13 As Gideon came close, there was a man telling his comrades about a dream. He said, 'I dreamt that I saw a barley loaf rolling over and over through the Midianite camp; it came to a tent, struck it, and the tent collapsed and turned upside down.' 14 The other answered, 'This can be none other than the sword of Gideon son of Joash the Israelite. God has delivered Midian and the whole army into his hands.'

15 When Gideon heard the account of the dream and its interpretation, he bowed down in worship. Then going back to the Israelite camp he said, 'Let us go! The LORD has delivered the camp of the Midianites into our hands.' 16 He divided the three hundred men into three companies, and furnished every man with a trumpet and an empty jar, with a torch inside each jar. 17 'Watch me,' he said to them. 'When I come to the edge of the camp, do exactly as I do. 18 When I and those with me blow our trumpets, you too all round the camp blow your trumpets and shout, "For the LORD and for Gideon!"'

19 Gideon and the hundred men who were with him reached the outskirts of the camp at the beginning of the middle watch, just after the posting of the sentries. They blew the trumpets and smashed the jars they were holding. 20 All three companies blew their trumpets and smashed their jars; then, grasping the torches in their left hands and the trumpets in their right, they shouted, 'A sword for the LORD and for Gideon!' 21 Every man stood where he was, all round the camp, and the whole camp leapt up in a panic and took flight. 22 When the three hundred blew their trumpets, the LORD set all the men in the camp fighting against each other. They fled as far as Beth-shittah in the direction of Zererah, as far as the ridge of Abel-meholah near Tabbath. 23 The Israelites from Naphtali and Asher and all Manasseh were called out to pursue the Midianites. 24 Gideon also sent messengers throughout the hill-country of Ephraim to say: 'Come down and cut off the Midianites. Hold the fords of the Jordan against them as far as Beth-barah.' So all the Ephraimites when called out held the fords of the Jordan as far as Beth-barah. 25 They captured the two Midianite princes, Oreb and Zeeb. Oreb they killed at the Rock of Oreb, and Zeeb by the Winepress of Zeeb, and they kept up the pursuit of the Midianites; afterwards they brought the heads of Oreb and Zeeb to Gideon on the other side of Jordan.

8 The men of Ephraim said to Gideon, 'Why have you treated us like this? Why did you not summon us when you went to fight Midian?' and they upbraided him fiercely. 2 But he replied, 'What have I now accomplished compared with you? Are not Ephraim's gleanings better than the whole grape harvest of Abiezer? 3 God delivered Oreb and Zeeb, the princes of Midian, into your hands. What have I been able to accomplish compared with you?' At that their anger against him died down.

4 Gideon came to the Jordan, and he and his three hundred men crossed over to continue the pursuit, exhausted though they were. 5 He said to the people of Succoth, 'Will you give my followers some bread? They are exhausted, and I am pursuing Zebah and Zalmunna, the kings of Midian.' 6 But the chief men of Succoth replied, 'Are Zebah and

---

y Another reading is *Zeredah*   *z* Gk: Heb *pursuing*

7:13 **struck it:** *prob. rdg; Heb.* adds and it fell.

11 When you hear what they are saying, you will have the courage to descend on the camp." So he went down with his aide Purah to the outposts of the camp. 12 The Midianites, Amalekites, and all the Kedemites lay in the valley, as numerous as locusts. Nor could their camels be counted, for these were as many as the sands on the seashore. 13 When Gideon arrived, one man was telling another about a dream. "I had a dream," he said, "that a round loaf of barley bread was rolling into the camp of Midian. It came to our tent and struck it, and as it fell it turned the tent upside down." 14 "This can only be the sword of the Israelite Gideon, son of Joash," the other replied. "God has delivered Midian and all the camp into his power." 15 When Gideon heard the description and explanation of the dream, he prostrated himself. Then returning to the camp of Israel, he said, "Arise, for the LORD has delivered the camp of Midian into your power."

16 He divided the three hundred men into three companies, and provided them all with horns and with empty jars and torches inside the jars. 17 "Watch me and follow my lead," he told them. "I shall go to the edge of the camp, and as I do, you must do also. 18 When I and those with me blow horns, you too must blow horns all around the camp and cry out, 'For the LORD and for Gideon!' " 19 So Gideon and the hundred men who were with him came to the edge of the camp at the beginning of the middle watch, just after the posting of the guards. They blew the horns and broke the jars they were holding. 20 All three companies blew horns and broke their jars. They held the torches in their left hands, and in their right the horns they were blowing, and cried out, "A sword for the LORD and Gideon!" 21 They all remained standing in place around the camp, while the whole camp fell to running and shouting and fleeing. 22 But the three hundred men kept blowing the horns, and throughout the camp the LORD set the sword of one against another. The army fled as far as Beth-shittah in the direction of Zarethan, near the border of Abel-meholah at Tabbath.

23 The Israelites were called to arms from Naphtali, from Asher, and from all Manasseh, and they pursued Midian. 24 Gideon also sent messengers throughout the mountain region of Ephraim to say, "Go down to confront Midian, and seize the water courses against them as far as Beth-barah, as well as the Jordan." So all the Ephraimites were called to arms, and they seized the water courses as far as Beth-barah, and the Jordan as well. 25 They captured the two princes of Midian, Oreb and Zeeb, killing Oreb at the rock of Oreb and Zeeb at the wine press of Zeeb. Then they pursued Midian and carried the heads of Oreb and Zeeb to Gideon beyond the Jordan.

8 But the Ephraimites said to him, "What have you done to us, not calling us when you went to fight against Midian?" And they quarrelled bitterly with him. 2 "What have I accomplished now in comparison with you?" he answered them. "Is not the gleaning of Ephraim better than the vintage of Abiezer? 3 Into your power God delivered the princes of Midian, Oreb and Zeeb. What have I been able to do in comparison with you?" When he said this, their anger against him subsided.

4 When Gideon reached the Jordan and crossed it with his three hundred men, they were exhausted and famished. 5 So he said to the men of Succoth, "Will you give my followers some loaves of bread? They are exhausted, and I am pursuing Zebah and Zalmunna, kings of Midian." 6 But the princes of Succoth replied, "Are the hands of Zebah and

ten to what they are saying, and that will encourage you to go down to the camp.' So, with his servant Purah, he went down to the edge of the outposts of the camp.

12 Midian, Amalek and all the sons of the East were deployed in the valley as thick as locusts; their camels were as innumerable as the sand on the seashore. 13 Gideon got there just as a man was telling his comrade a dream; he was saying, 'This was the dream I had: a cake made of barley bread came rolling into the camp of Midian; it came to a tent, struck against it and turned it upside down.' 14 His comrade replied, 'This can only be the sword of Gideon son of Joash the Israelite. God has put Midian and the whole camp into his power.' 15 When Gideon heard the dream thus told and interpreted, he bowed in reverence; he then went back to the camp of Israel and said, 'On your feet, for Yahweh has put the camp of Midian into your power!'

16 Gideon then divided his three hundred men into three groups. To each he gave a horn and an empty pitcher, with a torch inside each pitcher. 17 He said to them, 'Watch me, and do as I do. When I reach the edge of the camp, whatever I do, you must do also. 18 I shall blow my horn, and so will all those who are with me; you too will then blow your horns all round the camp and shout, "For Yahweh and for Gideon!" '

19 Gideon and his hundred companions reached the edge of the camp at the beginning of the middle watch, when the new sentries had just been posted; they blew their horns and smashed the pitchers in their hands. 20 The three groups blew their horns and smashed their pitchers; with their left hands they grasped the torches, with their right hands the horns for blowing them; and they shouted, 'The sword for Yahweh and for Gideon!' 21 And they stood still, spaced out round the camp. The whole camp was thrown into confusion and the Midianites fled, shouting. 22 While the three hundred blew their horns, Yahweh made each man turn his sword against his comrade throughout the entire camp. They all fled as far as Beth-ha-Shittah in the direction of Zarethan, as far as the bank of Abel-Meholah opposite Tabbath.

23 The men of Israel mustered from Naphtali, Asher and all Manasseh, and pursued Midian. 24 Gideon sent messengers throughout the highlands of Ephraim to say, 'Come down to meet Midian, seize the water-points ahead of them as far as Beth-Barah and the Jordan.' All the men of Ephraim mustered and seized the water-points as far as Beth-Barah and the Jordan. 25 They captured the two Midianite chieftains, Oreb and Zeeb; they killed Oreb at Oreb's Rock and Zeeb at Zeeb's Winepress.ʄ They pursued Midian; and they brought the heads of Oreb and Zeeb to Gideon on the other side of the Jordan.

8 Now the men of Ephraim said to Gideon, 'What do you mean by treating us like this, not summoning us when you went to fight Midian?' And they reproached him bitterly. 2 He replied, 'What have I achieved, compared with you? Is not the gleaning of Ephraim's grapes better than the vintage of Abiezer? 3 God delivered Oreb and Zeeb, the chieftains of Midian, into your power. What was I able to do, in comparison with what you have done?' At these words, their anger with him died down.

4 Gideon reached the Jordan and crossed it, but he and his three hundred companions were exhausted with the pursuit. 5 So he said to the men of Succoth, 'Please give my followers some loaves of bread, since they are exhausted, and I am pursuing Zebah and Zalmunna the kings of Midian.' 6 The headmen of Succoth replied, 'Are the hands of Zebah and

ʄ 7 Fragment explaining two place-names and independent of the main story.

you already have in your possession the hands of Zebah and Zalmunna, that we should give bread to your army?" 7 Gideon replied, "Well then, when the LORD has given Zebah and Zalmunna into my hand, I will trample your flesh on the thorns of the wilderness and on briers." 8 From there he went up to Penuel, and made the same request of them; and the people of Penuel answered him as the people of Succoth had answered. 9 So he said to the people of Penuel, "When I come back victorious, I will break down this tower."

10 Now Zebah and Zalmunna were in Karkor with their army, about fifteen thousand men, all who were left of all the army of the people of the east; for one hundred twenty thousand men bearing arms had fallen. 11 So Gideon went up by the caravan route east of Nobah and Jogbehah, and attacked the army; for the army was off its guard. 12 Zebah and Zalmunna fled; and he pursued them and took the two kings of Midian, Zebah and Zalmunna, and threw all the army into a panic.

13 When Gideon son of Joash returned from the battle by the ascent of Heres, 14 he caught a young man, one of the people of Succoth, and questioned him; and he listed for him the officials and elders of Succoth, seventy-seven people. 15 Then he came to the people of Succoth, and said, "Here are Zebah and Zalmunna, about whom you taunted me, saying, 'Do you already have in your possession the hands of Zebah and Zalmunna, that we should give bread to your troops who are exhausted?' " 16 So he took the elders of the city and he took thorns of the wilderness and briers and with them he trampled[a] the people of Succoth. 17 He also broke down the tower of Penuel, and killed the men of the city.

18 Then he said to Zebah and Zalmunna, "What about the men whom you killed at Tabor?" They answered, "As you are, so were they, every one of them; they resembled the sons of a king." 19 And he replied, "They were my brothers, the sons of my mother; as the LORD lives, if you had saved them alive, I would not kill you." 20 So he said to Jether his firstborn, "Go kill them!" But the boy did not draw his sword, for he was afraid, because he was still a boy. 21 Then Zebah and Zalmunna said, "You come and kill us; for as the man is, so is his strength." So Gideon proceeded to kill Zebah and Zalmunna; and he took the crescents that were on the necks of their camels.

22 Then the Israelites said to Gideon, "Rule over us, you and your son and your grandson also; for you have delivered us out of the hand of Midian." 23 Gideon said to them, "I will not rule over you, and my son will not rule over you; the LORD will rule over you." 24 Then Gideon said to them, "Let me make a request of you; each of you give me an earring he has taken as booty." (For the enemy[b] had golden earrings, because they were Ishmaelites.) 25 "We will willingly give them," they answered. So they spread a garment, and each threw into it an earring he had taken as booty. 26 The weight of the golden earrings that he requested was one thousand seven hundred shekels of gold (apart from the crescents and the pendants and the purple garments worn by the kings of Midian, and the collars that were on the necks of their camels). 27 Gideon made an ephod of it and put it in his town, in Ophrah; and all Israel prostituted themselves to it there, and it became a snare to Gideon and to his family. 28 So Midian was subdued before the Israelites, and they lifted up their heads no more. So the land had rest forty years in the days of Gideon.

29 Jerubbaal son of Joash went to live in his own house. 30 Now Gideon had seventy sons, his own offspring, for he had many wives. 31 His concubine who was in Shechem also bore him a son, and he named him Abimelech. 32 Then

Zalmunna already in your hands, that we should give bread to your troops?' 7 Gideon said, 'For that, when the LORD delivers Zebah and Zalmunna into my hands, I shall thresh your bodies with desert thorns and briars.' 8 He went on from there to Penuel and made the same request; the people of Penuel gave the same answer as had the people of Succoth. 9 He said to them, 'When I return victorious, I shall pull down your tower.'

10 Zebah and Zalmunna were at Karkor with an army of about fifteen thousand men. Those were all that remained of the entire host of the eastern tribes, a hundred and twenty thousand warriors having fallen in battle. 11 Gideon advanced along the track used by the tent-dwellers east of Nobah and Jogbehah, and his attack caught the enemy off guard. 12 Zebah and Zalmunna fled; but he went in pursuit of the Midianite kings and captured them both; and their whole army melted away.

13 As Gideon son of Joash was returning from battle by the ascent of Heres, 14 he caught a young man from Succoth. When questioned the young man listed for him the names of the rulers of Succoth and its elders, seventy-seven in all. 15 Gideon then came to the people of Succoth and said, 'Here are Zebah and Zalmunna, about whom you taunted me. "Are Zebah and Zalmunna already in your hands," you said, "that we should give your exhausted men bread?" ' 16 Then he took the elders of Succoth and inflicted punishment on them with desert thorns and briars. 17 He also pulled down the tower of Penuel and put the men of the town to death.

18 He said to Zebah and Zalmunna, 'What sort of men did you kill in Tabor?' They answered, 'They were like you; every one had the look of a king's son.' 19 'They were my brothers,' he said, 'my mother's sons. I swear by the LORD, if you had let them live I would not have killed you.' 20 Then he said to his eldest son Jether, 'Stand up and kill them.' But he was still only a lad, and did not draw his sword, because he was afraid. 21 Zebah and Zalmunna said, 'Rise up yourself and dispatch us, for you have a man's strength.' So Gideon got up and killed them both, and he took the crescents from the necks of their camels.

22 The Israelites said to Gideon, 'You have saved us from the Midianites; now you be our ruler, you and your son and your grandson.' 23 But Gideon replied, 'I shall not rule over you, nor will my son; the LORD will rule over you.' 24 He went on, 'I have a request to make: will every one of you give me an ear-ring from his booty?' — for the enemy, being Ishmaelites, wore gold ear-rings. 25 They said, 'Of course we shall give them.' So a cloak was spread out and every man threw on to it a gold ear-ring from his booty. 26 The ear-rings he asked for weighed seventeen hundred shekels of gold; this was in addition to the crescents and pendants and the purple robes worn by the Midianite kings, and not counting the chains on the necks of their camels. 27 Gideon made the gold into an ephod which he set up in his own town of Ophrah. All the Israelites went astray by worshipping it, and it became a snare for Gideon and his household.

28 Thus the Midianites were subdued by the Israelites; they could no longer hold up their heads. For forty years the land was at peace, all the lifetime of Gideon, 29 that is Jerubbaal son of Joash; and he retired to his own home. 30 Gideon had seventy sons, his own offspring, for he had many wives. 31 He had a concubine who lived in Shechem, and she also bore him a son, whom he named Abimelech.

---

[a] With verse 7, Compare Gk: Heb he taught   [b] Heb they

8:21 you have: so Gk; Heb. he has.

Zalmunna already in your possession, that we should give food to your army?" 7 Gideon said, "Very well; when the LORD has delivered Zebah and Zalmunna into my power, I will grind your flesh in with the thorns and briers of the desert." 8 He went up from there to Penuel and made the same request of them, but the men of Penuel answered him as had the men of Succoth. 9 So to the men of Penuel, too, he said, "When I return in triumph, I will demolish this tower."

10 Now Zebah and Zalmunna were in Karkor with their force of about fifteen thousand men; these were all who were left of the whole Kedemite army, a hundred and twenty thousand swordsmen having fallen. 11 Gideon went up by the route of the nomads east of Nobah and Jogbehah, and attacked the camp when it felt secure. 12 Zebah and Zalmunna fled. He pursued them and took the two kings of Midian, Zebah and Zalmunna, captive, throwing the entire army into panic.

13 Then Gideon, son of Joash, returned from battle by the pass of Heres. 14 He captured a young man of Succoth, who upon being questioned listed for him the seventy-seven princes and elders of Succoth. 15 So he went to the men of Succoth and said, "Here are Zebah and Zalmunna, with whom you taunted me, 'Are the hands of Zebah and Zalmunna already in your possession, that we should give food to your weary followers?' " 16 He took the elders of the city, and thorns and briers of the desert, and ground these men of Succoth into them. 17 He also demolished the tower of Penuel and slew the men of the city.

18 Then he said to Zebah and Zalmunna, "Where now are the men you killed at Tabor?" "They all resembled you," they replied. "They appeared to be princes." 19 "They were my brothers, my mother's sons," he said. "As the LORD lives, if you had spared their lives, I should not kill you." 20 Then he said to his first-born, Jether, "Go, kill them." Since Jether was still a boy, he was afraid and did not draw his sword. 21 Zebah and Zalmunna said, "Come, kill us yourself, for a man's strength is like the man." So Gideon stepped forward and killed Zebah and Zalmunna. He also took the crescents that were on the necks of their camels.

22 The Israelites then said to Gideon, "Rule over us — you, your son, and your son's son — for you rescued us from the power of Midian." 23 But Gideon answered them, "I will not rule over you, nor shall my son rule over you. The LORD must rule over you."

24 Gideon went on to say, "I should like to make a request of you. Will each of you give me a ring from his booty?" (For being Ishmaelites, the enemy had gold rings.) 25 "We will gladly give them," they replied, and spread out a cloak into which everyone threw a ring from his booty. 26 The gold rings that he requested weighed seventeen hundred gold shekels, in addition to the crescents and pendants, the purple garments worn by the kings of Midian, and the trappings that were on the necks of their camels. 27 Gideon made an ephod out of the gold and placed it in his city Ophrah. However, all Israel paid idolatrous homage to it there, and caused the ruin of Gideon and his family.

28 Thus was Midian brought into subjection by the Israelites; no longer did they hold their heads high. And the land had rest for forty years, during the lifetime of Gideon.

29 Then Jerubbaal, son of Joash, went back home to stay. 30 Now Gideon had seventy sons, his direct descendants, for he had many wives. 31 His concubine who lived in Shechem also bore him a son, whom he named Abimelech. 32 At a

Zalmunna already in your grasp, that we should give bread to your army?' 7 'Very well,' retorted Gideon, 'when Yahweh has put Zebah and Zalmunna into my power, I shall tear your flesh off with desert-thorn and thistles.' 8 From there he went up to Penuel and asked the men of Penuel the same thing; they replied as those of Succoth had done. 9 And to those of Penuel he made a similar retort, 'When I return victorious, I shall destroy this tower.'

10 Zebah and Zalmunna were in Karkor with their army, about fifteen thousand men, all that was left of the entire army of the sons of the East. Of men bearing arms, a hundred and twenty thousand had fallen. 11 Gideon approached them by the tent-dwellers' route, east of Nobah and Jogbehah, and attacked the army when it thought itself in safety. 12 Zebah and Zalmunna fled. He pursued them; he took the two kings of Midian prisoner — Zebah and Zalmunna — and the whole army he routed in panic.

13 After the battle Gideon came back by the Ascent of Heres. 14 He caught a young man, one of the people of Succoth, and questioned him, and the latter wrote down the names of the headmen and elders of Succoth for him — seventy-seven men. 15 Gideon son of Joash then went to the people of Succoth and said, 'Here you see Zebah and Zalmunna, about whom you taunted me and said, "Are the hands of Zebah and Zalmunna already in your grasp, that we should give bread to your exhausted troops?" ' 16 He then seized the elders of the town and, taking desert-thorn and thistles, tore the men of Succoth to pieces. 17 He destroyed the tower of Penuel and slaughtered the townsmen.

18 He then said to Zebah and Zalmunna, 'The men you killed at Tabor — what were they like?' They replied, 'They looked like you. Every one of them carried himself like the son of a king.' 19 Gideon replied, 'They were my brothers, the sons of my own mother; as Yahweh lives, if you had spared their lives I would not kill you.' 20 To Jether his eldest son he said, 'Stand up and kill them!' But the boy did not draw his sword; he dared not; he was still only a lad. 21 Zebah and Zalmunna then said, 'Stand up yourself, and strike us down; for as a man is, so is his strength.' Then Gideon stood up and killed Zebah and Zalmunna; and he took the crescents from round their camels' necks.

22 The men of Israel said to Gideon, 'Rule over us, you, your son and your grandson, since you have rescued us from the power of Midian.' 23 But Gideon replied, 'I will not rule you, neither will my son. Yahweh shall rule you.' 24 Gideon went on, however, 'Let me make you one request. Each of you give me one ring out of his booty' — for the vanquished had had gold rings, being Ishmaelites. 25 'We shall give them gladly,' they replied. So he spread out his cloak, and on it each of them threw a ring from his booty. 26 The weight of the gold rings which he had asked for amounted to seventeen hundred shekels of gold, besides the crescents and the earrings and purple garments worn by the kings of Midian, and besides the collars round their camels' necks. 27 From this Gideon made an *ephod*[g] and set it up in his town, in Ophrah. All Israel, following his example, prostituted themselves to it, and it was a snare for Gideon and his family.

28 Thus Midian was humbled before the Israelites. He did not raise his head again, and the country had peace for forty years, as long as Gideon lived. 29 So Jerubbaal son of Joash went to live at home. 30 Gideon had seventy sons begotten by him, for he had many wives. 31 His concubine, who lived in Shechem, also bore him a son, to whom he gave the name Abimelech. 32 Gideon son of Joash died after a happy

g 8 Here a cult-object, cf. Ex 28:6.

Gideon son of Joash died at a good old age, and was buried in the tomb of his father Joash at Ophrah of the Abiezrites.

33 As soon as Gideon died, the Israelites relapsed and prostituted themselves with the Baals, making Baal-berith their god. 34 The Israelites did not remember the LORD their God, who had rescued them from the hand of all their enemies on every side; 35 and they did not exhibit loyalty to the house of Jerubbaal (that is, Gideon) in return for all the good that he had done to Israel.

9 Now Abimelech son of Jerubbaal went to Shechem to his mother's kinsfolk and said to them and to the whole clan of his mother's family, 2 "Say in the hearing of all the lords of Shechem, 'Which is better for you, that all seventy of the sons of Jerubbaal rule over you, or that one rule over you?' Remember also that I am your bone and your flesh." 3 So his mother's kinsfolk spoke all these words on his behalf in the hearing of all the lords of Shechem; and their hearts inclined to follow Abimelech, for they said, "He is our brother." 4 They gave him seventy pieces of silver out of the temple of Baal-berith with which Abimelech hired worthless and reckless fellows, who followed him. 5 He went to his father's house at Ophrah, and killed his brothers the sons of Jerubbaal, seventy men, on one stone; but Jotham, the youngest son of Jerubbaal, survived, for he hid himself. 6 Then all the lords of Shechem and all Beth-millo came together, and they went and made Abimelech king, by the oak of the pillar[c] at Shechem.

7 When it was told to Jotham, he went and stood on the top of Mount Gerizim, and cried aloud and said to them, "Listen to me, you lords of Shechem, so that God may listen to you.

8 The trees once went out
to anoint a king over themselves.
So they said to the olive tree,
'Reign over us.'
9 The olive tree answered them,
'Shall I stop producing my rich oil
by which gods and mortals are honored,
and go to sway over the trees?'
10 Then the trees said to the fig tree,
'You come and reign over us.'
11 But the fig tree answered them,
'Shall I stop producing my sweetness
and my delicious fruit,
and go to sway over the trees?'
12 Then the trees said to the vine,
'You come and reign over us.'
13 But the vine said to them,
'Shall I stop producing my wine
that cheers gods and mortals,
and go to sway over the trees?'
14 So all the trees said to the bramble,
'You come and reign over us.'
15 And the bramble said to the trees,
'If in good faith you are anointing me king
over you,
then come and take refuge in my shade;
but if not, let fire come out of the bramble
and devour the cedars of Lebanon.'

16 "Now therefore, if you acted in good faith and honor when you made Abimelech king, and if you have dealt well with Jerubbaal and his house, and have done to him as his actions deserved — 17 for my father fought for you, and risked his life, and rescued you from the hand of Midian;

32 Gideon son of Joash died at a ripe old age and was buried in his father's grave at Ophrah-of-the-Abiezrites.

33 After Gideon's death the Israelites again went astray: they worshipped the baalim and made Baal-berith their god. 34 They were unmindful of the LORD their God who had delivered them from all their enemies around them, 35 nor did they show to the family of Jerubbaal, that is Gideon, the loyalty that was due to them for all the good he had done Israel.

9 ABIMELECH son of Jerubbaal went to Shechem to his mother's brothers, and spoke with them and with the rest of the clan of his mother's family. 2 'I beg you,' he said, 'whisper a word in the ears of all the people of Shechem. Ask them which is better for them: that seventy men, all the sons of Jerubbaal, should rule over them, or one man. Tell them to remember that I am their own flesh and blood.' 3 When his mother's kinsfolk repeated all this to every Shechemite on his behalf, they were moved to come over to Abimelech's side, because, as they said, he was their kinsman. 4 They gave him seventy pieces of silver from the temple of Baal-berith, and with these he hired good-for-nothing, reckless fellows as his followers. 5 He went to his father's house in Ophrah and butchered his seventy brothers, the sons of Jerubbaal, on a single stone block, all but Jotham, the youngest, who survived because he had gone into hiding. 6 Then all the inhabitants of Shechem and all Beth-millo came together and made Abimelech king beside the propped-up terebinth at Shechem.

7 When this was reported to Jotham, he climbed to the summit of Mount Gerizim, and standing there he cried at the top of his voice: 'Listen to me, you people of Shechem, and may God listen to you.

8 'Once upon a time the trees set out to anoint a king over them. They said to the olive tree: "Be king over us." 9 But the olive tree answered: "What, leave my rich oil by which gods and men are honoured, to go and hold sway over the trees?"

10 'So the trees said to the fig tree: "Then will you come and be king over us?" 11 But the fig tree answered: "What, leave my good fruit and all its sweetness, to go and hold sway over the trees?"

12 'So the trees said to the vine: "Then will you come and be king over us?" 13 But the vine answered: "What, leave my new wine which gladdens gods and men, to go and hold sway over the trees?"

14 'Then all the trees said to the thorn bush: "Will you come and be king over us?" 15 The thorn answered: "If you really mean to anoint me as your king, then come under the protection of my shadow; if not, fire will come out of the thorn and burn up the cedars of Lebanon." '

16 Jotham said, 'Now have you acted fairly and honourably in making Abimelech king? Have you done the right thing by Jerubbaal and his household? Have you given my father his proper due — 17 who fought for you, and risked his life to deliver you from the Midianites? 18 Today you have

---

[c] Cn: Meaning of Heb uncertain

good old age Gideon, son of Joash, died and was buried in the tomb of his father Joash in Ophrah of the Abiezrites. ³³ But after Gideon was dead, the Israelites again abandoned themselves to the Baals, making Baal of Berith their god ³⁴ and forgetting the LORD, their God, who had delivered them from the power of their enemies all around them. ³⁵ Nor were they grateful to the family of Jerubbaal [Gideon] for all the good he had done for Israel.

9 Abimelech, son of Jerubbaal, went to his mother's kinsmen in Shechem, and said to them and to the whole clan to which his mother's family belonged, ² "Put this question to all the citizens of Shechem: 'Which is better for you: that seventy men, or all Jerubbaal's sons, rule over you, or that one man rule over you?' You must remember that I am your own flesh and bone." ³ When his mother's kin repeated these words to them on his behalf, all the citizens of Shechem sympathized with Abimelech, thinking, "He is our kinsman." ⁴ They also gave him seventy silver shekels from the temple of Baal of Berith, with which Abimelech hired shiftless men and ruffians as his followers. ⁵ He then went to his ancestral house in Ophrah, and slew his brothers, the seventy sons of Jerubbaal, on one stone. Only the youngest son of Jerubbaal, Jotham, escaped, for he was hidden. ⁶ Then all the citizens of Shechem and all Beth-millo came together and proceeded to make Abimelech king by the terebinth at the memorial pillar in Shechem.

⁷ When this was reported to him, Jotham went to the top of Mount Gerizim, and standing there, cried out to them in a loud voice: "Hear me, citizens of Shechem, that God may then hear you! ⁸ Once the trees went to anoint a king over themselves. So they said to the olive tree, 'Reign over us.' ⁹ But the olive tree answered them, 'Must I give up my rich oil, whereby men and gods are honored, and go to wave over the trees?' ¹⁰ Then the trees said to the fig tree, 'Come; you reign over us!' ¹¹ But the fig tree answered them, 'Must I give up my sweetness and my good fruit, and go to wave over the trees?' ¹² Then the trees said to the vine, 'Come you, and reign over us.' ¹³ But the vine answered them, 'Must I give up my wine that cheers gods and men, and go to wave over the trees?' ¹⁴ Then all the trees said to the buckthorn, 'Come; you reign over us!' ¹⁵ But the buckthorn replied to the trees, 'If you wish to anoint me king over you in good faith, come and take refuge in my shadow. Otherwise, let fire come from the buckthorn and devour the cedars of Lebanon.'

¹⁶ "Now then, if you have acted in good faith and honorably in appointing Abimelech your king, if you have dealt well with Jerubbaal and with his family, and if you have treated him as he deserved — ¹⁷ for my father fought for you at the risk of his life when he saved you from the power of

old age and was buried in the tomb of Joash his father, at Ophrah of Abiezer.

³³ After Gideon's death, the people of Israel again began to prostitute themselves to the Baals, taking Baal-Berith for their god. ³⁴ The Israelites no longer remembered Yahweh their God, who had rescued them from all the enemies round them. ³⁵ And to the family of Jerubbaal — Gideon — they showed no faithful gratitude for all the good which it had done for Israel.

9 Abimelech son of Jerubbaal confronted his mother's brothers at Shechem and, to them and to the whole clan of his maternal grandfather's family, he said, ² 'Please put this question to the leading men of Shechem: Which is better for you: to be ruled by seventy people — all Jerubbaal's sons — or to be ruled by one? Remember too that I am your own flesh and bone.' ³ His mother's brothers said all this on his behalf to all the leading men of Shechem, and their feelings swayed them to follow Abimelech, since they argued, 'He is our brother.' ⁴ So they gave him seventy shekels of silver from the temple of Baal-Berith, and with this Abimelech paid violent adventurers to follow him. ⁵ He then went to his father's house at Ophrah and put his brothers, Jerubbaal's seventy sons, to death on one and the same stone. Jotham, however, Jerubbaal's youngest son, escaped by going into hiding. ⁶ All the leading men of Shechem and all Beth-Millo then met and proclaimed Abimelech king at the oak of the cultic stone at Shechem.

⁷ News of this was brought to Jotham. He went and stood on the top of Mount Gerizim and shouted at the top of his voice:

Hear me, leaders of Shechem,
so that God may also hear you!

⁸ One day the trees went out
to anoint a king to rule them.
They said to the olive tree, 'Be our king!'

⁹ The olive tree replied,
'Must I forgo my oil
which gives honour to gods and men,
to stand and sway over the trees?'

¹⁰ Then the trees said to the fig tree,
'You come and be our king!'

¹¹ The fig tree replied,
'Must I forgo my sweetness,
forgo my excellent fruit,
to go and sway over the trees?'

¹² Then the trees said to the vine,
'You come and be our king!'

¹³ The vine replied,
'Must I forgo my wine
which cheers gods and men,
to go and sway over the trees?'

¹⁴ Then the trees all said to the thorn bush,
'You come and be our king!'

¹⁵ And the thorn bush replied to the trees,
'If you are anointing me in good faith to be your king,
come and shelter in my shade.
But, if not, fire will come out of the thorn bush
and devour the cedars of Lebanon.'

¹⁶ 'Now then, if you have acted in sincerity and good faith in making Abimelech king, if you have dealt honourably with Jerubbaal and his family, and have treated him as his actions deserved, ¹⁷ my father having fought for you, risked his life and rescued you from the power of Midian, ¹⁸ and

18 but you have risen up against my father's house this day, and have killed his sons, seventy men on one stone, and have made Abimelech, the son of his slave woman, king over the lords of Shechem, because he is your kinsman — 19 if, I say, you have acted in good faith and honor with Jerubbaal and with his house this day, then rejoice in Abimelech, and let him also rejoice in you; 20 but if not, let fire come out from Abimelech, and devour the lords of Shechem, and Beth-millo; and let fire come out from the lords of Shechem, and from Beth-millo, and devour Abimelech." 21 Then Jotham ran away and fled, going to Beer, where he remained for fear of his brother Abimelech.

22 Abimelech ruled over Israel three years. 23 But God sent an evil spirit between Abimelech and the lords of Shechem; and the lords of Shechem dealt treacherously with Abimelech. 24 This happened so that the violence done to the seventy sons of Jerubbaal might be avenged*d* and their blood be laid on their brother Abimelech, who killed them, and on the lords of Shechem, who strengthened his hands to kill his brothers. 25 So, out of hostility to him, the lords of Shechem set ambushes on the mountain tops. They robbed all who passed by them along that way; and it was reported to Abimelech.

26 When Gaal son of Ebed moved into Shechem with his kinsfolk, the lords of Shechem put confidence in him. 27 They went out into the field and gathered the grapes from their vineyards, trod them, and celebrated. Then they went into the temple of their god, ate and drank, and ridiculed Abimelech. 28 Gaal son of Ebed said, "Who is Abimelech, and who are we of Shechem, that we should serve him? Did not the son of Jerubbaal and Zebul his officer serve the men of Hamor father of Shechem? Why then should we serve him? 29 If only this people were under my command! Then I would remove Abimelech; I would say*e* to him, 'Increase your army, and come out.'"

30 When Zebul the ruler of the city heard the words of Gaal son of Ebed, his anger was kindled. 31 He sent messengers to Abimelech at Arumah,*f* saying, "Look, Gaal son of Ebed and his kinsfolk have come to Shechem, and they are stirring up*g* the city against you. 32 Now therefore, go by night, you and the troops that are with you, and lie in wait in the fields. 33 Then early in the morning, as soon as the sun rises, get up and rush on the city; and when he and the troops that are with him come out against you, you may deal with them as best you can."

34 So Abimelech and all the troops with him got up by night and lay in wait against Shechem in four companies. 35 When Gaal son of Ebed went out and stood in the entrance of the gate of the city, Abimelech and the troops with him rose from the ambush. 36 And when Gaal saw them, he said to Zebul, "Look, people are coming down from the mountain tops!" And Zebul said to him, "The shadows on the mountains look like people to you." 37 Gaal spoke again and said, "Look, people are coming down from Tabbur-erez, and one company is coming from the direction of Elon-meonenim."*h* 38 Then Zebul said to him, "Where is your boast*i* now, you who said, 'Who is Abimelech, that we should serve him?' Are not these the troops you made light of? Go out now and fight with them." 39 So Gaal went out at the head of the lords of Shechem, and fought with Abimelech. 40 Abimelech chased him, and he fled before him. Many fell wounded, up to the entrance of the gate. 41 So Abimelech resided at Arumah; and Zebul drove out Gaal and his kinsfolk, so that they could not live on at Shechem.

risen against my father's family, butchered his sons, seventy on a single stone block, and made Abimelech, the son of his slave-girl, king over the inhabitants of Shechem just because he is your kinsman. 19 In this day's work have you acted fairly and honourably by Jerubbaal and his family? If so, I wish you joy in Abimelech and wish him joy in you! 20 If not, may fire come out of Abimelech and devour the inhabitants of Shechem and all Beth-millo; may fire also come out from the inhabitants of Shechem and Beth-millo to devour Abimelech.' 21 Jotham then slipped away and made his escape; he came to Be-er, and there he settled, to be out of reach of his brother Abimelech.

22 After Abimelech had been prince over Israel for three years, 23 God sent an evil spirit to create a breach between Abimelech and the inhabitants of Shechem, and they broke faith with him. 24 This was done in order that the violent murder of the seventy sons of Jerubbaal might recoil on their brother Abimelech who did the murder, and on the people of Shechem who encouraged him to do it. 25 The people of Shechem set men to lie in wait for him on the hilltops, and they robbed all who passed that way. But Abimelech had word of it.

26 Gaal son of Ebed came with his kinsmen to Shechem, and the people of Shechem gave him their allegiance. 27 They went out into the countryside, picked the early grapes in their vineyards, trod them in the winepress, and made merry. They went into the temple of their god, where they ate and drank and reviled Abimelech. 28 'Who is Abimelech,' said Gaal son of Ebed, 'and who are the Shechemites, that we should be his subjects? Have not this son of Jerubbaal and his lieutenant Zebul been subjects of the men of Hamor the father of Shechem? Why indeed should we be subject to him? 29 If only this people were in my charge I should know how to get rid of Abimelech! I should say to him, "Muster your force and come out."'

30 When Zebul the governor of the city heard what Gaal son of Ebed said, he was furious. 31 He resorted to a ruse and sent messengers to report to Abimelech, 'Gaal son of Ebed and his kinsmen have come to Shechem and are turning the city against you. 32 Set off by night, you and the people with you, and lie in wait out in the country. 33 Then in the morning start at sunrise, and advance with all speed on the city. When he and his people come out to you, do to him what the situation demands.'

34 So Abimelech and all the troops with him set out under cover of night, and lay in wait in four companies to attack Shechem. 35 Gaal son of Ebed came out and stood in the entrance of the city gate. When Abimelech and his men rose from their hiding-place, 36 and Gaal saw them, he said to Zebul, 'There are people coming down from the tops of the hills,' but Zebul replied, 'What you see that looks like men is the shadow of the hills.' 37 Once more Gaal said, 'There are people coming down from the central ridge, and another group is advancing along the road of the Soothsayers' Terebinth.' 38 Then Zebul said to him, 'Where are your brave words now? You said, "Who is Abimelech that we should be subject to him?" Are not these the people you despised? Go out and fight him.' 39 Gaal led out the men of Shechem and attacked Abimelech, 40 but Abimelech routed him and he fled. The ground was strewn with corpses all the way to the entrance of the gate. 41 Abimelech established himself in Arumah, and Zebul drove out Gaal and his kinsmen and allowed them no place in Shechem.

---

d Heb *might come* *e* Gk: Heb *and he said* *f* Cn See 9.41. Heb *Tormah* *g* Cn: Heb *are besieging* *h* That is *Diviners' Oak* *i* Heb *mouth*

9:29 **I should say:** *so Gk; Heb.* And he said. 9:37 **central ridge:** lit. navel of the land.

Midian; 18 but you have risen against his family this day and have killed his seventy sons upon one stone, and have made Abimelech, the son of his handmaid, king over the citizens of Shechem, because he is your kinsman— 19 if, then, you have acted in good faith and with honor toward Jerubbaal and his family this day, rejoice in Abimelech and may he in turn rejoice in you. 20 But if not, let fire come forth from Abimelech to devour the citizens of Shechem and Beth-millo, and let fire come forth from the citizens and from Beth-millo to devour Abimelech." 21 Then Jotham went in flight to Beer, where he remained for fear of his brother Abimelech.

22 When Abimelech had ruled Israel for three years, 23 God put bad feelings between Abimelech and the citizens of Shechem, who rebelled against Abimelech. 24 This was to repay the violence done to the seventy sons of Jerubbaal and to avenge their blood upon their brother Abimelech, who killed them, and upon the citizens of Shechem, who encouraged him to kill his brothers. 25 The citizens of Shechem then set men in ambush for him on the mountaintops, and these robbed all who passed them on the road. But it was reported to Abimelech.

26 Now Gaal, son of Ebed, came over to Shechem with his kinsmen. The citizens of Shechem put their trust in him, 27 and went out into the fields, harvested their grapes and trod them out. Then they held a festival and went to the temple of their god, where they ate and drank and cursed Abimelech. 28 Gaal, son of Ebed, said, "Who is Abimelech? And why should we of Shechem serve him? Were not the son of Jerubbaal and his lieutenant Zebul once subject to the men of Hamor, father of Shechem? Why should we serve him? 29 Would that this people were entrusted to my command! I would depose Abimelech. I would say to Abimelech, 'Get a larger army and come out!' "

30 At the news of what Gaal, son of Ebed, had said, Zebul, the ruler of the city, was angry 31 and sent messengers to Abimelech in Arumah with the information: "Gaal, son of Ebed, and his kinsmen have come to Shechem and are stirring up the city against you. 32 Now rouse yourself; set an ambush tonight in the fields, you and the men who are with you. 33 Promptly at sunrise tomorrow morning, make a raid on the city. When he and his followers come out against you, deal with him as best you can."

34 During the night Abimelech advanced with all his soldiers and set up an ambush for Shechem in four companies. 35 Gaal, son of Ebed, went out and stood at the entrance of the city gate. When Abimelech and his soldiers rose from their place of ambush, 36 Gaal saw them and said to Zebul, "There are men coming down from the hilltops!" But Zebul answered him, "You see the shadow of the hills as men." 37 But Gaal went on to say, "Men are coming down from the region of Tabbur-Haares, and one company is coming by way of Elon-Meonenim." 38 Zebul said to him, "Where now is the boast you uttered, 'Who is Abimelech that we should serve him?' Are these not the men for whom you expressed contempt? Go out now and fight with them." 39 So Gaal went out at the head of the citizens of Shechem and fought against Abimelech. 40 But Abimelech routed him, and he fled before him; and many fell slain right up to the entrance of the gate. 41 Abimelech returned to Arumah, but Zebul drove Gaal and his kinsmen from Shechem, which they had occupied.

you today having risen up against my father's family, murdered his sons — seventy of them on one and the same stone — and appointed Abimelech, his slave-girl's son, to rule the leading men of Shechem, because he is your brother! — 19 if, I say, you have acted in sincerity and good faith towards Jerubbaal and his family, then may Abimelech be your joy and may you be his! 20 If not, may fire come out of Abimelech and devour the leading men of Shechem and Beth-Millo, and fire come out of the leading men of Shechem and Beth-Millo to devour Abimelech!'

21 Jotham then took to his heels; he fled and made his way to Beer; and there he stayed, to be out of his brother Abimelech's reach.

22 Abimelech ruled Israel for three years. 23 God then sent a spirit of discord between Abimelech and the leaders of Shechem, and the leaders of Shechem betrayed Abimelech. 24 And this was so that the crime committed against Jerubbaal's seventy sons should be avenged, and their blood recoil on their brother Abimelech who had murdered them, and on those leaders of Shechem who had helped him to murder his brothers.

25 The leaders of Shechem put men to ambush him on the mountain tops, and these robbed anyone travelling their way. Abimelech was told of this. 26 Gaal son of Obed, with his brothers, happened to pass through Shechem and win the confidence of the leaders of Shechem. 27 These went out into the countryside to harvest their vineyards; they trod the grapes and made merry and went into the temple of their god. They ate and drank there and cursed Abimelech. 28 Gaal son of Obed said, 'Who is Abimelech, and what is Shechem, for us to be his slaves? Should not Jerubbaal's son and his lieutenant, Zebul, be serving the men of Hamor, father of Shechem? Why should we be his slaves? 29 Who will put this people under my command, so that I can expel Abimelech? I should say to him, "Reinforce your army and come out!"' 30 Zebul the governor of the town was told what Gaal son of Obed had said, and he was furious. 31 He sent messengers secretly to Abimelech to say, 'Look! Gaal son of Obed has come to Shechem with his brothers, and they are stirring up the town against you. 32 So, move under cover of dark, you and the men you have with you, and take up concealed positions in the countryside; 33 then in the morning at sunrise, break cover and rush on the town. When Gaal and his supporters come out to meet you, treat them as occasion offers.' 34 So Abimelech set off under cover of dark with all his own supporters and took up concealed positions over against Shechem, in four groups. 35 As Gaal son of Obed was coming out and pausing at the entrance of the town gate, Abimelech and his supporters rose from their ambush. 36 Gaal saw these men and said to Zebul, 'Look, there are men coming down from the tops of the mountains!' Zebul answered, 'You mistake the shadow of the mountains for men.' 37 But Gaal insisted, 'Look, there are men coming down from the Navel of the Earth and another group is coming from the direction of the Diviners' Oak.' 38 Zebul then said, 'Where are your mouthings now about "Who is Abimelech, for us to be his slaves?" Are not these the men you made light of? Sally out, then, and fight him.' 39 Gaal sallied out at the head of the leaders of Shechem and engaged Abimelech. 40 Abimelech drove Gaal off, who turned tail, many of his men falling dead before they could reach the gate. 41 Abimelech then stayed at Aruma, and Zebul expelled Gaal and his brothers and prevented them from living in Shechem.

NEW REVISED STANDARD VERSION

42 On the following day the people went out into the fields. When Abimelech was told, 43 he took his troops and divided them into three companies, and lay in wait in the fields. When he looked and saw the people coming out of the city, he rose against them and killed them. 44 Abimelech and the company that was *j* with him rushed forward and stood at the entrance of the gate of the city, while the two companies rushed on all who were in the fields and killed them. 45 Abimelech fought against the city all that day; he took the city, and killed the people that were in it; and he razed the city and sowed it with salt.

46 When all the lords of the Tower of Shechem heard of it, they entered the stronghold of the temple of El-berith. 47 Abimelech was told that all the lords of the Tower of Shechem were gathered together. 48 So Abimelech went up to Mount Zalmon, he and all the troops that were with him. Abimelech took an ax in his hand, cut down a bundle of brushwood, and took it up and laid it on his shoulder. Then he said to the troops with him, "What you have seen me do, do quickly, as I have done." 49 So every one of the troops cut down a bundle and following Abimelech put it against the stronghold, and they set the stronghold on fire over them, so that all the people of the Tower of Shechem also died, about a thousand men and women.

50 Then Abimelech went to Thebez, and encamped against Thebez, and took it. 51 But there was a strong tower within the city, and all the men and women and all the lords of the city fled to it and shut themselves in; and they went to the roof of the tower. 52 Abimelech came to the tower, and fought against it, and came near to the entrance of the tower to burn it with fire. 53 But a certain woman threw an upper millstone on Abimelech's head, and crushed his skull. 54 Immediately he called to the young man who carried his armor and said to him, "Draw your sword and kill me, so people will not say about me, 'A woman killed him.' " So the young man thrust him through, and he died. 55 When the Israelites saw that Abimelech was dead, they all went home. 56 Thus God repaid Abimelech for the crime he committed against his father in killing his seventy brothers; 57 and God also made all the wickedness of the people of Shechem fall back on their heads, and on them came the curse of Jotham son of Jerubbaal.

10 After Abimelech, Tola son of Puah son of Dodo, a man of Issachar, who lived at Shamir in the hill country of Ephraim, rose to deliver Israel. 2 He judged Israel twenty-three years. Then he died, and was buried at Shamir.

3 After him came Jair the Gileadite, who judged Israel twenty-two years. 4 He had thirty sons who rode on thirty donkeys; and they had thirty towns, which are in the land of Gilead, and are called Havvoth-jair to this day. 5 Jair died, and was buried in Kamon.

6 The Israelites again did what was evil in the sight of the LORD, worshiping the Baals and the Astartes, the gods of Aram, the gods of Sidon, the gods of Moab, the gods of the Ammonites, and the gods of the Philistines. Thus they abandoned the LORD, and did not worship him. 7 So the anger of the LORD was kindled against Israel, and he sold them into the hand of the Philistines and into the hand of the Ammonites, 8 and they crushed and oppressed the Israelites that year. For eighteen years they oppressed all the Israelites that were beyond the Jordan in the land of the Amorites, which is in Gilead. 9 The Ammonites also crossed the Jordan to fight against Judah and against Benjamin and against the house of Ephraim; so that Israel was greatly distressed. 10 So the Israelites cried to the LORD, saying, "We have sinned against you, because we have abandoned our God and have worshiped the Baals." 11 And the LORD said to the

REVISED ENGLISH BIBLE

42 Next day the people came out into the open country, and this was reported to Abimelech. 43 He took his supporters, divided them into three companies, and lay in wait in the open country; when he saw the people coming out of the city, he rose and attacked them. 44 Abimelech and the company with him advanced rapidly and took up position at the entrance of the city gate, while the other two companies made a dash against all those who were in the open and struck them down. 45 Abimelech kept up the attack on the city all that day, and, when he captured it, he slaughtered the people inside, razed the city to the ground, and sowed it with salt.

46 When news of this reached the occupants of the tower of Shechem, they took refuge in the crypt of the temple of Elberith. 47 It was reported to Abimelech that all the occupants of the tower of Shechem had flocked together, 48 so he and all his men went up Mount Zalmon, where with an axe he cut brushwood. He took it and, hoisting it on his shoulder, he said to his men, 'You see what I am doing; quick, do the same.' 49 Each man cut brushwood and then following Abimelech they laid the brushwood on the crypt. They burnt it over the heads of the occupants of the tower, and they all died, about a thousand men and women.

50 Abimelech proceeded to Thebez, which he besieged and captured. 51 There was a strong tower in the middle of the town, and all the townspeople, men and women, took refuge there. They shut themselves in and went up on the roof. 52 Abimelech came up to the tower and attacked it, and as he approached the entrance to set fire to it, 53 a woman threw a millstone down on his head and fractured his skull. 54 He called hurriedly to his armour-bearer and said, 'Draw your sword and dispatch me, or it will be said of me: A woman killed him.' So the young man ran him through, and he died. 55 When the Israelites saw that Abimelech was dead, they all went back to their homes. 56 In this way God repaid the crime which Abimelech had committed against his father by the murder of his seventy brothers, 57 and brought all the wickedness of the men of Shechem on their own heads. The curse of Jotham son of Jerubbaal overtook them.

10 After Abimelech there came forward to deliver Israel Tola son of Pua, son of Dodo, a man of Issachar who lived at Shamir in the hill-country of Ephraim. 2 He was judge over Israel for twenty-three years, and when he died he was buried in Shamir.

3 After him came Jair the Gileadite; he was judge over Israel for twenty-two years. 4 He had thirty sons, who rode on thirty donkeys; they had thirty towns in the land of Gilead, which to this day are called Havvoth-jair. 5 When Jair died, he was buried in Kamon.

6 Once more the Israelites did what was wrong in the eyes of the LORD, serving the baalim and the ashtaroth, the deities of Aram and of Sidon and of Moab, of the Ammonites and of the Philistines. They forsook the LORD and did not serve him. 7 The anger of the LORD was roused against Israel, and he sold them into the power of the Philistines and the Ammonites, 8 who for eighteen years harassed and oppressed all those Israelites who lived beyond the Jordan in Amorite territory in Gilead. 9 The Ammonites also crossed the Jordan to attack Judah, Benjamin, and Ephraim, so that Israel was in dire straits. 10 Then the Israelites cried to the LORD: 'We have sinned against you; we have forsaken our God and served the baalim.' 11 The LORD answered, 'The Egyptians, the Amorites,

---

j Vg and some Gk Mss: Heb *companies that were*

9:44 **company:** *so Lat.;* Heb. companies.   10:4 **Havvoth-jair:** *that is* Tent-villages of Jair.   10:8 **who for eighteen years:** *prob. rdg;* Heb. *adds* in that year.

NEW AMERICAN BIBLE

42 The next day, when the people were taking the field, it was reported to Abimelech, 43 who divided the men he had into three companies, and set up an ambush in the fields. He watched till he saw the people leave the city, and then rose against them for the attack. 44 Abimelech and the company with him dashed in and stood by the entrance of the city gate, while the other two companies rushed upon all who were in the field and attacked them. 45 That entire day Abimelech fought against the city, and captured it. He then killed its inhabitants and demolished the city, sowing the site with salt.

46 When they heard of this, all the citizens of Migdal-shechem went into the crypt of the temple of El-berith. 47 It was reported to Abimelech that all the citizens of Migdal-shechem were gathered together. 48 So he went up Mount Zalmon with all his soldiers, took his ax in his hand, and cut down some brushwood. This he lifted to his shoulder, then said to the men with him, "Hurry! Do just as you have seen me do." 49 So all the men likewise cut down brushwood, and following Abimelech, placed it against the crypt. Then they set the crypt on fire over their heads, so that every one of the citizens of Migdal-shechem, about a thousand men and women, perished.

50 Abimelech proceeded to Thebez, which he invested and captured. 51 Now there was a strong tower in the middle of the city, and all the men and women, in a word all the citizens of the city, fled there, shutting themselves in and going up to the roof of the tower. 52 Abimelech came up to the tower and fought against it, advancing to the very entrance of the tower to set it on fire. 53 But a certain woman cast the upper part of a millstone down on Abimelech's head, and it fractured his skull. 54 He immediately called his armor-bearer and said to him, "Draw your sword and dispatch me, lest they say of me that a woman killed me." So his attendant ran him through and he died. 55 When the Israelites saw that Abimelech was dead, they all left for their homes.

56 Thus did God requite the evil Abimelech had done to his father in killing his seventy brothers. 57 God also brought all their wickedness home to the Shechemites, for the curse of Jotham, son of Jerubbaal, overtook them.

10 After Abimelech there rose to save Israel the Issacharite Tola, son of Puah, son of Dodo, a resident of Shamir in the mountain region of Ephraim. 2 When he had judged Israel twenty-three years, he died and was buried in Shamir.

3 Jair the Gileadite came after him and judged Israel twenty-two years. 4 He had thirty sons who rode on thirty saddle-asses and possessed thirty cities in the land of Gilead; these are called Havvoth-jair to the present day. 5 Jair died and was buried in Kamon.

6 The Israelites again offended the LORD, serving the Baals and Ashtaroths, the gods of Aram, the gods of Sidon, the gods of Moab, the gods of the Ammonites, and the gods of the Philistines. Since they had abandoned the LORD and would not serve him, 7 the LORD became angry with Israel and allowed them to fall into the power of [the Philistines and] the Ammonites. 8 For eighteen years they afflicted and oppressed the Israelites in Bashan, and all the Israelites in the Amorite land beyond the Jordan in Gilead. 9 The Ammonites also crossed the Jordan to fight against Judah, Benjamin, and the house of Ephraim, so that Israel was in great distress.

10 Then the Israelites cried out to the LORD, "We have sinned against you; we have forsaken our God and have served the Baals." 11 The LORD answered the Israelites:

NEW JERUSALEM BIBLE

42 Next day, when the people went out into the countryside, Abimelech was told of this. 43 He took his men, divided them into three groups and lay in wait in the fields. When he saw the people leaving the town, he bore down on them and slaughtered them. 44 While Abimelech and his group rushed forward and took position at the entrance to the town gate, the two other groups fell on everyone in the fields and slaughtered them. 45 All that day Abimelech attacked the town. He stormed it and slaughtered the people inside, razed the town and sowed it with salt. 46 On hearing this, all the leading men inside Migdal-Shechem took refuge in the crypt of the temple of El-Berith. 47 As soon as Abimelech heard that the leading men inside Migdal-Shechem had all gathered there, 48 he went up Mount Zalmon with all his men. Then taking an axe in his hands, he cut off the branch of a tree, picked it up and put it on his shoulder, and said to the men with him, 'Hurry and do what you have seen me do.' 49 Each of his men similarly cut off a branch; then, following Abimelech, they piled the branches over the crypt and set it on fire over those who were inside; so that all the people in Migdal-Shechem died too, about a thousand men and women.

50 Abimelech then marched on Thebez, besieged it and captured it. 51 In the middle of the town there was a fortified tower in which all the men and women and all the leading men of the town took refuge. They locked the door behind them and climbed up to the roof of the tower. 52 Abimelech reached the tower and attacked it. As he was approaching the door of the tower to set it on fire, 53 a woman threw down a millstone on his head and cracked his skull. 54 He instantly called his young armour-bearer and said, 'Draw your sword and kill me, so that it will not be said of me that "A woman killed him".' His armour-bearer ran him through, and he died. 55 When the men of Israel saw that Abimelech was dead, they dispersed to their homes.

56 Thus God made to recoil on Abimelech the evil he had done his father by murdering his seventy brothers, 57 and all the evil that the men of Shechem had done God made recoil on their heads too. And so the curse of Jotham son of Jerubbaal came true for them.

10 After Abimelech, Tola son of Puah, son of Dodo, rose to deliver Israel. He belonged to Issachar and lived at Shamir in the mountain country of Ephraim. 2 He was judge in Israel for twenty-three years; he then died and was buried at Shamir.

3 After him rose Jair of Gilead, who judged Israel for twenty-two years. 4 He had thirty sons who rode on thirty young donkeys and who owned thirty towns, still known today as the Encampments of Jair, in the territory of Gilead. 5 Jair then died and was buried at Kamon.

6 The Israelites again began doing what is evil in Yahweh's eyes. They served Baal and Astarte, and the gods of Aram and Sidon, the gods of Moab and those of the Ammonites and Philistines. They deserted Yahweh and served him no more. 7 Yahweh's anger then grew hot against Israel and he gave them over into the power of the Philistines and the power of the Ammonites, 8 who from that year onwards crushed and oppressed the Israelites for eighteen years — all those Israelites living on the other side of the Jordan in Amorite territory, in Gilead. 9 Furthermore, the Ammonites would cross the Jordan and also make war on Judah, Benjamin and the House of Ephraim, so that Israel was in distress. 10 The Israelites then cried to Yahweh and said, 'We have sinned against you, because we have turned from Yahweh our God to serve Baals.' 11 And Yahweh said to the

NEW REVISED STANDARD VERSION

Israelites, "Did I not deliver you[k] from the Egyptians and from the Amorites, from the Ammonites and from the Philistines? 12 The Sidonians also, and the Amalekites, and the Maonites, oppressed you; and you cried to me, and I delivered you out of their hand. 13 Yet you have abandoned me and worshiped other gods; therefore I will deliver you no more. 14 Go and cry to the gods whom you have chosen; let them deliver you in the time of your distress." 15 And the Israelites said to the LORD, "We have sinned; do to us whatever seems good to you; but deliver us this day!" 16 So they put away the foreign gods from among them and worshiped the LORD; and he could no longer bear to see Israel suffer.

17 Then the Ammonites were called to arms, and they encamped in Gilead; and the Israelites came together, and they encamped at Mizpah. 18 The commanders of the people of Gilead said to one another, "Who will begin the fight against the Ammonites? He shall be head over all the inhabitants of Gilead."

11 Now Jephthah the Gileadite, the son of a prostitute, was a mighty warrior. Gilead was the father of Jephthah. 2 Gilead's wife also bore him sons; and when his wife's sons grew up, they drove Jephthah away, saying to him, "You shall not inherit anything in our father's house; for you are the son of another woman." 3 Then Jephthah fled from his brothers and lived in the land of Tob. Outlaws collected around Jephthah and went raiding with him.

4 After a time the Ammonites made war against Israel. 5 And when the Ammonites made war against Israel, the elders of Gilead went to bring Jephthah from the land of Tob. 6 They said to Jephthah, "Come and be our commander, so that we may fight with the Ammonites." 7 But Jephthah said to the elders of Gilead, "Are you not the very ones who rejected me and drove me out of my father's house? So why do you come to me now when you are in trouble?" 8 The elders of Gilead said to Jephthah, "Nevertheless, we have now turned back to you, so that you may go with us and fight with the Ammonites, and become head over us, over all the inhabitants of Gilead." 9 Jephthah said to the elders of Gilead, "If you bring me home again to fight with the Ammonites, and the LORD gives them over to me, I will be your head." 10 And the elders of Gilead said to Jephthah, "The LORD will be witness between us; we will surely do as you say." 11 So Jephthah went with the elders of Gilead, and the people made him head and commander over them; and Jephthah spoke all his words before the LORD at Mizpah.

12 Then Jephthah sent messengers to the king of the Ammonites and said, "What is there between you and me, that you have come to me to fight against my land?" 13 The king of the Ammonites answered the messengers of Jephthah, "Because Israel, on coming from Egypt, took away my land from the Arnon to the Jabbok and to the Jordan; now therefore restore it peaceably." 14 Once again Jephthah sent messengers to the king of the Ammonites 15 and said to him: "Thus says Jephthah: Israel did not take away the land of Moab or the land of the Ammonites, 16 but when they came up from Egypt, Israel went through the wilderness to the Red Sea[l] and came to Kadesh. 17 Israel then sent messengers to the king of Edom, saying, 'Let us pass through your land'; but the king of Edom would not listen. They also sent to the king of Moab, but he would not consent. So Israel remained at Kadesh. 18 Then they journeyed through the wilderness, went around the land of Edom and the land of Moab, arrived on the east side of the land of Moab, and camped on the other side of the Arnon. They did not enter the territory of Moab, for the Arnon was the boundary of Moab. 19 Israel then sent messengers to King Sihon of the

REVISED ENGLISH BIBLE

the Ammonites, the Philistines, 12 the Sidonians too, and the Amalekites and the Midianites — all these oppressed you and you cried to me for help; and did I not deliver you? 13 But you have forsaken me and served other gods; therefore I shall come to your rescue no more. 14 Go and cry for help to the gods you have chosen; let them save you in your day of distress.' 15 But the Israelites said to the LORD, 'We have sinned. Deal with us as you please; only save us this day, we implore you.' 16 They banished their foreign gods and served the LORD; and he could no longer bear the plight of Israel.

17 The Ammonites were called to arms and encamped in Gilead, while the Israelites assembled and encamped in Mizpah. 18 The people of Gilead and their chief men said to one another, 'Whoever strikes the first blow at the Ammonites shall be head over all the inhabitants of Gilead.'

11 JEPHTHAH the Gileadite was an intrepid warrior; he was the son of Gilead by a prostitute. 2 Gilead's wife also bore him sons, and when they grew up they drove Jephthah away, saying to him, 'You have no inheritance in our father's house; you are another woman's son.' 3 To escape his brothers, Jephthah fled and settled in the land of Tob, and a number of good-for-nothing fellows rallied to him and became his followers.

4 The time came when the Ammonites launched an offensive against Israel 5 and, when the fighting began, the elders of Gilead went to fetch Jephthah from the land of Tob. 6 'Come and be our commander so that we can fight the Ammonites,' they said to him. 7 But Jephthah answered, 'You drove me from my father's house in hatred. Why come to me now when you are in trouble?' 8 'It is because of that', they replied, 'that we have turned to you now. Come with us, fight the Ammonites, and become head over all the inhabitants of Gilead.' 9 Jephthah said to them, 'If you ask me back to fight the Ammonites and if the LORD delivers them into my hands, then I must become your head.' 10 The Gilead elders said to him, 'We swear by the LORD, who will be witness between us, that we will do what you say.' 11 Jephthah then went with the elders of Gilead, and the people made him their head and commander. And at Mizpah, in the presence of the LORD, Jephthah repeated the terms he had laid down.

12 Jephthah sent a mission to the king of Ammon to ask what quarrel he had with them that made him invade his country. 13 The king replied to the messengers: 'When the Israelites came up from Egypt, they seized our land all the way from the Arnon to the Jabbok and the Jordan. Now return these lands peaceably.' 14 Jephthah sent a second mission to the king of Ammon 15 to say, 'This is Jephthah's answer: Israel took neither Moabite nor Ammonite territory. 16 When they came up from Egypt, the Israelites passed through the wilderness to the Red Sea, and on to Kadesh. 17 They then sent envoys to the king of Edom asking him to grant them passage through his country, but the king of Edom would not consent. They sent also to the king of Moab, but he would not agree; so Israel remained at Kadesh. 18 'They then journeyed through the wilderness, skirting Edom and Moab, and kept to the east of Moab. They encamped beside the Arnon, but they did not enter Moabite territory, because the Arnon is the frontier of Moab. 19 Israel then sent envoys to the king of the Amorites, King Sihon

---

[k] Heb lacks *Did I not deliver you*   [l] Or *Sea of Reeds*

10:12 **the Midianites:** *so Gk; Heb.* Maon.   11:16 **Red Sea:** *or* sea of Reeds.

"Did not the Egyptians, the Amorites, the Ammonites, the Philistines, 12 the Sidonians, the Amalekites, and the Midianites oppress you? Yet when you cried out to me, and I saved you from their grasp, 13 you still forsook me and worshiped other gods. Therefore I will save you no more. 14 Go and cry out to the gods you have chosen; let them save you now that you are in distress." 15 But the Israelites said to the LORD, "We have sinned. Do to us whatever you please. Only save us this day." 16 And they cast out the foreign gods from their midst and served the LORD, so that he grieved over the misery of Israel.

17 The Ammonites had gathered for war and encamped in Gilead, while the Israelites assembled and encamped in Mizpah. 18 And among the people the princes of Gilead said to one another, "The one who begins the war against the Ammonites shall be leader of all the inhabitants of Gilead."

11 There was a chieftain, the Gileadite Jephthah, born to Gilead of a harlot. 2 Gilead's wife had also borne him sons, and on growing up the sons of the wife had driven Jephthah away, saying to him, "You shall inherit nothing in our family, for you are the son of another woman." 3 So Jephthah had fled from his brothers and had taken up residence in the land of Tob. A rabble had joined company with him, and went out with him on raids.

4 Some time later, the Ammonites warred on Israel. 5 When this occurred the elders of Gilead went to bring Jephthah from the land of Tob. 6 "Come," they said to Jephthah, "be our commander that we may be able to fight the Ammonites." 7 "Are you not the ones who hated me and drove me from my father's house?" Jephthah replied to the elders of Gilead. "Why do you come to me now, when you are in distress?" 8 The elders of Gilead said to Jephthah, "In any case, we have now come back to you; if you go with us to fight against the Ammonites, you shall be the leader of all of us who dwell in Gilead." 9 Jephthah answered the elders of Gilead, "If you bring me back to fight against the Ammonites and the LORD delivers them up to me, I shall be your leader." 10 The elders of Gilead said to Jephthah, "The LORD is witness between us that we will do as you say."

11 So Jephthah went with the elders of Gilead, and the people made him their leader and commander. In Mizpah, Jephthah settled all his affairs before the LORD. 12 Then he sent messengers to the king of the Ammonites to say, "What have you against me that you come to fight with me in my land?" 13 He answered the messengers of Jephthah, "Israel took away my land from the Arnon to the Jabbok and the Jordan when they came up from Egypt. Now restore the same peaceably."

14 Again Jephthah sent messengers to the king of the Ammonites, 15 saying to him, "This is what Jephthah says: Israel did not take the land of Moab or the land of the Ammonites. 16 For when they came up from Egypt, Israel went through the desert to the Red Sea and came to Kadesh. 17 Israel then sent messengers to the king of Edom saying, 'Let me pass through your land.' But the king of Edom did not give consent. They also sent to the king of Moab, but he too was unwilling. So Israel remained in Kadesh. 18 Then they went through the desert, and by-passing the land of Edom and the land of Moab, went east of the land of Moab and encamped across the Arnon. Thus they did not go through the territory of Moab, for the Arnon is the boundary of Moab. 19 Then Israel sent messengers to Sihon, king of

Israelites, 'When Egyptians and Amorites, Ammonites and Philistines, 12 when the Sidonians, Amalek and Midian oppressed you and you cried to me, did I not rescue you from their power? 13 But it is you who have forsaken me and served other gods; and so I shall rescue you no more. 14 Go and cry out to the gods whom you have chosen. Let them rescue you in your time of trouble.' 15 Yahweh replied to Yahweh, 'We have sinned. Treat us as you see fit, but please rescue us today.' 16 They got rid of their foreign gods and served Yahweh, who could bear Israel's suffering no longer.

17 The Ammonites gathered and pitched camp in Gilead. The Israelites rallied and pitched camp at Mizpah. 18 The people, the chieftains of Gilead, then said to one another, 'Who will volunteer to attack the Ammonites? He shall be chief of all who live in Gilead!'

11 Jephthah the Gileadite was a valiant warrior. He was a prostitute's son. Gilead was Jephthah's father, 2 but Gilead's wife also bore him sons, and the sons of this wife, when they grew up, drove Jephthah away, saying, 'No share of the paternal heritage for you, since you are a son of another woman.' 3 Jephthah fled far from his brothers and settled in the territory of Tob. Jephthah enlisted a group of adventurers who used to go raiding with him.

4 It was some time after this that the Ammonites made war on Israel. 5 And when the Ammonites had attacked Israel, the elders of Gilead went to fetch Jephthah from the territory of Tob. 6 'Come', they said, 'and be our commander, so that we can fight the Ammonites.' 7 Jephthah replied to the elders of Gilead, 'Didn't you hate me and drive me out of my father's house? Why come to me now, when you are in trouble?' 8 The elders of Gilead said to Jephthah, 'That is why we are turning to you now. Come with us; fight the Ammonites and be our chief, chief of all the people living in Gilead.' 9 Jephthah then said to the elders of Gilead, 'If you bring me home to fight the Ammonites and Yahweh defeats them for me, I am to be your chief?' 10 And the elders of Gilead then said to Jephthah, 'Yahweh be witness between us, if we do not do as you have said!' 11 So Jephthah set off with the elders of Gilead. The people put him at their head as chief and commander; and Jephthah repeated all his conditions at Mizpah in Yahweh's presence.

12 Jephthah sent messengers to the king of the Ammonites to say to him, 'What do you have against us, for you to come and make war on my country?' 13 The king of the Ammonites replied to Jephthah's messengers, 'The reason is that when Israel came up from Egypt, they seized my country from the Arnon to the Jabbok and to the Jordan; so now restore it to me peacefully.' 14 Jephthah sent messengers back to the king of the Ammonites 15 with this answer, 'Jephthah says this, "Israel seized neither the country of Moab nor the country of the Ammonites. 16 When Israel came out of Egypt, they marched through the desert as far as the Sea of Reeds and, having reached Kadesh, 17 Israel then sent messengers to the king of Edom to say: Please let me pass through your country, but the king of Edom would not listen. They sent similarly to the king of Moab, but he refused, and Israel remained at Kadesh; 18 later, moving on through the desert and skirting the countries of Edom and Moab until arriving to the east of Moabite territory, the people camped on the other side of the Arnon but did not enter Moabite territory, the Arnon being the Moabite frontier. 19 Israel then sent messengers to Sihon, king of the

NEW REVISED STANDARD VERSION

Amorites, king of Heshbon; and Israel said to him, 'Let us pass through your land to our country.' 20 But Sihon did not trust Israel to pass through his territory; so Sihon gathered all his people together, and encamped at Jahaz, and fought with Israel. 21 Then the LORD, the God of Israel, gave Sihon and all his people into the hand of Israel, and they defeated them; so Israel occupied all the land of the Amorites, who inhabited that country. 22 They occupied all the territory of the Amorites from the Arnon to the Jabbok and from the wilderness to the Jordan. 23 So now the LORD, the God of Israel, has conquered the Amorites for the benefit of his people Israel. Do you intend to take their place? 24 Should you not possess what your god Chemosh gives you to possess? And should we not be the ones to possess everything that the LORD our God has conquered for our benefit? 25 Now are you any better than King Balak son of Zippor of Moab? Did he ever enter into conflict with Israel, or did he ever go to war with them? 26 While Israel lived in Heshbon and its villages, and in Aroer and its villages, and in all the towns that are along the Arnon, three hundred years, why did you not recover them within that time? 27 It is not I who have sinned against you, but you are the one who does me wrong by making war on me. Let the LORD, who is judge, decide today for the Israelites or for the Ammonites." 28 But the king of the Ammonites did not heed the message that Jephthah sent him.

29 Then the spirit of the LORD came upon Jephthah, and he passed through Gilead and Manasseh. He passed on to Mizpah of Gilead, and from Mizpah of Gilead he passed on to the Ammonites. 30 And Jephthah made a vow to the LORD, and said, "If you will give the Ammonites into my hand, 31 then whoever comes out of the doors of my house to meet me, when I return victorious from the Ammonites, shall be the LORD's, to be offered up by me as a burnt offering." 32 So Jephthah crossed over to the Ammonites to fight against them; and the LORD gave them into his hand. 33 He inflicted a massive defeat on them from Aroer to the neighborhood of Minnith, twenty towns, and as far as Abel-keramim. So the Ammonites were subdued before the people of Israel.

34 Then Jephthah came to his home at Mizpah; and there was his daughter coming out to meet him with timbrels and with dancing. She was his only child; he had no son or daughter except her. 35 When he saw her, he tore his clothes, and said, "Alas, my daughter! You have brought me very low; you have become the cause of great trouble to me. For I have opened my mouth to the LORD, and I cannot take back my vow." 36 She said to him, "My father, if you have opened your mouth to the LORD, do to me according to what has gone out of your mouth, now that the LORD has given you vengeance against your enemies, the Ammonites." 37 And she said to her father, "Let this thing be done for me: Grant me two months, so that I may go and wander[m] on the mountains, and bewail my virginity, my companions and I." 38 "Go," he said and sent her away for two months. So she departed, she and her companions, and bewailed her virginity on the mountains. 39 At the end of two months, she returned to her father, who did with her according to the vow he had made. She had never slept with a man. So there arose an Israelite custom that 40 for four days every year the daughters of Israel would go out to lament the daughter of Jephthah the Gileadite.

12 The men of Ephraim were called to arms, and they crossed to Zaphon and said to Jephthah, "Why did you cross over to fight against the Ammonites, and did not call us to go with you? We will burn your house down over

REVISED ENGLISH BIBLE

of Heshbon, asking him to give them free passage through his country to their destination. 20 But Sihon refused to grant Israel passage through his territory; he mustered all his people, and from his camp in Jahaz he launched an attack on Israel. 21 But the LORD the God of Israel delivered Sihon and his whole army into the hands of Israel, who defeated the Amorites and occupied all their territory in that region. 22 They took possession of the entire Amorite country from the Arnon to the Jabbok and from the wilderness to the Jordan. 23 The LORD the God of Israel drove out the Amorites for the benefit of his people Israel. And do you now propose to take their place? 24 It is for you to possess whatever Kemosh your god gives you; and all that the LORD our God gave us as we advanced is ours.

25 'For that matter, are you any better than Balak son of Zippor, king of Moab? Did he ever pick a quarrel with Israel or attack them? 26 For three hundred years Israelites have lived in Heshbon and its dependent villages, in Aroer and its villages, and in all the towns by the Arnon. Why did you not retake them during all that time? 27 We have done you no wrong; it is you who are doing us wrong by attacking us. The LORD who is judge will decide this day between the Israelites and the Ammonites.' 28 But the king of the Ammonites would not listen to the message Jephthah sent him.

29 Then the spirit of the LORD came upon Jephthah, who passed through Gilead and Manasseh, by Mizpeh of Gilead, and from Mizpeh over to the Ammonites. 30 Jephthah made this vow to the LORD: 'If you will deliver the Ammonites into my hands, 31 then the first creature that comes out of the door of my house to meet me when I return from them safely shall be the LORD's; I shall offer that as a whole-offering.'

32 So Jephthah crossed over to attack the Ammonites, and the LORD delivered them into his hands. 33 He routed them with very great slaughter all the way from Aroer to near Minnith, taking twenty towns, and as far as Abel-keramim. Thus Ammon was subdued by Israel.

34 When Jephthah arrived home in Mizpah, it was his daughter who came out to meet him with tambourines and dancing. She was his only child; apart from her he had neither son nor daughter. 35 At the sight of her, he tore his clothes and said, 'Oh, my daughter, you have broken my heart! Such calamity you have brought on me! I have made a vow to the LORD and I cannot go back on it.'

36 She replied, 'Father, since you have made a vow to the LORD, do to me as your vow demands, now that the LORD has avenged you on the Ammonites, your enemies. 37 But, father, grant me this one favour: spare me for two months, that I may roam the hills with my companions and mourn that I must die a virgin.' 38 'Go,' he said, and he let her depart for two months. She went with her companions and mourned her virginity on the hills. 39 At the end of two months she came back to her father, and he fulfilled the vow he had made; she died a virgin. It became a tradition 40 that the daughters of Israel should go year by year and commemorate for four days the daughter of Jephthah the Gileadite.

12 The Ephraimites mustered their forces and, crossing over to Zaphon, said to Jephthah, 'Why did you march against the Ammonites and not summon us to go with you? We shall burn your house over your head.'

m Cn: Heb go down

11:37 **that ... roam:** or that I may go down country to.

the Amorites, king of Heshbon. Israel said to him, 'Let me pass through your land to my own place.' 20 But Sihon refused to let Israel pass through his territory. On the contrary, he gathered all his soldiers, who encamped at Jahaz and fought Israel. 21 But the LORD, the God of Israel, delivered Sihon and all his men into the power of Israel, who defeated them and occupied all the land of the Amorites dwelling in that region, 22 the whole territory from the Arnon to the Jabbok, from the desert to the Jordan. 23 If now the LORD, the God of Israel, has cleared the Amorites out of the way of his people, are you to dislodge Israel? 24 Should you not possess that which your god Chemosh gave you to possess, and should we not possess all that the LORD, our God, has cleared out for us? 25 Again, are you any better than Balak, son of Zippor, king of Moab? Did he ever quarrel with Israel, or did he war against them 26 when Israel occupied Heshbon and its villages, Aroer and its villages, and all the cities on the banks of the Arnon? Three hundred years have passed; why did you not recover them during that time? 27 I have not sinned against you, but you wrong me by warring against me. Let the LORD, who is judge, decide this day between the Israelites and the Ammonites!" 28 But the king of the Ammonites paid no heed to the message Jephthah sent him.

29 The spirit of the LORD came upon Jephthah. He passed through Gilead and Manasseh, and through Mizpah-Gilead as well, and from there he went on to the Ammonites. 30 Jephthah made a vow to the LORD. "If you deliver the Ammonites into my power," he said, 31 "whoever comes out of the doors of my house to meet me when I return in triumph from the Ammonites shall belong to the LORD. I shall offer him up as a holocaust."

32 Jephthah then went on to the Ammonites to fight against them, and the LORD delivered them into his power, 33 so that he inflicted a severe defeat on them, from Aroer to the approach of Minnith (twenty cities in all) and as far as Abel-keramim. Thus were the Ammonites brought into subjection by the Israelites. 34 When Jephthah returned to his house in Mizpah, it was his daughter who came forth, playing the tambourines and dancing. She was an only child: he had neither son nor daughter besides her. 35 When he saw her, he rent his garments and said, "Alas, daughter, you have struck me down and brought calamity upon me. For I have made a vow to the LORD and I cannot retract." 36 "Father," she replied, "you have made a vow to the LORD. Do with me as you have vowed, because the LORD has wrought vengeance for you on your enemies the Ammonites." 37 Then she said to her father, "Let me have this favor. Spare me for two months, that I may go off down the mountains to mourn my virginity with my companions." 38 "Go," he replied, and sent her away for two months. So she departed with her companions and mourned her virginity on the mountains. 39 At the end of the two months she returned to her father, who did to her as he had vowed. She had not been intimate with man. It then became a custom in Israel 40 for Israelite women to go yearly to mourn the daughter of Jephthah the Gileadite for four days of the year.

12 The men of Ephraim gathered together and crossed over to Zaphon. They said to Jephthah, "Why do you go on to fight with the Ammonites without calling us to go with you? We will burn your house over you." 2 Jeph-

Amorites, ruling in Heshbon. Israel's message was: Please let me pass through your country to my destination. 20 But Sihon would not let Israel pass through his territory; he mustered his whole army; they encamped at Jahaz, and he then joined battle with Israel. 21 Yahweh, God of Israel, delivered Sihon and his whole army into the power of Israel, who defeated them; as the result of which, Israel took possession of the entire territory of the Amorites living in that region. 22 Israel took possession of all the Amorite territory from the Arnon to the Jabbok and from the desert to the Jordan. 23 And now that Yahweh, God of Israel, has dispossessed the Amorites before his people Israel, do you think you can dispossess us? 24 Will you not keep as your possession whatever Chemosh, your god, has given you? And, just the same, we shall keep as ours whatever Yahweh our God has given us, to inherit from those who were before us! 25 Are you a better man than Balak son of Zippor, king of Moab? Did he pick a quarrel with Israel? Did he make war on them? 26 When Israel settled in Heshbon and its dependencies, and in Aroer and its dependencies, or in any of the towns on the banks of the Arnon (three hundred years ago), why did you not recover them then? 27 I for my part have done you no harm, but you are wronging me by making war on me. Let Yahweh the Judge give judgement today between the Israelites and the king of the Ammonites.' ' 28 But the king of the Ammonites took no notice of the message that Jephthah sent him.

29 The spirit of Yahweh was on Jephthah, who crossed Gilead and Manasseh, crossed by way of Mizpah in Gilead, and from Mizpah in Gilead crossed into Ammonite territory. 30 And Jephthah made a vow to Yahweh, 'If you deliver the Ammonites into my grasp, 31 the first thing to come out of the doors of my house to meet me when I return in triumph from fighting the Ammonites shall belong to Yahweh, and I shall sacrifice it as a burnt offering.' 32 Jephthah crossed into Ammonite territory to attack them, and Yahweh delivered them into his grasp. 33 He beat them from Aroer to the border of Minnith (twenty towns) and to Abel-Keramim. It was a very severe defeat, and the Ammonites were humbled by the Israelites.

34 As Jephthah returned to his house at Mizpah, his daughter came out to meet him, dancing to the sound of tambourines. She was his only child; apart from her, he had neither son nor daughter. 35 When he saw her, he tore his clothes and exclaimed, 'Oh my daughter, what misery you have brought upon me! You have joined those who bring misery into my life! I have made a promise before Yahweh which I cannot retract.' 36 She replied, 'Father, you have made a promise to Yahweh; treat me as the promise that you have made requires, since Yahweh has granted you vengeance on your enemies the Ammonites.' 37 She then said to her father, 'Grant me this! Let me be free for two months. I shall go and wander in the mountains, and with my companions bewail my virginity.' 38 He replied, 'Go,' and let her go away for two months. So she went away with her companions and bewailed her virginity in the mountains. 39 When the two months were over she went back to her father, and he treated her as the vow that he had uttered bound him. She had remained a virgin. And hence, the custom in Israel 40 for the daughters of Israel to leave home year by year and lament over the daughter of Jephthah the Gileadite for four days every year.

12 The men of Ephraim mobilised; they crossed the Jordan near Zaphon and said to Jephthah, 'Why did you go and make war on the Ammonites without asking us to go with you? We shall burn down your house over your

NEW REVISED STANDARD VERSION

REVISED ENGLISH BIBLE

you!" 2 Jephthah said to them, "My people and I were engaged in conflict with the Ammonites who oppressed usⁿ
severely. But when I called you, you did not deliver me
from their hand. 3 When I saw that you would not deliver
me, I took my life in my hand, and crossed over against the
Ammonites, and the LORD gave them into my hand. Why
then have you come up to me this day, to fight against me?"
4 Then Jephthah gathered all the men of Gilead and fought
with Ephraim; and the men of Gilead defeated Ephraim,
because they said, "You are fugitives from Ephraim, you
Gileadites—in the heart of Ephraim and Manasseh."^o
5 Then the Gileadites took the fords of the Jordan against the
Ephraimites. Whenever one of the fugitives of Ephraim
said, "Let me go over," the men of Gilead would say to
him, "Are you an Ephraimite?" When he said, "No," 6 they
said to him, "Then say Shibboleth," and he said, "Sibboleth," for he could not pronounce it right. Then they seized
him and killed him at the fords of the Jordan. Forty-two
thousand of the Ephraimites fell at that time.

7 Jephthah judged Israel six years. Then Jephthah the
Gileadite died, and was buried in his town in Gilead.^p

8 After him Ibzan of Bethlehem judged Israel. 9 He had
thirty sons. He gave his thirty daughters in marriage outside
his clan and brought in thirty young women from outside for
his sons. He judged Israel seven years. 10 Then Ibzan died,
and was buried at Bethlehem.

11 After him Elon the Zebulunite judged Israel; and he
judged Israel ten years. 12 Then Elon the Zebulunite died,
and was buried at Aijalon in the land of Zebulun.

13 After him Abdon son of Hillel the Pirathonite judged
Israel. 14 He had forty sons and thirty grandsons, who rode
on seventy donkeys; he judged Israel eight years. 15 Then
Abdon son of Hillel the Pirathonite died, and was buried at
Pirathon in the land of Ephraim, in the hill country of the
Amalekites.

13 The Israelites again did what was evil in the sight of
the LORD, and the LORD gave them into the hand of
the Philistines forty years.

2 There was a certain man of Zorah, of the tribe of the
Danites, whose name was Manoah. His wife was barren,
having borne no children. 3 And the angel of the LORD
appeared to the woman and said to her, "Although you are
barren, having borne no children, you shall conceive and
bear a son. 4 Now be careful not to drink wine or strong
drink, or to eat anything unclean, 5 for you shall conceive
and bear a son. No razor is to come on his head, for the boy
shall be a nazirite^q to God from birth. It is he who shall
begin to deliver Israel from the hand of the Philistines."
6 Then the woman came and told her husband, "A man of
God came to me, and his appearance was like that of an
angel^r of God, most awe-inspiring; I did not ask him where
he came from, and he did not tell me his name; 7 but he said
to me, 'You shall conceive and bear a son. So then drink no
wine or strong drink, and eat nothing unclean, for the boy
shall be a nazirite^q to God from birth to the day of his
death.' "

8 Then Manoah entreated the LORD, and said, "O,
LORD, I pray, let the man of God whom you sent come to
us again and teach us what we are to do concerning the boy
who will be born." 9 God listened to Manoah, and the angel
of God came again to the woman as she sat in the field; but
her husband Manoah was not with her. 10 So the woman ran
quickly and told her husband, "The man who came to me

2 Jephthah answered, 'I and my people had a grave feud
with the Ammonites, and had I appealed to you for help,
you would not have saved us from them. 3 When I saw that
we were not to look for help from you, I took my life in my
hands and marched against the Ammonites, and the LORD
delivered them into my power. So why do you now attack
me?' 4 Jephthah then mustered all the men of Gilead and
fought Ephraim, and the Gileadites defeated them. 5 The
Gileadites seized the fords of the Jordan and held them
against Ephraim. When any Ephraimite who had escaped
wished to cross, the men of Gilead would ask, 'Are you an
Ephraimite?' and if he said, 'No,' 6 they would retort, 'Say
"Shibboleth." ' He would say 'Sibboleth,' and because he
could not pronounce the word properly, they seized him and
killed him at the fords. At that time forty-two thousand men
of Ephraim lost their lives.

7 Jephthah was judge over Israel for six years; when he
died he was buried in his own town in Gilead. 8 After him
Ibzan of Bethlehem was made judge over Israel. 9 He had
thirty sons and thirty daughters. He gave away the thirty
girls in marriage and brought in thirty girls for his sons. He
was judge over Israel for seven years, 10 and when he died
he was buried in Bethlehem.

11 After him Elon the Zebulunite was judge over Israel for
ten years. 12 When he died, he was buried in Aijalon in
Zebulun territory.

13 Next Abdon son of Hillel the Pirathonite was judge
over Israel. 14 He had forty sons and thirty grandsons, each
of whom rode on his own donkey. He was judge over Israel
for eight years; 15 and when he died he was buried in Pirathon in Ephraim territory on the hill of the Amalekite.

13 ONCE more the Israelites did what was wrong in the
eyes of the LORD, and he delivered them into the
hands of the Philistines for forty years.

2 There was a certain man from Zorah of the tribe of Dan
whose name was Manoah and whose wife was barren; she
had no child. 3 The angel of the LORD appeared to her and
said, 'Though you are barren and have no child, you will
conceive and give birth to a son. 4 Now be careful to drink
no wine or strong drink, and to eat no forbidden food. 5 You
will conceive and give birth to a son, and no razor must
touch his head, for the boy is to be a Nazirite, consecrated
to God from birth. He will strike the first blow for Israel's
freedom from the power of the Philistines.'

6 The woman went and told her husband. 'A man of God
came to me,' she said to him; 'his appearance was that of
an angel of God, most terrible to see. I did not ask him
where he came from, nor did he tell me his name, 7 but he
said to me, "You are going to conceive and give birth to a
son. From now on drink no wine or strong drink and eat no
forbidden food, for the boy is to be a Nazirite, consecrated
to God from his birth to the day of his death." '

8 Manoah prayed to the LORD, 'If it is pleasing to you,
Lord, let the man of God whom you sent come again to tell
us what we are to do for the boy that is to be born.' 9 God
heard Manoah's prayer, and the angel of God came again to
the woman, as she was sitting in the field. Her husband not
being with her, 10 the woman ran quickly and said to him,
'The man who came to me the other day has appeared to me

ⁿGk OL, Syr H: Heb lacks who oppressed us   ^oMeaning of Heb
uncertain: Gk omits because . . . Manasseh   ^pGk: Heb in the
towns of Gilead   ^qThat is one separated or one consecrated
^rOr the angel

12:4 **defeated them:** so some Gk MSS; Heb. adds for they said,
'You are fugitives from Ephraim, Gilead, in the midst of Ephraim, in
the midst of Manasseh.'   13:4 **forbidden:** lit. unclean.
13:6 **an angel:** or the angel.

thah answered them, "My soldiers and I were engaged in a critical contest with the Ammonites. I summoned you, but you did not rescue me from their power. 3 When I saw that you would not effect a rescue, I took my life in my own hand and went on to the Ammonites, and the LORD delivered them into my power. Why, then, do you come up against me this day to fight with me?"

4 Then Jephthah called together all the men of Gilead and fought against Ephraim, whom they defeated; for the Ephraimites had said, "You of Gilead are Ephraimite fugitives in territory belonging to Ephraim and Manasseh." 5 The Gileadites took the fords of the Jordan toward Ephraim. When any of the fleeing Ephraimites said, "Let me pass," the men of Gilead would say to him, "Are you an Ephraimite?" If he answered, "No!" 6 they would ask him to say "Shibboleth." If he said "Sibboleth," not being able to give the proper pronunciation, they would seize him and kill him at the fords of the Jordan. Thus forty-two thousand Ephraimites fell at that time.

7 After having judged Israel for six years, Jephthah the Gileadite died and was buried in his city in Gilead.

8 After him Ibzan of Bethlehem judged Israel. 9 He had thirty sons. He also had thirty daughters married outside the family, and he brought in as wives for his sons thirty young women from outside the family. After having judged Israel for seven years, 10 Ibzan died and was buried in Bethlehem.

11 After him the Zebulunite Elon judged Israel. When he had judged Israel for ten years, 12 the Zebulunite Elon died and was buried in Elon in the land of Zebulun.

13 After him the Pirathonite Abdon, son of Hillel, judged Israel. 14 He had forty sons and thirty grandsons who rode on seventy saddle-asses. After having judged Israel for eight years, 15 the Pirathonite Abdon, son of Hillel, died and was buried in Pirathon in the land of Ephraim on the mountain of the Amalekites.

13 The Israelites again offended the LORD, who therefore delivered them into the power of the Philistines for forty years.

2 There was a certain man from Zorah, of the clan of the Danites, whose name was Manoah. His wife was barren and had borne no children. 3 An angel of the LORD appeared to the woman and said to her, "Though you are barren and have had no children, yet you will conceive and bear a son. 4 Now, then, be careful to take no wine or strong drink and to eat nothing unclean. 5 As for the son you will conceive and bear, no razor shall touch his head, for this boy is to be consecrated to God from the womb. It is he who will begin the deliverance of Israel from the power of the Philistines."

6 The woman went and told her husband, "A man of God came to me; he had the appearance of an angel of God, terrible indeed. I did not ask him where he came from, nor did he tell me his name. 7 But he said to me, 'You will be with child and will bear a son. So take neither wine nor strong drink, and eat nothing unclean. For the boy shall be consecrated to God from the womb, until the day of his death.' " 8 Manoah then prayed to the LORD. "O LORD, I beseech you," he said, "may the man of God whom you sent, return to us to teach us what to do for the boy who will be born."

9 God heard the prayer of Manoah, and the angel of God came again to the woman as she was sitting in the field. Since her husband Manoah was not with her, 10 the woman ran in haste and told her husband. "The man who came to me the other day has appeared to me," she said to him; 11 so

head!' 2 Jephthah replied, 'My people and I were in serious conflict with the Ammonites. I summoned you, but you did not come to rescue me from them. 3 When I saw that no one was coming to rescue me, I took my life in my hands and marched against the Ammonites, and Yahweh handed them over to me. So why advance on me today to make war on me?' 4 Jephthah then mustered all the men of Gilead and made war on Ephraim, and the men of Gilead defeated Ephraim — since the latter used to say, 'You are only fugitives from Ephraim, you Gileadites in the heart of Ephraim and Manasseh.' 5 Gilead then cut Ephraim off from the fords of the Jordan, and whenever Ephraimite fugitives said, 'Let me cross,' the men of Gilead would ask, 'Are you an Ephraimite?' If he said, 'No,' 6 they then said, 'Very well, say Shibboleth.' h If anyone said, "Sibboleth", because he could not pronounce it, then they would seize him and kill him by the fords of the Jordan.

Forty-two thousand Ephraimites fell on this occasion.

7 Jephthah judged Israel for six years. Jephthah the Gileadite then died and was buried in his town, in Gilead.

8 After him, Ibzan of Bethlehem was judge in Israel. 9 He had thirty sons and thirty daughters. He gave his daughters in marriage outside his clan and brought in thirty brides from outside for his sons. He was judge in Israel for seven years. 10 Ibzan then died and was buried in Bethlehem.

11 After him, Elon of Zebulun was judge in Israel. He was judge in Israel for ten years. 12 Elon of Zebulun then died and was buried at Aijalon in the territory of Zebulun.

13 After him, Abdon son of Hillel of Pirathon was judge in Israel. 14 He had forty sons and thirty grandsons who rode seventy young donkeys. He was judge in Israel for eight years. 15 Abdon son of Hillel of Pirathon then died and was buried at Pirathon in the territory of Ephraim, in the Amalekite highlands.

13 Again the Israelites began doing what is evil in Yahweh's eyes, and Yahweh delivered them into the power of the Philistines for forty years.

2 There was a man of Zorah of the tribe of Dan, called Manoah. His wife was barren; she had borne no children. 3 The Angel of Yahweh appeared to this woman and said to her, 'You are barren and have had no child, but you are going to conceive and give birth to a son. 4 From now on, take great care. Drink no wine or fermented liquor, and eat nothing unclean. 5 For you are going to conceive and give birth to a son. No razor is to touch his head, for the boy is to be God's nazirite from his mother's womb; and he will start rescuing Israel from the power of the Philistines.' 6 The woman then went and told her husband, 'A man of God has just come to me, who looked like the Angel of God, so majestic was he. I did not ask him where he came from, and he did not tell me his name. 7 But he said to me, "You are going to conceive and will give birth to a son. From now on, drink no wine or fermented liquor, and eat nothing unclean. For the boy is to be God's nazirite from his mother's womb to his dying day." '

8 Manoah then pleaded with Yahweh and said, 'I beg you, Lord, let the man of God that you sent come to us again and instruct us what to do about the child when he is born.' 9 Yahweh heard Manoah's prayer, and the Angel of Yahweh visited the woman again while she was sitting in a field and when her husband Manoah was not with her. 10 The woman quickly ran and told her husband, 'Look,' she said, 'the man who came to me the other day has ap-

---

h 12 The word (= 'ear of corn') is chosen simply to show up local pronunciation.

NEW REVISED STANDARD VERSION

the other day has appeared to me." 11 Manoah got up and followed his wife, and came to the man and said to him, "Are you the man who spoke to this woman?" And he said, "I am." 12 Then Manoah said, "Now when your words come true, what is to be the boy's rule of life; what is he to do?" 13 The angel of the LORD said to Manoah, "Let the woman give heed to all that I said to her. 14 She may not eat of anything that comes from the vine. She is not to drink wine or strong drink, or eat any unclean thing. She is to observe everything that I commanded her."

15 Manoah said to the angel of the LORD, "Allow us to detain you, and prepare a kid for you." 16 The angel of the LORD said to Manoah, "If you detain me, I will not eat your food; but if you want to prepare a burnt offering, then offer it to the LORD." (For Manoah did not know that he was the angel of the LORD.) 17 Then Manoah said to the angel of the LORD, "What is your name, so that we may honor you when your words come true?" 18 But the angel of the LORD said to him, "Why do you ask my name? It is too wonderful."

19 So Manoah took the kid with the grain offering, and offered it on the rock to the LORD, to him who works*s* wonders.*t* 20 When the flame went up toward heaven from the altar, the angel of the LORD ascended in the flame of the altar while Manoah and his wife looked on; and they fell on their faces to the ground. 21 The angel of the LORD did not appear again to Manoah and his wife. Then Manoah realized that it was the angel of the LORD. 22 And Manoah said to his wife, "We shall surely die, for we have seen God." 23 But his wife said to him, "If the LORD had meant to kill us, he would not have accepted a burnt offering and a grain offering at our hands, or shown us all these things, or now announced to us such things as these."

24 The woman bore a son, and named him Samson. The boy grew, and the LORD blessed him. 25 The spirit of the LORD began to stir him in Mahaneh-dan, between Zorah and Eshtaol.

14 Once Samson went down to Timnah, and at Timnah he saw a Philistine woman. 2 Then he came up, and told his father and mother, "I saw a Philistine woman at Timnah; now get her for me as my wife." 3 But his father and mother said to him, "Is there not a woman among your kin, or among all our*u* people, that you must go to take a wife from the uncircumcised Philistines?" But Samson said to his father, "Get her for me, because she pleases me." 4 His father and mother did not know that this was from the LORD; for he was seeking a pretext to act against the Philistines. At that time the Philistines had dominion over Israel.

5 Then Samson went down with his father and mother to Timnah. When he came to the vineyards of Timnah, suddenly a young lion roared at him. 6 The spirit of the LORD rushed on him, and he tore the lion apart barehanded as one might tear apart a kid. But he did not tell his father or his mother what he had done. 7 Then he went down and talked with the woman, and she pleased Samson. 8 After a while he returned to marry her, and he turned aside to see the carcass of the lion, and there was a swarm of bees in the body of the lion, and honey. 9 He scraped it out into his hands, and went on, eating as he went. When he came to his father and mother, he gave some to them, and they ate it. But he did not tell them that he had taken the honey from the carcass of the lion.

10 His father went down to the woman, and Samson made a feast there as the young men were accustomed to do. 11 When the people saw him, they brought thirty compan-

REVISED ENGLISH BIBLE

again.' 11 Manoah went with her at once and approached the man and said, 'Are you the man who talked with my wife?' 'Yes,' he replied, 'I am.' 12 'Now when your words come true,' Manoah said, 'what kind of boy will he be and what will he do?' 13 The angel of the LORD answered, 'Your wife must be careful to do all that I told her: 14 she must not taste anything that comes from the vine; she must drink no wine or strong drink, and she must eat no forbidden food. She must do whatever I say.'

15 Manoah said to the angel of the LORD, 'May we urge you to stay? Let us prepare a young goat for you.' 16 The angel replied, 'Though you urge me to stay, I shall not eat your food; but prepare a whole-offering if you will, and offer that to the LORD.' Manoah did not know that he was the angel of the LORD, 17 and said to him, 'What is your name? For we shall want to honour you when your words come true.' 18 The angel of the LORD said to him, 'How can you ask my name? It is a name of wonder.' 19 Manoah took a young goat with the proper grain-offering, and offered it on the rock to the LORD, to him whose works are full of wonder. While Manoah and his wife were watching, 20 the flame went up from the altar towards heaven, and the angel of the LORD ascended in the flame. Seeing this, Manoah and his wife fell face downward to the ground.

21 The angel of the LORD did not appear again to Manoah and his wife. When Manoah realized that it had been the angel of the LORD, 22 he said to his wife, 'We are doomed to die, for we have seen God.' 23 But she replied, 'If the LORD had wanted to kill us, he would not have accepted a whole-offering and a grain-offering at our hands; he would not now have let us see and hear all this.'

24-25 The woman gave birth to a son and named him Samson. The boy grew up in Mahaneh-dan between Zorah and Eshtaol, and the LORD blessed him, and the spirit of the LORD began to move him.

14 Samson went down to Timnah, and there a woman, one of the Philistines, caught his notice. 2 On his return he told his father and mother that he had seen this Philistine woman in Timnah and asked them to get her for him as his wife. 3 His parents protested, 'Is there no woman among your cousins or in all our own people? Must you go to the uncircumcised Philistines to find a wife?' But Samson said to his father, 'Get her for me, because she pleases me.' 4 Neither his father nor his mother knew that the LORD was at work in this, seeking an opportunity against the Philistines, who at that time held Israel in subjection.

5 Samson went down to Timnah and, when he reached the vineyards there, a young lion came at him growling. 6 The spirit of the LORD suddenly seized him and, without any weapon in his hand, Samson tore the lion to pieces as if it were a kid. He did not tell his parents what he had done. 7 Then he went down and spoke to the woman, and she pleased him.

8 When, after a time, he went down again to make her his wife, he turned aside to look at the carcass of the lion, and saw there was a swarm of bees in it, and honey. 9 He scraped the honey into his hands and went on, eating as he went. When he came to his father and mother, he gave them some and they ate it; but he did not tell them that he had scraped the honey out of the lion's carcass.

10 His father went down to see the woman, and Samson gave a feast there as the custom of young men was. 11 When the people saw him, they picked thirty companions to escort

---

s Gk Vg: Heb *and working*   *t* Heb *wonders, while Manoah and his wife looked on*   *u* Cn: Heb *my*

14:5 **Samson:** *prob. rdg; Heb.* adds and his father and mother. **he reached:** *so Gk; Heb.* they reached.

Manoah got up and followed his wife. When he reached the man, he said to him, "Are you the one who spoke to my wife?" "Yes," he answered. 12 Then Manoah asked, "Now, when that which you say comes true, what are we expected to do for the boy?" 13 The angel of the LORD answered Manoah, "Your wife is to abstain from all the things of which I spoke to her. 14 She must not eat anything that comes from the vine, nor take wine or strong drink, nor eat anything unclean. Let her observe all that I have commanded her." 15 Then Manoah said to the angel of the LORD, "Can we persuade you to stay, while we prepare a kid for you?" 16 But the angel of the LORD answered Manoah, "Although you press me, I will not partake of your food. But if you will, you may offer a holocaust to the LORD." Not knowing that it was the angel of the LORD, 17 Manoah said to him, "What is your name, that we may honor you when your words come true?" 18 The angel of the LORD answered him, "Why do you ask my name, which is mysterious?" 19 Then Manoah took the kid with a cereal offering and offered it on the rock to the LORD, whose works are mysteries. While Manoah and his wife were looking on, 20 as the flame rose to the sky from the altar, the angel of the LORD ascended in the flame of the altar. When Manoah and his wife saw this, they fell prostrate to the ground; 21 but the angel of the LORD was seen no more by Manoah and his wife. Then Manoah, realizing that it was the angel of the LORD, 22 said to his wife, "We will certainly die, for we have seen God." 23 But his wife pointed out to him, "If the LORD had meant to kill us, he would not have accepted a holocaust and cereal offering from our hands! Nor would he have let us see all this just now, or hear what we have heard."

24 The woman bore a son and named him Samson. The boy grew up and the LORD blessed him; 25 the spirit of the LORD first stirred him in Mahaneh-dan, which is between Zorah and Eshtaol.

14 Samson went down to Timnah and saw there one of the Philistine women. 2 On his return he told his father and mother, "There is a Philistine woman I saw in Timnah whom I wish you to get as a wife for me." 3 His father and mother said to him, "Can you find no wife among your kinsfolk or among all our people, that you must go and take a wife from the uncircumcised Philistines?" But Samson answered his father, "Get her for me, for she pleases me." 4 Now his father and mother did not know that this had been brought about by the LORD, who was providing an opportunity against the Philistines; for at that time they had dominion over Israel.

5 So Samson went down to Timnah with his father and mother. When they had come to the vineyards of Timnah, a young lion came roaring to meet him. 6 But the spirit of the LORD came upon Samson, and although he had no weapons, he tore the lion in pieces as one tears a kid. 7 However, on the journey to speak for the woman, he did not mention to his father or mother what he had done. 8 Later, when he returned to marry the woman who pleased him, he stepped aside to look at the remains of the lion and found a swarm of bees and honey in the lion's carcass. 9 So he scooped the honey out into his palms and ate it as he went along. When he came to his father and mother, he gave them some to eat, without telling them that he had scooped the honey from the lion's carcass.

10 His father also went down to the woman, and Samson gave a banquet there, since it was customary for the young men to do this. 11 When they met him, they brought thirty

peared to me again.' 11 Manoah got up, followed his wife, came to the man and said to him, 'Are you the man who spoke to this woman?' He replied, 'I am.' 12 Manoah then said, 'When your words come true, what will be the boy's way of life?' 13 The Angel of Yahweh replied to Manoah, 'From everything that I forbade this woman, let her abstain. 14 Let her swallow nothing that comes from the vine, let her drink no wine or fermented liquor, let her eat nothing unclean and let her obey all the orders that I have given her.' 15 Manoah then said to the Angel of Yahweh, 'Allow us to detain you while we prepare a kid for you' — 16b for Manoah did not know that this was the Angel of Yahweh. 16a The Angel of Yahweh said to Manoah, 'Even if you did detain me, I should not eat your food; but if you wish to prepare a burnt offering, offer it to Yahweh.' 17 Manoah then said to the Angel of Yahweh, 'What is your name, so that we may honour you when your words come true?' 18 The Angel of Yahweh replied, 'Why ask my name? It is a name of wonder.' 19 Manoah then took the kid and the oblation and offered it on the rock as a burnt offering to Yahweh the Wonderworker. Manoah and his wife looked on. 20 Now, as the flame rose heavenwards from the altar, the Angel of Yahweh ascended in this flame before the eyes of Manoah and his wife, and they fell face downwards on the ground. 21 After this, the Angel of Yahweh did not appear any more to Manoah and his wife, but Manoah understood that this had been the Angel of Yahweh. 22 And Manoah said to his wife, 'We are certain to die, because we have seen God.' 23 His wife replied, 'If Yahweh had meant to kill us, he would not have accepted a burnt offering and oblation from us, he would not have let us see all this and, at the same time, have told us such things.' 24 The woman gave birth to a son and called him Samson. The child grew, and Yahweh blessed him; 25 and the spirit of Yahweh began to stir him in the Camp of Dan, between Zorah and Eshtaol.

14 Samson went down to Timnah, and at Timnah he noticed a woman, a Philistine girl. 2 He went home again and told his father and mother this. 'At Timnah', he said, 'I noticed a woman, a Philistine girl. So now get her for me, to be my wife.' 3 His father and mother said to him, 'Is there no woman among your brothers' daughters or in our entire nation, for you to go and take a wife among these uncircumcised Philistines?' But Samson said to his father, 'Get that one for me; she is the one I am fond of.' 4 His father and mother did not know that all this came from Yahweh, who was seeking grounds for a quarrel with the Philistines, since at this time the Philistines dominated Israel.

5 Samson went down to Timnah and, as he reached the vineyards of Timnah, he saw a young lion coming roaring towards him. 6 The spirit of Yahweh seized on him and he tore the lion to pieces with his bare hands as though it were a kid; but he did not tell his father or mother what he had done. 7 He went down and talked to the woman, and he became fond of her. 8 Not long after this, Samson went back to marry her. He went out of his way to look at the carcase of the lion, and there was a swarm of bees in the lion's body, and honey. 9 He took up some honey in his hand and ate it as he went along. On returning to his father and mother, he gave some to them, which they ate too, but he did not tell them that he had taken it from the lion's carcase.

10 His father then went down to the woman, and Samson made a feast there, as is the custom for young men. 11 And when the Philistines saw him, they chose thirty companions to stay with him.

ions to be with him. 12 Samson said to them, "Let me now put a riddle to you. If you can explain it to me within the seven days of the feast, and find it out, then I will give you thirty linen garments and thirty festal garments. 13 But if you cannot explain it to me, then you shall give me thirty linen garments and thirty festal garments." So they said to him, "Ask your riddle; let us hear it." 14 He said to them,

"Out of the eater came something to eat.
Out of the strong came something sweet."

But for three days they could not explain the riddle.

15 On the fourth^v day they said to Samson's wife, "Coax your husband to explain the riddle to us, or we will burn you and your father's house with fire. Have you invited us here to impoverish us?" 16 So Samson's wife wept before him, saying, "You hate me; you do not really love me. You have asked a riddle of my people, but you have not explained it to me." He said to her, "Look, I have not told my father or my mother. Why should I tell you?" 17 She wept before him the seven days that their feast lasted; and because she nagged him, on the seventh day he told her. Then she explained the riddle to her people. 18 The men of the town said to him on the seventh day before the sun went down,

"What is sweeter than honey?
What is stronger than a lion?"

And he said to them,

"If you had not plowed with my heifer,
you would not have found out my riddle."

19 Then the spirit of the LORD rushed on him, and he went down to Ashkelon. He killed thirty men of the town, took their spoil, and gave the festal garments to those who had explained the riddle. In hot anger he went back to his father's house. 20 And Samson's wife was given to his companion, who had been his best man.

15 After a while, at the time of the wheat harvest, Samson went to visit his wife, bringing along a kid. He said, "I want to go into my wife's room." But her father would not allow him to go in. 2 Her father said, "I was sure that you had rejected her; so I gave her to your companion. Is not her younger sister prettier than she? Why not take her instead?" 3 Samson said to them, "This time, when I do mischief to the Philistines, I will be without blame." 4 So Samson went and caught three hundred foxes, and took some torches; and he turned the foxes^w tail to tail, and put a torch between each pair of tails. 5 When he had set fire to the torches, he let the foxes go into the standing grain of the Philistines, and burned up the shocks and the standing grain, as well as the vineyards and^x olive groves. 6 Then the Philistines asked, "Who has done this?" And they said, "Samson, the son-in-law of the Timnite, because he has taken Samson's wife and given her to his companion." So the Philistines came up, and burned her and her father. 7 Samson said to them, "If this is what you do, I swear I will not stop until I have taken revenge on you." 8 He struck them down hip and thigh with great slaughter; and he went down and stayed in the cleft of the rock of Etam.

9 Then the Philistines came up and encamped in Judah, and made a raid on Lehi. 10 The men of Judah said, "Why have you come up against us?" They said, "We have come up to bind Samson, to do to him as he did to us." 11 Then three thousand men of Judah went down to the cleft of the rock of Etam, and they said to Samson, "Do you not know that the Philistines are rulers over us? What then have you done to us?" He replied, "As they did to me, so I have done to them." 12 They said to him, "We have come down to bind

him. 12 Samson said to them, 'Let me ask you a riddle. If you can solve it during the seven days of the feast, I shall give you thirty lengths of linen and thirty changes of clothing; 13 but if you cannot guess the answer, then you will give me thirty lengths of linen and thirty changes of clothing.' 'Tell us your riddle,' they said; 'let us hear it.' 14 So he said to them:

'Out of the eater came something to eat;
out of the strong came something sweet.'

At the end of three days they had failed to guess the answer. 15 On the fourth day they said to Samson's wife, 'Coax your husband and make him explain the riddle to you, or we shall burn you and your father's house. Did you invite us here to beggar us?' 16 So Samson's wife wept on his shoulder and said, 'You really hate me, you do not love me. You have asked my kinsfolk a riddle and you have not told it to me.' He said to her, 'I have not told it even to my father and mother; and am I to tell it to you?' 17 But she wept on his shoulder every day until the seven feast days were ended, and on the seventh day, because she pestered him so, he told her, and she told the riddle to her kinsfolk. 18 So on the seventh day the men of the city said to Samson just before he entered the bridal chamber:

'What is sweeter than honey?
What is stronger than a lion?'

He replied, 'If you had not ploughed with my heifer, you would not have solved my riddle.' 19 Then the spirit of the LORD suddenly seized him, and he went down to Ashkelon, where he killed thirty men, took their belts, and gave their clothes to the men who had answered his riddle; then in a furious temper he went off to his father's house. 20 Samson's wife was given in marriage to the one who had been his groomsman.

15 After a while, during the time of wheat harvest, Samson went to visit his wife, taking a young goat as a present for her. He said, 'I am going to my wife in our bridal chamber,' but her father would not let him in. 2 He said, 'I was sure that you were really hostile to her, so I gave her in marriage to your groomsman. Her young sister is better than she is—take her instead.' 3 Samson said, 'This time I shall settle my score with the Philistines; I shall do them some real harm.' 4 He went and caught three hundred jackals and got some torches; he tied the jackals tail to tail and fastened a torch between each pair of tails. 5 He then lit the torches and turned the jackals loose in the standing grain of the Philistines, setting fire to standing grain and sheaves, as well as to vineyards and olive groves.

6 'Who has done this?' the Philistines demanded, and when they were told that it was Samson, because the Timnite, his father-in-law, had taken his wife and given her to his groomsman, they came and burnt her and her father to death. 7 Samson said to them, 'If you do things like that, I swear I will be revenged on you before I have done.' 8 He smote them hip and thigh, causing great slaughter; and after that he went down to live in a cave in the Rock of Etam.

9 The Philistines came up and pitched camp in Judah, and overran Lehi. 10 The Judahites said, 'Why have you attacked us?' They answered, 'We have come to take Samson prisoner, and do to him as he did to us.' 11 Then three thousand men from Judah went down to the cave in the Rock of Etam, where they said to Samson, 'Surely you know that the Philistines are our masters? Now look what you have done to us.' He answered, 'I only did to them as they had done to me.' 12 They told him, 'We have come

---

14:15 **fourth:** so Gk; Heb. seventh. **here:** so some MSS; others or not. 14:18 **he entered . . . chamber:** prob. rdg; Heb. the sun went down. 15:5 **and olive groves:** so Gk; Heb. omits and.

^v Gk Syr: Heb seventh   ^w Heb them   ^x Gk Tg Vg: Heb lacks and

men to be his companions. 12 Samson said to them, "Let me propose a riddle to you. If within the seven days of the feast you solve it for me successfully, I will give you thirty linen tunics and thirty sets of garments. 13 But if you cannot answer it for me, you must give me thirty tunics and thirty sets of garments." "Propose your riddle," they responded; "we will listen to it." 14 So he said to them,

"Out of the eater came forth food,
    and out of the strong came forth sweetness."

After three days' failure to answer the riddle, 15 they said on the fourth day to Samson's wife, "Coax your husband to answer the riddle for us, or we will burn you and your family. Did you invite us here to reduce us to poverty?" 16 At Samson's side, his wife wept and said, "You must hate me; you do not love me, for you have proposed a riddle to my countrymen, but have not told me the answer." He said to her, "If I have not told it even to my father or my mother, must I tell it to you?" 17 But she wept beside him during the seven days the feast lasted. On the seventh day, since she importuned him, he told her the answer, and she explained the riddle to her countrymen.

18 On the seventh day, before the sun set, the men of the city said to him,

"What is sweeter than honey,
    and what is stronger than a lion?"

He replied to them,

"If you had not plowed with my heifer,
    you would not have solved my riddle."

19 The spirit of the LORD came upon him, and he went down to Ashkelon, where he killed thirty of their men and despoiled them; he gave their garments to those who had answered the riddle. Then he went off to his own family in anger, 20 and Samson's wife was married to the one who had been best man at his wedding.

15 After some time, in the season of the wheat harvest, Samson visited his wife, bringing a kid. But when he said, "Let me be with my wife in private," her father would not let him enter, 2 saying, "I thought it certain you wished to repudiate her; so I gave her to your best man. Her younger sister is more beautiful than she; you may have her instead." 3 Samson said to them, "This time the Philistines cannot blame me if I harm them." 4 So Samson left and caught three hundred foxes. Turning them tail to tail, he tied between each pair of tails one of the torches he had at hand. 5 He then kindled the torches and set the foxes loose in the standing grain of the Philistines, thus burning both the shocks and the standing grain, and the vineyards and olive orchards as well.

6 When the Philistines asked who had done this, they were told, "Samson, the son-in-law of the Timnite, because his wife was taken and given to his best man." So the Philistines went up and destroyed her and her family by fire. 7 Samson said to them, "If this is how you act, I will not stop until I have taken revenge on you." 8 And with repeated blows, he inflicted a great slaughter on them. Then he went down and remained in a cavern of the cliff of Etam.

9 The Philistines went up and, from a camp in Judah, deployed against Lehi. 10 When the men of Judah asked, "Why have you come up against us?" they answered, "To take Samson prisoner; to do to him as he has done to us." 11 Three thousand men of Judah went down to the cavern in the cliff of Etam and said to Samson, "Do you not know that the Philistines are our rulers? Why, then, have you done this to us?" He answered them, "As they have done to me, so have I done to them." 12 They said to him, "We have come

12 Samson then said to them, 'Let me ask you a riddle. If you can give me the answer during the seven days of feasting, I shall give you thirty pieces of fine linen and thirty festal robes. 13 But if you cannot tell me the answer, then you in your turn must give me thirty pieces of fine linen and thirty festal robes.' 'Ask your riddle,' they replied, 'we are listening.' 14 So he said to them:

Out of the eater came what is eaten,
    and out of the strong came what is sweet.

But three days went by and they could not solve the riddle.

15 On the fourth day they said to Samson's wife, 'Cajole your husband into explaining the riddle to us, or we shall burn you and your father's family to death. Did you invite us here to rob us?' 16 Samson's wife then went to him in tears and said, 'You only hate me, you do not love me. You have asked my fellow-countrymen a riddle and told not even me the answer.' He said to her, 'I have not told even my father or mother; why should I tell you?' 17 She wept on his neck for the seven days that their feasting lasted. She was so persistent that on the seventh day he told her the answer, and she told her fellow-countrymen.

18 So on the seventh day, before he went into the bedroom, the men of the town said to him:

What is sweeter than honey,
    and what stronger than a lion?

He retorted:

If you had not ploughed with my heifer,
    you would never have solved my riddle.

19 Then the spirit of Yahweh seized on him. He went down to Ashkelon, killed thirty men there, took what they wore and gave the festal robes to those who had answered the riddle, then burning with rage returned to his father's house. 20 Samson's wife was then given to the companion who had acted as his best man.

15 Not long after this, at the time of the wheat harvest, Samson visited his wife, with a kid; he said, 'I wish to go to my wife in her room.' But her father would not let him enter. 2 'I felt sure', he said, 'that you had taken a real dislike to her, so I gave her to your companion. But would not her younger sister suit you better? Have her instead.' 3 But Samson answered them, 'I can get my revenge on the Philistines now only by doing them some damage.' 4 So Samson went off and caught three hundred foxes, then took torches and, turning the foxes tail to tail, put a torch between each pair of tails. 5 He lit the torches and set the foxes free in the Philistines' cornfields. In this way he burned both sheaves and standing corn, and the vines and olive trees as well.

6 The Philistines asked, 'Who has done this?' and received the answer, 'Samson, who married the Timnite's daughter; his father-in-law took the wife back again and gave her to his companion instead.' The Philistines then went and burned the woman and her father's family to death. 7 Samson said to them, 'If that is how you behave, I swear I will not rest till I have had my revenge on you.' 8 And he fell on them systematically and caused great havoc. Then he went down to the cave in the Rock of Etham and lived there.

9 The Philistines came up and encamped in Judah and made a foray against Lehi. 10 The men of Judah said to them, 'Why are you attacking us?' They replied, 'We have come to seize Samson and to treat him as he has treated us.' 11 Three thousand men of Judah then went down to the cave of the Rock of Etham and said to him, 'Don't you know that the Philistines have us in their power? Now what have you done to us?' He replied, 'I have treated them only as they treated me.' 12 They then

you, so that we may give you into the hands of the Philistines." Samson answered them, "Swear to me that you yourselves will not attack me." 13 They said to him, "No, we will only bind you and give you into their hands; we will not kill you." So they bound him with two new ropes, and brought him up from the rock.

14 When he came to Lehi, the Philistines came shouting to meet him; and the spirit of the LORD rushed on him, and the ropes that were on his arms became like flax that has caught fire, and his bonds melted off his hands. 15 Then he found a fresh jawbone of a donkey, reached down and took it, and with it he killed a thousand men. 16 And Samson said,

"With the jawbone of a donkey,
    heaps upon heaps,
with the jawbone of a donkey
    I have slain a thousand men."

17 When he had finished speaking, he threw away the jawbone; and that place was called Ramath-lehi.*y*

18 By then he was very thirsty, and he called on the LORD, saying, "You have granted this great victory by the hand of your servant. Am I now to die of thirst, and fall into the hands of the uncircumcised?" 19 So God split open the hollow place that is at Lehi, and water came from it. When he drank, his spirit returned, and he revived. Therefore it was named En-hakkore,*z* which is at Lehi to this day. 20 And he judged Israel in the days of the Philistines twenty years.

16 Once Samson went to Gaza, where he saw a prostitute and went in to her. 2 The Gazites were told,*a* "Samson has come here." So they circled around and lay in wait for him all night at the city gate. They kept quiet all night, thinking, "Let us wait until the light of the morning; then we will kill him." 3 But Samson lay only until midnight. Then at midnight he rose up, took hold of the doors of the city gate and the two posts, pulled them up, bar and all, put them on his shoulders, and carried them to the top of the hill that is in front of Hebron.

4 After this he fell in love with a woman in the valley of Sorek, whose name was Delilah. 5 The lords of the Philistines came to her and said to her, "Coax him, and find out what makes his strength so great, and how we may overpower him, so that we may bind him in order to subdue him; and we will each give you eleven hundred pieces of silver." 6 So Delilah said to Samson, "Please tell me what makes your strength so great, and how you could be bound, so that one could subdue you." 7 Samson said to her, "If they bind me with seven fresh bowstrings that are not dried out, then I shall become weak, and be like anyone else." 8 Then the lords of the Philistines brought her seven fresh bowstrings that had not dried out, and she bound him with them. 9 While men were lying in wait in an inner chamber, she said to him, "The Philistines are upon you, Samson!" But he snapped the bowstrings, as a strand of fiber snaps when it touches the fire. So the secret of his strength was not known.

10 Then Delilah said to Samson, "You have mocked me and told me lies; please tell me how you could be bound." 11 He said to her, "If they bind me with new ropes that have not been used, then I shall become weak, and be like anyone else." 12 So Delilah took new ropes and bound him with them, and said to him, "The Philistines are upon you, Samson!" (The men lying in wait were in an inner chamber.) But he snapped the ropes off his arms like a thread.

down to bind you and hand you over to the Philistines.' 'Swear to me that you will not set upon me yourselves,' he said. 13 'No, we shall not kill you,' they answered; 'we shall only bind you and hand you over to them.' They bound him with two new ropes and brought him up from the cave in the Rock.

14 When Samson came to Lehi, the Philistines met him with shouts of triumph; but the spirit of the LORD suddenly seized him, the ropes on his arms became like burnt tow, and his bonds melted away. 15 He came on the fresh jawbone of a donkey, and seizing it he slew a thousand men. 16 He made up this saying:

'With the jaw-bone of a donkey I have flayed them
    like donkeys;
with the jaw-bone of a donkey I have slain a
    thousand men.'

17 Having said this he threw away the jaw-bone; and he called that place Ramath-lehi.

18 He began to feel very thirsty and cried aloud to the LORD, 'You have let me, your servant, win this great victory, and must I now die of thirst and fall into the hands of the uncircumcised?' 19 God split open the Hollow of Lehi and water came out of it. Samson drank, his strength returned, and he revived. This is why to this day the spring in Lehi is called En-hakkore.

20 Samson was judge over Israel for twenty years in the days of the Philistines.

16 Samson went to Gaza, and seeing a prostitute there he lay with her. 2 The people of Gaza heard that Samson had come, and they gathered round and lay in wait for him all night at the city gate. During the night, however, they took no action, saying to themselves, 'When dawn comes we shall kill him.' 3 Samson stayed in bed till midnight; but then he rose, took hold of the doors of the city gate and the two gateposts, and pulled them out, bar and all; he hoisted them on his shoulders, and carried them to the top of the hill east of Hebron.

4 Afterwards Samson fell in love with a woman named Delilah, who lived by the wadi of Sorek. 5 The lords of the Philistines went up to her and said, 'Cajole him and find out what gives him his great strength, and how we can overpower and bind him and render him helpless. We shall each give you eleven hundred pieces of silver.' 6 Delilah said to Samson, 'Tell me, what gives you your great strength? How could you be bound and made helpless?' 7 'If I were bound with seven fresh bowstrings not yet dry,' replied Samson, 'then I should become no stronger than any other man.' 8 The lords of the Philistines brought her seven fresh bowstrings not yet dry, and she bound him with them. 9 She had men concealed in the inner room, and she cried, 'Samson, the Philistines are upon you!' Thereupon he snapped the bowstrings as a strand of tow snaps at the touch of fire, and his strength was not impaired.

10 Delilah said to Samson, 'You have made a fool of me and lied to me. Now tell me this time how you can be bound.' 11 He said to her, 'If I were tightly bound with new ropes that have never been used, then I should become no stronger than any other man.' 12 Delilah took new ropes and bound him with them. Then, with men concealed in the inner room, she cried, 'Samson, the Philistines are upon you!' But he snapped the ropes off his arms like thread.

---

y That is The Hill of the Jawbone   z That is The Spring of the One who Called   a Gk: Heb lacks were told

15:17 **Ramath-lehi:** *that is* Jaw-bone Hill.   15:19 **Hollow:** *lit.* Mortar. **En-hakkore:** *that is* the Crier's Spring.   16:2 **The people . . . heard:** *so* Gk; Heb. To the people of Gaza.

to take you prisoner, to deliver you over to the Philistines." Samson said to them, "Swear to me that you will not kill me yourselves." 13 "No," they replied, "we will certainly not kill you but will only bind you and deliver you over to them." So they bound him with two new ropes and brought him up from the cliff. 14 When he reached Lehi, and the Philistines came shouting to meet him, the spirit of the LORD came upon him: the ropes around his arms became as flax that is consumed by fire and his bonds melted away from his hands. 15 Near him was the fresh jawbone of an ass; he reached out, grasped it, and with it killed a thousand men. 16 Then Samson said,

"With the jawbone of an ass
    I have piled them in a heap;
With the jawbone of an ass
    I have slain a thousand men."

17 As he finished speaking he threw the jawbone from him; and so that place was named Ramath-lehi. 18 Being very thirsty, he cried to the LORD and said, "You have granted this great victory by the hand of your servant. Must I now die of thirst or fall into the hands of the uncircumcised?" 19 Then God split the cavity in Lehi, and water issued from it, which Samson drank till his spirit returned and he revived. Hence that spring in Lehi is called En-hakkore to this day.

20 Samson judged Israel for twenty years in the days of the Philistines.

16 Once Samson went to Gaza, where he saw a harlot and visited her. 2 Informed that Samson had come there, the men of Gaza surrounded him with an ambush at the city gate all night long. And all the night they waited, saying, "Tomorrow morning we will kill him." 3 Samson rested there until midnight. Then he rose, seized the doors of the city gate and the two gateposts, and tore them loose, bar and all. He hoisted them on his shoulders and carried them to the top of the ridge opposite Hebron.

4 After that he fell in love with a woman in the Wadi Sorek whose name was Delilah. 5 The lords of the Philistines came to her and said, "Beguile him and find out the secret of his great strength, and how we may overcome and bind him so as to keep him helpless. We will each give you eleven hundred shekels of silver."

6 So Delilah said to Samson, "Tell me the secret of your great strength and how you may be bound so as to be kept helpless." 7 "If they bind me with seven fresh bowstrings which have not dried," Samson answered her, "I shall be as weak as any other man." 8 So the lords of the Philistines brought her seven fresh bowstrings which had not dried, and she bound him with them. 9 She had men lying in wait in the chamber and so she said to him, "The Philistines are upon you, Samson!" But he snapped the strings as a thread of tow is severed by a whiff of flame; and the secret of his strength remained unknown.

10 Delilah said to Samson, "You have mocked me and told me lies. Now tell me how you may be bound." 11 "If they bind me tight with new ropes, with which no work has been done," he answered her, "I shall be as weak as any other man." 12 So Delilah took new ropes and bound him with them. Then she said to him, "The Philistines are upon you, Samson!" For there were men lying in wait in the chamber. But he snapped them off his arms like thread.

said, 'We have come down to take you, to hand you over to the Philistines.' He said, 'Swear to me not to kill me yourselves.' 13 They replied, 'No; we only want to bind you and hand you over to them; we certainly do not want to kill you.' They then bound him with two new ropes and brought him up from the Rock.

14 As he was approaching Lehi, and the Philistines came running towards him with triumphant shouts, the spirit of Yahweh was on him; the ropes on his arms became like burnt strands of flax and the cords round his hands came untied. 15 Coming across the fresh jawbone of a donkey, he reached out and snatched it up; and with it he slaughtered a thousand men. 16 And Samson said:

With the jawbone of a donkey I have laid them
    in heaps,
with the jawbone of a donkey I have felled a
    thousand men.

17 And with that he hurled the jawbone away; and that is why the place was called Ramath-Lehi.[i] 18 And as he was very thirsty, he called on Yahweh and said, 'You yourself have worked this great deliverance by the hand of your servant; and now must I die of thirst and fall into the hands of the uncircumcised?' 19 Then God opened a hollow in the ground, the hollow there is at Lehi, and water gushed out of it. Samson drank; his vigour returned and he revived. And therefore this spring was called En-ha-Kore;[j] it is still at Lehi today. 20 Samson was judge in Israel in the days of the Philistines for twenty years.

16 Samson then went to Gaza and, seeing a prostitute there, went in to her. 2 The men of Gaza being told, 'Samson has arrived,' surrounded the place and kept watch for him the whole night at the town gate. All that night they were going to make no move, thinking, 'Let us wait until daybreak, and then kill him.' 3 Till midnight, however, Samson stayed in bed, and then at midnight he got up, seized the doors of the town gate and the two posts as well; he tore them up, bar and all, hoisted them on to his shoulders and carried them to the top of the hill overlooking Hebron.

4 After this, he fell in love with a woman in the Vale of Sorek; she was called Delilah. 5 The Philistine chiefs visited her and said, 'Cajole him and find out where his great strength comes from, and how we can master him, so that we can bind him and subdue him. In return we shall each give you eleven hundred silver shekels.'

6 Delilah said to Samson, 'Please tell me where your great strength comes from, and what would be needed to bind and subdue you.' 7 Samson replied, 'If I were bound with seven new bowstrings which had not yet been dried, I should lose my strength and become like any other man.' 8 The Philistine chiefs brought Delilah seven new bowstrings which had not yet been dried and she took them and bound him with them. 9 She had men concealed in her room, and she shouted, 'The Philistines are on you, Samson!' Then he snapped the bowstrings as a strand of tow snaps at a touch of the fire. So the secret of his strength remained unknown.

10 Delilah then said to Samson, 'You have been laughing at me and telling me lies. But now please tell me what would be needed to bind you.' 11 He replied, 'If I were bound tightly with new ropes which have never been used, I should lose my strength and become like any other man.' 12 Delilah then took new ropes and bound him with them, and she shouted, 'The Philistines are on you, Samson!' She had men concealed in her room, but he snapped the ropes round his arms like thread.

---

i 15 Lit. 'hill of the jawbone'.　*j* 15 'The Spring of the Caller', where Samson called on Yahweh.

NEW REVISED STANDARD VERSION

REVISED ENGLISH BIBLE

13 Then Delilah said to Samson, "Until now you have mocked me and told me lies; tell me how you could be bound." He said to her, "If you weave the seven locks of my head with the web and make it tight with the pin, then I shall become weak, and be like anyone else." 14 So while he slept, Delilah took the seven locks of his head and wove them into the web,b and made them tight with the pin. Then she said to him, "The Philistines are upon you, Samson!" But he awoke from his sleep, and pulled away the pin, the loom, and the web.

15 Then she said to him, "How can you say, 'I love you,' when your heart is not with me? You have mocked me three times now and have not told me what makes your strength so great." 16 Finally, after she had nagged him with her words day after day, and pestered him, he was tired to death. 17 So he told her his whole secret, and said to her, "A razor has never come upon my head; for I have been a naziritec to God from my mother's womb. If my head were shaved, then my strength would leave me; I would become weak, and be like anyone else."

18 When Delilah realized that he had told her his whole secret, she sent and called the lords of the Philistines, saying, "This time come up, for he has told his whole secret to me." Then the lords of the Philistines came up to her, and brought the money in their hands. 19 She let him fall asleep on her lap; and she called a man, and had him shave off the seven locks of his head. He began to weaken,d and his strength left him. 20 Then she said, "The Philistines are upon you, Samson!" When he awoke from his sleep, he thought, "I will go out as at other times, and shake myself free." But he did not know that the LORD had left him. 21 So the Philistines seized him and gouged out his eyes. They brought him down to Gaza and bound him with bronze shackles; and he ground at the mill in the prison. 22 But the hair of his head began to grow again after it had been shaved.

23 Now the lords of the Philistines gathered to offer a great sacrifice to their god Dagon, and to rejoice; for they said, "Our god has given Samson our enemy into our hand." 24 When the people saw him, they praised their god; for they said, "Our god has given our enemy into our hand, the ravager of our country, who has killed many of us." 25 And when their hearts were merry, they said, "Call Samson, and let him entertain us." So they called Samson out of the prison, and he performed for them. They made him stand between the pillars; 26 and Samson said to the attendant who held him by the hand, "Let me feel the pillars on which the house rests, so that I may lean against them." 27 Now the house was full of men and women; all the lords of the Philistines were there, and on the roof there were about three thousand men and women, who looked on while Samson performed.

28 Then Samson called to the LORD and said, "Lord GOD, remember me and strengthen me only this once, O God, so that with this one act of revenge I may pay back the Philistines for my two eyes."e 29 And Samson grasped the two middle pillars on which the house rested, and he leaned his weight against them, his right hand on the one and his left hand on the other. 30 Then Samson said, "Let me die with the Philistines." He strained with all his might; and the house fell on the lords and all the people who were in it. So those he killed at his death were more than those he

13 Delilah said to him, 'You are still making a fool of me, still lying to me. Tell me: how can you be bound?' He said, 'Take the seven loose locks of my hair, weave them into the warp, and drive them tight with the beater; then I shall become no stronger than any other man.' So she lulled him to sleep, wove the seven loose locks of his hair into the warp, 14 drove them tight with the beater, and cried, 'Samson, the Philistines are upon you!' He woke from sleep and pulled away the warp and the loom with it.

15 She said to him, 'How can you say you love me when you do not confide in me? This is the third time you have made a fool of me and have not told me what gives you your great strength.' 16 She so pestered him with these words day after day, pressing him hard and wearying him to death, 17 that he told her the whole secret. 'No razor has touched my head,' he said, 'because I am a Nazirite, consecrated to God from the day of my birth. If my head were shaved, then my strength would leave me, and I should become no stronger than any other man.'

18 Delilah realized that he had told her his secret, and she sent word to the lords of the Philistines: 'Come up at once,' she said; 'he has told me his secret.' The lords of the Philistines came, bringing the money with them. 19 She lulled Samson to sleep on her lap, and then summoned a man to shave the seven locks of his hair. She was now making him helpless. When his strength had left him, 20 she cried, 'Samson, the Philistines are upon you!' He woke from his sleep and thought, 'I will go out as usual and shake myself'; he did not know that the LORD had left him. 21 Then the Philistines seized him, gouged out his eyes, and brought him down to Gaza. There they bound him with bronze fetters, and he was set to grinding grain in the prison. 22 But his hair, after it had been shaved, began to grow again.

23 The lords of the Philistines assembled to offer a great sacrifice to their god Dagon, and to rejoice and say,

'Our god has delivered into our hands
    Samson our enemy.'

24 The people, when they saw him, praised their god, chanting:

'Our god has delivered our enemy into our hands,
    the scourge of our land who piled it with our
        dead.'

25 When they grew merry, they said, 'Call Samson, and let him entertain us.' When Samson was summoned from prison, he was a source of entertainment to them. They then stood him between the pillars, 26 and Samson said to the boy who led him by the hand, 'Put me where I can feel the pillars which support the temple, so that I may lean against them.' 27 The temple was full of men and women, and all the lords of the Philistines were there, and there were about three thousand men and women on the roof watching the entertainment.

28 Samson cried to the LORD and said, 'Remember me, Lord GOD, remember me: for this one occasion, God, give me strength, and let me at one stroke be avenged on the Philistines for my two eyes.' 29 He put his arms round the two central pillars which supported the temple, his right arm round one and his left round the other and, bracing himself, 30 he said, 'Let me die with the Philistines.' Then Samson leaned forward with all his might, and the temple crashed down on the lords and all the people who were in it. So the dead whom he killed at his death were more than those he had killed in his life.

b Compare Gk: in verses 13-14, Heb lacks and make it tight . . . into the web   c That is one separated or one consecrated   d Gk: Heb She began to torment him   e Or so that I may be avenged upon the Philistines for one of my two eyes

16:13 and drive . . . warp: so Gk; Heb. omits.   16:14 the warp . . . with it: prob. rdg; Heb. adds an unintelligible word.

NEW AMERICAN BIBLE

13 Delilah said to Samson again, "Up to now you have mocked me and told me lies. Tell me how you may be bound." He said to her, "If you weave my seven locks of hair into the web and fasten them with the pin, I shall be as weak as any other man." 14 So while he slept, Delilah wove his seven locks of hair into the web, and fastened them in with the pin. Then she said, "The Philistines are upon you, Samson!" Awakening from his sleep, he pulled out both the weaver's pin and the web.

15 Then she said to him, "How can you say that you love me when you do not confide in me? Three times already you have mocked me, and not told me the secret of your great strength!" 16 She importuned him continually and vexed him with her complaints till he was deathly weary of them. 17 So he took her completely into his confidence and told her, "No razor has touched my head, for I have been consecrated to God from my mother's womb. If I am shaved, my strength will leave me, and I shall be as weak as any other man!" 18 When Delilah saw that he had taken her completely into his confidence, she summoned the lords of the Philistines, saying, "Come up this time, for he has opened his heart to me." So the lords of the Philistines came and brought up the money with them. 19 She had him sleep on her lap, and called for a man who shaved off his seven locks of hair. Then she began to mistreat him, for his strength had left him. 20 When she said, "The Philistines are upon you, Samson!", and he woke from his sleep, he thought he could make good his escape as he had done time and again, for he did not realize that the LORD had left him. 21 But the Philistines seized him and gouged out his eyes. Then they brought him down to Gaza and bound him with bronze fetters, and he was put to grinding in the prison. 22 But the hair of his head began to grow as soon as it was shaved off.

23 The lords of the Philistines assembled to offer a great sacrifice to their god Dagon and to make merry. They said,
"Our god has delivered into our power
Samson our enemy."
25 When their spirits were high, they said, "Call Samson that he may amuse us." So they called Samson from the prison, and he played the buffoon before them. 24 When the people saw him, they praised their god. For they said,
"Our god has delivered into our power
our enemy, the ravager of our land,
the one who has multiplied our slain."
Then they stationed him between the columns. 26 Samson said to the attendant who was holding his hand, "Put me where I may touch the columns that support the temple and may rest against them." 27 The temple was full of men and women: all the lords of the Philistines were there, and from the roof about three thousand men and women looked on as Samson provided amusement. 28 Samson cried out to the LORD and said, "O Lord GOD, remember me! Strengthen me, O God, this last time that for my two eyes I may avenge myself once and for all on the Philistines." 29 Samson grasped the two middle columns on which the temple rested and braced himself against them, one at his right hand, the other at his left. 30 And Samson said, "Let me die with the Philistines!" He pushed hard, and the temple fell upon the lords and all the people who were in it. Those he killed at his death were more than those he had killed during his lifetime.

NEW JERUSALEM BIBLE

13 Delilah then said to Samson, 'Up to now you have been laughing at me and telling me lies. Tell me what would be needed to bind you.' He replied, 'If you wove the seven locks of my hair into the warp of a cloth and beat them together tight with the reed, I should lose my strength and become like any other man.' 14 She lulled him to sleep, then wove the seven locks of his hair into the warp, beat them together tight with the reed and shouted, 'The Philistines are on you, Samson!' He woke from his sleep and pulled out both reed and warp. So the secret of his strength remained unknown.

15 Delilah said to him, 'How can you say that you love me, when your heart is not with me? Three times now you have laughed at me and have not told me where your great strength comes from.' 16 And day after day she pestered him with her talk, nagging him till he grew sick to death of it. 17 At last he confided everything to her; he said to her, 'A razor has never touched my head, because I have been God's nazirite from my mother's womb. If my head were shorn, then my power would leave me and I should lose my strength and become like any other man.' 18 Delilah then realized that he had really confided in her; she sent for the Philistine princes with the message, 'Come just once more: he has confided everything to me.' And the Philistine chiefs came to her with the money in their hands. 19 She lulled Samson to sleep in her lap, summoned a man and had him shear off the seven locks from his head. Thus for the first time she got control over him, and his strength left him. 20 She cried, 'The Philistines are on you, Samson!' He awoke from sleep, thinking, 'I shall break free as I have done time after time and shake myself clear.' But he did not know that Yahweh had left him. 21 The Philistines seized him, put out his eyes and took him down to Gaza. They fettered him with a double chain of bronze and he spent his time turning the mill in the prison.

22 But his hair began to grow again when it had been cut off.

23 The Philistine chiefs assembled to offer a great sacrifice to Dagon their god. And amid their festivities they said:
Into our hands our god has delivered
Samson our enemy.
24 And as soon as the people saw their god, they acclaimed him, shouting his praises:
Into our hands our god has delivered
Samson our enemy,
the man who laid our country waste
and killed so many of us.
25 And as their hearts were full of joy, they shouted, 'Summon Samson out to amuse us.' So Samson was summoned from prison, and he performed feats in front of them; then he was put to stand between the pillars. 26 Samson then said to the boy who was leading him by the hand, 'Lead me where I can touch the pillars supporting the building, so that I can lean against them.' 27 Now the building was crowded with men and women. All the Philistine chiefs were there, while about three thousand men and women were watching Samson's feats from the terrace. 28 Samson called on Yahweh and cried out, 'Lord Yahweh, I beg you, remember me; give me strength again this once, O God, and let me be revenged on the Philistines at one blow for my two eyes.' 29 And Samson took hold of the two central pillars supporting the building, and braced himself with his right arm round one and his left round the other; 30 and he shouted, 'Let me die with the Philistines!' He then heaved with all his might, and the building fell on the chiefs and on all the people there. Those whom he brought to their death by his death outnumbered those whom he had done to death during

had killed during his life. 31 Then his brothers and all his family came down and took him and brought him up and buried him between Zorah and Eshtaol in the tomb of his father Manoah. He had judged Israel twenty years.

17 There was a man in the hill country of Ephraim whose name was Micah. 2 He said to his mother, "The eleven hundred pieces of silver that were taken from you, about which you uttered a curse, and even spoke it in my hearing, — that silver is in my possession; I took it; but now I will return it to you."*f* And his mother said, "May my son be blessed by the LORD!" 3 Then he returned the eleven hundred pieces of silver to his mother; and his mother said, "I consecrate the silver to the LORD from my hand for my son, to make an idol of cast metal." 4 So when he returned the money to his mother, his mother took two hundred pieces of silver, and gave it to the silversmith, who made it into an idol of cast metal; and it was in the house of Micah. 5 This man Micah had a shrine, and he made an ephod and teraphim, and installed one of his sons, who became his priest. 6 In those days there was no king in Israel; all the people did what was right in their own eyes.

7 Now there was a young man of Bethlehem in Judah, of the clan of Judah. He was a Levite residing there. 8 This man left the town of Bethlehem in Judah, to live wherever he could find a place. He came to the house of Micah in the hill country of Ephraim to carry on his work.*g* 9 Micah said to him, "From where do you come?" He replied, "I am a Levite of Bethlehem in Judah, and I am going to live wherever I can find a place." 10 Then Micah said to him, "Stay with me, and be to me a father and a priest, and I will give you ten pieces of silver a year, a set of clothes, and your living."*h* 11 The Levite agreed to stay with the man; and the young man became to him like one of his sons. 12 So Micah installed the Levite, and the young man became his priest, and was in the house of Micah. 13 Then Micah said, "Now I know that the LORD will prosper me, because the Levite has become my priest."

18 In those days there was no king in Israel. And in those days the tribe of the Danites was seeking for itself a territory to live in; for until then no territory among the tribes of Israel had been allotted to them. 2 So the Danites sent five valiant men from the whole number of their clan, from Zorah and from Eshtaol, to spy out the land and to explore it; and they said to them, "Go, explore the land." When they came to the hill country of Ephraim, to the house of Micah, they stayed there. 3 While they were at Micah's house, they recognized the voice of the young Levite; so they went over and asked him, "Who brought you here? What are you doing in this place? What is your business here?" 4 He said to them, "Micah did such and such for me, and he hired me, and I have become his priest." 5 Then they said to him, "Inquire of God that we may know whether the mission we are undertaking will succeed." 6 The priest replied, "Go in peace. The mission you are on is under the eye of the LORD."

7 The five men went on, and when they came to Laish, they observed the people who were there living securely, after the manner of the Sidonians, quiet and unsuspecting, lacking*i* nothing on earth, and possessing wealth.*j* Furthermore, they were far from the Sidonians and had no dealings with Aram.*k* 8 When they came to their kinsfolk at Zorah and Eshtaol, they said to them, "What do you report?" 9 They said, "Come, let us go up against them; for we

31 His brothers and all his father's family came down, carried him up to the grave of his father Manoah between Zorah and Eshtaol, and buried him there. He had been judge over Israel for twenty years.

17 ONCE there was a man named Micah from the hill-country of Ephraim 2 who said to his mother, 'You remember the eleven hundred pieces of silver which were stolen from you, and how in my hearing you called down a curse on the thief? I have the money; I took it, and now I give it back to you.' His mother said, 'May the LORD bless you, my son!' 3 He gave back the eleven hundred pieces of silver to his mother, and she said, 'I now solemnly dedicate this silver to the LORD for the benefit of my son, to make a carved image and a cast idol.' 4 When he returned the money to his mother, she handed two hundred of the pieces of silver to a silversmith, who made them into an image and an idol, which were placed in Micah's house. 5 This man Micah had a shrine, and he made an ephod and teraphim and installed one of his sons to be his priest. 6 In those days there was no king in Israel and everyone did what was right in his own eyes.

7 There was a young man from Bethlehem in Judah, from the clan of Judah, a Levite named Ben-gershom. 8 He had left the town of Bethlehem to go and find somewhere to live. On his way he came to Micah's house in the hill-country of Ephraim. 9 Micah asked him, 'Where have you come from?' and he replied, 'I am a Levite from Bethlehem in Judah, and I am looking for somewhere to live.' 10 'Stay with me and be a father and priest to me,' Micah said. 'I shall give you ten pieces of silver a year, and provide you with food and clothes.' 11 The Levite agreed to stay with the man, who treated him as one of his own family. 12 Micah installed the Levite, and the young man became his priest and a member of his household. 13 Micah said, 'Now I know that the LORD will make me prosper, because I have a Levite as my priest.'

18 IN those days when Israel had no king, the tribe of Dan was looking for territory to occupy, because they had not so far come into possession of the territory allotted to them among the tribes of Israel. 2 The Danites therefore sent out five of their valiant fighters from Zorah and Eshtaol, instructing them to reconnoitre and explore the land. As they followed their instructions, they came to Micah's house in the hill-country of Ephraim and spent the night there. 3 While at the house, they recognized the speech of the young Levite, and turning they said, 'Who brought you here, and what are you doing? What is your business here?' 4 He explained, 'Micah did such and such: he hired me and I have become his priest.' 5 They said to him, 'Then enquire of God on our behalf whether our mission will be successful.' 6 The priest replied, 'Go and prosper. The LORD looks favourably on the mission you have undertaken.'

7 The five men went on their way and came to Laish. There they found the inhabitants living free of care in the same way as the Sidonians, quiet and carefree with nothing lacking in the country. They were a long way from the Sidonians, and had no contact with the Aramaeans.

8 On their return to Zorah and Eshtaol, the five men were asked by their kinsmen for their report, 9 and they replied,

*f*The words *but now I will return it to you* are transposed from the end of verse 3 in Heb   *g* Or *Ephraim, continuing his journey* *h*Heb *living, and the Levite went*   *i*Cn Compare 18.10: Meaning of Heb uncertain   *j*Meaning of Heb uncertain   *k*Symmachus: Heb *with anyone*

17:2 **and now . . . to you:** *transposed from verse 3.* 17:5 **teraphim:** *or* household gods.   17:7 **named Ben-gershom:** *prob. rdg, cp. 18:30; Heb.* he lodged there.   17:10 **food and clothes:** *so Lat.; Heb.* adds and the Levite went.   18:1 **they had . . . territory:** *so Gk; Heb.* obscure.   18:7 **with nothing . . . country:** *prob. rdg; Heb.* obscure. **Aramaeans:** *so some Gk MSS; Heb.* men.

31 All his family and kinsmen went down and bore him up for burial in the grave of his father Manoah between Zorah and Eshtaol. He had judged Israel for twenty years.

17

There was a man in the mountain region of Ephraim whose name was Micah. 2 He said to his mother, "The eleven hundred shekels of silver over which you pronounced a curse in my hearing when they were taken from you, are in my possession. It was I who took them; so now I will restore them to you." 3 When he restored the eleven hundred shekels of silver to his mother, she took two hundred of them and gave them to the silversmith, who made of them a carved idol overlaid with silver. 4 Then his mother said, "May the LORD bless my son! I have consecrated the silver to the LORD as my gift in favor of my son, by making a carved idol overlaid with silver." It remained in the house of Micah. 5 Thus the layman Micah had a sanctuary. He also made an ephod and household idols, and consecrated one of his sons, who became his priest. 6 In those days there was no king in Israel; everyone did what he thought best.

7 There was a young Levite who had resided within the tribe of Judah at Bethlehem of Judah. 8 From that city he set out to find another place of residence. On his journey he came to the house of Micah in the mountain region of Ephraim. 9 Micah said to him, "Where do you come from?" He answered him, "I am a Levite from Bethlehem in Judah, and am on my way to find some other place of residence." 10 "Stay with me," Micah said to him. "Be father and priest to me, and I will give you ten silver shekels a year, a set of garments, and your food." 11 So the young Levite decided to stay with the man, to whom he became as one of his own sons. 12 Micah consecrated the young Levite, who became his priest, remaining in his house. 13 Therefore Micah said, "Now I know that the LORD will prosper me, since the Levite has become my priest."

18

At that time there was no king in Israel. Moreover the tribe of Danites were in search of a district to dwell in, for up to that time they had received no heritage among the tribes of Israel.

2 So the Danites sent from their clan a detail of five valiant men of Zorah and Eshtaol, to reconnoiter the land and scout it. With their instructions to go and scout the land, they traveled as far as the house of Micah in the mountain region of Ephraim, where they passed the night. 3 Near the house of Micah, they recognized the voice of the young Levite and turned in that direction. "Who brought you here and what are you doing here?" they asked him. "What is your interest here?" 4 "This is how Micah treats me," he replied to them. "He pays me a salary and I am his priest." 5 They said to him, "Consult God, that we may know whether the undertaking we are engaged in will succeed." 6 The priest said to them, "Go and prosper: the LORD is favorable to the undertaking you are engaged in."

7 So the five men went on and came to Laish. They saw that the people dwelling there lived securely after the manner of the Sidonians, quiet and trusting, with no lack of any natural resources. They were distant from the Sidonians and had no contact with other people. 8 When the five returned to their kinsmen in Zorah and Eshtaol and were asked for a report, 9 they replied, "Come, let us attack them, for we

his life. 31 His brothers and the whole of his father's family came down and carried him away. They took him back and buried him between Zorah and Eshtaol in the tomb of Manoah his father. He had judged Israel for twenty years.

17

In the highlands of Ephraim there was a man called Micayehu. 2 He said to his mother, 'The eleven hundred silver shekels which were taken from you and concerning which you uttered a curse, having said in my hearing . . .k Look, I have got that silver. I was the one who took it.' His mother said, 'May Yahweh bless my boy!' 3 He gave the eleven hundred shekels back to his mother, who said, 'I have indeed vowed to give this silver to Yahweh for my son, to have a statue carved and an idol cast in metal, but now I should like to give it back to you.' He, however, returned the money to his mother.

4 His mother then took two hundred silver shekels and gave them to the metalworker. With them, he carved a statue (and cast an idol in metal) which was put in Micayehu's house. 5 This man Micah owned a shrine; he made an ephod and some domestic images, and installed one of his sons to be his priest. 6 In those days there was no king in Israel, and everyone did as he saw fit.

7 There was a young man of Bethlehem in Judah, of the clan of Judah, who was a Levite and resided there as a stranger. 8 This man left the town of Bethlehem in Judah to settle wherever he could find a home. On his travels he came to the highlands of Ephraim and to Micah's house. 9 Micah asked him, 'Where do you come from?' The other replied, 'I am a Levite from Bethlehem in Judah. I am travelling, and am going to settle wherever I can find a home.' 10 Micah said to him, 'Stay here with me; be my father and priest and I shall give you ten silver shekels a year, and clothing and food.' 11 The Levite agreed to remain in the man's house, and the young man became like one of his sons to him. 12 Micah installed the Levite; the young man became Micah's priest and stayed in his house. 13 And Micah said, 'Now I know that Yahweh will treat me well, since I have this Levite as priest.'

18

In those days there was no king in Israel. Now in those days the tribe of Dan was in search of a territory to live in, for until then no territory had fallen to them among the tribes of Israel. 2 From their clan the Danites sent five brave men from Zorah and Eshtaol to reconnoitre the country and explore it. They said to them, 'Go and explore the country.' The five men came to the highlands of Ephraim, as far as Micah's house, and spent the night there. 3 When they were near Micah's house, they recognised the voice of the young Levite and, going nearer, said to him, 'Who brought you here? What are you doing here? What is keeping you here?' 4 He replied, 'Micah has made certain arrangements with me. He pays me a wage and I act as his priest.' 5 They replied, 'Then consult God, so that we may know whether the journey we are on will lead to success.' 6 The priest replied, 'Go in peace; Yahweh is watching over your journey.'

7 The five men then left and, arriving at Laish, saw that the people living there had an untroubled existence, according to the customs of the Sidonians, peaceful and trusting, that there was no lack or shortage of any sort in the territory, that they were a long way away from the Sidonians and that they had no contact with the Aramaeans.

8 They then went back to their brothers at Zorah and Eshtaol and, when the latter asked them, 'What have you to report?' 9 they said, 'Up! we must go against them, since we

k 17 The words of the curse are omitted lest even to quote them might have its effect.

have seen the land, and it is very good. Will you do nothing? Do not be slow to go, but enter in and possess the land. 10 When you go, you will come to an unsuspecting people. The land is broad — God has indeed given it into your hands — a place where there is no lack of anything on earth."

11 Six hundred men of the Danite clan, armed with weapons of war, set out from Zorah and Eshtaol, 12 and went up and encamped at Kiriath-jearim in Judah. On this account that place is called Mahaneh-dan[l] to this day; it is west of Kiriath-jearim. 13 From there they passed on to the hill country of Ephraim, and came to the house of Micah.

14 Then the five men who had gone to spy out the land (that is, Laish) said to their comrades, "Do you know that in these buildings there are an ephod, teraphim, and an idol of cast metal? Now therefore consider what you will do." 15 So they turned in that direction and came to the house of the young Levite, at the home of Micah, and greeted him. 16 While the six hundred men of the Danites, armed with their weapons of war, stood by the entrance of the gate, 17 the five men who had gone to spy out the land proceeded to enter and take the idol of cast metal, the ephod, and the teraphim.[m] The priest was standing by the entrance of the gate with the six hundred men armed with weapons of war. 18 When the men went into Micah's house and took the idol of cast metal, the ephod, and the teraphim, the priest said to them, "What are you doing?" 19 They said to him, "Keep quiet! Put your hand over your mouth, and come with us, and be to us a father and a priest. Is it better for you to be priest to the house of one person, or to be priest to a tribe and clan in Israel?" 20 Then the priest accepted the offer. He took the ephod, the teraphim, and the idol, and went along with the people.

21 So they resumed their journey, putting the little ones, the livestock, and the goods in front of them. 22 When they were some distance from the home of Micah, the men who were in the houses near Micah's house were called out, and they overtook the Danites. 23 They shouted to the Danites, who turned around and said to Micah, "What is the matter that you come with such a company?" 24 He replied, "You take my gods that I made, and the priest, and go away, and what have I left? How then can you ask me, 'What is the matter?'" 25 And the Danites said to him, "You had better not let your voice be heard among us or else hot-tempered fellows will attack you, and you will lose your life and the lives of your household." 26 Then the Danites went their way. When Micah saw that they were too strong for him, he turned and went back to his home.

27 The Danites, having taken what Micah had made, and the priest who belonged to him, came to Laish, to a people quiet and unsuspecting, put them to the sword, and burned down the city. 28 There was no deliverer, because it was far from Sidon and they had no dealings with Aram.[n] It was in the valley that belongs to Beth-rehob. They rebuilt the city, and lived in it. 29 They named the city Dan, after their ancestor Dan, who was born to Israel; but the name of the city was formerly Laish. 30 Then the Danites set up the idol for themselves. Jonathan son of Gershom, son of Moses,[o] and his sons were priests to the tribe of the Danites until the time the land went into captivity. 31 So they maintained as their own Micah's idol that he had made, as long as the house of God was at Shiloh.

'Go and attack them at once. The land that we saw was very good. Why hang back? Do not hesitate to go there and take possession. 10 When you get there, you will find a people living a carefree life in a wide expanse of open country. It is a place where nothing on earth is lacking, and God has delivered it into your hands.'

11 Six hundred fully armed men from the Danite clan set out from Zorah and Eshtaol, 12 and went up country, where they encamped in Kiriath-jearim in Judah, which is why that place is called Mahaneh-dan to this day; it lies west of Kiriath-jearim. 13 From there they passed on to the hill-country of Ephraim until they came to Micah's house.

14 The five men who had been sent to reconnoitre the country round Laish addressed their kinsmen. 'Do you know', they said, 'that in one of these houses there are an ephod and teraphim, an image and an idol? Now consider what you had best do.' 15 They turned aside to Micah's house and greeted him. 16 As the six hundred armed Danites took their stand at the entrance of the gate, 17 the five men who had gone to explore the country went indoors to take the image and the idol, the ephod and the teraphim; the priest meanwhile was standing at the entrance with the six hundred armed men. 18 When the five men entered Micah's house and laid hands on the image and the idol, the ephod and the teraphim, the priest asked them what they were doing. 19 They said to him, 'Be quiet; not a word. Come with us and be to us a father and priest. Which is better, to be priest in the household of one man or to be priest to a tribe and clan in Israel?' 20 This pleased the priest, and carrying off the ephod and the teraphim, the image and the idol, he went with the people. 21 They set out on their way, putting their dependants, herds, and possessions in front.

22 The Danites had gone some distance from Micah's house, when his neighbours were called out in pursuit. As they caught up with them, 23 they shouted, and the Danites turned round and said to Micah, 'What is the matter with you that you have called out your men?' 24 'You have taken the gods which I made for myself and have taken the priest,' he answered; 'you have gone off and left me nothing. How can you ask, "What is the matter with you?"' 25 The Danites said to him, 'Not another word from you! We are desperate men and if we set about you it will be the death of you and your family.' 26 With that the Danites went on their way, and Micah, seeing that they were too strong for him, turned and went home.

27 Carrying off the things which Micah had made for himself along with his priest, the Danites then attacked Laish, whose people were quiet and carefree. They put the people to the sword and set fire to their town. 28 There was no one to save them, for it was a long way from Sidon and they had no contact with the Aramaeans; the town was in the valley near Beth-rehob. They rebuilt the town and settled in it, 29 naming it Dan after their forefather Dan, a son of Israel; its original name was Laish. 30 The Danites set up the image, and Jonathan son of Gershom, son of Moses, and his sons were priests to the tribe of Dan until the exile. 31 They set up for themselves the image which Micah had made, and it was there as long as the house of God was at Shiloh.

18:12 **Mahaneh-dan:** *that is* the Camp of Dan. 18:15 **turned aside to:** *so Gk (Luc.); Heb. adds* the house of the young Levite. 18:18 **the image . . . teraphim:** *prob. rdg; Heb.* the idol of the ephod, and teraphim and image. 18:20 **and the idol:** *so Gk; Heb. omits.* 18:28 **Aramaeans:** *prob. rdg, cp. verse 7; Heb.* men.

---

[l] That is *Camp of Dan* [m] Compare 17.4, 5; 18.14: Heb *teraphim and the cast metal* [n] Cn Compare verse 7: Heb *with anyone* [o] Another reading is *son of Manasseh*

NEW AMERICAN BIBLE

have seen the land and it is very good. Are you going to hesitate? Do not be slothful about beginning your expedition to possess the land. 10 Those against whom you go are a trusting people, and the land is ample. God has indeed given it into your power: a place where no natural resource is lacking."

11 So six hundred men of the clan of the Danites, fully armed with weapons of war, set out from where they were in Zorah and Eshtaol, 12 and camped in Judah, up near Kiriath-jearim; hence to this day the place, which lies west of Kiriath-jearim, is called Mahaneh-dan.

13 From there they went on to the mountain region of Ephraim and came to the house of Micah. 14 The five men who had gone to reconnoiter the land of Laish said to their kinsmen, "Do you know that in these houses there are an ephod, household idols, and a carved idol overlaid with silver? Now decide what you must do!" 15 So turning in that direction, they went to the house of the young Levite at the home of Micah and greeted him. 16 The six hundred men girt with weapons of war, who were Danites, stood by the entrance of the gate, and the priest stood there also. 17 Meanwhile the five men who had gone to reconnoiter the land went up and entered the house of Micah. 18 When they had gone in and taken the ephod, the household idols, and the carved idol overlaid with silver, the priest said to them, "What are you doing?" 19 They said to him, "Be still: put your hand over your mouth. Come with us and be our father and priest. Is it better for you to be priest for the family of one man or to be priest for a tribe and a clan in Israel?" 20 The priest, agreeing, took the ephod, household idols, and carved idol and went off in the midst of the band. 21 As they turned to depart, they placed their little ones, their livestock, and their goods at the head of the column.

22 The Danites had already gone some distance, when those in the houses near that of Micah took up arms and overtook them. 23 They called to the Danites, who turned about and said to Micah, "What do you want, that you have taken up arms?" 24 "You have taken my god, which I made, and have gone off with my priest as well," he answered. "What is left for me? How, then, can you ask me what I want?" 25 The Danites said to him, "Let us hear no further sound from you, lest fierce men fall upon you and you and your family lose your lives." 26 The Danites then went on their way, and Micah, seeing that they were stronger than he, returned home.

27 Having taken what Micah had made, and the priest he had had, they attacked Laish, a quiet and trusting people; they put them to the sword and destroyed their city by fire. 28 No one came to their aid, since the city was far from Sidon and they had no contact with other people. The Danites then rebuilt the city, which was in the valley that belongs to Beth-rehob, and lived there. 29 They named it Dan after their ancestor Dan, son of Israel. However, the name of the city was formerly Laish. 30 The Danites set up the carved idol for themselves, and Jonathan, son of Gershom, son of Moses, and his descendants were priests for the tribe of the Danites until the time of the captivity of the land. 31 They maintained the carved idol Micah had made as long as the house of God was in Shiloh.

have looked at the country and it is excellent, though you take no action! Waste no time in setting out and taking possession of the country. 10 When you get there, you will find a trusting people. The country is wide, and God has put it at your mercy. It is a place where there is no lack of anything on earth.'

11 From these places, consequently, from the clan of Danites at Zorah and Eshtaol, six hundred men set out equipped for war. 12 They went up and camped at Kiriath-Jearim in Judah; and for this reason the place is still called the Camp of Dan today. It lies to the west of Kiriath-Jearim. 13 From there they entered the highlands of Ephraim and came to Micah's house.

14 The five men who had been to reconnoitre the country then spoke to their brothers. 'Do you know', they said, 'that in these houses there is an ephod, some domestic images, a carved statue and an idol cast in metal? So now work out what you have got to do!'

15 So, turning off the road, they went to the young Levite's dwelling, to Micah's house, and greeted him peacefully. 16 While the six hundred men of the Danites, equipped for war, stood at the threshold of the gate, 17 the five who had been to reconnoitre the country went on into the house and took the carved statue, the ephod, the domestic images and the idol cast in metal; meanwhile the priest remained at the threshold of the gate with the six hundred men equipped for war. 18 These men, having entered Micah's house, took the carved statue, the ephod, the domestic images and the idol cast in metal. The priest, however, said, 'What are you doing?' 19 'Be quiet,' they replied. 'Put your hand over your mouth and come with us, and become our father and priest. Are you better off as domestic priest to one man, or as priest to a tribe and clan in Israel?' 20 The priest was delighted; he took the ephod, the domestic images and the carved statue, and went off among the people.

21 Resuming their original line of march, they set off, having put the women, children, livestock and baggage out in front. 22 They had gone some distance from Micah's house, when the people living in the houses near Micah's house raised the alarm and set off in pursuit of the Danites. 23 As they shouted after the Danites, the latter, turning about, said to Micah, 'What is the matter with you, that you are shouting like this?' 24 He replied, 'You have taken away my god, which I have had made, and the priest as well. You are going away, and what have I got left? And now you ask me, "What is the matter?"' 25 The Danites said, 'Let us hear no more from you, or quick-tempered men may set about you, and this might cost you your life and the lives of your family!' 26 So the Danites went on their way; and Micah, seeing that they were the stronger, turned and went home.

27 So, having taken the god made by Micah, and the priest who had been his, the Danites marched on Laish, on a peaceful and trusting people. They put it to the sword and they burned down the town. 28 There was no one to come to the rescue, since it was a long way from Sidon and had no contact with the Aramaeans. It lay in the valley running towards Beth-Rehob. They rebuilt the town and settled in it 29 and called it Dan, from the name of Dan their ancestor who had been born to Israel; originally, however, the town had been called Laish. 30 The Danites erected the carved statue for themselves. Jonathan son of Gershom, son of Moses, and his sons after him were priests for the tribe of Dan till the day when the inhabitants of the country were carried away into exile. 31 The carved statue made by Micah they installed for their own use, and there it stayed as long as the house of God remained at Shiloh.

19 In those days, when there was no king in Israel, a certain Levite, residing in the remote parts of the hill country of Ephraim, took to himself a concubine from Bethlehem in Judah. 2 But his concubine became angry with*p* him, and she went away from him to her father's house at Bethlehem in Judah, and was there some four months. 3 Then her husband set out after her, to speak tenderly to her and bring her back. He had with him his servant and a couple of donkeys. When he reached*q* her father's house, the girl's father saw him and came with joy to meet him. 4 His father-in-law, the girl's father, made him stay, and he remained with him three days; so they ate and drank, and he*r* stayed there. 5 On the fourth day they got up early in the morning, and he prepared to go; but the girl's father said to his son-in-law, "Fortify yourself with a bit of food, and after that you may go." 6 So the two men sat and ate and drank together; and the girl's father said to the man, "Why not spend the night and enjoy yourself?" 7 When the man got up to go, his father-in-law kept urging him until he spent the night there again. 8 On the fifth day he got up early in the morning to leave; and the girl's father said, "Fortify yourself." So they lingered*s* until the day declined, and the two of them ate and drank.*t* 9 When the man with his concubine and his servant got up to leave, his father-in-law, the girl's father, said to him, "Look, the day has worn on until it is almost evening. Spend the night. See, the day has drawn to a close. Spend the night here and enjoy yourself. Tomorrow you can get up early in the morning for your journey, and go home."

10 But the man would not spend the night; he got up and departed, and arrived opposite Jebus (that is, Jerusalem). He had with him a couple of saddled donkeys, and his concubine was with him. 11 When they were near Jebus, the day was far spent, and the servant said to his master, "Come now, let us turn aside to this city of the Jebusites, and spend the night in it." 12 But his master said to him, "We will not turn aside into a city of foreigners, who do not belong to the people of Israel; but we will continue on to Gibeah." 13 Then he said to his servant, "Come, let us try to reach one of these places, and spend the night at Gibeah or at Ramah." 14 So they passed on and went their way; and the sun went down on them near Gibeah, which belongs to Benjamin. 15 They turned aside there, to go in and spend the night at Gibeah. He went in and sat down in the open square of the city, but no one took them in to spend the night.

16 Then at evening there was an old man coming from his work in the field. The man was from the hill country of Ephraim, and he was residing in Gibeah. (The people of the place were Benjaminites.) 17 When the old man looked up and saw the wayfarer in the open square of the city, he said, "Where are you going and where do you come from?" 18 He answered him, "We are passing from Bethlehem in Judah to the remote parts of the hill country of Ephraim, from which I come. I went to Bethlehem in Judah; and I am going to my home.*u* Nobody has offered to take me in. 19 We your servants have straw and fodder for our donkeys, with bread and wine for me and the woman and the young man along with us. We need nothing more." 20 The old man said, "Peace be to you. I will care for all your wants; only do not spend the night in the square." 21 So he brought him into his house, and fed the donkeys; they washed their feet, and ate and drank.

19 IN those days when Israel had no king, a Levite residing in the heart of the hill-country of Ephraim had taken himself a concubine from Bethlehem in Judah. 2 In a fit of anger she had left him and gone to her father's house in Bethlehem in Judah. When she had been there four months, 3 her husband set out after her, with his servant and two donkeys, to appeal to her and bring her back. She brought him into the house of her father, who was delighted to see him and made him welcome. 4 Being pressed by his father-in-law, the girl's father, he stayed there three days, and they were regaled with food and drink during their visit. 5 On the fourth day, they rose early in the morning, and the Levite prepared to leave, but the father said to his son-in-law, 'Have a bite of something to sustain you before you go,' 6 and the two of them sat down and ate and drank together. The girl's father said to the man, 'Why not spend the night and enjoy yourself?' 7 The man, however, rose to go, but his father-in-law urged him to stay, and again he stayed for the night. 8 He rose early in the morning on the fifth day to depart, but the girl's father said, 'Have something to eat first.' So they lingered till late afternoon, eating and drinking together. 9 Then the man stood up to go with his concubine and his servant, but his father-in-law said, 'Look, the day is wearing on towards sunset. Spend the night here and enjoy yourself, and tomorrow rise early and set out for home.' 10 But the man would not stay the night; he set off on his journey.

He reached a point opposite Jebus, that is Jerusalem, with his two laden donkeys and his concubine. 11 Since they were close to Jebus and the day was nearly gone, the servant said to his master, 'Do let us turn into this Jebusite town for the night.' 12 His master replied, 'No, not into a strange town where the people are not Israelites; let us go on to Gibeah. 13 Come, we will go and find some other place, Gibeah or Ramah, to spend the night.' 14 So they went on until sunset overtook them; they were then near Gibeah which belongs to Benjamin. 15 They turned in there to spend the night, and went and sat down in the open square of the town; but nobody took them into his house for the night.

16 At nightfall an old man was coming home from his work in the fields. He was from the hill-country of Ephraim, though he lived in Gibeah, where the people were Benjamites. 17 When his eye lighted on the traveller in the town square, he asked him where he was going and where he came from. 18 He answered, 'We are travelling from Bethlehem in Judah to the heart of the hill-country of Ephraim. I come from there; I have been to Bethlehem in Judah and I am going home, but nobody has taken me into his house. 19 I have straw and provender for our donkeys, food and wine for myself, the girl, and the young man; we have all we need.' 20 The old man said, 'You are welcome. I shall supply all your wants; you must not spend the night in the open.' 21 He took him inside, where he provided fodder for the donkeys. Then, having bathed their feet, they all ate and drank.

---

p Gk OL: Heb *prostituted herself against*   *q* Gk: Heb *she brought him*   *r* Compare verse 7 and Gk: Heb *they*   *s* Cn: Heb *Linger*   *t* Gk: Heb lacks *and drank*   *u* Gk Compare 19.29. Heb *to the house of the LORD*

19:2 **In . . . anger:** *so Gk; Heb.* She was unfaithful.   19:8 **and drinking:** *so some Gk MSS; Heb.* omits.   19:9 **towards sunset:** *so Gk; Heb.* adds Spend the night: behold the camping of the day.   19:18 **home:** *so Gk; Heb.* to the house of the LORD.

19 At that time, when there was no king in Israel, there was a Levite residing in remote parts of the mountain region of Ephraim who had taken for himself a concubine from Bethlehem of Judah. 2 His concubine was unfaithful to him and left him for her father's house in Bethlehem of Judah, where she stayed for some four months. 3 Her husband then set out with his servant and a pair of asses, and went after her to forgive her and take her back. She brought him into her father's house, and on seeing him, the girl's father joyfully made him welcome. 4 He was detained by the girl's father, and so he spent three days with this father-in-law of his, eating and drinking and passing the night there. 5 On the fourth day they rose early in the morning and he prepared to go. But the girl's father said to his son-in-law, "Fortify yourself with a little food; you can go later on." 6 So they stayed and the two men ate and drank together. Then the girl's father said to the husband, "Why not decide to spend the night here and enjoy yourself?" 7 The man still made a move to go, but when his father-in-law pressed him he went back and spent the night there.

8 On the fifth morning he rose early to depart, but the girl's father said, "Fortify yourself and tarry until the afternoon." When he and his father-in-law had eaten, 9 and the husband was ready to go with his concubine and servant, the girl's father said to him, "It is already growing dusk. Stay for the night. See, the day is coming to an end. Spend the night here and enjoy yourself. Early tomorrow you can start your journey home." 10 The man, however, refused to stay another night; he and his concubine set out with a pair of saddled asses, and traveled till they came opposite Jebus, which is Jerusalem. 11 Since they were near Jebus with the day far gone, the servant said to his master, "Come, let us turn off to this city of the Jebusites and spend the night in it." 12 But his master said to him, "We will not turn off to a city of foreigners, who are not Israelites, but will go on to Gibeah. 13 Come," he said to his servant, "let us make for some other place, either Gibeah or Ramah, to spend the night." 14 So they continued on their way till the sun set on them when they were abreast of Gibeah of Benjamin.

15 There they turned off to enter Gibeah for the night. The man waited in the public square of the city he had entered, but no one offered them the shelter of his home for the night. 16 In the evening, however, an old man came from his work in the field; he was from the mountain region of Ephraim, though he lived among the Benjaminite townspeople of Gibeah. 17 When he noticed the traveler in the public square of the city, the old man asked where he was going, and whence he had come. 18 He said to him, "We are traveling from Bethlehem of Judah far up into the mountain region of Ephraim, where I belong. I have been to Bethlehem of Judah and am now going back home; but no one has offered me the shelter of his house. 19 We have straw and fodder for our asses, and bread and wine for the woman and myself and for our servant; there is nothing else we need." 20 "You are welcome," the old man said to him, "but let me provide for all your needs, and do not spend the night in the public square." 21 So he led them to his house and provided fodder for the asses. Then they washed their feet, and ate and drank.

19 In those days, when there was no king in Israel, there was a man, a Levite, whose home was deep in the highlands of Ephraim. He took as concubine a woman from Bethlehem in Judah. 2 In a fit of anger his concubine left him and went back to her father's house at Bethlehem in Judah, and she stayed there for some time — four months. 3 Her husband then set out after her, to appeal to her affections and fetch her back; he had his servant and two donkeys with him. As he was arriving at the house of the girl's father, the father saw him and came happily to meet him. 4 His father-in-law, the girl's father, kept him there; and he stayed with him for three days; they ate and drank and spent the nights there. 5 On the fourth day they got up early, and the Levite was preparing to leave when the girl's father said to his son-in-law, 'Have something to eat to gather strength; you can leave later.' 6 So they sat down and began eating and drinking, the two of them together; then the girl's father said to the young man, 'Please agree to spend tonight here too and enjoy yourself.' 7 And when the man got up to leave, the father-in-law pressed him again, and he spent another night there. 8 On the fifth day, the Levite got up early to leave, but the girl's father said to him, 'Please gather strength first!' So they stayed on until the sun began to go down, and the two men had a meal together. 9 The husband was getting up to leave with his concubine and his servant when his father-in-law, the girl's father, said, 'Look, day is fading into evening. Please spend the night here. Look, the day is nearly over. Spend the night here and enjoy yourself. Then, early tomorrow, you can leave on your journey and go back home.' 10 But the man, refusing to stay the night, got up and went on his way, until he arrived within sight of Jebus — that is, Jerusalem. He had with him two donkeys saddled, his concubine and his servant.

11 By the time they were near Jebus, the light was going fast. The servant said to his master, 'Come, on, please, let us turn off into this Jebusite town and spend the night there.' 12 His master replied, 'We shall not turn off into a town of foreigners, of people who are not Israelites; we shall go on to Gibeah.' 13 He then said to his servant, 'Come on, we shall try to reach one or other of those places, either Gibeah or Ramah, and spend the night there.' 14 So they kept going and went on with their journey. As they approached Gibeah in Benjamin, the sun was setting. 15 So they turned that way to spend the night in Gibeah. Once inside, the Levite sat down in the town square, but no one offered to take them in for the night.

16 Eventually, an old man came along at nightfall from his work in the fields. He too was from the highlands of Ephraim, although he was living in Gibeah; the people of the place, however, were Benjaminites. 17 Looking up, he saw the traveller in the town square. 'Where are you going?' said the old man, 'And where have you come from?' 18 'We are on our way', the other replied, 'from Bethlehem in Judah to a place deep in the highlands of Ephraim. That is where I come from. I have been to Bethlehem in Judah and now I am going home, but no one has offered to take me into his house, 19 although we have straw and provender for our donkeys, and I also have bread and wine for myself, and this maidservant and the young man who is travelling with your servant; we are short of nothing.' 20 'Welcome,' said the old man. 'I shall see that you have all you want. You cannot spend the night in the square.' 21 So he took him into his house and gave the donkeys provender. The travellers washed their feet, then ate and drank.

22 While they were enjoying themselves, the men of the city, a perverse lot, surrounded the house, and started pounding on the door. They said to the old man, the master of the house, "Bring out the man who came into your house, so that we may have intercourse with him." 23 And the man, the master of the house, went out to them and said to them, "No, my brothers, do not act so wickedly. Since this man is my guest, do not do this vile thing. 24 Here are my virgin daughter and his concubine; let me bring them out now. Ravish them and do whatever you want to them; but against this man do not do such a vile thing." 25 But the men would not listen to him. So the man seized his concubine, and put her out to them. They wantonly raped her, and abused her all through the night until the morning. And as the dawn began to break, they let her go. 26 As morning appeared, the woman came and fell down at the door of the man's house where her master was, until it was light.

27 In the morning her master got up, opened the doors of the house, and when he went out to go on his way, there was his concubine lying at the door of the house, with her hands on the threshold. 28 "Get up," he said to her, "we are going." But there was no answer. Then he put her on the donkey; and the man set out for his home. 29 When he had entered his house, he took a knife, and grasping his concubine he cut her into twelve pieces, limb by limb, and sent her throughout all the territory of Israel. 30 Then he commanded the men whom he sent, saying, "Thus shall you say to all the Israelites, 'Has such a thing ever happened[v] since the day that the Israelites came up from the land of Egypt until this day? Consider it, take counsel, and speak out.'"

20 Then all the Israelites came out, from Dan to Beer-sheba, including the land of Gilead, and the congregation assembled in one body before the LORD at Mizpah. 2 The chiefs of all the people, of all the tribes of Israel, presented themselves in the assembly of the people of God, four hundred thousand foot-soldiers bearing arms. 3 (Now the Benjaminites heard that the people of Israel had gone up to Mizpah.) And the Israelites said, "Tell us, how did this criminal act come about?" 4 The Levite, the husband of the woman who was murdered, answered, "I came to Gibeah that belongs to Benjamin, I and my concubine, to spend the night. 5 The lords of Gibeah rose up against me, and surrounded the house at night. They intended to kill me, and they raped my concubine until she died. 6 Then I took my concubine and cut her into pieces, and sent her throughout the whole extent of Israel's territory; for they have committed a vile outrage in Israel. 7 So now, you Israelites, all of you, give your advice and counsel here."

8 All the people got up as one, saying, "We will not any of us go to our tents, nor will any of us return to our houses. 9 But now this is what we will do to Gibeah: we will go up[w] against it by lot. 10 We will take ten men of a hundred throughout all the tribes of Israel, and a hundred of a thousand, and a thousand of ten thousand, to bring provisions for the troops, who are going to repay[x] Gibeah of Benjamin for all the disgrace that they have done in Israel." 11 So all the men of Israel gathered against the city, united as one.

22 While they were enjoying themselves, some of the most depraved scoundrels in the town surrounded the house, beating the door violently and shouting to the old man whose house it was, 'Bring out the man who has come to your house, for us to have intercourse with him.' 23 The owner of the house went outside to them and said, 'No, my friends, do nothing so wicked. This man is my guest; do not commit this outrage. 24 Here are my daughter, who is a virgin, and the man's concubine; let me bring them out to you. Abuse them and do what you please; but you must not commit such an outrage against this man.' 25 When the men refused to listen to him, the Levite took his concubine and thrust her outside for them. They raped and abused her all night till the morning; only when dawn broke did they let her go. 26 The woman came at daybreak and collapsed at the entrance of the man's house where her husband was, and lay there until it was light.

27 Her husband rose in the morning and opened the door of the house to be on his way, and there was his concubine lying at the door with her hands on the threshold. 28 He said to her, 'Get up and let us be off'; but there was no answer. So he lifted her on to his donkey and set off for home.

29 When he arrived there, he picked up a knife, took hold of his concubine, and cut her limb by limb into twelve pieces, which he then sent through the length and breadth of Israel. 30 He told the men he sent with them to say to every Israelite, 'Has the like of this happened or been seen from the time the Israelites came up from Egypt till today? Consider among yourselves and speak your minds.' Everyone who saw them said, 'Since that time no such thing has ever happened or been seen.'

20 ALL the Israelites, the whole community from Dan to Beersheba and also from Gilead, left their homes and as one man assembled before the LORD at Mizpah. 2 The leaders of the people and all the tribes of Israel presented themselves in the assembly of God's people, four hundred thousand foot-soldiers armed with swords. 3 That the Israelites had gone up to Mizpah became known to the Benjamites.

The Israelites asked how this wicked crime happened, 4 and the Levite, to whom the murdered woman belonged, answered, 'I and my concubine arrived at Gibeah in Benjamin to spend the night. 5 The townsmen of Gibeah rose against me that night and surrounded the house where I was, intending to kill me; and they raped my concubine so that she died. 6 I took her and cut her in pieces, and sent the pieces through the length and breadth of Israel, because of the abominable outrage they had committed in Israel. 7 It is for you, the whole of Israel, to come to a decision as to what action should be taken.'

8 As one man all the people stood up and declared, 'Not one of us will go back to his tent, not one will return home. 9 But this is what we shall do to Gibeah: we shall draw lots for the attack, 10 and in all the tribes of Israel we shall take ten men out of every hundred, a hundred out of every thousand, and a thousand out of every ten thousand, and they will collect provisions for the army, for those who have taken the field against Gibeah in Benjamin to avenge the outrage committed in Israel.' 11 Thus all the Israelites, united to a man, were massed against the town.

19:30 **He told . . . been seen from:** *prob. rdg, cp. Gk; Heb. omits*
He . . . seen. 20:2 **and:** *so Gk; Heb. omits.* 20:9 **we shall
draw . . . attack:** *so Gk; Heb.* against it by lot. 20:10 **who have
. . . to avenge:** *prob. rdg, cp. Gk; Heb.* to do when they come to
Geba in Benjamin.

v Compare Gk: Heb 30 *And all who saw it said, "Such a thing has not
happened or been seen* w Gk: Heb lacks *we will go up*
x Compare Gk: Meaning of Heb uncertain

NEW AMERICAN BIBLE

22 While they were enjoying themselves, the men of the city, who were corrupt, surrounded the house and beat on the door. They said to the old man whose house it was, "Bring out your guest, that we may abuse him." 23 The owner of the house went out to them and said, "No, my brothers; do not be so wicked. Since this man is my guest, do not commit this crime. 24 Rather let me bring out my maiden daughter or his concubine. Ravish them, or do whatever you want with them; but against the man you must not commit this wanton crime." 25 When the men would not listen to his host, the husband seized his concubine and thrust her outside to them. They had relations with her and abused her all night until the following dawn, when they let her go. 26 Then at daybreak the woman came and collapsed at the entrance of the house in which her husband was a guest, where she lay until the morning. 27 When her husband rose that day and opened the door of the house to start out again on his journey, there lay the woman, his concubine, at the entrance of the house with her hands on the threshold. 28 He said to her, "Come, let us go"; but there was no answer. So the man placed her on an ass and started out again for home.

29 On reaching home, he took a knife to the body of his concubine, cut her into twelve pieces, and sent them throughout the territory of Israel. 30 Everyone who saw this said, "Nothing like this has been done or seen from the day the Israelites came up from the land of Egypt to this day. Take note of it, and state what you propose to do."

20 So all the Israelites came out as one man: from Dan to Beer-sheba, and from the land of Gilead, the community was gathered to the LORD at Mizpah. 2 The leaders of all the people and all the tribesmen of Israel, four hundred thousand foot soldiers who were swordsmen, presented themselves in the assembly of the people of God. 3 Meanwhile, the Benjaminites heard that the Israelites had gone up to Mizpah. The Israelites asked to be told how the crime had taken place, 4 and the Levite, the husband of the murdered woman, testified: "My concubine and I went into Gibeah of Benjamin for the night. 5 But the citizens of Gibeah rose up against me by night and surrounded the house in which I was. Me they attempted to kill, and my concubine they abused so that she died. 6 So I took my concubine and cut her up and sent her through every part of the territory of Israel, because of the monstrous crime they had committed in Israel. 7 Now that you are all here, O Israelites, state what you propose to do." 8 All the people rose as one man to say, "None of us is to leave for his tent or return to his home. 9 Now as for Gibeah, this is what we will do: We will proceed against it by lot, 10 taking from all the tribes of Israel ten men for every hundred, a hundred for every thousand, a thousand for every ten thousand, and procuring supplies for the soldiers who will go to deal fully and suitably with Gibeah of Benjamin for the crime it committed in Israel."

11 When, therefore, all the men of Israel without excep-

NEW JERUSALEM BIBLE

22 While they were enjoying themselves, some townsmen, scoundrels, came crowding round the house; they battered on the door and said to the old man, master of the house, 'Send out the man who went into your house, we should like to have intercourse with him!' 23 The master of the house went out to them and said, 'No, brothers, please, do not be so wicked. Since this man is now under my roof, do not commit such an infamy. 24 Here is my daughter; she is a virgin; I shall bring her out to you. Ill-treat her, do what you please with her, but do not commit such an infamy against this man.' 25 But the men would not listen to him. So the Levite took hold of his concubine and brought her out to them. They had intercourse with her and ill-treated her all night till morning; when dawn was breaking they let her go.

26 At daybreak the girl came and fell on the threshold of her husband's host, and she stayed there until it was light. 27 In the morning her husband got up and, opening the door of the house, was going out to continue his journey when he saw the woman, his concubine, lying at the door of the house with her hands on the threshold. 28 'Get up,' he said, 'we must leave!' There was no answer. He then loaded her on his donkey and began the journey home. 29 Having reached his house, he took his knife, took hold of his concubine and cut her, limb by limb, into twelve pieces; he then sent her throughout the territory of Israel. 30 He gave instructions to his messengers, 'This is what you are to say to all the Israelites, "Has anything like this been done since the day when the Israelites came out of Egypt until today? Take this to heart, discuss it; then give your verdict." ' And all who saw it declared, 'Never has such a thing been done or been seen since the Israelites came out of Egypt until today.'

20 The Israelites then all turned out and, as one man, the entire community from Dan to Beersheba, including Gilead, assembled in Yahweh's presence at Mizpah. 2 The leaders of the entire people, of all the tribes of Israel, were present at this assembly of God's people, four hundred thousand trained infantry. 3 The Benjaminites heard that the Israelites had gone up to Mizpah. The Israelites then said, 'Tell us how this crime was committed.' 4 The Levite, husband of the murdered woman, spoke in reply and said, 5 'The men of Gibeah ganged up against me and, during the night, surrounded the house where I was lodging. They intended to murder me. They raped my concubine to death. 6 I then took my concubine, cut her up and sent her throughout the entire territory of the heritage of Israel, since these men had committed a shameful act, an infamy, in Israel. 7 Now, all you Israelites, discuss the matter and give your decision here and now.'

8 The whole people stood up as one man and said, 'None of us will go home, none of us will go back to his house! 9 And this is what we are now going to do to Gibeah. We shall draw lots 10 and, throughout the tribes of Israel, select ten men out of a hundred, a hundred out of a thousand and a thousand out of ten thousand to collect food for the people, so that, on their arrival, the latter may treat Gibeah in Benjamin as this infamy perpetrated in Israel deserves.' 11 Thus, as one man, all the men of Israel mustered against the town.

12 The tribes of Israel sent men through all the tribe of Benjamin, saying, "What crime is this that has been committed among you? 13 Now then, hand over those scoundrels in Gibeah, so that we may put them to death, and purge the evil from Israel." But the Benjaminites would not listen to their kinsfolk, the Israelites. 14 The Benjaminites came together out of the towns to Gibeah, to go out to battle against the Israelites. 15 On that day the Benjaminites mustered twenty-six thousand armed men from their towns, besides the inhabitants of Gibeah. 16 Of all this force, there were seven hundred picked men who were left-handed; every one could sling a stone at a hair, and not miss. 17 And the Israelites, apart from Benjamin, mustered four hundred thousand armed men, all of them warriors.

18 The Israelites proceeded to go up to Bethel, where they inquired of God, "Which of us shall go up first to battle against the Benjaminites?" And the LORD answered, "Judah shall go up first."

19 Then the Israelites got up in the morning, and encamped against Gibeah. 20 The Israelites went out to battle against Benjamin; and the Israelites drew up the battle line against them at Gibeah. 21 The Benjaminites came out of Gibeah, and struck down on that day twenty-two thousand of the Israelites. 23 yThe Israelites went up and wept before the LORD until the evening; and they inquired of the LORD, "Shall we again draw near to battle against our kinsfolk the Benjaminites?" And the LORD said, "Go up against them." 22 The Israelites took courage, and again formed the battle line in the same place where they had formed it on the first day.

24 So the Israelites advanced against the Benjaminites the second day. 25 Benjamin moved out against them from Gibeah the second day, and struck down eighteen thousand of the Israelites, all of them armed men. 26 Then all the Israelites, the whole army, went back to Bethel and wept, sitting there before the LORD; they fasted that day until evening. Then they offered burnt offerings and sacrifices of well-being before the LORD. 27 And the Israelites inquired of the LORD (for the ark of the covenant of God was there in those days, 28 and Phinehas son of Eleazar, son of Aaron, ministered before it in those days), saying, "Shall we go out once more to battle against our kinsfolk the Benjaminites, or shall we desist?" The LORD answered, "Go up, for tomorrow I will give them into your hand."

29 So Israel stationed men in ambush around Gibeah. 30 Then the Israelites went up against the Benjaminites on the third day, and set themselves in array against Gibeah, as before. 31 When the Benjaminites went out against the army, they were drawn away from the city. As before they began to inflict casualties on the troops, along the main roads, one of which goes up to Bethel and the other to Gibeah, as well as in the open country, killing about thirty men of Israel. 32 The Benjaminites thought, "They are being routed before us, as previously." But the Israelites said, "Let us retreat and draw them away from the city toward the roads." 33 The main body of the Israelites drew back its battle line to Baal-tamar, while those Israelites who were in ambush rushed out of their place westz of Geba. 34 There came against Gibeah ten thousand picked men out of all Israel, and the battle was fierce. But the Benjaminites did not realize that disaster was close upon them.

35 The LORD defeated Benjamin before Israel; and the Israelites destroyed twenty-five thousand one hundred men of Benjamin that day, all of them armed.

12 The tribes of Israel sent messengers throughout the tribe of Benjamin saying, 'What crime is this that has taken place among you? 13 Hand over to us now those scoundrels in Gibeah; we shall put them to death and purge Israel of this wickedness.' The Benjamites, however, refused to listen to their fellow-Israelites. 14 They flocked from their towns to Gibeah to do battle with the Israelites, 15 and that day they mustered out of their towns twenty-six thousand men armed with swords. There were also seven hundred picked men from Gibeah, 16 left-handed men, who could sling a stone and not miss by a hair's breadth. 17 The Israelites, without the Benjamites, numbered four hundred thousand men armed with swords, every one a warrior. 18 The Israelites at once moved on to Bethel and there sought an oracle from God. 'Which of us is to lead the attack on the Benjamites?' they enquired, and the LORD's answer was, 'Judah is to lead the attack.'

19 The Israelites set out at dawn and encamped opposite Gibeah. 20 They advanced to do battle with the Benjamites and drew up their forces before the town. 21 The Benjamites sallied out from Gibeah and laid low twenty-two thousand of Israel on the field that day. 23 The Israelites went up to Bethel, where they lamented before the LORD until evening, and enquired whether they should again attack their kinsmen the Benjamites. The LORD said, 'Go up to the attack.' 22 The Israelite army took fresh courage and formed up again on the same ground as the first day. 24 So on the second day they advanced against the Benjamites, 25 who sallied out from Gibeah to meet them and laid low on the field another eighteen thousand armed men.

26 The Israelites, the whole army, went back to Bethel, where they sat before the LORD lamenting and fasting until evening, and they offered whole-offerings and shared-offerings before the LORD. 27-28 In those days the Ark of the Covenant of God was there, and Phinehas son of Eleazar, son of Aaron, served before the LORD. The Israelites enquired of the LORD, 'Shall we again march out to battle against Benjamin our kin, or shall we desist?' The LORD answered, 'Attack! Tomorrow I shall deliver him into your hands.'

29 The Israelites posted men in ambush all round Gibeah, 30 and on the third day they advanced against the Benjamites and drew up their forces at Gibeah as before. 31 The Benjamites sallied out to meet them, and were drawn away from the town. They began the attack as before by killing a few Israelites, about thirty, on the highways which led across open country, one to Bethel and the other to Gibeon. 32 They thought that once again they were inflicting a defeat, but the Israelites had planned a retreat to draw them out on the highways away from the town. 33-34 Meanwhile the main body of Israelites left their positions and re-formed at Baal-tamar, while those in ambush, ten thousand picked men all told, burst out from their position in the neighbourhood of Gibeah and came in on the east of the town. There was some heavy fighting; yet the Benjamites did not suspect the disaster threatening them. 35 So the LORD put Benjamin to flight before Israel, and on that day the Israelites killed twenty-five thousand one hundred Benjamites, all armed with swords.

20:15 **from Gibeah:** *so Gk; Heb. adds* out of all this army there were seven hundred picked men.   20:22,23 *These verses transposed.*   20:23 **to Bethel:** *prob. rdg, cp. verses 18,26; Heb. omits.*   20:31 **a few . . . thirty:** *or* about thirty wounded men. **Gibeon:** *prob. rdg; Heb.* Gibeah.   20:33-34 **Gibeah:** *prob. rdg, cp. Gk; Heb.* Geba.

y Verses 22 and 23 are transposed   z Gk Vg: Heb *in the plain*

NEW AMERICAN BIBLE

NEW JERUSALEM BIBLE

tion were leagued together against the city, 12 the tribes of Israel sent men throughout the tribe of Benjamin to say, "What is this evil which has occurred among you? 13 Now give up these corrupt men of Gibeah, that we may put them to death and thus purge the evil from Israel." But the Benjaminites refused to accede to the demand of their brothers, the Israelites. 14 Instead, the Benjaminites assembled from their other cities to Gibeah, to do battle with the Israelites. 15 The number of the Benjaminite swordsmen from the other cities on that occasion was twenty-six thousand, in addition to the inhabitants of Gibeah. 16 Included in this total were seven hundred picked men who were left-handed, every one of them able to sling a stone at a hair without missing. 17 Meanwhile the other Israelites who, without Benjamin, mustered four hundred thousand swordsmen ready for battle, 18 moved on to Bethel and consulted God. When the Israelites asked who should go first in the attack on the Benjaminites, the LORD said, "Judah shall go first." 19 The next day the Israelites advanced on Gibeah with their forces.

20 On the day the Israelites drew up in battle array at Gibeah for the combat with Benjamin, 21 the Benjaminites came out of the city and felled twenty-two thousand men of Israel. 23 Then the Israelites went up and wept before the LORD until evening. "Shall I again engage my brother Benjamin in battle?" they asked the LORD; and the LORD answered that they should. 22 But though the Israelite soldiers took courage and again drew up for combat in the same place as on the previous day, 24 when they met the Benjaminites for the second time, 25 once again the Benjaminites who came out of Gibeah against them felled eighteen thousand Israelites, all of them swordsmen. 26 So the entire Israelite army went up to Bethel, where they wept and remained fasting before the LORD until evening of that day, besides offering holocausts and peace offerings before the LORD. 27 When the Israelites consulted the LORD (for the ark of the covenant of God was there in those days, 28 and Phinehas, son of Eleazar, son of Aaron, was ministering to him in those days), and asked, "Shall I go out again to battle with Benjamin, my brother, or shall I desist?" the LORD said, "Attack! for tomorrow I will deliver him into your power." 29 So Israel set men in ambush around Gibeah.

30 The Israelites went up against the Benjaminites for the third time and formed their line of battle at Gibeah as on other occasions. 31 The Benjaminites went out to meet them, and in the beginning they killed off about thirty of the Israelite soldiers in the open field, just as on the other occasions. 32 Therefore the Benjaminites thought, "We are defeating them as before"; not realizing that disaster was about to overtake them. The Israelites, however, had planned the flight so as to draw them away from the city onto the highways. They were drawn away from the city onto the highways, of which the one led to Bethel, the other to Gibeon. 33 And then all the men of Israel rose from their places. They re-formed their ranks at Baal-tamar, and the Israelites in ambush rushed from their place west of Gibeah, 34 ten thousand picked men from all Israel, and advanced against the city itself. In a fierce battle, 35 the LORD defeated Benjamin before Israel; and on that day the Israelites killed twenty-five thousand one hundred men of Benjamin, all of them swordsmen.

12 The tribes of Israel sent messengers throughout the tribe of Benjamin to say, 'What is this crime which has been committed in your territory? 13 Now, give up these men, these scoundrels, living in Gibeah, so that we can put them to death and wipe out this evil from Israel.' The Benjaminites, however, would not listen to their brother Israelites. 14 The Benjaminites left their towns and mustered at Gibeah to fight the Israelites. 15 At the time, a count was made of the Benjaminites from the various towns: there were twenty-six thousand swordsmen; and the count excluded the inhabitants of Gibeah. 16 In this great army there were seven hundred first-rate left-handers, every man of whom could sling a stone at a hair and not miss it.

17 A count was also held of the men of Israel, excluding Benjamin: there were four hundred thousand men, all experienced swordsmen. 18 They moved off, up to Bethel, to consult God. The Israelites put the question, 'Which of us is to go first into battle against the Benjaminites?' And Yahweh replied, 'Judah is to go first.'

19 In the morning, the Israelites moved off and pitched their camp over against Gibeah. 20 The men of Israel advanced to do battle with Benjamin; they drew up their battle line in front of Gibeah. 21 But the Benjaminites sallied out from Gibeah and that day massacred twenty thousand Israelites. 23 The Israelites went and wept before Yahweh until evening; they then consulted Yahweh; they asked, 'Shall we join battle again with the sons of our brother Benjamin?' Yahweh replied, 'March against him!' 22 The army of the men of Israel then took fresh heart and again drew up their battle line in the same place as the day before. 24 This second day, the Israelites advanced against the Benjaminites, 25 and, this second day, Benjamin sallied out from Gibeah to meet them and massacred another eighteen thousand Israelites, all experienced swordsmen.

26 Then all the Israelites and the whole people went off to Bethel; they wept and sat in Yahweh's presence; they fasted all day till the evening and presented burnt offerings and communion sacrifices before Yahweh. 27 The Israelites then consulted Yahweh. In those days, the ark of the covenant of God was there, 28 and Phinehas son of Eleazar, son of Aaron was its minister at the time. They said, 'Ought I to go into battle against the sons of my brother Benjamin again, or should I stop?' Yahweh replied, 'March! For tomorrow I shall deliver him into your hands.'

29 Israel then positioned troops in ambush all round Gibeah. 30 On the third day the Israelites marched against the Benjaminites and, as before, drew up their line in front of Gibeah. 31 The Benjaminites sallied out to engage the people and let themselves be drawn away from the town. As before, they began by killing those of the people who were on the roads, one of which runs up to Bethel, and the other to Gibeah through open country: some thirty men of Israel. 32 The Benjaminites thought, 'We have beaten them, as we did the first time,' but the Israelites had decided, 'We shall run away and draw them away from the town along the roads.'

33 All the Israelites then retreated and re-formed at Baal-Tamar, while the Israelite troops in ambush surged from their positions to the west of Gibeah. 34 Ten thousand picked men, chosen from the whole of Israel, launched their attack on Gibeah. The battle was fierce; and the others knew nothing of the disaster impending. 35 Yahweh defeated Benjamin before Israel and that day the Israelites killed twenty-five thousand one hundred men of Benjamin, all of them trained swordsmen.

NEW REVISED STANDARD VERSION

36 Then the Benjaminites saw that they were defeated.[a]

The Israelites gave ground to Benjamin, because they trusted to the troops in ambush that they had stationed against Gibeah. 37 The troops in ambush rushed quickly upon Gibeah. Then they put the whole city to the sword. 38 Now the agreement between the main body of Israel and the men in ambush was that when they sent up a cloud of smoke out of the city 39 the main body of Israel should turn in battle. But Benjamin had begun to inflict casualties on the Israelites, killing about thirty of them; so they thought, "Surely they are defeated before us, as in the first battle." 40 But when the cloud, a column of smoke, began to rise out of the city, the Benjaminites looked behind them — and there was the whole city going up in smoke toward the sky! 41 Then the main body of Israel turned, and the Benjaminites were dismayed, for they saw that disaster was close upon them. 42 Therefore they turned away from the Israelites in the direction of the wilderness; but the battle overtook them, and those who came out of the city[b] were slaughtering them in between.[c] 43 Cutting down[d] the Benjaminites, they pursued them from Nohah[e] and trod them down as far as a place east of Gibeah. 44 Eighteen thousand Benjaminites fell, all of them courageous fighters. 45 When they turned and fled toward the wilderness to the rock of Rimmon, five thousand of them were cut down on the main roads, and they were pursued as far as Gidom, and two thousand of them were slain. 46 So all who fell that day of Benjamin were twenty-five thousand arms-bearing men, all of them courageous fighters. 47 But six hundred turned and fled toward the wilderness to the rock of Rimmon, and remained at the rock of Rimmon for four months. 48 Meanwhile, the Israelites turned back against the Benjaminites, and put them to the sword — the city, the people, the animals, and all that remained. Also the remaining towns they set on fire.

21 Now the Israelites had sworn at Mizpah, "No one of us shall give his daughter in marriage to Benjamin." 2 And the people came to Bethel, and sat there until evening before God, and they lifted up their voices and wept bitterly. 3 They said, "O LORD, the God of Israel, why has it come to pass that today there should be one tribe lacking in Israel?" 4 On the next day, the people got up early, and built an altar there, and offered burnt offerings and sacrifices of well-being. 5 Then the Israelites said, "Which of all the tribes of Israel did not come up in the assembly to the LORD?" For a solemn oath had been taken concerning whoever did not come up to the LORD to Mizpah, saying, "That one shall be put to death." 6 But the Israelites had compassion for Benjamin their kin, and said, "One tribe is cut off from Israel this day. 7 What shall we do for wives for those who are left, since we have sworn by the LORD that we will not give them any of our daughters as wives?"

8 Then they said, "Is there anyone from the tribes of Israel who did not come up to the LORD to Mizpah?" It turned out that no one from Jabesh-gilead had come to the camp, to the assembly. 9 For when the roll was called among the people, not one of the inhabitants of Jabesh-gilead was there. 10 So the congregation sent twelve thousand soldiers there and commanded them, "Go, put the inhabitants of Jabesh-gilead to the sword, including the

REVISED ENGLISH BIBLE

36 The men of Benjamin now saw that they had suffered a defeat, for all that the Israelites, trusting in the ambush which they had set by Gibeah, had given ground before them. 37 The men in ambush made a sudden dash on Gibeah, fell on the town from all sides, and put all the inhabitants to the sword. 38 The agreed signal between the Israelites and those in ambush was to be a column of smoke sent up from the town, 39 and the Israelites would then face about in the battle. Benjamin began to cut down the Israelites, killing about thirty of them, in the belief that they were defeating the enemy as they had done in the first encounter. 40 But as the column of smoke began to go up from the town, the Benjamites looked back and thought the whole town was in flames. 41 Then the Israelites faced about, and the Benjamites saw that disaster had overtaken them. They were seized with panic, 42 and turned in flight before the Israelites in the direction of the wilderness; but the fighting caught up with them, and soon those from the town were among them, cutting them down. 43 They hemmed in the Benjamites, pursuing them without respite, and overtook them at a point to the east of Gibeah. 44 Eighteen thousand of the Benjamites fell, all of them valiant warriors. 45 The survivors turned and fled into the wilderness towards the Rock of Rimmon. The Israelites picked off the stragglers on the roads, five thousand of them, and continued the pursuit until they had cut down two thousand more. 46 Twenty-five thousand armed men of Benjamin fell in battle that day, all valiant warriors. 47 The six hundred who survived made off into the wilderness as far as the Rock of Rimmon, and there they remained for four months. 48 The Israelites then turned back to deal with the other Benjamites, and put to the sword the people in the towns and the cattle, every creature that they found; they also set fire to every town within their reach.

21 The Israelites had taken an oath at Mizpah that none of them would give his daughter in marriage to a Benjamite. 2 The people now came to Bethel and remained there in God's presence till sunset, raising their voices in bitter lamentation. 3 'LORD God of Israel,' they cried, 'why has it happened among us that one tribe should this day be lost to Israel?' 4 Early next morning the people built an altar there and offered whole-offerings and shared-offerings. 5 At that the Israelites asked themselves whether among all the tribes of Israel there was any who did not go up to the assembly before the LORD; for under the terms of the weighty oath they had sworn, anyone who had not gone up to the LORD at Mizpah was to be put to death. 6 The Israelites felt remorse over their brothers the Benjamites, because, as they said, 'This day one whole tribe has been lopped off Israel.'

7 They asked, 'What shall we do to provide wives for those who are left, as we ourselves have sworn to the LORD not to give any of our daughters to them in marriage? 8 Is there anyone in all the tribes of Israel who did not go up to the LORD at Mizpah?' Now it happened that no one from Jabesh-gilead had come to the camp for the assembly; 9 so when they held a roll-call of the people, they found that none of the inhabitants of Jabesh-gilead was present. 10 The community therefore sent off twelve thousand valiant fighting men with orders to go and put the inhabitants of Jabesh-gilead to the sword, men, women, and dependants. 11 'This

[a] This sentence is continued by verse 45.   [b] Compare Vg and some Gk Mss: Heb cities   [c] Compare Syr: Meaning of Heb uncertain   [d] Gk: Heb Surrounding   [e] Gk: Heb pursued them at their resting place

20:38 those in ambush: prob. rdg; Heb. adds an unintelligible word.   20:39 to cut ... of them: or to kill about thirty wounded men among the Israelites.   20:42 town: so Lat.; Heb. towns.   20:43 without respite: or from Nohah.   21:11 but spare ... they did: so Gk; Heb. omits.

36 To the Benjaminites it had looked as though the enemy were defeated, for the men of Israel gave ground to Benjamin, trusting in the ambush they had set at Gibeah. 37 But then the men in ambush made a sudden dash into Gibeah, overran it, and put the whole city to the sword. 38 Now, the other Israelites had agreed with the men in ambush on a smoke signal they were to send up from the city. 39 And though the men of Benjamin had begun by killing off some thirty of the men of Israel, under the impression that they were defeating them as surely as in the earlier fighting, the Israelites wheeled about to resist 40 as the smoke of the signal column began to rise up from the city. It was when Benjamin looked back and saw the whole city in flames against the sky 41 that the men of Israel wheeled about. Therefore the men of Benjamin were thrown into confusion, for they realized the disaster that had overtaken them. 42 They retreated before the men of Israel in the direction of the desert, with the fight being pressed against them. In their very midst, meanwhile, those who had been in the city were spreading destruction. 43 The men of Benjamin had been surrounded, and were now pursued to a point east of Gibeah, 44 while eighteen thousand of them fell, warriors to a man. 45 The rest turned and fled through the desert to the rock Rimmon. But on the highways the Israelites picked off five thousand men among them, and chasing them up to Gidom, killed another two thousand of them there. 46 Those of Benjamin who fell on that day were in all twenty-five thousand swordsmen, warriors to a man. 47 But six hundred others who turned and fled through the desert reached the rock Rimmon, where they remained for four months.

48 The men of Israel withdrew through the territory of the Benjaminites, putting to the sword the inhabitants of the cities, the livestock, and all they chanced upon. Moreover they destroyed by fire all the cities they came upon.

21 Now the men of Israel had sworn at Mizpah that none of them would give his daughter in marriage to anyone from Benjamin. 2 So the people went to Bethel and remained there before God until evening, raising their voices in bitter lament. 3 They said, "LORD, God of Israel, why has it come to pass in Israel that today one tribe of Israel should be lacking?" 4 Early the next day the people built an altar there and offered holocausts and peace offerings. 5 Then the Israelites asked, "Are there any among all the tribes of Israel who did not come up to the LORD for the assembly?" For they had taken a solemn oath that anyone who did not go up to the LORD at Mizpah should be put to death without fail.

6 The Israelites were disconsolate over their brother Benjamin and said, "Today one of the tribes of Israel has been cut off. 7 What can we do about wives for the survivors, since we have sworn by the LORD not to give them any of our daughters in marriage?" 8 And when they asked whether anyone among the tribes of Israel had not come up to the LORD in Mizpah, they found that none of the men of Jabesh-gilead had come to the encampment for the assembly. 9 A roll call of the army established that none of the inhabitants of that city were present. 10 The community, therefore, sent twelve thousand warriors with orders to go to Jabesh-gilead and put those who lived there to the sword, including the

36 The Benjaminites saw that they were beaten. The Israelites had given ground to Benjamin, since they were relying on the ambush which they had positioned close to Gibeah. 37 The troops in ambush threw themselves against Gibeah at top speed; fanning out, they put the whole town to the sword. 38 Now it had been agreed between the Israelites and those of the ambush that the latter should raise a smoke signal from the town, 39 whereupon the Israelites in the thick of the battle would turn about. Benjamin began by killing some of the Israelites, about thirty men, and thought, 'We have certainly beaten them, as we did in the first battle.' 40 But the signal, a column of smoke, began to rise from the town, and the Benjaminites looking back saw the whole town going up in flames to the sky. 41 The Israelites then turned about, and the Benjaminites were seized with terror, for they saw that disaster had struck them. 42 They broke before the Israelite onslaught and made for the desert, but the fighters pressed them hard, while the others coming out of the town took and slaughtered them from the rear. 43 They hemmed in the Benjaminites, pursued them relentlessly, crushing them opposite Gibeah on the east. 44 Of Benjamin, eighteen thousand men fell, all of them brave men. 45 They then turned tail and fled into the desert, towards the Rock of Rimmon. Five thousand of them were picked off on the roads, and the rest were relentlessly pursued as far as Gideon, two thousand of them being killed. 46 The total number of Benjaminites who fell that day was twenty-five thousand swordsmen, all of them brave men. 47 Six hundred men, however, turned tail and escaped into the desert, to the Rock of Rimmon, and there they stayed for four months.

48 The men of Israel then went back to the Benjaminites, and put them to the sword—people, livestock and everything else that came their way in the town. And they fired all the towns involved.

21 The men of Israel had sworn this oath at Mizpah, 'None of us is to give his daughter in marriage to Benjamin.' 2 The people went to Bethel and stayed there until evening, sitting before God and raising their voices, made a great lament, 3 and exclaiming, 'Yahweh, God of Israel, why has this happened in Israel that a tribe should be missing from Israel today? 4 The next day the people got up early and built an altar there; they presented burnt offerings and communion sacrifices. 5 The Israelites then said, 'Out of all the tribes of Israel, who has not come to Yahweh, to the assembly?'—for they had sworn a solemn oath that anyone who did not come to Yahweh at Mizpah would certainly die.

6 Now the Israelites felt sorry about Benjamin their brother. 'Today', they said, 'a tribe has been amputated from Israel. 7 What shall we do to provide wives for those who are left, since we have sworn by Yahweh not to give them any of our own daughters in marriage?'

8 They then asked, 'Out of the tribes of Israel, who is it that has not come to Yahweh at Mizpah?' It was discovered that no one from Jabesh in Gilead had come to the camp for the assembly; 9 for, a muster having been called of the people, none of the inhabitants of Jabesh in Gilead was present. 10 The community then despatched twelve thousand of their bravest men there, with these orders: 'Go and slaughter all the inhabitants of Jabesh in Gilead, including the women

women and the little ones. 11 This is what you shall do; every male and every woman that has lain with a male you shall devote to destruction." 12 And they found among the inhabitants of Jabesh-gilead four hundred young virgins who had never slept with a man and brought them to the camp at Shiloh, which is in the land of Canaan.

13 Then the whole congregation sent word to the Benjaminites who were at the rock of Rimmon, and proclaimed peace to them. 14 Benjamin returned at that time; and they gave them the women whom they had saved alive of the women of Jabesh-gilead; but they did not suffice for them.

15 The people had compassion on Benjamin because the LORD had made a breach in the tribes of Israel. 16 So the elders of the congregation said, "What shall we do for wives for those who are left, since there are no women left in Benjamin?" 17 And they said, "There must be heirs for the survivors of Benjamin, in order that a tribe may not be blotted out from Israel. 18 Yet we cannot give any of our daughters to them as wives." For the Israelites had sworn, "Cursed be anyone who gives a wife to Benjamin." 19 So they said, "Look, the yearly festival of the LORD is taking place at Shiloh, which is north of Bethel, on the east of the highway that goes up from Bethel to Shechem, and south of Lebonah." 20 And they instructed the Benjaminites, saying, "Go and lie in wait in the vineyards, 21 and watch; when the young women of Shiloh come out to dance in the dances, then come out of the vineyards and each of you carry off a wife for himself from the young women of Shiloh, and go to the land of Benjamin. 22 Then if their fathers or their brothers come to complain to us, we will say to them, 'Be generous and allow us to have them; because we did not capture in battle a wife for each man. But neither did you incur guilt by giving your daughters to them.' " 23 The Benjaminites did so; they took wives for each of them from the dancers whom they abducted. Then they went and returned to their territory, and rebuilt the towns, and lived in them. 24 So the Israelites departed from there at that time by tribes and families, and they went out from there to their own territories.

25 In those days there was no king in Israel; all the people did what was right in their own eyes.

is what you are to do,' they said: 'put to death every male person, and every woman who has had intercourse with a man, but spare any who are virgins.' This they did. 12 Among the inhabitants of Jabesh-gilead they found four hundred young women who were virgins and had not had intercourse with a man, and they brought them to the camp at Shiloh in Canaan. 13 The whole community sent messengers to the Benjamites at the Rock of Rimmon to parley with them, and peace was proclaimed. 14 The Benjamites came back then, and were given those of the women of Jabesh-gilead who had been spared; but these were not enough.

15 The people were still full of remorse over Benjamin because the LORD had made this gap in the tribes of Israel. 16 The elders of the community said, 'What can we do for wives for those who are left, as all the women in Benjamin have been wiped out?' 17 They said, 'Heirs there must be for the surviving Benjamites! Then Israel will not see one of its tribes destroyed. 18 Yet we cannot give them our own daughters in marriage, because we have sworn that there shall be a curse on the man who gives a wife to a Benjamite.'

19 They bethought themselves of the pilgrimage in honour of the LORD, made every year to Shiloh, the place which lies to the north of Bethel, on the east side of the highway from Bethel to Shechem and to the south of Lebonah. 20 They told the Benjamites to go and hide in the vineyards. 21 'Keep watch,' they said, 'and when the girls of Shiloh come out to take part in the dance, come from the vineyards, and each of you seize one of them for his wife; then be off to the territory of Benjamin. 22 If their fathers or brothers come and complain to us, we shall say to them, "Let them keep them with your approval, for none of us has captured a wife in battle. Had you yourselves given them the women, you would now have incurred guilt." '

23 The Benjamites did this; they carried off as many wives as they needed, snatching them from the dance; then they went their way back to their own territory, where they rebuilt their towns and settled in them. 24 The Israelites also dispersed by tribes and families, and every man returned to his own holding.

25 In those days there was no king in Israel; everyone did what was right in his own eyes.

women and children. 11 They were told to include under the ban all males and every woman who was not still a virgin. 12 Finding among the inhabitants of Jabesh-gilead four hundred young virgins, who had had no relations with men, they brought them to the camp at Shiloh in the land of Canaan. 13 Then the whole community sent a message to the Benjaminites at the rock Rimmon, offering them peace. 14 When Benjamin returned at that time, they gave them as wives the women of Jabesh-gilead whom they had spared; but these proved to be not enough for them.

15 The people were still disconsolate over Benjamin because the LORD had made a breach among the tribes of Israel. 16 And the elders of the community said, "What shall we do for wives for the survivors? For every woman in Benjamin has been put to death." 17 They said, "Those of Benjamin who survive must have heirs, else one of the Israelite tribes will be wiped out. 18 Yet we cannot give them any of our daughters in marriage, because the Israelites have sworn, 'Cursed be he who gives a woman to Benjamin!' " 19 Then they thought of the yearly feast of the LORD at Shiloh, north of Bethel, east of the highway that goes up from Bethel to Shechem, and south of Lebonah. 20 And they instructed the Benjaminites, "Go and lie in wait in the vineyards. 21 When you see the girls of Shiloh come out to do their dancing, leave the vineyards and each of you seize one of the girls of Shiloh for a wife, and go to the land of Benjamin. 22 When their fathers or their brothers come to complain to us, we shall say to them, 'Release them to us as a kindness, since we did not take a woman apiece in the war. Had you yourselves given them these wives, you would now be guilty.' "

23 The Benjaminites did this; they carried off a wife for each of them from their raid on the dancers, and went back to their own territory, where they rebuilt and occupied the cities. 24 Also at that time the Israelites dispersed; each of them left for his own heritage in his own clan and tribe.

25 In those days there was no king in Israel; everyone did what he thought best.

and children. 11 This is what you are to do. All males and all those women who have ever slept with a man, you will put under the curse of destruction, but the lives of the virgins you will spare.' And this they did. 12 Among the inhabitants of Jabesh in Gilead they found four hundred young virgins who had never slept with a man, and brought them to the camp (to Shiloh in the territory of Canaan).

13 The whole community then sent messengers to offer peace to the Benjaminites who were at the Rock of Rimmon. 14 Benjamin then came home: they were given those of the women of Jabesh in Gilead whose lives had been spared, but there were not enough for all.

15 The people felt sorry about Benjamin, Yahweh having made a breach in the tribes of Israel. 16 And the elders of the community said, 'What shall we do to provide wives for the survivors, since the women of Benjamin have been wiped out?' 17 They went on, 'How can we preserve a remnant for Benjamin so that a tribe may not be lost to Israel? 18 We cannot give them our own daughters in marriage' — for the Israelites had taken an oath, 'Accursed be the man who gives a wife to Benjamin!'

19 'However,' they said, 'there is the feast of Yahweh, held every year at Shiloh.' (The town lies north of Bethel, east of the highway that runs from Bethel up to Shechem, and south of Lebonah.) 20 So they told the Benjaminites to do as follows, 'Put yourselves in ambush in the vineyards. 21 Keep watch: when the girls of Shiloh come out in groups to dance, you then come out of the vineyards, each of you seize a wife from the girls of Shiloh and make for Benjaminite territory. 22 If their fathers or brothers come and complain to us, we shall say, "Let us have them, since we could not take wives for everyone in the battle; and you could not give them to them, or you would then have been guilty." '

23 The Benjaminites did this and, from the dancers whom they caught, took as many wives as there were men and then, setting off, went back to their heritage, rebuilt the towns and settled down in them.

24 The Israelites then dispersed, each man to rejoin his tribe and clan, each leaving that place for his own heritage.

25 In those days there was no king in Israel, and everyone did as he saw fit.

Ruth

1 In the days when the judges ruled, there was a famine in the land, and a certain man of Bethlehem in Judah went to live in the country of Moab, he and his wife and two sons. 2 The name of the man was Elimelech and the name of his wife Naomi, and the names of his two sons were Mahlon and Chilion; they were Ephrathites from Bethlehem in Judah. They went into the country of Moab and remained there. 3 But Elimelech, the husband of Naomi, died, and she was left with her two sons. 4 These took Moabite wives; the name of the one was Orpah and the name of the other Ruth. When they had lived there about ten years, 5 both Mahlon and Chilion also died, so that the woman was left without her two sons and her husband.

6 Then she started to return with her daughters-in-law from the country of Moab, for she had heard in the country of Moab that the LORD had considered his people and given them food. 7 So she set out from the place where she had been living, she and her two daughters-in-law, and they went on their way to go back to the land of Judah. 8 But Naomi said to her two daughters-in-law, "Go back each of you to your mother's house. May the LORD deal kindly with you, as you have dealt with the dead and with me. 9 The LORD grant that you may find security, each of you in the house of your husband." Then she kissed them, and they wept aloud. 10 They said to her, "No, we will return with you to your people." 11 But Naomi said, "Turn back, my daughters, why will you go with me? Do I still have sons in my womb that they may become your husbands? 12 Turn back, my daughters, go your way, for I am too old to have a husband. Even if I thought there was hope for me, even if I should have a husband tonight and bear sons, 13 would you then wait until they were grown? Would you then refrain from marrying? No, my daughters, it has been far more bitter for me than for you, because the hand of the LORD has turned against me." 14 Then they wept aloud again. Orpah kissed her mother-in-law, but Ruth clung to her.

15 So she said, "See, your sister-in-law has gone back to her people and to her gods; return after your sister-in-law." 16 But Ruth said,

"Do not press me to leave you
or to turn back from following you!
Where you go, I will go;
   where you lodge, I will lodge;
your people shall be my people,
   and your God my God.
17   Where you die, I will die —
   there will I be buried.
May the LORD do thus and so to me,
   and more as well,
if even death parts me from you!"

18 When Naomi saw that she was determined to go with her, she said no more to her.

19 So the two of them went on until they came to Bethlehem. When they came to Bethlehem, the whole town was stirred because of them; and the women said, "Is this Naomi?" 20 She said to them,

"Call me no longer Naomi,[a]
   call me Mara,[b]
for the Almighty[c] has dealt bitterly with me.

Ruth

1 ONCE, in the time of the Judges when there was a famine in the land, a man from Bethlehem in Judah went with his wife and two sons to live in Moabite territory. 2 The man's name was Elimelech, his wife was Naomi, and his sons were Mahlon and Chilion; they were Ephrathites from Bethlehem in Judah. They came to Moab and settled there.

3 Elimelech died, and Naomi was left a widow with her two sons. 4 The sons married Moabite women, one of whom was called Orpah and the other Ruth. They had lived there about ten years 5 when both Mahlon and Chilion died. Then Naomi, bereaved of her two sons as well as of her husband, 6 got ready to return to her own country with her daughters-in-law, because she heard in Moab that the LORD had shown his care for his people by giving them food. 7 Accompanied by her two daughters-in-law she left the place where she had been living, and they took the road leading back to Judah.

8 Naomi said to her daughters-in-law, 'Go back, both of you, home to your own mothers. May the LORD keep faith with you, as you have kept faith with the dead and with me; 9 and may he grant each of you the security of a home with a new husband.' And she kissed them goodbye. They wept aloud 10 and said, 'No, we shall return with you to your people.' 11 But Naomi insisted, 'Go back, my daughters. Why should you come with me? Am I likely to bear any more sons to be husbands for you? 12 Go back, my daughters, go; for I am too old to marry again. But if I could say that I had hope of a child, even if I were to be married tonight and were to bear sons, 13 would you then, wait until they grew up? Would you on their account remain unmarried? No, my daughters! For your sakes I feel bitter that the LORD has inflicted such misfortune on me.' 14 At this they wept still more. Then Orpah kissed her mother-in-law and took her leave, but Ruth clung to her.

15 'Look,' said Naomi, 'your sister-in-law has gone back to her people and her god. Go, follow her.' 16 Ruth answered, 'Do not urge me to go back and desert you. Where you go, I shall go, and where you stay, I shall stay. Your people will be my people, and your God my God. 17 Where you die, I shall die, and there be buried. I solemnly declare before the LORD that nothing but death will part me from you.' 18 When Naomi saw that Ruth was determined to go with her, she said no more.

19 The two of them went on until they came to Bethlehem, where their arrival set the whole town buzzing with excitement. The women cried, 'Can this be Naomi?' 20 'Do not call me Naomi,' she said; 'call me Mara, for the Almighty has made my life very bitter. 21 I went away full,

---

[a] That is *Pleasant*   [b] That is *Bitter*   [c] Traditional rendering of Heb *Shaddai*

1:13 **For . . . that:** *or* My lot is more bitter than yours, because. 1:20 **Naomi:** *that is* Pleasure. **Mara:** *that is* Bitter.

THE BOOK OF
Ruth

1 Once in the time of the judges there was a famine in the land; so a man from Bethlehem of Judah departed with his wife and two sons to reside on the plateau of Moab. 2 The man was named Elimelech, his wife Naomi, and his sons Mahlon and Chilion; they were Ephrathites from Bethlehem of Judah. Some time after their arrival on the Moabite plateau, 3 Elimelech, the husband of Naomi, died, and she was left with her two sons, 4 who married Moabite women, one named Orpah, the other Ruth. When they had lived there about ten years, 5 both Mahlon and Chilion died also, and the woman was left with neither her two sons nor her husband. 6 She then made ready to go back from the plateau of Moab because word reached her there that the LORD had visited his people and given them food.

7 She and her two daughters-in-law left the place where they had been living. Then as they were on the road back to the land of Judah, 8 Naomi said to her two daughters-in-law, "Go back, each of you, to your mother's house! May the LORD be kind to you as you were to the departed and to me! 9 May the LORD grant each of you a husband and a home in which you will find rest." She kissed them good-by, but they wept with loud sobs, 10 and told her they would return with her to her people. 11 "Go back, my daughters!" said Naomi. "Why should you come with me? Have I other sons in my womb who may become your husbands? 12 Go back, my daughters! Go, for I am too old to marry again. And even if I could offer any hopes, or if tonight I had a husband or had borne sons, 13 would you then wait and deprive yourselves of husbands until those sons grew up? No, my daughters! my lot is too bitter for you, because the LORD has extended his hand against me." 14 Again they sobbed aloud and wept; and Orpah kissed her mother-in-law good-by, but Ruth stayed with her.

15 "See now!" she said, "your sister-in-law has gone back to her people and her god. Go back after your sister-in-law!" 16 But Ruth said, "Do not ask me to abandon or forsake you! for wherever you go I will go, wherever you lodge I will lodge, your people shall be my people, and your God my God. 17 Wherever you die I will die, and there be buried. May the LORD do so and so to me, and more besides, if aught but death separates me from you!" 18 Naomi then ceased to urge her, for she saw she was determined to go with her.

19 So they went on together till they reached Bethlehem. On their arrival there, the whole city was astir over them, and the women asked, "Can this be Naomi?" 20 But she said to them, "Do not call me Naomi. Call me Mara, for the Almighty has made it very bitter for me. 21 I went away with

THE BOOK OF
Ruth

1 In the days when the Judges were governing, a famine occurred in the country and a certain man from Bethlehem of Judah went — he, his wife and his two sons — to live in the Plains of Moab. 2 The man was called Elimelech, his wife Naomi and his two sons Mahlon and Chilion;*a* they were Ephrathites from Bethlehem of Judah. Going to the Plains of Moab, they settled there. 3 Elimelech, Naomi's husband, died, and she and her two sons were left. 4 These married Moabite women: one was called Orpah and the other Ruth. They lived there for about ten years. 5 Mahlon and Chilion then both died too, and Naomi was thus bereft of her two sons and her husband. 6 She then decided to come back from the Plains of Moab with her daughters-in-law, having heard in the Plains of Moab that God had visited his people and given them food. 7 So, with her daughters-in-law, she left the place where she was living and they took the road back to Judah.

8 Naomi said to her two daughters-in-law, 'Go back, each of you to your mother's house. 9 May Yahweh show you faithful love, as you have done to those who have died and to me. Yahweh grant that you may each find happiness with a husband!' She then kissed them, but they began weeping loudly, 10 and said, 'No, we shall go back with you to your people.' 11 'Go home, daughters,' Naomi replied. 'Why come with me? Have I any more sons in my womb to make husbands for you?*b* 12 Go home, daughters, go, for I am now too old to marry again. Even if I said, "I still have a hope: I shall take a husband this very night and shall bear more sons," 13 would you be prepared to wait for them until they were grown up? Would you refuse to marry for their sake? No, daughters, I am bitterly sorry for your sakes that the hand of Yahweh should have been raised against me.' 14 They started weeping loudly all over again; Orpah then kissed her mother-in-law and went back to her people. But Ruth stayed with her.

15 Naomi then said, 'Look, your sister-in-law has gone back to her people and to her god. Go home, too; follow your sister-in-law.'

16 But Ruth said, 'Do not press me to leave you and to stop going with you, for

wherever you go, I shall go,
wherever you live, I shall live.
Your people will be my people,
and your God will be my God.
17 Where you die, I shall die
and there I shall be buried.
Let Yahweh bring unnameable ills*c* on me
and worse ills, too,
if anything but death
should part me from you!'

18 Seeing that Ruth was determined to go with her, Naomi said no more.

19 The two of them went on until they came to Bethlehem. Their arrival set the whole town astir, and the women said, 'Can this be Naomi?' 20 To this she replied, 'Do not call me Naomi, call me Mara,*d* for Shaddai has made my lot bitter.

---

a 1 The names are chosen for their meanings: Mahlon = sickness, Chilion = passing away.   *b* 1 A dead husband's nearest male relative must marry the childless widow and father heirs to his name.   *c* 1 The disasters are not named because mere mention might bring their effect.   *d* 1 Mara = the bitter one, Naomi = my sweetness.

NEW REVISED STANDARD VERSION

21 I went away full,
　　but the LORD has brought me back empty;
　why call me Naomi
　　when the LORD has dealt harshly with[d] me,
　　and the Almighty[e] has brought calamity upon
　　me?"

22 So Naomi returned together with Ruth the Moabite, her daughter-in-law, who came back with her from the country of Moab. They came to Bethlehem at the beginning of the barley harvest.

2 Now Naomi had a kinsman on her husband's side, a prominent rich man, of the family of Elimelech, whose name was Boaz. 2 And Ruth the Moabite said to Naomi, "Let me go to the field and glean among the ears of grain, behind someone in whose sight I may find favor." She said to her, "Go, my daughter." 3 So she went. She came and gleaned in the field behind the reapers. As it happened, she came to the part of the field belonging to Boaz, who was of the family of Elimelech. 4 Just then Boaz came from Bethlehem. He said to the reapers, "The LORD be with you." They answered, "The LORD bless you." 5 Then Boaz said to his servant who was in charge of the reapers, "To whom does this young woman belong?" 6 The servant who was in charge of the reapers answered, "She is the Moabite who came back with Naomi from the country of Moab. 7 She said, 'Please, let me glean and gather among the sheaves behind the reapers.' So she came, and she has been on her feet from early this morning until now, without resting even for a moment."[f]

8 Then Boaz said to Ruth, "Now listen, my daughter, do not go to glean in another field or leave this one, but keep close to my young women. 9 Keep your eyes on the field that is being reaped, and follow behind them. I have ordered the young men not to bother you. If you get thirsty, go to the vessels and drink from what the young men have drawn." 10 Then she fell prostrate, with her face to the ground, and said to him, "Why have I found favor in your sight, that you should take notice of me, when I am a foreigner?" 11 But Boaz answered her, "All that you have done for your mother-in-law since the death of your husband has been fully told me, and how you left your father and mother and your native land and came to a people that you did not know before. 12 May the LORD reward you for your deeds, and may you have a full reward from the LORD, the God of Israel, under whose wings you have come for refuge!" 13 Then she said, "May I continue to find favor in your sight, my lord, for you have comforted me and spoken kindly to your servant, even though I am not one of your servants."

14 At mealtime Boaz said to her, "Come here, and eat some of this bread, and dip your morsel in the sour wine." So she sat beside the reapers, and he heaped up for her some parched grain. She ate until she was satisfied, and she had some left over. 15 When she got up to glean, Boaz instructed his young men, "Let her glean even among the standing sheaves, and do not reproach her. 16 You must also pull out some handfuls for her from the bundles, and leave them for her to glean, and do not rebuke her."

17 So she gleaned in the field until evening. Then she beat out what she had gleaned, and it was about an ephah of barley. 18 She picked it up and came into the town, and her mother-in-law saw how much she had gleaned. Then she took out and gave her what was left over after she herself had been satisfied. 19 Her mother-in-law said to her,

REVISED ENGLISH BIBLE

and the LORD has brought me back empty. Why call me Naomi? The LORD has pronounced against me, the Almighty has brought me misfortune.'

22 That was how Naomi's daughter-in-law, Ruth the Moabite, returned with her from Moab; they arrived in Bethlehem just as the barley harvest was beginning.

2 NAOMI had a relative on her husband's side, a prominent and well-to-do member of Elimelech's family; his name was Boaz. 2 One day Ruth the Moabite asked Naomi, 'May I go to the harvest fields and glean behind anyone who will allow me?' 'Yes, go, my daughter,' she replied. 3 So Ruth went gleaning in the fields behind the reapers. As it happened, she was in that strip of the fields which belonged to Boaz of Elimelech's family, 4 and there was Boaz himself coming out from Bethlehem. He greeted the reapers, 'The LORD be with you!' and they responded, 'The LORD bless you!' 5 'Whose girl is this?' he asked the servant in charge of the reapers. The servant answered, 6 'She is a Moabite girl who has come back with Naomi from Moab. 7 She asked if she might glean, gathering among the sheaves behind the reapers. She came and has been on her feet from morning till now; she has hardly had a moment's rest in the shelter.'

8 Boaz said to Ruth, 'Listen, my daughter: do not go to glean in any other field. Do not look any farther, but stay close to my servant-girls. 9 Watch where the men reap, and follow the gleaners; I have told the men not to molest you. Any time you are thirsty, go and drink from the jars they have filled.' 10 She bowed to the ground and said, 'Why are you so kind as to take notice of me, when I am just a foreigner?' 11 Boaz answered, 'I have been told the whole story of what you have done for your mother-in-law since the death of your husband, how you left father and mother and homeland and came among a people you did not know before. 12 The LORD reward you for what you have done; may you be richly repaid by the LORD the God of Israel, under whose wings you have come for refuge.' 13 She said: 'I hope you will continue to be pleased with me, sir, for you have eased my mind by speaking kindly to me, though I am not one of your slave-girls.'

14 When mealtime came round, Boaz said to Ruth, 'Come over here and have something to eat. Dip your piece of bread in the vinegar.' She sat down beside the reapers, and he passed her some roasted grain. She ate all she wanted and still had some left. 15 When she got up to glean, Boaz instructed the men to allow her to glean right among the sheaves. 'Do not find fault with her,' he added; 16 'you may even pull out some ears of grain from the handfuls as you cut, and leave them for her to glean; do not check her.'

17 Ruth gleaned in the field until sunset, and when she beat out what she had gathered it came to about a bushel of barley. 18 She carried it into the town and showed her mother-in-law how much she had got; she also brought out and handed her what she had left over from the meal. 19 Her

---

[d] Or has testified against　[e] Traditional rendering of Heb Shaddai
[f] Compare Gk Vg: Meaning of Heb uncertain

2:17 bushel: Heb. ephah.

NEW AMERICAN BIBLE

an abundance, but the LORD has brought me back destitute. Why should you call me Naomi, since the LORD has pronounced against me and the Almighty has brought evil upon me?" 22 Thus it was that Naomi returned with the Moabite daughter-in-law, Ruth, who accompanied her back from the plateau of Moab. They arrived in Bethlehem at the beginning of the barley harvest.

2 Naomi had a prominent kinsman named Boaz, of the clan of her husband Elimelech. 2 Ruth the Moabite said to Naomi, "Let me go and glean ears of grain in the field of anyone who will allow me that favor." Naomi said to her, "Go, my daughter," 3 and she went. The field she entered to glean after the harvesters happened to be the section belonging to Boaz of the clan of Elimelech. 4 Boaz himself came from Bethlehem and said to the harvesters, "The LORD be with you!" and they replied, "The LORD bless you!" 5 Boaz asked the overseer of his harvesters, "Whose girl is this?" 6 The overseer of the harvesters answered, "She is the Moabite girl who returned from the plateau of Moab with Naomi. 7 She asked leave to gather the gleanings into sheaves after the harvesters; and ever since she came this morning she has remained here until now, with scarcely a moment's rest."

8 Boaz said to Ruth, "Listen, my daughter! Do not go to glean in anyone else's field; you are not to leave here. Stay here with my women servants. 9 Watch to see which field is to be harvested, and follow them; I have commanded the young men to do you no harm. When you are thirsty, you may go and drink from the vessels the young men have filled." 10 Casting herself prostrate upon the ground, she said to him, "Why should I, a foreigner, be favored with your notice?" 11 Boaz answered her: "I have had a complete account of what you have done for your mother-in-law after your husband's death; you have left your father and your mother and the land of your birth, and have come to a people whom you did not know previously. 12 May the LORD reward what you have done! May you receive a full reward from the LORD, the God of Israel, under whose wings you have come for refuge." 13 She said, "May I prove worthy of your kindness, my lord: you have comforted me, your servant, with your consoling words; would indeed that I were a servant of yours!" 14 At mealtime Boaz said to her, "Come here and have some food; dip your bread in the sauce." Then as she sat near the reapers, he handed her some roasted grain and she ate her fill and had some left over. 15 She rose to glean, and Boaz instructed his servants to let her glean among the sheaves themselves without scolding her, 16 and even to let drop some handfuls and leave them for her to glean without being rebuked.

17 She gleaned in the field until evening, and when she beat out what she had gleaned it came to about an ephah of barley, 18 which she took into the city and showed to her mother-in-law. Next she brought out and gave her what she had left over from lunch. 19 So her mother-in-law said to

NEW JERUSALEM BIBLE

21 I departed full,
and Yahweh has brought me home empty.
Why, then, call me Naomi,
since Yahweh has pronounced against me
and Shaddai has made me wretched?'
22 This was how Naomi came home with her daughter-in-law, Ruth the Moabitess, on returning from the Plains of Moab. They arrived in Bethlehem at the beginning of the barley harvest.

2 Naomi had a kinsman on her husband's side, well-to-do and of Elimelech's clan. His name was Boaz.

2 Ruth the Moabitess said to Naomi, 'Let me go into the fields and glean ears of corn in the footsteps of some man who will look on me with favour.' She replied, 'Go, daughter.' 3 So she set out and went to glean in the fields behind the reapers. Chance led her to a plot of land belonging to Boaz of Elimelech's clan. 4 Boaz, as it happened, had just come from Bethlehem. 'Yahweh be with you!' he said to the reapers. 'Yahweh bless you!' they replied. 5 Boaz said to a servant of his who was in charge of the reapers, 'To whom does this young woman belong?' 6 And the servant in charge of the reapers replied, 'The girl is the Moabitess, the one who came back with Naomi from the Plains of Moab. 7 She said, "Please let me glean and pick up what falls from the sheaves behind the reapers." Thus she came, and here she stayed, with hardly a rest from morning until now.'

8 Boaz said to Ruth, 'Listen to me, daughter. You must not go gleaning in any other field. You must not go away from here. Stay close to my work-women. 9 Keep your eyes on whatever part of the field they are reaping and follow behind. I have forbidden my men to molest you. And if you are thirsty, go to the pitchers and drink what the servants have drawn.' 10 Ruth fell on her face, prostrated herself and said, 'How have I attracted your favour, for you to notice me, who am only a foreigner?' 11 Boaz replied, 'I have been told all about the way you have behaved to your mother-in-law since your husband's death, and how you left your own father and mother and the land where you were born to come to a people of whom you previously knew nothing. 12 May Yahweh repay you for what you have done, and may you be richly rewarded by Yahweh, the God of Israel, under whose wings you have come for refuge!' 13 She said, 'My lord, I hope you will always look on me with favour! You have comforted and encouraged me, though I am not even the equal of one of your work-women.'

14 When it was time to eat, Boaz said to her, 'Come and eat some of this bread and dip your piece in the vinegar.' Ruth sat down beside the reapers and Boaz made a heap of roasted grain for her; she ate till her hunger was satisfied, and she had some left over. 15 When she had got up to glean, Boaz gave orders to his work-people, 'Let her glean among the sheaves themselves. Do not molest her. 16 And be sure you pull a few ears of corn out of the bundles and drop them. Let her glean them, and do not scold her.' 17 So she gleaned in the field till evening. Then she beat out what she had gleaned and it came to about a bushel of barley. 18 Taking it with her, she went back to the town. Her mother-in-law saw what she had gleaned. Ruth also took out what she had kept after eating all she wanted, and gave that to her. 19 Her mother-in-law said, 'Where have you

"Where did you glean today? And where have you worked? Blessed be the man who took notice of you." So she told her mother-in-law with whom she had worked, and said, "The name of the man with whom I worked today is Boaz." 20 Then Naomi said to her daughter-in-law, "Blessed be he by the LORD, whose kindness has not forsaken the living or the dead!" Naomi also said to her, "The man is a relative of ours, one of our nearest kin."g 21 Then Ruth the Moabite said, "He even said to me, 'Stay close by my servants, until they have finished all my harvest.' " 22 Naomi said to Ruth, her daughter-in-law, "It is better, my daughter, that you go out with his young women, otherwise you might be bothered in another field." 23 So she stayed close to the young women of Boaz, gleaning until the end of the barley and wheat harvests; and she lived with her mother-in-law.

3 Naomi her mother-in-law said to her, "My daughter, I need to seek some security for you, so that it may be well with you. 2 Now here is our kinsman Boaz, with whose young women you have been working. See, he is winnowing barley tonight at the threshing floor. 3 Now wash and anoint yourself, and put on your best clothes and go down to the threshing floor; but do not make yourself known to the man until he has finished eating and drinking. 4 When he lies down, observe the place where he lies; then, go and uncover his feet and lie down; and he will tell you what to do." 5 She said to her, "All that you tell me I will do."

6 So she went down to the threshing floor and did just as her mother-in-law had instructed her. 7 When Boaz had eaten and drunk, and he was in a contented mood, he went to lie down at the end of the heap of grain. Then she came stealthily and uncovered his feet, and lay down. 8 At midnight the man was startled, and turned over, and there, lying at his feet, was a woman! 9 He said, "Who are you?" And she answered, "I am Ruth, your servant; spread your cloak over your servant, for you are next-of-kin."g 10 He said, "May you be blessed by the LORD, my daughter; this last instance of your loyalty is better than the first; you have not gone after young men, whether poor or rich. 11 And now, my daughter, do not be afraid, I will do for you all that you ask, for all the assembly of my people know that you are a worthy woman. 12 But now, though it is true that I am a near kinsman, there is another kinsman more closely related than I. 13 Remain this night, and in the morning, if he will act as next-of-king for you, good; let him do it. If he is not willing to act as next-of-king for you, then, as the LORD lives, I will act as next-of-king for you. Lie down until the morning."

14 So she lay at his feet until morning, but got up before one person could recognize another; for he said, "It must not be known that the woman came to the threshing floor." 15 Then he said, "Bring the cloak you are wearing and hold it out." So she held it, and he measured out six measures of barley, and put it on her back; then he went into the city. 16 She came to her mother-in-law, who said, "How did things go with you,h my daughter?" Then she told her all that the man had done for her, 17 saying, "He gave me these six measures of barley, for he said, 'Do not go back to your mother-in-law empty-handed.' " 18 She replied, "Wait, my daughter, until you learn how the matter turns out, for the man will not rest, but will settle the matter today."

4 No sooner had Boaz gone up to the gate and sat down there than the next-of-kin,g of whom Boaz had spoken, came passing by. So Boaz said, "Come over, friend; sit down here." And he went over and sat down. 2 Then

mother-in-law asked, 'Where did you glean today? Which way did you go? Blessings on the man who took notice of you!' She told her mother-in-law in whose field she had been working. 'The owner of the field where I worked today', she said, 'is a man called Boaz.' 20 Naomi exclaimed, 'Blessings on him from the LORD, who has kept faith with the living and the dead! This man', she explained, 'is related to us; he is one of our very near kinsmen.' 21 'And what is more,' Ruth said, 'he told me to stay close to his workers until they had finished all his harvest.' 22 Naomi said, 'My daughter, it would be as well for you to go with his girls; in another field you might come to harm.' 23 So Ruth kept close to them, gleaning with them till the end of both barley and wheat harvests; but she lived with her mother-in-law.

3 One day Naomi, Ruth's mother-in-law, said to her, 'My daughter, I want to see you settled happily. 2 Now there is our kinsman Boaz, whose girls you have been with. 3 Tonight he will be winnowing barley at the threshing-floor. Bathe and anoint yourself with perfumed oil, then get dressed and go down to the threshing-floor; but do not make yourself known to the man until he has finished eating and drinking. 4 When he lies down make sure you know the place where he is. Then go in, turn back the covering at his feet and lie down. He will tell you what to do.' 5 'I will do everything you say,' replied Ruth.

6 She went down to the threshing-floor and did exactly as her mother-in-law had told her. 7 When Boaz had eaten and drunk, he felt at peace with the world and went and lay down to sleep at the far end of the heap of grain. Ruth came quietly, turned back the covering at his feet and lay down. 8 About midnight the man woke with a start; he turned over, and there, lying at his feet, was a woman! 9 'Who are you?' he said. 'Sir, it is I, Ruth,' she replied. 'Spread the skirt of your cloak over me, for you are my next-of-kin.' 10 Boaz said, 'The LORD bless you, my daughter! You are proving yourself more devoted to the family than ever by not running after any young man, whether rich or poor. 11 Set your mind at rest, my daughter: I shall do all you ask, for the whole town knows what a fine woman you are. 12 Yes, it is true that I am a near kinsman; but there is one even closer than I am. 13 Stay tonight, and then in the morning, if he is willing to act as your next-of-kin, well and good; but if he is not, then as sure as the LORD lives, I shall do so. Now lie down till morning.'

14 She lay at his feet till next morning, but rose before it was light enough for one man to recognize another; Boaz had it in mind that no one should know that the woman had been to the threshing-floor. 15 He said to her, 'Take the cloak you are wearing, and hold it out.' When she did so, he poured in six measures of barley and lifted it for her to carry, and she went off to the town.

16 When she came to her mother-in-law, Naomi asked, 'How did things go with you, my daughter?' Ruth related all that the man had done for her, 17 and she added, 'He gave me these six measures of barley; he would not let me come home to my mother-in-law empty-handed.' 18 Naomi said, 'Wait, my daughter, until you see what will come of it; he will not rest till he has settled the matter this very day.'

4 Boaz meanwhile had gone up to the town gate and was sitting there when the next-of-kin of whom he had spoken came past. Calling him by name, Boaz cried, 'Come over here and sit down.' He went over and sat down. 2 Boaz

---

g Or one with the right to redeem   h Or "Who are you,

3:15 she went: so many MSS; others he went.

NEW AMERICAN BIBLE

her, "Where did you glean today? Where did you go to work? May he who took notice of you be blessed!" Then she told her mother-in-law with whom she had worked. "The man at whose place I worked today is named Boaz," she said. 20 "May he be blessed by the LORD, who is ever merciful to the living and to the dead," Naomi exclaimed to her daughter-in-law; and she continued, "He is a relative of ours, one of our next of kin." 21 "He even told me," added Ruth the Moabite, "that I should stay with his servants until they complete his entire harvest." 22 "You would do well, my dear," Naomi rejoined, "to go out with his servants; for in someone else's field you might be insulted." 23 So she stayed gleaning with the servants of Boaz until the end of the barley and wheat harvests.

3 When she was back with her mother-in-law, 1 Naomi said to her, "My daughter, I must seek a home for you that will please you. 2 Now is not Boaz, with whose servants you were, a relative of ours? This evening he will be winnowing barley at the threshing floor. 3 So bathe and anoint yourself; then put on your best attire and go down to the threshing floor. Do not make yourself known to the man before he has finished eating and drinking. 4 But when he lies down, take note of the place where he does so. Then go, uncover a place at his feet, and lie down. He will tell you what to do." 5 "I will do whatever you advise," Ruth replied. 6 So she went down to the threshing floor and did just as her mother-in-law had instructed her.

7 Boaz ate and drank to his heart's content. Then when he went and lay down at the edge of the sheaves, she stole up, uncovered a place at his feet, and lay down. 8 In the middle of the night, however, the man gave a start and turned around to find a woman lying at his feet. 9 He asked, "Who are you?" And she replied, "I am your servant Ruth. Spread the corner of your cloak over me, for you are my next of kin." 10 He said, "May the LORD bless you, my daughter! You have been even more loyal now than before in not going after the young men, whether poor or rich. 11 So be assured, daughter, I will do for you whatever you say; all my townspeople know you for a worthy woman. 12 Now, though indeed I am closely related to you, you have another relative still closer. 13 Stay as you are for tonight, and to-morrow, if he wishes to claim you, good! let him do so. But if he does not wish to claim you, as the LORD lives, I will claim you myself. Lie there until morning." 14 So she lay at his feet until morning, but rose before men could recognize one another. Boaz said, "Let it not be known that this woman came to the threshing floor." 15 He then said to her, "Take off your cloak and hold it out." When she did so, he poured out six measures of barley, helped her lift the bundle, and left for the city.

16 Ruth went home to her mother-in-law, who asked, "How have you fared, my daughter?" So she told her all the man had done for her, 17 and concluded, "He gave me these six measures of barley because he did not wish me to come back to my mother-in-law empty-handed!" 18 Naomi then said, "Wait here, my daughter, until you learn what happens, for the man will not rest, but will settle the matter today."

4 Boaz went and took a seat at the gate; and when he saw the closer relative of whom he had spoken come along, he called to him by name, "Come and sit beside me!" And he did so. 2 Then Boaz picked out ten of the elders of the

NEW JERUSALEM BIBLE

been gleaning today? Where have you been working? Blessed be the man who took notice of you!' Ruth told her mother-in-law in whose field she had been working. 'The name of the man with whom I have been working today', she said, 'is Boaz.' 20 Naomi said to her daughter-in-law, 'May he be blessed by Yahweh who does not withhold his faithful love from living or dead! This man', Naomi added, 'is a close relation of ours. He is one of those who have the right of redemption over us.' 21 Ruth the Moabitess said to her mother-in-law, 'He also said, "Stay with my work-people until they have finished my whole harvest." ' 22 Naomi said to Ruth, her daughter-in-law, 'It is better for you, daughter, to go with his work-women than to go to some other field where you might be ill-treated.' 23 So she stayed with Boaz's work-women, and gleaned until the barley and wheat harvests were finished. And she went on living with her mother-in-law.

3 Her mother-in-law Naomi then said, 'Daughter, is it not my duty to see you happily settled? 2 And Boaz, the man with whose work-women you were, is he not our kinsman? Tonight he will be winnowing the barley on the threshing-floor. 3 So wash and perfume yourself, put on your cloak and go down to the threshing-floor. Don't let him recognise you while he is still eating and drinking. 4 But when he lies down, take note where he lies, then go and turn back the covering at his feet and lie down yourself. He will tell you what to do.' 5 Ruth said, 'I shall do everything you tell me.'

6 So she went down to the threshing-floor and did everything her mother-in-law had told her. 7 When Boaz had finished eating and drinking, he went off happily and lay down beside the pile of barley. Ruth then quietly went, turned back the covering at his feet and lay down. 8 In the middle of the night, he woke up with a shock and looked about him; and there lying at his feet was a woman. 9 'Who are you?' he said; and she replied, 'I am your servant Ruth. Spread the skirt of your cloak over your servant for you have the right of redemption over me.' 10 'May Yahweh bless you, daughter,' he said, 'for this second act of faithful love of yours is greater than the first, since you have not run after young men, poor or rich. 11 Don't be afraid, daughter, I shall do everything you ask, since the people at the gate of my town all know that you are a woman of great worth. 12 But, though it is true that I have the right of redemption over you, you have a kinsman closer than myself. 13 Stay here for tonight and, in the morning, if he wishes to exercise his right over you, very well, let him redeem you. But if he does not wish to do so, then as Yahweh lives, I shall redeem you. Lie here till morning.' 14 So she lay at his feet till morning, but got up before the hour when one man can recognise another; and he thought, 'It must not be known that this woman came to the threshing-floor.' 15 He then said, 'Let me have the cloak you are wearing, hold it out!' She held it out while he put six measures of barley into it and then loaded it on to her; and off she went to the town.

16 When Ruth got home, her mother-in-law asked her, 'How did things go with you, daughter?' She then told her everything that the man had done for her. 17 'He gave me these six measures of barley and said, "You must not go home empty-handed to your mother-in-law." ' 18 Naomi said, 'Do nothing, daughter, until you see how things have gone; I am sure he will not rest until he has settled the matter this very day.'

4 Boaz, meanwhile, had gone up to the gate and sat down, and the relative of whom he had spoken then came by. Boaz said to him, 'Here, my friend, come and sit down'; the man came and sat down. 2 Boaz then picked out

NEW REVISED STANDARD VERSION	REVISED ENGLISH BIBLE

Boaz took ten men of the elders of the city, and said, "Sit down here"; so they sat down. 3 He then said to the next-of-kin,[i] "Naomi, who has come back from the country of Moab, is selling the parcel of land that belonged to our kinsman Elimelech. 4 So I thought I would tell you of it, and say: Buy it in the presence of those sitting here, and in the presence of the elders of my people. If you will redeem it, redeem it; but if you will not, tell me, so that I may know; for there is no one prior to you to redeem it, and I come after you." So he said, "I will redeem it." 5 Then Boaz said, "The day you acquire the field from the hand of Naomi, you are also acquiring Ruth[j] the Moabite, the widow of the dead man, to maintain the dead man's name on his inheritance." 6 At this, the next-of-kin[i] said, "I cannot redeem it for myself without damaging my own inheritance. Take my right of redemption yourself, for I cannot redeem it."

7 Now this was the custom in former times in Israel concerning redeeming and exchanging: to confirm a transaction, the one took off a sandal and gave it to the other; this was the manner of attesting in Israel. 8 So when the next-of-kin[i] said to Boaz, "Acquire it for yourself," he took off his sandal. 9 Then Boaz said to the elders and all the people, "Today you are witnesses that I have acquired from the hand of Naomi all that belonged to Elimelech and all that belonged to Chilion and Mahlon. 10 I have also acquired Ruth the Moabite, the wife of Mahlon, to be my wife, to maintain the dead man's name on his inheritance, in order that the name of the dead may not be cut off from his kindred and from the gate of his native place; today you are witnesses." 11 Then all the people who were at the gate, along with the elders, said, "We are witnesses. May the LORD make the woman who is coming into your house like Rachel and Leah, who together built up the house of Israel. May you produce children in Ephrathah and bestow a name in Bethlehem; 12 and, through the children that the LORD will give you by this young woman, may your house be like the house of Perez, whom Tamar bore to Judah."

13 So Boaz took Ruth and she became his wife. When they came together, the LORD made her conceive, and she bore a son. 14 Then the women said to Naomi, "Blessed be the LORD, who has not left you this day without next-of-kin;[i] and may his name be renowned in Israel! 15 He shall be to you a restorer of life and a nourisher of your old age; for your daughter-in-law who loves you, who is more to you than seven sons, has borne him." 16 Then Naomi took the child and laid him in her bosom, and became his nurse. 17 The women of the neighborhood gave him a name, saying, "A son has been born to Naomi." They named him Obed; he became the father of Jesse, the father of David.

18 Now these are the descendants of Perez: Perez became the father of Hezron, 19 Hezron of Ram, Ram of Amminadab, 20 Amminadab of Nahshon, Nahshon of Salmon, 21 Salmon of Boaz, Boaz of Obed, 22 Obed of Jesse, and Jesse of David.

also stopped ten of the town's elders and asked them to sit there. When they were seated, 3 he addressed the next-of-kin: 'You will remember the strip of field that belonged to our kinsman Elimelech. Naomi is selling it, now that she has returned from Moab. 4 I promised to open the matter with you, to ask you to acquire it in the presence of those sitting here and in the presence of the elders of my people. If you are going to do your duty as next-of-kin, then do so; but if not, someone must do it. So tell me, and then I shall know, for I come after you as next-of-kin.' He answered, 'I shall act as next-of-kin.' 5 Boaz continued: 'On the day you take over the field from Naomi, I take over the widow, Ruth the Moabite, so as to perpetuate the name of the dead man on his holding.' 6 'Then I cannot act,' said the next-of-kin, 'lest it should be detrimental to my own holding; and as I cannot act, you yourself must take over my duty as next-of-kin.'

7 Now it used to be the custom when ratifying any transaction by which property was redeemed or transferred for a man to take off his sandal and give it to the other party; this was the form of attestation in Israel. 8 Accordingly when the next-of-kin said to Boaz, 'You must take it over,' he drew off his sandal and handed it over. 9 Then Boaz addressed the elders and all the other people there: 'You are witnesses this day that I have taken over from Naomi all that belonged to Elimelech and all that belonged to Chilion and Mahlon; 10 and, further, that I have taken over Mahlon's widow, Ruth the Moabite, to be my wife, in order to keep alive the dead man's name on his holding, so that his name may not be missing among his kindred and at the gate of his native town. You are witnesses this day.' 11 All who were at the gate, including the elders, replied, 'We are witnesses. May the LORD make this woman, who is about to come into your home, to be like Rachel and Leah, the two who built up the family of Israel. May you do a worthy deed in Ephrathah by keeping this name alive in Bethlehem. 12 Through the offspring the LORD gives you by this young woman may your family be like the family of Perez, whom Tamar bore to Judah.'

13 So Boaz took Ruth and she became his wife. When they had come together the LORD caused her to conceive, and she gave birth to a son. 14 The women said to Naomi, 'Blessed be the LORD, who has not left you this day without next-of-kin. May the name of your dead son be kept alive in Israel! 15 The child will give you renewed life and be your support and stay in your old age, for your devoted daughter-in-law, who has proved better to you than seven sons, has borne him.' 16 Naomi took the child and laid him in her own lap, and she became his foster-mother. 17 Her women neighbours gave him a name: 'Naomi has a son; we shall call him Obed,' they said. He became the father of Jesse, David's father.

18 THIS is the genealogy of Perez: Perez was the father of Hezron, 19 Hezron of Ram, Ram of Amminadab, 20 Amminadab of Nahshon, Nahshon of Salmon, 21 Salmon of Boaz, Boaz of Obed, 22 Obed of Jesse, and Jesse of David.

---

[i] Or one with the right to redeem   [j] OL Vg: Heb from the hand of Naomi and from Ruth

4:8 **and handed it over:** so Gk; Heb. omits.   4:14 **May ... son:** lit. May his name.   4:15 **The child:** lit. He.   4:20 **Salmon:** so some MSS; others Salmah.

city and asked them to sit nearby. When they had done this, 3 he said to the near relative: "Naomi, who has come back from the Moabite plateau, is putting up for sale the piece of land that belonged to our kinsman Elimelech. 4 So I thought I would inform you, bidding you before those here present, including the elders of my people, to put in your claim for it if you wish to acquire it as next of kin. But if you do not wish to claim it, tell me so, that I may be guided accordingly, for no one has a prior claim to yours, and mine is next." He answered, "I will put in my claim."

5 Boaz continued, "Once you acquire the field from Naomi, you must take also Ruth the Moabite, the widow of the late heir, and raise up a family for the departed on his estate." 6 The near relative replied, "I cannot exercise my claim lest I depreciate my own estate. Put in a claim yourself in my stead, for I cannot exercise my claim." 7 Now it used to be the custom in Israel that, to make binding a contract of redemption or exchange, one party would take off his sandal and give it to the other. This was the form of attestation in Israel. 8 So the near relative, in saying to Boaz, "Acquire it for yourself," drew off his sandal. 9 Boaz then said to the elders and to all the people, "You are witnesses today that I have acquired from Naomi all the holdings of Elimelech, Chilion and Mahlon. 10 I also take Ruth the Moabite, the widow of Mahlon, as my wife, in order to raise up a family for her late husband on his estate, so that the name of the departed may not perish among his kinsmen and fellow citizens. Do you witness this today?" 11 All those at the gate, including the elders, said, "We do so. May the LORD make this wife come into your house like Rachel and Leah, who between them built up the house of Israel. May you do well in Ephrathah and win fame in Bethlehem. 12 With the offspring the LORD will give you from this girl, may your house become like the house of Perez, whom Tamar bore to Judah."

13 Boaz took Ruth. When they came together as man and wife, the LORD enabled her to conceive and she bore a son. 14 Then the women said to Naomi, "Blessed is the LORD who has not failed to provide you today with an heir! May he become famous in Israel! 15 He will be your comfort and the support of your old age, for his mother is the daughter-in-law who loves you. She is worth more to you than seven sons!" 16 Naomi took the child, placed him on her lap, and became his nurse. 17 And the neighbor women gave him his name, at the news that a grandson had been born to Naomi. They called him Obed. He was the father of Jesse, the father of David.

18 These are the descendants of Perez: Perez was the father of Hezron, 19 Hezron was the father of Ram, Ram was the father of Amminadab, 20 Amminadab was the father of Nahshon, Nahshon was the father of Salmon, 21 Salmon was the father of Boaz, Boaz was the father of Obed, 22 Obed was the father of Jesse, and Jesse became the father of David.

ten of the town's elders and said, 'Sit down here'; they sat down. 3 Boaz then said to the man who had the right of redemption, 'Naomi, who has come back from the Plains of Moab, is selling the piece of land that belonged to our brother, Elimelech. 4 I thought I should tell you about this and say, "Acquire it in the presence of the men who are sitting here and in the presence of the elders of my people. If you want to use your right of redemption, redeem it; if you do not, tell me so that I know, for I am the only person to redeem it besides yourself, and I myself come after you."' The man said, 'I am willing to redeem it.' 5 Boaz then said, 'The day you acquire the field from Naomi, you also acquire Ruth the Moabitess, the wife of the man who has died, to perpetuate the dead man's name in his inheritance.' 6 The man with the right of redemption then said, 'I cannot use my right of redemption without jeopardising my own inheritance. Since I cannot use my right of redemption, exercise the right yourself.'

7 Now, in former times, it was the custom in Israel to confirm a transaction in matters of redemption or inheritance by one of the parties taking off his sandal and giving it to the other.e This was how agreements were ratified in Israel. 8 So, when the man with the right of redemption said to Boaz, 'Acquire it for yourself,' he took off his sandal.

9 Boaz then said to the elders and all the people there, 'Today you are witnesses that from Naomi I acquire everything that used to belong to Elimelech, and everything that used to belong to Mahlon and Chilion 10 and that I am also acquiring Ruth the Moabitess, Mahlon's widow, to be my wife, to perpetuate the dead man's name in his inheritance, so that the dead man's name will not be lost among his brothers and at the gate of his town. Today you are witnesses to this.' 11 All the people at the gate said, 'We are witnesses'; and the elders said, 'May Yahweh make the woman about to enter your family like Rachel and Leah who together built up the House of Israel.

Grow mighty in Ephrathah,
be renowned in Bethlehem!

12 And through the children Yahweh will give you by this young woman, may your family be like the family of Perez, whom Tamar bore to Judah.'

13 So Boaz took Ruth and she became his wife. And when they came together, Yahweh made her conceive and she bore a son. 14 And the women said to Naomi, 'Blessed be Yahweh who has not left you today without anyone to redeem you. May his name be praised in Israel! 15 The child will be a comfort to you and the prop of your old age, for he has been born to the daughter-in-law who loves you and is more to you than seven sons.' 16 And Naomi, taking the child, held him to her breast; and she it was who looked after him.

17 And the women of the neighbourhood gave him a name. 'A son', they said, 'has been born to Naomi,' and they called him Obed. This was the father of Jesse, the father of David.

18 These are the descendants of Perez. Perez fathered Hezron, 19 Hezron fathered Ram, Ram fathered Amminadab, 20 Amminadab fathered Nahshon, Nahshon fathered Salmon, 21 Salmon fathered Boaz, Boaz fathered Obed, 22 Obed fathered Jesse, and Jesse fathered David.

e 4 A distortion of the legislation given in Dt 25:9–10. To plant a sandal (or foot) on a field marks a claim to it. Here, taking off the sandal signifies renunciation of a claim.

THE FIRST BOOK OF

1 Samuel

Samuel

1 There was a certain man of Ramathaim, a Zuphite*a* from the hill country of Ephraim, whose name was Elkanah son of Jeroham son of Elihu son of Tohu son of Zuph, an Ephraimite. 2 He had two wives; the name of the one was Hannah, and the name of the other Peninnah. Peninnah had children, but Hannah had no children.

3 Now this man used to go up year by year from his town to worship and to sacrifice to the LORD of hosts at Shiloh, where the two sons of Eli, Hophni and Phinehas, were priests of the LORD. 4 On the day when Elkanah sacrificed, he would give portions to his wife Peninnah and to all her sons and daughters; 5 but to Hannah he gave a double portion,*b* because he loved her, though the LORD had closed her womb. 6 Her rival used to provoke her severely, to irritate her, because the LORD had closed her womb. 7 So it went on year by year; as often as she went up to the house of the LORD, she used to provoke her. Therefore Hannah wept and would not eat. 8 Her husband Elkanah said to her, "Hannah, why do you weep? Why do you not eat? Why is your heart sad? Am I not more to you than ten sons?"

9 After they had eaten and drunk at Shiloh, Hannah rose and presented herself before the LORD.*c* Now Eli the priest was sitting on the seat beside the doorpost of the temple of the LORD. 10 She was deeply distressed and prayed to the LORD, and wept bitterly. 11 She made this vow: "O LORD of hosts, if only you will look on the misery of your servant, and remember me, and not forget your servant, but will give to your servant a male child, then I will set him before you as a nazirite*d* until the day of his death. He shall drink neither wine nor intoxicants,*e* and no razor shall touch his head."

12 As she continued praying before the LORD, Eli observed her mouth. 13 Hannah was praying silently; only her lips moved, but her voice was not heard; therefore Eli thought she was drunk. 14 So Eli said to her, "How long will you make a drunken spectacle of yourself? Put away your wine." 15 But Hannah answered, "No, my lord, I am a woman deeply troubled; I have drunk neither wine nor strong drink, but I have been pouring out my soul before the LORD. 16 Do not regard your servant as a worthless woman, for I have been speaking out of my great anxiety and vexation all this time." 17 Then Eli answered, "Go in peace; the God of Israel grant the petition you have made to him." 18 And she said, "Let your servant find favor in your sight." Then the woman went to her quarters,*f* ate and drank with her husband,*g* and her countenance was sad no longer.*h*

19 They rose early in the morning and worshiped before the LORD; then they went back to their house at Ramah. Elkanah knew his wife Hannah, and the LORD remembered her. 20 In due time Hannah conceived and bore a son. She named him Samuel, for she said, "I have asked him of the LORD."

21 The man Elkanah and all his household went up to offer to the LORD the yearly sacrifice, and to pay his vow.

1 THERE was a certain man from Ramathaim, a Zuphite from the hill-country of Ephraim, named Elkanah son of Jeroham, son of Elihu, son of Tohu, son of Zuph an Ephraimite. 2 He had two wives, Hannah and Peninnah; Peninnah had children, but Hannah was childless. 3 Every year this man went up from his town to worship and sacrifice to the LORD of Hosts at Shiloh, where Eli's two sons, Hophni and Phinehas, were priests of the LORD.

4 When Elkanah sacrificed, he gave several shares of the meat to his wife Peninnah with all her sons and daughters; 5 but to Hannah he gave only one share; the LORD had not granted her children, yet it was Hannah whom Elkanah loved. 6 Hannah's rival also used to torment and humiliate her because she had no children. 7 This happened year after year when they went up to the house of the LORD; her rival used to torment her, until she was in tears and would not eat. 8 Her husband Elkanah said to her, 'Hannah, why are you crying and eating nothing? Why are you so miserable? Am I not more to you than ten sons?'

9–10 After they had finished eating and drinking at the sacrifice at Shiloh, Hannah rose in deep distress, and weeping bitterly stood before the LORD and prayed to him. Meanwhile Eli the priest was sitting on his seat beside the door of the temple of the LORD. 11 Hannah made this vow: 'LORD of Hosts, if you will only take notice of my trouble and remember me, if you will not forget me but grant me offspring, then I shall give the child to the LORD for the whole of his life, and no razor shall ever touch his head.'

12 For a long time she went on praying before the LORD, while Eli watched her lips. 13 Hannah was praying silently; her lips were moving although her voice could not be heard, and Eli took her for a drunken woman. 14 'Enough of this drunken behaviour!' he said to her. 'Leave off until the effect of the wine has gone.' 15 'Oh, sir!' she answered, 'I am a heart-broken woman; I have drunk neither wine nor strong drink, but I have been pouring out my feelings before the LORD. 16 Do not think me so devoid of shame, sir; all this time I have been speaking out of the depths of my grief and misery.' 17 Eli said, 'Go in peace, and may the God of Israel grant what you have asked of him.' 18 Hannah replied, 'May I be worthy of your kindness.' And no longer downcast she went away and had something to eat.

19 Next morning they were up early and, after prostrating themselves before the LORD, returned to their home at Ramah. Elkanah had intercourse with his wife Hannah, and the LORD remembered her; 20 she conceived, and in due time bore a son, whom she named Samuel, 'because', she said, 'I asked the LORD for him'.

21 Elkanah with his whole household went up to make the annual sacrifice to the LORD and to keep his vow. 22 Hannah

---

a Compare Gk and 1 Chr 6.35-36: Heb *Ramathaim-zophim*
b Syr: Meaning of Heb uncertain   *c* Gk: Heb lacks *and presented herself before the LORD*   *d* That is *one separated* or *one consecrated*
e Cn Compare Gk Q Ms 1.22: MT *then I will give him to the LORD all the days of his life*   *f* Gk: Heb *went her way*   *g* Gk: Heb lacks *and drank with her husband*   *h* Gk: Meaning of Heb uncertain

1:1 **a Zuphite:** *so Gk; Heb.* Zophim.   1:7 **they:** *so Lat.; Heb.* she.   1:9–10 **stood before the LORD:** *so Gk; Heb. omits.*
1:22 **come up . . . he is to:** *or* bring him up, and he will come into the presence of the LORD and.

THE FIRST BOOK OF
Samuel

1 There was a certain man from Ramathaim, Elkanah by name, a Zuphite from the hill country of Ephraim. He was the son of Jeroham, son of Elihu, son of Tohu, son of Zuph, an Ephraimite. 2 He had two wives, one named Hannah, the other Peninnah; Peninnah had children, but Hannah was childless. 3 This man regularly went on pilgrimage from his city to worship the LORD of hosts and to sacrifice to him at Shiloh, where the two sons of Eli, Hophni and Phinehas, were ministering as priests of the LORD. 4 When the day came for Elkanah to offer sacrifice, he used to give a portion each to his wife Peninnah and to all her sons and daughters, 5 but a double portion to Hannah because he loved her, though the LORD had made her barren. 6 Her rival, to upset her, turned it into a constant reproach to her that the LORD had left her barren. 7 This went on year after year; each time they made their pilgrimage to the sanctuary of the LORD, Peninnah would approach her, and Hannah would weep and refuse to eat. 8 Her husband Elkanah used to ask her: "Hannah, why do you weep, and why do you refuse to eat? Why do you grieve? Am I not more to you than ten sons?"

9 Hannah rose after one such meal at Shiloh, and presented herself before the LORD; at the time, Eli the priest was sitting on a chair near the doorpost of the LORD's temple. 10 In her bitterness she prayed to the LORD, weeping copiously, 11 and she made a vow, promising: "O LORD of hosts, if you look with pity on the misery of your handmaid, if you remember me and do not forget me, if you give your handmaid a male child, I will give him to the LORD for as long as he lives; neither wine nor liquor shall he drink, and no razor shall ever touch his head." 12 As she remained long at prayer before the LORD, Eli watched her mouth, 13 for Hannah was praying silently; though her lips were moving, her voice could not be heard. Eli, thinking her drunk, 14 said to her, "How long will you make a drunken show of yourself? Sober up from your wine!" 15 "It isn't that, my lord," Hannah answered. "I am an unhappy woman. I have had neither wine nor liquor; I was only pouring out my troubles to the LORD. 16 Do not think your handmaid a ne'er-do-well; my prayer has been prompted by my deep sorrow and misery." 17 Eli said, "Go in peace, and may the God of Israel grant you what you have asked of him." 18 She replied, "Think kindly of your maidservant," and left. She went to her quarters, ate and drank with her husband, and no longer appeared downcast. 19 Early the next morning they worshiped before the LORD, and then returned to their home in Ramah.

When Elkanah had relations with his wife Hannah, the LORD remembered her. 20 She conceived, and at the end of her term bore a son whom she called Samuel, since she had asked the LORD for him. 21 The next time her husband Elkanah was going up with the rest of his household to offer the customary sacrifice to the LORD and to fulfill his vows,

THE FIRST BOOK OF
Samuel

1 There was a man of Ramathaim, a Zuphite from the highlands of Ephraim whose name was Elkanah son of Jeroham, son of Elihu, son of Tohu, son of Zuph, an Ephraimite. 2 He had two wives, one called Hannah, the other Peninnah; Peninnah had children but Hannah had none. 3 Every year this man used to go up from his town to worship, and to sacrifice to Yahweh Sabaoth[a] at Shiloh. (The two sons of Eli, Hophni and Phinehas, were there as priests of Yahweh.) 4 One day Elkanah offered a sacrifice. Now he used to give portions to Peninnah and to all her sons and daughters; 5 to Hannah, however, he would give only one portion: for, although he loved Hannah more, Yahweh had made her barren. 6 Furthermore, her rival would taunt and provoke her, because Yahweh had made her womb barren. 7 And this went on year after year; every time they went up to the temple of Yahweh she used to taunt her. On that day she wept and would not eat anything; 8 so her husband Elkanah said, 'Hannah, why are you crying? Why are you not eating anything? Why are you so sad? Am I not more to you than ten sons?'

9 When they had finished eating in the room, Hannah got up and stood before Yahweh. Eli the priest was sitting on his seat by the doorpost of the temple of Yahweh. 10 In the bitterness of her soul she prayed to Yahweh with many tears, 11 and she made this vow, 'Yahweh Sabaoth! Should you condescend to notice the humiliation of your servant and keep her in mind instead of disregarding your servant, and give her a boy, I will give him to Yahweh for the whole of his life and no razor shall ever touch his head.' 12 While she went on praying to Yahweh, Eli was watching her mouth, 13 for Hannah was speaking under her breath; her lips were moving but her voice could not be heard, and Eli thought that she was drunk. 14 Eli said, 'How much longer are you going to stay drunk? Get rid of your wine.' 15 'No, my lord,' Hannah replied, 'I am a woman in great trouble; I have not been drinking wine or strong drink —I am pouring out my soul before Yahweh. 16 Do not take your servant for a worthless woman; all this time I have been speaking from the depth of my grief and my resentment.' 17 Eli then replied, 'Go in peace, and may the God of Israel grant what you have asked of him.' 18 To which she said, 'May your servant find favour in your sight.' With that, the woman went away; she began eating and was dejected no longer.

19 They got up early in the morning and, after worshipping Yahweh, set out and went home to Ramah. Elkanah lay with his wife Hannah, and Yahweh remembered her. 20 Hannah conceived and, in due course, gave birth to a son, whom she named Samuel,[b] 'since', she said, 'I asked Yahweh for him.' 21 Elkanah, the husband, went up with all his family to offer the annual sacrifice to Yahweh and to fulfil his vow. 22 However, Hannah did not go up, having said to

---

a 1 A mysterious title stemming from the shrine at Shiloh and interpreted as 'Lord of armies'.   *b* 1 Samuel is derived from *shem-'el* (=the Name of God), but is here related to *sha'al* (=ask).

NEW REVISED STANDARD VERSION

22 But Hannah did not go up, for she said to her husband, "As soon as the child is weaned, I will bring him, that he may appear in the presence of the LORD, and remain there forever; I will offer him as a nazirite[i] for all time."[j] 23 Her husband Elkanah said to her, "Do what seems best to you, wait until you have weaned him; only—may the LORD establish his word."[k] So the woman remained and nursed her son, until she weaned him. 24 When she had weaned him, she took him up with her, along with a three-year-old bull,[l] an ephah of flour, and a skin of wine. She brought him to the house of the LORD at Shiloh; and the child was young. 25 Then they slaughtered the bull, and they brought the child to Eli. 26 And she said, "Oh, my lord! As you live, my lord, I am the woman who was standing here in your presence, praying to the LORD. 27 For this child I prayed; and the LORD has granted me the petition that I made to him. 28 Therefore I have lent him to the LORD; as long as he lives, he is given to the LORD."

She left him there for[m] the LORD.

2 Hannah prayed and said,

"My heart exults in the LORD;
 my strength is exalted in my God.[n]
My mouth derides my enemies,
 because I rejoice in my[o] victory.

2 "There is no Holy One like the LORD,
 no one besides you;
 there is no Rock like our God.
3 Talk no more so very proudly,
 let not arrogance come from your mouth;
 for the LORD is a God of knowledge,
 and by him actions are weighed.
4 The bows of the mighty are broken,
 but the feeble gird on strength.
5 Those who were full have hired themselves out
  for bread,
 but those who were hungry are fat with spoil.
The barren has borne seven,
 but she who has many children is forlorn.
6 The LORD kills and brings to life;
 he brings down to Sheol and raises up.
7 The LORD makes poor and makes rich;
 he brings low, he also exalts.
8 He raises up the poor from the dust;
 he lifts the needy from the ash heap,
to make them sit with princes
 and inherit a seat of honor.[p]
For the pillars of the earth are the LORD's,
 and on them he has set the world.

9 "He will guard the feet of his faithful ones,
 but the wicked shall be cut off in darkness;
 for not by might does one prevail.
10 The LORD! His adversaries shall be shattered;
 the Most High[q] will thunder in heaven.
The LORD will judge the ends of the earth;
 he will give strength to his king,
 and exalt the power of his anointed."

11 Then Elkanah went home to Ramah, while the boy remained to minister to the LORD, in the presence of the priest Eli.

REVISED ENGLISH BIBLE

did not go; she said to her husband, 'After the child is weaned I shall come up with him to present him before the LORD; then he is to stay there always.' 23 Her husband Elkanah said to her, 'Do what you think best; stay at home until you have weaned him. Only, may the LORD indeed see your vow fulfilled.' So the woman stayed behind and nursed her son until she had weaned him.

24 When she had weaned him, she took him up with her. She took also a bull three years old, an ephah of flour, and a skin of wine, and she brought him, child as he was, into the house of the LORD at Shiloh. 25 When the bull had been slaughtered, Hannah brought the boy to Eli 26 and said, 'Sir, as sure as you live, I am the woman who stood here beside you praying to the LORD. 27 It was this boy that I prayed for and the LORD has granted what I asked. 28 Now I make him over to the LORD; for his whole life he is lent to the LORD.' And they prostrated themselves there before the LORD.

2 Then Hannah offered this prayer:

'My heart exults in the LORD,
 in the LORD I now hold my head high;
I gloat over my enemies,
 I rejoice because you have saved me.
2 There is none but you,
 none so holy as the LORD,
 none so righteous as our God.

3 'Cease your proud boasting,
 let no word of arrogance pass your lips,
 for the LORD is a God who knows;
 he governs what mortals do.
4 Strong men stand in mute dismay,
 but those who faltered put on new strength.
5 Those who had plenty sell themselves for a crust,
 and the hungry grow strong again.
The barren woman bears seven children,
 and the mother of many sons is left to languish.

6 'The LORD metes out both death and life:
 he sends down to Sheol, he can bring the dead up
  again.
7 Poverty and riches both come from the LORD;
 he brings low and he raises up.
8 He lifts the weak out of the dust
 and raises the poor from the refuse heap
to give them a place among the great,
 to assign them seats of honour.

'The foundations of the earth are the LORD's,
 and he has set the world upon them.
9 He will guard the footsteps of his loyal servants,
 while the wicked will be silenced in darkness;
 for it is not by strength that a mortal prevails.

10 'Those who oppose the LORD will be terrified
 when from the heavens he thunders against them.
The LORD is judge even to the ends of the earth;
 he will endow his king with strength
 and raise high the head of his anointed one.'

11 Then Elkanah went home to Ramah, but the boy remained behind in the service of the LORD under Eli the priest.

---

[i] That is *one separated* or *one consecrated*   [j] Cn Compare Q Ms:
MT lacks *I will offer him as a nazirite for all time*   [k] MT: Q Ms
Gk Compare Syr *that which goes out of your mouth*   [l] Q Ms Gk
Syr: MT *three bulls*   [m] Gk (Compare Q Ms) and Gk at 2.11: MT
And he (that is, Elkanah) *worshiped there before*   [n] Gk: Heb *the
LORD*   [o] Q Ms: MT *your*   [p] Gk (Compare Q Ms) adds *He grants
the vow of the one who vows, and blesses the years of the just*
[q] Cn Heb *against him he*

1:23 **your:** *so Gk; Heb.* his.   1:24 **a bull . . . old:** *so Gk; Heb.*
three bulls.   1:28 **they . . . themselves:** *so Syriac; Heb.* he . . .
himself.   2:2 **righteous:** *so Gk; Heb.* rock.   2:4 **in mute:**
prob. rdg; Heb. obscure.   2:6 **Sheol:** *or* the underworld.

22 Hannah did not go, explaining to her husband, "Once the child is weaned, I will take him to appear before the LORD and to remain there forever; I will offer him as a perpetual nazirite." 23 Her husband Elkanah answered her: "Do what you think best; wait until you have weaned him. Only, may the LORD bring your resolve to fulfillment!" And so she remained at home and nursed her son until she had weaned him.

24 Once he was weaned, she brought him up with her, along with a three-year-old bull, an ephah of flour, and a skin of wine, and presented him at the temple of the LORD in Shiloh. 25 After the boy's father had sacrificed the young bull, Hannah, his mother, approached Eli 26 and said: "Pardon, my lord! As you live, my lord, I am the woman who stood near you here, praying to the LORD. 27 I prayed for this child, and the LORD granted my request. 28 Now I, in turn, give him to the LORD; as long as he lives, he shall be dedicated to the LORD." She left him there;

2 1 and as she worshiped the LORD, she said:

"My heart exults in the LORD,
  my horn is exalted in my God.
I have swallowed up my enemies;
  I rejoice in my victory.
2 There is no Holy One like the LORD;
  there is no Rock like our God.

3 "Speak boastfully no longer,
  nor let arrogance issue from your mouths.
For an all-knowing God is the LORD,
  a God who judges deeds.
4 The bows of the mighty are broken,
  while the tottering gird on strength.
5 The well-fed hire themselves out for bread,
  while the hungry batten on spoil.
The barren wife bears seven sons,
  while the mother of many languishes.
6 "The LORD puts to death and gives life;
  he casts down to the nether world;
  he raises up again.
7 The LORD makes poor and makes rich,
  he humbles, he also exalts.
8 He raises the needy from the dust;
  from the ash heap he lifts up the poor,
To seat them with nobles
  and make a glorious throne their heritage.
He gives to the vower his vow,
  and blesses the sleep of the just.

"For the pillars of the earth are the LORD's,
  and he has set the world upon them.
9 He will guard the footsteps of his faithful ones,
  but the wicked shall perish in the darkness.
For not by strength does man prevail;
10   the LORD's foes shall be shattered.
The Most High in heaven thunders;
  The LORD judges the ends of the earth.
Now may he give strength to his king
  and exalt the horn of his anointed!"

11 When Elkanah returned home to Ramah, the child remained in the service of the LORD under the priest Eli.

her husband, 'Not before the child has been weaned. Then I shall bring him and present him before Yahweh and he will stay there for ever.' 23 Elkanah her husband then said to her, 'Do what you think fit; wait until you have weaned him. May Yahweh bring about what he has said.' So the woman stayed behind and nursed her child until she weaned him.

24 When she had weaned him, she took him up with her, as well as a three-year-old bull, an ephah of flour and a skin of wine, and took him into the temple of Yahweh at Shiloh; the child was very young. 25 They sacrificed the bull and led the child to Eli. 26 She said, 'If you please, my lord! As you live, my lord, I am the woman who stood beside you here, praying to Yahweh. 27 This is the child for which I was praying, and Yahweh has granted me what I asked of him. 28 Now I make him over to Yahweh for the whole of his life. He is made over to Yahweh.' They then worshipped Yahweh there.

2 Hannah then prayed as follows:

My heart exults in Yahweh,
  in my God is my strength lifted up,
my mouth derides my foes,
  for I rejoice in your deliverance.

2 There is no Holy One like Yahweh,
  (indeed, there is none but you)
  no Rock like our God.

3 Do not keep talking so proudly,
  let no arrogance come from your mouth,
for Yahweh is a wise God,
  his to weigh up deeds.
4 The bow of the mighty has been broken
  but those who were tottering are now braced with
    strength.
5 The full fed are hiring themselves out for bread
  but the hungry need labour no more;
the barren woman bears sevenfold
  but the mother of many is left desolate.

6 Yahweh gives death and life,
  brings down to Sheol and draws up;
7 Yahweh makes poor and rich,
  he humbles and also exalts.
8 He raises the poor from the dust,
  he lifts the needy from the dunghill
to give them a place with princes,
  to assign them a seat of honour;
for to Yahweh belong the pillars of the earth,
  on these he has poised the world.

9 He safeguards the steps of his faithful
  but the wicked vanish in darkness
  (for human strength can win no victories).
10 Yahweh, his enemies are shattered,
  the Most High thunders in the heavens.

Yahweh judges the ends of the earth,
  he endows his king with power,
  he raises up the strength of his Anointed.

11 Elkanah then went home to Ramah, but the child stayed in Yahweh's service, in the presence of Eli the priest.

12 Now the sons of Eli were scoundrels; they had no regard for the LORD 13 or for the duties of the priests to the people. When anyone offered sacrifice, the priest's servant would come, while the meat was boiling, with a three-pronged fork in his hand, 14 and he would thrust it into the pan, or kettle, or caldron, or pot; all that the fork brought up the priest would take for himself. *r* This is what they did at Shiloh to all the Israelites who came there. 15 Moreover, before the fat was burned, the priest's servant would come and say to the one who was sacrificing, "Give meat for the priest to roast; for he will not accept boiled meat from you, but only raw." 16 And if the man said to him, "Let them burn the fat first, and then take whatever you wish," he would say, "No, you must give it now; if not, I will take it by force." 17 Thus the sin of the young men was very great in the sight of the LORD; for they treated the offerings of the LORD with contempt.

18 Samuel was ministering before the LORD, a boy wearing a linen ephod. 19 His mother used to make for him a little robe and take it to him each year, when she went up with her husband to offer the yearly sacrifice. 20 Then Eli would bless Elkanah and his wife, and say, "May the LORD repay *s* you with children by this woman for the gift that she made to *t* the LORD"; and then they would return to their home.

21 And *u* the LORD took note of Hannah; she conceived and bore three sons and two daughters. And the boy Samuel grew up in the presence of the LORD.

22 Now Eli was very old. He heard all that his sons were doing to all Israel, and how they lay with the women who served at the entrance to the tent of meeting. 23 He said to them, "Why do you do such things? For I hear of your evil dealings from all these people. 24 No, my sons; it is not a good report that I hear the people of the LORD spreading abroad. 25 If one person sins against another, someone can intercede for the sinner with the LORD; *v* but if someone sins against the LORD, who can make intercession?" But they would not listen to the voice of their father; for it was the will of the LORD to kill them.

26 Now the boy Samuel continued to grow both in stature and in favor with the LORD and with the people.

27 A man of God came to Eli and said to him, "Thus the LORD has said, 'I revealed *w* myself to the family of your ancestor in Egypt when they were slaves *x* to the house of Pharaoh. 28 I chose him out of all the tribes of Israel to be my priest, to go up to my altar, to offer incense, to wear an ephod before me; and I gave to the family of your ancestor all my offerings by fire from the people of Israel. 29 Why then look with greedy eye *y* at my sacrifices and my offerings that I commanded, and honor your sons more than me by fattening yourselves on the choicest parts of every offering of my people Israel?' 30 Therefore the LORD the God of Israel declares: 'I promised that your family and the family of your ancestor should go in and out before me forever'; but now the LORD declares: 'Far be it from me; for those who honor me I will honor, and those who despise me shall be treated with contempt. 31 See, a time is coming when I will cut off your strength and the strength of your ancestor's family, so that no one in your family will live to old age. 32 Then in distress you will look with greedy eye *z* on all the prosperity that shall be bestowed upon Israel; and no one in your family shall ever live to old age. 33 The only one of you

12 Eli's sons were scoundrels with little regard for the LORD. 13 The custom of the priests in their dealings with the people was this: when anyone offered a sacrifice, the priest's servant would come while the flesh was stewing 14 and would thrust a three-pronged fork into the cauldron or pan or kettle or pot; and the priest would take whatever the fork brought out. This should have been their practice whenever Israelites came to sacrifice at Shiloh; but now, 15 even before the fat was burnt, the priest's servant would come and say to the person who was sacrificing, 'Give me meat to roast for the priest; he will not accept what has been already stewed, only raw meat.' 16 And if the man protested, 'Let them burn the fat first, and then take what you want,' the servant would say, 'No, hand it over now, or I shall take it by force.' 17 The young men's sin was very great in the LORD's sight, for they caused what was offered to him to be brought into general contempt.

18 Samuel continued in the service of the LORD, a mere boy with a linen ephod fastened round him. 19 Every year his mother made him a little cloak and took it to him when she went up with her husband to offer the annual sacrifice. 20 Eli would give his blessing to Elkanah and his wife and say, 'The LORD grant you children by this woman in place of the one whom you made over to the LORD.' Then they would return home.

21 The LORD showed his care for Hannah, and she conceived and gave birth to three sons and two daughters; meanwhile the boy Samuel grew up in the presence of the LORD.

22 When Eli, now a very old man, heard a detailed account of how his sons were treating all the Israelites, and how they lay with the women who were serving at the entrance to the Tent of Meeting, 23 he said to them, 'Why do you do such things? I hear from every quarter how wickedly you behave. 24 Do stop it, my sons; for this is not a good report that I hear spreading among the LORD's people. 25 If someone sins against another, God will intervene; but if someone sins against the LORD, who can intercede for him?' They would not listen, however, to their father's rebuke, for the LORD meant to bring about their death. 26 The young Samuel, as he grew up, increasingly commended himself to the LORD and to the people.

27 A man of God came to Eli and said, 'This is the word of the LORD: You know that I revealed myself to your forefather's house when he and his family were in Egypt in slavery to the house of Pharaoh. 28 You know that I chose your forefather out of all the tribes of Israel to be my priest, to go up to my altar, to burn incense, and to carry the ephod before me; and that I assigned all the food-offerings of the Israelites to your family. 29 Why then do you show disrespect for my sacrifices and the offerings which I have ordained? What makes you resent them? Why do you honour your sons more than me by letting them batten on the choicest offerings of my people Israel? 30 The LORD's word was: I promise that your house and your father's house will serve before me for all time. But now his word is: I shall have no such thing; I shall honour those who honour me, and those who despise me will meet with contempt. 31 The time is coming when I shall lop off every limb of your own and of your father's family, so that no one in your house will attain old age. 32 You will even resent the prosperity I give to Israel; never again will anyone in your house live to old age.

---

r Gk Syr Vg: Heb *with it*   *s* Q Ms Gk: MT *give*   *t* Q Ms Gk: MT *for the petition that she asked of*   *u* Q Ms Gk: MT *When*   *v* Gk Compare Q Ms: MT *another, God will mediate for him*   *w* Gk Tg Syr: Heb *Did I reveal*   *x* Q Ms Gk: MT lacks *slaves*   *y* Q Ms Gk: MT *then kick*   *z* Q Ms Gk: MT *will kick*

2:27 **in slavery:** *so Gk; Heb. omits.*   2:28 **carry:** *or wear.* 2:29 **What . . . them?:** *so Gk; Heb.* a dwelling-place.   2:32 **You . . . resent:** *prob. rdg; Heb. obscure.* **I give:** *so Aram. (Targ.); Heb.* he gives.

12 Now the sons of Eli were wicked; they had respect neither for the LORD 13 nor for the priests' duties toward the people. When someone offered a sacrifice, the priest's servant would come with a three-pronged fork, while the meat was still boiling, 14 and would thrust it into the basin, kettle, caldron, or pot. Whatever the fork brought up, the priest would keep. That is how all the Israelites were treated who came to the sanctuary at Shiloh. 15 In fact, even before the fat was burned, the priest's servant would come and say to the man offering the sacrifice, "Give me some meat to roast for the priest. He will not accept boiled meat from you, only raw meat." 16 And if the man protested to him, "Let the fat be burned first as is the custom, then take whatever you wish," he would reply, "No, give it to me now, or else I will take it by force." 17 Thus the young men sinned grievously in the presence of the LORD; they treated the offerings to the LORD with disdain.

18 Meanwhile the boy Samuel, girt with a linen apron, was serving in the presence of the LORD. 19 His mother used to make a little garment for him, which she would bring him each time she went up with her husband to offer the customary sacrifice. 20 And Eli would bless Elkanah and his wife, as they were leaving for home. He would say, "May the LORD repay you with children from this woman for the gift she has made to the LORD!" 21 The LORD favored Hannah so that she conceived and gave birth to three more sons and two daughters, while young Samuel grew up in the service of the LORD.

22 When Eli was very old, he heard repeatedly how his sons were treating all Israel [and that they were having relations with the women serving at the entry of the meeting tent.] 23 So he said to them: "Why are you doing such things? 24 No, my sons, you must not do these things! It is not a good report that I hear the people of the LORD spreading about you. 25 If a man sins against another man, one can intercede for him with the LORD; but if a man sins against the LORD, who can intercede for him?" But they disregarded their father's warning, since the LORD had decided on their death. 26 Meanwhile, young Samuel was growing in stature and in worth in the estimation of the LORD and of men.

27 A man of God came to Eli and said to him: "This is what the LORD says: 'I went so far as to reveal myself to your father's family when they were in Egypt as slaves to the house of Pharaoh. 28 I chose them out of all the tribes of Israel to be my priests, to go up to my altar, to burn incense, and to wear the ephod before me; and I assigned all the oblations of the Israelites to your father's family. 29 Why do you keep a greedy eye on my sacrifices and on the offerings which I have prescribed? And why do you honor your sons in preference to me, fattening yourselves with the choicest part of every offering of my people Israel?' 30 This, therefore, is the oracle of the LORD, the God of Israel: 'I said in the past that your family and your father's family should minister in my presence forever. But now,' the LORD declares, 'away with this! for I will honor those who honor me, but those who spurn me shall be accursed. 31 Yes, the time is coming when I will break your strength and the strength of your father's family, so that no man in your family shall reach old age. 32 You shall witness as a disappointed rival all the benefits enjoyed by Israel, but there shall never be an old man in your family. 33 I will permit

12 Now the sons of Eli were scoundrels; they cared nothing for Yahweh 13 nor for what was due to the priests from the people. Whenever anyone offered a sacrifice, the priest's servant would come with a three-pronged fork in his hand while the meat was being cooked; 14 he would thrust this into cauldron or pan, or dish or pot, and the priest claimed for his own whatever the fork brought up. That was how they behaved with all the Israelites who came there to Shiloh. 15 The priest's servant would even come up before the fat had been burnt and say to the person who was making the sacrifice, 'Give the priest some meat for him to roast. He will not accept boiled meat from you, only raw.' 16 Then, if the person replied, 'Let the fat be burnt first, and then take for yourself whatever you choose,' he would retort, 'No! You must give it to me now or I shall take it by force.' 17 The young men's sin was very great in Yahweh's eyes, because they treated with contempt the offering made to Yahweh.

18 Samuel was in Yahweh's service, a child wearing a linen loincloth. 19 His mother used to make him a little coat which she brought him each year when she came up with her husband to offer the yearly sacrifice. 20 Eli would bless Elkanah and his wife and say, 'May Yahweh grant you an heir by this woman in exchange for the one which she has made over to Yahweh,' and they would go home. 21 Yahweh visited Hannah; she conceived and gave birth to three sons and two daughters. Meanwhile, the child Samuel grew up in Yahweh's presence.

22 Although very old, Eli heard about everything that his sons were doing to all Israel, 23 and said, 'Why are you behaving as all the people say you are? 24 No, my sons, what I hear reported by the people of Yahweh is not good. 25 If one person sins against another, God will be the arbiter, but if he sins against Yahweh, who will intercede for him?' But they did not listen to their father's words, for Yahweh was bent on killing them.

26 Meanwhile, the child Samuel went on growing in stature and in favour both with Yahweh and with people.

27 A man of God came to Eli and said to him, 'This is what Yahweh says, "Did I not reveal myself to your father's family when they were in Egypt as slaves in Pharaoh's household? 28 Did I not single him out of all the tribes of Israel to be my priest, to go up to my altar, to burn the offering, to carry the *ephod*ᶜ in my presence; and did I not grant all the burnt offerings made by the Israelites to your father's family? 29 Why do you trample on the offering and on the sacrifice which I have ordered for my Dwelling, and honour your sons more than me, by growing fat on the best of the offerings of Israel, my people? 30 Whereas — this is what Yahweh, God of Israel, declares — I had promised that your family and your father's family would walk in my presence for ever, now, however — this is what Yahweh declares — nothing of the sort! Those who honour me I honour in my turn, and those who despise me will be an object of contempt. 31 Be sure, the days are coming when I shall cut off your strength and the strength of your father's family, so that no one in your family will live to old age. 32 Beside the Dwelling, you will see all the benefits that I shall confer on Israel, but no one in your family will ever live to old age. 33 I shall keep one of you at my altar for his

---

2, 22: The bracketed words, which recall Ex 38, 8, are a gloss in the received text; they are lacking in the oldest Greek translation, and in a Hebrew manuscript from Qumran.

ᶜ **2** Not a garment as elsewhere, but a holder for the sacred lots.

| NEW REVISED STANDARD VERSION | REVISED ENGLISH BIBLE |

whom I shall not cut off from my altar shall be spared to weep out his*a* eyes and grieve his*b* heart; all the members of your household shall die by the sword.*c* 34 The fate of your two sons, Hophni and Phinehas, shall be the sign to you — both of them shall die on the same day. 35 I will raise up for myself a faithful priest, who shall do according to what is in my heart and in my mind. I will build him a sure house, and he shall go in and out before my anointed one forever. 36 Everyone who is left in your family shall come to implore him for a piece of silver or a loaf of bread, and shall say, Please put me in one of the priest's places, that I may eat a morsel of bread.' "

3 Now the boy Samuel was ministering to the LORD under Eli. The word of the LORD was rare in those days; visions were not widespread.

2 At that time Eli, whose eyesight had begun to grow dim so that he could not see, was lying down in his room; 3 the lamp of God had not yet gone out, and Samuel was lying down in the temple of the LORD, where the ark of God was. 4 Then the LORD called, "Samuel! Samuel!"*d* and he said, "Here I am!" 5 and ran to Eli, and said, "Here I am, for you called me." But he said, "I did not call; lie down again." So he went and lay down. 6 The LORD called again, "Samuel!" Samuel got up and went to Eli, and said, "Here I am, for you called me." But he said, "I did not call, my son; lie down again." 7 Now Samuel did not yet know the LORD, and the word of the LORD had not yet been revealed to him. 8 The LORD called Samuel again, a third time. And he got up and went to Eli, and said, "Here I am, for you called me." Then Eli perceived that the LORD was calling the boy. 9 Therefore Eli said to Samuel, "Go, lie down; and if he calls you, you shall say, 'Speak, LORD, for your servant is listening.' " So Samuel went and lay down in his place.

10 Now the LORD came and stood there, calling as before, "Samuel! Samuel!" And Samuel said, "Speak, for your servant is listening." 11 Then the LORD said to Samuel, "See, I am about to do something in Israel that will make both ears of anyone who hears of it tingle. 12 On that day I will fulfill against Eli all that I have spoken concerning his house, from beginning to end. 13 For I have told him that I am about to punish his house forever, for the iniquity that he knew, because his sons were blaspheming God,*e* and he did not restrain them. 14 Therefore I swear to the house of Eli that the iniquity of Eli's house shall not be expiated by sacrifice or offering forever."

15 Samuel lay there until morning; then he opened the doors of the house of the LORD. Samuel was afraid to tell the vision to Eli. 16 But Eli called Samuel and said, "Samuel, my son." He said, "Here I am." 17 Eli said, "What was it that he told you? Do not hide it from me. May God do so to you and more also, if you hide anything from me of all that he told you." 18 So Samuel told him everything and hid nothing from him. Then he said, "It is the LORD; let him do what seems good to him."

19 As Samuel grew up, the LORD was with him and let none of his words fall to the ground. 20 And all Israel from Dan to Beer-sheba knew that Samuel was a trustworthy prophet of the LORD. 21 The LORD continued to appear at Shiloh, for the LORD revealed himself to Samuel at Shiloh

4 by the word of the LORD. 1 And the word of Samuel came to all Israel.

33 If I allow any to survive to serve my altar, his eyes will grow dim, his appetite fail, and his issue will be weaklings and die off. 34 The fate of your two sons will be a proof to you; Hophni and Phinehas will both die on the same day. 35 I shall appoint for myself a priest who will be faithful, who will do what I have in my mind and in my heart. I shall establish his family to serve in perpetual succession before my anointed king. 36 Any of your family still left will come and bow humbly before him to beg for a piece of silver and a loaf of bread, and ask for a turn of priestly duty to earn a crust.'

3 The boy Samuel was in the LORD's service under Eli. In those days the word of the LORD was rarely heard, and there was no outpouring of vision. 2 One night Eli, whose eyes were dim and his sight failing, was lying down in his usual place, 3 while Samuel slept in the temple of the LORD where the Ark of God was. Before the lamp of God had gone out, 4 the LORD called him, and Samuel answered, 'Here I am!' 5 and ran to Eli saying, 'You called me: here I am.' 'No, I did not call you,' said Eli; 'lie down again.' So he went and lay down. 6 The LORD called Samuel again, and he got up and went to Eli. 'Here I am!' he said. 'Surely you called me.' 'I did not call, my son,' he answered; 'lie down again.' 7 Samuel had not yet come to know the LORD, and the word of the LORD had not been disclosed to him. 8 When the LORD called him for the third time, he again went to Eli and said, 'Here I am! You did call me.' Then Eli understood that it was the LORD calling the boy; 9 he told Samuel to go and lie down and said, 'If someone calls once more, say, "Speak, LORD; your servant is listening." ' So Samuel went and lay down in his place.

10 Then the LORD came, and standing there called, 'Samuel, Samuel!' as before. Samuel answered, 'Speak, your servant is listening.' 11 The LORD said, 'Soon I shall do something in Israel which will ring in the ears of all who hear it. 12 When that day comes I shall make good every word from beginning to end that I have spoken against Eli and his family. 13 You are to tell him that my judgement on his house will stand for ever because he knew of his sons' blasphemies against God and did not restrain them. 14 Therefore I have sworn to the family of Eli that their abuse of sacrifices and offerings will never be expiated.'

15 Samuel lay down till morning, when he opened the doors of the house of the LORD; but he was afraid to tell Eli about the vision. 16 Eli called Samuel: 'Samuel, my son!' he said; and Samuel answered, 'Here I am!' 17 Eli asked, 'What did the LORD say to you? Do not hide it from me. God's curse upon you if you conceal from me one word of all that he said to you.' 18 Then Samuel told him everything, concealing nothing. Eli said, 'The LORD must do what is good in his eyes.'

19 As Samuel grew up, the LORD was with him, and none of his words went unfulfilled. 20 From Dan to Beersheba, all Israel recognized that Samuel was attested as a prophet of the LORD. 21 So the LORD continued to appear in Shiloh, because he had revealed himself there to Samuel.

4 1 Samuel's word had authority throughout Israel.

---

a Q Ms Gk: MT *your* *b* Q Ms Gk: Heb *your* *c* Q Ms See Gk: MT *die like mortals* *d* Q Ms See 3.10: MT *the LORD called Samuel* *e* Another reading is *for themselves*

2:33 **his:** *so Gk; Heb.* your. 3:13 **You are to:** *prob. rdg; Heb.* I shall. **because:** *prob. rdg; Heb.* in guilt. **against God:** *prob. original reading, altered in Heb. to* them. 3:21 **because . . . Samuel:** *prob. rdg; Heb.* adds according to the word of the LORD.

some of your family to remain at my altar, to wear out their eyes in consuming greed; but the rest of the men of your family shall die by the sword. 34 You shall have a sign in what will happen to your two sons, Hophni and Phinehas: both shall die on the same day. 35 I will choose a faithful priest who shall do what I have in heart and mind. I will establish a lasting house for him which shall function in the presence of my anointed forever. 36 Then whoever is left of your family will come to grovel before him for a piece of silver or a loaf of bread, and will say: Appoint me, I beg you, to a priestly function, that I may have a morsel of bread to eat.' "

3 During the time young Samuel was minister to the LORD under Eli, a revelation of the LORD was uncommon and vision infrequent. 2 One day Eli was asleep in his usual place. His eyes had lately grown so weak that he could not see. 3 The lamp of God was not yet extinguished, and Samuel was sleeping in the temple of the LORD where the ark of God was. 4 The LORD called to Samuel, who answered, "Here I am." 5 He ran to Eli and said, "Here I am. You called me." "I did not call you," Eli said. "Go back to sleep." So he went back to sleep. 6 Again the LORD called Samuel, who rose and went to Eli. "Here I am," he said. "You called me." But he answered, "I did not call you, my son. Go back to sleep."

7 At that time Samuel was not familiar with the LORD, because the LORD had not revealed anything to him as yet. 8 The LORD called Samuel again, for the third time. Getting up and going to Eli, he said, "Here I am. You called me." Then Eli understood that the LORD was calling the youth. 9 So he said to Samuel, "Go to sleep, and if you are called, reply, 'Speak, LORD, for your servant is listening.' " When Samuel went to sleep in his place, 10 the LORD came and revealed his presence, calling out as before, "Samuel, Samuel!" Samuel answered, "Speak, for your servant is listening." 11 The LORD said to Samuel: "I am about to do something in Israel that will cause the ears of everyone who hears it to ring. 12 On that day I will carry out in full against Eli everything I threatened against his family. 13 I announce to him that I am condemning his family once and for all, because of this crime: though he knew his sons were blaspheming God, he did not reprove them. 14 Therefore, I swear to the family of Eli that no sacrifice or offering will ever expiate its crime." 15 Samuel then slept until morning, when he got up early and opened the doors of the temple of the LORD. He feared to tell Eli the vision, 16 but Eli called to him, "Samuel, my son!" He replied, "Here I am." 17 Then Eli asked, "What did he say to you? Hide nothing from me! May God do thus and so to you if you hide a single thing he told you." 18 So Samuel told him everything, and held nothing back. Eli answered, "He is the LORD. He will do what he judges best."

19 Samuel grew up, and the LORD was with him, not permitting any word of his to be without effect. 20 Thus all Israel from Dan to Beer-sheba came to know that Samuel was an accredited prophet of the LORD. 21 The LORD continued to appear at Shiloh; he manifested himself to Samuel

4 Shiloh through his word, 1 and Samuel spoke to all Israel. At that time, the Philistines gathered for an at-

eyes to go blind and his soul to wither, but the bulk of your family will die by the sword.

34 ' "What happens to your two sons Hophni and Phinehas will be a sign for you: on the same day both will die. 35 I shall raise myself a faithful priest, who will do as I intend and as I desire. I shall build him an enduring House and he will walk in the presence of my Anointed for ever. 36 The members of your House who survive will come and beg him on their knees for a silver coin and a loaf of bread and say: Please give me some priestly work, so that I can have a scrap of bread to eat." '

3 Now, the boy Samuel was serving Yahweh in the presence of Eli; in those days it was rare for Yahweh to speak; visions were uncommon. 2 One day, it happened that Eli was lying down in his room. His eyes were beginning to grow dim; he could no longer see. 3 The lamp of God had not yet gone out, and Samuel was lying in Yahweh's sanctuary, where the ark of God was, 4 when Yahweh called, 'Samuel! Samuel!' He answered, 'Here I am,' 5 and, running to Eli, he said, 'Here I am, as you called me.' Eli said, 'I did not call. Go back and lie down.' So he went and lay down. 6 And again Yahweh called, 'Samuel! Samuel!' He got up and went to Eli and said, 'Here I am, as you called me.' He replied, 'I did not call, my son; go back and lie down.' 7 As yet, Samuel had no knowledge of Yahweh and the word of Yahweh had not yet been revealed to him. 8 Again Yahweh called, the third time. He got up and went to Eli and said, 'Here I am, as you called me.' Eli then understood that Yahweh was calling the child, 9 and he said to Samuel, 'Go and lie down, and if someone calls say, "Speak, Yahweh; for your servant is listening." ' So Samuel went and lay down in his place.

10 Yahweh then came and stood by, calling as he had done before, 'Samuel! Samuel!' Samuel answered, 'Speak, Yahweh; for your servant is listening.' 11 Yahweh then said to Samuel, 'I am going to do something in Israel which will make the ears of all who hear of it ring. 12 I shall carry out that day against Eli everything that I have said about his family, from beginning to end. 13 You are to tell him that I condemn his family for ever, since he is aware that his sons have been cursing God and yet has not corrected them. 14 Therefore — I swear it to the family of Eli — no sacrifice or offering shall ever expiate the guilt of Eli's family.'

15 Samuel lay where he was until morning and then opened the doors of Yahweh's temple. Samuel was afraid to tell Eli about the vision, 16 but Eli called Samuel and said, 'Samuel, my son.' 'Here I am,' he replied. 17 Eli asked, 'What message did he give you? Please do not hide it from me. May God bring unnameable ills on you and worse ones, too, if you hide from me anything of what he said to you.' 18 Samuel then told him everything, hiding nothing from him. Eli said, 'He is Yahweh; let him do what he thinks good.'

19 Samuel grew up. Yahweh was with him and did not let a single word fall to the ground of all that he had told him. 20 All Israel knew, from Dan to Beersheba, that Samuel was attested as a prophet of Yahweh. 21 Yahweh continued to manifest himself at Shiloh, revealing himself to Samuel

4 there, 1 and, for all Israel, the word of Samuel was as the word of Yahweh; since Eli was very old and his sons persisted in their wicked behaviour towards Yahweh.

NEW REVISED STANDARD VERSION	REVISED ENGLISH BIBLE

NEW REVISED STANDARD VERSION

In those days the Philistines mustered for war against Israel,*f* and Israel went out to battle against them;*g* they encamped at Ebenezer, and the Philistines encamped at Aphek. 2 The Philistines drew up in line against Israel, and when the battle was joined,*h* Israel was defeated by the Philistines, who killed about four thousand men on the field of battle. 3 When the troops came to the camp, the elders of Israel said, "Why has the LORD put us to rout today before the Philistines? Let us bring the ark of the covenant of the LORD here from Shiloh, so that he may come among us and save us from the power of our enemies." 4 So the people sent to Shiloh, and brought from there the ark of the covenant of the LORD of hosts, who is enthroned on the cherubim. The two sons of Eli, Hophni and Phinehas, were there with the ark of the covenant of God.

5 When the ark of the covenant of the LORD came into the camp, all Israel gave a mighty shout, so that the earth resounded. 6 When the Philistines heard the noise of the shouting, they said, "What does this great shouting in the camp of the Hebrews mean?" When they learned that the ark of the LORD had come to the camp, 7 the Philistines were afraid; for they said, "Gods have*i* come into the camp." They also said, "Woe to us! For nothing like this has happened before. 8 Woe to us! Who can deliver us from the power of these mighty gods? These are the gods who struck the Egyptians with every sort of plague in the wilderness. 9 Take courage, and be men, O Philistines, in order not to become slaves to the Hebrews as they have been to you; be men and fight."

10 So the Philistines fought; Israel was defeated, and they fled, everyone to his home. There was a very great slaughter, for there fell of Israel thirty thousand foot soldiers. 11 The ark of God was captured; and the two sons of Eli, Hophni and Phinehas, died.

12 A man of Benjamin ran from the battle line, and came to Shiloh the same day, with his clothes torn and with earth upon his head. 13 When he arrived, Eli was sitting upon his seat by the road watching, for his heart trembled for the ark of God. When the man came into the city and told the news, all the city cried out. 14 When Eli heard the sound of the outcry, he said, "What is this uproar?" Then the man came quickly and told Eli. 15 Now Eli was ninety-eight years old and his eyes were set, so that he could not see. 16 The man said to Eli, "I have just come from the battle; I fled from the battle today." He said, "How did it go, my son?" 17 The messenger replied, "Israel has fled before the Philistines, and there has also been a great slaughter among the troops; your two sons also, Hophni and Phinehas, are dead, and the ark of God has been captured." 18 When he mentioned the ark of God, Eli*j* fell over backward from his seat by the side of the gate; and his neck was broken and he died, for he was an old man, and heavy. He had judged Israel forty years.

19 Now his daughter-in-law, the wife of Phinehas, was pregnant, about to give birth. When she heard the news that the ark of God was captured, and that her father-in-law and her husband were dead, she bowed and gave birth; for her labor pains overwhelmed her. 20 As she was about to die, the women attending her said to her, "Do not be afraid, for you have borne a son." But she did not answer or give heed. 21 She named the child Ichabod, meaning, "The glory has departed from Israel," because the ark of God had been captured and because of her father-in-law and her husband. 22 She said, "The glory has departed from Israel, for the ark of God has been captured."

REVISED ENGLISH BIBLE

THE time came when the Philistines mustered for battle against Israel, and the Israelites, marching out to meet them, encamped near Eben-ezer, while the Philistines' camp was at Aphek. 2 The Philistines drew up their lines facing the Israelites, and when battle was joined the Israelites were defeated by the Philistines, who killed about four thousand men on the field. 3 When their army got back to camp, the Israelite elders asked, 'Why did the LORD let us be defeated today by the Philistines? Let us fetch the Ark of the Covenant of the LORD from Shiloh to go with us and deliver us from the power of our enemies.' 4 The army sent to Shiloh and fetched the Ark of the Covenant of the LORD of Hosts, who is enthroned upon the cherubim; Eli's two sons, Hophni and Phinehas, were there with the Ark.

5 When the Ark came into the camp it was greeted with such a great shout by all the Israelites that the earth rang. 6 The Philistines, hearing the noise, asked, 'What is this great shouting in the camp of the Hebrews?' When they learned that the Ark of the LORD had come into the camp, 7 they were alarmed. 'A god has come into the camp,' they cried. 'We are lost! No such thing has ever happened before. 8 We are utterly lost! Who can deliver us from the power of this mighty god? This is the god who broke the Egyptians and crushed them in the wilderness. 9 Courage, act like men, you Philistines, or you will become slaves to the Hebrews as they were to you. Be men, and fight!' 10 The Philistines then gave battle, and the Israelites were defeated and fled to their homes. It was a great defeat, and thirty thousand Israelite foot-soldiers fell. 11 The Ark of God was captured, and Eli's two sons, Hophni and Phinehas, perished.

12 A Benjamite ran from the battlefield and reached Shiloh on the same day, his clothes torn and dust on his head. 13 When he arrived Eli was sitting on a seat by the road to Mizpah, for he was deeply troubled about the Ark of God. The man entered the town with his news, and all the people cried out in horror. 14 When Eli heard the uproar, he asked, 'What does it mean?' The man hurried to Eli and told him. 15 Eli was ninety-eight years old and sat staring with sightless eyes. 16 The man said to him, 'I am the one who has just come from the battle. I fled from the field this very day.' Eli asked, 'What is the news, my son?' 17 The runner answered, 'The Israelites have fled before the Philistines; the army has suffered severe losses; your two sons, Hophni and Phinehas, are dead; and the Ark of God is taken.' 18 At the mention of the Ark of God, Eli fell backwards from his seat by the gate and broke his neck, for he was an old man and heavy. So he died; he had been judge over Israel for forty years.

19 His daughter-in-law, the wife of Phinehas, was pregnant and near her time, and when she heard of the capture of the Ark and the deaths of her father-in-law and her husband, she went into labour and she crouched down and was delivered. 20 As she lay dying, the women who attended her said, 'Do not be afraid; you have a son.' But she did not answer or heed what they said. 21 She named the boy Ichabod, saying, 'Glory has departed from Israel,' referring to the capture of the Ark of God and the deaths of her father-in-law and her husband; 22 'Glory has departed from Israel,' she said, 'because the Ark of God is taken.'

---

f Gk: Heb lacks *In those days the Philistines mustered for war against Israel*   *g* Gk: Heb *against the Philistines*   *h* Meaning of Heb uncertain   *i* Or *A god has*   *j* Heb *he*

4:1 **The time . . . Israel:** *so* Gk; Heb. omits.   4:21 **Ichabod:** *that is* No-glory.

NEW AMERICAN BIBLE

NEW JERUSALEM BIBLE

tack on Israel. Israel went out to engage them in battle and camped at Ebenezer, while the Philistines camped at Aphek. 2 The Philistines then drew up in battle formation against Israel. After a fierce struggle Israel was defeated by the Philistines, who slew about four thousand men on the battlefield. 3 When the troops retired to the camp, the elders of Israel said, "Why has the LORD permitted us to be defeated today by the Philistines? Let us fetch the ark of the LORD from Shiloh that it may go into battle among us and save us from the grasp of our enemies."

4 So the people sent to Shiloh and brought from there the ark of the LORD of hosts, who is enthroned upon the cherubim. The two sons of Eli, Hophni and Phinehas, were with the ark of God. 5 When the ark of the LORD arrived in the camp, all Israel shouted so loudly that the earth resounded. 6 The Philistines, hearing the noise of shouting, asked, "What can this loud shouting in the camp of the Hebrews mean?" On learning that the ark of the LORD had come into the camp, 7 the Philistines were frightened. They said, "Gods have come to their camp." They said also, "Woe to us! This has never happened before. 8 Woe to us! Who can deliver us from the power of these mighty gods? These are the gods that struck the Egyptians with various plagues and with pestilence. 9 Take courage and be manly, Philistines; otherwise you will become slaves to the Hebrews, as they were your slaves. So fight manfully!" 10 The Philistines fought and Israel was defeated; every man fled to his own tent. It was a disastrous defeat, in which Israel lost thirty thousand foot soldiers. 11 The ark of God was captured, and Eli's two sons, Hophni and Phinehas, were among the dead.

12 A Benjaminite fled from the battlefield and reached Shiloh that same day, with his clothes torn and his head covered with dirt. 13 When he arrived, Eli was sitting in his chair beside the gate, watching the road, for he was troubled at heart about the ark of God. The man, however, went into the city to divulge his news, which put the whole city in an uproar. 14 Hearing the outcry of the men standing near him, Eli inquired, "What does this commotion mean?" 15 (Eli was ninety-eight years old, and his eyes would not focus, so that he could not see.) 16 The man quickly came up to Eli and said, "It is I who have come from the battlefield; I fled from there today." He asked, "What happened, my son?" 17 And the messenger answered: "Israel fled from the Philistines; in fact, the troops suffered heavy losses. Your two sons, Hophni and Phinehas, are among the dead, and the ark of God has been captured." 18 At this mention of the ark of God, Eli fell backward from his chair into the gateway; since he was an old man and heavy, he died of a broken neck. He had judged Israel for forty years.

19 His daughter-in-law, the wife of Phinehas, was with child and at the point of giving birth. When she heard the news concerning the capture of the ark and the deaths of her father-in-law and her husband, she was seized with the pangs of labor, and gave birth. 20 She was about to die when the women standing around her said to her, "Never fear! You have given birth to a son." Yet she neither answered nor paid any attention. 21 [She named the child Ichabod, saying, "Gone is the glory from Israel," with reference to the capture of the ark of God and to her father-in-law and her husband.] 22 She said, "Gone is the glory from Israel," because the ark of God had been captured.

It happened at that time that the Philistines mustered to make war on Israel and Israel went out to meet them in war, pitching camp near Ebenezer while the Philistines pitched camp at Aphek. 2 The Philistines drew up their battle-line against Israel, the fighting was fierce, and Israel was beaten by the Philistines: about four thousand men in their ranks were killed on the field of battle. 3 When the troops returned to camp, the elders of Israel said, 'Why has Yahweh caused us to be beaten by the Philistines today? Let us fetch the ark of our God from Shiloh so that, when it goes with us, it may save us from the clutches of our enemies.' 4 So the troops sent to Shiloh and brought away the ark of Yahweh Sabaoth enthroned on the winged creatures; the two sons of Eli, Hophni and Phinehas, came with the ark. 5 When the ark of Yahweh arrived in the camp, all Israel raised a great war cry so that the earth resounded. 6 When the Philistines heard the noise of the war cry, they said, 'What can this great war cry in the Hebrew camp mean?' And they realised that the ark of Yahweh had come into the camp. 7 At this, the Philistines were afraid; for they said, 'God has come into the camp. Disaster!' they said. 'For nothing like this has ever happened before. 8 Disaster! Who will rescue us from the clutches of this mighty God? This was the God who struck down Egypt with every kind of misfortune in the desert. 9 But take courage and be men, Philistines, or you will become slaves to the Hebrews as they have been slaves to you. Be men and fight.' 10 So the Philistines gave battle and Israel was defeated, each man fleeing to his tent. The slaughter was very great: on the Israelite side, thirty thousand foot soldiers fell. 11 The ark of God was captured too, and Hophni and Phinehas the two sons of Eli died.

12 A Benjaminite ran from the battle-line and reached Shiloh the same day, his clothes torn and dust on his head. 13 When he arrived, Eli was sitting on his seat beside the gate watching the road, for his heart was trembling for the ark of God. The man came into the town and told the news, whereupon cries of anguish filled the town. 14 Eli heard the sound and asked, 'What does this uproar mean?' The man hurried on and told Eli. 15 Eli was ninety-eight years old; his gaze was fixed; he was blind. 16 The man said to Eli, 'I have come from the camp. I escaped from the battle-line today.' 'My son,' said Eli, 'what happened?' 17 The messenger replied, 'Israel has fled before the Philistines; the army has been utterly routed. What is worse, your two sons are dead and the ark of God has been captured.' 18 When he mentioned the ark of God, Eli fell backwards off his seat by the gate and broke his neck and died, for he was old and heavy. He had been judge of Israel for forty years.

19 Now his daughter-in-law, the wife of Phinehas, was with child and near her time. When she heard the news that the ark of God had been captured and that her father-in-law and husband were dead she crouched down and gave birth, for her labour pains had come on. 20 When she was at the point of death, the women at her side said, 'Do not be afraid; you have given birth to a son.' But she did not answer and took no notice. 21 She named the child Ichabod,[d] saying, 'The glory has gone from Israel,' alluding to the capture of the ark of God and to her father-in-law and husband. 22 She said, 'The glory has gone from Israel, because the ark of God has been captured.'

---

d 4 *Ei-kabod* = Where is the glory?

5 When the Philistines captured the ark of God, they brought it from Ebenezer to Ashdod; 2 then the Philistines took the ark of God and brought it into the house of Dagon and placed it beside Dagon. 3 When the people of Ashdod rose early the next day, there was Dagon, fallen on his face to the ground before the ark of the LORD. So they took Dagon and put him back in his place. 4 But when they rose early on the next morning, Dagon had fallen on his face to the ground before the ark of the LORD, and the head of Dagon and both his hands were lying cut off upon the threshold; only the trunk of k Dagon was left to him. 5 This is why the priests of Dagon and all who enter the house of Dagon do not step on the threshold of Dagon in Ashdod to this day.

6 The hand of the LORD was heavy upon the people of Ashdod, and he terrified and struck them with tumors, both in Ashdod and in its territory. 7 And when the inhabitants of Ashdod saw how things were, they said, "The ark of the God of Israel must not remain with us; for his hand is heavy on us and on our god Dagon." 8 So they sent and gathered together all the lords of the Philistines, and said, "What shall we do with the ark of the God of Israel?" The inhabitants of Gath replied, "Let the ark of God be moved on to us." l So they moved the ark of the God of Israel to Gath. m 9 But after they had brought it to Gath, n the hand of the LORD was against the city, causing a very great panic; he struck the inhabitants of the city, both young and old, so that tumors broke out on them. 10 So they sent the ark of the God of Israel o to Ekron. But when the ark of God came to Ekron, the people of Ekron cried out, "Why p have they brought around to us q the ark of the God of Israel to kill us q and our r people?" 11 They sent therefore and gathered together all the lords of the Philistines, and said, "Send away the ark of the God of Israel, and let it return to its own place, that it may not kill us and our people." For there was a deathly panic s throughout the whole city. The hand of God was very heavy there; 12 those who did not die were stricken with tumors, and the cry of the city went up to heaven.

6 The ark of the LORD was in the country of the Philistines seven months. 2 Then the Philistines called for the priests and the diviners and said, "What shall we do with the ark of the LORD? Tell us what we should send with it to its place." 3 They said, "If you send away the ark of the God of Israel, do not send it empty, but by all means return him a guilt offering. Then you will be healed and will be ransomed; t will not his hand then turn from you?" 4 And they said, "What is the guilt offering that we shall return to him?" They answered, "Five gold tumors and five gold mice, according to the number of the lords of the Philistines; for the same plague was upon all of you and upon your lords. 5 So you must make images of your tumors and images of your mice that ravage the land, and give glory to the God of Israel; perhaps he will lighten his hand on you and your gods and your land. 6 Why should you harden your hearts as the Egyptians and Pharaoh hardened their hearts? After he had made fools of them, did they not let the people go, and they departed? 7 Now then, get ready a new cart and two milch cows that have never borne a yoke, and yoke the cows to the cart, but take their calves home, away from them. 8 Take the ark of the LORD and place it on the cart,

5 After the Philistines had captured the Ark of God, they brought it from Eben-ezer to Ashdod, 2 where they carried it into the temple of Dagon and set it beside the god. 3 When the people of Ashdod rose next morning, there was Dagon fallen face downwards on the ground before the Ark of the LORD. They lifted him up and put him back in his place. 4 But next morning when they rose, Dagon had again fallen face downwards on the ground before the Ark of the LORD, with his head and his two hands lying broken off beside his platform; only Dagon's body remained on it. 5 That is why to this day the priests of Dagon and all who enter the temple of Dagon at Ashdod do not set foot on Dagon's platform.

6 The LORD's hand oppressed the people of Ashdod. He threw them into despair; he plagued them with tumours, and their territory swarmed with rats. There was death and destruction all through the city. 7 Seeing this, the men of Ashdod decided, 'The Ark of the God of Israel must not stay here, for his hand is pressing on us and on Dagon our god.' 8 When they called together all the Philistine lords to ask what should be done with the Ark, they were told, 'Let the Ark of the God of Israel be taken across to Gath.' They moved it there, 9 and after its removal there the LORD caused great havoc in that city; he plagued everybody, high and low alike, with the tumours which broke out. 10 So the Ark of God was sent on to Ekron, and when it arrived there, the people cried, 'They have moved the Ark of the God of Israel over to us, to kill us and our families.' 11 Summoning all the Philistine lords they said, 'Send the Ark of the God of Israel away; let it go back to its own place, or it will be the death of us all.' There was death and destruction all through the city; for the hand of God lay heavy upon it. 12 Those who did not die were plagued with tumours, and the cry of the city ascended to heaven.

6 When the Ark of the LORD had been in their territory for seven months, 2 the Philistines summoned the priests and soothsayers and asked, 'What shall we do with the Ark of the LORD? Tell us how we ought to send it back to its own place.' 3 Their answer was, 'If you send the Ark of the God of Israel back, do not let it go empty, but send it back with an offering by way of compensation; if you are then healed you will know why his hand had not been lifted from you.' 4 When they were asked, 'What should we send to him?' they answered, 'Send five tumours modelled in gold and five gold rats, one for each of the Philistine lords, for the same plague afflicted all of you and your lords. 5 Make models of your tumours and of the rats which are ravaging the land, and give honour to the God of Israel; perhaps he will relax the pressure of his hand on you, your god, and your land. 6 Why be stubborn like Pharaoh and the Egyptians? Remember how this God made sport of them until they let Israel go.

7 'Now make ready a new wagon with two milch cows which have never been yoked; harness the cows to the wagon, but take their calves away and keep them in their stall. 8 Fetch the Ark of the LORD and put it on the wagon, place

---

k Heb lacks the trunk of   l Gk Compare Q Ms: MT They answered, "Let the ark of the God of Israel be brought around to Gath."
m Gk: Heb lacks to Gath   n Q Ms: MT lacks to Gath   o Q Ms Gk: MT lacks of Israel   p Q Ms Gk: MT lacks Why   q Heb me
r Heb my   s Q Ms reads a panic from the LORD   t Q Ms Gk: MT and it will be known to you

5:4 beside his platform: or upon the threshold. Dagon's body: prob. rdg, cp. Gk; Heb. Dagon.   5:6 tumours: or, as otherwise read, haemorrhoids. and their . . . city: so Gk; Heb. Ashdod and its territory. rats: or mice.   6:4 you: so some MSS; others them.

5 The Philistines, having captured the ark of God, transferred it from Ebenezer to Ashdod. 2 They then took the ark of God and brought it into the temple of Dagon, placing it beside Dagon. 3 When the people of Ashdod rose early the next morning, Dagon was lying prone on the ground before the ark of the LORD. So they picked Dagon up and replaced him. 4 But the next morning early, when they arose, Dagon lay prone on the ground before the ark of the LORD, his head and hands broken off and lying on the threshold, his trunk alone intact. 5 For this reason, neither the priests of Dagon nor any others who enter the temple of Dagon tread on the threshold of Dagon in Ashdod to this very day; they always step over it.

6 Now the LORD dealt severely with the people of Ashdod. He ravaged and afflicted the city and its vicinity with hemorrhoids; he brought upon the city a great and deadly plague of mice that swarmed in their ships and overran their fields. 7 On seeing how matters stood, the men of Ashdod decided, "The ark of the God of Israel must not remain with us, for he is handling us and our god Dagon severely." 8 So they summoned all the Philistine lords and inquired of them, "What shall we do with the ark of the God of Israel?" The men of Gath replied, "Let them move the ark of the God of Israel on to us." 9 So they moved the ark of the God of Israel to Gath! But after it had been brought there, the LORD threw the city into utter turmoil: he afflicted its inhabitants, young and old, and hemorrhoids broke out on them. 10 The ark of God was next sent to Ekron; but as it entered that city, the people there cried out, "Why have they brought the ark of the God of Israel here to kill us and our kindred?" 11 Then they, too, sent a summons to all the Philistine lords and pleaded: "Send away the ark of the God of Israel. Let it return to its own place, that it may not kill us and our kindred." A deadly panic had seized the whole city, since the hand of God had been very heavy upon it. 12 Those who escaped death were afflicted with hemorrhoids, and the outcry from the city went up to the heavens.

6 The ark of the LORD had been in the land of the Philistines seven months 2 when they summoned priests and fortune-tellers to ask, "What shall we do with the ark of the LORD? Tell us what we should send back with it." 3 They replied: "If you intend to send away the ark of the God of Israel, you must not send it alone, but must, by all means, make amends to him through a guilt offering. Then you will be healed, and will learn why he continues to afflict you." 4 When asked further, "What guilt offering should be our amends to him?", they replied:

"Five golden hemorrhoids and five golden mice to correspond to the number of Philistine lords, since the same plague has struck all of you and your lords. 5 Therefore, make images of the hemorrhoids and of the mice that are infesting your land and give them as a tribute to the God of Israel. Perhaps then he will cease to afflict you, your gods, and your land. 6 Why should you become stubborn, as the Egyptians and Pharaoh were stubborn? Was it not after he had dealt ruthlessly with them that the Israelites were released and departed? 7 So now set to work and make a new cart. Then take two milch cows that have not borne the yoke; hitch them to the cart, but drive their calves indoors away from them. 8 You shall next take the ark of the LORD and place it on the cart, putting in a box beside it the golden

5 When the Philistines had captured the ark of God, they took it from Ebenezer to Ashdod. 2 Taking the ark of God, the Philistines put it in the temple of Dagon, setting it down beside Dagon. 3 When the people of Ashdod got up the following morning and went to the temple of Dagon, there lay Dagon face down on the ground before the ark of Yahweh. They picked Dagon up and put him back in his place. 4 But when they got up on the following morning, there lay Dagon face down on the ground before the ark of Yahweh, and Dagon's head and two hands lay severed on the threshold; only the trunk of Dagon was left in its place. 5 This is why the priests of Dagon and the people frequenting Dagon's temple never step on Dagon's threshold in Ashdod, even today.

6 Yahweh oppressed the people of Ashdod; he ravaged them and afflicted them with tumours — Ashdod and its territory. When the people of Ashdod saw what was happening they said, 7 'The ark of the God of Israel must not stay here with us, for he is oppressing us and our god Dagon.' 8 So they summoned all the Philistine chiefs to them, and said, 'What shall we do with the ark of the God of Israel?' They decided, 'The ark of the God of Israel shall be taken away to Gath.' So they took the ark of the God of Israel to Gath. 9 But after they had taken it there, Yahweh oppressed that town and a great panic broke out; afflicting the people of the town from highest to lowest, he brought them out in tumours too. 10 They then sent the ark of God to Ekron, but when it came to Ekron the Ekronites shouted, 'They have brought me the ark of the God of Israel to kill me and my people!' 11 They summoned all the Philistine chiefs and said, 'Send the ark of the God of Israel away; let it go back to where it belongs and not kill me and my people' — for there was mortal panic throughout the town; God was oppressing them. 12 The people who did not die were afflicted with tumours, and the wailing from the town rose to the sky.

6 The ark of Yahweh was in Philistine territory for seven months. 2 The Philistines then called for their priests and diviners and asked, 'What shall we do with the ark of Yahweh? Tell us how to send it back to where it belongs.' 3 They replied, 'If you send the ark of the God of Israel away, you must certainly not send it away without a gift; you must pay him a guilt offering. You will then recover and will realise why he continually oppressed you.' 4 They then asked, 'What guilt offering ought we to pay him?' They replied, 'Corresponding to the number of Philistine chiefs: five golden tumours and five golden rats, since the same plague afflicted your chiefs as the rest of you. 5 So make models of your tumours and models of your rats ravaging the territory, and pay honour to the God of Israel. Then perhaps he will stop oppressing you, your gods and your country. 6 Why should you be as stubborn as Egypt and Pharaoh were? After he had brought disasters on them, did they not let the people leave? 7 Now, then, take and fit out a new cart, and two milch cows that have never borne the yoke. Then harness the cows to the cart and take their calves back to the byre. 8 Then take the ark of Yahweh, place it on

NEW REVISED STANDARD VERSION	REVISED ENGLISH BIBLE

and put in a box at its side the figures of gold, which you are returning to him as a guilt offering. Then send it off, and let it go its way. 9 And watch; if it goes up on the way to its own land, to Beth-shemesh, then it is he who has done us this great harm; but if not, then we shall know that it is not his hand that struck us; it happened to us by chance."

10 The men did so; they took two milch cows and yoked them to the cart, and shut up their calves at home. 11 They put the ark of the LORD on the cart, and the box with the gold mice and the images of their tumors. 12 The cows went straight in the direction of Beth-shemesh along one highway, lowing as they went; they turned neither to the right nor to the left, and the lords of the Philistines went after them as far as the border of Beth-shemesh.

13 Now the people of Beth-shemesh were reaping their wheat harvest in the valley. When they looked up and saw the ark, they went with rejoicing to meet it.u 14 The cart came into the field of Joshua of Beth-shemesh, and stopped there. A large stone was there; so they split up the wood of the cart and offered the cows as a burnt offering to the LORD. 15 The Levites took down the ark of the LORD and the box that was beside it, in which were the gold objects, and set them upon the large stone. Then the people of Beth-shemesh offered burnt offerings and presented sacrifices on that day to the LORD. 16 When the five lords of the Philistines saw it, they returned that day to Ekron.

17 These are the gold tumors, which the Philistines returned as a guilt offering to the LORD: one for Ashdod, one for Gaza, one for Ashkelon, one for Gath, one for Ekron; 18 also the gold mice, according to the number of all the cities of the Philistines belonging to the five lords, both fortified cities and unwalled villages. The great stone, beside which they set down the ark of the LORD, is a witness to this day in the field of Joshua of Beth-shemesh.

19 The descendants of Jeconiah did not rejoice with the people of Beth-shemesh when they greetedv the ark of the LORD; and he killed seventy men of them.w The people mourned because the LORD had made a great slaughter among the people. 20 Then the people of Beth-shemesh said, "Who is able to stand before the LORD, this holy God? To whom shall he go so that we may be rid of him?" 21 So they sent messengers to the inhabitants of Kiriath-jearim, saying, "The Philistines have returned the ark of the LORD. 7 Come down and take it up to you." 1 And the people of Kiriath-jearim came and took up the ark of the LORD, and brought it to the house of Abinadab on the hill. They consecrated his son, Eleazar, to have charge of the ark of the LORD.

2 From the day that the ark was lodged at Kiriath-jearim, a long time passed, some twenty years, and all the house of Israel lamentedx after the LORD.

3 Then Samuel said to all the house of Israel, "If you are returning to the LORD with all your heart, then put away the foreign gods and the Astartes from among you. Direct your heart to the LORD, and serve him only, and he will deliver you out of the hand of the Philistines." 4 So Israel put away the Baals and the Astartes, and they served the LORD only.

5 Then Samuel said, "Gather all Israel at Mizpah, and I will pray to the LORD for you." 6 So they gathered at Mizpah, and drew water and poured it out before the LORD. They fasted that day, and said, "We have sinned against the LORD." And Samuel judged the people of Israel at Mizpah.

beside it in a casket the gold offerings that you are sending to him, and let it go where it will. 9 Watch: if it goes up towards its own territory to Beth-shemesh, then it was the LORD who has inflicted this great injury on us; but if not, then we shall know that it was not his hand that struck us, but that we have been the victims of chance.'

10 They did this: they took two milch cows and harnessed them to a wagon, meanwhile shutting up their calves in the stall; 11 they placed the Ark of the LORD on the wagon together with the casket containing the gold rats, and the models of their tumours. 12 The cows went straight in the direction of Beth-shemesh; they kept to the road, lowing as they went and turning neither right nor left, while the Philistine lords followed them as far as the territory of Beth-shemesh.

13 The people of Beth-shemesh, busy harvesting their wheat in the valley, looked up and saw the Ark, and they rejoiced at the sight. 14 The wagon came to the field of Joshua of Beth-shemesh and halted there, close by a great stone. The people chopped up the wood of the wagon and offered the cows as a whole-offering to the LORD. 15 The Levites who lifted down the Ark of the LORD and the casket containing the gold offerings laid them on the great stone; and the men of Beth-shemesh offered whole-offerings and shared-offerings that day to the LORD. 16 The five lords of the Philistines watched all this, and returned to Ekron the same day.

17 These golden tumours which the Philistines sent back as an offering to the LORD were for Ashdod, Gaza, Ashkelon, Gath, and Ekron, one for each city. 18 The gold rats were for all the towns of the Philistines governed by the five lords, both fortified towns and open settlements. The great stone where they deposited the Ark of the LORD stands witness on the farm of Joshua of Beth-shemesh to this day.

19 But the sons of Jeconiah did not rejoice with the rest of the men of Beth-shemesh when they welcomed the Ark of the LORD, and he struck down seventy of them. The people mourned because the LORD had struck them so heavy a blow, 20 and the men of Beth-shemesh said, 'No one is safe in the presence of the LORD, this holy God. To whom can we send the Ark, to be rid of him?' 21 So they sent this message to the inhabitants of Kiriath-jearim: 'The Philistines have returned the Ark of the LORD; come down and 7 take charge of it.' 1 The men of Kiriath-jearim came and took the Ark of the LORD away; they brought it into the house of Abinadab on the hill and consecrated his son Eleazar as its custodian.

2 For a long while, some twenty years in all, the Ark was housed in Kiriath-jearim. Then there was a movement throughout Israel to follow the LORD, 3 and Samuel addressed these words to the whole nation: 'If your return to the LORD is whole-hearted, banish the foreign gods and the ashtaroth from your shrines; turn to the LORD with heart and mind, and worship him alone, and he will deliver you from the Philistines.' 4 So the Israelites banished the baalim and the ashtaroth, and worshipped the LORD alone.

5 Samuel summoned all Israel to an assembly at Mizpah, so that he might intercede with the LORD for them. 6 When they had assembled, they drew water and poured it out before the LORD and fasted all day, confessing that they had sinned against the LORD. It was at Mizpah that Samuel acted as judge over Israel.

6:18 **The great stone:** *so Gk; Heb.* Abel-haggedolah.   6:19 **But ... seventy of them:** *prob. rdg, cp. Gk; Heb.* And he struck down some of the men of Beth-shemesh because they had gazed upon the Ark of the LORD; he struck down seventy men among the people, fifty thousand men.

u Gk: Heb *rejoiced to see it*   v Gk: Heb *And he killed some of the people of Beth-shemesh, because they looked into*   w Heb *killed seventy men, fifty thousand men*   x Meaning of Heb uncertain

articles that you are offering, as amends for your guilt. Start it on its way, and let it go. 9 Then watch! If it goes up to Beth-shemesh along the route to his own territory, he has brought this great calamity upon us; if not, we will know it was not he who struck us, but that an accident happened to us."

10 They acted upon this advice. Taking two milch cows, they hitched them to the cart but shut up their calves indoors. 11 Then they placed the ark of the LORD on the cart, along with the box containing the golden mice and the images of the hemorrhoids. 12 The cows went straight for the route to Beth-shemesh and continued along this road, mooing as they went, without turning right or left. The Philistine lords followed them as far as the border of Beth-shemesh. 13 The people of Beth-shemesh were harvesting the wheat in the valley. When they looked up and spied the ark, they greeted it with rejoicing. 14 The cart came to the field of Joshua the Beth-shemite and stopped there. At a large stone in the field, the wood of the cart was split up and the cows were offered as a holocaust to the LORD. 15 The Levites, meanwhile, had taken down the ark of God and the box beside it, in which the golden articles were, and had placed them on the great stone. The men of Beth-shemesh also offered other holocausts and sacrifices to the LORD that day. 16 After witnessing this, the five Philistine lords returned to Ekron the same day.

17 The golden hemorrhoids the Philistines sent back as a guilt offering to the LORD were as follows: one for Ashdod, one for Gaza, one for Ashkelon, one for Gath, and one for Ekron. 18 The golden mice, however, corresponded to the number of all the cities of the Philistines belonging to the five lords, including fortified cities and open villages. The large stone on which the ark of the LORD was placed is still in the field of Joshua the Beth-shemite at the present time.

19 The descendants of Jeconiah did not join in the celebration with the inhabitants of Beth-shemesh when they greeted the ark of the LORD, and seventy of them were struck down. The people went into mourning at this great calamity with which the LORD had afflicted them. 20 The men of Beth-shemesh asked, "Who can stand in the presence of this Holy One? To whom shall he go from us?" 21 They then sent messengers to the inhabitants of Kiriath-jearim, saying, "The Philistines have returned the ark of the LORD; come down and get it."

7 So the inhabitants of Kiriath-jearim came for the ark of the LORD and brought it into the house of Abinadab on the hill, appointing his son Eleazar as guardian of the ark of the LORD.

2 From the day the ark came to rest in Kiriath-jearim a long time, twenty years, elapsed, and the whole Israelite population turned to the LORD. 3 Samuel said to them: "If you wish with your whole heart to return to the LORD, put away your foreign gods and your Ashtaroth, devote yourselves to the LORD, and worship him alone. Then he will deliver you from the power of the Philistines." 4 So the Israelites put away their Baals and Ashtaroth, and worshiped the LORD alone. 5 Samuel then gave orders, "Gather all Israel to Mizpah, that I may pray to the LORD for you." 6 When they were gathered at Mizpah, they drew water and poured it out on the ground before the LORD, and they fasted that day, confessing, "We have sinned against the LORD." It was at Mizpah that Samuel began to judge the Israelites.

the cart, and put the golden objects which you are paying him as guilt offering in a box beside it; and then send it off on its own. 9 Watch it; if it goes up the road to its own territory, towards Beth-Shemesh, then he was responsible for this great harm to us; but if not, we shall know that it was not his hand that struck us, and that this has happened to us by chance.'

10 The people did this. They took two milch cows and harnessed them to the cart, shutting their calves in the byre. 11 They then put the ark of Yahweh on the cart, with the box and the golden rats and the models of their tumours.

12 The cows made straight for Beth-Shemesh, keeping to the one road, lowing as they went and turning neither to right nor to left. The Philistine chiefs followed them as far as the boundaries of Beth-Shemesh.

13 The people of Beth-Shemesh were reaping the wheat harvest in the plain when they looked up and saw the ark and went joyfully to meet it. 14 When the cart came to the field of Joshua of Beth-Shemesh, it stopped. There was a large stone there, and they cut up the wood of the cart and offered the cows as a burnt offering to Yahweh. 15 The Levites had taken down the ark of Yahweh and the box with it containing the golden objects and put these on the large stone. That day the people of Beth-Shemesh presented burnt offerings and made sacrifices to Yahweh. 16 The five chiefs of the Philistines, having witnessed this, went back to Ekron the same day.

17 The golden tumours paid by the Philistines as a guilt offering to Yahweh were as follows: one for Ashdod, one for Gaza, one for Ashkelon, one for Gath, one for Ekron; 18 and golden rats to the number of all the Philistine towns, those of the five chiefs, from fortified towns down to open villages: still to this day the large stone in the field of Joshua of Beth-Shemesh, on which they put the ark of Yahweh, is a witness. 19 Of the people of Beth-Shemesh the sons of Jeconiah had not rejoiced when they saw the ark of Yahweh, and Yahweh struck down seventy of them. The people mourned because Yahweh had struck them so fiercely.

20 The people of Beth-Shemesh then said, 'Who can stand his ground before Yahweh, this holy God? To whom shall he go, so that we are rid of him?' 21 So they sent messengers to the inhabitants of Kiriath-Jearim, to say, 'The Philistines have sent back the ark of Yahweh; come down and take it up to your town.'

7 The men of Kiriath-Jearim came and, taking up the ark of Yahweh, brought it to the house of Abinadab on the hill, and consecrated his son Eleazar to guard the ark of Yahweh.

2 From the day when the ark was installed at Kiriath-Jearim, a long time went by — twenty years — and the whole House of Israel longed for Yahweh. 3 Samuel then spoke as follows to the whole House of Israel, 'If you are returning to Yahweh with all your heart, banish the foreign gods and Astartes which you now have, and set your heart on Yahweh and serve him alone; and he will deliver you from the power of the Philistines.' 4 And the Israelites banished Baals and Astartes and served Yahweh alone.

5 Samuel then said, 'Muster all Israel at Mizpah and I shall plead with Yahweh for you.' 6 So they mustered at Mizpah and drew water and poured it out before Yahweh. They fasted that day and declared, 'We have sinned against Yahweh.' And Samuel was judge over the Israelites at Mizpah.

7 When the Philistines heard that the people of Israel had gathered at Mizpah, the lords of the Philistines went up against Israel. And when the people of Israel heard of it they were afraid of the Philistines. 8 The people of Israel said to Samuel, "Do not cease to cry out to the LORD our God for us, and pray that he may save us from the hand of the Philistines." 9 So Samuel took a sucking lamb and offered it as a whole burnt offering to the LORD; Samuel cried out to the LORD for Israel, and the LORD answered him. 10 As Samuel was offering up the burnt offering, the Philistines drew near to attack Israel; but the LORD thundered with a mighty voice that day against the Philistines and threw them into confusion; and they were routed before Israel. 11 And the men of Israel went out of Mizpah and pursued the Philistines, and struck them down as far as beyond Beth-car.

12 Then Samuel took a stone and set it up between Mizpah and Jeshanah,y and named it Ebenezer;z for he said, "Thus far the LORD has helped us." 13 So the Philistines were subdued and did not again enter the territory of Israel; the hand of the LORD was against the Philistines all the days of Samuel. 14 The towns that the Philistines had taken from Israel were restored to Israel, from Ekron to Gath; and Israel recovered their territory from the hand of the Philistines. There was peace also between Israel and the Amorites.

15 Samuel judged Israel all the days of his life. 16 He went on a circuit year by year to Bethel, Gilgal, and Mizpah; and he judged Israel in all these places. 17 Then he would come back to Ramah, for his home was there; he administered justice there to Israel, and built there an altar to the LORD.

8 When Samuel became old, he made his sons judges over Israel. 2 The name of his firstborn son was Joel, and the name of his second, Abijah; they were judges in Beer-sheba. 3 Yet his sons did not follow in his ways, but turned aside after gain; they took bribes and perverted justice.

4 Then all the elders of Israel gathered together and came to Samuel at Ramah, 5 and said to him, "You are old and your sons do not follow in your ways; appoint for us, then, a king to govern us, like other nations." 6 But the thing displeased Samuel when they said, "Give us a king to govern us." Samuel prayed to the LORD, 7 and the LORD said to Samuel, "Listen to the voice of the people in all that they say to you; for they have not rejected you, but they have rejected me from being king over them. 8 Just as they have done to me,a from the day I brought them up out of Egypt to this day, forsaking me and serving other gods, so also they are doing to you. 9 Now then, listen to their voice; only — you shall solemnly warn them, and show them the ways of the king who shall reign over them."

10 So Samuel reported all the words of the LORD to the people who were asking him for a king. 11 He said, "These will be the ways of the king who will reign over you: he will take your sons and appoint them to his chariots and to be his horsemen, and to run before his chariots; 12 and he will appoint for himself commanders of thousands and commanders of fifties, and some to plow his ground and to reap his harvest, and to make his implements of war and the equipment of his chariots. 13 He will take your daughters to be perfumers and cooks and bakers. 14 He will take the best of your fields and vineyards and olive orchards and give them to his courtiers. 15 He will take one-tenth of your grain and of your vineyards and give it to his officers and his courtiers. 16 He will take your male and female slaves, and the best of your cattleb and donkeys, and put them to his work. 17 He will take one-tenth of your flocks, and you shall

7 When the Philistines heard that the Israelites had assembled at Mizpah, their lords marched against them. The Israelites heard that the Philistines were advancing, and they were afraid 8 and begged Samuel, 'Do not cease to pray for us to the LORD our God to save us from the power of the Philistines.' 9 Samuel took a sucking-lamb, offered it up complete as a whole-offering, and prayed aloud to the LORD on behalf of Israel, and the LORD answered his prayer. 10 As Samuel was offering the sacrifice and the Philistines were advancing to the attack, the LORD with mighty thunder threw the Philistines into confusion. They fled in panic before the Israelites, 11 who set out from Mizpah in pursuit and kept up the slaughter of the Philistines till they reached a point below Beth-car.

12 There Samuel took a stone and set it up as a monument between Mizpah and Jeshanah, naming it Eben-ezer. 'This is a witness', he said, 'that the LORD has helped us.' 13 Thus the Philistines were subdued and no longer encroached on the territory of Israel; as long as Samuel lived, the hand of the LORD was against them. 14 The towns they had captured were restored to Israel, and from Ekron to Gath the borderland was freed from Philistine control. Between Israel and the Amorites also peace was maintained.

15 Samuel acted as judge in Israel as long as he lived, 16 and every year went on circuit to Bethel, Gilgal, and Mizpah; he dispensed justice at all these places. 17 But always he went back to Ramah; that was his home and the place from which he governed Israel, and there he built an altar to the LORD.

8 WHEN Samuel grew old, he appointed his sons to be judges in Israel. 2 The eldest son was called Joel and the second Abiah; they acted as judges in Beersheba. 3 His sons did not follow their father's ways but were intent on their own profit, taking bribes and perverting the course of justice. 4 So all the elders of Israel met, and came to Samuel at Ramah. 5 They said to him, 'You are now old and your sons do not follow your ways; appoint us a king to rule us, like all the other nations.' 6 But their request for a king displeased Samuel. He prayed to the LORD, 7 and the LORD told him, 'Listen to the people and all that they are saying; they have not rejected you, it is I whom they have rejected, I whom they will not have to be their king. 8 They are now doing to you just what they have done to me since I brought them up from Egypt: they have forsaken me and worshipped other gods. 9 Hear what they have to say now, but give them a solemn warning and tell them what sort of king will rule them.'

10 Samuel reported to the people who were asking him for a king all that the LORD had said to him. 11 'This will be the sort of king who will bear rule over you,' he said. 'He will take your sons and make them serve in his chariots and with his cavalry, and they will run before his chariot. 12 Some he will appoint officers over units of a thousand and units of fifty. Others will plough his fields and reap his harvest; others again will make weapons of war and equipment for the chariots. 13 He will take your daughters for perfumers, cooks, and bakers. 14 He will seize the best of your fields, vineyards, and olive groves, and give them to his courtiers. 15 He will take a tenth of your grain and your vintage to give to his eunuchs and courtiers. 16 Your slaves, both men and women, and the best of your cattle and your donkeys he will take for his own use. 17 He will take a tenth of your flocks,

---

7:12 **Jeshanah:** *prob. rdg* (cp. 2 *Chr. 13:19*); *Heb.* the tooth. **Eben-ezer:** *that is* Stone of Help.   8:16 **your cattle:** *so* Gk; *Heb.* your picked men.

y Gk Syr: Heb *Shen*   z That is *Stone of Help*   a Gk: Heb lacks *to me*   b Gk: Heb *young men*

NEW AMERICAN BIBLE

7 When the Philistines heard that the Israelites had gathered at Mizpah, their lords went up against Israel. Hearing this, the Israelites became afraid of the Philistines 8 and said to Samuel, "Implore the LORD our God unceasingly for us, to save us from the clutches of the Philistines." 9 Samuel therefore took an unweaned lamb and offered it entire as a holocaust to the LORD. He implored the LORD for Israel, and the LORD heard him. 10 While Samuel was offering the holocaust, the Philistines advanced to join battle with Israel. That day, however, the LORD thundered loudly against the Philistines, and threw them into such confusion that they were defeated by Israel. 11 Thereupon the Israelites sallied forth from Mizpah and pursued the Philistines, harrying them down beyond Beth-car. 12 Samuel then took a stone and placed it between Mizpah and Jeshanah; he named it Ebenezer, explaining, "To this point has the LORD helped us." 13 Thus were the Philistines subdued, never again to enter the territory of Israel, for the LORD was severe with them as long as Samuel lived. 14 The cities from Ekron to Gath which the Philistines had taken from Israel were restored to them. Israel also freed the territory of these cities from the dominion of the Philistines. Moreover there was peace between Israel and the Amorites.

15 Samuel judged Israel as long as he lived. 16 He made a yearly journey, passing through Bethel, Gilgal and Mizpah and judging Israel at each of these sanctuaries. 17 Then he used to return to Ramah, for that was his home. There, too, he judged Israel and built an altar to the LORD.

8 In his old age Samuel appointed his sons judges over Israel. 2 His first-born was named Joel, his second son, Abijah; they judged at Beer-sheba. 3 His sons did not follow his example but sought illicit gain and accepted bribes, perverting justice. 4 Therefore all the elders of Israel came in a body to Samuel at Ramah 5 and said to him, "Now that you are old, and your sons do not follow your example, appoint a king over us, as other nations have, to judge us."

6 Samuel was displeased when they asked for a king to judge them. He prayed to the LORD, however, 7 who said in answer: "Grant the people's every request. It is not you they reject, they are rejecting me as their king. 8 As they have treated me constantly from the day I brought them up from Egypt to this day, deserting me and worshiping strange gods, so do they treat you too. 9 Now grant their request; but at the same time, warn them solemnly and inform them of the rights of the king who will rule them."

10 Samuel delivered the message of the LORD in full to those who were asking him for a king. 11 He told them: "The rights of the king who will rule you will be as follows: He will take your sons and assign them to his chariots and horses, and they will run before his chariot. 12 He will also appoint from among them his commanders of groups of a thousand and of a hundred soldiers. He will set them to do his plowing and his harvesting, and to make his implements of war and the equipment of his chariots. 13 He will use your daughters as ointment-makers, as cooks, and as bakers. 14 He will take the best of your fields, vineyards, and olive groves, and give them to his officials. 15 He will tithe your crops and your vineyards, and give the revenue to his eunuchs and his slaves. 16 He will take your male and female servants, as well as your best oxen and your asses, and use them to do his work. 17 He will tithe your flocks and you

NEW JERUSALEM BIBLE

7 When the Philistines heard that the Israelites had mustered at Mizpah, the Philistine chiefs marched on Israel; and when the Israelites heard this, they were afraid of the Philistines. 8 They said to Samuel, 'Do not stop calling on Yahweh our God to rescue us from the power of the Philistines.' 9 Samuel took a sucking lamb and presented it as a burnt offering to Yahweh, and he called on Yahweh on behalf of Israel and Yahweh heard him. 10 While Samuel was in the act of presenting burnt offering, the Philistines joined battle with Israel, but that day Yahweh thundered violently over the Philistines, threw them into panic and Israel defeated them. 11 The men of Israel sallied out from Mizpah in pursuit of the Philistines and beat them all the way to below Beth-Car. 12 Samuel then took a stone and erected it between Mizpah and the Tooth, and gave it the name Ebenezer,e saying, 'Yahweh helped us as far as this.'

13 So the Philistines were humbled and no longer came into Israelite territory; Yahweh oppressed the Philistines throughout the life of Samuel. 14 The towns which the Philistines had taken from Israel were given back to Israel, from Ekron all the way to Gath, and Israel freed their territory from the power of the Philistines. There was peace, too, between Israel and the Amorites.

15 Samuel was judge over Israel throughout his life. 16 Each year he went on circuit through Bethel and Gilgal and Mizpah and judged Israel in all these places. 17 He would then return to Ramah, since his home was there; there too he judged Israel. And there he built an altar to Yahweh.

8 When Samuel grew old, he appointed his sons as judges of Israel. 2 His eldest son was called Joel and his second one, Abijah; they were judges at Beersheba. 3 His sons did not follow his example but, seduced by the love of money, took bribes and gave biased verdicts. 4 The elders of Israel all assembled, went back to Samuel at Ramah, and said, 5 'Look, you are old, and your sons are not following your example. So give us a king to judge us, like the other nations.' 6 Samuel thought that it was wrong of them to say, 'Let us have a king to judge us,' so he prayed to Yahweh. 7 But Yahweh said to Samuel, 'Obey the voice of the people in all that they say to you: it is not you they have rejected 8 but me, not wishing me to reign over them any more. They are now doing to you exactly what they have done to me since the day I brought them out of Egypt until now, deserting me and serving other gods. 9 So, do what they ask; only, you must give them a solemn warning, and must tell them what the king who is to reign over them will do.'

10 Everything that Yahweh had said, Samuel then repeated to the people who were asking him for a king. 11 He said, 'This is what the king who is to reign over you will do. He will take your sons and direct them to his chariotry and cavalry, and they will run in front of his chariot. 12 He will use them as leaders of a thousand and leaders of fifty; he will make them plough his fields and gather in his harvest and make his weapons of war and the gear for his chariots. 13 He will take your daughters as perfumers, cooks and bakers. 14 He will take the best of your fields, your vineyards and your olive groves and give them to his officials. 15 He will tithe your crops and vineyards to provide for his courtiers and his officials. 16 He will take the best of your servants, men and women, of your oxen and your donkeys, and make them work for him. 17 He will tithe your flocks,

---

e7 Eben-ezer = Stone of help.

NEW REVISED STANDARD VERSION

REVISED ENGLISH BIBLE

be his slaves. 18 And in that day you will cry out because of your king, whom you have chosen for yourselves; but the LORD will not answer you in that day."

19 But the people refused to listen to the voice of Samuel; they said, "No! but we are determined to have a king over us, 20 so that we also may be like other nations, and that our king may govern us and go out before us and fight our battles." 21 When Samuel had heard all the words of the people, he repeated them in the ears of the LORD. 22 The LORD said to Samuel, "Listen to their voice and set a king over them." Samuel then said to the people of Israel, "Each of you return home."

9 There was a man of Benjamin whose name was Kish son of Abiel son of Zeror son of Becorath son of Aphiah, a Benjaminite, a man of wealth. 2 He had a son whose name was Saul, a handsome young man. There was not a man among the people of Israel more handsome than he; he stood head and shoulders above everyone else.

3 Now the donkeys of Kish, Saul's father, had strayed. So Kish said to his son Saul, "Take one of the boys with you; go and look for the donkeys." 4 He passed through the hill country of Ephraim and passed through the land of Shalishah, but they did not find them. And they passed through the land of Shaalim, but they were not there. Then he passed through the land of Benjamin, but they did not find them.

5 When they came to the land of Zuph, Saul said to the boy who was with him, "Let us turn back, or my father will stop worrying about the donkeys and worry about us." 6 But he said to him, "There is a man of God in this town; he is a man held in honor. Whatever he says always comes true. Let us go there now; perhaps he will tell us about the journey on which we have set out." 7 Then Saul replied to the boy, "But if we go, what can we bring the man? For the bread in our sacks is gone, and there is no present to bring to the man of God. What have we?" 8 The boy answered Saul again, "Here, I have with me a quarter shekel of silver; I will give it to the man of God, to tell us our way." 9 (Formerly in Israel, anyone who went to inquire of God would say, "Come, let us go to the seer"; for the one who is now called a prophet was formerly called a seer.) 10 Saul said to the boy, "Good; come, let us go." So they went to the town where the man of God was.

11 As they went up the hill to the town, they met some girls coming out to draw water, and said to them, "Is the seer here?" 12 They answered, "Yes, there he is just ahead of you. Hurry; he has come just now to the town, because the people have a sacrifice today at the shrine. 13 As soon as you enter the town, you will find him, before he goes up to the shrine to eat. For the people will not eat until he comes, since he must bless the sacrifice; afterward those eat who are invited. Now go up, for you will meet him immediately." 14 So they went up to the town. As they were entering the town, they saw Samuel coming out toward them on his way up to the shrine.

15 Now the day before Saul came, the LORD had revealed to Samuel: 16 "Tomorrow about this time I will send to you a man from the land of Benjamin, and you shall anoint him to be ruler over my people Israel. He shall save my people from the hand of the Philistines; for I have seen the suffering of c my people, because their outcry has come to me." 17 When Samuel saw Saul, the LORD told him, "Here is the man of whom I spoke to you. It is who shall rule over my people." 18 Then Saul approached Samuel inside the gate, and said, "Tell me, please, where is the house of the seer?" 19 Samuel answered Saul, "I am the seer; go up

and you yourselves will become his slaves. 18 There will come a day when you will cry out against the king whom you have chosen; but the LORD will not answer you on that day.'

19 The people, however, refused to listen to Samuel. 'No,' they said, 'we must have a king over us; 20 then we shall be like other nations, with a king to rule us, to lead us out to war and fight our battles.' 21 When Samuel heard what the people had decided, he told the LORD, 22 who said, 'Take them at their word and appoint them a king.' Samuel then dismissed all the Israelites to their homes.

9 There was a man from the territory of Benjamin, whose name was Kish son of Abiel, son of Zeror, son of Bechorath, son of Aphiah a Benjamite. He was a man of substance, 2 and had a son named Saul, a young man in his prime; there was no better man among the Israelites than he. He stood a head taller than any of the people.

3 One day some donkeys belonging to Saul's father Kish had strayed, so he said to his son Saul, 'Take one of the servants with you, and go and look for the donkeys.' 4 They crossed the hill-country of Ephraim and went through the district of Shalisha but did not find them; they passed through the district of Shaalim but they were not there; they passed through the district of Benjamin but again did not find them. 5 When they reached the district of Zuph, Saul said to the servant who was with him, 'Come, we ought to turn back, or my father will stop thinking about the donkeys and begin to worry about us.' 6 The servant answered, 'There is a man of God in this town who has a great reputation, because everything he says comes true. Suppose we go there; he may tell us which way to take.' 7 Saul said, 'If we go, what shall we offer him? There is no food left in our packs and we have no present to give the man of God, nothing at all.' 8 The servant answered him again, 'Wait! I have here a quarter-shekel of silver. I can give that to the man, to tell us the way.' 10 Saul said, 'Good! Let us go to him.' So they went to the town where the man of God lived. 9 (In Israel in days gone by, when someone wished to consult God, he would say, 'Let us go to the seer.' For what is nowadays called a prophet used to be called a seer.)

11 As they were going up the ascent to the town they met some girls coming out to draw water and asked them, 'Shall we find the seer there?' 12 'Yes,' they answered, 'he is ahead of you; hurry now, for he has just arrived in the town because there is a feast at the shrine today. 13 As you enter the town you will meet him before he goes up to the shrine to eat; the people will not start until he comes, for he has to bless the sacrifice before the invited company can eat. Go up now, and you will find him at once.' 14 So they went up to the town and, just as they were going in, there was Samuel coming towards them on his way up to the shrine.

15 The day before Saul's arrival there, the LORD had disclosed his intention to Samuel: 16 'At this time tomorrow,' he said, 'I shall send you a man from the territory of Benjamin, and you are to anoint him prince over my people Israel. He will deliver my people from the Philistines; for I have seen the sufferings of my people, and their cry has reached my ears.' 17 The moment Saul appeared the LORD said to Samuel, 'Here is the man of whom I spoke to you. This man will govern my people.' 18 Saul came up to Samuel in the gateway and said, 'Tell me, please, where the seer lives.' 19 Samuel replied, 'I am the seer. Go on ahead of me

---

c Gk: Heb lacks *the suffering of*

9:9–10 *Verses 9 and 10 transposed.*   9:16 **the sufferings of:** *so Gk; Heb. omits.*

yourselves will become his slaves. 18 When this takes place, you will complain against the king whom you have chosen, but on that day the LORD will not answer you."

19 The people, however, refused to listen to Samuel's warning and said, "Not so! There must be a king over us. 20 We too must be like other nations, with a king to rule us and to lead us in warfare and fight our battles." 21 When Samuel had listened to all the people had to say, he repeated it to the LORD, 22 who then said to him, "Grant their request and appoint a king to rule them." Samuel thereupon said to the men of Israel, "Each of you go to his own city."

9 There was a stalwart man from Benjamin named Kish, who was the son of Abiel, son of Zeror, son of Becorath, son of Aphiah, a Benjaminite. 2 He had a son named Saul, who was a handsome young man. There was no other Israelite handsomer than Saul; he stood head and shoulders above the people.

3 Now the asses of Saul's father, Kish, had wandered off. Kish said to his son Saul, "Take one of the servants with you and go out and hunt for the asses." 4 Accordingly they went through the hill country of Ephraim, and through the land of Shalishah. Not finding them there, they continued through the land of Shaalim without success. They also went through the land of Benjamin, but they failed to find the animals. 5 When they came to the land of Zuph, Saul said to the servant who was with him, "Come, let us turn back, lest my father forget about the asses and become anxious about us." 6 The servant replied, "Listen! There is a man of God in this city, a man held in high esteem; all that he says is sure to come true. Let us go there now! Perhaps he can tell us how to accomplish our errand." 7 But Saul said to his servant, "If we go, what can we offer the man? There is no bread in our bags, and we have no present to give the man of God. What have we?" 8 Again the servant answered Saul, "I have a quarter of a silver shekel. If I give that to the man of God, he will tell us our way." ‡9.9: see below‡ 10 Saul then said to his servant, "Well said! Come on, let us go!" And they went to the city where the man of God lived.

11 As they were going up the ascent to the city, they met some girls coming out to draw water and inquired of them, "Is the seer in town?" 9 (In former times in Israel, anyone who sent to consult God used to say, "Come, let us go to the seer." For he who is now called prophet was formerly called seer.) 12 The girls answered, "Yes, there — straight ahead. Hurry now; just today he came to the city, because the people have a sacrifice today on the high place. 13 When you enter the city, you may reach him before he goes up to the high place to eat. The people will not eat until he arrives; only after he blesses the sacrifice will the invited guests eat. Go up immediately, for you should find him right now."

14 So they went up to the city. As they entered it, Samuel was coming toward them on his way to the high place. 15 The day before Saul's arrival, the LORD had given Samuel the revelation: 16 "At this time tomorrow I will send you a man from the land of Benjamin whom you are to anoint as commander of my people Israel. He shall save my people from the clutches of the Philistines, for I have witnessed their misery and accepted their cry for help." 17 When Samuel caught sight of Saul, the LORD assured him, "This is the man of whom I told you; he is to govern my people." 18 Saul met Samuel in the gateway and said, "Please tell me where the seer lives." 19 Samuel answered Saul: "I am the seer. Go

and you yourselves will become his slaves. 18 When that day comes, you will cry aloud because of the king you have chosen for yourselves, but on that day Yahweh will not hear you.'

19 The people, however, refused to listen to Samuel. They said, 'No! We are determined to have a king, 20 so that we can be like the other nations, with our own king to rule us and lead us and fight our battles.' 21 Samuel listened to all that the people had to say and repeated it in Yahweh's ear. 22 Yahweh then said to Samuel, 'Do as they ask and give them a king.' Samuel then said to the Israelites, 'Go home, each of you, to his own town.'

9 Among the men of Benjamin was a man called Kish son of Abiel, son of Zeror, son of Becorath, son of Aphiah; a Benjaminite and a person of rank. 2 He had a son called Saul, a handsome man in the prime of life. Of all the Israelites there was no one more handsome than he; he stood head and shoulders taller than anyone else.

3 Now since the donkeys belonging to Kish, Saul's father, had strayed, Kish said to his son Saul, 'My son, take one of the servants with you and be off; go and look for the donkeys.' 4 They went through the highlands of Ephraim, they went through the territory of Shalishah, and did not find them; they went through the territory of Shaalim but they were not there; they went through the territory of Benjamin and did not find them. 5 When they reached the territory of Zuph, Saul said to the servant who was with him, 'Come on, let us go back or my father will stop worrying over the donkeys and start being anxious about us.' 6 The servant, however, replied, 'Look, there is a man of God in this town, a man who is held in honour; everything he says comes true. Let us go there, then; perhaps he will be able to show us the way that we should take.' 7 Saul said to his servant, 'But if we do go, what can we take to the man? The food in our sacks is finished, and we have no present to offer the man of God. What else have we got?' 8 The servant spoke up again and said to Saul, 'Look, I happen to have a quarter of a silver shekel; I shall give that to the man of God, for him to tell us which way to go.' ‡9.9: see below‡ 10 Saul then said to his servant, 'Well said! Come on, let us go.' And they went off to the town where the man of God was.

11 As they were going up the slope to the town they came across some girls going out to draw water, and said to them, 'Is the seer there?' 9 In Israel, in olden days, when anyone used to go to consult God, he would say, 'Come on, let us go to the seer,' for a man who is now called a 'prophet' used to be called a 'seer' in olden days. 12 The girls replied, 'He is. He arrived a moment or two ahead of you. You had better hurry: he has just come to town because the people are having a sacrifice today on the high place. 13 You can catch him as soon as you go into the town, before he goes up to the high place for the meal. The people will not eat until he comes, since he must bless the sacrifice; after that, the guests will start eating. If you go up now, you will find him straight away.'

14 So they went up to the town and, as they were going through the gate, Samuel came out towards them on his way to the high place. 15 Now, Yahweh had given Samuel a revelation the day before Saul came, saying, 16 'About this time tomorrow, I shall send you a man from the territory of Benjamin; you are to anoint him as prince of my people Israel, and he will save my people from the power of the Philistines; for I have seen the misery of my people and their cries of anguish have come to me.' 17 When Samuel saw Saul, Yahweh told him, 'That is the man of whom I said to you, "He is to govern my people." ' 18 Saul accosted Samuel in the gateway and said, 'Tell me, please, where the seer's house is.' 19 Samuel replied to Saul, 'I am the seer.

NEW REVISED STANDARD VERSION | REVISED ENGLISH BIBLE

before me to the shrine, for today you shall eat with me, and in the morning I will let you go and will tell you all that is on your mind. 20 As for your donkeys that were lost three days ago, give no further thought to them, for they have been found. And on whom is all Israel's desire fixed, if not on you and on all your ancestral house?" 21 Saul answered, "I am only a Benjaminite, from the least of the tribes of Israel, and my family is the humblest of all the families of the tribe of Benjamin. Why then have you spoken to me in this way?"

22 Then Samuel took Saul and his servant-boy and brought them into the hall, and gave them a place at the head of those who had been invited, of whom there were about thirty. 23 And Samuel said to the cook, "Bring the portion I gave you, the one I asked you to put aside." 24 The cook took up the thigh and what went with it*d* and set them before Saul. Samuel said, "See, what was kept is set before you. Eat; for it is set*e* before you at the appointed time, so that you might eat with the guests."*f*

So Saul ate with Samuel that day. 25 When they came down from the shrine into the town, a bed was spread for Saul*g* on the roof, and he lay down to sleep.*h* 26 Then at the break of dawn*i* Samuel called to Saul upon the roof, "Get up, so that I may send you on your way." Saul got up, and both he and Samuel went out into the street.

27 As they were going down to the outskirts of the town, Samuel said to Saul, "Tell the boy to go on before us, and when he has passed on, stop here yourself for a while, that I may make known to you the word of God."

10 1 Samuel took a vial of oil and poured it on his head, and kissed him; he said, "The LORD has anointed you ruler over his people Israel. You shall reign over the people of the LORD and you will save them from the hand of their enemies all around. Now this shall be the sign to you that the LORD has anointed you ruler*j* over his heritage: 2 When you depart from me today you will meet two men by Rachel's tomb in the territory of Benjamin at Zelzah; they will say to you, 'The donkeys that you went to seek are found, and now your father has stopped worrying about them and is worrying about you, saying: What shall I do about my son?' 3 Then you shall go on from there further and come to the oak of Tabor; three men going up to God at Bethel will meet you there, one carrying three kids, another carrying three loaves of bread, and another carrying a skin of wine. 4 They will greet you and give you two loaves of bread, which you shall accept from them. 5 After that you shall come to Gibeath-elohim,*k* at the place where the Philistine garrison is; there, as you come to the town, you will meet a band of prophets coming down from the shrine with harp, tambourine, flute, and lyre playing in front of them; they will be in a prophetic frenzy. 6 Then the spirit of the LORD will possess you, and you will be in a prophetic frenzy along with them and be turned into a different person. 7 Now when these signs meet you, do whatever you see fit to do, for God is with you. 8 And you shall go down to Gilgal ahead of me; then I will come down to you to present burnt offerings and offer sacrifices of well-being. Seven days you shall wait, until I come to you and show you what you shall do."

9 As he turned away to leave Samuel, God gave him another heart; and all these signs were fulfilled that day.

to the shrine and eat with me today; in the morning I shall set you on your way, after telling you what you have on your mind. 20 Trouble yourself no more about the donkeys lost three days ago; they have been found. To whom does the tribute of all Israel belong? It belongs to you and to your whole ancestral house.' 21 'But I am a Benjamite,' said Saul, 'from the smallest of the tribes of Israel, and my family is the least important of all the families of the tribe of Benjamin. Why do you say this to me?'

22 Samuel brought Saul and his servant into the dining-hall and gave them a place at the head of the invited company, about thirty in number. 23 He said to the cook, 'Bring the portion that I gave you and told you to put on one side.' 24 The cook took up the whole haunch and leg and put it before Saul; and Samuel said, 'Here is the portion of meat kept for you. Eat it: it has been reserved for you at this feast to which I have invited the people.'

Saul dined with Samuel that day, 25 and when they came down from the shrine to the town a bed was spread on the roof for Saul, and he stayed there that night. 26 At dawn Samuel called to Saul on the roof, 'Get up, and I shall set you on your way.' When Saul rose, he and Samuel went outside together, 27 and as they came to the edge of the town, Samuel said to Saul, 'Tell the boy to go on ahead.' He did so; then Samuel said, 'Stay here a moment, and I shall tell you what God has said.'

10 Samuel took a flask of oil and poured it over Saul's head; he kissed him and said, 'The LORD anoints you prince over his people Israel. You are to rule the people of the LORD and deliver them from the enemies round about. You will receive a sign that the LORD has anointed you prince to govern his possession: 2 when you leave me today, you will meet two men by Rachel's tomb at Zelzah in the territory of Benjamin. They will tell you that the donkeys you set out to look for have been found and that your father is concerned for them no longer; he is anxious about you and keeps saying, "What shall I do about my son?" 3 From there go across country as far as the terebinth of Tabor, where three men going up to Bethel to worship God will meet you. One of them will be carrying three young goats, the second three loaves, and the third a skin of wine. 4 They will greet you and offer you two loaves, which you will accept. 5 Then when you reach the hill of God, where the Philistine governor resides, you will meet a company of prophets coming down from the shrine, led by lute, drum, fife, and lyre, and filled with prophetic rapture. 6 The spirit of the LORD will suddenly take possession of you, and you too will be rapt like a prophet and become another man. 7 When these signs happen, do whatever the occasion demands; God will be with you. 8 You are to go down to Gilgal ahead of me, and I shall come to you to sacrifice whole-offerings and shared-offerings. Wait seven days until I join you; then I shall tell you what you have to do.'

9 As Saul turned to leave Samuel, God made him a different person. On that same day all these signs happened.

---

d Meaning of Heb uncertain   *e* Q Ms Gk: MT *it was kept*
f Cn: Heb *it was kept for you, saying, I have invited the people*
g Gk: Heb *and he spoke with Saul*   *h* Gk: Heb lacks *and he lay down to sleep*   *i* Gk: Heb *and they arose early and at break of dawn*   *j* Gk: Heb lacks *over his people Israel. You shall . . . anointed you ruler*   *k* Or *the Hill of God*

9:24 **the portion of meat:** *prob. rdg; Heb.* what is left over. **to which:** *so Lat.; Heb.* saying.   9:25 **a bed . . . and he:** *so Gk; Heb.* he spoke with Saul on the roof and they.   10:1 **The LORD anoints . . . sign:** *so Gk; Heb.* omits.   10:5 **governor:** *or* garrison.

up ahead of me to the high place and eat with me today. In the morning, before dismissing you, I will tell you whatever you wish. 20 As for the asses you lost three days ago, do not worry about them, for they have been found. Whom does Israel desire ardently if not you and your father's family?" 21 Saul replied: "Am I not a Benjaminite, of one of the smallest tribes of Israel, and is not my clan the least among the clans of the tribe of Benjamin? Why say such things to me?"

22 Samuel then took Saul and his servant and brought them to the room, where he placed them at the head of the guests, of whom there were about thirty. 23 He said to the cook, "Bring the portion I gave you and told you to put aside." 24 So the cook took up the leg and what went with it, and placed it before Saul. Samuel said: "This is a reserved portion that has been set before you. Eat, for it was kept for you until your arrival; I explained that I was inviting some guests." Thus Saul dined with Samuel that day. 25 When they came down from the high place into the city, a mattress was spread for Saul on the roof, 26 and he slept there.

At daybreak Samuel called to Saul on the roof, "Get up, and I will start you on your journey." Saul rose, and he and Samuel went outside the city together. 27 As they were approaching the edge of the town, Samuel said to Saul, "Tell the servant to go on ahead of us, but stay here yourself for the moment, that I may give you a message from God."

10 Then, from a flask he had with him, Samuel poured oil on Saul's head; he also kissed him, saying: "The Lord anoints you commander over his heritage. You are to govern the Lord's people Israel, and to save them from the grasp of their enemies roundabout.

"This will be the sign for you that the Lord has anointed you commander over his heritage: 2 When you leave me today, you will meet two men near Rachel's tomb at Zelzah in the territory of Benjamin, who will say to you, 'The asses you went to look for have been found. Your father is no longer worried about the asses, but is anxious about you and says, What shall I do about my son?' 3 Farther on, when you arrive at the terebinth of Tabor, you will be met by three men going up to God at Bethel; one will be bringing three kids, another three loaves of bread, and the third a skin of wine. 4 They will greet you and offer you two wave offerings of bread, which you will take from them. 5 After that you will come to Gibeath-elohim, where there is a garrison of the Philistines. As you enter that city, you will meet a band of prophets, in a prophetic state, coming down from the high place preceded by lyres, tambourines, flutes and harps. The spirit of the Lord will rush upon you, and you will join them in their prophetic state and will be changed into another man. 7 When you see these signs fulfilled, do whatever you judge feasible, because God is with you. 8 Now go down ahead of me to Gilgal, for I shall come down to you, to offer holocausts and to sacrifice peace offerings. Wait seven days until I come to you; I shall then tell you what you must do."

9 As Saul turned to leave Samuel, God gave him another heart. That very day all these signs came to pass . . . .

Go up ahead of me to the high place. You must eat with me today. Tomorrow, when I let you go, I shall tell you whatever is on your mind. 20 As regards your donkeys, however, which strayed three days ago, do not worry about them; they have been found. And for whom is the whole wealth of Israel destined, if not for you and for all the members of your father's family?' 21 To this, Saul replied, 'Am I not a Benjaminite, from the smallest of the tribes of Israel? And is not my family the least of all the families of the tribe of Benjamin? Why are you saying a thing like this to me?'

22 Samuel then took Saul and his servant and brought them into the hall and gave them a place at the head of the guests, of whom there were about thirty. 23 Samuel then said to the cook, 'Serve the portion which I gave you and told you to put on one side.' 24 The cook then picked up the leg and the tail and put it in front of Saul, saying, 'This is for you. This is what was left. Make a good meal . . .' That day, Saul ate with Samuel.

25 They came down from the high place into the town. A bed was made for Saul on the roof and he lay down there. 26 At dawn, Samuel called to Saul on the roof, 'Get up, and I shall send you on your way.' Saul got up, and Samuel and he went outside together. 27 They had walked as far as the end of the town when Samuel said to Saul, 'Tell the servant to go on ahead of us, but you stand still for a moment, so that I can make known to you the word of God.'

10 Samuel took a phial of oil and poured it on Saul's head; he then kissed him and said, 'Has not Yahweh anointed you as leader of his people Israel? You are the man who is to govern Yahweh's people and save them from the power of the enemies surrounding them. The sign for you that Yahweh has anointed you as prince of his heritage is this: 2 after leaving me today, you will meet two men near the tomb of Rachel, on the frontier of Benjamin . . . and they will say to you, "The donkeys which you went looking for have been found, and your father has lost interest in the matter of the donkeys and is worrying about you and wondering, What am I to do about my son?" 3 Going on from there, you will come to the Oak of Tabor, where you will meet three men going up to God at Bethel; one will be carrying three kids, one three loaves of bread and the third a skin of wine. 4 They will greet you and give you two loaves of bread which you must accept from them. 5 After this, you will come to Gibeah of God (where the Philistine garrison is) and, when you are just outside the town, you will meet a group of prophets coming down from the high place, headed by lyre, tambourine, pipe and harp; they will be in a state of ecstasy. 6 The spirit of Yahweh will then seize on you, and you will go into ecstasy with them, and be changed into another man. 7 When these signs have occurred, act as occasion serves, for God is with you. 8 You will then go down, ahead of me, to Gilgal, and I shall join you there to make burnt offerings and to offer communion sacrifices. You must wait seven days for me to come to you, and I shall then reveal to you what you must do.'

9 As soon as he had turned his back to leave Samuel, God changed his heart. And all these signs occurred that very

| NEW REVISED STANDARD VERSION | REVISED ENGLISH BIBLE |

10 When they were going from there[l] to Gibeah,[m] a band of prophets met him; and the spirit of God possessed him, and he fell into a prophetic frenzy along with them. 11 When all who knew him before saw how he prophesied with the prophets, the people said to one another, "What has come over the son of Kish? Is Saul also among the prophets?" 12 A man of the place answered, "And who is their father?" Therefore it became a proverb, "Is Saul also among the prophets?" 13 When his prophetic frenzy had ended, he went home.[n]

14 Saul's uncle said to him and to the boy, "Where did you go?" And he replied, "To seek the donkeys; and when we saw they were not to be found, we went to Samuel." 15 Saul's uncle said, "Tell me what Samuel said to you." 16 Saul said to his uncle, "He told us that the donkeys had been found." But about the matter of the kingship, of which Samuel had spoken, he did not tell him anything.

17 Samuel summoned the people to the LORD at Mizpah 18 and said to them,[o] "Thus says the LORD, the God of Israel, 'I brought up Israel out of Egypt, and I rescued you from the hand of the Egyptians and from the hand of all the kingdoms that were oppressing you.' 19 But today you have rejected your God, who saves you from all your calamities and your distresses; and you have said, 'No! but set a king over us.' Now therefore present yourselves before the LORD by your tribes and by your clans."

20 Then Samuel brought all the tribes of Israel near, and the tribe of Benjamin was taken by lot. 21 He brought the tribe of Benjamin near by its families, and the family of the Matrites was taken by lot. Finally he brought the family of the Matrites near man by man,[p] and Saul the son of Kish was taken by lot. But when they sought him, he could not be found. 22 So they inquired again of the LORD, "Did the man come here?"[q] and the LORD said, "See, he has hidden himself among the baggage." 23 Then they ran and brought him from there. When he took his stand among the people, he was head and shoulders taller than any of them. 24 Samuel said to all the people, "Do you see the one whom the LORD has chosen? There is no one like him among all the people." And all the people shouted, "Long live the king!"

25 Samuel told the people the rights and duties of the kingship; and he wrote them in a book and laid it up before the LORD. Then Samuel sent all the people back to their homes. 26 Saul also went to his home at Gibeah, and with him went warriors whose hearts God had touched. 27 But some worthless fellows said, "How can this man save us?" They despised him and brought him no present. But he held his peace.

Now Nahash, king of the Ammonites, had been grievously oppressing the Gadites and the Reubenites. He would gouge out the right eye of each of them and would not grant Israel a deliverer. No one was left of the Israelites across the Jordan whose right eye Nahash, king of the Ammonites, had not gouged out. But there were seven thousand men who had escaped from the Ammonites and had entered Jabesh-gilead.[r]

11 About a month later,[s] Nahash the Ammonite went up and besieged Jabesh-gilead; and all the men of Jabesh said to Nahash, "Make a treaty with us, and we will serve you." 2 But Nahash the Ammonite said to them, "On this condition I will make a treaty with you, namely that I gouge out everyone's right eye, and thus put disgrace upon all Israel." 3 The elders of Jabesh said to him, "Give us

10 When they reached the hill there was a company of prophets coming to meet him, and the spirit of God suddenly took possession of him, so that he too was filled with prophetic rapture. 11 When people who had known him previously saw that he was rapt like the prophets, they said to one another, 'What can have happened to the son of Kish? Is Saul also among the prophets?' 12 One of the men of that place said, 'And whose sons are they?' Hence the proverb, 'Is Saul also among the prophets?' 13 When the prophetic rapture had passed, he went home. 14 Saul's uncle said to him and the boy, 'Where have you been?' Saul answered, 'To look for the donkeys, and when we could not find them, we went to Samuel.' 15 His uncle said, 'Tell me what Samuel said.' 16 'He told us that the donkeys had been found,' replied Saul; but he did not repeat what Samuel had said about his being king.

17 Samuel summoned the Israelites to the LORD at Mizpah 18 and said to them, 'This is the word of the LORD the God of Israel: I brought Israel up from Egypt; I delivered you from the Egyptians and from all the kingdoms that oppressed you. 19 But today you have rejected your God who saved you from all your misery and distress; you have said, "No, set a king over us." Therefore take up your positions now before the LORD tribe by tribe and clan by clan.'

20 Samuel presented all the tribes of Israel, and Benjamin was picked by lot. 21 Then he presented the tribe of Benjamin, family by family, and the family of Matri was picked. He presented the family of Matri, man by man, and Saul son of Kish was picked; but when search was made he was not to be found. 22 They went on to ask the LORD, 'Will the man be coming?' The LORD answered, 'There he is, hiding among the baggage.' 23 So some ran and fetched him out, and as he took his stand among the people, he was a head taller than anyone else. 24 Samuel said to the people, 'Look at the man whom the LORD has chosen; there is no one like him in this whole nation.' They all acclaimed him, shouting, 'Long live the king!'

25 Samuel explained to the people the nature of a king, and made a written record of it on a scroll which he deposited before the LORD. He then dismissed them to their homes. 26 Saul too went home to Gibeah, and with him went some fighting men whose hearts God had moved. 27 But there were scoundrels who said, 'How can this fellow deliver us?' They thought nothing of him and brought him no gifts.

11 About a month later Nahash the Ammonite attacked and besieged Jabesh-gilead. The men of Jabesh said to Nahash, 'Grant us terms and we will be your subjects.' 2 Nahash answered, 'On one condition only shall I grant you terms: that I gouge out the right eye of every one of you and bring disgrace on all Israel.' 3 The elders of Jabesh-gilead

---

[l] Gk: Heb they came there   [m] Or the hill   [n] Cn: Heb he came to the shrine   [o] Heb to the people of Israel   [p] Gk: Heb lacks Finally . . . man by man   [q] Gk: Heb Is there yet a man to come here?   [r] Q Ms Compare Josephus, Antiquities VI.v.1 (68-71): MT lacks Now Nahash . . . entered Jabesh-gilead.   [s] Q Ms Gk: MT lacks About a month later

10:13 **home:** prob. rdg; Heb. to the shrine.   10:19 **said, "No:** so many MSS; others said to him.   10:21 **He . . . by man:** so Gk; Heb. omits.   10:22 **the man:** so Gk; Heb. a man.   10:26 **some fighting men:** so Gk; Heb. the army.   11:1 **About . . . later:** so Scroll; Heb. But he was silent.

10 When they were going from there to Gibeah, a band of prophets met him, and the spirit of God rushed upon him, so that he joined them in their prophetic state. 11 When all who had known him previously saw him in a prophetic state among the prophets, they said to one another, "What has happened to the son of Kish? Is Saul also among the prophets?" 12 And someone from that district added, "And who is their father?" Thus the proverb arose, "Is Saul also among the prophets?" 13 When he came out of the prophetic state, he went home.

14 Saul's uncle inquired of him and his servant, "Where have you been?" Saul replied, "To look for the asses. When we could not find them, we went to Samuel." 15 Then Saul's uncle said, "Tell me, then, what Samuel said to you." 16 Saul said to his uncle, "He assured us that the asses had been found." But he mentioned nothing to him of what Samuel had said about the kingship.

17 Samuel called the people together to the LORD at Mizpah 18 and addressed the Israelites: "Thus says the LORD, the God of Israel, 'It was I who brought Israel up from Egypt and delivered you from the power of the Egyptians and from the power of all the kingdoms that oppressed you.' 19 But today you have rejected your God, who delivers you from all your evils and calamities, by saying to him, 'Not so, but you must appoint a king over us.' Now, therefore, take your stand before the LORD according to tribes and families." 20 So Samuel had all the tribes of Israel come forward, and the tribe of Benjamin was chosen. 21 Next he had the tribe of Benjamin come forward in clans, and the clan of Matri was chosen, and finally Saul, son of Kish, was chosen. But they looked for him in vain. 22 Again they consulted the LORD, "Has he come here?" The LORD answered, "He is hiding among the baggage." 23 They ran to bring him from there; and when he stood among the people, he was head and shoulders above all the crowd. 24 Samuel said to all the people, "Do you see the man whom the LORD has chosen? There is none like him among all the people!" Then all the people shouted, "Long live the king!"

25 Samuel next explained to the people the law of royalty and wrote it in a book, which he placed in the presence of the LORD. This done, Samuel dismissed the people, each to his own place. 26 Saul also went home to Gibeah, accompanied by warriors whose hearts the LORD had touched. 27 But certain worthless men said, "How can this fellow save us?" They despised him and brought him no present.

day . . . 10 From there, they came to Gibeah: and there was a group of prophets coming to meet him! The spirit of God seized on him and he fell into ecstasy with them. 11 Seeing him prophesying with the prophets, all the people who had known him previously said to one another, 'What has come over the son of Kish? Is Saul one of the prophets too?' 12 And one of the local people retorted, 'But who is their father?' Hence the origin of the proverb: Is Saul one of the prophets too?

13 When he came out of his ecstasy, he went into Gibeah. 14 Saul's uncle asked him and his servant, 'Where have you been?' 'Looking for the donkeys,' he replied, 'and when we could not find them anywhere, we went to Samuel.' 15 Saul's uncle said, 'Tell me please what Samuel said to you.' 16 Saul said to his uncle, 'He merely told us that the donkeys were already found,' but did not mention anything that Samuel had said about the kingship.

17 Samuel summoned the people to Yahweh at Mizpah 18 and said to the Israelites, 'Yahweh, God of Israel, says this, "I brought Israel out of Egypt and delivered you from the power of the Egyptians and of all the kingdoms that were oppressing you." 19 But today you have rejected your God, him who saves you from all your difficulties and troubles; and you have said, "No, you must set a king over us." Very well, take your positions before Yahweh, tribe by tribe and clan by clan.'

20 Samuel then made all the tribes of Israel come forward, and the lot indicated the tribe of Benjamin. 21 He then made the tribe of Benjamin come forward clan by clan, and the lot indicated the clan of Matri; he then made the clan of Matri come forward one by one, and the lot indicated Saul son of Kish, but when they looked for him, he was not to be found. 22 Again they consulted Yahweh, 'Has the man come here?' Yahweh replied, 'There he is, hiding among the baggage.' 23 So they ran and fetched him out and, as he stood among the people, he was head and shoulders taller than any of them. 24 Samuel then said to all the people, 'You have seen the man whom Yahweh has chosen, and that among the whole people he has no equal.' And all the people acclaimed him, shouting, 'Long live the king!'

25 Samuel then explained the king's constitutional position to the people and inscribed this in a book which he placed before Yahweh. Samuel then sent all the people away, everyone back to his home. 26 Saul too went home to Gibeah and with him went those strong men whose hearts God had touched. 27 But there were some scoundrels who said, 'How can this fellow save us?' These treated him with contempt and offered him no present.

11 About a month later, Nahash the Ammonite went up and laid siege to Jabesh-gilead. All the men of Jabesh begged Nahash, "Make a treaty with us, and we will be your subjects." 2 But Nahash the Ammonite replied, "This is my condition for a treaty with you: I must gouge out every man's right eye, that I may thus bring ignominy on all Israel." 3 The elders of Jabesh said to him: "Give us

11 About a month later, Nahash the Ammonite marched up and laid siege to Jabesh in Gilead. All the men of Jabesh said to Nahash, 'Make a treaty with us and we will be your subjects.' 2 Nahash the Ammonite replied, 'I shall make a treaty with you only on this condition, that I put out all your right eyes, and I will make it a taunt to the whole of Israel.' 3 The elders of Jabesh said to him,

seven days' respite that we may send messengers through all the territory of Israel. Then, if there is no one to save us, we will give ourselves up to you." 4 When the messengers came to Gibeah of Saul, they reported the matter in the hearing of the people; and all the people wept aloud.

5 Now Saul was coming from the field behind the oxen; and Saul said, "What is the matter with the people, that they are weeping?" So they told him the message from the inhabitants of Jabesh. 6 And the spirit of God came upon Saul in power when he heard these words, and his anger was greatly kindled. 7 He took a yoke of oxen, and cut them in pieces and sent them throughout all the territory of Israel by messengers, saying, "Whoever does not come out after Saul and Samuel, so shall it be done to his oxen!" Then the dread of the LORD fell upon the people, and they came out as one. 8 When he mustered them at Bezek, those from Israel were three hundred thousand, and those from Judah seventy[t] thousand. 9 They said to the messengers who had come, "Thus shall you say to the inhabitants of Jabesh-gilead: 'Tomorrow, by the time the sun is hot, you shall have deliverance.'" When the messengers came and told the inhabitants of Jabesh, they rejoiced. 10 So the inhabitants of Jabesh said, "Tomorrow we will give ourselves up to you, and you may do to us whatever seems good to you." 11 The next day Saul put the people in three companies. At the morning watch they came into the camp and cut down the Ammonites until the heat of the day; and those who survived were scattered, so that no two of them were left together.

12 The people said to Samuel, "Who is it that said, 'Shall Saul reign over us?' Give them to us so that we may put them to death." 13 But Saul said, "No one shall be put to death this day, for today the LORD has brought deliverance to Israel."

14 Samuel said to the people, "Come, let us go to Gilgal and there renew the kingship." 15 So all the people went to Gilgal, and there they made Saul king before the LORD in Gilgal. There they sacrificed offerings of well-being before the LORD, and there Saul and all the Israelites rejoiced greatly.

12 Samuel said to all Israel, "I have listened to you in all that you have said to me, and have set a king over you. 2 See, it is the king who leads you now; I am old and gray, but my sons are with you. I have led you from my youth until this day. 3 Here I am; testify against me before the LORD and before his anointed. Whose ox have I taken? Or whose donkey have I taken? Or whom have I defrauded? Whom have I oppressed? Or from whose hand have I taken a bribe to blind my eyes with it? Testify against me[u] and I will restore it to you." 4 They said, "You have not defrauded us or oppressed us or taken anything from the hand of anyone." 5 He said to them, "The LORD is witness against you, and his anointed is witness this day, that you have not found anything in my hand." And they said, "He is witness."

6 Samuel said to the people, "The LORD is witness, who[v] appointed Moses and Aaron and brought your ancestors up out of the land of Egypt. 7 Now therefore take your stand, so that I may enter into judgment with you before the LORD, and I will declare to you[w] all the saving deeds of the LORD that he performed for you and for your ancestors. 8 When Jacob went into Egypt and the Egyptians oppressed them,[x] then your ancestors cried to the LORD and the LORD sent Moses and Aaron, who brought forth your ancestors out of Egypt, and settled them in this place. 9 But they

said, 'Give us seven days' respite to send messengers throughout Israel and then, if no one relieves us, we shall surrender to you.' 4 The messengers came to Gibeah, where Saul lived, and delivered their message, and all the people broke into lamentation and weeping. 5 Saul was just coming from the field, driving in the oxen, and asked why the people were lamenting; and they told him what the men of Jabesh had said. 6 When Saul heard this, the spirit of God suddenly seized him; in anger 7 he took a pair of oxen, cut them in pieces, and sent messengers with the pieces all through Israel to proclaim that the same would be done to the oxen of any man who did not follow Saul and Samuel to battle. The fear of the LORD fell upon the people and they came out to a man. 8 Saul mustered them in Bezek, three hundred thousand men from Israel and thirty thousand from Judah. 9 He said to the messengers, 'Tell the men of Jabesh-gilead, "Victory will be yours tomorrow by the time the sun is hot."'

When they received this message, the men of Jabesh took heart; 10 but they said to Nahash, 'Tomorrow we shall surrender to you, and then you may deal with us as you think fit.' 11 Next day Saul with his men in three columns forced a way right into the enemy camp during the morning watch and massacred the Ammonites until the day grew hot; those who survived were scattered until no two of them were left together.

12 The people said to Samuel, 'Who said that Saul should not reign over us? Hand the men over to us to be put to death.' 13 But Saul said, 'No man is to be put to death on a day when the LORD has won such a victory in Israel.' 14 Samuel said to the people, 'Let us now go to Gilgal and there establish the kingship anew.' 15 So they all went to Gilgal and invested Saul there as king in the presence of the LORD. They sacrificed shared-offerings before the LORD, and Saul and all the Israelites celebrated with great joy.

12 SAMUEL thus addressed the assembled Israelites: 'I have listened to your request and installed a king to rule over you. 2 The king is now your leader, while I am old and white-haired and my sons are with you; but I have been your leader from my youth to the present. 3 Here I am! Cite your complaints against me in the presence of the LORD and of his anointed one. Whose ox have I taken, whose donkey have I taken? Whom have I wronged, whom have I oppressed? From whom have I taken a bribe to turn a blind eye? Tell me, and I shall make restitution to you.' 4 They answered, 'You have not wronged us, you have not oppressed us, nor have you taken anything from anyone.' 5 Samuel said to them, 'This day the LORD is witness among you, his anointed king is witness, that you have found nothing in my hands.' They said, 'He is witness.'

6 Samuel said to the people, 'The LORD is witness, the LORD who appointed Moses and Aaron and brought your fathers up from Egypt. 7 Now stand up, and here in the presence of the LORD I shall put the case against you and recite all the victories which he has won for you and for your forefathers. 8 After Jacob and his sons had gone down to Egypt and suffered at the hands of the Egyptians, your forefathers appealed to the LORD for help, and he sent Moses and Aaron, who brought them out of Egypt and settled them in this place. 9 But they forgot the LORD their God, and

---

[t] Q Ms Gk: MT thirty   [u] Gk: Heb lacks Testify against me
[v] Gk: Heb lacks is witness, who   [w] Gk: Heb lacks and I will declare to you   [x] Gk: Heb lacks and the Egyptians oppressed them

11:9 He: so Gk; Heb. They.   12:6 is witness: so Gk; Heb. omits.
12:7 and recite: so Gk; Heb. omits.   12:8 and his sons: so Gk; Heb. omits. suffered . . . Egyptians: so Gk; Heb. omits.

seven days to send messengers throughout the territory of Israel. If no one rescues us, we will surrender to you." 4 When the messengers arrived at Gibeah of Saul, they related the news to the people, all of whom wept aloud. 5 Just then Saul came in from the field, behind his oxen. "Why are the people weeping?" he asked. The message of the inhabitants of Jabesh was repeated to him. 6 As he listened to this report, the spirit of God rushed upon him and he became very angry. 7 Taking a yoke of oxen, he cut them into pieces, which he sent throughout the territory of Israel by couriers with the message, "If anyone does not come out to follow Saul [and Samuel], the same as this will be done to his oxen!" In dread of the LORD, the people turned out to a man. 8 When he reviewed them in Bezek, there were three hundred thousand Israelites and seventy thousand Judahites.

9 To the messengers who had come he said, "Tell the inhabitants of Jabesh-gilead that tomorrow, while the sun is hot, they will be rescued." The messengers came and reported this to the inhabitants of Jabesh, who were jubilant, 10 and said to Nahash, "Tomorrow we will surrender to you, and you may do whatever you please with us." 11 On the appointed day, Saul arranged his troops in three companies and invaded the camp during the dawn watch. They slaughtered Ammonites until the heat of the day; by then the survivors were so scattered that no two were left together.

12 The people then said to Samuel: "Who questioned whether Saul should rule over us? Hand over the men and we will put them to death." 13 But Saul broke in to say, "No man is to be put to death this day, for today the LORD has saved Israel." 14 Samuel said to the people, "Come, let us go to Gilgal to inaugurate the kingdom there." 15 So all the people went to Gilgal, where, in the presence of the LORD, they made Saul king. They also sacrificed peace offerings there before the LORD, and Saul and all the Israelites celebrated the occasion with great joy.

12 Samuel addressed all Israel: "I have granted your request in every respect," he said. "I have set a king over you 2 and now the king is your leader. As for me, I am old and gray, and have sons among you. I have lived with you from my youth to the present day. 3 Here I stand! Answer me in the presence of the LORD and of his anointed. Whose ox have I taken? Whose ass have I taken? Whom have I cheated? Whom have I oppressed? From whom have I accepted a bribe and overlooked his guilt? I will make restitution to you." 4 They replied, "You have neither cheated us, nor oppressed us, nor accepted anything from anyone." 5 So he said to them, "The LORD is witness against you this day, and his anointed as well, that you have found nothing in my possession." "He is witness," they agreed.

6 Continuing, Samuel said to the people: "The LORD is witness, who appointed Moses and Aaron, and who brought your fathers up from the land of Egypt. 7 Now, therefore, take your stand, and I shall arraign you before the LORD, and shall recount for you all the acts of mercy the LORD has done for you and your fathers. 8 When Jacob and his sons went to Egypt and the Egyptians oppressed them, your fathers appealed to the LORD, who sent Moses and Aaron to bring them out of Egypt, and he gave them this place to live in. 9 But they forgot the LORD their God; and he allowed

'Give us seven days' grace while we send messengers throughout the territory of Israel, and if no one comes to our help, we will come out to you.' 4 The messengers came to Gibeah of Saul, and reported this to the people, and all the people wept aloud.

5 Now Saul was just then coming in from the fields behind his oxen, and he said, 'What is wrong? Why are the people weeping?' They explained to him what the men of Jabesh had said. 6 And the spirit of Yahweh seized on Saul when he heard these words, and he fell into a fury. 7 He took a yoke of oxen, cut them into pieces and sent these by messengers throughout the territory of Israel with these words, 'Anyone who will not march with Saul will have the same done to his oxen!' At this, a panic from Yahweh swept on the people and they marched out as one man. 8 Saul inspected them at Bezek; there were three hundred thousand of Israel and thirty thousand of Judah. 9 Then he said to the messengers who had come, 'This is what you are to say to the people of Jabesh in Gilead, "Tomorrow, by the time that the sun is hot, help will reach you." ' The messengers went and reported this to the people of Jabesh who were overjoyed; 10 they said to Nahash, 'Tomorrow we shall come out to you and you can do whatever you like to us.'

11 The next day, Saul disposed the army in three contingents, which burst into the middle of the camp during the dawn watch and slaughtered the Ammonites until high noon. The survivors were so scattered that no two of them were left together.

12 The people then said to Samuel, 'Who said, "Must we have Saul reigning over us?" Hand the men over, for us to put them to death.' 13 'No one must be put to death today,' Saul said, 'for today Yahweh has intervened to rescue Israel.' 14 Samuel then said to the people, 'Let us now go to Gilgal and reaffirm the monarchy there.'

15 The people then all went to Gilgal. And there, at Gilgal, they proclaimed Saul king before Yahweh; they offered communion sacrifices before Yahweh, and there Saul and all the people of Israel gave themselves over to great rejoicing.

12 Samuel said to all Israel, 'I have faithfully done all that you asked of me, and have appointed you a king. 2 In future, the king will lead you. As for me, I am old and grey, and in any case you have my sons. I have been your leader ever since I was young until today. 3 Here I am. Bear witness against me before Yahweh and before his anointed. Whose ox have I taken? Whose donkey have I taken? Have I wronged or oppressed anyone? Have I taken a consideration from anyone for looking the other way? If so, I will make amends.' 4 They said, 'You have neither wronged nor oppressed us nor accepted anything from anyone.' 5 He said to them, 'Yahweh is your witness and his anointed is witness today that you have found nothing in my hands?' They replied, 'He is witness.'

6 Samuel then said to the people, 'Yahweh is witness, he who raised up Moses and Aaron and who brought your ancestors out of Egypt. 7 So now, stay where you are, while I plead with you before Yahweh and remind you of all the saving acts which he has done for you and for your ancestors. 8 After Jacob had arrived in Egypt, the Egyptians oppressed them, and your ancestors cried to Yahweh. Yahweh then sent Moses and Aaron, who brought your ancestors out of Egypt and gave them a settled home here. 9 They then

forgot the LORD their God; and he sold them into the hand of Sisera, commander of the army of King Jabin of *y* Hazor, and into the hand of the Philistines, and into the hand of the king of Moab; and they fought against them. 10 Then they cried to the LORD, and said, 'We have sinned, because we have forsaken the LORD, and have served the Baals and the Astartes; but now rescue us out of the hand of our enemies, and we will serve you.' 11 And the LORD sent Jerubbaal and Barak, *z* and Jephthah, and Samson, *a* and rescued you out of the hand of your enemies on every side; and you lived in safety. 12 But when you saw that King Nahash of the Ammonites came against you, you said to me, 'No, but a king shall reign over us,' though the LORD your God was your king. 13 See, here is the king whom you have chosen, for whom you have asked; see, the LORD has set a king over you. 14 If you will fear the LORD and serve him and heed his voice and not rebel against the commandment of the LORD, and if both you and the king who reigns over you will follow the LORD your God, it will be well; 15 but if you will not heed the voice of the LORD, but rebel against the commandment of the LORD, then the hand of the LORD will be against you and your king. *b* 16 Now therefore take your stand and see this great thing that the LORD will do before your eyes. 17 Is it not the wheat harvest today? I will call upon the LORD, that he may send thunder and rain; and you shall know and see that the wickedness that you have done in the sight of the LORD is great in demanding a king for yourselves." 18 So Samuel called upon the LORD, and the LORD sent thunder and rain that day; and all the people greatly feared the LORD and Samuel.

19 All the people said to Samuel, "Pray to the LORD your God for your servants, so that we may not die; for we have added to all our sins the evil of demanding a king for ourselves." 20 And Samuel said to the people, "Do not be afraid; you have done all this evil, yet do not turn aside from following the LORD, but serve the LORD with all your heart; 21 and do not turn aside after useless things that cannot profit or save, for they are useless. 22 For the LORD will not cast away his people, for his great name's sake, because it has pleased the LORD to make you a people for himself. 23 Moreover as for me, far be it from me that I should sin against the LORD by ceasing to pray for you; and I will instruct you in the good and the right way. 24 Only fear the LORD, and serve him faithfully with all your heart; for consider what great things he has done for you. 25 But if you still do wickedly, you shall be swept away, both you and your king."

13 Saul was . . . *c* years old when he began to reign; and he reigned . . . and two *d* years over Israel. 2 Saul chose three thousand out of Israel; two thousand were with Saul in Michmash and the hill country of Bethel, and a thousand were with Jonathan in Gibeah of Benjamin; the rest of the people he sent home to their tents. 3 Jonathan defeated the garrison of the Philistines that was at Geba; and the Philistines heard of it. And Saul blew the trumpet throughout all the land, saying, "Let the Hebrews hear!" 4 When all Israel heard that Saul had defeated the garrison of the Philistines, and also that Israel had become odious to the Philistines, the people were called out to join Saul at Gilgal.

he abandoned them to Sisera, commander-in-chief of King Jabin of Hazor, to the Philistines, and to the king of Moab, and they had to fight against them. 10 Then your forefathers cried to the LORD for help: "We have sinned in forsaking the LORD and worshipping the baalim and the ashtaroth. But now, deliver us from our enemies, and we shall worship you." 11 The LORD sent Jerubbaal and Barak, Jephthah and Samson, and delivered you from your enemies on every side; and you lived in security.

12 'Yet when you saw Nahash king of the Ammonites coming against you, you said to me, "No, let us have a king to rule over us," although the LORD your God was your king. 13 Now here is the king you chose; you asked for a king, and the LORD has set one over you. 14 If you will revere the LORD and give true and loyal service, if you do not rebel against his commands, and if you and the king who reigns over you are faithful to the LORD your God, well and good; 15 but if you do not obey the LORD, and if you rebel against his commands, then his hand will be against you and against your king.

16 'Stand now, and witness the great wonder which the LORD will perform before your eyes. 17 It is now wheat harvest. When I call upon the LORD and he sends thunder and rain, you will know and see how displeasing it was to the LORD for you to ask for a king.' 18 So Samuel called to the LORD and he sent thunder and rain that day; and all the people were in great fear of the LORD and of Samuel.

19 The people all said to Samuel, 'Pray for us your servants to the LORD your God, to save us from death; for we have added to all our other sins the great wickedness of asking for a king.' 20 Samuel answered, 'Do not be afraid; although you have been so wicked, do not give up the worship of the LORD, but serve him with all your heart. 21 Do not turn to the worship of sham gods which can neither help nor save, because they are a sham. 22 For his great name's sake the LORD will not cast you off, because he has resolved to make you his own people.

23 'As for me, God forbid that I should sin against the LORD by ceasing to pray for you. I shall show you what is right and good: 24 to revere the LORD and worship him faithfully with all your heart; for consider what great things he has done for you. 25 But if you persist in wickedness, both you and your king will be swept away.'

13 SAUL was thirty years old when he became king, and he reigned over Israel for twenty-two years. 2 Saul picked three thousand men from Israel, two thousand to be with him in Michmash and the hill-country of Bethel and a thousand to be with Jonathan in Gibeah of Benjamin; the rest of the army he dismissed to their homes.

3 Jonathan defeated the Philistine garrison in Geba, and the news spread among the Philistines that the Hebrews were in revolt. Saul sounded the trumpet all through the land; 4 and when the Israelites heard that Saul had defeated a Philistine garrison and that the very name of Israel was offensive among the Philistines, they answered the call to arms and rallied to Saul at Gilgal.

12:9 **King Jabin of:** *so Gk; Heb. omits.* 12:11 **Barak:** *so Gk; Heb.* Bedan. **Samson:** *so Gk (Luc.); Heb.* Samuel. 12:15 **your king:** *so Gk; Heb.* your fathers. 13:1 **thirty years:** *so some Gk MSS; Heb.* a year. **twenty-two:** *prob. rdg; Heb.* two. 13:2 **Gibeah:** Geba *in verse 3.* 13:3 **garrison:** *or* governors. **that . . . revolt:** *prob. rdg; Heb. has* saying, Let the Hebrews hear *after through the land.* 13:4 **they . . . Gilgal:** *or* they were summoned to follow Saul to Gilgal.

---

y Gk: Heb lacks *King Jabin of*   *z* Gk Syr: Heb *Bedan*   *a* Gk: Heb *Samuel*   *b* Gk: Heb *and your ancestors*   *c* The number is lacking in the Heb text (the verse is lacking in the Septuagint).   *d* Two is not the entire number; something has dropped out.

them to fall into the clutches of Sisera, the captain of the army of Jabin, king of Hazor, into the grasp of the Philistines, and into the grip of the king of Moab, who made war against them. 10 Each time they appealed to the LORD and said, 'We have sinned in forsaking the LORD and worshiping Baals and Ashtaroth; but deliver us now from the power of our enemies, and we will worship you.' 11 Accordingly, the LORD sent Jerubbaal, Barak, Jephthah, and Samson; he delivered you from the power of your enemies on every side, so that you were able to live in security. 12 Yet, when you saw Nahash, king of the Ammonites, advancing against you, you said to me, 'Not so, but a king must rule us,' even though the LORD your God is your king.

13 "Now you have the king you want, a king the LORD has given you. 14 If you fear the LORD and worship him, if you are obedient to him and do not rebel against the LORD's command, if both you and the king who rules you follow the LORD your God — well and good. 15 But if you do not obey the LORD and if you rebel against his command, the LORD will deal severely with you and your king, and destroy you. 16 Now then, stand ready to witness the great marvel the LORD is about to accomplish before your eyes. 17 Are we not in the harvest time for wheat? Yet I shall call to the LORD, and he will send thunder and rain. Thus you will see and understand how greatly the LORD is displeased that you have asked for a king." 18 Samuel then called to the LORD, and the LORD sent thunder and rain that day.

As a result, all the people dreaded the LORD and Samuel. 19 They said to Samuel, "Pray to the LORD your God for us, your servants, that we may not die for having added to all our other sins the evil of asking for a king." 20 "Do not fear," Samuel answered them. "It is true you have committed all this evil; still, you must not turn from the LORD, but must worship him with your whole heart. 21 Do not turn to meaningless idols which can neither profit nor save; they are nothing. 22 For the sake of his own great name the LORD will not abandon his people, since the LORD himself chose to make you his people. 23 As for me, far be it from me to sin against the LORD by ceasing to pray for you and to teach you the good and right way. 24 But you must fear the LORD and worship him faithfully with your whole heart; keep in mind the great things he has done among you. 25 If instead you continue to do evil, both you and your king shall perish."

13 [Saul was . . . years old when he became king and he reigned . . . (two) years over Israel.]
2 Saul chose three thousand men of Israel, of whom two thousand remained with him in Michmash and in the hill country of Bethel, and one thousand were with Jonathan in Gibeah of Benjamin. He sent the rest of the people back to their tents. 3 Now Jonathan overcame the Philistine garrison which was in Gibeah, and the Philistines got word of it. Then Saul sounded the horn throughout the land, with a proclamation, "Let the Hebrews hear!" 4 Thus all Israel learned that Saul had overcome the garrison of the Philistines and that Israel had brought disgrace upon the Philistines; and the soldiers were called up to Saul in Gilgal. 5 The

forgot Yahweh their God and he sold them into the power of Sisera, general of the army of Hazor, and also into the power of the Philistines and of the king of Moab, who made war on them. 10 They cried to Yahweh, "We have sinned," they said, "for we have deserted Yahweh and served the Baals and the Astartes. Rescue us now from the power of our enemies, and we will serve you." 11 Yahweh then sent Jerubbaal, Barak, Jephthah, and Samuel. He rescued you from the power of the enemies surrounding you, and you lived in security.

12 'But when you saw Nahash, king of the Ammonites, marching on you, you said to me, "No, we must have a king to rule us" — although Yahweh your God is your king. 13 So, here is the king whom you have chosen; Yahweh has appointed you a king. 14 If you fear and serve Yahweh and obey his voice and do not rebel against his commands, and if both you and the king who rules you follow Yahweh your God, all will be well. 15 But if you do not obey Yahweh's voice but rebel against his commands, Yahweh's hand will be against you and against your king.

16 'Stay where you are and see the wonder which Yahweh will do before your eyes. 17 Is it not now the wheat harvest? I shall call on Yahweh and he will send thunder and rain, so that you may clearly understand what a very wicked thing you have done, in Yahweh's eyes, by asking for a king.' 18 Samuel then called on Yahweh, and Yahweh sent thunder and rain the same day, and all the people held Yahweh and Samuel in great awe. 19 They all said to Samuel, 'Pray for your servants to Yahweh your God, to save us from death; for to all our sins we have added this wrong of asking for a king.'

20 Samuel said to the people, 'Do not be afraid. Although you have done all these wicked things, do not withdraw your allegiance from Yahweh. Instead, serve Yahweh with all your heart. 21 Do not transfer your allegiance to useless idols which, being useless, are futile and cannot save anybody; 22 Yahweh, for the sake of his great name, will not desert his people, for it has pleased Yahweh to make you his people. 23 For my part, far be it from me to sin against Yahweh by ceasing to pray for you or to instruct you in the good and right way. 24 Fear none but Yahweh, and serve him faithfully with all your heart, bearing in mind the wonder which he has just performed. But, if you persist in wickedness, you and your king will perish.'

13 Saul was . . . years old when he became king, and reigned over Israel for . . . years. 2 Saul selected three thousand men of Israel; two thousand of them were with Saul at Michmash and in the highlands of Bethel, and one thousand with Jonathan at Geba of Benjamin; the rest of the people Saul sent home, everyone to his tent.

3 Jonathan killed the Philistine governor stationed at Gibeah and the Philistines were informed that the Hebrews had risen in revolt. Saul had the trumpet sounded throughout the country, 4 and all Israel heard the news, 'Saul has killed the Philistine governor, and now Israel has antagonised the Philistines.' So all the people rallied behind Saul at Gilgal.

13, 1: A formula like that of 2 Sm 5, 4 was introduced here at some time; but the age of Saul when he became king remains a blank, and the two years assigned for his reign in the received text cannot be correct. Tradition (Acts 13, 21) offers the round number, "forty years."

NEW REVISED STANDARD VERSION

5 The Philistines mustered to fight with Israel, thirty thousand chariots, and six thousand horsemen, and troops like the sand on the seashore in multitude; they came up and encamped at Michmash, to the east of Beth-aven. 6 When the Israelites saw that they were in distress (for the troops were hard pressed), the people hid themselves in caves and in holes and in rocks and in tombs and in cisterns. 7 Some Hebrews crossed the Jordan to the land of Gad and Gilead. Saul was still at Gilgal, and all the people followed him trembling.

8 He waited seven days, the time appointed by Samuel; but Samuel did not come to Gilgal, and the people began to slip away from Saul.e 9 So Saul said, "Bring the burnt offering here to me, and the offerings of well-being." And he offered the burnt offering. 10 As soon as he had finished offering the burnt offering, Samuel arrived; and Saul went out to meet him and salute him. 11 Samuel said, "What have you done?" Saul replied, "When I saw that the people were slipping away from me, and that you did not come within the days appointed, and that the Philistines were mustering at Michmash, 12 I said, 'Now the Philistines will come down upon me at Gilgal, and I have not entreated the favor of the LORD'; so I forced myself, and offered the burnt offering." 13 Samuel said to Saul, "You have done foolishly; you have not kept the commandment of the LORD your God, which he commanded you. The LORD would have established your kingdom over Israel forever, 14 but now your kingdom will not continue; the LORD has sought out a man after his own heart; and the LORD has appointed him to be ruler over his people, because you have not kept what the LORD commanded you." 15 And Samuel left and went on his way from Gilgal.f The rest of the people followed Saul to join the army; they went up from Gilgal toward Gibeah of Benjamin.g

Saul counted the people who were present with him, about six hundred men. 16 Saul, his son Jonathan, and the people who were present with them stayed in Geba of Benjamin; but the Philistines encamped at Michmash. 17 And raiders came out of the camp of the Philistines in three companies; one company turned toward Ophrah, to the land of Shual, 18 another company turned toward Beth-horon, and another company turned toward the mountainh that looks down upon the valley of Zeboim toward the wilderness.

19 Now there was no smith to be found throughout all the land of Israel; for the Philistines said, "The Hebrews must not make swords or spears for themselves"; 20 so all the Israelites went down to the Philistines to sharpen their plowshare, mattocks, axes, or sickles;i 21 The charge was two-thirds of a shekelj for the plowshares and for the mattocks, and one-third of a shekel for sharpening the axes and for setting the goads.k 22 So on the day of the battle neither sword nor spear was to be found in the possession of any of the people with Saul and Jonathan; but Saul and his son Jonathan had them.

23 Now a garrison of the Philistines had gone out to **14** the pass of Michmash. 1 One day Jonathan son of Saul said to the young man who carried his armor, "Come, let us go over to the Philistine garrison on the other side." But he did not tell his father. 2 Saul was staying in the outskirts of Gibeah under the pomegranate tree that is at Migron; the troops that were with him were about six hundred men, 3 along with

REVISED ENGLISH BIBLE

5 The Philistines mustered to attack Israel; they had thirty thousand chariots and six thousand horse, with infantry as countless as sand on the seashore. They went up and camped at Michmash, to the east of Beth-aven. 6 The Israelites found themselves in sore straits, for the army was hard pressed, so they hid themselves in caves and holes and among the rocks, in pits and cisterns. 7 Some of them crossed the Jordan into the district of Gad and Gilead, but Saul remained at Gilgal, and all his followers were in a state of alarm. 8 He waited seven days for his meeting with Samuel, but Samuel failed to appear, and when the people began to drift away, 9 Saul said, 'Bring me the whole-offering and the shared-offerings,' and he offered up the whole-offering. 10 Saul had just finished the sacrifice, when Samuel arrived, and he went out to greet him. 11 Samuel said, 'What have you done?' Saul answered, 'I saw that the people were drifting away from me, and you yourself had not come at the time fixed, and the Philistines were mustering at Michmash; 12 and I thought, "The Philistines will now fall on me at Gilgal, and I have not ensured the LORD's favour"; so I felt compelled to make the whole-offering myself.' 13 Samuel said to Saul, 'You have acted foolishly! You have not kept the command laid on you by the LORD your God; if you had, he would have established your dynasty over Israel for all time. 14 But now your line will not endure; the LORD will seek out a man after his own heart, and appoint him prince over his people, because you have not kept the LORD's command.'

15 Without more ado Samuel left Gilgal and went on his way. The rest of the people followed Saul, as he moved from Gilgal towards the enemy. At Gibeah of Benjamin he mustered his followers; they were about six hundred men. 16 Saul, his son Jonathan, and their men took up their quarters in Gibeah of Benjamin, while the Philistines were encamped in Michmash. 17 Raiding parties went out from the Philistine camp in three directions. One party headed towards Ophrah in the district of Shual, 18 another towards Beth-horon, and the third towards the range of hills overlooking the valley of Zeboim and the wilderness beyond.

19 No blacksmith was to be found in the whole of Israel, for the Philistines were determined to prevent the Hebrews from making swords and spears. 20 The Israelites had all to go down to the Philistines for their ploughshares, mattocks, axes, and sickles to be sharpened. 21 The charge was two thirds of a shekel for ploughshares and mattocks, and one third of a shekel for sharpening the axes and pointing the goads. 22 So when war broke out the followers of Saul and Jonathan had neither sword nor spear; only Saul and Jonathan carried arms.

23 The Philistines had posted a company of troops to hold **14** the pass of Michmash. 1 and one day Saul's son Jonathan said to his armour-bearer, 'Come, let us go over to the Philistine outpost across there.' He did not tell his father, 2 who at the time had his tent under the pomegranate tree at Migron on the outskirts of Gibeah; with him were about six hundred men. 3 The ephod was carried by Ahijah son of Ahitub,

---

e Heb him   f Gk: Heb *went up from Gilgal to Gibeah of Benjamin*
g Gk: Heb lacks *The rest . . . of Benjamin*   h Cn Compare Gk: Heb
toward the border   i Gk: Heb *plowshare*   j Heb *was a pim*
k Cn: Meaning of Heb uncertain

13:7 **but . . . alarm:** *or* but Saul was still at Gilgal, and all the army joined him there.   13:15 **and went . . . enemy:** *prob. rdg, cp.*
Gk; Heb. omits.   13:16 **Gibeah:** *so Aram.* (Targ.); *Heb.* Geba.
13:20 **and sickles:** *so Gk; Heb.* and ploughshares.   13:21 **one third . . . goads:** *prob. rdg; Heb.* obscure.

Philistines also assembled for battle, with three thousand chariots, six thousand horsemen, and foot soldiers as numerous as the sands of the seashore. Moving up against Israel, they encamped in Michmash, east of Beth-aven. 6 Some Israelites, aware of the danger and of the difficult situation, hid themselves in caves, in thickets, among rocks, in caverns, and in cisterns, 7 and other Hebrews passed over the Jordan into the land of Gad and Gilead. Saul, however, held out at Gilgal, although all his followers were seized with fear. 8 He waited seven days — the time Samuel had determined. When Samuel did not arrive at Gilgal, the men began to slip away from Saul. 9 He then said, "Bring me the holocaust and peace offerings," and he offered up the holocaust.

10 He had just finished this offering when Samuel arrived. Saul went out to greet him, 11 and Samuel asked him, "What have you done?" Saul replied: "When I saw that the men were slipping away from me, since you had not come by the specified time, and with the Philistines assembled at Michmash, 12 I said to myself, 'Now the Philistines will come down against me at Gilgal, and I have not yet sought the LORD's blessing.' So in my anxiety I offered up the holocaust." 13 Samuel's response was: "You have been foolish! Had you kept the command the LORD your God gave you, the LORD would now establish your kingship in Israel as lasting; 14 but as things are, your kingdom shall not endure. The LORD has sought out a man after his own heart and has appointed him commander of his people, because you broke the LORD's command."

15 Then Samuel set out from Gilgal and went his own way; but the rest of the people went up after Saul to meet the soldiers, going from Gilgal to Gibeah of Benjamin. Saul then numbered the soldiers he had with him, who were about six hundred. 16 Saul, his son Jonathan, and the soldiers they had with them were now occupying Geba of Benjamin, and the Philistines were encamped at Michmash. 17 Meanwhile, raiders left the camp of the Philistines in three bands. One band took the Ophrah road toward the district of Shual; 18 another turned in the direction of Beth-horon; and the third took the road for Geba that overlooks the Valley of the Hyenas toward the desert.

19 Not a single smith was to be found in the whole land of Israel, for the Philistines had said, "Otherwise the Hebrews will make swords or spears." 20 All Israel, therefore, had to go down to the Philistines to sharpen their plowshares, mattocks, axes, and sickles. 21 The price for the plowshares and mattocks was two-thirds of a shekel, and a third of a shekel for sharpening the axes and for setting the ox-goads. 22 And so on the day of battle neither sword nor spear could be found in the possession of any of the soldiers with Saul or Jonathan. Only Saul and his son Jonathan had them.

23 An outpost of the Philistines had pushed forward to the pass of Michmash.

14 One day Jonathan, son of Saul, said to his armor-bearer, "Come, let us go over to the Philistine outpost on the other side." But he did not inform his father. 2 (Saul's command post was under the pomegranate tree near the threshing floor on the outskirts of Geba; those with him numbered about six hundred men. 3 Ahijah, son of

5 The Philistines mustered to make war on Israel, three thousand chariots, six thousand horse and a force as numerous as the sand on the seashore. They came up and pitched camp at Michmash, to the east of Beth-Aven. 6 When the Israelites saw that their plight was desperate, being so hard pressed, the people hid in caves, in holes, in crevices, in vaults, in wells. 7 Some also crossed the Jordan fords into the territory of Gad and Gilead.

Saul was still at Gilgal and all the people who followed him were trembling. 8 He waited for seven days, the period fixed by Samuel, but Samuel did not come to Gilgal, and the army, deserting Saul, began dispersing. 9 Saul then said, 'Bring me the burnt offering and the communion sacrifices.' And he presented the burnt offering. 10 Just as he had finished presenting the burnt offering, Samuel arrived, and Saul went out to meet and greet him. 11 Samuel said, 'What have you been doing?' Saul replied, 'I saw the army deserting me and dispersing, and you had not come at the time fixed, while the Philistines were mustering at Michmash. 12 So I thought: Now the Philistines are going to fall on me at Gilgal and I have not implored the favour of Yahweh. So I felt obliged to make the burnt offering myself.' 13 Samuel said to Saul, 'You have acted like a fool. You have not obeyed the order which Yahweh your God gave you. Otherwise, Yahweh would have confirmed your sovereignty over Israel for ever. 14 But now your sovereignty will not last; Yahweh has discovered a man after his own heart and designated him as leader of his people, since you have not carried out what Yahweh ordered you.' 15 Samuel then got up and left Gilgal to continue his journey.

Those people remaining followed Saul as he went to join the warriors, and went from Gilgal to Geba of Benjamin. Saul reviewed the force that was with him; there were about six hundred men.

16 Saul, his son Jonathan, and the force that was with them took up their quarters in Geba of Benjamin while the Philistines camped at Michmash. 17 The raiding company sallied out of the Philistine camp in three groups: one group made for Ophrah in the territory of Shual; 18 one group made for Beth-Horon; and one group made for the high ground overlooking the Valley of the Hyenas, in the direction of the desert.

19 There was not a single blacksmith throughout the territory of Israel, the Philistines' reasoning being, 'We do not want the Hebrews making swords or spears.' 20 Hence, the Israelites were all in the habit of going down individually to the Philistines to sharpen their ploughshares, axes, mattocks and scythes. 21 The price was two-thirds of a shekel for ploughshares and axes, and one-third for sharpening mattocks and straightening goads. 22 So it was that on the day of the battle, no one in the army with Saul and Jonathan was equipped with either sword or spear; only Saul and his son Jonathan were so equipped.

23 A Philistine unit set out for the Pass of Michmash.

14 One day, Jonathan son of Saul said to his armour-bearer, 'Come on, let us go across to the Philistine outpost over on the other side.' But he did not inform his father. 2 Saul was on the outskirts of Geba, sitting under the pomegranate tree that stands near the threshing-floor; the force with him numbered about six hundred men. 3 Ahijah

Ahijah son of Ahitub, Ichabod's brother, son of Phinehas son of Eli, the priest of the LORD in Shiloh, carrying an ephod. Now the people did not know that Jonathan had gone. 4 In the pass,*l* by which Jonathan tried to go over to the Philistine garrison, there was a rocky crag on one side and a rocky crag on the other; the name of the one was Bozez, and the name of the other Seneh. 5 One crag rose on the north in front of Michmash, and the other on the south in front of Geba.

6 Jonathan said to the young man who carried his armor, "Come, let us go over to the garrison of these uncircumcised; it may be that the LORD will act for us; for nothing can hinder the LORD from saving by many or by few." 7 His armor-bearer said to him, "Do all that your mind inclines to.*m* I am with you; as your mind is, so is mine."*n* 8 Then Jonathan said, "Now we will cross over to those men and will show ourselves to them. 9 If they say to us, 'Wait until we come to you,' then we will stand still in our place, and we will not go up to them. 10 But if they say, 'Come up to us,' then we will go up; for the LORD has given them into our hand. That will be the sign for us." 11 So both of them showed themselves to the garrison of the Philistines; and the Philistines said, "Look, Hebrews are coming out of the holes where they have hidden themselves." 12 The men of the garrison hailed Jonathan and his armor-bearer, saying, "Come up to us, and we will show you something." Jonathan said to his armor-bearer, "Come up after me; for the LORD has given them into the hand of Israel." 13 Then Jonathan climbed up on his hands and feet, with his armor-bearer following after him. The Philistines*o* fell before Jonathan, and his armor-bearer, coming after him, killed them. 14 In that first slaughter Jonathan and his armor-bearer killed about twenty men within an area about half a furrow long in an acre*p* of land. 15 There was a panic in the camp, in the field, and among all the people; the garrison and even the raiders trembled; the earth quaked; and it became a very great panic.

16 Saul's lookouts in Gibeah of Benjamin were watching as the multitude was surging back and forth.*q* 17 Then Saul said to the troops that were with him, "Call the roll and see who has gone from us." When they had called the roll, Jonathan and his armor-bearer were not there. 18 Saul said to Ahijah, "Bring the ark*r* of God here." For at that time the ark*r* of God went with the Israelites. 19 While Saul was talking to the priest, the tumult in the camp of the Philistines increased more and more; and Saul said to the priest, "Withdraw your hand." 20 Then Saul and all the people who were with him rallied and went into the battle; and every sword was against the other, so that there was very great confusion. 21 Now the Hebrews who previously had been with the Philistines and had gone up with them into the camp turned and joined the Israelites who were with Saul and Jonathan. 22 Likewise, when all the Israelites who had gone into hiding in the hill country of Ephraim heard that the Philistines were fleeing, they too followed closely after them in the battle. 23 So the LORD gave Israel the victory that day.

The battle passed beyond Beth-aven, and the troops with Saul numbered altogether about ten thousand men. The battle spread out over the hill country of Ephraim.

24 Now Saul committed a very rash act on that day.*s* He had laid an oath on the troops, saying, "Cursed be anyone who eats food before it is evening and I have avenged on my enemies." So none of the troops tasted food. 25 All the troops*t* came upon a honeycomb; and there was honey on the ground. 26 When the troops came upon the

Ichabod's brother, son of Phinehas son of Eli, the priest of the LORD at Shiloh. Nobody knew that Jonathan had gone. 4 On either side of the pass through which Jonathan sought to make his way to the Philistine post stood two sharp columns of rock, called Bozez and Seneh; 5 one of them was on the north towards Michmash, and the other on the south towards Geba. 6 Jonathan said to his armour-bearer, 'Let us go over and pay a visit to the post of the uncircumcised yonder. Perhaps the LORD will do something for us. Nothing can stop him from winning a victory, by many or by few.' 7 The armour-bearer answered, 'Do what you will, go ahead; I am with you whatever you do.' 8 Jonathan said, 'We shall cross over and let the men see us. 9 If they say, "Stay there till we come to you," then we shall stay where we are and not go up to them. 10 But if they say, "Come up to us," we shall go up; that will be the proof that the LORD has given them into our power.' 11 The two showed themselves to the Philistine outpost. 'Look!' said the Philistines. 'Hebrews coming out of the holes where they have been hiding!' 12 And they called across to Jonathan and his armour-bearer, 'Come up to us; we shall show you something.' Jonathan said to the armour-bearer, 'Come on, the LORD has put them into Israel's power.' 13 Jonathan climbed up on hands and feet, and the armour-bearer followed him. The Philistines fell before Jonathan, and the armour-bearer, coming behind, dispatched them. 14 In that first attack Jonathan and his armour-bearer killed about twenty of them, like men cutting a furrow across a half-acre field. 15 Terror spread throughout the army in the camp and in the field; the men at the post and the raiding parties were terrified. The very ground quaked, and there was great panic.

16 Saul's men on the watch in Gibeah of Benjamin saw the mob of Philistines surging to and fro in confusion. 17 Saul ordered his forces to call the roll to find out who was missing and, when it was called, they found that Jonathan and his armour-bearer were absent. 18 Saul said to Ahijah, 'Bring forward the ephod,' for it was he who at that time carried the ephod before Israel. 19 While Saul was speaking, the confusion in the Philistine camp kept increasing, and he said to the priest, 'Hold your hand.' 20 Then Saul and all his men made a concerted rush for the battlefield, where they found the enemy in complete disorder, every man's sword against his fellow. 21 Those Hebrews who up to now had been under the Philistines, and had been with them in camp, changed sides and joined the Israelites under Saul and Jonathan. 22 When all the Israelites in hiding in the hill-country of Ephraim heard that the Philistines were in flight, they also joined in and set off in close pursuit. 23 That day the LORD delivered Israel, and the fighting passed on beyond Beth-aven.

24 The Israelites had been driven to exhaustion on that day. Saul had issued this warning to the troops: 'A curse on any man who takes food before nightfall and before I have taken vengeance on my enemies.' So no one tasted any food. 25 There was honeycomb in the countryside; 26 but

---

l Heb *Between the passes*   *m* Gk: Heb *Do all that is in your mind.
Turn*   *n* Gk: Heb lacks *so is mine*   *o* Heb *They*   *p* Heb *yoke*
q Gk: Heb *they went and there*   *r* Gk *the ephod*   *s* Gk: Heb *The
Israelites were distressed that day*   *t* Heb *land*

14:4 **Bozez:** *that is* Shining. **Seneh:** *that is* Bramble Bush.
14:14 **like men cutting:** *so Syriac; Heb.* as in half of.   14:16 **to
and fro:** *so Gk; Heb.* and he went thither.   14:18 **'Bring . . .
Israel:** *so Gk; Heb.* 'Bring forward the Ark of God,' for the Ark of
God was on that day and the Israelites.   14:21 **changed sides:** *so
Gk; Heb.* round and also.   14:25 **There was honeycomb:** *prob.
rdg; Heb.* All the land went into the forest, and there was honey.

NEW AMERICAN BIBLE

Ahitub, brother of Ichabod, who was the son of Phinehas, son of Eli, the priest of the LORD at Shiloh, was wearing the ephod.) Nor did the soldiers know that Jonathan had gone. 4 Flanking the ravine through which Jonathan intended to get over to the Philistine outpost there was a rocky crag on each side, one called Bozez, the other Seneh. 5 One crag was to the north, toward Michmash, the other to the south, toward Geba. 6 Jonathan said to his armor-bearer: "Come, let us go over to that outpost of the uncircumcised. Perhaps the LORD will help us, because it is no more difficult for the LORD to grant victory through a few than through many." 7 His armor-bearer replied, "Do whatever you are inclined to do; I will match your resolve." 8 Jonathan continued: "We shall go over to those men and show ourselves to them. 9 If they say to us, 'Stay there until we can come to you,' we shall stop where we are; we shall not go up to them. 10 But if they say, 'Come up to us,' we shall go up, because the LORD has delivered them into our grasp. That will be our sign." 11 Accordingly, the two of them appeared before the outpost of the Philistines, who said, "Look, some Hebrews are coming out of the holes where they have been hiding." 12 The men of the outpost called to Jonathan and his armor-bearer. "Come up here," they said, "and we will teach you a lesson." So Jonathan said to his armor-bearer, "Climb up after me, for the LORD has delivered them into the grasp of Israel." 13 Jonathan clambered up with his armor-bearer behind him; as the Philistines turned to flee him, he cut them down, and his armor-bearer followed him and finished them off. 14 In this first exploit Jonathan and his armor-bearer slew about twenty men within half a furlong. 15 Then panic spread to the army and to the countryside, and all the soldiers, including the outpost and the raiding parties, were terror-stricken. The earth also shook, so that the panic was beyond human endurance.

16 The lookouts of Saul in Geba of Benjamin saw that the enemy camp had scattered and were running about in all directions. 17 Saul said to those around him, "Count the troops and find out if any of us are missing." When they had investigated, they found Jonathan and his armor-bearer missing. 18 Saul then said to Ahijah, "Bring the ephod here." (Ahijah was wearing the ephod in front of the Israelites at that time.) 19 While Saul was speaking to the priest, the tumult in the Philistine camp kept increasing. So he said to the priest, "Withdraw your hand." 20 And Saul and all his men shouted and rushed into the fight, where the Philistines, wholly confused, were thrusting swords at one another. 21 In addition, the Hebrews who had previously sided with the Philistines and had gone up with them to the camp, turned to join the Israelites under Saul and Jonathan. 22 Likewise, all the Israelites who were hiding in the hill country of Ephraim, on hearing that the Philistines were fleeing, pursued them in the rout. 23 Thus the LORD saved Israel that day.

The battle continued past Beth-horon; 24 the whole people, about ten thousand combatants, were with Saul, and there was scattered fighting in every town in the hill country of Ephraim. And Saul swore a very rash oath that day, putting the people under this ban: "Cursed be the man who takes food before evening, before I am able to avenge myself on my enemies." So none of the people tasted food. 25 Indeed, there was a honeycomb lying on the ground,

NEW JERUSALEM BIBLE

son of Ahitub, brother of Ichabod, son of Phinehas, son of Eli, the priest of Yahweh at Shiloh, was carrying the ephod.f The force did not know that Jonathan had left.

4 In the pass that Jonathan was trying to cross to reach the Philistine outpost, there is a rocky spur on one side and a rocky spur on the other; one is called Bozez, the other Seneh. 5 The first spur stands to the north facing Michmash, the other to the south facing Geba. 6 Jonathan said to his armour-bearer, 'Come on, let us go across to these uncircumcised people's outpost; perhaps Yahweh will do something for us, for Yahweh is free to grant deliverance through a few men, just as much as through many.' 7 His armour-bearer replied, 'Do exactly as you think. I am with you; our hearts are as one.' 8 Jonathan then said, 'Look, we will go across to these people and let ourselves be seen. 9 If they say, "Do not move until we come to you," we shall stay where we are and not go up to them. 10 But if they say, "Come up to us," we shall go up, for that will be the sign for us that Yahweh has given them into our power.'

11 When the two of them let themselves be seen by the Philistine outpost, the Philistines said, 'Look, the Hebrews are coming out of the holes where they have been hiding.' 12 The men of the outpost then hailed Jonathan and his armour-bearer. 'Come up to us,' they said, 'we have something to tell you.' Jonathan then said to his armour-bearer, 'Follow me up; Yahweh has given them into the power of Israel.' 13 Jonathan clambered up on hands and feet, with his armour-bearer behind him; the Philistines fell at Jonathan's onslaught, and his armour-bearer, coming behind, finished them off. 14 This first killing made by Jonathan and his armour-bearer accounted for about twenty men . . .

15 There was panic in the camp, in the field and throughout the army; outpost and raiding company too were panic-stricken; the earth quaked: it was a panic from Yahweh. 16 Saul's look-out men in Geba of Benjamin could see the camp scattering in all directions. 17 Saul then said to the force that was with him, 'Call the roll and see who has left us.' So they called the roll, and Jonathan and his armour-bearer were missing.

18 Saul then said to Ahijah, 'Bring the ephod,' since he was the man who carried the ephod in Israel. 19 But while Saul was speaking to the priest, the turmoil in the Philistine camp grew worse and worse; and Saul said to the priest, 'Withdraw your hand.' 20 Saul and the whole force with him then formed up and advanced to where the fighting was going on: and there they all were, drawing their swords on one another in wild confusion. 21 Those Hebrews who had earlier taken service with the Philistines and had accompanied them into camp, now defected to the Israelites who were with Saul and Jonathan. 22 Similarly, all those Israelites who had been hiding in the highlands of Ephraim, hearing that the Philistines were on the run, chased after them and joined in the fight. 23 That day Yahweh gave Israel the victory.

The fighting reached the other side of Beth-Horon. 24 As the men of Israel were hard pressed that day, Saul pronounced this imprecation over the people, 'A curse on anyone who eats food before evening, before I have taken revenge on my enemies!' So none of the people so much as tasted food.

25 Now there was a honeycomb out in the open. 26 The

_f_ **14** See note to 2:28.

honeycomb, the honey was dripping out; but they did not put their hands to their mouths, for they feared the oath. 27 But Jonathan had not heard his father charge the troops with the oath; so he extended the staff that was in his hand, and dipped the tip of it in the honeycomb, and put his hand to his mouth; and his eyes brightened. 28 Then one of the soldiers said, "Your father strictly charged the troops with an oath, saying, 'Cursed be anyone who eats food this day.' And so the troops are faint." 29 Then Jonathan said, "My father has troubled the land; see how my eyes have brightened because I tasted a little of this honey. 30 How much better if today the troops had eaten freely of the spoil taken from their enemies; for now the slaughter among the Philistines has not been great.

31 After they had struck down the Philistines that day from Michmash to Aijalon, the troops were very faint; 32 so the troops flew upon the spoil, and took sheep and oxen and calves, and slaughtered them on the ground; and the troops ate them with the blood. 33 Then it was reported to Saul, "Look, the troops are sinning against the LORD by eating with the blood." And he said, "You have dealt treacherously; roll a large stone before me here."u 34 Saul said, "Disperse yourselves among the troops, and say to them, 'Let all bring their oxen or their sheep, and slaughter them here, and eat; and do not sin against the LORD by eating with the blood.' " So all of the troops brought their oxen with them that night, and slaughtered them there. 35 And Saul built an altar to the LORD; it was the first altar that he built to the LORD.

36 Then Saul said, "Let us go down after the Philistines by night and despoil them until the morning light; let us not leave one of them." They said, "Do whatever seems good to you." But the priest said, "Let us draw near to God here." 37 So Saul inquired of God, "Shall I go down after the Philistines? Will you give them into the hand of Israel?" But he did not answer him that day. 38 Saul said, "Come here, all you leaders of the people; and let us find out how this sin has arisen today. 39 For as the LORD lives who saves Israel, even if it is in my son Jonathan, he shall surely die!" But there was no one among all the people who answered him. 40 He said to all Israel, "You shall be on one side, and I and my son Jonathan will be on the other side." The people said to Saul, "Do what seems good to you." 41 Then Saul said, "O LORD God of Israel, why have you not answered your servant today? If this guilt is in me or in my son Jonathan, O LORD God of Israel, give Urim; but if this guilt is in your people Israel,v give Thummim." And Jonathan and Saul were indicated by the lot, but the people were cleared. 42 Then Saul said, "Cast the lot between me and my son Jonathan." And Jonathan was taken.

43 Then Saul said to Jonathan, "Tell me what you have done." Jonathan told him, "I tasted a little honey with the tip of the staff that was in my hand; here I am, I will die." 44 Saul said, "God do so to me and more also; you shall surely die, Jonathan!" 45 Then the people said to Saul, "Shall Jonathan die, who has accomplished this great victory in Israel? Far from it! As the LORD lives, not one hair of his head shall fall to the ground; for he has worked with God today." So the people ransomed Jonathan, and he did not die. 46 Then Saul withdrew from pursuing the Philistines; and the Philistines went to their own place.

47 When Saul had taken the kingship over Israel, he fought against all his enemies on every side—against Moab, against the Ammonites, against Edom, against the kings of Zobah, and against the Philistines; wherever he turned he routed them. 48 He did valiantly, and struck down

when his men came upon it, dripping with honey though it was, not one of them put his hand to his mouth for fear of the curse. 27 Jonathan, however, had not heard his father's interdict to the army, and he stretched out the stick that was in his hand, dipped the end of it in the honeycomb, put it to his mouth, and was refreshed. 28 One of the people said to him, 'Your father strictly forbade this, saying, "A curse on the man who eats food today!" And the men are faint.' 29 Jonathan said, 'My father has done the people great harm; see how I am refreshed by this mere taste of honey. 30 How much better if the army had eaten today whatever they took from their enemies by way of spoil! Then there would indeed have been a great slaughter of Philistines.'

31 Israel defeated the Philistines that day, and pursued them from Michmash to Aijalon. But the troops were so faint with hunger 32 that they turned to plunder and seized sheep, cattle, and calves; they slaughtered them on the bare ground, and ate the meat with the blood in it. 33 Someone told Saul that the people were sinning against the LORD by eating meat with the blood in it. 'This is treacherous behaviour!' cried Saul. 'Roll a great stone here at once.' 34 He then said, 'Go about among the troops and tell them to bring their oxen and sheep, and to slaughter and eat them here; and so they will not sin against the LORD by eating meat with the blood in it.' So as night fell each man came, driving his own ox, and slaughtered it there. 35 Thus Saul came to erect an altar to the LORD, and this was the first altar to the LORD that he erected.

36 Saul said, 'Let us go down and make a night attack on the Philistines and harry them till daylight; we will not spare a single one of them.' His men answered, 'Do what you think best,' but the priest said, 'Let us first consult God.' 37 Saul enquired of God, 'Shall I pursue the Philistines? Will you put them into Israel's power?' But this time he received no answer. 38 So he said, 'Let all the leaders of the people come forward and let us find out where the sin lies this day. 39 As the LORD, the deliverer of Israel, lives, even if the sin lies in my son Jonathan, he shall die.' Not a soul answered him. 40 Then he said to the Israelites, 'All of you stand on one side, and I and my son Jonathan will stand on the other.' His men answered, 'Do what you think best.' 41 Saul said to the LORD the God of Israel, 'Why have you not answered your servant today? LORD God of Israel, if this guilt lies in me or in my son Jonathan, let the lot be Urim; if it lies in your people Israel, let it be Thummim.' Jonathan and Saul were taken, and the people were cleared. 42 Then Saul said, 'Cast lots between me and my son Jonathan'; and Jonathan was taken.

43 Saul said to Jonathan, 'Tell me what you have done.' Jonathan told him, 'True, I did taste a little honey on the tip of my stick. Here I am; I am ready to die.' 44 Then Saul swore a solemn oath that Jonathan should die. 45 But his men said to Saul, 'Shall Jonathan die, Jonathan who has won this great victory in Israel? God forbid! As the LORD lives, not a hair of his head shall fall to the ground, for he has been at work with God today.' So the army delivered Jonathan and he did not die. 46 Saul broke off the pursuit of the Philistines, who then made their way home.

47 When Saul had made his throne secure in Israel, he gave battle to his enemies on every side, the Moabites, the Ammonites, the Edomites, the king of Zobah, and the Philistines; and wherever he turned he met with victory. 48 He

---

u Gk: Heb *me this day*   v Vg Compare Gk: Heb *41 Saul said to the LORD, the God of Israel*

14:41 **Why . . . people Israel:** *so Gk; Heb. omits.*   14:47 **king:** *so Gk; Heb.* kings.

26 and when the soldiers came to the comb the swarm had left it; yet no one would raise a hand to his mouth from it, because the people feared the oath.

27 Jonathan, who had not heard that his father had put the people under oath, thrust out the end of the staff he was holding and dipped it into the honey. Then he raised it to his mouth and his eyes lit up. 28 At this one of the soldiers spoke up: "Your father put the people under a strict oath, saying, 'Cursed be the man who takes food this day!' As a result the people are weak." 29 Jonathan replied: "My father brings trouble to the land. Look how bright my eyes are from this small taste of honey I have had. 30 What is more, if the people had eaten freely today of their enemy's booty when they came across it, would not the slaughter of the Philistines by now have been the greater for it?"

31 After the Philistines were routed that day from Michmash to Aijalon, the people were completely exhausted. 32 So they pounced upon the spoil and took sheep, oxen and calves, slaughtering them on the ground and eating the flesh with blood. 33 Informed that the people were sinning against the LORD by eating the flesh with blood, Saul said: "You have broken faith. Roll a large stone here for me." 34 He continued: "Mingle with the people and tell each of them to bring his ox or his sheep to me. Slaughter it here and then eat, but you must not sin against the LORD by eating the flesh with blood." So everyone brought to the LORD whatever ox he had seized, and they slaughtered them there; 35 and Saul built an altar to the LORD—this was the first time he built an altar to the LORD.

36 Then Saul said, "Let us go down in pursuit of the Philistines by night, to plunder among them until daybreak and to kill them all off." They replied, "Do what you think best." But the priest said, "Let us consult God." 37 So Saul inquired of God: "Shall I go down in pursuit of the Philistines? Will you deliver them into the power of Israel?" But he received no answer on this occasion. 38 Saul then said, "Come here, all officers of the army. We must investigate and find out how this sin was committed today. 39 As the LORD lives who has given victory to Israel, even if my son Jonathan has committed it, he shall surely die!" But none of the people answered him. 40 So he said to all Israel, "Stand on one side, and I and my son Jonathan will stand on the other." The people responded, "Do what you think best." 41 And Saul said to the LORD, the God of Israel: "Why did you not answer your servant this time? If the blame for this resides in me or my son Jonathan, LORD, God of Israel, respond with Urim; but if this guilt is in your people Israel, respond with Thummim." Jonathan and Saul were designated, and the people went free. 42 Saul then said, "Cast lots between me and my son Jonathan." And Jonathan was designated. 43 Saul said to Jonathan, "Tell me what you have done." Jonathan replied, "I only tasted a little honey from the end of the staff I was holding. Am I to die for this?" 44 Saul said, "May God do thus and so to me if you do not indeed die, Jonathan!"

45 But the army said to Saul: "Is Jonathan to die, though it was he who brought Israel this great victory? This must not be! As the LORD lives, not a single hair of his head shall fall to the ground, for God was with him in what he did today!" Thus the soldiers were able to rescue Jonathan from death. 46 After that Saul gave up the pursuit of the Philistines, who returned to their own territory.

47 After taking over the kingship of Israel, Saul waged war on all their surrounding enemies—Moab, the Ammonites, Aram, Beth-rehob, the king of Zobah, and the Philistines. Wherever he turned, he was successful 48 and fought

people came to the honeycomb, the honey was dripping out, but no one put a hand to his mouth, the people being in awe of the oath. 27 Jonathan, however, not having heard his father bind the people with the oath, reached with the end of the stick which he was carrying, thrust it into the honeycomb and put it to his mouth; whereupon his eyes grew brighter. 28 One of the people then spoke up. 'Your father', he said, 'has bound the people with this oath: "A curse on anyone who eats anything today." ' 29 'My father has brought trouble on the country,' Jonathan replied. 'See how much brighter my eyes are for having eaten this mouthful of honey. 30 By the same token, if the people had been allowed to eat some of the booty which they had captured from the enemy today, would not the defeat of the Philistines have been all the greater?'

31 That day the Philistines were beaten from Michmash all the way to Aijalon, until the people were utterly exhausted. 32 The people flung themselves on the booty and, taking sheep, bullocks and calves, slaughtered them there on the ground and ate them with the blood. 33 Saul was informed, 'The people are sinning against Yahweh by eating with the blood!' He said, 'You have not kept faith! Roll me a large stone here!' 34 Saul then said, 'Scatter among the people and say, "Everyone is to bring his bullock or his sheep to me here." You will slaughter them here and eat, and not sin against Yahweh by eating with the blood.' Each individual brought what he happened to have that night, and they all slaughtered in the same place. 35 Saul built an altar to Yahweh; it was the first altar he had built to Yahweh.

36 Saul said, 'Let us go down under cover of dark and plunder the Philistines until dawn; we shall not leave one of them alive.' 'Do whatever you think right,' they replied. But the priest said, 'Let us approach God here.' 37 Saul consulted God, 'Shall I go down and pursue the Philistines? Will you hand them over to Israel?' But he gave him no reply that day. 38 Saul then said, 'Come forward, all you leaders of the people; consider carefully where today's sin may lie; 39 for as Yahweh lives who gives victory to Israel, even if the sin lies with Jonathan my son, he shall be put to death.' But not one out of all the people answered. 40 He then said to all Israel, 'Stand on one side, and I and Jonathan my son will stand on the other.' And the people replied to Saul, 'Do as you think right.' 41 Saul then said, 'Yahweh, God of Israel, why did you not answer your servant today? Yahweh, God of Israel, if the fault lies with me or with my son Jonathan, give *urim*: if the fault lies with your people Israel, give *thummim*.'g Jonathan and Saul were indicated and the people went free. 42 Saul said, 'Cast the lot between me and my son Jonathan,' and Jonathan was indicated.

43 'I only tasted a mouthful of honey off the end of the stick which I was carrying. But I am ready to die.' 44 Saul said, 'May God bring unnameable ills on me, and worse ones too, if you do not die, Jonathan!' 45 But the people said to Saul, 'Must Jonathan die after winning this great victory for Israel? We will never allow that! As Yahweh lives, not one hair of his head shall fall to the ground, for his deeds today have been done with the help of God.' And so the people ransomed Jonathan and he was not put to death.

46 Saul decided not to pursue the Philistines, and the Philistines retired to their own territory.

47 Saul consolidated his rule over Israel and made war on all his enemies on all fronts: on Moab, the Ammonites, Edom, the king of Zobah and the Philistines; whichever way he turned, he was victorious. 48 He did great deeds of

g 14 A simple yes/no answer is obtained by drawing one of the lots out of the *ephod*.

the Amalekites, and rescued Israel out of the hands of those who plundered them.

49 Now the sons of Saul were Jonathan, Ishvi, and Malchishua; and the names of his two daughters were these: the name of the firstborn was Merab, and the name of the younger, Michal. 50 The name of Saul's wife was Ahinoam daughter of Ahimaaz. And the name of the commander of his army was Abner son of Ner, Saul's uncle; 51 Kish was the father of Saul, and Ner the father of Abner was the son of Abiel.

52 There was hard fighting against the Philistines all the days of Saul; and when Saul saw any strong or valiant warrior, he took him into his service.

15 Samuel said to Saul, "The LORD sent me to anoint you king over his people Israel; now therefore listen to the words of the LORD. 2 Thus says the LORD of hosts, 'I will punish the Amalekites for what they did in opposing the Israelites when they came up out of Egypt. 3 Now go and attack Amalek, and utterly destroy all that they have; do not spare them, but kill both man and woman, child and infant, ox and sheep, camel and donkey.' "

4 So Saul summoned the people, and numbered them in Telaim, two hundred thousand foot soldiers, and ten thousand soldiers of Judah. 5 Saul came to the city of the Amalekites and lay in wait in the valley. 6 Saul said to the Kenites, "Go! Leave! Withdraw from among the Amalekites, or I will destroy you with them; for you showed kindness to all the people of Israel when they came up out of Egypt." So the Kenites withdrew from the Amalekites. 7 Saul defeated the Amalekites, from Havilah as far as Shur, which is east of Egypt. 8 He took King Agag of the Amalekites alive, but utterly destroyed all the people with the edge of the sword. 9 Saul and the people spared Agag, and the best of the sheep and of the cattle and of the fatlings, and the lambs, and all that was valuable, and would not utterly destroy them; all that was despised and worthless they utterly destroyed.

10 The word of the LORD came to Samuel: 11 "I regret that I made Saul king, for he has turned back from following me, and has not carried out my commands." Samuel was angry; and he cried out to the LORD all night. 12 Samuel rose early in the morning to meet Saul, and Samuel was told, "Saul went to Carmel, where he set up a monument for himself, and on returning he passed on down to Gilgal." 13 When Samuel came to Saul, Saul said to him, "May you be blessed by the LORD; I have carried out the command of the LORD." 14 But Samuel said, "What then is this bleating of sheep in my ears, and the lowing of cattle that I hear?" 15 Saul said, "They have brought them from the Amalekites; for the people spared the best of the sheep and the cattle, to sacrifice to the LORD your God; but the rest we have utterly destroyed." 16 Then Samuel said to Saul, "Stop! I will tell you what the LORD said to me last night." He replied, "Speak."

17 Samuel said, "Though you are little in your own eyes, are you not the head of the tribes of Israel? The LORD anointed you king over Israel. 18 And the LORD sent you on a mission, and said, 'Go, utterly destroy the sinners, the Amalekites, and fight against them until they are consumed.' 19 Why then did you not obey the voice of the LORD? Why did you swoop down on the spoil, and do what was evil in the sight of the LORD?" 20 Saul said to Samuel,

displayed his strength by defeating the Amalekites and freeing Israel from hostile raids.

49 Saul's sons were: Jonathan, Ishyo, and Malchishua. These were the names of his two daughters: Merab the elder and Michal the younger. 50 His wife was Ahinoam daughter of Ahimaaz, and his commander-in-chief was Abner, son of Saul's uncle, Ner; 51 Saul's father Kish and Abner's father Ner were sons of Abiel.

52 There was bitter warfare with the Philistines throughout Saul's lifetime; any strong man and any brave man that he found he took into his service.

15 SAMUEL said to Saul, 'The LORD sent me to anoint you king over his people Israel. Now listen to the voice of the LORD: 2 this is the very word of the LORD of Hosts: I shall punish the Amalekites for what they did to Israel, when they opposed them on their way up from Egypt. 3 Go now, fall upon the Amalekites, destroy them, and put their property under ban. Spare no one; put them all to death, men and women, children and babes in arms, herds and flocks, camels and donkeys.'

4 Saul called out the levy and reviewed them at Telaim: there were two hundred thousand foot-soldiers and another ten thousand from Judah. 5 When he reached the city of Amalek, he halted for a time in the valley. 6 Meanwhile he sent word to the Kenites to leave the Amalekites and come down, 'or', he said, 'I shall destroy you as well as them; but you were friendly to Israel as they came up from Egypt'. So the Kenites left the Amalekites.

7 Saul inflicted defeat on the Amalekites all the way from Havilah to Shur on the borders of Egypt. 8 Agag king of the Amalekites he took alive, but he destroyed all the people, putting them to the sword. 9 Saul and his army spared Agag and the best of the sheep and cattle, the fat beasts and the lambs, and everything worth keeping; these they were unwilling to destroy, but anything that was useless and of no value they destroyed.

10 The word of the LORD came to Samuel: 11 'I repent of having made Saul king, for he has turned away from me and has not obeyed my instructions.' Samuel was angry; all night long he cried aloud to the LORD. 12 Early next morning he went to meet Saul, but was told that he had gone to Carmel, for he had set up a monument to himself there, and then had turned and gone on down to Gilgal. 13 There Samuel found him, and Saul greeted him with the words, 'The LORD's blessing on you! I have carried out the LORD's instructions.' 14 'What then is this bleating of sheep in my ears?' demanded Samuel. 'How do I come to hear the lowing of cattle?' 15 Saul answered, 'The troops have taken them from the Amalekites. These are what they spared, the best of the sheep and cattle, to sacrifice to the LORD your God; the rest we completely destroyed.' 16 Samuel said to Saul, 'Be quiet! Let me tell you what the LORD said to me last night.' 'Tell me,' said Saul. 17 So Samuel went on, 'Once you thought little of yourself, but now you are head of the tribes of Israel. The LORD, who anointed you king over Israel, 18 charged you with the destruction of that wicked nation, the Amalekites; you were to go and wage war against them until you had wiped them out. 19 Why then did you not obey the LORD? Why did you swoop on the spoil, so doing what was wrong in the eyes of the LORD?' 20 Saul

14:49 **Ishyo**: *so Gk (Luc.); Heb.* Ishvi (Ishbosheth *in 2 Sam.* 2:8; Eshbaal *in 1 Chr.* 8:33). 14:51 **sons**: *prob. rdg; Heb.* son. 15:4 **another ... Judah**: *prob. rdg; Heb.* ten thousand with the men of Judah. 15:9 **the fat ... lambs**: *so Aram. (Targ.); Heb. obscure.*

bravely. He defeated Amalek and delivered Israel from the hands of those who were plundering them.

49 The sons of Saul were Jonathan, Ishvi, and Malchishua; his two daughters were named, the elder, Merob, and the younger, Michal. 50 Saul's wife, who was named Ahinoam, was the daughter of Ahimaaz. The name of his general was Abner, son of Saul's uncle, Ner; 51 Kish, Saul's father, and Ner, Abner's father, were sons of Abiel.

52 An unremitting war was waged against the Philistines during Saul's lifetime. When Saul saw any strong or brave man, he took him into his service.

15 Samuel said to Saul: "It was I the LORD sent to anoint you king over his people Israel. Now, therefore, listen to the message of the LORD. 2 This is what the LORD of hosts has to say: 'I will punish what Amalek did to Israel when he barred his way as he was coming up from Egypt. 3 Go, now, attack Amalek, and deal with him and all that he has under the ban. Do not spare him, but kill men and women, children and infants, oxen and sheep, camels and asses.'"

4 Saul alerted the soldiers, and at Telaim reviewed two hundred thousand foot soldiers and ten thousand men of Judah. 5 Saul went to the city of Amalek, and after setting an ambush in the wadi, 6 warned the Kenites: "Come! Leave Amalek and withdraw, that I may not have to destroy you with them, for you were kind to the Israelites when they came up from Egypt." After the Kenites left, 7 Saul routed Amalek from Havilah to the approaches of Shur, on the frontier of Egypt. 8 He took Agag, king of Amalek, alive, but on the rest of the people he put into effect the ban of destruction by the sword. 9 He and his troops spared Agag and the best of the fat sheep and oxen, and the lambs. They refused to carry out the doom on anything that was worthwhile, dooming only what was worthless and of no account.

10 Then the LORD spoke to Samuel: 11 "I regret having made Saul king, for he has turned from me and has not kept my command." At this Samuel grew angry and cried out to the LORD all night. 12 Early in the morning he went to meet Saul, but was informed that Saul had gone to Carmel, where he erected a trophy in his own honor, and that on his return he had passed on and gone down to Gilgal. 13 When Samuel came to him, Saul greeted him: "The LORD bless you! I have kept the command of the LORD." 14 But Samuel asked, "What, then, is the meaning of this bleating of sheep that comes to my ears, and the lowing of oxen that I hear?" 15 Saul replied: "They were brought from Amalek. The men spared the best sheep and oxen to sacrifice to the LORD, your God; but we have carried out the ban on the rest." 16 Samuel said to Saul: "Stop! Let me tell you what the LORD said to me last night." "Speak!" he replied. 17 Samuel then said: "Though little in your own esteem, are you not leader of the tribes of Israel? The LORD anointed you king of Israel 18 and sent you on a mission, saying, 'Go and put the sinful Amalekites under a ban of destruction. Fight against them until you have exterminated them.' 19 Why then have you disobeyed the LORD? You have pounced on the spoil, thus displeasing the LORD." 20 Saul answered

valour; he defeated the Amalekites and delivered Israel from those who used to pillage him.

49 Saul's sons were: Jonathan, Ishvi and Malchishua. The names of his two daughters were: the elder, Merab, and the younger, Michal. 50 The name of Saul's wife was Ahinoam daughter of Ahimaaz. The name of his army commander was Abner son of Ner, Saul's uncle. 51 Kish father of Saul, and Ner father of Abner were the sons of Abiel.

52 There was fierce warfare with the Philistines throughout Saul's life. Any strong or valiant man who caught Saul's eye, he recruited into his service.

15 Samuel said to Saul, 'I am the man whom Yahweh sent to anoint you as king of his people Israel, so now listen to the words of Yahweh. 2 This is what Yahweh Sabaoth says, "I intend to punish what Amalek did to Israel — laying a trap for him on the way as he was coming up from Egypt. 3 Now, go and crush Amalek; put him under the curse of destruction with all that he possesses. Do not spare him, but kill man and woman, babe and suckling, ox and sheep, camel and donkey."'

4 Saul summoned the people and reviewed them at Telaim: two hundred thousand foot soldiers (and ten thousand men of Judah). 5 Saul advanced on the town of Amalek and lay in ambush in the river bed. 6 Saul said to the Kenites, 'Go away, leave your homes among the Amalekites, in case I destroy you with them — you acted with faithful love towards all the Israelites when they were coming up from Egypt.' So the Kenites moved away from the Amalekites.

7 Saul then crushed the Amalekites, beginning at Havilah in the direction of Shur, which is to the east of Egypt. 8 He took Agag king of the Amalekites alive and, executing the curse of destruction, put all the people to the sword. 9 But Saul and the army spared Agag with the best of the sheep and cattle, the fatlings and lambs and all that was good. They did not want to consign these to the curse of destruction; they consigned only what was poor and worthless.

10 The word of Yahweh came to Samuel, 11 'I regret having made Saul king, since he has broken his allegiance to me and not carried out my orders.' Samuel was appalled and cried to Yahweh all night long.

12 In the morning, Samuel set off to find Saul. Samuel was told, 'Saul has been to Carmel, to raise himself a monument there, but now has turned about, moved on and gone down to Gilgal.' 13 When Samuel reached Saul, Saul said, 'May you be blessed by Yahweh! I have carried out Yahweh's orders.' 14 Samuel replied, 'Then what is this bleating of sheep in my ears and the lowing of cattle that I hear?' 15 Saul said, 'They have been brought from Amalek, the people having spared the best of the sheep and cattle to sacrifice them to Yahweh, your God; the rest we have consigned to the curse of destruction.'

16 Samuel then said to Saul, 'Stop! Let me tell you what Yahweh said to me last night.' He said, 'Go on.' 17 Samuel said, 'Small as you may be in your own eyes, are you not the leader of the tribes of Israel? Yahweh has anointed you as king of Israel. 18 When Yahweh sent you on a mission he said to you, "Go and put those sinners, the Amalekites, under the curse of destruction and make war on them until they are exterminated." 19 Why then did you not obey Yahweh's voice? Why did you fall on the booty and do what is wrong in Yahweh's eyes?' 20 Saul replied to Samuel, 'But

"I have obeyed the voice of the LORD, I have gone on the mission on which the LORD sent me, I have brought Agag the king of Amalek, and I have utterly destroyed the Amalekites. 21 But from the spoil the people took sheep and cattle, the best of the things devoted to destruction, to sacrifice to the LORD your God in Gilgal." 22 And Samuel said,
"Has the LORD as great delight in burnt offerings
and sacrifices,
as in obeying the voice of the LORD?
Surely, to obey is better than sacrifice,
and to heed than the fat of rams.
23 For rebellion is no less a sin than divination,
and stubbornness is like iniquity and idolatry.
Because you have rejected the word of the LORD,
he has also rejected you from being king."
24 Saul said to Samuel, "I have sinned; for I have transgressed the commandment of the LORD and your words, because I feared the people and obeyed their voice. 25 Now therefore, I pray, pardon my sin, and return with me, so that I may worship the LORD." 26 Samuel said to Saul, "I will not return with you; for you have rejected the word of the LORD, and the LORD has rejected you from being king over Israel." 27 As Samuel turned to go away, Saul caught hold of the hem of his robe, and it tore. 28 And Samuel said to him, "The LORD has torn the kingdom of Israel from you this very day, and has given it to a neighbor of yours, who is better than you. 29 Moreover the Glory of Israel will not recant[w] or change his mind; for he is not a mortal, that he should change his mind." 30 Then Saul[x] said, "I have sinned; yet honor me now before the elders of my people and before Israel, and return with me, so that I may worship the LORD your God." 31 So Samuel turned back after Saul; and Saul worshiped the LORD.
32 Then Samuel said, "Bring Agag king of the Amalekites here to me." And Agag came to him haltingly.[y] Agag said, "Surely this is the bitterness of death."[z] 33 But Samuel said,
"As your sword has made women childless,
so your mother shall be childless among
women."
And Samuel hewed Agag in pieces before the LORD in Gilgal.
34 Then Samuel went to Ramah; and Saul went up to his house in Gibeah of Saul. 35 Samuel did not see Saul again until the day of his death, but Samuel grieved over Saul. And the LORD was sorry that he had made Saul king over Israel.

16 The LORD said to Samuel, "How long will you grieve over Saul? I have rejected him from being king over Israel. Fill your horn with oil and set out; I will send you to Jesse the Bethlehemite, for I have provided for myself a king among his sons." 2 Samuel said, "How can I go? If Saul hears of it, he will kill me." And the LORD said, "Take a heifer with you, and say, 'I have come to sacrifice to the LORD.' 3 Invite Jesse to the sacrifice, and I will show you what you shall do; and you shall anoint for me the one whom I name to you." 4 Samuel did what the LORD commanded, and came to Bethlehem. The elders of the city came to meet him trembling, and said, "Do you come peaceably?" 5 He said, "Peaceably; I have come to sacrifice to the LORD; sanctify yourselves and come with me to the sacrifice." And he sanctified Jesse and his sons and invited them to the sacrifice.

answered, 'But I did obey the LORD; I went where the LORD sent me, and I have brought back Agag king of the Amalekites. 21 The rest of them I destroyed. Out of the spoil the troops took sheep and oxen, the choicest of the animals laid under ban, to sacrifice to the LORD your God at Gilgal.' 22 Samuel then said:
'Does the LORD desire whole-offerings and
sacrifices
as he desires obedience?
To obey is better than sacrifice,
and to listen to him better than the fat of rams.
23 Rebellion is as sinful as witchcraft,
arrogance as evil as idolatry.
Because you have rejected the word of the LORD,
he has rejected you as king.'
24 Saul said to Samuel, 'I have sinned. I have not complied with the LORD's command or with your instructions: I was afraid of the troops and gave in to them. 25 But now forgive my sin, I implore you, and come back with me, and I shall bow in worship before the LORD.' 26 Samuel answered, 'I shall not come back with you; you have rejected the word of the LORD and therefore the LORD has rejected you as king over Israel.' 27 As he turned to go, Saul caught the corner of his cloak and it tore. 28 And Samuel said to him, 'The LORD has torn the kingdom of Israel from your hand today and will give it to another, a better man than you. 29 God who is the Splendour of Israel does not deceive, nor does he change his mind, as a mortal might do.' 30 Saul pleaded, 'I have sinned; but honour me this once before the elders of my people and before Israel and come back with me, and I will bow in worship before the LORD our God.' 31 Samuel went back with Saul, and Saul worshipped the LORD.
32 Samuel said, 'Bring Agag king of the Amalekites.' So Agag came to him with faltering step and said, 'Surely the bitterness of death has passed.' 33 Samuel said,
'As your sword has made women childless,
so your mother will be childless among women.'
Then Samuel hewed Agag in pieces before the LORD at Gilgal.
34 Saul went to his own home at Gibeah, and Samuel went to Ramah; 35 and he never saw Saul again to his dying day, but he grieved for him, because the LORD had repented of having made him king over Israel.

16 THE LORD said to Samuel, 'How long will you grieve because I have rejected Saul as king of Israel? Fill your horn with oil and take it with you; I am sending you to Jesse of Bethlehem; for I have chosen myself a king from among his sons.' 2 Samuel answered, 'How can I go? If Saul hears of it, he will kill me.' 'Take a heifer with you,' said the LORD, 'say you have come to offer a sacrifice to the LORD, 3 and invite Jesse to the sacrifice; then I shall show you what you must do. You are to anoint for me the man whom I indicate to you.' 4 Samuel did as the LORD had told him, and went to Bethlehem, where the elders came in haste to meet him, saying, 'Why have you come? Is all well?' 5 'All is well,' said Samuel; 'I have come to sacrifice to the LORD. Purify yourselves and come with me to the sacrifice.' He himself purified Jesse and his sons and invited them to the sacrifice.

15:23 **as evil as:** *prob. rdg; Heb.* evil and. **idolatry:** *lit.* household gods; *Heb.* teraphim. 15:32 **with faltering step:** *prob. rdg, cp. Gk; Heb.* delicately. 16:3 **to the sacrifice:** *so Gk; Heb.* with the sacrifice. 16:5 **me to the sacrifice:** *so Lat.; Heb.* me with the sacrifice.

[w] Q Ms Gk: MT *deceive* [x] Heb *he* [y] Cn Compare Gk: Meaning of Heb uncertain [z] Q Ms Gk: MT *Surely the bitterness of death is past*

Samuel: "I did indeed obey the LORD and fulfill the mission on which the LORD sent me. I have brought back Agag, and I have destroyed Amalek under the ban. 21 But from the spoil the men took sheep and oxen, the best of what had been banned, to sacrifice to the LORD their God in Gilgal." 22 But Samuel said:

"Does the LORD so delight in holocausts
and sacrifices
as in obedience to the command of the LORD?
Obedience is better than sacrifice,
and submission than the fat of rams.
23 For a sin like divination is rebellion,
and presumption is the crime of idolatry.
Because you have rejected the command of
the LORD,
he, too, has rejected you as ruler."

24 Saul replied to Samuel: "I have sinned, for I have disobeyed the command of the LORD and your instructions. In my fear of the people, I did what they said. 25 Now forgive my sin, and return with me, that I may worship the LORD." 26 But Samuel said to Saul, "I will not return with you, because you rejected the command of the LORD and the LORD rejects you as king of Israel." 27 As Samuel turned to go, Saul seized a loose end of his mantle, and it tore off. 28 So Samuel said to him: "The LORD has torn the kingdom of Israel from you this day, and has given it to a neighbor of yours, who is better than you. 29 The Glory of Israel neither retracts nor repents, for he is not man that he should repent." 30 But he answered: "I have sinned, yet honor me now before the elders of my people and before Israel. Return with me that I may worship the LORD your God." 31 And so Samuel returned with him, and Saul worshiped the LORD.

32 Afterward Samuel commanded, "Bring Agag, king of Amalek, to me." Agag came to him struggling and saying, "So it is bitter death!" 33 And Samuel said,

"As your sword has made women childless,
so shall your mother be childless
among women."

Then he cut Agag down before the LORD in Gilgal.

34 Samuel departed for Ramah, while Saul went up to his home in Gibeah of Saul. 35 Never again, as long as he lived, did Samuel see Saul. Yet he grieved over Saul, because the LORD regretted having made him king of Israel.

16 The LORD said to Samuel: "How long will you grieve for Saul, whom I have rejected as king of Israel? Fill your horn with oil, and be on your way. I am sending you to Jesse of Bethlehem, for I have chosen my king from among his sons." 2 But Samuel replied: "How can I go? Saul will hear of it and kill me." To this the LORD answered: "Take a heifer along and say, 'I have come to sacrifice to the LORD.' 3 Invite Jesse to the sacrifice, and I myself will tell you what to do; you are to anoint for me the one I point out to you."

4 Samuel did as the LORD had commanded him. When he entered Bethlehem, the elders of the city came trembling to meet him and inquired, "Is your visit peaceful, O seer?" 5 He replied: "Yes! I have come to sacrifice to the LORD. So cleanse yourselves and join me today for the banquet." He also had Jesse and his sons cleanse themselves and invited them to the sacrifice. 6 As they came, he looked at Eliab and

I did obey Yahweh's voice. I went on the mission which Yahweh gave me; I brought back Agag king of the Amalekites; I put Amalek under the curse of destruction; 21 and from the booty the people have taken the best sheep and cattle of what was under the curse of destruction only to sacrifice them to Yahweh your God in Gilgal.' 22 To which, Samuel said:

Is Yahweh pleased by burnt offerings and sacrifices
or by obedience to Yahweh's voice?
Truly, obedience is better than sacrifice,
submissiveness than the fat of rams.
23 Rebellion is a sin of sorcery,
presumption a crime of idolatry!
'Since you have rejected Yahweh's word, he has rejected you as king.'

24 Saul then said to Samuel, 'I have sinned, having broken Yahweh's order and your instructions because I was afraid of the people and yielded to their demands. 25 Now, please forgive my sin and come back with me, so that I can worship Yahweh.' 26 Samuel said to Saul, 'I will not come back with you, since you have rejected Yahweh's word and Yahweh has rejected you as king of Israel.' 27 As Samuel turned away to leave, Saul caught at the hem of his cloak and it tore, 28 and Samuel said to him, 'Today Yahweh has torn the kingdom of Israel from you and given it to a neighbour of yours who is better than you.' 29 (The Glory of Israel, however, does not lie or go back on his word, not being human and liable to go back on his word.) 30 'I have sinned,' Saul said, 'but please still show me respect in front of my people's elders and in front of Israel, and come back with me, so that I can worship Yahweh your God.' 31 Samuel followed Saul back and Saul worshipped Yahweh.

32 Samuel then said, 'Bring me Agag king of the Amalekites!' Agag came towards him unsteadily saying, 'Truly death is bitter!' 33 Samuel said:

As your sword has left women childless,
so will your mother be left childless among
women!

Samuel then butchered Agag before Yahweh at Gilgal.

34 Samuel left for Ramah, and Saul went up home to Gibeah of Saul. 35 Samuel did not see Saul again till his dying day. Samuel indeed mourned over Saul, but Yahweh regretted having made Saul king of Israel.

16 Yahweh said to Samuel, 'How much longer do you mean to go on mourning over Saul, now that I myself have rejected him as ruler of Israel? Fill your horn with oil and go. I am sending you to Jesse of Bethlehem, for I have found myself a king from among his sons.' 2 Samuel replied, 'How can I go? When Saul hears of it he will kill me.' Yahweh then said, 'Take a heifer with you and say, "I have come to sacrifice to Yahweh." 3 Invite Jesse to the sacrifice, and I shall reveal to you what you must do; and you will anoint for me the one I indicate to you.'

4 Samuel did what Yahweh ordered and went to Bethlehem. The elders of the town came trembling to meet him and asked, 'Seer, is your coming favourable for us,' 5 'Yes,' he replied. 'I have come to sacrifice to Yahweh. Purify yourselves and come with me to the sacrifice.' He purified Jesse and his sons and invited them to the sacrifice.

| NEW REVISED STANDARD VERSION | REVISED ENGLISH BIBLE |

6 When they came, he looked on Eliab and thought, "Surely the LORD's anointed is now before the LORD."[a] 7 But the LORD said to Samuel, "Do not look on his appearance or on the height of his stature, because I have rejected him; for the LORD does not see as mortals see; they look on the outward appearance, but the LORD looks on the heart." 8 Then Jesse called Abinadab, and made him pass before Samuel. He said, "Neither has the LORD chosen this one." 9 Then Jesse made Shammah pass by. And he said, "Neither has the LORD chosen this one." 10 Jesse made seven of his sons pass before Samuel, and Samuel said to Jesse, "The LORD has not chosen any of these." 11 Samuel said to Jesse, "Are all your sons here?" And he said, "There remains yet the youngest, but he is keeping the sheep." And Samuel said to Jesse, "Send and bring him; for we will not sit down until he comes here." 12 He sent and brought him in. Now he was ruddy, and had beautiful eyes, and was handsome. The LORD said, "Rise and anoint him; for this is the one." 13 Then Samuel took the horn of oil, and anointed him in the presence of his brothers; and the spirit of the LORD came mightily upon David from that day forward. Samuel then set out and went to Ramah.

14 Now the spirit of the LORD departed from Saul, and an evil spirit from the LORD tormented him. 15 And Saul's servants said to him, "See now, an evil spirit from God is tormenting you. 16 Let our lord now command the servants who attend you to look for someone who is skillful in playing the lyre; and when the evil spirit from God is upon you, he will play it, and you will feel better." 17 So Saul said to his servants, "Provide for me someone who can play well, and bring him to me." 18 One of the young men answered, "I have seen a son of Jesse the Bethlehemite who is skillful in playing, a man of valor, a warrior, prudent in speech, and a man of good presence; and the LORD is with him." 19 So Saul sent messengers to Jesse, and said, "Send me your son David who is with the sheep." 20 Jesse took a donkey loaded with bread, a skin of wine, and a kid, and sent them by his son David to Saul. 21 And David came to Saul, and entered his service. Saul loved him greatly, and he became his armor-bearer. 22 Saul sent to Jesse, saying, "Let David remain in my service, for he has found favor in my sight." 23 And whenever the evil spirit from God came upon Saul, David took the lyre and played it with his hand, and Saul would be relieved and feel better, and the evil spirit would depart from him.

17 Now the Philistines gathered their armies for battle; they were gathered at Socoh, which belongs to Judah, and encamped between Socoh and Azekah, in Ephes-dammim. 2 Saul and the Israelites gathered and encamped in the valley of Elah, and formed ranks against the Philistines. 3 The Philistines stood on the mountain on the one side, and Israel stood on the mountain on the other side, with a valley between them. 4 And there came out from the camp of the Philistines a champion named Goliath, of Gath, whose height was six[b] cubits and a span. 5 He had a helmet of bronze on his head, and he was armed with a coat of mail; the weight of the coat was five thousand shekels of bronze. 6 He had greaves of bronze on his legs and a javelin of bronze slung between his shoulders. 7 The shaft of his spear was like a weaver's beam, and his spear's head weighed six hundred shekels of iron; and his shield-bearer went before him. 8 He stood and shouted to the ranks of Israel, "Why

6 When they came, and Samuel saw Eliab, he thought, 'Surely here, before the LORD, is his anointed king.' 7 But the LORD said to him, 'Pay no attention to his outward appearance and stature, for I have rejected him. The LORD does not see as a mortal sees; mortals see only appearances but the LORD sees into the heart.' 8 Then Jesse called Abinadab and had him pass before Samuel, but he said, 'No, the LORD has not chosen this one.' 9 Next he presented Shammah, of whom Samuel said, 'Nor has the LORD chosen him.' 10 Seven of his sons were presented to Samuel by Jesse, but he said, 'The LORD has not chosen any of these.' 11 Samuel asked, 'Are these all the sons you have?' 'There is still the youngest,' replied Jesse, 'but he is looking after the sheep.' Samuel said to Jesse, 'Send and fetch him; we will not sit down until he comes.' 12 So he sent and fetched him. He was handsome, with ruddy cheeks and bright eyes. The LORD said, 'Rise and anoint him: this is the man.' 13 Samuel took the horn of oil and anointed him in the presence of his brothers, and the spirit of the LORD came upon David and was with him from that day onwards. Then Samuel set out on his way to Ramah.

14 The spirit of the LORD had forsaken Saul, and at times an evil spirit from the LORD would seize him suddenly. 15 His servants said to him, 'You see how an evil spirit from God seizes you; 16 sir, why do you not command your servants here to go and find someone who can play on the lyre? Then, when an evil spirit from God comes on you, he can play and you will recover.' 17 Saul said to his servants, 'Find me someone who can play well and bring him to me.' 18 One of his attendants said, 'I have seen a son of Jesse of Bethlehem who can play; he is a brave man and a good fighter, wise in speech and handsome, and the LORD is with him.' 19 Saul therefore dispatched messengers to ask Jesse to send him his son David, who was with the sheep. 20 Jesse took a batch of bread, a skin of wine, and a kid, and sent them to Saul by his son David. 21 David came to Saul and entered his service; Saul loved him dearly, and David became his armour-bearer. 22 Saul sent word to Jesse: 'Allow David to stay in my service, for I am pleased with him.' 23 And whenever an evil spirit from God came upon Saul, David would take his lyre and play it, so that relief would come to Saul; he would recover and the evil spirit would leave him alone.

17 The Philistines mustered their forces for war; they massed at Socoh in Judah and encamped between Socoh and Azekah at Ephes-dammim. 2 Saul and the Israelites also mustered, and they encamped in the valley of Elah. They drew up their lines of battle facing the Philistines, 3 the Philistines occupying a position on one hill and the Israelites on another, with a valley between them.

4 A champion came out from the Philistine camp, a man named Goliath, from Gath; he was over nine feet in height. 5 He had a bronze helmet on his head, and he wore plate armour of bronze, weighing five thousand shekels. 6 On his legs were bronze greaves, and one of his weapons was a bronze dagger. 7 The shaft of his spear was like a weaver's beam, and its head, which was of iron, weighed six hundred shekels. His shield-bearer marched ahead of him.

8 The champion stood and shouted to the ranks of Israel,

---

thought, "Surely the LORD's anointed is here before him." 7 But the LORD said to Samuel: "Do not judge from his appearance or from his lofty stature, because I have rejected him. Not as man sees does God see, because man sees the appearance but the LORD looks into the heart." 8 Then Jesse called Abinadab and presented him before Samuel, who said, "The LORD has not chosen him." 9 Next Jesse presented Shammah, but Samuel said, "The LORD has not chosen this one either." 10 In the same way Jesse presented seven sons before Samuel, but Samuel said to Jesse, "The LORD has not chosen any one of these." 11 Then Samuel asked Jesse, "Are these all the sons you have?" Jesse replied, "There is still the youngest, who is tending the sheep." Samuel said to Jesse, "Send for him; we will not begin the sacrificial banquet until he arrives here." 12 Jesse sent and had the young man brought to them. He was ruddy, a youth handsome to behold and making a splendid appearance. The LORD said, "There — anoint him, for this is he!" 13 Then Samuel, with the horn of oil in hand, anointed him in the midst of his brothers; and from that day on, the spirit of the LORD rushed upon David. When Samuel took his leave, he went to Ramah.

14 The spirit of the LORD had departed from Saul, and he was tormented by an evil spirit sent by the LORD. 15 So the servants of Saul said to him: "Please! An evil spirit from God is tormenting you. 16 If your lordship will order it, we, your servants here in attendance on you, will look for a man skilled in playing the harp. When the evil spirit from God comes over you, he will play and you will feel better." 17 Saul then told his servants, "Find me a skillful harpist and bring him to me." 18 A servant spoke up to say: "I have observed that one of the sons of Jesse of Bethlehem is a skillful harpist. He is also a stalwart soldier, besides being an able speaker, and handsome. Moreover, the LORD is with him."

19 Accordingly, Saul dispatched messengers to ask Jesse to send him his son David, who was with the flock. 20 Then Jesse took five loaves of bread, a skin of wine, and a kid, and sent them to Saul by his son David. 21 Thus David came to Saul and entered his service. Saul became very fond of him, made him his armor-bearer, 22 and sent Jesse the message, "Allow David to remain in my service, for he meets with my approval." 23 Whenever the spirit from God seized Saul, David would take the harp and play, and Saul would be relieved and feel better, for the evil spirit would leave him.

17 The Philistines rallied their forces for battle at Socoh in Judah and camped between Socoh and Azekah at Ephes-dammim. 2 Saul and the Israelites also gathered and camped in the Vale of the Terebinth, drawing up their battle line to meet the Philistines. 3 The Philistines were stationed on one hill and the Israelites on an opposite hill, with a valley between them.

4 A champion named Goliath of Gath came out from the Philistine camp; he was six and a half feet tall. 5 He had a bronze helmet on his head and wore a bronze corselet of scale armor weighing five thousand shekels, 6 and bronze greaves, and had a bronze scimitar slung from a baldric. 7 The shaft of his javelin was like a weaver's heddle-bar, and its iron head weighed six hundred shekels. His shield-bearer went before him. 8 He stood and shouted to the ranks

6 When they arrived, he looked at Eliab and thought, 'This must be Yahweh's anointed now before him,' 7 but Yahweh said to Samuel, 'Take no notice of his appearance or his height, for I have rejected him; God does not see as human beings see; they look at appearances but Yahweh looks at the heart.' 8 Jesse then called Abinadab and presented him to Samuel, who said, 'Yahweh has not chosen this one either.' 9 Jesse then presented Shammah, but Samuel said, 'Yahweh has not chosen this one either.' 10 Jesse thus presented seven of his sons to Samuel, but Samuel said to Jesse, 'Yahweh has not chosen these.' 11 He then asked Jesse, 'Are these all the sons you have?' Jesse replied, 'There is still one left, the youngest; he is looking after the sheep.' Samuel then said to Jesse, 'Send for him, for we shall not sit down to eat until he arrives.' 12 Jesse had him sent for; he had ruddy cheeks, with fine eyes and an attractive appearance. Yahweh said, 'Get up and anoint him: he is the one!' 13 At this, Samuel took the horn of oil and anointed him, surrounded by his brothers; and the spirit of Yahweh seized on David from that day onwards. Samuel, for his part, set off and went to Ramah.

14 Now the spirit of Yahweh had withdrawn from Saul, and an evil spirit from Yahweh afflicted him with terrors. 15 Saul's servants said to him, 'An evil spirit from God is undoubtedly the cause of your terrors. 16 Let our lord give the order, and your servants who wait on you will look for a skilled harpist; when the evil spirit from God comes over you, he will play and it will do you good.' 17 Saul said to his attendants, 'Find me, please, a man who plays well, and bring him to me.' 18 One of the servants then spoke up and said, 'I have seen one of the sons of Jesse the Bethlehemite: he is a skilled player, a brave man and a fighter, well spoken, good-looking and Yahweh is with him.' 19 So Saul sent messengers to Jesse with the order, 'Send me your son David (who is with the sheep).' 20 Jesse took five loaves, a skin of wine and a kid, and sent them to Saul by his son David. 21 David went to Saul and entered his service;[h] Saul became very fond of him and David became his armour-bearer. 22 Saul then sent a message to Jesse, 'Let David stay in my service, since he has won my favour.' 23 And whenever the spirit from God came over Saul, David would take a harp and play; Saul would then be soothed; it would do him good, and the evil spirit would leave him.

17 The Philistines mustered their troops for war; they assembled at Socoh in Judah and pitched camp between Socoh and Azekah, in Ephes-Dammim. 2 Saul and the Israelites also mustered, pitching camp in the Valley of the Terebinth, and drew up their battle-line opposite the Philistines. 3 The Philistines occupied the high ground on one side and the Israelites occupied the high ground on the other side, with the valley between them.

4 A champion stepped out from the Philistine ranks; his name was Goliath, from Gath; he was six cubits and one span tall. 5 On his head was a bronze helmet and he wore a breastplate of scale-armour; the breastplate weighed five thousand shekels of bronze. 6 He had bronze greaves on his legs and a bronze scimitar slung across his shoulders. 7 The shaft of his spear was like a weaver's beam, and the head of his spear weighed six hundred shekels of iron. A shield-bearer walked in front of him.

8 Taking position in front of the Israelite lines, he

16, 18: Of the two traditions which describe the coming of David into Saul's service, the oldest Greek translation retains only the one comprised in 1 Sm 16, 14–23; 17, 1–11. 32–54. Though square brackets are used in this edition to indicate the passages lacking in the oldest translation, this is meant only to help the reader follow one account at a time. Both are equally a part of the inspired text, as are also the various amplifications and retouchings of the narrative given within brackets in chs 18 and 19.

h 16 There are two separate versions of David's early association with Saul: **1** David is a court musician; **2** He is a shepherd visiting his brothers. In this part of David's story there is a series of doublets: 18:11 = 19:8–10; 18:17–19 = 18:20–27; 19:1–7 = 20:1–42; 24 = 26; 21:11–16 = 27:1–12.

have you come out to draw up for battle? Am I not a Philistine, and are you not servants of Saul? Choose a man for yourselves, and let him come down to me. 9 If he is able to fight with me and kill me, then we will be your servants; but if I prevail against him and kill him, then you shall be our servants and serve us." 10 And the Philistine said, "Today I defy the ranks of Israel! Give me a man, that we may fight together." 11 When Saul and all Israel heard these words of the Philistine, they were dismayed and greatly afraid.

12 Now David was the son of an Ephrathite of Bethlehem in Judah, named Jesse, who had eight sons. In the days of Saul the man was already old and advanced in years.c 13 The three eldest sons of Jesse had followed Saul to the battle; the names of his three sons who went to the battle were Eliab the firstborn, and next to him Abinadab, and the third Shammah. 14 David was the youngest; the three eldest followed Saul, 15 but David went back and forth from Saul to feed his father's sheep at Bethlehem. 16 For forty days the Philistine came forward and took his stand, morning and evening.

17 Jesse said to his son David, "Take for your brothers an ephah of this parched grain and these ten loaves, and carry them quickly to the camp to your brothers; 18 also take these ten cheeses to the commander of their thousand. See how your brothers fare, and bring some token from them."

19 Now Saul, and they, and all the men of Israel, were in the valley of Elah, fighting with the Philistines. 20 David rose early in the morning, left the sheep with a keeper, took the provisions, and went as Jesse had commanded him. He came to the encampment as the army was going forth to the battle line, shouting the war cry. 21 Israel and the Philistines drew up for battle, army against army. 22 David left the things in charge of the keeper of the baggage, ran to the ranks, and went and greeted his brothers. 23 As he talked with them, the champion, the Philistine of Gath, Goliath by name, came up out of the ranks of the Philistines, and spoke the same words as before. And David heard him.

24 All the Israelites, when they saw the man, fled from him and were very much afraid. 25 The Israelites said, "Have you seen this man who has come up? Surely he has come up to defy Israel. The king will greatly enrich the man who kills him, and will give him his daughter and make his family free in Israel." 26 David said to the men who stood by him, "What shall be done for the man who kills this Philistine, and takes away the reproach from Israel? For who is this uncircumcised Philistine that he should defy the armies of the living God?" 27 The people answered him in the same way, "So shall it be done for the man who kills him."

28 His eldest brother Eliab heard him talking to the men; and Eliab's anger was kindled against David. He said, "Why have you come down? With whom have you left those few sheep in the wilderness? I know your presumption and the evil of your heart; for you have come down just to see the battle." 29 David said, "What have I done now? It was only a question." 30 He turned away from him toward another and spoke in the same way; and the people answered him again as before.

31 When the words that David spoke were heard, they repeated them before Saul; and he sent for him. 32 David said to Saul, "Let no one's heart fail because of him; your servant will go and fight with this Philistine." 33 Saul said to David, "You are not able to go against this Philistine to fight with him; for you are just a boy, and he has been a warrior from his youth." 34 But David said to Saul, "Your servant used to keep sheep for his father; and whenever a lion or a bear came, and took a lamb from the flock, 35 I

c Gk Syr: Heb *among men*

'Why do you come out to do battle? I am the Philistine champion and you are Saul's men. Choose your man to meet me. 9 If he defeats and kills me in fair fight, we shall become your slaves; but if I vanquish and kill him, you will be our slaves and serve us. 10 Here and now I challenge the ranks of Israel. Get me a man, and we will fight it out.' 11 When Saul and the Israelites heard what the Philistine said, they were all shaken and deeply afraid.

12 David was the son of an Ephrathite called Jesse, who had eight sons, and who by Saul's time had become old, well advanced in years. 13 His three eldest sons had followed Saul to the war; the eldest was called Eliab, the next Abinadab, and the third Shammah; 14 David was the youngest. When the three eldest followed Saul, 15 David used to go from attending Saul to minding his father's flocks at Bethlehem.

16 Morning and evening for forty days the Philistine came forward and took up his stance. 17 Then one day Jesse said to his son David, 'Take your brothers an ephah of this roasted grain and these ten loaves of bread, and go with them as quickly as you can to the camp. 18 These ten cream-cheeses are for you to take to their commanding officer. See if your brothers are well and bring back some token from them.' 19 Saul and the brothers and all the Israelites were in the valley of Elah, fighting the Philistines.

20 Early next morning David, having left someone in charge of the sheep, set out on his errand and went as Jesse had told him. He reached the lines just as the army was going out to take up position and was raising the war cry. 21 The Israelites and the Philistines drew up their ranks opposite each other. 22 David left his things in the charge of the quartermaster, ran to the line, and went up to his brothers to greet them. 23 While he was talking with them the Philistine champion, Goliath from Gath, came out from the Philistine ranks and issued his challenge in the same words as before; and David heard him. 24 When the Israelites saw the man they fell back before him in fear.

25 'Look at this man who comes out day after day to defy Israel,' they said. 'The king is to give a rich reward to the man who kills him; he will also give him his daughter in marriage and will exempt his family from service due in Israel.' 26 David asked the men near him, 'What is to be done for the man who kills this Philistine and wipes out this disgrace? And who is he, an uncircumcised Philistine, to defy the armies of the living God?' 27 The soldiers, repeating what had been said, told him what was to be done for the man who killed him.

28 David's elder brother Eliab overheard him talking with the men and angrily demanded, 'What are you doing here? And whom have you left to look after those few sheep in the wilderness? I know you, you impudent young rascal; you have only come to see the fighting.' 29 David answered, 'Now what have I done? I only asked a question.' 30 He turned away from him to someone else and repeated his question, but everybody gave him the same answer.

31 David's words were overheard and reported to Saul, who sent for him. 32 David said to him, 'Let no one lose heart! I shall go and fight this Philistine.' 33 Saul answered, 'You are not able to fight this Philistine; you are only a lad, and he has been a fighting man all his life.' 34 David said to Saul, 'Sir, I am my father's shepherd; whenever a lion or bear comes and carries off a sheep from the flock, 35 I go out

17:12 **Ephrathite:** *prob. rdg; Heb. adds* Is this the man from Bethlehem in Judah?

NEW AMERICAN BIBLE

NEW JERUSALEM BIBLE

of Israel: "Why come out in battle formation? I am a Philistine, and you are Saul's servants. Choose one of your men, and have him come down to me. 9 If he beats me in combat and kills me, we will be your vassals; but if I beat him and kill him, you shall be our vassals and serve us." 10 The Philistine continued: "I defy the ranks of Israel today. Give me a man and let us fight together." 11 Saul and all the men of Israel, when they heard this challenge of the Philistine, were dismayed and terror-stricken.

12 [David was the son of an Ephrathite named Jesse, who was from Bethlehem in Judah. He had eight sons, and in the days of Saul was old and well on in years. 13 The three oldest sons of Jesse had followed Saul to war; these three sons who had gone off to war were named, the first-born Eliab, the second son Abinadab, and the third Shammah. 14 David was the youngest. While the three oldest had joined Saul, 15 David would go and come from Saul to tend his father's sheep at Bethlehem.

16 [Meanwhile the Philistine came forward and took his stand morning and evening for forty days.

17 [Now Jesse said to his son David: "Take this ephah of roasted grain and these ten loaves for your brothers, and bring them quickly to your brothers in the camp. 18 Also take these ten cheeses for the field officer. Greet your brothers and bring home some token from them. 19 Saul, and they, and all Israel are fighting against the Philistines in the Vale of the Terebinth." 20 Early the next morning, having left the flock with a shepherd, David set out on his errand, as Jesse had commanded him. He reached the barricade of the camp just as the army, on their way to the battleground, were shouting their battle cry. 21 The Israelites and the Philistines drew up opposite each other in battle array. 22 David entrusted what he had brought to the keeper of the baggage and hastened to the battle line where he greeted his brothers. 23 While he was talking with them, the Philistine champion, by name Goliath of Gath, came up from the ranks of the Philistines and spoke as before, and David listened. 24 When the Israelites saw the man, they all retreated before him, very much afraid. 25 The Israelites had been saying: "Do you see this man coming up? He comes up to insult Israel. If anyone should kill him, the king would give him great wealth, and his daughter as well, and would grant exemption to his father's family in Israel." 26 David now said to the men standing by: "What will be done for the man who kills this Philistine and frees Israel of the disgrace? Who is this uncircumcised Philistine in any case, that he should insult the armies of the living God?" 27 They repeated the same words to him and said, "That is how the man who kills him will be rewarded." 28 When Eliab, his oldest brother, heard him speaking with the men, he grew angry with David and said: "Why did you come down? With whom have you left those sheep in the desert meanwhile? I know your arrogance and your evil intent. You came down to enjoy the battle!" 29 David replied, "What have I done now?—I was only talking." 30 Yet he turned from him to another and asked the same question; and everyone gave him the same answer as before. 31 The words that David had spoken were overheard and reported to Saul, who sent for him.]

32 Then David spoke to Saul: "Let your majesty not lose courage. I am at your service to go and fight this Philistine." 33 But Saul answered David, "You cannot go up against this Philistine and fight with him, for you are only a youth, while he has been a warrior from his youth." 34 Then David told Saul: "Your servant used to tend his father's sheep, and whenever a lion or bear came to carry off a sheep from the

shouted, 'Why have you come out to range yourselves for battle? Am I not a Philistine and are you not Saul's lackeys? Choose a man and let him come down to me. 9 If he can fight it out with me and kill me, we will be your servants; but if I can beat him and kill him, you become our servants and serve us.' 10 The Philistine then said, 'I challenge the ranks of Israel today. Give me a man and we will fight it out!' 11 When Saul and all Israel heard what the Philistine said, they were dismayed and terrified.

12 David was the son of an Ephrathite from Bethlehem of Judah whose name was Jesse; Jesse had eight sons and, by Saul's time, he was old and well on in years. 13 Jesse's eldest three sons followed Saul to the war. The names of the three sons who went to the war were: the eldest Eliab, the second Abinadab and the third Shammah. 14 David was the youngest; the eldest three followed Saul. 15 David alternated between serving Saul and looking after his father's sheep at Bethlehem. 16 Morning and evening, the Philistine advanced, presenting himself thus for forty days. 17 Jesse said to his son David, 'Take your brothers this *ephah* of roasted grain and these ten loaves, and hurry to the camp, to your brothers. 18 And take these ten cheeses to their commanding officer; find out how your brothers are and bring some token back from them; 19 they are with Saul and all the men of Israel in the Valley of the Terebinth, fighting the Philistines.'

20 David got up early in the morning and, leaving the sheep with someone to guard them, took up his load and went off as Jesse had ordered; he reached the encampment just as the troops were leaving to take up battle stations and shouting the war cry. 21 Israel and the Philistines drew up their lines facing one another. 22 David left his bundle in charge of the baggage guard and, running to the battle-line, went and asked his brothers how they were. 23 While he was talking to them, the champion (Goliath, the Philistine from Gath) came up from the Philistine ranks and made his usual speech, which David heard. 24 As soon as the Israelites saw this man, they all ran away from him and were terrified. 25 The Israelites said, 'You saw that man who just came up? He comes up to challenge Israel. The king will lavish riches on the man who kills him, he will give him his daughter in marriage and exempt his father's family from all taxes in Israel.'

26 David asked the men who were standing near him, 'What would be the reward for killing this Philistine and saving Israel from disgrace? Who is this uncircumcised Philistine, to challenge the armies of the living God?' 27 The people told him what they had been saying, 'That would be the reward for killing him,' they said. 28 His eldest brother Eliab heard David talking to the men and grew angry with him. 'Why have you come down here?' he said. 'Whom have you left in charge of those few sheep in the desert? I know how impudent and artful you are; you have come to watch the battle!' 29 David retorted, 'What have I done? May I not even speak?' 30 And he turned away from him to someone else and asked the same question, to which the people replied as before. 31 David's words were noted, however, and reported to Saul, who sent for him.

32 David said to Saul, 'Let no one be discouraged on his account; your servant will go and fight this Philistine.' 33 Saul said to David, 'You cannot go and fight the Philistine; you are only a boy and he has been a warrior since his youth.'

34 David said to Saul, 'Your servant used to look after the sheep for his father and whenever a lion or a bear came and

NEW REVISED STANDARD VERSION

REVISED ENGLISH BIBLE

went after it and struck it down, rescuing the lamb from its mouth; and if it turned against me, I would catch it by the jaw, strike it down, and kill it. 36 Your servant has killed both lions and bears; and this uncircumcised Philistine shall be like one of them, since he has defied the armies of the living God." 37 David said, "The LORD, who saved me from the paw of the lion and from the paw of the bear, will save me from the hand of this Philistine." So Saul said to David, "Go, and may the LORD be with you!"

38 Saul clothed David with his armor; he put a bronze helmet on his head and clothed him with a coat of mail. 39 David strapped Saul's sword over the armor, and he tried in vain to walk, for he was not used to them. Then David said to Saul, "I cannot walk with these; for I am not used to them." So David removed them. 40 Then he took his staff in his hand, and chose five smooth stones from the wadi, and put them in his shepherd's bag, in the pouch; his sling was in his hand, and he drew near to the Philistine.

41 The Philistine came on and drew near to David, with his shield-bearer in front of him. 42 When the Philistine looked and saw David, he disdained him, for he was only a youth, ruddy and handsome in appearance. 43 The Philistine said to David, "Am I a dog, that you come to me with sticks?" And the Philistine cursed David by his gods. 44 The Philistine said to David, "Come to me, and I will give your flesh to the birds of the air and to the wild animals of the field." 45 But David said to the Philistine, "You come to me with sword and spear and javelin; but I come to you in the name of the LORD of hosts, the God of the armies of Israel, whom you have defied. 46 This very day the LORD will deliver you into my hand, and I will strike you down and cut off your head; and I will give the dead bodies of the Philistine army this very day to the birds of the air and to the wild animals of the earth, so that all the earth may know that there is a God in Israel, 47 and that all this assembly may know that the LORD does not save by sword and spear; for the battle is the LORD's and he will give you into our hand."

48 When the Philistine drew nearer to meet David, David ran quickly toward the battle line to meet the Philistine. 49 David put his hand in his bag, took out a stone, slung it, and struck the Philistine on his forehead; the stone sank into his forehead, and he fell face down on the ground.

50 So David prevailed over the Philistine with a sling and a stone, striking down the Philistine and killing him; there was no sword in David's hand. 51 Then David ran and stood over the Philistine; he grasped his sword, drew it out of its sheath, and killed him; then he cut off his head with it.

When the Philistines saw that their champion was dead, they fled. 52 The troops of Israel and Judah rose up with a shout and pursued the Philistines as far as Gath*d* and the gates of Ekron, so that the wounded Philistines fell on the way from Shaaraim as far as Gath and Ekron. 53 The Israelites came back from chasing the Philistines, and they plundered their camp. 54 David took the head of the Philistine and brought it to Jerusalem; but he put his armor in his tent.

55 When Saul saw David go out against the Philistine, he said to Abner, the commander of the army, "Abner, whose son is this young man?" Abner said, "As your soul lives, O king, I do not know." 56 The king said, "Inquire whose son the stripling is." 57 On David's return from killing the Philistine, Abner took him and brought him before Saul, with the head of the Philistine in his hand. 58 Saul said to him, "Whose son are you, young man?" And David answered, "I am the son of your servant Jesse the Bethlehemite."

after it and attack it and rescue the victim from its jaws. Then if it turns on me, I seize it by the beard and batter it to death. 36 I have killed lions and bears, and this uncircumcised Philistine will fare no better than they; he has defied the ranks of the living God. 37 The LORD who saved me from the lion and the bear will save me from this Philistine.' 'Go then,' said Saul; 'and the LORD be with you.'

38 He put his own tunic on David, placed a bronze helmet on his head, and gave him a coat of mail to wear; 39 he then fastened his sword on David over his tunic. But David held back, because he had not tried them, and said to Saul, 'I cannot go with these, because I am not used to them.' David took them off, 40 then picked up his stick, chose five smooth stones from the wadi, and put them in a shepherd's bag which served as his pouch, and, sling in hand, went to meet the Philistine.

41 The Philistine, preceded by his shield-bearer, came on towards David. 42 He looked David up and down and had nothing but disdain for this lad with his ruddy cheeks and bright eyes. 43 He said to David, 'Am I a dog that you come out against me with sticks?' He cursed him in the name of his god, 44 and said, 'Come, I shall give your flesh to the birds and the beasts.' 45 David answered, 'You have come against me with sword and spear and dagger, but I come against you in the name of the LORD of Hosts, the God of the ranks of Israel which you have defied. 46 The LORD will put you into my power this day; I shall strike you down and cut your head off and leave your carcass and the carcasses of the Philistines to the birds and the wild beasts; the whole world will know that there is a God in Israel. 47 All those who are gathered here will see that the LORD saves without sword or spear; the battle is the LORD's, and he will put you all into our power.'

48 When the Philistine began moving closer to attack, David ran quickly to engage him. 49 Reaching into his bag, he took out a stone, which he slung and struck the Philistine on the forehead. The stone sank into his head, and he fell prone on the ground. 50 So with sling and stone David proved the victor; though he had no sword, he struck down the Philistine and gave him a mortal wound. 51 He ran up to the Philistine and stood over him; then, grasping his sword, he drew it out of the scabbard, dispatched him, and cut off his head.

When the Philistines saw the fate of their champion, they turned and fled. 52 The men of Israel and Judah at once raised the war cry and closely pursued them all the way to Gath and up to the gates of Ekron. The road that runs to Shaaraim, Gath, and Ekron was strewn with their dead. 53 On their return from the pursuit of the Philistines, the Israelites plundered their camp. 54 David took Goliath's head and carried it to Jerusalem, but he put Goliath's weapons in his own tent.

55 As Saul watched David go out to meet the Philistine, he said to Abner his commander-in-chief, 'That youth there, Abner, whose son is he?' 'By your life, your majesty,' replied Abner, 'I do not know.' 56 The king said, 'Go and find out whose son the stripling is.' 57 When David came back after killing the Philistine, Abner took him and presented him to Saul with the Philistine's head still in his hand. 58 Saul asked him, 'Whose son are you, young man?' and David answered, 'I am the son of your servant Jesse of Bethlehem.'

17:39 **he then . . . on David:** *so Gk; Heb.* David fastened on his sword. 17:40 **which . . . pouch:** *so Gk; Heb.* which was his and in the pouch. 17:42 **lad . . . eyes:** *prob. rdg; Heb. obscure.* 17:46 **leave . . . Philistines:** *so Gk; Heb.* leave the carcass of the Philistines. 17:52 **to Gath:** *so Gk; Heb.* to a valley.

d Gk Syr: Heb *Gai*

flock, 35 I would go after it and attack it and rescue the prey from its mouth. If it attacked me, I would seize it by the jaw, strike it, and kill it. 36 Your servant has killed both a lion and a bear, and this uncircumcised Philistine will be as one of them, because he has insulted the armies of the living God."

37 David continued: "The LORD, who delivered me from the claws of the lion and the bear, will also keep me safe from the clutches of this Philistine." Saul answered David, "Go! the LORD be with you."

38 Then Saul clothed David in his own tunic, putting a bronze helmet on his head and arming him with a coat of mail. 39 David also girded himself with Saul's sword over the tunic. He walked with difficulty, however, since he had never tried armor before. He said to Saul, "I cannot go in these, because I have never tried them before." So he took them off. 40 Then, staff in hand, David selected five smooth stones from the wadi and put them in the pocket of his shepherd's bag. With his sling also ready to hand, he approached the Philistine.

41 With his shield-bearer marching before him, the Philistine also advanced closer and closer to David. 42 When he had sized David up, and seen that he was youthful, and ruddy, and handsome in appearance, he held him in contempt. 43 The Philistine said to David, "Am I a dog that you come against me with a staff?" Then the Philistine cursed David by his gods 44 and said to him, "Come here to me, and I will leave your flesh for the birds of the air and the beasts of the field." 45 David answered him: "You come against me with sword and spear and scimitar, but I come against you in the name of the LORD of hosts, the God of the armies of Israel that you have insulted. 46 Today the LORD shall deliver you into my hand; I will strike you down and cut off your head. This very day I will leave your corpse and the corpses of the Philistine army for the birds of the air and the beasts of the field; thus the whole land shall learn that Israel has a God. 47 All this multitude, too, shall learn that it is not by sword or spear that the LORD saves. For the battle is the LORD's, and he shall deliver you into our hands."

48 The Philistine then moved to meet David at close quarters, while David ran quickly toward the battle line in the direction of the Philistine. 49 David put his hand into the bag and took out a stone, hurled it with the sling, and struck the Philistine on the forehead. The stone embedded itself in his brow, and he fell prostrate on the ground. 50 [Thus David overcame the Philistine with sling and stone; he struck the Philistine mortally, and did it without a sword.] 51 Then David ran and stood over him; with the Philistine's own sword [which he drew from its sheath] he dispatched him and cut off his head.

When they saw that their hero was dead, the Philistines took to flight. 52 Then the men of Israel and Judah, with loud shouts, went in pursuit of the Philistines to the approaches of Gath and to the gates of Ekron, and Philistines fell wounded along the road from Shaaraim as far as Gath and Ekron. 53 On their return from the pursuit of the Philistines, the Israelites looted their camp. 54 David took the head of the Philistine and brought it to Jerusalem; but he kept Goliath's armor in his own tent.

55 [When Saul saw David go out to meet the Philistine, he asked his general Abner, "Abner, whose son is that youth?" Abner replied, "As truly as your majesty is alive, I have no idea." 56 And the king said, "Find out whose son the lad is." 57 So when David returned from slaying the Philistine, Abner took him and presented him to Saul. David was still holding the Philistine's head. 58 Saul then asked him, "Whose son are you, young man?" David replied, "I am the son of your servant Jesse of Bethlehem."

took a sheep from the flock, 35 I used to follow it up, lay into it and snatch the sheep out of its jaws. If it turned on me, I would seize it by the beard and batter it to death. 36 Your servant has killed both lion and bear, and this uncircumcised Philistine will end up like one of them for having challenged the armies of the living God.' 37 'Yahweh,' David went on, 'who delivered me from the claws of lion and bear, will deliver me from the clutches of this Philistine.' Then Saul said to David, 'Go, and Yahweh be with you!'

38 Saul dressed David in his own armour; he put a bronze helmet on his head, dressed him in a breastplate 39 and buckled his own sword over David's armour. David tried to walk but, not being used to them, said to Saul, 'I cannot walk in these; I am not used to them.' So they took them off again.

40 He took his stick in his hand, selected five smooth stones from the river bed and put them in his shepherd's bag, in his pouch; then, sling in hand, he walked towards the Philistine. 41 The Philistine, preceded by his shield-bearer, came nearer and nearer to David. 42 When the Philistine looked David up and down, what he saw filled him with scorn, because David was only a lad, with ruddy cheeks and an attractive appearance. 43 The Philistine said to David, 'Am I a dog for you to come after me with sticks?' And the Philistine cursed David by his gods. 44 The Philistine said to David, 'Come over here and I will give your flesh to the birds of the air and the wild beasts!' 45 David retorted to the Philistine, 'You come to me with sword, spear and scimitar, but I come to you in the name of Yahweh Sabaoth, God of the armies of Israel, whom you have challenged. 46 Today, Yahweh will deliver you into my hand; I shall kill you, I shall cut off your head; today, I shall give your corpse and the corpses of the Philistine army to the birds of the air and the wild beasts, so that the whole world may know that there is a God in Israel, 47 and this whole assembly know that Yahweh does not give victory by means of sword and spear — for Yahweh is lord of the battle and he will deliver you into our power.'

48 No sooner had the Philistine started forward to confront David than David darted out of the lines and ran to meet the Philistine. 49 Putting his hand in his bag, he took out a stone, slung it and struck the Philistine on the forehead; the stone penetrated his forehead and he fell face downwards on the ground. 50 Thus David triumphed over the Philistine with a sling and a stone; he hit the Philistine and killed him, though he had no sword in his hand. 51 David ran and stood over the Philistine, seized his sword, pulled it from the scabbard, despatched him and cut off his head.

When the Philistines saw that their champion was dead, they fled. 52 The men of Israel and of Judah started forward, shouting their war cry, and pursued the Philistines as far as the approaches of Gath and the gates of Ekron. The Philistine dead lay all along the road from Shaaraim as far as Gath and Ekron. 53 Turning back from their ferocious pursuit of the Philistines, the Israelites plundered their camp. 54 And David took the Philistine's head and brought it to Jerusalem; his weapons, however, he put in his own tent.

55 When Saul saw David going to engage the Philistine he said to Abner, the army commander, 'Abner, whose son is that boy?' 'On your life, O king,' Abner replied, 'I do not know.' 56 The king said, 'Find out whose son the lad is.' 57 When David came back after killing the Philistine, Abner took him and brought him before Saul with the Philistine's head in his hand. 58 Saul asked him, 'Whose son are you, young man?' David replied, 'The son of your servant Jesse of Bethlehem.'

18 When David*e* had finished speaking to Saul, the soul of Jonathan was bound to the soul of David, and Jonathan loved him as his own soul. 2 Saul took him that day and would not let him return to his father's house. 3 Then Jonathan made a covenant with David, because he loved him as his own soul. 4 Jonathan stripped himself of the robe that he was wearing, and gave it to David, and his armor, and even his sword and his bow and his belt. 5 David went out and was successful wherever Saul sent him; as a result, Saul set him over the army. And all the people, even the servants of Saul, approved.

6 As they were coming home, when David returned from killing the Philistine, the women came out of all the towns of Israel, singing and dancing, to meet King Saul, with tambourines, with songs of joy, and with musical instruments.*f* 7 And the women sang to one another as they made merry,

"Saul has killed his thousands,
and David his ten thousands."

8 Saul was very angry, for this saying displeased him. He said, "They have ascribed to David ten thousands, and to me they have ascribed thousands; what more can he have but the kingdom?" 9 So Saul eyed David from that day on.

10 The next day an evil spirit from God rushed upon Saul, and he raved within his house, while David was playing the lyre, as he did day by day. Saul had his spear in his hand; 11 and Saul threw the spear, for he thought, "I will pin David to the wall." But David eluded him twice.

12 Saul was afraid of David, because the LORD was with him but had departed from Saul. 13 So Saul removed him from his presence, and made him a commander of a thousand; and David marched out and came in, leading the army. 14 David had success in all his undertakings; for the LORD was with him. 15 When Saul saw that he had great success, he stood in awe of him. 16 But all Israel and Judah loved David; for it was he who marched out and came in leading them.

17 Then Saul said to David, "Here is my elder daughter Merab; I will give her to you as a wife; only be valiant for me and fight the LORD's battles." For Saul thought, "I will not raise a hand against him; let the Philistines deal with him." 18 David said to Saul, "Who am I and who are my kinsfolk, my father's family in Israel, that I should be son-in-law to the king?" 19 But at the time when Saul's daughter Merab should have been given to David, she was given to Adriel the Meholathite as a wife.

20 Now Saul's daughter Michal loved David. Saul was told, and the thing pleased him. 21 Saul thought, "Let me give her to him that she may be a snare for him and that the hand of the Philistines may be against him." Therefore Saul said to David a second time,*g* "You shall now be my son-in-law." 22 Saul commanded his servants, "Speak to David in private and say, 'See, the king is delighted with you, and all his servants love you; now then, become the king's son-in-law.' " 23 So Saul's servants reported these words to David in private. And David said, "Does it seem to you a little thing to become the king's son-in-law, seeing that I am a poor man and of no repute?" 24 The servants of Saul told him, "This is what David said." 25 Then Saul said, "Thus shall you say to David, 'The king desires no marriage present except a hundred foreskins of the Philistines, that he may be avenged on the king's enemies.' " Now Saul planned to make David fall by the hand of the Philistines. 26 When his servants told David these words, David was well pleased to be the king's son-in-law. Before the time had expired, 27 David rose and went, along with his men,

18 1–2 That same day, when Saul had finished talking with David, he kept him and would not let him return any more to his father's house, for he saw that Jonathan had given his heart to David and had grown to love him as himself. 3 Jonathan and David made a solemn compact because each loved the other as dearly as himself. 4 Jonathan stripped off the cloak and tunic he was wearing, and gave them to David, together with his sword, his bow, and his belt.

5 David succeeded so well in every venture on which Saul sent him that he was given command of the fighting forces, and his promotion pleased all ranks, even the officials round Saul.

6 At the homecoming of the army and the return of David from slaying the Philistine, the women from all the cities and towns of Israel came out singing and dancing to meet King Saul, rejoicing with tambourines and three-stringed instruments. 7 The women as they made merry sang to one another:

'Saul struck down thousands,
but David tens of thousands.'

8 Saul was furious, and the words rankled. He said, 'They have ascribed to David tens of thousands and to me only thousands. What more can they do but make him king?' 9 From that time forward Saul kept a jealous eye on David.

10 Next day an evil spirit from God seized on Saul. He fell into a frenzy in the house, and David played the lyre to him as he had done before. Saul had a spear in his hand, 11 and he hurled it at David, meaning to pin him to the wall; but twice David dodged aside. 12 After this Saul was afraid of David, because he saw that the LORD had forsaken him and was with David. 13 He therefore removed David from his household and appointed him to the command of a thousand men. David led his men into action, 14 and succeeded in everything that he undertook, because the LORD was with him. 15 When Saul saw how successful he was, he was more afraid of him than ever. 16 But all Israel and Judah loved David because he took the field at their head.

17 Saul said to David, 'Here is my elder daughter Merab; I shall give her to you in marriage, but in return you must serve me valiantly and fight the LORD's battles.' For Saul meant David to meet his end not at his hands but at the hands of the Philistines. 18 David answered Saul, 'Who am I and what are my father's people, my kinsfolk, in Israel, that I should become the king's son-in-law?' 19 However, when the time came for Saul's daughter Merab to be married to David, she had already been given to Adriel of Meholah.

20 But Michal, Saul's other daughter, fell in love with David, and when Saul was told of this, he saw that it suited his plans. 21 Saul said to himself, 'I will give her to him; let her be the bait that lures him to his death at the hands of the Philistines.' So Saul proposed a second time to make David his son-in-law, 22 and ordered his courtiers to say to David privately, 'The king is well disposed to you and you are dear to us all; now is the time for you to marry into the king's family.' 23 When they spoke in this way to David, he said to them, 'Do you think that marrying the king's daughter is a matter of so little consequence that a poor man of no account, like myself, can do it?'

24 The courtiers reported what David had said, 25 and Saul replied, 'Tell David this: all the king wants as the bride-price is the foreskins of a hundred Philistines, by way of vengeance on his enemies.' Saul was counting on David's death at the hands of the Philistines. 26 The courtiers told David what Saul had said, and marriage with the king's daughter on these terms pleased him well. Before the appointed time, 27 David went out with his men and slew two

e Heb *he*   *f* Or *triangles,* or *three-stringed instruments*   *g* Heb *by two*

18:6 **singing:** or watching.   18:10 **a frenzy:** or prophetic rapture.

18 [By the time David finished speaking with Saul, Jonathan had become as fond of David as if his life depended on him; he loved him as he loved himself. ²Saul laid claim to David that day and did not allow him to return to his father's house. ³And Jonathan entered into a bond with David, because he loved him as himself. ⁴Jonathan divested himself of the mantle he was wearing and gave it to David, along with his military dress, and his sword, his bow and his belt. ⁵David then carried out successfully every mission on which Saul sent him. So Saul put him in charge of his soldiers, and this was agreeable to the whole army, even to Saul's own officers.]

⁶At the approach of Saul and David (on David's return after slaying the Philistine), women came out from each of the cities of Israel to meet King Saul, singing and dancing, with tambourines, joyful songs, and sistrums. ⁷The women played and sang:

"Saul has slain his thousands,
   and David his ten thousands."

⁸Saul was very angry and resentful of the song, for he thought: "They gave David ten thousands, but only thousands to me. All that remains for him is the kingship." ⁹[And from that day on, Saul was jealous of David.

¹⁰[The next day an evil spirit from God came over Saul, and he raged in his house. David was in attendance, playing the harp as at other times, while Saul was holding his spear. ¹¹Saul poised the spear, thinking to nail David to the wall, but twice David escaped him.] ¹²Saul then began to fear David, [because the LORD was with him, but had departed from Saul himself.] ¹³Accordingly, Saul removed him from his presence by appointing him a field officer. So David led the people on their military expeditions, ¹⁴and prospered in all his enterprises, for the LORD was with him. ¹⁵Seeing how successful he was, Saul conceived a fear of David; ¹⁶on the other hand, all Israel and Judah loved him, since he led them on their expeditions.

¹⁷[Saul said to David, "There is my older daughter, Merob, whom I will give you in marriage if you become my champion and fight the battles of the LORD." Saul had in mind, "I shall not touch him; let the Philistines strike him." ¹⁸But David answered Saul: "Who am I? And who are my kin or my father's clan in Israel that I should become the king's son-in-law?" ¹⁹However, when it was time for Saul's daughter Merob to be given to David, she was given in marriage to Adriel the Meholathite instead.]

²⁰Now Saul's daughter Michal loved David, and it was reported to Saul, who was pleased at this, ²¹for he thought, "I will offer her to him to become a snare for him, so that the Philistines may strike him." [Thus for the second time Saul said to David, "You shall become my son-in-law to-day."] ²²Saul then ordered his servants to speak to David privately and to say: "The king is fond of you, and all his officers love you. You should become the king's son-in-law." ²³But when Saul's servants mentioned this to David, he said: "Do you think it easy to become the king's son-in-law? I am poor and insignificant." ²⁴When his servants reported to him the nature of David's answer, ²⁵Saul commanded them to say this to David: "The king desires no other price for the bride than the foreskins of one hundred Philistines, that he may thus take vengeance on his enemies." Saul intended in this way to bring about David's death through the Philistines. ²⁶When the servants reported this offer to David, he was pleased with the prospect of becoming the king's son-in-law. [Before the year was up,] ²⁷David made preparations and sallied forth with his men

18 When David had finished talking to Saul, Jonathan felt an instant affection for David; Jonathan loved him like his very self; ²Saul engaged him that very day and would not let him go home to his father. ³Jonathan made a pact with David, since he loved him like his very self; ⁴Jonathan took off the cloak which he was wearing and gave it to David, and his armour too, even including his sword, his bow and his belt. ⁵Wherever David was sent on a mission by Saul, he was successful, and Saul put him in command of the fighting men; all the people respected him and so did Saul's staff.

⁶On their return, when David was coming back from killing the Philistine, the women came out of all the towns of Israel singing and dancing to meet King Saul, with tambourines, sistrums and cries of joy; ⁷and as they danced the women sang:

Saul has killed his thousands,
   and David his tens of thousands.

⁸Saul was very angry; the incident displeased him. 'They have given David the tens of thousands,' he said, 'but me only the thousands; what more can he have, except the throne?' ⁹And Saul watched David jealously from that day onwards.

¹⁰The following day, an evil spirit from God seized on Saul and he fell into a frenzy while he was indoors. David played the harp as on other occasions; Saul had a spear in his hand. ¹¹Saul brandished the spear; he said, 'I will pin David to the wall!' David evaded him twice.

¹²Saul feared David, since Yahweh was with him and had withdrawn from Saul. ¹³So Saul removed him from his presence and appointed him commander of a thousand; he led the people on campaign. ¹⁴In all his expeditions, David was successful and Yahweh was with him. ¹⁵And Saul, seeing how very successful he was, was afraid of him. ¹⁶All Israel and Judah loved David, however, since he was their leader on campaign.

¹⁷Saul said to David, 'This is my elder daughter Merab; I shall give her to you in marriage; but you must serve me bravely and fight Yahweh's wars.' Saul thought, 'Better than strike the blow myself, let the Philistines do it!' ¹⁸David replied to Saul, 'Who am I and what is my lineage — and my father's family — in Israel, for me to become the king's son-in-law?' ¹⁹When the time came for Merab daughter of Saul to be given to David, she was given to Adriel of Meholah instead.

²⁰Now Michal daughter of Saul fell in love with David. When Saul heard this he was pleased. ²¹He thought, 'Yes, I shall give her to him; she can be the snare for him, so that the Philistines will get him.' (On two occasions, Saul told David, 'Today, you shall be my son-in-law.') ²²Saul gave instructions to his servants, 'Have a private word with David and say, "Look, the king is fond of you and all his servants love you — why not be the king's son-in-law?" ' ²³Saul's servants repeated these words in David's ear, to which David replied, 'Do you think that becoming the king's son-in-law is a trivial matter; I have neither wealth nor position.' ²⁴Saul's servants then reported back, 'This is what David said.' ²⁵Saul replied, 'Tell David this, "The king desires no bride-price except one hundred Philistine foreskins, in vengeance on the king's enemies." ' Saul was counting on getting David killed by the Philistines.

²⁶When his servants repeated this to David, David thought it would be a fine thing to be the king's son-in-law. And no time was lost ²⁷before David got up to go, he and

and killed one hundred[h] of the Philistines; and David brought their foreskins, which were given in full number to the king, that he might become the king's son-in-law. Saul gave him his daughter Michal as a wife. 28 But when Saul realized that the LORD was with David, and that Saul's daughter Michal loved him, 29 Saul was still more afraid of David. So Saul was David's enemy from that time forward.

30 Then the commanders of the Philistines came out to battle; and as often as they came out, David had more success than all the servants of Saul, so that his fame became very great.

19 Saul spoke with his son Jonathan and with all his servants about killing David. But Saul's son Jonathan took great delight in David. 2 Jonathan told David, "My father Saul is trying to kill you; therefore be on guard tomorrow morning; stay in a secret place and hide yourself. 3 I will go out and stand beside my father in the field where you are, and I will speak to my father about you; if I learn anything I will tell you." 4 Jonathan spoke well of David to his father Saul, saying to him, "The king should not sin against his servant David, because he has not sinned against you, and because his deeds have been of good service to you; 5 for he took his life in his hand when he attacked the Philistine, and the LORD brought about a great victory for all Israel. You saw it, and rejoiced; why then will you sin against an innocent person by killing David without cause?" 6 Saul heeded the voice of Jonathan; Saul swore, "As the LORD lives, he shall not be put to death." 7 So Jonathan called David and related all these things to him. Jonathan then brought David to Saul, and he was in his presence as before.

8 Again there was war, and David went out to fight the Philistines. He launched a heavy attack on them, so that they fled before him. 9 Then an evil spirit from the LORD came upon Saul, as he sat in his house with his spear in his hand, while David was playing music. 10 Saul sought to pin David to the wall with the spear; but he eluded Saul, so that he struck the spear into the wall. David fled and escaped that night.

11 Saul sent messengers to David's house to keep watch over him, planning to kill him in the morning. David's wife Michal told him, "If you do not save your life tonight, tomorrow you will be killed." 12 So Michal let David down through the window; he fled away and escaped. 13 Michal took an idol[i] and laid it on the bed; she put a net[j] of goats' hair on its head, and covered it with the clothes. 14 When Saul sent messengers to take David, she said, "He is sick." 15 Then Saul sent the messengers to see David for themselves. He said, "Bring him up to me in the bed, that I may kill him." 16 When the messengers came in, the idol[k] was in the bed, with the covering[j] of goats' hair on its head. 17 Saul said to Michal, "Why have you deceived me like this, and let my enemy go, so that he has escaped?" Michal answered Saul, "He said to me, 'Let me go; why should I kill you?'"

18 Now David fled and escaped; he came to Samuel at Ramah, and told him all that Saul had done to him. He and Samuel went and settled at Naioth. 19 Saul was told, "David is at Naioth in Ramah." 20 Then Saul sent messengers to take David. When they saw the company of the prophets in a frenzy, with Samuel standing in charge of[j] them, the spirit of God came upon the messengers of Saul, and they also fell into a prophetic frenzy. 21 When Saul was told, he sent other messengers, and they also fell into a frenzy. Saul sent messengers again the third time, and they also fell into

hundred Philistines; he brought their foreskins and counted them out to the king in order to be accepted as his son-in-law. Saul then married his daughter Michal to David. 28 He saw clearly that the LORD was with David, and knew that Michal his daughter had fallen in love with him; 29 and he grew more and more afraid of David and was his enemy for the rest of his life.

30 The Philistine commanders continued to make forays, but whenever they took the field David had more success against them than all the rest of Saul's men, and he won a great name for himself.

19 SAUL incited Jonathan his son and all his household to kill David. 2 But Jonathan was devoted to David and told him that his father Saul was seeking to kill him. 'Be on your guard tomorrow morning,' he said; 'conceal yourself, and remain in hiding. 3 I shall come out and join my father in the open country where you are and speak to him about you, and if I discover anything I shall tell you.'

4 Jonathan spoke up for David to his father Saul and said to him, 'Sir, do not wrong your servant David; he has not wronged you; his achievements have all benefited you greatly. 5 Did he not take his life in his hands when he killed the Philistine, and the LORD brought about a great victory for all Israel? You saw it and shared in the rejoicing. Why should you wrong an innocent man and put David to death without cause?' 6 Saul heeded Jonathan's plea and swore solemnly by the LORD that David should not be put to death. 7 Jonathan called David and reported all this; then he brought him to Saul to be in attendance on the king as before.

8 When hostilities broke out again and David advanced to the attack, he inflicted such a severe defeat on the Philistines that they fled before him.

9 An evil spirit from the LORD came on Saul as he was sitting in the house with a spear in his hand; and David was playing on the lyre. 10 Saul tried to pin David to the wall with the spear, but he dodged the king's thrust so that Saul drove the spear into the wall. David escaped and got safely away.

That night 11 Saul sent servants to keep watch on David's house, intending to kill him in the morning. But David's wife Michal warned him to get away that night, 'or tomorrow', she said, 'you will be a dead man'. 12 She let David down through a window and he slipped away and escaped. 13 Michal then took their household god and put it on the bed; at its head she laid a goat's-hair rug and covered it all with a cloak. 14 When the men arrived to arrest David she told them he was ill. 15 Saul, however, sent them back to see David for themselves. 'Bring him to me, bed and all,' he ordered, 'so that I may kill him.' 16 When they came, there was the household god on the bed and the goat's-hair rug at its head. 17 Saul said to Michal, 'Why have you played this trick on me and let my enemy get away?' Michal answered, 'He said to me, "Help me to escape or I shall kill you."'

18 Meanwhile David made good his escape, and coming to Samuel at Ramah, he described how Saul had treated him. He and Samuel went to Naioth and stayed there. 19 When Saul was told that David was at Naioth, 20 he sent a party of men to seize him. But at the sight of the company of prophets in a frenzy, with Samuel standing at their head, the spirit of God came upon them and they fell into prophetic frenzy. 21 When this was reported to Saul he sent another party; these also fell into a frenzy, and when he sent men a

and slew two hundred Philistines. He brought back their foreskins and counted them out before the king, that he might thus become the king's son-in-law. So Saul gave him his daughter Michal in marriage. 28 Saul thus came to recognize that the LORD was with David; besides, his own daughter Michal loved David. 29 Therefore Saul feared David all the more [and was his enemy ever after].

30 [The Philistine chiefs continued to make forays, but each time they took the field, David was more successful against them than any other of Saul's officers, and as a result acquired great fame.]

19 Saul discussed his intention of killing David with his son Jonathan and with all his servants. But Saul's son Jonathan, who was very fond of David, 2 told him: "My father Saul is trying to kill you. Therefore, please be on your guard tomorrow morning; get out of sight and remain in hiding. 3 I, however, will go out and stand beside my father in the countryside where you are, and will speak to him about you. If I learn anything, I will let you know."

4 Jonathan then spoke well of David to his father Saul, saying to him: "Let not your majesty sin against his servant David, for he has committed no offense against you, but has helped you very much by his deeds. 5 When he took his life in his hands and slew the Philistine, and the LORD brought about a great victory for all Israel through him, you were glad to see it. Why, then, should you become guilty of shedding innocent blood by killing David without cause?" 6 Saul heeded Jonathan's plea and swore, "As the LORD lives, he shall not be killed." 7 So Jonathan summoned David and repeated the whole conversation to him. Jonathan then brought David to Saul, and David served him as before.

8 When war broke out again, David went out to fight against the Philistines and inflicted a great defeat upon them, putting them to flight. 9 Then an evil spirit from the LORD came upon Saul as he was sitting in his house with spear in hand and David was playing the harp nearby. 10 Saul tried to nail David to the wall with the spear, but David eluded Saul, so that the spear struck only the wall, and David got away safe.

11 The same night, Saul sent messengers to David's house to guard it, that he might kill him in the morning. David's wife Michal informed him, "Unless you save yourself tonight, tomorrow you will be killed." 12 Then Michal let David down through a window, and he made his escape in safety. 13 Michal took the household idol and laid it in the bed, putting a net of goat's hair at its head and covering it with a spread. 14 When Saul sent messengers to arrest David, she said, "He is sick." 15 Saul, however, sent the messengers back to see David and commanded them, "Bring him up to me in the bed, that I may kill him." 16 But when the messengers entered, they found the household idol in the bed, with the net of goat's hair at its head. 17 Saul therefore asked Michal: "Why did you play this trick on me? You have helped my enemy to get away!" Michal answered Saul: "He threatened me, 'Let me go or I will kill you.' "

18 Thus David got safely away; he went to Samuel in Ramah, informing him of all that Saul had done to him. Then he and Samuel went to stay in the sheds. 19 When Saul was told that David was in the sheds near Ramah, 20 he sent messengers to arrest David. But when they saw the band of prophets, presided over by Samuel, in a prophetic frenzy, they too fell into the prophetic state. 21 Informed of this, Saul sent other messengers, who also fell into the prophetic state. For the third time Saul sent messengers, but they too fell into the prophetic state.

his men, and killed two hundred of the Philistines. David brought their foreskins back and counted them out before the king, so that he could be the king's son-in-law. Saul then gave him his daughter Michal in marriage.

28 Saul could not but see that Yahweh was with David, and that the whole House of Israel loved him; 29 Saul became more afraid of David than ever, and became his inveterate enemy. 30 The Philistine chiefs kept mounting their campaigns but, whenever they did so, David proved more successful than any of Saul's staff; consequently he gained great renown.

19 Saul let his son Jonathan and all his servants know of his intention to kill David. But Jonathan, Saul's son, held David in great affection; 2 and Jonathan warned David, 'My father Saul is looking for a way to kill you, so be on your guard tomorrow morning; go into hiding, stay out of sight. 3 I shall go out and keep my father company in the countryside where you will be, and shall talk to my father about you; I shall see what the situation is and then tell you.'

4 Jonathan spoke highly of David to Saul his father and said, 'The king should not harm his servant David; far from harming you, what he has done has been greatly to your advantage. 5 He took his life in his hands, he killed the Philistine, and Yahweh brought about a great victory for all Israel. You saw for yourself. How pleased you were! Why then sin against innocent blood by killing David for no reason?' 6 Saul was impressed by Jonathan's words. Saul swore, 'As Yahweh lives, I will not kill him.' 7 Jonathan called David and told him all this. Jonathan then brought him to Saul, and David remained in attendance as before.

8 War broke out again and David sallied out to fight the Philistines; he inflicted a great defeat on them and they fled before him. 9 An evil spirit from Yahweh came over Saul while he was sitting in his house with his spear in hand; David was playing the harp. 10 Saul tried to pin David to the wall with his spear, but he avoided Saul's thrust and the spear stuck in the wall. David fled and made good his escape.

That same night 11 Saul sent agents to watch David's house, intending to kill him in the morning. But Michal, David's wife, warned him, 'If you do not escape tonight, you will be a dead man tomorrow!' 12 Michal then let David down through the window, and he made off, took to flight and so escaped.

13 Michal then took a domestic image, laid it on the bed, put a tress of goats' hair at the head of the bed and put a cover over it. 14 When Saul sent the agents to arrest David, she said, 'He is ill.' 15 Saul sent the agents back to see David, with the words, 'Bring him to me on his bed, for me to kill him!' 16 So in the agents went, and there in bed was the image, with the tress of goats' hair on its head! 17 Saul then said to Michal, 'Why have you deceived me like this and let my enemy go, and so make his escape?' Michal replied to Saul, 'He said, "Let me go, or I shall kill you!" '

18 David, having fled and made his escape, went to Samuel at Ramah and told him exactly how Saul had treated him; he and Samuel went and lived in the huts. 19 Word was brought to Saul, 'David is in the huts at Ramah.' 20 Saul accordingly sent agents to capture David; when they saw the community of prophets prophesying, and Samuel there as their leader, the spirit of God came over Saul's agents, and they too fell into frenzy. 21 When Saul was told of this, he sent other agents, and they too fell into frenzy; Saul then sent a third group of agents, and they fell into frenzy too.

NEW REVISED STANDARD VERSION

REVISED ENGLISH BIBLE

a frenzy. 22 Then he himself went to Ramah. He came to the great well that is in Secu;*l* he asked, "Where are Samuel and David?" And someone said, "They are at Naioth in Ramah." 23 He went there, toward Naioth in Ramah; and the spirit of God came upon him. As he was going, he fell into a prophetic frenzy, until he came to Naioth in Ramah. He too stripped off his clothes, and he too fell into a frenzy before Samuel. He lay naked all that day and all that night. Therefore it is said, "Is Saul also among the prophets?"

20 David fled from Naioth in Ramah. He came before Jonathan and said, "What have I done? What is my guilt? And what is my sin against your father that he is trying to take my life?" 2 He said to him, "Far from it! You shall not die. My father does nothing either great or small without disclosing it to me; and why should my father hide this from me? Never!" 3 But David also swore, "Your father knows well that you like me; and he thinks, 'Do not let Jonathan know this, or he will be grieved.' But truly, as the LORD lives and as you yourself live, there is but a step between me and death." 4 Then Jonathan said to David, "Whatever you say, I will do for you." 5 David said to Jonathan, "Tomorrow is the new moon, and I should not fail to sit with the king at the meal; but let me go, so that I may hide in the field until the third evening. 6 If your father misses me at all, then say, 'David earnestly asked leave of me to run to Bethlehem his city; for there is a yearly sacrifice there for all the family.' 7 If he says, 'Good!' it will be well with your servant; but if he is angry, then know that evil has been determined by him. 8 Therefore deal kindly with your servant, for you have brought your servant into a sacred covenant*m* with you. But if there is guilt in me, kill me yourself; why should you bring me to your father?" 9 Jonathan said, "Far be it from you! If I knew that it was decided by my father that evil should come upon you, would I not tell you?" 10 Then David said to Jonathan, "Who will tell me if your father answers you harshly?" 11 Jonathan replied to David, "Come, let us go out into the field." So they both went out into the field.

12 Jonathan said to David, "By the LORD, the God of Israel! When I have sounded out my father, about this time tomorrow, or on the third day, if he is well disposed toward David, shall I not then send and disclose it to you? 13 But if my father intends to do you harm, the LORD do so to Jonathan, and more also, if I do not disclose it to you, and send you away, so that you may go in safety. May the LORD be with you, as he has been with my father. 14 If I am still alive, show me the faithful love of the LORD; but if I die,*n* 15 never cut off your faithful love from my house, even if the LORD were to cut off every one of the enemies of David from the face of the earth." 16 Thus Jonathan made a covenant with the house of David, saying, "May the LORD seek out the enemies of David." 17 Jonathan made David swear again by his love for him; for he loved him as he loved his own life.

18 Jonathan said to him, "Tomorrow is the new moon; you will be missed, because your place will be empty. 19 On the day after tomorrow, you shall go a long way down; go to the place where you hid yourself earlier, and remain beside the stone there.*n* 20 I will shoot three arrows to the side of it, as though I shot at a mark. 21 Then I will send the boy, saying, 'Go, find the arrows.' If I say to the boy, 'Look, the arrows are on this side of you, collect them,' then you are to come, for, as the LORD lives, it is safe for you and there is no danger. 22 But if I say to the young man,

third time, they did the same. 22 Saul himself then set out for Ramah and came to the great cistern in Secu. He asked where Samuel and David were and was told that they were at Naioth in Ramah. 23 On his way there the spirit of God came upon him too and he went on, in a prophetic frenzy as he went, till he came to Naioth in Ramah. 24 There he too stripped off his clothes and like the rest fell into a frenzy before Samuel and lay down naked all that day and throughout that night. That is the reason for the saying, 'Is Saul also among the prophets?'

20 David made his escape from Naioth in Ramah and came to Jonathan. 'What have I done?' he asked. 'What is my offence? What wrong does your father think I have done, that he seeks my life?' 2 Jonathan answered, 'God forbid! There is no thought of putting you to death. I am sure my father will not do anything whatever without telling me. Why should my father hide such a thing from me? I cannot believe it!' 3 David said, 'I am ready to swear to it: your father has said to himself, "Jonathan must not know this or he will resent it," because he knows that you have a high regard for me. As the LORD lives, your life upon it, I am only a step away from death.' 4 Jonathan said to David, 'What do you want me to do for you?' 5 David answered, 'It is new moon tomorrow, and I am to dine with the king. But let me go and lie hidden in the fields until the third evening, 6 and if your father misses me, say, "David asked me for leave to hurry off on a visit to his home in Bethlehem, for it is the annual sacrifice there for the whole family." 7 If he says, "Good," it will be well for me; but if he flies into a rage, you will know that he is set on doing me harm. 8 My lord, keep faith with me; for you and I have entered into a solemn compact before the LORD. Kill me yourself if I am guilty, but do not let me fall into your father's hands.' 9 'God forbid!' cried Jonathan. 'If I find my father set on doing you harm, I shall tell you.' 10 David answered Jonathan, 'How will you let me know if he answers harshly?' 11 Jonathan said, 'Let us go into the fields,' and so they went there together.

12 Jonathan said, 'I promise you, David, in the sight of the LORD the God of Israel, this time tomorrow I shall sound my father for the third time and, if he is well disposed to you, I shall send and let you know. 13 If my father means mischief, may the LORD do the same to me and more, if I do not let you know and get you safely away. The LORD be with you as he has been with my father! 14 I know that as long as I live you will show me faithful friendship, as the LORD requires; and if I should die, 15 you will continue loyal to my family for ever. When the LORD rids the earth of all David's enemies, 16 may the LORD call him to account if he and his house are no longer my friends.' 17 Jonathan pledged himself afresh to David because of his love for him, for he loved him as himself.

18 Jonathan said, 'Tomorrow is the new moon, and you will be missed when your place is empty. 19 So the day after tomorrow go down at nightfall to the place where you hid on the day when the affair started; stay by the mound there. 20 I shall shoot three arrows towards it as though aiming at a target. 21 Then I shall send my boy to find the arrows. If I say to him, "Look, the arrows are on this side of you; pick them up," then you can come out of hiding. You will be quite safe, I swear it, for there will be nothing amiss. 22 But if I say to him, "Look, the arrows

20:12 **I promise . . . LORD:** *so Syriac; Heb.* David, the LORD. 20:16 **him:** *so Gk (Luc.); Heb.* David's enemies. **he . . . friends:** *so Gk; Heb. obscure.* 20:17 **pledged . . . David:** *so Gk; Heb.* made David swear. 20:19 **by . . . there:** *prob. rdg, cp. Gk; Heb.* by the Azel stone.

---

*l*Gk reads *to the well of the threshing floor on the bare height*
*m*Heb *a covenant of the LORD* *n*Meaning of Heb uncertain

22 Saul then went to Ramah himself. Arriving at the cistern of the threshing floor on the bare hilltop, he inquired, "Where are Samuel and David?", and was told, "At the sheds near Ramah." 23 As he set out from the hilltop toward the sheds, the spirit of God came upon him also, and he continued on in a prophetic condition until he reached the spot. At the sheds near Ramah 24 he, too, stripped himself of his garments and he, too, remained in the prophetic state in the presence of Samuel; all that day and night he lay naked. That is why they say, "Is Saul also among the prophets?"

20 David fled from the sheds near Ramah, and went to Jonathan. "What have I done?" he asked him. "What crime or what offense does your father hold against me that he seeks my life?" 2 Jonathan answered him: "Heaven forbid that you should die! My father does nothing, great or small, without disclosing it to me. Why, then, should my father conceal this from me? This cannot be so!" 3 But David replied: "Your father is well aware that I am favored with your friendship, so he has decided, 'Jonathan must not know of this lest he be grieved.' Nevertheless, as the LORD lives and as you live, there is but a step between me and death." 4 Jonathan then said to David, "I will do whatever you wish." 5 David answered: "Tomorrow is the new moon, when I should in fact dine with the king. Let me go and hide in the open country until evening. 6 If it turns out that your father misses me, say, 'David urged me to let him go on short notice to his city Bethlehem, because his whole clan is holding its seasonal sacrifice there.' 7 If he says, 'Very well,' your servant is safe. But if he becomes quite angry, you can be sure he has planned some harm. 8 Do this kindness for your servant because of the LORD's bond between us, into which you brought me: if I am guilty, kill me yourself! Why should you give me up to your father?" 9 But Jonathan answered: "Not I! If ever I find out that my father is determined to inflict injury upon you, I will certainly let you know." 10 David then asked Jonathan, "Who will tell me if your father gives you a harsh answer?"

11 [Jonathan replied to David, "Come, let us go out into the field." When they were out in the open country together, 12 Jonathan said to David: "As the LORD, the God of Israel, lives, I will sound out my father about this time tomorrow. Whether he is well disposed toward David or not, I will send you the information. 13 Should it please my father to bring any injury upon you, may the LORD do thus and so to Jonathan if I do not apprise you of it and send you on your way in peace. May the LORD be with you even as he was with my father. 14 Only this: if I am still alive, may you show me the kindness of the LORD. But if I die, 15 never withdraw your kindness from my house. And when the LORD exterminates all the enemies of David from the surface of the earth, 16 the name of Jonathan must never be allowed by the family of David to die out from among you, or the LORD will make you answer for it." 17 And in his love for David, Jonathan renewed his oath to him, because he loved him as his very self.]

18 Jonathan then said to him: "Tomorrow is the new moon; and you will be missed, since your place will be vacant. 19 On the following day you will be missed all the more. Go to the spot where you hid on the other occasion and wait near the mound there. 20 On the third day of the month I will shoot arrows, as though aiming at a target. 21 I will then send my attendant to go and recover the arrows. If in fact I say to him, 'Look, the arrow is this side of you; pick it up,' come, for you are safe. As the LORD lives, there will be nothing to fear. 22 But if I say to the boy, 'Look, the

22 He then went to Ramah himself and, arriving at the large storage-well at Seku, asked, 'Where are Samuel and David?' And someone said, 'Why, they are in the huts at Ramah!' 23 Making his way from there to the huts at Ramah, the spirit of God came over him too, and he went along in a frenzy until he arrived at the huts at Ramah. 24 He too stripped off his clothes and he too fell into a frenzy in Samuel's presence, then collapsed naked on the ground for the rest of that day and all night. Hence the saying: Is Saul one of the prophets too?

20 Fleeing from the huts at Ramah, David went and confronted Jonathan, 'What have I done, what is my guilt, how have I wronged your father, for him to want to take my life?' 2 He replied, 'You must not think that! You are not going to die. My father, you see, does nothing, important or unimportant, without confiding in me, so why should my father hide this from me? It is not true.' 3 In reply, David swore, 'Your father knows very well that I enjoy your favour, and thinks, "Jonathan must not know about this or he will be upset." But, as Yahweh lives and as you yourself live, there is only a step between me and death.'

4 At which, Jonathan said to David, 'Whatever you think best, I will certainly do for you.' 5 David replied, 'Look, tomorrow is New Moon and I ought to sit at table with the king, but you must let me go and hide in the countryside until the evening. 6 If your father notices my absence, you must say, "David insistently asked me for permission to hurry over to Bethlehem, his home town, because they are holding the annual sacrifice there for the whole clan." 7 If he says, "Very well," your servant is safe, but if he flies into a rage, you may be sure that he has some evil plan. 8 Show your servant faithful love, since you have bound your servant to you by a pact in Yahweh's name. But if I am guilty, then kill me yourself — why take me to your father?' 9 Jonathan replied, 'Perish the thought! If I knew for sure that my father was determined to do you a mischief, would I not have told you?' 10 David then said to Jonathan, 'Who will let me know if your father gives you a harsh answer?'

11 Jonathan then said to David, 'Come on, let us go out into the country,' and the pair of them went out into the country. 12 Jonathan then said to David, 'By Yahweh, God of Israel! I shall sound my father this time tomorrow; if all is well for David and I do not then send and inform you, 13 may Yahweh bring unnameable ills to Jonathan and worse ones too! If my father intends to do you a mischief, I shall tell you so and let you get away, so that you can be safe. And may Yahweh be with you as he used to be with my father! 14 If I am still alive, show your servant faithful love; if I die, 15 never withdraw your faithful love from my family. When Yahweh has exterminated every enemy of David's from the face of the earth, 16 do not let Jonathan's name be exterminated with Saul's family, or may Yahweh call David to account!' 17 Jonathan then renewed his oath to David, since he loved him like his very soul.

18 Jonathan then said to David, 'Tomorrow is New Moon; your absence will be noticed, since your place will be empty. 19 The day after tomorrow your absence will be very marked, and you must go to the place where you hid on the day of the deed, and stay beside that mound. 20 For my part, the day after tomorrow I shall shoot three arrows in that direction, as though at a target. 21 I shall then send a servant to go and find the arrows. If I say to him, "The arrows are this side of you, get them," come out, since all will be well for you and nothing the matter, as sure as Yahweh lives.

'Look, the arrows are beyond you,' then go; for the LORD has sent you away. 23 As for the matter about which you and I have spoken, the LORD is witness*o* between you and me forever."

24 So David hid himself in the field. When the new moon came, the king sat at the feast to eat. 25 The king sat upon his seat, as at other times, upon the seat by the wall. Jonathan stood, while Abner sat by Saul's side; but David's place was empty.

26 Saul did not say anything that day; for he thought, "Something has befallen him; he is not clean, surely he is not clean." 27 But on the second day, the day after the new moon, David's place was empty. And Saul said to his son Jonathan, "Why has the son of Jesse not come to the feast, either yesterday or today?" 28 Jonathan answered Saul, "David earnestly asked leave of me to go to Bethlehem; 29 he said, 'Let me go; for our family is holding a sacrifice in the city, and my brother has commanded me to be there. So now, if I have found favor in your sight, let me get away, and see my brothers.' For this reason he has not come to the king's table."

30 Then Saul's anger was kindled against Jonathan. He said to him, "You son of a perverse, rebellious woman! Do I not know that you have chosen the son of Jesse to your own shame, and to the shame of your mother's nakedness? 31 For as long as the son of Jesse lives upon the earth, neither you nor your kingdom shall be established. Now send and bring him to me, for he shall surely die." 32 Then Jonathan answered his father Saul, "Why should he be put to death? What has he done?" 33 But Saul threw his spear at him to strike him; so Jonathan knew that it was the decision of his father to put David to death. 34 Jonathan rose from the table in fierce anger and ate no food on the second day of the month, for he was grieved for David, and because his father had disgraced him.

35 In the morning Jonathan went out into the field to the appointment with David, and with him was a little boy. 36 He said to the boy, "Run and find the arrows that I shoot." As the boy ran, he shot an arrow beyond him. 37 When the boy came to the place where Jonathan's arrow had fallen, Jonathan called after the boy and said, "Is the arrow not beyond you?" 38 Jonathan called after the boy, "Hurry, be quick, do not linger." So Jonathan's arrow gathered up the arrows and came to his master. 39 But the boy knew nothing; only Jonathan and David knew the arrangement. 40 Jonathan gave his weapons to the boy and said to him, "Go and carry them to the city." 41 As soon as the boy had gone, David rose from beside the stone heap*p* and prostrated himself with his face to the ground. He bowed three times, and they kissed each other, and wept with each other; David wept the more. 42 Then Jonathan said to David, "Go in peace, since both of us have sworn in the name of the LORD, saying, 'The LORD shall be between me and you, and between my descendants and your descendants, forever.'" He got up and left; and Jonathan went into the city.*r*

21 *s* David came to Nob to the priest Ahimelech. Ahimelech came trembling to meet David, and said to him, "Why are you alone, and no one with you?" 2 David said to the priest Ahimelech, "The king has charged me with a matter, and said to me, 'No one must know anything of the matter about which I send you, and with which I have charged you.' I have made an appointment*t* with the young men for such and such a place. 3 Now then, what have you at hand? Give me five loaves of bread, or whatever is here."

are on the other side of you, farther on," then the LORD has said that you must go; 23 the LORD stands witness between us for ever to the pledges we have exchanged.'

24 David hid in the fields, and when the new moon came the king sat down to eat at mealtime. 25 Saul took his customary seat by the wall, and Abner sat beside him; Jonathan too was present, but David's place was empty. 26 That day Saul said nothing, for he thought that David was absent by some chance, perhaps because he was ritually unclean. 27 But on the second day, the day after the new moon, David's place was still empty, and Saul said to his son Jonathan, 'Why has the son of Jesse not come to the feast, either yesterday or today?' 28 Jonathan answered, 'David asked permission to go to Bethlehem. 29 He asked my leave and said, "Our family is holding a sacrifice in the town and my brother himself has told me to be there. Now, if you have any regard for me, let me slip away to see my brothers." That is why he has not come to the king's table.' 30 Saul's anger blazed up against Jonathan and he said, 'You son of a crooked and rebellious mother! I know perfectly well you have made a friend of the son of Jesse only to bring shame on yourself and dishonour on your mother. 31 But as long as Jesse's son remains alive on the earth, neither you nor your kingdom will be established. Send at once and fetch him; he deserves to die.' 32 Jonathan answered his father, 'Deserves to die? Why? What has he done?' 33 At that, Saul picked up his spear and threatened to kill him; and Jonathan knew that his father was bent on David's death. 34 He left the table in a rage and ate nothing on the second day of the festival; for he was indignant on David's behalf and because his father had humiliated him.

35 Next morning Jonathan, accompanied by a young boy, went out into the fields to keep the appointment with David. 36 He said to the boy, 'Run ahead and find the arrows I shoot.' As the boy ran on, he shot the arrows over his head. 37 When the boy reached the place where the arrows had fallen, Jonathan called out after him, 'Look, the arrows are beyond you. 38 Hurry! Go quickly! Do not delay.' The boy gathered up the arrows and brought them to his master; 39 but only Jonathan and David knew what this meant; the boy knew nothing. 40 Jonathan handed his weapons to the boy and told him to take them back to town.

41 When the boy had gone, David got up from behind the mound and bowed humbly three times. Then they kissed one another and shed tears together, until David's grief was even greater than Jonathan's. 42 Jonathan said to David, 'Go in safety; we have pledged each other in the name of the LORD who is witness for ever between you and me and between your descendants and mine.'

David went off at once, while Jonathan returned to the town.

21 1 David made his way to Nob to the priest Ahimelech, who hurried out to meet him and asked, 'Why are you alone and unattended?' 2 David answered Ahimelech, 'I am under orders from the king: I was to let no one know about the mission on which he was sending me or what these orders were. When I took leave of my men I told them to meet me in such and such a place. 3 Now, what have you got by you? Let me have five loaves, or as many as you can find.' 4 The priest answered David, 'I have no ordinary

---

o Gk: Heb lacks *witness*   *p* Gk: Heb *from beside the south*   *q* Vg: Meaning of Heb uncertain   *r* This sentence is 21.1 in Heb   *s* Ch 21.2 in Heb   *t* Q Ms Vg Compare Gk: Meaning of MT uncertain

20:27 on the second day: *so* Gk; *Heb.* the second.   **20:41 the mound:** *prob. rdg, cp.* Gk; *Heb.* the Negeb.   **20:42 David went off:** *in Heb.* 21:1 *begins here.*   **21:1** *In Heb.* 21:2.

arrow is beyond you,' go, for the LORD sends you away. 23 However, in the matter which you and I have discussed, the LORD shall be between you and me forever." 24 So David hid in the open country.

On the day of the new moon, when the king sat at table to dine, 25 taking his usual place against the wall, Jonathan sat facing him, while Abner sat at the king's side, and David's place was vacant. 26 Saul, however, said nothing that day, for he thought, "He must have become unclean by accident, and not yet have been cleansed." 27 On the next day, the second day of the month, David's place was vacant. Saul inquired of his son Jonathan, "Why has the son of Jesse not come to table yesterday or today?" 28 Jonathan answered Saul: "David urgently asked me to let him go to his city, Bethlehem. 29 'Please let me go,' he begged, 'for we are to have a clan sacrifice in our city, and my brothers insist on my presence. Now, therefore, if you think well of me, give me leave to visit my brothers.' That is why he has not come to the king's table." 30 But Saul was extremely angry with Jonathan and said to him: "Son of a rebellious woman, do I not know that, to your own shame and to the disclosure of your mother's shame, you are the companion of Jesse's son? 31 Why, as long as the son of Jesse lives upon the earth, you cannot make good your claim to the kingship! So send for him, and bring him to me, for he is doomed." 32 But Jonathan asked his father Saul: "Why should he die? What has he done?" 33 At this Saul brandished his spear to strike him, and thus Jonathan learned that his father was resolved to kill David. 34 Jonathan sprang up from the table in great anger and took no food that second day of the month, for he was grieved on David's account, since his father had railed against him.

35 The next morning Jonathan went out into the field with a little boy for his appointment with David. 36 There he said to the boy, "Run and fetch the arrow." And as the boy ran, he shot an arrow beyond him in the direction of the city. 37 When the boy made for the spot where Jonathan had shot the arrow, Jonathan called after him, "The arrow is farther on!" 38 Again he called to his lad, "Hurry, be quick, don't delay!" Jonathan's boy picked up the arrow and brought it to his master. 39 The boy knew nothing; only Jonathan and David knew what was meant. 40 Then Jonathan gave his weapons to this boy of his and said to him, "Go, take them to the city." 41 When the boy had left, David rose from beside the mound and prostrated himself on the ground three times before Jonathan in homage. They kissed each other and wept aloud together. 42 At length Jonathan said to David, "Go in peace, in keeping with what we two have sworn by the name of the LORD: 'The LORD shall be between you and me, and between your posterity and mine forever.' "

21 Then David departed on his way, while Jonathan went back into the city.

2 David went to Ahimelech, the priest of Nob, who came trembling to meet him and asked, "Why are you alone? Is there no one with you?" 3 David answered the priest: "The king gave me a commission and told me to let no one know anything about the business on which he sent me or the commission he gave me. For that reason I have arranged a meeting place with my men. 4 Now what have you on hand? Give me five loaves, or whatever you can find." 5 But the

22 But if I say to him, "The arrows are ahead of you," then be off, for Yahweh himself will be sending you away. 23 And as regards the agreement we made, you and I, why, Yahweh is witness between us for ever.'

24 So David hid in the country; New Moon came and the king sat down to his meal. 25 He sat in his usual place with his back to the wall, Jonathan sat facing him and Abner sat next to Saul; but David's place was empty. 26 Saul said nothing that day, thinking, 'It is sheer chance; he is unclean.' 27 On the day after New Moon, the second day, David's place was still empty. 28 Saul said to his son Jonathan, 'Why did not the son of Jesse come to the meal either yesterday or today?' 29 Jonathan answered Saul, 'David insistently asked me for permission to go to Bethlehem. "Please let me go," he said, "for we are holding the clan sacrifice in the town and my brothers have ordered me to attend. So now, if I enjoy your favour, let me get away and see my brothers." That is why he has not come to the king's table.'

30 Saul flew into a rage with Jonathan and said, 'Son of a rebellious slut! Don't I know that you side with the son of Jesse to your own shame and your mother's dishonour? 31 As long as the son of Jesse lives on earth, neither you nor your royal rights are secure. Now have him fetched and brought to me; he deserves to die.' 32 Jonathan retorted to his father Saul, 'Why should he die? What has he done?' 33 But Saul brandished his spear at him to strike him, and Jonathan realised that his father was determined that David should die. 34 Hot with anger, Jonathan got up from the table and ate nothing on the second day of the month, being upset about David — and because his father had insulted him.

35 Next morning, Jonathan went out into the country at the time agreed with David, taking a young servant with him. 36 He said to his servant, 'Run and find the arrows which I am going to shoot,' and the servant ran while Jonathan shot an arrow ahead of him. 37 When the servant reached the spot to which Jonathan had shot the arrow, Jonathan shouted after him, 'Is not the arrow ahead of you?' 38 Again Jonathan shouted after the servant, 'Quick! Hurry, do not stand around.' Jonathan's servant picked up the arrow and brought it back to his master. 39 The servant suspected nothing; only Jonathan and David knew what was meant.

40 Jonathan then gave his weapons to his servant and said, 'Go and carry them to the town.' 41 As soon as the servant had gone, David stood up beside the mound, threw himself to the ground, prostrating himself three times. They then embraced each other, both weeping copiously. 42 Jonathan then said to David, 'Go in peace. And as regards the oath that both of us have sworn by the name of Yahweh, may Yahweh be witness between you and me, between your descendants and mine for ever.'

21 David then got up and left, and Jonathan went back to the town.

2 David then went to Nob, to Ahimelech the priest. Ahimelech came out trembling to meet David and said, 'Why are you alone? Why is nobody with you?' 3 David replied to Ahimelech the priest, 'The king has given me an order and said to me, "Do not let anyone know anything about the mission on which I am sending you, or about the order which I have given you." I have arranged to meet the guards at such and such a place. 4 Meanwhile, if you have five loaves of bread to hand, give them to me, or whatever there is.' 5 The priest replied to David, 'I have no ordinary bread

4 The priest answered David, "I have no ordinary bread at hand, only holy bread — provided that the young men have kept themselves from women." 5 David answered the priest, "Indeed women have been kept from us as always when I go on an expedition; the vessels of the young men are holy even when it is a common journey; how much more today will their vessels be holy?" 6 So the priest gave him the holy bread; for there was no bread there except the bread of the Presence, which is removed from before the LORD, to be replaced by hot bread on the day it is taken away.

7 Now a certain man of the servants of Saul was there that day, detained before the LORD; his name was Doeg the Edomite, the chief of Saul's shepherds.

8 David said to Ahimelech, "Is there no spear or sword here with you? I did not bring my sword or my weapons with me, because the king's business required haste." 9 The priest said, "The sword of Goliath the Philistine, whom you killed in the valley of Elah, is here wrapped in a cloth behind the ephod; if you will take that, take it, for there is none here except that one." David said, "There is none like it; give it to me."

10 David rose and fled that day from Saul; he went to King Achish of Gath. 11 The servants of Achish said to him, "Is this not David the king of the land? Did they not sing to one another of him in dances,

'Saul has killed his thousands,
    and David his ten thousands'?"

12 David took these words to heart and was very much afraid of King Achish of Gath. 13 So he changed his behavior before them; he pretended to be mad when in their presence. *u* He scratched marks on the doors of the gate, and let his spittle run down his beard. 14 Achish said to his servants, "Look, you see the man is mad; why then have you brought him to me? 15 Do I lack madmen, that you have brought this fellow to play the madman in my presence? Shall this fellow come into my house?"

22 David left there and escaped to the cave of Adullam; when his brothers and all his father's house heard of it, they went down there to him. 2 Everyone who was in distress, and everyone who was in debt, and everyone who was discontented gathered to him; and he became captain over them. Those who were with him numbered about four hundred.

3 David went from there to Mizpeh of Moab. He said to the king of Moab, "Please let my father and mother come *v* to you, until I know what God will do for me." 4 He left them with the king of Moab, and they stayed with him all the time that David was in the stronghold. 5 Then the prophet Gad said to David, "Do not remain in the stronghold; leave, and go into the land of Judah." So David left, and went into the forest of Hereth.

6 Saul heard that David and those who were with him had been located. Saul was sitting at Gibeah, under the tamarisk tree on the height, with his spear in his hand, and all his servants were standing around him. 7 Saul said to his servants who stood around him, "Hear now, you Benjaminites; will the son of Jesse give every one of you fields and vineyards, will he make you all commanders of thousands and commanders of hundreds? 8 Is that why all of you have conspired against me? No one discloses to me when my son makes a league with the son of Jesse, none of you is sorry for me or discloses to me that my son has stirred up my servant against me, to lie in wait, as he is doing today." 9 Doeg the Edomite, who was in charge of Saul's servants, answered, "I saw the son of Jesse coming to Nob, to Ahimelech son of Ahitub; 10 he inquired of the LORD for him,

bread available. There is only the sacred bread; but have the young men kept themselves from women?' 5 David answered the priest, 'Women have been denied us as hitherto when I have been on campaign, even an ordinary campaign, and the young men's bodies have remained holy; and how much more will they be holy today!' 6 So, as there was no other bread there, the priest gave him the sacred bread, the Bread of the Presence, which had just been taken from the presence of the LORD to be replaced by freshly baked bread on the day that the old was removed. 7 One of Saul's servants happened to be there that day, detained before the LORD; his name was Doeg the Edomite, and he was the chief of Saul's herdsmen. 8 David said to Ahimelech, 'Have you a spear or sword here at hand? I have no sword or other weapon with me, because the king's business was urgent.' 9 The priest answered, 'There is the sword of Goliath the Philistine whom you slew in the valley of Elah; it is wrapped up in a cloak behind the ephod. If you want to take that, take it; there is no other weapon here.' David said, 'There is no sword like it; give it to me.'

10 That day David went on his way, fleeing from Saul, and came to King Achish of Gath. 11 The servants of Achish said to him, 'Surely this is David, the king of his country, the man of whom they sang as they danced:

"Saul struck down thousands,
    but David tens of thousands."'

12 These comments were not lost on David, and he became very much afraid of King Achish of Gath. 13 So he altered his behaviour in public and acted like a madman in front of them all, scrabbling on the double doors of the city gate and dribbling down his beard. 14 Achish said to his servants, 'The man is insane! Why bring him to me? 15 Am I short of madmen that you bring this one to plague me? Must I have this fellow in my house?'

22 DAVID stole away from there and went to the cave of Adullam, and, when his brothers and all the members of his family heard where he was, they went down and joined him there. 2 Everyone in any kind of distress or in debt or with a grievance gathered round him, about four hundred in number, and he became their chief. 3 From there David went to Mizpeh in Moab and said to the king of Moab, 'Let my father and mother come and take shelter with you until I know what God will do for me.' 4 He left them at the court of the king of Moab, and they stayed there as long as David remained in his stronghold.

5 The prophet Gad said to David, 'You must not stay in your stronghold; go at once into Judah.' David went as far as the forest of Hareth. 6 News that the whereabouts of David and his men was known reached Saul while he was in Gibeah, sitting under the tamarisk tree on the hilltop with his spear in his hand and all his retainers standing about him. 7 He said to them, 'Listen to me, you Benjamites: do you expect the son of Jesse to give you all fields and vineyards, or make you all officers over units of a thousand and a hundred? 8 Is that why you have all conspired against me? Not one of you told me when my son made a compact with the son of Jesse; none of you spared a thought for me or told me that my son had set against me my own servant, who is lying in wait for me now.'

9 Doeg the Edomite, who was standing with Saul's servants, spoke up: 'I saw the son of Jesse coming to Nob, to Ahimelech son of Ahitub. 10 Ahimelech consulted the LORD

---

u Heb *in their hands*   *v* Syr Vg: Heb *come out*

NEW AMERICAN BIBLE

NEW JERUSALEM BIBLE

priest replied to David, "I have no ordinary bread on hand, only holy bread; if the men have abstained from women, you may eat some of that." 6 David answered the priest: "We have indeed been segregated from women as on previous occasions. Whenever I go on a journey, all the young men are consecrated — even for a secular journey. All the more so today, when they are consecrated at arms!" 7 So the priest gave him holy bread, for no other bread was on hand except the showbread which had been removed from the LORD's presence and replaced by fresh bread when it was taken away. 8 One of Saul's servants was there that day, detained before the LORD; his name was Doeg the Edomite, and he was Saul's chief henchman.

9 David then asked Ahimelech: "Do you have a spear or a sword on hand? I brought along neither my sword nor my weapons, because the king's business was urgent." 10 The priest replied: "The sword of Goliath the Philistine, whom you killed in the Vale of the Terebinth, is here [wrapped in a mantle] behind an ephod. If you wish to take that, take it; there is no sword here except that one." David said: "There is none to match it. Give it to me!"

11 That same day David took to flight from Saul, going to Achish, king of Gath. 12 But the servants of Achish said, "Is this not David, the king of the land? During their dances do they not sing,

'Saul has slain his thousands,
but David his ten thousands'?"

13 David took note of these remarks and became very much afraid of Achish, king of Gath. 14 So, as they watched, he feigned insanity and acted like a madman in their hands, drumming on the doors of the gate and drooling onto his beard. 15 Finally Achish said to his servants: "You see the man is mad. Why did you bring him to me? 16 Do I not have enough madmen, that you bring in this one to carry on in my presence? Should this fellow come into my house?"

22 David left Gath and escaped to the cave of Adullam. When his brothers and the rest of his family heard about it, they came down to him there. 2 He was joined by all those who were in difficulties or in debt, or who were embittered, and he became their leader. About four hundred men were with him.

3 From there David went to Mizpeh of Moab and said to the king of Moab, "Let my father and mother stay with you, until I learn what God will do for me." 4 He left them with the king of Moab, and they stayed with him as long as David remained in the refuge.

5 But the prophet Gad said to David: "Do not remain in the refuge. Leave, and go to the land of Judah." And so David left and went to the forest of Hereth.

6 Now Saul heard that David and his men had been located. At the time he was sitting in Gibeah under a tamarisk tree on the high place, holding his spear, while all his servants were standing by. 7 So he said to them: "Listen, men of Benjamin! Will the son of Jesse give all of you fields and vineyards? Will he make each of you an officer over a thousand or a hundred men, 8 that you have all conspired against me and no one tells me that my son has made an agreement with the son of Jesse? None of you shows sympathy for me or discloses to me that my son has stirred up my servant to be an enemy against me, as is the case today." 9 Then Doeg the Edomite, who was standing with the officers of Saul, spoke up: "I saw the son of Jesse come to Ahimelech, son of Ahitub, in Nob. 10 He consulted the

to hand; there are only consecrated loaves of permanent offering — provided that the men have kept themselves from women?'

6 David replied to the priest, 'Certainly, women have been forbidden to us, as always when I set off on a campaign. The men's things are clean. Though this is a profane journey, they are certainly clean today as far as their things are concerned.' 7 The priest then gave him what had been consecrated, for the only bread there was the loaves of permanent offering, which is taken out of Yahweh's presence, to be replaced by warm bread on the day when it is removed.

8 Now one of Saul's servants happened to be there that day, detained in Yahweh's presence; his name was Doeg the Edomite and he was the strongest of Saul's shepherds.

9 David then said to Ahimelech, 'Have you no spear or sword here to hand? I did not bring either my sword or my weapons with me, because the king's business was urgent.' 10 The priest replied, 'The sword of Goliath the Philistine whom you killed in the Valley of the Terebinth is here, wrapped in a piece of clothing behind the *ephod;[i]* if you care to take it, do so, for that is the only one here.' David said, 'There is nothing like that one; give it to me.'

11 David journeyed on and that day fled out of Saul's reach, going to Achish king of Gath. 12 Achish's servants said to him, 'Is not this David, the king of the country? Was it not of him that they sang as they danced:

Saul has killed his thousands,
and David his tens of thousands?'

13 David pondered on these words and became very frightened of Achish king of Gath. 14 When their eyes were on him, he played the madman and, when they held him, he feigned lunacy. He drummed his feet on the doors of the gate and let his spittle run down his beard.

15 Achish said to his servants, 'You can see that this man is mad. Why bring him to me? 16 Have I not enough madmen, without your bringing me this one to weary me with his antics? Is he to join my household?'

22 David left there and took refuge in the Cave of Adullam; his brothers and his father's whole family heard this and joined him there. 2 All those in distress, all those in debt, all those who had a grievance, gathered round him and he became their leader. There were about four hundred men with him.

3 From there David went to Mizpah in Moab and said to the king of Moab, 'Allow my father and mother to stay with you until I know what God intends to do for me.' 4 He left them with the king of Moab and there they stayed all the time that David was in the stronghold.

5 The prophet Gad, however, said to David, 'Do not stay in the stronghold; leave and make your way into the territory of Judah.' David then left and went to the forest of Hereth.

6 When Saul heard that David and the men with him had been discovered, Saul was at Gibeah, seated under the tamarisk on the high place, spear in hand, with all his staff standing round him. 7 'Listen, Benjaminites!' said Saul to them, 'Is the son of Jesse going to give you all fields and vineyards and make all of you commanders of thousands and commanders of hundreds 8 that you all conspire against me? No one warned me when my son made a pact with the son of Jesse; none of you felt sorry for me or warned me when my son incited my servant to become my enemy, as he is now.'

9 Then, up spoke Doeg the Edomite, who was in command of Saul's staff, 'I saw the son of Jesse coming to Nob, to Ahimelech son of Ahitub. 10 That man consulted Yahweh

---

i **21** Here either the container of the sacred lots or some object used in worship.

| NEW REVISED STANDARD VERSION | REVISED ENGLISH BIBLE |

gave him provisions, and gave him the sword of Goliath the Philistine."

11 The king sent for the priest Ahimelech son of Ahitub and for all his father's house, the priests who were at Nob; and all of them came to the king. 12 Saul said, "Listen now, son of Ahitub." He answered, "Here I am, my lord." 13 Saul said to him, "Why have you conspired against me, you and the son of Jesse, by giving him bread and a sword, and by inquiring of God for him, so that he has risen against me, to lie in wait, as he is doing today?"

14 Then Ahimelech answered the king, "Who among all your servants is so faithful as David? He is the king's son-in-law, and is quick*w* to do your bidding, and is honored in your house. 15 Is today the first time that I have inquired of God for him? By no means! Do not let the king impute anything to his servant or to any member of my father's house; for your servant has known nothing of all this, much or little." 16 The king said, "You shall surely die, Ahimelech, you and all your father's house." 17 The king said to the guard who stood around him, "Turn and kill the priests of the LORD, because their hand also is with David; they knew that he fled, and did not disclose it to me." But the servants of the king would not raise their hand to attack the priests of the LORD. 18 Then the king said to Doeg, "You, Doeg, turn and attack the priests." Doeg the Edomite turned and attacked the priests; on that day he killed eighty-five who wore the linen ephod. 19 Nob, the city of the priests, he put to the sword; men and women, children and infants, oxen, donkeys, and sheep, he put to the sword.

20 But one of the sons of Ahimelech son of Ahitub, named Abiathar, escaped and fled after David. 21 Abiathar told David that Saul had killed the priests of the LORD. 22 David said to Abiathar, "I knew on that day, when Doeg the Edomite was there, that he would surely tell Saul. I am responsible*x* for the lives of all your father's house. 23 Stay with me, and do not be afraid; for the one who seeks my life seeks your life; you will be safe with me."

23 Now they told David, "The Philistines are fighting against Keilah, and are robbing the threshing floors." 2 David inquired of the LORD, "Shall I go and attack these Philistines?" The LORD said to David, "Go and attack the Philistines and save Keilah." 3 But David's men said to him, "Look, we are afraid here in Judah; how much more then if we go to Keilah against the armies of the Philistines?" 4 Then David inquired of the LORD again. The LORD answered him, "Yes, go down to Keilah; for I will give the Philistines into your hand." 5 So David and his men went to Keilah, fought with the Philistines, brought away their livestock, and dealt them a heavy defeat. Thus David rescued the inhabitants of Keilah.

6 When Abiathar son of Ahimelech fled to David at Keilah, he came down with an ephod in his hand. 7 Now it was told Saul that David had come to Keilah. And Saul said, "God has given*y* him into my hand; for he has shut himself in by entering a town that has gates and bars." 8 Saul summoned all the people to war, to go down to Keilah, to besiege David and his men. 9 When David learned that Saul was plotting evil against him, he said to the priest Abiathar, "Bring the ephod here." 10 David said, "O LORD, the God of Israel, your servant has heard that Saul seeks to come to Keilah, to destroy the city on my account. 11 And now, will*z* Saul come down as your servant has heard? O LORD, the God of Israel, I beseech you, tell your servant." The LORD said, "He will come down." 12 Then David said,

on his behalf, then gave him food and handed over to him the sword of Goliath the Philistine.' 11 The king sent for Ahimelech the priest and his whole family, who were priests at Nob, and they all came to him. 12 Saul said, 'Now listen, you son of Ahitub,' and the man answered, 'Yes, my lord?' 13 Saul said to him, 'Why have you and the son of Jesse plotted against me? You gave him food and a sword, and consulted God on his behalf; and now he has risen against me and is at this moment lying in wait for me.' 14 'And who among all your servants', answered Ahimelech, 'is like David, a man to be trusted, the king's son-in-law, appointed to your staff and holding an honourable place in your household? 15 Have I on this occasion done something profane in consulting God on his behalf? God forbid! I trust that my lord the king will not accuse me or my family; for I know nothing whatever about it.' 16 But the king said, 'Ahimelech, you shall die, you and all your family.' 17 He then said to the bodyguard attending him, 'Turn on the priests of the LORD and kill them; for they are in league with David, and, though they knew that he was a fugitive, they did not inform me.' The king's men, however, were unwilling to raise a hand against the priests of the LORD. 18 The king therefore said to Doeg the Edomite, 'You, Doeg, go and fall on the priests'; so Doeg went and fell upon the priests, killing that day with his own hand eighty-five men who wore the linen ephod. 19 He put to the sword every living thing in Nob, the town of the priests: men and women, children and babes in arms, oxen, donkeys, and sheep.

20 One of Ahimelech's sons named Abiathar made his escape and joined David. 21 He told David how Saul had killed the priests of the LORD, 22 and David said to him, 'When Doeg the Edomite was there that day, I knew that he would certainly tell Saul. I have brought this on all the members of your father's house. 23 Stay here with me, have no fear; he who seeks your life seeks mine, and you will be safe with me.'

23 The Philistines had launched an assault on Keilah and were plundering the threshing-floors. When this was reported to David, 2 he consulted the LORD and asked whether he should go and attack these Philistines. The LORD answered, 'Go, attack them, and relieve Keilah.' 3 But David's men said to him, 'Here in Judah we are afraid. How much worse if we challenge the Philistine forces at Keilah!' 4 David consulted the LORD once again and got the answer, 'Go down at once to Keilah; I shall give the Philistines into your hands.' 5 David and his men marched to Keilah, fought the Philistines, and carried off their livestock; they inflicted a heavy defeat on them and relieved the inhabitants of Keilah.

6 When Abiathar son of Ahimelech fled and joined David at Keilah, he brought an ephod with him. 7 It was reported to Saul that David had entered Keilah, and he said, 'God has put him into my hands; for he has walked into a trap by entering a walled town with its barred gates.' 8 He called out all the army to march on Keilah and besiege David and his men.

9 When David learnt how Saul planned his overthrow, he told Abiathar the priest to bring the ephod, 10 and then he prayed, 'LORD God of Israel, I your servant have heard that Saul intends to come to Keilah and destroy the town because of me. 11 Will the townspeople of Keilah surrender me to him? Will Saul come down as I have heard? LORD God of Israel, I pray you, tell your servant.' The LORD answered, 'He will come.' 12 David asked, 'Will the citi-

w Heb *and turns aside*   *x* Gk Vg: Meaning of Heb uncertain
y Gk Tg: Heb *made a stranger of*   *z* Q Ms Compare Gk: MT *Will the men of Keilah surrender me into his hand? Will*

LORD for him and gave him supplies, and the sword of Goliath the Philistine as well."

¹¹ At this the king sent a summons to Ahimelech the priest, son of Ahitub, and to all his family who were priests in Nob; and they all came to the king. ¹² Then Saul said, "Listen, son of Ahitub!" He replied, "Yes, my lord." ¹³ Saul asked him, "Why did you conspire against me with the son of Jesse by giving him food and a sword and by consulting God for him, that he might rebel against me and become my enemy, as is the case today?" ¹⁴ Ahimelech answered the king: "And who among all your servants is as loyal as David, the king's son-in-law, captain of your bodyguard, and honored in your own house? ¹⁵ Is this the first time I have consulted God for him? No indeed! Let not the king accuse his servant or anyone in my family of such a thing. Your servant knows nothing at all, great or small, about the whole matter." ¹⁶ But the king said, "You shall die, Ahimelech, with all your family." ¹⁷ The king then commanded his henchmen standing by: "Make the rounds and kill the priests of the LORD, for they assisted David. They knew he was a fugitive and yet failed to inform me." But the king's servants refused to lift a hand to strike the priests of the LORD.

¹⁸ The king therefore commanded Doeg, "You make the rounds and kill the priests!" So Doeg the Edomite went from one to the next and killed the priests himself, slaying on that day eighty-five who wore the linen ephod. ¹⁹ Saul also put the priestly city of Nob to the sword, including men and women, children and infants, and oxen, asses and sheep.

²⁰ One son of Ahimelech, son of Ahitub, named Abiathar, escaped and fled to David. ²¹ When Abiathar told David that Saul had slain the priests of the LORD, ²² David said to him: "I knew that day, when Doeg the Edomite was there, that he would surely tell Saul. I am responsible for the death of all your family. ²³ Stay with me. Fear nothing; he that seeks your life must seek my life also. You are under my protection."

23 David received information that the Philistines were attacking Keilah and plundering the threshing floors. ² So he consulted the LORD, inquiring, "Shall I go and defeat these Philistines?" The LORD answered, "Go, for you will defeat the Philistines and rescue Keilah." ³ But David's men said to him: "We are afraid here in Judah. How much more so if we go to Keilah against the forces of the Philistines!" ⁴ Again David consulted the LORD, who answered, "Go down to Keilah, for I will deliver the Philistines into your power." ⁵ David then went with his men to Keilah and fought with the Philistines. He drove off their cattle and inflicted a severe defeat on them, and thus rescued the inhabitants of Keilah.

⁶ Abiathar, son of Ahimelech, who had fled to David, went down with David to Keilah, taking the ephod with him.

⁷ When Saul was told that David had entered Keilah, he said: "God has put him in my grip. Now he has shut himself in, for he has entered a city with gates and bars." ⁸ Saul then called all the people to war, in order to go down to Keilah and besiege David and his men. ⁹ When David found out that Saul was planning to harm him, he said to the priest Abiathar, "Bring forward the ephod." ¹⁰ David then said: "O LORD God of Israel, your servant has heard a report that Saul plans to come to Keilah, to destroy the city on my account. ¹¹ Will they hand me over? And now: will Saul come down as your servant has heard? O LORD God of Israel, tell your servant." The LORD answered, "He will come down." ¹² David then asked, "Will the citizens of

on his behalf, gave him provisions and also the sword of Goliath the Philistine.' ¹¹ The king then sent for the priest Ahimelech son of Ahitub and his whole family, the priests of Nob; they all came to the king.

¹² Saul said, 'Now listen, son of Ahitub!' He replied, 'Here I am, my lord.' ¹³ 'Why have you conspired against me,' said Saul, 'you and the son of Jesse, giving him bread and a sword and consulting God on his behalf, for him to rebel against me as is now the case?' ¹⁴ Ahimelech replied to the king, 'Of all those in your service, who is more loyal than David son-in-law to the king, captain of your bodyguard, honoured in your household? ¹⁵ Was today the first time I ever consulted God on his behalf? Indeed it was not! The king has no grounds for bringing any charge against his servant or against his whole family, for your servant knew nothing whatever about all this.' ¹⁶ The king retorted, 'You must die, Ahimelech, you and your whole family.'

¹⁷ The king said to the scouts who were standing round him, 'Forward! and put the priests of Yahweh to death, for they too are on David's side, they knew that he was escaping, yet did not warn me of it.' The king's professional soldiers, however, would not lift a hand to strike the priests of Yahweh. ¹⁸ The king then said to Doeg, 'Forward, you! Fall on the priests!' Doeg the Edomite stepped forward and fell on the priests, himself that day killing eighty-five men who wore the linen *ephod*. ¹⁹ Nob, the town of the priests, Saul put to the sword: men and women, children and infants, cattle, donkeys and sheep.

²⁰ One son of Ahimelech son of Ahitub alone escaped. His name was Abiathar, and he fled away to join David. ²¹ When Abiathar told David that Saul had slaughtered the priests of Yahweh, ²² David said to Abiathar, 'I knew, that day when Doeg the Edomite was there, that he would be sure to inform Saul. I am responsible for the death of all your kinsmen. ²³ Stay with me, do not be afraid, for he who seeks your life seeks mine; you will be safe with me.'

23 News was then brought to David, 'The Philistines are besieging Keilah and plundering the threshing-floors'. ² David consulted Yahweh, 'Shall I go and fight these Philistines?' Yahweh replied to David, 'Go and fight the Philistines and save Keilah.' ³ But David's men said to him, 'We are already afraid here in Judah; how much more, then, if we go to Keilah to fight the Philistine troops!' ⁴ So David consulted Yahweh again and Yahweh replied, 'Be on your way; go down to Keilah, since I shall give the Philistines into your power.' ⁵ So David and his men went to Keilah and fought the Philistines and carried off their cattle and inflicted a great defeat on them. Thus David saved the inhabitants of Keilah. ⁶ When Abiathar son of Ahimelech took refuge with David, he went down to Keilah with the *ephod* in his hand.

⁷ When word was brought to Saul that David had gone to Keilah he said, 'God has delivered him into my power: he has trapped himself by going into a town with gates and bars.' ⁸ Saul called all the people to arms, to go down to Keilah and besiege David and his men. ⁹ David, however, was aware that Saul was plotting evil against him, and said to Abiathar the priest, 'Bring the *ephod*.' ¹⁰ David said, 'Yahweh, God of Israel, your servant has heard that Saul is preparing to come to Keilah and destroy the town because of me. ¹¹ Will Saul come down as your servant has heard? Yahweh, God of Israel, I beg you, let your servant know.' Yahweh replied, 'He will come down.' ¹² David then went

"Will the men of Keilah surrender me and my men into the hand of Saul?" The LORD said, "They will surrender you." 13 Then David and his men, who were about six hundred, set out and left Keilah; they wandered wherever they could go. When Saul was told that David had escaped from Keilah, he gave up the expedition. 14 David remained in the strongholds in the wilderness, in the hill country of the Wilderness of Ziph. Saul sought him every day, but the LORD a did not give him into his hand.

15 David was in the Wilderness of Ziph at Horesh when he learned that b Saul had come out to seek his life. 16 Saul's son Jonathan set out and came to David at Horesh; there he strengthened his hand through the LORD. c 17 He said to him, "Do not be afraid; for the hand of my father Saul shall not find you; you shall be king over Israel, and I shall be second to you; my father Saul also knows that this is so." 18 Then the two of them made a covenant before the LORD; David remained at Horesh, and Jonathan went home.

19 Then some Ziphites went up to Saul at Gibeah and said, "David is hiding among us in the strongholds of Horesh, on the hill of Hachilah, which is south of Jeshimon. 20 Now, O king, whenever you wish to come down, do so; and our part will be to surrender him into the king's hand." 21 Saul said, "May you be blessed by the LORD for showing me compassion! 22 Go and make sure once more; find out exactly where he is, and who has seen him there; for I am told that he is very cunning. 23 Look around and learn all the hiding places where he lurks, and come back to me with sure information. Then I will go with you; and if he is in the land, I will search him out among all the thousands of Judah." 24 So they set out and went to Ziph ahead of Saul.

David and his men were in the wilderness of Maon, in the Arabah to the south of Jeshimon. 25 Saul and his men went to search for him. When David was told, he went down to the rock and stayed in the wilderness of Maon. When Saul heard that, he pursued David into the wilderness of Maon. 26 Saul went on one side of the mountain, and David and his men on the other side of the mountain. David was hurrying to get away from Saul, while Saul and his men were closing in on David and his men to capture them. 27 Then a messenger came to Saul, saying, "Hurry and come; for the Philistines have made a raid on the land." 28 So Saul stopped pursuing David, and went against the Philistines; therefore that place was called the Rock of Escape. d 29 e David then went up from there, and lived in the strongholds of En-gedi.

24 When Saul returned from following the Philistines, he was told, "David is in the wilderness of En-gedi." 2 Then Saul took three thousand chosen men out of all Israel, and went to look for David and his men in the direction of the Rocks of the Wild Goats. 3 He came to the sheepfolds beside the road, where there was a cave; and Saul went in to relieve himself. f Now David and his men were sitting in the innermost parts of the cave. 4 The men of David said to him, "Here is the day of which the LORD said to you, 'I will give your enemy into your hand, and you shall do to him as it seems good to you.' " Then David went and stealthily cut off a corner of Saul's cloak. 5 Afterward David was stricken to the heart because he had cut off a corner of Saul's cloak. 6 He said to his men, "The LORD forbid that I should do this thing to my lord, the LORD's anointed, to raise my hand against him; for he is the LORD's anointed." 7 So David scolded his men severely and did not permit them to attack Saul. Then Saul got up and left the cave, and went on his way.

zens of Keilah surrender me and my men to Saul?' and the LORD answered, 'They will.' 13 At once David left Keilah with his men, who numbered about six hundred, and moved about from place to place. When it was reported to Saul that David had escaped from Keilah, he called off the operation.

14 David was living in the fastnesses of the wilderness of Ziph, in the hill-country, and though Saul went daily in search of him, God did not put him into his power. 15 David was at Horesh in the wilderness of Ziph, when he learnt that Saul had come out to seek his life. 16 Saul's son Jonathan came to David at Horesh and gave him fresh courage in God's name: 17 'Do not be afraid,' he said; 'my father's hand will not touch you. You will become king of Israel and I shall rank after you. This my father knows.' 18 After the two of them had made a solemn compact before the LORD, David remained in Horesh and Jonathan went home.

19 The Ziphites brought to Saul at Gibeah the news that David was in hiding among them in the fastnesses of Horesh on the hill of Hachilah, south of Jeshimon. 20 'Let your majesty come down whenever you will,' they said, 'and it will be our business to surrender him to you.' 21 Saul replied, 'The LORD's blessing on you; you have rendered me a service. 22 Go now and make further enquiry, and find out exactly where he is and who saw him there. They tell me that he is crafty enough to outwit me. 23 Find out which of his hiding-places he is using; then come back to me at such and such a place, and I shall go with you. So long as he stays in this country, I shall hunt him down, if I have to go through all the clans of Judah one by one.' 24 They left for Ziph without delay, ahead of Saul.

David and his men were in the wilderness of Maon in the Arabah to the south of Jeshimon. 25 Saul set off with his men to look for him; but David got word of it and went down to a refuge in the rocks, and there he stayed in the wilderness of Maon. On hearing this, Saul went into the wilderness after him; 26 he was on one side of the hill, David and his men on the other. While David and his men were trying desperately to get away, and Saul and his followers were closing in for the capture, 27 a runner brought a message to Saul: 'Come at once! The Philistines are invading the land.' 28 Saul called off the pursuit of David and turned back to face the Philistines. This is why that place is called the Dividing Rock. 29 David went up from there and lived in the fastnesses of En-gedi.

24 On his return from the pursuit of the Philistines, Saul learnt that David was in the wilderness of En-gedi. 2 Taking three thousand men picked from the whole of Israel, he went in search of David and his followers to the east of the Rocks of the Mountain Goats. 3 There beside the road were some sheepfolds, and nearby was a cave, in the inner recesses of which David and his men were concealed. Saul came to the cave and went in to relieve himself. 4-7 David's men said to him, 'The day has come: the LORD has put your enemy into your hands, as he promised he would. You may do what you please with him.' David said to his men, 'God forbid that I should harm my master, the LORD's anointed, or lift a hand against him. He is after all the LORD's anointed.' So David reproved his men and would not allow them to attack Saul. He himself got up stealthily and cut off a piece of Saul's cloak; but after he had cut it off, he was struck with remorse.

Saul left the cave and went on his way; 8 whereupon

a Q Ms Gk: MT God   b Or saw that   c Compare Q Ms Gk: MT God   d Or Rock of Division; Meaning of Heb uncertain   e Ch 24.1 in Heb   f Heb to cover his feet

23:29 In Heb. 24:1.   24:4–7 These verses are rearranged as follows: 4a,6,7a,4b,5,7b.

Keilah deliver me and my men into the grasp of Saul?" And the LORD answered, "Yes." 13 So David and his men, about six hundred in number, left Keilah and wandered from place to place. When Saul was informed that David had escaped from Keilah, he abandoned the expedition.

14 David now lived in the refuges in the desert, or in the barren hill country near Ziph. Though Saul sought him continually, the LORD did not deliver David into his grasp. 15 David was apprehensive because Saul had come out to seek his life; but while he was at Horesh in the barrens near Ziph, 16 Saul's son, Jonathan, came down there to David and strengthened his resolve in the LORD. 17 He said to him: "Have no fear, my father Saul shall not lay a hand to you. You shall be king of Israel and I shall be second to you. Even my father Saul knows this." 18 They made a joint agreement before the LORD in Horesh, where David remained, while Jonathan returned to his home.

19 Some of the Ziphites went up to Saul in Gibeah and said, "David is hiding among us, now in the refuges, and again at Horesh, or on the hill of Hachilah, south of the wasteland. 20 Therefore, whenever the king wishes to come down, let him do so. It will be our task to deliver him into the king's grasp." 21 Saul replied: "The LORD bless you for your sympathy toward me. 22 Go now and make sure once more! Take note of the place where he sets foot" (for he thought, perhaps they are playing some trick on me). 23 "Look around and learn in which of all the various hiding places he is holding out. Then come back to me with sure information, and I will go with you. If he is in the region, I will search him out among all the families of Judah." 24 So they went off to Ziph ahead of Saul. At this time David and his men were in the desert below Maon, in the Arabah south of the wasteland.

25 When Saul and his men came looking for him, David got word of it and went down to the gorge in the desert below Maon. Saul heard of this and pursued David into the desert below Maon. 26 As Saul moved along one rim of the gorge, David and his men took to the other. David was in anxious flight to escape Saul, and Saul and his men were attempting to outflank David and his men in order to capture them, 27 when a messenger came to Saul, saying, "Come quickly, because the Philistines have invaded the land." 28 Saul interrupted his pursuit of David and went to meet the Philistines. This is how that place came to be called the Gorge of Divisions.

24 David then went up from there and stayed in the refuges behind Engedi. 2 And when Saul returned from the pursuit of the Philistines, he was told that David was in the desert near Engedi. 3 So Saul took three thousand picked men from all Israel and went in search of David and his men in the direction of the wild goat crags. 4 When he came to the sheepfolds along the way, he found a cave, which he entered to ease nature. David and his men were occupying the inmost recesses of the cave.

5 David's servants said to him, "This is the day of which the LORD said to you, 'I will deliver your enemy into your grasp; do with him as you see fit.' " So David moved up and stealthily cut off an end of Saul's mantle. 6 Afterward, however, David regretted that he had cut off an end of Saul's mantle. 7 He said to his men, "The LORD forbid that I should do such a thing to my master, the LORD's anointed, as to lay a hand on him, for he is the LORD's anointed." 8 With these words David restrained his men and would not permit them to attack Saul. Saul then left the cave and went on his way.

on to ask, 'Will the notables of Keilah hand me and my men over to Saul?' Yahweh replied, 'They will hand you over.' 13 At this, David made off with his men, about six hundred in number; they left Keilah and went where they could. When Saul was told that David had escaped from Keilah, he abandoned the expedition.

14 David stayed in the desert, in the strongholds; he stayed in the mountains, in the desert of Ziph; Saul kept looking for him day after day, but God did not deliver him into his power. 15 David was aware that Saul had mounted an expedition to take his life. David was then at Horesh in the desert of Ziph. 16 Jonathan son of Saul set off and went to David at Horesh and encouraged him in the name of God. 17 'Do not be afraid,' he said, 'for my father Saul's hand will not reach you. You are to reign over Israel, and I shall be second to you. Saul my father is himself aware of this.' 18 And the two made a pact before Yahweh. David stayed at Horesh and Jonathan went home.

19 Some men from Ziph then went up to Saul at Gibeah and said, 'Look, David is hiding among us in the strongholds at Horesh, on the Hill of Hachilah to the south of the wastelands. 20 Now whenever you wish to go down, my lord king, do so; we shall make it our task to hand him over to the king.' 21 Saul replied, 'May you be blessed by Yahweh for sympathising with me. 22 Go and make doubly sure, find out exactly what place he frequents, for I have been told that he is very cunning. 23 Take careful note of all the hiding places where he lurks, and come back to me when you are certain. I shall then come with you and, if he is in the country, I shall track him down through every clan in Judah!'

24 Setting off they went to Ziph ahead of Saul. Meanwhile, David and his men were in the desert of Maon, in the plain to the south of the wastelands. 25 When Saul and his men set out in search, David was told and went down to the gorge running through the desert of Maon. 26 Saul and his men proceeded along one side of the mountain, David and his men along the other. David was hurrying to escape from Saul, while Saul and his men were trying to cross over to David and his men's side, to capture them, 27 when a messenger came to Saul and said, 'Come at once, the Philistines have invaded the country.' 28 So Saul broke off his pursuit of David and went to oppose the Philistines. That is why the place is called the Gorge of Separations.

24 From there David went up and installed himself in the strongholds of En-Gedi. 2 Once Saul was back from pursuing the Philistines, he was told, 'David is now in the desert of En-Gedi.' 3 Saul thereupon took three thousand men selected from all Israel and went in search of David and his men east of the Rocks of the Mountain Goats. 4 He came to the sheepfolds along the route, where there was a cave, and went in to cover his feet. Now David and his men were sitting in the recesses of the cave; 5 David's men said to him, 'Today is the day of which Yahweh said to you, "I shall deliver your enemy into your power; do what you like with him." ' David got up and, unobserved, cut off the border of Saul's cloak. 6 Afterwards David reproached himself for having cut off the border of Saul's cloak. 7 He said to his men, 'Yahweh preserve me from doing such a thing to my lord as to raise my hand against him, since he is Yahweh's anointed.' 8 By these words David restrained his men and would not let them attack Saul.

9 Saul then left the cave and went on his way. After this,

8 Afterwards David also rose up and went out of the cave and called after Saul, "My lord the king!" When Saul looked behind him, David bowed with his face to the ground, and did obeisance. 9 David said to Saul, "Why do you listen to the words of those who say, 'David seeks to do you harm'? 10 This very day your eyes have seen how the LORD gave you into my hand in the cave; and some urged me to kill you, but I spared*g* you. I said, 'I will not raise my hand against my lord; for he is the LORD's anointed.' 11 See, my father, see the corner of your cloak in my hand; for by the fact that I cut off the corner of your cloak, and did not kill you, you may know for certain that there is no wrong or treason in my hands. I have not sinned against you, though you are hunting me to take my life. 12 May the LORD judge between me and you! May the LORD avenge me on you; but my hand shall not be against you. 13 As the ancient proverb says, 'Out of the wicked comes forth wickedness'; but my hand shall not be against you. 14 Against whom has the king of Israel come out? Whom do you pursue? A dead dog? A single flea? 15 May the LORD therefore be judge, and give sentence between me and you. May he see to it, and plead my cause, and vindicate me against you."

16 When David had finished speaking these words to Saul, Saul said, "Is this your voice, my son David?" Saul lifted up his voice and wept. 17 He said to David, "You are more righteous than I; for you have repaid me good, whereas I have repaid you evil. 18 Today you have explained how you have dealt well with me, in that you did not kill me when the LORD put me into your hands. 19 For who has ever found an enemy, and sent the enemy safely away? So may the LORD reward you with good for what you have done to me this day. 20 Now I know that you shall surely be king, and that the kingdom of Israel shall be established in your hand. 21 Swear to me therefore by the LORD that you will not cut off my descendants after me, and that you will not wipe out my name from my father's house." 22 So David swore this to Saul. Then Saul went home; but David and his men went up to the stronghold.

25 Now Samuel died; and all Israel assembled and mourned for him. They buried him at his home in Ramah.

Then David got up and went down to the wilderness of Paran.

2 There was a man in Maon, whose property was in Carmel. The man was very rich; he had three thousand sheep and a thousand goats. He was shearing his sheep in Carmel. 3 Now the name of the man was Nabal, and the name of his wife Abigail. The woman was clever and beautiful, but the man was surly and mean; he was a Calebite. 4 David heard in the wilderness that Nabal was shearing his sheep. 5 So David sent ten young men; and David said to the young men, "Go up to Carmel, and go to Nabal, and greet him in my name. 6 Thus you shall salute him: 'Peace be to you, and peace be to your house, and peace be to all that you have. 7 I hear that you have shearers; now your shepherds have been with us, and we did them no harm, and they missed nothing, all the time they were in Carmel. 8 Ask your young men, and they will tell you. Therefore let my young men find favor in your sight; for we have come on a feast day. Please give whatever you have at hand to your servants and to your son David.' "

9 When David's young men came, they said all this to Nabal in the name of David; and then they waited. 10 But Nabal answered David's servants, "Who is David? Who is the son of Jesse? There are many servants today who are breaking away from their masters. 11 Shall I take my bread

David also came out of the cave and called after Saul, 'My lord king!' When Saul looked round, David prostrated himself in obeisance 9 and said to him, 'Why do you listen to those who say that David means to do you harm? 10 Today you can see for yourself that the LORD put you into my power in the cave. Though urged to kill you, I spared your life. "I cannot lift my hand against my master," I said, "for he is the LORD's anointed." 11 Look, my dear lord, see this piece of your cloak in my hand. I cut it off, but I did not kill you. This shows that I have no thought of violence or treachery against you, and that I have done you no wrong. Yet you are resolved to take my life. 12 May the LORD judge between us! But though he may take vengeance on you for my sake, my hand will not be against you. 13 As the old proverb has it, "One wrong begets another"; yet my hand will not be against you. 14 Against whom has the king of Israel come out? What are you pursuing? A dead dog? A flea? 15 May the LORD be judge and decide between us; let him consider my cause; he will plead for me and acquit me.'

16 When David had finished speaking, Saul said, 'Is that you, David my son?' and he burst into tears. 17 He said, 'The right is on your side, not mine: you have treated me so well; I have treated you so badly. 18 You have made plain today the good you have done me; the LORD put me at your mercy, but you did not kill me. 19 Not often does a man find his enemy and let him go unharmed. May the LORD reward you well for what you have done for me today! 20 I know now that you will surely become king, and that the kingdom of Israel will flourish under your rule. 21 Swear to me now by the LORD that you will not exterminate my descendants and blot out my name from my father's house.' 22 David swore this on oath to Saul. Then Saul went to his home, while David and his men went up to their fastness.

25 SAMUEL died, and all Israel gathered to mourn for him, and they buried him at his home in Ramah. Afterwards David went down to the wilderness of Paran.

2 There was a man in Maon who had property at Carmel and owned three thousand sheep and a thousand goats; and he was shearing his flocks in Carmel. 3 His name was Nabal and his wife's name Abigail; she was a beautiful and intelligent woman, but her husband, a Calebite, was surly and mean. 4 David heard in the wilderness that Nabal was shearing his flocks, 5 and sent ten of his young men, saying to them, 'Go up to Carmel, find Nabal, and give him my greetings. 6 You are to say, "All good wishes for the year ahead! Prosperity to yourself, your household, and all that is yours! 7 I hear that you are shearing. Your shepherds have been with us lately and we did not molest them; nothing of theirs was missing all the time they were in Carmel. 8 Ask your own men and they will tell you. Receive my men kindly, for this is an auspicious day with us, and give what you can to David your son and your servant." '

9 David's servants came and delivered this message to Nabal in David's name. When they paused, 10 Nabal answered, 'Who is David? Who is this son of Jesse? In these days there are many slaves who break away from their masters. 11 Am I to take my food and my wine and the meat

---

g Gk Syr Tg Vg: Heb *it* (my eye) *spared*

24:18 **You have made . . . done me:** or Your goodness to me this day has passed all bounds.   25:11 **wine:** *so Gk; Heb.* water.

NEW AMERICAN BIBLE

9 David also stepped out of the cave, calling to Saul, "My lord the king!" When Saul looked back, David bowed to the ground in homage 10 and asked Saul: "Why do you listen to those who say, 'David is trying to harm you'? 11 You see for yourself today that the LORD just now delivered you into my grasp in the cave. I had some thought of killing you, but I took pity on you instead. I decided, 'I will not raise a hand against my lord, for he is the LORD's anointed and a father to me.' 12 Look here at this end of your mantle which I hold. Since I cut off an end of your mantle and did not kill you, see and be convinced that I plan no harm and no rebellion. I have done you no wrong, though you are hunting me down to take my life. 13 The LORD will judge between me and you, and the LORD will exact justice from you in my case. I shall not touch you. 14 The old proverb says, 'From the wicked comes forth wickedness.' So I will take no action against you. 15 Against whom are you on campaign, O king of Israel? Whom are you pursuing? A dead dog, or a single flea! 16 The LORD will be the judge; he will decide between me and you. May he see this, and take my part, and grant me justice beyond your reach!"

17 When David finished saying these things to Saul, Saul answered, "Is that your voice, my son David?" And he wept aloud. 18 Saul then said to David: "You are in the right rather than I; you have treated me generously, while I have done you harm. 19 Great is the generosity you showed me today, when the LORD delivered me into your grasp and you did not kill me. 20 For if a man meets his enemy, does he send him away unharmed? May the LORD reward you generously for what you have done this day. 21 And now, since I know that you shall surely be king and that sovereignty over Israel shall come into your possession, 22 swear to me by the LORD that you will not destroy my descendants and that you will not blot out my name and family." 23 David gave Saul his oath and Saul returned home, while David and his men went up to the refuge.

25 Samuel died, and all Israel gathered to mourn him; they buried him at his home in Ramah.

2 Then David went down to the desert of Maon. There was a man of Maon who had property in Carmel; he was very wealthy, owning three thousand sheep and a thousand goats. At this time he was present for the shearing of his flock in Carmel. 3 The man was named Nabal, his wife, Abigail. The woman was intelligent and attractive, but Nabal himself, a Calebite, was harsh and ungenerous in his behavior. 4 When David heard in the desert that Nabal was shearing his flock, 5 he sent ten young men, instructing them: "Go up to Carmel. Pay Nabal a visit and greet him in my name. 6 Say to him, 'Peace be with you, my brother, and with your family, and with all who belong to you. 7 I have just heard that shearers are with you. Now, when your shepherds were with us, we did them no injury, neither did they miss anything all the while they were in Carmel. 8 Ask your servants and they will tell you so. Look kindly on these young men, since we come at a festival time. Please give your servants and your son David whatever you can manage.'"

9 When David's young men arrived, they delivered this message fully to Nabal in David's name, and then waited. 10 But Nabal answered the servants of David: "Who is David? Who is the son of Jesse? Nowadays there are many servants who run away from their masters. 11 Must I take

NEW JERUSALEM BIBLE

David too left the cave and called after Saul, 'My lord king!' Saul looked behind him and David, bowing to the ground, prostrated himself. 10 David then said to Saul, 'Why do you listen to people who say, "David intends your ruin"? 11 This very day you have seen for yourself how Yahweh put you in my power in the cave and how, refusing to kill you, I spared you saying, "I will not raise my hand against my lord, since he is Yahweh's anointed." 12 Look, father, look at the border of your cloak in my hand. Since, although I cut the border off your cloak, I did not kill you, surely you realise that I intend neither mischief nor crime. I have not wronged you, and yet you hunt me down to take my life. 13 May Yahweh be judge between me and you, and may Yahweh avenge me on you; but I shall never lay a hand on you! 14 (As the old proverb says: Wickedness comes out of wicked people, but I shall never lay a hand on you!) 15 On whose trail is the king of Israel campaigning? Whom are you pursuing? On the trail of a dead dog, of a flea! 16 May Yahweh be the judge and decide between me and you; may he examine and defend my cause and give judgement for me by rescuing me from your clutches!'

17 When David had finished saying this to Saul, Saul said, 'Is that your voice, my son David?' And Saul began to weep aloud. 18 'You are upright and I am not,' he said to David, 'since you have behaved well to me, whereas I have behaved badly to you. 19 And today you have shown how well you have behaved to me, since Yahweh had put me in your power but you did not kill me. 20 When a man comes on his enemy, does he let him go unmolested? May Yahweh reward you for the good you have done me today! 21 Now I know that you will indeed reign and that the sovereignty in Israel will pass into your hands. 22 Now swear to me by Yahweh that you will not suppress my descendants once I am gone, or blot my name out of my family.' 23 This David swore to Saul, and Saul went home while David and his men went back to the stronghold.

25 Samuel died and all Israel assembled to mourn for him. They buried him at his home in Ramah.

David then set off and went down to the desert of Maon. 2 Now, there was a man in Maon whose business was at Carmel; the man was very rich: he owned three thousand sheep and a thousand goats. He was then at Carmel, having his sheep shorn. 3 The man's name was Nabal and his wife's Abigail. She was a woman of intelligence and beauty, but the man was miserly and churlish. He was a Calebite. 4 When David heard in the desert that Nabal was at his sheepshearing, 5 he sent ten men off, having said to them, 'Go up to Carmel, visit Nabal and greet him from me. 6 And this is what you are to say to my brother, "Peace to you, peace to your family, peace to all that is yours! 7 I hear that you now have the shearers; your shepherds were with us recently: we did not molest them, nor did they lose anything all the while they were at Carmel. 8 Ask your young men and they will tell you. I hope that you will give the men a welcome, coming as we do on a festival. Whatever you have to hand please give to your servants and to your son David."'

9 David's men went and said all this to Nabal for David, and waited. 10 Nabal retorted to the men in David's service, 'Who is David? Who is the son of Jesse? There are many servants nowadays who run away from their masters. Am I

and my water and the meat that I have butchered for my shearers, and give it to men who come from I do not know where?" 12 So David's young men turned away, and came back and told him all this. 13 David said to his men, "Every man strap on his sword!" And every one of them strapped on his sword; David also strapped on his sword; and about four hundred men went up after David, while two hundred remained with the baggage.

14 But one of the young men told Abigail, Nabal's wife, "David sent messengers out of the wilderness to salute our master; and he shouted insults at them. 15 Yet the men were very good to us, and we suffered no harm, and we never missed anything when we were in the fields, as long as we were with them; 16 they were a wall to us both by night and by day, all the while we were with them keeping the sheep. 17 Now therefore know this and consider what you should do; for evil has been decided against our master and against all his house; he is so ill-natured that no one can speak to him."

18 Then Abigail hurried and took two hundred loaves, two skins of wine, five sheep ready dressed, five measures of parched grain, one hundred clusters of raisins, and two hundred cakes of figs. She loaded them on donkeys 19 and said to her young men, "Go on ahead of me; I am coming after you." But she did not tell her husband Nabal. 20 As she rode on the donkey and came down under cover of the mountain, David and his men came down toward her; and she met them. 21 Now David had said, "Surely it was in vain that I protected all that this fellow has in the wilderness, so that nothing was missed of all that belonged to him; but he has returned me evil for good. 22 God do so to David[h] and more also, if by morning I leave so much as one male of all who belong to him."

23 When Abigail saw David, she hurried and alighted from the donkey, fell before David on her face, bowing to the ground. 24 She fell at his feet and said, "Upon me alone, my lord, be the guilt; please let your servant speak in your ears, and hear the words of your servant. 25 My lord, do not take seriously this ill-natured fellow, Nabal; for as his name is, so is he; Nabal[i] is his name, and folly is with him; but I, your servant, did not see the young men of my lord, whom you sent.

26 Now then, my lord, as the LORD lives, and as you yourself live, since the LORD has restrained you from bloodguilt and from taking vengeance with your own hand, now let your enemies and those who seek to do evil to my lord be like Nabal. 27 And now let this present that your servant has brought to my lord be given to the young men who follow my lord. 28 Please forgive the trespass of your servant; for the LORD will certainly make my lord a sure house, because my lord is fighting the battles of the LORD; and evil shall not be found in you so long as you live. 29 If anyone should rise up to pursue you and to seek your life, the life of my lord shall be bound in the bundle of the living under the care of the LORD your God; but the lives of your enemies he shall sling out as from the hollow of a sling. 30 When the LORD has done to my lord according to all the good that he has spoken concerning you, and has appointed you prince over Israel, 31 my lord shall have no cause of grief, or pangs of conscience, for having shed blood without cause or for having saved himself. And when the LORD has dealt well with my lord, then remember your servant."

32 David said to Abigail, "Blessed be the LORD, the God of Israel, who sent you to meet me today! 33 Blessed be your good sense, and blessed be you, who have kept me today from bloodguilt and from avenging myself by my own hand! 34 For as surely as the LORD the God of Israel

I have provided for my shearers, and give it to men who come from I know not where?' 12 David's servants turned and made their way back to him and told him all this. 13 He said to his followers, 'Buckle on your swords, all of you.' So they buckled on their swords, as did David, and they followed him, four hundred of them, while two hundred stayed behind with the baggage.

14 One of Nabal's servants said to Abigail, Nabal's wife, 'David sent messengers from the wilderness to ask our master politely for a present, and he flared up at them. 15 The men have been very good to us and have not molested us, nor did we miss anything all the time we were going about with them in the open country. 16 They were as good as a wall round us, night and day, while we were minding the flocks. 17 Consider carefully what you had better do, for it is certain ruin for our master and his whole house; he is such a wretched fellow that it is no good talking to him.'

18 Abigail hastily collected two hundred loaves and two skins of wine, five sheep ready dressed, five measures of roasted grain, a hundred bunches of raisins, and two hundred cakes of dried figs, and loaded them on donkeys, 19 but told her husband nothing about it. She said to her servants, 'Go on ahead, I shall follow you.' 20 As she made her way on her donkey, hidden by the hill, there were David and his men coming down towards her, and she met them. 21 David had said, 'It was a waste of time to protect this fellow's property in the wilderness so well that nothing of his was missing. He has repaid me evil for good.' 22 David swore a solemn oath: 'God do the same to me and more if I leave him a single mother's son alive by morning!'

23 When Abigail saw David she dismounted in haste and prostrated herself before him, bowing low to the ground 24 at his feet, and said, 'Let me take the blame, my lord, but allow your humble servant to speak out, and let my lord give me a hearing. 25 How can you take any notice of this wretched fellow? He is just what his name Nabal means: "Churl" is his name, and churlish his behaviour. Sir, I did not myself see the men you sent. 26 And now, sir, the LORD has restrained you from starting a blood feud and from striking a blow for yourself. As the LORD lives, your life upon it, your enemies and all who want to see you ruined will be like Nabal. 27 Here is the present which I, your humble servant, have brought; give it to the young men under your command. 28 Forgive me, my lord, if I am presuming; for the LORD will establish your family for ever, because you have fought his battles. No calamity will overtake you as long as you live. 29 If anyone tries to pursue you and take your life, the LORD your God will wrap your life up and put it with his own treasure, but the lives of your enemies he will hurl away like stones from a sling. 30 When the LORD has made good all his promises to you, and has made you ruler of Israel, 31 there will be no reason why you should stumble or your courage should falter because you have shed innocent blood or struck a blow for yourself. Then when the LORD makes all you do prosper, remember me, your servant.'

32 David said to Abigail, 'Blessed be the LORD the God of Israel who today has sent you to meet me. 33 A blessing on your good sense, a blessing on you because you have saved me today from the guilt of bloodshed and from striking a blow for myself. 34 For I swear by the life of the LORD the

---

h Gk Compare Syr: Heb the enemies of David   i That is Fool

25:14 **flared up:** or railed.   25:17 **wretched fellow:** lit. son of Belial.   25:18 **measures:** Heb. seahs.   25:22 **David:** so Gk; Heb. David's enemies.   25:31 **because . . . shed:** so some MSS; others or you should shed.

my bread, my wine, my meat that I have slaughtered for my own shearers, and give them to men who come from I know not where?" 12 So David's young men retraced their steps and on their return reported to him all that had been said. 13 Thereupon David said to his men, "Let everyone gird on his sword." And so everyone, David included, girded on his sword. About four hundred men went up after David, while two hundred remained with the baggage.

14 But Nabal's wife Abigail was informed of this by one of the servants, who said: "David sent messengers from the desert to greet our master, but he flew at them screaming. 15 Yet these men were very good to us. We were done no injury, neither did we miss anything all the while we were living among them during our stay in the open country. 16 For us they were like a rampart night and day the whole time we were pasturing the sheep near them. 17 Now, see what you can do, for you must realize that otherwise evil is in store for our master and for his whole family. He is so mean that no one can talk to him." 18 Abigail quickly got together two hundred loaves, two skins of wine, five dressed sheep, five seahs of roasted grain, a hundred cakes of pressed raisins, and two hundred cakes of pressed figs, and loaded them on asses. 19 She then said to her servants, "Go on ahead; I will follow you." But she did not tell her husband Nabal.

20 As she came down through a mountain defile riding on an ass, David and his men were also coming down from the opposite direction. When she met them, 21 David had just been saying: "Indeed, it was in vain that I guarded all this man's possessions in the desert, so that he missed nothing. He has repaid good with evil. 22 May God do thus and so to David, if by morning I leave a single male alive among all those who belong to him." 23 As soon as Abigail saw David, she dismounted quickly from the ass and, falling prostrate on the ground before David, did him homage. 24 As she fell at his feet she said:

"My lord, let the blame be mine. Please let your handmaid speak to you, and listen to the words of your handmaid. 25 Let not my lord pay attention to that worthless man Nabal, for he is just like his name. Fool is his name, and he acts the fool. I, your handmaid, did not see the young men whom my lord sent. 26 Now, therefore, my lord, as the LORD lives, and as you live, it is the LORD who has kept you from shedding blood and from avenging yourself personally. May your enemies and those who seek to harm my lord become as Nabal! 27 Accept this present, then, which your maidservant has brought for my lord, and let it be given to the young men who follow my lord. 28 Please forgive the transgression of your handmaid, for the LORD shall certainly establish a lasting dynasty for my lord, because your lordship is fighting the battles of the LORD, and there is no evil to be found in you your whole life long. 29 If anyone rises to pursue you and to seek your life, may the life of my lord be bound in the bundle of the living in the care of the LORD your God; but may he hurl out the lives of your enemies as from the hollow of a sling. 30 And when the LORD carries out for my lord the promise of success he has made concerning you, and appoints you as commander over Israel, 31 you shall not have this as a qualm or burden on your conscience, my lord, for having shed innocent blood or for having avenged yourself personally. When the LORD confers this benefit on your lordship, remember your handmaid." 32 David said to Abigail: "Blessed be the LORD, the God of Israel, who sent you to meet me today. 33 Blessed be your good judgment and blessed be you yourself, who this day have prevented me from shedding blood and from avenging myself personally. 34 Otherwise, as the

to take my bread and my wine and the meat that I have slaughtered for my shearers and give it to men who come from I know not where?' 12 David's men turned on their heels and went back, and on their arrival told him exactly what had been said. 13 David then said to his men, 'Every man buckle on his sword!' And they buckled on their swords, and David buckled on his too; about four hundred followed David while two hundred stayed with the baggage.

14 Now one of the young men told Abigail, Nabal's wife. He said, 'David sent messengers from the desert to greet our master, but he flared up at them. 15 Now, these men were very good to us; they did not molest us and we lost nothing all the time we had anything to do with them while we were out in the country. 16 Night and day, they were like a rampart to us, all the time we were with them, minding the sheep. 17 So now make up your mind what you should do, for the ruin of our master and his whole family is a certainty, and he is such a brute that no one can say a word to him.'

18 Abigail hastily took two hundred loaves, two skins of wine, five sheep ready prepared, five measures of roasted grain, a hundred bunches of raisins and two hundred cakes of figs and loaded them on donkeys. 19 She said to her servants, 'Go on ahead, I shall follow you' — but she did not tell her husband Nabal.

20 As she was riding her donkey down behind a fold in the mountain, David and his men happened to be coming down in her direction; and she met them. 21 Now, David had decided, 'It was a waste of time my guarding all this man's property in the desert so that he lost nothing at all! He has repaid me bad for good. 22 May God bring unnameable ills on David and worse ones, too, if by morning I leave a single manjack alive of all who belong to him!' 23 As soon as Abigail saw David, she quickly dismounted from the donkey and, falling on her face in front of David, prostrated herself on the ground. 24 She fell at his feet and said, 'Let me take the blame, my lord. Let your servant speak in your ear; listen to what your servant has to say! 25 My lord, please pay no attention to this brute Nabal/ for his nature is like his name; "Brute" is his name and brutal he is. But I, your servant, did not see the men whom my lord sent. 26 And now, my lord, as Yahweh lives and as your soul lives, by Yahweh who kept you from the crime of bloodshed and from taking vengeance with your own hand, may your enemies and all those ill-disposed towards you become like Nabal. 27 As for the present which your servant has brought my lord, I should like this to be given to the men in your service. 28 Please forgive your servant for any offence I have given you, for Yahweh will certainly assure you of a lasting dynasty, since you are fighting Yahweh's battles and no fault has been found in you throughout your life. 29 Should anyone set out to hunt you down and try to kill you, your life will be kept close in the wallet of life with Yahweh your God, while your enemies' lives he will fling out of the pouch of the sling. 30 Once Yahweh has done for you all the good things which he has said he will do for you, and made you ruler of Israel, 31 you must have no anxiety, my lord, no remorse, over having wantonly shed blood, over having taken a revenge. When Yahweh has done well by you, then remember your servant.'

32 David said to Abigail, 'Blessed be Yahweh, God of Israel, who sent you to meet me today! 33 Blessed be your wisdom and blessed you yourself for today having restrained me from the crime of bloodshed and from exacting revenge! 34 But as Yahweh, God of Israel, lives, who pre-

j **25** *Nabal* = fool.

lives, who has restrained me from hurting you, unless you had hurried and come to meet me, truly by morning there would not have been left to Nabal so much as one male." 35 Then David received from her hand what she had brought him; he said to her, "Go up to your house in peace; see, I have heeded your voice, and I have granted your petition."

36 Abigail came to Nabal; he was holding a feast in his house, like the feast of a king. Nabal's heart was merry within him, for he was very drunk; so she told him nothing at all until the morning light. 37 In the morning, when the wine had gone out of Nabal, his wife told him these things, and his heart died within him; he became like a stone. 38 About ten days later the LORD struck Nabal, and he died.

39 When David heard that Nabal was dead, he said, "Blessed be the LORD who has judged the case of Nabal's insult to me, and has kept back his servant from evil; the LORD has returned the evildoing of Nabal upon his own head." Then David sent and wooed Abigail, to make her his wife. 40 When David's servants came to Abigail at Carmel, they said to her, "David has sent us to you to take you to him as his wife." 41 She rose and bowed down, with her face to the ground, and said, "Your servant is a slave to wash the feet of the servants of my lord." 42 Abigail got up hurriedly and rode away on a donkey; her five maids attended her. She went after the messengers of David and became his wife.

43 David also married Ahinoam of Jezreel; both of them became his wives. 44 Saul had given his daughter Michal, David's wife, to Palti son of Laish, who was from Gallim.

26 Then the Ziphites came to Saul at Gibeah, saying, "David is in hiding on the hill of Hachilah, which is opposite Jeshimon."*j* 2 So Saul rose and went down to the Wilderness of Ziph, with three thousand chosen men of Israel, to seek David in the Wilderness of Ziph. 3 Saul encamped on the hill of Hachilah, which is opposite Jeshimon*j* beside the road. But David remained in the wilderness. When he learned that Saul came after him into the wilderness, 4 David sent out spies, and learned that Saul indeed arrived. 5 Then David set out and came to the place where Saul had encamped; and David saw the place where Saul lay, with Abner son of Ner, the commander of his army. Saul was lying within the encampment, while the army was encamped around him.

6 Then David said to Ahimelech the Hittite, and to Joab's brother Abishai son of Zeruiah, "Who will go down with me into the camp to Saul?" Abishai said, "I will go down with you." 7 So David and Abishai went to the army by night; there Saul lay sleeping within the encampment, with his spear stuck in the ground at his head; and Abner and the army lay around him. 8 Abishai said to David, "God has given your enemy into your hand today; now therefore let me pin him to the ground with one stroke of the spear; I will not strike him twice." 9 But David said to Abishai, "Do not destroy him; for who can raise his hand against the LORD's anointed, and be guiltless?" 10 David said, "As the LORD lives, the LORD will strike him down; or his day will come to die; or he will go down into battle and perish. 11 The LORD forbid that I should raise my hand against the LORD's anointed; but now take the spear that is at his head, and the water jar, and let us go." 12 So David took the spear that was at Saul's head and the water jar, and they went away. No one saw it, or knew it, nor did anyone awake; for they were all asleep, because a deep sleep from the LORD had fallen upon them.

13 Then David went over to the other side, and stood on top of a hill far away, with a great distance between them. 14 David called to the army and to Abner son of Ner, saying,

God of Israel who has kept me from doing you wrong: if you had not come at once to meet me, not a man of Nabal's household, not a single mother's son, would have been left alive by morning.' 35 Then David accepted from her what she had brought him and said, 'Go home in peace; I have listened to you and I grant your request.'

36 On her return she found Nabal holding a right royal banquet in his house. He grew merry and became very drunk, so drunk that his wife said nothing at all to him till daybreak. 37 In the morning, when the wine had worn off, she told him everything, and he had a seizure and lay there like a log. 38 Some ten days later the LORD struck him and he died.

39 When David heard that Nabal was dead he said, 'Blessed be the LORD, who has himself punished Nabal for his insult, and has kept me his servant from doing wrong. The LORD has made Nabal's wrongdoing recoil on his own head.' David then sent a message to Abigail proposing that she should become his wife. 40 His servants came to her at Carmel and said, 'David has sent us to fetch you to be his wife.' 41 She rose and prostrated herself with her face to the ground, and said, 'I am his slave to command; I would wash the feet of my lord's servants.' 42 Abigail made her preparations with all speed and, with her five maids in attendance and accompanied by David's messengers, she set out on a donkey; and she became David's wife. 43 David had also married Ahinoam of Jezreel; both these women became his wives. 44 Saul meanwhile had given his daughter Michal, David's wife, to Palti son of Laish from Gallim.

26 THE Ziphites came to Saul at Gibeah with the news that David was in hiding on the hill of Hachilah overlooking Jeshimon. 2 Saul went down at once to the wilderness of Ziph, taking with him three thousand picked men, to search for David there. 3 He encamped beside the road on the hill of Hachilah overlooking Jeshimon, while David was still in the wilderness. As soon as David learnt that Saul had come to the wilderness in pursuit of him, 4 he sent out scouts and found that Saul had reached such and such a place. 5 He went at once to the place where Saul had pitched his camp, and observed where Saul and Abner son of Ner, the commander-in-chief, were lying. Saul lay within the lines with his troops encamped in a circle round him. 6 David turned to Ahimelech the Hittite and Abishai son of Zeruiah, Joab's brother, and said, 'Who will venture with me into the camp to Saul?' Abishai answered, 'I will.'

7 David and Abishai entered the camp at night, and there was Saul lying asleep within the lines with his spear thrust into the ground beside his head. Abner and the army were asleep all around him. 8 Abishai said to David, 'God has put your enemy into your power today. Let me strike him and pin him to the ground with one thrust of the spear. I shall not have to strike him twice.' 9 David said to him, 'Do him no harm. Who has ever lifted his hand against the LORD's anointed and gone unpunished? 10 As the LORD lives,' David went on, 'the LORD will strike him down; either his time will come and he will die, or he will go down to battle and meet his end. 11 God forbid that I should lift my hand against the LORD's anointed! But now let us take the spear which is by his head, and the water-jar, and go.' 12 So David took the spear and the water-jar from beside Saul's head, and they left. The whole camp was asleep; no one saw him, no one knew anything, no one woke. A deep sleep sent by the LORD had fallen on them.

13 Then David crossed over to the other side and stood on the top of a hill at some distance; there was a wide stretch between them. 14 David shouted across to the army and

j Or opposite the wasteland

LORD, the God of Israel, lives, who has restrained me from harming you, if you had not come so promptly to meet me, by dawn Nabal would not have had a single man or boy left alive." 35 David then took from her what she had brought him and said to her: "Go up to your home in peace! See, I have granted your request as a personal favor."

36 When Abigail came to Nabal, there was a drinking party in his house like that of a king, and Nabal was merry because he was very drunk. So she told him nothing at all before daybreak the next morning. 37 But then, when Nabal had become sober, his wife told him what had happened. At this his courage died within him, and he became like a stone. 38 About ten days later the LORD struck him and he died. 39 On hearing that Nabal was dead, David said: "Blessed be the LORD, who has requited the insult I received at the hand of Nabal, and who restrained his servant from doing evil, but has punished Nabal for his own evil deeds."

David then sent a proposal of marriage to Abigail. 40 When David's servants came to Abigail in Carmel, they said to her, "David has sent us to you that he may take you as his wife." 41 Rising and bowing to the ground, she answered, "Your handmaid would become a slave to wash the feet of my lord's servants." 42 She got up immediately, mounted an ass, and followed David's messengers, with her five maids following in attendance upon her. She became his wife, 43 and David also married Ahinoam of Jezreel. Thus both of them were his wives; but Saul gave David's wife Michal, Saul's own daughter, to Palti, son of Laish, who was from Gallim.

26 Men from Ziph came to Saul in Gibeah, reporting that David was hiding on the hill of Hachilah at the edge of the wasteland. 2 So Saul went off down to the desert of Ziph with three thousand picked men of Israel, to search for David in the desert of Ziph. 3 Saul camped beside the road on the hill of Hachilah, at the edge of the wasteland. David, who was living in the desert, saw that Saul had come into the desert after him 4 and sent out scouts, who confirmed Saul's arrival. 5 David himself then went to the place where Saul was encamped and examined the spot where Saul and Abner, son of Ner, the general, had their sleeping quarters. Saul's were within the barricade, and all his soldiers were camped around him. 6 David asked Ahimelech the Hittite, and Abishai, son of Zeruiah and brother of Joab, "Who will go down into the camp with me to Saul?" Abishai replied, "I will." 7 So David and Abishai went among Saul's soldiers by night and found Saul lying asleep within the barricade, with his spear thrust into the ground at his head and Abner and his men sleeping around him.

8 Abishai whispered to David: "God has delivered your enemy into your grasp this day. Let me nail him to the ground with one thrust of the spear; I will not need a second thrust!" 9 But David said to Abishai, "Do not harm him, for who can lay hands on the LORD's anointed and remain unpunished? 10 As the LORD lives," David continued, "it must be the LORD himself who will strike him, whether the time comes for him to die, or he goes out and perishes in battle. 11 But the LORD forbid that I touch his anointed! Now take the spear which is at his head and the water jug, and let us be on our way." 12 So David took the spear and the water jug from their place at Saul's head, and they got away without anyone's seeing or knowing or awakening. All remained asleep, because the LORD had put them into a deep slumber.

13 Going across to an opposite slope, David stood on a remote hilltop at a great distance from Abner, son of Ner, and the troops. 14 He then shouted, "Will you not answer,

vented me from harming you, had you not hurried out to meet me, I swear Nabal would not have had a single man-jack left alive by morning!' 35 David then accepted what she had brought him and said, 'Go home in peace; yes, I have listened to you and have pardoned you.'

36 Abigail returned to Nabal. He was holding a feast, a princely feast, in his house; Nabal was in high spirits, and as he was very drunk she told him nothing at all till it was daylight. 37 In the morning, when Nabal's wine had left him and his wife told him everything that had happened, his heart died within him and he became like a stone. 38 About ten days later Yahweh struck Nabal, and he died.

39 When David heard that Nabal was dead, he said, 'Blessed be Yahweh for having defended my cause over the insult which I received from Nabal, and for having restrained his servant from doing wrong! Yahweh has made Nabal's wickedness rebound on his own head!'

40 David then sent Abigail an offer of marriage. When the men in David's service came to Abigail at Carmel, they said, 'David has sent us to take you to him, to be his wife.' 41 She stood up, then prostrated herself on the ground. 'Consider your servant a slave', she said, 'to wash the feet of my lord's servants.' 42 Quickly Abigail stood up again and mounted a donkey; followed by five of her servant-girls, she followed David's messengers and became his wife.

43 David had also married Ahinoam of Jezreel and he kept them both as wives. 44 Saul had given his daughter Michal, David's wife, to Palti son of Laish, from Gallim.

26 Some men from Ziph went to Saul at Gibeah and said, 'Look, David is hiding on the Hill of Hachilah on the edge of the wastelands!' 2 So Saul set off and went down to the desert of Ziph, accompanied by three thousand picked men of Israel, to search for David in the desert of Ziph. 3 Saul pitched camp on the Hill of Hachilah, which is on the edge of the wastelands near the road. David was then living in the desert and saw that Saul had come after him into the desert. 4 Accordingly, David sent out spies and learned that Saul had indeed arrived. 5 Setting off, David went to the place where Saul had pitched camp. He saw the place where Saul and Abner son of Ner, commander of his army, had bedded down. Saul had bedded down inside the camp with the troops bivouacking round him.

6 Speaking to Ahimelech the Hittite and Abishai son of Zeruiah and brother of Joab, David said, 'Who will come down with me to the camp, to Saul?' Abishai answered, 'I will go down with you.' 7 So in the dark David and Abishai made their way towards the force, where they found Saul lying asleep inside the camp, his spear stuck in the ground beside his head, with Abner and the troops lying round him.

8 Abishai then said to David, 'Today God has put your enemy in your power; so now let me pin him to the ground with his own spear. Just one stroke! I shall not need to strike him twice.' 9 David said to Abishai, 'Do not kill him, for who could raise his hand against Yahweh's anointed and go unpunished? 10 As Yahweh lives,' David said, 'Yahweh himself will strike him down: either the day will come for him to die, or he will go into battle and perish then. 11 Yahweh forbid that I should raise my hand against Yahweh's anointed! But now let us take the spear beside his head and the pitcher of water, and let us go away.'

12 David took the spear and the pitcher of water from beside Saul's head, and they made off. No one saw, no one knew, no one woke up; they were all asleep, because a torpor from Yahweh had fallen on them.

13 David crossed to the other side and halted on the top of the mountain a long way off; there was a wide space between them. 14 David then called out to the troops and to

"Abner! Will you not answer?" Then Abner replied, "Who are you that calls to the king?" 15 David said to Abner, "Are you not a man? Who is like you in Israel? Why then have you not kept watch over your lord the king? For one of the people came in to destroy your lord the king. 16 This thing that you have done is not good. As the LORD lives, you deserve to die, because you have not kept watch over your lord, the LORD's anointed. See now, where is the king's spear, or the water jar that was at his head?"

17 Saul recognized David's voice, and said, "Is this your voice, my son David?" David said, "It is my voice, my lord, O king." 18 And he added, "Why does my lord pursue his servant? For what have I done? What guilt is on my hands? 19 Now therefore let my lord the king hear the words of his servant. If it is the LORD who has stirred you up against me, may he accept an offering; but if it is mortals, may they be cursed before the LORD, for they have driven me out today from my share in the heritage of the LORD, saying, 'Go, serve other gods.' 20 Now therefore, do not let my blood fall to the ground, away from the presence of the LORD; for the king of Israel has come out to seek a single flea, like one who hunts a partridge in the mountains."

21 Then Saul said, "I have done wrong; come back, my son David, for I will never harm you again, because my life was precious in your sight today; I have been a fool, and have made a great mistake." 22 David replied, "Here is the spear, O king! Let one of the young men come over and get it. 23 The LORD rewards everyone for his righteousness and his faithfulness; for the LORD gave you into my hand today, but I would not raise my hand against the LORD's anointed. 24 As your life was precious today in my sight, so may my life be precious in the sight of the LORD, and may he rescue me from all tribulation." 25 Then Saul said to David, "Blessed be you, my son David! You will do many things and will succeed in them." So David went his way, and Saul returned to his place.

27 David said in his heart, "I shall now perish one day by the hand of Saul; there is nothing better for me than to escape to the land of the Philistines; then Saul will despair of seeking me any longer within the borders of Israel, and I shall escape out of his hand." 2 So David set out and went over, he and the six hundred men who were with him, to King Achish son of Maoch of Gath. 3 David stayed with Achish at Gath, he and his troops, every man with his household, and David with his two wives, Ahinoam of Jezreel, and Abigail of Carmel, Nabal's widow. 4 When Saul was told that David had fled to Gath, he no longer sought for him.

5 Then David said to Achish, "If I have found favor in your sight, let a place be given me in one of the country towns, so that I may live there; for why should your servant live in the royal city with you?" 6 So that day Achish gave him Ziklag; therefore Ziklag has belonged to the kings of Judah to this day. 7 The length of time that David lived in the country of the Philistines was one year and four months.

8 Now David and his men went up and made raids on the Geshurites, the Girzites, and the Amalekites; for these were the landed settlements from Telam*k* on the way to Shur and on to the land of Egypt. 9 David struck the land, leaving neither man nor woman alive, but took away the sheep, the oxen, the donkeys, the camels, and the clothing, and came back to Achish. 10 When Achish asked, "Against whom*l* have you made a raid today?" David would say, "Against the Negeb of Judah," or "Against the Negeb of the Jerahmeelites," or, "Against the Negeb of the Kenites."

hailed Abner son of Ner, 'Answer me, Abner!' He answered, 'Who are you to shout to the king?' 15 David said to Abner, 'Do you call yourself a man? Is there anyone like you in Israel? Why, then, did you not keep watch over your lord the king, when someone came to harm your lord the king? 16 This was not well done. As the LORD lives, you deserve to die, all of you, because you have not kept watch over your master the LORD's anointed. Look! Where are the king's spear and the water-jar that were by his head?'

17 Saul recognized David's voice and said, 'Is that you, David my son?' 'Yes, your majesty, it is,' said David. 18 'Why must my lord pursue me? What have I done? What mischief am I plotting? 19 Listen, my lord king, to what I have to say. If it is the LORD who has set you against me, may an offering be acceptable to him; but if it is mortals, a curse on them in the LORD's name! For they have ousted me today from my share in the LORD's possession and have banished me to serve other gods! 20 Do not let my blood be shed on foreign soil, far from the presence of the LORD, just because the king of Israel came out to look for a flea, as one might hunt a partridge over the hills.'

21 Saul said, 'I have done wrong; come back, David my son. You have held my life precious this day, and I will never harm you again. I have been a fool, I have been sadly in the wrong.' 22 David answered, 'Here is the king's spear; let one of your men come across and fetch it. 23 The LORD who rewards uprightness and loyalty will reward the man into whose power he put you today, for I refused to lift my hand against the LORD's anointed. 24 As I held your life precious today, so may the LORD hold mine precious and deliver me from every distress.' 25 Saul said to David, 'A blessing on you, David my son! You will do great things and be triumphant.' With that David went on his way and Saul returned home.

27 DAVID thought to himself, 'One of these days I shall be killed by Saul. The best thing for me to do will be to escape into Philistine territory; then Saul will give up all further hope of finding me anywhere in Israel, search as he may, and I shall escape his clutches.' 2 So David and his six hundred men set out and crossed the frontier to Achish son of Maoch, king of Gath. 3 David settled in Gath with Achish, taking with him his men and their families and his two wives, Ahinoam of Jezreel and Abigail of Carmel, Nabal's widow. 4 Saul was told that David had escaped to Gath, and he abandoned the search.

5 David said to Achish, 'If I stand well in your opinion, grant me a place in one of your country towns where I may settle. Why should I remain in the royal city with your majesty?' 6 Achish granted him Ziklag on that day: that is why Ziklag still belongs to the kings of Judah.

7 David spent a year and four months in Philistine country. 8 He and his men would sally out and raid the Geshurites, the Gizrites, and the Amalekites, for it was they who inhabited the country from Telaim all the way to Shur and Egypt. 9 When David raided any territory he left no one alive, man or woman; he took flocks and herds, donkeys and camels, and clothes too, and then came back again to Achish. 10 Achish would ask, 'Where was your raid today?' and David would answer, 'The Negeb of Judah' or 'The Negeb of the Jerahmeelites' or 'The Negeb of the Kenites'.

---

k Compare Gk 15.4: Heb *from of old*   *l* Q Ms Gk Vg: MT lacks *whom*

27:8 **from Telaim:** *prob. rdg; Heb.* from of old.

Abner?" And Abner answered, "Who is it that calls me?" 15 David said no to Abner: "Are you not a man whose like does not exist in Israel? Why, then, have you not guarded your lord the king when one of his subjects went to kill the king, your lord? 16 This is no creditable service you have performed. As the LORD lives, you people deserve death because you have not guarded your lord, the LORD's anointed. Go, look: where are the king's spear and the water jug that was at his head?"

17 Saul recognized David's voice and asked, "Is that your voice, my son David?" David answered, "Yes, my lord the king." 18 He continued: "Why does my lord pursue his servant? What have I done? What evil do I plan? 19 Please, now, let my lord the king listen to the words of his servant. If the LORD has incited you against me, let an offering appease him; but if men, may they be cursed before the LORD, because they have exiled me so that this day I have no share in the LORD's inheritance, but am told: 'Go, serve other gods!' 20 Do not let my blood flow to the ground far from the presence of the LORD. For the king of Israel has come out to seek a single flea as if he were hunting partridge in the mountains." 21 Then Saul said: "I have done wrong. Come back, my son David, I will not harm you again, because you have held my life precious today. Indeed, I have been a fool and have made a serious mistake." 22 But David answered: "Here is the king's spear. Let an attendant come over to get it. 23 The LORD will reward each man for his justice and faithfulness. Today, though the LORD delivered you into my grasp, I would not harm the LORD's anointed. 24 As I valued your life highly today, so may the LORD value my life highly and deliver me from all difficulties." 25 Then Saul said to David: "Blessed are you, my son David! You shall certainly succeed in whatever you undertake." David went his way, and Saul returned to his home.

27 But David said to himself: "I shall perish some day at the hand of Saul. I have no choice but to escape to the land of the Philistines; then Saul will give up his continuous search for me throughout the land of Israel, and I shall be out of his reach." 2 Accordingly, David departed with his six hundred men and went over to Achish, son of Maoch, king of Gath. 3 David and his men lived in Gath with Achish; each one had his family, and David had his two wives, Ahinoam from Jezreel and Abigail, the widow of Nabal from Carmel. 4 When Saul was told that David had fled to Gath, he no longer searched for him.

5 David said to Achish: "If I meet with your approval, let me have a place to live in one of the country towns. Why should your servant live with you in the royal city?" 6 That same day Achish gave him Ziklag, which has, therefore, belonged to the kings of Judah up to the present time. 7 In all, David lived a year and four months in the country of the Philistines.

8 David and his men went up and made raids on the Geshurites, Girzites, and Amalekites — peoples living in the land between Telam, on the approach to Shur, and the land of Egypt. 9 In attacking the land David would not leave a man or woman alive, but would carry off sheep, oxen, asses, camels, and clothes. On his return he brought these to Achish, 10 who asked, "Whom did you raid this time?" And David answered, "The Negeb of Judah," or "The Negeb of Jarahmeel," or "The Negeb of the Kenites." 11 But

Abner son of Ner, 'Abner, why don't you answer?' Abner replied, 'Who is it that calling?' 15 David said to Abner, 'Are you not a man? Who is your equal in Israel? Why, then, did you not guard the king your lord? One of the people came to kill the king your lord. 16 What you did was not well done. As Yahweh lives, you all deserve to die since you did not guard your lord, Yahweh's anointed. Look where the king's spear is now, and the pitcher of water which was beside his head!'

17 Recognising David's voice, Saul said, 'Is that your voice, my son David?' David replied, 'It is my voice, my lord king. 18 Why is my lord pursuing his servant?' he said. 'What have I done? What crime have I committed? 19 May my lord king now listen to his servant's words: if Yahweh has incited you against me, may he be appeased with an offering; but if human beings have done it, may they be accursed before Yahweh, since they have as effectively banished me today from sharing in Yahweh's heritage as if they had said, "Go and serve other gods!" 20 So I pray now that my blood shall not be shed on soil remote from Yahweh's presence, when the king of Israel has mounted an expedition to take my life, as one might hunt a partridge in the mountains!'

21 Saul replied, 'I have done wrong! Come back, my son David; I shall never harm you again, since today you have shown respect for my life. Yes, I have behaved like a fool, I have been profoundly in the wrong.' 22 In reply, David said, 'Here is the king's spear. Let one of the men come across and get it. 23 May Yahweh reward each as each has been upright and loyal. Today Yahweh put you in my power but I would not raise my hand against Yahweh's anointed. 24 As today I set great value by your life, so may Yahweh set great value by my life and deliver me from every tribulation!'

25 Saul then said, 'May you be blessed, my son David! In what you undertake, you will certainly succeed.' David then went on his way and Saul returned home.

27 'One of these days,' David thought, 'I shall perish at the hand of Saul. The best thing that I can do is to get away into the country of the Philistines; then Saul will give up tracking me through the length and breadth of Israel and I shall be safe from him.' 2 So David set off and went over, he and his six hundred men, to Achish son of Maoch, king of Gath. 3 He settled at Gath with Achish, he and his men, each with his family and David with his two wives, Ahinoam of Jezreel and Abigail widow of Nabal of Carmel. 4 When news reached Saul that David had fled to Gath, he stopped searching for him.

5 David said to Achish, 'If I have won your favour, let me be given a place in one of the outlying towns, where I can live. Why should your servant live in the royal city with you?' 6 That very day Achish gave him Ziklag; and this is why Ziklag has been the property of the kings of Judah to the present day. 7 The time that David stayed in Philistine territory amounted to a year and four months.

8 David and his men went out on raids against the Geshurites, Girzites and Amalekites, for these are the tribes inhabiting the region which, from Telam, goes in the direction of Shur, as far as Egypt. 9 David laid the countryside waste and left neither man nor woman alive; he carried off the sheep and cattle, the donkeys, camels and clothing, and then came back again to Achish. 10 Achish would ask, 'Where did you go raiding today?' David would reply, 'Against the Negeb of Judah,' or 'the Negeb of Jerahmeel,' or 'the Negeb of the

11 David left neither man nor woman alive to be brought back to Gath, thinking, "They might tell about us, and say, 'David has done so and so.'" Such was his practice all the time he lived in the country of the Philistines. 12 Achish trusted David, thinking, "He has made himself utterly abhorrent to his people Israel; therefore he shall always be my servant."

28 In those days the Philistines gathered their forces for war, to fight against Israel. Achish said to David, "You know, of course, that you and your men are to go out with me in the army." 2 David said to Achish, "Very well, then you shall know what your servant can do." Achish said to David, "Very well, I will make you my bodyguard for life."

3 Now Samuel had died, and all Israel had mourned for him and buried him in Ramah, his own city. Saul had expelled the mediums and the wizards from the land. 4 The Philistines assembled, and came and encamped at Shunem. Saul gathered all Israel, and they encamped at Gilboa. 5 When Saul saw the army of the Philistines, he was afraid, and his heart trembled greatly. 6 When Saul inquired of the LORD, the LORD did not answer him, not by dreams, or by Urim, or by prophets. 7 Then Saul said to his servants, "Seek out for me a woman who is a medium, so that I may go to her and inquire of her." His servants said to him, "There is a medium at Endor."

8 So Saul disguised himself and put on other clothes and went there, he and two men with him. They came to the woman by night. And he said, "Consult a spirit for me, and bring up for me the one whom I name to you." 9 The woman said to him, "Surely you know what Saul has done, how he has cut off the mediums and the wizards from the land. Why then are you laying a snare for my life to bring about my death?" 10 But Saul swore to her by the LORD, "As the LORD lives, no punishment shall come upon you for this thing." 11 Then the woman said, "Whom shall I bring up for you?" He answered, "Bring up Samuel for me." 12 When the woman saw Samuel, she cried out with a loud voice; and the woman said to Saul, "Why have you deceived me? You are Saul!" 13 The king said to her, "Have no fear; what do you see?" The woman said to Saul, "I see a divine being[m] coming up out of the ground." 14 He said to her, "What is his appearance?" She said, "An old man is coming up; he is wrapped in a robe." So Saul knew that it was Samuel, and he bowed with his face to the ground, and did obeisance.

15 Then Samuel said to Saul, "Why have you disturbed me by bringing me up?" Saul answered, "I am in great distress, for the Philistines are warring against me, and God has turned away from me and answers me no more, either by prophets or by dreams; so I have summoned you to tell me what I should do." 16 Samuel said, "Why then do you ask me, since the LORD has turned from you and become your enemy? 17 The LORD has done to you just as he spoke by me; for the LORD has torn the kingdom out of your hand, and given it to your neighbor, David. 18 Because you did not obey the voice of the LORD, and did not carry out his fierce wrath against Amalek, therefore the LORD has done this thing to you today. 19 Moreover the LORD will give Israel along with you into the hands of the Philistines; and tomorrow you and your sons shall be with me; the LORD will also give the army of Israel into the hands of the Philistines."

20 Immediately Saul fell full length on the ground, filled with fear because of the words of Samuel; and there was no strength in him, for he had eaten nothing all day and

11 He let neither man nor woman survive to be brought back to Gath, for fear that they might denounce him and his men for what they had done. This was his practice as long as he remained with the Philistines. 12 Achish trusted him, thinking that David had made himself so obnoxious among his own people the Israelites that he would remain his vassal all his life.

28 AT that time the Philistines mustered their army for an attack on Israel, and Achish said to David, 'You know that you and your men must take the field with me.' 2 David answered, 'Good, you will learn what your servant can do.' Achish said, 'I will make you my bodyguard for life.'

3 By this time Samuel was dead, and all Israel had mourned for him and buried him in Ramah, his own town; and Saul had banished from the land all who trafficked with ghosts and spirits. 4 The Philistines mustered and encamped at Shunem, and Saul mustered all the Israelites and encamped at Gilboa. 5 At the sight of the Philistine forces, Saul was afraid, indeed struck to the heart by terror. 6 He enquired of the LORD, but the LORD did not answer him, neither by dreams, nor by Urim, nor by prophets. 7 So he said to his servants, 'Find a woman who has a familiar spirit, and I will go and enquire through her.' They told him that there was such a woman at En-dor.

8 Saul put on different clothes and went in disguise with two of his men. He came to the woman by night and said, 'Tell me my fortune by consulting the dead, and call up the man I name to you.' 9 The woman answered, 'Surely you know what Saul has done, how he has made away with those who call up ghosts and spirits; why do you press me to do what will lead to my death?' 10 Saul swore her an oath: 'As the LORD lives, no harm shall come to you for this.' 11 The woman asked whom she should call up, and Saul answered, 'Samuel.' 12 When the woman saw Samuel appear, she shrieked and said to Saul, 'Why have you deceived me? You are Saul!' 13 The king said to her, 'Do not be afraid. What do you see?' The woman answered, 'I see a ghostly form coming up from the earth.' 14 'What is it like?' he asked; she answered, 'Like an old man coming up, wrapped in a cloak.' Then Saul knew it was Samuel, and he bowed low with his face to the ground, and prostrated himself.

15 Samuel said to Saul, 'Why have you disturbed me and raised me?' Saul answered, 'I am in great trouble; the Philistines are waging war against me, and God has turned away; he no longer answers me through prophets or through dreams, and I have summoned you to tell me what I should do.' 16 Samuel said, 'Why do you ask me, now that the LORD has turned from you and become your adversary? 17 He has done what he foretold through me. He has wrested the kingdom from your hand and given it to another, to David. 18 You have not obeyed the LORD, or executed the judgement of his fierce anger against the Amalekites; that is why he has done this to you today. 19 For the same reason the LORD will let your people Israel fall along with you into the hands of the Philistines. What is more, tomorrow you and your sons will be with me. I tell you again: the LORD will give the Israelite army into the power of the Philistines.' 20 Saul was overcome, and terrified by Samuel's words he fell full length to the ground. He had no strength left, for he had eaten nothing all day and all night.

_____
[m] Or *a god*; or *gods*

David would not leave a man or woman alive to be brought to Gath, fearing that they would betray him by saying, "This is what David did." This was his custom as long as he lived in the country of the Philistines. 12 And Achish trusted David, thinking, "He must certainly be detested by his people Israel. I shall have him as my vassal forever."

28 In those days the Philistines mustered their military forces to fight against Israel. So Achish said to David, "You realize, of course, that you and your men must go out on campaign with me to Jezreel." 2 David answered Achish, "Good! Now you shall learn what your servant can do." Then Achish said to David, "I shall appoint you my permanent bodyguard."

3 Now Samuel had died and, after being mourned by all Israel, was buried in his city, Ramah. Meanwhile Saul had driven mediums and fortune-tellers out of the land.

4 The Philistine levies advanced to Shunem and encamped. Saul, too, mustered all Israel; they camped on Gilboa. 5 When Saul saw the camp of the Philistines, he was dismayed and lost heart completely. 6 He therefore consulted the Lord; but the Lord gave no answer, whether in dreams or by the Urim or through prophets. 7 Then Saul said to his servants, "Find me a woman who is a medium, to whom I can go to seek counsel through her." His servants answered him, "There is a woman in Endor who is a medium."

8 So he disguised himself, putting on other clothes, and set out with two companions. They came to the woman by night, and Saul said to her, "Tell my fortune through a ghost; conjure up for me the one I ask you to." 9 But the woman answered him, "You are surely aware of what Saul has done, in driving the mediums and fortune-tellers out of the land. Why, then, are you laying snares for my life, to have me killed?" 10 But Saul swore to her by the Lord, "As the Lord lives, you shall incur no blame for this." 11 Then the woman asked him, "Whom do you want me to conjure up?" and he answered, "Samuel."

12 When the woman saw Samuel, she shrieked at the top of her voice and said to Saul, "Why have you deceived me? You are Saul!" 13 But the king said to her, "Have no fear. What do you see?" The woman answered Saul, "I see a preternatural being rising from the earth." 14 "What does he look like?" asked Saul. And she replied, "It is an old man who is rising, clothed in a mantle." Saul knew that it was Samuel, and so he bowed face to the ground in homage.

15 Samuel then said to Saul, "Why do you disturb me by conjuring me up?" Saul replied: "I am in great straits, for the Philistines are waging war against me and God has abandoned me. Since he no longer answers me through prophets or in dreams, I have called you to tell me what I should do." 16 To this Samuel said: "But why do you ask me, if the Lord has abandoned you and is with your neighbor? 17 The Lord has done to you what he foretold through me: he has torn the kingdom from your grasp and has given it to your neighbor David.

18 "Because you disobeyed the Lord's directive and would not carry out his fierce anger against Amalek, the Lord has done this to you today. 19 Moreover, the Lord will deliver Israel, and you as well, into the clutches of the Philistines. By tomorrow you and your sons will be with me, and the Lord will have delivered the army of Israel into the hands of the Philistines." 20 Immediately Saul fell full length on the ground, for he was badly shaken by Samuel's message. Moreover, he had no bodily strength left, since he had eaten nothing all that

Kenites.' 11 David spared neither man nor woman to bring back alive to Gath, 'in case', as he thought, 'they inform on us and say, "David did such and such." ' This was the way David conducted his raids all the time he stayed in Philistine territory. 12 Achish trusted David. 'He has made himself detested by his own people Israel,' he thought, 'and so will be my servant for ever.'

28 It then happened that the Philistines mustered their forces for war, to fight Israel, and Achish said to David, 'It is understood that you and your men go into battle with me.' 2 David said to Achish, 'In that case, you will soon see what your servant can do.' Achish replied to David, 'Right, I shall appoint you as my permanent bodyguard.'

3 Now Samuel was dead, and all Israel had mourned him and buried him at Ramah, his own town. Saul had expelled the necromancers and wizards from the country.

4 Meanwhile the Philistines had mustered and had come and pitched camp at Shunem. Saul mustered all Israel and they encamped at Gilboa. 5 When Saul saw the Philistine camp, he was afraid and his heart trembled violently. 6 Saul consulted Yahweh, but Yahweh gave him no answer, either by dream, divination or prophet. 7 Saul then said to his servants, 'Find a necromancer for me, so that I can go and consult her.' His servants replied, 'There is a necromancer at En-Dor.'

8 And so Saul, disguising himself and changing his clothes, set out accompanied by two men; their visit to the woman took place at night. 'Disclose the future to me', he said, 'by means of a ghost. Conjure up the one I shall name to you.' 9 The woman replied, 'Look, you know what Saul has done, how he has outlawed necromancers and wizards from the country; why are you setting a trap for my life, then, to have me killed?' 10 But Saul swore to her by Yahweh, 'As Yahweh lives,' he said, 'no blame shall attach to you for this business.' 11 The woman asked, 'Whom shall I conjure up for you?' He replied, 'Conjure up Samuel.'

12 The woman saw Samuel and, giving a great cry, she said to Saul, 'Why have you deceived me? You are Saul!' 13 The king said, 'Do not be afraid! What do you see?' The woman replied to Saul, 'I see a ghost rising from the earth.' 14 'What is he like?' he asked. She replied, 'It is an old man coming up; he is wrapped in a cloak.' Saul then knew that it was Samuel and, bowing to the ground, prostrated himself.

15 Samuel said to Saul, 'Why have you disturbed my rest by conjuring me up?' Saul replied: 'I am in great distress; the Philistines are waging war on me, and God has abandoned me and no longer answers me either by prophet or by dream; and so I have summoned you to tell me what I ought to do.' 16 Samuel said, 'Why consult me, when Yahweh has abandoned you and has become your enemy? 17 Yahweh has treated you as he foretold through me; he has snatched the sovereignty from your hand and given it to your neighbour, David, 18 because you disobeyed Yahweh's voice and did not execute his fierce anger against Amalek. That is why Yahweh is treating you like this today. 19 What is more, Yahweh will deliver Israel and you too, into the power of the Philistines. Tomorrow you and your sons will be with me; and Yahweh will hand over the army of Israel into the power of the Philistines.'

20 Immediately Saul fell full length on the ground. He was terrified by what Samuel had said and was also weak from having eaten nothing all that day and night. 21 The

all night. 21 The woman came to Saul, and when she saw that he was terrified, she said to him, "Your servant has listened to you; I have taken my life in my hand, and have listened to what you have said to me. 22 Now therefore, you also listen to your servant; let me set a morsel of bread before you. Eat, that you may have strength when you go on your way." 23 He refused, and said, "I will not eat." But his servants, together with the woman, urged him; and he listened to their words. So he got up from the ground and sat on the bed. 24 Now the woman had a fatted calf in the house. She quickly slaughtered it, and she took flour, kneaded it, and baked unleavened cakes. 25 She put them before Saul and his servants, and they ate. Then they rose and went away that night.

29 Now the Philistines gathered all their forces at Aphek, while the Israelites were encamped by the fountain that is in Jezreel. 2 As the lords of the Philistines were passing on by hundreds and by thousands, and David and his men were passing on in the rear with Achish, 3 the commanders of the Philistines said, "What are these Hebrews doing here?" Achish said to the commanders of the Philistines, "Is this not David, the servant of King Saul of Israel, who has been with me now for days and years? Since he deserted to me I have found no fault in him to this day." 4 But the commanders of the Philistines were angry with him; and the commanders of the Philistines said to him, "Send the man back, so that he may return to the place that you have assigned to him; he shall not go down with us to battle, or else he may become an adversary to us in the battle. For how could this fellow reconcile himself to his lord? Would it not be with the heads of the men here? 5 Is this not David, of whom they sing to one another in dances,

'Saul has killed his thousands,
    and David his ten thousands'?"

6 Then Achish called David and said to him, "As the LORD lives, you have been honest, and to me it seems right that you should march out and in with me in the campaign; for I have found nothing wrong in you from the day of your coming to me until today. Nevertheless the lords do not approve of you. 7 So go back now; and go peaceably; do nothing to displease the lords of the Philistines." 8 David said to Achish, "But what have I done? What have you found in your servant from the day I entered your service until now, that I should not go and fight against the enemies of my lord the king?" 9 Achish replied to David, "I know that you are as blameless in my sight as an angel of God; nevertheless, the commanders of the Philistines have said, 'He shall not go up with us to the battle.' 10 Now then rise early in the morning, you and the servants of your lord who came with you, and go to the place that I appointed for you. As for the evil report, do not take it to heart, for you have done well before me.[n] Start early in the morning, and leave as soon as you have light." 11 So David set out with his men early in the morning, to return to the land of the Philistines. But the Philistines went up to Jezreel.

30 Now when David and his men came to Ziklag on the third day, the Amalekites had made a raid on the Negeb and on Ziklag. They had attacked Ziklag, burned it down, 2 and taken captive the women and all[o] who were in it, both small and great; they killed none of them, but carried them off, and went their way. 3 When David and his men came to the city, they found it burned down, and their wives and sons and daughters taken captive. 4 Then David and the people who were with him raised their voices and wept, until they had no more strength to weep. 5 David's two wives also had been taken captive, Ahinoam of Jezreel, and Abigail the widow of Nabal of Carmel. 6 David was in

[n] Gk: Heb lacks *and go to the place . . . done well before me*
[o] Gk: Heb lacks *and all*

21 The woman went to Saul and, seeing how deeply shaken he was, she said, 'I listened to what you said and I risked my life to obey you. 22 Now listen to me: let me set before you a little food to give you strength for your journey.' 23 He refused to eat anything, but when his servants joined the woman in pressing him, he yielded, rose from the ground, and sat on the couch. 24 The woman had a fattened calf at home, which she quickly slaughtered; she also took some meal, kneaded it, and baked unleavened loaves. 25 She set the food before Saul and his servants, and when they had eaten they set off that same night.

29 The Philistines mustered their entire army at Aphek; the Israelites encamped at En-harod in Jezreel. 2 While the Philistine lords were advancing with their troops in units of a hundred and a thousand, David and his men were in the rear of the column with Achish. 3 The Philistine commanders asked, 'What are those Hebrews doing here?' Achish answered, 'This is David, the servant of King Saul of Israel who has been with me now for a year or more. Ever since he came over to me I have had no fault to find with him.' 4 The commanders were indignant and said, 'Send the man back to the place you allotted to him. He must not fight side by side with us, for he may turn traitor in the battle. What better way to buy his master's favour, than at the price of our lives? 5 This is that David of whom they sang, as they danced:

"Saul struck down thousands,
    but David tens of thousands." '

6 Achish summoned David and said to him, 'As the LORD lives, you are an upright man and your service on my campaigns has well satisfied me. I have had no fault to find with you ever since you joined me, but the lords are not willing to accept you. 7 Now go home in peace, and you will then be doing nothing that they can regard as wrong.' 8 David protested, 'What have I done, or what fault have you found in me from the day I first entered your service till now, that I should not come and fight against the enemies of my lord the king?' 9 Achish answered, 'I agree that you have been as true to me as an angel of God, but the Philistine commanders insist that you are not to fight alongside them. 10 Now rise early tomorrow with those of your lord's subjects who have followed you, and go to the town which I allotted to you; harbour no resentment, for I am well satisfied with you. Be up early and start as soon as it is light.' 11 So in the morning David and his men made an early start to go back to the land of the Philistines, while the Philistines went on to Jezreel.

30 On the third day David and his men reached Ziklag. In the mean time the Amalekites had made a raid into the Negeb, attacked Ziklag, and set it on fire. 2 They had taken captive all the women, young and old. They did not put any to death, but carried them off as they continued their march. 3 When David and his men came to the town, they found it destroyed by fire, and their wives, their sons, and their daughters taken captive. 4 David and the people with him wept aloud until they could weep no more. 5 David's two wives, Ahinoam of Jezreel and Abigail widow of Nabal of Carmel, were among the captives. 6 David was in

28:23 **in pressing:** *prob. rdg, cp. Gk; Heb.* in breaking out on.
29:1 **at En-harod:** *prob. rdg; Heb.* at the spring.   29:10 **and go . . . with you:** *so Gk; Heb.* omits.

day and night. 21 Then the woman came to Saul, and seeing that he was quite terror-stricken, said to him: "Remember, your maidservant obeyed you: I took my life in my hands and fulfilled the request you made of me. 22 Now you, in turn, please listen to your maidservant. Let me set something before you to eat, so that you may have strength when you go on your way." 23 But he refused, saying, "I will not eat." However, when his servants joined the woman in urging him, he listened to their entreaties, got up from the ground, and sat on a couch. 24 The woman had a stall-fed calf in the house, which she now quickly slaughtered. Then taking flour, she kneaded it and baked unleavened bread. 25 She set the meal before Saul and his servants, and they ate. Then they stood up and left the same night.

29 Now the Philistines had mustered all their forces in Aphek, and the Israelites were encamped at the spring of Harod near Jezreel. 2 As the Philistine lords were marching their groups of a hundred and a thousand, David and his men were marching in the rear guard with Achish. 3 The Philistine chiefs asked, "What are those Hebrews doing here?" And Achish answered them: "Why, that is David, the officer of Saul, king of Israel. He has been with me now for a year or two, and I have no fault to find with him from the day he came over to me until the present." 4 But the Philistine chiefs were angered at this and said to him: "Send that man back! Let him return to the place you picked out for him. He must not go down into battle with us, lest during the battle he become our enemy. For how else can he win back his master's favor, if not with the heads of these men of ours? 5 Is this not the David of whom they sing during their dances,

'Saul has slain his thousands,
but David his ten thousands'?"

6 So Achish summoned David and said to him: "As the LORD lives, you are honest, and I should be pleased to have you active with me in the camp, for I have found nothing wrong with you from the day of your arrival to this day. But you are not welcome to the lords. 7 Withdraw peaceably, now, and do nothing that might displease the Philistine lords." 8 But David said to Achish: "What have I done? Or what have you against your servant from the first day I have been with you to this day, that I cannot go to fight against the enemies of my lord the king?" 9 "You know," Achish answered David, "that you are acceptable to me. But the Philistine chiefs have determined you are not to go up with us to battle. 10 So the first thing tomorrow, you and your lord's servants who came with you, go to the place I picked out for you. Do not decide to take umbrage at this; you are as acceptable to me as an angel of God. But make an early morning start, as soon as it grows light, and be on your way." 11 So David and his men left early in the morning to return to the land of the Philistines. The Philistines, however, went on up to Jezreel.

30 Before David and his men reached Ziklag on the third day, the Amalekites had raided the Negeb and Ziklag, had stormed the city, and had set it on fire. 2 They had taken captive the women and all who were in the city, young and old, killing no one; they had carried them off when they left. 3 David and his men arrived at the city to find it burned to the ground and their wives, sons and daughters taken captive. 4 Then David and those who were with him wept aloud until they could weep no more. 5 David's two wives, Ahinoam of Jezreel and Abigail, the widow of Nabal from Carmel, had also been carried off with the rest. 6 Now David found himself in great difficulty,

woman went to Saul and, seeing his terror, said, 'Look, your servant has obeyed your order; I have taken my life in my hands and obeyed the command which you gave me. 22 Now please, you in your turn listen to what your servant has to say. Let me offer you a piece of bread. Eat something and get some strength for your journey.' 23 But he refused. 'I will not eat,' he said. His servants however pressed him, and so did the woman. Allowing himself to be persuaded by them, he got up from the ground and sat on the bed. 24 The woman owned a fattened calf which she quickly slaughtered, and she took some flour and kneaded it and with it baked some unleavened cakes 25 which she served to Saul and his servants; they ate, and then set off and left the same night.

29 The Philistines mustered all their forces at Aphek while the Israelites pitched camp near the spring in Jezreel. 2 The Philistine commanders marched past with their hundreds and their thousands, and David and his men brought up the rear with Achish. 3 The Philistine chiefs asked, 'What are these Hebrews doing?' Achish replied to them, 'Why, this is David the servant of Saul, king of Israel, who has been with me for the last year or two. I have had no fault to find with him from the day he gave himself up to me until the present time.' 4 But the Philistine chiefs were angry with him. 'Send the man back,' they said, 'make him go back to the place which you assigned to him. He cannot go into battle with us, in case he turns on us once battle is joined. Would there be a better way for the man to regain his master's favour than with the heads of these men here? 5 Is not this the David of whom they sang as they danced:

Saul has killed his thousands,
and David his tens of thousands'?

6 So Achish called David and said, 'As Yahweh lives, you are loyal, and I am quite content with all your doings in our campaigning together, since I have found no fault with you from the day you came to me until the present time. But you are not acceptable to the chiefs. 7 So go home, in peace, rather than antagonise them.'

8 'But what have I done,' David asked Achish, 'what fault have you had to find with your servant from the day I entered your service to the present time, for me not to be allowed to go and fight the enemies of my lord the king?' 9 In reply, Achish said to David, 'In my opinion, it is true, you are as good as an angel of God; but the Philistine chiefs have said, "He must not go into battle with us." 10 So get up early tomorrow morning, with your master's servants who came with you, and go to the place which I assigned to you. Do not harbour resentment, since personally I have no fault to find with you. Get up early tomorrow morning and, as soon as it is light, be off.'

11 So David and his men got up early to leave at dawn and go back to Philistine territory. And the Philistines marched on Jezreel.

30 Now by the time David and his men reached Ziklag three days later, the Amalekites had raided the Negeb and Ziklag; they had sacked Ziklag and burnt it down. 2 They had taken the women prisoner, and everyone who was there, both small and great. They had not killed anyone, but had carried them off and gone away. 3 When David and his men arrived, they found the town burnt down and their wives and sons and daughters taken captive. 4 Then David and the people with him wept aloud till they were too weak to weep any more. 5 David's two wives had been captured: Ahinoam of Jezreel and Abigail widow of Nabal of Carmel.

NEW REVISED STANDARD VERSION

great danger; for the people spoke of stoning him, because all the people were bitter in spirit for their sons and daughters. But David strengthened himself in the LORD his God.

7 David said to the priest Abiathar son of Ahimelech, "Bring me the ephod." So Abiathar brought the ephod to David. 8 David inquired of the LORD, "Shall I pursue this band? Shall I overtake them?" He answered him, "Pursue; for you shall surely overtake and shall surely rescue." 9 So David set out, he and the six hundred men who were with him. They came to the Wadi Besor, where those stayed who were left behind. 10 But David went on with the pursuit, he and four hundred men; two hundred stayed behind, too exhausted to cross the Wadi Besor.

11 In the open country they found an Egyptian, and brought him to David. They gave him bread and he ate, they gave him water to drink; 12 they also gave him a piece of fig cake and two clusters of raisins. When he had eaten, his spirit revived; for he had not eaten bread or drunk water for three days and three nights. 13 Then David said to him, "To whom do you belong? Where are you from?" He said, "I am a young man of Egypt, servant to an Amalekite. My master left me behind because I fell sick three days ago. 14 We had made a raid on the Negeb of the Cherethites and on that which belongs to Judah and on the Negeb of Caleb; and we burned Ziklag down." 15 David said to him, "Will you take me down to this raiding party?" He said, "Swear to me by God that you will not kill me, or hand me over to my master, and I will take you down to them."

16 When he had taken him down, they were spread out all over the ground, eating and drinking and dancing, because of the great amount of spoil they had taken from the land of the Philistines and from the land of Judah. 17 David attacked them from twilight until the evening of the next day. Not one of them escaped, except four hundred young men, who mounted camels and fled. 18 David recovered all that the Amalekites had taken; and David rescued his two wives. 19 Nothing was missing, whether small or great, sons or daughters, spoil or anything that had been taken; David brought back everything. 20 David also captured all the flocks and herds, which were driven ahead of the other cattle; people said, "This is David's spoil."

21 Then David came to the two hundred men who had been too exhausted to follow David, and who had been left at the Wadi Besor. They went out to meet David and to meet the people who were with him. When David drew near to the people he saluted them. 22 Then all the corrupt and worthless fellows among the men who had gone with David said, "Because they did not go with us, we will not give them any of the spoil that we have recovered, except that each man may take his wife and children, and leave." 23 But David said, "You shall not do so, my brothers, with what the LORD has given us; he has preserved us and handed over to us the raiding party that attacked us. 24 Who would listen to you in this matter? For the share of the one who goes down into the battle shall be the same as the share of the one who stays by the baggage; they shall share alike." 25 From that day forward he made it a statute and an ordinance for Israel; it continues to the present day.

26 When David came to Ziklag, he sent part of the spoil to his friends, the elders of Judah, saying, "Here is a present for you from the spoil of the enemies of the LORD"; 27 it was for those in Bethel, in Ramoth of the Negeb, in Jattir, 28 in

REVISED ENGLISH BIBLE

a desperate position because the troops, embittered by the loss of their sons and daughters, threatened to stone him.

David sought strength in the LORD his God, 7 and told Abiathar the priest, son of Ahimelech, to bring the ephod. When Abiathar had brought the ephod, 8 David enquired of the LORD, 'Shall I pursue these raiders? And shall I overtake them?' The answer came, 'Pursue them: you will overtake them and rescue everyone.' 9 David and his six hundred men set out and reached the wadi of Besor. 10 Two hundred of them who were too exhausted to cross the wadi stayed behind, and David with four hundred pressed on in pursuit.

11 In the open country they came across an Egyptian and took him to David. They gave him food to eat and water to drink, 12 also a lump of dried figs and two bunches of raisins. When he had eaten he revived; for he had had nothing to eat or drink for three days and nights. 13 David asked him, 'Whose slave are you, and where have you come from?' 'I am an Egyptian,' he answered, 'the slave of an Amalekite, but my master left me behind because three days ago I fell ill. 14 We had raided the Negeb of the Kerethites, part of Judah, and the Negeb of Caleb; we also burned down Ziklag.' 15 David asked, 'Can you guide me to the raiders?' 'Swear to me by God', he answered, 'that you will not put me to death or hand me back to my master, and I shall guide you to them.' 16 He led him down, and there they found the Amalekites scattered everywhere, eating and drinking and celebrating the great mass of spoil taken from the Philistine and Judaean territories.

17 David attacked from dawn to dusk and continued till next day; only four hundred young men mounted on camels got away. 18 David rescued all those whom the Amalekites had taken captive, including his two wives. 19 No one was missing, young or old, sons or daughters, nor was any of the spoil missing, anything they had seized for themselves: David recovered everything. 20 They took all the flocks and herds, drove the cattle before him and said, 'This is David's spoil.'

21 When David returned to the two hundred men who had been too exhausted to follow him and whom he had left behind at the wadi of Besor, they came forward to meet him and his men. David greeted them all, enquiring how things were with them. 22 But some of those who had gone with David, rogues and scoundrels, broke in and said, 'These men did not go with us; we will not allot them any of the spoil that we have recaptured, except that each of them may take his wife and children and go.' 23 'That', said David, 'you must not do, considering what the LORD has given us, and how he has kept us safe and given the raiding party into our hands. 24 Who could agree with what you propose? Those who stayed with the stores are to have the same share as those who went into battle. All must share and share alike.' 25 From that time onwards, this has been the established custom in Israel down to this day.

26 When David reached Ziklag, he sent some of the spoil to the elders of Judah and to his friends, with this message: 'This is a present for you out of the spoil taken from the LORD's enemies.' 27 He sent to those in Bethuel, in Ramoth-

30:9 **Besor:** *prob. rdg; Heb. adds* those who were left over remained.   30:20 **They . . . before him:** *prob. rdg; Heb.* David took all the flocks and herds; they drove before that cattle. 30:22 **us:** *so some MSS; others* me.   30:23 **considering:** *prob. rdg, cp. Gk; Heb.* my brothers.   30:26 **and:** *so Gk; Heb. omits.* 30:28 **Ararah:** *prob. rdg; Heb.* Aroer.

for the men spoke of stoning him, so bitter were they over the fate of their sons and daughters. But with renewed trust in the LORD his God, 7 David said to Abiathar, the priest, son of Ahimelech, "Bring me the ephod!" When Abiathar brought him the ephod, 8 David inquired of the LORD, "Shall I pursue these raiders? Can I overtake them?" The LORD answered him, "Go in pursuit, for you shall surely overtake them and effect a rescue."

9 So David went off with his six hundred men and came as far as the Wadi Besor, where those who were to remain behind halted. 10 David continued the pursuit with four hundred men, but two hundred were too exhausted to cross the Wadi Besor and remained behind. 11 An Egyptian was found in the open country and brought to David. He was provided with food, which he ate, and given water to drink; 12 a cake of pressed figs and two cakes of pressed raisins were also offered to him. When he had eaten, he revived; he had not taken food nor drunk water for three days and three nights. 13 Then David asked him, "To whom do you belong, and where do you come from?" He replied: "I am an Egyptian, the slave of an Amalekite. My master abandoned me because I fell sick three days ago today. 14 We raided the Negeb of the Cherethites, the territory of Judah, and the Negeb of Caleb; and we set Ziklag on fire." 15 David then asked him, "Will you lead me down to this raiding party?" He answered, "Swear to me by God that you will not kill me or deliver me to my master, and I will lead you to the raiding party." 16 He did lead them, and there were the Amalekites scattered all over the ground, eating, drinking, and in a festive mood because of all the rich booty they had taken from the land of the Philistines and from the land of Judah.

17 From dawn to sundown David attacked them, putting them under the ban so that none escaped except four hundred young men, who mounted their camels and fled. 18 David recovered everything the Amalekites had taken, and rescued his two wives. 19 Nothing was missing, small or great, booty or sons or daughters, of all that the Amalekites had taken. David brought back everything. 20 Moreover, David took all the sheep and oxen, and as they drove them before him, they shouted, "This is David's spoil."

21 When David came to the two hundred men who had been too exhausted to follow him, and whom he had left behind at the Wadi Besor, they came out to meet David and the men with him. On nearing them David greeted them. 22 But all the stingy and worthless men among those who had accompanied David spoke up to say, "Since they did not accompany us, we will not give them anything from the booty, except to each man his wife and children. Let them take those along and be on their way." 23 But David said: "You must not do this, my brothers, after what the LORD has given us. He has protected us and delivered into our grip the band that came against us. 24 Who could agree with this proposal of yours? Rather, the share of the one who goes down to battle and that of the one who remains with the baggage shall be the same; they shall share alike." 25 And from that day forward he made it a law and a custom in Israel, as it still is today.

26 When David came to Ziklag, he sent part of the spoil to the elders of Judah, city by city, saying, "This is a gift to you from the spoil of the enemies of the LORD": 27 to those in Bethel, to those in Ramoth-negeb, to those in Jattir,

6 David was in great trouble, since the people were talking of stoning him; the people all felt very bitter, each man for his own sons and daughters. But David took courage from Yahweh his God. 7 To the priest Abiathar son of Ahimelech, David said, 'Bring me the ephod.' Abiathar brought the ephod to David. 8 David then consulted Yahweh, 'Shall I go in pursuit of these raiders? Will I overtake them?' The answer was, 'Go in pursuit; you will certainly overtake them and rescue the captives.' 9 David accordingly set off with the six hundred men who were with him and reached the torrent of Besor. 10 David then continued the pursuit with four hundred men, two hundred staying behind who were too exhausted to cross the torrent of Besor.

11 Out in the country they found an Egyptian and brought him to David. They gave him some bread to eat and some water to drink; 12 they also gave him a piece of fig cake and two bunches of raisins; he ate these and his spirits revived — he had had nothing to eat or drink for three days and three nights. 13 David then said to him, 'Whose man are you and where do you come from?' He replied, 'I am a young Egyptian, the slave of an Amalekite; my master abandoned me because I fell sick three days ago. 14 We raided the Negeb of the Cherethites, and the Negeb of Judah, and the Negeb of Caleb too, and we burnt Ziklag down.' 15 David said, 'Will you guide me to these raiders?' He replied, 'Swear to me by God not to kill me or hand me over to my master, and I will guide you to these raiders.'

16 He guided him to them, and there they were, scattered over the whole countryside, eating, drinking and celebrating, on account of the enormous booty which they had brought back from the territory of the Philistines and the territory of Judah. 17 David slaughtered them from dawn until the evening of the following day. No one escaped, except four hundred young men who mounted camels and fled. 18 He rescued everything that the Amalekites had taken — David also rescued his two wives. 19 Nothing of theirs was lost, whether small or great, from the booty or sons and daughters — everything that had been taken from them; David recovered everything. 20 They captured the flocks and herds as well and drove them in front of him. 'This is David's booty,' they shouted.

21 When David reached the two hundred men who had been too exhausted to follow him and whom he had left at the torrent of Besor, they came out to meet David and the party accompanying him; David approached with his party and greeted them. 22 But all the rogues and scoundrels among the men who had gone with David began saying, 'Since they did not go with us, we shall not give them any of the booty which we have rescued, except that each of them can have his wife and children. Let them take them away and be off.' 23 But David said, 'Do not behave like this, brothers, with what Yahweh has given us; he has protected us and has handed over to us the raiders who attacked us. 24 Who would agree with you on this? No:

As the share of the man who goes into battle,
so is the share of the man who stays with the
baggage.
They will share alike.' 25 And from that day on, he made that a rule and custom for Israel, which obtains to the present day.

26 When David reached Ziklag, he sent parts of the booty to the elders of Judah, town by town, with this message, 'Here is a present for you, taken from the booty of Yahweh's enemies':

27 to those in Bethel,
to those in Ramoth of the Negeb,

Aroer, in Siphmoth, in Eshtemoa, 29 in Racal, in the towns of the Jerahmeelites, in the towns of the Kenites, 30 in Hormah, in Bor-ashan, in Athach, 31 in Hebron, all the places where David and his men had roamed.

31 Now the Philistines fought against Israel; and the men of Israel fled before the Philistines, and many fell p on Mount Gilboa. 2 The Philistines overtook Saul and his sons; and the Philistines killed Jonathan and Abinadab and Malchishua, the sons of Saul. 3 The battle pressed hard upon Saul; the archers found him, and he was badly wounded by them. 4 Then Saul said to his armor-bearer, "Draw your sword and thrust me through with it, so that these uncircumcised may not come and thrust me through, and make sport of me." But his armor-bearer was unwilling; for he was terrified. So Saul took his own sword and fell upon it. 5 When his armor-bearer saw that Saul was dead, he also fell upon his sword and died with him. 6 So Saul and his three sons and his armor-bearer and all his men died together on the same day. 7 When the men of Israel who were on the other side of the valley and those beyond the Jordan saw that the men of Israel had fled and that Saul and his sons were dead, they forsook their towns and fled; and the Philistines came and occupied them.

8 The next day, when the Philistines came to strip the dead, they found Saul and his three sons fallen on Mount Gilboa. 9 They cut off his head, stripped off his armor, and sent messengers throughout the land of the Philistines to carry the good news to the houses of their idols and to the people. 10 They put his armor in the temple of Astarte; q and they fastened his body to the wall of Beth-shan. 11 But when the inhabitants of Jabesh-gilead heard what the Philistines had done to Saul, 12 all the valiant men set out, traveled all night long, and took the body of Saul and the bodies of his sons from the wall of Beth-shan. They came to Jabesh and burned them there. 13 Then they took their bones and buried them under the tamarisk tree in Jabesh, and fasted seven days.

p Heb and they fell slain   q Heb plural

negeb, in Jattir, 28 in Ararah, in Siphmoth, in Eshtemoa, 29 in Rachal, in the cities of the Jerahmeelites, in the towns of the Kenites, 30 in Hormah, in Borashan, in Athak, 31 in Hebron, and in all the places over which he and his men had ranged.

31 The Philistines engaged Israel in battle, and the Israelites were routed, leaving their dead on Mount Gilboa. 2 The Philistines closely pursued Saul and his sons, and Jonathan, Abinadab, and Malchishua, the sons of Saul, were killed. 3 The battle went hard for Saul, and when the archers caught up with him they wounded him severely. 4 He said to his armour-bearer, 'Draw your sword and run me through, so that these uncircumcised brutes may not come and taunt me and make sport of me.' But the armour-bearer refused; he dared not do it. Thereupon Saul took his own sword and fell on it. 5 When the armour-bearer saw that Saul was dead, he too fell on his sword and died with him. 6 So they died together on that day, Saul, his three sons, and his armour-bearer, as well as all his men. 7 When the Israelites in the neighbourhood of the valley and of the Jordan saw that the other Israelites had fled and that Saul and his sons had perished, they fled likewise, abandoning their towns; and the Philistines moved in and occupied them.

8 Next day, when the Philistines came to strip the slain, they found Saul and his three sons lying dead on Mount Gilboa. 9 They cut off his head and stripped him of his armour; then they sent messengers through the length and breadth of their land to carry the good news to idols and people alike. 10 They deposited his armour in the temple of Ashtoreth and nailed his body on the wall of Beth-shan. 11 When the inhabitants of Jabesh-gilead heard what the Philistines had done to Saul, 12 all the warriors among them set out and journeyed through the night to recover the bodies of Saul and his sons from the wall of Beth-shan. They brought them back to Jabesh and burned them; 13 they took the bones and buried them under the tamarisk tree in Jabesh, and for seven days they fasted.

31:1–13 *Cp. 1 Chr. 10:1–12.*   31:9 **idols:** *so Gk; Heb.* house of idols.   31:11 **heard:** *so Gk; Heb. adds* to him.   31:12 **They brought them:** *so Gk, cp. 1 Chr. 10:12; Heb.* they came.

28 to those in Aroer, to those in Siphmoth, to those in Eshtemoa, 29 to those in Racal, to those in the Jerahmeelite cities, to those in the Kenite cities, 30 to those in Hormah, to those in Borashan, to those in Athach, 31 to those in Hebron, and to all the places frequented by David and his men.

31 As they pressed their attack on Israel, with the Israelites fleeing before them and falling mortally wounded on Mount Gilboa, 2 the Philistines pursued Saul and his sons closely, and slew Jonathan, Abinadab, and Malchishua, sons of Saul. 3 The battle raged around Saul, and the archers hit him; he was pierced through the abdomen. 4 Then Saul said to his armor-bearer, "Draw your sword and run me through, lest these uncircumcised come and make sport of me." But his armor-bearer, badly frightened, refused to do it. So Saul took his own sword and fell upon it. 5 When the armor-bearer saw that Saul was dead, he too fell upon his sword and died with him. 6 Thus Saul, his three sons, and his armor-bearer died together on that same day.

7 When the Israelites on the slope of the valley and those along the Jordan saw that the men of Israel had fled and that Saul and his sons were dead, they too abandoned their cities and fled. Then the Philistines came and lived in those cities. 8 The day after the battle the Philistines came to strip the slain, and found Saul and his three sons lying on Mount Gilboa. 9 They cut off Saul's head and stripped him of his armor, and then sent the good news throughout the land of the Philistines to their idols and to the people. 10 They put his armor in the temple of Astarte, but impaled his body on the wall of Beth-shan.

11 When the inhabitants of Jabesh-gilead heard what the Philistines had done to Saul, 12 all their warriors set out, and after marching throughout the night, removed the bodies of Saul and his sons from the wall of Beth-shan, and brought them to Jabesh, where they cremated them. 13 Then they took their bones and buried them under the tamarisk tree in Jabesh, and fasted for seven days.

28 to those in Jattir,
 to those in Aroer,
 to those in Siphmoth,
 to those in Eshtemoa,
29 to those in Carmel,
 to those in the towns of Jerahmeel,
 to those in the towns of the Kenites,
30 to those in Hormah,
 to those in Borashan,
 to those in Athach,
31 to those in Hebron
and to all the places which David and his men had frequented.

31 The Philistines gave battle to Israel, and the Israelites, fleeing from the Philistines, fell and were slaughtered on Mount Gilboa. 2 The Philistines bore down on Saul and his sons, and they killed Jonathan, Abinadab and Malchishua, Saul's sons. 3 The fighting grew fiercer round Saul; the archers came upon him, and he was severely wounded 4 by the archers. Saul then said to his armour-bearer, 'Draw your sword and run me through with it; I do not want these uncircumcised men to come and make fun of me.' But his armour-bearer was very much afraid and would not do it. So Saul took his own sword and fell on it. 5 His armour-bearer, seeing that Saul was dead, fell on his sword too and died with him. 6 Thus died Saul, his three sons and his armour-bearer, together on the same day. 7 When the Israelites who were on the other side of the Jordan saw that the Israelites had been routed and that Saul and his sons were dead, they abandoned their towns and fled. The Philistines then came and occupied them.

8 When the Philistines came on the following day to strip the dead, they found Saul and his three sons lying on Mount Gilboa. 9 They cut off his head and, stripping him of his armour, had these carried round the territory of the Philistines to proclaim the good news to their idols and their people. 10 They put his armour in the temple of Astarte; and his body they fastened to the walls of Beth-Shean.

11 When the inhabitants of Jabesh in Gilead heard what the Philistines had done to Saul, 12 the warriors all set out and, having marched all night, took the bodies of Saul and his sons off the walls of Beth-Shean; they brought them to Jabesh and burned them there. 13 They then took their bones and buried them under the tamarisk of Jabesh, and fasted for seven days.

2 Samuel

THE SECOND BOOK OF
Samuel

1 After the death of Saul, when David had returned from defeating the Amalekites, David remained two days in Ziklag. 2 On the third day, a man came from Saul's camp, with his clothes torn and dirt on his head. When he came to David, he fell to the ground and did obeisance. 3 David said to him, "Where have you come from?" He said to him, "I have escaped from the camp of Israel." 4 David said to him, "How did things go? Tell me!" He answered, "The army fled from the battle, but also many of the army fell and died; and Saul and his son Jonathan also died." 5 Then David asked the young man who was reporting to him, "How do you know that Saul and his son Jonathan died?" 6 The young man reporting to him said, "I happened to be on Mount Gilboa; and there was Saul leaning on his spear, while the chariots and the horsemen drew close to him. 7 When he looked behind him, he saw me, and called to me. I answered, 'Here sir.' 8 And he said to me, 'Who are you?' I answered him, 'I am an Amalekite.' 9 He said to me, 'Come, stand over me and kill me; for convulsions have seized me, and yet my life still lingers.' 10 So I stood over him, and killed him, for I knew that he could not live after he had fallen. I took the crown that was on his head and the armlet that was on his arm, and I have brought them here to my lord."

11 Then David took hold of his clothes and tore them; and all the men who were with him did the same. 12 They mourned and wept, and fasted until evening for Saul and for his son Jonathan, and for the army of the LORD and for the house of Israel, because they had fallen by the sword. 13 David said to the young man who had reported to him, "Where do you come from?" He answered, "I am the son of a resident alien, an Amalekite." 14 David said to him, "Were you not afraid to lift your hand to destroy the LORD's anointed?" 15 Then David called one of the young men and said, "Come here and strike him down." So he struck him down and he died. 16 David said to him, "Your blood be on your head; for your own mouth has testified against you, saying, 'I have killed the LORD's anointed.'"

17 David intoned this lamentation over Saul and his son Jonathan. 18 (He ordered that The Song of the Bow*a* be taught to the people of Judah; it is written in the Book of Jashar.) He said:

19   Your glory, O Israel, lies slain upon your high
      places!
      How the mighty have fallen!

20   Tell it not in Gath,
      proclaim it not in the streets of Ashkelon;
      or the daughters of the Philistines will rejoice,
      the daughters of the uncircumcised will exult.

21   You mountains of Gilboa,
      let there be no dew or rain upon you,
      nor bounteous fields!*b*
      For there the shield of the mighty was defiled,
      the shield of Saul, anointed with oil no more.

22   From the blood of the slain,
      from the fat of the mighty,
      the bow of Jonathan did not turn back,
      nor the sword of Saul return empty.

1 AFTER Saul's death David returned from his victory over the Amalekites and spent two days in Ziklag. 2 On the third day a man came from Saul's camp; his clothes were torn and there was dust on his head. Coming into David's presence he fell to the ground and did obeisance. 3 David asked him where he had come from, and he replied, 'I have escaped from the Israelite camp.' 4 David said, 'What is the news? Tell me.' 'The army has been driven from the field,' he answered, 'many have fallen in battle, and Saul and Jonathan his son are dead.' 5 David said to the young man who brought the news, 'How do you know that Saul and Jonathan are dead?' 6 He answered, 'It so happened that I was on Mount Gilboa and saw Saul leaning on his spear with the chariots and horsemen closing in on him. 7 He turned and, seeing me, called to me. I said, "What is it, sir?" 8 He asked me who I was, and I said, "An Amalekite." 9 He said to me, "Come and stand over me and dispatch me. I still live, but the throes of death have seized me." 10 So I stood over him and dealt him the death blow, for I knew that, stricken as he was, he could not live. Then I took the crown from his head and the armlet from his arm, and I have brought them here to you, my lord.' 11 At that David and all the men with him took hold of their clothes and tore them. 12 They mourned and wept, and they fasted till evening because Saul and Jonathan his son and the army of the LORD and the house of Israel had fallen in battle.

13 David said to the young man who brought him the news, 'Where do you come from?' and he answered, 'I am the son of an alien, an Amalekite.' 14 'How is it', said David, 'that you were not afraid to raise your hand to kill the LORD's anointed?' 15 Summoning one of his own young men he ordered him to fall upon the Amalekite. The young man struck him down and he died. 16 David said, 'Your blood be on your own head; for out of your own mouth you condemned yourself by saying, "I killed the LORD's anointed."'

17 David raised this lament over Saul and Jonathan his son; 18 and he ordered that this dirge over them should be taught to the people of Judah. It was written down and may be found in the Book of Jashar:

19 Israel, upon your heights your beauty lies slain!
      How are the warriors fallen!

20 Do not tell it in Gath
      or proclaim it in the streets of Ashkelon,
      in case the Philistine maidens rejoice,
      and the daughters of the uncircumcised exult.

21 Hills of Gilboa, let no dew or rain fall on you,
      no showers on the uplands!
      For there the shields of the warriors lie tarnished,
      and the shield of Saul, no longer bright with oil.

22 The bow of Jonathan never held back
      from the breast of the foeman, from the blood of
        the slain;
      the sword of Saul never returned
      empty to the scabbard.

---

a Heb *that The Bow*   *b* Meaning of Heb uncertain

1:18 **Book of Jashar:** *or* Book of the Upright.   1:21 **showers on the uplands:** *prob. rdg; Heb.* fields of offerings.

THE SECOND BOOK OF
Samuel

1 After the death of Saul, David returned from his defeat of the Amalekites and spent two days in Ziklag. 2 On the third day a man came from Saul's camp, with his clothes torn and dirt on his head. Going to David, he fell to the ground in homage. 3 David asked him, "Where do you come from?" He replied, "I have escaped from the Israelite camp." 4 "Tell me what happened," David bade him. He answered that the soldiers had fled the battle and that many of them had fallen and were dead, among them Saul and his son Jonathan. 5 Then David said to the youth who was reporting to him, "How do you know that Saul and his son Jonathan are dead?" 6 The youthful informant replied: "It was by chance that I found myself on Mount Gilboa and saw Saul leaning on his spear, with chariots and horsemen closing in on him. 7 He turned around and, seeing me, called me to him. When I said, 'Here I am,' 8 he asked me, 'Who are you?' and I replied, 'An Amalekite.' 9 Then he said to me, 'Stand up to me, please, and finish me off, for I am in great suffering, yet fully alive.' 10 So I stood up to him and dispatched him, for I knew that he could not survive his wound. I removed the crown from his head and the armlet from his arm and brought them here to my lord."

11 David seized his garments and rent them, and all the men who were with him did likewise. 12 They mourned and wept and fasted until evening for Saul and his son Jonathan, and for the soldiers of the LORD of the clans of Israel, because they had fallen by the sword. 13 Then David said to the young man who had brought him the information, "Where are you from?" He replied, "I am the son of an Amalekite immigrant." 14 David said to him, "How is it that you were not afraid to put forth your hand to desecrate the LORD's anointed?" 15 David then called one of the attendants and said to him, "Come, strike him down"; and the youth struck him a mortal blow. 16 Meanwhile David said to him, "You are responsible for your own death, for you testified against yourself when you said, 'I dispatched the LORD's anointed.'"

17 Then David chanted this elegy for Saul and his son Jonathan, 18 which is recorded in the Book of Jashar to be taught to the Judahites. He sang:

19 "Alas! the glory of Israel, Saul,
 slain upon your heights;
how can the warriors have fallen!

20 "Tell it not in Gath,
 herald it not in the streets of Ashkelon,
Lest the Philistine maidens rejoice,
 lest the daughters of the strangers exult!
21 Mountains of Gilboa,
 may there be neither dew nor rain upon you,
 nor upsurgings of the deeps!
Upon you lie begrimed the warriors' shields,
 the shield of Saul, no longer anointed with oil.

22 "From the blood of the slain,
 from the bodies of the valiant,
The bow of Jonathan did not turn back,
 or the sword of Saul return unstained.

1 Saul was dead and David, returning after his victory over the Amalekites, had been at Ziklag for two days. 2 On the third day, a man arrived from Saul's camp with his clothes torn and earth on his head. When he came to David, he fell to the ground and prostrated himself. 3 David asked him, 'Where have you come from?' 'I have escaped from the Israelite camp,' he said. 4 David said, 'What has happened? Tell me.' He replied, 'The people fled from the battle, and many of them have fallen and are dead. Saul and his son Jonathan are dead too.'

5 Then David asked the young man who brought the news, 'How do you know that Saul and his son Jonathan are dead?' 6 The young man replied, 'I happened to be on Mount Gilboa, and there was Saul, leaning on his spear, with the chariots and the cavalry bearing down on him. 7 Glancing behind him and seeing me, he shouted to me. I replied, "Here I am!" 8 He said, "Who are you?" I replied, "I am an Amalekite." 9 He then said, "Come here and kill me. My head is swimming, although I still have all my strength." 10 So I went over to him and killed him, because I knew that once he fell he could not survive. I then took the crown he had on his head and the bracelet on his arm, and have brought them here to my lord.'

11 David then took hold of his clothes and tore them, and all the men with him did the same. 12 They mourned and wept and fasted until the evening for Saul and his son Jonathan, for the people of Yahweh and for the House of Israel, because they had fallen by the sword.

13 David said to the young man who had brought the news, 'Where are you from?' He replied, 'I am the son of a resident foreigner, an Amalekite.' 14 David said, 'How was it that you were not afraid to lift your hand to destroy Yahweh's anointed?' 15 Then David called one of the young men. 'Come here,' he said, 'strike him down.' The man struck him and he died. 16 David said, 'Your blood be on your own head. You convicted yourself out of your own mouth by saying, "I killed Yahweh's anointed."'

17 David sang the following lament over Saul and his son Jonathan 18 (it is for teaching archery to the children of Judah; it is written in the Book of the Just):[a]

19 Does the splendour of Israel
 lie dead on your heights?
How did the heroes fall?

20 Do not speak of it in Gath,
 nor broadcast it in the streets of Ashkelon,
 for fear the daughters of the Philistines rejoice,
 for fear the daughters of the uncircumcised gloat.

21 You mountains of Gilboa,
 no dew, no rain fall on you,
O treacherous fields
where the heroes' shield lies dishonoured!

Not greased with oil, the shield of Saul,
22 but with the blood of wounded men, the fat of
  warriors!
The bow of Jonathan never turned back,
 the sword of Saul never came home unsated!

---

a 1 Poetry from this book is quoted elsewhere too in the Bible.

23 Saul and Jonathan, beloved and lovely!
 In life and in death they were not divided;
they were swifter than eagles,
 they were stronger than lions.

24 O daughters of Israel, weep over Saul,
 who clothed you with crimson, in luxury,
 who put ornaments of gold on your apparel.

25 How the mighty have fallen
 in the midst of the battle!

Jonathan lies slain upon your high places.
26 I am distressed for you, my brother Jonathan;
greatly beloved were you to me;
 your love to me was wonderful,
 passing the love of women.

27 How the mighty have fallen,
 and the weapons of war perished!

2 After this David inquired of the LORD, "Shall I go up into any of the cities of Judah?" The LORD said to him, "Go up." David said, "To which shall I go up?" He said, "To Hebron." 2 So David went up there, along with his two wives, Ahinoam of Jezreel, and Abigail the widow of Nabal of Carmel. 3 David brought up the men who were with him, every one with his household; and they settled in the towns of Hebron. 4 Then the people of Judah came, and there they anointed David king over the house of Judah.

When they told David, "It was the people of Jabesh-gilead who buried Saul," 5 David sent messengers to the people of Jabesh-gilead, and said to them, "May you be blessed by the LORD, because you showed this loyalty to Saul your lord, and buried him! 6 Now may the LORD show steadfast love and faithfulness to you! And I too will reward you because you have done this thing. 7 Therefore let your hands be strong, and be valiant; for Saul your lord is dead, and the house of Judah has anointed me king over them."

8 But Abner son of Ner, commander of Saul's army, had taken Ishbaal*c* son of Saul, and brought him over to Mahanaim. 9 He made him king over Gilead, the Ashurites, Jezreel, Ephraim, and Benjamin, and over all Israel. 10 Ish-baal,*c* Saul's son, was forty years old when he began to reign over Israel, and he reigned two years. But the house of Judah followed David. 11 The time that David was king in Hebron over the house of Judah was seven years and six months.

12 Abner son of Ner, and the servants of Ishbaal*c* son of Saul, went out from Mahanaim to Gibeon. 13 Joab son of Zeruiah, and the servants of David, went out and met them at the pool of Gibeon. One group sat on one side of the pool, while the other sat on the other side of the pool. 14 Abner said to Joab, "Let the young men come forward and have a contest before us." Joab said, "Let them come forward." 15 So they came forward and were counted as they passed by, twelve for Benjamin and Ishbaal*c* son of Saul, and twelve of the servants of David. 16 Each grasped his opponent by the head, and thrust his sword in his opponent's side; so they fell down together. Therefore that place was called Helkath-hazzurim,*d* which is at Gibeon. 17 The battle was very fierce that day; and Abner and the men of Israel were beaten by the servants of David.

18 The three sons of Zeruiah were there, Joab, Abishai, and Asahel. Now Asahel was as swift of foot as a wild gazelle. 19 Asahel pursued Abner, turning neither to the right nor to the left as he followed him. 20 Then Abner looked back and said, "Is it you, Asahel?" He answered, "Yes, it is." 21 Abner said to him, "Turn to your right or to

23 Beloved and lovely were Saul and Jonathan;
neither in life nor in death were they parted.
They were swifter than eagles,
stronger than lions.

24 Daughters of Israel, weep for Saul,
who clothed you in scarlet and rich embroideries,
who spangled your attire with jewels of gold.

25 How are the warriors fallen on the field of battle!
Jonathan lies slain on your heights.
26 I grieve for you, Jonathan my brother;
you were most dear to me;
your love for me was wonderful,
surpassing the love of women.

27 How are the warriors fallen,
and their armour abandoned on the battlefield!

2 Afterwards David enquired of the LORD, 'Shall I go up into one of the towns of Judah?' The LORD answered, 'Go.' David asked, 'Where shall I go?' and the answer was, 'To Hebron.' 2 So David went up there with his two wives, Ahinoam of Jezreel and Abigail widow of Nabal of Carmel. 3 David also brought the men who had joined him, with their families, and they settled in Hebron and the neighbouring towns. 4 The men of Judah came, and there they anointed David king over the house of Judah.

It was reported to David that the men of Jabesh-gilead had buried Saul, 5 and he sent them this message: 'The LORD bless you because you kept faith with Saul your lord and buried him. 6 For this may the LORD keep faith and truth with you, and I for my part will show you favour too, because you have done this. 7 Be strong, be valiant, now that Saul your lord is dead, and the people of Judah have anointed me to be king over them.'

8 Meanwhile Saul's commander-in-chief, Abner son of Ner, had taken Saul's son Ishbosheth, brought him across to Mahanaim, 9 and made him king over Gilead, the Asherites, Jezreel, Ephraim, and Benjamin, and all Israel. 10 Ishbosheth was forty years old when he became king over Israel, and he reigned for two years. The tribe of Judah, however, followed David. 11 David's rule over Judah in Hebron lasted seven and a half years.

12 Abner son of Ner, with the troops of Saul's son Ishbosheth, marched out from Mahanaim to Gibeon, 13 and Joab son of Zeruiah marched out with David's troops from Hebron. They met at the pool of Gibeon and took up their positions, one force on one side of the pool and the other on the opposite side. 14 Abner said to Joab, 'Let the young men come forward and join in single combat before us.' Joab agreed. 15 So they came up, one by one, and took their places, twelve for Benjamin and Ishbosheth and twelve from David's men. 16 Each man seized his opponent by the head and thrust his sword into his opponent's side; and thus they fell together. That is why that place, which lies in Gibeon, was called the Field of Blades.

17 There ensued a very hard-fought battle that day, and Abner and the men of Israel were defeated by David's troops. 18 All three sons of Zeruiah were there, Joab, Abishai, and Asahel. Asahel, who was swift as a gazelle of the plains, 19 chased after Abner, swerving to neither right nor left in his pursuit. 20 Abner glanced back and said, 'Is it you, Asahel?' Asahel answered, 'It is.' 21 Abner said, 'Turn

---

c Gk Compare 1 Chr 8.33; 9.39: Heb *Ish-bosheth*, "man of shame"
d That is *Field of Sword-edges*

23 Saul and Jonathan, beloved and cherished,
    separated neither in life nor in death,
    swifter than eagles, stronger than lions!
24 Women of Israel, weep over Saul,
    who clothed you in scarlet and in finery,
    who decked your attire with ornaments of gold.

25 "How can the warriors have fallen —
    in the thick of the battle,
    slain upon your heights!
26 "I grieve for you, Jonathan my brother!
    most dear have you been to me;
  More precious have I held love for you
    than love for women.

27 "How can the warriors have fallen,
    the weapons of war have perished!"

2 After this David inquired of the LORD, "Shall I go up into one of the cities of Judah?" The LORD replied to him, "Yes." Then David asked, "Where shall I go?" He replied, "To Hebron." 2 So David went up there accompanied by his two wives, Ahinoam of Jezreel and Abigail, the widow of Nabal of Carmel. 3 David also brought up his men with their families, and they dwelt in the cities near Hebron. 4 Then the men of Judah came there and anointed David king of the Judahites.

A report reached David that the men of Jabesh-gilead had buried Saul. 5 So David sent messengers to the men of Jabesh-gilead and said to them: "May you be blessed by the LORD for having done this kindness to your lord Saul in burying him. 6 And now may the LORD be kind and faithful to you. I, too, will be generous to you for having done this. 7 Take courage, therefore, and prove yourselves valiant men, for though your lord Saul is dead, the Judahites have anointed me their king."

8 Abner, son of Ner, Saul's general, took Ishbaal, son of Saul, and brought him over to Mahanaim, 9 where he made him king over Gilead, the Ashurites, Jezreel, Ephraim, Benjamin, and the rest of Israel. 10 Ishbaal, son of Saul, was forty years old when he became king over Israel, and he reigned for two years. The Judahites alone followed David. 11 In all, David spent seven years and six months in Hebron as king of the Judahites.

12 Now Abner, son of Ner, and the servants of Ishbaal, Saul's son, left Mahanaim for Gibeon. 13 Joab, son of Zeruiah, and David's servants also set out and met them at the pool of Gibeon. And they sat down, one group on one side of the pool and the other on the opposite side. 14 Then Abner said to Joab, "Let the young men rise and perform for us." Joab replied, "All right!" 15 So they rose and were counted off: twelve of the Benjaminites of Ishbaal, son of Saul, and twelve of David's servants. 16 Then each one grasped his opponent's head and thrust his sword into his opponent's side, and all fell down together. And so that place, which is in Gibeon, was named the Field of the Sides.

17 After a very fierce battle that day, Abner and the men of Israel were defeated by David's servants. 18 The three sons of Zeruiah were there — Joab, Abishai, and Asahel. Asahel, who was as fleet of foot as a gazelle in the open field, 19 set out after Abner, turning neither right nor left in his pursuit. 20 Abner turned around and said, "Is that you, Asahel?" He replied, "Yes." 21 Abner said to him, "Turn

23 Saul and Jonathan, beloved and handsome,
    were divided neither in life, nor in death.
  Swifter than eagles were they,
    stronger than lions.

24 O daughters of Israel, weep for Saul
    who gave you scarlet and fine linen to wear,
    who pinned golden jewellery
    on your dresses!

25 How did the heroes fall
    in the thick of the battle?

  Jonathan, by your dying I too am stricken,
26 I am desolate for you, Jonathan my brother.
  Very dear you were to me,
    your love more wonderful to me
    than the love of a woman.

27 How did the heroes fall
    and the weapons of war succumb!

2 After this David consulted Yahweh, asking, 'Shall I go up to one of the towns of Judah?' Yahweh replied, 'Go up!' 'Which one shall I go to?' David asked. 'To Hebron,' was the reply. 2 So David went up, with his two wives Ahinoam of Jezreel and Abigail widow of Nabal of Carmel. 3 In addition David brought up the men who were with him, each with his family, and they settled in the towns of Hebron. 4 The men of Judah came, and there they anointed David as king of the House of Judah.

They told David that the people of Jabesh in Gilead had given Saul burial. 5 So David sent messengers to the people of Jabesh in Gilead. 'May you be blessed by Yahweh,' he said, 'for showing this faithful love to Saul your lord, and for burying him. 6 And now may Yahweh show faithful love and constancy towards you! I too shall treat you well because you have done this. 7 And now take courage and be men of valour. Saul your lord is dead, but the House of Judah has anointed me to be their king.'

8 Abner son of Ner, Saul's army commander, had taken Ishbaal son of Saul and brought him over to Mahanaim. 9 He had made him king of Gilead, of the Asherites, of Jezreel, of Ephraim, of Benjamin and indeed of all Israel. 10 Ishbaal of Saul was forty years old when he became king of Israel, and he reigned for two years. Only the House of Judah supported David. 11 The length of David's reign over Judah in Hebron was seven years and six months.

12 Abner son of Ner, with the retainers of Ishbaal son of Saul, marched out from Mahanaim to Gibeon. 13 Joab son of Zeruiah, with David's retainers, also took the field, encountering them at the pool of Gibeon. There they halted, one party on one side of the pool, and the other opposite.

14 Abner then said to Joab, 'Let the men come forward and fight it out between us!' Joab replied, 'Let them come forward.' 15 So they came forward and were numbered off, twelve from Benjamin for Ishbaal son of Saul, and twelve of David's retainers. 16 Each caught his opponent by the head and drove his sword into his side; and thus they all fell together. Hence the place was called the Field of Sides; it is at Gibeon.

17 That day a very fierce battle took place, and Abner and the men of Israel were beaten by David's retainers. 18 The three sons of Zeruiah were there, Joab, Abishai, and Asahel. Now Asahel could run like a wild gazelle. 19 Asahel chased Abner, not swerving to the right or left from pursuing him. 20 Abner turned and said, 'Asahel, is that you?' He replied, 'It is.' 21 Abner said, 'Turn to your right or your

NEW REVISED STANDARD VERSION

your left, and seize one of the young men, and take his spoil." But Asahel would not turn away from following him. 22 Abner said again to Asahel, "Turn away from following me; why should I strike you to the ground? How then could I show my face to your brother Joab?" 23 But he refused to turn away. So Abner struck him in the stomach with the butt of his spear, so that the spear came out at his back. He fell there, and died where he lay. And all those who came to the place where Asahel had fallen and died, stood still.

24 But Joab and Abishai pursued Abner. As the sun was going down they came to the hill of Ammah, which lies before Giah on the way to the wilderness of Gibeon. 25 The Benjaminites rallied around Abner and formed a single band; they took their stand on the top of a hill. 26 Then Abner called to Joab, "Is the sword to keep devouring forever? Do you not know that the end will be bitter? How long will it be before you order your people to turn from the pursuit of their kinsmen?" 27 Joab said, "As God lives, if you had not spoken, the people would have continued to pursue their kinsmen, not stopping until morning." 28 Joab sounded the trumpet, and all the people stopped; they no longer pursued Israel or engaged in battle any further.

29 Abner and his men traveled all that night through the Arabah; they crossed the Jordan, and, marching the whole forenoon,e they came to Mahanaim. 30 Joab returned from the pursuit of Abner; and when he had gathered all the people together, there were missing of David's servants nineteen men besides Asahel. 31 But the servants of David had killed of Benjamin three hundred sixty of Abner's men. 32 They took up Asahel and buried him in the tomb of his father, which was at Bethlehem. Joab and his men marched all night, and the day broke upon them at Hebron.

3 There was a long war between the house of Saul and the house of David; David grew stronger and stronger, while the house of Saul became weaker and weaker.

2 Sons were born to David at Hebron: his firstborn was Amnon, of Ahinoam of Jezreel; 3 his second, Chileab, of Abigail the widow of Nabal of Carmel; the third, Absalom son of Maacah, daughter of King Talmai of Geshur; 4 the fourth, Adonijah son of Haggith; the fifth, Shephatiah son of Abital; 5 and the sixth, Ithream, of David's wife Eglah. These were born to David in Hebron.

6 While there was war between the house of Saul and the house of David, Abner was making himself strong in the house of Saul. 7 Now Saul had a concubine whose name was Rizpah daughter of Aiah, and Ishbaalf said to Abner, "Why have you gone in to my father's concubine?" 8 The words of Ishbaalg made Abner very angry; he said, "Am I a dog's head for Judah? Today I keep showing loyalty to the house of your father Saul, to his brothers, and to his friends, and have not given you into the hand of David; and yet you charge me now with a crime concerning this woman. 9 So may God do to Abner and so may he add to it! For just what the LORD has sworn to David, that will I accomplish for him, 10 to transfer the kingdom from the house of Saul, and set up the throne of David over Israel and over Judah, from Dan to Beer-sheba." 11 And Ishbaalf could not answer Abner another word, because he feared him.

12 Abner sent messengers to David at Hebron,h saying, "To whom does the land belong? Make your covenant with me, and I will give you my support to bring all Israel over to you." 13 He said, "Good; I will make a covenant with you. But one thing I require of you: you shall never appear in my presence unless you bring Saul's daughter Michal when you come to see me." 14 Then David sent messengers

REVISED ENGLISH BIBLE

aside to right or left; tackle one of the young men and win his belt for yourself.' But Asahel would not abandon the pursuit. 22 Abner again urged him to give it up. 'Why should I kill you?' he said. 'How could I look Joab your brother in the face?' 23 When he still refused to turn away, Abner struck him in the belly with a back-thrust of his spear so that the spear came out through his back, and he fell dead in his tracks. All who came to the place where Asahel lay dead stopped there. 24 But Joab and Abishai kept up the pursuit of Abner, until, at sunset, they reached the hill of Ammah, opposite Giah on the road leading to the pastures of Gibeon.

25 The Benjamites rallied to Abner and, forming themselves into a single group, took their stand on the top of a hill. 26 Abner called to Joab, 'Must the slaughter go on for ever? Can you not see the bitterness that will result? How long before you recall the troops from the pursuit of their kinsmen?' 27 Joab answered, 'As God lives, if you had not spoken, they would not have given up the pursuit till morning.' 28 Then Joab sounded the trumpet, and the troops all halted; they abandoned the pursuit of the Israelites, and the fighting ceased.

29 Abner and his men moved along the Arabah all that night, crossed the Jordan, and continued all morning till they reached Mahanaim. 30 After Joab returned from the pursuit of Abner, he mustered his troops and found that, besides Asahel, nineteen of David's men were missing. 31 David's forces had routed the Benjamites and the followers of Abner, killing three hundred and sixty of them. 32 They took up Asahel and buried him in his father's tomb at Bethlehem. Joab and his men marched all night, and as day broke they reached Hebron.

3 THE war between the house of Saul and the house of David was long drawn out, David growing steadily stronger while the house of Saul became weaker.

2 Sons were born to David at Hebron. His eldest was Amnon, whose mother was Ahinoam from Jezreel; 3 his second Cileab, whose mother was Abigail widow of Nabal from Carmel; the third Absalom, whose mother was Maacah daughter of Talmai king of Geshur; 4 the fourth Adonijah, whose mother was Haggith; the fifth Shephatiah, whose mother was Abital; 5 and the sixth Ithream, whose mother was David's wife Eglah. These were born to David at Hebron.

6 As the war between the houses of Saul and David went on, Abner gradually strengthened his position in the house of Saul. 7 Now Saul had had a concubine named Rizpah daughter of Aiah. Ishbosheth challenged Abner, 'Why have you slept with my father's concubine?' 8 Abner, angered by this, exclaimed, 'Do you take me for a Judahite dog? Up to now I have been loyal to the house of your father Saul, to his brothers and friends, and I have not betrayed you into David's hands; yet you choose this moment to charge me with an offence over a woman. 9 But now, so help me God, I shall do all I can to bring about what the LORD swore to do for David: 10 I shall set to work to overthrow the house of Saul and to establish David's throne over Israel and Judah from Dan to Beersheba.' 11 Ishbosheth dared not say another word; he was too much afraid of Abner.

12 Abner sent envoys on his own behalf to David with the message, 'Who is to control the land? Let us come to terms, and you will have my support in bringing the whole of Israel over to you.' 13 David's answer was: 'Good, I will come to terms with you, but on one condition: that you do not come into my presence without bringing Saul's daughter Michal to me.' 14 David also sent messengers to Saul's son Ish-

---

e Meaning of Heb uncertain   f Heb And he   g Gk Compare 1 Chr 8.33; 9.39: Heb *Ish-bosheth*, "man of shame"   h Gk: Heb *where he was*

2:23 **a back-thrust of his spear:** *prob. rdg; Heb. obscure.*
3:2–5 *Cp. 1 Chr. 3:1–4.*

right or left; seize one of the young men and take what you can strip from him." But Asahel would not desist from his pursuit. 22 Once more Abner said to Asahel: "Stop pursuing me! Why must I strike you to the ground? How could I face your brother Joab?" 23 Still he refused to stop. So Abner struck him in the abdomen with the heel of his javelin, and the weapon protruded from his back. He fell there and died on the spot. And all who came to the place where Asahel had fallen and died, came to a halt. 24 Joab and Abishai, however, continued the pursuit of Abner. The sun had gone down when they came to the hill of Ammah which lies east of the valley toward the desert near Geba.

25 Here the Benjaminites rallied around Abner, forming a single group, and made a stand on the hilltop. 26 Then Abner called to Joab and said: "Must the sword destroy to the utmost? Do you not know that afterward there will be bitterness? How much longer will you refrain from ordering the people to stop the pursuit of their brothers?" 27 Joab replied, "As God lives, if you had not spoken, the soldiers would not have been withdrawn from the pursuit of their brothers until morning." 28 Joab then sounded the horn, and all the soldiers came to a halt, pursuing Israel no farther and fighting no more. 29 Abner and his men marched all night long through the Arabah, crossed the Jordan, marched all through the morning, and came to Mahanaim. 30 Joab, after interrupting the pursuit of Abner, assembled all the men. Besides Asahel, nineteen other servants of David were missing. 31 But David's servants had fatally wounded three hundred and sixty men of Benjamin, followers of Abner. 32 They took up Asahel and buried him in his father's tomb in Bethlehem. Joab and his men made an all-night march, and dawn found them in Hebron.

3 There followed a long war between the house of Saul and that of David, in which David grew stronger, but the house of Saul weaker.

2 Sons were born to David in Hebron: his first-born, Amnon, of Ahinoam from Jezreel; 3 the second, Chileab, of Abigail the widow of Nabal of Carmel; the third, Absalom, son of Maacah the daughter of Talmai, king of Geshur; 4 the fourth, Adonijah, son of Haggith; the fifth, Shephatiah, son of Abital; 5 and the sixth, Ithream, of David's wife Eglah. These were born to David in Hebron.

6 During the war between the house of Saul and of David, Abner was gaining power in the house of Saul. 7 Now Saul had had a concubine, Rizpah, the daughter of Aiah. And Ishbaal, son of Saul, said to Abner, "Why have you been intimate with my father's concubine?" 8 Enraged at the words of Ishbaal, Abner said, "Am I a dog's head in Judah? At present I am doing a kindness to the house of your father Saul, to his brothers and his friends, by keeping you out of David's clutches; yet this day you charge me with a crime involving a woman! 9 May God do thus and so to Abner if I do not carry out for David what the LORD swore to him — 10 that is, take away the kingdom from the house of Saul and establish the throne of David over Israel and over Judah from Dan to Beer-sheba." 11 In his fear of Abner, Ishbaal was no longer able to say a word to him.

12 Then Abner sent messengers to David in Telam, where he was at the moment, to say, "Make an agreement with me, and I will aid you by bringing all Israel over to you." 13 He replied, "Very well, I will make an agreement with you. But one thing I require of you. You must not appear before me unless you bring back Michal, Saul's daughter, when you come to present yourself to me." 14 At the same

left, catch one of the men and take his spoil!' But Asahel would not break off the pursuit. 22 Again Abner spoke to Asahel, 'Stop following me, unless you want me to strike you to the ground; and then how could I look your brother Joab in the face?' 23 But he refused to be diverted, so Abner struck him in the belly with the butt of his spear so that the shaft came out through his back; and he fell at his feet and died on the spot. On coming to the place where Asahel had fallen and died, everyone halted.

24 Joab and Abishai took up the pursuit of Abner and at sunset reached the Hill of Ammah, which is to the east of Giah on the road through the desert of Gibeon. 25 The Benjaminites gathered in close formation behind Abner and halted on the top of a hill. 26 Abner called out to Joab, 'Is the sword to go on devouring for ever? Surely you see that this can only end in bitterness? How long will it be before you order those people to stop pursuing their brothers?' 27 Joab replied, 'As Yahweh lives, if you had not spoken, these men would not have given up the pursuit of their brothers until morning.' 28 Joab then sounded the trumpet and all the troops halted; they pursued Israel no further and fought no more.

29 All that night Abner and his men made their way through the Arabah; they crossed the Jordan and, marching throughout the morning, came to Mahanaim. 30 Joab, having stopped pursuing Abner, mustered the whole contingent; David's retainers had lost nineteen men in addition to Asahel, 31 but had killed three hundred and sixty of Benjamin, Abner's men. 32 They took up Asahel and buried him in his father's tomb, which is at Bethlehem. Joab and his men then marched throughout the night, reaching Hebron at daybreak.

3 So the war dragged on between the House of Saul and the House of David, but David grew steadily stronger and the House of Saul steadily weaker.

2 The sons born to David at Hebron were: his first-born Amnon, by Ahinoam of Jezreel; 3 his second Chileab, by Abigail widow of Nabal of Carmel; the third Absalom son of Maacah, daughter of Talmai king of Geshur; 4 the fourth Adonijah son of Haggith; the fifth Shephatiah son of Abital; 5 the sixth Ithream, by David's wife, Eglah. These were born to David at Hebron.

6 This is what took place during the war between the House of Saul and the House of David. Abner took complete control in the House of Saul. 7 Now, there was a concubine of Saul's called Rizpah daughter of Aiah, and Abner took her. Ishbaal said to Abner, 'Why have you slept with my father's concubine?' 8 At these words of Ishbaal, Abner flew into a rage. 'Am I a dog's head?' he shouted. 'Here am I, full of faithful love towards the House of Saul your father, his brothers and his friends, not leaving you to the hands of David, and now you find fault with me over a woman! 9 May God bring unnameable ills on Abner, and worse ones, too, if I do not bring about what Yahweh has sworn to David: 10 to take the sovereignty from the House of Saul, and establish David's throne over Israel as well as Judah, from Dan to Beersheba!' 11 Ishbaal dared not say a single word to Abner in reply, as he was afraid of him.

12 Abner sent messengers on his own behalf to say to David, '. . . and furthermore, come to an agreement with me and I will give you my support to win all Israel over to you.' 13 'Very well,' David said, 'I will come to an agreement with you. I impose one condition however; you will not be admitted to my presence unless you bring me Michal, Saul's daughter, when you come to see me.' 14 David then

645

NEW REVISED STANDARD VERSION	REVISED ENGLISH BIBLE

to Saul's son Ishbaal,[i] saying, "Give me my wife Michal, to whom I became engaged at the price of one hundred foreskins of the Philistines." 15 Ishbaal[i] sent and took her from her husband Paltiel the son of Laish. 16 But her husband went with her, weeping as he walked behind her all the way to Bahurim. Then Abner said to him, "Go back home!" So he went back.

17 Abner sent word to the elders of Israel, saying, "For some time past you have been seeking David as king over you. 18 Now then bring it about; for the Lord has promised David: Through my servant David I will save my people Israel from the hand of the Philistines, and from all their enemies." 19 Abner also spoke directly to the Benjaminites; then Abner went to tell David at Hebron all that Israel and the whole house of Benjamin were ready to do.

20 When Abner came with twenty men to David at Hebron, David made a feast for Abner and the men who were with him. 21 Abner said to David, "Let me go and rally all Israel to my lord the king, in order that they may make a covenant with you, and that you may reign over all that your heart desires." So David dismissed Abner, and he went away in peace.

22 Just then the servants of David arrived with Joab from a raid, bringing much spoil with them. But Abner was not with David at Hebron, for David[i] had dismissed him, and he had gone away in peace. 23 When Joab and all the army that was with him came, it was told Joab, "Abner son of Ner came to the king, and he has dismissed him, and he has gone away in peace." 24 Then Joab went to the king and said, "What have you done? Abner came to you; why did you dismiss him, so that he got away? 25 You know that Abner son of Ner came to deceive you, and to learn your comings and goings and to learn all that you are doing."

26 When Joab came out from David's presence, he sent messengers after Abner, and they brought him back from the cistern of Sirah; but David did not know about it. 27 When Abner returned to Hebron, Joab took him aside in the gateway to speak with him privately, and there he stabbed him in the stomach. So he died for shedding[k] the blood of Asahel, Joab's[l] brother. 28 Afterward, when David heard of it, he said, "I and my kingdom are forever guiltless before the Lord for the blood of Abner son of Ner. 29 May the guilt[m] fall on the head of Joab, and on all his father's house; and may the house of Joab never be without one who has a discharge, or who is leprous,[n] or who holds a spindle, or who falls by the sword, or who lacks food!" 30 So Joab and his brother Abishai murdered Abner because he had killed their brother Asahel in the battle at Gibeon.

31 Then David said to Joab and to all the people who were with him, "Tear your clothes, and put on sackcloth, and mourn over Abner." And King David followed the bier. 32 They buried Abner at Hebron. The king lifted up his voice and wept at the grave of Abner, and all the people wept. 33 The king lamented for Abner, saying,

"Should Abner die as a fool dies?
34 Your hands were not bound,
        your feet were not fettered;
    as one falls before the wicked
        you have fallen."

And all the people wept over him again. 35 Then all the people came to persuade David to eat something while it was still day; but David swore, saying, "So may God do to me, and more, if I taste bread or anything else before the sun goes down!" 36 All the people took notice of it, and it pleased them; just as everything the king did pleased all the people. 37 So all the people and all Israel understood that

bosheth with the demand: 'Hand over to me my wife Michal for whom I gave a hundred Philistine foreskins as the bride-price.' 15 Thereupon Ishbosheth sent and took her from her husband, Paltiel son of Laish. 16 Her husband followed her as far as Bahurim, weeping all the way, until Abner ordered him back, and he went.

17 Abner conferred with the elders of Israel: 'For some time past', he said, 'you have wanted David for your king. 18 Now is the time to act, for this is the word of the Lord about David: "By the hand of my servant David I shall deliver my people Israel from the Philistines and from all their enemies." ' 19 Abner spoke also to the Benjamites and then went to report to David at Hebron all that the Israelites and the Benjamites had agreed. 20 When Abner, attended by twenty men, arrived, David gave a feast for him and his men. 21 Abner said to David, 'I shall now go and bring the whole of Israel over to your majesty. They will make a covenant with you, and you will be king over a realm after your own heart.' David dismissed Abner, granting him safe conduct.

22 Just then David's men and Joab returned from a raid, bringing a great quantity of plunder with them. Abner, having been dismissed, was no longer with David in Hebron. 23 Joab and the whole force with him were greeted on their arrival with the news that Abner son of Ner had been with the king and had departed under safe conduct.

24 Joab went in to the king and said, 'What have you done? You have had Abner here with you. How could you let him go and get clean away? 25 You know Abner son of Ner: his purpose in coming was to deceive you, to learn about your movements, and to find out everything you are doing.'

26 Leaving David's presence, Joab sent messengers after Abner, and they brought him back from the Pool of Sirah; but David knew nothing of this. 27 On Abner's return to Hebron, Joab drew him aside in the gateway, as though to speak privately with him, and there, in revenge for his brother Asahel, he stabbed him in the belly, and he died. 28 When David heard the news he said, 'In the sight of the Lord I and my kingdom are for ever innocent of the blood of Abner son of Ner. 29 May it recoil on the head of Joab and on all his family! May the house of Joab never be free from running sore or foul disease, nor lack a son fit only to ply the distaff or doomed to die by the sword or beg his bread!' 30 Joab and Abishai his brother slew Abner because he had killed their brother Asahel in battle at Gibeon. 31 Then David ordered Joab and all the troops with him to tear their clothes, put on sackcloth, and mourn for Abner, and the king himself walked behind the bier. 32 They buried Abner in Hebron and the king wept aloud at the tomb, while all the people wept with him. 33 The king made this lament for Abner:

    Must Abner die so base a death?
34 Your hands were not bound,
        your feet not fettered;
    you fell as one who falls at the hands of a
            criminal.

The people all wept again for him.

35 They came to urge David to eat something; but it was still day and he took an oath, 'So help me God! I refuse to touch food of any kind before sunset.' 36 The people noted this with approval; indeed, everything the king did pleased them all. 37 It was then known throughout Israel that the

---

[i] Heb Ish-bosheth   [j] Heb he   [k] Heb lacks shedding   [l] Heb his
[m] Heb May it   [n] A term for several skin diseases; precise meaning uncertain

time David sent messengers to Ishbaal, son of Saul, to say, "Give me my wife Michal, whom I espoused by paying a hundred Philistine foreskins." 15 Ishbaal sent for her and took her away from her husband Paltiel, son of Laish, 16 who followed her weeping as far as Bahurim. But Abner said to him, "Go back!" And he turned back.

17 Abner then said in discussion with the elders of Israel: "For a long time you have been seeking David as your king. 18 Now take action, for the LORD has said of David, 'By my servant David I will save my people Israel from the grasp of the Philistines and from the grasp of all their enemies.' " 19 Abner also spoke personally to Benjamin, and then went to make his own report to David in Hebron concerning all that would be agreeable to Israel and to the whole house of Benjamin. 20 When Abner, accompanied by twenty men, came to David in Hebron, David prepared a feast for Abner and for the men who were with him. 21 Then Abner said to David, "I will now go to assemble all Israel for my lord the king, that they may make an agreement with you; you will then be king over all whom you wish to rule." So David bade Abner farewell, and he went away in peace.

22 Just then David's servants and Joab were coming in from an expedition, bringing much plunder with them. Abner, having been dismissed by David, was no longer with him in Hebron but had gone his way in peace. 23 When Joab and the whole force he had with him arrived, he was informed, "Abner, son of Ner, came to David; he has been sent on his way in peace." 24 So Joab went to the king and said: "What have you done? Abner came to you. Why did you let him go peacefully on his way? 25 Are you not aware that Abner came to deceive you and to learn the ins and outs of all that you are doing?" 26 Joab then left David, and without David's knowledge sent messengers after Abner, who brought him back from the cistern of Sirah. 27 When Abner returned to Hebron, Joab took him aside within the city gate as though to speak with him privately. There he stabbed him in the abdomen, and he died in revenge for the killing of Joab's brother Asahel. 28 Later David heard of it and said: "Before the LORD, I and my kingdom are forever innocent. 29 May the full responsibility for the death of Abner, son of Ner, be laid to Joab and to all his family. May the men of Joab's family never be without one suffering from a discharge, or a leper, or one unmanly, one falling by the sword, or one in need of bread!" 30 [Joab and his brother Abishai had lain in wait for Abner because he killed their brother Asahel in battle at Gibeon.]

31 Then David said to Joab and to all the people who were with him, "Rend your garments, gird yourselves with sackcloth, and mourn over Abner." King David himself followed the bier. 32 When they had buried Abner in Hebron, the king wept aloud at the grave of Abner, and the people also wept. 33 And the king sang this elegy over Abner:

"Would Abner have died like a fool?
34 Your hands were not bound with chains,
 nor your feet placed in fetters;
As men fall before the wicked, you fell."
And all the people continued to weep for him. 35 Then they went to console David with food while it was still day. But David swore, "May God do thus and so to me if I eat bread or anything else before sunset." 36 All the people noted this with approval, just as they were pleased with everything that the king did. 37 So on that day all the people and all

sent messengers to say to Ishbaal son of Saul, 'Give me back my wife Michal, whom I acquired for a hundred foreskins of the Philistines.' 15 So Ishbaal sent for her to be taken from her husband Paltiel son of Laish. 16 Her husband set off with her and followed her, weeping as he went, as far as Bahurim; but Abner said to him, 'Go back!' and he went.

17 Now Abner conferred with the elders of Israel. 'For a long time now,' he said, 'you have wanted David as your king. 18 Now you must take action, since Yahweh has said of David, "By the hand of my servant David I shall deliver my people Israel from the clutches of the Philistines and all their enemies." ' 19 Abner also spoke to the men of Benjamin and then went to Hebron to tell David everything that had been agreed by Israel and the House of Benjamin.

20 Abner, accompanied by twenty men, came to David at Hebron, and David held a feast for Abner and the men who were with him. 21 Abner then said to David, 'I must get up and go. I am going to rally all Israel to my lord the king, so that they will make an alliance with you, and you will reign over all that you desire.' So David allowed Abner to go, and he went unmolested.

22 David's retainers were just then coming back with Joab from a raid, bringing a great quantity of booty with them. Abner was no longer with David at Hebron, since David had allowed him to go, and he had gone unmolested. 23 When Joab and the whole company with him had arrived, Joab was told, 'Abner son of Ner has been to the king, and the king has allowed Abner to go away unmolested.' 24 Joab then went to the king and said, 'What have you done? Abner comes to you and you let him go away and now he has gone — why? 25 You know Abner son of Ner! He came to trick you, to discover your every move, to find out what you are doing.'

26 Joab left David's presence and sent messengers after Abner and these, unknown to David, brought him back from the storage-well at Sirah. 27 When Abner reached Hebron, Joab took him aside in the town-gate, as if to have a quiet word with him, and there struck him a mortal blow in the belly to avenge the blood of his brother Asahel. 28 Afterwards, when David heard of this, he said, 'I and my kingdom are for ever innocent before Yahweh of the blood of Abner son of Ner; 29 may it fall on the head of Joab and on all his family! May the House of Joab never be free of men afflicted with haemorrhage or a virulent skin-disease, whose strength is in the distaff, who fall by the sword, who lack food.' 30 (Joab and his brother Abishai had murdered Abner because he killed their brother Asahel at the battle of Gibeon.) 31 David then said to Joab and the whole company with him, 'Tear your clothes, put on sackcloth, and mourn over Abner,' and King David walked behind the bier. 32 They buried Abner at Hebron, and the king wept aloud on his grave, and the people all wept too. 33 The king made this lament over Abner:

Should Abner have died as a brute dies?
34 Your hands were not tied, your feet not chained;
 you fell as a man falls at the hands of criminals.
And all the people wept for him louder than ever.

35 The people then all tried to persuade David to have some food while it was still daylight, but David swore this oath, 'May God bring unnameable ills on me, and worse ills, too, if I taste bread or anything whatever until the sun is down!' 36 All the people took note of this and it pleased them; indeed, everything the king did pleased the people. 37 That day, all the people and all Israel understood that the

NEW REVISED STANDARD VERSION

day that the king had no part in the killing of Abner son of Ner. 38 And the king said to his servants, "Do you not know that a prince and a great man has fallen this day in Israel? 39 Today I am powerless, even though anointed king; these men, the sons of Zeruiah, are too violent for me. The LORD pay back the one who does wickedly in accordance with his wickedness!"

4 When Saul's son Ishbaal⁰ heard that Abner had died at Hebron, his courage failed, and all Israel was dismayed. 2 Saul's son had two captains of raiding bands; the name of the one was Baanah, and the name of the other Rechab. They were sons of Rimmon a Benjaminite from Beeroth — for Beeroth is considered to belong to Benjamin. 3 (Now the people of Beeroth had fled to Gittaim and are there as resident aliens to this day).

4 Saul's son Jonathan had a son who was crippled in his feet. He was five years old when the news about Saul and Jonathan came from Jezreel. His nurse picked him up and fled; and, in her haste to flee, it happened that he fell and became lame. His name was Mephibosheth.ᵖ

5 Now the sons of Rimmon the Beerothite, Rechab and Baanah, set out, and about the heat of the day they came to the house of Ishbaal,ᑫ while he was taking his noonday rest. 6 They came inside the house as though to take wheat, and they struck him in the stomach; then Rechab and his brother Baanah escaped.ʳ 7 Now they had come into the house while he was lying on his couch in his bedchamber; they attacked him, killed him, and beheaded him. Then they took his head and traveled by way of the Arabah all night long. 8 They brought the head of Ishbaalᑫ to David at Hebron and said to the king, "Here is the head of Ishbaal,ᑫ son of Saul, your enemy, who sought your life; the LORD has avenged my lord the king this day on Saul and on his offspring."

9 David answered Rechab and his brother Baanah, the sons of Rimmon the Beerothite, "As the LORD lives, who has redeemed my life out of every adversity, 10 when the one who told me, 'See, Saul is dead,' thought he was bringing good news, I seized him and killed him at Ziklag — this was the reward I gave him for his news. 11 How much more then, when wicked men have killed a righteous man on his bed in his own house! And now shall I not require his blood at your hand, and destroy you from the earth?" 12 So David commanded the young men, and they killed them; they cut off their hands and feet, and hung their bodies beside the pool at Hebron. But the head of Ishbaalᑫ they took and buried in the tomb of Abner at Hebron.

5 Then all the tribes of Israel came to David at Hebron, and said, "Look, we are your bone and flesh. 2 For some time, while Saul was king over us, it was you who led out Israel and brought it in. The LORD said to you: It is you who shall be shepherd of my people Israel, you who shall be ruler over Israel." 3 So all the elders of Israel came to the king at Hebron; and King David made a covenant with them at Hebron before the LORD, and they anointed David king over Israel. 4 David was thirty years old when he began to reign, and he reigned forty years. 5 At Hebron he reigned over Judah seven years and six months; and at Jerusalem he reigned over all Israel and Judah thirty-three years.

6 The king and his men marched to Jerusalem against the Jebusites, the inhabitants of the land, who said to David, "You will not come in here, even the blind and the lame will turn you back" — thinking, "David cannot come in here."

REVISED ENGLISH BIBLE

king had had no hand in the murder of Abner son of Ner. 38 The king said to his servants, 'You must know that a warrior, a great man, has fallen this day in Israel. 39 Anointed king though I am, I feel weak and powerless in face of these ruthless sons of Zeruiah; they are too much for me. May the LORD requite the wrongdoer as his wrongdoing deserves.'

4 When Saul's son Ishbosheth heard that Abner had met his death in Hebron, his courage failed him, and all Israel was alarmed. 2 Ishbosheth had two officers, who were captains of raiding parties, and whose names were Baanah and Rechab; they were Benjamites, sons of Rimmon of Beeroth, Beeroth being reckoned part of Benjamin; 3 but the Beerothites had sought refuge in Gittaim, where they have lived as aliens ever since.

4 (Saul's son Jonathan had a son lame in both feet. He was five years old when word of the death of Saul and Jonathan came from Jezreel. His nurse had picked him up and fled, but as she hurried to get away he fell and was crippled. His name was Mephibosheth.)

5 Rechab and Baanah, the sons of Rimmon of Beeroth, came to Ishbosheth's house in the heat of the day, while he was taking his midday rest. 6 The door-keeper had been sifting wheat, but she had grown drowsy and fallen asleep, so Rechab and his brother Baanah slipped past, 7 found their way to the room where Ishbosheth was asleep on the bed, and attacked and killed him. They cut off his head and took it with them and, making their way along the Arabah all night, came to Hebron. 8 They brought Ishbosheth's head to David there and said to the king, 'Here is the head of Ishbosheth son of Saul, your enemy, who sought your life. The LORD has avenged your majesty today on Saul and on his family.' 9 David answered Rechab and his brother Baanah: 'As the LORD lives, who has delivered me from all my troubles, 10 I seized the man who brought me word that Saul was dead and thought he was bringing good news; I killed him in Ziklag. That was how I rewarded him for his news! 11 How much more shall I reward wicked men who have killed an innocent man on his bed in his own house! Am I not to take vengeance on you now for the blood you have shed, and rid the earth of you?' 12 David gave the word, and the young men killed them; they cut off their hands and feet and hung them up beside the pool in Hebron; but the head of Ishbosheth they took and buried in Abner's tomb at Hebron.

5 ALL the tribes of Israel came to David at Hebron and said to him, 'We are your own flesh and blood. 2 In the past, while Saul was still king over us, it was you that led the forces of Israel on their campaigns. To you the LORD said, "You are to be shepherd of my people Israel; you are to be their prince." ' 3 The elders of Israel all came to the king at Hebron; there David made a covenant with them before the LORD, and they anointed David king over Israel.

4 David came to the throne at the age of thirty and reigned for forty years. 5 In Hebron he had ruled over Judah for seven and a half years, and in Jerusalem he reigned over Israel and Judah combined for thirty-three years.

6 The king and his men went to Jerusalem to attack the Jebusites, the inhabitants of that region. The Jebusites said to David, 'You will never come in here, not till you have disposed of the blind and the lame,' stressing that David

---

4:2 **had:** *prob. rdg; Heb. omits.*   4:6 **The door-keeper . . . past:** *prob. rdg, cp. Gk; Heb.* They came right into the house carrying wheat, and they struck him in the belly; Rechab and his brother Baanah were acting stealthily. They.   5:1–3,6–10 *Cp. 1 Chr. 11:1–9.*

⁰ Heb lacks *Ishbaal*   ᵖ In 1 Chr 8.34 and 9.40, *Merib-baal*
ᑫ Heb *Ish-bosheth*   ʳ Meaning of Heb of verse 6 uncertain

Israel came to know that the king had no part in the killing of Abner, son of Ner. 38 The king then said to his servants: "You must recognize that a great general has fallen today in Israel. 39 Although I am the anointed king, I am weak this day, and these men, the sons of Zeruiah, are too ruthless for me. May the LORD requite the evildoer in accordance with his evil deed."

4 When Ishbaal, son of Saul, heard that Abner had died in Hebron, he ceased to resist and all Israel was alarmed. 2 Ishbaal, son of Saul, had two company leaders named Baanah and Rechab, sons of Rimmon the Beerothite, of the tribe of Benjamin. [Beeroth, too, was ascribed to Benjamin: 3 the Beerothites fled to Gittaim, where they have been resident aliens to this day. 4 Jonathan, son of Saul, had a son named Meribbaal with crippled feet. He was five years old when the news about Saul and Jonathan came from Jezreel, and his nurse took him up and fled. But in their hasty flight, he fell and became lame.] 5 The sons of Rimmon the Beerothite, Rechab and Baanah, came into the house of Ishbaal during the heat of the day, while he was taking his siesta. 6 The portress of the house had dozed off while sifting wheat, and was asleep. So Rechab and his brother Baanah slipped past 7 and entered the house while Ishbaal was lying asleep in his bedroom. They struck and killed him, and cut off his head. Then, taking the head, they traveled on the Arabah road all night long.

8 They brought the head of Ishbaal to David in Hebron and said to the king: "This is the head of Ishbaal, son of your enemy Saul, who sought your life. Thus has the LORD this day avenged my lord the king on Saul and his posterity." 9 But David replied to Rechab and his brother Baanah, sons of Rimmon the Beerothite: "As the LORD lives, who rescued me from all difficulty, 10 in Ziklag I seized and put to death the man who informed me of Saul's death, thinking himself the bearer of good news for which I ought to give him a reward. 11 How much more now, when wicked men have slain an innocent man in bed at home, must I hold you responsible for his death and destroy you from the earth!" 12 So at a command from David, the young men killed them and cut off their hands and feet, hanging them up near the pool in Hebron. But he took the head of Ishbaal and buried it in Abner's grave in Hebron.

5 All the tribes of Israel came to David in Hebron and said: "Here we are, your bone and your flesh. 2 In days past, when Saul was our king, it was you who led the Israelites out and brought them back. And the LORD said to you, 'You shall shepherd my people Israel and shall be commander of Israel.'" 3 When all the elders of Israel came to David in Hebron, King David made an agreement with them there before the LORD, and they anointed David king of Israel. 4 David was thirty years old when he became king, and he reigned for forty years: 5 seven years and six months in Hebron over Judah, and thirty-three years in Jerusalem over all Israel and Judah.

6 Then the king and his men set out for Jerusalem against the Jebusites who inhabited the region. David was told, "You cannot enter here: the blind and the lame will drive you away!" which was their way of saying, "David cannot

king had had no part in the murder of Abner son of Ner. 38 The king said to his retainers, 'Do you not realise that a prince, a great man, has fallen in Israel today? 39 I, though anointed king, am weak at present, and these men, the sons of Zeruiah, are too strong for me. May Yahweh repay the criminal as his crime deserves!'

4 When Saul's son heard that Abner had died at Hebron, his heart failed him, and all Israel was alarmed. 2 Now, Saul's son had two freebooting chieftains; one was called Baanah, the other Rechab. They were the sons of Rimmon of Beeroth, and Benjaminites—for Beeroth is regarded as belonging to Benjamin. 3 The people of Beeroth had taken refuge in Gittaim, where they have remained to this day as resident foreigners.

4 Jonathan son of Saul had a son with crippled feet. He was five years old when the news about Saul and Jonathan came from Jezreel. His nurse picked him up and fled but, as she hurried away, he fell and was lamed. His name was Meribbaal.

5 The sons of Rimmon of Beeroth, Rechab and Baanah, set out; they came to Ishbaal's house at the hottest part of the day when he was taking his midday rest. 6 The woman who kept the door had been cleaning wheat and had drowsed off to sleep. 7 Rechab and his brother Baanah stole past her and entered the house, where he was lying on his bed in his bedroom. They struck him and killed him, then cut off his head and, taking the head with them, travelled all night by way of the Arabah. 8 They brought Ishbaal's head to David at Hebron. 'Here', they said to the king, 'is the head of Ishbaal son of Saul, your enemy, who meant to take your life. Yahweh has avenged my lord the king today on Saul and on his offspring.'

9 But David answered Rechab and his brother Baanah, the sons of Rimmon, by saying, 'As Yahweh lives, who has rescued me from every danger, 10 when someone told me, "Saul is dead!" supposing himself to be bringing me good news, I seized and put him to death at Ziklag, and that was how I rewarded him for his news! 11 How much more when bandits have killed an upright man in his house, and on his bed! Am I not to demand an account of his blood from you, and rid the earth of you?' 12 David then gave an order to the men, who put them to death, cut off their hands and feet, and hung them up beside the pool of Hebron. Ishbaal's head they took and buried in Abner's grave at Hebron.

5 All the tribes of Israel then came to David at Hebron and said, 'Look, we are your own flesh and bone. 2 In days past when Saul was our king, it was you who led Israel on its campaigns, and to you it was that Yahweh promised, "You are to shepherd my people Israel and be leader of Israel."' 3 So all the elders of Israel came to the king at Hebron, and King David made a pact with them in Yahweh's presence at Hebron, and they anointed David as king of Israel.

4 David was thirty years old when he became king, and he reigned for forty years. 5 In Hebron he reigned over Judah for seven years and six months; then he reigned in Jerusalem over all Israel and Judah for thirty-three years.

6 The king and his men then marched on Jerusalem, on the Jebusites living in the territory. These said to David, 'You will not get in here. The blind and the lame will hold you off.' (That is to say: David will never get in here.) 7 But

NEW REVISED STANDARD VERSION

7 Nevertheless David took the stronghold of Zion, which is now the city of David. 8 David had said on that day, "Whoever would strike down the Jebusites, let him get up the water shaft to attack the lame and the blind, those whom David hates."*s* Therefore it is said, "The blind and the lame shall not come into the house." 9 David occupied the stronghold, and named it the city of David. David built the city all around from the Millo inward. 10 And David became greater and greater, for the LORD, the God of hosts, was with him.

11 King Hiram of Tyre sent messengers to David, along with cedar trees, and carpenters and masons who built David a house. 12 David then perceived that the LORD had established him king over Israel, and that he had exalted his kingdom for the sake of his people Israel.

13 In Jerusalem, after he came from Hebron, David took more concubines and wives; and more sons and daughters were born to David. 14 These are the names of those who were born to him in Jerusalem: Shammua, Shobab, Nathan, Solomon, 15 Ibhar, Elishua, Nepheg, Japhia, 16 Elishama, Eliada, and Eliphelet.

17 When the Philistines heard that David had been anointed king over Israel, all the Philistines went up in search of David; but David heard about it and went down to the stronghold. 18 Now the Philistines had come and spread out in the valley of Rephaim. 19 David inquired of the LORD, "Shall I go up against the Philistines? Will you give them into my hand?" The LORD said to David, "Go up; for I will certainly give the Philistines into your hand." 20 So David came to Baal-perazim, and David defeated them there. He said, "The LORD has burst forth against*t* my enemies before me, like a bursting flood." Therefore that place is called Baal-perazim.*u* 21 The Philistines abandoned their idols there, and David and his men carried them away.

22 Once again the Philistines came up, and were spread out in the valley of Rephaim. 23 When David inquired of the LORD, he said, "You shall not go up; go around to their rear, and come upon them opposite the balsam trees. 24 When you hear the sound of marching in the tops of the balsam trees, then be on the alert; for then the LORD has gone out before you to strike down the army of the Philistines." 25 David did just as the LORD had commanded him; and he struck down the Philistines from Geba all the way to Gezer.

6 David again gathered all the chosen men of Israel, thirty thousand. 2 David and all the people with him set out and went from Baale-judah, to bring up from there the ark of God, which is called by the name of the LORD of hosts who is enthroned on the cherubim. 3 They carried the ark of God on a new cart, and brought it out of the house of Abinadab, which was on the hill. Uzzah and Ahio,*v* the sons of Abinadab, were driving the new cart 4 with the ark of God;*w* and Ahio*v* went in front of the ark. 5 David and all the house of Israel were dancing before the LORD with all their might, with songs*x* and lyres and harps and tambourines and castanets and cymbals.

6 When they came to the threshing floor of Nacon, Uzzah reached out his hand to the ark of God and took hold of it, for the oxen shook it. 7 The anger of the LORD was

REVISED ENGLISH BIBLE

would never come in. 7 None the less David did capture the stronghold of Zion, and it is now known as the City of David. 8 On that day David had said, 'Everyone who is eager to attack the Jebusites, let him get up the water-shaft to reach the lame and the blind, David's bitter enemies.' That is why they say, 'No one who is blind or lame is to come into the LORD's house.'

9 David took up his residence in the stronghold and called it the City of David. He built up the city around it, starting at the Millo and working inwards. 10 David steadily grew more and more powerful, for the LORD the God of Hosts was with him.

11 KING Hiram of Tyre sent envoys to David with cedar logs, and with them carpenters and stonemasons, who built David a house. 12 David knew by now that the LORD had confirmed him as king over Israel and had enhanced his royal power for the sake of his people Israel.

13 After he had moved from Hebron he took more concubines and wives in Jerusalem, and more sons and daughters were born to him. 14 These are the names of the children born to him in Jerusalem: Shammua, Shobab, Nathan, Solomon, 15 Ibhar, Elishua, Nepheg, Japhia, 16 Elishama, Eliada, and Eliphelet.

17 When the Philistines learnt that David had been anointed king over Israel, they came up in force to seek him out. David, getting wind of this, went down to the stronghold for refuge. 18 When the Philistines had come and overrun the valley of Rephaim, 19 David enquired of the LORD, 'If I attack the Philistines, will you deliver them into my hands?' The LORD answered, 'Go, I shall deliver the Philistines into your hands.' 20 He went and attacked and defeated them at Baal-perazim. 'The LORD has broken through my enemies' lines', David said, 'as a river breaks its banks.' That is why the place was named Baal-perazim. 21 The Philistines abandoned their idols there, and David and his men carried them off.

22 The Philistines made another attack and overran the valley of Rephaim. 23 David enquired of the LORD, who said, 'Do not attack now but make a detour and come on them towards the rear opposite the aspens. 24 As soon as you hear a rustling sound in the treetops, move at once; for then the LORD will have gone out before you to defeat the Philistine army.' 25 David did as the LORD had commanded, and drove the Philistines in flight all the way from Geba to Gezer.

6 David again summoned the picked men of Israel, thirty thousand in all, 2 and went with the whole army that was then with him to Baalath-judah to fetch from there the Ark of God which bore the name of the LORD of Hosts, who is enthroned upon the cherubim. 3 They mounted the Ark of God on a new cart and conveyed it from Abinadab's house on the hill, with Uzzah and Ahio, sons of Abinadab, guiding the cart. 4 They led it with the Ark of God upon it from Abinadab's house on the hill, with Ahio walking in front. 5 David and all Israel danced for joy before the LORD with all their might to the sound of singing, of lyres, lutes, tambourines, castanets, and cymbals.

6 When they came to a certain threshing-floor, the oxen stumbled, and Uzzah reached out and held the Ark of God.

5:8 **the LORD's house:** *lit.* the house.   5:9 **the city:** *prob. rdg,* cp. *1 Chr. 11:8; Heb. omits.*   5:11–25 *Cp. 1 Chr. 14:1–16.* 5:14–16 *Cp. 1 Chr. 3:5–8; 14:4–7.*   5:20 **Baal-perazim:** *that is* Baal of Break-through.   5:25 **Geba:** *or, with 1 Chr. 14:16 and* Gk, Gibeon.   6:2–11 *Cp. 1 Chr. 13:6–14.*   6:2 **to** **Baalath-judah:** *prob. rdg,* cp. *1 Chr. 13:6; Heb.* from the lords of Judah.   6:5 **with . . . singing:** *prob. rdg,* cp. *1 Chr. 13:8; Heb.* to the beating of batons.

---

s Another reading is *those who hate David*   *t* Heb *paraz*   *u* That is *Lord of Bursting Forth*   *v* Or *and his brother*   *w* Compare Gk: Heb *and brought it out of the house of Abinadab, which was on the hill with the ark of God*   *x* Q Ms Gk 1 Chr 13.8: Heb *fir-trees*

enter here." 7 But David did take the stronghold of Zion, which is the City of David. 8 On that day David said: "All who wish to attack the Jebusites must strike at them through the water shaft. The lame and the blind shall be the personal enemies of David." That is why it is said, "The blind and the lame shall not enter the palace." 9 David then dwelt in the stronghold, which was called the City of David; he built up the area from Millo to the palace. 10 David grew steadily more powerful, for the LORD of hosts was with him. 11 Hiram, king of Tyre, sent ambassadors to David; he furnished cedar wood, as well as carpenters and masons, who built a palace for David. 12 And David knew that the LORD had established him as king of Israel and had exalted his rule for the sake of his people Israel.

13 David took more concubines and wives in Jerusalem after he had come from Hebron, and more sons and daughters were born to him in Jerusalem. 14 These are the names of those who were born to him in Jerusalem: Shammua, Shobab, Nathan, Solomon, 15 Ibhar, Elishua, Nepheg, Japhia, 16 Elishama, Baaliada, and Eliphelet.

17 When the Philistines heard that David had been anointed king of Israel, they all took the field in search of him. On hearing this, David went down to the refuge. 18 The Philistines came and overran the valley of Rephaim. 19 David inquired of the LORD, "Shall I attack the Philistines — will you deliver them into my grip?" The LORD replied to David, "Attack, for I will surely deliver the Philistines into your grip." 20 David then went to Baal-perazim, where he defeated them. He said, "The LORD has scattered my enemies before me like waters that have broken free." That is why the place is called Baal-perazim. 21 They abandoned their gods there, and David and his men carried them away. 22 But the Philistines came up again and overran the valley of Rephaim. 23 So David inquired of the LORD, who replied: "You must not attack frontally, but circle their rear and meet them before the mastic trees. 24 When you hear a sound of marching in the tops of the mastic trees, act decisively, for the LORD will have gone forth before you to attack the camp of the Philistines." 25 David obeyed the LORD's command and routed the Philistines from Gibeon as far as Gezer.

David captured the citadel of Zion, that is, the City of David. 8 That day, David said, 'Whoever gets up the tunnel and kills a Jebusite . . .'b As for the blind and the lame, David hated them with his whole being. (Hence the saying: the blind and the lame may not enter the Temple.) 9 David went to live in the citadel and called it the City of David. David then built a wall round it, from the Millo inwards. 10 David grew stronger and stronger, and Yahweh, God of Sabaoth, was with him.

11 Hiram king of Tyre sent envoys to David, with cedar wood, carpenters and stone-cutters, who built David a palace. 12 David then knew that Yahweh had confirmed him as king of Israel and, for the sake of his people Israel, had extended his sovereignty.

13 After coming from Hebron, David took other concubines and wives in Jerusalem, and sons and daughters were born to him. 14 These are the names of those born to him in Jerusalem: Shammua, Shobab, Nathan, Solomon, 15 Ibhar, Elishua, Nepheg, Japhia, 16 Elishama, Eliada, Eliphelet.

17 When the Philistines heard that David had been anointed as king of Israel, they all went up to seek him out. On hearing this, David went down to the stronghold. 18 When the Philistines arrived, they deployed in the Valley of the Rephaim. 19 David consulted Yahweh and asked, 'Shall I attack the Philistines? Will you deliver them into my power?' Yahweh replied to David, 'Attack! I shall certainly deliver the Philistines into your power.' 20 Accordingly, David went to Baal-Perazim and there David defeated them. He said, 'Yahweh has made a breach in my enemies for me, as though they had been breached by a flood.' This is why the place was given the name Baal-Perazim. 21 They had left their gods behind them there, and David and his men carried them off.

22 Again the Philistines invaded and deployed in the Valley of the Rephaim. 23 David consulted Yahweh, who replied, 'Do not attack them from the front; go round to their rear and engage them opposite the balsam trees. 24 When you hear the sound of footsteps in the tops of the balsam trees, advance, for that will be Yahweh going out ahead of you to defeat the Philistine army.' 25 David did as Yahweh had ordered and beat the Philistines from Gibeon to the Pass of Gezer.

6 David again assembled all the picked men of Israel, thirty thousand in number. 2 Then David and all the people who were with him set out for Baala of Judah to bring up from there the ark of God, which bears the name of the LORD of hosts enthroned above the cherubim. 3 The ark of God was placed on a new cart and taken away from the house of Abinadab on the hill. Uzzah and Ahio, sons of Abinadab, guided the cart, 4 with Ahio walking before it, 5 while David and all the Israelites made merry before the LORD with all their strength, with singing and with citharas, harps, tambourines, sistrums and cymbals. 6 When they came to the threshing floor of Nodan, Uzzah reached out his hand to the ark of God and steadied it, for the oxen were

6 David again mustered all the picked troops of Israel, thirty thousand men. 2 Setting off with the whole force then with him, David went to Baalah of Judah, from there to bring up the ark of God, who bears the title 'Yahweh Sabaoth, enthroned on the winged creatures'. 3 They transported the ark of God on a new cart and brought it out of Abinadab's house which is on the hill. Uzzah and Ahio, the sons of Abinadab, drove the cart, 4 Uzzah walked alongside the ark of God and Ahio went in front. 5 David and the whole House of Israel danced before Yahweh with all their might, singing to the accompaniment of harps, lyres, tambourines, sistrums and cymbals. 6 When they came to Nacon's threshing-floor, Uzzah reached his hand out to the ark of God and steadied it, as the oxen were making it tilt.

---

b 5 The sentence breaks off. The tunnel, a secret passage from the spring to the interior of the city, still exists.

NEW REVISED STANDARD VERSION

kindled against Uzzah; and God struck him there because he reached out his hand to the ark;*y* and he died there beside the ark of God. 8 David was angry because the LORD had burst forth with an outburst upon Uzzah; so that place is called Perez-uzzah,*z* to this day. 9 David was afraid of the LORD that day; he said, "How can the ark of the LORD come into my care?" 10 So David was unwilling to take the ark of the LORD into his care in the city of David; instead David took it to the house of Obed-edom the Gittite. 11 The ark of the LORD remained in the house of Obed-edom the Gittite three months; and the LORD blessed Obed-edom and all his household.

12 It was told King David, "The LORD has blessed the household of Obed-edom and all that belongs to him, because of the ark of God." So David went and brought up the ark of God from the house of Obed-edom to the city of David with rejoicing; 13 and when those who bore the ark of the LORD had gone six paces, he sacrificed an ox and a fatling. 14 David danced before the LORD with all his might; David was girded with a linen ephod. 15 So David and all the house of Israel brought up the ark of the LORD with shouting, and with the sound of the trumpet.

16 As the ark of the LORD came into the city of David, Michal daughter of Saul looked out of the window, and saw King David leaping and dancing before the LORD; and she despised him in her heart.

17 They brought in the ark of the LORD, and set it in its place, inside the tent that David had pitched for it; and David offered burnt offerings and offerings of well-being before the LORD. 18 When David had finished offering the burnt offerings and the offerings of well-being, he blessed the people in the name of the LORD of hosts, 19 and distributed food among all the people, the whole multitude of Israel, both men and women, to each a cake of bread, a portion of meat,*a* and a cake of raisins. Then all the people went back to their homes.

20 David returned to bless his household. But Michal the daughter of Saul came out to meet David, and said, "How the king of Israel honored himself today, uncovering himself today before the eyes of his servants' maids, as any vulgar fellow might shamelessly uncover himself!" 21 David said to Michal, "It was before the LORD, who chose me in place of your father and all his household, to appoint me as prince over Israel, the people of the LORD, that I have danced before the LORD. 22 I will make myself yet more contemptible than this, and I will be abased in my own eyes; but by the maids of whom you have spoken, by them I shall be held in honor." 23 And Michal the daughter of Saul had no child to the day of her death.

7 Now when the king was settled in his house, and the LORD had given him rest from all his enemies around him, 2 the king said to the prophet Nathan, "See now, I am living in a house of cedar, but the ark of God stays in a tent." 3 Nathan said to the king, "Go, do all that you have in mind; for the LORD is with you."

4 But that same night the word of the LORD came to Nathan: 5 Go and tell my servant David: Thus says the LORD: Are you the one to build me a house to live in? 6 I have not lived in a house since the day I brought up the people of Israel from Egypt to this day, but I have been moving about in a tent and a tabernacle. 7 Wherever I have moved about among all the people of Israel, did I ever speak a word with any of the tribal leaders*b* of Israel, whom I commanded to shepherd my people Israel, saying, "Why have you not built me a house of cedar?" 8 Now therefore

REVISED ENGLISH BIBLE

7 The LORD was angry with Uzzah and struck him down for his imprudent action, and he died there beside the Ark of God. 8 David was vexed because the LORD's anger had broken out on Uzzah, and he called the place Perez-uzzah, the name it still bears.

9 David was afraid of the LORD that day and said, 'How can the Ark of the LORD come to me?' 10 He felt he could not take the Ark of the LORD with him to the City of David; he turned aside and carried it to the house of Obed-edom the Gittite. 11 The Ark of the LORD remained at Obed-edom's house for three months, and the LORD blessed Obed-edom and his whole household.

12 When David was informed that the LORD had blessed Obed-edom's family and all that he possessed because of the Ark of God, he went and brought the Ark of God from the house of Obed-edom up to the City of David amid rejoicing. 13 When the bearers of the Ark of the LORD had gone six steps he sacrificed a bull and a buffalo. 14 He was wearing a linen ephod, and he danced with abandon before the LORD, 15 as he and all the Israelites brought up the Ark of the LORD with acclamation and blowing of trumpets. 16 As the Ark of the LORD was entering the City of David, Saul's daughter Michal looked down from a window and saw King David leaping and whirling before the LORD, and she despised him in her heart.

17 After they had brought the Ark of the LORD, they put it in its place inside the tent that David had set up for it, and David offered whole-offerings and shared-offerings before the LORD. 18 Having completed these sacrifices, David blessed the people in the name of the LORD of Hosts, 19 and distributed food to them all, a flat loaf of bread, a portion of meat, and a cake of raisins, to every man and woman in the whole gathering of the Israelites. Then all the people went home.

20 David returned to greet his household, and Michal, Saul's daughter, came out to meet him. She said, 'What a glorious day for the king of Israel, when he made an exhibition of himself in the sight of his servants' slave-girls, as any vulgar clown might do!' 21 David answered her, 'But it was done in the presence of the LORD, who chose me instead of your father and his family and appointed me prince over Israel, the people of the LORD. Before the LORD I shall dance for joy, yes, 22 and I shall earn yet more disgrace and demean myself still more in your eyes; but those slave-girls of whom you speak, they will hold me in honour for it.'

23 To her dying day Michal, Saul's daughter, was childless.

7 Once the king was established in his palace and the LORD had given him security from his enemies on all sides, 2 he said to Nathan the prophet, 'Here I am living in a house of cedar, while the Ark of God is housed in a tent.' 3 Nathan answered, 'Do whatever you have in mind, for the LORD is with you.' 4 But that same night the word of the LORD came to Nathan: 5 'Go and say to David my servant, This is the word of the LORD: Are you to build me a house to dwell in? 6 Down to this day I have never dwelt in a house since I brought Israel up from Egypt; I lived in a tent and a tabernacle. 7 Wherever I journeyed with Israel, did I ever ask any of the judges whom I appointed shepherds of my people Israel why they had not built me a cedar house?

y 1 Chr 13.10 Compare Q Ms: Meaning of Heb uncertain   *z* That is *Bursting Out Against Uzzah*   *a* Vg: Meaning of Heb uncertain
b Or *any of the tribes*

6:8 **Perez-uzzah:** *that is* Outbreak on Uzzah.   6:12–19 *Cp. 1 Chr. 15:25—16:3.*   6:19 **portion of meat:** *meaning of Heb. word uncertain.*   6:22 **your:** *so Gk; Heb.* my.   7:1–29 *Cp. 1 Chr. 17:1–27.*   7:7 **judges:** *prob. rdg, cp. 1 Chr. 17:6; Heb.* tribes.

making it tip. 7 But the LORD was angry with Uzzah; God struck him on that spot, and he died there before God. 8 David was disturbed because the LORD had vented his anger on Uzzah. (The place has been called Perez-uzzah down to the present day.) 9 David feared the LORD that day and said, "How can the ark of the LORD come to me?" 10 So David would not have the ark of the LORD brought to him in the City of David, but diverted it to the house of Obed-edom the Gittite.

11 The ark of the LORD remained in the house of Obed-edom the Gittite for three months, and the LORD blessed Obed-edom and his whole house. 12 When it was reported to King David that the LORD had blessed the family of Obed-edom and all that belonged to him, David went to bring up the ark of God from the house of Obed-edom into the City of David amid festivities. 13 As soon as the bearers of the ark of the LORD had advanced six steps, he sacrificed an ox and a fatling. 14 Then David, girt with a linen apron, came dancing before the LORD with abandon, 15 as he and all the Israelites were bringing up the ark of the LORD with shouts of joy and to the sound of the horn. 16 As the ark of the LORD was entering the City of David, Saul's daughter Michal looked down through the window and saw King David leaping and dancing before the LORD, and she despised him in her heart. 17 The ark of the LORD was brought in and set in its place within the tent David had pitched for it. Then David offered holocausts and peace offerings before the LORD. 18 When he finished making these offerings, he blessed the people in the name of the LORD of hosts. 19 He then distributed among all the people, to each man and each woman in the entire multitude of Israel, a loaf of bread, a cut of roast meat, and a raisin cake. With this, all the people left for their homes.

20 When David returned to bless his own family, Saul's daughter Michal came out to meet him and said, "How the king of Israel has honored himself today, exposing himself to the view of the slave girls of his followers, as a commoner might do!" 21 But David replied to Michal: "I was dancing before the LORD. As the LORD lives, who preferred me to your father and his whole family when he appointed me commander of the LORD's people, Israel, not only will I make merry before the LORD, 22 but I will demean myself even more. I will be lowly in your esteem, but in the esteem of the slave girls you spoke of I will be honored." 23 And so Saul's daughter Michal was childless to the day of her death.

7 When King David was settled in his palace, and the LORD had given him rest from his enemies on every side, 2 he said to Nathan the prophet, "Here I am living in a house of cedar, while the ark of God dwells in a tent!" 3 Nathan answered the king, "Go, do whatever you have in mind, for the LORD is with you." 4 But that night the LORD spoke to Nathan and said: 5 "Go, tell my servant David, 'Thus says the LORD: Should you build me a house to dwell in? 6 I have not dwelt in a house from the day on which I led the Israelites out of Egypt to the present, but I have been going about in a tent under cloth. 7 In all my wanderings everywhere among the Israelites, did I ever utter a word to any one of the judges whom I charged to tend my people Israel, to ask: Why have you not built me a house of cedar?'

7 This roused Yahweh's anger against Uzzah, and for this crime God struck him down on the spot, and there he died beside the ark of God. 8 David resented Yahweh's having broken out against Uzzah, and the place was given the name Perez-Uzzah,c which it still has today.

9 That day David felt afraid of Yahweh. 'How can the ark of Yahweh come to be with me?' he said. 10 So David decided not to take the ark of Yahweh with him into the city of David but diverted it to the house of Obed-Edom of Gath. 11 The ark of Yahweh remained in the house of Obed-Edom of Gath for three months, and Yahweh blessed Obed-Edom and his whole family.

12 King David was informed that Yahweh had blessed Obed-Edom's family and everything belonging to him on account of the ark of God. David accordingly went and, amid great rejoicing, brought the ark of God up from Obed-Edom's house to the City of David. 13 When the bearers of the ark of Yahweh had gone six paces, he sacrificed an ox and a fat sheep. 14 And David danced whirling round before Yahweh with all his might, wearing a linen loincloth. 15 Thus with war cries and blasts on the horn, David and the entire House of Israel brought up the ark of Yahweh. 16 Now as the ark of Yahweh entered the City of David, Michal daughter of Saul was watching from the window and when she saw King David leaping and whirling round before Yahweh, the sight of him filled her with contempt. 17 They brought the ark of Yahweh in and put it in position, inside the tent which David had erected for it; and David presented burnt offerings and communion sacrifices in Yahweh's presence. 18 And when David had finished presenting burnt offerings, he blessed the people in the name of Yahweh Sabaoth. 19 To all the people, to the whole multitude of Israelites, men and women, he then distributed to each a loaf of bread, a portion of dates and a raisin cake. Then the people all went back to their homes.

20 As David was coming back to bless his household, Michal daughter of Saul came out to meet him. 'Much honour the king of Israel has won today,' she said, 'making an exhibition of himself under the eyes of his servant-maids, making an exhibition of himself like a buffoon!' 21 David replied to Michal, 'I was dancing for Yahweh, not for them. As Yahweh lives, who chose me in preference to your father and his whole family to make me leader of Israel, Yahweh's people, I shall dance before Yahweh and 22 lower myself even further than that. In your eyes I may be base, but by the maids you speak of, by them, I shall be held in honour!' 23 And to the day of her death, Michal, daughter of Saul, had no children.

7 Once the king had settled into his palace and Yahweh had granted him rest from all the enemies surrounding him, 2 the king said to the prophet Nathan, 'Look, I am living in a cedar-wood palace, while the ark of God is under awnings.' 3 Nathan said to the king, 'Go and do whatever you have in mind, for Yahweh is with you.'

4 But that very night, the word of Yahweh came to Nathan:

5 'Go and tell my servant David, "Yahweh says this: Are you to build me a temple for me to live in? 6 I have never lived in a house from the day when I brought the Israelites out of Egypt until today, but have kept travelling with a tent for shelter. 7 In all my travels with all the Israelites, did I say to any of the judges of Israel, whom I had commanded to shepherd my people Israel: Why do you not build me a cedar-wood temple?" 8 This is what you must say to my

---

thus you shall say to my servant David: Thus says the LORD of hosts: I took you from the pasture, from following the sheep to be prince over my people Israel; 9 and I have been with you wherever you went, and have cut off all your enemies from before you; and I will make for you a great name, like the name of the great ones of the earth. 10 And I will appoint a place for my people Israel and will plant them, so that they may live in their own place, and be disturbed no more; and evildoers shall afflict them no more, as formerly, 11 from the time that I appointed judges over my people Israel; and I will give you rest from all your enemies. Moreover the LORD declares to you that the LORD will make you a house. 12 When your days are fulfilled and you lie down with your ancestors, I will raise up your offspring after you, who shall come forth from your body, and I will establish his kingdom. 13 He shall build a house for my name, and I will establish the throne of his kingdom forever. 14 I will be a father to him, and he shall be a son to me. When he commits iniquity, I will punish him with a rod such as mortals use, with blows inflicted by human beings. 15 But I will not take*c* my steadfast love from him, as I took it from Saul, whom I put away from before you. 16 Your house and your kingdom shall be made sure forever before me;*d* your throne shall be established forever. 17 In accordance with all these words and with all this vision, Nathan spoke to David.

18 Then King David went in and sat before the LORD, and said, "Who am I, O Lord GOD, and what is my house, that you have brought me thus far? 19 And yet this was a small thing in your eyes, O Lord GOD; you have spoken also of your servant's house for a great while to come. May this be instruction for the people,*e* O Lord GOD! 20 And what more can David say to you? For you know your servant, O Lord GOD! 21 Because of your promise, and according to your own heart, you have wrought all this greatness, so that your servant may know it. 22 Therefore you are great, O LORD God; for there is no one like you, and there is no God besides you, according to all that we have heard with our ears. 23 Who is like your people, like Israel? Is there another*f* nation on earth whose God went to redeem it as a people, and to make a name for himself, doing great and awesome things for them,*g* by driving out*h* before his people nations and their gods?*i* 24 And you established your people Israel for yourself to be your people forever; and you, O LORD, became their God. 25 And now, O LORD God, as for the word that you have spoken concerning your servant and concerning his house, confirm it forever; do as you have promised. 26 Thus your name will be magnified forever in the saying, 'The LORD of hosts is God over Israel'; and the house of your servant David will be established before you. 27 For you, O LORD of hosts, the God of Israel, have made this revelation to your servant, saying, 'I will build you a house'; therefore your servant has found courage to pray this prayer to you. 28 And now, O Lord GOD, you are God, and your words are true, and you have promised this good thing to your servant; 29 now therefore may it please you to bless the house of your servant, so that it may continue forever before you; for you, O Lord GOD, have spoken, and with your blessing shall the house of your servant be blessed forever."

8 Some time afterward, David attacked the Philistines and subdued them; David took Metheg-ammah out of the hand of the Philistines.

8 'Then say this to my servant David: This is the word of the LORD of Hosts: I took you from the pastures and from following the sheep to be prince over my people Israel. 9 I have been with you wherever you have gone, and have destroyed all the enemies in your path. I shall bring you fame like the fame of the great ones of the earth. 10 I shall assign a place for my people Israel; there I shall plant them to dwell in their own land. They will be disturbed no more; never again will the wicked oppress them as they did in the past, 11 from the day when I appointed judges over my people Israel; and I shall give you peace from all your enemies.

'The LORD has told you that he would build up your royal house. 12 When your life ends and you rest with your forefathers, I shall set up one of your family, one of your own children, to succeed you, and I shall establish his kingdom. 13 It is he who is to build a house in honour of my name, and I shall establish his royal throne for all time. 14 I shall be a father to him, and he will be my son. When he does wrong, I shall punish him as any father might, and not spare the rod. 15 But my love will never be withdrawn from him as I withdrew it from Saul, whom I removed from your path. 16 Your family and your kingdom will be established for ever in my sight; your throne will endure for all time.'

17 Nathan recounted to David all that had been said to him and all that had been revealed. 18 Then King David went into the presence of the LORD and, taking his place there, said, 'Who am I, Lord GOD, and what is my family, that you have brought me thus far? 19 It was a small thing in your sight, Lord GOD, to have planned for your servant's house in days long past. 20 What more can I say? Lord GOD, you yourself know your servant David. 21 For the sake of your promise and in accordance with your purpose you have done all this great thing to reveal it to your servant.

22 'Lord GOD, you are great. There is none like you; there is no God but you, as everything we have heard bears witness. 23 And your people Israel, to whom can they be compared? Is there any other nation on earth whom you, God, have set out to redeem from slavery to be your people? You have won renown for yourself by great and awesome deeds, driving out other nations and their gods to make way for your people whom you redeemed from Egypt. 24 You have established your people Israel as your own for ever, and you, LORD, have become their God.

25 'Now, LORD God, perform for all time what you have promised for your servant and his house; make good what you have promised. 26 May your fame be great for evermore, and let people say, "The LORD of Hosts is God over Israel"; and may the house of your servant David be established before you. 27 LORD of Hosts, God of Israel, you have shown me your purpose, in saying to your servant, "I shall build up your house"; therefore I have made bold to offer this prayer to you. 28 Now, Lord GOD, you are God and your promises will come true; you have made these noble promises to your servant. 29 Be pleased now to bless your servant's house so that it may continue always before you; you, Lord GOD, have promised, and may your blessing rest on your servant's house for ever.'

8 After this David attacked and subdued the Philistines, and took from them Metheg-ha-ammah. 2 He defeated

---

c Gk Syr Vg 1 Chr 17.13: Heb *shall not depart* *d* Gk Heb Mss: MT *before you*; Compare 2 Sam 7.26, 29 *e* Meaning of Heb uncertain *f* Gk: Heb *one* *g* Heb *you* *h* Gk 1 Chr 17.21: Heb *for your land* *i* Cn: Heb *before your people, whom you redeemed for yourself from Egypt, nations and its gods*

7:16 **my:** *so some MSS; others* your. 7:19 **long past:** *Heb. adds* This, Lord GOD, is a law for men. 7:23 **any other:** *so Gk; Heb.* one. **driving . . . people:** *so Gk, cp. 1 Chr. 17:21; Heb.* unintelligible. 8:1–14 *Cp. 1 Chr. 18:1–13.*

8 "Now then, speak thus to my servant David, 'The LORD of hosts has this to say: It was I who took you from the pasture and from the care of the flock to be commander of my people Israel. 9 I have been with you wherever you went, and I have destroyed all your enemies before you. And I will make you famous like the great ones of the earth. 10 I will fix a place for my people Israel; I will plant them so that they may dwell in their place without further disturbance. Neither shall the wicked continue to afflict them as they did of old, 11 since the time I first appointed judges over my people Israel. I will give you rest from all your enemies. The LORD also reveals to you that he will establish a house for you. 12 And when your time comes and you rest with your ancestors, I will raise up your heir after you, sprung from your loins, and I will make his kingdom firm. 13 It is he who shall build a house for my name. And I will make his royal throne firm forever. 14 I will be a father to him, and he shall be a son to me. And if he does wrong, I will correct him with the rod of men and with human chastisements; 15 but I will not withdraw my favor from him as I withdrew it from your predecessor Saul, whom I removed from my presence. 16 Your house and your kingdom shall endure forever before me; your throne shall stand firm forever.' " 17 Nathan reported all these words and this entire vision to David.

18 Then King David went in and sat before the LORD and said, "Who am I, Lord GOD, and who are the members of my house, that you have brought me to this point? 19 Yet even this you see as too little, Lord GOD; you have also spoken of the house of your servant for a long time to come: this too you have shown to man, Lord GOD! 20 What more can David say to you? You know your servant, Lord GOD! 21 For your servant's sake and as you have had at heart, you have brought about this entire magnificent disclosure to your servant. 22 And so —

"Great are you, Lord GOD! There is none like you and there is no God but you, just as we have heard it told. 23 What other nation on earth is there like your people Israel, which God has led, redeeming it as his people; so that you have made yourself renowned by doing this magnificent deed, and by doing awe-inspiring things as you have cleared nations and their gods out of the way of your people, which you redeemed for yourself from Egypt? 24 You have established for yourself your people Israel as yours forever, and you, LORD, have become their God. 25 And now, LORD God, confirm for all time the prophecy you have made concerning your servant and his house, and do as you have promised. 26 Your name will be forever great, when men say, 'The LORD of hosts is God of Israel,' and the house of your servant David stands firm before you. 27 It is you, LORD of hosts, God of Israel, who said in a revelation to your servant, 'I will build a house for you.' Therefore your servant now finds the courage to make this prayer to you. 28 And now, Lord GOD, you are God and your words are truth; you have made this generous promise to your servant. 29 Do, then, bless the house of your servant that it may be before you forever; for you, Lord GOD, have promised, and by your blessing the house of your servant shall be blessed forever."

8 After this David attacked the Philistines and conquered them, wresting . . . from the Philistines. 2 He also de-

servant David, "Yahweh Sabaoth says this: I took you from the pasture, from following the sheep, to be leader of my people Israel; 9 I have been with you wherever you went; I have got rid of all your enemies for you. I am going to make your fame as great as the fame of the greatest on earth. 10 I am going to provide a place for my people Israel; I shall plant them there, and there they will live and never be disturbed again; nor will they be oppressed by the wicked any more, as they were in former times 11 ever since the time when I instituted judges to govern my people Israel; and I shall grant you rest from all your enemies. Yahweh furthermore tells you that he will make you a dynasty. 12 And when your days are over and you fall asleep with your ancestors, I shall appoint your heir, your own son to succeed you (and I shall make his sovereignty secure). 13 He will build a temple for my name)d and I shall make his royal throne secure for ever. 14 I shall be a father to him and he a son to me; if he does wrong, I shall punish him with a rod such as men use, with blows such as mankind gives. 15 But my faithful love will never be withdrawn from him as I withdrew it from Saul, whom I removed from before you. 16 Your dynasty and your sovereignty will ever stand firm before me and your throne be for ever secure." '

17 Nathan related all these words and this whole revelation to David.

18 King David then went in, sat down in Yahweh's presence and said:

'Who am I, Lord Yahweh, and what is my lineage, for you to have led me as far as this? 19 Yet, to you, Lord Yahweh, this seemed too little, and now you extend your promises for your servant's family into the distant future. Such is human destiny, Lord Yahweh. 20 What more can David say to you, since you, Lord Yahweh, know all about your servant? 21 Because of your promise and since you were so inclined, you have had the generosity to reveal this to your servant. 22 That is why you are great, Lord Yahweh; there is no one like you, no God but you alone, as everything that we have heard confirms. 23 Is there another people on earth like your people, like Israel, whom a god proceeded to redeem, to make them his people and to make a name for himself by performing great and terrible things on their behalf, by driving out nations and their gods before his people? — 24 for you constituted your people Israel your own people for ever and you, Yahweh, became their God.

25 'Now, Yahweh God, may the promise which you have made for your servant and for his family stand firm forever as you have said, 26 so that your name will be exalted for ever and people will say, "Israel's God is Yahweh Sabaoth." Your servant David's dynasty will be secure before you, 27 since you, Yahweh Sabaoth, the God of Israel, have disclosed to your servant, "I am going to build you a dynasty." Hence, your servant has ventured to offer this prayer to you. 28 Yes, Lord Yahweh, you are God indeed, your words are true and you have made this generous promise to your servant. 29 What is more, you have deigned to bless your servant's dynasty, so that it may remain for ever before you; for you, Lord Yahweh, have spoken; and may your servant's dynasty be blessed with your blessing for ever.'

8 After this, David defeated the Philistines and subdued them. From the grip of the Philistines he wrested . . .

8, 1: Wresting . . .: the Hebrew text here gives "the bridle of the cubit;" 1 Chr 18, 1 understood "Gath and its dependent villages"; others implausibly read "dominion of the capital city."

d7 The words in brackets were probably added during Solomon's reign.

2 He also defeated the Moabites and, making them lie down on the ground, measured them off with a cord; he measured two lengths of cord for those who were to be put to death, and one length *j* for those who were to be spared. And the Moabites became servants to David and brought tribute.

3 David also struck down King Hadadezer son of Rehob of Zobah, as he went to restore his monument *k* at the river Euphrates. 4 David took from him one thousand seven hundred horsemen, and twenty thousand foot soldiers. David hamstrung all the chariot horses, but left enough for a hundred chariots. 5 When the Arameans of Damascus came to help King Hadadezer of Zobah, David killed twenty-two thousand men of the Arameans. 6 Then David put garrisons among the Arameans of Damascus; and the Arameans became servants to David and brought tribute. The LORD gave victory to David wherever he went. 7 David took the gold shields that were carried by the servants of Hadadezer, and brought them to Jerusalem. 8 From Betah and from Berothai, towns of Hadadezer, King David took a great amount of bronze.

9 When King Toi of Hamath heard that David had defeated the whole army of Hadadezer, 10 Toi sent his son Joram to King David, to greet him and to congratulate him because he had fought against Hadadezer and defeated him. Now Hadadezer had often been at war with Toi. Joram brought with him articles of silver, gold, and bronze; 11 these also King David dedicated to the LORD, together with the silver and gold that he dedicated from all the nations he subdued, 12 from Edom, Moab, the Ammonites, the Philistines, Amalek, and from the spoil of King Hadadezer son of Rehob of Zobah.

13 David won a name for himself. When he returned, he killed eighteen thousand Edomites *l* in the Valley of Salt. 14 He put garrisons in Edom; throughout all Edom he put garrisons, and all the Edomites became David's servants. And the LORD gave victory to David wherever he went.

15 So David reigned over all Israel; and David administered justice and equity to all his people. 16 Joab son of Zeruiah was over the army; Jehoshaphat son of Ahilud was recorder; 17 Zadok son of Ahitub and Ahimelech son of Abiathar were priests; Seraiah was secretary; 18 Benaiah son of Jehoiada was over *m* the Cherethites and the Pelethites; and David's sons were priests.

9 David asked, "Is there still anyone left of the house of Saul to whom I may show kindness for Jonathan's sake?" 2 Now there was a servant of the house of Saul whose name was Ziba, and he was summoned to David. The king said to him, "Are you Ziba?" And he said, "At your service!" 3 The king said, "Is there anyone remaining of the house of Saul to whom I may show the kindness of God?" Ziba said to the king, "There remains a son of Jonathan; he is crippled in his feet." 4 The king said to him, "Where is he?" Ziba said to the king, "He is in the house of Machir son of Ammiel, at Lo-debar." 5 Then King David sent and brought him from the house of Machir son of Ammiel, at Lo-debar. 6 Mephibosheth *n* son of Jonathan son of Saul came to David, and fell on his face and did obeisance. David said, "Mephibosheth!" *n* He answered, "I am your servant." 7 David said to him, "Do not be afraid, for I will

the Moabites and made them lie along the ground, where he measured them off with a length of cord; for every two lengths that were to be put to death one full length was spared. The Moabites became subject to him and paid tribute.

3 David also defeated Hadadezer the Rehobite, king of Zobah, who was on his way to restore his monument of victory by the river Euphrates. 4 From him David captured seventeen hundred horse and twenty thousand foot-soldiers; he hamstrung all the chariot-horses, except a hundred which he retained. 5 When the Aramaeans of Damascus came to the aid of King Hadadezer of Zobah, David destroyed twenty-two thousand of them, 6 and stationed garrisons among these Aramaeans; they became subject to him and paid tribute. Thus the LORD gave David victory wherever he went. 7 David took the gold shields borne by Hadadezer's attendants and brought them to Jerusalem; 8 he also removed from Hadadezer's cities, Betah and Berothai, a great quantity of bronze.

9 When King Toi of Hamath heard that David had defeated Hadadezer's entire army, 10 he sent his son Joram to King David to greet him and to congratulate him on his victory over Hadadezer, for Hadadezer had been at war with Toi; Joram brought with him vessels of silver, gold, and bronze. 11 These King David dedicated to the LORD, along with the silver and gold taken from all the nations he had subdued, 12 from Edom and Moab, from the Ammonites, the Philistines, and Amalek, as well as part of the spoil taken from Hadadezer the Rehobite, king of Zobah.

13 David made a great name for himself by the slaughter of eighteen thousand Edomites in the Valley of Salt. 14 He stationed garrisons throughout Edom, and all the Edomites became subject to him. The LORD gave David victory wherever he went.

15 David ruled over the whole of Israel and maintained law and justice among all his people. 16 Joab son of Zeruiah was in command of the army; Jehoshaphat son of Ahilud was secretary of state; 17 Zadok and Abiathar son of Ahimelech, son of Ahitub, were priests; Seraiah was adjutant-general; 18 Benaiah son of Jehoiada commanded the Kerethite and Pelethite guards. David's sons were priests.

9 David enquired, 'Is any member of Saul's family left, to whom I can show kindness for Jonathan's sake?' 2 A servant of Saul's family named Ziba was summoned to David, who asked, 'Are you Ziba?' He answered, 'Your servant, sir.' 3 The king asked, 'Is there any member of Saul's family still alive to whom I may show the kindness that God requires?' 'Yes,' said Ziba, 'there is still a son of Jonathan alive; he is a cripple, lame in both feet.' 4 'Where is he?' said the king, and Ziba answered, 'He is staying with Machir son of Ammiel in Lo-debar.' 5 The king had him fetched from Lodebar, from the house of Machir son of Ammiel, 6 and when Mephibosheth, son of Jonathan and grandson of Saul, entered David's presence, he prostrated himself and did obeisance. David said to him, 'Mephibosheth!' and he answered, 'Your servant, sir.' 7 Then David said, 'Do not be afraid; I mean to show you

8:3 **restore . . . victory by:** *or* recover control of the crossings of. 8:7 **shields:** *or* quivers. 8:8,10 **bronze:** *or* copper. 8:12 **Edom:** *so some MSS; others* Aram. 8:13 **Edomites:** *so some MSS; others* Aramaeans. 8:15–18 *Cp.* 20:23–26; *1 Kgs.* 4:2–6; *1 Chr.* 18:14–17. 8:17 **and Abiathar . . . Ahitub:** *prob. rdg, cp. 1 Sam.* 22:11,20; *2 Sam.* 20:25; *Heb.* son of Ahitub and Ahimelech son of Abiathar. 8:18 **commanded:** *so Lat., cp. 2 Sam.* 20:23; *1 Chr.* 18:17; *Heb.* and.

j Heb *one full length*   *k* Compare 1 Sam 15.12 and 2 Sam 18.18
l Gk: Heb *returned from striking down eighteen thousand Arameans*
m Syr Tg Vg 20.23; 1 Chr 18.17: Heb lacks *was over*
n Or *Merib-baal*: See 4.4 note

feated Moab and then measured them with a line, making them lie down on the ground. He told off two lengths of line for execution, and a full length to be spared. Thus the Moabites became tributary to David. 3 Next David defeated Hadadezer, son of Rehob, king of Zobah, when he went to reestablish his dominion at the Euphrates River. 4 David captured from him one thousand seven hundred horsemen and twenty thousand foot soldiers. And he hamstrung all the chariot horses, preserving only enough for a hundred chariots. 5 When the Arameans of Damascus came to the aid of Hadadezer, king of Zobah, David slew twenty-two thousand of them. 6 David then placed garrisons in Aram of Damascus, and the Arameans became subjects, tributary to David. The LORD brought David victory in all his undertakings. 7 David also took away the golden shields used by Hadadezer's servants and brought them to Jerusalem. [These Shishak, king of Egypt, took away when he came to Jerusalem in the days of Rehoboam, son of Solomon.] 8 From Tebah and Berothai, towns of Hadadezer, King David removed a very large quantity of bronze. 9 When Toi, king of Hamath, heard that David had defeated all the forces of Hadadezer, 10 he sent his son Hadoram to King David to greet him and to congratulate him for his victory over Hadadezer in battle, because Toi had been in many battles with Hadadezer. Hadoram also brought with him articles of silver, gold, and bronze. 11 These, too, King David consecrated to the LORD, together with the silver and gold he had taken from every nation he had conquered: 12 from Edom and Moab, from the Ammonites, from the Philistines, from the Amalekites, and from the plunder of Hadadezer, son of Rehob, king of Zobah.

13 On his return, David became famous for having slain eighteen thousand Edomites in the Salt Valley; 14 after which he placed garrisons in Edom. Thus all the Edomites became David's subjects, and the LORD brought David victory in all his undertakings.

15 David reigned over all Israel, judging and administering justice to all his people. 16 Joab, son of Zeruiah, was in command of the army. Jehoshaphat, son of Ahilud, was chancellor. 17 Zadok, son of Ahitub, and Ahimelech, son of Abiathar, were priests. Shawsha was scribe. 18 Benaiah, son of Jehoiada, was in command of the Cherethites and Pelethites. And David's sons were priests.

9 David asked, "Is there any survivor of Saul's house to whom I may show kindness for the sake of Jonathan?" 2 Now there was a servant of the family of Saul named Ziba. He was summoned to David, and the king asked him, "Are you Ziba?" He replied, "Your servant." 3 Then the king inquired, "Is there any survivor of Saul's house to whom I may show God's kindness?" Ziba answered the king, "There is still Jonathan's son, whose feet are crippled." 4 The king said to him, "Where is he?" and Ziba answered, "He is in the house of Machir, son of Ammiel, in Lodebar." 5 So King David sent for him and had him brought from the house of Machir, son of Ammiel, in Lodebar. 6 When Meribbaal, son of Jonathan, son of Saul, came to David, he fell prostrate in homage. David said, "Meribbaal," and he answered, "Your servant." 7 "Fear not," David said to him, "I

2 He also defeated the Moabites and, making them lie on the ground, measured them off by the line; he measured out two lines to be put to death and one full line to have their lives spared. The Moabites became David's subjects and paid him tribute.

3 David defeated Hadadezer son of Rehob, king of Zobah, when the latter mounted an expedition to extend his power over the River. 4 David captured one thousand seven hundred charioteers and twenty thousand foot soldiers from him; David hamstrung all the chariot teams, keeping only a hundred of them. 5 The Aramaeans of Damascus came to the help of Hadadezer king of Zobah, but David killed twenty-two thousand of the Aramaeans. 6 David then imposed governors on Aram of Damascus, and the Aramaeans became David's subjects and paid him tribute. Wherever David went, Yahweh gave him victory. 7 David took the golden shields carried by Hadadezer's guards and brought them to Jerusalem. 8 From Betah and Berothai, towns belonging to Hadadezer, King David captured a great quantity of bronze.

9 When Tou king of Hamath heard that David had defeated Hadadezer's entire army, 10 he sent his son Hadoram to King David to greet him and to congratulate him on having made war on Hadadezer and on having defeated him, since Hadadezer was at war with Tou. Hadoram brought with him objects made of silver, gold and bronze, 11 which King David also consecrated to Yahweh, as he had already consecrated the silver and gold taken from all the nations which he had subjugated — 12 from Aram, Moab, the Ammonites, the Philistines and Amalek; and from the spoil of Hadadezer son of Rehob, king of Zobah.

13 David became famous when he came home from defeating the Edomites in the Valley of Salt — eighteen thousand of them. 14 He imposed governors on Edom and all the Edomites became David's subjects. Wherever David went, Yahweh gave him victory.

15 David ruled over all Israel, administering law and justice to all his people. 16 e Joab son of Zeruiah was in command of the army; Jehoshaphat son of Ahilud was herald; 17 Zadok and Abiathar son of Ahimelech, son of Ahitub, were priests; Seraiah was secretary; 18 Benaiah son of Jehoiada was in command of the Cherethites and Pelethites; David's sons were priests.

9 David asked, 'Is there anyone belonging to Saul's family left, to whom I might show faithful love for Jonathan's sake?' 2 Now Saul's family had a servant whose name was Ziba. When he had been summoned to David, the king said, 'Are you Ziba?' 'At your service,' he replied. 3 The king said, 'Is there no one left, belonging to Saul's family, for me to treat with God's own faithful love?' Ziba said to the king, 'There is still one of Jonathan's sons. He has crippled feet.' 4 The king asked 'Where is he?' Ziba replied, 'He is living in the household of Machir son of Ammiel, at Lo-Debar.' 5 So King David sent for him to be fetched from the house of Machir son of Ammiel at Lo-Debar.

6 On entering David's presence, Meribbaal son of Jonathan, son of Saul, fell on his face and prostrated himself. David said, 'Meribbaal!' He replied, 'Here I am, at your service.' 7 David then said, 'Do not be afraid; I will indeed

show you kindness for the sake of your father Jonathan; I will restore to you all the land of your grandfather Saul, and you yourself shall eat at my table always." 8He did obeisance and said, "What is your servant, that you should look upon a dead dog such as I?"

9 Then the king summoned Saul's servant Ziba, and said to him, "All that belonged to Saul and to all his house I have given to your master's grandson. 10You and your sons and your servants shall till the land for him, and shall bring in the produce, so that your master's grandson may have food to eat; but your master's grandson Mephibosheth*o* shall always eat at my table." Now Ziba had fifteen sons and twenty servants. 11Then Ziba said to the king, "According to all that my lord the king commands his servant, so your servant will do." Mephibosheth*o* ate at David's*p* table, like one of the king's sons. 12Mephibosheth*o* had a young son whose name was Mica. And all who lived in Ziba's house became Mephibosheth's*q* servants. 13Mephibosheth*o* lived in Jerusalem, for he always ate at the king's table. Now he was lame in both his feet.

10 Some time afterward, the king of the Ammonites died, and his son Hanun succeeded him. 2David said, "I will deal loyally with Hanun son of Nahash, just as his father dealt loyally with me." So David sent envoys to console him concerning his father. When David's envoys came into the land of the Ammonites, 3the princes of the Ammonites said to their lord Hanun, "Do you really think that David is honoring your father just because he has sent messengers with condolences to you? Has not David sent his envoys to you to search the city, to spy it out, and to overthrow it?" 4So Hanun seized David's envoys, shaved off half the beard of each, cut off their garments in the middle at their hips, and sent them away. 5When David was told, he sent to meet them, for the men were greatly ashamed. The king said, "Remain at Jericho until your beards have grown, and then return."

6 When the Ammonites saw that they had become odious to David, the Ammonites sent and hired the Arameans of Beth-rehob and the Arameans of Zobah, twenty thousand foot soldiers, as well as the king of Maacah, one thousand men, and the men of Tob, twelve thousand men. 7When David heard of it, he sent Joab and all the army with the warriors. 8The Ammonites came out and drew up in battle array at the entrance of the gate; but the Arameans of Zobah and of Rehob, and the men of Tob and Maacah, were by themselves in the open country.

9 When Joab saw that the battle was set against him both in front and in the rear, he chose some of the picked men of Israel, and arrayed them against the Arameans; 10the rest of his men he put in the charge of his brother Abishai, and he arrayed them against the Ammonites. 11He said, "If the Arameans are too strong for me, then you shall help me; but if the Ammonites are too strong for you, then I will come and help you. 12Be strong, and let us be courageous for the sake of our people, and for the cities of our God; and may the LORD do what seems good to him." 13So Joab and the people who were with him moved forward into battle against the Arameans; and they fled before him. 14When the Ammonites saw that the Arameans fled, they likewise fled before Abishai, and entered the city. Then Joab returned from fighting against the Ammonites, and came to Jerusalem.

15 But when the Arameans saw that they had been defeated by Israel, they gathered themselves together. 16Hadadezer sent and brought out the Arameans who were beyond the Euphrates; and they came to Helam, with Shobach the commander of the army of Hadadezer at their head. 17When

kindness for your father Jonathan's sake; I shall restore to you the whole estate of your grandfather Saul and you will have a regular place at my table.' 8Mephibosheth prostrated himself again and said, 'Who am I that you should spare a thought for a dead dog like me?'

9David summoned Saul's servant Ziba and said, 'I assign to your master's grandson all the property that belonged to Saul and his family. 10You and your sons and your slaves must cultivate the land and bring in the harvest to provide for your master's household, but Mephibosheth your master's grandson shall have a regular place at my table.' Ziba, who had fifteen sons and twenty slaves, 11answered: 'I shall do all that your majesty commands.' So Mephibosheth took his place in the royal household like one of the king's sons. 12He had a young son, named Mica; and the members of Ziba's household were all Mephibosheth's servants, 13while Mephibosheth lived in Jerusalem and had his regular place at the king's table, crippled as he was in both feet.

10 SOME time afterwards the king of the Ammonites died and was succeeded by his son Hanun. 2David said, 'I must keep up the same loyal friendship with Hanun son of Nahash as his father showed me,' and he sent a mission to condole with him on the death of his father.

When David's envoys entered the country of the Ammonites, 3the Ammonite princes said to Hanun their lord, 'Do you suppose David means to do honour to your father when he sends envoys to condole with you? These men of his are spies whom he has sent to find out how to overthrow the city.' 4So Hanun took David's servants, shaved off half their beards and cut off half their garments up to the buttocks, and then dismissed them. 5Hearing how they had been treated, David ordered them to be met, for they were deeply humiliated; he told them to wait in Jericho and not return until their beards had grown again.

6The Ammonites, realizing they had given offence to David, hired the Aramaeans of Beth-rehob and of Zobah to come to their help with twenty thousand infantry; they hired also the king of Maacah with a thousand men, and twelve thousand men from Tob. 7When this was reported to David, he sent Joab out with all the fighting men. 8The Ammonites came on and took up their position at the entrance to the city gate, while the Aramaeans of Zobah and of Rehob and the men of Tob and Maacah took up theirs in the open country. 9When Joab saw that he was threatened from both front and rear, he detailed some picked Israelite troops and drew them up facing the Aramaeans. 10The rest of his forces he put under his brother Abishai, who took up a position facing the Ammonites. 11'If the Aramaeans prove too strong for me,' he said, 'you must come to my relief; and if the Ammonites prove too strong for you, I shall come to yours. 12Courage! Let us fight bravely for our people and for the cities of our God. And may the LORD's will be done.'

13Joab and his men engaged the Aramaeans closely and put them to flight; 14and when the Ammonites saw them in flight, they too fled before Abishai and withdrew into the city. Then Joab returned from the battle against the Ammonites and came to Jerusalem.

15The Aramaeans, reviewing their defeat by Israel, rallied their forces, 16and Hadadezer sent to summon other Aramaeans from the Great Bend of the Euphrates, and they advanced to Helam under Shobach, commander of Hadade-

---

o Or *Merib-baal*: See 4.4 note   *p* Gk: Heb *my*
q Or *Merib-baal's*: See 4.4 note

9:7 **grandfather:** *lit.* father.   9:9,10 **grandson:** *lit.* son.
9:10 **household:** *so some Gk MSS; Heb.* son.   9:11 **the royal:** *so Gk (Luc.); Heb.* my.   10:1–19 *Cp. 1 Chr.* 19:1–19.

will surely be kind to you for the sake of your father Jonathan. I will restore to you all the lands of your grandfather Saul, and you shall always eat at my table." 8 Bowing low, he answered, "What is your servant that you should pay attention to a dead dog like me?" 9 The king then called Ziba, Saul's attendant, and said to him: "I am giving your lord's son all that belonged to Saul and to all his family. 10 You and your sons and servants must till the land for him. You shall bring in the produce, which shall be food for your lord's family to eat. But Meribbaal, your lord's son, shall always eat at my table." Ziba, who had fifteen sons and twenty servants, 11 said to the king, "Your servant shall do just as my lord the king has commanded him." And so Meribbaal ate at David's table like one of the king's sons. 12 Meribbaal had a young son whose name was Mica; and all the tenants of Ziba's family worked for Meribbaal. 13 But Meribbaal lived in Jerusalem, because he always ate at the king's table. He was lame in both feet.

10 Some time later the king of the Ammonites died, and his son Hanun succeeded him as king. 2 David thought, "I will be kind to Hanun, son of Nahash, as his father was kind to me." So David sent his servants with condolences to Hanun for the loss of his father. But when David's servants entered the country of the Ammonites, 3 the Ammonite princes said to their lord Hanun: "Do you think that David is honoring your father by sending men with condolences? Is it not rather to explore the city, to spy on it, and to overthrow it, that David has sent his messengers to you?" 4 Hanun, therefore, seized David's servants and, after shaving off half their beards and cutting away the lower halves of their garments at the buttocks, sent them away. 5 When he was told of it, King David sent out word to them, since the men were quite ashamed. "Stay in Jericho until your beards grow," he said, "and then come back."

6 In view of the offense they had given to David, the Ammonites sent for and hired twenty thousand Aramean foot soldiers from Beth-rehob and Zobah, as well as the king of Maacah with one thousand men, and twelve thousand men from Tob. 7 On learning this, David sent out Joab with the entire levy of trained soldiers. 8 The Ammonites came out and drew up in battle formation at the entrance of their city gate, while the Arameans of Zobah and Rehob and the men of Tob and Maacah remained apart in the open country. 9 When Joab saw the battle lines drawn up against him, both front and rear, he made a selection from all the picked troops of Israel and arrayed them against the Arameans. 10 He placed the rest of the soldiers under the command of his brother Abishai, who arrayed them against the Ammonites. 11 Joab said, "If the Arameans are stronger than I, you shall help me. But if the Ammonites are stronger than you, I will come to help you. 12 Be brave; let us prove our valor for the sake of our people and the cities of our God; the LORD will do what he judges best." 13 When Joab and the soldiers who were with him approached the Arameans for battle, they fled before him. 14 The Ammonites, seeing that the Arameans had fled, also fled from Abishai and withdrew into the city. Joab then ceased his attack on the Ammonites and returned to Jerusalem.

15 Then the Arameans responded to their defeat by Israel with a full mustering of troops; 16 Hadadezer sent for and enlisted Arameans from beyond the Euphrates. They came to Helam, with Shobach, general of Hadadezer's army, at

treat you with faithful love for your father Jonathan's sake. I shall restore all your grandfather Saul's estates to you, and you will always eat at my table.' 8 Meribbaal prostrated himself and said, 'Who is your servant, for you to show favour to a dead dog like me?'

9 The king then summoned Saul's servant Ziba and said, 'Everything belonging to Saul and his family, I give to your master's son. 10 You must work the land for him, you and your sons and your slaves; you must harvest the produce to provide food for your mas ter's family to eat. But Meribbaal, your master's son, will always take his own meals at my table.' Now, Ziba had fifteen sons and twenty slaves. 11 Ziba said to the king, 'Your servant will do everything my lord the king has ordered his servant.'

So Meribbaal ate at David's table like one of the king's sons. 12 Meribbaal had a young son whose name was Micha. All the people living in Ziba's household entered Meribbaal's service. 13 Meribbaal lived in Jerusalem, since he always ate at the king's table. He was crippled in both feet.

10 After this, when the king of the Ammonites died and his son Hanun succeeded him, 2 David thought, 'I shall show Hanun son of Nahash the same faithful love as his father showed me.' And David sent his representatives to offer him condolences over his father. But, when David's representatives reached the Ammonites' country, 3 the Ammonite princes said to Hanun their master, 'Do you really think David means to honour your father when he sends you messengers with sympathy? On the contrary, the reason why David has sent his representatives to you is to explore the city, to reconnoitre and so overthrow it.' 4 Whereupon Hanun seized David's representatives, shaved off half their beards, cut their clothes off halfway up, at their buttocks, and sent them away. 5 When David was told, he sent someone to meet them, since the men were overcome with shame. 'Stay in Jericho', the king said, 'until your beards have grown again, and come back then.'

6 When the Ammonites realised that they had antagonised David, they sent agents to hire twenty thousand foot soldiers from the Aramaeans of Beth-Rehob and the Aramaeans of Zobah, one thousand men from the king of Maacah and twelve thousand men from the prince of Tob. 7 When David heard this, he sent Joab with the whole army, the champions. 8 The Ammonites marched out and drew up their line of battle at the city gate, while the Aramaeans of Zobah and of Rehob and the men of Tob and Maacah kept their distance in the open country. 9 Joab, seeing that he had to fight on two fronts, to his front and to his rear, chose the best of Israel's picked men and drew them up in line facing the Aramaeans. 10 He entrusted the rest of the army to his brother Abishai, and drew them up in line facing the Ammonites. 11 'If the Aramaeans prove too strong for me,' he said, 'you must come to my help; if the Ammonites prove too strong for you, I shall come to yours. 12 Be brave! Let us acquit ourselves like men for the sake of our people and for the cities of our God. And let Yahweh do as he thinks right!' 13 Joab and the force with him joined battle with the Aramaeans, who fled at his onslaught. 14 When the Ammonites saw that the Aramaeans had fled, they too fled from Abishai and withdrew into the city. Hence, Joab broke off his campaign against the Ammonites and returned to Jerusalem.

15 The Aramaeans, realising that Israel had got the better of them, concentrated their forces. 16 Hadadezer sent messengers and mobilised the Aramaeans living on the other side of the river; and these arrived at Helam, with Shobach the commander of Hadadezer's army, at their head. 17 Da-

NEW REVISED STANDARD VERSION | REVISED ENGLISH BIBLE

it was told David, he gathered all Israel together, and crossed the Jordan, and came to Helam. The Arameans arrayed themselves against David and fought with him. [18] The Arameans fled before Israel; and David killed of the Arameans seven hundred chariot teams, and forty thousand horsemen,[r] and wounded Shobach the commander of their army, so that he died there. [19] When all the kings who were servants of Hadadezer saw that they had been defeated by Israel, they made peace with Israel, and became subject to them. So the Arameans were afraid to help the Ammonites any more.

11 In the spring of the year, the time when kings go out to battle, David sent Joab with his officers and all Israel with him; they ravaged the Ammonites, and besieged Rabbah. But David remained at Jerusalem.

2 It happened, late one afternoon, when David rose from his couch and was walking about on the roof of the king's house, that he saw from the roof a woman bathing; the woman was very beautiful. [3] David sent someone to inquire about the woman. It was reported, "This is Bathsheba daughter of Eliam, the wife of Uriah the Hittite." [4] So David sent messengers to get her, and she came to him, and he lay with her. (Now she was purifying herself after her period.) Then she returned to her house. [5] The woman conceived; and she sent and told David, "I am pregnant."

6 So David sent word to Joab, "Send me Uriah the Hittite." And Joab sent Uriah to David. [7] When Uriah came to him, David asked how Joab and the people fared, and how the war was going. [8] Then David said to Uriah, "Go down to your house, and wash your feet." Uriah went out of the king's house, and there followed him a present from the king. [9] But Uriah slept at the entrance of the king's house with all the servants of his lord, and did not go down to his house. [10] When they told David, "Uriah did not go down to his house," David said to Uriah, "You have just come from a journey. Why did you not go down to your house?" [11] Uriah said to David, "The ark and Israel and Judah remain in booths;[s] and my lord Joab and the servants of my lord are camping in the open field; shall I then go to my house, to eat and to drink, and to lie with my wife? As you live, and as your soul lives, I will not do such a thing." [12] Then David said to Uriah, "Remain here today also, and tomorrow I will send you back." So Uriah remained in Jerusalem that day. On the next day, [13] David invited him to eat and drink in his presence and made him drunk; and in the evening he went out to lie on his couch with the servants of his lord, but he did not go down to his house.

14 In the morning David wrote a letter to Joab, and sent it by the hand of Uriah. [15] In the letter he wrote, "Set Uriah in the forefront of the hardest fighting, then draw back from him, so that he may be struck down and die." [16] As Joab was besieging the city, he assigned Uriah to the place where he knew there were valiant warriors. [17] The men of the city came out and fought with Joab; and some of the servants of David among the people fell. Uriah the Hittite was killed as well. [18] Then Joab sent and told David all the news about the fighting; [19] and he instructed the messenger, "When you have finished telling the king all the news about the fighting, [20] then, if the king's anger rises, and if he says to you, 'Why did you go so near the city to fight? Did you not know that they would shoot from the wall? [21] Who killed Abimelech son of Jerubbaal?[t] Did not a woman throw an upper millstone on him from the wall, so that he died at Thebez? Why did you go so near the wall?' then you shall say, 'Your servant Uriah the Hittite is dead too.' "

zer's army. [17] Their movement was reported to David, who immediately mustered all the forces of Israel, crossed the Jordan, and advanced to Helam. The Aramaeans took up positions facing David and engaged him, [18] but were put to flight by Israel. David slew seven hundred Aramaeans in chariots and forty thousand horsemen, mortally wounding Shobach, who died on the field. [19] When all the vassal kings of Hadadezer saw that they had been worsted by Israel, they sued for peace and submitted to the Israelites. The Aramaeans never dared to help the Ammonites again.

11 At the turn of the year, when kings go out to battle, David sent Joab out with his other officers and all the Israelite forces, and they ravaged Ammon and laid siege to Rabbah.

David remained in Jerusalem, 2 and one evening, as he got up from his couch and walked about on the roof of the palace, he saw from there a woman bathing, and she was very beautiful. [3] He made enquiries about the woman and was told, 'It must be Bathsheba daughter of Eliam and wife of Uriah the Hittite.' [4] He sent messengers to fetch her, and when she came to him, he had intercourse with her, though she was still purifying herself after her period, and then she went home. [5] She conceived, and sent word to David that she was pregnant.

6 David ordered Joab to send Uriah the Hittite to him. Joab did so, 7 and when Uriah arrived, David asked him for news of Joab and the troops and how the campaign was going, 8 and then said to him, 'Go down to your house and wash your feet after your journey.' As he left the palace, a present from the king followed him. 9 Uriah, however, did not return to his house; he lay down by the palace gate with all the king's servants. [10] David, learning that Uriah had not gone home, said to him, 'You have had a long journey; why did you not go home?' [11] Uriah answered, 'Israel and Judah are under canvas, and so is the Ark, and my lord Joab and your majesty's officers are camping in the open; how can I go home to eat and drink and to sleep with my wife? By your life, I cannot do this!' [12] David then said to Uriah, 'Stay here another day, and tomorrow I shall let you go.' So Uriah stayed in Jerusalem that day. [13] On the following day David invited him to eat and drink with him and made him drunk. But in the evening Uriah went out to lie down in his blanket among the king's servants and did not go home.

14 In the morning David wrote a letter to Joab and sent it with Uriah. [15] In it he wrote, 'Put Uriah opposite the enemy where the fighting is fiercest and then fall back, and leave him to meet his death.' [16] So Joab, during the siege of the city, stationed Uriah at a point where he knew the enemy had expert troops. [17] The men of the city sallied out and engaged Joab, and some of David's guards fell; Uriah the Hittite was also killed. [18] Joab sent David a dispatch with all the news of the battle [19] and gave the messenger these instructions: 'When you have finished your report to the king, [20] he may be angry and ask, "Why did you go so near the city during the fight? You must have known there would be shooting from the wall. [21] Remember who killed Abimelech son of Jerubbesheth. Was it not a woman who threw down an upper millstone on him from the wall of Thebez and killed him? Why did you go near the wall?" — if he asks this, then tell him, "Your servant Uriah the Hittite also is dead." '

---

[r] 1 Chr 19.18 and some Gk Mss read *foot soldiers* [s] Or *at Succoth*
[t] Gk Syr Judg 7.1: Heb *Jerubbesheth*

11:1 **when . . . battle:** *so some MSS, cp. 1 Chr. 20:1; others* when messengers set out.   11:11 **under canvas:** *or* at Succoth.
11:13 **in his blanket:** *or* on his pallet.

NEW AMERICAN BIBLE	NEW JERUSALEM BIBLE

their head. 17 On receiving this news, David assembled all Israel, crossed the Jordan, and went to Helam. The Arameans drew up in formation against David and fought with him. 18 But the Arameans gave way before Israel, and David's men killed seven hundred charioteers and forty thousand of the Aramean foot soldiers. Shobach, general of the army, was struck down and died on the field. 19 All of Hadadezer's vassal kings, in view of their defeat by Israel, then made peace with the Israelites and became their subjects. And the Arameans were afraid to give further aid to the Ammonites.

11 At the turn of the year, when kings go out on campaign, David sent out Joab along with his officers and the army of Israel, and they ravaged the Ammonites and besieged Rabbah. David, however, remained in Jerusalem. 2 One evening David rose from his siesta and strolled about on the roof of the palace. From the roof he saw a woman bathing, who was very beautiful. 3 David had inquiries made about the woman and was told, "She is Bathsheba, daughter of Eliam, and wife of [Joab's armor-bearer] Uriah the Hittite." 4 Then David sent messengers and took her. When she came to him, he had relations with her, at a time when she was just purified after her monthly period. She then returned to her house. 5 But the woman had conceived, and sent the information to David, "I am with child."

6 David therefore sent a message to Joab, "Send me Uriah the Hittite." So Joab sent Uriah to David. 7 When he came, David questioned him about Joab, the soldiers, and how the war was going, and Uriah answered that all was well. 8 David then said to Uriah, "Go down to your house and bathe your feet." Uriah left the palace, and a portion was sent out after him from the king's table. 9 But Uriah slept at the entrance of the royal palace with the other officers of his lord, and did not go down to his own house. 10 David was told that Uriah had not gone home. So he said to Uriah, "Have you not come from a journey? Why, then, did you not go down to your house?" 11 Uriah answered David, "The ark and Israel and Judah are lodged in tents, and my lord Joab and my majesty's servants are encamped in the open field. Can I go home to eat and to drink and to sleep with my wife? As the LORD lives and as you live, I will do no such thing." 12 Then David said to Uriah, "Stay here today also, I shall dismiss you tomorrow." So Uriah remained in Jerusalem that day. On the day following, 13 David summoned him, and he ate and drank with David, who made him drunk. But in the evening he went out to sleep on his bed among his lord's servants, and did not go down to his home. 14 The next morning David wrote a letter to Joab which he sent by Uriah. 15 In it he directed: "Place Uriah up front, where the fighting is fierce. Then pull back and leave him to be struck down dead." 16 So while Joab was besieging the city, he assigned Uriah to a place where he knew the defenders were strong. 17 When the men of the city made a sortie against Joab, some officers of David's army fell, and among them Uriah the Hittite died.

18 Then Joab sent David a report of all the details of the battle, 19 instructing the messenger, "When you have finished giving the king all the details of the battle, 20 the king may become angry and say to you: 'Why did you go near the city to fight? Did you not know that they would shoot from the wall above? 21 Who killed Abimelech, son of Jerubbaal? Was it not a woman who threw a millstone down on him from the wall above, so that he died in Thebez? Why did you go near the wall?' Then you in turn shall say, 'Your servant Uriah the Hittite is also dead.' " 22 The messenger

vid, being informed of this, mustered all Israel, crossed the Jordan and arrived at Helam. The Aramaeans drew up in line facing David and engaged him. 18 But the Aramaeans fled from Israel, and David killed seven hundred of their chariot teams and forty thousand men; he also cut down Shobach the commander of their army, who died there. 19 When all Hadadezer's vassal kings saw that Israel had got the better of them, they made peace with the Israelites and became their subjects. The Aramaeans were afraid to give any more help to the Ammonites.

11 At the turn of the year, at the time when kings go campaigning, David sent Joab and with him his guards and all Israel. They massacred the Ammonites and laid siege to Rabbah-of-the-Ammonites. David, however, remained in Jerusalem.

2 It happened towards evening when David had got up from resting and was strolling on the palace roof, that from the roof he saw a woman bathing; the woman was very beautiful. 3 David made enquiries about this woman and was told, 'Why, that is Bathsheba daughter of Eliam and wife of Uriah the Hittite.' 4 David then sent messengers to fetch her. She came to him, and he lay with her, just after she had purified herself from her period. She then went home again. 5 The woman conceived and sent word to David, 'I am pregnant.'

6 David then sent word to Joab, 'Send me Uriah the Hittite,' whereupon Joab sent Uriah to David. 7 When Uriah reached him, David asked how Joab was and how the army was and how the war was going. 8 David then said to Uriah, 'Go down to your house and wash your feet.' Uriah left the palace and was followed by a present from the king's table. 9 Uriah, however, slept at the palace gate with all his master's bodyguard and did not go down to his house.

10 This was reported to David; 'Uriah', they said 'has not gone down to his house.' So David asked Uriah, 'Haven't you just arrived from the journey? Why didn't you go down to your house?' 11 To which Uriah replied, 'The ark, Israel and Judah are lodged in huts; my master Joab and my lord's guards are camping in the open. Am I to go to my house, then, and eat and drink and sleep with my wife? As Yahweh lives, and as you yourself live, I shall do no such thing!' 12 David then said to Uriah, 'Stay on here today; tomorrow I shall send you off.' So Uriah stayed that day in Jerusalem. 13 The next day, David invited him to eat and drink in his presence and made him drunk. In the evening, Uriah went out and bedded down with his master's bodyguard, but did not go down to his house.

14 Next morning David wrote a letter to Joab and sent it by Uriah. 15 In the letter he wrote, 'Put Uriah out in front where the fighting is fiercest and then fall back, so that he gets wounded and killed.' 16 Joab, then besieging the city, stationed Uriah at a point where he knew that there would be tough fighters. 17 The people of the city sallied out and engaged Joab; there were casualties in the army, among David's guards, and Uriah the Hittite was killed as well.

18 Joab sent David a full account of the battle. 19 To the messenger he gave this order: 'When you have finished telling the king all about the battle, 20 if the king's anger is aroused and he says, "Why did you go near the town to give battle? Didn't you know that they would shoot from the ramparts? 21 Who killed Abimelech son of Jerubbaal? Wasn't it a woman who dropped a millstone on him from the ramparts, causing his death at Thebez? Why did you go near the ramparts?" you are to say, "Your servant Uriah the Hittite is dead too." '

22 So the messenger went, and came and told David all that Joab had sent him to tell. 23 The messenger said to David, "The men gained an advantage over us, and came out against us in the field; but we drove them back to the entrance of the gate. 24 Then the archers shot at your servants from the wall; some of the king's servants are dead; and your servant Uriah the Hittite is dead also." 25 David said to the messenger, "Thus you shall say to Joab, 'Do not let this matter trouble you, for the sword devours now one and now another; press your attack on the city, and overthrow it.' And encourage him."

26 When the wife of Uriah heard that her husband was dead, she made lamentation for him. 27 When the mourning was over, David sent and brought her to his house, and she became his wife, and bore him a son.

But the thing that David had done displeased the LORD.

12 ¹ and the LORD sent Nathan to David. He came to him, and said to him, "There were two men in a certain city, the one rich and the other poor. ² The rich man had very many flocks and herds; ³ but the poor man had nothing but one little ewe lamb, which he had bought. He brought it up, and it grew up with him and with his children; it used to eat of his meager fare, and drink from his cup, and lie in his bosom, and it was like a daughter to him. ⁴ Now there came a traveler to the rich man, and he was loath to take one of his own flock or herd to prepare for the wayfarer who had come to him, but he took the poor man's lamb, and prepared that for the guest who had come to him." ⁵ Then David's anger was greatly kindled against the man. He said to Nathan, "As the LORD lives, the man who has done this deserves to die; ⁶ he shall restore the lamb fourfold, because he did this thing, and because he had no pity."

7 Nathan said to David, "You are the man! Thus says the LORD, the God of Israel: I anointed you king over Israel, and I rescued you from the hand of Saul; ⁸ I gave you your master's house, and your master's wives into your bosom, and gave you the house of Israel and of Judah; and if that had been too little, I would have added as much more. ⁹ Why have you despised the word of the LORD, to do what is evil in his sight? You have struck down Uriah the Hittite with the sword, and have taken his wife to be your wife, and have killed him with the sword of the Ammonites. ¹⁰ Now therefore the sword shall never depart from your house, for you have despised me, and have taken the wife of Uriah the Hittite to be your wife. ¹¹ Thus says the LORD: I will raise up trouble against you from within your own house; and I will take your wives before your eyes, and give them to your neighbor, and he shall lie with your wives in the sight of this very sun. ¹² For you did it secretly; but I will do this thing before all Israel, and before the sun." ¹³ David said to Nathan, "I have sinned against the LORD." Nathan said to David, "Now the LORD has put away your sin; you shall not die. ¹⁴ Nevertheless, because by this deed you have utterly scorned the LORD, ᵘ the child that is born to you shall die."

22 The messenger set out and, when he came to David, he made his report as Joab had instructed him. David, angry with Joab, said to the messenger, 'Why did you go so near the city during the fight? You must have known you would be struck down from the wall. Remember who killed Abimelech son of Jerubbesheth. Was it not a woman who threw down an upper millstone on him from the wall of Thebez and killed him? Why did you go near the wall?' 23 He answered, 'The enemy massed against us and sallied out into the open; we drove them back as far as the gateway. 24 There the archers shot down at us from the wall and some of your majesty's men fell; and your servant Uriah the Hittite is dead.' 25 David told the messenger to say this to Joab: 'Do not let the matter distress you—there is no knowing where the sword will strike. Press home your attack on the city, take it, and raze it to the ground'; and to tell him to take heart.

26 When Uriah's wife heard that her husband was dead, she mourned for him. 27 Once the period of mourning was over, David sent for her and brought her into the palace; she became his wife and bore him a son. But what David had done was wrong in the eyes of the LORD.

12 The LORD sent Nathan the prophet to David, and when he entered the king's presence, he said, 'In a certain town there lived two men, one rich, the other poor. ² The rich man had large flocks and herds; ³ the poor man had nothing of his own except one little ewe lamb he had bought. He reared it, and it grew up in his home together with his children. It shared his food, drank from his cup, and nestled in his arms; it was like a daughter to him. ⁴ One day a traveller came to the rich man's house, and he, too mean to take something from his own flock or herd to serve to his guest, took the poor man's lamb and served that up.'

⁵ David was very angry, and burst out, 'As the LORD lives, the man who did this deserves to die! ⁶ He shall pay for the lamb four times over, because he has done this and shown no pity.'

⁷ Nathan said to David, 'You are the man! This is the word of the LORD the God of Israel to you: I anointed you king over Israel, I rescued you from the power of Saul, ⁸ I gave you your master's daughter and his wives to be your own, I gave you the daughters of Israel and Judah; and, had this not been enough, I would have added other favours as well. ⁹ Why then have you flouted the LORD's word by doing what is wrong in my eyes? You have struck down Uriah the Hittite with the sword; the man himself you murdered by the sword of the Ammonites, and you have stolen his wife. ¹⁰ Now, therefore, since you have despised me and taken the wife of Uriah the Hittite to be your own wife, your family will never again have rest from the sword. ¹¹ This is the word of the LORD: I shall bring trouble on you from within your own family. I shall take your wives and give them to another man before your eyes, and he will lie with them in broad daylight. ¹² What you did was done in secret; but I shall do this in broad daylight for all Israel to see.' ¹³ David said to Nathan, 'I have sinned against the LORD.' Nathan answered, 'The LORD has laid on another the consequences of your sin: you will not die, ¹⁴ but, since by this deed you have shown your contempt for the LORD, the child who will be born to you shall die.'

ᵘ Ancient scribal tradition: Compare 1 Sam 25.22 note: Heb *scorned the enemies of the LORD*

11:22 **David, angry . . . near the wall:** *so Gk; Heb. omits.*
12:1 **the prophet:** *so some MSS; others omit.*   12:8 **daughter:** *prob. rdg; Heb.* house. **daughters:** *so Syriac; Heb.* house.
12:14 **the LORD:** *prob. rdg; Heb.* the enemies of the LORD.

set out, and on his arrival he relayed to David all the details as Joab had instructed him. 23 He told David: "The men had us at a disadvantage and came out into the open against us, but we pushed them back to the entrance of the city gate. 24 Then the archers shot at your servants from the wall above, and some of the king's servants died, among them your servant Uriah." 25 David said to the messenger: "This is what you shall convey to Joab: 'Do not be chagrined at this, for the sword devours now here and now there. Strengthen your attack on the city and destroy it.' Encourage him."

26 When the wife of Uriah heard that her husband had died, she mourned her lord. 27 But once the mourning was over, David sent for her and brought her into his house. She became his wife and bore him a son. But the LORD was displeased with what David had done.

12 The LORD sent Nathan to David, and when he came to him, he said: "Judge this case for me! In a certain town there were two men, one rich, the other poor. 2 The rich man had flocks and herds in great numbers. 3 But the poor man had nothing at all except one little ewe lamb that he had bought. He nourished her, and she grew up with him and his children. She shared the little food he had and drank from his cup and slept in his bosom. She was like a daughter to him. 4 Now, the rich man received a visitor, but he would not take from his own flocks and herds to prepare a meal for the wayfarer who had come to him. Instead he took the poor man's ewe lamb and made a meal of it for his visitor." 5 David grew very angry with that man and said to Nathan: "As the LORD lives, the man who has done this merits death! 6 He shall restore the ewe lamb fourfold because he has done this and has had no pity."

7 Then Nathan said to David: "You are the man! Thus says the LORD God of Israel: 'I anointed you king of Israel. I rescued you from the hand of Saul. 8 I gave you your lord's house and your lord's wives for your own. I gave you the house of Israel and of Judah. And if this were not enough, I could count up for you still more. 9 Why have you spurned the LORD and done evil in his sight? You have cut down Uriah the Hittite with the sword; you took his wife as your own, and him you killed with the sword of the Ammonites. 10 Now, therefore, the sword shall never depart from your house, because you have despised me and have taken the wife of Uriah to be your wife.' 11 Thus says the LORD: 'I will bring evil upon you out of your own house. I will take your wives while you live to see it, and will give them to your neighbor. He shall lie with your wives in broad daylight. 12 You have done this deed in secret, but I will bring it about in the presence of all Israel, and with the sun looking down.' "

13 Then David said to Nathan, "I have sinned against the LORD." Nathan answered David: "The LORD on his part has forgiven your sin: you shall not die. 14 But since you have utterly spurned the LORD by this deed, the child born to you

22 So the messenger set off and, on his arrival, told David everything that Joab had instructed him to say. David flew into a rage with Joab and said to the messenger, 'Why did you go near the ramparts? Who killed Abimelech son of Jerubbaal? Wasn't it a woman who dropped a millstone on him from the ramparts, causing his death at Thebez? Why did you go near the ramparts?' 23 The messenger replied to David, 'Their men had won an initial advantage and then came out to engage us in the open. We then drove them back into the gateway, 24 but the archers shot at your retainers from the ramparts; some of the king's retainers lost their lives, and your servant Uriah the Hittite is dead too.' 25 David then said to the messenger, 'Say this to Joab, "Do not take the matter to heart; the sword devours now one and now another. Attack the town in greater force and destroy it." That will encourage him.' 26 When Uriah's wife heard that her husband Uriah was dead, she mourned for her husband. 27 When the period of mourning was over, David sent to have her brought to his house; she became his wife and bore him a son. But what David had done displeased Yahweh.

12 Yahweh sent the prophet Nathan to David. He came to him and said:

In the same town were two men,
  one rich, the other poor.
2 The rich man had flocks and herds
  in great abundance;
3 the poor man had nothing but a ewe lamb,
  only a single little one which he had bought.
He fostered it and it grew up with him and his
    children,
  eating his bread, drinking from his cup,
  sleeping in his arms; it was like a daughter to him.
4 When a traveller came to stay, the rich man
  would not take anything from his own flock or
    herd
  to provide for the wayfarer who had come to him.
  Instead, he stole the poor man's lamb
  and prepared that for his guest.

5 David flew into a great rage with the man. 'As Yahweh lives,' he said to Nathan 'the man who did this deserves to die. 6 For doing such a thing and for having shown no pity, he shall make fourfold restitution for the lamb.'

7 Nathan then said to David, 'You are the man! Yahweh, God of Israel, says this, "I anointed you king of Israel, I saved you from Saul's clutches, 8 I gave you your master's household and your master's wives into your arms, I gave you the House of Israel and the House of Judah; and, if this is still too little, I shall give you other things as well. 9 Why did you show contempt for Yahweh, by doing what displeases him? You put Uriah the Hittite to the sword, you took his wife to be your wife, causing his death by the sword of the Ammonites. 10 For this, your household will never be free of the sword, since you showed contempt for me and took the wife of Uriah the Hittite, to make her your wife."

11 'Yahweh says this, "Out of your own household I shall raise misfortune for you. Before your very eyes I shall take your wives and give them to your neighbour, who will lie with your wives in broad daylight. 12 You have worked in secret, but I shall work this for all Israel to see, in broad daylight." '

13 David said to Nathan, 'I have sinned against Yahweh.' Nathan then said to David, 'Yahweh, for his part, forgives your sin; you are not to die. 14 But, since you have outraged Yahweh by doing this, the child born to you will die.'

NEW REVISED STANDARD VERSION

15 Then Nathan went to his house.

The LORD struck the child that Uriah's wife bore to David, and it became very ill. 16 David therefore pleaded with God for the child; David fasted, and went in and lay all night on the ground. 17 The elders of his house stood beside him, urging him to rise from the ground; but he would not, nor did he eat food with them. 18 On the seventh day the child died. And the servants of David were afraid to tell him that the child was dead; for they said, "While the child was still alive, we spoke to him, and he did not listen to us; how then can we tell him the child is dead? He may do himself some harm." 19 But when David saw that his servants were whispering together, he perceived that the child was dead; and David said to his servants, "Is the child dead?" They said, "He is dead."

20 Then David rose from the ground, washed, anointed himself, and changed his clothes. He went into the house of the LORD, and worshiped; he then went to his own house; and when he asked, they set food before him and he ate. 21 Then his servants said to him, "What is this thing that you have done? You fasted and wept for the child while it was alive; but when the child died, you rose and ate food." 22 He said, "While the child was still alive, I fasted and wept; for I said, 'Who knows? The LORD may be gracious to me, and the child may live.' 23 But now he is dead; why should I fast? Can I bring him back again? I shall go to him, but he will not return to me."

24 Then David consoled his wife Bathsheba, and went to her, and lay with her; and she bore a son, and he named him Solomon. The LORD loved him, 25 and sent a message by the prophet Nathan; so he named him Jedidiah, v because of the LORD.

26 Now Joab fought against Rabbah of the Ammonites, and took the royal city. 27 Joab sent messengers to David, and said, "I have fought against Rabbah; moreover, I have taken the water city. 28 Now, then, gather the rest of the people together, and encamp against the city, and take it; or I myself will take the city, and it will be called by my name." 29 So David gathered all the people together and went to Rabbah, and fought against it and took it. 30 He took the crown of Milcom w from his head; the weight of it was a talent of gold, and in it was a precious stone; and it was placed on David's head. He also brought forth the spoil of the city, a very great amount. 31 He brought out the people who were in it, and set them to work with saws and iron picks and iron axes, or sent them to the brickworks. Thus he did to all the cities of the Ammonites. Then David and all the people returned to Jerusalem.

13 Some time passed. David's son Absalom had a beautiful sister whose name was Tamar; and David's son Amnon fell in love with her. 2 Amnon was so tormented that he made himself ill because of his sister Tamar, for she was a virgin and it seemed impossible to Amnon to do anything to her. 3 But Amnon had a friend whose name was Jonadab, the son of David's brother Shimeah; and Jonadab was a very crafty man. 4 He said to him, "O son of the king, why are you so haggard morning after morning? Will you not tell me?" Amnon said to him, "I love Tamar, my brother Absalom's sister." 5 Jonadab said to him, "Lie down on your bed, and pretend to be ill; and when your father comes to see you, say to him, 'Let my sister Tamar come and give me something to eat, and prepare the food in my sight, so that I may see it and eat it from her hand.' " 6 So Amnon lay down, and pretended to be ill;

REVISED ENGLISH BIBLE

15 After Nathan had gone home, the LORD struck the boy whom Uriah's wife had borne to David, and he became very ill. 16 David prayed to God for the child; he fasted and went in and spent the nights lying in sackcloth on the ground. 17 The older men of his household tried to get him to rise, but he refused and would eat no food with them. 18 On the seventh day the child died, and David's servants were afraid to tell him. 'While the boy was alive', they said, 'we spoke to him, and he did not listen to us; how can we now tell him that the boy is dead? He may do something desperate.' 19 David saw his servants whispering among themselves and realized that the boy was dead. He asked, 'Is the child dead?' and they answered, 'Yes, he is dead.'

20 David then rose from the ground, bathed and anointed himself, and put on fresh clothes; he entered the house of the LORD and prostrated himself there. Afterwards he returned home; he ordered food to be brought and, when it was set before him, ate it. 21 His servants asked him, 'What is this? While the boy lived you fasted and wept for him, but now that he is dead you rise and eat.' 22 'While the boy was still alive', he answered, 'I fasted and wept, thinking, "It may be that the LORD will be gracious to me, and the boy will live." 23 But now that he is dead, why should I fast? Can I bring him back again? I shall go to him; he will not come back to me.' 24 David consoled Bathsheba his wife; he went to her and had intercourse with her, and she gave birth to a son and called him Solomon. And because the LORD loved him, 25 he sent word through Nathan the prophet that for the LORD's sake he should be given the name Jedidiah.

26 Joab attacked the Ammonite city of Rabbah and took the King's Pool. 27 He sent this report to David: 'I have attacked Rabbah and have taken the pool. 28 Now muster the rest of the army, besiege the city, and take it; otherwise I myself shall take the city and the name to be proclaimed over it will be mine.' 29 David accordingly mustered his whole force, marched on Rabbah, and attacked and captured it. 30 The crown, which weighed a talent of gold and was set with a precious stone, was taken from the head of Milcom and placed on David's head; David also removed a vast quantity of booty from the city. 31 He brought out its inhabitants and set them to work with saws and other iron tools, sharp and toothed, and made them labour at the brickkilns. David did this to all the Ammonite towns; then he and all his army returned to Jerusalem.

13 THE following occurred some time later. David's son Absalom had a beautiful sister named Tamar, and David's son Amnon fell in love with her. 2 Amnon was so tormented that he became ill with love for his half-sister; for he thought it an impossible thing to approach her since she was a virgin. 3 But Amnon had a friend, a very shrewd man named Jonadab, son of David's brother Shimeah, 4 and he said to Amnon, 'Why are you, the king's son, so low-spirited morning after morning? Will you not tell me?' Amnon told him that he was in love with Tamar, his brother Absalom's sister. 5 Jonadab said to him, 'Take to your bed and pretend to be ill. When your father comes to visit you, say to him, "Please let my sister Tamar come and give me my food. Let her prepare it in front of me, so that I may watch her and then take it from her own hands." ' 6 So

---

v That is *Beloved of the LORD*　w Gk See 1 Kings 11.5, 33: Heb *their kings*

12:16 **in sackcloth:** *so Scroll; Heb. omits.*　12:24 **and called:** *or, as otherwise read, and he called.*　12:25 **Jedidiah:** *that is* Beloved of the LORD.　12:26–31 Cp. 1 Chr. 20:1–3.　12:30 **was set with:** *so Syriac; Heb. omits.* **Milcom:** *or their king.* 12:31 **labour at:** *prob. rdg; Heb.* pass through.

must surely die." 15 Then Nathan returned to his house. The LORD struck the child that the wife of Uriah had borne to David, and it became desperately ill. 16 David besought God for the child. He kept a fast, retiring for the night to lie on the ground clothed in sackcloth. 17 The elders of his house stood beside him urging him to rise from the ground; but he would not, nor would he take food with them. 18 On the seventh day, the child died. David's servants, however, were afraid to tell him that the child was dead, for they said: "When the child was alive, we spoke to him, but he would not listen to what we said. How can we tell him the child is dead? He may do some harm!" 19 But David noticed his servants whispering among themselves and realized that the child was dead. He asked his servants, "Is the child dead?" They replied, "Yes, he is." 20 Rising from the ground, David washed and anointed himself, and changed his clothes. Then he went to the house of the LORD and worshiped. He returned to his own house, where at his request food was set before him, and he ate. 21 His servants said to him: "What is this you are doing? While the child was living, you fasted and wept and kept vigil; now that the child is dead, you rise and take food." 22 He replied: "While the child was living, I fasted and wept, thinking, 'Perhaps the LORD will grant me the child's life.' 23 But now he is dead. Why should I fast? Can I bring him back again? I shall go to him, but he will not return to me." 24 Then David comforted his wife Bathsheba. He went and slept with her; and she conceived and bore him a son, who was named Solomon. The LORD loved him 25 and sent the prophet Nathan to name him Jedidiah, on behalf of the LORD.

26 Joab fought against Rabbah of the Ammonites and captured this royal city. 27 He sent messengers to David with the word: "I have fought against Rabbah and have taken the water-city. 28 Therefore, assemble the rest of the soldiers, join the siege against the city and capture it, lest it be I that capture the city and it be credited to me." 29 So David assembled the rest of the soldiers and went to Rabbah. When he had fought against it and captured it, 30 he took the crown from Milcom's head. It weighed a talent, of gold and precious stones; it was placed on David's head. He brought out immense booty from the city, 31 and also led away the inhabitants, whom he assigned to work with saws, iron picks, and iron axes, or put to work at the brickmold. This is what he did to all the Ammonite cities. David and all the soldiers then returned to Jerusalem.

13 Some time later the following incident occurred. David's son Absalom had a beautiful sister named Tamar, and David's son Amnon loved her. 2 He was in such straits over his sister Tamar that he became sick; since she was a virgin, Amnon thought it impossible to carry out his designs toward her. 3 Now Amnon had a friend named Jonadab, son of David's brother Shimeah, who was very clever. 4 He asked him, "Prince, why are you so dejected morning after morning? Why not tell me?" So Amnon said to him, "I am in love with Tamar, my brother Absalom's sister." 5 Then Jonadab replied, "Lie down on your bed and pretend to be sick. When your father comes to visit you, say to him, 'Please let my sister Tamar come and encourage me to take food. If she prepares something appetizing in my presence, for me to see, I will eat it from her hand.'" 6 So Amnon lay

15 And Nathan went home.

Yahweh struck the child which Uriah's wife had borne to David and it fell gravely ill. 16 David pleaded with Yahweh for the child; he kept a strict fast and went home and spent the night lying on the ground, covered with sacking. 17 The officials of his household stood round him, intending to get him off the ground, but he refused, nor would he take food with them. 18 On the seventh day the child died. David's retinue were afraid to tell him that the child was dead. 'Even when the child was alive', they thought, 'we reasoned with him and he would not listen to us. How can we tell him that the child is dead? He will do something desperate.' 19 David, however, noticed that his retinue were whispering among themselves, and realised that the child was dead. 'Is the child dead?' he asked the officers. They replied, 'He is dead.'

20 David got off the ground, bathed and anointed himself and put on fresh clothes. Then he went into Yahweh's sanctuary and prostrated himself. On returning to his house, he asked to be served with food and ate it. 21 His retinue said, 'Why are you acting like this? When the child was alive, you fasted and wept; now that the child is dead, you get up and take food!' 22 'When the child was alive', he replied, 'I fasted and wept because I kept thinking, "Who knows? Perhaps Yahweh will take pity on me and the child will live." 23 But now that he is dead, why should I fast? Can I bring him back again? I shall go to him but he cannot come back to me.'

24 David consoled his wife Bathsheba. He went to her and slept with her. She conceived and gave birth to a son, whom she called Solomon. Yahweh loved him 25 and made this known by means of the prophet Nathan, who named him Jedidiah, as Yahweh had instructed.

26 Joab assaulted Rabbah-of-the-Ammonites and captured the royal town. 27 He then sent messengers to tell David, 'I have assaulted Rabbah and captured the water supply. 28 So now muster the rest of the army, lay siege to the town and take it, or I will take it and the town will be called after me!' 29 So David mustered the whole army and marched on Rabbah; he assaulted the town and captured it. 30 He took the crown off Milcom's head; it weighed one talent of gold, and in it was set a precious stone which went on David's head instead. He carried off great quantities of booty from the town.' 31 And he expelled its inhabitants, setting them to work with saws, iron picks and iron axes, employing them at brickmaking. He treated all the Ammonite towns in the same way. David and the whole army returned to Jerusalem.

13 After this, the following events took place. Absalom son of David had a beautiful sister whose name was Tamar; Amnon son of David fell in love with her. 2 Amnon was so obsessed with his sister Tamar that it made him ill, since she was a virgin and Amnon thought it impossible to do anything to her. 3 But Amnon had a friend called Jonadab son of Shimeah, David's brother, and Jonadab was a very shrewd man. 4 'Son of the king,' he said, 'tell me why, morning after morning, you look so worn? Won't you tell me?' Amnon replied, 'I am in love with Tamar, my brother Absalom's sister.' 5 Then Jonadab said, 'Take to your bed, pretend to be ill and, when your father comes to visit you, say, "Please let my sister Tamar come and give me something to eat; let her prepare the food where I can see. What she gives me I shall eat."' 6 So Amnon lay down

NEW REVISED STANDARD VERSION	REVISED ENGLISH BIBLE

and when the king came to see him, Amnon said to the king, "Please let my sister Tamar come and make a couple of cakes in my sight, so that I may eat from her hand." 7 Then David sent home to Tamar, saying, "Go to your brother Amnon's house, and prepare food for him." 8 So Tamar went to her brother Amnon's house, where he was lying down. She took dough, kneaded it, made cakes in his sight, and baked the cakes. 9 Then she took the pan and set them*x* out before him, but he refused to eat. Amnon said, "Send out everyone from me." So everyone went out from him. 10 Then Amnon said to Tamar, "Bring the food into the chamber, so that I may eat from your hand." So Tamar took the cakes she had made, and brought them into the chamber to Amnon her brother. 11 But when she brought them near him to eat, he took hold of her, and said to her, "Come, lie with me, my sister." 12 She answered him, "No, my brother, do not force me; for such a thing is not done in Israel; do not do anything so vile! 13 As for me, where could I carry my shame? And as for you, you would be as one of the scoundrels in Israel. Now therefore, I beg you, speak to the king; for he will not withhold me from you." 14 But he would not listen to her; and being stronger than she, he forced her and lay with her.

15 Then Amnon was seized with a very great loathing for her; indeed, his loathing was even greater than the lust he had felt for her. Amnon said to her, "Get out!" 16 But she said to him, "No, my brother;*y* for this wrong in sending me away is greater than the other that you did to me." But he would not listen to her. 17 He called the young man who served him and said, "Put this woman out of my presence, and bolt the door after her." 18 (Now she was wearing a long robe with sleeves; for this is how the virgin daughters of the king were clothed in earlier times.*z*) So his servant put her out, and bolted the door after her. 19 But Tamar put ashes on her head, and tore the long robe that she was wearing; she put her hand on her head, and went away, crying aloud as she went.

20 Her brother Absalom said to her, "Has Amnon your brother been with you? Be quiet for now, my sister; he is your brother; do not take this to heart." So Tamar remained, a desolate woman, in her brother Absalom's house. 21 When King David heard of all these things, he became very angry, but he would not punish his son Amnon, because he loved him, for he was his firstborn.*a* 22 But Absalom spoke to Amnon neither good nor bad; for Absalom hated Amnon, because he had raped his sister Tamar.

23 After two full years Absalom had sheepshearers at Baal-hazor, which is near Ephraim, and Absalom invited all the king's sons. 24 Absalom came to the king, and said, "Your servant has sheepshearers; will the king and his servants please go with your servant?" 25 But the king said to Absalom, "No, my son, let us not all go, or else we will be burdensome to you." He pressed him, but he would not go but gave him his blessing. 26 Then Absalom said, "If not, please let my brother Amnon go with us." The king said to him, "Why should he go with you?" 27 But Absalom pressed him until he let Amnon and all the king's sons go with him. Absalom made a feast like a king's feast.*b* 28 Then Absalom commanded his servants, "Watch when Amnon's heart is merry with wine, and when I say to you, 'Strike Amnon,' then kill him. Do not be afraid; have I not myself commanded you? Be courageous and valiant." 29 So the servants of Absalom did to Amnon as Absalom had commanded. Then all the king's sons rose, and each mounted his mule and fled.

Amnon lay down and pretended to be ill. When the king came to visit him, he said, 'Sir, let my sister Tamar come and make a few bread-cakes in front of me, and serve them to me with her own hands.'

7 David sent a message to Tamar in the palace: 'Go to your brother Amnon's quarters and prepare a meal for him.' 8 Tamar came to her brother and found him lying down. She took some dough, kneaded it, and made cakes in front of him; having baked them, 9 she took the pan and turned them out before him. But Amnon refused to eat and ordered everyone out of the room. When they had all gone, 10 he said to Tamar, 'Bring the food over to the recess so that I may eat from your own hands.' Tamar took the cakes she had made and brought them to Amnon her brother in the recess. 11 When she offered them to him, he caught hold of her and said, 'Sister, come to bed with me.' 12 She answered, 'No, my brother, do not dishonour me. Such things are not done in Israel; do not behave so infamously. 13 Where could I go and hide my disgrace? You would sink as low as the most infamous in Israel. Why not speak to the king for me? He will not refuse you leave to marry me.' 14 But he would not listen; he overpowered and raped her.

15 Then Amnon was filled with intense revulsion; his revulsion for her was stronger than the love he had felt; he said to her, 'Get up and go.' 16 She answered, 'No, this great wrong, your sending me away, is worse than anything else you have done to me.' He would not listen to her; 17 he summoned the servant who attended him and said, 'Rid me of this woman; put her out and bolt the door after her.' 18 The servant turned her out and bolted the door. She had on a long robe with sleeves, the usual dress of unmarried princesses. 19 Tamar threw ashes over her head, tore the robe that she was wearing, put her hand on her head, and went away, sobbing as she went.

20 Her brother Absalom asked her, 'Has your brother Amnon been with you? Keep this to yourself; he is your brother. Do not take it to heart.' Forlorn and desolate, Tamar remained in her brother Absalom's house. 21 When King David heard the whole story he was very angry; but he would not hurt Amnon because he was his eldest son and he loved him. 22 Absalom did not speak a single word to Amnon, friendly or unfriendly, but he hated him for having dishonoured his sister Tamar.

23 Two years later Absalom invited all the king's sons to his sheep-shearing at Baal-hazor, near Ephron. 24 He approached the king and said, 'Sir, I am shearing; will your majesty and your servants come?' 25 The king answered, 'No, my son, we must not all come and be a burden to you.' Absalom pressed him, but David was still unwilling to go and dismissed him with his blessing. 26 Absalom said, 'If you will not come, may my brother Amnon come with us?' 'Why should he go with you?' the king asked; 27 but Absalom pressed him again, so he let Amnon and all the other princes go with him.

28 Absalom prepared a feast fit for a king, and gave this order to his servants: 'Watch your chance, and when Amnon is merry with wine and I say to you, "Strike Amnon," then kill him. You have nothing to fear; these are my orders. Be bold and resolute.' 29 Absalom's servants did to Amnon as Absalom had ordered, whereupon all the king's sons immediately mounted their mules and fled.

---

x Heb *and poured*   *y* Cn Compare Gk Vg: Meaning of Heb uncertain   *z* Cn: Heb *were clothed in robes*   *a* Q Ms Gk: MT lacks *but he would not punish . . . firstborn*   *b* Gk Compare Q Ms: MT lacks *Absalom made a feast like a king's feast*

13:18 **long . . . sleeves:** *or* ornamental robe.   13:21 **but he . . . loved him:** *so* Gk; Heb. omits.   13:23 **Ephron:** *prob. rdg; Heb.* Ephraim.   13:25 **pressed:** *so* Gk; Heb. broke out on. 13:28 **Absalom . . . king:** *so* Gk; Heb. omits.

down and pretended to be sick. When the king came to visit him, Amnon said to the king, "Please let my sister Tamar come and prepare some fried cakes before my eyes, that I may take nourishment from her hand."

7 David then sent home a message to Tamar, "Please go to the house of your brother Amnon and prepare some nourishment for him." 8 Tamar went to the house of her brother Amnon, who was in bed. Taking dough and kneading it, she twisted it into cakes before his eyes and fried the cakes. 9 Then she took the pan and set out the cakes before him. But Amnon would not eat; he said, "Have everyone leave me." When they had all left him, 10 Amnon said to Tamar, "Bring the nourishment into the bedroom, that I may have it from your hand." So Tamar picked up the cakes she had prepared and brought them to her brother Amnon in the bedroom. 11 But when she brought them to him to eat, he seized her and said to her, "Come! Lie with me, my sister!" 12 But she answered him, "No, my brother! Do not shame me! That is an intolerable crime in Israel. Do not commit this insensate deed. 13 Where would I take my shame? And you would be a discredited man in Israel. So please, speak to the king; he will not keep me from you."

14 Not heeding her plea, he overpowered her; he shamed her and had relations with her. 15 Then Amnon conceived an intense hatred for her, which far surpassed the love he had had for her. "Get up and leave," he said to her. 16 She replied, "No, brother, because to drive me out would be far worse than the first injury you have done me." He would not listen to her, 17 but called the youth who was his attendant and said, "Put her outside, away from me, and bar the door after her." 18 Now she had on a long tunic, for that is how maiden princesses dressed in olden days. When his attendant put her out and barred the door after her, 19 Tamar put ashes on her head and tore the long tunic in which she was clothed. Then, putting her hands to her head, she went away crying loudly. 20 Her brother Absalom said to her: "Has your brother Amnon been with you? Be still now, my sister; he is your brother. Do not take this affair to heart." But Tamar remained grief-stricken and forlorn in the house of her brother Absalom. 21 King David, who got word of the whole affair, became very angry. He did not, however, spark the resentment of his son Amnon, whom he favored because he was his first-born. 22 Absalom, moreover, said nothing at all to Amnon, although he hated him for having shamed his sister Tamar.

23 After a period of two years Absalom had shearers in Baal-hazor near Ephraim, and he invited all the princes. 24 Absalom went to the king and said: "Your servant is having shearers. Please, your majesty, come with all your retainers to your servant." 25 But the king said to Absalom, "No, my son, all of us should not go lest we be a burden to you." And though Absalom urged him, he refused to go and began to bid him goodbye. 26 Absalom then said, "If you will not come yourself, please let my brother Amnon come to us." The king asked him, "Why should he go to you?" 27 At Absalom's urging, however, he sent Amnon and all the other princes with him. Absalom prepared a banquet fit for royalty. 28 But he had instructed his servants: "Now watch! When Amnon is merry with wine and I say to you, 'Kill Amnon,' put him to death. Do not be afraid, for it is I who order you to do it. Be resolute and act manfully."

29 When the servants did to Amnon as Absalom had commanded, all the other princes rose, mounted their mules,

and pretended to be ill. The king then came to visit him and Amnon said to the king, 'Please let my sister Tamar come and make a cake or two where I can watch. What she gives me, I shall eat.' 7 David then sent word to Tamar at the palace, 'Go to your brother Amnon's house and prepare some food for him.' 8 Tamar went to the house of her brother Amnon who was lying there in bed. She took dough and kneaded it, and she made some cakes while he watched, and baked the cakes. 9 She then took the pan and dished them up in front of him, but he refused to eat. Amnon said, 'Let everyone leave me!' So everyone withdrew. 10 Amnon then said to Tamar, 'Bring the food to the inner room, so that I can eat what you give me.' So Tamar took the cakes which she had made and brought them to her brother Amnon in the inner room. 11 And as she was offering the food to him, he caught hold of her and said, 'Come to bed with me, sister!' 12 She replied, 'No, brother! Do not force me! This is no way to behave in Israel. Do not do anything so disgraceful! 13 Wherever should I go? I should be marked with this shame, while you would become disgraced in Israel. Why not go and speak to the king? He will not refuse to give me to you.' 14 But he would not listen to her; he overpowered her and raped her.

15 Amnon was then seized with extreme hatred for her; the hatred he now felt for her was greater than his earlier love. 'Get up and go!' he said. 16 She said, 'No, brother! To send me away would be worse than the other wrong you have done me!' But he would not listen to her. 17 He called his personal servant. 'Rid me of this woman!' he said. 'Throw her out and bolt the door behind her!' 18 (She was wearing a magnificent dress, for this was what the king's unmarried daughters wore in days gone by.) So the servant put her out and bolted the door behind her.

19 Tamar put dust on her head, tore the magnificent dress which she was wearing, laid her hand on her head, and went away, crying aloud as she went.

20 Her brother Absalom said to her, 'Has Amnon your brother been with you? Sister, be quiet; he is your brother; do not take the matter to heart!' Tamar, however, went back to her brother Absalom's house inconsolable.

21 When King David heard the whole story, he was very angry; but he had no wish to harm his son Amnon, whom he loved because he was his first-born. 22 Absalom, however, would not so much as speak to Amnon, since he hated Amnon for having raped his sister Tamar.

23 Two years later, when Absalom had the sheep-shearers at Baal-Hazor, which is near Ephraim, he invited all the king's sons. 24 Absalom went to the king and said, 'Now sir, your servant has the sheep-shearers. Will the king and his retinue be pleased to come with your servant?' 25 'No, my son,' the king replied, 'we must not all come and be a burden to you.' And though Absalom was insistent, he would not go but dismissed him. 26 Absalom persisted, 'Then at least let my brother Amnon come with us.' The king said, 'Why should he go with you?' 27 On Absalom's insistence, however, he let Amnon and all the king's sons to go with him.

Absalom prepared a royal banquet 28 and then gave this order to the servants, 'Listen carefully; when Amnon's heart is merry with wine and I say, "Strike Amnon down", then kill him. Don't be afraid. Have I not myself given you the order? Use your strength and show your mettle!' 29 Absalom's servants treated Amnon as Absalom had ordered. The king's sons all leapt to their feet, mounted their mules and fled.

30 While they were on the way, the report came to David that Absalom had killed all the king's sons, and not one of them was left. 31 The king rose, tore his garments, and lay on the ground; and all his servants who were standing by tore their garments. 32 But Jonadab, the son of David's brother Shimeah, said, "Let not my lord suppose that they have killed all the young men the king's sons; Amnon alone is dead. This has been determined by Absalom from the day Amnon[c] raped his sister Tamar. 33 Now therefore, do not let my lord the king take it to heart, as if all the king's sons were dead; for Amnon alone is dead."

34 But Absalom fled. When the young man who kept watch looked up, he saw many people coming from the Horonaim road[d] by the side of the mountain. 35 Jonadab said to the king, "See, the king's sons have come; as your servant said, so it has come about." 36 As soon as he had finished speaking, the king's sons arrived, and raised their voices and wept; and the king and all his servants also wept very bitterly.

37 But Absalom fled, and went to Talmai son of Ammihud, king of Geshur. David mourned for his son day after day. 38 Absalom, having fled to Geshur, stayed there three years. 39 And the heart of[e] the king went out, yearning for Absalom; for he was now consoled over the death of Amnon.

14 Now Joab son of Zeruiah perceived that the king's mind was on Absalom. 2 Joab sent to Tekoa and brought from there a wise woman. He said to her, "Pretend to be a mourner; put on mourning garments, do not anoint yourself with oil, but behave like a woman who has been mourning many days for the dead. 3 Go to the king and speak to him as follows." And Joab put the words into her mouth.

4 When the woman of Tekoa came to the king, she fell on her face to the ground and did obeisance, and said, "Help, O king!" 5 The king asked her, "What is your trouble?" She answered, "Alas, I am a widow; my husband is dead. 6 Your servant had two sons, and they fought with one another in the field; there was no one to part them, and one struck the other and killed him. 7 Now the whole family has risen against your servant. They say, 'Give up the man who struck his brother, so that we may kill him for the life of his brother whom he murdered, even if we destroy the heir as well.' Thus they would quench my one remaining ember, and leave to my husband neither name nor remnant on the face of the earth."

8 Then the king said to the woman, "Go to your house, and I will give orders concerning you." 9 The woman of Tekoa said to the king, "On me be the guilt, my lord the king, and on my father's house; let the king and his throne be guiltless." 10 The king said, "If anyone says anything to you, bring him to me, and he shall never touch you again." 11 Then she said, "Please, may the king keep the LORD your God in mind, so that the avenger of blood may kill no more, and my son not be destroyed." He said, "As the LORD lives, not one hair of your son shall fall to the ground."

12 Then the woman said, "Please let your servant speak a word to my lord the king." He said, "Speak." 13 The woman said, "Why then have you planned such a thing against the people of God? For in giving this decision the king convicts himself, inasmuch as the king does not bring his banished one home again. 14 We must all die; we are like water spilled on the ground, which cannot be gathered up. But God will not take away a life; he will devise plans so as not to keep an outcast banished forever from his presence.[f] 15 Now I have come to say this to my lord the king

30 While they were on their way, a rumour reached David that Absalom had murdered all the royal princes and that not one was left alive. 31 The king stood up and tore his clothes and then threw himself on the ground; all his servants were standing round him with their clothes torn. 32 Then Jonadab, son of David's brother Shimeah, said, 'My lord must not think that all the young princes have been murdered; only Amnon is dead. Absalom has gone about with a scowl on his face ever since Amnon ravished his sister Tamar. 33 Your majesty must not pay attention to what is no more than a rumour that all the princes are dead; only Amnon is dead.' 34 Absalom meanwhile had made good his escape.

The sentry on duty saw a crowd of people coming down the hill from the direction of Horonaim. He came and reported to the king, 'I see men coming down the hill from Horonaim.' 35 Jonadab said to the king, 'Here come the royal princes, just as I said they would.' 36 As he finished speaking, the princes came in and broke into loud lamentations; the king and all his servants also wept bitterly.

37 Absalom went to take refuge with Talmai son of Ammihud king of Geshur; and for a long while the king mourned for Amnon. 38 Absalom, having escaped to Geshur, stayed there for three years; 39 and David's heart went out to him with longing, as he became reconciled to the death of Amnon.

14 Joab son of Zeruiah saw that the king longed in his heart for Absalom, 2 so he sent for a wise woman from Tekoah and said to her, 'Pretend to be a mourner; put on mourning garb, go without anointing yourself, and behave like a woman who has been bereaved these many days. 3 Then go to the king and repeat what I tell you.' He told her exactly what she was to say.

4 When the woman from Tekoah came into the king's presence, she bowed to the ground in homage and cried, 'Help, your majesty!' 5 The king asked, 'What is it?' She answered, 'Sir, I am a widow; my husband is dead. 6 I had two sons; they came to blows out in the country where there was no one to part them, and one struck the other and killed him. 7 Now, sir, the kinsmen have confronted me with the demand, "Hand over the one who killed his brother, so that we can put him to death for taking his brother's life, and so cut off the succession." If they do this, they will stamp out my last live ember and leave my husband without name or descendant on the earth.' 8 'Go home,' said the king to the woman, 'and I shall settle your case.'

9 But the woman continued, 'The guilt be on me, your majesty, and on my father's house; let the king and his throne be blameless.' 10 The king said, 'If anyone says anything more to you, bring him to me and he will not trouble you again.' 11 Then the woman went on, 'Let your majesty call upon the LORD your God, to prevent the next-of-kin from doing their worst and destroying my son.' The king swore, 'As the LORD lives, not a hair of your son's head shall fall to the ground.'

12 The woman then said, 'May I add one word more, your majesty?' 'Say on,' said the king. 13 So she continued, 'How then could it enter your head to do this same wrong to God's people? By the decision you have pronounced, your majesty, you condemn yourself in that you have refused to bring back the one you banished. 14 We shall all die; we shall be like water that is spilt on the ground and lost; but God will spare the man who does not set himself to keep the outlaw in banishment.

13:34 **from the direction of Horonaim:** *prob. rdg; Heb.* from a road behind him. **He came . . . from Horonaim:** *so Gk; Heb.* omits. 13:39 **David's heart:** *so Aram.* (Targ.); *Heb.* David. 14:4 **came . . . presence:** *so some MSS; others* said to the king. 14:8 *See note on verses 15–17.*

[c] Heb *he*   [d] Cn Compare Gk: Heb *the road behind him*   [e] Q Ms Gk: MT *And David*   [f] Meaning of Heb uncertain

and fled. 30 While they were still on the road, a report reached David that Absalom had killed all the princes and that not one of them had survived. 31 The king stood up, rent his garments, and then lay on the ground. All his servants standing by him also rent their garments. 32 But Jonadab, son of David's brother Shimeah, spoke up: "Let not my lord think that all the young princes have been killed! Amnon alone is dead, for Absalom was determined on this ever since Amnon shamed his sister Tamar. 33 So let not my lord the king put faith in the report that all the princes are dead. Amnon alone is dead." 34 Meanwhile, Absalom had taken flight. Then the servant on watch looked about and saw a large group coming down the slope from the direction of Bahurim. He came in and reported this, telling the king that he had seen some men coming down the mountainside from the direction of Bahurim. 35 So Jonadab said to the king: "There! The princes have come. It is as your servant said." 36 No sooner had he finished speaking than the princes came in, weeping aloud. The king, too, and all his servants wept very bitterly. 37 But Absalom, who had taken flight, went to Talmai, son of Ammihud, king of Geshur, 38 and stayed in Geshur for three years.

39 The king continued during all that time to mourn over his son; but his longing reached out for Absalom as he became reconciled to the death of Amnon.

14 When Joab, son of Zeruiah, observed how the king felt toward Absalom, 2 he sent to Tekoa and brought from there a gifted woman, to whom he said: "Pretend to be in mourning. Put on mourning apparel and do not anoint yourself with oil, that you may appear to be a woman who has been long in mourning for a departed one. 3 Then go to the king and speak to him in this manner." And Joab instructed her what to say.

4 So the woman of Tekoa went to the king and fell prostrate to the ground in homage, saying, "Help, your majesty!" 5 The king said to her, "What do you want?" She replied: "Alas, I am a widow; my husband is dead. 6 Your servant had two sons, who quarreled in the field. There being no one to part them, one of them struck his brother and killed him. 7 Then the whole clan confronted your servant and demanded: 'Give up the one who killed his brother. We must put him to death for the life of his brother whom he has slain; we must extinguish the heir also.' Thus they will quench my remaining hope and leave my husband neither name nor posterity upon the earth." 8 The king then said to the woman: "Go home. I will issue a command on your behalf." 9 The woman of Tekoa answered him, "Let me and my family be to blame, my lord king; you and your throne are innocent." 10 Then the king said, "If anyone says a word to you, have him brought to me, and he shall not touch you again." 11 But she went on to say, "Please, your majesty, keep in mind the LORD your God, that the avenger of blood may not go too far in destruction and that my son may not be done away with." He replied, "As the LORD lives, not a hair of your son shall fall to the ground."

12 The woman continued, "Please let your servant say still another word to my lord the king." He replied, "Speak." 13 So the woman said: "Why, then, do you think of this same kind of thing against the people of God? In pronouncing as he has, the king shows himself guilty, for not bringing back his own banished son. 14 We must indeed die; we are then like water that is poured out on the ground and cannot be gathered up. Yet, though God does not bring back life, he does take thought how not to banish anyone from him. 15 And now, if I have presumed to speak of this matter

30 While they were on the road, word reached David, 'Absalom has killed all the king's sons; not one of them is left.' 31 The king stood up, tore his clothes and threw himself on the ground. All his officers tore their clothes too. 32 Jonadab son of Shimeah, David's brother, then spoke up and said, 'Do not let my lord take to heart the report that all the young men, the king's sons, have been killed, since only Amnon is dead: for Absalom has been promising himself to do this since the day when Amnon raped his sister Tamar. 33 So my lord the king must not imagine that all the king's sons are dead; only Amnon is dead 34 and Absalom has fled.'

The man on sentry duty looked up and saw a large troop coming along the road from Bahurim. The sentry came to tell the king, 'I have seen some people coming down the Bahurim road on the mountainside.' 35 Jonadab then said to the king, 'These are the king's sons arriving: what your servant said is exactly what happened.' 36 He had scarcely finished speaking when the king's sons arrived and wept aloud; the king and all his retinue wept aloud too. 37 Absalom had gone to Talmai son of Ammihud, king of Geshur. The king mourned for his son every day.

38 When Absalom had gone to Geshur, he stayed there for three years. 39 Once the king was consoled over Amnon's death, his anger against Absalom subsided.

14 Now, Joab son of Zeruiah observed that the king was favourably inclined to Absalom. 2 Joab therefore sent to Tekoa for a wise woman. 'Pretend to be in mourning,' he said. 'Dress yourself in mourning, do not perfume yourself; act like a woman who has long been mourning for the dead. 3 Then go to the king and say this to him.' And Joab put the words into her mouth which she was to say.

4 So the woman of Tekoa went to the king and, falling on her face to the ground, prostrated herself. 'Help, my lord king!' she said. 5 The king said, 'What is the matter?'

'As you see,' she replied, 'I am a widow; my husband is dead. 6 Your servant had two sons and out in the fields, where there was no one to intervene, they had a quarrel. And one of them struck the other and killed him. 7 And now the whole clan has risen against your servant. "Give up the man who killed his brother," they say, "so that we can put him to death, to atone for the life of the brother whom he has murdered; and thus we shall destroy the heir as well." By this means, they will extinguish the ember still left to me, leaving my husband neither name nor survivor on the face of the earth.' 8 Then the king said to the woman, 'Go home; I myself shall give orders about your case.' 9 The woman of Tekoa said to the king, 'My lord king! May the guilt be on me and on my family; the king and his throne are innocent of it.' 10 'Bring me the man who threatened you,' the king replied, 'and he shall never hurt you again.' 11 She then said, 'Let the king be pleased to pronounce the name of Yahweh your God, so that the avenger of blood may not do greater harm and destroy my son.' 'As Yahweh lives,' he said, 'not one of your son's hairs shall fall to the ground!'

12 Then the woman said, 'Permit your servant to say something else to my lord the king.' 'Go on,' he said. 13 The woman said, 'Why then has the king, who by giving this verdict has condemned himself, conceived the idea, against God's people's interests, of not bringing home the son whom he has banished? 14 We are all mortal; we are like water spilt on the ground, which cannot be gathered up again, nor does God raise up a corpse; let the king therefore make plans for his banished son not to remain far away from him in exile.

because the people have made me afraid; your servant thought, 'I will speak to the king; it may be that the king will perform the request of his servant. 16 For the king will hear, and deliver his servant from the hand of the man who would cut both me and my son off from the heritage of God.' 17 Your servant thought, 'The word of my lord the king will set me at rest'; for my lord the king is like the angel of God, discerning good and evil. The LORD your God be with you!"

18 Then the king answered the woman, "Do not withhold from me anything I ask you." The woman said, "Let my lord the king speak." 19 The king said, "Is the hand of Joab with you in all this?" The woman answered and said, "As surely as you live, my lord the king, one cannot turn right or left from anything that my lord the king has said. For it was your servant Joab who commanded me; it was he who put all these words into the mouth of your servant. 20 In order to change the course of affairs your servant Joab did this. But my lord has wisdom like the wisdom of the angel of God to know all things that are on the earth."

21 Then the king said to Joab, "Very well, I grant this; go, bring back the young man Absalom." 22 Joab prostrated himself with his face to the ground and did obeisance, and blessed the king; and Joab said, "Today your servant knows that I have found favor in your sight, my lord the king, in that the king has granted the request of his servant." 23 So Joab set off, went to Geshur, and brought Absalom to Jerusalem. 24 The king said, "Let him go to his own house; he is not to come into my presence." So Absalom went to his own house, and did not come into the king's presence.

25 Now in all Israel there was no one to be praised so much for his beauty as Absalom; from the sole of his foot to the crown of his head there was no blemish in him. 26 When he cut the hair of his head (for at the end of every year he used to cut it; when it was heavy on him, he cut it), he weighed the hair of his head, two hundred shekels by the king's weight. 27 There were born to Absalom three sons, and one daughter whose name was Tamar; she was a beautiful woman.

28 So Absalom lived two full years in Jerusalem, without coming into the king's presence. 29 Then Absalom sent for Joab to send him to the king; but Joab would not come to him. He sent a second time, but Joab would not come. 30 Then he said to his servants, "Look, Joab's field is next to mine, and he has barley there; go and set it on fire." So Absalom's servants set the field on fire. 31 Then Joab rose and went to Absalom at his house, and said to him, "Why have your servants set my field on fire?" 32 Absalom answered Joab, "Look, I sent word to you: Come here, that I may send you to the king with the question, 'Why have I come from Geshur? It would be better for me to be there still.' Now let me go into the king's presence; if there is guilt in me, let him kill me!" 33 Then Joab went to the king and told him; and he summoned Absalom. So he came to the king and prostrated himself with his face to the ground before the king; and the king kissed Absalom.

15 After this Absalom got himself a chariot and horses, and fifty men to run ahead of him. 2 Absalom used to rise early and stand beside the road into the gate; and when anyone brought a suit before the king for judgment, Absalom would call out and say, "From what city are you?" When the person said, "Your servant is of such and such a tribe in Israel," 3 Absalom would say, "See, your claims are good and right; but there is no one deputed by the king to hear you." 4 Absalom said moreover, "If only I

15 'I came to say this to your majesty because the people have threatened me: I thought, "If I can only speak to the king, perhaps he will attend to my case; 16 for he will listen, and he will save me from anyone who is seeking to cut off me and my son together from God's own possession." 17 I thought too that the words of my lord the king would be a comfort to me; for your majesty is like the angel of God and can decide between right and wrong. May the LORD your God be with you!'

18 The king said to the woman, 'Tell me no lies: I shall now ask you a question.' 'Let your majesty speak,' she said. 19 The king asked, 'Is the hand of Joab behind you in all this?' 'Your life upon it, sir!' she answered. 'When your majesty asks a question, there is no way round it, right or left. Yes, your servant Joab did prompt me; it was he who put the whole story into my mouth. 20 He did it to give a new turn to this affair. Your majesty is as wise as the angel of God and knows all that goes on in the land.'

21 The king said to Joab, 'You have my consent; go and bring back the young man Absalom.' 22 Then Joab humbly prostrated himself, took leave of the king with a blessing, and said, 'Now I know that I have found favour with your majesty, because you have granted my humble petition.' 23 Joab went at once to Geshur and brought Absalom to Jerusalem. 24 But the king said, 'Let him go to his own quarters; he shall not come into my presence.' So Absalom repaired to his own quarters and did not enter the king's presence.

25 In all Israel no man was so much admired for his beauty as Absalom; from the crown of his head to the sole of his foot he was without flaw. 26 When he cut his hair (as had to be done every year, for he found it heavy), it weighed two hundred shekels by the royal standard. 27 Three sons were born to Absalom, and a daughter named Tamar, who became a very beautiful woman.

28 Absalom lived in Jerusalem for two whole years without entering the king's presence. 29 Then he summoned Joab, intending to send a message by him to the king, but Joab refused to come; he sent for him a second time, but he still refused. 30 Absalom said to his servants, 'You know that Joab has a field next to mine with barley growing in it; go and set fire to it.' When Absalom's servants set fire to the field, 31 Joab promptly came to Absalom in his own quarters and demanded, 'Why have your servants set fire to my field?' 32 Absalom answered, 'I had sent for you to come here, so that I could ask you to give the king this message from me: "Why did I leave Geshur? It would be better for me if I were still there. Let me now come into your majesty's presence and, if I have done any wrong, put me to death."' 33 When Joab went to the king and told him, he summoned Absalom, who came and prostrated himself humbly, and the king greeted him with a kiss.

15 AFTER this Absalom provided himself with a chariot and horses and fifty outrunners. 2 He made it a practice to rise early and stand by the road leading through the city gate, and would hail everyone who had a case to bring before the king for judgement and ask him which town he came from. When he answered, 'I come, sir, from such and such a tribe of Israel,' 3 Absalom would say to him, 'I can see that you have a very good case, but you will get no hearing from the king.' 4 He would add, 'If only I

14:15–17 *Probably these verses are misplaced and should follow verse 7.* 14:16 **who is seeking:** *so Gk; Heb. omits.*

to your majesty, it is because the people have given me cause to fear. And so your servant thought: 'Let me speak to the king. Perhaps he will grant the petition of his maidservant. 16 For the king must surely consent to free his servant from the grasp of one who would seek to destroy me and my son as well from God's inheritance.' " 17 And the woman concluded: "Let the word of my lord the king provide a resting place; indeed, my lord the king is like an angel of God, evaluating good and bad. The LORD your God be with you."

18 The king answered the woman, "Now do not conceal from me anything I may ask you!" The woman said, "Let my lord the king speak." 19 So the king asked, "Is Joab involved with you in all this?" And the woman answered: "As you live, my lord the king, it is just as your majesty has said, and not otherwise. It was your servant Joab who instructed me and told your servant all these things she was to say. 20 Your servant Joab did this to come at the issue in a roundabout way. But my lord is as wise as an angel of God, so that he knows all things on earth."

21 Then the king said to Joab: "I hereby grant this request. Go, therefore, and bring back young Absalom." 22 Falling prostrate to the ground in homage and blessing the king, Joab said, "This day I know that I am in good favor with you, my lord the king, since the king has granted the request of his servant." 23 Joab then went off to Geshur and brought Absalom to Jerusalem. 24 But the king said, "Let him go to his own house; he shall not appear before me." So Absalom went off to his house and did not appear before the king.

25 In all Israel there was not a man who could so be praised for his beauty as Absalom, who was without blemish from the sole of his foot to the crown of his head. 26 When he shaved his head — which he used to do at the end of every year, because his hair became too heavy for him — the hair weighed two hundred shekels according to the royal standard. 27 Absalom had three sons born to him, besides a daughter named Tamar, who was a beautiful woman.

28 Absalom lived in Jerusalem for two years without appearing before the king. 29 Then he summoned Joab to send him to the king, but Joab would not come to him. Although he summoned him a second time, Joab refused to come. 30 He therefore instructed his servants: "You see Joab's field that borders mine, on which he has barley. Go, set it on fire." And so Absalom's servants set the field on fire. Joab's farmhands came to him with torn garments and reported to him what had been done. 31 At this, Joab went to Absalom in his house and asked him, "Why have your servants set my field on fire?" 32 Absalom answered Joab: "I was summoning you to come here, that I may send you to the king to say: 'Why did I come back from Geshur? I would be better off if I were still there!' Now, let me appear before the king. If I am guilty, let him put me to death." 33 Joab went to the king and reported this. The king then called Absalom, who came to him and in homage fell on his face to the ground before the king. Then the king kissed him.

15 After this Absalom provided himself with chariots, horses, and fifty henchmen. 2 Moreover, Absalom used to rise early and stand alongside the road leading to the gate. If someone had a lawsuit to be decided by the king, Absalom would call to him and say, "From what city are you?" And when he replied, "Your servant is of such and such a tribe of Israel," 3 Absalom would say to him, "Your suit is good and just, but there is no one to hear you in the king's name." 4 And he would continue: "If only I could be

15 'Now, the reason why I came to speak about this to my lord the king is that I was being intimidated, and your servant thought, "I shall speak to the king; perhaps the king will do what his servant asks. 16 Surely the king will consent to save his servant from the clutches of the man who is trying to cut both me and my son off from God's heritage. 17 Let a word from my lord the king, restore the peace!" your servant thought, "for my lord the king is like the Angel of God in understanding good and evil." May Yahweh your God be with you!'

18 Replying to the woman, the king said, 'Now do not evade the question which I am going to ask you.' The woman said, 'Let my lord the king ask his question.' 19 'Is not Joab's hand behind you in all this?' the king asked. The woman replied, 'As you live, my lord king, I cannot escape what my lord the king says, either to right or to left. Yes, it was your servant Joab who gave me my orders; he put all these words into your servant's mouth. 20 Your servant Joab did this to approach the matter indirectly, but my lord has the wisdom of the Angel of God; he knows everything that happens on earth!'

21 The king then said to Joab, 'Very well, the suit is granted. Go and bring the young man Absalom back.' 22 Joab fell on his face to the ground, prostrated himself and blessed the king. 'My lord king,' Joab said, 'today your servant knows that he has won your favour, since the king has done what his servant asked.' 23 Joab then set off, went to Geshur, and brought Absalom back to Jerusalem. 24 The king, however, said, 'Let him retire to his own house; he is not to appear in my presence.' So Absalom retired to his own house and was not received by the king.

25 In all Israel there was no one more praised for his beauty than Absalom; from the sole of his foot to the crown of his head, he could not be faulted. 26 When he cut his hair — he shaved it once a year because his hair got too heavy — he would weigh the hair: two hundred shekels, king's weight. 27 To Absalom were born three sons and one daughter called Tamar; she was a beautiful woman.

28 Absalom lived in Jerusalem for two years without being received by the king. 29 Absalom then summoned Joab, intending to send him to the king, but Joab would not come to him. He sent for him a second time, but still he would not come. 30 At this, Absalom said to his retainers, 'Look, Joab's field is next to mine and he has barley in it; go and set it on fire.' Absalom's retainers set fire to the field. 31 Joab then stirred himself, went to Absalom in his house and asked, 'Why have your retainers set my field on fire?' 32 Absalom replied to Joab, 'Look, I sent word to you: Come here, so that I can send you to the king to say, "Why come back from Geshur? Better for me to have been there still!" Now I want to be received by the king, and if I am guilty, let him put me to death!' 33 Joab went to the king and told him this. He then summoned Absalom, who prostrated himself with his face to the ground before the king. And the king kissed Absalom.

15 After this, Absalom procured a chariot and horses, with fifty men to run ahead of him. 2 He would get up early and stand beside the road leading to the city gate; and whenever a man with some lawsuit had to come before the king's tribunal, Absalom would call out to him and ask, 'Which town are you from?' If he answered, 'Your servant is from one of the tribes of Israel,' 3 then Absalom would say, 'Look, your case is sound and just, but not one of the king's deputies will listen to you.' 4 Absalom would say,

NEW REVISED STANDARD VERSION

I were judge in the land! Then all who had a suit or cause might come to me, and I would give them justice." 5 Whenever people came near to do obeisance to him, he would put out his hand and take hold of them, and kiss them. 6 Thus Absalom did to every Israelite who came to the king for judgment; so Absalom stole the hearts of the people of Israel.

7 At the end of four*g* years Absalom said to the king, "Please let me go to Hebron and pay the vow that I have made to the LORD. 8 For your servant made a vow while I lived at Geshur in Aram: If the LORD will indeed bring me back to Jerusalem, then I will worship the LORD in Hebron."*h* 9 The king said to him, "Go in peace." So he got up, and went to Hebron. 10 But Absalom sent secret messengers throughout all the tribes of Israel, saying, "As soon as you hear the sound of the trumpet, then shout: Absalom has become king at Hebron!" 11 Two hundred men from Jerusalem went with Absalom; they were invited guests, and they went in their innocence, knowing nothing of the matter. 12 While Absalom was offering the sacrifices, he sent for*i* Ahithophel the Gilonite, David's counselor, from his city Giloh. The conspiracy grew in strength, and the people with Absalom kept increasing.

13 A messenger came to David, saying, "The hearts of the Israelites have gone after Absalom." 14 Then David said to all his officials who were with him at Jerusalem, "Get up! Let us flee, or there will be no escape for us from Absalom. Hurry, or he will soon overtake us, and bring disaster down upon us, and attack the city with the edge of the sword." 15 The king's officials said to the king, "Your servants are ready to do whatever our lord the king decides." 16 So the king left, followed by all his household, except ten concubines whom he left behind to look after the house. 17 The king left, followed by all the people; and they stopped at the last house. 18 All his officials passed by him; and all the Cherethites, and all the Pelethites, and all the six hundred Gittites who had followed him from Gath, passed on before the king.

19 Then the king said to Ittai the Gittite, "Why are you also coming with us? Go back, and stay with the king; for you are a foreigner, and also an exile from your home. 20 You came only yesterday, and shall I today make you wander about with us, while I go wherever I can? Go back, and take your kinsfolk with you; and may the LORD show*j* steadfast love and faithfulness to you." 21 But Ittai answered the king, "As the LORD lives, and as my lord the king lives, wherever my lord the king may be, whether for death or for life, there also your servant will be." 22 David said to Ittai, "Go then, march on." So Ittai the Gittite marched on, with all his men and all the little ones who were with him. 23 The whole country wept aloud as all the people passed by; the king crossed the Wadi Kidron, and all the people moved on toward the wilderness.

24 Abiathar came up, and Zadok also, with all the Levites, carrying the ark of the covenant of God. They set down the ark of God, until the people had all passed out of the city. 25 Then the king said to Zadok, "Carry the ark of God back into the city. If I find favor in the eyes of the LORD, he will bring me back and let me see both it and the place where it stays. 26 But if he says, 'I take no pleasure in you,' here I am, let him do to me what seems good to him." 27 The king also said to the priest Zadok, "Look,*k* go back

REVISED ENGLISH BIBLE

were appointed judge in the land, it would be my business to see that everyone with a lawsuit or a claim got justice from me.' 5 Whenever a man approached to prostrate himself, Absalom would stretch out his hand, take hold of him, and kiss him. 6 By behaving like this to every Israelite who sought justice from the king, Absalom stole the affections of the people.

7 At the end of four years, Absalom said to the king, 'Give me leave to go to Hebron to fulfil a vow there that I made to the LORD. 8 When I lived at Geshur in Aram, I vowed, "If the LORD brings me back to Jerusalem, I shall worship the LORD in Hebron." ' 9 The king answered, 'You may go'; so he set off and went to Hebron.

10 Absalom sent runners through all the tribes of Israel with this message: 'As soon as you hear the sound of the trumpet, then say, "Absalom has become king in Hebron." ' 11 Two hundred men accompanied Absalom from Jerusalem; they were invited as guests and went in all innocence, knowing nothing of the affair. 12 Absalom also sent to summon Ahithophel the Gilonite, David's counsellor, from Giloh his town, where he was offering the customary sacrifices. The conspiracy gathered strength, and Absalom's supporters increased in number.

13 A messenger brought the news to David that the men of Israel had transferred their allegiance to Absalom. 14 The king said to those who were with him in Jerusalem, 'We must get away at once, or there will be no escape from Absalom for any of us. Make haste, or else he will soon be upon us, bringing disaster and putting the city to the sword.' 15 The king's servants said to him, 'Whatever your majesty thinks best; we are ready.' 16 The king set out, and all his household followed him except ten concubines whom he left in charge of the palace.

17 At the Far House the king and all the people who were with him halted. 18 His own servants then stood at his side, while the Kerethite and Pelethite guards and Ittai with the six hundred Gittites under him marched past the king. 19 The king said to Ittai the Gittite, 'Why should you come with us? Go back and stay with the new king, for you are a foreigner and, what is more, an exile from your own country. 20 You came only yesterday, and must you today be compelled to share my wanderings when I do not know where I am going? Go back home and take your countrymen with you; and may the LORD ever be your steadfast friend.' 21 Ittai answered, 'As the LORD lives, your life upon it, wherever you may be whether for life or death, I, your servant, shall be there.' 22 David said to Ittai, 'It is well, march on!' And Ittai the Gittite marched on with his whole company and all the dependants who were with him. 23 The whole countryside resounded with their weeping. The king remained standing while all the people crossed the wadi of the Kidron before him, by way of the olive tree in the wilderness.

24 Zadok also was there and all the Levites with him, carrying the Ark of the Covenant of God. They set it down beside Abiathar until all the army had passed out of the city. 25 The king said to Zadok, 'Take the Ark of God back into the city. If I find favour with the LORD, he will bring me back and let me see the Ark and its dwelling-place again. 26 But if he says he does not want me, then here I am; let him do what he pleases with me.' 27 The king went on to say

15:7 **four**: *so Gk (Luc.); Heb.* forty. 15:8 **in Hebron**: *so Gk (Luc.); Heb. omits.* 15:18 **stood**: *prob. rdg; Heb.* passed. **and Ittai**: *prob. rdg; Heb.* passed. 15:20 **and may . . . friend**: *so Gk; Heb.* constant love and truth. 15:23 **standing**: *prob. rdg; Heb.* passing. **by way . . . wilderness**: *prob. rdg; Heb.* obscure. 15:24 **beside Abiathar**: *prob. rdg; Heb.* and Abiathar went up.

g Gk Syr: Heb *forty*   *h* Gk Mss: Heb lacks *in Hebron*   *i* Or *he sent*   *j* Gk Compare 2.6: Heb lacks *may the LORD show*   *k* Gk: Heb *Are you a seer* or *Do you see?*

appointed judge in the land! Then everyone who has a lawsuit to be decided might come to me and I would render him justice." 5 Whenever a man approached him to show homage, he would extend his hand, hold him, and kiss him. 6 By behaving in this way toward all the Israelites who came to the king for judgment, Absalom was stealing away the loyalties of the men of Israel.

7 After a period of four years, Absalom said to the king: "Allow me to go to Hebron and fulfill a vow I made to the LORD. 8 For while living in Geshur in Aram, your servant made this vow: 'If the LORD ever brings me back to Jerusalem, I will worship him in Hebron.'" 9 The king wished him a safe journey, and he went off to Hebron. 10 Then Absalom sent spies throughout the tribes of Israel to say, "When you hear the sound of the horn, declare Absalom king in Hebron." 11 Two hundred men had accompanied Absalom from Jerusalem. They had been invited and went in good faith, knowing nothing of the plan. 12 Absalom also sent to Ahithophel the Gilonite, David's counselor, an invitation to come from his town, Giloh, for the sacrifices he was about to offer. So the conspiracy gained strength, and the people with Absalom increased in numbers.

13 An informant came to David with the report, "The Israelites have transferred their loyalty to Absalom." 14 At this, David said to all his servants who were with him in Jerusalem: "Up! Let us take flight, or none of us will escape from Absalom. Leave quickly, lest he hurry and overtake us, then visit disaster upon us and put the city to the sword." 15 The king's officers answered him, "Your servants are ready, whatever our lord the king chooses to do." 16 Then the king set out, accompanied by his entire household, except for ten concubines whom he left behind to take care of the palace. 17 As the king left the city, with all his officers accompanying him, they halted opposite the ascent of the Mount of Olives, at a distance, 18 while the whole army marched past him.

As all the Cherethites and Pelethites, and the six hundred men of Gath who had accompanied him from that city, were passing in review before the king, 19 he said to Ittai the Gittite: "Why should you also go with us? Go back and stay with the king, for you are a foreigner and you, too, are an exile from your own country. 20 You came only yesterday, and shall I have you wander about with us today, wherever I have to go? Return and take your brothers with you, and may the LORD be kind and faithful to you." 21 But Ittai answered the king, "As the LORD lives, and as my lord the king lives, your servant shall be wherever my lord the king may be, whether for death or for life." 22 So the king said to Ittai, "Go, then, march on." And Ittai the Gittite, with all his men and all the dependents that were with him, marched on. 23 Everyone in the countryside wept aloud as the last of the soldiers went by, and the king crossed the Kidron Valley with all the soldiers moving on ahead of him by way of the Mount of Olives, toward the desert.

24 Zadok, too [with all the Levite bearers of the ark of the covenant of God], and Abiathar brought the ark of God to a halt until the soldiers had marched out of the city. 25 Then the king said to Zadok: "Take the ark of God back to the city. If I find favor with the LORD, he will bring me back and permit me to see it and its lodging. 26 But if he should say, 'I am not pleased with you,' I am ready; let him do to me as he sees fit. 27 The king also said to the priest Zadok:

'Oh, who will appoint me judge in the land? Then anyone with a lawsuit or a plea could come to me and I should see he had justice!' 5 And whenever anyone came up to him to prostrate himself, he would stretch out his hand, draw him to him and kiss him. 6 Absalom acted like this with every Israelite who appealed to the king's tribunal, and so Absalom won the Israelites' hearts.

7 When four years had gone by, Absalom said to the king, 'Allow me to go to Hebron and fulfil the vow which I have made to Yahweh; 8 for, when I was in Geshur, in Aram, your servant made this vow, "If Yahweh brings me back to Jerusalem, I shall pay my devotions to Yahweh in Hebron." ' 9 The king said to him, 'Go in peace.' So he set off and went to Hebron.

10 Absalom sent couriers throughout the tribes of Israel to say, 'When you hear the trumpet sound, you are to say, "Absalom is king at Hebron!" ' 11 With Absalom went two hundred men from Jerusalem; they had been invited and had gone in all innocence, unaware of what was going on. 12 Absalom sent for Ahithophel the Gilonite, David's counsellor, from Giloh his town, and had him with him while offering the sacrifices. The conspiracy grew in strength, since Absalom's supporters grew in number.

13 A messenger came and told David, 'The men of Israel have shifted their allegiance to Absalom.' 14 David said to all his retinue then with him in Jerusalem, 'Up, let us flee, or we shall not escape from Absalom! Leave as quickly as you can, in case he mounts a sudden attack, overcomes us and puts the city to the sword.' 15 The king's retinue replied, 'Whatever my lord the king decides, we are at your service.' 16 The king set out on foot with his whole household, leaving ten concubines to look after the palace. 17 The king set out on foot with everyone following, and they halted at the last house. 18 All his officers stood at his side. All the Cherethites and all the Pelethites, with Ittai and all the six hundred Gittites who had come in his retinue from Gath, marched past the king. 19 The king said to Ittai the Gittite, 'You, why are you coming with us? Go back and stay with the king, for you are a foreigner, indeed an exile from your homeland. 20 You arrived only yesterday; should I take you wandering with us today, when I do not know myself where I am going? Go back, take your fellow countrymen with you, and may Yahweh show you mercy and faithful love!' 21 Ittai replied to the king, 'As Yahweh lives, and as my lord the king lives, wherever my lord the king may be, for death or life, your servant will be there too.' 22 David then said to Ittai, 'Go ahead, march past!' And Ittai of Gath marched past with all his men and with all his children too. 23 The entire population was weeping aloud as the king stood in the bed of the Kidron and everyone marched past him, making for the desert.

24 Zadok was there too, and all the Levites with him, carrying the ark of God. They set the ark of God down beside Abiathar until everyone had finished marching out of the town. 25 The king then said to Zadok, 'Take the ark of God back into the city. Should I win Yahweh's favour, he will bring me back and allow me to see it and its tent once more. 26 But should he say, "You displease me," here I am: let him treat me as he sees fit.' 27 The king said to Zadok the

to the city in peace, you and Abiathar,*l* with your two sons, Ahimaaz your son, and Jonathan son of Abiathar. 28 See, I will wait at the fords of the wilderness until word comes from you to inform me." 29 So Zadok and Abiathar carried the ark of God back to Jerusalem, and they remained there.

30 But David went up the ascent of the Mount of Olives, weeping as he went, with his head covered and walking barefoot; and all the people who were with him covered their heads and went up, weeping as they went. 31 David was told that Ahithophel was among the conspirators with Absalom. And David said, "O LORD, I pray you, turn the counsel of Ahithophel into foolishness."

32 When David came to the summit, where God was worshiped, Hushai the Archite came to meet him with his coat torn and earth on his head. 33 David said to him, "If you go on with me, you will be a burden to me. 34 But if you return to the city and say to Absalom, 'I will be your servant, O king; as I have been your father's servant in time past, so now I will be your servant,' then you will defeat for me the counsel of Ahithophel. 35 The priests Zadok and Abiathar will be with you there. So whatever you hear from the king's house, tell it to the priests Zadok and Abiathar. 36 Their two sons are with them there, Zadok's son Ahimaaz and Abiathar's son Jonathan; and by them you shall report to me everything you hear." 37 So Hushai, David's friend, came into the city, just as Absalom was entering Jerusalem.

16 When David had passed a little beyond the summit, Ziba the servant of Mephibosheth*m* met him, with a couple of donkeys saddled, carrying two hundred loaves of bread, one hundred bunches of raisins, one hundred of summer fruits, and one skin of wine. 2 The king said to Ziba, "Why have you brought these?" Ziba answered, "The donkeys are for the king's household to ride, the bread and summer fruit for the young men to eat, and the wine is for those to drink who faint in the wilderness." 3 The king said, "And where is your master's son?" Ziba said to the king, "He remains in Jerusalem; for he said, 'Today the house of Israel will give me back my grandfather's kingdom.'" 4 Then the king said to Ziba, "All that belonged to Mephibosheth*m* is now yours." Ziba said, "I do obeisance; let me find favor in your sight, my lord the king."

5 When King David came to Bahurim, a man of the family of the house of Saul came out whose name was Shimei son of Gera; he came out cursing. 6 He threw stones at David and at all the servants of King David; now all the people and all the warriors were on his right and on his left. 7 Shimei shouted while he cursed, "Out! Out! Murderer! Scoundrel! 8 The LORD has avenged on all of you the blood of the house of Saul, in whose place you have reigned; and the LORD has given the kingdom into the hand of your son Absalom. See, disaster has overtaken you; for you are a man of blood."

9 Then Abishai son of Zeruiah said to the king, "Why should this dead dog curse my lord the king? Let me go over and take off his head." 10 But the king said, "What have I to do with you, you sons of Zeruiah? If he is cursing because the LORD has said to him, 'Curse David,' who then shall say, 'Why have you done so?'" 11 David said to Abishai and to all his servants, "My own son seeks my life; how much more now may this Benjaminite! Let him alone, and let him curse; for the LORD has bidden him. 12 It may be that the LORD will look on my distress,*n* and the LORD will repay me with good for this cursing of me today." 13 So

to Zadok the priest, 'Are you not a seer? You may safely go back to the city, you and Abiathar, and take with you the two young men, Ahimaaz your son and Abiathar's son Jonathan. 28 I shall wait at the Fords of the Wilderness until you can send word to me.' 29 Then Zadok and Abiathar took the Ark of God back to Jerusalem and remained there.

30 David wept as he went up the slope of the mount of Olives; he was bareheaded and went barefoot. The people with him all had their heads uncovered and wept as they went. 31 David had been told that Ahithophel was among the conspirators with Absalom, and he prayed, 'LORD, frustrate the counsel of Ahithophel.'

32 As David was approaching the top of the ridge where it was the custom to prostrate oneself to God, Hushai the Archite was there to meet him with his tunic torn and dust on his head. 33 David said to him, 'If you come with me you will only be a hindrance; 34 but you can help me to frustrate Ahithophel's plans if you go back to the city and say to Absalom, "I shall be your majesty's servant. In the past I was your father's servant; now I shall be yours." 35 You will have with you, as you know, the priests Zadok and Abiathar; report to them everything that you hear in the royal palace. 36 They have with them Zadok's son Ahimaaz and Abiathar's son Jonathan, and through them you may pass on to me everything you hear.' 37 So Hushai, David's Friend, came to the city as Absalom was entering Jerusalem.

16 When David had moved on a little from the top of the ridge, he was met by Ziba the servant of Mephibosheth, who had with him a pair of donkeys saddled and loaded with two hundred loaves of bread, a hundred clusters of raisins, a hundred bunches of summer fruit, and a skin of wine. 2 The king asked, 'What are you doing with these?' Ziba answered, 'The donkeys are for the king's family to ride on, the bread and the summer fruit are for his servants to eat, and the wine for anyone who becomes exhausted in the wilderness.' 3 The king asked, 'Where is your master's grandson?' 'He is staying in Jerusalem,' said Ziba, 'for he thought that the Israelites might now restore to him his grandfather's kingdom.' 4 The king said to Ziba, 'You shall have everything that belongs to Mephibosheth.' Ziba said, 'I am your humble servant, sir; may I always find favour with your majesty.'

5 As King David approached Bahurim, a man of Saul's family, whose name was Shimei son of Gera, came out, cursing all the while. 6 He showered stones right and left on David and on all the king's servants and on everyone, soldiers and people alike. 7 With curses Shimei shouted: 'Get out, get out, you murderous scoundrel! 8 The LORD has taken vengeance on you for the blood of the house of Saul whose throne you took, and he has given the kingdom to your son Absalom. You murderer, see how your crimes have overtaken you!'

9 Abishai son of Zeruiah said to the king, 'Why let this dead dog curse your majesty? I will go across and strike off his head.' 10 But the king said, 'What has this to do with us, you sons of Zeruiah? If he curses because the LORD has told him to curse David, who can question it?' 11 David said to Abishai and to all his servants, 'If my very own son is out to kill me, who can wonder at this Benjamite? Let him be, let him curse; for the LORD has told him to. 12 Perhaps the LORD will mark my sufferings and bestow a blessing on me in place of the curse laid on me this day.' 13 David and his

---

l Cn: Heb lacks *and Abiathar*   *m* Or *Merib-baal:* See 4.4 note
n Gk Vg: Heb *iniquity*

15:27 **you and Abiathar:** *prob. rdg, cp. verse 29; Heb. omits.*
15:31 **David . . . told:** *so Gk; Heb.* David told.
16:12 **sufferings:** *so Gk; Heb.* wickedness.

"See to it that you and Abiathar return to the city in peace, and both your sons with you, your own son Ahimaaz, and Abiathar's son Jonathan. 28 Remember, I shall be waiting at the fords near the desert until I receive information from you." 29 So Zadok and Abiathar took the ark of God back to Jerusalem and remained there.

30 As David went up the Mount of Olives, he wept without ceasing. His head was covered, and he was walking barefoot. All those who were with him also had their heads covered and were weeping as they went. 31 When David was informed that Ahithophel was among the conspirators with Absalom, he said, "O LORD, turn the counsel of Ahithophel to folly!"

32 When David reached the top, where men used to worship God, Hushai the Archite was there to meet him, with rent garments and dirt upon his head. 33 David said to him: "If you come with me, you will be a burden to me. 34 But if you return to the city and say to Absalom, 'Let me be your servant, O king; I was formerly your father's servant, but now I will be yours,' you will undo for me the counsel of Ahithophel. 35 You will have the priests Zadok and Abiathar there with you. If you hear anything from the royal palace, you shall report it to the priests Zadok and Abiathar, 36 who have there with them both Zadok's son Ahimaaz and Abiathar's son Jonathan. Through them you shall send on to me whatever you hear." 37 So David's friend Hushai went into the city of Jerusalem as Absalom was about to enter it.

16 David had gone a little beyond the top when Ziba, the servant of Meribbaal, met him with saddled asses laden with two hundred loaves of bread, an ephah of cakes of pressed raisins, an ephah of summer fruits, and a skin of wine. 2 The king said to Ziba, "What do you plan to do with these?" Ziba replied: "The asses are for the king's household to ride on. The bread and summer fruits are for your servants to eat, and the wine for those to drink who are weary in the desert." 3 Then the king said, "And where is your lord's son?" Ziba answered the king, "He is staying in Jerusalem, for he said, 'Now the Israelites will restore to me my father's kingdom.'" 4 The king therefore said to Ziba, "So! Everything Meribbaal had is yours." Then Ziba said: "I pay you homage, my lord the king. May I find favor with you!"

5 As David was approaching Bahurim, a man named Shimei, the son of Gera of the same clan as Saul's family, was coming out of the place, cursing as he came. 6 He threw stones at David and at all the king's officers, even though all the soldiers, including the royal guard, were on David's right and on his left. 7 Shimei was saying as he cursed: "Away, away, you murderous and wicked man! 8 The LORD has requited you for all the bloodshed in the family of Saul, in whose stead you became king, and the LORD has given over the kingdom to your son Absalom. And now you suffer ruin because you are a murderer." 9 Abishai, son of Zeruiah, said to the king: "Why should this dead dog curse my lord the king? Let me go over, please, and lop off his head." 10 But the king replied: "What business is it of mine or of yours, sons of Zeruiah, that he curses? Suppose the LORD has told him to curse David; who then will dare to say, 'Why are you doing this?'" 11 Then the king said to Abishai and to all his servants: "If my own son, who came forth from my loins, is seeking my life, how much more might this Benjaminite do so! Let him alone and let him curse, for the LORD has told him to. 12 Perhaps the LORD will look upon my affliction and make it up to me with benefits for the curses he is uttering this day." 13 David and his men

priest, 'Look, you and Abiathar go back quietly into the city, with your two sons, your own son Ahimaaz and Jonathan son of Abiathar. 28 You see, I shall wait in the passes of the desert plain until word comes from you bringing me news.' 29 So Zadok and Abiathar took the ark of God back to Jerusalem and stayed there.

30 David then made his way up the Mount of Olives, weeping as he went, his head covered and his feet bare. And all the people with him had their heads covered and made their way up, weeping as they went. 31 David was then informed that Ahithophel was among the conspirators with Absalom. David said, 'I beg you, Yahweh, turn Ahithophel's advice to folly.'

32 As David reached the summit, where God is worshipped, he saw Hushai the Archite, his friend, coming to meet him with his tunic torn and with earth on his head. 33 David said, 'If you go along with me, you will be a burden to me. 34 But if you go back to the city and say to Absalom, "I am at your service, my lord king; once I was in your father's service, but now I shall serve you," you will be able to thwart Ahithophel's advice for me. 35 Surely the priests Zadok and Abiathar will be with you? Anything you hear from the palace you must report to the priests Zadok and Abiathar. 36 You see, their two sons are there with them, Zadok's son Ahimaaz, and Abiathar's son Jonathan; through these, you will send me word of everything you hear.' 37 Hushai, David's friend, entered the city just as Absalom was reaching Jerusalem.

16 When David had passed a little beyond the summit, Meribbaal's retainer, Ziba, met him with a pair of donkeys, saddled and laden with two hundred loaves of bread, a hundred bunches of raisins, a hundred of the season's fruits, and a skin of wine. 2 The king said to Ziba, 'What are you going to do with that?' 'The donkeys', Ziba replied, 'are for the king's family to ride, the bread and the fruit for the soldiers to eat, the wine for drinking by those who get exhausted in the desert.' 3 The king asked 'And where is your master's son?' Ziba replied to the king, 'Why, he has stayed in Jerusalem because, he says, "Today, the House of Israel will give me back my father's kingdom."' 4 Then the king said to Ziba, 'Everything owned by Meribbaal is yours.' Ziba said, 'I prostrate myself! May I be worthy of your favour, my lord king!'

5 As David was reaching Bahurim, out came a man of the same clan as Saul's family. His name was Shimei son of Gera and, as he came, he uttered curse after curse 6 and threw stones at David and at all King David's retinue, even though the whole army and all the champions formed an escort round the king on either side. 7 The words of his curse were these, 'Off with you, off with you, man of blood, scoundrel! 8 Yahweh has paid you back for all the spilt blood of the House of Saul whose sovereignty you have usurped; and Yahweh has transferred the sovereign power to Absalom your son. Now your wickedness has overtaken you, man of blood that you are.' 9 Abishai son of Zeruiah said to the king, 'Why should this dead dog curse my lord the king? Let me go over and cut his head off.' 10 But the king said, 'What concern is my business to you, sons of Zeruiah? Let him curse! If Yahweh has said to him, "Curse David!" what right has anyone to say, "Why have you done so?"' 11 David said to Abishai and all his retinue, 'Why, the son sprung from my own body is now seeking my life; all the more reason for this Benjaminite to do so! Let him curse on, if Yahweh has told him to! 12 Perhaps Yahweh will look on my wretchedness and will repay me with good for his curses today.' 13 So David and his men went on their way,

NEW REVISED STANDARD VERSION | REVISED ENGLISH BIBLE

David and his men went on the road, while Shimei went along on the hillside opposite him and cursed as he went, throwing stones and flinging dust at him. 14 The king and all the people who were with him arrived weary at the Jordan;o and there he refreshed himself.

15 Now Absalom and all the Israelitesp came to Jerusalem; Ahithophel was with him. 16 When Hushai the Archite, David's friend, came to Absalom, Hushai said to Absalom, "Long live the king! Long live the king!" 17 Absalom said to Hushai, "Is this your loyalty to your friend? Why did you not go with your friend?" 18 Hushai said to Absalom, "No; but the one whom the LORD and this people and all the Israelites have chosen, his I will be, and with him I will remain. 19 Moreover, whom should I serve? Should it not be his son? Just as I have served your father, so I will serve you."

20 Then Absalom said to Ahithophel, "Give us your counsel; what shall we do?" 21 Ahithophel said to Absalom, "Go in to your father's concubines, the ones he has left to look after the house; and all Israel will hear that you have made yourself odious to your father, and the hands of all who are with you will be strengthened." 22 So they pitched a tent for Absalom upon the roof; and Absalom went in to his father's concubines in the sight of all Israel. 23 Now in those days the counsel that Ahithophel gave was as if one consulted the oracle q of God; so all the counsel of Ahithophel was esteemed, both by David and by Absalom.

17 Moreover Ahithophel said to Absalom, "Let me choose twelve thousand men, and I will set out and pursue David tonight. 2 I will come upon him while he is weary and discouraged, and throw him into a panic; and all the people who are with him will flee. I will strike down only the king, 3 and I will bring all the people back to you as a bride comes home to her husband. You seek the life of only one man,r and all the people will be at peace." 4 The advice pleased Absalom and all the elders of Israel.

5 Then Absalom said, "Call Hushai the Archite also, and let us hear too what he has to say." 6 When Hushai came to Absalom, Absalom said to him, "This is what Ahithophel has said; shall we do as he advises? If not, you tell us." 7 Then Hushai said to Absalom, "This time the counsel that Ahithophel has given is not good." 8 Hushai continued, "You know that your father and his men are warriors, and that they are enraged, like a bear robbed of her cubs in the field. Besides, your father is expert in war; he will not spend the night with the troops. 9 Even now he has hidden himself in one of the pits, or in some other place. And when some of our troopss fall at the first attack, whoever hears it will say, 'There has been a slaughter among the troops who follow Absalom.' 10 Then even the valiant warrior, whose heart is like the heart of a lion, will utterly melt with fear; for all Israel knows that your father is a warrior, and that those who are with him are valiant warriors. 11 But my counsel is that all Israel be gathered to you, from Dan to Beer-sheba, like the sand by the sea for multitude, and that you go to battle in person. 12 So we shall come upon him in whatever place he may be found, and we shall light on him as the dew falls on the ground; and he will not survive, nor will any of those with him. 13 If he withdraws into a city, then all Israel will bring ropes to that city, and we shall drag it into the valley, until not even a pebble is to be found there." 14 Absalom and all the men of Israel said, "The

men continued on their way, and Shimei kept abreast along the ridge of the hill parallel to David's path, cursing as he went and hurling stones across the valley at him and covering him with dust. 14 When the king and all the people with him reached the Jordan, they rested there, for they were worn out.

15 By now Absalom and all his Israelites had reached Jerusalem, and Ahithophel was with him. 16 When Hushai the Archite, David's Friend, met Absalom he said, 'Long live the king! Long live the king!' 17 But Absalom retorted, 'Is this your loyalty to your friend? Why did you not go with him?' 18 Hushai answered, 'Because I mean to attach myself to the man chosen by the LORD and by this people and by all the men of Israel, and with him I shall stay. 19 After all, whom ought I to serve? Should I not serve the son? I shall serve you as I have served your father.'

20 Absalom said to Ahithophel, 'Give us your advice: how shall we act?' 21 Ahithophel answered, 'Lie with your father's concubines whom he left in charge of the palace. Then all Israel will come to hear that you have given great cause of offence to your father, and this will confirm the resolution of your followers.' 22 So they set up a tent for Absalom on the roof, and he lay with his father's concubines in the sight of all Israel.

23 In those days a man would seek counsel of Ahithophel as if he were making an enquiry of the word of God; that was how Ahithophel's counsel was esteemed by both David

17 and Absalom. 1 Ahithophel said to Absalom, 'Let me pick twelve thousand men to go in pursuit of David tonight. 2 If I overtake him when he is tired and dispirited I shall cut him off from his people and they will all scatter; I shall kill no one but the king. 3 I shall bring all the people over to you as a bride is brought to her husband. It is only one man's life that you are seeking; the rest of the people will be unharmed.' 4 Absalom and all the elders of Israel approved of Ahithophel's advice; 5 but Absalom said, 'Now summon Hushai the Archite and let us also hear what he has to say.' 6 When Hushai came, Absalom told him what Ahithophel had said and asked him, 'Shall we do as he advises? If not, speak up.'

7 Hushai said to Absalom, 'For once the counsel that Ahithophel has given is not good. 8 You know', he went on, 'that your father and the men with him are hardened warriors and savage as a bear in the wilds robbed of her cubs. Your father is an old campaigner and will not spend the night with the main body; 9 even now he will be lying hidden in a pit or in some such place. Then if any of your men are killed at the outset, whoever hears the news will say, "Disaster has overtaken Absalom's followers." 10 The courage of the most resolute and lion-hearted will melt away, for all Israel knows that your father is a man of war and has seasoned warriors with him.

11 'Here is my advice. Wait until the whole of Israel, from Dan to Beersheba, is gathered about you, countless as grains of sand on the seashore, and then march to battle with them in person. 12 When we come on him somewhere, wherever he may be, and descend on him like dew falling on the ground, not a man of his family or of his followers will be left alive. 13 If he retreats into a town, all Israel will bring ropes to that town, and we shall drag it into a ravine until not a stone can be found on the site.' 14 Absalom and

---

o Gk: Heb lacks at the Jordan   p Gk: Heb all the people, the men
of Israel   q Heb word   r Gk: Heb like the return of the whole (is)
the man whom you seek   s Gk Mss: Heb some of them

16:14 the Jordan: so Gk (Luc.); Heb. omits.   17:3 as a bride
. . . seeking: so Gk; Heb. as the whole returns, so is the man you are
seeking.

continued on the road, while Shimei kept abreast of them on the hillside, all the while cursing and throwing stones and dirt as he went. 14 The king and all the soldiers with him arrived at the Jordan tired out, and stopped there for a rest.

15 In the meantime Absalom, accompanied by Ahithophel, entered Jerusalem with all the Israelites. 16 When David's friend Hushai the Archite came to Absalom, he said to him: "Long live the king! Long live the king!" 17 But Absalom asked Hushai: "Is this your devotion to your friend? Why did you not go with your friend?" 18 Hushai replied to Absalom: "On the contrary, I am his whom the LORD and all this people and all Israel have chosen, and with him I will stay. 19 Furthermore, as I was in attendance upon your father, so will I be before you. Whom should I serve, if not his son?" 20 Then Absalom said to Ahithophel, "Offer your counsel on what we should do." 21 Ahithophel replied to Absalom: "Have relations with your father's concubines, whom he left behind to take care of the palace. When all Israel hears how odious you have made yourself to your father, all your partisans will take courage." 22 So a tent was pitched on the roof for Absalom, and he visited his father's concubines in view of all Israel.

23 Now the counsel given by Ahithophel at that time was as though one had sought divine revelation. Such was all his counsel both to David and to Absalom.

17 Ahithophel went on to say to Absalom: "Please let me choose twelve thousand men, and be off in pursuit of David tonight. 2 If I come upon him when he is weary and discouraged, I shall cause him to panic. When all the people with him flee, I shall strike down the king alone. 3 Then I can bring back the rest of the people to you, as a bride returns to her husband. It is the death of only one man you are seeking; then all the people will be at peace." 4 This plan was agreeable to Absalom and to all the elders of Israel.

5 Then Absalom said, "Now call Hushai the Archite also; let us hear what he too has to say." 6 When Hushai came to Absalom, Absalom said to him: "This is what Ahithophel proposed. Shall we follow his proposal? If not, speak up." 7 Hushai replied to Absalom, "This time Ahithophel has not given good counsel." 8 And he went on to say: "You know that your father and his men are warriors, and that they are as fierce as a bear in the wild robbed of her cubs. Moreover, since your father is skilled in warfare, he will not spend the night with the people. 9 Even now he lies hidden in one of the caves or in some other place. And if some of our soldiers should fall at the first attack, whoever hears of it will say, 'Absalom's followers have been slaughtered.' 10 Then even the brave man with the heart of a lion will lose courage. For all Israel knows that your father is a warrior and that those who are with him are brave.

11 "This is what I counsel: Let all Israel from Dan to Beer-sheba, who are as numerous as the sands by the sea, be called up for combat; and go with them yourself. 12 We can then attack him wherever we find him, settling down upon him as dew alights on the ground. None shall survive —neither he nor any of his followers. 13 And if he retires into a city, all Israel shall bring ropes to that city and we can drag it into the gorge, so that not even a pebble of it can be found." 14 Then Absalom and all the Israelites pronounced

and Shimei kept pace with him along the opposite mountainside, cursing as he went, throwing stones and flinging dust. 14 The king and all the people who were with him arrived exhausted at . . . f . . . and there they drew breath.

15 Absalom entered Jerusalem with all the men of Israel; with him was Ahithophel. 16 When Hushai the Archite, David's friend, reached Absalom, Hushai said to Absalom, 'Long live the king! Long live the king!' 17 Absalom said to Hushai, 'Is this your faithful love for your friend? Why didn't you go away with your friend?' 18 Hushai replied to Absalom, 'No, the man whom Yahweh and this people and all the men of Israel have chosen, he is the man for me, and with him will I stay! 19 Besides, whom should I serve, if not his son? As I served your father, so shall I serve you.'

20 Absalom said to Ahithophel, 'Think carefully. What shall we do?' 21 Ahithophel replied to Absalom, 'Go to your father's concubines whom he left to look after the palace; then all Israel will hear that you have thoroughly antagonised your father, and the resolution of all your supporters will be strengthened.' 22 So a tent was pitched for Absalom on the flat roof and, with all Israel watching, Absalom went to his father's concubines. 23 At the time, whatever advice Ahithophel gave was treated like a decision obtained from God; as by David, so by Absalom, was all Ahithophel's advice regarded.

17 Ahithophel said to Absalom, 'Let me choose twelve thousand men and set off this very night in pursuit of David. 2 I shall fall on him while he is tired and dispirited; I shall strike terror into him, and all the people who are with him will run away. I shall kill only the king, 3 and I shall then bring all the people back to you, like a bride returning to her husband. You seek the life of one individual only; the people as a whole will have peace.' 4 The suggestion seemed a good one to Absalom and all the elders of Israel.

5 Then Absalom said, 'Now call Hushai the Archite, for us to hear what he too has to say.' 6 When Hushai had come to Absalom, Absalom said, 'This is what Ahithophel says. Are we to do as he suggests? If not, suggest something yourself.' 7 Hushai said to Absalom, 'On this occasion the advice given by Ahithophel is not good. 8 You know', Hushai went on, 'that your father and his men are great fighters and that they are now as angry as a wild bear robbed of her cubs. Your father is a man of war: he will not let the army rest during the night. 9 At this moment he is concealed in some hollow or other place. If at the outset there are casualties among our troops, word will go round that the army supporting Absalom has met with disaster. 10 And then even the valiant, the truly lion-hearted, will be demoralized; for all Israel knows that your father is a champion and that the men with him are valiant. 11 For my part, I offer this advice: Summon all Israel, from Dan to Beersheba, to rally to you, as numerous as the sand on the seashore, and you take the field in person with them. 12 We shall reach him wherever he is to be found; we shall fall on him as the dew falls on the ground, and not leave him or any one of the men with him. 13 Should he retire into a town, all Israel will bring ropes to that town, and we shall drag it into the river-bed until not a pebble of it is to be found.' 14 Then Absalom and

f 16 A place-name is missing.

NEW REVISED STANDARD VERSION	REVISED ENGLISH BIBLE

counsel of Hushai the Archite is better than the counsel of Ahithophel." For the LORD had ordained to defeat the good counsel of Ahithophel, so that the LORD might bring ruin on Absalom.

15 Then Hushai said to the priests Zadok and Abiathar, "Thus and so did Ahithophel counsel Absalom and the elders of Israel; and thus and so I have counseled. 16 Therefore send quickly and tell David, 'Do not lodge tonight at the fords of the wilderness, but by all means cross over; otherwise the king and all the people who are with him will be swallowed up.' " 17 Jonathan and Ahimaaz were waiting at En-rogel; a servant-girl used to go and tell them, and they would go and tell King David; for they could not risk being seen entering the city. 18 But a boy saw them, and told Absalom; so both of them went away quickly, and came to the house of a man at Bahurim, who had a well in his courtyard; and they went down into it. 19 The man's wife took a covering, stretched it over the well's mouth, and spread out grain on it; and nothing was known of it. 20 When Absalom's servants came to the woman at the house, they said, "Where are Ahimaaz and Jonathan?" The woman said to them, "They have crossed over the brook *t* of water." And when they had searched and could not find them, they returned to Jerusalem.

21 After they had gone, the men came up out of the well, and went and told King David. They said to David, "Go and cross the water quickly; for thus and so has Ahithophel counseled against you." 22 So David and all the people who were with him set out and crossed the Jordan; by daybreak not one was left who had not crossed the Jordan.

23 When Ahithophel saw that his counsel was not followed, he saddled his donkey and went off home to his own city. He set his house in order, and hanged himself; he died and was buried in the tomb of his father.

24 Then David came to Mahanaim, while Absalom crossed the Jordan with all the men of Israel. 25 Now Absalom had set Amasa over the army in the place of Joab. Amasa was the son of a man named Ithra the Ishmaelite, *u* who had married Abigal daughter of Nahash, sister of Zeruiah, Joab's mother. 26 The Israelites and Absalom encamped in the land of Gilead.

27 When David came to Mahanaim, Shobi son of Nahash from Rabbah of the Ammonites, and Machir son of Ammiel from Lo-debar, and Barzillai the Gileadite from Rogelim, 28 brought beds, basins, and earthen vessels, wheat, barley, meal, parched grain, beans and lentils, *v* 29 honey and curds, sheep, and cheese from the herd, for David and the people with him to eat; for they said, "The troops are hungry and weary and thirsty in the wilderness."

18 Then David mustered the men who were with him, and set over them commanders of thousands and commanders of hundreds. 2 And David divided the army into three groups: *w* one third under the command of Joab, one third under the command of Abishai son of Zeruiah, Joab's brother, and one third under the command of Ittai the Gittite. The king said to the men, "I myself will also go out with you." 3 But the men said, "You shall not go out. For if we flee, they will not care about us. If half of us die, they will not care about us. But you are worth ten thousand of us; *x* therefore it is better that you send us help from the city." 4 The king said to them, "Whatever seems best to you

all the Israelites said, 'Hushai the Archite has given us better advice than Ahithophel.' It was the LORD's purpose to frustrate Ahithophel's good advice and so bring disaster on Absalom.

15 Hushai told Zadok and Abiathar the priests all the advice that Ahithophel had given to Absalom and the elders of Israel, and also what he himself had advised. 16 'Now send quickly to David', he said, 'and warn him not to spend the night at the Fords of the Wilderness but to cross the river at once, before an overwhelming blow can be launched at the king and his followers.' 17 Jonathan and Ahimaaz were waiting at En-rogel, and a servant-girl used to go and tell them what happened and they would pass it on to King David; for they dared not risk being seen entering the city. 18 But a lad saw them and told Absalom; so the two of them hurried to Bahurim to the house of a man who had a cistern in his courtyard, and they climbed down into it. 19 The man's wife took a covering, spread it over the mouth of the cistern, and scattered grain over it, so that nothing would be noticed. 20 Absalom's servants came to the house and asked the woman, 'Where are Ahimaaz and Jonathan?' She answered, 'They went past the pool.' The men searched, but not finding them they returned to Jerusalem. 21 As soon as they had gone the two climbed out of the cistern and went off to report to King David. They said to him, 'Get over the water at once, and with all speed!' and they told him Ahithophel's plan against him. 22 So David and all his company began at once to cross the Jordan; by daybreak there was not one who had not reached the other bank.

23 When Ahithophel saw that his advice had not been taken he saddled his donkey, went straight home to his own town, gave his last instructions to his household, and then hanged himself. So he died and was buried in his father's grave.

24 By the time that Absalom had crossed the Jordan with the Israelites, David was already at Mahanaim. 25 Absalom had appointed Amasa as commander-in-chief in Joab's place; he was the son of a man named Ithra, an Ishmaelite, by Abigal daughter of Nahash and sister to Joab's mother Zeruiah. 26 The Israelites and Absalom camped in the district of Gilead.

27 When David came to Mahanaim, he was met by Shobi son of Nahash from the Ammonite town Rabbah, Machir son of Ammiel from Lo-debar, and Barzillai the Gileadite from Rogelim, 28 bringing mattresses and blankets, bowls, and jugs. They brought also wheat and barley, flour and roasted grain, beans and lentils, 29 honey and curds, sheep and fat cattle, and offered them to David and his people to eat, knowing that the people must be hungry and thirsty and weary in the wilderness.

18 David reviewed the troops who were with him, and appointed officers over units of a thousand and of a hundred. 2 He divided his army in three, one division under the command of Joab, one under Joab's brother Abishai son of Zeruiah, and the third under Ittai the Gittite. The king announced to the troops that he himself was coming out with them. 3 But they said, 'No, you must not; if we take to flight, no one will care, nor will they even if half of us are killed; but you are worth ten thousand of us, and it would be better now for you to remain in the town in support.' 4 The king answered, 'I shall do what you think best.' He

---

17:20 **pool:** *Heb. word of uncertain meaning.*   17:25 **Ishmaelite:** *so one form of Gk, cp.* 1 Chr. 2:17; *Heb.* Israelite. 17:28 **bringing . . . jugs:** *prob. rdg; Heb.* a couch, bowls, and a potter's vessel. **lentils:** *so Gk; Heb.* adds and roasted grain. 18:3 **but you:** *so Gk; Heb.* but now. **in the town:** *so Gk; Heb.* from a town.

---

t Meaning of Heb uncertain   *u* 1 Chr 2.17: Heb *Israelite*
v Heb *and lentils and parched grain*   *w* Gk: Heb *sent forth the army*
x Gk Vg Symmachus: Heb *for now there are ten thousand such as we*

the counsel of Hushai the Archite better than that of Ahithophel. For the LORD had decided to undo Ahithophel's good counsel, in order thus to bring Absalom to ruin.

15 Then Hushai said to the priests Zadok and Abiathar: "This is the counsel Ahithophel gave Absalom and the elders of Israel, and this is what I counseled. 16 So send a warning to David immediately, not to spend the night at the fords near the desert, but to cross over without fail. Otherwise the king and all the people with him will be destroyed." 17 Now Jonathan and Ahimaaz were staying at En-rogel, since they could not risk being seen entering the city. A maidservant was to come with information for them, and they in turn were to go and report to King David. 18 But an attendant saw them and informed Absalom. They sped on their way and reached the house of a man in Bahurim who had a cistern in his courtyard. They let themselves down into this, 19 and the housewife took the cover and spread it over the cistern, strewing ground grain on the cover so that nothing could be noticed. 20 When Absalom's servants came to the woman at the house, they asked, "Where are Ahimaaz and Jonathan?" The woman replied, "They went by a short while ago toward the water." They searched, but found no one, and so returned to Jerusalem. 21 As soon as they left, Ahimaaz and Jonathan came up out of the cistern and went on to inform King David. They said to him: "Leave! Cross the water at once, for Ahithophel has given the following counsel in regard to you." 22 So David and all his people moved on and crossed the Jordan. By daybreak, there was no one left who had not crossed.

23 When Ahithophel saw that his counsel was not acted upon, he saddled his ass and departed, going to his home in his own city. Then, having left orders concerning his family, he hanged himself. And so he died and was buried in his father's tomb.

24 Now David had gone to Mahanaim when Absalom crossed the Jordan accompanied by all the Israelites. 25 Absalom had put Amasa in command of the army in Joab's place. Amasa was the son of an Ishmaelite named Ithra, who had married Abigail, daughter of Jesse and sister of Joab's mother Zeruiah. 26 Israel and Absalom encamped in the territory of Gilead.

27 When David came to Mahanaim, Shobi, son of Nahash from Rabbah of the Ammonites, Machir, son of Ammiel from Lodebar, and Barzillai, the Gileadite from Rogelim, 28 brought couches, coverlets, basins and earthenware, as well as wheat, barley, flour, roasted grain, beans, lentils, 29 honey, butter and cheese from the flocks and herds, for David and those who were with him to eat; for they said, "The people have been hungry and tired and thirsty in the desert."

18 After mustering the troops he had with him, David placed officers in command of groups of a thousand and groups of a hundred. 2 David then put a third part of the soldiers under Joab's command, a third under command of Abishai, son of Zeruiah and brother of Joab, and a third under command of Ittai the Gittite. The king then said to the soldiers, "I intend to go out with you myself." 3 But they replied: "You must not come out with us. For if we should flee, we shall not count; even if half of us should die, we shall not count. You are equal to ten thousand of us. Therefore it is better that we have you to help us from the city." 4 So the king said to them, "I will do what you think best";

all the people of Israel said, 'Hushai the Arkite's advice is better than Ahithophel's,' Yahweh having resolved to thwart Ahithophel's shrewd advice and so bring disaster on Absalom.

15 Hushai then told the priests Zadok and Abiathar, 'Ahithophel gave such and such advice to Absalom and the elders of Israel, but I advised so and so. 16 Send with all speed to David and say, "Do not camp in the desert passes tonight, but get through them as fast as you can, or the king and his whole army may be annihilated." '

17 Jonathan and Ahimaaz were posted at the Fuller's Spring; a servant-girl was to go and warn them and they in turn were to warn King David, since they could not give themselves away by coming into the city themselves. 18 A young man saw them nonetheless and told Absalom. The pair of them, however, made off quickly, reaching the house of a man in Bahurim. In his courtyard was a storage-well and they got down into it. 19 The woman took a piece of canvas and, spreading it over the mouth of the storage-well, scattered crushed grain on it so that nothing showed. 20 When Absalom's servants reached the woman at the house, they said, 'Where are Ahimaaz and Jonathan?' The woman said, 'They have gone further on, towards the water.' They searched but, having found nothing, went back to Jerusalem.

21 When they had gone, the men climbed out of the storage-well and went to warn King David. 'Set out!' they told David. 'Cross the water quickly, for Ahithophel has given such and such advice against you!' 22 So David and all the troops with him set off and crossed the Jordan. By dawn no one was left, all had crossed the Jordan.

23 When Ahithophel saw that his advice had not been followed, he saddled his donkey and set off and went home to his own town. Then, having set his house in order, he hanged himself. He was buried in his father's tomb.

24 David had reached Mahanaim by the time that Absalom crossed the Jordan with all the men of Israel. 25 Absalom had put Amasa in command of the army in place of Joab. This Amasa was the son of a man called Ithra the Ishmaelite, who had married Abigail, daughter of Jesse and sister of Zeruiah, mother of Joab. 26 Israel and Absalom pitched their camp in the territory of Gilead.

27 When David reached Mahanaim, Shobi son of Nahash from Rabbah-of-the-Ammonites, Machir son of Ammiel from Lo-Debar, and Barzillai the Gileadite from Rogelim 28 brought bedding, rugs, bowls and crockery; and wheat, barley, meal, roasted grain, beans, lentils, 29 honey, curds and cows' cheese and sheep's cheese, which they presented to David and the people with him for them to eat. 'The army', they said, 'must have been hungry, tired and thirsty in the desert.'

18 David reviewed the troops who were with him and appointed commanders of thousands and commanders of hundreds to lead them. 2 David divided the army into three groups, one under the command of Joab, another under the command of Abishai son of Zeruiah and brother of Joab, and the third under the command of Ittai the Gittite. David then said to the troops, 'I shall take the field in person with you.' 3 But the troops replied, 'You are not to take the field. No one will bother about us if we run away, they will not even bother about us if half of us are killed, but you are ten thousand times more valuable. So it is better if you stay inside the town, in case we need reinforcements.' 4 David said, 'I will do what you think best.' And the king stood

NEW REVISED STANDARD VERSION	REVISED ENGLISH BIBLE

I will do." So the king stood at the side of the gate, while all the army marched out by hundreds and by thousands. 5 The king ordered Joab and Abishai and Ittai, saying, "Deal gently for my sake with the young man Absalom." And all the people heard when the king gave orders to all the commanders concerning Absalom.

6 So the army went out into the field against Israel; and the battle was fought in the forest of Ephraim. 7 The men of Israel were defeated there by the servants of David, and the slaughter there was great on that day, twenty thousand men. 8 The battle spread over the face of all the country; and the forest claimed more victims that day than the sword.

9 Absalom happened to meet the servants of David. Absalom was riding on his mule, and the mule went under the thick branches of a great oak. His head caught fast in the oak, and he was left hanging *y* between heaven and earth, while the mule that was under him went on. 10 A man saw it, and told Joab, "I saw Absalom hanging in an oak." 11 Joab said to the man who told him, "What, you saw him! Why then did you not strike him there to the ground? I would have been glad to give you ten pieces of silver and a belt." 12 But the man said to Joab, "Even if I felt in my hand the weight of a thousand pieces of silver, I would not raise my hand against the king's son; for in our hearing the king commanded you and Abishai and Ittai, saying: For my sake protect the young man Absalom! 13 On the other hand, if I had dealt treacherously against his life *z* (and there is nothing hidden from the king), then you yourself would have stood aloof." 14 Joab said, "I will not waste time like this with you." He took three spears in his hand, and thrust them into the heart of Absalom, while he was still alive in the oak. 15 And ten young men, Joab's armor-bearers, surrounded Absalom and struck him, and killed him.

16 Then Joab sounded the trumpet, and the troops came back from pursuing Israel, for Joab restrained the troops. 17 They took Absalom, threw him into a great pit in the forest, and raised over him a very great heap of stones. Meanwhile all the Israelites fled to their homes. 18 Now Absalom in his lifetime had taken and set up for himself a pillar that is in the King's Valley, for he said, "I have no son to keep my name in remembrance"; he called the pillar by his own name. It is called Absalom's Monument to this day.

19 Then Ahimaaz son of Zadok said, "Let me run, and carry tidings to the king that the LORD has delivered him from the power of his enemies." 20 Joab said to him, "You are not to carry tidings today; you may carry tidings another day, but today you shall not do so, because the king's son is dead." 21 Then Joab said to a Cushite, "Go, tell the king what you have seen." The Cushite bowed before Joab, and ran. 22 Then Ahimaaz son of Zadok said again to Joab, "Come what may, let me also run after the Cushite." And Joab said, "Why will you run, my son, seeing that you have no reward *a* for the tidings?" 23 "Come what may," he said, "I will run." So he said to him, "Run." Then Ahimaaz ran by the way of the Plain, and outran the Cushite.

24 Now David was sitting between the two gates. The sentinel went up to the roof of the gate by the wall, and when he looked up, he saw a man running alone. 25 The sentinel shouted and told the king. The king said, "If he is alone, there are tidings in his mouth." He kept coming, and drew near. 26 Then the sentinel saw another man running; and the sentinel called to the gatekeeper and said, "See, another man running alone!" The king said, "He also is bringing tidings." 27 The sentinel said, "I think the running of the first one is like the running of Ahimaaz son of Zadok." The king said, "He is a good man, and comes with good tidings."

stood beside the gate, while all the army marched past by hundreds and by thousands, 5 and he gave this order to Joab, Abishai, and Ittai: 'Deal gently with the young man Absalom for my sake.' The whole army heard the king giving each of the officers the order about Absalom.

6 The army took the field against the Israelites, and a battle was fought in the forest of Ephron. 7 There the Israelites were routed before the onslaught of David's men, and the loss of life was great, for twenty thousand fell. 8 The fighting spread over the whole countryside, and the forest took toll of more people that day than the sword.

9 Some of David's men caught sight of Absalom; he was riding his mule and, as it passed beneath a large oak, his head was caught in its boughs; he was left in mid-air, while the mule went on from under him. 10 One of the men who saw this told Joab, 'I saw Absalom hanging from an oak.' 11 While the man was telling him, Joab broke in, 'You saw him? Why did you not strike him to the ground then and there? I would have given you ten pieces of silver and a belt.' 12 The man answered, 'If you were to put into my hands a thousand pieces of silver, I would not lift a finger against the king's son; we all heard the king giving orders to you and Abishai and Ittai to take care of the young man Absalom. 13 If I had dealt him a treacherous blow, the king would soon have known, and you would have kept well out of it.' 14 'That is a lie!' said Joab. 'I will make a start and show you.' He picked up three javelins and drove them into Absalom's chest while he was held fast in the tree and still alive. 15 Then ten young men who were Joab's armour-bearers closed in on Absalom, struck at him, and killed him. 16 Joab sounded the trumpet, and the army came back from the pursuit of Israel, because he had called on them to halt. 17 They took Absalom's body and flung it into a large pit in the forest, and raised over it a great cairn of stones. The Israelites all fled to their homes.

18 The pillar in the King's Valley had been set up by Absalom in his lifetime, for he said, 'I have no son to carry on my name.' He had named the pillar after himself, and to this day it is called Absalom's Monument.

19 Ahimaaz son of Zadok said, 'Let me run and take the news to the king that the LORD has avenged him and delivered him from his enemies.' 20 But Joab replied, 'This is no day for you to be the bearer of news. Another day you may have news to carry, but not today, because the king's son is dead.' 21 Joab told a Cushite to go and report to the king what he had seen. The Cushite bowed to Joab and set off running. 22 Ahimaaz pleaded again with Joab, 'Come what may,' he said, 'let me run after the Cushite.' 'Why should you, my son?' asked Joab. 'You will get no reward for your news.' 23 'Come what may,' he said, 'let me run.' 'Go, then,' said Joab. So Ahimaaz ran by the road through the plain of the Jordan and outstripped the Cushite.

24 David was sitting between the inner and outer gates and the watchman had gone up to the roof of the gatehouse by the wall of the town. Looking out and seeing a man running alone, 25 the watchman called to the king and told him. 'If he is alone,' said the king, 'then he is bringing news.' The man continued to approach, 26 and then the watchman saw another man running. He called down into the gate, 'Look, there is another man running alone.' The king said, 'He too brings news.' 27 The watchman said, 'I see by the way he runs that the first runner is Ahimaaz son of Zadok.' The king said, 'He is a good man and shall earn the reward for good news.'

y Gk Syr Tg: Heb *was put*   *z* Another reading is *at the risk of my life*   *a* Meaning of Heb uncertain

18:6 **Ephron:** *prob. rdg; Heb.* Ephraim.   18:9 **oak:** *or* terebinth.   18:14 **I . . . show you:** *or* I can waste no more time on you like this.   **javelins:** *so Gk; Heb.* clubs.

NEW AMERICAN BIBLE

and he stood by the gate as all the soldiers marched out in units of a hundred and of a thousand. 5 But the king gave this command to Joab, Abishai and Ittai: "Be gentle with young Absalom for my sake." All the soldiers heard the king instruct the various leaders with regard to Absalom. 6 David's army then took the field against Israel, and a battle was fought in the forest near Mahanaim. 7 The forces of Israel were defeated by David's servants, and the casualties there that day were heavy—twenty thousand men. 8 The battle spread out over that entire region, and the thickets consumed more combatants that day than did the sword.

9 Absalom unexpectedly came up against David's servants. He was mounted on a mule, and, as the mule passed under the branches of a large terebinth, his hair caught fast in the tree. He hung between heaven and earth while the mule he had been riding ran off. 10 Someone saw this and reported to Joab that he had seen Absalom hanging from a terebinth. 11 Joab said to his informant: "If you saw him, why did you not strike him to the ground on the spot? Then it would have been my duty to give you fifty pieces of silver and a belt." 12 But the man replied to Joab: "Even if I already held a thousand pieces of silver in my two hands, I would not harm the king's son, for the king charged you and Abishai and Ittai in our hearing to protect the youth Absalom for his sake. 13 Had I been disloyal and killed him, the whole matter would have come to the attention of the king, and you would stand aloof." 14 Joab replied, "I will not waste time with you in this way." And taking three pikes in hand, he thrust for the heart of Absalom, still hanging from the tree alive. 15 Next, ten of Joab's young armor-bearers closed in on Absalom, and killed him with further blows. 16 Joab then sounded the horn, and the soldiers turned back from the pursuit of the Israelites, because Joab called on them to halt. 17 Absalom was taken up and cast into a deep pit in the forest, and a very large mound of stones was erected over him. And all the Israelites fled to their own tents.

18 During his lifetime Absalom had taken a pillar and erected it for himself in the King's Valley, for he said, "I have no son to perpetuate my name." The pillar which he named for himself is called Yad-abshalom to the present day.

19 Then Ahimaaz, son of Zadok, said, "Let me run to take the good news to the king that the LORD has set him free from the grasp of his enemies." 20 But Joab said to him: "You are not the man to bring the news today. On some other day you may take the good news, but today you would not be bringing good news, for in fact the king's son is dead." 21 Then Joab said to a Cushite, "Go, tell the king what you have seen." The Cushite bowed to Joab and sped away. 22 But Ahimaaz, son of Zadok, said to Joab again, "Come what may, permit me also to run after the Cushite." Joab replied: "Why do you want to run, my son? You will receive no reward." 23 But he insisted, "Come what may, I want to run." Joab said to him, "Very well." Ahimaaz sped off by way of the Jordan plain and outran the Cushite.

24 Now David was sitting between the two gates, and a lookout mounted to the roof of the gate above the city wall, where he looked about and saw a man running all alone. 25 The lookout shouted to inform the king, who said, "If he is alone, he has good news to report." As he kept coming nearer, 26 the lookout spied another runner. From his place atop the gate he cried out, "There is another man running by himself." And the king responded, "He, too, is bringing good news." 27 Then the lookout said, "I notice that the first one runs like Ahimaaz, son of Zadok." The king replied, "He is a good man; he comes with good news." 28 Then

NEW JERUSALEM BIBLE

beside the gate as the troops marched out by their hundreds and their thousands. 5 The king gave orders to Joab, Abishai and Ittai, 'For my sake, treat young Absalom gently!' And the troops all heard the king give all the commanders these orders about Absalom. 6 So the troops marched out into the open to engage Israel, and the battle took place in the Forest of Ephraim. 7 There, the army of Israel was beaten by David's retainers; it was a great defeat that day, with twenty thousand casualties. 8 The fighting spread throughout the region and that day the forest claimed more victims than the sword.

9 Absalom happened to run into some of David's guards. Absalom was riding his mule and the mule passed under the thick branches of a great oak. Absalom's head got caught in the oak and he was left hanging between heaven and earth, while the mule he was riding went on. 10 Someone saw this and reported to Joab, 'I have just seen Absalom hanging from an oak.' 11 Joab said to the man who had informed him, 'If you saw him, why did you not strike him to the ground then and there? I would have made it my business to give you ten silver shekels and a belt!' 12 The man replied to Joab, 'Even if I could feel the weight of a thousand silver shekels in my hand, I would not lift my hand against the king's son. In our own hearing, the king gave you and Abishai and Ittai these orders, "For my sake, spare young Absalom." 13 Even if I had deceived myself, nothing stays hidden from the king and you would have dissociated yourself from me.' 14 Joab then said, 'I cannot waste time arguing with you!' And, taking three darts in his hand, he planted them in Absalom's heart, while he was still alive, deep in the oak-tree. 15 Ten soldiers, Joab's armour-bearers, then came in close, struck Absalom and killed him.

16 Joab then had the trumpet sounded, and the troops left off pursuing Israel, since Joab held the troops back. 17 They took Absalom, flung him into a deep pit in the forest and raised a huge cairn over him. All the Israelites had fled, dispersing to their homes.

18 Now, during his lifetime, Absalom had made and erected a pillar to himself, which is in the Valley of the King. 'I have no son,' he said, 'to preserve the memory of my name.' He gave his own name to the pillar, and today it is still called Absalom's Monument.

19 Ahimaaz son of Zadok said, 'Let me run and tell the king the good news that Yahweh has vindicated his cause by ridding him of his enemies.' 20 But Joab said, 'Today you would be no bearer of good news, some other day you may be; but today you would not be bringing good news, since the king's son is dead.' 21 Joab then said to the Cushite, 'Go and tell the king what you have seen.' The Cushite prostrated himself to Joab and ran off. 22 But Ahimaaz son of Zadok persisted. 'Come what may,' he said to Joab, 'please let me run after the Cushite.' 'My son,' Joab said, 'why run? You will get no reward for your news.' 23 But he replied, 'Come what may, let me run!' and Joab said 'Run, then!' So Ahimaaz ran off along the road through the Plain, outrunning the Cushite.

24 David was sitting between the two gates. The sentry, having gone up to the roof of the gate, looked out from the ramparts and saw a man running alone. 25 The sentry called down to the king and told him. The king said, 'If he is alone, he is bringing good news.' 26 As the man drew steadily nearer, the lookout saw another man running, and the sentry above the gate shouted, 'Here comes another man, running alone!' David said, 'He too is a bearer of good news.' 27 The sentry said, 'I recognise the way the first man runs; Ahimaaz son of Zadok runs like that.' 'He is a good man', said the king, 'and comes with good news.'

NEW REVISED STANDARD VERSION	REVISED ENGLISH BIBLE

28 Then Ahimaaz cried out to the king, "All is well!" He prostrated himself before the king with his face to the ground, and said, "Blessed be the LORD your God, who has delivered up the men who raised their hand against my lord the king." 29 The king said, "Is it well with the young man Absalom?" Ahimaaz answered, "When Joab sent your servant,*b* I saw a great tumult; but I do not know what it was." 30 The king said, "Turn aside, and stand here." So he turned aside, and stood still.

31 Then the Cushite came; and the Cushite said, "Good tidings for my lord the king! For the LORD has vindicated you this day, delivering you from the power of all who rose up against you." 32 The king said to the Cushite, "Is it well with the young man Absalom?" The Cushite answered, "May the enemies of my lord the king, and all who rise up to do you harm, be like that young man."

33*c* The king was deeply moved, and went up to the chamber over the gate, and wept; and as he went, he said, "O my son Absalom, my son, my son Absalom! Would I had died instead of you, O Absalom, my son, my son!"

19 It was told Joab, "The king is weeping and mourning for Absalom." 2 So the victory that day was turned into mourning for all the troops; for the troops heard that day, "The king is grieving for his son." 3 The troops stole into the city that day as soldiers steal in who are ashamed when they flee in battle. 4 The king covered his face, and the king cried with a loud voice, "O my son Absalom, O Absalom, my son, my son!" 5 Then Joab came into the house to the king, and said, "Today you have covered with shame the faces of all your officers who have saved your life today, and the lives of your sons and your daughters, and the lives of your wives and your concubines, 6 for love of those who hate you and for hatred of those who love you. You have made it clear today that commanders and officers are nothing to you; for I perceive that if Absalom were alive and all of us were dead today, then you would be pleased. 7 So go out at once and speak kindly to your servants; for I swear by the LORD, if you do not go, not a man will stay with you this night; and this will be worse for you than any disaster that has come upon you from your youth until now." 8 Then the king got up and took his seat in the gate. The troops were all told, "See, the king is sitting in the gate"; and all the troops came before the king.

Meanwhile, all the Israelites had fled to their homes. 9 All the people were disputing throughout all the tribes of Israel, saying, "The king delivered us from the hand of our enemies, and saved us from the hand of the Philistines; and now he has fled out of the land because of Absalom. 10 But Absalom, whom we anointed over us, is dead in battle. Now therefore why do you say nothing about bringing the king back?"

11 King David sent this message to the priests Zadok and Abiathar, "Say to the elders of Judah, 'Why should you be the last to bring the king back to his house? The talk of all Israel has come to the king.*d* 12 You are my kin, you are my bone and my flesh; why then should you be the last to bring back the king?' 13 And say to Amasa, 'Are you not my bone and my flesh? So may God do to me, and more, if you are not the commander of my army from now on, in place of Joab.'" 14 Amasa*e* swayed the hearts of all the people of Judah as one, and they sent word to the king, "Return, both you and all your servants." 15 So the king came back to the Jordan; and Judah came to Gilgal to meet the king and to bring him over the Jordan.

16 Shimei son of Gera, the Benjaminite, from Bahu-

28 Ahimaaz called out to the king, 'All is well!' He bowed low before him and said, 'Blessed be the LORD your God who has given into your hands the men who rebelled against your majesty.' 29 The king asked, 'Is all well with the young man Absalom?' Ahimaaz answered, 'Sir, when your servant Joab sent me, I saw a great commotion, but I did not know what had happened.' 30 The king told him to stand on one side; so he turned aside and waited there.

31 Then the Cushite came in and said, 'Good news for my lord the king! The LORD has avenged you this day on all those who rebelled against you.' 32 The king said to the Cushite, 'Is all well with the young man Absalom?' The Cushite answered, 'May all the king's enemies and all rebels intent on harming you be as that young man is.' 33 The king was deeply moved and went up to the roof-chamber over the gate and wept, crying out as he went, 'O, my son! Absalom my son, my son Absalom! Would that I had died instead of you! O Absalom, my son, my son.'

19 Joab was told that the king was weeping and mourning for Absalom; 2 and that day's victory was turned for the whole army into mourning, because the troops heard how the king grieved for his son; 3 they stole into the city like men ashamed to show their faces after fleeing from a battle. 4 The king covered his face and cried aloud, 'My son Absalom; O Absalom, my son, my son.'

5 Joab came into the king's quarters and said to him, 'All your servants, who have saved you and your sons and daughters, your wives and your concubines, you have covered with shame this day 6 by showing love for those who hate you and hate for those who love you. Today you have made it clear to officers and men alike that we are nothing to you; I realize that if Absalom were still alive and all of us dead, you would be content. 7 Now go at once and give your servants some encouragement; if you refuse, I swear by the LORD that by nightfall not a man will remain with you, and that would be a worse disaster than any you have suffered since your earliest days.' 8 At that the king rose and took his seat by the gate; and when the army was told that the king was sitting at the gate, they assembled before him there.

MEANWHILE the Israelites had scattered to their homes. 9 Throughout all the tribes of Israel people were discussing it among themselves and saying, 'The king has saved us from our enemies and freed us from the power of the Philistines, and now he has fled the country because of Absalom. 10 But Absalom, whom we anointed king, has fallen in battle; so now why have we no plans for bringing the king back?'

11 What all Israel was saying came to the king's ears, and he sent word to Zadok and Abiathar the priests: 'Ask the elders of Judah why they should be the last to bring the king back to his palace. 12 Tell them, "You are my brothers, my own flesh and blood; why are you last to bring me back?" 13 And say to Amasa, "You are my own flesh and blood. So help me God, you shall be my commander-in-chief for the rest of your life in place of Joab."' 14 Thus David swayed the hearts of all in Judah, and one and all they sent to the king, urging him and his men to return.

15 When on his way back the king reached the Jordan, the men of Judah came to Gilgal to meet him and escort him across the river. 16 Shimei son of Gera the Benjamite from

---

b Heb *the king's servant, your servant*   *c* Ch 19.1 in Heb
d Gk: Heb *to the king, to his house*   *e* Heb *He*

18:29 **Sir . . . sent me:** *prob. rdg; Heb.* At the sending of Joab the king's servant and your servant.   18:33 *In Heb. 19:1.*
19:11 **What . . . ears:** *prob. rdg; Heb.* has these words *after* back to his palace *and adds* to his palace.

Ahimaaz called out and greeted the king. With face to the ground he paid homage to the king and said, "Blessed be the LORD your God, who has delivered up the men who rebelled against my lord the king." 29 But the king asked, "Is the youth Absalom safe?" And Ahimaaz replied, "I saw a great disturbance when the king's servant Joab sent your servant on, but I do not know what it was." 30 The king said, "Step aside and remain in attendance here." So he stepped aside and remained there. 31 When the Cushite came in, he said, "Let my lord the king receive the good news that this day the LORD has taken your part, freeing you from the grasp of all who rebelled against you." 32 But the king asked the Cushite, "Is young Absalom safe?" The Cushite replied, "May the enemies of my lord the king and all who rebel against you with evil intent be as that young man!"

19 The king was shaken, and went up to the room over the city gate to weep. He said as he wept, "My son Absalom! My son, my son Absalom! If only I had died instead of you, Absalom, my son, my son!" 2 Joab was told that the king was weeping and mourning for Absalom; 3 and that day's victory was turned into mourning for the whole army when they heard that the king was grieving for his son. 4 The soldiers stole into the city that day like men shamed by flight in battle. 5 Meanwhile the king covered his face and cried out in a loud voice, "My son Absalom! Absalom! My son, my son!" 6 Then Joab went to his residence and said: "Though they saved your life and your sons' and daughters' lives, also the lives of your wives and those of your concubines, you have put all your servants to shame today 7 by loving those who hate you and hating those who love you. For you have shown today that officers and servants mean nothing to you. Indeed I am now certain that if Absalom were alive today and all of us dead, you would think that more suitable. 8 Now then, get up! Go out and speak kindly to your servants. I swear by the LORD that if you do not go out, not a single man will remain with you overnight, and this will be a far greater disaster for you than any that has afflicted you from your youth until now." 9 So the king stepped out and sat at the gate. When all the people were informed that the king was sitting at the gate, they came into his presence.

Now the Israelites had fled to their separate tents, 10 but throughout the tribes of Israel all the people were arguing among themselves, saying to one another: "The king delivered us from the clutches of our enemies, and it was he who rescued us from the grip of the Philistines. But now he has fled from the country before Absalom, 11 and Absalom, whom we anointed over us, died in battle. Why, then, should you remain silent about restoring the king to his palace?" When the talk of all Israel reached the king, 12 David sent word to the priests Zadok and Abiathar: "Say to the elders of Judah: 'Why should you be last to restore the king to his palace? 13 You are my brothers, you are my bone and flesh. Why should you be last to restore the king?' 14 Also say to Amasa: 'Are you not my bone and flesh? May God do thus and so to me, if you do not become my general permanently in place of Joab.'" 15 He won over all the Judahites as one man, and so they summoned the king to return, with all his servants.

16 When the king, on his return, reached the Jordan, Judah had come to Gilgal to meet him and to escort him across the Jordan. 17 Shimei, son of Gera, the Benjaminite from

28 Ahimaaz went up to the king. 'All hail!' he said, prostrating himself on the ground before the king. 'Blessed be Yahweh your God', he said, 'who has handed over the men who rebelled against my lord the king!' 29 'Is all well with young Absalom?' the king asked. Ahimaaz replied, 'I saw a great commotion when Joab, the king's servant, sent me off, but I do not know what it was.' 30 The king said, 'Go and stand over there.' He stood to one side and waited.

31 Then the Cushite arrived. 'Good news for my lord the king!' the Cushite shouted. 'Today Yahweh has vindicated your cause, by ridding you of all who had risen up against you.' 32 'Is all well with young Absalom?' the king asked the Cushite. 'May the enemies of my lord the king', the Cushite answered, 'and all who rise up to harm you, share the fate of that young man!'

19 The king shuddered. He went up to the room over the gate and burst into tears; and, as he wept, he kept saying, 'Oh, my son Absalom! My son! My son Absalom! If only I had died instead of you! Oh, Absalom my son, my son!' 2 Word was brought to Joab, 'The king is weeping and mourning for Absalom.' 3 And for the entire army that day, victory was turned to mourning, the troops having learnt that the king was grieving for his son. 4 And that day the troops came furtively back into town, like troops creeping shamefacedly away when deserting in battle. 5 The king had covered his face and kept crying aloud, 'My son Absalom! Oh, Absalom my son, my son!'

6 Joab went inside to the king and said, 'Today you have made all your servants feel ashamed — today, when they have saved your life, the lives of your sons and daughters, the lives of your wives and the lives of your concubines! — because you love those who hate you and hate those who love you. 7 Today you have made it plain that commanders and soldiers mean nothing to you — for today I can see that you would be content if we were all dead, provided that Absalom was alive! 8 Now get up, come out and reassure your soldiers; for if you do not come out, I swear by Yahweh, not one man will stay with you tonight; and this will be a worse misfortune for you than anything that has happened to you from your youth until now!' 9 The king got up and took his seat at the gate. An announcement was made to the whole army: 'The king is sitting at the gate.' And the whole army assembled in front of the king.

10 Israel had fled, dispersing to their homes. Throughout the tribes of Israel all was dissension and people began saying, 'The king, having freed us from the clutches of our enemies, having saved us from the clutches of the Philistines, has himself had to flee the country to escape from Absalom; 11 and now Absalom, whom we had anointed to reign over us, has died in battle. Why does no one suggest that the king should be brought back?'

12b What was being said throughout Israel reached the king. 12a King David then sent word to the priests Zadok and Abiathar, 'Say to the elders of Judah, "Why should you be the last to bring the king home? 13 You are my brothers, you are my own flesh and bone: why should you be the last to bring the king back?" 14 And say to Amasa, "Are you not my own flesh and bone? May God bring unnameable ills on me and worse ills, too, if you do not become my permanent army commander instead of Joab!"' 15 Thus he rallied the hearts of the men of Judah to a man and, as a result, they sent word to the king, 'Come back, you and all who serve you.'

16 So the king started home and reached the Jordan. Judah, coming to meet the king to escort him across the Jordan, had arrived at Gilgal. 17 Shimei son of Gera, the Benja-

NEW REVISED STANDARD VERSION | REVISED ENGLISH BIBLE

rim, hurried to come down with the people of Judah to meet King David; 17 with him were a thousand people from Benjamin. And Ziba, the servant of the house of Saul, with his fifteen sons and his twenty servants, rushed down to the Jordan ahead of the king, 18 while the crossing was taking place,*f* to bring over the king's household, and to do his pleasure.

Shimei son of Gera fell down before the king, as he was about to cross the Jordan, 19 and said to the king, "May my lord not hold me guilty or remember how your servant did wrong on the day my lord the king left Jerusalem; may the king not bear it in mind. 20 For your servant knows that I have sinned; therefore, see, I have come this day, the first of all the house of Joseph to come down to meet my lord the king." 21 Abishai son of Zeruiah answered, "Shall not Shimei be put to death for this, because he cursed the LORD's anointed?" 22 But David said, "What have I to do with you, you sons of Zeruiah, that you should today become an adversary to me? Shall anyone be put to death in Israel this day? For do I not know that I am this day king over Israel?" 23 The king said to Shimei, "You shall not die." And the king gave him his oath.

24 Mephibosheth*g* grandson of Saul came down to meet the king; he had not taken care of his feet, or trimmed his beard, or washed his clothes, from the day the king left until the day he came back in safety. 25 When he came from Jerusalem to meet the king, the king said to him, "Why did you not go with me, Mephibosheth?"*g* 26 He answered, "My lord, O king, my servant deceived me; for your servant said to him, 'Saddle a donkey for me,*h* so that I may ride on it and go with the king.' For your servant is lame. 27 He has slandered your servant to my lord the king. But my lord the king is like the angel of God; do therefore what seems good to you. 28 For all my father's house were doomed to death before my lord the king; but you set your servant among those who eat at your table. What further right have I, then, to appeal to the king?" 29 The king said to him, "Why speak any more of your affairs? I have decided: you and Ziba shall divide the land." 30 Mephibosheth*g* said to the king, "Let him take it all, since my lord the king has arrived home safely."

31 Now Barzillai the Gileadite had come down from Rogelim; he went on with the king to the Jordan, to escort him over the Jordan. 32 Barzillai was a very aged man, eighty years old. He had provided the king with food while he stayed at Mahanaim, for he was a very wealthy man. 33 The king said to Barzillai, "Come over with me, and I will provide for you in Jerusalem at my side." 34 But Barzillai said to the king, "How many years have I still to live, that I should go up with the king to Jerusalem? 35 Today I am eighty years old; can I discern what is pleasant and what is not? Can your servant taste what he eats or what he drinks? Can I still listen to the voice of singing men and singing women? Why then should your servant be an added burden to my lord the king? 36 Your servant will go a little way over the Jordan with the king. Why should the king recompense me with such a reward? 37 Please let your servant return, so that I may die in my own town, near the graves of my father and my mother. But here is your servant Chimham; let him go over with my lord the king; and do for him whatever seems good to you." 38 The king answered, "Chimham shall go over with me, and I will do for him whatever seems good to you; and all that you desire of me I will do for you." 39 Then all the people crossed over the Jordan, and the king crossed over; the king kissed Barzillai and blessed him, and he returned to his own home. 40 The

Bahurim hastened down among the men of Judah to meet King David 17 with a thousand men from Benjamin; Ziba was there too, the servant of Saul's family, with his fifteen sons and twenty servants. They rushed into the Jordan under the king's eyes 18 and crossed to and fro conveying his household in order to win his favour. Shimei son of Gera, when he had crossed the river, threw himself down before the king 19 and said, 'I beg your majesty not to remember how disgracefully your servant behaved when your majesty left Jerusalem; do not hold it against me. 20 I humbly acknowledge that I did wrong, and today I am the first of all the house of Joseph to come down to meet your majesty.' 21 Abishai son of Zeruiah objected. 'Ought not Shimei to be put to death', he said, 'because he cursed the LORD's anointed prince?' 22 David answered, 'What right have you, you sons of Zeruiah, to oppose me today? Should anyone be put to death this day in Israel? I know now that I am king of Israel.' 23 The king said to Shimei, 'You shall not die,' and he confirmed it with an oath.

24 Saul's grandson Mephibosheth also went down to meet the king. He had not bathed his feet, trimmed his beard, or washed his clothes, from the day the king went away until he returned victorious. 25 When he came from Jerusalem to meet the king, David said to him, 'Why did you not go with me, Mephibosheth?' 26 He answered, 'Sir, my servant deceived me; I did intend to harness my donkey and ride with the king (for I am lame), 27 but his stories set your majesty against me. Your majesty is like the angel of God; you must do what you think right. 28 My father's whole family, one and all, deserved to die at your majesty's hands, but you gave me, your servant, my place at your table. What further favour can I expect of the king?' 29 The king answered, 'You have said enough. My decision is that you and Ziba are to share the estate.' 30 Mephibosheth said, 'Let him have it all, now that your majesty has come home victorious.'

31 Barzillai the Gileadite too had come down from Rogelim, and he went as far as the Jordan with the king to escort him on his way. 32 Barzillai was very old, eighty years of age; it was he who had provided for the king while he was at Mahanaim, for he was a man of great wealth. 33 The king said to Barzillai, 'Cross over with me and I shall provide for you in my household in Jerusalem.' 34 Barzillai answered, 'Your servant is far too old to go up with your majesty to Jerusalem. 35 I am now eighty years old. I cannot tell what is pleasant and what is not; I cannot taste what I eat or drink; I can no longer listen to the voices of men and women singing. Why should I be a further burden on your majesty? 36 Your servant will attend the king for a short way across the Jordan; and why should the king reward me so handsomely? 37 Let me go back and end my days in my own town near the grave of my father and mother. Here is my son Kimham; let him cross over with your majesty, and do for him what you think best.' 38 The king answered, 'Let Kimham cross with me, and I shall do for him whatever you think best; and I shall do for you whatever you ask.'

39 All the people crossed the Jordan while the king waited. The king then kissed Barzillai and gave him his bless-

---

f Cn: Heb *the ford crossed*   *g* Or *Merib-baal*: See 4.4 note
h Gk Syr Vg: Heb *said, I will saddle a donkey for myself*

19.25 **from:** *so some Gk MSS; Heb.* to.   19.37 **my son:** *so Gk; Heb.* omits.   19.39 **waited:** *so Gk (Luc.); Heb.* crossed.

Bahurim, hurried down with the Judahites to meet King David, 18 accompanied by a thousand men from Benjamin. Ziba, too, the servant of the house of Saul, accompanied by his fifteen sons and twenty servants, hastened to the Jordan before the king. 19 They crossed over the ford to bring the king's household over and to do whatever he wished. When Shimei, son of Gera, crossed the Jordan, he fell down before the king 20 and said to him: "May my lord not hold me guilty, and may he not remember and take to heart the wrong that your servant did the day my lord the king left Jerusalem. 21 For your servant knows that he has done wrong. Yet realize that I have been the first of the whole house of Joseph to come down today to meet my lord the king." 22 But Abishai, son of Zeruiah, countered: "Shimei must be put to death for this. He cursed the LORD's anointed." 23 David replied: "What has come between you and me, sons of Zeruiah, that you would create enmity for me this day? Should anyone die today in Israel? Am I not aware that today I am king of Israel?" 24 Then the king said to Shimei, "You shall not die." And the king gave him his oath.

25 Meribbaal, son of Saul, also went down to meet the king. He had not washed his feet nor trimmed his mustache nor washed his clothes from the day the king left until he returned safely. 26 When he came from Jerusalem to meet the king, the king asked him, "Why did you not go with me, Meribbaal?" 27 He replied: "My lord the king, my servant betrayed me. For your servant, who is lame, said to him, 'Saddle the ass for me, that I may ride on it and go with the king.' 28 But he slandered your servant before my lord the king. But my lord the king is like an angel of God. Do what you judge best. 29 For though my father's entire house deserved only death from my lord the king, yet you placed your servant among the guests at your table. What right do I still have to make further appeal to the king?" 30 But the king said to him: "Why do you go on talking? I say, 'You and Ziba shall divide the property.'" 31 Meribbaal answered the king, "Indeed let him have it all, now that my lord the king has returned safely to his palace."

32 Barzillai the Gileadite also came down from Rogelim and escorted the king to the Jordan for his crossing, taking leave of him there. 33 It was Barzillai, a very old man of eighty and very wealthy besides, who had provisioned the king during his stay in Mahanaim. 34 The king said to Barzillai, "Cross over with me, and I will provide for your old age as my guest in Jerusalem." 35 But Barzillai answered the king: "How much longer have I to live, that I should go up to Jerusalem with the king? 36 I am now eighty years old. Can I distinguish between good and bad? Can your servant taste what he eats and drinks, or still appreciate the voices of singers and songstresses? Why should your servant be any further burden to my lord the king? 37 In escorting the king across the Jordan, your servant is doing little enough! Why should the king give me this reward? 38 Please let your servant go back to die in his own city by the tomb of his father and mother. Here is your servant Chimham. Let him cross over with my lord the king. Do for him whatever you will." 39 Then the king said to him, "Chimham shall come over with me, and I will do for him as you would wish. And anything else you would like me to do for you, I will do." 40 Then all the people crossed over the Jordan, but the king remained; he kissed Barzillai and bade him Godspeed as he

minite of Bahurim, hurried down with the men of Judah to meet King David. 18 With him were a thousand men from Benjamin. Ziba, servant of the House of Saul, with his fifteen sons and twenty servants, arrived at the Jordan before the king 19 and worked manfully ferrying the king's family across and doing whatever he required.

While the king was crossing the Jordan, Shimei son of Gera fell at the king's feet 20 and said to the king, 'I hope my lord does not regard me as guilty of a crime! Forget about the wrong your servant did on the day my lord the king left Jerusalem. Let my lord not hold my guilt against me. 21 For your servant is aware of having sinned, and that is why I have come today — the first member of the whole House of Joseph to come down to meet my lord the king.'

22 At this, Abishai son of Zeruiah spoke up and said, 'Does Shimei not deserve death for having cursed Yahweh's anointed?' 23 To which David replied, 'What concern is my business to you, sons of Zeruiah, that you should oppose my wishes today? Could anyone be put to death in Israel today? Today I know for sure that I am king of Israel?' 24 'Your life is spared,' the king said. And the king gave him his oath.

25 Meribbaal son of Saul also went down to meet the king. He had not cared for his feet or hands, he had not trimmed his moustache or washed his clothes from the day of the king's departure till the day of his peaceful return. 26 When he arrived from Jerusalem to greet the king, the king asked him, 'Why did you not come with me, Meribbaal?' 27 'My lord king,' he replied, 'my retainer deceived me. Your servant said to him, "Saddle the donkey for me to ride, so that I can go with the king," your servant being lame. 28 He has slandered your servant to my lord the king. My lord the king, however, is like the Angel of God, so do as you think right. 29 My father's entire family deserved no better than death from my lord the king, and yet you admitted your servant to the ranks of those who eat at your table. What right have I to make any further appeal to the king?' 30 The king said, 'You need say no more. I rule that you and Ziba divide the property between you.' 31 'Let him take it all,' Meribbaal said to the king, 'since my lord the king has come back home in peace!'

32 Barzillai the Gileadite had come down from Rogelim and accompanied the king towards the Jordan, intending to take leave of him at the Jordan. 33 Barzillai was a man of great age; he was eighty years old. He had kept the king in provisions during his stay at Mahanaim, being a very wealthy man. 34 'Come with me', the king said to Barzillai, 'and I will provide for you at my side in Jerusalem.' 35 Barzillai replied to the king, 'How many years have I left to live, for me to go up to Jerusalem with the king? 36 I am now eighty years old; can I tell the good from the bad? Has your servant any taste for his food and drink? Can I still hear the voices of men and women singers? Why should your servant be a further burden to my lord the king? 37 Your servant will go a little way across the Jordan with the king; but why should the king reward me so generously for that? 38 Please allow your servant to go home again, so that I can die in my own town near the grave of my father and mother. But here is your servant Chimham; let him go with my lord the king; treat him as you think right.' 39 The king said, 'Let Chimham come along with me then; I shall do whatever you wish for him, and anything you request I shall do for your sake.' 40 The people then all crossed the Jordan, and the king, having crossed, kissed Barzillai and blessed him, and the latter went home.

king went on to Gilgal, and Chimham went on with him; all the people of Judah, and also half the people of Israel, brought the king on his way.

41 Then all the people of Israel came to the king, and said to him, "Why have our kindred the people of Judah stolen you away, and brought the king and his household over the Jordan, and all David's men with him?" 42 All the people of Judah answered the people of Israel, "Because the king is near of kin to us. Why then are you angry over this matter? Have we eaten at all at the king's expense? Or has he given us any gift?" 43 But the people of Israel answered the people of Judah, "We have ten shares in the king, and in David also we have more than you. Why then did you despise us? Were we not the first to speak of bringing back our king?" But the words of the people of Judah were fiercer than the words of the people of Israel.

20 Now a scoundrel named Sheba son of Bichri, a Benjaminite, happened to be there. He sounded the trumpet and cried out,

> "We have no portion in David,
> no share in the son of Jesse!
> Everyone to your tents, O Israel!"

2 So all the people of Israel withdrew from David and followed Sheba son of Bichri; but the people of Judah followed their king steadfastly from the Jordan to Jerusalem.

3 David came to his house at Jerusalem; and the king took the ten concubines whom he had left to look after the house, and put them in a house under guard, and provided for them, but did not go in to them. So they were shut up until the day of their death, living as if in widowhood.

4 Then the king said to Amasa, "Call the men of Judah together to me within three days, and be here yourself." 5 So Amasa went to summon Judah; but he delayed beyond the set time that had been appointed him. 6 David said to Abishai, "Now Sheba son of Bichri will do us more harm than Absalom; take your lord's servants and pursue him, or he will find fortified cities for himself, and escape from us." 7 Joab's men went out after him, along with the Cherethites, the Pelethites, and all the warriors; they went out from Jerusalem to pursue Sheba son of Bichri. 8 When they were at the large stone that is in Gibeon, Amasa came to meet them. Now Joab was wearing a soldier's garment and over it was a belt with a sword in its sheath fastened at his waist; as he went forward it fell out. 9 Joab said to Amasa, "Is it well with you, my brother?" And Joab took Amasa by the beard with his right hand to kiss him. 10 But Amasa did not notice the sword in Joab's hand; Joab struck him in the belly so that his entrails poured out on the ground, and he died. He did not strike a second blow.

Then Joab and his brother Abishai pursued Sheba son of Bichri. 11 And one of Joab's men took his stand by Amasa, and said, "Whoever favors Joab, and whoever is for David, let him follow Joab." 12 Amasa lay wallowing in his blood on the highway, and the man saw that all the people were stopping. Since he saw that all who came by him were stopping, he carried Amasa from the highway into a field, and threw a garment over him. 13 Once he was removed from the highway, all the people went on after Joab to pursue Sheba son of Bichri.

14 Sheba[i] passed through all the tribes of Israel to Abel of Beth-maacah;[j] and all the Bichrites[k] assembled, and followed him inside. 15 Joab's forces[l] came and besieged

ing. Barzillai returned home; 40 the king crossed to Gilgal, Kimham with him.

The whole army of Judah had escorted the king over the river, as had also half the army of Israel. 41 But the Israelites all kept coming to the king and saying, 'Why should our brothers of Judah have got possession of the king's person by joining King David's own men and then escorting him and his household across the Jordan?' 42 The answer of all the men of Judah to the Israelites was, 'Because his majesty is our near kinsman. Why should you resent it? Have we eaten at the king's expense? Have we received any gifts?' 43 The men of Israel answered, 'We have ten times your interest in the king, and what is more, we are senior to you; why do you disparage us? Were we not the first to speak of bringing the king back?' The men of Judah used language even fiercer than the men of Israel.

20 A scoundrel named Sheba son of Bichri, a man of Benjamin, happened to be there. He sounded the trumpet and cried out:

> 'We have no share in David,
> no lot in the son of Jesse.
> Every man to his tent, O Israel!'

2 All the men of Israel deserted David to follow Sheba son of Bichri, but the men of Judah stood by their king and followed him from the Jordan to Jerusalem.

3 When David went up to his palace in Jerusalem he took the ten concubines whom he had left in charge of the palace and put them in a house under guard; he maintained them but did not have intercourse with them. They were kept in seclusion, living as if they were widows until the day of their death.

4 The king said to Amasa, 'Call up the men of Judah and appear before me again in three days' time.' 5 Amasa went to call up the men of Judah, but he took longer than the time fixed by the king. 6 David said to Abishai, 'Sheba son of Bichri will give us more trouble than Absalom; take the royal bodyguard and follow him closely in case he occupies some fortified cities and escapes us.' 7 Joab, along with the Kerethite and Pelethite guards and all the fighting men, marched out behind Abishai, and left Jerusalem in pursuit of Sheba son of Bichri.

8 When they reached the great stone in Gibeon, Amasa came to meet them. Joab was wearing his tunic and over it a belt supporting a sword in its scabbard. He came forward, concealing his treachery, 9 and said to Amasa, 'I hope you are well, my brother,' and with his right hand he grasped Amasa's beard to kiss him. 10 Amasa was not on his guard against the sword in Joab's hand. Joab struck him with it in the belly and his entrails poured out to the ground; he did not have to strike a second blow, for Amasa was dead. Joab with his brother Abishai went on in pursuit of Sheba son of Bichri. 11 One of Joab's men stood over Amasa and called out, 'Follow Joab, all who are for Joab and for David!' 12 Amasa's body lay soaked in blood in the middle of the road, and when the man saw how all the people stopped, he rolled him off the road into the field and threw a cloak over him; for everyone who came by stopped at the sight of the body. 13 When it had been removed from the road, they all went on and followed Joab in pursuit of Sheba son of Bichri.

14 Sheba passed through all the tribes of Israel until he came to Abel-beth-maacah, and all the clan of Bichri rallied to him and followed him into the city. 15 Joab's forces came

---

19:43 **senior:** *so Gk; Heb.* in David.   20:7 **behind Abishai:** *prob. rdg; Heb.* after him men.   20:14 **Abel-beth-maacah:** *prob. rdg, cp. verse 15; Heb.* Abel and Beth-maacah. **Bichri:** *prob. rdg; Heb.* Beri.

i Heb He   *j* Compare 20.15: Heb *and Beth-maacah*   *k* Compare Gk Vg: Heb *Berites*   *l* Heb *They*

returned to his district. ⁴¹ Finally the king crossed over to Gilgal, accompanied by Chimham.

All the people of Judah and half of the people of Israel had escorted the king across. ⁴² But all these Israelites began coming to the king and saying, "Why did our brothers the Judahites steal you away and escort the king and his household across the Jordan, along with all David's men?" ⁴³ All the Judahites replied to the men of Israel: "Because the king is our relative. Why are you angry over this affair? Have we had anything to eat at the king's expense? Or have portions from his table been given to us?" ⁴⁴ The Israelites answered the Judahites: "We have ten shares in the king. Also, we are the first-born rather than you. Why do you slight us? Were we not first to speak of restoring the king?" Then the Judahites in turn spoke even more fiercely than the Israelites.

20 Now a rebellious individual from Benjamin named Sheba, the son of Bichri, happened to be there. He sounded the horn and cried out,

"We have no portion in David,
    nor any share in the son of Jesse.
Every man to his tent, O Israel!"

² So all the Israelites left David for Sheba, son of Bichri. But from the Jordan to Jerusalem the Judahites remained loyal to their king. ³ When King David came to his palace in Jerusalem, he took the ten concubines whom he had left behind to take care of the palace and placed them in confinement. He provided for them, but had no further relations with them. And so they remained in confinement to the day of their death, lifelong widows.

⁴ Then the king said to Amasa: "Summon the Judahites for me within three days. Then present yourself here." ⁵ Accordingly Amasa set out to summon Judah, but delayed beyond the time set for him by David. ⁶ Then David said to Abishai: "Sheba, son of Bichri, may now do us more harm than Absalom did. Take your lord's servants and pursue him, lest he find fortified cities and take shelter while we look on." ⁷ So Joab and the Cherethites and Pelethites and all the warriors marched out behind Abishai from Jerusalem to campaign in pursuit of Sheba, son of Bichri. ⁸ They were at the great stone in Gibeon when Amasa met them. Now Joab had a belt over his tunic, from which was slung, in its sheath near his thigh, a sword that could be drawn with a downward movement. ⁹ And Joab asked Amasa, "How are you, my brother?" With his right hand Joab held Amasa's beard as if to kiss him. ¹⁰ And since Amasa was not on his guard against the sword in Joab's other hand, Joab stabbed him in the abdomen with it, so that his entrails burst forth to the ground, and he died without receiving a second thrust. Then Joab and his brother Abishai pursued Sheba, son of Bichri. ¹¹ One of Joab's attendants stood by Amasa and said, "Let him who favors Joab and is for David follow Joab." ¹² Amasa lay covered with blood in the middle of the highroad, and the man noticed that all the soldiers were stopping. So he removed Amasa from the road to the field and placed a garment over him, because all who came up to him were stopping. ¹³ When he had been removed from the road, everyone went on after Joab in pursuit of Sheba, son of Bichri.

¹⁴ Sheba passed through all the tribes of Israel to Abel Beth-maacah. Then all the Bichrites assembled and they too entered the city after him. ¹⁵ So David's servants came and

⁴¹ The king went on to Gilgal and Chimham went with him. All the people of Judah accompanied the king, and also half the people of Israel. ⁴² All the men of Israel then came to the king. 'Why', they asked the king, 'have our brothers, the men of Judah, carried you off and brought the king and his family across the Jordan, and all David's men with him?' ⁴³ All the men of Judah retorted to the men of Israel, 'Because the king is more closely related to us. Why do you take offence at this? Have we been eating at the king's expense? Have we taken any position for ourselves?' ⁴⁴ The men of Israel replied to the men of Judah, 'We have ten shares in the king and, what is more, we are your elder brothers, so why have you slighted us? Were we not the first to suggest bringing back our king?' The men of Judah's words were even more intemperate than those of the men of Israel.

20 Now there happened to be a scoundrel there called Sheba son of Bichri, a Benjaminite, who sounded the trumpet and shouted:

We have no share in David,
    we have no heritage in the son of Jesse.
Every man to his tents, O Israel!

² At this all the men of Israel deserted David and followed Sheba son of Bichri. But the men of Judah stuck close to their king, from the Jordan all the way to Jerusalem.

³ David returned to his palace in Jerusalem. The king took the ten concubines, whom he had left to look after the palace, and put them under guard. He provided for their upkeep but never went near them again; they were shut away until the day they died, widows, as it were, of a living man.

⁴ The king said to Amasa, 'Summon me the men of Judah and be here yourself within three days.' ⁵ Amasa went off to summon Judah, but he took longer than the time fixed by David. ⁶ David then said to Abishai, 'Sheba son of Bichri is now in a position to do us more damage even than Absalom. Take your master's retainers and be after him, before he can reach any fortified towns and elude us.' ⁷ Joab, the Cherethites, the Pelethites and all the champions took the field under Abishai, setting off from Jerusalem in pursuit of Sheba son of Bichri. ⁸ They were near the great stone at Gibeon when Amasa met them, coming the other way. Joab was wearing his uniform, over which he had buckled on a sword hanging from his waist in its scabbard; the sword came out and fell. ⁹ Joab said to Amasa, 'Are you well, brother?' and, with his right hand, took Amasa by the beard to kiss him. ¹⁰ Amasa paid no attention to the sword, which Joab had now picked up, and Joab struck him with it in the belly, spilling his entrails all over the ground. He did not need to strike a second blow; and Amasa died, while Joab and Abishai hurried on in pursuit of Sheba son of Bichri.

¹¹ One of Joab's men stood on guard beside Amasa, shouting, 'Whoever is on Joab's side, whoever is for David, follow Joab!' ¹² Amasa meanwhile lay wallowing in his blood in the middle of the road. Seeing that everyone was stopping, the man dragged Amasa off the road into the field and threw a cloak over him, having realised that everyone passing would stop. ¹³ Once Amasa had been taken off the road, the men all carried on, following Joab in pursuit of Sheba son of Bichri.

¹⁴ Sheba crossed all the tribes of Israel as far as Abel Beth-Maacah, and the Bichrites all . . . They formed up and followed him. ¹⁵ Laying siege to him in Abel Beth-Maacah,

him in Abel of Beth-maacah; they threw up a siege ramp against the city, and it stood against the rampart. Joab's forces were battering the wall to break it down. 16 Then a wise woman called from the city, "Listen! Listen! Tell Joab, 'Come here, I want to speak to you.' " 17 He came near her; and the woman said, "Are you Joab?" He answered, "I am." Then she said to him, "Listen to the words of your servant." He answered, "I am listening." 18 Then she said, "They used to say in the old days, 'Let them inquire at Abel'; and so they would settle a matter. 19 I am one of those who are peaceable and faithful in Israel; you seek to destroy a city that is a mother in Israel; why will you swallow up the heritage of the LORD?" 20 Joab answered, "Far be it from me, far be it, that I should swallow up or destroy! 21 That is not the case! But a man of the hill country of Ephraim, called Sheba son of Bichri, has lifted up his hand against King David; give him up alone, and I will withdraw from the city." The woman said to Joab, "His head shall be thrown over the wall to you." 22 Then the woman went to all the people with her wise plan. And they cut off the head of Sheba son of Bichri, and threw it out to Joab. So he blew the trumpet, and they dispersed from the city, and all went to their homes, while Joab returned to Jerusalem to the king.

23 Now Joab was in command of all the army of Israel;[m] Benaiah son of Jehoiada was in command of the Cherethites and the Pelethites; 24 Adoram was in charge of the forced labor; Jehoshaphat son of Ahilud was the recorder; 25 Sheva was secretary; Zadok and Abiathar were priests; 26 and Ira the Jairite was also David's priest.

21 Now there was a famine in the days of David for three years, year after year; and David inquired of the LORD. The LORD said, "There is bloodguilt on Saul and on his house, because he put the Gibeonites to death." 2 So the king called the Gibeonites and spoke to them. (Now the Gibeonites were not of the people of Israel, but of the remnant of the Amorites; although the people of Israel had sworn to spare them, Saul had tried to wipe them out in his zeal for the people of Israel and Judah.) 3 David said to the Gibeonites, "What shall I do for you? How shall I make expiation, that you may bless the heritage of the LORD?" 4 The Gibeonites said to him, "It is not a matter of silver or gold between us and Saul or his house; neither is it for us to put anyone to death in Israel." He said, "What do you say that I should do for you?" 5 They said to the king, "The man who consumed us and planned to destroy us, so that we should have no place in all the territory of Israel— 6 let seven of his sons be handed over to us, and we will impale them before the LORD at Gibeon on the mountain of the LORD."[n] The king said, "I will hand them over."

7 But the king spared Mephibosheth,[o] the son of Saul's son Jonathan, because of the oath of the LORD that was between them, between David and Jonathan son of Saul. 8 The king took the two sons of Rizpah daughter of Aiah, whom she bore to Saul, Armoni and Mephibosheth;[o] and the five sons of Merab[p] daughter of Saul, whom she bore to Adriel son of Barzillai the Meholathite; 9 he gave them into the hands of the Gibeonites, and they impaled them on the mountain before the LORD. The seven of them perished together. They were put to death in the first days of harvest, at the beginning of barley harvest.

up and besieged him in Abel-beth-maacah, raised a siege-ramp against it, and began undermining the wall to bring it down. 16 Then a wise woman stood on the rampart and called from the city, 'Listen, listen! Tell Joab to come here and let me speak with him.' 17 When he came forward the woman said, 'Are you Joab?' He answered, 'I am.' 'Listen to what I have to say, sir,' she said. 'I am listening,' he replied. 18 'In the old days', she went on, 'there was a saying, "Go to Abel for the answer," and that settled the matter. 19 My town is known to be one of the most peaceable and loyal in Israel; she is like a watchful mother in Israel, and you are seeking to kill her. Would you destroy the LORD's own possession?' 20 Joab answered, 'God forbid, far be it from me to ruin or destroy! 21 That is not our aim; but a man from the hill-country of Ephraim named Sheba son of Bichri has raised a revolt against King David. Surrender this one man, and I shall retire from the city.' The woman said to Joab, 'His head will be thrown over the wall to you.' 22 Then the woman went to the people, who, persuaded by her wisdom, cut off Sheba's head and threw it to Joab. He then sounded the trumpet, and the whole army withdrew from the town; they dispersed to their homes, while Joab went back to the king in Jerusalem.

23 JOAB was in command of the whole army in Israel, and Benaiah son of Jehoiada commanded the Kerethite and Pelethite guards. 24 Adoram was in charge of the forced levy, and Jehoshaphat son of Ahilud was secretary of state. 25 Sheva was adjutant-general, and Zadok and Abiathar were priests; 26 Ira the Jairite was David's priest.

21 IN David's reign there was a famine that lasted for three successive years. David consulted the LORD, who answered, 'Blood-guilt rests on Saul and on his family because he put the Gibeonites to death.' 2 (The Gibeonites were not of Israelite descent; they were a remnant of Amorite stock whom the Israelites had sworn that they would spare. Saul, however, in his zeal for Israel and Judah had sought to exterminate them.) King David summoned the Gibeonites, therefore, and said to them, 3 'What can be done for you? How can I make expiation, so that you may have cause to bless the LORD's own people?' 4 The Gibeonites answered, 'Our feud with Saul and his family cannot be settled in silver or gold, and there is no other man in Israel whose death would content us.' 'Then what do you want me to do for you?' asked David. 5 They answered, 'Let us make an end of the man who caused our undoing and ruined us, so that he will never again have his place within the borders of Israel. 6 Hand over to us seven of that man's descendants, and we shall hurl them down to their death before the LORD in Gibeah of Saul, the LORD's chosen one.' The king agreed to hand them over. 7 He spared Mephibosheth son of Jonathan, son of Saul, because of the oath that had been taken in the LORD's name by David and Saul's son Jonathan, 8 but the king took the two sons whom Rizpah daughter of Aiah had borne to Saul, Armoni and Mephibosheth, and the five sons whom Merab, Saul's daughter, had borne to Adriel son of Barzillai of Meholah. 9 He handed them over to the Gibeonites, and they flung them down from the mountain before the LORD; the seven of them fell together. They were put to death in the first days of harvest at the beginning of the barley harvest.

---

m Cn: Heb Joab to all the army, Israel   n Cn Compare Gk and 21.9: Heb at Gibeah of Saul, the chosen of the LORD
o Or Merib-baal: See 4.4 note   p Two Heb Mss Syr Compare Gk: MT Michal

20:16 stood . . . rampart: transposed from verse 15.   20:19 My town . . . loyal: prob. rdg; Heb. I am the requited ones of the loyal ones.   20:23–26 Cp. 8:16–18; 1 Kgs. 4:2–6; 1 Chr. 18:15–17.   21:6 before: or for.   21:8 Merab: so some MSS; others Michal.

besieged him in Abel Beth-maacah. They threw up a mound against the city, and all the soldiers who were with Joab began battering the wall to throw it down. 16 Then a wise woman from the city stood on the outworks and called out, "Listen, listen! Tell Joab to come here, that I may speak with him." 17 When Joab had come near her, the woman said, "Are you Joab?" And he replied, "Yes." She said to him, "Listen to what your maidservant has to say." He replied, "I am listening." 18 Then she went on to say: "There is an ancient saying, 'Let them ask if they will in Abel 19 or in Dan whether loyalty is finished or ended in Israel.' You are seeking to beat down a city that is a mother in Israel. Why do you wish to destroy the inheritance of the LORD?" 20 Joab answered, "Not at all, not at all! I do not wish to destroy or to ruin anything. 21 That is not the case at all. A man named Sheba, son of Bichri, from the hill country of Ephraim has rebelled against King David. Surrender him alone, and I will withdraw from the city." Then the woman said to Joab, "His head shall be thrown to you across the wall." 22 She went to all the people with her advice, and they cut off the head of Sheba, son of Bichri, and threw it out to Joab. He then sounded the horn, and they scattered from the city to their own tents, while Joab returned to Jerusalem to the king.

23 Joab was in command of the whole army of Israel. Banaiah, son of Jehoiada, was in command of the Cherethites and Pelethites. 24 Adoram was in charge of the forced labor. Jehoshaphat, son of Ahilud, was the chancellor. 25 Shawsha was the scribe. Zadok and Abiathar were priests. 26 Ira the Jairite was also David's priest.

21 During David's reign there was a famine for three successive years. David had recourse to the LORD, who said, "There is bloodguilt on Saul and his family because he put the Gibeonites to death." 2 So the king called the Gibeonites and spoke to them. (Now the Gibeonites were not Israelites, but survivors of the Amorites; and although the Israelites had given them their oath, Saul had attempted to kill them off in his zeal for the men of Israel and Judah.) 3 David said to the Gibeonites, "What must I do for you and how must I make atonement, that you may bless the inheritance of the LORD?" 4 The Gibeonites answered him, "We have no claim against Saul and his house for silver or gold, nor is it our place to put any man to death in Israel." Then he said, "I will do for you whatever you propose." 5 They said to the king, "As for the man who was exterminating us and who intended to destroy us that we might have no place in all the territory of Israel, 6 let seven men from among his descendants be given to us, that we may dismember them before the LORD in Gibeon, on the LORD'S mountain." The king replied, "I will give them up." 7 The king, however, spared Meribbaal, son of Jonathan, son of Saul, because of the LORD'S oath that formed a bond between David and Saul's son Jonathan. 8 But the king took Armoni and Meribbaal, the two sons that Aiah's daughter Rizpah had borne to Saul, and the five sons of Saul's daughter Merob that she had borne to Adriel, son of Barzillai the Meholathite, 9 and surrendered them to the Gibeonites. They then dismembered them on the mountain before the LORD. The seven fell at the one time; they were put to death during the first days of the harvest—that is, at the beginning of the barley harvest.

they threw up a ramp against the outer wall of the town, 16 while the whole army accompanying Joab undermined the wall to bring it down. A quick-witted woman shouted from the town, 'Listen! 17 Listen! Say to Joab, "Come here, I want to speak to you." ' He came forward, and the woman said, 'Are you Joab?' 'I am', he replied. She said, 'Listen to what your servant says.' 'I am listening,' he replied. 18 She then spoke as follows, 'In olden days people used to say, "Abel and Dan are where you should enquire 19 whether a tradition established by the faithful of Israel has finally died out." And yet you are trying to destroy a town, a metropolis of Israel. Why do you want to devour Yahweh's heritage?' 20 'The last thing I want to do', said Joab, 'is either to devour or to destroy. 21 This is not the issue; a man from the highlands of Ephraim, called Sheba son of Bichri, has revolted against the king, against David. Hand that one man over and I will raise the siege of the town.' 'Very well,' the woman said to Joab, 'his head will be thrown over the wall to you.' 22 The woman went and spoke to all the people as her wisdom dictated. They cut off the head of Sheba son of Bichri and threw it down to Joab. He had the trumpet sounded and they withdrew from the town and all went home, while Joab himself went back to the king in Jerusalem.

23 g Joab commanded the whole army; Benaiah son of Jehoiada commanded the Cherethites and Pelethites; 24 Adoram was in charge of forced labour; Jehoshaphat son of Ahilud was herald; 25 Shiya was secretary; Zadok and Abiathar were priests; 26 also: Ira the Jairite was David's priest.

21 h In the days of David there was a famine which lasted for three years on end. David consulted Yahweh, and Yahweh said, 'Saul and his family have incurred blood-guilt, by putting the Gibeonites to death.' 2 Then the king summoned the Gibeonites and said—now, the Gibeonites were not Israelites, but were a remnant of the Amorites, to whom the Israelites had bound themselves by oath; Saul, however, in his zeal for the Israelites and for Judah, had done his best to exterminate them—hence David said to the Gibeonites, 3 'What can I do for you? How can I make amends, so that you will call a blessing down on Yahweh's heritage?' 4 The Gibeonites replied, 'Our quarrel with Saul and his family cannot be settled for silver or gold, nor by putting to death one man in Israel.' David said, 'Say what you want and I will do it for you.' 5 Then they replied to the king, 'The man who dismembered us and planned to annihilate us, so that we should not exist anywhere in Israelite territory— 6 we want seven of his descendants handed over to us; and we shall dismember them before Yahweh at Gibeon on Yahweh's hill.' 'I shall hand them over,' said the king. 7 The king, however, spared Meribbaal son of Jonathan, son of Saul, on account of the oath by Yahweh binding them together, binding David and Jonathan son of Saul. 8 The king took the two sons born to Saul by Rizpah daughter of Aiah: Armoni and Meribbaal; and the five sons borne by Merab daughter of Saul to Adriel son of Barzillai, of Meholah. 9 He handed these over to the Gibeonites who dismembered them before Yahweh on the hill. The seven of them perished together; they were put to death in the first days of the harvest, at the beginning of the barley harvest.

g **20** 20:23seq. = 8:16–18.   h **21** Chh. 21—24 interrupt the succession narrative with 6 appendices in balancing pairs: famine and plague (21:1–14; 24), military exploits (21:15–22; 23:8–39), hymns of David (22; 23:1–7).

10 Then Rizpah the daughter of Aiah took sackcloth, and spread it on a rock for herself, from the beginning of harvest until rain fell on them from the heavens; she did not allow the birds of the air to come on the bodies*q* by day, or the wild animals by night. 11 When David was told what Rizpah daughter of Aiah, the concubine of Saul, had done, 12 David went and took the bones of Saul and the bones of his son Jonathan from the people of Jabesh-gilead, who had stolen them from the public square of Beth-shan, where the Philistines had hung them up, on the day the Philistines killed Saul on Gilboa. 13 He brought up from there the bones of Saul and the bones of his son Jonathan; and they gathered the bones of those who had been impaled. 14 They buried the bones of Saul and of his son Jonathan in the land of Benjamin in Zela, in the tomb of his father Kish; they did all that the king commanded. After that, God heeded supplications for the land.

15 The Philistines went to war again with Israel, and David went down together with his servants. They fought against the Philistines, and David grew weary. 16 Ishbi-benob, one of the descendants of the giants, whose spear weighed three hundred shekels of bronze, and who was fitted out with new weapons,*r* said he would kill David. 17 But Abishai son of Zeruiah came to his aid, and attacked the Philistine and killed him. Then David's men swore to him, "You shall not go out with us to battle any longer, so that you do not quench the lamp of Israel."

18 After this a battle took place with the Philistines, at Gob; then Sibbecai the Hushathite killed Saph, who was one of the descendants of the giants. 19 Then there was another battle with the Philistines at Gob; and Elhanan son of Jaare-oregim, the Bethlehemite, killed Goliath the Gittite, the shaft of whose spear was like a weaver's beam. 20 There was again war at Gath, where there was a man of great size, who had six fingers on each hand, and six toes on each foot, twenty-four in number; he too was descended from the giants. 21 When he taunted Israel, Jonathan son of David's brother Shimei, killed him. 22 These four were descended from the giants in Gath; they fell by the hands of David and his servants.

22 David spoke to the LORD the words of this song on the day when the LORD delivered him from the hand of all his enemies, and from the hand of Saul. 2 He said:

The LORD is my rock, my fortress, and my
    deliverer,
3   my God, my rock, in whom I take refuge,
my shield and the horn of my salvation,
    my stronghold and my refuge,
    my savior; you save me from violence.
4   I call upon the LORD, who is worthy to be
    praised,
and I am saved from my enemies.

5   For the waves of death encompassed me,
    the torrents of perdition assailed me;
6   the cords of Sheol entangled me,
    the snares of death confronted me.

7   In my distress I called upon the LORD;
    to my God I called.
From his temple he heard my voice,
    and my cry came to his ears.

8   Then the earth reeled and rocked;
    the foundations of the heavens trembled
and quaked, because he was angry.

10 Rizpah daughter of Aiah took sackcloth and spread it out as a bed for herself on the rock, from the beginning of harvest until the rains came and fell from the heavens on the bodies. She kept the birds away from them by day and the wild beasts by night. 11 When David was told what Rizpah the concubine of Saul had done, 12 he went and got the bones of Saul and his son Jonathan from the citizens of Jabesh-gilead, who had carried them off from the public square at Beth-shan, where the Philistines had hung them on the day they defeated Saul at Gilboa. 13 He removed the bones of Saul and Jonathan from there and gathered up the bones of the men who had been hurled to death. 14 They buried the bones of Saul and his son Jonathan at Zela in Benjamin, in the grave of his father Kish. Everything was done as the king ordered, and thereafter the LORD was willing to accept prayers offered for the country.

15 Once again war broke out between the Philistines and Israel. David and his men went down to the battle, but as he fought with the Philistines he fell exhausted. 16 When Benob, one of the race of the Rephaim, whose bronze spear weighed three hundred shekels and who wore a belt of honour, was about to kill David, 17 Abishai son of Zeruiah came to the king's aid; he struck the Philistine down and killed him. Then David's officers swore that he should never again go out with them to war, for fear that the lamp of Israel might be extinguished.

18 Some time later war with the Philistines broke out again in Gob: it was then that Sibbechai from Hushah killed Saph, a descendant of the Rephaim. 19 In another campaign against the Philistines in Gob, Elhanan son of Jair of Bethlehem killed Goliath of Gath, whose spear had a shaft like a weaver's beam. 20 In yet another campaign in Gath there appeared a giant with six fingers on each hand and six toes on each foot, twenty-four in all. He too was descended from the Rephaim; 21 when he defied Israel, Jonathan son of David's brother Shimeai killed him. 22 These four giants were the descendants of the Rephaim in Gath, and they all fell at the hands of David and his men.

22 THESE are the words of the song David sang to the LORD on the day when the LORD delivered him from the power of all his enemies and from the power of Saul:

2   The LORD is my lofty crag,
    my fortress, my champion,
3   my God, my rock in whom I find shelter,
    my shield and sure defender, my strong tower,
    my refuge, my deliverer who saves me from
        violence.
4   I shall call to the LORD to whom all praise is due;
    then I shall be made safe from my enemies.

5   When the waves of death encompassed me
    and destructive torrents overtook me,
6   the bonds of Sheol tightened about me,
    the snares of death were set to catch me.
7   When in anguish of heart I cried to the LORD
    and called to my God,
he heard me from his temple,
    and my cry reached his ears.

8   The earth shook and quaked.
Heaven's foundations trembled,
    shaking because of his anger.

21:16 **shekels:** *prob. rdg; Heb.* weight. **a belt of honour:** *lit.* a new belt.   21:18–22 *Cp. 1 Chr. 20:4–7.*   21:19 **Jair:** *prob. rdg, cp. 1 Chr. 20:5; Heb.* Jaare-oregim.   22:2–51 *Cp. Ps. 18:2–50.* 22:6 **Sheol:** *or* the underworld.

q Heb them   *r* Heb was belted anew

10 Then Rizpah, Aiah's daughter, took sackcloth and spread it out for herself on the rock from the beginning of the harvest until rain came down on them from the sky, fending off the birds of the sky from settling on them by day, and the wild animals by night. 11 When David was informed of what Rizpah, Aiah's daughter, the concubine of Saul, had done, 12 he went and obtained the bones of Saul and of his son Jonathan from the citizens of Jabesh-gilead, who had carried them off secretly from the public square of Beth-shan, where the Philistines had hanged them at the time they killed Saul on Gilboa. 13 When he had brought up from there the bones of Saul and of his son Jonathan, the bones of those who had been dismembered were also gathered up. 14 Then the bones of Saul and of his son Jonathan were buried in the tomb of his father Kish at Zela in the territory of Benjamin. After all that the king commanded had been carried out, God granted relief to the land.

15 There was another battle between the Philistines and Israel. David went down with his servants and fought the Philistines, but David grew tired. 16 Dadu, one of the Rephaim, whose bronze spear weighed three hundred shekels, was about to take him captive. Dadu was girt with a new sword and planned to kill David, 17 but Abishai, son of Zeruiah, came to his assistance and struck and killed the Philistine. Then David's men swore to him, "You must not go out to battle with us again, lest you quench the lamp of Israel."

18 After this there was another battle with the Philistines in Gob. On that occasion Sibbecai, from Husha, killed Saph, one of the Rephaim. 19 There was another battle with the Philistines in Gob, in which Elhanan, son of Jair from Bethlehem, killed Goliath of Gath, who had a spear with a shaft like a weaver's heddle-bar. 20 There was another battle at Gath in which there was a man of large stature with six fingers on each hand and six toes on each foot—twenty-four in all. He too was one of the Rephaim. 21 And when he insulted Israel, Jonathan, son of David's brother Shimei, killed him. 22 These four were Rephaim in Gath, and they fell at the hands of David and his servants.

22 David sang the words of this song to the LORD when the LORD had rescued him from the grasp of all his enemies and from the hand of Saul. 2 This is what he sang:

A

I

"O LORD, my rock, my fortress, my deliverer,
3   my God, my rock of refuge!
My shield, the horn of my salvation,
    my stronghold, my refuge,
    my savior, from violence you keep me safe.
4 'Praised be the LORD,' I exclaim,
    and I am safe from my enemies.

II

5 "The breakers of death surged round about me,
    the floods of perdition overwhelmed me;
6 The cords of the nether world enmeshed me,
    the snares of death overtook me.
7 In my distress I called upon the LORD
    and cried out to my God;
From his temple he heard my voice,
    and my cry reached his ears.

III

8 "The earth swayed and quaked;
    the foundations of the heavens trembled
    and shook when his wrath flared up.

10 Rizpah daughter of Aiah, wearing sacking and spreading some out on the rock, from the beginning of the barley harvest until the rain fell on them from heaven, kept the birds of the sky away from them in the daytime, and the wild animals away at night. 11 David was told of what Saul's concubine, Rizpah daughter of Aiah, had done.

12 David went and recovered the bones of Saul and his son Jonathan from the notables of Jabesh in Gilead. The latter had stolen them from the square in Beth-Shean, where the Philistines had hung them, when the Philistines had defeated Saul at Gilboa. 13 David fetched the bones of Saul and his son Jonathan. The bones of the men who had been dismembered were collected 14 and these, with the bones of Saul and his son Jonathan, were buried in the territory of Benjamin, at Zela, in the tomb of Saul's father, Kish. The king's orders were carried out to the letter and after that, God took pity on the country.

15 Once again the Philistines made war on Israel. David went down with his retainers; they fought the Philistines and David began to tire. 16 There was a champion, one of the sons of Rapha. His spear weighed three hundred shekels of bronze; he was wearing a new sword and was confident of killing David. 17 Abishai son of Zeruiah came to his rescue, however, attacking the Philistine and killing him. Then it was that David's men swore the following oath to him, 'You are never to go into battle with us again, in case you should extinguish the lamp of Israel!'

18 After this, war with the Philistines broke out again at Gob. This was when Sibbecai of Hushah killed Saph, one of the sons of Rapha.

19 Again, war with the Philistines broke out at Gob, and Elhanan son of Jair, of Bethlehem, killed Goliath of Gath, the shaft of whose spear was like a weaver's beam.

20 There was further warfare at Gath, where there was a man of huge stature with six fingers on each hand and six toes on each foot, twenty-four in all. He too was a son of Rapha. 21 When he defied Israel, Jonathan son of Shimea, brother of David cut him down.

22 These four were sons of Rapha in Gath and fell at the hands of David and his retainers.

22 *i*David addressed the words of this song to Yahweh, when Yahweh had delivered him from the clutches of all his enemies and from the clutches of Saul. 2 He said:

Yahweh is my rock and my fortress,
3 my deliverer is my God.
I take refuge in him, my rock,
    my shield, my saving strength,
    my stronghold, my place of refuge.

My Saviour, you have saved me from violence;
4 I call to Yahweh, who is worthy of praise,
    and I am saved from my foes.

5 With Death's breakers closing in on me,
    Belial's torrents ready to swallow me,
6 Sheol's snares on every side of me,
    Death's traps lying ahead of me,

7 I called to Yahweh in my anguish,
    I cried for help to my God,
    from his Temple he heard my voice,
    my cry came to his ears!

8 Then the earth quaked and rocked,
    the heavens' foundations shuddered,
    they quaked at his blazing anger.

i 22 = Ps 18.

NEW REVISED STANDARD VERSION

9 Smoke went up from his nostrils,
  and devouring fire from his mouth;
  glowing coals flamed forth from him.
10 He bowed the heavens, and came down;
  thick darkness was under his feet.
11 He rode on a cherub, and flew;
  he was seen upon the wings of the wind.
12 He made darkness around him a canopy,
  thick clouds, a gathering of water.
13 Out of the brightness before him
  coals of fire flamed forth.
14 The LORD thundered from heaven;
  the Most High uttered his voice.
15 He sent out arrows, and scattered them
  —lightning, and routed them.
16 Then the channels of the sea were seen,
  the foundations of the world were laid bare
at the rebuke of the LORD,
  at the blast of the breath of his nostrils.

17 He reached from on high, he took me,
  he drew me out of mighty waters.
18 He delivered me from my strong enemy,
  from those who hated me;
  for they were too mighty for me.
19 They came upon me in the day of my calamity,
  but the LORD was my stay.
20 He brought me out into a broad place;
  he delivered me, because he delighted in me.
21 The LORD rewarded me according to my
      righteousness;
  according to the cleanness of my hands he
      recompensed me.
22 For I have kept the ways of the LORD,
  and have not wickedly departed from my God.
23 For all his ordinances were before me,
  and from his statutes I did not turn aside.
24 I was blameless before him,
  and I kept myself from guilt.
25 Therefore the LORD has recompensed me
      according to my righteousness,
  according to my cleanness in his sight.

26 With the loyal you show yourself loyal;
  with the blameless you show yourself
      blameless;
27 with the pure you show yourself pure,
  and with the crooked you show yourself
      perverse.
28 You deliver a humble people,
  but your eyes are upon the haughty to bring
      them down.
29 Indeed, you are my lamp, O LORD,
  the LORD lightens my darkness.
30 By you I can crush a troop,
  and by my God I can leap over a wall.
31 This God—his way is perfect;
  the promise of the LORD proves true;
  he is a shield for all who take refuge in him.
32 For who is God, but the LORD?
  And who is a rock, except our God?
33 The God who has girded me with strength[s]
  has opened wide my path.[t]
34 He made my[u] feet like the feet of deer,
  and set me secure on the heights.
35 He trains my hands for war,
  so that my arms can bend a bow of bronze.

[s] Q Ms Gk Syr Vg Compare Ps 18.32: MT *God is my strong refuge*
[t] Meaning of Heb uncertain   [u] Another reading is *his*

REVISED ENGLISH BIBLE

9 Smoke went up from his nostrils,
  devouring fire from his mouth,
  glowing coals and searing heat.
10 He parted the heavens and came down;
  thick darkness lay under his feet.
11 He flew on the back of a cherub;
  he swooped on the wings of the wind.
12 He made darkness around him his covering,
  dense vapour his canopy.
13 Thick clouds came from the radiance before him;
  glowing coals burned brightly.
14 GOD thundered from the heavens;
  the Most High raised his voice.
15 He loosed arrows, he sped them far and wide,
  his lightning shafts, and sent them echoing.
16 The channels of the sea were exposed,
  earth's foundations laid bare
at the LORD's rebuke,
  at the blast of breath from his nostrils.

17 He reached down from on high and took me,
  he drew me out of mighty waters,
18 he delivered me from my enemies, strong as they
      were,
  from my foes when they grew too powerful for
      me.
19 They confronted me in my hour of peril,
  but the LORD was my buttress.
20 He brought me into untrammelled liberty;
  he rescued me because he delighted in me.
21 The LORD repaid me as my righteousness deserved;
  because my conduct was spotless he rewarded me,
22 for I have kept to the ways of the LORD
  and have not turned from my God to wickedness.
23 All his laws I keep before me,
  and have never failed to follow his decrees.
24 In his sight I was blameless
  and kept myself from wrongdoing;
25 because I was spotless in his eyes
  the LORD rewarded me as my righteousness
      deserved.

26 To the loyal you show yourself loyal
  and blameless to the blameless.
27 To the pure you show yourself pure,
  but skilful in your dealings with the perverse.
28 You bring humble folk to safety,
  but humiliate those who look so high and mighty.
29 LORD, you are my lamp;
  my God will lighten my darkness.
30 With your help I storm a rampart;
  by my God's aid I leap over a wall.
31 The way of God is blameless;
  the LORD's word has stood the test;
  he is the shield of all who take refuge in him.
32 What god is there but the LORD?
  What rock but our God:
33 the God who girds me with strength
  and makes my way free from blame,
34 who makes me swift as a hind
  and sets me secure on the heights,
35 who trains my hands for battle
  so that my arms can aim a bronze-tipped bow?

22:11 **swooped:** *prob. rdg, cp. Ps. 18:10; Heb.* was seen.
22:33 **who girds me:** *prob. rdg, cp. Ps. 18:32; Heb.* my refuge *or*
my strength. **and makes . . . blame:** *prob. rdg, cp. Ps. 18:32; Heb.*
unintelligible.   22:34 **the heights:** *Heb.* my heights.

9 Smoke rose from his nostrils,
and a devouring fire from his mouth;
he kindled coals into flame.
10 He inclined the heavens and came down,
with dark clouds under his feet.
11 He mounted a cherub and flew,
borne on the wings of the wind.
12 He made darkness the shelter about him,
with spattering rain and thickening clouds.
13 From the brightness of his presence
coals were kindled to flame.
14 "The LORD thundered from heaven;
the Most High gave forth his voice.
15 He sent forth arrows to put them to flight;
he flashed lightning and routed them.
16 Then the wellsprings of the sea appeared,
the foundations of the earth were laid bare,
At the rebuke of the LORD,
at the blast of the wind of his wrath.
17 "He reached out from on high and grasped me;
he drew me out of the deep waters.
18 He rescued me from my mighty enemy,
from my foes, who were too powerful for me.
19 They attacked me on my day of calamity,
but the LORD came to my support.
20 He set me free in the open,
and rescued me, because he loves me.

IV
21 "The LORD rewarded me according to my justice;
according to the cleanness of my hands he
requited me.
22 For I kept the ways of the LORD
and was not disloyal to my God.
23 For his ordinances were all present to me,
and his statutes I put not from me;
24 But I was wholehearted toward him,
and I was on my guard against guilt.
25 And the LORD requited me according to my justice,
according to my innocence in his sight.
26 "Toward the faithful you are faithful;
toward the wholehearted you are wholehearted;
27 Toward the sincere you are sincere;
but toward the crooked you are astute.
28 You save lowly people,
though on the lofty your eyes look down.
29 You are my lamp, O LORD!
O my God, you brighten the darkness about me.
30 For with your aid I run against an armed band,
and by the help of my God I leap over a wall.
31 God's way is unerring;
the promise of the LORD is fire-tried;
he is a shield to all who take refuge in him."

B
I
32 "For who is God except the LORD?
Who is a rock save our God?
33 The God who girded me with strength
and kept my way unerring;
34 Who made my feet swift as those of hinds
and set me on the heights;
35 Who trained my hands for war
till my arms could bend a bow of brass.

9 Smoke rose from his nostrils,
from his mouth devouring fire
(coals were kindled at it).
10 He parted the heavens and came down,
a storm-cloud underneath his feet;
11 riding one of the winged creatures, he flew,
soaring on the wings of the wind.
12 He wrapped himself in darkness,
his pavilion dark waters and dense cloud.
13 A brightness lit up before him,
hail and blazing fire.
14 Yahweh thundered from the heavens,
the Most High made his voice heard.
15 He shot his arrows and scattered them,
his lightning flashed and routed them.
16 The very springs of ocean were exposed,
the world's foundations were laid bare,
at the roaring of Yahweh,
at the blast of breath from his nostrils!
17 He reached down from on high, snatched me up,
pulled me from the watery depths,
18 rescued me from my mighty foe,
from my enemies who were stronger than I.
19 They assailed me on my day of disaster,
but Yahweh was there to support me,
20 he freed me, set me at large,
he rescued me, because he loves me.

21 Yahweh rewards me for my uprightness,
as my hands are pure so he repays me,
22 since I have kept the ways of Yahweh,
and not fallen away from my God.
23 His judgements are all before me,
his statutes I have not put away from me;
24 I am blameless before him,
I keep myself clear of evil.
25 Hence Yahweh repaid me for acting uprightly
because he could see I was pure.
26 Faithful you are to the faithful,
blameless with the blameless,
27 sincere to the sincere
but cunning to the crafty,
28 you save a people that is humble
and humiliate those with haughty looks.
29 Yahweh, you yourself are my lamp,
my God lights up my darkness;
30 with you I storm the rampart
with my God I can scale any wall.
31 This God, his way is blameless;
the word of Yahweh is refined in the furnace,
for he alone is the shield
of all who take refuge in him.

32 For who is God but Yahweh,
who is a rock but our God:
33 this God who girds me with strength,
who makes my way free from blame,
34 who makes me as swift as a deer
and sets me firmly on the heights,
35 who trains my hands for battle
my arms to bend a bow of bronze.

36 You have given me the shield of your salvation,
   and your help[v] has made me great.
37 You have made me stride freely,
   and my feet do not slip;
38 I pursued my enemies and destroyed them,
   and did not turn back until they were
      consumed.
39 I consumed them; I struck them down, so that
      they did not rise;
   they fell under my feet.
40 For you girded me with strength for the battle;
   you made my assailants sink under me.
41 You made my enemies turn their backs to me,
   those who hated me, and I destroyed them.
42 They looked, but there was no one to save them;
   they cried to the LORD, but he did not answer
      them.
43 I beat them fine like the dust of the earth,
   I crushed them and stamped them down like
      the mire of the streets.

44 You delivered me from strife with the peoples;[w]
   you kept me as the head of the nations;
   people whom I had not known served me.
45 Foreigners came cringing to me;
   as soon as they heard of me, they obeyed me.
46 Foreigners lost heart,
   and came trembling out of their strongholds.

47 The LORD lives! Blessed be my rock,
   and exalted be my God, the rock of my
      salvation,
48 the God who gave me vengeance
   and brought down peoples under me,
49 who brought me out from my enemies;
   you exalted me above my adversaries,
   you delivered me from the violent.
50 For this I will extol you, O LORD, among the
      nations,
   and sing praises to your name.
51 He is a tower of salvation for his king,
   and shows steadfast love to his anointed,
   to David and his descendants forever.

23 Now these are the last words of David:
   The oracle of David, son of Jesse,
   the oracle of the man whom God exalted,[x]
   the anointed of the God of Jacob,
   the favorite of the Strong One of Israel:

2 The spirit of the LORD speaks through me,
   his word is upon my tongue.
3 The God of Israel has spoken,
   the Rock of Israel has said to me:
   One who rules over people justly,
      ruling in the fear of God,
4 is like the light of morning,
   like the sun rising on a cloudless morning,
   gleaming from the rain on the grassy land.

5 Is not my house like this with God?
   For he has made with me an everlasting
      covenant,
   ordered in all things and secure.
   Will he not cause to prosper
   all my help and my desire?

36 You have given me the shield of your salvation;
   you stoop down to make me great.
37 You made room for my steps;
   my feet have not slipped.
38 I pursue and destroy my enemies,
   until I have made an end of them I do not turn
      back.
39 I make an end of them, I strike them down;
   they rise no more, but fall prostrate at my feet.
40 You gird me with strength for the battle
   and subdue my assailants beneath me.
41 You set my foot on my enemies' necks,
   and I wipe out those who hate me.
42 They cry, but there is no one to save them;
   they cry to the LORD, but he does not answer.
43 I shall beat them fine as dust on the ground,
   like mud in the streets I shall trample them.
44 You set me free from the people who challenge
      me,
   and make me master of nations.
   A people I never knew will be my subjects.
45 Foreigners will come fawning to me;
   as soon as they hear tell of me, they will submit.
46 Foreigners will be disheartened
   and come trembling from their strongholds.
47 The LORD lives! Blessed is my rock!
   High above all is God, my safe refuge.

48 You grant me vengeance, God,
   laying nations prostrate at my feet;
49 you free me from my enemies,
   setting me over my assailants;
   you are my deliverer from violent men.
50 Therefore, LORD, I shall praise you among the
      nations
   and sing psalms to your name,
51 to one who gives his king great victories
   and keeps faith with his anointed,
   with David and his descendants for ever.

23 These are the last words of David:

   The word of David son of Jesse,
   the word of the man whom the High God raised
      up,
   the anointed of the God of Jacob
   and the singer of Israel's psalms:

2 The spirit of the LORD has spoken through me,
   and his word is on my lips.
3 The God of Israel spoke,
   the Rock of Israel said of me:
   'He who rules people in justice,
   who rules in the fear of God,
4 is like the light of morning at sunrise,
   a morning that is cloudless after rain
   and makes the grass from the earth sparkle.'

5 Surely my house is true to God;
   for he has made an everlasting covenant with me,
   its terms spelled out and faithfully kept;
   that is my whole salvation, all my delight.

22:41 **You set:** *prob. rdg, cp. Ps. 18:40; Heb. unintelligible.*
22:42 **cry, but:** *prob. rdg, cp. Ps. 18:41; Heb. look, but.*
22:43 **trample them:** *prob. rdg, cp. Ps. 18:42; Heb. adds I will
stamp them down.* 22:44 **people who challenge me:** *so Gk and
Ps. 18:43; Heb. obscure.* **make:** *so Gk (Luc.) and Ps. 18:43; Heb.
keep.* 22:47 **God:** *Heb. adds rock.*

---

[v] Q Ms: MT *your answering*   [w] Gk: Heb *from strife with my people*
[x] Q Ms: MT *who was raised on high*

NEW AMERICAN BIBLE

II

36 "You have given me your saving shield,
  and your help has made me great.
37 You made room for my steps;
  unwavering was my stride.
38 I pursued my enemies and destroyed them,
  nor did I turn again till I made an end of them.
39 I smote them and they did not rise;
  they fell beneath my feet.

III

40 "You girded me with strength for war;
  you subdued my adversaries beneath me.
41 My enemies you put to flight before me
  and those who hated me I destroyed.
42 They cried for help—but no one saved them;
  to the LORD—but he answered them not.
43 I ground them fine as the dust of the earth;
  like the mud in the streets I trampled
    them down.

IV

44 "You rescued me from the strife of my people;
  you made me head over nations.
A people I had not known became my slaves;
45   as soon as they heard me, they obeyed.
46 The foreigners fawned and cringed before me;
  they staggered forth from their fortresses."

C

47 "The LORD live! And blessed be my Rock!
  Extolled be my God, Rock of my salvation.
48 O God, who granted me vengeance,
  who made peoples subject to me
49   and helped me escape from my enemies,
  Above my adversaries you exalt me
  and from the violent man you rescue me.
50 Therefore will I proclaim you, O LORD, among
    the nations,
  and I will sing praise to your name,
51 You who gave great victories to your king
  and showed kindness to your anointed,
  to David and his posterity forever."

23 These are the last words of David:
  "The utterance of David, son of Jesse;
  the utterance of the man God raised up,
Anointed of the God of Jacob,
  favorite of the Mighty One of Israel.
2 The spirit of the LORD spoke through me;
  his word was on my tongue.
3 The God of Israel spoke;
  of me the Rock of Israel said,
'He that rules over men in justice,
  that rules in the fear of God,
4 Is like the morning light at sunrise
  on a cloudless morning,
  making the greensward sparkle after rain.'
5 Is not my house firm before God?
  He has made an eternal covenant with me,
  set forth in detail and secured.
Will he not bring to fruition
  all my salvation and my every desire?

NEW JERUSALEM BIBLE

36 You give me your invincible shield,
  you never cease to listen to me,
37 you give me the strides of a giant,
  give me ankles that never weaken—

38 I pursue my enemies and exterminate them,
  not turning back till they are annihilated;
39 I strike them down, and they cannot rise,
  they fall, they are under my feet.

40 You have girded me with strength for the fight,
  bent down my assailants beneath me,
41 made my enemies retreat before me;
  and those who hate me I destroy.

42 They cry out, there is no one to save,
  to Yahweh, but no answer comes.
43 I crumble them like the dust of the squares,
  trample them like the mud of the streets.

44 You free me from the quarrels of my people,
  you place me at the head of the nations,
  a people I did not know are now my servants,

45 foreigners come wooing my favour,
  no sooner do they hear than they obey me,
46 foreigners grow faint of heart,
  they come trembling out of their fastnesses.

47 Life to Yahweh! Blessed be my rock!
  Exalted be the God of my salvation,
48 the God who gives me vengeance
  and crushes the peoples under me,

49 who takes me away from my enemies.
  You lift me high above those who attack me,
  you deliver me from the man of violence.

50 For this I will praise you, Yahweh, among the
    nations,
  and sing praise to your name.
51 He saves his king, time after time,
  displays faithful love for his anointed,
  for David and his heirs for ever.

23 These are the last words of David:

Thus speaks David son of Jesse,
  thus speaks the man raised to eminence,
  the anointed of the God of Jacob,
  the singer of the songs of Israel:

2 The spirit of Yahweh speaks through me,
  his word is on my tongue;
3 the God of Jacob has spoken,
  the Rock of Israel has said to me:

He whose rule is upright on earth,
  who rules in the fear of God,
4 is like the morning light at sunrise
  (on a cloudless morning)
  making the grass of the earth sparkle after rain.

5 Yes, my House stands firm with God:
  he has made an eternal covenant with me,
  all in order, well assured;
  does he not bring to fruition my every victory and
      desire?

NEW REVISED STANDARD VERSION	REVISED ENGLISH BIBLE

6 But the godless are^y all like thorns that are
  thrown away;
  for they cannot be picked up with the hand;
7 to touch them one uses an iron bar
  or the shaft of a spear.
  And they are entirely consumed in fire on the
    spot.^z

8 These are the names of the warriors whom David had: Josheb-basshebeth a Tahchemonite; he was chief of the Three;^a he wielded his spear^b against eight hundred whom he killed at one time.

9 Next to him among the three warriors was Eleazar son of Dodo son of Ahohi. He was with David when they defied the Philistines who were gathered there for battle. The Israelites withdrew, 10 but he stood his ground. He struck down the Philistines until his arm grew weary, though his hand clung to the sword. The LORD brought about a great victory that day. Then the people came back to him — but only to strip the dead.

11 Next to him was Shammah son of Agee, the Hararite. The Philistines gathered together at Lehi, where there was a plot of ground full of lentils; and the army fled from the Philistines. 12 But he took his stand in the middle of the plot, defended it, and killed the Philistines; and the LORD brought about a great victory.

13 Towards the beginning of harvest three of the thirty^c chiefs went down to join David at the cave of Adullam, while a band of Philistines was encamped in the valley of Rephaim. 14 David was then in the stronghold; and the garrison of the Philistines was then at Bethlehem. 15 David said longingly, "O that someone would give me water to drink from the well of Bethlehem that is by the gate!" 16 Then the three warriors broke through the camp of the Philistines, drew water from the well of Bethlehem that was by the gate, and brought it to David. But he would not drink of it; he poured it out to the LORD, 17 for he said, "The LORD forbid that I should do this. Can I drink the blood of the men who went at the risk of their lives?" Therefore he would not drink it. The three warriors did these things.

18 Now Abishai son of Zeruiah, the brother of Joab, was chief of the Thirty.^d With his spear he fought against three hundred men and killed them, and won a name beside the Three. 19 He was the most renowned of the Thirty,^e and became their commander; but he did not attain to the Three.

20 Benaiah son of Jehoiada was a valiant warrior^f from Kabzeel, a doer of great deeds; he struck down two sons of Ariel^g of Moab. He also went down and killed a lion in a pit on a day when snow had fallen. 21 And he killed an Egyptian, a handsome man. The Egyptian had a spear in his hand; but Benaiah went against him with a staff, snatched the spear out of the Egyptian's hand, and killed him with his own spear. 22 Such were the things Benaiah son of Jehoiada did, and won a name beside the three warriors. 23 He was renowned among the Thirty, but he did not attain to the Three. And David put him in charge of his bodyguard.

24 Among the Thirty were Asahel brother of Joab; Elhanan son of Dodo of Bethlehem; 25 Shammah of Harod; Elika of Harod; 26 Helez the Paltite; Ira son of Ikkesh of Tekoa; 27 Abiezer of Anathoth; Mebunnai the Hushathite; 28 Zalmon the Ahohite; Maharai of Netophah; 29 Heleb son of Baanah of Netophah; Ittai son of Ribai of Gibeah of the

---

6 But the ungodly put forth no shoots,
  they are all like briars thrown aside;
  none dare put out his hand to pick them up,
7 none touch them but with a tool of iron or wood;
  they are fit only for burning where they lie.

8 THESE are the names of David's heroes. First came Ishbosheth the Hachmonite, chief of the three; it was he who brandished his spear over eight hundred, all slain at one time. 9 Next to him was Eleazar son of Dodo the Ahohite, one of the heroic three. He was with David at Pasdammim where the Philistines had gathered for battle. When the Israelites fell back, 10 he stood his ground and rained blows on the Philistines until, from sheer weariness, his hand stuck to his sword. The LORD brought about a great victory that day. Afterwards the people rallied to him, but it was only to strip the dead. 11 Next to him was Shammah son of Agee a Hararite. The Philistines had gathered at Lehi, where there was a field with a fine crop of lentils; and, when the Philistines put the people to flight, 12 he stood his ground in the field, defended it, and defeated the foe. So the LORD brought about a great victory.

13 Towards the beginning of the harvest three of the thirty went down to join David at the cave of Adullam, while a band of Philistines was encamped in the valley of Rephaim. 14 David was then in the stronghold, and a Philistine garrison held Bethlehem. 15 One day David exclaimed with longing, 'If only I could have a drink of water from the well by the gate at Bethlehem!' 16 At this the heroic three made their way through the Philistine lines and drew water from the well by the gate of Bethlehem and brought it to David. But he refused to drink it; he poured it out to the LORD 17 saying, 'The LORD forbid that I should do such a thing! Can I drink the blood of these men who went at the risk of their lives?' So he would not drink it. Such were the exploits of the heroic three.

18 Abishai the brother of Joab son of Zeruiah was chief of the thirty; he it was who brandished his spear over three hundred dead. He was famous among the thirty, 19 and some think he surpassed in reputation the rest of the thirty; he became their captain, but he did not rival the three. 20 Benaiah son of Jehoiada, from Kabzeel, was a hero of many exploits. It was he who slew the two champions of Moab, and who once went down into a pit and killed a lion on a snowy day. 21 He also killed an Egyptian, a man of striking appearance armed with a spear. Benaiah went to meet him with a club, wrested the spear out of the Egyptian's hand, and killed him with his own weapon. 22 Such were the exploits of Benaiah son of Jehoiada, famous among the heroic thirty. 23 He was more famous than the rest of the thirty, but he did not rival the three. David appointed him to his household.

24 Asahel the brother of Joab was one of the thirty; Elhanan son of Dodo from Bethlehem; 25 Shammah from Harod; Elika from Harod; 26 Helez from a place unknown; Ira son of Ikkesh from Tekoa; 27 Abiezer from Anathoth; Mebunnai from Hushah; 28 Zalmon the Ahohite; Maharai from Netophah; 29 Heled son of Baanah from Netophah; Ittai son of

---

23:7 **but:** *prob. rdg; Heb.* he shall be filled. 23:8–39 *Cp. 1 Chr. 11:10–41.* 23:8 **Ishbosheth the Hachmonite:** *prob. rdg; Heb.* Josheb-basshebeth a Tahchemonite. **three:** *so Gk (Luc.); Heb.* third. **who . . . spear:** *prob. rdg, cp. 1 Chr. 11:11; Heb.* unintelligible. 23:9 **the Ahohite:** *prob. rdg, cp. 1 Chr. 11:12; Heb.* son of Ahohi. **He . . . Philistines:** *prob. rdg, cp. 1 Chr. 11:13; Heb.* With David they taunted them among the Philistines. 23:17 **I drink:** *prob. rdg, cp. 1 Chr. 11:19; Heb.* omits. 23:18 **thirty:** *so Syriac; Heb.* three. 23:19,22 **thirty:** *prob. rdg; Heb.* three. 23:24 **from:** *so some MSS; others omit.* 23:29 **Heled:** *so many MSS; others* Heleb.

---

^y Heb *But worthlessness*   ^z Heb *in sitting*   ^a Gk Vg Compare 1 Chr 11.11: Meaning of Heb uncertain   ^b 1 Chr 11.11: Meaning of Heb uncertain   ^c Heb adds *head*   ^d Two Heb Mss Syr: MT Three   ^e Syr Compare 1 Chr 11.25: Heb *Was he the most renowned of the Three?*   ^f Another reading is *the son of Ish-hai*   ^g Gk: Heb lacks *sons of*

NEW AMERICAN BIBLE

6 But the wicked are all like thorns to be cast
away;
they cannot be taken up by hand.
7 He who wishes to touch them
must arm himself with iron and the shaft of
a spear,
and they must be consumed by fire."
8 These are the names of David's warriors. Ishbaal, son of
Hachamoni, was the first of the Three. It was he who brandished his battle-ax over eight hundred slain in a single
encounter. 9 Next to him, among the Three warriors, was
Eleazar, son of Dodo the Ahohite. He was with David at
Ephesdammim when the Philistines assembled there for battle. The Israelites had retreated, 10 but he stood his ground
and fought the Philistines until his hand grew tired and
became cramped, holding fast to the sword. The LORD
brought about a great victory on that day; the soldiers turned
back after Eleazar, but only to strip the slain. 11 Next to him
was Shammah, son of Agee the Hararite. The Philistines
had assembled at Lehi, where there was a plot of land full
of lentils. When the soldiers fled from the Philistines, 12 he
took his stand in the middle of the plot and defended it. He
slew the Philistines, and the LORD brought about a great
victory. Such were the deeds of the Three warriors.
13 During the harvest three of the Thirty went down to
David in the cave of Adullam, while a Philistine clan was
encamped in the Vale of Rephaim. 14 At that time David
was in the refuge, and there was a garrison of Philistines in
Bethlehem. 15 Now David had a strong craving and said,
"Oh, that someone would give me a drink of water from the
cistern that is by the gate of Bethlehem!" 16 So the Three
warriors broke through the Philistine camp and drew water
from the cistern that is by the gate of Bethlehem. But when
they brought it to David he refused to drink it, and instead
poured it out to the LORD, 17 saying: "The LORD forbid that
I do this! Can I drink the blood of these men who went at
the risk of their lives?" So he refused to drink it.
18 Abishai, brother of Joab, son of Zeruiah, was at the
head of the Thirty. It was he who brandished his spear over
three hundred slain. He was listed among the Thirty 19 and
commanded greater respect than the Thirty, becoming their
leader. However, he did not attain to the Three.
20 Benaiah, son of Jehoiada, a stalwart from Kabzeel,
was a man of great achievements. It was he who slew the
two lions in Moab. He also went down and killed the lion
in the cistern at the time of the snow. 21 It was he, too, who
slew an Egyptian of large stature. Although the Egyptian
was armed with a spear, he went against him with a club
and wrested the spear from the Egyptian's hand, then killed
him with his own spear. 22 Such were the deeds performed
by Benaiah, son of Jehoiada. He was listed among the
Thirty warriors 23 and commanded greater respect than the
Thirty. However, he did not attain to the Three. David put
him in command of his bodyguard. 24 Asahel, brother of
Joab . . . .
Among the Thirty were: Elhanan, son of Dodo, from
Bethlehem; 25 Shammah from En-harod; Elika from En-
harod; 26 Helez from Beth-pelet; Ira, son of Ikkesh, from
Tekoa; 27 Abiezer from Anathoth; Sibbekai from Hushah;
28 Zalmon from Ahoh; Maharai from Netophah; 29 Heled,
son of Baanath, from Netophah; Ittai, son of Ribai, from

NEW JERUSALEM BIBLE

6 But men of Belial he rejects like thorns,
for these are never taken up in the hand:
7 no one touches them
except with a pitchfork or spear-shaft,
and then only to burn them to nothing!
8 These are the names of David's champions: Ishbaal the
Hachmonite leader of the Three; it was he who brandished
his spear over eight hundred men whom he had killed at one
time. 9 Next, there was Eleazar of Dodo, the Ahohite,
one of the three champions. He was with David at Pas-
Dammim when the Philistines mustered for battle there and
the men of Israel had disbanded. 10 But he stood his ground
and cut down the Philistines until his hand was so stiff that
he could not let go of the sword. Yahweh brought about a
great victory that day, and the people rallied behind him,
although only to plunder. 11 Next, there was Shamma son of
Elah, the Hararite. The Philistines had mustered at Lehi.
There was a field full of lentils there; the people fled from
the Philistines, 12 but he took his stand in the middle of the
field, held it, and cut down the Philistines; and Yahweh
brought about a great victory.
13 Three members of the Thirty went down at the beginning of the harvest and came to David at the Cave of Adullam while a company of Philistines was encamped in the
Valley of the Rephaim. 14 David was then in the stronghold,
and there was a Philistine garrison in Bethlehem. 15 Longingly David said, 'If only someone would fetch me a drink
of water from the well that stands by the gate at Bethlehem!'
16 At this, the three champions, forcing their way through
the Philistine camp, drew water from the well that stands by
the gate of Bethlehem and, taking it away, presented it to
David. He, however, would not drink any of it, but poured
it out as a libation to Yahweh. 17 'Yahweh preserve me', he
said, 'from doing such a thing! This is the blood of men
who went at risk of their lives.' That was why he would not
drink. Such were the deeds of these three champions.
18 Abishai, brother of Joab and son of Zeruiah, was leader
of the Thirty. It was he who brandished his spear over three
hundred men whom he had killed, winning himself a name
among the Thirty. 19 He was a most illustrious member of
the Thirty and became their captain, but he was not equal
to the Three.
20 Benaiah of Kabzeel was the son of Jehoiada and hero
of many exploits. He it was who slaughtered two formidable Moabites and, one snowy day, climbed down and
slaughtered the lion in the storage-well. 21 He was also
slaughtered an Egyptian of great stature. The Egyptian was
armed with a spear, but he took him on with a staff, tore the spear
from the Egyptian's hand and killed the man with it. 22 Such
were the exploits of Benaiah son of Jehoiada, winning him
a name among the thirty champions. 23 He was a most illustrious member of the Thirty, but he was not equal to the
Three. David put him in command of his bodyguard.
24 Asahel brother of Joab was one of the Thirty;
Elhanan son of Dodo, of Bethlehem;
25 Shammah of Harod;
Elika of Harod;
26 Helez of Beth-Pelet;
Ira son of Ikkesh, of Tekoa;
27 Abiezer of Anathoth;
Sibbecai of Hushah;
28 Zalmon of Ahoh;
Maharai of Netophah;
29 Heled son of Baanah, of Netophah;
Ittai son of Ribai, of Gibeah in Benjamin;

23, 24: A more complete notice about Asahel, who died early in his
career (2 Sm 2, 16–23), is to be presumed lost at this point.

Benjaminites; 30 Benaiah of Pirathon; Hiddai of the torrents of Gaash; 31 Abi-albon the Arbathite; Azmaveth of Bahurim; 32 Eliahba of Shaalbon; the sons of Jashen: Jonathan 33 son of*h* Shammah the Hararite; Ahiam son of Sharar the Hararite; 34 Eliphelet son of Ahasbai of Maacah; Eliam son of Ahithophel the Gilonite; 35 Hezro*i* of Carmel; Paarai the Arbite; 36 Igal son of Nathan of Zobah; Bani the Gadite; 37 Zelek the Ammonite; Naharai of Beeroth, the armor-bearer of Joab son of Zeruiah; 38 Ira the Ithrite; Gareb the Ithrite; 39 Uriah the Hittite — thirty-seven in all.

24 Again the anger of the LORD was kindled against Israel, and he incited David against them, saying, "Go, count the people of Israel and Judah." 2 So the king said to Joab and the commanders of the army,*j* who were with him, "Go through all the tribes of Israel, from Dan to Beer-sheba, and take a census of the people, so that I may know how many there are." 3 But Joab said to the king, "May the LORD your God increase the number of the people a hundredfold, while the eyes of my lord the king can still see it! But why does my lord the king want to do this?" 4 But the king's word prevailed against Joab and the commanders of the army. So Joab and the commanders of the army went out from the presence of the king to take a census of the people of Israel. 5 They crossed the Jordan, and began from*k* Aroer and from the city that is in the middle of the valley, toward Gad and on to Jazer. 6 Then they came to Gilead, and to Kadesh in the land of the Hittites;*l* and they came to Dan, and from Dan*m* they went around to Sidon, 7 and came to the fortress of Tyre and to all the cities of the Hivites and Canaanites; and they went out to the Negeb of Judah at Beer-sheba. 8 So when they had gone through all the land, they came back to Jerusalem at the end of nine months and twenty days. 9 Joab reported to the king the number of those who had been recorded: in Israel there were eight hundred thousand soldiers able to draw the sword, and those of Judah were five hundred thousand.

10 But afterward, David was stricken to the heart because he had numbered the people. David said to the LORD, "I have sinned greatly in what I have done. But now, O LORD, I pray you, take away the guilt of your servant; for I have done very foolishly." 11 When David rose in the morning, the word of the LORD came to the prophet Gad, David's seer, saying, 12 "Go and say to David: Thus says the LORD: Three things I offer*n* you; choose one of them, and I will do it to you." 13 So Gad came to David and told him; he asked him, "Shall three*o* years of famine come to you on your land? Or will you flee three months before your foes while they pursue you? Or shall there be three days' pestilence in your land? Now consider, and decide what answer I shall return to the one who sent me." 14 Then David said to Gad, "I am in great distress; let us fall into the hand of the LORD, for his mercy is great; but let me not fall into human hands."

Ribai from Gibeah of Benjamin; 30 Benaiah from Pirathon; Hiddai from the wadis of Gaash; 31 Abi-albon from Beth-arabah; Azmoth from Bahurim; 32 Eliahba from Shaalbon; Hashem the Gizonite; Jonathan son of 33 Shammah the Hararite; Ahiam son of Sharar the Hararite; 34 Eliphelet son of Ahasbai son of the Maacathite; Eliam son of Ahithophel the Gilonite; 35 Hezrai from Carmel; Paarai the Arbite; 36 Igal son of Nathan from Zobah; Bani the Gadite; 37 Zelek the Ammonite; Naharai from Beeroth, armour-bearer to Joab son of Zeruiah; 38 Ira the Ithrite; Gareb the Ithrite; 39 Uriah the Hittite: there were thirty-seven in all.

24 ONCE again the Israelites felt the LORD's anger, when he incited David against them and instructed him to take a census of Israel and Judah. 2 The king commanded Joab and the officers of the army with him to go round all the tribes of Israel, from Dan to Beersheba, and make a record of the people and report back the number to him. 3 Joab answered, 'Even if the LORD your God should increase the people a hundredfold and your majesty should live to see it, what pleasure would that give your majesty?' 4 But Joab and the officers, being overruled by the king, left his presence in order to take the census. 5 They crossed the Jordan and began at Aroer and the town at the wadi, proceeding towards Gad and Jazer. 6 They came to Gilead and to the land of the Hittites, to Kadesh, and then to Dan and Iyyon and so round towards Sidon. 7 They went as far as the walled city of Tyre and all the towns of the Hivites and Canaanites, and then went on to the Negeb of Judah at Beersheba. 8 They covered the whole country and arrived back at Jerusalem after nine months and twenty days. 9 Joab reported to the king the numbers recorded: the number of able-bodied men, capable of bearing arms, was eight hundred thousand in Israel and five hundred thousand in Judah.

10 After he had taken the census, David was overcome with remorse, and said to the LORD, 'I have acted very wickedly: I pray you, LORD, remove your servant's guilt, for I have been very foolish.' 11 When he rose next morning, the command of the LORD had come to the prophet Gad, David's seer, 12 to go and tell David: 'This is the word of the LORD: I offer you three things; choose one and I shall bring it upon you.' 13 Gad came to David and reported this to him and said, 'Is it to be three years of famine in your land, or three months of flight with the enemy in close pursuit, or three days of pestilence in your land? Consider carefully now what answer I am to take back to him who sent me.' 14 David said to Gad, 'This is a desperate plight I am in; let us fall into the hands of the LORD, for his mercy is great; and let me not fall into the hands of men.'

23:31 **Beth-arabah:** *prob. rdg, cp. Josh. 18:22; Heb.* Arabah. **Bahurim:** *prob. rdg, cp. 1 Chr. 11:33; Heb.* Barhum. 23:32 **Hashem . . . son of:** *prob. rdg, cp. 1 Chr. 11:34; Heb.* the sons of Jashen, Jonathan. 23:33 **Sharar the Hararite:** *prob. rdg, cp. 1 Chr. 11:35; Heb.* Sharar the Ararite. 24:1–25 *Cp. 1 Chr. 21:1–27.* 24:2 **Joab . . . army:** *prob. rdg, cp. 1 Chr. 21:2; Heb.* Joab the officer of the army. 24:5 **began . . . Gad:** *prob. rdg; Heb.* encamped in Aroer on the right of the level land of the wadi Gad. 24:6 **of the . . . Kadesh:** *so Gk (Luc.); Heb.* of Tahtim, Hodshi. **Iyyon:** *prob. rdg, cp. 1 Kgs. 15:20; Heb.* Yaan. **round:** *so Gk; Heb.* obscure. 24:13 **three years:** *so Gk, cp. 1 Chr. 21:12; Heb.* seven years.

h Gk: Heb lacks *son of*   *i* Another reading is *Hezrai*   *j* 1 Chr 21.2 Gk: Heb *to Joab the commander of the army*   *k* Gk Mss: Heb *encamped in Aroer south of*   *l* Gk: Heb *to the land of* *Tahtim-hodshi*   *m* Cn Compare Gk: Heb *they came to Dan-jaan and* *n* Or *hold over*   *o* 1 Chr 21.12 Gk: Heb *seven*

Gibeah of the Benjaminites; 30 Benaiah from Pirathon; Hiddai from Nahale-gaash; 31 Abibaal from Beth-arabah; Azmaveth from Bahurim; 32 Eliahba from Shaalbon; Jashen the Gunite; Jonathan, 33 son of Shammah the Hararite; Ahiam, son of Sharar the Hararite; 34 Eliphelet, son of Ahasbai, from Beth-maacah; Eliam, son of Ahithophel, from Gilo; 35 Hezrai from Carmel; Paarai the Arbite; 36 Igal, son of Nathan, from Zobah; Bani the Gadite; 37 Zelek the Ammonite; Naharai from Beeroth, armor-bearer of Joab, son of Zeruiah; 38 Ira from Jattir; Gareb from Jattir; 39 Uriah the Hittite — thirty-seven in all.

24 The LORD's anger against Israel flared again, and he incited David against the Israelites by prompting him to number Israel and Judah. 2 Accordingly the king said to Joab and the leaders of the army who were with him, "Tour all the tribes in Israel from Dan to Beer-sheba and register the people, that I may know their number." 3 But Joab said to the king: "May the LORD your God increase the number of people a hundredfold for your royal majesty to see it with his own eyes. But why does it please my lord the king to order a thing of this kind?" 4 The king, however, overruled Joab and the leaders of the army, so they left the king's presence in order to register the people of Israel. 5 Crossing the Jordan, they began near Aroer, south of the city in the wadi, and went in the direction of Gad, toward Jazer. 6 They continued on to Gilead and to the district below Mount Hermon. Then they proceeded to Dan; from there they turned toward Sidon, 7 going to the fortress of Tyre and to all the cities of the Hivites and Canaanites, and ending up at Beer-sheba in the Negeb of Judah. 8 Thus they toured the whole country, reaching Jerusalem again after nine months and twenty days. 9 Joab then reported to the king the number of people registered: in Israel, eight hundred thousand men fit for military service; in Judah, five hundred thousand.

10 Afterward, however, David regretted having numbered the people, and said to the LORD: "I have sinned grievously in what I have done. But now, LORD, forgive the guilt of your servant, for I have been very foolish." 11 When David rose in the morning, the LORD had spoken to the prophet Gad, David's seer, saying: 12 "Go and say to David, 'This is what the LORD says: I offer you three alternatives; choose one of them, and I will inflict it on you.'" 13 Gad then went to David to inform him. He asked: "Do you want a three years' famine to come upon your land, or to flee from your enemy three months while he pursues you, or to have a three days' pestilence in your land? Now consider and decide what I must reply to him who sent me." 14 David answered Gad: "I am in very serious difficulty. Let us fall by the hand of God, for he is most merciful; but let me not fall by the hand of man." 15 Thus David chose the pestilence.

30 Benaiah of Pirathon;
  Hiddai of the Torrents of Gaash;
31 Abibaal of Beth-ha-Arabah;
  Azmaveth of Bahurim;
32 Eliahba of Shaalbon;
  Jashen of Gimzo;
  Jonathan 33 son of Shammah, of Harar;
  Ahiam son of Sharar, of Harar;
34 Eliphelet son of Ahasbai, of Beth-Maacah;
  Eliam son of Ahithophel, of Gilo;
35 Hezro of Carmel;
  Paarai of Arab;
36 Igal son of Nathan, of Zobah;
  Bani the Gadite;
37 Zelek the Ammonite;
  Naharai of Beeroth squire to Joab, son of Zeruiah;
38 Ira of Jattir;
  Gareb of Jattir;
39 Uriah the Hittite —
thirty-seven in all.

24 Again, Yahweh's anger was aroused against Israel, and he incited David against them. 'Go,' he said, 'take a census of Israel and Judah.' 2 The king said to Joab and the senior army officers who were with him, 'Now, go through all the tribes of Israel from Dan to Beersheba, and take a census of the people; I wish to know the size of the population.' 3 Joab said to the king, 'May Yahweh your God multiply the people a hundred times — however many there are — while my lord the king still has eyes to see it, but why should my lord the king be set on this?' 4 The king nonetheless enforced his order on Joab and the senior officers, and Joab and the senior officers left the king's presence, to take a census of the people of Israel.

5 They crossed the Jordan and made a start with Aroer and the town in the middle of the valley, then moved on to the Gadites and to Jazer. 6 They then went to Gilead and the territory of the Hittites, to Kadesh; they then went to Dan and from Dan cut across to Sidon. 7 They then went to the fortress of Tyre and to all the towns of the Hittites and Canaanites ending up in the Negeb of Judah at Beersheba. 8 Having travelled throughout the country, after nine months and twenty days they returned to Jerusalem.

9 Joab gave the king the census results for the people; Israel had eight hundred thousand fighting men who could wield a sword, and Judah five hundred thousand.

10 But afterwards David's heart misgave him for having taken a census of the people. David then said to Yahweh, 'I have committed a grave sin by doing this. But now, Yahweh, I beg you to forgive your servant for this fault, for I have acted very foolishly.' 11 When, however, David got up next morning, the following message had come from Yahweh to the prophet Gad, David's seer, 12 'Go and say to David, "Yahweh says this: I offer you three things; choose which one of them I am to inflict on you."' 13 So Gad went to David and said, 'Which do you prefer: to have three years of famine befall your country; to flee for three months before a pursuing army; or to have three days of epidemic in your country? Now think, and decide how I am to answer him who sends me.' 14 David said to Gad, 'I am very apprehensive . . . Better to fall into Yahweh's hands, since his mercies are great, than to fall into the hands of men!' 15 So David chose the epidemic.

NEW REVISED STANDARD VERSION

15 So the LORD sent a pestilence on Israel from that morning until the appointed time; and seventy thousand of the people died, from Dan to Beer-sheba. 16 But when the angel stretched out his hand toward Jerusalem to destroy it, the LORD relented concerning the evil, and said to the angel who was bringing destruction among the people, "It is enough; now stay your hand." The angel of the LORD was then by the threshing floor of Araunah the Jebusite. 17 When David saw the angel who was destroying the people, he said to the LORD, "I alone have sinned, and I alone have done wickedly; but these sheep, what have they done? Let your hand, I pray, be against me and against my father's house."

18 That day Gad came to David and said to him, "Go up and erect an altar to the LORD on the threshing floor of Araunah the Jebusite." 19 Following Gad's instructions, David went up, as the LORD had commanded. 20 When Araunah looked down, he saw the king and his servants coming toward him; and Araunah went out and prostrated himself before the king with his face to the ground. 21 Araunah said, "Why has my lord the king come to his servant?" David said, "To buy the threshing floor from you in order to build an altar to the LORD, so that the plague may be averted from the people." 22 Then Araunah said to David, "Let my lord the king take and offer up what seems good to him; here are the oxen for the burnt offering, and the threshing sledges and the yokes of the oxen for the wood. 23 All this, O king, Araunah gives to the king." And Araunah said to the king, "May the LORD your God respond favorably to you."

24 But the king said to Araunah, "No, but I will buy them from you for a price; I will not offer burnt offerings to the LORD my God that cost me nothing." So David bought the threshing floor and the oxen for fifty shekels of silver. 25 David built there an altar to the LORD, and offered burnt offerings and offerings of well-being. So the LORD answered his supplication for the land, and the plague was averted from Israel.

REVISED ENGLISH BIBLE

15 The LORD sent a pestilence throughout Israel from the morning till the end of the appointed time; from Dan to Beersheba seventy thousand of the people died. 16 The angel stretched out his arm towards Jerusalem to destroy it; but the LORD repented of the evil and said to the angel who was destroying the people, 'Enough! Stay your hand.' At that moment the angel of the LORD was at the threshing-floor of Araunah the Jebusite.

17 When David saw the angel who was striking down the people, he said to the LORD, 'It is I who have sinned, I who committed the wrong; but these poor sheep, what have they done? Let your hand fall on me and on my family.'

18 Gad came to David that day and said, 'Go and set up an altar to the LORD on the threshing-floor of Araunah the Jebusite.' 19 David obeyed Gad's instructions, and went up as the LORD had commanded. 20 When Araunah looked down and saw the king and his servants coming towards him, he went out and, prostrating himself before the king, 21 said, 'Why has your majesty come to visit his servant?' David answered, 'To buy the threshing-floor from you so that I may build an altar to the LORD, and the plague which has attacked the people may be stopped.' 22 Araunah answered, 'I beg your majesty to take it and sacrifice what you think fit. See, here are the oxen for the whole-offering, and the threshing-sledges and the ox-yokes for fuel.' 23 Araunah gave it all to the king for his own use and said to him, 'May the LORD your God accept you.' 24 But the king said to Araunah, 'No, I shall buy it from you; I am not going to offer up to the LORD my God whole-offerings that have cost me nothing.' So David bought the threshing-floor and the oxen for fifty shekels of silver. 25 He built an altar to the LORD there and offered whole-offerings and shared-offerings. Then the LORD yielded to his prayer for the land, and the plague in Israel stopped.

24:23 **Araunah:** *prob. rdg; Heb. adds* the king.

Now it was the time of the wheat harvest when the plague broke out among the people. [The LORD then sent a pestilence over Israel from morning until the time appointed, and seventy thousand of the people from Dan to Beer-sheba died.] 16 But when the angel stretched forth his hand toward Jerusalem to destroy it, the LORD regretted the calamity and said to the angel causing the destruction among the people, "Enough now! Stay your hand." The angel of the LORD was then standing at the threshing floor of Araunah the Jebusite. 17 When David saw the angel who was striking the people, he said to the LORD: "It is I who have sinned; it is I, the shepherd, who have done wrong. But these are sheep; what have they done? Punish me and my kindred."

18 On the same day Gad went to David and said to him, "Go up and build an altar to the LORD on the threshing floor of Araunah the Jebusite." 19 Following Gad's bidding, David went up as the LORD had commanded. 20 Now Araunah looked down and noticed the king and his servants coming toward him while he was threshing wheat. So he went out and paid homage to the king, with face to the ground. 21 Then Araunah asked, "Why does my lord the king come to his servant?" David replied, "To buy the threshing floor from you, to build an altar to the LORD, that the plague may be checked among the people." 22 But Araunah said to David: "Let my lord the king take and offer up whatever he may wish. Here are oxen for holocausts, and threshing sledges and the yokes of the oxen for wood. 23 All this does Araunah give to the king." Araunah then said to the king, "May the LORD your God accept your offering." 24 The king, however, replied to Araunah, "No, I must pay you for it, for I cannot offer to the LORD my God holocausts that cost nothing." So David bought the threshing floor and the oxen for fifty silver shekels. 25 Then David built an altar there to the LORD, and offered holocausts and peace offerings. The LORD granted relief to the country, and the plague was checked in Israel.

It was the time of the wheat harvest. So Yahweh unleashed an epidemic on Israel from that morning until the time determined; plague ravaged the people and, of the people from Dan to Beersheba, seventy thousand died. 16 But when the angel stretched his hand towards Jerusalem to destroy it, Yahweh felt sorry about the calamity and said to the angel who was destroying the people, 'Enough now! Hold your hand!' The angel of Yahweh was standing by the threshing-floor of Araunah the Jebusite. 17 When David saw the angel who was ravaging the people, he said to Yahweh, 'I was the one who sinned. I was the one who acted wrongly. But these, the flock, what have they done? Let your hand lie heavy on me and on my family!'

18 Gad went to David that day and said, 'Go up and raise an altar to Yahweh on the threshing-floor of Araunah the Jebusite.' 19 So, at Gad's bidding, David went up, as Yahweh had ordered. 20 When Araunah looked up and saw the king and his retinue advancing towards him — Araunah was threshing the wheat — Araunah came forward and prostrated himself on the ground at the king's feet. 21 'Why has my lord the king come to his servant?' Araunah asked. David replied, 'To buy the threshing-floor from you, to build an altar to Yahweh, so that the plague may be lifted from the people.' 22 Araunah said to David, 'Let my lord the king take it and make what offerings he thinks fit. Here are the oxen for the burnt offering, the threshing-sleds and the oxen's yokes for the wood. 23 My lord the king's servant will give the king everything. And', Araunah said to the king, 'may Yahweh your God accept what you offer!'

24 'No,' said the king to Araunah, 'I shall give you a price for it; I will not offer Yahweh my God burnt offerings which have cost me nothing.' David bought the threshing-floor and the oxen for fifty shekels of silver. 25 David built an altar to Yahweh and offered burnt offerings and communion sacrifices. Yahweh then took pity on the country and the plague was lifted from Israel.

1 Kings

1 King David was old and advanced in years; and although they covered him with clothes, he could not get warm. 2 So his servants said to him, "Let a young virgin be sought for my lord the king, and let her wait on the king, and be his attendant; let her lie in your bosom, so that my lord the king may be warm." 3 So they searched for a beautiful girl throughout all the territory of Israel, and found Abishag the Shunammite, and brought her to the king. 4 The girl was very beautiful. She became the king's attendant and served him, but the king did not know her sexually.

5 Now Adonijah son of Haggith exalted himself, saying, "I will be king"; he prepared for himself chariots and horsemen, and fifty men to run before him. 6 His father had never at any time displeased him by asking, "Why have you done thus and so?" He was also a very handsome man, and he was born next after Absalom. 7 He conferred with Joab son of Zeruiah and with the priest Abiathar, and they supported Adonijah. 8 But the priest Zadok, and Benaiah son of Jehoiada, and the prophet Nathan, and Shimei, and Rei, and David's own warriors did not side with Adonijah.

9 Adonijah sacrificed sheep, oxen, and fatted cattle by the stone Zoheleth, which is beside En-rogel, and he invited all his brothers, the king's sons, and all the royal officials of Judah, 10 but he did not invite the prophet Nathan or Benaiah or the warriors or his brother Solomon.

11 Then Nathan said to Bathsheba, Solomon's mother, "Have you not heard that Adonijah son of Haggith has become king and our lord David does not know it? 12 Now therefore come, let me give you advice, so that you may save your own life and the life of your son Solomon. 13 Go in at once to King David, and say to him, 'Did you not, my lord the king, swear to your servant, saying: Your son Solomon shall succeed me as king, and he shall sit on my throne? Why then is Adonijah king?' 14 Then while you are still there speaking with the king, I will come in after you and confirm your words."

15 So Bathsheba went to the king in his room. The king was very old; Abishag the Shunammite was attending the king. 16 Bathsheba bowed and did obeisance to the king, and the king said, "What do you wish?" 17 She said to him, "My lord, you swore to your servant by the Lord your God, saying: Your son Solomon shall succeed me as king, and he shall sit on my throne. 18 But now suddenly Adonijah has become king, though you, my lord the king, do not know it. 19 He has sacrificed oxen, fatted cattle, and sheep in abundance, and has invited all the children of the king, the priest Abiathar, and Joab the commander of the army; but your servant Solomon he has not invited. 20 But you, my lord the king — the eyes of all Israel are on you to tell them who shall sit on the throne of my lord the king after him. 21 Otherwise it will come to pass, when my lord the king sleeps with his ancestors, that my son Solomon and I will be counted offenders."

22 While she was still speaking with the king, the prophet Nathan came in. 23 The king was told, "Here is the prophet Nathan." When he came in before the king, he did obeisance to the king, with his face to the ground. 24 Nathan said, "My lord the king, have you said, 'Adonijah shall succeed me as king, and he shall sit on my throne'? 25 For

Kings

1 King David was now a very old man, and, though they wrapped clothes round him, he could not keep warm. 2 His attendants said to him, 'Let us find a young virgin for your majesty, to attend you and take care of you; and let her lie in your arms, sir, and make you warm.' 3 After searching throughout Israel for a beautiful maiden, they found Abishag, a Shunammite, and brought her to the king. 4 She was a very beautiful girl. She took care of the king and waited on him, but he did not have intercourse with her.

5 Adonijah, whose mother was Haggith, was boasting that he was to be king. He provided himself with chariots and horses and fifty outrunners. 6 His father never corrected him or asked why he behaved as he did. He was next in age to Absalom, and was a very handsome man too. 7 He took counsel with Joab son of Zeruiah and with Abiathar the priest, and they assured him of their support; 8 but Zadok the priest, Benaiah son of Jehoiada, Nathan the prophet, Shimei, Rei, and David's bodyguard of heroes did not take his side. 9 Adonijah then held a sacrifice of sheep, oxen, and buffaloes at the stone Zoheleth beside En-rogel; he invited all his royal brothers and all those officers of the household who were of the tribe of Judah, 10 but he did not invite Nathan the prophet, Benaiah and the bodyguard, or Solomon his brother.

11 Nathan said to Bathsheba, Solomon's mother, 'Have you not heard that Adonijah son of Haggith has become king, without the knowledge of our lord David? 12 Now come, let me advise you what to do for your own safety and for the safety of your son Solomon. 13 Go in at once to the king and say to him, "Did not your majesty swear to me, your servant, that my son Solomon should succeed you as king, and that it was he who should sit on your throne? Why then has Adonijah become king?" 14 While you are still there speaking to the king, I shall come in after you and confirm your words.'

15 Bathsheba went to the king in his private chamber; he was now very old, and Abishag the Shunammite was waiting on him. 16 Bathsheba bowed before the king and did obeisance. 'What is your request?' asked the king. 17 She answered, 'My lord, you yourself swore to me your servant, by the Lord your God, that my son Solomon should succeed you as king and sit on your throne. 18 But now, here is Adonijah become king, all unknown to your majesty. 19 He has sacrificed great numbers of oxen, buffaloes, and sheep, and has invited to the feast all the king's sons, with Abiathar the priest and Joab the commander-in-chief, but he has not invited your servant Solomon. 20 Your majesty, all Israel is now looking to you to announce your successor on the throne. 21 Otherwise, when you, sir, rest with your forefathers, my son Solomon and I will be treated as criminals.'

22 Bathsheba was still addressing the king when Nathan the prophet arrived. 23 The king was informed that Nathan was there; he came into the king's presence and prostrated himself. 24 'My lord,' he said, 'has your majesty declared that Adonijah should succeed you and sit on your throne?

THE FIRST BOOK OF
Kings

1 When King David was old and advanced in years, though they spread covers over him he could not keep warm. ² His servants therefore said to him, "Let a young virgin be sought to attend you, lord king, and to nurse you. If she sleeps with your royal majesty, you will be kept warm." ³ So they sought for a beautiful girl throughout the territory of Israel, and found Abishag the Shunamite, whom they brought to the king. ⁴ The maiden, who was very beautiful, nursed the king and cared for him, but the king did not have relations with her.

⁵ Adonijah, son of Haggith, began to display his ambition to be king. He acquired chariots, drivers, and fifty henchmen. ⁶ Yet his father never rebuked him or asked why he was doing this. Adonijah was also very handsome, and next in age to Absalom by the same mother. ⁷ He conferred with Joab, son of Zeruiah, and with Abiathar the priest, and they supported him. ⁸ However, Zadok the priest, Benaiah, son of Jehoiada, Nathan the prophet, and Shimei and his companions, the pick of David's army, did not side with Adonijah. ⁹ When he slaughtered sheep, oxen, and fatlings at the stone Zoheleth, near En-rogel, Adonijah invited all his brothers, the king's sons, and all the royal officials of Judah. ¹⁰ But he did not invite the prophet Nathan, or Benaiah, or the pick of the army, or his brother Solomon.

¹¹ Then Nathan said to Bathsheba, Solomon's mother: "Have you not heard that Adonijah, son of Haggith, has become king without the knowledge of our lord David? ¹² Come now, let me advise you so that you may save your life and that of your son Solomon. ¹³ Go, visit King David, and say to him, 'Did you not, lord king, swear to your handmaid: Your son Solomon shall be king after me and shall sit upon my throne? Why, then, has Adonijah become king?' ¹⁴ And while you are still there speaking to the king, I will come in after you and confirm what you have said."

¹⁵ So Bathsheba visited the king in his room, while Abishag the Shunamite was attending him because of his advanced age. ¹⁶ Bathsheba bowed in homage to the king, who said to her, "What do you wish?" ¹⁷ She answered him: "My lord, you swore to me your handmaid by the LORD, your God, that my son Solomon should reign after you and sit upon your throne. ¹⁸ But now Adonijah has become king, and you, my lord king, do not know it. ¹⁹ He has slaughtered oxen, fatlings, and sheep in great numbers; he has invited all the king's sons, Abiathar the priest, and Joab, the general of the army, but not your servant Solomon. ²⁰ Now, my lord king, all Israel is waiting for you to make known to them who is to sit on the throne after your royal majesty. ²¹ If this is not done, when my lord the king sleeps with his fathers, I and my son Solomon will be considered criminals."

²² While she was still speaking to the king, the prophet Nathan came in. ²³ When he had been announced, the prophet entered the king's presence and, bowing to the floor, did him homage. ²⁴ Then Nathan said: "Have you decided, my lord king, that Adonijah is to reign after you

THE FIRST BOOK OF THE
Kings

1 King David was now a very old man, and though wrapped in bedclothes he could not keep warm. ² So his servants said to him, 'Let us find a young girl for my lord the king, to wait on the king and look after him; she will lie close beside you and this will keep my lord the king warm.' ³ Having searched for a beautiful girl throughout the territory of Israel, they found Abishag of Shunem and brought her to the king. ⁴ The girl was very beautiful. She looked after the king and waited on him but the king did not have intercourse with her. ⁵ Now Adonijah son of Haggith was growing pretentious and saying, 'I shall be king!' Accordingly, he procured a chariot and team with fifty guards to run ahead of him. ⁶ Never once in his life had his father crossed him by saying, 'Why are you behaving like that?' He was very handsome too; his mother had given birth to him after Absalom. ⁷ He conferred with Joab son of Zeruiah and with the priest Abiathar, who both rallied to Adonijah's cause; ⁸ but neither Zadok the priest, nor Benaiah son of Jehoiada, nor the prophet Nathan, nor Shimei and Rei, nor David's champions, supported Adonijah.

⁹ One day when Adonijah was sacrificing sheep, oxen and fattened calves at the Sliding Stone which is beside the Fuller's Spring, he invited all his brothers, the royal princes, and all the men of Judah in the king's service; ¹⁰ but he did not invite the prophet Nathan, or Benaiah, or the champions, or his brother Solomon.

¹¹ Nathan then said to Bathsheba, Solomon's mother, 'Have you not heard that, unknown to our lord David, Adonijah son of Haggith has become king? ¹² Well, this is my advice to you if you want to save your own life and the life of your son Solomon. ¹³ Go straight in to King David and say, "My lord king, did you not make your servant this promise on oath: Your son Solomon is to be king after me; he is the one who is to sit on my throne? How is it, then, that Adonijah is king?" ¹⁴ And while you are still there talking to the king, I shall come in after you and confirm what you say.'

¹⁵ So Bathsheba went to the king in his room (he was very old and Abishag of Shunem was in attendance on him). ¹⁶ She knelt, prostrated herself before the king, and the king said, 'What do you want?' ¹⁷ 'My lord,' she replied, 'you swore to your servant by Yahweh your God, "Your son Solomon is to be king after me; he is the one who is to sit on my throne." ¹⁸ And now here is Adonijah king, and you, my lord king, knowing nothing about it! ¹⁹ He has sacrificed quantities of oxen, fattened calves and sheep, and invited all the royal princes, the priest Abiathar, and Joab the army commander; but he has not invited your servant Solomon. ²⁰ Yet you are the man, my lord king, to whom all Israel looks, to tell them who is to succeed my lord the king. ²¹ And when my lord the king falls asleep with his ancestors, Solomon and I shall be made to suffer for this.'

²² She was still speaking to the king when the prophet Nathan came in. ²³ The king was told, 'The prophet Nathan is here'; and he came into the king's presence and prostrated himself on his face before the king. ²⁴ 'My lord king,' said Nathan, 'is this, then, your decree, "Adonijah is to be king after me; he is the one who is to sit on my throne"? ²⁵ For

NEW REVISED STANDARD VERSION

today he has gone down and has sacrificed oxen, fatted cattle, and sheep in abundance, and has invited all the king's children, Joab the commander[a] of the army, and the priest Abiathar, who are now eating and drinking before him, and saying, 'Long live King Adonijah!' 26 But he did not invite me, your servant, and the priest Zadok, and Benaiah son of Jehoiada, and your servant Solomon. 27 Has this thing been brought about by my lord the king and you have not let your servants know who should sit on the throne of my lord the king after him?"

28 King David answered, "Summon Bathsheba to me." So she came into the king's presence, and stood before the king. 29 The king swore, saying, "As the LORD lives, who has saved my life from every adversity, 30 as I swore to you by the LORD, the God of Israel, 'Your son Solomon shall succeed me as king, and he shall sit on my throne in my place,' so will I do this day." 31 Then Bathsheba bowed with her face to the ground, and did obeisance to the king, and said, "May my lord King David live forever!"

32 King David said, "Summon to me the priest Zadok, the prophet Nathan, and Benaiah son of Jehoiada." When they came before the king, 33 the king said to them, "Take with you the servants of your lord, and have my son Solomon ride on my own mule, and bring him down to Gihon. 34 There let the priest Zadok and the prophet Nathan anoint him king over Israel; then blow the trumpet, and say, 'Long live King Solomon!' 35 You shall go up following him. Let him enter and sit on my throne; he shall be king in my place; for I have appointed him to be ruler over Israel and over Judah." 36 Benaiah son of Jehoiada answered the king, "Amen! May the LORD, the God of my lord the king, so ordain. 37 As the LORD has been with my lord the king, so may he be with Solomon, and make his throne greater than the throne of my lord King David."

38 So the priest Zadok, the prophet Nathan, and Benaiah son of Jehoiada, and the Cherethites and the Pelethites, went down and had Solomon ride on King David's mule, and led him to Gihon. 39 There the priest Zadok took the horn of oil from the tent and anointed Solomon. Then they blew the trumpet, and all the people said, "Long live King Solomon!" 40 And all the people went up following him, playing on pipes and rejoicing with great joy, so that the earth quaked at their noise.

41 Adonijah and all the guests who were with him heard it as they finished feasting. When Joab heard the sound of the trumpet, he said, "Why is the city in an uproar?" 42 While he was still speaking, Jonathan son of the priest Abiathar arrived. Adonijah said, "Come in, for you are a worthy man and surely you bring good news." 43 Jonathan answered Adonijah, "No, for our lord King David has made Solomon king; 44 the king has sent with him the priest Zadok, the prophet Nathan, and Benaiah son of Jehoiada, and the Cherethites and the Pelethites; and they had him ride on the king's mule; 45 the priest Zadok and the prophet Nathan have anointed him king at Gihon; and they have gone up from there rejoicing, so that the city is in an uproar. This is the noise that you heard. 46 Solomon now sits on the royal throne. 47 Moreover the king's servants came to congratulate our lord King David, saying, 'May God make the name of Solomon more famous than yours, and make his throne greater than your throne.' The king bowed in worship on the bed 48 and went on to pray thus, 'Blessed be the LORD, the God of Israel, who today has granted one of my offspring[b] to sit on my throne and permitted me to witness it.'"

49 Then all the guests of Adonijah got up trembling and went their own ways. 50 Adonijah, fearing Solomon, got up and went to grasp the horns of the altar. 51 Solomon was

REVISED ENGLISH BIBLE

25 He has today gone down and sacrificed great numbers of oxen, buffaloes, and sheep, and has invited to the feast all the king's sons, the commanders of the army, and Abiathar the priest; and at this very moment they are eating and drinking in his presence and shouting, "Long live King Adonijah!" 26 But he has not invited me your servant, Zadok the priest, Benaiah son of Jehoiada, or your servant Solomon. 27 Has this been done by your majesty's authority? You have not told us your servants who should succeed you on the throne.'

28 King David said, 'Call Bathsheba,' and when she came into his presence and stood before him, 29 the king swore an oath to her: 'As the LORD lives, who has delivered me from all my troubles, 30 I swore by the LORD the God of Israel that Solomon your son should succeed me and that he should sit on my throne; this day I give effect to my oath.' 31 Bathsheba bowed low to the king, did obeisance, and said, 'May my lord King David live for ever!'

32 King David said, 'Summon Zadok the priest, Nathan the prophet, and Benaiah son of Jehoiada,' and, when they came into the king's presence, 33 he gave them this order: 'Take the officers of the household with you; mount my son Solomon on the king's mule and escort him down to Gihon. 34 There let Zadok the priest and Nathan the prophet anoint him king over Israel. Then sound the trumpet and shout, "Long live King Solomon!" 35 When you escort him home again let him come and sit on my throne and reign in my place; for he is the man that I have designated to be prince over Israel and Judah.' 36 Benaiah son of Jehoiada answered the king, 'It will be done. And may the LORD, the God of my lord the king, confirm it! 37 As the LORD has been with your majesty, so may he be with Solomon; may he make his throne even greater than the throne of my lord King David.'

38 Zadok the priest, Nathan the prophet, and Benaiah son of Jehoiada, together with the Kerethite and Pelethite guards, went down and, mounting Solomon on King David's mule, they escorted him to Gihon. 39 Zadok the priest took the horn of oil from the Tent of the LORD and anointed Solomon; they sounded the trumpet and all the people shouted, 'Long live King Solomon!' 40 Then all the people escorted him home in procession, with great rejoicing and playing of pipes, so that the very earth split with the noise.

41 Adonijah and his guests had just finished their banquet when the noise reached their ears. On hearing the sound of the trumpet, Joab exclaimed, 'What is the meaning of this uproar in the city?' 42 Even as he was speaking, Jonathan son of Abiathar the priest arrived. 'Come in,' said Adonijah. 'You are an honourable man and must be a bringer of good news.' 43 'Far from it,' Jonathan replied; 'our lord King David has made Solomon king. 44 He has sent with him Zadok the priest, Nathan the prophet, and Benaiah son of Jehoiada, together with the Kerethite and Pelethite guards, and they have mounted Solomon on the king's mule, 45 and Zadok the priest and Nathan the prophet have anointed him king at Gihon. They have now escorted him home rejoicing, and the city is in an uproar. That was the noise you heard. 46 More than that, Solomon has taken his seat on the royal throne. 47 Yes, and the officers of the household have been to our lord, King David, and greeted him in this fashion: "May your God make the name of Solomon your son more famous than your own and his throne even greater than yours," and the king bowed upon his couch. 48 What is more, he said this: "Blessed be the LORD the God of Israel who has set a successor on my throne this day while I am still alive to see it."'

49 Adonijah's guests all rose in panic and dispersed. 50 Adonijah himself, in fear of Solomon, went at once to the altar and grasped hold of its horns. 51 A message was sent

---

[a] Gk: Heb the commanders   [b] Gk: Heb one

1:39 the Tent ... LORD: lit. the tent, cp. 2:28.

and sit on your throne? 25 He went down today and slaughtered oxen, fatlings, and sheep in great numbers; he invited all the king's sons, the commanders of the army, and Abiathar the priest, and they are eating and drinking in his company and saying, 'Long live King Adonijah!' 26 But me, your servant, he did not invite; nor Zadok the priest, nor Benaiah, son of Jehoiada, nor your servant Solomon. 27 Was this done by my royal master's order without my being told who was to succeed to your majesty's kingly throne?"

28 King David answered, "Call Bathsheba here." When she re-entered the king's presence and stood before him, 29 the king swore, "As the LORD lives, who has delivered me from all distress, 30 this very day I will fulfill the oath I swore to you by the LORD, the God of Israel, that your son Solomon should reign after me and should sit upon my throne in my place." 31 Bowing to the floor in homage to the king, Bathsheba said, "May my lord, King David, live forever!" 32 Then King David summoned Zadok the priest, Nathan the prophet, and Benaiah, son of Jehoiada. When they had entered the king's presence, 33 he said to them: "Take with you the royal attendants. Mount my son Solomon upon my own mule and escort him down to Gihon. 34 There Zadok the priest and Nathan the prophet are to anoint him king of Israel, and you shall blow the horn and cry, 'Long live King Solomon!' 35 When you come back in his train, he is to go in and sit upon my throne and reign in my place. I designate him ruler of Israel and of Judah." 36 In answer to the king, Benaiah, son of Jehoiada, said: "So be it! May the LORD, the God of my lord the king, so decree! 37 As the LORD has been with your royal majesty, so may he be with Solomon, and exalt his throne even more than that of my lord, King David!"

38 So Zadok the priest, Nathan the prophet, Benaiah, son of Jehoiada, and the Cherethites and Pelethites went down, and mounting Solomon on King David's mule, escorted him to Gihon. 39 Then Zadok the priest took the horn of oil from the tent and anointed Solomon. They blew the horn and all the people shouted, "Long live King Solomon!" 40 Then all the people went up after him, playing flutes and rejoicing so much as to split open the earth with their shouting.

41 Adonijah and all the guests who were with him heard it, just as they ended their banquet. When Joab heard the sound of the horn, he asked, "What does this uproar in the city mean?" 42 As he was speaking, Jonathan, son of Abiathar the priest, arrived. "Come," said Adonijah, "you are a man of worth and must bring good news." 43 "On the contrary!" Jonathan answered him. "Our lord, King David, has made Solomon king. 44 The king sent with him Zadok the priest, Nathan the prophet, Benaiah, son of Jehoiada, and the Cherethites and Pelethites, and they mounted him upon the king's own mule. 45 Zadok the priest and Nathan the prophet anointed him king at Gihon, and they went up from there rejoicing, so that the city is in an uproar. That is the noise you heard. 46 Besides, Solomon took his seat on the royal throne, 47 and the king's servants went in and paid their respects to our lord, King David, saying, 'May God make Solomon more famous than you and exalt his throne more than your own!' And the king in his bed worshiped God, 48 and this is what he said: 'Blessed be the LORD, the God of Israel, who has this day seated one of my sons upon my throne, so that I see it with my own eyes.'"

49 All the guests of Adonijah left in terror, each going his own way. 50 Adonijah, in fear of Solomon, also left; he went and seized the horns of the altar. 51 It was reported to

he has gone down today and sacrificed quantities of oxen, fattened calves and sheep, and invited all the royal princes, the army commanders, and the priest Abiathar; and they are there now, eating and drinking in his presence and shouting, "Long live King Adonijah!" 26 He has not, however, invited me your servant, Zadok the priest, Benaiah son of Jehoiada, or your servant Solomon. 27 Can it be that this is done with my lord the king's approval and that you have not told those loyal to you who is to succeed to the throne of my lord the king?'

28 King David then spoke. 'Call Bathsheba to me,' he said. And she came into the king's presence and stood before him. 29 Then the king swore this oath, 'As Yahweh lives, who has delivered me from all adversity, 30 just as I swore to you by Yahweh, God of Israel, that your son Solomon should be king after me and take my place on my throne, so I shall bring it about this very day.' 31 Bathsheba knelt down, prostrated herself on her face before the king and said, 'May my lord King David live for ever!' 32 Then King David said, 'Summon Zadok the priest, the prophet Nathan and Benaiah son of Jehoiada.' So they came into the king's presence. 33 'Take the royal guard with you,' said the king, 'mount my son Solomon on my own mule and escort him down to Gihon. 34 There Zadok the priest and the prophet Nathan are to anoint him king of Israel; then sound the trumpet and shout, "Long live King Solomon!" 35 Then you are to escort him back, and he is then to assume my throne and be king in place of me, for he is the man whom I have appointed as ruler of Israel and of Judah.' 36 Benaiah son of Jehoiada answered the king. 'Amen!' he said. 'And may Yahweh, God of my lord the king, confirm it! 37 As Yahweh has been with my lord the king, so may he be with Solomon and make his throne even greater than the throne of my lord King David!'

38 Zadok the priest, the prophet Nathan, Benaiah son of Jehoiada, and the Cherethites and Pelethites then went down; they mounted Solomon on King David's mule and escorted him to Gihon. 39 Zadok the priest took the horn of oil from the Tent and anointed Solomon. They sounded the trumpet and all the people shouted, 'Long live King Solomon!' 40 The people all escorted him back, with pipes playing and loud rejoicing and shouts to split the earth.

41 Adonijah and his guests, who had by then finished their meal, all heard the noise. Joab too heard the sound of the trumpet and said, 'What is that noise of uproar in the city?' 42 While he was still speaking, Jonathan son of Abiathar the priest arrived. 'Come in,' Adonijah said, 'you are an honest man, so you must be bringing good news.' 43 'The truth is,' Jonathan answered, 'our lord King David has made Solomon king. 44 With him, the king sent Zadok the priest, the prophet Nathan, Benaiah son of Jehoiada and the Cherethites and Pelethites; they mounted him on the king's mule, 45 and Zadok the priest and the prophet Nathan have anointed him king at Gihon; and they have gone back again with shouts of joy and the city is now in an uproar; that was the noise you heard. 46 What is more, Solomon is seated on the royal throne. 47 And further, the king's officers have been to congratulate our lord King David with the words, "May your God make the name of Solomon more glorious than yours, and his throne more exalted than your own!" And the king bowed down on his bed, 48 and then said, "Blessed be Yahweh, God of Israel, for setting one of my own sons on the throne while I am still alive to see it!"'

49 At this, all Adonijah's guests, taking fright, got up and made off in their several directions. 50 Adonijah, in terror of Solomon, got up and ran off to cling to the horns of the altar. 51 Solomon was told, 'You should know that Adonijah

| NEW REVISED STANDARD VERSION | REVISED ENGLISH BIBLE |

informed, "Adonijah is afraid of King Solomon; see, he has laid hold of the horns of the altar, saying, 'Let King Solomon swear to me first that he will not kill his servant with the sword.' " 52 So Solomon responded, "If he proves to be a worthy man, not one of his hairs shall fall to the ground; but if wickedness is found in him, he shall die." 53 Then King Solomon sent to have him brought down from the altar. He came to do obeisance to King Solomon; and Solomon said to him, "Go home."

2 When David's time to die drew near, he charged his son Solomon, saying: 2 "I am about to go the way of all the earth. Be strong, be courageous, 3 and keep the charge of the LORD your God, walking in his ways and keeping his statutes, his commandments, his ordinances, and his testimonies, as it is written in the law of Moses, so that you may prosper in all that you do and wherever you turn. 4 Then the LORD will establish his word that he spoke concerning me: 'If your heirs take heed to their way, to walk before me in faithfulness with all their heart and with all their soul, there shall not fail you a successor on the throne of Israel.'

5 "Moreover you know also what Joab son of Zeruiah did to me, how he dealt with the two commanders of the armies of Israel, Abner son of Ner, and Amasa son of Jether, whom he murdered, retaliating in time of peace for blood that had been shed in war, and putting the blood of war on the belt around his waist, and on the sandals on his feet. 6 Act therefore according to your wisdom, but do not let his gray head go down to Sheol in peace. 7 Deal loyally, however, with the sons of Barzillai the Gileadite, and let them be among those who eat at your table; for with such loyalty they met me when I fled from your brother Absalom. 8 There is also with you Shimei son of Gera, the Benjaminite from Bahurim, who cursed me with a terrible curse on the day when I went to Mahanaim; but when he came down to meet me at the Jordan, I swore to him by the LORD, 'I will not put you to death with the sword.' 9 Therefore do not hold him guiltless, for you are a wise man; you will know what you ought to do to him, and you must bring his gray head down with blood to Sheol."

10 Then David slept with his ancestors, and was buried in the city of David. 11 The time that David reigned over Israel was forty years; he reigned seven years in Hebron, and thirty-three years in Jerusalem. 12 So Solomon sat on the throne of his father David; and his kingdom was firmly established.

13 Then Adonijah son of Haggith came to Bathsheba, Solomon's mother. She asked, "Do you come peaceably?" He said, "Peaceably." 14 Then he said, "May I have a word with you?" She said, "Go on." 15 He said, "You know that the kingdom was mine, and that all Israel expected me to reign; however, the kingdom has turned about and become my brother's, for it was his from the LORD. 16 And now I have one request to make of you; do not refuse me." She said to him, "Go on." 17 He said, "Please ask King Solomon — he will not refuse you — to give me Abishag the Shunammite as my wife." 18 Bathsheba said, "Very well; I will speak to the king on your behalf."

19 So Bathsheba went to King Solomon, to speak to him on behalf of Adonijah. The king rose to meet her, and bowed down to her; then he sat on his throne, and had a throne brought for the king's mother, and she sat on his right. 20 Then she said, "I have one small request to make of you; do not refuse me." And the king said to her, "Make your request, my mother; for I will not refuse you." 21 She said, "Let Abishag the Shunammite be given to your brother Adonijah as his wife." 22 King Solomon answered his

to Solomon: 'Adonijah, in his fear of King Solomon, is clinging to the horns of the altar; he says, "Let King Solomon swear to me here and now that he will not put his servant to the sword." ' 52 Solomon said, 'If he proves himself an honourable man, not a hair of his head will fall to the ground; but if he is found making trouble, he must die.' 53 Then King Solomon sent and had him brought down from the altar. He came in and prostrated himself before the king, and Solomon said to him, 'Go to your house.'

2 As the time of David's death drew near, he gave this charge to his son Solomon: 2 'I am about to go the way of all the earth. Be strong and show yourself a man. 3 Fulfil your duty to the LORD your God; conform to his ways, observe his statutes and his commandments, his judgements and his solemn precepts, as they are written in the law of Moses, so that you may prosper in whatever you do and whichever way you turn, 4 and that the LORD may fulfil this promise that he made about me: "If your descendants are careful to walk faithfully in my sight with all their heart and with all their soul, you shall never lack a successor on the throne of Israel."

5 'You know how Joab son of Zeruiah treated me and what he did to two commanders-in-chief in Israel, Abner son of Ner and Amasa son of Jether. He killed them both, breaking the peace by bloody acts of war; and with that blood he stained the belt about his waist and the sandals on his feet. 6 Act as your wisdom prompts you, and do not let his grey hairs go down to the grave in peace. 7 Show constant friendship to the family of Barzillai of Gilead; let them have their place at your table; they rallied to me when I was a fugitive from your brother Absalom. 8 Do not forget Shimei son of Gera, the Benjamite from Bahurim, who cursed me bitterly the day I went to Mahanaim. True, he came down to meet me at the Jordan, and I swore by the LORD that I would not put him to death. 9 But you do not need to let him go unpunished now; you are a wise man and will know how to deal with him; bring down his grey hairs in blood to the grave.'

10 So David rested with his forefathers and was buried in the city of David, 11 having reigned over Israel for forty years, seven in Hebron and thirty-three in Jerusalem; 12 and Solomon succeeded his father David as king and was firmly established on the throne.

13 Then Adonijah son of Haggith came to Bathsheba, Solomon's mother. 'Do you come as a friend?' she asked. 'As a friend,' he answered; 14 'I have something to discuss with you.' 'Tell me,' she said. 15 'You know,' he went on, 'that the throne was mine and that all Israel was looking to me to be king; but I was passed over and the throne has gone to my brother; it was his by the will of the LORD. 16 Now I have one request to make of you; do not refuse me.' 'What is it?' she said. 17 He answered, 'Will you ask King Solomon (he will never refuse you) to give me Abishag the Shunammite in marriage?' 18 'Very well,' said Bathsheba, 'I shall speak to the king on your behalf.'

19 When Bathsheba went in to King Solomon to speak for Adonijah, the king rose to meet her and do obeisance to her. Then he seated himself on his throne, and a throne was set for the king's mother at his right hand. 20 She said, 'I have one small request to make of you; do not refuse me.' 'What is it, mother?' he replied. 'I will not refuse you.' 21 'It is this,' she said, 'that Abishag the Shunammite be given in marriage to your brother Adonijah.' 22 At that King Solo-

2:6,9 the grave: lit. Sheol (the underworld).

Solomon that Adonijah, in his fear of King Solomon, had seized the horns of the altar and said, "Let King Solomon first swear that he will not kill me, his servant, with the sword." 52 Solomon answered, "If he proves himself worthy, not a hair shall fall from his head. But if he is found guilty of crime, he shall die." 53 King Solomon sent to have him brought down from the altar, and he came and paid homage to the king. Solomon then said to him, "Go to your home."

2 When the time of David's death drew near, he gave these instructions to his son Solomon: 2 "I am going the way of all mankind. Take courage and be a man. 3 Keep the mandate of the Lord, your God, following his ways and observing his statutes, commands, ordinances, and decrees as they are written in the law of Moses, that you may succeed in whatever you do, wherever you turn, 4 and the Lord may fulfill the promise he made on my behalf when he said, 'If your sons so conduct themselves that they remain faithful to me with their whole heart and with their whole soul, you shall always have someone of your line on the throne of Israel.' 5 You yourself know what Joab, son of Zeruiah, did to me when he slew the two generals of Israel's armies, Abner, son of Ner, and Amasa, son of Jether. He took revenge for the blood of war in a time of peace, and put blood shed without provocation on the belt about my waist and on the sandal on my foot. 6 Act with the wisdom you possess; you must not allow him to go down to the grave in peaceful old age.

7 "But be kind to the sons of Barzillai the Gileadite, and have them eat at your table. For they received me kindly when I was fleeing your brother Absalom.

8 "You also have with you Shimei, son of Gera, the Benjaminite of Bahurim, who cursed me balefully when I was going to Mahanaim. Because he came down to meet me at the Jordan, I swore to him by the Lord that I would not put him to the sword. 9 But you must not let him go unpunished. You are a prudent man and will know how to deal with him to send down his hoary head in blood to the grave."

10 David rested with his ancestors and was buried in the City of David. 11 The length of David's reign over Israel was forty years: he reigned seven years in Hebron and thirty-three years in Jerusalem.

12 When Solomon was seated on the throne of his father David, with his sovereignty firmly established, 13 Adonijah, son of Haggith, went to Bathsheba, the mother of Solomon. "Do you come as a friend?" she asked. "Yes," he answered, 14 and added, "I have something to say to you." She replied, "Say it." 15 So he said: "You know that the kingdom was mine, and all Israel expected me to be king. But the kingdom escaped me and became my brother's, for the Lord gave it to him. 16 But now there is one favor I would ask of you. Do not refuse me." And she said, "Speak on." 17 He said, "Please ask King Solomon, who will not refuse you, to give me Abishag the Shunamite for my wife." 18 "Very well," replied Bathsheba, "I will speak to the king for you."

19 Then Bathsheba went to King Solomon to speak to him for Adonijah, and the king stood up to meet her and paid her homage. Then he sat down upon his throne, and a throne was provided for the king's mother, who sat at his right. 20 "There is one small favor I would ask of you," she said. "Do not refuse me." "Ask it, my mother," the king said to her, "for I will not refuse you." 21 So she said, "Let Abishag the Shunamite be given to your brother Adonijah for his

is terrified of King Solomon and is now clinging to the horns of the altar, saying, "Let King Solomon first swear to me that he will not have his servant executed." ' 52 'Should he bear himself honourably,' Solomon answered, 'not one hair of his shall fall to the ground; but if he proves difficult, he shall die.' 53 King Solomon then sent for him to be brought down from the altar; he came and threw himself prostrate before King Solomon; Solomon said to him, 'Go to your house.'

2 As David's life drew to its close he laid this charge on his son Solomon, 2 'I am going the way of all the earth. Be strong and show yourself a man. 3 Observe the injunctions of Yahweh your God, following his ways and keeping his laws, his commandments, his ordinances and his decrees, as stands written in the Law of Moses, so that you may be successful in everything you do and undertake, 4 and that Yahweh may fulfil the promise which he made me, "If your sons are careful how they behave, and walk loyally before me with all their heart and soul, you will never want for a man on the throne of Israel."

5 'You know too what Joab son of Zeruiah did to me, and what he did to the two commanders of the army of Israel, Abner son of Ner and Amasa son of Jether; how he murdered them, shedding the blood of war in time of peace and staining the belt round my waist and the sandals on my feet with the blood of war. 6 You will be wise not to let his grey head go down to Sheol in peace. 7 As regards the sons of Barzillai of Gilead, treat them with faithful love, let them be among those who eat at your table, for they were as kind to me when I was fleeing from your brother Absalom. 8 You also have with you Shimei son of Gera, the Benjaminite from Bahurim. He called down a terrible curse on me the day I left for Mahanaim, but he came down to meet me at the Jordan and I swore to him by Yahweh that I would not put him to death. 9 But you, you must not let him go unpunished; you are a wise man and will know how to deal with him, to bring his grey head down to Sheol in blood.'

10 So David fell asleep with his ancestors and was buried in the City of David. 11 David was king of Israel for a period of forty years: he reigned at Hebron for seven years, and in Jerusalem for thirty-three.

12 Solomon then sat on the throne of David, and his sovereignty was securely established.

13 Adonijah son of Haggith went to Bathsheba mother of Solomon. 'Do you bring peace?' she asked. He replied, 'Yes, peace.' 14 Then he said, 'I have something to say to you.' 'Say on,' she replied. 15 'You know', he said, 'that the kingdom should have come to me, and that all Israel expected me to be king; but the crown eluded me and fell to my brother, since it came to him from Yahweh. 16 Now I have one request to make you; do not refuse me.' 'Go on,' she said. 17 He went on, 'Please ask King Solomon—for he will not refuse you—to give me Abishag of Shunem in marriage.' 18 'Very well,' Bathsheba replied, 'I shall speak to the king about you.' 19 So Bathsheba went to King Solomon to speak to him about Adonijah; the king got up to meet her and bowed before her; he then sat down on his throne; a seat was brought for the king's mother, and she sat down on his right. 20 She said, 'I have one small request to make you; do not refuse me.' 'Mother,' the king replied, 'make your request, for I shall not refuse you.' 21 'Let Abishag of Shunem', she said, 'be given in marriage to your brother Adonijah.' 22 King Solomon replied to his mother,

mother, "And why do you ask Abishag the Shunammite for Adonijah? Ask for him the kingdom as well! For he is my elder brother; ask not only for him but also for the priest Abiathar and for Joab son of Zeruiah!" 23 Then King Solomon swore by the LORD, "So may God do to me, and more also, for Adonijah has devised this scheme at the risk of his life! 24 Now therefore as the LORD lives, who has established me and placed me on the throne of my father David, and who has made me a house as he promised, today Adonijah shall be put to death." 25 So King Solomon sent Benaiah son of Jehoiada; he struck him down, and he died.

26 The king said to the priest Abiathar, "Go to Anathoth, to your estate; for you deserve death. But I will not at this time put you to death, because you carried the ark of the Lord GOD before my father David, and because you shared in all the hardships my father endured." 27 So Solomon banished Abiathar from being priest to the LORD, thus fulfilling the word of the LORD that he had spoken concerning the house of Eli in Shiloh.

28 When the news came to Joab — for Joab had supported Adonijah though he had not supported Absalom — Joab fled to the tent of the LORD and grasped the horns of the altar. 29 When it was told King Solomon, "Joab has fled to the tent of the LORD and now is beside the altar," Solomon sent Benaiah son of Jehoiada, saying, "Go, strike him down." 30 So Benaiah came to the tent of the LORD and said to him, "The king commands, 'Come out.' " But he said, "No, I will die here." Then Benaiah brought the king word again, saying, "Thus said Joab, and thus he answered me." 31 The king replied to him, "Do as he has said, strike him down and bury him; and thus take away from me and from my father's house the guilt for the blood that Joab shed without cause. 32 The LORD will bring back his bloody deeds on his own head, because, without the knowledge of my father David, he attacked and killed with the sword two men more righteous and better than himself, Abner son of Ner, commander of the army of Israel, and Amasa son of Jether, commander of the army of Judah. 33 So shall their blood come back on the head of Joab and on the head of his descendants forever; but to David, and to his descendants, and to his house, and to his throne, there shall be peace from the LORD forevermore." 34 Then Benaiah son of Jehoiada went up and struck him down and killed him; and he was buried at his own house near the wilderness. 35 The king put Benaiah son of Jehoiada over the army in his place, and the king put the priest Zadok in the place of Abiathar.

36 Then the king sent and summoned Shimei, and said to him, "Build yourself a house in Jerusalem, and live there, and do not go out from there to any place whatever. 37 For on the day you go out, and cross the Wadi Kidron, know for certain that you shall die; your blood shall be on your own head." 38 And Shimei said to the king, "The sentence is fair; as my lord the king has said, so will your servant do." So Shimei lived in Jerusalem many days.

39 But it happened at the end of three years that two of Shimei's slaves ran away to King Achish son of Maacah of Gath. When it was told Shimei, "Your slaves are in Gath," 40 Shimei arose and saddled a donkey, and went to Achish in Gath, to search for his slaves; Shimei went and brought his slaves from Gath. 41 When Solomon was told that Shimei had gone from Jerusalem to Gath and returned, 42 the king sent and summoned Shimei, and said to him, "Did I not make you swear by the LORD, and solemnly adjure you, saying, 'Know for certain that on the day you go out and go to any place whatever, you shall die'? And you said to me, 'The sentence is fair; I accept.' 43 Why then have you not kept your oath to the LORD and the commandment with which I charged you?" 44 The king also said to

mon answered, 'Why do you ask that Abishag the Shunammite be given to Adonijah? You might as well ask the kingdom for him; he is my elder brother and has both Abiathar the priest and Joab son of Zeruiah on his side.' 23 Then he swore by the LORD: 'So help me God, Adonijah must pay for this with his life. 24 As the LORD lives, who has established me and set me on the throne of David my father and has founded a house for me as he promised, this very day Adonijah must be put to death!' 25 King Solomon sent Benaiah son of Jehoiada with orders to strike him down; so Adonijah died.

26 Abiathar the priest was told by the king to go to Anathoth to his estate. 'You deserve to die,' he said, 'but in spite of this day's work I shall not put you to death, for you carried the Ark of the Lord GOD before my father David, and you shared in all the hardships he endured.' 27 Solomon deposed Abiathar from his office as priest of the LORD, so fulfilling the sentence pronounced by the LORD against the house of Eli in Shiloh.

28 When news of all this reached Joab, he fled to the Tent of the LORD and laid hold of the horns of the altar; for he had sided with Adonijah, though not with Absalom. 29 When King Solomon was told that Joab had fled to the Tent of the LORD and was beside the altar, he sent Benaiah son of Jehoiada with orders to strike him down. 30 Benaiah came to the Tent of the LORD and ordered Joab in the king's name to come away. But he said, 'No, I will die here.' Benaiah reported Joab's answer to the king, 31 and the king said, 'Let him have his way; strike him down and bury him, and so rid me and my father's house of the guilt for the blood that he wantonly shed. 32 The LORD will hold him responsible for his own death, because he struck down two innocent men who were better men than he, Abner son of Ner, commander of the army of Israel, and Amasa son of Jether, commander of the army of Judah, and ran them through with the sword, without my father David's knowledge. 33 Let the guilt of their blood recoil on Joab and his descendants for all time; but may David and his descendants, his house and his throne, enjoy perpetual prosperity from the LORD.' 34 Benaiah son of Jehoiada went up to the altar and struck Joab down and killed him, and he was buried at his house out in the country. 35 The king appointed Benaiah to command the army in place of Joab, and installed Zadok the priest in the place of Abiathar.

36 Next the king sent for Shimei and said to him, 'Build yourself a house in Jerusalem and stay there; you are not to leave the city for any other place. 37 If ever you leave and cross the wadi Kidron, know for certain that you will die. Your blood will be on your own head.' 38 Shimei replied, 'I accept your sentence; I shall do as your majesty commands.'

For a long time Shimei remained in Jerusalem. 39 But when three years later two of his slaves ran away to Achish son of Maacah, king of Gath, and this was reported to Shimei, 40 he at once saddled his donkey and went to Achish in search of his slaves; he reached Gath and brought them back. 41 When King Solomon was informed that Shimei had gone from Jerusalem to Gath and back, 42 he sent for him and said, 'Did I not require you to swear by the LORD? Did I not give you this solemn warning: "If ever you leave this city for any other place, know for certain that you will die"? You said, "I accept your sentence; I shall obey." 43 Why then have you not kept the oath which you swore by the LORD, and the order which I gave you? 44 Shimei, you know

wife." 22 "And why do you ask Abishag the Shunamite for Adonijah?" King Solomon answered his mother. "Ask the kingdom for him as well, for he is my elder brother and has with him Abiathar the priest and Joab, son of Zeruiah." 23 And King Solomon swore by the LORD: "May God do thus and so to me, and more besides, if Adonijah has not proposed this at the cost of his life. 24 And now, as the LORD lives, who has seated me firmly on the throne of my father David and made of me a dynasty as he promised, this day shall Adonijah be put to death." 25 Then King Solomon sent Benaiah, son of Jehoiada, who struck him dead.

26 The king said to Abiathar the priest: "Go to your land in Anathoth. Though you deserve to die, I will not put you to death this time, because you carried the ark of the Lord GOD before my father David and shared in all the hardships my father endured." 27 So Solomon deposed Abiathar from his office of priest of the LORD, thus fulfilling the prophecy which the LORD had made in Shiloh about the house of Eli.

28 When the news came to Joab, who had sided with Adonijah, though not with Absalom, he fled to the tent of the LORD and seized the horns of the altar. 29 King Solomon was told that Joab had fled to the tent of the LORD and was at the altar. He sent Benaiah, son of Jehoiada, with the order, "Go, strike him down." 30 Benaiah went to the tent of the LORD and said to him, "The king says 'Come out.'" But he answered, "No! I will die here." Benaiah reported to the king, "This is what Joab said to me in reply." 31 The king answered him: "Do as he has said. Strike him down and bury him, and you will remove from me and from my family the blood which Joab shed without provocation. 32 The LORD will hold him responsible for his own blood, because he struck down two men better and more just than himself, and slew them with the sword without my father David's knowledge: Abner, son of Ner, general of Israel's army, and Amasa, son of Jether, general of Judah's army. 33 Joab and his descendants shall be responsible forever for their blood. But there shall be the peace of the LORD forever for David, and his descendants, and his house, and his throne." 34 Benaiah, son of Jehoiada, went back, struck him down and killed him; he was buried in his house in the desert. 35 The king appointed Benaiah, son of Jehoiada, over the army in his place, and put Zadok the priest in place of Abiathar.

36 Then the king summoned Shimei and said to him: "Build yourself a house in Jerusalem and live there. Do not go anywhere else. 37 For if you leave, and cross the Kidron Valley, be certain you shall die without fail. You shall be responsible for your own blood." 38 Shimei answered the king: "I accept. Your servant will do just as the king's majesty has said." So Shimei stayed in Jerusalem for a long time. 39 But three years later, two of Shimei's servants ran away to Achish, son of Maacah, king of Gath, and Shimei was informed that his servants were in Gath. 40 So Shimei rose, saddled his ass, and went to Achish in Gath in search of his servants, whom he brought back. 41 When Solomon was informed that Shimei had gone from Jerusalem to Gath, and had returned, 42 the king summoned Shimei and said to him: "Did I not have you swear by the LORD to your clear understanding of my warning that, if you left and went anywhere else, you should die without fail? And you answered, 'I accept and obey.' 43 Why, then, have you not kept the oath of the LORD and the command that I gave you?" 44 And the king said to Shimei: "You know in your

'And why do you request Abishag of Shunem for Adonijah? You might as well request the kingdom for him, since he is my elder brother and Abiathar the priest and Joab son of Zeruiah are on his side.' 23 And King Solomon swore by Yahweh: 'May God bring unnameable ills on me, and worse ills, too,' he said, 'if Adonijah does not pay for these words of his with his life.' 24 As Yahweh lives who has set me securely on the throne of my father David, and who, as he promised, has given me a dynasty, Adonijah shall be put to death this very day.' 25 And King Solomon commissioned Benaiah son of Jehoiada to strike him down, and that was how he died.

26 As for Abiathar the priest, the king said to him, 'Go to Anathoth to your estate. You deserve to die, but I am not going to put you to death now, since you carried the ark of Yahweh in the presence of my father David and shared all my father's hardships.' 27 Solomon deprived Abiathar of the priesthood of Yahweh, thus fulfilling the prophecy which Yahweh had uttered against the House of Eli at Shiloh.

28 When the news reached Joab — for Joab had lent his support to Adonijah, though he had not supported Absalom — he fled to the Tent of Yahweh and clung to the horns of the altar. 29 King Solomon was told, 'Joab has fled to the Tent of Yahweh; he is there beside the altar.' On this, Solomon sent word to Joab, 'What reason did you have for fleeing to the altar?' Joab replied, 'I was afraid of you and fled to Yahweh.' Solomon then sent Benaiah son of Jehoiada. 'Go', he said, 'and strike him down.' 30 Accordingly Benaiah went to the Tent of Yahweh. 'By order of the king,' he said, 'come out!' 'No,' he said, 'I will die here.' So Benaiah brought word back to the king, 'This is what Joab said, and the answer he gave me.' 31 'Do as he says,' the king replied. 'Strike him down and bury him, and so rid me and my family today of the innocent blood which Joab has shed. 32 Yahweh will bring his blood down on his own head, because he struck down two more upright and better men than he, and, without my father David's knowledge, put to the sword Abner son of Ner, commander of the army of Israel, and Amasa son of Jether, commander of the army of Judah. 33 May their blood come down on the head of Joab and his descendants for ever, but may David, his descendants, his dynasty, his throne, have peace for ever from Yahweh.' 34 Whereupon Benaiah son of Jehoiada went out, struck Joab down and put him to death; he was buried at his home in the desert. 35 In his place as head of the army the king appointed Benaiah son of Jehoiada and, in place of Abiathar, the priest Zadok.

36 The king had Shimei summoned to him. 'Build yourself a house in Jerusalem,' he told him. 'You are to live there; do not leave it to go anywhere at all. 37 The day you go out and cross the ravine of the Kidron, be sure you will certainly die. Your blood will be on your own head.' 38 'That is a fair demand,' Shimei replied to the king, 'your servant will do as my lord the king orders.' And for a long time Shimei lived in Jerusalem.

39 But when three years had gone by, it happened that two of Shimei's slaves ran away to Achish son of Maacah, king of Gath; Shimei was told, 'Your slaves are in Gath.' 40 On this, Shimei got up and saddled his donkey and went to Akish at Gath to find his slaves. He went off and brought his slaves back from Gath. 41 Solomon was informed that Shimei had left Jerusalem for Gath and come back again.

42 The king had Shimei summoned to him. 'Did I not make you swear by Yahweh,' he said, 'and did I not warn you, "The day you leave to go anywhere at all, be sure you will certainly die"? To which you replied, "That is a fair demand." 43 Why did you not keep the oath to Yahweh and the order which I imposed on you?' 44 The king then said to

Shimei, "You know in your own heart all the evil that you did to my father David; so the Lord will bring back your evil on your own head. 45 But King Solomon shall be blessed, and the throne of David shall be established before the Lord forever." 46 Then the king commanded Benaiah son of Jehoiada; and he went out and struck him down, and he died.

So the kingdom was established in the hand of Solomon.

3 Solomon made a marriage alliance with Pharaoh king of Egypt; he took Pharaoh's daughter and brought her into the city of David, until he had finished building his own house and the house of the Lord and the wall around Jerusalem. 2 The people were sacrificing at the high places, however, because no house had yet been built for the name of the Lord.

3 Solomon loved the Lord, walking in the statutes of his father David; only, he sacrificed and offered incense at the high places. 4 The king went to Gibeon to sacrifice there, for that was the principal high place; Solomon used to offer a thousand burnt offerings on that altar. 5 At Gibeon the Lord appeared to Solomon in a dream by night; and God said, "Ask what I should give you." 6 And Solomon said, "You have shown great and steadfast love to your servant my father David, because he walked before you in faithfulness, in righteousness, and in uprightness of heart toward you; and you have kept for him this great and steadfast love, and have given him a son to sit on his throne today. 7 And now, O Lord my God, you have made your servant king in place of my father David, although I am only a little child; I do not know how to go out or come in. 8 And your servant is in the midst of the people whom you have chosen, a great people, so numerous they cannot be numbered or counted. 9 Give your servant therefore an understanding mind to govern your people, able to discern between good and evil; for who can govern this your great people?"

10 It pleased the Lord that Solomon had asked this. 11 God said to him, "Because you have asked this, and have not asked for yourself long life or riches, or for the life of your enemies, but have asked for yourself understanding to discern what is right, 12 I now do according to your word. Indeed I give you a wise and discerning mind; no one like you has been before you and no one like you shall arise after you. 13 I give you also what you have not asked, both riches and honor all your life; no other king shall compare with you. 14 If you will walk in my ways, keeping my statutes and my commandments, as your father David walked, then I will lengthen your life."

15 Then Solomon awoke; it had been a dream. He came to Jerusalem where he stood before the ark of the covenant of the Lord. He offered up burnt offerings and offerings of well-being, and provided a feast for all his servants.

16 Later, two women who were prostitutes came to the king and stood before him. 17 The one woman said, "Please, my lord, this woman and I live in the same house; and I gave birth while she was in the house. 18 Then on the third day after I gave birth, this woman also gave birth. We were together; there was no one else with us in the house, only the two of us were in the house. 19 Then this woman's son died in the night, because she lay on him. 20 She got up in the middle of the night and took my son from beside me while your servant slept. She laid him at her breast, and laid her dead son at my breast. 21 When I rose in the morning to nurse my son, I saw that he was dead; but when I looked at him closely in the morning, clearly it was not the son I had borne." 22 But the other woman said, "No, the living son is

in your heart what mischief you did to my father David; the Lord is now making that mischief recoil on your own head. 45 But King Solomon is blessed, and the throne of David will be secure before the Lord for all time.' 46 The king then gave orders to Benaiah son of Jehoiada, who went out and struck Shimei down, and he died. Thus Solomon's royal power was securely established.

3 Solomon allied himself to Pharaoh king of Egypt by marrying his daughter. He brought her to the City of David, until he had finished building his palace and the house of the Lord and the wall round Jerusalem. 2 The people however continued to sacrifice at the shrines, for up to that time no house had been built for the name of the Lord. 3 Solomon himself loved the Lord, conforming to the precepts laid down by his father David; but he too slaughtered and burnt sacrifices at the shrines.

4 The king went to Gibeon to offer a sacrifice, for that was the chief shrine, where he used to offer a thousand whole-offerings on the altar. 5 That night the Lord appeared to Solomon there in a dream. God said, 'What shall I give you? Tell me.' 6 He answered, 'You have shown great and constant love to your servant David my father, because he walked before you in loyalty, righteousness, and integrity of heart; and you have maintained this great and constant love towards him and now you have given him a son to succeed him on the throne.

7 'Now, Lord my God, you have made your servant king in place of my father David, though I am a mere child, unskilled in leadership. 8 Here I am in the midst of your people, the people of your choice, too many to be numbered or counted. 9 Grant your servant, therefore, a heart with skill to listen, so that he may govern your people justly and distinguish good from evil. Otherwise who is equal to the task of governing this great people of yours?'

10 The Lord was well pleased that this was what Solomon had asked for, 11 and God said, 'Because you have asked for this, and not for long life, or for wealth, or for the lives of your enemies, but have asked for discernment in administering justice, 12 I grant your request; I give you a heart so wise and so understanding that there has been none like you before your time, nor will there be after you. 13 What is more, I give you those things for which you did not ask, such wealth and glory as no king of your time can match. 14 If you conform to my ways and observe my ordinances and commandments, as your father David did, I will also give you long life.' 15 Then Solomon awoke, and realized it was a dream.

Solomon came to Jerusalem and stood before the Ark of the Covenant of the Lord, where he sacrificed whole-offerings and brought shared-offerings, and gave a banquet for all his household.

16 Two women who were prostitutes approached the king at that time, and as they stood before him 17 one said, 'My lord, this woman and I share a house, and I gave birth to a child when she was there with me. 18 On the third day after my baby was born she too gave birth to a child. We were alone; no one else was with us in the house; only the two of us were there. 19 During the night this woman's child died because she lay on it, 20 and she got up in the middle of the night, took my baby from my side while I, your servant, was asleep, and laid it on her bosom, putting her dead child on mine. 21 When I got up in the morning to feed my baby, I found him dead; but when I looked at him closely, I found that it was not the child that I had borne.' 22 The other

heart the evil that you did to my father David. Now the LORD requites you for your own wickedness. 45 But King Solomon shall be blessed, and David's throne shall endure before the LORD forever." 46 The king then gave the order to Benaiah, son of Jehoiada, who struck him dead as he left.

3 With the royal power firmly in his grasp, Solomon allied himself by marriage with Pharaoh, king of Egypt. The daughter of Pharaoh, whom he married, he brought to the City of David, until he should finish building his palace, and the temple of the LORD, and the wall around Jerusalem.

2 However, the people were sacrificing on the high places, for up to that time no temple had been built to the name of the LORD. 3 Solomon loved the LORD, and obeyed the statutes of his father David; yet he offered sacrifice and burned incense on the high places.

4 The king went to Gibeon to sacrifice there, because that was the most renowned high place. Upon its altar Solomon offered a thousand holocausts. 5 In Gibeon the LORD appeared to Solomon in a dream at night. God said, "Ask something of me and I will give it to you." 6 Solomon answered: "You have shown great favor to your servant, my father David, because he behaved faithfully toward you, with justice and an upright heart; and you have continued this great favor toward him, even today, seating a son of his on his throne. 7 O LORD, my God, you have made me, your servant, king to succeed my father David; but I am a mere youth, not knowing at all how to act. 8 I serve you in the midst of the people whom you have chosen, a people so vast that it cannot be numbered or counted. 9 Give your servant, therefore, an understanding heart to judge your people and to distinguish right from wrong. For who is able to govern this vast people of yours?"

10 The LORD was pleased that Solomon made this request. 11 So God said to him: "Because you have asked for this — not for a long life for yourself, nor for riches, nor for the life of your enemies, but for understanding so that you may know what is right — 12 I do as you requested. I give you a heart so wise and understanding that there has never been anyone like you up to now, and after you there will come no one to equal you. 13 In addition, I give you what you have not asked for, such riches and glory that among kings there is not your like. 14 And if you follow me by keeping my statutes and commandments, as your father David did, I will give you a long life."

15 When Solomon awoke from his dream, he went to Jerusalem, stood before the ark of the covenant of the LORD, offered holocausts and peace offerings, and gave a banquet for all his servants.

16 Later, two harlots came to the king and stood before him. 17 One woman said: "By your leave, my lord, this woman and I live in the same house, and I gave birth in the house while she was present. 18 On the third day after I gave birth, this woman also gave birth. We were alone in the house; there was no one there but us two. 19 This woman's son died during the night; she smothered him by lying on him. 20 Later that night she got up and took my son from my side, as I, your handmaid, was sleeping. Then she laid him in her bosom, after she had laid her dead child in my bosom. 21 I rose in the morning to nurse my child, and I found him dead. But when I examined him in the morning light, I saw it was not the son whom I had borne."

Shimei, 'You know well all the evil you did to my father David. Yahweh is about to bring your wickedness down on your own head. 45 But may King Solomon be blessed, and may the throne of David be kept secure before Yahweh for ever!' 46 The king gave orders to Benaiah son of Jehoiada; he went out and struck Shimei down; and that was how he died. And now the kingdom was securely in Solomon's hands.

3 Solomon became the son-in-law of Pharaoh king of Egypt; he married Pharaoh's daughter, and took her to the City of David until he could complete the building of his palace, the Temple of Yahweh and the ramparts of Jerusalem. 2 The people, however, were still sacrificing on the high places, because at that time a dwelling-place for the name of Yahweh had not yet been built. 3 Solomon loved Yahweh: he followed the precepts of his father David, except that he offered sacrifice and incense on the high places.

4 The king went to Gibeon to sacrifice there, since that was the principal high place — Solomon presented a thousand burnt offerings on that altar. 5 At Gibeon Yahweh appeared to Solomon in a dream during the night. God said, 'Ask what you would like me to give you.' 6 Solomon replied, 'You showed most faithful love to your servant David, my father, when he lived his life before you in faithfulness and uprightness and integrity of heart; you have continued this most faithful love to him by allowing a son of his to sit on his throne today. 7 Now, Yahweh my God, you have made your servant king in succession to David my father. But I am a very young man, unskilled in leadership. 8 And here is your servant, surrounded with your people whom you have chosen, a people so numerous that its number cannot be counted or reckoned. 9 So give your servant a heart to understand how to govern your people, how to discern between good and evil, for how could one otherwise govern such a great people as yours?' 10 It pleased Yahweh that Solomon should have asked for this. 11 'Since you have asked for this,' God said, 'and not asked for long life for yourself or riches or the lives of your enemies but have asked for a discerning judgement for yourself, 12 here and now I do what you ask. I give you a heart wise and shrewd as no one has had before and no one will have after you. 13 What you have not asked I shall give you too: such riches and glory as no other king can match. 14 And I shall give you a long life, if you follow my ways, keeping my laws and commandments, as your father David followed them.' 15 Then Solomon woke up; it had been a dream. He returned to Jerusalem and stood before the ark of the covenant of Yahweh; he presented burnt offerings and communion sacrifices and held a banquet for all those in his service.

16 Later two prostitutes came to the king and stood before him. 17 'If it please you, my lord,' one of the women said, 'this woman and I live in the same house, and while she was in the house I gave birth to a child. 18 Now it happened on the third day after my delivery that this woman also gave birth to a child. We were alone together; there was no one else in the house with us; just the two of us in the house. 19 Now one night this woman's son died; she overlaid him. 20 And in the middle of the night she got up and took my son from beside me while your servant was asleep; she took him in her arms and put her own dead son in mine. 21 When I got up to suckle my child, there he was, dead. But in the morning I looked at him carefully, and he was not the child I had borne at all.' 22 Then the other woman spoke. 'That is not

NEW REVISED STANDARD VERSION	REVISED ENGLISH BIBLE

mine, and the dead son is yours." The first said, "No, the dead son is yours, and the living son is mine." So they argued before the king. 23 Then the king said, "The one says, 'This is my son that is alive, and your son is dead'; while the other says, 'Not so! Your son is dead, and my son is the living one.'" 24 So the king said, "Bring me a sword," and they brought a sword before the king. 25 The king said, "Divide the living boy in two; then give half to the one, and half to the other." 26 But the woman whose son was alive said to the king — because compassion for her son burned within her — "Please, my lord, give her the living boy; certainly do not kill him!" The other said, "It shall be neither mine nor yours; divide it." 27 Then the king responded: "Give the first woman the living boy; do not kill him. She is his mother." 28 All Israel heard of the judgment that the king had rendered; and they stood in awe of the king, because they perceived that the wisdom of God was in him, to execute justice.

4 King Solomon was king over all Israel, 2 and these were his high officials: Azariah son of Zadok was the priest; 3 Elihoreph and Ahijah sons of Shisha were secretaries; Jehoshaphat son of Ahilud was recorder; 4 Benaiah son of Jehoiada was in command of the army; Zadok and Abiathar were priests; 5 Azariah son of Nathan was over the officials; Zabud son of Nathan was priest and king's friend; 6 Ahishar was in charge of the palace; and Adoniram son of Abda was in charge of the forced labor.

7 Solomon had twelve officials over all Israel, who provided food for the king and his household; each one had to make provision for one month in the year. 8 These were their names: Ben-hur, in the hill country of Ephraim; 9 Bendeker, in Makaz, Shaalbim, Beth-shemesh, and Elon-beth-hanan; 10 Ben-hesed, in Arubboth (to him belonged Socoh and all the land of Hepher); 11 Ben-abinadab, in all Naphath-dor (he had Taphath, Solomon's daughter, as his wife); 12 Baana son of Ahilud, in Taanach, Megiddo, and all Beth-shean, which is beside Zarethan below Jezreel, and from Beth-shean to Abel-meholah, as far as the other side of Jokmeam; 13 Ben-geber, in Ramoth-gilead (he had the villages of Jair son of Manasseh, which are in Gilead, and he had the region of Argob, which is in Bashan, sixty great cities with walls and bronze bars); 14 Ahinadab son of Iddo, in Mahanaim; 15 Ahimaaz, in Naphtali (he had taken Basemath, Solomon's daughter, as his wife); 16 Baana son of Hushai, in Asher and Bealoth; 17 Jehoshaphat son of Paruah, in Issachar; 18 Shimei son of Ela, in Benjamin; 19 Geber son of Uri, in the land of Gilead, the country of King Sihon of the Amorites and of King Og of Bashan. And there was one official in the land of Judah.

woman broke in, 'No, the living child is mine; yours is the dead one,' while the first insisted, 'No, the dead child is yours; mine is the living one.' So they went on arguing before the king. 23 The king thought to himself, 'One of them says, "This is my child, the living one; yours is the dead one." The other says, "No, it is your child that is dead and mine that is alive."' 24 Then he said, 'Fetch me a sword.' When a sword was brought, 25 the king gave the order: 'Cut the living child in two and give half to one woman and half to the other.' 26 At this the woman who was the mother of the living child, moved with love for her child, said to the king, 'Oh, sir, let her have the baby! Whatever you do, do not kill it.' The other said, 'Let neither of us have it; cut it in two.' 27 The king then spoke up: 'Give the living baby to the first woman,' he said; 'do not kill it. She is its mother.' 28 When Israel heard the judgement which the king had given, they all stood in awe of him; for they saw that he possessed wisdom from God for administering justice.

4 King Solomon reigned over Israel. 2 His officers were as follows:
In charge of the calendar: Azariah son of Zadok the priest.
3 Adjutant-general: Ahijah son of Shisha.
Secretary of state: Jehoshaphat son of Ahilud.
4 Commander of the army: Benaiah son of Jehoiada.
Priests: Zadok and Abiathar.
5 Superintendent of the regional governors: Azariah son of Nathan.
King's Friend: Zabud son of Nathan.
6 Comptroller of the household: Ahishar.
Superintendent of the forced levy: Adoniram son of Abda.

7 Solomon had twelve regional governors over Israel and they supplied the food for the king and the royal household, each being responsible for one month's provision in the year. 8 These were their names:
Ben-hur in the hill-country of Ephraim.
9 Ben-dekar in Makaz, Shaalbim, Beth-shemesh, Elon, and Beth-hanan.
10 Ben-hesed in Aruboth; he had charge also of Socoh and all the land of Hepher.
11 Ben-abinadab, who had married Solomon's daughter Taphath, in all the district of Dor.
12 Baana son of Ahilud in Taanach and Megiddo, all Beth-shean as far as Abel-meholah beside Zartanah, and from Beth-shean below Jezreel as far as Jokmeam.
13 Ben-geber in Ramoth-gilead, including the tent-villages of Jair son of Manasseh in Gilead and the region of Argob in Bashan, sixty large walled towns with bronze gate-bars.
14 Ahinadab son of Iddo in Mahanaim.
15 Ahimaaz in Naphtali; he also had married a daughter of Solomon, Basmath.
16 Baanah son of Hushai in Asher and Aloth.
17 Jehoshaphat son of Paruah in Issachar.
18 Shimei son of Elah in Benjamin.
19 Geber son of Uri in Gilead, the country of Sihon king of the Amorites and of Og king of Bashan.
In addition, one governor over all the governors in the land.

4:2–6 Cp. 2 Sam. 8:16–18; 20:23–26; 1 Chr. 18:15–17.   4:2 In
... calendar: prob. rdg; Heb. Elihoreph (verse 3).
4:3 Adjutant-general: prob. rdg, cp. 1 Chr. 18:16; Heb.
Adjutants-general. son of Shisha: prob. rdg; Heb. sons of Shisha.
4:5 Zabud . . . Nathan: so Gk; Heb. adds priest.   4:9 Elon, and
Beth-hanan: so some MSS; others Elon-beth-hanan.   4:19 over
... governors: prob. rdg; Heb. omits.

NEW AMERICAN BIBLE	NEW JERUSALEM BIBLE

22 The other woman answered, "It is not so! The living one is my son, the dead one is yours." But the first kept saying, "No, the dead one is your child, the living one is mine!" Thus they argued before the king. 23 Then the king said: "One woman claims, 'This, the living one, is my child, and the dead one is yours.' The other answers, 'No! The dead one is your child; the living one is mine.'" 24 The king continued, "Get me a sword." When they brought the sword before him, 25 he said, "Cut the living child in two, and give half to one woman and half to the other." 26 The woman whose son it was, in the anguish she felt for it, said to the king, "Please, my lord, give her the living child — please do not kill it!" The other, however, said, "It shall be neither mine nor yours. Divide it!" 27 The king then answered, "Give the first one the living child! By no means kill it, for she is the mother."

28 When all Israel heard the judgment the king had given, they were in awe of him, because they saw that the king had in him the wisdom of God for giving judgment.

4 Solomon was king over all Israel, 2 and these were the officials he had in his service:
Azariah, son of Zadok, priest;
3 Elihoreph and Ahijah, sons of Shisha, scribes;
Jehoshaphat, son of Ahilud, chancellor;
4 [Benaiah, son of Jehoiada, commander of the army;
Zadok and Abiathar, priests;]
5 Azariah, son of Nathan, chief of the commissaries;
Zabud, son of Nathan, companion to the king;
6 Ahishar, major-domo of the palace; and
Adoniram, son of Abda, superintendent of the forced labor.
7 Solomon had twelve commissaries for all Israel who supplied food for the king and his household, each having to provide for one month in the year. 8 Their names were:
the son of Hur in the hill country of Ephraim;
9 the son of Deker in Makaz, Shaalbim, Beth-shemesh, Elon and Beth-hanan;
10 the son of Hesed in Arubboth, as well as in Socoh and the whole region of Hepher;
11 the son of Abinadab, who was married to Solomon's daughter Taphath, in all the Naphath-dor;
12 Baana, son of Ahilud, in Taanach and Megiddo, and beyond Jokmeam, and in all Beth-shean, and in the country around Zarethan below Jezreel from Beth-shean to Abel-meholah;
13 the son of Geber in Ramoth-Gilead, having charge of the villages of Jair, son of Manasseh, in Gilead; and of the district of Argob in Bashan — sixty large walled cities with gates barred with bronze;
14 Ahinadab, son of Iddo, in Mahanaim;
15 Ahimaaz, who was married to Basemath, another daughter of Solomon, in Naphtali;
16 Baana, son of Hushai, in Asher and along the rocky coast;
17 Jehoshaphat, son of Paruah, in Issachar;
18 Shimei, son of Ela, in Benjamin;
19 Geber, son of Uri, in the land of Gilead, the land of Sihon, king of the Amorites, and of Og, king of Bashan.
There was one prefect besides, in the king's own land.
‡4.20: see below in ch.5‡
5 7 These commissaries, one for each month, provided food for King Solomon and for all the guests at the royal table. They left nothing unprovided. 8 For the chariot

true! My son is the live one, yours is the dead one'; and the first retorted, 'That is not true! Your son is the dead one, mine is the live one.' And so they wrangled before the king. 23 'This one says,' the king observed, ' "My son is the one who is alive; your son is dead," while the other says, "That is not true! Your son is the dead one, mine is the live one." 24 Bring me a sword,' said the king; and a sword was brought into the king's presence. 25 'Cut the living child in two,' the king said, 'and give half to one, half to the other.' 26 At this the woman who was the mother of the living child addressed the king, for she felt acutely for her son. 'I beg you, my lord,' she said, 'let them give her the live child; on no account let them kill him!' But the other said, 'He shall belong to neither of us. Cut him in half!' 27 Then the king gave his decision. 'Give the live child to the first woman,' he said, 'and do not kill him. She is his mother.' 28 All Israel came to hear of the judgement which the king had pronounced and held the king in awe, recognising that he possessed divine wisdom for dispensing justice.

4 King Solomon was king of all Israel, 2 and these were his high officials:
Azariah son of Zadok, priest;
3 Elihaph and Ahijah sons of Shisha, secretaries;
Jehoshaphat son of Ahilud, herald.
4 (Benaiah son of Jehoiada, commander of the army.
Zadok and Abiathar, priests);
5 Azariah son of Nathan, chief administrator;
Zabud son of Nathan, Friend of the King;
6 Ahishar, master of the palace;
Eliab son of Joab, commander of the army;
Adoram son of Abda, in charge of forced labour.
7 Solomon had twelve administrators for all Israel who saw to the provisioning of the king and his household; each had to provide for one month in the year.
8 These are their names:
Son of Hur, in the mountain country of Ephraim.
9 Son of Deker, in Makaz, Shaalbim, Beth-Shemesh, Aijalon, Beth-Hanan.
10 Son of Hesed, in Arubboth; his district was Socoh and the whole territory of Hepher.
11 Son of Abinadab, all the Slopes of Dor. Tabaath Solomon's daughter was his wife.
12 Baana son of Ahilud, in Taanach and Megiddo as far as the other side of Jokmeam, and all Beth-Shean below Jezreel, from Beth-Shean as far as Abel-Meholah by Zarethan.
13 Son of Geber, in Ramoth-Gilead: his district was the Encampments of Jair son of Manasseh, which are in Gilead; he had the region of Argob, which is in Bashan: sixty fortified towns, walled and with bolts of bronze.
14 Ahinadab son of Iddo, in Mahanaim.
15 Ahimaaz in Naphtali; he too married a daughter of Solomon, Basemath.
16 Baana son of Hushai, in Asher and in the highlands.
17 Jehoshaphat son of Paruah, in Issachar.
18 Shimei son of Ela, in Benjamin.
19 Geber son of Uri, in the territory of Gad, the territory of Sihon king of the Amorites and of Og king of Bashan. In addition, there was one administrator in the country.
‡4.20: see below‡

5 7 These[a] administrators provided the food for Solomon and for all those who were admitted by him to the royal table, each for the period of a month; they ensured that nothing was wanting. 8 They also provided the barley and

a 5 This edition follows the order of the Gk, as more logical.

NEW REVISED STANDARD VERSION

REVISED ENGLISH BIBLE

20 Judah and Israel were as numerous as the sand by the sea; they ate and drank and were happy. 21 *c* Solomon was sovereign over all the kingdoms from the Euphrates to the land of the Philistines, even to the border of Egypt; they brought tribute and served Solomon all the days of his life. 22 Solomon's provision for one day was thirty cors of choice flour, and sixty cors of meal, 23 ten fat oxen, and twenty pasture-fed cattle, one hundred sheep, besides deer, gazelles, roebucks, and fatted fowl. 24 For he had dominion over all the region west of the Euphrates from Tiphsah to Gaza, over all the kings west of the Euphrates; and he had peace on all sides. 25 During Solomon's lifetime Judah and Israel lived in safety, from Dan even to Beer-sheba, all of them under their vines and fig trees. 26 Solomon also had forty thousand stalls of horses for his chariots, and twelve thousand horsemen. 27 Those officials supplied provisions for King Solomon and for all who came to King Solomon's table, each one in his month; they let nothing be lacking. 28 They also brought to the required place barley and straw for the horses and swift steeds, each according to his charge.

29 God gave Solomon very great wisdom, discernment, and breadth of understanding as vast as the sand on the seashore, 30 so that Solomon's wisdom surpassed the wisdom of all the people of the east, and all the wisdom of Egypt. 31 He was wiser than anyone else, wiser than Ethan the Ezrahite, and Heman, Calcol, and Darda, children of Mahol; his fame spread throughout all the surrounding nations. 32 He composed three thousand proverbs, and his songs numbered a thousand and five. 33 He would speak of trees, from the cedar that is in the Lebanon to the hyssop that grows in the wall; he would speak of animals, and birds, and reptiles, and fish. 34 People came from all the nations to hear the wisdom of Solomon; they came from all the kings of the earth who had heard of his wisdom.

5 *d* Now King Hiram of Tyre sent his servants to Solomon, when he heard that they had anointed him king in place of his father; for Hiram had always been a friend to David. 2 Solomon sent word to Hiram, saying, 3 "You know that my father David could not build a house for the name of the LORD his God because of the warfare with which his enemies surrounded him, until the LORD put them under the soles of his feet. *e* 4 But now the LORD my God has given me rest on every side; there is neither adversary nor misfortune. 5 So I intend to build a house for the name of the LORD my God, as the LORD said to my father David, 'Your son, whom I will set on your throne in your place, shall build the house for my name.' 6 Therefore command that cedars from the Lebanon be cut for me. My servants will join your servants, and I will give you whatever wages you set for your servants; for you know that there is no one among us who knows how to cut timber like the Sidonians."

20 THE people of Judah and Israel were countless as the sands of the sea; they ate and drank and enjoyed life. 21 Solomon ruled over all the kingdoms from the river Euphrates to Philistia and as far as the frontier of Egypt; they paid tribute and were subject to him all his life. 22 Solomon's provisions for one day were thirty kor of flour and sixty kor of meal, 23 ten fat oxen and twenty oxen from the pastures and a hundred sheep, as well as stags, gazelles, roebucks, and fattened fowl. 24 For he was paramount over all the region west of the Euphrates from Tiphsah to Gaza, ruling all the kings west of the river; and he enjoyed peace on all sides. 25 All through his reign the people of Judah and Israel lived in peace, everyone from Dan to Beersheba under his own vine and his own fig tree.

26 Solomon had forty thousand chariot-horses in his stables and twelve thousand cavalry horses. 27 The regional governors, each for a month in turn, supplied provisions for King Solomon and all who came to his table; they never fell short in their deliveries. 28 They provided also barley and straw, each according to his duty, for the horses and chariot-horses where it was required.

29 God gave Solomon deep wisdom and insight, and understanding as wide as the sand on the seashore, 30 so that Solomon's wisdom surpassed that of all the men of the east and of all Egypt. 31 For he was wiser than any man, wiser than Ethan the Ezrahite, and Heman, Calcol, and Darda, the sons of Mahol; his fame spread among all the surrounding nations. 32 He propounded three thousand proverbs, and his songs numbered a thousand and five. 33 He discoursed of trees, from the cedar of Lebanon down to the marjoram that grows out of the wall, of beasts and birds, of reptiles and fish. 34 People of all races came to listen to the wisdom of Solomon, and he received gifts from all the kings in the world who had heard of his wisdom.

5 WHEN Hiram king of Tyre heard that Solomon had been anointed king in his father's place, he sent envoys to him, because he had always been friendly with David. 2 Solomon sent this message to Hiram: 3 'You know that my father David could not build a house for the name of the LORD his God, because of the armed nations surrounding him, until the LORD made them subject to him. 4 But now on every side the LORD my God has given me peace; there is no one to oppose me, I fear no attack. 5 So I propose to build a house for the name of the LORD my God, following the promise given by the LORD to my father David: "Your son whom I shall set on the throne in your place will build the house for my name." 6 If therefore you will now give orders that cedars be felled and brought from Lebanon, my men will work with yours, and I shall pay you for your men whatever sum you fix; for, as you know, we have none so skilled at felling trees as your Sidonians.'

c Ch 5.1 in Heb *d* Ch 5.15 in Heb *e* Gk Tg Vg: Heb *my feet or his feet*

4:21 *In Heb. 5:1.* 4:34 **he received gifts:** *so Gk (Luc.); Heb. omits.* 5:1 *In Heb. 5:15.* 5:2–11 *Cp. 2 Chr. 2:3–16.*

horses and draft animals also, each brought his quota of barley and straw to the required place.

4,20 Judah and Israel were as numerous as the sands by the sea; they ate and drank and made merry. 1 Solomon ruled over all the kingdoms from the River to the land of the Philistines, down to the border of Egypt; they paid Solomon tribute and were his vassals as long as he lived.

2 Solomon's supplies for each day were thirty kors of fine flour, sixty kors of meal, 3 ten fatted oxen, twenty pasture-fed oxen, and a hundred sheep, not counting harts, gazelles, roebucks, and fatted fowl.

4 He ruled over all the land west of the Euphrates, from Tiphsah to Gaza, and over all its kings, and he had peace on all his borders round about. 5 Thus Judah and Israel lived in security, every man under his vine or under his fig tree from Dan to Beer-sheba, as long as Solomon lived.

6 Solomon had four thousand stalls for his twelve thousand chariot horses.

‡5.7–8: see above‡

9 Moreover, God gave Solomon wisdom and exceptional understanding and knowledge, as vast as the sand on the seashore. 10 Solomon surpassed all the Cedemites and all the Egyptians in wisdom. 11 He was wiser than all other men — than Ethan the Ezrahite, or Heman, Chalcol, and Darda, the musicians — and his fame spread throughout the neighboring nations. 12 Solomon also uttered three thousand proverbs, and his songs numbered a thousand and five. 13 He discussed plants, from the cedar on Lebanon to the hyssop growing out of the wall, and he spoke about beasts, birds, reptiles, and fishes. 14 Men came to hear Solomon's wisdom from all nations, sent by all the kings of the earth who had heard of his wisdom.

15 When Hiram, king of Tyre, heard that Solomon had been anointed king in place of his father, he sent an embassy to him; for Hiram had always been David's friend. 16 Solomon sent back this message to Hiram: 17 "You know that my father David, because of the enemies surrounding him on all sides, could not build a temple in honor of the LORD, his God, until such a time as the LORD should put these enemies under the soles of his feet. 18 But now the LORD, my God, has given me peace on all sides. There is no enemy or threat of danger. 19 So I propose to build a temple in honor of the LORD, my God, as the LORD predicted to my father David when he said: 'It is your son whom I will put upon your throne in your place who shall build the temple in my honor.' 20 Give orders, then, to have cedars from the Lebanon cut down for me. My servants shall accompany yours, since you know that there is no one among us who is skilled in cutting timber like the Sidonians, and I will pay you whatever you say for your servants' salary."

straw for the horses and draught animals, where required, each according to the quota demanded of him. 2 The daily provisions for Solomon were: thirty measures of fine flour and sixty measures of meal, 3 ten fattened oxen, twenty free-grazing oxen, one hundred sheep, besides deer and gazelles, roebucks and fattened poultry. 4 For he was master of all Transeuphrates — of all the kings of Transeuphrates from Tiphsah to Gaza — and he enjoyed peace on all his frontiers. 5 Judah and Israel lived in security, everyone under his vine and his fig tree, from Dan to Beersheba, throughout the lifetime of Solomon.

4 20 Judah and Israel were numerous, as numerous as the sand on the sea-shore; they ate and drank and were happy.

5 1 Solomon was overlord of all the kingdoms from the River[b] to the territory of the Philistines and the Egyptian border. They brought tribute and served him all his life long.

‡5.2–5: see above‡

6 And Solomon had four thousand stalls of horses for his chariots and twelve thousand cavalrymen.

‡5.7–8: see above‡

9 God gave Solomon immense wisdom and understanding, and a heart as vast as the sand on the sea-shore. 10 The wisdom of Solomon surpassed the wisdom of all the sons of the East and all the wisdom of Egypt. 11 He was wiser than anyone else, wiser than Ethan the Ezrahite, than the sons of Mahol, Heman, Calcol and Darda; his fame spread to all the surrounding nations. 12 He composed three thousand proverbs, and his songs numbered a thousand and five. 13 He could discourse on plants, from the cedar in Lebanon to the hyssop growing on the wall; and he could discourse on animals and birds and reptiles and fish. 14 Men from all nations came to hear Solomon's wisdom, and he received gifts from all the kings in the world, who had heard of his wisdom.

15 Hiram king of Tyre sent an embassy to Solomon, having learnt that he had been anointed king in succession to his father and because Hiram had always been a friend of David. 16 And Solomon sent this message to Hiram, 17 'You are aware that my father David was unable to build a temple for the name of Yahweh his God, on account of the wars waged on him from every side, until Yahweh put his enemies under the soles of his feet. 18 But now Yahweh my God has given me peace on every side: not one enemy, no calamities. 19 I propose, then, to build a temple for the name of Yahweh my God, in accordance with what Yahweh told my father David, "Your son whom I shall place on your throne to succeed you will be the man to build a temple for my name." 20 So now have cedars of Lebanon cut down for me; my servants will work with your servants, and I shall pay for the hire of your servants at whatever rate you fix. As you know, we have no one as skilled in felling

b 5 The Euphrates.

NEW REVISED STANDARD VERSION

7 When Hiram heard the words of Solomon, he rejoiced greatly, and said, "Blessed be the LORD today, who has given to David a wise son to be over this great people." 8 Hiram sent word to Solomon, "I have heard the message that you have sent to me; I will fulfill all your needs in the matter of cedar and cypress timber. 9 My servants shall bring it down to the sea from the Lebanon; I will make it into rafts to go by sea to the place you indicate. I will have them broken up there for you to take away. And you shall meet my needs by providing food for my household." 10 So Hiram supplied Solomon's every need for timber of cedar and cypress. 11 Solomon in turn gave Hiram twenty thousand cors of wheat as food for his household, and twenty cors of fine oil. Solomon gave this to Hiram year by year. 12 So the LORD gave Solomon wisdom, as he promised him. There was peace between Hiram and Solomon; and the two of them made a treaty.

13 King Solomon conscripted forced labor out of all Israel; the levy numbered thirty thousand men. 14 He sent them to the Lebanon, ten thousand a month in shifts; they would be a month in the Lebanon and two months at home; Adoniram was in charge of the forced labor. 15 Solomon also had seventy thousand laborers and eighty thousand stonecutters in the hill country, 16 besides Solomon's three thousand three hundred supervisors who were over the work, having charge of the people who did the work. 17 At the king's command, they quarried out great, costly stones in order to lay the foundation of the house with dressed stones. 18 So Solomon's builders and Hiram's builders and the Gebalites did the stonecutting and prepared the timber and the stone to build the house.

6 In the four hundred eightieth year after the Israelites came out of the land of Egypt, in the fourth year of Solomon's reign over Israel, in the month of Ziv, which is the second month, he began to build the house of the LORD. 2 The house that King Solomon built for the LORD was sixty cubits long, twenty cubits wide, and thirty cubits high. 3 The vestibule in front of the nave of the house was twenty cubits wide, across the width of the house. Its depth was ten cubits in front of the house. 4 For the house he made windows with recessed frames. f 5 He also built a structure against the wall of the house, running around the walls of the house, both the nave and the inner sanctuary; and he made side chambers all around. 6 The lowest story g was five cubits wide, the middle one was six cubits wide, and the third was seven cubits wide; for around the outside of the house he made offsets on the wall in order that the supporting beams should not be inserted into the walls of the house.

7 The house was built with stone finished at the quarry, so that neither hammer nor ax nor any tool of iron was heard in the temple while it was being built.

8 The entrance for the middle story was on the south side of the house: one went up by winding stairs to the middle story, and from the middle story to the third. 9 So he built the house, and finished it; he roofed the house with beams and planks of cedar. 10 He built the structure against the whole house, each story h five cubits high, and it was joined to the house with timbers of cedar.

11 Now the word of the LORD came to Solomon, 12 "Concerning this house that you are building, if you will walk in my statutes, obey my ordinances, and keep all my commandments by walking in them, then I will establish my promise with you, which I made to your father David.

REVISED ENGLISH BIBLE

7 Hiram was greatly pleased to receive Solomon's message, and said, 'Blessed be the LORD today who has given David a wise son to rule over this great people.' 8 He sent Solomon this reply: 'I have received your message. In this matter of timber, both cedar and pine, I shall do all you wish. 9 My men will bring down the logs from Lebanon to the sea and I shall make them up into rafts to be floated to the place you appoint; I shall have them broken up there and you can remove them. You, for your part, will meet my wishes if you provide the food for my household.' 10 So Hiram kept Solomon supplied with all the cedar and pine that he wanted, 11 and Solomon supplied Hiram with twenty thousand kor of wheat as food for his household and twenty kor of oil of pounded olives; Solomon gave this yearly to Hiram. 12 The LORD bestowed wisdom on Solomon as he had promised him; there was peace between Hiram and Solomon and they concluded a treaty.

13 King Solomon raised a forced levy from the whole of Israel amounting to thirty thousand men. 14 He sent them to Lebanon in monthly relays of ten thousand, so that the men spent one month in Lebanon and two at home; Adoniram was superintendent of the levy. 15 Solomon had also seventy thousand hauliers and eighty thousand quarrymen, 16 apart from the three thousand three hundred foremen in charge of the work who superintended the labourers. 17 By the king's orders they quarried huge, costly blocks for laying the foundation of the LORD's house in hewn stone. 18 The builders supplied by Solomon and Hiram, together with the Gebalites, shaped the blocks and prepared both timber and stone for the building of the house.

6 It was in the four hundred and eightieth year after the Israelites had come out of Egypt, in the fourth year of Solomon's reign over Israel, in the second month of that year, the month of Ziv, that he began to build the house of the LORD. 2 The house which King Solomon built for the LORD was sixty cubits long by twenty cubits broad, and its height was thirty cubits. 3 The vestibule in front of the sanctuary was twenty cubits long, spanning the whole breadth of the house, while it projected ten cubits in front of the house; 4 and he fitted the house with embrasures. 5 Then he built a terrace against its wall round both the sanctuary and the inner shrine. He made arcades all round: 6 the lowest arcade was five cubits in depth, the middle six, and the highest seven; for he made rebatements all round the outside of the main wall so that the bearer beams might not be fixed into the walls. 7 In the building of the house, only blocks of stone dressed at the quarry were used; no hammer or axe or any iron tool whatever was heard in the house while it was being built.

8 The entrance to the lowest arcade was in the right-hand corner of the house; there was access by a spiral stairway from that to the middle arcade, and from the middle arcade to the highest. 9-10 So Solomon built the house and finished it, having constructed the terrace five cubits high against the whole building, braced the house with struts of cedar, and roofed it with beams and coffering of cedar.

11 Then the word of the LORD came to Solomon, saying, 12 'As for this house which you are building, if you are obedient to my ordinances and conform to my precepts and loyally observe all my commands, then I will fulfil my promise to you, the promise I gave to your father David,

6,7 *In these chapters there are several Hebrew technical terms whose meaning is not certain and has to be determined, as well as may be, from the context.*   6:1–3 *Cp.* 2 *Chr.* 3:2–4.   6:5 **against its wall:** *so* Gk; *Heb.* adds *round the walls of the house.*
6:6 **arcade:** *so* Gk; *Heb.* platform. **the bearer beams:** *so Aram.* (*Targ.*); *Heb. omits.*   6:8 **lowest:** *so* Gk; *Heb.* middle.

f Gk: Meaning of Heb uncertain   g Gk: Heb *structure*
h Heb lacks *each story*

21 When he had heard the words of Solomon, Hiram was pleased and said, "Blessed be the LORD this day, who has given David a wise son to rule this numerous people." 22 Hiram then sent word to Solomon, "I agree to the proposal you sent me, and I will provide all the cedars and fir trees you wish. 23 My servants shall bring them down from the Lebanon to the sea, and I will arrange them into rafts in the sea and bring them wherever you say. There I will break up the rafts, and you shall take the lumber. You, for your part, shall furnish the provisions I desire for my household."

24 So Hiram continued to provide Solomon with all the cedars and fir trees he wished; 25 while Solomon every year gave Hiram twenty thousand kors of wheat to provide for his household, and twenty thousand measures of pure oil. 26 The LORD, moreover, gave Solomon wisdom as he promised him, and there was peace between Hiram and Solomon, since they were parties to a treaty.

27 King Solomon conscripted thirty thousand workmen from all Israel. 28 He sent them to the Lebanon each month in relays of ten thousand, so that they spent one month in the Lebanon and two months at home. Adoniram was in charge of the draft. 29 Solomon had seventy thousand carriers and eighty thousand stonecutters in the mountain, 30 in addition to three thousand three hundred overseers, answerable to Solomon's prefects for the work, directing the people engaged in the work. 31 By order of the king, fine, large blocks were quarried to give the temple a foundation of hewn stone. 32 Solomon's and Hiram's builders, along with the Gebalites, hewed them out, and prepared the wood and stones for building the temple.

6 In the four hundred and eightieth year from the departure of the Israelites from the land of Egypt, in the fourth year of Solomon's reign over Israel, in the month of Ziv, which is the second month, the construction of the temple of the LORD was begun.

2 The temple which King Solomon built for the LORD was sixty cubits long, twenty wide, and twenty-five high. 3 The porch in front of the temple was twenty cubits from side to side, along the width of the nave, and ten cubits deep in front of the temple. 4 Splayed windows with trellises were made for the temple, 5 and adjoining the wall of the temple, which enclosed the nave and the sanctuary, an annex of several stories was built. 6 Its lowest story was five cubits wide, the middle one six cubits wide, the third seven cubits wide, because there were offsets along the outside of the temple so that the beams would not be fastened into the walls of the temple. 7 (The temple was built of stone dressed at the quarry, so that no hammer, axe, or iron tool was to be heard in the temple during its construction.) 8 The entrance to the lowest floor of the annex was at the right side of the temple, and stairs with intermediate landings led up to the middle story and from the middle story to the third. 9 When the temple was built to its full height, it was roofed in with rafters and boards of cedar. 10 The annex, with its lowest story five cubits high, was built all along the outside of the temple, to which it was joined by cedar beams.

11 This word of the LORD came to Solomon: 12 "As to this temple you are building — if you observe all my statutes, carry out my ordinances, keep and obey all my commands, I will fulfill toward you the promise I made to your father David.

trees as the Sidonians.' 21 When Hiram heard what Solomon had said, he was delighted. 'Now blessed be Yahweh,' he said, 'who has given David a wise son to rule over this great people!' 22 And Hiram sent word to Solomon, 'I have received your message. For my part, I shall supply you with all you require in the way of cedar wood and juniper. 23 Your servants will bring these down from Lebanon to the sea, and I shall have them towed by sea to any place you name; I shall discharge them there, and you will take them over. For your part, you will see to the provisioning of my household as I desire.' 24 So Hiram provided Solomon with all the cedar wood and juniper he wanted 25 while Solomon gave Hiram twenty thousand kor of wheat to feed his household, and twenty thousand kor of pure oil. Solomon gave Hiram this every year. 26 Yahweh gave Solomon wisdom as he had promised him; good relations persisted between Solomon and Hiram, and the two of them concluded a treaty. 27 King Solomon raised a levy throughout Israel for forced labour: the levy numbered thirty thousand men. 28 He sent these to Lebanon in relays, ten thousand a month; they spent one month in Lebanon and two months at home. Adoram was in charge of the forced labour. 29 Solomon also had seventy thousand porters and eighty thousand quarrymen in the mountains, 30 as well as the administrators, officials who supervised the work, three thousand three hundred of them in charge of the men employed in the work. 31 At the king's orders they quarried huge stones, special stones for the laying of the temple foundations, dressed stones. 32 Solomon's workmen and Hiram's workmen and the Giblites cut and assembled the wood and stone for the building of the Temple.

6 In the four hundred and eightieth year after the Israelites came out of Egypt, in the fourth year of Solomon's reign over Israel, in the month of Ziv, which is the second month, he began building the Temple of Yahweh. 2 The temple which King Solomon built for Yahweh was sixty cubits long, twenty cubits wide and twenty-five high. 3 The portico in front of the Hekal of the Temple was twenty cubits long across the width of the Temple and ten cubits wide along the length of the Temple. 4 He made windows for the Temple with frames and latticework. 5 He also built an annex against the Temple wall, right round the Hekal and Debir. He built lateral storeys all round; 6 the lowest lateral storey was five cubits wide, the middle one six cubits, and the third seven cubits, for he had made the outside of the Temple wall correspondingly stepped back all round, so that the annex was not attached to the Temple walls. 7 (The building of the Temple was done with quarry-dressed stone; no sound of hammer or pick or any iron tool was to be heard in the Temple while it was being built.) 8 The entrance to the lowest storey was at the right-hand corner of the Temple; access to the middle storey was by a spiral staircase, and so from the middle storey to the third. 9 Having finished building the Temple, he roofed the Temple with a coffered ceiling of cedar wood. 10 Round the outside of the Temple he then built the annex which was five cubits high and was joined to the Temple by cedar-wood beams. 11 And the word of Yahweh came to Solomon, 12 'With regard to this temple which you are now building, if you follow my statutes and obey my ordinances and faithfully follow my commandments, I shall fulfil the promise which I made about you to your father David. 13 And I shall make my home

13 I will dwell among the children of Israel, and will not forsake my people Israel."

14 So Solomon built the house, and finished it. 15 He lined the walls of the house on the inside with boards of cedar; from the floor of the house to the rafters of the ceiling, he covered them on the inside with wood; and he covered the floor of the house with boards of cypress. 16 He built twenty cubits of the rear of the house with boards of cedar from the floor to the rafters, and he built this within as an inner sanctuary, as the most holy place. 17 The house, that is, the nave in front of the inner sanctuary, was forty cubits long. 18 The cedar within the house had carvings of gourds and open flowers; all was cedar, no stone was seen. 19 The inner sanctuary he prepared in the innermost part of the house, to set there the ark of the covenant of the LORD. 20 The interior of the inner sanctuary was twenty cubits long, twenty cubits wide, and twenty cubits high; he overlaid it with pure gold. He also overlaid the altar with cedar. i 21 Solomon overlaid the inside of the house with pure gold, then he drew chains of gold across, in front of the inner sanctuary, and overlaid it with gold. 22 Next he overlaid the whole house with gold, in order that the whole house might be perfect; even the whole altar that belonged to the inner sanctuary he overlaid with gold.

23 In the inner sanctuary he made two cherubim of olivewood, each ten cubits high. 24 Five cubits was the length of one wing of the cherub, and five cubits the length of the other wing of the cherub; it was ten cubits from the tip of one wing to the tip of the other. 25 The other cherub also measured ten cubits; both cherubim had the same measure and the same form. 26 The height of one cherub was ten cubits, and so was that of the other cherub. 27 He put the cherubim in the innermost part of the house; the wings of the cherubim were spread out so that a wing of one was touching the one wall, and a wing of the other cherub was touching the other wall; their other wings toward the center of the house were touching wing to wing. 28 He also overlaid the cherubim with gold.

29 He carved the walls of the house all around about with carved engravings of cherubim, palm trees, and open flowers, in the inner and outer rooms. 30 The floor of the house he overlaid with gold, in the inner and outer rooms.

31 For the entrance to the inner sanctuary he made doors of olivewood; the lintel and the doorposts were five-sided. i 32 He covered the two doors of olivewood with carvings of cherubim, palm trees, and open flowers; he overlaid them with gold, and spread gold on the cherubim and on the palm trees.

33 So also he made for the entrance to the nave doorposts of olivewood, four-sided each, 34 and two doors of cypress wood; the two leaves of the one door were folding, and the two leaves of the other door were folding. 35 He carved cherubim, palm trees, and open flowers, overlaying them with gold evenly applied upon the carved work. 36 He built the inner court with three courses of dressed stone to one course of cedar beams.

37 In the fourth year the foundation of the house of the LORD was laid, in the month of Ziv. 38 In the eleventh year, in the month of Bul, which is the eighth month, the house was finished in all its parts, and according to all its specifications. He was seven years in building it.

13 and I will dwell among the Israelites and never forsake my people Israel.'

14 So Solomon built the LORD's house and finished it. 15 He panelled the inner walls of the house with cedar boards, covering the interior from floor to rafters with wood; the floor he laid with boards of pine. 16 In the innermost part of the house he partitioned off a space of twenty cubits with cedar boards from floor to rafters and made of it an inner shrine, to be the Most Holy Place. 17 The sanctuary in front of this was forty cubits long. 18 The cedar inside the house was carved with open flowers and gourds; all was cedar, no stone was left visible.

19 He prepared an inner shrine in the farthest recesses of the house to receive the Ark of the Covenant of the LORD. 20 This inner shrine was twenty cubits square and it stood twenty cubits high; he overlaid it with red gold and made an altar of cedar. 21 Solomon overlaid the inside of the house with red gold and drew a veil with golden chains across in front of the inner shrine. 22 The whole house he overlaid with gold until it was all covered; and the whole of the altar by the inner shrine he overlaid with gold.

23 In the inner shrine he carved two cherubim of wild olive wood, each ten cubits high. 24 Each wing of the cherubim was five cubits long, and from wingtip to wingtip was ten cubits. 25 Similarly, the second cherub measured ten cubits; the two cherubim were alike in size and shape, 26 and each ten cubits high. 27 He put the cherubim within the inner shrine and their wings were spread, so that a wing of one cherub touched the wall on one side and a wing of the other touched the wall on the other side, and their other wings met in the middle; 28 he overlaid the cherubim with gold.

29 Round all the walls of the house he carved figures of cherubim, palm trees, and open flowers, both in the inner chamber and in the outer. 30 The floor of the house he overlaid with gold, both in the inner chamber and in the outer. 31 At the entrance to the inner shrine he made a double door of wild olive wood; the pilasters and the doorposts were pentagonal. 32 The doors were of wild olive, and he carved cherubim, palms, and open flowers on them, overlaying them with gold and hammering the gold upon the cherubim and the palms. 33 Similarly for the doorway of the sanctuary he made a square frame of wild olive 34 and a double door of pine, each leaf having two swivel-pins. 35 On them he carved cherubim, palms, and open flowers, overlaying them evenly with gold over the carving.

36 He built the inner court with three courses of dressed stone and one course of lengths of cedar.

37 In the fourth year of Solomon's reign, in the month of Ziv, the foundation of the house of the LORD was laid; 38 and in the eleventh year, in the month of Bul, which is the eighth month, the house was finished in all its details according to the specification. It had taken seven years to build.

6:15 **rafters:** *so Gk; Heb.* walls.   6:17 **The sanctuary . . . this:** *so Gk; Heb.* The house, that is the sanctuary, before me.   6:20 **This inner:** *so Lat.; Heb. prefixes* Before. **made:** *so Gk; Heb.* overlaid. 6:21 **a veil:** *prob. rdg; Heb. omits.* **inner shrine:** *prob. rdg; Heb. adds* and overlaid it with gold.   6:23–28 *Cp.* 2 Chr. 3:10–13. 6:29,30 **inner chamber:** *so Gk; Heb.* inwards.   6:31 **and the:** *prob. rdg; Heb. omits.* **pentagonal:** *so Gk; Heb.* fifth.   6:33 **a square:** *so Gk; Heb.* from with a fourth.

---

i Meaning of Heb uncertain

13 I will dwell in the midst of the Israelites and will not forsake my people Israel."

14 When Solomon finished building the temple, 15 its walls were lined from floor to ceiling beams with cedar paneling, and its floor was laid with fir planking. 16 At the rear of the temple a space of twenty cubits was set off by cedar partitions from the floor to the rafters, enclosing the sanctuary, the holy of holies. 17 The nave, or part of the temple in front of the sanctuary, was forty cubits long. 18 The cedar in the interior of the temple was carved in the form of gourds and open flowers; all was of cedar, and no stone was to be seen.

19 In the innermost part of the temple was located the sanctuary to house the ark of the LORD's covenant, 20 twenty cubits long, twenty wide, and twenty high. 21 Solomon overlaid the interior of the temple with pure gold. He made in front of the sanctuary a cedar altar, overlaid it with gold, and looped it with golden chains. 22 The entire temple was overlaid with gold so that it was completely covered with it; the whole altar before the sanctuary was also overlaid with gold. 23 In the sanctuary were two cherubim, each ten cubits high, made of olive wood. 24 Each wing of a cherub measured five cubits so that the space from wing tip to wing tip of each was ten cubits. 25 The cherubim were identical in size and shape, 26 and each was exactly ten cubits high. 27 The cherubim were placed in the inmost part of the temple, with their wings spread wide, so that one wing of each cherub touched a side wall while the other wing, pointing toward the middle of the room, touched the corresponding wing of the second cherub. 28 The cherubim, too, were overlaid with gold.

29 The walls on all sides of both the inner and the outer rooms had carved figures of cherubim, palm trees, and open flowers. 30 The floor of both the inner and the outer rooms was overlaid with gold. 31 At the entrance of the sanctuary, doors of olive wood were made; the doorframes had beveled posts. 32 The two doors were of olive wood, with carved figures of cherubim, palm trees, and open flowers. The doors were overlaid with gold, which was also molded to the cherubim and the palm trees. 33 The same was done at the entrance to the nave, where the doorposts of olive wood were rectangular. 34 The two doors were of fir wood; each door was banded by a metal strap, front and back, 35 and had carved cherubim, palm trees, and open flowers, over which gold was evenly applied.

36 The inner court was walled off by means of three courses of hewn stones and one course of cedar beams.

37 The foundations of the LORD's temple were laid in the month of Ziv 38 in the fourth year, and it was completed in all particulars, exactly according to plan, in the month of Bul, the eighth month, in the eleventh year. Thus it took Solomon seven years to build it.

among the Israelites and never forsake Israel my people.'
14 Solomon finished building the Temple.

15 He lined the inside of the Temple walls with panels of cedar wood — panelling them on the inside from the floor of the Temple to the beams of the ceiling — and laid the floor of the Temple with juniper planks. 16 The twenty cubits measured from the end of the Temple he built of cedar planks from the floor to the beams, and this part was reserved as the Debir, the Holy of Holies. 17 The Temple measured forty cubits — the Hekal — in front of the Debir. 18 There was cedar wood round the inside of the Temple, ornamentally carved with gourds and rosettes; all was cedar wood, with no stone showing. 19 In the inner part of the Temple he designed a Debir, to contain the ark of the covenant of Yahweh. 20 The Debir was twenty cubits long, twenty cubits wide, and twenty high, and he overlaid it on the inside with pure gold. He made an altar of cedar wood 21 in front of the Debir and overlaid it with gold. 22 He overlaid the whole Temple with gold, the whole Temple entirely.

23 In the Debir he made two great winged creatures of wild-olive wood . . . It was ten cubits high. 24 One winged creature's wing was five cubits long and the other wing five cubits: ten cubits from wing tip to wing tip. 25 The other winged creature also measured ten cubits; both had the same measurements and the same shape. 26 The height of one was the same as the other's. 27 He placed them in the middle of the inner chamber; their wings were spread out so that the wing of one touched one of the walls and the wing of the other touched the other wall, while their wings met in the middle of the chamber wing to wing. 28 And he overlaid them with gold. 29 All round the Temple walls he carved figures of winged creatures, palm trees and rosettes, both inside and outside. 30 He overlaid the floor of the Temple with gold, both inside and outside.

31 He made the door of the Debir with uprights of wild-olive wood, and door jambs with five indented sections, 32 and the two leaves of wild-olive wood. He carved figures of great winged creatures, palm trees and rosettes which he overlaid with gold, and he gilded winged creatures and palm trees. 33 Similarly, he made uprights of wild-olive wood for the door of the Hekal, and door jambs with four indented sections, 34 and the two leaves of juniper: one leaf had two ribs binding it, and the other had two ribs binding it. 35 He carved winged creatures, palm trees and rosettes, which he overlaid with gold laid evenly over the carvings.

36 He built the wall of the inner court in three courses of dressed stone and one course of cedar beams.

37 In the fourth year, in the month of Ziv, the foundations of the Temple were laid; 38 in the eleventh year, in the month of Bul — that is, the eighth month — the Temple was completed exactly as it had been planned and designed. Solomon took seven years to build it.

NEW REVISED STANDARD VERSION

7 Solomon was building his own house thirteen years, and he finished his entire house.

2 He built the House of the Forest of the Lebanon one hundred cubits long, fifty cubits wide, and thirty cubits high, built on four rows of cedar pillars, with cedar beams on the pillars. 3 It was roofed with cedar on the forty-five rafters, fifteen in each row, which were on the pillars. 4 There were window frames in the three rows, facing each other in the three rows. 5 All the doorways and doorposts had four-sided frames, opposite, facing each other in the three rows.

6 He made the Hall of Pillars fifty cubits long and thirty cubits wide. There was a porch in front with pillars, and a canopy in front of them.

7 He made the Hall of the Throne where he was to pronounce judgment, the Hall of Justice, covered with cedar from floor to floor.

8 His own house where he would reside, in the other court back of the hall, was of the same construction. Solomon also made a house like this hall for Pharaoh's daughter, whom he had taken in marriage.

9 All these were made of costly stones, cut according to measure, sawed with saws, back and front, from the foundation to the coping, and from outside to the great court. 10 The foundation was of costly stones, huge stones, stones of eight and ten cubits. 11 There were costly stones above, cut to measure, and cedarwood. 12 The great court had three courses of dressed stone to one layer of cedar beams all around; so had the inner court of the house of the LORD, and the vestibule of the house.

13 Now King Solomon invited and received Hiram from Tyre. 14 He was the son of a widow of the tribe of Naphtali, whose father, a man of Tyre, had been an artisan in bronze; he was full of skill, intelligence, and knowledge in working bronze. He came to King Solomon, and did all his work.

15 He cast two pillars of bronze. Eighteen cubits was the height of the one, and a cord of twelve cubits would encircle it; the second pillar was the same.*j* 16 He also made two capitals of molten bronze, to set on the tops of the pillars; the height of the one capital was five cubits, and the height of the other capital was five cubits. 17 There were nets of checker work with wreaths of chain work for the capitals on the tops of the pillars; seven*k* for the one capital, and seven*k* for the other capital. 18 He made the columns with two rows around each latticework to cover the capitals that were above the pomegranates; he did the same with the other capital. 19 Now the capitals that were on the tops of the pillars in the vestibule were of lily-work, four cubits high. 20 The capitals were on the two pillars and also above the rounded projection that was beside the latticework; there were two hundred pomegranates in rows all around; and so with the other capital. 21 He set up the pillars at the vestibule of the temple; he set up the pillar on the south and called it Jachin; and he set up the pillar on the north and called it Boaz. 22 On the tops of the pillars was lily-work. Thus the work of the pillars was finished.

23 Then he made the molten sea; it was round, ten cu-

REVISED ENGLISH BIBLE

7 By the time he had finished, Solomon had been engaged on building for thirteen years. 2 He built the House of the Forest of Lebanon, a hundred cubits long, fifty broad, and thirty high, constructed of four rows of cedar columns, on top of which were laid lengths of cedar. 3 It had a cedar roof, extending over the beams, which rested on the columns, fifteen in each row; and the number of the beams was forty-five. 4 There were three rows of window-frames, and the windows corresponded to each other at three levels. 5 All the doorways and the windows had square frames, and window corresponded to window at three levels.

6 Solomon made also the portico, fifty cubits long and thirty broad, with a cornice above.

7 He built the Portico of Judgement, the portico containing the throne where he was to give judgement; this was panelled in cedar from floor to rafters.

8 His own house where he was to reside, in another courtyard set back from the portico, and the house he made for Pharaoh's daughter whom he had married, were constructed like this portico.

9 All these were made of costly blocks of stone, hewn to measure and trimmed with the saw on the inner and outer sides, from foundation to coping and from the court of the house as far as the great court. 10 At the base were costly stones, huge blocks, some ten and some eight cubits in size, 11 and above were costly stones dressed to measure, and cedar. 12 The great court had three courses of dressed stone all around and a course of lengths of cedar; so had the inner court of the house of the LORD, and so had the vestibule of the house.

13 King Solomon fetched from Tyre Hiram, 14 the son of a widow of the tribe of Naphtali. His father, a native of Tyre, had been a worker in bronze, and he himself was a man of great skill and ingenuity, versed in every kind of craftsmanship in bronze. After he came to King Solomon, Hiram carried out all his works.

15 He cast in a mould the two bronze pillars. One stood eighteen cubits high and it took a cord of twelve cubits long to go round it, it was hollow, and the metal was four fingers thick. The second pillar was the same. 16 He made two capitals of solid bronze to set on the tops of the pillars, each capital five cubits high. 17 He made two bands of ornamental network, in festoons of chain-work, for the capitals on the tops of the pillars, a band of network for each capital. 18 He made pomegranates in two rows all round on top of the ornamental network of the one pillar; he did the same with the other capital. 19 The capitals at the tops of the pillars in the vestibule were shaped like lilies and were four cubits high. 20 On the capitals at the tops of the two pillars, immediately above the cushion, extending beyond the network upwards, were two hundred pomegranates in rows all round on the two capitals. 21 Then he erected the pillars at the vestibule of the sanctuary. When he had erected the pillar on the right side, he named it Jachin, and when he erected the one on the left side, he named it Boaz. 22 On the tops of the pillars was lily-work. Thus the work of the pillars was finished.

23 He made the Sea of cast metal; it was round in shape,

7:5 **windows:** *so Gk; Heb.* doorposts.   7:6 **fifty . . . broad:** *prob. rdg; Heb. adds* and a colonnade and pillars in front of them.   7:7 **rafters:** *so Lat.; Heb.* floor.   7:9 **from the . . . house:** *prob. rdg, cp. verse 12; Heb.* from outside.   7:15–21 *Cp. 2 Chr. 3:15–17.*   7:15 **it was . . . thick:** *prob. rdg, cp. Jer. 52:21; Heb. omits.* **the same:** *so Gk; Heb. omits.*   7:17 **He made two:** *so Gk; Heb. omits.* **a band of network:** *so Gk; Heb.* seven.   7:18 **pomegranates:** *so some MSS; others* pillars. **one pillar:** *so Gk; Heb. adds* to cover the capitals on the top of the pomegranates.   7:20 **the two capitals:** *prob. rdg; Heb.* the second capital.   7:21 **Jachin:** *that is* He shall establish. **Boaz:** *that is* In him is strength.   7:23–26 *Cp. 2 Chr. 4:2–5.*

j Cn: Heb *and a cord of twelve cubits encircled the second pillar*; Compare Jer 52.21   *k* Heb: Gk *a net*

7 His own palace Solomon completed after thirteen years of construction. 2 He built the hall called the Forest of Lebanon one hundred cubits long, fifty wide, and thirty high; it was supported by four rows of cedar columns, with cedar capitals upon the columns. 3 Moreover, it had a ceiling of cedar above the beams resting on the columns; these beams numbered forty-five, fifteen to a row. 4 There were three window frames at either end, with windows in strict alignment. 5 The posts of all the doorways were rectangular, and the doorways faced each other, three at either end. 6 The porch of the columned hall he made fifty cubits long and thirty wide. The porch extended the width of the columned hall, and there was a canopy in front. 7 He also built the vestibule of the throne where he gave judgment — that is, the tribunal; it was paneled with cedar from floor to ceiling beams. 8 His living quarters were in another court, set in deeper than the tribunal and of the same construction. A palace like this tribunal was built for Pharaoh's daughter, whom Solomon had married.

9 All these buildings were of fine stones, hewn to size and trimmed front and back with a saw, from the foundation to the bonding course. 10 (The foundation was made of fine, large blocks, some ten cubits and some eight cubits. 11 Above were fine stones hewn to size, and cedar wood.) 12 The great court was enclosed by three courses of hewn stones and a bonding course of cedar beams. So also were the inner court of the temple of the LORD and the temple porch.

13 King Solomon had Hiram brought from Tyre. 14 He was a bronze worker, the son of a widow from the tribe of Naphtali; his father had been from Tyre. He was endowed with skill, understanding, and knowledge of how to produce any work in bronze. He came to King Solomon and did all his metal work.

15 Two hollow bronze columns were cast, each eighteen cubits high and twelve cubits in circumference; their metal was of four fingers' thickness. 16 There were also two capitals cast in bronze, to place on top of the columns, each of them five cubits high. 17 Two pieces of network with a chainlike mesh were made to cover the (nodes of the) capitals on top of the columns, one for each capital. 18 Four hundred pomegranates were also cast; two hundred of them in a double row encircled the piece of network on each of the two capitals. 19 The capitals on top of the columns were finished wholly in a lotus pattern 20 above the level of the nodes and their enveloping network. 21 The columns were then erected adjacent to the porch of the temple, one to the right, called Jachin, and the other to the left, called Boaz. 22 Thus the work on the columns was completed.

23 The sea was then cast; it was made with a circular rim,

7 As regards his palace, Solomon spent thirteen years on it before the building was completed. 2 He built the House of the Forest of Lebanon, a hundred cubits long, fifty cubits wide, and thirty cubits high, on four rows of cedarwood pillars, 3 with lengths of cedar wood laid horizontally on the pillars. The upper part was panelled with cedar right down to the tie-beams on forty-five pillars, fifteen in each row. 4 There were three rows of window-frames, with the windows corresponding to one another at three levels. 5 All the doorways and windows were rectangular, with the windows corresponding to one another at three levels. 6 He also made the Colonnade, fifty cubits long and thirty cubits broad, with a cornice in front. 7 He also made the Hall of the Throne where he used to dispense justice, that is, the Hall of Justice; it was panelled in cedar from floor to beams. 8 His own living quarters, in the other court and inwards from the Hall, were of the same construction. And there was a house similar to this Hall for Pharaoh's daughter whom he had taken in marriage.

9 All these buildings were of special stones cut to measure, trimmed on the inner and outer sides with the saw, from the foundations to the coping — 10 the foundations were of special stones, huge stones, of ten and eight cubits, 11 and, above these, special stones, cut to measure, and cedar wood — 12 and, on the outside, the great court had three courses of dressed stone round it and one course of cedar beams; so also had the inner court of the Temple of Yahweh and the vestibule of the Temple.

13 King Solomon sent for Hiram of Tyre; 14 he was the son of a widow of the tribe of Naphtali, but his father had been a Tyrian, a bronzeworker. He was a highly intelligent craftsman, skilled in all types of bronzework. He came to King Solomon and did all this work for him.

15 He cast the two bronze pillars; the height of one pillar was eighteen cubits, and a cord twelve cubits long gave the measurement of its girth; so also was the second pillar. 16 He made two capitals of cast bronze for the tops of the pillars; the height of one capital was five cubits, and the height of the other five cubits. 17 He made two sets of filigree to cover the moulding of the two capitals surmounting the pillars, one filigree for one capital and one filigree for the other. 18 He also made pomegranates: two rows of them round each filigree, 19b four hundred in all, 20 applied on the raised moulding behind the filigree; there were two hundred pomegranates round one capital and the same round the other capital. 19a The capitals surrounding the pillars were lily-shaped. 21 He erected the pillars in front of the portico of the Temple, he erected the right-hand pillar and named it Jachin; he erected the left-hand pillar and named it Boaz. 22 Thus, the work on the pillars was completed.

23 He made the Sea of cast metal, ten cubits from rim to

bits from brim to brim, and five cubits high. A line of thirty cubits would encircle it completely. 24 Under its brim were panels all around it, each of ten cubits, surrounding the sea; there were two rows of panels, cast when it was cast. 25 It stood on twelve oxen, three facing north, three facing west, three facing south, and three facing east; the sea was set on them. The hindquarters of each were toward the inside. 26 Its thickness was a handbreadth; its brim was made like the brim of a cup, like the flower of a lily; it held two thousand baths.¹

27 He also made the ten stands of bronze; each stand was four cubits long, four cubits wide, and three cubits high. 28 This was the construction of the stands: they had borders; the borders were within the frames; 29 on the borders that were set in the frames were lions, oxen, and cherubim. On the frames, both above and below the lions and oxen, there were wreaths of beveled work. 30 Each stand had four bronze wheels and axles of bronze; at the four corners were supports for a basin. The supports were cast with wreaths at the side of each. 31 Its opening was within the crown whose height was one cubit; its opening was round, as a pedestal is made; it was a cubit and a half wide. At its opening there were carvings; its borders were four-sided, not round. 32 The four wheels were underneath the borders; the axles of the wheels were in the stands; and the height of a wheel was a cubit and a half. 33 The wheels were made like a chariot wheel; their axles, their rims, their spokes, and their hubs were all cast. 34 There were four supports at the four corners of each stand; the supports were of one piece with the stands. 35 On the top of the stand there was a round band half a cubit high; on the top of the stand, its stays and its borders were of one piece with it. 36 On the surfaces of its stays and on its borders he carved cherubim, lions, and palm trees, where each had space, with wreaths all around. 37 In this way he made the ten stands; all of them were cast alike, with the same size and the same form.

38 He made ten basins of bronze; each basin held forty baths,¹ each basin measured four cubits; there was a basin for each of the ten stands. 39 He set five of the stands on the south side of the house, and five on the north side of the house; he set the sea on the southeast corner of the house.

40 Hiram also made the pots, the shovels, and the basins. So Hiram finished all the work that he did for King Solomon on the house of the LORD: 41 the two pillars, the two bowls of the capitals that were on the tops of the pillars, the two latticeworks to cover the two bowls of the capitals that were on the tops of the pillars; 42 the four hundred pomegranates for the two latticeworks, two rows of pomegranates for each latticework, to cover the two bowls of the capitals that were on the pillars; 43 the ten stands, the ten basins on the stands; 44 the one sea, and the twelve oxen underneath the sea.

45 The pots, the shovels, and the basins, all these vessels that Hiram made for King Solomon for the house of the LORD were of burnished bronze. 46 In the plain of the Jordan the king cast them, in the clay ground between Succoth and Zarethan. 47 Solomon left all the vessels unweighed, because there were so many of them; the weight of the bronze was not determined.

48 So Solomon made all the vessels that were in the house of the LORD: the golden altar, the golden table for the bread of the Presence, 49 the lampstands of pure gold, five on the south side and five on the north, in front of the inner

the diameter from rim to rim being ten cubits; it stood five cubits high, and it took a line thirty cubits long to go round it. 24 All round the Sea on the outside under its rim, completely surrounding the thirty cubits of its circumference, were two rows of gourds, cast in one piece with the Sea itself. 25 It was mounted on twelve oxen, three facing north, three west, three south, and three east, their hindquarters turned inwards; the Sea rested on top of them. 26 Its thickness was a hand's breadth; its rim was made like that of a cup, shaped like the calyx of a lily; it held two thousand bath.

27 Hiram also made the ten trolleys of bronze; each trolley was four cubits long, four wide, and three high. 28 This was the construction of the trolleys: they had panels set in frames; 29 on these panels were portrayed lions, oxen, and cherubim, and the same on the frames; above and below the lions, oxen, and cherubim were fillets of hammered work of spiral design. 30 Each trolley had four bronze wheels with bronze axles; it also had four flanges and handles beneath the laver, and these handles were of cast metal with a spiral design on their sides. 31 The opening for the basin was set within a crown which projected one cubit; the opening was round with a level edge, and it had decorations in relief. The panels of the trolleys were square, not round. 32 The four wheels were beneath the panels, and the wheel-forks were made in one piece with the trolleys; the height of each wheel was one and a half cubits. 33 The wheels were constructed like those of a chariot, their axles, hubs, spokes, and felloes being all of cast metal. 34 The four handles were at the four corners of each trolley, of one piece with the trolley. 35 At the top of the trolley there was a circular band half a cubit high; the struts and panels on the trolley were of one piece with it. 36 On the plates, that is on the panels, he carved cherubim, lions, and palm trees, wherever there was a blank space, with spiral work all round it. 37 This is how the ten trolleys were made; all of them were cast alike, having the same size and the same shape.

38 Hiram then made ten bronze basins, each holding forty bath and measuring four cubits; there was a basin for each of the ten trolleys. 39 He put five trolleys on the right side of the house and five on the left side; and he placed the Sea in the south-east corner of it.

40 Hiram made the pots, the shovels, and the tossing-bowls. With them he finished all the work which he had undertaken for King Solomon in the house of the LORD: 41 the two pillars; the two bowl-shaped capitals on the tops of the pillars; the two ornamental networks to cover the two bowl-shaped capitals on the tops of the pillars; 42 the four hundred pomegranates for the two networks, two rows of pomegranates for each network, to cover the bowl-shaped capitals on the two pillars; 43 the ten trolleys and the ten basins on the trolleys; 44 the one Sea and the twelve oxen which supported it; 45 the pots, the shovels, and the tossing-bowls—all these objects in the house of the LORD which Hiram made for King Solomon being of burnished bronze. 46 The king cast them in the foundry between Succoth and Zarethan in the plain of the Jordan.

47 Solomon put all these objects in their places; so great was the quantity of bronze used in their making that the weight of it was beyond all reckoning. 48 He made also all the furnishings for the house of the LORD: the golden altar and the golden table upon which was set the Bread of the Presence; 49 the lampstands of red gold, five on the right

7:24 **thirty:** *prob. rdg; Heb.* ten. 7:29 **and cherubim were fillets:** *prob. rdg; Heb. omits* and cherubim. 7:31 **level edge:** *prob. rdg; Heb. adds* one and a half cubits *(cp. verse 32).* 7:35 **on:** *prob. rdg; Heb. adds* the head of. 7:36 **the panels:** *prob. rdg; Heb. adds* its struts. 7:40–51 *Cp.* 2 *Chr.* 4:11—5:1. 7:40 **pots:** *so many MSS; others* basins. 7:42 **on the two:** *so Gk; Heb.* on the surface of.

¹A Heb measure of volume

and measured ten cubits across, five in height, and thirty in circumference. 24 Under the brim, gourds encircled it, ten to the cubit all the way around; the gourds were in two rows and were cast in one mold with the sea. 25 This rested on twelve oxen, three facing north, three facing west, three facing south, and three facing east, with their haunches all toward the center, where the sea was set upon them. 26 It was a handbreadth thick, and its brim resembled that of a cup, being lily-shaped. Its capacity was two thousand measures.

27 Ten stands were also made of bronze, each four cubits long, four wide, and three high. 28 When these stands were constructed, panels were set within the framework. 29 On the panels between the frames there were lions, oxen, and cherubim; and on the frames likewise, above and below the lions and oxen, there were wreaths in relief.

30 Each stand had four bronze wheels and bronze axles. ‡7.31: see below‡ 32 The four wheels were below the paneling, and the axletrees of the wheels and the stand were of one piece. Each wheel was a cubit and a half high. 33 The wheels were constructed like chariot wheels; their axles, fellies, spokes, and hubs were all cast.

The four legs of each stand had cast braces, which were under the basin; they had wreaths on each side. 34 These four braces, extending to the corners of each stand, were of one piece with the stand.

35 On top of the stand there was a raised collar half a cubit high, with supports and panels which were of one piece with the top of the stand. 31 This was surmounted by a crown one cubit high within which was a rounded opening to provide a receptacle a cubit and a half in depth. There was carved work at the opening, on panels that were angular, not curved. 36 On the surfaces of the supports and on the panels, wherever there was a clear space, cherubim, lions, and palm trees were carved, as well as wreaths all around. 37 This was how the ten stands were made, all of the same casting, the same size, the same shape. 38 Ten bronze basins were then made, each four cubits in diameter with a capacity of forty measures, one basin for the top of each of the ten stands. 39 The stands were placed, five on the south side of the temple and five on the north. The sea was placed off to the southeast from the south side of the temple.

40 When Hiram made the pots, shovels, and bowls, he therewith completed all his work for King Solomon in the temple of the LORD: 41 two columns, two nodes for the capitals on top of the columns, two pieces of network covering the nodes for the capitals on top of the columns, 42 four hundred pomegranates in double rows on both pieces of network that covered the two nodes of the capitals where they met the columns, 43 ten stands, ten basins on the stands, 44 one sea, twelve oxen supporting the sea, 45 pots, shovels, and bowls. All these articles which Hiram made for King Solomon in the temple of the LORD were of burnished bronze. 46 The king had them cast in the neighborhood of the Jordan, in the clayey ground between Succoth and Zarethan. 47 Solomon did not weigh all the articles because they were so numerous; the weight of the bronze, therefore, was not determined.

48 Solomon had all the articles made for the interior of the temple of the LORD: the golden altar; the golden table on which the showbread lay; 49 the lampstands of pure gold,

rim, circular in shape and five cubits high; a cord thirty cubits long gave the measurement of its girth. 24 Under its rim and completely encircling it were gourds surrounding the Sea; over a length of thirty cubits the gourds were in two rows, of one and the same casting with the rest. 25 It rested on twelve oxen, three facing north, three facing west, three facing south, three facing east; on these, their hindquarters all turned inwards, stood the Sea. 26 It was a hand's breadth in thickness, and its rim was shaped like the rim of a cup, lily-shaped. It could hold two thousand measures.

27 He made the ten bronze stands; each stand was four cubits long, four cubits wide, and three high. 28 They were designed as follows; they had an undercarriage and crosspieces to the undercarriage. 29 On the crosspieces of the undercarriage were lions and bulls and winged creatures, and on top of the undercarriage was a support; under the lions and oxen there were scrolls in the style of . . . 30 Each stand had four bronze wheels with bronze axles; its four feet had shoulderings under the basin, and the shoulderings were cast . . . 31 Its mouth measured one and a half cubits from where the shoulderings met to the top; its mouth was round like a stand for a vessel, and on the mouth there were engravings too; the crosspieces, however, were rectangular and not round. 32 The four wheels were under the crosspieces. The axles of the wheels were inside the stands; the height of the wheels was one and a half cubits. 33 The wheels were designed like chariot wheels: their axles, felloes, spokes and naves had all been cast. 34 There were four shoulderings at the four corners of each stand: the stand and the shoulderings were all of a piece. 35 At the top of the stand there was a support, circular in shape and half a cubit high; and on top of the stand there were lugs. The crosspieces were of a piece with the stand. 36 On the bands he engraved winged creatures and lions and palm leaves . . . and scrolls right round. 37 He made the ten stands like this: the same casting and the same measurements for all.

38 He made ten bronze basins; each basin held forty measures and each basin measured four cubits, one basin to each of the ten stands. 39 He arranged the stands, five on the right-hand side of the Temple, five on the left-hand side of the Temple; the Sea he placed on the right-hand side of the Temple, to the south east.

40 Hiram made the ash containers, the scoops and the sprinkling bowls. He finished all the work that he did for King Solomon on the Temple of Yahweh:

41 Two pillars; the two mouldings of the capitals surrounding the pillars; the two sets of filigree to cover the two mouldings of the capitals surmounting the pillars; 42 the four hundred pomegranates for the two sets of filigree — two rows of pomegranates for each set of filigree;

43 the ten stands and the ten basins on the stands;

44 the one Sea and the twelve oxen beneath the Sea;

45 the ash containers, the scoops, and sprinkling bowls.

All these objects made by Hiram for King Solomon for the Temple of Yahweh were of burnished bronze. 46 He made them by the process of sand casting, in the plain of the Jordan between Succoth and Zarethan. 47 There were so many of them, that the weight of the bronze was never calculated.

48 Solomon made all the objects designed for the Temple of Yahweh: the golden altar and the gold table for the loaves of permanent offering; 49 the lamp-stands, five on the right

sanctuary; the flowers, the lamps, and the tongs, of gold; 50 the cups, snuffers, basins, dishes for incense, and fire-pans, of pure gold; the sockets for the doors of the inner-most part of the house, the most holy place, and for the doors of the nave of the temple, of gold.

51 Thus all the work that King Solomon did on the house of the LORD was finished. Solomon brought in the things that his father David had dedicated, the silver, the gold, and the vessels, and stored them in the treasuries of the house of the LORD.

8 Then Solomon assembled the elders of Israel and all the heads of the tribes, the leaders of the ancestral houses of the Israelites, before King Solomon in Jerusalem, to bring up the ark of the covenant of the LORD out of the city of David, which is Zion. 2 All the people of Israel assembled to King Solomon at the festival in the month Ethanim, which is the seventh month. 3 And all the elders of Israel came, and the priests carried the ark. 4 So they brought up the ark of the LORD, the tent of meeting, and all the holy vessels that were in the tent; the priests and the Levites brought them up. 5 King Solomon and all the con-gregation of Israel, who had assembled before him, were with him before the ark, sacrificing so many sheep and oxen that they could not be counted or numbered. 6 Then the priests brought the ark of the covenant of the LORD to its place, in the inner sanctuary of the house, in the most holy place, underneath the wings of the cherubim. 7 For the cher-ubim spread out their wings over the place of the ark, so that the cherubim made a covering above the ark and its poles. 8 The poles were so long that the ends of the poles were seen from the holy place in front of the inner sanctuary; but they could not be seen from outside; they are there to this day. 9 There was nothing in the ark except the two tablets of stone that Moses had placed there at Horeb, where the LORD made a covenant with the Israelites, when they came out of the land of Egypt. 10 And when the priests came out of the holy place, a cloud filled the house of the LORD, 11 so that the priests could not stand to minister because of the cloud; for the glory of the LORD filled the house of the LORD.

12 Then Solomon said,
   "The LORD has said that he would dwell in thick
      darkness.
13 I have built you an exalted house,
      a place for you to dwell in forever."

14 Then the king turned around and blessed all the as-sembly of Israel, while all the assembly of Israel stood. 15 He said, "Blessed be the LORD, the God of Israel, who with his hand has fulfilled what he promised with his mouth to my father David, saying, 16 'Since the day that I brought my people Israel out of Egypt, I have not chosen a city from any of the tribes of Israel in which to build a house, that my name might be there; but I chose David to be over my people Israel.' 17 My father David had it in mind to build a house for the name of the LORD, the God of Israel. 18 But the LORD said to my father David, 'You did well to consider building a house for my name; 19 nevertheless you shall not build the house, but your son who shall be born to you shall build the house for my name.' 20 Now the LORD has upheld the promise that he made; for I have risen in the place of my father David; I sit on the throne of Israel, as the LORD promised, and have built the house for the name of the LORD, the God of Israel. 21 There I have provided a place for the ark, in which is the covenant of the LORD that he made with our ancestors when he brought them out of the land of Egypt."

22 Then Solomon stood before the altar of the LORD in the presence of all the assembly of Israel, and spread out his

side and five on the left side of the inner shrine; the flowers, lamps, and tongs of gold; 50 the cups, snuffers, tossing-bowls, saucers, and firepans of red gold; and the panels for the doors of the inner sanctuary, the Most Holy Place, and for the doors of the house, of gold.

51 When all the work which King Solomon did for the house of the LORD was completed, he brought in the sacred treasures of his father David, the silver, the gold, and the vessels, and deposited them in the treasuries of the house of the LORD.

8 THEN Solomon summoned to him at Jerusalem the elders of Israel, all the heads of the tribes who were chiefs of families in Israel, in order to bring up the Ark of the Covenant of the LORD from the City of David, which is called Zion. 2 All the men of Israel assembled in King Solo-mon's presence at the pilgrim-feast in the month Ethanim, the seventh month. 3 When the elders of Israel had all ar-rived, the priests lifted the Ark of the LORD 4 and carried it up; the Tent of Meeting and all the sacred furnishings of the Tent were carried by the priests and the Levites. 5 King Solomon and the whole congregation of Israel assembled with him before the Ark sacrificed sheep and oxen in num-bers past counting or reckoning.

6 The priests brought in the Ark of the Covenant of the LORD to its place in the inner shrine of the house, the Most Holy Place, beneath the wings of the cherubim. 7 The cheru-bim, whose wings were spread over the place of the Ark, formed a canopy above the Ark and its poles. 8 The poles projected, and their ends were visible from the Holy Place immediately in front of the inner shrine, but from nowhere else outside; they are there to this day. 9 There was nothing inside the Ark but the two stone tablets which Moses had deposited there at Horeb, when the LORD made the covenant with the Israelites after they left Egypt.

10 The priests came out of the Holy Place, since the cloud was filling the house of the LORD, 11 and they could not continue to minister because of it, for the glory of the LORD filled his house. 12 Then Solomon said:

   'The LORD has caused his sun to shine in the
      heavens,
   but he has said he would dwell in thick darkness.
13 I have built you a lofty house,
   a dwelling-place for you to occupy for ever.'

14 While the whole assembly of Israelites stood, the king turned and blessed them: 15 'Blessed be the LORD the God of Israel who spoke directly to my father David and has himself fulfilled his promise. For he said, 16 "From the day when I brought my people Israel out of Egypt, I chose no city out of all the tribes of Israel where I should build a house for my name to be, but I chose Jerusalem where my name should be, and David to be over my people Israel." 17 'My father David had it in mind to build a house for the name of the LORD the God of Israel, 18 but the LORD said to him, "You purposed to build a house for my name, and your purpose was good. 19 Nevertheless, you are not to build it; but the son who is to be born to you, he is to build the house for my name." 20 The LORD has now fulfilled his promise: I have succeeded my father David and taken his place on the throne of Israel, as the LORD promised; and I have built the house for the name of the LORD the God of Israel. 21 I have assigned a place in it for the Ark containing the covenant of the LORD, which he made with our forefathers when he brought them out of Egypt.'

22 Standing in front of the altar of the LORD in the pres-ence of the whole assembly of Israel, Solomon spread out

7:50 **the house:** prob. rdg; Heb. adds for the temple.
8:1–9 Cp. 2 Chr. 5:2–10.   8:12–50 Cp. 2 Chr. 6:1–39.
8:12 **has caused . . . but he:** prob. rdg, cp. Gk; Heb. omits.
8:16 **Jerusalem . . . and:** so Gk; Heb. omits.

NEW AMERICAN BIBLE

five to the right and five to the left before the sanctuary, with their flowers, lamps, and tongs of gold; 50 basins, snuffers, bowls, cups, and fire pans of pure gold; and hinges of gold for the doors of the inner room, or holy of holies, and for the doors of the outer room, the nave. 51 When all the work undertaken by King Solomon in the temple of the LORD was completed, he brought in the dedicated offerings of his father David, putting the silver, gold, and other articles in the treasuries of the temple of the LORD.

8 At the order of Solomon, the elders of Israel and all the leaders of the tribes, the princes in the ancestral houses of the Israelites, came to King Solomon in Jerusalem, to bring up the ark of the LORD's covenant from the City of David [which is Zion]. 2 All the men of Israel assembled before King Solomon during the festival in the month of Ethanim (the seventh month). 3 When all the elders of Israel had arrived, the priests took up the ark; 4 they carried the ark of the LORD and the meeting tent with all the sacred vessels that were in the tent. (The priests and Levites carried them.) 5 King Solomon and the entire community of Israel present for the occasion sacrificed before the ark sheep and oxen too many to number or count. 6 The priests brought the ark of the covenant of the LORD to its place beneath the wings of the cherubim in the sanctuary, the holy of holies of the temple. 7 The cherubim had their wings spread out over the place of the ark, sheltering the ark and its poles from above. 8 The poles were so long that their ends could be seen from that part of the holy place adjoining the sanctuary; however, they could not be seen beyond. (They have remained there to this day.) 9 There was nothing in the ark but the two stone tablets which Moses had put there at Horeb, when the LORD made a covenant with the Israelites at their departure from the land of Egypt.

10 When the priests left the holy place, the cloud filled the temple of the LORD 11 so that the priests could no longer minister because of the cloud, since the LORD's glory had filled the temple of the LORD. 12 Then Solomon said, "The LORD intends to dwell in the dark cloud; 13 I have truly built you a princely house, a dwelling where you may abide forever."

14 The king turned and greeted the whole community of Israel as they stood. 15 He said to them: "Blessed be the LORD, the God of Israel, who with his own mouth made a promise to my father David and by his hand has brought it to fulfillment. It was he who said, 16 'Since the day I brought my people Israel out of Egypt, I have not chosen a city out of any tribe of Israel for the building of a temple to my honor; but I choose David to rule my people Israel.' 17 When my father David wished to build a temple to the honor of the LORD, the God of Israel, 18 the Lord said to him, 'In wishing to build a temple to my honor, you do well. 19 It will not be you, however, who will build the temple; but the son who will spring from you, he shall build the temple to my honor.' 20 And now the LORD has fulfilled the promise that he made: I have succeeded my father David and sit on the throne of Israel, as the LORD foretold, and I have built this temple to honor the LORD, the God of Israel. 21 I have provided in it a place for the ark in which is the covenant of the LORD, which he made with our fathers when he brought them out of the land of Egypt."

22 Solomon stood before the altar of the LORD in the presence of the whole community of Israel, and stretching forth

NEW JERUSALEM BIBLE

and five on the left in front of the Debir, of pure gold; the floral work, the lamps, the tongs, of gold; 50 the basins, the snuffers, the sprinkling bowls, the incense ladles and the pans, of real gold; the door panels — for the inner shrine — that is, the Holy of Holies — and for the Hekal, of gold. 51 Thus all the work done by King Solomon for the Temple of Yahweh was completed, and Solomon brought in the gifts which his father David had consecrated; and he had the silver, the gold and the utensils put into the treasuries of the Temple of Yahweh.

8 Solomon then summoned the elders of Israel to Jerusalem to bring the ark of the covenant of Yahweh up from the City of David, that is, Zion. 2 All the men of Israel assembled round King Solomon in the month of Ethanim, at the time of the feast (that is, the seventh month). 3 When all the elders of Israel had arrived, the priests took up the ark 4 and the Tent of Meeting and all the sacred utensils which were in the Tent. 5 King Solomon and all Israel, present with him before the ark, sacrificed countless, innumerable sheep and oxen. 6 The priests brought the ark of the covenant of Yahweh to its place, in the Debir of the Temple, that is, in the Holy of Holies, under the wings of the winged creatures 7 for the winged creatures spread their wings over the place where the ark stood, forming a canopy over the ark and its shafts. 8 These were so long, however, that the ends of the shafts could be seen from the Holy Place in front of the Debir, though they could not be seen from outside. They are still there today. 9 There was nothing in the ark except the two stone tablets which Moses had placed in it at Horeb, the tablets of the covenant which Yahweh made with the Israelites when they came out of Egypt.

10 Now when the priests came out of the Holy Place, the cloud filled the Temple of Yahweh, 11 and because of the cloud the priests could not stay and perform their duties. For the glory of Yahweh filled the Temple of Yahweh.

12 Then Solomon said:

Yahweh has chosen to dwell in thick cloud.
13 I have built you a princely dwelling,
a residence for you for ever.

14 The king then turned round and blessed the whole assembly of Israel, while the whole assembly of Israel stood. 15 He said, 'Blessed be Yahweh, God of Israel, who has carried out by his hand what he promised with his mouth to my father David, when he said, 16 "From the day I brought my people Israel out of Egypt I chose no city, in any of the tribes of Israel, to have a temple built where my name should be; but I did choose David to rule my people Israel." 17 My father David had set his heart on building a temple for the name of Yahweh, God of Israel, 18 but Yahweh said to my father David, "You have set your heart on building a temple for my name, and in this you have done well; 19 and yet, you are not the man to build the temple; but your son, yet to be born to you, will be the one to build the temple for my name." 20 Yahweh has kept the promise which he made: I have succeeded my father David and am seated on the throne of Israel, as Yahweh promised; I have built the temple for the name of Yahweh, God of Israel, 21 and in it I have made a place for the ark containing the covenant of Yahweh which he made with our ancestors when he brought them out of Egypt.'

22 Then, in the presence of the whole assembly of Israel, Solomon stood facing the altar of Yahweh and, stretching

|

hands to heaven. 23 He said, "O LORD, God of Israel, there is no God like you in heaven above or on earth beneath, keeping covenant and steadfast love for your servants who walk before you with all their heart, 24 the covenant that you kept for your servant my father David as you declared to him; you promised with your mouth and have this day fulfilled with your hand. 25 Therefore, O LORD, God of Israel, keep for your servant my father David that which you promised him, saying, 'There shall never fail you a successor before me to sit on the throne of Israel, if only your children look to their way, to walk before me as you have walked before me.' 26 Therefore, O God of Israel, let your word be confirmed, which you promised to your servant my father David.

27 "But will God indeed dwell on the earth? Even heaven and the highest heaven cannot contain you, much less this house that I have built! 28 Regard your servant's prayer and his plea, O LORD my God, heeding the cry and the prayer that your servant prays to you today; 29 that your eyes may be open night and day toward this house, the place of which you said, 'My name shall be there,' that you may heed the prayer that your servant prays toward this place. 30 Hear the plea of your servant and of your people Israel when they pray toward this place; O hear in heaven your dwelling place; heed and forgive.

31 "If someone sins against a neighbor and is given an oath to swear, and comes and swears before your altar in this house, 32 then hear in heaven, and act, and judge your servants, condemning the guilty by bringing their conduct on their own head, and vindicating the righteous by rewarding them according to their righteousness.

33 "When your people Israel, having sinned against you, are defeated before an enemy but turn again to you, confess your name, pray and plead with you in this house, 34 then hear in heaven, forgive the sin of your people Israel, and bring them again to the land that you gave to their ancestors.

35 "When heaven is shut up and there is no rain because they have sinned against you, and then they pray toward this place, confess your name, and turn from their sin, because you punish[m] them, 36 then hear in heaven, and forgive the sin of your servants, your people Israel, when you teach them the good way in which they should walk; and grant rain on your land, which you have given to your people as an inheritance.

37 "If there is famine in the land, if there is plague, blight, mildew, locust, or caterpillar; if their enemy besieges them in any[n] of their cities; whatever plague, whatever sickness there is; 38 whatever prayer, whatever plea there is from any individual or from all your people Israel, all knowing the afflictions of their own hearts so that they stretch out their hands toward this house; 39 then hear in heaven your dwelling place, forgive, act, and render to all whose hearts you know — according to all their ways, for only you know what is in every human heart — 40 so that they may fear you all the days that they live in the land that you gave to our ancestors.

41 "Likewise when a foreigner, who is not of your people Israel, comes from a distant land because of your name 42 — for they shall hear of your great name, your mighty hand, and your outstretched arm — when a foreigner comes and prays toward this house, 43 then hear in heaven your dwelling place, and do according to all that the foreigner calls to you, so that all the peoples of the earth may know your name and fear you, as do your people Israel, and so that they may know that your name has been invoked on this house that I have built.

his hands towards heaven 23 and said, 'LORD God of Israel, there is no God like you in heaven above or on earth beneath, keeping covenant with your servants and showing them constant love while they continue faithful to you with all their hearts. 24 You have kept your promise to your servant David my father; by your deeds this day you have fulfilled what you said to him in words. 25 Now, therefore, LORD God of Israel, keep this promise of yours to your servant David my father, when you said: "You will never want for a man appointed by me to sit on the throne of Israel, if only your sons look to their ways and walk before me as you have done." 26 God of Israel, let the promise which you made to your servant David my father be confirmed.

27 'But can God indeed dwell on earth? Heaven itself, the highest heaven, cannot contain you; how much less this house that I have built! 28 Yet attend, LORD my God, to the prayer and the supplication of your servant; listen to the cry and the prayer which your servant makes before you this day, 29 that your eyes may ever be on this house night and day, this place of which you said, "My name will be there." Hear your servant when he prays towards this place. 30 Hear the supplication of your servant and your people Israel when they pray towards this place. Hear in heaven your dwelling and, when you hear, forgive.

31 'Should anyone wrong a neighbour and be adjured to take an oath, and come to take the oath before your altar in this house, 32 then hear in heaven and take action: be your servants' judge, condemning the guilty person and bringing his deeds on his own head, acquitting the innocent and rewarding him as his innocence may deserve.

33 'Should your people Israel be defeated by an enemy because they have sinned against you, and then turn back to you, confessing your name and making their prayer and supplication to you in this house, 34 hear in heaven; forgive the sin of your people Israel and restore them to the land which you gave to their forefathers.

35 'Should the heavens be shut up and there be no rain, because your servant and your people Israel have sinned against you, and they then pray towards this place, confessing your name and forsaking their sin when they feel your punishment, 36 hear in heaven and forgive their sin; so teach them the good way which they are to follow, and grant rain on your land which you have given to your people as their own possession.

37 'Should there be famine in the land, or pestilence, or blight either black or red, or locusts developing or fully grown, or should their enemies besiege them in any of their cities, or plague or sickness befall them, 38 then hear the prayer or supplication of everyone among your people Israel, as each, prompted by the remorse of his own heart, spreads out his hands towards this house: 39 hear it in heaven your dwelling-place, forgive, and take action. As you know a person's heart, reward him according to his deeds, for you alone know the hearts of all; 40 and so they will fear you throughout their lives in the land you gave to our forefathers.

41 'The foreigner too, anyone who does not belong to your people Israel, but has come from a distant land because of your fame 42 (for your great fame and your strong hand and outstretched arm will be widely known), when such a one comes and prays towards this house, 43 hear in heaven your dwelling-place and respond to the call which the foreigner makes to you, so that like your people Israel all the peoples of the earth may know your fame and fear you, and learn that this house which I have built bears your name.

---

[m] Or when you answer   [n] Gk Syr: Heb in the land

8:35 **servant:** so Gk; Heb. servants.   8:37 **in any:** so Gk; Heb. in the land.

his hands toward heaven, 23 he said, "LORD, God of Israel, there is no God like you in heaven above or on earth below; you keep your covenant of kindness with your servants who are faithful to you with their whole heart. 24 You have kept the promise you made to my father David, your servant. You who spoke that promise, have this day, by your own power, brought it to fulfillment. 25 Now, therefore, LORD, God of Israel, keep the further promise you made to my father David, your servant, saying, 'You shall always have someone from your line to sit before me on the throne of Israel, provided only that your descendants look to their conduct so that they live in my presence, as you have lived in my presence.' 26 Now, LORD, God of Israel, may this promise which you made to my father David, your servant, be confirmed.

27 "Can it indeed be that God dwells among men on earth? If the heavens and the highest heavens cannot contain you, how much less this temple which I have built! 28 Look kindly on the prayer and petition of your servant, O LORD, my God, and listen to the cry of supplication which I, your servant, utter before you this day. 29 May your eyes watch night and day over this temple, the place where you have decreed you shall be honored; may you heed the prayer which I, your servant, offer in this place. 30 Listen to the petitions of your servant and of your people Israel which they offer in this place. Listen from your heavenly dwelling and grant pardon.

31 "If a man sins against his neighbor and is required to take an oath sanctioned by a curse, when he comes and takes the oath before your altar in this temple, 32 listen in heaven; take action and pass judgment on your servants. Condemn the wicked and punish him for his conduct, but acquit the just and establish his innocence.

33 "If your people Israel sin against you and are defeated by an enemy, and if then they return to you, praise your name, pray to you, and entreat you in this temple, 34 listen in heaven and forgive the sin of your people Israel, and bring them back to the land you gave their fathers.

35 "If the sky is closed, so that there is no rain, because they have sinned against you and you afflict them, and if then they repent of their sin, and pray, and praise your name in this place, 36 listen in heaven and forgive the sin of your servant and of your people Israel, teaching them the right way to live and sending rain upon this land of yours which you have given to your people as their heritage.

37 "If there is famine in the land or pestilence; or if blight comes, or mildew, or a locust swarm, or devouring insects; if an enemy of your people besieges them in one of their cities; whatever plague or sickness there may be, 38 if then any one [of your entire people Israel] has remorse of conscience and offers some prayer or petition, stretching out his hands toward this temple, 39 listen from your heavenly dwelling place and forgive. You who alone know the hearts of all men, render to each one of them according to his conduct; knowing their hearts, so treat them 40 that they may fear you as long as they live on the land you gave our fathers.

41 "To the foreigner, likewise, who is not of your people Israel, but comes from a distant land to honor you 42 (since men will learn of your great name and your mighty hand and your outstretched arm), when he comes and prays toward this temple, 43 listen from your heavenly dwelling. Do all that the foreigner asks of you, that all the peoples of the earth may know your name, may fear you as do your people Israel, and may acknowledge that this temple which I have built is dedicated to your honor.

out his hands towards heaven, 23 said, 'Yahweh, God of Israel, there is no god like you in heaven above or on earth beneath, as loyal to the covenant and faithful in love to your servants as long as they walk wholeheartedly in your way. 24 You have kept the promise you made to your servant, my father David, as you promised him you would. Today you have carried it out by your power. 25 And now, Yahweh, God of Israel, keep the promise which you made to your servant David when you said, "You will never lack for a man to sit before me on the throne of Israel, provided that your sons are careful how they behave, walking before me as you yourself have done." 26 So now, God of Israel, let the words come true which you spoke to your servant, my father David. 27 Yet will God really live with human beings on earth? Why, the heavens, the highest of the heavens, cannot contain you. How much less this temple built by me! 28 Even so, listen favourably to the prayer and entreaty of your servant, Yahweh my God; listen to the cry and to the prayer which your servant makes to you today: 29 day and night may your eyes watch over this temple, over this place of which you have said, "My name will be there." Listen to the prayer which your servant offers in this place.

30 'Listen to the entreaty of your servant and of your people Israel; whenever they pray in this place, listen from the place where you reside in heaven; and when you hear, forgive.

31 'If someone has wronged his neighbour and a curse is laid on him to make him swear an oath here before your altar in this Temple, 32 then listen from the place where you reside in heaven and do justice between your servants: condemning the guilty one by making him suffer for his conduct, and acquitting the upright by rewarding him as his uprightness deserves.

33 'When your people Israel are defeated by the enemy because they have sinned against you, but then return to you and acknowledge your name, and pray and seek your favours in this Temple, 34 then listen from the place where you reside in heaven; forgive the sin of your people Israel, and bring them back to the country which you gave to their ancestors.

35 'When the heavens are shut and there is no rain because they have sinned against you, if they pray in this place and praise your name and, having been humbled by you, desist from their sin, 36 then listen from the place where you reside in heaven and forgive the sin of your servant and your people Israel — for you are constantly showing them the good way which they must follow — and send rain on your country, which you have given to your people as their heritage.

37 'Should there be famine in the country, or pestilence, wind-blast or mildew, locust or caterpillar; should their enemy lay siege to one of their gates; should there be any plague or any disease: 38 whatever be the prayer or entreaty of any individual aware of a particular affliction: when that person stretches out the hands towards this Temple, 39 then listen from heaven where you reside; forgive and, since you know what is in the heart, deal with each as their conduct deserves — for you alone know what is in every human heart — 40 so that they may reverence you throughout their lives in the country which you gave to our ancestors.

41 'Even the foreigner, not belonging to your people Israel but coming from a distant country, attracted by your name — 42 for they too will hear of your name, of your mighty hand and outstretched arm — if a foreigner comes and prays in this Temple, 43 listen from heaven where you reside, and grant all that the foreigner asks of you, so that all the peoples of the earth may acknowledge your name and, like your people Israel, revere you and know that this Temple, which I have built, bears your name.

44 "If your people go out to battle against their enemy, by whatever way you shall send them, and they pray to the LORD toward the city that you have chosen and the house that I have built for your name, 45 then hear in heaven their prayer and their plea, and maintain their cause.

46 "If they sin against you—for there is no one who does not sin—and you are angry with them and give them to an enemy, so that they are carried away captive to the land of the enemy, far off or near; 47 yet if they come to their senses in the land to which they have been taken captive, and repent, and plead with you in the land of their captors, saying, 'We have sinned, and have done wrong; we have acted wickedly'; 48 if they repent with all their heart and soul in the land of their enemies, who took them captive, and pray to you toward their land, which you gave to their ancestors, the city that you have chosen, and the house that I have built for your name; 49 then hear in heaven your dwelling place their prayer and their plea, maintain their cause 50 and forgive your people who have sinned against you, and all their transgressions that they have committed against you; and grant them compassion in the sight of their captors, so that they may have compassion on them 51 (for they are your people and heritage, which you brought out of Egypt, from the midst of the iron-smelter). 52 Let your eyes be open to the plea of your servant, and to the plea of your people Israel, listening to them whenever they call to you. 53 For you have separated them from among all the peoples of the earth, to be your heritage, just as you promised through Moses, your servant, when you brought our ancestors out of Egypt, O Lord GOD."

54 Now when Solomon finished offering all this prayer and this plea to the LORD, he arose from facing the altar of the LORD, where he had knelt with hands outstretched toward heaven; 55 he stood and blessed all the assembly of Israel with a loud voice:

56 "Blessed be the LORD, who has given rest to his people Israel according to all that he promised; not one word has failed of all his good promise, which he spoke through his servant Moses. 57 The LORD our God be with us, as he was with our ancestors; may he not leave us or abandon us, 58 but incline our hearts to him, to walk in all his ways, and to keep his commandments, his statutes, and his ordinances, which he commanded our ancestors. 59 Let these words of mine, with which I pleaded before the LORD, be near to the LORD our God day and night, and may he maintain the cause of his servant and the cause of his people Israel, as each day requires; 60 so that all the peoples of the earth may know that the LORD is God; there is no other. 61 Therefore devote yourselves completely to the LORD our God, walking in his statutes and keeping his commandments, as at this day."

62 Then the king, and all Israel with him, offered sacrifice before the LORD. 63 Solomon offered as sacrifices of well-being to the LORD twenty-two thousand oxen and one hundred twenty thousand sheep. So the king and all the people of Israel dedicated the house of the LORD. 64 The same day the king consecrated the middle of the court that was in front of the house of the LORD; for there he offered the burnt offerings and the grain offerings and the fat pieces of the sacrifices of well-being, because the bronze altar that was before the LORD was too small to receive the burnt offerings and the grain offerings and the fat pieces of the sacrifices of well-being.

65 So Solomon held the festival at that time, and all Israel with him—a great assembly, people from Lebo-hamath to the Wadi of Egypt—before the LORD our God, seven days.o 66 On the eighth day he sent the people away;

o Compare Gk: Heb seven days and seven days, fourteen days

44 'When your people go to war against an enemy, wherever you send them, and when they pray to the LORD, turning towards this city which you have chosen and towards this house which I have built for your name, 45 then hear in heaven their prayer and supplication, and maintain their cause.

46 'Should they sin against you (and who is free from sin?) and should you in your anger give them over to an enemy who carries them captive to his own land, far or near, 47 and should they then in the land of their captivity have a change of heart and make supplication to you there and say, "We have sinned and acted perversely and wickedly," 48 and turn back to you wholeheartedly in the land of their enemies who took them captive, and pray to you, turning towards their land which you gave to their forefathers and towards this city which you chose and this house which I have built for your name, 49 then in heaven your dwelling-place hear their prayer and supplication, and maintain their cause. 50 Forgive your people their sins and transgressions against you; put pity for them in their captors' hearts. 51 For they are your possession, your people whom you brought out of Egypt, from the smelting furnace. 52 Let your eyes be ever open to the entreaty of your servant and of your people Israel, and hear whenever they call to you. 53 You yourself have singled them out from all the peoples of the earth to be your possession; so, Lord GOD, you promised through your servant Moses when you brought our forefathers from Egypt.'

54 As Solomon finished all this prayer and supplication to the LORD, he rose from before the altar of the LORD, where he had been kneeling with his hands spread out to heaven; 55 he stood up and in a loud voice blessed the whole assembly of Israel: 56 'Blessed be the LORD who has given his people Israel rest, as he promised: not one of the promises he made through his servant Moses has failed. 57 May the LORD our God be with us as he was with our forefathers; may he never leave us or forsake us. 58 May he turn our hearts towards him, so that we may conform to all his ways, observing his commandments, statutes, and judgements, as he commanded our forefathers. 59 And may the words of my supplication to the LORD be with the LORD our God day and night, that, as the need arises day by day, he may maintain the cause of his servant and of his people Israel. 60 So all the peoples of the earth will know that the LORD is God, he and no other, 61 and you will be perfect in loyalty to the LORD our God as you are this day, conforming to his statutes and observing his commandments.'

62 The king and all Israel with him offered sacrifices before the LORD; 63 Solomon offered as shared-offerings to the LORD twenty-two thousand oxen and a hundred and twenty thousand sheep. Thus the king and the Israelites dedicated the house of the LORD. 64 On that day also the king consecrated the centre of the court which lay in front of the house of the LORD; there he offered the whole-offering, the grain-offering, and the fat portions of the shared-offerings, because the bronze altar which stood before the LORD was too small to accommodate the whole-offering, the grain-offering, and the fat portions of the shared-offerings.

65 So Solomon and with him all Israel, a great assembly from Lebo-hamath to the wadi of Egypt, celebrated the pilgrim-feast at that time before the LORD our God for seven days. 66 On the eighth day he dismissed the people; and they

8:64–66 Cp. 2 Chr. 7:7–10. 8:64 in front: or to the east.
8:65 for seven days: so Gk; Heb. adds and seven days, fourteen days.

44 "Whatever the direction in which you may send your people forth to war against their enemies, if they pray to you, O LORD, toward the city you have chosen and the temple I have built in your honor, 45 listen in heaven to their prayer and petition, and defend their cause.

46 "When they sin against you (for there is no man who does not sin), and in your anger against them you deliver them to the enemy, so that their captors deport them to a hostile land, far or near, 47 may they repent in the land of their captivity and be converted. If then they entreat you in the land of their captors and say, 'We have sinned and done wrong; we have been wicked'; 48 if with their whole heart and soul they turn back to you in the land of the enemies who took them captive, pray to you toward the land you gave their fathers, the city you have chosen, and the temple I have built in your honor, 49 listen from your heavenly dwelling, 50 Forgive your people their sins and all the offenses they have committed against you, and grant them mercy before their captors, so that these will be merciful to them. 51 For they are your people and your inheritance, whom you brought out of Egypt, from the midst of an iron furnace.

52 "Thus may your eyes be open to the petition of your servant and to the petition of your people Israel. Hear them whenever they call upon you, 53 because you have set them apart among all the peoples of the earth for your inheritance, as you declared through your servant Moses when you brought our fathers out of Egypt, O Lord GOD."

54 When Solomon finished offering this entire prayer of petition to the LORD, he rose from before the altar of the LORD, where he had been kneeling with his hands outstretched toward heaven. 55 He stood and blessed the whole community of Israel, saying in a loud voice: 56 "Blessed be the LORD who has given rest to his people Israel, just as he promised. Not a single word has gone unfulfilled of the entire generous promise he made through his servant Moses. 57 May the LORD, our God, be with us as he was with our fathers and may he not forsake us nor cast us off. 58 May he draw our hearts to himself, that we may follow him in everything and keep the commands, statutes, and ordinances which he enjoined on our fathers. 59 May this prayer I have offered to the LORD, our God, be present to him day and night, that he may uphold the cause of his servant and of his people Israel as each day requires, 60 that all the peoples of the earth may know the LORD is God and there is no other. 61 You must be wholly devoted to the LORD, our God, observing his statutes and keeping his commandments, as on this day."

62 The king and all Israel with him offered sacrifices before the LORD. 63 Solomon offered as peace offerings to the LORD twenty-two thousand oxen and one hundred twenty thousand sheep. Thus the king and all the Israelites dedicated the temple of the LORD. 64 On that day the king consecrated the middle of the court facing the temple of the LORD; he offered there the holocausts, the cereal offerings, and the fat of the peace offerings, because the bronze altar before the LORD was too small to hold these offerings.

65 On this occasion Solomon and all the Israelites, who had assembled in large numbers from Labo of Hamath to the wadi of Egypt, celebrated the festival before the LORD, our God, for seven days. 66 On the eighth day he dismissed

44 'If your people go out to war against the enemy, on whatever missions you send them, and they pray to Yahweh, turning towards the city which you have chosen and towards the Temple which I have built for your name, 45 then listen from heaven to their prayer and their entreaty, and uphold their cause.

46 'When they sin against you — for there is no one who does not sin — and you are angry with them and abandon them to the enemy, and their captors carry them off to a hostile country, be it far away or near, 47 if they come to their senses in the country to which they have been taken as captives and repent and entreat you in the country of their captors, saying, "We have sinned, we have acted perversely and wickedly," 48 and turn back to you with all their heart and soul in the country of the enemies who have taken them captive, and pray to you, turning towards the country which you gave to their ancestors, towards the city which you have chosen and towards the Temple which I have built for your name, 49 listen to their prayer and their entreaty from the place where you reside in heaven, uphold their cause, 50 forgive your people for having sinned against you and for all the crimes against you of which they have been guilty, and allow them to arouse the pity of their captors so that these may have pity on them: 51 for they are your people and your heritage whom you brought out of Egypt, that iron foundry!

52 'May your eyes be open to the entreaty of your servant and the entreaty of your people Israel, to listen to them, whatever they ask of you. 53 For you it was who set them apart from all the peoples of the earth to be your heritage, as you declared through your servant Moses when you brought our ancestors out of Egypt, Lord Yahweh.'

54 When Solomon had finished offering to Yahweh this whole prayer and entreaty, he rose from where he was kneeling with hands stretched out towards heaven before the altar of Yahweh, 55 and stood upright. And in a loud voice he blessed the whole assembly of Israel. 56 'Blessed be Yahweh,' he said, 'who has granted rest to his people Israel, keeping all his promises. Of all the promises of good that he made through his servant Moses, not one has failed. 57 May Yahweh our God be with us, as he was with our ancestors; may he never desert us or cast us off. 58 May he turn our hearts towards him so that we may follow all his ways and keep the commandments and laws and ordinances which he gave to our ancestors. 59 May these words of mine, of my entreaty before Yahweh, be present with Yahweh our God day and night, that he may uphold the cause of his servant and the cause of Israel his people, as each day requires, 60 so that all the peoples of the earth may come to know that Yahweh is God indeed and that there is no other. 61 May your hearts be wholly with Yahweh our God, following his laws and keeping his commandments as at this present day.'

62 The king and all Israel with him offered sacrifice before Yahweh. 63 Solomon offered a communion sacrifice of twenty-two thousand oxen and a hundred and twenty thousand sheep to Yahweh; and thus the king and all the Israelites dedicated the Temple of Yahweh. 64 On the same day the king consecrated the middle part of the court in front of the Temple of Yahweh; for that was where he presented the burnt offerings, oblations and fatty parts of the communion sacrifices, since the bronze altar which stood before Yahweh was too small to hold the burnt offering, oblation and the fatty parts of the communion sacrifice. 65 And then Solomon and with him all Israel from the Pass of Hamath to the Torrent of Egypt — a great assembly — celebrated the feast before Yahweh our God for seven days. 66 On the eighth

NEW REVISED STANDARD VERSION

and they blessed the king, and went to their tents, joyful and in good spirits because of all the goodness that the LORD had shown to his servant David and to his people Israel.

9 When Solomon had finished building the house of the LORD and the king's house and all that Solomon desired to build, 2 the LORD appeared to Solomon a second time, as he had appeared to him at Gibeon. 3 The LORD said to him, "I have heard your prayer and your plea, which you made before me; I have consecrated this house that you have built, and put my name there forever; my eyes and my heart will be there for all time. 4 As for you, if you will walk before me, as David your father walked, with integrity of heart and uprightness, doing according to all that I have commanded you, and keeping my statutes and my ordinances, 5 then I will establish your royal throne over Israel forever, as I promised your father David, saying, 'There shall not fail you a successor on the throne of Israel.'

6 "If you turn aside from following me, you or your children, and do not keep my commandments and my statutes that I have set before you, but go and serve other gods and worship them, 7 then I will cut Israel off from the land that I have given them; and the house that I have consecrated for my name I will cast out of my sight; and Israel will become a proverb and a taunt among all peoples. 8 This house will become a heap of ruins;*p* everyone passing by it will be astonished, and will hiss; and they will say, 'Why has the LORD done such a thing to this land and to this house?' 9 Then they will say, 'Because they have forsaken the LORD their God, who brought their ancestors out of the land of Egypt, and embraced other gods, worshiping them and serving them; therefore the LORD has brought this disaster upon them.' "

10 At the end of twenty years, in which Solomon had built the two houses, the house of the LORD and the king's house, 11 King Hiram of Tyre having supplied Solomon with cedar and cypress timber and gold, as much as he desired, King Solomon gave to Hiram twenty cities in the land of Galilee. 12 But when Hiram came from Tyre to see the cities that Solomon had given him, they did not please him. 13 Therefore he said, "What kind of cities are these that you have given me, my brother?" So they are called the land of Cabul*q* to this day. 14 But Hiram had sent to the king one hundred twenty talents of gold.

15 This is the account of the forced labor that King Solomon conscripted to build the house of the LORD and his own house, the Millo and the wall of Jerusalem, Hazor, Megiddo, Gezer 16 (Pharaoh king of Egypt had gone up and captured Gezer and burned it down, had killed the Canaanites who lived in the city, and had given it as dowry to his daughter, Solomon's wife; 17 so Solomon rebuilt Gezer), Lower Beth-horon, 18 Baalath, Tamar in the wilderness, within the land, 19 as well as all of Solomon's storage cities, the cities for his chariots, the cities for his cavalry, and whatever Solomon desired to build, in Jerusalem, in Lebanon, and in all the land of his dominion. 20 All the people who were left of the Amorites, the Hittites, the Perizzites, the Hivites, and the Jebusites, who were not of the people of Israel — 21 their descendants who were still left in the land, whom the Israelites were unable to destroy completely — these Solomon conscripted for slave labor, and so they are to this day. 22 But of the Israelites Solomon made no slaves; they were the soldiers, they were his officials, his commanders, his captains, and the commanders of his chariotry and cavalry.

REVISED ENGLISH BIBLE

blessed the king, and went home happy and glad at heart for all the prosperity granted by the LORD to his servant David and to his people Israel.

9 WHEN Solomon had completed the house of the LORD and the palace and all the plans for building on which he had set his heart, 2 the LORD again appeared to him, as he had appeared to him at Gibeon, 3 and said, 'I have heard the prayer and supplication which you have offered me. I have consecrated this house which you have built to receive my name for all time, and my eyes and my heart will be fixed on it for ever. 4 If you, for your part, live in my sight as your father David lived, in integrity and uprightness, doing all I command you and observing my statutes and my judgements, 5 then I shall establish the throne of your kingdom over Israel for ever, as I promised your father David when I said, "You shall never want for a man on the throne of Israel." 6 But if you or your sons turn away from following me and do not observe my commandments and my statutes which I have set before you, and if you go and serve other gods and bow down before them, 7 then I shall cut off Israel from the land which I gave them; I shall renounce this house which I have consecrated to my name, and Israel will become a byword and an object-lesson among all peoples. 8 This house will become a ruin; every passer-by will be appalled and gasp at the sight of it; and they will ask, "Why has the LORD so treated this land and this house?" 9 The answer will be, "Because they forsook the LORD their God, who brought their forefathers out of Egypt, and they clung to other gods, bowing down before them and serving them; that is why the LORD has brought all this misfortune on them." '

10 At the end of the twenty years it had taken Solomon to build the two houses, the house of the LORD and the palace, 11 he made over to Hiram king of Tyre twenty towns in Galilee, for Hiram had supplied him with the timber, both cedar and pine, and the gold, all he requested. 12 But when Hiram went from Tyre to inspect the towns, they did not satisfy him, 13 and he said, 'My brother, what kind of towns are these you have given me?' And so he called them the Land of Cabul, the name they still bear. 14 Hiram had sent a hundred and twenty talents of gold to the king.

15 This is the record of the forced labour which King Solomon conscripted to build the house of the LORD, his own palace, the Millo, the wall of Jerusalem, and Hazor, Megiddo, and Gezer. 16 Gezer had been attacked and captured by Pharaoh king of Egypt, who had burnt it to the ground, put its Canaanite inhabitants to death, and given it as a marriage gift to his daughter, Solomon's wife. 17 Solomon rebuilt it. He also built Lower Beth-horon, 18 Baalath, and Tamar in the wilderness, 19 as well as all his store-cities, and the towns where he quartered his chariots and horses; and he carried out all his cherished plans for building in Jerusalem, in the Lebanon, and throughout his whole dominion. 20 All the survivors of the Amorites, Hittites, Perizzites, Hivites, and Jebusites who did not belong to Israel — 21 that is those of their descendants who survived in the land, wherever the Israelites had been unable to exterminate them — all were employed by Solomon on perpetual forced labour, as they still are. 22 None of the Israelites were put to forced labour; they were his fighting men, his captains and lieutenants, and the commanders of his chariots

9:1–9 *Cp. 2 Chr. 7:11–22.* 9:8 **become a ruin:** *so Syriac; Heb.* be high. **gasp:** *lit.* hiss. 9:10–28 *Cp. 2 Chr. 8:1–18.* 9:13 **Cabul:** *that is* Sterile. 9:18 **Tamar:** *or, as otherwise read,* Tadmor. **wilderness:** *so Gk; Heb. adds* in the land. 9:19 **horses:** *or* cavalry. 9:22 **fighting men:** *prob. rdg; Heb. adds* and his servants.

p Syr Old Latin: Heb *will become high good for nothing*   *q* Perhaps meaning *a land*

the people, who bade the king farewell and went to their homes, rejoicing and happy over all the blessings the LORD had given to his servant David and to his people Israel.

9 After Solomon finished building the temple of the LORD, the royal palace, and everything else that he had planned, 2 the LORD appeared to him a second time, as he had appeared to him in Gibeon. 3 The LORD said to him: "I have heard the prayer of petition which you offered in my presence. I have consecrated this temple which you have built; I confer my name upon it forever, and my eyes and my heart shall be there always. 4 As for you, if you live in my presence as your father David lived, sincerely and uprightly, doing just as I have commanded you, keeping my statutes and decrees, 5 I will establish your throne of sovereignty over Israel forever, as I promised your father David when I said, 'You shall always have someone from your line on the throne of Israel.' 6 But if you and your descendants ever withdraw from me, fail to keep the commandments and statutes which I set before you, and proceed to venerate and worship strange gods, 7 I will cut off Israel from the land I gave them and repudiate the temple I have consecrated to my honor. Israel shall become a proverb and a byword among all nations, 8 and this temple shall become a heap of ruins. Every passerby shall catch his breath in amazement, and ask, 'Why has the LORD done this to the land and to this temple?' 9 Men will answer: 'They forsook the LORD, their God, who brought their fathers out of the land of Egypt; they adopted strange gods which they worshiped and served. That is why the LORD has brought down upon them all this evil.' "

10 After the twenty years during which Solomon built the two houses, the temple of the LORD and the palace of the king — 11 Hiram, king of Tyre, supplying Solomon with all the cedar wood, fir wood, and gold he wished — King Solomon gave Hiram twenty cities in the land of Galilee. 12 Hiram left Tyre to see the cities Solomon had given him, but was not satisfied with them. 13 So he said, "What are these cities you have given me, my brother?" And he called them the land of Cabul, as they are called to this day. 14 Hiram, however, had sent King Solomon one hundred and twenty talents of gold.

15 This is an account of the forced labor which King Solomon levied in order to build the temple of the LORD, his palace, Millo, the wall of Jerusalem, Hazor, Megiddo, Gezer 16 (Pharaoh king of Egypt, had come up and taken Gezer and, after destroying it by fire and slaying all the Canaanites living in the city, had given it as dowry to his daughter, Solomon's wife; 17 Solomon then rebuilt Gezer), Lower Beth-horon, 18 Baalath, Tamar in the desert of Judah, 19 all his cities for supplies, cities for chariots and for horses, and whatever else Solomon decided should be built in Jerusalem, in Lebanon, and in the entire land under his dominion. 20 All the non-Israelite people who remained in the land, descendants of the Amorites, Hittites, Perizzites, Hivites, and Jebusites 21 whose doom the Israelites had been unable to accomplish, Solomon conscripted as forced laborers, as they are to this day. 22 But Solomon enslaved none of the Israelites, for they were his fighting force, his ministers, commanders, adjutants, chariot officers, and charioteers.

day he dismissed the people, who bade farewell to the king and went home joyful and happy of heart over all the goodness which Yahweh had shown to his servant and his people Israel.

9 When Solomon had finished building the Temple of Yahweh, the royal palace and everything else which Solomon had wanted to do, 2 Yahweh appeared to Solomon a second time, as he had appeared to him at Gibeon. 3 Yahweh said to him, 'I have heard your prayer and the entreaty which you have before me. I consecrate this temple which you have built: I place my name there for ever; my eyes and my heart will be there always. 4 For your part, if you walk before me in innocence of heart and in honesty, like your father David, if you do everything that I command and keep my laws and my ordinances, 5 I shall make your royal throne secure over Israel for ever, as I promised your father David when I said, "You will never lack for a man on the throne of Israel." 6 But if you turn away from me, either you or your descendants, and instead of keeping my commandments and laws which I have laid down for you, you go and serve other gods and worship them, 7 then I shall banish Israel from the country which I have given them, and shall disown this Temple which I have consecrated for my name, and Israel will be a proverb and a byword among all peoples. 8 As for this once-exalted Temple, everyone who passes by will be appalled, and they will whistle and say, "Why has Yahweh treated this country and this Temple like this?" 9 And the answer will be, "Because they deserted Yahweh their God who brought their ancestors out of Egypt, and they adopted other gods and worshipped and served them; that is why Yahweh has brought all these disasters on them." '

10 At the end of the twenty years that it took Solomon to erect the two buildings, the Temple of Yahweh and the royal palace 11 (Hiram king of Tyre had provided Solomon with all the cedar wood, juniper wood and gold that he wanted), King Solomon gave Hiram twenty towns in the territory of Galilee. 12 But when Hiram came from Tyre to view the towns that Solomon had given him, he was not pleased with them. 13 He said, 'What kind of towns are these you have given me, brother?' And to this day they are known as 'cabul-land'. 14 Hiram sent the king one hundred and twenty talents of gold.

15 This is an account of the forced labour levied by King Solomon for building the Temple of Yahweh, his own palace, the Millo and the fortifications of Jerusalem, Hazor, Megiddo, Gezer 16 (Pharaoh king of Egypt mounted an expedition, captured Gezer, burnt it down and massacred the Canaanites living there; he then gave the town as a dowry to his daughter, Solomon's wife, 17 and Solomon rebuilt Gezer), Lower Beth-Horon, 18 Baalath, Tamar in the desert, inside the country, 19 all Solomon's storage towns owned by Solomon, all the towns for his chariots and horses, and whatever Solomon was pleased to build in Jerusalem, in the Lebanon and in all the countries under his rule. 20 All those who survived of the Amorite, Hittite, Perizzite, Hivite and Jebusite peoples, who were not Israelites — 21 their descendants still remaining in the country on whom the Israelites had not been able to enforce the curse of destruction — these Solomon levied as forced labourers, as is still the case today. 22 Solomon did not, however, impose forced labour on the Israelites; for they were soldiers, his officials, his administrators, his officers and his chariot and cavalry com-

23 These were the chief officers who were over Solomon's work: five hundred fifty, who had charge of the people who carried on the work.

24 But Pharaoh's daughter went up from the city of David to her own house that Solomon had built for her; then he built the Millo.

25 Three times a year Solomon used to offer up burnt offerings and sacrifices of well-being on the altar that he built for the LORD, offering incense[r] before the LORD. So he completed the house.

26 King Solomon built a fleet of ships at Ezion-geber, which is near Eloth on the shore of the Red Sea,[s] in the land of Edom. 27 Hiram sent his servants with the fleet, sailors who were familiar with the sea, together with the servants of Solomon. 28 They went to Ophir, and imported from there four hundred twenty talents of gold, which they delivered to King Solomon.

10 When the queen of Sheba heard of the fame of Solomon, (fame due to[t] the name of the LORD), she came to test him with hard questions. 2 She came to Jerusalem with a very great retinue, with camels bearing spices, and very much gold, and precious stones; and when she came to Solomon, she told him all that was on her mind. 3 Solomon answered all her questions; there was nothing hidden from the king that he could not explain to her. 4 When the queen of Sheba had observed all the wisdom of Solomon, the house that he had built, 5 the food of his table, the seating of his officials, and the attendance of his servants, their clothing, his valets, and his burnt offerings that he offered at the house of the LORD, there was no more spirit in her.

6 So she said to the king, "The report was true that I heard in my own land of your accomplishments and of your wisdom, 7 but I did not believe the reports until I came and my own eyes had seen it. Not even half had been told me; your wisdom and prosperity far surpass the report that I had heard. 8 Happy are your wives![u] Happy are these your servants, who continually attend you and hear your wisdom! 9 Blessed be the LORD your God, who has delighted in you and set you on the throne of Israel! Because the LORD loved Israel forever, he has made you king to execute justice and righteousness." 10 Then she gave the king one hundred twenty talents of gold, a great quantity of spices, and precious stones; never again did spices come in such quantity as that which the queen of Sheba gave to King Solomon.

11 Moreover, the fleet of Hiram, which carried gold from Ophir, brought from Ophir a great quantity of almug wood and precious stones. 12 From the almug wood the king made supports for the house of the LORD, and for the king's house, lyres also and harps for the singers; no such almug wood has come or been seen to this day.

13 Meanwhile King Solomon gave to the queen of Sheba every desire that she expressed, as well as what he gave her out of Solomon's royal bounty. Then she returned to her own land, with her servants.

14 The weight of gold that came to Solomon in one year was six hundred sixty-six talents of gold, 15 besides that which came from the traders and from the business of the merchants, and from all the kings of Arabia and the gover-

and of his cavalry. 23 The number of officers in charge of the foremen over Solomon's work was five hundred and fifty; these superintended the people engaged on the work.

24 Solomon brought Pharaoh's daughter up from the City of David to her own house which he had built for her; later he built the Millo.

25 Three times a year Solomon used to offer whole-offerings and shared-offerings on the altar which he had built to the LORD, burning the offerings before the LORD. So he completed the house.

26 King Solomon built a fleet of ships at Ezion-geber, near Eloth on the shore of the Red Sea, in Edom. 27 Hiram sent men of his own to serve with the fleet, experienced seamen, to work with Solomon's men. 28 They went to Ophir and brought back four hundred and twenty talents of gold, which they delivered to King Solomon.

10 THE queen of Sheba heard of Solomon's fame and came to test him with enigmatic questions. 2 She arrived in Jerusalem with a very large retinue, camels laden with spices, gold in vast quantity, and precious stones. When she came to Solomon, she talked to him about everything she had on her mind. 3 Solomon answered all her questions; not one of them was too hard for the king to answer. 4 When the queen of Sheba observed all the wisdom of Solomon, the palace he had built, 5 the food on his table, the courtiers sitting around him, and his attendants standing behind in their livery, his cupbearers, and the whole-offerings which he used to offer in the house of the LORD, she was overcome with amazement. 6 She said to the king, 'The account which I heard in my own country about your achievements and your wisdom was true, 7 but I did not believe what they told me until I came and saw for myself. Indeed I was not told half of it; your wisdom and your prosperity far surpass all I had heard of them. 8 Happy are your wives, happy these courtiers of yours who are in attendance on you every day and hear your wisdom! 9 Blessed be the LORD your God who has delighted in you and has set you on the throne of Israel; because he loves Israel unendingly, he has made you king to maintain law and justice.' 10 She presented the king with a hundred and twenty talents of gold, spices in great abundance, and precious stones. Never again did such a quantity of spices come as the queen of Sheba gave to King Solomon.

11 Besides all this, Hiram's fleet of ships, which had brought gold from Ophir, brought also from Ophir huge cargoes of almug wood and precious stones. 12 The king used the wood to make stools for the house of the LORD and for the palace, as well as lyres and lutes for the singers. No such quantities of almug wood have ever been imported or even seen since that time.

13 King Solomon gave the queen of Sheba whatever she desired and asked for, in addition to all that he gave her of his royal bounty. Then she departed with her retinue and went back to her own land.

14 The weight of gold which Solomon received in any one year was six hundred and sixty-six talents, 15 in addition to the tolls levied by the customs officers, the profits on foreign trade, and the tribute of the kings of Arabia and the regional governors.

9:24 **Solomon . . . up:** *so Gk; Heb.* However, Pharaoh's daughter had gone up.   9:25 **the offerings:** *so Gk; Heb. adds* with it which.   9:26 **Red Sea:** *or* sea of Reeds.   10:1–25 *Cp. 2 Chr.* 9:1–24.   10:1 **The queen . . . fame:** *prob. rdg, cp. 2 Chr.* 9:1; *Heb. adds* to the name of the LORD.   10:8 **wives:** *so Gk; Heb.* men.   10:12 **stools:** *meaning of Heb. word uncertain.* 10:15 **tolls levied by:** *so Gk; Heb.* men of. **and the tribute of:** *prob. rdg; Heb.* and all.

[r] Gk: Heb *offering incense with it that was*   [s] Or *Sea of Reeds*
[t] Meaning of Heb uncertain   [u] Gk Syr: Heb *men*

23 The supervisors of Solomon's works who policed the people engaged in the work numbered five hundred and fifty.

24 As soon as Pharaoh's daughter went up from the City of David to her palace, which he had built for her, Solomon built Millo.

25 Three times a year Solomon used to offer holocausts and peace offerings on the altar which he had built to the LORD, and to burn incense before the LORD; and he kept the temple in repair.

26 King Solomon also built a fleet at Ezion-geber, which is near Elath on the shore of the Red Sea in the land of Edom. 27 In this fleet Hiram placed his own expert seamen with the servants of Solomon. 28 They went to Ophir, and brought back four hundred and twenty talents of gold to King Solomon.

10 The queen of Sheba, having heard of Solomon's fame, came to test him with subtle questions. 2 She arrived in Jerusalem with a very numerous retinue, and with camels bearing spices, a large amount of gold, and precious stones. She came to Solomon and questioned him on every subject in which she was interested. 3 King Solomon explained everything she asked about, and there remained nothing hidden from him that he could not explain to her.

4 When the queen of Sheba witnessed Solomon's great wisdom, the palace he had built, 5 the food at his table, the seating of his ministers, the attendance and garb of his waiters, his banquet service, and the holocausts he offered in the temple of the LORD, she was breathless. 6 "The report I heard in my country about your deeds and your wisdom is true," she told the king. 7 "Though I did not believe the report until I came and saw with my own eyes, I have discovered that they were not telling me the half. Your wisdom and prosperity surpass the report I heard. 8 Happy are your men, happy these servants of yours, who stand before you always and listen to your wisdom. 9 Blessed be the LORD, your God, whom it has pleased to place you on the throne of Israel. In his enduring love for Israel, the LORD has made you king to carry out judgment and justice." 10 Then she gave the king one hundred and twenty gold talents, a very large quantity of spices, and precious stones. Never again did anyone bring such an abundance of spices as the queen of Sheba gave to King Solomon.

11 Hiram's fleet, which used to bring gold from Ophir, also brought from there a large quantity of cabinet wood and precious stones. 12 With the wood the king made supports for the temple of the LORD and for the palace of the king, and harps and lyres for the chanters. No more such wood was brought or seen to the present day.

13 King Solomon gave the queen of Sheba everything she desired and asked for, besides such presents as were given her from Solomon's royal bounty. Then she returned with her servants to her own country.

14 The gold that Solomon received every year weighed six hundred and sixty-six gold talents, 15 in addition to what came from the Tarshish fleet, from the traffic of merchants, and from all the kings of Arabia and the governors of the

manders. 23 There were five hundred and fifty officials in charge of the foremen over Solomon's work, who supervised the people employed on the work.

24 After Pharaoh's daughter had moved from the City of David up to the palace which he had built for her, he then built the Millo.

25 Three times a year Solomon presented burnt offerings and communion sacrifices on the altar which he had built for Yahweh and set his burnt offerings smoking before Yahweh.

Thus he completed the Temple.

26 King Solomon equipped a fleet at Ezion-Geber, which is near Elath on the shores of the Red Sea, in Edom. 27 For this fleet Hiram sent men of his, experienced sailors, to serve with those in Solomon's service. 28 They went to Ophir and took on four hundred and twenty talents of gold, which they brought back to Solomon.

10 The queen of Sheba heard of Solomon's fame and came to test him with difficult questions. 2 She arrived in Jerusalem with a very large retinue, with camels laden with spices and an immense quantity of gold and precious stones. Having reached Solomon, she discussed with him everything that she had in mind, 3 and Solomon had an answer for all her questions; not one of them was too obscure for the king to answer for her. 4 When the queen of Sheba saw how very wise Solomon was, the palace which he had built, 5 the food at his table, the accommodation for his officials, the organisation of his staff and the way they were dressed, his cupbearers, and the burnt offerings which he presented in the Temple of Yahweh, it left her breathless, 6 and she said to the king, 'The report I heard in my own country about your wisdom in handling your affairs was true then! 7 Until I came and saw for myself, I did not believe the reports, but clearly I was told less than half: for wisdom and prosperity, you surpass what was reported to me. 8 How fortunate your wives are! How fortunate these courtiers of yours, continually in attendance on you and listening to your wisdom! 9 Blessed be Yahweh your God who has shown you his favour by setting you on the throne of Israel! Because of Yahweh's everlasting love for Israel, he has made you king to administer law and justice.' 10 And she presented the king with a hundred and twenty talents of gold and great quantities of spices and precious stones; no such wealth of spices ever came again as those which the queen of Sheba gave to King Solomon. 11 Similarly, Hiram's fleet, which brought the gold from Ophir, also brought back great cargoes of *almug* timber and precious stones. 12 Of the *almug* timber the king made supports for the Temple of Yahweh and for the royal palace, and harps and lyres for the musicians; no more of this *almug* timber has since come or been seen to this day. 13 And King Solomon, in his turn, presented the queen of Sheba with everything that she expressed a wish for, besides those presents which he gave her with a munificence worthy of King Solomon. After which, she went home to her own country, she and her servants.

14 The weight of gold received annually by Solomon amounted to six hundred and sixty-six talents of gold, 15 besides what tolls and foreign trade, as well as everything the Arab kings and the provincial governors brought in. 16 King

nors of the land. 16 King Solomon made two hundred large shields of beaten gold; six hundred shekels of gold went into each large shield. 17 He made three hundred shields of beaten gold; three minas of gold went into each shield; and the king put them in the House of the Forest of Lebanon. 18 The king also made a great ivory throne, and overlaid it with the finest gold. 19 The throne had six steps. The top of the throne was rounded in the back, and on each side of the seat were arm rests and two lions standing beside the arm rests, 20 while twelve lions were standing, one on each end of a step on the six steps. Nothing like it was ever made in any kingdom. 21 All King Solomon's drinking vessels were of gold, and all the vessels of the House of the Forest of Lebanon were of pure gold; none were of silver — it was not considered as anything in the days of Solomon. 22 For the king had a fleet of ships of Tarshish at sea with the fleet of Hiram. Once every three years the fleet of ships of Tarshish used to come bringing gold, silver, ivory, apes, and peacocks. ^{v}

23 Thus King Solomon excelled all the kings of the earth in riches and in wisdom. 24 The whole earth sought the presence of Solomon to hear his wisdom, which God had put into his mind. 25 Every one of them brought a present, objects of silver and gold, garments, weaponry, spices, horses, and mules, so much year by year.

26 Solomon gathered together chariots and horses; he had fourteen hundred chariots and twelve thousand horses, which he stationed in the chariot cities and with the king in Jerusalem. 27 The king made silver as common in Jerusalem as stones, and he made cedars as numerous as the sycamores of the Shephelah. 28 Solomon's import of horses was from Egypt and Kue, and the king's traders received them from Kue at a price. 29 A chariot could be imported from Egypt for six hundred shekels of silver, and a horse for one hundred fifty; so through the king's traders they were exported to all the kings of the Hittites and the kings of Aram.

11 King Solomon loved many foreign women along with the daughter of Pharaoh: Moabite, Ammonite, Edomite, Sidonian, and Hittite women, 2 from the nations concerning which the Lord had said to the Israelites, "You shall not enter into marriage with them, neither shall they with you; for they will surely incline your heart to follow their gods"; Solomon clung to these in love. 3 Among his wives were seven hundred princesses and three hundred concubines; and his wives turned away his heart. 4 For when Solomon was old, his wives turned away his heart after other gods; and his heart was not true to the Lord his God, as was the heart of his father David. 5 For Solomon followed Astarte the goddess of the Sidonians, and Milcom the abomination of the Ammonites. 6 So Solomon did what was evil in the sight of the Lord, and did not completely follow the Lord, as his father David had done. 7 Then Solomon built a high place for Chemosh the abomination of Moab, and for Molech the abomination of the Ammonites, on the mountain east of Jerusalem. 8 He did the same for all his foreign wives, who offered incense and sacrificed to their gods.

9 Then the Lord was angry with Solomon, because his heart had turned away from the Lord, the God of Israel, who had appeared to him twice, 10 and had commanded him concerning this matter, that he should not follow other gods; but he did not observe what the Lord commanded. 11 Therefore the Lord said to Solomon, "Since this has been your mind and you have not kept my covenant and my statutes that I have commanded you, I will surely tear the kingdom from you and give it to your servant. 12 Yet for the

16 King Solomon made two hundred shields of beaten gold, and six hundred shekels of gold went to the making of each one; 17 he also made three hundred bucklers of beaten gold, and three minas of gold went to the making of each buckler. The king put these into the House of the Forest of Lebanon.

18 The king also made a great throne inlaid with ivory and overlaid with fine gold. 19 Six steps led up to the throne; at the back of the throne there was the head of a calf. There were armrests on each side of the seat, with a lion standing beside each of them, 20 while twelve lions stood on the six steps, one at either end of each step. Nothing like it had ever been made for any monarch. 21 All Solomon's drinking vessels were of gold, and all the plate in the House of the Forest of Lebanon was of red gold; no silver was used, for it was reckoned of no value in the days of Solomon. 22 The king had a fleet of merchantmen at sea with Hiram's fleet; once every three years this fleet of merchantmen came home, bringing gold and silver, ivory, apes, and monkeys.

23 Thus King Solomon outdid all the kings of the earth in wealth and wisdom, 24 and the whole world courted him to hear the wisdom with which God had endowed his mind. 25 Each one brought his gift with him, vessels of silver and gold, garments, perfumes and spices, horses and mules in annual tribute.

26 Solomon amassed chariots and horses; he had fourteen hundred chariots and twelve thousand horses; he stationed some in the chariot-towns, while others he kept at hand in Jerusalem. 27 He made silver as common in Jerusalem as stone, and cedar as plentiful as the sycomore-fig is in the Shephelah. 28 Horses were imported from Egypt and Kue for Solomon; the merchants of the king obtained them from Kue by purchase. 29 Chariots were imported from Egypt for six hundred silver shekels each, and horses for a hundred and fifty; in the same way the merchants obtained them for export from all the kings of the Hittites and the kings of Aram.

11 King Solomon loved many foreign women; in addition to Pharaoh's daughter there were Moabite, Ammonite, Edomite, Sidonian, and Hittite women, 2 from the nations with whom the Lord had forbidden the Israelites to intermarry, 'because', he said, 'they will entice you to serve their gods'. But Solomon was devoted to them and loved them dearly. 3 He had seven hundred wives, all princesses, and three hundred concubines, and they influenced him, 4 for as he grew old, his wives turned his heart to follow other gods, and he did not remain wholly loyal to the Lord his God as his father David had been. 5 He followed Ashtoreth, goddess of the Sidonians, and Milcom, the loathsome god of the Ammonites. 6 Thus Solomon did what was wrong in the eyes of the Lord, and was not wholehearted in his loyalty to the Lord as his father David had been. 7 He built a shrine for Kemosh, the loathsome god of Moab, on the heights to the east of Jerusalem, and one for Milcom, the loathsome god of the Ammonites. 8 These things he did for the gods to whom all his foreign wives burnt offerings and made sacrifices.

9 The Lord was angry with Solomon because his heart had turned away from the Lord the God of Israel, who had appeared to him twice 10 and had strictly commanded him not to follow other gods; but he disobeyed the Lord's command. 11 The Lord therefore said to Solomon, 'Because you have done this and have not kept my covenant and my statutes as I commanded you, I will tear the kingdom from you and give it to your servant. 12 Nevertheless, for the sake

---

10:22 **merchantmen:** *lit.* ships of Tarshish.　　10:26 **horses:** *or* cavalry.　　10:26–29 *Cp. 2 Chr. 1:14–17; 9:25–28.*　　10:28 **Kue:** *or* Cilicia.　　11:7 **Milcom:** *so Gk; Heb.* Molech.

^{v} Or *baboons*

country. 16 Moreover, King Solomon made two hundred shields of beaten gold (six hundred gold shekels went into each shield) 17 and three hundred bucklers of beaten gold (three minas of gold went into each buckler); and he put them in the hall of the Forest of Lebanon. 18 The king also had a large ivory throne made, and overlaid it with refined gold. 19 The throne had six steps, a back with a round top, and an arm on each side of the seat. Next to each arm stood a lion; 20 and twelve other lions stood on the steps, two to a step, one on either side of each step. Nothing like this was produced in any other kingdom. 21 In addition, all King Solomon's drinking vessels were of gold, and all the utensils in the hall of the Forest of Lebanon were of pure gold. There was no silver, for in Solomon's time it was considered worthless. 22 The king had a fleet of Tarshish ships at sea with Hiram's fleet. Once every three years the fleet of Tarshish ships would come with a cargo of gold, silver, ivory, apes, and monkeys. 23 Thus King Solomon surpassed in riches and wisdom all the kings of the earth. 24 And the whole world sought audience with Solomon, to hear from him the wisdom which God had put in his heart. 25 Each one brought his yearly tribute: silver or gold articles, garments, weapons, spices, horses and mules.

26 Solomon collected chariots and drivers; he had one thousand four hundred chariots and twelve thousand drivers; these he allocated among the chariot cities and to the king's service in Jerusalem. 27 The king made silver as common in Jerusalem as stones, and cedars as numerous as the sycamores of the foothills. 28 Solomon's horses were imported from Cilicia, where the king's agents purchased them. 29 A chariot imported from Egypt cost six hundred shekels, a horse one hundred and fifty shekels; they were exported at these rates to all the Hittite and Aramean kings.

11 King Solomon loved many foreign women besides the daughter of Pharaoh (Moabites, Ammonites, Edomites, Sidonians, and Hittites), 2 from nations with which the LORD had forbidden the Israelites to intermarry, "because," he said, "they will turn your hearts to their gods." 3 But Solomon fell in love with them. He had seven hundred wives of princely rank and three hundred concubines, and his wives turned his heart.

4 When Solomon was old his wives had turned his heart to strange gods, and his heart was not entirely with the LORD, his God, as the heart of his father David had been. 5 By adoring Astarte, the goddess of the Sidonians, and Milcom, the idol of the Ammonites, 6 Solomon did evil in the sight of the LORD; he did not follow him unreservedly as his father David had done. 7 Solomon then built a high place to Chemosh, the idol of Moab, and to Molech, the idol of the Ammonites, on the hill opposite Jerusalem. 8 He did the same for all his foreign wives who burned incense and sacrificed to their gods. 9 The LORD, therefore, became angry with Solomon, because his heart was turned away from the LORD, the God of Israel, who had appeared to him twice 10 (for though the LORD had forbidden him this very act of following strange gods, Solomon had not obeyed him).

11 So the LORD said to Solomon: "Since this is what you want, and you have not kept my covenant and my statutes which I enjoined on you, I will deprive you of the kingdom and give it to your servant. 12 I will not do this during your

Solomon made two hundred great shields of beaten gold, six hundred shekels of gold going into one shield; 17 also three hundred small shields of beaten gold, three *mina* of gold going into one shield; and the king put these into the House of the Forest of Lebanon. 18 The king also made a great ivory throne which he overlaid with refined gold. 19 The throne had six steps, a back with a rounded top, and arms on each side of the seat; two lions stood beside the arms, 20 and twelve lions stood on each side of the six steps. Nothing like it has ever been made in any other kingdom.

21 All King Solomon's drinking vessels were of gold, and all the plate in the House of the Forest of Lebanon was of pure gold; silver was little thought of in Solomon's days, 22 since the king had a fleet of Tarshish[c] at sea with Hiram's fleet, and once every three years the fleet of Tarshish would come back laden with gold and silver, ivory, apes and baboons. 23 For riches and for wisdom, King Solomon surpassed all kings on earth, 24 and the whole world consulted Solomon to hear the wisdom which God had implanted in his heart; 25 and everyone would bring a present with him: things made of silver, things made of gold, robes, armour, spices, horses and mules; and this went on year after year.

26 Solomon then built up a force of chariots and cavalry; he had one thousand four hundred chariots and twelve thousand horses, these he stationed in the chariot towns and near the king in Jerusalem. 27 In Jerusalem the king made silver as common as stones, and cedar wood as plentiful as sycamore in the lowlands. 28 Solomon's horses were imported from Muzur and Cilicia. The king's dealers acquired them from Cilicia at the prevailing price. 29 A chariot was imported from Egypt for six hundred silver shekels and a horse from Cilicia for a hundred and fifty. They also supplied the Hittite and Aramaean kings, who all used them as middlemen.

11 King Solomon loved many foreign women: not only Pharaoh's daughter but Moabites, Edomites, Sidonians and Hittites, 2 from those peoples of whom Yahweh had said to the Israelites, 'You are not to go among them nor they among you, or they will be sure to sway your hearts to their own gods.' But Solomon was deeply attached to them. 3 He had seven hundred wives of royal rank and three hundred concubines. 4 When Solomon grew old his wives swayed his heart to other gods; and his heart was not wholly with Yahweh his God as his father David's had been. 5 Solomon became a follower of Astarte, the goddess of the Sidonians, and of Milcom, the Ammonite abomination. 6 He did what was displeasing to Yahweh, and was not a wholehearted follower of Yahweh, as his father David had been. 7 Then it was that Solomon built a high place for Chemosh, the abomination of Moab, on the mountain to the east of Jerusalem, and to Milcom, the abomination of the Ammonites. 8 He did the same for all his foreign wives, who offered incense and sacrifice to their gods.

9 Yahweh was angry with Solomon because his heart had turned away from Yahweh, God of Israel, who had twice appeared to him 10 and had forbidden him to follow other gods; but he did not carry out Yahweh's order. 11 Yahweh therefore said to Solomon, 'Since you have behaved like this and have not kept my covenant or the laws which I laid down for you, I shall tear the kingdom away from you and give it to one of your servants. 12 For your father David's

c **10** Meaning uncertain, perhaps a place-name. Or 'refinery ships', so ships for carrying metal.

NEW REVISED STANDARD VERSION

sake of your father David I will not do it in your lifetime; I will tear it out of the hand of your son. 13 I will not, however, tear away the entire kingdom; I will give one tribe to your son, for the sake of my servant David and for the sake of Jerusalem, which I have chosen."

14 Then the LORD raised up an adversary against Solomon, Hadad the Edomite; he was of the royal house in Edom. 15 For when David was in Edom, and Joab the commander of the army went up to bury the dead, he killed every male in Edom 16 (for Joab and all Israel remained there six months, until he had eliminated every male in Edom); 17 but Hadad fled to Egypt with some Edomites who were servants of his father. He was a young boy at that time. 18 They set out from Midian and came to Paran; they took people with them from Paran and came to Egypt, to Pharaoh king of Egypt, who gave him a house, assigned him an allowance of food, and gave him land. 19 Hadad found great favor in the sight of Pharaoh, so that he gave him his sister-in-law for a wife, the sister of Queen Tahpenes. 20 The sister of Tahpenes gave birth by him to his son Genubath, whom Tahpenes weaned in Pharaoh's house; Genubath was in Pharaoh's house among the children of Pharaoh. 21 When Hadad heard in Egypt that David slept with his ancestors and that Joab the commander of the army was dead, Hadad said to Pharaoh, "Let me depart, that I may go to my own country." 22 But Pharaoh said to him, "What do you lack with me that you now seek to go to your own country?" And he said, "No, do let me go."

23 God raised up another adversary against Solomon,w Rezon son of Eliada, who had fled from his master, King Hadadezer of Zobah. 24 He gathered followers around him and became leader of a marauding band, after the slaughter by David; they went to Damascus, settled there, and made him king in Damascus. 25 He was an adversary of Israel all the days of Solomon, making trouble as Hadad did; he despised Israel and reigned over Aram.

26 Jeroboam son of Nebat, an Ephraimite of Zeredah, a servant of Solomon, whose mother's name was Zeruah, a widow, rebelled against the king. 27 The following was the reason he rebelled against the king. Solomon built the Millo, and closed up the gap in the wallx of the city of his father David. 28 The man Jeroboam was very able, and when Solomon saw that the young man was industrious he gave him charge over all the forced labor of the house of Joseph. 29 About that time, when Jeroboam was leaving Jerusalem, the prophet Ahijah the Shilonite found him on the road. Ahijah had clothed himself with a new garment. The two of them were alone in the open country 30 when Ahijah laid hold of the new garment he was wearing and tore it into twelve pieces. 31 He then said to Jeroboam: Take for yourself ten pieces; for thus says the LORD, the God of Israel, "See, I am about to tear the kingdom from the hand of Solomon, and will give you ten tribes. 32 One tribe will remain his, for the sake of my servant David and for the sake of Jerusalem, the city that I have chosen out of all the tribes of Israel. 33 This is because he hasy forsaken me, worshiped Astarte the goddess of the Sidonians, Chemosh the god of Moab, and Milcom the god of the Ammonites, and hasy not walked in my ways, doing what is right in my sight and keeping my statutes and my ordinances, as his father David did. 34 Nevertheless I will not take the whole

REVISED ENGLISH BIBLE

of your father David I will not do this in your day; I will tear it out of your son's hand. 13 Even so not the whole kingdom; I will leave him one tribe for the sake of my servant David and for the sake of Jerusalem, my chosen city.'

14 The LORD raised up an adversary for Solomon, Hadad the Edomite, of the royal house of Edom. 15 At the time when David reduced Edom, his commander-in-chief Joab had destroyed every male in the country when he went into it to bury the slain. 16 He and the Israelite armies remained there for six months, until he had slain every male in Edom. 17 But Hadad, who was still a boy, fled the country with some of his father's Edomite servants; their goal was Egypt. 18 They set out from Midian, made their way to Paran, and, taking some men from there, came to Pharaoh king of Egypt, who assigned Hadad a house and maintenance and made him a grant of land. 19 Hadad found great favour with Pharaoh, who gave him in marriage a sister of his wife, Queen Tahpenes. 20 She bore him his son Genubath; Tahpenes weaned the child in Pharaoh's palace, and he lived there with Pharaoh's sons.

21 When Hadad heard in Egypt that David rested with his forefathers and that his commander-in-chief Joab was also dead, he said to Pharaoh, 'Give me leave to go, so that I may return to my own country.' 22 'What is it that you find wanting in my country', said Pharaoh, 'that you want to go back to your own?' 'Nothing,' replied Hadad, 'but do let me go.' 25 He remained an adversary for Israel all through Solomon's reign. This is the harm that Hadad caused: he maintained a stranglehold on Israel and became king of Edom.

23 Another adversary God raised up against Solomon was Rezon son of Eliada, who had fled from his master Hadadezer king of Zobah. 24 He gathered men about him and became a captain of freebooters; he went to Damascus, occupied it, and became king there. ‡11.25: see above‡

26 Jeroboam son of Nebat, one of Solomon's courtiers, an Ephrathite from Zeredah, whose widowed mother was named Zeruah, rebelled against the king. 27 This is the story of his rebellion. When Solomon built the Millo and closed the breach in the wall of the city of his father David, 28 he saw how the young man worked, for Jeroboam was a man of great ability, and the king put him in charge of all the labour-gangs in the tribal district of Joseph. 29 On one occasion when Jeroboam left Jerusalem, the prophet Ahijah from Shiloh met him on the road. The prophet was wearing a new cloak and, when the two of them were alone out in the open country, 30 Ahijah, taking hold of the new cloak he was wearing, tore it into twelve pieces, 31 and said to Jeroboam, 'Take for yourself ten pieces, for the LORD the God of Israel has declared that he is about to tear the kingdom from the hand of Solomon and give you ten tribes. 32 But, says the LORD, one tribe will remain Solomon's, for the sake of my servant David and for the sake of Jerusalem, the city I have chosen out of all the tribes of Israel. 33 I shall do this because Solomon has forsaken me; he has bowed down before Ashtoreth goddess of the Sidonians, Kemosh god of Moab, and Milcom god of the Ammonites, and has not conformed to my ways. He has not done what is right in my eyes or observed my statutes and judgements as David his father did.

34 'Nevertheless I shall not take the whole kingdom from

11:22–26 Verse 25 transposed to follow verse 22.   11:25 This: so Gk; Heb. obscure. maintained . . . on: so Syriac; Heb. loathed. Edom: so Gk; Heb. Aram.   11:24 freebooters: so Gk; Heb. adds when David killed them. he: so Gk; Heb. they.   11:33 has forsaken . . . has bowed down . . . has not conformed: so Gk; Heb. has plural.

w Heb him   x Heb lacks in the wall   y Gk Syr Vg: Heb they have

lifetime, however, for the sake of your father David; it is your son whom I will deprive. 13 Nor will I take away the whole kingdom. I will leave your son one tribe for the sake of my servant David and of Jerusalem, which I have chosen."

14 The LORD then raised up an adversary to Solomon: Hadad the Edomite, who was of the royal line in Edom. 15 Earlier, when David had conquered Edom, Joab, the general of the army, while going to bury the slain, put to death every male in Edom. 16 Joab and all Israel remained there six months until they had killed off every male in Edom. 17 Meanwhile, Hadad, who was only a boy, fled toward Egypt with some Edomite servants of his father. 18 They left Midian and passing through Paran, where they picked up additional men, they went into Egypt to Pharaoh, king of Egypt, who gave Hadad a house, appointed him rations, and assigned him land.

19 Hadad won great favor with Pharaoh, so that he gave him in marriage the sister of Queen Tahpenes, his own wife. 20 Tahpenes' sister bore Hadad a son, Genubath. After his weaning, the queen kept him in Pharaoh's palace, where he then lived with Pharaoh's own sons. 21 When Hadad in Egypt heard that David rested with his ancestors and that Joab, the general of the army, was dead, he said to Pharaoh, "Give me leave to return to my own country." 22 Pharaoh said to him, "What do you lack with me, that you are seeking to return to your own country?" "Nothing," he said, "but please let me go!"

23 God raised up against Solomon another adversary, in Rezon, the son of Eliada, who had fled from his lord, Hadadezer, king of Zobah, 24 when David defeated them with slaughter. Rezon gathered men about him and became leader of a band, went to Damascus, settled there, and became king in Damascus. 25 He was an enemy of Israel as long as Solomon lived; this added to the harm done by Hadad, who made a rift in Israel by becoming king over Edom.

26 Solomon's servant Jeroboam, son of Nebat, an Ephraimite from Zeredah with a widowed mother, Zeruah, also rebelled against the king. 27 This is why he rebelled. King Solomon was building Millo, closing up the breach of his father's City of David. 28 Jeroboam was a man of means, and when Solomon saw that he was also an industrious young man, he put him in charge of the entire labor force of the house of Joseph. 29 At that time Jeroboam left Jerusalem, and the prophet Ahijah the Shilonite met him on the road. The two were alone in the area, and the prophet was wearing a new cloak. 30 Ahijah took off his new cloak, tore it into twelve pieces, 31 and said to Jeroboam:

"Take ten pieces for yourself; the LORD, the God of Israel, says: 'I will tear away the kingdom from Solomon's grasp and will give you ten of the tribes. 32 One tribe shall remain to him for the sake of David my servant, and of Jerusalem, the city I have chosen out of all the tribes of Israel. 33 The ten I will give you because he has forsaken me and has worshiped Astarte, goddess of the Sidonians, Chemosh, god of Moab, and Milcom, god of the Ammonites; he has not followed my ways or done what is pleasing to me according to my statutes and my decrees, as his father David did. 34 Yet I will not take any of the kingdom from

sake, however, I shall not do this during your lifetime, but shall tear it out of your son's hands. 13 Even so, I shall not tear the whole kingdom from him. For the sake of my servant David, and for the sake of Jerusalem which I have chosen, I shall leave your son one tribe.'

14 Yahweh raised an enemy against Solomon, Hadad the Edomite, of the kingly stock of Edom. 15 After David had crushed Edom, Joab the army commander had gone to bury the dead and had slaughtered the entire male population of Edom 16 (Joab stayed there with all Israel for six months until he had exterminated the entire male population of Edom), 17 but Hadad with a number of Edomites in his father's service had fled to Egypt. Hadad had been only a boy at the time. 18 They set out from Midian, and on reaching Paran, took a number of men from Paran with them and went on to Egypt, to Pharaoh the king of Egypt, who provided him with a house, undertook to maintain him, and assigned him an estate. 19 Hadad became a great favourite of Pharaoh who gave him his own wife's sister in marriage, the sister of the Great Lady Tahpenes. 20 The sister of Tahpenes bore him his son Genubath whom Tahpenes brought up in Pharaoh's palace, Genubath living in Pharaoh's palace with Pharaoh's own children. 21 But when news reached Hadad in Egypt that David had fallen asleep with his ancestors and that Joab the army commander was dead, he said to Pharaoh, 'Give me leave to go that I may return to my own country.' 22 'What do you want here with me,' Pharaoh said, 'for you to want to go back to your country?' 'Nothing,' he replied, 'but please let me go.' 25b Hence the harm which Hadad caused: he loathed Israel and ruled Edom.

23 God raised a second enemy against Solomon, Rezon son of Eliada. He had fled from his master, Hadadezer king of Zobah. 24 A number of men having rallied to him, he became leader of a marauding band (which was then massacred by David). Rezon captured Damascus and settled there and became king of Damascus. 25a He was hostile to Israel as long as Solomon lived. ‡11.25b: see above‡

26 Jeroboam was the son of Nebat, an Ephraimite from Zeredah; the name of his mother, a widow, was Zeruah; he was in Solomon's service but revolted against the king. 27 This is the account of his revolt.

Solomon was building the Millo and closing the breach in the City of David his father. 28 Now this Jeroboam was a man of great energy; Solomon, noticing how the young man set about his work, put him in charge of all the forced labour of the House of Joseph. 29 One day when Jeroboam had gone out of Jerusalem, the prophet Ahijah of Shiloh accosted him on the road. Ahijah was wearing a new cloak; the two of them were in the open country by themselves. 30 Ahijah took the new cloak which he was wearing and tore it into twelve strips, 31 saying to Jeroboam: 'Take ten strips for yourself, for Yahweh, God of Israel, says this, "I am going to tear the kingdom from Solomon's hand and give ten tribes to you. 32 He will keep one tribe for the sake of my servant David and for the sake of Jerusalem, the city which I have chosen out of all the tribes of Israel; 33 for he has forsaken me to worship Astarte the goddess of the Sidonians, Chemosh the god of Moab, Milcom the god of the Ammonites; he has not followed my ways by doing what I regard as right, or by keeping my laws and ordinances as his father David did. 34 But it is not from his hands that I will

kingdom away from him but will make him ruler all the days of his life, for the sake of my servant David whom I chose and who did keep my commandments and my statutes; 35 but I will take the kingdom away from his son and give it to you — that is, the ten tribes. 36 Yet to his son I will give one tribe, so that my servant David may always have a lamp before me in Jerusalem, the city where I have chosen to put my name. 37 I will take you, and you shall reign over all that your soul desires; you shall be king over Israel. 38 If you will listen to all that I command you, walk in my ways, and do what is right in my sight by keeping my statutes and my commandments, as David my servant did, I will be with you, and will build you an enduring house, as I built for David, and I will give Israel to you. 39 For this reason I will punish the descendants of David, but not forever." 40 Solomon sought therefore to kill Jeroboam; but Jeroboam promptly fled to Egypt, to King Shishak of Egypt, and remained in Egypt until the death of Solomon.

41 Now the rest of the acts of Solomon, all that he did as well as his wisdom, are they not written in the Book of the Acts of Solomon? 42 The time that Solomon reigned in Jerusalem over all Israel was forty years. 43 Solomon slept with his ancestors and was buried in the city of his father David; and his son Rehoboam succeeded him.

12 Rehoboam went to Shechem, for all Israel had come to Shechem to make him king. 2 When Jeroboam son of Nebat heard of it (for he was still in Egypt, where he had fled from King Solomon), then Jeroboam returned fromᶻ Egypt. 3 And they sent and called him; and Jeroboam and all the assembly of Israel came and said to Rehoboam, 4 "Your father made our yoke heavy. Now therefore lighten the hard service of your father and his heavy yoke that he placed on us, and we will serve you." 5 He said to them, "Go away for three days, then come again to me." So the people went away.

6 Then King Rehoboam took counsel with the older men who had attended his father Solomon while he was still alive, saying, "How do you advise me to answer this people?" 7 They answered him, "If you will be a servant to this people today and serve them, and speak good words to them when you answer them, then they will be your servants forever." 8 But he disregarded the advice that the older men gave him, and consulted with the young men who had grown up with him and now attended him. 9 He said to them, "What do you advise that we answer this people who have said to me, 'Lighten the yoke that your father put on us'?" 10 The young men who had grown up with him said to him, "Thus you should say to this people who spoke to you, 'Your father made our yoke heavy, but you must lighten it for us'; thus you should say to them, 'My little finger is thicker than my father's loins. 11 Now, whereas my father laid on you a heavy yoke, I will add to your yoke. My father disciplined you with whips, but I will discipline you with scorpions.' "

12 So Jeroboam and all the people came to Rehoboam the third day, as the king had said, "Come to me again the third day." 13 The king answered the people harshly. He disregarded the advice that the older men had given him 14 and spoke to them according to the advice of the young men, "My father made your yoke heavy, but I will add to your yoke; my father disciplined you with whips, but I will discipline you with scorpions." 15 So the king did not listen to the people, because it was a turn of affairs brought about by the LORD that he might fulfill his word, which the LORD had spoken by Ahijah the Shilonite to Jeroboam son of Nebat.

him, but shall maintain his rule as long as he lives, for the sake of my chosen servant David, who did observe my commandments and statutes. 35 But I shall take the kingdom, that is the ten tribes, from his son and give it to you. 36 To his son I shall give one tribe, that my servant David may always have a lamp burning before me in Jerusalem, the city which I chose to receive my name. 37 I shall appoint you to rule over all that you can desire, and to be king over Israel. 38 If you pay heed to all my commands, if you conform to my ways and do what is right in my eyes, observing my statutes and commandments as my servant David did, then I shall be with you. I shall establish your family for ever as I did for David; I shall give Israel to you, 39 and punish David's descendants as they have deserved, but not for ever.'

40 After this Solomon sought to kill Jeroboam, but he fled to King Shishak in Egypt and remained there till Solomon's death.

41 The other acts and events of Solomon's reign, and all his wisdom, are recorded in the annals of Solomon. 42 The reign of King Solomon in Jerusalem over the whole of Israel lasted forty years. 43 Then he rested with his forefathers and was buried in the city of David his father; he was succeeded by his son Rehoboam.

12 REHOBOAM went to Shechem, for all Israel had gone there to make him king. 2 When Jeroboam son of Nebat, who was still in Egypt, heard of it, he remained there, having taken refuge in Egypt to escape King Solomon. 3 The people now recalled him, and he and all the assembly of Israel came to Rehoboam and said, 4 'Your father laid a harsh yoke upon us; but if you will now lighten the harsh labour he imposed and the heavy yoke he laid on us, we shall serve you.' 5 'Give me three days,' he said, 'and then come back.'

When the people had gone, 6 King Rehoboam consulted the elders who had been in attendance during the lifetime of his father Solomon: 'What answer do you advise me to give to this people?' 7 They said, 'If today you are willing to serve this people, show yourself their servant now and speak kindly to them, and they will be your servants ever after.' 8 But he rejected the advice given him by the elders, and consulted the young men who had grown up with him, and were now in attendance; 9 he asked them, 'What answer do you advise me to give to this people's request that I should lighten the yoke which my father laid on them?' 10 The young men replied, 'Give this answer to the people who say that your father made their yoke heavy and ask you to lighten it; tell them: "My little finger is thicker than my father's loins. 11 My father laid a heavy yoke on you, but I shall make it heavier. My father whipped you, but I shall flay you." '

12 Jeroboam and the people all came to Rehoboam on the third day, as the king had ordered. 13 The king gave them a harsh answer; he rejected the advice which the elders had given him 14 and spoke to the people as the young men had advised: 'My father made your yoke heavy, but I shall make it heavier. My father whipped you, but I shall flay you.' 15 The king would not listen to the people; for the LORD had given this turn to the affair in order that the word he had spoken by Ahijah of Shiloh to Jeroboam son of Nebat might be fulfilled.

ᶻ Gk Vg Compare 2 Chr 10.2: Heb *lived in*

12:1–19 *Cp.* 2 *Chr.* 10:1–19.

Solomon himself, but will keep him a prince as long as he lives for the sake of my servant David, whom I chose, who kept my commandments and statutes. 35 But I will take the kingdom from his son and will give it to you — that is, the ten tribes. 36 I will give his son one tribe, that my servant David may always have a lamp before me in Jerusalem, the city in which I choose to be honored. 37 I will take you; you shall reign over all that you desire and shall become king of Israel. 38 If, then, you heed all that I command you, follow my ways, and please me by keeping my statutes and my commandments like my servant David, I will be with you. I will establish for you, as I did for David, a lasting dynasty; I will give Israel to you. 39 I will punish David's line for this, but not forever.' "

40 When Solomon tried to have Jeroboam killed for his rebellion, he escaped to King Shishak, in Egypt, where he remained until Solomon's death.

41 The rest of the acts of Solomon, with all his deeds and his wisdom, are recorded in the book of the chronicles of Solomon. 42 The time that Solomon reigned in Jerusalem over all Israel was forty years. 43 Solomon rested with his ancestors; he was buried in his father's City of David, and his son Rehoboam succeeded him as king.

12 Rehoboam went to Shechem, where all Israel had come to proclaim him king. ‡12.2: see below‡ 3 They said to Rehoboam: 4 "Your father put on us a heavy yoke. If you now lighten the harsh service and the heavy yoke your father imposed on us, we will serve you." 5 "Come back to me in three days," he answered them. When the people had departed, 6 King Rehoboam consulted the elders who had been in his father's service while he was alive, and asked, "What answer do you advise me to give this people?" 7 They replied, "If today you will be the servant of this people and submit to them, giving them a favorable answer, they will be your servants forever." 8 But he ignored the advice the elders had given him, and consulted the young men who had grown up with him and were in his service. 9 He said to them, "What answer do you advise me to give this people, who have asked me to lighten the yoke my father imposed on them?" 10 The young men who had grown up with him replied, "This is what you must say to this people who have asked you to lighten the yoke your father put on them: 'My little finger is thicker than my father's body. 11 Whereas my father put a heavy yoke on you, I will make it heavier. My father beat you with whips, but I will beat you with scorpions.' "

12 On the third day all Israel came back to King Rehoboam, as he had instructed them to do. 13 Ignoring the advice the elders had given him, the king gave the people a harsh answer. 14 He said to them, as the young men had advised: "My father put on you a heavy yoke, but I will make it heavier. My father beat you with whips, but I will beat you with scorpions." 15 The king did not listen to the people, for the LORD brought this about to fulfill the prophecy he had uttered to Jeroboam, son of Nebat, through Ahijah the Shilonite.

take the kingdom, since I have made him a prince for as long as he lives, for the sake of my servant David who kept my commandments and laws. 35 I shall, however, take the kingdom from the hand of his son, and I shall give it to you, that is, the ten tribes. 36 I shall give one tribe to his son, so that my servant David may always have a lamp in my presence in Jerusalem, the city which I have chosen as a dwelling-place for my name. 37 You nonetheless I shall appoint to rule over as much as you wish, and you will be king of Israel. 38 If you listen to all my orders and follow my ways, by doing what I regard as right and by keeping my laws and commandments as my servant David did, then I shall be with you and shall build you as enduring a dynasty as the one which I built for David. I shall give Israel to you, 39 and I shall humble the descendants of David, but not for ever." '

40 Solomon tried to kill Jeroboam but he made off and fled to Egypt, to Shishak king of Egypt, and he remained in Egypt until Solomon's death.

41 The rest of the history of Solomon, his entire career, his wisdom, is this not recorded in the Book of the Annals of Solomon? 42 Solomon's reign in Jerusalem over all Israel lasted forty years. 43 When Solomon fell asleep with his ancestors, he was buried in the City of David his father; his son Rehoboam succeeded him.

12 Rehoboam then went to Shechem, all Israel having come to Shechem to proclaim him king. 2 (As soon as Jeroboam son of Nebat heard the news — he was still in Egypt, where he had taken refuge from King Solomon — he returned from Egypt. 3 They now sent for him, and Jeroboam and the whole assembly of Israel came.) And they spoke as follows to Rehoboam, 4 'Your father laid a cruel yoke on us; if you will lighten your father's cruel slavery, that heavy yoke which he imposed on us, we are willing to serve you.' 5 He said to them, 'Go away for three days and then come back to me.' And the people went away.

6 King Rehoboam then consulted the elders who had been in attendance on his father Solomon while he was alive, and said, 'How do you advise me to answer this people?' 7 They replied, 'If you become the servant of this people today, and submit to them and give them a fair reply, then they will remain your servants for ever.' 8 But he rejected the advice given him by the elders and consulted the young men in attendance on him, who had grown up with him. 9 He said, 'How do you advise us to answer these people who have been saying, "Lighten the yoke which your father imposed on us!"? ' 10 The young men who had grown up with him replied, 'This is the way to answer these people who have been saying, "Your father made our yoke heavy, you must lighten it for us!" This is the right thing to say to them, "My little finger is thicker than my father's loins. 11 Although my father laid a heavy yoke on you, I shall make it heavier still. My father controlled you with the whip, but I shall apply a spiked lash!" '

12 On the third day Jeroboam and all the people came to Rehoboam in obedience to the king's instruction: 'Come back to me in three days' time.' 13 And the king gave the people a harsh answer, rejecting the advice given him by the elders 14 and speaking to them as the young men had recommended, 'My father made your yoke heavy, I shall make it heavier still! My father controlled you with the whip, but I shall apply a spiked lash!'

15 Thus the king refused to listen to the people, and this was brought about by Yahweh to fulfil the promise which he had made through Ahijah of Shiloh to Jeroboam son of

16 When all Israel saw that the king would not listen to them, the people answered the king,

> "What share do we have in David?
> We have no inheritance in the son of Jesse.
> To your tents, O Israel!
> Look now to your own house, O David."

So Israel went away to their tents. 17 But Rehoboam reigned over the Israelites who were living in the towns of Judah. 18 When King Rehoboam sent Adoram, who was taskmaster over the forced labor, all Israel stoned him to death. King Rehoboam then hurriedly mounted his chariot to flee to Jerusalem. 19 So Israel has been in rebellion against the house of David to this day.

20 When all Israel heard that Jeroboam had returned, they sent and called him to the assembly and made him king over all Israel. There was no one who followed the house of David, except the tribe of Judah alone.

21 When Rehoboam came to Jerusalem, he assembled all the house of Judah and the tribe of Benjamin, one hundred eighty thousand chosen troops to fight against the house of Israel, to restore the kingdom to Rehoboam son of Solomon. 22 But the word of God came to Shemaiah the man of God: 23 Say to King Rehoboam of Judah, son of Solomon, and to all the house of Judah and Benjamin, and to the rest of the people, 24 "Thus says the LORD, You shall not go up or fight against your kindred the people of Israel. Let everyone go home, for this thing is from me." So they heeded the word of the LORD and went home again, according to the word of the LORD.

25 Then Jeroboam built Shechem in the hill country of Ephraim, and resided there; he went out from there and built Penuel. 26 Then Jeroboam said to himself, "Now the kingdom may well revert to the house of David. 27 If this people continues to go up to offer sacrifices in the house of the LORD at Jerusalem, the heart of this people will turn again to their master, King Rehoboam of Judah; they will kill me and return to King Rehoboam of Judah." 28 So the king took counsel, and made two calves of gold. He said to the people,*a* "You have gone up to Jerusalem long enough. Here are your gods, O Israel, who brought you up out of the land of Egypt." 29 He set one in Bethel, and the other he put in Dan. 30 And this thing became a sin, for the people went to worship before the one at Bethel and before the other as far as Dan.*b* 31 He also made houses*c* on high places, and appointed priests from among all the people, who were not Levites. 32 Jeroboam appointed a festival on the fifteenth day of the eighth month like the festival that was in Judah, and he offered sacrifices on the altar; so he did in Bethel, sacrificing to the calves that he had made. And he placed in Bethel the priests of the high places that he had made. 33 He went up to the altar that he had made in Bethel on the fifteenth day in the eighth month, in the month that he alone had devised; he appointed a festival for the people of Israel, and he went up to the altar to offer incense.

13 While Jeroboam was standing by the altar to offer incense, a man of God came out of Judah by the word of the LORD to Bethel 2 and proclaimed against the altar by the word of the LORD, and said, "O altar, altar, thus says the LORD: 'A son shall be born to the house of David, Josiah by name; and he shall sacrifice on you the priests of the high places who offer incense on you, and human bones shall be burned on you.'" 3 He gave a sign the same day, saying, "This is the sign that the LORD has spoken: 'The altar shall be torn down, and the ashes that are on it shall be poured out.'" 4 When the king heard what the man of God

---

16 When all Israel saw that the king would not listen to them, they answered:

> 'What share have we in David?
> We have no lot in the son of Jesse.
> Away to your tents, Israel!
> Now see to your own house, David!'

With that Israel went off to their homes. 17 Rehoboam ruled only over those Israelites who lived in the cities and towns of Judah.

18 King Rehoboam sent out Adoram, the commander of the forced levies, but when the Israelites stoned him to death, the king hastily mounted his chariot and fled to Jerusalem. 19 From that day to this Israel has been in rebellion against the house of David.

20 When the men of Israel heard that Jeroboam had returned, they sent and called him to the assembly and made him king over the whole of Israel. The tribe of Judah alone stayed loyal to the house of David.

21 When Rehoboam reached Jerusalem, he mustered the tribes of Judah and Benjamin, a hundred and eighty thousand chosen warriors, to fight against Israel and recover his kingdom. 22 But this word of God came to Shemaiah the man of God: 23 'Say to Rehoboam son of Solomon, king of Judah, and to all Judah and Benjamin and the rest of the people, 24 This is the word of the LORD: You are not to go up to make war on your kinsmen the Israelites. Return to your homes, for this is my doing.' They listened to the word of the LORD and went back, as the LORD had told them.

25 JEROBOAM rebuilt Shechem in the hill-country of Ephraim and took up residence there; from there he went out and built Penuel. 26 'As things now stand', he said to himself, 'the kingdom will revert to the house of David. 27 If these people go up to sacrifice in the house of the LORD in Jerusalem, it will revive their allegiance to their lord King Rehoboam of Judah, and they will kill me and return to King Rehoboam.' 28 After taking counsel about the matter he made two calves of gold and said to the people, 'You have gone up to Jerusalem long enough; here are your gods, Israel, that brought you up from Egypt.' 29 One he set up at Bethel and the other he put at Dan, 30 and this thing became a sin in Israel; the people went to Bethel to worship the one, and all the way to Dan to worship the other. 31 He also erected temple buildings at shrines and appointed priests who did not belong to the Levites, from every class of the people. 32 He instituted a pilgrim-feast on the fifteenth day of the eighth month like that in Judah, and he offered sacrifices on the altar. This he did at Bethel, sacrificing to the calves that he had made and compelling the priests of the shrines, which he had set up, to serve at Bethel. 33 He went up on the fifteenth day of the eighth month to the altar that he had made at Bethel; there, in a month of his own choosing, he instituted for the Israelites a pilgrim-feast and himself went up to the altar to burn the sacrifice.

13 As Jeroboam stood by the altar to burn the sacrifice, a man of God from Judah, moved by the word of the LORD, appeared at Bethel. 2 He inveighed against the altar in the LORD's name, crying out, 'O altar, altar! This is the word of the LORD: Listen! To the house of David a child shall be born named Josiah. On you he will sacrifice the priests of the shrines who make offerings on you, and he will burn human bones on you.' 3 He gave a sign the same day: 'This is the sign which the LORD has ordained: This altar will be split asunder and the ashes on it will be scattered.' 4 When King Jeroboam heard the sentence which the

---

a Gk: Heb *to them*   *b* Compare Gk: Heb *went to the one as far as Dan*   *c* Gk Vg Compare 13.32: Heb *a house*

12:21–24 Cp. 2 *Chr.* 11:1–4.   12:30 **in Israel . . . one, and:** *so Gk (Luc.); Heb.* the people went.   13:2 **he will burn:** *so Gk; Heb.* they will burn.

16 When all Israel saw that the king did not listen to them, the people answered the king:

"What share have we in David?
We have no heritage in the son of Jesse.
To your tents, O Israel!
Now look to your own house, David."

So Israel went off to their tents, 17 but Rehoboam reigned over the Israelites who lived in the cities of Judah. 18 King Rehoboam then sent out Adoram, superintendent of the forced labor, but all Israel stoned him to death. Rehoboam managed to mount his chariot to flee to Jerusalem, 19 and Israel went into rebellion against David's house to this day. 2 Jeroboam, son of Nebat, who was still in Egypt, where he had fled from King Solomon, returned from Egypt as soon as he learned this. 20 When all Israel heard that Jeroboam had returned, they summoned him to an assembly and made him king over all Israel. None remained loyal to David's house except the tribe of Judah alone.

21 On his arrival in Jerusalem, Rehoboam gathered together all the house of Judah and the tribe of Benjamin—one hundred eighty thousand seasoned warriors—to fight against the house of Israel, to restore the kingdom to Rehoboam, son of Solomon. 22 However, the LORD spoke to Shemaiah, a man of God: 23 "Say to Rehoboam, son of Solomon, king of Judah, and to the house of Judah and to Benjamin, and to the rest of the people: 24 'Thus says the LORD: You must not march out to fight against your brother Israelites. Let every man return home, for I have brought this about.'" They accepted this message of the LORD and gave up the expedition accordingly.

25 Jeroboam built up Shechem in the hill country of Ephraim and lived there. Then he left it and built up Penuel.

26 Jeroboam thought to himself: "The kingdom will return to David's house. 27 If now this people go up to offer sacrifices in the temple of the LORD in Jerusalem, the hearts of this people will return to their master, Rehoboam, king of Judah, and they will kill me." 28 After taking counsel, the king made two calves of gold and said to the people: "You have been going up to Jerusalem long enough. Here is your God, O Israel, who brought you up from the land of Egypt." 29 And he put one in Bethel, the other in Dan. 30 This led to sin, because the people frequented these calves in Bethel and in Dan. 31 He also built temples on the high places and made priests from among the people who were not Levites. 32 Jeroboam established a feast in the eighth month on the fifteenth day of the month to duplicate in Bethel the pilgrimage feast of Judah, with sacrifices to the calves he had made; and he stationed in Bethel priests of the high places he had built.

33 Jeroboam ascended the altar he built in Bethel on the fifteenth day of the eighth month, the month in which he arbitrarily chose to establish a feast for the Israelites; he was going to offer sacrifice.

13 A man of God came from Judah to Bethel by the word of the LORD, while Jeroboam was standing at the altar to offer sacrifice. 2 He cried out against the altar by the word of the LORD: "O altar, altar, the LORD says, 'A child shall be born to the house of David, Josiah by name, who shall slaughter upon you the priests of the high places who offer sacrifice upon you, and he shall burn human bones upon you.'" 3 He gave a sign that same day and said: "This is the sign that the LORD has spoken: The altar shall break up and the ashes on it shall be strewn about."

4 When King Jeroboam heard what the man of God was

Nebat. 16 When all Israel saw that the king refused to listen to them, the people answered the king thus:

What share have we in David?
— No heritage in the son of Jesse!
Away to your tents, Israel!
Now look after your own House, David!

So Israel went home again. 17 Rehoboam, however, reigned over those Israelites who lived in the towns of Judah. 18 When King Rehoboam sent Adoram, who was in charge of forced labour, all Israel stoned him to death, while King Rehoboam managed to mount his chariot and escape to Jerusalem. 19 And Israel has remained in rebellion against the House of David from that day to this.

20 When all Israel heard that Jeroboam had returned, they summoned him to the assembly and made him king of all Israel; no one remained loyal to the House of David, except the tribe of Judah.

21 When Rehoboam reached Jerusalem he mustered the whole House of Judah and the tribe of Benjamin, a hundred and eighty thousand picked warriors, to fight the House of Israel and win back the kingdom for Rehoboam son of Solomon. 22 But the word of Yahweh came to Shemaiah, man of God, 23 'Say this to Rehoboam son of Solomon, king of Judah, to the whole House of Judah, to Benjamin and to the rest of the people, 24 "Yahweh says this: Do not go and make war on your brothers, the Israelites; let everyone go home, for this is my doing."' They obeyed the command of Yahweh and turned back in accordance with his word.

25 Jeroboam fortified Shechem in the mountain country of Ephraim and made that his residence. Then, leaving there, he fortified Penuel.

26 Jeroboam thought to himself, 'As things are, the kingdom will revert to the House of David. 27 If this people continues to go up to the Temple of Yahweh in Jerusalem to offer sacrifices, the people's heart will turn back again to their lord, Rehoboam king of Judah, and they will put me to death.' 28 So the king thought this over and then made two golden calves; he said to the people, 'You have been going up to Jerusalem long enough. Here is your God, Israel, who brought you out of Egypt!' 29 He set one up at Bethel, 30 and the people went in procession in front of the other one all the way to Dan. In Israel this gave rise to sin, for the people went to Bethel to worship the one, and all the way to Dan to worship the other. 31 He set up shrines on the high places and appointed priests from ordinary families, who were not of levitical descent. 32 Jeroboam also instituted a feast in the eighth month, on the fifteenth of the month, like the feast kept in Judah, when he offered sacrifices on the altar. This he did at Bethel, offering sacrifices to the calves which he had made and, at Bethel, installing the priests of the high places which he had set up. 33 On the fifteenth of the eighth month, the month which he had chosen deliberately, he offered sacrifices on the altar which he had made at Bethel; he instituted a feast for the Israelites and himself went up to the altar to burn the sacrifice.

13 There came to Bethel at Yahweh's command a man of God from Judah, just as Jeroboam was standing by the altar to offer the sacrifice, and at Yahweh's command this man denounced the altar. 'Altar, altar,' he said, 'Yahweh says this, "A son is to be born to the House of David, Josiah by name, and on you he will slaughter the priests of the high places who have offered sacrifice on you, and on you he will burn human bones."' 3 At the same time he gave a sign. 'This is the sign', he said, 'that Yahweh has spoken, "This altar will burst apart and the ashes which are on it will be spilt."' 4 When the king heard how the man of

cried out against the altar at Bethel, Jeroboam stretched out his hand from the altar, saying, "Seize him!" But the hand that he stretched out against him withered so that he could not draw it back to himself. 5 The altar also was torn down, and the ashes poured out from the altar, according to the sign that the man of God had given by the word of the LORD. 6 The king said to the man of God, "Entreat now the favor of the LORD your God, and pray for me, so that my hand may be restored to me." So the man of God entreated the LORD; and the king's hand was restored to him, and became as it was before. 7 Then the king said to the man of God, "Come home with me and dine, and I will give you a gift." 8 But the man of God said to the king, "If you give me half your kingdom, I will not go in with you; nor will I eat food or drink water in this place. 9 For thus I was commanded by the word of the LORD: You shall not eat food, or drink water, or return by the way that you came." 10 So he went out another way, and did not return by the way that he had come to Bethel.

11 Now there lived an old prophet in Bethel. One of his sons came and told him all that the man of God had done that day in Bethel; the words also that he had spoken to the king, they told to their father. 12 Their father said to them, "Which way did he go?" And his sons showed him the way that the man of God who came from Judah had gone. 13 Then he said to his sons, "Saddle a donkey for me." So they saddled a donkey for him, and he mounted it. 14 He went after the man of God, and found him sitting under an oak tree. He said to him, "Are you the man of God who came from Judah?" He answered, "I am." 15 Then he said to him, "Come home with me and eat some food." 16 But he said, "I cannot return with you, or go in with you; nor will I eat food or drink water with you in this place; 17 for it was said to me by the word of the LORD: You shall not eat food or drink water there, or return by the way that you came." 18 Then the other[d] said to him, "I also am a prophet as you are, and an angel spoke to me by the word of the LORD: Bring him back with you into your house so that he may eat food and drink water." But he was deceiving him. 19 Then the man of God[d] went back with him, and ate food and drank water in his house.

20 As they were sitting at the table, the word of the LORD came to the prophet who had brought him back; 21 and he proclaimed to the man of God who came from Judah, "Thus says the LORD: Because you have disobeyed the word of the LORD, and have not kept the commandment that the LORD your God commanded you, 22 but have come back and have eaten food and drunk water in the place of which he said to you, 'Eat no food, and drink no water,' your body shall not come to your ancestral tomb." 23 After the man of God[d] had eaten food and had drunk, they saddled for him a donkey belonging to the prophet who had brought him back. 24 Then as he went away, a lion met him on the road and killed him. His body was thrown in the road, and the donkey stood beside it; the lion also stood beside the body. 25 People passed by and saw the body thrown in the road, with the lion standing by the body. And they came and told it in the town where the old prophet lived.

26 When the prophet who had brought him back from the way heard of it, he said, "It is the man of God who disobeyed the word of the LORD; therefore the LORD has given him to the lion, which has torn him and killed him according to the word that the LORD spoke to him." 27 Then he said to his sons, "Saddle a donkey for me." So they saddled one, 28 and he went and found the body thrown in the road, with the donkey and the lion standing beside the body. The lion had not eaten the body or attacked the donkey. 29 The prophet took up the body of the man of God,

man of God pronounced against the altar at Bethel, he pointed to him from the altar and cried, 'Seize him!' Immediately the hand which he had pointed at him became paralysed, so that he could not draw it back. 5 The altar too was split asunder and the ashes were scattered, in fulfilment of the sign that the man of God had given at the LORD's command. 6 The king appealed to the man of God to placate the LORD his God and pray for him that his hand might be restored. The man of God did as he asked; the king's hand was restored and became as it had been before. 7 He said to the man of God, 'Come home with me and have some refreshment, and let me give you a reward.' 8 But he answered, 'If you were to give me half your house, I would not enter it with you: I will eat and drink nothing in this place, 9 for the LORD's command to me was to eat and drink nothing, and not to go back by the way I came.' 10 So he went back another way, not returning by the road he had taken to Bethel.

11 At that time there was an aged prophet living in Bethel. His sons came and told him all that the man of God had done there that day, and what he had said to the king. 12 Their father asked, 'Which road did he take?' They pointed out the direction taken by the man of God who had come from Judah. 13 He said to his sons, 'Saddle the donkey for me.' They saddled the donkey, and, mounted on it, 14 he went after the man of God.

He came on him seated under a terebinth and asked, 'Are you the man of God who came from Judah?' 'I am,' he replied. 15 'Come home and eat with me,' said the prophet. 16 'I may not go back with you or enter your house,' said the other; 'I may neither eat nor drink with you in this place, 17 for it was told me by the word of the LORD: You are to eat and drink nothing there, nor are you to go back the way you came.' 18 The old man urged him, 'I also am a prophet, as you are; and an angel commanded me by the word of the LORD to bring you to my home to eat and drink with me.' He was lying. 19 but the man of Judah went back with him and ate and drank in his house. 20 While they were still seated at table the word of the LORD came to the prophet who had brought him back, 21 and he cried out to the man of God from Judah, 'This is the word of the LORD: You have defied the word of the LORD your God and have not obeyed his command; 22 you have gone back to eat and drink in the place where he forbade it; therefore your body will not be laid in the grave of your forefathers.'

23 After the man of God had eaten and drunk, the prophet who had brought him back saddled the donkey for him. 24 As he rode on his way a lion met him and killed him, and his body was left lying in the road, with the donkey and the lion both standing beside it. 25 Some passers-by saw the body lying in the road and the lion standing beside it, and they brought the news to the town where the old prophet lived. 26 When the prophet who had caused him to break his journey heard it, he said, 'It is the man of God who defied the word of the LORD. The LORD has given him to the lion, and it has broken his neck and killed him in fulfilment of the word of the LORD.' 27 He told his sons to saddle the donkey and, when they did so, 28 he set out and found the body lying in the road with the donkey and the lion standing beside it; the lion had neither devoured the body nor broken the back of the donkey. 29 The prophet lifted the body of the

---

[d] Heb he

13:11 **His sons came:** *so Gk; Heb.* His son came.

crying out against the altar, he stretched forth his hand from the altar and said, "Seize him!" But the hand he stretched forth against him withered, so that he could not draw it back. 5 Moreover, the altar broke up and the ashes from it were strewn about—the sign the man of God had given as the word of the LORD. 6 Then the king appealed to the man of God. "Entreat the LORD, your God," he said, "and intercede for me that I may be able to withdraw my hand." So the man of God entreated the LORD, and the king recovered the normal use of his hand. 7 "Come home with me for some refreshment," the king invited the man of God, "and I will give you a present." 8 "If you gave me half your kingdom," the man of God said to the king, "I would not go with you, nor eat bread or drink water in this place. 9 For I was instructed by the word of the LORD not to eat bread or drink water and not to return by the way I came." 10 So he departed by another road and did not go back the way he had come to Bethel.

11 There was an old prophet living in the city, whose sons came and told him all that the man of God had done that day in Bethel. When they repeated to their father the words he had spoken to the king, 12 the father asked them, "Which way did he go?" And his sons pointed out to him the road taken by the man of God who had come from Judah. 13 Then he said to his sons, "Saddle the ass for me." When they had saddled it, he mounted 14 and followed the man of God, whom he found seated under a terebinth. When he asked him, "Are you the man of God who came from Judah?" he answered, "Yes." 15 Then he said, "Come home with me and have some bread." 16 "I cannot go back with you, and I cannot eat bread or drink water with you in this place," he answered, 17 "for I was told by the word of the LORD neither to eat bread nor drink water here, and not to go back the way I came." 18 But he said to him, "I, too, am a prophet like you, and an angel told me in the word of the LORD to bring you back with me to my house and to have you eat bread and drink water." He was lying to him, however.

19 So he went back with him, and ate bread and drank water in his house. 20 But while they were sitting at table, the LORD spoke to the prophet who had brought him back, 21 and he cried out to the man of God who had come from Judah: "The LORD says, 'Because you rebelled against the command of the LORD and did not keep the command which the LORD, your God, gave you, 22 but returned and ate bread and drank water in the place where he told you to do neither, your corpse shall not be brought to the grave of your ancestors.'"

23 After he had eaten bread and drunk water, the ass was saddled for him, and he again 24 set out. But a lion met him on the road, and killed him. His corpse lay sprawled on the road, and the ass remained standing by it, and so did the lion. 25 Some passers-by saw the body lying in the road, with the lion standing beside it, and carried the news to the city where the old prophet lived. 26 On hearing it, the prophet who had brought him back from his journey said: "It is the man of God who rebelled against the command of the LORD. He has delivered him to a lion, which mangled and killed him, as the LORD predicted to him." 27 Then he said to his sons, "Saddle the ass for me." When they had saddled it, 28 he went off and found the body lying in the road with the ass and the lion standing beside it. The lion had not eaten the body nor had it harmed the ass. 29 The prophet

God denounced the altar of Bethel, he stretched out his hand from the altar, saying, 'Seize him!' But the hand he stretched out against the man withered, and he could not draw it back, 5 and the altar burst apart and the ashes from the altar were spilt, in accordance with the sign given by the man of God at Yahweh's command. 6 The king said to the man of God, 'I beg you to placate Yahweh your God, and so restore me the use of my hand.' The man of God placated Yahweh; the king's hand was restored as it had been before. 7 The king then said to the man of God, 'Come home with me and refresh yourself, and I shall give you a present,' 8 but the man of God replied to the king, 'Were you to give me half your palace, I would not go with you. I will eat and drink nothing here, 9 for I have had Yahweh's order, "You are to eat or drink nothing, nor to return by the way you came." ' 10 And he left by another road and did not return by the way he had come to Bethel.

11 Now there was an old prophet living in Bethel, and his sons came to tell him all that the man of God had done in Bethel that day; and the words which he had said to the king, they told these to their father too. 12 'Which road did he take?' their father asked. His sons showed him the road which the man of God who came from Judah had taken. 13 'Saddle the donkey for me,' he said to his sons; they saddled the donkey for him and he mounted. 14 He followed the man of God and found him sitting under a terebinth. 'Are you the man of God', he said, 'who came from Judah?' 'I am,' he replied. 15 'Come home with me,' he said, 'and take some food.' 16 'I cannot go back with you,' he answered, 'or eat or drink anything here, 17 for I have received Yahweh's order, "You are to eat or drink nothing there, nor to return by the way you came." ' 18 'I too am a prophet like you,' the other replied, 'and an angel told me this by Yahweh's command, "Bring him back with you to your house to eat and drink." ' He was lying to him. 19 The man of God went back with him; he ate and drank at his house.

20 As they were sitting at table a word of Yahweh came to the prophet who had brought him back, 21 and he addressed the man of God who came from Judah. 'Yahweh says this,' he said. 'Since you have defied Yahweh's command and not obeyed the orders which Yahweh your God gave you, 22 but have come back and eaten and drunk where he forbade you to eat and drink, your corpse will never reach the tomb of your ancestors.'' 23 After he had eaten and drunk, the prophet saddled the donkey for him, and he turned about and went away. 24 A lion met him on the road and killed him; his corpse lay stretched out on the road; the donkey stood there beside it; the lion stood by the corpse too. 25 People going by saw the corpse lying on the road and the lion standing by the corpse, and went and spoke about it in the town where the old prophet lived. 26 When the prophet who had made the man turn back heard about it, he said, 'That is the man of God who defied Yahweh's command! Yahweh has handed him over to the lion, which has mauled and killed him, just as Yahweh had foretold it would.' 27 He said to his sons, 'Saddle the donkey for me,' and they saddled it. 28 He set off and found the man's corpse lying on the road with the donkey and the lion standing beside the corpse; the lion had neither eaten the corpse nor mauled the donkey. 29 The prophet lifted the corpse of the

laid it on the donkey, and brought it back to the city,[e] to mourn and to bury him. 30 He laid the body in his own grave; and they mourned over him, saying, "Alas, my brother!" 31 After he had buried him, he said to his sons, "When I die, bury me in the grave in which the man of God is buried; lay my bones beside his bones. 32 For the saying that he proclaimed by the word of the LORD against the altar in Bethel, and against all the houses of the high places that are in the cities of Samaria, shall surely come to pass."

33 Even after this event Jeroboam did not turn from his evil way, but made priests for the high places again from among all the people; any who wanted to be priests he consecrated for the high places. 34 This matter became sin to the house of Jeroboam, so as to cut it off and to destroy it from the face of the earth.

14 At that time Abijah son of Jeroboam fell sick. 2 Jeroboam said to his wife, "Go, disguise yourself, so that it will not be known that you are the wife of Jeroboam, and go to Shiloh; for the prophet Ahijah is there, who said of me that I should be king over this people. 3 Take with you ten loaves, some cakes, and a jar of honey, and go to him; he will tell you what shall happen to the child." 4 Jeroboam's wife did so; she set out and went to Shiloh, and came to the house of Ahijah. Now Ahijah could not see, for his eyes were dim because of his age. 5 But the LORD said to Ahijah, "The wife of Jeroboam is coming to inquire of you concerning her son; for he is sick. Thus and thus you shall say to her."

When she came, she pretended to be another woman. 6 But when Ahijah heard the sound of her feet, as she came in at the door, he said, "Come in, wife of Jeroboam; why do you pretend to be another? For I am charged with heavy tidings for you. 7 Go, tell Jeroboam, 'Thus says the LORD, the God of Israel: Because I exalted you from among the people, made you leader over my people Israel, 8 and tore the kingdom away from the house of David to give it to you; yet you have not been like my servant David, who kept my commandments and followed me with all his heart, doing only that which was right in my sight, 9 but you have done evil above all those who were before you and have gone and made for yourself other gods, and cast images, provoking me to anger, and have thrust me behind your back; 10 therefore, I will bring evil upon the house of Jeroboam. I will cut off from Jeroboam every male, both bond and free in Israel, and will consume the house of Jeroboam, just as one burns up dung until it is all gone. 11 Anyone belonging to Jeroboam who dies in the city, the dogs shall eat; and anyone who dies in the open country, the birds of the air shall eat; for the LORD has spoken.' 12 Therefore set out, go to your house. When your feet enter the city, the child shall die. 13 All Israel shall mourn for him and bury him; for he alone of Jeroboam's family shall come to the grave, because in him there is found something pleasing to the LORD, the God of Israel, in the house of Jeroboam. 14 Moreover the LORD will raise up for himself a king over Israel, who shall cut off the house of Jeroboam today, even right now![f]

15 "The LORD will strike Israel, as a reed is shaken in the water; he will root up Israel out of this good land that he gave to their ancestors, and scatter them beyond the Euphrates, because they have made their sacred poles,[g] provoking the LORD to anger. 16 He will give Israel up because of the sins of Jeroboam, which he sinned and which he caused Israel to commit."

17 Then Jeroboam's wife got up and went away, and she came to Tirzah. As she came to the threshold of the house, the child died. 18 All Israel buried him and mourned

man of God, laid it on the donkey, and brought it back to his own town to mourn over it and bury it. 30 He laid the body in his own grave and they mourned for him, saying, 'Oh, my brother!' 31 After burying him, he said to his sons, 'When I die, bury me in the grave where the man of God lies buried; lay my bones beside his; 32 for the sentence which he pronounced at the LORD's command against the altar in Bethel and all the temples at shrines throughout Samaria will surely come true.'

33 After this Jeroboam still did not abandon his evil ways, but went on appointing priests for the shrines from all classes of the people; any man who offered himself he would consecrate to be priest of a shrine. 34 By doing this he brought guilt on his own house and doomed it to utter destruction.

14 At that time Jeroboam's son Abijah fell ill, 2 and Jeroboam said to his wife, 'Go at once to Shiloh, but disguise yourself so that people will not recognize you as my wife. Ahijah the prophet is there, he who said I was to be king over this people. 3 Take with you ten loaves, some raisins, and a jar of honey. Go to him and he will tell you what will happen to the boy.' 4 Jeroboam's wife did so; she set off at once for Shiloh and came to Ahijah's house. Now as Ahijah could not see, for his eyes were fixed in the blindness of old age, 5 the LORD had said to him, 'Jeroboam's wife is on her way to consult you about her son, who is ill; you are to give her such and such an answer.'

When she came in, concealing who she was, 6 and Ahijah heard her footsteps at the door, he said, 'Come in, wife of Jeroboam. Why conceal who you are? I have heavy news for you. 7 Go, tell Jeroboam: "This is the word of the LORD the God of Israel: I raised you out of the people and appointed you prince over my people Israel; 8 I tore the kingdom from the house of David and gave it to you. But you have not been like my servant David, who kept my commands and followed me with his whole heart, doing only what was right in my eyes. 9 You have outdone all your predecessors in wickedness; you have provoked me to anger by making for yourself other gods and images of cast metal; and you have turned your back on me. 10 For this I am going to bring disaster on the house of Jeroboam; I shall destroy them all, every mother's son, whether still under the protection of the family or not, and I shall sweep away the house of Jeroboam in Israel, as one sweeps away dung until none is left. 11 Those of that house who die in the town shall be food for the dogs, and those who die in the country shall be food for the birds. It is the word of the LORD."

12 'Go home now; the moment you set foot in the town, the child will die. 13 All Israel will mourn for him and bury him; he alone of all Jeroboam's family will have proper burial, because in him alone could the LORD the God of Israel find anything good.

14 'The LORD will set up a king over Israel who will put an end to the house of Jeroboam. This first; and what next? 15 The LORD will strike Israel, till it trembles like a reed in the water; he will uproot its people from this good land which he gave to their forefathers and scatter them beyond the Euphrates, because they have made their sacred poles, thus provoking the LORD's anger. 16 He will abandon Israel because of the sins that Jeroboam has committed and has led Israel to commit.'

17 Jeroboam's wife went away back to Tirzah and, as she crossed the threshold of the house, the boy died. 18 They

---

[e] Gk: Heb he came to the town of the old prophet [f] Meaning of Heb uncertain [g] Heb Asherim

14:14 **next:** so Aram. (Targ.); Heb. now.   14:15 **sacred poles:** Heb. asherim.

NEW AMERICAN BIBLE

lifted up the body of the man of God and put it on the ass, and brought it back to the city to mourn over it and to bury it. 30 He laid the man's body in his own grave, and they mourned over it: "Alas, my brother!" 31 After he had buried him, he said to his sons, "When I die, bury me in the grave where the man of God is buried. Lay my remains beside his. 32 For the word of the LORD which he proclaimed against the altar in Bethel and against all the shrines on the high places in the cities of Samaria shall certainly come to pass."

33 Jeroboam did not give up his evil ways after this event, but again made priests for the high places from among the common people. Whoever desired it was consecrated and became a priest of the high places. 34 This was a sin on the part of the house of Jeroboam for which it was to be cut off and destroyed from the earth.

14 At that time Abijah, son of Jeroboam, took sick. 2 So Jeroboam said to his wife, "Get ready and disguise yourself so that none will recognize you as Jeroboam's wife. Then go to Shiloh, where you will find the prophet Ahijah. It is he who predicted my reign over this people. 3 Take along ten loaves, some cakes, and a jar of preserves, and go to him. He will tell you what will happen to the child." 4 The wife of Jeroboam obeyed. She made the journey to Shiloh and entered the house of Ahijah who could not see because age had dimmed his sight.

5 The LORD had said to Ahijah: "Jeroboam's wife is coming to consult you about her son, for he is sick. This is what you must tell her. When she comes, she will be in disguise." 6 So Ahijah, hearing the sound of her footsteps as she entered the door, said, "Come in, wife of Jeroboam. Why are you in disguise? I have been commissioned to give you bitter news. 7 Go, tell Jeroboam, 'This is what the LORD, the God of Israel, says: I exalted you from among the people and made you ruler of my people Israel. 8 I deprived the house of David of the kingdom and gave it to you. Yet you have not been like my servant David, who kept my commandments and followed me with his whole heart, doing only what pleased me. 9 You have done worse than all who preceded you: you have gone and made for yourself strange gods and molten images to provoke me; but me you have cast behind your back. 10 Therefore, I am bringing evil upon the house of Jeroboam: I will cut off every male in Jeroboam's line, whether slave or freeman in Israel, and will burn up the house of Jeroboam completely, as though dung were being burned. 11 When one of Jeroboam's line dies in the city, dogs will devour him; when one of them dies in the field, he will be devoured by the birds of the sky. For the LORD has spoken!' 12 So leave; go home! As you step inside the city, the child will die, 13 and all Israel will mourn him and bury him, for he alone of Jeroboam's line will be laid in the grave, since in him alone of Jeroboam's house has something pleasing to the LORD, the God of Israel, been found. 14 Today, at this very moment, the LORD will raise up for himself a king of Israel who will destroy the house of Jeroboam. 15 The LORD will strike Israel like a reed tossed about in the water and will pluck out Israel from this good land which he gave their fathers, scattering them beyond the River, because they made sacred poles for themselves and thus provoked the LORD. 16 He will give up Israel because of the sins Jeroboam has committed and caused Israel to commit."

17 So Jeroboam's wife started back; when she reached Tirzah and crossed the threshold of her house, the child died. 18 He was buried with all Israel mourning him, as the

NEW JERUSALEM BIBLE

man of God and put it on the donkey and brought it back to the town where he lived to hold mourning for him and bury him. 30 He laid the corpse in his own tomb, and they raised the mourning cry for him, 'Alas, my brother!' 31 After burying him, the prophet said to his sons, 'When I die, bury me in the same tomb as the man of God, lay my bones beside his. 32 For the word he uttered at Yahweh's command against the altar of Bethel and against all the shrines of the high places in the towns of Samaria will certainly come true.'

33 Jeroboam did not give up his wicked ways after this incident, but went on appointing priests for the high places from the common people. He consecrated as priests of the high places any who wished to be. 34 Such conduct made the House of Jeroboam a sinful House, and caused its ruin and extinction from the face of the earth.

14 At that time Abijah, Jeroboam's son, fell sick. 2 and Jeroboam said to his wife, 'Come, please disguise yourself so that no one will recognise you as Jeroboam's wife, and go to Shiloh; the prophet Ahijah is there, the man who said I was to be king of this people. 3 Go to him, and take ten loaves and some savoury food and a jar of honey; he will tell you what will happen to the child.' 4 Jeroboam's wife did this: she set out, went to Shiloh and came to Ahijah's house. 5 Now Ahijah could not see, his eyes were fixed with age, but Yahweh had told him, 'Jeroboam's wife is now on her way to ask you for a prophecy about her son, as he is sick. You will tell her such and such. When she comes, she will pretend to be some other woman.' 6 So when Ahijah heard her footsteps at the door, he called, 'Come in, wife of Jeroboam; why pretend to be someone else? I have bad news for you. 7 Go and tell Jeroboam, "Yahweh, God of Israel, says this: I raised you from the people and made you leader of my people Israel; 8 I tore the kingdom from the House of David and gave it to you. But you have not been like my servant David who kept my commandments and followed me with all his heart, doing only what I regard as right; 9 you have done more evil than all your predecessors, you have gone and made yourself other gods, idols of cast metal, provoking my anger, and you have turned your back on me. 10 For this I shall bring disaster on the House of Jeroboam, I shall wipe out every manjack of the family of Jeroboam, fettered or free in Israel, I shall sweep away the House of Jeroboam as a man sweeps dung away till none is left. 11 Those of Jeroboam's family who die in the city, the dogs will eat; and those who die in the open country, the birds of the air will eat, for Yahweh has spoken." 12 Now get up and go home; at the moment your feet enter the town, the child will die. 13 All Israel will mourn for him, and bury him; and he alone of Jeroboam's family will have a proper burial, for in him alone of the House of Jeroboam can Yahweh, God of Israel, find anything good. 14 Yahweh will set a king over Israel, who will put an end to the House of Jeroboam. 15 Yahweh will make Israel shake, till it quivers like a reed in the water; he will uproot Israel from this prosperous land which he gave to their ancestors and scatter them beyond the River for provoking Yahweh to anger by making their sacred poles. 16 He will abandon Israel for the sins which Jeroboam has committed and made Israel commit.' 17 Jeroboam's wife rose and left. She arrived at Tirzah, and when she crossed the threshold of the palace, the child was already dead.

for him, according to the word of the LORD, which he spoke by his servant the prophet Ahijah.

19 Now the rest of the acts of Jeroboam, how he warred and how he reigned, are written in the Book of the Annals of the Kings of Israel. 20 The time that Jeroboam reigned was twenty-two years; then he slept with his ancestors, and his son Nadab succeeded him.

21 Now Rehoboam son of Solomon reigned in Judah. Rehoboam was forty-one years old when he began to reign, and he reigned seventeen years in Jerusalem, the city that the LORD had chosen out of all the tribes of Israel, to put his name there. His mother's name was Naamah the Ammonite. 22 Judah did what was evil in the sight of the LORD; they provoked him to jealousy with their sins that they committed, more than all that their ancestors had done. 23 For they also built for themselves high places, pillars, and sacred poles[h] on every high hill and under every green tree; 24 there were also male temple prostitutes in the land. They committed all the abominations of the nations that the LORD drove out before the people of Israel.

25 In the fifth year of King Rehoboam, King Shishak of Egypt came up against Jerusalem; 26 he took away the treasures of the house of the LORD and the treasures of the king's house; he took everything. He also took away all the shields of gold that Solomon had made; 27 so King Rehoboam made shields of bronze instead, and committed them to the hands of the officers of the guard, who kept the door of the king's house. 28 As often as the king went into the house of the LORD, the guard carried them and brought them back to the guardroom.

29 Now the rest of the acts of Rehoboam, and all that he did, are they not written in the Book of the Annals of the Kings of Judah? 30 There was war between Rehoboam and Jeroboam continually. 31 Rehoboam slept with his ancestors and was buried with his ancestors in the city of David. His mother's name was Naamah the Ammonite. His son Abijam succeeded him.

15 Now in the eighteenth year of King Jeroboam son of Nebat, Abijam began to reign over Judah. 2 He reigned for three years in Jerusalem. His mother's name was Maacah daughter of Abishalom. 3 He committed all the sins that his father did before him; his heart was not true to the LORD his God, like the heart of his father David. 4 Nevertheless for David's sake the LORD his God gave him a lamp in Jerusalem, setting up his son after him, and establishing Jerusalem; 5 because David did what was right in the sight of the LORD, and did not turn aside from anything that he commanded him all the days of his life, except in the matter of Uriah the Hittite. 6 The war begun between Rehoboam and Jeroboam continued all the days of his life. 7 The rest of the acts of Abijam, and all that he did, are they not written in the Book of the Annals of the Kings of Judah? There was war between Abijam and Jeroboam. 8 Abijam slept with his ancestors, and they buried him in the city of David. Then his son Asa succeeded him.

9 In the twentieth year of King Jeroboam of Israel, Asa began to reign over Judah; 10 he reigned forty-one years in Jerusalem. His mother's name was Maacah daughter of Abishalom. 11 Asa did what was right in the sight of the LORD, as his father David had done. 12 He put away the male temple prostitutes out of the land, and removed all the idols that his ancestors had made. 13 He also removed his

buried him, and all Israel mourned over him; and thus the word of the LORD was fulfilled which he had spoken through his servant Ahijah the prophet.

19 The other events of Jeroboam's reign, in war and peace, are recorded in the annals of the kings of Israel. 20 After reigning for twenty-two years, he rested with his forefathers and was succeeded by his son Nadab.

21 IN Judah Rehoboam son of Solomon had become king. He was forty-one years old when he came to the throne, and he reigned for seventeen years in Jerusalem, the city where the LORD had chosen, out of all the tribes of Israel, to set his name. Rehoboam's mother was a woman of Ammon called Naamah. 22 Judah did what was wrong in the eyes of the LORD, rousing his jealous indignation by the sins they committed, which were beyond anything that their forefathers had done. 23 They erected shrines, sacred pillars, and sacred poles on every high hill and under every spreading tree. 24 Worse still, all over the country there were male prostitutes attached to the shrines, and the people adopted all the abominable practices of the nations whom the LORD had dispossessed in favour of Israel.

25 In the fifth year of Rehoboam's reign King Shishak of Egypt attacked Jerusalem, 26 and carried away the treasures of the house of the LORD and of the king's palace; he seized everything, including all the gold shields made for Solomon. 27 King Rehoboam replaced them with bronze shields and entrusted them to the officers of the escort who guarded the entrance of the palace. 28 Whenever the king entered the house of the LORD, the escort carried them; afterwards they returned them to the guardroom.

29 The other acts and events of Rehoboam's reign are recorded in the annals of the kings of Judah. 30 There was continual fighting between him and Jeroboam. 31 He rested with his forefathers and was buried with them in the city of David. Rehoboam's mother was an Ammonite called Naamah. He was succeeded by his son Abijam.

15 In the eighteenth year of the reign of Jeroboam son of Nebat, Abijam became king of Judah. 2 He reigned in Jerusalem for three years; his mother was Maacah granddaughter of Abishalom. 3 All the sins that his father before him had committed he also committed, nor was he faithful to the LORD his God as his ancestor David had been. 4 But for David's sake the LORD his God gave him a lamp to burn in Jerusalem, by establishing his dynasty and making Jerusalem secure, 5 because David had done what was right in the eyes of the LORD and had not disobeyed any of his commandments all his life, except in the matter of Uriah the Hittite. 7 The other acts and events of Abijam's reign are recorded in the annals of the kings of Judah. There was war between Abijam and Jeroboam. 8 Abijam rested with his forefathers and was buried in the city of David; his son Asa succeeded him.

9 In the twentieth year of King Jeroboam of Israel, Asa became king of Judah. 10 He reigned in Jerusalem for forty-one years; his grandmother was Maacah granddaughter of Abishalom. 11 Asa did what was right in the eyes of the LORD, as his ancestor David had done. 12 He expelled from the land the male prostitutes attached to the shrines and removed all the idols which his predecessors had made.

14:25–28 Cp. 2 Chr. 12:9–11.   14:29–31 Cp. 2 Chr. 12:13–16.
15:2 granddaughter: lit. daughter.   15:5 except . . . Hittite: prob. rdg; Heb. adds 6 There was war between Rehoboam and Jeroboam all his days (cp. 14:30).   15:10 grandmother: lit. mother. granddaughter: lit. daughter.

h Heb Asherim

NEW AMERICAN BIBLE

LORD had prophesied through his servant the prophet Ahijah.

19 The rest of the acts of Jeroboam, with his warfare and his reign, are recorded in the book of the chronicles of the kings of Israel. 20 The length of Jeroboam's reign was twenty-two years. He rested with his ancestors, and his son Nadab succeeded him as king.

21 Rehoboam, son of Solomon, reigned in Judah. He was forty-one years old when he became king, and he reigned seventeen years in Jerusalem, the city in which, out of all the tribes of Israel, the LORD chose to be honored. His mother was the Ammonite named Naamah.

22 Judah did evil in the sight of the LORD, and by their sins angered him even more than their fathers had done. 23 They, too, built for themselves high places, pillars, and sacred poles, upon every high hill and under every green tree. 24 There were also cult prostitutes in the land. Judah imitated all the abominable practices of the nations whom the LORD had cleared out of the Israelites' way.

25 In the fifth year of King Rehoboam, Shishak, king of Egypt, attacked Jerusalem. 26 He took everything, including the treasures of the temple of the LORD and those of the royal palace, as well as all the gold shields made under Solomon. 27 To replace them, King Rehoboam had bronze shields made, which he entrusted to the officers of the guard on duty at the entrance of the royal palace. 28 Whenever the king visited the temple of the LORD, those on duty would carry the shields, and then return them to the guardroom.

29 The rest of the acts of Rehoboam, with all that he did, are recorded in the book of the chronicles of the kings of Judah. 30 There was constant warfare between Rehoboam and Jeroboam. 31 Rehoboam rested with his ancestors; he was buried with them in the City of David. His mother was the Ammonite named Naamah. His son Abijam succeeded him as king.

15 In the eighteenth year of King Jeroboam, son of Nebat, Abijam became king of Judah; 2 he reigned three years in Jerusalem. His mother's name was Maacah, daughter of Abishalom. 3 He imitated all the sins his father had committed before him, and his heart was not entirely with the LORD, his God, like the heart of his grandfather David. 4 Yet for David's sake the LORD, his God, gave him a lamp in Jerusalem, raising up his son after him and permitting Jerusalem to endure; 5 because David had pleased the LORD and did not disobey any of his commands as long as he lived, except in the case of Uriah the Hittite.

7 The rest of Abijam's acts, with all that he did, are written in the book of the chronicles of the kings of Judah. 6 There was war between Abijam and Jeroboam. 8 Abijam rested with his ancestors; he was buried in the City of David, and his son Asa succeeded him as king.

9 In the twentieth year of Jeroboam, king of Israel, Asa, king of Judah, began to reign; 10 he reigned forty-one years in Jerusalem. His grandmother's name was Maacah, daughter of Abishalom. 11 Asa pleased the LORD like his forefather David, 12 banishing the temple prostitutes from the land and removing all the idols his father had made. 13 He also

NEW JERUSALEM BIBLE

18 They buried him, and all Israel mourned for him, just as Yahweh had foretold through his servant Ahijah the prophet.

19 The rest of the history of Jeroboam, what wars he waged, how he governed, this is recorded in the Book of the Annals of the Kings of Israel. 20 Jeroboam's reign lasted twenty-two years. Then he fell asleep with his ancestors; his son Nadab succeeded him.

21 In Judah, Rehoboam son of Solomon became king; he was forty-one years old when he came to the throne and he reigned for seventeen years in Jerusalem, the city which Yahweh had chosen out of all the tribes of Israel, to give his name a home there. His mother's name was Naamah, the Ammonite. 22 He did what is displeasing to Yahweh, arousing his resentment more than his ancestors by all the sins which they had committed; 23 they had built themselves high places, and had set up pillars and sacred poles on every high hill and under every spreading tree. 24 There were even male sacred prostitutes in the country. He copied all the shameful practices of the nations whom Yahweh had dispossessed for the Israelites.

25 And so it happened that in the fifth year of King Rehoboam, Shishak king of Egypt advanced on Jerusalem 26 and carried off all the treasures of the Temple of Yahweh and the treasures of the royal palace; he took everything away, including all the golden shields which Solomon had made. 27 To replace those King Rehoboam made bronze shields, entrusting them to the commanders of the guard who guarded the king's palace gate. 28 Whenever the king went to the Temple of Yahweh, the guards would carry them, returning them to the guardroom afterwards.

29 The rest of the history of Rehoboam, his entire career, is this not recorded in the Book of the Annals of the Kings of Judah? 30 Warfare between Rehoboam and Jeroboam went on throughout the period. 31 When Rehoboam fell asleep with his ancestors, he was buried in the City of David; his son Abijam succeeded him.

15 In the eighteenth year of King Jeroboam son of Nebat, Abijam became king of Judah 2 and reigned for three years in Jerusalem. His mother's name was Maacah descendant of Absalom. 3 In everything he followed the sinful example of his father before him; his heart was not wholly with Yahweh his God, as the heart of David his ancestor had been. 4 However, for David's sake, Yahweh his God gave him a lamp in Jerusalem, with a son to succeed him, so keeping Jerusalem secure; 5 for David had done what Yahweh regarded as right and had never in all his life disobeyed whatever he commanded him (except in the matter of Uriah the Hittite). *d*

7 The rest of the history of Abijam, his entire career, is this not recorded in the Book of the Annals of the Kings of Judah? Abijam and Jeroboam made war on each other. 8 When Abijam fell asleep with his ancestors, he was buried in the City of David; his son Asa succeeded him.

9 In the twentieth year of Jeroboam king of Israel, Asa became king of Judah 10 and reigned for forty-one years in Jerusalem. His mother's name was Maacah descendant of Absalom. 11 Asa did what Yahweh regards as right, as his ancestor David had done. 12 He drove the male prostitutes out of the country and got rid of all the idols which his ancestors had made. 13 He even deprived his grandmother

d **15** v. 6 is omitted as in some Gk texts; it doubles 14:30.

mother Maacah from being queen mother, because she had made an abominable image for Asherah; Asa cut down her image and burned it at the Wadi Kidron. [14] But the high places were not taken away. Nevertheless the heart of Asa was true to the LORD all his days. [15] He brought into the house of the LORD the votive gifts of his father and his own votive gifts — silver, gold, and utensils.

[16] There was war between Asa and King Baasha of Israel all their days. [17] King Baasha of Israel went up against Judah, and built Ramah, to prevent anyone from going out or coming in to King Asa of Judah. [18] Then Asa took all the silver and the gold that were left in the treasures of the house of the LORD and the treasures of the king's house, and gave them into the hands of his servants. King Asa sent them to King Ben-hadad son of Tabrimmon son of Hezion of Aram, who resided in Damascus, saying, [19] "Let there be an alliance between me and you, like that between my father and your father: I am sending you a present of silver and gold; go, break your alliance with King Baasha of Israel, so that he may withdraw from me." [20] Ben-hadad listened to King Asa, and sent the commanders of his armies against the cities of Israel. He conquered Ijon, Dan, Abel-beth-maacah, and all Chinneroth, with all the land of Naphtali. [21] When Baasha heard of it, he stopped building Ramah and lived in Tirzah. [22] Then King Asa made a proclamation to all Judah, none was exempt: they carried away the stones of Ramah and its timber, with which Baasha had been building; with them King Asa built Geba of Benjamin and Mizpah. [23] Now the rest of all the acts of Asa, all his power, all that he did, and the cities that he built, are they not written in the Book of the Annals of the Kings of Judah? But in his old age he was diseased in his feet. [24] Then Asa slept with his ancestors, and was buried with his ancestors in the city of his father David; his son Jehoshaphat succeeded him.

[25] Nadab son of Jeroboam began to reign over Israel in the second year of King Asa of Judah; he reigned over Israel two years. [26] He did what was evil in the sight of the LORD, walking in the way of his ancestor and in the sin that he caused Israel to commit.

[27] Baasha son of Ahijah, of the house of Issachar, conspired against him; and Baasha struck him down at Gibbethon, which belonged to the Philistines; for Nadab and all Israel were laying siege to Gibbethon. [28] So Baasha killed Nadab[i] in the third year of King Asa of Judah, and succeeded him. [29] As soon as he was king, he killed all the house of Jeroboam; he left to the house of Jeroboam not one that breathed, until he had destroyed it, according to the word of the LORD that he spoke by his servant Ahijah the Shilonite — [30] because of the sins of Jeroboam that he committed and that he caused Israel to commit, and because of the anger to which he provoked the LORD, the God of Israel.

[31] Now the rest of the acts of Nadab, and all that he did, are they not written in the Book of the Annals of the Kings of Israel? [32] There was war between Asa and King Baasha of Israel all their days.

[33] In the third year of King Asa of Judah, Baasha son of Ahijah began to reign over all Israel at Tirzah; he reigned twenty-four years. [34] He did what was evil in the sight of the LORD, walking in the way of Jeroboam and in the sin that he caused Israel to commit.

16 The word of the LORD came to Jehu son of Hanani against Baasha, saying, [2] "Since I exalted you out of the dust and made you leader over my people Israel, and you have walked in the way of Jeroboam, and have caused my people Israel to sin, provoking me to anger with their sins, [3] therefore, I will consume Baasha and his house, and

[13] He even deprived Maacah his grandmother of her rank as queen mother because she had an obscene object made for the worship of Asherah; Asa cut it down and burnt it in the wadi Kidron. [14] Although the shrines were allowed to remain, Asa himself remained faithful to the LORD all his life. [15] He brought into the house of the LORD all his father's votive offerings and his own, the silver and gold and the sacred vessels.

[16] There was war between Asa and King Baasha of Israel all through their reigns. [17] King Baasha invaded Judah and fortified Ramah to prevent anyone leaving or entering the kingdom of Asa of Judah. [18] Asa took all the silver and gold that remained in the treasuries of the house of the LORD and the palace, and sent his servants with them to Ben-hadad son of Tabrimmon, son of Hezion, king of Aram, whose capital was Damascus, with instructions to say, [19] 'Let there be an alliance between us, as there was between our fathers. Herewith I send you a present of silver and gold; break off your alliance with King Baasha of Israel, so that he will abandon his campaign against me.' [20] Ben-hadad listened with approval to King Asa; he ordered his army commanders to move against the towns of Israel, and they attacked Iyyon, Dan, Abel-beth-maacah, and that part of Kinnereth which marches with the land of Naphtali. [21] When Baasha heard of it, he discontinued the fortifying of Ramah and fell back on Tirzah. [22] Then King Asa issued a proclamation requiring every man in Judah without exception to join in removing the stones of Ramah and the timbers with which Baasha had fortified it, and he used them to fortify Geba of Benjamin and Mizpah.

[23] All the other events of Asa's reign, his exploits and achievements, and the towns he built, are recorded in the annals of the kings of Judah. But in his old age he was afflicted with disease in his feet. [24] He rested with his forefathers and was buried with them in the city of his ancestor David; he was succeeded by his son Jehoshaphat.

[25] Nadab son of Jeroboam became king of Israel in the second year of King Asa of Judah, and he reigned for two years. [26] He did what was evil in the eyes of the LORD and followed in his father's footsteps, repeating the sin which Jeroboam had led Israel to commit. [27] Baasha son of Ahijah, of the house of Issachar, conspired against him and attacked him at Gibbethon, a Philistine town which Baasha was besieging with all his forces. [28] Baasha slew him and usurped the throne in the third year of King Asa of Judah. [29] As soon as he became king, he struck down the whole family of Jeroboam, destroying every living soul and leaving not one survivor. Thus the word of the LORD was fulfilled which he spoke through his servant Ahijah the Shilonite. [30] This happened because of the sins of Jeroboam and the sins which he led Israel to commit, and because he had provoked the anger of the LORD the God of Israel. [31] The other events of Nadab's reign and all his acts are recorded in the annals of the kings of Israel. [32] There was war between Asa and King Baasha of Israel throughout their reigns.

[33] In the third year of King Asa of Judah, Baasha son of Ahijah became king of all Israel in Tirzah and reigned for twenty-four years. [34] He did what was wrong in the eyes of the LORD and followed in Jeroboam's footsteps, repeating the sin which Jeroboam had led Israel to commit.

16 [1] This word of the LORD against Baasha came to Jehu son of Hanani: [2] 'I raised you from the dust and made you a prince over my people Israel, but you have followed in the footsteps of Jeroboam and have led my people Israel into sin, so provoking me to anger with their sins. [3] Therefore I am about to sweep away Baasha and his

[i] Heb *him*

15:13–15 *Cp. 2 Chr. 15:16–18.* 15:17–22 *Cp. 2 Chr. 16:1–6.*
15:23–24 *Cp. 2 Chr. 16:11–14.*

NEW AMERICAN BIBLE

NEW JERUSALEM BIBLE

deposed his grandmother Maacah from her position as queen mother, because she had made an outrageous object for Asherah. Asa cut down this object and burned it in the Kidron Valley. 14 The high places did not disappear; yet Asa's heart was entirely with the LORD as long as he lived. 15 He brought into the temple of the LORD his father's and his own votive offerings of silver, gold, and various utensils.

16 There was war between Asa and Baasha, king of Israel, as long as they both reigned. 17 Baasha, king of Israel, attacked Judah and fortified Ramah to prevent communication with Asa, king of Judah. 18 Asa then took all the silver and gold remaining in the treasuries of the temple of the LORD and of the royal palace. Entrusting them to his ministers, King Asa sent them to Ben-hadad, son of Tabrimmon, son of Hezion, king of Aram, resident in Damascus. He said: 19 "There is a treaty between you and me, as there was between your father and my father. I am sending you a present of silver and gold. Go, break your treaty with Baasha, king of Israel, that he may withdraw from me." 20 Ben-hadad agreed with King Asa and sent the leaders of his troops against the cities of Israel. They attacked Ijon, Dan, Abel-beth-maacah, and all Chinnereth, besides all the land of Naphtali. 21 When Baasha heard of it, he left off fortifying Ramah, and stayed in Tirzah. 22 Then King Asa summoned all Judah without exception, and they carried away the stones and beams with which Baasha was fortifying Ramah. With them King Asa built Geba of Benjamin and Mizpeh.

23 The rest of the acts of Asa, with all his valor and accomplishments, and the cities he built, are written in the book of the chronicles of the kings of Judah. In his old age, Asa had an infirmity in his feet. 24 He rested with his ancestors; he was buried in his forefather's City of David, and his son Jehoshaphat succeeded him as king.

25 In the second year of Asa, king of Judah, Nadab, son of Jeroboam, became king of Israel; he reigned over Israel two years. 26 He did evil in the LORD's sight, imitating his father's conduct and the sin which he had caused Israel to commit. 27 Baasha, son of Ahijah, of the house of Issachar, plotted against him and struck him down at Gibbethon of the Philistines, which Nadab and all Israel were besieging. 28 Baasha killed him in the third year of Asa, king of Judah, and reigned in his stead. 29 Once he was king, he killed off the entire house of Jeroboam, not leaving a single soul to Jeroboam but destroying him utterly, according to the warning which the LORD had pronounced through his servant, Ahijah the Shilonite, 30 because of the sins Jeroboam committed and caused Israel to commit, by which he provoked the LORD, the God of Israel, to anger.

31 The rest of the acts of Nadab, with all that he did, are written in the book of the chronicles of the kings of Israel. 32 [There was war between Asa and Baasha, king of Israel, as long as they lived.]

33 In the third year of Asa, king of Judah, Baasha, son of Ahijah, began his twenty-four-year reign over Israel in Tirzah. 34 He did evil in the LORD's sight, imitating the conduct of Jeroboam and the sin he had caused Israel to commit.

16

The LORD spoke against Baasha to Jehu, son of Hanani, and said: 2 "Inasmuch as I lifted you up from the dust and made you ruler of my people Israel, but you have imitated the conduct of Jeroboam and have caused my people Israel to sin, provoking me to anger by their sins,

Maacah of the dignity of Great Lady for having made an obscenity for Asherah; Asa cut down her obscenity and burnt it in the ravine of the Kidron. 14 Though the high places were not abolished, Asa's heart was loyal to Yahweh throughout his life. 15 He deposited his father's and his own dedicated gifts of silver, gold and sacred vessels in the Temple of Yahweh.

16 Asa and Baasha king of Israel were at war with each other throughout their reigns. 17 Baasha king of Israel marched on Judah and fortified Ramah to blockade Asa king of Judah. 18 Asa then took all the remaining silver and gold left in the treasuries of the Temple of Yahweh and the royal palace. Entrusting this to his servants, King Asa sent them with the following message to Ben-Hadad son of Tabrimmon, son of Hezion, the king of Aram who lived in Damascus, 19 'Let us make an alliance between myself and yourself, between my father and your father! Look, I have sent you a gift of silver and gold. Come, break off your alliance with Baasha king of Israel, which will make him withdraw from me.' 20 Ben-Hadad listened favourably to King Asa, and sent the generals of his armies to attack the towns of Israel; he ravaged Ijon, Dan, Abel-Beth-Maacah, all Chinneroth, and the whole territory of Naphtali. 21 When Baasha heard this he gave up fortifying Ramah and retired to Tirzah. 22 King Asa then summoned all Judah, no one was exempt; they took away the stones and timber with which Baasha had been fortifying Ramah, and King Asa used them to fortify Geba of Benjamin and Mizpah.

23 The rest of the history of Asa, all his valour, his entire career, is this not recorded in the Book of the Annals of the Kings of Judah? In his old age, however, he contracted a disease of his feet. 24 When Asa fell asleep with his ancestors, he was buried with his ancestors in the City of his ancestor David; his son Jehoshaphat succeeded him.

25 Nadab son of Jeroboam became king of Israel in the second year of Asa king of Judah, and he reigned over Israel for two years. 26 He did what is displeasing to Yahweh; he copied his father's example and the sin into which he had led Israel. 27 Baasha son of Ahijah, of the House of Issachar, plotted against him and murdered him at Gibbethon, a Philistine town which Nadab and all Israel were besieging. 28 Baasha killed Nadab and succeeded him in the third year of Asa king of Judah. 29 No sooner was he king than he butchered the entire House of Jeroboam, not sparing a soul, and put an end to it, just as Yahweh had foretold through his servant Ahijah of Shiloh, 30 because of the sins which he had committed and into which he had led Israel, and because he had provoked the anger of Yahweh, God of Israel.

31 The rest of the history of Nadab, his entire career, is this not recorded in 32 the Book of the Annals of the Kings of Israel?

33 In the third year of Asa king of Judah, Baasha son of Ahijah became king of Israel at Tirzah for twenty-four years. 34 He did what is displeasing to Yahweh; he copied the example of Jeroboam and the sin into which he had led Israel.

16

The word of Yahweh came to Jehu son of Hanani against Baasha: 2 'I raised you from the dust and made you leader of my people Israel, but you have followed Jeroboam's example and led my people Israel into sins which provoke my anger. 3 Now I shall sweep away Baasha

NEW REVISED STANDARD VERSION

REVISED ENGLISH BIBLE

I will make your house like the house of Jeroboam son of Nebat. 4 Anyone belonging to Baasha who dies in the city the dogs shall eat; and anyone of his who dies in the field the birds of the air shall eat."

5 Now the rest of the acts of Baasha, what he did, and his power, are they not written in the Book of the Annals of the Kings of Israel? 6 Baasha slept with his ancestors, and was buried at Tirzah; and his son Elah succeeded him. 7 Moreover the word of the LORD came by the prophet Jehu son of Hanani against Baasha and his house, both because of all the evil that he did in the sight of the LORD, provoking him to anger with the work of his hands, in being like the house of Jeroboam, and also because he destroyed it.

8 In the twenty-sixth year of King Asa of Judah, Elah son of Baasha began to reign over Israel in Tirzah; he reigned two years. 9 But his servant Zimri, commander of half his chariots, conspired against him. When he was at Tirzah, drinking himself drunk in the house of Arza, who was in charge of the palace at Tirzah, 10 Zimri came in and struck him down and killed him, in the twenty-seventh year of King Asa of Judah, and succeeded him.

11 When he began to reign, as soon as he had seated himself on his throne, he killed all the house of Baasha; he did not leave him a single male of his kindred or his friends. 12 Thus Zimri destroyed all the house of Baasha, according to the word of the LORD, which he spoke against Baasha by the prophet Jehu — 13 because of all the sins of Baasha and the sins of his son Elah that they committed, and that they caused Israel to commit, provoking the LORD God of Israel to anger with their idols. 14 Now the rest of the acts of Elah, and all that he did, are they not written in the Book of the Annals of the Kings of Israel?

15 In the twenty-seventh year of King Asa of Judah, Zimri reigned seven days in Tirzah. Now the troops were encamped against Gibbethon, which belonged to the Philistines, 16 and the troops who were encamped heard it said, "Zimri has conspired, and he has killed the king"; therefore all Israel made Omri, the commander of the army, king over Israel that day in the camp. 17 So Omri went up from Gibbethon, and all Israel with him, and they besieged Tirzah. 18 When Zimri saw that the city was taken, he went into the citadel of the king's house; he burned down the king's house over himself with fire, and died — 19 because of the sins that he committed, doing evil in the sight of the LORD, walking in the way of Jeroboam, and for the sin that he committed, causing Israel to sin. 20 Now the rest of the acts of Zimri, and the conspiracy that he made, are they not written in the Book of the Annals of the Kings of Israel?

21 Then the people of Israel were divided into two parts; half of the people followed Tibni son of Ginath, to make him king, and half followed Omri. 22 But the people who followed Omri overcame the people who followed Tibni son of Ginath; so Tibni died, and Omri became king. 23 In the thirty-first year of King Asa of Judah, Omri began to reign over Israel; he reigned for twelve years, six of them in Tirzah.

24 He bought the hill of Samaria from Shemer for two talents of silver; he fortified the hill, and called the city that he built, Samaria, after the name of Shemer, the owner of the hill.

25 Omri did what was evil in the sight of the LORD; he did more evil than all who were before him. 26 For he walked in all the way of Jeroboam son of Nebat, and in the sins that he caused Israel to commit, provoking the LORD, the God of Israel, to anger by their idols. 27 Now the rest of the acts of Omri that he did, and the power that he showed, are they not written in the Book of the Annals of the Kings of Israel? 28 Omri slept with his ancestors, and was buried in Samaria; his son Ahab succeeded him.

house and deal with it as I dealt with the house of Jeroboam son of Nebat. 4 Those of Baasha's family who die in a town will be food for the dogs, and those who die in the country will be food for the birds.' 5 The other events of Baasha's reign, his achievements and his exploits, are recorded in the annals of the kings of Israel. 6 Baasha rested with his forefathers and was buried in Tirzah; he was succeeded by his son Elah.

7 The word of the LORD concerning Baasha and his family came also through the prophet Jehu son of Hanani, because of all the wrong that he had done in the eyes of the LORD, thereby provoking his anger: he had not only sinned like the house of Jeroboam, but had also brought destruction upon it.

8 In the twenty-sixth year of King Asa of Judah, Elah son of Baasha became king of Israel and he reigned in Tirzah for two years. 9 Zimri, who was in his service commanding half the chariotry, plotted against him. The king was in Tirzah drinking himself into insensibility in the house of Arza, comptroller of the household there, 10 when Zimri broke in, attacked and assassinated him, and made himself king. This took place in the twenty-seventh year of King Asa of Judah.

11 As soon as Zimri had become king and was enthroned, he struck down all the household of Baasha; he left him not a single mother's son alive, neither kinsman nor friend. 12 By destroying the whole household of Baasha he fulfilled the word of the LORD concerning Baasha, spoken through the prophet Jehu. 13 This was what came of all the sins which Baasha and his son Elah had committed and the sins into which they had led Israel, provoking the anger of the LORD the God of Israel with their worthless idols. 14 The other events and acts of Elah's reign are recorded in the annals of the kings of Israel.

15 In the twenty-seventh year of King Asa of Judah, Zimri reigned in Tirzah for seven days. At the time the army was investing the Philistine city of Gibbethon. 16 When the Israelite troops in the camp heard of Zimri's conspiracy and the murder of the king, there and then they made their commander Omri king of Israel by common consent. 17 Omri and his whole force then withdrew from Gibbethon and laid siege to Tirzah. 18 As soon as Zimri saw that the city had fallen, he retreated to the keep of the royal palace, set the whole of it on fire over his head, and so perished. 19 This was what came of the sin he had committed by doing what was wrong in the eyes of the LORD and following in the footsteps of Jeroboam, repeating the sin into which he had led Israel. 20 The other events of Zimri's reign, and his conspiracy, are recorded in the annals of the kings of Israel.

21 Thereafter the people of Israel were split into two factions: one supported Tibni son of Ginath, determined to make him king; the other supported Omri. 22 Omri's party proved the stronger; Tibni lost his life, and Omri became king.

23 It was in the thirty-first year of King Asa of Judah that Omri became king of Israel and he reigned for twelve years, six of them in Tirzah. 24 He bought the hill of Samaria from Shemer for two talents of silver, and built a city on it which he named Samaria after Shemer the owner of the hill. 25 Omri did what was wrong in the eyes of the LORD; he outdid all his predecessors in wickedness. 26 He followed in the footsteps of Jeroboam son of Nebat, repeating the sins which he had led Israel to commit, so that they provoked the anger of the LORD their God with their worthless idols. 27 The other events of Omri's reign, and his exploits, are recorded in the annals of the kings of Israel. 28 So Omri rested with his forefathers and was buried in Samaria; he was succeeded by his son Ahab.

NEW AMERICAN BIBLE

3 I will destroy you, Baasha, and your house; 4 I will make your house like that of Jeroboam, son of Nebat. If anyone of Baasha's line dies in the city, dogs shall devour him; if he dies in the field, he shall be devoured by the birds of the sky."

5 The rest of the acts of Baasha, with all his valor and accomplishments, are written in the book of the chronicles of the kings of Israel. 6 Baasha rested with his ancestors; he was buried in Tirzah, and his son Elah succeeded him as king. 7 [Through the prophet Jehu, son of Hanani, the LORD had threatened Baasha and his house, because of all the evil Baasha did in the sight of the LORD, provoking him to anger by his evil deeds, so that he became like the house of Jeroboam; and because he killed Nadab.]

8 In the twenty-sixth year of Asa, king of Judah, Elah, son of Baasha, began his two-year reign over Israel in Tirzah. 9 His servant Zimri, commander of half his chariots, plotted against him. As he was in Tirzah, drinking to excess in the house of Arza, superintendent of his palace in Tirzah, 10 Zimri entered; he struck and killed him in the twenty-seventh year of Asa, king of Judah, and reigned in his place. 11 Once he was seated on the royal throne, he killed off the whole house of Baasha, not sparing a single male relative or friend of his. 12 Zimri destroyed the entire house of Baasha, as the LORD had prophesied to Baasha through the prophet Jehu, 13 because of all the sins which Baasha and his son Elah committed and caused Israel to commit, provoking the LORD, the God of Israel, to anger by their idols.

14 The rest of the acts of Elah, with all that he did, are written in the book of the chronicles of the kings of Israel.

15 In the twenty-seventh year of Asa, king of Judah, Zimri reigned seven days in Tirzah. The army was besieging Gibbethon of the Philistines 16 when they heard that Zimri had formed a conspiracy and had killed the king. So that day in the camp all Israel proclaimed Omri, general of the army, king of Israel. 17 Omri marched up from Gibbethon, accompanied by all Israel, and laid siege to Tirzah. 18 When Zimri saw the city was captured, he entered the citadel of the royal palace and burned down the palace over him. He died 19 because of the sins he had committed, doing evil in the sight of the LORD by imitating the sinful conduct of Jeroboam, thus causing Israel to sin.

20 The rest of the acts of Zimri, with the conspiracy he carried out, are written in the book of the chronicles of the kings of Israel.

21 At that time the people of Israel were divided, half following Tibni, son of Ginath, to make him king, and half for Omri. 22 The partisans of Omri prevailed over those of Tibni, son of Ginath. Tibni died and Omri became king.

23 In the thirty-first year of Asa, king of Judah, Omri became king; he reigned over Israel twelve years, the first six of them in Tirzah. 24 He then bought the hill of Samaria from Shemer for two silver talents and built upon the hill, naming the city he built Samaria after Shemer, the former owner. 25 But Omri did evil in the LORD's sight beyond any of his predecessors. 26 He closely imitated the sinful conduct of Jeroboam, son of Nebat, causing Israel to sin and to provoke the LORD, the God of Israel, to anger by their idols.

27 The rest of the acts of Omri, with all his valor and accomplishments, are written in the book of the chronicles of the kings of Israel. 28 Omri rested with his ancestors; he was buried in Samaria, and his son Ahab succeeded him as king.

NEW JERUSALEM BIBLE

and his House; I shall make your House like the House of Jeroboam son of Nebat. 4 Those of Baasha's family who die in the city, the dogs will eat; and those who die in the open country, the birds of the air will eat.'

5 The rest of the history of Baasha, his career, his valour, is this not recorded in the Book of the Annals of the Kings of Israel? 6 When Baasha fell asleep with his ancestors, he was buried in Tirzah; his son Elah succeeded him.

7 Furthermore, the word of Yahweh was delivered through the prophet Jehu son of Hanani against Baasha and his House, first because of the many ways in which he had displeased Yahweh, provoking him to anger by his actions and becoming like the House of Jeroboam; secondly because he had destroyed that House.

8 In the twenty-sixth year of Asa king of Judah, Elah son of Baasha became king of Israel at Tirzah, for two years. 9 Zimri, one of his officers, captain of half his chariotry, plotted against him. While he was at Tirzah, drinking himself senseless in the house of Arza who was master of the palace in Tirzah, 10 Zimri came in, struck him down and killed him in the twenty-seventh year of Asa king of Judah, and succeeded him. 11 On his accession, as soon as he was seated on the throne, he butchered Baasha's entire family, not leaving him one manjack of them alive, neither relative nor friend. 12 Zimri destroyed the whole House of Baasha, in accordance with the word which Yahweh had spoken against Baasha through the prophet Jehu, 13 because of all the sins of Baasha and his son Elah into which they had led Israel, provoking the anger of Yahweh, God of Israel, with their worthless idols.

14 The history of Elah, his entire career, is this not recorded in the Book of the Annals of the Kings of Israel?

15 In the twenty-seventh year of Asa king of Judah, Zimri became king for seven days, at Tirzah. The people were then encamped in front of Gibbethon, a Philistine town. 16 When news reached the camp of how Zimri had not only plotted against but actually killed the king, all Israel proclaimed the army commander Omri as king of Israel in the camp that very day. 17 Omri, and all Israel with him, raised the siege of Gibbethon and laid siege to Tirzah. 18 When Zimri saw that the town had been captured, he went into the keep of the royal palace, burned the palace over his own head, and died. 19 This was because of the sin which he had committed in doing what is displeasing to Yahweh, by copying the example of Jeroboam and the sin into which he had led Israel.

20 The rest of the history of Zimri and of his conspiracy, is this not recorded in the Book of the Annals of the Kings of Israel?

21 The people of Israel then split into two factions: one half following Tibni son of Ginath to make him king, the other half following Omri. 22 But the faction of Omri proved stronger than that of Tibni son of Ginath; thus Tibni lost his life and Omri became king.

23 In the thirty-first year of Asa king of Judah, Omri became king of Israel and reigned for twelve years. He reigned for six years at Tirzah. 24 Then for two talents of silver he bought the hill of Samaria from Shemer and on it built a town which he named Samaria after Shemer who had owned the hill. 25 Omri did what is displeasing to Yahweh, and was worse than all his predecessors. 26 In every way he copied the example of Jeroboam son of Nebat and the sins into which he had led Israel, provoking the anger of Yahweh, God of Israel, with their worthless idols.

27 The rest of the history of Omri, his career, his valour, is this not recorded in the Book of the Annals of the Kings of Israel? 28 When Omri fell asleep with his ancestors, he was buried in Samaria; his son Ahab succeeded him.

NEW REVISED STANDARD VERSION

29 In the thirty-eighth year of King Asa of Judah, Ahab son of Omri began to reign over Israel; Ahab son of Omri reigned over Israel in Samaria twenty-two years. 30 Ahab son of Omri did evil in the sight of the LORD more than all who were before him.

31 And as if it had been a light thing for him to walk in the sins of Jeroboam son of Nebat, he took as his wife Jezebel daughter of King Ethbaal of the Sidonians, and went and served Baal, and worshiped him. 32 He erected an altar for Baal in the house of Baal, which he built in Samaria. 33 Ahab also made a sacred pole.*j* Ahab did more to provoke the anger of the LORD, the God of Israel, than had all the kings of Israel who were before him. 34 In his days Hiel of Bethel built Jericho; he laid its foundation at the cost of Abiram his firstborn, and set up its gates at the cost of his youngest son Segub, according to the word of the LORD, which he spoke by Joshua son of Nun.

17 Now Elijah the Tishbite, of Tishbe*k* in Gilead, said to Ahab, "As the LORD the God of Israel lives, before whom I stand, there shall be neither dew nor rain these years, except by my word." 2 The word of the LORD came to him, saying, 3 "Go from here and turn eastward, and hide yourself by the Wadi Cherith, which is east of the Jordan. 4 You shall drink from the wadi, and I have commanded the ravens to feed you there." 5 So he went and did according to the word of the LORD; he went and lived by the Wadi Cherith, which is east of the Jordan. 6 The ravens brought him bread and meat in the morning, and bread and meat in the evening; and he drank from the wadi. 7 But after a while the wadi dried up, because there was no rain in the land.

8 Then the word of the LORD came to him, saying, 9 "Go now to Zarephath, which belongs to Sidon, and live there; for I have commanded a widow there to feed you." 10 So he set out and went to Zarephath. When he came to the gate of the town, a widow was there gathering sticks; he called to her and said, "Bring me a little water in a vessel, so that I may drink." 11 As she was going to bring it, he called to her and said, "Bring me a morsel of bread in your hand." 12 But she said, "As the LORD your God lives, I have nothing baked, only a handful of meal in a jar, and a little oil in a jug; I am now gathering a couple of sticks, so that I may go home and prepare it for myself and my son, that we may eat it, and die." 13 Elijah said to her, "Do not be afraid; go and do as you have said; but first make me a little cake of it and bring it to me, and afterwards make something for yourself and your son. 14 For thus says the LORD the God of Israel: The jar of meal will not be emptied and the jug of oil will not fail until the day that the LORD sends rain on the earth." 15 She went and did as Elijah said, so that she as well as he and her household ate for many days. 16 The jar of meal was not emptied, neither did the jug of oil fail, according to the word of the LORD that he spoke by Elijah.

17 After this the son of the woman, the mistress of the house, became ill; his illness was so severe that there was no breath left in him. 18 She then said to Elijah, "What have you against me, O man of God? You have come to me to bring my sin to remembrance, and to cause the death of my son!" 19 But he said to her, "Give me your son." He took him from her bosom, carried him up into the upper chamber where he was lodging, and laid him on his own bed. 20 He cried out to the LORD, "O LORD my God, have you brought calamity even upon the widow with whom I am staying, by killing her son?" 21 Then he stretched himself upon the child three times, and cried out to the LORD, "O LORD my God, let this child's life come into him again." 22 The LORD lis-

REVISED ENGLISH BIBLE

29 AHAB son of Omri became king of Israel in the thirty-eighth year of King Asa of Judah, and he reigned over Israel in Samaria for twenty-two years. 30 More than any of his predecessors he did what was wrong in the eyes of the LORD. 31 As if it were not enough for him to follow the sinful ways of Jeroboam son of Nebat, he took as his wife Jezebel daughter of King Ethbaal of Sidon, and went and served Baal; he prostrated himself before him 32 and erected an altar to him in the temple of Baal which he built in Samaria. 33 He also set up a sacred pole; indeed he did more to provoke the anger of the LORD the God of Israel than all the kings of Israel before him.

34 During Ahab's reign Hiel of Bethel rebuilt Jericho; laying its foundations cost him his eldest son Abiram, and the setting up of its gates cost him Segub his youngest son. Thus was fulfilled what the LORD had spoken through Joshua son of Nun.

17 Elijah the Tishbite from Tishbe in Gilead said to Ahab, 'I swear by the life of the LORD the God of Israel, whose servant I am, that there will be neither dew nor rain these coming years unless I give the word.' 2 Then the word of the LORD came to him: 3 'Leave this place, turn eastwards, and go into hiding in the wadi of Kerith east of the Jordan. 4 You are to drink from the stream, and I have commanded the ravens to feed you there.' 5 Elijah did as the LORD had told him: he went and stayed in the wadi of Kerith east of the Jordan, 6 and the ravens brought him bread and meat morning and evening, and he drank from the stream.

7 After a while the stream dried up, for there had been no rain in the land. 8 Then the word of the LORD came to him: 9 'Go now to Zarephath, a village of Sidon, and stay there; I have commanded a widow there to feed you.' 10 He went off to Zarephath, and when he reached the entrance to the village, he saw a widow gathering sticks. He called to her, 'Please bring me a little water in a pitcher to drink.' 11 As she went to fetch it, he called after her, 'Bring me, please, a piece of bread as well.' 12 But she answered, 'As the LORD your God lives, I have no food baked, only a handful of flour in a jar and a little oil in a flask. I am just gathering two or three sticks to go and cook it for my son and myself before we die.' 13 'Have no fear,' said Elijah; 'go and do as you have said. But first make me a small cake from what you have and bring it out to me, and after that make something for your son and yourself. 14 For this is the word of the LORD the God of Israel: The jar of flour will not give out, nor the flask of oil fail, until the LORD sends rain on the land.' 15 She went and did as Elijah had said, and there was food for him and for her and for her family for a long time. 16 The jar of flour did not give out, nor did the flask of oil fail, as the word of the LORD foretold through Elijah.

17 Afterwards the son of the woman, the owner of the house, fell ill and was in a very bad way, until at last his breathing stopped. 18 The woman said to Elijah, 'What made you interfere, you man of God? You came here to bring my sins to light and cause my son's death!' 19 'Give me your son,' he said. He took the boy from her arms and carried him up to the roof-chamber where his lodging was, and laid him on his bed. 20 He called out to the LORD, 'LORD my God, is this your care for the widow with whom I lodge, that you have been so cruel to her son?' 21 Then he breathed deeply on the child three times and called to the LORD, 'I pray, LORD my God, let the breath of life return to the body

---

j Heb *Asherah*   *k* Gk: Heb *of the settlers*   17:21 **breathed deeply:** *or* stretched himself.

NEW AMERICAN BIBLE

29 In the thirty-eighth year of Asa, king of Judah, Ahab, son of Omri, became king of Israel; he reigned over Israel in Samaria for twenty-two years. 30 Ahab, son of Omri, did evil in the sight of the LORD more than any of his predecessors. 31 It was not enough for him to imitate the sins of Jeroboam, son of Nebat. He even married Jezebel, daughter of Ethbaal, king of the Sidonians, and went over to the veneration and worship of Baal. 32 Ahab erected an altar to Baal in the temple of Baal which he built in Samaria, 33 and also made a sacred pole. He did more to anger the LORD, the God of Israel, than any of the kings of Israel before him.

34 During his reign, Hiel from Bethel rebuilt Jericho. He lost his first-born son, Abiram, when he laid the foundation, and his youngest son, Segub, when he set up the gates, as the LORD had foretold through Joshua, son of Nun.

17 Elijah the Tishbite, from Tishbe in Gilead, said to Ahab: "As the LORD, the God of Israel, lives, whom I serve, during these years there shall be no dew or rain except at my word." 2 The LORD then said to Elijah: 3 "Leave here, go east and hide in the Wadi Cherith, east of the Jordan. 4 You shall drink of the stream, and I have commanded ravens to feed you there." 5 So he left and did as the LORD had commanded. He went and remained by the Wadi Cherith, east of the Jordan. 6 Ravens brought him bread and meat in the morning, and bread and meat in the evening, and he drank from the stream.

7 After some time, however, the brook ran dry, because no rain had fallen in the land. 8 So the LORD said to him: 9 "Move on to Zarephath of Sidon and stay there. I have designated a widow there to provide for you." 10 He left and went to Zarephath. As he arrived at the entrance of the city, a widow was gathering sticks there; he called out to her, "Please bring me a small cupful of water to drink." 11 She left to get it, and he called out after her, "Please bring along a bit of bread." 12 "As the LORD, your God, lives," she answered, "I have nothing baked; there is only a handful of flour in my jar and a little oil in my jug. Just now I was collecting a couple of sticks, to go in and prepare something for myself and my son; when we have eaten it, we shall die." 13 "Do not be afraid," Elijah said to her. "Go and do as you propose. But first make me a little cake and bring it to me. Then you can prepare something for yourself and your son. 14 For the LORD, the God of Israel, says, 'The jar of flour shall not go empty, nor the jug of oil run dry, until the day when the LORD sends rain upon the earth.'" 15 She left and did as Elijah had said. She was able to eat for a year, and he and her son as well; 16 the jar of flour did not go empty, nor the jug of oil run dry, as the LORD had foretold through Elijah.

17 Some time later the son of the mistress of the house fell sick, and his sickness grew more severe until he stopped breathing. 18 So she said to Elijah, "Why have you done this to me, O man of God? Have you come to me to call attention to my guilt and to kill my son?" 19 "Give me your son," Elijah said to her. Taking him from her lap, he carried him to the upper room where he was staying, and laid him on his own bed. 20 He called out to the LORD: "O LORD, my God, will you afflict even the widow with whom I am staying by killing her son?" 21 Then he stretched himself out upon the child three times and called out to the LORD: "O LORD, my God, let the life breath return to the body of this child."

NEW JERUSALEM BIBLE

29 Ahab son of Omri became king of Israel in the thirty-eighth year of Asa king of Judah, and reigned over Israel for twenty-two years in Samaria. 30 Ahab son of Omri did what is displeasing to Yahweh, and was worse than all his predecessors. 31 The least that he did was to follow the sinful example of Jeroboam son of Nebat: he married Jezebel daughter of Ethbaal, king of the Sidonians, and then proceeded to serve Baal and worship him. 32 He erected an altar to him in the temple of Baal which he built in Samaria. 33 Ahab also put up a sacred pole and committed other crimes as well, provoking the anger of Yahweh, God of Israel, more than all the kings of Israel his predecessors. 34 It was in his time that Hiel of Bethel rebuilt Jericho. Laying its foundations cost him his eldest son Abiram and erecting its gates cost him his youngest son Segub, just as Yahweh had foretold through Joshua son of Nun.*e*

17 Elijah the Tishbite, of Tishbe in Gilead, said to Ahab, 'By the life of Yahweh, God of Israel, whom I serve, there will be neither dew nor rain these coming years unless I give the word.'

2 The word of Yahweh came to him, 3 'Go away from here, go east and hide by the torrent of Cherith, east of the Jordan. 4 You can drink from the stream, and I have ordered the ravens to bring you food there.' 5 So he set out and did as Yahweh had said; he went and stayed by the torrent of Cherith, east of the Jordan. 6 The ravens brought him bread in the morning and meat in the evening, and he quenched his thirst at the stream.

7 But after a while the stream dried up, for the country had had no rain. 8*f* And then the word of Yahweh came to him, 9 'Up and go to Zarephath in Sidonia, and stay there. I have ordered a widow there to give you food.' 10 So he went off to Sidon. And when he reached the city gate, there was a widow gathering sticks. Addressing her he said, 'Please bring a little water in a pitcher for me to drink.' 11 She was on her way to fetch it when he called after her. 'Please', he said, 'bring me a scrap of bread in your hand.' 12 'As Yahweh your God lives,' she replied, 'I have no baked bread, but only a handful of meal in a jar and a little oil in a jug; I am just gathering a stick or two to go and prepare this for myself and my son to eat, and then we shall die.' 13 But Elijah said to her, 'Do not be afraid, go and do as you have said; but first make a little scone of it for me and bring it to me, and then make some for yourself and for your son. 14 For Yahweh, God of Israel, says this:

Jar of meal shall not be spent,
jug of oil shall not be emptied,
before the day when Yahweh sends
rain on the face of the earth.'

15 The woman went and did as Elijah told her and they ate the food, she, himself and her son. 16 The jar of meal was not spent nor the jug of oil emptied, just as Yahweh had foretold through Elijah.

17*g* It happened after this that the son of the mistress of the house fell sick; his illness was so severe that in the end he expired. 18 And the woman said to Elijah, 'What quarrel have you with me, man of God? Have you come here to bring my sins home to me and to kill my son?' 19 'Give me your son,' he said and, taking him from her lap, he carried him to the upper room where he was staying and laid him on his bed. 20 He cried out to Yahweh, 'Yahweh my God, by killing her son do you mean to bring grief even to the widow who is looking after me?' 21 He stretched himself on the child three times and cried out to Yahweh, 'Yahweh my God, may the soul of this child, I beg you, come into him

e 16 Jos 6:26.   *f* 17 17:8seq. // 2 K 4:1–7.
g 17 17:17seq. // 2 K 4:18–37.

753

NEW REVISED STANDARD VERSION

tened to the voice of Elijah; the life of the child came into him again, and he revived. 23 Elijah took the child, brought him down from the upper chamber into the house, and gave him to his mother; then Elijah said, "See, your son is alive." 24 So the woman said to Elijah, "Now I know that you are a man of God, and that the word of the LORD in your mouth is truth."

18 After many days the word of the LORD came to Elijah, in the third year of the drought,[1] saying, "Go, present yourself to Ahab; I will send rain on the earth." 2 So Elijah went to present himself to Ahab. The famine was severe in Samaria. 3 Ahab summoned Obadiah, who was in charge of the palace. (Now Obadiah revered the LORD greatly; 4 when Jezebel was killing off the prophets of the LORD, Obadiah took a hundred prophets, hid them fifty to a cave, and provided them with bread and water.) 5 Then Ahab said to Obadiah, "Go through the land to all the springs of water and to all the wadis; perhaps we may find grass to keep the horses and mules alive, and not lose some of the animals." 6 So they divided the land between them to pass through it; Ahab went in one direction by himself, and Obadiah went in another direction by himself.

7 As Obadiah was on the way, Elijah met him; Obadiah recognized him, fell on his face, and said, "Is it you, my lord Elijah?" 8 He answered him, "It is I. Go, tell your lord that Elijah is here." 9 And he said, "How have I sinned, that you would hand your servant over to Ahab, to kill me? 10 As the LORD your God lives, there is no nation or kingdom to which my lord has not sent to seek you; and when they would say, 'He is not here,' he would require an oath of the kingdom or nation, that they had not found you. 11 But now you say, 'Go, tell your lord that Elijah is here.' 12 As soon as I have gone from you, the spirit of the LORD will carry you I know not where; so, when I come and tell Ahab and he cannot find you, he will kill me, although I your servant have revered the LORD from my youth. 13 Has it not been told my lord what I did when Jezebel killed the prophets of the LORD, how I hid a hundred of the LORD's prophets fifty to a cave, and provided them with bread and water? 14 Yet now you say, 'Go, tell your lord that Elijah is here'; he will surely kill me." 15 Elijah said, "As the LORD of hosts lives, before whom I stand, I will surely show myself to him today." 16 So Obadiah went to meet Ahab, and told him; and Ahab went to meet Elijah.

17 When Ahab saw Elijah, Ahab said to him, "Is it you, you troubler of Israel?" 18 He answered, "I have not troubled Israel; but you have, and your father's house, because you have forsaken the commandments of the LORD and followed the Baals. 19 Now therefore have all Israel assemble for me at Mount Carmel, with the four hundred fifty prophets of Baal and the four hundred prophets of Asherah, who eat at Jezebel's table."

20 So Ahab sent to all the Israelites, and assembled the prophets at Mount Carmel. 21 Elijah then came near to all the people, and said, "How long will you go limping with two different opinions? If the LORD is God, follow him; but if Baal, then follow him." The people did not answer him a word. 22 Then Elijah said to the people, "I, even I only, am left a prophet of the LORD; but Baal's prophets number four hundred fifty. 23 Let two bulls be given to us; let them choose one bull for themselves, cut it in pieces, and lay it on the wood, but put no fire to it; I will prepare the other bull and lay it on the wood, but put no fire to it. 24 Then you

REVISED ENGLISH BIBLE

of this child.' 22 The LORD listened to Elijah's cry, and the breath of life returned to the child's body, and he revived.

23 Elijah lifted him and took him down from the roof-chamber into the house, and giving him to his mother he said, 'Look, your son is alive.' 24 She said to Elijah, 'Now I know for certain that you are a man of God and that the word of the LORD on your lips is truth.'

18 Time went by, and in the third year the word of the LORD came to Elijah: 'Go, appear before Ahab, and I shall send rain on the land.' 2 So Elijah went to show himself to Ahab.

At this time the famine in Samaria was at its height, 3 and Ahab summoned Obadiah, the comptroller of his household, a devout worshipper of the LORD. 4 When Jezebel massacred the prophets of the LORD, he had taken a hundred of them, hidden them in caves, fifty by fifty, and sustained them with food and drink. 5 Ahab said to Obadiah, 'Let us go throughout the land to every spring and wadi; if we can find enough grass we may keep the horses and mules alive and not lose any of our animals.' 6 They divided the land between them for their survey, Ahab himself going one way and Obadiah another.

7 As Obadiah was on his journey, Elijah suddenly confronted him. Obadiah recognized Elijah and prostrated himself before him. 'Can it really be you, my lord Elijah?' he said. 8 'Yes,' he replied, 'it is I. Go and tell your master that Elijah is here.' 9 'What wrong have I done?' protested Obadiah. 'Why should you give me into Ahab's hands? He will put me to death. 10 As the LORD your God lives, there is no region or kingdom to which my master has not sent in search of you. If they said, "He is not here," he made that kingdom or region swear on oath that you could not be found. 11 Yet now you say, "Go and tell your master that Elijah is here." 12 What will happen? As soon as I leave you, the spirit of the LORD will carry you away, who knows where? I shall go and tell Ahab, and when he fails to find you, he will kill me. Yet I, your servant, have been a worshipper of the LORD from boyhood. 13 Have you not been told, my lord, what I did when Jezebel put the LORD's prophets to death, how I hid a hundred of them in caves, fifty by fifty, and kept them alive with food and drink? 14 And now you say, "Go and tell your master that Elijah is here"! He will kill me.' 15 Elijah answered, 'As the LORD of Hosts lives, whose servant I am, I swear that I shall show myself to him this day.' 16 So Obadiah went to find Ahab and gave him the message, and Ahab went to confront Elijah.

17 As soon as Ahab saw Elijah, he said to him, 'Is it you, you troubler of Israel?' 18 'It is not I who have brought trouble on Israel,' Elijah replied, 'but you and your father's family, by forsaking the commandments of the LORD and following Baal. 19 Now summon all Israel to meet me on Mount Carmel, including the four hundred and fifty prophets of Baal and the four hundred prophets of the goddess Asherah, who are attached to Jezebel's household.' 20 So Ahab sent throughout the length and breadth of Israel and assembled the prophets on Mount Carmel.

21 Elijah stepped forward towards all the people there and said, 'How long will you sit on the fence? If the LORD is God, follow him; but if Baal, then follow him.' Not a word did they answer. 22 Then Elijah said, 'I am the only prophet of the LORD still left, but there are four hundred and fifty prophets of Baal. 23 Bring two bulls for us. Let them choose one for themselves, cut it up, and lay it on the wood without setting fire to it, and I shall prepare the other and lay it on the wood without setting fire to it. 24 Then invoke your god

18:5 **Let . . . throughout:** *so Gk; Heb.* Go into. 18:21 **sit on the fence:** *lit.* bestride two branches.

[1] Heb lacks *of the drought*

NEW AMERICAN BIBLE

22 The LORD heard the prayer of Elijah; the life breath returned to the child's body and he revived. 23 Taking the child, Elijah brought him down into the house from the upper room and gave him to his mother. "See!" Elijah said to her, "your son is alive." 24 "Now indeed I know that you are a man of God," the woman replied to Elijah. "The word of the LORD comes truly from your mouth."

18 Long afterward, in the third year, the LORD spoke to Elijah. "Go, present yourself to Ahab," he said, "that I may send rain upon the earth." 2 So Elijah went to present himself to Ahab.

3 Now the famine in Samaria was bitter, 4 and Ahab had summoned Obadiah, his vizier, who was a zealous follower of the LORD. When Jezebel was murdering the prophets of the LORD, Obadiah took a hundred prophets, hid them away fifty each in two caves, and supplied them with food and drink. 5 Ahab said to Obadiah, "Come, let us go through the land to all sources of water and to all the streams. We may find grass and save the horses and mules, so that we shall not have to slaughter any of the beasts." 6 Dividing the land to explore between them, Ahab went one way by himself, Obadiah another way by himself.

7 As Obadiah was on his way, Elijah met him. Recognizing him, Obadiah fell prostrate and asked, "Is it you, my lord Elijah?" 8 "Yes," he answered. "Go tell your master, 'Elijah is here!'" 9 But Obadiah said, "What sin have I committed, that you are handing me over to Ahab to have me killed? 10 As the LORD, your God, lives, there is no nation or kingdom where my master has not sent in search of you. When they replied, 'He is not here,' he made each kingdom and nation swear they could not find you. 11 And now you say, 'Go tell your master: Elijah is here!' 12 After I leave you, the spirit of the LORD will carry you to some place I do not know, and when I go to inform Ahab and he does not find you, he will kill me. Your servant has revered the LORD from his youth. 13 Have you not been told, my lord, what I did when Jezebel was murdering the prophets of the LORD — that I hid a hundred of the prophets of the LORD, fifty each in two caves, and supplied them with food and drink? 14 And now you say, 'Go tell your master: Elijah is here!' He will kill me!" 15 Elijah answered, "As the LORD of hosts lives, whom I serve, I will present myself to him today."

16 So Obadiah went to meet Ahab and informed him. Ahab came to meet Elijah, 17 and when he saw Elijah, said to him, "Is it you, you disturber of Israel?" 18 "It is not I who disturb Israel," he answered, "but you and your family, by forsaking the commands of the LORD and following the Baals. 19 Now summon all Israel to me on Mount Carmel, as well as the four hundred and fifty prophets of Baal and the four hundred prophets of Asherah who eat at Jezebel's table." 20 So Ahab sent to all the Israelites and had the prophets assemble on Mount Carmel.

21 Elijah appealed to all the people and said, "How long will you straddle the issue? If the LORD is God, follow him; if Baal, follow him." The people, however, did not answer him. 22 So Elijah said to the people, "I am the only surviving prophet of the LORD, and there are four hundred and fifty prophets of Baal. 23 Give us two young bulls. Let them choose one, cut it into pieces, and place it on the wood, but start no fire. I shall prepare the other and place it on the wood, but shall start no fire. 24 You shall call on your gods,

NEW JERUSALEM BIBLE

again!' 22 Yahweh heard Elijah's prayer and the child's soul came back into his body and he revived. 23 Elijah took the child, brought him down from the upper room into the house, and gave him to his mother. 'Look,' Elijah said, 'your son is alive.' 24 And the woman replied, 'Now I know you are a man of God and the word of Yahweh in your mouth is truth itself.'

18 A long time went by, and the word of Yahweh came to Elijah in the third year, 'Go, present yourself to Ahab, and I will send rain on the country.' 2 So Elijah set off to present himself to Ahab.

As the famine was particularly severe in Samaria, 3 Ahab summoned Obadiah, the master of the palace — Obadiah held Yahweh in great reverence: 4 when Jezebel was butchering the prophets of Yahweh, Obadiah took a hundred of them and hid them, fifty at a time, in a cave, and kept them provided with food and water — 5 and Ahab said to Obadiah, 'Come along, we must scour the country, all the springs and all the ravines in the hope of finding grass to keep horses and mules alive, or we shall have to slaughter some of our stock.' 6 They divided the country for the purpose of their survey; Ahab went one way by himself and Obadiah went another way by himself. 7 While Obadiah was on his way, whom should he meet but Elijah. Recognising him he fell on his face and said, 'So it is you, my lord Elijah!' 8 'Yes,' he replied, 'go and tell your master, "Elijah is here."' 9 But Obadiah said, 'What sin have I committed, for you to put your servant into Ahab's power and cause my death? 10 As Yahweh your God lives, there is no nation or kingdom where my master has not sent in search of you; and when they said, "He is not there," he made the kingdom or nation swear an oath that they did not know where you were. 11 And now you say to me, "Go and tell your master: Elijah is here." 12 But as soon as I leave you, the spirit of Yahweh will carry you away and I shall not know where; I shall go and tell Ahab; he will not be able to find you, and then he will kill me. Yet from his youth your servant has revered Yahweh. 13 Has no one told my lord what I did when Jezebel butchered the prophets of Yahweh, how I hid a hundred of them in a cave, fifty at a time, and kept them provided with food and water? 14 And now you say to me, "Go and tell your master: Elijah is here." Why, he will kill me!' 15 Elijah replied, 'As Yahweh Sabaoth lives, whom I serve, I shall present myself to him today!'

16 Obadiah went to find Ahab and tell him the news, and Ahab then went to find Elijah. 17 When he saw Elijah, Ahab said, 'So there you are, you scourge of Israel!' 18 'Not I,' he replied, 'I am not the scourge of Israel, you and your family are; because you have deserted Yahweh and followed Baal. 19 Now give orders for all Israel to gather round me on Mount Carmel, and also the four hundred prophets of Baal who eat at Jezebel's table.'

20 Ahab called all Israel together and assembled the prophets on Mount Carmel. 21 Elijah stepped out in front of all the people. 'How long', he said, 'do you mean to hobble first on one leg then on the other? If Yahweh is God, follow him; if Baal, follow him.' But the people had nothing to say. 22 Elijah then said to them, 'I, alone, am left as a prophet of Yahweh, while the prophets of Baal are four hundred and fifty. 23 Let two bulls be given us; let them choose one for themselves, dismember it but not set fire to it. I in my turn shall prepare the other bull, but not set fire to it. 24 You must call on the name of your god, and I shall

call on the name of your god and I will call on the name of the LORD; the god who answers by fire is indeed God." All the people answered, "Well spoken!" 25 Then Elijah said to the prophets of Baal, "Choose for yourselves one bull and prepare it first, for you are many; then call on the name of your god, but put no fire to it." 26 So they took the bull that was given them, prepared it, and called on the name of Baal from morning until noon, crying, "O Baal, answer us!" But there was no voice, and no answer. They limped about the altar that they had made. 27 At noon Elijah mocked them, saying, "Cry aloud! Surely he is a god; either he is meditating, or he has wandered away, or he is on a journey, or perhaps he is asleep and must be awakened." 28 Then they cried aloud and, as was their custom, they cut themselves with swords and lances until the blood gushed out over them. 29 As midday passed, they raved on until the time of the offering of the oblation, but there was no voice, no answer, and no response.

30 Then Elijah said to all the people, "Come closer to me"; and all the people came closer to him. First he repaired the altar of the LORD that had been thrown down; 31 Elijah took twelve stones, according to the number of the tribes of the sons of Jacob, to whom the word of the LORD came, saying, "Israel shall be your name"; 32 with the stones he built an altar in the name of the LORD. Then he made a trench around the altar, large enough to contain two measures of seed. 33 Next he put the wood in order, cut the bull in pieces, and laid it on the wood. He said, "Fill four jars with water and pour it on the burnt offering and on the wood." 34 Then he said, "Do it a second time"; and they did it a second time. Again he said, "Do it a third time"; and they did it a third time, 35 so that the water ran all around the altar, and filled the trench also with water.

36 At the time of the offering of the oblation, the prophet Elijah came near and said, "O LORD, God of Abraham, Isaac, and Israel, let it be known this day that you are God in Israel, that I am your servant, and that I have done all these things at your bidding. 37 Answer me, O LORD, answer me, so that this people may know that you, O LORD, are God, and that you have turned their hearts back." 38 Then the fire of the LORD fell and consumed the burnt offering, the wood, the stones, and the dust, and even licked up the water that was in the trench. 39 When all the people saw it, they fell on their faces and said, "The LORD indeed is God; the LORD indeed is God." 40 Elijah said to them, "Seize the prophets of Baal; do not let one of them escape." Then they seized them; and Elijah brought them down to the Wadi Kishon, and killed them there.

41 Elijah said to Ahab, "Go up, eat and drink; for there is a sound of rushing rain." 42 So Ahab went up to eat and to drink. Elijah went up to the top of Carmel; there he bowed himself down upon the earth and put his face between his knees. 43 He said to his servant, "Go up now, look toward the sea." He went up and looked, and said, "There is nothing." Then he said, "Go again seven times." 44 At the seventh time he said, "Look, a little cloud no bigger than a person's hand is rising out of the sea." Then he said, "Go say to Ahab, 'Harness your chariot and go down before the rain stops you.'" 45 In a little while the heavens grew black with clouds and wind; there was a heavy rain. Ahab rode off and went to Jezreel. 46 But the hand of the LORD was on Elijah; he girded up his loins and ran in front of Ahab to the entrance of Jezreel.

19 Ahab told Jezebel all that Elijah had done, and how he had killed all the prophets with the sword. 2 Then

by name and I shall invoke the LORD by name; the god who answers by fire, he is God.' The people all shouted their approval.

25 Elijah said to the prophets of Baal, 'Choose one of the bulls and offer it first, for there are more of you; invoke your god by name, but do not set fire to the wood.' 26 They took the bull provided for them and offered it, and they invoked Baal by name from morning until noon, crying, 'Baal, answer us'; but there was no sound, no answer. They danced wildly by the altar they had set up. 27 At midday Elijah mocked them: 'Call louder, for he is a god. It may be he is deep in thought, or engaged, or on a journey; or he may have gone to sleep and must be woken up.' 28 They cried still louder and, as was their custom, gashed themselves with swords and spears until the blood flowed. 29 All afternoon they raved and ranted till the hour of the regular offering, but still there was no sound, no answer, no sign of attention.

30 Elijah said to the people, 'Come here to me,' and they all came to him. He repaired the altar of the LORD which had been torn down. 31 He took twelve stones, one for each tribe of the sons of Jacob, him who was named Israel by the word of the LORD. 32 With these stones he built an altar in the name of the LORD, and dug a trench round it big enough to hold two measures of seed; 33 he arranged the wood, cut up the bull, and laid it on the wood. 34 Then he said, 'Fill four jars with water and pour it on the whole-offering and on the wood.' They did so; he said, 'Do it again.' They did it again; he said, 'Do it a third time.' They did it a third time, 35 and the water ran all round the altar and even filled the trench.

36 At the hour of the regular offering the prophet Elijah came forward and prayed, 'LORD God of Abraham, of Isaac, and of Israel, let it be known today that you are God in Israel and that I am your servant and have done all these things at your command. 37 Answer me, LORD, answer me and let this people know that you, LORD, are God and that it is you who have brought them back to their allegiance.' 38 The fire of the LORD fell, consuming the whole-offering, the wood, the stones, and the earth, and licking up the water in the trench. 39 At the sight the people all bowed with their faces to the ground and cried, 'The LORD is God, the LORD is God.' 40 Elijah said to them, 'Seize the prophets of Baal; let not one of them escape.' They were seized, and Elijah took them down to the Kishon and slaughtered them there in the valley.

41 Elijah said to Ahab, 'Go back now, eat and drink, for I hear the sound of heavy rain.' 42 He did so, while Elijah himself climbed to the crest of Carmel, where he bowed down to the ground and put his face between his knees. 43 He said to his servant, 'Go and look toward the west.' He went and looked; 'There is nothing to see,' he said. Seven times Elijah ordered him back, and seven times he went. 44 The seventh time he said, 'I see a cloud no bigger than a man's hand, coming up from the west.' 'Now go', said Elijah, 'and tell Ahab to harness his chariot and be off, or the rain will stop him.' 45 Meanwhile the sky grew black with clouds, the wind rose, and heavy rain began to fall. Ahab mounted his chariot and set off for Jezreel; 46 and the power of the LORD was on Elijah: he tucked up his robe and ran before Ahab all the way to Jezreel.

19 When Ahab told Jezebel all that Elijah had done and how he had put all the prophets to the sword,

---

18:32 **measures:** *the Heb. measure called* seah.   18:34 **They did so:** *so Gk; Heb. omits.*   18:43 **and seven . . . went:** *so Gk; Heb. omits.*

and I will call on the LORD. The God who answers with fire is God." All the people answered, "Agreed!" 25 Elijah then said to the prophets of Baal, "Choose one young bull and prepare it first, for there are more of you. Call upon your gods, but do not start the fire." 26 Taking the young bull that was turned over to them, they prepared it and called on Baal from morning to noon, saying, "Answer us, Baal!" But there was no sound, and no one answering. And they hopped around the altar they had prepared. 27 When it was noon, Elijah taunted them: "Call louder, for he is a god and may be meditating, or may have retired, or may be on a journey. Perhaps he is asleep and must be awakened." 28 They called out louder and slashed themselves with swords and spears, as was their custom, until blood gushed over them. 29 Noon passed and they remained in a prophetic state until the time for offering sacrifice. But there was not a sound; no one answered, and no one was listening.

30 Then Elijah said to all the people, "Come here to me." When they had done so, he repaired the altar of the LORD which had been destroyed. 31 He took twelve stones, for the number of tribes of the sons of Jacob, to whom the LORD had said, "Your name shall be Israel." 32 He built an altar in honor of the LORD with the stones, and made a trench around the altar large enough for two seahs of grain. 33 When he had arranged the wood, he cut up the young bull and laid it on the wood. 34 "Fill four jars with water," he said, "and pour it over the holocaust and over the wood." "Do it again," he said, and they did it again. "Do it a third time," he said, and they did it a third time. 35 The water flowed around the altar, and the trench was filled with the water.

36 At the time for offering sacrifice, the prophet Elijah came forward and said, "LORD, God of Abraham, Isaac, and Israel, let it be known this day that you are God in Israel and that I am your servant and have done all these things by your command. 37 Answer me, LORD! Answer me, that this people may know that you, LORD, are God and that you have brought them back to their senses." 38 The LORD's fire came down and consumed the holocaust, wood, stones, and dust, and it lapped up the water in the trench. 39 Seeing this, all the people fell prostrate and said, "The LORD is God! The LORD is God!" 40 Then Elijah said to them, "Seize the prophets of Baal. Let none of them escape!" They were seized, and Elijah had them brought down to the brook Kishon and there he slit their throats.

41 Elijah then said to Ahab, "Go up, eat and drink, for there is the sound of a heavy rain." 42 So Ahab went up to eat and drink, while Elijah climbed to the top of Carmel, crouched down to the earth, and put his head between his knees. 43 "Climb up and look out to sea," he directed his servant, who went up and looked, but reported, "There is nothing." Seven times he said, "Go, look again!" 44 And the seventh time the youth reported, "There is a cloud as small as a man's hand rising from the sea." Elijah said, "Go and say to Ahab, 'Harness up and leave the mountain before the rain stops you.'" 45 In a trice, the sky grew dark with clouds and wind, and a heavy rain fell. Ahab mounted his chariot and made for Jezreel. 46 But the hand of the LORD was on Elijah, who girded up his clothing and ran before Ahab as far as the approaches to Jezreel.

19 Ahab told Jezebel all that Elijah had done — that he had put all the prophets to the sword. 2 Jezebel then

call on the name of Yahweh; the god who answers with fire, is God indeed.' The people all answered, 'Agreed!' 25 Elijah then said to the prophets of Baal, 'Choose one bull and begin, for there are more of you. Call on the name of your god but light no fire.' 26 They took the bull and prepared it, and from morning to midday they called on the name of Baal. 'O Baal, answer us!' they cried, but there was no voice, no answer, as they performed their hobbling dance round the altar which they had made. 27 Midday came, and Elijah mocked them. 'Call louder,' he said, 'for he is a god: he is preoccupied or he is busy, or he has gone on a journey; perhaps he is asleep and needs to be woken up!' 28 So they shouted louder and gashed themselves, as their custom was, with swords and spears until the blood flowed down them. 29 Midday passed, and they ranted on until the time when the offering is presented; but there was no voice, no answer, no sign of attention.

30 Then Elijah said to all the people, 'Come over to me,' and all the people came over to him. He repaired Yahweh's altar which had been torn down. 31 Elijah took twelve stones, corresponding to the number of tribes of the sons of Jacob, to whom the word of Yahweh had come, 'Israel is to be your name,' 32 and built an altar in the name of Yahweh. Round the altar he dug a trench of a size to hold two measures of seed. 33 He then arranged the wood, dismembered the bull, and laid it on the wood. 34 Then he said, 'Fill four jars with water and pour it on the burnt offering and on the wood.' They did this. He said, 'Do it a second time;' they did it a second time. He said, 'Do it a third time;' they did it a third time. 35 The water flowed round the altar until even the trench itself was full of water. 36 At the time when the offering is presented, Elijah the prophet stepped forward. 'Yahweh, God of Abraham, Isaac and Israel,' he said, 'let them know today that you are God in Israel, and that I am your servant, that I have done all these things at your command. 37 Answer me, Yahweh, answer me, so that this people may know that you, Yahweh, are God and are winning back their hearts.'

38 Then Yahweh's fire fell and consumed the burnt offering and the wood and licked up the water in the trench. 39 When all the people saw this they fell on their faces. 'Yahweh is God,' they cried, 'Yahweh is God!' 40 Elijah said, 'Seize the prophets of Baal: do not let one of them escape.' They seized them, and Elijah took them down to the Kishon, and there he slaughtered them.

41 Elijah said to Ahab, 'Go back now, eat and drink; for I hear the approaching sound of rain.' 42 While Ahab went back to eat and drink, Elijah climbed to the top of Carmel and bowed down to the ground, putting his face between his knees. 43 'Now go up', he told his servant, 'and look out to sea.' He went up and looked. 'There is nothing at all,' he said. Seven times Elijah told him to go back. 44 The seventh time, the servant said, 'Now there is a cloud, small as a man's hand, rising from the sea.' Elijah said, 'Go and say to Ahab, "Harness the chariot and go down before the rain stops you."' 45 And with that the sky grew dark with cloud and storm, and rain fell in torrents. Ahab mounted his chariot and made for Jezreel. 46 But the hand of Yahweh had come on Elijah and, hitching up his clothes, he ran ahead of Ahab all the way to Jezreel.

19 When Ahab told Jezebel everything that Elijah had done, and how he had put all the prophets to the

NEW REVISED STANDARD VERSION

Jezebel sent a messenger to Elijah, saying, "So may the gods do to me, and more also, if I do not make your life like the life of one of them by this time tomorrow." ³ Then he was afraid; he got up and fled for his life, and came to Beer-sheba, which belongs to Judah; he left his servant there.

4 But he himself went a day's journey into the wilderness, and came and sat down under a solitary broom tree. He asked that he might die: "It is enough; now, O LORD, take away my life, for I am no better than my ancestors." ⁵ Then he lay down under the broom tree and fell asleep. Suddenly an angel touched him and said to him, "Get up and eat." ⁶ He looked, and there at his head was a cake baked on hot stones, and a jar of water. He ate and drank, and lay down again. ⁷ The angel of the LORD came a second time, touched him, and said, "Get up and eat, otherwise the journey will be too much for you." ⁸ He got up, and ate and drank; then he went in the strength of that food forty days and forty nights to Horeb the mount of God. ⁹ At that place he came to a cave, and spent the night there.

Then the word of the LORD came to him, saying, "What are you doing here, Elijah?" ¹⁰ He answered, "I have been very zealous for the LORD, the God of hosts; for the Israelites have forsaken your covenant, thrown down your altars, and killed your prophets with the sword. I alone am left, and they are seeking my life, to take it away."

11 He said, "Go out and stand on the mountain before the LORD, for the LORD is about to pass by." Now there was a great wind, so strong that it was splitting mountains and breaking rocks in pieces before the LORD, but the LORD was not in the wind; and after the wind an earthquake, but the LORD was not in the earthquake; ¹² and after the earthquake a fire, but the LORD was not in the fire; and after the fire a sound of sheer silence. ¹³ When Elijah heard it, he wrapped his face in his mantle and went out and stood at the entrance of the cave. Then there came a voice to him that said, "What are you doing here, Elijah?" ¹⁴ He answered, "I have been very zealous for the LORD, the God of hosts; for the Israelites have forsaken your covenant, thrown down your altars, and killed your prophets with the sword. I alone am left, and they are seeking my life, to take it away." ¹⁵ Then the LORD said to him, "Go, return on your way to the wilderness of Damascus; when you arrive, you shall anoint Hazael as king over Aram. ¹⁶ Also you shall anoint Jehu son of Nimshi as king over Israel; and you shall anoint Elisha son of Shaphat of Abel-meholah as prophet in your place. ¹⁷ Whoever escapes from the sword of Hazael, Jehu shall kill; and whoever escapes from the sword of Jehu, Elisha shall kill. ¹⁸ Yet I will leave seven thousand in Israel, all the knees that have not bowed to Baal, and every mouth that has not kissed him."

19 So he set out from there, and found Elisha son of Shaphat, who was plowing. There were twelve yoke of oxen ahead of him, and he was with the twelfth. Elijah passed by him and threw his mantle over him. ²⁰ He left the oxen, ran after Elijah, and said, "Let me kiss my father and my mother, and then I will follow you." Then Elijah*m* said to him, "Go back again; for what have I done to you?" ²¹ He returned from following him, took the yoke of oxen, and slaughtered them; using the equipment from the oxen, he boiled their flesh, and gave it to the people, and they ate. Then he set out and followed Elijah, and became his servant.

20 King Ben-hadad of Aram gathered all his army together; thirty-two kings were with him, along with horses and chariots. He marched against Samaria, laid siege to it, and attacked it. ² Then he sent messengers into the city

REVISED ENGLISH BIBLE

² she sent this message to Elijah, 'The gods do the same to me and more, unless by this time tomorrow I have taken your life as you took theirs.' ³ In fear he fled for his life, and when he reached Beersheba in Judah he left his servant there, ⁴ while he himself went a day's journey into the wilderness. He came to a broom bush, and sitting down under it he prayed for death: 'It is enough,' he said; 'now, LORD, take away my life, for I am no better than my fathers before me.' ⁵ He lay down under the bush and, while he slept, an angel touched him and said, ⁶ 'Rise and eat.' He looked, and there at his head was a cake baked on hot stones, and a pitcher of water. He ate and drank and lay down again. ⁷ The angel of the LORD came again and touched him a second time, saying, 'Rise and eat; the journey is too much for you.' ⁸ He rose and ate and drank and, sustained by this food, he went on for forty days and forty nights to Horeb, the mount of God. ⁹ There he entered a cave where he spent the night.

The word of the LORD came to him: 'Why are you here, Elijah?' ¹⁰ 'Because of my great zeal for the LORD the God of Israel,' he replied. 'The people of Israel have forsaken your covenant, torn down your altars, and put your prophets to the sword. I alone am left, and they seek to take my life.' ¹¹ To this the answer came: 'Go and stand on the mount before the LORD.' The LORD was passing by: a great and strong wind came, rending mountains and shattering rocks before him, but the LORD was not in the wind; and after the wind there was an earthquake, but the LORD was not in the earthquake; ¹² and after the earthquake fire, but the LORD was not in the fire; and after the fire a faint murmuring sound. ¹³ When Elijah heard it, he wrapped his face in his cloak and went out and stood at the entrance to the cave. There came a voice: 'Why are you here, Elijah?' ¹⁴ 'Because of my great zeal for the LORD the God of Hosts,' he replied. 'The people of Israel have forsaken your covenant, torn down your altars, and put your prophets to the sword. I alone am left, and they seek to take my life.'

¹⁵ The LORD said to him, 'Go back by way of the wilderness of Damascus, enter the city, and anoint Hazael to be king of Aram; ¹⁶ anoint also Jehu son of Nimshi to be king of Israel, and Elisha son of Shaphat of Abel-meholah to be prophet in your place. ¹⁷ Whoever escapes the sword of Hazael Jehu will slay, and whoever escapes the sword of Jehu Elisha will slay. ¹⁸ But I shall leave seven thousand in Israel, all who have not bowed the knee to Baal, all whose lips have not kissed him.'

¹⁹ Elijah departed and found Elisha son of Shaphat ploughing; there were twelve pair of oxen ahead of him, and he himself was with the last of them. As Elijah passed, he threw his cloak over him. ²⁰ Elisha, leaving his oxen, ran after Elijah and said, 'Let me kiss my father and mother goodbye, and then I shall follow you.' 'Go back,' he replied; 'what have I done to prevent you?' ²¹ He followed him no farther but went home, took his pair of oxen, slaughtered them, and burnt the wooden yokes to cook the flesh, which he gave to the people to eat. He then followed Elijah and became his disciple.

20 KING Ben-hadad of Aram, having mustered all his forces, and taking with him thirty-two kings with their horses and chariots, marched up against Samaria to take it by siege and assault. ² He sent envoys into the city

m Heb *he*

19:16 **son of Nimshi:** *or* grandson of Nimshi *(cp. 2 Kgs. 9:2).*

sent a messenger to Elijah and said, "May the gods do thus and so to me if by this time tomorrow I have not done with your life what was done to each of them." ³Elijah was afraid and fled for his life, going to Beer-sheba of Judah. He left his servant there ⁴and went a day's journey into the desert, until he came to a broom tree and sat beneath it. He prayed for death: "This is enough, O LORD! Take my life, for I am no better than my fathers." ⁵He lay down and fell asleep under the broom tree, but then an angel touched him and ordered him to get up and eat. ⁶He looked and there at his head was a hearth cake and a jug of water. After he ate and drank, he lay down again, ⁷but the angel of the LORD came back a second time, touched him, and ordered, "Get up and eat, else the journey will be too long for you!" ⁸He got up, ate and drank; then strengthened by that food, he walked forty days and forty nights to the mountain of God, Horeb.

⁹There he came to a cave, where he took shelter. But the word of the LORD came to him, "Why are you here, Elijah?" ¹⁰He answered: "I have been most zealous for the LORD, the God of hosts, but the Israelites have forsaken your covenant, torn down your altars, and put your prophets to the sword. I alone am left, and they seek to take my life." ¹¹Then the LORD said, "Go outside and stand on the mountain before the LORD; the LORD will be passing by." A strong and heavy wind was rending the mountains and crushing rocks before the LORD—but the LORD was not in the wind. After the wind there was an earthquake—but the LORD was not in the earthquake. ¹²After the earthquake there was fire—but the LORD was not in the fire. After the fire there was a tiny whispering sound. ¹³When he heard this, Elijah hid his face in his cloak and went and stood at the entrance of the cave. A voice said to him, "Elijah, why are you here?" ¹⁴He replied, "I have been most zealous for the LORD, the God of hosts. But the Israelites have forsaken your covenant, torn down your altars, and put your prophets to the sword. I alone am left, and they seek to take my life." ¹⁵"Go, take the road back to the desert near Damascus," the LORD said to him. "When you arrive, you shall anoint Hazael as king of Aram. ¹⁶Then you shall anoint Jehu, son of Nimshi, as king of Israel, and Elisha, son of Shaphat of Abel-meholah, as prophet to succeed you. ¹⁷If anyone escapes the sword of Hazael, Jehu will kill him. If he escapes the sword of Jehu, Elisha will kill him. ¹⁸Yet I will leave seven thousand men in Israel—all those who have not knelt to Baal or kissed him."

¹⁹Elijah set out, and came upon Elisha, son of Shaphat, as he was plowing with twelve yoke of oxen; he was following the twelfth. Elijah went over to him and threw his cloak over him. ²⁰Elisha left the oxen, ran after Elijah, and said, "Please, let me kiss my father and mother goodbye, and I will follow you." "Go back!" Elijah answered. "Have I done anything to you?" ²¹Elisha left him and, taking the yoke of oxen, slaughtered them; he used the plowing equipment for fuel to boil their flesh, and gave it to his people to eat. Then he left and followed Elijah as his attendant.

20 Ben-hadad, king of Aram, gathered all his forces, and accompanied by thirty-two kings with horses and chariotry, proceeded to invest and attack Samaria. ²He

sword, ²Jezebel sent a messenger to Elijah to say, 'May the gods bring unnameable ills on me and worse ills too, if by this time tomorrow I have not made your life like one of theirs!' ³He was afraid and fled for his life. He came to Beersheba, a town of Judah, where he left his servant. ⁴He himself went on into the desert, a day's journey, and sitting under a furze bush wished he were dead. 'Yahweh,' he said, 'I have had enough. Take my life; I am no better than my ancestors.' ⁵Then he lay down and went to sleep. Then all of a sudden an angel touched him and said, 'Get up and eat.' ⁶He looked round, and there at his head was a scone baked on hot stones, and a jar of water. He ate and drank and then lay down again. ⁷But the angel of Yahweh came back a second time and touched him and said, 'Get up and eat, or the journey will be too long for you.' ⁸So he got up and ate and drank, and strengthened by that food he walked for forty days and forty nights until he reached Horeb, God's mountain.

⁹There he went into a cave and spent the night there. Then the word of Yahweh came to him saying, 'What are you doing here, Elijah?' ¹⁰He replied, 'I am full of jealous zeal for Yahweh Sabaoth, because the Israelites have abandoned your covenant, have torn down your altars and put your prophets to the sword. I am the only one left, and now they want to kill me.' ¹¹Then he was told, 'Go out and stand on the mountain before Yahweh.' For at that moment Yahweh was going by. A mighty hurricane split the mountains and shattered the rocks before Yahweh. But Yahweh was not in the hurricane. And after the hurricane, an earthquake. But Yahweh was not in the earthquake. ¹²And after the earthquake, fire. But Yahweh was not in the fire. And after the fire, a light murmuring sound. ¹³And when Elijah heard this, he covered his face with his cloak and went out and stood at the entrance of the cave. Then a voice came to him, which said, 'What are you doing here, Elijah?' ¹⁴He replied, 'I am full of jealous zeal for Yahweh, God Sabaoth, because the Israelites have abandoned your covenant, have torn down your altars and put your prophets to the sword. I am the only one left and now they want to kill me.' ¹⁵'Go,' Yahweh said, 'go back by the same way to the desert of Damascus. You must go and anoint Hazael as king of Aram. ¹⁶You must anoint Jehu son of Nimshi as king of Israel, and anoint Elisha son of Shaphat, of Abel-Meholah, as prophet to succeed you. ¹⁷Anyone who escapes the sword of Hazael will be put to death by Jehu; and anyone who escapes the sword of Jehu will be put to death by Elisha. ¹⁸But I shall spare seven thousand in Israel; all the knees that have not bent before Baal, all the mouths that have not kissed him.'

¹⁹Leaving there, he came on Elisha son of Shaphat as he was ploughing behind twelve yoke of oxen, he himself being with the twelfth. Elijah passed near to him and threw his cloak over him. ²⁰Elisha left his oxen and ran after Elijah. 'Let me kiss my father and my mother, then I will follow you,' he said. Elijah answered, 'Go, go back; for have I done anything to you?' ²¹Elisha turned away, took a yoke of oxen and slaughtered them. He used the oxen's tackle for cooking the meat, which he gave the people to eat. He then rose and, following Elijah, became his servant.

20 Ben-Hadad king of Aram mustered his whole army —thirty-two kings were with him, and horses and chariots—and marched on Samaria, to besiege it and take it by assault. ²He sent messengers into the city to Ahab king

NEW REVISED STANDARD VERSION

to King Ahab of Israel, and said to him: "Thus says Ben-hadad: 3 Your silver and gold are mine; your fairest wives and children also are mine." 4 The king of Israel answered, "As you say, my lord, O king, I am yours, and all that I have." 5 The messengers came again and said: "Thus says Ben-hadad: I sent to you, saying, 'Deliver to me your silver and gold, your wives and children'; 6 nevertheless I will send my servants to you tomorrow about this time, and they shall search your house and the houses of your servants, and lay hands on whatever pleases them,*n* and take it away."

7 Then the king of Israel called all the elders of the land, and said, "Look now! See how this man is seeking trouble; for he sent to me for my wives, my children, my silver, and my gold; and I did not refuse him." 8 Then all the elders and all the people said to him, "Do not listen or consent." 9 So he said to the messengers of Ben-hadad, "Tell my lord the king: All that you first demanded of your servant I will do; but this thing I cannot do." The messengers left and brought him word again. 10 Ben-hadad sent to him and said, "The gods do so to me, and more also, if the dust of Samaria will provide a handful for each of the people who follow me." 11 The king of Israel answered, "Tell him: One who puts on armor should not brag like one who takes it off." 12 When Ben-hadad heard this message — now he had been drinking with the kings in the booths — he said to his men, "Take your positions!" And they took their positions against the city.

13 Then a certain prophet came up to King Ahab of Israel and said, "Thus says the LORD, Have you seen all this great multitude? Look, I will give it into your hand today; and you shall know that I am the LORD." 14 Ahab said, "By whom?" He said, "Thus says the LORD, By the young men who serve the district governors." Then he said, "Who shall begin the battle?" He answered, "You." 15 Then he mustered the young men who serve the district governors, two hundred thirty-two; after them he mustered all the people of Israel, seven thousand.

16 They went out at noon, while Ben-hadad was drinking himself drunk in the booths, he and the thirty-two kings allied with him. 17 The young men who serve the district governors went out first. Ben-hadad had sent out scouts,*o* and they reported to him, "Men have come out from Samaria." 18 He said, "If they have come out for peace, take them alive; if they have come out for war, take them alive."

19 But these had already come out of the city: the young men who serve the district governors, and the army that followed them. 20 Each killed his man; the Arameans fled and Israel pursued them, but King Ben-hadad of Aram escaped on a horse with the cavalry. 21 The king of Israel went out, attacked the horses and chariots, and defeated the Arameans with a great slaughter.

22 Then the prophet approached the king of Israel and said to him, "Come, strengthen yourself, and consider well what you have to do; for in the spring the king of Aram will come up against you."

23 The servants of the king of Aram said to him, "Their gods are gods of the hills, and so they were stronger than we; but let us fight against them in the plain, and surely we shall be stronger than they. 24 Also do this: remove the kings, each from his post, and put commanders in place of them; 25 and muster an army like the army that you have lost, horse for horse, and chariot for chariot; then we will fight against them in the plain, and surely we shall be stronger than they." He heeded their voice, and did so.

26 In the spring Ben-hadad mustered the Arameans and went up to Aphek to fight against Israel. 27 After the Israel-

REVISED ENGLISH BIBLE

to King Ahab of Israel to say, 'Hear what Ben-hadad says: 3 Your silver and gold are mine, your wives and fine children are mine.' 4 The king of Israel answered, 'As you say, my lord king, I and all that I have are yours.' 5 The envoys came again and said, 'Hear what Ben-hadad says: I demand that you hand over your silver and gold, your wives and your children. 6 This time tomorrow I shall send my servants to ransack your palace and your subjects' houses to take possession of everything you prize, and carry it off.'

7 The king of Israel summoned all the elders of the land and said, 'You can see the man is bent on picking a quarrel; for I did not demur when he sent to claim my wives and my children, my silver and gold.' 8 The elders and people all answered, 'Do not listen to him; you must not consent.' 9 So he gave this reply to Ben-hadad's envoys: 'Say to my lord the king: I accepted your majesty's demands on the first occasion; but what you now ask I cannot do.' The envoys went away and reported to their master, 10 and Ben-hadad sent back word: 'The gods do the same to me and more, if enough dust is left in Samaria to provide a handful for each of my men.' 11 The king of Israel made reply, 'Tell him of the saying: "The time for boasting is after the battle." ' 12 This message reached Ben-hadad while he and the kings were feasting in their quarters, and he at once ordered his men to position themselves for an attack on the city, and they did so.

13 Meanwhile a prophet had come to King Ahab of Israel and announced, 'This is the word of the LORD: You see this great host? Today I shall give it into your hands and you will know that I am the LORD.' 14 'Whom will you use for that?' asked Ahab. 'The LORD says: The young men who serve the district officers,' was the answer. 'Who will launch the attack?' asked the king. 'You,' said the prophet. 15 Then Ahab mustered these young men, two hundred and thirty-two all told, and behind them the people of Israel, seven thousand in all.

16 They marched out at midday, while Ben-hadad and his allies, those thirty-two kings, were drinking themselves into insensibility in their quarters. 17 The young men sallied out first, and word was sent to Ben-hadad that men had come out of Samaria. 18 'If they have come out for peace,' he said, 'take them alive; if for battle, take them alive.'

19 With the army following behind them, the young men went out from the city; 20 each struck down his man, and the Aramaeans fled, with the Israelites in pursuit. Ben-hadad the king of Aram escaped on horseback with some of the cavalry. 21 The king of Israel advanced and captured the horses and chariots, inflicting a heavy defeat on the Aramaeans.

22 The prophet came to the king of Israel and advised him, 'Build up your forces; you know what you must do. At the turn of the year the king of Aram will renew the attack.' 23 The ministers of the king of Aram gave him this advice: 'Their gods are gods of the hills; that is why they are too strong for us. Let us fight them in the plain, and then we shall have the upper hand. 24 What you must do is to relieve the kings of their command and appoint other officers in their place. 25 Raise another army like the one you have lost. Bring your cavalry and chariots up to their former strength, and then let us fight Israel in the plain; then assuredly we shall have the upper hand.' He listened to their advice and acted on it.

26 At the turn of the year Ben-hadad mustered the Aramaeans and advanced to Aphek to launch their attack on

---

n Gk Syr Vg: Heb *you*   *o* Heb lacks *scouts*

20:16 **in their quarters:** *or* at Succoth.   20:21 **captured:** *so Gk; Heb.* destroyed.   20:23 **gods are gods:** *or* God is a god.

sent couriers to Ahab, king of Israel, within the city, 3 and said to him, "This is Ben-hadad's message: 'Your silver and gold are mine, and your wives and your promising sons are mine.' " 4 The king of Israel answered, "As you say, my lord king, I and all I have are yours." 5 But the couriers came again and said, "This is Ben-hadad's message: 'I sent you word to give me your silver and gold, your wives and your sons. 6 Now, however, at this time tomorrow I will send my servants to you, and they shall ransack your house and the houses of your servants. They shall seize and take away whatever they consider valuable.' "

7 The king of Israel then summoned all the elders of the land and said: "Understand clearly that this man wants to ruin us. When he sent to me for my wives and sons, my silver and my gold, I did not refuse him." 8 All the elders and all the people said to him, "Do not listen. Do not give in." 9 Accordingly he directed the couriers of Ben-hadad, "Say to my lord the king, 'I will do all that you demanded of your servant the first time. But this I cannot do.' " The couriers left and reported this. 10 Ben-hadad then sent him the message, "May the gods do thus and so to me if there is enough dust in Samaria to make handfuls for all my followers." 11 The king of Israel replied, "Tell him, 'It is not for the man who is buckling his armor to boast as though he were taking it off.' " 12 Ben-hadad was drinking in the pavilions with the kings when he heard this reply. "Prepare the assault," he commanded his servants; and they made ready to storm the city.

13 Then a prophet came up to Ahab, king of Israel, and said: "The LORD says, 'Do you see all this huge army? When I deliver it up to you today, you will know that I am the LORD.' " 14 But Ahab asked, "Through whom will it be delivered up?" He answered, "The LORD says, 'Through the retainers of the governors of the provinces.' " Then Ahab asked, "Who is to attack?" He replied, "You are." 15 So Ahab called up the retainers of the governors of the provinces, two hundred thirty-two of them. Behind them he mustered all the Israelite soldiery, who numbered seven thousand. 16 They marched out at noon, while Ben-hadad was drinking heavily in the pavilions with the thirty-two kings who were his allies. 17 When the retainers of the governors of the provinces marched out first, Ben-hadad received word that some men had marched out of Samaria. 18 He answered, "Whether they have come out for peace or for war, in any case take them alive." 19 But when these had come out of the city—the soldiers of the governors of the provinces with the army following them— 20 each of them struck down his man. The Arameans fled with Israel pursuing them, while Ben-hadad, king of Aram, escaped on a chariot steed. 21 The king of Israel went out, took the horses and chariots, and inflicted a severe defeat on Aram.

22 Then the prophet went up to the king of Israel and said to him: "Go, regroup your forces. Mark well what you do, for at the beginning of the year the king of Aram will attack you." 23 On the other hand, the servants of the king of Aram said to him: "Their gods are gods of mountains. That is why they defeated us. But if we fight them on level ground, we shall be sure to defeat them. 24 This is what you must do: Take the kings from their posts and put prefects in their places. 25 Mobilize an army as large as the army that has deserted you, horse for horse, chariot for chariot. Let us fight them on level ground, and we shall surely defeat them." He took their advice and did this.

26 At the beginning of the year, Ben-hadad mobilized Aram and went up to Aphek to fight against Israel. 27 The

of Israel to tell him, 'Ben-Hadad says this, 3 "Your silver and gold are mine. Your wives and children remain yours." ' 4 The king of Israel replied, 'As you command, my lord king. Myself and all I have are yours.'

5 The messengers came again, this time they said, 'Ben-Hadad says this, "I have already sent you an order to hand over your silver and your gold, your wives and your children; 6 but I swear, this time tomorrow, I shall send my servants to ransack your house and your servants' houses and lay hands on everything that they value and take it away." '

7 The king of Israel summoned all the elders of the country and said, 'You can see clearly how this man intends to ruin us. He has already demanded my wives and my children, although I have not refused him my silver and gold.' 8 All the elders and all the people said, 'Take no notice. Do not consent.' 9 So he gave this answer to Ben-Hadad's messengers, 'Say to my lord the king, "All you first required of your servant I will do, but this I cannot do." ' And the messengers went back with the answer.

10 Ben-Hadad then sent him the following message, 'May the gods bring unnameable ills on me and worse ills too, if there is enough dust in Samaria for each of my followers to have a handful!' 11 But the king of Israel returned this answer, 'Say: the man who puts on his armour is not the one to boast, but the man who takes it off.' 12 When Ben-Hadad heard this message—he was under the awnings drinking with the kings—he gave orders to his servants, 'Take up position!' And they took up their positions against the city.

13 A prophet then arrived, looking for Ahab king of Israel, he said. ' "You have seen this huge army? This very day I shall deliver it into your hands, and you will know that I am Yahweh." ' 14 'By whose means?' Ahab asked. The prophet replied, 'Yahweh says this, "By means of the guards of the district governors." ' 'Who will co-ordinate the attack?' Ahab asked. 'You will,' the prophet replied.

15 So Ahab inspected the guards of the district governors: there were two hundred and thirty-two. After these he reviewed the army, all the Israelites: there were seven thousand. 16 They made a sortie at midday, when Ben-Hadad was drinking himself senseless under the awnings, he and the thirty-two kings who were allies. 17 The guards of the district governors led the sortie. A report was made to Ben-Hadad: 'Some men have come out of Samaria.' 18 He said, 'If they have come out for peace, take them alive; if they have come out for war, take them alive too.' 19 So they made a sortie from the city, the district governors' guards and behind them the army, 20 and each struck down his man. Aram took to flight and Israel pursued; Ben-Hadad king of Aram escaped on horseback. 21 The king of Israel then advanced, capturing horses and chariots and inflicting a great defeat on Aram.

22 The prophet then went to the king of Israel and said, 'Now is the time to be resolute and think carefully about what you should do, for at the turn of the year the king of Aram will march against you.'

23 The servants of the king of Aram said to him, 'Their gods are gods of the mountains; that is why they have proved stronger than we are. But if we fight them on level ground, we shall certainly beat them. 24 This is what you must do: remove all these kings from their commands and appoint professional soldiers in their place. 25 You, for your part, must recruit an army as large as the one which deserted you, with as many horses and as many chariots; then if we fight them on level ground, we shall certainly beat them.' He listened to their advice and acted accordingly.

26 At the turn of the year, Ben-Hadad mustered the Aramaeans and marched on Aphek to fight Israel. 27 The Israel-

ites had been mustered and provisioned, they went out to engage them; the people of Israel encamped opposite them like two little flocks of goats, while the Arameans filled the country. 28 A man of God approached and said to the king of Israel, "Thus says the LORD: Because the Arameans have said, 'The LORD is a god of the hills but he is not a god of the valleys,' therefore I will give all this great multitude into your hand, and you shall know that I am the LORD." 29 They encamped opposite one another seven days. Then on the seventh day the battle began; the Israelites killed one hundred thousand Aramean foot soldiers in one day. 30 The rest fled into the city of Aphek; and the wall fell on twenty-seven thousand men that were left.

Ben-hadad also fled, and entered the city to hide. 31 His servants said to him, "Look, we have heard that the kings of the house of Israel are merciful kings; let us put sackcloth around our waists and ropes on our heads, and go out to the king of Israel; perhaps he will spare your life." 32 So they tied sackcloth around their waists, put ropes on their heads, went to the king of Israel, and said, "Your servant Ben-hadad says, 'Please let me live.'" And he said, "Is he still alive? He is my brother." 33 Now the men were watching for an omen; they quickly took it up from him and said, "Yes, Ben-hadad is your brother." Then he said, "Go and bring him." So Ben-hadad came out to him; and he had him come up into the chariot. 34 Ben-hadad *p* said to him, "I will restore the towns that my father took from your father; and you may establish bazaars for yourself in Damascus, as my father did in Samaria." The king of Israel responded,*q* "I will let you go on those terms." So he made a treaty with him and let him go.

35 At the command of the LORD a certain member of a company of prophets*r* said to another, "Strike me!" But the man refused to strike him. 36 Then he said to him, "Because you have not obeyed the voice of the LORD, as soon as you have left me, a lion will kill you." And when he had left him, a lion met him and killed him. 37 Then he found another man and said, "Strike me!" So the man hit him, striking and wounding him. 38 Then the prophet departed, and waited for the king along the road, disguising himself with a bandage over his eyes. 39 As the king passed by, he cried to the king and said, "Your servant went out into the thick of the battle; then a soldier turned and brought a man to me, and said, 'Guard this man; if he is missing, your life shall be given for his life, or else you shall pay a talent of silver.' 40 While your servant was busy here and there, he was gone." The king of Israel said to him, "So shall your judgment be; you yourself have decided it." 41 Then he quickly took the bandage away from his eyes. The king of Israel recognized him as one of the prophets. 42 Then he said to him, "Thus says the LORD, 'Because you have let the man go whom I had devoted to destruction, therefore your life shall be for his life, and your people for his people.'" 43 The king of Israel set out toward home, resentful and sullen, and came to Samaria.

21 Later the following events took place: Naboth the Jezreelite had a vineyard in Jezreel, beside the palace of King Ahab of Samaria. 2 And Ahab said to Naboth, "Give me your vineyard, so that I may have it for a vegetable garden, because it is near my house; I will give you a better vineyard for it; or, if it seems good to you, I will give you its value in money." 3 But Naboth said to Ahab, "The LORD forbid that I should give you my ancestral inheritance." 4 Ahab went home resentful and sullen because of

Israel. 27 The Israelites too were mustered and formed into companies, and then went to meet the enemy. When the Israelites encamped opposite them, they seemed no better than a pair of new-born goats, while the Aramaeans covered the countryside. 28 The man of God came to the king of Israel and said, 'This is the word of the LORD: The Aramaeans may think that the LORD is a god of the hills and not a god of the valleys; but I shall give all this great host into your hands and you will know that I am the LORD.'

29 They lay in camp opposite one another for seven days; on the seventh day battle was joined and the Israelites destroyed a hundred thousand of the Aramaean infantry in one day. 30 The survivors fled to Aphek, into the citadel, and the city wall fell upon the twenty-seven thousand men who were left. Ben-hadad took refuge in the citadel, retreating into an inner room.

31 His attendants said to him, 'We have heard that the Israelite kings are men to be trusted. Let us therefore put sackcloth round our waists and wind rough cord round our heads and go out to the king of Israel. It may be that he will spare your life.' 32 So they fastened on the sackcloth and the cord, and went to the king of Israel and said, 'Your servant Ben-hadad pleads for his life.' 'My royal cousin,' he said, 'is he still alive?' 33 The man, taking the word for a favourable omen, caught it up at once and said, 'Your cousin Ben-hadad, yes.' 'Go and fetch him,' he said. When Ben-hadad came out Ahab invited him into his chariot. 34 Ben-hadad said to him, 'I shall give back the towns which my father took from your father, and you may establish for yourself a trading quarter in Damascus, as my father did in Samaria.' 'On these terms', said Ahab, 'I shall let you go.' So he granted him a treaty and let him go.

35 One of a company of prophets, at the command of the LORD, ordered a certain man to strike him, but the man refused. 36 'Because you have not obeyed the LORD,' said the prophet, 'when you leave me a lion will attack you.' When the man left, a lion did come upon him and attack him. 37 The prophet met another man and ordered him to strike him. This man struck and wounded him. 38 The prophet went off, with a bandage over his eyes, and thus disguised waited by the wayside for the king. 39 As the king was passing, he called out to him, 'Sir, I went into the thick of the battle, and a soldier came over to me with a prisoner and said, "Take charge of this fellow. If by any chance he gets away, your life will be forfeit, or you must pay a talent of silver." 40 While I was busy with one thing and another, sir, he disappeared.' The king of Israel said to him, 'You have passed sentence on yourself.' 41 At that the prophet tore the bandage from his eyes, and the king saw that he was one of the prophets. 42 He said to the king, 'This is the word of the LORD: Because you let that man go when I had put him under a ban, your life shall be forfeit for his life, your people for his people.' 43 The king of Israel went off home and entered Samaria sullen and angry.

21 SOME time later there occurred an incident involving Naboth of Jezreel, who had a vineyard in Jezreel adjoining the palace of King Ahab of Samaria. 2 Ahab made a proposal to Naboth: 'Your vineyard is close to my palace; let me have it for a garden, and I shall give you a better vineyard in exchange for it or, if you prefer, I shall give you its value in silver.' 3 But Naboth answered, 'The LORD forbid that I should surrender to you land which has always been in my family.' 4 Ahab went home sullen and

p Heb *He*   *q* Heb lacks *The king of Israel responded*   *r* Heb *of the sons of the prophets*

Israelites, too, were called to arms and supplied with provisions; then they went out to engage the foe. The Israelites, encamped opposite them, seemed like a couple of small flocks of goats, while Aram covered the countryside. 28 A man of God came up and said to the king of Israel: "The LORD says, 'Because Aram has said the LORD is a god of mountains, not a god of plains, I will deliver up to you all this large army, that you may know I am the LORD.' " 29 They were encamped opposite each other for seven days. On the seventh day battle was joined, and the Israelites struck down one hundred thousand foot soldiers of Aram in one day. 30 The survivors, twenty-seven thousand of them, fled into the city of Aphek, and there the wall collapsed. Ben-hadad, too, fled, and took refuge within the city, in an inside room.

31 His servants said to him: "We have heard that the kings of the land of Israel are merciful kings. Allow us, therefore, to garb ourselves in sackcloth, with cords around our heads, and go out to the king of Israel. Perhaps he will spare your life." 32 So they dressed in sackcloth girded at the waist, and wearing cords around their heads, they went to the king of Israel. "Your servant Ben-hadad pleads for his life," they said. "Is he still alive?" the king asked. "He is my brother." 33 Hearing this as a good omen, the men quickly took him at his word and said, "Ben-hadad is your brother." He answered, "Go and get him." When Ben-hadad came out to him, the king had him mount his chariot. 34 Ben-hadad said to him, "I will restore the cities which my father took from your father, and you may make yourself bazaars in Damascus, as my father did in Samaria." "On these terms," Ahab replied, "I will set you free." So he made an agreement with him and then set him free.

35 One of the guild prophets was prompted by the LORD to say to his companion, "Strike me." But he refused to strike him. 36 Then he said to him, "Since you did not obey the voice of the LORD, a lion will kill you when you leave me." When they parted company, a lion came upon him and killed him. 37 The prophet met another man and said, "Strike me." The man struck him a blow and wounded him. 38 The prophet went on and waited for the king on the road, having disguised himself with a bandage over his eyes. 39 As the king was passing, he called out to the king and said, "Your servant went into the thick of the battle, and suddenly someone turned and brought me a man and said, 'Guard this man. If he is missing, you shall have to pay for his life with your life or pay out a talent of silver.' 40 But while your servant was looking here and there, the man disappeared." The king of Israel said to him, "That is your sentence. You have decided it yourself." 41 He immediately removed the bandage from his eyes, and the king of Israel recognized him as one of the prophets. 42 He said to him: "The LORD says, 'Because you have set free the man I doomed to destruction, your life shall pay for his life, your people for his people.' " Disturbed and angry, the king of Israel went off homeward and entered Samaria.

21 Some time after this, as Naboth the Jezreelite had a vineyard in Jezreel next to the palace of Ahab, king of Samaria, 2 Ahab said to Naboth, "Give me your vineyard to be my vegetable garden, since it is close by, next to my house. I will give you a better vineyard in exchange, or, if you prefer, I will give you its value in money." 3 "The LORD forbid," Naboth answered him, "that I should give you my ancestral heritage." 4 Ahab went home disturbed and angry

ites were already mobilised and provisioned, and marched out to meet them. Encamped opposite them, the Israelites looked like two herds of goats, whereas the Aramaeans filled the countryside. 28 The man of God then went to the king of Israel and said, 'Yahweh says this, "Since Aram has said that Yahweh is a god of the mountains and not a god of the plains, I shall put the whole of this huge army into your power, and you will know that I am Yahweh." ' 29 For seven days they were encamped opposite each other. On the seventh day battle was joined and the Israelites slaughtered the Aramaeans, a hundred thousand foot soldiers in one day. 30 The rest fled to Aphek, into the citadel, but the city walls collapsed on twenty-seven thousand of the survivors.

Now Ben-Hadad had fled and taken refuge in an inner room inside the citadel. 31 'Look,' his servants said to him, 'we have heard that the kings of Israel are faithful and kind kings. Let us put sackcloth round our waists and cords round our heads and go out to the king of Israel; perhaps he will spare your life.' 32 So they wrapped sackcloth round their waists and put cords round their heads and went to the king of Israel, and said, 'Your servant Ben-Hadad says, "Spare my life." ' 33 'So he is still alive?' he replied. 'He is my brother.' The men took this for a good omen and quickly seized on his words. 'Yes,' they said, 'Ben-Hadad is your brother.' Ahab said, 'Go and fetch him.' Then Ben-Hadad came out to him and Ahab made him get up into his chariot. 34 Ben-Hadad said, 'I shall restore the towns which my father took from your father and you may set up a trading quarter for yourself in Damascus as my father did in Samaria.' 'With a treaty,' Ahab said, 'I shall set you free.' Granting him a treaty, Ahab let him go.

35 At Yahweh's command a member of the brotherhood of prophets said to a companion of his, 'Strike me,' but the man refused to strike him. 36 So he said to him, 'Since you have disobeyed Yahweh's order, the very moment you leave me a lion will kill you.' And no sooner had he left him than he met a lion, which killed him. 37 The prophet then went to find another man and said, 'Strike me,' and the man struck him and wounded him. 38 The prophet then went and stood waiting for the king on the road, disguising himself with a bandage over his eyes. 39 As the king passed, he called out to him, 'Your servant was making his way to where the fight was thickest when someone left the fighting to bring a man to me, and said, "Guard this man; if he is found missing, your life will pay for his, or else you will have to pay one talent of silver." 40 But your servant was busy with one thing and another, the man disappeared.' The king of Israel said, 'That is your sentence then. You have pronounced it yourself.' 41 At this the man quickly pulled off the bandage over his eyes, and the king of Israel recognised him as one of the prophets. 42 He said to the king, 'Yahweh says this, "Since you have let the man escape who was under my curse of destruction, your life will pay for his, your people for his people." ' 43 And the king of Israel went home, gloomy and out of temper, back to Samaria.

21 This is what happened next: Naboth of Jezreel had a vineyard close by the palace of Ahab king of Samaria, 2 and Ahab said to Naboth, 'Give me your vineyard to be my vegetable garden, since it adjoins my palace; I will give you a better vineyard for it or, if you prefer, I will give you its value in money.' 3 Naboth, however, said to Ahab, 'Yahweh forbid that I should give you my ancestral heritage!'

4 Ahab went home gloomy and out of temper at the words

NEW REVISED STANDARD VERSION | REVISED ENGLISH BIBLE

what Naboth the Jezreelite had said to him; for he had said, "I will not give you my ancestral inheritance." He lay down on his bed, turned away his face, and would not eat.

5 His wife Jezebel came to him and said, "Why are you so depressed that you will not eat?" 6 He said to her, "Because I spoke to Naboth the Jezreelite and said to him, 'Give me your vineyard for money; or else, if you prefer, I will give you another vineyard for it'; but he answered, 'I will not give you my vineyard.'" 7 His wife Jezebel said to him, "Do you now govern Israel? Get up, eat some food, and be cheerful; I will give you the vineyard of Naboth the Jezreelite."

8 So she wrote letters in Ahab's name and sealed them with his seal; she sent the letters to the elders and the nobles who lived with Naboth in his city. 9 She wrote in the letters, "Proclaim a fast, and seat Naboth at the head of the assembly; 10 seat two scoundrels opposite him, and have them bring a charge against him, saying, 'You have cursed God and the king.' Then take him out, and stone him to death." 11 The men of his city, the elders and the nobles who lived in his city, did as Jezebel had sent word to them. Just as it was written in the letters that she had sent to them, 12 they proclaimed a fast and seated Naboth at the head of the assembly. 13 The two scoundrels came in and sat opposite him; and the scoundrels brought a charge against Naboth, in the presence of the people, saying, "Naboth cursed God and the king." So they took him outside the city, and stoned him to death. 14 Then they sent to Jezebel, saying, "Naboth has been stoned; he is dead."

15 As soon as Jezebel heard that Naboth had been stoned and was dead, Jezebel said to Ahab, "Go, take possession of the vineyard of Naboth the Jezreelite, which he refused to give you for money; for Naboth is not alive, but dead." 16 As soon as Ahab heard that Naboth was dead, Ahab set out to go down to the vineyard of Naboth the Jezreelite, to take possession of it.

17 Then the word of the LORD came to Elijah the Tishbite, saying: 18 Go down to meet King Ahab of Israel, who rules[s] in Samaria; he is now in the vineyard of Naboth, where he has gone to take possession. 19 You shall say to him, "Thus says the LORD: Have you killed, and also taken possession?" You shall say to him, "Thus says the LORD: In the place where dogs licked up the blood of Naboth, dogs will also lick up your blood."

20 Ahab said to Elijah, "Have you found me, O my enemy?" He answered, "I have found you. Because you have sold yourself to do what is evil in the sight of the LORD, 21 I will bring disaster on you; I will consume you, and will cut off from Ahab every male, bond or free, in Israel; 22 and I will make your house like the house of Jeroboam son of Nebat, and like the house of Baasha son of Ahijah, because you have provoked me to anger and have caused Israel to sin. 23 Also concerning Jezebel the LORD said, 'The dogs shall eat Jezebel within the bounds of Jezreel.' 24 Anyone belonging to Ahab who dies in the city the dogs shall eat; and anyone of his who dies in the open country the birds of the air shall eat."

25 (Indeed, there was no one like Ahab, who sold himself to do what was evil in the sight of the LORD, urged on by his wife Jezebel. 26 He acted most abominably in going after idols, as the Amorites had done, whom the LORD drove out before the Israelites.)

27 When Ahab heard those words, he tore his clothes and put sackcloth over his bare flesh; he fasted, lay in the sackcloth, and went about dejectedly. 28 Then the word of the LORD came to Elijah the Tishbite: 29 "Have you seen

angry because Naboth had refused to let him have his ancestral holding. He took to his bed, covered his face, and refused to eat. 5 When his wife Jezebel came in to him and asked, 'Why this sullenness, and why do you refuse to eat?' 6 he replied, 'I proposed that Naboth of Jezreel should let me have his vineyard at its value or, if he liked, in exchange for another; but he refused to let me have it.' 7 'Are you or are you not king in Israel?' retorted Jezebel. 'Come, eat and take heart; I shall make you a gift of the vineyard of Naboth of Jezreel.'

8 She wrote letters in Ahab's name, sealed them with his seal, and sent them to the elders and notables of Naboth's city, who sat in council with him. 9 She wrote: 'Proclaim a fast and give Naboth the seat of honour among the people. 10 Opposite him seat two unprincipled rogues to charge him with cursing God and the king; then take him out and stone him to death.' 11 The elders and notables of Naboth's city carried out the instructions Jezebel had sent them in her letter: 12 they proclaimed a fast and gave Naboth the seat of honour. 13 The two unprincipled rogues came in, sat opposite him, and charged him publicly with cursing God and the king. He was then taken outside the city and stoned, 14 and word was sent to Jezebel that Naboth had been stoned to death.

15 As soon as Jezebel heard of the death of Naboth, she said to Ahab, 'Get up and take possession of the vineyard which Naboth refused to sell you, for he is no longer alive; Naboth of Jezreel is dead.' 16 On hearing that Naboth was dead, Ahab got up and went to the vineyard to take possession.

17 The word of the LORD came to Elijah the Tishbite: 18 'Go down at once to King Ahab of Israel, who is in Samaria; you will find him in Naboth's vineyard, where he has gone to take possession. 19 Say to him, "This is the word of the LORD: Have you murdered and seized property?" Say to him, "This is the word of the LORD: Where dogs licked the blood of Naboth, there dogs will lick your blood."' 20 Ahab said to Elijah, 'So you have found me, my enemy.' 'Yes,' he said, 'because you have sold yourself to do what is wrong in the eyes of the LORD. 21 I shall bring disaster on you; I shall sweep you away and destroy every mother's son of the house of Ahab in Israel, whether under protection of the family or not. 22 I shall deal with your house as I dealt with the house of Jeroboam son of Nebat and that of Baasha son of Ahijah, because you have provoked my anger and led Israel into sin.' 23 The LORD went on to say of Jezebel, 'Jezebel will be eaten by dogs near the rampart of Jezreel. 24 Of the house of Ahab, those who die in the city will be food for the dogs, and those who die in the country food for the birds.'

25 (Never was there a man who sold himself to do what is wrong in the LORD's eyes as Ahab did, and all at the prompting of Jezebel his wife. 26 He committed gross abominations in going after false gods, doing everything that had been done by the Amorites, whom the LORD dispossessed in favour of Israel.)

27 When Ahab heard Elijah's words, he tore his clothes, put on sackcloth, and fasted; he lay down in his sackcloth and went about moaning. 28 The word of the LORD came to Elijah the Tishbite: 29 'Have you seen how Ahab has hum-

21:10,13 cursing: *lit.* bidding farewell to. 21:20–21 he said ... LORD. I shall bring: *or* he said. 'Because you ... LORD, I am bringing. 21:23 near the rampart of: *or, with some MSS,* in the plot of ground at (*cp. 2 Kgs. 9:36*).

[s] Heb *who is*

at the answer Naboth the Jezreelite had made to him: "I will not give you my ancestral heritage." Lying down on his bed, he turned away from food and would not eat.

5 His wife Jezebel came to him and said to him, "Why are you so angry that you will not eat?" 6 He answered her, "Because I spoke to Naboth the Jezreelite and said to him, 'Sell me your vineyard, or, if you prefer, I will give you a vineyard in exchange.' But he refused to let me have his vineyard." 7 "A fine ruler over Israel you are indeed!" his wife Jezebel said to him. "Get up. Eat and be cheerful. I will obtain the vineyard of Naboth the Jezreelite for you."

8 So she wrote letters in Ahab's name and, having sealed them with his seal, sent them to the elders and to the nobles who lived in the same city with Naboth. 9 This is what she wrote in the letters: "Proclaim a fast and set Naboth at the head of the people. 10 Next, get two scoundrels to face him and accuse him of having cursed God and king. Then take him out and stone him to death." 11 His fellow citizens — the elders and the nobles who dwelt in his city — did as Jezebel had ordered them in writing, through the letters she had sent them. 12 They proclaimed a fast and placed Naboth at the head of the people. 13 Two scoundrels came in and confronted him with the accusation, "Naboth has cursed God and king." And they led him out of the city and stoned him to death. 14 Then they sent the information to Jezebel that Naboth had been stoned to death.

15 When Jezebel learned that Naboth had been stoned to death, she said to Ahab, "Go on, take possession of the vineyard of Naboth the Jezreelite which he refused to sell you, because Naboth is not alive, but dead." 16 On hearing that Naboth was dead, Ahab started off on his way down to the vineyard of Naboth the Jezreelite, to take possession of it.

17 But the LORD said to Elijah the Tishbite: 18 "Start down to meet Ahab, king of Israel, who rules in Samaria. He will be in the vineyard of Naboth, of which he has come to take possession. 19 This is what you shall tell him, 'The LORD says: After murdering, do you also take possession? For this, the LORD says: In the place where the dogs licked up the blood of Naboth, the dogs shall lick up your blood, too.'" 20 "Have you found me out, my enemy?" Ahab said to Elijah. "Yes," he answered. "Because you have given yourself up to doing evil in the LORD's sight, 21 I am bringing evil upon you: I will destroy you and will cut off every male in Ahab's line, whether slave or freeman, in Israel. 22 I will make your house like that of Jeroboam, son of Nebat, and like that of Baasha, son of Ahijah, because of how you have provoked me by leading Israel into sin." 23 (Against Jezebel, too, the LORD declared, "The dogs shall devour Jezebel in the district of Jezreel.") 24 "When one of Ahab's line dies in the city, dogs will devour him; when one of them dies in the field, the birds of the sky will devour him." 25 Indeed, no one gave himself up to the doing of evil in the sight of the LORD as did Ahab, urged on by his wife Jezebel. 26 He became completely abominable by following idols, just as the Amorites had done, whom the LORD drove out before the Israelites.

27 When Ahab heard these words, he tore his garments and put on sackcloth over his bare flesh. He fasted, slept in the sackcloth, and went about subdued. 28 Then the LORD said to Elijah the Tishbite, 29 "Have you seen that Ahab has

of Naboth of Jezreel, 'I will not give you my heritage from my ancestors.' He lay down on his bed and turned his face away and refused to eat. 5 His wife Jezebel came to him. 'Why are you so dispirited,' she said, 'that you refuse to eat?' 6 He said, 'I have been talking to Naboth of Jezreel. I said, "Give me your vineyard either for money or, if you prefer, for another vineyard in exchange." But he said, "I will not give you my vineyard."' 7 Then his wife Jezebel said, 'Some king of Israel you make! Get up, eat and take heart; I myself shall get you the vineyard of Naboth the Jezreelite.'

8 So she wrote a letter in Ahab's name and sealed it with his seal, sending the letter to the elders and notables of the city where Naboth lived. 9 In the letter, she wrote, 'Proclaim a fast, and put Naboth in a prominent place among the people. 10 There confront him with a couple of scoundrels who will accuse him as follows, "You have cursed God and the king." Then take him outside and stone him to death.' 11 The men of Naboth's city, the elders and notables living in his city, did what Jezebel ordered, as was written in the letter which she had sent him. 12 They proclaimed a fast and put Naboth in a prominent place among the people. 13 The two scoundrels then came and confronted him, and the scoundrels then publicly accused Naboth as follows, 'Naboth has cursed God and the king.' He was then taken outside the city and stoned to death. 14 They then sent word to Jezebel, 'Naboth has been stoned to death.' 15 When Jezebel heard that Naboth had been stoned to death, she said to Ahab, 'Get up! Take possession of the vineyard which Naboth of Jezreel refused to sell you, for Naboth is no longer alive, he is dead.' 16 When Ahab heard that Naboth was dead, he got up to go down to the vineyard of Naboth of Jezreel and take possession of it.

17 Then the word of Yahweh came to Elijah the Tishbite, 18 'Up! Go down to meet Ahab king of Israel, in Samaria. You will find him in Naboth's vineyard; he has gone down to take possession of it. 19 You are to say this to him, "Yahweh says this: You have committed murder and now you usurp as well. For this — and Yahweh says this — in the place where the dogs licked the blood of Naboth, the dogs will lick your blood too." ' [h] 20 Ahab said to Elijah, 'So you have caught me, O my enemy!' Elijah answered, 'I have caught you! For your double dealing, and since you have done what is displeasing to Yahweh, 21 I shall now bring disaster down on you; I shall sweep away your descendants and wipe out every manjack of the House of Ahab, fettered or free in Israel. 22 I shall treat your House as I treated the house of Jeroboam son of Nebat and Baasha son of Ahijah, for provoking my anger and leading Israel into sin. 23 (Against Jezebel too Yahweh spoke these words, "The dogs will eat Jezebel in the Field of Jezreel.") 24 Those of Ahab's family who die in the city, the dogs will eat; and those who die in the open country, the birds of the air will eat.'

25 And indeed there never was anyone like Ahab for double dealing and for doing what is displeasing to Yahweh, urged on by Jezebel his wife. 26 He behaved in the most abominable way, adhering to idols, just as the Amorites had, whom Yahweh had dispossessed for the Israelites.

27 When Ahab heard these words, he tore his garments and put sackcloth next to his skin and fasted; he slept in the sackcloth; he walked with slow steps. 28 Then the word of Yahweh came to Elijah the Tishbite, 29 'Have you seen how

how Ahab has humbled himself before me? Because he has humbled himself before me, I will not bring the disaster in his days; but in his son's days I will bring the disaster on his house."

22 For three years Aram and Israel continued without war. 2 But in the third year King Jehoshaphat of Judah came down to the king of Israel. 3 The king of Israel said to his servants, "Do you know that Ramoth-gilead belongs to us, yet we are doing nothing to take it out of the hand of the king of Aram?" 4 He said to Jehoshaphat, "Will you go with me to battle at Ramoth-gilead?" Jehoshaphat replied to the king of Israel, "I am as you are; my people are your people, my horses are your horses."

5 But Jehoshaphat also said to the king of Israel, "Inquire first for the word of the LORD." 6 Then the king of Israel gathered the prophets together, about four hundred of them, and said to them, "Shall I go to battle against Ramoth-gilead, or shall I refrain?" They said, "Go up; for the LORD will give it into the hand of the king." 7 But Jehoshaphat said, "Is there no other prophet of the LORD here of whom we may inquire?" 8 The king of Israel said to Jehoshaphat, "There is still one other by whom we may inquire of the LORD, Micaiah son of Imlah; but I hate him, for he never prophesies anything favorable about me, but only disaster." Jehoshaphat said, "Let the king not say such a thing." 9 Then the king of Israel summoned an officer and said, "Bring quickly Micaiah son of Imlah." 10 Now the king of Israel and King Jehoshaphat of Judah were sitting on their thrones, arrayed in their robes, at the threshing floor at the entrance of the gate of Samaria; and all the prophets were prophesying before them. 11 Zedekiah son of Chenaanah made for himself horns of iron, and he said, "Thus says the LORD: With these you shall gore the Arameans until they are destroyed." 12 All the prophets were prophesying the same and saying, "Go up to Ramoth-gilead and triumph; the LORD will give it into the hand of the king."

13 The messenger who had gone to summon Micaiah said to him, "Look, the words of the prophets with one accord are favorable to the king; let your word be like the word of one of them, and speak favorably." 14 But Micaiah said, "As the LORD lives, whatever the LORD says to me, that I will speak."

15 When he had come to the king, the king said to him, "Micaiah, shall we go to Ramoth-gilead to battle, or shall we refrain?" He answered him, "Go up and triumph; the LORD will give it into the hand of the king." 16 But the king said to him, "How many times must I make you swear to tell me nothing but the truth in the name of the LORD?" 17 Then Micaiah[t] said, "I saw all Israel scattered on the mountains, like sheep that have no shepherd; and the LORD said, 'These have no master; let each one go home in peace.' " 18 The king of Israel said to Jehoshaphat, "Did I not tell you that he would not prophesy anything favorable about me, but only disaster?"

19 Then Micaiah[t] said, "Therefore hear the word of the LORD: I saw the LORD sitting on his throne, with all the host of heaven standing beside him to the right and to the left of him. 20 And the LORD said, 'Who will entice Ahab, so that he may go up and fall at Ramoth-gilead?' Then one said one thing, and another said another, 21 until a spirit came forward and stood before the LORD, saying, 'I will entice him.' 22 'How?' the LORD asked him. He replied, 'I will go out and be a lying spirit in the mouth of all his prophets.' Then the LORD[t] said, 'You are to entice him, and you shall succeed; go out and do it.' 23 So you see, the LORD has put a lying spirit in the mouth of all these your prophets; the LORD has decreed disaster for you."

bled himself before me? Because he has thus humbled himself, I shall not bring disaster on his house in his own lifetime, but in that of his son.'

22 FOR three years there was no war between the Aramaeans and the Israelites. 2 In the third year King Jehoshaphat of Judah went down to visit the king of Israel, 3 who had said to his ministers, 'You know that Ramoth-gilead belongs to us, and yet we do nothing to recover it from the king of Aram'; 4 and to Jehoshaphat he said, 'Will you join me in attacking Ramoth-gilead?' Jehoshaphat replied, 'What is mine is yours: myself, my people, and my horses,' 5 but he said to the king of Israel, 'First let us seek counsel from the LORD.'

6 The king of Israel assembled the prophets, some four hundred of them, and asked, 'Shall I attack Ramoth-gilead or not?' 'Attack,' was the answer; 'the Lord will deliver it into your majesty's hands.' 7 Jehoshaphat asked, 'Is there no other prophet of the LORD here through whom we may seek guidance?' 8 'There is one more', the king of Israel answered, 'through whom we may seek guidance of the LORD, but I hate the man, because he never prophesies good for me, never anything but evil. His name is Micaiah son of Imlah.' Jehoshaphat exclaimed, 'My lord king, let no such word pass your lips!' 9 So the king of Israel called one of his eunuchs and told him to fetch Micaiah son of Imlah with all speed.

10 The king of Israel and King Jehoshaphat of Judah in their royal robes were seated on their thrones at the entrance to the gate of Samaria, and all the prophets were prophesying before them. 11 One of them, Zedekiah son of Kenaanah, made himself iron horns and declared, 'This is the word of the LORD: With horns like these you will gore the Aramaeans and make an end of them.' 12 In the same vein all the prophets prophesied, 'Attack Ramoth-gilead and win the day; the LORD will deliver it into your hands.'

13 The messenger sent to fetch Micaiah told him that the prophets had unanimously given the king a favourable answer. 'And mind you agree with them,' he added. 14 'As the LORD lives,' said Micaiah, 'I shall say only what the LORD tells me to say.' 15 When he came into the king's presence, the king asked, 'Micaiah, shall I attack Ramoth-gilead, or shall I refrain?' 'Attack and win the day,' he replied; 'the LORD will deliver it into your hands.' 16 'How often must I adjure you', said the king, 'to tell me nothing but the truth in the name of the LORD?' 17 Then Micaiah said,

'I saw all Israel scattered on the mountains,
    like sheep without a shepherd;
and I heard the LORD say, "They have no master;
    let them go home in peace." '

18 The king of Israel said to Jehoshaphat, 'Did I not tell you that he never prophesies good for me, never anything but evil?' 19 Micaiah went on, 'Listen now to the word of the LORD: I saw the LORD seated on his throne, with all the host of heaven in attendance on his right and on his left. 20 The LORD said, "Who will entice Ahab to go up and attack Ramoth-gilead?" One said one thing and one said another, 21 until a spirit came forward and, standing before the LORD, said, "I shall entice him." 22 "How?" said the LORD. "I shall go out", he answered, "and be a lying spirit in the mouths of all his prophets." "Entice him; you will succeed," said the LORD. "Go and do it." 23 You see, then, how the LORD has put a lying spirit in the mouths of all these prophets of yours, because he has decreed disaster for you.'

---

[t] Heb *he*

22:2–35 *Cp. 2 Chr. 18:2–34.*   22:15 **I:** *so Gk; Heb.* we.

766

humbled himself before me? Since he has humbled himself before me, I will not bring the evil in his time. I will bring the evil upon his house during the reign of his son."

22 Three years passed without war between Aram and Israel. ²In the third year, however, King Jehoshaphat of Judah came down to the king of Israel, ³who said to his servants, "Do you not know that Ramoth-gilead is ours and we are doing nothing to take it from the king of Aram?" ⁴He asked Jehoshaphat, "Will you come with me to fight against Ramoth-gilead?" Jehoshaphat answered the king of Israel, "You and I are as one, and your people and my people, your horses and my horses as well." ⁵Jehoshaphat also said to the king of Israel, "Seek the word of the LORD at once."

⁶The king of Israel gathered together the prophets, about four hundred of them, and asked, "Shall I go to attack Ramoth-gilead or shall I refrain?" "Go up," they answered. "The LORD will deliver it over to the king." ⁷But Jehoshaphat said, "Is there no other prophet of the LORD here whom we may consult?" ⁸The king of Israel answered, "There is one other through whom we might consult the LORD, Micaiah, son of Imlah; but I hate him because he prophesies not good but evil about me." Jehoshaphat said, "Let not your majesty speak of evil against you."

⁹So the king of Israel called an official and said to him, "Get Micaiah, son of Imlah, at once." ¹⁰The king of Israel and King Jehoshaphat of Judah were seated, each on his throne, clothed in their robes of state on a threshing floor at the entrance of the gate of Samaria, and all the prophets were prophesying before them. ¹¹Zedekiah, son of Chenaanah, made himself horns of iron and said, "The LORD says, 'With these you shall gore Aram until you have destroyed them.'" ¹²The other prophets prophesied in a similar vein, saying: "Go up to Ramoth-gilead; you shall succeed. The LORD will deliver it over to the king."

¹³The messenger who had gone to call Micaiah said to him, "Look now, the prophets are unanimously predicting good for the king. Let your word be the same as any of theirs; predict good." ¹⁴"As the LORD lives," Micaiah answered, "I shall say whatever the LORD tells me."

¹⁵When he came to the king, the king said to him, "Micaiah, shall we go to fight against Ramoth-gilead, or shall we refrain?" "Go up," he answered, "you shall succeed! The LORD will deliver it over to the king." ¹⁶But the king answered him, "How many times must I adjure you to tell me nothing but the truth in the name of the LORD?" ¹⁷So Micaiah said:

"I see all Israel
scattered on the mountains,
like sheep without a shepherd,
and the LORD saying, 'These have no master!
Let each of them go back home in peace.'"

¹⁸The king of Israel said to Jehoshaphat, "Did I not tell you he prophesies not good but evil about me?" ¹⁹Micaiah continued: "Therefore hear the word of the LORD: I saw the LORD seated on his throne, with the whole host of heaven standing by to his right and to his left. ²⁰The LORD asked, 'Who will deceive Ahab, so that he will go up and fall at Ramoth-gilead?' And one said this, another that, ²¹until one of the spirits came forth and presented himself to the LORD, saying, 'I will deceive him.' The LORD asked, 'How?' ²²He answered, 'I will go forth and become a lying spirit in the mouths of all his prophets.' The LORD replied, 'You shall succeed in deceiving him. Go forth and do this.' ²³So now, the LORD has put a lying spirit in the mouths of all these prophets of yours, but the LORD himself has decreed evil against you."

Ahab has humbled himself before me? Since he has humbled himself before me, I shall not bring the disaster in his days; I shall bring the disaster down on his House in his son's days.'ⁱ

22 There was a lull of three years, with no fighting between Aram and Israel. ²Then, in the third year, Jehoshaphat king of Judah paid a visit to the king of Israel. ³The king of Israel said to his officers, 'You are aware that Ramoth in Gilead belongs to us? And yet we do nothing to wrest it away from the king of Aram.' ⁴He said to Jehoshaphat, 'Will you come with me to attack Ramoth in Gilead?' Jehoshaphat replied to the king of Israel, 'I will be as you, my men as yours, my horses as yours.'

⁵Jehoshaphat, however, said to the king of Israel, 'First, please enquire what the word of Yahweh is.' ⁶The king of Israel then called the prophets together, about four hundred of them. 'Should I go and attack Ramoth in Gilead,' he asked, 'or should I hold back?' 'Go ahead,' they replied, 'for Yahweh has already given it to the king.' ⁷Jehoshaphat, however, said, 'Is there no other prophet of Yahweh here, so that we can enquire through him?' ⁸The king of Israel said to Jehoshaphat, 'There is one more man through whom we can consult Yahweh, but I hate him because he never has a favourable prophecy for me, only unfavourable ones; he is Micaiah son of Imlah.' 'I hope the king's words are unjustified,' said Jehoshaphat. ⁹The king of Israel then summoned a court official and said, 'Bring Micaiah son of Imlah immediately.'

¹⁰The king of Israel and Jehoshaphat king of Judah were sitting each on his throne, wearing their robes, in an open space just outside the gate of Samaria, with all the prophets in a state of ecstasy before them. ¹¹Zedekiah son of Kenaanah, who had made himself some iron horns, said, 'Yahweh says, "With horns like these you will gore the Aramaeans till you make an end of them."' ¹²And all the prophets cried ecstatically in the same vein, 'March on Ramoth in Gilead! Success is sure, for Yahweh has already given it to the king!'

¹³The messenger who had gone to summon Micaiah said to him, 'Look here, what the prophets are saying is uniformly favourable to the king. I hope you will say the same as they do and speak favourably.' ¹⁴Micaiah said, 'As Yahweh lives, I shall speak as Yahweh tells me!' ¹⁵When he came to the king, the king said, 'Micaiah, should we go and attack Ramoth in Gilead, or should we hold back?' He replied, 'Go ahead! Success is sure, for Yahweh has already given it to the king!' ¹⁶The king then said, 'How often must I put you on oath to tell me nothing but the truth in the name of Yahweh?' ¹⁷Then he spoke out:

I saw all Israel scattered on the mountains
like sheep without a shepherd.
And Yahweh said, 'These have no master,
let them all go safely home!'

¹⁸At this the king of Israel said to Jehoshaphat, 'Did I not tell you that he never gives me favourable prophecies, but only unfavourable ones?' ¹⁹Micaiah went on, 'Now listen to the word of Yahweh. I saw Yahweh seated on his throne with the whole array of heaven standing by him, on his right and on his left. ²⁰Yahweh said, "Who will entice Ahab into marching to his death at Ramoth in Gilead?" At which some answered one way, and some another. ²¹A spirit then came forward and stood before Yahweh and said, "I will entice him." ²²"How?" Yahweh asked. He replied, "I shall go and be a deceptive spirit in the mouths of all his prophets." Yahweh said, "You will succeed in enticing him. Go and do it." ²³And now, you see, Yahweh has put a deceptive spirit into the mouths of all your prophets here, for in fact Yahweh has pronounced disaster on you.'

ⁱ**21** See 2 K 9–10.

24 Then Zedekiah son of Chenaanah came up to Micaiah, slapped him on the cheek, and said, "Which way did the spirit of the LORD pass from me to speak to you?" 25 Micaiah replied, "You will find out on that day when you go in to hide in an inner chamber." 26 The king of Israel then ordered, "Take Micaiah, and return him to Amon the governor of the city and to Joash the king's son, 27 and say, 'Thus says the king: Put this fellow in prison, and feed him on reduced rations of bread and water until I come in peace.' " 28 Micaiah said, "If you return in peace, the LORD has not spoken by me." And he said, "Hear, you peoples, all of you!"

29 So the king of Israel and King Jehoshaphat of Judah went up to Ramoth-gilead. 30 The king of Israel said to Jehoshaphat, "I will disguise myself and go into battle, but you wear your robes." So the king of Israel disguised himself and went into battle. 31 Now the king of Aram had commanded the thirty-two captains of his chariots, "Fight with no one small or great, but only with the king of Israel." 32 When the captains of the chariots saw Jehoshaphat, they said, "It is surely the king of Israel." So they turned to fight against him; and Jehoshaphat cried out. 33 When the captains of the chariots saw that it was not the king of Israel, they turned back from pursuing him. 34 But a certain man drew his bow and unknowingly struck the king of Israel between the scale armor and the breastplate; so he said to the driver of his chariot, "Turn around, and carry me out of the battle, for I am wounded." 35 The battle grew hot that day, and the king was propped up in his chariot facing the Arameans, until at evening he died; the blood from the wound had flowed into the bottom of the chariot. 36 Then about sunset a shout went through the army, "Every man to his city, and every man to his country!"

37 So the king died, and was brought to Samaria; they buried the king in Samaria. 38 They washed the chariot by the pool of Samaria; the dogs licked up his blood, and the prostitutes washed themselves in it, [u] according to the word of the LORD that he had spoken. 39 Now the rest of the acts of Ahab, and all that he did, and the ivory house that he built, and all the cities that he built, are they not written in the Book of the Annals of the Kings of Israel? 40 So Ahab slept with his ancestors; and his son Ahaziah succeeded him.

41 Jehoshaphat son of Asa began to reign over Judah in the fourth year of King Ahab of Israel. 42 Jehoshaphat was thirty-five years old when he began to reign, and he reigned twenty-five years in Jerusalem. His mother's name was Azubah daughter of Shilhi. 43 He walked in all the way of his father Asa; he did not turn aside from it, doing what was right in the sight of the LORD; yet the high places were not taken away, and the people still sacrificed and offered incense on the high places. 44 Jehoshaphat also made peace with the king of Israel.

45 Now the rest of the acts of Jehoshaphat, and his power that he showed, and how he waged war, are they not written in the Book of the Annals of the Kings of Judah? 46 The remnant of the male temple prostitutes who were still in the land in the days of his father Asa, he exterminated. 47 There was no king in Edom; a deputy was king. 48 Jehoshaphat made ships of the Tarshish type to go to Ophir for gold; but they did not go, for the ships were wrecked at Ezion-geber. 49 Then Ahaziah son of Ahab said to Jehoshaphat, "Let my servants go with your servants in the ships," but Jehoshaphat was not willing. 50 Jehoshaphat slept with his ancestors and was buried with his ancestors in the city of his father David; his son Jehoram succeeded him.

[u] Heb lacks in it

24 At that, Zedekiah son of Kenaanah came up to Micaiah and struck him in the face: 'And how did the spirit of the LORD pass from me to speak to you?' he demanded. 25 Micaiah retorted, 'That you will find out on the day when you run into an inner room to hide.' 26 The king of Israel ordered Micaiah to be arrested and committed to the custody of Amon the governor of the city and Joash the king's son. 27 'Throw this fellow into prison,' he said, 'and put him on a prison diet of bread and water until I come home in safety.' 28 Micaiah declared, 'If you do return in safety, the LORD has not spoken by me.'

29 The king of Israel and King Jehoshaphat of Judah marched on Ramoth-gilead. 30 The king of Israel went into battle in disguise, for he had said to Jehoshaphat, 'I shall disguise myself to go into battle, but you must wear your royal robes.' 31 The king of Aram had ordered the thirty-two captains of his chariots not to engage all and sundry, but the king of Israel alone. 32 When the captains saw Jehoshaphat, they thought he was the king of Israel and turned to attack him, but Jehoshaphat cried out, 33 and when the captains saw that he was not the king of Israel, they broke off the attack on him. 34 One man, however, drew his bow at random and hit the king of Israel where the breastplate joins the plates of the armour. The king said to his driver, 'Turn about and take me out of the line; I am wounded.' 35 When the day's fighting reached its height, the king was facing the Aramaeans, propped up in his chariot, and the blood from his wound flowed down to the floor of the chariot; and in the evening he died. 36 At sunset the herald went through the ranks, crying, 'Every man to his city, every man to his country.' 37 Thus the king died. He was brought to Samaria and buried there. 38 The chariot was swilled out at the pool of Samaria where the prostitutes washed themselves, and dogs licked up the blood, in fulfilment of the word the LORD had spoken.

39 The other acts and events of Ahab's reign, the palace he decorated with ivory and all the towns he built, are recorded in the annals of the kings of Israel. 40 Ahab rested with his forefathers and was succeeded by his son Ahaziah.

41 Jehoshaphat son of Asa had become king of Judah in the fourth year of King Ahab of Israel. 42 He was thirty-five years old when he came to the throne, and he reigned in Jerusalem for twenty-five years; his mother was Azubah daughter of Shilhi. 43 He followed in the footsteps of Asa his father and did not deviate from them; he did what was right in the eyes of the LORD. But the shrines were allowed to remain; the people continued to sacrifice and burn offerings there. 44 Jehoshaphat remained at peace with the king of Israel. 45 The other events of Jehoshaphat's reign, his exploits and his wars, are recorded in the annals of the kings of Judah. 46 He expelled from the land such of the male prostitutes attached to the shrines as were still left from the days of Asa his father.

47 There was no king in Edom, only a viceroy of Jehoshaphat; 48 he built merchantmen to sail to Ophir for gold, but they never made the voyage because they were wrecked at Ezion-geber. 49 Ahaziah son of Ahab proposed to Jehoshaphat that his men should go to sea with Jehoshaphat's; but Jehoshaphat would not agree.

50 Jehoshaphat rested with his forefathers and was buried with them in the city of David his father; he was succeeded by his son Joram.

22:26 **son:** or deputy.   22:28 **by me:** so Gk; Heb. adds and he said, 'Listen, peoples, all together.' Cp. 2 Chr. 20:31–33.   22:43 **But . . . there:** verse 44 in Heb.
22:47 **only:** prob. rdg; Heb. omits.   22:48 **merchantmen:** lit. ships of Tarshish.

24 Thereupon Zedekiah, son of Chenaanah, came up and slapped Micaiah on the cheek, saying, "Has the spirit of the LORD, then, left me to speak with you?" 25 "You shall find out," Micaiah replied, "on that day when you retreat into an inside room to hide." 26 The king of Israel then said, "Seize Micaiah and take him back to Amon, prefect of the city, and to Joash, the king's son, 27 and say, 'This is the king's order: Put this man in prison and feed him scanty rations of bread and water until I return in safety.'" 28 But Micaiah said, "If ever you return in safety, the LORD has not spoken through me."

29 The king of Israel and King Jehoshaphat of Judah went up to Ramoth-gilead, 30 and the king of Israel said to Jehoshaphat, "I will disguise myself and go into battle, but you put on your own clothes." So the king of Israel disguised himself and entered the fray. 31 In the meantime the king of Aram had given his thirty-two chariot commanders the order, "Do not fight with anyone at all except the king of Israel." 32 When the chariot commanders saw Jehoshaphat, they cried out, "That must be the king of Israel!" and shifted to fight him. But Jehoshaphat shouted his battle cry, 33 and the chariot commanders, aware that he was not the king of Israel, gave up pursuit of him. 34 Someone, however, drew his bow at random, and hit the king of Israel between the joints of his breastplate. He ordered his charioteer, "Rein about and take me out of the ranks, for I am disabled." 35 The battle grew fierce during the day, and the king, who was propped up in his chariot facing the Arameans, died in the evening. The blood from his wound flowed to the bottom of the chariot. 36 At sunset a cry went through the army, "Every man to his city, every man to his land, 37 for the king is dead!" So they went to Samaria, where they buried the king. 38 When the chariot was washed at the pool of Samaria, the dogs licked up his blood and harlots bathed there, as the LORD had prophesied.

39 The rest of the acts of Ahab, with all that he did, including the ivory palace and all the cities he built, are recorded in the book of the chronicles of the kings of Israel. 40 Ahab rested with his ancestors, and his son Ahaziah succeeded him as king.

41 Jehoshaphat, son of Asa, began to reign over Judah in the fourth year of Ahab, king of Israel. 42 Jehoshaphat was thirty-five years old when he began to reign, and he reigned twenty-five years in Jerusalem. His mother's name was Azubah, daughter of Shilhi. 43 He followed all the ways of his father Asa unswervingly, doing what was right in the LORD's sight. 44 Nevertheless, the high places did not disappear, and the people continued to sacrifice and to burn incense on the high places. 45 Jehoshaphat also made peace with the king of Israel. 46 The rest of the acts of Jehoshaphat, with his prowess, what he did and how he fought, are recorded in the book of the chronicles of the kings of Judah.

47 He removed from the land the rest of the cult prostitutes who had remained in the reign of his father Asa. 48 There was no king in Edom, but an appointed regent. 49 Jehoshaphat made Tarshish ships to go to Ophir for gold; but in fact the ships did not go, because they were wrecked at Ezion-geber. 50 Then Ahaziah, son of Ahab, said to Jehoshaphat, "Let my servants accompany your servants in the ships." But Jehoshaphat would not agree. 51 Jehoshaphat rested with his ancestors; he was buried in his forefathers' City of David. His son Jehoram succeeded him as king.

24 Zedekiah son of Chenaanah then came up, struck Micaiah on the cheek and said, 'Which way did Yahweh's spirit leave me, to speak to you?' 25 'That is what you will find out,' Micaiah retorted, 'the day you go from room to room, trying to hide.' 26 The king of Israel said, 'Seize Micaiah and hand him over to Amon, governor of the city, and Joash, the king's son, 27 and say, "These are the king's orders: Put this man in prison and feed him on nothing but bread and water until I am safely home." ' 28 Micaiah said, 'If you ever do get home safely, Yahweh has not spoken through me.'

29 The king of Israel and Jehoshaphat king of Judah marched on Ramoth in Gilead. 30 The king of Israel said to Jehoshaphat, 'I shall disguise myself to go into battle, but you put on your robes.' So the king of Israel disguised himself and went into battle. 31 Now, the king of Aram had given his chariot commanders the following order, 'Do not attack anyone of whatever rank, except the king of Israel.' 32 So, when the chariot commanders saw Jehoshaphat, they thought, 'That is obviously the king of Israel,' and surrounded him to attack. But when Jehoshaphat shouted his war cry 33 the chariot commanders, realising that he was not the king of Israel, broke off their pursuit.

34 Someone, however, drawing his bow without any special aim, shot the king of Israel between the joints of his armour. 'Turn about!' said the king to his charioteer. 'Get me out of the fighting; I am collapsing.' 35 But the battle grew fiercer as the day went on and the king had to be held upright in his chariot facing the Aramaeans, the blood from the wound running into the bottom of the chariot, until in the evening he died. 36 At sundown a shout ran through the ranks, 'Every man back to his town, every man back to his country!' 37 The king is dead.' He was taken to Samaria and in Samaria the king was buried. 38 They washed the chariot at the Pool of Samaria; the dogs licked up the blood, and the prostitutes washed in it, in accordance with the word which Yahweh had spoken.

39 The rest of the history of Ahab, his entire career, the ivory house he erected, all the towns he built, is this not recorded in the Book of the Annals of the Kings of Israel? 40 When Ahab fell asleep with his ancestors, his son Ahaziah succeeded him.

41 Jehoshaphat son of Asa became king of Judah in the fourth year of Ahab king of Israel. 42 Jehoshaphat was thirty-five years old when he came to the throne, and he reigned for twenty-five years in Jerusalem. His mother's name was Azubah daughter of Shilhi. 43 In every way he followed the example of his father Asa undeviatingly, doing what is pleasing to Yahweh. 44 The high places, however, were not abolished; the people still offered sacrifice and incense on the high places. 45 Jehoshaphat was at peace with the king of Israel.

46 The rest of the history of Jehoshaphat, the valour he showed, the wars he waged, is this not recorded in the Book of the Annals of the Kings of Judah? 47 The few male sacred prostitutes left over from the days of his father Asa, he expelled from the country. 48 At the time, Edom had no king, and King 49 Jehoshaphat built ships of Tarshish to go to Ophir for gold, but they never made the voyage since the ships were wrecked at Ezion-Geber. 50 Ahaziah son of Ahab then proposed to Jehoshaphat, 'Let my men go to sea with yours.' But Jehoshaphat would not agree. 51 When Jehoshaphat fell asleep with his ancestors he was buried in the City of his ancestor, David; his son Jehoram succeeded him.

NEW REVISED STANDARD VERSION

REVISED ENGLISH BIBLE

51 Ahaziah son of Ahab began to reign over Israel in Samaria in the seventeenth year of King Jehoshaphat of Judah; he reigned two years over Israel. 52 He did what was evil in the sight of the LORD, and walked in the way of his father and mother, and in the way of Jeroboam son of Nebat, who caused Israel to sin. 53 He served Baal and worshiped him; he provoked the LORD, the God of Israel, to anger, just as his father had done.

51 Ahaziah son of Ahab became king of Israel in Samaria in the seventeenth year of King Jehoshaphat of Judah, and reigned over Israel for two years. 52 He did what was wrong in the eyes of the LORD, following in the footsteps of his father and mother and in those of Jeroboam son of Nebat, who had led Israel into sin. 53 He served Baal and worshipped him, and provoked the anger of the LORD the God of Israel, as his father had done.

52 Ahaziah, son of Ahab, began to reign over Israel in Samaria in the seventeenth year of Jehoshaphat, king of Judah; he reigned two years over Israel. 53 He did evil in the sight of the LORD, behaving like his father, his mother, and Jeroboam, son of Nebat, who caused Israel to sin. 54 He served and worshiped Baal, thus provoking the LORD, the God of Israel, just as his father had done.

52 Ahaziah son of Ahab became king of Israel in Samaria in the seventeenth year of Jehoshaphat king of Judah, and reigned over Israel for two years. 53 He did what is displeasing to Yahweh, by following the example of his father and mother, and of Jeroboam son of Nebat who had led Israel into sin. 54 He served Baal and worshipped him, and provoked the anger of Yahweh God of Israel just as his father had done.

2 Kings

THE SECOND BOOK OF
Kings

1 After the death of Ahab, Moab rebelled against Israel. 2 Ahaziah had fallen through the lattice in his upper chamber in Samaria, and lay injured; so he sent messengers, telling them, "Go, inquire of Baal-zebub, the god of Ekron, whether I shall recover from this injury." 3 But the angel of the LORD said to Elijah the Tishbite, "Get up, go to meet the messengers of the king of Samaria, and say to them, 'Is it because there is no God in Israel that you are going to inquire of Baal-zebub, the god of Ekron?' 4 Now therefore thus says the LORD, 'You shall not leave the bed to which you have gone, but you shall surely die.' " So Elijah went.

5 The messengers returned to the king, who said to them, "Why have you returned?" 6 They answered him, "There came a man to meet us, who said to us, 'Go back to the king who sent you, and say to him: Thus says the LORD: Is it because there is no God in Israel that you are sending to inquire of Baal-zebub, the god of Ekron? Therefore you shall not leave the bed to which you have gone, but shall surely die.' " 7 He said to them, "What sort of man was he who came to meet you and told you these things?" 8 They answered him, "A hairy man, with a leather belt around his waist." He said, "It is Elijah the Tishbite."

9 Then the king sent to him a captain of fifty with his fifty men. He went up to Elijah, who was sitting on the top of a hill, and said to him, "O man of God, the king says, 'Come down.' " 10 But Elijah answered the captain of fifty, "If I am a man of God, let fire come down from heaven and consume you and your fifty." Then fire came down from heaven, and consumed him and his fifty.

11 Again the king sent to him another captain of fifty with his fifty. He went up*a* and said to him, "O man of God, this is the king's order: Come down quickly!" 12 But Elijah answered them, "If I am a man of God, let fire come down from heaven and consume you and your fifty." Then the fire of God came down from heaven and consumed him and his fifty.

13 Again the king sent the captain of a third fifty with his fifty. So the third captain of fifty went up, and came and fell on his knees before Elijah, and entreated him, "O man of God, please let my life, and the life of these fifty servants of yours, be precious in your sight. 14 Look, fire came down from heaven and consumed the two former captains of fifty men with their fifties; but now let my life be precious in your sight." 15 Then the angel of the LORD said to Elijah, "Go down with him; do not be afraid of him." So he set out and went down with him to the king, 16 and said to him, "Thus says the LORD: Because you have sent messengers to inquire of Baal-zebub, the god of Ekron, — is it because there is no God in Israel to inquire of his word? — therefore you shall not leave the bed to which you have gone, but you shall surely die."

17 So he died according to the word of the LORD that Elijah had spoken. His brother,*b* Jehoram succeeded him as king in the second year of King Jehoram son of Jehoshaphat of Judah, because Ahaziah had no son. 18 Now the rest of the acts of Ahaziah that he did, are they not written in the Book of the Annals of the Kings of Israel?

2 Now when the LORD was about to take Elijah up to heaven by a whirlwind, Elijah and Elisha were on their way from Gilgal. 2 Elijah said to Elisha, "Stay here; for the

1 AFTER Ahab's death Moab rebelled against Israel. 2 When Ahaziah fell through a latticed window in his roof-chamber in Samaria and injured himself, he sent messengers to enquire of Baal-zebub the god of Ekron whether he would recover from this injury. 3 The angel of the LORD ordered Elijah the Tishbite to go and meet the messengers of the king of Samaria and say to them, 'Is there no God in Israel, that you go to consult Baal-zebub the god of Ekron? 4 For what you have done the word of the LORD to your master is this: You will not rise from the bed where you are lying; you will die.' With that Elijah departed.

5 When the messengers returned to the king, he asked them why they had come back. 6 They answered that a man had come to meet them and had ordered them to return to the king who had sent them and say, 'This is the word of the LORD: Is there no God in Israel, that you send to enquire of Baal-zebub the god of Ekron? In consequence, you will not rise from the bed where you are lying; you will die.' 7 The king asked them what kind of man it was who had come to meet them and given them this message. 8 'A hairy man', they answered, 'with a leather belt round his waist.' 'It is Elijah the Tishbite,' said the king.

9 The king sent a captain with his company of fifty men to Elijah. He went up to the prophet, who was sitting on a hilltop, and said, 'Man of God, the king orders you to come down.' 10 Elijah answered, 'If I am a man of God, may fire fall from heaven and consume you and your company!' Fire fell from heaven and consumed the officer and his fifty men.

11 The king sent another captain of fifty with his company, and he went up and said to the prophet, 'Man of God, this is the king's command: Come down at once.' 12 Elijah answered, 'If I am a man of God, may fire fall from heaven and consume you and your company!' Fire from God fell from heaven and consumed the man and his company.

13 The king sent the captain of a third company with his fifty men, and this third captain went up the hill to Elijah and knelt down before him. 'Man of God,' he pleaded, 'consider me and these fifty servants of yours, and have some regard for our lives. 14 Fire fell from heaven and consumed the other two captains of fifty and their companies; but now have regard for my life.' 15 The angel of the LORD said to Elijah, 'Go down with him; do not be afraid.' At that he rose and went down with him to the king, 16 to whom he said, 'This is the word of the LORD: You have sent to consult Baal-zebub the god of Ekron. Is that because there is no God in Israel you could consult? For what you have done you will not rise from the bed where you are lying; you will die.' 17 Ahaziah's death fulfilled the word of the LORD which Elijah had spoken. Because Ahaziah had no son, his brother Jehoram succeeded him; that was in the second year of Joram son of King Jehoshaphat of Judah.

18 The other events of Ahaziah's reign are recorded in the annals of the kings of Israel.

2 When the LORD was about to take Elijah up to heaven in a whirlwind, Elijah and Elisha had set out from Gilgal. 2 Elijah said to Elisha, 'Stay here; for the LORD has

---

a Gk Compare verses 9, 13: Heb *He answered His brother*   *b* Gk Syr: Heb lacks *His brother*

1:11 **went up:** *so Gk (Luc.); Heb.* answered.   1:17 **his brother:** *so Gk (Luc.); Heb.* omits.

THE SECOND BOOK OF THE
Kings

1 After Ahab's death, Moab rebelled against Israel. 2 Ahaziah had fallen through the lattice of his roof terrace at Samaria and had been injured. So he sent messengers with the instructions: "Go and inquire of Baalzebub, the god of Ekron, whether I shall recover from this injury."

3 Meanwhile, the angel of the LORD said to Elijah the Tishbite: "Go, intercept the messengers of Samaria's king, and ask them, 'Is it because there is no God in Israel that you are going to inquire of Baalzebub, the god of Ekron?' 4 For this, the LORD says: 'You shall not leave the bed upon which you lie; instead, you shall die.'" And with that, Elijah departed. 5 The messengers then returned to Ahaziah, who asked them, "Why have you returned?" 6 "A man came up to us," they answered, "who said to us, 'Go back to the king who sent you and tell him: The LORD says, Is it because there is no God in Israel that you are sending to inquire of Baalzebub, the god of Ekron? For this you shall not leave the bed upon which you lie; instead, you shall die.'" 7 The king asked them, "What was the man like who came up to you and said these things to you?" 8 "Wearing a hairy garment," they replied, "with a leather girdle about his loins." "It is Elijah the Tishbite!" he exclaimed.

9 Then the king sent a captain with his company of fifty men after Elijah. The prophet was seated on a hilltop when he found him. "Man of God," he ordered, "the king commands you to come down." 10 "If I am a man of God," Elijah answered the captain, "may fire come down from heaven and consume you and your fifty men." And fire came down from heaven and consumed him and his fifty men. 11 Ahaziah sent another captain with his company of fifty men after Elijah. "Man of God," he called out to Elijah, "the king commands you to come down immediately." 12 "If I am a man of God," Elijah answered him, "May fire come down from heaven and consume you and your fifty men." And divine fire came down from heaven, consuming him and his fifty men.

13 Again, for the third time, Ahaziah sent a captain with his company of fifty men. When the third captain arrived, he fell to his knees before Elijah, pleading with him. "Man of God," he implored him, "let my life and the lives of these fifty men, your servants, count for something in your sight! 14 Already fire has come down from heaven, consuming two captains with their companies of fifty men. But now, let my life mean something to you!" 15 Then the angel of the LORD said to Elijah, "Go down with him; you need not be afraid of him."

16 So Elijah left and went down with him and stated to the king: "Thus says the LORD: 'Because you sent messengers to inquire of Baalzebub, the god of Ekron, you shall not leave the bed upon which you lie; instead you shall die.'"

17 Ahaziah died in fulfillment of the prophecy of the LORD spoken by Elijah. Since he had no son, his brother Joram succeeded him as king, in the second year of Jehoram, son of Jehoshaphat, king of Judah. 18 The rest of the acts of Ahaziah are recorded in the book of chronicles of the kings of Israel.

2 When the LORD was about to take Elijah up to heaven in a whirlwind, he and Elisha were on their way from Gilgal. 2 "Stay here, please," Elijah said to Elisha. "The

THE SECOND BOOK OF THE
Kings

1 After Ahab's death Moab rebelled against Israel. 2 Ahaziah had fallen from the balcony of his upper room in Samaria, and was lying ill; so he sent messengers, saying to them, 'Go and consult Baal-Zebub*a* god of Ekron and ask whether I shall recover from my illness.' 3 But the angel of Yahweh said to Elijah the Tishbite, 'Up! Go and intercept the king of Samaria's messengers. Say to them, "Is there no God in Israel, for you to go and consult Baal-Zebub god of Ekron? 4 Yahweh says this: You will never leave the bed you have got into; you are certainly going to die." ' And Elijah set out.

5 The messengers returned to the king, who said, 'Why have you come back?' 6 'A man came to meet us,' they answered. 'He said, "Go back to the king who sent you and tell him: Yahweh says this: Is there no God in Israel, for you to go and consult Baal-Zebub god of Ekron? For this, you will never leave the bed you have got into; you are certainly going to die." '

7 He said, 'This man who met you and said all this, what was he like?' 8 'A man wearing a hair cloak', they answered, 'and a leather loincloth.' 'It was Elijah the Tishbite,' he said.

9 He then sent a captain of fifty soldiers with his fifty men to Elijah, whom they found sitting on top of a hill; the captain went up to him and said, 'Man of God, the king says, "Come down." ' 10 Elijah answered the captain, 'If I am a man of God, may fire fall from heaven and destroy both you and your fifty men.' And fire fell from heaven and destroyed him and his fifty men. 11 The king sent a second captain of fifty to him, again with fifty men, and he too went up and said, 'Man of God, this is the king's order, "Come down at once." ' 12 Elijah answered them, 'If I am a man of God, may fire fall from heaven and destroy both you and your fifty men.' And lightning fell from heaven and destroyed him and his fifty men. 13 The king then sent a third captain of fifty to him, with another fifty men. The third captain of fifty came up to Elijah, fell on his knees before him and pleaded with him. 'Man of God,' he said, 'may my life and the lives of these fifty servants of yours count for something in your eyes. 14 Fire has fallen from heaven and destroyed two captains of fifties and their companies, but this time may my life count for something in your eyes!' 15 The angel of Yahweh said to Elijah, 'Go down with him; do not be afraid of him.' He rose and accompanied him down to the king, 16 and said to him, 'Yahweh says this, "Since you sent messengers to consult Baal-Zebub god of Ekron, you will never leave the bed you have got into; you are certainly going to die." '

17 And, in accordance with the word of Yahweh which Elijah had uttered, he died. Since he had no son, his brother Jehoram succeeded him, in the second year of Jehoram son of Jehoshaphat, king of Judah. 18 The rest of the history of Ahaziah, and his career, is this not recorded in the Book of the Annals of the Kings of Israel?

2 This is what happened when Yahweh took Elijah up to heaven in the whirlwind: Elijah and Elisha set out from Gilgal. 2 and Elijah said to Elisha, 'You stay here, for Yah-

---

a 1 A mocking pun (= Baal of Flies). The god's real name was Baal-Zebul (= Baal the Prince).

NEW REVISED STANDARD VERSION

LORD has sent me as far as Bethel." But Elisha said, "As the LORD lives, and as you yourself live, I will not leave you." So they went down to Bethel. 3 The company of prophets^c who were in Bethel came out to Elisha, and said to him, "Do you know that today the LORD will take your master away from you?" And he said, "Yes, I know; keep silent."

4 Elijah said to him, "Elisha, stay here; for the LORD has sent me to Jericho." But he said, "As the LORD lives, and as you yourself live, I will not leave you." So they came to Jericho. 5 The company of prophets^c who were at Jericho drew near to Elisha, and said to him, "Do you know that today the LORD will take your master away from you?" And he answered, "Yes, I know; be silent."

6 Then Elijah said to him, "Stay here; for the LORD has sent me to the Jordan." But he said, "As the LORD lives, and as you yourself live, I will not leave you." So the two of them went on. 7 Fifty men of the company of prophets^c also went, and stood at some distance from them, as they both were standing by the Jordan. 8 Then Elijah took his mantle and rolled it up, and struck the water; the water was parted to the one side and to the other, until the two of them crossed on dry ground.

9 When they had crossed, Elijah said to Elisha, "Tell me what I may do for you, before I am taken from you." Elisha said, "Please let me inherit a double share of your spirit." 10 He responded, "You have asked a hard thing; yet, if you see me as I am being taken from you, it will be granted you; if not, it will not." 11 As they continued walking and talking, a chariot of fire and horses of fire separated the two of them, and Elijah ascended in a whirlwind into heaven. 12 Elisha kept watching and crying out, "Father, father! The chariots of Israel and its horsemen!" But when he could no longer see him, he grasped his own clothes and tore them in two pieces.

13 He picked up the mantle of Elijah that had fallen from him, and went back and stood on the bank of the Jordan. 14 He took the mantle of Elijah that had fallen from him, and struck the water, saying, "Where is the LORD, the God of Elijah?" When he had struck the water, the water was parted to the one side and to the other, and Elisha went over.

15 When the company of prophets^c who were at Jericho saw him at a distance, they declared, "The spirit of Elijah rests on Elisha." They came to meet him and bowed to the ground before him. 16 They said to him, "See now, we have fifty strong men among your servants; please let them go and seek your master; it may be that the spirit of the LORD has caught him up and thrown him down on some mountain or into some valley." He responded, "No, do not send them." 17 But when they urged him until he was ashamed, he said, "Send them." So they sent fifty men who searched for three days but did not find him. 18 When they came back to him (he had remained at Jericho), he said to them, "Did I not say to you, Do not go?"

19 Now the people of the city said to Elisha, "The location of this city is good, as my lord sees; but the water is bad, and the land is unfruitful." 20 He said, "Bring me a new bowl, and put salt in it." So they brought it to him. 21 Then he went to the spring of water and threw the salt into it, and said, "Thus says the LORD, I have made this water wholesome; from now on neither death nor miscarriage shall come from it." 22 So the water has been wholesome to this day, according to the word that Elisha spoke.

23 He went up from there to Bethel; and while he was going up on the way, some small boys came out of the city and jeered at him, saying, "Go away, baldhead! Go away, baldhead!" 24 When he turned around and saw them, he

^c Heb sons of the prophets

REVISED ENGLISH BIBLE

sent me to Bethel.' Elisha replied, 'As the LORD lives, your life upon it, I shall not leave you.' They went down country to Bethel, 3 and there a company of prophets came out to Elisha and said to him, 'Do you know that the LORD is going to take your lord and master from you today?' 'I do know,' he replied; 'say nothing.'

4 Elijah said to him, 'Stay here, Elisha; for the LORD has sent me to Jericho.' He replied, 'As the LORD lives, your life upon it, I shall not leave you.' So they went to Jericho, 5 and there a company of prophets came up to Elisha and said to him, 'Do you know that the LORD is going to take your lord and master from you today?' 'I do know,' he replied; 'say nothing.'

6 Then Elijah said to him, 'Stay here; for the LORD has sent me to the Jordan.' The other replied, 'As the LORD lives, your life upon it, I shall not leave you.' So the two of them went on. 7 Fifty of the prophets followed, and stood watching from a distance as the two of them stopped by the Jordan. 8 Elijah took his cloak, rolled it up, and struck the water with it. The water divided to right and left, and both crossed over on dry ground.

9 While they were crossing, Elijah said to Elisha, 'Tell me what I can do for you before I am taken from you.' Elisha said, 'Let me inherit a double share of your spirit.' 10 'You have asked a hard thing,' said Elijah. 'If you see me taken from you, your wish will be granted; if you do not, it will not be granted.' 11 They went on, talking as they went, and suddenly there appeared a chariot of fire and horses of fire, which separated them from one another, and Elijah was carried up to heaven in a whirlwind. 12 At the sight Elisha cried out, 'My father, my father, the chariot and the horsemen of Israel!' and he saw him no more.

He clutched hold of his mantle and tore it in two. 13 He picked up the cloak which had fallen from Elijah, and went back and stood on the bank of the Jordan. 14 There he struck the water with Elijah's cloak, saying as he did so, 'Where is the LORD, the God of Elijah?' As he too struck the water, it divided to right and left, and he crossed over.

15 The prophets from Jericho, who were watching, said, 'The spirit of Elijah has settled on Elisha.' They came to meet him, bowed to the ground before him, 16 and said, 'Your servants have fifty stalwart men. Let them go and search for your master; perhaps the spirit of the LORD has lifted him up and cast him on some mountain or into some valley.' But he said, 'No, you must not send them.' 17 They pressed him, however, until he had not the heart to refuse. So they sent out the fifty men but, though they searched for three days, they did not find him. 18 When they came back to Elisha, who had remained at Jericho, he said to them, 'Did I not tell you not to go?'

19 The people of the city said to Elisha, 'Lord, you can see how pleasantly situated our city is, but the water is polluted and the country is sterile.' 20 He said, 'Fetch me a new, unused bowl and put salt in it.' When they had brought it, 21 he went out to the spring and, throwing the salt into it, he said, 'This is the word of the LORD: I purify this water. It shall no longer cause death or sterility.' 22 The water has remained pure till this day, in fulfilment of Elisha's word.

23 From there he went up to Bethel and, as he was on his way, some small boys came out of the town and jeered at him, saying, 'Get along with you, bald head, get along.'

LORD has sent me on to Bethel." "As the LORD lives, and as you yourself live," Elisha replied, "I will not leave you." So they went down to Bethel, 3 where the guild prophets went out to Elisha and asked him, "Do you know that the LORD will take your master from over you today?" "Yes, I know it," he replied. "Keep still."

4 Then Elijah said to him, "Stay here, please, Elisha, for the LORD has sent me on to Jericho." "As the LORD lives, and as you yourself live," Elisha replied, "I will not leave you." 5 They went on to Jericho, where the guild prophets approached Elisha and asked him, "Do you know that the LORD will take your master from over you today?" "Yes, I know it," he replied. "Keep still."

6 Elijah said to Elisha, "Please stay here; the LORD has sent me on to the Jordan." "As the LORD lives, and as you yourself live," Elisha replied, "I will not leave you." And so the two went on together. 7 Fifty of the guild prophets followed, and when the two stopped at the Jordan, stood facing them at a distance. 8 Elijah took his mantle, rolled it up and struck the water, which divided, and both crossed over on dry ground.

9 When they had crossed over, Elijah said to Elisha, "Ask for whatever I may do for you, before I am taken from you." Elisha answered, "May I receive a double portion of your spirit." 10 "You have asked something that is not easy," he replied. "Still, if you see me taken up from you, your wish will be granted; otherwise not." 11 As they walked on conversing, a flaming chariot and flaming horses came between them, and Elijah went up to heaven in a whirlwind. 12 When Elisha saw it happen he cried out, "My father! my father! Israel's chariots and drivers!" But when he could no longer see him, Elisha gripped his own garment and tore it in two.

13 Then he picked up Elijah's mantle which had fallen from him, and went back and stood at the bank of the Jordan. 14 Wielding the mantle which had fallen from Elijah, he struck the water in his turn and said, "Where is the LORD, the God of Elijah?" When Elisha struck the water it divided and he crossed over.

15 The guild prophets in Jericho, who were on the other side, saw him and said, "The spirit of Elijah rests on Elisha." They went to meet him, bowing to the ground before him. 16 "Among your servants are fifty brave men," they said. "Let them go in search of your master. Perhaps the spirit of the LORD has carried him away to some mountain or some valley." "Do not send them," he answered. 17 However, they kept urging him, until he was embarrassed and said, "Send them." So they sent the fifty men, who searched for three days without finding him. 18 When they returned to Elisha in Jericho, where he was staying, he said to them, "Did I not tell you not to go?"

19 Once the inhabitants of the city complained to Elisha, "The site of the city is fine indeed, as my lord can see, but the water is bad and the land unfruitful." 20 "Bring me a new bowl," Elisha said, "and put salt into it." When they had brought it to him, 21 he went out to the spring and threw salt into it, saying, "Thus says the LORD, 'I have purified this water. Never again shall death or miscarriage spring from it.'" 22 And the water has stayed pure even to this day, just as Elisha prophesied.

23 From there Elisha went up to Bethel. While he was on the way, some small boys came out of the city and jeered at him. "Go up, baldhead," they shouted, "go up, baldhead!" 24 The prophet turned and saw them, and he cursed

weh is only sending me to Bethel.' But Elisha replied, 'As Yahweh lives and as you yourself live, I will not leave you!' and they went down to Bethel. 3 The brotherhood of prophets living at Bethel came out to meet Elisha and said, 'Do you know that Yahweh will carry your lord and master away today?' 'Yes, I know,' he said, 'be quiet.' 4 Elijah said, 'Elisha, you stay here, Yahweh is only sending me to Jericho.' But he replied, 'As Yahweh lives and as you yourself live, I will not leave you!' and they went on to Jericho. 5 The brotherhood of prophets living at Jericho went up to Elisha and said, 'Do you know that Yahweh will carry your lord and master away today?' 'Yes, I know,' he said, 'be quiet.' 6 Elijah said, 'Elisha, you stay here, Yahweh is only sending me to the Jordan.' But he replied, 'As Yahweh lives and as you yourself live, I will not leave you!' And they went on together.

7 Fifty of the brotherhood of prophets followed them, halting some distance away as the two of them stood beside the Jordan. 8 Elijah took his cloak, rolled it up and struck the water; and the water divided to left and right, and the two of them crossed over dry-shod. 9 When they had crossed, Elijah said to Elisha, 'Make your request. What can I do for you before I am snatched away from you?' Elisha answered, 'Let me inherit a double share of your spirit.' 10 'Your request is difficult,' Elijah said. 'If you see me while I am being snatched away from you, it will be as you ask; if not, it will not be so.' 11 Now as they walked on, talking as they went, a chariot of fire appeared and horses of fire coming between the two of them; and Elijah went up to heaven in the whirlwind. 12 Elisha saw it, and shouted, 'My father! My father! Chariot of Israel and its chargers!' Then he lost sight of him, and taking hold of his own clothes he tore them in half. 13 He picked up Elijah's cloak which had fallen, and went back and stood on the bank of the Jordan.

14 He took Elijah's cloak and struck the water. 'Where is Yahweh, the God of Elijah?' he cried. As he struck the water it divided to right and left, and Elisha crossed over.

15 The brotherhood of prophets saw him in the distance, and said, 'The spirit of Elijah has come to rest on Elisha'; they went to meet him and bowed to the ground before him. 16 'Look,' they said, 'your servants have fifty strong men with them, let them go and look for your master; the Spirit of Yahweh may have taken him up and thrown him down on a mountain or into a valley.' 'Send no one,' he replied. 17 But they so shamed him with their insistence that he consented. So they sent fifty men who searched for three days without finding him. 18 They then came back to Elisha who had stayed in Jericho; he said, 'Didn't I tell you not to go?'

19 The people of the city said to Elisha, 'The city is pleasant to live in, as my lord indeed can see, but the water is foul and the country suffers from miscarriages.' 20 'Bring me a new bowl,' he said, 'and put some salt in it.' They brought it to him. 21 Then he went to the source of the water, threw salt into it and said, 'Yahweh says this, "I make this water wholesome: neither death nor miscarriage shall come from it any more."' 22 And the water became wholesome, as it is today, exactly as Elisha had said it would.

23 From there he went up to Bethel, and while he was on the road, some small boys came out of the town and jeered at him. 'Hurry up, baldy!' they shouted. 'Come on up, baldy!' 24 He turned round and looked at them; and he

cursed them in the name of the LORD. Then two she-bears came out of the woods and mauled forty-two of the boys. 25 From there he went on to Mount Carmel, and then returned to Samaria.

3 In the eighteenth year of King Jehoshaphat of Judah, Jehoram son of Ahab became king over Israel in Samaria; he reigned twelve years. 2 He did what was evil in the sight of the LORD, though not like his father and mother, for he removed the pillar of Baal that his father had made. 3 Nevertheless he clung to the sin of Jeroboam son of Nebat, which he caused Israel to commit; he did not depart from it.

4 Now King Mesha of Moab was a sheep breeder, who used to deliver to the king of Israel one hundred thousand lambs, and the wool of one hundred thousand rams. 5 But when Ahab died, the king of Moab rebelled against the king of Israel. 6 So King Jehoram marched out of Samaria at that time and mustered all Israel. 7 As he went he sent word to King Jehoshaphat of Judah, "The king of Moab has rebelled against me; will you go with me to battle against Moab?" He answered, "I will; I am with you, my people are your people, my horses are your horses." 8 Then he asked, "By which way shall we march?" Jehoram answered, "By the way of the wilderness of Edom."

9 So the king of Israel, the king of Judah, and the king of Edom set out; and when they had made a roundabout march of seven days, there was no water for the army or for the animals that were with them. 10 Then the king of Israel said, "Alas! The LORD has summoned us, three kings, only to be handed over to Moab." 11 But Jehoshaphat said, "Is there no prophet of the LORD here, through whom we may inquire of the LORD?" Then one of the servants of the king of Israel answered, "Elisha son of Shaphat, who used to pour water on the hands of Elijah, is here." 12 Jehoshaphat said, "The word of the LORD is with him." So the king of Israel and Jehoshaphat and the king of Edom went down to him.

13 Elisha said to the king of Israel, "What have I to do with you? Go to your father's prophets or to your mother's." But the king of Israel said to him, "No; it is the LORD who has summoned us, three kings, only to be handed over to Moab." 14 Elisha said, "As the LORD of hosts lives, whom I serve, were it not that I have regard for King Jehoshaphat of Judah, I would give you neither a look nor a glance. 15 But get me a musician." And then, while the musician was playing, the power of the LORD came on him. 16 And he said, "Thus says the LORD, 'I will make this wadi full of pools.' 17 For thus says the LORD, 'You shall see neither wind nor rain, but the wadi shall be filled with water, so that you shall drink, you, your cattle, and your animals.' 18 This is only a trifle in the sight of the LORD, for he will also hand Moab over to you. 19 You shall conquer every fortified city and every choice city; every good tree you shall fell, all springs of water you shall stop up, and every good piece of land you shall ruin with stones." 20 The next day, about the time of the morning offering, suddenly water began to flow from the direction of Edom, until the country was filled with water.

21 When all the Moabites heard that the kings had come up to fight against them, all who were able to put on armor, from the youngest to the oldest, were called out and were drawn up at the frontier. 22 When they rose early in the morning, and the sun shone upon the water, the Moabites saw the water opposite them as red as blood. 23 They said, "This is blood; the kings must have fought together, and killed one another. Now then, Moab, to the spoil!" 24 But when they came to the camp of Israel, the Israelites rose up and attacked the Moabites, who fled before them; as they

24 He turned round, looked at them, and cursed them in the name of the LORD; and two she-bears came out of a wood and mauled forty-two of them. 25 From there he went on to Mount Carmel, and thence back to Samaria.

3 In the eighteenth year of King Jehoshaphat of Judah, Jehoram son of Ahab became king of Israel in Samaria, and he reigned for twelve years. 2 He did what was wrong in the eyes of the LORD, though not as his father and his mother had done; he did remove the sacred pillar of Baal which his father had made. 3 Yet he persisted in the sins into which Jeroboam son of Nebat had led Israel, and did not give them up.

4 KING Mesha of Moab was a sheep-breeder, and he had to supply the king of Israel regularly with the wool of a hundred thousand lambs and a hundred thousand rams. 5 When Ahab died, the king of Moab rebelled against the king of Israel, 6 and King Jehoram marched out from Samaria and mustered all Israel. 7 He also sent this message to King Jehoshaphat of Judah: 'The king of Moab has rebelled against me. Will you join me in a campaign against Moab?' 'I will join you,' he replied; 'what is mine is yours: myself, my people, and my horses.' 8 'From which direction shall we attack?' he asked. 'Through the wilderness of Edom,' replied the other.

9 The king of Israel set out with the king of Judah and the king of Edom, and when they had been seven days on the indirect route they were following, they had no water left for the army or their pack-animals. 10 The king of Israel cried, 'Alas, the LORD has brought together three kings, only to put us at the mercy of the Moabites.' 11 Jehoshaphat said, 'Is there not a prophet of the LORD here through whom we may seek the LORD's guidance?' One of the officers of the king of Israel answered, 'Elisha son of Shaphat is here, the man who poured water on Elijah's hands.' 12 'The word of the LORD is with him,' said Jehoshaphat. When the king of Israel and Jehoshaphat and the king of Edom went down to Elisha, 13 he said to the king of Israel, 'Why do you come to me? Go to your father's prophets or your mother's.' 'No,' answered the king of Israel; 'it is the LORD who has called us three kings out to put us at the mercy of the Moabites.' 14 'As the LORD of Hosts lives, whom I serve,' said Elisha, 'I would not spare a look or a glance for you, if it were not for my regard for King Jehoshaphat of Judah. 15 But now fetch me a minstrel'; and while the minstrel played, the power of the LORD came on Elisha, 16 and he said, 'This is the word of the LORD: Pools will form all over this wadi. 17 The LORD has decreed that you will see neither wind nor rain, yet this wadi will be filled with water for you and your army and your pack-animals to drink. 18 That is a mere trifle in the sight of the LORD; what he will also do is to put Moab at your mercy. 19 You will raze to the ground every fortified town and every noble city; you will cut down all their fine trees; you will stop up all the springs of water; and you will spoil every good piece of land by littering it with stones.' 20 In the morning at the hour of the regular offering they saw water flowing in from the direction of Edom, and the land was flooded.

21 Meanwhile all Moab had heard that the kings had come up to wage war against them, and every man, young and old, who could bear arms was called out and stationed on the frontier. 22 When they got up next morning and the sun was shining over the water, the Moabites saw the water in front of them red like blood 23 and cried out, 'It is blood! The kings must have quarrelled and attacked one another. Now to the plunder, Moab!' 24 But when they came to the Israelite camp, the Israelites sallied out and attacked them, driving the Moabites in headlong flight. The Israelites

3:17 **army:** so Gk (Luc.); Heb. cattle.

them in the name of the LORD. Then two she-bears came out of the woods and tore forty-two of the children to pieces. 25 From there he went to Mount Carmel, and thence he returned to Samaria.

3 Joram, son of Ahab, became king of Israel in Samaria [in the eighteenth year of Jehoshaphat, king of Judah, and he reigned for twelve years]. 2 He did evil in the LORD's sight, though not as much as his father and mother. He did away with the pillar of Baal, which his father had made, 3 but he still clung to the sin to which Jeroboam, son of Nebat, had lured Israel; this he did not give up.

4 Now Mesha, king of Moab, who raised sheep, used to pay the king of Israel as tribute a hundred thousand lambs and the wool of a hundred thousand rams. 5 But when Ahab died, the king of Moab had rebelled against the king of Israel. 6 Joram as king mustered all Israel, and when he set out on a campaign from Samaria, 7 he sent the king of Judah the message: "The king of Moab is in rebellion against me. Will you join me in battle against Moab?" "I will," he replied. "You and I shall be as one, your people and mine, and your horses and mine as well." 8 They discussed the route for their attack, and settled upon the route through the desert of Edom.

9 So the king of Israel set out, accompanied by the king of Judah and the king of Edom. After their roundabout journey of seven days the water gave out for the army and for the animals with them. 10 "Alas!" exclaimed the king of Israel. "The LORD has called together these three kings to put them in the grasp of Moab." 11 But the king of Judah asked, "Is there no prophet of the LORD here through whom we may inquire of the LORD?" One of the officers of the king of Israel replied, "Elisha, son of Shaphat, who poured water on the hands of Elijah, is here." 12 "He has the word of the LORD," the king of Judah agreed. So the kings of Israel, Judah, and Edom went down to Elisha. 13 "What do you want with me?" Elisha asked the king of Israel. "Go to the prophets of your father and to the prophets of your mother." "No," the king of Israel replied. "The LORD has called these three kings together to put them in the grasp of Moab." 14 Then Elisha said, "As the LORD of hosts lives, whom I serve, were it not that I respect the king of Judah, I should neither look at you nor notice you at all. 15 Now get me a minstrel."

When the minstrel played, the power of the LORD came upon Elisha 16 and he announced: "Thus says the LORD, 'Provide many catch basins in this wadi.' 17 For the LORD says, 'Though you will see neither wind nor rain, yet this wadi will be filled with water for you, your livestock, and your pack animals to drink.' 18 And since the LORD does not consider this enough, he will also deliver Moab into your grasp. 19 You shall destroy every fortified city, fell every fruit tree, stop up all the springs, and ruin every fertile field with stones."

20 In the morning, at the time of the sacrifice, water came from the direction of Edom and filled the land. 21 Meanwhile, all Moab heard that the kings had come to give them battle; every man capable of bearing arms was called up and stationed at the border. 22 Early that morning, when the sun shone on the water, the Moabites saw the water at a distance as red as blood. 23 "This is blood!" they exclaimed. "The kings have fought among themselves and killed one another. Quick! To the spoils, Moabites!" 24 But when they reached the camp of Israel, the Israelites rose up and attacked the Moabites, who fled from them. They ranged

cursed them in the name of Yahweh. And two bears came out of the forest and savaged forty-two of the boys. 25 From there he went on to Mount Carmel and then returned to Samaria.

3 Jehoram son of Ahab became king of Israel in Samaria in the eighteenth year of Jehoshaphat king of Judah, and reigned for twelve years. 2 He did what is displeasing to Yahweh, though not like his father and mother, for he did away with the pillar to Baal which his father had made. 3 Nonetheless, he continued to practise the sins into which Jeroboam son of Nebat had led Israel and did not give them up.

4 Mesha king of Moab was a sheep-breeder and used to pay the king of Israel in tribute a hundred thousand lambs and a hundred thousand rams with their wool. 5 But when Ahab died, the king of Moab rebelled against the king of Israel.

6 At once King Jehoram left Samaria and mustered all Israel. 7 After this he sent word to the king of Judah, 'The king of Moab has rebelled against me. Will you go to war with me against Moab?' 'I will,' he replied. 'I will be as you, my men as yours, my horses as yours,' 8 and added, 'Which way are we to attack?' 'Through the desert of Edom,' the other answered.

9 So they set out, the king of Israel, the king of Judah and the king of Edom. They carried out a flanking movement for seven days, until there was no water left for the troops or for the beasts of their baggage train. 10 'Alas!' the king of Israel exclaimed, 'Yahweh has summoned us three kings, only to put us into the power of Moab.' 11 But the king of Judah said, 'Is there no prophet of Yahweh here for us to consult Yahweh through him?' One of the king of Israel's servants answered, 'Elisha son of Shaphat is here, who used to pour water on the hands of Elijah.' 12 'The word of Yahweh is with him,' the king of Judah said. So the king of Israel, the king of Judah and the king of Edom went to consult him. 13 But Elisha said to the king of Israel, 'What business have you with me? Go to your father's and your mother's prophets.' 'No,' the king of Israel answered, 'Yahweh is the one who has summoned us three kings, only to put us into the power of Moab.' Elisha replied, 14 'By the life of Yahweh Sabaoth whom I serve, if I did not respect the king of Judah, I would take no notice of you, nor so much as look at you. 15 Now bring me someone who can play the lyre.' And as the musician played, the hand of Yahweh came on him 16 and he said, 'Yahweh says this, "Dig in this valley ditch after ditch," 17 for Yahweh says, "You will see no wind, you will see no rain, but this valley will become full of water, and you and your troops and your baggage animals will drink." 18 But this is only a trifle in Yahweh's eyes, for he will put Moab itself into your power. 19 You will storm every fortified town, fell every productive tree, block every water-hole, ruin all the best fields with stones.' 20 Next morning at the time when the oblation was being offered, water came from the direction of Edom, and the whole terrain was flooded.

21 When the Moabites learned that the kings were advancing to fight them, all those of an age to bear arms were mobilised; they took up position on the frontier. 22 In the morning when they got up, the sun was shining on the water; and in the distance the Moabites saw the water as red as blood. 23 'This is blood!' they said. 'The kings must have fought among themselves and killed one another. So now for the booty, Moab!' 24 But when they reached the Israelite camp, the Israelites launched their attack and the Moabites

| NEW REVISED STANDARD VERSION | REVISED ENGLISH BIBLE |

entered Moab they continued the attack. *d* 25 The cities they overturned, and on every good piece of land everyone threw a stone, until it was covered; every spring of water they stopped up, and every good tree they felled. Only at Kir-hareseth did the stone walls remain, until the slingers surrounded and attacked it. 26 When the king of Moab saw that the battle was going against him, he took with him seven hundred swordsmen to break through, opposite the king of Edom; but they could not. 27 Then he took his firstborn son who was to succeed him, and offered him as a burnt offering on the wall. And great wrath came upon Israel, so they withdrew from him and returned to their own land.

4 Now the wife of a member of the company of prophets*e* cried to Elisha, "Your servant my husband is dead; and you know that your servant feared the LORD, but a creditor has come to take my two children as slaves." 2 Elisha said to her, "What shall I do for you? Tell me, what do you have in the house?" She answered, "Your servant has nothing in the house, except a jar of oil." 3 He said, "Go outside, borrow vessels from all your neighbors, empty vessels and not just a few. 4 Then go in, and shut the door behind you and your children, and start pouring into all these vessels; when each is full, set it aside." 5 So she left him and shut the door behind her and her children; they kept bringing vessels to her, and she kept pouring. 6 When the vessels were full, she said to her son, "Bring me another vessel." But he said to her, "There are no more." Then the oil stopped flowing. 7 She came and told the man of God, and he said, "Go sell the oil and pay your debts, and you and your children can live on the rest."

8 One day Elisha was passing through Shunem, where a wealthy woman lived, who urged him to have a meal. So whenever he passed that way, he would stop there for a meal. 9 She said to her husband, "Look, I am sure that this man who regularly passes our way is a holy man of God. 10 Let us make a small roof chamber with walls, and put there for him a bed, a table, a chair, and a lamp, so that he can stay there whenever he comes to us."

11 One day when he came there, he went up to the chamber and lay down there. 12 He said to his servant Gehazi, "Call the Shunammite woman." When he had called her, she stood before him. 13 He said to him, "Say to her, Since you have taken all this trouble for us, what may be done for you? Would you have a word spoken on your behalf to the king or to the commander of the army?" She answered, "I live among my own people." 14 He said, "What then may be done for her?" Gehazi answered, "Well, she has no son, and her husband is old." 15 He said, "Call her." When he had called her, she stood at the door. 16 He said, "At this season, in due time, you shall embrace a son." She replied, "No, my lord, O man of God; do not deceive your servant."

17 The woman conceived and bore a son at that season, in due time, as Elisha had declared to her.

18 When the child was older, he went out one day to his father among the reapers. 19 He complained to his father, "Oh, my head, my head!" The father said to his servant, "Carry him to his mother." 20 He carried him and brought him to his mother; the child sat on her lap until noon, and he died. 21 She went up and laid him on the bed of the man of God, closed the door on him, and left. 22 Then she called to her husband, and said, "Send me one of the servants and

pushed forward into Moab, destroying as they went. 25 They razed the towns to the ground; they littered every good piece of land with stones, each man casting a stone on it; they stopped up every spring of water; they cut down all the fine trees; and they harried Moab until only in Kir-hareseth were any buildings left standing, and even this city the slingers surrounded and attacked.

26 When the Moabite king saw that the war had gone against him, he took with him seven hundred men armed with swords to cut a way through to the king of Aram, but the attempt failed. 27 Then he took his eldest son, who would have succeeded him, and offered him as a whole-offering on the city wall. There was such great consternation among the Israelites that they struck camp and returned to their own land.

4 The wife of one of the prophets appealed to Elisha. 'My husband, your servant, has died,' she said, 'and you know that he was a man who feared the LORD. Now a creditor has come to take away my two boys as slaves.' 2 Elisha asked her, 'How can I help you? Tell me what you have in the house.' 'Nothing at all,' she answered, 'except a flask of oil.' 3 'Go out', he said, 'and borrow vessels from everyone in the neighbourhood; get as many empty ones as you can. 4 When you come home, shut yourself in with your sons; then pour from the flask into all the vessels and, as they are filled, set them aside.' 5 She left him and shut herself indoors with her sons. As they brought her the vessels she filled them. 6 When they were all full, she said to one of her sons, 'Bring me another.' 'There are none left,' he replied. Then the flow of oil ceased. 7 She came out and told the man of God, and he said, 'Go, sell the oil and pay off your debt, and you and your sons can live on what is left.'

8 IT happened once that Elisha went over to Shunem. There was a well-to-do woman there who pressed him to accept hospitality, and afterwards whenever he came that way, he stopped there for a meal. 9 One day she said to her husband, 'I know that this man who comes here regularly is a holy man of God. 10 Why not build up the wall to make him a small roof-chamber, and put in it a bed, a table, a seat, and a lamp, and let him stay there whenever he comes to us?'

11 One time when he arrived there and went to this roof-chamber to lie down, 12 he said to Gehazi, his servant, 'Call this Shunammite woman.' When he called her and she appeared before the prophet, 13 Elisha said to his servant, 'Say to her, "You have taken all this trouble for us. What can I do for you? Shall I speak for you to the king or to the commander-in-chief?"' But she replied, 'I am content where I am, among my own people.' 14 He said, 'Then what can be done for her?' Gehazi said, 'There is only this: she has no child and her husband is old.' 15 'Call her back,' Elisha said. When she was called and appeared in the doorway, 16 he said, 'In due season, this time next year, you will have a son in your arms.' But she said, 'No, no, my lord, you are a man of God and would not lie to your servant.'

17 Next year in due season the woman conceived and bore a son, as Elisha had foretold.

18 When the child was old enough, he went out one day to his father among the reapers. 19 All of a sudden he cried out to his father, 'Oh, my head, my head!' His father told a servant to carry the child to his mother, 20 and when he was brought to her, he sat on her lap till midday, and then he died. 21 She went up, laid him on the bed of the man of God, shut the door, and went out. 22 She called her husband and said, 'Send me one of the servants and a she-donkey;

---

d Compare Gk Syr: Meaning of Heb uncertain   *e* Heb *the sons of the prophets*

3:24 **pushed . . . into:** *so Gk; Heb.* destroyed.   3:25 **and . . . Moab:** *so Gk (Luc.); Heb.* omits.   3:26 **Aram:** *so Old Latin; Heb.* Edom.

through the countryside striking down the Moabites, and [25] destroying the cities; each of them cast stones onto every fertile field till they had loaded it down; all the springs they stopped up and every useful tree they felled. Finally only Kir-hareseth was left behind its stone walls, and the slingers had surrounded it and were attacking it. [26] When he saw that he was losing the battle, the king of Moab took seven hundred swordsmen to break through to the king of Aram, but he failed. [27] So he took his first-born, his heir apparent, and offered him as a holocaust upon the wall. The wrath against Israel was so great that they gave up the siege and returned to their own land.

4 A certain woman, the widow of one of the guild prophets, complained to Elisha: "My husband, your servant, is dead. You know that he was a God-fearing man, yet now his creditor has come to take my two children as his slaves." [2] "How can I help you?" Elisha answered her. "Tell me what you have in the house." "This servant of yours has nothing in the house but a jug of oil," she replied. [3] "Go out," he said, "borrow vessels from all your neighbors — as many empty vessels as you can. [4] Then come back and close the door on yourself and your children; pour the oil into all the vessels, and as each is filled, set it aside." [5] She went and did so, closing the door on herself and her children. As they handed her the vessels, she would pour in oil. [6] When all the vessels were filled, she said to her son, "Bring me another vessel." "There is none left," he answered her. And then the oil stopped. [7] She went and told the man of God, who said, "Go and sell the oil to pay off your creditor; with what remains, you and your children can live."

[8] One day Elisha came to Shunem, where there was a woman of influence, who urged him to dine with her. Afterward, whenever he passed by, he used to stop there to dine. [9] So she said to her husband, "I know that he is a holy man of God. Since he visits us often, [10] let us arrange a little room on the roof and furnish it for him with a bed, table, chair, and lamp, so that when he comes to us he can stay there." [11] Some time later Elisha arrived and stayed in the room overnight. [12] Then he said to his servant Gehazi, "Call this Shunammite woman." He did so, and when she stood before Elisha, [13] he told Gehazi, "Say to her, 'You have lavished all this care on us; what can we do for you? Can we say a good word for you to the king or to the commander of the army?'" She replied, "I am living among my own people." [14] Later Elisha asked, "Can something be done for her?" "Yes!" Gehazi answered. "She has no son, and her husband is getting on in years." [15] "Call her," said Elisha. When she had been called, and stood at the door, [16] Elisha promised, "This time next year you will be fondling a baby son." "Please, my lord," she protested, "you are a man of God; do not deceive your servant." [17] Yet the woman conceived, and by the same time the following year she had given birth to a son, as Elisha promised.

[18] The day came when the child was old enough to go out to his father among the reapers. [19] "My head hurts!" he complained to his father. "Carry him to his mother," the father said to a servant. [20] The servant picked him up and carried him to his mother; he stayed with her until noon, when he died in her lap. [21] The mother took him upstairs and laid him on the bed of the man of God. Closing the door on him, she went out [22] and called to her husband, "Let me

fled before them, and as they advanced they cut the Moabites to pieces. [25] They laid the towns in ruins, and each man threw a stone into all the best fields to fill them up, and they blocked every water-hole and felled every productive tree. In the end, there was only Kir-Hareseth left, which the slingers surrounded and bombarded. [26] When the king of Moab saw that the battle had turned against him, he mustered seven hundred swordsmen in the hope of breaking a way out and going to the king of Aram, but he failed. [27] Then he took his eldest son who was to succeed him and offered him as a sacrifice on the city wall. Alarmed at this, the Israelites withdrew and retired to their own territory.

4 [b] The wife of a member of the prophetic brotherhood appealed to Elisha. 'Your servant my husband is dead,' she said, 'and you know how your servant revered Yahweh. A creditor has now come to take my two children and make them his slaves.' [2] Elisha said, 'What can I do for you? Tell me, what have you got in the house?' 'Your servant has nothing in the house,' she replied, 'except a flask of oil.' [3] Then he said, 'Go outside and borrow jars from all your neighbours, empty jars and not too few. [4] When you come back, shut the door on yourself and your sons, and pour the oil into all these jars, putting each aside when it is full.' [5] So she left him; and she shut the door on herself and her sons; they passed her the jars and she went on pouring. [6] When the jars were full, she said to her son, 'Pass me another jar.' 'There are no more,' he replied. Then the oil stopped flowing. [7] She went and told the man of God, who said, 'Go and sell the oil and redeem your pledge; you and your children can live on the remainder.'

[8] One day as Elisha was on his way to Shunem, a woman of rank who lived there pressed him to stay and eat there. After this he always broke his journey for a meal when he passed that way. [9] She said to her husband, 'Look, I am sure the man who is constantly passing our way must be a holy man of God. [10] Let us build him a small walled room, and put him a bed in it, and a table and chair and lamp; whenever he comes to us he can rest there.' [11] One day when he came, he retired to the upper room and lay down. [12] He said to his servant Gehazi, 'Call our Shunammite.' He called her and when she appeared, Elisha said, [13] 'Tell her this: "Look, you have gone to all this trouble for us, what can we do for you? Is there anything you would like said for you to the king or to the commander of the army?"' But she replied, 'I live with my own people about me.' [14] 'What can I do for you then?' he asked. Gehazi replied, 'Well, she has no son and her husband is old.' [15] Elisha said, 'Call her.' The servant called her and she stood at the door. [16] 'This time next year', he said, 'you will hold a son in your arms.' But she said, 'No, my lord, do not deceive your servant.' [17] But the woman did conceive, and she gave birth to a son at the time that Elisha had said she would.

[18] The child grew up; one day he went to his father who was with the reapers, [19] and exclaimed to his father, 'Oh, my head! My head!' The father told a servant to carry him to his mother. [c] [20] He lifted him up and took him to his mother, and the boy lay on her lap until midday, when he died. [21] She went upstairs, laid him on the bed of the man of God, shut the door on him and went out. [22] She called her husband and said, 'Send me one of the servants with a

one of the donkeys, so that I may quickly go to the man of God and come back again." 23 He said, "Why go to him today? It is neither new moon nor sabbath." She said, "It will be all right." 24 Then she saddled the donkey and said to her servant, "Urge the animal on; do not hold back for me unless I tell you." 25 So she set out, and came to the man of God at Mount Carmel.

When the man of God saw her coming, he said to Gehazi his servant, "Look, there is the Shunammite woman; 26 run at once to meet her, and say to her, Are you all right? Is your husband all right? Is the child all right?" She answered, "It is all right." 27 When she came to the man of God at the mountain, she caught hold of his feet. Gehazi approached to push her away. But the man of God said, "Let her alone, for she is in bitter distress; the LORD has hidden it from me and has not told me." 28 Then she said, "Did I ask my lord for a son? Did I not say, Do not mislead me?" 29 He said to Gehazi, "Gird up your loins, and take my staff in your hand, and go. If you meet anyone, give no greeting, and if anyone greets you, do not answer; and lay my staff on the face of the child." 30 Then the mother of the child said, "As the LORD lives, and as you yourself live, I will not leave without you." So he rose up and followed her. 31 Gehazi went on ahead and laid the staff on the face of the child, but there was no sound or sign of life. He came back to meet him and told him, "The child has not awakened."

32 When Elisha came into the house, he saw the child lying dead on his bed. 33 So he went in and closed the door on the two of them, and prayed to the LORD. 34 Then he got up on the bed[f] and lay upon the child, putting his mouth upon his mouth, his eyes upon his eyes, and his hands upon his hands; and while he lay bent over him, the flesh of the child became warm. 35 He got down, walked once to and fro in the room, then got up again and bent over him; the child sneezed seven times, and the child opened his eyes. 36 Elisha[g] summoned Gehazi and said, "Call the Shunammite woman." So he called her. When she came to him, he said, "Take your son." 37 She came and fell at his feet, bowing to the ground; then she took her son and left.

38 When Elisha returned to Gilgal, there was a famine in the land. As the company of prophets was[h] sitting before him, he said to his servant, "Put the large pot on, and make some stew for the company of prophets."[i] 39 One of them went out into the field to gather herbs; he found a wild vine and gathered from it a lapful of wild gourds, and came and cut them up into the pot of stew, not knowing what they were. 40 They served some for the men to eat. But while they were eating the stew, they cried out, "O man of God, there is death in the pot!" They could not eat it. 41 He said, "Then bring some flour." He threw it into the pot, and said, "Serve the people and let them eat." And there was nothing harmful in the pot.

42 A man came from Baal-shalishah, bringing food from the first fruits to the man of God: twenty loaves of barley and fresh ears of grain in his sack. Elisha said, "Give it to the people and let them eat." 43 But his servant said, "How can I set this before a hundred people?" So he repeated, "Give it to the people and let them eat, for thus says the LORD, 'They shall eat and have some left.'" 44 He set it before them, they ate, and had some left, according to the word of the LORD.

5 Naaman, commander of the army of the king of Aram, was a great man and in high favor with his master, because by him the LORD had given victory to Aram. The man, though a mighty warrior, suffered from leprosy.[j]

I must go to the man of God as fast as I can, and come straight back.' 23 'Why go to him today?' he asked. 'It is neither new moon nor sabbath.' 'Never mind that,' she answered. 24 When the donkey was saddled, she said to her servant, 'Lead on and do not slacken pace unless I tell you.' 25 So she set out and came to the man of God on Mount Carmel.

The man of God spied her in the distance and said to Gehazi, his servant, 'That is the Shunammite woman coming. 26 Run and meet her, and ask, "Is all well with you? Is all well with your husband? Is all well with the boy?" ' She answered, 'All is well.' 27 When she reached the man of God on the hill, she clutched his feet. Gehazi came forward to push her away, but the man of God said, 'Let her alone; she is in great distress, and the LORD has concealed it from me and not told me.' 28 'My lord,' she said, 'did I ask for a son? Did I not beg you not to raise my hopes and then dash them?' 29 Elisha turned to Gehazi: 'Hitch up your cloak; take my staff with you and run. If you meet anyone on the way, do not stop to greet him; if anyone greets you, do not answer. Lay my staff on the boy's face.' 30 But the mother cried, 'As the LORD lives, your life upon it, I shall not leave you.' So he got up and followed her.

31 Gehazi went on ahead and laid the staff on the boy's face, but there was no sound or sign of life, so he went back to meet Elisha and told him that the boy had not stirred. 32 When Elisha entered the house, there was the dead boy, where he had been laid on the bed. 33 He went into the room, shut the door on the two of them, and prayed to the LORD. 34 Then, getting on to the bed, he lay upon the child, put his mouth to the child's mouth, his eyes to his eyes, and his hands to his hands; as he crouched upon him, the child's body grew warm. 35 Elisha got up and walked once up and down the room; getting on to the bed again, he crouched upon him and breathed into him seven times, and the boy opened his eyes. 36 The prophet summoned Gehazi and said, 'Call the Shunammite woman.' She answered his call and the prophet said, 'Take up your child.' 37 She came in and prostrated herself before him. Then she took up her son and went out.

38 ELISHA returned to Gilgal at a time when there was a famine in the land. One day, when a group of prophets was sitting at his feet, he said to his servant, 'Set the big pot on the fire and prepare broth for the company.' 39 One of them went out into the fields to gather herbs and found a wild vine, and filled the skirt of his garment with wild gourds. He came back and sliced them into the pot, not knowing what they were. 40 The broth was poured out for the men to eat but, on tasting it, they cried out, 'Man of God, there is death in the pot,' and they could not eat it. 41 The prophet said, 'Fetch some meal.' He threw it into the pot and said, 'Now pour out for the people to eat.' This time there was no harm in the pot.

42 A MAN came from Baal-shalisha, bringing the man of God some of the new season's bread, twenty barley loaves, and fresh ripe ears of grain. Elisha said, 'Give this to the people to eat.' 43 His attendant protested, 'I cannot set this before a hundred people.' Still he insisted, 'Give it to the people to eat; for this is the word of the LORD: They will eat and there will be some left over.' 44 So he set it before them, and they ate and had some left over, as the LORD had said.

5 NAAMAN, commander of the king of Aram's army, was a great man and highly esteemed by his master, because through him the LORD had given victory to Aram; he was a mighty warrior, but he was a leper. 2 On one of

---

[f] Heb lacks *on the bed*   [g] Heb *he*   [h] Heb *sons of the prophets* [i] Heb *sons of the prophets* [j] A term for several skin diseases; precise meaning uncertain

4:35 **and breathed into him:** *or* and the boy sneezed.   4:42 **fresh ... grain:** *prob. rdg; Heb.* unintelligible.   5:1 **he was a leper:** *or* his skin was diseased.

have a servant and a donkey. I must go quickly to the man of God, and I will be back." 23 "Why are you going to him today?" he asked. "It is neither the new moon nor the sabbath." But she bade him good-bye, 24 and when the donkey was saddled, said to her servant: "Lead on! Do not stop my donkey unless I tell you to." 25 She kept going till she reached the man of God on Mount Carmel. When he spied her at a distance, the man of God said to his servant Gehazi: "There is the Shunammite! 26 Hurry to meet her, and ask if all is well with her, with her husband, and with the boy." "Greetings," she replied. 27 But when she reached the man of God on the mountain, she clasped his feet. Gehazi came near to push her away, but the man of God said: "Let her alone, she is in bitter anguish; the LORD hid it from me and did not let me know." 28 "Did I ask my lord for a son?" she cried out. "Did I not beg you not to deceive me?" 29 "Gird your loins," Elisha said to Gehazi, "take my staff with you and be off; if you meet anyone, do not greet him, and if anyone greets you, do not answer. Lay my staff upon the boy." 30 But the boy's mother cried out: "As the LORD lives and as you yourself live, I will not release you." So he started to go back with her.

31 Meanwhile, Gehazi had gone on ahead and had laid the staff upon the boy, but there was no sound or sign of life. He returned to meet Elisha and informed him that the boy had not awakened. 32 When Elisha reached the house, he found the boy lying dead. 33 He went in, closed the door on them both, and prayed to the LORD. 34 Then he lay upon the child on the bed, placing his mouth upon the child's mouth, his eyes upon the eyes, and his hands upon the hands. As Elisha stretched himself over the child, the body became warm. 35 He arose, paced up and down the room, and then once more lay down upon the boy, who now sneezed seven times and opened his eyes. 36 Elisha summoned Gehazi and said, "Call the Shunammite." She came at his call, and Elisha said to her, "Take your son." 37 She came in and fell at his feet in gratitude; then she took her son and left the room.

38 When Elisha returned to Gilgal, there was a famine in the land. Once, when the guild prophets were seated before him, he said to his servant, "Put the large pot on, and make some vegetable stew for the guild prophets." 39 Someone went out into the field to gather herbs and found a wild vine, from which he picked a clothful of wild gourds. On his return he cut them up into the pot of vegetable stew without anybody's knowing it. 40 The stew was poured out for the men to eat, but when they began to eat it, they exclaimed, "Man of God, there is poison in the pot!" And they could not eat it. 41 "Bring some meal," Elisha said. He threw it into the pot and said, "Serve it to the people to eat." And there was no longer anything harmful in the pot.

42 A man came from Baal-shalishah bringing the man of God twenty barley loaves made from the first-fruits, and fresh grain in the ear. "Give it to the people to eat," Elisha said. 43 But his servant objected, "How can I set this before a hundred men?" "Give it to the people to eat," Elisha insisted. "For thus says the LORD, 'They shall eat and there shall be some left over.'" 44 And when they had eaten, there was some left over, as the LORD had said.

5 Naaman, the army commander of the king of Aram, was highly esteemed and respected by his master, for through him the LORD had brought victory to Aram. But valiant as he was, the man was a leper. 2 Now the Arameans

donkey. I must hurry to the man of God and back.' 23 'Why go to him today?' he asked. 'It is not New Moon or Sabbath.' But she replied, 'Never mind.' 24 She had the donkey saddled and said to her servant, 'Lead on, go! Do not draw rein until I give the order.' 25 She set off and made her way to the man of God at Mount Carmel. When the man of God saw her in the distance, he said to his servant Gehazi, 'Look, here comes our Shunammite! 26 Now run and meet her and ask her, "Are you well? Is your husband well? Your child well?"' 'Yes,' she replied. 27 When she came to the man of God there on the mountain, she took hold of his feet. Gehazi stepped forward to push her away, but the man of God said, 'Leave her; there is bitterness in her soul and Yahweh has hidden it from me, he has not told me.' 28 She said, 'Did I ask my lord for a son? Did I not say: Don't deceive me?'

29 Elisha said to Gehazi, 'Hitch up your clothes, take my staff in your hand and go. If you meet anyone, do not greet him; if anyone greets you, do not answer him. You are to stretch out my staff over the child.' 30 But the child's mother said, 'As Yahweh lives and as you yourself live, I will not leave you.' Then he stood up and followed her. 31 Gehazi had gone ahead of them and had stretched out the staff over the child, but there was no sound or response. He went back to meet Elisha and told him. 'The child has not woken up,' he said. 32 Elisha then went to the house, and there on his bed lay the child, dead. 33 He went in and shut the door on the two of them and prayed to Yahweh. 34 Then he climbed on to the bed and stretched himself on top of the child, putting his mouth on his mouth, his eyes to his eyes, and hands on his hands, and as he lowered himself on to him, the child's flesh grew warm. 35 Then he got up and walked to and fro inside the house, and then climbed on to the bed again and lowered himself on to the child seven times in all; then the child sneezed and opened his eyes. 36 He then summoned Gehazi. 'Call our Shunammite,' he said. He called her. When she came to him, he said, 'Pick up your son.' 37 She went in and, falling at his feet, prostrated herself on the floor and then picked up her son and went out.

38 Elisha went back to Gilgal while there was famine in the country. As the brotherhood of prophets were sitting with him, he said to his servant, 'Put the large pot on the fire and cook some soup for the brotherhood.' 39 One of them went into the fields to gather herbs and came on some wild vine, off which he gathered enough gourds to fill his lap. On his return, he cut them up into the pot of soup; they did not know what they were. 40 They then poured the soup out for the men to eat, but they had no sooner tasted the soup than they cried, 'Man of God, there is death in the pot!' And they could not eat it. 41 'Bring some meal then,' Elisha said. This he threw into the pot, and said, 'Pour out, for the company to eat!' And there was nothing harmful in the pot.

42 A man came from Baal-Shalishah, bringing the man of God bread from the first-fruits, twenty barley loaves and fresh grain still in the husk. 'Give it to the company to eat,' Elisha said. 43 But his servant replied, 'How can I serve this to a hundred men?' 'Give it to the company to eat,' he insisted, 'for Yahweh says this, "They will eat and have some left over."' 44 He served them; they ate and had some left over, as Yahweh had said.

5 Naaman, army commander to the king of Aram, was a man who enjoyed his master's respect and favour, since through him Yahweh had granted victory to the Aramaeans. 2 But the man suffered from a virulent skin-disease.

2 Now the Arameans on one of their raids had taken a young girl captive from the land of Israel, and she served Naaman's wife. 3 She said to her mistress, "If only my lord were with the prophet who is in Samaria! He would cure him of his leprosy."*k* 4 So Naaman*l* went in and told his lord just what the girl from the land of Israel had said. 5 And the king of Aram said, "Go then, and I will send along a letter to the king of Israel."

He went, taking with him ten talents of silver, six thousand shekels of gold, and ten sets of garments. 6 He brought the letter to the king of Israel, which read, "When this letter reaches you, know that I have sent to you my servant Naaman, that you may cure him of his leprosy."*k* 7 When the king of Israel read the letter, he tore his clothes and said, "Am I God, to give death or life, that this man sends word to me to cure a man of his leprosy?*k* Just look and see how he is trying to pick a quarrel with me."

8 But when Elisha the man of God heard that the king of Israel had torn his clothes, he sent a message to the king, "Why have you torn your clothes? Let him come to me, that he may learn that there is a prophet in Israel." 9 So Naaman came with his horses and chariots, and halted at the entrance of Elisha's house. 10 Elisha sent a messenger to him, saying, "Go, wash in the Jordan seven times, and your flesh shall be restored and you shall be clean." 11 But Naaman became angry and went away, saying, "I thought that for me he would surely come out, and stand and call on the name of the LORD his God, and would wave his hand over the spot, and cure the leprosy!*k* 12 Are not Abana*m* and Pharpar, the rivers of Damascus, better than all the waters of Israel? Could I not wash in them, and be clean?" He turned and went away in a rage. 13 But his servants approached and said to him, "Father, if the prophet had commanded you to do something difficult, would you not have done it? How much more, when all he said to you was, 'Wash, and be clean'?" 14 So he went down and immersed himself seven times in the Jordan, according to the word of the man of God; his flesh was restored like the flesh of a young boy, and he was clean.

15 Then he returned to the man of God, he and all his company; he came and stood before him and said, "Now I know that there is no God in all the earth except in Israel; please accept a present from your servant." 16 But he said, "As the LORD lives, whom I serve, I will accept nothing!" He urged him to accept, but he refused. 17 Then Naaman said, "If not, please let two mule-loads of earth be given to your servant; for your servant will no longer offer burnt offering or sacrifice to any god except the LORD. 18 But may the LORD pardon your servant on one count: when my master goes into the house of Rimmon to worship there, leaning on my arm, and I bow down in the house of Rimmon, when I do bow down in the house of Rimmon, may the LORD pardon your servant on this one count." 19 He said to him, "Go in peace."

But when Naaman had gone from him a short distance, 20 Gehazi, the servant of Elisha the man of God, thought, "My master has let that Aramean Naaman off too lightly by not accepting from him what he offered. As the LORD lives, I will run after him and get something out of him." 21 So Gehazi went after Naaman. When Naaman saw someone running after him, he jumped down from the chariot to meet him and said, "Is everything all right?" 22 He replied, "Yes, but my master has sent me to say, 'Two members of a company of prophets*n* have just come to me from the hill country of Ephraim; please give them a talent of silver and two changes of clothing.' " 23 Naaman said, "Please accept

their raids the Aramaeans brought back as a captive from the land of Israel a young girl, who became a servant to Naaman's wife. 3 She said to her mistress, 'If only my master could meet the prophet who lives in Samaria, he would cure him of the leprosy.' 4 Naaman went and reported to his master what the Israelite girl had said. 5 'Certainly you may go,' said the king of Aram, 'and I shall send a letter to the king of Israel.'

Naaman set off, taking with him ten talents of silver, six thousand shekels of gold, and ten changes of clothing. 6 He delivered the letter to the king of Israel; it read: 'This letter is to inform you that I am sending to you my servant Naaman, and I beg you to cure him of his leprosy.' 7 When the king of Israel read the letter, he tore his clothes and said, 'Am I God to kill and to make alive, that this fellow sends to me to cure a man of his disease? See how he picks a quarrel with me.' 8 When Elisha, the man of God, heard how the king of Israel had torn his clothes, he sent this message: 'Why did you tear your clothes? Let the man come to me, and he will know that there is a prophet in Israel.' 9 When Naaman came with his horses and chariots and halted at the entrance to Elisha's house, 10 Elisha sent out a messenger to say to him, 'If you go and wash seven times in the Jordan, your flesh will be restored and you will be clean.'

11 At this Naaman was furious and went away, saying, 'I thought he would at least have come out and stood, and invoked the LORD his God by name, waved his hand over the place, and cured me of the leprosy. 12 Are not Abana and Pharpar, rivers of Damascus, better than all the waters of Israel? Can I not wash in them and be clean?' So he turned and went off in a rage.

13 But his servants came to him and said, 'If the prophet had told you to do something difficult, would you not do it? How much more should you, then, if he says to you, "Wash and be clean"!' 14 So he went down and dipped himself in the Jordan seven times as the man of God had told him, and his flesh was restored so that it was like a little child's, and he was clean.

15 Accompanied by his retinue he went back to the man of God and standing before him said, 'Now I know that there is no God anywhere in the world except in Israel. Will you accept a token of gratitude from your servant?' 16 'As the LORD lives, whom I serve,' said the prophet, 'I shall accept nothing.' Though pressed to accept, he refused. 17 'Then if you will not,' said Naaman, 'let me, sir, have two mules' load of earth, for I shall no longer offer whole-offering or sacrifice to any god but the LORD. 18 In one matter only may the LORD pardon me: when my master goes to the temple of Rimmon to worship, leaning on my arm, and I worship in the temple of Rimmon when he worships there, for this let the LORD pardon me.' 19 Elisha bade him go in peace.

Naaman had gone only a short distance on his way, 20 when Gehazi, the servant of Elisha the man of God, said to himself, 'Has my master let this Aramaean, Naaman, go without accepting what he brought? As the LORD lives, I shall run after him and get something from him.' 21 So Gehazi hurried after Naaman. When Naaman saw him running after him, he alighted from his chariot to meet him saying, 'Is anything wrong?' 22 'Nothing,' replied Gehazi, 'but my master sent me to say that two young men of the company of prophets from the hill-country of Ephraim have just arrived. Could you provide them with a talent of silver and two changes of clothing?' 23 Naaman said, 'By all

---

|

had captured from the land of Israel in a raid a little girl, who became the servant of Naaman's wife. 3 "If only my master would present himself to the prophet in Samaria," she said to her mistress, "he would cure him of his leprosy." 4 Naaman went and told his lord just what the slave girl from the land of Israel had said. 5 "Go," said the king of Aram. "I will send along a letter to the king of Israel." So Naaman set out, taking along ten silver talents, six thousand gold pieces, and ten festal garments. 6 To the king of Israel he brought the letter, which read: "With this letter I am sending my servant Naaman to you, that you may cure him of his leprosy."

7 When he read the letter, the king of Israel tore his garments and exclaimed: "Am I a god with power over life and death, that this man should send someone to me to be cured of leprosy? Take note! You can see he is only looking for a quarrel with me!" 8 When Elisha, the man of God, heard that the king of Israel had torn his garments, he sent word to the king: "Why have you torn your garments? Let him come to me and find out that there is a prophet in Israel."

9 Naaman came with his horses and chariots and stopped at the door of Elisha's house. 10 The prophet sent him the message: "Go and wash seven times in the Jordan, and your flesh will heal, and you will be clean." 11 But Naaman went away angry, saying, "I thought that he would surely come out and stand there to invoke the LORD his God, and would move his hand over the spot, and thus cure the leprosy. 12 Are not the rivers of Damascus, the Abana and the Pharpar, better than all the waters of Israel? Could I not wash in them and be cleansed?" With this, he turned about in anger and left.

13 But his servants came up and reasoned with him. "My father," they said, "if the prophet had told you to do something extraordinary, would you not have done it? All the more now, since he said to you, 'Wash and be clean,' should you do as he said." 14 So Naaman went down and plunged into the Jordan seven times at the word of the man of God. His flesh became again like the flesh of a little child, and he was clean.

15 He returned with his whole retinue to the man of God. On his arrival he stood before him and said, "Now I know that there is no God in all the earth, except in Israel. Please accept a gift from your servant."

16 "As the LORD lives whom I serve, I will not take it," Elisha replied; and despite Naaman's urging, he still refused. 17 Naaman said: "If you will not accept, please let me, your servant, have two mule-loads of earth, for I will no longer offer holocaust or sacrifice to any other god except to the LORD. 18 But I trust the LORD will forgive your servant this: when my master enters the temple of Rimmon to worship there, then I, too, as his adjutant, must bow down in the temple of Rimmon. May the LORD forgive your servant this." 19 "Go in peace," Elisha said to him.

20 Naaman had gone some distance when Gehazi, the servant of Elisha, the man of God, thought to himself: "My master was too easy with this Aramean Naaman, not accepting what he brought. As the LORD lives, I will run after him and get something out of him." 21 So Gehazi hurried after Naaman. Aware that someone was running after him, Naaman alighted from his chariot to wait for him. "Is everything all right?" he asked. 22 "Yes," Gehazi replied, "but my master sent me to say, 'Two young men have just come to me, guild prophets from the hill country of Ephraim. Please give them a talent of silver and two festal garments.' "

Now, on one of their raids into Israelite territory, the Aramaeans had carried off a little girl, who became a servant of Naaman's wife. 3 She said to her mistress, 'If only my master would approach the prophet of Samaria! He would cure him of his skin-disease.' 4 Naaman went and told his master. 'This and this,' he reported, 'is what the girl from Israel has said.' 5 'Go by all means,' said the king of Aram, 'I shall send a letter to the king of Israel.' So Naaman left, taking with him ten talents of silver, six thousand shekels of gold and ten festal robes. 6 He presented the letter to the king of Israel. It read, 'With this letter, I am sending my servant Naaman to you for you to cure him of his skin-disease.' 7 When the king of Israel read the letter, he tore his clothes. 'Am I a god to give death and life,' he said, 'for him to send a man to me and ask me to cure him of his skin-disease? Listen to this and take note of it and see how he intends to pick a quarrel with me.'

8 When Elisha heard that the king of Israel had torn his clothes, he sent word to the king, 'Why have you torn your clothes? Let him come to me, and he will find there is a prophet in Israel.' 9 So Naaman came with his team and chariot and drew up at the door of Elisha's house. 10 And Elisha sent him a messenger to say, 'Go and bathe seven times in the Jordan, and your flesh will become clean once more.' 11 But Naaman was indignant and went off, saying, 'Here was I, thinking he would be sure to come out to me, and stand there, and call on the name of Yahweh his God, and wave his hand over the spot and cure the part that was diseased. 12 Surely, Abana and Parpar, the rivers of Damascus, are better than any water in Israel? Could I not bathe in them and become clean?' And he turned round and went off in a rage. 13 But his servants approached him and said, 'Father, if the prophet had asked you to do something difficult, would you not have done it? All the more reason, then, when he says to you, "Bathe, and you will become clean." ' 14 So he went down and immersed himself seven times in the Jordan, as Elisha had told him to do. And his flesh became clean once more like the flesh of a little child.

15 Returning to Elisha with his whole escort, he went in and, presenting himself, said, 'Now I know that there is no God anywhere on earth except in Israel. Now, please, accept a present from your servant.' 16 But Elisha replied, 'As Yahweh lives, whom I serve, I will accept nothing.' Naaman pressed him to accept, but he refused. 17 Then Naaman said, 'Since your answer is "No," allow your servant to be given as much earth as two mules may carry, since your servant will no longer make burnt offerings or sacrifice to any god except Yahweh. 18 Only — and may Yahweh forgive your servant for this — when my master goes to the temple of Rimmon to worship there, he leans on my arm, and I bow down in the temple of Rimmon when he does; may Yahweh forgive your servant for doing this!' 19 'Go in peace,' Elisha replied.

20 Naaman had gone a small distance, when Gehazi, Elisha's servant, said to himself, 'My master has let this Aramaean Naaman off lightly, by not accepting what he offered. As Yahweh lives, I will run after him and get something out of him.' 21 So Gehazi set off in pursuit of Naaman. When Naaman saw him running after him, he jumped down from his chariot to meet him. 'Is all well?' he asked. 22 'All is well,' he said. 'My master has sent me to say, "This very moment two young men of the prophetic brotherhood have arrived from the highlands of Ephraim. Be kind enough to give them a talent of silver and two festal robes." ' 23 'Please accept two talents,' Naaman replied,

two talents." He urged him, and tied up two talents of silver in two bags, with two changes of clothing, and gave them to two of his servants, who carried them in front of Gehazi.*o* 24 When he came to the citadel, he took the bags *p* from them, and stored them inside; he dismissed the men; and they left.

25 He went in and stood before his master; and Elisha said to him, "Where have you been, Gehazi?" He answered, "Your servant has not gone anywhere at all." 26 But he said to him, "Did I not go with you in spirit when someone left his chariot to meet you? Is this a time to accept money and to accept clothing, olive orchards and vineyards, sheep and oxen, and male and female slaves? 27 Therefore the leprosy*q* of Naaman shall cling to you, and to your descendants forever." So he left his presence leprous,*q* as white as snow.

6 Now the company of prophets*r* said to Elisha, "As you see, the place where we live under your charge is too small for us. 2 Let us go to the Jordan, and let us collect logs there, one for each of us, and build a place there for us to live." He answered, "Do so." 3 Then one of them said, "Please come with your servants." And he answered, "I will." 4 So he went with them. When they came to the Jordan, they cut down trees. 5 But as one was felling a log, his ax head fell into the water; he cried out, "Alas, master! It was borrowed." 6 Then the man of God said, "Where did it fall?" When he showed him the place, he cut off a stick, and threw it in there, and made the iron float. 7 He said, "Pick it up." So he reached out his hand and took it.

8 Once when the king of Aram was at war with Israel, he took counsel with his officers. He said, "At such and such a place shall be my camp." 9 But the man of God sent word to the king of Israel, "Take care not to pass this place, because the Arameans are going down there." 10 The king of Israel sent word to the place of which the man of God spoke. More than once or twice he warned such a place*s* so that it was on the alert.

11 The mind of the king of Aram was greatly perturbed because of this; he called his officers and said to them, "Now tell me who among us sides with the king of Israel?" 12 Then one of his officers said, "No one, my lord king. It is Elisha, the prophet in Israel, who tells the king of Israel the words that you speak in your bedchamber." 13 He said, "Go and find where he is; I will send and seize him." He was told, "He is in Dothan." 14 So he sent horses and chariots there and a great army; they came by night, and surrounded the city.

15 When an attendant of the man of God rose early in the morning and went out, an army with horses and chariots was all around the city. His servant said, "Alas, master! What shall we do?" 16 He replied, "Do not be afraid, for there are more with us than there are with them." 17 Then Elisha prayed: "O Lord, please open his eyes that he may see." So the Lord opened the eyes of the servant, and he saw; the mountain was full of horses and chariots of fire all around Elisha. 18 When the Arameans*t* came down against him, Elisha prayed to the Lord, and said, "Strike this people, please, with blindness." So he struck them with blindness as Elisha had asked. 19 Elisha said to them, "This is not the way, and this is not the city; follow me, and I will bring you to the man whom you seek." And he led them to Samaria.

20 As soon as they entered Samaria, Elisha said, "O Lord, open the eyes of these men so that they may see." The Lord opened their eyes, and they saw that they were inside Samaria. 21 When the king of Israel saw them he said

means; take two talents.' He pressed him to take them; then he tied up the two talents of silver in two bags, and the two changes of clothing, and gave them to two of his servants, and they walked ahead carrying them. 24 When Gehazi came to the citadel he took them from the two servants, deposited them in the house, and dismissed the men; and they went away.

25 When he went in and stood before his master, Elisha said, 'Where have you been, Gehazi?' 'Nowhere,' said Gehazi. 26 But he said to him, 'Was I not present in spirit when the man turned and got down from his chariot to meet you? Was it a time to get money and garments, olive trees and vineyards, sheep and oxen, slaves and slave-girls?' 27 Naaman's leprosy will fasten on you and on your descendants for ever.' Gehazi left Elisha's presence, his skin diseased, white as snow.

6 The company of prophets who were with Elisha said to him, 'As you see, this place where we live with you is too cramped for us. 2 Let us go to the Jordan and each fetch a log, and make ourselves a place to live in.' The prophet said, 'Yes, go.' 3 One of them said, 'Please, sir, come with us.' 'I shall come,' he said, 4 and he went with them. When they reached the Jordan and began cutting down trees 5 it chanced that, as one of them was felling a trunk, the head of his axe flew off into the water. 'Oh, master!' he exclaimed. 'It was borrowed.' 6 'Where did it fall?' asked the man of God. When shown the place, he cut off a piece of wood and threw it into the water and made the iron float. 7 Elisha said, 'Lift it out.' So he reached down and picked it up.

8 Once, when the king of Aram was at war with Israel, he held a conference with his staff at which he said, 'I mean to attack in such and such a direction.' 9 The man of God warned the king of Israel: 'Take care to avoid this place, for the Aramaeans are going down there.' 10 The king of Israel sent word to the place about which the man of God had given him this warning; and the king took special precautions every time he found himself near that place. 11 The king of Aram was greatly incensed at this and, summoning his staff, he said to them, 'Tell me, which of us is for the king of Israel?' 12 'There is no one, my lord king,' said one of his staff; 'but Elisha, the prophet in Israel, tells the king of Israel the very words you speak in your bedchamber.' 13 'Go, find out where he is,' said the king, 'and I shall send and seize him.' It was reported to him that the prophet was at Dothan, 14 and he sent a strong force there with horses and chariots. They came by night and surrounded the town.

15 When the attendant of the man of God rose and went out early next morning, he saw a force with horses and chariots surrounding the town. 'Oh, master,' he said, 'which way are we to turn?' 16 Elisha answered, 'Do not be afraid, for those on our side are more than those on theirs.' 17 He offered this prayer: 'Lord, open his eyes and let him see.' The Lord opened the young man's eyes, and he saw the hills covered with horses and chariots of fire all around Elisha. 18 As the Aramaeans came down towards him, Elisha prayed to the Lord: 'Strike this host, I pray, with blindness'; and they were struck blind as Elisha had asked. 19 Elisha said to them, 'You are on the wrong road; this is not the town. Follow me and I will lead you to the man you are looking for.' And he led them to Samaria. 20 As soon as they had entered Samaria, Elisha prayed, 'Lord, open the eyes of these men and let them see again.' He opened their eyes, and they saw that they were inside Samaria. 21 When the king of Israel saw them, he said to

---

o Heb *him*   *p* Heb lacks *the bags*   *q* A term for several skin diseases; precise meaning uncertain   *r* Heb *sons of the prophets*   *s* Heb *warned it*   *t* Heb *they*

5:23 **pressed:** *prob. rdg; Heb.* broke out on.   5:24 **citadel:** *or* hill.   6:2 **make ourselves:** *so Syriac; Heb.* adds there.

23 "Please take two talents," Naaman said, and pressed them upon him. He tied up these silver talents in bags and gave them, with the two festal garments, to two of his servants, who carried them before Gehazi. 24 When they reached the hill, Gehazi took what they had, carried it into the house, and sent the men on their way.

25 He went in and stood before Elisha his master, who asked him, "Where have you been, Gehazi?" He answered, "Your servant has not gone anywhere." 26 But Elisha said to him: "Was I not present in spirit when the man alighted from his chariot to wait for you? Is this a time to take money or to take garments, olive orchards or vineyards, sheep or cattle, male or female servants? 27 The leprosy of Naaman shall cling to you and your descendants forever." And Gehazi left Elisha, a leper white as snow.

6 The guild prophets once said to Elisha: "There is not enough room for us to continue to live here with you. 2 Let us go to the Jordan, where by getting one beam apiece we can build ourselves a place to live." "Go," Elisha said. 3 "Please agree to accompany your servants," one of them requested. "Yes, I will come," he replied.

4 So he went with them, and when they arrived at the Jordan they began to fell trees. 5 While one of them was felling a tree trunk, the iron axhead slipped into the water. "O master," he cried out, "it was borrowed!" 6 "Where did it fall?" asked the man of God. When he pointed out the spot, Elisha cut off a stick, threw it into the water, and brought the iron to the surface. 7 "Pick it up," he said. And the man reached down and grasped it.

8 When the king of Aram was waging war on Israel, he would make plans with his servants to attack a particular place. 9 But the man of God would send word to the king of Israel, "Be careful! Do not pass by this place, for Aram will attack there." 10 So the king of Israel would send word to the place which the man of God had indicated, and alert it; then they would be on guard. This happened several times.

11 Greatly disturbed over this, the king of Aram called together his officers. "Will you not tell me," he asked them, "who among us is for the king of Israel?" 12 "No one, my lord king," answered one of the officers. "The Israelite prophet Elisha can tell the king of Israel the very words you speak in your bedroom." 13 "Go, find out where he is," he said, "so that I may take him captive."

Informed that Elisha was in Dothan, 14 he sent there a strong force with horses and chariots. They arrived by night and surrounded the city. 15 Early the next morning, when the attendant of the man of God arose and went out, he saw the force with its horses and chariots surrounding the city. "Alas!" he said to Elisha. "What shall we do, my lord?" 16 "Do not be afraid," Elisha answered. "Our side outnumbers theirs." 17 Then he prayed, "O LORD, open his eyes, that he may see." And the LORD opened the eyes of the servant, so that he saw the mountainside filled with horses and fiery chariots around Elisha.

18 When the Arameans came down to get him, Elisha prayed to the LORD, "Strike this people blind, I pray you." And in answer to the prophet's prayer the LORD struck them blind. 19 Then Elisha said to them: "This is the wrong road, and this is the wrong city. Follow me! I will take you to the man you want." And he led them to Samaria. 20 When they entered Samaria, Elisha prayed, "O LORD, open their eyes that they may see." The LORD opened their eyes, and they saw that they were inside Samaria. 21 When the king of

and pressed him, tying up the two talents of silver in two bags with the two festal robes and consigning them to two of his servants who carried them ahead of Gehazi. 24 When he reached Ophel, he took these from them and put them away in the house. He then dismissed the men, who went away.

25 He, for his part, went and presented himself to his master. Elisha said, 'Gehazi, where have you been?' 'Your servant has not been anywhere,' he replied. 26 But Elisha said to him, 'Was not my heart present there when someone left his chariot to meet you? Now you have taken the money, you can buy gardens with it, and olive groves, sheep and oxen, male and female slaves. 27 But Naaman's disease of the skin will cling to you and your descendants for ever.' And Gehazi left his presence white as snow from skin-disease.

6 The brotherhood of prophets said to Elisha, 'Look, the place where we are living with you is too small for us. 2 Let us go to the Jordan, then, and each of us cut a beam there, and we will make our living quarters there.' He replied, 'Go.' 3 'Be good enough to go with your servants,' one of them said. 'I will go,' he replied, 4 and went with them. On reaching the Jordan they began cutting down timber. 5 But, as one of them was felling his beam, the iron axehead fell into the water. 'Alas, my lord,' he exclaimed, 'and it was a borrowed one too!' 6 'Where did it fall?' the man of God asked; and he showed him the spot. Then, cutting a stick, Elisha threw it in at that point and made the iron axehead float. 7 'Lift it out,' he said; and the man stretched out his hand and took it.

8 The king of Aram was at war with Israel. He conferred with his officers and said, 'You must attack at such and such a place.' 9 Elisha, however, sent word to the king of Israel, 'Be on your guard about such and such a place, because the Aramaeans are going to attack it.' 10 The king of Israel accordingly sent men to the place which Elisha had named. And he kept warning the king, and the king stayed on the alert; and this happened more than once or twice.

11 The king of Aram grew very much disturbed over this. He summoned his officers, and said, 'Tell me which of you is betraying us to the king of Israel.' 12 'No one, my lord king,' one of his officers replied. 'It is Elisha, the prophet in Israel. The words you utter in your bedchamber, he reveals to the king of Israel.' 13 'Go and find out where he is,' the king said, 'so that I can send people to capture him.' Word was brought to him, 'He is now in Dothan.' 14 So he sent horses and chariots there, and a large force; and these, arriving during the night, surrounded the town.

15 Next day, Elisha got up early and went out; and there surrounding the town was an armed force with horses and chariots. 'Oh, my lord,' his servant said, 'what are we to do?' 16 'Do not be afraid,' he replied, 'for there are more on our side than on theirs.' 17 And Elisha prayed. 'Yahweh,' he said, 'open his eyes and make him see.' Yahweh opened the servant's eyes, and he saw the mountain covered in fiery horses and chariots surrounding Elisha.

18 As the Aramaeans came down towards him, Elisha prayed to Yahweh, 'I beg you to strike these people sun-blind.' And, at Elisha's word, he struck them sun-blind. 19 Then Elisha said to them, 'This is not the road, nor is this the town. Follow me; I shall lead you to the man you are looking for.' But he led them to Samaria. 20 As they entered Samaria, Elisha said, 'Yahweh, open these people's eyes, and let them see.' Yahweh opened their eyes and they saw; they were inside Samaria.

21 When the king of Israel saw them, he said to Elisha,

NEW REVISED STANDARD VERSION	REVISED ENGLISH BIBLE

to Elisha, "Father, shall I kill them? Shall I kill them?" 22 He answered, "No! Did you capture with your sword and your bow those whom you want to kill? Set food and water before them so that they may eat and drink; and let them go to their master." 23 So he prepared for them a great feast; after they ate and drank, he sent them on their way, and they went to their master. And the Arameans no longer came raiding into the land of Israel.

24 Some time later King Ben-hadad of Aram mustered his entire army; he marched against Samaria and laid siege to it. 25 As the siege continued, famine in Samaria became so great that a donkey's head was sold for eighty shekels of silver, and one-fourth of a kab of dove's dung for five shekels of silver. 26 Now as the king of Israel was walking on the city wall, a woman cried out to him, "Help, my lord king!" 27 He said, "No! Let the LORD help you. How can I help you? From the threshing floor or from the wine press?" 28 But then the king asked her, "What is your complaint?" She answered, "This woman said to me, 'Give up your son; we will eat him today, and we will eat my son tomorrow.' 29 So we cooked my son and ate him. The next day I said to her, 'Give up your son and we will eat him.' But she has hidden her son." 30 When the king heard the words of the woman he tore his clothes—now since he was walking on the city wall, the people could see that he had sackcloth on his body underneath— 31 and he said, "So may God do to me, and more, if the head of Elisha son of Shaphat stays on his shoulders today." 32 So he dispatched a man from his presence.

Now Elisha was sitting in his house, and the elders were sitting with him. Before the messenger arrived, Elisha said to the elders, "Are you aware that this murderer has sent someone to take off my head? When the messenger comes, see that you shut the door and hold it closed against him. Is not the sound of his master's feet behind him?" 33 While he was still speaking with them, the king[u] came down to him and said, "This trouble is from the LORD! Why should I hope in the LORD any longer?"

7 1 But Elisha said, "Hear the word of the LORD: thus says the LORD, Tomorrow about this time a measure of choice meal shall be sold for a shekel, and two measures of barley for a shekel, at the gate of Samaria." 2 Then the captain on whose hand the king leaned said to the man of God, "Even if the LORD were to make windows in the sky, could such a thing happen?" But he said, "You shall see it with your own eyes, but you shall not eat from it."

3 Now there were four leprous[v] men outside the city gate, who said to one another, "Why should we sit here until we die? 4 If we say, 'Let us enter the city,' the famine is in the city, and we shall die there; but if we sit here, we shall also die. Therefore, let us desert to the Aramean camp; if they spare our lives, we shall live; and if they kill us, we shall but die." 5 So they arose at twilight to go to the Aramean camp; but when they came to the edge of the Aramean camp, there was no one there at all. 6 For the Lord had caused the Aramean army to hear the sound of chariots, and of horses, the sound of a great army, so that they said to one another, "The king of Israel has hired the kings of the Hittites and the kings of Egypt to fight against us." 7 So they fled away in the twilight and abandoned their tents, their horses, and their donkeys leaving the camp just as it was, and fled for their lives. 8 When these leprous[v] men had

Elisha, 'My father, am I to destroy them?' 22 'No, you must not do that,' he answered. 'Would you destroy those whom you have not taken prisoner with your own sword and bow? As for these men, provide them with food and water, and let them eat and drink and go back to their master.' 23 So he prepared a great feast for them; they ate and drank and then were sent back to their master. From that time Aramaean raids on Israel ceased.

24 BUT later, Ben-hadad king of Aram mustered his whole army and marched to the siege of Samaria. 25 The city was near starvation, and they were besieging it so closely that a donkey's head was sold for eighty shekels of silver, and a quarter of a kab of locust-beans for five shekels. 26 One day, as the king of Israel was walking along the city wall, a woman called to him, 'Help, my lord king!' 27 He said, 'If the LORD does not bring you help, where can I find help for you? From threshing-floor or from winepress? 28 What is your trouble?' She replied, 'This woman said to me, "Give up your child for us to eat today, and we will eat mine tomorrow." 29 So we cooked my son and ate him; but when I said to her the next day, "Now give up your child for us to eat," she had hidden him.' 30 When he heard the woman's story, the king tore his clothes. He was walking along the wall at the time, and, when the people looked, they saw that he had sackcloth underneath, next to his skin. 31 He said, 'The LORD do the same to me and more, if the head of Elisha son of Shaphat stays on his shoulders today.'

32 Elisha was sitting at home, the elders with him. The king had dispatched one of those at court, but, before the messenger arrived, Elisha said to the elders, 'See how this son of a murderer has sent to behead me! When the messenger comes, be sure to close the door and hold it fast against him. Can you not hear his master following on his heels?' 33 While he was still speaking, the king arrived and said, 'Look at our plight! This is the LORD's doing. Why should I wait any longer for him to help us?'

7 1 Elisha answered, 'Hear this word from the LORD: By this time tomorrow a shekel will buy a measure of flour or two measures of barley at the gate of Samaria.' 2 The officer on whose arm the king leaned said to the man of God, 'Even if the LORD were to open windows in the sky, such a thing could not happen!' He answered, 'You will see it with your own eyes, but you will not eat any of it.'

3 At the city gate were four lepers. They said to one another, 'Why should we stay here and wait for death? 4 If we say we will go into the city, the famine is there, and we shall die; if we stay here, we shall die. Well then, let us go to the camp of the Aramaeans and give ourselves up: if they spare us, we shall live; if they put us to death, we can but die.'

5 At dusk they set out for the Aramaean camp, and when they reached the outskirts, they found no one there. 6 The LORD had caused the Aramaean army to hear a sound like that of chariots and horses and a great host, so that the word went round: 'The king of Israel has hired the kings of the Hittites and the kings of Egypt to attack us.' 7 They had taken to flight in the dusk, abandoning their tents, horses, and donkeys. Leaving the camp as it stood, they had fled for their lives. 8 Those lepers came to the outskirts of the camp,

6:22 **[have] not**: so Gk (Luc.); Heb. omits.   6:27 **If the LORD does not**: so Aram. (Targ.); Heb. Let the LORD not.   6:33 **king**: prob. rdg; Heb. messenger.   7:1 **measure**: Heb. seah. 7:3 **lepers**: or men suffering from skin disease.

u See 7.2: Heb messenger   v A term for several skin diseases; precise meaning uncertain

Israel saw them, he asked, "Shall I kill them, my father?" 22 "You must not kill them," replied Elisha. "Do you slay those whom you have taken captive with your sword or bow? Serve them bread and water. Let them eat and drink, and then go back to their master." 23 The king spread a great feast for them. When they had eaten and drunk he sent them away, and they went back to their master. No more Aramean raiders came into the land of Israel.

24 After this, Ben-hadad, king of Aram, mustered his whole army and laid seige to Samaria. 25 Because of the seige the famine in Samaria was so severe that an ass's head sold for eighty pieces of silver, and a fourth of a kab of wild onion for five pieces of silver.

26 One day, as the king of Israel was walking on the city wall, a woman cried out to him, "Help, my lord king!" 27 "No," he replied, "the Lord help you! Where could I find help for you: from the threshing floor or the winepress?" 28 Then the king asked her, "What is your trouble?" She replied: "This woman said to me, 'Give up your son that we may eat him today; then tomorrow we will eat my son.' 29 So we boiled my son and ate him. The next day I said to her, 'Now give up your son that we may eat him.' But she hid her son." 30 When the king heard the woman's words, he tore his garments. And as he was walking on the wall, the people saw that he was wearing sackcloth underneath, next to his skin.

31 "May God do thus and so to me," the king exclaimed, "if the head of Elisha, son of Shaphat, stays on him today!" 32 Meanwhile, Elisha was sitting in his house in conference with the elders. The king had sent a man ahead before he himself should come to him. Elisha had said to the elders: "Do you know that this son of a murderer is sending someone to cut off my head? When the messenger comes, see that you close the door and hold it fast against him. His master's footsteps are echoing behind him." 33 While Elisha was still speaking, the king came down to him and said, "This evil is from the Lord. Why should I trust in the Lord any longer?"

7 Elisha said: "Hear the word of the Lord! Thus says the Lord, 'At this time tomorrow a seah of fine flour will sell for a shekel, and two seahs of barley for a shekel, in the market of Samaria.' " 2 But the adjutant on whose arm the king leaned, answered the man of God, "Even if the Lord were to make windows in heaven, how could this happen?" "You shall see it with your own eyes," Elisha said, "but you shall not eat of it."

3 At the city gate were four lepers who were deliberating, "Why should we sit here until we die? 4 If we decide to go into the city, we shall die there, for there is famine in the city. If we remain here, we shall die too. Come, let us desert to the camp of the Arameans. If they spare us, we live; if they kill us, we die." 5 At twilight they left for the Arameans; but when they reached the edge of the camp, no one was there. 6 The Lord had caused the army of the Arameans to hear the sound of chariots and horses, the din of a large army, and they had reasoned among themselves, "The king of Israel has hired the kings of the Hittites and the kings of the borderlands to fight us." 7 Then in the twilight they fled, abandoning their tents, their horses, and their asses, the whole camp just as it was, and fleeing for their lives.

'Shall I kill them, father?' 22 'Do not kill them,' he replied. 'Do you kill your own prisoners with sword and bow? Offer them food and water, so that they can eat and drink, and then let them go back to their master.' 23 So the king provided a great feast for them; and when they had eaten and drunk, he sent them off and they went back to their master. Aramaean raiding parties never invaded the territory of Israel again.

24 It happened after this that Ben-Hadad king of Aram, mustering his whole army, marched on and laid siege to Samaria. 25 In Samaria there was great famine, and so strict was the siege that the head of a donkey sold for eighty shekels of silver, and one quarter-*kab* of wild onions for five shekels of silver.

26 Now as the king was passing along the city wall, a woman shouted, 'Help, my lord king!' 27 'If Yahweh does not help you,' he retorted, 'where can I find help for you? From the threshing-floor? From the winepress?' 28 Then the king asked, 'What is the matter?' 'This woman here', she answered, 'said to me, "Give up your son; we will eat him today, and eat my son tomorrow." 29 So we cooked my son and ate him. Next day, I said to her, "Give up your son for us to eat." But she has hidden her son.' 30 On hearing the woman's words, the king tore his clothes; the king was walking on the wall, and the people saw that underneath he was wearing sackcloth next his body. 31 'May God bring unnameable ills on me, and worse ills, too,' he said, 'if the head of Elisha son of Shaphat remains on his shoulders today!'

32 Elisha was sitting in his house, and the elders were sitting with him. The king sent a messenger ahead but, before the man arrived, Elisha had said to the elders, 'Do you see how this son of a murderer has given orders to cut off my head? Look, when the messenger comes, shut the door; hold the door against him. Isn't that the sound of his master's step behind him?' 33 He was still actually speaking, when the king arrived and said, 'This misery plainly comes from Yahweh. Why should I still trust in Yahweh?'

7 'Listen to the word of Yahweh,' Elisha said. 'Yahweh says this, "By this time tomorrow a measure of finest flour will sell for one shekel, and two measures of barley for one shekel, at the gate of Samaria." 2 The equerry on whose arm the king was leaning retorted to Elisha, 'Even if Yahweh made windows in the sky, could this word come true?' 'You will see it with your own eyes,' Elisha replied, 'though you will eat none of it.'

3 Now at the entrance to the gate — for they were afflicted with virulent skin-disease — there were four men and they debated among themselves, 'Why sit here waiting for death? 4 If we decide to go into the city, what with the famine in it, we shall die there; if we stay where we are, we shall die just the same. Come on, let us go over to the Aramaean camp; if they spare our lives, we live; if they kill us, well, then we die.' 5 So at dusk they set out and made for the Aramaean camp, but when they reached the confines of the camp there was not a soul there. 6 For Yahweh had caused the Aramaeans in their camp to hear a noise of chariots and horses, the noise of a great army; and they had said to one another, 'Listen! The king of Israel has hired the Hittite and Egyptian kings against us, to attack us.' 7 So in the dusk they had made off and fled, abandoning their tents, their horses and their donkeys; leaving the camp just as it was, they had fled for their lives. 8 The men with skin-

come to the edge of the camp, they went into a tent, ate and drank, carried off silver, gold, and clothing, and went and hid them. Then they came back, entered another tent, carried off things from it, and went and hid them. 9 Then they said to one another, "What we are doing is wrong. This is a day of good news; if we are silent and wait until the morning light, we will be found guilty; therefore let us go and tell the king's household." 10 So they came and called to the gatekeepers of the city, and told them, "We went to the Aramean camp, but there was no one to be seen or heard there, nothing but the horses tied, the donkeys tied, and the tents as they were." 11 Then the gatekeepers called out and proclaimed it to the king's household. 12 The king got up in the night, and said to his servants, "I will tell you what the Arameans have prepared against us. They know that we are starving; so they have left the camp to hide themselves in the open country, thinking, 'When they come out of the city, we shall take them alive and get into the city.'" 13 One of his servants said, "Let some men take five of the remaining horses, since those left here will suffer the fate of the whole multitude of Israel that have perished already;w let us send and find out." 14 So they took two mounted men, and the king sent them after the Aramean army, saying, "Go and find out." 15 So they went after them as far as the Jordan; the whole way was littered with garments and equipment that the Arameans had thrown away in their haste. So the messengers returned, and told the king.

16 Then the people went out, and plundered the camp of the Arameans. So a measure of choice meal was sold for a shekel, and two measures of barley for a shekel, according to the word of the LORD. 17 Now the king had appointed the captain on whose hand he leaned to have charge of the gate; the people trampled him to death in the gate, just as the man of God had said when the king came down to him. 18 For when the man of God had said to the king, "Two measures of barley shall be sold for a shekel, and a measure of choice meal for a shekel, about this time tomorrow in the gate of Samaria," 19 the captain had answered the man of God, "Even if the LORD were to make windows in the sky, could such a thing happen?" And he had answered, "You shall see it with your own eyes, but you shall not eat from it." 20 It did indeed happen to him; the people trampled him to death in the gate.

8 Now Elisha had said to the woman whose son he had restored to life, "Get up and go with your household, and settle wherever you can; for the LORD has called for a famine, and it will come on the land for seven years." 2 So the woman got up and did according to the word of the man of God; she went with her household and settled in the land of the Philistines seven years. 3 At the end of the seven years, when the woman returned from the land of the Philistines, she set out to appeal to the king for her house and her land. 4 Now the king was talking with Gehazi the servant of the man of God, saying, "Tell me all the great things that Elisha has done." 5 While he was telling the king how Elisha had restored a dead person to life, the woman whose son he had restored to life appealed to the king for her house and her land. Gehazi said, "My lord king, here is the woman, and here is her son whom Elisha restored to life." 6 When the king questioned the woman, she told him. So the king appointed an official for her, saying, "Restore all that was hers, together with all the revenue of the fields from the day that she left the land until now."

7 Elisha went to Damascus while King Ben-hadad of Aram was ill. When it was told him, "The man of God has come here," 8 the king said to Hazael, "Take a present with

where they went into a tent. They ate and drank, looted silver and gold and clothing, and made off and hid them. Then they came back, went into another tent and rifled it, and made off and hid the loot. 9 But they said to one another, 'What we are doing is not right. This is a day of good news and we are keeping it to ourselves. If we wait till morning, we shall be held to blame. We must go now and give the news to the king's household.' 10 So they went and called to the watch at the city gate and described how they had gone to the Aramaean camp and found not one man in it and had heard no human voice: nothing but horses and donkeys tethered, and the tents left as they were. 11 The watch called out and announced the news to the king's household in the palace. 12 The king rose in the night and said to his staff, 'I shall tell you what the Aramaeans have done. They know we are starving, so they have left their camp to go and hide in the open country, expecting us to come out, and then they can take us alive and enter the city.' 13 One of his staff said, 'Send out a party of men with some of the horses that are left; if they live, they will be as well off as all the other Israelites who are still left; if they die, they will be no worse off than all those who have already perished. Let them go and see what has happened.' 14 They picked two mounted men, and the king dispatched them in the track of the Aramaean army with the order to go and find out what had happened. 15 Having followed as far as the Jordan and found the whole road littered with clothing and equipment which the Aramaeans had discarded in their haste, the messengers returned and made their report to the king.

16 The people went out and plundered the Aramaean camp, and a measure of flour was sold for a shekel and two measures of barley for a shekel, so that the word of the LORD came true. 17 The king had appointed the officer on whose arm he leaned to take charge of the gate, and the crowd trampled him to death there, just as the man of God had foretold when the king visited him. 18 For when the man of God said to the king, 'By this time tomorrow a shekel will buy two measures of barley or one measure of flour at the gate of Samaria,' 19 the officer had answered, 'Even if the LORD were to open windows in the sky, such a thing could not happen!' And the man of God had said, 'You will see it with your own eyes, but you will not eat any of it.' 20 This is what happened to him: he was trampled to death at the gate by the crowd.

8 Elisha said to the woman whose son he had restored to life, 'Go away at once with your household and find lodging where you can, for the LORD has decreed a seven years' famine and it has already come on the land.' 2 The woman acted at once on the word of the man of God and went away with her household to Philistine territory, where she stayed for seven years. 3 On her return at the end of that time she sought an audience of the king to beg for her house and land. 4 The king was questioning Gehazi, the servant of the man of God, about all the great things Elisha had done; 5 and, as he was describing to the king how he had brought the dead to life, the selfsame woman began her appeal to the king for her house and land. 'My lord king,' said Gehazi, 'this is the woman, and this is her son whom Elisha restored to life.' 6 The king questioned the woman, and she told him about it. Then he entrusted her case to an official, ordering him to restore all her property to her, together with all the revenues from her land from the time she left till that day.

7 Elisha came to Damascus, at a time when King Ben-hadad of Aram was ill; and when the king was told that the man of God had arrived, 8 he ordered Hazael to take a gift

---

w Compare Gk Syr Vg: Meaning of Heb uncertain

7:13 if they live . . . if they die: prob. rdg; Heb. obscure.
7:14 two mounted men: so Gk; Heb. two horse-chariots.
7:17 had foretold: so Syriac; Heb. adds which he had foretold.

8 After the lepers reached the edge of the camp, they went first into one tent, ate and drank, and took silver, gold, and clothing from it, and went out and hid them. Back they came into another tent, took things from it, and again went out and hid them. 9 Then they said to one another: "We are not doing right. This is a day of good news, and we are keeping silent. If we wait until morning breaks, we shall be blamed. Come, let us go and inform the palace."

10 They came and summoned the city gatekeepers. "We went to the camp of the Arameans," they said, "but no one was there—not a human voice, only the horses and asses tethered, and the tents just as they were left." 11 The gatekeepers announced this and it was reported within the palace. 12 Though it was night, the king got up; he said to his servants: "Let me tell you what the Arameans have done to us. Knowing that we are in famine, they have left their camp to hide in the field, hoping to take us alive and enter our city when we leave it." 13 One of his servants, however, suggested: "Since those who are left in the city are no better off than all the throng that has perished, let some of us take five of the abandoned horses and send scouts to investigate."

14 They took two chariots, and horses, and the king sent them to reconnoiter the Aramean army. "Go and find out," he ordered. 15 They followed the Arameans as far as the Jordan, and the whole route was strewn with garments and other objects that the Arameans had thrown away in their haste. The messengers returned and told the king. 16 The people went out and plundered the camp of the Arameans; and then a seah of fine flour sold for a shekel and two seahs of barley for a shekel, as the LORD had said.

17 The king put in charge of the gate the officer who was his adjutant; but the people trampled him to death at the gate, just as the man of God had predicted when the king visited him. 18 Thus was fulfilled the prophecy of the man of God to the king, "Two seahs of barley will sell for a shekel, and one seah of fine flour for a shekel at this time tomorrow at the gate of Samaria." 19 The adjutant had answered the man of God, "Even if the LORD were to make windows in heaven, how could this happen?" And Elisha has replied, "You shall see it with your own eyes, but you shall not eat of it." 20 And that is what happened to him, for the people trampled him to death at the gate.

8 Elisha once said to the woman whose son he had restored to life: "Get ready! Leave with your family and settle wherever you can, because the LORD has decreed a seven-year famine which is coming upon the land." 2 The woman got ready and did as the man of God said, setting out with her family and settling in the land of the Philistines for seven years. 3 At the end of the seven years, the woman returned from the land of the Philistines and went out to the king to claim her house and her field. 4 The king was talking with Gehazi, the servant of the man of God. "Tell me," he said, "all the great things that Elisha has done." 5 Just as he was relating to the king how his master had restored a dead person to life, the very woman whose son Elisha had restored to life came to the king to claim her house and field. "My lord king," Gehazi said, "this is the woman, and this is that son of hers whom Elisha restored to life." 6 The king questioned the woman, and she told him her story. With that the king placed an official at her disposal, saying, "Restore all her property to her, with all that the field produced from the day she left the land until now."

7 Elisha came to Damascus at a time when Ben-hadad, king of Aram, lay sick. When he was told that the man of God had come there, 8 the king said to Hazael, "Take a gift

disease, then, reached the confines of the camp. They went into one of the tents and ate and drank, and from it carried off silver and gold and clothing; these they took and hid. Then they came back and, entering another tent, looted it too, and took and hid their booty.

9 Then they said to one another, 'We are doing wrong. This is a day of good news, yet we are holding our tongues! If we wait till morning, we shall certainly be punished. Come on, let us go and take the news to the palace.' 10 Off they went and shouted out to the guards on the city gate, 'We have been to the Aramaean camp. There was not a soul there, no sound of anyone, only tethered horses and tethered donkeys, and their tents just as they were.' 11 The gatekeepers shouted the news, which was reported inside the palace. 12 The king got up while it was still dark and said to his officers, 'I can tell you what the Aramaeans have done to us. They know we are starving, so they have left the camp to hide in the open country. "They will come out of the city," they think, "we shall catch them alive and get into the city." ' 13 One of his officers replied, 'Five of the surviving horses still left us had better be taken—they would die in any case like all the rest. Let us send them and see.' 14 So they took two chariot teams and the king sent them after the Aramaean army, saying, 'Go and see.' 15 They followed them as far as the Jordan, finding the whole way strewn with clothes and gear which the Aramaeans had thrown away in their panic. The scouts returned and informed the king. 16 Then the people went out and plundered the Aramaean camp: a measure of finest flour sold for one shekel, and two measures of barley for one shekel, as Yahweh had promised they would. 17 The king had detailed the equerry, on whose arm he leaned, as commander of the guard on the gate, but the people trampled on him in the gateway and he died, as the man of God had foretold when the king had come down to him. 18 (What Elisha had said to the king came true, 'Two measures of barley will sell for one shekel, and a measure of finest flour for one shekel, by this time tomorrow at the gate of Samaria.' 19 And the equerry in question had replied to the man of God, 'Even if Yahweh made windows in the sky, could this word come true?' 'You will see it with your own eyes,' Elisha had answered, 'though you will eat none of it.' 20 And that was what happened to him: for the people trampled on him in the gateway and he died.)

8 Elisha had said to the woman whose son he had raised to life, 'Move away with your family, and live where you can in some foreign country, for Yahweh has called up a famine—it is already coming on the country—for seven years.' 2 The woman hurried to do what the man of God had told her: she set out, she and her family, and for seven years she lived in Philistine territory. 3 When the seven years were over, the woman returned from Philistine territory and went to lodge a claim with the king for her house and land.

4 Now the king was talking to Gehazi, the servant of the man of God. 'Tell me', he was saying, 'all about the marvels which Elisha did.' 5 Gehazi was just telling the king how Elisha had raised the dead child to life, when the woman whose son Elisha had raised lodged her claim with the king for her house and land. 'My lord king,' Gehazi said, 'this is the very woman, and that is her son whom Elisha raised to life.' 6 The king questioned the woman, who told him the story. The king then delegated one of the officials to her with this order, 'See that all her property is restored to her, and all the revenue from her land from the day she left the country until now.'

7 Elisha went to Damascus. Ben-Hadad king of Aram was ill, and was told, 'The man of God has come all the way to us.' 8 Then the king said to Hazael, 'Take a present with you

NEW REVISED STANDARD VERSION

you and go to meet the man of God. Inquire of the LORD through him, whether I shall recover from this illness." 9 So Hazael went to meet him, taking a present with him, all kinds of goods of Damascus, forty camel loads. When he entered and stood before him, he said, "Your son King Ben-hadad of Aram has sent me to you, saying, 'Shall I recover from this illness?' " 10 Elisha said to him, "Go, say to him, 'You shall certainly recover'; but the LORD has shown me that he shall certainly die." 11 He fixed his gaze and stared at him, until he was ashamed. Then the man of God wept. 12 Hazael asked, "Why does my lord weep?" He answered, "Because I know the evil that you will do to the people of Israel; you will set their fortresses on fire, you will kill their young men with the sword, dash in pieces their little ones, and rip up their pregnant women." 13 Hazael said, "What is your servant, who is a mere dog, that he should do this great thing?" Elisha answered, "The LORD has shown me that you are to be king over Aram." 14 Then he left Elisha, and went to his master Ben-hadad,*x* who said to him, "What did Elisha say to you?" And he answered, "He told me that you would certainly recover." 15 But the next day he took the bed-cover and dipped it in water and spread it over the king's face, until he died. And Hazael succeeded him.

16 In the fifth year of King Joram son of Ahab of Israel,*y* Jehoram son of King Jehoshaphat of Judah began to reign. 17 He was thirty-two years old when he became king, and he reigned eight years in Jerusalem. 18 He walked in the way of the kings of Israel, as the house of Ahab had done, for the daughter of Ahab was his wife. He did what was evil in the sight of the LORD. 19 Yet the LORD would not destroy Judah, for the sake of his servant David, since he had promised to give a lamp to him and to his descendants forever.

20 In his days Edom revolted against the rule of Judah, and set up a king of their own. 21 Then Joram crossed over to Zair with all his chariots. He set out by night and attacked the Edomites and their chariot commanders who had surrounded him;*z* but his army fled home. 22 So Edom has been in revolt against the rule of Judah to this day. Libnah also revolted at the same time. 23 Now the rest of the acts of Joram, and all that he did, are they not written in the Book of the Annals of the Kings of Judah? 24 So Joram slept with his ancestors, and was buried with them in the city of David; his son Ahaziah succeeded him.

25 In the twelfth year of King Joram son of Ahab of Israel, Ahaziah son of King Jehoram of Judah began to reign. 26 Ahaziah was twenty-two years old when he began to reign; he reigned one year in Jerusalem. His mother's name was Athaliah, a granddaughter of King Omri of Israel. 27 He also walked in the way of the house of Ahab, doing what was evil in the sight of the LORD, as the house of Ahab had done, for he was son-in-law to the house of Ahab.

28 He went with Joram son of Ahab to wage war against King Hazael of Aram at Ramoth-gilead, where the Arameans wounded Joram. 29 King Joram returned to be healed in Jezreel of the wounds that the Arameans had inflicted on him at Ramah, when he fought against King Hazael of Aram. King Ahaziah son of Jehoram of Judah went down to see Joram son of Ahab in Jezreel, because he was wounded.

9 Then the prophet Elisha called a member of the company of prophets*a* and said to him, "Gird up your loins; take this flask of oil in your hand, and go to Ramoth-

REVISED ENGLISH BIBLE

with him and go to the man of God and through him enquire of the LORD whether he would recover from his illness. 9 Hazael went, taking with him as a gift forty camel-loads of all kinds of Damascus wares. When he came into the prophet's presence, he said, 'Your son King Ben-hadad of Aram has sent me to you to ask whether he will recover from his illness.' 10 'Go and tell him that he will recover,' he answered; 'but the LORD has revealed to me that in fact he will die.' 11 The man of God stood staring with set face until Hazael became disconcerted; then the man of God wept. 12 'Why do you weep, sir?' said Hazael. He answered, 'Because I know the harm you will do to the Israelites: you will set their fortresses on fire and put their young men to the sword; you will dash their children to the ground and rip open their pregnant women.' 13 Hazael said, 'But I am a dog, a mere nobody; how can I do this great thing?' Elisha answered, 'The LORD has revealed to me that you will become king of Aram.' 14 Hazael left Elisha and returned to his master, who asked what Elisha had said. 'He told me that you would recover,' he replied. 15 But the next day he took a blanket and, after dipping it in water, laid it over the king's face, so that he died; and Hazael succeeded him.

16 In the fifth year of Jehoram son of King Ahab of Israel, Joram son of King Jehoshaphat of Judah became king. 17 He was thirty-two years old when he came to the throne, and he reigned in Jerusalem for eight years. 18 He followed the practices of the kings of Israel as the house of Ahab had done, for he had married Ahab's daughter; he did what was wrong in the eyes of the LORD. 19 Yet for his servant David's sake the LORD was unwilling to destroy Judah, as he had promised to give him and his descendants a lamp for all time.

20 During Joram's reign Edom revolted against Judah and set up its own king. 21 Joram with all his chariots pushed on to Zair. When the Edomites encircled him and his chariot-commanders he made a sortie by night, and broke out; his main force, however, fled to their homes. 22 To this day Edom has remained independent of Judah. Libnah also revolted at the same time. 23 The other acts and events of Joram's reign are recorded in the annals of the kings of Judah. 24 Joram rested with his forefathers and was buried with them in the city of David. His son Ahaziah succeeded him.

25 In the twelfth year of Jehoram son of Ahab king of Israel, Ahaziah son of King Joram of Judah became king. 26 Ahaziah was twenty-two years old when he came to the throne, and he reigned in Jerusalem for one year; his mother was Athaliah granddaughter of King Omri of Israel. 27 He followed the practices of the house of Ahab and did what was wrong in the eyes of the LORD like the house of Ahab, for he was connected with that house by marriage. 28 He allied himself with Jehoram son of Ahab to fight against King Hazael of Aram at Ramoth-gilead. But King Jehoram was wounded by the Aramaeans, 29 and retired to Jezreel to recover from the wounds inflicted on him at Ramoth in battle with King Hazael. Because of Jehoram's injury Ahaziah son of Joram king of Judah went down to Jezreel to visit him.

9 ELISHA the prophet summoned one of the company of prophets and said to him, 'Get ready for the road; take this flask of oil with you and go to Ramoth-gilead. 2 When

---

8:16 **King . . . Israel:** *so some Gk MSS; Heb. adds* and Jehoshaphat king of Judah. 8:17–22 *Cp.* 2 Chr. 21:5–10. 8:19 **him and:** *so many MSS; others omit.* 8:25–29 *Cp.* 2 Chr. 22:1–6. 8:26 **grand-daughter:** *lit.* daughter. 8:29 **Ramoth:** *so Gk; Heb.* Ramah.

---

x Heb lacks *Ben-hadad* *y* Gk Syr: Heb adds *Jehoshaphat being king of Judah,* *z* Meaning of Heb uncertain *a* Heb *sons of the prophets*

| NEW AMERICAN BIBLE | NEW JERUSALEM BIBLE |

with you and go call on the man of God. Have him consult the LORD as to whether I shall recover from this sickness." 9 Hazael went to visit him, carrying a present, and with forty camel loads of the best goods of Damascus. On his arrival, he stood before the prophet and said, "Your son Ben-hadad, king of Aram, has sent me to ask you whether he will recover from his sickness." 10 "Go and tell him," Elisha answered, "that he will surely recover. However, the LORD has showed me that he will in fact die." 11 Then he stared him down until Hazael became ill at ease. The man of God wept, 12 and Hazael asked, "Why are you weeping, my lord?" Elisha replied, "Because I know the evil that you will inflict upon the Israelites. You will burn their fortresses, you will slay their youth with the sword, you will dash their little children to pieces, you will rip open their pregnant women."

13 Hazael exclaimed, "How can a dog like me, your servant, do anything so important?" "The LORD has showed you to me as king over Aram," replied Elisha.

14 Hazael left Elisha and returned to his master. "What did Elisha tell you?" asked Ben-hadad. "He told me that you would surely recover," replied Hazael. 15 The next day, however, Hazael took a cloth, dipped it in water, and spread it over the king's face, so that he died. And Hazael reigned in his stead.

16 In the fifth year of Joram, son of Ahab, king of Israel, Jehoram, son of Jehoshaphat, king of Judah, became king. 17 He was thirty-two years old when he began to reign, and he reigned eight years in Jerusalem. 18 He conducted himself like the kings of Israel of the line of Ahab, since the sister of Ahab was his wife; and he did evil in the LORD's sight. 19 Even so, the LORD was unwilling to destroy Judah, because of his servant David. For he had promised David that he would leave him a lamp in the LORD's presence for all time. 20 During Jehoram's reign, Edom revolted against the sovereignty of Judah and chose a king of its own. 21 Thereupon Jehoram with all his chariots crossed over to Zair. He arose by night and broke through the Edomites when they had surrounded him and the commanders of his chariots. Then his army fled homeward. 22 To this day Edom has been in revolt against the rule of Judah. Libnah also revolted at that time. 23 The rest of the acts of Jehoram, with all that he did, are recorded in the book of the chronicles of the kings of Judah. 24 Jehoram rested with his ancestors and was buried with them in the City of David. His son Ahaziah succeeded him as king.

25 Ahaziah, son of Jehoram, king of Judah, became king in the twelfth year of Joram, son of Ahab, king of Israel. 26 He was twenty-two years old when he began his reign, and he reigned one year in Jerusalem. His mother's name was Athaliah; she was the daughter of Omri, king of Israel. 27 He conducted himself like the house of Ahab, doing evil in the LORD's sight as they did, since he was related to them by marriage. 28 He joined Joram, son of Ahab, in battle against Hazael, king of Aram, at Ramoth-gilead, where the Arameans wounded Joram. 29 King Joram returned to Jezreel to be healed of the wounds which the Arameans had inflicted on him at Ramah in his battle against Hazael, king of Aram. Then Ahaziah, son of Jehoram, king of Judah, went down to Jezreel to visit him there in his illness.

9 The prophet Elisha called one of the guild prophets and said to him: "Gird your loins, take this flask of oil with you, and go to Ramoth-gilead. 2 When you get there, look

and go and meet the man of God; consult Yahweh through him, and find out if I shall recover from my illness.' 9 So Hazael went to meet Elisha, taking with him as a present the best that Damascus could offer, a load for forty camels. He arrived and, presenting himself, said, 'Your son Ben-Hadad king of Aram has sent me to ask you, "Shall I recover from my illness?"' 10 Elisha replied, 'Go and tell him, "You might recover," though Yahweh has shown me that he will certainly die.' 11 Then the face of the man of God went rigid, and his look grew strangely fixed, and he wept. 12 'Why', Hazael asked, 'does my lord weep?' 'Because I know', Elisha replied, 'what harm you will do to the Israelites: you will burn down their fortresses, put their picked warriors to the sword, dash their little children to pieces, disembowel their pregnant women.' 13 'But what is your servant?' Hazael said. 'How could this dog achieve anything so great?' 'In a vision from Yahweh,' Elisha replied, 'I have seen you king of Aram.'

14 Leaving Elisha, Hazael went back to his master who asked, 'What did Elisha say to you?' He replied, 'He told me that you might recover.' 15 Next day he took a blanket, soaked it in water, and spread it over his face. So died Ben-Hadad, and Hazael succeeded him.

16 In the fifth year of Jehoram son of Ahab, king of Israel, Jehoram son of Jehoshaphat became king of Judah. 17 He was thirty-two years old when he came to the throne, and he reigned for eight years in Jerusalem. 18 He followed the example of the kings of Israel as the House of Ahab were doing; he had married one of Ahab's daughters; and he did what is displeasing to Yahweh. 19 But Yahweh was unwilling to destroy Judah, because of his servant David, and was faithful to the promise which he had made him to leave him a lamp for ever in his presence.

20 In his time Edom threw off the domination of Judah and set up a king for itself. 21 Jehoram crossed to Zair, and with him all the chariots . . . Under cover of dark, he and his chariot commanders broke through the Edomites surrounding him; the people fled to their tents. 22 Even so, Edom threw off the domination of Judah, remaining free to the present day. Libnah also revolted at that time.

23 The rest of the history of Jehoram, his entire career, is this not recorded in the Book of the Annals of the Kings of Judah? 24 Then Jehoram fell asleep with his ancestors and was buried with them in the City of David; his son Ahaziah succeeded him.

25 In the twelfth year of Jehoram son of Ahab, king of Israel, Ahaziah son of Jehoram, king of Judah, became king. 26 Ahaziah was twenty-two years old when he came to the throne, and he reigned for one year in Jerusalem. His mother's name was Athaliah granddaughter of Omri king of Israel. 27 He followed the example of the House of Ahab and did what is displeasing to Yahweh, as the House of Ahab were doing, to whom he was related by marriage.

28 He went with Jehoram son of Ahab to make war on Hazael king of Aram at Ramoth in Gilead, but the Aramaeans wounded Jehoram. 29 King Jehoram returned to Jezreel to recover from the wounds which he had received at Ramah, fighting against Hazael king of Aram. Ahaziah son of Jehoram, king of Judah, went down to Jezreel to visit Jehoram son of Ahab because he was ailing.

9 The prophet Elisha summoned a member of the prophetic brotherhood to him, 'Hitch up your clothes, take this flask of oil, and go to Ramoth in Gilead. 2 When you

gilead. 2 When you arrive, look there for Jehu son of Jehoshaphat, son of Nimshi; go in and get him to leave his
companions, and take him into an inner chamber. 3 Then
take the flask of oil, pour it on his head, and say, 'Thus says
the LORD: I anoint you king over Israel.' Then open the door
and flee; do not linger."

4 So the young man, the young prophet, went to
Ramoth-gilead. 5 He arrived while the commanders of the
army were in council, and he announced, "I have a message
for you, commander." "For which one of us?" asked Jehu.
"For you, commander." 6 So Jehu b got up and went inside;
the young man poured the oil on his head, saying to him,
"Thus says the LORD the God of Israel: I anoint you king
over the people of the LORD, over Israel. 7 You shall strike
down the house of your master Ahab, so that I may avenge
on Jezebel the blood of my servants the prophets, and the
blood of all the servants of the LORD. 8 For the whole house
of Ahab shall perish; I will cut off from Ahab every male,
bond or free, in Israel. 9 I will make the house of Ahab like
the house of Jeroboam son of Nebat, and like the house of
Baasha son of Ahijah. 10 The dogs shall eat Jezebel in the
territory of Jezreel, and no one shall bury her." Then he
opened the door and fled.

11 When Jehu came back to his master's officers, they
said to him, "Is everything all right? Why did that madman
come to you?" He answered them, "You know the sort and
how they babble." 12 They said, "Liar! Come on, tell us!"
So he said, "This is just what he said to me: 'Thus says the
LORD, I anoint you king over Israel.'" 13 Then hurriedly
they all took their cloaks and spread them for him on the
bare c steps; and they blew the trumpet, and proclaimed,
"Jehu is king."

14 Thus Jehu son of Jehoshaphat son of Nimshi conspired against Joram. Joram with all Israel had been on
guard at Ramoth-gilead against King Hazael of Aram; 15 but
King Joram had returned to be healed in Jezreel of the
wounds that the Arameans had inflicted on him, when he
fought against King Hazael of Aram. So Jehu said, "If this
is your wish, then let no one slip out of the city to go and
tell the news in Jezreel." 16 Then Jehu mounted his chariot
and went to Jezreel, where Joram was lying ill. King Ahaziah of Judah had come down to visit Joram.

17 In Jezreel, the sentinel standing on the tower spied
the company of Jehu arriving, and said, "I see a company."
Joram said, "Take a horseman; send him to meet them, and
let him say, 'Is it peace?'" 18 So the horseman went to meet
him; he said, "Thus says the king, 'Is it peace?'" Jehu
responded, "What have you to do with peace? Fall in behind
me." The sentinel reported, saying, "The messenger
reached them, but he is not coming back." 19 Then he sent
out a second horseman, who came to them and said, "Thus
says the king, 'Is it peace?'" Jehu answered, "What have
you to do with peace? Fall in behind me." 20 Again the
sentinel reported, "He reached them, but he is not coming
back. It looks like the driving of Jehu son of Nimshi; for he
drives like a maniac."

21 Joram said, "Get ready." And they got his chariot
ready. Then King Joram of Israel and King Ahaziah of
Judah set out, each in his chariot, and went to meet Jehu;
they met him at the property of Naboth the Jezreelite.
22 When Joram saw Jehu, he said, "Is it peace, Jehu?" He
answered, "What peace can there be, so long as the many
whoredoms and sorceries of your mother Jezebel continue?"
23 Then Joram reined about and fled, saying to Ahaziah,
"Treason, Ahaziah!" 24 Jehu drew his bow with all his
strength, and shot Joram between the shoulders, so that the
arrow pierced his heart; and he sank in his chariot. 25 Jehu

you arrive, look there for Jehu son of Jehoshaphat, son of
Nimshi; go in and call him aside from his fellow-officers,
and lead him through to an inner room. 3 Take the flask and
pour the oil on his head and say, "This is the word of the
LORD: I anoint you king over Israel." After that open the
door and flee for your life.'

4 The young prophet went to Ramoth-gilead, 5 and when
he arrived, he found the officers sitting together. He said,
'Sir, I have a word for you.' 'For which of us?' asked Jehu.
'For you, sir,' he said. 6 Jehu rose and went into the house,
where the prophet poured the oil on his head, saying, 'This
is the word of the LORD the God of Israel: I anoint you king
over Israel, the people of the LORD. 7 You are to strike down
the house of Ahab your master, and I shall take vengeance
on Jezebel for the blood of my servants the prophets and for
the blood of all the LORD's servants. 8 The entire house of
Ahab will perish; I shall destroy every mother's son of his
house in Israel, whether under the protection of the family
or not. 9 I shall make Ahab's house like the house of Jeroboam son of Nebat and the house of Baasha son of Ahijah.
10 Jezebel will be devoured by dogs in the plot of ground at
Jezreel and no one will bury her.' With that he opened the
door and fled.

11 When Jehu rejoined the king's officers, they said to
him, 'Is all well? What did this crazy fellow want with
you?' 'You know him and his ideas,' he said. 12 'That is no
answer!' they replied. 'Tell us what happened.' 'I shall tell
you exactly what he said: "This is the word of the LORD: I
anoint you king over Israel."' 13 They snatched up their
cloaks and spread them under him at the top of the steps,
and they sounded the trumpet and shouted, 'Jehu is king.'

14 Jehu son of Jehoshaphat, son of Nimshi, organized a
conspiracy against Jehoram, while Jehoram and all the Israelites were defending Ramoth-gilead against King Hazael of
Aram. 15 King Jehoram had returned to Jezreel to recover
from the wounds inflicted on him by the Aramaeans in his
battle against Hazael. Jehu said to his colleagues, 'If you
are on my side, see that no one escapes from the city to
carry the news to Jezreel.' 16 He mounted his chariot and
drove to Jezreel, for Jehoram was laid up there and King
Ahaziah of Judah had gone down to visit him.

17 The watchman standing on the watch-tower in Jezreel
saw Jehu's troops approaching and called out, 'I see a troop
of men.' Jehoram said, 'Fetch a horseman and send to meet
them and ask if they come peaceably.' 18 The horseman
went to meet him and said, 'The king asks, "Is it peace?"'
Jehu said, 'Peace? What is that to do with you? Fall in
behind me.' The watchman reported, 'The messenger has
met them but is not coming back.' 19 A second horseman
was sent; when he met them, he also said, 'The king asks,
"Is it peace?"' 'Peace?' said Jehu. 'What is that to do with
you? Fall in behind me.' 20 The watchman reported, 'He has
met them but is not coming back. The driving is like the
driving of Jehu son of Nimshi, for he drives furiously.'

21 'Harness my chariot,' said Jehoram. When it was ready
King Jehoram of Israel and King Ahaziah of Judah went out
each in his own chariot to meet Jehu, and they met him by
the plot of Naboth of Jezreel. 22 When Jehoram saw Jehu,
he said, 'Is it peace, Jehu?' He replied, 'Do you call it peace
while your mother Jezebel keeps up her obscene idol-worship and monstrous sorceries?' 23 Jehoram wheeled about
and fled, crying out, 'Treachery, Ahaziah!' 24 Jehu drew his
bow and shot Jehoram between the shoulders; the arrow
pierced his heart and he slumped down in his chariot.

b Heb he   c Meaning of Heb uncertain

9:15 **on my side:** so Gk; Heb. omits.   9:20 **son:** or grandson (cp.
verse 2).

for Jehu, son of Jehoshaphat, son of Nimshi. Enter and take him away from his companions into an inner chamber. ³From the flask you have, pour oil on his head, and say, 'Thus says the LORD: I anoint you king over Israel.' Then open the door and flee without delay." ⁴The young man (the guild prophet) went to Ramoth-gilead. ⁵When he arrived, the commanders of the army were in session. "I have a message for you, commander," he said. "For which one of us?" asked Jehu. "For you, commander," he answered. ⁶Jehu got up and went into the house. Then the young man poured the oil on his head and said, "Thus says the LORD, the God of Israel: 'I anoint you king over the people of the LORD, over Israel. ⁷You shall destroy the house of Ahab your master; thus will I avenge the blood of my servants the prophets, and the blood of all the other servants of the LORD shed by Jezebel, ⁸and by all the rest of the family of Ahab. I will cut off every male in Ahab's line, whether slave or freeman in Israel. ⁹I will deal with the house of Ahab as I dealt with the house of Jeroboam, son of Nebat, and with the house of Baasha, son of Ahijah. ¹⁰Dogs shall devour Jezebel at the confines of Jezreel, so that no one can bury her.' " Then he opened the door and fled.

¹¹When Jehu rejoined his master's servants, they asked him, "Is all well? Why did that madman come to you?" "You know that kind of man and his talk," he replied. ¹²But they said, "Not at all! Come, tell us." So he told them what the young man had said to him, and finally, "Thus says the LORD: 'I anoint you king over Israel.' " ¹³At once each took his garment, spread it under Jehu on the bare steps, blew the trumpet, and cried out, "Jehu is king!"

¹⁴Thus Jehu, son of Jehoshaphat, son of Nimshi, formed a conspiracy against Joram. Joram, with all Israel, had been besieging Ramoth-gilead against Hazael, king of Aram, ¹⁵but had returned to Jezreel to be healed of the wounds the Arameans had inflicted on him in the battle against Hazael, king of Aram.

"If you are truly with me," Jehu said, "see that no one escapes from the city to report in Jezreel." ¹⁶Then Jehu mounted his chariot and drove to Jezreel, where Joram lay ill and Ahaziah, king of Judah, had come to visit him.

¹⁷The watchman standing on the tower in Jezreel saw the troop of Jehu coming and reported, "I see chariots." "Get a driver," Joram said, "and send him to meet them and to ask whether all is well." ¹⁸So a driver went out to meet him and said, "The king asks whether all is well." "What does it matter to you how things are?" Jehu said. "Get behind me." The watchman reported to the king, "The messenger has reached them, but is not returning."

¹⁹Joram sent a second driver, who went to them and said, "The king asks whether all is well." "What does it matter to you how things are?" Jehu replied. "Get behind me."

²⁰The watchman reported, "The messenger has reached them, but is not returning. The driving is like that of Jehu, son of Nimshi, in its fury." ²¹"Prepare my chariot," said Joram. When they had done so, Joram, king of Israel, and Ahaziah, king of Judah, set out, each in his own chariot, to meet Jehu. They reached him near the field of Naboth the Jezreelite. ²²When Joram recognized Jehu, he asked, "Is all well, Jehu?" "How can all be well," Jehu replied, "as long as the many fornications and witchcrafts of your mother Jezebel continue?" ²³Joram reined about and fled, crying to Ahaziah, "Treason, Ahaziah!" ²⁴But Jehu drew his bow and shot Joram between the shoulders, so that the arrow went through his heart and he collapsed in his chariot.

arrive there, look for Jehu son of Jehoshaphat, son of Nimshi. Then, when you find him, tell him to get up and leave his companions, and take him into an inner room. ³Take the flask of oil then and pour it over his head, and say, "Yahweh says this: I have anointed you king of Israel." Then open the door and flee as fast as you can.'

⁴The young man left for Ramoth in Gilead ⁵and when he arrived, found the senior officers of the army sitting together. 'I have a message for you, commander,' he said. 'For which of us?' asked Jehu. 'For you, commander,' he answered. ⁶Jehu then got up and went into the house. And the young man poured the oil on his head, saying, 'Yahweh, God of Israel, says this, "I have anointed you king of Yahweh's people, of Israel. ⁷You will strike down the family of Ahab your master, and I shall avenge the blood of my servants the prophets and all of Yahweh's servants, on Jezebel ⁸and on the whole family of Ahab. I shall destroy every manjack of Ahab's family, fettered or free in Israel. ⁹I shall make the House of Ahab like the House of Jeroboam son of Nebat and of Baasha son of Ahijah. ¹⁰As for Jezebel, the dogs will eat her in the field of Jezreel; no one will bury her." ' With this, he opened the door and made his escape.

¹¹Jehu came out to his master's officers. 'Is all well?' they asked him. 'Why did this madman come to you?' 'You know the fellow and how he talks,' he answered. ¹²'Evasion!' they cried, 'Come on, tell us.' He replied, 'He said this and that to me. He said, "Yahweh says this: I have anointed you king of Israel." ' ¹³Whereupon they all took their cloaks and spread them under him on the bare steps; they sounded the trumpet and shouted, 'Jehu is king!'

¹⁴Jehu son of Jehoshaphat, son of Nimshi plotted against Jehoram. (At the time, Jehoram, with all Israel, was holding Ramoth in Gilead against an attack by Hazael king of Aram, ¹⁵but King Jehoram had gone back to Jezreel to recover from the wounds which he had received from the Aramaeans while he was fighting against Hazael king of Aram.) 'If you agree,' Jehu said, 'let no one leave the town to go and take the news to Jezreel.' ¹⁶Jehu then mounted his chariot and left for Jezreel; Jehoram had taken to his bed there, and Ahaziah king of Judah had gone down to visit him.

¹⁷The lookout posted on the tower of Jezreel saw Jehu's troop approaching. 'I can see a body of men,' he shouted. Jehoram gave the order: 'Have a horseman sent to meet them and ask, "Is all well?" ' ¹⁸The horseman went to meet Jehu and said, 'The king says, "Is all well?" ' 'What has it to do with you whether all is well?' Jehu replied, 'Fall in behind me.' The lookout reported, 'The messenger has reached them and is not coming back.' ¹⁹The king sent a second horseman who reached them and said, 'The king says, "Is all well?" ' 'What has it to do with you whether all is well?' Jehu replied. 'Fall in behind me.' ²⁰The lookout reported, 'He has reached them and is not coming back. The manner of driving is like that of Jehu son of Nimshi: he drives like a madman.' ²¹'Harness!' Jehoram cried; and they harnessed his chariot. Then Jehoram king of Israel and Ahaziah king of Judah, each in his chariot, set out to meet Jehu. They reached him in the field of Naboth of Jezreel.

²²As soon as Jehoram saw Jehu he asked, 'Is all well, Jehu?' 'What a question!' he replied, 'when all the while the prostitutions and countless sorceries of your mother Jezebel go on.' ²³At this, Jehoram wheeled and fled, saying to Ahaziah, 'Treason, Ahaziah!' ²⁴But Jehu had drawn his bow; he struck Jehoram between the shoulder-blades, the arrow went through the king's heart, and he sank down in

said to his aide Bidkar, "Lift him out, and throw him on the plot of ground belonging to Naboth the Jezreelite; for remember, when you and I rode side by side behind his father Ahab how the LORD uttered this oracle against him: 26 'For the blood of Naboth and for the blood of his children that I saw yesterday, says the LORD, I swear I will repay you on this very plot of ground.' Now therefore lift him out and throw him on the plot of ground, in accordance with the word of the LORD."

27 When King Ahaziah of Judah saw this, he fled in the direction of Beth-haggan. Jehu pursued him, saying, "Shoot him also!" And they shot him*d* in the chariot at the ascent to Gur, which is by Ibleam. Then he fled to Megiddo, and died there. 28 His officers carried him in a chariot to Jerusalem, and buried him in his tomb with his ancestors in the city of David.

29 In the eleventh year of Joram son of Ahab, Ahaziah began to reign over Judah.

30 When Jehu came to Jezreel, Jezebel heard of it; she painted her eyes, and adorned her head, and looked out of the window. 31 As Jehu entered the gate, she said, "Is it peace, Zimri, murderer of your master?" 32 He looked up to the window and said, "Who is on my side? Who?" Two or three eunuchs looked out at him. 33 He said, "Throw her down." So they threw her down; some of her blood spattered on the wall and on the horses, which trampled on her. 34 Then he went in and ate and drank; he said, "See to that cursed woman and bury her; for she is a king's daughter." 35 But when they went to bury her, they found no more of her than the skull and the feet and the palms of her hands. 36 When they came back and told him, he said, "This is the word of the LORD, which he spoke by his servant Elijah the Tishbite, 'In the territory of Jezreel the dogs shall eat the flesh of Jezebel; 37 the corpse of Jezebel shall be like dung on the field in the territory of Jezreel, so that no one can say, This is Jezebel.' "

10 Now Ahab had seventy sons in Samaria. So Jehu wrote letters and sent them to Samaria, to the rulers of Jezreel,*e* to the elders, and to the guardians of the sons of*f* Ahab, saying, 2 "Since your master's sons are with you and you have at your disposal chariots and horses, a fortified city, and weapons, 3 select the son of your master who is the best qualified, set him on his father's throne, and fight for your master's house." 4 But they were utterly terrified and said, "Look, two kings could not withstand him; how then can we stand?" 5 So the steward of the palace, and the governor of the city, along with the elders and the guardians, sent word to Jehu: "We are your servants; we will do anything you say. We will not make anyone king; do whatever you think right." 6 Then he wrote them a second letter, saying, "If you are on my side, and if you are ready to obey me, take the heads of your master's sons and come to me at Jezreel tomorrow at this time." Now the king's sons, seventy persons, were with the leaders of the city, who were charged with their upbringing. 7 When the letter reached them, they took the king's sons and killed them, seventy persons; they put their heads in baskets and sent them to him at Jezreel. 8 When the messenger came and told him, "They have brought the heads of the king's sons," he said, "Lay them in two heaps at the entrance of the gate until the

25 Jehu said to Bidkar, his lieutenant, 'Pick him up and throw him into the plot of land belonging to Naboth of Jezreel; remember how, when you and I were riding side by side behind Ahab his father, the LORD pronounced this sentence against him: 26 "It is the word of the LORD: as surely as I saw yesterday the blood of Naboth and the blood of his sons, I will requite you on this plot of land." Pick him up, therefore, and throw him into the plot and so fulfil the word of the LORD.' 27 When King Ahaziah of Judah saw this he fled by the road to Beth-haggan. Jehu pursued him and said, 'Get him too.' They shot him down in his chariot on the road up the valley near Ibleam, but he escaped to Megiddo and died there. 28 His servants conveyed his body to Jerusalem by chariot and buried him in his tomb with his forefathers in the city of David.

29 It was in the eleventh year of Jehoram son of Ahab that Ahaziah became king over Judah.

30 Then Jehu came to Jezreel. When Jezebel heard what had happened she painted her eyes and adorned her hair, and she stood looking down from a window. 31 As Jehu entered the gate, she said, 'Is it peace, you Zimri, you murderer of your master?' 32 He looked up at the window and said, 'Who is on my side? Who?' Two or three eunuchs looked out to him, 33 and he said, 'Throw her down.' They threw her down, and some of her blood splashed on to the wall and the horses, which trampled her underfoot. 34 Jehu went in and ate and drank. 'See to this accursed woman,' he said, 'and bury her; for she is a king's daughter.' 35 But when they went to bury her they found nothing of her but the skull, the feet, and the palms of her hands. 36 When they went back and told him, Jehu said, 'It is the word of the LORD which his servant Elijah the Tishbite spoke, when he said, "In the plot of ground at Jezreel the dogs will devour the flesh of Jezebel, 37 and Jezebel's corpse will lie like dung on the ground in the plot at Jezreel so that no one will be able to say: This is Jezebel." '

10 There were seventy sons of Ahab left in Samaria. Jehu therefore sent a letter to Samaria, addressed to the rulers of the city, the elders, and the guardians of Ahab's sons, in which he wrote: 2 'You have in your care your master's family as well as his chariots and horses, fortified cities, and weapons; therefore, whenever this letter reaches you, 3 choose the best and the most suitable of your master's sons, set him on his father's throne, and fight for your master's house.' 4 They were panic-stricken and said, 'If two kings could not stand against him, what hope is there that we can?' 5 Therefore the comptroller of the household and the governor of the city, with the elders and the children's guardians, sent this message to Jehu: 'We are your servants. Whatever you tell us we shall do; but we shall not make anyone king. Do as you think fit.'

6 So in a second letter to them Jehu wrote: 'If you are on my side and will obey my orders, then bring the heads of your master's sons to me at Jezreel by this time tomorrow.' The royal princes, seventy in all, were with the nobles of the city who had charge of their upbringing. 7 When the letter arrived, they took the royal princes and killed all seventy; they piled their heads in baskets and sent the heads to Jehu in Jezreel. 8 When the messenger came to him and reported that they had brought the heads of the royal princes, he ordered them to be piled in two heaps and left till morning at the entrance to the city gate.

9:27 They . . . down: so Syriac; Heb. omits. the valley: prob. rdg; Heb. to Gur.   10:1 of the city: so Gk (Luc.); Heb. of Jezreel. Ahab's sons: so some Gk MSS; Heb. omits sons.   10:2 cities: so some MSS; others city.   10:6 the heads of: so Gk (Luc.); Heb. adds the men of.

---

d Syr Vg Compare Gk: Heb lacks *and they shot him*   *e* Or *of the city*; Vg Compare Gk   *f* Gk: Heb lacks *of the sons of*

25 Then Jehu said to his adjutant Bidkar, "Take him and throw him into the field of Naboth the Jezreelite. For I remember that when we were driving teams behind his father Ahab, the LORD delivered this oracle against him: 26 'As surely as I saw yesterday the blood of Naboth and the blood of his sons,' says the LORD, 'I will repay you for it in that very plot of ground, says the LORD.' So now take him into this plot of ground, in keeping with the word of the LORD."

27 Seeing what was happening, Ahaziah, king of Judah, fled toward Beth-haggan. Jehu pursued him, shouting, "Kill him too!" And they pierced him as he rode through the pass of Gur near Ibleam. He continued his flight as far as Megiddo and died there. 28 His servants brought him in a chariot to Jerusalem and buried him in the tomb of his ancestors in the City of David. 29 Ahaziah had become king of Judah in the eleventh year of Joram, son of Ahab.

30 When Jezebel learned that Jehu had arrived in Jezreel, she shadowed her eyes, adorned her hair, and looked down from her window. 31 As Jehu came through the gate, she cried out, "Is all well, Zimri, murderer of your master?" 32 Jehu looked up to the window and shouted, "Who is on my side? Anyone?" At this, two or three eunuchs looked down toward him. 33 "Throw her down," he ordered. They threw her down, and some of her blood spurted against the wall and against the horses. Jehu rode in over her body 34 and, after eating and drinking, he said: "Attend to that accursed woman and bury her; after all, she was a king's daughter." 35 But when they went to bury her, they found nothing of her but the skull, the feet, and the hands. 36 They returned to Jehu, and when they told him, he said, "This is the sentence which the LORD pronounced through his servant Elijah the Tishbite: 'In the confines of Jezreel dogs shall eat the flesh of Jezebel. 37 The corpse of Jezebel shall be like dung in the field in the confines of Jezreel, so that no one can say: This was Jezebel.' "

10 Ahab had seventy descendants in Samaria. Jehu prepared letters and sent them to the city rulers, to the elders, and to the guardians of Ahab's descendants in Samaria. 2 "Since your master's sons are with you," he wrote, "and you have the chariots, the horses, a fortified city, and the weapons, when this letter reaches you 3 decide which is the best and the fittest of your master's offspring, place him on his father's throne, and fight for your master's house." 4 They were overcome with fright and said, "If two kings could not withstand him, how can we?" 5 So the vizier and the ruler of the city, along with the elders and the guardians, sent this message to Jehu: "We are your servants, and we will do everything you tell us. We will proclaim no one king; do whatever you think best." 6 So Jehu wrote them a second letter: "If you are on my side and will obey me, count the heads of your master's sons and come to me in Jezreel at this time tomorrow." [The seventy princes were in the care of prominent men of the city, who were rearing them.]

7 When the letter arrived, they took the princes and slew all seventy of them, put their heads in baskets, and sent them to Jehu in Jezreel. 8 "They have brought the heads of the princes," a messenger came in and told him. "Pile them in two heaps at the entrance of the city until morning," he

his chariot. 25 'Pick him up,' Jehu said to Bidkar, his equerry, 'and throw him into the field of Naboth of Jezreel. Remember how, when you and I manned a chariot together behind Ahab his father, Yahweh pronounced this sentence against him, d 26 "This I swear. Yesterday I saw the blood of Naboth and the blood of his sons — Yahweh says this. And in this same field I shall requite you — Yahweh says this." So pick him up, and throw him into the field, as Yahweh declared should happen!'

27 When Ahaziah king of Judah saw this, he fled along the Beth-ha-Gan road, but Jehu went in pursuit of him. 'Strike him down too,' he said. And they wounded him in his chariot at the slope of Gur, which is near Ibleam, and he took refuge in Megiddo, where he died. 28 His servants carried him in a chariot to Jerusalem and buried him in his tomb in the City of David. 29 Ahaziah had become king of Judah in the eleventh year of Jehoram son of Ahab.

30 When Jehu went back to Jezreel, Jezebel was told. She made up her eyes with mascara, adorned her head and appeared at the window. 31 As Jehu came through the gateway she said, 'How did Zimri get on after killing his master?' 32 Jehu looked up to the window and said, 'Who is on my side? Who?' And two or three officials looked down at him. 33 'Throw her down,' he said. They threw her down and her blood spattered the walls and the horses; and Jehu rode over her. 34 He went in and ate and drank, then said, 'See to this accursed woman, and give her burial; after all, she was a king's daughter.' 35 But when they went to bury her, they found nothing but her skull, feet and hands. 36 They came back and told Jehu, who said, 'This is the word of Yahweh which he spoke through his servant Elijah the Tishbite, "The dogs will eat the flesh of Jezebel in the field of Jezreel; 37 the corpse of Jezebel will be like dung spread on the fields, so that no one will be able to say: This was Jezebel." '

10 There were seventy of Ahab's sons in Samaria. Jehu sent to Samaria, to the authorities of the city, to the elders and to the guardians of Ahab's children. He said, 2 'Now, when this letter reaches you, you have your master's sons with you; you also have chariots and horses, a fortified city and weapons. 3 See which of your master's sons is the best and worthiest, put him on his father's throne and fight for your master's dynasty!' 4 They were utterly terrified. 'We have seen how the two kings could not stand up to him,' they said, 'so how could we?' 5 Consequently the master of the palace, the governor of the city, the elders and the guardians sent word to Jehu, 'We are your servants. We shall do whatever you order us. We shall not proclaim a king; act as you think best.'

6 Jehu then wrote them a second letter. He said, 'If you are for me and if you are prepared to accept orders from me, take the heads of the men of your master's family and come to me at Jezreel by this time tomorrow.' (There were seventy of Ahab's sons being educated there by the leading men of the city.) 7 When this letter reached them, they took the king's sons and butchered all seventy of them, put their heads in baskets and sent them to him at Jezreel.

8 The messenger came and told Jehu, 'They have brought the heads of the king's sons.' 'Leave them in two heaps at the entrance to the gate until morning,' he replied. 9 When

d 9 // 1 K 21:19.

morning." 9 Then in the morning when he went out, he stood and said to all the people, "You are innocent. It was I who conspired against my master and killed him; but who struck down all these? 10 Know then that there shall fall to the earth nothing of the word of the LORD, which the LORD spoke concerning the house of Ahab; for the LORD has done what he said through his servant Elijah." 11 So Jehu killed all who were left of the house of Ahab in Jezreel, all his leaders, close friends, and priests, until he left him no survivor.

12 Then he set out and went to Samaria. On the way, when he was at Beth-eked of the Shepherds, 13 Jehu met relatives of King Ahaziah of Judah and said, "Who are you?" They answered, "We are kin of Ahaziah; we have come down to visit the royal princes and the sons of the queen mother." 14 He said, "Take them alive." They took them alive, and slaughtered them at the pit of Beth-eked, forty-two in all; he spared none of them.

15 When he left there, he met Jehonadab son of Rechab coming to meet him; he greeted him, and said to him, "Is your heart as true to mine as mine is to yours?"g Jehonadab answered, "It is." Jehu said,h "If it is, give me your hand." So he gave him his hand. Jehu took him up with him into the chariot. 16 He said, "Come with me, and see my zeal for the LORD." So hei had him ride in his chariot. 17 When he came to Samaria, he killed all who were left to Ahab in Samaria, until he had wiped them out, according to the word of the LORD that he spoke to Elijah.

18 Then Jehu assembled all the people and said to them, "Ahab offered Baal small service; but Jehu will offer much more. 19 Now therefore summon to me all the prophets of Baal, all his worshipers, and all his priests; let none be missing, for I have a great sacrifice to offer to Baal; whoever is missing shall not live." But Jehu was acting with cunning in order to destroy the worshipers of Baal. 20 Jehu decreed, "Sanctify a solemn assembly for Baal." So they proclaimed it. 21 Jehu sent word throughout all Israel; all the worshipers of Baal came, so that there was no one left who did not come. They entered the temple of Baal, until the temple of Baal was filled from wall to wall. 22 He said to the keeper of the wardrobe, "Bring out the vestments for all the worshipers of Baal." So he brought out the vestments for them. 23 Then Jehu entered the temple of Baal with Jehonadab son of Rechab; he said to the worshipers of Baal, "Search and see that there is no worshiper of the LORD here among you, but only worshipers of Baal." 24 Then they proceeded to offer sacrifices and burnt offerings.

Now Jehu had stationed eighty men outside, saying, "Whoever allows any of those to escape whom I deliver into your hands shall forfeit his life." 25 As soon as he had finished presenting the burnt offering, Jehu said to the guards and to the officers, "Come in and kill them; let no one escape." So they put them to the sword. The guards and the officers threw them out, and then went into the citadel of the temple of Baal. 26 They brought out the pillarj that was in the temple of Baal, and burned it. 27 Then they demolished the pillar of Baal, and destroyed the temple of Baal, and made it a latrine to this day.

28 Thus Jehu wiped out Baal from Israel. 29 But Jehu did not turn aside from the sins of Jeroboam son of Nebat, which he caused Israel to commit — the golden calves that were in Bethel and in Dan. 30 The LORD said to Jehu, "Be-

9 In the morning Jehu went out, and standing there said to all the people, 'You are fair-minded judges. I conspired against my master and killed him, but who put all these to death? 10 Be sure then that every word which the LORD has spoken against the house of Ahab will be fulfilled, and that the LORD has now done what he promised through his servant Elijah.' 11 So Jehu put to death all who were left of the house of Ahab in Jezreel, as well as all Ahab's nobles, his close friends, and priests, until he had left not one survivor.

12 Then he set out for Samaria, and on the way there, when he had reached a shepherds' shelter, 13 he came upon the kinsmen of King Ahaziah of Judah and demanded to know who they were. 'We are kinsmen of Ahaziah,' they replied, 'and we have come down to pay our respects to the families of the king and of the queen mother.' 14 'Take them alive,' he said. They were taken alive, all forty-two of them, then slain, and flung into a pit that was there; he did not leave a single survivor.

15 When he had left that place, he found Jehonadab son of Rechab coming to meet him. Jehu greeted him and said, 'Are you with me wholeheartedly, as I am with you?' 'I am,' replied Jehonadab. 'Then if you are,' said Jehu, 'give me your hand,' and he did so. Jehu had him come up into his chariot. 16 'Come with me,' he said, 'and you will see my zeal for the LORD.' So he took him with him in his chariot. 17 When he came to Samaria, he put to death all of Ahab's house who were left there and so blotted it out, in fulfilment of the word which the LORD had spoken to Elijah.

18 Jehu called all the people together and said to them, 'Ahab served the Baal a little; Jehu will serve him much. 19 Now summon all the prophets of Baal, all his ministers and priests; not one must be missing. For I am holding a great sacrifice to Baal, and no one who is missing from it shall live.' In this way Jehu outwitted the ministers of Baal in order to destroy them. 20 Jehu gave the order, 'Proclaim a sacred ceremony for Baal.' This was done, 21 and Jehu himself sent word throughout Israel. All the ministers of Baal came; there was not a man left who did not come, and when they went into the temple of Baal, it was filled from end to end. 22 Jehu said to the person who had charge of the wardrobe, 'Bring out robes for all the ministers of Baal'; and he brought them out. 23 Then Jehu and Jehonadab son of Rechab went into the temple of Baal and said to the ministers, 'Look carefully and make sure that there are no servants of the LORD here with you, but only the ministers of Baal.' 24 Then they went in to offer sacrifices and whole-offerings.

Jehu had stationed eighty of his men outside and warned them, 'I shall hold you responsible for these men, and if anyone of you lets one of them escape he will pay for it with his own life.' 25 When he had finished offering the whole-offering, Jehu ordered the guards and officers to go in and cut them all down, and let not one of them escape. They were slain without quarter, and the guard and the officers threw them out. Then going into the keep of the temple of Baal, 26 they brought out the sacred pole from the temple and burnt it; 27 they overthrew the sacred pillar of the Baal and pulled down the temple itself and made a privy of it — as it is today. 28 Thus Jehu stamped out the worship of Baal in Israel. 29 He did not however abandon the sins of Jeroboam son of Nebat who led Israel into sin: he maintained the worship of the golden calves of Bethel and Dan.

---

g Gk: Heb Is it right with your heart, as my heart is with your heart? h Gk: Heb lacks Jehu said i Gk Syr Tg: Heb they j Gk Vg Syr Tg: Heb pillars

10:12 a shepherds' shelter: or Beth-eked of the Shepherds. 10:15 said Jehu: so Gk; Heb. omits. 10:16 he took: so Gk; Heb. they took. 10:26 sacred pole: prob. rdg; Heb. sacred pillars.

ordered. 9 Going out in the morning, he stopped and said to all the people: "You are not responsible, and although I conspired against my lord and slew him, yet who killed all these? 10 Know that not a single word which the LORD has spoken against the house of Ahab shall go unfulfilled. The LORD has accomplished all that he foretold through his servant Elijah." 11 Thereupon Jehu slew all who were left of the family of Ahab in Jezreel, as well as all his powerful supporters, intimates, and priests, leaving him no survivor.

12 Then he set out for Samaria, and at Beth-eked-haroim on the way, 13 he came across kinsmen of Ahaziah, king of Judah. "Who are you?" he asked. "We are kinsmen of Ahaziah," they replied. "We are going down to visit the princes and the family of the queen mother." 14 "Take them alive," Jehu ordered. They were taken alive, forty-two in number, then slain at the pit of Beth-eked. Not one of them was spared.

15 When he had left there, Jehu met Jehonadab, son of Rechab, on the road. He greeted him and asked, "Are you sincerely disposed toward me, as I am toward you?" "Yes," replied Jehonadab. "If you are," continued Jehu, "give me your hand." Jehonadab gave him his hand, and Jehu drew him up into his chariot. 16 "Come with me," he said, "and see my zeal for the LORD." And he took him along in his own chariot.

17 When he arrived in Samaria, Jehu slew all who remained there of Ahab's line, doing away with them completely and thus fulfilling the prophecy which the LORD had spoken to Elijah.

18 Jehu gathered all the people together and said to them: "Ahab served Baal to some extent, but Jehu will serve him yet more. 19 Now summon for me all Baal's prophets, all his worshipers, and all his priests. See that no one is absent, for I have a great sacrifice for Baal. Whoever is absent shall not live." This Jehu did as a trick, so that he might destroy the worshipers of Baal. 20 Jehu said further, "Proclaim a solemn assembly in honor of Baal." They did so, 21 and Jehu sent word of it throughout the land of Israel. All the worshipers of Baal without exception came into the temple of Baal, which was filled to capacity. 22 Then Jehu said to the custodian of the wardrobe, "Bring out the garments for all the worshipers of Baal." When he had brought out the garments for them, 23 Jehu, with Jehonadab, son of Rechab, entered the temple of Baal and said to the worshipers of Baal, "Search and be sure that there is no worshiper of the LORD here with you, but only worshipers of Baal." 24 Then they proceeded to offer sacrifices and holocausts. Now Jehu had stationed eighty men outside with this warning, "If one of you lets anyone escape of those whom I shall deliver into your hands, he shall pay for it with his life." 25 As soon as he finished offering the holocaust, Jehu said to the guards and officers, "Go in and slay them. Let no one escape." So the guards and officers put them to the sword and cast them out. Afterward they went into the inner shrine of the temple of Baal, 26 took out the stele of Baal, and burned the shrine. 27 Then they smashed the stele of Baal, tore down the building, and turned it into a latrine, as it remains today.

28 Thus Jehu rooted out the worship of Baal from Israel. 29 However, he did not desist from the sins which Jeroboam, son of Nebat, had caused Israel to commit, as regards the golden calves at Bethel and at Dan. 30 The LORD

morning came, he went out and, standing, said to all the people, 'No guilt attaches to you! I did indeed plot against my master and have killed him; but what about all these? Who struck them? 10 Know, then, that nothing will fail to be fulfilled of the prophecy uttered by Yahweh against the House of Ahab; Yahweh has done what he said through his servant Elijah.' 11 Jehu then killed every member of the House of Ahab surviving in Jezreel, all his leading men, his close friends, his priests; he did not leave a single one alive.

12 Jehu then set out for Samaria. As he was on his way, at Beth-Eked of the Shepherds, 13 he met the brothers of Ahaziah king of Judah. 'Who are you?' he asked. 'We are Ahaziah's brothers,' they replied, 'and we are on our way to pay our respects to the king's sons and the queen mother's sons.' 14 'Take them alive,' he said. They took them alive, and he slaughtered them at the storage-well of Beth-Eked, forty-two of them; he did not spare a single one.

15 Leaving there, he came on Jehonadab son of Rechab who was on his way to meet him. He greeted him and said, 'Is your heart true to mine, as my heart is to yours?' Jehonadab replied, 'Yes.' 'If so,' Jehu said, 'give me your hand.' Jehonadab gave him his hand, and Jehu took him up beside him in his chariot. 16 'Come with me,' he said, 'and witness my zeal for Yahweh,' and took him along in his chariot. 17 When he entered Samaria, he killed all the survivors of Ahab's family there; he destroyed it, as Yahweh had told Elijah it would happen.

18 Then Jehu assembled all the people. 'Ahab did Baal some small service,' he said, 'but Jehu will do him a great one. 19 Now call me all the prophets of Baal and all his priests. Not one is to be absent: I have a great sacrifice to offer to Baal. If anyone is absent, he will forfeit his life.' This was a trick on Jehu's part to destroy the devotees of Baal. 20 'Summon a sacred assembly for Baal,' he commanded; and they summoned it. 21 Jehu sent messengers throughout Israel, and all the devotees of Baal arrived, not a man was left who did not attend. They crowded into the temple of Baal until it was full from wall to wall. 22 Jehu then said to the keeper of the wardrobe, 'Bring out vestments for all the devotees of Baal'; he brought out the vestments for them. 23 Jehu then went into the temple of Baal with Jehonadab son of Rechab and said to Baal's devotees, 'Make quite sure that there are no devotees of Yahweh in here with you, but only devotees of Baal.' 24 He then proceeded to present sacrifices and burnt offerings.

Now Jehu had stationed eighty of his men outside, having said, 'Whoever lets one of the people go whom I am now putting within your clutches, will pay for it with his life.' 25 When he had finished making the burnt offering, he gave the order to the guards and equerries, 'Go in, strike them down! Let no one out!' The guards and equerries went in, putting everyone to the sword all the way to the sanctuary of Baal's temple. 26 They took the sacred pole out of Baal's temple and burned it. 27 They demolished Baal's image and demolished Baal's temple too, making it into a latrine, which it still is today.

28 Thus Jehu rid Israel of Baal. 29 Even so, Jehu did not give up the sins into which Jeroboam son of Nebat had led Israel, the golden calves of Bethel and Dan. 30 Yahweh said

| NEW REVISED STANDARD VERSION | REVISED ENGLISH BIBLE |

cause you have done well in carrying out what I consider right, and in accordance with all that was in my heart have dealt with the house of Ahab, your sons of the fourth generation shall sit on the throne of Israel." 31 But Jehu was not careful to follow the law of the LORD the God of Israel with all his heart; he did not turn from the sins of Jeroboam, which he caused Israel to commit.

32 In those days the LORD began to trim off parts of Israel. Hazael defeated them throughout the territory of Israel: 33 from the Jordan eastward, all the land of Gilead, the Gadites, the Reubenites, and the Manassites, from Aroer, which is by the Wadi Arnon, that is, Gilead and Bashan. 34 Now the rest of the acts of Jehu, all that he did, and all his power, are they not written in the Book of the Annals of the Kings of Israel? 35 So Jehu slept with his ancestors, and they buried him in Samaria. His son Jehoahaz succeeded him. 36 The time that Jehu reigned over Israel in Samaria was twenty-eight years.

11 Now when Athaliah, Ahaziah's mother, saw that her son was dead, she set about to destroy all the royal family. 2 But Jehosheba, King Joram's daughter, Ahaziah's sister, took Joash son of Ahaziah, and stole him away from among the king's children who were about to be killed; she put*k* him and his nurse in a bedroom. Thus she*l* hid him from Athaliah, so that he was not killed; 3 he remained with her six years, hidden in the house of the LORD, while Athaliah reigned over the land.

4 But in the seventh year Jehoiada summoned the captains of the Carites and of the guards and had them come to him in the house of the LORD. He made a covenant with them and put them under oath in the house of the LORD; then he showed them the king's son. 5 He commanded them, "This is what you are to do: one-third of you, those who go off duty on the sabbath and guard the king's house 6 (another third being at the gate Sur and a third at the gate behind the guards), shall guard the palace; 7 and your two divisions that come on duty in force on the sabbath and guard the house of the LORD*m* 8 shall surround the king, each with weapons in hand; and whoever approaches the ranks is to be killed. Be with the king in his comings and goings."

9 The captains did according to all that the priest Jehoiada commanded; each brought his men who were to go off duty on the sabbath, with those who were to come on duty on the sabbath, and came to the priest Jehoiada. 10 The priest delivered to the captains the spears and shields that had been King David's, which were in the house of the LORD; 11 the guards stood, every man with his weapons in his hand, from the south side of the house to the north side of the house, around the altar and the house, to guard the king on every side. 12 Then he brought out the king's son, put the crown on him, and gave him the covenant;*n* they proclaimed him king, and anointed him; they clapped their hands and shouted, "Long live the king!"

13 When Athaliah heard the noise of the guard and of the people, she went into the house of the LORD to the people; 14 when she looked, there was the king standing by the pillar, according to custom, with the captains and the trumpeters beside the king, and all the people of the land rejoicing and blowing trumpets. Athaliah tore her clothes and cried, "Treason! Treason!" 15 Then the priest Jehoiada

30 The LORD said to Jehu, 'You have done well in carrying out what is right in my eyes, and you have done to the house of Ahab all that it was in my mind to do. Therefore your sons to the fourth generation will occupy the throne of Israel.' 31 But Jehu was not careful to follow the law of the LORD the God of Israel with all his heart; he did not abandon the sins of Jeroboam who led Israel into sin.

32 IN those days the LORD began to cut down Israel. Hazael struck at them in every corner of their territory 33 eastwards from the Jordan: all the land of Gilead, Gad, Reuben, and Manasseh, from Aroer which is by the wadi of the Arnon, including Gilead and Bashan.

34 The other events of Jehu's reign, his achievements and his exploits, are recorded in the annals of the kings of Israel. 35 Jehu rested with his forefathers and was buried in Samaria. His son Jehoahaz succeeded him. 36 Jehu had reigned over Israel in Samaria for twenty-eight years.

11 As SOON as Athaliah mother of Ahaziah saw that her son was dead, she set out to destroy the whole royal line. 2 But Jehosheba, the daughter of King Joram, the sister of Ahaziah, took Ahaziah's son Joash and stole him away from among the princes who were being murdered; she put him and his nurse in a bedchamber where he was hidden from Athaliah and escaped death. 3 He remained concealed with her in the house of the LORD for six years, while Athaliah ruled the country.

4 In the seventh year Jehoiada sent for the captains of units of a hundred, both of the Carites and of the guards, and he brought them to him in the house of the LORD, where he made a compact with them and put them on oath; he showed them the king's son, 5 and gave them these orders: 'One third of you who are on duty on the sabbath are to be on guard in the palace; 6 the rest of you are to be on special duty in the house of the LORD, one third at the Sur Gate and the other third at the gate with the outrunners. 7 Your two companies who are off duty on the sabbath are to be on duty for the king in the house of the LORD. 8 Mount guard round the king, each man holding his weapons, and anyone who comes near the ranks is to be put to death. You are to stay with the king wherever he goes.'

9 The captains carried out the orders of Jehoiada the priest to the letter: each took his men, both those who came on duty on the sabbath and those who went off, and they reported to Jehoiada. 10 The priest handed out to the captains King David's spears and shields, which were kept in the house of the LORD. 11 The guards took up their stations round the king, each man holding his weapons, from corner to corner of the house to north and south. 12 Then Jehoiada brought out the king's son, put the crown on his head, handed him the testimony, and anointed him king. The people clapped their hands and shouted, 'Long live the king.'

13 When Athaliah heard the noise made by the guards and the people, she came into the house of the LORD where the people were; 14 she found the king standing by the pillar, as was the custom, amidst outbursts of song and fanfares of trumpets in his honour; all the populace were rejoicing and blowing trumpets. Athaliah tore her clothes and cried, 'Treason! Treason!' 15 Jehoiada the priest gave orders to the

---

11:1–20 *Cp. 2 Chr. 22:10—23:21.*   11:2 **she put:** *prob. rdg, cp. 2 Chr. 22:11; Heb. omits.*   11:5 **are to . . . guard:** *so Syriac; Heb.* who keep guard.   11:10 **spears:** *so Gk, cp. 2 Chr. 23:9; Heb.* spear.   11:11 **north and south:** *prob. rdg; Heb. adds* of the altar and the house.   11:12 **The people:** *so Gk (Luc.); Heb. omits.*   11:13 **and the people:** *so Syriac; Heb. omits* and.   11:14 **by the pillar:** *or* on the dais *(cp. Lat.).*

---

k With 2 Chr 22.11: Heb lacks *she put*   *l* Gk Syr Vg Compare 2 Chr 22.11: Heb *they*   *m* Heb *the LORD to the king*   *n* Or *treaty* or *testimony*; Heb *eduth*

said to Jehu, "Because you have done well what I deem right, and have treated the house of Ahab as I desire, your sons to the fourth generation shall sit upon the throne of Israel." 31 But Jehu was not careful to observe wholeheartedly the law of the LORD, the God of Israel, since he did not desist from the sins which Jeroboam caused Israel to commit.

32 At that time the LORD began to dismember Israel. Hazael defeated the Israelites throughout their territory 33 east of the Jordan (all the land of Gilead, of the Gadites, Reubenites and Manassehites), from Aroer on the river Arnon up through Gilead and Bashan.

34 The rest of the acts of Jehu, his valor and all his accomplishments, are written in the book of the chronicles of the kings of Israel. 35 Jehu rested with his ancestors and was buried in Samaria. His son Jehoahaz succeeded him as king. 36 The length of Jehu's reign over Israel in Samaria was twenty-eight years.

11 When Athaliah, the mother of Ahaziah, saw that her son was dead, she began to kill off the whole royal family. 2 But Jehosheba, daughter of King Jehoram and sister of Ahaziah, took Joash, his son, and spirited him away, along with his nurse, from the bedroom where the princes were about to be slain. She concealed him from Athaliah, and so he did not die. 3 For six years he remained hidden in the temple of the LORD, while Athaliah ruled the land.

4 But in the seventh year, Jehoiada summoned the captains of the Carians and of the guards. He had them come to him in the temple of the LORD, exacted from them a sworn commitment, and then showed them the king's son. 5 He gave them these orders: "This is what you must do: the third of you who come on duty on the sabbath shall guard the king's palace; 6 another third shall be at the gate Sur; and the last third shall be at the gate behind the guards. 7 The two of your divisions who are going off duty that week shall keep guard over the temple of the LORD for the king. 8 You shall surround the king, each with drawn weapons, and if anyone tries to approach the cordon, kill him; stay with the king, whatever he may do."

9 The captains did just as Jehoiada the priest commanded. Each one with his men, both those going on duty for the sabbath and those going off duty that week, came to Jehoiada the priest. 10 He gave the captains King David's spears and shields, which were in the temple of the LORD. 11 And the guards, with drawn weapons, lined up from the southern to the northern limit of the enclosure, surrounding the altar and the temple on the king's behalf. 12 Then Jehoiada led out the king's son and put the crown and the insignia upon him. They proclaimed him king and anointed him, clapping their hands and shouting, "Long live the king!"

13 Athaliah heard the noise made by the people, and appeared before them in the temple of the LORD. 14 When she saw the king standing by the pillar, as was the custom, and the captains and trumpeters near him, with all the people of the land rejoicing and blowing trumpets, she tore her garments and cried out, "Treason, treason!" 15 Then Jehoiada

to Jehu, 'Since you have done well in carrying out what pleases me, and have done everything I required to be done to the House of Ahab, your sons will occupy the throne of Israel down to the fourth generation.' 31 Jehu, however, did not faithfully and wholeheartedly follow the law of Yahweh, God of Israel; he did not give up the sins into which Jeroboam son of Nebat had led Israel.

32 At that time Yahweh began to whittle Israel down, and Hazael defeated the Israelites throughout the territory east of the Jordan: 33 the whole territory of Gilead — of the Gadites, the Reubenites and the Manassehites — from Aroer on the River Arnon: Gilead and Bashan.

34 The rest of the history of Jehu, his entire career, all his prowess, is this not recorded in the Book of the Annals of the Kings of Israel? 35 Then he fell asleep with his ancestors and was buried in Samaria; his son Jehoahaz succeeded him. 36 Jehu's reign over Israel in Samaria lasted twenty-eight years.

11 When Athaliah mother of Ahaziah learned that her son was dead, she promptly murdered all those of royal stock.

2 But Jehosheba, daughter of King Jehoram and sister of Ahaziah, surreptitiously rescued Jehoash son of Ahaziah from among the princes who were to be murdered, and put him with his nurse in the sleeping quarters; in this way she hid him from Athaliah, and he was not killed. 3 He stayed, hidden with her in the Temple of Yahweh for six years, while Athaliah governed the country.

4 In the seventh year, Jehoiada sent for the regimental commanders of the Carians and the guards, and had them brought to him in the Temple of Yahweh. He made a pact with them, put them on oath, then showed them the king's son. He gave them this order, 5 'This is what you must do: a third of you who come on duty on the Sabbath must mount guard at the royal palace, *e* 7 and your two other sections who come off duty on the Sabbath and mount guard at the Temple of Yahweh 8 must surround the king, each man with his weapons in his hand; anyone forcing his way through the ranks is to be killed. And you will escort the king as he leaves and as he comes in.'

9 The regimental commanders did everything as Jehoiada the priest had ordered, and each one brought his men, those coming on duty on the Sabbath and those going off duty on the Sabbath, and reported to Jehoiada the priest. 10 The priest then issued the regimental commanders with King David's spears and shields, which were kept in the Temple of Yahweh. 11 The guards then took position, each man with his weapons in his hand, from the south corner of the Temple to the north corner of the Temple, all round the altar and the Temple. 12 Then Jehoiada brought the king's son out — crowned him and gave him a copy of the covenant; and they made him king and anointed him, and they clapped their hands and shouted, 'Long live the king!'

13 On hearing the people shouting, Athaliah joined the people in the Temple of Yahweh. 14 When she looked, there stood the king on a dais, as the custom was, with the officers and trumpeters at the king's side, and all the people of the country rejoicing and blowing the trumpets; then Athaliah tore her clothes and shouted, 'Treason, treason!' 15 Jehoiada the priest then gave the orders to the commanders in

---

e **11** v. 6 is omitted as a confused gloss.

NEW REVISED STANDARD VERSION

commanded the captains who were set over the army, "Bring her out between the ranks, and kill with the sword anyone who follows her." For the priest said, "Let her not be killed in the house of the LORD." 16 So they laid hands on her; she went through the horses' entrance to the king's house, and there she was put to death.

17 Jehoiada made a covenant between the LORD and the king and people, that they should be the LORD's people; also between the king and the people. 18 Then all the people of the land went to the house of Baal, and tore it down; his altars and his images they broke in pieces, and they killed Mattan, the priest of Baal, before the altars. The priest posted guards over the house of the LORD. 19 He took the captains, the Carites, the guards, and all the people of the land; then they brought the king down from the house of the LORD, marching through the gate of the guards to the king's house. He took his seat on the throne of the kings. 20 So all the people of the land rejoiced; and the city was quiet after Athaliah had been killed with the sword at the king's house.

21 o Jehoash p was seven years old when he began to reign.

12 In the seventh year of Jehu, Jehoash began to reign; he reigned forty years in Jerusalem. His mother's name was Zibiah of Beer-sheba. 2 Jehoash did what was right in the sight of the LORD all his days, because the priest Jehoiada instructed him. 3 Nevertheless the high places were not taken away; the people continued to sacrifice and make offerings on the high places.

4 Jehoash said to the priests, "All the money offered as sacred donations that is brought into the house of the LORD, the money for which each person is assessed — the money from the assessment of persons — and the money from the voluntary offerings brought into the house of the LORD, 5 let the priests receive from each of the donors; and let them repair the house wherever any need of repairs is discovered." 6 But by the twenty-third year of King Jehoash the priests had made no repairs on the house. 7 Therefore King Jehoash summoned the priest Jehoiada with the other priests and said to them, "Why are you not repairing the house? Now therefore do not accept any more money from your donors but hand it over for the repair of the house." 8 So the priests agreed that they would neither accept more money from the people nor repair the house.

9 Then the priest Jehoiada took a chest, made a hole in its lid, and set it beside the altar on the right side as one entered the house of the LORD; the priests who guarded the threshold put in it all the money that was brought into the house of the LORD. 10 Whenever they saw that there was a great deal of money in the chest, the king's secretary and the high priest went up, counted the money that was found in the house of the LORD, and tied it up in bags. 11 They would give the money that was weighed out into the hands of the workers who had the oversight of the house of the LORD; then they paid it out to the carpenters and the builders who worked on the house of the LORD, 12 to the masons and the stonecutters, as well as to buy timber and quarried stone for making repairs on the house of the LORD, as well as for any outlay for repairs of the house. 13 But for the house of the LORD no basins of silver, snuffers, bowls, trumpets, or any vessels of gold, or of silver, were made from the money that was brought into the house of the LORD, 14 for that was given to the workers who were repairing the house of the LORD with it. 15 They did not ask an accounting from those into whose hand they delivered the money to pay out to the workers, for they dealt honestly. 16 The money from the

REVISED ENGLISH BIBLE

captains in command of the troops: 'Bring her outside the precincts and put to the sword anyone in attendance on her'; for the priest said, 'Let her not be put to death in the house of the LORD.' 16 They took her and brought her out by the entry for horses to the palace, and there she was put to death.

17 Jehoiada made a covenant, between the LORD on one side and the king and people on the other, that they should be the LORD's people, and a covenant also between the king and the people. 18 The people all went to the temple of Baal and pulled it down; they smashed to pieces its altars and images, and they slew Mattan the priest of Baal before the altars.

Jehoiada set a guard over the house of the LORD; 19 he took the captains of units of a hundred, the Carites and the guards, and all the people, and they escorted the king from the house of the LORD through the Gate of the Guards to the palace, and seated him on the royal throne. 20 The whole people rejoiced and the city had quiet. That is how Athaliah was put to the sword in the palace.

21 Joash was seven years old when he became king.

12 1 It was in the seventh year of Jehu that Joash became king, and he reigned in Jerusalem for forty years; his mother was Zibiah from Beersheba. 2 He did what was right in the eyes of the LORD all his days, as Jehoiada the priest had taught him. 3 The shrines, however, were allowed to remain; the people continued to sacrifice and burn offerings there.

4 Joash ordered that all the silver brought as holy-gifts into the house of the LORD, the silver for which each man was assessed, the silver for the persons assessed under his name, and any silver brought voluntarily to the house of the LORD, 5 should be taken by the priests, each receiving it from a treasurer; he also ordered them to repair the house wherever it was found necessary. 6 But in the twenty-third year of Joash's reign the priests had still not carried out the repairs. 7 The king summoned Jehoiada the priest along with the other priests and asked, 'Why are you not repairing the house? Henceforth you need not receive the money from your treasurers, but hand it over for the repair of the house.' 8 The priests agreed neither to receive money from the people nor to undertake the repairs of the house themselves.

9 Jehoiada the priest took a chest, bored a hole in the lid, and put it beside the sacrificial slaughtering-place on the right side going into the house of the LORD. The priests on duty at the entrance put in it all the money brought to the house of the LORD. 10 Whenever they saw that the chest was well filled, the king's secretary and the high priest came and melted down the silver found in the house of the LORD and weighed it. 11 When it had been checked, they handed over the silver to those supervising the work in the house of the LORD, and they paid the carpenters and the builders working there 12 and the masons and the stone-cutters; they used it also to purchase timber and hewn stone for the repairs and for all other expenses connected with them. 13 They did not use the money brought into the house of the LORD to make silver cups, snuffers, tossing-bowls, trumpets, or any gold or silver vessels; 14 but they used it for paying the workmen and for the repairs. 15 No account was asked from the men to whom the money was given for the payment of the workers; they were acting on trust. 16 Money from reparation-

11:21 *In Heb. 12:1.*   11:21—12:15 *Cp. 2 Chr. 24:1–14.*
12:4 **all the silver . . . was assessed:** *prob. rdg; Heb. obscure.*
12:9 **sacrificial slaughtering-place:** *prob. rdg; Heb. altar.*

o Ch 12.1 in Heb   p Another spelling is *Joash*; see verse 19

the priest instructed the captains in command of the force: "Bring her outside through the ranks. If anyone follows her," he added, "let him die by the sword." He had given orders that she should not be slain in the temple of the LORD. 16 She was led out forcibly to the horse gate of the royal palace, where she was put to death.

17 Then Jehoiada made a covenant between the LORD as one party and the king and the people as the other, by which they would be the LORD's people; and another covenant, between the king and the people. 18 Thereupon all the people of the land went to the temple of Baal and demolished it. They shattered its altars and images completely, and slew Mattan, the priest of Baal, before the altars. After appointing a detachment for the temple of the LORD, Jehoiada 19 with the captains, the Carians, the guards, and all the people of the land, led the king down from the temple of the LORD through the guards' gate to the palace, where Joash took his seat on the royal throne. 20 All the people of the land rejoiced and the city was quiet, now that Athaliah had been slain with the sword at the royal palace.

12 Joash was seven years old when he became king. 2 Joash began to reign in the seventh year of Jehu, and he reigned forty years in Jerusalem. His mother, who was named Zibiah, was from Beer-sheba. 3 Joash did what was pleasing to the LORD as long as he lived, because the priest Jehoiada guided him. 4 Still, the high places did not disappear; the people continued to sacrifice and to burn incense there.

5 For the priests Joash made this rule: "All the funds for sacred purposes that are brought to the temple of the LORD —the census tax, personal redemption money, and whatever funds are freely brought to the temple of the LORD— 6 the priests may take for themselves, each from his own clients. However, they must make whatever repairs on the temple may prove necessary. 7 Nevertheless, as late as the twenty-third year of the reign of King Joash, the priests had not made needed repairs on the temple. 8 Accordingly, King Joash summoned the priest Jehoiada and the other priests. "Why do you not repair the temple?" he asked them. "You must no longer take funds from your clients, but you shall turn them over for the repairs." 9 So the priests agreed that they would neither take funds from the people nor make the repairs on the temple.

10 The priest Jehoiada then took a chest, bored a hole in its lid, and set it beside the stele, on the right as one entered the temple of the LORD. The priests who guarded the entry would put into it all the funds that were brought to the temple of the LORD. 11 When they noticed that there was a large amount of silver in the chest, the royal scribe [and the priest] would come up, and they would melt down all the funds that were in the temple of the LORD, and weigh them. 12 The amount thus realized they turned over to the master workmen in the temple of the LORD. They in turn would give it to the carpenters and builders working in the temple of the LORD, 13 and to the lumbermen and stone cutters, and for the purchase of the wood and hewn stone used in repairing the breaches, and for any other expenses that were necessary to repair the temple. 14 None of the funds brought to the temple of the LORD were used there to make silver cups, snuffers, basins, trumpets, or any gold or silver article. 15 Instead, they were given to the workmen, and with them they repaired the temple of the LORD. 16 Moreover, no reckoning was asked of the men who were provided with the funds to give to the workmen, because they held positions of trust. 17 The funds from guilt-offerings and from

charge of the troops, 'Take her out under guard and put to death anyone who follows her.' 'For', the priest had already said, 'she must not be killed inside the Temple of Yahweh.' 16 They seized her, and when she reached the horses' entry to the palace, she was killed there.

17 Jehoiada made a covenant between Yahweh, the king and the people that they would remain Yahweh's people; and another one between the king and the people. 18 All the people of the country then went to the temple of Baal and demolished it; they smashed its altars and its images and killed Mattan the priest of Baal in front of the altars.

The priest made arrangements for the security of the Temple of Yahweh. 19 He then took the regimental commanders, the Carians, the guards and all the people of the country, and they escorted the king down from the Temple of Yahweh, entering the palace through the Gate of the Guards. Jehoash took his seat on the throne of the kings. 20 All the people of the country were delighted; the city, however, made no move. And Athaliah was put to death inside the palace.

12 Jehoash was seven years old when he came to the throne. 2 Jehoash became king in the seventh year of Jehu, and reigned for forty years in Jerusalem. His mother's name was Zibiah of Beersheba. 3 All his life Jehoash did what Yahweh regards as right, having been instructed by Jehoiada the priest. 4 The high places, however, were not abolished, and the people still offered sacrifices and incense on the high places.

5 Jehoash said to the priests, 'All the money from the sacred revenues brought to the Temple of Yahweh, the money from personal taxes, and all the money voluntarily offered to the Temple— 6 the priests are to receive this individually from people of their acquaintance and will carry out all the repairs to the Temple which need to be made.' 7 Now in the twenty-third year of King Jehoash the priests had done no repairs to the Temple; 8 so King Jehoash summoned Jehoiada the priest and the other priests. 'Why are you not repairing the Temple?' he asked. 'You are no longer to accept money from people of your acquaintance but are to hand it over for the Temple repairs.' 9 The priests agreed to accept no money from the people and no longer to be responsible for repairs to the Temple.

10 Jehoiada the priest took a chest, bored a hole in the lid and placed it beside the pillar, to the right of the entry to the Temple of Yahweh; in it the priests who guarded the threshold put all the money which was given for the Temple of Yahweh. 11 Whenever they saw that there was a great deal of money in the chest, the king's secretary would come, and they would empty it out and reckon the money then in the Temple of Yahweh. 12 Once checked, they paid this money over to the masters of works attached to the Temple of Yahweh, and these in turn spent it on carpenters and builders working on the Temple of Yahweh, 13 on masons and stonecutters, and on buying timber and dressed stone to be used for repairs to the Temple of Yahweh; in short, for all the costs of the Temple repairs. 14 But no silver basins, knives, sprinkling bowls, trumpets or gold or silver objects were made for the Temple of Yahweh out of the money presented, 15 which was all given to the masters of works for repairing the Temple of Yahweh. 16 No accounts were kept with the men to whom the money was paid over to be spent on the workmen, since they were honest in their work.

guilt offerings and the money from the sin offerings was not brought into the house of the LORD; it belonged to the priests.

17 At that time King Hazael of Aram went up, fought against Gath, and took it. But when Hazael set his face to go up against Jerusalem, 18 King Jehoash of Judah took all the votive gifts that Jehoshaphat, Jehoram, and Ahaziah, his ancestors, the kings of Judah, had dedicated, as well as his own votive gifts, all the gold that was found in the treasuries of the house of the LORD and of the king's house, and sent these to King Hazael of Aram. Then Hazael withdrew from Jerusalem.

19 Now the rest of the acts of Joash, and all that he did, are they not written in the Book of the Annals of the Kings of Judah? 20 His servants arose, devised a conspiracy, and killed Joash in the house of Millo, on the way that goes down to Silla. 21 It was Jozacar son of Shimeath and Jehozabad son of Shomer, his servants, who struck him down, so that he died. He was buried with his ancestors in the city of David; then his son Amaziah succeeded him.

13 In the twenty-third year of King Joash son of Ahaziah of Judah, Jehoahaz son of Jehu began to reign over Israel in Samaria; he reigned seventeen years. 2 He did what was evil in the sight of the LORD, and followed the sins of Jeroboam son of Nebat, which he caused Israel to sin; he did not depart from them. 3 The anger of the LORD was kindled against Israel, so that he gave them repeatedly into the hand of King Hazael of Aram, then into the hand of Ben-hadad son of Hazael. 4 But Jehoahaz entreated the LORD, and the LORD heeded him; for he saw the oppression of Israel, how the king of Aram oppressed them. 5 Therefore the LORD gave Israel a savior, so that they escaped from the hand of the Arameans; and the people of Israel lived in their homes as formerly. 6 Nevertheless they did not depart from the sins of the house of Jeroboam, which he caused Israel to sin, but walked*q* in them; the sacred pole*r* also remained in Samaria. 7 So Jehoahaz was left with an army of not more than fifty horsemen, ten chariots and ten thousand footmen; for the king of Aram had destroyed them and made them like the dust at threshing. 8 Now the rest of the acts of Jehoahaz and all that he did, including his might, are they not written in the Book of the Annals of the Kings of Israel? 9 So Jehoahaz slept with his ancestors, and they buried him in Samaria; then his son Joash succeeded him.

10 In the thirty-seventh year of King Joash of Judah, Jehoash son of Jehoahaz began to reign over Israel in Samaria; he reigned sixteen years. 11 He also did what was evil in the sight of the LORD; he did not depart from all the sins of Jeroboam son of Nebat, which he caused Israel to sin, but he walked in them. 12 Now the rest of the acts of Joash, and all that he did, as well as the might with which he fought against King Amaziah of Judah, are they not written in the Book of the Annals of the Kings of Judah? 13 So Joash slept with his ancestors, and Jeroboam sat upon his throne; Joash was buried in Samaria with the kings of Israel.

14 Now when Elisha had fallen sick with the illness of which he was to die, King Joash of Israel went down to him, and wept before him, crying, "My father, my father! The chariots of Israel and its horsemen!" 15 Elisha said to him, "Take a bow and arrows"; so he took a bow and arrows. 16 Then he said to the king of Israel, "Draw the bow"; and he drew it. Elisha laid his hands on the king's hands. 17 Then he said, "Open the window eastward"; and he opened it. Elisha said, "Shoot"; and he shot. Then he said, "The LORD's arrow of victory, the arrow of victory over Aram! For you shall fight the Arameans in Aphek until you have made an end of them." 18 He continued, "Take the

offerings and purification-offerings was not brought into the house of the LORD: it belonged to the priests.

17 King Hazael of Aram came up at that time and attacked Gath, and after its capture he moved on against Jerusalem. 18 Thereupon King Joash of Judah took all the holy-gifts that Jehoshaphat, Joram, and Ahaziah his forefathers, kings of Judah, had dedicated, and his own holy-gifts, and all the gold that was in the treasuries of the house of the LORD and in the royal palace, and sent them to Hazael; and he withdrew from Jerusalem.

19 The other acts and events of the reign of Joash are recorded in the annals of the kings of Judah. 20 His servants rose against him in a conspiracy and assassinated him in the house of Millo on the descent to Silla; 21 it was his servants Jozachar son of Shimeath and Jehozabad son of Shomer who struck the fatal blow. He was buried with his forefathers in the city of David. His son Amaziah succeeded him.

13 In the twenty-third year of Joash son of Ahaziah king of Judah, Jehoahaz son of Jehu became king over Israel in Samaria and he reigned for seventeen years. 2 He did what was wrong in the eyes of the LORD and continued the sinful practices of Jeroboam son of Nebat who led Israel into sin, and did not give them up. 3 This roused the anger of the LORD against Israel, and he made them subject for some years to King Hazael of Aram and Ben-hadad his son. 4 When Jehoahaz sought to placate the LORD, the LORD heard his prayer, for he saw how the king of Aram oppressed Israel. 5 The LORD appointed a deliverer for Israel, and they escaped from the power of Aram and settled down again in their own homes. 6 But they did not give up the sinful practices of the house of Jeroboam who led Israel into sin, but continued in them; the goddess Asherah remained in Samaria. 7 Hazael had left Jehoahaz no armed force except fifty horsemen, ten chariots, and ten thousand infantry; all the rest the king of Aram had destroyed and made like dust under foot.

8 The other events of the reign of Jehoahaz, and all his achievements and exploits, are recorded in the annals of the kings of Israel. 9 He rested with his forefathers and was buried in Samaria. His son Jehoash succeeded him.

10 In the thirty-ninth year of King Joash of Judah, Jehoash son of Jehoahaz became king over Israel in Samaria and reigned for sixteen years. 11 He did what was wrong in the eyes of the LORD; he did not give up any of the sinful practices of Jeroboam son of Nebat who led Israel into sin, but continued in them. 12 The other events of the reign of Jehoash, all his achievements, his exploits, and his war with King Amaziah of Judah, are recorded in the annals of the kings of Israel. 13 Jehoash rested with his forefathers and was buried in Samaria with the kings of Israel. Jeroboam ascended the throne.

14 When Elisha fell ill and lay on his deathbed, King Jehoash of Israel went down to him and, weeping over him, said, 'My father! My father! The chariots and horsemen of Israel!' 15 Elisha said, 'Take a bow and arrows,' and he did so. 16 'Put your hand to the bow,' said the prophet. He did so, and Elisha laid his hands on those of the king. 17 Then he said, 'Open the window towards the east'; he opened it and Elisha told him to shoot, and he did so. Then the prophet said, 'An arrow for the LORD's victory, an arrow for victory over Aram! You will utterly defeat Aram at

12:20–21 Cp. 2 Chr. 24:25–27.   12:21 **Jozachar:** so some MSS; others Jozabad.   13:6 **but continued:** so Gk; Heb. he continued. **the goddess Asherah:** or the sacred pole.   13:10 **thirty-ninth:** so some Gk MSS; Heb. thirty-seventh.

q Gk Syr Tg Vg: Heb *he walked*   *r* Heb *Asherah*

sin-offerings, however, were not brought to the temple of the LORD; they belonged to the priests. [18] Then King Hazael of Aram mounted a siege against Gath. When he had taken it, Hazael decided to go on to attack Jerusalem. [19] But King Jehoash of Judah took all the dedicated offerings presented by his forebears, Jehoshaphat, Jehoram, and Ahaziah, kings of Judah, as well as his own, and all the gold there was in the treasuries of the temple and the palace, and sent them to King Hazael of Aram, who then led his forces away from Jerusalem. [20] The rest of the acts of Joash, with all that he did, are recorded in the book of the chronicles of the kings of Judah. [21] Certain of his officials entered into a plot against him and killed him at Beth-millo. [22] Jozacar, son of Shimeath, and Jehozabad, son of Shomer, were the officials who killed him. He was buried in his forefathers' City of David, and his son Amaziah succeeded him as king.

[13] In the twenty-third year of Joash, son of Ahaziah, king of Judah, Jehoahaz, son of Jehu, began his seventeen-year reign over Israel in Samaria. [2] He did evil in the LORD's sight, conducting himself like Jeroboam, son of Nebat, and not renouncing the sin he had caused Israel to commit. [3] The LORD was angry with Israel and for a long time left them in the power of Hazael, king of Aram, and of Ben-hadad, son of Hazael. [4] Then Jehoahaz entreated the LORD, who heard him, since he saw the oppression to which the king of Aram had subjected Israel. [5] So the LORD gave Israel a savior, and the Israelites, freed from the power of Aram, dwelt in their own homes as formerly. [6] Nevertheless, they did not desist from the sins which the house of Jeroboam had caused Israel to commit, but persisted in them. The sacred pole also remained standing in Samaria. [7] No soldiers were left to Jehoahaz, except fifty horsemen with ten chariots and ten thousand foot soldiers, since the king of Aram had destroyed them and trampled them like dust. [8] The rest of the acts of Jehoahaz, with all his valor and accomplishments, are recorded in the book of the chronicles of the kings of Israel. [9] Jehoahaz rested with his ancestors and was buried in Samaria. His son Joash succeeded him as king.

[10] In the thirty-seventh year of Joash, king of Judah, Jehoash, son of Jehoahaz, began his sixteen-year reign over Israel in Samaria. [11] He did evil in the sight of the LORD; he did not desist from any of the sins which Jeroboam, son of Nebat, had caused Israel to commit, but persisted in them. [12] [The rest of the acts of Joash, the valor with which he fought against Amaziah, king of Judah, and all his accomplishments, are recorded in the book of the chronicles of the kings of Israel. [13] Joash rested with his ancestors, and Jeroboam occupied the throne. Joash was buried with the kings of Israel in Samaria.]

[14] When Elisha was suffering from the sickness of which he was to die, King Joash of Israel went down to visit him. "My father, my father!" he exclaimed, weeping over him. "Israel's chariots and horsemen!" [15] "Take a bow and some arrows," Elisha said to him. When he had done so, [16] Elisha said to the king of Israel, "Put your hand on the bow." As the king held the bow, Elisha placed his hands over the king's hands [17] and said, "Open the window toward the east." He opened it, Elisha said, "Shoot," and he shot. The prophet exclaimed, "The LORD's arrow of victory! The arrow of victory over Aram! You will completely conquer Aram at Aphec."

[17] Money offered in expiation of an offence or of a sin was not given to the Temple of Yahweh; that was for the priests. [18] At that time Hazael king of Aram went to war against Gath, and captured it; he then prepared to attack Jerusalem. [19] Jehoash king of Judah took all the sacred offerings dedicated by his ancestors, the kings of Judah, Jehoshaphat, Jehoram and Ahaziah, with those which he himself had dedicated, and all the gold which was to be found in the treasuries of the Temple of Yahweh and of the palace; he sent it all to Hazael king of Aram, who retired from Jerusalem. [20] The rest of the history of Joash, his entire career, is this not recorded in the Book of the Annals of the Kings of Judah? [21] His own retainers rebelled and hatched a plot; they murdered Joash in the palace of the Millo . . . [22] Jozacar son of Shimeath and Jehozabad son of Shomer were the retainers who struck the blows from which he died. He was buried with his ancestors in the City of David; his son Amaziah succeeded him.

[13] In the twenty-third year of Joash son of Ahaziah, king of Judah, Jehoahaz son of Jehu became king of Israel in Samaria. He reigned for seventeen years. [2] He did what is displeasing to Yahweh and copied the sin into which Jeroboam son of Nebat had led Israel; he did not give it up. [3] This aroused Yahweh's anger against the Israelites, and he delivered them without respite into the power of Hazael king of Aram and of Ben-Hadad son of Hazael. [4] Jehoahaz, however, tried to placate Yahweh, and Yahweh heard him, for he had seen the oppression which the king of Aram was inflicting on Israel. [5] Yahweh gave Israel a saviour who freed them from the grip of Aram, and the Israelites lived in their tents as in the past. [6] But they did not give up the sin into which Jeroboam had led Israel; they persisted in it, and even the sacred pole stayed standing in Samaria. [7] Of Jehoahaz's army Yahweh left only fifty horsemen, ten chariots and ten thousand foot soldiers. The king of Aram had destroyed them, making them like dust trampled under foot. [8] The rest of the history of Jehoahaz, his entire career, his prowess, is this not recorded in the Book of the Annals of the Kings of Israel? [9] Then Jehoahaz fell asleep with his ancestors, and was buried in Samaria; his son Joash succeeded him.

[10] In the thirty-seventh year of Joash king of Judah, Jehoash son of Jehoahaz, became king of Israel in Samaria. He reigned for sixteen years. [11] He did what is displeasing to Yahweh, he did not give up the sin into which Jeroboam son of Nebat had led Israel; he persisted in it. [12] The rest of the history of Joash, his entire career, his prowess, how he waged war on Amaziah king of Judah, is this not recorded in the Book of the Annals of the Kings of Israel? [13] Then Joash fell asleep with his ancestors, and Jeroboam ascended his throne. Joash was buried in Samaria with the kings of Israel.

[14] When Elisha had fallen ill of the illness of which he was to die, Joash king of Israel went down to him and shedding tears over him said, 'Father! Father! Chariot of Israel and its chargers!' [15] Elisha said to him, 'Bring bow and arrows,' and he sent for a bow and arrows. [16] Then Elisha said to the king, 'Draw the bow,' and he drew it. Elisha put his hands over the hands of the king, [17] then he said, 'Open the window towards the east,' and he opened it. Then Elisha said, 'Shoot!' And he shot. Elisha said, 'Arrow of victory over Aram! You will defeat Aram at Aphek — completely.'

13, 12f: The conclusion to the reign of Joash is given again in 2 Kgs 14, 15f, where it is more appropriate.

arrows"; and he took them. He said to the king of Israel, "Strike the ground with them"; he struck three times, and stopped. 19 Then the man of God was angry with him, and said, "You should have struck five or six times; then you would have struck down Aram until you had made an end of it, but now you will strike down Aram only three times."

20 So Elisha died, and they buried him. Now bands of Moabites used to invade the land in the spring of the year. 21 As a man was being buried, a marauding band was seen and the man was thrown into the grave of Elisha; as soon as the man touched the bones of Elisha, he came to life and stood on his feet.

22 Now King Hazael of Aram oppressed Israel all the days of Jehoahaz. 23 But the LORD was gracious to them and had compassion on them; he turned toward them, because of his covenant with Abraham, Isaac, and Jacob, and would not destroy them; nor has he banished them from his presence until now.

24 When King Hazael of Aram died, his son Ben-hadad succeeded him. 25 Then Jehoash son of Jehoahaz took again from Ben-hadad son of Hazael the towns that he had taken from his father Jehoahaz in war. Three times Joash defeated him and recovered the towns of Israel.

14 In the second year of King Joash son of Joahaz of Israel, King Amaziah son of Joash of Judah, began to reign. 2 He was twenty-five years old when he began to reign, and he reigned twenty-nine years in Jerusalem. His mother's name was Jehoaddin of Jerusalem. 3 He did what was right in the sight of the LORD, yet not like his ancestor David; in all things he did as his father Joash had done. 4 But the high places were not removed; the people still sacrificed and made offerings on the high places. 5 As soon as the royal power was firmly in his hand he killed his servants who had murdered his father the king. 6 But he did not put to death the children of the murderers; according to what is written in the book of the law of Moses, where the LORD commanded, "The parents shall not be put to death for the children, or the children be put to death for the parents; but all shall be put to death for their own sins."

7 He killed ten thousand Edomites in the Valley of Salt and took Sela by storm; he called it Jokthe-el, which is its name to this day.

8 Then Amaziah sent messengers to King Jehoash son of Jehoahaz, son of Jehu, of Israel, saying, "Come, let us look one another in the face." 9 King Jehoash of Israel sent word to King Amaziah of Judah, "A thornbush on Lebanon sent to a cedar on Lebanon, saying, 'Give your daughter to my son for a wife'; but a wild animal of Lebanon passed by and trampled down the thornbush. 10 You have indeed defeated Edom, and your heart has lifted you up. Be content with your glory, and stay at home; for why should you provoke trouble so that you fall, you and Judah with you?"

11 But Amaziah would not listen. So King Jehoash of Israel went up; he and King Amaziah of Judah faced one another in battle at Beth-shemesh, which belongs to Judah. 12 Judah was defeated by Israel; everyone fled home. 13 King Jehoash of Israel captured King Amaziah of Judah son of Jehoash, son of Ahaziah, at Beth-shemesh; he came to Jerusalem, and broke down the wall of Jerusalem from the Ephraim Gate to the Corner Gate, a distance of four hundred cubits. 14 He seized all the gold and silver, and all the vessels that were found in the house of the LORD and in the treasuries of the king's house, as well as hostages; then he returned to Samaria.

15 Now the rest of the acts that Jehoash did, his might, and how he fought with King Amaziah of Judah, are they not written in the Book of the Annals of the Kings of Israel?

Aphek.' 18 He went on, 'Now take up your arrows.' When he did so, Elisha said, 'Strike the ground with them.' He struck three times and stopped. 19 The man of God was angry with him and said, 'You should have struck five or six times; then you would have defeated Aram utterly; as it is, you will strike Aram three times and no more.'

20 Elisha died and was buried.

Year after year Moabite raiders used to invade the land. 21 Once some men were burying a dead man when they caught sight of the raiders, and they threw the body into the grave of Elisha and made off. When the body touched the prophet's bones, the man came to life and rose to his feet.

22 All through the reign of Jehoahaz, King Hazael of Aram oppressed Israel. 23 But the LORD was gracious and took pity on them; because of his covenant with Abraham, Isaac, and Jacob, he looked on them with favour and was unwilling to destroy them; nor has he even yet banished them from his sight. 24 When King Hazael of Aram died and was succeeded by his son Ben-hadad, 25 Jehoash son of Jehoahaz recaptured the towns which Ben-hadad had taken in war from Jehoahaz his father; three times Jehoash defeated him and so recovered the towns of Israel.

14 In the second year of Jehoash son of Jehoahaz king of Israel, Amaziah son of King Joash of Judah succeeded his father. 2 He was twenty-five years old when he came to the throne, and he reigned in Jerusalem for twenty-nine years; his mother was Jehoaddin from Jerusalem. 3 He did what was right in the eyes of the LORD, yet not as his ancestor David had done; he followed his father Joash in everything. 4 The shrines were not abolished; the people continued to sacrifice and burn offerings there. 5 As soon as the royal power was firmly in his grasp, he put to death those of his servants who had murdered the king his father; 6 but he spared the murderers' children in obedience to the LORD's command written in the law of Moses: 'Parents are not to be put to death for their children, nor children for their parents; each one may be put to death only for his own sin.' 7 He defeated ten thousand Edomites in the valley of Salt and captured Sela; he gave it the name Joktheel, which it still bears.

8 Amaziah sent envoys to Jehoash son of Jehoahaz, son of Jehu, king of Israel, to propose a confrontation. 9 King Jehoash of Israel sent back this answer to King Amaziah of Judah: 'A thistle in Lebanon sent to a cedar in Lebanon to say, "Give your daughter in marriage to my son." But a wild beast in Lebanon, passing by, trampled on the thistle. 10 You have defeated Edom, it is true; but it has gone to your head. Stay at home and enjoy your triumph. Why should you involve yourself in disaster and bring yourself to the ground, and drag down Judah with you?'

11 When, however, Amaziah would not listen, King Jehoash of Israel marched out, and he and King Amaziah of Judah clashed at Beth-shemesh in Judah. 12 The men of Judah were routed by Israel and fled to their homes. 13 King Jehoash of Israel captured Amaziah king of Judah, son of Joash, son of Ahaziah, at Beth-shemesh. He marched on Jerusalem, where he broke down the city wall from the Ephraim Gate to the Corner Gate, a distance of four hundred cubits. 14 He took all the gold and silver and all the vessels found in the house of the LORD and in the treasuries of the palace, as well as hostages, and then returned to Samaria.

15 The other events of the reign of Jehoash, and all his achievements, his exploits, and his wars with King Amaziah of Judah, are recorded in the annals of the kings of Israel.

13:21 and made off: so Gk (Luc.); Heb. and he made off.
14:1–6 Cp. 2 Chr. 25:1–4.   14:8–14 Cp. 2 Chr. 25:17–24.

NEW AMERICAN BIBLE

NEW JERUSALEM BIBLE

18 Then he said to the king of Israel, "Take the arrows," which he did. Elisha said to him, "Strike the ground!" He struck the ground three times and stopped. 19 Angry with him, the man of God said: "You should have struck five or six times; you would have defeated Aram completely. Now, you will defeat Aram only three times." 20 Elisha died and was buried. At the time, bands of Moabites used to raid the land each year. 21 Once some people were burying a man, when suddenly they spied such a raiding band. So they cast the dead man into the grave of Elisha, and everyone went off. But when the man came in contact with the bones of Elisha, he came back to life and rose to his feet. 22 King Hazael of Aram oppressed Israel during the entire reign of Jehoahaz. 23 But the LORD was merciful with Israel and looked on them with compassion because of his covenant with Abraham, Isaac, and Jacob. He was unwilling to destroy them or to cast them out from his presence. 24 So when King Hazael of Aram died and his son Ben-hadad succeeded him as king, 25 Joash, son of Jehoahaz, took back from Ben-hadad, son of Hazael, the cities which Hazael had taken in battle from his father Jehoahaz. Joash defeated Ben-hadad three times, and thus recovered the cities of Israel.

14 In the second year of Joash, son of Jehoahaz, king of Israel, Amaziah, son of Joash, king of Judah, began to reign. 2 He was twenty-five years old when he became king, and he reigned twenty-nine years in Jerusalem. His mother, whose name was Jehoaddin, was from Jerusalem. 3 He pleased the LORD, yet not like his forefather David, since he did just as his father Joash had done. 4 Thus the high places did not disappear, but the people continued to sacrifice and to burn incense on them. 5 When Amaziah had the kingdom firmly in hand, he slew the officials who had murdered the king, his father. 6 But the children of the murderers he did not put to death, obeying the LORD's command written in the book of the law of Moses, "Fathers shall not be put to death for their children, nor shall children be put to death for their fathers; each one shall die for his own sin."

7 Amaziah slew ten thousand Edomites in the Salt Valley, and took Sela in battle. He renamed it Joktheel, the name it has to this day.

8 Then Amaziah sent messengers to Jehoash, son of Jehoahaz, son of Jehu, king of Israel, with this challenge, "Come, let us meet face to face." 9 King Jehoash of Israel sent this reply to the king of Judah: "The thistle of Lebanon sent word to the cedar of Lebanon, 'Give your daughter to my son in marriage,' but an animal of Lebanon passed by and trampled the thistle underfoot. 10 You have indeed conquered Edom, and you have become ambitious. Enjoy your glory, but stay at home! Why involve yourself and Judah with you in misfortune and failure?"

11 But Amaziah would not listen. King Jehoash of Israel then advanced, and he and King Amaziah of Judah met in battle at Beth-shemesh of Judah. 12 Judah was defeated by Israel, and all the Judean soldiery fled homeward. 13 King Jehoash of Israel captured Amaziah, son of Jehoash, son of Ahaziah, king of Judah, at Beth-shemesh. He went on to Jerusalem where he tore down four hundred cubits of the city wall, from the Gate of Ephraim to the Corner Gate. 14 He took all the gold and silver and all the utensils there were in the temple of the LORD and in the treasuries of the palace, and hostages as well. Then he returned to Samaria. 15 The rest of the acts of Jehoash, his valor, and how he fought Amaziah, king of Judah, are recorded in the book of the chronicles of the kings of Israel. 16 Jehoash rested with

18 Elisha said, 'Take the arrows,' and he took them. Then he said to the king, 'Strike the ground,' and he struck it three times, then stopped. 19 At this the man of God grew angry with him. 'You should have struck half a dozen times,' he said, 'and you would have beaten Aram completely; now you will beat Aram only three times.' 20 Elisha died and was buried. Bands of Moabites were making incursions into the country every year. 21 Some people happened to be carrying a man out for burial; at the sight of one of these bands, they flung the man into the tomb of Elisha and made off. The man had no sooner touched the bones of Elisha than he came to life and stood up on his feet. 22 Hazael king of Aram had oppressed the Israelites throughout the lifetime of Jehoahaz, 23 but Yahweh was kind and took pity on them. Because of the covenant which he had made with Abraham, Isaac and Jacob, he relented towards them; he had no wish to destroy them, he did not cast them out of his presence. 24 Hazael king of Aram died, and his son Ben-Hadad succeeded him. 25 From Ben-Hadad son of Hazael, Jehoash son of Jehoahaz recaptured the towns which Hazael had seized from his father Jehoahaz by force of arms. Joash defeated him three times and recovered the Israelite towns.

14 In the second year of Joash son of Jehoahaz, king of Israel, Amaziah son of Joash became king of Judah. 2 He was twenty-five years old when he came to the throne, and he reigned for twenty-nine years in Jerusalem. His mother's name was Jehoaddin of Jerusalem. 3 He did what Yahweh regards as right, though not like his ancestor David; he imitated his father Joash in all respects. 4 The high places, however, were not abolished, and the people still offered sacrifices and incense on the high places.

5 Once the kingdom was firmly under his control, he killed those of his retainers who had murdered the king his father. 6 But he did not put the murderers' sons to death, in accordance with what is written in the Book of Moses, where Yahweh has commanded: 'Parents may not be put to death for their children, nor children for parents, but each must be put to death for his own crime.' f

7 It was he who slaughtered the Edomites in the Valley of Salt, ten thousand of them, and captured the Rock; he gave it the name Joktheel, which it bears to the present day.

8 Amaziah then sent messengers to Jehoash son of Jehoahaz, king of Israel, saying, 'Come and make a trial of strength!' 9 Jehoash king of Israel sent back word to Amaziah king of Judah, 'The thistle of Lebanon sent a message to the cedar of Lebanon, saying, "Give my son your daughter in marriage"; but a wild animal of the Lebanon ran over the thistle and squashed it. 10 You have conquered Edom and now aspire to even greater glory. Stay where you belong! Why provoke disaster, to your own and Judah's ruin?'

11 But Amaziah would not listen, so Jehoash king of Israel marched to the attack. And at Beth-Shemesh, which belongs to Judah, he and Amaziah king of Judah made their trial of strength. 12 Judah was defeated by Israel, and everyone fled to his tent. 13 The king of Judah, Amaziah son of Jehoash, son of Ahaziah, was taken prisoner at Beth-Shemesh by Jehoash king of Israel who led him off to Jerusalem, where he demolished four hundred cubits of the city wall between the Ephraim Gate and the Corner Gate; 14 all the gold and silver, and all the vessels to be found in the Temple of Yahweh and in the palace treasury, and hostages besides, he then took back with him to Samaria.

15 The rest of the history of Jehoash, his entire career, his prowess, how he waged war on Amaziah king of Judah, is this not recorded in the Book of the Annals of the Kings of Israel? 16 Then Joash fell asleep with his ancestors, and was

f **14** Dt 24:16.

16 Jehoash slept with his ancestors, and was buried in Samaria with the kings of Israel; then his son Jeroboam succeeded him.

17 King Amaziah son of Joash of Judah lived fifteen years after the death of King Jehoash son of Jehoahaz of Israel. 18 Now the rest of the deeds of Amaziah, are they not written in the Book of the Annals of the Kings of Judah? 19 They made a conspiracy against him in Jerusalem, and he fled to Lachish. But they sent after him to Lachish, and killed him there. 20 They brought him on horses; he was buried in Jerusalem with his ancestors in the city of David. 21 All the people of Judah took Azariah, who was sixteen years old, and made him king to succeed his father Amaziah. 22 He rebuilt Elath and restored it to Judah, after King Amaziah^s slept with his ancestors.

23 In the fifteenth year of King Amaziah son of Joash of Judah, King Jeroboam son of Joash of Israel began to reign in Samaria; he reigned forty-one years. 24 He did what was evil in the sight of the LORD; he did not depart from all the sins of Jeroboam son of Nebat, which he caused Israel to sin. 25 He restored the border of Israel from Lebo-hamath as far as the Sea of the Arabah, according to the word of the LORD, the God of Israel, which he spoke by his servant Jonah son of Amittai, the prophet, who was from Gath-hepher. 26 For the LORD saw that the distress of Israel was very bitter; there was no one left, bond or free, and no one to help Israel. 27 But the LORD had not said that he would blot out the name of Israel from under heaven, so he saved them by the hand of Jeroboam son of Joash.

28 Now the rest of the acts of Jeroboam, and all that he did, and his might, how he fought, and how he recovered for Israel Damascus and Hamath, which had belonged to Judah, are they not written in the Book of the Annals of the Kings of Israel? 29 Jeroboam slept with his ancestors, the kings of Israel; his son Zechariah succeeded him.

15 In the twenty-seventh year of King Jeroboam of Israel King Azariah son of Amaziah of Judah began to reign. 2 He was sixteen years old when he began to reign, and he reigned fifty-two years in Jerusalem. His mother's name was Jecoliah of Jerusalem. 3 He did what was right in the sight of the LORD, just as his father Amaziah had done. 4 Nevertheless the high places were not taken away; the people still sacrificed and made offerings on the high places. 5 The LORD struck the king, so that he was leprous^t to the day of his death, and lived in a separate house. Jotham the king's son was in charge of the palace, governing the people of the land. 6 Now the rest of the acts of Azariah, and all that he did, are they not written in the Book of the Annals of the Kings of Judah? 7 Azariah slept with his ancestors; they buried him with his ancestors in the city of David; his son Jotham succeeded him.

8 In the thirty-eighth year of King Azariah of Judah, Zechariah son of Jeroboam reigned over Israel in Samaria six months. 9 He did what was evil in the sight of the LORD, as his ancestors had done. He did not depart from the sins of Jeroboam son of Nebat, which he caused Israel to sin. 10 Shallum son of Jabesh conspired against him, and struck him down in public and killed him, and reigned in place of him. 11 Now the rest of the deeds of Zechariah are written in the Book of the Annals of the Kings of Israel. 12 This was the promise of the LORD that he gave to Jehu, "Your sons shall sit on the throne of Israel to the fourth generation." And so it happened.

16 He rested with his forefathers and was buried in Samaria with the kings of Israel. His son Jeroboam succeeded him.

17 Amaziah son of Joash, king of Judah, outlived Jehoash son of Jehoahaz, king of Israel, by fifteen years. 18 The other events of Amaziah's reign are recorded in the annals of the kings of Judah. 19 A conspiracy was formed against him in Jerusalem and he fled to Lachish; but the conspirators sent after him to Lachish and put him to death there. 20 His body was conveyed on horseback to Jerusalem, and there he was buried with his forefathers in the city of David.

21 The people of Judah, acting together, took Azariah, now sixteen years old, and made him king in succession to his father Amaziah. 22 It was he who built Elath and restored it to Judah after the king rested with his forefathers.

23 In the fifteenth year of Amaziah son of Joash, king of Judah, Jeroboam son of Jehoash, king of Israel, became king in Samaria and reigned for forty-one years. 24 He did what was wrong in the eyes of the LORD; he did not give up the sinful practices of Jeroboam son of Nebat who led Israel into sin. 25 He re-established the frontiers of Israel from Lebo-hamath to the sea of the Arabah, in fulfilment of the word of the LORD the God of Israel spoken by his servant the prophet Jonah son of Amittai, from Gath-hepher. 26 For the LORD had seen how bitterly Israel had suffered; no one was safe, whether under the protection of his family or not, and Israel was left defenceless. 27 But the LORD had made no threat to blot out the name of Israel under heaven, and he saved them through Jeroboam son of Jehoash.

28 The other events of Jeroboam's reign, and all his achievements, his exploits, the wars he fought, and how he recovered Damascus and Hamath in Jaudi for Israel, are recorded in the annals of the kings of Israel. 29 Jeroboam rested with his forefathers the kings of Israel, and he was succeeded by his son Zechariah.

15 In the twenty-seventh year of King Jeroboam of Israel, Azariah son of King Amaziah of Judah became king. 2 He was sixteen years old when he came to the throne, and he reigned in Jerusalem for fifty-two years; his mother was Jecoliah from Jerusalem. 3 He did what was right in the eyes of the LORD, as Amaziah his father had done. 4 But the shrines were not abolished; the people still continued to sacrifice and burn offerings there. 5 The LORD struck the king with leprosy, which he had till the day of his death; he was relieved of all duties and lived in his palace, while his son Jotham was comptroller of the household and regent over the country. 6 The other acts and events of Azariah's reign are recorded in the annals of the kings of Judah. 7 He rested with his forefathers and was buried with them in the city of David. His son Jotham succeeded him.

8 In the thirty-eighth year of King Azariah of Judah, Zechariah son of Jeroboam became king over Israel in Samaria and reigned for six months. 9 He did what was wrong in the eyes of the LORD, as his forefathers had done; he did not give up the sinful practices of Jeroboam son of Nebat who led Israel into sin. 10 Shallum son of Jabesh formed a conspiracy against him, attacked and killed him in Ibleam, and usurped the throne. 11 The other events of Zechariah's reign are recorded in the annals of the kings of Israel. 12 Thus the word of the LORD spoken to Jehu was fulfilled: 'Your sons to the fourth generation will occupy the throne of Israel.'

14:17–22 Cp. 2 Chr. 25:25—26:2. 14:28 in Jaudi for: prob. rdg; Heb. to Judah in. 15:1 Azariah: Uzziah in verses 13,30,32,34. 15:2–3 Cp. 2 Chr. 26:3–4. 15:5–7 Cp. 2 Chr. 26:21–23. 15:5 leprosy: or a skin disease. 15:10 in Ibleam: so Gk (Luc.); Heb. before people.

^s Heb the king   ^t A term for several skin diseases; precise meaning uncertain

NEW AMERICAN BIBLE

his ancestors; he was buried in Samaria with the kings of Israel. His son Jeroboam succeeded him as king.

17 Amaziah, son of Joash, king of Judah, survived Jehoash, son of Jehoahaz, king of Israel, by fifteen years. 18 The rest of the acts of Amaziah are written in the book of the chronicles of the kings of Judah. 19 When a conspiracy was formed against him in Jerusalem, he fled to Lachish. But he was pursued to Lachish and killed there. 20 He was brought back on horses and buried with his ancestors in the City of David in Jerusalem. 21 Thereupon all the people of Judah took the sixteen-year-old Azariah and proclaimed him king to succeed his father Amaziah. 22 It was Azariah who rebuilt Elath and restored it to Judah, after King Amaziah rested with his ancestors.

23 In the fifteenth year of Amaziah, son of Joash, king of Judah, Jeroboam, son of Joash, king of Israel, began his forty-one-year reign in Samaria. 24 He did evil in the sight of the LORD; he did not desist from any of the sins which Jeroboam, son of Nebat, had caused Israel to commit. 25 He restored the boundaries of Israel from Labo-of-Hamath to the sea of the Arabah, just as the LORD, the God of Israel, had prophesied through his servant, the prophet Jonah, son of Amittai, from Gath-hepher. 26 For the LORD saw the very bitter affliction of Israel, where there was neither slave nor freeman, no one at all to help Israel. 27 Since the LORD had not determined to blot out the name of Israel from under the heavens, he saved them through Jeroboam, son of Joash. 28 The rest of the acts of Jeroboam, his valor and all his accomplishments, how he fought with Damascus and turned back Hamath from Israel, are recorded in the book of the chronicles of the kings of Israel. 29 Jeroboam rested with his ancestors, the kings of Israel, and his son Zechariah succeeded him as king.

15 Azariah, son of Amaziah, king of Judah, became king in the twenty-seventh year of Jeroboam, king of Israel. 2 He was sixteen years old when he began to reign, and he reigned fifty-two years in Jerusalem. His mother, whose name was Jecholiah, was from Jerusalem. 3 He pleased the LORD just as his father Amaziah had done. 4 Yet the high places did not disappear; the people continued to sacrifice and to burn incense on them. 5 The LORD afflicted the king, and he was a leper to the day of his death. He lived in a house apart, while Jotham, the king's son, was vizier and regent for the people of the land. 6 The rest of the acts of Azariah, and all his accomplishments, are recorded in the book of the chronicles of the kings of Judah. 7 Azariah rested with his ancestors, and was buried with them in the City of David. His son Jotham succeeded him as king.

8 In the thirty-eighth year of Azariah, king of Judah, Zechariah, son of Jeroboam, was king of Israel in Samaria for six months. 9 He did evil in the sight of the LORD as his fathers had done, and did not desist from the sins which Jeroboam, son of Nebat, had caused Israel to commit. 10 Shallum, son of Jabesh, conspired against Zechariah, attacked and killed him at Ibleam, and reigned in his place. 11 The rest of the acts of Zechariah are recorded in the book of the chronicles of the kings of Israel. 12 Thus the LORD's promise to Jehu, "Your descendants to the fourth generation shall sit upon the throne of Israel," was fulfilled.

NEW JERUSALEM BIBLE

buried in Samaria with the kings of Israel; his son Jeroboam succeeded him.

17 Amaziah son of Joash, king of Judah, lived for fifteen years after the death of Jehoash son of Jehoahaz, king of Israel. 18 The rest of the history of Amaziah, is this not recorded in the Book of the Annals of the Kings of Judah? 19 A plot having been hatched against him in Jerusalem, he fled to Lachish; but he was followed to Lachish where he was murdered. 20 He was then transported by horse and buried in Jerusalem with his ancestors in the City of David. 21 All the people of Judah then chose Uzziah, who was sixteen years old, and made him king in succession to his father Amaziah. 22 It was he who rebuilt Elath, recovering it for Judah, after the king had fallen asleep with his ancestors.

23 In the fifteenth year of Amaziah son of Joash, king of Judah, Jeroboam son of Joash became king of Israel in Samaria. He reigned for forty-one years. 24 He did what is displeasing to Yahweh and did not give up any of the sins into which Jeroboam son of Nebat had led Israel. 25 It was he who recovered the territory of Israel from the Pass of Hamath to the Sea of the Arabah, in accordance with the word which Yahweh, God of Israel, had spoken through his servant Jonah son of Amittai, the prophet from Gath-Hepher. 26 For Yahweh had seen how very bitter the affliction of Israel was, with no one, either fettered or free, to come to Israel's help. 27 But Yahweh had resolved not to blot out the name of Israel under heaven; he rescued them by means of Jeroboam son of Joash. 28 The rest of the history of Jeroboam, his entire career, his prowess, what wars he waged, how he brought Damascus and Hamath back to their allegiance to Judah and Israel, is this not recorded in the Book of the Annals of the Kings of Israel? 29 Then Jeroboam fell asleep with his ancestors and was buried in Samaria with the kings of Israel; his son Zechariah succeeded him.

15 In the seventeenth year of Jeroboam king of Israel, Uzziah son of Amaziah became king of Judah. 2 He was sixteen years old when he came to the throne, and he reigned for fifty-two years in Jerusalem. His mother's name was Jecoliah of Jerusalem. 3 He did what Yahweh regards as right, just as his father Amaziah had done. 4 The high places, however, were not abolished, and the people still offered sacrifices and incense on the high places.

5 But Yahweh struck the king, and he was afflicted with a virulent skin-disease till his dying day. He lived confined to his room, while Jotham the king's son, who was master of the palace, governed the country. 6 The rest of the history of Uzziah, his entire career, is this not recorded in the Book of the Annals of the Kings of Judah? 7 Then Uzziah fell asleep with his ancestors and was buried in the City of David; his son Jotham then succeeded him.

8 In the thirty-eighth year of Uzziah king of Judah, Zechariah son of Jeroboam became king of Israel in Samaria for six months. 9 He did what is displeasing to Yahweh, as his fathers had done; he did not give up the sins into which Jeroboam son of Nebat had led Israel. Shallum son of Jabesh plotted against him, murdered him at Ibleam, 10 and succeeded him. 11 The rest of the history of Zechariah is recorded in the Book of the Annals of the Kings of Israel. 12 This was the word which Yahweh had spoken to Jehu, 'Your sons will sit on the throne of Israel to the fourth generation.' And so it turned out.

NEW REVISED STANDARD VERSION	REVISED ENGLISH BIBLE

NEW REVISED STANDARD VERSION

13 Shallum son of Jabesh began to reign in the thirty-ninth year of King Uzziah of Judah; he reigned one month in Samaria. 14 Then Menahem son of Gadi came up from Tirzah and came to Samaria; he struck down Shallum son of Jabesh in Samaria and killed him; he reigned in place of him. 15 Now the rest of the deeds of Shallum, including the conspiracy that he made, are written in the Book of the Annals of the Kings of Israel. 16 At that time Menahem sacked Tiphsah, all who were in it and its territory from Tirzah on; because they did not open it to him, he sacked it. He ripped open all the pregnant women in it.

17 In the thirty-ninth year of King Azariah of Judah, Menahem son of Gadi began to reign over Israel; he reigned ten years in Samaria. 18 He did what was evil in the sight of the LORD; he did not depart all his days from any of the sins of Jeroboam son of Nebat, which he caused Israel to sin. 19 King Pul of Assyria came against the land; Menahem gave Pul a thousand talents of silver, so that he might help him confirm his hold on the royal power. 20 Menahem exacted the money from Israel, that is, from all the wealthy, fifty shekels of silver from each one, to give to the king of Assyria. So the king of Assyria turned back, and did not stay there in the land. 21 Now the rest of the deeds of Menahem, and all that he did, are they not written in the Book of the Annals of the Kings of Israel? 22 Menahem slept with his ancestors, and his son Pekahiah succeeded him.

23 In the fiftieth year of King Azariah of Judah, Pekahiah son of Menahem began to reign over Israel in Samaria; he reigned two years. 24 He did what was evil in the sight of the LORD; he did not turn away from the sins of Jeroboam son of Nebat, which he caused Israel to sin. 25 Pekah son of Remaliah, his captain, conspired against him with fifty of the Gileadites, and attacked him in Samaria, in the citadel of the palace along with Argob and Arieh; he killed him, and reigned in place of him. 26 Now the rest of the deeds of Pekahiah, and all that he did, are written in the Book of the Annals of the Kings of Israel.

27 In the fifty-second year of King Azariah of Judah, Pekah son of Remaliah began to reign over Israel in Samaria; he reigned twenty years. 28 He did what was evil in the sight of the LORD; he did not depart from the sins of Jeroboam son of Nebat, which he caused Israel to sin.

29 In the days of King Pekah of Israel, King Tiglath-pileser of Assyria came and captured Ijon, Abel-beth-maacah, Janoah, Kedesh, Hazor, Gilead, and Galilee, all the land of Naphtali; and he carried the people captive to Assyria. 30 Then Hoshea son of Elah made a conspiracy against Pekah son of Remaliah, attacked him, and killed him; he reigned in place of him, in the twentieth year of Jotham son of Uzziah. 31 Now the rest of the acts of Pekah, and all that he did, are written in the Book of the Annals of the Kings of Israel.

32 In the second year of King Pekah son of Remaliah of Israel, King Jotham son of Uzziah of Judah began to reign. 33 He was twenty-five years old when he began to reign and reigned sixteen years in Jerusalem. His mother's name was Jerusha daughter of Zadok. 34 He did what was right in the sight of the LORD, just as his father Uzziah had done. 35 Nevertheless the high places were not removed; the people still sacrificed and made offerings on the high places. He built the upper gate of the house of the LORD. 36 Now the rest of the acts of Jotham, and all that he did, are they not written in the Book of the Annals of the Kings of Judah?

REVISED ENGLISH BIBLE

13 Shallum son of Jabesh became king in the thirty-ninth year of King Uzziah of Judah, and he reigned for one full month in Samaria. 14 Menahem son of Gadi came up from Tirzah to Samaria, attacked Shallum son of Jabesh there, killed him, and usurped the throne. 15 The other events of Shallum's reign and the conspiracy that he formed are recorded in the annals of the kings of Israel.

16 Then Menahem, starting out from Tirzah, destroyed Tappuah and everything in it and ravaged its territory; he ravaged it because it had not opened its gates to him, and he ripped open every pregnant woman there.

17 In the thirty-ninth year of King Azariah of Judah, Menahem son of Gadi became king over Israel and he reigned in Samaria for ten years. 18-19 He did what was wrong in the eyes of the LORD; he did not give up the sinful practices of Jeroboam son of Nebat who led Israel into sin. In Menahem's time King Pul of Assyria invaded the country, and Menahem gave him a thousand talents of silver to obtain his help in strengthening his hold on the kingdom. 20 Menahem laid a levy on all the men of wealth in Israel; each had to give the king of Assyria fifty silver shekels, and he withdrew without occupying the country. 21 The other acts and events of Menahem's reign are recorded in the annals of the kings of Israel. 22 He rested with his forefathers, and was succeeded by his son Pekahiah.

23 In the fiftieth year of King Azariah of Judah, Pekahiah son of Menahem became king over Israel in Samaria and reigned for two years. 24 He did what was wrong in the eyes of the LORD; he did not give up the sinful practices of Jeroboam son of Nebat who led Israel into sin. 25 Pekah son of Remaliah, his lieutenant, formed a conspiracy against him and, with the help of fifty Gileadites, attacked and killed him in the citadel of the royal palace in Samaria, and usurped the throne. 26 The other acts and events of Pekahiah's reign are recorded in the annals of the kings of Israel.

27 In the fifty-second year of King Azariah of Judah, Pekah son of Remaliah became king over Israel in Samaria and reigned for twenty years. 28 He did what was wrong in the eyes of the LORD; he did not give up the sinful practices of Jeroboam son of Nebat who led Israel into sin. 29 In the days of King Pekah of Israel, King Tiglath-pileser of Assyria came and seized Iyyon, Abel-beth-maacah, Janoah, Kedesh, Hazor, Gilead, and Galilee, with all the land of Naphtali, and deported the people to Assyria. 30 Then Hoshea son of Elah formed a conspiracy against Pekah son of Remaliah, attacked and killed him, and usurped the throne in the twentieth year of Jotham son of Uzziah. 31 The other acts and events of Pekah's reign are recorded in the annals of the kings of Israel.

32 In the second year of Pekah son of Remaliah, king of Israel, Jotham son of King Uzziah of Judah became king. 33 He was twenty-five years old when he came to the throne, and he reigned in Jerusalem for sixteen years; his mother was Jerusha daughter of Zadok. 34 He did what was right in the eyes of the LORD, as his father Uzziah had done; 35 but the shrines were not abolished and the people continued to sacrifice and burn offerings there. It was he who constructed the Upper Gate of the house of the LORD. 36 The other acts and events of Jotham's reign are recorded in the annals of the kings of Judah. 37 In those days the LORD began to

15:16 **Tappuah:** *so Gk (Luc.); Heb.* Tiphsah.   15:25 **the citadel ... palace:** *prob. rdg; Heb. adds* Argob and Arieh.
15:33–38 *Cp.* 2 Chr. 27:1–9.

13 Shallum, son of Jabesh, became king in the thirty-ninth year of Uzziah, king of Judah; he reigned one month in Samaria. 14 Menahem, son of Gadi, came up from Tirzah to Samaria, where he attacked and killed Shallum, son of Jabesh, and reigned in his place. 15 The rest of the acts of Shallum, and the fact of his conspiracy, are recorded in the book of the chronicles of the kings of Israel. 16 At that time, Menahem punished Tappuah, all the inhabitants of the town and of its whole district, because on his way from Tirzah they did not let him in. He punished them even to ripping open all the pregnant women.

17 In the thirty-ninth year of Azariah, king of Judah, Menahem, son of Gadi, began his ten-year reign over Samaria. 18 He did evil in the sight of the LORD, not desisting from the sins which Jeroboam, son of Nebat, had caused Israel to commit. During his reign, 19 Pul, king of Assyria, invaded the land, and Menahem gave him a thousand talents of silver to have his assistance in strengthening his hold on the kingdom. 20 Menahem secured the money to give to the king of Assyria by exacting it from all the men of substance in the country, fifty silver shekels from each. The king of Assyria did not remain in the country but withdrew. 21 The rest of the acts of Menahem, and all his accomplishments, are recorded in the book of the chronicles of the kings of Israel. 22 Menahem rested with his ancestors, and his son Pekahiah succeeded him as king.

23 In the fiftieth year of Azariah, king of Judah, Pekahiah, son of Menahem, began his two-year reign over Israel in Samaria. 24 He did evil in the sight of the LORD, not desisting from the sins which Jeroboam, son of Nebat, had caused Israel to commit. 25 His adjutant Pekah, son of Remaliah, who had with him fifty men from Gilead, conspired against him, killed him within the palace stronghold in Samaria, and reigned in his place. 26 The rest of the acts of Pekahiah, and all his accomplishments, are recorded in the book of the chronicles of the kings of Israel.

27 In the fifty-second year of Azariah, king of Judah, Pekah, son of Remaliah, began his twenty-year reign over Israel in Samaria. 28 He did evil in the sight of the LORD, not desisting from the sins which Jeroboam, son of Nebat, had caused Israel to commit. 29 During the reign of Pekah, king of Israel, Tiglath-pileser, king of Assyria, came and took Ijon, Abel-beth-maacah, Janoah, Kedesh, Hazor, all the territory of Naphtali, Gilead, and Galilee, deporting the inhabitants to Assyria. 30 Hoshea, son of Elah, conspired against Pekah, son of Remaliah; he attacked and killed him, and reigned in his place [in the twentieth year of Jotham, son of Uzziah]. 31 The rest of the acts of Pekah, and all his accomplishments, are recorded in the book of the chronicles of the kings of Israel.

32 In the second year of Pekah, son of Remaliah, king of Israel, Jotham, son of Uzziah, king of Judah, began to reign. 33 He was twenty-five years old when he became king, and he reigned sixteen years in Jerusalem. His mother's name was Jerusha, daughter of Zadok. 34 He pleased the LORD, just as his father Uzziah had done. 35 Nevertheless the high places did not disappear and the people continued to sacrifice and to burn incense on them. It was he who built the Upper Gate of the temple of the LORD. 36 The rest of the acts of Jotham, and all his accomplishments, are recorded in the book of the chronicles of the kings of Judah. 37 It was at that time that the LORD first

13 Shallum son of Jabesh became king in the thirty-ninth year of Uzziah king of Judah and reigned for one month in Samaria. 14 Then Menahem son of Gadi marched from Tirzah, entered Samaria, murdered Shallum son of Jabesh there and succeeded him. 15 The rest of the history of Shallum, and the plot he hatched, is recorded in the Book of the Annals of the Kings of Israel. 16 Menahem then sacked Tappuah — killing all who were in it — and its territory from Tirzah onwards, because it had not opened its gates to him; he sacked the town and disembowelled all the pregnant women.

17 In the thirty-ninth year of Uzziah king of Judah, Menahem son of Gadi became king of Israel. He reigned for ten years in Samaria. 18 He did what is displeasing to Yahweh, he did not give up the sins into which Jeroboam son of Nebat had led Israel.

In his days 19 Pul$g$ king of Assyria invaded the country. Menahem gave Pul a thousand talents of silver in return for his support in strengthening his hold on the royal power. 20 Menahem levied this sum from Israel, from all the men of rank, at the rate of fifty shekels a head, to be given to the king of Assyria, who then withdrew and did not stay in the country.

21 The rest of the history of Menahem, his entire career, is this not recorded in the Book of the Annals of the Kings of Israel? 22 Then Menahem fell asleep with his ancestors; his son Pekahiah succeeded him.

23 In the fiftieth year of Uzziah king of Judah, Pekahiah son of Menahem became king of Israel in Samaria. He reigned for two years. 24 He did what is displeasing to Yahweh; he did not give up the sins into which Jeroboam son of Nebat had led Israel. 25 Pekah son of Remaliah, his equerry, plotted against him and assassinated him in the palace keep . . .h He had fifty Gileadites with him. He killed the king and succeeded him.

26 The rest of the history of Pekahiah, his entire career, is recorded in the Book of the Annals of the Kings of Israel. 27 In the fifty-second year of Uzziah king of Judah, Pekah son of Remaliah became king of Israel in Samaria. He reigned for twenty years. 28 He did what is displeasing to Yahweh; he did not give up the sins into which Jeroboam son of Nebat had led Israel.

29 In the days of Pekah king of Israel, Tiglath-Pileser king of Assyria came and captured Ijon, Abel-Beth-Maacah, Janoah, Kedesh, Hazor, Gilead and Galilee — the whole territory of Naphtali and deported the population to Assyria. 30 Hoshea son of Elah hatched a plot against Pekah son of Remaliah; he murdered the king and succeeded him.

31 The rest of the history of Pekah, his entire career, is recorded in the Book of the Annals of the Kings of Israel.

32 In the second year of Pekah son of Remaliah, king of Israel, Jotham son of Uzziah became king of Judah. 33 He was twenty-five years old when he came to the throne, and he reigned for sixteen years in Jerusalem. His mother's name was Jerusha daughter of Zadok. 34 He did what Yahweh regards as right, just as his father Uzziah had done. 35 The high places, however, were not abolished, and the people still offered sacrifices and incense on the high places.

It was he who built the Upper Gate of the Temple of Yahweh.

36 The rest of the history of Jotham, his entire career, is this not recorded in the Book of the Annals of the Kings of Judah? 37 At that time Yahweh began sending Razon king of

g 15 Name taken by Tiglath-Pileser III of Assyria when he assumed power also in Babylon.   h 15 Hebr. adds 'Argob and Arieh', a gloss on 'Gileadites'.

| NEW REVISED STANDARD VERSION | REVISED ENGLISH BIBLE |

37 In those days the LORD began to send King Rezin of Aram and Pekah son of Remaliah against Judah. 38 Jotham slept with his ancestors, and was buried with his ancestors in the city of David, his ancestor; his son Ahaz succeeded him.

16 In the seventeenth year of Pekah son of Remaliah, King Ahaz son of Jotham of Judah began to reign. 2 Ahaz was twenty years old when he began to reign; he reigned sixteen years in Jerusalem. He did not do what was right in the sight of the LORD his God, as his ancestor David had done, 3 but he walked in the way of the kings of Israel. He even made his son pass through fire, according to the abominable practices of the nations whom the LORD drove out before the people of Israel. 4 He sacrificed and made offerings on the high places, on the hills, and under every green tree.

5 Then King Rezin of Aram and King Pekah son of Remaliah of Israel came up to wage war on Jerusalem; they besieged Ahaz but could not conquer him. 6 At that time the king of Edom^u recovered Elath for Edom,^{v} and drove the Judeans from Elath; and the Edomites came to Elath, where they live to this day. 7 Ahaz sent messengers to King Tiglath-pileser of Assyria, saying, "I am your servant and your son. Come up, and rescue me from the hand of the king of Aram and from the hand of the king of Israel, who are attacking me." 8 Ahaz also took the silver and gold found in the house of the LORD and in the treasures of the king's house, and sent a present to the king of Assyria. 9 The king of Assyria listened to him; the king of Assyria marched up against Damascus, and took it, carrying its people captive to Kir; then he killed Rezin.

10 When King Ahaz went to Damascus to meet King Tiglath-pileser of Assyria, he saw the altar that was at Damascus. King Ahaz sent to the priest Uriah a model of the altar, and its pattern, exact in all its details. 11 The priest Uriah built the altar; in accordance with all that King Ahaz had sent from Damascus, just so did the priest Uriah build it, before King Ahaz arrived from Damascus. 12 When the king came from Damascus, the king viewed the altar. Then the king drew near to the altar, went up on it, 13 and offered his burnt offering and his grain offering, poured his drink offering, and dashed the blood of his offerings of well-being against the altar. 14 The bronze altar that was before the LORD he removed from the front of the house, from the place between his altar and the house of the LORD, and put it on the north side of his altar. 15 King Ahaz commanded the priest Uriah, saying, "Upon the great altar offer the morning burnt offering, and the evening grain offering, and the king's burnt offering, and his grain offering, with the burnt offering of all the people of the land, their grain offering, and their drink offering; then dash against it all the blood of the burnt offering, and all the blood of the sacrifice; but the bronze altar shall be for me to inquire by." 16 The priest Uriah did everything that King Ahaz commanded.

17 Then King Ahaz cut off the frames of the stands, and removed the laver from them; he removed the sea from the bronze oxen that were under it, and put it on a pediment of stone. 18 The covered portal for use on the sabbath that had been built inside the palace, and the outer entrance for the king he removed from^w the house of the LORD. He did this because of the king of Assyria. 19 Now the rest of the acts of Ahaz that he did, are they not written in the Book of the Annals of the Kings of Judah? 20 Ahaz slept with his ancestors, and was buried with his ancestors in the city of David; his son Hezekiah succeeded him.

send King Rezin of Aram and Pekah son of Remaliah to attack Judah. 38 Jotham rested with his forefathers and was buried with them in the city of David his forefather. His son Ahaz succeeded him.

16 IN the seventeenth year of Pekah son of Remaliah, Ahaz son of King Jotham of Judah became king. 2 Ahaz was twenty years old when he came to the throne, and he reigned in Jerusalem for sixteen years. He did not do what was right in the eyes of the LORD his God like his forefather David, 3 but followed in the footsteps of the kings of Israel; he even passed his son through the fire according to the abominable practice of the nations whom the LORD had dispossessed in favour of the Israelites. 4 He sacrificed and burned offerings at the shrines and on the hilltops and under every spreading tree.

5 Then King Rezin of Aram and Pekah son of Remaliah, king of Israel, attacked Jerusalem and besieged Ahaz but could not bring him to battle. 6 At that time the king of Edom recovered Elath by driving the Judaeans out of it; the Edomites entered the city and have occupied it to this day. 7 Ahaz sent messengers to King Tiglath-pileser of Assyria to say, 'I am your servant and your son. Come and save me from the king of Aram and from the king of Israel, who are attacking me.' 8 Ahaz took the silver and gold found in the house of the LORD and in the treasuries of the royal palace and sent them as a gift to the king of Assyria, 9 who listened to him; he advanced on Damascus, captured it, deported its inhabitants to Kir, and put Rezin to death.

10 When King Ahaz went to meet King Tiglath-pileser of Assyria at Damascus, he saw there an altar of which he sent a sketch and a detailed plan to Uriah the priest. 11 Accordingly, Uriah built an altar, following all the instructions that the king had sent him from Damascus, and had it ready against the king's return. 12 When the king came back from Damascus, he saw the altar, approached it, and mounted the steps; 13 there he burnt his whole-offering and his grain-offering and poured out his drink-offering, and he flung the blood of his shared-offerings against it. 14 The bronze altar that was before the LORD he removed from the front of the house, from between this new altar and the house of the LORD, and put it on the north side of this altar.

15 King Ahaz gave these instructions to Uriah the priest: 'Burn on the great altar the morning whole-offering and the evening grain-offering, and the king's whole-offering and his grain-offering, and the whole-offering of all the people of the land, their grain-offering and their drink-offerings, and fling against it all the blood of the sacrifices. But the bronze altar shall be for me, to offer morning sacrifice.' 16 Uriah the priest carried out all the king's orders.

17 King Ahaz stripped the trolleys and removed the panels, and he took down the basin and the Sea of bronze from the oxen which supported it and put it on a stone base. 18 In the house of the LORD he removed the structure they had erected for use on the sabbath, and the outer gate for the king, to satisfy the king of Assyria. 19 The other acts and events of the reign of Ahaz are recorded in the annals of the kings of Judah. 20 Ahaz rested with his forefathers and was buried with them in the city of David. His son Hezekiah succeeded him.

^{u} Cn: Heb *King Rezin of Aram* ^{v} Cn: Heb *Aram* ^{w} Cn: Heb lacks *from*

16:2–4 *Cp. 2 Chr. 28:1–4.*   16:6 **the king of Edom:** *prob. rdg; Heb.* Rezin king of Aram.   16:18 **structure:** *meaning uncertain.* 16:19–20 *Cp. 2 Chr. 28:26–27.*

NEW AMERICAN BIBLE | NEW JERUSALEM BIBLE

loosed Rezin, king of Aram, and Pekah, son of Remaliah, against Judah. 38 Jotham rested with his ancestors and was buried with them in his forefather's City of David. His son Ahaz succeeded him as king.

16 In the seventeenth year of Pekah, son of Remaliah, Ahaz, son of Jotham, king of Judah, began to reign. 2 Ahaz was twenty years old when he became king, and he reigned sixteen years in Jerusalem. He did not please the LORD, his God, like his forefather David, 3 but conducted himself like the kings of Israel, and even immolated his son by fire, in accordance with the abominable practice of the nations whom the LORD had cleared out of the way of the Israelites. 4 Further, he sacrificed and burned incense on the high places, on hills, and under every leafy tree.

5 Then Rezin, king of Aram, and Pekah, son of Remaliah, king of Israel, came up to Jerusalem to attack it. Although they besieged Ahaz, they were unable to conquer him. 6 At the same time the king of Edom recovered Elath for Edom, driving the Judeans out of it. The Edomites then entered Elath, which they have occupied until the present. 7 Meanwhile, Ahaz sent messengers to Tiglath-pileser, king of Assyria, with the plea: "I am your servant and your son. Come up and rescue me from the clutches of the king of Aram and the king of Israel, who are attacking me." 8 Ahaz took the silver and gold that were in the temple of the LORD and in the palace treasuries and sent them as a present to the king of Assyria, 9 who listened to him and moved against Damascus, which he captured. He deported its inhabitants to Kir and put Rezin to death.

10 King Ahaz went to Damascus to meet Tiglath-pileser, king of Assyria. When he saw the altar in Damascus, King Ahaz sent to Uriah the priest a model of the altar and a detailed design of its construction. 11 Uriah the priest built an altar according to the plans which King Ahaz sent him from Damascus, and had it completed by the time the king returned home. 12 On his arrival from Damascus, the king inspected this altar, then went up to it and offered sacrifice on it, 13 burning his holocaust and cereal-offering, pouring out his libation, and sprinkling the blood of his peace-offerings on the altar. 14 The bronze altar that stood before the LORD he brought from the front of the temple — that is, from the space between the new altar and the temple of the Lord — and set it on the north side of his altar. 15 "Upon the large altar," King Ahaz commanded Uriah the priest, "burn the morning holocaust and the evening cereal-offering, the royal holocaust and cereal-offering, as well as the holocausts, cereal-offerings, and libations of the people. You must also sprinkle on it all the blood of holocausts and sacrifices. But the old bronze altar shall be mine for consultation." 16 Uriah the priest did just as King Ahaz had commanded. 17 King Ahaz detached the frames from the bases and removed the lavers from them; he also took down the bronze sea from the bronze oxen that supported it, and set it on a stone pavement. 18 In deference to the king of Assyria he removed from the temple of the LORD the emplacement which had been built in the temple for a throne, and the outer entrance for the king. 19 The rest of the acts of Ahaz are recorded in the book of the chronicles of the kings of Judah. 20 Ahaz rested with his ancestors and was buried with them in the City of David. His son Hezekiah succeeded him as king.

Aram and Pekah son of Remaliah against Judah. 38 Then Jotham fell asleep with his ancestors and was buried in the City of David, his ancestor; his son Ahaz succeeded him.

16 In the seventeenth year of Pekah son of Remaliah, Ahaz son of Jotham became king of Judah. 2 Ahaz was twenty years old when he came to the throne, and he reigned for sixteen years in Jerusalem. He did not do what Yahweh his God regards as right, as his ancestor David had done. 3 He followed the example of the kings of Israel, even causing his son to pass through the fire of sacrifice, also copying the disgusting practices of the nations whom Yahweh had dispossessed for the Israelites. 4 He offered sacrifices and incense on the high places, on the hills and under every luxuriant tree.

5 Then it was that Razon king of Aram and Pekah son of Remaliah, king of Israel, launched their campaign against Jerusalem. They besieged it but could not reduce it. 6 (At that time, the king of Edom recovered Elath for Edom; he drove the Judaeans out of Elath, and the Edomites occupied it and have been there ever since.) 7 Ahaz then sent messengers to Tiglath-Pileser king of Assyria to say, 'I am your servant and your son. Come and rescue me from the king of Aram and the king of Israel who are making war on me.' 8 And Ahaz took what silver and gold was to be found in the Temple of Yahweh and in the palace treasury, and sent this as a present to the king of Assyria. 9 The king of Assyria granted his request and, marching on Damascus, captured it; he deported its population to Kir and put Razon to death.

10 When King Ahaz went to Damascus to meet Tiglath-Pileser king of Assyria, he saw the altar which was in Damascus. King Ahaz then sent a picture and model of the altar, with details of its construction, to Uriah the priest. 11 Uriah the priest constructed the altar; all the instructions sent by King Ahaz from Damascus were carried out by Uriah the priest before King Ahaz returned from Damascus. 12 When the king arrived from Damascus, he inspected the altar, he approached it and ascended it. 13 And on the altar he made his burnt offering and his oblation; he poured out his libation and sprinkled the blood of his communion sacrifices. 14 The altar which used to stand before Yahweh he removed from the front of the Temple, where it had stood between the new altar and the Temple of Yahweh, and placed it at the north side of the new altar. 15 King Ahaz gave this order to Uriah the priest, 'In future you will present the morning burnt offering, the evening oblation, the king's burnt offering and oblation, the burnt offering, the oblation and the libations of all the people of the country on the large altar; on it you will pour out all the blood of the burnt offerings and sacrifices. As regards the bronze altar, I shall see to that.' 16 Uriah the priest did everything that King Ahaz had ordered.

17 King Ahaz broke up the wheeled stands; removed the crosspieces and the basins from them, and took the bronze Sea off the oxen supporting it, and rested it on the stone pavement. 18 And from the Temple of Yahweh, in deference to the king of Assyria, he removed the dais for the throne which had been built inside, and the royal entrance on the outside.

19 The rest of the history of Ahaz, his entire career, is this not recorded in the Book of the Annals of the Kings of Judah? 20 Then Ahaz fell asleep with his ancestors and was buried in the City of David; his son Hezekiah succeeded him.

NEW REVISED STANDARD VERSION

17 In the twelfth year of King Ahaz of Judah, Hoshea son of Elah began to reign in Samaria over Israel; he reigned nine years. 2 He did what was evil in the sight of the LORD, yet not like the kings of Israel who were before him. 3 King Shalmaneser of Assyria came up against him; Hoshea became his vassal, and paid him tribute. 4 But the king of Assyria found treachery in Hoshea; for he had sent messengers to King So of Egypt, and offered no tribute to the king of Assyria, as he had done year by year; therefore the king of Assyria confined him and imprisoned him.

5 Then the king of Assyria invaded all the land and came to Samaria; for three years he besieged it. 6 In the ninth year of Hoshea the king of Assyria captured Samaria; he carried the Israelites away to Assyria. He placed them in Halah, on the Habor, the river of Gozan, and in the cities of the Medes.

7 This occurred because the people of Israel had sinned against the LORD their God, who had brought them up out of the land of Egypt from under the hand of Pharaoh king of Egypt. They had worshiped other gods 8 and walked in the customs of the nations whom the LORD drove out before the people of Israel, and in the customs that the kings of Israel had introduced.x 9 The people of Israel secretly did things that were not right against the LORD their God. They built for themselves high places at all their towns, from watchtower to fortified city; 10 they set up for themselves pillars and sacred poles y on every high hill and under every green tree; 11 there they made offerings on all the high places, as the nations did whom the LORD carried away before them. They did wicked things, provoking the LORD to anger; 12 they served idols, of which the LORD had said to them, "You shall not do this." 13 Yet the LORD warned Israel and Judah by every prophet and every seer, saying, "Turn from your evil ways and keep my commandments and my statutes, in accordance with all the law that I commanded your ancestors and that I sent to you by my servants the prophets." 14 They would not listen but were stubborn, as their ancestors had been, who did not believe in the LORD their God. 15 They despised his statutes, and his covenant that he made with their ancestors, and the warnings that he gave them. They went after false idols and became false; they followed the nations that were around them, concerning whom the LORD had commanded them that they should not do as they did. 16 They rejected all the commandments of the LORD their God and made for themselves cast images of two calves; they made a sacred pole,z worshiped all the host of heaven, and served Baal. 17 They made their sons and their daughters pass through fire; they used divination and augury; and they sold themselves to do evil in the sight of the LORD, provoking him to anger. 18 Therefore the LORD was very angry with Israel and removed them out of his sight; none was left but the tribe of Judah alone.

19 Judah also did not keep the commandments of the LORD their God but walked in the customs that Israel had introduced. 20 The LORD rejected all the descendants of Israel; he punished them and gave them into the hand of plunderers, until he had banished them from his presence.

21 When he had torn Israel from the house of David, they made Jeroboam son of Nebat king. Jeroboam drove Israel from following the LORD and made them commit great sin. 22 The people of Israel continued in all the sins that Jeroboam committed; they did not depart from them 23 until the LORD removed Israel out of his sight, as he had foretold through all his servants the prophets. So Israel was exiled from their own land to Assyria until this day.

REVISED ENGLISH BIBLE

17 In the twelfth year of King Ahaz of Judah, Hoshea son of Elah became king over Israel and he reigned in Samaria for nine years. 2 He did what was wrong in the eyes of the LORD, but not as previous kings of Israel had done. 3 King Shalmaneser of Assyria marched up against Hoshea, who had been tributary to him, 4 but when the king of Assyria discovered that Hoshea was being disloyal to him, sending envoys to the king of Egypt at So, and withholding the annual tribute which he had been paying, the king of Assyria seized and imprisoned him. 5 He overran the whole country and, reaching Samaria, besieged it for three years. 6 In the ninth year of Hoshea he captured Samaria and deported its people to Assyria, and settled them in Halah and on the Habor, the river of Gozan, and in the towns of Media.

7 All this came about because the Israelites had sinned against the LORD their God who brought them up from Egypt, from the despotic rule of Pharaoh king of Egypt; they paid homage to other gods 8 and observed the laws and customs of the nations whom the LORD had dispossessed before them, 9 and uttered blasphemies against the LORD their God; they built shrines for themselves in all their settlements, from watch-tower to fortified city; 10 they set up for themselves sacred pillars and sacred poles on every high hill and under every spreading tree, 11 and burnt offerings at all the shrines there, as the nations did whom the LORD had displaced before them. By this wickedness of theirs they provoked the LORD's anger. 12 They worshipped idols, a thing which the LORD had forbidden them to do.

13 Still the LORD solemnly charged Israel and Judah by every prophet and seer, saying, 'Give up your evil ways; keep my commandments and statutes given in all the law which I enjoined on your forefathers and delivered to you through my servants the prophets.' 14 They would not listen, however, but were as stubborn and rebellious as their forefathers had been, for they too refused to put their trust in the LORD their God. 15 They rejected his statutes and the covenant which he had made with their forefathers and the solemn warnings which he had given to them. Following worthless idols they became worthless themselves and imitated the nations round about them, which the LORD had forbidden them to do. 16 Forsaking every commandment of the LORD their God, they made themselves images, two calves of cast metal, and also a sacred pole. They prostrated themselves to all the host of heaven and worshipped Baal; 17 they made their sons and daughters pass through the fire. They practised augury and divination; they sold themselves to do what was wrong in the eyes of the LORD and so provoked his anger.

18 Thus it was that the LORD was incensed against Israel and banished them from his presence; only the tribe of Judah was left. 19 Even Judah did not keep the commandments of the LORD their God but followed the practices adopted by Israel; 20 so the LORD rejected all the descendants of Israel and punished them and gave them over to plunderers and finally flung them out from his presence. 21 When he tore Israel from the house of David, they made Jeroboam son of Nebat king, and he seduced Israel from their allegiance to the LORD and led them into grave sin. 22 The Israelites persisted in all the sins that Jeroboam had committed and did not give them up, 23 until finally the LORD banished the Israelites from his presence, as he had threatened through all his servants the prophets, and they were deported from their own land to exile in Assyria; and there they are to this day.

17:4 **to the . . . So:** *prob. rdg; Heb.* to So king of Egypt.
17:8 **before them:** *so Syriac; Heb. adds* and those of the kings of Egypt which they practised.

---

x Meaning of Heb uncertain   y Heb *Asherim*   z Heb *Asherah*

17 In the twelfth year of Ahaz, king of Judah, Hoshea, son of Elah, began his nine-year reign over Israel in Samaria. 2 He did evil in the sight of the LORD, yet not to the extent of the kings of Israel before him. 3 Shalmaneser, king of Assyria, advanced against him, and Hoshea became his vassal and paid him tribute. 4 But the king of Assyria found Hoshea guilty of conspiracy for sending envoys to the king of Egypt at Sais, and for failure to pay the annual tribute to his Assyrian overlord. 5 For this, the king of Assyria arrested and imprisoned Hoshea; he then occupied the whole land and attacked Samaria, which he besieged for three years. 6 In the ninth year of Hoshea, the king of Assyria took Samaria, and deported the Israelites to Assyria, settling them in Halah, at the Habor, a river of Gozan, and in the cities of the Medes.

7 This came about because the Israelites sinned against the LORD, their God, who had brought them up from the land of Egypt, from under the domination of Pharaoh, king of Egypt, and because they venerated other gods. 8 They followed the rites of the nations whom the LORD had cleared out of the way of the Israelites [and the kings of Israel whom they set up]. 9 They adopted unlawful practices toward the LORD, their God. They built high places in all their settlements, the watchtowers as well as the walled cities. 10 They set up pillars and sacred poles for themselves on every high hill and under every leafy tree. 11 There, on all the high places, they burned incense like the nations whom the LORD had sent into exile at their coming. They did evil things that provoked the LORD, 12 and served idols, although the LORD had told them, "You must not do this."

13 And though the LORD warned Israel and Judah by every prophet and seer, "Give up your evil ways and keep my commandments and statutes, in accordance with the entire law which I enjoined on your fathers and which I sent you by my servants the prophets," 14 they did not listen, but were as stiff-necked as their fathers, who had not believed in the LORD, their God. 15 They rejected his statutes, the covenant which he had made with their fathers, and the warnings which he had given them. The vanity they pursued, they themselves became: they followed the surrounding nations whom the LORD had commanded them not to imitate. 16 They disregarded all the commandments of the LORD, their God, and made for themselves two molten calves; they also made a sacred pole and worshiped all the host of heaven, and served Baal. 17 They immolated their sons and daughters by fire, practiced fortune-telling and divination, and sold themselves into evildoing in the LORD's sight, provoking him 18 till, in his great anger against Israel, the LORD put them away out of his sight. Only the tribe of Judah was left.

19 Even the people of Judah, however, did not keep the commandments of the LORD, their God, but followed the rites practiced by Israel. 20 So the LORD rejected the whole race of Israel. He afflicted them and delivered them over to plunderers, finally casting them out from before him. 21 When he tore Israel away from the house of David, they made Jeroboam, son of Nebat, king: he drove the Israelites away from the LORD, causing them to commit a great sin. 22 The Israelites imitated Jeroboam in all the sins he committed, nor would they desist from them. 23 Finally, the LORD put Israel away out of his sight as he had foretold through all his servants, the prophets; and Israel went into exile from their native soil to Assyria, an exile lasting to the present.

17 In the twelfth year of Ahaz king of Judah, Hoshea son of Elah became king of Israel in Samaria, and reigned for nine years. 2 He did what is displeasing to Yahweh, though not like the preceding kings of Israel.

3 Shalmaneser king of Assyria made war on Hoshea who submitted to him and paid him tribute. 4 But the king of Assyria discovered that Hoshea was playing a double game with him; he had sent messengers to Sais, to the king of Egypt, and had not, as in previous years, handed over the tribute to the king of Assyria. For this the king of Assyria imprisoned him in chains.

5 The king of Assyria invaded the whole country and, coming to Samaria, laid siege to it for three years. 6 In the ninth year of Hoshea the king of Assyria captured Samaria and deported the Israelites to Assyria. He settled them in Halah on the Habor, a river of Gozan, and in the cities of the Medes.

7 This happened because the Israelites had sinned against Yahweh their God who had brought them out of Egypt, out of the grip of Pharaoh king of Egypt. They worshipped other gods, 8 they followed the practices of the nations which Yahweh had dispossessed for them. 9 The Israelites spoke slightingly of Yahweh their God. They built themselves high places wherever they lived, from watchtower to fortified town. 10 They set up pillars and sacred poles for themselves on every high hill and under every luxuriant tree. 11 They sacrificed on all the high places like the nations which Yahweh had expelled for them, and did wicked things there, provoking Yahweh's anger. 12 They served idols, although Yahweh had told them, 'This you must not do.'

13 And yet through all the prophets and the seers, Yahweh had given Israel and Judah this warning, 'Turn from your wicked ways and keep my commandments and my laws in accordance with the entire Law which I laid down for your fathers and delivered to them through my servants the prophets.' 14 But they would not listen, they were as stubborn as their ancestors, who had no faith in Yahweh their God. 15 They despised his laws and the covenant which he had made with their ancestors and the warnings which he had given them. Pursuing futility, they themselves became futile through copying the nations round them, although Yahweh had ordered them not to act as they did. 16 They rejected all the commandments of Yahweh their God and cast themselves metal idols, two calves; they made themselves sacred poles, they worshipped the whole array of heaven, and they served Baal. 17 They caused their sons and daughters to pass through the fire of sacrifice, also they practised divination and sorcery, they sold themselves to doing what displeases Yahweh, provoking his anger. 18 Because of which, Yahweh became enraged with Israel and thrust them away from him. The tribe of Judah was the only one left.

19 Judah did not keep the commandments of Yahweh their God either but copied the practices which Israel had introduced. 20 Yahweh rejected the whole race of Israel; he brought them low, delivering them into the hands of marauders, until at length he thrust them away from him. 21 And indeed he had torn Israel away from the House of David, and they had made Jeroboam son of Nebat king; Jeroboam had drawn Israel away from Yahweh and led them into a great sin. 22 The Israelites copied the sin which Jeroboam had committed; they did not give it up, 23 until at length Yahweh thrust Israel away from him, as he had foretold through all his servants the prophets; he deported the Israelites from their own country to Assyria, where they have been ever since.

24 The king of Assyria brought people from Babylon, Cuthah, Avva, Hamath, and Sepharvaim, and placed them in the cities of Samaria in place of the people of Israel; they took possession of Samaria, and settled in its cities. 25 When they first settled there, they did not worship the LORD; therefore the LORD sent lions among them, which killed some of them. 26 So the king of Assyria was told, "The nations that you have carried away and placed in the cities of Samaria do not know the law of the god of the land; therefore he has sent lions among them; they are killing them, because they do not know the law of the god of the land." 27 Then the king of Assyria commanded, "Send there one of the priests whom you carried away from there; let him*a* go and live there, and teach them the law of the god of the land." 28 So one of the priests whom they had carried away from Samaria came and lived in Bethel; he taught them how they should worship the LORD.

29 But every nation still made gods of its own and put them in the shrines of the high places that the people of Samaria had made, every nation in the cities in which they lived; 30 the people of Babylon made Succoth-benoth, the people of Cuth made Nergal, the people of Hamath made Ashima; 31 the Avvites made Nibhaz and Tartak; the Sepharvites burned their children in the fire to Adrammelech and Anammelech, the gods of Sepharvaim. 32 They also worshiped the LORD and appointed from among themselves all sorts of people as priests of the high places, who sacrificed for them in the shrines of the high places. 33 So they worshiped the LORD but also served their own gods, after the manner of the nations from among whom they had been carried away. 34 To this day they continue to practice their former customs.

They do not worship the LORD and they do not follow the statutes or the ordinances or the law or the commandment that the LORD commanded the children of Jacob, whom he named Israel. 35 The LORD had made a covenant with them and commanded them, "You shall not worship other gods or bow yourselves to them or serve them or sacrifice to them, 36 but you shall worship the LORD, who brought you out of the land of Egypt with great power and with an outstretched arm; you shall bow yourselves to him, and to him you shall sacrifice. 37 The statutes and the ordinances and the law and the commandment that he wrote for you, you shall always be careful to observe. You shall not worship other gods; 38 you shall not forget the covenant that I have made with you. You shall not worship other gods, 39 but you shall worship the LORD your God; he will deliver you out of the hand of all your enemies." 40 They would not listen, however, but they continued to practice their former custom.

41 So these nations worshiped the LORD, but also served their carved images; to this day their children and their children's children continue to do as their ancestors did.

18 In the third year of King Hoshea son of Elah of Israel, Hezekiah son of King Ahaz of Judah began to reign. 2 He was twenty-five years old when he began to reign; he reigned twenty-nine years in Jerusalem. His mother's name was Abi daughter of Zechariah. 3 He did what was right in the sight of the LORD just as his ancestor David had done. 4 He removed the high places, broke down the pillars, and cut down the sacred pole.*b* He broke in pieces the bronze serpent that Moses had made, for until those days the people of Israel had made offerings to it; it

24 Then the king of Assyria brought people from Babylon, Cuthah, Avva, Hamath, and Sepharvaim, and settled them in the towns of Samaria in place of the Israelites; so they occupied Samaria and lived in its towns. 25 In the early years of their settlement they did not pay homage to the LORD, so the LORD sent lions among them to prey on them. 26 The king of Assyria was told that the deported peoples whom he had settled in the towns of Samaria did not know the established usage of the God of the country, and that he had sent lions among them which were preying on them because they did not know this. 27 The king, therefore, gave orders that one of the priests taken captive from Samaria should be sent back to live there and teach the people the usage of the God of the country. 28 So one of the deported priests came and lived at Bethel, and taught them how to worship the LORD.

29 But each of the nations went on making its own god. They set them up in niches at the shrines which the Samaritans had made, each nation in its own settlements. 30 Succoth-benoth was worshipped by the men of Babylon, Nergal by the men of Cuth, Ashima by the men of Hamath, 31 Nibhaz and Tartak by the Avvites; and the Sepharvites burnt their children as offerings to Adrammelech and Anammelech, the gods of Sepharvaim. 32 While still paying homage to the LORD, they appointed all sorts of people to act as priests of the shrines and they resorted to them there. 33 They paid homage to the LORD, while at the same time they served their own gods, according to the custom of the nations from which they had been carried into exile.

34 They keep up these old practices to this day; they do not pay homage to the LORD, for they do not keep his statutes and his judgements, the law and commandment, which he enjoined on the descendants of Jacob whom he named Israel. 35 When the LORD made a covenant with them, he gave them this commandment: 'Do not pay homage to other gods or bow down to them or serve them or sacrifice to them, 36 but pay homage to the LORD who brought you up from Egypt with great power and with outstretched arm; to him alone you are to bow down, to him alone you are to offer sacrifice. 37 You must faithfully keep the statutes, the judgements, the law, and the commandments which he wrote for you; you must not pay homage to other gods. 38 Do not forget the covenant which I made with you; do not pay homage to other gods. 39 But to the LORD your God you are to pay homage; it is he who will preserve you from all your enemies.' 40 However, they would not listen but continued their former practices. 41 While these nations paid homage to the LORD they continued to serve their images, and their children and their children's children have maintained the practice of their forefathers to this day.

18 In the third year of Hoshea son of Elah, king of Israel, Hezekiah son of King Ahaz of Judah became king. 2 He was twenty-five years old when he came to the throne, and he reigned in Jerusalem for twenty-nine years; his mother was Abi daughter of Zechariah. 3 He did what was right in the eyes of the LORD, as his ancestor David had done. 4 It was he who suppressed the shrines, smashed the sacred pillars, cut down every sacred pole, and broke up the bronze serpent that Moses had made, for up to that time the Israelites had been in the habit of burning sacrifices to it;

---

a Syr Vg: Heb *them*   *b* Heb *Asherah*   17:34 **his:** *prob. rdg; Heb.* their.   18:1–3 *Cp. 2 Chr. 29:1–2.*

24 The king of Assyria brought people from Babylon, Cuthah, Avva, Hamath, and Sepharvaim, and settled them in the cities of Samaria in place of the Israelites. They took possession of Samaria and dwelt in its cities. 25 When they first settled there, they did not venerate the LORD, so he sent lions among them that killed some of their number. 26 A report reached the king of Assyria: "The nations whom you deported and settled in the cities of Samaria do not know how to worship the God of the land, and he has sent lions among them that are killing them, since they do not know how to worship the God of the land." 27 The king of Assyria gave the order, "Send back one of the priests whom I deported, to go there and settle, to teach them how to worship the God of the land." 28 So one of the priests who had been deported from Samaria returned and settled in Bethel, and taught them how to venerate the LORD.

29 But these peoples began to make their own gods in the various cities in which they were living; in the shrines on the high places which the Samaritans had made, each people set up gods. 30 Thus the Babylonians made Marduk and his consort; the men of Cuth made Nergal; the men of Hamath made Ashima; 31 the men of Avva made Nibhaz and Tartak; and the men of Sepharvaim immolated their children by fire to their city gods, King Hadad and his consort Anath. 32 They also venerated the LORD, choosing from their number priests for the high places, who officiated for them in the shrines on the high places. 33 But, while venerating the LORD, they served their own gods, following the worship of the nations from among whom they had been deported.

34 To this day they worship according to their ancient rites. [They did not venerate the LORD nor observe the statutes and regulations, the law and commandments, which the LORD enjoined on the descendants of Jacob, whom he had named Israel. 35 When he made a covenant with them, he commanded them: "You must not venerate other gods, nor worship them, nor serve them, nor offer sacrifice to them. 36 The LORD, who brought you up from the land of Egypt with great power and outstretched arm: him shall you venerate, him shall you worship, and to him shall you sacrifice. 37 You must be careful to observe forever the statutes and regulations, the law and commandment, which he wrote for you, and you must not venerate other gods. 38 The covenant which I made with you, you must not forget; you must not venerate other gods. 39 But the LORD, your God, you must venerate; it is he who will deliver you from the power of all your enemies." 40 They did not listen, however, but continued in their earlier manner.] 41 Thus these nations venerated the LORD, but also served their idols. And their sons and grandsons, to this day, are doing as their fathers did.

18 In the third year of Hoshea, son of Elah, king of Israel, Hezekiah, son of Ahaz, king of Judah, began to reign. 2 He was twenty-five years old when he became king, and he reigned twenty-nine years in Jerusalem. His mother's name was Abi, daughter of Zechariah. 3 He pleased the LORD, just as his forefather David had done. 4 It was he who removed the high places, shattered the pillars, and cut down the sacred poles. He smashed the bronze serpent called Nehushtan which Moses had made, because up to that time the Israelites were burning incense to it. 5 He

24 The king of Assyria brought people from Babylon, Cuthah, Avva, Hamath and Sepharvaim, and settled them in the towns of Samaria to replace the Israelites; these took possession of Samaria and lived in its towns.

25 When they first came to live there, they did not worship Yahweh; hence, Yahweh sent lions on them, which killed a number of them. 26 Consequently, the king of Assyria was informed as follows, 'The nations whom you deported and settled in the towns of Samaria do not know how to worship the local god, and he has set lions on them; and now these are killing them because they do not know how to worship the local god.' 27 So the king of Assyria gave this order, 'Send back one of the priests whom I deported from there; let him go and live there and teach them how to worship the local god.' 28 Accordingly, one of the priests who had been deported from Samaria came to live in Bethel; he taught them how to worship Yahweh.

29 Each nationality made gods of its own and put them in the shrines on the high places built by the Samaritans; each nationality did this in the towns where it lived. 30 The people from Babylon had made a Succoth-Benoth, the people from Cuthah a Nergal, the people from Hamath an Ashima, 31 the Avvites a Nibhaz and a Tartak; while the Sepharvites caused their children to pass through the fire of sacrifice to Adrammelech and Anammelech, gods of Sepharvaim. 32 They worshipped Yahweh as well, and they appointed priests out of their own number for the high places, and these officiated in the shrines on the high places. 33 They worshipped Yahweh and served their own gods at the same time, with the rites of the countries from which they had been deported. 34 They still follow their old rites even now.

They did not worship Yahweh and did not conform to his statutes or ritual, or the law or the commandments, which Yahweh had laid down for the sons of Jacob to whom he gave the name Israel. 35 Yahweh had made a covenant with them and given them this command, 'You are not to worship alien gods, you are not to bow down to them or serve them or offer them sacrifices. 36 You are to bow down and offer sacrifice only to Yahweh who brought you out of Egypt with great power and outstretched arm. 37 You are to observe the statutes and ritual, the law and the commandments which he has given you in writing and to which you are always to conform; you are not to worship alien gods. 38 Do not forget the covenant which I have made with you, and do not venerate alien gods. 39 But venerate Yahweh your God, and he will deliver you from the clutches of all your enemies.' 40 But they would not listen and still followed their old rites.

41 These nationalities, then, worshipped Yahweh and served their idols as well, as did their children; and their children's children still behave today as their ancestors behaved in the past.

18 In the third year of Hoshea son of Elah, king of Israel, Hezekiah son of Ahaz became king of Judah. 2 He was twenty-five years old when he came to the throne, and he reigned for twenty-nine years in Jerusalem. His mother's name was Abijah daughter of Zechariah. 3 He did what Yahweh regards as right, just as his ancestor David had done. 4 He abolished the high places, broke the pillars, cut down the sacred poles and smashed the bronze serpent which Moses had made; for up to that time the Israelites had offered sacrifices to it; it was called Nehushtan.

17, 34–40: They did not . . . earlier manner: this passage is an adaptation of language denouncing the Israelites to make it applicable to the later Samaritan sect of post-exilic times. The original bearing of the discourse (vv 13–15) can be seen by reading it between vv 22 and 23.

was called Nehushtan. 5 He trusted in the LORD the God of Israel; so that there was no one like him among all the kings of Judah after him, or among those who were before him. 6 For he held fast to the LORD; he did not depart from following him but kept the commandments that the LORD commanded Moses. 7 The LORD was with him; wherever he went, he prospered. He rebelled against the king of Assyria and would not serve him. 8 He attacked the Philistines as far as Gaza and its territory, from watchtower to fortified city.

9 In the fourth year of King Hezekiah, which was the seventh year of King Hoshea son of Elah of Israel, King Shalmaneser of Assyria came up against Samaria, besieged it, 10 and at the end of three years, took it. In the sixth year of Hezekiah, which was the ninth year of King Hoshea of Israel, Samaria was taken. 11 The king of Assyria carried the Israelites away to Assyria, settled them in Halah, on the Habor, the river of Gozan, and in the cities of the Medes, 12 because they did not obey the voice of the LORD their God but transgressed his covenant — all that Moses the servant of the LORD had commanded; they neither listened nor obeyed.

13 In the fourteenth year of King Hezekiah, King Sennacherib of Assyria came up against all the fortified cities of Judah and captured them. 14 King Hezekiah of Judah sent to the king of Assyria at Lachish, saying, "I have done wrong; withdraw from me; whatever you impose on me I will bear." The king of Assyria demanded of King Hezekiah of Judah three hundred talents of silver and thirty talents of gold. 15 Hezekiah gave him all the silver that was found in the house of the LORD and in the treasuries of the king's house. 16 At that time Hezekiah stripped the gold from the doors of the temple of the LORD, and from the doorposts that King Hezekiah of Judah had overlaid and gave it to the king of Assyria. 17 The king of Assyria sent the Tartan, the Rabsaris, and the Rabshakeh with a great army from Lachish to King Hezekiah at Jerusalem. They went up and came to Jerusalem. When they arrived, they came and stood by the conduit of the upper pool, which is on the highway to the Fuller's Field. 18 When they called for the king, there came out to them Eliakim son of Hilkiah, who was in charge of the palace, and Shebnah the secretary, and Joah son of Asaph, the recorder.

19 The Rabshakeh said to them, "Say to Hezekiah: Thus says the great king, the king of Assyria: On what do you base this confidence of yours? 20 Do you think that mere words are strategy and power for war? On whom do you now rely, that you have rebelled against me? 21 See, you are relying now on Egypt, that broken reed of a staff, which will pierce the hand of anyone who leans on it. Such is Pharaoh king of Egypt to all who rely on him. 22 But if you say to me, 'We rely on the LORD our God,' is it not he whose high places and altars Hezekiah has removed, saying to Judah and to Jerusalem, 'You shall worship before this altar in Jerusalem'? 23 Come now, make a wager with my master the king of Assyria: I will give you two thousand horses, if you are able on your part to set riders on them. 24 How then can you repulse a single captain among the least of my master's servants, when you rely on Egypt for chariots and for horsemen? 25 Moreover, is it without the LORD that I have come up against this place to destroy it? The LORD said to me, Go up against this land, and destroy it."

they called it Nehushtan. 5 He put his trust in the LORD the God of Israel; there was nobody like him among all the kings of Judah who succeeded him or among those who had gone before him. 6 He remained loyal to the LORD and did not fail in his allegiance to him, and he kept the commandments which the LORD had given to Moses. 7 The LORD was with him and he prospered in all that he undertook. He rebelled against the king of Assyria and was no longer subject to him; 8 he conquered the Philistine country as far as Gaza and its boundaries, from watch-tower to fortified city.

9 In the fourth year of Hezekiah's reign, which was the seventh year of Hoshea son of Elah, king of Israel, King Shalmaneser of Assyria marched up against Samaria, laid siege to it, 10 and captured it at the end of three years; it was in the sixth year of Hezekiah, that is the ninth year of King Hoshea of Israel, that Samaria was captured. 11 The king of Assyria deported the Israelites to Assyria and settled them in Halah and on the Habor, the river of Gozan, and in the cities of Media, 12 because they did not obey the LORD their God but violated his covenant and every commandment that Moses the servant of the LORD had given them; they would not listen and they would not obey.

13 In the fourteenth year of King Hezekiah's reign, King Sennacherib of Assyria attacked and captured all the fortified towns of Judah. 14 Hezekiah sent a message to the king of Assyria at Lachish: 'I have done wrong; withdraw from me, and I shall pay any penalty you impose upon me.' The king of Assyria laid on Hezekiah king of Judah a penalty of three hundred talents of silver and thirty talents of gold; 15 and Hezekiah gave him all the silver found in the house of the LORD and in the treasuries of the palace. 16 At that time Hezekiah stripped of their gold the doors of the temple of the LORD and the door-frames which he himself had plated, and gave it to the king of Assyria.

17 From Lachish the king of Assyria sent the commander-in-chief, the chief eunuch, and the chief officer with a strong force to King Hezekiah at Jerusalem. They marched up and when they reached Jerusalem they halted by the conduit of the Upper Pool on the causeway leading to the Fuller's Field. 18 When they called for the king, the comptroller of the household, Eliakim son of Hilkiah, came out to them with Shebna, the adjutant-general, and Joah son of Asaph, the secretary of state.

19 The chief officer said to them, 'Tell Hezekiah that this is the message of the Great King, the king of Assyria: "What ground have you for this confidence of yours? 20 Do you think words can take the place of skill and military strength? On whom then do you rely for support in your rebellion against me? 21 On Egypt? Egypt is a splintered cane that will run into a man's hand and pierce it if he leans on it. That is what Pharaoh king of Egypt proves to all who rely on him. 22 And if you tell me that you are relying on the LORD your God, is he not the god whose shrines and altars Hezekiah has suppressed, telling Judah and Jerusalem they must worship at this altar in Jerusalem?"

23 'Now, make a deal with my master the king of Assyria: I shall give you two thousand horses if you can find riders for them. 24 How then can you reject the authority of even the least of my master's servants and rely on Egypt for chariots and horsemen? 25 Do you think that I have come to attack this place and destroy it without the consent of the LORD? No; the LORD himself said to me, "Go up and destroy this land." '

18:13–37 Cp. Isa. 36:1–22; 2 Chr. 32:1–19.   18:17 the commander-in-chief . . . officer: or Tartan, Rab-saris, and Rab-shakeh. reached Jerusalem: so Gk; Heb. adds and went up and came.

put his trust in the LORD, the God of Israel; and neither before him nor after him was there anyone like him among all the kings of Judah. 6 Loyal to the LORD, Hezekiah never turned away from him, but observed the commandments which the LORD had given Moses. 7 The LORD was with him, and he prospered in all that he set out to do. He rebelled against the king of Assyria and did not serve him. 8 He also subjugated the watchtowers and walled cities of the Philistines, all the way to Gaza and its territory.

9 In the fourth year of King Hezekiah, which was the seventh year of Hoshea, son of Elah, king of Israel, Shalmaneser, king of Assyria, attacked Samaria, laid siege to it, 10 and after three years captured it. In the sixth year of Hezekiah, the ninth year of Hoshea, king of Israel, Samaria was taken. 11 The king of Assyria then deported the Israelites to Assyria and settled them in Halah, at the Habor, a river of Gozan, and in the cities of the Medes. 12 This came about because they had not heeded the warning of the LORD, their God, but violated his covenant, not heeding and not fulfilling the commandments of Moses, the servant of the LORD.

13 In the fourteenth year of King Hezekiah, Sennacherib, king of Assyria, went on an expedition against all the fortified cities of Judah and captured them. 14 Hezekiah, king of Judah, sent this message to the king of Assyria at Lachish: "I have done wrong. Leave me, and I will pay whatever tribute you impose on me." The king of Assyria exacted three hundred talents of silver and thirty talents of gold from Hezekiah, king of Judah. 15 Hezekiah paid him all the funds there were in the temple of the LORD and in the palace treasuries. 16 He broke up the door panels and the uprights of the temple of the LORD which he himself had ordered to be overlaid with gold, and gave the gold to the king of Assyria.

17 The king of Assyria sent the general, the lord chamberlain, and the commander from Lachish with a great army to King Hezekiah at Jerusalem. They went up, and on their arrival in Jerusalem, stopped at the conduit of the upper pool on the highway of the fuller's field. 18 They called for the king, who sent out to them Eliakim, son of Hilkiah, the master of the palace; Shebnah the scribe; and the herald Joah, son of Asaph. 19 The commander said to them, "Tell Hezekiah, 'Thus says the great king, the king of Assyria: On what do you base this confidence of yours? 20 Do you think mere words substitute for strategy and might in war? On whom, then, do you rely, that you rebel against me? 21 This Egypt, the staff on which you rely, is in fact a broken reed which pierces the hand of anyone who leans on it. That is what Pharaoh, king of Egypt, is to all who rely on him. 22 But if you say to me, We rely on the LORD, our God, is not he the one whose high places and altars Hezekiah had removed, commanding Judah and Jerusalem to worship before this altar in Jerusalem?'

23 "Now, make a wager with my lord, the king of Assyria: I will give you two thousand horses if you can put riders on them. 24 How then can you repulse even one of the least servants of my lord, relying as you do on Egypt for chariots and horsemen? 25 Was it without the LORD's will that I have come up to destroy this place? The LORD said to me, 'Go up and destroy that land!' "

5 He put his trust in Yahweh, God of Israel. No king of Judah after him could be compared with him — nor any of those before him. 6 He was devoted to Yahweh, never turning from him, but keeping the commandments which Yahweh had laid down for Moses. 7 And so Yahweh was with him, and he was successful in all that he undertook. He rebelled against the king of Assyria and refused to serve him. 8 He beat the Philistines back to Gaza, laying their territory waste from watchtower to fortified town.

9 In the fourth year of Hezekiah, which was the seventh year of Hoshea son of Elah, king of Israel, Shalmaneser king of Assyria marched on Samaria and laid siege to it. 10 He captured it after three years. Samaria fell in the sixth year of Hezekiah, which was the ninth year of Hoshea king of Israel. 11 The king of Assyria deported the Israelites to Assyria and settled them in Halah on the Habor, a river of Gozan, and in the cities of the Medes. 12 This happened because they had not obeyed the voice of Yahweh their God and had broken his covenant, everything that Moses servant of Yahweh had laid down. They neither listened to it nor put it into practice.

13 iIn the fourteenth year of King Hezekiah, Sennacherib king of Assyria advanced on all the fortified towns of Judah and captured them. 14 Then Hezekiah king of Judah sent this message to the king of Assyria at Lachish, 'I have been at fault. Call off the attack, and I will submit to whatever you impose on me.' The king of Assyria exacted three hundred talents of silver and thirty talents of gold from Hezekiah king of Judah, 15 and Hezekiah gave him all the silver in the Temple of Yahweh and in the palace treasury. 16 At which time, Hezekiah stripped the facing from the leaves and jambs of the doors of the Temple of Yahweh, which an earlier king of Judah had put on, and gave it to the king of Assyria.

17 From Lachish the king of Assyria sent the cupbearer-in-chief with a large force to King Hezekiah in Jerusalem. He marched on Jerusalem and, on his arrival, took up position near the conduit of the upper pool which is on the road to the Fuller's Field. 18 He summoned the king. The master of the palace, Eliakim son of Hilkiah, Shebnah the secretary and the herald Joah son of Asaph went out to him. 19 The cupbearer-in-chief said to them, 'Say to Hezekiah, "The great king, the king of Assyria, says this: What makes you so confident? 20 Do you think empty words are as good as strategy and military strength? Who are you relying on, to dare to rebel against me? 21 There you are, relying on that broken reed Egypt, which pricks and pierces the hand of whoever leans on it. That is what Pharaoh king of Egypt is like to all who rely on him. 22 You may say to me: We rely on Yahweh our God. But have his high places and altars not been suppressed by Hezekiah who told Judah and Jerusalem: Here, in Jerusalem, is the altar before which you must worship? 23 Very well, then, make a wager with my lord the king of Assyria: I will give you two thousand horses if you can find horsemen to ride them. 24 How could you repel a single one of the least of my master's soldiers? And yet you have relied on Egypt for chariots and horsemen. 25 And lastly, have I marched on this place to lay it waste without warrant from Yahweh? Yahweh himself said to me: March on this country and lay it waste." '

i 18 The whole of 18:13—20:19 is repeated with minor variations in Is 36—39.

NEW REVISED STANDARD VERSION

26 Then Eliakim son of Hilkiah, and Shebnah, and Joah said to the Rabshakeh, "Please speak to your servants in the Aramaic language, for we understand it; do not speak to us in the language of Judah within the hearing of the people who are on the wall." 27 But the Rabshakeh said to them, "Has my master sent me to speak these words to your master and to you, and not to the people sitting on the wall, who are doomed with you to eat their own dung and to drink their own urine?"

28 Then the Rabshakeh stood and called out in a loud voice in the language of Judah, "Hear the word of the great king, the king of Assyria! 29 Thus says the king: 'Do not let Hezekiah deceive you, for he will not be able to deliver you out of my hand. 30 Do not let Hezekiah make you rely on the LORD by saying, The LORD will surely deliver us, and this city will not be given into the hand of the king of Assyria.' 31 Do not listen to Hezekiah; for thus says the king of Assyria: 'Make your peace with me and come out to me; then every one of you will eat from your own vine and your own fig tree, and drink water from your own cistern, 32 until I come and take you away to a land like your own land, a land of grain and wine, a land of bread and vineyards, a land of olive oil and honey, that you may live and not die. Do not listen to Hezekiah when he misleads you by saying, The LORD will deliver us. 33 Has any of the gods of the nations ever delivered its land out of the hand of the king of Assyria? 34 Where are the gods of Hamath and Arpad? Where are the gods of Sepharvaim, Hena, and Ivvah? Have they delivered Samaria out of my hand? 35 Who among all the gods of the countries have delivered their countries out of my hand, that the LORD should deliver Jerusalem out of my hand?' "

36 But the people were silent and answered him not a word, for the king's command was, "Do not answer him." 37 Then Eliakim son of Hilkiah, who was in charge of the palace, and Shebna the secretary, and Joah son of Asaph, the recorder, came to Hezekiah with their clothes torn and told him the words of the Rabshakeh.

19 When King Hezekiah heard it, he tore his clothes, covered himself with sackcloth, and went into the house of the LORD. 2 And he sent Eliakim, who was in charge of the palace, and Shebna the secretary, and the senior priests, covered with sackcloth, to the prophet Isaiah son of Amoz. 3 They said to him, "Thus says Hezekiah, This day is a day of distress, of rebuke, and of disgrace; children have come to the birth, and there is no strength to bring them forth. 4 It may be that the LORD your God heard all the words of the Rabshakeh, whom his master the king of Assyria has sent to mock the living God, and will rebuke the words that the LORD your God has heard; therefore lift up your prayer for the remnant that is left." 5 When the servants of King Hezekiah came to Isaiah, 6 Isaiah said to them, "Say to your master, 'Thus says the LORD: Do not be afraid because of the words that you have heard, with which the servants of the king of Assyria have reviled me. 7 I myself will put a spirit in him, so that he shall hear a rumor and return to his own land; I will cause him to fall by the sword in his own land.' "

8 The Rabshakeh returned, and found the king of Assyria fighting against Libnah; for he had heard that the king had left Lachish. 9 When the king[c] heard concerning King Tirhakah of Ethiopia,[d] "See, he has set out to fight against you," he sent messengers again to Hezekiah, saying, 10 "Thus shall you speak to King Hezekiah of Judah: Do not let your God on whom you rely deceive you by promising that Jerusalem will not be given into the hand of the king of

REVISED ENGLISH BIBLE

26 Eliakim son of Hilkiah, Shebna, and Joah said to the chief officer, 'Please speak to us in Aramaic, for we understand it; do not speak Hebrew to us within earshot of the people on the city wall.' 27 The chief officer answered, 'Is it to your master and to you that my master has sent me to say this? Is it not to the people sitting on the wall who, like you, will have to eat their own dung and drink their own urine?'

28 Then he stood and shouted in Hebrew, 'Hear the message of the Great King, the king of Assyria! 29 These are the king's words: "Do not be taken in by Hezekiah. He is powerless to save you from me. 30 Do not let him persuade you to rely on the LORD, and tell you that the LORD will surely save you and that this city will never be surrendered to the king of Assyria." 31 Do not listen to Hezekiah, for this is what the king of Assyria says: "Make your peace with me, and surrender. Then every one of you will eat the fruit of his own vine and of his own fig tree, and drink the water of his own cistern, 32 until I come and take you to a land like your own, a land of grain and new wine, of bread and vineyards, of olives, fine oil, and honey — life for you all, instead of death. Do not listen to Hezekiah; he will only mislead you by telling you that the LORD will save you. 33 Did any god of the nations save his land from the king of Assyria's power? 34 Where are the gods of Hamath and Arpad? Where are the gods of Sepharvaim, Hena, and Ivvah? Where are the gods of Samaria? Did they save Samaria from me? 35 Among all the gods of the nations is there one who saved his land from me? So how is the LORD to save Jerusalem?" '

36 The people remained silent and said not a word in reply, for the king had given orders that no one was to answer him. 37 Eliakim son of Hilkiah, comptroller of the household, Shebna the adjutant-general, and Joah son of Asaph, secretary of state, came to Hezekiah with their clothes torn and reported the words of the chief officer.

19 When King Hezekiah heard their report, he tore his clothes, put on sackcloth, and went into the house of the LORD. 2 He sent Eliakim comptroller of the household, Shebna the adjutant-general, and the senior priests, all wearing sackcloth, to the prophet Isaiah son of Amoz, 3 to give him this message from the king: 'Today is a day of trouble for us, a day of reproof and contumely. We are like a woman who has no strength to bring to birth the child she is carrying. 4 It may be that the LORD your God will give heed to all the words of the chief officer whom his master the king of Assyria sent to taunt the living God, and will confute the words which the LORD your God heard. Offer a prayer for those who still survive.'

5 When King Hezekiah's servants came to Isaiah, 6 they were given this answer for their master: 'Here is the word of the LORD: Do not be alarmed at what you heard when the Assyrian king's minions blasphemed me. 7 I shall sap his morale till at a mere rumour he will withdraw to his own country; and there I shall make him fall by the sword.'

8 Meanwhile the chief officer went back, and having heard that the king of Assyria had moved camp from Lachish, he found him attacking Libnah. 9 But when the king learnt that King Tirhakah of Cush was on the way to engage him in battle, he sent messengers again to King Hezekiah of Judah 10 to say to him, 'How can you be deluded by your God on whom you rely when he promises that Jerusalem will not fall into the hands of the king of Assyria? 11 You

---

18:34 **Where are the gods of Samaria?:** *so Gk (Luc.); Heb. omits.*
19:1–37 *Cp. Isa. 37:1–38; 2 Chr. 32:20–22.*   19:7 **I shall sap his morale:** *lit.* I shall put a spirit in him.

[c] Heb *he*   [d] Or *Nubia;* Heb *Cush*

26 Then Eliakim, son of Hilkiah, and Shebnah and Joah said to the commander: "Please speak to your servants in Aramaic; we understand it. Do not speak to us in Judean within earshot of the people who are on the wall."
27 But the commander replied: "Was it to your master and to you that my lord sent me to speak these words? Was it not rather to the men sitting on the wall, who, with you, will have to eat their own excrement and drink their urine?" 28 Then the commander stepped forward and cried out in a loud voice in Judean, "Listen to the words of the great king, the king of Assyria. 29 Thus says the king: 'Do not let Hezekiah deceive you, since he cannot deliver you out of my hand. 30 Let not Hezekiah induce you to rely on the LORD, saying, The LORD will surely save us; this city will not be handed over to the king of Assyria. 31 Do not listen to Hezekiah, for the king of Assyria says: Make peace with me and surrender! Then each of you will eat of his own vine and of his own fig-tree, and drink the water of his own cistern, 32 until I come to take you to a land like your own, a land of grain and wine, of bread and orchards, of olives, oil and fruit syrup. Choose life, not death. Do not listen to Hezekiah when he would seduce you by saying, The LORD will rescue us. 33 Has any of the gods of the nations ever rescued his land from the hand of the king of Assyria? 34 Where are the gods of Hamath and Arpad? Where are the gods of Sepharvaim, Hena, and Avva? Where are the gods of the land of Samaria? 35 Which of the gods for all these lands ever rescued his land from my hand? Will the LORD then rescue Jerusalem from my hand?' " 36 But the people remained silent and did not answer him one word, for the king had ordered them not to answer him.
37 Then the master of the palace, Eliakim, son of Hilkiah, Shebnah the scribe, and the herald Joah, son of Asaph, came to Hezekiah with their garments torn, and reported to him what the commander had said.

19 When King Hezekiah heard this, he tore his garments, wrapped himself in sackcloth, and went into the temple of the LORD. 2 He sent Eliakim, the master of the palace, Shebnah the scribe, and the elders of the priests, wrapped in sackcloth, to tell the prophet Isaiah, son of Amoz, 3 "Thus says Hezekiah: 'This is a day of distress, of rebuke, and of disgrace. Children are at the point of birth, but there is no strength to bring them forth. 4 Perhaps the LORD, your God, will hear all the words of the commander, whom his master, the king of Assyria, sent to taunt the living God, and will rebuke him for the words which the LORD, your God, has heard. So send up a prayer for the remnant that is here.' " 5 When the servants of King Hezekiah had come to Isaiah, 6 he said to them, "Tell this to your master: 'Thus says the LORD: Do not be frightened by the words you have heard, with which the servants of the king of Assyria have blasphemed me. 7 I am about to put in him such a spirit that, when he hears a certain report, he will return to his own land, and there I will cause him to fall by the sword.' "
8 When the commander, on his return, heard that the king of Assyria had withdrawn from Lachish, he found him besieging Libnah. 9 The king of Assyria heard a report that Tirhakah, king of Ethiopia, had come out to fight against him. Again he sent envoys to Hezekiah with this message: 10 "Thus shall you say to Hezekiah, king of Judah: 'Do not let your God on whom you rely deceive you by saying that Jerusalem will not be handed over to the king of Assyria.

26 Eliakim, Shebnah and Joah said to the cupbearer-in-chief, 'Please speak to your servants in Aramaic, for we understand it; do not speak to us in the Judaean language within earshot of the people on the ramparts.' 27 But the cupbearer-in-chief said, 'Do you think my lord sent me here to say these things to your master or to you? On the contrary, it was to the people sitting on the ramparts who, like you, are doomed to eat their own dung and drink their own urine.'
28 The cupbearer-in-chief then drew himself up and shouted loudly in the Judaean language, 'Listen to the word of the great king, the king of Assyria. 29 The king says this, "Do not let Hezekiah delude you. He will be powerless to save you from my clutches. 30 Do not let Hezekiah persuade you to rely on Yahweh by saying: Yahweh is sure to save us; this city will not fall into the king of Assyria's clutches. 31 Do not listen to Hezekiah, for the king of Assyria says this: Make peace with me, surrender to me, and every one of you will be free to eat the fruit of his own vine and of his own fig tree and to drink the water of his own storage-well 32 until I come and take you away to a country like your own, a land of corn and good wine, a land of bread and vineyards, a land of oil and honey: and so you will survive and not die. Do not listen to Hezekiah; he is deluding you when he says: Yahweh will save us. 33 Has any god of any nation been able to save his country from the king of Assyria's clutches? 34 Where are the gods of Hamath and Arpad? Where are the gods of Sepharvaim and Hena and Ivvah? Where are the local gods of Samaria? Did they save Samaria from my clutches? 35 Of all the local gods, which ones have saved their countries from my clutches, for Yahweh to be able to save Jerusalem from my clutches?" '
36 The people, however, kept quiet and said nothing in reply, since the king had given the order, 'You are not to answer him.' 37 The master of the palace, Eliakim son of Hilkiah, Shebnah the secretary and the herald Joah son of Asaph, with their clothes torn, went to Hezekiah and reported what the cupbearer-in-chief had said.

19 On hearing this, King Hezekiah tore his clothes, put on sackcloth and went to the Temple of Yahweh. 2 He sent Eliakim master of the palace, Shebnah the secretary and the elders of the priests, wearing sackcloth, to the prophet Isaiah son of Amoz. 3 They said to him, 'This is what Hezekiah says, "Today is a day of suffering, of punishment, of disgrace. Children come to birth, and there is no strength to bring them forth. 4 May Yahweh your God hear the words of the cupbearer-in-chief whom his master, the king of Assyria, has sent to insult the living God, and may Yahweh your God punish the words he has heard. Offer your prayer for the remnant still remaining." '
5 King Hezekiah's ministers went to Isaiah, 6 and Isaiah said to them, 'Say to your master, "Yahweh says this: Do not be afraid of the words which you have heard or the blasphemies which the king of Assyria's minions have uttered against me. 7 Look, I am going to put a spirit in him and, on the strength of a rumour, he will go back to his own country, and in that country I shall make him fall by the sword." '
8 The cupbearer turned about and rejoined the king of Assyria, who was then attacking Libnah, as the cupbearer had learnt that the king had already left Lachish 9 on hearing that Tirhakah king of Cush was on his way to attack him.
10 Sennacherib again sent messengers to Hezekiah, saying, 'Tell Hezekiah king of Judah this, "Do not let your God on whom you are relying deceive you with the promise: Jerusalem will not fall into the king of Assyria's clutches.

NEW REVISED STANDARD VERSION

Assyria. 11 See, you have heard what the kings of Assyria have done to all lands, destroying them utterly. Shall you be delivered? 12 Have the gods of the nations delivered them, the nations that my predecessors destroyed, Gozan, Haran, Rezeph, and the people of Eden who were in Telassar? 13 Where is the king of Hamath, the king of Arpad, the king of the city of Sepharvaim, the king of Hena, or the king of Ivvah?"

14 Hezekiah received the letter from the hand of the messengers and read it; then Hezekiah went up to the house of the LORD and spread it before the LORD. 15 And Hezekiah prayed before the LORD, and said: "O LORD the God of Israel, who are enthroned above the cherubim, you are God, you alone, of all the kingdoms of the earth; you have made heaven and earth. 16 Incline your ear, O LORD, and hear; open your eyes, O LORD, and see; hear the words of Sennacherib, which he has sent to mock the living God. 17 Truly, O LORD, the kings of Assyria have laid waste the nations and their lands, 18 and have hurled their gods into the fire, though they were no gods but the work of human hands—wood and stone—and so they were destroyed. 19 So now, O LORD our God, save us, I pray you, from his hand, so that all the kingdoms of the earth may know that you, O LORD, are God alone."

20 Then Isaiah son of Amoz sent to Hezekiah, saying, "Thus says the LORD, the God of Israel: I have heard your prayer to me about King Sennacherib of Assyria. 21 This is the word that the LORD has spoken concerning him:

> She despises you, she scorns you—
>   virgin daughter Zion;
> she tosses her head—behind your back,
>   daughter Jerusalem.

22 Whom have you mocked and reviled?
>   Against whom have you raised your voice
> and haughtily lifted your eyes?
>   Against the Holy One of Israel!
23 By your messengers you have mocked the Lord,
>   and you have said, 'With my many chariots
> I have gone up the heights of the mountains,
>   to the far recesses of Lebanon;
> I felled its tallest cedars,
>   its choicest cypresses;
> I entered its farthest retreat,
>   its densest forest.
24 I dug wells
>   and drank foreign waters,
> I dried up with the sole of my foot
>   all the streams of Egypt.'
25 Have you not heard
>   that I determined it long ago?
> I planned from days of old
>   what now I bring to pass,
> that you should make fortified cities
>   crash into heaps of ruins,
26 while their inhabitants, shorn of strength,
>   are dismayed and confounded;
> they have become like plants of the field
>   and like tender grass,
> like grass on the housetops,
>   blighted before it is grown.
27 "But I know your rising[e] and your sitting,
>   your going out and coming in,
>   and your raging against me.

[e] Gk Compare Isa 37.27 Q Ms: MT lacks *rising*

REVISED ENGLISH BIBLE

yourself must have heard what the kings of Assyria have done to all countries: they utterly destroyed them. Can you then hope to escape? 12 Did their gods save the nations which my predecessors wiped out: Gozan, Harran, Rezeph, and the people of Eden living in Telassar? 13 Where are the kings of Hamath, of Arpad, and of Lahir, Sepharvaim, Hena, and Ivvah?'

14 Hezekiah received the letter from the messengers and, having read it, he went up to the house of the LORD and spread it out before the LORD 15 with this prayer: 'LORD God of Israel, enthroned on the cherubim, you alone are God of all the kingdoms of the world; you made heaven and earth. 16 Incline your ear, LORD, and listen; open your eyes, LORD, and see; hear the words that Sennacherib has sent to taunt the living God. 17 LORD, it is true that the kings of Assyria have laid waste the nations and their lands 18 and have consigned their gods to the flames. They destroyed them, because they were no gods but the work of men's hands, mere wood and stone. 19 Now, LORD our God, save us from his power, so that all the kingdoms of the earth may know that you alone, LORD, are God.'

20 Isaiah son of Amoz sent Hezekiah the following message: 'This is the word of the LORD the God of Israel: I have heard your prayer to me concerning King Sennacherib of Assyria, 21 and this is the word which the LORD has spoken against him:

> The virgin daughter of Zion disdains you,
>   she laughs you to scorn;
> the daughter of Jerusalem tosses her head
>   as you retreat.
22 Whom have you taunted and blasphemed?
>   Against whom did you raise an outcry,
> casting haughty glances at the Holy One of Israel?
23 You sent your messengers to taunt the Lord, and said:
> "I have mounted my chariot and performed mighty deeds;
> I have ascended the mountain heights,
>   gone to the remote recesses of Lebanon.
> I have felled its tallest cedars,
>   the finest of its pines;
> I have reached its farthest corners,
>   the most luxuriant forest.
24 I have dug wells
>   and drunk the waters of a foreign land,
> and with the sole of my foot I have dried up
>   all the streams of Egypt."
25 'Have you not heard?
>   Long ago I did it all.
> In days gone by I planned it
>   and now I have brought it about,
> till your fortified cities have crashed
>   into heaps of rubble.
26 Their inhabitants, shorn of strength,
>   disheartened and put to shame,
> were but as plants in the field, frail as green herbs,
>   as grass on the rooftops blasted by the east wind.
27 I know your rising up and your sitting down,
>   your going out and your coming in.

19:23 **and performed mighty deeds:** so Gk (Luc.); Heb. omits.
19:25 **heaps of rubble:** prob. rdg, cp. Isa. 37:26; Heb. obscure.
19:26 **by the east wind:** prob. rdg, cp. Isa. 37:27; Heb. before it is mature.   19:27 **your rising up:** prob. rdg, cp. Isa. 37:28; Heb. omits.

11 You have heard what the kings of Assyria have done to all other countries: they doomed them! Will you, then, be saved? 12 Did the gods of the nations whom my fathers destroyed save them? Gozan, Haran, Rezeph, or the Edenites in Telassar? 13 Where are the king of Hamath, the king of Arpad, or the kings of the cities Sepharvaim, Hena and Avva?' "

14 Hezekiah took the letter from the hand of the messengers and read it; then he went up to the temple of the LORD, and spreading it out before him, 15 he prayed in the LORD's presence: "O LORD, God of Israel, enthroned upon the cherubim! You alone are God over all the kingdoms of the earth. You have made the heavens and the earth. 16 Incline your ear, O LORD, and listen! Open your eyes, O LORD, and see! Hear the words of Sennacherib which he sent to taunt the living God. 17 Truly, O LORD, the kings of Assyria have laid waste the nations and their lands, 18 and cast their gods into the fire; they destroyed them because they were not gods, but the work of human hands, wood and stone. 19 Therefore, O LORD, our God, save us from the power of this man, that all the kingdoms of the earth may know that you alone, O LORD, are God."

20 Then Isaiah, son of Amoz, sent this message to Hezekiah: "Thus says the LORD, the God of Israel, in answer to your prayer for help against Sennacherib, king of Assyria: I have listened! 21 This is the word the LORD has spoken concerning him:

" 'She despises you, laughs you to scorn,
    the virgin daughter Zion!
Behind you she wags her head,
    daughter Jerusalem.
22 Whom have you insulted and blasphemed,
    against whom have you raised your voice
And lifted up your eyes on high?
    Against the Holy One of Israel!
23 Through your servants you have insulted the LORD.
    You said: With my many chariots
I climbed the mountain heights,
    the recesses of Lebanon;
I cut down its lofty cedars,
    its choice cypresses;
I reached the remotest heights,
    its forest park.
24 I dug wells and drank water in foreign lands;
    I dried up with the soles of my feet
    all the rivers of Egypt.

25 " 'Have you not heard?
    Long ago I prepared it,
From days of old I planned it.
    Now I have brought it to pass:
That you should reduce fortified cities
    into heaps of ruins,
26 While their inhabitants, shorn of power,
    are dismayed and ashamed,
Becoming like the plants of the field, like the
        green growth,
    like the scorched grass on the housetops.
27 I am aware whether you stand or sit;
    I know whether you come or go,
28   and also your rage against me.

11 You have learnt by now what the kings of Assyria have done to all the other countries, devoting them to destruction. Are you likely to be saved? 12 Did the gods of the nations whom my ancestors devastated save them — Gozan, Haran, Rezeph and the Edenites who were in Tel Basar? 13 Where is the king of Hamath, the king of Arpad, the king of Lair, of Sepharvaim, of Hena, of Ivvah?" '

14 Hezekiah took the letter from the messengers' hands and read it; he then went up to the Temple of Yahweh and spread it out before Yahweh. 15 Hezekiah said this prayer in the presence of Yahweh, 'Yahweh Sabaoth, God of Israel, enthroned on the winged creatures, you alone are God of all the kingdoms of the world, you made heaven and earth. 16 Give ear, Yahweh, and listen; open your eyes, Yahweh, and see! Hear the words of Sennacherib, who has sent to insult the living God. 17 It is true, Yahweh, that the kings of Assyria have destroyed the nations, 18 they have thrown their gods on the fire, for these were not gods but human artefacts — wood and stone — and hence they have destroyed them. 19 But now, Yahweh our God, save us from his clutches, I beg you, and let all the kingdoms of the world know that you alone are God, Yahweh.'

20 Isaiah son of Amoz then sent the following message to Hezekiah, 'Yahweh, God of Israel, says this, "I have heard the prayer which you have addressed to me about Sennacherib king of Assyria." 21 Here is the pronouncement which Yahweh has made about him:

"She despises you, she scorns you,
    the virgin daughter of Zion;
she tosses her head at you,
    the daughter of Jerusalem!
22 Whom have you insulted, whom have you
        blasphemed?
Against whom raised your voice
    and lifted your haughty eyes?
Against the Holy One of Israel!
23 Through your envoys you have insulted the Lord,
    thinking: With my many chariots
I have climbed the mountain-tops,
    the utmost peaks of Lebanon.
I have felled
    its mighty cedars,
    its finest cypresses,
have reached its furthest recesses,
    its forest garden.
24 Yes, I have dug
    and drunk of foreign waters;
under the soles of my feet
    I have dried up all Egypt's rivers.

25 "Do you hear? Long ago
    I prepared this,
from days of old I actually planned it,
    now I carry it out.
You were to lay walled cities
    in heaps of ruins;
26 that was why their inhabitants,
    feeble of hand,
were dismayed and discomfited,
    were weak as grass,
    were frail as plants,
    were like grass of housetop and meadow
    under the east wind.
27 But whether you stand up or you sit down,
    whether you go out or you come in, I know it.

NEW REVISED STANDARD VERSION

REVISED ENGLISH BIBLE

28 Because you have raged against me
and your arrogance has come to my ears,
I will put my hook in your nose
and my bit in your mouth;
I will turn you back on the way
by which you came.

29 "And this shall be the sign for you: This year you shall eat what grows of itself, and in the second year what springs from that; then in the third year sow, reap, plant vineyards, and eat their fruit. 30 The surviving remnant of the house of Judah shall again take root downward, and bear fruit upward; 31 for from Jerusalem a remnant shall go out, and from Mount Zion a band of survivors. The zeal of the LORD of hosts will do this.
32 "Therefore thus says the LORD concerning the king of Assyria: He shall not come into this city, shoot an arrow there, come before it with a shield, or cast up a siege ramp against it. 33 By the way that he came, by the same he shall return; he shall not come into this city, says the LORD. 34 For I will defend this city to save it, for my own sake and for the sake of my servant David."
35 That very night the angel of the LORD set out and struck down one hundred eighty-five thousand in the camp of the Assyrians; when morning dawned, they were all dead bodies. 36 Then King Sennacherib of Assyria left, went home, and lived at Nineveh. 37 As he was worshiping in the house of his god Nisroch, his sons Adrammelech and Sharezer killed him with the sword, and they escaped into the land of Ararat. His son Esar-haddon succeeded him.

28 The frenzy of your rage against me
and your arrogance have come to my ears.
I shall put a ring in your nose
and a bridle in your mouth,
and I shall take you back
by the way on which you came.

29 'This will be the sign for you: this year you will eat the leavings of the grain and in the second year what is self-sown; but in the third year you will sow and reap, plant vineyards and eat their fruit. 30 The survivors left in Judah will strike fresh root below ground and yield fruit above ground, 31 for a remnant will come out of Jerusalem and survivors from Mount Zion. The zeal of the LORD will perform this.
32 'Therefore, this is the word of the LORD about the king of Assyria:
He will not enter this city
or shoot an arrow there,
he will not advance against it with shield
or cast up a siege-ramp against it.
33 By the way he came he will go back;
he will not enter this city.
This is the word of the LORD.
34 I shall shield this city to deliver it
for my own sake and for the sake of my servant David.'
35 That night the angel of the LORD went out and struck down a hundred and eighty-five thousand in the Assyrian camp; when morning dawned, there they all lay dead. 36 King Sennacherib of Assyria broke camp and marched away; he went back to Nineveh and remained there. 37 One day, while he was worshipping in the temple of his god Nisroch, Adrammelech and Sharezer his sons assassinated him and made their escape to the land of Ararat. His son Esarhaddon succeeded him.

20 In those days Hezekiah became sick and was at the point of death. The prophet Isaiah son of Amoz came to him, and said to him, "Thus says the LORD: Set your house in order, for you shall die; you shall not recover." 2 Then Hezekiah turned his face to the wall and prayed to the LORD: 3 "Remember now, O LORD, I implore you, how I have walked before you in faithfulness with a whole heart, and have done what is good in your sight." Hezekiah wept bitterly. 4 Before Isaiah had gone out of the middle court, the word of the LORD came to him: 5 "Turn back, and say to Hezekiah prince of my people, Thus says the LORD, the God of your ancestor David: I have heard your prayer, I have seen your tears; indeed, I will heal you; on the third day you shall go up to the house of the LORD. 6 I will add fifteen years to your life. I will deliver you and this city out of the hand of the king of Assyria; I will defend this city for my own sake and for my servant David's sake." 7 Then Isaiah said, "Bring a lump of figs. Let them take it and apply it to the boil, so that he may recover."
8 Hezekiah said to Isaiah, "What shall be the sign that the LORD will heal me, and that I shall go up to the house of the LORD on the third day?" 9 Isaiah said, "This is the sign to you from the LORD, that the LORD will do the thing that he has promised: the shadow has now advanced ten intervals; shall it retreat ten intervals?" 10 Hezekiah answered, "It is normal for the shadow to lengthen ten intervals; rather let the shadow retreat ten intervals." 11 The prophet Isaiah

20 At this time Hezekiah became mortally ill, and the prophet Isaiah son of Amoz came to him with this message from the LORD: 'Give your last instructions to your household, for you are dying; you will not recover.' 2 Hezekiah turned his face to the wall and offered this prayer to the LORD: 3 'LORD, remember how I have lived before you, faithful and loyal in your service, doing always what was pleasing to you.' And he wept bitterly. 4 But before Isaiah had left the citadel, the word of the LORD came to him: 5 'Go back and say to Hezekiah, the prince of my people: This is the word of the LORD the God of your father David: I have heard your prayer and seen your tears; I shall heal you, and on the third day you will go up to the house of the LORD. 6 I shall add fifteen years to your life and deliver you and this city from the king of Assyria. I shall protect this city for my own sake and for the sake of my servant David.'
7 Isaiah told them to prepare a fig-plaster; when it was made and applied to the inflammation, Hezekiah recovered. 8 He asked Isaiah what proof there was that the LORD would cure him and that he would go up to the house of the LORD on the third day. 9 Isaiah replied, 'This will be your proof from the LORD that he will do what he has promised; will the shadow go forward ten steps or back ten steps?' 10 Hezekiah answered, 'It is an easy thing for the shadow to move forward ten steps; rather let it go back ten steps.' 11 Isaiah

19:28 against me: prob. rdg, cp. Isa. 37:29; Heb. repeats the frenzy of your rage against me. 19:33 came: so some MSS; others comes. 20:1–11 Cp. Isa. 38:1–8,21,22. 20:9 will the shadow go: so Aram. (Targ.); Heb. has the shadow gone.

Because of your rage against me
and your fury which has reached my ears,
I will put my hook in your nose
and my bit in your mouth,
and make you return the way you came.

29 " 'This shall be a sign for you:
this year you shall eat the aftergrowth,
next year, what grows of itself;
But in the third year, sow and reap,
plant vineyards and eat their fruit!
30 The remaining survivors of the house of Judah
shall again strike root below
and bear fruit above.
31 For out of Jerusalem shall come a remnant,
and from Mount Zion, survivors.
The zeal of the LORD of hosts shall do this.'

32 "Therefore, thus says the LORD concerning the king of Assyria: 'He shall not reach this city, nor shoot an arrow at it, nor come before it with a shield, nor cast up siege-works against it. 33 He shall return by the same way he came, without entering the city, says the LORD. 34 I will shield and save this city for my own sake, and for the sake of my servant David.' "

35 That night the angel of the LORD went forth and struck down one hundred and eighty-five thousand men in the Assyrian camp. Early the next morning, there they were, all the corpses of the dead. 36 So Sennacherib, the king of Assyria, broke camp, and went back home to Nineveh.

37 When he was worshiping in the temple of his god Nisroch, his sons Adrammelech and Sharezer slew him with the sword and fled into the land of Ararat. His son Esarhaddon reigned in his stead.

20 In those days, when Hezekiah was mortally ill, the prophet Isaiah, son of Amoz, came and said to him: "Thus says the LORD: 'Put your house in order, for you are about to die; you shall not recover.' " 2 He turned his face to the wall and prayed to the LORD: 3 "O LORD, remember how faithfully and wholeheartedly I conducted myself in your presence, doing what was pleasing to you!" And Hezekiah wept bitterly.

4 Before Isaiah had left the central courtyard, the word of the LORD came to him: 5 "Go back and tell Hezekiah, the leader of my people: 'Thus says the LORD, the God of your forefather David: I have heard your prayer and seen your tears. I will heal you. In three days you shall go up to the LORD's temple; 6 I will add fifteen years to your life. I will rescue you and this city from the hand of the king of Assyria; I will be a shield to this city for my own sake, and for the sake of my servant David.' "

7 Isaiah then ordered a poultice of figs to be brought and applied to the boil, that he might recover. 8 Then Hezekiah asked Isaiah, "What is the sign that the LORD will heal me and that I shall go up to the temple of the LORD on the third day?" 9 Isaiah replied, "This will be the sign for you from the LORD that he will do what he has promised: Shall the shadow go forward or back ten steps?"

10 "It is easy for the shadow to advance ten steps," Hezekiah answered. "Rather, let it go back ten steps." 11 So the

28 Because you have raved against me,
and your arrogance has reached my ears,
I shall put a hook through your nostrils
and a muzzle on your lips,
and make you return by the road
by which you came.

29 And this will be the sign for you:
this year will be eaten the self-sown grain,
next year what sprouts in the fallow;
but in the third year sow and reap,
plant vineyards and eat their fruit.
30 The surviving remnant of the House of Judah will
bring forth
new roots below and fruits above;
31 for a remnant will issue from Jerusalem,
and survivors from Mount Zion.
Yahweh Sabaoth's jealous love will accomplish
this.

32 "This, then, is what Yahweh says about the king of Assyria:
"He will not enter this city,
will shoot no arrow at it,
confront it with no shield,
throw up no earthwork against it.
33 By the road by which he came, by that he will
return;
he will not enter this city, declares Yahweh.
34 I shall protect this city and save it
for my sake and my servant David's sake." '

35 That same night the angel of Yahweh went out and struck down a hundred and eighty-five thousand men in the Assyrian camp. In the early morning when it was time to get up, there they lay, so many corpses.

36 Sennacherib struck camp and left; he returned home and stayed in Nineveh. 37 One day when he was worshipping in the temple of his god Nisroch, his sons Adrammelech and Sharezer struck him down with the sword and escaped into the territory of Ararat. His son Esarhaddon succeeded him.

20 About then Hezekiah fell ill and was at the point of death. The prophet Isaiah son of Amoz came and said to him, 'Yahweh says this, "Put your affairs in order, for you are going to die, you will not live." ' 2 Hezekiah turned his face to the wall and addressed this prayer to Yahweh, 3 'Ah, Yahweh, remember, I beg you, that I have behaved faithfully and with sincerity of heart in your presence and done what you regard as right.' And Hezekiah shed many tears.

4 Isaiah had not left the middle court, before the word of Yahweh came to him, 5 'Go back and say to Hezekiah, prince of my people, "Yahweh, the God of your ancestor David, says this: I have heard your prayer and seen your tears. I shall cure you: in three days' time you will go up to the Temple of Yahweh. 6 I shall add fifteen years to your life. I shall save you and this city from the king of Assyria's clutches and defend this city for my sake and my servant David's sake." '

7 'Bring a fig poultice,' Isaiah said; they brought one, applied it to the ulcer, and the king recovered.

8 Hezekiah said to Isaiah, 'What is the sign to tell me that Yahweh will cure me and that I shall be going up to the Temple of Yahweh in three days' time?' 9 'Here', Isaiah replied, 'is the sign from Yahweh that he will do what he has said; would you like the shadow to go forward ten steps, or to go back ten steps?' 10 'It is easy for the shadow to lengthen ten steps,' Hezekiah replied. 'No, I would rather the shadow went back ten steps.' 11 The prophet Isaiah then

NEW REVISED STANDARD VERSION	REVISED ENGLISH BIBLE

cried to the LORD; and he brought the shadow back the ten intervals, by which the sun*f* had declined on the dial of Ahaz.

12 At that time King Merodach-baladan son of Baladan of Babylon sent envoys with letters and a present to Hezekiah, for he had heard that Hezekiah had been sick. 13 Hezekiah welcomed them;*g* he showed them all his treasure house, the silver, the gold, the spices, the precious oil, his armory, all that was found in his storehouses; there was nothing in his house or in all his realm that Hezekiah did not show them. 14 Then the prophet Isaiah came to King Hezekiah, and said to him, "What did these men say? From where did they come to you?" Hezekiah answered, "They have come from a far country, from Babylon." 15 He said, "What have they seen in your house?" Hezekiah answered, "They have seen all that is in my house; there is nothing in my storehouses that I did not show them."

16 Then Isaiah said to Hezekiah, "Hear the word of the LORD: 17 Days are coming when all that is in your house, and that which your ancestors have stored up until this day, shall be carried to Babylon; nothing shall be left, says the LORD. 18 Some of your own sons who are born to you shall be taken away; they shall be eunuchs in the palace of the king of Babylon." 19 Then Hezekiah said to Isaiah, "The word of the LORD that you have spoken is good." For he thought, "Why not, if there will be peace and security in my days?"

20 The rest of the deeds of Hezekiah, all his power, how he made the pool and the conduit and brought water into the city, are they not written in the Book of the Annals of the Kings of Judah? 21 Hezekiah slept with his ancestors; and his son Manasseh succeeded him.

21 Manasseh was twelve years old when he began to reign; he reigned fifty-five years in Jerusalem. His mother's name was Hephzibah. 2 He did what was evil in the sight of the LORD, following the abominable practices of the nations that the LORD drove out before the people of Israel. 3 For he rebuilt the high places that his father Hezekiah had destroyed; he erected altars for Baal, made a sacred pole, *h* as King Ahab of Israel had done, worshiped all the host of heaven, and served them. 4 He built altars in the house of the LORD, of which the LORD had said, "In Jerusalem I will put my name." 5 He built altars for all the host of heaven in the two courts of the house of the LORD. 6 He made his son pass through fire; he practiced soothsaying and augury, and dealt with mediums and with wizards. He did much evil in the sight of the LORD, provoking him to anger. 7 The carved image of Asherah that he had made he set in the house of which the LORD said to David and to his son Solomon, "In this house, and in Jerusalem, which I have chosen out of all the tribes of Israel, I will put my name forever; 8 I will not cause the feet of Israel to wander any more out of the land that I gave to their ancestors, if only they will be careful to do according to all that I have commanded them, and according to all the law that my servant Moses commanded them." 9 But they did not listen; Manasseh misled them to do more evil than the nations had done that the LORD destroyed before the people of Israel.

10 The LORD said by his servants the prophets, 11 "Because King Manasseh of Judah has committed these abominations, has done things more wicked than all that the Amorites did, who were before him, and has caused Judah also to sin with his idols; 12 therefore thus says the LORD, the God of Israel, I am bringing upon Jerusalem and Judah such evil that the ears of everyone who hears of it will tingle. 13 I

the prophet called to the LORD, and he made the shadow go back ten steps where it had advanced down the stairway of Ahaz.

12 At that time the king of Babylon, Merodach-baladan son of Baladan, sent envoys with a gift to Hezekiah, for he heard that he had been ill. 13 Hezekiah welcomed them and showed them all his treasury, the silver and gold, the spices and fragrant oil, his armoury, and everything to be found among his treasures; there was nothing in his palace or in his whole realm that Hezekiah did not show them. 14 The prophet Isaiah came to King Hezekiah and asked, 'What did these men say? Where did they come from?' 'They came from a distant country,' Hezekiah answered, 'from Babylon.' 15 'What did they see in your palace?' Isaiah demanded. 'They saw everything,' was the reply; 'there was nothing among my treasures that I did not show them.'

16 Isaiah said to Hezekiah, 'Hear the word of the LORD: 17 The time is coming, says the LORD, when everything in your palace, and all that your forefathers have amassed till the present day, will be carried away to Babylon; not a thing will be left. 18 And some of your sons, your own offspring, will be taken from you to serve as eunuchs in the palace of the king of Babylon.' 19 Hezekiah answered, 'The word of the LORD which you have spoken is good,' for he was thinking to himself that peace and security would last out his lifetime.

20 The other events of Hezekiah's reign, his exploits, and how he made the pool and the conduit and brought water into the city, are recorded in the annals of the kings of Judah. 21 Hezekiah rested with his forefathers, and his son Manasseh succeeded him.

21 MANASSEH was twelve years old when he came to the throne, and he reigned in Jerusalem for fifty-five years; his mother was Hephzibah. 2 He did what was wrong in the eyes of the LORD, in following the abominable practices of the nations which the LORD had dispossessed in favour of the Israelites. 3 He rebuilt the shrines which his father Hezekiah had destroyed, he erected altars to the Baal, made a sacred pole as Ahab king of Israel had done, and prostrated himself before all the host of heaven and served them. 4 He built altars in the house of the LORD, that house of which the LORD had said, 'I shall set my name in Jerusalem.' 5 He built altars for all the host of heaven in the two courts of the house of the LORD; 6 he made his son pass through the fire, he practised soothsaying and divination, and dealt with ghosts and spirits. He did much wrong in the eyes of the LORD and provoked his anger. 7 He made an image of the goddess Asherah and set it up in the house of which the LORD had said to David and Solomon his son, 'In this house and Jerusalem, which I chose out of all the tribes of Israel, I shall establish my name for all time. 8 I shall not again make Israel outcasts from the land which I gave to their forefathers, if only they are careful to observe all my commands and all the law that my servant Moses gave them.' 9 But they did not obey, and Manasseh led them astray into wickedness far worse than that of the nations which the LORD had exterminated in favour of the Israelites.

10 The LORD spoke through his servants the prophets: 11 'Because King Manasseh of Judah has done these abominable things, outdoing the Amorites before him in wickedness, and because he has led Judah into sin with his idols, 12 this is the word of the LORD the God of Israel: I am about to bring such disaster on Jerusalem and Judah that it will ring in the ears of all who hear of it. 13 I shall use against

f Syr See Isa 38.8 and Tg: Heb *it*   *g* Gk Vg Syr: Heb *When Hezekiah heard about them*   *h* Heb *Asherah*

20:12–19 *Cp. Isa. 39:1–8.*   20:12 **Merodach:** *so some MSS, cp. Isa. 39:1; others* Berodach.   20:13 **welcomed:** *so some MSS, cp. Isa. 39:2; others* heard.   21:1–9 *Cp. 2 Chr. 33:1–9.*

prophet Isaiah invoked the LORD, who made the shadow retreat the ten steps it had descended on the staircase to the terrace of Ahaz.

12 At that time, when Merodach-baladan, son of Baladan, king of Babylon, heard that Hezekiah had been ill, he sent letters and gifts to him. 13 Hezekiah was pleased at this, and therefore showed the messengers his whole treasury, the silver, gold, spices and fine oil, his armory, and all that was in his storerooms; there was nothing in his house or in all his realm that Hezekiah did not show them.

14 Then Isaiah the prophet came to King Hezekiah and asked him: "What did these men say to you? Where did they come from?" "They came from a distant land, from Babylon," replied Hezekiah. 15 "What did they see in your house?" the prophet asked. "They saw everything in my house," answered Hezekiah. "There is nothing in my storerooms that I did not show them."

16 Then Isaiah said to Hezekiah: "Hear the word of the LORD: 17 The time is coming when all that is in your house, and everything that your fathers have stored up until this day, shall be carried off to Babylon; nothing shall be left, says the LORD. 18 Some of your own bodily descendants shall be taken and made servants in the palace of the king of Babylon."

19 Hezekiah replied to Isaiah, "The word of the LORD which you have spoken is favorable." For he thought, "There will be peace and security in my lifetime."

20 The rest of the acts of Hezekiah, all his valor, and his construction of the pool and conduit by which water was brought into the city, are written in the book of the chronicles of the kings of Judah. 21 Hezekiah rested with his ancestors and his son Manasseh succeeded him as king.

21 Manasseh was twelve years old when he began to reign, and he reigned fifty-five years in Jerusalem. His mother's name was Hephzibah. 2 He did evil in the sight of the LORD, following the abominable practices of the nations whom the LORD had cleared out of the way of the Israelites. 3 He rebuilt the high places which his father Hezekiah had destroyed. He erected altars to Baal, and also set up a sacred pole, as Ahab, king of Israel, had done. He worshiped and served the whole host of heaven. 4 He built altars in the temple of the LORD, about which the LORD had said, "I will establish my name in Jerusalem" — 5 altars for the whole host of heaven, in the two courts of the temple.

6 He immolated his son by fire. He practiced soothsaying and divination, and reintroduced the consulting of ghosts and spirits. He did much evil in the LORD's sight and provoked him to anger.

7 The Asherah idol he had made, he set up in the temple, of which the LORD had said to David and to his son Solomon: "In this temple and in Jerusalem, which I have chosen out of all the tribes of Israel, I shall place my name forever. 8 I will not in future allow Israel to be driven off the land I gave their fathers, provided that they are careful to observe all I have commanded them, the entire law which my servant Moses enjoined upon them." 9 But they did not listen, and Manasseh misled them into doing even greater evil than the nations whom the LORD had destroyed at the coming of the Israelites.

10 Then the LORD spoke through his servants the prophets: 11 "Because Manasseh, king of Judah, has practiced these abominations and has done greater evil than all that was done by the Amorites before him, and has led Judah into sin by his idols, 12 therefore thus says the LORD, the God of Israel: 'I will bring such evil on Jerusalem and Judah that, whenever anyone hears of it, his ears shall ring. 13 I will

called on Yahweh, who made the shadow cast by the declining sun on the steps — the steps to Ahaz's roof-room — go back ten steps.

12 At that time the king of Babylon, Merodach-Baladan son of Baladan, sent letters and a gift to Hezekiah, for he had heard of his illness and his recovery. 13 Hezekiah was delighted at this and showed the ambassadors his entire treasury, the silver, gold, spices, precious oil, his armoury too, and everything to be seen in his storehouses. There was nothing in his palace or in his whole domain that Hezekiah did not show them.

14 The prophet Isaiah then came to King Hezekiah and asked him, 'What have these men said, and where have they come from?' Hezekiah answered, 'They have come from a distant country, from Babylon.' 15 Isaiah said, 'What have they seen in your palace?' 'They have seen everything in my palace,' Hezekiah answered. 'There is nothing in my storehouses that I have not shown them.'

16 Then Isaiah said to Hezekiah, 'Listen to the word of Yahweh, 17 "The days are coming when everything in your palace, everything that your ancestors have amassed until now, will be carried off to Babylon. Not a thing will be left," Yahweh says. 18 "Sons sprung from you, sons fathered by you, will be abducted to be eunuchs in the palace of the king of Babylon." ' 19 Hezekiah said to Isaiah, 'This word of Yahweh that you announce is reassuring,' for he was thinking, 'And why not? So long as there is peace and security during my lifetime.'

20 The rest of the history of Hezekiah, all his prowess, how he constructed the pool and the conduit to bring water into the city, is this not recorded in the Book of the Annals of the Kings of Judah? 21 Then Hezekiah fell asleep with his ancestors; his son Manasseh succeeded him.

21 Manasseh was twelve years old when he came to the throne and he reigned for fifty-five years in Jerusalem. His mother's name was Hephzibah. 2 He did what is displeasing to Yahweh, copying the disgusting practices of the nations whom Yahweh had dispossessed for the Israelites.

3 He rebuilt the high places which his father Hezekiah had destroyed, he set up altars to Baal and made a sacred pole as Ahab king of Israel had done, he worshipped the whole array of heaven and served it. 4 He built altars in the Temple of Yahweh of which Yahweh had said, 'Jerusalem is where I shall put my name.' 5 He built altars to the whole array of heaven in the two courts of the Temple of Yahweh. 6 He caused his son to pass through the fire of sacrifice, he also practised soothsaying and divination and set up mediums and spirit guides. He did very many more things displeasing to Yahweh, thus provoking his anger. 7 He had an image of Asherah carved and placed it inside the Temple of which Yahweh had said to David and his son Solomon, 'In this Temple and in Jerusalem, the city which I have chosen out of all the tribes of Israel, I shall put my Name for ever. 8 Nor shall I ever again set Israel's footsteps wandering outside the country which I gave to their ancestors, provided they are careful to observe all I have commanded them as laid down in the whole Law which my servant Moses prescribed for them.' 9 But they would not listen, and Manasseh misled them into doing worse things than the nations whom Yahweh had destroyed for the Israelites.

10 Then Yahweh spoke through his servants the prophets as follows, 11 'Since Manasseh king of Judah has done these shameful deeds, doing more wicked deeds than anything which the Amorites did before him, and has led Judah too into sin with his idols, 12 Yahweh, God of Israel, says this, "Look, I shall bring such disaster on Jerusalem and Judah as will make the ears of all who hear of it tingle. 13 Over

NEW REVISED STANDARD VERSION

will stretch over Jerusalem the measuring line for Samaria, and the plummet for the house of Ahab; I will wipe Jerusalem as one wipes a dish, wiping it and turning it upside down. 14 I will cast off the remnant of my heritage, and give them into the hand of their enemies; they shall become a prey and a spoil to all their enemies, 15 because they have done what is evil in my sight and have provoked me to anger, since the day their ancestors came out of Egypt, even to this day."

16 Moreover Manasseh shed very much innocent blood, until he had filled Jerusalem from one end to another, besides the sin that he caused Judah to sin so that they did what was evil in the sight of the LORD.

17 Now the rest of the acts of Manasseh, all that he did, and the sin that he committed, are they not written in the Book of the Annals of the Kings of Judah? 18 Manasseh slept with his ancestors, and was buried in the garden of his house, in the garden of Uzza. His son Amon succeeded him.

19 Amon was twenty-two years old when he began to reign; he reigned two years in Jerusalem. His mother's name was Meshullemeth daughter of Haruz of Jotbah. 20 He did what was evil in the sight of the LORD, as his father Manasseh had done. 21 He walked in all the way in which his father walked, served the idols that his father served, and worshiped them; 22 he abandoned the LORD, the God of his ancestors, and did not walk in the way of the LORD. 23 The servants of Amon conspired against him, and killed the king in his house. 24 But the people of the land killed all those who had conspired against King Amon, and the people of the land made his son Josiah king in place of him. 25 Now the rest of the acts of Amon that he did, are they not written in the Book of the Annals of the Kings of Judah? 26 He was buried in his tomb in the garden of Uzza; then his son Josiah succeeded him.

22 Josiah was eight years old when he began to reign; he reigned thirty-one years in Jerusalem. His mother's name was Jedidah daughter of Adaiah of Bozkath. 2 He did what was right in the sight of the LORD, and walked in all the way of his father David; he did not turn aside to the right or to the left.

3 In the eighteenth year of King Josiah, the king sent Shaphan son of Azaliah, son of Meshullam, the secretary, to the house of the LORD, saying, 4 "Go up to the high priest Hilkiah, and have him count the entire sum of the money that has been brought into the house of the LORD, which the keepers of the threshold have collected from the people; 5 let it be given into the hand of the workers who have the oversight of the house of the LORD; let them give it to the workers who are at the house of the LORD, repairing the house, 6 that is, to the carpenters, to the builders, to the masons; and let them use it to buy timber and quarried stone to repair the house. 7 But no accounting shall be asked from them for the money that is delivered into their hand, for they deal honestly."

8 The high priest Hilkiah said to Shaphan the secretary, "I have found the book of the law in the house of the LORD." When Hilkiah gave the book to Shaphan, he read it. 9 Then Shaphan the secretary came to the king, and reported to the king, "Your servants have emptied out the money that was found in the house, and have delivered it into the hand of the workers who have oversight of the house of the LORD." 10 Shaphan the secretary informed the king, "The priest Hilkiah has given me a book." Shaphan then read it aloud to the king.

11 When the king heard the words of the book of the law, he tore his clothes. 12 Then the king commanded the

REVISED ENGLISH BIBLE

Jerusalem the measuring line used against Samaria and the plummet used against the house of Ahab. I shall wipe Jerusalem as one wipes a plate and turns it upside down. 14 I shall cast off what is left of my people, my own possession, and hand them over to their enemies. They will be plundered, a prey to all their enemies, 15 for they have done what is wrong in my eyes and have provoked my anger from the day their forefathers left Egypt up to the present day. 16 This Manasseh shed so much innocent blood that he filled Jerusalem with it from end to end, not to mention the sin into which he led Judah by doing what is wrong in my eyes.'

17 The other events and acts of Manasseh's reign, and the sin that he committed, are recorded in the annals of the kings of Judah. 18 Manasseh rested with his forefathers and was buried in the garden-tomb of his family, in the garden of Uzza. His son Amon succeeded him.

19 Amon was twenty-two years old when he came to the throne, and he reigned in Jerusalem for two years; his mother was Meshullemeth daughter of Haruz from Jotbah. 20 He did what was wrong in the eyes of the LORD as his father Manasseh had done. 21 Following in his father's footsteps he served the idols that his father had served and prostrated himself before them. 22 He forsook the LORD the God of his forefathers and did not conform to the LORD's ways. 23 Amon's courtiers conspired against him and assassinated him in the palace; 24 but the people of the land killed all the conspirators and made his son Josiah king in his place. 25 The other events of Amon's reign are recorded in the annals of the kings of Judah. 26 He was buried in his grave in the garden of Uzza. His son Josiah succeeded him.

22 JOSIAH was eight years old when he came to the throne, and he reigned in Jerusalem for thirty-one years; his mother was Jedidah daughter of Adaiah of Bozkath. 2 He did what was right in the eyes of the LORD, following in the footsteps of his forefather David and deviating neither to the right nor to the left.

3 In the eighteenth year of his reign, Josiah sent Shaphan son of Azaliah, son of Meshullam, the adjutant-general, to the house of the LORD. 4 'Go to the high priest Hilkiah,' he said, 'and tell him to melt down the silver that has been brought into the house of the LORD, which those on duty at the entrance have received from the people; 5 tell him to hand it over to those supervising in the house of the LORD, to pay the workmen who are carrying out repairs in it, 6 the carpenters, builders, and masons, and to purchase timber and hewn stones for its repair. 7 They are not to be asked to account for the money that has been given them; they are acting on trust.'

8 The high priest Hilkiah told Shaphan the adjutant-general that he had discovered the scroll of the law in the house of the LORD, and he gave it to him to read. 9 When Shaphan came to report to the king that his servants had melted down the silver in the house of the LORD and handed it over to those supervising there, 10 he told the king of the scroll the high priest Hilkiah had given him, and he read it in the king's presence. 11 When the king heard what was written in the book of the law, he tore his clothes. 12 He ordered the

21:19–24 *Cp. 2 Chr. 33:21–25.*   22:1–2 *Cp. 2 Chr. 34:1–2.*
22:3—23:3 *Cp. 2 Chr. 34:8–32.*   22:4 **melt down:** *so Gk (Luc.);*
Heb. complete.

826

measure Jerusalem with the same cord as I did Samaria, and with the plummet I used for the house of Ahab. I will wipe Jerusalem clean as one wipes a dish, wiping it inside and out. 14 I will cast off the survivors of my inheritance and deliver them into enemy hands, to become a prey and a booty for all their enemies, 15 because they have done evil in my sight and provoked me from the day their fathers came forth from Egypt until today.' "

16 In addition to the sin which he caused Judah to commit, Manasseh did evil in the sight of the LORD, shedding so much innocent blood as to fill the length and breadth of Jerusalem. 17 The rest of the acts of Manasseh, the sin he committed and all that he did, are written in the book of the chronicles of the kings of Judah. 18 Manasseh rested with his ancestors and was buried in his palace garden, the garden of Uzza. His son Amon succeeded him as king.

19 Amon was twenty-two years old when he began to reign, and he reigned two years in Jerusalem. His mother's name was Meshullemeth, daughter of Haruz of Jotbah. 20 He did evil in the sight of the LORD, as his father Manasseh had done. 21 He followed exactly the path his father had trod, serving and worshiping the idols his father had served. 22 He abandoned the LORD, the God of his fathers, and did not follow the path of the LORD. 23 Subjects of Amon conspired against him and slew the king in his palace, 24 but the people of the land then slew all who had conspired against King Amon, and proclaimed his son Josiah king in his stead. 25 The rest of the acts that Amon did are written in the book of the chronicles of the kings of Judah. 26 He was buried in his own grave in the garden of Uzza, and his son Josiah succeeded him as king.

22 Josiah was eight years old when he began to reign, and he reigned thirty-one years in Jerusalem. His mother's name was Jedidah, daughter of Adaiah of Bozkath. 2 He pleased the LORD and conducted himself unswervingly just as his ancestor David had done.

3 In his eighteenth year, King Josiah sent the scribe Shaphan, son of Azaliah, son of Meshullam, to the temple of the LORD with orders to 4 go to the high priest Hilkiah and have him smelt down the precious metals that had been donated to the temple of the Lord, which the doorkeepers had collected from the people. 5 They were to be consigned to the master workmen in the temple of the LORD, who should then pay them out to the carpenters, builders, and lumbermen making repairs on the temple, 6 and for the purchase of wood and hewn stone for the temple repairs. 7 No reckoning was asked of them regarding the funds consigned to them, because they held positions of trust.

8 The high priest Hilkiah informed the scribe Shaphan, "I have found the book of the law in the temple of the LORD." Hilkiah gave the book to Shaphan, who read it. 9 Then the scribe Shaphan went to the king and reported, "Your servants have smelted down the metals available in the temple and have consigned them to the master workmen in the temple of the LORD." 10 The scribe Shaphan also informed the king that the priest Hilkiah had given him a book, and then read it aloud to the king. 11 When the king had heard the contents of the book of the law, he tore his garments

Jerusalem I shall stretch the same measuring line as over Samaria, the same plumb-rule as for the House of Ahab; I shall scour Jerusalem as someone scours a dish and, having scoured it, turns it upside down. 14 I shall cast away the remnant of my heritage, delivering them into the clutches of their enemies and making them the prey and booty of all their enemies, 15 because they have done what is displeasing to me and have provoked my anger from the day their ancestors came out of Egypt until now." '

16 Manasseh shed innocent blood, too, in such great quantity that he flooded Jerusalem from one end to the other, besides the sins into which he led Judah by doing what is displeasing to Yahweh. 17 The rest of the history of Manasseh, his entire career, the sins he committed, is this not recorded in the Book of the Annals of the Kings of Judah? 18 Then Manasseh fell asleep with his ancestors and was buried in the garden of his palace, the Garden of Uzza; his son Amon succeeded him.

19 Amon was twenty-two years old when he came to the throne, and he reigned for two years in Jerusalem. His mother's name was Meshullemeth daughter of Haruz, of Jotbah. 20 He did what is displeasing to Yahweh, as Manasseh his father had done. 21 In every respect he followed the example of his father, serving the idols which his father had served, and worshipping them. 22 He abandoned Yahweh, God of his ancestors; he did not follow the way of Yahweh. 23 Amon's retinue plotted against the king and killed him in his own palace. 24 The people of the country, however, slaughtered all those who had plotted against King Amon and proclaimed his son Josiah as his successor. 25 The rest of the history of Amon, his entire career, is this not recorded in the Book of the Annals of the Kings of Judah? 26 He was buried in his father's tomb in the Garden of Uzza; his son Josiah succeeded him.

22 Josiah was eight years old when he came to the throne, and he reigned for thirty-one years in Jerusalem. His mother's name was Jedidah daughter of Adaiah, of Bozkath. 2 He did what Yahweh regards as right, and in every respect followed the example of his ancestor David, not deviating from it to right or left.

3 In the eighteenth year of King Josiah, the king sent the secretary Shaphan son of Azaliah, son of Meshullam to the Temple of Yahweh. 4 'Go to Hilkiah the high priest,' he told him, 'and tell him to melt down the silver contributed to the Temple of Yahweh and collected by the guardians of the threshold from the people. 5 He is to hand it over to the masters of works attached to the Temple of Yahweh, for them to pay it over to men working on the Temple of Yahweh, to repair the damaged parts of the Temple: 6 to the carpenters, builders and masons, and for buying timber and dressed stone for the Temple repairs.' 7 The latter were not required to render account of the money handed over to them, since they were conscientious in their work.

8 The high priest Hilkiah said to Shaphan the secretary, 'I have found the Book of the Law in the Temple of Yahweh.' And Hilkiah gave the book to Shaphan, who read it. 9 Shaphan the secretary went to the king, reporting furthermore to him as follows, 'Your servants have melted down the silver which was in the Temple and have handed it over to the masters of works attached to the Temple of Yahweh.' 10 Then Shaphan the secretary informed the king, 'The priest Hilkiah has given me a book'; and Shaphan read it aloud in the king's presence.

11 On hearing the words of the Book of the Law he tore his clothes. 12 Then the king gave the following order to the

| NEW REVISED STANDARD VERSION | REVISED ENGLISH BIBLE |

priest Hilkiah, Ahikam son of Shaphan, Achbor son of Micaiah, Shaphan the secretary, and the king's servant Asaiah, saying, 13 "Go, inquire of the LORD for me, for the people, and for all Judah, concerning the words of this book that has been found; for great is the wrath of the LORD that is kindled against us, because our ancestors did not obey the words of this book, to do according to all that is written concerning us."

14 So the priest Hilkiah, Ahikam, Achbor, Shaphan, and Asaiah went to the prophetess Huldah the wife of Shallum son of Tikvah, son of Harhas, keeper of the wardrobe; she resided in Jerusalem in the Second Quarter, where they consulted her. 15 She declared to them, "Thus says the LORD, the God of Israel: Tell the man who sent you to me, 16 Thus says the LORD, I will indeed bring disaster on this place and on its inhabitants — all the words of the book that the king of Judah has read. 17 Because they have abandoned me and have made offerings to other gods, so that they have provoked me to anger with all the work of their hands, therefore my wrath will be kindled against this place, and it will not be quenched. 18 But as to the king of Judah, who sent you to inquire of the LORD, thus shall you say to him, Thus says the LORD, the God of Israel: Regarding the words that you have heard, 19 because your heart was penitent, and you humbled yourself before the LORD, when you heard how I spoke against this place, and against its inhabitants, that they should become a desolation and a curse, and because you have torn your clothes and wept before me, I also have heard you, says the LORD. 20 Therefore, I will gather you to your ancestors, and you shall be gathered to your grave in peace; your eyes shall not see all the disaster that I will bring on this place." They took the message back to the king.

23 Then the king directed that all the elders of Judah and Jerusalem should be gathered to him. 2 The king went up to the house of the LORD, and with him went all the people of Judah, all the inhabitants of Jerusalem, the priests, the prophets, and all the people, both small and great; he read in their hearing all the words of the book of the covenant that had been found in the house of the LORD. 3 The king stood by the pillar and made a covenant before the LORD, to follow the LORD, keeping his commandments, his decrees, and his statutes, with all his heart and all his soul, to perform the words of this covenant that were written in this book. All the people joined in the covenant.

4 The king commanded the high priest Hilkiah, the priests of the second order, and the guardians of the threshold, to bring out of the temple of the LORD all the vessels made for Baal, for Asherah, and for all the host of heaven; he burned them outside Jerusalem in the fields of the Kidron, and carried their ashes to Bethel. 5 He deposed the idolatrous priests whom the kings of Judah had ordained to make offerings in the high places at the cities of Judah and around Jerusalem; those also who made offerings to Baal, to the sun, the moon, the constellations, and all the host of the heavens. 6 He brought out the image of[i] Asherah from the house of the LORD, outside Jerusalem, to the Wadi Kidron, burned it at the Wadi Kidron, beat it to dust and threw the dust of it upon the graves of the common people. 7 He broke down the houses of the male temple prostitutes that were in the house of the LORD, where the women did weaving for Asherah. 8 He brought all the priests out of the

priest Hilkiah, Ahikam son of Shaphan, Akbor son of Micaiah, Shaphan the adjutant-general, and Asaiah the king's attendant 13 to go and seek guidance of the LORD for himself, for the people, and for all Judah, about the contents of this book that had been discovered. 'Great must be the wrath of the LORD', he said, 'that has been kindled against us, because our forefathers did not obey the commands in this scroll and do all that is laid on us.'

14 Hilkiah the priest, Ahikam, Akbor, Shaphan, and Asaiah went to Huldah the prophetess, wife of Shallum son of Tikvah, son of Harhas, the keeper of the wardrobe, and consulted her at her home in the Second Quarter of Jerusalem. 15 'This is the word of the LORD the God of Israel,' she answered: 'Tell the man who sent you to me, 16 that this is what the LORD says: I am about to bring disaster on this place and its inhabitants as foretold in the scroll which the king of Judah has read, 17 because they have forsaken me and burnt sacrifices to other gods, provoking my anger with all the idols they have made with their own hands; for this my wrath is kindled against this place and will not be quenched. 18 Tell the king of Judah who sent you to seek guidance of the LORD that this is what the LORD the God of Israel says: You have listened to my words 19 and shown a willing heart and humbled yourself before the LORD when you heard me say that this place and its inhabitants would become objects of loathing and scorn, and have torn your clothes and wept before me. Because of this, I for my part have listened to you. This is the word of the LORD. 20 Therefore I shall gather you to your forefathers, and you will be gathered to your grave in peace; you will not live to see all the disaster which I am bringing on this place.' They brought back this answer to the king.

23 At the king's summons all the elders of Judah and Jerusalem were assembled, 2 and he went up to the house of the LORD, taking with him all the men of Judah, the inhabitants of Jerusalem, the priests, and the prophets, the entire population, high and low. There he read out to them the whole scroll of the covenant which had been discovered in the house of the LORD. 3 Then, standing by the pillar, the king entered into a covenant before the LORD to obey him and keep his commandments, his testimonies, and his statutes, with all his heart and soul, and so carry out the terms of the covenant written in the scroll. All the people pledged themselves to the covenant.

4 The king ordered the high priest Hilkiah, the deputy high priest, and those on duty at the entrance to remove from the house of the LORD all the objects made for Baal, for Asherah, and for all the host of heaven, and he burnt these outside Jerusalem on the slope by the Kidron, and carried the ashes to Bethel. 5 He suppressed the heathen priests whom the kings of Judah had appointed to burn sacrifices at the shrines in the towns of Judah and in the neighbourhood of Jerusalem, as well as those who burnt sacrifices to Baal, to the sun and moon, to the planets and all the host of heaven. 6 He took the Asherah from the house of the LORD to the wadi of the Kidron outside Jerusalem, burnt it there, and pounded it to dust, which was then scattered over the common burial-ground. 7 He also pulled down the quarters of the male prostitutes attached to the house of the LORD, where the women wove vestments in honour of Asherah.

23:4 **deputy high priest:** *prob. rdg; Heb.* deputy high priests.
23:5 **to burn:** *so Gk (Luc.); Heb.* and he burnt.   23:6 **Asherah:** *or* sacred pole.

[i] Heb lacks *image of*

NEW AMERICAN BIBLE

NEW JERUSALEM BIBLE

12 and issued this command to Hilkiah the priest, Ahikam, son of Shaphan, Achbor, son of Micaiah, the scribe Shaphan, and the king's servant Asaiah: 13 "Go, consult the LORD for me, for the people, for all Judah, about the stipulations of this book that has been found, for the anger of the LORD has been set furiously ablaze against us, because our fathers did not obey the stipulations of this book, nor fulfill our written obligations."

14 So Hilkiah the priest, Ahikam, Achbor, Shaphan, and Asaiah betook themselves to the Second Quarter in Jerusalem, where the prophetess Huldah resided. She was the wife of Shallum, son of Tikvah, son of Harhas, keeper of the wardrobe. When they had spoken to her, 15 she said to them, "Thus says the LORD, the God of Israel: 'Say to the man who sent you to me, 16 Thus says the LORD: I will bring upon this place and upon its inhabitants all the evil that is threatened in the book which the king of Judah has read. 17 Because they have forsaken me and have burned incense to other gods, provoking me by everything to which they turn their hands, my anger is ablaze against this place and it cannot be extinguished.'

18 "But to the king of Judah who sent you to consult the LORD, give this response: 'Thus says the LORD, the God of Israel: As for the threats you have heard, 19 because you were heartsick and have humbled yourself before the LORD when you heard my threats that this place and its inhabitants would become a desolation and a curse; because you tore your garments and wept before me; I in turn have listened, says the LORD. 20 I will therefore gather you to your ancestors; you shall go to your grave in peace, and your eyes shall not see all the evil I will bring upon this place.' " This they reported to the king.

23 The king then had all the elders of Judah and of Jerusalem summoned together before him. 2 The king went up to the temple of the LORD with all the men of Judah and all the inhabitants of Jerusalem: priests, prophets, and all the people, small and great. He had the entire contents of the book of the covenant that had been found in the temple of the LORD, read out to them. 3 Standing by the column, the king made a covenant before the LORD that they would follow him and observe his ordinances, statutes and decrees with their whole hearts and souls, thus reviving the terms of the covenant which were written in this book. And all the people stood as participants in the covenant.

4 Then the king commanded the high priest Hilkiah, his vicar, and the doorkeepers to remove from the temple of the LORD all the objects that had been made for Baal, Asherah, and the whole host of heaven. He had these burned outside Jerusalem on the slopes of the Kidron and their ashes carried to Bethel. 5 He also put an end to the pseudo-priests whom the kings of Judah had appointed to burn incense on the high places in the cities of Judah and in the vicinity of Jerusalem, as well as those who burned incense to Baal, to the sun, moon, and signs of the Zodiac, and to the whole host of heaven. 6 From the temple of the LORD he also removed the sacred pole, to the Kidron Valley, outside Jerusalem; there he had it burned and beaten to dust, which was then scattered over the common graveyard. 7 He tore down the apartments of the cult prostitutes which were in the temple of the LORD, and in which the women wove garments for the Asherah.

priest Hilkiah, Ahikam son of Shaphan, Achbor son of Micaiah, Shaphan the secretary and Asaiah the king's minister: 13 'Go and consult Yahweh on behalf of me and the people about the words of the book that has been discovered; for Yahweh's furious wrath has been kindled against us because our ancestors disobeyed the word of Yahweh by not doing what this book says they ought to have done.'

14 The priest Hilkiah, Ahikam, Achbor, Shaphan and Asaiah went to the prophetess Huldah wife of Shallum son of Tikvah, son of Harhas the keeper of the wardrobe; she lived in Jerusalem in the new town. They put the matter to her, 15 and she replied, 'Yahweh, God of Israel, says this, "To the man who sent you to me say this: 16 Yahweh says this: I am going to bring disaster on this place and the people who live in it — all the words of the book read by the king of Judah. 17 Because they have abandoned me and sacrificed to other gods, so as to provoke my anger by their every action, my wrath is kindled against this place, and nothing can stop it. 18 As for the king of Judah who sent you to consult Yahweh, say this to him: As regards the words you have heard . . . 19 But since your heart has been touched and you have humbled yourself before Yahweh on hearing what I have decreed against this place and the people who live in it, how they will become an object of horror and cursing, and have torn your clothes and wept before me, I too have heard — Yahweh says this. 20 So look, when I gather you to your ancestors, you will be gathered into your grave in peace; you will not live to see the great disaster that I am going to bring on this place." ' They took this answer to the king.

23 The king then had all the elders of Judah and of Jerusalem summoned to him, 2 and the king went up to the Temple of Yahweh with all the people of Judah and all the inhabitants of Jerusalem, priests, prophets and the whole populace, high and low. In their hearing he read out the entire contents of the Book of the Covenant discovered in the Temple of Yahweh. 3 The king then, standing on the dais, bound himself by the covenant before Yahweh, to follow Yahweh, to keep his commandments, decrees and laws with all his heart and soul, and to carry out the terms of the covenant as written in this book. All the people pledged their allegiance to the covenant.

4 The king ordered Hilkiah with the priest next in rank and the guardians of the threshold to remove all the cult objects which had been made for Baal, Asherah and the whole array of heaven; he burnt them outside Jerusalem in the fields of the Kidron and had the ashes taken to Bethel. 5 He exterminated the spurious priests whom the kings of Judah had appointed and who offered sacrifice on the high places, in the towns of Judah and the neighbourhood of Jerusalem; also those who offered sacrifice to Baal, to the sun, the moon, the constellations and the whole array of heaven. 6 And from the Temple of Yahweh he took the sacred pole outside Jerusalem to the Kidron valley and in the Kidron valley he burnt it, reducing it to ashes and throwing its ashes on the common burial-ground. 7 He pulled down the house of the sacred male prostitutes which was in the Temple of Yahweh and where the women wove veils for Asherah.

NEW REVISED STANDARD VERSION

towns of Judah, and defiled the high places where the priests had made offerings, from Geba to Beer-sheba; he broke down the high places of the gates that were at the entrance of the gate of Joshua the governor of the city, which were on the left at the gate of the city. 9 The priests of the high places, however, did not come up to the altar of the LORD in Jerusalem, but ate unleavened bread among their kindred. 10 He defiled Topheth, which is in the valley of Ben-hinnom, so that no one would make a son or a daughter pass through fire as an offering to Molech. 11 He removed the horses that the kings of Judah had dedicated to the sun, at the entrance to the house of the LORD, by the chamber of the eunuch Nathan-melech, which was in the precincts;*j* then he burned the chariots of the sun with fire. 12 The altars on the roof of the upper chamber of Ahaz, which the kings of Judah had made, and the altars that Manasseh had made in the two courts of the house of the LORD, he pulled down from there and broke in pieces, and threw the rubble into the Wadi Kidron. 13 The king defiled the high places that were east of Jerusalem, to the south of the Mount of Destruction, which King Solomon of Israel had built for Astarte the abomination of the Sidonians, for Chemosh the abomination of Moab, and for Milcom the abomination of the Ammonites. 14 He broke the pillars in pieces, cut down the sacred poles,*k* and covered the sites with human bones.

15 Moreover, the altar at Bethel, the high place erected by Jeroboam son of Nebat, who caused Israel to sin — he pulled down that altar along with the high place. He burned the high place, crushing it to dust; he also burned the sacred pole.*l* 16 As Josiah turned, he saw the tombs there on the mount; and he sent and took the bones out of the tombs, and burned them on the altar, and defiled it, according to the word of the LORD that the man of God proclaimed,*m* when Jeroboam stood by the altar at the festival; he turned and looked up at the tomb of the man of God who had predicted these things. 17 Then he said, "What is that monument that I see?" The people of the city told him, "It is the tomb of the man of God who came from Judah and predicted these things that you have done against the altar at Bethel." 18 He said, "Let him rest; let no one move his bones." So they let his bones alone, with the bones of the prophet who came out of Samaria. 19 Moreover, Josiah removed all the shrines of the high places that were in the towns of Samaria, which kings of Israel had made, provoking the LORD to anger; he did to them just as he had done at Bethel. 20 He slaughtered on the altars all the priests of the high places who were there, and burned human bones on them. Then he returned to Jerusalem.

21 The king commanded all the people, "Keep the passover to the LORD your God as prescribed in this book of the covenant." 22 No such passover had been kept since the days of the judges who judged Israel, or during all the days of the kings of Israel or of the kings of Judah; 23 but in the eighteenth year of King Josiah this passover was kept to the LORD in Jerusalem.

24 Moreover Josiah put away the mediums, wizards, teraphim,*n* idols, and all the abominations that were seen in the land of Judah and in Jerusalem, so that he established the words of the law that were written in the book that the priest Hilkiah had found in the house of the LORD. 25 Before him there was no king like him, who turned to the LORD with all his heart, with all his soul, and with all his might, according to all the law of Moses; nor did any like him arise after him.

REVISED ENGLISH BIBLE

8 The king brought in all the priests from the towns of Judah and desecrated the shrines where they had burnt sacrifices, from Geba to Beersheba, and dismantled the shrines of the demons in front of the gate of Joshua, the city governor, which is to the left of the city gate. 9 These priests, however, never came up to the altar of the LORD in Jerusalem but used to eat unleavened bread with the priests of their clan. 10 He desecrated Topheth in the valley of Ben-hinnom, so that no one might make his son or daughter pass through the fire for Molech. 11 He did away with the horses that the kings of Judah had set up in honour of the sun at the entrance to the house of the LORD, beside the room of the eunuch Nathan-melech in the colonnade, and he burnt the chariots of the sun. 12 He demolished the altars made by the kings of Judah on the roof by the upper chamber of Ahaz and the altars made by Manasseh in the two courts of the house of the LORD; he pounded them to dust and threw it into the wadi of the Kidron. 13 Also, on the east of Jerusalem, to the south of the mount of Olives, the king desecrated the shrines which Solomon the king of Israel had built for Ashtoreth the loathsome goddess of the Sidonians, and for Kemosh the loathsome god of Moab, and for Milcom the abominable god of the Ammonites; 14 he smashed the sacred pillars and cut down the sacred poles and filled the places where they had stood with human bones.

15 At Bethel he dismantled the altar by the shrine made by Jeroboam son of Nebat who led Israel into sin, together with the shrine itself; he broke its stones in pieces, crushed them to dust, and burnt the sacred pole. 16 When Josiah saw the graves which were there on the hill, he sent and had the bones taken from them, and he burnt them on the altar to desecrate it, thus fulfilling the word of the LORD announced by the man of God when Jeroboam stood by the altar at the feast. When Josiah saw the grave of the man of God who had foretold these things, 17 he asked, 'What is that monument I see?' The people of the town answered, 'It is the grave of the man of God who came from Judah and foretold all that you have done to the altar at Bethel.' 18 'Leave it alone,' he said; 'let no one disturb his bones.' So they spared his bones along with those of the prophet who came from Samaria. 19 Josiah also suppressed all the temples at the shrines in the towns of Samaria, which the kings of Israel had set up and thereby provoked the LORD's anger, and he did to them what he had done at Bethel. 20 He slaughtered on the altars all the priests of the shrines who were there, and he burnt human bones on them. Then he went back to Jerusalem.

21 The king ordered all the people to keep the Passover to the LORD their God, as this scroll of the covenant prescribed; 22 no Passover like it had been kept either when the judges were ruling Israel or during the times of the kings of Israel and of Judah, 23 until in the eighteenth year of Josiah's reign this Passover was kept to the LORD in Jerusalem.

24 Further, Josiah got rid of all who called up ghosts and spirits, and of all household gods and idols and all the loathsome objects to be seen in the land of Judah and in Jerusalem, so that he might fulfil the requirements of the law written in the scroll which the priest Hilkiah had discovered in the house of the LORD. 25 No king before him had turned to the LORD as he did, with all his heart and soul and strength, following the whole law of Moses; nor did any king like him appear again.

23:13 **mount of Olives:** *so Aram. (Targ.); Heb.* mount of the Destroyer.   23:15 **by the shrine:** *prob. rdg; Heb.* omits by. **he broke . . . pieces:** *so Gk; Heb.* he burnt the shrine.   23:16 **when Jeroboam . . . man of God:** *so Gk; Heb.* omits.   23:19 **the LORD's:** *so Gk; Heb.* omits.   23:24 **household gods:** *Heb.* teraphim.

j Meaning of Heb uncertain   *k* Heb *Asherim*   *l* Heb *Asherah*   *m* Gk: Heb *proclaimed, who had predicted these things*   *n* Or *household gods*

8 He brought in all the priests from the cities of Judah, and then defiled, from Geba to Beer-sheba, the high places where they had offered incense. He also tore down the high place of the satyrs, which was at the entrance of the Gate of Joshua, governor of the city, to the left as one enters the city gate. 9 The priests of the high places could not function at the altar of the LORD in Jerusalem; but they, along with their relatives, ate the unleavened bread.

10 The king also defiled Topheth in the Valley of Ben-hinnom, so that there would no longer be any immolation of sons or daughters by fire in honor of Molech. 11 He did away with the horses which the kings of Judah had dedicated to the sun; these were at the entrance of the temple of the LORD, near the chamber of Nathan-melech the eunuch, which was in the large building. The chariots of the sun he destroyed by fire. 12 He also demolished the altars made by the kings of Judah on the roof (the roof terrace of Ahaz), and the altars made by Manasseh in the two courts of the temple of the LORD. He pulverized them and threw the dust into the Kidron Valley. 13 The king defiled the high places east of Jerusalem, south of the Mount of Misconduct, which Solomon, king of Israel, had built in honor of Astarte, the Sidonian horror, of Chemosh, the Moabite horror, and of Milcom, the idol of the Ammonites. 14 He broke to pieces the pillars, cut down the sacred poles, and filled the places where they had been with human bones. 15 Likewise the altar which was at Bethel, the high place built by Jeroboam, son of Nebat, who caused Israel to sin — this same altar and high place he tore down, breaking up the stones and grinding them to powder, and burning the Asherah.

16 When Josiah turned and saw the graves there on the mountainside, he ordered the bones taken from the graves and burned on the altar, and thus defiled it in fulfillment of the word of the LORD which the man of God had proclaimed as Jeroboam was standing by the altar on the feast day. When the king looked up and saw the grave of the man of God who had proclaimed these words, 17 he asked, "What is that tombstone I see?" The men of the city replied, "It is the grave of the man of God who came from Judah and predicted the very things you have done to the altar of Bethel." 18 "Let him be," he said, "let no one move his bones." So they left his bones undisturbed together with the bones of the prophet who had come from Samaria.

19 Josiah also removed all the shrines on the high places near the cities of Samaria which the kings of Israel had erected, thereby provoking the LORD; he did the very same to them as he had done in Bethel. 20 He slaughtered upon the altars all the priests of the high places that were at the shrines, and burned human bones upon them. Then he returned to Jerusalem.

21 The king issued a command to all the people to observe the Passover of the LORD, their God, as it was prescribed in that book of the covenant. 22 No Passover such as this had been observed during the period when the Judges ruled Israel, or during the entire period of the kings of Israel and the kings of Judah, 23 until the eighteenth year of King Josiah, when this Passover of the LORD was kept in Jerusalem.

24 Further, Josiah did away with the consultation of ghosts and spirits, with the household gods, idols, and all the other horrors to be seen in the land of Judah and in Jerusalem, so that he might carry out the stipulations of the law written in the book that the priest Helkiah had found in the temple of the LORD.

25 Before him there had been no king who turned to the LORD as he did, with his whole heart, his whole soul, and his whole strength, in accord with the entire law of Moses; nor could any after him compare with him.

8 He brought all the priests in from the towns of Judah, and from Geba to Beersheba he rendered unsanctified the high places where these priests had offered sacrifice. He pulled down the High Place of the Gates, which stood at the gate of Joshua, the governor of the city, to the left of the entry to the city. 9 The priests of the high places, however, did not officiate at the altar of Yahweh in Jerusalem, although they did share the unleavened bread of their brother-priests. 10 He rendered unsanctified Tophet in the Valley of Ben-Hinnom, so that no one could pass his son or daughter through the fire of sacrifice to Molech. 11 He destroyed the horses which the kings of Judah had dedicated to the sun at the entrance to the Temple of Yahweh, near the apartment of Nathan-Melech the official, in the precincts, and he burned the solar chariot. 12 The king pulled down altars which the kings of Judah had built on the roof and those which Manasseh had built in the two courts of the Temple of Yahweh, and broke them to pieces on the spot, throwing their rubble into the Kidron valley. 13 The king rendered unsanctified the high places facing Jerusalem, to the south of the Mount of Olives, which Solomon king of Israel had built for Astarte the Sidonian abomination, for Chemosh the Moabite abomination, and for Milcom the Ammonite abomination. 14 He also smashed the sacred pillars, cut down the sacred poles, and covered with human bones the places where they had stood.

15 As for the altar which was at Bethel, the high place built by Jeroboam son of Nebat who had led Israel into sin, he demolished this altar and this high place as well, in the same way, breaking up its stones and reducing them to powder. The sacred pole he burned.

16 On looking round, Josiah saw the tombs there on the hillside; he had the bones fetched from the tombs and burned them on the altar. This he rendered unsanctified, in accordance with the word of Yahweh which the man of God had proclaimed when Jeroboam was standing by the altar at the time of the feast. On looking round, Josiah caught sight of the tomb of the man of God who had foretold these things. 17 'What is that monument I see?' he asked. The townspeople replied, 'It is the tomb of the man of God who came from Judah and foretold what you have done to the altar.' 18 'Let him rest,' the king said, 'and let no one disturb his bones.' So they left his bones untouched, with the bones of the prophet who came from Samaria.

19 Josiah also destroyed all the shrines on the high places which were in the towns of Samaria and which the kings of Israel had built to provoke Yahweh's anger; he treated these places exactly as he had treated the one at Bethel. 20 All the priests of the high places who were there he slaughtered on the altars, and on those altars burned human bones. Then he returned to Jerusalem.

21 The king gave this order to the whole people: 'Celebrate a Passover to Yahweh your God, as prescribed in this Book of the Covenant.' 22 No Passover like this had ever been celebrated since the days when the judges ruled Israel, nor throughout the entire period of the kings of Israel and the kings of Judah. 23 The eighteenth year of King Josiah was the only time when such a Passover was celebrated in Yahweh's honour in Jerusalem.

24 What is more, the spirit-guides and mediums, the household gods and idols, and all the abominations to be seen in the country of Judah and in Jerusalem, were swept away by Josiah to give effect to the words of the Law written in the book found by the priest Hilkiah in the Temple of Yahweh. 25 No king before him turned to Yahweh as he did, with all his heart, all his soul, all his strength, in perfect loyalty to the Law of Moses; nor did any king like him arise again.

26 Still the LORD did not turn from the fierceness of his great wrath, by which his anger was kindled against Judah, because of all the provocations with which Manasseh had provoked him. 27 The LORD said, "I will remove Judah also out of my sight, as I have removed Israel; and I will reject this city that I have chosen, Jerusalem, and the house of which I said, My name shall be there."

28 Now the rest of the acts of Josiah, and all that he did, are they not written in the Book of the Annals of the Kings of Judah? 29 In his days Pharaoh Neco king of Egypt went up to the king of Assyria to the river Euphrates. King Josiah went to meet him; but when Pharaoh Neco met him at Megiddo, he killed him. 30 His servants carried him dead in a chariot from Megiddo, brought him to Jerusalem, and buried him in his own tomb. The people of the land took Jehoahaz son of Josiah, anointed him, and made him king in place of his father.

31 Jehoahaz was twenty-three years old when he began to reign; he reigned three months in Jerusalem. His mother's name was Hamutal daughter of Jeremiah of Libnah. 32 He did what was evil in the sight of the LORD, just as his ancestors had done. 33 Pharaoh Neco confined him at Riblah in the land of Hamath, so that he might not reign in Jerusalem, and imposed tribute on the land of one hundred talents of silver and a talent of gold. 34 Pharaoh Neco made Eliakim son of Josiah king in place of his father Josiah, and changed his name to Jehoiakim. But he took Jehoahaz away; he came to Egypt, and died there. 35 Jehoiakim gave the silver and the gold to Pharaoh, but he taxed the land in order to meet Pharaoh's demand for money. He exacted the silver and the gold from the people of the land, from all according to their assessment, to give it to Pharaoh Neco.

36 Jehoiakim was twenty-five years old when he began to reign; he reigned eleven years in Jerusalem. His mother's name was Zebidah daughter of Pedaiah of Rumah. 37 He did what was evil in the sight of the LORD, just as all his ancestors had done.

24 In his days King Nebuchadnezzar of Babylon came up; Jehoiakim became his servant for three years; then he turned and rebelled against him. 2 The LORD sent against him bands of the Chaldeans, bands of the Arameans, bands of the Moabites, and bands of the Ammonites; he sent them against Judah to destroy it, according to the word of the LORD that he spoke by his servants the prophets. 3 Surely this came upon Judah at the command of the LORD, to remove them out of his sight, for the sins of Manasseh, for all that he had committed, 4 and also for the innocent blood that he had shed; for he filled Jerusalem with innocent blood, and the LORD was not willing to pardon. 5 Now the rest of the deeds of Jehoiakim, and all that he did, are they not written in the Book of the Annals of the Kings of Judah? 6 So Jehoiakim slept with his ancestors; then his son Jehoiachin succeeded him. 7 The king of Egypt did not come again out of his land, for the king of Babylon had taken over all that belonged to the king of Egypt from the Wadi of Egypt to the River Euphrates.

8 Jehoiachin was eighteen years old when he began to reign; he reigned three months in Jerusalem. His mother's name was Nehushta daughter of Elnathan of Jerusalem. 9 He did what was evil in the sight of the LORD, just as his father had done.

10 At that time the servants of King Nebuchadnezzar of Babylon came up to Jerusalem, and the city was besieged.

26 Yet the LORD did not abate his fierce anger; it still burned against Judah because of all the provocation which Manasseh had given him. 27 'Judah also I shall banish from my presence', he declared, 'as I banished Israel; and I shall reject this city of Jerusalem which once I chose, and the house where I promised that my name should be.'

28 The other events and acts of Josiah's reign are recorded in the annals of the kings of Judah. 29 It was in his reign that Pharaoh Necho king of Egypt set out for the river Euphrates to help the king of Assyria. King Josiah went to meet him; and when they met at Megiddo, Pharaoh Necho slew him. 30 His attendants conveyed his body in a chariot from Megiddo to Jerusalem and buried him in his own burial-place. Then the people of the land took Josiah's son Jehoahaz and anointed him king in place of his father.

31 JEHOAHAZ was twenty-three years old when he came to the throne, and he reigned in Jerusalem for three months; his mother was Hamital daughter of Jeremiah from Libnah. 32 He did what was wrong in the eyes of the LORD, as his forefathers had done. 33 Pharaoh Necho removed him from the throne in Jerusalem, and imposed on the land an indemnity of a hundred talents of silver and one talent of gold. 34 He made Josiah's son Eliakim king in place of his father and changed his name to Jehoiakim. He carried Jehoahaz away to Egypt, where he died. 35 Jehoiakim handed over the silver and gold to Pharaoh, taxing the country to meet Pharaoh's demands; he exacted it from the people, from every man according to his assessment, so that he could pay Pharaoh Necho.

36 Jehoiakim was twenty-five years old when he came to the throne, and he reigned in Jerusalem for eleven years; his mother was Zebidah daughter of Pedaiah of Rumah. 37 He did what was wrong in the eyes of the LORD as his forefathers had done.

24 1 During his reign an attack was launched by King Nebuchadnezzar of Babylon, and Jehoiakim became his vassal; three years later, however, he broke with him and revolted. 2 The LORD sent against him raiding parties of Chaldaeans, Aramaeans, Moabites, and Ammonites, letting them range through Judah and ravage it, as the LORD had foretold through his servants the prophets. 3 All this happened to Judah in fulfilment of the LORD's purpose, to banish them from his presence because of all the sin Manasseh had committed 4 and because of the innocent blood he had shed; he had flooded Jerusalem with innocent blood, and the LORD would not forgive him. 5 The other events and acts of Jehoiakim's reign are recorded in the annals of the kings of Judah. 6 He rested with his forefathers, and his son Jehoiachin succeeded him. 7 The Egyptian king did not leave his own land again, because the king of Babylon had stripped him of all he possessed from the wadi of Egypt to the river Euphrates.

8 JEHOIACHIN was eighteen years old when he came to the throne, and he reigned in Jerusalem for three months; his mother was Nehushta daughter of Elnathan from Jerusalem. 9 He did what was wrong in the eyes of the LORD, as his father had done.

10 At that time the troops of King Nebuchadnezzar of Babylon advanced on Jerusalem and the city came under

23:30–34 Cp. 2 Chr. 36:1–4.   23:33 removed . . . throne: prob. rdg, cp. 2 Chr. 36:3; Heb. bound him at Riblah in the land of Hamath when he was king.   24:8–17 Cp. 2 Chr. 36:9–10.

26 Yet, because of all the provocations that Manasseh had given, the LORD did not desist from his fiercely burning anger against Judah. 27 The LORD said: "Even Judah will I put out of my sight as I did Israel. I will reject this city, Jerusalem, which I chose, and the temple of which I said, 'There shall my name be.' "

28 The rest of the acts of Josiah, with all that he did, are written in the book of the chronicles of the kings of Judah. 29 In his time Pharaoh Neco, king of Egypt, went up toward the river Euphrates to the king of Assyria. King Josiah set out to confront him, but was slain at Megiddo at the first encounter. 30 His servants brought his body on a chariot from Megiddo to Jerusalem, where they buried him in his own grave. Then the people of the land took Jehoahaz, son of Josiah, anointed him, and proclaimed him king to succeed his father.

31 Jehoahaz was twenty-three years old when he began to reign, and he reigned three months in Jerusalem. His mother, whose name was Hamutal, daughter of Jeremiah, was from Libnah. 32 He did evil in the sight of the LORD, just as his forebears had done. 33 Pharaoh Neco took him prisoner at Riblah in the land of Hamath, thus ending his reign in Jerusalem. He imposed a fine upon the land of a hundred talents of silver and a talent of gold. 34 Pharaoh Neco then appointed Eliakim, son of Josiah, king in place of his father Josiah; he changed his name to Jehoiakim. Jehoahaz he took away with him to Egypt, where he died. 35 Jehoiakim gave the silver and gold to Pharaoh, but taxed the land to raise the amount Pharaoh demanded. He exacted the silver and gold from the people of the land, from each proportionately, to pay Pharaoh Neco.

36 Jehoiakim was twenty-five years old when he began to reign, and he reigned eleven years in Jerusalem. His mother's name was Zebidah, daughter of Pedaiah, from Rumah. 37 He did evil in the sight of the LORD, just as his forebears had done.

24 During his reign Nebuchadnezzar, king of Babylon, moved against him, and Jehoiakim became his vassal for three years. Then Jehoiakim turned and rebelled against him. 2 The LORD loosed against him bands of Chaldeans, Arameans, Moabites, and Ammonites; he loosed them against Judah to destroy it, as the LORD had threatened through his servants the prophets. 3 This befell Judah because the LORD stated that he would inexorably put them out of his sight for the sins Manasseh had committed in all that he did; 4 and especially because of the innocent blood he shed, with which he filled Jerusalem, the LORD would not forgive.

5 The rest of the acts of Jehoiakim, with all that he did, are written in the book of the chronicles of the kings of Judah. 6 Jehoiakim rested with his ancestors, and his son Jehoiachin succeeded him as king. 7 The king of Egypt did not again leave his own land, for the king of Babylon had taken all that belonged to the king of Egypt from the wadi of Egypt to the Euphrates River.

8 Jehoiachin was eighteen years old when he began to reign, and he reigned three months in Jerusalem. His mother's name was Nehushta, daughter of Elnathan of Jerusalem. 9 He did evil in the sight of the LORD, just as his forebears had done.

10 At that time the officials of Nebuchadnezzar, king of Babylon, attacked Jerusalem, and the city came under

26 Yet Yahweh did not renounce the heat of his great anger which had been aroused against Judah by all the provocations which Manasseh had caused him. 27 Yahweh said, 'I shall thrust Judah away from me too, as I have already thrust Israel; I shall cast off Jerusalem, this city which I have chosen, and the Temple of which I have said: My Name shall be there.'

28 The rest of the history of Josiah, his entire career, is this not recorded in the Book of the Annals of the Kings of Judah?

29 In his times, Pharaoh Necho king of Egypt was advancing to meet the king of Assyria at the River Euphrates, and King Josiah went to intercept him; but Necho killed him at Megiddo in the first encounter. 30 His retainers carried his body from Megiddo by chariot; they brought him to Jerusalem and buried him in his own tomb. The people of the country then took Jehoahaz son of Josiah and anointed him, proclaiming him king in succession to his father.

31 Jehoahaz was twenty-three years old when he came to the throne, and he reigned for three months in Jerusalem. His mother's name was Hamutal daughter of Jeremiah, of Libnah. 32 He did what is displeasing to Yahweh, just as his ancestors had done.

33 Pharaoh Necho put him in chains at Riblah in Hamath, to prevent his reigning any longer in Jerusalem, and imposed a levy of a hundred talents of silver and ten talents of gold on the country. 34 Pharaoh Necho then made Eliakim son of Josiah king in succession to Josiah his father, and changed his name to Jehoiakim. Carrying off Jehoahaz, he took him to Egypt, where he died.

35 Jehoiakim paid over the silver and gold to Pharaoh, but first had to tax the people of the country before he could raise the sum which Pharaoh demanded: he levied the silver and gold to be paid over to Pharaoh Necho from each according to his means.

36 Jehoiakim was twenty-five years old when he came to the throne, and he reigned for eleven years in Jerusalem. His mother's name was Zebidah daughter of Pedaiah of Rumah. 37 He did what is displeasing to Yahweh, just as his ancestors had done.

24 In his times, Nebuchadnezzar king of Babylon invaded, and Jehoiakim became his vassal for three years, but then rebelled against him a second time. 2 So he sent armed bands of Chaldaeans, Arameans, Moabites and Ammonites against him; he sent these against Judah to destroy it, in accordance with the word which Yahweh had spoken through his servants the prophets. 3 It was entirely due to Yahweh's anger that this happened to Judah; he had resolved to thrust them away from him because of Manasseh's sins and all that he had done, 4 and also because of the innocent blood which he had shed, flooding Jerusalem with innocent blood. Yahweh would not forgive.

5 The rest of the history of Jehoiakim, his entire career, is this not recorded in the Book of the Annals of the Kings of Judah? 6 Then Jehoiakim fell asleep with his ancestors; his son Jehoiachin succeeded him.

7 The king of Egypt did not leave his own country again, because the king of Babylon had conquered everywhere belonging to the king of Egypt, from the Torrent of Egypt to the River Euphrates.

8 Jehoiachin was eighteen years old when he came to the throne, and he reigned for three months in Jerusalem. His mother's name was Nehushta daughter of Elnathan of Jerusalem. 9 He did what is displeasing to Yahweh, just as his father had done.

10 At that time the troops of Nebuchadnezzar king of Babylon advanced on Jerusalem, and the city was besieged.

NEW REVISED STANDARD VERSION

REVISED ENGLISH BIBLE

11 King Nebuchadnezzar of Babylon came to the city, while his servants were besieging it; 12 King Jehoiachin of Judah gave himself up to the king of Babylon, himself, his mother, his servants, his officers, and his palace officials. The king of Babylon took him prisoner in the eighth year of his reign.

13 He carried off all the treasures of the house of the LORD, and the treasures of the king's house; he cut in pieces all the vessels of gold in the temple of the LORD, which King Solomon of Israel had made, all this as the LORD had foretold. 14 He carried away all Jerusalem, all the officials, all the warriors, ten thousand captives, all the artisans and the smiths; no one remained, except the poorest people of the land. 15 He carried away Jehoiachin to Babylon; the king's mother, the king's wives, his officials, and the elite of the land, he took into captivity from Jerusalem to Babylon. 16 The king of Babylon brought captive to Babylon all the men of valor, seven thousand, the artisans and the smiths, one thousand, all of them strong and fit for war. 17 The king of Babylon made Mattaniah, Jehoiachin's uncle, king in his place, and changed his name to Zedekiah.

18 Zedekiah was twenty-one years old when he began to reign; he reigned eleven years in Jerusalem. His mother's name was Hamutal daughter of Jeremiah of Libnah. 19 He did what was evil in the sight of the LORD, just as Jehoiakim had done. 20 Indeed, Jerusalem and Judah so angered the LORD that he expelled them from his presence.

Zedekiah rebelled against the king of Babylon.

25 1 And in the ninth year of his reign, in the tenth month, on the tenth day of the month, King Nebuchadnezzar of Babylon came with all his army against Jerusalem, and laid siege to it; they built siegeworks against it all around. 2 So the city was besieged until the eleventh year of King Zedekiah. 3 On the ninth day of the fourth month the famine became so severe in the city that there was no food for the people of the land. 4 Then a breach was made in the city wall;*o* the king with all the soldiers fled*p* by night by the way of the gate between the two walls, by the king's garden, though the Chaldeans were all around the city. They went in the direction of the Arabah. 5 But the army of the Chaldeans pursued the king, and overtook him in the plains of Jericho; all his army was scattered, deserting him. 6 Then they captured the king and brought him up to the king of Babylon at Riblah, who passed sentence on him. 7 They slaughtered the sons of Zedekiah before his eyes, then put out the eyes of Zedekiah; they bound him in fetters and took him to Babylon.

8 In the fifth month, on the seventh day of the month — which was the nineteenth year of King Nebuchadnezzar, king of Babylon — Nebuzaradan, the captain of the bodyguard, a servant of the king of Babylon, came to Jerusalem. 9 He burned the house of the LORD, the king's house, and all the houses of Jerusalem; every great house he burned down. 10 All the army of the Chaldeans who were with the captain of the guard broke down the walls around Jerusalem. 11 Nebuzaradan the captain of the guard carried into exile the rest of the people who were left in the city and the deserters who had defected to the king of Babylon — all the rest of the population. 12 But the captain of the guard left some of the poorest people of the land to be vinedressers and tillers of the soil.

siege. 11 Nebuchadnezzar arrived while his troops were besieging it, 12 and King Jehoiachin of Judah, along with his mother, his courtiers, his officers, and his eunuchs surrendered to the king of Babylon. The king of Babylon, now in the eighth year of his reign, made him a prisoner; 13 and, as the LORD had foretold, he carried off all the treasures of the house of the LORD and of the palace and broke up all the vessels of gold which King Solomon of Israel had made for the temple of the LORD. 14 He took into exile the people of Jerusalem, the officers and all the fighting men, ten thousand in number, together with all the craftsmen and smiths; only the poorest class of the people was left. 15 He deported Jehoiachin to Babylon; he also took into exile from Jerusalem to Babylon the king's mother and his wives, his eunuchs, and the foremost men of the land. 16 He took also all the people of substance, seven thousand in number, and a thousand craftsmen and smiths, all of them able-bodied men and skilled armourers. 17 He made Mattaniah, uncle of Jehoiachin, king in his place and changed his name to Zedekiah.

18 Zedekiah was twenty-one years old when he came to the throne, and he reigned in Jerusalem for eleven years; his mother was Hamital daughter of Jeremiah from Libnah. 19 He did what was wrong in the eyes of the LORD, as Jehoiakim had done. 20 Jerusalem and Judah so angered the LORD that in the end he banished them from his sight.

Zedekiah rebelled against the king of Babylon.

25 1 In the ninth year of his reign, on the tenth day of the tenth month, King Nebuchadnezzar of Babylon advanced with his whole army against Jerusalem, invested it, and erected siege-towers against it on every side; 2 the siege lasted till the eleventh year of King Zedekiah. 3 In the fourth month of that year, on the ninth day of the month, when famine was severe in the city and there was no food for the people, 4 the city capitulated. When King Zedekiah of Judah saw this, he and all his armed escort left the city and, fleeing by night through the gate called Between the Two Walls, near the king's garden, they made their escape towards the Arabah, although the Chaldaeans were surrounding the city. 5 The Chaldaean army pursued the king and overtook him in the lowlands of Jericho. His men all forsook him and scattered, 6 and the king was captured and, having been brought before the king of Babylon at Riblah, he was put on trial and sentenced. 7 Zedekiah's sons were slain before his eyes; then his eyes were put out, and he was brought to Babylon bound in bronze fetters.

8 In the fifth month, on the seventh day of the month, in the nineteenth year of King Nebuchadnezzar of Babylon, Nebuzaradan, captain of the king of Babylon's bodyguard, came to Jerusalem. 9 He set fire to the house of the LORD and the royal palace, indeed all the houses in the city; every notable's house was burnt down. 10 The whole Chaldaean force which was with the captain of the guard razed to the ground the walls on every side of Jerusalem. 11 Nebuzaradan captain of the guard deported the people who were left in the city, those who had deserted to the king of Babylon, and any remaining artisans. 12 He left only the poorest class of the people, to be vine-dressers and labourers.

24:18 — 25:21 *Cp. Jer. 52:1–27.* 25:1–12 *Cp. Jer. 39:1–10; verses 1–17, cp. 2 Chr. 36:17–20.* 25:3 **In . . . year:** *prob. rdg, cp. Jer. 52:6; Heb. omits.* 25:4 **When . . . this:** *prob. rdg, cp. Jer. 39:4; Heb. omits.* **left . . . fleeing:** *so Syriac, cp. Jer. 52:7; Heb. omits.* 25:10 **The . . . was with:** *so many MSS, cp. Jer. 52:14; others omit.* 25:11 **any . . . artisans:** *prob. rdg, cp. Jer. 52:15; Heb.* the remaining crowd.

o Heb lacks *wall*   *p* Gk Compare Jer 39.4; 52.7: Heb lacks *the king* and lacks *fled*

siege. 11 Nebuchadnezzar, king of Babylon, himself arrived at the city while his servants were besieging it. 12 Then Jehoiachin, king of Judah, together with his mother, his ministers, officers, and functionaries, surrendered to the king of Babylon, who, in the eighth year of his reign, took him captive. 13 He carried off all the treasures of the temple of the LORD and those of the palace, and broke up all the gold utensils that Solomon, king of Israel, had provided in the temple of the LORD, as the LORD had foretold. 14 He deported all Jerusalem: all the officers and men of the army, ten thousand in number, and all the craftsmen and smiths. None were left among the people of the land except the poor. 15 He deported Jehoiachin to Babylon, and also led captive from Jerusalem to Babylon the king's mother and wives, his functionaries, and the chief men of the land. 16 The king of Babylon also led captive to Babylon all seven thousand men of the army, and a thousand craftsmen and smiths, all of them trained soldiers. 17 In place of Jehoiachin, the king of Babylon appointed his uncle Mattaniah king, and changed his name to Zedekiah.

18 Zedekiah was twenty-one years old when he became king, and he reigned eleven years in Jerusalem. His mother's name was Hamutal, daughter of Jeremiah of Libnah. 19 He also did evil in the sight of the LORD, just as Jehoiakim had done. 20 The LORD's anger befell Jerusalem and Judah till he cast them out from his presence. Thus Zedekiah rebelled against the king of Babylon.

25 In the tenth month of the ninth year of Zedekiah's reign, on the tenth day of the month, Nebuchadnezzar, king of Babylon, and his whole army advanced against Jerusalem, encamped around it, and built siege walls on every side. 2 The siege of the city continued until the eleventh year of Zedekiah. 3 On the ninth day of the fourth month, when famine had gripped the city, and the people had no more bread, 4 the city walls were breached. Then the king and all the soldiers left the city by night through the gate between the two walls which was near the king's garden. Since the Chaldeans had the city surrounded, they went in the direction of the Arabah. 5 But the Chaldean army pursued the king and overtook him in the desert near Jericho, abandoned by his whole army.

6 The king was therefore arrested and brought to Riblah to the king of Babylon, who pronounced sentence on him. 7 He had Zedekiah's sons slain before his eyes. Then he blinded Zedekiah, bound him with fetters, and had him brought to Babylon.

8 On the seventh day of the fifth month (this was in the nineteenth year of Nebuchadnezzar, king of Babylon), Nebuzaradan, captain of the bodyguard, came to Jerusalem as the representative of the king of Babylon. 9 He burned the house of the LORD, the palace of the king, and all the houses of Jerusalem; every large building was destroyed by fire. 10 Then the Chaldean troops who were with the captain of the guard tore down the walls that surrounded Jerusalem.

11 Then Nebuzaradan, captain of the guard, led into exile the last of the people remaining in the city, and those who had deserted to the king of Babylon, and the last of the artisans. 12 But some of the country's poor, Nebuzaradan, captain of the guard, left behind as vinedressers and farmers.

11 Nebuchadnezzar king of Babylon advanced on the city and his generals laid siege to it. 12 Jehoiachin king of Judah — he, his mother, his retinue, his nobles and his officials — then surrendered to the king of Babylon, and the king of Babylon took them prisoner in the eighth year of his reign.

13 The latter carried off all the treasures of the Temple of Yahweh and the treasures of the palace and broke up all the golden furnishings which Solomon king of Israel had made for the sanctuary of Yahweh, as Yahweh had foretold. 14 He carried all Jerusalem off into exile, all the nobles and all the notables, ten thousand of these were exiled, with all the blacksmiths and metalworkers; only the poorest people in the country were left behind. 15 He deported Jehoiachin to Babylon, as also the king's mother, his officials and the nobility of the country; he made them all leave Jerusalem for exile in Babylon. 16 All the men of distinction, seven thousand of them, the blacksmiths and metalworkers, one thousand of them, all the men capable of bearing arms, were led off into exile in Babylon by the king of Babylon.

17 The king of Babylon deposed Jehoiachin in favour of his paternal uncle Mattaniah, whose name he changed to Zedekiah.

18 j Zedekiah was twenty-one years old when he came to the throne, and he reigned for eleven years in Jerusalem. His mother's name was Hamital daughter of Jeremiah, of Libnah. 19 He did what is displeasing to Yahweh, just as Jehoiakim had done. 20 It was entirely due to Yahweh's anger that this happened to Jerusalem and Judah. It resulted in his casting them from his presence. Zedekiah rebelled against the king of Babylon.

25 In the ninth year of his reign, in the tenth month, on the tenth day of the month, Nebuchadnezzar king of Babylon advanced on Jerusalem with his entire army; he pitched camp in front of the city and threw up earthworks round it. 2 The city lay under siege till the eleventh year of King Zedekiah. 3 In the fourth month, on the ninth day of the month, when famine was raging in the city and there was no food for the populace, 4 a breach was made in the city wall. The king then made his escape under cover of dark, with all the fighting men, by way of the gate between the two walls, which is near the king's garden — the Chaldaeans had surrounded the city — and made his way towards the Arabah. 5 The Chaldaean troops pursued the king and caught up with him in the Plains of Jericho, where all his troops deserted. 6 The Chaldaeans captured the king and took him to the king of Babylon at Riblah, who passed sentence on him. 7 He had Zedekiah's sons slaughtered before his eyes, then put out Zedekiah's eyes and, loading him with chains, carried him off to Babylon.

8 In the fifth month, on the seventh day of the month — it was in the nineteenth year of Nebuchadnezzar king of Babylon — Nebuzaradan commander of the guard, a member of the king of Babylon's staff, entered Jerusalem. 9 He burned down the Temple of Yahweh, the royal palace and all the houses in Jerusalem. 10 The Chaldaean troops who accompanied the commander of the guard demolished the walls surrounding Jerusalem. 11 Nebuzaradan commander of the guard deported the remainder of the population left in the city, the deserters who had gone over to the king of Babylon, and the rest of the common people. 12 But the commander of the guard left some of the poor country people behind as vineyard workers and ploughmen.

NEW REVISED STANDARD VERSION

13 The bronze pillars that were in the house of the LORD, as well as the stands and the bronze sea that were in the house of the LORD, the Chaldeans broke in pieces, and carried the bronze to Babylon. 14 They took away the pots, the shovels, the snuffers, the dishes for incense, and all the bronze vessels used in the temple service, 15 as well as the firepans and the basins. What was made of gold the captain of the guard took away for the gold, and what was made of silver, for the silver. 16 As for the two pillars, the one sea, and the stands, which Solomon had made for the house of the LORD, the bronze of all these vessels was beyond weighing. 17 The height of the one pillar was eighteen cubits, and on it was a bronze capital; the height of the capital was three cubits; latticework and pomegranates, all of bronze, were on the capital all around. The second pillar had the same, with the latticework.

18 The captain of the guard took the chief priest Seraiah, the second priest Zephaniah, and the three guardians of the threshold; 19 from the city he took an officer who had been in command of the soldiers, and five men of the king's council who were found in the city; the secretary who was the commander of the army who mustered the people of the land; and sixty men of the people of the land who were found in the city. 20 Nebuzaradan the captain of the guard took them, and brought them to the king of Babylon at Riblah. 21 The king of Babylon struck them down and put them to death at Riblah in the land of Hamath. So Judah went into exile out of its land.

22 He appointed Gedaliah son of Ahikam son of Shaphan as governor over the people who remained in the land of Judah, whom King Nebuchadnezzar of Babylon had left. 23 Now when all the captains of the forces and their men heard that the king of Babylon had appointed Gedaliah as governor, they came with their men to Gedaliah at Mizpah, namely, Ishmael son of Nethaniah, Johanan son of Kareah, Seraiah son of Tanhumeth the Netophathite, and Jaazaniah son of the Maacathite. 24 Gedaliah swore to them and their men, saying, "Do not be afraid because of the Chaldean officials; live in the land, serve the king of Babylon, and it shall be well with you." 25 But in the seventh month, Ishmael son of Nethaniah son of Elishama, of the royal family, came with ten men; they struck down Gedaliah so that he died, along with the Judeans and Chaldeans who were with him at Mizpah. 26 Then all the people, high and low*q* and the captains of the forces set out and went to Egypt; for they were afraid of the Chaldeans.

27 In the thirty-seventh year of the exile of King Jehoiachin of Judah, in the twelfth month, on the twenty-seventh day of the month, King Evil-merodach of Babylon, in the year that he began to reign, released King Jehoiachin of Judah from prison; 28 he spoke kindly to him, and gave him a seat above the other seats of the kings who were with him in Babylon. 29 So Jehoiachin put aside his prison clothes. Every day of his life he dined regularly in the king's presence. 30 For his allowance, a regular allowance was given him by the king, a portion every day, as long as he lived.

q Or young and old

REVISED ENGLISH BIBLE

13 The Chaldeans broke up the bronze pillars in the house of the LORD, the trolleys, and the bronze Sea, and took the metal to Babylon. 14 They took also the pots, shovels, snuffers, saucers, and all the bronze vessels used in the service of the temple. 15 The captain of the guard took away the precious metal, whether gold or silver, of which the firepans and the tossing-bowls were made. 16 The bronze of the two pillars, the one Sea, and the trolleys, which Solomon had made for the house of the LORD, was beyond weighing. 17 One pillar was eighteen cubits high and its capital was bronze; the capital was three cubits high, and a decoration of network and pomegranates ran all round it, wholly of bronze. The other pillar, with its network, was exactly like it.

18 The captain of the guard took Seraiah the chief priest, Zephaniah the deputy chief priest, and the three on duty at the entrance; 19 he took also from the city a eunuch who was in charge of the fighting men, five of those with right of access to the king who were still in the city, the adjutant-general whose duty was to muster the people for war, and sixty men of the people who were still there. 20 These Nebuzaradan captain of the guard brought to the king of Babylon at Riblah. 21 There, in the land of Hamath, the king had them flogged and put to death. So Judah went into exile from her own land.

22 King Nebuchadnezzar of Babylon appointed Gedaliah son of Ahikam, son of Shaphan, governor over the people whom he had left in Judah. 23 When the captains of the armed bands and their men heard that the king of Babylon had appointed Gedaliah governor, they all gathered to him at Mizpah: Ishmael son of Nethaniah, Johanan son of Kareah, Seraiah son of Tanhumeth of Netophah, and Jaazaniah of Beth-maacah. 24 Gedaliah gave them and their men this assurance: 'Have no fear of the Chaldaean officers. Settle down in the land and serve the king of Babylon; and all will be well with you.' 25 But in the seventh month Ishmael son of Nethaniah, son of Elishama, who was a member of the royal house, came with ten men and assassinated Gedaliah and the Jews and Chaldaeans who were with him at Mizpah. 26 Thereupon all the people, high and low, and the captains of the armed forces, fled to Egypt for fear of the Chaldaeans.

27 In the thirty-seventh year of the exile of King Jehoiachin of Judah, on the twenty-seventh day of the twelfth month, King Evil-merodach of Babylon in the year of his accession showed favour to King Jehoiachin. He released him from prison, 28 treated him kindly, and gave him a seat at table above the kings with him in Babylon. 29 Jehoiachin, discarding his prison clothes, lived as a pensioner of the king for the rest of his life. 30 For his maintenance as long as he lived a regular daily allowance was given him by the king.

25:19 **adjutant-general:** *prob. rdg; Heb. adds* commander-in-chief.
25:27–30 *Cp. Jer. 52:31–34.*   25:27 **He released him:** *so Gk,*
cp. Jer. 52:31; Heb. omits.

13 The bronze pillars that belonged to the house of the LORD, and the wheeled carts and the bronze sea in the house of the LORD, the Chaldeans broke into pieces; they carried away the bronze to Babylon. 14 They took also the pots, the shovels, the snuffers, the bowls, the pans and all the bronze vessels used for service. 15 The fire-holders and the bowls which were of gold or silver the captain of the guard also carried off. 16 The weight in bronze of the two pillars, the bronze sea, and the wheeled carts, all of them furnishings which Solomon had made for the house of the LORD, was never calculated. 17 Each of the pillars was eighteen cubits high; a bronze capital five cubits high surmounted each pillar, and a network with pomegranates encircled the capital, all of bronze; and so for the other pillar, as regards the network.

18 The captain of the guard also took Seraiah the high priest, Zephaniah the second priest, and the three keepers of the entry. 19 And from the city he took one courtier, a commander of soldiers, five men in the personal service of the king who were still in the city, the scribe of the army commander, who mustered the people of the land, and sixty of the common people still remaining in the city. 20 The captain of the guard, Nebuzaradan, arrested these and brought them to the king of Babylon at Riblah; 21 the king had them struck down and put to death in Riblah, in the land of Hamath. Thus was Judah exiled from her land.

22 As for the people whom he had allowed to remain in the land of Judah, Nebuchadnezzar, king of Babylon, appointed as their governor Gedaliah, son of Ahikam, son of Shaphan. 23 Hearing that the king of Babylon had appointed Gedaliah governor, all the army commanders with their men came to him at Mizpah: Ishmael, son of Nethaniah, Johanan, son of Kareah, Seraiah, son of Tanhumeth the Netophathite, and Jaazaniah, from Beth-maacah. 24 Gedaliah gave the commanders and their men his oath. "Do not be afraid of the Chaldean officials," he said to them. "Remain in the country and serve the king of Babylon, and all will be well with you."

25 But in the seventh month Ishmael, son of Nethaniah, son of Elishama, of royal descent, came with ten men, attacked Gedaliah and killed him, along with the Jews and Chaldeans who were in Mizpah with him. 26 Then all the people, great and small, left with the army commanders and went to Egypt for fear of the Chaldeans.

27 In the thirty-seventh year of the exile of Jehoiachin, king of Judah, on the twenty-seventh day of the twelfth month, Evil-merodach, king of Babylon, in the inaugural year of his own reign, raised up Jehoiachin, king of Judah, from prison. 28 He spoke kindly to him and gave him a throne higher than that of the other kings who were with him in Babylon. 29 Jehoiachin took off his prison garb and ate at the king's table as long as he lived. 30 The allowance granted him by the king was a perpetual allowance, in fixed daily amounts, for as long as he lived.

13 The Chaldaeans broke up the bronze pillars from the Temple of Yahweh, the wheeled stands and the bronze Sea, which were in the Temple of Yahweh, and took the bronze away to Babylon. 14 They also took the ash containers, the scoops, the knives, the incense boats, and all the bronze furnishings used in worship. 15 The commander of the guard also took the censers and the sprinkling bowls, everything made of gold and everything made of silver. 16 As regards the two pillars, the one Sea and the wheeled stands, which Solomon had made for the Temple of Yahweh, there was no reckoning the weight of bronze in all these objects. 17 The height of one pillar was eighteen cubits, and on it stood a capital of bronze, the height of the capital being five cubits; round the capital were filigree and pomegranates, all in bronze. So also for the second pillar.

18 The commander of the guard took prisoner Seraiah the chief priest, Zephaniah the priest next in rank, and the three guardians of the threshold. 19 In the city he took prisoner an official who was in command of the fighting men, five of the king's personal friends who were discovered in the city, the secretary to the army commander, responsible for military conscription, and sixty men of distinction discovered in the city. 20 Nebuzaradan commander of the guard took these men and brought them to the king of Babylon at Riblah, 21 and at Riblah in the territory of Hamath the king of Babylon had them put to death. Thus Judah was deported from its country.

22 For the people remaining in the country of Judah whom Nebuchadnezzar king of Babylon had left behind, he appointed Gedaliah son of Ahikam, son of Shaphan as governor. 23 When the military leaders and their men all heard that the king of Babylon had appointed Gedaliah as governor, they went to him at Mizpah: Ishmael son of Nethaniah, Johanan son of Kareah, Seraiah son of Tanhumeth the Netophathite, Jaazaniah the Maacathite, they and their men. 24 To them and to their men Gedaliah swore an oath. 'Do not be afraid of the Chaldaeans,' he said, 'stay in the country, serve the king of Babylon, and all will go well with you.'

25 But in the seventh month, Ishmael son of Nethaniah, son of Elishama, who was of royal descent, and ten men with him, came and murdered Gedaliah, as well as the Judaeans and Chaldaeans who were with him at Mizpah. 26 Then all the people, high and low, with the military leaders, set off and went to Egypt, being afraid of the Chaldaeans.

27 In the thirty-seventh year of the exile of Jehoiachin king of Judah, in the twelfth month, on the twenty-seventh day of the month, Evil-Merodach king of Babylon, in the year he came to the throne, pardoned Jehoiachin king of Judah and released him from prison. 28 He treated him with kindness and allotted him a seat above those of the other kings who were with him in Babylon. 29 So Jehoiachin laid aside his prisoner's garb, and for the rest of his life always ate at the king's table. 30 And his upkeep was permanently ensured by the king, day after day, for the rest of his life.

THE FIRST BOOK OF THE

1 Chronicles

Chronicles

1 Adam, Seth, Enosh; [2] Kenan, Mahalalel, Jared; [3] Enoch, Methuselah, Lamech; [4] Noah, Shem, Ham, and Japheth.

5 The descendants of Japheth: Gomer, Magog, Madai, Javan, Tubal, Meshech, and Tiras. [6] The descendants of Gomer: Ashkenaz, Diphath,[a] and Togarmah. [7] The descendants of Javan: Elishah, Tarshish, Kittim, and Rodanim.[b]

8 The descendants of Ham: Cush, Egypt, Put, and Canaan. [9] The descendants of Cush: Seba, Havilah, Sabta, Raama, and Sabteca. The descendants of Raamah: Sheba and Dedan. [10] Cush became the father of Nimrod; he was the first to be a mighty one on the earth.

11 Egypt became the father of Ludim, Anamim, Lehabim, Naphtuhim, [12] Pathrusim, Casluhim, and Caphtorim, from whom the Philistines come.[c]

13 Canaan became the father of Sidon his firstborn, and Heth, [14] and the Jebusites, the Amorites, the Girgashites, [15] the Hivites, the Arkites, the Sinites, [16] the Arvadites, the Zemarites, and the Hamathites.

17 The descendants of Shem: Elam, Asshur, Arpachshad, Lud, Aram, Uz, Hul, Gether, and Meshech.[d] [18] Arpachshad became the father of Shelah; and Shelah became the father of Eber. [19] To Eber were born two sons: the name of the one was Peleg (for in his days the earth was divided), and the name of his brother Joktan. [20] Joktan became the father of Almodad, Sheleph, Hazarmaveth, Jerah, [21] Hadoram, Uzal, Diklah, [22] Ebal, Abimael, Sheba, [23] Ophir, Havilah, and Jobab; all these were the descendants of Joktan.

24 Shem, Arpachshad, Shelah; [25] Eber, Peleg, Reu; [26] Serug, Nahor, Terah; [27] Abram, that is, Abraham.

28 The sons of Abraham: Isaac and Ishmael. [29] These are their genealogies: the firstborn of Ishmael, Nebaioth; and Kedar, Adbeel, Mibsam, [30] Mishma, Dumah, Massa, Hadad, Tema, [31] Jetur, Naphish, and Kedemah. These are the sons of Ishmael. [32] The sons of Keturah, Abraham's concubine: she bore Zimran, Jokshan, Medan, Midian, Ishbak, and Shuah. The sons of Jokshan: Sheba and Dedan. [33] The sons of Midian: Ephah, Epher, Hanoch, Abida, and Eldaah. All these were the descendants of Keturah.

34 Abraham became the father of Isaac. The sons of Isaac: Esau and Israel. [35] The sons of Esau: Eliphaz, Reuel, Jeush, Jalam, and Korah. [36] The sons of Eliphaz: Teman, Omar, Zephi, Gatam, Kenaz, Timna, and Amalek. [37] The sons of Reuel: Nahath, Zerah, Shammah, and Mizzah.

1 ADAM, Seth, Enosh, [2] Kenan, Mahalalel, Jared, [3] Enoch, Methuselah, Lamech, [4] Noah.
The sons of Noah: Shem, Ham, and Japheth.

[5] The sons of Japheth: Gomer, Magog, Madai, Javan, Tubal, Meshech, and Tiras. [6] The sons of Gomer: Ashkenaz, Diphath, and Togarmah. [7] The sons of Javan: Elishah, Tarshish, Kittim, and Rodanim.

[8] The sons of Ham: Cush, Mizraim, Put, and Canaan. [9] The sons of Cush: Seba, Havilah, Sabta, Raama, and Sabtecha. The sons of Raama: Sheba and Dedan. [10] Cush was the father of Nimrod, who began to show himself a man of might on earth. [11] From Mizraim sprang the Lydians, Anamites, Lehabites, Naphtuhites, [12] Pathrusites, Casluhites, and the Caphtorites, from whom the Philistines were descended.

[13] Canaan was the father of Sidon, who was his eldest son, and Heth, [14] the Jebusites, the Amorites, the Girgashites, [15] the Hivites, the Arkites, the Sinites, [16] the Arvadites, the Zemarites, and the Hamathites.

[17] The sons of Shem: Elam, Asshur, Arphaxad, Lud, and Aram. The sons of Aram: Uz, Hul, Gether, and Mash. [18] Arphaxad was the father of Shelah, and Shelah the father of Eber. [19] Eber had two sons: one was named Peleg, because in his time the earth was divided, and his brother's name was Joktan. [20] Joktan was the father of Almodad, Sheleph, Hazarmoth, Jerah, [21] Hadoram, Uzal, Diklah, [22] Ebal, Abimael, Sheba, [23] Ophir, Havilah, and Jobab. All these were sons of Joktan.

[24] The line of Shem: Arphaxad, Shelah, [25] Eber, Peleg, Reu, [26] Serug, Nahor, Terah, [27] Abram, also known as Abraham, [28] whose sons were Isaac and Ishmael.

[29] The sons of Ishmael in the order of their birth: Nebaioth the eldest, then Kedar, Adbeel, Mibsam, [30] Mishma, Dumah, Massa, Hadad, Teman, [31] Jetur, Naphish, and Kedemah. These were Ishmael's sons.

[32] The sons of Keturah, Abraham's concubine: she bore him Zimran, Jokshan, Medan, Midian, Ishbak, and Shuah. The sons of Jokshan: Sheba and Dedan. [33] The sons of Midian: Ephah, Epher, Enoch, Abida, and Eldaah. All these were descendants of Keturah.

[34] Abraham was the father of Isaac, and Isaac's sons were Esau and Israel. [35] The sons of Esau: Eliphaz, Reuel, Jeush, Jaalam, and Korah. [36] The sons of Eliphaz: Teman, Omar, Zephi, Gatam, Kenaz, Timna, and Amalek. [37] The sons of Reuel: Nahath, Zerah, Shammah, and Mizzah.

1:2–4 Cp. Gen. 5:9–32.   1:4 **The sons of:** so Gk; Heb. omits.
1:5–7 Cp. Gen. 10:2–4.   1:5 **Javan:** or Greece.
1:6 **Diphath:** or, with many MSS, Riphath (cp. Gen. 10:3).
1:7 **Tarshish, Kittim:** or Tarshish of the Kittians. **Rodanim:** or, with many MSS, Dodanim (cp. Gen. 10:4).   1:8–10 Cp. Gen. 10:6–8.   1:8 **Mizraim:** or Egypt.   1:11–16 Cp. Gen. 10:13–18.   1:12 **and the Caphtorites:** transposed from end of verse; cp. Amos 9:7.   1:13 **Heth:** or the Hittites.   1:17–23 Cp. Gen. 10:22–29.   1:17 **Lud:** or the Lydians. **The sons of Aram:** so one MS, cp. Gen. 10:23; others omit. **Mash:** so some MSS, cp. Gen. 10:23; others Meshech.   1:19 **Peleg:** that is Division.
1:22 **Ebal:** so some MSS; others Obal.   1:24–27 Cp. Gen.11:10–26.   1:24 **The line of:** prob. rdg; Heb. omits.
1:29–31 Cp. Gen. 25:13–16.   1:29 **The sons of:** prob. rdg, cp. Gen. 25:13; Heb. omits.   1:30 **Hadad:** or, possibly, Hadar (cp. Gen. 25:15).   **Teman:** so Gk; Heb. Tema.   1:32–33 Cp. Gen. 25:1–4.   1:35–37 Cp. Gen. 36:4–5,9–13.

a Gen 10.3 Ripath; See Gk Vg   b Gen 10.4 Dodanim; See Syr Vg
c Heb Casluhim, from which the Philistines come, Caphtorim; See Am 9.7, Jer 47.4   d Mash in Gen 10.23

THE FIRST BOOK OF
Chronicles

1 Adam, Seth, Enosh, [2] Kenan, Mahalalel, Jared, [3] Enoch, Methuselah, Lamech, [4] Noah, Shem, Ham, and Japheth. [5] The descendants of Japheth were Gomer, Magog, Madai, Javan, Tubal, Meshech, and Tiras. [6] The descendants of Gomer were Ashkenaz, Riphath, and Togarmah. [7] The descendants of Javan were Elishah, Tarshis, the Kittim, and the Rodanim.

[8] The descendants of Ham were Cush, Mesraim, Put, and Canaan. [9] The descendants of Cush were Seba, Havilah, Sabta, Raama, and Sabteca. The descendants of Raama were Sheba and Dedan. [10] Cush became the father of Nimrod, who was the first to be a conqueror on the earth. [11] Mesraim became the father of the Ludim, Anamim, Lehabim, Naphtuhim, [12] Pathrusim, Casluhim, and Caphtorim, from whom the Philistines sprang. [13] Canaan became the father of Sidon, his first-born, and Heth, [14] and the Jebusite, the Amorite, the Girgashite, [15] the Hivite, the Arkite, the Sinite, [16] the Arvadite, the Zemarite, and the Hamathite.

[17] The descendants of Shem were Elam, Asshur, Arpachshad, Lud, and Aram. The descendants of Aram were Uz, Hul, Gether, and Mash. [18] Arpachshad became the father of Shelah, and Shelah became the father of Eber. [19] Two sons were born to Eber; the first was named Peleg (for in his time the world was divided), and his brother was Joktan. [20] Joktan became the father of Almodad, Sheleph, Hazarmaveth, Jerah, [21] Hadoram, Uzal, Diklah, [22] Ebal, Abimael, Sheba, [23] Ophir, Havilah, and Jobab; all these were the sons of Joktan.

[24] Shem, Arpachshad, Shelah, [25] Eber, Peleg, Reu, [26] Serug, Nahor, Terah, [27] Abram, who was Abraham.

[28] The sons of Abraham were Isaac and Ishmael. [29] These were their descendants:

Nebaioth, the first-born of Ishmael, then Kedar, Adbeel, Mibsam, [30] Mishma, Dumah, Massa, Hadad, Tema, [31] Jetur, Naphish, and Kedemah. These were the descendants of Ishmael.

[32] The descendants of Keturah, Abraham's concubine: she bore Zimran, Jokshan, Medan, Midian, Ishbak, and Shuah. The sons of Jokshan were Sheba and Dedan. The descendants of Midian were Ephah, Epher, Hanoch, Abida, and Eldaah. All these were the descendants of Keturah.

[34] Abraham became the father of Isaac. The sons of Isaac were Esau and Israel.

[35] The sons of Esau were Eliphaz, Reuel, Jeush, Jalam, and Korah. [36] The sons of Eliphaz were Teman, Omar, Zephi, Gatam, Kenaz, [Timna,] and Amalek. [37] The sons of Reuel were Nahath, Zerah, Shammah, and Mizzah.

THE FIRST BOOK OF
Chronicles

1 Adam, Seth, Enosh, [2] Kenan, Mahalalel, Jared, [3] Enoch, Methuselah, Lamech, [4] Noah, Shem, Ham and Japheth.

[5] Sons of Japheth: Gomer, Magog, the Medes, Javan, Tubal, Meshech, Tiras.

[6] Sons of Gomer: Ashkenaz, Riphath, Togarmah. [7] Sons of Javan: Elishah, Tarshish, the Kittim, the Dananites.

[8] Sons of Ham: Cush, Mizraim, Put, Canaan. [9] Sons of Cush: Seba, Havilah, Sabta, Raama, Sabteca. Sons of Raamah: Sheba, Dedan. [10] Cush fathered Nimrod, the first mighty warrior on earth.

[11] Mizraim fathered the people of Lud, of Anam, of Lehab, of Naphtuh, [12] of Pathros, Casluh and Caphtor, from which the Philistines came. [13] Canaan fathered Sidon, his first-born, then Heth, [14] and the Jebusites, the Amorites, Girgashites, [15] Hivites, Arkites, Sinites, [16] Arvadites, Zemarites, Hamathites.

[17] Sons of Shem: Elam, Asshur, Arpachshad, Lud, Aram. Sons of Aram: Uz, Hul, Gether and Meshech.

[18] Arpachshad fathered Shelah and Shelah fathered Eber. [19] To Eber were born two sons; the first was called Peleg, because it was in his time that the earth was divided into districts, and his brother was called Joktan.

[20] Joktan fathered Almodad, Sheleph, Hazarmaveth, Jerah, [21] Hadoram, Uzal, Diklah, [22] Ebal, Abimael, Sheba, [23] Ophir, Havilah, Jobab; all these are sons of Joktan.

[24] Arpachshad, Shelah, [25] Eber, Peleg, Reu, [26] Serug, Nahor, Terah, [27] Abram, that is, Abraham. [28] Sons of Abraham: Isaac and Ishmael. [29] These are their descendants:

The first-born of Ishmael, Nebaioth; then Kedar, Adbeel, Mibsam, [30] Mishma, Dumah, Massa, Hada, Tema, [31] Jetur, Naphish and Kedemah. These are the sons of Ishmael.

[32] Sons of Keturah, Abraham's concubine: she gave birth to Zimran, Jokshan, Medan, Midian, Ishbak, and Shuah. Sons of Jokshan: Sheba and Dedan. [33] Sons of Midian: Ephah, Epher, Hanoch, Abida, Eldaah. All these are sons of Keturah.

[34] Abraham fathered Isaac. Sons of Isaac: Esau and Israel.

[35] Sons of Esau: Eliphaz, Reuel, Jeush, Jalam and Korah. [36] Sons of Eliphaz: Teman, Omar, Zephi, Gatam, Kenaz, Timna, Amalek. [37] Sons of Reuel: Nahath, Zerah, Shammah, Mizzah.

38 The sons of Seir: Lotan, Shobal, Zibeon, Anah, Dishon, Ezer, and Dishan. 39 The sons of Lotan: Hori and Homam; and Lotan's sister was Timna. 40 The sons of Shobal: Alian, Manahath, Ebal, Shephi, and Onam. The sons of Zibeon: Aiah and Anah. 41 The sons of Anah: Dishon. The sons of Dishon: Hamran, Eshban, Ithran, and Cheran. 42 The sons of Ezer: Bilhan, Zaavan, and Jaakan.*e* The sons of Dishan:*f* Uz and Aran.

43 These are the kings who reigned in the land of Edom before any king reigned over the Israelites: Bela son of Beor, whose city was called Dinhabah. 44 When Bela died, Jobab son of Zerah of Bozrah succeeded him. 45 When Jobab died, Husham of the land of the Temanites succeeded him. 46 When Husham died, Hadad son of Bedad, who defeated Midian in the country of Moab, succeeded him; and the name of his city was Avith. 47 When Hadad died, Samlah of Masrekah succeeded him. 48 When Samlah died, Shaul*g* of Rehoboth on the Euphrates succeeded him. 49 When Shaul*g* died, Baal-hanan son of Achbor succeeded him. 50 When Baal-hanan died, Hadad succeeded him; the name of his city was Pai, and his wife's name Mehetabel daughter of Matred, daughter of Me-zahab. 51 And Hadad died.

The clans*h* of Edom were: clans*h* Timna, Aliah,*i* Jetheth, 52 Oholibamah, Elah, Pinon, 53 Kenaz, Teman, Mibzar, 54 Magdiel, and Iram; these are the clans*h* of Edom.

2 These are the sons of Israel: Reuben, Simeon, Levi, Judah, Issachar, Zebulun, 2 Dan, Joseph, Benjamin, Naphtali, Gad, and Asher. 3 The sons of Judah: Er, Onan, and Shelah; these three the Canaanite woman Bath-shua bore to him. Now Er, Judah's firstborn, was wicked in the sight of the LORD, and he put him to death. 4 His daughter-in-law Tamar also bore him Perez and Zerah. Judah had five sons in all.

5 The sons of Perez: Hezron and Hamul. 6 The sons of Zerah: Zimri, Ethan, Heman, Calcol, and Dara,*j* five in all. 7 The sons of Carmi: Achar, the troubler of Israel, who transgressed in the matter of the devoted thing; 8 and Ethan's son was Azariah.

9 The sons of Hezron, who were born to him: Jerahmeel, Ram, and Chelubai. 10 Ram became the father of Amminadab, and Amminadab became the father of Nahshon, prince of the sons of Judah. 11 Nahshon became the father of Salma, Salma of Boaz, 12 Boaz of Obed, Obed of Jesse. 13 Jesse became the father of Eliab his firstborn, Abinadab the second, Shimea the third, 14 Nethanel the fourth, Raddai the fifth, 15 Ozem the sixth, David the seventh; 16 and their sisters were Zeruiah and Abigail. The sons of Zeruiah: Abishai, Joab, and Asahel, three. 17 Abigail bore Amasa, and the father of Amasa was Jether the Ishmaelite.

18 Caleb son of Hezron had children by his wife Azubah, and by Jerioth; these were her sons: Jesher, Shobab, and Ardon. 19 When Azubah died, Caleb married Ephrath, who bore him Hur. 20 Hur became the father of Uri, and Uri became the father of Bezalel.

21 Afterward Hezron went in to the daughter of Machir father of Gilead, whom he married when he was sixty years old; and she bore him Segub. 22 and Segub became the father of Jair, who had twenty-three towns in the land of Gilead. 23 But Geshur and Aram took from them Havvoth-

38 The sons of Seir: Lotan, Shobal, Zibeon, Anah, Dishon, Ezer, and Dishan. 39 The sons of Lotan: Hori and Homam; and Lotan had a sister named Timna. 40 The sons of Shobal: Alvan, Manahath, Ebal, Shephi, and Onam. The sons of Zibeon: Aiah and Anah. 41 The son of Anah: Dishon. The sons of Dishon: Hamran, Eshban, Ithran, and Cheran. 42 The sons of Ezer: Bilhan, Zaavan, and Akan. The sons of Dishan: Uz and Aran.

43 These are the kings who ruled over Edom before there were kings in Israel: Bela son of Beor, whose city was named Dinhabah. 44 When he died, he was succeeded by Jobab son of Zerah from Bozrah. 45 When Jobab died, he was succeeded by Husham from Teman. 46 When Husham died, he was succeeded by Hadad son of Bedad, who defeated Midian in Moabite country. His city was named Avith. 47 When Hadad died, he was succeeded by Samlah from Masrekah. 48 When Samlah died, he was succeeded by Saul from Rehoboth on the River. 49 When Saul died, he was succeeded by Baal-hanan son of Akbor. 50 When Baal-hanan died, he was succeeded by Hadad. His city was named Pai; his wife's name was Mehetabel daughter of Matred, a woman of Me-zahab.

51 After Hadad died the chiefs in Edom were: Timna, Aliah, Jetheth, 52 Oholibamah, Elah, Pinon, 53 Kenaz, Teman, Mibzar, 54 Magdiel, and Iram. These were the chiefs of Edom.

2 These were the sons of Israel: Reuben, Simeon, Levi, Judah, Issachar, Zebulun, 2 Dan, Joseph, Benjamin, Naphtali, Gad, and Asher. 3 The sons of Judah: Er, Onan, and Shelah; the mother of these three was a Canaanite woman, Bathshua. Er, Judah's eldest son, displeased the LORD and the LORD slew him. 4 Then Tamar, Judah's daughter-in-law, bore him Perez and Zerah, making in all five sons of Judah. 5 The sons of Perez: Hezron and Hamul. 6 The sons of Zerah: Zimri, Ethan, Heman, Calcol, and Darda, five in all. 7 The son of Zimri: Carmi. The son of Carmi: Achar, who brought trouble on Israel by his violation of the sacred ban. 8 The son of Ethan: Azariah. 9 The sons of Hezron: Jerahmeel, Ram, and Caleb. 10 Ram was the father of Amminadab, Amminadab father of Nahshon, prince of Judah. 11 Nahshon was the father of Salma, Salma father of Boaz, 12 Boaz father of Obed, Obed father of Jesse. 13 The eldest son of Jesse was Eliab, the second Abinadab, the third Shimea, 14 the fourth Nethanel, the fifth Raddai, 15 the sixth Ozem, the seventh David; 16 their sisters were Zeruiah and Abigail. The sons of Zeruiah: Abishai, Joab, and Asahel, three in all. 17 Abigail was the mother of Amasa; his father was Jether the Ishmaelite.

18 Caleb son of Hezron had Jerioth by Azubah his wife; these were her sons: Jesher, Shobab, and Ardon. 19 When Azubah died, Caleb married Ephrath, who bore him Hur. 20 Hur was the father of Uri, and Uri father of Bezalel. 21 Later, Hezron, then sixty years of age, married and had intercourse with the daughter of Machir, father of Gilead, and she bore Segub. 22 Segub was the father of Jair, who had twenty-three towns in Gilead. 23 Geshur and Aram took

1:38–42 Cp. Gen. 36:20–28.   1:40 **Alvan:** so many MSS, cp. Gen. 36:23; others Alian.   1:41 **son:** prob. rdg; Heb. sons; the same correction is made in several other places in chapters 1–9. 1:42 **and Akan:** so many MSS, cp. Gen. 36:27; others Jaakan. 1:43–54 Cp. Gen. 36:31–43.   1:50 **woman of Me-zahab:** or daughter of Mezahab.   2:3 **Bathshua:** or daughter of Shua. 2:6 **Darda:** so many MSS; others Dara.   2:7 **The son of Zimri: Carmi:** prob. rdg (cp. Josh. 7:1,18); Heb. omits.   2:9 **Caleb:** so Gk; Heb. Celubai.   2:18 **his wife:** prob. rdg; Heb. a woman and.

e Or and Akan; See Gen 36.27   *f* See 1.38: Heb Dishon
g Or Saul   *h* Or chiefs   *i* Or Alvah; See Gen 36.40   *j* Or Darda; Compare Syr Tg some Gk Mss; See 1 Kings 4.31

NEW AMERICAN BIBLE

38 The descendants of Seir were Lotan, Shobal, Zibeon, Anah, Dishon, Ezer, and Dishan. 39 The sons of Lotan were Hori and Homam; Timna was the sister of Lotan. 40 The sons of Shobal were Alian, Manahath, Ebal, Shephi, and Onam. The sons of Zibeon were Aiah and Anah. 41 The sons of Anah: Dishon. The sons of Dishon were Hemdan, Eshban, Ithran, and Cheran. 42 The sons of Ezer were Bilhan, Zaavan, and Jaakan. The sons of Dishan were Uz and Aran.

43 The kings who reigned in the land of Edom before they had Israelite kings were the following: Bela, son of Beor, the name of whose city was Ninhabah. 44 When Bela died, Jobab, son of Zerah, from Bozrah, succeeded him. 45 When Jobab died, Husham, from the land of the Temanites, succeeded him. 46 Husham died and Hadad, son of Bedad, succeeded him. He overthrew the Midianites on the Moabite plateau, and the name of his city was Avith. 47 Hadad died and Samlah of Masrekah succeeded him. 48 Samlah died and Shaul from Rehoboth-han-nahar succeeded him. 49 When Shaul died, Baalhanan, son of Achbor, succeeded him. 50 Baalhanan died and Hadad succeeded him. The name of his city was Pai, and his wife's name was Mehetabel. She was the daughter of Matred, who was the daughter of Mezahab. 51 After Hadad died. . . .

These were the chiefs of Edom: the chiefs of Timna, Aliah, Jetheth, 52 Oholibamah, Elah, Pinon, 53 Kenaz, Teman, Mibzar, 54 Magdiel, and Iram were the chiefs of Edom.

2 These were the sons of Israel: Reuben, Simeon, Levi, Judah, Issachar, Zebulun, 2 Dan, Joseph, Benjamin, Naphtali, Gad, and Asher.

3 The sons of Judah were: Er, Onan, and Shelah; these three were born to him of Bathshua, a Canaanite woman. But Judah's first-born, Er, was wicked in the sight of the LORD, so he killed him. 4 Judah's daughter-in-law Tamar bore him Perez and Zerah, so that he had five sons in all.

5 The sons of Perez were Hezron and Hamul. 6 The sons of Zerah were Zimri, Ethan, Heman, Calcol, and Darda — five in all. 7 The sons of Zimri: Carmi. The sons of Carmi: Achar, who brought trouble upon Israel by violating the ban. 8 The sons of Ethan: Azariah. 9 The sons born to Hezron were Jerahmeel, Ram, and Chelubai.

10 Ram became the father of Amminadab, and Amminadab became the father of Nahshon, a prince of the Judahites. 11 Nahshon became the father of Salma. Salma became the father of Boaz. 12 Boaz became the father of Obed. Obed became the father of Jesse. 13 Jesse became the father of Eliab, his first-born, of Abinadab, the second son, Shimea, the third, 14 Nethanel, the fourth, Raddai, the fifth, 15 Ozem, the sixth, and David, the seventh. 16 Their sisters were Zeruiah and Abigail. Zeruiah had three sons: Abishai, Joab, and Asahel. 17 Abigail bore Amasa, whose father was Jether the Ishmaelite.

18 By his wife Azubah, Caleb, son of Hezron, became the father of a daughter, Jerioth. Her sons were Jesher, Shobab, and Ardon. 19 When Azubah died, Caleb married Ephrath, who bore him Hur. 20 Hur became the father of Uri, and Uri became the father of Bezalel. 21 Then Hezron had relations with the daughter of Machir, the father of Gilead, having married her when he was sixty years old. She bore him Segub. 22 Segub became the father of Jair, who possessed twenty-three cities in the land of Gilead. 23 Geshur and

NEW JERUSALEM BIBLE

38 Sons of Seir: Lotan, Shobal, Zibeon, Anah, Dishon, Ezer, Dishan. 39 Sons of Lotan: Hori and Homam. Sister of Lotan: Timna. 40 Sons of Shobal: Alian, Manahath, Ebal, Shephi, Onam. Sons of Zibeon: Aiah and Anah. 41 Son of Anah: Dishon. Sons of Dishon: Hamran, Eshban, Ithran, Cheran. 42 Sons of Ezer: Bilhan, Zaavan, Jaakan. Sons of Dishan: Uz and Aran.

43 These are the kings who ruled in Edom before an Israelite king ruled: Bela son of Beor; his city was called Dinhabah. 44 Bela died and Jobab son of Zerah, from Bozrah, succeeded. 45 Jobab died and Husham from the territory of the Temanites succeeded. 46 Husham died and Hada son of Bedad succeeded; he defeated the Midianites in Moab, and his city was called Avith. 47 Hadad died and Samlah of Masrekah succeeded. 48 Samlah died and Shaul of Rehoboth-ha-Nahar succeeded. 49 Shaul died and Baal-Hanan son of Achbor succeeded. 50 Baal-Hanan died and Hadad succeeded. His city was called Pai; his wife's name was Mehetabel daughter of Matred, daughter of Mezahab.

51 Hadad died, and then there were chiefs in Edom: Chief Timna, Chief Aliah, Chief Jetheth, 52 Chief Oholibamah, Chief Elah, Chief Pinon, 53 Chief Kenaz, Chief Teman, Chief Mibzar, 54 Chief Magdiel, Chief Iram. These were the chiefs of Edom.

2 These are the sons of Israel: Reuben, Simeon, Levi, Judah, Issachar, and Zebulun. 2 Dan, Joseph, and Benjamin, Naphtali, Gad, and Asher.

3 Sons of Judah: Er, Onan and Shelah. These three were born to him by Bath-shua the Canaanite woman. Er, Judah's first-born, displeased Yahweh who put him to death. 4 Tamar, Judah's daughter-in-law, bore him Perez and Zerah. Judah had five sons in all.

5 Sons of Perez: Hezron and Hamul.

6 Sons of Zerah: Zimri, Ethan, Heman, Calcol and Dara, five in all.

7 Sons of Carmi: Achar, who brought trouble on Israel by being unfaithful to the curse of destruction.

8 Sons of Ethan: Azariah.

9 Sons of Hezron: there were born to him Jerahmeel, Ram, Chelubai.

10 Ram fathered Amminadab, Amminadab fathered Nahshon chief of the sons of Judah, 11 Nahshon fathered Salma, Salma fathered Boaz. 12 Boaz fathered Obed, Obed fathered Jesse. 13 Jesse fathered Eliab, his first-born, Abinadab second, Shimea third, 14 Nethanel fourth, Raddai fifth, 15 Ozem sixth, David seventh. 16 Their sisters were Zeruiah and Abigail. Sons of Zeruiah: Abishai, Joab and Asahel: three. 17 Abigail gave birth to Amasa; father of Amasa was Jether the Ishmaelite.

18 Caleb son of Hezron fathered Jerioth by Azubah his wife; these are her sons: Jesher, Shobab and Ardon. 19 Azubah died, and Caleb married Ephrath, who bore him Hur. 20 Hur fathered Uri, Uri fathered Bezalel.

21 Afterwards, Hezron married the daughter of Machir, father of Gilead; he married her when he was sixty years old and she bore him Segub. 22 Segub fathered Jair who held twenty-three towns in the territory of Gilead. 23 From them,

NEW REVISED STANDARD VERSION	REVISED ENGLISH BIBLE

jair, Kenath and its villages, sixty towns. All these were descendants of Machir, father of Gilead. 24 After the death of Hezron, in Caleb-ephrathah, Abijah wife of Hezron bore him Ashhur, father of Tekoa.

25 The sons of Jerahmeel, the firstborn of Hezron: Ram his firstborn, Bunah, Oren, Ozem, and Ahijah. 26 Jerahmeel also had another wife, whose name was Atarah; she was the mother of Onam. 27 The sons of Ram, the firstborn of Jerahmeel: Maaz, Jamin, and Eker. 28 The sons of Onam: Shammai and Jada. The sons of Shammai: Nadab and Abishur. 29 The name of Abishur's wife was Abihail, and she bore him Ahban and Molid. 30 The sons of Nadab: Seled and Appaim; and Seled died childless. 31 The son*k* of Appaim: Ishi. The son*k* of Ishi: Sheshan. The son*k* of Sheshan: Ahlai. 32 The sons of Jada, Shammai's brother: Jether and Jonathan; and Jether died childless. 33 The sons of Jonathan: Peleth and Zaza. These were the descendants of Jerahmeel. 34 Now Sheshan had no sons, only daughters; but Sheshan had an Egyptian slave, whose name was Jarha. 35 So Sheshan gave his daughter in marriage to his slave Jarha; and she bore him Attai. 36 Attai became the father of Nathan, and Nathan of Zabad. 37 Zabad became the father of Ephlal, and Ephlal of Obed. 38 Obed became the father of Jehu, and Jehu of Azariah. 39 Azariah became the father of Helez, and Helez of Eleasah. 40 Eleasah became the father of Sismai, and Sismai of Shallum. 41 Shallum became the father of Jekamiah, and Jekamiah of Elishama.

42 The sons of Caleb brother of Jerahmeel: Mesha*l* his firstborn, who was father of Ziph. The sons of Mareshah father of Hebron. 43 The sons of Hebron: Korah, Tappuah, Rekem, and Shema. 44 Shema became father of Raham, father of Jorkeam; and Rekem became the father of Shammai. 45 The son of Shammai: Maon; and Maon was the father of Beth-zur. 46 Ephah also, Caleb's concubine, bore Haran, Moza, and Gazez; and Haran became the father of Gazez. 47 The sons of Jahdai: Regem, Jotham, Geshan, Pelet, Ephah, and Shaaph. 48 Maacah, Caleb's concubine, bore Sheber and Tirhanah. 49 She also bore Shaaph father of Madmannah, Sheva father of Machbenah and father of Gibea; and the daughter of Caleb was Achsah. 50 These were the descendants of Caleb.

The sons*m* of Hur the firstborn of Ephrathah: Shobal father of Kiriath-jearim, 51 Salma father of Bethlehem, and Hareph father of Beth-gader. 52 Shobal father of Kiriath-jearim had other sons: Haroeh, half of the Menuhoth. 53 And the families of Kiriath-jearim: the Ithrites, the Puthites, the Shumathites, and the Mishraites; from these came the Zorathites and the Eshtaolites. 54 The sons of Salma: Bethlehem, the Netophathites, Atroth-beth-joab, and half of the Manahathites, the Zorites. 55 The families also of the scribes that lived at Jabez: the Tirathites, the Shimeathites, and the Sucathites. These are the Kenites who came from Hammath, father of the house of Rechab.

from them Havvoth-jair, and Kenath and its dependent villages, a total of sixty places. All these were descendants of Machir father of Gilead. 24 After the death of Hezron, Caleb had intercourse with Ephrathah and she bore him Ashhur the founder of Tekoa.

25 The sons of Jerahmeel, eldest son of Hezron by Ahijah, were Ram the eldest, Bunah, Oren, and Ozem. 26 Jerahmeel had another wife, whose name was Atarah; she was the mother of Onam. 27 The sons of Ram, eldest son of Jerahmeel: Maaz, Jamin, and Eker. 28 The sons of Onam: Shammai and Jada. The sons of Shammai: Nadab and Abishur. 29 The name of Abishur's wife was Abihail; she bore him Ahban and Molid. 30 The sons of Nadab: Seled and Ephraim; Seled died without children. 31 Ephraim's son was Ishi, Ishi's son Sheshan, Sheshan's son Ahlai. 32 The sons of Jada brother of Shammai: Jether and Jonathan; Jether died without children. 33 The sons of Jonathan: Peleth and Zaza. These were the descendants of Jerahmeel.

34 Sheshan had daughters but no sons. He had an Egyptian servant named Jarha; 35 he gave him in marriage to this Jarha, and she bore him Attai. 36 Attai was the father of Nathan, Nathan father of Zabad, 37 Zabad father of Ephlal, Ephlal father of Obed, 38 Obed father of Jehu, Jehu father of Azariah, 39 Azariah father of Helez, Helez father of Elasah, 40 Elasah father of Sisamai, Sisamai father of Shallum, 41 Shallum father of Jekamiah, and Jekamiah father of Elishama.

42 The sons of Caleb brother of Jerahmeel: Mesha the eldest, founder of Ziph, and Mareshah, founder of Hebron. 43 The sons of Hebron: Korah, Tappuah, Rekem, and Shema. 44 Shema was the father of Raham father of Jorkoam, and Rekem was the father of Shammai. 45 The son of Shammai was Maon, and Maon was the founder of Beth-zur. 46 Ephah, Caleb's concubine, was the mother of Haran, Moza, and Gazez; Haran was the father of Gazez. 47 The sons of Jahdai: Regem, Jotham, Geshan, Pelet, Ephah, and Shaaph. 48 Maacah, Caleb's concubine, was the mother of Sheber and Tirhanah; 49 she bore also Shaaph, founder of Madmannah, and Sheva, founder of Machbenah and Gibea. Caleb also had a daughter named Achsah.

50 The descendants of Caleb: the sons of Hur, the eldest son of Ephrathah: Shobal the founder of Kiriath-jearim, 51 Salma the founder of Bethlehem, and Hareph the founder of Beth-gader. 52 Shobal the founder of Kiriath-jearim was the father of Reaiah and the ancestor of half the Manahethites. 53 The clans of Kiriath-jearim: Ithrites, Puthites, Shumathites, and Mishraites, from whom were descended the Zorathites and the Eshtaulites. 54 The descendants of Salma: Bethlehem, the Netophathites, Ataroth, Beth-joab, half the Manahethites, and the Zorites. 55 The clans of Sophrites living at Jabez: Tirathites, Shimeathites, and Suchathites. These were Kenites who were connected by marriage with the ancestor of the Rechabites.

2:24 **Caleb had intercourse:** *so Gk; Heb.* in Caleb. **Ephrathah:** *so Syriac; Heb. adds* and Abiah Hezron's wife. **founder:** *lit.* father *and similarly several times in chapters 2–4.* 2:25 **by:** *prob. rdg; Heb. omits.* 2:30 **Ephraim:** *so one MS; others* Appaim. **and:** *prob. rdg; Heb. adds* the sons of. 2:50 **sons:** *so Gk; Heb.* son. 2:52 **Reaiah:** *prob. rdg, cp. 4:2; Heb.* the seer. **Manahethites:** *prob. rdg, cp. verse 54; Heb.* Menuhoth. 2:55 **Sophrites:** *or* secretaries. **Kenites:** *lit.* Kinites.

k Heb *sons*   *l* Gk reads *Mareshah*   *m* Gk Vg: Heb *son*

Aram took from them the villages of Jair, that is, Kenath and its towns, sixty cities in all, which had belonged to the sons of Machir, the father of Gilead. 24 After the death of Hezron, Caleb had relations with Ephrathah, the widow of his father Hezron, and she bore him Ashhur, the father of Tekoa.

25 The sons of Jerahmeel, the first-born of Hezron, were Ram, the first-born, then Bunah, Oren, and Ozem, his brothers. 26 Jerahmeel also had another wife, Atarah by name, who was the mother of Onam. 27 The sons of Ram, the first-born of Jerahmeel, were Maaz, Jamin, and Eker. 28 The sons of Onam were Shammai and Jada. The sons of Shammai were Nadab and Abishur. 29 Abishur's wife, who was named Abihail, bore him Ahban and Molid. 30 The sons of Nadab were Seled and Appaim. Seled died without sons. 31 The sons of Appaim: Ishi. The sons of Ishi: Sheshan. The sons of Sheshan: Ahlai. 32 The sons of Jada, the brother of Shammai, were Jether and Jonathan. Jether died without sons. 33 The sons of Jonathan were Peleth and Zaza. These were the descendants of Jerahmeel. 34 Sheshan, who had no sons, only daughters, had an Egyptian slave named Jarha. 35 Sheshan gave his daughter in marriage to his slave Jarha, and she bore him Attai. 36 Attai became the father of Nathan. Nathan became the father of Zabad. 37 Zabad became the father of Ephlal. Ephlal became the father of Obed. 38 Obed became the father of Jehu. Jehu became the father of Azariah. 39 Azariah became the father of Helez. Helez became the father of Eleasah. 40 Eleasah became the father of Sismai. Sismai became the father of Shallum. 41 Shallum became the father of Jekamiah. Jekamiah became the father of Elishama.

42 The descendants of Caleb, the brother of Jerahmeel: [Mesha] his first-born, who was the father of Ziph. Then the sons of Mareshah, who was the father of Hebron. 43 The sons of Hebron were Korah, Tappuah, Rekem, and Shema. 44 Shema became the father of Raham, who was the father of Jorkeam. Rekem became the father of Shammai. 45 The sons of Shammai: Maon, who was the father of Beth-zur. 46 Ephah, Caleb's concubine, bore Haran, Moza, and Gazez. Haran became the father of Gazez. 47 The sons of Jahdai were Regem, Jotham, Geshan, Pelet, Ephah, and Shaaph. 48 Maacah, Caleb's concubine, bore Sheber and Tirhanah. 49 She also bore Shaaph, the father of Madmannah, Sheva, the father of Machbenah, and the father of Gibea. Achsah was Caleb's daughter.

50 These were descendants of Caleb, sons of Hur, the first-born of Ephrathah: Shobal, the father of Kiriath-jearim, 51 Salma, the father of Bethlehem, and Hareph, the father of Bethgader. 52 The sons of Shobal, the father of Kiriath-jearim, were Reaiah, half the Manahathites, 53 and the clans of Kiriath-jearim: the Ithrites, the Puthites, the Shumathites, and the Mishraites. From these the people of Zorah and the Eshtaolites derived. 54 The descendants of Salma were Bethlehem, the Netophathites, Atroth-beth-Joab, half the Manahathites, and the Zorites. 55 The clans of the Sopherim dwelling in Jabez were the Tirathites, the Shimeathites, and the Sucathites. They were the Kenites, who came from Hammath of the ancestor of the Rechabites.

however, Geshur and Aram took the Encampments of Jair and Kenath with its dependencies: sixty towns. All these used to belong to the sons of Machir father of Gilead.

24 After Hezron's death, Caleb married Ephrathah, wife of Hezron his father, who bore him Ashhur father of Tekoa.

25 Jerahmeel, Hezron's eldest son, fathered Hezron, his first-born, Ram, Bunah, Oren, Ozem, Ahijah. 26 Jerahmeel had another wife called Atarah; she was the mother of Onam.

27 Sons of Ram, Jerahmeel's first-born: Maaz, Jamin and Eker.

28 Sons of Onam: Shammai and Jada. Sons of Shammai: Nadab and Abishur. 29 Abishur's wife was called Abihail; she bore him Ahban and Molid. 30 Sons of Nadab: Seled and Ephraim. Seled died leaving no son. 31 Son of Ephraim: Ishi; son of Ishi: Sheshan; son of Sheshan: Ahlai. 32 Sons of Jada, Shammai's brother: Jether and Jonathan. Jether died leaving no sons. 33 Sons of Jonathan: Peleth and Zaza.

These were the sons of Jerahmeel.

34 Sheshan had no sons, only daughters. He had an Egyptian slave Jarha 35 to whom Sheshan gave his daughter in marriage. She bore him Attai. 36 Attai fathered Nathan, Nathan fathered Zabad, 37 Zabad fathered Ephlal, Ephlal fathered Obed, 38 Obed fathered Jehu, Jehu fathered Azariah, 39 Azariah fathered Helez, Helez fathered Eleasah, 40 Eleasah fathered Sismai, Sismai fathered Shallum, 41 Shallum fathered Jekamiah, Jekamiah fathered Elishama.

42 Sons of Caleb, Jerahmeel's brother: Mesha, his first-born, who fathered Ziph. His son was Mareshah, father of Hebron. 43 Sons of Hebron: Korah, Tappuah, Rekem and Shema. 44 Shema fathered Raham, father of Jorkeam. Rekem fathered Shammai. 45 Shammai's son was Maon, and Maon fathered Beth-Zur.

46 Ephah, Caleb's concubine, gave birth to Haran, Moza and Gazez. Haran fathered Gazez.

47 Sons of Jahdai: Regem, Jotham, Geshan, Pelet, Ephah and Shaaph.

48 Maacah, Caleb's concubine, gave birth to Sheber and Tirhanah. 49 She gave birth to Shaaph, who fathered Madmannah, and Sheva, who fathered Machbenah and Gibea. The daughter of Caleb was Achsah.

50 These were the sons of Caleb.

Sons of Hur, the first-born of Ephrathah: Shobal fathered Kiriath-Jearim; 51 Salma fathered Bethlehem; Hareph fathered Beth-Gader. 52 Shobal, father of Kiriath-Jearim, had sons: Haroeh, that is, half of the Manahathites, 53 and the clans of Kiriath-Jearim: the Ithrites, Puthites, Shumathites and Mishraites. Their descendants are the people of Zorah and Eshtaol.

54 Sons of Salma: Bethlehem, the Netophathites, Atroth Beth-Joab, half of the Manahathites, the Zorathites, 55 the Sophrite clans living at Jabez, the Tirathites, the Shimeathites, the Sucathites. They were the Kenites descended from Hammath, father of the House of Rechab.

3 These are the sons of David who were born to him in Hebron: the firstborn Amnon, by Ahinoam the Jezreelite; the second Daniel, by Abigail the Carmelite; 2 the third Absalom, son of Maacah, daughter of King Talmai of Geshur; the fourth Adonijah, son of Haggith; 3 the fifth Shephatiah, by Abital; the sixth Ithream, by his wife Eglah; 4 six were born to him in Hebron, where he reigned for seven years and six months. And he reigned thirty-three years in Jerusalem. 5 These were born to him in Jerusalem: Shimea, Shobab, Nathan, and Solomon, four by Bath-shua, daughter of Ammiel; 6 then Ibhar, Elishama, Eliphelet, 7 Nogah, Nepheg, Japhia, 8 Elishama, Eliada, and Eliphelet, nine. 9 All these were David's sons, besides the sons of the concubines; and Tamar was their sister.

10 The descendants of Solomon: Rehoboam, Abijah his son, Asa his son, Jehoshaphat his son, 11 Joram his son, Ahaziah his son, Joash his son, 12 Amaziah his son, Azariah his son, Jotham his son, 13 Ahaz his son, Hezekiah his son, Manasseh his son, 14 Amon his son, Josiah his son. 15 The sons of Josiah: Johanan the firstborn, the second Jehoiakim, the third Zedekiah, the fourth Shallum. 16 The descendants of Jehoiakim: Jeconiah his son, Zedekiah his son; 17 and the sons of Jeconiah, the captive: Shealtiel his son, 18 Malchiram, Pedaiah, Shenazzar, Jekamiah, Hoshama, and Nedabiah; 19 The sons of Pedaiah: Zerubbabel and Shimei; and the sons of Zerubbabel: Meshullam and Hananiah, and Shelomith was their sister; 20 and Hashubah, Ohel, Berechiah, Hasadiah, and Jushab-hesed, five. 21 The sons of Hananiah: Pelatiah and Jeshaiah, his son[n] Rephaiah, his son[n] Arnan, his son[n] Obadiah, his son[n] Shecaniah. 22 The son[o] of Shecaniah: Shemaiah. And the sons of Shemaiah: Hattush, Igal, Bariah, Neariah, and Shaphat, six. 23 The sons of Neariah: Elioenai, Hizkiah, and Azrikam, three. 24 The sons of Elioenai: Hodaviah, Eliashib, Pelaiah, Akkub, Johanan, Delaiah, and Anani, seven.

4 The sons of Judah: Perez, Hezron, Carmi, Hur, and Shobal. 2 Reaiah son of Shobal became the father of Jahath, and Jahath became the father of Ahumai and Lahad. These were the families of the Zorathites. 3 These were the sons[p] of Etam: Jezreel, Ishma, and Idbash; and the name of their sister was Hazzelelponi, 4 and Penuel was the father of Gedor, and Ezer the father of Hushah. These were the sons of Hur, the firstborn of Ephrathah, the father of Bethlehem. 5 Ashhur father of Tekoa had two wives, Helah and Naarah; 6 Naarah bore him Ahuzzam, Hepher, Temeni, and Haahashtari.[q] These were the sons of Naarah. 7 The sons of Helah: Zereth, Izhar,[r] and Ethnan. 8 Koz became the father of Anub, Zobebah, and the families of Aharhel son of Harum. 9 Jabez was honored more than his brothers; and his mother named him Jabez, saying, "Because I bore him in pain." 10 Jabez called on the God of Israel, saying, "Oh that you would bless me and enlarge my border, and that your hand might be with me, and that you would keep me from hurt and harm!" And God granted what he asked. 11 Chelub the brother of Shuhah became the father of Mehir, who was the father of Eshton. 12 Eshton became the father of Beth-

3 These were the sons of David who were born at Hebron: the eldest Amnon, whose mother was Ahinoam from Jezreel; the second Daniel, whose mother was Abigail from Carmel; 2 the third Absalom, whose mother was Maacah daughter of Talmai king of Geshur; the fourth Adonijah, whose mother was Haggith; 3 the fifth Shephatiah, whose mother was Abital; the sixth Ithream, whose mother was David's wife Eglah. 4 These six were born at Hebron, where David reigned for seven years and six months.

In Jerusalem he reigned for thirty-three years, 5 and there the following sons were born to him: Shimea, Shobab, Nathan, and Solomon; these four were sons of Bathsheba daughter of Ammiel. 6-8 There were nine others: Ibhar, Elishama, Eliphelet, Nogah, Nepheg, Japhia, Elishama, Eliada, and Eliphelet. 9 These were all the sons of David, with their sister Tamar, in addition to his sons by concubines.

10 Solomon's son was Rehoboam, his son Abijah, his son Asa, his son Jehoshaphat, 11 his son Joram, his son Ahaziah, his son Joash, 12 his son Amaziah, his son Azariah, his son Jotham, 13 his son Ahaz, his son Hezekiah, his son Manasseh, 14 his son Amon, and his son Josiah. 15 The sons of Josiah: the eldest Johanan, the second Jehoiakim, the third Zedekiah, the fourth Shallum. 16 The sons of Jehoiakim: Jeconiah and Zedekiah. 17 The sons of Jeconiah, a prisoner: Shealtiel, 18 Malchiram, Pedaiah, Shenazzar, Jekamiah, Hoshama, and Nedabiah. 19 The sons of Pedaiah: Zerubbabel and Shimei. The sons of Zerubbabel: Meshullam and Hananiah; they had a sister, Shelomith. 20 There were five others: Hashubah, Ohel, Berechiah, Hasadiah, and Jushab-hesed. 21 The sons of Hananiah: Pelatiah and Isaiah; his son was Rephaiah, his son Arnan, his son Obadiah, his son Shecaniah. 22 The sons of Shecaniah: Shemaiah, Hattush, Igal, Bariah, Neariah, and Shaphat, six in all. 23 The sons of Neariah: Elioenai, Hezekiah, and Azrikam, three in all. 24 The sons of Elioenai: Hodaiah, Eliashib, Pelaiah, Akkub, Johanan, Delaiah, and Anani, seven in all.

4 The sons of Judah: Perez, Hezron, Carmi, Hur, and Shobal. 2 Reaiah son of Shobal was the father of Jahath, Jahath father of Ahumai and Lahad. These were the clans of the Zorathites.

3-4 The sons of Etam: Jezreel, Ishma, Idbash, Penuel the founder of Gedor, and Ezer the founder of Hushah; they had a sister named Hazelelponi. These were the sons of Hur: Ephrathah the eldest, the founder of Bethlehem.

5 Ashhur the founder of Tekoa had two wives, Helah and Naarah. 6 Naarah bore him Ahuzzam, Hepher, Temeni, and Haahashtari. These were the sons of Naarah. 7 The sons of Helah: Zereth, Jezoar, Ethnan, and Coz. 8 Coz was the father of Anub and Zobebah and the clans of Aharhel son of Harum.

9 Jabez ranked higher than his brothers; his mother called him Jabez because, as she said, she had borne him in pain. 10 Jabez called to the God of Israel, 'I pray you, bless me and grant me wide territories. May your hand be with me; do me no harm, I pray you, and let me be free from pain'; and God granted his petition.

11 Kelub brother of Shuah was the father of Mehir the father of Eshton. 12 Eshton was the father of Beth-rapha,

3:1–4 *Cp. 2 Sam. 3:2–5.*   3:5–8 *Cp. 1 Chr. 14:4–7; 2 Sam. 5:14–16.*
3:5 **Bathsheba:** *so Lat.*; *Heb.* Bathshua.   3:17 **Jeconiah, a**
prisoner: *or* Jeconiah. Assir. **Shealtiel:** *so Gk; Heb.* adds his son.
3:19 **sons of Zerubbabel:** *so some MSS; others* son of Zerubbabel.
3:21 **his son was:** *so Gk, throughout verse; Heb.* the sons of.
3:22 **Shemaiah:** *prob. rdg; Heb.* adds and the sons of Shemaiah.
4:3–4 **sons of Etam:** *so Gk; Heb.* father of Etam.   4:6 **Temeni,**
and Haahashtari: *or* the Temanite and the Ahashtarite.   4:7 **and**
Coz: *so Aram. (Targ.); Heb.* omits.

[n]Gk Compare Syr Vg: Heb *sons of*   [o]Heb *sons*   [p]Gk Compare
Vg: Heb *the father*   [q]Or *Ahashtari*   [r]Another reading is *Zohar*

3 The following were the sons of David who were born to him in Hebron: the first-born, Amnon, by Ahinoam of Jezreel; the second, Daniel, by Abigail of Carmel; ²the third, Absalom, son of Maacah, who was the daughter of Talmai, king of Geshur; the fourth, Adonijah, son of Haggith; ³the fifth, Shephatiah, by Abital; the sixth, Ithream, by his wife Eglah. ⁴Six in all were born to him in Hebron, where he reigned seven years and six months. Then he reigned thirty-three years in Jerusalem, ⁵where the following were born to him: Shimea, Shobab, Nathan, Solomon —four by Bathsheba, the daughter of Ammiel, ⁶Ibhar, Elishua, Eliphelet, ⁷Nogah, Nepheg, Japhia, ⁸Elishama, Eliada, and Eliphelet—nine. ⁹All these were sons of David, in addition to other sons by concubines; and Tamar was their sister.

¹⁰The son of Solomon was Rehoboam, whose son was Abijah, whose son was Asa, whose son was Jehoshaphat, ¹¹whose son was Joram, whose son was Ahaziah, whose son was Joash, ¹²whose son was Amaziah, whose son was Azariah, whose son was Jotham, ¹³whose son was Ahaz, whose son was Hezekiah, whose son was Manasseh, ¹⁴whose son was Amon, whose son was Josiah. ¹⁵The sons of Josiah were: the first-born, Johanan; the second, Jehoiakim; the third, Zedekiah; the fourth, Shallum. ¹⁶The sons of Jehoiakim were: Jeconiah, his son; Zedekiah, his son.

¹⁷The sons of Jeconiah the captive were: Shealtiel, ¹⁸Malchiram, Pedaiah, Shenazzar, Jekamiah, Shama, and Nedabiah. ¹⁹The sons of Pedaiah were Zerubbabel and Shimei. The sons of Zerubbabel were Meshullam and Hananiah; Shelomith was their sister. ²⁰The sons of Meshullam were Hashubah, Ohel, Berechiah, Hasadiah, Jushab-hesed —five. ²¹The sons of Hananiah were Pelatiah, Jeshaiah, Rephaiah, Arnan, Obadiah, and Shecaniah. ²²The sons of Shecaniah were Shemiah, Hattush, Igal, Bariah, Neariah, Shaphat —six. ²³The sons of Neariah were Elioenai, Hizkiah, and Azrikam—three. ²⁴The sons of Elioenai were Hodaviah, Eliashib, Pelaiah, Akkub, Johanan, Delaiah, and Anani —seven.

4 The descendants of Judah were: Perez, Hezron, Carmi, Hur, and Shobal. ²Reaiah, the son of Shobal, became the father of Jahath, and Jahath became the father of Ahumai and Lahad. These were the clans of the Zorathites.

³These were the descendants of Hareph, the father of Etam: Jezreel, Ishma, and Idbash; their sister was named Hazzelelponi. ⁴Penuel was the father of Gedor, and Ezer the father of Hushah. These were the descendants of Hur, the first-born of Ephrathah, the father of Bethlehem.

⁵Ashhur, the father of Tekoa, had two wives, Helah and Naarah. ⁶Naarah bore him Ahuzzam, Hepher, the Temenites and the Ahashtarites. These were the descendants of Naarah. ⁷The sons of Helah were Zereth, Izhar, Ethnan, and Koz. ⁸Koz became the father of Anub and Zobebah, as well as of the clans of Aharhel, son of Harum. ⁹Jabez was the most distinguished of the brothers. His mother had named him Jabez, saying, "I bore him with pain." ¹⁰Jabez prayed to the God of Israel: "Oh, that you may truly bless me and extend my boundaries! Help me and free me from of misfortune, without pain!" And God granted his prayer.

¹¹Chelub, the brother of Shuhah, became the father of Mehir, who was the father of Eshton. ¹²Eshton became the

3 These are the sons of David who were born to him in Hebron: the first-born Amnon, by Ahinoam of Jezreel; second, Daniel, by Abigail of Carmel; ²third, Absalom son of Maacah, daughter of Talmai king of Geshur; fourth, Adonijah son of Haggith; ³fifth, Shephatiah by Abital, sixth, Ithream by his wife Eglah. ⁴Six, therefore, were born to him in Hebron, where he reigned for three years and six months.

He reigned for thirty-three years in Jerusalem. ⁵These are the sons who were born to him in Jerusalem: Shimea, Shobab, Nathan, Solomon, the four of them children of Bath-Shua daughter of Ammiel; ⁶Ibhar, Elishama, Eliphelet, ⁷Nogah, Nepheg, Japhia, ⁸Elishama, Eliada, Eliphelet: nine.

⁹All these were sons of David, not counting the sons of the concubines. Tamar was their sister.

¹⁰Sons of Solomon: Rehoboam; Abijah his son, Asa his son, Jehoshaphat his son, ¹¹Joram his son, Ahaziah his son, Joash his son, ¹²Amaziah his son, Azariah his son, Jotham his son, ¹³Ahaz his son, Hezekiah his son, Manasseh his son, ¹⁴Amon his son, Josiah his son. ¹⁵Sons of Josiah: Johanan, the first-born, Jehoiakim second, Zedekiah third, Shallum fourth. ¹⁶The sons of Jehoiakim: Jeconiah his son, Zedekiah his son.

¹⁷Sons of Jeconiah the captive: Shealtiel his son, ¹⁸then Malchiram, Pedaiah, Shenazzar, Jechamiah, Hoshama, Nedabiah. ¹⁹Sons of Pedaiah: Zerubbabel and Shimei. Sons of Zerubbabel: Meshullam and Hananiah; Shelomith was their sister. ²⁰Sons of Meshullam: Hashubah, Ohel, Berechiah, Hasadiah, Jushab-Hesed: five. ²¹Sons of Hananiah: Pelatiah; Jeshaiah his son, Rephaiah his son, Arnan his son, Obadiah his son, Shecaniah his son. ²²Sons of Shecaniah: Shemaiah, Hattush, Igal, Bariah, Neariah, Shaphat: six. ²³Sons of Neariah: Elioenai, Hizkiah, Azrikam: three. ²⁴Sons of Elioenai: Hodaviah, Eliashib, Pelaiah, Akkub, Johanan, Delaiah, Anani: seven.

4 Sons of Judah: Perez, Hezron, Carmi, Hur, Shobal. ²Reaiah son of Shobal fathered Jahath, and Jahath fathered Ahumai and Lahad. These are the Zoreathite clans. ³These are Abi-Etam, Jezreel, Ishma, and Idbash, whose sister was called Hazzelelponi. ⁴Penuel fathered Gedor, and Ezer fathered Hushah.

These were the sons of Hur, first-born of Ephrathah and father of Bethlehem.

⁵Ashhur, father of Tekoa, had two wives: Helah and Naarah. ⁶Naarah bore him Ahuzzam, Hepher, the Timnites, and the Ahashtarites—these were the sons of Naarah. ⁷Sons of Helah: Zereth, Zohar, Ethnan.

⁸Koz fathered Anub, Hazzobebah and the clans of Aharhel son of Harum. ⁹Jabez was better known than his brothers. His mother gave him the name Jabez, 'because', she said, 'in distress I gave birth to him.' ¹⁰Jabez called on the God of Israel. 'If you truly bless me,' he said, 'you will extend my lands, your hand will be with me, you will keep harm away and my distress will cease.' God granted him what he had asked.

¹¹Chelub, Shuhah's brother, fathered Mehir, who fathered Eshton. ¹²Eshton fathered Bethrapha, Paseah and

rapha, Paseah, and Tehinnah the father of Ir-nahash. These are the men of Recah. 13 The sons of Kenaz: Othniel and Seraiah; and the sons of Othniel: Hathath and Meonothai.*s*
14 Meonothai became the father of Ophrah; and Seraiah became the father of Joab father of Ge-harashim,*t* so-called because they were artisans. 15 The sons of Caleb son of Jephunneh: Iru, Elah, and Naam; and the son*u* of Elah: Kenaz. 16 The sons of Jehallelel: Ziph, Ziphah, Tiria, and Asarel. 17 The sons of Ezrah: Jether, Mered, Epher, and Jalon. These are the sons of Bithiah, daughter of Pharaoh, whom Mered married;*v* and she conceived and bore*w* Miriam, Shammai, and Ishbah father of Eshtemoa. 18 And his Judean wife bore Jered father of Gedor, Heber father of Soco, and Jekuthiel father of Zanoah. 19 The sons of the wife of Hodiah, the sister of Naham, were the fathers of Keilah the Garmite and Eshtemoa the Maacathite. 20 The sons of Shimon: Amnon, Rinnah, Ben-hanan, and Tilon. The sons of Ishi: Zoheth and Ben-zoheth. 21 The sons of Shelah son of Judah: Er father of Lecah, Laadah father of Mareshah, and the families of the guild of linen workers at Beth-ashbea; 22 and Jokim, and the men of Cozeba, and Joash, and Saraph, who married into Moab but returned to Lehem*x* (now the records*y* are ancient). 23 These were the potters and inhabitants of Netaim and Gederah; they lived there with the king in his service.

24 The sons of Simeon: Nemuel, Jamin, Jarib, Zerah, Shaul;*z* 25 Shallum was his son, Mibsam his son, Mishma his son. 26 The sons of Mishma: Hammuel his son, Zaccur his son, Shimei his son. 27 Shimei had sixteen sons and six daughters; but his brothers did not have many children, nor did all their family multiply like the Judeans. 28 They lived in Beer-sheba, Moladah, Hazar-shual, 29 Bilhah, Ezem, Tolad, 30 Bethuel, Hormah, Ziklag, 31 Beth-marcaboth, Hazar-susim, Beth-biri, and Shaaraim. These were their towns until David became king. 32 And their villages were Etam, Ain, Rimmon, Tochen, and Ashan, five towns, 33 along with all their villages that were around these towns as far as Baal. These were their settlements. And they kept a genealogical record.

34 Meshobab, Jamlech, Joshah son of Amaziah, 35 Joel, Jehu son of Joshibiah son of Seraiah son of Asiel, 36 Elioenai, Jaakobah, Jeshohaiah, Asaiah, Adiel, Jesimiel, Benaiah, 37 Ziza son of Shiphi son of Allon son of Jedaiah son of Shimri son of Shemaiah— 38 these mentioned by name were leaders in their families, and their clans increased greatly. 39 They journeyed to the entrance of Gedor, to the east side of the valley, to seek pasture for their flocks, 40 where they found rich, good pasture, and the land was very broad, quiet, and peaceful; for the former inhabitants there belonged to Ham. 41 These, registered by name, came in the days of King Hezekiah of Judah, and attacked their tents and the Meunim who were found there, and exterminated them to this day, and settled in their place, because there was pasture there for their flocks. 42 And some of

Paseah, and Tehinnah father of Irnahash. These were the men of Rechah.
13 The sons of Kenaz: Othniel and Seraiah. The sons of Othniel: Hathath and Meonothai.
14 Meonothai was the father of Ophrah.
Seraiah was the father of Joab founder of Ge-harashim, for they were craftsmen.
15 The sons of Caleb son of Jephunneh: Iru, Elah, and Naam. The son of Elah: Kenaz.
16 The sons of Jehallelel: Ziph and Ziphah, Tiria, and Asarel.
17–18 The sons of Ezra: Jether, Mered, Epher, and Jalon. These were the sons of Bithiah daughter of Pharaoh, whom Mered had married; she conceived and gave birth to Miriam, Shammai, and Ishbah founder of Eshtemoa. His Jewish wife was the mother of Jered founder of Gedor, Heber founder of Soco, and Jekuthiel founder of Zanoah. 19 The sons of his wife Hodiah sister of Naham were Daliah father of Keilah the Garmite, and Eshtemoa the Maacathite.
20 The sons of Shimon: Amnon, Rinnah, Ben-hanan, and Tilon.
The sons of Ishi: Zoheth and Ben-zoheth.
21 The sons of Shelah son of Judah: Er founder of Lecah, Laadah founder of Mareshah, the clans of the guild of linen-workers at Ashbea, 22 Jokim, the men of Kozeba, Joash, and Saraph who fell out with Moab and came back to Bethlehem. (The records are ancient.) 23 They were the potters, and those who lived at Netaim and Gederah were there on the king's service.

24 The sons of Simeon: Nemuel, Jamin, Jarib, Zerah, Saul, his son Shallum, his son Mibsam, and his son Mishma. 26 The sons of Mishma: his son Hammuel, his son Zaccur, and his son Shimei. 27 Shimei had sixteen sons and six daughters, but others of his family had fewer children, and the clan as a whole did not increase as much as the tribe of Judah. 28 They lived at Beersheba, Moladah, Hazar-shual, 29 Bilhah, Ezem, Tolad, 30 Bethuel, Hormah, Ziklag, 31 Beth-marcaboth, Hazar-susim, Beth-biri, and Shaaraim. These were their towns until David came to the throne. 32 Their settlements were Etam, Ain, Rimmon, Tochen, and Ashan, five towns in all. 33 They had also hamlets round these towns as far as Baal. These were the places where they lived.

34 The names on their register were: Meshobab, Jamlech, Joshah son of Amaziah, 35 Joel, Jehu son of Joshibiah, son of Seraiah, son of Asiel, 36 Elioenai, Jaakobah, Jeshohaiah, Asaiah, Adiel, Jesimiel, Benaiah, 37 Ziza son of Shiphi, son of Allon, son of Jedaiah, son of Shimri, son of Shemaiah, 38 whose names are recorded as princes in their clans, and their families had greatly increased. 39 They then went from the approaches to Gedor east of the valley in search of pasture for their flocks. 40 They found rich and good pasture in a wide stretch of open country where everything was quiet and peaceful; before then it had been occupied by Hamites. 41 During the reign of King Hezekiah of Judah those whose names are written above came and destroyed the tribes of Ham and the Meunites where they found them. They annihilated them so that no trace of them has remained to this day; and they occupied the land in their place, for there was pasture for their flocks. 42 Of their number five

4:13 **The sons of Othniel . . . Meonothai:** so *Lat.; Heb*. The sons of Othniel: Hathath. 4:14 **Ge-harashim:** *or* the valley of Craftsmen. 4:15 **Kenaz:** *so some MSS; others* and Kenaz. 4:17–18 **and gave birth to:** *prob. rdg; Heb. omits*. 4:19 **his:** *prob. rdg; Heb. omits*. **Daliah:** *so Gk; Heb. omits*. 4:22 **and came . . . Bethlehem:** *prob. rdg; Heb. unintelligible*. 4:32 **settlements:** *prob. rdg; Heb.* hamlets. 4:41 **the tribes of Ham:** *prob. rdg, cp. verse 40; Heb.* their tribes.

s Gk Vg: Heb lacks *and Meonothai* *t* That is *Valley of artisans* *u* Heb *sons* *v* The clause: *These are . . . married* is transposed from verse 18 *w* Heb lacks *and bore* *x* Vg Compare Gk: Heb *and Jashubi-lehem* *y* Or *matters* *z* Or *Saul*

father of Beth-rapha, Paseah, and Tehinnah, the father of the city of Nahash. These were the men of Recah. 13 The sons of Kenaz were Othniel and Seraiah. The sons of Othniel were Hathath and Meonothai; 14 Meonothai became the father of Ophrah. Seraiah became the father of Joab, the father of Geharashim, so called because they were craftsmen. 15 The sons of Caleb, son of Jephunneh, were Ir, Elah, and Naam. The sons of Elah were . . . and Kenaz. 16 The sons of Jehallelel were Ziph, Ziphah, Tiria, and Asarel. 17 The sons of Ezrah were Jether, Mered, Epher, and Jalon. Jether became the father of Miriam, Shammai, and Ishbah, the father of Eshtemoa. [. . . . . .] 18 His (Mered's) Egyptian wife bore Jared, the father of Gedor, Heber, the father of Soco, and Jekuthiel, the father of Zanoah. These were the sons of Bithiah, the daughter of Pharaoh, whom Mered married. 19 The sons of his Jewish wife, the sister of Naham, the father of Keilah, were Shimon the Garmite and Ishi the Maacathite. 20 The sons of Shimon were Amnon, Rinnah, Benhanan, and Tilon. The son of Ishi was Zoheth and the son of Zoheth. . . .

21 The descendants of Shelah, son of Judah, were: Er, the father of Lecah; Laadah, the father of Mareshah; the clans of the linen weavers' guild in Beth-ashbea; 22 Jokim; the men of Cozeba; and Joash and Saraph, who held property in Moab, but returned to Bethlehem. [These are events of old.] 23 They were potters and inhabitants of Netaim and Gederah, where they lived in the king's service.

24 The sons of Simeon were Nemuel, Jamin, Jachin, Zerah, and Shaul, 25 whose son was Shallum, whose son was Mibsam, whose son was Mishma. 26 The descendants of Mishma were his son Hammuel, whose son was Zaccur, whose son was Shimei. 27 Shimei had sixteen sons and six daughters. His brothers, however, did not have many sons, and as a result all their clans did not equal the number of the Judahites. 28 They dwelt in Beer-sheba, Moladah, Hazar-shual, 29 Bilhah, Ezem, Tolad, 30 Bethuel, Hormah, Ziklag, 31 Bethmarcaboth, Hazar-susim, Bethbiri, and Shaaraim. Until David came to reign, these were their cities 32 and their villages. Etam, also, and Ain, Rimmon, Tochen, and Ashan — five cities, 33 together with all their outlying villages as far as Baal. Here is where they dwelt, and so it was inscribed of them in their family records.

34 Meshobab, Jamlech, Joshah, son of Amaziah, 35 Joel, Jehu, son of Joshibiah, son of Seraiah, son of Asiel, 36 Elioenai, Jaakobath, Jeshohaiah, Asaiah, Adiel, Jesimiel, Benaiah, 37 Ziza, son of Shiphi, son of Allon, son of Jedaiah, son of Shimri, son of Shemaiah — 38 these just named were princes in their clans, and their ancestral houses spread out to such an extent 39 that they went to the approaches of Gedor, east of the valley, seeking pasture for their flocks. 40 They found abundant and good pastures, and the land was spacious, quiet, and peaceful. 41 They who have just been listed by name set out during the reign of Hezekiah, king of Judah, and attacked the tents of Ham (for Hamites dwelt there formerly) and also the Meunites who were there. They pronounced against them the ban that is still in force and dwelt in their place because they found pasture there for their flocks.

Tehinnah father of Irnahash. These were the men of Recab. 13 Sons of Kenaz: Othniel and Seraiah. Sons of Othniel: Hathath and Meonothai; 14 Meonothai fathered Ophrah. Seraiah fathered Joab, father of Geharashim — for they were craftsmen. 15 Sons of Caleb son of Jephunneh: Iru, Elah and Naam. Sons of Elah: Kenaz. 16 Sons of Jehallelel: Ziph, Ziphah, Tiria, Asarel. 17 Sons of Ezrah: Jether, Mered, Epher, Jalon. She conceived Miriam, Shammai, and Ishbah, the father of Eshtemoa, 18 whose Judaean wife gave birth to Jered father of Gedor, Heber father of Soco, and Jekuthiel, father of Zanoah. These were the sons of Bithiah the daughter of Pharaoh whom Mered had married. 19 The sons of Hodiah's wife, sister of Naham father of Keilah the Garmite and of Eshtemoa the Maacathite . . . 20 Sons of Shimon: Amnon, Rinnah, Ben-Hanan, Tilon. Sons of Ishi: Zoheth and Ben-Zoheth.

21 Sons of Shelah son of Judah: Er father of Lecah, Laadah father of Mareshah, and the clans of linenworkers at Beth-Ashbea, 22 Jokim, the men of Cozeba, Joash and Saraph where Moab found wives and then returned to Bethlehem. (These are old traditions.) 23 These were potters and lived at Netaim and Gederah; they resided there, working for the king.

24 Sons of Simeon: Nemuel, Jamin, Jarib, Zerah, Saul; 25 Shallum was his son, Mibsam his son, Mishma his son. 26 The sons of Mishma: Hammuel his son, Zaccur his son, Shimei his son. 27 Shimei had sixteen sons and six daughters, but his brothers did not have many children, and the sum of their clans did not multiply as the sons of Judah did. 28 They lived in Beersheba, Moladah and Hazar-Shual, 29 Bilhah, Ezem and Tolad, 30 Bethuel, Hormah and Ziklag, 31 Beth-Marcaboth, Hazar-Susim, Beth-Biri, Shaaraim. 32 These were their towns until the reign of David. Their settlements were: Etam, Ain, Rimmon, Tochen and Ashan, five towns, 33 and all the dependencies surrounding these towns as far as Baalath. That was where they lived and they had an official genealogy. 34 Meshobab, Jamlech, Joshah son of Amaziah, 35 Joel, Jehu son of Joshibiah, son of Seraiah, son of Asiel, 36 Elioenai, Jaakobah, Jeshohaiah, Asaiah, Adiel, Jesimiel, Benaiah, 37 Ziza, Ben-Shiphi, Ben-Allon, Ben-Jedaiah, Ben-Shimri, Ben-Shemaiah — 38 these above named were princes in their clans in their ancestral home. Their numbers increased enormously. 39 In search of pasture for their flocks, they spread from the Pass of Gerar to the eastern end of the valley, 40 where they found good, fat pasture; the land was broad, untroubled, peaceful. Hamites had been living there before them. 41 These Simeonites, recorded by name, arrived there in the time of Hezekiah king of Judah; they overran their tents and the dwellings which they found there. They put them under a curse of destruction still in force today and settled in their place, since there was pasturage for their flocks.

NEW REVISED STANDARD VERSION | REVISED ENGLISH BIBLE

them, five hundred men of the Simeonites, went to Mount Seir, having as their leaders Pelatiah, Neariah, Rephaiah, and Uzziel, sons of Ishi; 43 they destroyed the remnant of the Amalekites that had escaped, and they have lived there to this day.

5 The sons of Reuben the firstborn of Israel. (He was the firstborn, but because he defiled his father's bed his birthright was given to the sons of Joseph son of Israel, so that he is not enrolled in the genealogy according to the birthright; 2 though Judah became prominent among his brothers and a ruler came from him, yet the birthright belonged to Joseph.) 3 The sons of Reuben, the firstborn of Israel: Hanoch, Pallu, Hezron, and Carmi. 4 The sons of Joel: Shemaiah his son, Gog his son, Shimei his son, 5 Micah his son, Reaiah his son, Baal his son, 6 Beerah his son, whom King Tilgath-pilneser of Assyria carried away into exile; he was a chieftain of the Reubenites. 7 And his kindred by their families, when the genealogy of their generations was reckoned: the chief, Jeiel, and Zechariah, 8 and Bela son of Azaz, son of Shema, son of Joel, who lived in Aroer, as far as Nebo and Baal-meon. 9 He also lived to the east as far as the beginning of the desert this side of the Euphrates, because their cattle had multiplied in the land of Gilead. 10 And in the days of Saul they made war on the Hagrites, who fell by their hand; and they lived in their tents throughout all the region east of Gilead.

11 The sons of Gad lived beside them in the land of Bashan as far as Salecah: 12 Joel the chief, Shapham the second, Janai, and Shaphat in Bashan. 13 And their kindred according to their clans: Michael, Meshullam, Sheba, Jorai, Jacan, Zia, and Eber, seven. 14 These were the sons of Abihail son of Huri, son of Jaroah, son of Gilead, son of Michael, son of Jeshishai, son of Jahdo, son of Buz; 15 Ahi son of Abdiel, son of Guni, was chief in their clan; 16 and they lived in Gilead, in Bashan and in its towns, and in all the pasture lands of Sharon to their limits. 17 All of these were enrolled by genealogies in the days of King Jotham of Judah, and in the days of King Jeroboam of Israel.

18 The Reubenites, the Gadites, and the half-tribe of Manasseh had valiant warriors, who carried shield and sword, and drew the bow, expert in war, forty-four thousand seven hundred sixty, ready for service. 19 They made war on the Hagrites, Jetur, Naphish, and Nodab; 20 and when they received help against them, the Hagrites and all who were with them were given into their hands, for they cried to God in the battle, and he granted their entreaty because they trusted in him. 21 They captured their livestock: fifty thousand of their camels, two hundred fifty thousand sheep, two thousand donkeys, and one hundred thousand captives. 22 Many fell slain, because the war was of God. And they lived in their territory until the exile.

23 The members of the half-tribe of Manasseh lived in the land; they were very numerous from Bashan to Baal-hermon, Senir, and Mount Hermon. 24 These were the heads of their clans: Epher,[a] Ishi, Eliel, Azriel, Jeremiah, Hodaviah, and Jahdiel, mighty warriors, famous men, heads of their clans. 25 But they transgressed against the God of their ancestors, and prostituted themselves to the gods of the peoples of the land, whom God had destroyed before them. 26 So the God of Israel stirred up the spirit of

hundred Simeonites invaded the hill-country of Seir, led by Pelatiah, Neariah, Rephaiah, and Uzziel, the sons of Ishi. 43 They destroyed all who were left of the surviving Amalekites; and they live there still.

5 The sons of Reuben, the eldest of Israel's sons. (He had been, in fact, the first son born, but because he committed incest with a wife of his father's the status of the eldest was transferred to the sons of Joseph, Israel's son, who, however, could not be registered as the eldest son. 2 Judah held the leading place among his brothers because he fathered a ruler, and the status of the eldest was his, not Joseph's.) 3 The sons of Reuben, the eldest of Israel's sons: Enoch, Pallu, Hezron, and Carmi. 4 The sons of Joel: his son Shemaiah, his son Gog, his son Shimei, 5 his son Micah, his son Reaia, his son Baal, 6 his son Beerah, whom King Tiglath-pileser of Assyria carried away into exile; he was a prince of the Reubenites. 7 His kinsmen, family by family, as registered in their tribal lists: Jeiel the chief, Zechariah, 8 Bela son of Azaz, son of Shema, son of Joel. They lived in Aroer, and their lands stretched as far as Nebo and Baal-meon. 9 Eastwards they occupied territory as far as the edge of the desert which stretches from the river Euphrates, for they had large numbers of cattle in Gilead. 10 During Saul's reign they made war on the Hagarites, whom they conquered, occupying their encampments over all the territory east of Gilead.

11 Adjoining them were the Gadites, occupying the district of Bashan as far as Salcah: 12 Joel the chief; second in rank, Shapham; then Jaanai and Shaphat in Bashan. 13 Their fellow-tribesmen belonged to the families of Michael, Meshullam, Sheba, Jorai, Jachan, Zia, and Heber, seven in all. 14 These were the sons of Abihail son of Huri, son of Jaroah, son of Gilead, son of Michael, son of Jeshishai, son of Jahdo, son of Buz. 15 Ahi son of Abdiel, son of Guni, was head of their family; 16 they lived in Gilead, in Bashan and its villages, in all the common land of Sharon as far as it stretched. 17 These registers were all compiled in the reigns of King Jotham of Judah and King Jeroboam of Israel.

18 The sons of Reuben, Gad, and half the tribe of Manasseh: of their fighting men armed with shield and sword, their archers and their battle-trained soldiers, forty-four thousand seven hundred and sixty were ready for active service. 19 They made war on the Hagarites, Jetur, Nephish, and Nodab. 20 They were given help against them, for they cried to their God for help in the battle, and because they trusted him he listened to their prayer, and the Hagarites and all their allies surrendered to them. 21 They drove off their cattle, fifty thousand camels, two hundred and fifty thousand sheep, and two thousand donkeys, and they took a hundred thousand captives. 22 Many Hagarites had been killed, for the war was of God's making, and they occupied their land until the exile.

23 Half the tribe of Manasseh lived in the land from Bashan to Baal-hermon, Senir, and Mount Hermon, and were numerous also in Lebanon. 24 The heads of their families were: Epher, Ishi, Eliel, Azriel, Jeremiah, Hodaviah, and Jahdiel, all men of ability and repute, heads of their families. 25 But they sinned against the God of their fathers, and turned wantonly to worship the gods of the peoples whom God had destroyed before them. 26 So the God of Israel

---

5:2 **his, not:** prob. rdg.; Heb. omits. 5:6 **Tiglath-pileser:** so Gk (Luc.); Heb. Tiglath-pileser. 5:16 **as far as:** so Gk; Heb. upon. 5:20 **They were . . . to them:** or They attacked them boldly, and the Hagarites and all their allies surrendered to them, for they cried . . . to their prayer. 5:23 **in Lebanon:** so Gk; Heb. omits. 5:24 **Epher:** so Gk; Heb. and Epher. 5:26 **Tiglath-pileser:** so Syriac; Heb. Tilgath-pilneser.

a Gk Vg: Heb and Epher

42 Five hundred of them (the Simeonites) went to Mount Seir under the leadership of Pelatiah, Neariah, Rephaiah, and Uzziel, sons of Ishi. 43 They attacked the surviving Amalekites who had escaped, and have resided there to the present day.

5 The sons of Reuben, the first-born of Israel. (He was indeed the first-born, but because he disgraced the couch of his father his birthright was given to the sons of Joseph, son of Israel, so that he is not listed in the family records according to birthright. 2 Judah, in fact, became powerful among his brothers, so that the ruler came from him, though the birthright had been Joseph's.) 3 The sons of Reuben, the first-born of Israel, were Hanoch, Pallu, Hezron, and Carmi. 4 His son was Joel, whose son was Shemaiah, whose son was Gog, whose son was Shimei, 5 whose son was Micah, whose son was Reaiah, whose son was Baal, 6 whose son was Beerah, whom Tiglath-pileser, the king of Assyria, took into exile; he was a prince of the Reubenites. 7 His brothers who belonged to his clans, when they were listed in the family records according to their descendants, were: Jeiel, the chief, and Zechariah, 8 and Bela, son of Azaz, son of Shema, son of Joel. The Reubenites lived in Aroer and as far as Nebo and Baal-meon; 9 toward the east they dwelt as far as the desert which extends from the Euphrates River, for they had much livestock in the land of Gilead. 10 During the reign of Saul they waged war with the Hagrites, and when they had defeated them they occupied their tents throughout the region east of Gilead.

11 The Gadites lived alongside them in the land of Bashan as far as Salecah. 12 Joel was chief, Shapham was second in command, and Janai was judge in Bashan. 13 Their brothers, corresponding to their ancestral houses, were: Michael, Meshullam, Sheba, Jorai, Jacan, Zia, and Eber — seven. 14 These were the sons of Abihail, son of Huri, son of Jaroah, son of Gilead, son of Michael, son of Jeshishai, son of Jahdo, son of Buz. 15 Ahi, son of Abdiel, son of Guni, was the head of their ancestral houses. 16 They dwelt in Gilead, in Bashan and its towns, and in all the pasture lands of Sirion to the borders. 17 All were listed in the family records in the time of Jotham, king of Judah, and of Jeroboam, king of Israel.

18 The Reubenites, Gadites, and half-tribe of Manasseh were warriors, men who bore shield and sword and who drew the bow, trained in warfare — forty-four thousand seven hundred and sixty men fit for military service. 19 When they waged war against the Hagrites and against Jetur, Naphish, and Nodab, 20 they received help so that they mastered the Hagrites and all who were with them. For during the battle they called on God, and he heard them because they had put their trust in him. 21 Along with one hundred thousand men they also captured their livestock: fifty thousand camels, two hundred fifty thousand sheep, and two thousand asses. 22 Many had fallen in battle, for victory is from God; and they took over their dwelling place until the time of the exile.

23 The numerous members of the half-tribe of Manasseh lived in the land of Bashan as far as Baal-hermon, Senir, and Mount Hermon. 24 The following were the heads of their ancestral houses: Epher, Ishi, Eliel, Azriel, Jeremiah, Hodaviah, and Jahdiel — men who were warriors, famous men, and heads over their ancestral houses. 25 However, they offended the God of their fathers by lusting after the gods of the natives of the land, whom God had cleared out of their way. 26 Therefore the God of Israel

42 Five hundred of them, of the Simeonites, went to Mount Seir, their leaders being Pelatiah, Neariah, Rephaiah, and Uzziel, the sons of Ishi.

43 They defeated the surviving fugitives of Amalek and still live there today.

5 Sons of Reuben, first-born of Israel. He was indeed first-born but, when he defiled his father's bed, his birthright was given to the sons of Joseph son of Israel, and he was no longer reckoned as the eldest son.

2 Although Judah grew greater than his brothers and a leader came from him, the birthright was Joseph's.

3 Sons of Reuben, first-born of Israel: Henoch, Pallu, Hezron, Carmi.

4 Sons of Joel: Shemaiah his son, Gog his son, Shimei his son, 5 Micah his son, Reaiah his son, Baal his son. 6 Beerah his son, whom Tiglath-Pileser king of Assyria carried off into exile, was the chief of the Reubenites.

7 His brothers, by families, were grouped according to relationship. Jeiel was first, then Zechariah 8 and Bela son of Azaz, son of Shema, son of Joel.

It was Reuben who lived in Aroer and his territory extended as far as Nebo and Baal-Meon. 9 To eastward, what he occupied extended to the edge of the desert and the River Euphrates, for they had many herds in Gilead.

10 In the time of Saul, they made war on the Hagrites, whom they defeated and who were then living in their tents throughout the eastern front of Gilead.

11 Next to them, in Bashan as far as Salecah, lived the sons of Gad. 12 Joel was the first, Shapham the second, then Janai and Shaphat in Bashan.

13 Their brothers, by families, were Michael, Meshullam, Sheba, Jorai, Jacan, Zia, Eber: seven. 14 These were the sons of Abihail: Ben-Huri, Ben-Jaroah, Ben-Gilead, Ben-Michael, Ben-Jeshishai, Ben-Jahdo, Ben-Buz. 15 Ahi son of Abdiel, son of Guni, was the head of their families. 16 They inhabited Gilead, Bashan and its dependencies, as well as all the pasture lands of Sharon on their extremities. 17 In the time of Jotham king of Judah and in the time of Jeroboam king of Israel, all of them were included in the official genealogy.

18 The sons of Reuben, the Gadites and the half-tribe of Manasseh had warriors, men armed with shield and sword who could handle the bow and were trained for war, to the number of forty-four thousand seven hundred and sixty fit for service. 19 They made war on the Hagrites, on Jetur, Naphish and Nodab. 20 God came to their help, and the Hagrites and all their allies fell into their hands, for they called on God as they fought, and because they put their trust in him he heard their prayer. 21 Of their livestock they carried off fifty thousand camels, two hundred and fifty thousand sheep, two thousand donkeys and a hundred thousand people. 22 Because the war was of God, the slaughter was great. They continued to live in their territory until the exile.

23 The sons of the half-tribe of Manasseh lived in the territory between Bashan and Baal-Hermon, Senir and Mount Hermon.

They were numerous. 24 These were the heads of their families: Epher, Ishi, Eliel, Azriel, Jeremiah, Hodaviah, Jahdiel — stout fighting men, men of renown, heads of their families.

25 But since they were unfaithful to the God of their ancestors and prostituted themselves to the gods of the peoples of the country whom God had destroyed before them, 26 the

King Pul of Assyria, the spirit of King Tilgath-pilneser of Assyria, and he carried them away, namely, the Reubenites, the Gadites, and the half-tribe of Manasseh, and brought them to Halah, Habor, Hara, and the river Gozan, to this day.

6 [b] The sons of Levi: Gershom, [c] Kohath, and Merari. 2 The sons of Kohath: Amram, Izhar, Hebron, and Uzziel. 3 The children of Amram: Aaron, Moses, and Miriam. The sons of Aaron: Nadab, Abihu, Eleazar, and Ithamar. 4 Eleazar became the father of Phinehas, Phinehas of Abishua, 5 Abishua of Bukki, Bukki of Uzzi, 6 Uzzi of Zerahiah, Zerahiah of Meraioth, 7 Meraioth of Amariah, Amariah of Ahitub, 8 Ahitub of Zadok, Zadok of Ahimaaz, 9 Ahimaaz of Azariah, Azariah of Johanan, 10 and Johanan of Azariah (it was he who served as priest in the house that Solomon built in Jerusalem). 11 Azariah became the father of Amariah, Amariah of Ahitub, 12 Ahitub of Zadok, Zadok of Shallum, 13 Shallum of Hilkiah, Hilkiah of Azariah, 14 Azariah of Seraiah, Seraiah of Jehozadak; 15 and Jehozadak went into exile when the LORD sent Judah and Jerusalem into exile by the hand of Nebuchadnezzar.

stirred up King Pul of Assyria, that is King Tiglath-pileser of Assyria, and he carried away Reuben, Gad, and half the tribe of Manasseh. He took them to Halah, Habor, Hara, and the river Gozan, where they are to this day.

6 THE sons of Levi: Gershon, Kohath, and Merari. 2 The sons of Kohath: Amram, Izhar, Hebron, and Uzziel. 3 The children of Amram: Aaron, Moses, and Miriam. The sons of Aaron: Nadab, Abihu, Eleazar, and Ithamar. 4 Eleazar was the father of Phinehas, Phinehas father of Abishua, 5 Abishua father of Bukki, Bukki father of Uzzi, 6 Uzzi father of Zerahiah, Zerahiah father of Meraioth, 7 Meraioth father of Amariah, Amariah father of Ahitub, 8 Ahitub father of Zadok, Zadok father of Ahimaaz, 9 Ahimaaz father of Azariah, Azariah father of Johanan, 10 and Johanan father of Azariah, the priest who officiated in the LORD's house which Solomon built at Jerusalem. 11 Azariah was the father of Amariah, Amariah father of Ahitub, 12 Ahitub father of Zadok, Zadok father of Shallum, 13 Shallum father of Hilkiah, Hilkiah father of Azariah, 14 Azariah father of Seraiah, and Seraiah father of Jehozadak. 15 Jehozadak was deported when the LORD sent Judah and Jerusalem into exile under Nebuchadnezzar.

16 [d] The sons of Levi: Gershom, Kohath, and Merari. 17 These are the names of the sons of Gershom: Libni and Shimei. 18 The sons of Kohath: Amram, Izhar, Hebron, and Uzziel. 19 The sons of Merari: Mahli and Mushi. These are the clans of the Levites according to their ancestry. 20 Of Gershom: Libni his son, Jahath his son, Zimmah his son, 21 Joah his son, Iddo his son, Zerah his son, Jeatherai his son. 22 The sons of Kohath: Amminadab his son, Korah his son, Assir his son, 23 Elkanah his son, Ebiasaph his son, Assir his son, 24 Tahath his son, Uriel his son, Uzziah his son, and Shaul his son. 25 The sons of Elkanah: Amasai and Ahimoth, 26 Elkanah his son, Zophai his son, Nahath his son, 27 Eliab his son, Jeroham his son, Elkanah his son. 28 The sons of Samuel: Joel [e] his firstborn, the second Abijah. [f] 29 The sons of Merari: Mahli, Libni his son, Shimei his son, Uzzah his son, 30 Shimea his son, Haggiah his son, and Asaiah his son.

31 These are the men whom David put in charge of the service of song in the house of the LORD, after the ark came to rest there. 32 They ministered with song before the tabernacle of the tent of meeting, until Solomon had built the house of the LORD in Jerusalem; and they performed their service in due order. 33 These are the men who served; and their sons were: Of the Kohathites: Heman, the singer, son of Joel, son of Samuel, 34 son of Elkanah, son of Jeroham, son of Eliel, son of Toah, 35 son of Zuph, son of Elkanah, son of Mahath, son of Amasai, 36 son of Elkanah, son of Joel, son of Azariah, son of Zephaniah, 37 son of Tahath, son of Assir, son of Ebiasaph, son of Korah, 38 son of Izhar, son of Kohath, son of Levi, son of Israel, 39 and his brother Asaph, who stood on his right, namely, Asaph son of Berechiah, son of Shimea, 40 son of Michael, son of Baaseiah, son of Malchijah, 41 son of Ethni, son of Zerah, son of

16 The sons of Levi: Gershom, Kohath, and Merari. 17 The sons of Gershom: Libni and Shimei. 18 The sons of Kohath: Amram, Izhar, Hebron, and Uzziel. 19 The sons of Merari: Mahli and Mushi. The clans of Levi, family by family: 20 Gershom: his son Libni, his son Jahath, his son Zimmah, 21 his son Joah, his son Iddo, his son Zerah, his son Jeaterai. 22 The sons of Kohath: his son Amminadab, his son Korah, his son Assir, 23 his son Elkanah, his son Ebiasaph, his son Assir, 24 his son Tahath, his son Uriel, his son Uzziah, his son Saul. 25 The sons of Elkanah: Amasai and Ahimoth, 26 his son Elkanah, his son Zophai, his son Nahath, 27 his son Eliab, his son Jeroham, his son Elkanah. 28 The sons of Samuel: Joel the eldest and Abiah the second. 29 The sons of Merari: his son Mahli, his son Libni, his son Uzza, his son Shimea, his son Haggiah, his son Asaiah.

31 These are the men whom David appointed to take charge of the music in the house of the LORD when the Ark should be deposited there. 32 They performed their musical duties at the front of the Tent of Meeting before Solomon built the house of the LORD in Jerusalem; they took their turns of duty as was laid down for them. 33 The following, with their descendants, took this duty. Of the line of Kohath: Heman the musician, son of Joel, son of Samuel, 34 son of Elkanah, son of Jeroham, son of Eliel, son of Toah, 35 son of Zuph, son of Elkanah, son of Mahath, son of Amasai, 36 son of Elkanah, son of Joel, son of Azariah, son of Zephaniah, 37 son of Tahath, son of Assir, son of Ebiasaph, son of Korah, 38 son of Izhar, son of Kohath, son of Levi, son of Israel. 39 Heman's colleague Asaph stood at his right hand. He was the son of Berechiah, son of Shimea, 40 son of Michael, son of Baaseiah, son of Malchiah, 41 son

6:1 In Heb. 5:27. Gershon: Gershom in verses 16,17,20.
6:4–8 Cp. verses 50–53.   6:16 In Heb. 6:1.   6:16–19 Cp.
Exod. 6:16–19.   6:20–21 Cp. verses 41–43.   6:22–28 Cp.
verses 33–38.   6:26 his son Elkanah: so Gk; Heb. Elkanah, the
sons of Elkanah.   6:28 Joel ... second: so Gk (Luc.); Heb. the
eldest Vashni and Abiah.   6:29 his son Mahli: so Syriac; Heb.
omits his son.   6:41–43 Cp. verses 20–21.

b Ch 5.27 in Heb   c Heb Gershon, variant of Gershom; See 6.16
d Ch 6.1 in Heb   e Gk Syr Compare verse 33 and 1 Sam 8.2: Heb
lacks Joel   f Heb reads Vashni, and Abijah for the second Abijah,
taking the second as a proper name

NEW AMERICAN BIBLE

incited against them the anger of Pul, king of Assyria, and of Tiglath-pileser, king of Assyria, who deported the Reubenites, the Gadites, and the half-tribe of Manasseh and brought them to Halah, Habor, and Hara, and to the river Gozan, where they have remained to this day. ²⁷The sons of Levi were Gershon, Kohath, and Merari. ²⁸The sons of Kohath were Amram, Izhar, Hebron, and Uzziel. ²⁹The children of Amram were Aaron, Moses, and Miriam. The sons of Aaron were Nadab, Abihu, Eleazar, and Ithamar. ³⁰Eleazar, became the father of Phinehas. Phinehas became the father of Abishua. ³¹Abishua became the father of Bukki. Bukki became the father of Uzzi. ³²Uzzi became the father of Zerahiah. Zerahiah became the father of Meraioth. ³³Meraioth became the father of Amariah. Amariah became the father of Ahitub. ³⁴Ahitub became the father of Zadok. Zadok became the father of Ahimaaz. ³⁵Ahimaaz became the father of Azariah. Azariah became the father of Johanan. ³⁶Johanan became the father of Azariah, who served as priest in the temple Solomon built in Jerusalem. ³⁷Azariah became the father of Amariah. Amariah became the father of Ahitub. ³⁸Ahitub became the father of Zadok. Zadok became the father of Shallum. ³⁹Shallum became the father of Hilkiah. Hilkiah became the father of Azariah. ⁴⁰Azariah became the father of Seraiah. Seraiah became the father of Jehozadak. ⁴¹Jehozadak was one of those who went into the exile which the LORD inflicted on Judah and Jerusalem through Nebuchadnezzar.

6 The sons of Levi were Gershon, Kohath, and Merari. ²The sons of Gershon were named Libni and Shimei. ³The sons of Kohath were Amram, Izhar, Hebron, and Uzziel. ⁴The sons of Merari were Mahli and Mushi. The following were the clans of Levi, distributed according to their ancestors: ⁵of Gershon: his son Libni, whose son was Jahath, whose son was Zimmah, ⁶whose son was Joah, whose son was Iddo, whose son was Zerah, whose son was Jetherai.

⁷The descendants of Kohath were: his son Amminadab, whose son was Korah, whose son was Assir, ⁸whose son was Elkanah, whose son was Ebiasaph, whose son was Assir, ⁹whose son was Tahath, whose son was Uriel, whose son was Uzziah, whose son was Shaul. ¹⁰The sons of Elkanah were Amasai and Ahimoth, ¹¹whose son was Elkanah, whose son was Zophai, whose son was Nahath, ¹²whose son was Eliab, whose son was Jeroham, whose son was Elkanah, whose son was Samuel. ¹³The sons of Samuel were Joel, the first-born, and Abijah, the second. ¹⁴The descendants of Merari were Mahli, whose son was Libni, whose son was Shimei, whose son was Uzzah, ¹⁵whose son was Shimea, whose son was Haggiah, whose son was Asaiah.

¹⁶The following were entrusted by David with the choir services in the LORD's house from the time when the ark had obtained a permanent resting place. ¹⁷They served as singers before the Dwelling of the meeting tent until Solomon built the temple of the LORD in Jerusalem, and they performed their services in an order prescribed for them. ¹⁸Those who so performed are the following, together with their descendants.

Among the Kohathites: Heman, the chanter, son of Joel, son of Samuel, ¹⁹son of Elkanah, son of Jeroham, son of Eliel, son of Toah, ²⁰son of Zuth, son of Elkanah, son of Mahath, son of Amasi, ²¹son of Elkanah, son of Joel, son of Azariah, son of Zephaniah, ²²son of Tahath, son of Assir, son of Ebiasaph, son of Korah, ²³son of Izhar, son of Kohath, son of Levi, son of Israel.

²⁴His brother Asaph stood at his right hand. Asaph was the son of Berechiah, son of Shimea, ²⁵son of Michael, son of Baaseiah, son of Malchijah, ²⁶son of Ethni, son of Ze-

NEW JERUSALEM BIBLE

God of Israel roused the hostility of Pul, king of Assyria, that is the wrath of Tiglath-Pileser, king of Assyria who deported them — the Reubenites, the Gadites and the half-tribe of Manasseh — taking them off to Halah, Habor, Hara and the river of Gozan. They are still there today. ²⁷Sons of Levi: Gershom, Kohath and Merari. ²⁸Sons of Kohath: Amram, Izhar, Hebron, Uzziel. ²⁹Children of Amram: Aaron, Moses and Miriam. Sons of Aaron: Nadab and Abihu, Eleazar and Ithamar.

³⁰Eleazar fathered Phinehas, Phinehas fathered Abishua, ³¹Abishua fathered Bukki, Bukki fathered Uzzi. ³²Uzzi fathered Zerahiah, Zerahiah fathered Meraioth. ³³Meraioth fathered Amariah, Amariah fathered Ahitub, ³⁴Ahitub fathered Zadok, Zadok fathered Ahimaaz. ³⁵Ahimaaz fathered Azariah, Azariah fathered Johanan. ³⁶Johanan fathered Azariah. He it was who officiated as priest in the Temple which Solomon built in Jerusalem. ³⁷Azariah fathered Amariah, Amariah fathered Ahitub, ³⁸Ahitub fathered Zadok, Zadok fathered Shallum, ³⁹Shallum fathered Hilkiah, Hilkiah fathered Azariah, ⁴⁰Azariah fathered Seraiah, Seraiah fathered Jehozadak, ⁴¹and Jehozadak went into exile when, at the hands of Nebuchadnezzar, Yahweh exiled Judah and Jerusalem.

6 Sons of Levi: Gershom, Kohath and Merari. ²These are the names of the sons of Gershom: Libni and Shimei. ³Sons of Kohath: Amram, Izhar, Hebron, Uzziel. ⁴Sons of Merari: Mahli and Mushi.

These are the levitical clans according to their father.

⁵Of Gershom: Libni his son, Jahath his son, Zimmah his son, ⁶Joah his son, Iddo his son, Zerah his son, Jeatherai his son.

⁷Sons of Kohath: Amminadab his son, Korah his son, Assir his son, ⁸Elkanah his son, Ebiasaph his son, Assir his son. ⁹Tahath his son, Uriel his son, Uzziah his son, Shaul his son. ¹⁰Sons of Elkanah: Amasai and Ahimoth. ¹¹Elkanah his son, Zophai his son, Nahath his son, ¹²Eliab his son, Jeroham his son, Elkanah his son. ¹³Sons of Elkanah: Samuel his first-born, the second Abijah.

¹⁴Sons of Merari: Mahli, Libni his son, ¹⁵Shimei his son, Haggiah his son, Asaiah his son.

¹⁶These are the men whom David nominated to lead the singing in the Temple of Yahweh after the ark had come to rest there. ¹⁷They were responsible for the singing before the Dwelling, the Tent of Meeting, until Solomon had built the Temple of Yahweh in Jerusalem and then continued their customary duties.

¹⁸These were the persons in office, with their sons:

Of the sons of Kohath: Heman the singer, son of Joel, son of Samuel, ¹⁹son of Elkanah, son of Jeroham, son of Eliel, son of Toah, ²⁰son of Zuph, son of Elkanah, son of Mahath, son of Amasai, ²¹son of Elkanah, son of Joel, son of Azariah, son of Zephaniah, ²²son of Tahath, son of Assir, son of Ebiasaph, son of Korah, ²³son of Izhar, son of Kohath, son of Levi, son of Israel.

²⁴His brother Asaph stood on his right: Asaph son of Berechiah, son of Shimea, ²⁵son of Michael, son of Baaseiah, son of Malchijah, ²⁶son of Ethni, son of Zerah, son of

| NEW REVISED STANDARD VERSION | REVISED ENGLISH BIBLE |

Adaiah, [42] son of Ethan, son of Zimmah, son of Shimei, [43] son of Jahath, son of Gershom, son of Levi. [44] On the left were their kindred the sons of Merari: Ethan son of Kishi, son of Abdi, son of Malluch, [45] son of Hashabiah, son of Amaziah, son of Hilkiah, [46] son of Amzi, son of Bani, son of Shemer, [47] son of Mahli, son of Mushi, son of Merari, son of Levi; [48] and their kindred the Levites were appointed for all the service of the tabernacle of the house of God.

[49] But Aaron and his sons made offerings on the altar of burnt offering and on the altar of incense, doing all the work of the most holy place, to make atonement for Israel, according to all that Moses the servant of God had commanded. [50] These are the sons of Aaron: Eleazar his son, Phinehas his son, Abishua his son, [51] Bukki his son, Uzzi his son, Zerahiah his son, [52] Meraioth his son, Amariah his son, Ahitub his son, [53] Zadok his son, Ahimaaz his son.

[54] These are their dwelling places according to their settlements within their borders: to the sons of Aaron of the families of Kohathites — for the lot fell to them first — [55] to them they gave Hebron in the land of Judah and its surrounding pasture lands, [56] but the fields of the city and its villages they gave to Caleb son of Jephunneh. [57] To the sons of Aaron they gave the cities of refuge: Hebron, Libnah with its pasture lands, Jattir, Eshtemoa with its pasture lands, [58] Hilen[g] with its pasture lands, Debir with its pasture lands, [59] Ashan with its pasture lands, and Bethshemesh with its pasture lands. [60] From the tribe of Benjamin, Geba with its pasture lands, Alemeth with its pasture lands, and Anathoth with its pasture lands. All their towns throughout their families were thirteen.

[61] To the rest of the Kohathites were given by lot out of the family of the tribe, out of the half-tribe, the half of Manasseh, ten towns. [62] To the Gershomites according to their families were allotted thirteen towns out of the tribes of Issachar, Asher, Naphtali, and Manasseh in Bashan. [63] To the Merarites according to their families were allotted twelve towns out of the tribes of Reuben, Gad, and Zebulun. [64] So the people of Israel gave the Levites the towns with their pasture lands. [65] They also gave them by lot out of the tribes of Judah, Simeon, and Benjamin these towns that are mentioned by name.

[66] And some of the families of the sons of Kohath had towns of their territory out of the tribe of Ephraim. [67] They were given the cities of refuge: Shechem with its pasture lands in the hill country of Ephraim, Gezer with its pasture lands, [68] Jokmeam with its pasture lands, Beth-horon with its pasture lands, [69] Aijalon with its pasture lands, Gathrimmon with its pasture lands; [70] and out of the half-tribe of Manasseh, Aner with its pasture lands, and Bileam with its pasture lands, for the rest of the families of the Kohathites.

[71] To the Gershomites: out of the half-tribe of Manasseh: Golan in Bashan with its pasture lands and Ashtaroth with its pasture lands; [72] and out of the tribe of Issachar: Kedesh with its pasture lands, Daberath[h] with its pasture lands, [73] Ramoth with its pasture lands, and Anem with its pasture lands; [74] out of the tribe of Asher: Mashal with its pasture lands, Abdon with its pasture lands, [75] Hukok with its pasture lands, and Rehob with its pasture lands; [76] and out of the tribe of Naphtali: Kedesh in Galilee with its pasture lands, Hammon with its pasture lands, and Kiriathaim with its pasture lands. [77] To the rest of the Merarites

of Ethni, son of Zerah, son of Adaiah, [42] son of Ethan, son of Zimmah, son of Shimei, [43] son of Jahath, son of Gershom, son of Levi. [44] On their left stood their colleague of the line of Merari: Ethan son of Kishi, son of Abdi, son of Malluch, [45] son of Hashabiah, son of Amaziah, son of Hilkiah, [46] son of Amzi, son of Bani, son of Shemer, [47] son of Mahli, son of Mushi, son of Merari, son of Levi. [48] Their kinsmen the Levites were dedicated to all the service of the Tabernacle, the house of God.

[49] But it was Aaron and his descendants who burnt the sacrifices on the altar of whole-offering and the altar of incense, in fulfilment of all the duties connected with the most sacred gifts, and to make expiation for Israel, exactly as Moses the servant of God had commanded. [50] The sons of Aaron: his son Eleazar, his son Phinehas, his son Abishua, [51] his son Bukki, his son Uzzi, his son Zerahiah, [52] his son Meraioth, his son Amariah, his son Ahitub, [53] his son Zadok, his son Ahimaaz.

[54] These are their settlements in encampments in the districts assigned to the descendants of Aaron, to the clan of Kohath, for it was to them that the lot had fallen: [55] they were given Hebron in Judah, with the common land round it, [56] but to Caleb son of Jephunneh were assigned the open country belonging to the town and its hamlets. [57] To the sons of Aaron were given: Hebron the city of refuge, Libnah, Jattir, Eshtemoa, [58] Hilen, Debir, [59] Ashan, and Bethshemesh, each with its common land. [60] And from the tribe of Benjamin: Geba, Alemeth, and Anathoth, each with its common land, making thirteen towns in all by their clans.

[61] To the remaining clans of the sons of Kohath ten towns were allotted from the half tribe of Manasseh. [62] To the sons of Gershom according to their clans they gave thirteen towns from the tribes of Issachar, Asher, Naphtali, and Manasseh in Bashan. [63] To the sons of Merari according to their clans they gave by lot twelve towns from the tribes of Reuben, Gad, and Zebulun. [64] Israel gave these towns, each with its common land, to the Levites. [65] (The towns mentioned above, from the tribes of Judah, Simeon, and Benjamin, were assigned by lot.)

[66] Some of the clans of Kohath had towns allotted to them. [67] They gave them the city of refuge Shechem in the hill-country of Ephraim, Gezer, [68] Jokmeam, Beth-horon, [69] Aijalon, and Gath-rimmon, each with its common land. [70] From the half tribe of Manasseh, Aner and Bileam, each with its common land, were given to the rest of the clans of Kohath.

[71] To the sons of Gershom they gave from the half tribe of Manasseh: Golan in Bashan, and Ashtaroth, each with its common land. [72] From the tribe of Issachar: Kedesh, Daberath, [73] Ramoth, and Anem, each with its common land. [74] From the tribe of Asher: Mashal, Abdon, [75] Hukok, and Rehob, each with its common land. [76] From the tribe of Naphtali: Kedesh in Galilee, Hammon, and Kiriathaim, each with its common land.

6:50–53 Cp. verses 4–8.   6:57–81 Cp. Josh. 21:13–39.
6:57 **city**: prob. rdg., cp. Josh. 21:13; Heb. cities.   6:58 **Hilen:** so many MSS; others Hilez.   6:61 **half tribe**: so Lat.; Heb. adds half.   6:66 **allotted**: prob. rdg, cp. Josh. 21:20; Heb. of their frontier.   6:67 **city**: prob. rdg, cp. Josh. 21:21; Heb. cities.

[g] Other readings Hilez, Holon; See Josh 21.15   [h] Or Dobrath

rah, son of Adaiah, 27 son of Ethan, son of Zimmah, son of Shimei, 28 son of Jahath, son of Gershon, son of Levi.

29 Their brothers, the Merarites, stood at the left: Ethan, son of Kishi, son of Abdi, son of Malluch, 30 son of Hashabiah, son of Amaziah, son of Hilkiah, 31 son of Amzi, son of Bani, son of Shemer, 32 son of Mahli, son of Mushi, son of Merari, son of Levi.

33 Their brother Levites were appointed to all other services of the Dwelling of the house of God. 34 However, it was Aaron and his descendants who burnt the offerings on the altar of holocausts and on the altar of incense; they alone had charge of the holy of holies and of making atonement for Israel, as Moses, the servant of God, had ordained.

35 These were the descendants of Aaron: his son Eleazer, whose son was Phinehas, whose son was Abishua, 36 whose son was Bukki, whose son was Uzzi, whose son was Zerahiah, 37 whose son was Meraioth, whose son was Amariah, whose son was Ahitub, 38 whose son was Zadok, whose son was Ahimaaz.

39 The following were their dwelling places to which their encampment was limited. To the descendants of Aaron who belonged to the clan of the Kohathites, since the first lot fell to them, 40 was assigned Hebron with its adjacent pasture lands in the land of Judah, 41 although the open country and the villages belonging to the city had been given to Caleb, the son of Jephunneh. 42 There were assigned to the descendants of Aaron: Hebron, a city of asylum, Libnah with its pasture lands, Jattir with its pasture lands, Eshtemoa with its pasture lands, 43 Holon with its pasture lands, Debir with its pasture lands, 44 Ashan with its pasture lands, Jetta with its pasture lands, and Beth-shemesh with its pasture lands. 45 Also from the tribe of Benjamin: Gibeon with its pasture lands, Geba with its pasture lands, Almon with its pasture lands, Anathoth with its pasture lands. In all, they had thirteen cities with their pasture lands. 49 The Israelites assigned these cities with their pasture lands to the Levites, 50 designating them by name and assigning them by lot from the tribes of the Judahites, Simeonites, and Benjaminites.

46 The other Kohathites obtained ten cities by lot for their clans from the tribe of Ephraim, from the tribe of Dan, and from the half-tribe of Manasseh. 47 The clans of the Gershonites obtained thirteen cities from the tribes of Issachar, Asher, and Naphtali, and from the half-tribe of Manasseh in Bashan. 48 The clans of the Merarites obtained twelve cities by lot from the tribes of Reuben, Gad, and Zebulun. ‡6.49–50: see above‡

51 The clans of the Kohathites obtained cities by lot from the tribe of Ephraim. 52 They were assigned: Shechem in the mountain region of Ephraim, a city of asylum, with its pasture lands, Gezer with its pasture lands, 53 Kibzaim with its pasture lands, and Beth-horon with its pasture lands. 54 From the tribe of Dan: Elteke with its pasture lands, Gibbethon with its pasture lands, Aijalon with its pasture lands, and Gath-rimmon with its pasture lands. 55 From the half-tribe of Manasseh: Taanach with its pasture lands and Ibleam with its pasture lands. These belonged to the rest of the Kohathite clan.

56 The clans of the Gershonites received from the half-tribe of Manasseh: Golan in Bashan with its pasture lands and Ashtaroth with its pasture lands. 57 From the tribe of Issachar: Kedesh with its pasture lands, Daberath with its pasture lands, 58 Ramoth with its pasture lands, and Enganim with its pasture lands. 59 From the tribe of Asher: Mashal with its pasture lands, Abdon with its pasture lands, 60 Hilkath with its pasture lands, and Rehob with its pasture lands. 61 From the tribe of Naphtali: Kedesh in Galilee with its pasture lands, Hammon with its pasture lands, and Kiriathaim with its pasture lands.

Adaiah, 27 son of Ethan, son of Zimmah, son of Shimei, 28 son of Jahath, son of Gershom, son of Levi.

29 On the left, the sons of Merari: Ethan son of Kishi, son of Abdi, son of Malluch, 30 son of Hashabiah, son of Amaziah, son of Hilkiah, 31 son of Amzi, son of Bani, son of Shemer, 32 son of Mahli, son of Mushi, son of Merari, son of Levi.

33 Their brother Levites were dedicated for all the other duties of the Dwelling, the Temple of God, 34 but Aaron and his sons burned the offerings on the altar of burnt offering and on the altar of incense; they were entirely responsible for the most holy things and for the ritual of expiation for Israel, in accordance with all that Moses, servant of God, had commanded.

35 These were the sons of Aaron: Eleazar his son, Phinehas his son, Abishua his son, 36 Bukki his son, Uzzi his son, Zerahiah his son, 37 Meraioth his son, Amariah his son, Ahitub his son, 38 Zadok his son, Ahimaaz his son.

39 These were their places of settlement within their prescribed territory:

The sons of Aaron of the Kohathite clan — for to these the first lot fell — 40 were given Hebron in the territory of Judah with its surrounding pasture lands. 41 But the open country of the town and its dependencies were given to Caleb son of Jephunneh. 42 The sons of Aaron were also given the cities of refuge, Hebron, Libnah with its pasture lands, Jattir, Eshtemoa with its pasture lands. 43 Hilen with its pasture lands, Debir with its pasture lands, 44 Ashan with its pasture lands and Beth-Shemesh with its pasture lands; 45 and, from the tribe of Benjamin, Geba with its pasture lands, Alemeth with its pasture lands and Anathoth with its pasture lands. In all, the towns distributed among their clans numbered thirteen.

46 The remaining sons of Kohath were allotted ten towns from the clans of the tribe, that is, from the half-tribe of Manasseh. 47 The sons of Gershom and their clans were allotted thirteen towns from the tribe of Issachar, from the tribe of Asher, from the tribe of Naphtali and from the tribe of Manasseh in Bashan. 48 The sons of Merari and their clans were allotted twelve towns from the tribe of Reuben, from the tribe of Gad and from the tribe of Zebulun. 49 The Israelites gave these towns with their pasture lands to the Levites. 50 From the tribe of the sons of Judah, from the tribe of the sons of Simeon and from the tribe of the sons of Benjamin, they also allotted them those towns to which they gave their names.

51 Towns from the tribe of Ephraim were also assigned to the territory of some clans of the sons of Kohath. 52 They were given the cities of refuge: Shechem in the highlands of Ephraim with its pasture lands, Gezer and its pasture lands, 53 Jokmeam with its pasture lands, Beth-Horon with its pasture lands, 54 Aijalon with its pasture lands and Gath-Rimmon with its pasture lands 55 and from the half-tribe of Manasseh, Aner with its pasture lands and Bileam with its pasture lands. So much was given to the remaining families of the sons of Kohath.

56 From the half-tribe of Manasseh, the sons of Gershom according to family were given Golan in Bashan with its pasture lands and Ashtaroth with its pasture lands; 57 from the tribe of Issachar, Kedesh with its pasture lands, Daberath with its pasture lands, 58 Ramoth with its pasture lands and Anem with its pasture lands; 59 from the tribe of Asher: Mashal with its pasture lands, Abdon with its pasture lands. 60 Hukok with its pasture lands and Rehob with its pasture lands; 61 from the tribe of Naphtali, Kedesh in Galilee with its pasture lands, Hammon with its pasture lands and Kiriataim with its pasture lands.

out of the tribe of Zebulun: Rimmono with its pasture lands, Tabor with its pasture lands, [78] and across the Jordan from Jericho, on the east side of the Jordan, out of the tribe of Reuben: Bezer in the steppe with its pasture lands, Jahzah with its pasture lands, [79] Kedemoth with its pasture lands, and Mephaath with its pasture lands; [80] and out of the tribe of Gad: Ramoth in Gilead with its pasture lands, Mahanaim with its pasture lands, [81] Heshbon with its pasture lands, and Jazer with its pasture lands.

7 The sons[i] of Issachar: Tola, Puah, Jashub, and Shimron, four. [2] The sons of Tola: Uzzi, Rephaiah, Jeriel, Jahmai, Ibsam, and Shemuel, heads of their ancestral houses, namely of Tola, mighty warriors of their generations, their number in the days of David being twenty-two thousand six hundred. [3] The son[j] of Uzzi: Izrahiah. And the sons of Izrahiah: Michael, Obadiah, Joel, and Isshiah, five, all of them chiefs; [4] and along with them, by their generations, according to their ancestral houses, were units of the fighting force, thirty-six thousand, for they had many wives and sons. [5] Their kindred belonging to all the families of Issachar were in all eighty-seven thousand mighty warriors, enrolled by genealogy.

6 The sons of Benjamin: Bela, Becher, and Jediael, three. [7] The sons of Bela: Ezbon, Uzzi, Uzziel, Jerimoth, and Iri, five, heads of ancestral houses, mighty warriors; and their enrollment by genealogies was twenty-two thousand thirty-four. [8] The sons of Becher: Zemirah, Joash, Eliezer, Elioenai, Omri, Jeremoth, Abijah, Anathoth, and Alemeth. All these were the sons of Becher; [9] and their enrollment by genealogies, according to their generations, as heads of their ancestral houses, mighty warriors, was twenty thousand two hundred. [10] The sons of Jediael: Bilhan. And the sons of Bilhan: Jeush, Benjamin, Ehud, Chenaanah, Zethan, Tarshish, and Ahishahar. [11] All these were the sons of Jediael according to the heads of their ancestral houses, mighty warriors, seventeen thousand two hundred, ready for service in war. [12] And Shuppim and Huppim were the sons of Ir, Hushim the son[j] of Aher.

13 The descendants of Naphtali: Jahziel, Guni, Jezer, and Shallum, the descendants of Bilhah.

14 The sons of Manasseh: Asriel, whom his Aramean concubine bore; she bore Machir the father of Gilead. [15] And Machir took a wife for Huppim and for Shuppim. The name of his sister was Maacah. And the name of the second was Zelophehad; and Zelophehad had daughters. [16] Maacah the wife of Machir bore a son, and she named him Peresh; the name of his brother was Sheresh; and his sons were Ulam and Rekem. [17] The son[j] of Ulam: Bedan. These were the sons of Gilead son of Machir, son of Manasseh. [18] And his sister Hammolecheth bore Ishhod, Abiezer, and Mahlah. [19] The sons of Shemida were Ahian, Shechem, Likhi, and Aniam.

20 The sons of Ephraim: Shuthelah, and Bered his son, Tahath his son, Eleadah his son, Tahath his son, [21] Zabad his son, Shuthelah his son, and Ezer and Elead. Now the people of Gath, who were born in the land, killed them, because they came down to raid their cattle. [22] And their father Ephraim mourned many days, and his brothers came to comfort him. [23] Ephraim[k] went in to his wife, and she

[77] To the rest of the sons of Merari they gave from the tribe of Zebulun: Rimmon and Tabor, each with its common land. [78] On the east of Jordan, opposite Jericho, from the tribe of Reuben: Bezer-in-the-wilderness, Jahaz, [79] Kedemoth, and Mephaath, each with its common land. [80] From the tribe of Gad: Ramoth in Gilead, Mahanaim, [81] Heshbon, and Jazer, each with its common land.

7 The sons of Issachar: Tola, Pua, Jashub, and Shimron, four. [2] The sons of Tola: Uzzi, Rephaiah, Jeriel, Jahmai, Jibsam, and Samuel, all able men and heads of families by paternal descent from Tola according to their tribal lists; their number in David's time was twenty-two thousand six hundred. [3] The son of Uzzi: Izrahiah, and the sons of Izrahiah — Michael, Obadiah, Joel, and Isshiah — making a total of five, all of them chiefs. [4] In addition there were bands of fighting men recorded by families according to their tribal lists to the number of thirty-six thousand, for they had many wives and children. [5] Their fellow-tribesmen in all the clans of Issachar were able men, eighty-seven thousand; every one of them was registered.

6 The sons of Benjamin: Bela, Becher, and Jediael, three. [7] The sons of Bela: Ezbon, Uzzi, Uzziel, Jerimoth, and Iri, five. They were heads of their families and able men; the number registered was twenty-two thousand and thirty-four. [8] The sons of Becher: Zemira, Joash, Eliezer, Elioenai, Omri, Jeremoth, Abijah, Anathoth, and Alemeth; all these were sons of Becher [9] according to their tribal lists, heads of their families and able men; and the number registered was twenty thousand two hundred. [10] The son of Jediael: Bilhan. The sons of Bilhan: Jeush, Benjamin, Ehud, Kenaanah, Zethan, Tarshish, and Ahishahar. [11] All these were descendants of Jediael, heads of families and able men. The number was seventeen thousand two hundred men, fit for active service in war.

[12] The sons of Dan: Hushim and the sons of Aher.

[13] The sons of Naphtali: Jahziel, Guni, Jezer, Shallum. These were sons of Bilhah.

[14] The sons of Manasseh, born of his concubine, an Aramaean: Machir father of Gilead. [15] Machir married a woman whose name was Maacah. The second son was named Zelophehad, and Zelophehad had daughters. [16] Maacah wife of Machir had a son whom she named Peresh. His brother's name was Sheresh, and his sons were Ulam and Rakem. [17] The son of Ulam: Bedan. These were the sons of Gilead son of Machir, son of Manasseh. [18] His sister Hammoleketh was the mother of Ishhod, Abiezer, and Mahlah. [19] The sons of Shemida: Ahian, Shechem, Likhi, and Aniam.

[20] The sons of Ephraim: Shuthelah, his son Bered, his son Tahath, his son Eladah, his son Tahath, [21] his son Zabad, his son Shuthelah. Ephraim's other sons Ezer and Elead were killed by the native Gittites when they came down to lift their cattle. [22] Their father Ephraim mourned for them a long while, and his kinsmen came to comfort him. [23] Then

6:77 **Rimmon:** *so Gk; Heb.* his Rimmon.   7:1,6,13,30 and 8:1–5 *Cp. Gen. 46:13,17,21–24.*   7:1 **The sons of:** *so Syriac; Heb.* To the sons of.   7:6 **The sons of:** *so some MSS; others omit.*   7:11 **heads of:** *prob. rdg; Heb.* to the heads of.
7:12 **The sons of Dan:** *prob. rdg, cp. Gen. 46:23; Heb.* And Shuppim and Huppim, the sons of Ir. **Aher:** *or* another.
7:14–19 *Cp. Num. 26:29–33.*   7:14 **Manasseh:** *prob. rdg; Heb. adds* Asriel.   7:15 **whose name was:** *prob. rdg; Heb.* to Huppim and Shuppim, and his sister's name was. **The second . . . daughters:** *possibly to be transposed to follow* Gilead *at the end of verse 14.*

[i] Syr Compare Vg: Heb *And to the sons*   [j] Heb *sons*   [k] Heb *He*

62 The rest of the Merarites received from the tribe of Zebulun: Jokneam with its pasture lands, Kartah with its pasture lands, Rimmon with its pasture lands, and Tabor with its pasture lands. 63 Across the Jordan at Jericho [that is, east of the Jordan] they received from the tribe of Reuben: Bezer in the desert with its pasture lands, Jahzah with its pasture lands, 64 Kedemoth with its pasture lands, and Mephaath with its pasture lands. 65 From the tribe of Gad: Ramoth in Gilead with its pasture lands, Mahanaim with its pasture lands, 66 Heshbon with its pasture lands, and Jazer with its pasture lands.

7 The sons of Issachar were Tola, Puah, Jashub, and Shimron: four. 2 The sons of Tola were Uzzi, Rephaiah, Jeriel, Jahmai, Ibsam, and Shemuel, warrior heads of the ancestral houses of Tola. Their kindred numbered twenty-two thousand six hundred in the time of David. 3 The sons of Uzzi: Izrahiah. The sons of Izarahiah were Michael, Obadiah, Joel, and Isshiah. All five of these were chiefs. 4 Their kindred, by ancestral houses, numbered thirty-six thousand men in organized military troops, since they had more wives and sons 5 than their fellow tribesmen. In all the clans of Issachar there was a total of eighty-seven thousand warriors in their family records. 6 The sons of Benjamin were Bela, Becher, and Jediael — three. 7 The sons of Bela were Ezbon, Uzzi, Uzziel, Jerimoth, and Iri — five. They were heads of their ancestral houses and warriors. Their family records listed twenty-two thousand and thirty-four. 8 The sons of Becher were Zemirah, Joash, Eliezer, Elioenai, Omri, Jeremoth, Abijah, Anathoth, and Alemeth — all these were sons of Becher. 9 Their family records listed twenty thousand two hundred of their kindred who were heads of their ancestral houses and warriors. 10 The sons of Jediael: Bilhan. The sons of Bilhan were Jeush, Benjamin, Ehud, Chenaanah, Zethan, Tarshish, and Ahishahar. 11 All these were descendants of Jediael, heads of ancestral houses and warriors. They numbered seventeen thousand two hundred men fit for military service . . . Shupham and Hupham. 12 The sons of Dan: Hushim. 13 The sons of Naphtali were Jahziel, Guni, Jezer, and Shallum. These were descendants of Bilhah. 14 The sons of Manasseh, whom his Aramean concubine bore: she bore Machir, the father of Gilead. 15 Machir took a wife whose name was Maacah; his sister's name was Molecheth. Manasseh's second son was named Zelophehad, but to Zelophehad only daughters were born. 16 Maacah, Machir's wife, bore a son whom she named Peresh. He had a brother named Sheresh, whose sons were Ulam and Rakem. 17 The sons of Ulam: Bedan. These were the descendants of Gilead, the son of Machir, the son of Manasseh. 18 His sister Molecheth bore Ishhod, Abiezer, and Mahlah. 19 The sons of Shemida were Ahian, Shechem, Likhi, and Aniam. 20 The sons of Ephraim: Shuthelah, whose son was Bered, whose son was Tahath, whose son was Eleadah, whose son was Tahath, 21 whose son was Zabad. Ephraim's son Shuthelah, and Ezer and Elead, who were born in the land, were slain by the inhabitants of Gath because they had gone down to take away their livestock. 22 Their father Ephraim mourned a long time, but after his kinsmen had come and comforted him, 23 he visited his wife, who conceived and

62 To the remainder of the sons of Merari: from the tribe of Zebulun, Rimmon with its pasture lands and Tabor with its pasture lands; 63 in Transjordan, near Jericho, east of the Jordan, from the tribe of Reuben: Bezer in the desert with its pasture lands, Jahzah with its pasture lands, 64 Kedemoth with its pasture lands and Mephaath with its pasture lands; 65 from the tribe of Gad: Ramoth in Gilead with its pasture lands, Mahanaim with its pasture lands, 66 Heshbon with its pasture lands and Jazer with its pasture lands.

7 For the sons of Issachar: Tola, Puah, Jashub, Shimron: four. 2 Sons of Tola: Uzzi, Rephaiah, Jeriel, Jahmai, Ibsam, Shemuel, heads of their families of Tola. In the time of David, these numbered twenty-two thousand six hundred stout fighting men, grouped according to their kinship. 3 Sons of Uzzi: Izrahiah. Sons of Izrahiah: Michael, Obadiah, Joel, Isshiah. In all five chiefs, 4 responsible for fighting companies amounting to thirty-six thousand troops, according to relationship and family, for they had many women and children. 5 They had kinsmen belonging to all the clans of Issachar, eighty-seven thousand stout fighting men, all belonging to one related group.

6 Sons of Benjamin: Bela, Becher, Jediael: three. 7 Sons of Bela: Ezbon, Uzzi, Uzziel, Jerimoth and Iri: five, chiefs of families and warriors. Their official genealogy included twenty-two thousand and thirty-four members.

8 Sons of Becher: Zemirah, Joash, Eliezar, Elioenai, Omri, Jeremoth, Abijah, Anathoth, Alemeth, all these were the sons of Becher. 9 The official genealogy of the descendants of the chiefs of their families included twenty thousand two hundred warriors.

10 Sons of Jediael: Bilhan. Sons of Bilhan: Jeush, Benjamin, Ehud, Chenaanah, Zethan, Tarshish, Ahishahar. 11 All these sons of Jediael, became heads of families, stout fighting men, numbering seventeen thousand two hundred men fit for active service.

12 Shuppim and Huppim. Son of Ir: Hushim; his son: Aher.

13 Sons of Naphtali: Jahziel, Guni, Jezer, Shallum.

These were the sons of Bilhah.

14 Sons of Manasseh: Asriel, born of his Aramaean concubine. She gave birth to Machir, father of Gilead. 15 Machir took a wife for Huppim and Shuppim. His sister's name was Maacah.

The name of the second son was Zelophehad. Zelophehad had daughters.

16 Maacah the wife of Machir gave birth to a son whom she called Peresh. His brother was called Sheresh and his sons Ulam and Rakem.

17 Sons of Ulam: Bedan. These were the sons of Gilead son of Machir, son of Manasseh.

18 His sister Hammoleketh gave birth to Ishod, Abiezer and Mahlah.

19 Shemida had sons: Ahian, Shechem, Likhi and Aniam.

20 Sons of Ephraim: Shuthelah, Bered his son, Tahath his son, Eleadah his son, Tahath his son, 21 Zabad his son, Shuthelah his son and Ezer and Elead whom the men of Gath, natives of the country, killed when they came down to raid their cattle. 22 Their father Ephraim mourned for a long time and his brothers came to comfort him. 23 He had

conceived and bore a son; and he named him Beriah, because disaster[l] had befallen his house. 24 His daughter was Sheerah, who built both Lower and Upper Beth-horon, and Uzzen-sheerah. 25 Rephah was his son, Resheph his son, Telah his son, Tahan his son, 26 Ladan his son, Ammihud his son, Elishama his son, 27 Nun[m] his son, Joshua his son. 28 Their possessions and settlements were Bethel and its towns, and eastward Naaran, and westward Gezer and its towns, Shechem and its towns, as far as Ayyah and its towns; 29 also along the borders of the Manassites, Beth-shean and its towns, Taanach and its towns, Megiddo and its towns, Dor and its towns. In these lived the sons of Joseph son of Israel.

30 The sons of Asher: Imnah, Ishvah, Ishvi, Beriah, and their sister Serah. 31 The sons of Beriah: Heber and Malchiel, who was the father of Birzaith. 32 Heber became the father of Japhlet, Shomer, Hotham, and their sister Shua. 33 The sons of Japhlet: Pasach, Bimhal, and Ashvath. These are the sons of Japhlet. 34 The sons of Shemer: Ahi, Rohgah, Hubbah, and Aram. 35 The sons of Helem[n] his brother: Zophah, Imna, Shelesh, and Amal. 36 The sons of Zophah: Suah, Harnepher, Shual, Beri, Imrah, 37 Bezer, Hod, Shamma, Shilshah, Ithran, and Beera. 38 The sons of Jether: Jephunneh, Pispa, and Ara. 39 The sons of Ulla: Arah, Hanniel, and Rizia. 40 All of these were men of Asher, heads of ancestral houses, select mighty warriors, chief of the princes. Their number enrolled by genealogies, for service in war, was twenty-six thousand men.

8 Benjamin became the father of Bela his firstborn, Ashbel the second, Aharah the third, 2 Nohah the fourth, and Rapha the fifth. 3 And Bela had sons: Addar, Gera, Abihud,[o] 4 Abishua, Naaman, Ahoah, 5 Gera, Shephuphan, and Huram. 6 These are the sons of Ehud (they were heads of ancestral houses of the inhabitants of Geba, and they were carried into exile to Manahath): 7 Naaman,[p] Ahijah, and Gera, that is, Heglam,[q] who became the father of Uzza and Ahihud. 8 And Shaharaim had sons in the country of Moab after he had sent away his wives Hushim and Baara. 9 He had sons by his wife Hodesh: Jobab, Zibia, Mesha, Malcam, 10 Jeuz, Sachia, and Mirmah. These were his sons, heads of ancestral houses. 11 He also had sons by Hushim: Abitub and Elpaal. 12 The sons of Elpaal: Eber, Misham, and Shemed, who built Ono and Lod with its towns, 13 and Beriah and Shema (they were heads of ancestral houses of the inhabitants of Aijalon, who put to flight the inhabitants of Gath); 14 and Ahio, Shashak, and Jeremoth. 15 Zebadiah, Arad, Eder, 16 Michael, Ishpah, and Joha were sons of Beriah. 17 Zebadiah, Meshullam, Hizki, Heber, 18 Ishmerai, Izliah, and Jobab were the sons of Elpaal. 19 Jakim, Zichri, Zabdi, 20 Elienai, Zillethai, Eliel, 21 Adaiah, Beraiah, and Shimrath were the sons of Shimei. 22 Ishpan, Eber, Eliel, 23 Abdon, Zichri, Hanan, 24 Hananiah, Elam, Anthothijah, 25 Iphdeiah, and Penuel were the sons of Shashak. 26 Shamsherai, Shehariah, Athaliah, 27 Jaareshiah, Elijah, and Zichri were the sons of Jeroham. 28 These were the heads of ancestral houses, according to their generations, chiefs. These lived in Jerusalem.

29 Jeiel[r] the father of Gibeon lived in Gibeon, and the name of his wife was Maacah. 30 His firstborn son: Abdon,

he had intercourse with his wife; she conceived and had a son whom he named Beriah (because disaster had come on his family). 24 He had a daughter named Sherah; she built Lower and Upper Beth-horon and Uzzen-sherah. 25 He also had a son named Rephah; his son was Resheph, his son Telah, his son Tahan, 26 his son Laadan, his son Ammihud, his son Elishama, 27 his son Nun, his son Joshua. 28 Their lands and settlements were: Bethel and its dependent villages, to the east Naaran, to the west Gezer, Shechem, and Gaza, with their villages. 29 In the possession of Manasseh were Beth-shean, Taanach, Megiddo, and Dor, with their villages. In all of these lived the descendants of Joseph the son of Israel.

30 The sons of Asher: Imnah, Ishvah, Ishvi, and Beriah, together with their sister Serah. 31 The sons of Beriah: Heber and Malchiel father of Birzavith. 32 Heber was the father of Japhlet, Shomer, Hotham, and their sister Shua. 33 The sons of Japhlet: Pasach, Bimhal, and Ashvath. These were the sons of Japhlet. 34 The sons of Shomer: Ahi, Rohgah, Jehubbah, and Aram. 35 The sons of his brother Hotham: Zophah, Imna, Shelesh, and Amal. 36 The sons of Zophah: Suah, Harnepher, Shual, Beri, Imrah, 37 Bezer, Hod, Shamma, Shilshah, Ithran, and Beera. 38 The sons of Jether: Jephunneh, Pispah, and Ara. 39 The sons of Ulla: Arah, Hanniel, and Rezia. 40 All these were descendants of Asher, heads of families, picked men of ability, leading princes. They were enrolled among the fighting troops; the total number was twenty-six thousand men.

8 The sons of Benjamin were: the eldest Bela, the second Ashbel, the third Aharah, 2 the fourth Nohah, and the fifth Rapha. 3 The sons of Bela: Addar, Gera father of Ehud, 4 Abishua, Naaman, Ahoah, 5 Gera, Shephuphan, and Huram. 6 These were the sons of Ehud, heads of families living in Geba, who were removed to Manahath: 7 Naaman, Ahiah, and Gera—it was who removed them; he was the father of Uzza and Ahihud. 8 Shaharaim had sons born to him in Moabite country, after putting away his wives Mahasham and Baara. 9 By his wife Hodesh he had Jobab, Zibia, Mesha, Malcham, 10 Jeuz, Sachiah, and Mirmah. These were his sons, heads of families. 11 By Mahasham he had had Abitub and Elpaal. 12 The sons of Elpaal: Eber, Misham, Shamed who built Ono and Lod with its villages, 13 also Beriah and Shema who were heads of families living in Aijalon, having cleared out the inhabitants of Gath. 14 Ahio, Shashak, Jeremoth, 15 Zebadiah, Arad, Eder, 16 Michael, Ishpah, and Joha were sons of Beriah; 17 Zebadiah, Meshullam, Hizki, Heber, 18 Ishmerai, Jezliah, and Jobab were sons of Elpaal; 19 Jakim, Zichri, Zabdi, 20 Elienai, Zillethai, Eliel, 21 Adaiah, Beraiah, and Shimrath were sons of Shimei; 22 Ishpan, Heber, Eliel, 23 Abdon, Zichri, Hanan, 24 Hananiah, Elam, Antothiah, 25 Iphedeiah, and Penuel were sons of Shashak; 26 Shamsherai, Shehariah, Athaliah, 27 Jaareshiah, Elijah, and Zichri were sons of Jeroham. 28 These were enrolled in the tribal lists as heads of families, chiefs living in Jerusalem.

29 Jehiel founder of Gibeon lived at Gibeon; his wife's name was Maacah. 30 His eldest son was Abdon, followed

7:23 **disaster:** *Heb.* beraah.   7:25 **his son was:** *so Gk (Luc.)*; *Heb. omits.*   7:28 **Gaza:** *so some MSS; others* Aiah.   7:35 **Hotham:** *prob. rdg., cp. verse 32; Heb.* Helem.   8:3 **father of Ehud:** *prob. rdg., cp. Judg. 3:15; Heb.* Abihud.   8:8 **Mahasham:** *prob. rdg., cp. Gk (Luc.) in verse 11; Heb.* Hushim.   8:11 **Mahasham:** *prob. rdg., cp. Gk (Luc.); Heb.* Hushim.   8:29–38 *Cp. 9:35–44.*   8:29 **Jehiel:** *so Gk (Luc.), cp. 9:35; Heb. omits.*

[l] Heb beraah   [m] Here spelled *Non;* see Ex 33.11   [n] Or *Hotham;* see 7.32   [o] Or *father of Ehud;* see 8.6   [p] Heb *and Naaman*   [q] Or *he carried them into exile*   [r] Compare 9.35: Heb lacks *Jeiel*

bore a son whom he named Beriah, since evil had befallen his house. 24 He had a daughter, Sheerah, who built lower and upper Beth-horon and Uzzen-sheerah. 25 Zabad's son was Rephah, whose son was Resheph, whose son was Telah, whose son was Tahan, 26 whose son was Ladan, whose son was Ammihud, whose son was Elishama, 27 whose son was Nun, whose son was Joshua.

28 Their property and their dwellings were in Bethel and its towns, Naaran to the east, Gezer and its towns to the west, and also Shechem and its towns as far as Ayyah and its towns. 29 Manasseh, however, had possession of Beth-shean and its towns, Taanach and its towns, Megiddo and its towns, and Dor and its towns. In these dwelt the descendants of Joseph, the son of Israel.

30 The sons of Asher were Imnah, Iishvah, Ishvi, and Beriah; their sister was Serah. 31 Beriah's sons were Heber and Malchiel, who was the father of Birzaith. 32 Heber became the father of Japhlet, Shomer, Hotham, and their sister Shua. 33 The sons of Japhlet were Pasach, Bimhal, and Ashvath; these were the sons of Japhlet. 34 The sons of Shomer were Ahi, Rohgah, Jehubbah, and Aram. 35 The sons of his brother Hotham were Zophah, Imna, Shelesh, and Amal. 36 The sons of Zophah were Suah, Harnepher, Shual, Beri, Imrah, 37 Bezer, Hod, Shamma, Shilshah, Ithran, and Beera. 38 The sons of Jether were Jephunneh, Pispa, and Ara. 39 The sons of Ulla were Arah, Hanniel, and Rizia. 40 All these were descendants of Asher, heads of ancestral houses, distinguished men, warriors, and chiefs among the princes. Their family records numbered twenty-six thousand men fit for military service.

8 Benjamin became the father of Bela, his first-born, Ashbel, the second son, Aharah, the third, 2 Nohah, the fourth, and Rapha, the fifth. 3 The sons of Bela were Addar and Gera, the father of Ehud. 4 The sons of Ehud were Abishua, Naaman, Ahoah, 5 Gera, Shephuphan, and Huram. 6 These were the sons of Ehud, family heads over those who dwelt in Geba and were deported to Manahath. 7 Also Naaman, Ahijah, and Gera. The last, who led them into exile, became the father of Uzza and Ahihud. 8 Shaharaim became a father on the Moabite plateau after he had put away his wives Hushim and Baara. 9 By his wife Hodesh he became the father of Jobab, Zibia, Mesha, Malcam, 10 Jeuz, Sachia, and Mirmah. These were his sons, family heads. 11 By Hushim he became the father of Abitub and Elpaal. 12 The sons of Elpaal were Eber, Misham, Shemed, who built Ono and Lod with its nearby towns, 13 Beriah, and Shema. They were family heads of those who dwelt in Aijalon, and they put the inhabitants of Gath to flight. 14 Their brethren were Elpaal, Shashak, and Jeremoth. 15 Zebadiah, Arad, Eder, 16 Michael, Ishpah, and Joha were the sons of Beriah. 17 Zebadiah, Meshullam, Hizki, Heber, 18 Ishmerai, Izliah, and Jobab were the sons of Elpaal. 19 Jakim, Zichri, Zabdi, 20 Elienai, Zillethai, Eliel, 21 Adaiah, Beraiah, and Shimrath were the sons of Shimei. 22 Ishpan, Eber, Eliel, 23 Abdon, Zichri, Hanan, 24 Hananiah, Elam, Anthothijah, 25 Iphdeiah, and Penuel were the sons of Shashak. 26 Shamsherai, Shehariah, Athaliah, 27 Jaareshiah, Elijah, and Zichri were the sons of Jeroham. 28 These were family heads over their kindred, chiefs who dwelt in Jerusalem.

29 In Gibeon dwelt Jeiel, the founder of Gibeon, whose wife's name was Maacah; 30 also his first-born son, Abdon,

intercourse with his wife, who conceived and gave birth to a son whom he called Beriah because his house was in misfortune. 24 He had a daughter, Sheerah, who built Upper and Lower Beth-Horon and Uzzen-Sheerah.

25 Rephah was his son, Shuthelah his son, Tahan his son, 26 Ladan his son, Ammihud his son, Elishama his son, 27 Nun his son, Joshua his son.

28 They had lands and settlements in Bethel and its dependencies from Naaran on the east to Gezer and its dependencies on the west, as well as Shechem and its dependencies as far as Ayyah and its dependencies. 29 Beth-Shean with its dependencies, Taanach and its dependencies, Megiddo and its dependencies and Dor with its dependencies were in the hands of the sons of Manasseh. There lived the sons of Joseph son of Israel.

30 Sons of Asher: Imnah, Ishvah, Ishvi, Beriah; their sister Serah. 31 Sons of Beriah: Heber and Malchiel. He fathered Birzaith. 32 Heber fathered Japhlet, Shomer, Hotham and their sister Shua. 33 Sons of Japhlet: Pasach, Bimhal and Ashvath. These were the sons of Japhlet. 34 Sons of Shomer his brother: Rohgah, Hubbah and Aram. 35 Sons of Helem his brother: Zophah, Imna, Shelesh and Amal. 36 Sons of Zophah: Suah, Harnepher, Shual, Beri and Imrah. 37 Bezer, Hod, Shamma, Shilshah, Ithran and Beerah. 38 Sons of Ithran: Jephunneh, Pispa, Ara. 39 Sons of Ulla: Arah, Hanniel, Rizia.

40 All these were the sons of Asher, heads of families, picked men, warriors and senior princes. They were registered in fighting companies to the number of twenty-six thousand men.

8 Benjamin was father of Bela, his first-born, Ashbel second, Ahiram third, 2 Nohah fourth, Rapha fifth. 3 Bela had sons: Addar, Gera father of Ehud, 4 Abishua, Naaman, Ahoah, 5 Gera, Shephuphan and Huram. 6 These are the sons of Ehud. They were heads of families of the inhabitants of Geba and led them into exile at Manahath: 7 Naaman, Ahijah and Gera. It was he who led them into exile; he became the father of Uzza and Ahihud. 8 Shaharaim had children in the Plains of Moab after he had dismissed his wives, Hushim and Baara. 9 By his new wife he had sons: Jobab, Zibia, Mesha, Malcam, 10 Jeuz, Sachia, Mirmah. These were his sons, heads of families. 11 By Hushim he had sons: Abitub and Elpaal. 12 The sons of Elpaal were Eber, Misham and Shemed, who built Ono and Lud and its dependencies.

13 Beriah and Shema were the chiefs of the families who lived at Aijalon; they routed the inhabitants of Gath. 14 His brother was Shashak. Jeremoth, 15 Zebadiah, Arad, Eder, 16 Michael, Ishpah, Joha were the sons of Beriah. 17 Zebadiah, Meshullam, Hizki, Haber, 18 Ishmerai, Izliah, Jobab were the sons of Elpaal. 19 Jakim, Zichri, Zabdi, 20 Elienai, Zillethai, Eliel, 21 Adaiah, Beraiah, Shimrath were the sons of Shimei. 22 Ishpan, Eber, Eliel, 23 Abdon, Zichri, Hanan, 24 Hananiah, Elam, Anthothijah, 25 Iphdeiah, Penuel were the sons of Shashak. 26 Shamsherai, Shehariah, Athaliah, 27 Jaareshaiah, Elijah, Zichri were the sons of Jeroham. 28 These were chiefs of families according to their relationship. They lived in Jerusalem.

29 At Gibeon lived Jeiel the father of Gibeon, whose wife was called Maacah. 30 His first-born son was Abdon, then

NEW REVISED STANDARD VERSION	REVISED ENGLISH BIBLE

then Zur, Kish, Baal,[s] Nadab, 31 Gedor, Ahio, Zecher, 32 and Mikloth, who became the father of Shimeah. Now these also lived opposite their kindred in Jerusalem, with their kindred. 33 Ner became the father of Kish, Kish of Saul,[t] Saul[t] of Jonathan, Malchishua, Abinadab, and Esh-baal; 34 and the son of Jonathan was Merib-baal; and Merib-baal became the father of Micah. 35 The sons of Micah: Pithon, Melech, Tarea, and Ahaz. 36 Ahaz became the father of Jehoaddah; and Jehoaddah became the father of Alemeth, Azmaveth, and Zimri; Zimri became the father of Moza. 37 Moza became the father of Binea; Raphah was his son, Eleasah his son, Azel his son. 38 Azel had six sons, and these are their names: Azrikam, Bocheru, Ishmael, Sheariah, Obadiah, and Hanan; all these were the sons of Azel. 39 The sons of his brother Eshek: Ulam his firstborn, Jeush the second, and Eliphelet the third. 40 The sons of Ulam were mighty warriors, archers, having many children and grandchildren, one hundred fifty. All these were Benjaminites.

9 So all Israel was enrolled by genealogies; and these are written in the Book of the Kings of Israel. And Judah was taken into exile in Babylon because of their unfaithfulness. 2 Now the first to live again in their possessions in their towns were Israelites, priests, Levites, and temple servants.

3 And some of the people of Judah, Benjamin, Ephraim, and Manasseh lived in Jerusalem: 4 Uthai son of Ammihud, son of Omri, son of Imri, son of Bani, from the sons of Perez son of Judah. 5 And of the Shilonites: Asaiah the firstborn, and his sons. 6 Of the sons of Zerah: Jeuel and their kin, six hundred ninety. 7 Of the Benjaminites: Sallu son of Meshullam, son of Hodaviah, son of Hassenuah, 8 Ibneiah son of Jeroham, Elah son of Uzzi, son of Michri, and Meshullam son of Shephatiah, son of Reuel, son of Ibnijah; 9 and their kindred according to their generations, nine hundred fifty-six. All these were heads of families according to their ancestral houses.

10 Of the priests: Jedaiah, Jehoiarib, Jachin, 11 and Azariah son of Hilkiah, son of Meshullam, son of Zadok, son of Meraioth, son of Ahitub, the chief officer of the house of God; 12 and Adaiah son of Jeroham, son of Pashhur, son of Malchijah, and Maasai son of Adiel, son of Jahzerah, son of Meshullam, son of Meshillemith, son of Immer; 13 besides their kindred, heads of their ancestral houses, one thousand seven hundred sixty, qualified for the work of the service of the house of God.

14 Of the Levites: Shemaiah son of Hasshub, son of Azrikam, son of Hashabiah, of the sons of Merari; 15 and Bakbakkar, Heresh, Galal, and Mattaniah son of Mica, son of Zichri, son of Asaph; 16 and Obadiah son of Shemaiah, son of Galal, son of Jeduthun, and Berechiah son of Asa, son of Elkanah, who lived in the villages of the Netophathites.

17 The gatekeepers were: Shallum, Akkub, Talmon, Ahiman; and their kindred Shallum was the chief, 18 stationed previously in the king's gate on the east side. These were the gatekeepers of the camp of the Levites. 19 Shallum son of Kore, son of Ebiasaph, son of Korah, and his kindred of his ancestral house, the Korahites, were in charge of the work of the service, guardians of the thresholds of the tent, as their ancestors had been in charge of the camp of the LORD, guardians of the entrance. 20 And Phinehas son of Eleazar was chief over them in former times; the LORD was with him. 21 Zechariah son of Meshelemiah was gatekeeper at the entrance of the tent of meeting. 22 All these, who were

by Zur, Kish, Baal, Nadab, 31 Gedor, Ahio, Zecher, and Mikloth. 32 Mikloth was the father of Shimeah; they lived alongside their kinsmen in Jerusalem.

33 Ner was the father of Kish, Kish father of Saul, Saul father of Jonathan, Malchishua, Abinadab, and Eshbaal. 34 Jonathan's son was Meribbaal, who was the father of Micah. 35 The sons of Micah: Pithon, Melech, Tarea, and Ahaz. 36 Ahaz was the father of Jehoaddah, Jehoaddah father of Alemeth, Azmoth, and Zimri. Zimri was the father of Moza, 37 and Moza father of Binea; his son was Raphah, his son Elasah, and his son Azel. 38 Azel had six sons, whose names were Azrikam, Bocheru, Ishmael, Sheariah, Obadiah, and Hanan. All these were sons of Azel. 39 The sons of his brother Eshek: the eldest Ulam, the second Jeush, the third Eliphelet. 40 The sons of Ulam were able men, archers, and they had many sons and grandsons, a hundred and fifty. All these were descendants of Benjamin.

9 ALL Israel were registered and recorded in the book of the kings of Israel; but Judah for their sins were carried away to exile in Babylon. 2 The first to occupy their ancestral land in their towns were lay Israelites, priests, Levites, and temple servitors. 3 Jerusalem was occupied partly by Judahites, partly by Benjamites, and partly by men of Ephraim and Manasseh. 4 Judahites: Uthai son of Ammihud, son of Omri, son of Imri, son of Bani, a descendant of Perez son of Judah. 5 Shelanites: Asaiah the eldest and his sons. 6 The sons of Zerah: Jeuel and six hundred and ninety of their kinsmen. 7 Benjamites: Sallu son of Meshullam, son of Hodaviah, son of Hassenuah, 8 Ibneiah son of Jeroham, Elah son of Uzzi, son of Micri, Meshullam son of Shephatiah, son of Reuel, son of Ibnijah, 9 and their recorded kinsmen numbering nine hundred and fifty-six, all heads of families.

10 Priests: Jedaiah, Jehoiarib, Jachin, 11 Azariah son of Hilkiah, son of Meshullam, son of Zadok, son of Meraioth, son of Ahitub, the official in charge of the house of God, 12 Adaiah son of Jeroham, son of Pashhur, son of Malchiah, Maasai son of Adiel, son of Jahzerah, son of Meshullam, son of Meshillemith, son of Immer, 13 and their colleagues, heads of families numbering one thousand seven hundred and sixty, men of substance with responsibility for the work connected with the service of the house of God.

14 Levites: Shemaiah son of Hasshub, son of Azrikam, son of Hashabiah, a descendant of Merari, 15 Bakbakkar, Heresh, Galal, Mattaniah son of Mica, son of Zichri, son of Asaph, 16 Obadiah son of Shemaiah, son of Galal, son of Jeduthun, and Berechiah son of Asa, son of Elkanah, who lived in the hamlets of the Netophathites.

17 The door-keepers were Shallum, Akkub, Talmon, and Ahiman; their brother Shallum was the chief. 18 Until then they had all been door-keepers in the quarters of the Levites at the King's Gate, on the east. 19 Shallum son of Kore, son of Ebiasaph, son of Korah, and his kinsmen of the Korahite family were responsible for service as guards of the thresholds of the Tabernacle; their ancestors had performed the duty of guarding the entrances to the camp of the LORD. 20 Phinehas son of Eleazar had been their overseer in the past — the LORD was with him. 21 Zechariah son of Meshelemiah was the door-keeper of the Tent of Meeting.

8:31 and Mikloth: so Gk, cp. 9:37; Heb. omits.   8:32 in Jerusalem: so Syriac; Heb. adds with their kinsmen.   9:2–22 Cp. Neh. 11:3–22.   9:2 temple servitors: Heb. Nethinim.   9:4 Judahites: prob. rdg; Heb. omits.   9:19 Tabernacle: lit. Tent.

[s] Gk Ms adds Ner; Compare 8.33 and 9.36   [t] Or Shaul

858

and Zur, Kish, Baal, Ner, Nadab, 31 Gedor, Ahio, Zecher, and Mikloth. 32 Mikloth became the father of Shimeah. These, too, dwelt with their relatives in Jerusalem, opposite their fellow tribesmen. 33 Ner became the father of Kish, and Kish became the father of Saul. Saul became the father of Jonathan, Malchishua, Abinadab, and Eshbaal. 34 The son of Jonathan was Meribbaal, and Meribbaal became the father of Micah. 35 The sons of Micah were Pithon, Melech, Tarea, and Ahaz. 36 Ahaz became the father of Jehoaddah, and Jehoaddah became the father of Alemeth, Azmaveth, and Zimri. Zimri became the father of Moza. 37 Moza became the father of Binea, whose son was Raphah, whose son was Eleasah, whose son was Azel. 38 Azel had six sons, whose names were Azrikam, his first-born, Ishmael, Sheariah, Azariah, Obadiah, and Hanan; all these were the sons of Azel. 39 The sons of Eshek, his brother, were Ulam, his first-born, Jeush, the second son, and Eliphelet, the third. 40 The sons of Ulam were combat archers, and many were their sons and grandsons: one hundred and fifty. All these were the descendants of Benjamin.

9 Thus all Israel was inscribed in its family records which are recorded in the book of the kings of Israel. Now Judah had been carried in captivity to Babylon because of its rebellion. 2 The first to settle again in their cities and dwell there were certain lay Israelites, the priests, the Levites, and the temple slaves.

3 In Jerusalem lived Judahites and Benjaminites; also Ephraimites and Manassehites. 4 Among the Judahites was Uthai, son of Ammihud, son of Omri, son of Imri, son of Bani, one of the descendants of Perez, son of Judah. 5 Among the Shelanites were Asaiah, the first-born, and his sons. 6 Among the Zerahites were Jeuel and six hundred and ninety of their brethren. 7 Among the Benjaminites were Sallu, son of Meshullam, son of Hodaviah, son of Hassenuah; 8 Ibneiah, son of Jeroham; Elah, son of Uzzi, son of Michri; Meshullam, son of Shephatiah, son of Reuel, son of Ibnijah. 9 Their kindred of various families were nine hundred and fifty-six. All those named were heads of their ancestral houses.

10 Among the priests were Jedaiah; Jehoiarib; Jachin; 11 Azariah, son of Hilkiah, son of Meshullam, son of Zadok, son of Meraioth, son of Ahitub, the ruler of the house of God; 12 Adaiah, son of Jeroham, son of Pashhur, son of Malchijah; Maasai, son of Adiel, son of Jahzerah, son of Meshullam, son of Meshillemith, son of Immer. 13 Their brethren, heads of their ancestral houses, were one thousand seven hundred and sixty, valiant for the work of the service of the house of God.

14 Among the Levites were Shemaiah, son of Hasshub, son of Azrikam, son of Hashabiah, one of the descendants of Merari; 15 Bakbakkar; Heresh; Galal; Mattaniah, son of Mica, son of Zichri, a descendant of Asaph; 16 Obadiah, son of Shemaiah, son of Galal, a descendant of Jeduthun; and Berechiah, son of Asa, son of Elkanah, whose family lived in the villages of the Netophathites.

17 The gatekeepers were Shallum, Akkub, Talmon, Ahiman, and their brethren; Shallum was the chief. 18 Previously they had stood guard at the king's gate on the east side; now they became gatekeepers for the encampments of the Levites. 19 Shallum, son of Kore, son of Ebiasaph, a descendant of Korah, and his brethren of the same ancestral house of the Korahites had as their assigned task the guarding of the threshold of the tent, just as their fathers had guarded the entrance to the encampment of the LORD. 20 Phinehas, son of Eleazar, had been their chief in times past — the LORD be with him! 21 Zechariah, son of Meshelemiah, guarded the gate of the meeting tent. 22 In all, those

Zur, Kish, Baal, Ner, Nadab, 31 Gedor, Ahio, Zecher 32 and Mikloth. Mikloth fathered Shimeah. But they, unlike their brothers, lived at Jerusalem with their brothers.

33 Ner fathered Kish, Kish fathered Saul, Saul fathered Jonathan, Malchishua, Abinadab and Eshbaal. 34 Son of Jonathan: Meribbaal. Meribbaal fathered Micah. 35 Sons of Micah: Pithon, Melech, Tarea, Ahaz. 36 Ahaz fathered Jehoaddah, Jehoaddah fathered Alemeth, Azmaveth and Zimri. Zimri fathered Moza, 37 Moza fathered Binea, Raphah his son, Eleasah his son and Azel his son. 38 Azel had six sons, whose names were these: Azrikam, his first-born, then Ishmael, Sheariah, Obadiah, Hanan. All these were sons of Azel.

39 Sons of Eshek his brother: Ulam, his first-born, Jeush second, Eliphelet third.

40 The sons of Ulam were warriors — archers. They had as many as a hundred and fifty sons and grandsons.

All these belonged to the sons of Benjamin.

9 Thus, all Israel's official genealogies had been entered in the records of the kings of Israel and Judah before they were deported to Babylon for their infidelity.

2 Now the first citizens to return to their property in their cities were the Israelites, the priests, the Levites and the temple slaves. 3 In Jerusalem, there settled Judaeans, Benjaminites, Ephraimites and Manassehites.

4 Uthai son of Ammihud, son of Omri, son of Imri, son of Bani, one of the sons of Perez son of Judah. 5 Of the descendants of Shelah: Asaiah, the first-born, and his sons. 6 Of the sons of Zerah: Jeuel. And six hundred and ninety of their kinsmen.

7 And of the sons of Benjamin: Sallu son of Meshullam, son of Hodaviah, son of Hassenuah; 8 Ibneiah son of Jeroham; Elah son of Uzzi, son of Michri; and Meshullam son of Shephatiah, son of Reuel, son of Ibnijah. 9 Their kinsmen, according to their relationship, numbered nine hundred and fifty-six. All these men were chiefs of their families.

10 Of the priests there were Jedaiah, Jehoiarib, Jachin, 11 Azariah son of Hilkiah, son of Meshullam, son of Zadok, son of Meraioth, son of Ahitub, the chief of the Temple of God; 12 Adaiah son of Jeroham, son of Pashhur, son of Malchijah; and Maasai son of Adiel, son of Jahzerah, son of Meshullam, son of Meshillemith, son of Immer. 13 Their kinsmen, heads of families, numbered one thousand seven hundred and sixty — men expert in the ministerial service of the Temple of God.

14 Of the Levites there were Shemaiah son of Hasshub, son of Azrikam, son of Hashabiah of the sons of Merari, 15 Bakbakar, Heresh, Galai, Mattaniah son of Mica, son of Zichri, son of Asaph. 16 Obadiah son of Shemaiah, son of Galal, son of Jeduthun and Berechiah son of Asa, son of Elkanah, who lived in the dependencies of the Netophathites.

17 The gatekeepers were Shallum, Akkub, Talmon, Ahiman and their kinsmen. Shallum was the chief 18 and is still gatekeeper of the King's Gate to the east. They were the gatekeepers of the camps of the sons of Levi.

19 Shallum son of Kore, son of Ebiasaph, son of Korah, and his brothers belonging to his family, the Korahites, were also in charge of the ministerial service as doorkeepers of the Tent, as their ancestors had been keepers of the entrance to the camp of Yahweh. 20 Formerly, Phinehas son of Eleazar had been in charge of them — Yahweh be with him! 21 Zechariah son of Meshelemiah was gatekeeper at the door of the Tent of Meeting. 22 All the keepers of the gate

chosen as gatekeepers at the thresholds, were two hundred twelve. They were enrolled by genealogies in their villages. David and the seer Samuel established them in their office of trust. 23 So they and their descendants were in charge of the gates of the house of the LORD, that is, the house of the tent, as guards. 24 The gatekeepers were on the four sides, east, west, north, and south; 25 and their kindred who were in their villages were obliged to come in every seven days, in turn, to be with them; 26 for the four chief gatekeepers, who were Levites, were in charge of the chambers and the treasures of the house of God. 27 And they would spend the night near the house of God; for on them lay the duty of watching, and they had charge of opening it every morning.

28 Some of them had charge of the utensils of service, for they were required to count them when they were brought in and taken out. 29 Others of them were appointed over the furniture, and over all the holy utensils, also over the choice flour, the wine, the oil, the incense, and the spices. 30 Others, of the sons of the priests, prepared the mixing of the spices, 31 and Mattithiah, one of the Levites, the firstborn of Shallum the Korahite, was in charge of making the flat cakes. 32 Also some of their kindred of the Kohathites had charge of the rows of bread, to prepare them for each sabbath.

33 Now these are the singers, the heads of ancestral houses of the Levites, living in the chambers of the temple free from other service, for they were on duty day and night. 34 These were heads of ancestral houses of the Levites, according to their generations; these leaders lived in Jerusalem.

35 In Gibeon lived the father of Gibeon, Jeiel, and the name of his wife was Maacah. 36 His firstborn son was Abdon, then Zur, Kish, Baal, Ner, Nadab, 37 Gedor, Ahio, Zechariah, and Mikloth; 38 and Mikloth became the father of Shimeam; and these also lived opposite their kindred in Jerusalem, with their kindred. 39 Ner became the father of Kish, Kish of Saul, Saul of Jonathan, Malchishua, Abinadab, and Esh-baal; 40 and the son of Jonathan was Merib-baal; and Merib-baal became the father of Micah. 41 The sons of Micah: Pithon, Melech, Tahrea, and Ahaz;*u* 42 and Ahaz became the father of Jarah, and Jarah of Alemeth, Azmaveth, and Zimri; and Zimri became the father of Moza. 43 Moza became the father of Binea; and Rephaiah was his son, Eleasah his son, Azel his son. 44 Azel had six sons, and these are their names: Azrikam, Bocheru, Ishmael, Sheariah, Obadiah, and Hanan; these were the sons of Azel.

10 Now the Philistines fought against Israel; and the men of Israel fled before the Philistines, and fell slain on Mount Gilboa. 2 The Philistines overtook Saul and his sons; and the Philistines killed Jonathan and Abinadab and Malchishua, sons of Saul. 3 The battle pressed hard on Saul; and the archers found him, and he was wounded by the archers. 4 Then Saul said to his armor-bearer, "Draw your sword, and thrust me through with it, so that these uncircumcised may not come and make sport of me." But his armor-bearer was unwilling, for he was terrified. So Saul took his own sword and fell on it. 5 When his armor-bearer saw that Saul was dead, he also fell on his sword and died. 6 Thus Saul died; he and his three sons and all his house died together. 7 When all the men of Israel who were in the valley saw that the army*v* had fled and that Saul and his sons were dead, they abandoned their towns and fled; and the Philistines came and occupied them.

8 The next day when the Philistines came to strip the dead, they found Saul and his sons fallen on Mount Gilboa.

22 Those picked to be door-keepers numbered two hundred and twelve in all, registered in their hamlets. David and Samuel the seer had installed them because they were trustworthy. 23 They and their sons had charge, by watches, of the gates of the house, the tent-dwelling of the LORD. 24 The door-keepers were to be on four sides, east, west, north, and south. 25 Their kinsmen from their hamlets had to come on duty with them for seven days at a time in turn. 26 The four principal door-keepers were chosen for their trustworthiness; they were Levites and had charge of the rooms and the stores in the house of God. 27 They always slept in the precincts of the house of God (for the watch was their duty) and they had charge of the key for opening the gates every morning.

28 Some of them had charge of the vessels used in the service of the temple, keeping count of them as they were brought in and taken out. 29 Some of them were detailed to take charge of the furniture and all the sacred vessels, the flour, the wine, the oil, the incense, and the spices. 30 Some of the priests compounded the ointment for the perfumes. 31 Mattithiah the Levite, the eldest son of Shallum the Korahite, was in charge of the preparation of the wafers because he was trustworthy. 32 Some of their Kohathite kinsmen were in charge of setting out the rows of the Bread of the Presence every sabbath.

33 These are the musicians, heads of Levite families, who were lodged in rooms set apart for them, because they were liable for duty by day and by night. 34 These are the heads of Levite families, chiefs according to their tribal lists, living in Jerusalem.

35 Jehiel founder of Gibeon lived at Gibeon; his wife's name was Maacah, 36 and his sons were Abdon the eldest, Zur, Kish, Baal, Ner, Nadab, 37 Gedor, Ahio, Zechariah, and Mikloth. 38 Mikloth was the father of Shimeam; they lived alongside their kinsmen in Jerusalem. 39 Ner was the father of Kish, Kish father of Saul, Saul father of Jonathan, Malchishua, Abinadab, and Eshbaal. 40 The son of Jonathan was Meribbaal, and Meribbaal was the father of Micah. 41 The sons of Micah: Pithon, Melech, Tahrea, and Ahaz. 42 Ahaz was the father of Jarah, Jarah father of Alemeth, Azmoth, and Zimri; Zimri father of Moza, 43 and Moza father of Binea; his son was Rephaiah, his son Elasah, his son Azel. 44 Azel had six sons, whose names were Azrikam, Bocheru, Ishmael, Sheariah, Obadiah, and Hanan. These were the sons of Azel.

10 THE Philistines engaged Israel in battle, and the Israelites were routed, leaving their dead on Mount Gilboa. 2 The Philistines closely pursued Saul and his sons, and Jonathan, Abinadab, and Malchishua, the sons of Saul, were killed. 3 The battle went hard for Saul, and when the archers caught up with him they wounded him. 4 He said to his armour-bearer, 'Draw your sword and run me through, so that these uncircumcised brutes may not come and make sport of me.' But the armour-bearer refused; he dared not. Thereupon Saul took his own sword and fell on it. 5 When the armour-bearer saw that Saul was dead, he too fell on his sword and died. 6 Thus Saul and his three sons died; his whole house perished together. 7 When all the Israelites in the valley saw that their army had fled and that Saul and his sons had perished, they fled likewise, abandoning their towns; and the Philistines moved in and occupied them.

8 Next day, when the Philistines came to strip the slain, they found Saul and his sons lying dead on Mount Gilboa.

---

*u*Compare 8.35: Heb lacks *and Ahaz*   *v*Heb *they*

9:22 **numbered:** *so Syriac; Heb.* at the thresholds.   9:35–44 *Cp.* 8:29–38.   9:38 **in Jerusalem:** *prob. rdg; Heb adds* with their kinsmen.   9:41 **and Ahaz:** *so Gk (Luc.), cp.* 8:35; *Heb.* omits.   10:1–12 *Cp. 1 Sam. 31:1–13.*

who were chosen for gatekeepers at the threshold were two hundred and twelve. They were inscribed in the family records of their villages. David and Samuel the seer had established them in their position of trust. 23 Thus they and their sons kept guard over the gates of the house of the LORD, the house which was then a tent. 24 The gatekeepers were stationed at the four sides, to the east, the west, the north, and the south. 25 Their kinsmen who lived in their own villages took turns in assisting them for seven-day periods, 26 while the four chief gatekeepers were on constant duty. These were the Levites who also had charge of the chambers and treasures of the house of God. 27 At night they lodged about the house of God, for it was in their charge and they had the duty of opening it each morning. 28 Some of them had charge of the liturgical equipment, tallying it as it was brought in and taken out. 29 Others were appointed to take care of the utensils and all the sacred vessels, as well as the fine flour, the wine, the oil, the frankincense, and the spices. 30 It was the sons of priests, however, who mixed the spiced ointments. 31 Mattithiah, one of the Levites, the first-born of Shallum the Koreite, was entrusted with preparing the cakes. 32 Benaiah the Kohathite, one of their brethren, was in charge of setting out the showbread each sabbath.

33 These were the chanters and the gatekeepers, family heads over the Levites. They stayed in the chambers when free of duty, for day and night they had to be ready for service. 34 These were the levitical family heads over their kindred, chiefs who dwelt in Jerusalem.

35 In Gibeon dwelt Jeiel, the founder of Gibeon, whose wife's name was Maacah. 36 His first-born son was Abdon; then came Zur, Kish, Baal, Ner, Nadab, 37 Gedor, Ahio, Zechariah, and Mikloth. 38 Mikloth became the father of Shimeam. These, too, with their brethren, dwelt opposite their brethren in Jerusalem. 39 Ner became the father of Kish, and Kish became the father of Saul. Saul became the father of Jonathan, Malchishua, Abinadab, and Eshbaal. 40 The son of Jonathan was Meribbaal, and Meribbaal became the father of Micah. 41 The sons of Micah were Pithon, Melech, Tahrea, and Ahaz. 42 Ahaz became the father of Jehoaddah, and Jehoaddah became the father of Alemeth, Azmaveth, and Zimri. Zimri became the father of Moza. 43 Moza became the father of Binea, whose son was Rephaiah, whose son was Eleasah, whose son was Azel. 44 Azel had six sons, whose names were Azrikam, his first-born, Ishmael, Sheariah, Azariah, Obadiah, and Hanan; these were the sons of Azel.

10 Now the Philistines were at war with Israel; the Israelites fled before the Philistines, and a number of them fell, slain on Mount Gilboa. 2 The Philistines pressed hard after Saul and his sons. When the Philistines had killed Jonathan, Abinadab, and Malchishua, sons of Saul, 3 the whole fury of the battle descended upon Saul. Then the archers found him, and wounded him with their arrows.

4 Saul said to his armor-bearer, "Draw your sword and thrust me through with it, that these uncircumcised may not come and maltreat me." But the armor-bearer, in great fear, refused. So Saul took his own sword and fell on it; 5 and seeing him dead, the armor-bearer also fell on his sword and died. 6 Thus, with Saul and his three sons, his whole house died at one time. 7 When all the Israelites who were in the valley saw that Saul and his sons had died in the rout, they left their cities and fled; thereupon the Philistines came and occupied them.

8 On the following day, when the Philistines came to strip the slain, they found Saul and his sons where they had fallen

at the thresholds were picked men; there were two hundred and twelve of them. They were grouped by relationship in their various villages. These were confirmed in office by David and Samuel the seer because of their dependability. 23 They and their sons continued in charge as guards of the gates of the Temple of Yahweh, the house of the Tent. 24 The gatekeepers were assigned to the four sides, east, west, north and south, 25 and their brothers in their villages were required to assist them from time to time for a week, 26 since the four head gatekeepers were permanently on duty.

They were Levites and were in charge of the accommodation and supplies of the Temple of God. 27 They spent the night in the precincts of the Temple of God, their duties being to guard it and open it every morning. 28 Some of them were in charge of the implements of worship, having to count them when they took them out and when they put them away. 29 Others of them were put in charge of the implements, of all the objects in the sanctuary and of the flour, the wine, the oil, the incense and the perfume. 30 Members of the priestly caste, however, mixed the ointment for the perfume.

31 One of the Levites, Mattithiah — he was the first-born of Shallum the Korahite — had regular charge of baking operations. 32 Some of their kinsmen the Kohathites were responsible for the loaves to be set out in rows Sabbath by Sabbath.

33 In addition, there were the singers, the heads of the levitical families, who were accommodated in the Temple, free of other responsibilities because they were on duty day and night.

34 Such were the chiefs of the levitical families, according to their relationship; these lived in Jerusalem.

35 Jeiel father of Gibeon lived at Gibeon and his wife was called Maacah. 36 His first-born son was Abdon, then Zur, Kish, Baal, Ner, Nadab, 37 Gedor, Ahio, Zechariah and Mikloth. 38 Mikloth fathered Shimeam. But they, unlike their brothers, lived at Jerusalem with their brothers.

39 Ner fathered Kish, Kish fathered Saul, Saul fathered Jonathan, Malchishua, Abinadab and Eshbaal. 40 Son of Jonathan: Meribbaal. Meribbaal fathered Micah. 41 Sons of Micah: Pithon, Melech, Tahrea. 42 Ahaz fathered Jarah, Jarah fathered Alemeth, Azmaveth and Zimri; Zimri fathered Moza, 43 Moza fathered Binea, Rephaiah his son, Eleasah his son and Azel his son. 44 Azel had six sons; their names were these: Azrikam his first-born, Ishmael, Sheariah, Obadiah, Hanan. These were the sons of Azel.

10 The Philistines gave battle to Israel and the Israelites, fleeing from the Philistines, fell and were slaughtered on Mount Gilboa. 2 The Philistines bore down on Saul and his sons, and they killed Jonathan, Abinadab and Malchishua, Saul's sons. 3 The fighting grew fiercer round Saul; the archers came upon him, and he was wounded by the archers. 4 Saul then said to his armour-bearer, 'Draw your sword and run me through with it. I do not want these uncircumcised men to come and make fun of me.' But his armour-bearer was very much afraid and would not do it. So Saul took his own sword and fell on it. 5 His armour-bearer, seeing that Saul was dead, fell on his sword too and died with him. 6 Thus died Saul, his three sons and his entire household together. 7 When all the Israelites who were in the valley saw that the Israelites had been routed and that Saul and his sons were dead, they abandoned their towns and fled. The Philistines then came and occupied them.

8 When the Philistines came on the following day to strip the dead, they found Saul and his sons lying on Mount

9 They stripped him and took his head and his armor, and sent messengers throughout the land of the Philistines to carry the good news to their idols and to the people. 10 They put his armor in the temple of their gods, and fastened his head in the temple of Dagon. 11 But when all Jabesh-gilead heard everything that the Philistines had done to Saul, 12 all the valiant warriors got up and took away the body of Saul and the bodies of his sons, and brought them to Jabesh. Then they buried their bones under the oak in Jabesh, and fasted seven days.

13 So Saul died for his unfaithfulness; he was unfaithful to the LORD in that he did not keep the command of the LORD; moreover, he had consulted a medium, seeking guidance, 14 and did not seek guidance from the LORD. Therefore the LORD ^{w} put him to death and turned the kingdom over to David son of Jesse.

11 Then all Israel gathered together to David at Hebron and said, "See, we are your bone and flesh. 2 For some time now, even while Saul was king, it was you who commanded the army of Israel. The LORD your God said to you: It is you who shall be shepherd of my people Israel, you who shall be ruler over my people Israel." 3 So all the elders of Israel came to the king at Hebron, and David made a covenant with them at Hebron before the LORD. And they anointed David king over Israel, according to the word of the LORD by Samuel.

4 David and all Israel marched to Jerusalem, that is Jebus, where the Jebusites were, the inhabitants of the land. 5 The inhabitants of Jebus said to David, "You will not come in here." Nevertheless David took the stronghold of Zion, now the city of David. 6 David had said, "Whoever attacks the Jebusites first shall be chief and commander." And Joab son of Zeruiah went up first, so he became chief. 7 David resided in the stronghold; therefore it was called the city of David. 8 He built the city all around, from the Millo in complete circuit; and Joab repaired the rest of the city. 9 And David became greater and greater, for the LORD of hosts was with him.

10 Now these are the chiefs of David's warriors, who gave him strong support in his kingdom, together with all Israel, to make him king, according to the word of the LORD concerning Israel. 11 This is an account of David's mighty warriors: Jashobeam, son of Hachmoni, ^{x} was chief of the Three; ^{y} he wielded his spear against three hundred whom he killed at one time.

12 And next to him among the three warriors was Eleazar son of Dodo, the Ahohite. 13 He was with David at Pas-dammim when the Philistines were gathered there for battle. There was a plot of ground full of barley. Now the people had fled from the Philistines, 14 but he and David took their stand in the middle of the plot, defended it, and killed the Philistines; and the LORD saved them by a great victory.

15 Three of the thirty chiefs went down to the rock to David at the cave of Adullam, while the army of Philistines was encamped in the valley of Rephaim. 16 David was then in the stronghold; and the garrison of the Philistines was then at Bethlehem. 17 David said longingly, "O that someone would give me water to drink from the well of Bethlehem that is by the gate!" 18 Then the Three broke through the camp of the Philistines, and drew water from the well of Bethlehem that was by the gate, and they brought it to David. But David would not drink of it; he poured it out to the LORD, 19 and said, "My God forbid that I should do this.

9 They stripped him, cut off his head, and took away his armour; then they sent messengers through the length and breadth of their land to carry the good news to idols and people alike. 10 They deposited his armour in the temple of their god, and nailed up his skull in the temple of Dagon. 11 When the people of Jabesh-gilead heard everything the Philistines had done to Saul, 12 all the warriors among them set out to recover the bodies of Saul and his sons. They brought them back to Jabesh and buried their bones under the oak tree there, and for seven days they fasted. 13 Thus Saul paid with his life for his unfaithfulness: he had disobeyed the word of the LORD and had resorted to ghosts for guidance. 14 He had not sought guidance of the LORD, who therefore destroyed him and transferred the kingdom to David son of Jesse.

11 ALL Israel assembled and came to David at Hebron. 'We are your own flesh and blood,' they said. 2 'In the past, while Saul was still king, it was you that led the forces of Israel on their campaigns. To you the LORD your God said, "You are to be shepherd of my people Israel; you are to be their prince." ' 3 The elders of Israel all came to the king at Hebron; there David made a covenant with them before the LORD, and they anointed David king over Israel, as the LORD had said through the lips of Samuel.

4 David and all Israel went to Jerusalem, that is Jebus, where the Jebusites, the inhabitants of the region, lived. 5 The people of Jebus said to David, 'You will never come in here'; none the less David did capture the stronghold of Zion, and it is now known as the City of David. 6 David had said, 'The first man to kill a Jebusite will become a commander or an officer,' and the first man to go up was Joab son of Zeruiah; so he was given the command.

7 David took up his residence in the stronghold: that is why it was called the City of David. 8 He built the city around it: David started at the Millo and included its neighbourhood, while Joab reconstructed the rest of the city. 9 David steadily grew more and more powerful, for the LORD of Hosts was with him.

10 These were the chief of David's heroes, men who lent their full strength to his government and, with all Israel, joined in making him king; such was the LORD's decree for Israel. 11 First came Jashobeam the Hachmonite, chief of the three; it was he who brandished his spear over three hundred, all slain at one time. 12 Next to him was Eleazar son of Dodo the Ahohite, one of the heroic three. 13 He was with David at Pas-dammim where the Philistines had gathered for battle in a field carrying a good crop of barley. When the people had fled from the Philistines 14 he stood his ground in the field, defended it, and defeated them. So the LORD brought about a great victory.

15 Three of the thirty went down to the rock to join David at the cave of Adullam, while the Philistines were encamped in the valley of Rephaim. 16 David was then in the stronghold, and a Philistine garrison held Bethlehem. 17 One day David exclaimed with longing, 'If only I could have a drink of water from the well by the gate at Bethlehem!' 18 At this the three made their way through the Philistine lines and drew water from the well by the gate of Bethlehem and brought it to David. But he refused to drink it; he poured it out to the LORD, 19 saying, 'God forbid that

---

10:10 **god:** or gods. 11:1–9 Cp. 2 Sam. 5:1–3, 6–10. 11:10–41 Cp. 2 Sam. 23:8–39. 11:11 **Jashobeam:** some Gk MSS have Ishbaal. **the three:** so Gk (Luc.); Heb. the thirty or the lieutenants. 11:14 **he . . . ground:** so Gk, cp. 2 Sam. 23:12; Heb. they stood their ground. 11:17 **well:** or cistern.

---

^{w} Heb *he* ^{x} Or *a Hachmonite* ^{y} Compare 2 Sam 23.8: Heb *Thirty* or *captains*

on Mount Gilboa. 9 They stripped him, cut off his head, and took his armor; these they sent throughout the land of the Philistines to convey the good news to their idols and their people. 10 His armor they put in the house of their gods, but his skull they impaled on the temple of Dagon.

11 When all the inhabitants of Jabesh-gilead had heard what the Philistines had done to Saul, 12 its warriors rose to a man, recovered the bodies of Saul and his sons, and brought them to Jabesh. They buried their bones under the oak of Jabesh, and fasted seven days.

13 Thus Saul died because of his rebellion against the LORD in disobeying his command, and also because he had sought counsel of a necromancer, 14 and had not rather inquired of the LORD. Therefore the LORD slew him, and transferred his kingdom to David, the son of Jesse.

11 Then all Israel gathered about David in Hebron, and they said: "Surely, we are of the same bone and flesh as you. 2 Even formerly, when Saul was still the king, it was you who led Israel in all its battles. And now the LORD, your God, has said to you, 'You shall shepherd my people Israel and be ruler over them.' " 3 Then all the elders of Israel came to the king at Hebron, and there David made a covenant with them in the presence of the LORD; and they anointed him king over Israel, in accordance with the word of the LORD as revealed through Samuel.

4 Then David and all Israel went to Jerusalem, that is, Jebus, where the natives of the land were called Jebusites. 5 The inhabitants of Jebus said to David, "You shall not enter here." David nevertheless captured the fortress of Sion, which is the City of David. 6 David said, "Whoever strikes the Jebusites first shall be made the chief commander." Joab, the son of Zeruiah, was the first to go up; and so he became chief. 7 David took up his residence in the fortress, which thenceforth was called the City of David. 8 He rebuilt the city on all sides, from the Millo all the way around, while Joab restored the rest of the city. 9 David became more and more powerful, for the LORD of hosts was with him.

10 These were David's chief warriors who, together with all Israel, supported him in his reign in order to make him true king, even as the LORD had commanded concerning Israel. 11 Here is the list of David's warriors:

Ishbaal, the son of Hachamoni, chief of the Three. He brandished his spear against three hundred, whom he slew in a single encounter.

12 Next to him Eleazar, the son of Dodo the Ahohite, one of the Three warriors. 13 He was with David at Pasdammim, where the Philistines had massed for battle. The plowland was fully planted with barley, but its defenders were retreating before the Philistines. 14 He made a stand on the sown ground, kept it safe, and cut down the Philistines. Thus the LORD brought about a great victory.

15 Three of the Thirty chiefs went down to the rock, to David, who was in the cave of Adullam while the Philistines were encamped in the valley of Rephaim. 16 David was then in the stronghold, and a Philistine garrison was at Bethlehem. 17 David expressed a desire: "Oh, that someone would give me a drink from the cistern that is by the gate at Bethlehem!" 18 Thereupon the Three broke through the encampment of the Philistines, drew water from the cistern by the gate at Bethlehem, and carried it back to David. But David refused to drink it. Instead, he poured it out as a libation to the LORD, 19 saying, "God forbid that I should do

Gilboa. 9 They stripped him and, taking his head and his armour, had these carried round the territory of the Philistines to proclaim the good news to their idols and their people. 10 They placed his armour in the temple of their gods and nailed his head up in the temple of Dagon.

11 When all the inhabitants of Jabesh in Gilead heard everything that the Philistines had done to Saul, 12 the warriors all set out and took the bodies of Saul and his sons away; they brought them to Jabesh and buried their bones under the tamarisk of Jabesh and fasted for seven days.

13 Thus died Saul in the infidelity of which he had been guilty towards Yahweh, in that he had not obeyed the word of Yahweh and because he had consulted a necromancer for guidance. 14 He had not consulted Yahweh, who therefore caused his death and transferred the monarchy to David son of Jesse.

11 All Israel then rallied to David at Hebron and said, 'Look, we are your own flesh and bone. 2 In days past when Saul was king, it was you who led Israel on its campaigns, and Yahweh your God promised you, "You are to shepherd my people Israel and be leader of my people Israel." ' 3 So all the elders of Israel came to the king at Hebron, and David made a pact with them in Yahweh's presence at Hebron, and they anointed David as king of Israel, in accordance with the word of Yahweh through Samuel.

4 David and all Israel then marched on Jerusalem (that is to say, Jebus); the inhabitants of the territory were the Jebusites. 5 The inhabitants of Jebus said to David, 'You will not get in here.' But David captured the citadel of Zion, that is, the City of David. 6 David said, 'The first man to kill a Jebusite will be made army commander and chief.' Joab son of Zeruiah was the first man to go up, and was made commander of the army. 7 David went to live in the citadel, and that is how it came to be called the City of David. 8 He then built a wall round the city, all round, beginning from the Millo, and Joab restored the rest of the city. 9 Thus David grew stronger and stronger, for Yahweh Sabaoth was with him.

10 These are David's principal champions who joined forces with him in his kingdom, with all Israel, to make him king in accordance with the word of Yahweh concerning Israel. 11 This is the roll of David's champions: Jashobeam son of Hachmoni, head of the Three; he it was who brandished his spear over three hundred men whom he had killed at one time.

12 Next, there was Eleazar son of Dodo, the Ahohite, one of the three champions. 13 He was with David at Pas-Dammim when the Philistines mustered for battle there. There was a field full of barley there; and the people fled from the Philistines. 14 And they took their stand in the middle of the field, held it and cut down the Philistines; and Yahweh brought about a great victory.

15 Three members of the Thirty went down to David at the rock near the Cave of Adullam while a company of Philistines was encamped in the Valley of the Rephaim. 16 David was then in the stronghold and there was a Philistine garrison in Bethlehem. 17 Longingly, David said, 'If only someone would fetch me a drink of water from the well that stands by the gate at Bethlehem!' 18 At this the three champions, forcing their way through the Philistine camp, drew water from the well that stands by the gate of Bethlehem and, bringing it away, presented it to David. David, however, would not drink any of it, but poured it out as a libation to Yahweh. 19 'God preserve me', he said, 'from

Can I drink the blood of these men? For at the risk of their lives they brought it." Therefore he would not drink it. The three warriors did these things.

20 Now Abishai,ᶻ the brother of Joab, was chief of the Thirty.ᵃ With his spear he fought against three hundred and killed them, and won a name beside the Three. 21 He was the most renownedᵇ of the Thirty,ᵃ and became their commander; but he did not attain to the Three.

22 Benaiah son of Jehoiada was a valiant manᶜ of Kabzeel, a doer of great deeds; he struck down two sons ofᵈ Ariel of Moab. He also went down and killed a lion in a pit on a day when snow had fallen. 23 And he killed an Egyptian, a man of great stature, five cubits tall. The Egyptian had in his hand a spear like a weaver's beam; but Benaiah went against him with a staff, snatched the spear out of the Egyptian's hand, and killed him with his own spear. 24 Such were the things Benaiah son of Jehoiada did, and he won a name beside the three warriors. 25 He was renowned among the Thirty, but he did not attain to the Three. And David put him in charge of his bodyguard.

26 The warriors of the armies were Asahel brother of Joab, Elhanan son of Dodo of Bethlehem, 27 Shammoth of Harod,ᵉ Helez the Pelonite, 28 Ira son of Ikkesh of Tekoa, Abiezer of Anathoth, 29 Sibbecai the Hushathite, Ilai the Ahohite, 30 Maharai of Netophah, Heled son of Baanah of Netophah, 31 Ithai son of Ribai of Gibeah of the Benjaminites, Benaiah of Pirathon, 32 Hurai of the wadis of Gaash, Abiel the Arbathite, 33 Azmaveth of Baharum, Eliahba of Shaalbon, 34 Hashemᶠ the Gizonite, Jonathan son of Shagee the Hararite, 35 Ahiam son of Sachar the Hararite, Eliphal son of Ur, 36 Hepher the Mecherathite, Ahijah the Pelonite, 37 Hezro of Carmel, Naarai son of Ezbai, 38 Joel the brother of Nathan, Mibhar son of Hagri, 39 Zelek the Ammonite, Naharai of Beeroth, the armor-bearer of Joab son of Zeruiah, 40 Ira the Ithrite, Gareb the Ithrite, 41 Uriah the Hittite, Zabad son of Ahlai, 42 Adina son of Shiza the Reubenite, a leader of the Reubenites, and thirty with him, 43 Hanan son of Maacah, and Joshaphat the Mithnite, 44 Uzzia the Ashterathite, Shama and Jeiel sons of Hotham the Aroerite, 45 Jediael son of Shimri, and his brother Joha the Tizite, 46 Eliel the Mahavite, and Jeribai and Joshaviah sons of Elnaam, and Ithmah the Moabite, 47 Eliel, and Obed, and Jaasiel the Mezobaite.

I should do such a thing! Can I drink the blood of these men? They have brought it at the risk of their lives.' So he would not drink it. Such were the exploits of the heroic three.

20 Abishai the brother of Joab was chief of the thirty; he it was who brandished his spear over three hundred dead. He was famous among the thirty. 21 He surpassed in reputation the rest of the thirty; he became their captain, but he did not rival the three. 22 Benaiah son of Jehoiada, from Kabzeel, was a hero of many exploits. It was he who slew the two champions of Moab, and who once went down into a pit and killed a lion on a snowy day. 23 He also killed an Egyptian, a giant seven and a half feet high armed with a spear as big as the beam of a loom. Benaiah went to meet him with a club, wrested the spear out of the Egyptian's hand, and killed him with his own weapon. 24 Such were the exploits of Benaiah son of Jehoiada, famous among the heroic thirty. 25 He was more famous than the rest of the thirty, but he did not rival the three. David appointed him to his household.

26 These were his valiant heroes: Asahel the brother of Joab; Elhanan son of Dodo from Bethlehem; 27 Shammoth from Harod; Helez from a place unknown; 28 Ira son of Ikkesh from Tekoa; Abiezer from Anathoth; 29 Sibbechai from Hushah; Ilai the Ahohite; 30 Maharai from Netophah; Heled son of Baanah from Netophah; 31 Ithai son of Ribai from Gibeah of Benjamin; Benaiah from Pirathon; 32 Hurai from the wadis of Gaash; Abiel from Beth-arabah; 33 Azmoth from Bahurim; Eliahba from Shaalbon; 34 Hashem the Gizonite; Jonathan son of Shage the Hararite; 35 Ahiam son of Sacar the Hararite; Eliphal son of Ur; 36 Hepher from Mecherah; Ahijah from a place unknown; 37 Hezro from Carmel; Naarai son of Ezbai; 38 Joel brother of Nathan; Mibhar son of Hageri; 39 Zelek the Ammonite; Naharai from Beroth, armour-bearer to Joab son of Zeruiah; 40 Ira the Ithrite; Gareb the Ithrite; 41 Uriah the Hittite; Zabad son of Ahlai. 42 Adina son of Shiza the Reubenite, a chief of the Reubenites, was over these thirty. 43 Also Hanan son of Maacah, and Joshaphat the Mithnite; 44 Uzzia from Ashtaroth, Shama and Jeiel the sons of Hotham from Aroer; 45 Jediael son of Shimri, and his brother Joha the Tizite; 46 Eliel the Mahavite, and Jeribai and Joshaviah sons of Elnaam, and Ithmah the Moabite; 47 Eliel and Obed, and Jaasiel from Zobah.

ᶻGk Vg Tg Compare 2 Sam 23.18: Heb Abshai   ᵃSyr: Heb Three
ᵇCompare 2 Sam 23.19: Heb more renowned among the two
ᶜSyr: Heb the son of a valiant man   ᵈSee 2 Sam 23.20: Heb lacks sons of   ᵉCompare 2 Sam 23.25: Heb the Harorite   ᶠCompare Gk and 2 Sam 23.32: Heb the sons of Hashem

11:19 these men: so Lat.; Heb. adds at the risk of their lives.   11:20,21 thirty: so Syriac; Heb. three.   11:22 Kabzeel, was: so Syriac; Heb. adds the son of.   11:23 seven . . . feet: lit. five cubits.   11:24 thirty: prob. rdg; Heb. three.   11:27 Harod: prob. rdg, cp. 2 Sam. 23:25; Heb. Haror.   11:34 Hashem: so some Gk MSS, cp. 2 Sam. 23:32; Heb. the sons of Hashem.   11:42 was . . . thirty: so Syriac; Heb. had thirty over him.   11:47 from Zobah: prob. rdg; Heb. obscure.

such a thing! Could I drink the blood of these men who risked their lives?" For at the risk of their lives they brought it; and so he refused to drink. Such deeds as these the Three warriors performed.

20 Abishai, the brother of Joab. He was the chief of the Thirty; he brandished his spear against three hundred, and slew them. Thus he had a reputation like that of the Three. 21 He was twice as famous as any of the Thirty and became their commander, but he did not attain to the Three.

22 Benaiah, the son of Jehoiada, a valiant man of mighty deeds, from Kabzeel. He killed the two sons of Ariel of Moab, and also, on a snowy day, he went down and killed the lion in the cistern. 23 He likewise slew the Egyptian, a huge man five cubits tall. The Egyptian carried a spear that was like a weaver's heddle-bar, but he came against him with a staff, wrested the spear from the Egyptian's hand, and killed him with his own spear. 24 Such deeds as these of Benaiah, the son of Jehoiada, gave him a reputation like that of the Three. 25 He was more famous than any of the Thirty, but he did not attain to the Three. David put him in charge of his bodyguard.

26 Also these warriors: Asahel, the brother of Joab; Elhanan, son of Dodo, from Bethlehem; 27 Shammoth, from En-harod; Helez, from Palti; 28 Ira, son of Ikkesh, from Tekoa; Abiezer, from Anathoth; 29 Sibbecai, from Husha; Ilai, from Ahoh; 30 Maharai, from Netophah; Heled, son of Baanah, from Netophah; 31 Ithai, son of Ribai, from Gibeah of Benjamin; Benaiah, from Pirathon; 32 Hurai, from the valley of Gaash; Abiel, from Beth-arabah; 33 Azmaveth, from Bahurim; Eliahba, from Shaalbon; 34 Jashen the Gunite; Jonathan, son of Shagee, from En-harod; 35 Ahiam, son of Sachar, from En-harod; Elipheleth, son of 36 Ahasabi, from Beth-maacah; Ahijah, from Gilo; 37 Hezro, from Carmel; Naarai, the son of Ezbai; 38 Joel, brother of Nathan, from Rehob, the Gadite; 39 Zelek the Ammonite; Naharai, from Beeroth, the armor-bearer of Joab, son of Zeruiah; 40 Ira, from Jattir; Gareb, from Jattir; 41 Uriah the Hittite; Zabad, son of Ahlai, 42 and, in addition to the Thirty, Adina, son of Shiza, the Reubenite, chief of the tribe of Reuben; 43 Hanan, from Beth-maacah; Joshaphat the Mithnite; 44 Uzzia, from Ashterath; Shama and Jeiel, sons of Hotham, from Aroer; 45 Jediael, son of Shimri, and Joha, his brother, the Tizite; 46 Eliel the Mahavite; Jeribai and Joshaviah, sons of Elnaam; Ithmam, from Moab; 47 Eliel, Obed, and Jaasiel the Mezobian.

doing such a thing! Am I to drink these men's blood? For at the risk of their lives they brought it.' And so he would not drink. Such were the deeds of the three champions.

20 Abishai, brother of Joab, was leader of the Thirty. He it was who brandished his spear over three hundred men whom he had killed, winning himself a name among the Thirty. 21 He was a most illustrious member of the Thirty and became their captain, but he was not equal to the Three.

22 Benaiah son of Jehoiada from Kabzeel was the hero of many exploits; he it was who slaughtered two formidable Moabites and, one snowy day, climbed down and slaughtered the lion in the storage-well. 23 He also slaughtered an Egyptian, a man who was seven and a half feet tall. The Egyptian was armed with a spear in his hand like a weaver's beam, but he took him on with a staff, tore the spear from the Egyptian's hand and killed the man with it. 24 Such were the exploits of Benaiah son of Jehoiada, winning him a name among the thirty champions. 25 He was a most illustrious member of the Thirty, but he was not equal to the Three. David put him in command of his bodyguard.

26 The military champions were:
   Asahel brother of Joab;
   Elhanan son of Dodo, of Bethlehem;
27 Shammoth of Haror;
   Helez the Pelonite;
28 Ira son of Ikkesh, of Tekoa;
   Abiezer of Anathoth;
29 Sibbecai of Hushah;
   Ilai of Ahoh;
30 Maharai of Netophah;
   Heled son of Baanah, of Netophah.
31 Ithai son of Ribai, of Gibeah in Benjamin.
   Benaiah of Pirathon;
32 Hurai of the Torrents of Gaash;
   Abiel of Beth-ha-Arabah;
33 Azmaveth of Bahurim;
   Eliahba of Shaalbon;
34 the sons of Hashem of Gizon;
   Jonathan son of Shagee, of Harar;
35 Ahiam son of Sachar, of Harar;
   Eliphelet son of Ur;
36 Hepher of Mecherah;
   Ahijah the Pelonite;
37 Hezro of Carmel;
   Naarai son of Ezbai;
38 Joel brother of Nathan;
   Mibhar son of Hagri;
39 Zelek the Ammonite;
   Naharai of Beeroth, armour-bearer to Joab son of Zeruiah;
40 Ira of Jattir;
   Gareb of Jattir;
41 Uriah the Hittite;
   Zabad son of Ahlai;
42 Adina son of Shiza the Reubenite, chief of the Reubenites and commander of the Thirty;
43 Hanan son of Maacah;
   Joshaphat the Mithnite;
44 Uzzia of Ashteroth;
   Shama and Jeiel sons of Hotham of Aroer;
45 Jediael son of Shimri, and Joha his brother, the Tizite;
46 Eliel the Mahavite;
   Jeribai and Joshaviah sons of Elnaam;
   Ithmah the Moabite;
47 Eliel, Obed, and Jaasiel of Zobah.

NEW REVISED STANDARD VERSION

REVISED ENGLISH BIBLE

12 The following are those who came to David at Ziklag, while he could not move about freely because of Saul son of Kish; they were among the mighty warriors who helped him in war. 2 They were archers, and could shoot arrows and sling stones with either the right hand or the left; they were Benjaminites, Saul's kindred. 3 The chief was Ahiezer, then Joash, both sons of Shemaah of Gibeah; also Jeziel and Pelet sons of Azmaveth; Beracah, Jehu of Anathoth, 4 Ishmaiah of Gibeon, a warrior among the Thirty and a leader over the Thirty; Jeremiah,g Jahaziel, Johanan, Jozabad of Gederah, 5 Eluzai,h Jerimoth, Bealiah, Shemariah, Shephatiah the Haruphite; 6 Elkanah, Isshiah, Azarel, Joezer, and Jashobeam, the Korahites; 7 and Joelah and Zebadiah, sons of Jeroham of Gedor.

8 From the Gadites there went over to David at the stronghold in the wilderness mighty and experienced warriors, expert with shield and spear, whose faces were like the faces of lions, and who were swift as gazelles on the mountains: 9 Ezer the chief, Obadiah second, Eliab third, 10 Mishmannah fourth, Jeremiah fifth, 11 Attai sixth, Eliel seventh, 12 Johanan eighth, Elzabad ninth, 13 Jeremiah tenth, Machbannai eleventh. 14 These Gadites were officers of the army, the least equal to a hundred and the greatest to a thousand. 15 These are the men who crossed the Jordan in the first month, when it was overflowing all its banks, and put to flight all those in the valleys, to the east and to the west.

16 Some Benjaminites and Judahites came to the stronghold to David. 17 David went out to meet them and said to them, "If you have come to me in friendship, to help me, then my heart will be knit to you; but if you have come to betray me to my adversaries, though my hands have done no wrong, then may the God of our ancestors see and give judgment." 18 Then the spirit came upon Amasai, chief of the Thirty, and he said,

"We are yours, O David;
  and with you, O son of Jesse!
Peace, peace to you,
  and peace to the one who helps you!
For your God is the one who helps you."

Then David received them, and made them officers of his troops.

19 Some of the Manassites deserted to David when he came with the Philistines for the battle against Saul. (Yet he did not help them, for the rulers of the Philistines took counsel and sent him away, saying, "He will desert to his master Saul at the cost of our heads.") 20 As he went to Ziklag these Manassites deserted to him: Adnah, Jozabad, Jediael, Michael, Jozabad, Elihu, and Zillethai, chiefs of the thousands in Manasseh. 21 They helped David against the band of raiders,i for they were all warriors and commanders in the army. 22 Indeed from day to day people kept coming to David to help him, until there was a great army, like an army of God.

23 These are the numbers of the divisions of the armed troops who came to David in Hebron to turn the kingdom of Saul over to him, according to the word of the LORD. 24 The people of Judah bearing shield and spear numbered six thousand eight hundred armed troops. 25 Of the Simeonites, mighty warriors, seven thousand one hundred. 26 Of the Levites four thousand six hundred. 27 Jehoiada, leader of the house of Aaron, and with him three thousand seven hundred. 28 Zadok, a young warrior, and twenty-two commanders from his own ancestral house. 29 Of the Benjamin-

12 These are the men who joined David at Ziklag while he was banned from the presence of Saul son of Kish. They ranked among the warriors valiant in battle; 2 they carried bows and could sling stones or shoot arrows with the left hand or the right. They were Benjamites, kinsmen of Saul. 3 The foremost were Ahiezer and Joash, the sons of Shemaah of Gibeah; Jeziel and Pelet, men of Beth-azmoth; Berakah and Jehu from Anathoth; 4 Ishmaiah the Gibeonite, a hero among the thirty and a chief among them; Jeremiah, Jahaziel, Johanan, and Jozabad from Gederah; 5 Eluzai, Jerimoth, Bealiah, Shemariah, and Shephatiah the Hariphite; 6 Elkanah, Isshiah, Azarel, Joezer, Jashobeam, the Korahites; 7 and Joelah and Zebadiah sons of Jeroham from Gedor.

8 Some Gadites also joined David at the stronghold in the wilderness, valiant men trained for war, experts with the heavy shield and spear, grim as lions and swift as gazelles on the mountains. 9 Ezer was their chief, Obadiah the second, Eliab the third; 10 Mishmannah the fourth and Jeremiah the fifth; 11 Attai the sixth and Eliel the seventh; 12 Johanan the eighth and Elzabad the ninth; 13 Jeremiah the tenth and Machbanai the eleventh. 14 These were chiefs of the Gadites in the army, the least of them a match for a hundred, the greatest a match for a thousand. 15 These were the men who in the first month crossed the Jordan, which was in full flood in all its reaches; they cleared the valleys, east and west.

16 Some men of Benjamin and Judah came to David at the stronghold. 17 David went out to them and said, 'If you come as friends to help me, join me and welcome; but if you come to betray me to my enemies, innocent though I am of any crime of violence, may the God of our fathers see and judge.' 18 At that a spirit took possession of Amasai, the chief of the thirty, and he said:

'We are on your side, David!
We are with you, son of Jesse!
All prosperity to you
  and to him who helps you,
for your God is your helper.'

So David welcomed them and attached them to the columns of his raiding parties.

19 Some men of Manasseh had deserted to David when he went with the Philistines to war against Saul, though he did not, in fact, fight on the side of the Philistines. Their lords dismissed him, saying to themselves that he would desert them for his master Saul, and that would cost them their heads. 20 The men of Manasseh who deserted to him when he went to Ziklag were these: Adnah, Jozabad, Jediael, Michael, Jozabad, Elihu, and Zillethai, each commanding his thousand in Manasseh. 21 It was they who stood valiantly by David against the raiders, for they were all good fighters, and they were given commands in his forces. 22 Day by day men came in to help David, until he had gathered an immense army.

23 These are the numbers of the armed bands which joined David at Hebron to transfer the sovereignty to him in succession to Saul, as the LORD had said: 24 men of Judah, bearing heavy shield and spear, six thousand eight hundred drafted for active service; 25 of Simeon, fighting men drafted for active service, seven thousand one hundred; 26 of Levi, four thousand six hundred, 27 together with Jehoiada prince of the house of Aaron and three thousand seven hundred men, 28 and Zadok, a valiant fighter, with twenty-two officers of his own clan; 29 of Benjamin, Saul's kins-

12:3 **men of Beth-azmoth:** *lit.* sons of Azmoth. 12:4 *In Heb. verses 4 and 5.* 12:5 *In Heb. verse 6.* 12:18 **took possession of:** *lit.* clothed itself with. **and he said:** *so Gk; Heb. omits.*
12:22 **an immense army:** *lit.* a great army like the army of God.
12:28 **of:** *so Gk; Heb. omits.*

g Heb verse 5   h Heb verse 6   i Or *as officers of his troops*

12 The following men came to David in Ziklag while he was still under banishment from Saul, son of Kish; they, too, were among the warriors who helped him in his battles. 2 They were archers who could use either the right or the left hand, both in slinging stones and in shooting arrows with the bow. They were some of Saul's kinsmen, from Benjamin. 3 Ahiezer was their chief, along with Joash, both sons of Shemaah of Gibeah; also Jeziel and Pelet, sons of Azmaveth; Beracah; Jehu, from Anathoth; 4 Ishmaiah the Gibeonite, a warrior on the level of the Thirty, and in addition to their number: 5 Jeremiah; Jahaziel; Johanan; Jozabad, from Gederah; 6 Eluzai; Jerimoth; Bealiah; Shemariah; Shephatiah the Haruphite; 7 Elkanah, Isshiah, Azarel, Joezer, and Ishbaal, who were Korahites; 8 Joelah, finally, and Zebadiah, sons of Jeroham, from Gedor.

9 Some of the Gadites also went over to David when he was at the stronghold in the wilderness. They were valiant warriors, experienced soldiers equipped with shield and spear, who bore themselves like lions, and were as swift as the gazelles on the mountains. 10 Ezer was their chief, Obadiah was second, Eliab third, 11 Mishmannah fourth, Jeremiah fifth, 12 Attai sixth, Eliel seventh, 13 Johanan eighth, Elzabad ninth, 14 Jeremiah tenth, and Machbannai eleventh. 15 These Gadites were army commanders, the lesser placed over hundreds and the greater over thousands. 16 It was they who crossed over the Jordan when it was overflowing both its banks in the first month, and dispersed all who were in the valleys to the east and to the west.

17 Some Benjaminites and Judahites also came to David at the stronghold. 18 David went out to meet them and addressed them in these words: "If you come peacefully, to help me, I am of a mind to have you join me. But if you have come to betray me to my enemies though my hands have done no wrong, may the God of our fathers see and punish you."

19 Then spirit enveloped Amasai, the chief of the Thirty, who spoke:

"We are yours, O David,
    we are with you, O son of Jesse.
Peace, peace to you,
    and peace to him who helps you;
    your God it is who helps you."

So David received them and placed them among the leaders of his troops.

20 Men from Manasseh also deserted to David when he came with the Philistines to battle against Saul. However, he did not help the Philistines, for their lords took counsel and sent him home, saying, "At the cost of our heads he will desert to his master Saul." 21 As he was returning to Ziklag, therefore, these deserted to him from Manasseh: Adnah, Jozabad, Jediael, Michael, Jozabad, Elihu, and Zillethai, chiefs of thousands of Manasseh. 22 They helped David by taking charge of his troops, for they were all warriors and became commanders of his army. 23 And from day to day men kept coming to David's help until there was a vast encampment, like an encampment of angels.

24 This is the muster of the detachments of armed troops that came to David at Hebron to transfer to him Saul's kingdom, as the LORD had ordained. 25 Judahites bearing shields and spears: six thousand eight hundred armed troops. 26 Of the Simeonites, warriors fit for battle: seven thousand one hundred. 27 Of the Levites: four thousand six hundred, 28 along with Jehoiada, leader of the line of Aaron, with another three thousand seven hundred, 29 and Zadok, a young warrior, with twenty-two princes of his father's house. 30 Of the Benjaminites, the brethren of Saul: three

12 These are the men who rallied to David at Ziklag while he was still being kept away from Saul son of Kish; they were among the champions, the warriors. 2 They were equipped with bows and could sling stones or shoot arrows from the bow with either right hand or left.

Of Saul's fellow-tribesmen from Benjamin: 3 Ahiezer the leader, and Joash, sons of Hassemar of Gibeah, Jeziel and Peleth, sons of Azmaveth, Berachah and Jehu of Anathoth, 4 Ishmaiah of Gibeon, one of the champions in the Thirty and commander of the Thirty, 5 Jeremiah, Jahaziel, Johanan and Jozabed of Gederoth, 6 Eluzai, Jerimoth, Bealiah, Shemariah, Shephatiah of Hariph, 7 Elkanah, Isshiah, Azarel, Joezer and Jashobeam the Korahites, 8 Joelah, Zebadiah, sons of Jeroham of Gedor.

9 From the Gadites, some good, capable fighting men defected and came to David at the stronghold in the desert —all skilled with shield and spear, fierce as lions and nimble as mountain gazelles. 10 Ezer was the leader, Obadiah second, Eliab third, 11 Mishmannah fourth, Jeremiah fifth, 12 Attai sixth, Eliel seventh, 13 Johanan eighth, Elzabad ninth, 14 Jeremiah tenth, Machbannai eleventh. 15 These Gadites were the leaders of the troops, the least of them a match for a hundred men and the greatest a match for a thousand. 16 These were the men who once crossed the Jordan in the first month, when it had overflowed its banks and had driven out all the lowlanders to east and west.

17 Some of the Benjaminites and Judahites also joined David at the stronghold. 18 When David came forward to meet them, he responded to them by saying, 'If you have come to me with peaceful intent to help me, you will find me a good friend. But if it is to betray me to my enemies, seeing that I have done nothing wrong, may the God of our ancestors take note and condemn you.'

19 Then the Spirit invested Amasai the leader of the Thirty:

'We are your men, David; with you, son of Jesse!
Peace be with you, peace be with you; peace be
    with those who help you!
For your God has helped you!'

And David accepted them, including them among his more senior officers.

20 Some Manassehites also defected to David as he was setting out with the Philistines to fight Saul. But he did not help the Philistines because, after consultation, their chiefs sent him away, saying, 'He will defect to his master Saul and it will cost us our heads!' 21 He was on his way to Ziklag when these Manassehites deserted to him: Adnah, Jozabad, Jediael, Michael, Jozabad, Elihu, Zillethai, chiefs of thousands in Manasseh. 22 They helped David and his band, since they were all men of standing and became officers in the army.

23 Indeed reinforcements reached David day after day, so that his camp grew into a camp of prodigious size.

24 These are the numbers of fully armed men who joined David at Hebron to transfer Saul's kingdom to him in accordance with the order of Yahweh:

25 Judahites carrying shield and spear: six thousand eight hundred fully armed warriors;

26 Simeonites; seven thousand one hundred champions valiant in war;

27 Levites: four thousand six hundred, 28 in addition to Jehoiada, in command of the Aaronites, with three thousand seven hundred of these, 29 Zadok, a young and valiant champion, and twenty-two commanders of his family;

ites, the kindred of Saul, three thousand, of whom the majority had continued to keep their allegiance to the house of Saul. 30 Of the Ephraimites, twenty thousand eight hundred, mighty warriors, notables in their ancestral houses. 31 Of the half-tribe of Manasseh, eighteen thousand, who were expressly named to come and make David king. 32 Of Issachar, those who had understanding of the times, to know what Israel ought to do, two hundred chiefs, and all their kindred under their command. 33 Of Zebulun, fifty thousand seasoned troops, equipped for battle with all the weapons of war, to help David *j* with singleness of purpose. 34 Of Naphtali, a thousand commanders, with whom there were thirty-seven thousand armed with shield and spear. 35 Of the Danites, twenty-eight thousand six hundred equipped for battle. 36 Of Asher, forty thousand seasoned troops ready for battle. 37 Of the Reubenites and Gadites and the half-tribe of Manasseh from beyond the Jordan, one hundred twenty thousand armed with all the weapons of war.

38 All these, warriors arrayed in battle order, came to Hebron with full intent to make David king over all Israel; likewise all the rest of Israel were of a single mind to make David king. 39 They were there with David for three days, eating and drinking, for their kindred had provided for them. 40 And also their neighbors, from as far away as Issachar and Zebulun and Naphtali, came bringing food on donkeys, camels, mules, and oxen — abundant provisions of meal, cakes of figs, clusters of raisins, wine, oil, oxen, and sheep, for there was joy in Israel.

13 David consulted with the commanders of the thousands and of the hundreds, with every leader. 2 David said to the whole assembly of Israel, "If it seems good to you, and if it is the will of the LORD our God, let us send abroad to our kindred who remain in all the land of Israel, including the priests and Levites in the cities that have pasture lands, that they may come together to us. 3 Then let us bring again the ark of our God to us; for we did not turn to it in the days of Saul." 4 The whole assembly agreed to do so, for the thing pleased all the people.

5 So David assembled all Israel from the Shihor of Egypt to Lebo-hamath, to bring the ark of God from Kiriath-jearim. 6 And David and all Israel went up to Baalah, that is, to Kiriath-jearim, which belongs to Judah, to bring up from there the ark of God, the LORD, who is enthroned on the cherubim, which is called by his*k* name. 7 They carried the ark of God on a new cart, from the house of Abinadab, and Uzzah and Ahio*l* were driving the cart. 8 David and all Israel were dancing before God with all their might, with song and lyres and harps and tambourines and cymbals and trumpets.

9 When they came to the threshing floor of Chidon, Uzzah put out his hand to hold the ark, for the oxen shook it. 10 The anger of the LORD was kindled against Uzzah; he struck him down because he put out his hand to the ark; and he died there before God. 11 David was angry because the LORD had burst out against Uzzah; so that place is called Perez-uzzah*m* to this day. 12 David was afraid of God that day; he said, "How can I bring the ark of God into my care?" 13 So David did not take the ark into his care into the city of David; he took it instead to the house of Obed-edom the Gittite. 14 The ark of God remained with the household

men, three thousand, though most of them had hitherto remained loyal to the house of Saul; 30 of Ephraim, twenty thousand eight hundred fighting men, famous in their own clans; 31 of the half tribe of Manasseh, eighteen thousand, who had been nominated to come and make David king; 32 of Issachar, whose tribesmen were skilled in reading the signs of the times to discover what course Israel should follow, two hundred chiefs with all their kinsmen under their command; 33 of Zebulun, fifty thousand troops well-drilled for battle, armed with every kind of weapon, bold and single-minded; 34 of Naphtali, a thousand officers with thirty-seven thousand men equipped with heavy shield and spear; 35 of the Danites, twenty-eight thousand six hundred well-drilled for battle; 36 of Asher, forty thousand troops well-drilled for battle; 37 of the Reubenites and the Gadites and the half tribe of Manasseh east of Jordan, a hundred and twenty thousand armed with every kind of weapon.

38 All these valiant men trained for war came to Hebron, fully determined to make David king over the whole of Israel; the rest of Israel, too, were of one mind to make him king. 39 They spent three days there with David, eating and drinking, for their kinsmen made provision for them. 40 Also their neighbours round about, as far away as Issachar, Zebulun, and Naphtali, brought food on donkeys and camels, on mules and oxen: supplies of meal, fig-cakes, raisin-cakes, wine and oil, oxen and sheep in plenty; for there was rejoicing in Israel.

13 DAVID consulted the officers over units of a thousand and a hundred on every matter brought forward. 2 Then he said to the whole assembly of Israel, 'If you approve, and if the LORD our God opens a way, let us send to our kinsmen who have stayed behind in all the districts of Israel, and also to the priests and Levites in the cities and towns where they have common lands, bidding them join us. 3 Let us fetch the Ark of our God, for while Saul lived we never resorted to it.' 4 With the approval of the whole nation the assembly resolved unanimously to do this.

5 So David assembled all Israel from the Shihor in Egypt to Lebo-hamath, in order to fetch the Ark of God from Kiriath-jearim. 6 David and all Israel went up to Baalah, to Kiriath-jearim, which belonged to Judah, to fetch from there the Ark of God, the LORD enthroned upon the cherubim, the Ark which bore his name. 7 They mounted the Ark on a new cart and conveyed it from the house of Abinadab, with Uzza and Ahio guiding the cart. 8 David and all Israel danced for joy before God with all their might to the sound of singing, of lyres, lutes, tambourines, cymbals, and trumpets. 9 When they came to the threshing-floor of Kidon, the oxen stumbled, and Uzza reached out his hand to hold the Ark. 10 The LORD was angry with Uzza and struck him down because he had put out his hand to the Ark. So he died there before God. 11 David was vexed because the LORD's anger had broken out on Uzza, and he called the place Perez-uzza, the name it still bears.

12 David was afraid of God that day and said, 'How can the Ark of God come to me?' 13 So he did not take the Ark with him into the City of David; he turned aside and carried it to the house of Obed-edom the Gittite. 14 The Ark of God

13:2 **and if . . . let us:** or and if it is from the LORD our God, let us seize the opportunity and.   13:6–14 Cp. 2 Sam. 6:2–11.
13:6 **which bore his name:** prob. rdg; Heb. obscure.
13:11 **Perez-uzza:** that is Outbreak on Uzza.

j Gk: Heb lacks David   *k* Heb lacks his   *l* Or and his brother
m That is Bursting Out Against Uzzah

thousand — until this time, most of them had held their allegiance to the house of Saul. 31 Of the Ephraimites: twenty thousand eight hundred warriors, men renowned in their ancestral houses. 32 Of the half-tribe of Manasseh: eighteen thousand, designated by name to come and make David king. 33 Of the Issacharites, their chiefs who were endowed with an understanding of the times and who knew what Israel had to do: two hundred chiefs, together with all their brethren under their command. 34 From Zebulun, men fit for military service, set in battle array with every kind of weapon for war: fifty thousand men rallying with a single purpose. 35 From Naphtali: one thousand captains, and with them, armed with shield and lance, thirty-seven thousand men. 36 Of the Danites, set in battle array: twenty-eight thousand six hundred. 37 From Asher, fit for military service and set in battle array: forty thousand. 38 From the other side of the Jordan, of the Reubenites, Gadites, and the half-tribe of Manasseh, men equipped with every kind of weapon of war: one hundred and twenty thousand.

39 All these soldiers, drawn up in battle order, came to Hebron with the resolute intention of making David king over all Israel. The rest of Israel was likewise of one mind to make David king. 40 They remained with David for three days, feasting and drinking, for their brethren had prepared for them. 41 Moreover, their neighbors from as far as Issachar, Zebulun, and Naphtali came bringing food on asses, camels, mules, and oxen — provisions in great quantity of meal, pressed figs, raisins, wine, oil, oxen, and sheep. For there was rejoicing in Israel.

13 After David had taken counsel with his commanders of thousands and of hundreds, that is to say, with every one of his leaders, 2 he said to the whole assembly of Israel: "If it seems good to you, and is so decreed by the LORD our God, let us summon the rest of our brethren from all the districts of Israel, and also the priests and the Levites from their cities with pasture lands, that they may join us; 3 and let us bring the ark of our God here among us, for in the days of Saul we did not visit it." 4 And the whole assembly agreed to do this, for the idea was pleasing to all the people.

5 Then David assembled all Israel, from Shihor of Egypt to Labo of Hamath, to bring the ark of God from Kiriath-jearim. 6 David and all Israel went up to Baalah, that is, to Kiriath-jearim, of Judah, to bring back the ark of God, which was known by the name "LORD enthroned upon the cherubim." 7 They transported the ark of God on a new cart from the house of Abinadab; Uzzah and Ahio were guiding the cart, 8 while David and all Israel danced before God with great enthusiasm, amid songs and music on lyres, harps, tambourines, cymbals, and trumpets.

9 As they reached the threshing floor of Chidon, Uzzah stretched out his hand to steady the ark, for the oxen were upsetting it. 10 Then the LORD became angry with Uzzah and struck him; he died there in God's presence, because he had laid his hand on the ark. 11 David was disturbed because the LORD's anger had broken out against Uzzah. Therefore that place has been called Perez-uzza even to this day.

12 David was now afraid of God, and he said, "How can I bring the ark of God with me?" 13 Therefore he did not take the ark back with him to the City of David, but he took it instead to the house of Obed-edom the Gittite. 14 The ark

30 Benjaminites: three thousand kinsmen of Saul, most of them hitherto in the service of the House of Saul;

31 Ephraimites: twenty thousand eight hundred valiant champions, men famous in their families;

32 of the half-tribe of Manasseh: eighteen thousand men assigned by name to go and proclaim David king;

33 Issacharites, sound judges of the times when Israel should take action, and the way to do it: two hundred chiefs and all their kinsmen under their command;

34 Zebulunites: fifty thousand men fit for service, marshalled for battle, with warlike weapons of every kind, staunch-hearted auxiliaries;

35 Naphtalites: a thousand commanders, and with them thirty-seven thousand men armed with shield and spear;

36 Danites: twenty-eight thousand six hundred men marshalled for battle;

37 Asherites: forty thousand men fit for service, marshalled for battle;

38 from Transjordan: a hundred and twenty thousand men of Reuben, Gad and the half-tribe of Manasseh, with warlike weapons of every kind.

39 All these warriors in battle array came to David at Hebron with the firm determination of making David king of all Israel; and the rest of Israel, too, was of one mind in wanting to make David king. 40 For three days they stayed there with David, eating and drinking, their fellow-tribesmen having made preparations for them; 41 their neighbours too, from as far away as Issachar and Zebulun and Naphtali, came bringing food on donkeys, camels, mules and oxen — supplies of flour, fig cakes, bunches of raisins, wine, oil, quantities of oxen and sheep — for there was joy in Israel.

13 David conferred with the commanders of the thousands and the hundreds, in fact with all the leaders. 2 Then, to the whole assembly of Israel, David said, 'If this has your approval, and if Yahweh our God wills it so, we shall send messengers to the rest of our brothers throughout the territories of Israel, and also to the priests and Levites in their towns and pasture lands, bidding them join us. 3 And then we will go and recover the ark of our God, for in the days of Saul we neglected to do it.'

4 The whole assembly agreed to this, because all the people thought that this was the right thing to do. 5 So David summoned all Israel from the Shihor of Egypt to the Pass of Hamath, to bring the ark of God from Kiriath-Jearim. 6 David and all Israel then went up to Baalah, to Kiriath-Jearim in Judah, from there to bring up the ark of God, which bears the title 'Yahweh enthroned on the winged creatures'. 7 They transported the ark of God out of Abinadab's house on a new cart. Uzzah and Ahio drove the cart. 8 David and all Israel danced before God with all their might, singing to the accompaniment of harps, lyres, tambourines, cymbals and trumpets. 9 When they came to the threshing-floor of the Javelin, Uzzah reached out his hand to steady the ark, as the oxen were making it tilt. 10 This roused Yahweh's anger against Uzzah, and he struck him down because he had laid his hand on the Ark, and there he died before God. 11 David resented Yahweh's having broken out against Uzzah, and the place was given the name Perez-Uzzah, which it still has today.

12 That day David felt afraid of God. 'How can I bring the ark of God to be with me?' he said. 13 So David did not take the ark with him into the City of David but had it put in the house of Obed-Edom of Gath. 14 The ark of God remained

of Obed-edom in his house three months, and the LORD blessed the household of Obed-edom and all that he had.

14 King Hiram of Tyre sent messengers to David, along with cedar logs, and masons and carpenters to build a house for him. 2 David then perceived that the LORD had established him as king over Israel, and that his kingdom was highly exalted for the sake of his people Israel.

3 David took more wives in Jerusalem, and David became the father of more sons and daughters. 4 These are the names of the children whom he had in Jerusalem: Shammua, Shobab, and Nathan; Solomon, 5 Ibhar, Elishua, and Elpelet; 6 Nogah, Nepheg, and Japhia; 7 Elishama, Beeliada, and Eliphelet.

8 When the Philistines heard that David had been anointed king over all Israel, all the Philistines went up in search of David; and David heard of it and went out against them. 9 Now the Philistines had come and made a raid in the valley of Rephaim. 10 David inquired of God, "Shall I go up against the Philistines? Will you give them into my hand?" The LORD said to him, "Go up, and I will give them into your hand." 11 So he went up to Baal-perazim, and David defeated them there. David said, "God has burst out*n* against my enemies by my hand, like a bursting flood." Therefore that place is called Baal-perazim.*o* 12 They abandoned their gods there, and at David's command they were burned.

13 Once again the Philistines made a raid in the valley. 14 When David again inquired of God, God said to him, "You shall not go up after them; go around and come on them opposite the balsam trees. 15 When you hear the sound of marching in the tops of the balsam trees, then go out to battle; for God has gone out before you to strike down the army of the Philistines." 16 David did as God had commanded him, and they struck down the Philistine army from Gibeon to Gezer. 17 The fame of David went out into all lands, and the LORD brought the fear of him on all nations.

15 David*p* built houses for himself in the city of David, and he prepared a place for the ark of God and pitched a tent for it. 2 Then David commanded that no one but the Levites were to carry the ark of God, for the LORD had chosen them to carry the ark of the LORD and to minister to him forever. 3 David assembled all Israel in Jerusalem to bring up the ark of the LORD to its place, which he had prepared for it. 4 Then David gathered together the descendants of Aaron and the Levites: 5 of the sons of Kohath, Uriel the chief, with one hundred twenty of his kindred; 6 of the sons of Merari, Asaiah the chief, with two hundred twenty of his kindred; 7 of the sons of Gershom, Joel the chief, with one hundred thirty of his kindred; 8 of the sons of Elizaphan, Shemaiah the chief, with two hundred of his kindred; 9 of the sons of Hebron, Eliel the chief, with eighty of his kindred; 10 of the sons of Uzziel, Amminadab the chief, with one hundred twelve of his kindred.

11 David summoned the priests Zadok and Abiathar, and the Levites Uriel, Asaiah, Joel, Shemaiah, Eliel, and Amminadab. 12 He said to them, "You are the heads of families of the Levites; sanctify yourselves, you and your kindred, so that you may bring up the ark of the LORD, the God of Israel, to the place that I have prepared for it. 13 Because you did not carry it the first time,*q* the LORD our God burst out against us, because we did not give it proper care." 14 So the priests and the Levites sanctified themselves

remained in its tent beside Obed-edom's house for three months, and the LORD blessed the family of Obed-edom and all that he had.

14 King Hiram of Tyre sent envoys to David with cedar logs, and with them masons and carpenters to build him a house. 2 David knew by now that the LORD had confirmed him as king over Israel and had enhanced his royal power for the sake of his people Israel.

3 David married more wives in Jerusalem, and more sons and daughters were born to him. 4 These are the names of the children born to him in Jerusalem: Shammua, Shobab, Nathan, Solomon, 5 Ibhar, Elishua, Elpelet, 6 Nogah, Nepheg, Japhia, 7 Elishama, Beeliada, and Eliphelet.

8 When the Philistines learnt that David had been anointed king over the whole of Israel, they came up in force to seek him out. David, getting wind of this, went out to face them. 9 When the Philistines came and raided the valley of Rephaim, 10 David enquired of God, 'If I attack the Philistines, will you deliver them into my hands?' The LORD answered, 'Go, I shall deliver them into your hands.' 11 He went up and attacked and defeated them at Baal-perazim. 'God has used me to break through my enemies' lines', David said, 'as a river breaks through its banks.' That is why the place was named Baal-perazim. 12 The Philistines abandoned their gods there, and by David's orders these were burnt.

13 The Philistines made another raid on the valley. 14 Again David enquired of God, who said to him, 'No, you must attack towards their rear; make a detour without making contact and come upon them opposite the aspens. 15 As soon as you hear a rustling sound in the treetops, then give battle at once, for God will have gone out before you to defeat the Philistine army.' 16 David did as God had commanded, and the Philistine army was driven in flight all the way from Gibeon to Gezer. 17 David's fame spread through every land, and the LORD inspired all nations with dread of him.

15 DAVID built himself quarters in the City of David, and prepared a place for the Ark of God and pitched a tent for it. 2 He decreed that only Levites should carry the Ark of God, since they had been chosen by the LORD to carry it and to serve him for ever. 3 David assembled all Israel at Jerusalem to bring up the Ark of the LORD to the place he had prepared for it. 4 He gathered together the descendants of Aaron and the Levites: 5 of the descendants of Kohath, Uriel the chief with a hundred and twenty of his kinsmen; 6 of the descendants of Merari, Asaiah the chief with two hundred and twenty of his kinsmen; 7 of the descendants of Gershom, Joel the chief with a hundred and thirty of his kinsmen; 8 of the descendants of Elizaphan, Shemaiah the chief with two hundred of his kinsmen; 9 of the descendants of Hebron, Eliel the chief with eighty of his kinsmen; 10 of the descendants of Uzziel, Amminadab the chief with a hundred and twelve of his kinsmen.

11 David summoned Zadok and Abiathar the priests, together with the Levites Uriel, Asaiah, Joel, Shemaiah, Eliel, and Amminadab, 12 and said to them, 'You are heads of families of the Levites; hallow yourselves, you and your kinsmen, and bring up the Ark of the LORD the God of Israel to the place which I have prepared for it. 13 It was because you were not present the first time that the LORD our God broke out upon us. For we had not sought his guidance as we should have done.' 14 The priests and the Levites then

13:14 **its:** or his.   14:1–16 Cp. 2 Sam. 5:11–25.   14:2 **and:** so Aram. (Targ.), cp. 2 Sam. 5:12; Heb. omits.   14:4–7 Cp. 7:3–8. 14:11 **He:** so Gk, cp. 2 Sam. 5:20; Heb. They. **Baal-perazim:** that is Baal of Break-through.   14:14 **No . . . contact and:** or Do not go up to the attack; withdraw from them and then.   15:2 **him:** or it.

n Heb paraz   *o* That is Lord of Bursting Out   *p* Heb He
q Meaning of Heb uncertain

of God remained in the house of Obed-edom with his family for three months, and the LORD blessed Obed-edom's household and all that he possessed.

14 Hiram, king of Tyre, sent envoys to David along with masons and carpenters, and cedar wood to build him a house. 2 David now understood that the LORD had truly confirmed him as king over Israel, for his kingdom was greatly exalted for the sake of his people Israel. 3 David took other wives in Jerusalem and became the father of more sons and daughters. 4 These are the names of those who were born to him in Jerusalem: Shammua, Shobab, Nathan, Solomon, 5 Ibhar, Elishua, Elpelet, 6 Nogah, Nepheg, Japhia, 7 Elishama, Beeliada, and Eliphelet.

8 When the Philistines had heard that David was anointed king over all Israel, they went up in unison to seek him out. But when David heard of this, he marched out against them. 9 Meanwhile the Philistines had come and raided the valley of Rephaim. 10 David inquired of God, "Shall I advance against the Philistines, and will you deliver them into my power?" The LORD answered him, "Advance, for I will deliver them into your power." 11 They advanced, therefore, to Baal-perazim, and David defeated them there. Then David said, "God has used me to break through my enemies just as water breaks through a dam." Therefore that place was called Baal-perazim. 12 The Philistines had left their gods there, and David ordered them to be burnt.

13 Once again the Philistines raided the valley, 14 and again David inquired of God. But God answered him: "Do not try to pursue them, but go around them and come upon them from the direction of the mastic trees. 15 When you hear the sound of marching in the tops of the mastic trees, then go forth to battle, for God has already gone before you to strike the army of the Philistines." 16 David did as God commanded him, and they routed the Philistine army from Gibeon to Gezer.

17 Thus David's fame was spread abroad through every land, and the LORD made all the nations fear him.

15 David built houses for himself in the City of David and prepared a place for the ark of God, pitching a tent for it there. 2 At that time he said, "No one may carry the ark of God except the Levites, for the LORD chose them to carry the ark of the LORD and to minister to him forever." 3 Then David assembled all Israel in Jerusalem to bring the ark of the LORD to the place which he had prepared for it. 4 David also called together the sons of Aaron and the Levites: 5 of the sons of Kohath, Uriel, their chief, and one hundred and twenty of his brethren; 6 of the sons of Merari, Asaiah, their chief, and two hundred and twenty of his brethren; 7 of the sons of Gershon, Joel, their chief, and one hundred and thirty of his brethren; 8 of the sons of Elizaphan, Shemaiah, their chief, and two hundred of his brethren; 9 of the sons of Hebron, Eliel, their chief, and eighty of his brethren; 10 of the sons of Uzziel, Amminadab, their chief, and one hundred and twelve of his brethren. 11 David summoned the priests Zadok and Abiathar, and the Levites Uriel, Asaiah, Joel, Shemaiah, Eliel, and Amminadab, 12 and said to them: "You, the heads of the levitical families, must sanctify yourselves along with your brethren and bring the ark of the LORD, the God of Israel, to the place which I have prepared for it. 13 Because you were not with us the first time, the wrath of the LORD our God burst upon us, for we did not seek him aright." 14 Ac-

with Obed-Edom, in his house, for three months, and Yahweh blessed Obed-Edom's family and everything that belonged to him.

14 Hiram king of Tyre sent envoys to David, with cedar wood, stone-cutters and carpenters, to build him a palace. 2 David then knew that Yahweh had confirmed him as king of Israel and, for the sake of his people, had extended his sovereignty. 3 David took more wives in Jerusalem and fathered more sons and daughters. 4 These are the names of the children born to him in Jerusalem: Shammua, Shobab, Nathan, Solomon, 5 Ibhar, Elishua, Elpelet, 6 Nogah, Nepheg, Japhia, 7 Elishama, Beeliada, Eliphelet.

8 When the Philistines heard that David had been anointed as king of all Israel, they all invaded to seek him out. On hearing this, David marched out towards them. 9 When the Philistines arrived, they deployed in the Valley of the Rephaim. 10 David consulted God and asked, 'Shall I attack the Philistines? Will you deliver them into my power?' Yahweh replied to him, 'Attack! I shall deliver them into your power.' 11 Accordingly, they went up to Baal-Perazim and there David defeated them. David said, 'Through me God has made a breach in my enemies, as though they had been breached by a flood.' This is why the place was given the name Baal-Perazim. 12 They had left their gods behind there, and David ordered them to be burnt.

13 Again the Philistines deployed in the valley. 14 David again consulted God, and God replied, 'Do not attack them from the front; go round and engage them opposite the balsam trees. 15 When you hear the sound of footsteps in the tops of the balsam trees, launch your attack, for that will be God going out ahead of you to defeat the Philistine army.' 16 David did as God had ordered, and they beat the Philistine army from Gibeon to Gezer.

17 David's fame then spread to every country, and Yahweh made him feared by every nation.

15 After he had put up buildings for himself in the City of David, he prepared a place for the ark of God and pitched a tent for it. 2 David then said, 'No one but the Levites should carry the ark of God, since Yahweh has chosen them to carry the ark of Yahweh and to minister to him for ever.' 3 David then summoned all Israel to Jerusalem, to move the ark of Yahweh to the place which he had prepared for it. 4 David also called the sons of Aaron and the Levites together: 5 of the sons of Kohath: Uriel the chief and his hundred and twenty kinsmen; 6 of the sons of Merari: Asaiah the chief and his two hundred and twenty kinsmen; 7 of the sons of Gershom: Joel the chief and his hundred and thirty kinsmen; 8 of the sons of Elizaphan: Shemaiah the chief and his two hundred kinsmen; 9 of the sons of Hebron: Eliel the chief and eighty kinsmen; 10 of the sons of Uzziel: Amminadab the chief and his hundred and twelve kinsmen.

11 David then sent for the priests Zadok and Abiathar, and the Levites Uriel, Asaiah, Joel, Shemaiah, Eliel and Amminadab. 12 To them he said, 'You are the heads of the levitical families. Sanctify yourselves, you and your kinsmen, so that you can move the ark of Yahweh, God of Israel, to the place which I have prepared for it. 13 Because you were not there the first time, Yahweh our God broke out at us because we did not handle it properly.' 14 So the

to bring up the ark of the LORD, the God of Israel. 15 And the Levites carried the ark of God on their shoulders with the poles, as Moses had commanded according to the word of the LORD.

16 David also commanded the chiefs of the Levites to appoint their kindred as the singers to play on musical instruments, on harps and lyres and cymbals, to raise loud sounds of joy. 17 So the Levites appointed Heman son of Joel; and of his kindred Asaph son of Berechiah; and of the sons of Merari, their kindred, Ethan son of Kushaiah; 18 and with them their kindred of the second order, Zechariah, Jaaziel, Shemiramoth, Jehiel, Unni, Eliab, Benaiah, Maaseiah, Mattithiah, Eliphelehu, and Mikneiah, and the gatekeepers Obed-edom and Jeiel. 19 The singers Heman, Asaph, and Ethan were to sound bronze cymbals; 20 Zechariah, Aziel, Shemiramoth, Jehiel, Unni, Eliab, Maaseiah, and Benaiah were to play harps according to Alamoth; 21 but Mattithiah, Eliphelehu, Mikneiah, Obed-edom, Jeiel, and Azaziah were to lead with lyres according to the Sheminith. 22 Chenaniah, leader of the Levites in music, was to direct the music, for he understood it. 23 Berechiah and Elkanah were to be gatekeepers for the ark. 24 Shebaniah, Joshaphat, Nethanel, Amasai, Zechariah, Benaiah, and Eliezer, the priests, were to blow the trumpets before the ark of God. Obed-edom and Jehiah also were to be gatekeepers for the ark.

25 So David and the elders of Israel, and the commanders of the thousands, went to bring up the ark of the covenant of the LORD from the house of Obed-edom with rejoicing. 26 And because God helped the Levites who were carrying the ark of the covenant of the LORD, they sacrificed seven bulls and seven rams. 27 David was clothed with a robe of fine linen, as also were all the Levites who were carrying the ark, and the singers, and Chenaniah the leader of the music of the singers; and David wore a linen ephod. 28 So all Israel brought up the ark of the covenant of the LORD with shouting, to the sound of the horn, trumpets, and cymbals, and made loud music on harps and lyres.

29 As the ark of the covenant of the LORD came to the city of David, Michal daughter of Saul looked out of the window, and saw King David leaping and dancing; and she despised him in her heart.

16 They brought in the ark of God, and set it inside the tent that David had pitched for it; and they offered burnt offerings and offerings of well-being before God. 2 When David had finished offering the burnt offerings and the offerings of well-being, he blessed the people in the name of the LORD; 3 and he distributed to every person in Israel — man and woman alike — to each a loaf of bread, a portion of meat,r and a cake of raisins.

4 He appointed certain of the Levites as ministers before the ark of the LORD, to invoke, to thank, and to praise the LORD, the God of Israel. 5 Asaph was the chief, and second to him Zechariah, Jeiel, Shemiramoth, Jehiel, Mattithiah, Eliab, Benaiah, Obed-edom, and Jeiel, with harps and lyres; Asaph was to sound the cymbals, 6 and the priests Benaiah and Jahaziel were to blow trumpets regularly, before the ark of the covenant of God.

7 Then on that day David first appointed the singing of praises to the LORD by Asaph and his kindred.

8 O give thanks to the LORD, call on his name,
make known his deeds among the peoples.

hallowed themselves to bring up the Ark of the LORD the God of Israel, 15 and the Levites carried the Ark of God, bearing it on their shoulders with poles as Moses had ordered on instructions from the LORD.

16 David ordered the chiefs of the Levites to install as musicians those of their kinsmen who were players skilled in making joyful music on their instruments — lutes, lyres, and cymbals. 17 The Levites installed Heman son of Joel and, from his kinsmen, Asaph son of Berechiah; and from their kinsmen the Merarites, Ethan son of Kushaiah, 18 together with their kinsmen of the second degree Zechariah, Jaaziel, Shemiramoth, Jehiel, Unni, Eliab, Benaiah, Maaseiah, Mattithiah, Eliphelehu, and Mikneiah, and the doorkeepers Obed-edom and Jeiel. 19 They installed the musicians Heman, Asaph, and Ethan to sound the bronze cymbals; 20 Zechariah, Jaaziel, Shemiramoth, Jehiel, Unni, Eliab, Maaseiah, and Benaiah to play on lutes; 21 Mattithiah, Eliphelehu, Mikneiah, Obed-edom, Jeiel, and Azaziah to play on lyres. 22 Kenaniah, officer of the Levites, was precentor in charge of the music because of his proficiency.

23 Berechiah and Elkanah were door-keepers for the Ark, 24 while the priests Shebaniah, Joshaphat, Nethanel, Amasai, Zechariah, Benaiah, and Eliezer sounded the trumpets before the Ark of God; and Obed-edom and Jehiah also were door-keepers for the Ark.

25 Then David and the elders of Israel and the captains of units of a thousand went to bring up the Ark of the Covenant of the LORD with much rejoicing from the house of Obededom. 26 Because God had helped the Levites who carried the Ark of the Covenant of the LORD, they sacrificed seven bulls and seven rams. 27 David and all the Levites who carried the Ark, and the musicians, and Kenaniah the precentor, were arrayed in robes of fine linen; and David had on a linen ephod. 28 All Israel escorted the Ark of the Covenant of the LORD with acclamation, blowing on horns and trumpets, clashing cymbals, and playing on lutes and lyres. 29 As the Ark of the Covenant of the LORD was entering the City of David, Saul's daughter Michal looked down from a window and saw King David dancing and making merry, and she despised him in her heart.

16 After they had brought the Ark of God, they put it inside the tent that David had set up for it, and they offered whole-offerings and shared-offerings before God. 2 Having completed these sacrifices, David blessed the people in the name of the LORD 3 and distributed food, a loaf of bread, a portion of meat, and a cake of raisins, to each Israelite, man or woman. 4 He appointed certain Levites to serve before the Ark of the LORD, to celebrate, to give thanks, and to praise the LORD the God of Israel. 5 Their leader was Asaph; second to him was Zechariah; then came Jaaziel, Shemiramoth, Jehiel, Mattithiah, Eliab, Benaiah, Obed-edom, and Jeiel, with lutes and lyres; Asaph, who sounded the cymbals; 6 and Benaiah and Jahaziel the priests, who blew the trumpets regularly before the Ark of the Covenant of God.

7 It was then that David first ordained the offering of thanks to the LORD by Asaph and his kinsmen:

8 Give thanks to the LORD, invoke him by name,
make known his deeds among the peoples.

15:18 Zechariah: so some MSS, cp. verse 20; others add a son.
15:20 on lutes: prob. rdg; Heb. adds al alamoth, possibly a musical term.   15:21 on lyres: prob. rdg; Heb. adds al hashsheminith lenasseah, probably musical terms.   15:25–29 Cp. 2 Sam. 6:12–16.   15:27 the precentor: prob. rdg; Heb. obscure. 16:1–3 Cp. 2 Sam. 6:17–19.   16:3 portion of meat: meaning of Heb. word uncertain.   16:5 Jaaziel: prob. rdg, cp. 15:18,20; Heb. Jeiel.   16:8–22 Cp. Ps. 105:1–15.

r Compare Gk Syr Vg: Meaning of Heb uncertain

cordingly, the priests and the Levites sanctified themselves to bring up the ark of the LORD, the God of Israel. 15 The Levites bore the ark of God on their shoulders with poles, as Moses had ordained according to the word of the LORD.

16 David commanded the chiefs of the Levites to appoint their brethren as chanters, to play on musical instruments, harps, lyres, and cymbals, to make a loud sound of rejoicing. 17 Therefore the Levites appointed Heman, son of Joel, and, among his brethren, Asaph, son of Berechiah; and among the sons of Merari, their brethren, Ethan, son of Kushaiah; 18 and, together with these, their brethren of the second rank: the gatekeepers Zechariah, Uzziel, Shemiramoth, Jehiel, Unni, Eliab, Benaiah, Maaseiah, Mattithiah, Eliphelehu, Mikneiah, Obed-edom, and Jeiel. 19 The chanters, Heman, Asaph, and Ethan, sounded brass cymbals. 20 Zechariah, Uzziel, Shemiramoth, Jehiel, Unni, Eliab, Maaseiah, and Benaiah played on harps set to "Alamoth." 21 But Mattithiah, Eliphelehu, Mikneiah, Obed-edom, and Jeiel led the chant on lyres set to "the eighth." 22 Chenaniah was the chief of the Levites in the chanting; he directed the chanting, for he was skillful. 23 Berechiah and Elkanah were gatekeepers before the ark. 24 The priests, Shebaniah, Joshaphat, Nethanel, Amasai, Zechariah, Benaiah, and Eliezer, sounded the trumpets before the ark of God. Obed-edom and Jeiel were also gatekeepers before the ark.

25 Thus David, the elders of Israel, and the commanders of thousands went to bring up the ark of the covenant of the LORD with joy from the house of Obed-edom. 26 While the Levites, with God's help, were bearing the ark of the covenant of the LORD, seven bulls and seven rams were sacrificed. 27 David was clothed in a robe of fine linen, as were all the Levites who carried the ark, the singers, and Chenaniah, the leader of the chant; David was also wearing a linen ephod. 28 Thus all Israel brought back the ark of the covenant of the LORD with joyful shouting, and to the sound of horns, trumpets, and cymbals, and the music of harps and lyres. 29 But as the ark of the covenant of the LORD was entering the City of David, Michal, daughter of Saul, looked down from her window, and when she saw King David leaping and dancing, she despised him in her heart.

16 They brought in the ark of God and set it within the tent which David had pitched for it. Then they offered up holocausts and peace offerings to God. 2 When David had finished offering up the holocausts and peace offerings, he blessed the people in the name of the LORD, 3 and distributed to every Israelite, to every man and to every woman, a loaf of bread, a piece of meat, and a raisin cake.

4 He now appointed certain Levites to minister before the ark of the LORD, to celebrate, thank, and praise the LORD, the God of Israel. 5 Asaph was their chief, and second to him were Zechariah, Uzziel, Shemiramoth, Jehiel, Mattithiah, Eliab, Benaiah, Obed-edom, and Jeiel. These were to play on harps and lyres, while Asaph was to sound the cymbals, 6 and the priests Benaiah and Jahaziel were to be the regular trumpeters before the ark of the covenant of God.

7 Then, on that same day, David appointed Asaph and his brethren to sing for the first time these praises of the LORD:

8 Give thanks to the LORD, invoke his name;
   make known among the nations his deeds.

priests and the Levites sanctified themselves, to move the ark of Yahweh, God of Israel, 15 and the Levites carried the ark of God with the shafts on their shoulders, as Moses had ordered in accordance with the word of Yahweh.

16 David also told the heads of the Levites to appoint their kinsmen as singers with the accompaniment of musical instruments, lyres, harps, and cymbals to play joyfully. 17 The Levites then appointed Heman son of Joel, Asaph son of Berechiah, one of his brothers, Ethan son of Kushaiah, one of their Merarite kinsmen; 18 and with them their kinsmen of the second rank: Zechariah, Uzziel, Shemiramoth, Jehiel, Unni, Eliab, Benaiah, Maaseiah, Mattithiah, Eliphelehu, Mikneiah, and Obed-Edom and Jehiel the gatekeepers. 19 The singers, Heman, Asaph and Ethan, were to play the bronze cymbals. 20 Zechariah, Uzziel, Shemiramoth, Jehiel, Unni, Eliab, Maaseiah and Benaiah were to play the lyre. 21 Mattithiah, Eliphelehu, Mikneiah, Obed-Edom, Jehiel and Azaziah, giving the beat, were to play the harp. 22 Chenaniah, the levitical director of transport was in charge of the transport, being skilful at it. 23 Berechiah and Elkanah were gatekeepers for the ark. 24 The priests Shebaniah, Joshaphat, Nethanel, Amasai, Zechariah, Benaiah and Eliezer blew trumpets before the ark of God, while Obed-Edom and Jehiah were also gatekeepers for the ark.

25 David, the elders of Israel and the commanders of the thousands accordingly went, amid great rejoicing, to bring the ark of the covenant of Yahweh up from Obed-Edom's house, 26 and since God was helping the Levites who carried the ark of the covenant of Yahweh, they sacrificed seven bulls and seven rams. 27 David, all the Levites who carried the ark, the singers and Chenaniah, director of transport, wore cloaks of fine linen. David also wore a linen *ephod*. 28 Thus, with war-cries and the sounding of the horn, the trumpets and the cymbals, and the music of lyres and harps, all Israel transported the ark of the covenant of Yahweh. 29 Now, as the ark of the covenant of Yahweh entered the City of David, Michal daughter of Saul was watching from the window and, when she saw King David dancing and playing, the sight of him filled her with contempt.

16 They brought the ark of God in and put it inside the tent which David had erected for it, and brought burnt offerings and made communion sacrifices in God's presence. 2 And when David had finished making burnt offerings and communion sacrifices, he blessed the people in the name of Yahweh. 3 To all the Israelites, both men and women, to each, he then distributed a loaf of bread, a portion of meat and a raisin cake.

4 He appointed some of the Levites as ministers before the ark of Yahweh, to extol, glorify and praise Yahweh, God of Israel; 5 first Asaph, second Zechariah, then Uzziel, Shemiramoth, Jehiel, Mattithiah, Eliab, Benaiah, Obed-Edom and Jeiel, who played the lyre and harp, while Asaph played the cymbals. 6 The priests Benaiah and Jahaziel continually blew the trumpet before the ark of the covenant of God. 7 On that day, David was the first to assign to Asaph and his kinsmen the giving of thanks to Yahweh:

8 Give thanks to Yahweh, call his name aloud,
   proclaim his deeds to the peoples.

9 Sing to him, sing praises to him,
  tell of all his wonderful works.
10 Glory in his holy name;
  let the hearts of those who seek the LORD
    rejoice.
11 Seek the LORD and his strength,
  seek his presence continually.
12 Remember the wonderful works he has done,
  his miracles, and the judgments he uttered,
13 O offspring of his servant Israel,*s*
  children of Jacob, his chosen ones.

14 He is the LORD our God;
  his judgments are in all the earth.
15 Remember his covenant forever,
  the word that he commanded, for a thousand
    generations,
16 the covenant that he made with Abraham,
  his sworn promise to Isaac,
17 which he confirmed to Jacob as a statute,
  to Israel as an everlasting covenant,
18 saying, "To you I will give the land of Canaan
  as your portion for an inheritance."

19 When they were few in number,
  of little account, and strangers in the land,*t*
20 wandering from nation to nation,
  from one kingdom to another people,
21 he allowed no one to oppress them;
  he rebuked kings on their account,
22 saying, "Do not touch my anointed ones;
  do my prophets no harm."

23 Sing to the LORD, all the earth.
  Tell of his salvation from day to day.
24 Declare his glory among the nations,
  his marvelous works among all the peoples.
25 For great is the LORD, and greatly to be praised;
  he is to be revered above all gods.
26 For all the gods of the peoples are idols,
  but the LORD made the heavens.
27 Honor and majesty are before him;
  strength and joy are in his place.

28 Ascribe to the LORD, O families of the peoples,
  ascribe to the LORD glory and strength.
29 Ascribe to the LORD the glory due his name;
  bring an offering, and come before him.
  Worship the LORD in holy splendor;
30 tremble before him, all the earth.
  The world is firmly established; it shall never
    be moved.
31 Let the heavens be glad, and let the earth rejoice,
  and let them say among the nations, "The
    LORD is king!"
32 Let the sea roar, and all that fills it;
  let the field exult, and everything in it.
33 Then shall the trees of the forest sing for joy
  before the LORD, for he comes to judge the
    earth.
34 O give thanks to the LORD, for he is good;
  for his steadfast love endures forever.

35 Say also:
  "Save us, O God of our salvation,
    and gather and rescue us from among the
      nations,
  that we may give thanks to your holy name,
    and glory in your praise.

9 Pay him honour with song and psalm
  and tell of all his marvellous deeds.
10 Exult in his hallowed name;
  let those who seek the LORD be joyful in heart.
11 Look to the LORD and be strong;
  at all times seek his presence.
12 Remember the marvels he has wrought,
  his portents and the judgements he has given,
13 you descendants of Israel, his servants,
  you children of Jacob, his chosen ones!

14 He is the LORD our God;
  his judgements cover the whole world.
15 He is ever mindful of his covenant,
  the promise he ordained for a thousand
    generations,
16 the covenant made with Abraham,
  his oath given to Isaac,
17 and confirmed as a statute for Jacob,
  as an everlasting covenant for Israel:
18 'I shall give you the land of Canaan', he said,
  'as your allotted holding.'

19 A small company it was,
  few in number, strangers in that land,
20 wandering from nation to nation,
  from one kingdom to another;
21 but he let no one oppress them;
  on their account he rebuked kings:
22 'Do not touch my anointed servants,' he said;
  'do no harm to my prophets.'

23 Sing to the LORD, all the earth,
  proclaim his victory day by day.
24 Declare his glory among the nations,
  his marvellous deeds to every people.
25 Great is the LORD and most worthy of praise;
  he is more to be feared than all gods.
26 For the gods of the nations are idols every one;
  but the LORD made the heavens.
27 Majesty and splendour attend him,
  might and joy are in his dwelling.

28 Ascribe to the LORD, you families of nations,
  ascribe to the LORD glory and might;
29 ascribe to the LORD the glory due to his name.
  Bring an offering and come before him.
  Worship the LORD in holy attire.
30 Tremble before him, all the earth.
  He has established the earth immovably.
31 Let the heavens rejoice and the earth be glad;
  let it be declared among the nations, 'The LORD is
    king.'
32 Let the sea resound and everything in it,
  let the fields exult and all that is in them;
33 let the trees of the forest shout for joy
  before the LORD, when he comes to judge the
    earth.
34 It is good to give thanks to the LORD,
  for his love endures for ever.
35 Cry, 'Deliver us, God our saviour;
  gather us in and save us from the nations
  that we may give thanks to your holy name
  and make your praise our pride.'

16:11 **and be strong:** *or* the symbol of his strength; *lit.* and his
strength.   16:13 **servants:** *so Gk; Heb.* servant.   16:15 **He is
. . . covenant:** *so some Gk MSS, cp. Ps. 105:8; Heb.* For ever call
his covenant to mind.   16:19 **it was:** *so some MSS, cp. Ps.
105:12; others* you were.   16:23–33 *Cp. Ps. 96:1–13.*
16:34 *Cp. Ps. 107:1.*   16:35–36 *Cp. Ps. 106:47–48.*

---

s Another reading is *Abraham* (compare Ps 105.6)   *t* Heb *in it*

NEW AMERICAN BIBLE	NEW JERUSALEM BIBLE

NEW AMERICAN BIBLE

9 Sing to him, sing his praise,
   proclaim all his wondrous deeds.
10 Glory in his holy name;
   rejoice, O hearts that seek the LORD!
11 Look to the LORD in his strength;
   seek to serve him constantly.
12 Recall the wondrous deeds that he has wrought,
   his portents, and the judgments he has uttered,
13 You descendants of Israel, his servants,
   sons of Jacob, his chosen ones!

14 He, the LORD, is our God;
   throughout the earth his judgments prevail.
15 He remembers forever his covenant
   which he made binding for a
      thousand generations —
16 Which he entered into with Abraham
   and by his oath to Isaac;
17 Which he established for Jacob by statute,
   for Israel as an everlasting covenant,
18 Saying, "To you will I give the land of Canaan
   as your alloted inheritance."

19 When they were few in number,
   a handful, and strangers there,
20 Wandering from nation to nation,
   from one kingdom to another people,
21 He let no one oppress them,
   and for their sake he rebuked kings:
22 "Touch not my anointed,
   and to my prophets do no harm."

23 Sing to the LORD, all the earth,
   announce his salvation, day after day.
24 Tell his glory among the nations;
   among all peoples, his wondrous deeds.
25 For great is the LORD and highly to be praised;
   and awesome is he, beyond all gods.
26 For all the gods of the nations are things
      of nought,
   but the LORD made the heavens.
27 Splendor and majesty go before him;
   praise and joy are in his holy place.

28 Give to the LORD, you families of nations,
   give to the LORD glory and praise;
29 Give to the LORD the glory due his name!
   Bring gifts, and enter his presence;
   worship the LORD in holy attire.
30 Tremble before him, all the earth;
   he has made the world firm, not to be moved.

31 Let the heavens be glad and the earth rejoice;
   let them say among the nations: The LORD
      is king.
32 Let the sea and what fills it resound;
   let the plains rejoice and all that is in them!
33 Then shall all the trees of the forest exult
   before the LORD, for he comes:
   he comes to rule the earth.

34 Give thanks to the LORD, for he is good,
   for his kindness endures forever;
35 And say, "Save us, O God, our savior,
   gather us and deliver us from the nations,
   That we may give thanks to your holy name
   and glory in praising you."

NEW JERUSALEM BIBLE

9 Chant to him, play to him,
   sing about all his wonders!
10 Take pride in his holy name,
   let your heart rejoice, you seekers of Yahweh!
11 Seek out Yahweh, seek his strength,
   continually seek out his presence!
12 Remember what wonders he has done,
   what miracles, what rulings he has given,
13 you offspring of Israel his servant,
   you children of Jacob his chosen one!

14 For he is Yahweh our God,
   his authority extends throughout the world.
15 For ever remember his covenant,
   the pact imposed for a thousand generations,
16 which he concluded with Abraham,
   which was sworn by him to Isaac,
17 since he confirmed it as a law for Jacob,
   as an eternal covenant for Israel,
18 saying, 'I will give you the country;
   Canaan is the measure of your inheritance,

19 'though you are few in number,
   only a few strangers there!'

20 As they wandered from nation to nation,
   from this kingdom to that people,
21 he would not let anyone oppress them
   and on their account he admonished kings,
22 'You are not to touch my anointed ones,
   my prophets are not to be harmed!'

23 Sing to Yahweh, all the earth,
   day after day proclaim his salvation!
24 Declare his glory among the nations,
   his marvels to every people!
25 Great is Yahweh, worthy of all praise,
   more awesome than any of the gods.
26 Nothingness, all the gods of the nations.

   Yahweh it was who made the heavens,
27 in his presence are splendour and majesty,
   in his sanctuary strength and joy.

28 Give Yahweh his due, families of peoples,
   give Yahweh his due of glory and power,
29 give Yahweh the glory due to his name!

   Bring an offering and enter his courts,
   bow down to Yahweh in his sacred court,
30 tremble before him, all the earth!

   The world is firm, it cannot be moved,
31 let the heavens rejoice and earth be glad!
   Say among the nations, 'Yahweh is king!'
32 Let the sea thunder and all it holds,
   the countryside exult and everything that is in it,
33 and all the trees of the forest cry out for joy
   at Yahweh's approach, for he is coming to judge
      the earth.

34 Give thanks to Yahweh, for he is good,
   for his faithful love lasts for ever!
35 Say, 'Save us, God of our salvation,
   gather us together and free us from the nations —
   so that we may give thanks to your holy name —
   to be extolled whenever you are praised!'

36 Blessed be the LORD, the God of Israel,
from everlasting to everlasting."

Then all the people said "Amen!" and praised the LORD.

37 David left Asaph and his kinsfolk there before the ark of the covenant of the LORD to minister regularly before the ark as each day required, 38 and also Obed-edom and his*u* sixty-eight kinsfolk; while Obed-edom son of Jeduthun and Hosah were to be gatekeepers. 39 And he left the priest Zadok and his kindred the priests before the tabernacle of the LORD in the high place that was at Gibeon, 40 to offer burnt offerings to the LORD on the altar of burnt offering regularly, morning and evening, according to all that is written in the law of the LORD that he commanded Israel. 41 With them were Heman and Jeduthun, and the rest of those chosen and expressly named to render thanks to the LORD, for his steadfast love endures forever. 42 Heman and Jeduthun had with them trumpets and cymbals for the music, and instruments for sacred song. The sons of Jeduthun were appointed to the gate.

43 Then all the people departed to their homes, and David went home to bless his household.

17 Now when David settled in his house, David said to the prophet Nathan, "I am living in a house of cedar, but the ark of the covenant of the LORD is under a tent." 2 Nathan said to David, "Do all that you have in mind, for God is with you."

3 But that same night the word of the LORD came to Nathan, saying: 4 Go and tell my servant David: Thus says the LORD: You shall not build me a house to live in. 5 For I have not lived in a house since the day I brought out Israel to this very day, but I have lived in a tent and a tabernacle.*v* 6 Wherever I have moved about among all Israel, did I ever speak a word with any of the judges of Israel, whom I commanded to shepherd my people, saying, Why have you not built me a house of cedar? 7 Now therefore thus you shall say to my servant David: Thus says the LORD of hosts: I took you from the pasture, from following the sheep, to be ruler over my people Israel; 8 and I have been with you wherever you went, and have cut off all your enemies before you; and I will make for you a name, like the name of the great ones of the earth. 9 I will appoint a place for my people Israel, and will plant them, so that they may live in their own place, and be disturbed no more; and evildoers shall wear them down no more, as they did formerly, 10 from the time that I appointed judges over my people Israel; and I will subdue all your enemies.

Moreover I declare to you that the LORD will build you a house. 11 When your days are fulfilled to go to be with your ancestors, I will raise up your offspring after you, one of your own sons, and I will establish his kingdom. 12 He shall build a house for me, and I will establish his throne forever. 13 I will be a father to him, and he shall be a son to me. I will not take my steadfast love from him, as I took it from him who was before you, 14 but I will confirm him in my house and in my kingdom forever, and his throne shall be established forever. 15 In accordance with all these words and all this vision, Nathan spoke to David.

16 Then King David went in and sat before the LORD, and said, "Who am I, O LORD God, and what is my house, that you have brought me thus far? 17 And even this was a small thing in your sight, O God; you have also spoken of your servant's house for a great while to come. You regard me as someone of high rank,*w* O LORD God! 18 And what more can David say to you for honoring your servant? You know your servant. 19 For your servant's sake, O LORD, and

36 Blessed be the LORD, the God of Israel,
from everlasting to everlasting.

And all the people said 'Amen' and 'Praise the LORD.'

37 David left Asaph and his kinsmen there before the Ark of the Covenant of the LORD, to perform regular service before the Ark as each day's duty required. 38 As door-keepers he left Obed-edom son of Jeduthun, and Hosah. Obed-edom and his kinsmen were sixty-eight in number. 39 He left Zadok the priest and his kinsmen the priests before the Tabernacle of the LORD at the shrine in Gibeon, 40 to make offerings there to the LORD upon the altar of whole-offering regularly morning and evening, exactly as it is written in the law enjoined by the LORD on Israel. 41 With them he left Heman and Jeduthun and the other men chosen by name to give thanks to the LORD, 'for his love endures for ever'. 42 They had trumpets and cymbals for the players, and the instruments used for sacred song. The sons of Jeduthun kept the gate.

43 So all the people went home, and David returned to greet his household.

17 ONCE David was established in his palace, he said to Nathan the prophet, 'Here I am living in a house of cedar, while the Ark of the Covenant of the LORD is housed in a tent.' 2 Nathan answered, 'Do whatever you have in mind, for God is with you.' 3 But that same night the word of God came to Nathan: 4 'Go and say to David my servant, This is the word of the LORD: It is not you who are to build me a house to dwell in. 5 Down to this day I have never dwelt in a house since I brought Israel up from Egypt; I lived in a tent and a tabernacle. 6 Wherever I journeyed with Israel, did I ever ask any of the judges whom I appointed shepherds of my people why they had not built me a cedar house?

7 'Then say this to my servant David: This is the word of the LORD of Hosts: I took you from the pastures and from following the sheep to be prince over my people Israel. 8 I have been with you wherever you have gone, and have destroyed all the enemies in your path. I shall bring you fame like the fame of the great ones of the earth. 9 I shall assign a place for my people Israel; there I shall plant them to dwell in their own land. They will be disturbed no more; never again will the wicked wear them down as they did 10 in the past from the day when I appointed judges over my people Israel; and I shall subdue all your enemies.

'But I shall make you great and the LORD will build up your royal house. 11 When your life ends and you go to join your forefathers, I shall set up one of your family, one of your own sons, to succeed you, and I shall establish his kingdom. 12 It is he who will build me a house, and I shall establish his throne for all time. 13 I shall be a father to him, and he will be my son. I shall never withdraw my love from him as I withdrew it from your predecessor. 14 But I shall give him a sure place in my house and kingdom for all time, and his throne will endure for ever.'

15 Nathan recounted to David all that had been said to him and all that had been revealed. 16 Then King David went into the presence of the LORD and, taking his place there, said, 'Who am I, LORD God, and what is my family, that you have brought me thus far? 17 It was a small thing in your sight, God, to have planned for your servant's house in days long past, and now you look on me as a man already embarked on a high career, LORD God. 18 What more can David say to you of the honour you have done your servant? You yourself know your servant. 19 For the sake of your

---

16:38 **his:** *so Gk; Heb.* their.   16:42 **They:** *so Gk; Heb. adds* Heman and Jeduthun.   17:1–27 *Cp. 2 Sam. 7:1–29.*   17:5 **I lived ... tabernacle:** *prob. rdg; Heb.* I have been from tent to tent and from a tabernacle.

u Gk Syr Vg: Heb *their*   *v* Gk 2 Sam 7.6: Heb *but I have been from tent to tent and from tabernacle*   *w* Meaning of Heb uncertain

NEW AMERICAN BIBLE

36 Blessed be the LORD, the God of Israel,
through all eternity!
Let all the people say, Amen! Alleluia.

37 Then David left Asaph and his brethren there before the ark of the covenant of the LORD to minister before the ark regularly according to the daily ritual; 38 he also left there Obed-edom and sixty-eight of his brethren, including Obed-edom, son of Jeduthun, and Hosah, to be gatekeepers. 39 But the priest Zadok and his priestly brethren he left before the Dwelling of the LORD on the high place at Gibeon, 40 to offer holocausts to the LORD on the altar of holocausts regularly, morning and evening, and to do all that is written in the law of the LORD which he has decreed for Israel. 41 With them were Heman and Jeduthun and the others who were chosen and designated by name to give thanks to the LORD, "because his kindness endures forever," 42 with trumpets and cymbals for accompaniment, and instruments for the sacred chant. The sons of Jeduthun kept the gate. 43 Then all the people departed, each to his own home, and David returned to bless his household.

17 After David had taken up residence in his house, he said to Nathan the prophet, "See, I am living in a house of cedar, but the ark of the covenant of the LORD dwells under tentcloth." 2 Nathan replied to David, "Do, therefore, whatever you desire, for God is with you."

3 But that same night the word of God came to Nathan: 4 "Go and tell my servant David, Thus says the LORD: It is not you who are to build a house for me to dwell in. 5 For I have never dwelt in a house, from the time when I led Israel onward, even to this day, but I have been lodging in tent or pavilion 6 as long as I have wandered about with all of Israel. Did I ever say a word to any of the judges of Israel whom I commanded to guide my people, such as, 'Why have you not built me a house of cedar?' 7 Therefore, tell my servant David, Thus says the LORD of hosts: I took you from the pasture, from following the sheep, that you might become ruler over my people Israel. 8 I was with you wherever you went, and I cut down all your enemies before you. I will make your name great like that of the greatest on the earth. 9 I will assign a place for my people Israel and I will plant them in it to dwell there henceforth undisturbed; nor shall wicked men ever again oppress them, as they did at first, 10 and during all the time when I appointed judges over my people Israel. And I will subdue all your enemies. Moreover, I declare to you that I, the LORD, will build you a house; 11 so that when your days have been completed and you must join your fathers, I will raise up your offspring after you who will be one of your own sons, and I will establish his kingdom. 12 He it is who shall build me a house, and I will establish his throne forever. 13 I will be a father to him, and he shall be a son to me, and I will not withdraw my favor from him as I withdrew it from him who preceded you; 14 but I will maintain him in my house and in my kingdom forever, and his throne shall be firmly established forever."

15 All these words and this whole vision Nathan related exactly to David.

16 Then David came in and sat in the LORD's presence, saying: "Who am I, O LORD God, and what is my family, that you should have brought me as far as I have come? 17 And yet, even this you now consider too little, O God! For you have made a promise regarding your servant's family reaching into the distant future, and you have looked on me as henceforth the most notable of men, O LORD God. 18 What more can David say to you? You know your servant. 19 O LORD, for your servant's sake and in keeping

NEW JERUSALEM BIBLE

36 Blessed be Yahweh, God of Israel,
from everlasting to everlasting!

To which all the people said, 'Amen, Alleluia!'

37 There before the ark of the covenant of Yahweh David left Asaph and his kinsmen to maintain a permanent ministry before the ark as each day's ritual required, 38 and also Obed-Edom with his sixty-eight kinsmen. Obed-Edom son of Jeduthun, and Hosah were gatekeepers. 39 Zadok the priest and the priests, his kinsmen, he left before the dwelling of Yahweh on the high place at Gibeon 40 to bring burnt offerings to Yahweh unfailingly, morning and evening, on the altar of burnt offering, and to carry out all that is written in the Law of Yahweh laid down for Israel. 41 With them were Heman and Jeduthun and the rest of those who were chosen and assigned by name to give thanks to Yahweh, 'for his faithful love lasts for ever'. 42 With them were Heman and Jeduthun to play trumpets and cymbals, as well as instruments for accompanying sacred song. The sons of Jeduthun were in charge of the gates. 43 Then all the people went back to their homes, and David went back to bless his household.

17 It happened, once David had settled into his palace, that David said to the prophet Nathan, 'Here am I living in a cedar-wood palace, while the ark of the covenant of Yahweh is under awnings.' 2 Nathan said to David, 'Do whatever you have in mind, for God is with you.'

3 But that very night the word of God came to Nathan, as follows:

4 'Go and tell my servant David, "Yahweh says this: You must not build a temple for me to live in. 5 I have never lived in a house from the day when I brought Israel out until today, but have kept travelling from tent to tent and from shelter to shelter. 6 In all my travels with all Israel, did I say to any of the judges of Israel, whom I had commanded to shepherd my people: Why do you not build me a cedar-wood temple? 7 This is what you must say to my servant David: Yahweh Sabaoth says this: I took you from the pasture, from following the sheep, to be leader of my people Israel. 8 I have been with you wherever you went; I have got rid of all your enemies for you. I am going to make your fame like that of the greatest men on earth. 9 I am going to provide a place for my people Israel; I shall plant them there and there they will live and never be disturbed again; nor will they be oppressed by the wicked as they were in former times 10 ever since I instituted judges to govern my people Israel; I shall subdue all your enemies. Yahweh moreover tells you that he will build you a dynasty. 11 And when your days are over and you have gone to join your ancestors, I shall appoint your heir — who will be one of your sons — to succeed you, and I shall make his sovereignty secure. 12 He will build a temple for me and I shall make his throne secure for ever. 13 I shall be his father and he will be my son, and I shall not withdraw my favour from him, as I withdrew it from your predecessor. 14 I shall set him over my temple and kingdom for ever and his throne will be for ever secure."'

15 Nathan related all these words and this whole revelation to David.

16 King David then went in, sat down in Yahweh's presence and said:
'Who am I, Yahweh God, and what is my lineage, that you have led me as far as this? 17 Yet, to you, O God, this seemed too little, and now you extend your promises for your servant's family into the distant future, making me see as it were a whole succession of men, and it is Yahweh God himself who raises it up. 18 What more can David reply to you for the honour you have given to your servant? You yourself have singled out your servant. 19 For your servant,

| NEW REVISED STANDARD VERSION | REVISED ENGLISH BIBLE |

according to your own heart, you have done all these great deeds, making known all these great things. 20 There is no one like you, O LORD, and there is no God besides you, according to all that we have heard with our ears. 21 Who is like your people Israel, one nation on the earth whom God went to redeem to be his people, making for yourself a name for great and terrible things, in driving out nations before your people whom you redeemed from Egypt? 22 And you made your people Israel to be your people forever; and you, O LORD, became their God.

23 "And now, O LORD, as for the word that you have spoken concerning your servant and concerning his house, let it be established forever, and do as you have promised. 24 Thus your name will be established and magnified forever in the saying, 'The LORD of hosts, the God of Israel, is Israel's God'; and the house of your servant David will be established in your presence. 25 For you, my God, have revealed to your servant that you will build a house for him; therefore your servant has found it possible to pray before you. 26 And now, O LORD, you are God, and you have promised this good thing to your servant; 27 therefore may it please you to bless the house of your servant, that it may continue forever before you. For you, O LORD, have blessed and are blessed[x] forever."

18 Some time afterward, David attacked the Philistines and subdued them; he took Gath and its villages from the Philistines.

2 He defeated Moab, and the Moabites became subject to David and brought tribute.

3 David also struck down King Hadadezer of Zobah, toward Hamath,[y] as he went to set up a monument at the river Euphrates. 4 David took from him one thousand chariots, seven thousand cavalry, and twenty thousand foot soldiers. David hamstrung all the chariot horses, but left one hundred of them. 5 When the Arameans of Damascus came to help King Hadadezer of Zobah, David killed twenty-two thousand Arameans. 6 Then David put garrisons[z] in Aram of Damascus; and the Arameans became subject to David, and brought tribute. The LORD gave victory to David wherever he went. 7 David took the gold shields that were carried by the servants of Hadadezer, and brought them to Jerusalem. 8 From Tibhath and from Cun, cities of Hadadezer, David took a vast quantity of bronze; with it Solomon made the bronze sea and the pillars and the vessels of bronze.

9 When King Tou of Hamath heard that David had defeated the whole army of King Hadadezer of Zobah, 10 he sent his son Hadoram to King David, to greet him and to congratulate him, because he had fought against Hadadezer and defeated him. Now Hadadezer had often been at war with Tou. He sent all sorts of articles of gold, of silver, and of bronze; 11 these also King David dedicated to the LORD, together with the silver and gold that he had carried off from all the nations, from Edom, Moab, the Ammonites, the Philistines, and Amalek.

12 Abishai son of Zeruiah killed eighteen thousand Edomites in the Valley of Salt. 13 He put garrisons in Edom; and all the Edomites became subject to David. And the LORD gave victory to David wherever he went.

14 So David reigned over all Israel; and he administered justice and equity to all his people. 15 Joab son of Zeruiah was over the army; Jehoshaphat son of Ahilud was recorder;

servant, LORD, in accordance with your purpose, you have done this great thing and revealed all the great things to come.

20 'There is none like you, LORD; there is no God but you, as everything we have heard bears witness. 21 And your people Israel, to whom can they be compared? Is there any other nation on earth whom you, God, have set out to redeem from slavery to be your people? You have won renown for yourself by great and awesome deeds, driving out nations to make way for your people whom you redeemed from Egypt. 22 You have made your people Israel your own for ever, and you, LORD, have become their God.

23 'But now, LORD, let what you have promised for your servant and his house stand fast for all time; make good what you have promised. 24 Let it stand fast, that your fame may be great for evermore, and let people say, "The LORD of Hosts, the God of Israel, is Israel's God"; and may the house of your servant David be established before you. 25 You, my God, have shown me your purpose, to build up your servant's house; therefore I have been able to pray before you. 26 LORD, you are God, and you have made these noble promises to your servant. 27 Be pleased now to bless your servant's house, so that it may continue always before you; you it is who have blessed it, and it shall be blessed for ever.'

18 AFTER this David attacked and subdued the Philistines, and took from them Gath with its villages. 2 He defeated the Moabites, and they became subject to him and paid him tribute. 3 He also defeated King Hadadezer of Zobah-hamath, who was on his way to set up his monument of victory by the river Euphrates. 4 From him David captured a thousand chariots, seven thousand horsemen, and twenty thousand foot-soldiers; he hamstrung all the chariot-horses, except a hundred which he retained. 5 When the Aramaeans of Damascus came to the aid of King Hadadezer of Zobah, David destroyed twenty-two thousand of them, 6 and stationed garrisons among these Aramaeans; they became subject to him and paid him tribute. Thus the LORD gave David victory wherever he went. 7 David took the gold shields borne by Hadadezer's servants and brought them to Jerusalem; 8 he also removed from Hadadezer's cities Tibhath and Kun a great quantity of bronze, from which Solomon made the bronze Sea, the pillars, and the bronze vessels.

9 When King Tou of Hamath heard that David had defeated the entire army of King Hadadezer of Zobah, 10 he sent his son Hadoram to King David to greet him and to congratulate him on his victory over Hadadezer in battle, for Hadadezer had been at war with Tou; Hadoram brought with him vessels of gold, silver, and bronze. 11 These King David dedicated to the LORD, along with the silver and gold which he had carried away from all the nations, from Edom and Moab, from the Ammonites and Philistines, and from Amalek.

12 Abishai son of Zeruiah killed eighteen thousand of the Edomites in the valley of Salt; 13 he stationed garrisons throughout Edom, and all the Edomites became subject to David. The LORD gave David victory wherever he went.

14 David ruled over the whole of Israel and maintained law and justice among all his people. 15 Joab son of Zeruiah was in command of the army; Jehoshaphat son of Ahilud

17:21 **any other:** *so Gk; Heb.* one.   18:1–13 *Cp. 2 Sam. 8:1–14.*
18:7 **shields:** *or* quivers.   18:10 **Hadoram brought with him:** *so Syriac and 2 Sam. 8:10; Heb. omits.* **vessels:** *so Syriac and 2 Sam. 8:10; Heb.* all vessels.   18:14–17 *Cp. 2 Sam. 8:15–18; 20:23–26; 1 Kgs. 4:2–4.*

x Or *and it is blessed*   y Meaning of Heb uncertain
z Gk Vg 2 Sam 8.6 Compare Syr: Heb lacks *garrisons*

with your purpose, you have done this great thing. 20 O LORD, there is no one like you and there is no God but you, just as we have always understood.

21 "Is there, like your people Israel, whom you redeemed from Egypt, another nation on earth whom a god went to redeem as his people? You won for yourself a name for great and awesome deeds by driving out the nations before your people. 22 You made your people Israel your own forever, and you, O LORD, became their God. 23 Therefore, O LORD, may the promise that you have uttered concerning your servant and his house remain firm forever. Bring about what you have promised, 24 that your renown as LORD of hosts, God of Israel, may be great and abide forever, while the house of David, your servant, is established in your presence.

25 "Because you, O my God, have revealed to your servant that you will build him a house, your servant has made bold to pray before you. 26 Since you, O LORD, are truly God and have promised this good thing to your servant, 27 and since you have deigned to bless the house of your servant, so that it will remain forever — since it is you, O LORD, who blessed it, it is blessed forever."

18 After this, David defeated the Philistines and subdued them; and he took Gath and its towns away from the control of the Philistines. 2 He also defeated Moab, and the Moabites became his subjects, paying tribute.

3 David then defeated Hadadezer, king of Zobah toward Hamath, when the latter was on his way to set up his victory stele at the river Euphrates. 4 David took from him twenty thousand foot soldiers, one thousand chariots, and seven thousand horsemen. Of the chariot horses, David hamstrung all but one hundred. 5 The Arameans of Damascus came to the aid of Hadadezer, king of Zobah, but David also slew twenty-two thousand of their men. 6 Then David set up garrisons in the Damascus region of Aram, and the Arameans became his subjects, paying tribute. Thus the LORD made David victorious in all his campaigns.

7 David took the golden shields that were carried by Hadadezer's attendants and brought them to Jerusalem. 8 He likewise took away from Tibhath and Cun, cities of Hadadezer, large quantities of bronze, which Solomon later used to make the bronze sea and the pillars and the vessels of bronze.

9 When Tou, king of Hamath, heard that David had defeated the entire army of Hadadezer, king of Zobah, 10 he sent his son Hadoram to wish King David well and to congratulate him on having waged a victorious war against Hadadezer; for Hadadezer had been at war with Tou. He also sent David gold, silver and bronze utensils of every sort. 11 These also King David consecrated to the LORD along with all the silver and gold that he had taken from the nations: from Edom, Moab, the Ammonites, the Philistines, and Amalek.

12 Abishai, the son of Zeruiah, also slew eighteen thousand Edomites in the Valley of Salt. 13 He set up garrisons in Edom, and all the Edomites became David's subjects. Thus the LORD made David victorious in all his campaigns.

14 David reigned over all Israel and dispensed justice and right to all his people. 15 Joab, son of Zeruiah, was in command of the army; Jehoshaphat, son of Ahilud, was herald;

and since you were so inclined, you have had the generosity to reveal all this greatness to come. 20 Yahweh, there is no one like you, no God but you alone, as everything that we have heard confirms. 21 Is there another people on earth like your people Israel, whom a god has proceeded to redeem, to make them his people and to make them famous and do for them great and terrible deeds, by driving out nations before your people, whom you redeemed from Egypt? — 22 for you made your people Israel your own people for ever and you, Yahweh, became their God.

23 'Now, Yahweh, may the promise which you have made for your servant and as regards his family hold good for ever, and do as you have said. 24 May it hold good, so your name will be exalted for ever and people will say, "Israel's God is Yahweh Sabaoth; he is God for Israel." Your servant David's dynasty will be secure before you 25 since you, my God, have disclosed to your servant that you are going to build him a dynasty. Hence, your servant has ventured to offer this prayer to you. 26 Yes, Yahweh, you are God indeed, and you have made this generous promise to your servant. 27 What is more, you have deigned to bless your servant's dynasty, so that it may remain for ever before you; and since you, Yahweh, have blessed it, blessed will it be for ever.'

18 After this David defeated the Philistines and subdued them. From the grip of the Philistines he wrested Gath and its dependencies. 2 He also defeated the Moabites; the Moabites became David's subjects and paid him tribute.

3 David also defeated Hadadezer king of Zobah, which lies in the direction of Hamath, when the latter mounted an expedition to assert his rule on the River Euphrates. 4 David captured one thousand chariots, seven thousand charioteers and twenty thousand foot soldiers from him; David hamstrung all the chariot teams, keeping only a hundred of them. 5 The Aramaeans of Damascus came to the help of Hadadezer king of Zobah, but David killed twenty-two thousand of the Aramaeans. 6 David then imposed governors in Aram of Damascus, and the Aramaeans became David's subjects and paid him tribute. Wherever David went, Yahweh gave him victory. 7 David took the golden shields carried by Hadadezer's guards and brought them to Jerusalem. 8 From Tibhath and from Cun, towns belonging to Hadadezer, David captured a great quantity of bronze, with which Solomon made the bronze Sea, the pillars and the bronze implements.

9 When Tou king of Hamath heard that David had defeated the entire army of Hadadezer king of Zobah, 10 he sent his son Hadoram to King David to greet him and to congratulate him on having made war on Hadadezer and on having defeated him, since Hadadezer was at war with Tou. He also sent all sorts of objects made of gold, silver and bronze, 11 which King David also consecrated to Yahweh, as well as the silver and gold which he had levied from all the nations, from Edom, Moab, the Ammonites, the Philistines and Amalek.

12 Abishai son of Zeruiah defeated the Edomites in the Valley of Salt — eighteen thousand of them. 13 He stationed garrisons in Edom, and all the Edomites became David's subjects. Wherever David went, Yahweh gave him victory.

14 David ruled over all Israel, administering law and justice to all his people. 15 Joab son of Zeruiah was in command of the army; Jehoshaphat son of Ahilud was herald;

<table>
<tr><td>NEW REVISED STANDARD VERSION</td><td>REVISED ENGLISH BIBLE</td></tr>
</table>

16 Zadok son of Ahitub and Ahimelech son of Abiathar were priests; Shavsha was secretary; 17 Benaiah son of Jehoiada was over the Cherethites and the Pelethites; and David's sons were the chief officials in the service of the king.

19 Some time afterward, King Nahash of the Ammonites died, and his son succeeded him. 2 David said, "I will deal loyally with Hanun son of Nahash, for his father dealt loyally with me." So David sent messengers to console him concerning his father. When David's servants came to Hanun in the land of the Ammonites, to console him, 3 the officials of the Ammonites said to Hanun, "Do you think, because David has sent consolers to you, that he is honoring your father? Have not his servants come to you to search and to overthrow and to spy out the land?" 4 So Hanun seized David's servants, shaved them, cut off their garments in the middle at their hips, and sent them away; 5 and they departed. When David was told about the men, he sent messengers to them, for they felt greatly humiliated. The king said, "Remain at Jericho until your beards have grown, and then return."

6 When the Ammonites saw that they had made themselves odious to David, Hanun and the Ammonites sent a thousand talents of silver to hire chariots and cavalry from Mesopotamia, from Aram-maacah and from Zobah. 7 They hired thirty-two thousand chariots and the king of Maacah with his army, who came and camped before Medeba. And the Ammonites were mustered from their cities and came to battle. 8 When David heard of it, he sent Joab and all the army of the warriors. 9 The Ammonites came out and drew up in battle array at the entrance of the city, and the kings who had come were by themselves in the open country.

10 When Joab saw that the line of battle was set against him both in front and in the rear, he chose some of the picked men of Israel and arrayed them against the Arameans; 11 the rest of his troops he put in the charge of his brother Abishai, and they were arrayed against the Ammonites. 12 He said, "If the Arameans are too strong for me, then you shall help me; but if the Ammonites are too strong for you, then I will help you. 13 Be strong, and let us be courageous for our people and for the cities of our God; and may the LORD do what seems good to him." 14 So Joab and the troops who were with him advanced toward the Arameans for battle; and they fled before him. 15 When the Ammonites saw that the Arameans fled, they likewise fled before Abishai, Joab's brother, and entered the city. Then Joab came to Jerusalem.

16 But when the Arameans saw that they had been defeated by Israel, they sent messengers and brought out the Arameans who were beyond the Euphrates, with Shophach the commander of the army of Hadadezer at their head. 17 When David was informed, he gathered all Israel together, crossed the Jordan, came to them, and drew up his forces against them. When David set the battle in array against the Arameans, they fought with him. 18 The Arameans fled before Israel; and David killed seven thousand Aramean charioteers and forty thousand foot soldiers, and also killed Shophach the commander of their army. 19 When the servants of Hadadezer saw that they had been defeated by Israel, they made peace with David, and became subject to him. So the Arameans were not willing to help the Ammonites any more.

was secretary of state; 16 Zadok and Abiathar son of Ahimelech, son of Ahitub, were priests; Shavsha was adjutant-general; 17 Benaiah son of Jehoiada commanded the Kerethite and Pelethite guards. The eldest sons of David were in attendance on the king.

19 Some time afterwards Nahash king of the Ammonites died and was succeeded by his son. 2 David said, 'I must keep up the same loyal friendship with Hanun son of Nahash as his father showed me,' and he sent a mission to condole with him on the death of his father. When David's envoys entered the country of the Ammonites to condole with Hanun, 3 the Ammonite princes said to Hanun, 'Do you suppose David means to do honour to your father when he sends envoys to condole with you? These men of his are spies whom he has sent to find out how to overthrow the country.' 4 So Hanun took David's servants, shaved them, and cut off half their garments up to the buttocks, and then dismissed them. 5 Hearing how they had been treated, David ordered them to be met, for they were deeply humiliated; he told them to wait in Jericho and not return until their beards had grown again.

6 The Ammonites realized that they had given offence to David, so Hanun and the Ammonites sent a thousand talents of silver to hire chariots and horsemen from Aram-naharaim, Maacah, and Aram-zobah. 7 They hired thirty-two thousand chariots and the king of Maacah and his people, who came and encamped before Medeba, while the Ammonites came from their cities and mustered for battle. 8 When this was reported to David, he sent Joab out with all the fighting men. 9 The Ammonites came on and took up their position at the entrance to the city, while the allied kings took up theirs in the open country. 10 When Joab saw that he was threatened from both front and rear, he detailed some picked Israelite troops and drew them up facing the Aramaeans. 11 The rest of his forces he put under his brother Abishai, who took up a position facing the Ammonites. 12 'If the Aramaeans prove too strong for me,' he said, 'you must come to my relief; and if the Ammonites prove too strong for you, I shall come to yours. 13 Courage! Let us fight bravely for our people and for the cities of our God. And may the LORD's will be done.'

14 Joab and his men engaged with the Aramaeans closely and put them to flight; 15 and when the Ammonites saw them in flight, they too fled before his brother Abishai and withdrew into the city. Then Joab came to Jerusalem.

16 The Aramaeans, reviewing their defeat by Israel, sent messengers to summon other Aramaeans from the Great Bend of the Euphrates under Shophach, commander of Hadadezer's army. 17 Their movement was reported to David, who immediately mustered all the forces of Israel, crossed the Jordan, and advanced against them and took up battle positions. The Aramaeans likewise took up positions facing David and engaged him, 18 but were put to flight by Israel. David slew seven thousand Aramaeans in chariots and forty thousand infantry, killing Shophach the commander of the army. 19 When Hadadezer's men saw that they had been worsted by Israel, they sued for peace and submitted to David. The Aramaeans were never willing to help the Ammonites again.

<hr>

18:16 **and Abiathar . . . Ahitub:** *prob. rdg, cp. 2 Sam. 8:17; Heb.* son of Ahitub and Abimelech son of Abiathar.   19:1–19 *Cp. 2 Sam. 10:1–19.*   19:6 **Aram-naharaim:** *that is* Aram of Two Rivers. **Maacah, and Aram-zobah:** *prob. rdg; Heb.* Aram-maacah, and Zobah. 19:13 **cities:** *or* altars.   19:17 **The Aramaeans . . . him:** *so Gk; Heb.* When David had taken up positions facing the Aramaeans, they engaged him.

16 Zadok, son of Ahitub, and Ahimelech, son of Abiathar, were priests; Shavsha was scribe; 17 Benaiah, son of Jehoiada, was in command of the Cherethites and the Pelethites; and David's sons were the chief assistants to the king.

19 Afterward Nahash, king of the Ammonites, died and his son succeeded him as king. 2 David said, "I will show kindness to Hanun, the son of Nahash, for his father treated me with kindness." Therefore he sent envoys to him to comfort him over the death of his father. But when David's servants had entered the land of the Ammonites to comfort Hanun, 3 the Ammonite princes said to Hanun, "Do you think David is doing this — sending you these consolers — to honor your father? Have not his servants rather come to you to explore the land, spying it out for its overthrow?" 4 Thereupon Hanun seized David's servants and had them shaved and their garments cut off half-way at the hips. Then he sent them away. 5 When David was informed of what had happened to his men, he sent messengers to meet them, for the men had been greatly disgraced. "Remain at Jericho," the king told them, "until your beards have grown again; and then you may come back here."

6 When the Ammonites realized that they had put themselves in bad odor with David, Hanun and the Ammonites sent a thousand talents of silver to hire chariots and horsemen from Aram Naharaim, from Aram-maacah, and from Zobah. 7 They hired thirty-two thousand chariots along with the king of Maacah and his army, who came and encamped before Medeba. The Ammonites also assembled from their cities and came out for war.

8 When David heard of this, he sent Joab and his whole army of warriors against them. 9 The Ammonites marched out and lined up for battle at the gate of the city, while the kings who had come to their help remained apart in the open field. 10 When Joab saw that there was a battle line both in front of and behind him, he chose some of the best fighters among the Israelites and set them in array against the Arameans; 11 the rest of the army, which he placed under the command of his brother Abishai, then lined up to oppose the Ammonites. 12 And he said: "If the Arameans prove too strong for me, you must come to my help; and if the Ammonites prove too strong for you, I will save you. 13 Hold steadfast and let us show ourselves courageous for the sake of our people and the cities of our God; then may the LORD do what seems best to him." 14 Joab therefore advanced with his men to engage the Arameans in battle; but they fled before him. 15 And when the Ammonites saw that the Arameans had fled, they also took to flight before his brother Abishai, and reentered the city. Joab then returned to Jerusalem.

16 Seeing themselves vanquished by Israel, the Arameans sent messengers to bring out the Arameans from the other side of the River, with Shophach, the general of Hadadezer's army, at their head. 17 When this was reported to David, he gathered all Israel together, crossed the Jordan, and met them. With the army of David drawn up to fight the Arameans, they gave battle. 18 But the Arameans fled before Israel, and David slew seven thousand of their chariot fighters and forty thousand of their foot soldiers; he also killed Shophach, the general of the army. 19 When the vassals of Hadadezer saw themselves vanquished by Israel, they made peace with David and became his subjects. After this, the Arameans refused to come to the aid of the Ammonites.

16 Zadok son of Ahitub and Abiathar son of Ahimelech were priests; Shusha was secretary; 17 Benaiah son of Jehoiada was in command of the Cherethites and Pelethites; David's sons took first place after the king.

19 After this, when Nahash king of the Ammonites died and his son Hanun succeeded him, 2 David thought, 'I shall show Hanun son of Nahash the same faithful love as his father showed me.' And David sent representatives to offer him condolences over his father. But when David's representatives reached Hanun in the Ammonites' country to present these condolences, 3 the Ammonite leaders said to Hanun, 'Do you really think David means to honour your father when he sends you messengers with sympathy? On the contrary, the reason why his representatives have come to you is to explore, overthrow and reconnoitre the country.' 4 Whereupon Hanun seized David's representatives, shaved them, cut their clothes off half-way up, right by their buttocks, and sent them away. 5 As soon as David was told how the men had been treated, he sent someone to meet them, since the men were overcome with shame. 'Stay in Jericho,' the king said, 'until your beards have grown, and come back then.'

6 When the Ammonites realised that they had antagonised David, Hanun and the Ammonites sent a thousand talents of silver to hire chariots and cavalry from the Aramaeans of Upper Mesopotamia, of Maacah and of Zobah. 7 They hired thirty-two thousand chariots and the king of Maacah with his people, who came and encamped before Medeba, while the Ammonites, having left their towns and mustered, were advancing to the war. 8 When David heard this, he sent Joab with the whole army, the champions. 9 The Ammonites marched out and drew up their line of battle at the city gate, while the kings who had come kept their distance in the open country. 10 Joab, seeing that he had to fight on two fronts, to his front and to his rear, chose the best of Israel's picked men and drew them up in line facing the Aramaeans. 11 He entrusted the rest of the army to his brother Abishai, and drew them up in line facing the Ammonites. 12 'If the Aramaeans prove too strong for me,' he said, 'you must come to my help; if the Ammonites prove too strong for you, I shall come to yours. 13 Be brave and let us fight valiantly, for the sake of our people and for the cities of our God! And let Yahweh dispose as he thinks fit!' 14 Joab and the force with him joined battle with the Aramaeans, who fled at his onslaught. 15 When the Ammonites saw that the Aramaeans had fled, they too fled from his brother Abishai and withdrew into the city. Joab then returned to Jerusalem.

16 The Aramaeans, realising that Israel had got the better of them, sent messengers and mobilised the Aramaeans living on the other side of the River, with Shophach, commander of Hadadezer's army, at their head. 17 David, being informed of this, mustered all Israel, crossed the Jordan, made contact with them and took up position near them. David drew up his line of battle facing the Aramaeans, who then engaged him. 18 But the Aramaeans fled from Israel, and David killed seven thousand of their chariot teams and forty thousand men; and also Shophach, the commander of the army. 19 When Hadadezer's vassals saw that Israel had got the better of them, they made peace with David and became his subjects. The Aramaeans were unwilling to give any more help to the Ammonites.

20 In the spring of the year, the time when kings go out to battle, Joab led out the army, ravaged the country of the Ammonites, and came and besieged Rabbah. But David remained at Jerusalem. Joab attacked Rabbah, and overthrew it. 2 David took the crown of Milcom*a* from his head; he found that it weighed a talent of gold, and in it was a precious stone; and it was placed on David's head. He also brought out the booty of the city, a very great amount. 3 He brought out the people who were in it, and set them to work*b* with saws and iron picks and axes.*c* Thus David did to all the cities of the Ammonites. Then David and all the people returned to Jerusalem.

4 After this, war broke out with the Philistines at Gezer; then Sibbecai the Hushathite killed Sippai, who was one of the descendants of the giants; and the Philistines were subdued. 5 Again there was war with the Philistines; and Elhanan son of Jair killed Lahmi the brother of Goliath the Gittite, the shaft of whose spear was like a weaver's beam. 6 Again there was war at Gath, where there was a man of great size, who had six fingers on each hand, and six toes on each foot, twenty-four in number; he also was descended from the giants. 7 When he taunted Israel, Jonathan son of Shimea, David's brother, killed him. 8 These were descended from the giants in Gath; they fell by the hand of David and his servants.

21 Satan stood up against Israel, and incited David to count the people of Israel. 2 So David said to Joab and the commanders of the army, "Go, number Israel, from Beer-sheba to Dan, and bring me a report, so that I may know their number." 3 But Joab said, "May the LORD increase the number of his people a hundredfold! Are they not, my lord the king, all of them my lord's servants? Why then should my lord require this? Why should he bring guilt on Israel?" 4 But the king's word prevailed against Joab. So Joab departed and went throughout all Israel, and came back to Jerusalem. 5 Joab gave the total count of the people to David. In all Israel there were one million one hundred thousand men who drew the sword, and in Judah four hundred seventy thousand who drew the sword. 6 But he did not include Levi and Benjamin in the numbering, for the king's command was abhorrent to Joab.

7 But God was displeased with this thing, and he struck Israel. 8 David said to God, "I have sinned greatly in that I have done this thing. But now, I pray you, take away the guilt of your servant; for I have done very foolishly." 9 The LORD spoke to Gad, David's seer, saying, 10 "Go and say to David, 'Thus says the LORD: Three things I offer you; choose one of them, so that I may do it to you.'" 11 So Gad came to David and said to him, "Thus says the LORD, 'Take your choice: 12 either three years of famine; or three months of devastation by your foes, while the sword of your enemies overtakes you; or three days of the sword of the LORD, pestilence on the land, and the angel of the LORD destroying throughout all the territory of Israel.' Now decide what answer I shall return to the one who sent me." 13 Then David said to Gad, "I am in great distress; let me fall into the hand of the LORD, for his mercy is very great; but let me not fall into human hands."

14 So the LORD sent a pestilence on Israel; and seventy thousand persons fell in Israel. 15 And God sent an angel to

20 AT the turn of the year, when kings go out to battle, Joab led the army out and ravaged the Ammonite country, while David remained in Jerusalem. Joab came to Rabbah and laid siege to it, and after reducing it he razed it to the ground. 2 David took the crown from the head of Milcom and found that it weighed a talent of gold and was set with a precious stone, and it was placed on David's head; he also removed a vast quantity of booty from the city. 3 He brought out its inhabitants and set them to work with saws and other iron tools, sharp and toothed. David did this to all the Ammonite towns; then he and all his army returned to Jerusalem.

4 Some time later war with the Philistines broke out in Gezer; it was then that Sibbechai from Hushah killed Sippai, a descendant of the Rephaim, and the Philistines were reduced to submission. 5 In another campaign against the Philistines, Elhanan son of Jair killed Lahmi brother of Goliath of Gath, whose spear had a shaft like a weaver's beam. 6 In yet another campaign in Gath there appeared a giant with six fingers on each hand and six toes on each foot, twenty-four in all. He too was descended from the Rephaim; 7 when he defied Israel, Jonathan son of David's brother Shimea killed him. 8 These giants were the descendants of the Rephaim in Gath, and they all fell at the hands of David and his men.

21 NOW SATAN, setting himself against Israel, incited David to make a census of the people. 2 The king commanded Joab and the officers of the army to go out and number Israel from Beersheba to Dan, and to report back the number to him. 3 Joab answered, 'Even if the LORD should increase his people a hundredfold, would not your majesty still be king and all the people your slaves? Why should your majesty want to do this? It will only bring guilt on Israel.' 4 But Joab was overruled by the king; he set out and went up and down the whole country. He then came to Jerusalem 5 and reported to David the numbers recorded: those capable of bearing arms were one million one hundred thousand in Israel, and four hundred and seventy thousand in Judah. 6 Levi and Benjamin were not counted by Joab, so deep was his repugnance against the king's order.

7 God also was displeased with the order, and he proceeded to punish Israel. 8 David said to God, 'I have acted very wickedly: I pray you remove your servant's guilt, for I have been very foolish.' 9 The LORD said to Gad, David's seer, 10 'Go and tell David, This is the word of the LORD: I offer three things; choose one and I shall bring it on you.' 11 Gad came to David and said, 'This is the word of the LORD: Make your choice: 12 three years of famine, three months of harrying by your foes and close pursuit by the sword of your enemy, or three days of the LORD's own sword, bringing pestilence throughout the land, and the LORD's angel working destruction in all the territory of Israel. Consider now what answer I am to take back to him who sent me.' 13 David said to Gad, 'This is a desperate plight I am in; let me fall into the hands of the LORD, for his mercy is very great; and let me not fall into the hands of man.'

14 The LORD sent a pestilence throughout Israel, and seventy thousand Israelites died. 15 God sent an angel to Jerusa-

---

a Gk Vg See 1 Kings 11.5, 33: MT *of their king*   *b* Compare 2 Sam 12.31: Heb *and he sawed*   *c* Compare 2 Sam 12.31: Heb *saws*

20:1–3 *Cp. 2 Sam. 11:1; 12:26–31.*   20:3 **toothed:** *so one MS, cp. 2 Sam. 12:31; others* saws.   20:4–8 *Cp. 2 Sam. 21:18–22.* 21:1–27 *Cp. 2 Sam. 24:1–25.*

20 At the beginning of the following year, the time when kings go to war, Joab led the army out in force, laid waste the land of the Ammonites, and went on to besiege Rabbah, while David himself remained in Jerusalem. When Joab had attacked Rabbah and destroyed it, 2 David took the crown of Milcom from the idol's head. It was found to weigh a talent of gold; and it contained precious stones, which David wore on his own head. He also brought out a great amount of booty from the city. 3 He deported the people of the city and set them to work with saws, iron picks, and axes. Thus David dealt with all the cities of the Ammonites. Then he and his whole army returned to Jerusalem.

4 Afterward there was another battle with the Philistines, at Gezer. At that time, Sibbecai the Hushathite slew Sippai, one of the descendants of the Raphaim, and the Philistines were subdued. 5 Once again there was war with the Philistines, and Elhanan, the son of Jair, slew Lahmi, the brother of Goliath of Gath, whose spear shaft was like a weaver's heddle-bar.

6 In still another battle, at Gath, they encountered a giant, also a descendant of the Raphaim, who had six fingers to each hand and six toes to each foot; twenty-four in all. 7 He defied Israel, and Jonathan, the son of Shimea, David's brother, slew him. 8 These were the descendants of the Raphaim of Gath who died at the hands of David and his servants.

21 A satan rose up against Israel, and he enticed David into taking a census of Israel. 2 David therefore said to Joab and to the other generals of the army, "Go, find out the number of the Israelites from Beer-sheba to Dan, and report back to me that I may know their number." 3 But Joab replied: "May the LORD increase his people a hundredfold! My lord king, are not all of them my lord's subjects? Why does my lord seek to do this thing? Why will he bring guilt upon Israel?" 4 However, the king's command prevailed over Joab, who departed and traversed all of Israel, and then returned to Jerusalem. 5 Joab reported the result of the census to David: of men capable of wielding a sword, there were in all Israel one million one hundred thousand, and in Judah four hundred and seventy thousand. 6 Levi and Benjamin, however, he did not include in the census, for the king's command was repugnant to Joab. 7 This command displeased God, who began to punish Israel. 8 Then David said to God, "I have sinned greatly in doing this thing. Take away your servant's guilt, for I have acted very foolishly."

9 Then the LORD spoke to Gad, David's seer, in these words: 10 "Go, tell David: Thus says the LORD: I offer you three alternatives; choose one of them, and I will inflict it on you." 11 Accordingly, Gad went to David and said to him: "Thus says the LORD: Decide now — 12 will it be three years of famine; or three months of fleeing your enemies, with the sword of your foes ever at your back; or three days of the LORD's own sword, a pestilence in the land, with the LORD's destroying angel in every part of Israel? Therefore choose: What answer am I to give him who sent me?" 13 Then David said to Gad: "I am in dire straits. But I prefer to fall into the hand of the LORD, whose mercy is very great, than into the hands of men."

14 Therefore the LORD sent pestilence upon Israel, and seventy thousand men of Israel died. 15 God also sent an

20 At the turn of the year, at the time when kings go campaigning, Joab led out the troops and, having ravaged the Ammonites' territory, proceeded to lay siege to Rabbah. David, however, remained in Jerusalem. Joab reduced Rabbah and dismantled it. 2 David took the crown off Milcom's head and found that it weighed a talent of gold, and in it was set a precious stone which went on David's head instead. He carried off great quantities of booty from the city. 3 And he expelled its inhabitants, setting them to work with saws, iron picks and axes. David treated all the Ammonite towns in the same way. David and all the people then returned to Jerusalem.

4 After this war broke out with the Philistines at Gezer. This was when Sibbecai of Hushah killed Sippai, one of the Rephaim, and the Philistines were subdued.

5 Again, war with the Philistines broke out, and Elhanan son of Jair killed Lahmi brother of Goliath of Gath, the shaft of whose spear was like a weaver's beam.

6 There was further warfare at Gath, where there was a man of huge stature with six fingers on each hand and six toes on each foot, twenty-four in all. He too was a son of Rapha. 7 When he defied Israel, Jonathan son of Shimea, brother of David cut him down.

8 These men were sons of Rapha in Gath and fell at the hands of David and his guards.

21 Satan took his stand against Israel and incited David to take a census of Israel. 2 David said to Joab and the people's princes, 'Go, and take a census of Israel, from Beersheba to Dan, then bring it back to me and let me know the total.' 3 Joab replied, 'May Yahweh multiply his people to a hundred times what they are today! But my lord king, are they not all my lord's servants in any case? Why should my lord insist on this? Why should he involve Israel in guilt?' 4 But the king enforced his order on Joab, and Joab set out, travelled throughout all Israel, and then returned to Jerusalem. 5 Joab gave David the census results for the people: all Israel had eleven hundred thousand men who could wield a sword; Judah had four hundred and seventy thousand men who could wield a sword. 6 Joab had found the king's command so distasteful that he did not include Levi and Benjamin.

7 God looked with displeasure on this and punished Israel in consequence. 8 David then said to God, 'I have committed a grave sin by doing this. But now I beg you to forgive your servant for this fault, for I have acted very foolishly.'

9 Yahweh then spoke to Gad, David's seer, 10 'Go and say to David, "Yahweh says this: I offer you three things; choose which one of them I am to inflict on you." ' 11 So Gad went to David and said, 'Yahweh says this, 12 "Take your choice between three years of famine; or three months of disaster at the hands of your enemies, with your enemies' sword overtaking you; or three days of Yahweh's sword, an epidemic in the country, while the angel of Yahweh wreaks havoc throughout the territory of Israel." Now decide how I am to answer him who sends me.' 13 David said to Gad, 'I am very apprehensive. Better for me to fall into Yahweh's hand, since his mercies are very great, than for me to fall into the hands of human enemies.'

14 So Yahweh unleashed an epidemic on Israel, and seventy Israelites succumbed. 15 Next, God sent the

Jerusalem to destroy it; but when he was about to destroy it, the LORD took note and relented concerning the calamity; he said to the destroying angel, "Enough! Stay your hand." The angel of the LORD was then standing by the threshing floor of Ornan the Jebusite. 16 David looked up and saw the angel of the LORD standing between earth and heaven, and in his hand a drawn sword stretched out over Jerusalem. Then David and the elders, clothed in sackcloth, fell on their faces. 17 And David said to God, "Was it not I who gave the command to count the people? It is I who have sinned and done very wickedly. But these sheep, what have they done? Let your hand, I pray, O LORD my God, be against me and against my father's house; but do not let your people be plagued!"

18 Then the angel of the LORD commanded Gad to tell David that he should go up and erect an altar to the LORD on the threshing floor of Ornan the Jebusite. 19 So David went up following Gad's instructions, which he had spoken in the name of the LORD. 20 Ornan turned and saw the angel; and while his four sons who were with him hid themselves, Ornan continued to thresh wheat. 21 As David came to Ornan, Ornan looked and saw David; he went out from the threshing floor, and did obeisance to David with his face to the ground. 22 David said to Ornan, "Give me the site of the threshing floor that I may build on it an altar to the LORD — give it to me at its full price — so that the plague may be averted from the people." 23 Then Ornan said to David, "Take it; and let my lord the king do what seems good to him; see, I present the oxen for burnt offerings, and the threshing sledges for the wood, and the wheat for a grain offering. I give it all." 24 But King David said to Ornan, "No; I will buy them for the full price. I will not take for the LORD what is yours, nor offer burnt offerings that cost me nothing." 25 So David paid Ornan six hundred shekels of gold by weight for the site. 26 David built there an altar to the LORD and presented burnt offerings and offerings of well-being. He called upon the LORD, and he answered him with fire from heaven on the altar of burnt offering. 27 Then the LORD commanded the angel, and he put his sword back into its sheath.

28 At that time, when David saw that the LORD had answered him at the threshing floor of Ornan the Jebusite, he made his sacrifices there. 29 For the tabernacle of the LORD, which Moses had made in the wilderness, and the altar of burnt offering were at that time in the high place at Gibeon; 30 but David could not go before it to inquire of God, for he was afraid of the sword of the angel of the LORD. 22 1 Then David said, "Here shall be the house of the LORD God and here the altar of burnt offering for Israel."

2 David gave orders to gather together the aliens who were residing in the land of Israel, and he set stonecutters to prepare dressed stones for building the house of God. 3 David also provided great stores of iron for nails for the doors of the gates and for clamps, as well as bronze in quantities beyond weighing, 4 and cedar logs without number — for the Sidonians and Tyrians brought great quantities of cedar to David. 5 For David said, "My son Solomon is young and inexperienced, and the house that is to be built for the LORD must be exceedingly magnificent, famous and glorified throughout all lands; I will therefore make preparation for it." So David provided materials in great quantity before his death.

6 Then he called for his son Solomon and charged him to build a house for the LORD, the God of Israel. 7 David

lem to destroy it; but, as he was destroying it, the LORD saw and repented of the evil, and said to the destroying angel at the moment when he was standing at the threshing-floor of Ornan the Jebusite, 'Enough! Stay your hand.'

16 When David looked up and saw the angel of the LORD standing between earth and heaven, and in his hand a drawn sword stretched out over Jerusalem, he and the elders, clothed in sackcloth, fell prostrate to the ground. 17 David said to God, 'It was I who gave the order to count the people. It is I who have sinned, I, the shepherd, who have committed the wrong; but these poor sheep, what have they done? LORD my God, let your hand fall on me and on my family, but check this plague on the people.'

18 The angel of the LORD, speaking through the lips of Gad, commanded David to go to the threshing-floor of Ornan the Jebusite and to set up there an altar to the LORD. 19 David went up as Gad had bidden him in the LORD's name. 20 Ornan's four sons who were with him hid themselves, but he was busy threshing his wheat when he turned and saw the angel. 21 As David approached, Ornan looked up and, seeing the king, came out from the threshing-floor and prostrated himself before him. 22 David said to Ornan, 'Let me have the site of the threshing-floor, so that I may build on it an altar to the LORD; sell it to me at the full price, so that the plague which has attacked the people may be stopped.' 23 Ornan answered, 'Take it and let your majesty do as he thinks fit; see, here are the oxen for whole-offerings, the threshing-sledges for the fuel, and the wheat for the grain-offering; I give you everything.' 24 But King David said to Ornan, 'No, I shall pay the full price; I am not going to present to the LORD what is yours, or offer a whole-offering which has cost me nothing.' 25 So David gave Ornan six hundred shekels of gold for the site. 26 He built an altar to the LORD there, and offered whole-offerings and shared-offerings. He called to the LORD, who answered him with fire falling from heaven on the altar of whole-offering. 27 Then, at the LORD's command, the angel sheathed his sword.

28 It was when David saw that the LORD had answered him at the threshing-floor of Ornan the Jebusite that he offered sacrifice there. 29 The Tabernacle of the LORD and the altar of whole-offering which Moses had made in the wilderness were then at the shrine in Gibeon; 30 but David had been unable to go there and seek God's guidance, so shocked and shaken was he at the sight of the angel's 22 sword. 1 Then David said, 'This is to be the house of the LORD God, and this is to be an altar of whole-offering for Israel.'

2 DAVID now gave orders to assemble the aliens resident in Israel, and he set them as masons to dress hewn stones for building the house of God. 3 He laid in a great store of iron to make nails and clamps for the doors, and more bronze than could be weighed, 4 and cedar-wood without limit; the men of Sidon and Tyre brought David an ample supply of cedar. 5 David said, 'My son Solomon is a boy of tender years, and the house that is to be built for the LORD must be exceedingly magnificent, renowned and celebrated in every land; therefore I must make provision for it myself.' So David before his death made abundant provision.

6 He sent for Solomon his son and charged him with building a house for the LORD the God of Israel. 7 'Solo-

21:17 I, the shepherd: prob. rdg; Heb. doing wrong. check . . . people: prob. rdg; Heb. among your people, not for a plague.

angel to destroy Jerusalem; but as he was on the point of destroying it, the LORD saw and decided against the calamity, and said to the destroying angel, "Enough now! Stay your hand!"

The angel of the LORD was then standing by the threshing floor of Ornan the Jebusite. 16 When David raised his eyes, he saw the angel of the LORD standing between earth and heaven, with a naked sword in his hand stretched out against Jerusalem. David and the elders, clothed in sackcloth, prostrated themselves face to the ground, 17 and David prayed to God: "Was it not I who ordered the census of the people? I am the one who sinned, I did this wicked thing. But these sheep, what have they done? O LORD, my God, strike me and my father's family, but do not afflict your people with this plague!"

18 Then the angel of the LORD commanded Gad to tell David to go up and erect an altar to the LORD on the threshing floor of Ornan the Jebusite. 19 David went up at Gad's command, given in the name of the LORD. 20 While Ornan was threshing wheat, he turned around and saw the king, and his four sons who were with him, without recognizing them. 21 But as David came on toward him, he looked up and saw that it was David. Then he left the threshing floor and bowed down before David, his face to the ground. 22 David said to Ornan: "Sell me the ground of this threshing floor, that I may build on it an altar to the LORD. Sell it to me at its full price, that the plague may be stayed from the people." 23 But Ornan said to David: "Take it as your own, and let my lord the king do what seems best to him. See, I also give you the oxen for the holocausts, the threshing sledges for the wood, and the wheat for the cereal offering. I give it all to you." 24 But King David replied to Ornan: "No! I will buy it from you properly, at its full price. I will not take what is yours for the LORD, nor offer up holocausts that cost me nothing." 25 So David paid Ornan six hundred shekels of gold for the place.

26 David then built an altar there to the LORD, and offered up holocausts and peace offerings. When he called upon the LORD, he answered him by sending down fire from heaven upon the altar of holocausts. 27 Then the LORD gave orders to the angel to return his sword to its sheath.

28 Once David saw that the LORD had heard him on the threshing floor of Ornan the Jebusite, he continued to offer sacrifices there. 29 The Dwelling of the LORD, which Moses had built in the desert, and the altar of holocausts were at that time on the high place at Gibeon. 30 But David could not go there to worship God, for he was fearful of the sword

22 of the angel of the LORD. 1 Therefore David said, "This is the house of the LORD God, and this is the altar of holocausts for Israel."

2 David then ordered that all the aliens who lived in the land of Israel be brought together, and he appointed them stonecutters to hew out stone blocks for building the house of God. 3 He also laid up large stores of iron to make nails for the doors of the gates, and clamps, together with so much bronze that it could not be weighed, 4 and cedar trees without number. The Sidonians and Tyrians brought great stores of cedar logs to David, 5 who said: "My son Solomon is young and immature; but the house that is to be built for the LORD must be made so magnificent that it will be renowned and glorious in all countries. Therefore I will make preparations for it." Thus before his death David laid up materials in abundance.

6 Then he called for his son Solomon and commanded him to build a house for the LORD, the God of Israel. 7 Da-

angel to Jerusalem to destroy it, but as he was about to destroy it, Yahweh looked down and felt sorry about the calamity; and he said to the destroying angel, 'Enough now! Hold your hand!' The angel of Yahweh was standing by the threshing-floor of Ornan the Jebusite. 16 David, raising his eyes, saw the angel of Yahweh standing between earth and heaven, a drawn sword in his hand stretched out towards Jerusalem. David and the elders then put on sackcloth and fell on their faces, 17 and David said to God, 'Did I not order the people to be counted? I was the one who sinned and actually committed the wrong. But these, the flock, what have they done? Yahweh my God, let your hand lie heavy on me and on my family; but spare your people from the plague!'

18 The angel of Yahweh then ordered Gad to tell David that David should go up and erect an altar to Yahweh on the threshing-floor of Ornan the Jebusite. 19 So, at Gad's bidding, given in Yahweh's name, David went up. 20 Ornan had turned round and seen the angel, and he and his four sons with him had hidden. 21 When David arrived Ornan was threshing wheat. He looked up and saw David and came off the threshing-floor and prostrated himself on the ground at David's feet. 22 David then said to Ornan, 'Let me have the site of the threshing-floor, so that I can build an altar to Yahweh on it; let me have it at the full price — so that the plague may be lifted from the people.' Ornan said to David, 23 'Take it, and let my lord the king do what he thinks fit. Look, I shall give you the oxen for burnt offerings, the threshing-sleds for the wood and the wheat for the oblation. I shall give everything.'

24 'No,' said King David to Ornan, 'I insist on buying it at the full price. I will not offer Yahweh what belongs to you or bring burnt offerings which have cost me nothing.' 25 So David gave Ornan six hundred shekels of gold by weight for the site.

26 There David built an altar to Yahweh and brought burnt offerings and peace offerings. He called on Yahweh, and Yahweh answered him with fire from heaven on the altar of burnt offering. 27 Then Yahweh ordered the angel to sheathe his sword. 28 Whereupon, seeing that Yahweh had answered him on the threshing-floor of Ornan the Jebusite, David offered sacrifice there. 29 The Dwelling which Moses had made in the desert and the altar of burnt offering were at that time on the high place at Gibeon, 30 but David could not go there to consult God because he was terrified of the angel's sword.

22 David then said, 'This is to be the house of Yahweh God and this the altar of burnt offering for Israel.'

2 David then gave orders for all foreigners in Israel to be rounded up, and appointed quarrymen to cut dressed stone for building the house of God. 3 David also prepared great quantities of iron to make nails for the leaves of the doors and for the clamps, and more bronze than could be weighed, 4 as well as innumerable cedar-wood logs, as the Sidonians and Tyrians had brought cedar logs to David in great quantities.

5 David then said, 'My son Solomon is young and immature, and the house to be built for Yahweh must be superlatively fine, the most famous and splendid in any country. I shall now make the preparations for it.' And so, before he died, David made ample preparations. 6 He then summoned his son Solomon and commanded him to build a house for Yahweh, God of Israel. 7 'My son,' David said to Solomon,

NEW REVISED STANDARD VERSION | REVISED ENGLISH BIBLE

said to Solomon, "My son, I had planned to build a house to the name of the LORD my God. 8 But the word of the LORD came to me, saying, 'You have shed much blood and have waged great wars; you shall not build a house to my name, because you have shed so much blood in my sight on the earth. 9 See, a son shall be born to you; he shall be a man of peace. I will give him peace from all his enemies on every side; for his name shall be Solomon,*d* and I will give peace*e* and quiet to Israel in his days. 10 He shall build a house for my name. He shall be a son to me, and I will be a father to him, and I will establish his royal throne in Israel forever.' 11 Now, my son, the LORD be with you, so that you may succeed in building the house of the LORD your God, as he has spoken concerning you. 12 Only, may the LORD grant you discretion and understanding, so that when he gives you charge over Israel you may keep the law of the LORD your God. 13 Then you will prosper if you are careful to observe the statutes and the ordinances that the LORD commanded Moses for Israel. Be strong and of good courage. Do not be afraid or dismayed. 14 With great pains I have provided for the house of the LORD one hundred thousand talents of gold, one million talents of silver, and bronze and iron beyond weighing, for there is so much of it; timber and stone too I have provided. To these you must add more. 15 You have an abundance of workers: stonecutters, masons, carpenters, and all kinds of artisans without number, skilled in working 16 gold, silver, bronze, and iron. Now begin the work, and the LORD be with you."

17 David also commanded all the leaders of Israel to help his son Solomon, saying, 18 "Is not the LORD your God with you? Has he not given you peace on every side? For he has delivered the inhabitants of the land into my hand; and the land is subdued before the LORD and his people. 19 Now set your mind and heart to seek the LORD your God. Go and build the sanctuary of the LORD God so that the ark of the covenant of the LORD and the holy vessels of God may be brought into a house built for the name of the LORD."

23 When David was old and full of days, he made his son Solomon king over Israel.

2 David assembled all the leaders of Israel and the priests and the Levites. 3 The Levites, thirty years old and upward, were counted, and the total was thirty-eight thousand. 4 "Twenty-four thousand of these," David said, "shall have charge of the work in the house of the LORD, six thousand shall be officers and judges, 5 four thousand gatekeepers, and four thousand shall offer praises to the LORD with the instruments that I have made for praise." 6 And David organized them in divisions corresponding to the sons of Levi: Gershon,*f* Kohath, and Merari.

7 The sons of Gershon*g* were Ladan and Shimei. 8 The sons of Ladan: Jehiel the chief, Zetham, and Joel, three. 9 The sons of Shimei: Shelomoth, Haziel, and Haran, three. These were the heads of families of Ladan. 10 And the sons of Shimei: Jahath, Zina, Jeush, and Beriah. These four were the sons of Shimei. 11 Jahath was the chief, and Zizah the second; but Jeush and Beriah did not have many sons, so they were enrolled as a single family.

12 The sons of Kohath: Amram, Izhar, Hebron, and Uzziel, four. 13 The sons of Amram: Aaron and Moses. Aaron was set apart to consecrate the most holy things, so that he and his sons forever should make offerings before the LORD, and minister to him and pronounce blessings in his name forever; 14 but as for Moses the man of God, his

mon, my son,' he said, 'it was my intention to build a house for the name of the LORD my God; 8 but the LORD forbade me and said, "You have shed much blood in my sight and waged great wars; for this reason you are not to build a house for my name. 9 But you will have a son who will be a man of peace; I shall give him peace from all his enemies on every side; his name will be Solomon, 'Man of Peace', and I shall grant peace and quiet to Israel in his days. 10 It is he who will build a house for my name; he will be my son and I shall be a father to him, and I shall establish his royal throne over Israel for ever."

11 'Now, my son, may the LORD be with you! May you prosper and build the house of the LORD your God as he promised you would. 12 May the LORD grant you insight and understanding, so that when he gives you authority in Israel you may keep the law of the LORD your God. 13 You will prosper only if you are careful to observe the decrees and ordinances which the LORD enjoined upon Moses for Israel; be strong and resolute, neither faint-hearted nor dismayed.

14 'At the cost of some trouble, I have here ready for the house of the LORD a hundred thousand talents of gold and a million talents of silver, with great quantities of bronze and iron, more than can be weighed; timber and stone, too, I have got ready; and you may add to them. 15 Besides, you have at your disposal a large force of workmen, masons, sculptors, and carpenters, and every kind of skilled craftsmen 16 in gold and silver, bronze and iron. Set to work, and the LORD be with you!'

17 David ordered all the officers of Israel to help Solomon his son: 18 'Is not the LORD your God with you? Will he not give you peace on every side? For he has given the inhabitants of the land into my power; the land will be subdued before the LORD and his people. 19 Devote yourselves, therefore, heart and soul, to seeking guidance of the LORD your God, and set about building his sanctuary, so that the Ark of the Covenant of the LORD and God's holy vessels may be brought into the house built for his name.'

23 David was now an old man, weighed down with years, and he appointed Solomon his son king over Israel. 2 He assembled all the officers of Israel, the priests, and the Levites. 3 The Levites were enrolled from the age of thirty upwards, their males being thirty-eight thousand in all. 4 Of these, twenty-four thousand were to be responsible for the maintenance and service of the house of the LORD, six thousand to act as officers and magistrates, 5 four thousand to be door-keepers, and four thousand to praise the LORD with the musical instruments which David had produced for the service of praise. 6 David organized them in divisions, called after Gershon, Kohath, and Merari, the sons of Levi.

7 The sons of Gershon: Laadan and Shimei. 8 The sons of Laadan: Jehiel the chief, Zetham, and Joel, three. 9 These were the heads of the families grouped under Laadan. 10 The sons of Shimei: Jahath, Ziza, Jeush, and Beriah, four. 11 Jahath was the chief and Ziza the second, but Jeush and Beriah, having few children, were reckoned for duty as a single family.

12 The sons of Kohath: Amram, Izhar, Hebron, and Uzziel, four. 13 The sons of Amram: Aaron and Moses. Aaron was set apart, he and his sons in perpetuity, to dedicate the most holy gifts, to burn sacrifices before the LORD, to serve him, and to give the blessing in his name for ever, 14 but the

22:9 *Cp. 1 Kgs. 5:4.* **peace:** *Heb.* shalom. 23:5 **David:** *so Gk; Heb.* I. 23:8 **three:** *prob. rdg; Heb.* adds The sons of Shimei: Shelomith, Haziel, and Haran, three. 23:10 **Ziza:** *so Gk; Heb.* Zina. 23:13 **to dedicate . . . gifts:** *or* to be hallowed as most holy.

d Heb *Shelomoh* *e* Heb *shalom* *f* Or *Gershom*; See 1 Chr 6.1, note, and 23.15 *g* Vg Compare Gk Syr: Heb *to the Gershonite*

NEW AMERICAN BIBLE

NEW JERUSALEM BIBLE

vid said to Solomon: "My son, it was my purpose to build a house myself for the honor of the LORD, my God. 8 But this word of the LORD came to me: 'You have shed much blood, and you have waged great wars. You may not build a house in my honor, because you have shed too much blood upon the earth in my sight. 9 However, a son is to be born to you. He will be a peaceful man, and I will give him rest from all his enemies on every side. For Solomon shall be his name, and in his time I will bestow peace and tranquility on Israel. 10 It is he who shall build a house in my honor; he shall be a son to me, and I will be a father to him, and I will establish the throne of his kingship over Israel forever.' 11 Now, my son, the LORD be with you, and may you succeed in building the house of the LORD your God, as he has said you shall. 12 May the LORD give you prudence and discernment when he brings you to rule over Israel, so that you keep the law of the LORD, your God. 13 Only then shall you succeed, if you are careful to observe the precepts and decrees which the LORD gave Moses for Israel. Be brave and steadfast; do not fear or lose heart. 14 See, with great effort I have laid up for the house of the LORD a hundred thousand talents of gold, a million talents of silver, and bronze and iron in such great quantities that they cannot be weighed. I have also stored up wood and stones, to which you may add. 15 Moreover, you have available an unlimited supply of workmen, stonecutters, masons, carpenters, and every kind of craftsman 16 skilled in gold, silver, bronze, and iron. Set to work, therefore, and the LORD be with you!"

17 David also commanded all of Israel's leaders to help his son Solomon: 18 "Is not the LORD your God with you? Has he not given you rest on every side? Indeed, he has delivered the occupants of the land into my power, and the land is subdued before the LORD and his people. 19 Therefore, devote your hearts and souls to seeking the LORD your God. Proceed to build the sanctuary of the LORD God, that the ark of the covenant of the LORD and God's sacred vessels may be brought into the house built in honor of the LORD."

23 When David had grown old and was near the end of his days, he made his son Solomon king over Israel. 2 He then gathered together all the leaders of Israel, together with the priests and the Levites.

3 The Levites thirty years old and above were counted, and their total number was found to be thirty-eight thousand men. 4 Of these, twenty-four thousand were to direct the service of the house of the LORD, six thousand were to be officials and judges, 5 four thousand were to be gatekeepers, and four thousand were to praise the LORD with the instruments which David had devised for praise. 6 David divided them into classes according to the sons of Levi: Gershon, Kohath, and Merari.

7 To the Gershonites belonged Ladan and Shimei. 8 The sons of Ladan: Jehiel the chief, then Zetham and Joel; three in all. 9 The sons of Shimei were Shelomoth, Haziel, and Haran; three. These were the heads of the families of Ladan. 10 The sons of Shimei were Jahath, Zizah, Jeush, and Beriah; these were the sons of Shimei, four in all. 11 Jahath was the chief and Zizah was second to him; but Jeush and Beriah had not many sons, and therefore they were classed as a single family, fulfilling a single office. 12 The sons of Kohath: Amram, Izhar, Hebron, and Uzziel; four in all. 13 The sons of Amran were Aaron and Moses. Aaron was set apart to be consecrated as most holy, he and his sons forever, to offer sacrifice before the LORD, to minister to him, and to bless his name forever. 14 As for

'my heart was set on building a house for the name of Yahweh my God. 8 But the word of Yahweh came to me, "You have shed much blood and fought great wars; it is not for you to build a house for my name, since you have shed much blood in my sight on earth. 9 Look, a son will be born to you. He will be a man of peace, and I shall give him peace from his enemies on all sides; for Solomon is to be his name,[a] and in his days I shall give Israel peace and tranquillity. 10 He must build a house for my name; he will be my son and I shall be his father, and I shall make the throne of his kingdom secure over Israel for ever." 11 Now, my son, may Yahweh be with you and give you success in building a house for Yahweh your God, as he has promised about you. 12 And especially, may Yahweh give you discretion and discernment, may he give you his orders for Israel, so that you may observe the Law of Yahweh your God. 13 Success will be yours, only if you observe the statutes and ordinances which Yahweh gave Moses as regulations for Israel. Be strong and stand fast, be fearless, be dauntless. 14 Now, poor as I am, I have set aside for the house of Yahweh a hundred thousand talents of gold, a million talents of silver and more bronze and iron than can be weighed, there being so much. I have also provided timber and stone, to which you may add more. 15 Furthermore, you have a large number of workmen, quarrymen, masons, carpenters and all sorts of craftsmen for every kind of work, 16 while your gold and silver, bronze and iron will be beyond reckoning. Set to work, then, and may Yahweh be with you!'

17 David then commanded all the leaders of Israel to help his son Solomon. 18 'Has not Yahweh your God been with you and given you peace on all sides, having put the inhabitants of the country into my power and the country now having been subdued for Yahweh and his people? 19 So now devote heart and soul to searching for Yahweh your God. Set to and build the sanctuary of Yahweh God, so that you can bring the ark of the covenant of Yahweh and the holy vessels of God into the house built for the name of Yahweh.'

23 When David had become old and full of days, he made his son Solomon king of Israel, 2 and then summoned all the leaders of Israel, with the priests and Levites.

3 A census was taken of those Levites thirty years old and upwards. On a count of heads, they numbered thirty-eight thousand men; 4 twenty-four thousand were responsible for the service of the House of Yahweh, six thousand were officials and judges, 5 four thousand were gatekeepers and four thousand praised Yahweh on the instruments which David had made for praising him.

6 David then divided the Levites into classes: Gershon, Kohath and Merari.

7 Of the Gershonites there were Ladan and Shimei. 8 Sons of Ladan: Jehiel first, Zetham, Joel; three in all. 9 Sons of Shimei: Shelomoth, Haziel, Haran; three in all. These are the heads of families of Ladan. 10 Sons of Shimei: Jahath, Zina, Jeush, Beriah; these were the sons of Shimei; four in all. 11 Jahath was the eldest, Zizah the second, then Jeush and Beriah, who had not many children and were reckoned as one family.

12 Sons of Kohath: Amram, Izhar, Hebron, Uzziel; four in all. 13 Sons of Amram: Aaron and Moses. Aaron was set apart to consecrate the things that were especially holy, he and his sons for ever, to burn incense in the presence of Yahweh, to serve him and to bless in his name for ever.

a 22 The name is here derived from *shalom* = peace.

| NEW REVISED STANDARD VERSION | REVISED ENGLISH BIBLE |

sons were to be reckoned among the tribe of Levi. 15 The sons of Moses: Gershom and Eliezer. 16 The sons of Gershom: Shebuel the chief. 17 The sons of Eliezer: Rehabiah the chief; Eliezer had no other sons, but the sons of Rehabiah were very numerous. 18 The sons of Izhar: Shelomith the chief. 19 The sons of Hebron: Jeriah the chief, Amariah the second, Jahaziel the third, and Jekameam the fourth. 20 The sons of Uzziel: Micah the chief and Isshiah the second.

21 The sons of Merari: Mahli and Mushi. The sons of Mahli: Eleazar and Kish. 22 Eleazar died having no sons, but only daughters; their kindred, the sons of Kish, married them. 23 The sons of Mushi: Mahli, Eder, and Jeremoth, three.

24 These were the sons of Levi by their ancestral houses, the heads of families as they were enrolled according to the number of the names of the individuals from twenty years old and upward who were to do the work for the service of the house of the LORD. 25 For David said, "The LORD, the God of Israel, has given rest to his people; and he resides in Jerusalem forever. 26 And so the Levites no longer need to carry the tabernacle or any of the things for its service" — 27 for according to the last words of David these were the number of the Levites from twenty years old and upward — 28 "but their duty shall be to assist the descendants of Aaron for the service of the house of the LORD, having the care of the courts and the chambers, the cleansing of all that is holy, and any work for the service of the house of God; 29 to assist also with the rows of bread, the choice flour for the grain offering, the wafers of unleavened bread, the baked offering, the offering mixed with oil, and all measures of quantity or size. 30 And they shall stand every morning, thanking and praising the LORD, and likewise at evening, 31 and whenever burnt offerings are offered to the LORD on sabbaths, new moons, and appointed festivals, according to the number required of them, regularly before the LORD. 32 Thus they shall keep charge of the tent of meeting and the sanctuary, and shall attend the descendants of Aaron, their kindred, for the service of the house of the LORD."

24 The divisions of the descendants of Aaron were these. The sons of Aaron: Nadab, Abihu, Eleazar, and Ithamar. 2 But Nadab and Abihu died before their father, and had no sons; so Eleazar and Ithamar became the priests. 3 Along with Zadok of the sons of Eleazar, and Ahimelech of the sons of Ithamar, David organized them according to the appointed duties in their service. 4 Since more chief men were found among the sons of Eleazar than among the sons of Ithamar, they organized them under sixteen heads of ancestral houses of the sons of Eleazar, and eight of the sons of Ithamar. 5 They organized them by lot, all alike, for there were officers of the sanctuary and officers of God among both the sons of Eleazar and the sons of Ithamar. 6 The scribe Shemaiah son of Nethanel, a Levite, recorded them in the presence of the king, the officers, and Zadok the priest, and Ahimelech son of Abiathar, and the heads of ancestral houses of the priests and of the Levites; one ancestral house being chosen for Eleazar and one chosen for Ithamar.

7 The first lot fell to Jehoiarib, the second to Jedaiah, 8 the third to Harim, the fourth to Seorim, 9 the fifth to Malchijah, the sixth to Mijamin, 10 the seventh to Hakkoz, the eighth to Abijah, 11 the ninth to Jeshua, the tenth to Shecaniah, 12 the eleventh to Eliashib, the twelfth to Jakim, 13 the thirteenth to Huppah, the fourteenth to Jeshebeab, 14 the fifteenth to Bilgah, the sixteenth to Immer, 15 the sev-

sons of Moses, the man of God, were to keep the name of Levite. 15 The sons of Moses: Gershom and Eliezer. 16 The sons of Gershom: Shubael the chief. 17 The sons of Eliezer: Rehabiah the chief. Eliezer had no other sons, but Rehabiah had very many. 18 The sons of Izhar: Shelomoth the chief. 19 The sons of Hebron: Jeriah the chief, Amariah the second, Jahaziel the third, and Jekameam the fourth. 20 The sons of Uzziel: Micah the chief and Isshiah the second.

21 The sons of Merari: Mahli and Mushi. The sons of Mahli: Eleazar and Kish. 22 When Eleazar died, he left daughters but no sons, and their cousins, the sons of Kish, married them. 23 The sons of Mushi: Mahli, Eder, and Jeremoth, three.

24 Such were the Levites, grouped by families in the father's line whose heads were named in the detailed list; they performed duties in the service of the house of the LORD, from the age of twenty upwards. 25 For David said, 'The LORD the God of Israel has given his people peace and has made his dwelling in Jerusalem for ever. 26 The Levites will no longer have to carry the Tabernacle or any of the vessels for its service.' 27 According to these last instructions of David the Levites were enrolled from the age of twenty upwards. 28 Their duty was to help the descendants of Aaron in the service of the house of the LORD: they were responsible for the care of the courts and the rooms, for the cleansing of all holy things, and for the general service of the house of God; 29 for the rows of the Bread of the Presence, the flour for the grain-offerings, unleavened wafers, cakes baked on the griddle, and pastry, and for the weights and measures. 30 They were to be on duty continually before the LORD every morning and evening, giving thanks and praise to him, 31 and whenever whole-offerings were presented to the LORD, on sabbaths, new moons, and at the appointed seasons, according to their prescribed number. 32 The Levites were to have charge of the Tent of Meeting and of the sanctuary, but Aaron's descendants, their kinsmen, were charged with the service of worship in the house of the LORD.

24 The divisions of the sons of Aaron: his sons were Nadab and Abihu, Eleazar and Ithamar. 2 Nadab and Abihu died before their father, leaving no sons; therefore Eleazar and Ithamar held the office of priest. 3 David, acting with Zadok of the sons of Eleazar and with Ahimelech of the sons of Ithamar, organized them in divisions for the discharge of the duties of their office. 4 The male heads of families proved to be more numerous in the line of Eleazar than in that of Ithamar, so that sixteen heads of families were grouped under the line of Eleazar and eight under that of Ithamar. 5 He organized them by drawing lots among them, for there were sacred officers and officers of God in the line of Eleazar and in that of Ithamar. 6 Shemaiah the clerk, a Levite, son of Nethanel, wrote down the names in the presence of the king, the officers, Zadok the priest, and Ahimelech son of Abiathar, and of the heads of the priestly and levitical families, one priestly family being taken from the line of Eleazar and one from that of Ithamar. 7 The first lot fell to Jehoiarib, the second to Jedaiah, 8 the third to Harim, the fourth to Seorim, 9 the fifth to Malchiah, the sixth to Mijamin, 10 the seventh to Hakkoz, the eighth to Abijah, 11 the ninth to Jeshua, the tenth to Shecaniah, 12 the eleventh to Eliashib, the twelfth to Jakim, 13 the thirteenth to Huppah, the fourteenth to Jeshebeab, 14 the fifteenth to Bilgah, the sixteenth to Immer, 15 the

23:16 **Shubael:** *so Gk; Heb.* Shebuel.   23:18 **Shelomoth:** *so one MS; others* Shelomith.   24:5 **sacred officers:** *or* officers of the sanctuary.   24:6 **one from that:** *so some MSS; others* taken from that.   24:13 **Jeshebeab:** *one form of Gk has* Ishbaal.

NEW AMERICAN BIBLE

Moses, however, the man of God, his sons were counted as part of the tribe of Levi. 15 The sons of Moses were Gershon and Eliezer. 16 The sons of Gershon: Shubael the chief. 17 The sons of Eliezer were Rehabiah the chief — Eliezer had no other sons, but the sons of Rehabiah were very numerous. 18 The sons of Izhar: Shelomith the chief. 19 The sons of Hebron: Jeriah, the chief, Amariah, the second, Jahaziel, the third, and Jekameam, the fourth. 20 The sons of Uzziel: Micah, the chief, and Isshiah, the second.

21 The sons of Merari: Mahli and Mushi. The sons of Mahli: Eleazar and Kish. 22 Eleazar died leaving no sons, only daughters; the sons of Kish, their kinsmen, married them. 23 The sons of Mushi: Mahli, Eder, and Jeremoth; three in all.

24 These were the sons of Levi according to their ancestral houses, the family heads as they were enrolled one by one according to their names. They performed the work of the service of the house of the LORD from twenty years of age upward, 27 for David's final orders were to enlist the Levites from the time they were twenty years old.

25 David said: "The LORD, the God of Israel, has given rest to his people, and has taken up his dwelling in Jerusalem. 26 Henceforth the Levites need not carry the Dwelling or any of its furnishings or equipment. ‡23.27: see above‡ 28 Rather, their duty shall be to assist the sons of Aaron in the service of the house of the LORD, having charge of the courts, the chambers, and the preservation of everything holy: they shall take part in the service of the house of God. 29 They shall also have charge of the showbread, of the fine flour for the cereal offering, of the wafers of unleavened bread, and of the baking and mixing, and of all measures of quantity and size. 30 They must be present every morning to offer thanks and to praise the LORD, and likewise in the evening; 31 and at every offering of holocausts to the LORD on sabbaths, new moons, and feast days, in such numbers as are prescribed, they must always be present before the LORD. 32 They shall observe what is prescribed for them concerning the meeting tent, the sanctuary, and the sons of Aaron, their brethren, in the service of the house of the LORD."

24 The descendants of Aaron also were divided into classes. The sons of Aaron were Nadab, Abihu, Eleazar, and Ithamar. 2 Nadab and Abihu died before their father, leaving no sons; therefore only Eleazar and Ithamar served as priests. 3 David, with Zadok, a descendant of Eleazar, and Ahimelech, a descendant of Ithamar, assigned the functions for the priestly service. 4 But since the descendants of Eleazar were found to be more numerous than those of Ithamar, the former were divided into sixteen groups, and the latter into eight groups, each under its family head. 5 Their functions were assigned impartially by lot, for there were officers of the holy place, and officers of the divine presence, descended both from Eleazar and from Ithamar. 6 The scribe Shemaiah, son of Nethanel, a Levite, made a record of it in the presence of the king, and of the leaders, of Zadok the priest, and of Ahimelech, son of Abiathar, and of the heads of the ancestral houses of the priests and of the Levites, listing two successive family groups from Eleazar before each one from Ithamar.

7 The first lot fell to Jehoiarib, the second to Jedaiah, 8 the third to Harim, the fourth to Seorim, 9 the fifth to Malchijah, the sixth to Mijamin, 10 the seventh to Hakkoz, the eighth to Abijah, 11 the ninth to Jeshua, the tenth to Shecaniah, 12 the eleventh to Eliashib, the twelfth to Jakim, 13 the thirteenth to Huppah, the fourteenth to Ishbaal, 14 the fifteenth to Bilgah, the sixteenth to Immer, 15 the seventeenth

NEW JERUSALEM BIBLE

14 Moses, man of God, and his sons were reckoned with the tribe of Levi. 15 Sons of Moses: Gershom and Eliezer. 16 Sons of Gershom: Shebuel, the first. 17 Of the sons of Eliezer, Rehabiah was the first. Eliezer had no other sons, but the sons of Rehabiah were very numerous. 18 Sons of Izhar: Shelomith, the first. 19 Sons of Hebron: Jeriah first, Amariah second, Jahaziel third, Jekameam fourth. 20 Sons of Uzziel: Micah first, Isshiah second.

21 Sons of Merari: Mahli and Mushi. Sons of Mahli: Eleazar and Kish. 22 Eleazar died without sons, but he did have daughters, whom their cousins, the sons of Kish, married. 23 Sons of Mushi: Mahli, Eder, Jeremoth: three in all.

24 These were the sons of Levi by their families, the heads of families, and those registered by name, individually; whoever was twenty years old or upwards had his function in the service of the Temple of Yahweh.

25 For David said, 'Since Yahweh, God of Israel, has given rest to his people Israel and has taken up residence in Jerusalem for ever, 26 the Levites need no longer carry the Dwelling or any of the objects required for its service.' 27 For, according to the last words of David, the Levites who had been registered were of twenty years and upwards. 28 Their duty now is to help the sons of Aaron in the service of the House of Yahweh, in the care of the courts and rooms, the purification of all the holy things, the work for the service of the House of God, 29 the loaves of permanent offering, the flour for the oblation, the wafers of unleavened bread, the pan-baked materials, the unmixed materials and all measures of volume and length. 30 Furthermore, they have to be present every morning to give thanks and praise to Yahweh, and also in the evening; 31 and at the bringing of every burnt offering to Yahweh on Sabbath, New Moon or solemn feast, appearing regularly before Yahweh in accordance with the numbers required of them. 32 In serving the Temple of Yahweh they observe the ritual of the Tent of Meeting, the ritual of the sanctuary and the ritual of their kinsmen, the sons of Aaron.'

24 Orders of the sons of Aaron: Sons of Aaron: Nadab, Abihu, Eleazar, Ithamar. 2 Nadab and Abihu died in their father's lifetime leaving no children, so Eleazar and Ithamar filled the office of priest. 3 With Zadok of the sons of Eleazar, and Ahimelech of the sons of Ithamar, David allocated them according to the classification of their duties. 4 Since the sons of Eleazar were found to have more headmen than the sons of Ithamar, they allocated sixteen heads of families to the sons of Eleazar and eight heads of families to the sons of Ithamar. 5 They allocated them by lot, both alike, there being religious officials and officials of God among the sons of Eleazar, as among the sons of Ithamar. 6 The levitical scribe Shemaiah son of Nethanel, recorded them in the presence of the king, the leaders, Zadok the priest, Ahimelech son of Abiathar and the heads of the priestly and levitical families, so that two families were selected for Eleazar for each one selected for Ithamar.

7 The first lot fell to Jehoiarib, the second to Jedaiah, 8 the third to Harim, the fourth to Seorim, 9 the fifth to Malchijah, the sixth to Mijamin, 10 the seventh to Hakkoz, the eighth to Abijah, 11 the ninth to Jeshua, the tenth to Shecaniah, 12 the eleventh to Eliashib, the twelfth to Jakim, 13 the thirteenth to Huppah, the fourteenth to Ishbaal, 14 the fifteenth to Bilgah, the sixteenth to Immer, 15 the seventeenth

enteenth to Hezir, the eighteenth to Happizzez, 16 the nineteenth to Pethahiah, the twentieth to Jehezkel, 17 the twenty-first to Jachin, the twenty-second to Gamul, 18 the twenty-third to Delaiah, the twenty-fourth to Maaziah. 19 These had as their appointed duty in their service to enter the house of the LORD according to the procedure established for them by their ancestor Aaron, as the LORD God of Israel had commanded him.

20 And of the rest of the sons of Levi: of the sons of Amram, Shubael; of the sons of Shubael, Jehdeiah. 21 Of Rehabiah: of the sons of Rehabiah, Isshiah the chief. 22 Of the Izharites, Shelomoth; of the sons of Shelomoth, Jahath. 23 The sons of Hebron:*h* Jeriah the chief,*i* Amariah the second, Jahaziel the third, Jekameam the fourth. 24 The sons of Uzziel, Micah; of the sons of Micah, Shamir. 25 The brother of Micah, Isshiah; of the sons of Isshiah, Zechariah. 26 The sons of Merari: Mahli and Mushi. The sons of Jaaziah: Beno.*j* 27 The sons of Merari: of Jaaziah, Beno,*j* Shoham, Zaccur, and Ibri. 28 Of Mahli: Eleazar, who had no sons. 29 Of Kish, the sons of Kish: Jerahmeel. 30 The sons of Mushi: Mahli, Eder, and Jerimoth. These were the sons of the Levites according to their ancestral houses. 31 These also cast lots corresponding to their kindred, the descendants of Aaron, in the presence of King David, Zadok, Ahimelech, and the heads of ancestral houses of the priests and of the Levites, the chief as well as the youngest brother.

25 David and the officers of the army also set apart for the service the sons of Asaph, and of Heman, and of Jeduthun, who should prophesy with lyres, harps, and cymbals. The list of those who did the work and of their duties was: 2 Of the sons of Asaph: Zaccur, Joseph, Nethaniah, and Asarelah, sons of Asaph, under the direction of Asaph, who prophesied under the direction of the king. 3 Of Jeduthun, the sons of Jeduthun: Gedaliah, Zeri, Jeshaiah, Shimei,*k* Hashabiah, and Mattithiah, six, under the direction of their father Jeduthun, who prophesied with the lyre in thanksgiving and praise to the LORD. 4 Of Heman, the sons of Heman: Bukkiah, Mattaniah, Uzziel, Shebuel, and Jerimoth, Hananiah, Hanani, Eliathah, Giddalti, and Romamti-ezer, Joshbekashah, Mallothi, Hothir, Mahazioth. 5 All these were the sons of Heman the king's seer, according to the promise of God to exalt him; for God had given Heman fourteen sons and three daughters. 6 They were all under the direction of their father for the music in the house of the LORD with cymbals, harps, and lyres for the service of the house of God. Asaph, Jeduthun, and Heman were under the order of the king. 7 They and their kindred, who were trained in singing to the LORD, all of whom were skillful, numbered two hundred eighty-eight. 8 And they cast lots for their duties, small and great, teacher and pupil alike.

9 The first lot fell for Asaph to Joseph; the second to Gedaliah, to him and his brothers and his sons, twelve; 10 the third to Zaccur, his sons and his brothers, twelve; 11 the fourth to Izri, his sons and his brothers, twelve; 12 the fifth to Nethaniah, his sons and his brothers, twelve; 13 the

seventeenth to Hezir, the eighteenth to Aphses, 16 the nineteenth to Pethahiah, the twentieth to Jehezkel, 17 the twenty-first to Jachin, the twenty-second to Gamul, 18 the twenty-third to Delaiah, and the twenty-fourth to Maaziah. 19 This was their order of duty for the discharge of their service when they entered the house of the LORD, according to the rule prescribed for them by their ancestor Aaron, who had received his instructions from the LORD the God of Israel.

20 Of the remaining Levites: of the sons of Amram: Shubael. Of the sons of Shubael: Jehdeiah. 21 Of Rehabiah: Isshiah, the chief of Rehabiah's sons. 22 Of the line of Izhar: Shelomoth. Of the sons of Shelomoth: Jahath. 23 The sons of Hebron: Jeriah the chief, Amariah the second, Jahaziel the third, and Jekameam the fourth. 24 The sons of Uzziel: Micah. Of the sons of Micah: Shamir; 25 Micah's brother: Isshiah. Of the sons of Isshiah: Zechariah. 26 The sons of Merari: Mahli and Mushi and also Jaaziah his son. 27 The sons of Merari: of Jaaziah: Beno, Shoham, Zaccur, and Ibri. 28 Of Mahli: Eleazar, who had no sons; 29 of Kish: the sons of Kish: Jerahmeel; 30 and the sons of Mushi: Mahli, Eder, and Jerimoth. These were the Levites by families. 31 These also, side by side with their kinsmen the descendants of Aaron, cast lots in the presence of King David, Zadok, Ahimelech, and the heads of the priestly and levitical families, the senior and junior houses casting lots side by side.

25 David and his chief officers assigned special duties to the sons of Asaph, of Heman, and of Jeduthun, leaders in inspired prophecy to the accompaniment of lyres, lutes, and cymbals; the list of those who performed this work in the temple was as follows. 2 Of the sons of Asaph: Zaccur, Joseph, Nethaniah, and Asarelah; these were under Asaph, a leader in inspired prophecy under the king. 3 Of the sons of Jeduthun: Gedaliah, Izri, Isaiah, Shimei, Hashabiah, Mattithiah, these six under their father Jeduthun, a leader in inspired prophecy to the accompaniment of the lyre, giving thanks and praise to the LORD. 4 Of the sons of Heman: Bukkiah, Mattaniah, Uzziel, Shubael, Jerimoth, Hananiah, Hanani, Eliathah, Giddalti, Romamti-ezer, Joshbekashah, Mallothi, Hothir, and Mahazioth; 5 all these were sons of Heman the king's seer, given to him through the promises of God for his greater glory. God had given Heman fourteen sons and three daughters, 6 and they all served under their father for the singing in the house of the LORD; they took part in the service of the house of God, with cymbals, lutes, and lyres, while Asaph, Jeduthun, and Heman were under the king. 7 Reckoned with their kinsmen, trained singers of the LORD, they brought the total number of skilled musicians up to two hundred and eighty-eight. 8 They cast lots for their duties, young and old, master-singer and apprentice side by side.

9 The first lot fell to Joseph: he and his brothers and his sons, twelve. The second to Gedaliah: he and his brothers and his sons, twelve. 10 The third to Zaccur: his sons and his brothers, twelve. 11 The fourth to Izri: his sons and his brothers, twelve. 12 The fifth to Nethaniah: his sons and his brothers, twelve. 13 The sixth to Bukkiah: his sons and his

24:23 **Hebron:** *so one MS; others omit.* **the chief:** *so Gk (Luc.); Heb. omits.* 24:26 and also: *prob. rdg; Heb.* the sons of. 25:3 Izri: *prob. rdg, cp. verse 11; Heb.* Zeri. **Shimei:** *so one MS; others omit.* 25:4 **Shubael:** *so Gk, cp. verse 20; Heb.* Shebuel. **Hananiah . . . Mahazioth:** *these nine proper names may have been originally the words of a prayer:* Be gracious to me, LORD, be gracious to me; you are my God; I will magnify and exalt you, my helper. Lingering in hardship, I faint. Grant me vision after vision. 25:9 **fell:** *prob. rdg; Heb. adds* to Asaph. **Joseph: he and his brothers and his sons, twelve:** *prob. rdg; Heb. omits* he . . . twelve.

h See 23.19: Heb lacks *Hebron*   *i* See 23.19: Heb lacks *the chief*   *j* Or *his son:* Meaning of Heb uncertain   *k* One Ms: Gk: MT lacks *Shimei*

to Hezir, the eighteenth to Happizzez, 16 the nineteenth to Pethahiah, the twentieth to Jehezkel, 17 the twenty-first to Jachin, the twenty-second to Gamul, 18 the twenty-third to Delaiah, the twenty-fourth to Maaziah. 19 This was the appointed order of their service when they functioned in the house of the LORD in keeping with the precepts given them by Aaron, their father, as the LORD, the God of Israel, had commanded him.

20 Of the remaining Levites, there were Shubael, of the descendants of Amram, and Jehdeiah, of the descendants of Shubael; 21 Isshiah, the chief, of the descendants of Rehabiah; 22 Shelomith of the Izharites, and Jahath of the descendants of Shelomith. 23 The descendants of Hebron were Jeriah, the chief, Amariah, the second, Jahaziel, the third, Jekameam, the fourth. 24 The descendants of Uzziel were Micah; Shamir, of the descendants of Micah; 25 Isshiah, the brother of Micah; and Zechariah, a descendant of Isshiah. 26 The descendants of Merari were Mahli, Mushi, and the descendants of his son Uzziah. 27 The descendants of Merari through his son Uzziah: Shoham, Zaccur, and Ibri. 28 Descendants of Mahli were Eleazar, who had no sons, 29 and Jerahmeel, of the descendants of Kish. 30 The descendants of Mushi were Mahli, Eder, and Jerimoth.

These were the descendants of the Levites according to their ancestral houses. 31 They too, in the same manner as their relatives, the descendants of Aaron, cast lots in the presence of King David, Zadok, Ahimelech, and the heads of the priestly and levitical families; the more important family did so in the same way as the less important one.

25 David and the leaders of the liturgical cult set apart for service the descendants of Asaph, Heman, and Jeduthun, as singers of inspired song to the accompaniment of lyres and harps and cymbals.

This is the list of those who performed this service: 2 Of the sons of Asaph: Zaccur, Joseph, Nethaniah, and Asharelah, sons of Asaph, under the direction of Asaph, who sang inspired songs under the guidance of the king. 3 Of Jeduthun, these sons of Jeduthun: Gedaliah, Zeri, Jeshaiah, Shimei, Hashabiah, and Mattithiah; six, under the direction of their father Jeduthun, who sang inspired songs to the accompaniment of a lyre, to give thanks and praise to the LORD. 4 Of Heman, these sons of Heman: Bukkiah, Mattaniah, Uzziel, Shubael, and Jerimoth; Hananiah, Hanani, Eliathah, Giddalti, Romamti-ezer, Joshbekashah, Mallothi, Hothir, and Mahazioth. 5 All these were the sons of Heman, the king's seer in divine matters; to enhance his prestige, God gave Heman fourteen sons and three daughters. 6 All these, whether of Asaph, Jeduthun, or Heman, were under their fathers' direction in the singing in the house of the LORD to the accompaniment of cymbals, harps and lyres, serving in the house of God, under the guidance of the king. 7 Their number, together with that of their brethren who were trained in singing to the LORD, all of them skilled men, was two hundred and eighty-eight. 8 They cast lots for their functions equally, young and old, master and pupil alike.

9 The first lot fell to Asaph, the family of Joseph; he and his sons and his brethren were twelve. Gedaliah was the second; he and his brethren and his sons were twelve. 10 The third was Zaccur, his sons and his brethren: twelve. 11 The fourth fell to Izri, his sons, and his brethren: twelve. 12 The fifth was Nethaniah, his sons, and his brethren: twelve.

to Hezir, the eighteenth to Happizzez, 16 the nineteenth to Pethahiah, the twentieth to Jehezkel, 17 the twenty-first to Jachin, the twenty-second to Gamul, 18 the twenty-third to Delaiah and the twenty-fourth to Maaziah.

19 These were their classifications for their duties when they entered the House of Yahweh in accordance with prescriptions laid down by Aaron their ancestor as Yahweh, God of Israel, had commanded him.

20 As regards the rest of the sons of Levi:

Of the sons of Amram: Shubael. Of the sons of Shubael: Jehdeiah. 21 As regards Rehabiah, of the sons of Rehabiah: Isshiah, the first one. 22 Of the sons of Izhar: Shelomoth; of the sons of Shelomoth: Jahath. 23 Of the sons of Hebron: Jeriah the first, Amariah the second, Jahaziel the third, Jekameam the fourth. 24 The son of Uzziel was Micah; of the sons of Micah: Shamir. 25 The brother of Micah was Isshiah; of the sons of Isshiah, Zechariah. 26 The sons of Merari were Mahli and Mushi; of his sons: Jaaziah his son. 27 The sons of Merari by his son Jaaziah were Shoham, Zaccur and Ibri. 28 Of Mahli, there was Eleazar who had no sons, 29 and Kish; and of the sons of Kish: Jerahmeel. 30 The sons of Mushi were Mahli, Eder and Jerimoth.

These were the Levites according to families. 31 Like their kinsmen, the sons of Aaron, these heads of families, senior and junior alike, also drew lots in the presence of King David, Zadok, Ahimelech, and the heads of the priestly and levitical families.

25 For the liturgy, David and the religious officials selected the sons of Asaph, of Heman and of Jeduthun, who were to prophesy to the accompaniment of harps, lyres and cymbals. The list of ministrants for this service was as follows:

2 Of the sons of Asaph: Zaccur, Joseph, Nethaniah, Asharelah; the sons of Asaph were under the direction of Asaph who prophesied at the king's direction.

3 Of Jeduthun there were the sons of Jeduthun: Gedaliah, Zeri, Jeshaiah, Hashabiah and Mattithiah, six, under the direction of their father Jeduthun who, with the harp, prophesied when thanks and praise were to be given to Yahweh.

4 Of Heman there were the sons of Heman: Bukkiah, Mattaniah, Uzziel, Shebuel, Jerimoth, Hananiah, Hanani, Eliathah, Giddalti, Romamti-Ezer, Joshbekashah, Mallothi, Hothir, Mahazioth. 5 All these were sons of Heman, the king's seer; at God's word they blew the horn. God gave Heman fourteen sons and three daughters. 6 Under the king's direction all these had the duty of singing to the accompaniment of cymbal, lyre and harp for the liturgy of the house of God under the direction of their fathers.

Asaph, Jeduthun and Heman, 7 trained in the songs of Yahweh, with their brothers, numbered two hundred and eighty-eight, all expert. 8 Junior and senior, master and pupil alike, they drew lots for their term of duty. 9 The first to whom the lot fell was the Asaphite, Joseph. The second was Gedaliah, who with his sons and brothers made twelve. 10 The third was Zaccur, who with his sons and brothers made twelve. 11 The fourth was Izri, who with his sons and brothers made twelve. 12 The fifth was Nethaniah, who with his sons and brothers made twelve. 13 The sixth was Buk-

sixth to Bukkiah, his sons and his brothers, twelve; 14the seventh to Jesarelah,*l* his sons and his brothers, twelve; 15the eighth to Jeshaiah, his sons and his brothers, twelve; 16the ninth to Mattaniah, his sons and his brothers, twelve; 17the tenth to Shimei, his sons and his brothers, twelve; 18the eleventh to Azarel, his sons and his brothers, twelve; 19the twelfth to Hashabiah, his sons and his brothers, twelve; 20to the thirteenth, Shubael, his sons and his brothers, twelve; 21to the fourteenth, Mattithiah, his sons and his brothers, twelve; 22to the fifteenth, to Jeremoth, his sons and his brothers, twelve; 23to the sixteenth, to Hananiah, his sons and his brothers, twelve; 24to the seventeenth, to Joshbekashah, his sons and his brothers, twelve; 25to the eighteenth, to Hanani, his sons and his brothers, twelve; 26to the nineteenth, to Mallothi, his sons and his brothers, twelve; 27to the twentieth, to Eliathah, his sons and his brothers, twelve; 28to the twenty-first, to Hothir, his sons and his brothers, twelve; 29to the twenty-second, to Giddalti, his sons and his brothers, twelve; 30to the twenty-third, to Mahazioth, his sons and his brothers, twelve; 31to the twenty-fourth, to Romamti-ezer, his sons and his brothers, twelve.

26 As for the divisions of the gatekeepers: of the Korahites, Meshelemiah son of Kore, of the sons of Asaph. 2Meshelemiah had sons: Zechariah the firstborn, Jediael the second, Zebadiah the third, Jathniel the fourth, 3Elam the fifth, Jehohanan the sixth, Eliehoenai the seventh. 4Obed-edom had sons: Shemaiah the firstborn, Jehozabad the second, Joah the third, Sachar the fourth, Nethanel the fifth, 5Ammiel the sixth, Issachar the seventh, Peullethai the eighth; for God blessed him. 6Also to his son Shemaiah sons were born who exercised authority in their ancestral houses, for they were men of great ability. 7The sons of Shemaiah: Othni, Rephael, Obed, and Elzabad, whose brothers were able men, Elihu and Semachiah. 8All these, sons of Obed-edom with their sons and brothers, were able men qualified for the service; sixty-two of Obed-edom. 9Meshelemiah had sons and brothers, able men, eighteen. 10Hosah, of the sons of Merari, had sons: Shimri the chief (for though he was not the firstborn, his father made him chief), 11Hilkiah the second, Tebaliah the third, Zechariah the fourth: all the sons and brothers of Hosah totaled thirteen.

12 These divisions of the gatekeepers, corresponding to their leaders, had duties, just as their kindred did, ministering in the house of the Lord; 13and they cast lots by ancestral houses, small and great alike, for their gates. 14The lot for the east fell to Shelemiah. They cast lots also for his son Zechariah, a prudent counselor, and his lot came out for the north. 15Obed-edom's came out for the south, and to his sons was allotted the storehouse. 16For Shuppim and Hosah it came out for the west, at the gate of Shallecheth on the ascending road. Guard corresponded to guard. 17On the east there were six Levites each day,*m* on the north four each day, on the south four each day, as well as two and two at the storehouse; 18and for the colonnade*n* on the west there were four at the road and two at the colonnade.*n* 19These were the divisions of the gatekeepers among the Korahites and the sons of Merari.

20 And of the Levites, Ahijah had charge of the treasuries of the house of God and the treasuries of the dedicated gifts. 21The sons of Ladan, the sons of the Gershonites

brothers, twelve. 14The seventh to Asarelah: his sons and his brothers, twelve. 15The eighth to Isaiah: his sons and his brothers, twelve. 16The ninth to Mattaniah: his sons and his brothers, twelve. 17The tenth to Shimei: his sons and his brothers, twelve. 18The eleventh to Azarel: his sons and his brothers, twelve. 19The twelfth to Hashabiah: his sons and his brothers, twelve. 20The thirteenth to Shubael: his sons and his brothers, twelve. 21The fourteenth to Mattithiah: his sons and his brothers, twelve. 22The fifteenth to Jeremoth: his sons and his brothers, twelve. 23The sixteenth to Hananiah: his sons and his brothers, twelve. 24The seventeenth to Joshbekashah: his sons and his brothers, twelve. 25The eighteenth to Hanani: his sons and his brothers, twelve. 26The nineteenth to Mallothi: his sons and his brothers, twelve. 27The twentieth to Eliathah: his sons and his brothers, twelve. 28The twenty-first to Hothir: his sons and his brothers, twelve. 29The twenty-second to Giddalti: his sons and his brothers, twelve. 30The twenty-third to Mahazioth: his sons and his brothers, twelve. 31The twenty-fourth to Romamti-ezer: his sons and his brothers, twelve.

26 The divisions of the door-keepers: Korahites: Meshelemiah son of Kore, son of Ebiasaph. 2Sons of Meshelemiah: Zechariah the eldest, Jediael the second, Zebadiah the third, Jathniel the fourth, 3Elam the fifth, Jehohanan the sixth, Eliehoenai the seventh. 4Sons of Obed-edom: Shemaiah the eldest, Jehozabad the second, Joah the third, Sacar the fourth, Nethanel the fifth, 5Ammiel the sixth, Issachar the seventh, Peulthai the eighth (for God had blessed him). 6Shemaiah, his son, was the father of sons who had authority in their family, for they were men of great ability. 7Sons of Shemaiah: Othni, Rephael, Obed, Elzabad, and his brothers Elihu and Semachiah, men of ability. 8All these belonged to the family of Obed-edom; they, their sons and brothers, were men of ability, fit for service in the temple; total: sixty-two. 9Sons and brothers of Meshelemiah, all men of ability, eighteen. 10Sons of Hosah, a Merarite: Shimri the chief (he was not the eldest, but his father had made him chief), 11Hilkiah the second, Tebaliah the third, Zechariah the fourth. Total of Hosah's sons and brothers: thirteen.

12The male heads of families constituted the divisions of the door-keepers; their duty was to serve in the house of the Lord side by side with their kinsmen. 13Young and old, family by family, they cast lots for the gates. 14The lot for the east gate fell to Shelemiah; then lots were cast for his son Zechariah, a prudent councillor, and he was allotted the north gate. 15To Obed-edom was allotted the south gate, and the gatehouse to his sons. 16Hosah was allotted the west gate, together with the Shalleketh gate on the ascending causeway. Guard corresponded to guard. 17Six Levites were on duty daily on the east side, four on the north and four on the south, and two at each gatehouse; 18at the western colonnade there were four at the causeway and two at the colonnade itself. 19These were the divisions of the door-keepers, Korahites and Merarites.

20Fellow-Levites were in charge of the stores of the house of God and of the stores of sacred gifts. 21Of the

25:14 **Asarelah:** *so one form of Gk, cp. verse 2; Heb.* Yesarelah. 26:1 **son of Ebiasaph:** *prob. rdg; Heb.* from the sons of Asaph. 26:7 **Elzabad, and:** *so some MSS; others omit* and. 26:10 **the chief:** *or* the fratriarch. 26:16 **Hosah:** *prob. rdg; Heb.* Shuppim and Hosah. 26:20 **Fellow-Levites:** *so Gk; Heb.* Levites, Ahijah.

*l*Or *Asarelah;* see 25.2   *m*Gk: Heb lacks *each day*
*n*Heb *parbar:* meaning uncertain

13 The sixth was Bukkiah, his sons, and his brethren: twelve. 14 The seventh was Jesarelah, his sons, and his brethren: twelve. 15 The eighth was Jeshaiah, his sons, and his brethren: twelve. 16 The ninth was Mattaniah, his sons, and his brethren: twelve. 17 The tenth was Shimei, his sons, and his brethren: twelve. 18 The eleventh was Uzziel, his sons, and his brethren: twelve. 19 The twelfth fell to Hashabiah, his sons, and his brethren: twelve. 20 The thirteenth was Shubael, his sons, and his brethren: twelve. 21 The fourteenth was Mattithiah, his sons, and his brethren: twelve. 22 The fifteenth fell to Jeremoth, his sons, and his brethren: twelve. 23 The sixteenth fell to Hananiah, his sons, and his brethren: twelve. 24 The seventeenth fell to Joshbekashah, his sons, and his brethren: twelve. 25 The eighteenth fell to Hanani, his sons, and his brethren: twelve. 26 The nineteenth fell to Mallothi, his sons, and his brethren: twelve. 27 The twentieth fell to Eliathah, his sons, and his brethren: twelve. 28 The twenty-first fell to Hothir, his sons, and his brethren: twelve. 29 The twenty-second fell to Giddalti, his sons, and his brethren: twelve. 30 The twenty-third fell to Mahazioth, his sons, and his brethren: twelve. 31 The twenty-fourth fell to Romamti-ezer, his sons, and his brethren: twelve.

26 As for the classes of gatekeepers. Of the Korahites was Meshelemiah, the son of Kore, one of the sons of Abiasaph. 2 Meshelemiah's sons: Zechariah, the first-born, Jediael, the second son, Zebadiah, the third, Jathniel, the fourth, 3 Elam, the fifth, Jehohanan, the sixth, Eliehoenai, the seventh. 4 Obed-edom's sons: Shemaiah, the first-born, Jehozabad, a second son, Joah, the third, Sachar, the fourth, Nethanel, the fifth, 5 Ammiel, the sixth, Issachar, the seventh, Peullethai, the eighth, for God blessed him. 6 To his son Shemaiah were born sons who ruled over their family, for they were warriors. 7 The sons of Shemaiah were Othni, Rephael, Obed, and Elzabad; also his brethren who were men of might, Elihu and Semachiah. 8 All these were of the sons of Obed-edom, who, together with their sons and their brethren, were mighty men, fit for the service. Of Obed-edom, sixty-two. 9 Of Meshelemiah, eighteen sons and brethren, mighty men.

10 Hosah, a descendant of Merari, had these sons: Shimri, the chief (for though he was not the first-born, his father made him chief), 11 Hilkiah, the second son, Tebaliah, the third, Zechariah, the fourth. All the sons and brethren of Hosah were thirteen.

12 To these classes of gatekeepers, under their chief men, were assigned watches in the service of the house of the LORD, for each group in the same way. 13 They cast lots for each gate, the small and the large families alike. 14 When the lot was cast for the east side, it fell to Meshelemiah. Then they cast lots for his son Zechariah, a prudent counselor, and the north side fell to his lot. 15 To Obed-edom fell the south side, and to his sons the storehouse. 16 To Hosah fell the west side with the Shallecheth gate at the ascending highway. For each family, watches were established. 17 On the east, six watched each day, on the north, four each day, on the south, four each day, and at the storehouse they were two and two; 18 as for the large building on the west, there were four at the highway and two at the large building. 19 These were the classes of the gatekeepers, descendants of Kore and Merari.

20 Their brother Levites superintended the stores for the house of God and the stores of votive offerings. 21 Among

kiah, who with his sons and brothers made twelve. 14 The seventh was Jesharelah, who with his sons and brothers made twelve. 15 The eighth was Jeshaiah, who with his sons and brothers made twelve. 16 The ninth was Mattaniah, who with his sons and brothers made twelve. 17 The tenth was Shimei, who with his sons and brothers made twelve. 18 The eleventh was Azarel, who with his sons and brothers made twelve. 19 The twelfth was Hashabiah, who with his sons and brothers made twelve. 20 The thirteenth was Shubael, who with his sons and brothers made twelve. 21 The fourteenth was Mattithiah, who with his sons and brothers made twelve. 22 The fifteenth was Jeremoth, who with his sons and brothers made twelve. 23 The sixteenth was Hananiah, who with his sons and brothers made twelve. 24 The seventeenth was Joshbekashah, who with his sons and brothers made twelve. 25 The eighteenth was Hanani, who with his sons and brothers made twelve. 26 The nineteenth was Mallothi, who with his sons and brothers made twelve. 27 The twentieth was Eliathah, who with his sons and brothers made twelve. 28 The twenty-first was Hothir, who with his sons and brothers made twelve. 29 The twenty-second was Giddalti, who with his sons and brothers made twelve. 30 The twenty-third was Mahazioth, who with his sons and brothers made twelve. 31 The twenty-fourth was Romamti-Ezer, who with his sons and brothers made twelve.

26 As regards the orders of the gate keepers: Of the Korahites there was Meshelemiah son of Kore, one of the sons of Ebiasaph, 2 and Meshelemiah's sons: Zechariah the first-born, Jediael the second, Zebadiah the third, Jathniel the fourth, 3 Elam the fifth, Jehohanan the sixth, Elioenai the seventh.

4 Obed-Edom's sons were: Shemaiah the first-born, Jehozabad the second, Joah the third, Sacar the fourth, Nethanel the fifth, 5 Ammiel the sixth, Issachar the seventh, Peullethai the eighth; God had indeed blessed him. 6 His son Shemaiah also had sons who wielded authority in their family, because they were men of outstanding quality. 7 The sons of Shemaiah were: Othni, Rephael, Obed and Elzabad, whose brothers Elihu and Semachiah were outstanding men. 8 All these were sons of Obed-Edom, who with their sons and brothers were men of standing, well fitted for their task. Obed-Edom had sixty-two.

9 Meshelemiah had eighteen outstanding sons and brothers.

10 Hosah, one of the sons of Merari, had sons: Shimri was the first, for although he was not the first-born his father had made him the chief. 11 Hilkiah was the second, Tebaliah the third, Zechariah the fourth: Hosah had thirteen sons and brothers in all.

12 These orders of gatekeepers, allocated according to their headmen, had duties, just like their brothers, of serving in the house of Yahweh. 13 Similarly, they drew lots for each gate, whether their families were large or small. 14 For the eastern one, the lot fell to Shelemiah; and when they drew lots for Zechariah his son, a shrewd counsellor, his lot came out for the north. 15 To Obed-Edom went the south, and to his sons the storehouses. 16 To Shuppim and Hosah went the west with the Gate of the Felled Tree-trunk on the upper road. The corresponding guards were as follows: 17 for the east gate, six per day; for the north gate, four per day; for the south gate, four per day; for the storehouses, two each; 18 for the Parbar at the west gate, four by the road and two for the Parbar. 19 These were the orders of the gatekeepers of the sons of Korah and the sons of Merari.

20 The Levites, their brothers, who were responsible for the treasures of the house of God and for the treasures of consecrated gifts, 21 were the sons of Ladan and belonged to

belonging to Ladan, the heads of families belonging to La-dan the Gershonite: Jehieli.*o*

22 The sons of Jehieli, Zetham and his brother Joel, were in charge of the treasuries of the house of the LORD. 23 Of the Amramites, the Izharites, the Hebronites, and the Uzzielites: 24 Shebuel son of Gershom, son of Moses, was chief officer in charge of the treasuries. 25 His brothers: from Eliezer were his son Rehabiah, his son Jeshaiah, his son Joram, his son Zichri, and his son Shelomoth. 26 This Shelomoth and his brothers were in charge of all the treasuries of the dedicated gifts that King David, and the heads of families, and the officers of the thousands and the hundreds, and the commanders of the army, had dedicated. 27 From booty won in battles they dedicated gifts for the mainte-nance of the house of the LORD. 28 Also all that Samuel the seer, and Saul son of Kish, and Abner son of Ner, and Joab son of Zeruiah had dedicated—all dedicated gifts were in the care of Shelomoth*p* and his brothers.

29 Of the Izharites, Chenaniah and his sons were ap-pointed to outside duties for Israel, as officers and judges. 30 Of the Hebronites, Hashabiah and his brothers, one thou-sand seven hundred men of ability, had the oversight of Israel west of the Jordan for all the work of the LORD and for the service of the king. 31 Of the Hebronites, Jerijah was chief of the Hebronites. (In the fortieth year of David's reign search was made, of whatever genealogy or family, and men of great ability among them were found at Jazer in Gilead.) 32 King David appointed him and his brothers, two thousand seven hundred men of ability, heads of families, to have the oversight of the Reubenites, the Gadites, and the half-tribe of the Manassites for everything pertaining to God and for the affairs of the king.

27 This is the list of the people of Israel, the heads of families, the commanders of the thousands and the hundreds, and their officers who served the king in all mat-ters concerning the divisions that came and went, month after month throughout the year, each division numbering twenty-four thousand:

2 Jashobeam son of Zabdiel was in charge of the first division in the first month; in his division were twenty-four thousand. 3 He was a descendant of Perez, and was chief of all the commanders of the army for the first month. 4 Dodai the Ahohite was in charge of the division of the second month; Mikloth was the chief officer of his division. In his division were twenty-four thousand. 5 The third com-mander, for the third month, was Benaiah son of the priest Jehoiada, as chief; in his division were twenty-four thou-sand. 6 This is the Benaiah who was a mighty man of the Thirty and in command of the Thirty; his son Ammizabad was in charge of his division.*q* 7 Asahel brother of Joab was fourth, for the fourth month, and his son Zebadiah after him; in his division were twenty-four thousand. 8 The fifth commander, for the fifth month, was Shamhut, the Izra-hite; in his division were twenty-four thousand. 9 Sixth, for the sixth month, was Ira son of Ikkesh the Tekoite; in his division were twenty-four thousand. 10 Seventh, for the sev-enth month, was Helez the Pelonite, of the Ephraimites; in his division were twenty-four thousand. 11 Eighth, for the eighth month, was Sibbecai the Hushathite, of the Zera-hites; in his division were twenty-four thousand. 12 Ninth,

children of Laadan, descendants of the Gershonite line through Laadan, heads of families in the group of Laadan the Gershonite: Jehiel 22 and his brothers Zetham and Joel were in charge of the stores of the house of the LORD. 23 Of the families of Amram, Izhar, Hebron, and Uzziel, 24 Shu-bael son of Gershom, son of Moses, was overseer of the stores. 25 The line of Eliezer his brother: his son Rehabiah, his son Isaiah, his son Joram, his son Zichri, and his son Shelomoth. 26 This Shelomoth and his kinsmen were in charge of all the stores of the sacred gifts dedicated by King David, the heads of families, the officers over units of a thousand and a hundred, and other officers of the army. 27 They had dedicated some of the spoils taken in the wars for the upkeep of the house of the LORD. 28 Everything which Samuel the seer, Saul son of Kish, Abner son of Ner, and Joab son of Zeruiah had dedicated, in short every sacred gift, was under the charge of Shelomoth and his kinsmen. 29 Of the family of Izhar: Kenaniah and his sons acted as clerks and magistrates in the secular affairs of Israel. 30 Of the family of Hebron: Hashabiah and his kinsmen, men of ability to the number of seventeen hundred, had the over-sight of Israel west of the Jordan, both in the work of the LORD and in the service of the king. 31 Also of the family of Hebron, Jeriah was the chief. (In the fortieth year of Da-vid's reign search was made in the family histories of the Hebronites, and men of great ability were found among them at Jazer in Gilead.) 32 His kinsmen, all men of ability, two thousand seven hundred of them, heads of families, were charged by King David with the oversight of the Reu-benites, the Gadites, and the half tribe of Manasseh, in religious and civil affairs alike.

27 THE number of the Israelites—that is to say, of the heads of families, the officers over units of a thou-sand and a hundred, and the clerks who had their share in the king's service in the various divisions which took monthly turns of duty throughout the year—was twenty-four thousand in each division.

2 First, Jashobeam son of Zabdiel commanded the divi-sion for the first month with twenty-four thousand in his division; 3 a member of the house of Perez, he was chief officer of the temple staff for the first month. 4 Eleazar son of Dodai the Ahohite commanded the division for the sec-ond month with twenty-four thousand in his division. 5 Third, Benaiah son of Jehoiada the chief priest, command-er of the army, was the officer for the third month with twenty-four thousand in his division 6 (he was the Benaiah who was one of the thirty warriors and was a chief among the thirty); but his son Ammizabad commanded his divi-sion. 7 Fourth, Asahel, the brother of Joab, was the officer commanding for the fourth month with twenty-four thou-sand in his division; and his successor was Zebadiah his son. 8 Fifth, Shamhuth the Zerahite was the officer com-manding for the fifth month with twenty-four thousand in his division. 9 Sixth, Ira son of Ikkesh, a man of Tekoa, was the officer commanding for the sixth month with twenty-four thousand in his division. 10 Seventh, Helez, an Ephra-imite from a place unknown, was the officer commanding for the seventh month with twenty-four thousand in his division. 11 Eighth, Sibbechai from Hushah, of the family of Zerah, was the officer commanding for the eighth month with twenty-four thousand in his division. 12 Ninth, Abie-

---

26:21–22 **Jehiel and:** *prob. rdg; Heb.* Jehieli. The sons of Jehieli. 26:24 **Shubael:** *so Lat.; Heb.* Shebuel. 26:25 **The line . . . brother:** *so Gk; Heb.* obscure. 27:4 **Eleazar son of:** *prob. rdg, cp. 11:12; Heb.* omits. **the Ahohite:** *so Gk; Heb.* adds and his division and Mikloth the prince. 27:6 **commanded:** *so Gk; Heb.* omits. 27:8 **the Zerahite:** *prob. rdg; Heb.* the Izrah.

the descendants of Ladan the Gershonite, the family heads were descendants of Jehiel: the descendants of Jehiel, 22 Zetham and his brother Joel, who superintended the treasures of the house of the LORD. 23 From the Amramites, Izharites, Hebronites, and Uzzielites, 24 Shubael, son of Gershon, son of Moses, was chief superintendent over the treasures. 25 His associate pertained to Eliezer, whose son was Rehabiah, whose son was Jeshaiah, whose son was Joram, whose son was Zichri, whose son was Shelomith. 26 This Shelomith and his brethren superintended all the stores of the votive offerings dedicated by King David, the heads of the families, the commanders of thousands and of hundreds, and the commanders of the army, 27 from the booty they had taken in the wars, for the enhancement of the house of the LORD. 28 Also, whatever Samuel the seer, Saul, son of Kish, Abner, son of Ner, Joab, son of Zeruiah, and all others had consecrated, was under the charge of Shelomith and his brethren.

29 Among the Izharites, Chananiah and his sons were in charge of Israel's civil affairs as officials and judges. 30 Among the Hebronites, Hashabiah and his brethren, one thousand seven hundred police officers, had the administration of Israel on the western side of the Jordan in all the work of the LORD and in the service of the king. 31 Among the Hebronites, Jerijah was their chief according to their family records. In the fortieth year of David's reign search was made, and there were found among them outstanding officers at Jazer of Gilead. 32 His brethren were also police officers, two thousand seven hundred heads of families. King David appointed them to the administration of the Reubenites, the Gadites, and the half-tribe of Manasseh in everything pertaining to God and to the king.

27 This is the list of the Israelite family heads, commanders of thousands and of hundreds, and other officers who served the king in all that pertained to the divisions, of twenty-four thousand men each, that came and went month by month throughout the year.

2 Over the first division for the first month was Ishbaal, son of Zabdiel, and in his division were twenty-four thousand men; 3 a descendant of Perez, he was chief over all the commanders of the army for the first month. 4 Over the division of the second month was Eleazar, son of Dodo, from Ahoh, and in his division were twenty-four thousand men. 5 The third army commander, chief for the third month, was Benaiah, son of Jehoiada the priest, and in his division were twenty-four thousand men. 6 This Benaiah was a warrior among the Thirty and over the Thirty. His son Ammizabad was over his division. 7 Fourth, for the fourth month, was Asahel, brother of Joab, and after him his son Zebadiah, and in his division were twenty-four thousand men. 8 Fifth, for the fifth month, was the commander Shamhuth, a descendant of Zerah, and in his division were twenty-four thousand men. 9 Sixth, for the sixth month, was Ira, son of Ikkesh, from Tekoa, and in his division were twenty-four thousand men. 10 Seventh, for the seventh month, was Helles, from Beth-pheleth, of the sons of Ephraim, and in his division were twenty-four thousand men. 11 Eighth, for the eighth month, was Sibbecai the Hushathite, a descendant of Zerah, and in his division were twenty-four thousand men. 12 Ninth, for the ninth month,

the Gershonites — the heads of the families of Ladan were descended from Ladan the Gershonite — that is to say, the Jehielites. 22 The sons of the Jehielites, Zetham and Joel his brother, were responsible for the treasures of the house of Yahweh.

23 Over the Amramites, Izharites, Hebronites, and Uzzielites 24 was Shebuel son of Gershom, son of Moses, who was governor of the treasures; 25 and his brothers of the line of Eliezer were Rehabiah his son, Jeshaiah his son, Joram his son, Zichri his son and Shelomoth his son. 26 This Shelomoth and his kinsmen were responsible for all the consecrated treasures dedicated by King David, by the heads of families, by the commanders of the thousands and hundreds and by the commanders of the army, 27 who had dedicated a part of the spoils of war to the service of the house of Yahweh, 28 and also for all that Samuel the seer, Saul son of Kish, Abner son of Ner and Joab son of Zeruiah had dedicated. In fact, whatever was dedicated was the responsibility of Shelomoth and his kinsmen.

29 Of the Izharites, Chananiah and his sons were assigned to secular duties for Israel as officials and judges.

30 Of the Hebronites, Hashabiah and his kinsmen, one thousand seven hundred outstanding men were in charge of Israel west of Jordan in everything pertaining to Yahweh and to the service of the king. 31 Of the Hebronites, Jerijah was the head. In the fortieth year of David's reign research was done on the lineage and relationships of the Hebronites, and men of outstanding quality from among them were found at Jazer in Gilead. 32 There were twenty-seven hundred outstanding men, heads of families, whom King David put in charge of the Reubenites, the Gadites and the half-tribe of Manasseh in all matters pertaining to God and the king.

27 The Israelites listed according to heads of families, commanders of thousands and hundreds, with their officials in the king's service who dealt with all matters affecting the companies on monthly duty, month by month throughout the year, each company consisting of twenty-four thousand men:

2 The commander of the first company detailed for the first month was Jashobeam son of Zabdiel, whose company consisted of twenty-four thousand men. 3 He belonged to the family of Perez and was the senior military officer of all those detailed for the first month.

4 The commander of the company for the second month was Dodai the Ahohite, whose company consisted of twenty-four thousand men.

5 The officer commanding the third body of men for the third month was Benaiah son of Jehoiada, the chief priest, whose company consisted of twenty-four thousand men. 6 This was the Benaiah who was an important member of the Thirty and his company. His son was Ammizabad.

7 The fourth for the fourth month was Asahel brother of Joab, and his son Zebadiah after him, whose company consisted of twenty-four thousand men.

8 The fifth officer commanding for the fifth month was Shamhuth the Zerahite, whose company consisted of twenty-four thousand men.

9 The sixth for the sixth month was Ira son of Ikkesh of Tekoa, whose company consisted of twenty-four thousand men.

10 The seventh for the seventh month was Helez the Pelonite, one of the Ephraimites, whose company consisted of twenty-four thousand men.

11 The eighth for the eighth month was Sibbecai of Hushah, a Zerahite, whose company consisted of twenty-four thousand men.

for the ninth month, was Abiezer of Anathoth, a Benjaminite; in his division were twenty-four thousand. 13 Tenth, for the tenth month, was Maharai of Netophah, of the Zerahites; in his division were twenty-four thousand. 14 Eleventh, for the eleventh month, was Benaiah of Pirathon, of the Ephraimites; in his division were twenty-four thousand. 15 Twelfth, for the twelfth month, was Heldai the Netophathite, of Othniel; in his division were twenty-four thousand.

16 Over the tribes of Israel, for the Reubenites, Eliezer son of Zichri was chief officer; for the Simeonites, Shephatiah son of Maacah; 17 for Levi, Hashabiah son of Kemuel; for Aaron, Zadok; 18 for Judah, Elihu, one of David's brothers; for Issachar, Omri son of Michael; 19 for Zebulun, Ishmaiah son of Obadiah; for Naphtali, Jerimoth son of Azriel; 20 for the Ephraimites, Hoshea son of Azaziah; for the half-tribe of Manasseh, Joel son of Pedaiah; 21 for the half-tribe of Manasseh in Gilead, Iddo son of Zechariah; for Benjamin, Jaasiel son of Abner; 22 for Dan, Azarel son of Jeroham. These were the leaders of the tribes of Israel. 23 David did not count those below twenty years of age, for the LORD had promised to make Israel as numerous as the stars of heaven. 24 Joab son of Zeruiah began to count them, but did not finish; yet wrath came upon Israel for this, and the number was not entered into the account of the Annals of King David.

25 Over the king's treasuries was Azmaveth son of Adiel. Over the treasuries in the country, in the cities, in the villages and in the towers, was Jonathan son of Uzziah. 26 Over those who did the work of the field, tilling the soil, was Ezri son of Chelub. 27 Over the vineyards was Shimei the Ramathite. Over the produce of the vineyards for the wine cellars was Zabdi the Shiphmite. 28 Over the olive and sycamore trees in the Shephelah was Baal-hanan the Gederite. Over the stores of oil was Joash. 29 Over the herds that pastured in Sharon was Shitrai the Sharonite. Over the herds in the valleys was Shaphat son of Adlai. 30 Over the camels was Obil the Ishmaelite. Over the donkeys was Jehdeiah the Meronothite. Over the flocks was Jaziz the Hagrite. 31 All these were stewards of King David's property.

32 Jonathan, David's uncle, was a counselor, being a man of understanding and a scribe; Jehiel son of Hachmoni attended the king's sons. 33 Ahithophel was the king's counselor, and Hushai the Archite was the king's friend. 34 After Ahithophel came Jehoiada son of Benaiah, and Abiathar. Joab was commander of the king's army.

28 David assembled at Jerusalem all the officials of Israel, the officials of the tribes, the officers of the divisions that served the king, the commanders of the thousands, the commanders of the hundreds, the stewards of all the property and cattle of the king and his sons, together with the palace officials, the mighty warriors, and all the warriors. 2 Then King David rose to his feet and said: "Hear me, my brothers and my people. I had planned to build a house of rest for the ark of the covenant of the LORD, for the footstool of our God; and I made preparations for building. 3 But God said to me, 'You shall not build a house for my name, for you are a warrior and have shed blood.' 4 Yet the

zer, from Anathoth in Benjamin, was the officer commanding for the ninth month with twenty-four thousand in his division. 13 Tenth, Maharai the Netophathite, of the family of Zerah, was the officer commanding for the tenth month with twenty-four thousand in his division. 14 Eleventh, Benaiah the Pirathonite, from Ephraim, was the officer commanding for the eleventh month with twenty-four thousand in his division. 15 Twelfth, Heldai the Netophathite, of the family of Othniel, was the officer commanding for the twelfth month with twenty-four thousand in his division.

16 The following were the principal officers in charge of the tribes of Israel: of Reuben, Eliezer son of Zichri; of Simeon, Shephatiah son of Maacah; 17 of Levi, Hashabiah son of Kemuel; of Aaron, Zadok; 18 of Judah, Elihu a kinsman of David; of Issachar, Omri son of Michael; 19 of Zebulun, Ishmaiah son of Obadiah; of Naphtali, Jerimoth son of Azriel; 20 of Ephraim, Hoshea son of Azaziah; of the half tribe of Manasseh, Joel son of Pedaiah; 21 of the half of Manasseh in Gilead, Iddo son of Zechariah; of Benjamin, Jaasiel son of Abner; 22 of Dan, Azarel son of Jeroham. These were the officers in charge of the tribes of Israel. 23 David took no census of those under twenty years of age, for the LORD had promised to make the Israelites as many as the stars in the sky. 24 Joab son of Zeruiah did begin to take a census but he did not finish it; the census brought down wrath on Israel, and it was not entered in the annals of King David's reign.

25 Azmoth son of Adiel was in charge of the king's stores; Jonathan son of Uzziah was in charge of the stores in the country, in the cities, in the villages, and in the fortresses. 26 Ezri son of Kelub had oversight of the workers on the land; 27 Shimei from Ramah was in charge of the vine-dressers, while Zabdi from Shephem had charge of the produce of the vineyards for the wine cellars. 28 Baal-hanan the Gederite supervised the wild olives and the sycomore-figs in the Shephelah; Joash was in charge of the oil stores. 29 Shitrai from Sharon was in charge of the herds grazing in Sharon, Shaphat son of Adlai of the herds in the valleys. 30 Obil the Ishmaelite was in charge of the camels, Jehdeiah the Meronothite of the donkeys. 31 Jaziz the Hagarite was in charge of the flocks. All these were the officers in charge of King David's possessions. 32 David's favourite nephew Jonathan, a counsellor, a discreet and learned man, and Jehiel the Hachmonite, were tutors to the king's sons. 33 Ahithophel was a king's counsellor; Hushai the Archite was the king's Friend. 34 Ahithophel was succeeded by Jehoiada son of Benaiah and by Abiathar. Joab was commander of the army.

28 DAVID assembled at Jerusalem all the officers of Israel, the officers over the tribes, over the divisions engaged in the king's service, over the units of a thousand and a hundred, and officials in charge of all the property and the cattle of the king and of his sons, as well as the eunuchs, the heroes, and all the men of ability. 2 King David stood up and addressed them: 'Hear me, my kinsmen and my people. I had it in mind to build a house as a resting-place for the Ark of the Covenant of the LORD which might serve as a footstool for our God, and I made preparations to build it. 3 But God said to me, "You are not to build a house for my name, because you have been a fighting man and you have shed blood." 4 Nevertheless, the

was Abiezer from Anathoth, of Benjamin, and in his division were twenty-four thousand men. 13 Tenth, for the tenth month, was Maharai from Netophah, a descendant of Zerah, and in his division were twenty-four thousand men. 14 Eleventh, for the eleventh month, was Benaiah the Pirathonite, of Ephraim, and in his division were twenty-four thousand men. 15 Twelfth, for the twelfth month, was Heldai the Netophathite, of the family of Othniel, and in his division were twenty-four thousand men.

16 Over the tribes of Israel, for the Reubenites the leader was Eliezer, son of Zichri; for the Simeonites, Shephatiah, son of Maacah; 17 for Levi, Hashabiah, son of Kemuel; for Aaron, Zadok; 18 for Judah, Eliab, one of David's brothers; for Issachar, Omri, son of Michael; 19 for Zebulun, Ishmaiah, son of Obadiah; for Naphtali, Jeremoth, son of Azriel; 20 for the sons of Ephraim, Hoshea, son of Azaziah; for the half-tribe of Manasseh, Joel, son of Pedaiah; 21 for the half-tribe of Manasseh in Gilead, Iddo, son of Zechariah; for Benjamin, Jaasiel, son of Abner; 22 for Dan, Azarel, son of Jeroham. These were the commanders of the tribes of Israel.

23 David did not count those who were twenty years of age or younger, for the LORD had promised to multiply Israel like the stars of the heavens. 24 Joab, son of Zeruiah, began to take the census, but he did not complete it, for because of it wrath fell upon Israel. Therefore the number did not enter into the book of chronicles of King David.

25 Over the treasures of the king was Azmaveth, the son of Adiel. Over the stores in the country, the cities, the villages, and the towers was Jonathan, son of Uzziah. 26 Over the farm workers who tilled the soil was Ezri, son of Chelub. 27 Over the vineyards was Shimei from Ramah, and over their produce for the wine cellars was Zabdi the Shiphmite. 28 Over the olive trees and sycamores of the foothills was Baal-hanan the Gederite, and over the stores of oil was Joash. 29 Over the cattle that grazed in Sharon was Shitrai the Sharonite, and over the cattle in the valleys was Shaphat, the son of Adlai; 30 over the camels was Obil the Ishmaelite; over the she-asses was Jehdeiah the Meronothite; 31 and over the flocks was Jaziz the Hagrite. All these were the overseers of King David's possessions.

32 Jonathan, David's uncle and a man of intelligence, was counselor and scribe; he and Jehiel, the son of Hachmoni, were tutors of the king's sons. 33 Ahithophel was also the king's counselor, and Hushai the Archite was the king's confidant. 34 After Ahithophel came Jehoiada, the son of Benaiah, and Abiathar. The commander of the king's army was Joab.

28 David assembled at Jerusalem all the leaders of Israel, the heads of the tribes, the commanders of the divisions who were in the service of the king, the commanders of thousands and of hundreds, the overseers of all the king's estates and possessions, and his sons, together with the courtiers, the warriors, and every important man. 2 King David rose to his feet and said: "Hear me, my brethren and my people. It was my purpose to build a house of repose myself for the ark of the covenant of the LORD, the footstool for the feet of our God; and I was preparing to build it. 3 But God said to me, 'You may not build a house in my honor, for you are a man who fought wars and shed blood.' 4 How-

12 The ninth for the ninth month was Abiezer of Anathoth, a Benjaminite, whose company consisted of twenty-four thousand men.

13 The tenth for the tenth month was Maharai of Netophah, a Zerahite, whose company consisted of twenty-four thousand men.

14 The eleventh for the eleventh month was Benaiah of Pirathon, an Ephraimite, whose company consisted of twenty-four thousand men.

15 The twelfth for the twelfth month was Heldai of Netophah, of Othniel, whose company consisted of twenty-four thousand men.

16 Responsible for the tribes of Israel were chief Eliezer son of Zichri for the Reubenites, Shephatiah son of Maacah for the Simeonites, 17 Hashabiah son of Kemuel for the Levites, Zadok for the Aaronites, 18 Elihu, one of David's brothers, for Judah, Omri son of Michael for Issachar, 19 Ishmaiah son of Obadiah for Zebulun, Jerimoth son of Azriel for Naphtali, 20 Hoshea son of Azaziah for the Ephraimites, Joel son of Pedaiah for the half-tribe of Manasseh, 21 Iddo son of Zechariah for the half-tribe of Manasseh in Gilead, Jaasiel son of Abner for Benjamin, 22 and Azarel son of Jeroham for Dan.

These were the tribal chiefs of Israel.

23 Now in the census David did not include those who were twenty years old and under, since Yahweh had promised to make Israel as numerous as the stars of heaven. 24 Joab son of Zeruiah began the count but never finished. This is why retribution came upon Israel, and the number did not come up to that recorded in the annals of King David.

25 Overseer of the king's supplies: Azmaveth son of Adiel. Overseer of supplies in the countryside, towns, villages and fortresses: Jonathan son of Uzziah. 26 Overseer of the farmers who tilled the land: Ezri son of Chelub. 27 Overseer of vineyards: Shimei of Ramah. Overseer of those in the vineyards who looked after the wine cellars: Zabdi of Shepham. 28 Overseer of olive and sycamore trees in the Shephelah: Baal-Hanan of Geder. Overseer of oil supplies: Joash. 29 Overseer of cattle at pasture in the plains of Sharon: Shitrai of Sharon. Overseer of cattle in the valleys: Shaphat son of Adlai. 30 Overseer of camels: Obil the Ishmaelite. 31 Overseer of donkeys: Jehdeiah of Meranoth. Overseer of flocks: Jaziz the Hagrite.

All the above supervised the property belonging to King David.

32 Jonathan, David's uncle, a councillor, wise man and scribe, and Jehiel son of Hachmoni took care of the king's sons. 33 Ahitophel was the king's counsellor and Hushai, the Archite, was Friend of the King. 34 Jehoiada son of Benaiah and Abiathar succeeded Ahitophel — Joab was commander of the king's army.

28 David then summoned to Jerusalem all the officials of Israel — the tribal chiefs, the senior officials in the royal service, the commanders of the thousands, the commanders of the hundreds and the overseers of all the property and livestock belonging to the king and to his sons — including the court officials, the champions and all the men of standing. 2 King David then rose to his feet and said:

'My brothers and my people, listen to me. I have set my heart on building a settled home for the ark of the covenant of Yahweh, for the footstool for our God, but when I was ready to build it, 3 God said to me, "You must not build a house for my name, for you have been a man of war and have shed blood."'

LORD God of Israel chose me from all my ancestral house to be king over Israel forever; for he chose Judah as leader, and in the house of Judah my father's house, and among my father's sons he took delight in making me king over all Israel. 5 And of all my sons, for the LORD has given me many, he has chosen my son Solomon to sit upon the throne of the kingdom of the LORD over Israel. 6 He said to me, 'It is your son Solomon who shall build my house and my courts, for I have chosen him to be a son to me, and I will be a father to him. 7 I will establish his kingdom forever if he continues resolute in keeping my commandments and my ordinances, as he is today.' 8 Now therefore in the sight of all Israel, the assembly of the LORD, and in the hearing of our God, observe and search out all the commandments of the LORD your God; that you may possess this good land, and leave it for an inheritance to your children after you forever.

9 "And you, my son Solomon, know the God of your father, and serve him with single mind and willing heart; for the LORD searches every mind, and understands every plan and thought. If you seek him, he will be found by you; but if you forsake him, he will abandon you forever. 10 Take heed now, for the LORD has chosen you to build a house as the sanctuary; be strong, and act."

11 Then David gave his son Solomon the plan of the vestibule of the temple, and of its houses, its treasuries, its upper rooms, and its inner chambers, and of the room for the mercy seat;r 12 and the plan of all that he had in mind: for the courts of the house of the LORD, all the surrounding chambers, the treasuries of the house of God, and the treasuries for dedicated gifts; 13 for the divisions of the priests and of the Levites, and all the work of the service in the house of the LORD; for all the vessels for the service in the house of the LORD, 14 the weight of gold for all golden vessels for each service, the weight of silver vessels for each service, 15 the weight of the golden lampstands and their lamps, the weight of gold for each lampstand and its lamps, the weight of silver for a lampstand and its lamps, according to the use of each in the service, 16 the weight of gold for each table for the rows of bread, the silver for the silver tables, 17 and pure gold for the forks, the basins, and the cups; for the golden bowls and the weight of each; for the silver bowls and the weight of each; 18 for the altar of incense made of refined gold, and its weight; also his plan for the golden chariot of the cherubim that spread their wings and covered the ark of the covenant of the LORD.

19 "All this, in writing at the LORD's direction, he made clear to me — the plan of all the works."

20 David said further to his son Solomon, "Be strong and of good courage, and act. Do not be afraid or dismayed; for the LORD God, my God, is with you. He will not fail you or forsake you, until all the work for the service of the house of the LORD is finished. 21 Here are the divisions of the priests and the Levites for all the service of the house of God; and with you in all the work will be every volunteer who has skill for any kind of service; also the officers and all the people will be wholly at your command."

LORD the God of Israel chose me out of all my father's family to be king over Israel for ever. For it was Judah that he chose as ruling tribe, and, out of the house of Judah, my father's family; and among my father's sons it was I whom he was pleased to make king over all Israel. 5 And out of all my sons — for the LORD gave me many sons — he has chosen Solomon to sit on the throne of the LORD's sovereignty over Israel; 6 he said to me, "It is Solomon your son who is to build my house and my courts, for I have chosen him to be a son to me and I shall be a father to him. 7 I shall establish his sovereignty for ever, if he steadfastly obeys my commandments and my laws as he now does."

8 'Now therefore, in the sight of all Israel, the assembly of the LORD, and in the hearing of our God, I say to you: Study carefully all the commandments of the LORD your God, in order that you may possess this good land and hand it down as an inheritance for all time to your children after you.

9 'And you, Solomon my son, acknowledge your father's God and serve him with whole heart and willing mind, for the LORD searches all hearts and discerns whatever plan may be devised. If you search for him, he will let you find him, but if you forsake him, he will cast you off for ever. 10 Remember, then, that the LORD has chosen you to build a house as a sanctuary: be steadfast and do it.'

11 David gave Solomon his son the plan of the porch of the temple and its buildings, strong-rooms, roof-chambers and inner courts, and the shrine of expiation; 12 also the plans of all he had in mind for the courts of the house of the LORD and for all the rooms around it, for the stores of God's house, and for the stores of the sacred gifts. 13 He gave directions for the divisions of the priests and Levites, for all the work connected with the service of the house of the LORD, and for all the vessels used in its service. 14 He prescribed the weight of gold for all the gold vessels used in the various services, and the weight of silver for all the silver vessels used in the various services; 15 and the weight of gold for the gold lampstands and their lamps; and the weight of silver for the silver lampstands, the weight required for each lampstand and its lamps according to the use of each; 16 and the weight of gold for each of the tables for the rows of the Bread of the Presence, and of silver for the silver tables. 17 He prescribed also the weight of pure gold for the forks, tossing-bowls, and cups, the weight of gold for each of the golden dishes, and of silver for each of the silver dishes; 18 the weight also of refined gold for the altar of incense, and of gold for the model of the chariot, that is the cherubim with their wings spread to screen the Ark of the Covenant of the LORD. 19 'All this was drafted by the LORD's own hand,' said David; 'my part was to consider the detailed working out of the plan.'

20 Then David said to Solomon his son, 'Be steadfast and resolute and carry it out; be neither faint-hearted nor dismayed, for the LORD God, my God, will be with you; he will neither fail you nor forsake you, until you have finished all the work needed for the service of the house of the LORD. 21 Here are the divisions of the priests and the Levites, ready for all the service of the house of God. In all the work you will have the help of every willing craftsman for any task; and the officers and all the people are entirely at your command.'

28:11 of the temple: prob. rdg; Heb. omits. the shrine of expiation: or the place for the Ark with its cover. 28:14 for ... gold vessels: prob. rdg; Heb. for gold. of silver: prob. rdg; Heb. omits. 28:17 of silver: prob. rdg; Heb. omits.

ever, the LORD, the God of Israel, chose me from all my father's family to be king over Israel forever. For he chose Judah as leader, then one family of Judah, that of my father; and finally, among all the sons of my father, it pleased him to make me king over all Israel. 5 And of all my sons — for the LORD has given me many sons — he has chosen my son Solomon to sit on the LORD's royal throne over Israel. 6 For he said to me: 'It is your son Solomon who shall build my house and my courts, for I have chosen him for my son, and I will be a father to him. 7 I will establish his kingdom forever, if he perseveres in keeping my commandments and decrees as he keeps them now.' 8 Therefore in the presence of all Israel, the assembly of the LORD, and in the hearing of our God, I exhort you to keep and to carry out all the commandments of the LORD, your God, that you may continue to possess this good land and afterward leave it as an inheritance to your children forever.

9 "As for you, Solomon, my son, know the God of your father and serve him with a perfect heart and a willing soul, for the LORD searches all hearts and understands all the mind's thoughts. If you seek him, he will let himself be found by you; but if you abandon him, he will cast you off forever. 10 See, then! The LORD has chosen you to build a house as his sanctuary. Take courage and set to work."

11 Then David gave to his son Solomon the pattern of the portico and of the building itself, with its storerooms, its upper rooms and inner chambers, and the room with the propitiatory. 12 He provided also the pattern for all else that he had in mind by way of courts for the house of the LORD, with the surrounding compartments for the stores for the house of God and the stores of the votive offerings, 13 as well as for the divisions of the priests and Levites, for all the work of the service of the house of the LORD, and for all the liturgical vessels of the house of the LORD. 14 He specified the weight of gold to be used in the golden vessels for the various services and the weight of silver to be used in the silver vessels for the various services; 15 likewise for the golden lampstands and their lamps he specified the weight of gold for each lampstand and its lamps, and for the silver lampstands he specified the weight of silver for each lampstand and its lamps, depending on the use to which each lampstand was to be put. 16 He specified the weight of gold for each table to hold the showbread, and the silver for the silver tables; 17 the pure gold to be used for the forks and pitchers; the amount of gold for each golden bowl and the silver for each silver bowl; 18 the refined gold, and its weight, to be used for the altar of incense; and, finally, gold for what would suggest a chariot throne: the cherubim that spread their wings and covered the ark of the covenant of the LORD. 19 He had successfully committed to writing the exact specifications of the pattern, because the hand of the LORD was upon him.

20 Then David said to his son Solomon: "Be firm and steadfast; go to work without fear or discouragement, for the LORD God, my God, is with you. He will not fail you or abandon you before you have completed all the work for the service of the house of the LORD. 21 The classes of the priests and Levites are ready for all the service of the house of God; they will help you in all your work with all those who are eager to show their skill in every kind of craftsmanship. Also the leaders and all the people will do everything that you command."

4 'Even so, out of my entire family, it was I whom Yahweh, God of Israel, chose to reign over Israel for ever. Having chosen Judah as leader, and my family out of the House of Judah, it pleased him out of all my father's sons to make me king of all Israel. 5 Out of all my sons — for Yahweh has given me many — he has chosen my son Solomon to sit on Yahweh's sovereign throne over Israel. 6 Furthermore, he has told me, "Solomon your son is the man to build my house and my courts, for I have chosen him to be my son and I shall be his father. 7 I shall make his sovereignty secure for ever if he sturdily carries out my commandments and ordinances as he does now."

8 'So now in the sight of all Israel, the assembly of Yahweh, and in the hearing of our God, I charge you to observe and adhere strictly to all the commandments of Yahweh your God, so that you may retain possession of this fine country and leave it to your sons after you as a heritage for ever.

9 'And you, Solomon my son, know the God of your father and serve him with an undivided heart and willing mind; for Yahweh scrutinises all hearts and understands whatever plans they may devise. If you seek him, he will let you find him; but forsake him and he will cast you off for ever. 10 So, since Yahweh has chosen you to build a house for his sanctuary, go resolutely to work!'

11 David then gave his son Solomon the plans for the portico, the plans for the buildings, its storehouses, its upper rooms, its inner rooms and the room for the throne of mercy 12 as well as the plans for everything that he had in mind: for the courts of the house of Yahweh, for all the surrounding rooms, for the treasuries of the house of God and for the sacred treasuries, 13 for the orders of priests and Levites, for all the duties to be carried out in the service of the house of Yahweh, and for all the liturgical objects to be used in the house of Yahweh; 14 for the gold bullion, for all the golden liturgical objects of various uses; for the silver bullion, for all the silver liturgical objects of various uses; 15 for the gold bullion for the golden lamp-stands and for their lamps, for the silver bullion for the silver lampstands and their lights, depending on the function of each lamp-stand; 16 for the gold bullion for each of the tables for the loaves of permanent offering and the silver for the silver tables; 17 for the pure gold for the forks, the bowls and the jars, for the gold bullion for each of the golden basins and for the silver bullion for each of the silver basins; 18 and for the refined gold bullion for the altar of incense; also for the gold for the model of the chariot and of the great winged creatures which cover the ark of the covenant of Yahweh with wings outspread — 19 all this was in the document conveying Yahweh's instructions, by which he revealed the pattern of what was to be done.

20 David then said to his son Solomon, 'Be resolute and courageous in your work, do not be afraid or disheartened, because Yahweh God, my God, is with you. He will not fail you or forsake you before you have finished all the work to be done for the house of Yahweh. 21 And besides, there are the orders of priests and Levites for whatever is needed in connection with the house of God, and you have at your disposal every kind of craftsman for whatever has to be done, as well as the officials and all the people entirely at your command.'

NEW REVISED STANDARD VERSION

29 King David said to the whole assembly, "My son Solomon, whom alone God has chosen, is young and inexperienced, and the work is great; for the temple*s* will not be for mortals but for the LORD God. 2 So I have provided for the house of my God, so far as I was able, the gold for the things of gold, the silver for the things of silver, and the bronze for the things of bronze, the iron for the things of iron, and wood for the things of wood, besides great quantities of onyx and stones for setting, antimony, colored stones, all sorts of precious stones, and marble in abundance. 3 Moreover, in addition to all that I have provided for the holy house, I have a treasure of my own of gold and silver, and because of my devotion to the house of my God I give it to the house of my God: 4 three thousand talents of gold, of the gold of Ophir, and seven thousand talents of refined silver, for overlaying the walls of the house, 5 and for all the work to be done by artisans, gold for the things of gold and silver for the things of silver. Who then will offer willingly, consecrating themselves today to the LORD?"

6 Then the leaders of ancestral houses made their freewill offerings, as did also the leaders of the tribes, the commanders of the thousands and of the hundreds, and the officers over the king's work. 7 They gave for the service of the house of God five thousand talents and ten thousand darics of gold, ten thousand talents of silver, eighteen thousand talents of bronze, and one hundred thousand talents of iron. 8 Whoever had precious stones gave them to the treasury of the house of the LORD, into the care of Jehiel the Gershonite. 9 Then the people rejoiced because these had given willingly, for with single mind they had offered freely to the LORD; King David also rejoiced greatly.

10 Then David blessed the LORD in the presence of all the assembly; David said: "Blessed are you, O LORD, the God of our ancestor Israel, forever and ever. 11 Yours, O LORD, are the greatness, the power, the glory, the victory, and the majesty; for all that is in the heavens and on the earth is yours; yours is the kingdom, O LORD, and you are exalted as head above all. 12 Riches and honor come from you, and you rule over all. In your hand are power and might; and it is in your hand to make great and to give strength to all. 13 And now, our God, we give thanks to you and praise your glorious name.

14 "But who am I, and what is my people, that we should be able to make this freewill offering? For all things come from you, and of your own have we given you. 15 For we are aliens and transients before you, as were all our ancestors; our days on the earth are like a shadow, and there is no hope. 16 O LORD our God, all this abundance that we have provided for building you a house for your holy name comes from your hand and is all your own. 17 I know, my God, that you search the heart, and take pleasure in uprightness; in the uprightness of my heart I have freely offered all these things, and now I have seen your people, who are present here, offering freely and joyously to you. 18 O LORD, the God of Abraham, Isaac, and Israel, our ancestors, keep forever such purposes and thoughts in the hearts of your people, and direct their hearts toward you. 19 Grant to my son Solomon that with single mind he may keep your commandments, your decrees, and your statutes, performing all of them, and that he may build the temple*s* for which I have made provision."

REVISED ENGLISH BIBLE

29 KING David said to the whole assembly, 'My son Solomon is the one chosen by God, Solomon alone, a boy of tender years; and this is a great work, for it is a habitation not for man but for the LORD God. 2 Now to the best of my ability I have made ready for the house of my God gold for the gold work, silver for the silver, bronze for the bronze, iron for the iron, and wood for the woodwork, together with cornelian and other gems for setting, stones for mosaic work, precious stones of every sort, and marble in plenty. 3 Further, because I delight in the house of my God, I have given my own private store of gold and silver for the house of my God—over and above all the store which I have collected for the sanctuary—4 namely three thousand talents of gold from Ophir, and seven thousand talents of fine silver for overlaying the walls of the buildings, 5 for providing gold for the gold work, silver for the silver, and for any work to be done by skilled craftsmen. Now who is willing to give with open hand to the LORD today?'

6 Then the heads of families, the officers administering the tribes of Israel, the officers over units of a thousand and a hundred, and the officers in charge of the king's service, responded willingly 7 and gave for the work of the house of God five thousand talents of gold, ten thousand darics, ten thousand talents of silver, eighteen thousand talents of bronze, and a hundred thousand talents of iron. 8 Further, those who possessed precious stones gave them to the treasury of the house of the LORD, into the charge of Jehiel the Gershonite. 9 The people rejoiced at this willing response, because in the loyalty of their hearts they had given willingly to the LORD; King David also was full of joy.

10 David blessed the LORD in the presence of all the assembly, saying:

'Blessed are you, LORD God of our father Israel,
 from of old and for ever.
11 Yours, LORD, is the greatness and the power,
 the glory, the splendour, and the majesty;
 for everything in heaven and on earth is yours;
 yours, LORD, is the sovereignty,
 and you are exalted over all as head.
12 Wealth and honour come from you; you rule over all;
 might and power are of your disposing;
 yours it is to give power and strength to all.
13 Now, our God, we give you thanks
 and praise your glorious name.

14 'But who am I, and who are my people, that we should be able to give willingly like this? For everything comes from you, and it is only of your gifts that we give to you. 15 We are aliens before you and settlers, as were all our fathers; our days on earth are like a shadow, and we have no abiding place. 16 LORD our God, from you comes all this wealth that we have laid up to build a house in honour of your holy name, and it is all yours. 17 I know that you test the heart and that integrity pleases you, my God; with an honest heart I have given all these gifts willingly, and have rejoiced now to see your people who are here present give willingly to you. 18 LORD God of Abraham, Isaac, and Israel, our forefathers, maintain this purpose for ever in your people's thoughts and direct their hearts toward yourself. 19 Grant that Solomon my son may loyally keep your commandments, your solemn charge, and your statutes, that he may fulfil them all, and build the palace for which I have made provision.'

---

s Heb *fortress*

29:11 **is yours:** *prob. rdg; Heb. omits.*

29 King David then said to the whole assembly: "My son Solomon, whom alone God has chosen, is still young and immature; the work, however, is great, for this castle is not intended for man, but for the LORD God. 2 For this reason I have stored up for the house of my God, as far as I was able, gold for what will be made of gold, silver for what will be made of silver, bronze for what will be made of bronze, iron for what will be made of iron, wood for what will be made of wood, onyx stones and settings for them, carnelian and mosaic stones, every other kind of precious stone, and great quantities of marble. 3 But now, because of the delight I take in the house of my God, in addition to all that I stored up for the holy house, I give to the house of my God my personal fortune in gold and silver: 4 three thousand talents of Ophir gold, and seven thousand talents of refined silver, for overlaying the walls of the rooms, 5 for the various utensils to be made of gold and silver, and for every work that is to be done by artisans. Now, who else is willing to contribute generously this day to the LORD?"

6 Then the heads of the families, the leaders of the tribes of Israel, the commanders of thousands and of hundreds, and the overseers of the king's affairs came forward willingly 7 and contributed for the service of the house of God five thousand talents and ten thousand darics of gold, ten thousand talents of silver, eighteen thousand talents of bronze, and one hundred thousand talents of iron. 8 Those who had precious stones gave them into the keeping of Jehiel the Gershonite for the treasury of the house of the LORD. 9 The people rejoiced over these free-will offerings, which had been contributed to the LORD wholeheartedly. King David also rejoiced greatly.

10 Then David blessed the LORD in the presence of the whole assembly, praying in these words:

"Blessed may you be, O LORD,
God of Israel our father,
from eternity to eternity.

11 "Yours, O LORD, are grandeur and power,
majesty, splendor, and glory.
For all in heaven and on earth is yours;
yours, O LORD, is the sovereignty;
you are exalted as head over all.

12 "Riches and honor are from you,
and you have dominion over all.
In your hand are power and might;
it is yours to give grandeur and strength to all.

13 Therefore, our God, we give you thanks
and we praise the majesty of your name."

14 "But who am I, and who are my people, that we should have the means to contribute so freely? For everything is from you, and we only give you what we have received from you. 15 For we stand before you as aliens: we are only your guests, like all our fathers. Our life on earth is like a shadow that does not abide. 16 O LORD our God, all this wealth that we have brought together to build you a house in honor of your holy name comes from you and is entirely yours. 17 I know, O my God, that you put hearts to the test and that you take pleasure in uprightness. With a sincere heart I have willingly given all these things, and now with joy I have seen your people here present also giving to you generously. 18 O LORD, God of our fathers Abraham, Isaac, and Israel, keep such thoughts in the hearts and minds of your people forever, and direct their hearts toward you. 19 Give to my son Solomon a wholehearted desire to keep your commandments, precepts, and statutes, that he may carry out all these plans and build the castle for which I have made preparation."

29 David then addressed the whole assembly, 'Solomon my son, whom Yahweh has specifically chosen, is young and immature, and the work is great; this palace is not for any human being but for Yahweh God. 2 With all the resources I can command, for the house of my God I have provided gold for what must be made of gold, silver for what must be made of silver, bronze for what must be made of bronze, iron for what must be made of iron, wood for what must be made of wood, as well as cornelian for inlay work, slabs of multi-coloured mosaic, every kind of precious stone and quantities of alabaster. 3 Furthermore, because my affections are set on the house of my God, I have also given what gold and silver I personally own for the house of my God, over and above everything which I have already provided for the holy Temple — 4 that is to say, three thousand talents of gold of Ophir, and seven thousand talents of refined silver for overlaying the walls of the buildings, 5 the gold being for what must be made of gold, and the silver for what must be made of silver: and for whatever the craftsmen must make. Who, then, is willing to devote himself to Yahweh's service today?'

6 At this, the heads of families, the tribal chiefs of Israel, the commanders of the thousands and the hundreds and those who managed the king's affairs, 7 volunteered a gift of five thousand talents and ten thousand darics of gold, ten thousand talents of silver, eighteen thousand talents of bronze and a hundred thousand talents of iron, 8 while those who owned precious stones presented them to the treasury of the house of Yahweh in the custody of Jehiel the Gershonite. 9 The people rejoiced at what these had given so readily, since they had presented their freewill offerings wholeheartedly to Yahweh. King David too was filled with joy.

10 Hence, in the presence of the whole assembly David blessed Yahweh. David said:

'May you be blessed, Yahweh, God of Israel our ancestor, for ever and for ever! 11 Yours, Yahweh, is the greatness, the power, the splendour, length of days and glory, everything in heaven and on earth is yours. Yours is the sovereignty, Yahweh; you are exalted, supreme over all. 12 Wealth and riches come from you, you are ruler of all, in your hand lie strength and power, and you bestow greatness and might on whomsoever you please. 13 So now, our God, we give thanks to you and praise your majestic name, 14 for who am I and what is my people, for us to be able to volunteer offerings like this? — since everything has come from you and we have given you only what you bestowed in the first place, 15 and we are guests before you, and passing visitors as were all our ancestors, our days on earth fleeting as a shadow and without hope. 16 Yahweh our God, all this wealth, which we have provided to build a house for your holy name, has come from you and all belongs to you.

17 'Knowing, my God, how you examine our motives and how you delight in integrity, with integrity of motive I have willingly given all this and have been overjoyed to see your people, now present here, willingly offering their gifts to you. 18 Yahweh, God of Abraham, Isaac and Israel our ancestors, watch over this for ever, shape the purpose of your people's heart and direct their hearts to you, 19 and give an undivided heart to Solomon my son to keep your commandments, your decrees and your statutes, to put them all into effect and to build the palace for which I have made provision.'

20 Then David said to the whole assembly, "Bless the LORD your God." And all the assembly blessed the LORD, the God of their ancestors, and bowed their heads and prostrated themselves before the LORD and the king. 21 On the next day they offered sacrifices and burnt offerings to the LORD, a thousand bulls, a thousand rams, and a thousand lambs, with their libations, and sacrifices in abundance for all Israel; 22 and they ate and drank before the LORD on that day with great joy.

They made David's son Solomon king a second time; they anointed him as the LORD's prince, and Zadok as priest. 23 Then Solomon sat on the throne of the LORD, succeeding his father David as king; he prospered, and all Israel obeyed him. 24 All the leaders and the mighty warriors, and also all the sons of King David, pledged their allegiance to King Solomon. 25 The LORD highly exalted Solomon in the sight of all Israel, and bestowed upon him such royal majesty as had not been on any king before him in Israel.

26 Thus David son of Jesse reigned over all Israel. 27 The period that he reigned over Israel was forty years; he reigned seven years in Hebron, and thirty-three years in Jerusalem. 28 He died in a good old age, full of days, riches, and honor; and his son Solomon succeeded him. 29 Now the acts of King David, from first to last, are written in the records of the seer Samuel, and in the records of the prophet Nathan, and in the records of the seer Gad, 30 with accounts of all his rule and his might and of the events that befell him and Israel and all the kingdoms of the earth.

20 Turning to the whole assembly, David said, 'Now bless the LORD your God.' Then all the assembly blessed the LORD the God of their forefathers, bowing low and prostrating themselves before the LORD and the king. 21 The next day they sacrificed to the LORD and offered whole-offerings to him: a thousand oxen, a thousand rams, a thousand lambs, with the prescribed drink-offerings, and abundant sacrifices for all Israel. 22 So they ate and drank before the LORD that day with great rejoicing.

They then appointed Solomon, David's son, king a second time and anointed him as the LORD's prince, and Zadok as priest. 23 So Solomon sat on the LORD's throne as king in place of his father David, and he prospered and all Israel obeyed him. 24 All the officers and the warriors, as well as all the sons of King David, swore fealty to King Solomon. 25 The LORD made Solomon stand very high in the eyes of all Israel, and bestowed upon him sovereignty such as no king in Israel had had before him.

26 David son of Jesse had ruled over the whole of Israel, 27 and the length of his reign over Israel was forty years, seven years in Hebron and thirty-three in Jerusalem. 28 He died in ripe old age, full of years, wealth, and honour; and Solomon his son ruled in his stead. 29 The events of King David's reign from first to last are recorded in the books of Samuel the seer, of Nathan the prophet, and of Gad the seer, 30 with a full account of his reign, his prowess, and the times through which he and Israel and all the kingdoms of the world had passed.

NEW AMERICAN BIBLE

20 Then David besought the whole assembly, "Now bless the LORD your God!" And the whole assembly blessed the LORD, the God of their fathers, bowing down and prostrating themselves before the LORD and before the king. 21 On the following day they offered sacrifices and holocausts to the LORD, a thousand bulls, a thousand rams, and a thousand lambs, together with their libations and many other sacrifices for all Israel; 22 and on that day they ate and drank in the LORD's presence with great rejoicing.

Then for a second time they proclaimed David's son Solomon king, and they anointed him as the LORD's prince, and Zadok as priest. 23 Thereafter Solomon sat on the throne of the LORD as king in place of his father David; he prospered, and all Israel obeyed him. 24 All the leaders and warriors, and also all the other sons of King David, swore allegiance to King Solomon. 25 And the LORD exalted Solomon greatly in the eyes of all Israel, giving him a glorious reign such as had not been enjoyed by any king over Israel before him.

26 Thus David, the son of Jesse, had reigned over all Israel. 27 The time that he reigned over Israel was forty years: in Hebron he reigned seven years, and in Jerusalem thirty-three. 28 He died at a ripe old age, rich in years and wealth and glory, and his son Solomon succeeded him as king.

29 Now the deeds of King David, first and last, can be found written in the history of Samuel the seer, the history of Nathan the prophet, and the history of Gad the seer, 30 together with the particulars of his reign and valor, and of the events that affected him and all Israel and all the kingdoms of the surrounding lands.

NEW JERUSALEM BIBLE

20 David then addressed the whole assembly: 'Now bless Yahweh your God!' And the whole assembly blessed Yahweh, God of their ancestors, bowing down in homage to Yahweh, and to the king.

21 On the day following this, they slaughtered sacrifices and brought burnt offerings to Yahweh on behalf of Israel —a thousand bulls, a thousand rams, a thousand lambs with their libations, as well as many other sacrifices— 22 and they ate and drank that day in Yahweh's presence with great joy. They then made Solomon son of David king a second time, anointing him as leader for Yahweh, and Zadok as priest. 23 Solomon took his seat on Yahweh's throne, to reign in succession to David his father. He prospered, and all Israel obeyed him. 24 All the chiefs, all the leading citizens and all King David's other sons pledged allegiance to King Solomon. 25 Yahweh made Solomon exceedingly powerful, as all Israel could see, and gave him a reign of such splendour as no previous king of Israel ever had.

26 David son of Jesse was king of all Israel. 27 He was king of Israel for a period of forty years; he reigned at Hebron for seven years, and in Jerusalem for thirty-three. 28 He died at a good old age, full of days, riches and honour. Then his son Solomon succeeded him. 29 The history of King David, from first to last, is all written down in the records of Samuel the seer, the records of Nathan the prophet and the records of Gad the seer, 30 with his entire reign, his mighty deeds and the times which he, Israel and all the kings of other countries, had experienced.

2 Chronicles

1 Solomon son of David established himself in his kingdom; the LORD his God was with him and made him exceedingly great.

2 Solomon summoned all Israel, the commanders of the thousands and of the hundreds, the judges, and all the leaders of all Israel, the heads of families. 3 Then Solomon, and the whole assembly with him, went to the high place that was at Gibeon; for God's tent of meeting, which Moses the servant of the LORD had made in the wilderness, was there. 4 (But David had brought the ark of God up from Kiriath-jearim to the place that David had prepared for it; for he had pitched a tent for it in Jerusalem.) 5 Moreover the bronze altar that Bezalel son of Uri, son of Hur, had made, was there in front of the tabernacle of the LORD. And Solomon and the assembly inquired at it. 6 Solomon went up there to the bronze altar before the LORD, which was at the tent of meeting, and offered a thousand burnt offerings on it.

7 That night God appeared to Solomon, and said to him, "Ask what I should give you." 8 Solomon said to God, "You have shown great and steadfast love to my father David, and have made me succeed him as king. 9 O LORD God, let your promise to my father David now be fulfilled, for you have made me king over a people as numerous as the dust of the earth. 10 Give me now wisdom and knowledge to go out and come in before this people, for who can rule this great people of yours?" 11 God answered Solomon, "Because this was in your heart, and you have not asked for possessions, wealth, honor, or the life of those who hate you, and have not even asked for long life, but have asked for wisdom and knowledge for yourself that you may rule my people over whom I have made you king, 12 wisdom and knowledge are granted to you. I will also give you riches, possessions, and honor, such as none of the kings who were before you, and none after you shall have the like." 13 So Solomon came from*a* the high place at Gibeon, from the tent of meeting, to Jerusalem. And he reigned over Israel.

14 Solomon gathered together chariots and horses; he had fourteen hundred chariots and twelve thousand horses, which he stationed in the chariot cities and with the king in Jerusalem. 15 The king made silver and gold as common in Jerusalem as stone, and he made cedar as plentiful as the sycamore of the Shephelah. 16 Solomon's horses were imported from Egypt and Kue; the king's traders received them from Kue at the prevailing price. 17 They imported from Egypt, and then exported, a chariot for six hundred shekels of silver, and a horse for one hundred fifty; so through them these were exported to all the kings of the Hittites and the kings of Aram.

2 *b* Solomon decided to build a temple for the name of the LORD, and a royal palace for himself. 2 *c* Solomon conscripted seventy thousand laborers and eighty thousand stonecutters in the hill country, with three thousand six hundred to oversee them.

3 Solomon sent word to King Huram of Tyre: "Once you dealt with my father David and sent him cedar to build himself a house to live in. 4 I am now about to build a house

THE SECOND BOOK OF THE
Chronicles

1 KING Solomon, David's son, strengthened his hold on the kingdom, for the LORD his God was with him and made him very great.

2 Solomon addressed all Israel, the officers over units of a thousand and of a hundred, the judges, and all the leading men of Israel, the heads of families. 3 Then he, together with all the assembled people, went to the shrine at Gibeon, for the Tent of Meeting, which Moses the LORD's servant had made in the wilderness, was there. 4 (The Ark of God had been brought up from Kiriath-jearim by David to the place which he had prepared for it; he had pitched a tent for it in Jerusalem.) 5 The bronze altar also, which Bezalel son of Uri, son of Hur, had made, was at Gibeon in front of the Tabernacle of the LORD; and Solomon and the assembly resorted to it. 6 Solomon went up to this bronze altar before the LORD in the Tent of Meeting and offered on it a thousand whole-offerings.

7 God appeared to Solomon that night and said, 'What shall I give you? Tell me.' 8 He answered, 'You have shown great and constant love to David my father and you have made me king in his place. 9 Now, LORD God, let your promise to David my father be confirmed, for you have made me king over a people as numerous as the dust on the earth; 10 now grant me wisdom and knowledge, that I may lead this people; otherwise who can govern this great people of yours?'

11 God said to Solomon, 'Because this is what you desire, because you have not asked for wealth or possessions or honour, or the lives of those hostile to you, or even long life for yourself, but have asked for wisdom and knowledge to govern my people over whom I have made you king, 12 wisdom and knowledge are granted to you; I shall also give you wealth and possessions and glory, such as no king before you has had, and none after you shall have.' 13 Then Solomon returned to Jerusalem from before the Tent of Meeting at the shrine at Gibeon, and reigned over Israel.

14 Solomon amassed chariots and horses; he had fourteen hundred chariots and twelve thousand horses; he stationed some in the chariot-towns, while others he kept at hand in Jerusalem. 15 The king made silver and gold as plentiful as stone, and cedar as plentiful as the sycamore-fig is in the Shephelah. 16 Horses were imported from Egypt and Kue for Solomon; the merchants of the king obtained them from Kue by purchase. 17 Chariots were imported from Egypt for six hundred silver shekels each, and horses for a hundred and fifty; in the same way the merchants obtained them for export from all the kings of the Hittites and the kings of Aram.

2 Solomon resolved to build a house for the name of the LORD and a royal palace for himself. 2 He engaged seventy thousand bearers and eighty thousand quarrymen, and three thousand six hundred men to superintend them. 3 He sent this message to King Huram of Tyre: 'You were so good as to send my father David cedar-wood to build his royal residence. 4 Now I am about to build a house for the

---

1:5 **was at Gibeon:** *lit.* was there; *some MSS read* he placed.
resorted to it: *or* worshipped him.   1:7–12 *Cp. 1 Kgs. 3:5–14.*
1:14 **horses:** *or* cavalry.   1:14–17 *Cp. 9:25–28; 1 Kgs. 10:26–29.*
1:16 **Kue:** *or* Cilicia.   2:1 *In Heb. 1:18.*   2:2 *In Heb. 2:1*
2:3–16 *Cp. 1 Kgs. 5:2–11.*

---

*a*Gk Vg: Heb *to*   *b*Ch 1.18 in Heb   *c*Ch 2.1 in Heb

THE SECOND BOOK OF
Chronicles

1 Solomon, son of David, strengthened his hold on the kingdom, for the LORD, his God, was with him, constantly making him more renowned. [2] He sent a summons to all Israel, to the commanders of thousands and of hundreds, the judges, the princes of all Israel, and the family heads; [3] and, accompanied by the whole assembly, he went to the high place at Gibeon, because the meeting tent of God, made in the desert by Moses, the LORD's servant, was there. [4] (The ark of God, however, David had brought up from Kiriath-jearim to Jerusalem, where he had provided a place and pitched a tent for it.) [5] The bronze altar made by Bezalel, son of Uri, son of Hur, he put in front of the LORD's Dwelling on the high place. There Solomon and the assembly consulted the LORD, [6] and Solomon offered sacrifice in the LORD's presence on the bronze altar at the meeting tent; he offered a thousand holocausts upon it.

[7] That night God appeared to Solomon and said to him, "Make a request of me, and I will grant it to you." [8] Solomon answered God: "You have shown great favor to my father David, and you have allowed me to succeed him as king. [9] Now, LORD God, may your promise to my father David be fulfilled, for you have made me king over a people as numerous as the dust of the earth. [10] Give me, therefore, wisdom and knowledge to lead this people, for otherwise who could rule this great people of yours?" [11] God then replied to Solomon: "Since this has been your wish and you have not asked for riches, treasures and glory, nor for the life of those who hate you, nor even for a long life for yourself, but have asked for wisdom and knowledge in order to rule my people over whom I have made you king, [12] wisdom and knowledge are given you; but I will also give you riches, treasures and glory, such as kings before you never had, nor will those have them who come after you."

[13] Solomon returned to Jerusalem from the high place at Gibeon, from the meeting tent, and became king over Israel. [14] He gathered together chariots and drivers, so that he had one thousand four hundred chariots and twelve thousand drivers he could station in the chariot cities and with the king in Jerusalem. [15] The king made silver and gold as common in Jerusalem as stones, while cedars became as numerous as the sycamores of the foothills. [16] Solomon also imported horses from Egypt and Cilicia. The king's agents would acquire them by purchase from Cilicia, [17] and would then bring up chariots from Egypt and export them at six hundred silver shekels, with the horses going for a hundred and fifty shekels. At these rates they served as middlemen for all the Hittite and Aramean kings.

[18] Solomon gave orders for the building of a house to honor the LORD and also of a house for his own royal estate.
2 He conscripted seventy thousand men to carry stone and eighty thousand to cut the stone in the mountains, and over these he placed three thousand six hundred overseers. [2] Moreover, Solomon sent this message to Huram, king of Tyre: "As you dealt with my father David, sending him cedars to build a house for his dwelling, so deal with me. [3] I intend to build a house for the honor of the LORD,

THE SECOND BOOK OF
Chronicles

1 Solomon son of David then made himself secure over his kingdom. Yahweh his God was with him, making him more and more powerful. [2] Solomon then spoke to all Israel, to the commanders of thousands and of hundreds, to the judges and to every leader in all Israel, the heads of families. [3] Solomon, and the whole assembly with him, then went to the high place at Gibeon, where God's Tent of Meeting was, which Moses, servant of God, had made in the desert. [4] The ark of the covenant, however, David had brought from Kiriath-Jearim to the place which he had prepared for it, having pitched a tent for it in Jerusalem. [5] The bronze altar which Bezalel son of Uri, son of Hur, had made was there, in front of Yahweh's Dwelling, where Solomon and the assembly consulted him. [6] There Solomon presented a burnt offering before Yahweh on the bronze altar of the Tent of Meeting, making on it one thousand burnt offerings.

[7] That night God appeared to Solomon and said, 'Ask what you would like me to give you.' [8] Solomon replied to God, 'You showed most faithful love to David my father, and you have made me king in succession to him. [9] Yahweh God, the promise you made to David my father has now been fulfilled, since you have made me king over a people as numerous as the dust of the earth. [10] Therefore give me wisdom and knowledge to act as leader of this people, for how otherwise could such a great people as yours be governed?'

[11] 'Since that is what you want,' God said to Solomon, 'since you have asked, not for riches, treasure, honour, the lives of your enemies, or even for a long life, but for wisdom and knowledge to govern my people of whom I have made you king, [12] therefore wisdom and knowledge are granted you. I give you riches too, and treasure, and honour such as no king had before you and none will have after you.'

[13] So Solomon came away from the high place at Gibeon, from the Tent of Meeting, to Jerusalem and reigned over Israel.

[14] Solomon then built up a force of chariots and cavalry; he had one thousand four hundred chariots and twelve thousand horses; these he kept in the chariot towns and near the king at Jerusalem. [15] In Jerusalem the king made silver and gold as common as stones, and cedar wood as plentiful as sycamore in the lowlands. [16] Solomon's horses were imported from Muzur and Cilicia. The king's dealers acquired them in Cilicia at the prevailing price. [17] A chariot was imported from Egypt for six hundred silver shekels and a horse from Cilicia for a hundred and fifty. They also supplied the Hittite and Aramaean kings, who all used them as middlemen.

[18] Solomon then gave the order to build a house for the name of Yahweh and a palace in which to reign.
2 And Solomon allocated seventy thousand men to be porters and eighty thousand to quarry in the hills and three thousand six hundred overseers for them. [2] And Solomon sent this message to Huram king of Tyre, 'Do as you did for my father David when you sent him cedars for him to build himself a palace to live in. [3] You see, I am building

for the name of the LORD my God and dedicate it to him for offering fragrant incense before him, and for the regular offering of the rows of bread, and for burnt offerings morning and evening, on the sabbaths and the new moons and the appointed festivals of the LORD our God, as ordained forever for Israel. 5 The house that I am about to build will be great, for our God is greater than other gods. 6 But who is able to build him a house, since heaven, even highest heaven, cannot contain him? Who am I to build a house for him, except as a place to make offerings before him? 7 So now send me an artisan skilled to work in gold, silver, bronze, and iron, and in purple, crimson, and blue fabrics, trained also in engraving, to join the skilled workers who are with me in Judah and Jerusalem, whom my father David provided. 8 Send me also cedar, cypress, and algum timber from Lebanon, for I know that your servants are skilled in cutting Lebanon timber. My servants will work with your servants 9 to prepare timber for me in abundance, for the house I am about to build will be great and wonderful. 10 I will provide for your servants, those who cut the timber, twenty thousand cors of crushed wheat, twenty thousand cors of barley, twenty thousand baths*d* of wine, and twenty thousand baths of oil."

11 Then King Huram of Tyre answered in a letter that he sent to Solomon, "Because the LORD loves his people he has made you king over them." 12 Huram also said, "Blessed be the LORD God of Israel, who made heaven and earth, who has given King David a wise son, endowed with discretion and understanding, who will build a temple for the LORD, and a royal palace for himself.

13 "I have dispatched Huram-abi, a skilled artisan, endowed with understanding, 14 the son of one of the Danite women, his father a Tyrian. He is trained to work in gold, silver, bronze, iron, stone, and wood, and in purple, blue, and crimson fabrics and fine linen, and to do all sorts of engraving and execute any design that may be assigned him, with your artisans, the artisans of my lord, your father David. 15 Now, as for the wheat, barley, oil, and wine, of which my lord has spoken, let him send them to his servants. 16 We will cut whatever timber you need from Lebanon, and bring it to you as rafts by sea to Joppa; you will take it up to Jerusalem."

17 Then Solomon took a census of all the aliens who were residing in the land of Israel, after the census that his father David had taken; and there were found to be one hundred fifty-three thousand six hundred. 18 Seventy thousand of them he assigned as laborers, eighty thousand as stonecutters in the hill country, and three thousand six hundred as overseers to make the people work.

3 Solomon began to build the house of the LORD in Jerusalem on Mount Moriah, where the LORD had appeared to his father David, at the place that David had designated, on the threshing floor of Ornan the Jebusite. 2 He began to build on the second day of the second month of the fourth year of his reign. 3 These are Solomon's measurements*e* for building the house of God: the length, in cubits of the old standard, was sixty cubits, and the width twenty cubits. 4 The vestibule in front of the nave of the house was twenty

name of the LORD my God and to consecrate it to him, so that I may burn fragrant incense in it before him, and present the rows of the Bread of the Presence regularly, and whole-offerings morning and evening, on the sabbaths and at the new moons and appointed festivals of the LORD our God; for this is a duty laid on Israel for ever. 5 The house I am about to build must be great, because our God is greater than all gods. 6 But who is able to build a house for him when heaven itself, the highest heaven, cannot contain him? Who am I that I should build him a house, except to burn sacrifices before him? 7 Send me now a skilled craftsman, one able to work in gold and silver, bronze, and iron, and in purple, crimson, and violet yarn, one who is also an expert engraver and will work in Judah and in Jerusalem with my skilled workmen who were provided by David my father. 8 Send me also cedar, pine, and algum timber from Lebanon, for I know that your men are expert at felling the trees of Lebanon; my men will work with yours 9 to get an ample supply of timber ready for me, for the house which I shall build will be great and wonderful. 10 I shall supply provisions for your servants, the woodmen who fell the trees: twenty thousand kor of wheat and twenty thousand kor of barley, with twenty thousand bath of wine and twenty thousand bath of oil.'

11 King Huram of Tyre sent this letter in reply: 'It is because of the love which the LORD has for his people that he has made you king over them.' 12 The letter continued, 'Blessed be the LORD the God of Israel, maker of heaven and earth, who has given to King David a wise son, endowed with insight and understanding, to build a house for the LORD and a royal palace for himself.

13 'I now send you my expert Huram, a skilful and experienced craftsman. 14 He is the son of a Danite woman and a Tyrian father; he is an experienced worker in gold and silver, bronze and iron, stone and wood, as well as in purple, violet, and crimson yarn, and in fine linen; he is also a trained engraver who will be able to work with your own skilled craftsmen and those of my lord David your father, to any design submitted to him. 15 Now let my lord send his servants the wheat and the barley, the oil and the wine, which he promised; 16 we shall fell all the timber in Lebanon that you need and float it as rafts to the roadstead at Joppa; you can convey it up to Jerusalem.'

17 Solomon took a census of all the aliens resident in Israel, similar to the census which David his father had taken; these were found to be a hundred and fifty-three thousand six hundred. 18 He made seventy thousand of them bearers, and eighty thousand quarrymen, and three thousand six hundred superintendents to make the people work.

3 Then Solomon began to build the house of the LORD in Jerusalem on Mount Moriah, where the LORD had appeared to his father David; it was the site which David had prepared on the threshing-floor of Ornan the Jebusite. 2 He began to build in the second month of the fourth year of his reign. 3 These are the foundations which Solomon laid for building the house of God: according to the old standard of measurement the length was sixty cubits and the breadth twenty. 4 The vestibule in front of the house was twenty

2:7 **bronze:** *or* copper.　　2:8 **algum:** almug *in 1 Kgs. 10:11.*
2:10 **provisions:** *so Lat., cp. 1 Kgs. 5:11; Heb.* plagues.
2:14 **bronze:** *or* copper.　　3:1 **it was . . . prepared:** *so Gk; Heb.* which he had prepared on David's site.　　3:2–4 *Cp. 1 Kgs. 6:1–3.*
3:2 **in . . . month:** *so some MSS; others add* on the second.
3:4 **house was:** *prob. rdg; Heb.* length was.

d A Hebrew measure of volume　　*e* Syr: Heb *foundations*

NEW AMERICAN BIBLE

NEW JERUSALEM BIBLE

my God, and to consecrate it to him, for the burning of fragrant incense in his presence, for the perpetual display of the showbread, for holocausts morning and evening, and for the sabbaths, new moons, and festivals of the LORD, our God: such is Israel's perpetual obligation. 4 And the house I intend to build must be large, for our God is greater than all other gods. 5 Yet who is really able to build him a house, since the heavens and even the highest heavens cannot contain him? And who am I that I should build him a house, unless it be to offer incense in his presence? 6 Now, send me men skilled at work in gold, silver, bronze and iron, in purple, crimson, and violet fabrics, and who know how to do engraved work, to join the craftsmen who are with me in Judah and Jerusalem, whom my father David appointed. 7 Also send me boards of cedar, cypress and cabinet wood from Lebanon, for I realize that your servants know how to cut the wood of the Lebanon. My servants will labor with yours 8 in order to prepare for me a great quantity of wood, since the house I intend to build must be lofty and wonderful. 9 I will furnish as food for your servants, the hewers who cut the wood, twenty thousand kors of wheat, twenty thousand kors of barley, twenty thousand measures of wine, and twenty thousand measures of oil."

10 Huram, king of Tyre, wrote an answer which he sent to Solomon: "Because the LORD loves his people, he has placed you over them as king." 11 He added: "Blessed be the LORD, the God of Israel, who made heaven and earth, for having given King David a wise son of intelligence and understanding, who will build a house for the LORD and also a house for his royal estate. 12 I am now sending you a craftsman of great skill, Huram-abi, 13 son of a Danite woman and of a father from Tyre; he knows how to work with gold, silver, bronze and iron, with stone and wood, with purple, violet, fine linen and crimson, and also how to do all kinds of engraved work and to devise every type of artistic work that may be given him and your craftsmen and the craftsmen of my lord David your father. 14 And now, let my lord send to his servants the wheat, barley, oil and wine which he has promised. 15 For our part, we will cut trees on Lebanon, as many as you need, and float them down to you at the port of Joppa, whence you may take them up to Jerusalem."

16 Thereupon Solomon took a census of all the alien men who were in the land of Israel (following the census David his father had taken of them), who were found to number one hundred fifty-three thousand six hundred. 17 Of these he made seventy thousand carriers and eighty thousand cutters in the mountains, and three thousand six hundred overseers to keep the people working.

3 Then Solomon began to build the house of the LORD in Jerusalem on Mount Moriah, which had been pointed out to his father David, on the spot which David had selected, the threshing-floor of Ornan the Jebusite. 2 He began to build in the second month of the fourth year of his reign. 3 These were the specifications laid down by Solomon for building the house of God: the length was sixty cubits according to the old measure, and the width was twenty cubits; 4 the porch which lay before the nave along the width

a house for the name of Yahweh my God, to acknowledge his holiness so that perfumed incense may be burnt before him, the loaves of permanent offering be perpetually laid out and the burnt offerings be made morning and evening, on the Sabbaths, New Moons and solemn festivals of Yahweh our God, as prescribed to Israel for ever; 4 and the house which I am building must be large, for our God is greater than all gods; 5 even so, who would not find it an impossible task to build a house for him, when the heavens and the heavens of the heavens cannot contain him? And who am I to build a house for him except to burn incense before him? 6 So now send me a man skilled at working in gold, silver, bronze, iron, scarlet, crimson and violet materials, and who knows the art of engraving too; he is to work with my skilled men in Judah and Jerusalem, whom my father David has provided. 7 Also send me cedar, juniper and algum trunks from the Lebanon, for I know that your servants know the art of felling timber in the Lebanon. And, my servants will work with your servants 8 in preparing a vast quantity of timber for me, since the house which I intend to build is to be of a size to marvel at. 9 Furthermore, for the upkeep of the woodcutters whom you employ to cut the timber, I shall provide twenty thousand kor of wheat, twenty thousand kor of barley, twenty thousand bat of wine and twenty thousand bat of oil.'

10 In a letter sent to King Solomon, Huram king of Tyre replied, 'Because Yahweh loves his people he has made you their king!' 11 Huram went on to say, 'Praised be Yahweh, God of Israel, who made heaven and earth and has given King David a wise son, endowed with discretion and discernment, to build a house for Yahweh and a palace in which to reign! — 12 I am now sending you a skilled and intelligent man, Huram-Abi 13 the son of a Danite woman by a Tyrian father. He knows the arts of working in gold, silver, bronze, stone, wood, scarlet, violet, fine linen and crimson materials, and is competent to carry out any kind of engraving and to execute any design which may be entrusted to him, in collaboration with your skilled men and those of my lord David, your father.

14 'So now let my lord send his servants the wheat, barley, oil and wine as promised 15 and we will fell all the wood you need from Lebanon, and bring it to you in rafts by sea to Jaffa; and it will be your responsibility to transport it to Jerusalem.'

16 Solomon then took a census of all the aliens resident in Israel similar to the census which his father David had taken; it was found that there were a hundred and fifty-three thousand six hundred. 17 He impressed seventy thousand of them as porters, eighty thousand as quarrymen in the hills and three thousand six hundred as overseers to make sure the people worked.

3 Solomon then began building the house of Yahweh in Jerusalem on Mount Moriah where David his father had had a vision — on the site which David had prepared — on the threshing-floor of Ornan the Jebusite. 2 He began building it on the second day of the second month of the fourth year of his reign. 3 These are the dimensions which Solomon fixed for the structure of the house of God: its length in cubits, according to the old standard, was sixty cubits and its width twenty cubits; 4 and the portico in front

NEW REVISED STANDARD VERSION

cubits long, across the width of the house;f and its height was one hundred twenty cubits. He overlaid it on the inside with pure gold. 5 The nave he lined with cypress, covered it with fine gold, and made palms and chains on it. 6 He adorned the house with settings of precious stones. The gold was gold from Parvaim. 7 So he lined the house with gold — its beams, its thresholds, its walls, and its doors; and he carved cherubim on the walls.

8 He made the most holy place; its length, corresponding to the width of the house, was twenty cubits, and its width was twenty cubits; he overlaid it with six hundred talents of fine gold. 9 The weight of the nails was fifty shekels of gold. He overlaid the upper chambers with gold.

10 In the most holy place he made two carved cherubim and overlaidg them with gold. 11 The wings of the cherubim together extended twenty cubits: one wing of the one, five cubits long, touched the wall of the house, and its other wing, five cubits long, touched the wing of the other cherub; 12 and of this cherub, one wing, five cubits long, touched the wall of the house, and the other wing, also five cubits long, was joined to the wing of the first cherub. 13 The wings of these cherubim extended twenty cubits; the cherubimh stood on their feet, facing the nave. 14 And Solomoni made the curtain of blue and purple and crimson fabrics and fine linen, and worked cherubim into it.

15 In front of the house he made two pillars thirty-five cubits high, with a capital of five cubits on the top of each. 16 He made encirclingj chains and put them on the tops of the pillars; and he made one hundred pomegranates, and put them on the chains. 17 He set up the pillars in front of the temple, one on the right, the other on the left; the one on the right he called Jachin, and the one on the left, Boaz.

4 He made an altar of bronze, twenty cubits long, twenty cubits wide, and ten cubits high. 2 Then he made the molten sea; it was round, ten cubits from rim to rim, and five cubits high. A line of thirty cubits would encircle it completely. 3 Under it were panels all around, each of ten cubits, surrounding the sea; there were two rows of panels, cast when it was cast. 4 It stood on twelve oxen, three facing north, three facing west, three facing south, and three facing east; the sea was set on them. The hindquarters of each were toward the inside. 5 Its thickness was a handbreadth; its rim was made like the rim of a cup, like the flower of a lily; it held three thousand baths.k 6 He also made ten basins in which to wash, and set five on the right side, and five on the left. In these they were to rinse what was used for the burnt offering. The sea was for the priests to wash in.

7 He made ten golden lampstands as prescribed, and set them in the temple, five on the south side and five on the north. 8 He also made ten tables and placed them in the temple, five on the right side and five on the left. And he made one hundred basins of gold. 9 He made the court of the priests, and the great court, and doors for the court; he overlaid their doors with bronze. 10 He set the sea at the southeast corner of the house.

REVISED ENGLISH BIBLE

cubits long, spanning the whole breadth of the house, and its height was twenty; on the inside he overlaid it with pure gold. 5 He panelled the large chamber with pine, covered it with fine gold, and carved on it palm trees and chain-work. 6 He adorned the house with precious stones for decoration and with gold from Parvaim. 7 He overlaid the whole house with gold, its rafters and frames, its walls and doors; and he carved cherubim on the walls.

8 He made the Most Holy Place twenty cubits long, corresponding to the breadth of the house, and twenty cubits broad. He overlaid it all with six hundred talents of fine gold, 9 and the weight of the gold nails was fifty shekels. He also covered the upper chambers with gold.

10 In the Most Holy Place he carved two images of cherubim and overlaid them with gold. 11 The total span of the wings of the cherubim was twenty cubits. A wing of one cherub extended five cubits to touch the wall of the house, while its other wing reached out five cubits to meet a wing of the other cherub. 12 Similarly, a wing of the second cherub extended five cubits to touch the other wall of the house, while its other wing met a wing of the first cherub. 13 The wings of these cherubim extended twenty cubits; they stood with their feet on the ground, facing the outer chamber. 14 He made the veil of violet, purple, and crimson yarn, and fine linen, and embroidered cherubim on it.

15 In front of the house he erected two pillars eighteen cubits high, with a capital five cubits high on top of each. 16 He made chain-work like a necklace and set it round the tops of the pillars, and he carved a hundred pomegranates and set them in the chain-work. 17 He erected the pillars in front of the temple, one on the right and one on the left; the one on the right he named Jachin and the one on the left Boaz.

4 He made an altar of bronze, twenty cubits long, twenty cubits broad, and ten cubits high. 2 He made the Sea of cast metal; it was round in shape, the diameter from rim to rim being ten cubits; it stood five cubits high, and it took a line thirty cubits long to go round it. 3 Under the Sea, on every side, completely surrounding the thirty cubits of its circumference, were what looked like gourds, two rows of them, cast in one piece with the Sea itself. 4 It was mounted on twelve oxen, three facing north, three west, three south, and three east, their hindquarters turned inwards; the Sea rested on top of them. 5 Its thickness was a hand's breadth; its rim was made like that of a cup, shaped like the calyx of a lily; when full it held three thousand bath. 6 He also made ten basins for washing, setting five on the left side and five on the right; in these they rinsed everything used for the whole-offering. The Sea was for the priests to wash in.

7 He made ten gold lampstands in the prescribed manner and set them in the temple, five on the right side and five on the left. 8 He also made ten tables and placed them in the temple, five on the right and five on the left; and he made a hundred gold tossing-bowls. 9 He made the court of the priests and the great precinct and the doors for it, and overlaid the doors of both with copper; 10 he put the Sea at the right side, at the south-east corner of the temple.

3:4 **height was twenty:** *so Gk; Heb.* heights was a hundred and twenty. 3:9 **gold . . . shekels:** *prob. rdg; Heb.* nails was fifty shekels of gold. 3:10–13 *Cp. 1 Kgs. 6:23–28.* 3:10 **images:** *mng of Heb. word uncertain.* 3:15–17 *Cp. 1 Kgs. 7:15–21.* 3:15 **eighteen:** *so Syriac, cp. 1 Kgs. 7:15; Heb.* thirty-five. 3:16 **necklace:** *prob. rdg; Heb. obscure.* 3:17 **Jachin:** *or* Jachun, *that is* It shall stand. **Boaz:** *or* Booz, *that is* In Strength. 4:2–5 *Cp. 1 Kgs. 7:23–26.* 4:3 **thirty:** *prob. rdg; Heb.* ten. **gourds:** *prob. rdg, cp. 1 Kgs. 7:24; Heb.* oxen.

fCompare 1 Kings 6.3: Meaning of Heb uncertain   gHeb *they overlaid*   hHeb *they*   iHeb *he*   jCn: Heb *in the inner sanctuary*   kA Hebrew measure of volume

of the house was also twenty cubits, and it was twenty cubits high. He overlaid its interior with pure gold. 5 The nave he overlaid with cypress wood which he covered with fine gold, embossing on it palms and chains. 6 He also decorated the building with precious stones. 7 The house; its beams and thresholds, as well as its walls and its doors, he overlaid with gold, and he engraved cherubim upon the walls. (The gold was from Parvaim.) 8 He also made the room of the holy of holies. Its length corresponded to the width of the house, twenty cubits, and its width was also twenty cubits. He overlaid it with fine gold to the amount of six hundred talents. 9 The weight of the nails was fifty gold shekels. The upper chambers he likewise covered with gold.

10 For the room of the holy of holies he made two cherubim of carved workmanship, which were then overlaid with gold. 11 The wings of the cherubim spanned twenty cubits: 12 one wing of each cherub, five cubits in length, extended to a wall of the building, while the other wing, also five cubits in length, touched the corresponding wing of the second cherub. 13 The combined wingspread of the two cherubim was thus twenty cubits. They stood upon their own feet, facing toward the nave. 14 He made the veil of violet, purple, crimson and fine linen, and had cherubim embroidered upon it.

15 In front of the building he set two columns thirty-five cubits high; the capital topping each was of five cubits. 16 He worked out chains in the form of a collar with which he encircled the capitals of the columns, and he made a hundred pomegranates which he set on the chains. 17 He set up the columns to correspond with the nave, one for the right side and the other for the left, and he called the one to the right Jachin and the one to the left Boaz.

4 Then he made a bronze altar twenty cubits long, twenty cubits wide and ten cubits high. 2 He also made the molten sea. It was perfectly round, ten cubits in diameter, five in depth, and thirty in circumference; 3 below the rim a ring of figures of oxen encircled the sea, ten to the cubit, all the way around; there were two rows of these cast in the same mold with the sea. 4 It rested on twelve oxen, three facing north, three west, three south, and three east, with their haunches all toward the center; the sea rested on their backs. 5 It was a handbreadth thick, and its brim was made like that of a cup, being lily-shaped. It had a capacity of three thousand measures.

6 Then he made ten basins for washing, placing five of them to the right and five to the left. Here were cleansed the victims for the holocausts; but the sea was for the priests to wash in.

7 He made the lampstands of gold, ten of them as was prescribed, and placed them in the nave, five to the right and five to the left. 8 He made ten tables and had them set in the nave, five to the right and five to the left; and he made a hundred golden bowls. 9 He made the court of the priests and the great courtyard and the gates of the courtyard; the gates he overlaid with bronze. 10 The sea was placed off to the southeast from the right side of the temple.

of the house was the full width of the house, that is, twenty cubits, and its height was a hundred and twenty cubits; on the inside he overlaid it with pure gold. 5 The Great Hall he lined with juniper, which he overlaid with fine gold and ornamented with palm trees and festoons, 6 and he decorated the hall beautifully with precious stones and with gold from Parvaim, 7 overlaying the hall, its beams and its thresholds, its walls and its doors, with gold and engraving the walls with great winged creatures.

8 He also made the Holy of Holies, the length of which corresponded to the width of the Great Hall, being twenty cubits, with a width of twenty cubits, and this he overlaid with fine gold weighing six hundred talents, 9 while the weight of the gold nails was fifty shekels. He also overlaid the upper rooms with gold. 10 In the Holy of Holies he modelled two winged creatures of wrought metal work and overlaid them with gold. 11 The total span of their wings was twenty cubits; one wing, being five cubits long, touched the wall of the house and the other wing, being five cubits long, touched the wing of the other winged creature; 12 while one wing of the other, five cubits long, touched the other wall of the house and the other wing, five cubits long, touched the wing of the other winged creature. 13 The spread of these creatures' wings was twenty cubits. They stood in an upright position, with their faces towards the Hall.

14 He also made the Curtain of violet, scarlet, crimson and fine linen, working a design of winged creatures on it.

15 In front of the Hall he made two pillars thirty-five cubits high, and on the top of each a capital measuring five cubits. 16 He made festoons, in the Debir, to go at the tops of the pillars, and made a hundred pomegranates to go on the festoons. 17 He erected the pillars in front of the Temple, one on the right, the other on the left; the one on the right he called Jachin and the one on the left, Boaz.

4 He made a bronze altar, twenty cubits long, twenty cubits wide and ten cubits high. 2 He made the Sea of cast metal, ten cubits from rim to rim, circular in shape and five cubits high; a cord thirty cubits long gave the measurement of its girth. 3 Under it and completely encircling it were things like oxen, ten to the cubit round the entire Sea; the oxen were in two rows, of one and the same casting with the rest. 4 It rested on twelve oxen, three facing north, three facing west, three facing south, three facing east; on these, their hindquarters all turned inwards, stood the Sea. 5 It was a hand's breadth in thickness, and its rim was shaped like the rim of a cup — lily-shaped. It could hold three thousand *bat.*

6 He made ten basins, putting five on the right and five on the left, for washing in; the things to be offered as burnt offerings were to be rinsed in these, but the Sea was for the priests to wash in. 7 He made the ten golden lamp-stands according to the pattern and placed them in the Hekal, five on the right and five on the left. 8 He made ten tables which he set up in the Hekal, five on the right and five on the left. He also made a hundred golden sprinkling bowls.

9 He made the court of the priests and the great court with its gates and plated the gates with bronze. 10 The Sea he placed on the right-hand side of the Temple, to the south-east.

| NEW REVISED STANDARD VERSION | REVISED ENGLISH BIBLE |

11 And Huram made the pots, the shovels, and the basins. Thus Huram finished the work that he did for King Solomon on the house of God: 12 the two pillars, the bowls, and the two capitals on the top of the pillars; and the two latticeworks to cover the two bowls of the capitals that were on the top of the pillars; 13 the four hundred pomegranates for the two latticeworks, two rows of pomegranates for each latticework, to cover the two bowls of the capitals that were on the pillars. 14 He made the stands, the basins on the stands, 15 the one sea, and the twelve oxen underneath it. 16 The pots, the shovels, the forks, and all the equipment for these Huram-abi made of burnished bronze for King Solomon for the house of the LORD. 17 In the plain of the Jordan the king cast them, in the clay ground between Succoth and Zeredah. 18 Solomon made all these things in great quantities, so that the weight of the bronze was not determined.

19 So Solomon made all the things that were in the house of God: the golden altar, the tables for the bread of the Presence, 20 the lampstands and their lamps of pure gold to burn before the inner sanctuary, as prescribed; 21 the flowers, the lamps, and the tongs, of purest gold; 22 the snuffers, basins, ladles, and firepans, of pure gold. As for the entrance to the temple: the inner doors to the most holy place and the doors of the nave of the temple were of gold.

5 Thus all the work that Solomon did for the house of the LORD was finished. Solomon brought in the things that his father David had dedicated, and stored the silver, the gold, and all the vessels in the treasuries of the house of God.

2 Then Solomon assembled the elders of Israel and all the heads of the tribes, the leaders of the ancestral houses of the people of Israel, in Jerusalem, to bring up the ark of the covenant of the LORD out of the city of David, which is Zion. 3 And all the Israelites assembled before the king at the festival that is in the seventh month. 4 And all the elders of Israel came, and the Levites carried the ark. 5 So they brought up the ark, the tent of meeting, and all the holy vessels that were in the tent; the priests and the Levites brought them up. 6 King Solomon and all the congregation of Israel, who had assembled before him, were before the ark, sacrificing so many sheep and oxen that they could not be numbered or counted. 7 Then the priests brought the ark of the covenant of the LORD to its place, in the inner sanctuary of the house, in the most holy place, underneath the wings of the cherubim. 8 For the cherubim spread out their wings over the place of the ark, so that the cherubim made a covering above the ark and its poles. 9 The poles were so long that the ends of the poles were seen from the holy place in front of the inner sanctuary; but they could not be seen from outside; they are there to this day. 10 There was nothing in the ark except the two tablets that Moses put there at Horeb, where the LORD made a covenant[l] with the people of Israel after they came out of Egypt.

11 Now when the priests came out of the holy place (for all the priests who were present had sanctified themselves, without regard to their divisions, 12 and all the levitical sing-

11 Huram made the pots, the shovels, and the tossing-bowls. With them he finished the work which he had undertaken for King Solomon on the house of God: 12 the two pillars; the two bowl-shaped capitals on the tops of the pillars; the two ornamental networks to cover the two bowl-shaped capitals on the tops of the pillars; 13 the four hundred pomegranates for the two networks, two rows of pomegranates for each network, to cover the two bowl-shaped capitals on the two pillars; 14 the ten trolleys and the ten basins on the trolleys; 15 the one Sea and the twelve oxen which supported it; 16 the pots, the shovels, and the tossing-bowls — all these objects Master Huram made of burnished bronze for King Solomon for the house of the LORD. 17 The king cast them in the foundry between Succoth and Zeredah in the plain of Jordan. 18 Solomon made great quantities of all these objects; the weight of the bronze used was beyond reckoning.

19 Solomon made also all the furnishings for the house of God: the golden altar, the tables upon which was set the Bread of the Presence, 20 the lampstands of red gold whose lamps burned before the inner shrine in the prescribed manner, 21 the flowers, lamps, and tongs of solid gold, 22 the snuffers, tossing-bowls, saucers, and firepans of red gold, and, at the entrance to the house, the inner doors leading to the Most Holy Place and those leading to the sanctuary, of gold.

5 When all the work which Solomon did for the house of the LORD was completed, he brought in the treasures dedicated by his father David, the silver, the gold, and the vessels, and deposited them in the treasuries of the house of God.

2 THEN Solomon summoned the elders of Israel, and all the heads of the tribes who were chiefs of families in Israel, to assemble in Jerusalem, in order to bring up the Ark of the Covenant of the LORD from the City of David, which is called Zion. 3 All the men of Israel were assembled in the king's presence at the pilgrim-feast in the seventh month. 4 When the elders of Israel had all arrived, the Levites lifted the Ark 5 and carried it up; the Tent of Meeting and all the sacred furnishings of the Tent were carried by the priests and the Levites. 6 King Solomon and the whole congregation of Israel assembled with him before the Ark sacrificed sheep and oxen in numbers past counting or reckoning.

7 The priests brought in the Ark of the Covenant of the LORD to its place, in the inner shrine of the house, the Most Holy Place, beneath the wings of the cherubim. 8 The cherubim, whose wings were spread over the place of the Ark, formed a canopy above the Ark and its poles. 9 The poles projected, and their ends were visible from the Holy Place immediately in front of the inner shrine, but from nowhere else outside; they are there to this day. 10 There was nothing inside the Ark but the two tablets which Moses had put there at Horeb, when the LORD made the covenant with the Israelites after they left Egypt.

11 When the priests came out of the Holy Place (for all the priests who were present had hallowed themselves without keeping to their divisions), 12 all the levitical singers,

4:11—5:1 Cp. 1 Kgs. 7:40—51. 4:12 **bowl-shaped capitals:** prob. rdg, cp. 1 Kgs. 7:41; Heb. the bowls and the capitals. 4:13 **two pillars:** prob. rdg, cp. 1 Kgs. 7:42; Heb. surface of the pillars. 4:14 **the ten:** prob. rdg, cp. 1 Kgs. 7:43; Heb. he made the. 4:16 **tossing-bowls:** prob. rdg, cp. 1 Kgs. 7:45; Heb. forks. **these:** prob. rdg, cp. 1 Kgs. 7:45; Heb. their. 4:18 **bronze:** or copper. 4:21 **solid:** mng of Heb. word uncertain. 5:2–10 Cp. 1 Kgs. 8:1–9. 5:5 **priests and:** so some MSS; others omit and. 5:9 **Holy Place:** so Gk; Heb. Ark. **they are:** so many MSS; others it is.

l Heb lacks a covenant

11 Huram also made the pots, the shovels and the bowls. Huram thus completed the work he had to do for King Solomon in the house of God: 12 two columns, two nodes for the capitals topping these two columns, and two networks covering the nodes of the capitals topping the columns; 13 also four hundred pomegranates for the two networks, with two rows of pomegranates to each network, to cover the two nodes of the capitals topping the columns. 14 He made the stands, and the basins on the stands; 15 one sea, and the twelve oxen under it; 16 likewise the pots, the shovels and the forks. Huram-abi made all these articles for King Solomon from polished bronze for the house of the LORD. 17 The king had them cast in the Jordan region, in the clayey ground between Succoth and Zeredah. 18 Solomon made all these vessels, so many in number that the weight of the bronze was not ascertained.

19 Solomon had all these articles for the house of God: the golden altar, the tables on which the showbread lay, 20 the lampstands and their lamps of pure gold which were to burn according to prescription before the sanctuary, 21 flowers, lamps and gold tongs [this was the purest gold], 22 snuffers, bowls, cups and firepans of pure gold. As for the entry to the house, its inner doors to the holy of holies, as well as the doors to the nave, were of gold.

5 When all the work undertaken by Solomon for the temple of the LORD had been completed, he brought in the dedicated offerings of his father David, putting the silver, the gold and all the other articles in the treasuries of the house of God. 2 At Solomon's order the elders of Israel and all the leaders of the tribes, the princes of the Israelite ancestral houses, came to Jerusalem to bring up the ark of the LORD's covenant from the City of David (which is Zion). 3 All the men of Israel assembled before the king during the festival of the seventh month. 4 When all the elders of Israel had arrived, the Levites took up the ark, 5 and they carried the ark and the meeting tent with all the sacred vessels that were in the tent; it was the levitical priests who carried them.

6 King Solomon and the entire community of Israel gathered about him before the ark were sacrificing sheep and oxen so numerous that they could not be counted or numbered. 7 The priests brought the ark of the covenant of the LORD to its place beneath the wings of the cherubim in the sanctuary, the holy of holies of the temple. 8 The cherubim had their wings spread out over the place of the ark, sheltering the ark and its poles from above. 9 The poles were long enough so that their ends could be seen from that part of the holy place nearest the sanctuary; however, they could not be seen beyond. The ark has remained there to this day. 10 There was nothing in it but the two tablets which Moses put there on Horeb, the tablets of the covenant which the LORD made with the Israelites at their departure from Egypt.

11 When the priests came out of the holy place (all the priests who were present had purified themselves without reference to the rotation of their various classes), 12 the Le-

11 Huram made the ash containers, the scoops and the sprinkling bowls. Thus Huram completed all the work done for King Solomon for the Temple of God: 12 the two pillars; the mouldings of the capitals surmounting the two pillars; the two sets of filigree to cover the two mouldings of the capitals surmounting the pillars; 13 the four hundred pomegranates for the two sets of filigree — two rows of pomegranates for each set of filigree; 14 the ten stands and the ten basins on the stands; 15 the one Sea and the twelve oxen beneath it; 16 the ash containers, scoops and forks.

All these utensils made by Huram-Abi for King Solomon for the Temple of Yahweh were of burnished bronze. 17 The King made them by the process of sand casting, in the plain of the Jordan between Succoth and Zeredah. 18 There was such an enormous quantity of them that the weight of the bronze could not be calculated.

19 Solomon made all the objects designed for the Temple of God, as well as the golden altar and the tables for the loaves of permanent offering; 20 the lamp-stands with their lamps to burn, as prescribed, in front of the Debir, of pure gold; 21 the floral work, the lamps, the tongs, of gold (and it was pure gold); 22 the snuffers, the sprinkling bowls, incense ladles and the pans, of real gold; and the entrance to the Temple, the inner doors (for the Holy of Holies) and the doors of the Temple itself, that is of the Hekal, were also made of gold.

5 Thus all the work done by Solomon for the Temple of Yahweh was completed, and Solomon brought in the gifts which his father David had consecrated; and he had the silver, the gold and all the utensils put into the treasuries of the Temple of God.

2 Solomon then assembled the elders of Israel to Jerusalem, all the tribal chiefs, the princes of the families of Israel, to bring the ark of the covenant of Yahweh up from the City of David, that is, Zion. 3 All the men of Israel assembled round the king at the time of the feast, that is, in the seventh month. 4 When all the elders of Israel had arrived, the Levites took up the ark; 5 they brought up the ark and the Tent of Meeting and all the sacred utensils which were in the Tent; the levitical priests brought them up.

6 King Solomon and the whole assembly of Israel present with him before the ark sacrificed countless, innumerable sheep and oxen. 7 The priests brought the ark of the covenant of Yahweh to its place, in the Debir of the Temple, that is, in the Holy of Holies, under the wings of the winged creatures; 8 for they spread their wings over the place where the ark stood, forming a canopy over the ark and its shafts. 9 The shafts were so long, however, that the ends of the shafts of the ark could be seen in front of the Holy Place in front of the Debir, though they could not be seen from outside. They are still there today. 10 There was nothing in the ark except the two tablets which Moses had placed in it at Horeb, when Yahweh made a covenant with the Israelites when they came out of Egypt.

11 Now when the priests came out of the Holy Place — for all the priests present had sanctified themselves regardless of the orders to which they belonged, 12 and all the levitical

ers, Asaph, Heman, and Jeduthun, their sons and kindred, arrayed in fine linen, with cymbals, harps, and lyres, stood east of the altar with one hundred twenty priests who were trumpeters). 13 It was the duty of the trumpeters and singers to make themselves heard in unison in praise and thanksgiving to the LORD, and when the song was raised, with trumpets and cymbals and other musical instruments, in praise to the LORD,

> "For he is good,
> for his steadfast love endures forever,"

the house, the house of the LORD, was filled with a cloud, 14 so that the priests could not stand to minister because of the cloud; for the glory of the LORD filled the house of God.

6 Then Solomon said, "The LORD has said that he would reside in thick darkness. 2 I have built you an exalted house, a place for you to reside in forever."

3 Then the king turned around and blessed all the assembly of Israel, while all the assembly of Israel stood. 4 And he said, "Blessed be the LORD, the God of Israel, who with his hand has fulfilled what he promised with his mouth to my father David, saying, 5 'Since the day that I brought my people out of the land of Egypt, I have not chosen a city from any of the tribes of Israel in which to build a house, so that my name might be there, and I chose no one as ruler over my people Israel; 6 but I have chosen Jerusalem in order that my name may be there, and I have chosen David to be over my people Israel.' 7 My father David had it in mind to build a house for the name of the LORD, the God of Israel. 8 But the LORD said to my father David, 'You did well to consider building a house for my name; 9 nevertheless you shall not build the house, but your son who shall be born to you shall build the house for my name.' 10 Now the LORD has fulfilled his promise that he made; for I have succeeded my father David, and sit on the throne of Israel, as the LORD promised, and have built the house for the name of the LORD, the God of Israel. 11 There I have set the ark, in which is the covenant of the LORD that he made with the people of Israel."

12 Then Solomon[m] stood before the altar of the LORD in the presence of the whole assembly of Israel, and spread out his hands. 13 Solomon had made a bronze platform five cubits long, five cubits wide, and three cubits high, and had set it in the court; and he stood on it. Then he knelt on his knees in the presence of the whole assembly of Israel, and spread out his hands toward heaven. 14 He said, "O LORD, God of Israel, there is no God like you, in heaven or on earth, keeping covenant in steadfast love with your servants who walk before you with all their heart— 15 you who have kept for your servant, my father David, what you promised to him. Indeed, you promised with your mouth and this day have fulfilled with your hand. 16 Therefore, O LORD, God of Israel, keep for your servant, my father David, that which you promised him, saying, 'There shall never fail you a successor before me to sit on the throne of Israel, if only your children keep to their way, to walk in my law as you have walked before me.' 17 Therefore, O LORD, God of Israel, let your word be confirmed, which you promised to your servant David.

18 "But will God indeed reside with mortals on earth? Even heaven and the highest heaven cannot contain you, how much less this house that I have built! 19 Regard your servant's prayer and his plea, O LORD my God, heeding the cry and the prayer that your servant prays to you. 20 May

Asaph, Heman, and Jeduthun, their sons, and their kinsmen, attired in fine linen, stood with cymbals, lutes, and lyres to the east of the altar, together with a hundred and twenty priests who blew trumpets. 13 Now the trumpeters and the singers joined in unison to sound forth praise and thanksgiving to the LORD, and the song was raised with trumpets, cymbals, and musical instruments, in praise of the LORD, because 'it is good, for his love endures for ever'; and the house was filled with the cloud of the glory of the LORD. 14 The priests could not continue to minister because of the cloud, for the glory of the LORD filled the house of God. 1 Then Solomon said:

6 'The LORD has caused the sun to shine in the heavens; but he has said he would dwell in thick darkness. 2 I have built you a lofty house, a dwelling-place for you to occupy for ever.'

3 While the whole assembly of Israelites stood, the king turned and blessed them. 4 'Blessed be the LORD the God of Israel who spoke directly to my father David and has himself fulfilled his promise. For he said, 5 "From the day when I brought my people out of Egypt, I chose no city out of all the tribes of Israel where I should build a house for my name to be, nor did I choose any man to be prince over my people Israel. 6 But I chose Jerusalem where my name should be, and David to be over my people Israel."

7 'My father David had it in mind to build a house for the name of the LORD the God of Israel, 8 but the LORD said to him, "You purposed to build a house for my name, and your purpose was good. 9 Nevertheless you are not to build it; but the son who is to be born to you, he is to build the house for my name." 10 The LORD has now fulfilled his promise: I have succeeded my father David and taken his place on the throne of Israel, as the LORD promised; and I have built the house for the name of the LORD the God of Israel. 11 I have installed there the Ark containing the covenant of the LORD, which he made with Israel.'

12 Standing in front of the altar of the LORD in the presence of the whole assembly of Israel, Solomon spread out his hands. 13 He had made a bronze platform, five cubits long, five cubits broad, and three cubits high, and had placed it in the centre of the precinct. He mounted it and knelt down in the presence of the assembly and, spreading out his hands towards heaven, 14 he said, 'LORD God of Israel, there is no God like you in heaven or on earth, keeping covenant with your servants and showing them constant love while they continue faithful to you with all their heart. 15 You have kept your promise to your servant David my father; by your deeds this day you have fulfilled what you said to him in words. 16 Now, therefore, LORD God of Israel, keep this promise of yours to your servant David my father, when you said: "You will never want for a man appointed by me to sit on the throne of Israel, if only your sons look to their ways and conform to my law, as you have walked before me." 17 LORD God of Israel, let the promise which you made to your servant David be now confirmed.

18 'But can God indeed dwell with mortals on earth? Heaven itself, the highest heaven, cannot contain you; how much less this house that I have built! 19 Yet attend, LORD my God, to the prayer and the supplication of your servant; listen to the cry and the prayer which your servant makes before you, 20 that your eyes may ever be on this house day

5:13 **it:** *or* he. **glory:** *so Gk; Heb.* house.   6:1–39 *Cp. 1 Kgs. 8:12–50.*   6:1 **The LORD . . . heavens:** *prob. rdg, cp. 1 Kgs. 8:12.*

[m] Heb *he*

vites who were singers, all who belonged to Asaph, Heman, Jeduthun, and their sons and brothers, clothed in fine linen, with cymbals, harps and lyres, stood east of the altar, and with them a hundred and twenty priests blowing trumpets. 13 When the trumpeters and singers were heard as a single voice praising and giving thanks to the LORD, and when they raised the sound of the trumpets, cymbals and other musical instruments to "give thanks to the LORD, for he is good, for his mercy endures forever," the building of the LORD's temple was filled with a cloud. 14 The priests could not continue to minister because of the cloud, since the LORD's glory filled the house of God.

6 Then Solomon said: "The LORD intends to dwell in the dark cloud. 2 I have truly built you a princely house and dwelling, where you may abide forever." 3 Turning about, the king greeted the whole community of Israel as they stood. 4 He said: "Blessed be the LORD, the God of Israel, who with his own mouth made a promise to my father David and by his own hands brought it to fulfillment. He said: 5 'Since the day I brought my people out of the land of Egypt, I have not chosen any city from among all the tribes of Israel for the building of a temple to my honor, nor have I chosen any man to be commander of my people Israel; 6 but now I choose Jerusalem, where I shall be honored, and I choose David to rule my people Israel.' 7 My father David wished to build a temple to the honor of the LORD, the God of Israel, 8 but the LORD said to him: 'In wishing to build a temple to my honor, you do well. 9 However, you shall not build the temple; rather, your son whom you will beget shall build the temple to my honor.'

10 "Now the LORD has fulfilled the promise that he made. I have succeeded my father David and have taken my seat on the throne of Israel, as the LORD foretold, and I have built the temple to the honor of the LORD, the God of Israel. 11 And I have placed there the ark, in which abides the covenant of the LORD which he made with the Israelites."

12 Solomon then took his place before the altar of the LORD in the presence of the whole community of Israel and stretched forth his hands. 13 He had made a bronze platform five cubits long, five cubits wide, and three cubits high, which he had placed in the middle of the courtyard. Having ascended it, Solomon knelt in the presence of the whole of Israel and stretched forth his hands toward heaven. 14 Thus he prayed: "LORD, God of Israel, there is no god like you in heaven or on earth; you keep your covenant and show kindness to your servants who are wholeheartedly faithful to you. 15 You have kept the promise you made to my father David, your servant. With your own mouth you spoke it, and by your own hand you have brought it to fulfillment this day. 16 Now, therefore, LORD, God of Israel, keep the further promise you made to my father David, your servant, when you said, 'You shall always have someone from your line to sit before me on the throne of Israel, provided only that your descendants look to their conduct so as always to live according to my law, even as you have lived in my presence.' 17 Now, LORD, God of Israel, may this promise which you made to your servant David be confirmed.

18 "Can it indeed be that God dwells with mankind on earth? If the heavens and the highest heavens cannot contain you, how much less this temple which I have built! 19 Look kindly on the prayer and petition of your servant, O LORD, my God, and listen to the cry of supplication your servant makes before you. 20 May your eyes watch day and night

singers, Asaph, Heman and Jeduthun with their sons and brothers, dressed in linen, were standing to the east of the altar with cymbals, lyres and harps and with them one hundred and twenty priests blowing the trumpets, 13 and the harmony between trumpeters and singers was such that only one melody could be heard as they praised and gave thanks to Yahweh — and the singing began, to the accompaniment of trumpets, cymbals and musical instruments, and they praised Yahweh 'for he is good, for his faithful love is everlasting' — then the Temple was filled with the cloud of the glory of Yahweh, 14 and because of the cloud the priests could not stay and perform their duties. For the glory of Yahweh filled the Temple of God.

6 Then Solomon said:

Yahweh has chosen to dwell in thick cloud,
2 and I have built you a princely dwelling,
a residence for you for ever.

3 Then the king turned round and blessed the whole assembly of Israel, while the whole assembly of Israel stood. 4 He said, 'Blessed be Yahweh, God of Israel, who has carried out by his hand what he promised verbally to my father David, when he said, 5 "From the day I brought my people out of Egypt I chose no city, in any of the tribes of Israel, to have a temple built where my name should be, nor did I choose anyone to be prince of my people Israel; 6 but I did choose Jerusalem for my name to be there, and I did choose David to rule my people Israel." 7 My father David had set his heart on building a temple for the name of Yahweh, God of Israel, 8 but Yahweh said to my father David, "You have set your heart on building a temple for my name, and in this you have done well; 9 and yet, you are not the man to build the temple; but your son, yet to be born to you, will be the one to build the temple for my name." 10 Yahweh has kept the promise which he made: I have succeeded my father David and am seated on the throne of Israel, as Yahweh promised; I have built the temple for the name of Yahweh, God of Israel, 11 and I have placed in it the ark containing the covenant of Yahweh, which he made with the Israelites.'

12 Then in the presence of the whole assembly of Israel, he stood facing the altar of Yahweh and stretched out his hands — 13 for Solomon had made a bronze platform, five cubits long, five cubits wide and five cubits high, which he had placed in the middle of the court and on which he was standing; he knelt down in front of the whole assembly of Israel, stretched out his hands to heaven — 14 and said, 'Yahweh, God of Israel, there is no god like you in heaven or on earth, you who are loyal to the covenant and show faithful love to your servants as long as they walk wholeheartedly in your way. 15 You have kept it with your servant, my father David, as you promised him you would. What you promised verbally today you have carried out by your hand. 16 And now, Yahweh, God of Israel, keep the promise which you made to your servant David when you said, "You will never lack for a man to sit in my presence before me on the throne of Israel, provided that your sons are careful how they behave, following my law as you yourself have done." 17 So now, God of Israel, let the words come true which you spoke to your servant, my father David. 18 Yet will God really live with the people on earth? Why, the heavens and the heavens of the heavens cannot contain you! How much less this temple built by me! 19 Even so, listen favourably to the prayer and entreaty of your servant, Yahweh my God; listen to the cry and to the prayer which your servant makes to you: 20 Day and night,

your eyes be open day and night toward this house, the place where you promised to set your name, and may you heed the prayer that your servant prays toward this place. 21 And hear the plea of your servant and of your people Israel, when they pray toward this place; may you hear from heaven your dwelling place; hear and forgive.

22 "If someone sins against another and is required to take an oath and comes and swears before your altar in this house, 23 may you hear from heaven, and act, and judge your servants, repaying the guilty by bringing their conduct on their own head, and vindicating those who are in the right by rewarding them in accordance with their righteousness.

24 "When your people Israel, having sinned against you, are defeated before an enemy but turn again to you, confess your name, pray and plead with you in this house, 25 may you hear from heaven, and forgive the sin of your people Israel, and bring them again to the land that you gave to them and to their ancestors.

26 "When heaven is shut up and there is no rain because they have sinned against you, and then they pray toward this place, confess your name, and turn from their sin, because you punish them, 27 may you hear in heaven, forgive the sin of your servants, your people Israel, when you teach them the good way in which they should walk; and send down rain upon your land, which you have given to your people as an inheritance.

28 "If there is famine in the land, if there is plague, blight, mildew, locust, or caterpillar; if their enemies besiege them in any of the settlements of the lands; whatever suffering, whatever sickness there is; 29 whatever prayer, whatever plea from any individual or from all your people Israel, all knowing their own suffering and their own sorrows so that they stretch out their hands toward this house; 30 may you hear from heaven, your dwelling place, forgive, and render to all whose heart you know, according to all their ways, for only you know the human heart. 31 Thus may they fear you and walk in your ways all the days that they live in the land that you gave to our ancestors.

32 "Likewise when foreigners, who are not of your people Israel, come from a distant land because of your great name, and your mighty hand, and your outstretched arm, when they come and pray toward this house, 33 may you hear from heaven your dwelling place, and do whatever the foreigners ask of you, in order that all the peoples of the earth may know your name and fear you, as do your people Israel, and that they may know that your name has been invoked on this house that I have built.

34 "If your people go out to battle against their enemies, by whatever way you shall send them, and they pray to you toward this city that you have chosen and the house that I have built for your name, 35 then hear from heaven their prayer and their plea, and maintain their cause.

36 "If they sin against you—for there is no one who does not sin—and you are angry with them and give them to an enemy, so that they are carried away captive to a land far or near; 37 then if they come to their senses in the land to which they have been taken captive, and repent, and plead with you in the land of their captivity, saying, 'We have sinned, and have done wrong; we have acted wickedly'; 38 if they repent with all their heart and soul in the land of their captivity, to which they were taken captive, and pray toward their land, which you gave to their ancestors, the city that you have chosen, and the house that I have built for your name, 39 then hear from heaven your dwelling place their prayer and their pleas, maintain their cause and forgive your people who have sinned against you. 40 Now,

and night, this place where you said you would set your name. Hear your servant when he prays towards this place. 21 Hear the supplications of your servant and of your people Israel when they pray towards this place. Hear from heaven your dwelling and, when you hear, forgive.

22 'Should anyone wrong a neighbour and be adjured to take an oath, and come to take the oath before your altar in this house, 23 then hear from heaven and take action: be your servants' judge, requiting the guilty person and bringing his deeds on his own head, acquitting the innocent and rewarding him as his innocence may deserve.

24 'Should your people Israel be defeated by an enemy because they have sinned against you, and then turn back to you, confessing your name and making their prayer and supplication before you in this house, 25 hear from heaven; forgive the sin of your people Israel and restore them to the land which you gave to them and to their forefathers.

26 'Should the heavens be shut up and there be no rain, because your servant and your people Israel have sinned against you, and they then pray towards this place, confessing your name and forsaking their sin when they feel your punishment, 27 hear in heaven and forgive their sin; so teach them the good way which they are to follow, and grant rain on your land which you have given to your people as their own possession.

28 'Should there be famine in the land, or pestilence, or black blight or red, or locusts developing or fully grown, or should their enemies besiege them in any of their cities, or plague or sickness befall them, 29 then hear the prayer or supplication of everyone among your people Israel, as each, prompted by his own suffering and misery, spreads out his hands towards this house; 30 hear it from heaven your dwelling-place and forgive. As you know a person's heart, reward him according to his deeds, for you alone know the hearts of all; 31 and so they will fear and obey you throughout their lives in the land you gave to our forefathers.

32 'The foreigner too, anyone who does not belong to your people Israel, but has come from a distant land because of your great fame and your strong hand and out-stretched arm, when such a one comes and prays towards this house, 33 hear from heaven your dwelling-place and respond to the call which the foreigner makes to you, so that like your people Israel all the peoples of the earth may know your fame and fear you, and learn that this house which I have built bears your name.

34 'When your people go to war against their enemies, wherever you send them, and when they pray to you, turning towards this city which you have chosen and towards this house which I have built for your name, 35 then hear from heaven their prayer and supplication, and maintain their cause.

36 'Should they sin against you (and who is free from sin?) and should you in your anger give them over to an enemy who carries them captive to a land far or near; 37 and should they then in the land of their captivity have a change of heart and turn back and make supplication to you there and say, "We have sinned and acted perversely and wickedly," 38 and turn back to you wholeheartedly in the land of their captivity to which they have been taken, and pray, turning towards their land which you gave to their forefathers and towards this city which you chose and this house which I have built for your name; 39 then from heaven your dwelling-place hear their prayer and supplications and maintain their cause. Forgive your people their sins against

6:26 **servant:** *so Syriac; Heb*. servants.   6:27 **in:** *or, with Gk,* from.   6:28 **in any:** *prob. rdg; Heb.* in the land.

over this temple, the place where you have decreed you shall be honored; may you heed the prayer which I your servant offer toward this place. 21 Listen to the petitions of your servant and of your people Israel which they direct toward this place. Listen from your heavenly dwelling, and when you have heard, pardon.

22 "When any man sins against his neighbor and is required to take an oath of execration against himself, and when he comes for the oath before your altar in this temple, 23 listen from heaven: take action and pass judgment on your servants, requiting the wicked man and holding him responsible for his conduct, but absolving the innocent and rewarding him according to his virtue. 24 When your people Israel have sinned against you and are defeated by the enemy, but afterward they return and praise your name, and they pray to you and entreat you in this temple, 25 listen from heaven and forgive the sin of your people Israel, and bring them back to the land which you gave them and their fathers. 26 When the sky is closed so that there is no rain, because they have sinned against you, but then they pray toward this place and praise your name, and they withdraw from sin because you afflict them, 27 listen in heaven and forgive the sin of your servants and of your people Israel. But teach them the right way to live, and send rain upon your land which you gave your people as their heritage. 28 When there is famine in the land, when there is pestilence, or blight, or mildew, or locusts, or caterpillars; when their enemies besiege them at any of their gates; whenever there is a plague or sickness of any kind; 29 when any Israelite of all your people offers a prayer or petition of any kind, and in awareness of his affliction and pain, stretches out his hands toward this temple, 30 listen from your heavenly dwelling place, and forgive. Knowing his heart, render to everyone according to his conduct, for you alone know the hearts of men. 31 So may they fear you and walk in your ways as long as they live on the land you gave our fathers.

32 "For the foreigner, too, who is not of your people Israel, when he comes from a distant land to honor your great name, your mighty power, and your outstretched arm, when they come in prayer to this temple, 33 listen from your heavenly dwelling place, and do whatever the foreigner entreats you, that all the peoples of the earth may know your name, fearing you as do your people Israel, and knowing that this house which I have built is dedicated to your honor.

34 "When your people go forth to war against their enemies, wherever you send them, and pray to you in the direction of this city and of the house I have built to your honor, 35 listen from heaven to their prayer and petition, and defend their cause. 36 When they sin against you (for there is no man who does not sin), and in your anger against them you deliver them to the enemy, so that their captors deport them to another land, far or near, 37 when they repent in the land where they are captive and are converted, when they entreat you in the land of their captivity and say, 'We have sinned and done wrong; we have been wicked,' 38 and with their whole heart and with their whole soul they turn back to you in the land of those who hold them captive, when they pray in the direction of their land which you gave their fathers, and of the city you have chosen, and of the house which I have built to your honor, 39 listen from your heavenly dwelling place, hear their prayer and petitions, and uphold their cause. Forgive your people who have sinned

may your eyes watch over this temple, over this place in which you have promised to put your name. Listen to the prayer which your servant offers in this place.

21 'Listen to the entreaties of your servant and of your people Israel; whenever they pray in this place, listen from the place where you reside in heaven; and when you hear, forgive.

22 'If someone has wronged his neighbour and a curse is laid on him to make him swear here before your altar in this Temple, 23 then listen from heaven and do justice between your servants, paying back the guilty one by making him suffer for his conduct, and acquitting the upright by rewarding him as his uprightness deserves.

24 'If your people Israel are defeated by the enemy because they have sinned against you, but then return to you and acknowledge your name, and pray and seek your favour in this temple, 25 then listen from heaven; forgive the sin of your people Israel, and bring them back to the country which you gave to them and their ancestors.

26 'When the heavens are shut and there is no rain because they have sinned against you, if they pray in this place and praise your name and, having been humbled by you, desist from their sin, 27 then listen from heaven and forgive the sin of your servant and of your people Israel — for you are constantly showing them the good way which they must follow — and send rain on your country, which you have given to your people as their heritage.

28 'Should there be famine in the country, or pestilence, wind-blast or mildew, locust or caterpillar; should their enemy lay siege to their territory; should there be any plague or any disease; 29 whatever be the prayer or entreaty of any individual, or of all your people Israel, each being aware of his own affliction and pain; when he stretches out his hands towards this Temple, 30 then listen from heaven where you reside; forgive, and, since you know what is in his heart, deal with each as his conduct deserves — for you alone know what is in the human heart — 31 so that they may revere you by following your directions, which you gave to our ancestors, throughout their lives on earth.

32 'Even the foreigner, not belonging to your people Israel but coming from a distant country, attracted by your great name, your mighty hand and outstretched arm, if he comes and prays in this Temple, 33 then listen from heaven where you reside, and grant all that the foreigner asks of you, so that all the peoples of the earth may acknowledge your name, and, like your people Israel, revere you, and know that this Temple, which I have built, bears your name.

34 'If your people go out to war against their enemies, on whatever mission you send them, and they pray to you, turning towards this city which you have chosen and towards the Temple which I have built for your name, 35 then listen from heaven to their prayer and their entreaty, and uphold their cause.

36 'When they sin against you — for there is no one who does not sin — and you are angry with them and abandon them to the enemy, and their captors carry them off to a country be it far away or near, 37 if they come to their senses in the country to which they have been taken as captives and pray to you once again in the country of their captivity, saying, "We have sinned, we have acted wrongly and wickedly," 38 and turn back to you with all their heart and soul in the country of their captivity to which they have been carried away as captives, and pray, turning towards the country which you gave to their ancestors, towards the city you have chosen, and towards the Temple which I have built for your name, 39 then listen from heaven where you reside, hear their prayer and entreaties, uphold their cause and forgive your people for having sinned against you.

O my God, let your eyes be open and your ears attentive to prayer from this place.

41 "Now rise up, O LORD God, and go to your
    resting place,
    you and the ark of your might.
Let your priests, O LORD God, be clothed with
    salvation,
    and let your faithful rejoice in your goodness.
42 O LORD God, do not reject your anointed one.
    Remember your steadfast love for your servant
    David."

7 When Solomon had ended his prayer, fire came down from heaven and consumed the burnt offering and the sacrifices; and the glory of the LORD filled the temple. 2 The priests could not enter the house of the LORD, because the glory of the LORD filled the LORD's house. 3 When all the people of Israel saw the fire come down and the glory of the LORD on the temple, they bowed down on the pavement with their faces to the ground, and worshiped and gave thanks to the LORD, saying,
    "For he is good,
        for his steadfast love endures forever."
4 Then the king and all the people offered sacrifice before the LORD. 5 King Solomon offered as a sacrifice twenty-two thousand oxen and one hundred twenty thousand sheep. So the king and all the people dedicated the house of God. 6 The priests stood at their posts; the Levites also, with the instruments for music to the LORD that King David had made for giving thanks to the LORD — for his steadfast love endures forever — whenever David offered praises by their ministry. Opposite them the priests sounded trumpets; and all Israel stood.
7 Solomon consecrated the middle of the court that was in front of the house of the LORD; for there he offered the burnt offerings and the fat of the offerings of well-being because the bronze altar Solomon had made could not hold the burnt offering and the grain offering and the fat parts.
8 At that time Solomon held the festival for seven days, and all Israel with him, a very great congregation, from Lebo-hamath to the Wadi of Egypt. 9 On the eighth day they held a solemn assembly; for they had observed the dedication of the altar seven days and the festival seven days. 10 On the twenty-third day of the seventh month he sent the people away to their homes, joyful and in good spirits because of the goodness that the LORD had shown to David and to Solomon and to his people Israel.
11 Thus Solomon finished the house of the LORD and the king's house; all that Solomon had planned to do in the house of the LORD and in his own house he successfully accomplished.
12 Then the LORD appeared to Solomon in the night and said to him: "I have heard your prayer, and have chosen this place for myself as a house of sacrifice. 13 When I shut up the heavens so that there is no rain, or command the locust to devour the land, or send pestilence among my people, 14 if my people who are called by my name humble themselves, pray, seek my face, and turn from their wicked ways, then I will hear from heaven, and will forgive their sin and heal their land. 15 Now my eyes will be open and my ears attentive to the prayer that is made in this place. 16 For now I have chosen and consecrated this house so that my name may be there forever; my eyes and my heart will be there for all time. 17 As for you, if you walk before me, as your father David walked, doing according to all that I have commanded you and keeping my statutes and my ordinances, 18 then I will establish your royal throne, as I made

you. 40 Now, my God, let your eyes be open and your ears attentive to the prayer made in this place.

41 'Arise now, LORD God, and come to your
    resting-place,
    you and your powerful Ark.
Let your priests, LORD God, be clothed with
    salvation
    and your loyal servants rejoice in prosperity.
42 LORD God, do not reject your anointed one;
    remember the loyal service of David your servant.'

7 As Solomon finished this prayer, fire came down from heaven and consumed the whole-offering and the sacrifices, while the glory of the LORD filled the house. 2 The priests were unable to enter the house of the LORD because the glory of the LORD had filled it. 3 All the Israelites witnessed the fire coming down with the glory of the LORD on the house, and where they were on the paved court they bowed low to the ground and worshipped and gave thanks to the LORD, because 'it is good, for his love endures for ever'.
4 The king and all the people offered sacrifice before the LORD; 5 King Solomon offered a sacrifice of twenty-two thousand oxen and a hundred and twenty thousand sheep. Thus the king and all the people dedicated the house of God. 6 The priests stood at their appointed posts; so too the Levites with their musical instruments for the LORD's service, which King David had made for giving thanks to the LORD — 'for his love endures for ever' — whenever he rendered praise with their help; opposite them, the priests sounded their trumpets, while all the Israelites were standing. 7 Then Solomon consecrated the centre of the court which lay in front of the house of the LORD; there he offered the whole-offerings and the fat portions of the shared-offerings, because the bronze altar which he had made could not accommodate the whole-offering, the grain-offering, and the fat portions.
8 So Solomon and with him all Israel, a very great assembly from Lebo-hamath to the wadi of Egypt, celebrated the pilgrim-feast at that time for seven days. 9 On the eighth day they held a closing ceremony; for they had celebrated the dedication of the altar for seven days, and the pilgrim-feast lasted seven days. 10 On the twenty-third day of the seventh month he dismissed the people to their homes, happy and glad at heart for all the prosperity granted by the LORD to David, to Solomon, and to his people Israel.
11 When Solomon had completed the house of the LORD and the palace and had carried out successfully all that he had planned for the house of the LORD and the palace, 12 the LORD appeared to him by night and said: 'I have heard your prayer and I have chosen this place to be my house of sacrifice. 13 When I shut up the heavens and there is no rain, or command the locusts to consume the land, or send a pestilence on my people, 14 and then my people whom I have named my own submit and pray to me and seek me and turn back from their evil ways, I shall hear from heaven and forgive their sins and restore their land. 15 Now my eyes will be open and my ears attentive to the prayers which are made in this place. 16 I have chosen and consecrated this house, so that my name may be there for all time and my eyes and my heart may be fixed on it for ever. 17 If you, for your part, live in my sight as your father David lived, doing all I command you, and observing my statutes and my judgements, 18 then I shall establish the throne of your king-

NEW AMERICAN BIBLE

NEW JERUSALEM BIBLE

against you. 40 My God, may your eyes be open and your ears attentive to the prayer of this place. 41 And now,
"Advance, LORD God, to your resting place,
you and the ark of your majesty.
May your priests, LORD God, be clothed
with salvation,
may your faithful ones rejoice in good things.
42 LORD God, reject not the plea of your anointed,
remember the devotion of David, your servant."

40 'Now, O my God, may your eyes be open and your ears attentive to prayer offered in this place. 41 And now Yahweh God, go up to your resting-place,
you and your fortress, the Ark!
Let your priests, Yahweh God, be robed in
salvation,
let your faithful rejoice in what is good!
42 Yahweh God, do not rebuff your Anointed —
remember the faithful love of your servant David!'

7 When Solomon had ended his prayer, fire came down from heaven and consumed the holocaust and the sacrifices, and the glory of the LORD filled the house. 2 But the priests could not enter the house of the LORD, for the glory of the LORD had filled the house of the LORD. 3 All the Israelites looked on while the fire came down and the glory of the LORD was upon the house, and they fell down upon the pavement with their faces to the earth and adored, praising the LORD, "for he is good, for his mercy endures forever." 4 The king and all the people were offering sacrifices before the LORD. 5 King Solomon offered as sacrifice twenty-two thousand oxen, and one hundred twenty thousand sheep.

6 Thus the king and all the people dedicated the house of God. The priests were standing at their stations, as were the Levites, with the musical instruments of the LORD which King David had made for "praising the LORD, for his mercy endures forever," when David used them to accompany the hymns. Across from them the priests blew the trumpets and all Israel stood.

7 Then Solomon consecrated the middle part of the court which lay before the house of the LORD; there he offered the holocausts and the fat of the peace offerings, since the bronze altar which Solomon had made could not hold the holocausts, the cereal offerings and the fat.

8 On this occasion Solomon and with him all Israel, who had assembled in very large numbers from Labo of Hamath to the Wadi of Egypt, celebrated the festival for seven days. 9 On the eighth day they held a special meeting, for they had celebrated the dedication of the altar for seven days and the feast for seven days. 10 On the twenty-third day of the seventh month he sent the people back to their tents, rejoicing and glad at heart at the good things the LORD had done for David, for Solomon, and for his people Israel. 11 Solomon completed the house of the LORD and the royal palace; he successfully accomplished everything he had planned to do in regard to the house of the LORD and his own house.

12 The LORD appeared to Solomon during the night and said to him: "I have heard your prayer, and I have chosen this place for my house of sacrifice. 13 If I close heaven so that there is no rain, if I command the locust to devour the land, if I send pestilence among my people, 14 and if my people, upon whom my name has been pronounced, humble themselves and pray, and seek my presence and turn from their evil ways, I will hear them from heaven and pardon their sins and revive their land. 15 Now my eyes shall be open and my ears attentive to the prayer of this place. 16 And now I have chosen and consecrated this house that my name may be there forever; my eyes and my heart also shall be there always.

17 "As for you, if you live in my presence as your father David did, doing all that I have commanded you and keeping my statutes and ordinances, 18 I will establish your royal

7 When Solomon had finished his prayer, fire came down from heaven and consumed the burnt offering and the sacrifices; and the glory of Yahweh filled the Temple. 2 The priests could not enter the Temple of Yahweh, because the glory of Yahweh filled the Temple of Yahweh. 3 When all the Israelites saw the fire come down and the glory of Yahweh resting on the Temple, they bowed down on the pavement with their faces to the earth, worshipping and praising Yahweh with 'For he is good, for his faithful love lasts for ever!'

4 Then the king and all the people offered sacrifices before Yahweh. 5 King Solomon offered a sacrifice of twenty-two thousand oxen and a hundred and twenty thousand sheep; and thus the king and all the people dedicated the Temple of God. 6 The priests stood in their places, as did the Levites with Yahweh's musical instruments which King David had provided, to render 'Give thanks to Yahweh, for his faithful love lasts for ever!' whenever David offered praise to their accompaniment. Opposite them, the priests blew trumpets, while all Israel stood.

7 Solomon also consecrated the middle part of the court in front of the Temple of Yahweh; for that was where he presented the burnt offerings and the fatty parts of the communion sacrifices, since the bronze altar which Solomon had made could not hold the burnt offering, the oblation and the fatty parts. 8 And then Solomon and with him all Israel from the Pass of Hamath to the Torrent of Egypt — a very great assembly — celebrated the feast for seven days. 9 On the eighth day they held the assembly, for they had devoted seven days to the dedication of the altar and seven days to the feast. 10 On the twenty-third day of the seventh month Solomon dismissed the people to their homes, rejoicing and happy of heart over the goodness which Yahweh had shown to David, to Solomon and to his people Israel.

11 Thus Solomon finished the Temple of Yahweh and the royal palace, and he successfully concluded everything that he was of a mind to do in the Temple of Yahweh and in his own palace. 12 Then Yahweh appeared to Solomon in the night and said, 'I have heard your prayer and have chosen this place for myself as a house of sacrifice. 13 If I shut the heavens so that there is no rain, or if I command the locusts to devour the country, or if I send pestilence among my people, 14 if my people who bear my name humble themselves, and pray and seek my presence and turn from their wicked ways, then I will listen from heaven and forgive their sins and restore their country. 15 Now and for the future my eyes are open and my ears attentive to prayer offered in this place, 16 for now I have chosen and consecrated this Temple, for my name to be there for ever; my eyes and my heart will constantly be there. 17 And if, for your part, you walk before me as your father David did, and do everything that I have commanded you to do, and keep my laws and my ordinances, 18 I shall make your royal throne secure,

covenant with your father David saying, 'You shall never lack a successor to rule over Israel.'

19 "But if you[n] turn aside and forsake my statutes and my commandments that I have set before you, and go and serve other gods and worship them, 20 then I will pluck you[o] up from the land that I have given you;[o] and this house, which I have consecrated for my name, I will cast out of my sight, and will make it a proverb and a byword among all peoples. 21 And regarding this house, now exalted, everyone passing by will be astonished, and say, 'Why has the LORD done such a thing to this land and to this house?' 22 Then they will say, 'Because they abandoned the LORD the God of their ancestors who brought them out of the land of Egypt, and they adopted other gods, and worshiped them and served them; therefore he has brought all this calamity upon them.' "

8 At the end of twenty years, during which Solomon had built the house of the LORD and his own house, 2 Solomon rebuilt the cities that Huram had given to him, and settled the people of Israel in them.

3 Solomon went to Hamath-zobah, and captured it. 4 He built Tadmor in the wilderness and all the storage towns that he built in Hamath. 5 He also built Upper Beth-horon and Lower Beth-horon, fortified cities, with walls, gates, and bars, 6 and Baalath, as well as all Solomon's storage towns, and all the towns for his chariots, the towns for his cavalry, and whatever Solomon desired to build, in Jerusalem, in Lebanon, and in all the land of his dominion. 7 All the people who were left of the Hittites, the Amorites, the Perizzites, the Hivites, and the Jebusites, who were not of Israel, 8 from their descendants who were still left in the land, whom the people of Israel had not destroyed — these Solomon conscripted for forced labor, as is still the case today. 9 But of the people of Israel Solomon made no slaves for his work; they were soldiers, and his officers, the commanders of his chariotry and cavalry. 10 These were the chief officers of King Solomon, two hundred fifty of them, who exercised authority over the people.

11 Solomon brought Pharaoh's daughter from the city of David to the house that he had built for her, for he said, "My wife shall not live in the house of King David of Israel, for the places to which the ark of the LORD has come are holy."

12 Then Solomon offered up burnt offerings to the LORD on the altar of the LORD that he had built in front of the vestibule, 13 as the duty of each day required, offering according to the commandment of Moses for the sabbaths, the new moons, and the three annual festivals — the festival of unleavened bread, the festival of weeks, and the festival of booths. 14 According to the ordinance of his father David, he appointed the divisions of the priests for their service, and the Levites for their offices of praise and ministry alongside the priests as the duty of each day required, and the gatekeepers in their divisions for the several gates; for so David the man of God had commanded. 15 They did not turn away from what the king had commanded the priests and Levites regarding anything at all, or regarding the treasuries.

16 Thus all the work of Solomon was accomplished from[p] the day the foundation of the house of the LORD was laid until the house of the LORD was finished completely.

17 Then Solomon went to Ezion-geber and Eloth on the shore of the sea, in the land of Edom. 18 Huram sent him,

dom, as I promised by a covenant granted to your father David when I said, "You will never want for a man to rule Israel." 19 But if you turn away and forsake my statutes and my commandments which I have set before you, and if you go and serve other gods and bow down before them, 20 then I shall uproot you from my land which I gave you; I shall reject this house which I have consecrated to my name, and make it a byword and an object-lesson among all peoples. 21 This house will become a ruin; every passer-by will be appalled at the sight of it, and they will ask, "Why has the LORD so treated this land and this house?" 22 The answer will be, "Because they forsook the LORD the God of their forefathers, who brought them out of Egypt, and they clung to other gods, bowing down before them and serving them; that is why the LORD has brought all this misfortune on them." '

8 At the end of the twenty years Solomon had taken to build the house of the LORD and his own palace, 2 he rebuilt the towns which Huram had given him and he settled Israelites in them. 3 He went to Hamath-zobah and seized it. 4 He strengthened Tadmor in the wilderness and all the store-cities which he had built in Hamath. 5 He also built Upper Beth-horon and Lower Beth-horon as fortified cities with walls and barred gates, 6 and Baalath, as well as all his store-cities, and all the towns where he quartered his chariots and horses. He carried out all his cherished plans for building in Jerusalem, in the Lebanon, and throughout his whole dominion. 7 All the survivors of the Hittites, Amorites, Perizzites, Hivites, and Jebusites, who did not belong to Israel — 8 that is those of their descendants who survived in the land, wherever the Israelites had been unable to exterminate them — all were employed by Solomon on forced labour, as they still are. 9 None of the Israelites were put to forced labour for his public works; they were his fighting men, his captains and lieutenants, and the commanders of his chariots and of his cavalry. 10 These were King Solomon's officers, two hundred and fifty of them, in charge of the foremen who superintended the people.

11 Solomon brought Pharaoh's daughter up from the City of David to the house he had built for her, for he said, 'No wife of mine shall live in the house of King David of Israel, because this place which the Ark of the LORD has entered is holy.'

12 Then Solomon offered whole-offerings to the LORD on the altar which he had built to the east of the vestibule, 13 according to what was required for each day, making offerings according to the law of Moses for the sabbaths, the new moons, and the three annual appointed feasts — the pilgrim-feasts of Unleavened Bread, of Weeks, and of Booths. 14 Following the practice of his father David, he drew up the roster of service for the priests and that for the Levites for leading the praise and for waiting upon the priests, as each day required, and that for the door-keepers at each gate; for such was the instruction which David the man of God had given. 15 The instructions which David had given concerning the priests and the Levites and concerning the treasuries were never disregarded.

16 By this time all Solomon's work was achieved, from the foundation of the house of the LORD to its completion; the house of the LORD was completed. 17 Then Solomon went to Ezion-geber and to Eloth on the coast of Edom, 18 and Huram sent ships under the command of his own

---

7:20 **you:** *so Gk; Heb.* them. 7:21 **will become a ruin:** *so Syriac; Heb.* which was high. 8:1–18 *Cp. 1 Kgs. 9:10–28.* 8:6 **horses:** *or* cavalry. 8:9 **his captains and lieutenants:** *so Gk; Heb.* the captains of his lieutenants. 8:11 **this place which . . . is:** *prob. rdg; Heb.* those which . . . are. 8:13 **Booths:** *or* Tabernacles.

---

[n] The word *you* in this verse is plural [o] Heb *them* [p] Gk Syr Vg: Heb *to*

throne as I covenanted with your father David when I said, 'There shall never be lacking someone of yours as ruler in Israel.' 19 But if you turn away and forsake my statutes and commands which I placed before you, if you proceed to venerate and worship strange gods, 20 then I will uproot the people from the land I gave them; I will cast from my sight this house which I have consecrated to my honor, and I will make it a proverb and a byword among all peoples. 21 This temple which is so exalted — everyone passing by it will be amazed and ask: 'Why has the LORD done this to this land and to this house?' 22 And men will answer: 'They forsook the LORD, the God of their fathers, who brought them out of the land of Egypt, and they adopted strange gods and worshiped them and served them. That is why he has brought down upon them all this evil.' "

8 After the twenty years during which Solomon built the house of the LORD and his own house, 2 he built up the cities which Huram had given him, and settled Israelites there. 3 Then Solomon went to Hamath of Zoba and conquered it. 4 He built Tadmor in the desert region and all the supply cities, which he built in Hamath. 5 He built Upper Beth-horon and Lower Beth-horon, fortified cities with walls, gates and bars; 6 also Baalath, all the supply cities belonging to Solomon, and all the cities for the chariots, the cities for the horsemen, and whatever else Solomon decided should be built in Jerusalem, in the Lebanon, and in the entire land under his dominion. 7 All the people that remained of the Hittites, Amorites, Perizzites, Hivites, and Jebusites, who were not of Israel — 8 that is, their descendants remaining in the land, whom the Israelites had not destroyed — Solomon subjected to forced labor, as they continue to this day. 9 But Solomon did not enslave the Israelites for his works. They became soldiers, commanders of his warriors, and commanders of his chariots and his horsemen. 10 They were also King Solomon's two hundred and fifty overseers who had charge of the people.

11 Solomon brought the daughter of Pharaoh up from the City of David to the palace which he had built for her, for he said, "No wife of mine shall dwell in the house of David, king of Israel, for the places where the ark of the LORD has come are holy."

12 In those times Solomon offered holocausts to the LORD upon the altar of the LORD which he had built in front of the porch, 13 as was required day by day according to the command of Moses, and in particular on the sabbaths, at the new moons, and on the fixed festivals three times a year: on the feast of the Unleavened Bread, the feast of Weeks and the feast of Booths.

14 And according to the ordinance of his father David he appointed the various classes of the priests for their service, and the Levites according to their functions of praise and ministry alongside the priests, as the daily duty required. The gatekeepers of the various classes stood guard at each gate, since such was the command of David, the man of God. 15 There was no deviation from the king's command in any respect relating to the priests and Levites or the treasuries. 16 All of Solomon's work was carried out successfully from the day the foundation of the house of the LORD was laid until the house of the LORD had been completed in every detail.

17 In those times Solomon went to Ezion-geber and to Elath on the seashore of the land of Edom. 18 Huram,

as I covenanted with your father David when I said: You will never lack for a male to rule in Israel. 19 But if you turn away and forsake my laws and commandments which I have laid down for you, and go and serve other gods and worship them, 20 then I shall uproot them from the country which I have given them, and shall disown this Temple which I have consecrated for my name and make it a proverb and a byword among all the peoples. 21 And at this once-exalted Temple, everyone who passes by will be appalled, and will say, "Why has Yahweh treated this country and this Temple like this?" 22 And the answer will be, "Because they deserted Yahweh, the God of their ancestors, who brought them out of Egypt, and adopted other gods and worshipped and served them; that is why he has brought all these disasters on them." '

8 At the end of the twenty years which it took Solomon to build the Temple of Yahweh and his own palace, 2 and to rebuild the towns which Huram had given him and settle them with Israelites, 3 Solomon mounted an expedition against Hamath-Zobah and captured it. 4 He also fortified Tadmor in the desert and all the storage towns which he had built in Hamath. 5 He also built Upper Beth-Horon and Lower Beth-Horon as fortified towns with walls and gates and bars, 6 also Baalath and all Solomon's storage towns, all the towns for his chariots and horses, and everything which Solomon was pleased to build in Jerusalem, in the Lebanon and throughout the territory under his rule. 7 All those who survived of the Hittite, Amorite, Perizzite, Hivite and Jebusite peoples, who did not belong to Israel — 8 those of their descendants still remaining in the country, whom the Israelites had not exterminated, these Solomon levied for forced labour, as is still the case today. 9 Solomon did not, however, impose forced labour on the Israelites for his work — for they were soldiers, his senior officers and his chariot and cavalry commanders. 10 There were two hundred and fifty of King Solomon's officials in charge of the foremen who supervised the people.

11 Solomon moved Pharaoh's daughter up from the City of David to the palace which he had built for her. 'I must not be responsible', he said, 'for a woman living in the palace of David king of Israel, for these buildings to which the ark of Yahweh has come are sacred.'

12 Thereafter, Solomon made burnt offerings to Yahweh on the altar of Yahweh which he had built in front of the portico, 13 in accordance with the regular prescriptions for burnt sacrifice as commanded by Moses, on the Sabbaths, New Moons and the three annual feasts; the feast of Unleavened Bread, the feast of Weeks and the feast of Shelters. 14 Following the prescriptions of his father David, he assigned the orders of priests to their duties and the Levites to their tasks of praise and of assisting the priests in accordance with day-to-day requirements; as also the gatekeepers in their various orders to each gate — for such was the command of David, man of God. 15 Nor was there deviation on any point from the king's command as regards the priests, the Levites or even the storehouses.

16 Thus, all the work was over which Solomon had put in hand when the Temple of Yahweh was founded until it was finished. The Temple of Yahweh was complete in every detail.

17 Solomon then mounted an expedition to Ezion-Geber and Elath on the sea-coast of Edom. 18 Huram sent him

NEW REVISED STANDARD VERSION

in the care of his servants, ships and servants familiar with the sea. They went to Ophir, together with the servants of Solomon, and imported from there four hundred fifty talents of gold and brought it to King Solomon.

9 When the queen of Sheba heard of the fame of Solomon, she came to Jerusalem to test him with hard questions, having a very great retinue and camels bearing spices and very much gold and precious stones. When she came to Solomon, she discussed with him all that was on her mind. 2 Solomon answered all her questions; there was nothing hidden from Solomon that he could not explain to her. 3 When the queen of Sheba had observed the wisdom of Solomon, the house that he had built, 4 the food of his table, the seating of his officials, and the attendance of his servants, and their clothing, his valets, and their clothing, and his burnt offerings*q* that he offered at the house of the LORD, there was no more spirit left in her.

5 So she said to the king, "The report was true that I heard in my own land of your accomplishments and of your wisdom, 6 but I did not believe the*r* reports until I came and my own eyes saw it. Not even half of the greatness of your wisdom had been told to me; you far surpass the report that I had heard. 7 Happy are your people! Happy are these your servants, who continually attend you and hear your wisdom! 8 Blessed be the LORD your God, who has delighted in you and set you on his throne as king for the LORD your God. Because your God loved Israel and would establish them forever, he has made you king over them, that you may execute justice and righteousness." 9 Then she gave the king one hundred twenty talents of gold, a very great quantity of spices, and precious stones: there were no spices such as those that the queen of Sheba gave to King Solomon.

10 Moreover the servants of Huram and the servants of Solomon who brought gold from Ophir brought algum wood and precious stones. 11 From the algum wood, the king made steps*s* for the house of the LORD and for the king's house, lyres also and harps for the singers; there never was seen the like of them before in the land of Judah.

12 Meanwhile King Solomon granted the queen of Sheba every desire that she expressed, well beyond what she had brought to the king. Then she returned to her own land, with her servants.

13 The weight of gold that came to Solomon in one year was six hundred sixty-six talents of gold, 14 besides that which the traders and merchants brought; and all the kings of Arabia and the governors of the land brought gold and silver to Solomon. 15 King Solomon made two hundred large shields of beaten gold; six hundred shekels of beaten gold went into each large shield. 16 He made three hundred shields of beaten gold; three hundred shekels of gold went into each shield; and the king put them in the House of the Forest of Lebanon. 17 The king also made a great ivory throne, and overlaid it with pure gold. 18 The throne had six steps and a footstool of gold, which were attached to the throne, and on each side of the seat were arm rests and two lions standing beside the arm rests, 19 while twelve lions were standing, one on each end of a step on the six steps. The like of it was never made in any kingdom. 20 All King

REVISED ENGLISH BIBLE

officers and manned by crews of experienced seamen; and these, in company with Solomon's servants, went to Ophir and brought back four hundred and fifty talents of gold, which they delivered to King Solomon.

9 THE queen of Sheba heard of Solomon's fame and came to test him with enigmatic questions. She arrived in Jerusalem with a very large retinue, camels laden with spices, much gold, and precious stones. When she came to Solomon, she talked to him about everything she had on her mind. 2 Solomon answered all her questions; not one of them was too hard for him to answer. 3 When the queen of Sheba observed the wisdom of Solomon, the palace he had built, 4 the food on his table, the courtiers sitting around him, his attendants and his cupbearers in their livery standing behind, and the stairs by which he went up to the house of the LORD, she was overcome with amazement. 5 She said to the king, 'The account which I heard in my own country about your achievements and your wisdom was true, 6 but I did not believe what they told me until I came and saw for myself. Indeed, I was not told half of the greatness of your wisdom; you surpass all I had heard of you. 7 Happy are your wives, happy these courtiers of yours who are in attendance on you every day and hear your wisdom! 8 Blessed be the LORD your God who has delighted in you and has set you on his throne as his king; because in his love your God has elected Israel to make it endure for ever, he has made you king over it to maintain law and justice.' 9 She presented the king with a hundred and twenty talents of gold, spices in great abundance, and precious stones. There had never been any spices to equal those which the queen of Sheba gave to King Solomon.

10 Besides all this, the servants of Huram and of Solomon, who had brought gold from Ophir, brought also cargoes of algum-wood and precious stones. 11 The king used the wood to make stands for the house of the LORD and for the palace, as well as lyres and lutes for the singers. The like of them had never before been seen in the land of Judah.

12 King Solomon gave the queen of Sheba whatever she desired and asked for, in addition to his gifts in return for what she had brought him. Then she departed with her retinue and went back to her own land.

13 The weight of gold which Solomon received in any one year was six hundred and sixty-six talents, 14 in addition to the tolls levied on merchants and on traders who imported goods; all the kings of Arabia and the regional governors also brought gold and silver to the king.

15 King Solomon made two hundred large shields of beaten gold, and six hundred shekels of gold went to the making of each one; 16 he also made three hundred bucklers of beaten gold, and three hundred shekels of gold went to the making of each buckler. The king put these into the House of the Forest of Lebanon.

17 The king also made a great throne inlaid with ivory and overlaid with pure gold. 18 Six steps and a footstool for the throne were all encased in gold. There were armrests on each side of the seat, with a lion standing beside each of them, 19 while twelve lions stood on the six steps, one at either end of each step. Nothing like it had ever been made for any monarch. 20 All Solomon's drinking vessels were of

q Gk Syr Vg 1 Kings 10.5: Heb *ascent*   *r* Heb *their*   *s* Gk Vg: Meaning of Heb uncertain

through his servants, sent him ships and crewmen acquainted with the sea, who accompanied Solomon's servants to Ophir and brought back from there four hundred and fifty talents of gold to King Solomon.

9 When the queen of Sheba heard of Solomon's fame, she came to Jerusalem to test him with subtle questions, accompanied by a very numerous retinue and by camels bearing spices, much gold, and precious stones. She came to Solomon and questioned him on every subject in which she was interested. 2 Solomon explained to her everything she asked about, and there remained nothing hidden from Solomon that he could not explain to her.

3 When the queen of Sheba witnessed Solomon's wisdom, the palace he had built, 4 the food at his table, the seating of his ministers, the attendance of his servants and their dress, his cupbearers and their dress, and the holocausts he offered in the house of the LORD, it took her breath away. 5 "The account I heard in my country about your deeds and your wisdom is true," she told the king. 6 "Yet I did not believe the report until I came and saw with my own eyes. I have discovered that they did not tell me the half of your great wisdom; you have surpassed the stories I heard. 7 Happy are your men, happy these servants of yours, who stand before you always and listen to your wisdom. 8 Blessed be the LORD, your God, who has been so pleased with you as to place you on his throne as king for the LORD, your God. Because your God has so loved Israel as to will to make it last forever, he has appointed you over them as king to administer right and justice." 9 Then she gave the king one hundred and twenty gold talents and a very large quantity of spices, as well as precious stones. There was no other spice like that which the queen of Sheba gave to King Solomon.

10 The servants of Huram and of Solomon who brought gold from Ophir also brought cabinet wood and precious stones. 11 With the cabinet wood the king made stairs for the temple of the LORD and the palace of the king; also lyres and harps for the chanters. The like of these had not been seen before in the land of Judah.

12 King Solomon gave the queen of Sheba everything she desired and asked him for, more than she had brought to the king. Then she returned to her own country with her servants.

13 The gold that Solomon received each year weighed six hundred and sixty-six gold talents, 14 in addition to what was collected from travelers and what the merchants brought. All the kings of Arabia also, and the governors of the country, brought gold and silver to Solomon.

15 Moreover, King Solomon made two hundred large shields of beaten gold, six hundred shekels of beaten gold going into each shield, 16 and three hundred bucklers of beaten gold, three hundred shekels of gold going into each buckler; these the king put in the hall of the Forest of Lebanon.

17 King Solomon also made a large ivory throne which he overlaid with fine gold. 18 The throne had six steps; a footstool of gold was fastened to it, and there was an arm on each side of the seat, with two lions standing beside the arms. 19 Twelve other lions also stood there, one on either side of each step. Nothing like this had ever been produced in any other kingdom. 20 Furthermore, all of King Solo-

9 The queen of Sheba heard of Solomon's fame and came to Jerusalem to test Solomon with difficult questions, with a very large retinue with camels laden with spices and an immense quantity of gold and precious stones. Having reached Solomon, she discussed everything that she had in mind with him, 2 and Solomon had an answer for all her questions; not one of them was too obscure for Solomon to answer for her. 3 When the queen of Sheba saw how wise Solomon was, the palace which he had built, 4 the food at his table, the accommodation for his officials, the organisation of his staff and the way they were dressed, his cupbearers and the way they were dressed, and the burnt offerings, which he made in the Temple of Yahweh, it left her breathless, 5 and she said to the king, 'The report I heard in my own country about you and about your wisdom in handling your affairs was true, then! 6 Until I came and saw for myself, I did not believe the reports, but clearly I was told less than half about the true extent of your wisdom. You surpass what was reported to me. 7 How fortunate your people are! How fortunate your courtiers, continually in attendance on you and listening to your wisdom! 8 Blessed be Yahweh your God. Because your God loved Israel and meant to keep it secure for ever, he has made you its king to administer law and justice.' 9 And she presented the king with a hundred and twenty talents of gold and great quantities of spices and precious stones. There never were such spices as those which the queen of Sheba gave to King Solomon. 10 Similarly, the men employed by Huram and the men employed by Solomon, who brought the gold from Ophir, also brought back *algum* wood and precious stones. 11 Of the *algum* wood the king made steps for the Temple of Yahweh and for the royal palace, and harps and lyres for the musicians, the like of which had never before been seen in Judah. 12 And King Solomon, in his turn, presented the queen of Sheba with everything that she expressed a wish for, besides what he gave her in exchange for what she had brought to the king. After which, she went home to her own country, she and her servants.

13 The weight of the gold received annually by Solomon amounted to six hundred and sixty-six talents of gold, 14 besides what tolls and foreign trade brought in; all the Arab kings and the provincial governors also brought gold and silver to Solomon. 15 King Solomon made two hundred great shields of beaten gold, six hundred shekels of beaten gold going into one shield; 16 also three hundred small shields of beaten gold, three hundred shekels of gold going into one shield; and the king put these into the House of the Forest of Lebanon. 17 The king also made a great ivory throne which he overlaid with refined gold. 18 The throne had six steps with a golden foot-rest attached to the throne, and arms on each side of the seat and two lions standing beside the arms, 19 and twelve lions stood on either side of the six steps. Nothing like it had ever been made in any other kingdom.

Solomon's drinking vessels were of gold, and all the vessels of the House of the Forest of Lebanon were of pure gold; silver was not considered as anything in the days of Solomon. 21 For the king's ships went to Tarshish with the servants of Huram; once every three years the ships of Tarshish used to come bringing gold, silver, ivory, apes, and peacocks. ᶠ

22 Thus King Solomon excelled all the kings of the earth in riches and in wisdom. 23 All the kings of the earth sought the presence of Solomon to hear his wisdom, which God had put into his mind. 24 Every one of them brought a present, objects of silver and gold, garments, weaponry, spices, horses, and mules, so much year by year. 25 Solomon had four thousand stalls for horses and chariots, and twelve thousand horses, which he stationed in the chariot cities and with the king in Jerusalem. 26 He ruled over all the kings from the Euphrates to the land of the Philistines, and to the border of Egypt. 27 The king made silver as common in Jerusalem as stone, and cedar as plentiful as the sycamore of the Shephelah. 28 Horses were imported for Solomon from Egypt and from all lands.

29 Now the rest of the acts of Solomon, from first to last, are they not written in the history of the prophet Nathan, and in the prophecy of Ahijah the Shilonite, and in the visions of the seer Iddo concerning Jeroboam son of Nebat? 30 Solomon reigned in Jerusalem over all Israel forty years. 31 Solomon slept with his ancestors and was buried in the city of his father David; and his son Rehoboam succeeded him.

10 Rehoboam went to Shechem, for all Israel had come to Shechem to make him king. 2 When Jeroboam son of Nebat heard of it (for he was in Egypt, where he had fled from King Solomon), then Jeroboam returned from Egypt. 3 They sent and called him; and Jeroboam and all Israel came and said to Rehoboam, 4 "Your father made our yoke heavy. Now therefore lighten the hard service of your father and his heavy yoke that he placed on us, and we will serve you." 5 He said to them, "Come to me again in three days." So the people went away.

6 Then King Rehoboam took counsel with the older men who had attended his father Solomon while he was still alive, saying, "How do you advise me to answer this people?" 7 They answered him, "If you will be kind to this people and please them, and speak good words to them, then they will be your servants forever." 8 But he rejected the advice that the older men gave him, and consulted the young men who had grown up with him and now attended him. 9 He said to them, "What do you advise that we answer this people who have said to me, 'Lighten the yoke that your father put on us'?" 10 The young men who had grown up with him said to him, "Thus should you speak to the people who said to you, 'Your father made our yoke heavy, but you must lighten it for us'; tell them, 'My little finger is thicker than my father's loins. 11 Now, whereas my father laid on you a heavy yoke, I will add to your yoke. My father disciplined you with whips, but I will discipline you with scorpions.'"

12 So Jeroboam and all the people came to Rehoboam the third day, as the king had said, "Come to me again the third day." 13 The king answered them harshly. King Rehoboam rejected the advice of the older men; 14 he spoke to them in accordance with the advice of the young men, "My father made your yoke heavy, but I will add to it; my father disciplined you with whips, but I will discipline you with scorpions." 15 So the king did not listen to the people, because it was a turn of affairs brought about by God so that the LORD might fulfill his word, which he had spoken by Ahijah the Shilonite to Jeroboam son of Nebat.

ᶠ Or baboons

gold, and all the plate in the House of the Forest of Lebanon was of red gold; silver was reckoned of no value in the days of Solomon. 21 The king had a fleet of ships plying to Tarshish with Huram's men; once every three years this fleet of merchantmen came home, bringing gold and silver, ivory, apes, and monkeys.

22 Thus King Solomon outdid all the kings of the earth in wealth and wisdom, 23 and all the kings of the earth courted him, to hear the wisdom with which God had endowed his mind. 24 Each one brought his gift with him, vessels of silver and gold, garments, perfumes and spices, horses and mules in annual tribute.

25 Solomon had standing for four thousand horses and chariots, and twelve thousand cavalry horses; he stationed some in the chariot-towns, while others he kept at hand in Jerusalem. 26 He ruled over all the kings from the Euphrates to the land of the Philistines and the border of Egypt. 27 He made silver as common in Jerusalem as stone, and cedar as plentiful as the sycomore-fig is in the Shephelah. 28 Horses were imported from Egypt and from all countries for Solomon.

29 The rest of the acts of Solomon's reign, from first to last, are recorded in the history of Nathan the prophet, in the prophecy of Ahijah of Shiloh, and in the visions of Iddo the seer concerning Jeroboam son of Nebat. 30 Solomon ruled in Jerusalem over the whole of Israel for forty years. 31 Then he rested with his forefathers and was buried in the city of David his father; he was succeeded by his son Rehoboam.

10 REHOBOAM went to Shechem, for all Israel had gone there to make him king. 2 When Jeroboam son of Nebat heard of it in Egypt, where he had taken refuge to escape Solomon, he returned from Egypt. 3 The people now recalled him, and he and all Israel came to Rehoboam and said, 4 'Your father laid a harsh yoke upon us; but if you will now lighten the harsh labour he imposed and the heavy yoke he laid on us, we shall serve you.' 5 'Give me three days,' he said, 'and then come back.'

When the people had gone, 6 King Rehoboam consulted the elders who had been in attendance during the lifetime of his father Solomon: 'What answer do you advise me to give to this people?' 7 They said, 'If you show yourself well-disposed to this people and gratify them by speaking kindly to them, they will be your servants ever after.' 8 But rejecting the advice given him by the elders he consulted the young men who had grown up with him and were now in attendance; 9 he asked them, 'What answer do you advise me to give to this people's request that I should lighten the yoke which my father laid on them?' 10 The young men replied, 'Give this answer to the people who say that your father made their yoke heavy and ask you to lighten it; tell them: "My little finger is thicker than my father's loins. 11 My father laid a heavy yoke on you; but I shall make it heavier. My father whipped you; but I shall flay you."'

12 Jeroboam and the people all came to Rehoboam on the third day, as the king had ordered. 13 The king gave them a harsh answer; he rejected the advice which the elders had given him 14 and spoke to the people as the young men had advised: 'My father made your yoke heavy; but I shall make it heavier. My father whipped you; but I shall flay you.' 15 The king would not listen to the people, for the LORD had given this turn to the affair in order that the word he had spoken by Ahijah of Shiloh to Jeroboam son of Nebat might be fulfilled.

9:21 **merchantmen:** *lit.* ships of Tarshish.　　9:25–28 *Cp. 1:14–17; 1 Kgs. 10:26–29.*　　9:29–31 *Cp. 1 Kgs. 11:41–43.*
10:1–19 *Cp. 1 Kgs. 12:1–19.*　　10:14 **My father made:** *so some MSS; others* I shall make.

mon's drinking vessels were of gold, and all the utensils in the hall of the Forest of Lebanon were of pure gold; silver was not considered of value in Solomon's time. 21 For the king had ships that went to Tarshish with the servants of Huram. Once every three years the fleet of Tarshish would return with a cargo of gold and silver, ivory, apes and monkeys. 22 Thus King Solomon surpassed all the other kings of the earth in riches as well as in wisdom.

23 All the kings of the earth sought audience with Solomon, to hear from him the wisdom which God had put in his heart. 24 Year in and year out, each one would bring his tribute — silver and gold articles, garments, weapons, spices, horses and mules. 25 Solomon also had four thousand stalls of horses, chariots, and twelve thousand horsemen, which he assigned to the chariot cities and to the king in Jerusalem. 26 He was ruler over all the kings from the River to the land of the Philistines and down to the border of Egypt. 27 The king made silver as common in Jerusalem as stones, while cedars became as numerous as the sycamores of the foothills. 28 Horses were imported for Solomon from Egypt and from all the lands.

29 The rest of the acts of Solomon, first and last, are written, as is well known, in the acts of Nathan the prophet, in the prophecy of Ahijah the Shilonite, and in the visions of Iddo the seer which concern Jeroboam, son of Nebat. 30 Solomon reigned in Jerusalem over all Israel for forty years. 31 He rested with his ancestors; he was buried in his father's City of David, and his son Rehoboam succeeded him as king.

10 Rehoboam went to Shechem, for all Israel had come to Shechem to proclaim him king. 2 When Jeroboam, son of Nebat, heard of this in Egypt where he had fled from King Solomon, he returned from Egypt. 3 Jeroboam was summoned to the assembly, and he and all Israel said to Rehoboam: 4 "Your father laid a heavy yoke upon us. If you now lighten the harsh service and the heavy yoke that your father imposed on us, we will serve you." 5 "In three days," he answered them, "come back to me."

When the people had departed, 6 King Rehoboam consulted the elders who had been in the service of his father during Solomon's lifetime, asking, "What answer do you advise me to give this people?" 7 They replied, "If you will deal kindly with this people and give in to them, acceding to their request, they will be your servants forever." 8 But he ignored the advice the elders had given him and consulted the young men who had grown up with him and were in his service. 9 He said to them, "What answer do you advise me to give this people, who have asked me to lighten the yoke my father imposed on them?" 10 The young men who had grown up with him replied: "This is the answer you should give to this people who have said to you, 'Your father laid a heavy yoke upon us, but do you lighten our yoke'; this you should say to them: 'My little finger is thicker than my father's body. 11 Whereas my father put a heavy yoke on you, I will make it heavier! My father beat you with whips, but I will beat you with scorpions!'"

12 On the third day, Jeroboam and all the people came back to King Rehoboam as he had instructed them to do. 13 Ignoring the advice the elders had given him, the king gave them a harsh answer, 14 speaking to them according to the advice of the young men: "My father laid a heavy yoke on you, but I will make it heavier. My father beat you with whips, but I will beat you with scorpions." 15 The king would not listen to the people, for this turn of events was divinely ordained to fulfill the prophecy the LORD had uttered to Jeroboam, the son of Nebat, through Ahijah the Shilonite.

20 All King Solomon's drinking vessels were of gold, and all the plate in the House of the Forest of Lebanon was of pure gold; silver was little thought of in Solomon's days, 21 since the king's ships went to Tarshish with Huram's employees, and once every three years the merchantmen would come back laden with gold and silver, ivory, apes and baboons. 22 For riches and for wisdom, King Solomon surpassed all kings on earth, 23 and all the kings in the world consulted Solomon to hear the wisdom which God had implanted in his heart, 24 and everyone would bring a present with him: objects of silver and of gold, robes, armour, spices, horses and mules; and this went on year after year. 25 Solomon also had four thousand stalls for horses and chariots, and twelve thousand cavalrymen; these he stationed in the chariot towns and near the king in Jerusalem. 26 He was overlord of all the kings from the River to the territory of the Philistines and the Egyptian border. 27 In Jerusalem the king made silver as common as stones, and cedar wood as plentiful as sycamore in the Lowlands. 28 Horses were imported for Solomon from Muzur and all the other countries too.

29 The rest of the history of Solomon, from first to last, is this not all written down in the records of Nathan the prophet, in the Prophecy of Ahijah of Shiloh, and in the Vision of Iddo the seer concerning Jeroboam son of Nebat? 30 Solomon reigned in Jerusalem over all Israel for forty years. 31 When Solomon fell asleep with his ancestors, he was buried in the City of his father David; Rehoboam his son succeeded him.

10 Rehoboam then went to Shechem, all Israel having come to Shechem to proclaim him king. 2 As soon as Jeroboam son of Nebat heard the news — he was in Egypt, where he had taken refuge from King Solomon — he returned from Egypt. 3 They now sent for him, so Jeroboam and all Israel came and spoke as follows to Rehoboam, 4 'Your father laid a cruel yoke on us; if you will lighten your father's cruel slavery, that heavy yoke which he imposed on us, we are willing to serve you.' 5 He said to them, 'Come back to me in three days' time.' And the people went away.

6 King Rehoboam then consulted the elders, who had been in attendance on his father Solomon while he was alive, and said, 'How do you advise me to answer this people?' 7 They replied, 'If you are fair to these people, pleasant to them and give them a fair reply, they will remain your servants for ever.' 8 But he rejected the advice given him by the elders and consulted the young men in attendance on him, who had grown up with him. 9 He said, 'How do you advise us to answer these people who have been saying, "Lighten the yoke which your father imposed on us"?' 10 The young men who had grown up with him replied, 'This is the way to answer the people who have been saying, "Your father made our yoke heavy, you must lighten it for us!" This is the right thing to say to them, "My little finger is thicker than my father's loins! 11 Although my father laid a heavy yoke on you, I shall make it heavier still! My father controlled you with the whip, but I shall apply a spiked lash!"' 12 On the third day, Jeroboam and all the people came to Rehoboam in obedience to the king's instructions, 'Come back to me in three days' time.' 13 And the king gave them a harsh answer. King Rehoboam, rejecting the advice of the elders, 14 spoke to them as the young men had recommended, 'My father made your yoke heavy, but I shall add to it. My father controlled you with the whip, but I shall apply a spiked lash.' 15 Thus the king refused to listen to the people, and this was brought about by God, so that Yahweh might fulfil the promise which he had made through Ahijah of Shiloh to Jeroboam son of Nebat.

NEW REVISED STANDARD VERSION

REVISED ENGLISH BIBLE

16 When all Israel saw that the king would not listen to them, the people answered the king,
"What share do we have in David?
We have no inheritance in the son of Jesse.
Each of you to your tents, O Israel!
Look now to your own house, O David."
So all Israel departed to their tents. 17 But Rehoboam reigned over the people of Israel who were living in the cities of Judah. 18 When King Rehoboam sent Hadoram, who was taskmaster over the forced labor, the people of Israel stoned him to death. King Rehoboam hurriedly mounted his chariot to flee to Jerusalem. 19 So Israel has been in rebellion against the house of David to this day.

11 When Rehoboam came to Jerusalem, he assembled one hundred eighty thousand chosen troops of the house of Judah and Benjamin to fight against Israel, to restore the kingdom to Rehoboam. 2 But the word of the LORD came to Shemaiah the man of God: 3 Say to King Rehoboam of Judah, son of Solomon, and to all Israel in Judah and Benjamin, 4 "Thus says the LORD: You shall not go up or fight against your kindred. Let everyone return home, for this thing is from me." So they heeded the word of the LORD and turned back from the expedition against Jeroboam.

5 Rehoboam resided in Jerusalem, and he built cities for defense in Judah. 6 He built up Bethlehem, Etam, Tekoa, 7 Beth-zur, Soco, Adullam, 8 Gath, Mareshah, Ziph, 9 Adoraim, Lachish, Azekah, 10 Zorah, Aijalon, and Hebron, fortified cities that are in Judah and in Benjamin. 11 He made the fortresses strong, and put commanders in them, and stores of food, oil, and wine. 12 He also put large shields and spears in all the cities, and made them very strong. So he held Judah and Benjamin.

13 The priests and the Levites who were in all Israel presented themselves to him from all their territories. 14 The Levites had left their common lands and their holdings and had come to Judah and Jerusalem, because Jeroboam and his sons had prevented them from serving as priests of the LORD, 15 and had appointed his own priests for the high places, and for the goat-demons, and for the calves that he had made. 16 Those who had set their hearts to seek the LORD God of Israel came after them from all the tribes of Israel to Jerusalem to sacrifice to the LORD, the God of their ancestors. 17 They strengthened the kingdom of Judah, and for three years they made Rehoboam son of Solomon secure, for they walked for three years in the way of David and Solomon.

18 Rehoboam took as his wife Mahalath daughter of Jerimoth son of David, and of Abihail daughter of Eliab son of Jesse. 19 She bore him sons: Jeush, Shemariah, and Zaham. 20 After her he took Maacah daughter of Absalom, who bore him Abijah, Attai, Ziza, and Shelomith. 21 Rehoboam loved Maacah daughter of Absalom more than all his other wives and concubines (he took eighteen wives and sixty concubines, and became the father of twenty-eight sons and sixty daughters). 22 Rehoboam appointed Abijah son of Maacah as chief prince among his brothers, for he intended to make him king. 23 He dealt wisely, and distributed some of his sons through all the districts of Judah and Benjamin, in all the fortified cities; he gave them abundant provisions, and found many wives for them.

16 When all Israel saw that the king would not listen to them, they answered:
'What share have we in David?
We have no lot in the son of Jesse.
Away to your tents, Israel!
Now see to your own house, David.'
With that all Israel went off to their homes. 17 Rehoboam ruled only over those Israelites who lived in the cities and towns of Judah.

18 King Rehoboam sent out Hadoram, the commander of the forced levies, but when the Israelites stoned him to death, the king hastily mounted his chariot and fled to Jerusalem. 19 From that day to this Israel has been in rebellion against the house of David.

11 When Rehoboam reached Jerusalem, he mustered the tribes of Judah and Benjamin, a hundred and eighty thousand chosen warriors, to fight against Israel and recover his kingdom. 2 But this word of the LORD came to Shemaiah the man of God: 3 'Say to Rehoboam son of Solomon, king of Judah, and to all the Israelites in Judah and Benjamin, 4 This is the word of the LORD: You are not to go up to make war on your kinsmen. Return to your homes, for this is my doing.' They listened to the word of the LORD and abandoned their campaign against Jeroboam.

5 Rehoboam resided in Jerusalem and built up the defences of certain towns in Judah. 6 The towns in Judah and Benjamin which he fortified were Bethlehem, Etam, Tekoa, 7 Beth-zur, Soco, Adullam, 8 Gath, Mareshah, Ziph, 9 Adoraim, Lachish, Azekah, 10 Zorah, Aijalon, and Hebron. 11 He strengthened the defences of these fortified towns, and put governors in them, as well as supplies of food, oil, and wine. 12 Also he stored shields and spears in each of them, and made them very strong. Thus he retained possession of Judah and Benjamin.

13 The priests and the Levites throughout the whole of Israel resorted to Rehoboam from all their territories; 14 for the Levites had left all their common land and their own property and had gone to Judah and Jerusalem, because Jeroboam and his sons rejected their services as priests of the LORD, 15 and he appointed his own priests for the shrines, for the demons, and for the calves which he had made. 16 Out of all the tribes of Israel, those who were resolved to seek the LORD the God of Israel followed the Levites to Jerusalem to sacrifice to the LORD the God of their fathers. 17 They strengthened the kingdom of Judah and for three years made Rehoboam son of Solomon secure, because he followed the example of David and Solomon during that time.

18 Rehoboam married Mahalath, whose father was Jerimoth son of David and whose mother was Abihail daughter of Eliab son of Jesse. 19 His sons by her were: Jeush, Shemariah, and Zaham. 20 Next he married Maacah granddaughter of Absalom, who bore him Abijah, Attai, Ziza, and Shelomith. 21 Of all his wives and concubines, Rehoboam loved Maacah most; he had in all eighteen wives and sixty concubines and became the father of twenty-eight sons and sixty daughters. 22 He appointed Abijah son of Maacah chief among his brothers, making him crown prince and planning to make him his successor on the throne. 23 He showed prudence in detailing his sons to take charge of all the fortified towns throughout the whole territory of Judah and Benjamin; he also made generous provision for them and obtained wives for them.

10:16 **saw:** *prob. rdg, cp. 1 Kgs. 12:16; Heb. omits.*   11:1–4 *Cp. 1 Kgs. 12:21–24.*   11:15 **demons:** *or* satyrs.   11:17 **he:** *so Gk; Heb.* they.   11:20 **granddaughter:** *lit.* daughter.   11:22 **planning:** *so Lat.; Heb. omits.*   11:23 **obtained . . . them:** *prob. rdg; Heb.* asked for a multitude of wives.

16 When all Israel saw that the king would not listen to them, the people answered the king,
"What share have we in David?
We have no heritage in the son of Jesse.
Everyone to your tents, O Israel!
Now look to your own house, David!"
So all Israel went off to their tents. 17 Rehoboam, therefore, reigned over only those Israelites who lived in the cities of Judah. 18 King Rehoboam then sent out Hadoram, who was superintendent of the forced labor, but the Israelites stoned him to death. Rehoboam himself managed to mount his chariot and flee to Jerusalem. 19 Thus Israel has been in rebellion against David's house to this day.

11 On his arrival in Jerusalem Rehoboam gathered together the house of Judah and Benjamin, a hundred and eighty thousand seasoned warriors, to have them fight against Israel and restore the kingdom to him. 2 However, the word of the LORD came to Shemiah, a man of God: 3 "Say to Rehoboam, son of Solomon, king of Judah, and to all the Israelites in Judah and Benjamin: 4 'Thus says the LORD: You must not march out to fight against your brothers. Let every man return home, for what has occurred I have brought about.' " They obeyed this message of the LORD and gave up the expedition against Jeroboam.
5 Rehoboam took up residence in Jerusalem and built fortified cities in Judah. 6 He built up Bethlehem, Etam, Tekoa, 7 Beth-zur, Soco, Adullam, 8 Gath, Mareshah, Ziph, 9 Adoraim, Lachish, Azekah, 10 Zorah, Aijalon, and Hebron; these were fortified cities in Judah and Benjamin. 11 Then he strengthened the fortifications and put commanders in them, with supplies of food, oil and wine. 12 In every city were shields and spears, and he made them very strong. Thus Judah and Benjamin remained his.
13 Now the priests and Levites throughout Israel presented themselves to him from all parts of their land, 14 for the Levites left their assigned pasture lands and their holdings and came to Judah and Jerusalem, because Jeroboam and his sons repudiated them as priests of the LORD. 15 In their place, he himself appointed priests for the high places and satyrs and calves he had made. 16 After them, all those of the Israelite tribes who firmly desired to seek the LORD, the God of Israel, came to Jerusalem to sacrifice to the LORD, the God of their fathers. 17 Thus they strengthened the kingdom of Judah and made Rehoboam, son of Solomon, prevail for three years; for they walked in the way of David and Solomon three years.
18 Rehoboam took to himself as wife Mahalath, daughter of Jerimoth, son of David and of Abihail, daughter of Eliab, son of Jesse. 19 She bore him sons: Jehush, Shemariah and Zaham. 20 After her, he married Maacah, daughter of Absalom, who bore him Abijah, Attai, Ziza and Shelomith. 21 Rehoboam loved Maacah, daughter of Absalom, more than all his other wives and concubines; he had taken eighteen wives and sixty concubines, and he fathered twenty-eight sons and sixty daughters. 22 Rehoboam constituted Abijah, son of Maacah, commander among his brothers, for he intended to make him king. 23 He acted prudently, distributing various of his sons throughout all the districts of Judah and Benjamin, in all the fortified cities; and he furnished them with copious provisions and sought an abundance of wives for them.

16 When all Israel saw that the king refused to listen to them, the people answered the king thus:
What share have we in David?
— no heritage in the son of Jesse!
Each of you, to your tents, Israel!
Now look to your own house, David!
So Israel went home again. 17 Rehoboam, however, reigned over those Israelites who lived in the towns of Judah. 18 When King Rehoboam sent Adoram who was in charge of forced labour, the Israelites stoned him to death, while King Rehoboam managed to mount his chariot and escape to Jerusalem. 19 And Israel has remained in rebellion against the House of David from that day to this.

11 When Rehoboam reached Jerusalem, he mustered a hundred and eighty thousand picked warriors of the House of Judah and Benjamin to fight Israel and win back the kingdom for Rehoboam. 2 But the word of Yahweh came to Shemaiah, man of God, 3 'Say this to Rehoboam son of Solomon king of Judah, and to all Israel in Judah and Benjamin, 4 "Yahweh says this: Do not go and make war on your brothers; let everyone go home, for this is my doing." ' They obeyed Yahweh's command and went back instead of marching against Jeroboam.
5 Rehoboam, residing in Jerusalem, fortified a number of towns for the defence of Judah. 6 He built Bethlehem, Etam, Tekoa, 7 Beth-Zur, Soco, Adullam, 8 Gath, Mareshah, Ziph, 9 Adoraim, Lachish, Azekah, 10 Zorah, Aijalon, Hebron, these being the fortified towns in Judah and Benjamin. 11 He equipped these fortresses, stationing commanders in them, with supplies of food, oil and wine, 12 and shields and spears in each of these towns, making them extremely strong and thus retaining control of Judah and Benjamin.
13 The priests and the Levites from all over Israel left their districts to put themselves at his disposal. 14 The Levites, indeed, abandoned their pasture lands and their holdings and came to Judah and Jerusalem because Jeroboam and his sons had excluded them from the priesthood of Yahweh. 15 Jeroboam had appointed his own priests for the high places dedicated to the satyrs and calves which he had made. 16 And those members of all the tribes of Israel who were determined to seek Yahweh, God of Israel, followed those priests and Levites to Jerusalem to sacrifice to Yahweh, God of their ancestors. 17 These added strength to the kingdom of Judah and gave their support to Rehoboam son of Solomon for three years. For three years they remained loyal to David and Solomon.
18 Rehoboam married Mahalath daughter of Jerimoth, son of David, and of Abihail daughter of Eliab son of Jesse, 19 and she bore him sons: Jeush, Shemariah and Zaham. 20 After her, he married Maacah daughter of Absalom, who bore him Abijah, Attai, Ziza and Shelomith. 21 Rehoboam loved Maacah daughter of Absalom, more than all his other wives and concubines. He had in fact a total of eighteen wives and sixty concubines and fathered twenty-eight sons and sixty daughters. 22 Rehoboam named Abijah son of Maacah as head, hence leader, of his brothers, with a view to making him king, 23 and acted wisely by distributing his sons throughout the territories of Judah and Benjamin, some in each fortified town, where he provided plenty of food for them and found them wives.

NEW REVISED STANDARD VERSION | REVISED ENGLISH BIBLE

12 When the rule of Rehoboam was established and he grew strong, he abandoned the law of the LORD, he and all Israel with him. 2 In the fifth year of King Rehoboam, because they had been unfaithful to the LORD, King Shishak of Egypt came up against Jerusalem 3 with twelve hundred chariots and sixty thousand cavalry. A countless army came with him from Egypt—Libyans, Sukkiim, and Ethiopians.ᵘ 4 He took the fortified cities of Judah and came as far as Jerusalem. 5 Then the prophet Shemaiah came to Rehoboam and to the officers of Judah, who had gathered at Jerusalem because of Shishak, and said to them, "Thus says the LORD: You abandoned me, so I have abandoned you to the hand of Shishak." 6 Then the officers of Israel and the king humbled themselves and said, "The LORD is in the right." 7 When the LORD saw that they humbled themselves, the word of the LORD came to Shemaiah, saying: "They have humbled themselves; I will not destroy them, but I will grant them some deliverance, and my wrath shall not be poured out on Jerusalem by the hand of Shishak. 8 Nevertheless they shall be his servants, so that they may know the difference between serving me and serving the kingdoms of other lands."

9 So King Shishak of Egypt came up against Jerusalem; he took away the treasures of the house of the LORD and the treasures of the king's house; he took everything. He also took away the shields of gold that Solomon had made; 10 but King Rehoboam made in place of them shields of bronze, and committed them to the hands of the officers of the guard, who kept the door of the king's house. 11 Whenever the king went into the house of the LORD, the guard would come along bearing them, and would then bring them back to the guardroom. 12 Because he humbled himself the wrath of the LORD turned from him, so as not to destroy them completely; moreover, conditions were good in Judah.

13 So King Rehoboam established himself in Jerusalem and reigned. Rehoboam was forty-one years old when he began to reign; he reigned seventeen years in Jerusalem, the city that the LORD had chosen out of all the tribes of Israel to put his name there. His mother's name was Naamah the Ammonite. 14 He did evil, for he did not set his heart to seek the LORD.

15 Now the acts of Rehoboam, from first to last, are they not written in the records of the prophet Shemaiah and of the seer Iddo, recorded by genealogy? There were continual wars between Rehoboam and Jeroboam. 16 Rehoboam slept with his ancestors and was buried in the city of David; and his son Abijah succeeded him.

13 In the eighteenth year of King Jeroboam, Abijah began to reign over Judah. 2 He reigned for three years in Jerusalem. His mother's name was Micaiah daughter of Uriel of Gibeah.

Now there was war between Abijah and Jeroboam. 3 Abijah engaged in battle, having an army of valiant warriors, four hundred thousand picked men; and Jeroboam drew up his line of battle against him with eight hundred thousand picked mighty warriors. 4 Then Abijah stood on the slope of Mount Zemaraim that is in the hill country of Ephraim, and said, "Listen to me, Jeroboam and all Israel! 5 Do you not know that the LORD God of Israel gave the kingship over Israel forever to David and his sons by a covenant of salt? 6 Yet Jeroboam son of Nebat, a servant of Solomon son of David, rose up and rebelled against his lord; 7 and certain

12 When Rehoboam's kingdom was firmly established and he grew powerful, he along with all Israel forsook the law of the LORD. 2 In the fifth year of Rehoboam's reign, because of this disloyalty to the LORD, King Shishak of Egypt attacked Jerusalem 3 with twelve hundred chariots and sixty thousand horsemen; he also brought with him from Egypt an innumerable following of Libyans, Sukkites, and Cushites. 4 He captured the fortified towns of Judah and reached Jerusalem. 5 Then Shemaiah the prophet came to Rehoboam and the leading men of Judah, who had collected together at Jerusalem in the face of the advance of Shishak, and said, 'This is the word of the LORD: You have abandoned me; therefore I now abandon you to Shishak.' 6 The princes of Israel and the king submitted and said, 'The LORD is just.' 7 When the LORD saw that they had submitted, there came from him this word to Shemaiah: 'Because they have submitted I shall not destroy them; I shall grant them some measure of relief: my wrath will not be poured out on Jerusalem by means of Shishak, 8 but they will become his servants; then they will know the difference between serving me and serving the rulers of other countries.' 9 King Shishak of Egypt in his attack on Jerusalem carried away the treasures of the house of the LORD and of the king's palace, and seized everything, including the gold shields made for Solomon. 10 King Rehoboam replaced them with bronze shields and entrusted them to the officers of the escort who guarded the entrance of the palace. 11 Whenever the king entered the house of the LORD, the escort entered, carrying the shields; afterwards they returned them to the guardroom. 12 Because Rehoboam submitted, the LORD's wrath was averted from him, and he was not utterly destroyed; Judah enjoyed prosperity.

13 King Rehoboam increased his power in Jerusalem. He was forty-one years old when he came to the throne, and he reigned for seventeen years in Jerusalem, the city which the LORD had chosen out of all the tribes of Israel as the place to receive his name. Rehoboam's mother was an Ammonite woman called Naamah. 14 He did what was wrong; he did not make a practice of seeking guidance of the LORD. 15 The events of Rehoboam's reign, from first to last, are recorded in the histories of Shemaiah the prophet and Iddo the seer. There was continual fighting between Rehoboam and Jeroboam. 16 Rehoboam rested with his forefathers and was buried in the city of David. His son Abijah succeeded him.

13 IN the eighteenth year of King Jeroboam's reign Abijah became king of Judah. 2 He reigned in Jerusalem for three years; his mother was Maacah daughter of Uriel of Gibeah.

When war broke out between Abijah and Jeroboam, 3 Abijah drew up his army of four hundred thousand picked troops in order of battle, while Jeroboam formed up against him with eight hundred thousand picked troops. 4 Abijah stood up on the slopes of Mount Zemaraim in the hill-country of Ephraim and called out, 'Jeroboam and all Israel, hear me: 5 Do you not know that the LORD the God of Israel gave the kingship over Israel to David and his descendants for ever by a covenant of salt? 6 Yet Jeroboam son of Nebat, a servant of Solomon son of David, rose in rebellion against his lord, 7 and certain worthless scoundrels gathered round

12:3 **Cushites:** *or* Nubians.   12:9–11 *Cp. 1 Kgs. 14:25–28.*
12:13–16 *Cp. 1 Kgs. 14:29–31.*   12:15 **and . . . seer:** *prob. rdg;*
Heb. adds to be enrolled by genealogy.   13:2 **Maacah:** *so Gk, cp.*
1 Kgs. 15:2; Heb. Micaiah.

ᵘ Or *Nubians*; Heb *Cushites*

12 After Rehoboam had consolidated his rule and had become powerful, he abandoned the law of the LORD, he and all Israel with him. 2 Thus it happened that in the fifth year of King Rehoboam, Shishak, king of Egypt, attacked Jerusalem, for they had been unfaithful to the LORD. 3 He came up with twelve hundred chariots and sixty thousand horsemen, and there was no counting the army that came with him from Egypt—Libyans, Sukkites and Ethiopians. 4 They captured the fortified cities of Judah and came as far as Jerusalem. 5 Then Shemaiah the prophet came to Rehoboam and the commanders of Judah who had gathered at Jerusalem because of Shishak, and said to them: "Thus says the LORD: 'You have abandoned me, and therefore I have abandoned you to the power of Shishak.' "

6 However, the commanders of Israel and the king humbled themselves, saying, "The LORD is just." 7 When the LORD saw that they had humbled themselves, the word of the LORD came to Shemaiah: "Because they have humbled themselves, I will not destroy them; I will give them some deliverance, and my wrath shall not be poured out upon Jerusalem through Shishak. 8 But they shall be his servants, that they may know what it is to serve me and what it is to serve earthly kingdoms." 9 Therefore Shishak, king of Egypt, attacked Jerusalem and carried off the treasures of the temple of the LORD and of the king's palace. He took everything, including the gold bucklers that Solomon had made. 10 (To replace them, King Rehoboam made bronze bucklers, which he entrusted to the officers of the guard on duty at the entrance of the royal palace. 11 Whenever the king visited the temple of the LORD, the troops would come bearing them, and then they would return them to the guardroom.) 12 Because he had humbled himself, the anger of the LORD turned from him so that it did not destroy him completely; and in Judah, moreover, good deeds were found.

13 King Rehoboam consolidated his power in Jerusalem and continued to rule; he was forty-one years old when he became king, and he reigned seventeen years in Jerusalem, the city in which, out of all the tribes of Israel, the LORD chose to be honored. Rehoboam's mother was named Naamah, an Ammonite. 14 He did evil, for he had not truly resolved to seek the LORD. 15 The acts of Rehoboam, first and last, are written, as is well known, in the history of Shemaiah the prophet and of Iddo the seer [his family record]. There was war continually between Rehoboam and Jeroboam. 16 Rehoboam rested with his ancestors; he was buried in the City of David. His son Abijah succeeded him as king.

13 In the eighteenth year of King Jeroboam, Abijah became king of Judah; 2 he reigned three years in Jerusalem. His mother was named Michaiah, daughter of Uriel of Gibeah. There was war between Abijah and Jeroboam. 3 Abijah joined battle with a force of four hundred thousand picked warriors, while Jeroboam lined up against him in battle with eight hundred thousand picked and valiant warriors. 4 Abijah stood on Mount Zemaraim, which is in the highlands of Ephraim, and said: "Listen to me, Jeroboam and all Israel! 5 Do you not know that the LORD, the God of Israel, has given the kingdom of Israel to David forever, to him and to his sons, by a covenant made in salt? 6 Yet Jeroboam, son of Nebat, the servant of Solomon, son of David, has stood up and rebelled against his lord!

12 When Rehoboam had consolidated the kingdom and become strong, he, and all Israel with him, abandoned the Law of Yahweh; 2 and thus it happened that in the fifth year of King Rehoboam, Shishak king of Egypt marched on Jerusalem, because they had been unfaithful to Yahweh, 3 with twelve hundred chariots and sixty thousand cavalry and countless hordes of Libyans, Sukkiim and Cushites who came from Egypt with him. 4 They captured the fortified towns of Judah and reached Jerusalem. 5 The prophet Shemaiah then came to Rehoboam and the generals of Judah, who had fallen back on Jerusalem before Shishak's advance, and said to them, 'Yahweh says this, "You have abandoned me and so I have abandoned you into Shishak's clutches." ' 6 At this, the Israelite generals and the king humbled themselves and said, 'Yahweh is just!' 7 When Yahweh saw that they had humbled themselves, the word of Yahweh came to Shemaiah as follows, 'They have humbled themselves. I shall not destroy them but shall grant them some degree of deliverance. My retribution will not be poured out on Jerusalem by means of Shishak; 8 they are nonetheless to become his slaves, so that they may learn the difference between serving me and serving kings of other countries.'

9 So Shishak king of Egypt advanced on Jerusalem and carried off the treasures of the Temple and the treasures of the royal palace. He took everything away, including the golden shields which Solomon had made. 10 To replace these, King Rehoboam made bronze shields, entrusting them to the commanders of the guard who guarded the king's palace gate. 11 Whenever the king went to the Temple of Yahweh, the guards would come out carrying them, returning them to the guardroom afterwards. 12 Because King Rehoboam had humbled himself, the retribution of Yahweh turned away from him so as not to destroy him completely; and there were also some good features in Judah. 13 Thus he was able to strengthen his position in Jerusalem and continue as king; for Rehoboam was forty-one years old when he came to the throne and remained king for seventeen years in Jerusalem, the city chosen by Yahweh from all the tribes of Israel to put his name there. His mother's name was Naamah the Ammonite. 14 But he did wrong in not setting his heart on seeking Yahweh.

15 The history of Rehoboam, from first to last, is this not all written down in the records of Shemaiah the prophet and of Iddo the seer? Warfare between Rehoboam and Jeroboam went on throughout the period. 16 When Rehoboam fell asleep with his ancestors, he was buried in the City of David; his son Abijah succeeded him.

13 In the eighteenth year of King Jeroboam, Abijah became king of Judah 2 and reigned for three years in Jerusalem. His mother's name was Micaiah daughter of Uriel of Gibeah. When war broke out between Abijah and Jeroboam, 3 Abijah took the field with an army of four hundred thousand picked warriors, while Jeroboam took the field against him with eight hundred thousand picked warriors. 4 Abijah took position on Mount Zemaraim, in the highlands of Ephraim. 'Jeroboam and all Israel,' he cried, 'listen to me! 5 Do you not know that Yahweh, God of Israel, has given eternal sovereignty of Israel to David and his sons by an inviolable covenant? 6 Yet Jeroboam son of Nebat, the slave of Solomon son of David, rose in revolt against his

NEW REVISED STANDARD VERSION	REVISED ENGLISH BIBLE

worthless scoundrels gathered around him and defied Rehoboam son of Solomon, when Rehoboam was young and irresolute and could not withstand them.

8 "And now you think that you can withstand the kingdom of the LORD in the hand of the sons of David, because you are a great multitude and have with you the golden calves that Jeroboam made as gods for you. 9 Have you not driven out the priests of the LORD, the descendants of Aaron, and the Levites, and made priests for yourselves like the peoples of other lands? Whoever comes to be consecrated with a young bull or seven rams becomes a priest of what are no gods. 10 But as for us, the LORD is our God, and we have not abandoned him. We have priests ministering to the LORD who are descendants of Aaron, and Levites for their service. 11 They offer to the LORD every morning and every evening burnt offerings and fragrant incense, set out the rows of bread on the table of pure gold, and care for the golden lampstand so that its lamps may burn every evening; for we keep the charge of the LORD our God, but you have abandoned him. 12 See, God is with us at our head, and his priests have their battle trumpets to sound the call to battle against you. O Israelites, do not fight against the LORD, the God of your ancestors; for you cannot succeed."

13 Jeroboam had sent an ambush around to come on them from behind; thus his troops[v] were in front of Judah, and the ambush was behind them. 14 When Judah turned, the battle was in front of them and behind them. They cried out to the LORD, and the priests blew the trumpets. 15 Then the people of Judah raised the battle shout. And when the people of Judah shouted, God defeated Jeroboam and all Israel before Abijah and Judah. 16 The Israelites fled before Judah, and God gave them into their hands. 17 Abijah and his army defeated them with great slaughter; five hundred thousand picked men of Israel fell slain. 18 Thus the Israelites were subdued at that time, and the people of Judah prevailed, because they relied on the LORD, the God of their ancestors. 19 Abijah pursued Jeroboam, and took cities from him: Bethel with its villages and Jeshanah with its villages and Ephron[w] with its villages. 20 Jeroboam did not recover his power in the days of Abijah; the LORD struck him down, and he died. 21 But Abijah grew strong. He took fourteen wives, and became the father of twenty-two sons and sixteen daughters. 22 The rest of the acts of Abijah, his behavior and his deeds, are written in the story of the prophet Iddo.

14 [x] So Abijah slept with his ancestors, and they buried him in the city of David. His son Asa succeeded him. In his days the land had rest for ten years. 2 [y] Asa did what was good and right in the sight of the LORD his God. 3 He took away the foreign altars and the high places, broke down the pillars, hewed down the sacred poles,[z] 4 and commanded Judah to seek the LORD, the God of their ancestors, and to keep the law and the commandment. 5 He also removed from all the cities of Judah the high places and the incense altars. And the kingdom had rest under him. 6 He built fortified cities in Judah while the land had rest. He had no war in those years, for the LORD gave him peace. 7 He said to Judah, "Let us build these cities, and surround them with walls and towers, gates and bars; the land is still ours because we have sought the LORD our God; we have sought him, and he has given us peace on every side." So they built and prospered. 8 Asa had an army of three hundred thousand

---

him, who stubbornly opposed Solomon's son Rehoboam when he was young and inexperienced, and he was no match for them.

8 'Now you propose to match yourselves against the kingdom of the LORD as ruled by David's sons, you with your mob of supporters and the golden calves which Jeroboam has made to be your gods. 9 Have you not dismissed from office the Aaronites, priests of the LORD, and the Levites, and followed the practice of other lands in appointing your own priests? If any man comes for ordination with an offering of a young bull and seven rams, you accept him as a priest to a god who is no god.

10 'But as for us, the LORD is our God and we have not forsaken him. We have Aaronites as priests ministering to the LORD with the Levites, duly discharging their office. 11 Morning and evening, these burn whole-offerings and fragrant incense to the LORD and offer the Bread of the Presence arranged in rows on a table ritually clean; they also kindle the lamps on the gold lampstand every evening. Thus we do indeed keep the charge of the LORD our God, whereas you have forsaken him. 12 God is with us at our head, and his priests stand there with trumpets to signal the battle cry against you. Men of Israel, do not fight the LORD the God of your forefathers; you will have no success.'

13 Jeroboam sent a detachment of his troops to go round and lay an ambush in the rear, so that his main body faced Judah while the ambush lay behind them. 14 The men of Judah turned to find that they were engaged front and rear. They cried to the LORD for help; the priests sounded their trumpets, 15 and the men of Judah raised their battle cry; and when they shouted, God put Jeroboam and all Israel to rout before Abijah and Judah. 16 The Israelites fled before the men of Judah, and God delivered them into their power. 17 Abijah and his men defeated them with very heavy losses: five hundred thousand picked men of Israel fell in the battle. 18 On that occasion the Israelites had to submit; Judah prevailed because they relied on the LORD the God of their forefathers. 19 Abijah pressed home his victory over Jeroboam by capturing from him the cities of Bethel, Jeshanah, and Ephron with their villages. 20 Jeroboam did not regain his power all the days of Abijah; finally the LORD struck him down and he died.

21 But Abijah established his position; he married fourteen wives and became the father of twenty-two sons and sixteen daughters. 22 The other events of Abijah's reign, both what he said and what he did, are recorded in the discourse of the prophet Iddo. 1 Abijah rested with his forefathers and was buried in the city of David. His son Asa succeeded him, and in his time the land had peace for ten years.

14 2 Asa did what was good and right in the eyes of the LORD his God. 3 He suppressed the foreign altars and the shrines, smashed the sacred pillars and hacked down the sacred poles, 4 and ordered Judah to seek guidance of the LORD God of their forefathers and to keep the law and the commandments. 5 In all the towns he suppressed the shrines and the incense-altars, and the kingdom was at peace under him. 6 He built fortified towns in Judah, for the land was at peace. He had no war on his hands during those years, because the LORD had given him security. 7 Asa said to the men of Judah, 'Let us build these towns and fortify them, with walls round them, and towers and barred gates. The land still lies open before us. Because we have sought guidance of the LORD our God, he has sought us and given us security on every side.' So they built and prospered.

---

v Heb they   w Another reading is Ephrain   x Ch 13.23 in Heb
y Ch 14.1 in Heb   z Heb Asherim

13:10 **duly . . . office:** so Gk; Heb. in the work.   14:1 In Heb.
13:23.   14:2 In Heb. 14:1.

928

7 Worthless men, scoundrels, joined him and overcame Rehoboam, son of Solomon, when Rehoboam was young and unthinking, and no match for them. 8 But now, do you think you are a match for the kingdom of the LORD commanded by the sons of David, simply because you are a huge multitude and have with you the golden calves which Jeroboam made you for gods?

9 "Have you not expelled the priests of the LORD, the sons of Aaron, and the Levites, and made for yourselves priests like the peoples of foreign lands? Everyone who comes to consecrate himself with a young bull and seven rams becomes a priest of no-gods. 10 But as for us, the LORD is our God, and we have not forsaken him. The priests ministering to the LORD are sons of Aaron, and the Levites also have their offices. 11 They burn holocausts to the LORD and fragrant incense morning after morning and evening after evening; they display the showbread on the pure table, and the lamps of the golden lampstand burn evening after evening; for we observe our duties to the LORD, our God, but you have abandoned him. 12 See, God is with us, at our head, and his priests are here with trumpets to sound the attack against you. Do not battle against the LORD, the God of your fathers, O Israelites, for you will not succeed!"

13 But Jeroboam had an ambush go around them to come at them from the rear; so that while his army faced Judah, his ambush lay behind them. 14 When Judah turned and saw that they had to battle on both fronts, they cried out to the LORD and the priests sounded the trumpets. 15 Then the men of Judah shouted; and when they did so, God defeated Jeroboam and all Israel before Abijah and Judah. 16 The Israelites fled before Judah, and God delivered them into their hands. 17 Abijah and his people inflicted a severe defeat upon them; five hundred thousand picked men of Israel fell slain. 18 The Israelites were subdued on that occasion and the Judahites were victorious because they relied on the LORD, the God of their fathers. 19 Abijah pursued Jeroboam and took cities from him: Bethel and its dependencies, Jeshanah and its dependencies, and Ephron and its dependencies. 20 Jeroboam did not regain power during the time of Abijah; the LORD struck him down and he died, 21 while Abijah continued to grow stronger. He took to himself fourteen wives and fathered twenty-two sons and sixteen daughters.

22 The rest of Abijah's acts, his deeds and his words, are written in the midrash of the prophet Iddo. 23 Abijah rested with his ancestors; they buried him in the City of David. His son Asa succeeded him as king. During his time, ten years of peace began in the land.

14 Asa did what was good and pleasing to the LORD, his God, 2 removing the heathen altars and the high places, breaking to pieces the sacred pillars, and cutting down the sacred poles. 3 He commanded Judah to seek the LORD, the God of their fathers, and to observe the law and its commands. 4 He removed the high places and incense stands from all the cities of Judah, and under him the kingdom had peace. 5 He built fortified cities in Judah, for the land had peace and no war was waged against him during these years, because the LORD had given him peace. 6 He said to Judah: "Let us build these cities and surround them with walls, towers, gates and bars. The land is still ours, for we have sought the LORD, our God; we sought him, and he has given us rest on every side." So they built and prospered.

master. 7 Worthless men, scoundrels, rallied to him, proving too strong for Rehoboam son of Solomon, as Rehoboam was then inexperienced and timid and unable to resist them. 8 And now you propose to resist Yahweh's sovereignty as exercised by the sons of David because there is a great number of you and you have the golden calves that Jeroboam made you for gods! 9 Have you not driven out the priests of Yahweh, the sons of Aaron and the Levites, to make priests of your own like the peoples of foreign countries? Anyone who comes with a bull and seven rams to get himself consecrated can become priest of these gods that are no gods. 10 But for our part, our God is Yahweh, and we have not abandoned him; our priests are sons of Aaron who minister to Yahweh, and those who serve are Levites; 11 morning after morning, evening after evening, they present burnt offerings and perfumed incense to Yahweh, they put the bread of permanent offering on the clean table and nightly light the lamps on the golden lamp-stand; for we keep the decree of Yahweh our God, although you have abandoned him. 12 See how God is with us, at our head, and his priests with trumpets to sound the alarm against you! Israelites, do not make war on Yahweh, God of your ancestors, for you will not succeed.'

13 Now Jeroboam had sent a party round to ambush them from the rear; thus the main force confronted Judah and the ambush lay to their rear. 14 And when Judah looked round, they found themselves being attacked from front and rear. They called on Yahweh, the priests sounded the trumpets, 15 and the men of Judah raised the war cry and, as they raised the cry, God routed Jeroboam and all Israel before Abijah and Judah. 16 So the Israelites fled before Judah, because God had given Judah the upper hand, 17 and Abijah and his army inflicted a great slaughter on them: five hundred thousand of Israel's picked men fell, killed. 18 So the Israelites were humbled on that occasion, while the Judaeans won, since they had relied on Yahweh, God of their ancestors.

19 Abijah pursued Jeroboam, taking from him the towns of Bethel with its dependencies, Jeshanah with its dependencies and Ephron with its dependencies, 20 nor did Jeroboam regain strength during Abijah's lifetime. Eventually Yahweh struck him and he died, 21 but Abijah grew stronger than ever; he married fourteen wives and fathered twenty-two sons and sixteen daughters. 22 The rest of the history of Abijah, his conduct and his sayings, are recorded in the midrash of the prophet Iddo. 23 When Abijah fell asleep with his ancestors, he was buried in the City of David; his son Asa succeeded him.

In his time the country was at peace for ten years.

14 Asa did what Yahweh his God regards as good and right. 2 He abolished the foreign altars and the high places, broke the pillars, cut down the sacred poles, 3 and urged Judah to seek Yahweh, God of their ancestors, and to observe the law and commandment. 4 Because he abolished the high places and incense altars through the towns of Judah, the kingdom under him was undisturbed. 5 He rebuilt the fortified towns of Judah, since the country was at peace and free of war during those years, because Yahweh had granted him peace. 6 'Let us rebuild these towns,' he told Judah, 'let us surround them with wall and tower, with gate and bar while the country is still ours, for we have sought Yahweh our God and he has sought us and given us peace all around.' They built and prospered.

from Judah, armed with large shields and spears, and two hundred eighty thousand troops from Benjamin who carried shields and drew bows; all these were mighty warriors. 9 Zerah the Ethiopian*a* came out against them with an army of a million men and three hundred chariots, and came as far as Mareshah. 10 Asa went out to meet him, and they drew up their lines of battle in the valley of Zephathah at Mareshah. 11 Asa cried to the LORD his God, "O LORD, there is no difference for you between helping the mighty and the weak. Help us, O LORD our God, for we rely on you, and in your name we have come against this multitude. O LORD, you are our God; let no mortal prevail against you." 12 So the LORD defeated the Ethiopians*b* before Asa and before Judah, and the Ethiopians*b* fled. 13 Asa and the army with him pursued them as far as Gerar, and the Ethiopians*b* fell until no one remained alive; for they were broken before the LORD and his army. The people of Judah*c* carried away a great quantity of booty. 14 They defeated all the cities around Gerar, for the fear of the LORD was on them. They plundered all the cities; for there was much plunder in them. 15 They also attacked the tents of those who had livestock,*d* and carried away sheep and goats in abundance, and camels. Then they returned to Jerusalem.

15 The spirit of God came upon Azariah son of Oded. 2 He went out to meet Asa and said to him, "Hear me, Asa, and all Judah and Benjamin: The LORD is with you, while you are with him. If you seek him, he will be found by you, but if you abandon him, he will abandon you. 3 For a long time Israel was without the true God, and without a teaching priest, and without law; 4 but when in their distress they turned to the LORD, the God of Israel, and sought him, he was found by them. 5 In those times it was not safe for anyone to go or come, for great disturbances afflicted all the inhabitants of the lands. 6 They were broken in pieces, nation against nation and city against city, for God troubled them with every sort of distress. 7 But you, take courage! Do not let your hands be weak, for your work shall be rewarded."

8 When Asa heard these words, the prophecy of Azariah son of Oded,*e* he took courage, and put away the abominable idols from all the land of Judah and Benjamin and from the towns that he had taken in the hill country of Ephraim. He repaired the altar of the LORD that was in front of the vestibule of the house of the LORD.*f* 9 He gathered all Judah and Benjamin, and those from Ephraim, Manasseh, and Simeon who were residing as aliens with them, for great numbers had deserted to him from Israel when they saw that the LORD his God was with him. 10 They were gathered at Jerusalem in the third month of the fifteenth year of the reign of Asa. 11 They sacrificed to the LORD on that day, from the booty that they had brought, seven hundred oxen and seven thousand sheep. 12 They entered into a covenant to seek the LORD, the God of their ancestors, with all their heart and with all their soul. 13 Whoever would not seek the LORD, the God of Israel, should be put to death, whether young or old, man or woman. 14 They took an oath to the LORD with a loud voice, and with shouting, and with trumpets, and with horns. 15 All Judah rejoiced over the oath; for they had sworn with all their heart, and had sought him with their whole desire, and he was found by them, and the LORD gave them rest all around.

8 Asa had an army equipped with large shields and with spears; three hundred thousand men came from Judah, and two hundred and eighty thousand from Benjamin, archers carrying bucklers; all were valiant warriors. 9 Zerah the Cushite marched out against them with an army a million strong and three hundred chariots. When he reached Mareshah, 10 Asa came out to meet him and they took up position in the valley of Zephathah at Mareshah. 11 Asa called to the LORD his God and said, 'There is none like you, LORD, to help men, whether strong or weak; help us, LORD our God, for on you we rely and in your name we have come out against this horde. LORD, you are our God; no mere mortal can vie with you.' 12 The LORD gave Asa and Judah victory over the Cushites, who fled, 13 with Asa and his men in pursuit as far as Gerar. The Cushites broke before the LORD and his army, and many of them fell mortally wounded. Judah carried off great loads of spoil. 14 They destroyed all the towns around Gerar, for the LORD had struck the people with panic; and they plundered the towns, finding rich spoil in them all. 15 They also killed the herdsmen and seized many sheep and camels, and then they returned to Jerusalem.

15 The spirit of God came upon Azariah son of Oded. 2 He went out to meet Asa and said, 'Hear me, Asa and all Judah and Benjamin. The LORD is with you when you are with him; if you seek him, he will let himself be found, but if you forsake him, he will forsake you. 3 For a long time Israel was without the true God, without a priest to interpret the law, and without law. 4 But when, in their distress, they turned to the LORD the God of Israel and sought him, he let himself be found by them. 5 At those times there was no safety for people as they went about their business; the inhabitants of every land had their fill of trouble; 6 there was ruin on every side, nation at odds with nation, city with city, for God harassed them with every kind of distress. 7 But now you must be strong and not let your courage fail; for your work will be rewarded.'

8 When Asa heard these words, this prophecy of Oded the prophet, he resolutely suppressed the loathsome idols in all Judah and Benjamin and in the towns which he had captured in the hill-country of Ephraim, and he repaired the altar of the LORD which stood before the vestibule of the LORD's house. 9 Then he assembled all the people of Judah and Benjamin and all who had come from Ephraim, Manasseh, and Simeon to reside among them, for great numbers had come over to him from Israel, when they saw that the LORD his God was with him. 10 They assembled at Jerusalem in the third month of the fifteenth year of Asa's reign, 11 and that day they sacrificed to the LORD seven hundred oxen and seven thousand sheep from the spoil which they had brought. 12 They entered wholeheartedly into a covenant to seek guidance of the LORD the God of their fathers; 13 all who would not seek the LORD the God of Israel were to be put to death, whether young or old, men and women alike. 14 Then they bound themselves by an oath to the LORD, with loud shouts of acclamation while trumpets and horns sounded. 15 All Judah rejoiced at the oath, because they had bound themselves with all their heart and had sought the LORD earnestly; he had let himself be found by them, and he gave them security

a Or *Nubian*; Heb *Cushite*   *b* Or *Nubians*; Heb *Cushites*
c Heb *They*   *d* Meaning of Heb uncertain   *e* Compare Syr Vg:
Heb *the prophecy, the prophet Obed*   *f* Heb *the vestibule of the*
LORD

15:3 **without law:** *or* without the law.   15:8 **house:** *prob. rdg;*
Heb. omits.   15:16–18 Cp. *1 Kgs. 15:13–15.*

7 Asa had an army of three hundred thousand shield- and lance-bearers from Judah, and two hundred and eighty thousand from Benjamin who carried bucklers and were archers, all of them valiant warriors. 8 Zerah the Ethiopian moved against them with a force of one million men and three hundred chariots, and he came as far as Mareshah. 9 Asa went out to meet him and set himself in battle array in the valley of Zephathah, near Mareshah. 10 Asa called upon the LORD, his God, praying: "O LORD, there is none like you to help the powerless against the strong. Help us, O LORD, our God, for we rely on you, and in your name we have come against this multitude. You are the LORD, our God; let no man prevail against you." 11 And so the LORD defeated the Ethiopians before Asa and Judah, and they fled. 12 Asa and those with him pursued them as far as Gerar, and the Ethiopians fell until there were no survivors, for they were crushed before the LORD and his army, which carried away enormous spoils. 13 Then the Judahites conquered all the cities around Gerar, for the fear of the LORD was upon them; they despoiled all the cities, for there was much booty in them. 14 They attacked also the tents of the cattle-herders and carried off a great number of sheep and camels. Then they returned to Jerusalem.

15 Upon Azariah, son of Oded, came the spirit of God. 2 He went forth to meet Asa and said to him: "Hear me, Asa and all Judah and Benjamin! The LORD is with you when you are with him, and if you seek him he will be present to you; but if you abandon him, he will abandon you. 3 For a long time Israel had no true God, no priest-teacher and no law, 4 but when in their distress they turned to the LORD, the God of Israel, and sought him, he was present to them. 5 In that former time there was no place for anyone to go or come, but there were many terrors upon the inhabitants of the lands. 6 Nation crushed nation and city crushed city, for God destroyed them by every kind of adversity. 7 But as for you, be strong and do not relax, for your work shall be rewarded."

8 When Asa heard these words and the prophecy [Oded the prophet], he was encouraged to remove the detestable idols from the whole land of Judah and Benjamin and from the cities he had taken in the highlands of Ephraim, and to restore the altar of the LORD which was before the vestibule of the LORD. 9 Then he convened all Judah and Benjamin, together with those of Ephraim, Manasseh and Simeon who sojourned with them; for many had fled to him from Israel when they saw that the LORD, his God, was with him. 10 They gathered at Jerusalem in the third month of the fifteenth year of Asa's reign, 11 and sacrificed to the LORD at that time seven hundred oxen and seven thousand sheep of the booty they had brought. 12 They entered into a covenant to seek the LORD, the God of their fathers, with all their heart and soul; 13 and everyone who would not seek the LORD, the God of Israel, was to be put to death, whether small or great, whether man or woman. 14 They swore to the LORD with a loud voice, with shouting and with trumpets and horns. 15 All Judah rejoiced over the oath, for they had sworn with their whole heart and sought him with complete desire, so that he was present to them. And the LORD gave them rest on every side.

7 Asa had an army of three hundred thousand men of Judah armed with shields and spears and two hundred and eighty thousand men of Benjamin armed with shields and bows, all of them outstanding soldiers. 8 Zerah the Cushite took the field against them with an army a million strong and three hundred chariots, and penetrated to Mareshah. 9 Asa took the field against him and the battle-lines were drawn up in the Valley of Zephathah, at Mareshah. 10 Asa then called on Yahweh his God and said, 'Yahweh, numbers and strength make no difference to you when you give your help. Help us, Yahweh our God, for, relying on you, we are confronting this horde in your name. Yahweh, you are our God. Human strength cannot prevail against you!'

11 Yahweh routed the Cushites before Asa and Judah. The Cushites fled, 12 and Asa pursued them with his army as far as Gerar. So many of the Cushites fell that they were unable to survive. They were cut to pieces by Yahweh and his army.

They carried off a great deal of booty, 13 they destroyed all the towns round Gerar — for a panic from Yahweh had seized the towns — and plundered all the towns since they were full of loot. 14 They also routed the cattle-owners and carried off great numbers of sheep and camels; then they returned to Jerusalem.

15 The spirit of God then came on Azariah son of Oded; 2 he went out to meet Asa and said, 'Listen to me, Asa, and all you in Judah and in Benjamin: Yahweh will be with you so long as you are with him. If you seek him, he will let you find him; but if you desert him, he will desert you. 3 For a long time Israel did not have the true God or a teacher-priest or a law, 4 but when in their distress they turned to Yahweh, God of Israel, and sought him, he let them find him. 5 In those times there was no security for people as they went about their business, but great unrest affecting the inhabitants of all countries, 6 nation being crushed by nation and city by city, since God caused confusion among them by every kind of distress. 7 So be strong, do not be discouraged, for your deeds will be rewarded.'

8 When Asa heard these words and the prophecy, he took courage and removed the abominable idols throughout the land of Judah and Benjamin as well as from the towns which he had captured in the highlands of Ephraim, and repaired the altar of Yahweh which stood in front of the portico of Yahweh. 9 He summoned all Judah and Benjamin as well as those Ephraimites, Manassehites and Simeonites who had settled with them — for a great many people from Israel had gone over to Asa when they saw that Yahweh his God was with him. 10 They assembled in Jerusalem in the third month of the fifteenth year of Asa's reign, 11 that day sacrificing to Yahweh seven hundred oxen and seven thousand sheep from the booty which they had brought back. 12 They then made a covenant to seek Yahweh, God of their ancestors, with all their heart and soul; 13 anyone who would not seek Yahweh, God of Israel, was to be put to death, whether high or low, man or woman. 14 They pledged their oath to Yahweh in ringing tones, with shouts of joy, to the sound of trumpet and horn; 15 all Judah rejoiced over the oath, for they had sworn it wholeheartedly, and sought him so earnestly that he allowed them to find him; Yahweh gave them peace all round.

16 King Asa even removed his mother Maacah from being queen mother because she had made an abominable image for Asherah. Asa cut down her image, crushed it, and burned it at the Wadi Kidron. 17 But the high places were not taken out of Israel. Nevertheless the heart of Asa was true all his days. 18 He brought into the house of God the votive gifts of his father and his own votive gifts — silver, gold, and utensils. 19 And there was no more war until the thirty-fifth year of the reign of Asa.

16 In the thirty-sixth year of the reign of Asa, King Baasha of Israel went up against Judah, and built Ramah, to prevent anyone from going out or coming into the territory of*g* King Asa of Judah. 2 Then Asa took silver and gold from the treasures of the house of the LORD and the king's house, and sent them to King Ben-hadad of Aram, who resided in Damascus, saying, 3 "Let there be an alliance between me and you, like that between my father and your father; I am sending to you silver and gold; go, break your alliance with King Baasha of Israel, so that he may withdraw from me." 4 Ben-hadad listened to King Asa, and sent the commanders of his armies against the cities of Israel. They conquered Ijon, Dan, Abel-maim, and all the store-cities of Naphtali. 5 When Baasha heard of it, he stopped building Ramah, and let his work cease. 6 Then King Asa brought all Judah, and they carried away the stones of Ramah and its timber, with which Baasha had been building, and with them he built up Geba and Mizpah.

7 At that time the seer Hanani came to King Asa of Judah, and said to him, "Because you relied on the king of Aram, and did not rely on the LORD your God, the army of the king of Aram has escaped you. 8 Were not the Ethiopians*h* and the Libyans a huge army with exceedingly many chariots and cavalry? Yet because you relied on the LORD, he gave them into your hand. 9 For the eyes of the LORD range throughout the entire earth, to strengthen those whose heart is true to him. You have done foolishly in this; for from now on you will have wars." 10 Then Asa was angry with the seer, and put him in the stocks, in prison, for he was in a rage with him because of this. And Asa inflicted cruelties on some of the people at the same time.

11 The acts of Asa, from first to last, are written in the Book of the Kings of Judah and Israel. 12 In the thirty-ninth year of his reign Asa was diseased in his feet, and his disease became severe; yet even in his disease he did not seek the LORD, but sought help from physicians. 13 Then Asa slept with his ancestors, dying in the forty-first year of his reign. 14 They buried him in the tomb that he had hewn out for himself in the city of David. They laid him on a bier that had been filled with various kinds of spices prepared by the perfumer's art; and they made a very great fire in his honor.

17 His son Jehoshaphat succeeded him, and strengthened himself against Israel. 2 He placed forces in all the fortified cities of Judah, and set garrisons in the land of Judah, and in the cities of Ephraim that his father Asa had taken. 3 The LORD was with Jehoshaphat, because he walked in the earlier ways of his father;*i* he did not seek the Baals, 4 but sought the God of his father and walked in his commandments, and not according to the ways of Israel. 5 Therefore the LORD established the kingdom in his hand. All Judah brought tribute to Jehoshaphat, and he had great

on every side. 16 King Asa even deprived Maacah his grandmother of her rank as queen mother because she had an obscene object made for the worship of Asherah; Asa cut it down, ground it to powder, and burnt it in the wadi of the Kidron. 17 Although the shrines were allowed to remain in Israel, Asa himself remained faithful all his life. 18 He brought into the house of God all his father's votive offerings and his own, gold and silver and sacred vessels. 19 And there was no more war until the thirty-fifth year of Asa's reign.

16 In the thirty-sixth year of the reign of Asa, King Baasha of Israel invaded Judah and fortified Ramah to prevent anyone leaving or entering the kingdom of Asa of Judah. 2 Asa brought out silver and gold from the treasuries of the house of the LORD and the king's palace, and sent them to Ben-hadad king of Aram, whose capital was Damascus, with this request: 3 'Let there be an alliance between us, as there was between our fathers. Herewith I send you silver and gold; break off your alliance with King Baasha of Israel, so that he may abandon his campaign against me.' 4 Ben-hadad listened with approval to King Asa; he ordered his army commanders to move against the towns of Israel, and they attacked Iyyon, Dan, Abel-mayim, and all the store-cities of Naphtali. 5 When Baasha heard of it, he discontinued the fortifying of Ramah and stopped all work on it. 6 Then King Asa took with him all the men of Judah and they removed the stones of Ramah and the timbers with which Baasha had fortified it, and he used them to fortify Geba and Mizpah.

7 At that time the seer Hanani came to King Asa of Judah and said to him, 'Because you relied on the king of Aram and not on the LORD your God, the army of the king of Israel has escaped. 8 Did not the Cushites and the Libyans have a great army with a vast number of chariots and horsemen? Yet, because you relied on the LORD, he delivered them into your power. 9 The eyes of the LORD range through the whole world, to bring aid and comfort to those whose hearts are loyal to him. You have acted foolishly in this affair; you will have wars from now on.' 10 Asa was vexed with the seer and had him put in the stocks; for those words had made the king very indignant. At the same time he treated some of the people with great brutality.

11 The events of Asa's reign, from beginning to end, are recorded in the annals of the kings of Judah and Israel. 12 In the thirty-ninth year of his reign Asa became gravely affected with disease in his feet; he did not seek guidance of the LORD but resorted to physicians. 13 He rested with his forefathers, in the forty-first year of his reign, 14 and was buried in the tomb which he had bought for himself in the city of David, being laid on a bier which had been heaped with all kinds of spices skilfully compounded; and a great fire was kindled in his honour.

17 ASA was succeeded by his son Jehoshaphat, who strengthened his position against Israel, 2 posting troops in all the fortified towns of Judah and stationing garrisons throughout Judah and in the towns of Ephraim which his father Asa had captured. 3 The LORD was with Jehoshaphat, for he followed the example his father had set in his early years and did not resort to the baalim; 4 he sought guidance of the God of his father and obeyed his commandments and did not follow the practices of Israel. 5 The LORD established the kingdom under his control; all Judah brought him gifts, and his wealth and fame became

---

15:16 **grandmother:** *lit.* mother.   16:1–6 *Cp. 1 Kgs. 15:17–22.*
16:7 **Israel:** *so Gk (Luc.); Heb.* Aram.   16:11–14 *Cp.*
1 Kgs. 15:23–24.   16:14 **bought:** *or* dug. **on a bier:** *or*
in a niche.   17:2 **garrisons:** *or* officers.   17:3 **father:** *so some*
MSS; others add David. **the baalim:** *or* Baal.   17:5 **fame:** *or* riches.

---

g Heb lacks *the territory of*   *h* Or *Nubians*; Heb *Cushites*
i Another reading is *his father David*

16 Maacah, the mother of King Asa, he deposed as queen mother because she had made an outrageous object for Asherah; Asa cut this down, smashed it, and burnt it in the Kidron Valley. 17 Although the high places did not disappear from Israel, yet Asa's heart was undivided as long as he lived. 18 He brought into the house of God his father's votive offerings and his own: silver, gold, and various utensils. 19 There was no war until the thirty-fifth year of Asa's reign.

16 In the thirty-sixth year of Asa's reign, Baasha, king of Israel, attacked Judah and fortified Ramah to prevent any communication with Asa, king of Judah. 2 Asa then brought out silver and gold from the treasuries of the temple of the LORD and of the royal palace and sent them to Ben-hadad, king of Aram, who lived in Damascus, with this message: 3 "There is a treaty between you and me, as there was between your father and my father. See, I am sending you silver and gold. Go, break your treaty with Baasha, king of Israel, that he may withdraw from me." 4 Ben-hadad agreed to King Asa's request and sent the leaders of his troops against the cities of Israel. They attacked Ijon, Dan, Abel-maim, and all the store cities of Naphtali. 5 When Baasha heard of it, he left off fortifying Ramah; he stopped his work. 6 Then King Asa commandeered all of Judah to carry away the stone and wood with which Baasha had been fortifying Ramah, and with them he fortified Geba and Mizpah.

7 At that time Hanani the seer came to Asa, king of Judah, and said to him: "Because you relied on the king of Aram and did not rely on the LORD, your God, the army of the king of Aram has escaped your hand. 8 Were not the Ethiopians and Libyans a vast army, with great numbers of chariots and drivers? And yet, because you relied on the LORD, he delivered them into your power. 9 The eyes of the LORD roam over the whole earth, to encourage those who are devoted to him wholeheartedly. You have acted foolishly in this matter, for from now on you will have wars." 10 But Asa became angry with the seer and imprisoned him in the stocks, so greatly was he enraged at him over this. Asa also oppressed some of his people at this time.

11 Now the acts of Asa, first and last, can be found recorded in the book of the kings of Judah and Israel. 12 In the thirty-ninth year of his reign, Asa contracted a serious disease in his feet. But even in his sickness he did not seek the LORD, but only the physicians. 13 Asa rested with his ancestors; he died in the forty-first year of his reign. 14 They buried him in the tomb he had hewn for himself in the City of David, having laid him upon a couch which was filled with spices and various kinds of aromatics compounded into an ointment. They also burned a very great funeral pyre for him.

17 His son Jehoshaphat succeeded him as king and strengthened his hold against Israel. 2 He placed armed forces in all the fortified cities of Judah, and put garrisons in the land of Judah and in the cities of Ephraim which his father Asa had taken. 3 The LORD was with Jehoshaphat, for he walked in the ways his father had pursued in the beginning, and he did not consult the Baals. 4 Rather, he sought the God of his father and observed his commands, and not the practices of Israel. 5 As a result, the LORD made his kingdom secure, and all Judah gave Jehoshaphat gifts, so that he enjoyed great wealth and glory. 6 Thus he was

16 King Asa even deprived his mother Maacah of the dignity of Great Lady for having made an obscenity for Asherah; Asa cut down her obscenity, smashed it and burnt it in the ravine of the Kidron. 17 Though the high places were not abolished in Israel, Asa's heart was loyal throughout his life. 18 He deposited his father's and his own dedicated gifts of silver, gold and sacred vessels, in the Temple of Yahweh.

19 Up to the thirty-fifth year of Asa's reign there was no war.

16 In the thirty-sixth year of Asa's reign, Baasha king of Israel marched on Judah and fortified Ramah to block the communications of Asa king of Judah. 2 Asa then took silver and gold from the treasuries of the Temple of Yahweh and the royal palace and sent this with the following message to Ben-Hadad king of Aram, who lived in Damascus, 3 'Let us make an alliance between me and you, between my father and your father! Look, I have sent you silver and gold. Come, break off your alliance with Baasha king of Israel, which will make him withdraw from me.' 4 Ben-Hadad listened favourably to King Asa and sent the generals of his armies to attack the towns of Israel; he ravaged Ijon, Dan, Abel-Maim and all the storage towns of Naphtali. 5 When Baasha heard this he gave up fortifying Ramah, abandoning this work. 6 King Asa then had all Judah carry away the stones and timber with which Baasha had been fortifying Ramah, and used them to fortify Geba and Mizpah.

7 Then it was that Hanani the seer came to Asa king of Judah and said, 'Because you relied on the king of Aram and not on Yahweh your God, the king of Aram's army will slip through your fingers. 8 Did not the Cushites and Libyans form a vast army with great numbers of chariots and cavalry? Even so, because you relied on Yahweh, he gave you the upper hand; 9 for Yahweh's eyes rove to and fro across the whole world to support those whose hearts are loyal to him. You have acted like a fool in this respect; hence, from now on you will have wars.' 10 Enraged with the seer, Asa had him put in the stocks in prison, being angry with him over this; at the same time Asa ill-treated some of the people too.

11 The history of Asa, from first to last, is recorded in the Book of the Kings of Judah and Israel. 12 In the thirty-ninth year of his reign, Asa contracted a disease in his feet, which became very severe; in his illness, however, he consulted not Yahweh but the doctors. 13 Asa then fell asleep with his ancestors, dying in the forty-first year of his reign. 14 He was buried in the tomb which he had ordered to be cut for him in the City of David. He was laid in the burial chamber which was filled with perfume blended from all sorts of oils, and a very great funeral fire was made for him.

17 When his son Jehoshaphat succeeded him, he made himself stronger against Israel 2 by stationing troops in all the fortified towns in Judah and by garrisoning Judah and the towns of Ephraim which his father Asa had captured.

3 Yahweh was with Jehoshaphat because he followed the example of his father's earlier days and did not have recourse to Baal, 4 but sought Yahweh, the God of his father, following his commandments and not behaving as Israel did. 5 Because of this, Yahweh put him in secure control of the kingdom, while all Judah gave Jehoshaphat presents until ample riches and honour were his. 6 He was so en-

riches and honor. 6 His heart was courageous in the ways of the LORD; and furthermore he removed the high places and the sacred poles *j* from Judah.

7 In the third year of his reign he sent his officials, Ben-hail, Obadiah, Zechariah, Nethanel, and Micaiah, to teach in the cities of Judah. 8 With them were the Levites, Shemaiah, Nethaniah, Zebadiah, Asahel, Shemiramoth, Jehonathan, Adonijah, Tobijah, and Tob-adonijah; and with these Levites, the priests Elishama and Jehoram. 9 They taught in Judah, having the book of the law of the LORD with them; they went around through all the cities of Judah and taught among the people.

10 The fear of the LORD fell on all the kingdoms of the lands around Judah, and they did not make war against Jehoshaphat. 11 Some of the Philistines brought Jehoshaphat presents, and silver for tribute; and the Arabs also brought him seven thousand seven hundred rams and seven thousand seven hundred male goats. 12 Jehoshaphat grew steadily greater. He built fortresses and storage cities in Judah. 13 He carried out great works in the cities of Judah. He had soldiers, mighty warriors, in Jerusalem. 14 This was the muster of them by ancestral houses: Of Judah, the commanders of the thousands: Adnah the commander, with three hundred thousand mighty warriors, 15 and next to him Jehohanan the commander, with two hundred eighty thousand, 16 and next to him Amasiah son of Zichri, a volunteer for the service of the LORD, with two hundred thousand mighty warriors. 17 Of Benjamin: Eliada, a mighty warrior, with two hundred thousand armed with bow and shield, 18 and next to him Jehozabad with one hundred eighty thousand armed for war. 19 These were in the service of the king, besides those whom the king had placed in the fortified cities throughout all Judah.

18 Now Jehoshaphat had great riches and honor; and he made a marriage alliance with Ahab. 2 After some years he went down to Ahab in Samaria. Ahab slaughtered an abundance of sheep and oxen for him and for the people who were with him, and induced him to go up against Ramoth-gilead. 3 King Ahab of Israel said to Jehoshaphat of Judah, "Will you go with me to Ramoth-gilead?" He answered him, "I am with you, my people are your people. We will be with you in the war."

4 But Jehoshaphat also said to the king of Israel, "Inquire first for the word of the LORD." 5 Then the king of Israel gathered the prophets together, four hundred of them, and said to them, "Shall we go to battle against Ramoth-gilead, or shall I refrain?" They said, "Go up; for God will give it into the hand of the king." 6 But Jehoshaphat said, "Is there no other prophet of the LORD here of whom we may inquire?" 7 The king of Israel said to Jehoshaphat, "There is still one other by whom we may inquire of the LORD, Micaiah son of Imlah; but I hate him, for he never prophesies anything favorable about me, but only disaster." Jehoshaphat said, "Let the king not say such a thing." 8 Then the king of Israel summoned an officer and said, "Bring quickly Micaiah son of Imlah." 9 Now the king of Israel and King Jehoshaphat of Judah were sitting on their thrones, arrayed in their robes; and they were sitting at the threshing floor at the entrance of the gate of Samaria; and all the prophets were prophesying before them. 10 Zedekiah son of Chenaa-

very great. 6 He took pride in the service of the LORD; he again suppressed the shrines and the sacred poles in Judah.

7 In the third year of his reign he sent his officers Benhayil, Obadiah, Zechariah, Nethanel, and Micaiah to teach in the towns of Judah, 8 together with the Levites Shemaiah, Nethaniah, Zebadiah, Asahel, Shemiramoth, Jehonathan, Adonijah, Tobiah, and Tob-adonijah, accompanied by the priests Elishama and Jehoram. 9 They taught in Judah, having with them the scroll of the law of the LORD; they went round the towns of Judah teaching the people.

10 The dread of the LORD fell upon all the rulers of the lands surrounding Judah, and they did not make war on Jehoshaphat. 11 Certain Philistines brought him a gift of a great quantity of silver; the Arabs too brought him seven thousand seven hundred rams and seven thousand seven hundred he-goats. 12 Jehoshaphat grew ever more powerful. He built fortresses and store-towns in Judah, 13 and was engaged on much work in her towns.

He kept regular, seasoned troops in Jerusalem, 14 enrolled according to their clans in this way: of Judah, the officers over units of a thousand: Adnah the commander, together with three hundred thousand seasoned troops; 15 next to him the commander Johanan, with two hundred and eighty thousand; 16 next to him Amasiah son of Zichri, who had volunteered for the service of the LORD, with two hundred thousand seasoned troops; 17 and of Benjamin: an experienced soldier Eliada, with two hundred thousand men armed with bows and shields; 18 next to him Jehozabad, with a hundred and eighty thousand fully armed men. 19 These were the men who served the king, apart from those whom the king had posted in the fortified towns throughout Judah.

18 When Jehoshaphat had become very wealthy and famous, he allied himself with Ahab by marriage. 2 Some years afterwards he went down to Samaria to visit Ahab, who slaughtered many sheep and oxen for him and his retinue, and incited him to attack Ramoth-gilead. 3 What King Ahab of Israel said to King Jehoshaphat of Judah was: 'Will you join me in attacking Ramoth-gilead?' Jehoshaphat replied, 'What is mine is yours: myself and my people; I shall join you in the war,' 4 but he said to the king of Israel, 'First let us seek counsel from the LORD.'

5 The king of Israel assembled the prophets, some four hundred of them, and asked them, 'Shall we attack Ramoth-gilead or not?' 'Attack,' was the answer; 'God will deliver it into your majesty's hands.' 6 Jehoshaphat asked, 'Is there no other prophet of the LORD here through whom we may seek guidance?' 7 'There is one more,' the king of Israel answered, 'through whom we may seek guidance of the LORD, but I hate the man, because he never prophesies good for me, never anything but evil. His name is Micaiah son of Imla.' Jehoshaphat exclaimed, 'Let your majesty say no such thing!' 8 The king of Israel called one of his eunuchs and told him to fetch Micaiah son of Imla with all speed.

9 The king of Israel and King Jehoshaphat of Judah, clothed in their royal robes and in shining armour, were seated on their thrones at the entrance to the gate of Samaria, and all the prophets were prophesying before them.

j Heb *Asherim*

17:8 **Tob-adonijah:** *prob. rdg; Heb. adds* the Levites.
18:1 **famous:** *or* rich. 18:2–34 *Cp. 1 Kgs.* 22:2–35.

934

encouraged to follow the LORD's ways, and again he removed the high places and the sacred poles from Judah. 7 In the third year of his reign he sent his leading men, Ben-hail, Obadiah, Zechariah, Nethanel and Micaiah, to teach in the cities of Judah. 8 With them he sent the Levites Shemaiah, Nethaniah, Zebadiah, Asahel, Shemiramoth, Jehonathan, Adonijah and Tobijah, together with the priests Elishama and Jehoram. 9 They taught in Judah, having with them the book containing the law of the LORD; they traveled through all the cities of Judah and taught among the people.

10 Now the fear of the LORD was upon all the kingdoms of the countries surrounding Judah, so that they did not war against Jehoshaphat. 11 Some of the Philistines brought Jehoshaphat gifts and a tribute of silver; and the Arabs also brought him a flock of seven thousand seven hundred rams and seven thousand seven hundred he-goats.

12 Jehoshaphat grew steadily greater. He built strongholds and store cities in Judah. 13 He carried out many works in the cities of Judah, and he had soldiers, valiant warriors, in Jerusalem. 14 This was their mustering according to their ancestral houses. Of Judah, the commanders of thousands: Adnah the commander, and with him three hundred thousand valiant warriors. 15 Next to him, Jehohanan the commander, and with him two hundred eighty thousand. 16 Next to him, Amasiah, son of Zichri, who offered himself to the LORD, and with him two hundred thousand valiant warriors. 17 From Benjamin: Eliada, a valiant warrior, and with him two hundred thousand armed with bow and buckler. 18 Next to him, Jozabad, and with him one hundred and eighty thousand equipped for war. 19 These were at the service of the king; in addition were those whom the king had placed in the fortified cities throughout all Judah.

18 Jehoshaphat therefore had wealth and glory in abundance; but he became related to Ahab by marriage. 2 After some years he went down to Ahab at Samaria; Ahab offered numerous sheep and oxen for him and the people with him, and persuaded him to go up against Ramoth-gilead. 3 Ahab, king of Israel, asked Jehoshaphat, king of Judah, "Will you come with me to Ramoth-gilead?" "You and I are as one," was his answer; "your people and my people as well. We will be with you in the battle." 4 But Jehoshaphat also said to the king of Israel, "Seek the word of the LORD at once."

5 The king of Israel gathered his prophets, four hundred in number, and asked them, "Shall we go to attack Ramothgilead, or shall I refrain?" "Go up," they answered. "God will deliver it over to the king." 6 But Jehoshaphat said, "Is there no other prophet of the LORD here whom we may consult?" 7 The king of Israel answered Jehoshaphat, "There is still another through whom we may consult the LORD, but I hate him, for he prophesies not good but always evil about me. That is Micaiah, son of Imlah." Jehoshaphat said, "Let not your Majesty speak of evil against you." 8 So the king of Israel called an official, to whom he said, "Get Micaiah, son of Imlah, at once." 9 The king of Israel and King Jehoshaphat of Judah were seated each on his throne, clothed in their robes of state on a threshing floor at the entrance of the gate of Samaria, and all the prophets were prophesying before them.

thusiastic about obeying Yahweh that once again he abolished the high places and sacred poles in Judah. 7 In the third year of his reign he sent his leading men — Ben-Hail, Obadiah, Zechariah, Nethanel and Micaiah, to give instruction in the towns of Judah. 8 With them went the Levites: Shemaiah, Nethaniah, Zebadiah, Asahel, Shemiramoth, Jehonathan, Adonijah and Tobijah, the Levites; Elishama and Jehoram the priests went with them. 9 They gave instruction in Judah, having with them the book of the Law of Yahweh, and went round all the towns of Judah instructing the people.

10 A panic from Yahweh seized all the kings of the countries surrounding Judah, as a result of which they did not make war on Jehoshaphat. 11 Some of the Philistines brought Jehoshaphat presents and a load of silver and the Arabs brought him seven thousand seven hundred rams and seven thousand seven hundred he-goats.

12 Jehoshaphat became more and more powerful. He built fortresses and storage towns in Judah.

13 He accumulated ample supplies in the towns of Judah. He also had warriors, outstanding men, in Jerusalem. 14 According to family, this is how they were classified: Over the commanders of the thousands of Judah was General Adnah, who had three hundred thousand outstanding men;

15 Under him was General Jehohanan, who had two hundred and eighty thousand;

16 Under him was Amasiah son of Zichri, who had volunteered for Yahweh and who had two hundred thousand outstanding men;

17 That outstanding soldier, Eliada, represented Benjamin, and he had two hundred thousand men armed with bow and shield;

18 And under him Jehozabad, who had one hundred and eighty thousand equipped for war.

19 These were in attendance on the king, apart from those whom the king had stationed in the fortified towns all over Judah.

18 Although Jehoshaphat enjoyed great wealth and honour, he allied himself by marriage to Ahab. 2 After some years he paid a visit to Ahab in Samaria. Ahab slaughtered an immense number of sheep and oxen for him and his retinue, to induce him to attack Ramoth-Gilead. 3 Ahab king of Israel then said to Jehoshaphat king of Judah, 'Will you come with me to Ramoth-Gilead?' He replied, 'I will share in battle with you, my men with yours.'

4 Jehoshaphat, however, said to the king of Israel, 'First, please consult the word of Yahweh.' 5 So the king of Israel called the prophets together, four hundred of them. 'Should we go and attack Ramoth-Gilead,' he asked, 'or should I hold back?' 'March,' they replied, 'for God will deliver it into the king's power.' 6 Jehoshaphat, however, said, 'Is there no other prophet of Yahweh here, for us to consult?' 7 The king of Israel answered Jehoshaphat, 'There is one more man through whom we can consult Yahweh, but I hate him because he never has a favourable prophecy for me, always unfavourable ones; he is Micaiah son of Imlah.' 'The king should not say such things,' said Jehoshaphat. 8 The king of Israel then summoned a court official and said, 'Bring Micaiah son of Imlah immediately.'

9 The king of Israel and Jehoshaphat king of Judah were sitting each on his throne, wearing their robes; in an open space just outside the gate of Samaria, with all the prophets prophesying before them, 10 Zedekiah son of Chenaanah,

nah made for himself horns of iron, and he said, "Thus says the LORD: With these you shall gore the Arameans until they are destroyed." 11 All the prophets were prophesying the same and saying, "Go up to Ramoth-gilead and triumph; the LORD will give it into the hand of the king."

12 The messenger who had gone to summon Micaiah said to him, "Look, the words of the prophets with one accord are favorable to the king; let your word be like the word of one of them, and speak favorably." 13 But Micaiah said, "As the LORD lives, whatever my God says, that I will speak."

14 When he had come to the king, the king said to him, "Micaiah, shall we go to Ramoth-gilead to battle, or shall I refrain?" He answered, "Go up and triumph; they will be given into your hand." 15 But the king said to him, "How many times must I make you swear to tell me nothing but the truth in the name of the LORD?" 16 Then Micaiah[k] said, "I saw all Israel scattered on the mountains, like sheep without a shepherd; and the LORD said, 'These have no master; let each one go home in peace.' " 17 The king of Israel said to Jehoshaphat, "Did I not tell you that he would not prophesy anything favorable about me, but only disaster?"

18 Then Micaiah[k] said, "Therefore hear the word of the LORD: I saw the LORD sitting on his throne, with all the host of heaven standing to the right and to the left of him. 19 And the LORD said, 'Who will entice King Ahab of Israel, so that he may go up and fall at Ramoth-gilead?' Then one said one thing, and another said another, 20 until a spirit came forward and stood before the LORD, saying, 'I will entice him.' The LORD asked him, 'How?' 21 He replied, 'I will go out and be a lying spirit in the mouth of all his prophets.' Then the LORD[k] said, 'You are to entice him, and you shall succeed; go out and do it.' 22 So you see, the LORD has put a lying spirit in the mouth of these your prophets; the LORD has decreed disaster for you."

23 Then Zedekiah son of Chenaanah came up to Micaiah, slapped him on the cheek, and said, "Which way did the spirit of the LORD pass from me to speak to you?" 24 Micaiah replied, "You will find out on that day when you go in to hide in an inner chamber." 25 The king of Israel then ordered, "Take Micaiah, and return him to Amon the governor of the city and to Joash the king's son; 26 and say, 'Thus says the king: Put this fellow in prison, and feed him on reduced rations of bread and water until I return in peace.' " 27 Micaiah said, "If you return in peace, the LORD has not spoken by me." And he said, "Hear, you peoples, all of you!"

28 So the king of Israel and King Jehoshaphat of Judah went up to Ramoth-gilead. 29 The king of Israel said to Jehoshaphat, "I will disguise myself and go into battle, but you wear your robes." So the king of Israel disguised himself, and they went into battle. 30 Now the king of Aram had commanded the captains of his chariots, "Fight with no one small or great, but only with the king of Israel." 31 When the captains of the chariots saw Jehoshaphat, they said, "It is the king of Israel." So they turned to fight against him; and Jehoshaphat cried out, and the LORD helped him. God drew them away from him, 32 for when the captains of the chariots saw that it was not the king of Israel, they turned back from pursuing him. 33 But a certain man drew his bow and unknowingly struck the king of Israel between the scale armor and the breastplate; so he said to the driver of his chariot, "Turn around, and carry me out of the battle, for I am wounded." 34 The battle grew hot that day, and the king of Israel propped himself up in his chariot facing the Arameans until evening; then at sunset he died.

10 One of them, Zedekiah son of Kenaanah, made himself iron horns and declared, 'This is the word of the LORD: "With horns like these you will gore the Aramaeans and make an end of them." ' 11 In the same vein all the prophets prophesied, 'Attack Ramoth-gilead and win the day; the LORD will deliver it into your hands.'

12 The messenger sent to fetch Micaiah told him that the prophets had unanimously given the king a favourable answer. 'And mind you agree with them,' he added. 13 'As the LORD lives,' said Micaiah, 'I shall say only what my God tells me to say.' 14 When he came into the king's presence, the king asked him, 'Micaiah, shall we attack Ramoth-gilead or not?' 'Attack and win the day,' he replied; 'it will fall into your hands.' 15 'How often must I adjure you', said the king, 'to tell me nothing but the truth in the name of the LORD?' 16 Then Micaiah said,

'I saw all Israel scattered on the mountains,
like sheep without a shepherd;
and I heard the LORD say: "They have no master;
let them go home in peace." '

17 The king of Israel said to Jehoshaphat, 'Did I not tell you that he never prophesies good for me, never anything but evil?' 18 Micaiah went on, 'Listen now to the word of the LORD: I saw the LORD seated on his throne, with all the host of heaven in attendance on his right and on his left. 19 The LORD said, "Who will entice King Ahab of Israel to go up and attack Ramoth-gilead?" One said one thing and one said another, 20 until a spirit came forward and, standing before the LORD, said, "I shall entice him." "How?" said the LORD. 21 "I shall go out", he answered, "and be a lying spirit in the mouths of all his prophets." "Entice him; you will succeed," said the LORD. "Go and do it." 22 You see, then, how the LORD has put a lying spirit in the mouths of all these prophets of yours, because he has decreed disaster for you.'

23 At that Zedekiah son of Kenaanah came up to Micaiah and struck him in the face: 'And how did the spirit of the LORD pass from me to speak to you?' he demanded. 24 Micaiah retorted, 'That you will find out on the day when you run into an inner room to hide.' 25 The king of Israel ordered Micaiah to be arrested and committed to the custody of Amon the governor of the city and Joash the king's son. 26 'Throw this fellow into prison,' he said, 'and put him on a prison diet of bread and water until I come home in safety.' 27 Micaiah declared, 'If you do return in safety, the LORD has not spoken by me.'

28 The king of Israel and King Jehoshaphat of Judah marched on Ramoth-gilead. 29 The king of Israel went into battle in disguise, for he had said to Jehoshaphat, 'I shall disguise myself to go into battle, but you must wear your royal robes.' 30 The king of Aram had ordered the captains of his chariots not to engage all and sundry, but the king of Israel alone. 31 When the captains saw Jehoshaphat, they thought he was the king of Israel and wheeled to attack him, but Jehoshaphat cried out, and the LORD came to his help; God drew them away from him. 32 When the captains saw that he was not the king of Israel, they broke off the attack on him. 33 One man, however, drew his bow at random and hit the king of Israel where the breastplate joins the plates of the armour. The king said to his driver, 'Turn about and take me out of the line; I am wounded.' 34 When the day's fighting reached its height, the king of Israel was facing the Aramaeans, propped up in his chariot; he remained so till evening, and at sunset he died.

k Heb he

10 Zedekiah, son of Chenaanah, made iron horns for himself and said: "The LORD says, 'With these you shall gore Aram until you have destroyed them.' " 11 The other prophets prophesied in the same vein, saying: "Go up to Ramoth-gilead. You shall succeed; the LORD will deliver it over to the king." 12 The messenger who had gone to call Micaiah said to him: "Look now, the prophets unanimously predict good for the king. Let your word, like each of theirs, predict good." 13 "As the LORD lives," Micaiah answered, "I will say what my God tells me."

14 When he came to the king, the king said to him, "Micaiah, shall we go to fight against Ramoth-gilead, or shall I refrain?" "Go up," he answered, "and succeed; they will be delivered into your power." 15 But the king said to him, "How many times must I adjure you to tell me nothing but the truth in the name of the LORD?" 16 Then Micaiah answered:

"I see all Israel
        scattered on the mountains,
    like sheep without a shepherd,
        and the LORD saying, 'These have no master!
Let each of them go back home in peace.' "

17 The king of Israel said to Jehoshaphat, "Did I not tell you that he prophesies no good about me, but only evil?" 18 But Micaiah continued: "Therefore hear the word of the LORD: I saw the LORD seated on his throne, with the whole host of heaven standing by to his right and to his left. 19 The LORD asked, 'Who will deceive Ahab, king of Israel, so that he will go up and fall at Ramoth-gilead?' And one said this, another that, 20 until a spirit came forward and presented himself to the LORD, saying, 'I will deceive him.' The LORD asked, 'How?' 21 He answered, 'I will go forth and become a lying spirit in the mouths of all his prophets.' The LORD agreed: 'You shall succeed in deceiving him. Go forth and do this.' 22 So now the LORD has put a lying spirit in the mouths of these your prophets, but the LORD himself has decreed evil against you."

23 Thereupon Zedekiah, son of Chenaanah, came up and slapped Micaiah on the cheek, saying, "Which way did the spirit of the LORD go when he left me to speak to you?" 24 "You shall find out," Micaiah replied, "on that day when you enter an innermost chamber to hide." 25 The king of Israel then said: "Seize Micaiah and take him back to Amon, prefect of the city, and to Joash the king's son, 26 and say, 'This is the king's order: Put this man in prison and feed him scanty rations of bread and water until I return in safety!' " 27 But Micaiah said, "If ever you return in safety, the LORD has not spoken through me." And he said, "Hear, O peoples, all of you!"

28 The king of Israel and King Jehoshaphat of Judah went up to Ramoth-gilead 29 and the king of Israel said to Jehoshaphat, "I will go into battle disguised, but you put on your own clothes." So the king of Israel disguised himself and they entered the fray. 30 Meanwhile, the king of Aram had given his chariot commanders the order, "Fight with no one, small or great, except the king of Israel." 31 When the commanders saw Jehoshaphat, they exclaimed, "That must be the king of Israel!" and shifted to fight him. But Jehoshaphat cried out and the LORD helped him; God induced them to leave him. 32 The chariot commanders became aware that he was not the king of Israel and gave up their pursuit of him. 33 Someone, however, drew his bow at random and hit the king of Israel between the joints of his breastplate. He ordered his charioteer, "Rein about and take me out of the ranks, for I am disabled." 34 The battle grew fierce during the day, and the king of Israel braced himself up on his chariot facing the Arameans until evening. He died as the sun was setting.

who had made himself some iron horns, said, 'Yahweh says, "With horns like these, you will gore the Aramaeans till you make an end of them." ' 11 And all the prophets prophesied in the same vein, saying, 'March on Ramoth-Gilead! Success is sure, for Yahweh has already given it to the king!'

12 The messenger who had gone to summon Micaiah said to him, 'Look! What the prophets are saying is uniformly favourable to the king. So I hope you will say the same as they do and speak favourably.' 13 Micaiah said, 'As Yahweh lives, I shall speak exactly as Yahweh tells me!' 14 When I came to the king, the king said, 'Micaiah, should we march to attack Ramoth-Gilead, or should I hold back?' He replied, 'Go and conquer, Yahweh will deliver them into your power!' 15 The king went on, 'How often must I put you on oath to tell me nothing but the truth in the name of Yahweh?' 16 Then he spoke out.

    I saw all Israel scattered on the mountains
        like sheep without a shepherd.
    And Yahweh said, 'These have no master,
        let them all go peacefully home!'

17 At this the king of Israel said to Jehoshaphat, 'Did I not tell you that he never gives me favourable prophecies, but only unfavourable ones?' 18 Micaiah went on, 'Now listen to the word of Yahweh. I saw Yahweh seated on his throne with the whole array of heaven standing on his right and on his left. 19 Yahweh said, "Who will entice Ahab king of Israel into marching to his death at Ramoth-Gilead?" At which some answered one way, and some another. 20 A spirit then came forward and stood before Yahweh and said, "I will entice him." "How?" Yahweh asked. 21 He replied, "I shall go and be a deceptive spirit in the mouths of all his prophets." Yahweh said, "You will succeed in enticing him. Go and do it." 22 And now, you see, Yahweh has put a deceptive spirit into the mouths of your prophets here, for in fact Yahweh has pronounced disaster on you.'

23 Zedekiah son of Chenaanah then came up, struck Micaiah on the cheek and said, 'Which way did Yahweh's spirit leave me, to speak to you?' 24 'That is what you will find out,' Micaiah retorted, 'the day you go from room to room, trying to hide.' 25 The king of Israel said, 'Seize Micaiah and hand him over to Amon governor of the city, and to Joash the king's son, 26 and say, "These are the king's orders: Put this man in prison and feed him on nothing but bread and water until I am safely home." ' 27 Micaiah said, 'If you ever do get home safely, Yahweh has not spoken through me.'

28 The king of Israel and Jehoshaphat king of Judah marched on Ramoth-Gilead. 29 The king of Israel said to Jehoshaphat, 'I shall disguise myself to go into battle, but you put on your robes.' So the king of Israel disguised himself, and they went into battle. 30 Now, the king of Aram had given his chariot commanders the following order, 'Do not attack anyone of whatever rank, except the king of Israel.' 31 So, when the chariot commanders saw Jehoshaphat, they thought, 'That is the king of Israel,' and surrounded him to attack. But when Jehoshaphat shouted his war cry, Yahweh came to his help, God drew them away from him, 32 for the chariot commanders, realising that he was not the king of Israel, broke off their pursuit.

33 Someone, however, drawing his bow without any special aim, shot the king of Israel between the joints of his armour. 'Turn about!' he said to his charioteer. 'Get me out of the fighting; I am collapsing.' 34 But the battle grew fiercer as the day went on, and the king of Israel had to be held upright in his chariot facing the Aramaeans until the evening, and at sunset he died.

19 King Jehoshaphat of Judah returned in safety to his house in Jerusalem. 2 Jehu son of Hanani the seer went out to meet him and said to King Jehoshaphat, "Should you help the wicked and love those who hate the LORD? Because of this, wrath has gone out against you from the LORD. 3 Nevertheless, some good is found in you, for you destroyed the sacred poles[i] out of the land, and have set your heart to seek God."

4 Jehoshaphat resided at Jerusalem; then he went out again among the people, from Beer-sheba to the hill country of Ephraim, and brought them back to the LORD, the God of their ancestors. 5 He appointed judges in the land in all the fortified cities of Judah, city by city, 6 and said to the judges, "Consider what you are doing, for you judge not on behalf of human beings but on the LORD's behalf; he is with you in giving judgment. 7 Now, let the fear of the LORD be upon you; take care what you do, for there is no perversion of justice with the LORD our God, or partiality, or taking of bribes."

8 Moreover in Jerusalem Jehoshaphat appointed certain Levites and priests and heads of families of Israel, to give judgment for the LORD and to decide disputed cases. They had their seat at Jerusalem. 9 He charged them: "This is how you shall act: in the fear of the LORD, in faithfulness, and with your whole heart; 10 whenever a case comes to you from your kindred who live in their cities, concerning bloodshed, law or commandment, statutes or ordinances, then you shall instruct them, so that they may not incur guilt before the LORD and wrath may not come on you and your kindred. Do so, and you will not incur guilt. 11 See, Amariah the chief priest is over you in all matters of the LORD; and Zebadiah son of Ishmael, the governor of the house of Judah, in all the king's matters; and the Levites will serve you as officers. Deal courageously, and may the LORD be with the good!"

20 After this the Moabites and Ammonites, and with them some of the Meunites,[m] came against Jehoshaphat for battle. 2 Messengers[n] came and told Jehoshaphat, "A great multitude is coming against you from Edom,[o] from beyond the sea; already they are at Hazazon-tamar" (that is, En-gedi). 3 Jehoshaphat was afraid; he set himself to seek the LORD, and proclaimed a fast throughout all Judah. 4 Judah assembled to seek help from the LORD; from all the towns of Judah they came to seek the LORD.

5 Jehoshaphat stood in the assembly of Judah and Jerusalem, in the house of the LORD, before the new court, 6 and said, "O LORD, God of our ancestors, are you not God in heaven? Do you not rule over all the kingdoms of the nations? In your hand are power and might, so that no one is able to withstand you. 7 Did you not, O our God, drive out the inhabitants of this land before your people Israel, and give it forever to the descendants of your friend Abraham? 8 They have lived in it, and in it have built you a sanctuary for your name, saying, 9 'If disaster comes upon us, the sword, judgment,[p] or pestilence, or famine, we will stand before this house, and before you, for your name is in this house, and cry to you in our distress, and you will hear and save.' 10 See now, the people of Ammon, Moab, and Mount Seir, whom you would not let Israel invade when they came from the land of Egypt, and whom they avoided and did not destroy— 11 they reward us by coming to drive us out of your possession that you have given us to inherit. 12 O our

19 As King Jehoshaphat of Judah returned in safety to his palace in Jerusalem, 2 Jehu son of Hanani, the seer, went out to meet him and said, 'Do you take delight in helping the wicked and befriending the enemies of the LORD? For this the LORD's wrath will strike you. 3 Yet there is some good in you, for you have swept away the sacred poles from the land and have made a practice of seeking guidance of God.'

4 Jehoshaphat had his residence in Jerusalem, but he went out again among his people from Beersheba to the hill-country of Ephraim and brought them back to the LORD the God of their forefathers. 5 He appointed judges throughout the land, one in each of the fortified towns of Judah, 6 and said to them, 'Be careful what you do; you are there as judges, to please not man but the LORD, who is with you when you pass sentence. 7 Now let the dread of the LORD be on you; take care what you do, for the LORD our God will not tolerate injustice, partiality, or bribery.'

8 In Jerusalem Jehoshaphat appointed some of the Levites and priests and some heads of Israelite families by paternal descent to administer the law of the LORD and to arbitrate in lawsuits among the inhabitants of the towns. 9 He gave them these instructions: 'You must at all times act in the fear of the LORD, faithfully and with singleness of mind. 10 In every suit which comes before you from your kinsmen, in whatever town they live, whether cases of bloodshed or offences against the law or the commandments, against statutes or regulations, you must warn them to commit no offence against the LORD; otherwise the LORD's wrath will strike you and your kinsmen. If you act thus, you will be free of all offence. 11 Your authority in all matters which concern the LORD is Amariah the chief priest, and in those which concern the king is Zebadiah son of Ishmael, the prince of the house of Judah; the Levites are your officers. Be strong and resolute, and may the LORD be on the side of the good!'

20 It happened some time afterwards that the Moabites, the Ammonites, and some of the Meunites came to make war on Jehoshaphat. 2 News was brought to him of an attack by a great horde from beyond the Dead Sea, from Edom; they were already at Hazazon-tamar, which is En-gedi. 3 Jehoshaphat in alarm resolved to seek guidance of the LORD, and proclaimed a fast for all Judah. 4 The Judahites gathered to ask counsel of the LORD, coming from every town in the land to consult him.

5 Jehoshaphat stood in the assembly of Judah and Jerusalem in the house of the LORD in front of the new court, 6 and said, 'LORD God of our forefathers, are you not the God who is in heaven? You rule over all the kingdoms of the nations; in your hand are strength and power, and there is none who can withstand you. 7 You, our God, dispossessed the inhabitants of this land in favour of your people Israel, and gave it for ever to the descendants of your friend Abraham. 8 They have lived in it and built a sanctuary in it for your name, saying, 9 "Should any disaster befall us, whether war or flood, pestilence or famine, we shall stand before this house and before you, for in this house is your name, and we shall cry to you in our distress, and you will hear and save." 10 You did not allow the Israelites, when they came out of Egypt, to enter the land of the Ammonites, the Moabites, and the people of the hill-country of Seir, so they turned aside and left them alone and did not destroy them. 11 Now see how these people repay us: they are coming to drive us out of your possession which you gave to us.

19:8 in . . . inhabitants: prob. rdg, cp. Gk; Heb. obscure.
20:1 Meunites: prob. rdg, cp. Gk; Heb. Ammonites.
20:2 Edom: so one MS; others Aram.   20:9 flood: prob. rdg;
Heb. judgement.

[i] Heb Asheroth   [m] Compare 26.7: Heb Ammonites   [n] Heb They
[o] One Ms: MT Aram   [p] Or the sword of judgment

19 King Jehoshaphat of Judah returned in safety to his house in Jerusalem. 2 Jehu the seer, son of Hanani, met King Jehoshaphat and said to him: "Should you help the wicked and love those who hate the LORD? For this reason, wrath is upon you from the LORD. 3 Yet some good things are to be found in you, since you have removed the sacred poles from the land and have been determined to seek God."

4 Jehoshaphat dwelt in Jerusalem; but he went out again among the people from Beer-sheba to the highlands of Ephraim and brought them back to the LORD, the God of their fathers. 5 He appointed judges in the land, in all the fortified cities of Judah, city by city, 6 and he said to them: "Take care what you do, for you are judging, not on behalf of man, but on behalf of the LORD; he judges with you. 7 And now, let the fear of the LORD be upon you. Act carefully, for with the LORD, our God, there is no injustice, no partiality, no bribe-taking." 8 In Jerusalem also, Jehoshaphat appointed some Levites and priests and some of the family heads of Israel to judge in the name of the LORD and to settle quarrels among the inhabitants of Jerusalem. 9 He gave them this command: "You shall act faithfully and wholeheartedly in the fear of the LORD. 10 And in every dispute that your brethren living in their cities bring to you, whether it concerns bloodguilt or questions of law, command, statutes, or judgments, warn them lest they become guilty before the LORD and his wrath come upon you and your brethren. Do that and you shall be guiltless. 11 See now, Amariah is high priest over you in everything that pertains to the LORD, and Zebadiah, son of Ishmael, is leader of the house of Judah in all that pertains to the king; and the Levites will be your officials. Act firmly, and the LORD will be with the good."

20 After this the Moabites, the Ammonites, and with them some Meunites came to fight against Jehoshaphat. 2 The message was brought to Jehoshaphat: "A great multitude is coming against you from across the sea, from Edom; they are already in Hazazontamar" (which is En-gedi). 3 Jehoshaphat was frightened, and he hastened to consult the LORD. He proclaimed a fast for all Judah. 4 Then Judah gathered to seek help from the LORD; from every one of the cities of Judah they came to seek the LORD.

5 Jehoshaphat stood up in the assembly of Judah and Jerusalem in the house of the LORD before the new court, 6 and he said: "LORD, God of our fathers, are you not the God in heaven, and do you not rule over all the kingdoms of the nations? In your hand is power and might, and no one can withstand you. 7 Was it not you, our God, who drove out the inhabitants of this land before your people Israel and gave it forever to the descendants of Abraham, your friend? 8 They have dwelt in it and they built in it a sanctuary to your honor, saying, 9 'When evil comes upon us, the sword of judgment, or pestilence, or famine, we will stand before this house and before you, for your name is in this house, and we will cry out to you in our affliction, and you will hear and save!' 10 And now, see the Ammonites, Moabites, and those of Mount Seir whom you did not allow Israel to invade when they came from the land of Egypt, but instead they passed them by and did not destroy them. 11 See how they are now repaying us by coming to drive us out of the possession you have given us. 12 O our God, will you not

19 Jehoshaphat king of Judah returned home safely, however, to Jerusalem. 2 Jehu son of Hanani the seer went to meet him and said to King Jehoshaphat, 'Should a man give help to the wicked? Should you love those who hate Yahweh and so bring his retribution on yourself? 3 All the same, there are good things to your credit, since you have removed the sacred poles from the country and have set your heart on seeking God.'

4 Jehoshaphat resided in Jerusalem but regularly went on progress among the people, from Beersheba to the highlands of Ephraim, to convert them to Yahweh, God of their ancestors. 5 He also appointed judges in the country in every one of the fortified towns of Judah, 6 saying to the judges, 'Be careful what you do, since you are judging not by any human power but in the name of Yahweh, who will be with you when you pronounce sentence. 7 This being so, let fear of Yahweh govern you; be careful what you do, for Yahweh our God will not tolerate malpractice, partiality or the taking of bribes.'

8 Jehoshaphat also appointed some of the Levites, priests and heads of Israelite families in Jerusalem to settle disputes. They lived in Jerusalem 9 and Jehoshaphat gave them the following charge: 'In fear of Yahweh and with conscientious integrity, this is how you are to act: 10 whatever case your brothers living in other towns refer to you, whether involving blood feuds or law and commandment, statutes and judgements, you are to instruct them in such manner that they do not incur guilt before Yahweh and that you and your brothers do not incur his anger. If you act thus, you will not incur guilt. 11 Amariah the chief priest himself will be your president in all religious cases, and Zebadiah son of Ishmael, leader of the House of Judah, in all civil ones, while the Levites will act as officers of the court. Be firm, put this into practice and may Yahweh protect the right!'

20 Some time later, the Moabites and Ammonites, and with them the Meunites, advanced to war against Jehoshaphat. 2 Jehoshaphat received the following intelligence, 'A vast horde is advancing on you from the other side of the Sea, from Edom; they are already at Hazazon-Tamar, that is, En-Gedi.'

3 Jehoshaphat was alarmed and resolved to have recourse to Yahweh; he proclaimed a fast throughout all Judah. 4 So Judah assembled to seek help from Yahweh; to seek Yahweh they came from every town in Judah.

5 Then, standing in the Temple of Yahweh in front of the new court among the assembled people of Judah and Jerusalem, Jehoshaphat 6 said, 'Yahweh, God of our ancestors, are you not God in heaven, and do you not rule all the kingdoms of the nations? Your power and might are such that no one can resist you. 7 Did not you, our God, dispossess the inhabitants of this country for your people Israel and give it to the descendants of Abraham, your friend, for ever? 8 They have lived in it and built you a sanctuary there for your name, 9 saying, "If disaster, war, flood, pestilence or famine befall us, and we stand in front of this Temple, before you—for your name is in this Temple—and cry to you in our distress, then you will listen and rescue us."

10 'Now see, the Ammonites and Moabites and the people of Mount Seir, whom you would not allow Israel to invade when they came out of Egypt—on the contrary, Israel avoided them, and did not destroy them— 11 see how they reward us, by coming to drive us out of your possession which you allotted to us! 12 Our God, will you not pass

NEW REVISED STANDARD VERSION

God, will you not execute judgment upon them? For we are
powerless against this great multitude that is coming against
us. We do not know what to do, but our eyes are on you."
13 Meanwhile all Judah stood before the LORD, with
their little ones, their wives, and their children. 14 Then the
spirit of the LORD came upon Jahaziel son of Zechariah, son
of Benaiah, son of Jeiel, son of Mattaniah, a Levite of the
sons of Asaph, in the middle of the assembly. 15 He said,
"Listen, all Judah and inhabitants of Jerusalem, and King
Jehoshaphat: Thus says the LORD to you: 'Do not fear or be
dismayed at this great multitude; for the battle is not yours
but God's. 16 Tomorrow go down against them; they will
come up by the ascent of Ziz; you will find them at the end
of the valley, before the wilderness of Jeruel. 17 This battle
is not for you to fight; take your position, stand still, and see
the victory of the LORD on your behalf, O Judah and Jerusalem.' Do not fear or be dismayed; tomorrow go out against
them, and the LORD will be with you."
18 Then Jehoshaphat bowed down with his face to the
ground, and all Judah and the inhabitants of Jerusalem fell
down before the LORD, worshiping the LORD. 19 And the
Levites, of the Kohathites and the Korahites, stood up to
praise the LORD, the God of Israel, with a very loud voice.
20 They rose early in the morning and went out into the
wilderness of Tekoa; and as they went out, Jehoshaphat
stood and said, "Listen to me, O Judah and inhabitants of
Jerusalem! Believe in the LORD your God and you will be
established; believe his prophets." 21 When he had taken
counsel with the people, he appointed those who were to
sing to the LORD and praise him in holy splendor, as they
went before the army, saying,

"Give thanks to the LORD,
for his steadfast love endures forever."

22 As they began to sing and praise, the LORD set an ambush
against the Ammonites, Moab, and Mount Seir, who had
come against Judah, so that they were routed. 23 For the
Ammonites and Moab attacked the inhabitants of Mount
Seir, destroying them utterly; and when they had made an
end of the inhabitants of Seir, they all helped to destroy one
another.
24 When Judah came to the watchtower of the wilderness, they looked toward the multitude; they were corpses
lying on the ground; no one had escaped. 25 When Jehoshaphat and his people came to take the booty from them, they
found livestock[q] in great numbers, goods, clothing, and
precious things, which they took for themselves until they
could carry no more. They spent three days taking the
booty, because of its abundance. 26 On the fourth day they
assembled in the Valley of Beracah, for there they blessed
the LORD; therefore that place has been called the Valley of
Beracah[r] to this day. 27 Then all the people of Judah and
Jerusalem, with Jehoshaphat at their head, returned to Jerusalem with joy, for the LORD had enabled them to rejoice
over their enemies. 28 They came to Jerusalem, with harps
and lyres and trumpets, to the house of the LORD. 29 The
fear of God came on all the kingdoms of the countries when
they heard that the LORD had fought against the enemies of
Israel. 30 And the realm of Jehoshaphat was quiet, for his
God gave him rest all around.
31 So Jehoshaphat reigned over Judah. He was thirty-
five years old when he began to reign; he reigned twenty-
five years in Jerusalem. His mother's name was Azubah
daughter of Shilhi. 32 He walked in the way of his father Asa

[q] Gk: Heb *among them* [r] That is *Blessing*

REVISED ENGLISH BIBLE

12 Judge them, God our God, for we have not the strength
to face this great host which is invading our land; we do not
know what we ought to do, but our eyes look to you.'
13 As all the men of Judah stood before the LORD, with
their dependants, their wives, and their children, 14 there, in
the midst of the assembly, the spirit of the LORD came upon
Jahaziel son of Zechariah, son of Benaiah, son of Jeiel, son
of Mattaniah, a Levite of the line of Asaph, 15 and he said,
'Pay attention, all Judah and you inhabitants of Jerusalem
and King Jehoshaphat; this is the word of the LORD to you:
Do not fear or be dismayed by this great horde, for the battle
is in God's hands, not yours. 16 Go down to engage them
tomorrow as they come up by the ascent of Ziz; you will
find them at the end of the wadi, east of the wilderness of
Jeruel. 17 It is not you who will fight this battle; stand firm
and wait, and you will see the deliverance worked by the
LORD for you, Judah and Jerusalem. Do not fear or be
dismayed; go out tomorrow to face them, for the LORD is
with you.' 18 Jehoshaphat bowed low to the ground, and all
Judah and the inhabitants of Jerusalem fell down before the
LORD in obeisance to him. 19 Then the Levites of the lines
of Kohath and Korah stood up and praised the LORD the
God of Israel with mighty voice.
20 They rose early next morning to go out to the wilderness of Tekoa. As they were about to start, Jehoshaphat
stood up and said, 'Hear me, Judah and you inhabitants of
Jerusalem: hold firmly to your faith in the LORD your God
and you will be upheld; have faith in his prophets and you
will succeed.' 21 After consulting with the people, he appointed men to sing to the LORD and praise the splendour of
his holiness as they marched out before the armed troops,
singing:

'Give thanks to the LORD,
for his love endures for ever.'

22 As soon as their loud shouts of praise were heard, the
LORD misled the Ammonites and Moabites and the men of
the hill-country of Seir who were invading Judah, and they
were defeated. 23 It turned out that the Ammonites and Moabites had taken up a position against the men of the hill-
country of Seir, and set themselves to annihilate and destroy
them; and when they had exterminated the men of Seir, they
savagely attacked one another.
24 When Judah came to the watch-tower in the wilderness
and looked towards the enemy host, there they were all
lying dead on the ground; none had escaped. 25 Jehoshaphat
and his men, coming to collect the booty, found many cattle
and a large quantity of equipment, clothing, and articles of
value, which they plundered until they could carry away no
more. They spent three days gathering the booty, there was
so much of it. 26 On the fourth day they assembled in the
valley of Berakah, the name that it bears to this day because
there they blessed the LORD. 27 Afterwards, with Jehoshaphat at their head, all the men of Judah and Jerusalem
returned home to the city in triumph; for the LORD had given
them cause to triumph over their enemies. 28 They entered
Jerusalem with lutes, lyres, and trumpets playing, and went
into the house of the LORD. 29 The dread of God fell upon
the rulers of every country, when they heard that the LORD
had fought against the enemies of Israel. 30 With God giving
Jehoshaphat security on all sides, his realm enjoyed peace.
31 Thus Jehoshaphat reigned over Judah. He was thirty-
five years old when he came to the throne, and he reigned
in Jerusalem for twenty-five years; his mother was Azubah
daughter of Shilhi. 32 He followed in the footsteps of Asa

20:21 **men . . . holiness:** *or* singers in sacred vestments to praise the LORD. 20:25 **cattle:** *so Gk; Heb.* among them. **clothing:** *so some MSS; others* effigies. 20:26 **Berakah:** *that is* Blessing. 20:31–33 *Cp. 1 Kgs. 22:41–43.*

pass judgment on them? We are powerless before this vast multitude that comes against us. We are at a loss what to do, hence our eyes are turned toward you."

13 All Judah was standing before the LORD, with their little ones, their wives, and their young sons. 14 And the spirit of the LORD came upon Jahaziel, son of Zechariah, son of Benaiah, son of Jeiel, son of Mattaniah, a Levite of the clan of Asaph, in the midst of the assembly, 15 and he said: "Listen, all of Judah, inhabitants of Jerusalem, and King Jehoshaphat! The LORD says to you: 'Do not fear or lose heart at the sight of this vast multitude, for the battle is not yours but God's. 16 Go down against them tomorrow. You will see them coming up by the ascent of Ziz, and you will come upon them at the end of the wadi which opens on the wilderness of Jeruel. 17 You will not have to fight in this encounter. Take your places, stand firm, and see how the LORD will be with you to deliver you, Judah and Jerusalem. Do not fear or lose heart. Tomorrow go out to meet them, and the LORD will be with you.' " 18 Then Jehoshaphat knelt down with his face to the ground, and all Judah and the inhabitants of Jerusalem fell down before the LORD in worship. 19 Levites from among the Kohathites and Korahites rose to sing the praises of the LORD, the God of Israel, in a resounding chorus.

20 In the early morning they hastened out to the wilderness of Tekoa. As they were going out, Jehoshaphat halted and said: "Listen to me, Judah and inhabitants of Jerusalem! Trust in the LORD, your God, and you will be found firm. Trust in his prophets and you will succeed." 21 After consulting with the people, he appointed some to sing to the LORD and some to praise the holy Appearance as it went forth at the head of the army. They sang: "Give thanks to the LORD, for his mercy endures forever." 22 At the moment they began their jubilant hymn, the LORD laid an ambush against the Ammonites, Moabites, and those of Mount Seir who were coming against Judah, so that they were vanquished. 23 For the Ammonites and Moabites set upon the inhabitants of Mount Seir and completely exterminated them. And when they had finished with the inhabitants of Seir, they began to destroy each other.

24 When Judah came to the watchtower of the desert and looked toward the throng, they saw only corpses fallen on the ground, with no survivors. 25 Jehoshaphat and his people came to take plunder, and they found an abundance of cattle and personal property, garments and precious vessels. They took so much that they were unable to carry it all; they were three days taking the spoil, so great was it. 26 On the fourth day they held an assembly in the Valley of Beracah — for there they blessed the LORD; therefore that place has ever since been called the Valley of Beracah. 27 Then all the men of Judah and Jerusalem, with Jehoshaphat at their head, turned back toward Jerusalem celebrating the joyful victory the LORD had given them over their enemies. 28 They came to Jerusalem, to the house of the LORD, with harps, lyres and trumpets. 29 And the fear of God came upon all the kingdoms of the surrounding lands when they heard how the LORD had fought against the enemies of Israel. 30 Thereafter Jehoshaphat's kingdom enjoyed peace, for his God gave him rest on every side.

31 Thus Jehoshaphat reigned over Judah. He was thirty-five years old when he became king, and he reigned twenty-five years in Jerusalem. His mother was named Azubah, daughter of Shilhi. 32 He followed the path of his father Asa

sentence on them, since we are helpless against this vast horde about to attack us? Because we do not know what to do, we look to you.'

13 All Judah, including their families, wives and children, were standing before Yahweh, 14 when, in the middle of the assembly, the spirit of Yahweh came on Jahaziel son of Zechariah, son of Benaiah, son of Jeiel, son of Mattaniah the Levite, a member of the clan of Asaph, 15 who then cried, 'Listen, all Judah and you citizens of Jerusalem, and you, King Jehoshaphat! Yahweh says this to you, "Do not be afraid, do not be daunted by this vast horde, for the war is not your affair but God's. 16 Go down against them tomorrow; they are coming up by the Slope of Ziz and you will encounter them at the end of the ravine near the desert of Jeruel. 17 You will not need to fight in this battle. Take up your position, stand firm, and see what salvation Yahweh has in store for you. Judah and Jerusalem, be fearless, be dauntless; march out against them tomorrow and Yahweh will be with you." ' 18 Jehoshaphat bowed his head, his face to the ground, and all Judah and the citizens of Jerusalem fell down before Yahweh to worship Yahweh. 19 Then the Levites — both the Kohathites and Korahites — stood up to praise Yahweh, God of Israel, at the top of their voices.

20 Early next morning they prepared to set out for the desert of Tekoa. As they were setting out, Jehoshaphat stood up and said, 'Listen to me, Judah and you citizens of Jerusalem! Believe in Yahweh your God and you will be secure; believe in his prophets and you will be successful.' 21 Then, having conferred with the people, he appointed singers who were to praise Yahweh and go out ahead of the army in sacred vestments, singing

Praise Yahweh,
for his faithful love endures for ever!

22 The moment they began their shouts of praise, Yahweh sprang an ambush on the Ammonites, Moabites and the people of Mount Seir who were invading Judah, and that was the end of them, 23 for the Ammonites and Moabites turned on the people of Mount Seir, and put them under the curse of destruction and then, having finished off the people of Seir, set to work slaughtering one another.

24 When Judah reached the point overlooking the desert and looked towards the horde, there were nothing but corpses lying on the ground; no one escaped. 25 When Jehoshaphat arrived to take the booty, they found quantities of cattle and innumerable possessions, clothes and valuables, which they seized for themselves; it was impossible to carry it, and it took them three days to collect it. 26 On the fourth day they assembled in the Valley of Beracah, where they blessed Yahweh — hence the place was given the name Valley of Beracah, which it still has today. 27 Then all the men of Judah and Jerusalem returned joyfully to Jerusalem with Jehoshaphat at their head as Yahweh had given them cause to rejoice over their enemies. 28 To the sound of lyre, harp and trumpet they came to Jerusalem, to the Temple of Yahweh, 29 and a panic from Yahweh seized all the neighbouring kings when they heard how Yahweh had fought against the enemies of Israel. 30 And henceforth Jehoshaphat's reign was undisturbed, for his God gave him peace all round.

31 So Jehoshaphat reigned over Judah. He was thirty-five years old when he came to the throne and he reigned for twenty-five years in Jerusalem. His mother's name was Azubah daughter of Shilhi. 32 He followed the example of

and did not turn aside from it, doing what was right in the sight of the LORD. 33 Yet the high places were not removed; the people had not yet set their hearts upon the God of their ancestors.

34 Now the rest of the acts of Jehoshaphat, from first to last, are written in the Annals of Jehu son of Hanani, which are recorded in the Book of the Kings of Israel.

35 After this King Jehoshaphat of Judah joined with King Ahaziah of Israel, who did wickedly. 36 He joined him in building ships to go to Tarshish; they built the ships in Ezion-geber. 37 Then Eliezer son of Dodavahu of Mareshah prophesied against Jehoshaphat, saying, "Because you have joined with Ahaziah, the LORD will destroy what you have made." And the ships were wrecked and were not able to go to Tarshish.

21 Jehoshaphat slept with his ancestors and was buried with his ancestors in the city of David; his son Jehoram succeeded him. 2 He had brothers, the sons of Jehoshaphat: Azariah, Jehiel, Zechariah, Azariah, Michael, and Shephatiah; all these were the sons of King Jehoshaphat of Judah.ⁱ 3 Their father gave them many gifts, of silver, gold, and valuable possessions, together with fortified cities in Judah; but he gave the kingdom to Jehoram, because he was the firstborn. 4 When Jehoram had ascended the throne of his father and was established, he put all his brothers to the sword, and also some of the officials of Israel. 5 Jehoram was thirty-two years old when he began to reign; he reigned eight years in Jerusalem. 6 He walked in the way of the kings of Israel, as the house of Ahab had done; for the daughter of Ahab was his wife. He did what was evil in the sight of the LORD. 7 Yet the LORD would not destroy the house of David because of the covenant that he had made with David, and since he had promised to give a lamp to him and to his descendants forever.

8 In his days Edom revolted against the rule of Judah and set up a king of their own. 9 Then Jehoram crossed over with his commanders and all his chariots. He set out by night and attacked the Edomites, who had surrounded him and his chariot commanders. 10 So Edom has been in revolt against the rule of Judah to this day. At that time Libnah also revolted against his rule, because he had forsaken the LORD, the God of his ancestors.

11 Moreover he made high places in the hill country of Judah, and led the inhabitants of Jerusalem into unfaithfulness, and made Judah go astray. 12 A letter came to him from the prophet Elijah, saying: "Thus says the LORD, the God of your father David: Because you have not walked in the ways of your father Jehoshaphat or in the ways of King Asa of Judah, 13 but have walked in the way of the kings of Israel, and have led Judah and the inhabitants of Jerusalem into unfaithfulness, as the house of Ahab led Israel into unfaithfulness, and because you also have killed your brothers, members of your father's house, who were better than yourself, 14 see, the LORD will bring a great plague on your people, your children, your wives, and all your possessions, 15 and you yourself will have a severe sickness with a disease of your bowels, until your bowels come out, day after day, because of the disease."

16 The LORD aroused against Jehoram the anger of the Philistines and of the Arabs who are near the Ethiopians.ⁱ 17 They came up against Judah, invaded it, and carried away all the possessions they found that belonged to the king's house, along with his sons and his wives, so that no son was left to him except Jehoahaz, his youngest son.

18 After all this the LORD struck him in his bowels with an incurable disease. 19 In course of time, at the end of two

his father and did not deviate from them; he did what was right in the eyes of the LORD. 33 But the shrines were allowed to remain, and the people did not set their hearts on the God of their forefathers. 34 The other events of Jehoshaphat's reign, from first to last, are recorded in the history of Jehu son of Hanani, which is included in the annals of the kings of Israel.

35 Later King Jehoshaphat of Judah allied himself with King Ahaziah of Israel: he did wrong 36 in joining with him to build ships for trade with Tarshish; these were built in Ezion-geber. 37 But Eliezer son of Dodavahu of Mareshah denounced Jehoshaphat with this prophecy: 'Because you have joined with Ahaziah, the LORD will bring your work to nothing.' So the ships were wrecked and could not make the voyage to Tarshish.

21 JEHOSHAPHAT rested with his forefathers and was buried with them in the city of David. He was succeeded by his son Joram, 2 whose brothers, sons of Jehoshaphat, were Azariah, Jehiel, Zechariah, Azariah, Michael, and Shephatiah. All of them were sons of King Jehoshaphat of Judah, 3 and their father gave them many gifts, silver and gold and other costly things, as well as fortified towns in Judah; the kingship he gave to Joram because he was the eldest.

4 When Joram was firmly established on his father's throne, he put to the sword all his brothers, as well as some of the leading figures in Israel. 5 He was thirty-two years old when he came to the throne, and he reigned in Jerusalem for eight years. 6 He followed the practices of the kings of Israel as the house of Ahab had done, for he had married Ahab's daughter; he did what was wrong in the eyes of the LORD. 7 Yet for the sake of the covenant which he had made with David, the LORD was unwilling to destroy the house of David, as he had promised to give him and his descendants a lamp for all time.

8 During Joram's reign Edom revolted against Judah and set up its own king. 9 Joram, with his commanders and all his chariots, pushed on into Edom. When the Edomites encircled him and his chariot-commanders he made a sortie by night and broke out. 10 To this day Edom has remained independent of Judah. Libnah revolted against him at the same time, because he had forsaken the LORD the God of his fathers, 11 and because he had built shrines in the hill-country of Judah and had seduced the inhabitants of Jerusalem into idolatrous practices and corrupted Judah.

12 A letter reached Joram from Elijah the prophet, which read: 'This is the word of the LORD the God of David your father: You have not followed in the footsteps of Jehoshaphat your father and of King Asa of Judah, 13 but have followed the kings of Israel and have led astray Judah and the inhabitants of Jerusalem, as the house of Ahab did; and you have murdered your own brothers, sons of your father's house, men better than yourself. 14 Because of all this, the LORD is about to strike a heavy blow at your people, your children, your wives, and all your possessions; 15 you yourself will suffer from a chronic disease of the bowels, so that they prolapse and become severely ulcerated.'

16 The LORD aroused against Joram the hostility of the Philistines and of the Arabs who live near the Cushites, 17 and they invaded Judah. Overrunning it, they carried off all the property which they found in the king's palace, as well as his sons and wives; not a son was left to him except the youngest, Jehoahaz. 18 After this the LORD struck down the king with an incurable disease of the bowels. 19 It con-

21:2 **Judah:** so many MSS; others Israel.   21:5–10 Cp. 2 Kgs. 8:17–22.

ⁱGk Syr: Heb Israel   ⁱOr Nubians; Heb Cushites

unswervingly, doing what was right in the LORD's sight. ³³ But the high places were not removed, nor as yet had the people fixed their hearts on the God of their fathers.

³⁴ The rest of the acts of Jehoshaphat, first and last, can be found written in the chronicle of Jehu, son of Hanani, which is inserted in the book of the kings of Israel. ³⁵ After this, King Jehoshaphat of Judah allied himself with King Ahaziah of Israel, who did evil. ³⁶ He joined with him in building ships to sail to Tarshish; the fleet was built at Ezion-geber. ³⁷ But Eliezer, son of Dodavahu from Mareshah, prophesied against Jehoshaphat, saying, "Because you have joined with Ahaziah, the LORD will shatter your work." And the ships were wrecked and were unable to sail to Tarshish.

21 Jehoshaphat rested with his ancestors; he was buried with them in the City of David. Jehoram, his son, succeeded him as king. ² His brothers, sons of Jehoshaphat, were Azariah, Jehiel, Zechariah, Azariah, Michael and Shephatiah; all these were sons of King Jehoshaphat of Judah. ³ Their father gave them numerous gifts of silver, gold and precious objects, together with fortified cities in Judah, but the kingship he gave to Jehoram because he was the first-born.

⁴ When Jehoram had come into his father's kingdom and had consolidated his power, he put to the sword all his brothers and also some of the princes of Israel. ⁵ Jehoram was thirty-two years old when he became king, and he reigned eight years in Jerusalem. ⁶ He conducted himself like the kings of Israel of the line of Ahab, because one of Ahab's daughters was his wife. He did evil in the sight of the LORD, ⁷ but the LORD would not destroy the house of David because of the covenant he had made with David and because of his promise to give him and his sons a lamp for all time.

⁸ During his time Edom revolted against the sovereignty of Judah; they chose a king of their own. ⁹ Thereupon Jehoram crossed over with his officers and all the chariots he had. He arose by night and broke through the Edomites when they had surrounded him and the commanders of his chariots. ¹⁰ However, Edom has continued in revolt against the sovereignty of Judah down to the present time. Libnah also revolted at that time against Jehoram's sovereignty because he had forsaken the LORD, the God of his fathers. ¹¹ He also set up high places in the mountains of Judah; he led the inhabitants of Jerusalem into idolatry and seduced Judah.

¹² He received a letter from the prophet Elijah with this message: Thus says the LORD, the God of your ancestor David: 'Because you have not followed the path of your father Jehoshaphat, nor of Asa, king of Judah, ¹³ but instead have walked in the way of the kings of Israel and have led Judah and the inhabitants of Jerusalem into idolatry, as did the house of Ahab, and also because you have murdered your brothers of your father's house who were better than you, ¹⁴ the LORD will strike your people, your children, your wives, and all that is yours with a great plague; ¹⁵ and you shall have severe pains from a disease in your bowels, while your bowels issue forth because of the disease, day after day.' "

¹⁶ Then the LORD stirred up against Jehoram the animosity of the Philistines and of the Arabs who bordered on the Ethiopians. ¹⁷ They came up against Judah, invaded it, and carried away all the wealth found in the king's palace, along with his sons and his wives; there was left to him only one son, Jehoahaz, his youngest. ¹⁸ After these events, the LORD afflicted him with an incurable disease of the bowels. ¹⁹ As time went on until a period of two years had

his father Asa undeviatingly, doing what Yahweh regards as right. ³³ The high places, however, were not abolished; the people had still not set their hearts on the God of their ancestors. ³⁴ The rest of the history of Jehoshaphat, from first to last, is written down in the records of Jehu son of Hanani, which are quoted in the Book of the Kings of Israel.

³⁵ Afterwards, Jehoshaphat formed a partnership with Ahaziah king of Israel, which was very wrong of him. ³⁶ He joined him in building some ships to go to Tarshish; they built them at Ezion-Geber. ³⁷ Eliezer son of Dodavahu of Mareshah then prophesied against Jehoshaphat as follows, 'Because you have become Ahaziah's partner, Yahweh has wrecked your efforts.' The ships were wrecked and were never fit to sail for Tarshish.

21 Then Jehoshaphat fell asleep with his ancestors and was buried with them in the city of David; his son Jehoram succeeded him.

² Jehoram's brothers, sons of Jehoshaphat, were Azariah, Jehiel, Zechariah, Azariahu, Michael and Shephatiah — all of them sons of Jehoshaphat king of Israel. ³ Their father had lavishly given them presents of silver, gold and other valuables as well as fortified towns in Judah; but the throne he bequeathed to Jehoram since he was the first-born. ⁴ Jehoram, having taken control of his father's kingdom and secured his own position, put all his brothers to the sword and some officials of Israel too.

⁵ Jehoram was thirty-two years old when he came to the throne, and he reigned for eight years in Jerusalem. ⁶ He followed the example of the kings of Israel as the House of Ahab were doing, he having married one of Ahab's daughters; and he did what is displeasing to Yahweh. ⁷ But Yahweh would not destroy the House of David, because of the covenant which he had made with David, promising to provide him and his sons with a lamp for ever.

⁸ In his time Edom threw off the domination of Judah and set up a king for itself. ⁹ Jehoram crossed the frontier, and with him his commanders and all his chariots. Under cover of dark, he and his chariot commanders broke through the Edomites surrounding him. ¹⁰ Thus Edom threw off the domination of Judah and has remained free to the present day. Libnah revolted against him at the same time, because he had abandoned Yahweh, God of his ancestors. ¹¹ What is more, he set up high places in the highlands of Judah, leading the citizens of Jerusalem and the people of Judah into apostasy.

¹² Something written by the prophet Elijah then came into his hands. It said, 'Yahweh, God of your ancestor David, says this, "Since you have not followed the example of your father Jehoshaphat or of Asa king of Judah, ¹³ but have followed the example of the kings of Israel and have led Judah and the citizens of Jerusalem into apostasy, just as the House of Ahab has led Israel into apostasy, and have even murdered your brothers, your own family, who were better men than you, ¹⁴ Yahweh is going to afflict your people, your sons, your wives and all your property with a great calamity, ¹⁵ and you yourself with a severe disease affecting your bowels, as a result of which disease, continuing day after day, you will suffer protrusion of your bowels." '

¹⁶ Yahweh then roused the hostility of the Philistines and of the Arabs living near the Cushites against Jehoram. ¹⁷ They invaded Judah, forcing their way into it and carrying off all the property to be found in the king's palace, as well as his sons and his wives, so that he was left no sons at all except his youngest son Jehoahaz. ¹⁸ And after all this, Yahweh afflicted him with an incurable disease of the bowels; ¹⁹ in due time, after about two years, his bowels pro-

| NEW REVISED STANDARD VERSION | REVISED ENGLISH BIBLE |

years, his bowels came out because of the disease, and he died in great agony. His people made no fire in his honor, like the fires made for his ancestors. 20 He was thirty-two years old when he began to reign; he reigned eight years in Jerusalem. He departed with no one's regret. They buried him in the city of David, but not in the tombs of the kings.

22 The inhabitants of Jerusalem made his youngest son Ahaziah king as his successor; for the troops who came with the Arabs to the camp had killed all the older sons. So Ahaziah son of Jehoram reigned as king of Judah. 2 Ahaziah was forty-two years old when he began to reign; he reigned one year in Jerusalem. His mother's name was Athaliah, a granddaughter of Omri. 3 He also walked in the ways of the house of Ahab, for his mother was his counselor in doing wickedly. 4 He did what was evil in the sight of the LORD, as the house of Ahab had done; for after the death of his father they were his counselors, to his ruin. 5 He even followed their advice, and went with Jehoram son of King Ahab of Israel to make war against King Hazael of Aram at Ramoth-gilead. The Arameans wounded Joram, 6 and he returned to be healed in Jezreel of the wounds that he had received at Ramah, when he fought King Hazael of Aram. And Ahaziah son of King Jehoram of Judah went down to see Joram son of Ahab in Jezreel, because he was sick.

7 But it was ordained by God that the downfall of Ahaziah should come about through his going to visit Joram. For when he came there he went out with Jehoram to meet Jehu son of Nimshi, whom the LORD had anointed to destroy the house of Ahab. 8 When Jehu was executing judgment on the house of Ahab, he met the officials of Judah and the sons of Ahaziah's brothers, who attended Ahaziah, and he killed them. 9 He searched for Ahaziah, who was captured while hiding in Samaria and was brought to Jehu, and put to death. They buried him, for they said, "He is the grandson of Jehoshaphat, who sought the LORD with all his heart." And the house of Ahaziah had no one able to rule the kingdom.

10 Now when Athaliah, Ahaziah's mother, saw that her son was dead, she set about to destroy all the royal family of the house of Judah. 11 But Jehoshabeath, the king's daughter, took Joash son of Ahaziah, and stole him away from among the king's children who were about to be killed; she put him and his nurse in a bedroom. Thus Jehoshabeath, daughter of King Jehoram and wife of the priest Jehoiada — because she was a sister of Ahaziah — hid him from Athaliah, so that she did not kill him; 12 he remained with them six years, hidden in the house of God, while Athaliah reigned over the land.

23 But in the seventh year Jehoiada took courage, and entered into a compact with the commanders of the hundreds, Azariah son of Jeroham, Ishmael son of Jehohanan, Azariah son of Obed, Maaseiah son of Adaiah, and Elishaphat son of Zichri. 2 They went around through Judah and gathered the Levites from all the towns of Judah, and the heads of families of Israel, and they came to Jerusalem. 3 Then the whole assembly made a covenant with the king in the house of God. Jehoiada[u] said to them, "Here is the king's son! Let him reign, as the LORD promised concerning the sons of David. 4 This is what you are to do: one third of

tinued for some time, and towards the end of the second year the disease caused his bowels to prolapse, and the painful ulceration brought on his death. But his people kindled no fire in his honour as they had done for his fathers.

20 Joram was thirty-two years old when he became king, and he reigned in Jerusalem for eight years. His passing went unsung, and he was buried in the city of David, but not in the burial-place of the kings.

22 Then the inhabitants of Jerusalem made Ahaziah, his youngest son, king in his place, for the raiders who had joined the Arabs in the campaign had killed all the older sons. So Ahaziah son of Joram became king of Judah. 2 He was twenty-two years old when he came to the throne, and he reigned in Jerusalem for one year; his mother Athaliah granddaughter of Omri. 3 He too followed the practices of the house of Ahab, for his mother was his counsellor in wickedness. 4 He did what was wrong in the eyes of the LORD like the house of Ahab, for they had been his counsellors after his father's death, to his undoing. 5 He followed their counsel also in the alliance he made with Jehoram son of Ahab king of Israel, to fight against King Hazael of Aram at Ramoth-gilead. But Jehoram was wounded by the Aramaeans, 6 and retired to Jezreel to recover from the wounds inflicted on him at Ramoth in battle with King Hazael.

Because of Jehoram's injury Ahaziah son of Joram king of Judah went down to Jezreel to visit him. 7 It was God's will that the visit of Ahaziah to Jehoram should be the occasion of his downfall. During the visit he went out with Jehoram to meet Jehu son of Nimshi, whom the LORD had anointed to bring the house of Ahab to an end. 8 So it came about that Jehu, who was then at variance with the house of Ahab, found the officers of Judah and the kinsmen of Ahaziah who were his attendants, and killed them. 9 He then searched out Ahaziah himself, and his men captured him in Samaria, where he had gone into hiding. They brought him to Jehu and put him to death; they gave him burial, for they said, 'He was descended from Jehoshaphat who sought the guidance of the LORD with his whole heart.' There was no one left of the house of Ahaziah strong enough to rule.

10 As soon as Athaliah mother of Ahaziah saw that her son was dead, she set out to get rid of the whole royal line of the house of Judah. 11 But Jehosheba the daughter of King Joram took Ahaziah's son Joash and stole him away from among the princes who were being murdered; she put him and his nurse in a bedchamber. Thus Jehosheba daughter of King Joram and wife of Jehoiada the priest, because she was Ahaziah's sister, hid Joash from Athaliah so that she did not put him to death. 12 He remained concealed with them in the house of God for six years, while Athaliah ruled the country.

23 In the seventh year Jehoiada felt himself strong enough to make an agreement with Azariah son of Jeroham, Ishmael son of Jehohanan, Azariah son of Obed, Maaseiah son of Adaiah, and Elishaphat son of Zichri, all captains of units of a hundred. 2 They went throughout Judah and gathered to Jerusalem the Levites from all the cities of Judah and the heads of clans in Israel, and they came to Jerusalem. 3 The whole assembly made a compact with the king in the house of God, and Jehoiada said to them, 'Here is the king's son! He will be king, as the LORD promised that David's descendants should be. 4 This is what you must

22:1–6 Cp. 2 Kgs. 8:25–29.   22:1 **campaign:** lit. camp.
22:2 **twenty-two:** prob. rdg, cp. 2 Kgs. 8:26; Heb. forty-two.
granddaughter: lit. daughter.   22:6 **from:** so some MSS; others
because. **Ramoth:** so Gk (Luc.); Heb. Ramah. **Ahaziah:** so some
MSS, cp. 2 Kgs. 8:29; others Azariah.   22:8 **Judah and:** so Gk;
Heb. adds the sons of.   22:10 – 23:21 Cp. 2 Kgs. 11:1–20.
22:11 **Jehosheba:** so Gk, cp. 2 Kgs. 11:2; Heb. Jehoshabeath.

u Heb He

elapsed, his bowels issued forth because of the disease and he died in great pain. His people did not make a pyre for him like that of his fathers. 20 He was thirty-two years old when he became king, and he reigned eight years in Jerusalem. He departed unloved and was buried in the City of David, but not in the tombs of the kings.

22 Then the inhabitants of Jerusalem made Ahaziah, his youngest son, king in his stead, since all the older sons had been slain by the band that had come into the fort with the Arabs. Thus Ahaziah, son of Jehoram, reigned as king of Judah. 2 He was twenty-two years old when he became king, and he reigned one year in Jerusalem. His mother was named Athaliah, daughter of Omri. 3 He, too, followed the ways of the house of Ahab, because his mother counseled him to act sinfully. 4 To his own destruction, he did evil in the sight of the LORD, as did the house of Ahab, since they were his counselors after the death of his father.

5 He was also following their counsel when he accompanied Jehoram, son of Ahab, king of Israel, to battle against Hazael, king of Aram, at Ramoth-gilead. There Jehoram was wounded by the Arameans. 6 He returned to Jezreel to be healed of the wounds he had received at Rama in his battle against Hazael, king of Aram. Because of this illness, Ahaziah, son of Jehoram, king of Judah, went down to visit Jehoram, son of Ahab, in Jezreel. 7 Now it was willed by God for Ahaziah's downfall that he should join Jehoram, for after his arrival he rode out with Jehoram to Jehu, son of Nimshi, whom the LORD had anointed to cut down the house of Ahab. 8 While Jehu was executing judgment on the house of Ahab, he also encountered the princes of Judah and the nephews of Ahaziah who were his attendants, and he slew them. 9 Then he looked for Ahaziah himself. They caught him where he was hiding in Samaria and brought him to Jehu, who put him to death. They buried him, for they said, "He was the grandson of Jehoshaphat, who sought the LORD with his whole heart." There remained in Ahaziah's house no one powerful enough to wield the kingship.

10 When Athaliah, mother of Ahaziah, learned that her son was dead, she proceeded to kill off all the royal offspring of the house of Judah. 11 But Jehosheba, a royal princess, secretly took Ahaziah's son Joash from among the king's sons who were about to be slain, and put him and his nurse in a bedroom. In this way Jehosheba, who was the daughter of King Jehoram, a sister of Ahaziah, and wife of Jehoiada the priest, hid the child from Athaliah's sight, so that she did not put him to death. 12 For six years he remained hidden with them in the house of God, while Athaliah ruled over the land.

23 In the seventh year, Jehoiada took courage and entered a conspiracy with certain captains: Azariah, son of Jehoram; Ishmael, son of Jehohanan; Azariah, son of Obed; Masseiah, son of Adaiah; and Elishaphat, son of Zichri. 2 They journeyed about Judah, gathering the Levites from all the cities of Judah and also the heads of the Israelite families. When they had come to Jerusalem, 3 the whole assembly made a covenant with the king in the house of God. Jehoiada said to them: "Here is the king's son who must reign, as the LORD promised concerning the sons of David. 4 This is what you must do: a third of your number,

truded as a result of his disease and he died in acute pain. His people did not make a funeral pyre for him, as they had for his ancestors.

20 He was thirty-two years old when he came to the throne and he reigned for eight years in Jerusalem. He passed away unlamented and was buried in the City of David, though not in the tombs of the kings.

22 The inhabitants of Jerusalem then made his youngest son Ahaziah king in succession to him, since the marauders who had attacked the camp with the Arabs had killed all the older ones. That was why Ahaziah son of Jehoram, king of Judah became king. 2 Ahaziah was forty-two years old when he came to the throne and he reigned for one year in Jerusalem. His mother's name was Athaliah, descendant of Omri. 3 He too followed the example of the House of Ahab, for his mother being his adviser brought about his condemnation. 4 He did what is displeasing to Yahweh as the House of Ahab did, for they were his advisers after his father's death, to his undoing. 5 He followed their advice and went with Jehoram son of Ahab, king of Israel, to make war on Hazael king of Aram at Ramoth-Gilead. But the Aramaeans wounded Jehoram, 6 who returned to Jezreel to recover from the wounds which he had received at Ramoth, fighting against Hazael king of Aram. Ahaziah son of Jehoram, king of Judah, went down to Jezreel to visit Jehoram son of Ahab because he was ailing. 7 Through this visit to Jehoram God brought ruin on Ahaziah. On his arrival he went out with Jehoram to meet Jehu son of Nimshi whom Yahweh had anointed to make an end of the House of Ahab. 8 While Jehu was executing sentence on the House of Ahab and came across the officers of Judah and Ahaziah's nephews who were in attendance on Ahaziah, he killed them, 9 and then went in search of Ahaziah. The latter was captured while hiding in Samaria, and taken to Jehu who put him to death. But they gave him burial because, they said, 'He was the grandson of Jehoshaphat who sought Yahweh with all his heart.'

As a result, there was no member of Ahaziah's family left who was strong enough to rule the kingdom.

10 When Athaliah mother of Ahaziah learned that her son was dead, she promptly did away with all the royal stock of the House of Judah. 11 But Jehosheba the king's daughter, surreptitiously rescued Joash son of Ahaziah from among the chiefs who were to be murdered, and put him with his nurse in the sleeping quarters; in this way Jehosheba daughter of King Joram and wife of Jehoiada the priest — she was the sister of Ahaziah — hid him from Athaliah, and he was not put to death. 12 He stayed hidden with them in the Temple of God for six years while Athaliah governed the country.

23 In the seventh year Jehoiada decided to take action and made a pact with the regimental commanders, Azariah son of Jeroham, Ishmael son of Jehohanan, Azariah son of Obed, Maaseiah son of Adaiah and Elishaphat son of Zichri. 2 These went all over Judah, gathering the Levites from all the towns of Judah, and the heads of the Israelite families, who then came to Jerusalem, 3 and the whole assembly made a pact with the king in the Temple of God. Jehoiada said to them, 'Look, the king's son is now to be king, as Yahweh has promised of the sons of David! 4 This

you, priests and Levites, who come on duty on the sabbath, shall be gatekeepers, 5 one third shall be at the king's house, and one third at the Gate of the Foundation; and all the people shall be in the courts of the house of the LORD. 6 Do not let anyone enter the house of the LORD except the priests and ministering Levites; they may enter, for they are holy, but all the other^v people shall observe the instructions of the LORD. 7 The Levites shall surround the king, each with his weapons in his hand; and whoever enters the house shall be killed. Stay with the king in his comings and goings."

8 The Levites and all Judah did according to all that the priest Jehoiada commanded; each brought his men, who were to come on duty on the sabbath, with those who were to go off duty on the sabbath; for the priest Jehoiada did not dismiss the divisions. 9 The priest Jehoiada delivered to the captains the spears and the large and small shields that had been King David's, which were in the house of God; 10 and he set all the people as a guard for the king, everyone with weapon in hand, from the south side of the house to the north side of the house, around the altar and the house. 11 Then he brought out the king's son, put the crown on him, and gave him the covenant;^w they proclaimed him king, and Jehoiada and his sons anointed him; and they shouted, "Long live the king!"

12 When Athaliah heard the noise of the people running and praising the king, she went into the house of the LORD to the people; 13 and when she looked, there was the king standing by his pillar at the entrance, and the captains and the trumpeters beside the king, and all the people of the land rejoicing and blowing trumpets, and the singers with their musical instruments leading in the celebration. Athaliah tore her clothes, and cried, "Treason! Treason!" 14 Then the priest Jehoiada brought out the captains who were set over the army, saying to them, "Bring her out between the ranks; anyone who follows her is to be put to the sword." For the priest said, "Do not put her to death in the house of the LORD." 15 So they laid hands on her; she went into the entrance of the Horse Gate of the king's house, and there they put her to death.

16 Jehoiada made a covenant between himself and all the people and the king that they should be the LORD's people. 17 Then all the people went to the house of Baal, and tore it down; his altars and his images they broke in pieces, and they killed Mattan, the priest of Baal, in front of the altars. 18 Jehoiada assigned the care of the house of the LORD to the levitical priests whom David had organized to be in charge of the house of the LORD, to offer burnt offerings to the LORD, as it is written in the law of Moses, with rejoicing and with singing, according to the order of David. 19 He stationed the gatekeepers at the gates of the house of the LORD so that no one should enter who was in any way unclean. 20 And he took the captains, the nobles, the governors of the people, and all the people of the land, and they brought the king down from the house of the LORD, marching through the upper gate to the king's house. They set the king on the royal throne. 21 So all the people of the land rejoiced, and the city was quiet after Athaliah had been killed with the sword.

24 Joash was seven years old when he began to reign; he reigned forty years in Jerusalem; his mother's name was Zibiah of Beer-sheba. 2 Joash did what was right

do: one third of you, priests and Levites, as you come on duty on the sabbath, are to be on guard at the threshold gates, 5 another third are to be in the royal palace, and another third are to be at the Foundation Gate, while all the people will be in the courts of the house of the LORD. 6 No one must enter the house of the LORD except the priests and the attendant Levites; they may enter, for they are holy, but all the people must continue to keep the LORD's charge. 7 The Levites must mount guard round the king, each man holding his weapons, and anyone who tries to enter the house is to be put to death. They are to stay with the king wherever he goes.'

8 The Levites and all Judah carried out the orders of Jehoiada the priest to the letter: each captain took his men, both those who came on duty on the sabbath and those who went off, for Jehoiada the priest had not released the outgoing divisions. 9 Jehoiada the priest handed out to the captains King David's spears, shields, and bucklers, which were kept in the house of God. 10 He stationed all the troops round the king, each man holding his weapon, from corner to corner of the house to north and south. 11 Then they brought out the king's son, put the crown on his head, handed him the testimony, and proclaimed him king. When Jehoiada and his sons anointed him, a shout went up: 'Long live the king.'

12 When Athaliah heard the noise made by the people as they ran and cheered the king, she came into the house of the LORD where the people were, 13 and found the king standing by the pillar at the entrance, amidst outbursts of song and fanfares of trumpets in his honour; all the populace were rejoicing and blowing trumpets, and singers with musical instruments were leading the celebrations. Athaliah tore her clothes and cried, 'Treason! Treason!' 14 Jehoiada the priest gave orders to the captains in command of the troops: 'Bring her outside the precincts and put to the sword anyone in attendance on her'; for the priest said, 'Do not kill her in the house of the LORD.' 15 They took her and brought her to the royal palace and there at the passage to the Horse Gate they put her to death.

16 Jehoiada made a covenant between the LORD on one side and the whole people and the king on the other, that they should be the LORD's people. 17 The people all went to the temple of Baal and pulled it down; they smashed its altars and images, and they slew Mattan the priest of Baal before the altars.

18 Jehoiada committed the supervision of the house of the LORD to the charge of the priests and the Levites whom David had allocated to the house of the LORD, to offer whole-offerings to the LORD as prescribed in the law of Moses, with the singing and rejoicing as handed down from David. 19 He stationed the door-keepers at the gates of the house of the LORD, to prevent anyone entering who was in any way unclean. 20 Then he took the captains of units of a hundred, the nobles, and the governors of the people, and all the people of the land, and they escorted the king from the house of the LORD through the Upper Gate to the palace, and seated him on the royal throne. 21 The whole people rejoiced and the city had quiet. That is how Athaliah was put to death.

24 Joash was seven years old when he became king, and he reigned in Jerusalem for forty years; his mother was Zibiah from Beersheba. 2 He did what was right

23:9 **bucklers:** *mng of Heb. word uncertain.* 23:10 **north and south:** *prob. rdg; Heb. adds of the altar and the house.* 23:13 **by the pillar:** *prob. rdg, cp. 2 Kgs. 11:14; Heb. on the dais.* 23:14 **gave orders to:** *prob. rdg, cp. 2 Kgs. 11:15; Heb. brought out.* 23:16 **the LORD:** *prob. rdg, cp. 2 Kgs. 11:17; Heb. him.* 23:18 **priests and:** *so some MSS; others omit and.* 24:1–14 *Cp. 2 Kgs. 11:21–12:15.*

^v Heb lacks *other*   ^w Or *treaty,* or *testimony;* Heb *eduth*

both priests and Levites, who come in on the sabbath must guard the thresholds, 5 another third must be at the king's palace, and the final third at the Foundation Gate, when all the people will be in the courts of the LORD's temple. 6 Let no one enter the LORD's house except the priests and those Levites who are ministering. They may enter because they are holy; but all the other people must observe the prescriptions of the LORD. 7 The Levites shall surround the king on all sides, each with his weapon drawn. Whoever tries to enter the house must be slain. Stay with the king wherever he goes."

8 The Levites and all Judah did just as Jehoiada the priest commanded. Each brought his men, those who were to come in on the sabbath as well as those who were to depart on the sabbath, since Jehoiada the priest had not dismissed any of the divisions. 9 Jehoiada the priest gave the captains the spears, shields and bucklers of King David which were in the house of God. 10 He stationed all the people, each with his spear in hand, from the southern to the northern extremity of the enclosure, around the altar and the temple on the king's behalf. 11 Then they brought out the king's son, set the crown and the insignia upon him, and made him king. Jehoiada and his sons anointed him, and they cried, "Long live the king!"

12 When Athaliah heard the din of the people running and acclaiming the king, she went to the people in the temple of the LORD. 13 She looked, and there was the king standing beside his pillar at the entrance, the officers and the trumpeters around him, and all the people of the land rejoicing and blowing trumpets, while the singers with their musical instruments were leading the acclaim. Athaliah tore her garments and cried out, "Treason! treason!" 14 Then Jehoiada the priest sent out the captains who were in command of the army; he said to them: "Take her outside through the ranks, and if anyone tries to follow her, let him die by the sword. For," the priest continued, "you must not put her to death in the LORD's temple." 15 So they seized her, and when she arrived at the entrance to the Horse Gate of the palace, they put her to death there.

16 Then Jehoiada made a covenant between himself and all the people and the king, that they should be the LORD's people. 17 And all the people went to the temple of Baal and tore it down. They smashed its altars and images, and they slew Mattan, the priest of Baal, before the altars. 18 Then Jehoiada gave the charge of the LORD's temple into the hands of the levitical priests, to whom David had assigned turns in the temple for offering the holocausts of the LORD, as is written in the law of Moses, with rejoicing and song, as David had provided. 19 Moreover, he stationed guards at the gates of the LORD's temple, so that no one unclean in any respect might enter. 20 Then he took the captains, the nobles, the rulers among the people, and all the people of the land, and led the king out of the LORD's house. When they had come within the upper gate of the king's house, they seated the king upon the royal throne. 21 All the people of the land rejoiced and the city was quiet, now that Athaliah had been put to death by the sword.

24 Joash was seven years old when he became king, and he reigned forty years in Jerusalem. His mother, named Zibiah, was from Beer-sheba. 2 Joash did

is what you must do: a third of you priests and Levites who come on duty on the Sabbath must guard the gates, 5 a third the royal palace, a third the Foundation Gate, while the people must all stay in the courts of the Temple of Yahweh. 6 No one must enter the Temple of Yahweh except the priests and the ministering Levites; they may come in because they are consecrated. But the people must all observe Yahweh's regulations. 7 The Levites must surround the king, each man with his weapons in his hands; anyone who enters the Temple must be killed. And you will escort the king when he comes in and when he leaves.'

8 The Levites and all Judah did everything as Jehoiada the priest had ordered, and each one brought his men, those coming on duty on the Sabbath and those going off duty on the Sabbath, for Jehoiada the priest had not released any of the divisions from duty. 9 Jehoiada the priest then issued the regimental commanders with King David's spears and large and small shields, which were kept in the Temple of God. 10 He then positioned all the people, each man with his weapon in his hand, from the south side of the Temple to the north side of the Temple, close to the altar and the Temple, to form a circle round the king. 11 Then they brought the king's son out, crowned him, gave him a copy of the covenant and made him king. When Jehoiada and his sons had anointed him, they shouted, 'Long live the king!'

12 On hearing the people shouting as they ran to acclaim the king, Athaliah joined the people in the Temple of Yahweh. 13 When she looked, there stood the king on his dais by the entrance, with the officers and trumpeters at the king's side, and all the people of the country rejoicing and blowing the trumpets, and the singers with their musical instruments leading the hymns of praise. Then Athaliah tore her clothes and shouted, 'Treason, treason!' 14 Jehoiada the priest then gave the order to the regimental commanders in charge of the troops, 'Take her out between the ranks and put to the sword anyone who follows her.' For the priest had already said, 'Do not kill her inside the Temple of Yahweh.' 15 So they made way for her, and when she reached the entrance to the Horses' Gate of the palace, they killed her there.

16 Jehoiada made a covenant between himself, all the people and the king to remain Yahweh's people. 17 All the people then went to the temple of Baal and demolished it; they smashed its altars and its images and killed Mattan the priest of Baal in front of the altars. 18 Jehoiada entrusted the security of the Temple of Yahweh to the priests and Levites, whom David had put in charge of the Temple of Yahweh to present the burnt offerings of Yahweh as laid down in the Law of Moses, with joy and song as ordained by David. 19 He also appointed gatekeepers for the gates of the Temple of Yahweh, so that no one who was unclean might enter for any purpose at all. 20 He then took the regimental commanders, the nobles, the government officials and all the people of the land and he escorted the king down from the Temple of Yahweh. Entering the palace through the Upper Gate, they placed the king on the royal throne. 21 All the people of the land were delighted, and the city made no move after Athaliah had been put to death.

24 Joash was seven years old when he came to the throne and he reigned for forty years in Jerusalem. His mother's name was Zibiah of Beersheba. 2 Joash did

in the sight of the LORD all the days of the priest Jehoiada. 3 Jehoiada got two wives for him, and he became the father of sons and daughters.

4 Some time afterward Joash decided to restore the house of the LORD. 5 He assembled the priests and the Levites and said to them, "Go out to the cities of Judah and gather money from all Israel to repair the house of your God, year by year; and see that you act quickly." But the Levites did not act quickly. 6 So the king summoned Jehoiada the chief, and said to him, "Why have you not required the Levites to bring in from Judah and Jerusalem the tax levied by Moses, the servant of the LORD, on^x the congregation of Israel for the tent of the covenant?"^y 7 For the children of Athaliah, that wicked woman, had broken into the house of God, and had even used all the dedicated things of the house of the LORD for the Baals.

8 So the king gave command, and they made a chest, and set it outside the gate of the house of the LORD. 9 A proclamation was made throughout Judah and Jerusalem to bring in for the LORD the tax that Moses the servant of God laid on Israel in the wilderness. 10 All the leaders and all the people rejoiced and brought their tax and dropped it into the chest until it was full. 11 Whenever the chest was brought to the king's officers by the Levites, when they saw that there was a large amount of money in it, the king's secretary and the officer of the chief priest would come and empty the chest and take it and return it to its place. So they did day after day, and collected money in abundance. 12 The king and Jehoiada gave it to those who had charge of the work of the house of the LORD, and they hired masons and carpenters to restore the house of the LORD, and also workers in iron and bronze to repair the house of the LORD. 13 So those who were engaged in the work labored, and the repairing went forward at their hands, and they restored the house of God to its proper condition and strengthened it. 14 When they had finished, they brought the rest of the money to the king and Jehoiada, and with it were made utensils for the house of the LORD, utensils for the service and for the burnt offerings, and ladles, and vessels of gold and silver. They offered burnt offerings in the house of the LORD regularly all the days of Jehoiada.

15 But Jehoiada grew old and full of days, and died; he was one hundred thirty years old at his death. 16 And they buried him in the city of David among the kings, because he had done good in Israel, and for God and his house.

17 Now after the death of Jehoiada the officials of Judah came and did obeisance to the king; then the king listened to them. 18 They abandoned the house of the LORD, the God of their ancestors, and served the sacred poles^z and the idols. And wrath came upon Judah and Jerusalem for this guilt of theirs. 19 Yet he sent prophets among them to bring them back to the LORD; they testified against them, but they would not listen.

20 Then the spirit of God took possession of^a Zechariah son of the priest Jehoiada; he stood above the people and said to them, "Thus says God: Why do you transgress the commandments of the LORD, so that you cannot prosper? Because you have forsaken the LORD, he has also forsaken you." 21 But they conspired against him, and by command of the king they stoned him to death in the court of the house of the LORD. 22 King Joash did not remember the kindness that Jehoiada, Zechariah's father, had shown him, but killed his son. As he was dying, he said, "May the LORD see and avenge!"

in the eyes of the LORD as long as Jehoiada the priest was alive. 3 Jehoiada chose him two wives, and he had a family of sons and daughters.

4 Some time afterwards, Joash decided to renovate the house of the LORD. 5 He assembled the priests and Levites and said to them, 'Go through the cities and towns of Judah and collect without delay the annual tax from all the Israelites for the restoration of the house of your God.' But the Levites did not act quickly. 6 The king summoned Jehoiada the chief priest and asked him, 'Why have you not required the Levites to bring in from Judah and Jerusalem the tax imposed by Moses the servant of the LORD and by the assembly of Israel for the Tent of the Testimony?' 7 For the wicked Athaliah and her adherents had broken into the house of God and had even devoted all its holy things to the service of the baalim.

8 The king ordered a chest to be made and placed outside the gate of the house of the LORD; 9 and proclamation was made throughout Judah and Jerusalem that the people should bring to the LORD the tax imposed on Israel in the wilderness by Moses the servant of God. 10 All the leaders and the people gladly brought their taxes and dropped them into the chest until it was full. 11 Whenever the chest was brought by the Levites to the king's officers and they saw that it was well filled, the king's secretary and the chief priest's officer would come to empty it, after which it was returned to its place. This they did daily, and a large sum of money was collected. 12 The king and Jehoiada handed it over to those responsible for carrying out the work in the house of the LORD, and they hired masons and carpenters to do the renovation, as well as craftsmen in iron and copper to restore the house. 13 The workmen got on with their task and the work progressed under their hands; they restored the house of God according to its original design and strengthened it. 14 When they had finished, they brought what was left of the money to the king and Jehoiada, and it was made into vessels for the house of the LORD, both for service and for sacrificing, saucers and other articles of gold and silver. During Jehoiada's lifetime whole-offerings were offered regularly in the house of the LORD.

15 Jehoiada, now old and weighed down with years, died at the age of a hundred and thirty 16 and was buried with the kings in the city of David, because he had done good in Israel in the service of God and of his house.

17 After the death of Jehoiada the leading men of Judah came and made obeisance to the king. He listened to them, 18 and they forsook the house of the LORD the God of their forefathers and worshipped sacred poles and idols. For this wickedness Judah and Jerusalem suffered. 19 The LORD sent prophets to bring them back to himself, prophets who denounced them but were not heeded. 20 Then the spirit of God took possession of Zechariah son of Jehoiada the priest. Taking his stance looking down on the people he declared, 'This is the word of God: Why do you disobey the commands of the LORD and court disaster? Because you have forsaken the LORD, he has forsaken you.' 21 But they made common cause against him, and on orders from the king they stoned him to death in the court of the house of the LORD. 22 King Joash, forgetful of the loyalty of Zechariah's father Jehoiada, killed his son. As he was dying he said, 'May the LORD see this and exact the penalty.'

---

x Compare Vg: Heb and   y Or treaty, or testimony; Heb eduth
z Heb Asherim   a Heb clothed itself with

24:7 **Athaliah and:** so Gk; Heb. omits and. **her adherents:** lit. her sons.   24:12 **copper:** or bronze.   24:20 **took possession of:** lit. clothed itself with.

what was pleasing to the LORD as long as Jehoiada the priest lived. 3 Jehoiada provided him with two wives, and he became the father of sons and daughters.

4 After some time, Joash decided to restore the LORD's temple. 5 He called together the priests and Levites and said to them: "Go out to all the cities of Judah and collect money from all Israel that you may repair the house of your God over the years. You must hasten this affair." But the Levites did not hasten. 6 Then the king summoned Jehoiada, who was in charge, and said to him: "Why have you not required the Levites to bring in from Judah and Jerusalem the tax levied by Moses, the servant of the LORD, and by the assembly of Israel, for the tent of the testimony?" 7 For the wicked Athaliah and her sons had damaged the house of God and had even turned over to the Baals the dedicated resources of the LORD's temple.

8 At the king's command, therefore, they made a chest, which they put outside the gate of the LORD's temple. 9 They had it proclaimed throughout Judah and Jerusalem that the tax which Moses, the servant of God, had imposed on Israel in the desert should be brought to the LORD. 10 All the princes and the people rejoiced; they brought what was asked and cast it into the chest until it was filled. 11 Whenever the chest was brought to the royal officials by the Levites and they saw that it contained much money, the royal scribe and an overseer for the high priest came, emptied the chest, then took it back and returned it to its place. This they did day after day until they had collected a large sum of money. 12 Then the king and Jehoiada gave it to the workmen in charge of the labor on the LORD's temple, who hired masons and carpenters to restore the temple, and also iron- and bronze-smiths to repair it. 13 The workmen labored, and the task of restoration progressed under their hands. They restored the house of God according to its original form, and reinforced it. 14 After they had finished, they brought the rest of the money to the king and to Jehoiada, who had it made into utensils for the LORD's temple, utensils for the service and the holocausts, and basins and other gold and silver utensils. They offered holocausts in the LORD's temple continually throughout the lifetime of Jehoiada. 15 Jehoiada lived to a ripe old age; he was a hundred and thirty years old when he died. 16 He was buried in the City of David with the kings, because he had done good in Israel, in particular with respect to God and his temple.

17 After the death of Jehoiada, the princes of Judah came and paid homage to the king, and the king then listened to them. 18 They forsook the temple of the LORD, the God of their fathers, and began to serve the sacred poles and the idols; and because of this crime of theirs, wrath came upon Judah and Jerusalem. 19 Although prophets were sent to them to convert them to the LORD, the people would not listen to their warnings. 20 Then the spirit of God possessed Zechariah, son of Jehoiada the priest. He took his stand above the people and said to them: "God says, 'Why are you transgressing the LORD's commands, so that you cannot prosper? Because you have abandoned the LORD, he has abandoned you.' " 21 But they conspired against him, and at the king's order they stoned him to death in the court of the LORD's temple. 22 Thus King Joash was unmindful of the devotion shown him by Jehoiada, Zechariah's father, and slew his son. And as he was dying, he said, "May the LORD see and avenge."

what Yahweh regards as right throughout the lifetime of Jehoiada the priest. 3 Jehoiada found him two wives and he fathered several sons and daughters.

4 Later, Joash made up his mind to repair the Temple of Yahweh. 5 Calling the priests and the Levites together, he said, 'Go out to the towns of Judah and collect money from all Israel for annual repairs to the Temple of Yahweh. Do this quickly.' But the Levites were in no hurry, 6 so the king summoned Jehoiada the chief priest and said, 'Why have you not insisted on the Levites' bringing in the tax from Judah and Jerusalem for the Tent of Witness, as imposed by Moses servant of Yahweh and the community of Israel?' — 7 Athaliah and her sons, whom she corrupted, despoiled the Temple of God and even assigned all the sacred revenues of the Temple of Yahweh to Baal. 8 So, at the king's order, a chest was made and put outside the gate of the Temple of Yahweh, 9 and a proclamation was issued throughout Judah and Jerusalem that the tax, which Moses servant of God had imposed on Israel in the desert, was to be brought to Yahweh. 10 Then all the officials and all the people gladly brought in their contributions, depositing them in the chest until the payment was complete.

11 Whenever the chest was brought by the Levites for royal inspection and found to contain a large sum of money, the king's secretary and the chief priest's representative would come and empty the chest and then have it returned to its place. This was done day after day and a great deal of money was collected. 12 The king and Jehoiada handed it over to the foreman attached to the Temple of Yahweh, and the hired masons and carpenters set about repairing Temple of Yahweh; and iron-workers and bronze-workers laboured to repair the Temple of Yahweh. 13 The workmen got on with the task — the repair work made good progress at their hands — until they had restored the Temple of God to its former state and reconditioned it. 14 When they had finished, they brought the balance of the money to the king and Jehoiada, and with this vessels were made for the Temple of Yahweh, vessels for the liturgy and for the burnt offerings, bowls and other gold and silver vessels. And the perpetual burnt offering was offered in the Temple of Yahweh throughout Jehoiada's lifetime.

15 But Jehoiada, growing old, had his fill of days and died. He died at the age of a hundred and thirty years, 16 and was buried with the kings in the City of David because he had served Israel and God and his Temple well.

17 After Jehoiada's death the officials of Judah came to pay court to the king, and the king listened to their advice, 18 and they abandoned the Temple of Yahweh, God of their ancestors, for the worship of sacred poles and idols. Judah and Jerusalem incurred wrath because of this guilt of theirs. 19 He sent their prophets to lead them back to Yahweh; these put the case against them, but they would not listen. 20 The spirit of God then invested Zechariah son of Jehoiada the priest. He stood up before the people and said, 'God says this, "Why transgress Yahweh's commands to your certain ruin? For if you abandon Yahweh, he will abandon you." ' 21 They then plotted against him and, at the king's order, stoned him in the court of the Temple of Yahweh. 22 Thus King Joash, forgetful of the devotion which Jehoiada father of Zechariah had displayed on his behalf, murdered his son, who cried out as he died, 'Yahweh will see this and avenge it!'

23 At the end of the year the army of Aram came up against Joash. They came to Judah and Jerusalem, and destroyed all the officials of the people from among them, and sent all the booty they took to the king of Damascus. 24 Although the army of Aram had come with few men, the LORD delivered into their hand a very great army, because they had abandoned the LORD, the God of their ancestors. Thus they executed judgment on Joash.

25 When they had withdrawn, leaving him severely wounded, his servants conspired against him because of the blood of the son*b* of the priest Jehoiada, and they killed him on his bed. So he died; and they buried him in the city of David, but they did not bury him in the tombs of the kings. 26 Those who conspired against him were Zabad son of Shimeath the Ammonite, and Jehozabad son of Shimrith the Moabite. 27 Accounts of his sons, and of the many oracles against him, and of the rebuilding*c* of the house of God are written in the Commentary on the Book of the Kings. And his son Amaziah succeeded him.

25 Amaziah was twenty-five years old when he began to reign, and he reigned twenty-nine years in Jerusalem. His mother's name was Jehoaddan of Jerusalem. 2 He did what was right in the sight of the LORD, yet not with a true heart. 3 As soon as the royal power was firmly in his hand he killed his servants who had murdered his father the king. 4 But he did not put their children to death, according to what is written in the law, in the book of Moses, where the LORD commanded, "The parents shall not be put to death for the children, or the children be put to death for the parents; but all shall be put to death for their own sins."

5 Amaziah assembled the people of Judah, and set them by ancestral houses under commanders of the thousands and of the hundreds for all Judah and Benjamin. He mustered those twenty years old and upward, and found that they were three hundred thousand picked troops fit for war, able to handle spear and shield. 6 He also hired one hundred thousand mighty warriors from Israel for one hundred talents of silver. 7 But a man of God came to him and said, "O king, do not let the army of Israel go with you, for the LORD is not with Israel — all these Ephraimites. 8 Rather, go by yourself and act; be strong in battle, or God will fling you down before the enemy; for God has power to help or to overthrow." 9 Amaziah said to the man of God, "But what shall we do about the hundred talents that I have given to the army of Israel?" The man of God answered, "The LORD is able to give you much more than this." 10 Then Amaziah discharged the army that had come to him from Ephraim, letting them go home again. But they became very angry with Judah, and returned home in fierce anger.

11 Amaziah took courage, and led out his people; he went to the Valley of Salt, and struck down ten thousand men of Seir. 12 The people of Judah captured another ten thousand alive, took them to the top of Sela, and threw them down from the top of Sela, so that all of them were dashed to pieces. 13 But the men of the army whom Amaziah sent back, not letting them go with him to battle, fell on the cities of Judah from Samaria to Beth-horon; they killed three thousand people in them, and took much booty.

14 Now after Amaziah came from the slaughter of the Edomites, he brought the gods of the people of Seir, set them up as his gods, and worshiped them, making offerings to them. 15 The LORD was angry with Amaziah and sent to him a prophet, who said to him, "Why have you resorted to a people's gods who could not deliver their own people from your hand?" 16 But as he was speaking the king*d* said

23 At the turn of the year a force of Aramaeans advanced against Joash; they invaded Judah and Jerusalem and massacred all the officers of the army, so that it ceased to exist, and they sent all their spoil to the king of Damascus. 24 Although the Aramaeans had invaded with a small force, the LORD delivered a very great army into their power, because the people had forsaken the LORD the God of their forefathers; and Joash suffered just punishment.

25 When the Aramaeans had withdrawn, leaving the king severely wounded, his servants conspired against him to avenge the death of the son of Jehoiada the priest, and they murdered him on his bed. Thus he died and was buried in the city of David, but not in the burial-place of the kings. 26 The conspirators were Zabad son of Shimeath an Ammonite woman and Jehozabad son of Shimrith a Moabite woman. 27 His children, the many oracles about him, and his reconstruction of the house of God are all on record in the discourse given in the annals of the kings. His son Amaziah succeeded him.

25 AMAZIAH was twenty-five years old when he came to the throne, and he reigned in Jerusalem for twenty-nine years; his mother was Jehoaddan from Jerusalem. 2 He did what was right in the eyes of the LORD, yet not wholeheartedly. 3 As soon as the royal power was firmly in his grasp, he put to death those of his servants who had murdered the king his father; 4 but he spared their children, in obedience to the LORD's command written in the law of Moses: 'Parents are not to be put to death for their children, nor children for their parents; each one may be put to death only for his own sin.'

5 Amaziah assembled the men of Judah and drew them up by families, and Benjamin as well as all Judah, under officers over units of a thousand and a hundred. He mustered those of twenty years and upwards and found their number to be three hundred thousand, all picked troops ready for service, able to handle spear and shield. 6 He also hired a hundred thousand seasoned troops from Israel for a hundred talents of silver. 7 But a man of God came to him and said, 'My lord king, do not let the Israelite army march with you; the LORD is not with Israel — all these Ephraimites! 8 For, if you make these people your allies in the war, God will overthrow you in battle, for God has the power to help or to overthrow.' 9 Amaziah said to the man of God, 'What am I to do about the hundred talents which I have spent on the Israelite army?' The man answered, 'It is in the LORD's power to give you much more than that.' 10 Amaziah detached the troops which had come to him from Ephraim and sent them home; that made them furious against Judah and they went home in a rage.

11 Amaziah led his men with resolution to the valley of Salt and there killed ten thousand men of Seir. 12 The men of Judah captured another ten thousand men alive, brought them to the top of a cliff, and hurled them over so that they were all dashed to pieces. 13 Meanwhile the troops which Amaziah had sent home without allowing them to take part in the battle raided the towns of Judah from Samaria to Beth-horon, massacred three thousand people in them, and carried off rich spoil.

14 After Amaziah had returned from the defeat of the Edomites, he brought the gods of the people of Seir and, setting them up as his own gods, worshipped them and burnt sacrifices to them. 15 The LORD was angry with Amaziah for this and sent a prophet who said to him, 'Why have you resorted to gods who could not save their own people from you?' 16 While he was speaking, the king said to him,

24:25–27 Cp. 2 Kgs.12:20–21.   24:25 son: so Gk; Heb. sons.
25:1–4 Cp. 2 Kgs. 14:1–6.   25:8 these people: prob. rdg; Heb.
obscure.   25:12 a cliff: or Sela.

b Gk Vg: Heb sons   *c* Heb founding   *d* Heb he

23 At the turn of the year a force of Arameans came up against Joash. They invaded Judah and Jerusalem, did away with all the princes of the people, and sent all their spoil to the king of Damascus. 24 Though the Aramean force came with few men, the LORD surrendered a very large force into their power, because Judah had abandoned the LORD, the God of their fathers. So punishment was meted out to Joash. 25 After the Arameans had departed from him, leaving him in grievous suffering, his servants conspired against him because of the murder of the son of Jehoiada the priest. They killed him on his sickbed. He was buried in the City of David, but not in the tombs of the kings. 26 These conspired against him: Zabad, son of Shimeath from Ammon, and Jehozabad, son of Shimrith from Moab. 27 Of his sons, and the great tribute imposed on him, and of his rebuilding of the house of God, there is a written account in the midrash of the book of the kings. His son Amaziah succeeded him as king.

25 Amaziah was twenty-five years old when he became king, and he reigned twenty-nine years in Jerusalem. His mother, named Jehoaddan, was from Jerusalem. 2 He did what was pleasing in the sight of the LORD, though not wholeheartedly. 3 After he had strengthened his hold on the kingdom, he slew those of his servants who had killed the king, his father; 4 but he did not put their children to death, for he acted according to what is written in the law, in the Book of Moses, as the LORD commanded: "Fathers shall not be put to death for their children, nor children for their fathers; but only for his own guilt shall a man be put to death."

5 Amaziah mustered Judah and placed them, out of all Judah and Benjamin according to their ancestral houses, under leaders of thousands and of hundreds. When he had counted those of twenty years and over, he found them to be three hundred thousand picked men fit for war, capable of handling lance and shield. 6 He also hired a hundred thousand valiant warriors from Israel for a hundred talents of silver. 7 But a man of God came to him and said: "O king, let not the army of Israel go with you, for the LORD is not with Israel, with any Ephraimite. 8 Instead, go on your own, strongly prepared for the conflict; otherwise the LORD will defeat you in the face of the enemy. It is God who has the power to reinforce or to defeat." 9 Amaziah answered the man of God, "But what is to be done about the hundred talents that I paid for the troops of Israel?" The man of God replied, "The LORD can give you much more than that." 10 Amaziah then disbanded the troops that had come to him from Ephraim, and sent them home. They, however, became furiously angry with Judah, and returned home blazing with resentment.

11 Amaziah now assumed command of his army. They proceeded to the Valley of Salt, and there they killed ten thousand men of Seir. 12 The Judahites also brought back another ten thousand alive, whom they led to the summit of the Rock and then cast down, so that they were all crushed. 13 Meanwhile, the mercenaries whom Amaziah had dismissed from battle service with him raided the cities of Judah from Samaria to Beth-horon. They killed three thousand of the inhabitants and took away much booty.

14 When Amaziah returned from his conquest of the Edomites he brought back with him the gods of the people of Seir, which he set up as his own gods; he bowed down before them and offered sacrifice to them. 15 Then the anger of the LORD blazed out against Amaziah, and he sent a prophet to him who said: "Why have you had recourse to this people's gods that could not save their own people from your hand?" 16 While he was still speaking, however, the

23 At the turn of the year, the Aramaean army made war on Joash. When they reached Judah and Jerusalem, they massacred all the nation's government officials and sent all their booty to the king of Damascus. 24 Although the invading Aramaean army was only a small body of men, Yahweh allowed them to defeat a very large army because they had abandoned Yahweh, God of their ancestors; thus they executed judgement on Joash.

After they had retired — for they left him seriously wounded — 25 his own retainers plotted against him to avenge the blood of the son of Jehoiada the priest and murdered him in his bed. When he died he was buried in the City of David, but not in the tombs of the kings. 26 These were the conspirators: Zabad son of Shimeath the Ammonite and Jehozabad son of Shimrith the Moabite. 27 As regards his sons, the heavy tribute imposed on him, and the restoration of the Temple of God, this is recorded in the Commentary on the Book of the Kings. His son Amaziah succeeded him.

25 Amaziah was twenty-five years old when he came to the throne and he reigned for twenty-nine years in Jerusalem. His mother's name was Jehoaddan of Jerusalem. 2 He did what Yahweh regards as right, though not wholeheartedly. 3 Once the kingdom was firmly under his control, he killed those of his retainers who had murdered the king his father. 4 But he did not put their sons to death; this was in accordance with what is written in the Law, in the book of Moses, where Yahweh had commanded, 'Parents may not be put to death for children, nor children for parents, but each must be put to death for his own crime.' a 5 Amaziah summoned Judah and organised all Judah and Benjamin by families under commanders of thousands and commanders of hundreds. He also made a register of those who were twenty years old and upwards, and found there were three hundred thousand picked men, ready for service and capable of wielding spear and shield. 6 Furthermore, he hired a hundred thousand tough fighting men from Israel for a hundred talents of silver. 7 A man of God then came to him and said, 'My lord king, do not let the Israelite troops march with you, for Yahweh is not with Israel or with any of the Ephraimites. 8 For however valiantly you act in war, God will bring you down before the enemy, for God has the power to uphold or to throw down.' 9 Amaziah said to the man of God, 'But what about the hundred talents which I have paid for the Israelite troops?' 'Yahweh can give you far more than that,' said the man of God. 10 At this, Amaziah dismissed the troops who had come to him from Ephraim and sent them home again. They were furious with Judah and went home in a great rage.

11 Amaziah then, coming to a decision, led out his own troops and, having reached the Valley of Salt, struck down ten thousand Seirites. 12 The men of Judah captured ten thousand more alive, taking them to the summit of the Rock, threw them off the summit of the Rock so that they were all dashed to pieces. 13 Meanwhile, the troops whom Amaziah had dismissed and not allowed to go into battle with him rased the towns of Judah, from Samaria to Beth-Horon, killing three thousand of their inhabitants and capturing great quantities of plunder.

14 On returning from his slaughter of the Edomites, Amaziah brought the gods of the Seirites with him; he set these up as his gods, bowing down before them and burning incense to them. 15 Yahweh's anger was aroused by Amaziah and he sent him a prophet, who said to him, 'Why do you consult those people's gods when they could not save their own people from your clutches?' 16 He was still speak-

to him, "Have we made you a royal counselor? Stop! Why should you be put to death?" So the prophet stopped, but said, "I know that God has determined to destroy you, because you have done this and have not listened to my advice."

17 Then King Amaziah of Judah took counsel and sent to King Joash son of Jehoahaz son of Jehu of Israel, saying, "Come, let us look one another in the face." 18 King Joash of Israel sent word to King Amaziah of Judah, "A thornbush on Lebanon sent to a cedar on Lebanon, saying, 'Give your daughter to my son for a wife'; but a wild animal of Lebanon passed by and trampled down the thornbush. 19 You say, 'See, I have defeated Edom,' and your heart has lifted you up in boastfulness. Now stay at home; why should you provoke trouble so that you fall, you and Judah with you?"

20 But Amaziah would not listen — it was God's doing, in order to hand them over, because they had sought the gods of Edom. 21 So King Joash of Israel went up; he and King Amaziah of Judah faced one another in battle at Beth-shemesh, which belongs to Judah. 22 Judah was defeated by Israel; everyone fled home. 23 King Joash of Israel captured King Amaziah of Judah, son of Joash, son of Ahaziah, at Beth-shemesh; he brought him to Jerusalem, and broke down the wall of Jerusalem from the Ephraim Gate to the Corner Gate, a distance of four hundred cubits. 24 He seized all the gold and silver, and all the vessels that were found in the house of God, and Obed-edom with them; he seized also the treasuries of the king's house, also hostages; then he returned to Samaria.

25 King Amaziah son of Joash of Judah, lived fifteen years after the death of King Joash son of Jehoahaz of Israel. 26 Now the rest of the deeds of Amaziah, from first to last, are they not written in the Book of the Kings of Judah and Israel? 27 From the time that Amaziah turned away from the LORD they made a conspiracy against him in Jerusalem, and he fled to Lachish. But they sent after him to Lachish, and killed him there. 28 They brought him back on horses; he was buried with his ancestors in the city of David.

26 Then all the people of Judah took Uzziah, who was sixteen years old, and made him king to succeed his father Amaziah. 2 He rebuilt Eloth and restored it to Judah, after the king slept with his ancestors. 3 Uzziah was sixteen years old when he began to reign, and he reigned fifty-two years in Jerusalem. His mother's name was Jecoliah of Jerusalem. 4 He did what was right in the sight of the LORD, just as his father Amaziah had done. 5 He set himself to seek God in the days of Zechariah, who instructed him in the fear of God; and as long as he sought the LORD, God made him prosper.

6 He went out and made war against the Philistines, and broke down the wall of Gath and the wall of Jabneh and the wall of Ashdod; he built cities in the territory of Ashdod and elsewhere among the Philistines. 7 God helped him against the Philistines, against the Arabs who lived in Gur-baal, and against the Meunites. 8 The Ammonites paid tribute to Uzziah, and his fame spread even to the border of Egypt, for he became very strong. 9 Moreover Uzziah built towers in Jerusalem at the Corner Gate, at the Valley Gate, and at the Angle, and fortified them. 10 He built towers in the wilder-

'Have we appointed you counsellor to the king? Stop! Why risk your life?' The prophet did stop, but first he said, 'I know that God has determined to destroy you because you do this and do not listen to my counsel.'

17 King Amaziah of Judah, after consultation, sent envoys to Jehoash son of Jehoahaz son of Jehu, king of Israel, to propose a confrontation. 18 King Jehoash of Israel sent back this answer to King Amaziah of Judah: 'A thistle in Lebanon sent to a cedar in Lebanon to say, "Give your daughter in marriage to my son." But a wild beast in Lebanon, passing by, trampled on the thistle. 19 You have defeated Edom, I see, but it has gone to your head. Stay at home and enjoy your triumph. Why should you involve yourself in disaster and bring yourself to the ground, and drag down Judah with you?'

20 Amaziah, however, would not listen; and this was God's doing in order to give Judah into the power of Jehoash, because they had resorted to the gods of Edom. 21 So King Jehoash of Israel marched out, and he and King Amaziah of Judah clashed at Beth-shemesh in Judah. 22 The men of Judah were routed by Israel and fled to their homes. 23 King Jehoash of Israel captured Amaziah king of Judah, son of Joash, son of Jehoahaz, at Beth-shemesh. He brought him to Jerusalem, where he broke down the city wall from the Ephraim Gate to the Corner Gate, a distance of four hundred cubits. 24 He took all the gold and silver and all the vessels found in the house of God, in the care of Obed-edom, and the treasures of the palace, as well as hostages, and then returned to Samaria.

25 Amaziah son of Joash, king of Judah, outlived Jehoash son of Jehoahaz, king of Israel, by fifteen years. 26 The other events of Amaziah's reign, from first to last, are recorded in the annals of the kings of Judah and Israel. 27 From the time when he turned away from the LORD, a conspiracy was formed against him in Jerusalem, and he fled to Lachish; the conspirators sent after him to Lachish and put him to death there. 28 His body was conveyed on horseback to Jerusalem, and there he was buried with his forefathers in the city of David.

26 The people of Judah, acting together, took Uzziah, now sixteen years old, and made him king in succession to his father Amaziah. 2 It was he who built Eloth and restored it to Judah after the king rested with his forefathers.

3 Uzziah was sixteen years old when he came to the throne, and he reigned in Jerusalem for fifty-two years; his mother was Jecoliah from Jerusalem. 4 He did what was right in the eyes of the LORD, as Amaziah his father had done. 5 He set himself to seek the guidance of God in the days of Zechariah, who instructed him in the fear of God; as long as he sought guidance from the LORD, God caused him to prosper.

6 He took the field against the Philistines. He broke down the walls of Gath, Jabneh, and Ashdod, and built towns in the territory of Ashdod and among the Philistines. 7 God aided him against them, as well as against the Arabs who lived in Gur-baal, and against the Meunites. 8 The Ammonites brought tribute to Uzziah and his fame spread to the borders of Egypt, for he had become very powerful. 9 He erected towers in Jerusalem at the Corner Gate, at the Valley Gate, and at the escarpment, and fortified them. 10 He

25:17–24 *Cp. 2 Kgs. 14:8–14.* 25:20 **of Jehoash:** *so Gk (Luc.); Heb. omits.* 25:24 **He took:** *prob. rdg, cp. 2 Kgs. 14:14; Heb. omits.* 25:25—26:2 *Cp. 2 Kgs. 14:17–22.* 25:28 **David:** *so some MSS; others Judah.* 26:3–4 *Cp. 2 Kgs. 15:2–3.* 26:5 **in the fear of:** *so some MSS; others on seeing.*

king said to him: "Have you been made the king's counselor? Be silent! Why should it be necessary to kill you?" Therefore the prophet desisted. "I know, however," he said, "that God has let you take counsel to your own destruction, because you have done this thing and have refused to hear my counsel."

17 Having taken counsel, King Amaziah of Judah sent messengers to Joash, son of Jehoahaz, son of Jehu, the king of Israel, saying, "Come, let us meet each other face to face." 18 King Joash of Israel sent this reply to King Amaziah of Judah: "The thistle of the Lebanon sent a message to the cedar of the Lebanon, saying, 'Give your daughter to my son for his wife.' But the wild beasts of the Lebanon passed by and trampled the thistle down. 19 You are thinking, 'See, I have beaten Edom!,' and thus ambition makes you proud. Remain at home. Why involve yourself, and Judah with you, in misfortune and failure?" 20 But Amaziah would not listen, for God had determined to hand them over because they had had recourse to the gods of Edom.

21 Therefore King Joash of Israel advanced and he and King Amaziah met in battle at Beth-shemesh of Judah. 22 There Judah was defeated by Israel, and all the Judean soldiers fled homeward. 23 King Joash of Israel captured Amaziah, king of Judah, son of Joash, son of Jehoahaz, at Beth-shemesh and brought him to Jerusalem. Then he tore down the wall of Jerusalem from the Ephraim Gate to the Corner Gate, a distance of four hundred cubits. 24 He took away all the gold and silver and all the vessels he found in the house of God with Obed-edom, together with the treasures of the palace, and hostages as well. Then he returned to Samaria.

25 Amaziah, son of Joash, king of Judah, survived Joash, son of Jehoahaz, king of Israel, by fifteen years. 26 The rest of the acts of Amaziah, first and last, can be found written, as is well known, in the book of the kings of Judah and Israel. 27 Now from the time that Amaziah ceased to follow the LORD, a conspiracy was formed against him in Jerusalem; hence he fled to Lachish. But they pursued him to Lachish and put him to death there. 28 They brought him back on horses and buried him with his ancestors in the City of Judah.

26 All the people of Judah chose Uzziah, though he was but sixteen years of age, and proclaimed him king to succeed his father Amaziah. 2 He rebuilt Elath and restored it to Judah; this was after King Amaziah had gone to rest with his ancestors. 3 Uzziah was sixteen years old when he became king, and he reigned fifty-two years in Jerusalem. His mother, named Jecoliah, was from Jerusalem. 4 He pleased the LORD, just as his father Amaziah had done.

5 He was prepared to seek God as long as Zechariah lived, who taught him to fear God; and as long as he sought the LORD, God made him prosper. 6 He went out and fought the Philistines and razed the walls of Gath, Jabneh and Ashdod [and built cities in the district of Ashdod and in Philistia]. 7 God helped him against the Philistines, against the Arabs who dwelt in Gurbaal, and against the Meunites. 8 The Ammonites paid tribute to Uzziah and his fame spread as far as Egypt, for he grew stronger and stronger. 9 Moreover, Uzziah built towers in Jerusalem at the Corner Gate, at the Valley Gate, and at the Angle, and he fortified them. 10 He

ing when Amaziah interrupted him. 'Have we appointed you a royal counsellor? Stop, as you value your life!' So the prophet stopped, and then said, 'I know that God has decided to destroy you for having done this and for not listening to my advice.'

17 After consultation, Amaziah king of Judah then sent a message to Joash son of Jehoahaz son of Jehu, king of Israel, saying, 'Come and make a trial of strength!' 18 Joash king of Israel sent back word to Amaziah king of Judah, 'The thistle of Lebanon sent a message to the cedar of Lebanon, saying, "Give my son your daughter in marriage"; but a wild animal of the Lebanon ran over the thistle and squashed it. 19 "Look at me, the conqueror of Edom," you say, and now aspire to even greater glory. But stay where you belong! Why challenge disaster, to your own and Judah's ruin?'

20 But Amaziah would not listen, for this was an act of God to deliver them up for having consulted the gods of Edom. 21 So Joash king of Israel marched to the attack. And at Beth-Shemesh, which belongs to Judah, he and Amaziah king of Judah made their trial of strength. 22 Judah was defeated by Israel, and everyone fled to his tent. 23 The king of Judah, Amaziah son of Joash, son of Ahaziah, was taken prisoner at Beth-Shemesh by Joash king of Israel who led him off to Jerusalem, where he demolished four hundred cubits of the city wall between the Ephraim Gate and the Corner Gate; 24 he then took back with him to Samaria all the gold and silver, and all the vessels to be found in the Temple of God in the care of Obed-Edom, the treasures in the palace, and hostages besides.

25 Amaziah son of Joash, king of Judah, lived for fifteen years after the death of Joash son of Jehoahaz, king of Israel.

26 The rest of the history of Amaziah, from first to last, is this not recorded in the Book of the Kings of Judah and Israel? 27 Some time after Amaziah had defected from Yahweh, a plot having been hatched against him in Jerusalem, he fled to Lachish where he was murdered. 28 He was then transported by horse and buried with his ancestors in the city of David.

26 All the people then chose Uzziah, who was sixteen years old, and made him king in succession to his father Amaziah. 2 It was he who rebuilt Elath, recovering it for Judah, after the king had fallen asleep with his ancestors. 3 Uzziah was sixteen years old when he came to the throne and he reigned for fifty-two years in Jerusalem. His mother's name was Jecoliah of Jerusalem. 4 He did what is pleasing to Yahweh, just as his father Amaziah had done; 5 he consulted God throughout the lifetime of Zechariah, who instructed him in the fear of God. And as long as he consulted Yahweh, God gave him success.

6 He went on campaign against the Philistines, demolished the walls of Gath, the walls of Jabneh and the walls of Ashdod, and built towns in the area of Ashdod and elsewhere in Philistine territory. 7 God helped him against the Philistines, the Arabs living at Gur-Baal and the Meunites. 8 The Meunites paid tribute to Uzziah and his fame spread as far as the frontier of Egypt, since he kept growing stronger and stronger.

9 Uzziah built towers in Jerusalem, at the Corner Gate, at the Valley Gate and at the Angle, and fortified them. 10 He

NEW REVISED STANDARD VERSION	REVISED ENGLISH BIBLE

ness and hewed out many cisterns, for he had large herds, both in the Shephelah and in the plain, and he had farmers and vinedressers in the hills and in the fertile lands, for he loved the soil. 11 Moreover Uzziah had an army of soldiers, fit for war, in divisions according to the numbers in the muster made by the secretary Jeiel and the officer Maaseiah, under the direction of Hananiah, one of the king's commanders. 12 The whole number of the heads of ancestral houses of mighty warriors was two thousand six hundred. 13 Under their command was an army of three hundred seven thousand five hundred, who could make war with mighty power, to help the king against the enemy. 14 Uzziah provided for all the army the shields, spears, helmets, coats of mail, bows, and stones for slinging. 15 In Jerusalem he set up machines, invented by skilled workers, on the towers and the corners for shooting arrows and large stones. And his fame spread far, for he was marvelously helped until he became strong.

16 But when he had become strong he grew proud, to his destruction. For he was false to the LORD his God, and entered the temple of the LORD to make offering on the altar of incense. 17 But the priest Azariah went in after him, with eighty priests of the LORD who were men of valor; 18 they withstood King Uzziah, and said to him, "It is not for you, Uzziah, to make offering to the LORD, but for the priests the descendants of Aaron, who are consecrated to make offering. Go out of the sanctuary; for you have done wrong, and it will bring you no honor from the LORD God." 19 Then Uzziah was angry. Now he had a censer in his hand to make offering, and when he became angry with the priests a leprous*e* disease broke out on his forehead, in the presence of the priests in the house of the LORD, by the altar of incense. 20 When the chief priest Azariah, and all the priests, looked at him, he was leprous*e* in his forehead. They hurried him out, and he himself hurried to get out, because the LORD had struck him. 21 King Uzziah was leprous*e* to the day of his death, and being leprous*e* lived in a separate house, for he was excluded from the house of the LORD. His son Jotham was in charge of the palace of the king, governing the people of the land.

22 Now the rest of the acts of Uzziah, from first to last, the prophet Isaiah son of Amoz wrote. 23 Uzziah slept with his ancestors; they buried him near his ancestors in the burial field that belonged to the kings, for they said, "He is leprous."*e* His son Jotham succeeded him.

27 Jotham was twenty-five years old when he began to reign; he reigned sixteen years in Jerusalem. His mother's name was Jerushah daughter of Zadok. 2 He did what was right in the sight of the LORD just as his father Uzziah had done — only he did not invade the temple of the LORD. But the people still followed corrupt practices. 3 He built the upper gate of the house of the LORD, and did extensive building on the wall of Ophel. 4 Moreover he built cities in the hill country of Judah, and forts and towers on the wooded hills. 5 He fought with the king of the Ammonites and prevailed against them. The Ammonites gave him that year one hundred talents of silver, ten thousand cors of wheat and ten thousand of barley. The Ammonites paid him the same amount in the second and the third years. 6 So Jotham became strong because he ordered his ways before the LORD his God. 7 Now the rest of the acts of Jotham, and all his wars and his ways, are written in the Book of the Kings of Israel and Judah. 8 He was twenty-five years old

erected other towers in the wilderness and dug many cisterns, for he had large herds of cattle both in the Shephelah and in the plain. He also had farmers and vine-dressers in the hill-country and in the fertile lands, for he loved the soil.

11 Uzziah had an army of soldiers trained and ready for service, mustered in divisions according to the numbering made by Jeiel the adjutant-general and Maaseiah the clerk, under the direction of Hananiah, one of the king's commanders. 12 The total number of heads of families which supplied seasoned warriors was two thousand six hundred. 13 Under their command was an army of three hundred and seven thousand five hundred, a powerful fighting force to aid the king against his enemies. 14 Uzziah provided for the whole army shields, spears, helmets, coats of armour, bows, and sling-stones. 15 In Jerusalem he had machines designed by engineers for use on towers and battlements to discharge arrows and large stones. His fame spread far and wide, for he was so wonderfully gifted that he became very powerful.

16 But when he grew powerful his pride became great and led to his own undoing: he offended against the LORD his God by entering the temple of the LORD to burn incense on the incense-altar. 17 Azariah the priest and eighty others of the LORD's priests, courageous men, went in after King Uzziah, 18 confronted him, and said, 'It is not for you, Uzziah, to burn incense to the LORD, but for the Aaronite priests who have been consecrated for that office. Leave the sanctuary; for you have offended, and that will certainly bring you no honour from the LORD God.' 19 The king, who had a censer in his hand ready to burn incense, was enraged; but while he was raging at the priests, leprosy broke out on his forehead in the presence of the priests, there in the house of the LORD, beside the altar of incense. 20 When Azariah the chief priest and the other priests looked towards him, they saw that his forehead was leprous. They hurried him out of the temple, and indeed he himself hastened to leave, because the LORD had struck him with the disease. 21 King Uzziah remained a leper till the day of his death; he lived in his palace as a leper, relieved of all duties and excluded from the house of the LORD, while his son Jotham was comptroller of the household and regent over the country. 22 The other events of Uzziah's reign, from first to last, are recorded by the prophet Isaiah son of Amoz. 23 He rested with his forefathers and was buried with them, but in the field adjoining the royal tombs, for they said, 'He is a leper.' His son Jotham succeeded him.

27 Jotham was twenty-five years old when he came to the throne, and he reigned in Jerusalem for sixteen years; his mother was Jerushah daughter of Zadok. 2 He did what was right in the eyes of the LORD, as his father Uzziah had done, but unlike him he did not enter the temple of the LORD; the people, however, continued their corrupt practices. 3 He constructed the Upper Gate of the house of the LORD and built extensions on the wall at Ophel. 4 He built towns in the hill-country of Judah, and forts and towers on the wooded hills. 5 He made war on the king of the Ammonites and defeated him; and that year the Ammonites delivered to him a hundred talents of silver, ten thousand kor of wheat, and ten thousand of barley. They paid him the same tribute in the second and third years. 6 Jotham became very powerful because he maintained a steady course of obedience to the LORD his God. 7 The other events of Jotham's reign, all that he did in war and in peace, are recorded in the annals of the kings of Israel and Judah. 8 He was twenty-five

26:14 **and:** *prob. rdg; Heb. adds* for.   26:16 **his pride . . . undoing:** *or* he became so proud that he acted corruptly.
27:1–9 *Cp. 2 Kgs. 15:33–38.*

e A term for several skin diseases; precise meaning uncertain

|

built towers in the desert and dug numerous cisterns, for he had many cattle. He had plowmen in the foothills and the plains, and vinedressers in the highlands and the garden land. He was a lover of the soil.

11 Uzziah also had a standing army of fit soldiers divided into bands according to the number in which they were mustered by Jeiel the scribe and Maaseiah the recorder, under the command of Hananiah, one of the king's officials. 12 The entire number of family heads over these valiant warriors was two thousand six hundred, 13 and at their disposal was a mighty army of three hundred seven thousand five hundred fighting men of great valor to help the king against his enemies. 14 Uzziah provided for them — for the entire army — bucklers, lances, helmets, breastplates, bows and slingstones. 15 He also built machines in Jerusalem, devices contrived to stand on the towers and at the angles of the walls to shoot arrows and cast large stones. His fame spread far and wide, and his power was ascribed to the marvelous help he had received.

16 But after he had become strong, he became proud to his own destruction and broke faith with the LORD, his God. He entered the temple of the LORD to make an offering on the altar of incense. 17 But Azariah the priest, and with him eighty other priests of the LORD, courageous men, followed him. 18 They opposed King Uzziah, saying to him: "It is not for you, Uzziah, to burn incense to the LORD, but for the priests, the sons of Aaron, who have been consecrated for this purpose. Leave the sanctuary, for you have broken faith and no longer have a part in the glory that comes from the LORD God." 19 Uzziah, who was holding a censer for burning the incense, became angry, but at the moment he showed his anger to the priests, while they were looking at him in the house of the LORD beside the altar of incense, leprosy broke out on his forehead. 20 Azariah the chief priest and all the other priests examined him, and when they saw that his forehead was leprous, they expelled him from the temple. He himself fled willingly, for the LORD had afflicted him. 21 King Uzziah remained a leper to the day of his death. As a leper he dwelt in a segregated house, for he was excluded from the house of the LORD. Therefore his son Jotham was regent of the palace and ruled the people of the land.

22 The prophet Isaiah, son of Amos, wrote the rest of the acts of Uzziah, first and last. 23 Uzziah rested with his ancestors; he was buried with them in the field adjoining the royal cemetery, for they said, "He was a leper." His son Jotham succeeded him as king.

27 Jotham was twenty-five years old when he became king, and he reigned sixteen years in Jerusalem. His mother was named Jerusa, daughter of Zadok. 2 He pleased the LORD just as his father Uzziah had done, though he did not enter the temple of the LORD; the people, however, continued to act sinfully.

3 He built the upper gate of the LORD's house and had much construction done on the wall of Ophel. 4 Moreover, he built cities in the hill country of Judah, and in the forest land he set up fortresses and towers. 5 He fought with the king of the Ammonites and conquered them. That year the Ammonites paid him one hundred talents of silver, together with ten thousand kors of wheat and ten thousand of barley. They brought the same to him also in the second and in the third year. 6 Thus Jotham continued to grow strong because he lived resolutely in the presence of the LORD, his God. 7 The rest of the acts of Jotham, his wars and his activities, can be found written in the book of the kings of Israel and Judah. 8 He was twenty-five years old when he became

built towers in the desert too, and dug many storage-wells, for he had large herds in the lowlands and on the tableland, and farmers and vine dressers in the hills and fertile lands: for he loved the land.

11 Uzziah had a trained army ready to go on campaign, organised in companies manned as detailed by the scribe Jeiel and the staff-officer Maaseiah, and commanded by Hananiah one of the king's generals. 12 The heads of families of the military champions numbered in all two thousand six hundred. 13 Under them was an army of three hundred and seven thousand five hundred men ready for war, a powerful force to support the king against the enemy. 14 Uzziah provided shields, spears, helmets, armour, bows and sling-stones for the entire army. 15 He also erected expertly contrived devices for the towers and angles of Jerusalem from which to shoot arrows and drop large stones. His fame spread far and wide, for he was miraculously helped to become strong.

16 But once he was strong, his arrogance was such that it led to his downfall; he was unfaithful to Yahweh his God by entering the Temple of Yahweh to burn incense on the altar of incense. 17 Azariah the priest with eight brave priests of Yahweh followed him in; 18 confronting King Uzziah, they said to him, 'Uzziah, you are not allowed to burn incense to Yahweh; only the Aaronite priests consecrated for the purpose may burn incense. Leave the sanctuary, for you have been unfaithful and will have no honour from Yahweh God.' 19 Uzziah, censer in hand to burn incense, flew into a rage. But while he was raging at the priests, a virulent skin-disease broke out on his forehead in the presence of the priests, in the Temple of Yahweh, there by the altar of incense. 20 When Azariah the chief priest and all the other priests turned towards him, there was skin-disease on his forehead and they hurried him outside, and he himself was equally anxious to get out, because Yahweh had struck him.

21 King Uzziah was afflicted with skin-disease till his dying day. Because of this, he lived confined to his room and was excluded from the Temple of Yahweh, while Jotham his son, who was master of the palace, governed the people of the country.

22 The rest of the history of Uzziah, from first to last, has been written by the prophet Isaiah son of Amoz. 23 Then Uzziah fell asleep with his ancestors and was buried with them in the field beside the burial ground of the kings since, it was reasoned, he was afflicted with virulent skin-disease. His son Jotham then succeeded him.

27 Jotham was twenty-five years old when he came to the throne and he reigned for sixteen years in Jerusalem. His mother's name was Jerushah daughter of Zadok. 2 He did what Yahweh regards as right, just as his father Uzziah had done. Only he did not enter Yahweh's sanctuary. But the people continued to do wrong.

3 It was he who built the Upper Gate of the Temple of Yahweh and carried out considerable work on the wall of the Ophel. 4 He also built towns in the highlands of Judah and built forts and towers in the wooded areas. 5 He also went to war against the king of the Ammonites and defeated them; and the Ammonites had to give him a hundred talents of silver, ten thousand kor of wheat and ten thousand of barley that year. And the Ammonites paid him the same amount, the second and third years afterwards. 6 Jotham became powerful because he kept an unswerving course before Yahweh his God.

7 The rest of the history of Jotham, all his wars and his policy, are recorded in the Book of the Kings of Israel and Judah. 8 He was twenty-five years old when he came to the

when he began to reign; he reigned sixteen years in Jerusalem. 9 Jotham slept with his ancestors, and they buried him in the city of David; and his son Ahaz succeeded him.

28 Ahaz was twenty years old when he began to reign; he reigned sixteen years in Jerusalem. He did not do what was right in the sight of the LORD, as his ancestor David had done, 2 but he walked in the ways of the kings of Israel. He even made cast images for the Baals; 3 and he made offerings in the valley of the son of Hinnom, and made his sons pass through fire, according to the abominable practices of the nations whom the LORD drove out before the people of Israel. 4 He sacrificed and made offerings on the high places, on the hills, and under every green tree.

5 Therefore the LORD his God gave him into the hand of the king of Aram, who defeated him and took captive a great number of his people and brought them to Damascus. He was also given into the hand of the king of Israel, who defeated him with great slaughter. 6 Pekah son of Remaliah killed one hundred twenty thousand in Judah in one day, all of them valiant warriors, because they had abandoned the LORD, the God of their ancestors. 7 And Zichri, a mighty warrior of Ephraim, killed the king's son Maaseiah, Azrikam the commander of the palace, and Elkanah the next in authority to the king.

8 The people of Israel took captive two hundred thousand of their kin, women, sons, and daughters; they also took much booty from them and brought the booty to Samaria. 9 But a prophet of the LORD was there, whose name was Oded; he went out to meet the army that came to Samaria, and said to them, "Because the LORD, the God of your ancestors, was angry with Judah, he gave them into your hand, but you have killed them in a rage that has reached up to heaven. 10 Now you intend to subjugate the people of Judah and Jerusalem, male and female, as your slaves. But what have you except sins against the LORD your God? 11 Now hear me, and send back the captives whom you have taken from your kindred, for the fierce wrath of the LORD is upon you." 12 Moreover, certain chiefs of the Ephraimites, Azariah son of Johanan, Berechiah son of Meshillemoth, Jehizkiah son of Shallum, and Amasa son of Hadlai, stood up against those who were coming from the war, 13 and said to them, "You shall not bring the captives in here, for you propose to bring on us guilt against the LORD in addition to our present sins and guilt. For our guilt is already great, and there is fierce wrath against Israel." 14 So the warriors left the captives and the booty before the officials and all the assembly. 15 Then those who were mentioned by name got up and took the captives, and with the booty they clothed all that were naked among them; they clothed them, gave them sandals, provided them with food and drink, and anointed them; and carrying all the feeble among them on donkeys, they brought them to their kindred at Jericho, the city of palm trees. Then they returned to Samaria.

16 At that time King Ahaz sent to the king *f* of Assyria for help. 17 For the Edomites had again invaded and defeated Judah, and carried away captives. 18 And the Philistines had made raids on the cities in the Shephelah and the Negeb of Judah, and had taken Beth-shemesh, Aijalon, Gederoth, Soco with its villages, Timnah with its villages, and Gimzo with its villages; and they settled there. 19 For the LORD brought Judah low because of King Ahaz of Israel, for he had behaved without restraint in Judah and had been faithless to the LORD. 20 So King Tilgath-pilneser of Assyria came against him, and oppressed him instead of

f Gk Syr Vg Compare 2 Kings 16.7: Heb *kings*

years old when he came to the throne, and he reigned in Jerusalem for sixteen years. 9 He rested with his forefathers and was buried in the city of David. His son Ahaz succeeded him.

28 AHAZ was twenty years old when he came to the throne, and he reigned in Jerusalem for sixteen years. He did not do what was right in the eyes of the LORD like his forefather David, 2 but followed in the footsteps of the kings of Israel, and cast metal images for the baalim. 3 He also burnt sacrifices in the valley of Ben-hinnom; he even burnt his sons in the fire according to the abominable practice of the nations whom the LORD had dispossessed in favour of the Israelites. 4 He sacrificed and burned offerings at the shrines and on the hilltops and under every spreading tree.

5 The LORD his God let Ahaz suffer at the hands of the king of Aram: the Aramaeans defeated him, took many captives, and brought them to Damascus. He was also made to suffer at the hands of the king of Israel, who inflicted a severe defeat on him. 6 This was Pekah son of Remaliah, who killed in one day a hundred and twenty thousand men of Judah, seasoned troops, for they had forsaken the LORD the God of their forefathers. 7 Zichri, an Ephraimite hero, killed Maaseiah the king's son and Azrikam the comptroller of the household and Elkanah the king's chief minister. 8 The Israelites took captive from their kinsmen two hundred thousand women and children; they also removed a large amount of booty and brought it to Samaria.

9 A prophet of the LORD was there, Oded by name; he went out to meet the army as it returned to Samaria and said to them, 'It is because the LORD the God of your forefathers is angry with Judah that he has given them into your power. But you have massacred them in a rage that has towered up to heaven. 10 You now propose to force the people of Judah and Jerusalem, male and female, into slavery. Are you not also guilty men before the LORD your God? 11 Now listen to me. Send back those you have taken captive from your kinsmen, for the anger of the LORD is roused against you.'

12 Next, some Ephraimite chiefs, Azariah son of Jehohanan, Berechiah son of Meshillemoth, Hezekiah son of Shallum, and Amasa son of Hadlai, met those who were returning from the war 13 and said to them, 'You must not bring these captives into our country; what you are proposing would make us guilty before the LORD and add to our sins and transgressions. We are guilty enough already, and there is fierce anger against Israel.' 14 So the armed men left the captives and the spoil with the officers and the assembled people. 15 The captives were put in the charge of men nominated for this duty, who found clothes from the spoil for all who were naked; they clothed and shod them, gave them food and drink, and anointed them. All who were tottering on their last legs they mounted on donkeys, and took them to their kinsmen in Jericho, the city of palm trees. Then they themselves returned to Samaria.

16 At that time King Ahaz sent to the king of Assyria for help. 17 The Edomites had invaded again and defeated Judah and carried away prisoners, 18 while the Philistines had raided towns of the Shephelah and of the Negeb of Judah; they had captured and occupied Beth-shemesh, Aijalon, and Gederoth, as well as Soco, Timnah, and Gimzo with their villages. 19 The LORD had reduced Judah to submission because of Ahaz king of Judah; for his actions in Judah had been unbridled and he had been grossly unfaithful to the LORD. 20 Then King Tiglath-pileser of Assyria came to him and, far from assisting him, pressed him hard. 21 Ahaz

28:1–4 Cp. *2 Kgs. 16:2–4.* 28:7 **son:** *or* deputy. 28:12 **Hezekiah:** *or* Jehizkiah. 28:16 **the king:** *so Gk; Heb.* the kings. 28:19 **king of Judah:** *so some MSS; others* king of Israel. 28:20 **Tiglath-pileser:** *so Syriac; Heb.* Tilgath-pilneser.

king, and he reigned sixteen years in Jerusalem. ⁹Jotham rested with his ancestors and was buried in the City of David, and his son Ahaz succeeded him as king.

28 Ahaz was twenty years old when he became king, and he reigned sixteen years in Jerusalem. He did not please the LORD as his forefather David had done, ²but conducted himself like the kings of Israel and even made molten idols of the Baals. ³Moreover, he offered sacrifice in the Valley of Ben-hinnom, and immolated his sons by fire according to the abominable practice of the nations which the LORD had cleared out before the Israelites. ⁴He offered sacrifice and incense on the high places, on hills, and under every leafy tree.

⁵Therefore the LORD, his God, delivered him into the power of the king of Aram. The Arameans defeated him and carried away captive a large number of his people, whom they brought to Damascus. He was also delivered into the power of the king of Israel, who defeated him with great slaughter. ⁶For Pekah, son of Remaliah, slew one hundred and twenty thousand of Judah in a single day, all of them valiant men, because they had abandoned the LORD, the God of their fathers. ⁷Zichri, an Ephraimite warrior, killed Maaseiah, the king's son, and Azrikam, the master of the palace, and also Elkanah, who was second to the king. ⁸The Israelites took away as captives two hundred thousand of their brethren's wives, sons and daughters; they also took from them much plunder, which they brought to Samaria.

⁹In Samaria there was a prophet of the LORD by the name of Oded. He went out to meet the army returning to Samaria and said to them: "It was because the LORD, the God of your fathers, was angry with Judah that he delivered them into your hands. You, however, have slaughtered them with a fury that has reached up to heaven. ¹⁰And now you are planning to make the children of Judah and Jerusalem your slaves and bondwomen. Are not you yourselves, therefore, guilty of a crime against the LORD, your God? ¹¹Now listen to me: send back the captives you have carried off from among your brethren, for the burning anger of the LORD is upon you."

¹²At this, some of the Ephraimite leaders, Azariah, son of Johanan, Berechiah, son of Meshillemoth, Jehizkiah, son of Shallum, and Amasa, son of Hadlai, themselves stood up in opposition to those who had returned from the war. ¹³They said to them: "Do not bring the captives here, for what you propose will make us guilty before the LORD and increase our sins and our guilt. Our guilt is already great, and there is a burning anger upon Israel." ¹⁴Therefore the soldiers left their captives and the plunder before the princes and the whole assembly. ¹⁵Then the men just named proceeded to help the captives. All of them who were naked they clothed from the booty; they clothed them, put sandals on their feet, gave them food and drink, anointed them, and all who were weak they set on asses. They brought them to Jericho, the city of palms, to their brethren. Then they returned to Samaria.

¹⁶At that time King Ahaz sent an appeal for help to the kings of Assyria. ¹⁷The Edomites had returned, attacked Judah, and carried off captives. ¹⁸The Philistines too had raided the cities of the foothills and the Negeb of Judah; they captured Beth-shemesh, Aijalon, Gederoth, Soco and its dependencies, Timnah and its dependencies, and Gimzo and its dependencies, and occupied them. ¹⁹For the LORD had brought Judah low because of Ahaz, king of Israel, who let Judah go its own way and proved utterly faithless to the LORD. ²⁰Tilgath-pilneser, king of Assyria, did indeed come to him, but to oppress him rather than to help him.

throne and he reigned for sixteen years in Jerusalem. ⁹Then Jotham fell asleep with his ancestors, and was buried in the City of David; his son Ahaz succeeded him.

28 Ahaz was twenty years old when he came to the throne and he reigned for sixteen years in Jerusalem. He did not do what Yahweh regards as right, as his ancestor David had done. ²He followed the example of the kings of Israel, even having images cast for the Baals; ³he burned incense in the Valley of Ben-Hinnom, caused his sons to pass through the fire of sacrifice, copying the disgusting practices of the nations whom Yahweh had dispossessed for the Israelites. ⁴He offered sacrifices and incense on the high places, on the hills and under every green tree.

⁵So Yahweh his God put him at the mercy of the king of Aram, who defeated him and took large numbers of captives, carrying them off to Damascus. He also put him at the mercy of the king of Israel, who inflicted heavy casualties on him. ⁶In a single day, Pekah son of Remaliah killed a hundred and twenty thousand in Judah, all of them prominent men, because they had abandoned Yahweh, God of their ancestors. ⁷Zichri, an Ephraimite champion, killed Maaseiah the king's son, Azrikam the controller of the household and Elkanah the king's second-in-command. ⁸Of their brothers, the Israelites took two hundred thousand captive including wives, sons, daughters; they also took quantities of booty, carrying everything off to Samaria.

⁹Now there was a prophet of Yahweh there by the name of Oded, who went out to meet the troops returning to Samaria and said, 'Look, because Yahweh, God of your ancestors, was angry with Judah, he put them at your mercy, but you have slaughtered them with such fury as reached to heaven, ¹⁰and now you propose to reduce the children of Judah and Jerusalem to being your male and female slaves! Have you not yourselves committed sins against Yahweh your God? ¹¹Now listen to me: release the captives you have taken from your brothers, for the fierce anger of Yahweh hangs over you.'

¹²Some of the Ephraimite chieftains—Azariah son of Jehohanan, Berechaiah son of Meshillemoth, Jehizkiah son of Shallum and Amasa son of Hadlai—then protested to those returning from the war ¹³and said to them, 'You must not bring the captives here, for we have already sinned against Yahweh and you propose to add to our sin and guilt, although our guilt is already great, and fierce anger is hanging over Israel.' ¹⁴So in the presence of the officials and whole assembly, the soldiers gave up the captives and booty. ¹⁵Men nominated for the purpose then took charge of the captives. From the booty they clothed all those of them who were naked; they gave them clothing and sandals, provided them with food and drink, mounted on donkeys all those who were infirm and took them back to Jericho, the city of palm trees, to their brothers. Then they returned to Samaria.

¹⁶This was when King Ahaz sent asking the king of Assyria to come to his assistance. ¹⁷The Edomites again invaded, defeated Judah, and carried off captives, ¹⁸while the Philistines raided the towns in the lowlands and in the Negeb of Judah, capturing Beth-Shemesh, Aijalon, Gederoth, Soco and its dependencies, Timnah and its dependencies and Gimzo and its dependencies, and settled there. ¹⁹For Yahweh brought Judah low because of Ahaz king of Israel, since he behaved without restraint in Judah and had been unfaithful to Yahweh. ²⁰Tiglath-Pileser king of Assyria attacked and besieged him; but he could not overpower him. ²¹Although Ahaz

NEW REVISED STANDARD VERSION

strengthening him. 21 For Ahaz plundered the house of the LORD and the houses of the king and of the officials, and gave tribute to the king of Assyria; but it did not help him.

22 In the time of his distress he became yet more faithless to the LORD — this same King Ahaz. 23 For he sacrificed to the gods of Damascus, which had defeated him, and said, "Because the gods of the kings of Aram helped them, I will sacrifice to them so that they may help me." But they were the ruin of him, and of all Israel. 24 Ahaz gathered together the utensils of the house of God, and cut in pieces the utensils of the house of God. He shut up the doors of the house of the LORD and made himself altars in every corner of Jerusalem. 25 In every city of Judah he made high places to make offerings to other gods, provoking to anger the LORD, the God of his ancestors. 26 Now the rest of his acts and all his ways, from first to last, are written in the Book of the Kings of Judah and Israel. 27 Ahaz slept with his ancestors, and they buried him in the city, in Jerusalem; but they did not bring him into the tombs of the kings of Israel. His son Hezekiah succeeded him.

29 Hezekiah began to reign when he was twenty-five years old; he reigned twenty-nine years in Jerusalem. His mother's name was Abijah daughter of Zechariah. 2 He did what was right in the sight of the LORD, just as his ancestor David had done.

3 In the first year of his reign, in the first month, he opened the doors of the house of the LORD and repaired them. 4 He brought in the priests and the Levites and assembled them in the square on the east. 5 He said to them, "Listen to me, Levites! Sanctify yourselves, and sanctify the house of the LORD, the God of your ancestors, and carry out the filth from the holy place. 6 For our ancestors have been unfaithful and have done what was evil in the sight of the LORD our God; they have forsaken him, and have turned away their faces from the dwelling of the LORD, and turned their backs. 7 They also shut the doors of the vestibule and put out the lamps, and have not offered incense or made burnt offerings in the holy place to the God of Israel. 8 Therefore the wrath of the LORD came upon Judah and Jerusalem, and he has made them an object of horror, of astonishment, and of hissing, as you see with your own eyes. 9 Our fathers have fallen by the sword and our sons and our daughters and our wives are in captivity for this. 10 Now it is in my heart to make a covenant with the LORD, the God of Israel, so that his fierce anger may turn away from us. 11 My sons, do not now be negligent, for the LORD has chosen you to stand in his presence to minister to him, and to be his ministers and make offerings to him."

12 Then the Levites arose, Mahath son of Amasai, and Joel son of Azariah, of the sons of the Kohathites; and of the sons of Merari, Kish son of Abdi, and Azariah son of Jehallelel; and of the Gershonites, Joah son of Zimmah, and Eden son of Joah; 13 and of the sons of Elizaphan, Shimri and Jeuel; and of the sons of Asaph, Zechariah and Mattaniah; 14 and of the sons of Heman, Jehuel and Shimei; and of the sons of Jeduthun, Shemaiah and Uzziel. 15 They gathered their brothers, sanctified themselves, and went in as the king had commanded, by the words of the LORD, to cleanse the house of the LORD. 16 The priests went into the inner part of the house of the LORD to cleanse it, and they brought out all the unclean things that they found in the temple of the LORD into the court of the house of the LORD; and the Levites took them and carried them out to the Wadi Kidron. 17 They began to sanctify on the first day of the first

REVISED ENGLISH BIBLE

stripped the house of the LORD, the king's palace, and the houses of his officers, and gave the plunder to the king of Assyria; but all to no purpose.

22 This king, Ahaz, when hard pressed, became more and more unfaithful to the LORD; 23 he sacrificed to the gods of Damascus who had defeated him, for he said, 'The gods of the kings of Aram helped them; I shall sacrifice to them so that they may help me.' But in fact they caused his downfall and that of all Israel. 24 Then Ahaz gathered together the vessels of the house of God and broke them up, and shut up the doors of the house of the LORD; he made himself altars at every corner in Jerusalem, 25 and at every town of Judah he made shrines to burn sacrifices to other gods and provoked the anger of the LORD the God of his forefathers.

26 The other acts and all the events of his reign, from first to last, are recorded in the annals of the kings of Judah and Israel. 27 Ahaz rested with his forefathers and was buried in the city of Jerusalem, but he was not given burial with the kings of Judah. His son Hezekiah succeeded him.

29 HEZEKIAH was twenty-five years old when he came to the throne, and he reigned in Jerusalem for twenty-nine years; his mother was Abijah daughter of Zechariah. 2 He did what was right in the eyes of the LORD, as his ancestor David had done.

3 In the first year of his reign, in the first month, he opened and repaired the doors of the house of the LORD. 4 He brought in the priests and Levites and, assembling them in the square on the east side, 5 said to them, 'Levites, listen to me. Hallow yourselves now, hallow the house of the LORD the God of your forefathers, and remove all defilement from the sanctuary. 6 For our forefathers were unfaithful and did what was wrong in the eyes of the LORD our God: they forsook him, they faced about, and they turned their backs on his dwelling-place. 7 They shut the doors of the porch and extinguished the lamps; they ceased to burn incense and offer whole-offerings in the sanctuary to the God of Israel. 8 Therefore the anger of the LORD fell on Judah and Jerusalem and he made them repugnant, an object of horror and derision, as you see for yourselves. 9 That is why our fathers fell by the sword, why our sons and daughters and our wives are in captivity. 10 Now I intend that we should pledge ourselves to the LORD the God of Israel, in order that his anger may be averted from us. 11 My sons, let no time be lost; for the LORD has chosen you to serve him and to minister to him, to be his ministers and to burn sacrifices.'

12 The Levites set to work; they were Mahath son of Amasai and Joel son of Azariah of the family of Kohath; of the family of Merari, Kish son of Abdi and Azariah son of Jehallelel; of the family of Gershon, Joah son of Zimmah and Eden son of Joah; 13 of the family of Elizaphan, Shimri and Jeiel; of the family of Asaph, Zechariah and Mattaniah; 14 of the family of Heman, Jehiel and Shimei; and of the family of Jeduthun, Shemaiah and Uzziel. 15 They assembled their kinsmen and hallowed themselves, and then went in, as at the LORD's command the king had instructed them, to purify the house of the LORD. 16 The priests went inside to purify the house of the LORD; they removed all defilement they found in the temple into the court of the house of the LORD, where the Levites received it and carried it outside to the wadi of the Kidron. 17 They began the rites on the

---

28:26–27 *Cp. 2 Kgs. 16:19–20.* 28:27 **Judah:** *so Syriac; Heb.* Israel. 29:1–2 *Cp. 2 Kgs. 18:2–3.*

21 Though Ahaz plundered the LORD's house and the houses of the king and the princes to make payment to the king of Assyria, it availed him nothing.

22 While he was already in distress, the same King Ahaz became even more unfaithful to the LORD. 23 He sacrificed to the gods of Damascus who had defeated him, saying, "Since it was the gods of the kings of Aram who helped them, I will sacrifice to them that they may help me also." However, they only caused further disaster to him and to all Israel. 24 Ahaz gathered up the utensils of God's house and broke them in pieces. He closed the doors of the LORD's house and had altars made for himself in every corner of Jerusalem. 25 In every city throughout Judah he set up high places to offer sacrifice to other gods. Thus he angered the LORD, the God of his fathers.

26 The rest of his deeds and his activities, first and last, can be found written in the book of the kings of Judah and Israel. 27 Ahaz rested with his ancestors and was buried in Jerusalem — in the city, for they did not bring him to the tombs of the kings of Israel. His son Hezekiah succeeded him as king.

29 Hezekiah was twenty-five years old when he became king, and he reigned twenty-nine years in Jerusalem. His mother was named Abia, daughter of Zechariah. 2 He pleased the LORD just as his forefather David had done. 3 It was he who, in the first month of the first year of his reign, opened the doors of the LORD's house and repaired them. 4 He summoned the priests and Levites, gathered them in the open space to the east, 5 and said to them: "Listen to me, you Levites! Sanctify yourselves now and sanctify the house of the LORD, the God of your fathers, and clean out the filth from the sanctuary. 6 Our fathers acted faithlessly and did evil in the eyes of the LORD, our God. They abandoned him, turned away their faces from the LORD's dwelling, and turned their backs on him. 7 They also closed the doors of the vestibule, extinguished the lamps, and refused to burn incense and offer holocausts in the sanctuary to the honor of the God of Israel. 8 Therefore the anger of the LORD has come upon Judah and Jerusalem; he has made them an object of terror, astonishment and mockery, as you see with your own eyes. 9 For our fathers, as you know, fell by the sword, and our sons, our daughters and our wives have been taken captive because of this. 10 Now, I intend to make a covenant with the LORD, the God of Israel, that his burning anger may withdraw from us. 11 My sons, be not negligent any longer, for it is you whom the LORD has chosen to stand before him, to minister to him, to be his ministers and to offer incense."

12 Then the Levites arose: Mahath, son of Amasai, and Joel, son of Azariah, descendants of the Kohathites; of the sons of Merari: Kish, son of Abdi, and Azariah, son of Jehallel; of the Gershonites: Joah, son of Zimmah, and Eden, son of Joah; 13 of the sons of Elizaphan: Shimri and Jeuel; of the sons of Asaph: Zechariah and Mattaniah; 14 of the sons of Heman: Jehuel and Shimei; of the sons of Jeduthun: Shemiah and Uzziel. 15 They gathered their brethren together and sanctified themselves; then they came as the king had ordered, to cleanse the LORD's house in keeping with his words.

16 The priests entered the interior of the LORD's house to cleanse it; and whatever they found in the LORD's temple that was unclean they brought out to the court of the LORD's house, where the Levites took it from them and carried it out to the Kidron Valley. 17 They began the work of conse-

robbed the Temple of Yahweh and the palaces of the king and princes and gave the proceeds to the king of Assyria, he received no help from him.

22 During the time when he was under siege he disobeyed Yahweh even more grossly, this King Ahaz. 23 For he offered sacrifices to the gods of Damascus who had defeated him. 'Since the gods of the kings of Aram', he thought, 'have supported them, I shall sacrifice to them, and perhaps they will help me.' But they proved to be his and all Israel's downfall.

24 Ahaz then collected the equipment of the Temple of God, broke up the equipment of the Temple of God, sealed the doors of the Temple of Yahweh and put his own altars in every corner of Jerusalem; 25 he set up high places in every town of Judah to burn incense to other gods, thus provoking the anger of Yahweh, God of his ancestors.

26 The rest of his history, his whole policy, from first to last, is recorded in the Book of the Kings of Judah and Israel. 27 Then Ahaz fell asleep with his ancestors and was buried in the City, in Jerusalem, though he was not taken to the tombs of the kings of Israel. His son Hezekiah succeeded him.

29 Hezekiah was twenty-five years old when he came to the throne and he reigned for twenty-nine years in Jerusalem. His mother's name was Abijah daughter of Zechariah. 2 He did what Yahweh regards as right, just as his ancestor David had done.

3 In the first month of the first year of his reign, he opened the doors of the Temple of Yahweh, having repaired them. 4 He then brought in the priests and the Levites, assembled them in the eastern square, 5 and said to them,

'Listen to me, Levites! First sanctify yourselves, then sanctify the Temple of Yahweh, God of your ancestors, and remove the filth from the sanctuary. 6 Our ancestors were unfaithful, and did what is displeasing to Yahweh our God. They abandoned him, turned their faces away from Yahweh's home and turned their backs on him. 7 They even closed the doors of the portico, put out the lamps and stopped burning incense and making burnt offerings in the sanctuary of the God of Israel. 8 This was why Yahweh's anger fell on Judah and Jerusalem and he made them an object of terror, astonishment and derision, as you can see for yourselves. 9 Yes, our ancestors were put to the sword, and our sons, our daughters and our wives were taken captive because of this. 10 I am now determined to make a covenant with Yahweh, God of Israel, so that his fierce anger may turn away from us. 11 Now, my sons, do not be remiss, for Yahweh has chosen you to stand in his presence and serve him by conducting his worship and offering him incense.'

12 The Levites set about it — Mahath son of Amasai and Joel son of Azariah, from the Kohathites; Kish son of Abdi and Azariah son of Jehallel, from the Merarites; Joah son of Zimmah and Eden son of Joah, from the Gershonites; 13 Shimri and Jeuel, of the sons of Elizaphan; Zechariah and Mattaniah of the sons of Asaph; 14 Jehiel and Shimei of the sons of Heman; Shemaiah and Uzziel of the sons of Jeduthun — 15 and gathered their brothers together; they sanctified themselves, and in obedience to the king's order, in accordance with the words of Yahweh, they came to purify the Temple of Yahweh.

16 The priests went into the inner part of the Temple of Yahweh to purify it. They brought all the unclean things which they found in Yahweh's sanctuary, out into the court of the Temple of Yahweh, where the Levites collected them and took them out to the Kidron Valley. 17 They began

NEW REVISED STANDARD VERSION	REVISED ENGLISH BIBLE

month, and on the eighth day of the month they came to the vestibule of the LORD; then for eight days they sanctified the house of the LORD, and on the sixteenth day of the first month they finished. 18 Then they went inside to King Hezekiah and said, "We have cleansed all the house of the LORD, the altar of burnt offering and all its utensils, and the table for the rows of bread and all its utensils. 19 All the utensils that King Ahaz repudiated during his reign when he was faithless, we have made ready and sanctified; see, they are in front of the altar of the LORD."

20 Then King Hezekiah rose early, assembled the officials of the city, and went up to the house of the LORD. 21 They brought seven bulls, seven rams, seven lambs, and seven male goats for a sin offering for the kingdom and for the sanctuary and for Judah. He commanded the priests the descendants of Aaron to offer them on the altar of the LORD. 22 So they slaughtered the bulls, and the priests received the blood and dashed it against the altar; they slaughtered the rams and their blood was dashed against the altar; they also slaughtered the lambs and their blood was dashed against the altar. 23 Then the male goats for the sin offering were brought to the king and the assembly; they laid their hands on them, 24 and the priests slaughtered them and made a sin offering with their blood at the altar, to make atonement for all Israel. For the king commanded that the burnt offering and the sin offering should be made for all Israel.

25 He stationed the Levites in the house of the LORD with cymbals, harps, and lyres, according to the commandment of David and of Gad the king's seer and of the prophet Nathan, for the commandment was from the LORD through his prophets. 26 The Levites stood with the instruments of David, and the priests with the trumpets. 27 Then Hezekiah commanded that the burnt offering be offered on the altar. When the burnt offering began, the song to the LORD began also, and the trumpets, accompanied by the instruments of King David of Israel. 28 The whole assembly worshiped, the singers sang, and the trumpeters sounded; all this continued until the burnt offering was finished. 29 When the offering was finished, the king and all who were present with him bowed down and worshiped. 30 King Hezekiah and the officials commanded the Levites to sing praises to the LORD with the words of David and of the seer Asaph. They sang praises with gladness, and they bowed down and worshiped.

31 Then Hezekiah said, "You have now consecrated yourselves to the LORD; come near, bring sacrifices and thank offerings to the house of the LORD." The assembly brought sacrifices and thank offerings; and all who were of a willing heart brought burnt offerings. 32 The number of the burnt offerings that the assembly brought was seventy bulls, one hundred rams, and two hundred lambs; all these were for a burnt offering to the LORD. 33 The consecrated offerings were six hundred bulls and three thousand sheep. 34 But the priests were too few and could not skin all the burnt offerings, so, until other priests had sanctified themselves, their kindred, the Levites, helped them until the work was finished—for the Levites were more conscientious[g] than the priests in sanctifying themselves. 35 Besides the great number of burnt offerings there was the fat of the offerings of well-being, and there were the drink offerings for the burnt offerings. Thus the service of the house of the LORD was restored. 36 And Hezekiah and all the people rejoiced because of what God had done for the people; for the thing had come about suddenly.

first day of the first month, and on the eighth day they reached the porch; then for eight days they consecrated the house of the LORD, and on the sixteenth day of the first month they finished.

18 When they went into the palace they reported to King Hezekiah, 'We have purified the whole of the house of the LORD, the altar of whole-offering with all its vessels, and the table of the Bread of the Presence arranged in rows with all its vessels. 19 We have also put in order and consecrated all the vessels which King Ahaz cast aside during his reign, when he was unfaithful. They are now in place before the altar of the LORD.'

20 Early next morning King Hezekiah assembled the officers of the city and went up to the house of the LORD. 21 They brought seven bulls, seven rams, and seven lambs for the whole-offering, and seven he-goats as a purification-offering for the kingdom, for the sanctuary, and for Judah; these he commanded the priests of Aaron's line to offer on the altar of the LORD. 22 When the bulls were slaughtered, the priests took the blood and flung it against the altar; the rams were slaughtered, and their blood was flung against the altar; the lambs were slaughtered, and their blood flung against the altar. 23 The he-goats for the purification-offering were brought before the king and the assembly, who laid their hands on them; 24 and the priests slaughtered them and used their blood as a purification-offering on the altar to make expiation for all Israel. For the king had commanded that the whole-offering and the purification-offering should be made for all Israel.

25 He stationed the Levites in the house of the LORD with cymbals, lutes, and lyres, according to the rule prescribed by David, by Gad the king's seer, and Nathan the prophet; for this rule had come from the LORD through his prophets. 26 The Levites stood ready with the instruments of David, and the priests with the trumpets. 27 Hezekiah gave the order that the whole-offering should be offered on the altar. At the moment when the whole-offering began, the song to the LORD began too, with the trumpets, led by the instruments of David king of Israel. 28 The whole assembly prostrated themselves, the singers sang, and the trumpeters sounded; all this continued until the whole-offering was complete. 29 When the offering was complete, the king and all his company bowed down and prostrated themselves. 30 King Hezekiah and his officers commanded the Levites to praise the LORD in the words of David and of Asaph the seer. They praised him most joyfully and bowed down and prostrated themselves.

31 Hezekiah said, 'Now that you are consecrated to the LORD, approach with your sacrifices and thank-offerings for the house of the LORD.' So the assembly brought sacrifices and thank-offerings; and everyone of willing spirit brought whole-offerings. 32 The number of whole-offerings which the assembly brought was seventy bulls, a hundred rams, and two hundred lambs; all these made a whole-offering to the LORD. 33 The consecrated offerings were six hundred bulls and three thousand sheep. 34 But the priests were too few and could not flay all the whole-offerings; so their colleagues the Levites helped them until the work was completed and all the priests had hallowed themselves—for the Levites had been more scrupulous than the priests in hallowing themselves. 35 There were indeed whole-offerings in abundance, besides the fat of the shared-offerings and the drink-offerings for the whole-offerings. In this way the service of the house of the LORD was restored; 36 and Hezekiah and all the people rejoiced over what God had done for the people and because it had come about so speedily.

---

g Heb upright in heart

29:21 for the whole-offering: prob. rdg; Heb. omits.

cration on the first day of the first month, and on the eighth day of the month they arrived at the vestibule of the LORD; they consecrated the LORD's house during eight days, and on the sixteenth day of the first month, they had finished.

18 Then they went inside to King Hezekiah and said: "We have cleansed the entire house of the LORD, the altar of holocausts with all its utensils, and the table for the show-bread with all its utensils. 19 All the articles which King Ahaz during his reign had thrown away because of his apostasy, we have restored and consecrated, and they are now before the LORD's altar."

20 Then King Hezekiah hastened to convoke the princes of the city and went up to the LORD's house. 21 Seven bulls, seven rams, seven lambs and seven he-goats were brought for a sin offering for the kingdom, for the sanctuary, and for Judah, and he ordered the sons of Aaron, the priests, to offer them on the altar of the LORD. 22 They slaughtered the bulls, and the priests collected the blood and cast it on the altar. Then they slaughtered the rams and cast the blood on the altar; then they slaughtered the lambs and cast the blood on the altar. 23 Then the he-goats for the sin offering were led before the king and the assembly, who laid their hands upon them. 24 The priests then slaughtered them and offered their blood on the altar to atone for the sin of all Israel; for "The holocaust and the sin offering," the king had said, "is for all Israel."

25 He stationed the Levites in the LORD's house with cymbals, harps and lyres according to the prescriptions of David, of Gad the king's seer, and of Nathan the prophet; for the prescriptions were from the LORD through his prophets. 26 The Levites were stationed with the instruments of David, and the priests with the trumpets. 27 Then Hezekiah ordered the holocaust to be sacrificed on the altar, and in the same instant that the holocaust began, they also began the song of the LORD, to the accompaniment of the trumpets and the instruments of David, king of Israel. 28 The entire assembly prostrated itself, and they continued to sing the song and to sound the trumpets until the holocaust had been completed. 29 As the holocaust was completed, the king and all who were with him knelt and prostrated themselves. 30 King Hezekiah and the princes then commanded the Levites to sing the praises of the LORD in the words of David and of Asaph the seer. They sang praises till their joy was full, then fell down and prostrated themselves.

31 Hezekiah now spoke out this command: "You have undertaken a work for the LORD. Approach, and bring forward the sacrifices and thank offerings for the house of the LORD." Then the assembly brought forward the sacrifices and thank offerings and all the holocausts which were free-will offerings. 32 The number of holocausts that the assembly brought forward was seventy oxen, one hundred rams, and two hundred lambs: all of these as a holocaust to the LORD. 33 As consecrated gifts there were six hundred oxen and three thousand sheep. 34 Since the priests were too few in number to be able to skin all the victims for the holocausts, their brethren the Levites assisted them until the task was completed and the priests had sanctified themselves; the Levites, in fact, were more willing than the priests to sanctify themselves. 35 Also, the holocausts were many, along with the fat of the peace offerings and the libations for the holocausts. Thus the service of the house of the LORD was reestablished. 36 Hezekiah and all the people rejoiced over what God had reestablished for the people, and at how suddenly this had been done.

sanctifying on the first day of the first month, and by the eighth day of the month had reached Yahweh's portico; thus they took eight days to sanctify the Temple of Yahweh, and by the sixteenth day of the first month everything was finished.

18 They then waited on King Hezekiah and said, 'We have purified the whole Temple of Yahweh, the altar of burnt offering with all its equipment and the table for the loaves of permanent offering with all their equipment. 19 We have also got ready and sanctified all the equipment which King Ahaz in his infidelity had removed during his reign. It is all ready in front of Yahweh's altar.'

20 King Hezekiah lost no time but called the officials of the city together and went up to the Temple of Yahweh. 21 They brought seven bulls, seven rams, seven lambs and seven goats as a sin sacrifice for the royal house, for the sanctuary and for Judah, and he ordered the Aaronite priests to offer them on Yahweh's altar. 22 So they slaughtered the bulls and the priests took the blood and sprinkled it over the altar. They then slaughtered the rams and sprinkled the blood over the altar; and they slaughtered the lambs and sprinkled the blood over the altar. 23 Then they brought the goats, the sacrifice for sin, before the king and the assembly who laid their hands on them. 24 The priests slaughtered them and made a sacrifice for sin with their blood at the altar to expiate for all Israel, since the king had ordered the burnt offering and the sacrifice for sin on behalf of all Israel.

25 He positioned the Levites in the Temple of Yahweh with cymbals, lyres and harps, in accordance with the ordinance of David, of Gad the king's seer and of Nathan the prophet, for such was Yahweh's order conveyed through his prophets. 26 When the Levites stood with David's musical instruments, and the priests with the trumpets, 27 Hezekiah ordered the burnt offering to be presented on the altar. And as the burnt offering began, the hymns of Yahweh began too, and the trumpets sounded, to the accompaniment of the instruments of David king of Israel, 28 while the whole congregation worshipped, the singers singing and the trumpeters sounding the trumpets, continuously until the burnt offering was over.

29 When the burnt offering was finished, the king and all those present with him fell to their knees and worshipped. 30 Then King Hezekiah and the officials told the Levites to sing praise to Yahweh in the words of David and Asaph the seer; and joyfully they sang their praises, then knelt in worship.

31 Hezekiah spoke again, 'Now that you have consecrated yourselves to Yahweh, come forward and bring thanksgiving sacrifices to the Temple of Yahweh.' Then the congregation brought thanksgiving sacrifices and those who were generous brought burnt offerings. 32 The number of burnt offerings brought by the congregation was seventy bulls, a hundred rams and two hundred lambs, all as burnt offerings for Yahweh. 33 The consecrated gifts amounted to six hundred bulls and three thousand sheep. 34 The priests were too few, however, and were unable to dismember all the burnt offerings, so their brothers, the Levites, helped them until the work was finished and the priests had sanctified themselves; for the Levites had been more conscientious about sanctifying themselves than the priests had. 35 In addition to the abundance of burnt offerings, there were also the fatty pieces for communion sacrifices and the libations for the burnt offerings.

And so the liturgy of Yahweh's Temple was restored, 36 and Hezekiah and all the people rejoiced over what God had provided for the people, since everything had happened so suddenly.

NEW REVISED STANDARD VERSION

30 Hezekiah sent word to all Israel and Judah, and wrote letters also to Ephraim and Manasseh, that they should come to the house of the LORD at Jerusalem, to keep the passover to the LORD the God of Israel. 2 For the king and his officials and all the assembly in Jerusalem had taken counsel to keep the passover in the second month 3 (for they could not keep it at its proper time because the priests had not sanctified themselves in sufficient number, nor had the people assembled in Jerusalem). 4 The plan seemed right to the king and all the assembly. 5 So they decreed to make a proclamation throughout all Israel, from Beer-sheba to Dan, that the people should come and keep the passover to the LORD the God of Israel, at Jerusalem; for they had not kept it in great numbers as prescribed. 6 So couriers went throughout all Israel and Judah with letters from the king and his officials, as the king had commanded, saying, "O people of Israel, return to the LORD, the God of Abraham, Isaac, and Israel, so that he may turn again to the remnant of you who have escaped from the hand of the kings of Assyria. 7 Do not be like your ancestors and your kindred, who were faithless to the LORD God of their ancestors, so that he made them a desolation, as you see. 8 Do not now be stiff-necked as your ancestors were, but yield yourselves to the LORD and come to his sanctuary, which he has sanctified forever, and serve the LORD your God, so that his fierce anger may turn away from you. 9 For as you return to the LORD, your kindred and your children will find compassion with their captors, and return to this land. For the LORD your God is gracious and merciful, and will not turn away his face from you, if you return to him."

10 So the couriers went from city to city through the country of Ephraim and Manasseh, and as far as Zebulun; but they laughed them to scorn, and mocked them. 11 Only a few from Asher, Manasseh, and Zebulun humbled themselves and came to Jerusalem. 12 The hand of God was also on Judah to give them one heart to do what the king and the officials commanded by the word of the LORD.

13 Many people came together in Jerusalem to keep the festival of unleavened bread in the second month, a very large assembly. 14 They set to work and removed the altars that were in Jerusalem, and all the altars for offering incense they took away and threw into the Wadi Kidron. 15 They slaughtered the passover lamb on the fourteenth day of the second month. The priests and the Levites were ashamed, and they sanctified themselves and brought burnt offerings into the house of the LORD. 16 They took their accustomed posts according to the law of Moses the man of God; the priests dashed the blood that they received[h] from the hands of the Levites. 17 For there were many in the assembly who had not sanctified themselves; therefore the Levites had to slaughter the passover lamb for everyone who was not clean, to make it holy to the LORD. 18 For a multitude of the people, many of them from Ephraim, Manasseh, Issachar, and Zebulun, had not cleansed themselves, yet they ate the passover otherwise than as prescribed. But Hezekiah prayed for them, saying, "The good LORD pardon all 19 who set their hearts to seek God, the LORD the God of their ancestors, even though not in accordance with the sanctuary's rules of cleanness." 20 The LORD heard Hezekiah, and healed the people. 21 The people of Israel who were present at Jerusalem kept the festival of unleavened bread seven days with great gladness; and the Levites and the priests praised the LORD day by day, accompanied by loud instruments for the LORD. 22 Hezekiah spoke encouragingly to all

REVISED ENGLISH BIBLE

30 Hezekiah sent word to all Israel and Judah, and also wrote letters to Ephraim and Manasseh, inviting them to come to the house of the LORD in Jerusalem to keep the Passover of the LORD the God of Israel. 2 The king and his officers and all the assembly in Jerusalem had agreed to keep the Passover in the second month, 3 but they had not been able to keep it at that time, because not enough priests had hallowed themselves and the people had not assembled in Jerusalem. 4 The proposal being acceptable to the king and the whole assembly, 5 they resolved to make a proclamation throughout all Israel, from Beersheba to Dan, that the people should come to Jerusalem to keep the Passover of the LORD the God of Israel. Never before had so many kept it according to the prescribed form. 6 Couriers went throughout all Israel and Judah with letters from the king and his officers, proclaiming the royal command: 'Turn back, you Israelites, to the LORD the God of your forefathers, Abraham, Isaac, and Israel, so that he may turn back to those of you who escaped capture by the kings of Assyria. 7 Do not be like your forefathers and your kinsmen, who were unfaithful to the LORD the God of their fathers, so that he made them an object of horror, as you yourselves saw. 8 Do not be stubborn as your forefathers were; submit yourselves to the LORD and enter his sanctuary which he has sanctified for ever, and worship the LORD your God, so that his anger may be averted from you. 9 For when you turn back to the LORD, your kinsmen and your children will win compassion from their captors and return to this land. The LORD your God is gracious and compassionate, and he will not turn away from you if you turn back to him.'

10 As the couriers passed from town to town throughout the land of Ephraim and Manasseh and as far as Zebulun, they were treated with scorn and ridicule. 11 However, a few people from Asher, Manasseh, and Zebulun submitted and came to Jerusalem. 12 Further, the hand of God moved the people in Judah with one accord to carry out what the king and his officers had ordered at the LORD's command.

13 It was a very large assembly that gathered in Jerusalem to keep the pilgrim-feast of Unleavened Bread in the second month. 14 They began by removing the altars in Jerusalem, and the incense-altars they removed and threw into the wadi of the Kidron. 15 They killed the Passover lamb on the fourteenth day of the second month. The priests and the Levites were bitterly ashamed, and they hallowed themselves and brought whole-offerings to the house of the LORD. 16 They took their accustomed places, according to the direction laid down for them in the law of Moses the man of God, and the priests flung against the altar the blood which they received from the Levites.

17 Because many in the assembly had not hallowed themselves, the Levites had to kill Passover lambs for all who were unclean, in order to hallow them to the LORD. 18 For a majority of the people, many from Ephraim, Manasseh, Issachar, and Zebulun, had not kept themselves ritually clean, and therefore kept the Passover irregularly. But Hezekiah prayed for them, saying, 'May the good LORD grant pardon to everyone 19 who makes a practice of seeking guidance of God, the LORD the God of his forefathers, even if he has not observed the rules of purification for the sanctuary.' 20 The LORD heard Hezekiah and healed the people. 21 The Israelites who were present in Jerusalem kept the feast of Unleavened Bread for seven days with great rejoicing, and the Levites and the priests praised the LORD every day with unrestrained fervour. 22 Hezekiah spoke encourag-

---

h Heb lacks *that they received*

30:21 **with unrestrained fervour:** *prob. rdg; Heb.* with powerful instruments.

30 Hezekiah sent a message to all Israel and Judah, and even wrote letters to Ephraim and Manasseh saying that they should come to the house of the LORD in Jerusalem to celebrate the Passover in honor of the LORD, the God of Israel. 2 The king, his princes, and the entire assembly in Jerusalem had agreed to celebrate the Passover during the second month, 3 for they could not celebrate it at the time of the restoration: the priests had not sanctified themselves in sufficient numbers, and the people were not gathered at Jerusalem. 4 When this proposal had been approved by the king and the entire assembly, 5 they issued a decree to be proclaimed throughout all Israel from Beersheba to Dan, that everyone should come to Jerusalem to celebrate the Passover in honor of the LORD, the God of Israel; for not many had kept it in the manner prescribed. 6 Accordingly the couriers, with the letters written by the king and his princes, traversed all Israel and Judah, and at the king's command they said: "Israelites, return to the LORD, the God of Abraham, Isaac and Israel, that he may return to you, the remnant left from the hands of the Assyrian kings. 7 Be not like your fathers and your brethren who proved faithless to the LORD, the God of their fathers, so that he delivered them over to desolation, as you yourselves now see. 8 Be not obstinate, as your fathers were; extend your hands to the LORD and come to his sanctuary that he has consecrated forever, and serve the LORD, your God, that he may turn away his burning anger from you. 9 For when you return to the LORD, your brethren and your children will find mercy with their captors and return to this land; for merciful and compassionate is the LORD, your God, and he will not turn away his face from you if you return to him."

10 So the couriers passed from city to city in the land of Ephraim and Manasseh and as far as Zebulun, but they were derided and scoffed at. 11 Nevertheless, some from Asher, Manasseh and Zebulun humbled themselves and came to Jerusalem. 12 In Judah, however, the power of God brought it about that the people were of one mind to carry out the command of the king and the princes in accordance with the word of the LORD. 13 Thus many people gathered in Jerusalem to celebrate the feast of Unleavened Bread in the second month; it was a very great assembly.

14 They proceeded to take down the altars that were in Jerusalem; also they removed all the altars of incense and cast them into the Kidron Valley. 15 They slaughtered the Passover on the fourteenth day of the second month. The priests and Levites, touched with shame, sanctified themselves and brought holocausts into the house of the LORD. 16 They stood in the places prescribed for them according to the law of Moses, the man of God. The priests sprinkled the blood given them by the Levites; 17 for many in the assembly had not sanctified themselves, and the Levites were in charge of slaughtering the Passover victims for all who were unclean and therefore could not consecrate them to the LORD. 18 The greater part of the people, in fact, chiefly from Ephraim, Manasseh, Issachar and Zebulun, had not cleansed themselves. Nevertheless they ate the Passover, contrary to the prescription; for Hezekiah prayed for them, saying, "May the LORD, who is good, grant pardon 19 everyone who has resolved to seek God, the LORD, the God of his fathers, though he be not clean as holiness requires." 20 The LORD heard Hezekiah and spared the people.

21 Thus the Israelites who were in Jerusalem celebrated the feast of Unleavened Bread with great rejoicing for seven days, and the Levites and the priests sang the praises of the LORD day after day with all their strength. 22 Hezekiah

30 Hezekiah sent messengers to all Israel and Judah, and also wrote letters to Ephraim and Manasseh, bidding them come to the Temple of Yahweh in Jerusalem to celebrate the Passover in honour of Yahweh, God of Israel. 2 For the king and his officials and the whole congregation in Jerusalem had agreed to celebrate the Passover in the second month, 3 having been unable to celebrate it at the proper time, since the priests had not purified themselves in sufficient number, and the people were not assembled in Jerusalem. 4 And since this arrangement seemed fitting to the king and the whole congregation, 5 they resolved to send a proclamation throughout Israel, from Dan to Beersheba, calling on the people to come to Jerusalem and celebrate a Passover in honour of Yahweh, God of Israel, since they had not celebrated it in a body as prescribed. 6 So, by order of the king, courtiers set out with letters from the king and his officials for every part of Israel and Judah, saying, 'Israelites, return to Yahweh, God of Abraham, Isaac and Israel, and he will return to those of you who are left and have escaped the grasp of the kings of Assyria. 7 Do not be like your fathers and brothers who were unfaithful to Yahweh, God of their ancestors; he brought them to ruin, as you can see. 8 Do not be stubborn like your ancestors. Submit to Yahweh, come to his sanctuary which he has consecrated for ever, and serve Yahweh your God, so that his fierce anger may turn away from you. 9 For if you return to Yahweh, your brothers and your sons will be treated mercifully by their captors and be allowed to return to this country; for Yahweh your God is gracious and merciful and will not turn his face away from you, if you return to him.'

10 The courtiers went from town to town through the territory of Ephraim and Manasseh and as far as Zebulon but the people laughed and scoffed at them; 11 even so, some people from Asher and Manasseh and Zebulon were humble enough to come to Jerusalem, 12 while in Judah the hand of God was also at work inspiring a unanimous desire to obey the order of the king and the officials in accordance with the word of Yahweh.

13 A huge crowd assembled in Jerusalem to celebrate the feast of Unleavened Bread in the second month. An immense crowd 14 set to work removing the altars then in Jerusalem; they also removed all the incense altars and threw them into the Kidron Valley. 15 They then slaughtered the Passover victims on the fourteenth day of the second month. Ashamed of themselves, the priests and Levites had in the meanwhile sanctified themselves and brought burnt offerings to the Temple of Yahweh, 16 so they now stood in their positions prescribed in the Law of Moses man of God, the priests sprinkling the blood handed to them by the Levites. 17 Since many people in the congregation had not sanctified themselves, the Levites took care of the slaughter of the Passover victims to consecrate them to Yahweh for all who were not clean. 18 For a great many people, especially from Ephraim, Manasseh, Issachar and Zebulon, had not purified themselves, since they did not eat the Passover as prescribed. But Hezekiah prayed for them as follows, 'May Yahweh in his goodness pardon 19 everyone whose heart is set on seeking God, Yahweh, God of his ancestors, even if he has not been purified as holy things demand.' 20 Yahweh listened to Hezekiah and left the people unharmed.

21 Amid great rejoicing, the Israelites present in Jerusalem celebrated the feast of Unleavened Bread for seven days, while day after day the Levites and the priests praised Yahweh with all their might. 22 Hezekiah then encouraged

|

the Levites who showed good skill in the service of the LORD. So the people ate the food of the festival for seven days, sacrificing offerings of well-being and giving thanks to the LORD the God of their ancestors.

23 Then the whole assembly agreed together to keep the festival for another seven days; so they kept it for another seven days with gladness. 24 For King Hezekiah of Judah gave the assembly a thousand bulls and seven thousand sheep for offerings, and the officials gave the assembly a thousand bulls and ten thousand sheep. The priests sanctified themselves in great numbers. 25 The whole assembly of Judah, the priests and the Levites, and the whole assembly that came out of Israel, and the resident aliens who came out of the land of Israel, and the resident aliens who lived in Judah, rejoiced. 26 There was great joy in Jerusalem, for since the time of Solomon son of King David of Israel there had been nothing like this in Jerusalem. 27 Then the priests and the Levites stood up and blessed the people, and their voice was heard; their prayer came to his holy dwelling in heaven.

31 Now when all this was finished, all Israel who were present went out to the cities of Judah and broke down the pillars, hewed down the sacred poles,[i] and pulled down the high places and the altars throughout all Judah and Benjamin, and in Ephraim and Manasseh, until they had destroyed them all. Then all the people of Israel returned to their cities, all to their individual properties.

2 Hezekiah appointed the divisions of the priests and of the Levites, division by division, everyone according to his service, the priests and the Levites, for burnt offerings and offerings of well-being, to minister in the gates of the camp of the LORD and to give thanks and praise. 3 The contribution of the king from his own possessions was for the burnt offerings: the burnt offerings of morning and evening, and the burnt offerings for the sabbaths, the new moons, and the appointed festivals, as it is written in the law of the LORD. 4 He commanded the people who lived in Jerusalem to give the portion due to the priests and the Levites, so that they might devote themselves to the law of the LORD. 5 As soon as the word spread, the people of Israel gave in abundance the first fruits of grain, wine, oil, honey, and of all the produce of the field; they brought in abundantly the tithe of everything. 6 The people of Israel and Judah who lived in the cities of Judah also brought in the tithe of cattle and sheep, and the tithe of the dedicated things that had been consecrated to the LORD their God, and laid them in heaps. 7 In the third month they began to pile up the heaps, and finished them in the seventh month. 8 When Hezekiah and the officials came and saw the heaps, they blessed the LORD and his people Israel. 9 Hezekiah questioned the priests and the Levites about the heaps. 10 The chief priest Azariah, who was of the house of Zadok, answered him, "Since they began to bring the contributions into the house of the LORD, we have had enough to eat and have plenty to spare; for the LORD has blessed his people, so that we have this great supply left over."

11 Then Hezekiah commanded them to prepare storechambers in the house of the LORD; and they prepared them. 12 Faithfully they brought in the contributions, the tithes and the dedicated things. The chief officer in charge of them was Conaniah the Levite, with his brother Shimei as second; 13 while Jehiel, Azaziah, Nahath, Asahel, Jerimoth, Jozabad, Eliel, Ismachiah, Mahath, and Benaiah were overseers assisting Conaniah and his brother Shimei, by the appointment of King Hezekiah and of Azariah the chief officer of the house of God. 14 Kore son of Imnah the Le-

ingly to all the Levites who had shown true insight in the service of the LORD. The seven days of the festival they spent sacrificing shared-offerings and making confession to the LORD the God of their forefathers.

23 The whole assembly agreed to keep the feast for another seven days, and they kept it with general rejoicing. 24 For Hezekiah king of Judah set aside for the assembly a thousand bulls and seven thousand sheep, and his officers set aside for the assembly a thousand bulls and ten thousand sheep; and priests hallowed themselves in great numbers. 25 The whole assembly of Judah, including the priests and the Levites, rejoiced along with all who had assembled from Israel, and the resident aliens from Israel as well as those who lived in Judah. 26 There was great rejoicing in Jerusalem, the like of which had not been known there since the days of Solomon son of David king of Israel. 27 The priests and the Levites stood to bless the people, and their voice was heard when their prayer reached God's holy dwellingplace in heaven.

31 When this was over, all the Israelites present went out into the towns and cities of Judah and smashed the sacred pillars, hacked down the sacred poles, and demolished the shrines and the altars throughout Judah and Benjamin, and in Ephraim and Manasseh, until they had made an end of them all. That done, the Israelites returned, each to his own holding in his own town.

2 Hezekiah installed the priests and the Levites in office, division by division, allotting to each priest and each Levite his own particular duty, for whole-offerings or shared-offerings, to serve, to give thanks, and to sing praise at the gates of the several quarters in the LORD's house.

3 The king provided from his own resources, as the share due from him, the whole-offerings for both morning and evening, and for sabbaths, new moons, and appointed seasons, as prescribed in the law of the LORD. 4 He ordered the people living in Jerusalem to provide the share due to the priests and the Levites, so that these might devote themselves entirely to the law of the LORD. 5 As soon as the king's order was issued to the Israelites, they gave generously from the firstfruits of their grain, new wine, oil, and honey, all the produce of their land; they brought a full tithe of everything. 6 The Israelites and Judaeans living in the towns of Judah also brought a tithe of cattle and sheep, and a tithe of all produce as offerings dedicated to the LORD their God, and they stacked the produce in heaps. 7 They began to deposit the heaps in the third month and completed them in the seventh.

8 When Hezekiah and his officers came and saw the heaps, they praised the LORD and his people Israel. 9 Hezekiah consulted the priests and the Levites about these heaps, 10 and Azariah the chief priest, who was of the line of Zadok, answered, 'From the time when the people began to bring their contribution into the house of the LORD, they have had enough to eat, enough and to spare; indeed, the LORD has so greatly blessed them that they have this great store left over.'

11 Hezekiah gave orders for storerooms to be prepared in the house of the LORD, and when this was done 12 the people faithfully brought in their contributions, the tithe, and their dedicated gifts. The overseer in charge of them was Conaniah the Levite, with Shimei his brother as his deputy; 13 Jehiel, Azaziah, Nahath, Asahel, Jerimoth, Jozabad, Eliel, Ismachiah, Mahath, and Benaiah were appointed by King Hezekiah and Azariah, the chief overseer of the house of God, to assist Conaniah and Shimei his brother. 14 Kore son

30:22 **making confession to:** or confessing. 30:27 **and the Levites:** so many MSS; others omit and. 31:2 **in the LORD's house:** so Gk; Heb. of the LORD.

[i] Heb Asherim

spoke encouragingly to all the Levites who had shown themselves well skilled in the service of the LORD. And when they had completed the seven days of festival, slaying peace offerings and singing praises to the LORD, the God of their fathers, 23 the whole assembly agreed to celebrate another seven days. With joy, therefore, they continued the festivity seven days longer. 24 King Hezekiah of Judah had contributed a thousand bulls and seven thousand sheep to the assembly, and the princes had contributed to the assembly a thousand bulls and ten thousand sheep. The priests sanctified themselves in great numbers, 25 and the whole assembly of Judah rejoiced, together with the priests and Levites and the rest of the assembly that had come from Israel, as well as the sojourners from the land of Israel and those that lived in Judah. 26 There was great rejoicing in Jerusalem, for since the days of Solomon, son of David, king of Israel, there had not been the like in the city. 27 Then the levitical priests rose and blessed the people; their voice was heard and their prayer reached heaven, God's holy dwelling.

31 After all this was over, those Israelites who had been present went forth to the cities of Judah and smashed the sacred pillars, cut down the sacred poles, and tore down the high places and altars throughout Judah, Benjamin, Ephraim and Manasseh, until all were destroyed. Then the Israelites returned to their various cities, each to his own possession.

2 Hezekiah reestablished the classes of the priests and the Levites according to their former classification, assigning to each priest and Levite his proper service, whether in regard to holocausts or peace offerings, thanksgiving or praise, or ministering in the gates of the encampment of the LORD. 3 From his own wealth the king allotted a portion for holocausts, those of morning and evening and those on sabbaths, new moons and festivals, as prescribed in the law of the LORD. 4 He also commanded the people living in Jerusalem to provide the support of the priests and Levites, that they might devote themselves entirely to the law of the LORD.

5 As soon as the order was promulgated, the Israelites brought, in great quantities, the best of their grain, wine, oil and honey, and all the produce of the fields; they gave a generous tithe of everything. 6 Israelites and Judahites living in other cities of Judah also brought in tithes of oxen, sheep, and things that had been consecrated to the LORD, their God; these they brought in and set out in heaps. 7 It was in the third month that they began to establish these heaps, and they completed them in the seventh month. 8 When Hezekiah and the princes had come and seen the heaps, they blessed the LORD and his people Israel. 9 Then Hezekiah questioned the priests and the Levites concerning the heaps, 10 and the priest Azariah, head of the house of Zadoc, answered him, "Since they began to bring the offerings to the house of the LORD, we have eaten to the full and have had much left over, for the LORD has blessed his people. This great supply is what was left over."

11 Hezekiah then gave orders that chambers should be constructed in the house of the LORD. When this had been done, 12 the offerings, tithes and consecrated things were deposited there in safekeeping. The overseer of these things was Conaniah the Levite, and his brother Shimei was second in charge. 13 Jehiel, Azaziah, Nathan, Asahel, Jerimoth, Jozabad, Eliel, Ismachiah, Mahath and Benaiah were supervisors subject to Conaniah and his brother Shimei by appointment of King Hezekiah and of Azariah, the prefect of the house of God. 14 Kore, the son of Imnah, a Levite and

all the Levites who had such understanding of Yahweh.

Having finished the seven-day festival, during which they sacrificed communion sacrifices and praised Yahweh, God of their ancestors, 23 the whole congregation decided to celebrate for a further seven days. So they joyfully celebrated for another seven days, 24 Hezekiah king of Judah contributing a thousand bulls and seven thousand sheep for the congregation, and the officials another thousand bulls and ten thousand sheep. And a large number of priests sanctified themselves. 25 The whole congregation of Judah, the priests, the Levites, the whole congregation coming from Israel and the foreigners coming from the territory of Israel as well as those resident in Judah, rejoiced. 26 There was great rejoicing in Jerusalem, for since the days of Solomon son of David, king of Israel, nothing comparable had ever occurred in Jerusalem. 27 The levitical priests then stood up and blessed the people and their voice was heard, and their prayer reached his holy dwelling in heaven.

31 When all this was complete, all Israel present went out to the towns of Judah, broke the pillars, cut down the sacred poles, wrecked the high places and the altars, and did away with them entirely throughout Judah, Benjamin, Ephraim, and Manasseh. Then all the Israelites returned to their towns, everyone to his property.

2 Hezekiah re-established the priestly and levitical orders, each man in his proper order according to his duties, whether priest or Levite, to bring burnt offerings and communion sacrifices, to serve and to give thanks and praise within the gates of Yahweh's camp. 3 He also established a king's portion from his possessions for the morning and evening burnt offerings, and the burnt offerings for the Sabbaths, New Moons and festivals, as laid down in the Law of Yahweh. 4 He furthermore requested the people living in Jerusalem to present the portion for the priests and Levites so that they might devote themselves to the Law of Yahweh. 5 As soon as the order had been promulgated, the Israelites provided the first fruits of grain, new wine, olive oil, honey and every other kind of agricultural produce in abundance; they brought in an abundant tithe of everything. 6 The Israelites and Judaeans living in the towns of Judah also brought in the tithe of cattle and sheep, and the tithe of sacred gifts consecrated to Yahweh their God, laying them in heaps. 7 They began accumulating the heaps in the third month and had finished them by the seventh. 8 When Hezekiah and the officials came to inspect the heaps they praised Yahweh and his people Israel.

9 While Hezekiah was questioning the priests and Levites about the heaps, 10 Azariah, the chief priest, of the family of Zadok, replied as follows, 'Since they began bringing the contributions to the Temple of Yahweh,' he said, 'we have had enough to eat and quantities left over, for Yahweh has blessed his people; this mass of stuff is left.' 11 Hezekiah then ordered them to have storerooms prepared in the Temple of Yahweh and, when they had got them ready, 12 they conscientiously brought in the contributions, tithes and consecrated gifts, Conaniah the Levite was put in charge of them, with Shimei his brother as his assistant, 13 and with Jehiel, Azaziah, Nahath, Asahel, Jeremith, Jozabad, Eliel, Ismachiah, Mahath, and Benaiah as overseers under Conaniah and his brother Shimei, by order of King Hezekiah and of Azariah, the chief of the Temple of God. 14 Kore son of

| NEW REVISED STANDARD VERSION | REVISED ENGLISH BIBLE |

vite, keeper of the east gate, was in charge of the freewill offerings to God, to apportion the contribution reserved for the LORD and the most holy offerings. 15 Eden, Miniamin, Jeshua, Shemaiah, Amariah, and Shecaniah were faithfully assisting him in the cities of the priests, to distribute the portions to their kindred, old and young alike, by divisions, 16 except those enrolled by genealogy, males from three years old and upwards, all who entered the house of the LORD as the duty of each day required, for their service according to their offices, by their divisions. 17 The enrollment of the priests was according to their ancestral houses; that of the Levites from twenty years old and upwards was according to their offices, by their divisions. 18 The priests were enrolled with all their little children, their wives, their sons, and their daughters, the whole multitude; for they were faithful in keeping themselves holy. 19 And for the descendants of Aaron, the priests, who were in the fields of common land belonging to their towns, town by town, the people designated by name were to distribute portions to every male among the priests and to everyone among the Levites who was enrolled.

20 Hezekiah did this throughout all Judah; he did what was good and right and faithful before the LORD his God. 21 And every work that he undertook in the service of the house of God, and in accordance with the law and the commandments, to seek his God, he did with all his heart; and he prospered.

32 After these things and these acts of faithfulness, King Sennacherib of Assyria came and invaded Judah and encamped against the fortified cities, thinking to win them for himself. 2 When Hezekiah saw that Sennacherib had come and intended to fight against Jerusalem, 3 he planned with his officers and his warriors to stop the flow of the springs that were outside the city; and they helped him. 4 A great many people were gathered, and they stopped all the springs and the wadi that flowed through the land, saying, "Why should the Assyrian kings come and find water in abundance?" 5 Hezekiah*j* set to work resolutely and built up the entire wall that was broken down, and raised towers on it,*k* and outside it he built another wall; he also strengthened the Millo in the city of David, and made weapons and shields in abundance. 6 He appointed combat commanders over the people, and gathered them together to him in the square at the gate of the city and spoke encouragingly to them, saying, 7 "Be strong and of good courage. Do not be afraid or dismayed before the king of Assyria and all the horde that is with him; for there is one greater with us than with him. 8 With him is an arm of flesh; but with us is the LORD our God, to help us and to fight our battles." The people were encouraged by the words of King Hezekiah of Judah.

9 After this, while King Sennacherib of Assyria was at Lachish with all his forces, he sent his servants to Jerusalem to King Hezekiah of Judah and to all the people of Judah that were in Jerusalem, saying, 10 "Thus says King Sennacherib of Assyria: On what are you relying, that you undergo the siege of Jerusalem? 11 Is not Hezekiah misleading you, handing you over to die by famine and by thirst, when he tells you, 'The LORD our God will save us from the hand of the king of Assyria'? 12 Was it not this same Hezekiah who took away his high places and his altars and commanded Judah and Jerusalem, saying, 'Before one altar you shall worship, and upon it you shall make your offerings'? 13 Do you not know what I and my ancestors have done to all the peoples of other lands? Were the gods of the nations of those lands at all able to save their lands out of my hand? 14 Who among all the gods of those nations that

of Imnah the Levite, keeper of the East Gate, was in charge of the freewill-offerings to God, to apportion the contributions made to the LORD and the most sacred offerings. 15 Eden, Miniamin, Jeshua, Shemaiah, Amariah, and Shecaniah in the priestly cities and towns assisted him in the fair distribution of portions to their kinsmen, young and old alike, by divisions. 16 Irrespective of their registration, shares were distributed to all males three years of age and upwards who would enter the house of the LORD to take their daily part in the service, according to their divisions, as their office demanded. 17 The priests were registered by families, the Levites of twenty years of age and upwards by their offices in their divisions. 18 They were registered with all their dependants, their wives, their sons, and their daughters, the whole company of them, because in virtue of their permanent standing they had to keep themselves duly hallowed. 19 As for the priests of Aaron's line in the common lands attached to their cities and towns, in every place men were nominated to distribute portions to every male among the priests and to everyone among the Levites who was on the register.

20 Such was the action taken by Hezekiah throughout Judah; he did what was good and right and loyal in the sight of the LORD his God. 21 Whatever he undertook in the service of the house of God and in obedience to the law and the commandment to seek guidance of his God, he did with all his heart, and he prospered.

32 It was after these events and this example of loyal conduct that King Sennacherib of Assyria invaded Judah and encamped against the fortified towns, believing that he could gain entry and secure them for himself. 2 When Hezekiah saw that he had come determined to attack Jerusalem, 3 he consulted his civil and military officers about blocking up the springs outside the city; and they supported him. 4 They brought together a large number of people to block up all the springs and the stream which flowed through the land. 'Why should Assyrian kings come here and find plenty of water?' they said. 5 Acting with resolution the king made good every breach in the city wall, erecting towers on it and building another wall outside it. He strengthened the Millo of the city of David, and got together a large quantity of weapons and shields.

6 He appointed military commanders over the people and, assembling them in the public square by the city gate, he spoke these words of encouragement: 7 'Be strong; be brave. Do not let the king of Assyria or the rabble he has brought with him strike terror or panic into your hearts, for we have more on our side than he has. 8 He has human strength; but we have the LORD our God to help us and to fight our battles.' The people were buoyed up by the speech of King Hezekiah.

9 After this, while King Sennacherib of Assyria and his high command were at Lachish, he sent envoys to Jerusalem to deliver this message to King Hezekiah of Judah and to all the Judaeans in Jerusalem: 10 'King Sennacherib of Assyria says, "What gives you the confidence to stay in Jerusalem under siege? 11 Hezekiah is deluding you into risking death by famine or thirst where you are, when he tells you that the LORD your God will save you from the clutches of the Assyrian king. 12 Was it not Hezekiah himself who suppressed the LORD's shrines and altars and told the people of Judah and Jerusalem that they must worship at one altar only and burn sacrifices there?

13 "You know very well what I and my forefathers have done to all the peoples of other lands. Were the gods of these nations able to save their lands from me? 14 Not one

---

31:15 **young and old:** or high and low.   32:1–19 Cp. 2 Kgs. 18:13–37; Isa. 36:1–22.   32:5 **towers on it:** so Aram. (Targ.); Heb. on the towers.

j Heb He   *k* Vg: Heb and raised on the towers

NEW AMERICAN BIBLE

the keeper of the eastern gate, was in charge of the free-will gifts made to God; he distributed the offerings made to the LORD and the most holy of the consecrated things. 15 Under him in the priestly cities were Eden, Miniamin, Jeshua, Shemaiah, Amariah and Shecaniah, who faithfully made the distribution to their brethren, great and small alike, according to their classes.

16 There was also a register by ancestral houses of males thirty years of age and over, for all priests who were eligible to enter the house of the LORD according to the daily rule to fulfill their service in the order of their classes. 17 The priests were inscribed in their family records according to their ancestral houses, and the Levites of twenty years and over according to their various offices and classes. 18 A distribution was also made to all who were inscribed in the family records, for their little ones, wives, sons and daughters — thus for the entire assembly, since they were to sanctify themselves by sharing faithfully in the consecrated things. 19 The sons of Aaron, the priests who lived on the lands attached to their cities, had in every city men designated by name to distribute portions to every male among the priests and to every Levite listed in the family records.

20 This Hezekiah did in all Judah. He did what was good, upright and faithful before the LORD, his God. 21 Everything that he undertook, for the service of the house of God or for the law and the commandments, was to do the will of his God. He did this wholeheartedly, and he prospered.

32 But after he had proved his fidelity by such deeds, Sennacherib, king of Assyria, came. He invaded Judah, besieged the fortified cities, and proposed to take them by storm. 2 When Hezekiah saw that Sennacherib was coming with the intention of attacking Jerusalem, 3 he decided in counsel with his princes and warriors to stop the waters of the springs outside the city. When they had pledged him their support, 4 a large crowd was gathered which stopped all the springs and also the running stream in the valley nearby. For they said, "Why should the kings of Assyria come and find an abundance of water?" 5 He then looked to his defenses: he rebuilt the wall where it was broken down, raised towers upon it, and built another wall outside. He strengthened the Millo of the City of David and had a great number of spears and shields prepared. 6 Then he appointed army commanders over the people. He gathered them together in his presence in the open space at the gate of the city and encouraged them with these words: 7 "Be brave and steadfast; do not be afraid or dismayed because of the king of Assyria and all the throng that is coming with him, for there is more with us than with him. 8 For he has only an arm of flesh, but we have the LORD, our God, to help us and to fight our battles." And the people took confidence from the words of King Hezekiah of Judah.

9 After this, while Sennacherib, king of Assyria, himself remained at Lachish with all his forces, he sent his officials to Jerusalem with this message for King Hezekiah of Judah, and all the Judahites who were in Jerusalem: 10 "King Sennacherib of Assyria has this to say: On what are you relying, while you remain under siege in Jerusalem? 11 Has not Hezekiah deceived you, delivering you over to a death of famine and thirst, by his claim that 'the LORD, our God, will save us from the grasp of the king of Assyria'? 12 Has not this same Hezekiah removed his high places and altars and commanded Judah and Jerusalem, 'You shall prostrate yourselves before one altar only, and on it alone you shall offer incense'? 13 Do you not know what my fathers and I have done to all the peoples of other lands? Were the gods of the nations in those lands able to save their lands from my hand? 14 Who among all the gods of those nations which my

NEW JERUSALEM BIBLE

Jimnah the Levite, keeper of the eastern gate, was made responsible for the voluntary offerings to God and for providing the portion set aside for Yahweh and the most holy gifts. 15 Supporting him loyally in the priestly towns were Eden, Miniamin, Jeshua, Shemaiah, Amariah and Shechaniah, who made the distributions to their brothers in their various orders, whether high or low, 16 irrespective of their official genealogy, to the males of thirty years and upwards — to each one who attended the Temple of Yahweh to fulfil his daily obligations — for the performance of their duties appropriate to their orders: 17 the priests being registered according to family and the Levites of twenty years and upwards according to their duties within their orders. 18 And the official genealogy included all their household, their wives, their sons and their daughters, throughout the community, since these men were obliged to keep sanctifying themselves anew. 19 The Aaronite priests who lived on the pasture lands belonging to their towns, had men named in every town to distribute portions to every male among the priests and to everyone included in the official genealogy of the Levites.

20 Hezekiah did this throughout all Judah. He did what Yahweh his God regards as good and right and loyal. 21 Everything that he undertook, whether in the service of the Temple of God or in connection with the law or the commandments, he did in absolute devotion to his God, and so succeeded.

32 After these loyal actions, Sennacherib king of Assyria advanced and invaded Judah, and laid siege to the fortified towns, intending to demolish them. 2 Hezekiah, realising that Sennacherib's advance was the preliminary to an attack on Jerusalem, 3 consulted his officers and warriors about sealing off the waters of the springs outside the city, and they supported him. 4 So a large number of people were called out to block all the springs and cut off the watercourse flowing through the country. 'Why', they said, 'should the kings of Assyria find plenty of water when they arrive?'

5 Acting with determination, he also repaired all the damaged parts of the wall, built towers on it, constructed a second wall on the outer side, strengthened the Millo of the City of David and made quantities of missiles and shields. 6 He then appointed generals to command the people, summoned them to him in the square by the city gate and spoke as follows to encourage them, 7 'Be strong and brave; do not be afraid or tremble when you face the king of Assyria and the whole horde he brings with him, for there are more on our side than on his. 8 He has only human strength, but we have Yahweh our God to help us and fight our battles.' The people took heart at the words of Hezekiah king of Judah.

9 Next, Sennacherib king of Assyria, who was then besieging Lachish with all his forces, sent his representatives to Jerusalem, to Hezekiah king of Judah, and all Judah at Jerusalem, with the following message, 10 'Sennacherib king of Assyria says this, "What gives you the confidence to remain in the fortress of Jerusalem? 11 Isn't Hezekiah deluding you, only to condemn you to die of famine and thirst, when he says: Yahweh our God will save us from the King of Assyria's clutches? 12 Isn't Hezekiah the very man who has suppressed his high places and altars, and given the order to Judah and to Jerusalem: You must worship before one altar and on that alone offer incense? 13 Don't you know what I and my ancestors have done to all the peoples of the other countries? Have the national gods of those countries had the slightest success in saving their countries from my clutches? 14 Of all the gods of those nations whom my an-

my ancestors utterly destroyed was able to save his people from my hand, that your God should be able to save you from my hand? 15 Now therefore do not let Hezekiah deceive you or mislead you in this fashion, and do not believe him, for no god of any nation or kingdom has been able to save his people from my hand or from the hand of my ancestors. How much less will your God save you out of my hand!"

16 His servants said still more against the Lord God and against his servant Hezekiah. 17 He also wrote letters to throw contempt on the LORD the God of Israel and to speak against him, saying, "Just as the gods of the nations in other lands did not rescue their people from my hands, so the God of Hezekiah will not rescue his people from my hand." 18 They shouted it with a loud voice in the language of Judah to the people of Jerusalem who were on the wall, to frighten and terrify them, in order that they might take the city. 19 They spoke of the God of Jerusalem as if he were like the gods of the peoples of the earth, which are the work of human hands.

20 Then King Hezekiah and the prophet Isaiah son of Amoz prayed because of this and cried to heaven. 21 And the LORD sent an angel who cut off all the mighty warriors and commanders and officers in the camp of the king of Assyria. So he returned in disgrace to his own land. When he came into the house of his god, some of his own sons struck him down there with the sword. 22 So the LORD saved Hezekiah and the inhabitants of Jerusalem from the hand of King Sennacherib of Assyria and from the hand of all his enemies; he gave them rest*l* on every side. 23 Many brought gifts to the LORD in Jerusalem and precious things to King Hezekiah of Judah, so that he was exalted in the sight of all nations from that time onward.

24 In those days Hezekiah became sick and was at the point of death. He prayed to the LORD, and he answered him and gave him a sign. 25 But Hezekiah did not respond according to the benefit done to him, for his heart was proud. Therefore wrath came upon him and upon Judah and Jerusalem. 26 Then Hezekiah humbled himself for the pride of his heart, both he and the inhabitants of Jerusalem, so that the wrath of the LORD did not come upon them in the days of Hezekiah.

27 Hezekiah had very great riches and honor; and he made for himself treasuries for silver, for gold, for precious stones, for spices, for shields, and for all kinds of costly objects; 28 storehouses also for the yield of grain, wine, and oil; and stalls for all kinds of cattle, and sheepfolds.*m* 29 He likewise provided cities for himself, and flocks and herds in abundance; for God had given him very great possessions. 30 This same Hezekiah closed the upper outlet of the waters of Gihon and directed them down to the west side of the city of David. Hezekiah prospered in all his works. 31 So also in the matter of the envoys of the officials of Babylon, who had been sent to him to inquire about the sign that had been done in the land, God left him to himself, in order to test him and to know all that was in his heart.

32 Now the rest of the acts of Hezekiah, and his good deeds, are written in the vision of the prophet Isaiah son of Amoz in the Book of the Kings of Judah and Israel. 33 Hezekiah slept with his ancestors, and they buried him on the ascent to the tombs of the descendants of David; and all Judah and the inhabitants of Jerusalem did him honor at his death. His son Manasseh succeeded him.

of the gods of these nations, which my predecessors exterminated, was able to save his people from me. Much less will your God save you! 15 Now, can you let Hezekiah deceive and delude you like this? Can you put any trust in him, for no god of any nation or kingdom has been able to save his people from me or my forefathers? Much less will your gods save you!" '

16 Sennacherib's envoys spoke still more against the LORD God and against his servant Hezekiah. 17 The king also wrote a letter insulting the LORD the God of Israel in these terms: 'Just as the gods of other nations could not save their people from me, so Hezekiah's God cannot save his people from me.' 18 Then they shouted in Hebrew at the tops of their voices at the people of Jerusalem on the wall, to strike them with fear and terror, hoping thus to capture the city. 19 They described the God of Jerusalem as being like the gods of the other peoples of the earth—things made by the hands of men.

20 In this plight King Hezekiah and the prophet Isaiah son of Amoz cried to heaven in prayer. 21 So the LORD sent an angel who cut down every fighting man, leader, and commander in the camp of the king of Assyria, so that he withdrew disgraced to his own land. When he entered the temple of his god, certain of his own sons put him to the sword.

22 Thus the LORD saved Hezekiah and the inhabitants of Jerusalem from King Sennacherib of Assyria and from all their enemies; he gave them respite on every side. 23 Many people brought to Jerusalem offerings for the LORD and costly gifts for King Hezekiah of Judah. From then on he was held in high honour by all the nations.

24 In those days Hezekiah fell dangerously ill and prayed to the LORD, who said, 'I shall heal you,' and granted him a sign. 25 But, being a proud man, he was not grateful for the good done to him, and the LORD's wrath fell on him and on Judah and Jerusalem. 26 Then, proud though he was, Hezekiah submitted, and the people of Jerusalem with him, and the LORD's anger did not fall on them again in Hezekiah's time.

27 Hezekiah enjoyed great wealth and fame. He built treasuries for silver, gold, precious stones, spices, shields, and other costly things; 28 and barns for the harvests of grain, new wine, and oil; and stalls for various kinds of cattle, as well as sheepfolds. 29 He amassed a great many flocks and herds; God had indeed given him vast riches. 30 It was this same Hezekiah who blocked the upper outflow of the waters of Gihon and directed them downwards and westwards to the city of David. In fact, Hezekiah was successful in everything he attempted, 31 even in the affair of the envoys sent by the king of Babylon, the envoys who came to enquire about the portent which had been seen in the land at the time when God left him to himself, in order to test him and to discover all that was in his mind.

32 The other events of Hezekiah's reign, and his works of piety, are recorded in the vision of the prophet Isaiah son of Amoz and in the annals of the kings of Judah and Israel. 33 Hezekiah rested with his forefathers and was buried in the upper part of the graves of David's sons; all Judah and the people of Jerusalem paid him honour when he died. His son Manasseh succeeded him.

32:15 **gods:** or, with some MSS, God.   32:19 **God:** or gods. 32:20–22 Cp. 2 Kgs. 19:1–37; Isa. 37:1–38.   32:24 **I . . . you:** prob. rdg, cp. 2 Kgs. 20:5; Heb. omits.   32:28 **sheepfolds:** so Gk; Heb. sheep for the folds.   32:29 **He amassed:** prob. rdg; Heb. adds cities.   32:31 **king:** prob. rdg, cp. 2 Kgs. 20:12; Heb. officers.   32:32 **and in:** so Gk; Heb. omits and.

l Gk Vg: Heb guided them   *m* Gk Vg: Heb flocks for folds

NEW AMERICAN BIBLE

NEW JERUSALEM BIBLE

fathers put under the ban was able to save his people from my hand? Will your god, then, be able to save you from my hand? 15 Let not Hezekiah mislead you further and deceive you in any such way. Do not believe him! Since no other god of any other nation or kingdom has been able to save his people from my hand or the hands of my fathers, how much the less shall your god save you from my hand!"

16 His officials said still more against the LORD God and against his servant Hezekiah, 17 for he had written letters to deride the LORD, the God of Israel, speaking of him in these terms: "As the gods of the nations in other lands have not saved their people from my hand, neither shall Hezekiah's god save his people from my hand." 18 In a loud voice they shouted in the Judean language to the people of Jerusalem who were on the wall, to frighten and terrify them so that they might capture their city. 19 They spoke of the God of Israel as though he were one of the gods of the other peoples of the earth, a work of human hands. 20 But because of this, King Hezekiah and the prophet Isaiah, son of Amos, prayed and called out to heaven.

21 Then the LORD sent an angel, who destroyed every valiant warrior, leader and commander in the camp of the Assyrian king, so that he had to return shamefaced to his own country. And when he entered the temple of his god, some of his own offspring struck him down there with the sword. 22 Thus the LORD saved Hezekiah and the inhabitants of Jerusalem from the hand of Sennacherib, king of Assyria, as from every other power; he gave them rest on every side. 23 Many brought gifts for the LORD to Jerusalem and costly objects for King Hezekiah of Judah, who thereafter was exalted in the eyes of all the nations.

24 In those days Hezekiah became mortally ill. He prayed to the LORD, who answered him by giving him a sign. 25 Hezekiah, however, did not then discharge his debt of gratitude, for he had become proud. Therefore anger descended upon him and upon Judah and Jerusalem. 26 But then Hezekiah humbled himself for his pride — both he and the inhabitants of Jerusalem; and therefore the LORD did not vent his anger upon them during the time of Hezekiah.

27 Hezekiah possessed very great wealth and glory. He had treasuries made for his silver, gold, precious stones, spices, jewels, and other precious things of all kinds; 28 also storehouses for the harvest of grain, for wine and oil, and barns for the various kinds of cattle and for the flocks. 29 He built cities for himself, and he acquired sheep and oxen in great numbers, for God gave him very great riches. 30 This same Hezekiah stopped the upper outflow of water from Gihon and led it underground westward to the City of David. Hezekiah prospered in all his undertakings. 31 Nevertheless, in respect to the ambassadors [princes] sent to him from Babylon to investigate the sign that had occurred in the land, God forsook him to test him, that he might know all that was in his heart.

32 The rest of Hezekiah's acts, including his pious works, can be found written in the Vision of the Prophet Isaiah, son of Amos, and in the book of the kings of Judah and Israel. 33 Hezekiah rested with his ancestors; he was buried at the approach to the tombs of the descendants of David. All Judah and the inhabitants of Jerusalem paid him honor at his death. His son Manasseh succeeded him as king.

cestors devoted to destruction, which one has been able to save his people from my clutches, for your god to be able to save you from my clutches? 15 Do not let Hezekiah mislead you. Do not let him delude you like this. Do not believe him, for no god of any nation or country has been able to save his people from me or from my ancestors' clutches. No more will your god be able to save you from my clutches." ' 16 And his representatives said a great deal more, maligning Yahweh God, and his servant Hezekiah.

17 He also wrote a letter to insult Yahweh, God of Israel, maligning him as follows, 'Just as the national gods of the other countries could not save their peoples from my clutches, so Hezekiah's god cannot save his people from my clutches.' 18 They then shouted loudly in the Judaean language to the people of Jerusalem on the ramparts to frighten and confuse them, in the hope of capturing the city, 19 maligning the God of Jerusalem as though he were one of the man-made gods of other peoples in the world.

20 Then King Hezekiah and the prophet Isaiah son of Amoz prayed and cried out to Heaven about this, 21 and Yahweh sent an angel who destroyed every warrior, commander and officer in the king of Assyria's camp. So he had to retire shamefacedly to his own country and when he went into the temple of his god, some of his own sons there struck him down with the sword. 22 So Yahweh saved Hezekiah and the inhabitants of Jerusalem from the clutches of Sennacherib king of Assyria and of everyone else, and gave them peace on every side. 23 Many people then brought gifts to Yahweh in Jerusalem and valuable presents to Hezekiah king of Judah; from then on, all the other nations held him in high esteem.

24 About then Hezekiah fell ill and was at the point of death. He prayed to Yahweh, who heard him and granted him a sign. 25 But Hezekiah made no return for the benefit which he had received; he became proud and brought retribution on himself and on Judah and Jerusalem. 26 Then, however, Hezekiah did humble himself in his pride, and so did the inhabitants of Jerusalem; as a result of which, Yahweh's retribution did not overtake them during Hezekiah's lifetime.

27 Hezekiah enjoyed immense riches and honour. He built himself treasuries for gold, silver, precious stones, spices, jewels and every kind of desirable object, 28 as well as storehouses for his returns of grain, new wine and olive oil, and stalls for all kinds of cattle and pens for the flocks. 29 He also provided himself with donkeys in addition to his immense wealth of flocks and herds, since God had made him immensely wealthy.

30 It was Hezekiah who stopped the upper outlet of the waters of Gihon and directed them straight down on the west side of the City of David. Hezekiah succeeded in all that he undertook, 31 although when the envoys were sent to him by the rulers of Babylon to enquire about the extraordinary thing which had taken place in the country, God left him alone to test him and discover what lay in his heart.

32 The rest of the history of Hezekiah, and his deeds of faithful love, are recorded in the Vision of the prophet Isaiah son of Amoz, in the Book of the Kings of Judah and Israel. 33 Then Hezekiah fell asleep with his ancestors and was buried in the upper section of the tombs of the sons of David. All Judah and the inhabitants of Jerusalem paid him honours at his death. His son Manasseh succeeded him.

| NEW REVISED STANDARD VERSION | REVISED ENGLISH BIBLE |

33 Manasseh was twelve years old when he began to reign; he reigned fifty-five years in Jerusalem. 2 He did what was evil in the sight of the LORD, according to the abominable practices of the nations whom the LORD drove out before the people of Israel. 3 For he rebuilt the high places that his father Hezekiah had pulled down, and erected altars to the Baals, made sacred poles,*n* worshiped all the host of heaven, and served them. 4 He built altars in the house of the LORD, of which the LORD had said, "In Jerusalem shall my name be forever." 5 He built altars for all the host of heaven in the two courts of the house of the LORD. 6 He made his son pass through fire in the valley of the son of Hinnom, practiced soothsaying and augury and sorcery, and dealt with mediums and with wizards. He did much evil in the sight of the LORD, provoking him to anger. 7 The carved image of the idol that he had made he set in the house of God, of which God said to David and to his son Solomon, "In this house, and in Jerusalem, which I have chosen out of all the tribes of Israel, I will put my name forever; 8 I will never again remove the feet of Israel from the land that I appointed for your ancestors, if only they will be careful to do all that I have commanded them, all the law, the statutes, and the ordinances given through Moses." 9 Manasseh misled Judah and the inhabitants of Jerusalem, so that they did more evil than the nations whom the LORD had destroyed before the people of Israel.

10 The LORD spoke to Manasseh and to his people, but they gave no heed. 11 Therefore the LORD brought against them the commanders of the army of the king of Assyria, who took Manasseh captive in manacles, bound him with fetters, and brought him to Babylon. 12 While he was in distress he entreated the favor of the LORD his God and humbled himself greatly before the God of his ancestors. 13 He prayed to him, and God received his entreaty, heard his plea, and restored him again to Jerusalem and to his kingdom. Then Manasseh knew that the LORD indeed was God.

14 Afterward he built an outer wall for the city of David west of Gihon, in the valley, reaching the entrance at the Fish Gate; he carried it around Ophel, and raised it to a very great height. He also put commanders of the army in all the fortified cities in Judah. 15 He took away the foreign gods and the idol from the house of the LORD, and all the altars that he had built on the mountain of the house of the LORD and in Jerusalem, and he threw them out of the city. 16 He also restored the altar of the LORD and offered on it sacrifices of well-being and of thanksgiving; and he commanded Judah to serve the LORD the God of Israel. 17 The people, however, still sacrificed at the high places, but only to the LORD their God.

18 Now the rest of the acts of Manasseh, his prayer to his God, and the words of the seers who spoke to him in the name of the LORD God of Israel, these are in the Annals of the Kings of Israel. 19 His prayer, and how God received his entreaty, all his sin and his faithlessness, the sites on which he built high places and set up the sacred poles*o* and the images, before he humbled himself, these are written in the records of the seers.*p* 20 So Manasseh slept with his ancestors, and they buried him in his house. His son Amon succeeded him.

21 Amon was twenty-two years old when he began to reign; he reigned two years in Jerusalem. 22 He did what was evil in the sight of the LORD, as his father Manasseh had done. Amon sacrificed to all the images that his father Manasseh had made, and served them. 23 He did not humble

33 MANASSEH was twelve years old when he came to the throne, and he reigned in Jerusalem for fifty-five years. 2 He did what was wrong in the eyes of the LORD, in following the abominable practices of the nations which the LORD had dispossessed in favour of the Israelites. 3 He rebuilt the shrines which his father Hezekiah had demolished, he erected altars to the baalim, made sacred poles, and prostrated himself before all the host of heaven and served them. 4 He built altars in the house of the LORD, that house of which the LORD had said, 'In Jerusalem my name will be for ever.' 5 He built altars for all the host of heaven in the two courts of the house of the LORD; 6 he made his sons pass through the fire in the valley of Ben-hinnom, he practised soothsaying, divination, and sorcery, and dealt with ghosts and spirits. He did much wrong in the eyes of the LORD and provoked his anger. 7 The image that he had had carved in relief he set up in the house of God, of which God had said to David and Solomon his son, 'In this house and Jerusalem, which I chose out of all the tribes of Israel, I shall establish my name for all time. 8 I shall not again displace Israel from the land which I assigned to their forefathers, if only they are careful to observe all that I commanded them through Moses, all the law, the statutes, and the rules.' 9 But Manasseh led Judah and the inhabitants of Jerusalem astray into wickedness far worse than that of the nations which the LORD had exterminated in favour of the Israelites.

10 The LORD spoke to Manasseh and his people, but when they paid no heed, 11 he brought against them the commanders of the army of the king of Assyria; they captured Manasseh with spiked weapons, put him in bronze fetters, and brought him to Babylon. 12 In his distress he prayed to the LORD his God and sought to placate him, and made his humble submission before the God of his forefathers. 13 When he prayed, God accepted his petition and heard his supplication; he brought him back to Jerusalem and restored him to the throne. Thus Manasseh learnt that the LORD was God.

14 After this he built an outer wall for the city of David, west of Gihon in the valley, and extended it to the entrance by the Fish Gate, enclosing Ophel; and he raised it to a great height. He also stationed military commanders in all the fortified towns of Judah. 15 He removed the foreign gods and the carved image from the house of the LORD as well as all the altars which he had erected on the temple mount and in Jerusalem, and threw them out of the city. 16 He repaired the altar of the LORD and sacrificed at it shared-offerings and thank-offerings, and commanded Judah to serve the LORD the God of Israel. 17 But the people still continued to sacrifice at the shrines, though only to the LORD their God.

18 The rest of the acts of Manasseh, his prayer to his God, and the discourses of the seers who spoke to him in the name of the LORD the God of Israel, are recorded in the chronicles of the kings of Israel. 19 His prayer and the answer to it he received, all his sin and unfaithfulness, and the places where he built shrines and set up sacred poles and carved idols before he submitted, are recorded in the chronicles of the seers. 20 Manasseh rested with his forefathers and was buried in the garden-tomb of his family. His son Amon succeeded him.

21 Amon was twenty-two years old when he came to the throne, and he reigned in Jerusalem for two years. 22 He did what was wrong in the eyes of the LORD as his father Manasseh had done. He sacrificed to all the images that his father Manasseh had made, and worshipped them. 23 He

---

33:1–9 *Cp. 2 Kgs. 21:1–9.*   33:15 **temple mount:** *lit.* mount of the house of the LORD.   33:19 **the seers:** *so one MS; others* my seers.   33:20 **the garden-tomb of:** *prob. rdg, cp. 2 Kgs. 21:18; Heb. omits.*   33:21–25 *Cp. 2 Kgs. 21:19–24.*

n Heb Asheroth   *o Heb Asherim*   *p One Ms Gk: MT of Hozai*

33 Manasseh was twelve years old when he became king, and he reigned fifty-five years in Jerusalem. 2 He did evil in the sight of the LORD, following the abominable practices of the nations whom the LORD had cleared out of the way of the Israelites. 3 He rebuilt the high places which his father Hezekiah had torn down, erected altars for the Baals, made sacred poles, and prostrated himself before the whole host of heaven and worshiped them. 4 He even built altars in the temple of the LORD, of which the LORD had said, "In Jerusalem shall my name be forever": 5 he built altars to the whole host of heaven in the two courts of the LORD's house. 6 It was he, too, who immolated his sons by fire in the Valley of Ben-hinnom. He practiced augury, divination and magic, and appointed necromancers and diviners of spirits, so that he provoked the LORD with the great evil that he did in his sight. 7 He placed an idol that he had carved in the house of God, of which God had said to David and his son Solomon: "In this house and in Jerusalem which I have chosen from all the tribes of Israel I shall place my name forever. 8 I will not again allow Israel's feet to leave the land which I assigned to your fathers, provided they are careful to observe all that I commanded them, keeping the whole law and the statutes and the ordinances given by Moses." 9 Manasseh misled Judah and the inhabitants of Jerusalem into doing even greater evil than the nations which the LORD had destroyed at the coming of the Israelites. 10 The LORD spoke to Manasseh and his people, but they paid no attention.

11 Therefore the LORD brought against them the army commanders of the Assyrian king; they took Manasseh with hooks, shackled him with chains, and transported him to Babylon. 12 In this distress, he began to appease the LORD, his God. He humbled himself abjectly before the God of his fathers 13 and prayed to him. The LORD let himself be won over: he heard his prayer and restored him to his kingdom in Jerusalem. Then Manasseh understood that the LORD is indeed God.

14 Afterward he built an outer wall for the City of David to the west of Gihon in the valley, extending to the Fish Gate and encircling Ophel; he built it very high. He stationed army officers in all the fortified cities of Judah. 15 He removed the foreign gods and the idol from the LORD's house and all the altars he had built on the mount of the LORD's house and in Jerusalem, and he cast them outside the city. 16 He restored the altar of the LORD, and sacrificed on it peace offerings and thank offerings, and commanded Judah to serve the LORD, the God of Israel. 17 Though the people continued to sacrifice on the high places, they now did so to the LORD, their God.

18 The rest of the acts of Manasseh, his prayer to his God, and the words of the seers who spoke to him in the name of the LORD, the God of Israel, can be found written in the chronicles of the kings of Israel. 19 His prayer and how his supplication was heard, all his sins and his infidelity, the sites where he built high places and erected sacred poles and carved images before he humbled himself, all can be found written down in the history of his seers. 20 Manasseh rested with his ancestors and was buried in his own palace. His son Amon succeeded him as king.

21 Amon was twenty-two years old when he became king, and he reigned two years in Jerusalem. 22 He did evil in the sight of the LORD, just as his father Manasseh had done. Amon offered sacrifice to all the idols which his father Manasseh had made, and worshiped them. 23 Moreover, he

33 Manasseh was twelve years old when he came to the throne, and he reigned for fifty-five years in Jerusalem. 2 He did what is displeasing to Yahweh, copying the disgusting practices of the nations whom Yahweh had dispossessed for the Israelites.

3 He rebuilt the high places which his father Hezekiah had demolished, he set up altars to Baal and made sacred poles, he worshipped the whole array of heaven and served it. 4 He built altars in the Temple of Yahweh, of which Yahweh had said, 'My name will be in Jerusalem for ever.' 5 He built altars to the whole array of heaven in the two courts of the Temple of Yahweh. 6 He caused his sons to pass through the fire of sacrifice in the Valley of Ben-Hinnom. He practised soothsaying, divination and sorcery, and had dealings with mediums and spirit-guides. He did very many more things displeasing to Yahweh, thus provoking his anger. 7 He put a sculpted image, an idol which he had had made, inside the Temple of which God had said to David and his son Solomon, 'In this Temple and in Jerusalem, the city which I have chosen out of all the tribes of Israel, I shall put my name for ever. 8 Nor shall I ever again remove Israel's foot from the soil on which I established your ancestors on condition that they were careful to observe all I commanded them as laid down in the whole Law, the statutes and the ordinances, given through Moses.' 9 But Manasseh misled Judah and the inhabitants of Jerusalem into doing worse things than the nations which Yahweh had destroyed for the Israelites. 10 When Yahweh spoke to Manasseh and his people, they would not listen.

11 Yahweh then brought down on them the generals of the king of Assyria's army who captured Manasseh with hooks, put him in chains and took him to Babylon. 12 While in his distress, he placated Yahweh his God by genuinely humbling himself before the God of his ancestors. 13 When he prayed to him, he was moved by his entreaty, heard his supplication and brought him back to Jerusalem to his kingdom. Manasseh realised then that Yahweh is God.

14 Afterwards, he rebuilt the outer wall of the City of David, to the west of Gihon, in the valley, up to the Fish Gate and round the Ophel, and made it very much higher. And he stationed military governors in all the fortified towns of Judah.

15 He also removed the foreign gods and the idol from the Temple of Yahweh, as well as all the altars which he had built on the mountain of the Temple of Yahweh and in Jerusalem, and threw them out of the city. 16 He repaired the altar of Yahweh and offered communion sacrifices and thanksgiving offerings on it, and commanded Judah to serve Yahweh, God of Israel. 17 The people, however, went on sacrificing at the high places, although only to Yahweh their God.

18 The rest of the history of Manasseh, his prayer to his God, and the prophecies of the seers who spoke to him in the name of Yahweh, God of Israel, can be found in the Annals of the Kings of Israel. 19 His prayer and how God was moved by his entreaty, all his sins, his infidelity, the sites where he built high places and set up sacred poles and idols before humbling himself, are set down in the records of Hozai. 20 Then Manasseh fell asleep with his ancestors and was buried in the garden of his palace. His son Amon succeeded him.

21 Amon was twenty-two years old when he came to the throne, and he reigned for two years in Jerusalem. 22 He did what is displeasing to Yahweh, as his father Manasseh had done, for Amon sacrificed to all the images which his father Manasseh had made, and served them. 23 He did not humble

himself before the LORD, as his father Manasseh had humbled himself, but this Amon incurred more and more guilt. 24 His servants conspired against him and killed him in his house. 25 But the people of the land killed all those who had conspired against King Amon; and the people of the land made his son Josiah king to succeed him.

34 Josiah was eight years old when he began to reign; he reigned thirty-one years in Jerusalem. 2 He did what was right in the sight of the LORD, and walked in the ways of his ancestor David; he did not turn aside to the right or to the left. 3 For in the eighth year of his reign, while he was still a boy, he began to seek the God of his ancestor David, and in the twelfth year he began to purge Judah and Jerusalem of the high places, the sacred poles,q and the carved and the cast images. 4 In his presence they pulled down the altars of the Baals; he demolished the incense altars that stood above them. He broke down the sacred poles$q$ and the carved and the cast images; he made dust of them and scattered it over the graves of those who had sacrificed to them. 5 He also burned the bones of the priests on their altars, and purged Judah and Jerusalem. 6 In the towns of Manasseh, Ephraim, and Simeon, and as far as Naphtali, in their ruins$r$ all around, 7 he broke down the altars, beat the sacred poles$q$ and the images into powder, and demolished all the incense altars throughout all the land of Israel. Then he returned to Jerusalem.

8 In the eighteenth year of his reign, when he had purged the land and the house, he sent Shaphan son of Azaliah, Maaseiah the governor of the city, and Joah son of Joahaz, the recorder, to repair the house of the LORD his God. 9 They came to the high priest Hilkiah and delivered the money that had been brought into the house of God, which the Levites, the keepers of the threshold, had collected from Manasseh and Ephraim and from all the remnant of Israel and from all Judah and Benjamin and from the inhabitants of Jerusalem. 10 They delivered it to the workers who had the oversight of the house of the LORD, and the workers who were working in the house of the LORD gave it for repairing and restoring the house. 11 They gave it to the carpenters and the builders to buy quarried stone, and timber for binders, and beams for the buildings that the kings of Judah had let go to ruin. 12 The people did the work faithfully. Over them were appointed the Levites Jahath and Obadiah, of the sons of Merari, along with Zechariah and Meshullam, of the sons of the Kohathites, to have oversight. Other Levites, all skillful with instruments of music, 13 were over the burden bearers and directed all who did work in every kind of service; and some of the Levites were scribes, and officials, and gatekeepers.

14 While they were bringing out the money that had been brought into the house of the LORD, the priest Hilkiah found the book of the law of the LORD given through Moses. 15 Hilkiah said to the secretary Shaphan, "I have found the book of the law in the house of the LORD"; and Hilkiah gave the book to Shaphan. 16 Shaphan brought the book to the king, and further reported to the king, "All that was committed to your servants they are doing. 17 They have emptied out the money that was found in the house of the LORD and have delivered it into the hand of the overseers and the workers." 18 The secretary Shaphan informed the king, "The priest Hilkiah has given me a book." Shaphan then read it aloud to the king.

19 When the king heard the words of the law he tore his clothes. 20 Then the king commanded Hilkiah, Ahikam son of Shaphan, Abdon son of Micah, the secretary Shaphan, and the king's servant Asaiah: 21 "Go, inquire of the LORD

was not submissive before the LORD like his father Manasseh; his guilt was much greater. 24 His courtiers conspired against him and assassinated him in the palace; 25 but the people of the land killed all the conspirators and made his son Josiah king in his place.

34 JOSIAH was eight years old when he came to the throne, and he reigned in Jerusalem for thirty-one years. 2 He did what was right in the eyes of the LORD, following in the footsteps of his forefather David, and deviating neither to the right nor to the left. 3 In the eighth year of his reign, when he was still a youth, he began to seek guidance of the God of his forefather David; and in the twelfth year he began to purge Judah and Jerusalem of the shrines and the sacred poles, and the carved idols and the metal images. 4 He saw to it that the altars for the baalim were destroyed and he hacked down the incense-altars which stood above them; he broke in pieces the sacred poles and the carved and metal images, grinding them to powder and scattering it on the graves of those who had sacrificed to them. 5 He burnt the bones of the priests on their altars and purged Judah and Jerusalem. 6 In the towns of Manasseh, Ephraim, and Simeon, and as far as Naphtali, he burnt down their houses wherever he found them; 7 he destroyed the altars and the sacred poles, ground the idols to powder, and hacked down the incense-altars throughout the land of Israel. Then he returned to Jerusalem.

8 In the eighteenth year of his reign, after he had purified the land and the house of the LORD, Josiah sent Shaphan son of Azaliah and Maaseiah the governor of the city and Joah son of Joahaz the secretary of state to repair the house of the LORD his God. 9 They came to Hilkiah the high priest and delivered to him the silver that had been brought to the house of God, the silver which the Levites, on duty at the threshold, had received from Manasseh, Ephraim, and all the rest of Israel, as well as from Judah and Benjamin and the inhabitants of Jerusalem. 10 It was then handed over to those supervising the work in the house of the LORD, and these men, working in the house, used it for repairing and strengthening the fabric; 11 they gave it also to the carpenters and builders to purchase hewn stone, and timber for rafters and beams, for the buildings which the kings of Judah had allowed to fall into disrepair. 12-13 The men did their work faithfully under the supervision of Jahath and Obadiah, Levites of the line of Merari, and Zechariah and Meshullam, members of the family of Kohath. These also had control of the bearers and directed the workmen of every trade. The Levites were all skilled musicians, and some of them were secretaries, clerks, or door-keepers.

14 When they were fetching out the silver which had been brought to the house of the LORD, the priest Hilkiah discovered the scroll of the law of the LORD which had been given through Moses. 15 Hilkiah told Shaphan the adjutant-general that he had discovered the scroll of the law in the house of the LORD; he gave the scroll to Shaphan, who brought it to the king and reported to him: 'Your servants are doing all that was entrusted to them. 17 They have melted down the silver in the house of the LORD and have handed it over to the supervisors of the work and the workmen.'

18 Shaphan the adjutant-general also told the king of the scroll that the priest Hilkiah had given him; and he read from it in the king's presence. 19 When the king heard what was written in the scroll of the law, he tore his clothes. 20 He ordered Hilkiah, Ahikam son of Shaphan, Abdon son of Micah, Shaphan the adjutant-general, and Asaiah the king's attendant 21 to go and seek guidance of the LORD for himself

---

q Heb *Asherim* r Meaning of Heb uncertain

34:1-2 *Cp. 2 Kgs. 22:1-2.*   34:8-32 *Cp. 2 Kgs. 22:3-23:3.*

did not humble himself before the LORD as his father Manasseh had done; on the contrary, Amon only increased his guilt. 24 His servants conspired against him and put him to death in his own house. 25 But the people of the land slew all those who had conspired against King Amon, and then they, the people of the land, made his son Josiah king in his stead.

34 Josiah was eight years old when he became king, and he reigned thirty-one years in Jerusalem. 2 He pleased the LORD, following the path of his ancestor David. 3 In the eighth year of his reign, while he was still a youth, he began to seek after the God of his forefather David, and in his twelfth year he began to purge Judah and Jerusalem of the high places, the sacred poles and the carved and molten images. 4 In his presence, the altars of the Baals were destroyed; the incense stands erected above them were torn down; the sacred poles and the carved and molten images were shattered and beaten into dust, which was strewn over the tombs of those who had sacrificed to them; 5 and the bones of the priests he burned upon their altars. Thus he purged Judah and Jerusalem. 6 He did likewise in the cities of Manasseh, Ephraim, Simeon, and in the ruined villages of the surrounding country as far as Naphtali; 7 he destroyed the altars, broke up the sacred poles and carved images and beat them into dust, and tore down the incense stands throughout the land of Israel. Then he returned to Jerusalem.

8 In the eighteenth year of his reign, in order to cleanse the temple as well as the land, he sent Shaphan, son of Azaliah, Maaseiah, the ruler of the city, and Joah, son of Joahaz, the chamberlain, to restore the house of the LORD, his God. 9 They came to Hilkiah the high priest and turned over the money brought to the house of God which the Levites, the guardians of the threshold, had collected from Manasseh, Ephraim, and all the remnant of Israel, as well as from all of Judah, Benjamin, and the inhabitants of Jerusalem. 10 They turned it over to the master workmen in the house of the LORD, and these in turn used it to pay the workmen in the LORD's house who were restoring and repairing the temple. 11 They also gave it to the carpenters and the masons to buy hewn stone and timber for the tie beams and rafters of the buildings which the kings of Judah had allowed to fall into ruin. 12 The men worked faithfully at their tasks; their overseers were Jahath and Obadiah, Levites of the line of Merari, and Zechariah and Meshullam, of the Kohathites, who directed them. All those Levites who were skillful with musical instruments 13 were in charge of the men who carried the burdens, and they directed all the workers in every kind of labor. Some of the other Levites were scribes, officials and gatekeepers.

14 When they brought out the money that had been deposited in the house of the LORD, Hilkiah the priest found the book of the law of the LORD given through Moses. 15 He reported this to Shaphan the scribe, saying, "I have found the book of the law in the house of the LORD." Hilkiah gave the book to Shaphan, 16 who brought it to the king at the same time that he was making his report to him. He said, "Your servants are doing everything that has been entrusted to them; 17 they have turned into bullion the metals deposited in the LORD's house and have handed it over to the overseers and the workmen." 18 Then Shaphan the scribe announced to the king, "Hilkiah the priest has given me a book." And Shaphan read from it before the king.

19 When the king heard the words of the law, he tore his garments 20 and issued this command to Hilkiah, to Ahikam, son of Shaphan, to Abdon, son of Michah, to Shaphan the scribe, and to Asaiah, the king's servant: 21 "On behalf

himself before Yahweh as his father Manasseh had done; on the contrary, Amon wilfully added to his guilt. 24 His retinue plotted against him and killed him in his own palace. 25 The people of the country, however, slaughtered all those who had plotted against King Amon and proclaimed his son Josiah as his successor.

34 Josiah was eight years old when he came to the throne, and he reigned for thirty-one years in Jerusalem. 2 He did what is pleasing to Yahweh, and followed the example of his ancestor David, not deviating from it to right or to left.

3 In the eighth year of his reign, when he was still a youth, he began to seek the God of his ancestor David. In the twelfth year he began to purge Judah and Jerusalem of the high places, the sacred poles and the sculpted and cast images. 4 He superintended the smashing of the altars of Baal, he broke up the incense altars standing above them, he shattered the sacred poles and the sculpted and cast images and reduced them to powder, scattering the powder on the graves of those who had sacrificed to them. 5 He burned the bones of their priests on their altars and so purified Judah and Jerusalem. 6 In the towns of Manasseh, Ephraim and Simeon, as far as Naphtali, and round their open spaces, 7 he smashed the altars and sacred poles, reduced the sculpted images to powder and broke up all the incense altars throughout the territory of Israel. Then he returned to Jerusalem.

8 In the eighteenth year of his reign, after purging the country and the Temple, he commissioned Shaphan son of Azaliah, Maaseiah governor of the city and the herald Joah son of Joahaz, to repair the Temple of Yahweh his God. 9 When they came to the high priest Hilkiah, they handed over the money contributed to the Temple of God and collected by the levitical guardians of the threshold from Manasseh and Ephraim, from all the rest of Israel, from all Judah and Benjamin, and from the inhabitants of Jerusalem. 10 They handed it over to the masters of works attached to the Temple of Yahweh, and these gave it to the men working on the Temple of Yahweh to repair and restore the Temple; 11 they gave it to the craftsmen and builders for buying dressed stone and timber for beams, to underpin the buildings which the kings of Judah had allowed to fall into decay.

12 The men were conscientious in doing their work; their foremen were Jahath and Obadiah, Levites descended from Merari, and Zechariah and Meshullam, descended from Kohath, who supervised. The Levites—all of whom were skilled instrumentalists— 13 were in charge of the carriers and supervised all the workmen at their various jobs, while some of the Levites acted as secretaries, book-keepers and gatekeepers.

14 While bringing out the money contributed to the Temple of Yahweh, the priest Hilkiah found the book of the Law of Yahweh given through Moses. 15 Hilkiah then said to Shaphan the secretary, 'I have found the Book of the Law in the Temple of Yahweh.' And Hilkiah gave the book to Shaphan. 16 Shaphan took the book to the king, reporting furthermore to him as follows, 'Your servants have done everything entrusted to them. 17 They have melted down the silver which was in the Temple of Yahweh and have handed it over to the supervisors and the masters of works.' 18 Shaphan the secretary also informed the king, 'The priest Hilkiah has given me a book'; and Shaphan read extracts from it in the king's presence.

19 On hearing the words of the Law, the king tore his clothes. 20 Then the king gave the following order to Hilkiah, Ahikam son of Shaphan, Abdon son of Micah, Shaphan the secretary and Asaiah the king's minister, 21 'Go

for me and for those who are left in Israel and in Judah, concerning the words of the book that has been found; for the wrath of the LORD that is poured out on us is great, because our ancestors did not keep the word of the LORD, to act in accordance with all that is written in this book."

22 So Hilkiah and those whom the king had sent went to the prophet Huldah, the wife of Shallum son of Tokhath son of Hasrah, keeper of the wardrobe (who lived in Jerusalem in the Second Quarter) and spoke to her to that effect. 23 She declared to them, "Thus says the LORD, the God of Israel: Tell the man who sent you to me, 24 Thus says the LORD: I will indeed bring disaster upon this place and upon its inhabitants, all the curses that are written in the book that was read before the king of Judah. 25 Because they have forsaken me and have made offerings to other gods, so that they have provoked me to anger with all the works of their hands, my wrath will be poured out on this place and will not be quenched. 26 But as to the king of Judah, who sent you to inquire of the LORD, thus shall you say to him: Thus says the LORD, the God of Israel: Regarding the words that you have heard, 27 because your heart was penitent and you humbled yourself before God when you heard his words against this place and its inhabitants, and you have humbled yourself before me, and have torn your clothes and wept before me, I also have heard you, says the LORD. 28 I will gather you to your ancestors and you shall be gathered to your grave in peace; your eyes shall not see all the disaster that I will bring on this place and its inhabitants." They took the message back to the king.

29 Then the king sent word and gathered together all the elders of Judah and Jerusalem. 30 The king went up to the house of the LORD, with all the people of Judah, the inhabitants of Jerusalem, the priests and the Levites, all the people both great and small; he read in their hearing all the words of the book of the covenant that had been found in the house of the LORD. 31 The king stood in his place and made a covenant before the LORD, to follow the LORD, keeping his commandments, his decrees, and his statutes, with all his heart and all his soul, to perform the words of the covenant that were written in this book. 32 Then he made all who were present in Jerusalem and in Benjamin pledge themselves to it. And the inhabitants of Jerusalem acted according to the covenant of God, the God of their ancestors. 33 Josiah took away all the abominations from all the territory that belonged to the people of Israel, and made all who were in Israel worship the LORD their God. All his days they did not turn away from following the LORD the God of their ancestors.

35 Josiah kept a passover to the LORD in Jerusalem; they slaughtered the passover lamb on the fourteenth day of the first month. 2 He appointed the priests to their offices and encouraged them in the service of the house of the LORD. 3 He said to the Levites who taught all Israel and who were holy to the LORD, "Put the holy ark in the house that Solomon son of David, king of Israel, built; you need no longer carry it on your shoulders. Now serve the LORD your God and his people Israel. 4 Make preparations by your ancestral houses by your divisions, following the written directions of King David of Israel and the written directions of his son Solomon. 5 Take position in the holy place according to the groupings of the ancestral houses of your kindred the people, and let there be Levites for each division of an ancestral house.ˢ 6 Slaughter the passover lamb, sanctify yourselves, and on behalf of your kindred make preparations, acting according to the word of the LORD by Moses."

and for all who still remained in Israel and Judah, about the contents of the scroll that had been discovered. 'Great must be the wrath of the LORD,' he said, 'and it has been poured out on us, because our forefathers did not observe the LORD's command and do all that is written in this scroll.' 22 Hilkiah and those whom the king had instructed went to Huldah the prophetess, wife of Shallum son of Tikvah, son of Hasrah, the keeper of the wardrobe, and consulted her at her home in the Second Quarter of Jerusalem. 23 'This is the word of the LORD the God of Israel,' she answered: 'Tell the man who sent you to me 24 that this is what the LORD says: I am about to bring disaster on this place and its inhabitants, fulfilling all the imprecations recorded in the scroll which was read in the presence of the king of Judah, 25 because they have forsaken me and burnt sacrifices to other gods, provoking my anger with all the idols they have made with their own hands; for this my wrath will be poured out on this place and will not be quenched. 26 Tell the king of Judah who sent you to seek guidance of the LORD that this is what the LORD the God of Israel says: You have listened to my words 27 and shown a willing heart and humbled yourself before God when you heard what I said about this place and its inhabitants; you humbled yourself and tore your clothes and wept before me. Because of this, I for my part have listened to you. This is the word of the LORD. 28 Therefore I shall gather you to your forefathers, and you will be gathered to your grave in peace; you will not live to see all the disaster which I am bringing on this place and its inhabitants.' They brought back this answer to the king.

29 At the king's summons all the elders of Judah and Jerusalem were assembled, 30 and he went up to the house of the LORD, taking with him all the men of Judah, the inhabitants of Jerusalem, the priests, and the Levites, the entire population, high and low. There he read out to them the whole scroll of the covenant which had been discovered in the house of the LORD. 31 Then, standing by the pillar, the king entered into a covenant before the LORD to obey him and keep his commandments, his testimonies, and his statutes with all his heart and soul, and so carry out the terms of the covenant written in the scroll. 32 Then he took an oath, swearing with all who were present in Jerusalem to keep the covenant. Thereafter the inhabitants of Jerusalem did obey the covenant of God, the God of their forefathers. 33 Josiah removed all the abominable idols from the whole territory of the Israelites, so that everyone living in Israel might serve the LORD his God. As long as he lived they did not fail in their allegiance to the LORD the God of their forefathers.

35 Josiah kept a Passover to the LORD in Jerusalem, the Passover lamb being killed on the fourteenth day of the first month. 2 He appointed the priests to their offices and encouraged them in the service of the house of the LORD. 3 He said to the Levites, who instructed Israel and were dedicated to the LORD, 'Put the sacred Ark in the house which Solomon son of David king of Israel built. As it is not to be carried about on your shoulders, you are now to serve the LORD your God and his people Israel: 4 prepare yourselves by families according to your divisions, following the written instructions of David king of Israel and those of Solomon his son. 5 Stand in the Holy Place as representatives of the family groups of the lay people, your brothers, one division of Levites to each family group. 6 Kill the Passover lamb and hallow yourselves, and prepare for your brothers to fulfil the word of the LORD given through Moses.'

34:22 **had instructed:** *so Gk; Heb. omits.* **Tikvah:** *prob. rdg, cp.* 2 Kgs. 22:14; *Heb.* Tokhath.   34:31 **by the pillar:** *or* on the dais.   34:32 **to keep the covenant:** *prob. rdg, cp.* 2 Kgs. 23:3; *Heb.* and Benjamin.

ˢ Meaning of Heb uncertain

of myself and those who are left in Israel and Judah, go, consult the LORD concerning the words of the book that has been found. For the anger of the LORD has been set furiously ablaze against us, since our fathers have not kept the word of the LORD and have not done all that is written in this book." 22 Then Hilkiah and the other men from the king went to the prophetess Huldah, the wife of Shallum, son of Tokhath, son of Hasrah, the guardian of the wardrobe; she dwelt in Jerusalem, in the new quarter. They spoke to her as they had been instructed, 23 and she said to them: "Thus says the LORD, the God of Israel: 'Tell the one who sent you to me, 24 The LORD says: I am prepared to bring evil upon this place and upon its inhabitants, all the curses written in the book that has been read before the king of Judah. 25 Because they have abandoned me and have offered incense to other gods, provoking me by every deed that they have performed, my anger is ablaze against this place and cannot be extinguished.'

26 "But to the king of Judah who sent you to consult the LORD, give this response: 'Thus says the LORD, the God of Israel, concerning the threats you have heard: 27 Because you were heartsick and have humbled yourself before God on hearing his words spoken against this place and its inhabitants; because you have humbled yourself before me, have torn your garments, and have wept before me, I in turn have listened — so declares the LORD. 28 I will gather you to your ancestors and you shall be taken to your grave in peace. Your eyes shall not see all the evil I will bring upon this place and upon its inhabitants.'"

They brought back this message to the king.

29 The king now convened all the elders of Judah and Jerusalem. 30 He went up to the house of the LORD with all the men of Judah and the inhabitants of Jerusalem, the priests, the Levites, and all the people, great and small; and he had read aloud to them the entire text of the book of the covenant that had been found in the house of the LORD. 31 Standing at his post, the king made a covenant before the LORD to follow the LORD and to keep his commandments, decrees, and statutes with his whole heart and soul, thus observing the terms of the covenant written in this book. 32 He thereby committed all who were of Jerusalem and Benjamin, and the inhabitants of Jerusalem conformed themselves to the covenant of God, the God of their fathers. 33 Josiah removed every abominable thing from all the territory belonging to the Israelites, and he obliged all who were in Israel to serve the LORD, their God. During their lifetime they did not desert the LORD, the God of their fathers.

35 Josiah celebrated in Jerusalem a Passover to honor the LORD; the Passover sacrifice was slaughtered on the fourteenth day of the first month. 2 He reappointed the priests to their duties and encouraged them in the service of the LORD's house. 3 He said to the Levites who were to instruct all Israel, and who were consecrated to the LORD: "Put the holy ark in the house built by Solomon, son of David, king of Israel. It shall no longer be a burden on your shoulders. Serve now the LORD, your God, and his people Israel. 4 Prepare yourselves in your ancestral houses and your classes according to the prescriptions of King David of Israel and his son Solomon. 5 Stand in the sanctuary according to the divisions of the ancestral houses of your brethren, the common people, so that the distribution of the Levites and the families may be the same. 6 Slay the Passover sacrifice, sanctify yourselves, and be at the disposition of your brethren, that all may be carried out according to the word of the LORD given through Moses."

and consult Yahweh on behalf of me and of those left in Israel and Judah about the words of the book that has been discovered: for Yahweh's furious wrath has been pouring down on us because our ancestors did not obey the word of Yahweh by doing what this book says they ought to have done.'

22 Hilkiah and those whom the king had designated went to the prophetess Huldah wife of Shallum, son of Tokhath, son of Hasrah, the keeper of the wardrobe; she lived in Jerusalem in the new town. They spoke to her about this, 23 and she replied, 'Yahweh, God of Israel, says this, "To the man who sent you to me reply: 24 Yahweh says this: I am going to bring disaster on this place and the people who live in it — all the curses set down in the book read in the king of Judah's presence. 25 Because they have abandoned me and burnt incense to other gods, so as to provoke my anger by their every action, my wrath is about to be poured down on this place, and nothing can stop it. 26 As for the king of Judah who sent you to consult Yahweh, say this to him: Yahweh, God of Israel, says this: The words you have heard . . . 27 But since your heart has been touched and you have humbled yourself before God on hearing what he has decreed against this place and the people who live in it, have torn your clothes and wept before me, I too have heard" — Yahweh says this. 28 "Look, when I gather you to your ancestors, you will be gathered into your grave in peace; you will not live to see the great disaster that I am going to bring on this place and on the people who live in it." ' They took this answer to the king.

29 The king then had all the elders of Judah and of Jerusalem summoned, 30 and the king went up to the temple of Yahweh, with all the men of Judah and all the inhabitants of Jerusalem, priests, Levites and all the people, high and low. In their hearing he read out the entire contents of the Book of the Covenant discovered in the Temple of Yahweh. 31 The king then, standing on the dais, bound himself by the covenant before Yahweh, to follow Yahweh, to keep his commandments, decrees and laws with all his heart and soul and to carry out the terms of the covenant as written in this book. 32 He made all those present in Jerusalem and Benjamin pledge their allegiance to it.

The citizens of Jerusalem took action in keeping with the covenant of God, the God of their ancestors, 33 while Josiah removed all the abominations throughout the territories belonging to the Israelites and required all inhabitants of Israel to serve Yahweh their God; throughout his lifetime they did not deviate from following Yahweh, God of their ancestors.

35 Josiah then celebrated a Passover to Yahweh in Jerusalem. The Passover victims were slaughtered on the fourteenth day of the first month.

2 He assigned the priests to their posts, encouraging them to do their duty in the Temple of Yahweh. 3 Then he said to the Levites, who had understanding for all Israel and were consecrated to Yahweh, 'Put the sacred ark in the Temple built by Solomon son of David, king of Israel. You need not carry it about on your shoulders any more. Now serve Yahweh your God and Israel his people! 4 Prepare yourselves by families according to your orders, as laid down in the decree of David king of Israel and that of Solomon his son, 5 and take up positions in the sanctuary corresponding to the family divisions of your brothers the laity, so that there are Levites for each family division. 6 Slaughter the Passover, sanctify yourselves and prepare it so that your brothers can observe it in the way the word of Yahweh through Moses requires.'

7 Then Josiah contributed to the people, as passover offerings for all that were present, lambs and kids from the flock to the number of thirty thousand, and three thousand bulls; these were from the king's possessions. 8 His officials contributed willingly to the people, to the priests, and to the Levites. Hilkiah, Zechariah, and Jehiel, the chief officers of the house of God, gave to the priests for the passover offerings two thousand six hundred lambs and kids and three hundred bulls. 9 Conaniah also, and his brothers Shemaiah and Nethanel, and Hashabiah and Jeiel and Jozabad, the chiefs of the Levites, gave to the Levites for the passover offerings five thousand lambs and kids and five hundred bulls.

10 When the service had been prepared for, the priests stood in their place, and the Levites in their divisions according to the king's command. 11 They slaughtered the passover lamb, and the priests dashed the blood that they received[t] from them, while the Levites did the skinning. 12 They set aside the burnt offerings so that they might distribute them according to the groupings of the ancestral houses of the people, to offer to the LORD, as it is written in the book of Moses. And they did the same with the bulls. 13 They roasted the passover lamb with fire according to the ordinance; and they boiled the holy offerings in pots, in caldrons, and in pans, and carried them quickly to all the people. 14 Afterward they made preparations for themselves and for the priests, because the priests the descendants of Aaron were occupied in offering the burnt offerings and the fat parts until night; so the Levites made preparations for themselves and for the priests, the descendants of Aaron. 15 The singers, the descendants of Asaph, were in their place according to the command of David, and Asaph, and Heman, and the king's seer Jeduthun. The gatekeepers were at each gate; they did not need to interrupt their service, for their kindred the Levites made preparations for them.

16 So all the service of the LORD was prepared that day, to keep the passover and to offer burnt offerings on the altar of the LORD, according to the command of King Josiah. 17 The people of Israel who were present kept the passover at that time, and the festival of unleavened bread seven days. 18 No passover like it had been kept in Israel since the days of the prophet Samuel; none of the kings of Israel kept such a passover as was kept by Josiah, by the priests and the Levites, by all Judah and Israel who were present, and by the inhabitants of Jerusalem. 19 In the eighteenth year of the reign of Josiah this passover was kept.

20 After all this, when Josiah had set the temple in order, King Neco of Egypt went up to fight at Carchemish on the Euphrates, and Josiah went out against him. 21 But Neco[u] sent envoys to him, saying, "What have I to do with you, king of Judah? I am not coming against you today, but against the house with which I am at war; and God has commanded me to hurry. Cease opposing God, who is with me, so that he will not destroy you." 22 But Josiah would not turn away from him, but disguised himself in order to fight with him. He did not listen to the words of Neco from the mouth of God, but joined battle in the plain of Megiddo. 23 The archers shot King Josiah; and the king said to his servants, "Take me away, for I am badly wounded." 24 So his servants took him out of the chariot and carried him in his second chariot[v] and brought him to Jerusalem. There he died, and was buried in the tombs of his ancestors. All Judah and Jerusalem mourned for Josiah. 25 Jeremiah also uttered a lament for Josiah, and all the singing men and singing women have spoken of Josiah in their laments to this day. They made these a custom in Israel; they are recorded in the Laments. 26 Now the rest of the acts of

7 Josiah contributed on behalf of all the lay people present thirty thousand small livestock, that is young rams and goats, for the Passover, in addition to three thousand bulls; all these were from the king's own resources. 8 His officers contributed willingly for the people, the priests, and the Levites. Hilkiah, Zechariah, and Jehiel, the chief officers of the house of God, gave on behalf of the priests two thousand six hundred small livestock for the Passover, in addition to three hundred bulls. 9 Conaniah, Shemaiah and Nethanel his brothers, and Hashabiah, Jeiel, and Jozabad, the chiefs of the Levites, gave on behalf of the Levites for the Passover five thousand small livestock in addition to five hundred bulls.

10 When the service had been arranged, the priests stood in their places and the Levites in their divisions according to the king's command. 11 The Levites killed the Passover victims, and the priests flung the blood against the altar, while the Levites flayed the animals. 12 Then they removed the fat flesh, which they allocated to the people by groups of families for them to offer to the LORD, as prescribed in the book of Moses; and so with the bulls. 13 They cooked the Passover victims over the fire according to custom, and boiled the holy offerings in pots, cauldrons, and pans, and served them quickly to all the people.

14 After that they made the necessary preparations for themselves and the priests, because the priests of Aaron's line were engaged till nightfall in offering whole-offerings and the fat portions; so the Levites made the necessary preparations for themselves and for the priests of Aaron's line. 15 The Asaphite singers were in their places according to the rules laid down by David and by Asaph, Heman, and Jeduthun, the king's seers. The door-keepers stood, each at his gate; there was no need for them to leave their posts, because their kinsmen the Levites had made the preparations for them.

16 In this manner all the service of the LORD was arranged that day, to keep the Passover and to offer whole-offerings on the altar of the LORD, according to the command of King Josiah. 17 The people of Israel who were present kept the Passover at that time and the pilgrim-feast of Unleavened Bread for seven days. 18 No Passover like it had been kept in Israel since the days of the prophet Samuel; none of the kings of Israel had ever kept such a Passover as Josiah kept, with the priests and Levites and all Judah and Israel who were present and the inhabitants of Jerusalem. 19 This Passover was kept in the eighteenth year of Josiah's reign.

20 Some time after Josiah had thus organized the entire service of the house of the LORD, King Necho marched up from Egypt to attack Carchemish on the Euphrates; Josiah went out to confront him. 21 Necho sent envoys, saying, 'King of Judah, what do you want with me? I have no quarrel with you today, only with those with whom I am at war. God has purposed, to speed me on my way, and God is on my side. Do not stand in his way, or he will destroy you.' 22 Josiah would not be deflected from his purpose but determined to fight; he refused to listen to Necho's words spoken at God's command, and he sallied out to join battle in the vale of Megiddo. 23 The archers shot at him; he was severely wounded and told his bodyguard to take him away. 24 They lifted him out of his chariot and conveyed him in his viceroy's chariot to Jerusalem. There he died and was buried among the tombs of his ancestors, and all Judah and Jerusalem mourned for him. 25 Jeremiah also made a lament for Josiah; and to this day the minstrels, both men and women, commemorate Josiah in their lamentations. Such laments have become traditional in Israel, and they are found in the written collections.

---

[t] Heb lacks *that they received*   [u] Heb *he*   [v] Or *the chariot of his deputy*

35:11 **the blood:** *so Syriac; Heb.* from their hand.   35:12 **fat flesh:** *or* whole-offering.   35:15 **seers:** *so some MSS; others* seer.

7 Josiah contributed to the common people a flock of lambs and kids, thirty thousand in number, each to serve as a Passover victim for any who were present, and also three thousand oxen; these were from the king's property. 8 His princes also gave a free-will gift to the people, the priests and the Levites. Hilkiah, Zechariah and Jehiel, prefects of the house of God, gave to the priests two thousand six hundred Passover victims together with three hundred oxen. 9 Conaniah and his brothers Shemaiah, Nethanel, Hashabiah, Jehiel and Jozabad, the rulers of the Levites, contributed to the Levites five thousand Passover victims, together with five hundred oxen.

10 When the service had been arranged, the priests took their places, as did the Levites in their classes according to the king's command. 11 The Passover sacrifice was slaughtered, whereupon the priests sprinkled some of the blood and the Levites proceeded to the skinning. 12 They separated what was destined for the holocaust and gave it to various groups of the ancestral houses of the common people to offer to the LORD, as is prescribed in the book of Moses. They did the same with the oxen. 13 They cooked the Passover on the fire as prescribed, and also cooked the sacred meals in pots, cauldrons and pans, then brought them quickly to all the common people. 14 Afterward they prepared the Passover for themselves and for the priests. Indeed the priests, the sons of Aaron, were busy offering holocausts and the fatty portions until night; therefore the Levites prepared for themselves and for the priests, the sons of Aaron. 15 The singers, the sons of Asaph, were at their posts as prescribed by David: Asaph, Heman and Jeduthun, the king's seer. The gatekeepers were at every gate; there was no need for them to leave their stations, for their brethren, the Levites, prepared for them. 16 Thus the entire service of the Lord was arranged that day so that the Passover could be celebrated and the holocausts offered on the altar of the Lord, as King Josiah had commanded. 17 The Israelites who were present on that occasion kept the Passover and the feast of the Unleavened Bread for seven days. 18 No such Passover had been observed in Israel since the time of the prophet Samuel, nor had any king of Israel kept a Passover like that of Josiah, the priests and Levites, all of Judah and Israel that were present, and the inhabitants of Jerusalem. 19 It was in the eighteenth year of Josiah's reign that this Passover was observed.

20 After Josiah had done all this to restore the temple, Neco, king of Egypt, came up to fight at Carchemish on the Euphrates, and Josiah went out to intercept him. 21 Neco sent messengers to him, saying: "What quarrel is between us, king of Judah? I have not come against you this day, for my war is with another kingdom, and God has told me to hasten. Do not interfere with God who is with me, as otherwise he will destroy you." 22 But Josiah would not withdraw from him, for he had sought a pretext for fighting with him. Therefore he would not listen to the words of Neco that came from the mouth of God, but went out to fight in the plain of Megiddo. 23 Then the archers shot King Josiah, who said to his servants, "Take me away, for I am seriously wounded." 24 His servants removed him from his own chariot, placed him in another he had in reserve, and brought him to Jerusalem, where he died. He was buried in the tombs of his ancestors, and all Judah and Jerusalem mourned him. 25 Jeremiah also composed a lamentation over Josiah, which is recited to this day by all the male and female singers in their lamentations over Josiah. These have been made obligatory for Israel, and can be found written in the Lamentations.

7 For the laity Josiah provided small livestock, that is, lambs and young goats — everything for the Passover offerings for all who attended — to the number of thirty thousand, as well as three thousand bullocks; these were from the king's own possessions. 8 His officials also made voluntary contributions for the people, the priests and the Levites; and Hilkiah, Zechariah and Jehiel, the chiefs of the Temple of God, gave two thousand six hundred lambs and three hundred bullocks to the priests for the Passover offerings; 9 while Conaniah, Shemaiah, Nethanel his brother, Hashabiah, Jeiel and Jozabad, the head Levites, provided five thousand lambs and five hundred bullocks as Passover offerings for the Levites.

10 So the service was arranged, the priests stood in their places and the Levites in their orders as the king had commanded. 11 Then they slaughtered the Passover victims and while the priests sprinkled the blood as they received it from the Levites, the latter did the skinning. 12 Next they put the burnt offering aside for presentation to the family divisions of the laity, so that they could offer it to Yahweh in the way prescribed in the Book of Moses; they did the same with the bullocks. 13 They roasted the Passover victim over an open fire in accordance with the regulation and boiled the consecrated offerings in pots, kettles and pans, which they then distributed to all the laity as quickly as they could. 14 Afterwards they provided for themselves and the priests, since the Aaronite priests were kept busy till nightfall making the burnt offerings and offering the fat; that was why the Levites prepared the Passover for themselves and for the Aaronite priests. 15 The Asaphite singers were at their places, in accordance with the command of David and Asaph, Heman and Jeduthun the king's seer; so were the gatekeepers at each gate. Because they could not leave their duties, their brothers the Levites prepared the Passover for them.

16 So the whole service of Yahweh was arranged that day to celebrate the Passover and to bring burnt offerings on the altar of Yahweh, in accordance with King Josiah's command. 17 On that occasion the Israelites who were present celebrated the Passover and the feast of Unleavened Bread for seven days. 18 No Passover like this one had ever been celebrated in Israel since the days of the prophet Samuel, nor had any of the kings of Israel ever celebrated a Passover like the one celebrated by Josiah, the priests, the Levites, all Judah and Israel who were present, and the inhabitants of Jerusalem.

19 This Passover was celebrated in the eighteenth year of Josiah's reign.

20 After all this, when Josiah had provided for the Temple, Necho king of Egypt advanced to give battle at Carchemish on the Euphrates and Josiah went to intercept him. 21 Necho however sent him messengers to say, 'Why be concerned about me, king of Judah? I have not come today to attack you; my quarrel is with another dynasty. God has commanded me to move quickly, so keep well clear of the god who is with me!' 22 But Josiah was not to be deflected from his determination to fight him, and would not listen to Necho's words, which came from the mouth of God. He gave battle in the plain of Megiddo. 23 The archers shot King Josiah. The king then said to his retainers, 'Take me away; I am badly wounded.' 24 So his retainers lifted him out of his own chariot, transferred him to one which he had in reserve and brought him to Jerusalem, where he died and was buried in the tombs of his ancestors. All Judah and Jerusalem held mourning for Josiah. 25 Jeremiah composed a lament for Josiah and all the male and female singers to this day lament Josiah in their dirges; they have made it a rule in Israel; they are recorded in the Lamentations.

NEW REVISED STANDARD VERSION REVISED ENGLISH BIBLE

Josiah and his faithful deeds in accordance with what is written in the law of the LORD, 27 and his acts, first and last, are written in the Book of the Kings of Israel and Judah.

36 The people of the land took Jehoahaz son of Josiah and made him king to succeed his father in Jerusalem. 2 Jehoahaz was twenty-three years old when he began to reign; he reigned three months in Jerusalem. 3 Then the king of Egypt deposed him in Jerusalem and laid on the land a tribute of one hundred talents of silver and one talent of gold. 4 The king of Egypt made his brother Eliakim king over Judah and Jerusalem, and changed his name to Jehoiakim; but Neco took his brother Jehoahaz and carried him to Egypt.

5 Jehoiakim was twenty-five years old when he began to reign; he reigned eleven years in Jerusalem. He did what was evil in the sight of the LORD his God. 6 Against him King Nebuchadnezzar of Babylon came up, and bound him with fetters to take him to Babylon. 7 Nebuchadnezzar also carried some of the vessels of the house of the LORD to Babylon and put them in his palace in Babylon. 8 Now the rest of the acts of Jehoiakim, and the abominations that he did, and what was found against him, are written in the Book of the Kings of Israel and Judah; and his son Jehoiachin succeeded him.

9 Jehoiachin was eight years old when he began to reign; he reigned three months and ten days in Jerusalem. He did what was evil in the sight of the LORD. 10 In the spring of the year King Nebuchadnezzar sent and brought him to Babylon, along with the precious vessels of the house of the LORD, and made his brother Zedekiah king over Judah and Jerusalem.

11 Zedekiah was twenty-one years old when he began to reign; he reigned eleven years in Jerusalem. 12 He did what was evil in the sight of the LORD his God. He did not humble himself before the prophet Jeremiah who spoke from the mouth of the LORD. 13 He also rebelled against King Nebuchadnezzar, who had made him swear by God; he stiffened his neck and hardened his heart against turning to the LORD, the God of Israel. 14 All the leading priests and the people also were exceedingly unfaithful, following all the abominations of the nations; and they polluted the house of the LORD that he had consecrated in Jerusalem.

15 The LORD, the God of their ancestors, sent persistently to them by his messengers, because he had compassion on his people and on his dwelling place; 16 but they kept mocking the messengers of God, despising his words, and scoffing at his prophets, until the wrath of the LORD against his people became so great that there was no remedy.

17 Therefore he brought up against them the king of the Chaldeans, who killed their youths with the sword in the house of their sanctuary, and had no compassion on young man or young woman, the aged or the feeble; he gave them all into his hand. 18 All the vessels of the house of God, large and small, and the treasures of the house of the LORD, and the treasures of the king and of his officials, all these he brought to Babylon. 19 They burned the house of God, broke down the wall of Jerusalem, burned all its palaces with fire, and destroyed all its precious vessels. 20 He took into exile in Babylon those who had escaped from the sword, and they became servants to him and to his sons until the establishment of the kingdom of Persia, 21 to fulfill

26 The other events of Josiah's reign, and his works of piety, all performed in accordance with what is laid down in the law of the LORD, 27 and his acts from first to last are recorded in the annals of the kings of Israel and Judah.

36 THE people of the land took Josiah's son Jehoahaz and made him king at Jerusalem in place of his father. 2 He was twenty-three years old when he came to the throne, and he reigned in Jerusalem for three months. 3 Then Necho king of Egypt removed him from the throne in Jerusalem and imposed on the land an indemnity of a hundred talents of silver and one talent of gold. 4 He made Jehoahaz's brother Eliakim king over Judah and Jerusalem in his place, and changed his name to Jehoiakim. He carried away his brother Jehoahaz to Egypt.

5 Jehoiakim was twenty-five years old when he came to the throne, and he reigned in Jerusalem for eleven years. He did what was wrong in the eyes of the LORD his God. 6 King Nebuchadnezzar of Babylon launched an attack against him, put him in bronze fetters, and took him to Babylon. 7 Nebuchadnezzar also removed to Babylon some of the vessels of the house of the LORD and put them into his own palace there. 8 The other events of Jehoiakim's reign, including the abominations he committed, and everything of which he was held guilty, are recorded in the annals of the kings of Israel and Judah. His son Jehoiachin succeeded him.

9 Jehoiachin was eight years old when he came to the throne, and he reigned in Jerusalem for three months and ten days. He did what was wrong in the eyes of the LORD. 10 At the turn of the year King Nebuchadnezzar sent and brought him to Babylon, together with the choicest vessels of the house of the LORD, and made his father's brother Zedekiah king over Judah and Jerusalem.

11 Zedekiah was twenty-one years old when he came to the throne, and he reigned in Jerusalem for eleven years. 12 He did what was wrong in the eyes of the LORD his God; he did not defer to the guidance of the prophet Jeremiah, the spokesman of the LORD. 13 He also rebelled against King Nebuchadnezzar, who had laid on him a solemn oath of allegiance. He was stubborn and obstinate and refused to return to the LORD the God of Israel. 14 All the chiefs of Judah and the priests and the people became more and more unfaithful, following all the abominable practices of the other nations; and they defiled the house of the LORD which he had hallowed in Jerusalem.

15 The LORD God of their forefathers had warned them time and again through his messengers, for he took pity on his people and on his dwelling-place; 16 but they never ceased to deride his messengers, scorn his words, and scoff at his prophets, until the anger of the LORD burst out against his people and could not be appeased. 17 He brought against them the king of the Chaldaeans, who put their young men to the sword in the sanctuary and spared neither young man nor maiden, neither the old nor the weak; God gave them all into his power.

18 Nebuchadnezzar took all the vessels of the house of God, great and small, and the treasures of the house of the LORD and of the king and his officers — all these he took to Babylon. 19 They set fire to the house of God, razed to the ground the city wall of Jerusalem, and burnt down all its stately mansions and all the cherished possessions in them until everything was destroyed. 20 Those who escaped the sword he carried captive to Babylon, and they became slaves to him and his sons until the sovereignty passed to the Persians, 21 while the land of Israel ran the full term of its

36:1–4 Cp. 2 Kgs. 23:30–34.   36:9–10 Cp. 2 Kgs. 24:8–17.
36:10 father's brother: so Gk; Heb. brother.   36:14 Judah and: so Gk; Heb. omits.   36:17–20 Cp. 2 Kgs. 25:1–17.

26 The rest of the chronicle of Josiah, his pious deeds in regard to what is written in the law of the LORD, and his acts, first and last, can be found written in the book of the kings of Israel and Judah.

36 The people of the land took Jehoahaz, son of Josiah, and made him king in Jerusalem in his father's stead.

2 Jehoahaz was twenty-three years old when he became king, and he reigned three months in Jerusalem. 3 The king of Egypt deposed him in Jerusalem and fined the land one hundred talents of silver and a talent of gold. 4 Then the king of Egypt made his brother Eliakim king over Judah and Jerusalem, and changed his name to Jehoiakim. Neco took his brother Jehoahaz away and brought him to Egypt.

5 Jehoiakim was twenty-five years old when he became king, and he reigned eleven years in Jerusalem. He did evil in the sight of the LORD, his God. 6 Nebuchadnezzar, king of Babylon, came up against him and bound him with chains to take him to Babylon. 7 Nebuchadnezzar also carried away to Babylon some of the vessels of the house of the LORD and put them in his palace in Babylon. 8 The rest of the acts of Jehoiakim, the abominable things that he did, and what therefore happened to him, can be found written in the book of the kings of Israel and Judah. His son Jehoiachin succeeded him as king.

9 Jehoiachin was eighteen years old when he became king, and he reigned three months [and ten days] in Jerusalem. He did evil in the sight of the LORD. 10 At the turn of the year, King Nebuchadnezzar sent for him and had him brought to Babylon, along with precious vessels from the temple of the LORD. He made his brother Zedekiah king over Judah and Jerusalem.

11 Zedekiah was twenty-one years old when he became king, and he reigned eleven years in Jerusalem. 12 He did evil in the sight of the LORD, his God, and he did not humble himself before the prophet Jeremiah, who spoke the word of the Lord. 13 He also rebelled against King Nebuchadnezzar, who had made him swear by God. He became stiff-necked and hardened his heart rather than return to the LORD, the God of Israel. 14 Likewise all the princes of Judah, the priests and the people added infidelity to infidelity, practicing all the abominations of the nations and polluting the LORD's temple which he had consecrated in Jerusalem. 15 Early and often did the LORD, the God of their fathers, send his messengers to them, for he had compassion on his people and his dwelling place. 16 But they mocked the messengers of God, despised his warnings, and scoffed at his prophets, until the anger of the LORD against his people was so inflamed that there was no remedy. 17 Then he brought up against them the king of the Chaldeans, who slew their young men in their own sanctuary building, sparing neither young man nor maiden, neither the aged nor the decrepit; he delivered all of them over into his grip. 18 All the utensils of the house of God, the large and the small, and the treasures of the LORD's house and of the king and his princes, all these he brought to Babylon. 19 They burnt the house of God, tore down the walls of Jerusalem, set all its palaces afire, and destroyed all its precious objects. 20 Those who escaped the sword he carried captive to Babylon, where they became his and his sons' servants until the kingdom of the Persians came to power. 21 All this was to fulfill the

26 The rest of the history of Josiah, his deeds of faithful love conforming to what is prescribed in the Law of Yahweh, 27 his history from first to last, are recorded in the Book of the Kings of Israel and Judah.

36 The people of the land then took Jehoahaz son of Josiah and proclaimed him king of Jerusalem in succession to his father. 2 Jehoahaz was twenty-three years old when he came to the throne, and he reigned for three months in Jerusalem. 3 The king of Egypt deposed him in Jerusalem and imposed a levy of a hundred talents of silver and one talent of gold on the country. 4 The king of Egypt then made his brother Eliakim king of Judah and Jerusalem, and changed his name to Jehoiakim. Carrying off his brother Jehoahaz, Necho took him to Egypt.

5 Jehoiakim was twenty-five years old when he came to the throne, and he reigned for eleven years in Jerusalem. He did what is displeasing to Yahweh his God. 6 Nebuchadnezzar king of Babylon attacked him, loaded him with chains and took him to Babylon. 7 To Babylon Nebuchadnezzar also took some of the objects belonging to the Temple of Yahweh and put them in his palace in Babylon. 8 The rest of the history of Jehoiakim, the shameful things he did and what happened to him in consequence, these are recorded in the Book of the Kings of Israel and Judah. His son Jehoiachin succeeded him.

9 Jehoiachin was eighteen years old when he came to the throne, and he reigned for three months and ten days in Jerusalem. He did what is displeasing to Yahweh. 10 At the turn of the year, King Nebuchadnezzar sent for him and had him taken to Babylon, with the valuables belonging to the Temple of Yahweh, and made his brother Zedekiah king of Judah and Jerusalem.

11 Zedekiah was twenty-one years old when he came to the throne, and he reigned for eleven years in Jerusalem. 12 He did what is displeasing to Yahweh his God. He did not listen humbly to the prophet Jeremiah who spoke for Yahweh. 13 Furthermore, he rebelled against King Nebuchadnezzar who had made him swear allegiance to him by God. He became stubborn, and obstinately refused to return to Yahweh, God of Israel. 14 Furthermore, all the leaders of Judah, the priests and the people too, added infidelity to infidelity, copying all the shameful practices of the nations and defiling the Temple of Yahweh which he himself had consecrated in Jerusalem. 15 Yahweh, God of their ancestors, continuously sent them word through his messengers because he felt sorry for his people and his dwelling, 16 but they ridiculed the messengers of God, they despised his words, they laughed at his prophets, until Yahweh's wrath with his people became so fierce that there was no further remedy.

17 So against them he summoned the king of the Chaldaeans and he put their young men to the sword within the very building of their Temple, not sparing young man or girl, or the old and infirm; he put them all at his mercy. 18 All the things belonging to the Temple of God, whether large or small, the treasures of the Temple of Yahweh, the treasures of the king and his officials, everything he took to Babylon. 19 He burned down the temple of God, demolished the walls of Jerusalem, burned all its palaces to the ground and destroyed everything of value in it. 20 And those who had escaped the sword he deported to Babylon, where they were enslaved by him and his descendants until the rise of the kingdom of Persia, 21 to fulfil Yahweh's prophecy through

NEW REVISED STANDARD VERSION

the word of the LORD by the mouth of Jeremiah, until the land had made up for its sabbaths. All the days that it lay desolate it kept sabbath, to fulfill seventy years.

22 In the first year of King Cyrus of Persia, in fulfillment of the word of the LORD spoken by Jeremiah, the LORD stirred up the spirit of King Cyrus of Persia so that he sent a herald throughout all his kingdom and also declared in a written edict: 23 "Thus says King Cyrus of Persia: The LORD, the God of heaven, has given me all the kingdoms of the earth, and he has charged me to build him a house at Jerusalem, which is in Judah. Whoever is among you of all his people, may the LORD his God be with him! Let him go up."

REVISED ENGLISH BIBLE

sabbaths. All the time that it lay desolate it kept the sabbath rest, to complete seventy years in fulfilment of the word of the LORD by the prophet Jeremiah.

22 In the first year of King Cyrus of Persia, the LORD, to fulfil his word spoken through Jeremiah, inspired the king to issue throughout his kingdom the following proclamation, which he also put in writing:

23 The decree of King Cyrus of Persia: The LORD the God of heaven has given me all the kingdoms of the earth, and he himself has charged me to build him a house at Jerusalem in Judah. Whoever among you belongs to his people, may the LORD his God be with him, and let him go up.

36:22–23 *Cp. Ezra 1:1–3.*   36:23 **be:** *prob. rdg, cp. Ezra 1:3; Heb. omits.*

NEW AMERICAN BIBLE

NEW JERUSALEM BIBLE

word of the LORD spoken by Jeremiah: "Until the land has retrieved its lost sabbaths, during all the time it lies waste it shall have rest while seventy years are fulfilled."

22 In the first year of Cyrus, king of Persia, in order to fulfill the word of the LORD spoken by Jeremiah, the LORD inspired King Cyrus of Persia to issue this proclamation throughout his kingdom, both by word of mouth and in writing: 23 "Thus says Cyrus, king of Persia: 'All the kingdoms of the earth the LORD, the God of heaven, has given to me, and he has also charged me to build him a house in Jerusalem, which is in Judah. Whoever, therefore, among you belongs to any part of his people, let him go up, and may his God be with him!' "

Jeremiah: *Until the country has paid off its Sabbaths, it will lie fallow for all the days of its desolation—until the seventy years are complete.* [b]

22 In the first year of Cyrus king of Persia—to fulfil the word of Yahweh through Jeremiah—Yahweh roused the spirit of Cyrus king of Persia to issue a proclamation and to have it publicly displayed throughout his kingdom: 23 'Cyrus king of Persia says this, "Yahweh, the God of Heaven, has given me all the kingdoms of the earth and has appointed me to build him a Temple in Jerusalem, which is in Judah. Whoever there is among you of all his people, may his God be with him! Let him go up." '

[b] 36 A combination of Lv 26:34–35 and Jr 25:11; 29:10.

THE BOOK OF

Ezra

Ezra

1 In the first year of King Cyrus of Persia, in order that the word of the LORD by the mouth of Jeremiah might be accomplished, the LORD stirred up the spirit of King Cyrus of Persia so that he sent a herald throughout all his kingdom, and also in a written edict declared:
2 "Thus says King Cyrus of Persia: The LORD, the God of heaven, has given me all the kingdoms of the earth, and he has charged me to build him a house at Jerusalem in Judah. 3 Any of those among you who are of his people — may their God be with them! — are now permitted to go up to Jerusalem in Judah, and rebuild the house of the LORD, the God of Israel — he is the God who is in Jerusalem; 4 and let all survivors, in whatever place they reside, be assisted by the people of their place with silver and gold, with goods and with animals, besides freewill offerings for the house of God in Jerusalem."

5 The heads of the families of Judah and Benjamin, and the priests and the Levites — everyone whose spirit God had stirred — got ready to go up and rebuild the house of the LORD in Jerusalem. 6 All their neighbors aided them with silver vessels, with gold, with goods, with animals, and with valuable gifts, besides all that was freely offered. 7 King Cyrus himself brought out the vessels of the house of the LORD that Nebuchadnezzar had carried away from Jerusalem and placed in the house of his gods. 8 King Cyrus of Persia had them released into the charge of Mithredath the treasurer, who counted them out to Sheshbazzar the prince of Judah. 9 And this was the inventory: gold basins, thirty; silver basins, one thousand; knives, *a* twenty-nine; 10 gold bowls, thirty; other silver bowls, four hundred ten; other vessels, one thousand; 11 the total of the gold and silver vessels was five thousand four hundred. All these Sheshbazzar brought up, when the exiles were brought up from Babylonia to Jerusalem.

2 Now these were the people of the province who came from those captive exiles whom King Nebuchadnezzar of Babylon had carried captive to Babylonia; they returned to Jerusalem and Judah, all to their own towns. 2 They came with Zerubbabel, Jeshua, Nehemiah, Seraiah, Reelaiah, Mordecai, Bilshan, Mispar, Bigvai, Rehum, and Baanah.
The number of the Israelite people: 3 the descendants of Parosh, two thousand one hundred seventy-two. 4 Of Shephatiah, three hundred seventy-two. 5 Of Arah, seven hundred seventy-five. 6 Of Pahath-moab, namely the descendants of Jeshua and Joab, two thousand eight hundred twelve. 7 Of Elam, one thousand two hundred fifty-four. 8 Of Zattu, nine hundred forty-five. 9 Of Zaccai, seven hundred sixty. 10 Of Bani, six hundred forty-two. 11 Of Bebai, six hundred twenty-three. 12 Of Azgad, one thousand two hundred twenty-two. 13 Of Adonikam, six hundred sixty-six. 14 Of Bigvai, two thousand fifty-six. 15 Of Adin, four hundred fifty-four. 16 Of Ater, namely of Hezekiah, ninety-eight. 17 Of Bezai, three hundred twenty-three. 18 Of Jorah, one hundred twelve. 19 Of Hashum, two hundred twenty-

1 IN the first year of King Cyrus of Persia the LORD, to fulfil his word spoken through Jeremiah, inspired the king to issue throughout his kingdom the following proclamation, which he also put in writing:
2 The decree of King Cyrus of Persia.
The LORD the God of the heavens has given me all the kingdoms of the earth, and he himself has charged me to build him a house at Jerusalem in Judah. 3 Whoever among you belongs to his people, may his God be with him; and let him go up to Jerusalem in Judah, and build the house of the LORD the God of Israel, the God who is in Jerusalem. 4 Let every Jew left among us, wherever he is settled throughout the country, be helped by his neighbours with silver and gold, goods and livestock, in addition to the voluntary offerings for the house of God in Jerusalem.

5 Thereupon the heads of families of Judah and Benjamin came forward, along with the priests and the Levites, all whom God had moved to go up and rebuild the house of the LORD in Jerusalem. 6 Their neighbours all supported them with gifts of every kind, silver and gold, goods and livestock and valuable gifts in abundance, in addition to everything given as a freewill-offering. 7 Moreover, King Cyrus brought out the vessels of the house of the LORD which Nebuchadnezzar had removed from Jerusalem and placed in the temple of his gods. 8 When King Cyrus of Persia brought them out he gave them into the charge of Mithredath the treasurer, who made an inventory of them for Sheshbazzar the ruler of Judah. 9 The list was as follows: thirty gold basins, a thousand silver basins, twenty-nine vessels of various kinds, 10 thirty gold dishes, four hundred and ten silver dishes of various types, and a thousand other vessels. 11 In all there were five thousand four hundred gold and silver vessels; and Sheshbazzar took them all up to Jerusalem, when the exiles were brought back there from Babylon.

2 Of the captives whom King Nebuchadnezzar of Babylon had taken into exile in Babylon, these were the people of the province who returned to Jerusalem and Judah, each to his own town. 2 They were led by Zerubbabel, Jeshua, Nehemiah, Seraiah, Reelaiah, Mordecai, Bilshan, Mispar, Bigvai, Rehum, and Baanah.
The number of the men of the Israelite nation: 3 the line of Parosh two thousand one hundred and seventy-two; 4 the line of Shephatiah three hundred and seventy-two; 5 the line of Arah seven hundred and seventy-five; 6 the line of Pahath-moab, namely the lines of Jeshua and Joab, two thousand eight hundred and twelve; 7 the line of Elam one thousand two hundred and fifty-four; 8 the line of Zattu nine hundred and forty-five; 9 the line of Zaccai seven hundred and sixty; 10 the line of Bani six hundred and forty-two; 11 the line of Bebai six hundred and twenty-three; 12 the line of Azgad one thousand two hundred and twenty-two; 13 the line of Adonikam six hundred and sixty-six; 14 the line of Bigvai two thousand and fifty-six; 15 the line of Adin four hundred and fifty-four; 16 the line of Ater, namely that of Hezekiah, ninety-eight; 17 the line of Bezai three hundred and twenty-three; 18 the line of Jorah one hundred and twelve; 19 the line of Hashum two hundred and twenty-

---

1:4,6 **goods:** *or* pack-animals.   1:6 **with gifts . . . silver:** *prob. rdg, cp. 1 Esd. 2:9; Heb.* with vessels of silver. **in abundance:** *prob. rdg, cp. 1 Esd. 2:9; Heb.* apart.   2:1–70 *Cp. Neh. 7:6–73.*
2:6 **and Joab:** *prob. rdg, cp. Neh. 7:11; Heb. omits* and.

a Vg: Meaning of Heb uncertain

THE BOOK OF
Ezra

1 In the first year of Cyrus, king of Persia, in order to fulfill the word of the LORD spoken by Jeremiah, the LORD inspired King Cyrus of Persia to issue this proclamation throughout his kingdom, both by word of mouth and in writing: ² "Thus says Cyrus, king of Persia: 'All the kingdoms of the earth the LORD, the God of heaven, has given to me, and he has also charged me to build him a house in Jerusalem, which is in Judah. ³ Whoever, therefore, among you belongs to any part of his people, let him go up, and may his God be with him! ⁴ Let everyone who has survived, in whatever place he may have dwelt, be assisted by the people of that place with silver, gold, goods, and cattle, together with free will offerings for the house of God in Jerusalem.' "

⁵ Then the family heads of Judah and Benjamin and the priests and Levites — everyone, that is, whom God had inspired to do so — prepared to go up to build the house of the LORD in Jerusalem. ⁶ All their neighbors gave them help in every way, with silver, gold, goods, and cattle, and with many precious gifts besides all their free-will offerings. ⁷ King Cyrus, too, had the utensils of the house of the LORD brought forth which Nebuchadnezzar had taken away from Jerusalem and placed in the house of his god. ⁸ Cyrus, king of Persia, had them brought forth by the treasurer Mithredath, and counted out to Sheshbazzar, the prince of Judah. ⁹ This was the inventory: sacks of goldware, thirty; sacks of silverware, one thousand and twenty-nine; ¹⁰ golden bowls, thirty; silver bowls, four hundred and ten; other ware, one thousand pieces. ¹¹ Total of the gold- and silverware: five thousand four hundred pieces. All these Sheshbazzar took with him when the exiles were brought back from Babylon to Jerusalem.

2 These are the inhabitants of the province who returned from the captivity of the exiles, whom Nebuchadnezzar, king of Babylon, had carried away to Babylon, and who came back to Jerusalem and Judah, each man in his own city ² (those who returned with Zerubbabel, Jeshua, Nehemiah, Seraiah, Reelaiah, Mordecai, Bilshan, Mispereth, Bigvai, Rehum, and Baanah):

The census of the men of Israel: ³ sons of Parosh, two thousand one hundred and seventy-two; ⁴ sons of Shephatiah, three hundred and seventy-two; ⁵ sons of Arah, seven hundred and seventy-five; ⁶ sons of Pahath-moab, who were sons of Jeshua and Joab, two thousand eight hundred and twelve; ⁷ sons of Elam, one thousand two hundred and fifty-four; ⁸ sons of Zattu, nine hundred and forty-five; ⁹ sons of Zaccai, seven hundred and sixty; ¹⁰ sons of Bani, six hundred and forty-two; ¹¹ sons of Bebai, six hundred and twenty-three; ¹² sons of Azgad, one thousand two hundred and twenty-two; ¹³ sons of Adonikam, six hundred and sixty-six; ¹⁴ sons of Bigvai, two thousand and fifty-six; ¹⁵ sons of Adin, four hundred and fifty-four; ¹⁶ sons of Ater, who were sons of Hezekiah, ninety-eight; ¹⁷ sons of Bezai, three hundred and twenty-three; ¹⁸ sons of Jorah, one hundred and twelve; ¹⁹ sons of Hashum, two hundred and

THE BOOK OF
Ezra

1 In the first year of Cyrus king of Persia — to fulfil the word of Yahweh spoken through Jeremiah[a] — Yahweh roused the spirit of Cyrus king of Persia to issue a proclamation and to have it publicly displayed throughout his kingdom:

² 'Cyrus king of Persia says this, "Yahweh, the God of heaven, has given me all the kingdoms of the earth and has appointed me to build him a Temple in Jerusalem, in Judah. ³ Whoever among you belongs to the full tally of his people, may his God be with him! Let him go up to Jerusalem, in Judah, and build the Temple of Yahweh, God of Israel, who is the God in Jerusalem. ⁴ And let each survivor, wherever he lives, be helped by the people of his locality with silver, gold, equipment and riding beasts, as well as voluntary offerings for the Temple of God which is in Jerusalem." '

⁵ Then the heads of families of Judah and of Benjamin, the priests and the Levites, in fact all whose spirit had been roused by God, prepared to go and rebuild the Temple of Yahweh in Jerusalem; ⁶ and all their neighbours gave them every kind of help: silver, gold, equipment, riding beasts and valuable presents, in addition to their voluntary offerings.

⁷ Furthermore, King Cyrus handed over the articles belonging to the Temple of Yahweh which Nebuchadnezzar had carried away from Jerusalem and put in the temple of his god. ⁸ Cyrus king of Persia handed them over to Mithredath the treasurer who checked them out to Sheshbazzar the prince of Judah. ⁹ The inventory was as follows: thirty gold dishes; one thousand silver dishes, twenty-nine repaired; ¹⁰ thirty gold bowls; a thousand silver bowls, four hundred and ten damaged; one thousand other articles. ¹¹ In all, five thousand four hundred articles of gold and silver. Sheshbazzar took all these with him when he led the exiles back from Babylon to Jerusalem.

2 These were the people of the province who returned[b] from the captivity of the Exile, those whom Nebuchadnezzar king of Babylon had deported to Babylon, and who returned to Jerusalem and Judah, each to his own town. ² They were the ones who arrived with Zerubbabel, Jeshua, Nehemiah, Seraiah, Reelaiah, Nahamani, Mordecai, Bilshan, Mispar, Bigvai, Rehum and Baanah.

The number of the men of the people of the country of Israel: ³ sons of Parosh, two thousand one hundred and seventy-two; ⁴ sons of Shephatiah, three hundred and seventy-two; ⁵ sons of Arah, seven hundred and seventy-five; ⁶ sons of Pahath-Moab, that is to say the sons of Jeshua and Joab, two thousand eight hundred and twelve; ⁷ sons of Elam, one thousand two hundred and fifty-four; ⁸ sons of Zattu, nine hundred and forty-five; ⁹ sons of Zaccai, seven hundred and sixty; ¹⁰ sons of Bani, six hundred and forty-two; ¹¹ sons of Bebai, six hundred and twenty-three; ¹² sons of Azgad, one thousand two hundred and twenty-two; ¹³ sons of Adonikam, six hundred and sixty-six; ¹⁴ sons of Bigvai, two thousand and fifty-six; ¹⁵ sons of Adin, four hundred and fifty-four; ¹⁶ sons of Ater, that is to say of Hezekiah, ninety-eight; ¹⁷ sons of Bezai, three hundred and twenty-three; ¹⁸ sons of Jorah, one hundred and twelve;

a 1 Jr 25:11–12; 29:10.   b 2 // Ne 7:6–72.

three. 20 Of Gibbar, ninety-five. 21 Of Bethlehem, one hundred twenty-three. 22 The people of Netophah, fifty-six. 23 Of Anathoth, one hundred twenty-eight. 24 The descendants of Azmaveth, forty-two. 25 Of Kiriatharim, Chephirah, and Beeroth, seven hundred forty-three. 26 Of Ramah and Geba, six hundred twenty-one. 27 The people of Michmas, one hundred twenty-two. 28 Of Bethel and Ai, two hundred twenty-three. 29 The descendants of Nebo, fifty-two. 30 Of Magbish, one hundred fifty-six. 31 Of the other Elam, one thousand two hundred fifty-four. 32 Of Harim, three hundred twenty. 33 Of Lod, Hadid, and Ono, seven hundred twenty-five. 34 Of Jericho, three hundred forty-five. 35 Of Senaah, three thousand six hundred thirty.

36 The priests: the descendants of Jedaiah, of the house of Jeshua, nine hundred seventy-three. 37 Of Immer, one thousand fifty-two. 38 Of Pashhur, one thousand two hundred forty-seven. 39 Of Harim, one thousand seventeen.

40 The Levites: the descendants of Jeshua and Kadmiel, of the descendants of Hodaviah, seventy-four. 41 The singers: the descendants of Asaph, one hundred twenty-eight. 42 The descendants of the gatekeepers: of Shallum, of Ater, of Talmon, of Akkub, of Hatita, and of Shobai, in all one hundred thirty-nine.

43 The temple servants: the descendants of Ziha, Hasupha, Tabbaoth, 44 Keros, Siaha, Padon, 45 Lebanah, Hagabah, Akkub, 46 Hagab, Shamlai, Hanan, 47 Giddel, Gahar, Reaiah, 48 Rezin, Nekoda, Gazzam, 49 Uzza, Paseah, Besai, 50 Asnah, Meunim, Nephisim, 51 Bakbuk, Hakupha, Harhur, 52 Bazluth, Mehida, Harsha, 53 Barkos, Sisera, Temah, 54 Neziah, and Hatipha.

55 The descendants of Solomon's servants: Sotai, Hassophereth, Peruda, 56 Jaalah, Darkon, Giddel, 57 Shephatiah, Hattil, Pochereth-hazzebaim, and Ami.

58 All the temple servants and the descendants of Solomon's servants were three hundred ninety-two.

59 The following were those who came up from Telmelah, Tel-harsha, Cherub, Addan, and Immer, though they could not prove their families or their descent, whether they belonged to Israel: 60 the descendants of Delaiah, Tobiah, and Nekoda, six hundred fifty-two. 61 Also, of the descendants of the priests: the descendants of Habaiah, Hakkoz, and Barzillai (who had married one of the daughters of Barzillai the Gileadite, and was called by their name). 62 These looked for their entries in the genealogical records, but they were not found there, and so they were excluded from the priesthood as unclean; 63 the governor told them that they were not to partake of the most holy food, until there should be a priest to consult Urim and Thummim.

64 The whole assembly together was forty-two thousand three hundred sixty, 65 besides their male and female

three; 20 the line of Gibbar ninety-five. 21 The men of Bethlehem one hundred and twenty-three; 22 the men of Netophah fifty-six; 23 the men of Anathoth one hundred and twenty-eight; 24 the men of Beth-azmoth forty-two; 25 the men of Kiriath-jearim, Kephirah, and Beeroth seven hundred and forty-three; 26 the men of Ramah and Geba six hundred and twenty-one; 27 the men of Michmas one hundred and twenty-two; 28 the men of Bethel and Ai two hundred and twenty-three; 29 the men of Nebo fifty-two; 30 the men of Magbish one hundred and fifty-six; 31 the men of the other Elam one thousand two hundred and fifty-four; 32 the men of Harim three hundred and twenty; 33 the men of Lod, Hadid, and Ono seven hundred and twenty-five; 34 the men of Jericho three hundred and forty-five; 35 the men of Senaah three thousand six hundred and thirty.

36 The priests: the line of Jedaiah, of the house of Jeshua, nine hundred and seventy-three; 37 the line of Immer one thousand and fifty-two; 38 the line of Pashhur one thousand two hundred and forty-seven; 39 the line of Harim one thousand and seventeen.

40 The Levites: the lines of Jeshua and Kadmiel, of the house of Hodaviah, seventy-four. 41 The singers: the line of Asaph one hundred and twenty-eight. 42 The guild of doorkeepers: the line of Shallum, the line of Ater, the line of Talmon, the line of Akkub, the line of Hatita, and the line of Shobai, one hundred and thirty-nine in all.

43 The temple servitors: the line of Ziha, the line of Hasupha, the line of Tabbaoth, 44 the line of Keros, the line of Siaha, the line of Padon, 45 the line of Lebanah, the line of Hagabah, the line of Akkub, 46 the line of Hagab, the line of Shamlai, the line of Hanan, 47 the line of Giddel, the line of Gahar, the line of Reaiah, 48 the line of Rezin, the line of Nekoda, the line of Gazzam, 49 the line of Uzza, the line of Paseah, the line of Besai, 50 the line of Asnah, the line of the Meunim, the line of the Nephusim, 51 the line of Bakbuk, the line of Hakupha, the line of Harhur, 52 the line of Bazluth, the line of Mehida, the line of Harsha, 53 the line of Barkos, the line of Sisera, the line of Temah, 54 the line of Neziah, and the line of Hatipha.

55 The descendants of Solomon's servants: the line of Sotai, the line of Hassophereth, the line of Peruda, 56 the line of Jaalah, the line of Darkon, the line of Giddel, 57 the line of Shephatiah, the line of Hattil, the line of Pocherethhazzebaim, and the line of Ami.

58 The temple servitors and the descendants of Solomon's servants amounted to three hundred and ninety-two in all.

59 The following returned from Tel-melah, Tel-harsha, Kerub, Addan, and Immer, but could not prove by their father's line or their descent that they were Israelites: 60 the line of Delaiah, the line of Tobiah, and the line of Nekoda, six hundred and fifty-two. 61 Also of the priests: the line of Hobaiah, the line of Hakkoz, and the line of Barzillai who had married a daughter of Barzillai the Gileadite and went by his name. 62 When these searched for their names among those enrolled in the genealogies, they could not be traced, and so they were deemed disqualified and debarred from officiating. 63 The governor forbade them to partake of the most sacred food until there should be a priest able to consult the Urim and Thummim.

64 The whole assembled people numbered forty-two thousand three hundred and sixty, 65 apart from their slaves,

---

2:21 **men:** *prob. rdg, cp. Neh. 7:26; Heb.* line. 2:24 **the men of Beth-azmoth:** *prob. rdg, cp. Neh. 7:28; Heb.* the line of Azmoth. 2:25 **the men of Kiriath-jearim:** *prob. rdg, cp. Neh. 7:29; Heb.* the line of Kiriath-arim. 2:26 **men:** *prob. rdg, cp. Neh. 7:30; Heb.* line. 2:29–35 **men:** *prob. rdg; Heb.* line. 2:46 **Shamlai:** *or* Shalmai *(cp. Neh. 7:48).*

twenty-three; 20 sons of Gibeon, ninety-five; 21 sons of Bethlehem, one hundred and twenty-three; 22 men of Netophah, fifty-six; 23 men of Anathoth, one hundred and twenty-eight; 24 men of Beth-azmaveth, forty-two; 25 men of Kiriath-jearim, Chephirah, and Beeroth, seven hundred and forty-three; 26 men of Ramah and Geba, six hundred and twenty-one; 27 men of Michmas, one hundred and twenty-two; 28 men of Bethel and Ai, two hundred and twenty-three; 29 sons of Nebo, fifty-two; 30 sons of Magbish, one hundred and fifty-six; 31 sons of the other Elam, one thousand two hundred and fifty-four; 32 sons of Harim, three hundred and twenty; 33 sons of Lod, Hadid, and Ono, seven hundred and twenty-five; 34 sons of Jericho, three hundred and forty-five; 35 sons of Senaah, three thousand six hundred and thirty.

36 The priests: sons of Jedaiah, who were of the house of Jeshua, nine hundred and seventy-three; 37 sons of Immer, one thousand and fifty-two; 38 sons of Pashhur, one thousand two hundred and forty-seven; 39 sons of Harim, one thousand and seventeen.

40 The Levites: sons of Jeshua, Kadmiel, Binnui, and Hodaviah, seventy-four.

41 The singers: sons of Asaph, one hundred and twenty-eight.

42 The gatekeepers: sons of Shallum, sons of Ater, sons of Talmon, sons of Akkub, sons of Hatita, sons of Shobai, one hundred and thirty-nine in all.

43 The temple slaves: sons of Ziha, sons of Hasupha, sons of Tabbaoth, 44 sons of Keros, sons of Siaha, sons of Padon, 45 sons of Lebanah, sons of Hagabah, sons of Akkub, 46 sons of Hagab, sons of Shamlai, sons of Hanan, 47 sons of Giddel, sons of Gahar, sons of Reaiah, 48 sons of Rezin, sons of Nekoda, sons of Gazzam, 49 sons of Uzza, sons of Paseah, sons of Besai, 50 sons of Asnah, sons of the Meunites, sons of the Nephusites, 51 sons of Bakbuk, sons of Hakupha, sons of Harhur, 52 sons of Bazluth, sons of Mehida, sons of Harsha, 53 sons of Barkos, sons of Sisera, sons of Temah, 54 sons of Neziah, sons of Hatipha.

55 Descendants of the slaves of Solomon: sons of Sotai, sons of Hassophereth, sons of Peruda, 56 sons of Jaalah, sons of Darkon, sons of Giddel, 57 sons of Shephatiah, sons of Hattil, sons of Pochereth-hazzebaim, sons of Ami. 58 The total of the temple slaves and the descendants of the slaves of Solomon was three hundred and ninety-two.

59 The following who returned from Telmelah, Telharsha, Cherub, Addan, and Immer were unable to prove that their ancestral houses and their descent were Israelite: 60 sons of Delaiah, sons of Tobiah, sons of Nekoda, six hundred and fifty-two. 61 Also, of the priests: sons of Habaiah, sons of Hakkoz, sons of Barzillai (he had married one of the daughters of Barzillai the Gileadite and became known by his name). 62 These men searched their family records, but their names could not be found written there; hence they were degraded from the priesthood, 63 and His Excellency ordered them not to partake of the most holy foods until there should be a priest bearing the Urim and Thummim.

64 The entire assembly taken together came to forty-two thousand three hundred and sixty, 65 not counting their male

19 sons of Hashum, two hundred and twenty-three; 20 sons of Gibbar, ninety-five; 21 sons of Bethlehem, one hundred and twenty-three; 22 men of Netophah, fifty-six; 23 men of Anathoth, one hundred and twenty-eight; 24 sons of Azmaveth, forty-two; 25 sons of Kiriath-Jearim, Chephirah and Beeroth, seven hundred and forty-three; 26 sons of Ramah and Geba, six hundred and twenty-one; 27 men of Michmas, one hundred and twenty-two; 28 men of Bethel and Ai, two hundred and twenty-three; 29 sons of Nebo, fifty-two; 30 of Magbish, one hundred and fifty-six; 31 sons of the other Elam, one thousand two hundred and fifty-four; 32 sons of Harim, three hundred and twenty; 33 sons of Lod, Hadid and Ono, seven hundred and twenty-five; 34 sons of Jericho, three hundred and forty-five; 35 sons of Senaah, three thousand six hundred and thirty.

36 The priests: sons of Jedaiah, of the House of Jeshua, nine hundred and seventy-three; 37 sons of Immer, one thousand and fifty-two; 38 sons of Pashhur, one thousand two hundred and forty-seven; 39 sons of Harim, one thousand and seventeen.

40 The Levites: sons of Jeshua and Kadmiel, of the line of Hodaviah, seventy-four.

41 The singers: sons of Asaph, one hundred and twenty-eight.

42 The sons of the gatekeepers: sons of Shallum, sons of Ater, sons of Talmon, sons of Akkub, sons of Hatita, sons of Shobai: in all, one hundred and thirty-nine.

43 The temple slaves: sons of Ziha, sons of Hasupha, sons of Tabbaoth, 44 sons of Keros, sons of Siaha, sons of Padon, 45 sons of Lebanah, sons of Hagabah, sons of Akkub, 46 sons of Hagab, sons of Shamlai, sons of Hanan, 47 sons of Giddel, sons of Gahar, sons of Reaiah, 48 sons of Rezin, sons of Nekoda, sons of Gazzam, 49 sons of Uzza, sons of Paseah, sons of Besai, 50 sons of Asnah, sons of the Meunites, sons of the Nephisites, 51 sons of Bakbuk, sons of Hakupha, sons of Harhur, 52 sons of Bazluth, sons of Mehida, sons of Harsha, 53 sons of Barkos, sons of Sisera, sons of Temah, 54 sons of Neziah, sons of Hatipha.

55 The sons of Solomon's slaves: sons of Sotai, sons of Hassophereth, sons of Peruda, 56 sons of Jaalah, sons of Darkon, sons of Giddel, 57 sons of Shephatiah, sons of Hattil, sons of Pochereth-ha-Zebaim, sons of Ami. 58 The total of the temple slaves and the sons of Solomon's slaves: three hundred and ninety-two.

59 The following, who came from Tel-Melah, Tel-Harsha, Cherub, Addan and Immer, could not prove that their families and ancestry were of Israelite origin: 60 the sons of Delaiah, the sons of Tobiah, the sons of Nekoda: six hundred and fifty-two. 61 And among the sons of the priests: the sons of Habaiah, the sons of Hakkoz, the sons of Barzillai—who had married one of the daughters of Barzillai the Gileadite, whose name he adopted. 62 These had looked for their entries in the official genealogies but were not to be found there, and were hence disqualified from the priesthood. 63 Consequently, His Excellency forbade them to eat any of the consecrated food until a priest appeared who could consult urim and thummim.

64 The whole assembly numbered forty-two thousand, three hundred and sixty people, 65 not counting their male

NEW REVISED STANDARD VERSION	REVISED ENGLISH BIBLE

servants, of whom there were seven thousand three hundred thirty-seven; and they had two hundred male and female singers. 66 They had seven hundred thirty-six horses, two hundred forty-five mules, 67 four hundred thirty-five camels, and six thousand seven hundred twenty donkeys.

68 As soon as they came to the house of the LORD in Jerusalem, some of the heads of families made freewill offerings for the house of God, to erect it on its site. 69 According to their resources they gave to the building fund sixty-one thousand darics of gold, five thousand minas of silver, and one hundred priestly robes.

70 The priests, the Levites, and some of the people lived in Jerusalem and its vicinity;*b* and the singers, the gatekeepers, and the temple servants lived in their towns, and all Israel in their towns.

3 When the seventh month came, and the Israelites were in the towns, the people gathered together in Jerusalem. 2 Then Jeshua son of Jozadak, with his fellow priests, and Zerubbabel son of Shealtiel with his kin set out to build the altar of the God of Israel, to offer burnt offerings on it, as prescribed in the law of Moses the man of God. 3 They set up the altar on its foundation, because they were in dread of the neighboring peoples, and they offered burnt offerings upon it to the LORD, morning and evening. 4 And they kept the festival of booths,*c* as prescribed, and offered the daily burnt offerings by number according to the ordinance, as required for each day, 5 and after that the regular burnt offerings, the offerings at the new moon and at all the sacred festivals of the LORD, and the offerings of everyone who made a freewill offering to the LORD. 6 From the first day of the seventh month they began to offer burnt offerings to the LORD. But the foundation of the temple of the LORD was not yet laid. 7 So they gave money to the masons and the carpenters, and food, drink, and oil to the Sidonians and the Tyrians to bring cedar trees from Lebanon to the sea, to Joppa, according to the grant that they had from King Cyrus of Persia.

8 In the second year after their arrival at the house of God at Jerusalem, in the second month, Zerubbabel son of Shealtiel and Jeshua son of Jozadak made a beginning, together with the rest of their people, the priests and the Levites and all who had come to Jerusalem from the captivity. They appointed the Levites, from twenty years and upward, to have the oversight of the work on the house of the LORD. 9 And Jeshua with his sons and his kin, and Kadmiel and his sons, Binnui and Hodaviah*d* along with the sons of Henadad, the Levites, their sons and kin, together took charge of the workers in the house of God.

10 When the builders laid the foundation of the temple of the LORD, the priests in their vestments were stationed to praise the LORD with trumpets, and the Levites, the sons of Asaph, with cymbals, according to the directions of King David of Israel; 11 and they sang responsively, praising and giving thanks to the LORD,

"For he is good,
for his steadfast love endures forever toward Israel."

And all the people responded with a great shout when they praised the LORD, because the foundation of the house of

male and female, of whom there were seven thousand three hundred and thirty-seven; and they had two hundred male and female singers. 66 Their horses numbered seven hundred and thirty-six, their mules two hundred and forty-five, 67 their camels four hundred and thirty-five, and their donkeys six thousand seven hundred and twenty.

68 On their arrival at the house of the LORD in Jerusalem, certain of the heads of families offered to rebuild the house of God on its original site. 69 According to their ability they gave to the treasury for the fabric a total of sixty-one thousand drachmas of gold, five thousand minas of silver, and one hundred priestly vestments.

70 The priests, the Levites, and some of the people stayed in Jerusalem and the neighbourhood; the singers, the door-keepers and the temple servitors, and all the rest of the Israelites, lived in their own towns.

3 WHEN the seventh month came, the Israelites now being settled in their towns, the people came together with one accord to Jerusalem, 2 and Jeshua son of Jozadak along with his fellow-priests, and Zerubbabel son of Shealtiel, with his colleagues, set to work to build the altar of the God of Israel, in order to offer on it whole-offerings as prescribed in the law of Moses, the man of God. 3 They put the altar in place first, because they lived in fear of the foreign population; and they offered on it whole-offerings to the LORD, both morning and evening offerings. 4 They kept the pilgrim-feast of Booths as decreed, and offered whole-offerings every day in the number prescribed for each day; 5 in addition to these, they made the regular whole-offerings and the offerings for sabbaths, for new moons, and for all the sacred seasons appointed by the LORD, and all voluntary offerings made to the LORD. 6 The presentation of whole-offerings began from the first day of the seventh month, although the foundations of the temple of the LORD had not yet been laid. 7 Money was contributed for the masons and carpenters; the Sidonians and the Tyrians were supplied with food and drink and oil for bringing cedar trees from the Lebanon to the roadstead at Joppa. This was done by authority of King Cyrus of Persia.

8 In the second month of the second year, after they came to the house of God in Jerusalem, Zerubbabel son of Shealtiel and Jeshua son of Jozadak began the work. They were aided by all their fellow-Israelites, the priests and the Levites and all who had returned to Jerusalem from captivity. Levites who were aged twenty years and upwards were appointed to supervise the work of the house of the LORD. 9 Jeshua, with his sons and his kinsmen Kadmiel, Binnui, and Hodaviah, together assumed control of those doing the work on the house of God.

10 When the builders had laid the foundation of the temple of the LORD, the priests in their robes took their places with their trumpets, and the Levites, the sons of Asaph, with cymbals, to praise the LORD in the manner prescribed by King David of Israel. 11 They chanted praises and thanksgiving to the LORD, singing, 'It is good to give thanks to the LORD, for his love towards Israel endures for ever.' The whole people raised a great shout of praise to the LORD because the foundation of the LORD's house had been laid.

2:70 **in ... neighbourhood:** *prob. rdg, cp. 1 Esd. 5:46; Heb. omits.*
temple servitors: *prob. rdg; Heb. adds in their towns.* 3:5 **for sabbaths:** *prob. rdg, cp. 1 Esd. 5:52; Heb. omits.* 3:9 **Binnui, and Hodaviah:** *prob. rdg; Heb. and his sons the line of Judah.*
house of God: *prob. rdg; Heb. adds the line of Henadad, their sons, and their kinsmen the Levites.* 3:11 **to give thanks to the LORD:** *prob. rdg, cp. Ps. 106:1; Heb. omits.*

---

b 1 Esdras 5.46: Heb lacks *lived in Jerusalem and its vicinity*
c Or *tabernacles*; Heb *succoth*   *d* Compare 2.40; Neh 7.43;
1 Esdras 5.58: Heb *sons of Judah*

and female slaves, who were seven thousand three hundred and thirty-seven. They also had two hundred male and female singers. 66 Their horses were seven hundred and thirty-six, their mules two hundred and forty-five, 67 their camels four hundred and thirty-five, their asses six thousand seven hundred and twenty.

68 When they arrived at the house of the LORD in Jerusalem, some of the family heads made free-will offerings for the house of God, to rebuild it in its place. 69 According to their means they contributed to the treasury for the temple service: sixty-one thousand drachmas of gold, five thousand minas of silver, and one hundred garments for the priests. 70 The priests, the Levites, and some of the common people took up residence in Jerusalem; but the singers, the gatekeepers, and the temple slaves dwelt in their cities. Thus all the Israelites dwelt in their cities.

3 Now when the seventh month came, after the Israelites had settled in their cities, the people gathered at Jerusalem as one man. 2 Then Jeshua, son of Jozadak, together with his brethren the priests, and Zerrubbabel, son of Shealtiel, together with his brethren, set about rebuilding the altar of the God of Israel in order to offer on it the holocausts prescribed in the law of Moses, the man of God. 3 Despite their fear of the peoples of the land, they replaced the altar on its foundations and offered holocausts to the LORD on it, both morning and evening. 4 They also kept the feast of Booths in the manner prescribed, and they offered the daily holocausts in the proper number required for each day. 5 Thereafter they offered the established holocaust, the sacrifices prescribed for the new moons and all the festivals sacred to the LORD, and those which anyone might offer as a free-will gift to the LORD. 6 From the first day of the seventh month they began to offer holocausts to the LORD, though the foundation of the temple of the LORD had not yet been laid.

7 Then they hired stonecutters and carpenters, and sent food and drink and oil to the Sidonians and Tyrians that they might ship cedar trees from the Lebanon to the port of Joppa, as Cyrus, king of Persia, had authorized. 8 In the year after their coming to the house of God in Jerusalem, in the second month, Zerubbabel, son of Shealtiel, and Jeshua, son of Jozadak, together with the rest of their brethren, the priests and Levites and all who had come from the captivity to Jerusalem, began by appointing the Levites twenty years of age and over to supervise the work on the house of the LORD. 9 Jeshua and his sons and brethren, with Kadmiel and Binnui, son of Henadad, and their sons and their brethren, the Levites, stood as one man to supervise those who were engaged in the work on the house of God. 10 When the builders had laid the foundation of the LORD's temple, the vested priests with the trumpets and the Levites, sons of Asaph, were stationed there with the cymbals to praise the LORD in the manner laid down by David, king of Israel. 11 They alternated in songs of praise and thanksgiving to the LORD, "for he is good, for his kindness to Israel endures forever"; and all the people raised a great shout of joy, praising the LORD because the foundation of the LORD's

and female slaves to the number of seven thousand three hundred and thirty-seven. They also had two hundred male and female singers. 66 Their horses numbered seven hundred and thirty-six, their mules two hundred and forty-five, 67 their camels four hundred and thirty-five and their donkeys six thousand seven hundred and twenty.

68 When they arrived at the Temple of Yahweh in Jerusalem, a certain number of heads of families made voluntary offerings for the Temple of God, for its rebuilding on its site. 69 In accordance with their means they gave sixty-one thousand gold drachmas, five thousand silver minas and one hundred priestly robes to the sacred treasury. 70 The priests, the Levites and some of the people settled in Jerusalem; the singers, the gatekeepers and the temple slaves in their appropriate towns; and all the other Israelites in their own towns.

3 When the seventh month came after the Israelites had been resettled in their towns, the people gathered as one person in Jerusalem. 2 Then Jeshua son of Jozadak, with his brother priests, and Zerubbabel son of Shealtiel, with his brothers, set about rebuilding the altar of the God of Israel, to offer burnt offerings on it as prescribed in the Law of Moses man of God. 3 They erected the altar on its old site, despite their fear of the people of the country, and on it they presented burnt offerings to Yahweh, burnt offerings morning and evening; 4 they celebrated the feast of Shelters as prescribed,c offering daily the number of burnt offerings required from day to day, 5 and in addition presented the continual burnt offerings prescribed for the Sabbaths, for the New Moons and for all the festivals sacred to Yahweh, as well as those voluntary offerings made by individuals to Yahweh. 6 From the first day of the seventh month they began presenting burnt offerings to Yahweh, though the foundations of the Temple of Yahweh had not yet been laid.

7 They also contributed money for the masons and carpenters, and food, drink and oil for the Sidonians and Tyrians for bringing cedar wood from Lebanon by sea to Jaffa, for which Cyrus king of Persia had given permission. 8 It was in the second month of the second year after their arrival at the Temple of God in Jerusalem that Zerubbabel son of Shealtiel and Jeshua son of Jozadak, with the rest of their brothers, the priests, the Levites and all the people who had returned to Jerusalem from captivity, began the work by appointing some of the Levites who were twenty years old or more to superintend the work on the Temple of Yahweh. 9 The Levites, Jeshua, his sons and his brothers, with Kadmiel, Binnui and his sons, the sons of Hodaviah, agreed to superintend the men working on the Temple of God. 10 When the builders had laid the foundations of the Temple of Yahweh, the priests in their robes stood forward with trumpets, and the Levites, the sons of Asaph, with cymbals, to praise Yahweh according to the ordinances of David king of Israel. 11 They chanted praise and thanksgiving to Yahweh because for Israel, they said, 'he is good, and everlasting in his faithful love.' Then all the people raised a mighty shout of praise to Yahweh, since the foundations of the Temple of Yahweh had now been laid.

c 3 Ex 23:14.

the LORD was laid. 12 But many of the priests and Levites and heads of families, old people who had seen the first house on its foundations, wept with a loud voice when they saw this house, though many shouted aloud for joy, 13 so that the people could not distinguish the sound of the joyful shout from the sound of the people's weeping, for the people shouted so loudly that the sound was heard far away.

4 When the adversaries of Judah and Benjamin heard that the returned exiles were building a temple to the LORD, the God of Israel, 2 they approached Zerubbabel and the heads of families and said to them, "Let us build with you, for we worship your God as you do, and we have been sacrificing to him ever since the days of King Esar-haddon of Assyria who brought us here." 3 But Zerubbabel, Jeshua, and the rest of the heads of families in Israel said to them, "You shall have no part with us in building a house to our God; but we alone will build to the LORD, the God of Israel, as King Cyrus of Persia has commanded us."

4 Then the people of the land discouraged the people of Judah, and made them afraid to build, 5 and they bribed officials to frustrate their plan throughout the reign of King Cyrus of Persia and until the reign of King Darius of Persia.

6 In the reign of Ahasuerus, in his accession year, they wrote an accusation against the inhabitants of Judah and Jerusalem.

7 And in the days of Artaxerxes, Bishlam and Mithredath and Tabeel and the rest of their associates wrote to King Artaxerxes of Persia; the letter was written in Aramaic and translated. *e* 8 Rehum the royal deputy and Shimshai the scribe wrote a letter against Jerusalem to King Artaxerxes as follows 9 (then Rehum the royal deputy, Shimshai the scribe, and the rest of their associates, the judges, the envoys, the officials, the Persians, the people of Erech, the Babylonians, the people of Susa, that is, the Elamites, 10 and the rest of the nations whom the great and noble Osnappar deported and settled in the cities of Samaria and in the rest of the province Beyond the River wrote — and now 11 this is a copy of the letter that they sent):

"To King Artaxerxes: Your servants, the people of the province Beyond the River, send greeting. And now 12 may it be known to the king that the Jews who came up from you to us have gone to Jerusalem. They are rebuilding that rebellious and wicked city; they are finishing the walls and repairing the foundations. 13 Now may it be known to the king that, if this city is rebuilt and the walls finished, they will not pay tribute, custom, or toll, and the royal revenue will be reduced. 14 Now because we share the salt of the palace and it is not fitting for us to witness the king's dishonor, therefore we send and inform the king, 15 so that a search may be made in the annals of your ancestors. You will discover in the annals that this is a rebellious city, hurtful to kings and provinces, and that sedition was stirred up in it from long ago. On that account this city was laid waste. 16 We make known to the king that, if this city is rebuilt and its walls finished, you will then have no possession in the province Beyond the River."

12 Many of the priests and Levites and heads of families, who were old enough to have seen the former house, wept and wailed aloud when they saw the foundation of this house laid, while many others shouted for joy at the tops of their voices. 13 The people could not distinguish the sound of the shout of joy from that of the weeping and wailing, so great was the shout which the people were raising, and the sound could be heard a long way off.

4 When those who were hostile to Judah and Benjamin heard that the returned exiles were building a temple to the LORD the God of Israel, 2 they approached Zerubbabel and Jeshua and the heads of families. 'Let us build with you,' they said, 'for like you we seek your God, and have sacrificed to him ever since the days of King Esarhaddon of Assyria who brought us here.' 3 But Zerubbabel and Jeshua and the rest of the heads of the Israelite families replied, 'It is not for you to share in building the house for our God; we alone are to build it for the LORD the God of Israel, as his majesty King Cyrus of Persia commanded us.'

4 Then the people of the land caused the Jews to lose heart and made them afraid to continue building; 5 and, in order to thwart the purpose of the Jews, those people bribed officials at court to act against them. This continued throughout the lifetime of King Cyrus of Persia and into the reign of King Darius.

6 At the beginning of the reign of Ahasuerus, the people of the land brought a charge in writing against the inhabitants of Judah and Jerusalem. 7 In the days of King Artaxerxes of Persia, Tabeel and all his colleagues, with the agreement of Mithredath, wrote to the king; the letter was written in Aramaic and translated. (The following text is in Aramaic.)

8 Rehum the high commissioner and Shimshai the secretary wrote a letter to King Artaxerxes concerning Jerusalem as follows:

9 From Rehum the High Commissioner, Shimshai the Secretary, and all their colleagues, the judges, the commissioners, the overseers and chief officers, the men of Erech and Babylon, and the Elamites in Susa, 10 and the other peoples whom the great and renowned Asnappar deported and settled in the city of Samaria and in the rest of the province of Beyond-Euphrates.

11 Here follows a copy of their letter:

To King Artaxerxes from his servants, the men of the province of Beyond-Euphrates.

12 Be it known to your majesty that the Jews who left you to come here have arrived in Jerusalem. They are rebuilding that rebellious and wicked city; they are restoring the walls and repairing the foundations of the temple. 13 Be it known to your majesty that, if their city is rebuilt and the walls are completed, they will pay neither general levy, nor poll tax, nor land tax, and in the end your royal house will suffer harm. 14 Now, because we eat the king's salt and it is not right that we should witness the king's dishonour, therefore we have sent to bring it to your majesty's notice, 15 in order that search may be made in the records left by your predecessors. You will discover by searching the records that this has been a rebellious city, harmful to the royal house and to the provinces, and that from earliest times sedition has been rife within its walls. For that reason it was laid in ruins. 16 We submit to your majesty that, if this city is rebuilt and its walls are completed, the result will be that you will be denied a footing in the province of Beyond-Euphrates.

---

e Heb adds *in Aramaic*, indicating that 4.8–6.18 is in Aramaic. Another interpretation is *The letter was written in the Aramaic script and set forth in the Aramaic language*

4:8 *The text in Aramaic continues to 6:18.*

house had been laid. 12 Many of the priests, Levites, and family heads, the old men who had seen the former house, cried out in sorrow as they watched the foundation of the present house being laid. Many others, however, lifted up their voices in shouts of joy, 13 and no one could distinguish the sound of the joyful shouting from the sound of those who were weeping; for the people raised a mighty clamor which was heard afar off.

4 When the enemies of Judah and Benjamin heard that the exiles were building a temple for the LORD, the God of Israel, 2 they approached Zerubbabel and the family heads and said to them, "Let us build with you, for we seek your God just as you do, and we have sacrificed to him since the days of Esarhaddon, king of Assyria, who had us brought here." 3 But Zerubbabel, Jeshua, and the rest of the family heads of Israel answered them, "It is not your responsibility to build with us a house for our God, but we alone must build it for the LORD, the God of Israel, as King Cyrus of Persia has commanded us." 4 Thereupon the people of the land set out to intimidate and dishearten the people of Judah so as to keep them from building. 5 They also suborned counselors to work against them and thwart their plans during the remaining years of Cyrus, king of Persia, and until the reign of Darius, king of Persia.

6 Also at the beginning of the reign of Ahasuerus they prepared a written accusation against the inhabitants of Judah and Jerusalem.

7 Again, in the time of Artaxerxes, Mithredath wrote in concert with Tabeel and the rest of his fellow officials to Artaxerxes, king of Persia. The document was written in Aramaic and was accompanied by a translation. [Aramaic:]

8 Then Rehum, the governor, and Shimshai, the scribe, wrote the following letter against Jerusalem to King Artaxerxes: 9 "Rehum, the governor, Shimshai, the scribe, and their fellow judges, officials, and agents from among the Persian, Urukian, Babylonian, Susian (that is, Elamite), 10 and the other peoples whom the great and illustrious Assurbanipal transported and settled in the city of Samaria and elsewhere in the province West-of-Euphrates, as follows. . . ." 11 This is a copy of the letter that they sent to him:

"To King Artaxerxes, your servants, the men of West-of-Euphrates, as follows: 12 Let it be known to the king that the Jews who came up from you to us have arrived at Jerusalem and are now rebuilding this rebellious and evil city. They are raising up its walls, and the foundations have already been laid. 13 Now let it be known to the king that if this city is rebuilt and its walls are raised up again, they will no longer pay taxes, tributes, or tolls; thus it can only result in harm to the throne. 14 Now, since we partake of the salt of the palace, we ought not simply to look on while the king is being dishonored. Therefore we have sent this message to inform you, O king, 15 so that inquiry may be made in the historical records of your fathers. In the historical records you can discover and verify that this city is a rebellious city which has proved fatal to kings and provinces, and that sedition has been fostered there since ancient times. For that reason this city was destroyed. 16 We inform you, O king, that if this city is rebuilt and its walls are raised up again, by that very fact you will no longer own any part of West-of-Euphrates."

12 Many of the older priests, Levites and heads of families, who had seen the first temple, wept very loudly when the foundations of this one were laid before their eyes, but many others shouted aloud for joy, 13 so that nobody could distinguish the noise of the joyful shout from the noise of the people's weeping; for the people shouted so loudly that the noise could be heard far away.

4 When the enemies of Judah and Benjamin heard that the exiles were building the Temple of Yahweh, God of Israel, 2 they came to Zerubbabel and Jeshua and the heads of families and said, 'Let us help you build, for we resort to your God as you do and we have been sacrificing to him since the time of Esarhaddon king of Assyria, who brought us here.' 3 Zerubbabel, Jeshua, and the other heads of Israelite families replied, 'It is out of the question that you should join us in building a Temple for our God. We shall build for Yahweh, God of Israel, on our own, as King Cyrus king of Persia has commanded us.' 4 The people of the country then set about demoralising the people of Judah and deterring them from building; 5 they also bribed counsellors against them to frustrate their purpose throughout the lifetime of Cyrus king of Persia right on into the reign of Darius king of Persia.

6 d In the reign of Xerxes, at the beginning of his reign, they drew up an accusation against the inhabitants of Judah and Jerusalem.

7 In the days of Artaxerxes, Mithredath, Tabeel and their other associates wrote to Artaxerxes king of Persia against Jerusalem; the text of the letter was written in Aramaic writing and dialect.

8 Then Rehum the governor and Shimshai the secretary wrote a letter to King Artaxerxes, denouncing Jerusalem as follows:

9 'From Rehum the governor and Shimshai the secretary and their other associates, the judges, the legates, the Persian officials, the people of Uruk, Babylon and Susa — that is, the Elamites — 10 and the other peoples whom the great and illustrious Ashurbanipal deported and settled in the towns of Samaria and in the rest of Transeuphrates.'

11 This is the text of the letter which they sent him:

'To King Artaxerxes, from your servants the people of Transeuphrates:

12 'May the king now please be informed that the Jews, who have come up from you to us, have arrived in Jerusalem and are rebuilding the rebellious and evil city; they have begun rebuilding the walls and are laying the foundations; 13 and now the king should be informed that once this city is rebuilt and the walls are restored, they will refuse to pay tribute, tax or toll, thus the king will incur a loss; 14 and now, because we eat the palace salt, it is not proper for us to see this affront offered to the king; we therefore send this information to the king 15 so that a search may be made in the archives of your ancestors: in which archives you will find and learn that this city is a rebellious city, the bane of kings and provinces, and that sedition has been stirred up there from ancient times; that is why this city was destroyed. 16 We inform the king that if this city is rebuilt and its walls are restored, you will soon have no territories left in Transeuphrates.'

4, 7: Aramaic: this word in the original text seems to be a note indicating a change of language from Hebrew to Aramaic, which in fact takes place here. The Aramaic section ends with Ezr 6, 18, but again in Ezr 7, 12–26 a royal letter is cited in Aramaic.

d 4 The passage 4:6–6:18 is written in Aramaic.

17 The king sent an answer: "To Rehum the royal deputy and Shimshai the scribe and the rest of their associates who live in Samaria and in the rest of the province Beyond the River, greeting. And now 18 the letter that you sent to us has been read in translation before me. 19 So I made a decree, and someone searched and discovered that this city has risen against kings from long ago, and that rebellion and sedition have been made in it. 20 Jerusalem has had mighty kings who ruled over the whole province Beyond the River, to whom tribute, custom, and toll were paid. 21 Therefore issue an order that these people be made to cease, and that this city not be rebuilt, until I make a decree. 22 Moreover, take care not to be slack in this matter; why should damage grow to the hurt of the king?"

23 Then when the copy of King Artaxerxes' letter was read before Rehum and the scribe Shimshai and their associates, they hurried to the Jews in Jerusalem and by force and power made them cease. 24 At that time the work on the house of God in Jerusalem stopped and was discontinued until the second year of the reign of King Darius of Persia.

5 Now the prophets, Haggai *f* and Zechariah son of Iddo, prophesied to the Jews who were in Judah and Jerusalem, in the name of the God of Israel who was over them. 2 Then Zerubbabel son of Shealtiel and Jeshua son of Jozadak set out to rebuild the house of God in Jerusalem; and with them were the prophets of God, helping them.

3 At the same time Tattenai the governor of the province Beyond the River and Shethar-bozenai and their associates came to them and spoke to them thus, "Who gave you a decree to build this house and to finish this structure?" 4 They *g* also asked them this, "What are the names of the men who are building this building?" 5 But the eye of their God was upon the elders of the Jews, and they did not stop them until a report reached Darius and then answer was returned by letter in reply to it.

6 The copy of the letter that Tattenai the governor of the province Beyond the River and Shethar-bozenai and his associates the envoys who were in the province Beyond the River sent to King Darius; 7 they sent him a report, in which was written as follows: "To Darius the king, all peace! 8 May it be known to the king that we went to the province of Judah, to the house of the great God. It is being built of hewn stone, and timber is laid in the walls; this work is being done diligently and prospers in their hands. 9 Then we spoke to those elders and asked them, 'Who gave you a decree to build this house and to finish this structure?' 10 We also asked them their names, for your information, so that we might write down the names of the men at their head. 11 This was their reply to us: 'We are the servants of the God of heaven and earth, and we are rebuilding the house that was built many years ago, which a great king of Israel built and finished. 12 But because our ancestors had angered the God of heaven, he gave them into the hand of King Nebuchadnezzar of Babylon, the Chaldean, who destroyed this house and carried away the people to Babylonia. 13 However, King Cyrus of Babylon, in the first year of his reign, made a decree that this house of God should be rebuilt.

17 The king sent this reply:

To Rehum the High Commissioner, Shimshai the Secretary, and all your colleagues resident in Samaria and in the rest of the province of Beyond-Euphrates.

Greeting.

18 The letter which you sent to me has now been translated and read in my presence. 19 I ordered search to be made and that city, it was discovered, has a long history of opposition to the royal house, and rebellion and sedition have been rife in it. 20 There have been powerful kings ruling in Jerusalem and exercising authority over the whole province of Beyond-Euphrates; and general levy, poll tax, and land tax have been paid to them. 21 Therefore, issue orders that these men must desist; this city is not to be rebuilt until a decree to that effect is issued by me. 22 See that you do not neglect your duty in this matter, lest more damage and harm result to the royal house.

23 When the copy of the letter from King Artaxerxes was read before Rehum the high commissioner, Shimshai the secretary, and their colleagues, they went at once to Jerusalem and forcibly compelled the Jews to stop work. 24 From then onwards the work on the house of God in Jerusalem ceased; it remained at a standstill till the second year of the reign of King Darius of Persia.

5 The prophets Haggai and Zechariah son of Iddo prophesied to the Jews in Judah and Jerusalem, rebuking them in the name of the God of Israel. 2 Then Zerubbabel son of Shealtiel and Jeshua son of Jozadak, with the prophets of God at their side to help them, began at once to rebuild the house of God in Jerusalem. 3 Immediately Tattenai, governor of the province of Beyond-Euphrates, Shethar-bozenai, and their colleagues came to them and asked, 'Who has given you authority to rebuild this house and complete its furnishings?' 4 They also asked for the names of the men engaged in the building. 5 But the elders of the Jews were under God's watchful eye, and they were not prevented from continuing the work, until such time as a report should reach Darius and an official reply should be returned.

6 Here follows a copy of the letter to King Darius sent by Tattenai, governor of the province of Beyond-Euphrates, Shethar-bozenai, and his colleagues, the inspectors in the province of Beyond-Euphrates. 7 This is the written report that they sent:

To King Darius.

All greetings.

8 Be it known to your majesty that we went to the province of Judah and found the house of the great God being rebuilt, with massive stones and beams set in the walls. The work was being done energetically and was making rapid headway under the direction of the elders. 9 We then enquired of them by whose authority they were building this house and completing the furnishings. 10 We also asked them for their names, so that we might provide for your information a list of those in charge. 11 Their reply was as follows: 'We are servants of the God of heaven and earth, and we are rebuilding the house first erected many years ago; it was built and completed by a great king of Israel. 12 But because our forefathers provoked the anger of the God of heaven, he delivered them into the power of the Chaldaean, King Nebuchadnezzar of Babylon. The house was demolished and the people carried away captive to Babylon.

13 'But King Cyrus of Babylon in the first year of his reign issued a decree that this house of God should be

17 The king sent this answer: "To Rehum, the governor, Shimshai, the scribe, and their fellow officials living in Samaria and elsewhere in the province West-of-Euphrates, greetings and the following: 18 The communication which you sent us has been read plainly in my presence. 19 When at my command inquiry was made, it was verified that from ancient times this city has risen up against kings and that rebellion and sedition have been fostered there. 20 Powerful kings were once in Jerusalem who ruled over all West-of-Euphrates, and taxes, tributes, and tolls were paid to them. 21 Give orders, therefore, that will stop the work of these men. This city may not be rebuilt until a further decree has been issued by me. 22 Take care that you do not neglect this matter, lest the evil grow to the detriment of the throne."

23 As soon as a copy of King Artaxerxes' letter had been read before Rehum, the governor, Shimshai, the scribe, and their fellow officials, they went in all haste to the Jews in Jerusalem and stopped their work by force of arms.

24 Thus it was that the work on the house of God in Jerusalem was halted. This inaction lasted until the second year of the reign of Darius, king of Persia.

5 Then the prophets Haggai and Zechariah, son of Iddo, began to prophesy to the Jews in Judah and Jerusalem in the name of the God of Israel. 2 Thereupon Zerubbabel, son of Shealtiel, and Jeshua, son of Jozadak, began again to build the house of God in Jerusalem, with the prophets of God giving them support. 3 At that time there came to them Tattenai, governor of West-of-Euphrates, and Shethar-bozenai, and their fellow officials, who asked of them: "Who issued the decree for you to build this house and raise this edifice? 4 What are the names of the men who are building this structure?" 5 But their God watched over the elders of the Jews so that they were not hindered, until a report could go to Darius and then a written order be sent back concerning this matter.

6 A copy of the letter sent to King Darius by Tattenai, governor of West-of-Euphrates, and Shethar-bozenai, and their fellow officials from West-of-Euphrates; 7 they sent him a report in which was written the following:

"To King Darius, all good wishes! 8 Let it be known to the king that we have visited the province of Judah and the house of the great God: it is being rebuilt of cut stone and the walls are being reinforced with timber; the work is being carried on diligently and is making good progress under their hands. 9 We then questioned the elders, addressing to them the following words: 'Who issued the decree for you to build this house and raise this edifice?' 10 We also asked them their names, to report them to you in a list of the men who are their leaders. 11 This was their answer to us: 'We are the servants of the God of heaven and earth, and we are rebuilding the house built here long years ago, which a great king of Israel built and finished. 12 But because our fathers provoked the wrath of the God of heaven, he delivered them into the power of the Chaldean, Nebuchadnezzar, king of Babylon, who destroyed this house and led the people captive to Babylon. 13 However, in the first year of Cyrus, king of Babylon, King Cyrus issued a decree for the rebuilding

17 The king sent this reply:

'To Rehum the governor, to Shimshai the secretary, and to their other associates resident in Samaria and elsewhere in Transeuphrates: Greetings!

18 'And now, the document which you sent us has been accurately translated for me, 19 and by my orders search has been made, and it has been found that this city has rebelled against the kings in the past and that revolt and sedition have been contrived in it; 20 and that powerful kings have reigned in Jerusalem, governing the whole of Transeuphrates and exacting tribute, tax and toll; 21 now give orders for these men to cease work; this city is not to be rebuilt until I give the order. 22 Beware of acting negligently in this matter. Why should the harm grow, to endanger the king?'

23 As soon as the text of King Artaxerxes' document had been read to Rehum the governor, Shimshai the secretary and their associates, they hurried to the Jews in Jerusalem and stopped their work by force of arms.

24 Work on the Temple of God in Jerusalem then ceased, and was discontinued until the second year of the reign of Darius King of Persia.

5 When the prophets Haggai and Zechariah son of Iddo prophesied to the Jews who were in Judah and Jerusalem in the name of the God of Israel who was over them, 2 Zerubbabel son of Shealtiel and Jeshua son of Jozadak began rebuilding the Temple of God in Jerusalem; with them were the prophets of God, supporting them.

3 It was then that Tattenai governor of Transeuphrates, Shethar-Bozenai and their associates came to them and asked, 'Who gave you the order to rebuild this Temple and complete this structure? 4 What are the names of the men putting up this building?' 5 But the eyes of their God were watching over the elders of the Jews, so they were not forced to stop until a report could reach Darius and an official reply about the matter could be received from him.

6 A copy of the letter which Tattenai, governor of Transeuphrates, Shethar-Bozenai and his associates, the officials in Transeuphrates, sent to King Darius. 7 They sent him a report which ran as follows:

'To King Darius, hearty greetings!

8 'The king should be informed that we went to the province of Judah, to the Temple of the great God, which is being rebuilt with large stones; beams are being embedded in the walls; the work is being carried out energetically and is making good progress. 9 Questioning these elders, we asked them, "Who gave you permission to rebuild this Temple and complete this structure?" 10 We also asked them their names, to inform you, so that we could record the names of the men who were their leaders.

11 'They gave us the following answer, "We are the servants of the God of heaven and earth; we are rebuilding the Temple built many years ago, which a great king of Israel had built and completed. 12 But because our ancestors angered the God of heaven, he handed them over to Nebuchadnezzar the Chaldaean king of Babylon who destroyed this Temple and deported the people to Babylon. 13 In the first year of Cyrus king of Babylon, however, King Cyrus issued an official order that this Temple of God should be rebuilt; 14 furthermore, those

NEW REVISED STANDARD VERSION

14 Moreover, the gold and silver vessels of the house of God, which Nebuchadnezzar had taken out of the temple in Jerusalem and had brought into the temple of Babylon, these King Cyrus took out of the temple of Babylon, and they were delivered to a man named Sheshbazzar, whom he had made governor. 15 He said to him, "Take these vessels; go and put them in the temple in Jerusalem, and let the house of God be rebuilt on its site." 16 Then this Sheshbazzar came and laid the foundations of the house of God in Jerusalem; and from that time until now it has been under construction, and it is not yet finished.' 17 And now, if it seems good to the king, have a search made in the royal archives there in Babylon, to see whether a decree was issued by King Cyrus for the rebuilding of this house of God in Jerusalem. Let the king send us his pleasure in this matter."

6 Then King Darius made a decree, and they searched the archives where the documents were stored in Babylon. 2 But it was in Ecbatana, the capital in the province of Media, that a scroll was found on which this was written: "A record. 3 In the first year of his reign, King Cyrus issued a decree: Concerning the house of God at Jerusalem, let the house be rebuilt, the place where sacrifices are offered and burnt offerings are brought;h its height shall be sixty cubits and its width sixty cubits, 4 with three courses of hewn stones and one course of timber; let the cost be paid from the royal treasury. 5 Moreover, let the gold and silver vessels of the house of God, which Nebuchadnezzar took out of the temple in Jerusalem and brought to Babylon, be restored and brought back to the temple in Jerusalem, each to its place; you shall put them in the house of God."

6 "Now you, Tattenai, governor of the province Beyond the River, Shethar-bozenai, and you, their associates, the envoys in the province Beyond the River, keep away; 7 let the work on this house of God alone; let the governor of the Jews and the elders of the Jews rebuild this house of God on its site. 8 Moreover I make a decree regarding what you shall do for these elders of the Jews for the rebuilding of this house of God: the cost is to be paid to these people, in full and without delay, from the royal revenue, the tribute of the province Beyond the River. 9 Whatever is needed — young bulls, rams, or sheep for burnt offerings to the God of heaven, wheat, salt, wine, or oil, as the priests in Jerusalem require — let that be given to them day by day without fail, 10 so that they may offer pleasing sacrifices to the God of heaven, and pray for the life of the king and his children. 11 Furthermore I decree that if anyone alters this edict, a beam shall be pulled out of the house of the perpetrator, who then shall be impaled on it. The house shall be made a dunghill. 12 May the God who has established his name there overthrow any king or people that shall put forth a hand to alter this, or to destroy this house of God in Jerusalem. I, Darius, make a decree; let it be done with all diligence."

13 Then, according to the word sent by King Darius, Tattenai, the governor of the province Beyond the River, Shethar-bozenai, and their associates did with all diligence what King Darius had ordered. 14 So the elders of the Jews

REVISED ENGLISH BIBLE

rebuilt. 14 He brought out from the temple in Babylon the gold and silver vessels of the house of God, which Nebuchadnezzar had taken from the temple in Jerusalem and put in the temple in Babylon, and he delivered them to a man named Sheshbazzar, whom he had appointed governor. 15 He said to him, "Take these vessels; go and restore them to the temple in Jerusalem, and let the house of God be rebuilt on its original site." 16 Then this Sheshbazzar came and laid the foundations of the house of God in Jerusalem; and from that time until now the rebuilding has continued, and is still not completed.'

17 Now, therefore, if it please your majesty, let search be made in the royal treasury in Babylon, to discover whether a decree was issued by King Cyrus for the rebuilding of the house of God in Jerusalem, and let the king convey to us his wishes in the matter.

6 King Darius ordered search to be made in the archives where treasures were deposited in Babylon, 2 and there was found in Ecbatana, in the royal residence in the province of Media, a scroll on which was written the following memorandum:

3 In the first year of his reign King Cyrus issued this decree concerning the house of God in Jerusalem: Let the house be rebuilt as a place where sacrifices are offered and fire-offerings brought. Its height is to be sixty cubits and its breadth sixty cubits, 4 with three courses of massive stones to one course of timber, the cost to be defrayed from the royal treasury. 5 Also the gold and silver vessels of the house of God, which Nebuchadnezzar carried away from the temple in Jerusalem and brought to Babylon, are to be returned; they are all to be taken back to the temple in Jerusalem, and restored each to its place in the house of God.

6 Then King Darius issued this instruction:

Now, Tattenai, governor of the province of Beyond-Euphrates, Shethar-bozenai, and your colleagues, the inspectors in the province of Beyond-Euphrates, you are to keep away from the place, 7 and to leave the governor of the Jews and their elders free to rebuild this house of God; let them rebuild it on its original site. 8 I also issue an order prescribing what you are to do for these elders of the Jews, so that the said house of God may be rebuilt. Their expenses are to be defrayed in full from the royal funds accruing from the taxes of the province of Beyond-Euphrates, so that the work may not be brought to a standstill.

9 Let there be provided for them daily without fail whatever they need, young bulls, rams, and lambs as whole-offerings for the God of heaven, and wheat, salt, wine, and oil, as the priests in Jerusalem require, 10 so that they may offer soothing sacrifices to the God of heaven, and pray for the life of the king and his sons. 11 Furthermore, I decree that whoever tampers with this edict will have a beam torn out of his house, and he will be fastened erect to it and flogged; in addition, his house is to be razed to the ground. 12 May the God who made that place a dwelling for his name overthrow any king or people that presumes to tamper with this edict or to destroy this house of God in Jerusalem.

I Darius have decreed it; let it be strictly obeyed.

13 Then Tattenai, governor of the province of Beyond-Euphrates, Shethar-bozenai, and their colleagues carried out to the letter the instructions which King Darius had sent them,

6:4 one: prob. rdg; cp. 1 Esd. 6:25; Aram. new.   6:6 Then . . . instruction: prob. rdg, cp. 1 Esd. 6:27; Aram. omits.

h Meaning of Aram uncertain

of this house of God. 14 Moreover, the gold and silver utensils of the house of God which Nebuchadnezzar had taken from the temple in Jerusalem and carried off to the temple in Babylon, King Cyrus ordered to be removed from the temple in Babylon and consigned to a certain Sheshbazzar, whom he named governor. 15 And he commanded him: Take these utensils and deposit them in the temple of Jerusalem, and let the house of God be rebuilt on its former site. 16 Then this same Sheshbazzar came and laid the foundations of the house of God in Jerusalem. Since that time the building has been going on, and it is not yet completed.' 17 Now, if it please the king, let a search be made in the royal archives of Babylon to discover whether a decree really was issued by King Cyrus for the rebuilding of this house of God in Jerusalem. And may the king's pleasure in this matter be communicated to us."

6 Thereupon King Darius issued an order to search the archives in which the Babylonian records were stored away; 2 and in Ecbatana, the stronghold in the province of Media, a scroll was found containing the following text: "Memorandum. 3 In the first year of King Cyrus, King Cyrus issued a decree: The house of God in Jerusalem. The house is to be rebuilt as a place for offering sacrifices and bringing burnt offerings. Its height is to be sixty cubits and its width sixty cubits. 4 It shall have three courses of cut stone for each one of timber. The costs are to be borne by the royal palace. 5 Also, the gold and silver utensils of the house of God which Nebuchadnezzar took from the temple of Jerusalem and brought to Babylon are to be sent back: to be returned to their place in the temple of Jerusalem and deposited in the house of God.

6 "Now, therefore, Tattenai, governor of West-of-Euphrates, and Shethar-bozenai, and you, their fellow officials in West-of-Euphrates, do not interfere in that place. 7 Let the governor and the elders of the Jews continue the work on that house of God; they are to rebuild it on its former site. 8 I also issue this decree concerning your dealing with these elders of the Jews in the rebuilding of that house of God: From the royal revenue, the taxes of West-of-Euphrates, let these men be repaid for their expenses, in full and without delay. 9 Whatever else is required — young bulls, rams, and lambs for holocausts to the God of heaven, wheat, salt, wine, and oil, according to the requirements of the priests who are in Jerusalem — is to be delivered to them day by day without fail, 10 that they may continue to offer sacrifices of pleasing odor to the God of heaven and pray for the life of the king and his sons. 11 I also issue this decree: If any man violates this edict, a beam is to be taken from his house, and he is to be lifted up and impaled on it; and his house is to be reduced to rubble for this offense. 12 And may the God who causes his name to dwell there overthrow every king or people who may undertake to alter this or to destroy this house of God in Jerusalem. I, Darius, have issued this decree; let it be carefully executed."

13 Then Tattenai, the governor of West-of-Euphrates, and Shethar-bozenai, and their fellow officials carried out fully the instructions King Darius had sent them. 14 The elders of

gold and silver articles belonging to the Temple of God, which Nebuchadnezzar had removed from the temple in Jerusalem and brought to the temple of Babylon, King Cyrus in turn removed from the temple of Babylon and handed back to a certain Sheshbazzar whom he had appointed governor. 15 He said to him, 'Take these articles; go and return them to the Temple which is in Jerusalem and let the Temple of God be rebuilt on its original site;' 16 this Sheshbazzar then came and laid the foundations of the Temple of God in Jerusalem, and it has been under construction ever since, and is not yet finished."

17 'Hence, if it please the king, let search be made in the royal treasuries in Babylon, to find out if it is true that an official order was issued by King Cyrus for this temple of God in Jerusalem to be rebuilt; and let the king's decision on this matter be sent to us.'

6 Then, on the order of King Darius, search was made in the archives deposited in the treasuries in Babylon 2 and a scroll was found in the fortress of Ecbatana, which ran as follows:

'Memorandum.

3 'In the first year of King Cyrus, King Cyrus issued this order:

"Temple of God in Jerusalem.

"The Temple is to be rebuilt as a place of offering sacrifice and its foundations retained. Its height is to be sixty cubits, its width sixty cubits, 4 with three layers of large stones and one layer of timber. The cost is to be met by the royal treasury. 5 Furthermore, the gold and silver articles belonging to the Temple of God which Nebuchadnezzar took from the Temple in Jerusalem and brought to Babylon are to be given back and returned to the temple in Jerusalem, each to its proper place, and deposited in the Temple of God."

6 'Hence, Tattenai governor of Transeuphrates, Shethar-Bozenai and your associates, the officials of Transeuphrates, keep away from there! 7 Leave the governor of the Jews and the elders of the Jews alone, to get on with their work on that Temple of God; they are permitted to rebuild that Temple of God on that site. 8 And herewith are my instructions as to how you will assist these elders of the Jews in the rebuilding of that Temple of God: the cost is to be paid in full to these men from the royal revenue, that is, from the taxes of Transeuphrates, and without interruption. 9 And whatever is required — young bulls, rams, lambs for burnt offerings to the God of heaven, wheat, salt, wine, oil, as the priests in Jerusalem request — is to be given them day by day without fail, 10 so that they may offer sacrifices acceptable to the God of heaven and pray for the life of the king and his sons. 11 Furthermore I have issued an instruction that if anyone disobeys this order, a beam is to be torn from his house, he is to be impaled on it and his house is to be reduced to a rubbish-heap for his offence; 12 and may the God who has caused his name to live there overthrow the king of any people who dares to defy this and destroy that Temple of God in Jerusalem! I, Darius, have issued this order. Let it be punctiliously obeyed!'

13 Tattenai governor of Transeuphrates, Shethar-Bozenai and their associates punctiliously obeyed the instructions sent by King Darius; 14 and the elders of the Jews made

NEW REVISED STANDARD VERSION	REVISED ENGLISH BIBLE

built and prospered, through the prophesying of the prophet Haggai and Zechariah son of Iddo. They finished their building by command of the God of Israel and by decree of Cyrus, Darius, and King Artaxerxes of Persia; 15 and this house was finished on the third day of the month of Adar, in the sixth year of the reign of King Darius.

16 The people of Israel, the priests and the Levites, and the rest of the returned exiles, celebrated the dedication of this house of God with joy. 17 They offered at the dedication of this house of God one hundred bulls, two hundred rams, four hundred lambs, and as a sin offering for all Israel, twelve male goats, according to the number of the tribes of Israel. 18 Then they set the priests in their divisions and the Levites in their courses for the service of God at Jerusalem, as it is written in the book of Moses.

19 On the fourteenth day of the first month the returned exiles kept the passover. 20 For both the priests and the Levites had purified themselves; all of them were clean. So they killed the passover lamb for all the returned exiles, for their fellow priests, and for themselves. 21 It was eaten by the people of Israel who had returned from exile, and also by all who had joined them and separated themselves from the pollutions of the nations of the land to worship the LORD, the God of Israel. 22 With joy they celebrated the festival of unleavened bread seven days; for the LORD had made them joyful, and had turned the heart of the king of Assyria to them, so that he aided them in the work on the house of God, the God of Israel.

7 After this, in the reign of King Artaxerxes of Persia, Ezra son of Seraiah, son of Azariah, son of Hilkiah, 2 son of Shallum, son of Zadok, son of Ahitub, 3 son of Amariah, son of Azariah, son of Meraioth, 4 son of Zerahiah, son of Uzzi, son of Bukki, 5 son of Abishua, son of Phinehas, son of Eleazar, son of the chief priest Aaron — 6 this Ezra went up from Babylonia. He was a scribe skilled in the law of Moses that the LORD the God of Israel had given; and the king granted him all that he asked, for the hand of the LORD his God was upon him.

7 Some of the people of Israel, and some of the priests and Levites, the singers and gatekeepers, and the temple servants also went up to Jerusalem, in the seventh year of King Artaxerxes. 8 They came to Jerusalem in the fifth month, which was in the seventh year of the king. 9 On the first day of the first month the journey up from Babylon was begun, and on the first day of the fifth month he came to Jerusalem, for the gracious hand of his God was upon him. 10 For Ezra had set his heart to study the law of the LORD, and to do it, and to teach the statutes and ordinances in Israel.

11 This is a copy of the letter that King Artaxerxes gave to the priest Ezra, the scribe, a scholar of the text of the commandments of the LORD and his statutes for Israel: 12 "Artaxerxes, king of kings, to the priest Ezra, the scribe of the law of the God of heaven: Peace.*i* And now 13 I decree that any of the people of Israel or their priests or Levites in my kingdom who freely offers to go to Jerusalem may go with you. 14 For you are sent by the king and his seven counselors to make inquiries about Judah and Jerusalem according to the law of your God, which is in your hand, 15 and also to convey the silver and gold that the king and his counselors have freely offered to the God of Israel, whose dwelling is in Jerusalem, 16 with all the silver and

14 and the elders of the Jews went on with the rebuilding. Good progress was made with the sacred works, as the result of the prophecies of Haggai and Zechariah son of Iddo, and they finished the rebuilding as commanded by the God of Israel and according to the decrees of Cyrus and Darius and King Artaxerxes of Persia. 15 The house was completed on the third day of the month of Adar, in the sixth year of the reign of King Darius.

16 Then the Israelites, priests, Levites, and all the other exiles who had returned, celebrated the rededication of this house of God with great rejoicing. 17 At its rededication they offered one hundred bulls, two hundred rams, and four hundred lambs, and as a purification-offering for all Israel twelve he-goats, corresponding to the number of the tribes of Israel. 18 They re-established the priests in their groups and the Levites in their divisions for the service of God in Jerusalem, as prescribed in the book of Moses.

19 On the fourteenth day of the first month the returned exiles observed the Passover. 20 The priests and the Levites, one and all, had purified themselves; all of them were ritually clean, and they killed the Passover lamb for all the exiles who had returned, for their fellow-priests, and for themselves. 21 It was eaten by the Israelites who had returned from exile and by all who had held aloof from the peoples of the land and their uncleanness, and had sought the LORD the God of Israel. 22 They observed the pilgrim-feast of Unleavened Bread for seven days with rejoicing; for the LORD had given them cause for joy by changing the disposition of the Assyrian king towards them, so that he supported them in the work of the house of God, the God of Israel.

7 IT was after these events, in the reign of King Artaxerxes of Persia, that Ezra came. He was the son of Seraiah, son of Azariah, son of Hilkiah, 2 son of Shallum, son of Zadok, son of Ahitub, 3 son of Amariah, son of Azariah, son of Meraioth, 4 son of Zerahiah, son of Uzzi, son of Bukki, 5 son of Abishua, son of Phinehas, son of Eleazar, son of Aaron the chief priest. 6 Ezra had come up from Babylon; he was a scribe, expert in the law of Moses which the LORD the God of Israel had given them. The king granted him everything he requested, for the favour of the LORD his God was with him.

7 He was accompanied to Jerusalem by some Israelites, priests, Levites, temple singers, door-keepers, and temple servitors in the seventh year of King Artaxerxes. 8 They reached Jerusalem in the fifth month, in the seventh year of the king. 9 On the first day of the first month Ezra fixed the day for departure from Babylon, and on the first day of the fifth month he arrived at Jerusalem; the favour of God was with him, 10 for he had devoted himself to the study and observance of the law of the LORD and to teaching statute and ordinance in Israel.

11 This is a copy of the letter which King Artaxerxes had given to Ezra the priest and scribe, a scribe versed in questions concerning the commandments and the statutes of the LORD laid upon Israel:

12 Artaxerxes, King of Kings, to Ezra the priest and scribe learned in the law of the God of heaven.

This is my decision. 13 I hereby issue a decree that any of the people of Israel or of its priests or Levites in my kingdom who volunteer to go to Jerusalem may go with you. 14 You are sent by the king and his seven counsellors to consider the situation in Judah and Jerusalem with regard to the law of your God with which you are entrusted. 15 You are also to convey the silver and gold which the king and his counsellors have freely offered to the God of Israel whose dwelling is in Jerusalem, 16 together

---

the Jews continued to make progress in the building, supported by the message of the prophets, Haggai and Zechariah, son of Iddo. They finished the building according to the command of the God of Israel and the decrees of Cyrus and Darius [and of Artaxerxes, king of Persia]. 15 They completed this house on the third day of the month Adar, in the sixth year of the reign of King Darius. 16 The Israelites — priests, Levites, and the other returned exiles — celebrated the dedication of this house of God with joy. 17 For the dedication of this house of God, they offered one hundred bulls, two hundred rams, and four hundred lambs, together with twelve he-goats as a sin-offering for all Israel, in keeping with the number of the tribes of Israel. 18 Finally, they set up the priests in their classes and the Levites in their divisions for the service of God in Jerusalem, as is prescribed in the book of Moses.

19 The exiles kept the Passover on the fourteenth day of the first month. 20 The Levites, every one of whom had purified himself for the occasion, sacrificed the Passover for the rest of the exiles, for their brethren the priests, and for themselves. 21 The Israelites who had returned from the exile partook of it together with all those who had separated themselves from the uncleanness of the peoples of the land to join them in seeking the LORD, the God of Israel. 22 They joyfully kept the feast of Unleavened Bread for seven days, for the LORD had filled them with joy by making the king of Assyria favorable to them, so that he gave them help in their work on the house of God, the God of Israel.

7 After these events, during the reign of Artaxerxes, king of Persia, Ezra, son of Seraiah, son of Azariah, son of Hilkiah, 2 son of Shallum, son of Zadok, son of Ahitub, 3 son of Amariah, son of Azariah, son of Meraioth, 4 son of Zerahiah, son of Uzzi, son of Bukki, 5 son of Abishua, son of Phinehas, son of Eleazar, son of the high priest Aaron— 6 this Ezra came up from Babylon. He was a scribe, well-versed in the law of Moses which was given by the LORD, the God of Israel. Because the hand of the LORD, his God, was upon him, the king granted him all that he requested.

7 Some of the Israelites and some priests, Levites, singers, gatekeepers, and temple slaves also came up to Jerusalem in the seventh year of King Artaxerxes. 8 Ezra came to Jerusalem in the fifth month of that seventh year of the king. 9 On the first day of the first month he resolved on the journey up from Babylon, and on the first day of the fifth month he arrived at Jerusalem, for the favoring hand of his God was upon him. 10 Ezra had set his heart on the study and practice of the law of the LORD and on teaching statutes and ordinances in Israel.

11 This is a copy of the rescript which King Artaxerxes gave to Ezra the priest-scribe, the scribe of the text of the LORD's commandments and statutes for Israel:

12 "Artaxerxes, king of kings, to Ezra the priest, scribe of the law of the God of heaven (then, after greetings): 13 I have issued this decree, that anyone in my kingdom belonging to the people of Israel, its priests or Levites, who is minded to go up to Jerusalem with you, may do so. 14 You are the envoy from the king and his seven counselors to supervise Judah and Jerusalem in respect of the law of your God which is in your possession, 15 and to bring with you the silver and gold which the king and his counselors have freely contributed to the God of Israel, whose dwelling is in Jerusalem, 16 as well as all the silver and gold which you

good progress over their building, thanks to the prophetic activity of the prophet Haggai and Zechariah son of Iddo, completing the reconstruction in accordance with the command of the God of Israel and the order of Cyrus and of Darius. 15 This Temple was completed on the twenty-third day of the month of Adar, in the sixth year of the reign of King Darius. 16 The Israelites — the priests, the Levites and the remainder of the exiles — joyfully celebrated the dedication of this Temple of God; 17 for the dedication of this Temple of God they offered one hundred bulls, two hundred rams, four hundred lambs and, as a sin offering for all Israel, twelve he-goats, corresponding to the number of the tribes of Israel. 18 Then they installed the priests in their orders and the Levites in their positions for the ministry of the Temple of God in Jerusalem, as prescribed in the Book of Moses.

19 The exiles celebrated the Passover on the fourteenth day of the first month. 20 The Levites, as one man, had purified themselves; all were pure, so they sacrificed the Passover for all the exiles, for their brothers the priests and for themselves. 21 So the Israelites who had returned from exile and all those who had renounced the filthy practices of the people of the country to join them in resorting to Yahweh, God of Israel, ate the Passover. 22 For seven days they joyfully celebrated the feast of Unleavened Bread, for Yahweh had given them cause to rejoice, having moved the heart of the king of Assyria in their favour to support them in their work on the Temple of God, the God of Israel.

7 After these events, in the reign of Artaxerxes king of Persia, Ezra son of Seraiah, son of Azariah, son of Hilkiah, 2 son of Shallum, son of Zadok, son of Ahitub, 3 son of Amariah, son of Azariah, son of Meraioth, 4 son of Zerahiah, son of Uzzi, son of Bukki, 5 son of Abishua, son of Phinehas, son of Eleazar, son of the chief priest Aaron— 6 this Ezra came up from Babylon. He was a scribe versed in the Law of Moses, which Yahweh, God of Israel, had given. The king gave him everything that he asked for, since the hand of Yahweh his God was over him. 7 A number of Israelites, priests, Levites, singers, gatekeepers and temple slaves went up to Jerusalem in the seventh year of the reign of King Artaxerxes. 8 Ezra arrived in Jerusalem in the fifth month, in the seventh year of the king's reign; 9 for he had ordered the departure from Babylon on the first day of the first month, and he arrived in Jerusalem on the first day of the fifth month, since the kindly hand of his God was over him. 10 For Ezra had devoted himself to studying the Law of Yahweh so as to put into practice and teach its statutes and rulings.

11 This is the text of the document which King Artaxerxes gave to Ezra, the priest-scribe, a student of matters pertaining to Yahweh's commandments and statutes relating to Israel:

12 'Artaxerxes, king of kings, to the priest Ezra, Secretary of the Law of the God of heaven: greetings!

13 'Now here are my orders. All members of the people of Israel in my kingdom, including their priests and Levites, who freely choose to go to Jerusalem, may go with you, 14 for you are being sent by the king and his seven counsellors to investigate how the Law of your God, in which you are expert, is being applied in Judah and Jerusalem, 15 and to transport the silver and gold which the king and his counsellors have voluntarily offered to the God of Israel who resides in Jerusalem, 16 as well as all the silver and gold which you receive throughout the

NEW REVISED STANDARD VERSION

REVISED ENGLISH BIBLE

gold that you shall find in the whole province of Babylonia, and with the freewill offerings of the people and the priests, given willingly for the house of their God in Jerusalem. 17 With this money, then, you shall with all diligence buy bulls, rams, and lambs, and their grain offerings and their drink offerings, and you shall offer them on the altar of the house of your God in Jerusalem. 18 Whatever seems good to you and your colleagues to do with the rest of the silver and gold, you may do, according to the will of your God. 19 The vessels that have been given you for the service of the house of your God, you shall deliver before the God of Jerusalem. 20 And whatever else is required for the house of your God, which you are responsible for providing, you may provide out of the king's treasury.

21 "I, King Artaxerxes, decree to all the treasurers in the province Beyond the River: Whatever the priest Ezra, the scribe of the law of the God of heaven, requires of you, let it be done with all diligence, 22 up to one hundred talents of silver, one hundred cors of wheat, one hundred baths^j of wine, one hundred baths^j of oil, and unlimited salt. 23 Whatever is commanded by the God of heaven, let it be done with zeal for the house of the God of heaven, or wrath will come upon the realm of the king and his heirs. 24 We also notify you that it shall not be lawful to impose tribute, custom, or toll on any of the priests, the Levites, the singers, the doorkeepers, the temple servants, or other servants of this house of God.

25 "And you, Ezra, according to the God-given wisdom you possess, appoint magistrates and judges who may judge all the people in the province Beyond the River who know the laws of your God; and you shall teach those who do not know them. 26 All who will not obey the law of your God and the law of the king, let judgment be strictly executed on them, whether for death or for banishment or for confiscation of their goods or for imprisonment."

27 Blessed be the LORD, the God of our ancestors, who put such a thing as this into the heart of the king to glorify the house of the LORD in Jerusalem, 28 and who extended to me steadfast love before the king and his counselors, and before all the king's mighty officers. I took courage, for the hand of the LORD my God was upon me, and I gathered leaders from Israel to go up with me.

8 These are their family heads, and this is the genealogy of those who went up with me from Babylonia, in the reign of King Artaxerxes: 2 Of the descendants of Phinehas, Gershom. Of Ithamar, Daniel. Of David, Hattush, 3 of the descendants of Shecaniah. Of Parosh, Zechariah, with whom were registered one hundred fifty males. 4 Of the descendants of Pahath-moab, Eliehoenai son of Zerahiah, and with him two hundred males. 5 Of the descendants of Zattu,^k Shecaniah son of Jahaziel, and with him three hundred males. 6 Of the descendants of Adin, Ebed son of Jonathan, and with him fifty males. 7 Of the descendants of Elam, Jeshaiah son of Athaliah, and with him seventy males. 8 Of the descendants of Shephatiah, Zebadiah son of Michael, and with him eighty males. 9 Of the descendants of Joab, Obadiah son of Jehiel, and with him two hundred eighteen males. 10 Of the descendants of Bani,^l Shelomith son of Josiphiah, and with him one hundred sixty males.

with any silver and gold that you may find throughout the province of Babylon, and the voluntary offerings of the people and of the priests which they freely offer for the house of their God in Jerusalem. 17 In pursuance of this decree you are to expend the money solely on the purchase of bulls, rams, and lambs, and the proper grain-offerings and drink-offerings, to be offered on the altar in the house of your God in Jerusalem. 18 Further, should any silver and gold be left over, it may be put to such use as you and your colleagues think fit, according to the will of your God. 19 In the presence of the God of Jerusalem you are to hand over the vessels which have been given you for the service of the house of your God. 20 Any other expenses you may incur for the needs of the house of your God will be defrayed from the royal treasury.

21 I, King Artaxerxes, hereby issue an order to all treasurers in the province of Beyond-Euphrates, to supply exactly to Ezra the priest, a scribe learned in the law of the God of heaven, whatever he may request of you, 22 up to one hundred talents of silver, one hundred kor of wheat, one hundred bath of wine, one hundred bath of oil, and salt without a set limit. 23 Let all the commands of the God of heaven be diligently fulfilled for the house of the God of heaven; otherwise wrath may befall the realm of the king and his sons. 24 You are informed that you have no authority to impose a general levy, poll tax, or land tax on any of the priests, Levites, musicians, door-keepers, temple servitors, or other servants of this house of God.

25 You, Ezra, in accordance with the wisdom of your God with which you are entrusted, are to appoint arbitrators and judges to administer justice for all your people in the province of Beyond-Euphrates, all who acknowledge the laws of your God, and you with them are to instruct those who do not know those laws. 26 Whoever will not obey the law of your God and the law of the king, let judgement be rigorously executed on him, be it death, banishment, confiscation of property, or imprisonment. 27 Then Ezra the scribe said, 'Blessed is the LORD the God of our fathers who has put such a thing as this into the king's mind, to glorify the house of the LORD in Jerusalem, 28 and has made the king and his counsellors and all his high officers well disposed towards me!'

Encouraged by the help of the LORD my God, I gathered leading men out of Israel to go up with me. 1 These 8 are the heads of families, as registered, family by family, of those who went up with me from Babylon in the reign of King Artaxerxes: 2 of the line of Phinehas, Gershom; of the line of Ithamar, Daniel; of the line of David, Hattush 3 son of Shecaniah; of the line of Parosh, Zechariah, and with him a hundred and fifty males in the register; 4 of the line of Pahath-moab, Elihoenai son of Zerahiah, and with him two hundred males; 5 of the line of Zattu, Shecaniah son of Jahaziel, and with him three hundred males; 6 of the line of Adin, Ebed son of Jonathan, and with him fifty males; 7 of the line of Elam, Isaiah son of Athaliah, and with him seventy males; 8 of the line of Shephatiah, Zebadiah son of Michael, and with him eighty males; 9 of the line of Joab, Obadiah son of Jehiel, and with him two hundred and eighteen males; 10 of the line of Bani, Shelomith son of Josiphiah, and with him a hundred and sixty

7:25 to administer . . . your God: or all of them versed in the laws of your God, to judge all the people in the province of Beyond-Euphrates. 7:27 Then . . . said: prob. rdg, cp. 1 Esd. 8:25; Heb. omits. 8:3 son of: prob. rdg; Heb. of the family of. 8:5 of Zattu: prob. rdg, cp. 1 Esd. 8:32; Heb. omits. 8:10 of Bani: prob. rdg, cp. 1 Esd. 8:36; Heb. omits.

j A Heb measure of volume   k Gk 1 Esdras 8.32: Heb lacks of Zattu
l Gk 1 Esdras 8.36: Heb lacks Bani

may receive throughout the province of Babylon, together with the free-will offerings which the people and priests freely contribute for the house of their God in Jerusalem. 17 You must take care, therefore, to use this money to buy bulls, rams, lambs, and the cereal offerings and libations proper to these, and offer them on the altar of the house of your God in Jerusalem. 18 You and your brethren may do whatever seems best to you with the remainder of the silver and gold, conformably to the will of your God. 19 The utensils consigned to you for the service of the house of your God you are to deposit before the God of Jerusalem. 20 Whatever else you may be required to supply for the needs of the house of your God, you may draw from the royal treasury. 21 I, Artaxerxes the king, issue this decree to all the treasurers of West-of-Euphrates: Whatever Ezra the priest, scribe of the law of the God of heaven, requests of you, dispense to him accurately, 22 within these limits: silver, one hundred talents; wheat, one hundred kors; wine, one hundred baths; oil, one hundred baths; salt, without limit. 23 Let everything that is ordered by the God of heaven be carried out exactly for the house of the God of heaven, that wrath may not come upon the realm of the king and his sons. 24 We also inform you that it is not permitted to impose taxes, tributes, or tolls on any priest, Levite, singer, gatekeeper, temple slave, or any other servant of that house of God.

25 "As for you, Ezra, in accordance with the wisdom of your God which is in your possession, appoint magistrates and judges to administer justice to all the people in West-of-Euphrates, to all, that is, who know the laws of your God. Instruct those who do not know these laws. 26 Whoever does not obey the law of your God and the law of the king, let strict judgment be executed upon him, whether death, or corporal punishment, or a fine on his goods, or imprisonment."

27 Blessed be the LORD, the God of our fathers, who thus disposed the mind of the king to glorify the house of the LORD in Jerusalem, 28 and who let me find favor with the king, with his counselors, and with all the most influential royal officials. I therefore took courage and, with the hand of the LORD, my God, upon me, I gathered together Israelite family heads to make the return journey with me.

8 This is the list of the family heads who returned with me from Babylon during the reign of King Artaxerxes: 2 Of the sons of Phinehas, Gershon; of the sons of Ithamar, Daniel; of the sons of David, Hattush, 3 son of Shecaniah; of the sons of Parosh, Zechariah, and with him one hundred and fifty males were enrolled; 4 of the sons of Pahath-moab, Eliehoenai, son of Zerahiah, and with him two hundred males; 5 of the sons of Zattu, Shecaniah, son of Jahaziel, and with him three hundred males; 6 of the sons of Adin, Ebed, son of Jonathan, and with him fifty males; 7 of the sons of Elam, Jeshaiah, son of Athaliah, and with him seventy males; 8 of the sons of Shephatiah, Zebadiah, son of Michael, and with him eighty males; 9 of the sons of Joab, Obadiah, son of Jehiel, and with him two hundred and eighteen males; 10 of the sons of Bani, Shelomith, son of Josiphiah, and with him one hundred and sixty males; 11 of

province of Babylon and the voluntary offerings freely contributed by the people and the priests for the Temple of their God in Jerusalem.

17 'This money you will punctiliously use for the purchase of bulls, rams, lambs and the materials for the oblations and libations which go with them, offering these on the altar of the Temple of your God in Jerusalem, 18 and using the remainder of the silver and gold in accordance with the will of your God as you and your brothers may think fit.

19 'You will deliver the articles which have been given you for the ministry of the Temple of your God, to the God of Jerusalem, 20 and whatever else is needed and you are obliged to supply for the Temple of your God, you will supply from the royal treasury.

21 'I, King Artaxerxes, have issued the following instruction to all the treasurers of Transeuphrates: Whatever the priest Ezra, Secretary of the Law of the God of heaven, may request of you is to be punctiliously complied with: 22 up to one hundred talents of silver, one hundred *kor* of wheat, one hundred *bat* of wine, one hundred *bat* of oil, and unlimited salt. 23 Whatever the God of heaven demands for the Temple of the God of heaven must be diligently provided; why should retribution come on the realm of the king and of his sons? 24 You are further informed that it is against the law to impose tribute, tax or toll on any of the priests, Levites, singers, gatekeepers, temple slaves or other servants of this temple of God.

25 'And you, Ezra, by virtue of the wisdom of your God, which you possess, are to appoint magistrates and scribes to administer justice for the whole people of Transeuphrates, that is, for all who know the Law of your God; and you are to teach it to those who do not know it. 26 And on anyone who will not comply with the Law of your God and the Law of the king let sentence be swiftly executed, whether it be death, banishment, fine or imprisonment.'

27 Blessed be Yahweh, God of our ancestors, who moved the king's heart in this way to restore the beauty of the Temple of Yahweh in Jerusalem, 28 won for me the faithful love of the king, his counsellors and all the most powerful of the king's officials! Taking heart since the hand of Yahweh my God was over me, I assembled those Israelite heads of families who were to go with me.

8 These, with their genealogies, were the heads of families who set out from Babylon with me in the reign of King Artaxerxes: 2 Of the sons of Phinehas: Gershom; of the sons of Ithamar: Daniel; of the sons of David: Hattush 3 son of Shechaniah; of the sons of Parosh: Zechariah, and with him a hundred and fifty males officially registered; 4 of the sons of Pahath-Moab: Elioenai son of Zerahiah, and with him two hundred males; 5 of the sons of Zattu: Shechaniah son of Jahaziel, and with him three hundred males; 6 of the sons of Adin: Ebed son of Jonathan, and with him fifty males; 7 of the sons of Elam: Jeshaiah son of Athaliah, and with him seventy males; 8 of the sons of Shephatiah: Zebadiah son of Michael, and with him eighty males; 9 of the sons of Joab: Obadiah son of Jehiel, and with him two hundred and eighteen males; 10 of the sons of Bani: Shelomith son of Josiphiah, and with him a hundred and sixty males; 11 of the

11 Of the descendants of Bebai, Zechariah son of Bebai, and with him twenty-eight males. 12 Of the descendants of Azgad, Johanan son of Hakkatan, and with him one hundred ten males. 13 Of the descendants of Adonikam, those who came later, their names being Eliphelet, Jeuel, and Shemaiah, and with them sixty males. 14 Of the descendants of Bigvai, Uthai and Zaccur, and with them seventy males.

15 I gathered them by the river that runs to Ahava, and there we camped three days. As I reviewed the people and the priests, I found there none of the descendants of Levi. 16 Then I sent for Eliezer, Ariel, Shemaiah, Elnathan, Jarib, Elnathan, Nathan, Zechariah, and Meshullam, who were leaders, and for Joiarib and Elnathan, who were wise, 17 and sent them to Iddo, the leader at the place called Casiphia, telling them what to say to Iddo and his colleagues the temple servants at Casiphia, namely, to send us ministers for the house of our God. 18 Since the gracious hand of our God was upon us, they brought us a man of discretion, of the descendants of Mahli son of Levi son of Israel, namely Sherebiah, with his sons and kin, eighteen; 19 also Hashabiah and with him Jeshaiah of the descendants of Merari, with his kin and their sons, twenty; 20 besides two hundred twenty of the temple servants, whom David and his officials had set apart to attend the Levites. These were all mentioned by name.

21 Then I proclaimed a fast there, at the river Ahava, that we might deny ourselves*m* before our God, to seek from him a safe journey for ourselves, our children, and all our possessions. 22 For I was ashamed to ask the king for a band of soldiers and cavalry to protect us against the enemy on our way, since we had told the king that the hand of our God is gracious to all who seek him, but his power and his wrath are against all who forsake him. 23 So we fasted and petitioned our God for this, and he listened to our entreaty.

24 Then I set apart twelve of the leading priests: Sherebiah, Hashabiah, and ten of their kin with them. 25 And I weighed out to them the silver and the gold and the vessels, the offering for the house of our God that the king, his counselors, his lords, and all Israel there present had offered; 26 I weighed out into their hand six hundred fifty talents of silver, and one hundred silver vessels worth . . . talents,*n* and one hundred talents of gold, 27 twenty gold bowls worth a thousand darics, and two vessels of fine polished bronze as precious as gold. 28 And I said to them, "You are holy to the LORD, and the vessels are holy; and the silver and the gold are a freewill offering to the LORD, the God of your ancestors. 29 Guard them and keep them until you weigh them before the chief priests and the Levites and the heads of families in Israel at Jerusalem, within the chambers of the house of the LORD." 30 So the priests and the Levites took over the silver, the gold, and the vessels as they were weighed out, to bring them to Jerusalem, to the house of our God.

31 Then we left the river Ahava on the twelfth day of the first month, to go to Jerusalem; the hand of our God was upon us, and he delivered us from the hand of the enemy and from ambushes along the way. 32 We came to Jerusalem and remained there three days. 33 On the fourth day, within the house of our God, the silver, the gold, and the vessels were weighed into the hands of the priest Meremoth son of Uriah, and with him was Eleazar son of Phinehas, and with them were the Levites, Jozabad son of Jeshua and Noadiah son of Binnui. 34 The total was counted and weighed, and the weight of everything was recorded.

males; 11 of the line of Bebai, Zechariah son of Bebai, and with him twenty-eight males; 12 of the line of Azgad, Johanan son of Hakkatan, and with him a hundred and ten males. 13 The last were the line of Adonikam, and these were their names: Eliphelet, Jeiel, and Shemaiah, and with them sixty males; 14 and the line of Bigvai, Uthai and Zabbud, and with them seventy males.

15 I assembled them by the river which flows towards Ahava, and we encamped there for three days. I checked the people and the priests, and finding no one there who was a Levite, 16 I sent to Eliezer, Ariel, Shemaiah, Elnathan, Jarib, Elnathan, Nathan, Zechariah, and Meshullam, prominent men, and Joiarib and Elnathan, men of discretion, 17 and instructed them to go to Iddo, the head of the settlement at Casiphia; and I gave them a message for him and his colleagues, the temple servitors there, asking that there should be sent to us men to serve in the house of our God. 18 Under the providence of God they sent us Sherebiah, a man of discretion, of the line of Mahli son of Levi, son of Israel, together with his sons and kinsmen, eighteen men in all; 19 also Hashabiah, together with Isaiah of the line of Merari, his kinsmen and their sons, twenty men; 20 besides two hundred and twenty temple servitors, an order instituted by David and his officers to assist the Levites. These were all indicated by name.

21 I proclaimed a fast there by the river Ahava, so that we might mortify ourselves before our God and ask him for a straightforward journey for ourselves, our dependants, and all our possessions. 22 I was ashamed to apply to the king for an escort of infantry and cavalry to protect us against enemies on the way, for we had told him that the might of our God would ensure a successful outcome for all those who looked to him; but his fierce anger is on all who forsake him. 23 So we fasted and asked our God for a safe journey, and he answered our prayer.

24 Then I set apart twelve of the chiefs of the priests, together with Sherebiah and Hashabiah and ten of their kinsmen. 25 I weighed out for them the silver and gold and the vessels, the contribution for the house of our God presented by the king, his counsellors and officers, and by all the Israelites there present, as their contribution to the house of our God. 26 After weighing it, I handed over to them six hundred and fifty talents of silver, a hundred silver vessels weighing two talents, a hundred talents of gold, 27 twenty gold dishes worth a thousand darics, and two vessels of a fine red copper, precious as gold. 28 I said, 'Just as you are consecrated to the LORD, so too are the sacred vessels; the silver and gold are a voluntary offering to the LORD the God of your fathers. 29 Guard them with all vigilance until you weigh them at Jerusalem in the rooms of the LORD's house in the presence of the chiefs of the priests, the Levites, and the heads of the families of Israel.' 30 So the priests and the Levites received the consignment of silver and gold and vessels, to be taken to the house of God in Jerusalem.

31 On the twelfth day of the first month we struck camp at the river Ahava and set out for Jerusalem. Under the protection of our God, who saved us from enemy attack and ambush on the way, 32 we reached Jerusalem and rested there for three days. 33 On the fourth day the silver and gold and vessels were weighed and handed over in the house of our God into the charge of Meremoth son of Uriah the priest, with whom was Eleazar son of Phinehas; present with them were the Levites Jozabad son of Jeshua and Noadiah son of Binnui. 34 Everything was counted and weighed and every weight recorded then and there.

8:14 **Zabbud:** *or, as otherwise read,* Zaccur. 8:24 **together with:** *prob. rdg; cp. 1 Esd. 8:54; Heb. omits.*

m Or *might fast*   *n* The number of talents is lacking

the sons of Bebai, Zechariah, son of Bebai, and with him twenty-eight males; 12 of the sons of Azgad, Johanan, son of Hakkatan, and with him one hundred and ten males; 13 of the sons of Adonikam, younger sons, whose names were Eliphelet, Jeiel, and Shemaiah, and with them sixty males; 14 of the sons of Bigvai, Uthai, son of Zakkur, and with him seventy males.

15 I had them assemble by the river that flows toward Ahava, where we made camp for three days. There I perceived that both laymen and priests were present, but I could not discover a single Levite. 16 Therefore I sent Eliezer, Ariel, Shemaiah, Jarib, Elnathan, Nathan, Zechariah, and Meshullam, wise leaders, 17 with a command for Iddo, the leader in the place Casiphia, instructing them what to say to Iddo and his brethren, and to the temple slaves in Casiphia, in order to procure for us ministers for the house of our God. 18 They sent to us — for the favoring hand of our God was upon us — a well-instructed man, one of the sons of Mahli, son of Levi, son of Israel, namely Sherebiah, with his sons and brethren, eighteen men. 19 They also sent us Hashabiah, and with him Jeshaiah, sons of Merari, and their brethren and their sons, twenty men. 20 Of the temple slaves (those whom David and the princes appointed to serve the Levites) there were two hundred and twenty. All these men were enrolled by name.

21 Then I proclaimed a fast, there by the river of Ahava, that we might humble ourselves before our God to petition from him a safe journey for ourselves, our children, and all our possessions. 22 For I would have been ashamed to ask the king for troops and horsemen to protect us against enemies along the way, since we had said to the king, "The favoring hand of our God is upon all who seek him, but his mighty wrath is against all who forsake him." 23 So we fasted, and prayed to our God for this, and our petition was granted. 24 Next I selected twelve of the priestly leaders along with Sherebiah, Hashabiah, and ten of their brethren, 25 and I weighed out before them the silver and the gold and the utensils offered for the house of our God by the king, his counselors, his officials, and all the Israelites of that region. I consigned it to them in these amounts: 26 silver, six hundred and fifty talents; silver utensils, one hundred; gold, one hundred talents; 27 twenty golden bowls valued at a thousand darics; two vases of excellent polished bronze, as precious as gold. 28 I addressed them in these words: "You are consecrated to the LORD, and the utensils are also consecrated; the silver and the gold are a free-will offering to the LORD, the God of your fathers. 29 Keep good watch over them till you weigh them out in Jerusalem in the presence of the chief priests and Levites and the family leaders of Israel, in the chambers of the house of the LORD." 30 The priests and the Levites then took over the silver, the gold, and the utensils that had been weighted out, to bring them to Jerusalem, to the house of our God.

31 We set out for Jerusalem from the river of Ahava on the twelfth day of the first month. The hand of our God remained upon us, and he protected us from enemies and bandits along the way. 32 Thus we arrived at Jerusalem, where we first rested for three days. 33 On the fourth day, the silver, the gold, and the utensils were weighed out in the house of our God and consigned to the priest Meremoth, son of Uriah, who was assisted by Eleazar, son of Phinehas; they were assisted by the Levites Jozazar, son of Jeshua, and Noadiah, son of Binnui. 34 Everything was in order as to number and weight, and the total weight was registered.

sons of Bebai: Zechariah son of Bebai, and with him twenty-eight males; 12 of the sons of Azgad: Johanan son of Hakkatan, and with him a hundred and ten males; 13 of the sons of Adonikam: the younger sons, whose names are: Eliphelet, Jeiel and Shemaiah, and with them sixty males; 14 and of the sons of Bigvai: Uthai son of Zabud, and with him seventy males.

15 I assembled them near the canal which runs to Ahava, where we camped for three days. I noticed laymen and priests, but I could not discover any Levites there. 16 I then sent for Eliezer, Ariel, Shemaiah, Elnathan, Jarib, Elnathan, Nathan, Zechariah and Meshullam, judicious men, 17 and sent them to Iddo, the leading man of a place called Casiphia; I told them what they were to say to Iddo and his kinsmen, living at the place called Casiphia, that is, to provide us with people to serve the Temple of our God. 18 And because the hand of God was good to us, they sent us a wise man of the sons of Mahli son of Levi, son of Israel, a certain Sherebiah with his sons and kinsmen: eighteen men; 19 also Hashabiah and with him his brother Jeshaiah of the sons of Merari with his kinsmen and sons: twenty men; 20 and two hundred and twenty temple slaves — descendants of the temple slaves whom David and the princes had assigned to serve the Levites — all of them designated by name.

21 There, beside the Ahava Canal, I then proclaimed a fast, to humble ourselves before our God and to pray to him for a successful journey for us, our dependants and all our belongings. 22 For I should have been ashamed to ask the king for a company of cavalry to protect us from hostile people on our road, as we had already said to the king, 'The hand of our God is over all who seek him for their protection, but his mighty retribution befalls all those who forsake him.' 23 So we fasted and pleaded with our God about this, and he heard us.

24 I next chose twelve of the leading priests, and also Sherebiah and Hashabiah with ten of their kinsmen. 25 To them I weighed out the silver, the gold and the utensils, the contributions which the king, his counsellors, his notables and all the Israelites there present had made for the Temple of our God. 26 To them I weighed out and handed over six hundred and fifty talents of silver, one hundred utensils of silver valued at two talents, one hundred talents of gold, 27 twenty golden bowls valued at a thousand darics and two utensils of fine burnished copper as precious as gold. 28 I said to them, 'You are consecrated to Yahweh; these utensils are consecrated too; the silver and gold are a voluntary offering to Yahweh, God of your ancestors. 29 Guard them carefully until you weigh them out to the leading priests, the Levites, and the heads of families of Israel in the rooms of the Temple of Yahweh.' 30 The priests and Levites then took charge of the silver, the gold and the utensils thus weighed, to bring them to Jerusalem to the Temple of our God.

31 On the twelfth day of the first month we left the Ahava Canal to make our way to Jerusalem; the hand of our God was over us and protected us from enemies and surprise attacks on our way. 32 When we arrived in Jerusalem, we rested for three days. 33 On the fourth day the silver, the gold and the utensils were weighed in the Temple of our God and handed over to the priest Meremoth son of Uriah and, with him, Eleazar son of Phinehas; with them were the Levites Jozabad son of Jeshua and Noadiah son of Binnui. 34 By number and weight all was there. The total weight was recorded at the same time.

NEW REVISED STANDARD VERSION	REVISED ENGLISH BIBLE

35 At that time those who had come from captivity, the returned exiles, offered burnt offerings to the God of Israel, twelve bulls for all Israel, ninety-six rams, seventy-seven lambs, and as a sin offering twelve male goats; all this was a burnt offering to the LORD. 36 They also delivered the king's commissions to the king's satraps and to the governors of the province Beyond the River; and they supported the people and the house of God.

9 After these things had been done, the officials approached me and said, "The people of Israel, the priests, and the Levites have not separated themselves from the peoples of the lands with their abominations, from the Canaanites, the Hittites, the Perizzites, the Jebusites, the Ammonites, the Moabites, the Egyptians, and the Amorites. 2 For they have taken some of their daughters as wives for themselves and for their sons. Thus the holy seed has mixed itself with the peoples of the lands, and in this faithlessness the officials and leaders have led the way." 3 When I heard this, I tore my garment and my mantle, and pulled hair from my head and beard, and sat appalled. 4 Then all who trembled at the words of the God of Israel, because of the faithlessness of the returned exiles, gathered around me while I sat appalled until the evening sacrifice.

5 At the evening sacrifice I got up from my fasting, with my garments and my mantle torn, and fell on my knees, spread out my hands to the LORD my God, 6 and said,

"O my God, I am too ashamed and embarrassed to lift my face to you, my God, for our iniquities have risen higher than our heads, and our guilt has mounted up to the heavens. 7 From the days of our ancestors to this day we have been deep in guilt, and for our iniquities we, our kings, and our priests have been handed over to the kings of the lands, to the sword, to captivity, to plundering, and to utter shame, as is now the case. 8 But now for a brief moment favor has been shown by the LORD our God, who has left us a remnant, and given us a stake in his holy place, in order that he*o* may brighten our eyes and grant us a little sustenance in our slavery. 9 For we are slaves; yet our God has not forsaken us in our slavery, but has extended to us his steadfast love before the kings of Persia, to give us new life to set up the house of our God, to repair its ruins, and to give us a wall in Judea and Jerusalem.

10 "And now, our God, what shall we say after this? For we have forsaken your commandments, 11 which you commanded by your servants the prophets, saying, 'The land that you are entering to possess is a land unclean with the pollutions of the peoples of the lands, with their abominations. They have filled it from end to end with their uncleanness. 12 Therefore do not give your daughters to their sons, neither take their daughters for your sons, and never seek their peace or prosperity, so that you may be strong and eat the good of the land and leave it for an inheritance to your children forever.' 13 After all that has come upon us for our evil deeds and for our great guilt, seeing that you, our God, have punished us less than our iniquities deserved and have given us such a remnant as this, 14 shall we break your commandments again and intermarry with the peoples who practice these abominations? Would you not be angry with us until you destroy us without remnant or survivor? 15 O LORD, God of Israel, you are just, but we have escaped as a remnant, as is now the case. Here we are before you in our guilt, though no one can face you because of this."

10 While Ezra prayed and made confession, weeping and throwing himself down before the house of God, a very great assembly of men, women, and children gathered to him out of Israel; the people also wept bitterly.

o Heb *our God*

35 Those who had returned from captivity offered as whole-offerings to the God of Israel twelve bulls for all Israel, ninety-six rams, and seventy-seven lambs, with twelve he-goats as a purification-offering; all these were offered as a whole-offering to the LORD. 36 They also delivered the king's commission to the royal satraps and governors in the province of Beyond-Euphrates; and these gave support to the people and the house of God.

9 ONCE this business had been concluded, the leaders came to me and said, 'The people of Israel, including even priests and Levites, have not kept themselves apart from the alien population and from the abominable practices of the Canaanites, Hittites, Perizzites, Jebusites, Ammonites, Moabites, Egyptians, and Amorites. 2 They have taken women of these nations as wives for themselves and their sons, so that the holy race has become mixed with the alien population; and the leaders and magistrates have been the chief offenders.'

3 At this news I tore my robe and mantle; I plucked tufts from my beard and the hair of my head and sat appalled. 4 All who went in fear of the words of the God of Israel gathered round me because of the offence of these exiles; and I sat appalled until the evening sacrifice. 5 Then, at the evening sacrifice, with my robe and mantle torn, I rose from my self-abasement, and kneeling down, held out my hands in prayer to the LORD my God.

6 'I am humiliated, my God,' I said, 'I am ashamed, my God, to lift my face to you. Our sins tower above us, and our guilt is so great that it reaches high heaven. 7 From the days of our forefathers down to this present day our guilt has been great. Because of our iniquities we and our kings and priests have been given into the power of foreign rulers to be killed, taken captive, pillaged, and humiliated to this very day. 8 But now, for a brief moment, the LORD our God has been gracious to us, leaving us some survivors and giving us a foothold in his holy place; our God has brought light to our eyes again and given us some chance to renew our lives in our slavery. 9 For slaves we are; nevertheless, our God has not forsaken us in our slavery, but has secured for us the favour of the kings of Persia: they have provided us with the means of renewal, so that we may repair the house of our God and rebuild its ruins, thereby giving us a wall of defence for Judah and Jerusalem.

10 'Now, our God, in the face of this, what are we to say? For we have neglected your commandments, 11 given us through your servants the prophets. You said: "The land which you are going to occupy is a land defiled with the pollution of its heathen population and their abominable practices; they have filled it with their impure ways from end to end. 12 Now therefore do not marry your daughters to their sons or take their daughters for your sons; nor must you ever seek their welfare or prosperity. Only thus will you be strong and enjoy the good things of the land, and hand it on as an everlasting possession to your descendants." 13 After all that has come upon us through our evil deeds and great guilt—although you, our God, have punished us less than our iniquities deserved and have allowed us to survive as now we do—14 shall we once again disobey your commands and intermarry with peoples who indulge in such abominable practices? Would you not be so angry with us as to destroy us till no remnant, no survivor was left? 15 LORD God of Israel, you are just; for we today are a remnant that has survived. In all our guilt we are here before you; because of it we can no longer stand in your presence.'

10 While Ezra was praying and making confession, prostrate in tears before the house of God, there gathered round him a vast throng of Israelites, men, women, and children, and there was widespread lamentation

NEW AMERICAN BIBLE

At that same time, 35 those who had returned from the captivity, the exiles, offered as holocausts to the God of Israel twelve bulls for all Israel, ninety-six rams, seventy-seven lambs, and twelve goats as sin-offerings: all these as a holocaust to the LORD. 36 Finally, the orders of the king were presented to the king's satraps and to the governors in West-of-Euphrates, who gave their support to the people and to the house of God.

9 When these matters had been concluded, the leaders approached me with this report: "Neither the Israelite laymen nor the priests nor the Levites have kept themselves aloof from the peoples of the land and their abominations [Canaanites, Hittites, Perizzites, Jebusites, Ammonites, Moabites, Egyptians, and Amorites]; 2 for they have taken some of their daughters as wives for themselves and their sons, and thus they have desecrated the holy race with the peoples of the land. Furthermore, the leaders and rulers have taken a leading part in this apostasy!"

3 When I had heard this thing, I tore my cloak and my mantle, plucked hair from my head and beard, and sat there stupefied. 4 Around me gathered all who were in dread of the sentence of the God of Israel on this apostasy of the exiles, while I remained motionless until the evening sacrifice. 5 Then, at the time of the evening sacrifice, I rose in my wretchedness, and with cloak and mantle torn I fell on my knees, stretching out my hands to the LORD, my God.

6 I said: "My God, I am too ashamed and confounded to raise my face to you, O my God, for our wicked deeds are heaped up above our heads and our guilt reaches up to heaven. 7 From the time of our fathers even to this day great has been our guilt, and for our wicked deeds we have been delivered over, we and our kings and our priests, to the will of the kings of foreign lands, to the sword, to captivity, to pillage, and to disgrace, as is the case today.

8 "And now, but a short time ago, mercy came to us from the LORD, our God, who left us a remnant and gave us a stake in his holy place; thus our God has brightened our eyes and given us relief in our servitude. 9 For slaves we are, but in our servitude our God has not abandoned us; rather, he has turned the good will of the kings of Persia toward us. Thus he has given us new life to raise again the house of our God and restore its ruins, and has granted us a fence in Judah and Jerusalem. 10 But now, O our God, what can we say after all this? For we have abandoned your commandments, 11 which you gave through your servants the prophets: the land which you are entering to take as your possession is a land unclean with the filth of the peoples of the land, with the abominations with which they have filled it from one end to the other in their uncleanness. 12 Do not, then, give your daughters to their sons in marriage, and do not take their daughters for your sons. Never promote their peace and prosperity; thus you will grow strong, enjoy the produce of the land, and leave it as an inheritance to your children forever.

13 "After all that has come upon us for our evil deeds and our great guilt — though you, our God, have made less of our sinfulness than it deserved and have allowed us to survive as we do — 14 shall we again violate your commandments by intermarrying with these abominable peoples? Would you not become so angered with us as to destroy us without remnant or survivor? 15 O LORD, God of Israel, you are just; yet we have been spared, the remnant we are today. Here we are before you in our sins. Because of all this, we can no longer stand in your presence."

10 While Ezra prayed and acknowledged their guilt, weeping and prostrate before the house of God, a very large assembly of Israelites gathered about him, men, women, and children; and the people wept profusely. 2 Then

NEW JERUSALEM BIBLE

35 When the exiles arrived from their captivity, they offered burnt offerings to the God of Israel — twelve bulls on behalf of all Israel, ninety-six rams, seventy-two lambs, and as a sin offering twelve he-goats: the whole of this as a burnt offering to Yahweh.

36 They also delivered the king's instructions to the king's satraps and the governors of Transeuphrates, who then supported the people and the Temple of God.

9 Once this was done, the officials approached me to say, 'The people of Israel, the priests and the Levites, have not renounced the disgusting practices of the people of the country — the Canaanites, the Hittites, the Perizzites, the Jebusites, the Moabites, the Egyptians and the Amorites — 2 since they and their sons have married some of their women, as a result of which the holy race has been contaminated by the people of the country. The officials and leaders have been the worst offenders in this act of infidelity.' 3 On hearing this, I tore my clothes and my cloak; I pulled hair from my head and beard and sat down in horror. 4 All who trembled at the words of the God of Israel gathered round me, when faced with the infidelity of the exiles, while I went on sitting there in horror until the evening sacrifice. 5 At the evening sacrifice I came out of my stupor and, falling on my knees in my torn clothes and cloak, stretched out my hands to Yahweh my God, 6 and said:

'My God, I am ashamed, I blush to lift my face to you, my God. For our iniquities have increased, until they are higher than our heads, and our guilt has risen as high as heaven. 7 From the days of our ancestors until now we have been deeply guilty and, because of our iniquities, we, our kings and our priests, have been handed over to the kings of other countries, to the sword, to captivity, to pillage, to shame, as is the case today. 8 And now, for a brief moment, the favour of Yahweh our God has allowed a remnant of us to escape and given us a stable home in his holy place, so that our God can raise our spirits and revive us a little in our slavery. 9 For we are slaves; but God has not forgotten us in our slavery; he has extended his faithful love to us even under the kings of Persia and revived us to rebuild the Temple of our God, restore its ruins and provide us with a refuge in Judah and in Jerusalem. 10 But now, our God, what can we say after this? For we have abandoned your commandments, 11 which you gave through your servants the prophets in these terms, "The country which you are about to possess is a polluted country, polluted by the people of the country and their disgusting practices, which have filled it with their filth from end to end. 12 Hence you are not to give your daughters in marriage to their sons, or let their daughters marry your sons, or ever concern yourselves about peace or good relations with them, if you want to grow stronger, to live off the fat of the land and bequeath it to your sons for ever."

13 'After all that has befallen us because of our evil deeds and our deep guilt — though you, our God, have punished us less than our iniquities deserved and have allowed us to escape like this — 14 are we to break your commandments again and intermarry with people with these disgusting practices? Would you not be enraged with us to the point of destroying us, leaving neither remnant nor survivor? 15 Yahweh, God of Israel, you are upright. We survive only as the remnant we are today. We come before you in our guilt; because of it we cannot stand in your presence.'

10 While Ezra, weeping and prostrating himself in front of the Temple of God, was praying and making confession, a very large crowd of men, women and children of Israel gathered round him, the people weeping

2 Shecaniah son of Jehiel, of the descendants of Elam, addressed Ezra, saying, "We have broken faith with our God and have married foreign women from the peoples of the land, but even now there is hope for Israel in spite of this. 3 So now let us make a covenant with our God to send away all these wives and their children, according to the counsel of my lord and of those who tremble at the commandment of our God; and let it be done according to the law. 4 Take action, for it is your duty, and we are with you; be strong, and do it." 5 Then Ezra stood up and made the leading priests, the Levites, and all Israel swear that they would do as had been said. So they swore.

6 Then Ezra withdrew from before the house of God, and went to the chamber of Jehohanan son of Eliashib, where he spent the night.*p* He did not eat bread or drink water, for he was mourning over the faithlessness of the exiles. 7 They made a proclamation throughout Judah and Jerusalem to all the returned exiles that they should assemble at Jerusalem, 8 and that if any did not come within three days, by order of the officials and the elders all their property should be forfeited, and they themselves banned from the congregation of the exiles.

9 Then all the people of Judah and Benjamin assembled at Jerusalem within the three days; it was the ninth month, on the twentieth day of the month. All the people sat in the open square before the house of God, trembling because of this matter and because of the heavy rain. 10 Then Ezra the priest stood up and said to them, "You have trespassed and married foreign women, and so increased the guilt of Israel. 11 Now make confession to the LORD the God of your ancestors, and do his will; separate yourselves from the peoples of the land and from the foreign wives." 12 Then all the assembly answered with a loud voice, "It is so; we must do as you have said. 13 But the people are many, and it is a time of heavy rain; we cannot stand in the open. Nor is this a task for one day or for two, for many of us have transgressed in this matter. 14 Let our officials represent the whole assembly, and let all in our towns who have taken foreign wives come at appointed times, and with them the elders and judges of every town, until the fierce wrath of our God on this account is averted from us." 15 Only Jonathan son of Asahel and Jahzeiah son of Tikvah opposed this, and Meshullam and Shabbethai the Levites supported them.

16 Then the returned exiles did so. Ezra the priest selected men,*q* heads of families, according to their families, each of them designated by name. On the first day of the tenth month they sat down to examine the matter. 17 By the first day of the first month they had come to the end of all the men who had married foreign women.

18 There were found of the descendants of the priests who had married foreign women, of the descendants of Jeshua son of Jozadak and his brothers: Maaseiah, Eliezer, Jarib, and Gedaliah. 19 They pledged themselves to send away their wives, and their guilt offering was a ram of the flock for their guilt. 20 Of the descendants of Immer: Hanani and Zebadiah. 21 Of the descendants of Harim: Maaseiah, Elijah, Shemaiah, Jehiel, and Uzziah. 22 Of the descendants of Pashhur: Elioenai, Maaseiah, Ishmael, Nethanel, Jozabad, and Elasah.

23 Of the Levites: Jozabad, Shimei, Kelaiah (that is, Kelita), Pethahiah, Judah, and Eliezer. 24 Of the singers: Eliashib. Of the gatekeepers: Shallum, Telem, and Uri.

among the crowd. 2 Shecaniah son of Jehiel, one of the family of Elam, spoke up and said to Ezra, 'We have broken faith with our God in taking foreign wives from the peoples of the land. But in spite of this, there is still hope for Israel. 3 Let us now pledge ourselves to our God to get rid of all such wives with their children, according to your counsel, my lord, and the counsel of those who go in fear of the command of our God; and let the law take its course. 4 Rise up, the matter is in your hands; and we are with you. Take strong action!' 5 Ezra got up and put the chiefs of the priests, the Levites, and all the Israelites on oath to act in this way, and they took the oath. 6 Ezra then left the forecourt of the house of God and went to the room of Jehohanan grandson of Eliashib. He stayed there, eating no bread and drinking no water, for he was still mourning for the unfaithfulness of the returned exiles.

7 A proclamation was issued throughout Judah and Jerusalem directing all the returned exiles to assemble at Jerusalem. 8 If any failed to arrive within three days, as decided by the chief officers and the elders, they were to have all their property confiscated and would themselves be excluded from the community that had come from exile.

9 Three days later, on the twentieth day of the ninth month, all the men of Judah and Benjamin had assembled in Jerusalem, where they all sat in the open space before the house of God, full of apprehension and shivering in the heavy rain. 10 Ezra the priest stood up and addressed them: 'You have broken faith in marrying foreign women,' he said 'and have added to Israel's guilt. 11 Now, make confession to the LORD the God of your fathers; do his will, cut yourselves off from the peoples of the land and from your foreign wives.'

12 The whole company assented loudly, saying, 'We shall do as you say! 13 But', they added, 'our numbers are great; it is the rainy season and we cannot stay out in the open. Besides, this is not the work of one or two days only, for the offence is rife amongst us. 14 Let our leading men act for the whole assembly, and let all those who have married foreign wives present themselves at stated times, accompanied by the elders and judges for each town, until our God's fierce anger at what has been done is averted from us.' 15 Only Jonathan son of Asahel and Jahzeiah son of Tikvah, supported by Meshullam and Shabbethai the Levite, opposed this.

16 The returned exiles duly put this into effect, and Ezra the priest selected, each by name, certain men, heads of households representing their families. They met in session to investigate the matter on the first day of the tenth month, 17 and by the first day of the first month the enquiry into all the marriages with foreign women was brought to a conclusion.

18 Among the members of priestly families who had married foreign women were found Maaseiah, Eliezer, Jarib, and Gedaliah, of the line of Jeshua son of Jozadak, and his brothers. 19 They pledged themselves to dismiss their wives, and to offer a ram from the flock as a reparation-offering for their offence. 20 Of the line of Immer: Hanani and Zebadiah. 21 Of the line of Harim: Maaseiah, Elijah, Shemaiah, Jehiel, and Uzziah. 22 Of the line of Pashhur: Elioenai, Maaseiah, Ishmael, Nethanel, Jozabad, and Elasah.

23 Of the Levites: Jozabad, Shimei, Kelaiah (that is Kelita), Pethahiah, Judah, and Eliezer. 24 Of the singers: Eliashib. Of the door-keepers: Shallum, Telem, and Uri.

---

p 1 Esdras 9.2: Heb *where he went*   *q* 1 Esdra 9.16: Syr: Heb *And there were selected Ezra,*

10:6 **stayed:** *prob. rdg, cp. 1 Esd. 9:2; Heb.* went.   10:16 **and . . . selected:** *prob. rdg, cp. 1 Esd. 9:16; Heb. obscure.*

Shecaniah, the son of Jehiel, one of the sons of Elam, made this appeal to Ezra: "We have indeed betrayed our God by taking as wives foreign women of the peoples of the land. Yet even now there remains a hope for Israel. 3 Let us therefore enter into a covenant before our God to dismiss all our foreign wives and the children born of them, in keeping with what you, my lord, advise, and those who fear the commandments of our God. Let the law be observed! 4 Rise, then, for this is your duty! We will stand by you, so have courage and take action!"

5 Ezra rose to his feet and demanded an oath from the chiefs of the priests, from the Levites and from all Israel that they would do as had been proposed; and they swore it. 6 Then Ezra retired from his place before the house of God and entered the chamber of Johanan, son of Eliashib, where he spent the night neither eating food nor drinking water, for he was in mourning over the betrayal by the exiles. 7 A proclamation was made throughout Judah and Jerusalem that all the exiles should gather together in Jerusalem, 8 and that whoever failed to appear within three days would, according to the judgment of the leaders and elders, suffer the confiscation of all his possessions, and himself be excluded from the assembly of the exiles.

9 All the men of Judah and Benjamin gathered together in Jerusalem within the three-day period: it was in the ninth month, on the twentieth day of the month. All the people, standing in the open place before the house of God, were trembling both over the matter at hand and because it was raining. 10 Then Ezra, the priest, stood up and said to them: "Your unfaithfulness in taking foreign women as wives has added to Israel's guilt. 11 But now, give praise to the LORD, the God of your fathers, and do his will: separate yourselves from the peoples of the land and from these foreign women." 12 In answer, the whole assembly cried out with a loud voice: "Yes, it is our duty to do as you say! 13 But the people are numerous and it is the rainy season, so that we cannot remain out-of-doors; besides, this is not a task that can be performed in a single day or even two, for those of us who have sinned in this regard are many. 14 Let our leaders represent the whole assembly; then let all those in our cities who have taken foreign women for wives appear at appointed times, accompanied by the elders and magistrates of each city in question, till we have turned away from us our God's burning anger over this affair." 15 Only Jonathan, son of Asahel, and Jahzeiah, son of Tikvah, were against this proposal, with Meshullam and Shabbethai the Levite supporting them.

16 The exiles did as agreed. Ezra appointed as his assistants men who were family heads, one for each family, all of them designated by name. They held sessions to examine the matter, beginning with the first day of the tenth month. 17 By the first day of the first month they had passed judgment on all the men who had taken foreign women for wives.

18 Among the priests, the following were found to have taken foreign women for wives: Of the sons of Jeshua, son of Jozadak, and his brethren: Maaseiah, Eliezer, Jarib, and Gedaliah. 19 They pledged themselves to dismiss their wives, and as a guilt-offering for their guilt they gave a ram from the flock. 20 Of the sons of Immer: Hanani and Zebadiah; 21 of the sons of Harim: Maaseiah, Elijah, Shemaiah, Jehiel, and Uzziah; 22 of the sons of Pashhur: Elioenai, Maaseiah, Ishmael, Nethanel, Jozabad, and Elasah.

23 Of the Levites: Jozabad, Shemei, Kelaiah (also called Kelita), Pethahiah, Judah, and Eliezer.

24 Of the singers: Eliashib and Zakkur; of the gatekeepers: Shallum, Telem, and Uri.

bitterly. 2 Then Shechaniah son of Jehiel, one of the sons of Elam, spoke up and said to Ezra, 'We have been unfaithful to our God by marrying foreign women from the people of the country. But, in spite of this, there is still some hope for Israel. 3 We will make a covenant with our God to send away all the foreign wives and their children in obedience to the advice of my lord and of those who tremble at the commandment of our God. Let us act in accordance with the Law. 4 Go ahead, do your duty; we support you. Be brave, take action!' 5 Then Ezra stood up and put the leading priests and Levites and all Israel on oath to do what had been said. They took the oath. 6 Ezra then left his place in front of the Temple of God and went to the room of Jehohanan son of Eliashib, where he spent the night without eating food or drinking water, because he was still mourning over the exiles' infidelity.

7 A proclamation was issued throughout Judah and Jerusalem that all the exiles were to assemble in Jerusalem, 8 and that anyone who failed within three days to answer the summons of the officials and elders was to forfeit all his possessions and himself be excluded from the community of the exiles. 9 As a result, all the men of Judah and Benjamin assembled in Jerusalem within the three days; it was the twentieth day of the ninth month. All the people sat down in the square in front of the Temple of God, trembling because of the matter in hand and because of the heavy rain. 10 The priest Ezra then stood up and said to them, 'You have been unfaithful and have married foreign wives, thus adding to Israel's guilt. 11 So now give thanks to Yahweh, God of your ancestors, and do his will by holding aloof from the people of the country and from foreign wives.' 12 In ringing tones, the whole assembly answered, 'Yes, our duty is to do as you say. 13 But there are many people here and it is the rainy season; we cannot stay out in the open; besides, this is not something that can be dealt with in one or two days, since many of us have been unfaithful over this. 14 Let our officials deputise for the whole community, and all the people in our towns who have married foreign wives can come at stated times, accompanied by elders and judges from each town, until our God's fierce anger over this is turned away from us.' 15 Only Jonathan son of Asahel and Jahzeiah son of Tikvah, supported by Meshullam and Shabbethai the Levite, were opposed to this. 16 The exiles did as had been proposed. And the priest Ezra selected the family heads of the various families, all of them by name, who began their sittings on the first day of the tenth month to look into the matter. 17 And by the first day of the first month they had dealt with all the men who had married foreign women.

18 Among the priests who were found to have married foreign wives were:

of the sons of Jeshua son of Jozadak and his brothers: Maaseiah, Eliezer, Jarib and Gedaliah, 19 who agreed to send their wives away; their guilt offering was a ram from the flock for their guilt;

20 of the sons of Immer: Hanani and Zebadiah;

21 of the sons of Harim: Maaseiah, Elijah, Shemaiah, Jehiel and Uzziah;

22 of the sons of Pashhur: Elioenai, Maaseiah, Ishmael, Nethanel, Jozabad and Elasah;

23 of the Levites: Jozabad, Shimei, Kelaiah — that is, Kelita — Pethahiah, Judah, and Eliezer;

24 of the singers: Eliashib and Zaccur;

of the gatekeepers: Shallum, Telem and Uri;

NEW REVISED STANDARD VERSION	REVISED ENGLISH BIBLE

25 And of Israel: of the descendants of Parosh: Ramiah, Izziah, Malchijah, Mijamin, Eleazar, Hashabiah,*r* and Benaiah. 26 Of the descendants of Elam: Mattaniah, Zechariah, Jehiel, Abdi, Jeremoth, and Elijah. 27 Of the descendants of Zattu: Elioenai, Eliashib, Mattaniah, Jeremoth, Zabad, and Aziza. 28 Of the descendants of Bebai: Jehohanan, Hananiah, Zabbai, and Athlai. 29 Of the descendants of Bani: Meshullam, Malluch, Adaiah, Jashub, Sheal, and Jeremoth. 30 Of the descendants of Pahath-moab: Adna, Chelal, Benaiah, Maaseiah, Mattaniah, Bezalel, Binnui, and Manasseh. 31 Of the descendants of Harim: Eliezer, Isshijah, Malchijah, Shemaiah, Shimeon, 32 Benjamin, Malluch, and Shemariah. 33 Of the descendants of Hashum: Mattenai, Mattattah, Zabad, Eliphelet, Jeremai, Manasseh, and Shimei. 34 Of the descendants of Bani: Maadai, Amram, Uel, 35 Benaiah, Bedeiah, Cheluhi, 36 Vaniah, Meremoth, Eliashib, 37 Mattaniah, Mattenai, and Jaasu. 38 Of the descendants of Binnui:*s* Shimei, 39 Shelemiah, Nathan, Adaiah, 40 Machnadebai, Shashai, Sharai, 41 Azarel, Shelemiah, Shemariah, 42 Shallum, Amariah, and Joseph. 43 Of the descendants of Nebo: Jeiel, Mattithiah, Zabad, Zebina, Jaddai, Joel, and Benaiah. 44 All these had married foreign women, and they sent them away with their children.*t*

r 1 Esdras 9.26 Gk: Heb *Malchijah*   *s* Gk: Heb *Bani, Binnui*
t 1 Esdras 9.36; Meaning of Heb uncertain

25 And of Israel: of the line of Parosh: Ramiah, Izziah, Malchiah, Mijamin, Eleazar, Malchiah, and Benaiah. 26 Of the line of Elam: Mattaniah, Zechariah, Jehiel, Abdi, Jeremoth, and Elijah. 27 Of the line of Zattu: Elioenai, Eliashib, Mattaniah, Jeremoth, Zabad, and Aziza. 28 Of the line of Bebai: Jehohanan, Hananiah, Zabbai, and Athlai. 29 Of the line of Bani: Meshullam, Malluch, Adaiah, Jashub, Sheal, and Jeremoth. 30 Of the line of Pahath-moab: Adna, Kelal, Benaiah, Maaseiah, Mattaniah, Bezalel, Binnui and Manasseh. 31 Of the line of Harim: Eliezer, Isshiah, Malchiah, Shemaiah, Simeon, 32 Benjamin, Malluch, and Shemariah. 33 Of the line of Hashum: Mattenai, Mattattah, Zabad, Eliphelet, Jeremai, Manasseh, and Shimei. 34 Of the line of Bani: Maadai, Amram and Uel, 35 Benaiah, Bedeiah and Keluhi, 36 Vaniah, Meremoth, Eliashib, 37 Mattaniah, Mattenai, and Jaasau. 38 Of the line of Binnui: Shimei, 39 Shelemiah, Nathan and Adaiah, 40 Maknadebai, Shashai and Sharai, 41 Azarel, Shelemiah and Shemariah, 42 Shallum, Amariah, and Joseph. 43 Of the line of Nebo: Jeiel, Mattithiah, Zabad, Zebina, Jaddai, Joel, and Benaiah. 44 All these had married foreign women, and they dismissed them, together with their children.

10:38 **Of the line of:** *prob. rdg, cp. 1 Esd. 9:34; Heb.* and Bani and.   10:44 **and they ... children:** *prob. rdg, cp. 1 Esd. 9:36; Heb.* and some of them were women; and they had borne sons.

Nehemiah

1 The words of Nehemiah son of Hacaliah. In the month of Chislev, in the twentieth year, while I was in Susa the capital, 2 one of my brothers, Hanani, came with certain men from Judah; and I asked them about the Jews that survived, those who had escaped the captivity, and about Jerusalem. 3 They replied, "The survivors there in the province who escaped captivity are in great trouble and shame; the wall of Jerusalem is broken down, and its gates have been destroyed by fire."

4 When I heard these words I sat down and wept, and mourned for days, fasting and praying before the God of heaven. 5 I said, "O LORD God of heaven, the great and awesome God who keeps covenant and steadfast love with those who love him and keep his commandments; 6 let your ear be attentive and your eyes open to hear the prayer of your servant that I now pray before you day and night for the people of Israel your servants, confessing the sins of the people of Israel, which we have sinned against you. Both I and my family have sinned. 7 We have offended deeply against you, and have not kept the commandments, the statutes, and the ordinances that you commanded your servant Moses. 8 Remember the word that you commanded your servant Moses, 'If you are unfaithful, I will scatter you among the peoples; 9 but if you return to me and keep my commandments and do them, though your outcasts are under the farthest skies, I will gather them from there and bring them to the place at which I have chosen to establish my name.' 10 They are your servants and your people, whom you redeemed by your great power and your strong hand. 11 O Lord, let your ear be attentive to the prayer of your servant, and to the prayer of your servants who delight in revering your name. Give success to your servant today, and grant him mercy in the sight of this man!"

At the time, I was cupbearer to the king.

2 In the month of Nisan, in the twentieth year of King Artaxerxes, when wine was served him, I carried the wine and gave it to the king. Now, I had never been sad in his presence before. 2 So the king said to me, "Why is your face sad, since you are not sick? This can only be sadness of the heart." Then I was very much afraid. 3 I said to the king, "May the king live forever! Why should my face not be sad, when the city, the place of my ancestors' graves, lies waste, and its gates have been destroyed by fire?" 4 Then the king said to me, "What do you request?" So I prayed to the God of heaven. 5 Then I said to the king, "If it pleases the king, and if your servant has found favor with you, I ask that you send me to Judah, to the city of my ancestors' graves, so that I may rebuild it." 6 The king said to me (the queen also was sitting beside him), "How long will you be gone, and when will you return?" So it pleased the king to send me, and I set him a date. 7 Then I said to the king, "If it pleases the king, let letters be given me to the governors of the province Beyond the River, that they may grant me passage until I arrive in Judah; 8 and a letter to Asaph, the keeper of the king's forest, directing him to give me timber to make beams for the gates of the temple fortress, and for the wall of the city, and for the house that I shall occupy." And the king granted me what I asked, for the gracious hand of my God was upon me.

THE BOOK OF

Nehemiah

1 The narrative of Nehemiah son of Hacaliah.
In the month of Kislev in the twentieth year, when I was in Susa the capital city, it happened 2 that one of my brothers, Hanani, arrived with some other Judaeans. I asked them about Jerusalem and about the Jews, the families still remaining of those who survived the captivity. 3 They told me that those who had survived the captivity and still lived in the province were facing dire trouble and derision; the wall of Jerusalem was broken down and its gates had been destroyed by fire.

4 When I heard this, I sat down and wept, mourning for several days, fasting and praying to the God of heaven. 5 This was my prayer. 'LORD God of heaven, great and terrible God faithfully keeping covenant with those who love him and observe his commandments, 6 let your ear be attentive and your eyes open to hear your servant's humble prayer, which I now offer in your presence on behalf of your servants the Israelites, confessing the sins which we Israelites have committed against you, my father's family and I. 7 We have wronged you and have not observed the commandments, statutes, and rules which you enjoined on your servant Moses. 8 'Remember what you imposed on him when you said: "If you are unfaithful, I shall disperse you among the peoples; 9 but if you return to me and observe my commandments and fulfil them, I shall gather your scattered people, however far away they may be, and bring them to the place I have chosen as a dwelling for my name." 10 They are your servants and your people whom you redeemed with your great strength and might. 11 Lord, let your ear be attentive to my prayer, and to the prayer of your servants who delight to revere your name. Grant me success this day, and put it into this man's heart to show me kindness.' I was then cupbearer to the king.

2 One day, in the month of Nisan, in the twentieth year of King Artaxerxes, when his wine was ready, I took it and handed it to the king, and as I stood before him my face revealed my unhappiness. 2 The king asked, 'Why do you look so unhappy? You are not ill; it can be nothing but a feeling of unhappiness.' I was very much afraid, 3 but I answered, 'May the king live for ever! But how can I help looking unhappy when the city where my forefathers are buried lies in ruins with its gates burnt down?' 4 'What then do you want?' asked the king. With a prayer to the God of heaven, 5 I answered, 'If it please your majesty, and if I enjoy your favour, I beg you to send me to Judah, to the city where my forefathers are buried, so that I may rebuild it.' 6 The king, with the queen consort sitting beside him, asked me, 'How long will the journey last, and when will you return?' When I told him how long I should be, the king approved the request and let me go.

7 I then said to him 'If it please your majesty, let letters be given me for the governors in the province of Beyond-Euphrates, with orders to grant me safe passage until I reach Judah. 8 Let me have also a letter for Asaph, the keeper of your royal forests, instructing him to supply me with timber to make beams for the gates of the citadel, which adjoins the temple, and for the city wall, and for the temple which is the object of my journey.' The king granted my requests, for the gracious hand of my God was upon me.

25 Among the other Israelites: Of the sons of Parosh: Ramiah, Izziah, Malchijah, Mijamin, Eleazar, Malchijah, and Benaiah; 26 of the sons of Elam: Mattaniah, Zechariah, Jehiel, Abdi, Jeremoth, and Elijah; 27 of the sons of Zattu: Elioenai, Eliashib, Mattaniah, Jeremoth, Zabad, and Aziza; 28 of the sons of Bebai: Jehohanan, Hananiah, Zabbai, and Athlai; 29 of the sons of Bani: Meshullam, Malluch, Adaiah, Jashub, Sheal, and Jeremoth; 30 of the sons of Pahath-moab: Adna, Chelal, Benaiah, Maaseiah, Mattaniah, Bezalel, Binnui, and Manasseh; 31 of the sons of Harim: Eliezer, Isshijah, Malchijah, Shemaiah, Shimeon, 32 Benjamin, Malluch, Shemariah; 33 of the sons of Hashum: Mattenai, Mattattah, Zabad, Eliphelet, Jeremai, Manasseh, Shimei; 34 of the sons of Begu: Maadai, Amram, Uel, 35 Benaiah, Bedeiah, Cheluhi, 36 Vaniah, Meremoth, Eliashib, 37 Mattaniah, Mattenai, and Jaasu, 38 of the sons of Nebo: Jeiel, Matti-39 Shelemiah, Nathan, Shashai, Sh... Joseph... lum, A... Zabad, Zebina, Jadd... thia... 44 ... these had tak... away, b... the w...

25 and of the Israelites:
of the sons of Parosh: Ramiah, Izziah, Malchijah, Mijamin, Eleazar, Malchijah and Benaiah;
26 of the sons of Elam: Mattaniah, Zechariah, Jehiel, Abdi, Jeremoth and Elijah;
27 of the sons of Zattu: Elioenai, Eliashib, Mattaniah, Jeremoth, Zabad and Aziza;
28 of the sons of Bebai: Jehohanan, Hananiah, Zabbai, Atlai;
29 of the sons of Bigvai: Meshullam, Malluch, Jedaiah, Jashub, Sheal, Jeremoth;
30 of the sons of Pahath-Moab: Adna, Chelal, Benaiah, Maaseiah, Mattaniah, Bezalel, Binnui and Manasseh;
31 of the sons of Harim: Eliezer, Isshijah, Malchijah, Shemaiah, Shimeon, 32 Benjamin, Malluch, Shemariah;
33 of the sons of Hashum: Mattenai, Mattattah, Zabad, Eliphelet, ... the sons of Manasseh, Shimei;
34 of the sons of Bani: Maadai, Amram, Uel, 35 Benaiah, Bediah, Jeluhi, 36 Vaniah, Meremoth, Eliashib, 37 Mattaniah, Mattenai, ... 38 ... Shallum, Amariah, ... nan
43 of the sons of Nebo: Jeiel, Mattithiah, ... Azarel, Shel... Jaddai, Joel, Benaiah. Zeb... Zebina,
44 All these had married foreign wives but sent them away, with their children.

THE BOOK OF
Nehemiah

1 The words of Nehemiah, the son of Hacaliah.

In the month Chislev of the twentieth year, I was in the citadel of Susa 2 when Hanani, one of my brothers, came with other men from Judah. I asked them about the Jews, the remnant preserved after the captivity, and about Jerusalem, 3 and they answered me: "The survivors of the captivity there in the province are in great distress and under reproach. Also, the wall of Jerusalem lies breached, and its gates have been gutted with fire." 4 When I heard this report, I began to weep and continued mourning for several days; I fasted and prayed before the God of heaven.

5 I prayed: "O LORD, God of heaven, great and awesome God, you who preserve your covenant of mercy toward those who love you and keep your commandments, 6 may your ear be attentive, and your eyes open, to heed the prayer which I, your servant, now offer in your presence day and night for your servants the Israelites, confessing the sins which we of Israel have committed against you, I and my father's house included. 7 Grievously have we offended you, not keeping the commandments, the statutes, and the ordinances which you committed to your servant Moses. 8 But remember, I pray, the promise which you gave through Moses, your servant, when you said: 'Should you prove faithless, I will scatter you among the nations; 9 but should you return to me and carefully keep my commandments, even though your outcasts have been driven to the farthest corner of the world, I will gather them from there, and bring them back to the place which I have chosen as the dwelling place for my name.' 10 They are your servants, your people, whom you freed by your great might and your strong hand. 11 O LORD, may your ear be attentive to my prayer and that of all your willing servants who revere your name. Grant success to your servant this day, and let him find favor with this man" — for I was cupbearer to the king.

2 In the month Nisan of the twentieth year of King Artaxerxes, when the wine was in my charge, I took some and offered it to the king. As I had never before been sad in his presence, 2 the king asked me, "Why do you look sad? If you are not sick, you must be sad at heart." Though I was seized with great fear, 3 I answered the king: "May the king live forever! How could I not look sad when the city where my ancestors are buried lies in ruins, and its gates have been eaten out by fire?" 4 The king asked me, "What is it, then, that you wish?" I prayed to the God of heaven 5 and then answered the king: "If it please the king, and if your servant is deserving of your favor, send me to Judah, to the city of my ancestors' graves, to rebuild it." 6 Then the king, and the queen seated beside him, asked me how long my journey would take and when I would return. I set a date that was acceptable to him, and the king agreed that I might go.

7 I asked the king further: "If it please the king, let letters be given to me for the governors of West-of-Euphrates, that they may afford me safe-conduct till I arrive in Judah; 8 also a letter for Asaph, the keeper of the royal park, that he may give me wood for timbering the gates of the temple-citadel and for the city wall and the house that I shall occupy." The king granted my requests, for the favoring hand of my God was upon me. 9 Thus I proceeded to the governors of West-

1 The words of Nehemiah son of Hacaliah.

It happened in the month of Chislev, in the twentieth year, while I was in the citadel of Susa, 2 that Hanani, one of my brothers, arrived with some men from Judah. I asked them about the Jews — those who had escaped and those who survived from the captivity — and about Jerusalem. 3 They replied, 'The survivors remaining there in the province since the captivity are in a very bad and demoralised condition: the walls of Jerusalem are in ruins and its gates have been burnt down.' 4 On hearing this I sat down and wept; for some days I mourned, fasting and praying before the God of heaven.

5 I said, 'Yahweh, God of heaven — the great and awe-inspiring God who keeps a covenant of faithful love with those who love him and obey his commandments — 6 let your ear be attentive and your eyes open, to listen to your servant's prayer, which I now offer you day and night on behalf of your servants the Israelites. I admit the sins of the Israelites, which we have committed against you. Both I and my father's House have sinned; 7 we have acted very wickedly towards you by not keeping the commandments, laws and rulings which you enjoined on your servant Moses. a 8 Remember, I beg you, the promise which you solemnly made to your servant Moses, "If you are unfaithful, I shall scatter you among the peoples; 9 but if you come back to me and keep my commandments and practise them, even though those who have been banished are at the very sky's end, I shall gather them from there and bring them back to the place which I have chosen as a dwelling-place for my name." 10 Since they are your servants, your people, whom you have redeemed with your mighty power and strong hand, 11 O Lord, let your ear now be attentive to your servant's prayer and to the prayer of your servants who want to revere your name. I beg you let your servant be successful today and win this man's compassion.'

At the time I was cupbearer to the king.

2 In the month of Nisan, in the twentieth year of King Artaxerxes, since I was in charge of the wine, I took the wine and offered it to the king. Now, he had never seen me looking depressed before. 2 So the king said to me, 'Why are you looking depressed? You are not sick! This must be a sadness of the heart.' Thoroughly alarmed by this, 3 I said to the king, 'May the king live for ever! How can I not look depressed when the city where the tombs of my ancestors are lies in ruins and its gates have been burnt down?' 4 The king then said to me, 'What would you like me to do?' Praying to the God of heaven, 5 I said to the king, 'If the king approves and your servant enjoys your favour, send me to Judah, to the city of the tombs of my ancestors, so that I can rebuild it.' 6 The king — with the queen sitting beside him — said, 'How long will your journey take, and when will you come back?' Once I had given him a definite time, the king approved my mission.

7 I then said to the king, 'If the king approves, may I be given orders for the governors of Transeuphrates to let me pass through on my way to Judah? 8 Also an order for Asaph, keeper of the king's forest, to supply me with timber for the beams of the gates of the citadel of the Temple, for the city walls and for the house which I am to occupy?' These the king granted me because the kindly hand of my God was over me.

a 1 Dt 30:1–4.

NEW REVISED STANDARD VERSION

9 Then I came to the governors of the province Beyond the River, and gave them the king's letters. Now the king had sent officers of the army and cavalry with me. 10 When Sanballat the Horonite and Tobiah the Ammonite official heard this, it displeased them greatly that someone had come to seek the welfare of the people of Israel.

11 So I came to Jerusalem and was there for three days. 12 Then I got up during the night, I and a few men with me; I told no one what my God had put into my heart to do for Jerusalem. The only animal I took was the animal I rode. 13 I went out by night by the Valley Gate past the Dragon's Spring and to the Dung Gate, and I inspected the walls of Jerusalem that had been broken down and its gates that had been destroyed by fire. 14 Then I went on to the Fountain Gate and to the King's Pool; but there was no place for the animal I was riding to continue. 15 So I went up by way of the valley by night and inspected the wall. Then I turned back and entered by the Valley Gate, and so returned. 16 The officials did not know where I had gone or what I was doing; I had not yet told the Jews, the priests, the nobles, the officials, and the rest that were to do the work.

17 Then I said to them, "You see the trouble we are in, how Jerusalem lies in ruins with its gates burned. Come, let us rebuild the wall of Jerusalem, so that we may no longer suffer disgrace." 18 I told them that the hand of my God had been gracious upon me, and also the words that the king had spoken to me. Then they said, "Let us start building!" So they committed themselves to the common good. 19 But when Sanballat the Horonite and Tobiah the Ammonite official, and Geshem the Arab heard of it, they mocked and ridiculed us, saying, "What is this that you are doing? Are you rebelling against the king?" 20 Then I replied to them, "The God of heaven is the one who will give us success, and we his servants are going to start building; but you have no share or claim or historic right in Jerusalem."

3 Then the high priest Eliashib set to work with his fellow priests and rebuilt the Sheep Gate. They consecrated it and set up its doors; they consecrated it as far as the Tower of the Hundred and as far as the Tower of Hananel. 2 And the men of Jericho built next to him. And next to them*a* Zaccur son of Imri built.

3 The sons of Hassenaah built the Fish Gate; they laid its beams and set up its doors, its bolts, and its bars. 4 Next to them Meremoth son of Uriah son of Hakkoz made repairs. Next to them Meshullam son of Berechiah son of Meshezabel made repairs. Next to them Zadok son of Baana made repairs. 5 Next to them the Tekoites made repairs; but their nobles would not put their shoulders to the work of their Lord.*b*

6 Joiada son of Paseah and Meshullam son of Besodeiah repaired the Old Gate; they laid its beams and set up its doors, its bolts, and its bars. 7 Next to them repairs were made by Melatiah the Gibeonite and Jadon the Meronothite — the men of Gibeon and of Mizpah — who were under the jurisdiction of*c* the governor of the province Beyond the River. 8 Next to them Uzziel son of Harhaiah, one of the goldsmiths, made repairs. Next to him Hananiah, one of the perfumers, made repairs; and they restored Jerusalem as far as the Broad Wall. 9 Next to them Rephaiah son of Hur, ruler of half the district of*d* Jerusalem, made repairs. 10 Next to them Jedaiah son of Harumaph made repairs opposite his house; and next to him Hattush son of Hashabneiah made repairs. 11 Malchijah son of Harim and Hasshub

REVISED ENGLISH BIBLE

9 I CAME in due course to the governors in the province of Beyond-Euphrates and presented the king's letters to them; the king had given me an escort of army officers with cavalry. 10 But when Sanballat the Horonite and the slave Tobiah, an Ammonite, heard this, they were greatly displeased that someone should have come to promote the interests of the Israelites.

11 WHEN I arrived in Jerusalem, I waited three days. 12 Then I set out by night, taking a few men with me, but without telling anyone what my God was prompting me to do for Jerusalem. Taking no beast with me except the one on which I myself rode, 13 I went out by night through the Valley Gate towards the Dragon Spring and the Dung Gate; and I inspected the places where the walls of Jerusalem had been broken down, and its gates, which had been destroyed by fire. 14 Then I passed on to the Fountain Gate and the King's Pool; but there was no room for me to ride through. 15 I went up the valley by night and inspected the city wall; then I re-entered the city through the Valley Gate. So I arrived back 16 without the magistrates knowing where I had been or what I was doing, for I had not yet told the Jews, neither the priests, the nobles, the magistrates, nor any of those who would be responsible for the work.

17 Then I said to them, 'You see what trouble we are in: Jerusalem lies in ruins, its gates destroyed by fire. Come, let us rebuild the wall of Jerusalem and suffer derision no more.' 18 I told them also how the gracious hand of my God had been upon me and also what the king had said to me. They replied, 'Let us start the rebuilding,' and they set about the work vigorously and to good purpose.

19 But when Sanballat the Horonite, Tobiah the Ammonite slave, and Geshem the Arab heard of it, they jeered at us, asking contemptuously, 'What is this you are doing? Is this a rebellion against the king?' 20 But I answered, 'The God of heaven will grant us success. We, his servants, are making a start with the rebuilding. But you have no stake, or claim, or traditional right in Jerusalem.'

3 Eliashib the high priest and his fellow-priests set to work and rebuilt the Sheep Gate. They laid its beams and put its doors in place; they carried the work as far as the Tower of the Hundred and the Tower of Hananel, and consecrated it. 2 The men of Jericho worked next to Eliashib; and next to them Zaccur son of Imri.

3 The Fish Gate was built by the sons of Hassenaah; they laid its tie-beams and put its doors in place with their bolts and bars. 4 Next to them Meremoth son of Uriah, son of Hakkoz, repaired his section; next to them Meshullam son of Berechiah, son of Meshezabel; next to them Zadok son of Baana did the repairs; 5 and next again the men of Tekoa did the repairs, but their nobles would not demean themselves to serve their governor.

6 The Jeshanah Gate was repaired by Joiada son of Paseah and Meshullam son of Besodeiah; they laid its tie-beams and put its doors in place with their bolts and bars. 7 Next to them Melatiah the Gibeonite and Jadon the Meronothite, the men of Gibeon and Mizpah, did the repairs in the service of the governor of the province of Beyond-Euphrates. 8 Next to them Uzziel son of Harhaiah, a goldsmith, did the repairs, and next Hananiah of the perfumers' guild; they reconstructed Jerusalem as far as the Broad Wall. 9 Next to them Rephaiah son of Hur, ruler of half the district of Jerusalem, did the repairs. 10 Next to them Jedaiah son of Harumaph did the repairs opposite his own house; and next Hattush son of Hashabniah. 11 Malchiah son of Harim and

---

a Heb *him*   *b* Or *lords*   *c* Meaning of Heb uncertain
d Or *supervisor of half the portion assigned to*

3:1 **laid its beams:** *prob. rdg; Heb.* consecrated it.
3:6 **Jeshanah Gate:** *or* gate of the Old City.   3:8 **a goldsmith:** *so Syriac; Heb.* goldsmiths.

of-Euphrates and presented the king's letters to them. The king also sent with me army officers and cavalry.

10 When Sanballat the Horonite and Tobiah the Ammonite slave had heard of this, they were very much displeased that someone had come to seek the welfare of the Israelites.

11 When I had arrived in Jerusalem, I first rested for three days. 12 Then I set out by night with only a few other men (for I had not told anyone what my God had inspired me to do for Jerusalem) and with no other animals but my own mount. 13 I rode out at night by the Valley Gate, passed by the Dragon Spring, and came to the Dung Gate, observing how the walls of Jerusalem lay in ruins and its gates had been eaten out by fire. 14 Then I passed over to the Spring Gate and to the King's Pool. Since there was no room here for my mount to pass with me astride, 15 I continued on foot up the wadi by night, inspecting the wall all the while till I once more reached the Valley Gate, by which I went back in. 16 The magistrates knew nothing of where I had gone or what I was doing, for as yet I had disclosed nothing to the Jews, neither to the priests, nor to the nobles, nor to the magistrates, nor to the others who would be concerned about the matter.

17 Afterward I said to them: "You see the evil plight in which we stand: how Jerusalem lies in ruins and its gates have been gutted by fire. Come, let us rebuild the wall of Jerusalem, so that we may no longer be an object of derision!" 18 Then I explained to them how the favoring hand of my God had rested upon me, and what the king had said to me. They replied, "Let us be up and building!" And they undertook the good work with vigor.

19 On hearing of this, Sanballat the Horonite, Tobiah the Ammonite slave, and Geshem the Arab mocked us and ridiculed us. "What is this that you are about?" they asked. "Are you rebelling against the king?" 20 My answer to them was this: "It is the God of heaven who will grant us success. We, his servants, shall set about the rebuilding; but for you there is to be neither share nor claim nor memorial in Jerusalem."

3 Eliashib the high priest and his priestly brethren took up the task of rebuilding the Sheep Gate. They timbered it and set up its doors, its bolts, and its bars, then continued the rebuilding to the Tower of Hananel. 2 At their side the men of Jericho were rebuilding, and next to them was Zaccur, son of Imri. 3 The Fish Gate was rebuilt by the sons of Hassenaah; they timbered it and set up its doors, its bolts, and its bars. 4 At their side Meremoth, son of Uriah, son of Hakkoz, carried out the work of repair; next to him was Meshullam, son of Berechiah, son of Meshezabel; and next to him was Zadok, son of Baana. 5 Next to him the Tekoites carried out the work of repair; however, some of their outstanding men would not submit to the labor asked by their lords. 6 The New City Gate was repaired by Joiada, son of Paseah; and Meshullam, son of Besodeiah; they timbered it and set up its doors, its bolts, and its bars. 7 At their side were Melatiah the Gibeonite, Jadon the Meronothite, and the men of Gibeon and of Mizpah, who were under the jurisdiction of the governor of West-of-Euphrates. 8 Next to them the work of repair was carried out by Uzziel, son of Harhaiah, a member of the goldsmiths' guild, and at his side was Hananiah, one of the perfumers' guild. They restored Jerusalem as far as the wall of the public square. 9 Next to them the work of repair was carried out by Repha-iah, son of Hur, leader of half the district of Jerusalem, 10 and at his side was Jedaiah, son of Harumaph, who repaired opposite his own house. Next to him Hattush, son of Hashabneiah, carried out the work of repair. 11 The adjoin-

9 When I reached the governors of Transeuphrates, I gave them the king's orders. The king had sent an escort of army officers and cavalry along with me.

10 When Sanballat the Horonite and Tobiah the official of Ammon heard about this, they were exceedingly displeased that someone had come to promote the welfare of the Israelites.

11 And so I reached Jerusalem. After I had been there three days, 12 I got up during the night with a few other men—I had not told anyone what my God had inspired me to do for Jerusalem—taking no animal with me other than my own mount. 13 Under cover of dark I went out through the Valley Gate towards the Dragon's Fountain as far as the Dung Gate, and examined the wall of Jerusalem where it was broken down and its gates burnt out. 14 I then crossed to the Fountain Gate and the King's Pool, but it was impassable to my mount. 15 So I went up the Valley in the dark, examining the wall; I then went in again through the Valley Gate, coming back 16 without the officials knowing where I had gone or what I had been doing. So far I had said nothing to the Jews: neither to the priests, the nobles, the officials nor any other persons involved in the undertaking.

17 I then said to them, 'You see what a sorry state we are in: Jerusalem is in ruins and its gates have been burnt down. Come on, we must rebuild the walls of Jerusalem and put an end to our humiliating position!' 18 And I told them how the kindly hand of my God had been over me, and the words which the king had said to me. At this they said, 'Let us start building at once!' and they set their hands to the good work.

19 When Sanballat the Horonite, Tobiah the official of Ammon, and Geshem the Arab heard about this, they laughed at us and jeered. They said, 'What is this you are doing? Are you going to revolt against the king?' 20 But I gave them this answer, 'The God of heaven will grant us success and we, his servants, mean to start building; as for you, you have neither share nor right nor memorial in Jerusalem.'

3 Eliashib the high priest with his brother priests then set to work and rebuilt the Sheep Gate; they made the framework, hung its doors, fixed its bolts and bars and proceeded as far as the Tower of the Hundred and the Tower of Hananel. 2 The men of Jericho built next to him; Zaccur son of Imri built next to them. 3 The sons of Ha-Senaah rebuilt the Fish Gate; they made the framework, hung its doors and fixed its bolts and bars. 4 Meremoth son of Uriah, son of Hakkoz, carried out repairs next to them; Meshullam son of Berechiah, son of Meshezabel, carried out repairs next to him; and Zadok son of Baana carried out repairs next to him. 5 The men of Tekoa carried out repairs next to him, though their nobles would not demean themselves to help their masters. 6 Joiada son of Paseah and Meshullam son of Besodeiah repaired the gate of the New Quarter; they made the framework, hung its doors and fixed its bolts and bars. 7 Next to them repairs were carried out by Melatiah of Gibeon, Jadon of Meronoth, and the men of Gibeon and Mizpah, for the sake of the governor of Transeuphrates. 8 Next to them repairs were carried out by Uzziel son of Harhaiah, a member of the metal-workers' guild, and next to him repairs were carried out by Hananiah of the perfumers' guild. These renovated the wall of Jerusalem as far as the Broad Wall.

9 Next to them repairs were carried out by Rephaiah son of Hur, who was head of one half of the district of Jerusalem. 10 Next to them Jedaiah son of Harumaph carried out repairs opposite his own house; next to him repairs were carried out by Hattush son of Hashabneiah. 11 Malchijah son

NEW REVISED STANDARD VERSION	REVISED ENGLISH BIBLE

son of Pahath-moab repaired another section and the Tower of the Ovens. 12 Next to him Shallum son of Hallohesh, ruler of half the district of[e] Jerusalem, made repairs, he and his daughters.

13 Hanun and the inhabitants of Zanoah repaired the Valley Gate; they rebuilt it and set up its doors, its bolts, and its bars, and repaired a thousand cubits of the wall, as far as the Dung Gate.

14 Malchijah son of Rechab, ruler of the district of[f] Beth-haccherem, repaired the Dung Gate; he rebuilt it and set up its doors, its bolts, and its bars.

15 And Shallum son of Col-hozeh, ruler of the district of[f] Mizpah, repaired the Fountain Gate; he rebuilt it and covered it and set up its doors, its bolts, and its bars; and he built the wall of the Pool of Shelah of the king's garden, as far as the stairs that go down from the City of David.

16 After him Nehemiah son of Azbuk, ruler of half the district of[e] Beth-zur, repaired from a point opposite the graves of David, as far as the artificial pool and the house of the warriors. 17 After him the Levites made repairs: Rehum son of Bani; next to him Hashabiah, ruler of half the district of[e] Keilah, made repairs for his district. 18 After him their kin made repairs: Binnui,[g] son of Henadad, ruler of half the district of[e] Keilah; 19 next to him Ezer son of Jeshua, ruler[h] of Mizpah, repaired another section opposite the ascent to the armory at the Angle. 20 After him Baruch son of Zabbai repaired another section from the Angle to the door of the house of the high priest Eliashib. 21 After him Meremoth son of Uriah son of Hakkoz repaired another section from the door of the house of Eliashib to the end of the house of Eliashib. 22 After him the priests, the men of the surrounding area, made repairs. 23 After them Benjamin and Hasshub made repairs opposite their house. After them Azariah son of Maaseiah son of Ananiah made repairs beside his own house. 24 After him Binnui son of Henadad repaired another section, from the house of Azariah to the Angle and to the corner. 25 Palal son of Uzai repaired opposite the Angle and the tower projecting from the upper house of the king at the court of the guard. After him Pedaiah son of Parosh 26 and the temple servants living[i] on Ophel made repairs up to a point opposite the Water Gate on the east and the projecting tower. 27 After him the Tekoites repaired another section opposite the great projecting tower as far as the wall of Ophel.

28 Above the Horse Gate the priests made repairs, each one opposite his own house. 29 After them Zadok son of Immer made repairs opposite his own house. After him Shemaiah son of Shecaniah, the keeper of the East Gate, made repairs. 30 After him Hananiah son of Shelemiah and Hanun sixth son of Zalaph repaired another section. After him Meshullam son of Berechiah made repairs opposite his living quarters. 31 After him Malchijah, one of the goldsmiths, made repairs as far as the house of the temple servants and of the merchants, opposite the Muster Gate,[j] and to the upper room of the corner. 32 And between the upper room of the corner and the Sheep Gate the goldsmiths and the merchants made repairs.

Hasshub son of Pahath-moab repaired a second section including the Tower of the Ovens. 12 Next to them Shallum son of Hallohesh, ruler of half the district of Jerusalem, did the repairs with the help of his daughters.

13 The Valley Gate was repaired by Hanun and the inhabitants of Zanoah; they rebuilt it and put its doors in place with their bolts and bars, and they repaired a thousand cubits of the wall as far as the Dung Gate. 14 The Dung Gate itself was repaired by Malchiah son of Rechab, ruler of the district of Beth-hakkerem; he rebuilt it and put its doors in place with their bolts and bars. 15 The Fountain Gate was repaired by Shallun son of Col-hozeh, ruler of the district of Mizpah; he rebuilt it and roofed it and put its doors in place with their bolts and bars; and he built the wall of the Pool of Shelah next to the king's garden and onwards as far as the steps leading down from the City of David.

16 After him Nehemiah son of Azbuk, ruler of half the district of Beth-zur, did the repairs as far as a point opposite the burial-place of David, as far as the artificial pool and the barracks. 17 After him the Levites did the repairs: Rehum son of Bani and next to him Hashabiah, ruler of half the district of Keilah, did the repairs for his district. 18 After him their kinsmen did the repairs: Binnui son of Henadad, ruler of half the district of Keilah; 19 next to him Ezer son of Jeshua, ruler of Mizpah, repaired a second section opposite the point at which the ascent meets the escarpment; 20 after him Baruch son of Zabbai repaired a second section, from the escarpment to the door of the house of Eliashib the high priest. 21 After him Meremoth son of Uriah, son of Hakkoz, repaired a second section, from the door of Eliashib's house to the end of his house.

22 After him the priests of the neighbourhood of Jerusalem did the repairs. 23 Next Benjamin and Hasshub did the repairs opposite their own house; and next Azariah son of Maaseiah, son of Ananiah, did the repairs beside his own house. 24 After him Binnui son of Henadad repaired a second section, from the house of Azariah as far as the escarpment and the corner. 25 Palal son of Uzai worked opposite the escarpment and the upper tower which projects from the king's house and belongs to the court of the guard. After him Pedaiah son of Parosh 26 worked as far as a point on the east opposite the Water Gate and the projecting tower. 27 Next the men of Tekoa repaired a second section, from a point opposite the great projecting tower as far as the wall of Ophel.

28 Above the Horse Gate the priests did the repairs opposite their own houses. 29 After them Zadok son of Immer did the repairs opposite his own house; after him Shemaiah son of Shecaniah, the keeper of the East Gate, did the repairs. 30 After him Hananiah son of Shelemiah, along with Hanun, sixth son of Zalaph, repaired a second section. After him Meshullam son of Berechiah did the repairs opposite his room. 31 After him Malchiah, a goldsmith, did the repairs as far as the house of the temple servitors and the merchants, opposite the Mustering Gate, as far as the roof-chamber at the corner. 32 Between the roof-chamber at the corner and the Sheep Gate the goldsmiths and merchants did the repairs.

[e] Or supervisor of half the portion assigned to   [f] Or supervisor of the portion assigned to   [g] Gk Syr Compare verse 24, 10.9: Heb Bavvai   [h] Or supervisor   [i] Cn: Heb were living   [j] Or Hammiphkad Gate

3:14 **rebuilt**: prob. rdg; Heb. will rebuild.   3:15 **rebuilt**: prob. rdg; Heb. will rebuild.   3:20 **son of Zabbai**: so some MSS; others add inflamed.   3:25 **son of Parosh**: prob. rdg; Heb. adds and the temple servitors lodged on Ophel (cp. 11:21).

ing sector, as far as the Oven Tower, was repaired by Malchijah, son of Harim, and Hasshub, of Pahath-moab. 12 At their side the work of repair was carried out by Shallum, son of Hallohesh, leader of half the district of Jerusalem, by himself and his daughters. 13 The Valley Gate was repaired by Hanun and the inhabitants of Zanoah; they rebuilt it and set up its doors, its bolts, and its bars. They also repaired a thousand cubits of the wall up to the Dung Gate. 14 The Dung Gate was repaired by Malchijah, son of Rechab, leader of the district of Beth-haccherem; he rebuilt it and set up its doors, its bolts, and its bars. 15 The Spring Gate was repaired by Shallum, son of Colhozeh, leader of the district of Mizpah; he rebuilt it, roofed it over, and set up its doors, its bolts, and its bars. He also repaired the wall of the Aqueduct Pool near the king's garden as far as the steps that lead down from the City of David. 16 After him, the work of repair was carried out by Nehemiah, son of Azbuk, leader of half the district of Beth-zur, to a place opposite the tombs of David, as far as the artificial pool and the barracks.

17 After him, the Levites carried out the work of repair: Rehum, son of Bani. Next to him, for his own district, was Hashabiah, leader of half the district of Keilah. 18 After him, their brethren carried out the work of repair: Binnui, son of Henadad, leader of half the district of Keilah; 19 next to him Ezer, son of Jeshua, leader of Mizpah, who repaired the adjoining sector, the Corner, opposite the ascent to the arsenal. 20 After him, Baruch, son of Zabbai, repaired the adjoining sector from the Corner to the entrance of the house of Eliashib, the high priest. 21 After him, Meremoth, son of Uriah, son of Hakkoz, repaired the adjoining sector from the entrance of Eliashib's house to the end of the house.

22 After him, the work of repair was carried out by the priests, men of the surrounding country. 23 After them, Benjamin and Hasshub carried out the repair in front of their houses; after them, Azariah, son of Maaseiah, son of Ananiah, made the repairs alongside his house. 24 After him, Binnui, son of Henadad, repaired the adjoining sector from the house of Azariah to the Corner [that is, to the Angle]. 25 After him, Palal, son of Uzai, carried out the work of repair opposite the Corner and the tower projecting from the Upper Palace at the quarters of the guard. After him, Pedaiah, son of Parosh, carried out the work of repair 26 to a point opposite the Water Gate on the east, and the projecting tower. 27 After him, the Tekoites repaired the adjoining sector opposite the great projecting tower, to the wall of Ophel [the temple slaves were dwelling on Ophel].

28 Above the Horse Gate the priests carried out the work of repair, each before his own house. 29 After them Zadok, son of Immer, carried out the repair before his house, and after him the repair was carried out by Shemaiah, son of Shecaniah, keeper of the East Gate. 30 After him, Hananiah, son of Shelemiah, and Hanun, the sixth son of Zalaph, repaired the adjoining sector; after them, Meshullam, son of Berechiah, repaired the place opposite his own lodging. 31 After him, Malchijah, a member of the goldsmiths' guild, carried out the work of repair as far as the quarters of the temple slaves and the merchants, before the Gate of Inspection and as far as the upper chamber of the Angle. 32 Between the upper chamber of the Angle and the Sheep Gate, the goldsmiths and the merchants carried out the work of repair.

of Harim and Hasshub son of Pahath-Moab repaired another section as far as the Furnace Tower. 12 Next to them repairs were carried out by Shallum son of Hallohesh, head of the other half of the district of Jerusalem, by him and his sons. 13 Hanun and the inhabitants of Zanoah repaired the Valley Gate: they rebuilt it, hung its doors and fixed its bolts and bars; they also repaired a thousand cubits of wall up to the Dung Gate. 14 Malchijah son of Rechab, head of the district of Beth-ha-Cherem, repaired the Dung Gate; he rebuilt it, hung its doors and fixed its bolts and bars.

15 Shallum son of Col-Hozeh, head of the district of Mizpah, repaired the Fountain Gate; he rebuilt it, roofed it, hung its doors and fixed its bolts and bars. He also rebuilt the wall of the Pool of Siloah, adjoining the king's garden, as far as the steps going down from the City of David. 16 After him, Nehemiah son of Azbuk, head of half the district of Beth-Zur, carried out repairs from a point opposite the Davidic Tombs to the artificial pool and the House of the Champions. 17 After him, repairs were carried out by the Levites: Rehum son of Bani; and next to him Hashabiah, head of one half of the district of Keilah, carried out repairs for his own district. 18 After him, repairs were carried out by their brothers: Binnui son of Henadad, head of the other half of the district of Keilah. 19 Next to him, Ezer son of Jeshua, headman of Mizpah, repaired another section in front of the ascent to the armoury at the Angle.

20 After him, Baruch son of Zabbai repaired another section from the Angle to the door of the house of Eliashib the high priest. 21 After him, Meremoth son of Uriah, son of Hakkoz, repaired another section from the door of Eliashib's house as far as the end of Eliashib's house. 22 And after him repairs were carried out by the priests who lived in the district. 23 After them repairs were carried out by Benjamin and Hasshub, opposite their own house. After them repairs were carried out by Azariah son of Maaseiah, son of Ananiah, beside his own house. 24 After him, Binnui son of Henadad repaired another section from Azariah's house as far as the Angle at the corner. 25 After him, Palal son of Uzai carried out repairs in front of the Angle and the tower projecting from the king's Upper Palace by the Court of the Guard; and after him, Pedaiah son of Parosh carried out the repairs 26 to a point by the Water Gate to the east and the projecting tower. 27 After him, the men of Tekoa repaired another section from in front of the great projecting tower as far as the wall of Ophel.

28 From the Horse Gate onwards repairs were carried out by the priests, each in front of his own house. 29 After them repairs were carried out by Zadok son of Immer in front of his house, and after him repairs were carried out by Shemaiah son of Shechaniah, keeper of the East Gate. 30 After him Hananiah son of Shelemiah and Hanun sixth son of Zalaph repaired another section, after whom repairs were carried out by Meshullam son of Berechiah in front of his room. 31 After him Malchijah, of the metal-workers' guild, repaired as far as the Hall of the temple slaves and merchants, in front of the Muster Gate, as far as the upper room at the corner. 32 And between the upper room at the corner and the Sheep Gate repairs were carried out by the goldsmiths and the merchants.

NEW REVISED STANDARD VERSION	REVISED ENGLISH BIBLE

NEW REVISED STANDARD VERSION

4 [k] Now when Sanballat heard that we were building the wall, he was angry and greatly enraged, and he mocked the Jews. 2 He said in the presence of his associates and of the army of Samaria, "What are these feeble Jews doing? Will they restore things? Will they sacrifice? Will they finish it in a day? Will they revive the stones out of the heaps of rubbish — and burned ones at that?" 3 Tobiah the Ammonite was beside him, and he said, "That stone wall they are building — any fox going up on it would break it down!" 4 Hear, O our God, for we are despised; turn their taunt back on their own heads, and give them over as plunder in a land of captivity. 5 Do not cover their guilt, and do not let their sin be blotted out from your sight; for they have hurled insults in the face of the builders.

6 So we rebuilt the wall, and all the wall was joined together to half its height; for the people had a mind to work.

7 [l] But when Sanballat and Tobiah and the Arabs and the Ammonites and the Ashdodites heard that the repairing of the walls of Jerusalem was going forward and the gaps were beginning to be closed, they were very angry, 8 and all plotted together to come and fight against Jerusalem and to cause confusion in it. 9 So we prayed to our God, and set a guard as a protection against them day and night.

10 But Judah said, "The strength of the burden bearers is failing, and there is too much rubbish so that we are unable to work on the wall." 11 And our enemies said, "They will not know or see anything before we come upon them and kill them and stop the work." 12 When the Jews who lived near them came, they said to us ten times, "From all the places where they live[m] they will come up against us."[n] 13 So in the lowest parts of the space behind the wall, in open places, I stationed the people according to their families,[o] with their swords, their spears, and their bows. 14 After I looked these things over, I stood up and said to the nobles and the officials and the rest of the people, "Do not be afraid of them. Remember the LORD, who is great and awesome, and fight for your kin, your sons, your daughters, your wives, and your homes."

15 When our enemies heard that their plot was known to us, and that God had frustrated it, we all returned to the wall, each to his work. 16 From that day on, half of my servants worked on construction, and half held the spears, shields, bows, and body-armor; and the leaders posted themselves behind the whole house of Judah, 17 who were building the wall. The burden bearers carried their loads in such a way that each labored on the work with one hand and with the other held a weapon. 18 And each of the builders had his sword strapped at his side while he built. The man who sounded the trumpet was beside me. 19 And I said to the nobles, the officials, and the rest of the people, "The work is great and widely spread out, and we are separated far from one another on the wall. 20 Rally to us wherever you hear the sound of the trumpet. Our God will fight for us."

21 So we labored at the work, and half of them held the spears from break of dawn until the stars came out. 22 I also said to the people at that time, "Let every man and his servant pass the night inside Jerusalem, so that they may be a guard for us by night and may labor by day." 23 So neither I nor my brothers nor my servants nor the men of the guard who followed me ever took off our clothes; each kept his weapon in his right hand.[p]

REVISED ENGLISH BIBLE

4 THE news that we were rebuilding the wall roused the indignation of Sanballat, and angrily he jeered at the Jews, 2 saying in front of his companions and of the garrison in Samaria, 'What do these feeble Jews think they are doing? Do they mean to reconstruct the place? Do they hope to offer sacrifice and finish the work in a day? Can they make stones again out of heaps of rubble, and burnt rubble at that?' 3 Tobiah the Ammonite, who was beside him, said, 'Whatever it is they are building, if a fox climbs up their stone walls, it will break them down.'

4 Hear, our God, how we are treated with contempt. Make their derision recoil on their own heads; let them become objects of contempt in a land of captivity. 5 Do not condone their guilt or let their sin be struck off the record, for they have openly provoked the builders.

6 We built up the wall until it was continuous all round up to half its height; and the people worked with a will. 7 But when Sanballat and Tobiah, and the Arabs and Ammonites and Ashdodites, heard that the new work on the walls of Jerusalem had made progress and that the closing up of the breaches had gone ahead, they were furious, 8 and all banded together to launch an attack on Jerusalem and create confusion. 9 So we prayed to our God, and posted a guard against them day and night.

10 In Judah it was said:

'The labourers' strength has failed,
and there is too much rubble;
by ourselves we shall never be able
to rebuild the wall.'

11 Our adversaries said, 'Before they know it or see anything, we shall be upon them, killing them and putting an end to the work.' 12 When the Jews living nearby came into the city, they warned us a dozen times that our adversaries would gather from every place where they lived to attack us, 13 and that they would station themselves on the lowest levels below the wall, on patches of open ground. Accordingly I posted my people by families, armed with swords, spears, and bows. 14 Then having surveyed the position I addressed the nobles, the magistrates, and the rest of the people. 'Do not be afraid of them,' I said. 'Remember the Lord, great and terrible, and fight for your brothers, your sons and daughters, your wives and your homes.' 15 When our enemies heard that everything was known to us, and that God had frustrated their plans, we all returned to the wall, each to his task.

16 From that day forward half the men under me were engaged in the actual building, while the other half stood by holding their spears, shields, and bows, and wearing coats of mail; and officers supervised all the people of Judah 17 who were engaged on the wall. The porters carrying the loads held their load with one hand and a weapon with the other. 18 The builders had their swords attached to their belts as they built. The trumpeter stayed beside me, 19 and I said to the nobles, the magistrates, and all the people: 'The work is great and extends over much ground, and we are widely separated on the wall, each man at some distance from his neighbour. 20 Wherever you hear the trumpet sound, rally to us there, and our God will fight for us.' 21 So with half the men holding spears we continued the work from daybreak until the stars came out. 22 At the same time I had said to the people, 'Let every man and his servant remain all night inside Jerusalem, to act as a guard for us by night and a working party by day.' 23 Neither I nor my kinsmen nor the men under me nor my bodyguard ever took off our clothes; each one kept his right hand on his spear.

---

[k] Ch 3.33 in Heb   [l] Ch 4.1 in Heb   [m] Cn: Heb *you return*
[n] Compare Gk Syr: Meaning of Heb uncertain   [o] Meaning of Heb uncertain   [p] Cn: Heb *each his weapon the water*

4:1 *In Heb. 3:33*.   4:7 *In Heb. 4:1*.   4:12–13 **where . . .**
themselves: *so Gk; Heb.* which you return against us and I stationed.
4:23 **kept . . . on:** *prob. rdg; Heb. obscure.*

33 When Sanballat heard that we were rebuilding the wall, it roused his anger and he became very much incensed. He ridiculed the Jews, 34 saying in the presence of his brethren and the troops of Samaria: "What are these miserable Jews trying to do? Will they complete their restoration in a single day? Will they recover these stones, burnt as they are, from the heaps of dust?" 35 Tobiah the Ammonite was beside him, and he said: "It is a rubble heap they are building. Any fox that attacked it would breach their wall of stones!" 36 Take note, O our God, how we were mocked! Turn back their derision upon their own heads and let them be carried away to a land of captivity! 37 Hide not their crime and let not their sin be blotted out in your sight, for they insulted the builders to their face! 38 We, however, continued to build the wall, which was soon filled in and completed up to half its height. The people worked with a will.

4 When Sanballat, Tobiah, the Arabs, the Ammonites, and the Ashdodites heard that the restoration of the walls of Jerusalem was progressing — for the gaps were beginning to be closed up — they became extremely angry. 2 Thereupon they all plotted together to come and fight against Jerusalem and thus to throw us into confusion. 3 We prayed to our God and posted a watch against them day and night for fear of what they might do. 4 Meanwhile the Judahites were saying:

"Slackened is the bearers' strength,
    there is no end to the rubbish;
Never shall we be able
    the wall to rebuild."

5 Our enemies thought, "Before they are aware of it or see us, we shall come into their midst, kill them, and put an end to the work."

6 When the Jews who lived near them had come to us from one place after another, and had told us ten times over that they were about to attack us, 7 I stationed guards down below, behind the wall, near the exposed points, assigning them by family groups with their swords, their spears, and their bows. 8 I made an inspection, then addressed these words to the nobles, the magistrates, and the rest of the people: "Have no fear of them! Keep in mind the LORD, who is great and to be feared, and fight for your brethren, your sons and daughters, your wives and your homes." 9 When our enemies became aware that we had been warned and that God had upset their plan, we all went back, each to his own task at the wall.

10 From that time on, however, only half my able men took a hand in the work, while the other half, armed with spears, bucklers, bows, and breastplates, stood guard behind the whole house of Judah 11 as they rebuilt the wall. The load carriers, too, were armed; each did his work with one hand and held a weapon with the other. 12 Every builder, while he worked, had his sword girt at his side. Also, a trumpeter stood beside me, 13 for I had said to the nobles, the magistrates, and the rest of the people: "Our work is scattered and extensive, and we are widely separated from one another along the wall; 14 wherever you hear the trumpet sound, join us there; our God will fight with us." 15 Thus we went on with the work, half of the men with spears at the ready, from daybreak till the stars came out.

16 At the same time I told the people to spend the nights inside Jerusalem, each man with his own attendant, so that they might serve as a guard by night and a working force by day. 17 Neither I, nor my kinsmen, nor any of my attendants, nor any of the bodyguard that accompanied me took off his clothes; everyone kept his weapon at his right hand.

33 When Sanballat heard that we were rebuilding the wall, he became furiously angry. 34 He ridiculed the Jews and in front of his kinsmen and the aristocracy of Samaria he exclaimed, 'What are these pathetic Jews doing . . . ? Are they going to give up? Or offer sacrifices? Or complete the work in a day? Can they put new life into stones taken from rubbish heaps and even charred?' 35 And beside him Tobiah of Ammon remarked, 'If a jackal were to jump on what they are building, it would knock their stone wall down!' 36 Listen, our God, for we are despised! Make their sneers fall back on their own heads! Send them as booty to a land of captivity! 37 Do not pardon their wickedness, may their sin never be erased before you, for they have insulted the builders to their face!

38 Meanwhile we were rebuilding the wall, which was soon joined up all the way round to mid-height; the people put their hearts into the work.

4 When Sanballat, Tobiah, the Arabs, the Ammonites and the Ashdodites heard that repairs to the walls of Jerusalem were going forward — that the gaps were beginning to fill up — they became very angry, 2 and they all plotted to come and attack Jerusalem and upset my plans.

3 We, however, prayed to our God and organised a guard day and night to protect the city from them. 4 But in Judah the saying went, 'The strength of the carrier falters, the rubbish heap is so vast that by ourselves we cannot rebuild the wall!' 5 And our opponents said, 'They will never know or see a thing, until we are in there among them, and then we shall massacre them and put a stop to the work.'

6 Now when the Jews who lived near them had warned us ten times over, 'They are coming up against us from every place they live in,' 7 men took up position in the space behind the wall at those points where it was lowest, and I organised the people by families with their swords, spears and bows. 8 Aware of their anxiety, I then addressed the nobles, the officials and the rest of the people, 'Do not be afraid of them. Remember the great and awe-inspiring Lord and fight for your kinsmen, your sons, your daughters, your wives and your homes.' 9 Once our enemies heard that we were forewarned and that God had thwarted their plan, they withdrew and we all went back to the wall, each one to his work.

10 From then on, half my own retainers went on working, while the other half stood by, armed with spears, shields, bows and armour to protect the whole House of Judah as they rebuilt the wall. 11 The carriers were armed, working with one hand and holding a spear in the other. 12 Each builder had his sword strapped to his side as he built. Beside me stood a trumpeter. 13 I then said to the nobles, the officials and the rest of the people, 'The work is great and widely spread out, and we are deployed along the wall some way from one another. 14 Rally to us wherever you hear the trumpet sounding; our God will fight for us.' 15 And so we went on with the work from break of day until the stars came out. 16 At the same time I also told the people, 'Let every man, with his attendant, spend the night inside Jerusalem; we shall spend the night on guard and the day at work.' 17 Neither I, nor my brothers, nor my attendants, nor my bodyguards, ever took off our clothes; each one kept his spear in his right hand.

5 Now there was a great outcry of the people and of their wives against their Jewish kin. 2 For there were those who said, "With our sons and our daughters, we are many; we must get grain, so that we may eat and stay alive." 3 There were also those who said, "We are having to pledge our fields, our vineyards, and our houses in order to get grain during the famine." 4 And there were those who said, "We are having to borrow money on our fields and vineyards to pay the king's tax. 5 Now our flesh is the same as that of our kindred; our children are the same as their children; and yet we are forcing our sons and daughters to be slaves, and some of our daughters have been ravished; we are powerless, and our fields and vineyards now belong to others."

6 I was very angry when I heard their outcry and these complaints. 7 After thinking it over, I brought charges against the nobles and the officials; I said to them, "You are all taking interest from your own people." And I called a great assembly to deal with them, 8 and said to them, "As far as we were able, we have bought back our Jewish kindred who had been sold to other nations; but now you are selling your own kin, who must then be bought back by us!" They were silent, and could not find a word to say. 9 So I said, "The thing that you are doing is not good. Should you not walk in the fear of our God, to prevent the taunts of the nations our enemies? 10 Moreover I and my brothers and my servants are lending them money and grain. Let us stop this taking of interest. 11 Restore to them, this very day, their fields, their vineyards, their olive orchards, and their houses, and the interest on money, grain, wine, and oil that you have been exacting from them." 12 Then they said, "We will restore everything and demand nothing more from them. We will do as you say." And I called the priests, and made them take an oath to do as they had promised. 13 I also shook out the fold of my garment and said, "So may God shake out everyone from house and from property who does not perform this promise. Thus may they be shaken out and emptied." And all the assembly said, "Amen," and praised the LORD. And the people did as they had promised.

14 Moreover from the time that I was appointed to be their governor in the land of Judah, from the twentieth year to the thirty-second year of King Artaxerxes, twelve years, neither I nor my brothers ate the food allowance of the governor. 15 The former governors who were before me laid heavy burdens on the people, and took food and wine from them, besides forty shekels of silver. Even their servants lorded it over the people. But I did not do so, because of the fear of God. 16 Indeed, I devoted myself to the work on this wall, and acquired no land; and all my servants were gathered there for the work. 17 Moreover there were at my table one hundred fifty people, Jews and officials, besides those who came to us from the nations around us. 18 Now that which was prepared for one day was one ox and six choice sheep; also fowls were prepared for me, and every ten days skins of wine in abundance; yet with all this I did not demand the food allowance of the governor, because of the heavy burden of labor on the people. 19 Remember for my good, O my God, all that I have done for this people.

6 Now when it was reported to Sanballat and Tobiah and to Geshem the Arab and to the rest of our enemies that I had built the wall and that there was no gap left in it (though up to that time I had not set up the doors in the

5 THERE came a time when the common people, both men and women, raised a great outcry against their fellow-Jews. 2 Some complained that they had to give their sons and daughters as pledges for food to eat to keep themselves alive; 3 others that they were mortgaging their fields, vineyards, and homes to buy grain during the famine; 4 still others that they were borrowing money on their fields and vineyards to pay the king's tax. 5 'But', they said, 'our bodily needs are the same as other people's, our children are as good as theirs; yet here we are, forcing our sons and daughters into slavery. Some of our daughters are already enslaved, and there is nothing we can do, because our fields and vineyards now belong to others.'

6 When I heard their outcry and the story they told, I was greatly incensed, 7 but I controlled my feelings and reasoned with the nobles and the magistrates. I said to them, 'You are holding your fellow-Jews as pledges for debt.' I rebuked them severely 8 and said, 'As far as we have been able, we have bought back our fellow-Jews who had been sold to foreigners; but you are now selling your own fellow-countrymen, and they will have to be bought back by us!' They were silent and had not a word to say.

9 I went on, 'What you are doing is wrong. You ought to live so much in the fear of our God that you are above reproach in the eyes of the nations who are our enemies. 10 Speaking for myself, I and my kinsmen and the men under me are advancing them money and grain. Let us give up this taking of pledges for debt. 11 This very day give them back their fields and vineyards, their olive groves and houses, as well as the income in money, in grain, new wine, and oil.' 12 'We shall give them back', they promised, 'and exact nothing more. We shall do as you say.' Then after summoning the priests I put the offenders on oath to do as they had promised. 13 Also I shook out the fold of my robe and said, 'So may God shake out from house and property every man who fails to keep this promise. May he be shaken out like this and emptied!' All the assembled people said 'Amen' and praised the LORD; and they did as they had promised.

14 Moreover, from the twentieth year of King Artaxerxes, the time when I was appointed governor in Judah, until his thirty-second year, a period of twelve years, neither I nor my kinsmen drew the governor's allowance of food. 15 Former governors, my predecessors, had laid a heavy burden on the people, exacting from them a daily toll of bread and wine to the value of forty shekels of silver, while the men under them had also tyrannized over the people. But, because I feared God, I did not behave like this. 16 Further, I put all my energy into working on the wall; I acquired no land, and all my men were gathered there for the work. 17 At my table I had as guests a hundred and fifty Jews, including the magistrates, as well as men who came to us from the surrounding nations. 18 The provision which had to be made each day was an ox and six prime sheep; fowls also were prepared for me, and every ten days skins of wine in abundance. Yet even so I did not draw the governor's allowance, because the people were so heavily burdened.

19 God, remember me favourably for all that I have done for this people!

6 When it was reported to Sanballat, Tobiah, Geshem the Arab, and the rest of our enemies that I had rebuilt the wall and not a single gap remained in it — although I had not yet set up the gates in the gateways — 2 Sanballat and

5:2 that they . . . pledges: prob. rdg; Heb. that they, their sons and daughters were many. 5:4 on: so Gk (Luc.); Heb. omits. 5:7 I rebuked . . . severely: or I called a great assembly to deal with them. 5:11 income: prob. rdg; Heb. hundredth. 5:15 a daily toll: prob. rdg; Heb. obscure.

5 Then there rose a great outcry of the common people and their wives against certain of their fellow Jews. ² Some said: "We are forced to pawn our sons and daughters in order to get grain to eat that we may live." ³ Others said: "We are forced to pawn our fields, our vineyards, and our houses, that we may have grain during the famine." ⁴ Still others said: "To pay the king's tax we have borrowed money on our fields and our vineyards. ⁵ And though these are our own kinsmen and our children are as good as theirs, we have had to reduce our sons and daughters to slavery, and violence has been done to some of our daughters! Yet we can do nothing about it, for our fields and our vineyards belong to others."

⁶ I was extremely angry when I heard the reasons they had for complaint. ⁷ After some deliberation, I called the nobles and magistrates to account, saying to them, "You are exacting interest from your own kinsmen!" I then rebuked them severely, ⁸ saying to them: "As far as we were able, we bought back our fellow Jews who had been sold to Gentiles; you, however, are selling your own brothers, to have them bought back by us." They remained silent, for they could find no answer. ⁹ I continued: "What you are doing is not good. Should you not walk in the fear of our God, and put an end to the derision of our Gentile enemies? ¹⁰ I myself, my kinsmen, and my attendants have lent the people money and grain without charge. Let us put an end to this usury! ¹¹ I ask that you return to them this very day their fields, their vineyards, their olive groves, and their houses, together with the interest on the money, the grain, the wine, and the oil that you have lent them." ¹² They answered: "We will return everything and exact nothing further from them. We will do just what you ask." Then I called for the priests and had them administer an oath to these men that they would do as they had promised. ¹³ I also shook out the folds of my garment, saying, "Thus may God shake from his home and his fortune every man who fails to keep this promise, and may he thus be shaken out and emptied!" And the whole assembly answered, "Amen," and praised the LORD. Then the people did as they had promised.

¹⁴ Moreover, from the time that King Artaxerxes appointed me governor in the land of Judah, from his twentieth to his thirty-second year — during these twelve years neither I nor my brethren lived from the governor's allowance. ¹⁵ The earlier governors, my predecessors, had laid a heavy burden on the people, taking from them each day forty silver shekels for their food; then too, their men oppressed the people. But I, because I feared God, did not act thus. ¹⁶ Moreover, though I had acquired no land of my own, I did my part in this work on the wall, and all my men were gathered there for the work. ¹⁷ Though I set my table for a hundred and fifty persons, Jews and magistrates, as well as those who came to us from the nations round about, ¹⁸ and though the daily preparations were made at my expense — one beef, six choice muttons, poultry — besides all kinds of wine in abundance every ten days, despite this I did not claim the governor's allowance, for the labor lay heavy upon this people. ¹⁹ Keep in mind, O my God, in my favor all that I did for this people.

6 When it had been reported to Sanballat, Tobiah, Geshem the Arab, and our other enemies that I had rebuilt the wall and that there was no breach left in it (though up to that time I had not yet set up the doors in the gates),

5 There was a great outcry from the people, and from their wives, against their brother Jews. ² Some said, 'We are having to pledge our sons and daughters to get enough grain to eat and keep us alive.' ³ Others said, 'We are having to mortgage our fields, our vineyards and our houses to get grain because of the shortage.' ⁴ Still others said, 'We have had to borrow money on our fields and our vineyards to pay the royal tax; ⁵ and though we belong to the same race as our brothers, and our children are as good as theirs, we shall have to sell our sons and our daughters into slavery; some of our daughters have been sold into slavery already. We can do nothing about it, since our fields and our vineyards now belong to others.'

⁶ When I heard their complaints and these words I was very angry. ⁷ Having turned the matter over in my mind, I reprimanded the nobles and the officials as follows, 'Each of you is imposing a burden on his brother.' Summoning a great assembly to deal with them, ⁸ I said to them, 'To the best of our power, we have redeemed our brother Jews who were forced to sell themselves to foreigners, and now you in turn are selling your brothers, for them to be bought back by us!' They were silent and could find nothing to say. ⁹ 'What you are doing', I went on, 'is wrong. Do you not want to walk in the fear of our God and escape the sneers of the nations, our enemies? ¹⁰ I too, with my brothers and retainers, have lent them money and grain. Let us cancel these pledges. ¹¹ This very day return them their fields, their vineyards, their olive groves and their houses, and cancel the claim on the money, grain, new wine and olive oil, which you have lent them.' ¹² 'We shall make restitution,' they replied, 'we shall claim nothing more from them; we shall do as you say.' Summoning the priests, I then made them swear to do as they had promised. ¹³ Then, shaking out the fold of my garment, I said, 'May God thus shake out of house and possessions anyone who does not make good this promise; may he be shaken out thus and left empty!' And the whole assembly answered, 'Amen' and praised Yahweh. And the people kept this promise.

¹⁴ What is more, from the time when the king appointed me to be their governor in Judah, from the twentieth to the thirty-second year of King Artaxerxes, for twelve years, neither I nor my brothers ever levied the governor's subsistence allowance, ¹⁵ whereas the former governors, my predecessors, had been a burden on the people, from whom they took forty silver shekels a day for food and wine, while their attendants oppressed the people too. But I, fearing God, never did this. ¹⁶ Also, not acquiring any land, I concentrated on the work of this wall and all my attendants joined in the work together, too.

¹⁷ Furthermore, magistrates and officials to the number of a hundred and fifty ate at my table, not to mention those who came to us from the surrounding nations. ¹⁸ Every day, one ox, six fine sheep, as well as poultry, were prepared for me; every ten days, skins of wine were brought in bulk. But even so, I never claimed the governor's subsistence allowance, since the people already had burden enough to bear.

¹⁹ To my credit, my God, remember all I have done for this people.

6 When Sanballat, Tobiah, Geshem the Arab and our other enemies heard that I had rebuilt the wall and that not a single gap was left — though at that time I had not fixed the doors to the gates — ² Sanballat and Geshem sent

NEW REVISED STANDARD VERSION	REVISED ENGLISH BIBLE

gates), 2 Sanballat and Geshem sent to me, saying, "Come and let us meet together in one of the villages in the plain of Ono." But they intended to do me harm. 3 So I sent messengers to them, saying, "I am doing a great work and I cannot come down. Why should the work stop while I leave it to come down to you?" 4 They sent to me four times in this way, and I answered them in the same manner. 5 In the same way Sanballat for the fifth time sent his servant to me with an open letter in his hand. 6 In it was written, "It is reported among the nations — and Geshem*q* also says it — that you and the Jews intend to rebel; that is why you are building the wall; and according to this report you wish to become their king. 7 You have also set up prophets to proclaim in Jerusalem concerning you, 'There is a king in Judah!' And now it will be reported to the king according to these words. So come, therefore, and let us confer together." 8 Then I sent to him, saying, "No such things as you say have been done; you are inventing them out of your own mind" 9 — for they all wanted to frighten us, thinking, "Their hands will drop from the work, and it will not be done." But now, O God, strengthen my hands.

10 One day when I went into the house of Shemaiah son of Delaiah son of Mehetabel, who was confined to his house, he said, "Let us meet together in the house of God, within the temple, and let us close the doors of the temple, for they are coming to kill you; indeed, tonight they are coming to kill you." 11 But I said, "Should a man like me run away? Would a man like me go into the temple to save his life? I will not go in!" 12 Then I perceived and saw that God had not sent him at all, but he had pronounced the prophecy against me because Tobiah and Sanballat had hired him. 13 He was hired for this purpose, to intimidate me and make me sin by acting in this way, and so they could give me a bad name, in order to taunt me. 14 Remember Tobiah and Sanballat, O my God, according to these things that they did, and also the prophetess Noadiah and the rest of the prophets who wanted to make me afraid.

15 So the wall was finished on the twenty-fifth day of the month Elul, in fifty-two days. 16 And when all our enemies heard of it, all the nations around us were afraid*r* and fell greatly in their own esteem; for they perceived that this work had been accomplished with the help of our God. 17 Moreover in those days the nobles of Judah sent many letters to Tobiah, and Tobiah's letters came to them. 18 For many in Judah were bound by oath to him, because he was the son-in-law of Shecaniah son of Arah: and his son Jehohanan had married the daughter of Meshullam son of Berechiah. 19 Also they spoke of his good deeds in my presence, and reported my words to him. And Tobiah sent letters to intimidate me.

7 Now when the wall had been built and I had set up the doors, and the gatekeepers, the singers, and the Levites had been appointed, 2 I gave my brother Hanani charge over Jerusalem, along with Hananiah the commander of the citadel — for he was a faithful man and feared God more than many. 3 And I said to them, "The gates of Jerusalem are not to be opened until the sun is hot; while the gatekeepers*s* are still standing guard, let them shut and bar the doors. Appoint guards from among the inhabitants of Jerusalem, some at their watch posts, and others before their own houses." 4 The city was wide and large, but the people within it were few and no houses had been built.

Geshem sent me an invitation to come and confer with them at Hakkephirim in the plain of Ono; their intention was to do me some harm. 3 So I sent messengers to them with this reply: 'I have important work on my hands at the moment and am unable to come down. Why should the work be brought to a standstill while I leave it and come down to you?' 4 Four times they sent me a similar invitation, and each time I gave them the same answer. 5 On a fifth occasion Sanballat made a similar approach, but this time his servant came with an open letter. 6 It ran as follows: 'It is reported among the nations, and Gashmu confirms it, that you and the Jews are plotting rebellion, and that is why you are building the wall; it is further reported that you yourself want to be king, 7 and have even appointed prophets to make this proclamation concerning you in Jerusalem: "Judah has a king!" Such matters will certainly get to the king's notice; so come at once and let us talk them over.' 8 I sent this reply: 'No such thing as you allege has taken place; your imagination has invented the whole story.' 9 They were all trying to intimidate us, in the hope that we should then relax our efforts and that the work would never be completed. Strengthen me for the work, was my prayer.

10 One day I went to the house of Shemaiah son of Delaiah, son of Mehetabel, for he was confined to his house. He said,

'Let us meet in the house of God,
within the sanctuary,
and let us shut the doors,
for they are coming to kill you,
and they will come to do it by night.'

11 But I said, 'Should a man like me run away? Can a man like me go into the sanctuary to save his life? I will not go.' 12 Then it dawned on me: God had not sent him. His prophecy aimed at harming me, and Tobiah and Sanballat had bribed him to utter it. 13 He had been bribed to frighten me into compliance and into committing sin; then they could give me a bad name and discredit me.

14 God, remember Tobiah and Sanballat for what they have done, and also the prophetess Noadiah and all the other prophets who tried to intimidate me!

15 On the twenty-fifth day of the month of Elul the wall was finished; it had taken fifty-two days. 16 When all our enemies heard of it, and all the surrounding nations saw it, they thought it a very wonderful achievement, and recognized it was by the help of our God that this work had been accomplished.

17 In those days the nobles in Judah kept sending letters to Tobiah, and receiving replies from him, 18 for many in Judah were in league with him, because he was a son-in-law of Shecaniah son of Arah, and his son Jehohanan had married a daughter of Meshullam son of Berechiah. 19 They were always praising him in my presence and repeating to him what I said. Tobiah also wrote to me to intimidate me.

7 WHEN the wall had been rebuilt, and I had put the gates in place and the gate-keepers had been appointed, 2 I gave the charge of Jerusalem to my brother Hanani and to Hananiah, the governor of the citadel, for he was trustworthy and godfearing above other men. 3 I said to them, 'The entrances to Jerusalem are not to be left open during the heat of the day; the gates must be kept shut and barred while the gate-keepers are standing at ease. Appoint guards from among the inhabitants of Jerusalem, some on sentry duty and others posted in front of their own homes.'

4 The city was large and spacious; there were few people in it and no houses had yet been rebuilt. 5 Then God prompt-

---

q Heb *Gashmu*   *r* Another reading is *saw*   *s* Heb *while they*

6:6 **Gashmu:** Geshem *elsewhere.*   7:1 **gate-keepers:** *prob. rdg;* Heb. *adds* the singers and the Levites.

2 Sanballat and Geshem sent me this message: "Come, let us hold council together at Caphirim in the plain of Ono." They were planning to do me harm. 3 However, I sent messengers to them with this reply: "I am engaged in a great enterprise and am unable to come down; why should the work stop, while I leave it to come down to you?" 4 Four times they sent me this same proposal, and each time I gave the same reply. 5 Then, the fifth time, Sanballat sent me the same message by one of his servants, who bore an unsealed letter 6 containing this text: "Among the nations it has been reported — Geshem is witness to this — that you and the Jews are planning a rebellion; that for this reason you are rebuilding the wall; and that you are to be their king" — and so on. 7 "Also, that you have set up prophets in Jerusalem to proclaim you king of Judah. Now, since matters like these must reach the ear of the king, come, let us hold council together." 8 I sent him this answer: "Nothing of what you report has taken place; rather, it is the invention of your own mind." 9 They were all trying to frighten us, thinking, "Their hands will slacken in the work, and it will never be completed." But instead, I now redoubled my efforts.

10 I went to the house of Shemaiah, son of Delaiah, son of Mehetabel, who was unable to go about, and he said:

"Let us meet in the house of God,
  inside the temple building;
  let us lock the doors of the temple.
For men are coming to kill you;
  by night they are coming coming to kill you."

11 My answer was: "A man like me take flight? Can a man like me enter the temple to save his life? I will not go!" 12 For on consideration it was plain to me that God had not sent him; rather, because Tobiah and Sanballat had bribed him, he voiced this prophecy concerning me 13 that I might act on it out of fear and commit this sin. Then they would have had a shameful story with which to discredit me. 14 Keep in mind Tobiah and Sanballat, O my God, because of these things they did; keep in mind as well Noadiah the prophetess and the other prophets who were trying to frighten me.

15 The wall was finished on the twenty-fifth day of Elul; it had taken fifty-two days. 16 When all our enemies had heard of this, and all the nations round about had taken note of it, our enemies lost much face in the eyes of the nations, for they knew that it was with our God's help that this work had been completed. 17 At that same time, however, many letters were going to Tobiah from the nobles of Judah, and Tobiah's letters were reaching them, 18 for many in Judah were in league with him, since he was the son-in-law of Shecaniah, son of Arah, and his son Jehohanan had married the daughter of Meshullam, son of Berechiah. 19 Thus they would praise his good deeds in my presence and relate to him whatever I said; and Tobiah sent letters trying to frighten me.

7 When the wall had been rebuilt, I had the doors set up, and the gatekeepers [and the singers and the Levites] were put in charge of them. 2 Over Jerusalem I placed Hanani, my brother, and Hananiah, the commander of the citadel, who was a more trustworthy and God-fearing man than most. 3 I said to them: "The gates of Jerusalem are not to be opened until the sun is hot, and while the sun is still shining they shall shut and bar the doors. Appoint as watchmen the inhabitants of Jerusalem, some at their watch posts, and others before their own houses."

4 Now the city was quite wide and spacious, but its population was small, and none of the houses had been rebuilt.

me this message, 'Come and meet us at Ha-Chephirim in the Vale of Ono.' But they had evil designs on me. 3 So I sent messengers to them to say, 'I am engaged in a great undertaking, so I cannot come down. Why should the work stop while I leave it and come down to you?' 4 Four times they sent me the same invitation and I made them the same reply. 5 The fifth time, with the same purpose in mind, Sanballat sent me his servant bearing an open letter. 6 It ran, 'There is a rumour among the nations — and Gashmu confirms it — that you and the Jews are thinking of rebelling, which is why you are rebuilding the wall, and you intend to become their king; 7 and that you have even briefed prophets to acclaim you in Jerusalem with the cry, "There is a king in Judah!" Now, these rumours are going to reach the king; so you had better come and discuss them with us.' 8 To this I sent him the following reply, 'As regards what you say, nothing of the sort has occurred; it is a figment of your own imagination.' 9 For they were all trying to terrorise us, thinking, 'They will become demoralised over the work and it will not get finished.' But my morale rose even higher.

10 Then, when I went to visit Shemaiah son of Delaiah, son of Mehetabel, since he was prevented from coming to me, he said:

We must gather at the Temple of God,
  inside the sanctuary itself;
we must shut the sanctuary doors,
  for they are coming to kill you,
they are coming to kill you tonight!

11 But I retorted, 'Should a man like me run away? Would a man like me go into the Temple to save his life? I shall not go in!' 12 I realised that God had not sent him to say this, but that he had produced this prophecy for me because Tobiah was paying him 13 to terrorise me into doing as he said and committing a sin, so that they would have grounds for blackening my reputation and blaming me.

14 Remember Tobiah, my God, for what he did; and Noadiah the prophetess, and the other prophets who tried to terrorise me.

15 The wall was finished within fifty-two days, on the twenty-fifth of Elul. 16 When all our enemies heard about it and all the surrounding nations saw it, they thought it a wonderful thing, because they realised that this work had been accomplished by the power of our God.

17 During this same period, the nobles of Judah kept sending letter after letter to Tobiah, and letters from Tobiah kept arriving for them; 18 for he had many sworn to his interest in Judah, since he was son-in-law to Shecaniah son of Arah, and his son Jehohanan had married the daughter of Meshullam son of Berechiah. 19 They even cried up his good deeds in my presence, and they reported what I said back to him. And Tobiah kept sending letters to terrorise me.

7 Now, when the wall had been rebuilt and I had hung the doors, the gatekeepers (the singers and the Levites) were then appointed. 2 I entrusted the administration of Jerusalem to my brother Hanani, and to Hananiah the commander of the citadel, for he was a more trustworthy, Godfearing man than many others. 3 I said to them, 'The gates of Jerusalem must not be opened until the sun gets hot; and the doors must be shut and barred before it begins to go down. Detail guards from the residents of Jerusalem, each to his post, in front of his own house.'

4 The city was large and spacious but the population was small, and the houses had not been rebuilt. 5 My God then

5 Then my God put it into my mind to assemble the nobles and the officials and the people to be enrolled by genealogy. And I found the book of the genealogy of those who were the first to come back, and I found the following written in it:

6 These are the people of the province who came up out of the captivity of those exiles whom King Nebuchadnezzar of Babylon had carried into exile; they returned to Jerusalem and Judah, each to his town. 7 They came with Zerubbabel, Jeshua, Nehemiah, Azariah, Raamiah, Nahamani, Mordecai, Bilshan, Mispereth, Bigvai, Nehum, Baanah.

The number of the Israelite people: 8 the descendants of Parosh, two thousand one hundred seventy-two. 9 Of Shephatiah, three hundred seventy-two. 10 Of Arah, six hundred fifty-two. 11 Of Pahath-moab, namely the descendants of Jeshua and Joab, two thousand eight hundred eighteen. 12 Of Elam, one thousand two hundred fifty-four. 13 Of Zattu, eight hundred forty-five. 14 Of Zaccai, seven hundred sixty. 15 Of Binnui, six hundred forty-eight. 16 Of Bebai, six hundred twenty-eight. 17 Of Azgad, two thousand three hundred twenty-two. 18 Of Adonikam, six hundred sixty-seven. 19 Of Bigvai, two thousand sixty-seven. 20 Of Adin, six hundred fifty-five. 21 Of Ater, namely of Hezekiah, ninety-eight. 22 Of Hashum, three hundred twenty-eight. 23 Of Bezai, three hundred twenty-four. 24 Of Hariph, one hundred twelve. 25 Of Gibeon, ninety-five. 26 The people of Bethlehem and Netophah, one hundred eighty-eight. 27 Of Anathoth, one hundred twenty-eight. 28 Of Beth-azmaveth, forty-two. 29 Of Kiriath-jearim, Chephirah, and Beeroth, seven hundred forty-three. 30 Of Ramah and Geba, six hundred twenty-one. 31 Of Michmas, one hundred twenty-two. 32 Of Bethel and Ai, one hundred twenty-three. 33 Of the other Nebo, fifty-two. 34 The descendants of the other Elam, one thousand two hundred fifty-four. 35 Of Harim, three hundred twenty. 36 Of Jericho, three hundred forty-five. 37 Of Lod, Hadid, and Ono, seven hundred twenty-one. 38 Of Senaah, three thousand nine hundred thirty.

39 The priests: the descendants of Jedaiah, namely the house of Jeshua, nine hundred seventy-three. 40 Of Immer, one thousand fifty-two. 41 Of Pashhur, one thousand two hundred forty-seven. 42 Of Harim, one thousand seventeen.

43 The Levites: the descendants of Jeshua, namely of Kadmiel of the descendants of Hodevah, seventy-four. 44 The singers: the descendants of Asaph, one hundred forty-eight. 45 The gatekeepers: the descendants of Shallum, of Ater, of Talmon, of Akkub, of Hatita, of Shobai, one hundred thirty-eight.

46 The temple servants: the descendants of Ziha, of Hasupha, of Tabbaoth, 47 of Keros, of Sia, of Padon, 48 of Lebana, of Hagaba, of Shalmai, 49 of Hanan, of Giddel, of Gahar, 50 of Reaiah, of Rezin, of Nekoda, 51 of Gazzam, of Uzza, of Paseah, 52 of Besai, of Meunim, of Nephushesim, 53 of Bakbuk, of Hakupha, of Harhur, 54 of Bazlith, of Mehida, of Harsha, 55 of Barkos, of Sisera, of Temah, 56 of Neziah, of Hatipha.

ed me to assemble the nobles, the magistrates, and the people, to be enrolled family by family. I discovered the register of the genealogies of those who had been the first to come back, and this is what I found written in it:

6 Of the captives whom King Nebuchadnezzar of Babylon had taken into exile, these are the people of the province who have returned to Jerusalem and Judah, each to his own town, 7 led by Zerubbabel, Jeshua, Nehemiah, Azariah, Raamiah, Nahamani, Mordecai, Bilshan, Mispereth, Bigvai, Nehum, and Baanah.

The roll of the men of the people of Israel: 8 the line of Parosh two thousand one hundred and seventy-two; 9 the line of Shephatiah three hundred and seventy-two; 10 the line of Arah six hundred and fifty-two; 11 the line of Pahath-moab, namely the lines of Jeshua and Joab, two thousand eight hundred and eighteen; 12 the line of Elam one thousand two hundred and fifty-four; 13 the line of Zattu eight hundred and forty-five; 14 the line of Zaccai seven hundred and sixty; 15 the line of Binnui six hundred and forty-eight; 16 the line of Bebai six hundred and twenty-eight; 17 the line of Azgad two thousand three hundred and twenty-two; 18 the line of Adonikam six hundred and sixty-seven; 19 the line of Bigvai two thousand and sixty-seven; 20 the line of Adin six hundred and fifty-five; 21 the line of Ater, namely that of Hezekiah, ninety-eight; 22 the line of Hashum three hundred and twenty-eight; 23 the line of Bezai three hundred and twenty-four; 24 the line of Hariph one hundred and twelve; 25 the line of Gibeon ninety-five. 26 The men of Bethlehem and Netophah one hundred and eighty-eight; 27 the men of Anathoth one hundred and twenty-eight; 28 the men of Beth-azmoth forty-two; 29 the men of Kiriath-jearim, Kephirah, and Beeroth seven hundred and forty-three; 30 the men of Ramah and Geba six hundred and twenty-one; 31 the men of Michmas one hundred and twenty-two; 32 the men of Bethel and Ai one hundred and twenty-three; 33 the men of Nebo fifty-two; 34 the men of the other Elam one thousand two hundred and fifty-four; 35 the men of Harim three hundred and twenty; 36 the men of Jericho three hundred and forty-five; 37 the men of Lod, Hadid, and Ono seven hundred and twenty-one; 38 the men of Senaah three thousand nine hundred and thirty.

39 Priests: the line of Jedaiah, of the house of Jeshua, nine hundred and seventy-three; 40 the line of Immer one thousand and fifty-two; 41 the line of Pashhur one thousand two hundred and forty-seven; 42 the line of Harim one thousand and seventeen.

43 Levites: the lines of Jeshua and Kadmiel, of the house of Hodvah, seventy-four. 44 Singers: the line of Asaph one hundred and forty-eight. 45 Door-keepers: the line of Shallum, the line of Ater, the line of Talmon, the line of Akkub, the line of Hatita, and the line of Shobai, one hundred and thirty-eight in all.

46 Temple servitors: the line of Ziha, the line of Hasupha, the line of Tabbaoth, 47 the line of Keros, the line of Sia, the line of Padon, 48 the line of Lebanah, the line of Hagabah, the line of Shalmai, 49 the line of Hanan, the line of Giddel, the line of Gahar, 50 the line of Reaiah, the line of Rezin, the line of Nekoda, 51 the line of Gazzam, the line of Uzza, the line of Paseah, 52 the line of Besai, the line of the Meunim, the line of the Nephishesim, 53 the line of Bakbuk, the line of Hakupha, the line of Harhur, 54 the line of Bazlith, the line of Mehida, the line of Harsha, 55 the line of Barkos, the line of Sisera, the line of Temah, 56 the line of Neziah, and the line of Hatipha.

7:6–73 Cp. Ezra 2:1–70. 7:33 **the men of:** prob. rdg, cp. Ezra 2:29; Heb. adds the other. 7:34 **men:** prob. rdg; Heb. line (also in verses 35–38). 7:43 **and:** prob. rdg, cp. Ezra 2:40; Heb. to.

5 When my God had put it into my mind to gather together the nobles, the magistrates, and the common people, and to examine their family records, I came upon the family list of those who had returned in the earliest period. There I found the following written:

6 These are the inhabitants of the province who returned from the captivity of the exiles whom Nebuchadnezzar, king of Babylon, had carried away, and who came back to Jerusalem and Judah, each man to his own city 7 (those who returned with Zerubbabel, Jeshua, Nehemiah, Azariah, Raamiah, Nahamani, Mordecai, Bilshan, Mispereth, Bigvai, Nehum, and Baanah).

The census of the men of Israel: 8 sons of Parosh, two thousand one hundred and seventy-two; 9 sons of Shephatiah, three hundred and seventy-two; 10 sons of Arah, six hundred and fifty-two; 11 sons of Pahath-moab who were sons of Jeshua and Joab, two thousand eight hundred and eighteen; 12 sons of Elam, one thousand two hundred and fifty-four; 13 sons of Zattu, eight hundred and forty-five; 14 sons of Zaccai, seven hundred and sixty; 15 sons of Binnui, six hundred and forty-eight; 16 sons of Bebai, six hundred and twenty-eight; 17 sons of Azgad, two thousand three hundred and twenty-two; 18 sons of Adonikam, six hundred and sixty-seven; 19 sons of Bigvai, two thousand and sixty-seven; 20 sons of Adin, six hundred and fifty-five; 21 sons of Ater who were sons of Hezekiah, ninety-eight; 22 sons of Hashum, three hundred and twenty-eight; 23 sons of Bezai, three hundred and twenty-four; 24 sons of Hariph, one hundred and twelve; 25 sons of Gibeon, ninety-five; 26 men of Bethlehem and Netophah, one hundred and eighty-eight; 27 men of Anathoth, one hundred and twenty-eight; 28 men of Beth-azmaveth, forty-two; 29 men of Kiriath-jearim, Chephirah, and Beeroth, seven hundred and forty-three; 30 men of Ramah and Geba, six hundred and twenty-one; 31 men of Michmas, one hundred and twenty-two; 32 men of Bethel and Ai, one hundred and twenty-three; 33 men of Nebo, fifty-two; 34 sons of another Elam, one thousand two hundred and fifty-four; 35 sons of Harim, three hundred and twenty; 36 sons of Jericho, three hundred and forty-five; 37 sons of Lod, Hadid, and Ono, seven hundred and twenty-one; 38 sons of Senaah, three thousand nine hundred and thirty.

39 The priests: sons of Jedaiah who were of the house of Jeshua, nine hundred and seventy-three; 40 sons of Immer, one thousand and fifty-two; 41 sons of Pashhur, one thousand two hundred and forty-seven; 42 sons of Harim, one thousand and seventeen.

43 The Levites: sons of Jeshua, Kadmiel, Binnui, Hodeviah, seventy-four.

44 The singers: sons of Asaph, one hundred and forty-eight.

45 The gatekeepers: sons of Shallum, sons of Ater, sons of Talmon, sons of Akkub, sons of Hatita, sons of Shobai, one hundred and thirty-eight.

46 The temple slaves: sons of Ziha, sons of Hasupha, sons of Tabbaoth, 47 sons of Keros, sons of Sia, sons of Padon, 48 sons of Lebana, sons of Hagaba, sons of Shalmai, 49 sons of Hanan, sons of Giddel, sons of Gahar, 50 sons of Reaiah, sons of Rezin, sons of Nekoda, 51 sons of Gazzam, sons of Uzza, sons of Paseah, 52 sons of Besai, sons of the Meunites, sons of the Nephusites, 53 sons of Bakbuk, sons of Hakupha, sons of Harhur, 54 sons of Bazlith, sons of Mehida, sons of Harsha, 55 sons of Barkos, sons of Sisera, sons of Temah, 56 sons of Neziah, sons of Hatipha.

inspired me to assemble the nobles, the officials and the people for the purpose of taking a census by families. I discovered the genealogical register of those who had returned in the first group, and there I found entered:

6 b These are the people of the province who returned from the captivity of the Exile, those whom Nebuchadnezzar king of Babylon had deported, and who returned to Jerusalem and Judah, each to his own town. 7 They were the ones who arrived with Zerubbabel, Jeshua, Nehemiah, Azariah, Raamiah, Nahamani, Mordecai, Bilshan, Mispereth, Bigvai, Nehum, Baanah.

The number of the men of the people of Israel: 8 sons of Parosh, two thousand one hundred and seventy-two; 9 sons of Shephatiah, three hundred and seventy-two; 10 sons of Arah, six hundred and fifty-two; 11 sons of Pahath-Moab, that is to say sons of Jeshua and Joab, two thousand eight hundred and eighteen; 12 sons of Elam, one thousand two hundred and fifty-four; 13 sons of Zattu, eight hundred and forty-five; 14 sons of Zaccai, seven hundred and sixty; 15 sons of Binnui, six hundred and forty-eight; 16 sons of Bebai, six hundred and twenty-eight; 17 sons of Azgad, two thousand three hundred and twenty-two; 18 sons of Adonikam, six hundred and sixty-seven; 19 sons of Bigvai, two thousand and sixty-seven; 20 sons of Adin, six hundred and fifty-five; 21 sons of Ater, that is to say of Hezekiah, ninety-eight; 22 sons of Hashum, three hundred and twenty-eight; 23 sons of Bezai, three hundred and twenty-four; 24 sons of Hariph, one hundred and twelve; 25 sons of Gibeon, ninety-five; 26 men of Bethlehem and Netophah, one hundred and eighty-eight; 27 men of Anathoth, one hundred and twenty-eight; 28 men of Beth-Azmaveth, forty-two; 29 men of Kiriath-Jearim, Chephirah and Beeroth, seven hundred and forty-three; 30 men of Ramah and Geba, six hundred and twenty-one; 31 men of Michmas, one hundred and twenty-two; 32 men of Bethel and Ai, one hundred and twenty-three; 33 men of the other Nebo, fifty-two; 34 sons of the other Elam, one thousand two hundred and fifty-four; 35 sons of Harim, three hundred and twenty; 36 sons of Jericho, three hundred and forty-five; 37 sons of Lod, Hadid and Ono, seven hundred and twenty-one; 38 sons of Senaah, three thousand nine hundred and thirty.

39 The priests: sons of Jedaiah, of the House of Jeshua, nine hundred and seventy-three; 40 sons of Immer, one thousand and fifty-two; 41 sons of Pashhur, one thousand two hundred and forty-seven; 42 sons of Harim, one thousand and seventeen.

43 The Levites: sons of Jeshua, of Kadmiel, of the sons of Hodiah, seventy-four.

44 The singers: sons of Asaph, one hundred and forty-eight.

45 The gatekeepers: sons of Shallum, sons of Ater, sons of Talmon, sons of Akkub, sons of Hatita, sons of Shobai, one hundred and thirty-eight.

46 The temple slaves: sons of Ziha, sons of Hasupha, sons of Tabbaoth, 47 sons of Keros, sons of Sia, sons of Padon, 48 sons of Lebana, sons of Hagaba, sons of Shalmai, 49 sons of Hanan, sons of Giddel, sons of Gahar, 50 sons of Reaiah, sons of Rezin, sons of Nekoda, 51 sons of Gazzam, sons of Uzza, sons of Paseah, 52 sons of Besai, sons of the Meunites, sons of the Nephusites, 53 sons of Bakbuk, sons of Hakupha, sons of Harhur, 54 sons of Bazlith, sons of Mehida, sons of Harsha, 55 sons of Barkos, sons of Sisera, sons of Temah, 56 sons of Nezaiah, sons of Hatipha.

57 The descendants of Solomon's servants: of Sotai, of Sophereth, of Perida, 58 of Jaala, of Darkon, of Giddel, 59 of Shephatiah, of Hattil, of Pochereth-hazzebaim, of Amon.

60 All the temple servants and the descendants of Solomon's servants were three hundred ninety-two.

61 The following were those who came up from Tel-melah, Tel-harsha, Cherub, Addon, and Immer, but they could not prove their ancestral houses or their descent, whether they belonged to Israel: 62 the descendants of Delaiah, of Tobiah, of Nekoda, six hundred forty-two. 63 Also, of the priests: the descendants of Hobaiah, of Hakkoz, of Barzillai (who had married one of the daughters of Barzillai the Gileadite and was called by their name). 64 These sought their registration among those enrolled in the genealogies, but it was not found there, so they were excluded from the priesthood as unclean; 65 the governor told them that they were not to partake of the most holy food, until a priest with Urim and Thummim should come.

66 The whole assembly together was forty-two thousand three hundred sixty, 67 besides their male and female slaves, of whom there were seven thousand three hundred thirty-seven; and they had two hundred forty-five singers, male and female. 68 They had seven hundred thirty-six horses, two hundred forty-five mules,[r] 69 four hundred thirty-five camels, and six thousand seven hundred twenty donkeys.

70 Now some of the heads of ancestral houses contributed to the work. The governor gave to the treasury one thousand darics of gold, fifty basins, and five hundred thirty priestly robes. 71 And some of the heads of ancestral houses gave into the building fund twenty thousand darics of gold and two thousand two hundred minas of silver. 72 And what the rest of the people gave was twenty thousand darics of gold, two thousand minas of silver, and sixty-seven priestly robes.

73 So the priests, the Levites, the gatekeepers, the singers, some of the people, the temple servants, and all Israel settled in their towns.

8 When the seventh month came — the people of Israel being settled in their towns — 1 all the people gathered together into the square before the Water Gate. They told the scribe Ezra to bring the book of the law of Moses, which the LORD had given to Israel. 2 Accordingly, the priest Ezra brought the law before the assembly, both men and women and all who could hear with understanding. This was on the first day of the seventh month. 3 He read from it facing the square before the Water Gate from early morning until midday, in the presence of the men and the women and those who could understand; and the ears of all the people were attentive to the book of the law. 4 The scribe Ezra stood on a wooden platform that had been made for the purpose; and beside him stood Mattithiah, Shema, Anaiah, Uriah, Hilkiah, and Maaseiah on his right hand; and Pedaiah, Mishael, Malchijah, Hashum, Hash-baddanah, Zechariah, and Meshullam on his left hand. 5 And Ezra opened the book in the sight of all the people, for he was standing above all the people; and when he opened it, all the people

57 Descendants of Solomon's servants: the line of Sotai, the line of Sophereth, the line of Perida, 58 the line of Jaalah, the line of Darkon, the line of Giddel, 59 the line of Shephatiah, the line of Hattil, the line of Pochereth-hazzebaim, and the line of Amon.

60 The temple servitors and the descendants of Solomon's servants amounted to three hundred and ninety-two in all.

61 The following were those who returned from Tel-melah, Tel-harsha, Kerub, Addon, and Immer, but could not establish their father's line nor whether by descent they belonged to Israel: 62 the line of Delaiah, the line of Tobiah, the line of Nekoda, six hundred and forty-two. 63 Also of the priests: the line of Hobaiah, the line of Hakkoz, and the line of Barzillai who had married a daughter of Barzillai the Gileadite and went by his name. 64 These searched for their names among those enrolled in the genealogies, but they could not be found; they were disqualified for the priesthood as unclean, 65 and the governor forbade them to partake of the most sacred food until there should be a priest able to consult the Urim and the Thummim.

66 The whole assembled people numbered forty-two thousand three hundred and sixty, 67 apart from their slaves, male and female, of whom there were seven thousand three hundred and thirty-seven; and they had two hundred and forty-five singers, men and women. 68 Their horses numbered seven hundred and thirty-six, their mules two hundred and forty-five, 69 their camels four hundred and thirty-five, and their donkeys six thousand seven hundred and twenty.

70 Some of the heads of families gave contributions for the work. The governor gave to the treasury a thousand gold drachmas, fifty tossing-bowls, and five hundred and thirty priestly vestments. 71 Some of the heads of families gave for the fabric fund twenty thousand gold drachmas and two thousand two hundred silver minas. 72 What the rest of the people gave us was twenty thousand gold drachmas, two thousand silver minas, and sixty-seven priestly vestments.

73 The priests and Levites, with some of the people, lived in Jerusalem and its neighbourhood; the door-keepers, the singers, the temple servitors, and all other Israelites lived in their own towns.

8 WHEN the seventh month came, and the Israelites were now settled in their towns, 1 all the people assembled with one accord in the broad space in front of the Water Gate, and requested Ezra the scribe to bring the book of the law of Moses, which the LORD had enjoined upon Israel. 2 On the first day of the seventh month, Ezra the priest brought the law before the whole assembly, both men and women, and all who were capable of understanding what they heard. 3 From early morning till noon he read aloud from it, facing the square in front of the Water Gate, in the presence of the men and the women, and those who could understand; the people all listened attentively to the book of the law.

4 Ezra the scribe stood on a wooden platform which had been made for this purpose; beside him stood Mattithiah, Shema, Anaiah, Uriah, Hilkiah, and Maaseiah on his right hand, and on his left Pedaiah, Mishael, Malchiah, Hashum, Hashbaddanah, Zechariah, and Meshullam. 5 Then Ezra opened the book in the sight of all the people, for he was standing above them; and when he opened it, they all stood.

---

[r] Ezra 2.66 and the margins of some Hebrew Mss: MT lacks *They had . . . forty-five mules*

7:68 **Their horses . . . forty-five:** *so some MSS; others omit.*
7:73 **in . . . neighbourhood:** *prob. rdg, cp. 1 Esd. 5:46; Heb. omits.*
8:1 **scribe:** *or doctor of the law.*

NEW AMERICAN BIBLE

NEW JERUSALEM BIBLE

57 Descendants of the slaves of Solomon: sons of Sotai, sons of Sophereth, sons of Perida, 58 sons of Jaala, sons of Darkon, sons of Giddel, 59 sons of Shephatiah, sons of Hattil, sons of Pochereth-hazzebaim, sons of Amon. 60 The total of the temple slaves and the descendants of the slaves of Solomon was three hundred and ninety-two.

61 The following who returned from Telmelah, Telharsha, Cherub, Addon, and Immer were unable to prove that their ancestral houses and their descent were Israelite: 62 sons of Delaiah, sons of Tobiah, sons of Nekoda, six hundred and forty-two. 63 Also, of the priests: sons of Hobaiah, sons of Hakkoz, sons of Barzillai (he had married one of the daughters of Barzillai the Gileadite and became known by his name). 64 These men searched their family records, but their names could not be found written there; hence they were degraded from the priesthood, 65 and His Excellency ordered them not to partake of the most holy foods until there should be a priest bearing the Urim and Thummim.

66 The entire assembly taken together came to forty-two thousand three hundred and sixty, 67 not counting their male and female slaves, who were seven thousand three hundred and thirty-seven. They also had two hundred male and female singers. Their horses were seven hundred and thirty-six, their mules two hundred and forty-five, 68 their camels four hundred and thirty-five, their asses six thousand seven hundred and twenty.

69 Certain of the family heads contributed to the service. His Excellency put into the treasury one thousand drachmas of gold, fifty basins, thirty garments for priests, and five hundred minas of silver. 70 Some of the family heads contributed to the treasury for the temple service: twenty thousand drachmas of gold and two thousand two hundred minas of silver. 71 The contributions of the rest of the people amounted to twenty thousand drachmas of gold, two thousand minas of silver, and sixty-seven garments for priests.

72 The priests, the Levites, the gatekeepers, the singers, the temple slaves, and all Israel took up residence in their cities.

57 The sons of Solomon's slaves: sons of Sotai, sons of Sophereth, sons of Perida, 58 sons of Jaala, sons of Darkon, sons of Giddel, 59 sons of Shephatiah, sons of Hattil, sons of Pochereth-ha-Zebaim, sons of Amon. 60 The total of the temple slaves and the sons of Solomon's slaves: three hundred and ninety-two.

61 The following, who came from Tel-Melah, Tel-Harsha, Cherub, Addon and Immer, could not prove that their families and ancestry were of Israelite origin: 62 the sons of Delaiah, the sons of Tobiah, the sons of Nekoda: six hundred and forty-two. 63 And among the priests: the sons of Hobaiah, the sons of Hakkoz, the sons of Barzillai — who had married one of the daughters of Barzillai the Gileadite, whose name he adopted. 64 These had looked for their entries in the official genealogies but were not to be found there, and were hence disqualified from the priesthood. 65 Consequently, His Excellency forbade them to eat any of the consecrated food until a priest appeared who could consult *urim* and *thummim*.

66 The whole assembly numbered forty-two thousand three hundred and sixty people, 67 not counting their slaves and maidservants to the number of seven thousand three hundred and thirty-seven. They also had two hundred and forty-five male and female singers. 68 They had four hundred and thirty-five camels and six thousand seven hundred and twenty donkeys.

69 A certain number of heads of families contributed to the work. His Excellency contributed one thousand gold drachmas, fifty bowls, and thirty priestly robes to the fund. 70 And heads of families gave twenty thousand gold drachmas and two thousand two hundred silver minas to the work fund. 71 The gifts made by the rest of the people amounted to twenty thousand gold drachmas, two thousand silver minas, and sixty-seven priestly robes.

72 The priests, the Levites and some of the people lived in Jerusalem and thereabouts; the singers, the gatekeepers, and the temple slaves in their appropriate towns; and all the other Israelites, in their own towns.

8 Now when the seventh month came, 1 the whole people gathered as one man in the open space before the Water Gate, and they called upon Ezra the scribe to bring forth the book of the law of Moses which the LORD prescribed for Israel. 2 On the first day of the seventh month, therefore, Ezra the priest brought the law before the assembly, which consisted of men, women, and those children old enough to understand. 3 Standing at one end of the open place that was before the Water Gate, he read out of the book from daybreak till midday, in the presence of the men, the women, and those children old enough to understand; and all the people listened attentively to the book of the law. 4 Ezra the scribe stood on a wooden platform that had been made for the occasion; at his right side stood Mattithiah, Shema, Anaiah, Uriah, Hilkiah, and Maaseiah, and on his left Pedaiah, Mishael, Malchijah, Hashum, Hashbaddanah, Zechariah, Meshullam. 5 Ezra opened the scroll so that all the people might see it (for he was standing higher up than any of the people); and, as he opened it, all the people rose.

8 Now when the seventh month came round — the Israelites being in their towns — 1 all the people gathered as one man in the square in front of the Water Gate, and asked the scribe Ezra to bring the Book of the Law of Moses which Yahweh had prescribed for Israel. 2 Accordingly, on the first day of the seventh month, the priest Ezra brought the Law before the assembly, consisting of men, women and all those old enough to understand. 3 In the square in front of the Water Gate, in the presence of the men and women, and of those old enough to understand, he read from the book from dawn till noon; all the people listened attentively to the Book of the Law. 4 The scribe Ezra stood on a wooden dais erected for the purpose; beside him stood, on his right, Mattithiah, Shema, Anaiah, Uriah, Hilkiah and Maaseiah; on his left, Pedaiah, Mishael, Malchijah, Hashum, Hashbaddanah, Zechariah, and Meshullam. 5 In full view of all the people — since he stood higher than them all — Ezra opened the book; and when he opened it, all the people stood up. 6 Then Ezra

7, 72b—8, 18: to be read after Ezr 8, 36. The gloss mentioning Nehemiah in v 9 was inserted in this Ezra section after the dislocation of several parts of Ezra-Nehemiah had occurred. There is no clear evidence of a simultaneous presence of Nehemiah and Ezra in Jerusalem; Neh. 12, 26 and 12, 36 are also scribal glosses.

stood up. 6 Then Ezra blessed the LORD, the great God, and all the people answered, "Amen, Amen," lifting up their hands. Then they bowed their heads and worshiped the LORD with their faces to the ground. 7 Also Jeshua, Bani, Sherebiah, Jamin, Akkub, Shabbethai, Hodiah, Maaseiah, Kelita, Azariah, Jozabad, Hanan, Pelaiah, the Levites, ᵘhelped the people to understand the law, while the people remained in their places. 8 So they read from the book, from the law of God, with interpretation. They gave the sense, so that the people understood the reading.

9 And Nehemiah, who was the governor, and Ezra the priest and scribe, and the Levites who taught the people said to all the people, "This day is holy to the LORD your God; do not mourn or weep." For all the people wept when they heard the words of the law. 10 Then he said to them, "Go your way, eat the fat and drink sweet wine and send portions of them to those for whom nothing is prepared, for this day is holy to our LORD; and do not be grieved, for the joy of the LORD is your strength." 11 So the Levites stilled all the people, saying, "Be quiet, for this day is holy; do not be grieved." 12 And all the people went their way to eat and drink and to send portions and to make great rejoicing, because they had understood the words that were declared to them.

13 On the second day the heads of ancestral houses of all the people, with the priests and the Levites, came together to the scribe Ezra in order to study the words of the law. 14 And they found it written in the law, which the LORD had commanded by Moses, that the people of Israel should live in boothsᵛ during the festival of the seventh month, 15 and that they should publish and proclaim in all their towns and in Jerusalem as follows, "Go out to the hills and bring branches of olive, wild olive, myrtle, palm, and other leafy trees to make booths,ᵛ as it is written." 16 So the people went out and brought them, and made boothsᵛ for themselves, each on the roofs of their houses, and in their courts and in the courts of the house of God, and in the square at the Water Gate and in the square at the Gate of Ephraim. 17 And all the assembly of those who had returned from the captivity made boothsᵛ and lived in them; for from the days of Jeshua son of Nun to that day the people of Israel had not done so. And there was very great rejoicing. 18 And day by day, from the first day to the last day, he read from the book of the law of God. They kept the festival seven days; and on the eighth day there was a solemn assembly, according to the ordinance.

9 Now on the twenty-fourth day of this month the people of Israel were assembled with fasting and in sackcloth, and with earth on their heads.ʷ 2 Then those of Israelite descent separated themselves from all foreigners, and stood and confessed their sins and the iniquities of their ancestors. 3 They stood up in their place and read from the book of the law of the LORD their God for a fourth part of the day, and for another fourth they made confession and worshiped the LORD their God. 4 Then Jeshua, Bani, Kadmiel, Shebaniah, Bunni, Sherebiah, Bani, and Chenani stood on the stairs of the Levites and cried out with a loud voice to the LORD their God. 5 Then the Levites, Jeshua, Kadmiel, Bani, Hashabneiah, Sherebiah, Hodiah, Shebaniah, and Pethahiah, said, "Stand up and bless the LORD your God from everlasting to everlasting. Blessed be your glorious name, which is exalted above all blessing and praise."

6 Ezra blessed the LORD, the great God, and all the people raised their hands and responded, 'Amen, Amen'; then they bowed their heads and prostrated themselves before the LORD. 7 Jeshua, Bani, Sherebiah, Jamin, Akkub, Shabbethai, Hodiah, Maaseiah, Kelita, Azariah, Jozabad, Hanan, and Pelaiah, the Levites, expounded the law to the people while the people remained in their places. 8 They read from the book of the law of God clearly, made its sense plain, and gave instruction in what was read.

9 Then Nehemiah the governor and Ezra the priest and scribe, and the Levites who instructed the people, said to them all, 'This day is holy to the LORD your God; do not mourn or weep'; for the people had all been weeping while they listened to the words of the law. 10 'Go now,' he continued, 'feast yourselves on rich food and sweet drinks, and send a share to all who cannot provide for themselves, for the day is holy to our Lord. Let there be no sadness, for joy in the LORD is your strength.' 11 The Levites calmed the people, saying, 'Be quiet, for this day is holy; let there be no sadness.' 12 So all the people went away to eat and to drink, to send shares to others, and to celebrate the day with great rejoicing, because they had understood what had been explained to them.

13 On the second day the heads of families of the whole people, with the priests and the Levites, assembled before Ezra the scribe to study the law. 14 They found written in the law that the LORD had given commandment through Moses that the Israelites were to live in booths during the feast of the seventh month; 15 they should issue this proclamation throughout all their towns and in Jerusalem: 'Go out to the hills and fetch branches of olive and wild olive, myrtle and palm, and other leafy boughs, to make booths as prescribed.' 16 So the people went and fetched branches and made booths for themselves, each on his own roof, and in their courtyards and in the precincts of the house of God, and in the square at the Water Gate and the square at the Ephraim Gate. 17 The whole community of those who had returned from the captivity made booths and lived in them, a thing that the Israelites had not done from the days of Joshua son of Nun until that day; and there was very great rejoicing. 18 The book of the law of God was read day by day, from the first day to the last. They kept the feast for seven days, and on the eighth day there was a closing ceremony, according to the rule.

9 On the twenty-fourth day of this month the Israelites, clothed in sackcloth and with dust on their heads, assembled for a fast. 2 Those who were of Israelite descent separated themselves from all who were foreigners; they stood and confessed their sins and the iniquities of their forefathers. 3 Then, while they stood up where they were, the book of the law of the LORD their God was read for one quarter of the day, and another quarter of the day they spent in confession and in worshipping the LORD their God. 4 On the steps assigned to the Levites stood Jeshua, Bani, Kadmiel, Shebaniah, Bunni, Sherebiah, Bani, and Kenani, and they cried aloud to the LORD their God. 5 Then the Levites, Jeshua, Kadmiel, Bani, Hashabniah, Sherebiah, Hodiah, Shebaniah, and Pethahiah, said, 'Stand up and bless the LORD your God in these words: From everlasting to everlasting may your glorious name be blessed and exalted above all blessing and praise.

ᵘ 1 Esdras 9.48 Vg: Heb and the Levites   ᵛ Or tabernacles; Heb succoth   ʷ Heb on them

8:7 the Levites: prob. rdg; Heb. and the Levites.

NEW AMERICAN BIBLE

6 Ezra blessed the LORD, the great God, and all the people, their hands raised high, answered, "Amen, amen!" Then they bowed down and prostrated themselves before the LORD, their faces to the ground. 7 [The Levites Jeshua, Bani, Sherebiah, Jamin, Akkub, Shabbethai, Hodiah, Maaseiah, Kelita, Azariah, Jozabad, Hanan, and Pelaiah explained the law to the people, who remained in their places.] 8 Ezra read plainly from the book of the law of God, interpreting it so that all could understand what was read. 9 Then [Nehemiah, that is, His Excellency, and] Ezra the priest-scribe [and the Levites who were instructing the people] said to all the people: "Today is holy to the LORD your God. Do not be sad, and do not weep" — for all the people were weeping as they heard the words of the law. 10 He said further: "Go, eat rich foods and drink sweet drinks, and allot portions to those who had nothing prepared; for today is holy to our LORD. Do not be saddened this day, for rejoicing in the LORD must be your strength!" 11 [And the Levites quieted all the people, saying, "Hush, for today is holy, and you must not be saddened."] 12 Then all the people went to eat and drink, to distribute portions, and to celebrate with great joy, for they understood the words that had been expounded to them.

13 On the second day, the family heads of the whole people and also the priests and the Levites gathered around Ezra the scribe and examined the words of the law more closely. 14 They found it written in the law prescribed by the LORD through Moses that the Israelites must dwell in booths during the feast of the seventh month; 15 and that they should have this proclamation made throughout their cities and in Jerusalem: "Go out into the hill country and bring in branches of olive trees, oleasters, myrtle, palm, and other leafy trees, to make booths, as the law prescribes." 16 The people went out and brought in branches with which they made booths for themselves, on the roofs of their houses, in their courtyards, in the courts of the house of God, and in the open spaces of the Water Gate and the Gate of Ephraim. 17 Thus the entire assembly of the returned exiles made booths and dwelt in them. Now the Israelites had done nothing of this sort from the days of Jeshua, son of Nun, until this occasion; therefore there was very great joy. 18 Ezra read from the book of the law of God day after day, from the first day to the last. They kept the feast for seven days, and the solemn assembly on the eighth day, as was required.

9 On the twenty-fourth day of this month, the Israelites gathered together fasting and in sackcloth, their heads covered with dust. 2 Those of Israelite descent separated themselves from all who were of foreign extraction, then stood forward and confessed their sins and the guilty deeds of their fathers. 3 When they had taken their places, they read from the book of the law of the LORD their God, for a fourth part of the day, and during another fourth part they made their confession and prostrated themselves before the LORD their God. 4 Standing on the platform of the Levites were Jeshua, Binnui, Kadmiel, Shebaniah, Bunni, Sherebiah, Bani, and Chenani, who cried out to the LORD their God with a loud voice. 5 The Levites Jeshua, Kadmiel, Bani, Hashabneiah, Sherebiah, Hodiah, Shebaniah, and Pethahiah said,

"Arise, bless the LORD, your God,
    from eternity to eternity!"
The Israelites answered with the blessing,
    "Blessed is your glorious name,
        and exalted above all blessing and praise."

NEW JERUSALEM BIBLE

blessed Yahweh, the great God, and all the people raised their hands and answered, 'Amen! Amen!'; then they bowed down and, face to the ground, prostrated themselves before Yahweh. 7 And Jeshua, Bani, Sherebiah, Jamin, Akkub, Shabbethai, Hodiah, Maaseiah, Kelita, Azariah, Jozabab, Hanan, Pelaiah, who were Levites, explained the Law to the people, while the people all kept their places. 8 Ezra read from the book of the Law of God, translating and giving the sense; so the reading was understood.

9 Then His Excellency Nehemiah and the priest-scribe Ezra and the Levites who were instructing the people said to all the people, 'Today is sacred to Yahweh your God. Do not be mournful, do not weep.' For the people were all in tears as they listened to the words of the Law.

10 He then said, 'You may go; eat what is rich, drink what is sweet and send a helping to the man who has nothing prepared. For today is sacred to our Lord. Do not be sad: the joy of Yahweh is your stronghold.' 11 And the Levites calmed all the people down, saying, 'Keep quiet; this is a sacred day. Do not be sad.' 12 Then all the people went off to eat and drink and give helpings away and enjoy themselves to the full, since they had understood the meaning of what had been proclaimed to them.

13 On the second day, the heads of families of the whole people, and the priests and Levites, gathered round the scribe Ezra to study the words of the Law. 14 And written in the Law that Yahweh had prescribed through Moses[c] they found that the Israelites were to live in shelters during the feast of the seventh month. 15 So they issued a proclamation and had it circulated in all their towns and in Jerusalem: 'Go into the hills and bring branches of olive, pine, myrtle, palm and other leafy trees to make shelters, as it says in the book.' 16 The people went out; they brought branches and made shelters for themselves, each man on his roof, in their courtyards, in the precincts of the Temple of God, in the square of the Water Gate and in the square of the Ephraim Gate. 17 The whole assembly, all who had returned from the captivity, put up shelters and lived in them; this the Israelites had not done from the days of Joshua son of Nun till that day, and there was very great merrymaking.

18 Each day, from the first day to the last one, Ezra read from the Book of the Law of God. They celebrated the feast for seven days; on the eighth day, as prescribed, they held a solemn assembly.

9 On the twenty-fourth day of this month the Israelites, in sackcloth and with dust on their heads, assembled for a fast. 2 Then those of Israelite stock who had severed relations with all foreigners stood up and confessed their sins and the iniquities of their ancestors. 3 Standing, each man in his place, they read from the Book of the Law of Yahweh their God for one quarter of the day; for another quarter they confessed their sins and worshipped Yahweh their God. 4 On the Levites' platform stood Jeshua, Binnui, Kadmiel, Shebaniah, Bunni, Sherebiah, Bani and Chenani, calling to Yahweh their God in ringing tones. 5 The Levites, Jeshua, Kadmiel, Bani, Hashabneiah, Sherebiah, Hodiah, Shebaniah and Pethahiah said, 'Stand up and bless Yahweh your God!

'Blessed are you, Yahweh our God
    from everlasting to everlasting,
    and blessed be your glorious name,
    surpassing all blessing and praise!

c 8 Lv 23:33–43.

1023

6 And Ezra said:*x* "You are the LORD, you alone; you have made heaven, the heaven of heavens, with all their host, the earth and all that is on it, the seas and all that is in them. To all of them you give life, and the host of heaven worships you. 7 You are the LORD, the God who chose Abram and brought him out of Ur of the Chaldeans and gave him the name Abraham; 8 and you found his heart faithful before you, and made with him a covenant to give to his descendants the land of the Canaanite, the Hittite, the Amorite, the Perizzite, the Jebusite, and the Girgashite; and you have fulfilled your promise, for you are righteous.

9 "And you saw the distress of our ancestors in Egypt and heard their cry at the Red Sea.*y* 10 You performed signs and wonders against Pharaoh and all his servants and all the people of his land, for you knew that they acted insolently against our ancestors. You made a name for yourself, which remains to this day. 11 And you divided the sea before them, so that they passed through the sea on dry land, but you threw their pursuers into the depths, like a stone into mighty waters. 12 Moreover, you led them by day with a pillar of cloud, and by night with a pillar of fire, to give them light on the way in which they should go. 13 You came down also upon Mount Sinai, and spoke with them from heaven, and gave them right ordinances and true laws, good statutes and commandments, 14 and you made known your holy sabbath to them and gave them commandments and statutes and a law through your servant Moses. 15 For their hunger you gave them bread from heaven, and for their thirst you brought water for them out of the rock, and you told them to go in to possess the land that you swore to give them.

16 "But they and our ancestors acted presumptuously and stiffened their necks and did not obey your commandments; 17 they refused to obey, and were not mindful of the wonders that you performed among them; but they stiffened their necks and determined to return to their slavery in Egypt. But you are a God ready to forgive, gracious and merciful, slow to anger and abounding in steadfast love, and you did not forsake them. 18 Even when they had cast an image of a calf for themselves and said, 'This is your God who brought you up out of Egypt,' and had committed great blasphemies, 19 you in your great mercies did not for-

6 'You alone are the LORD;
you created the heavens,
the highest heavens with all their host,
the earth and all that is on it,
the seas and all that is in them.
You give life to them all,
and the heavenly host worships you.

7 'You are the LORD,
the God who chose Abram,
who brought him from Ur of the Chaldees
and named him Abraham.
8 Finding him faithful you made a covenant with him
to give to his descendants
the land of the Canaanites,
Hittites, Amorites, and Perizzites,
Jebusites, and Girgashites;
you fulfilled your promise,
for you are just.

9 'You saw the misery of our forefathers in Egypt
and heard their cry at the Red Sea.
10 You worked signs and portents against Pharaoh,
against all his courtiers and the people of his land,
for you knew how arrogantly
they treated our forefathers;
and you won for yourself renown
that lives to this day.
11 You divided asunder the sea before them,
and they passed through on dry ground;
but their pursuers you flung into the depths,
like a stone flung into turbulent waters.
12 By a pillar of cloud you guided them in the
daytime,
and at night by a pillar of fire
to light the road they were to travel.
13 You came down on Mount Sinai
and spoke to them from heaven;
you gave them right judgements and true laws,
statutes and commandments which were good.
14 You made known to them your holy sabbath,
and through Moses your servant
you gave them commandments, statutes, and laws.
15 You gave them bread from heaven to stay their
hunger
and brought water out from a rock to quench their
thirst.
You bade them enter and take possession of the
land
which you had solemnly sworn to give them.

16 'But they, our forefathers, were arrogant;
stubbornly they flouted your commandments.
17 They refused to listen,
forgetful of the miracles you had accomplished
among them.
In their stubbornness they appointed a leader
to bring them back to slavery in Egypt.
But you are a forgiving God,
gracious and compassionate,
long-suffering and ever constant,
and you did not abandon them.
18 'Even when they made for themselves
the metal image of a bull-calf
and said, "This is your god
who brought you up from Egypt,"
and were guilty of gross blasphemies,

9:9 **Red Sea:** *or* sea of Reeds. 9:17 **in Egypt:** *so some MSS; others* in their rebellion.

x Gk: Heb lacks *And Ezra said* *y* Or *Sea of Reeds*

6 Then Ezra said: "It is you, O Lord, you are the only one; you made the heavens, the highest heavens and all their host, the earth and all that is upon it, the seas and all that is in them. To all of them you give life, and the heavenly hosts bow down before you.

7 "You, O Lord, are the God who chose Abram, who brought him out from Ur of the Chaldees, and named him Abraham. 8 When you had found his heart faithful in your sight, you made the covenant with him to give to him and his posterity the land of the Canaanites, Hittites, Amorites, Perizzites, Jebusites, and Girgashites. These promises of yours you fulfilled, for you are just.

9 "You saw the affliction of our fathers in Egypt,
you heard their cry by the Red Sea;
10 You worked signs and wonders against Pharoah,
against all his servants and the people of
his land,
Because you knew of their insolence toward them;
thus you made for yourself a name even to
this day.
11 The sea you divided before them,
on dry ground they passed through the midst of
the sea;
Their pursuers you hurled into the depths,
like a stone into the mighty waters.
12 With a column of cloud you led them by day,
and by night with a column of fire,
To light the way of their journey,
the way in which they must travel.
13 On Mount Sinai you came down,
you spoke with them from heaven;
You gave them just ordinances, firm laws,
good statutes, and commandments;
14 Your holy sabbath you made known to them,
commandments, statutes, and law you prescribed
for them,
by the hand of Moses your servant.
15 Food from heaven you gave them in their hunger,
water from a rock you sent them in their thirst.
You bade them enter and occupy the land
which you had sworn with upraised hand to
give them.

16 "But they, our fathers, proved to be insolent; they held their necks stiff and would not obey your commandments. 17 They refused to obey and no longer remembered the miracles you had worked for them. They stiffened their necks and turned their heads to return to their slavery in Egypt. But you are a God of pardons, gracious and compassionate, slow to anger and rich in mercy; you did not forsake them. 18 Though they made for themselves a molten calf, and proclaimed, 'Here is your God who brought you up out of Egypt,' and were guilty of great effronteries, 19 yet in your

6 'You, Yahweh, are the one, only Yahweh,
you have created the heavens,
the heaven of heavens and all their array,
the earth and all it bears,
the seas and all they hold.
To all of them you give life,
and the array of heaven worships you.

7 'You are Yahweh God,
who chose Abram,
brought him out of Ur in Chaldaea
and changed his name to Abraham.
8 Finding his heart was faithful to you,
you made a covenant with him,
to give the country of the Canaanites,
the Hittites, the Amorites,
the Perizzites, the Jebusites and the Girgashites
to him and his descendants.
And you have made good your promises,
for you are upright.

9 'You saw the distress of our ancestors in Egypt,
you heard their cry by the Sea of Reeds.
10 You displayed signs and wonders against Pharaoh,
against all his servants and all the people of his
land;
for you knew how arrogantly they treated them.
You won a reputation which you keep to this day.
11 You opened up the sea in front of them:
they walked on dry ground right through the sea.
Into the depths you hurled their pursuers
like a stone into the raging waters.
12 With a pillar of cloud you led them by day,
with a pillar of fire by night:
to light the way ahead of them
by which they were to go.
13 You came down on Mount Sinai
and spoke with them from heaven;
you gave them right rules, reliable laws,
good statutes and commandments;
14 you revealed your holy Sabbath to them;
you laid down commandments, statutes and law for
them
through your servant Moses.
15 For their hunger you gave them bread from
heaven,
for their thirst you brought them water out of a
rock,
and you told them to go in and take possession of
the country
which you had sworn to give them.

16 'But they and our ancestors acted arrogantly,
grew obstinate and flouted your commands.
17 They refused to obey,
forgetful of the wonders which you had worked for
them;
they grew obstinate
and made up their minds to return
to their slavery in Egypt.
But because you are a forgiving God,
gracious and compassionate,
patient and rich in faithful love,
you did not abandon them!

18 'Even when they cast themselves a calf out of
molten metal
and said, "This is your God
who brought you up from Egypt!"
and committed monstrous impieties,

sake them in the wilderness; the pillar of cloud that led them in the way did not leave them by day, nor the pillar of fire by night that gave them light on the way by which they should go. 20 You gave your good spirit to instruct them, and did not withhold your manna from their mouths, and gave them water for their thirst. 21 Forty years you sustained them in the wilderness so that they lacked nothing; their clothes did not wear out and their feet did not swell. 22 And you gave them kingdoms and peoples, and allotted to them every corner,ᶻ so they took possession of the land of King Sihon of Heshbon and the land of King Og of Bashan. 23 You multiplied their descendants like the stars of heaven, and brought them into the land that you had told their ancestors to enter and possess. 24 So the descendants went in and possessed the land, and you subdued before them the inhabitants of the land, the Canaanites, and gave them into their hands, with their kings and the peoples of the land, to do with them as they pleased. 25 And they captured fortress cities and a rich land, and took possession of houses filled with all sorts of goods, hewn cisterns, vineyards, olive orchards, and fruit trees in abundance; so they ate, and were filled and became fat, and delighted themselves in your great goodness.

26 "Nevertheless they were disobedient and rebelled against you and cast your law behind their backs and killed your prophets, who had warned them in order to turn them back to you, and they committed great blasphemies. 27 Therefore you gave them into the hands of their enemies, who made them suffer. Then in the time of their suffering they cried out to you and you heard them from heaven, and according to your great mercies you gave them saviors who saved them from the hands of their enemies. 28 But after they had rest, they again did evil before you, and you abandoned them to the hands of their enemies, so that they had dominion over them; yet when they turned and cried to you, you heard from heaven, and many times you rescued them according to your mercies. 29 And you warned them in order

19 you in your great compassion
did not abandon them in the wilderness.
The pillar of cloud never failed
to guide them on their journey by day,
nor did the pillar of fire fail by night
to light the road they were to travel.
20 You gave them your good spirit to instruct them;
you did not withhold your manna,
and you gave them water for their thirst.
21 During forty years you sustained them;
in the wilderness they lacked nothing,
their clothes did not wear out,
and their feet were not swollen.

22 'You gave them kings and their people as spoils of
war.
They took possession
of the land of King Sihon of Heshbon
and the land of King Og of Bashan.
23 You made their descendants numerous,
countless as the stars in the sky,
and brought them into the land
you had promised their forefathers
they would enter and possess.
24 When their descendants came into the land
to take possession of it,
you subdued the Canaanite inhabitants before them,
giving kings and peoples into their hands
to do with them as they pleased.
25 They captured fortified towns and fertile land,
taking possession of houses
filled with all good things,
of rock-hewn cisterns, vineyards, olive groves,
and fruit trees in abundance.
They ate and were satisfied and grew fat;
they found delight in your great goodness.

26 'In growing defiance, they rebelled
and turned their backs on your law.
They killed your prophets,
who with warnings admonished them
to bring them again to you;
they were guilty of great blasphemies.
27 You handed them over to enemies to be oppressed.
But when they, under oppression, appealed to you,
from heaven you heard them
and in your great compassion sent saviours
to save them from their enemies.
28 After some respite
again they did what was wrong in your eyes,
and you abandoned them to their enemies,
who held them in subjection.
Yet once more they appealed to you,
and time after time you heard them from heaven
and in your compassion saved them.

great mercy you did not forsake them in the desert. The column of cloud did not cease to lead them by day on their journey, nor did the column of fire by night cease to light for them the way by which they were to travel.

20 "Your good spirit you bestowed on them, to give them understanding; your manna you did not withhold from their mouths, and you gave them water in their thirst. 21 Forty years in the desert you sustained them: they did not want; their garments did not become worn, and their feet did not become swollen. 22 You gave them kingdoms and peoples, which you divided up among them as border lands. They possessed the land of Sihon, king of Heshbon, and the land of Og, king of Bashan.

23 "You made their children as numerous as the stars of the heavens, and you brought them into the land which you had commanded their fathers to enter and possess. 24 The sons went in to take possession of the land, and you humbled before them the Canaanite inhabitants of the land and delivered them over into their power, their kings as well as the peoples of the land, to do with them as they would. 25 They captured fortified cities and fertile land; they took possession of houses filled with all good things, cisterns already dug, vineyards, olive groves, and fruit trees in abundance. They could eat and have their fill, fatten and feast themselves on your immense good gifts.

26 "But they were contemptuous and rebellious: they cast your law behind their backs, they slew your prophets who bore witness against them in order to bring them back to you, and they were guilty of great effronteries. 27 Therefore you delivered them into the power of their enemies, who oppressed them. But in the time of their oppression they would cry out to you, and you would hear them from heaven, and according to your great mercy give them saviors to deliver them from the power of their enemies.

28 "As soon as they had relief, they would go back to doing evil in your sight. Then again you abandoned them to the power of their enemies, who crushed them. Then they cried out to you, and you heard them from heaven and delivered them according to your mercy, many times over.

19 you, in your great compassion,
did not abandon them in the desert:
the pillar of cloud did not leave them,
leading them on their path by day,
nor the pillar of fire by night,
lighting the way ahead of them
by which they were to go.
20 You gave them your good spirit to instruct them,
you did not withhold your manna from their
mouths,
you gave them water for their thirst.
21 For forty years you cared for them in the desert,
so that they went short of nothing,
their clothes did not wear out,
nor were their feet swollen.
22 'You gave them kingdoms and peoples,
allotting them these as frontier lands;
they occupied the country of Sihon king of
Heshbon,
and the country of Og king of Bashan.
23 You gave them as many children
as there are stars in the sky,
and brought them into the country
which you had promised their ancestors
that they would enter and possess.
24 The children entered
and took possession of the country
and before them you subdued
the country's inhabitants, the Canaanites,
whom you put at their mercy,
with their kings and the peoples of the country,
for them to treat as they pleased;
25 they captured fortified towns
and a fertile countryside,
they took possession of houses
stocked with all kinds of goods,
of storage-wells ready-hewn, of vineyards, olive
groves
and fruit trees in profusion;
so they ate, were full, grew fat
and revelled in your great goodness.

26 'But they grew disobedient, rebelled against you
and thrust your law behind their backs;
they slaughtered your prophets
who had reproved them
to bring them back to you,
and committed monstrous impieties.
27 So you put them at the mercy of their enemies
who oppressed them.
But when they were being oppressed and called to
you,
you heard them from heaven
and because of your great compassion
you gave them deliverers
who rescued them from their oppressors' clutches.
28 But once at peace again,
again they did what was wrong before you;
so you put them at the mercy of their enemies
who then became their rulers.
When they called to you again,
you heard them from heaven
and, because of your compassion, rescued them
many times.

to turn them back to your law. Yet they acted presumptuously and did not obey your commandments, but sinned against your ordinances, by the observance of which a person shall live. They turned a stubborn shoulder and stiffened their neck and would not obey. 30 Many years you were patient with them, and warned them by your spirit through your prophets; yet they would not listen. Therefore you handed them over to the peoples of the lands. 31 Nevertheless, in your great mercies you did not make an end of them or forsake them, for you are a gracious and merciful God.

32 "Now therefore, our God — the great and mighty and awesome God, keeping covenant and steadfast love — do not treat lightly all the hardship that has come upon us, upon our kings, our officials, our priests, our prophets, our ancestors, and all your people, since the time of the kings of Assyria until today. 33 You have been just in all that has come upon us, for you have dealt faithfully and we have acted wickedly; 34 our kings, our officials, our priests, and our ancestors have not kept your law or heeded the commandments and the warnings that you gave them. 35 Even in their own kingdom, and in the great goodness you bestowed on them, and in the large and rich land that you set before them, they did not serve you and did not turn from their wicked works. 36 Here we are, slaves to this day — slaves in the land that you gave to our ancestors to enjoy its fruit and its good gifts. 37 Its rich yield goes to the kings whom you have set over us because of our sins; they have power also over our bodies and over our livestock at their pleasure, and we are in great distress."

38a Because of all this we make a firm agreement in writing, and on that sealed document are inscribed the names of our officials, our Levites, and our priests.

10b Upon the sealed document are the names of Nehemiah the governor, son of Hacaliah, and Zedekiah; 2 Seraiah, Azariah, Jeremiah, 3 Pashhur, Amariah, Malchijah, 4 Hattush, Shebaniah, Malluch, 5 Harim, Meremoth, Obadiah, 6 Daniel, Ginnethon, Baruch, 7 Meshullam, Abijah, Mijamin, 8 Maaziah, Bilgai, Shemaiah; these are the priests. 9 And the Levites: Jeshua son of Azaniah, Binnui of the sons of Henadad, Kadmiel; 10 and their associates, Shebaniah, Hodiah, Kelita, Pelaiah, Hanan, 11 Mica, Rehob, Hashabiah, 12 Zaccur, Sherebiah, Shebaniah, 13 Hodiah, Bani, Beninu. 14 The leaders of the people: Parosh,

29 To bring them back to your law
  you solemnly warned them,
  but arrogantly they flouted your commandments,
  sinning against the ordinances
  which bring life to those who keep them.
  Stubbornly they turned aside;
  in their obstinacy they would not obey.
30 For many years you were patient
  and your spirit admonished them through the
      prophets.
  Still they would not listen,
  and so you handed them over
  to the peoples of other countries.
31 Nevertheless in your great compassion
  you did not make an end of them or forsake them;
  for you are a gracious and compassionate God.

32 'Now, great and mighty and terrible God,
  faithfully keeping covenant, our God,
  do not regard as a small thing the hardships
  that have befallen us, our kings and princes,
  our priests, our prophets, our forefathers,
  and all your people from the time of the kings of
      Assyria
  up to the present day.
33 In all that has come upon us
  you have been just,
  for you have kept faith
  while we have done wrong.
34 Our kings, our princes, our priests, and our
      forefathers
  did not keep your law;
  they paid no heed to your commandments
  and the warnings you gave them.
35 Even in their own kingdom,
  while they were enjoying
  the great prosperity you gave them,
  and the broad, fertile land you bestowed on them,
  they did not serve you or renounce their evil ways.

36 'Today we are slaves,
  slaves here in the land
  which you gave to our forefathers
  so that they might eat its fruits
  and enjoy its good things.
37 All its produce now goes to the kings
  whom you have set over us
  because of our sins.
  They have power over our bodies,
  and they do as they please with our livestock:
  we are in dire distress.

38 'Because of all this we make a binding declaration in writing, and our princes, our Levites, and our priests witness the sealing.

10 'Those who witness the sealing are Nehemiah the governor, son of Hacaliah, Zedekiah, 2 Seraiah, Azariah, Jeremiah, 3 Pashhur, Amariah, Malchiah, 4 Hattush, Shebaniah, Malluch, 5 Harim, Meremoth, Obadiah, 6 Daniel, Ginnethon, Baruch, 7 Meshullam, Abiah, Mijamin, 8 Maaziah, Bilgai, Shemaiah; these are the priests. 9 The Levites: Jeshua son of Azaniah, Binnui of the line of Henadad, Kadmiel; 10 and their brethren, Shebaniah, Hodiah, Kelita, Pelaiah, Hanan, 11 Mica, Rehob, Hashabiah, 12 Zaccur, Sherebiah, Shebaniah, 13 Hodiah, Bani, Beninu.

a Ch 10.1 in Heb   b Ch 10.2 in Heb   9:38 In Heb. 10:1.   10:9 Jeshua: prob. rdg; Heb. and Jeshua.

1028

29 You bore witness against them, in order to bring them back to your law. But they were insolent and would not obey your commandments; they sinned against your ordinances, from which men draw life when they practice them. They turned stubborn backs, stiffened their necks, and would not obey. 30 You were patient with them for many years, bearing witness against them through your spirit, by means of your prophets; still they would not listen. Thus you delivered them over into the power of the peoples of the lands. 31 Yet in your great mercy you did not completely destroy them and you did not forsake them, for you are a kind and merciful God.

32 "Now, therefore, O our God, great, mighty, and awesome God, you who in your mercy preserve the covenant, take into account all the disasters that have befallen us, our kings, our princes, our priests, our prophets, our fathers, and your entire people, from the time of the kings of Assyria until this day! 33 In all that has come upon us you have been just, for you kept faith while we have done evil. 34 Yes, our kings, our princes, our priests, and our fathers have not kept your law; they paid no attention to your commandments and the obligations of which you reminded them. 35 While they were yet in their kingdom, in the midst of the many good things that you had given them and in the wide and fertile land that you had spread out before them, they did not serve you nor did they turn away from their evil deeds. 36 But, see, we today are slaves; and as for the land which you gave our fathers that they might eat its fruits and good things — see, we have become slaves upon it! 37 Its rich produce goes to the kings whom you set over us because of our sins, who rule over our bodies and our cattle as they please. We are in great distress!"

10 In view of all this, we are entering into a firm pact, which we are putting into writing. On the sealed document appear the names of our princes, our Levites, and our priests.

2 On the sealed document: His Excellency Nehemiah, son of Hacaliah, and Zedekiah.

3 Seraiah, Azariah, Jeremiah, 4 Pashhur, Amariah, Malchijah, 5 Hattush, Shebaniah, Malluch, 6 Harim, Meremoth, Obadiah, 7 Daniel, Ginnethon, Baruch, 8 Meshullam, Abijah, Mijamin, 9 Maaziah, Bilgai, Shemaiah: these are the priests.

10 The Levites: Jeshua, son of Azaniah; Binnui, of the sons of Henadad; Kadmiel; 11 and their brethren Shebaniah, Hodiah, Kelita, Pelaiah, Hanan, 12 Mica, Rehob, Hashabiah, 13 Zaccur, Sherebiah, Shebaniah, 14 Hodiah, Bani, Beninu.

29 You warned them, to bring them back to your law,
but they became arrogant,
did not obey your commandments
and sinned against your rules,
in whose observance is life;
they turned a stubborn shoulder,
were obstinate, and disobeyed.
30 You were patient with them for many years
and warned them by your spirit
through your prophets,
but they would not listen:
so you put them at the mercy of the people of the
country.
31 But, because of your great compassion,
you did not destroy them completely
nor abandon them,
for you are a gracious, compassionate God.
32 Now, our God — the great God,
the Mighty and Awe-inspiring One,
maintaining the covenant and your faithful love —
count as no small thing this misery
which has befallen us, our kings, our princes,
our priests, our prophets, and all your people
from the times of the Assyrian kings
to the present day.
33 You have been upright
in all that has happened to us,
for you acted faithfully,
while we did wrong.
34 Our kings, our princes, our priests
and our ancestors did not keep your law
or pay attention to your commandments and
obligations
which you imposed upon them.
35 Even in their own kingdom,
despite your great goodness
which you bestowed on them,
despite the wide and fertile country
which you had lavished on them,
they did not serve you
or renounce their evil deeds.
36 See, we are slaves today,
slaves in the country which you gave to our
ancestors
for them to eat the good things it produces.
37 Its abundant produce goes to the kings
whom, for our sins, you have set over us,
who rule over our persons
and over our cattle as they please.
We are in great distress.'

10 In view of all this we make a firm agreement, in writing. Our princes, our Levites, our priests and the rest of the people have put their names to the document under seal.

2 On the sealed document were the names of: Nehemiah, son of Hacaliah, and Zedekiah; 3 Seraiah, Azariah, Jeremiah, 4 Pashhur, Amariah, Malchijah, 5 Hattush, Shebaniah, Malluch, 6 Harim, Meremoth, Obadiah, 7 Daniel, Ginnethon, Baruch, 8 Meshullam, Abijah, Mijamin, 9 Maaziah, Bilgai, Shemaiah: these were the priests.

10 The Levites were: Jeshua son of Azaniah, Binnui of the sons of Henadad, Kadmiel, 11 and their kinsmen Shebaniah, Hodaviah, Kelita, Pelaiah, Hanan, 12 Mica, Rehob, Hashabiah, 13 Zaccur, Sherebiah, Shebaniah, 14 Hodiah, Bani, Chenani.

NEW REVISED STANDARD VERSION	REVISED ENGLISH BIBLE

NEW REVISED STANDARD VERSION

Pahath-moab, Elam, Zattu, Bani, 15 Bunni, Azgad, Bebai, 16 Adonijah, Bigvai, Adin, 17 Ater, Hezekiah, Azzur, 18 Hodiah, Hashum, Bezai, 19 Hariph, Anathoth, Nebai, 20 Magpiash, Meshullam, Hezir, 21 Meshezabel, Zadok, Jaddua, 22 Pelatiah, Hanan, Anaiah, 23 Hoshea, Hananiah, Hasshub, 24 Hallohesh, Pilha, Shobek, 25 Rehum, Hashabnah, Maaseiah, 26 Ahiah, Hanan, Anan, 27 Malluch, Harim, and Baanah.

28 The rest of the people, the priests, the Levites, the gatekeepers, the singers, the temple servants, and all who have separated themselves from the peoples of the lands to adhere to the law of God, their wives, their sons, their daughters, all who have knowledge and understanding, 29 join with their kin, their nobles, and enter into a curse and an oath to walk in God's law, which was given by Moses the servant of God, and to observe and do all the commandments of the LORD our Lord and his ordinances and his statutes. 30 We will not give our daughters to the peoples of the land or take their daughters for our sons; 31 and if the peoples of the land bring in merchandise or any grain on the sabbath day to sell, we will not buy it from them on the sabbath or on a holy day; and we will forego the crops of the seventh year and the exaction of every debt.

32 We also lay on ourselves the obligation to charge ourselves yearly one-third of a shekel for the service of the house of our God: 33 for the rows of bread, the regular grain offering, the regular burnt offering, the sabbaths, the new moons, the appointed festivals, the sacred donations, and the sin offerings to make atonement for Israel, and for all the work of the house of our God. 34 We have also cast lots among the priests, the Levites, and the people, for the wood offering, to bring it into the house of our God, by ancestral houses, at appointed times, year by year, to burn on the altar of the LORD our God, as it is written in the law. 35 We obligate ourselves to bring the first fruits of our soil and the first fruits of all fruit of every tree, year by year, to the house of the LORD; 36 also to bring to the house of our God, to the priests who minister in the house of our God, the firstborn of our sons and of our livestock, as it is written in the law, and the firstlings of our herds and of our flocks; 37 and to bring the first of our dough, and our contributions, the fruit of every tree, the wine and the oil, to the priests, to the chambers of the house of our God; and to bring to the Levites the tithes from our soil, for it is the Levites who collect the tithes in all our rural towns. 38 And the priest, the descendant of Aaron, shall be with the Levites when the Levites receive the tithes; and the Levites shall bring up a tithe of the tithes to the house of our God, to the chambers of the storehouse. 39 For the people of Israel and the sons of Levi shall bring the contribution of grain, wine, and oil to the storerooms where the vessels of the sanctuary are, and where the priests that minister, and the gatekeepers and the singers are. We will not neglect the house of our God.

11 Now the leaders of the people lived in Jerusalem; and the rest of the people cast lots to bring one out of ten to live in the holy city Jerusalem, while nine-tenths remained in the other towns. 2 And the people blessed all those who willingly offered to live in Jerusalem.

3 These are the leaders of the province who lived in Jerusalem; but in the towns of Judah all lived on their property in their towns: Israel, the priests, the Levites, the temple servants, and the descendants of Solomon's servants.

REVISED ENGLISH BIBLE

14 The chiefs of the people: Parosh, Pahath-moab, Elam, Zattu, Bani, 15 Bunni, Azgad, Bebai, 16 Adonijah, Bigvai, Adin, 17 Ater, Hezekiah, Azzur, 18 Hodiah, Hashum, Bezai, 19 Hariph, Anathoth, Nebai, 20 Magpiash, Meshullam, Hezir, 21 Meshezabel, Zadok, Jaddua, 22 Pelatiah, Hanan, Anaiah, 23 Hoshea, Hananiah, Hasshub, 24 Hallohesh, Pilha, Shobek, 25 Rehum, Hashabnah, Maaseiah, 26 Ahiah, Hanan, Anan, 27 Malluch, Harim, Baanah.

28 'The rest of the people, the priests, the Levites, the door-keepers, the singers, the temple servitors, with their wives, their sons and their daughters, all who are capable of understanding, all who for the sake of the law of God have kept themselves apart from the foreign population, 29 join with the leading brethren, when the oath is put to them, in swearing to obey God's law given by Moses the servant of God, and to observe and fulfil all the commandments of the LORD our Lord, his rules and his statutes. 30 'We shall not give our daughters in marriage to the foreign population or take their daughters for our sons. 31 If on the sabbath these people bring in merchandise or grain for sale, we shall not buy from them on the sabbath or on any holy day. We shall forgo the crops of the seventh year and release every person still held as a pledge for debt.

32 'We hereby undertake the duty of giving yearly one third of a shekel for the service of the house of our God: 33 for the rows of the Bread of the Presence, the regular grain-offering and whole-offering, the sabbaths, the new moons, the appointed seasons, the holy-gifts, and the purification-offerings to make expiation on behalf of Israel, and for all else that has to be done in the house of our God. 34 We, the priests, the Levites, and the people, have cast lots for the wood-offering, so that it may be brought into the house of our God by each family in turn, at appointed times, year by year, to burn upon the altar of the LORD our God, as prescribed in the law. 35 We undertake to bring the first-fruits of our land and the firstfruits of every fruit tree, year by year, to the house of the LORD; 36 also to bring to the house of our God, to the priests who minister in the house of our God, the firstborn of our sons and of our cattle, as prescribed in the law, and the firstborn of our herds and of our flocks; 37 and to bring to the priests the first kneading of our dough, and the first of the fruit of every tree, of the new wine and of the oil, to the storerooms in the house of our God; and to bring to the Levites the tithes from our land, for it is the Levites who collect the tithes in all our farming villages. 38 An Aaronite priest must be with the Levites when they collect the tithes; and the Levites are to bring up one tenth of the tithes to the house of our God, to the appropriate rooms in the storehouse. 39 For the Israelites and the Levites must bring the contribution of grain, new wine, and oil to the rooms where the vessels of the sanctuary are kept, and where the ministering priests, the door-keepers, and the singers are lodged. We shall not neglect the house of our God.'

11 THE leaders of the people settled in Jerusalem; and the rest of the people cast lots to bring one in every ten to live in Jerusalem, the Holy City, while the remaining nine lived in other towns. 2 The people invoked a blessing on all those who volunteered to settle in Jerusalem.

3 These are the chiefs of the province who lived in Jerusalem; but, in the towns of Judah, other Israelites, priests, Levites, temple servitors, and descendants of Solomon's servants lived on their own property, in their own towns.

10:37 **our dough:** so Gk; Heb. adds and our contributions.

15 The leaders of the people: Parosh, Pahath-moab, Elam, Zattu, Bani, 16 Bunni, Azgad, Bebai, 17 Adonijah, Bigvai, Adin, 18 Ater, Hezekiah, Azzur, 19 Hodiah, Hashum, Bezai, 20 Hariph, Anathoth, Nebai, 21 Magpiash, Meshullam, Hazir, 22 Meshezabel, Zadok, Jaddua, 23 Pelatiah, Hanan, Anaiah, 24 Hoshea, Hananiah, Hasshub, 25 Hallohesh, Pilha, Shobek, 26 Rehum, Hashabnah, Maaseiah, 27 Ahiah, Hanan, Anan, 28 Malluch, Harim, Baanah.

29 The rest of the people, priests, Levites, gatekeepers, singers, temple slaves, and all others who have separated themselves from the peoples of the lands in favor of the law of God, with their wives, their sons, their daughters, all who are of the age of discretion, 30 join with their brethren who are their princes, and with the sanction of a curse take this oath to follow the law of God which was given through Moses, the servant of God, and to observe carefully all the commandments of the LORD, our Lord, his ordinances and his statutes.

31 Agreed, that we will not marry our daughters to the peoples of the land, and that we will not take their daughters for our sons.

32 When the peoples of the land bring in merchandise or any kind of grain for sale on the sabbath day, we will not buy from them on the sabbath or on any other holyday. We will forgo the seventh year, as well as every kind of debt.

33 We impose these commandments on ourselves: to give a third of a shekel each year for the service of the house of our God, 34 for the showbread, for the daily cereal offering, for the daily holocaust, for the sabbaths, new moons, and festivals, for the holy offerings, for sin offerings to make atonement for Israel, and for every service of the house of our God. 35 We, priests, Levites, and people, have determined by lot concerning the procurement of wood: it is to be brought to the house of our God by each of our family houses at stated times each year, to be burnt on the altar of the LORD, our God, as the law prescribes. 36 We have agreed to bring each year to the house of the LORD the first fruits of our fields and of our fruit trees, of whatever kind; 37 also, as is prescribed in the law, to bring to the house of our God, to the priests who serve in the house of our God, the first-born of our children and our animals, including the first-born of our flocks and herds. 38 The first batch of our dough, and our offerings of the fruit of every tree, of wine and of oil, we will bring to the priests, to the chambers of the house of our God. The tithe of our fields we will bring to the Levites; they, the Levites, shall take the tithe in all the cities of our service. 39 An Aaronite priest shall be with the Levites when they take the tithe, and the Levites shall bring the tithe of the tithes to the house of our God, to the chambers of the treasury. 40 For to these chambers the Israelites and Levites bring the offerings of grain, wine, and oil; there also are housed the utensils of the sanctuary, and the ministering priests, the gatekeepers, and the singers. We will not neglect the house of our God.

11 The leaders of the people took up residence in Jerusalem, and the rest of the people cast lots to bring one man in ten to reside in Jerusalem, the holy city, while the other nine would remain in the other cities. 2 The people applauded all those men who willingly agreed to take up residence in Jerusalem.

3 These are the heads of the province who took up residence in Jerusalem. (In the cities of Judah dwelt lay Israelites, priests, Levites, temple slaves, and the descendants of the slaves of Solomon, each man on the property he owned in his own city.)

15 The leaders of the people were: Parosh, Pahath-Moab, Elam, Zattu, Bani, 16 Bunni, Azgad, Bebai, 17 Adonijah, Bigvai, Adin, 18 Ater, Hezekiah, Azzur, 19 Hodiah, Hashum, Bezai, 20 Hariph, Anathoth, Nebai, 21 Magpiash, Meshullam, Hezir, 22 Meshezabel, Zadok, Jaddua, 23 Pelatiah, Hanan, Anaiah, 24 Hoshea, Hananiah, Hasshub, 25 Hallohesh, Pilha, Shobek, 26 Rehum, Hashabnah, Maaseiah, 27 Ahijah, Hanan, Anan, 28 Malluch, Harim, Baanah.

29 And the rest of the people, the priests, the Levites, the gatekeepers, the singers, the temple slaves and all those who had severed relations with the people of the country to adhere to the law of God, as also their wives, their sons, their daughters, that is, all those who had reached the age of discretion, 30 have joined their esteemed brothers in a solemn oath to follow the law of God given through Moses, servant of God, and to observe and practise all the commandments of Yahweh our Lord, with his rules and his statutes.

31 We will not give our daughters in marriage to the peoples of the country, nor allow their daughters to marry our sons.

32 If the people of the country bring goods or foodstuff of any kind to sell on the Sabbath day, we will buy nothing from them on Sabbath or holy day.

In the seventh year, we will forgo the produce of the soil and the exaction of all debts.

33 We recognise the following obligations:

to give one-third of a shekel yearly for the service of the Temple of our God: 34 for the loaves of permanent offering, for the perpetual oblation, for the perpetual burnt offering, for the sacrifices on Sabbaths, on New Moons and on festivals, for the consecrated gifts, the sin offerings to expiate for Israel, in short, for the whole work of the Temple of our God; d ‡10.35: see below‡

36 and further, to bring yearly to the Temple of our God the first-fruits of our soil and the first-fruits of all our orchards, 37 also the first-born of our sons and of our cattle, as the law prescribes, the first-born of our herds and flocks should be taken to the Temple of our God for the priests officiating in the Temple of our God. 38 Furthermore, we shall bring the best of our dough, of every kind of fruit, of the new wine and of the oil to the priests, to the storerooms of the Temple of our God, and the tithe on our soil to the Levites — the Levites will themselves collect the tithes from all the towns of our religion. 39 An Aaronite priest will accompany the Levites when they collect the tithes, and the Levites will bring a tenth part 40a,b of the tithes to the Temple of our God, into the treasury storerooms; for these rooms are where the Israelites and the Levites are to bring the contributions of corn, wine and oil, and where the vessels of the sanctuary are, and the officiating priests, the gatekeepers and the singers.

35 Furthermore, as regards deliveries of wood for burning on the altar of our God as the law prescribes, we have arranged, by drawing lots, how these deliveries are to be made at the Temple of our God by the priests, the Levites and the people by families, at stated times every year.

40c We will no longer neglect the Temple of our God.

11 Now the leaders of the people took up residence in Jerusalem; so the rest of the people drew lots: one man in ten was to come and live in Jerusalem, the holy city, while the other nine were to stay in the towns outside. 2 The people praised all those who volunteered to live in Jerusalem.

3 In the towns of Judah each man lived on his own property, but these are the provincial leaders, the Israelites, the priests, the Levites, the temple slaves and the descendants of Solomon's slaves, who made their homes in Jerusalem:

d 10 v. 35 is found after v. 40b.

4 And in Jerusalem lived some of the Judahites and of the Benjaminites. Of the Judahites: Athaiah son of Uzziah son of Zechariah son of Amariah son of Shephatiah son of Mahalalel, of the descendants of Perez; 5 and Maaseiah son of Baruch son of Col-hozeh son of Hazaiah son of Adaiah son of Joiarib son of Zechariah son of the Shilonite. 6 All the descendants of Perez who lived in Jerusalem were four hundred sixty-eight valiant warriors.

7 And these are the Benjaminites: Sallu son of Meshullam son of Joed son of Pedaiah son of Kolaiah son of Maaseiah son of Ithiel son of Jeshaiah. 8 And his brothers c Gabbai, Sallai: nine hundred twenty-eight. 9 Joel son of Zichri was their overseer; and Judah son of Hassenuah was second in charge of the city.

10 Of the priests: Jedaiah son of Joiarib, Jachin, 11 Seraiah son of Hilkiah son of Meshullam son of Zadok son of Meraioth son of Ahitub, officer of the house of God, 12 and their associates who did the work of the house, eight hundred twenty-two; and Adaiah son of Jeroham son of Pelaliah son of Amzi son of Zechariah son of Pashhur son of Malchijah, 13 and his associates, heads of ancestral houses, two hundred forty-two; and Amashsai son of Azarel son of Ahzai son of Meshillemoth son of Immer, 14 and their associates, valiant warriors, one hundred twenty-eight; their overseer was Zabdiel son of Haggedolim.

15 And of the Levites: Shemaiah son of Hasshub son of Azrikam son of Hashabiah son of Bunni; 16 and Shabbethai and Jozabad, of the leaders of the Levites, who were over the outside work of the house of God; 17 and Mattaniah son of Mica son of Zabdi son of Asaph, who was the leader to begin the thanksgiving in prayer, and Bakbukiah, the second among his associates; and Abda son of Shammua son of Galal son of Jeduthun. 18 All the Levites in the holy city were two hundred eighty-four.

19 The gatekeepers, Akkub, Talmon and their associates, who kept watch at the gates, were one hundred seventy-two. 20 And the rest of Israel, and of the priests and the Levites, were in all the towns of Judah, all of them in their inheritance. 21 But the temple servants lived on Ophel; and Ziha and Gishpa were over the temple servants.

22 The overseer of the Levites in Jerusalem was Uzzi son of Bani son of Hashabiah son of Mattaniah son of Mica, of the descendants of Asaph, the singers, in charge of the work of the house of God. 23 For there was a command from the king concerning them, and a settled provision for the singers, as was required every day. 24 And Pethahiah son of Meshezabel, of the descendants of Zerah son of Judah, was at the king's hand in all matters concerning the people.

25 And as for the villages, with their fields, some of the people of Judah lived in Kiriath-arba and its villages, and in Dibon and its villages, and in Jekabzeel and its villages, 26 and in Jeshua and in Moladah and Beth-pelet, 27 in Hazar-shual, in Beer-sheba and its villages, 28 in Ziklag, in Meconah and its villages, 29 in En-rimmon, in Zorah, in Jarmuth, 30 Zanoah, Adullam, and their villages, Lachish and its fields, and Azekah and its villages. So they camped from Beer-sheba to the valley of Hinnom. 31 The people of Benjamin also lived from Geba onward, at Michmash, Aija, Bethel and its villages, 32 Anathoth, Nob, Ananiah, 33 Hazor, Ramah, Gittaim, 34 Hadid, Zeboim, Neballat, 35 Lod, and Ono, the valley of artisans. 36 And certain divisions of the Levites in Judah were joined to Benjamin.

4 Some members of the tribes of Judah and Benjamin lived in Jerusalem. Of Judah: Athaiah son of Uzziah, son of Zechariah, son of Amariah, son of Shephatiah, son of Mahalalel of the line of Perez, 6 all of whose family, to the number of four hundred and sixty-eight men of substance, lived in Jerusalem; 5 and Maaseiah son of Baruch, son of Col-hozeh, son of Hazaiah, son of Adaiah, son of Joiarib, son of Zechariah of the Shelanite family.

7 These were the Benjamites: Sallu son of Meshullam, son of Joed, son of Pedaiah, son of Kolaiah, son of Maaseiah, son of Ithiel, son of Isaiah, 8 and his kinsmen Gabbai and Sallai, nine hundred and twenty-eight in all. 9 Joel son of Zichri was their overseer, and Judah son of Hassenuah was second over the city.

10 Of the priests: Jedaiah son of Joiarib, son of 11 Seraiah, son of Hilkiah, son of Meshullam, son of Zadok, son of Meraioth, son of Ahitub, supervisor of the house of God, 12 and his brethren responsible for the work in the temple, eight hundred and twenty-two in all; and Adaiah son of Jeroham, son of Pelaliah, son of Amzi, son of Zechariah, son of Pashhur, son of Malchiah, 13 and his brethren, heads of fathers' houses, two hundred and forty-two in all; and Amashai son of Azarel, son of Ahzai, son of Meshillemoth, son of Immer, 14 and his brethren, men of substance, a hundred and twenty-eight in all; their overseer was Zabdiel son of Haggedolim.

15 And of the Levites: Shemaiah son of Hasshub, son of Azrikam, son of Hashabiah, son of Bunni; 16 and Shabbethai and Jozabad, of the chiefs of the Levites, who had charge of the external business of the house of God; 17 and Mattaniah son of Micah, son of Zabdi, son of Asaph, who as precentor led the prayer of thanksgiving, and Bakbukiah who held the second place among his brethren; and Abda son of Shammua, son of Galal, son of Jeduthun. 18 The number of Levites in the Holy City was two hundred and eighty-four in all.

19 The gate-keepers who kept guard at the gates were Akkub, Talmon, and their brethren, a hundred and seventy-two. 20 The rest of the Israelites were in all the towns of Judah, each man on his own inherited property. 21 But the temple servitors lodged on Mount Ophel, and Ziha and Gishpa were in charge of them.

22 The overseer of the Levites in Jerusalem was Uzzi son of Bani, son of Hashabiah, son of Mattaniah, son of Mica, of the line of Asaph, the singers, for the supervision of the business of the house of God. 23 For they were under the king's orders, and there was obligatory duty for the singers every day. 24 Pethahiah son of Meshezabel, of the line of Zerah son of Judah, was the king's adviser on all matters affecting the people.

25 As for the hamlets with their surrounding fields: some of the men of Judah lived in Kiriath-arba and its villages, in Dibon and its villages, and in Jekabzeel and its hamlets, 26 in Jeshua, Moladah, and Bethpelet, 27 in Hazar-shual, and in Beersheba and its villages, 28 in Ziklag and in Meconah and its villages, 29 in Enrimmon, Zorah, and Jarmuth, 30 in Zanoah, Adullam, and their hamlets, in Lachish and its fields, and Azekah and its villages. Thus they occupied the country from Beersheba to the valley of Hinnom. 31 The men of Benjamin lived in Geba, Michmash, Aiah, and Bethel with its villages, 32 in Anathoth, Nob, and Ananiah, 33 in Hazor, Ramah, and Gittaim, 34 in Hadid, Zeboim, and Neballat, 35 in Lod, Ono, and Ge-harashim. 36 Certain divisions of the Levites in Judah were attached to Benjamin.

11:8 his kinsmen: so Gk (Luc.); Heb. after him.   11:10 son of [Seraiah]: prob. rdg; Heb. obscure.   11:20 The rest ... Israelites: prob. rdg; Heb. adds the levitical priests.   11:31 lived in: prob. rdg; Heb. from.

c Gk Mss: Heb And after him

4 In Jerusalem dwelt both Judahites and Benjaminites. Of the Judahites: Athaiah, son of Uzziah, son of Zechariah, son of Amariah, son of Shephatiah, son of Mehallalel, of the sons of Perez; 5 Maaseiah, son of Baruch, son of Colhozeh, son of Hazaiah, son of Adaiah, son of Joiarib, son of Zechariah, a son of the Shelanites. 6 The total of the sons of Perez who dwelt in Jerusalem was four hundred and sixty-eight valiant men.

7 These were the Benjaminites: Sallu, son of Meshullam, son of Joed, son of Pedaiah, son of Kolaiah, son of Maaseiah, son of Ithiel, son of Jeshaiah, 8 and his brethren, warriors, nine hundred and twenty-eight in number. 9 Joel, son of Zichri, was their commander, and Judah, son of Hassenuah, was second in charge of the city.

10 Among the priests were: Jedaiah; Joiarib; Jachin; 11 Seraiah, son of Hilkiah, son of Meshullam, son of Zadok, son of Meraioth, son of Ahitub, the ruler of the house of God, 12 and their brethren who carried out the temple service, eight hundred and twenty-two; Adaiah, son of Jeroham, son of Pelaliah, son of Amzi, son of Zechariah, son of Pashhur, son of Malchijah, 13 and his brethren, family heads, two hundred and forty-two; and Amasai, son of Azarel, son of Ahzai, son of Meshillemoth, son of Immer, 14 and his brethren, warriors, one hundred and twenty-eight. Their commander was Zabdiel, son of Haggadol.

15 Among the Levites were Shemaiah, son of Hasshub, son of Azrikam, son of Hashabiah, son of Bunni; 16 Shabbethai and Jozabad, levitical chiefs who were placed over the external affairs of the house of God; 17 Mattaniah, son of Micah, son of Zabdi, son of Asaph, director of the psalms, who led the thanksgiving at prayer; Bakbukiah, second in rank among his brethren; and Abda, son of Shammua, son of Galal, son of Jeduthun. 18 The total of the Levites in the holy city was two hundred and eighty-four.

19 The gatekeepers were Akkub, Talmon, and their brethren, who kept watch over the gates; one hundred and seventy-two in number.

20 The rest of Israel, including priests and Levites, were in all the other cities of Judah, each man in his inheritance.

21 The temple slaves lived on Ophel. Ziha and Gishpa were in charge of the temple slaves.

22 The prefect of the Levites in Jerusalem was Uzzi, son of Bani, son of Hashabiah, son of Mattaniah, son of Mica; he was one of the sons of Asaph, the singers appointed to the service of the house of God— 23 for they had been appointed by royal decree, and there was a fixed schedule for the singers assigning them their daily duties.

24 Pethahiah, son of Meshezabel, a descendant of Zerah, son of Judah, was royal deputy in all affairs that concerned the people.

25 As concerns their villages in the country: Judahites lived in Kiriath-arba and its dependencies, in Dibon and its dependencies, in Jekabzeel and its villages, 26 in Jeshua, Moladah, Beth-pelet, 27 in Hazar-shual, in Beer-sheba and its dependencies, 28 in Ziklag, in Meconah and its dependencies, 29 in En-rimmon, Zorah, Jarmuth, 30 Zanoah, Adullam, and their villages, Lachish and its countryside, Azekah and its dependencies. They were settled from Beer-sheba to Ge-hinnom.

31 Benjaminites were in Geba, Michmash, Aija, Bethel and its dependencies, 32 Anathoth, Nob, Ananiah, 33 Hazor, Ramah, Gittaim, 34 Hadid, Zeboim, Neballat, 35 Lod, Ono, and the Valley of the Artisans.

36 Some sections of the Levites from Judah settled in Benjamin.

4 Of the sons of Judah and the sons of Benjamin who made their homes in Jerusalem there were:

Of the sons of Judah: Athaiah son of Uzziah, son of Zechariah, son of Amariah, son of Shephatiah, son of Mehalalel, of the descendants of Perez; 5 and Maaseiah son of Baruch, son of Col-Hozeh, son of Hazaiah, son of Adaiah, son of Joiarib, son of Zechariah, descendant of Shelah. 6 The total number of the descendants of Perez living in Jerusalem was four hundred and sixty-eight outstanding people.

7 These are the sons of Benjamin: Sallu son of Meshullam, son of Joed, son of Pedaiah, son of Kolaiah, son of Maaseiah, son of Ithiel, son of Jeshaiah, 8 and his brothers Gabbai and Sallai; nine hundred and twenty-eight. 9 Joel son of Zichri was their chief, and Judah son of Hassenuah was second in command of the city.

10 Of the priests there were Jedaiah son of Joiakim, 11 Seraiah, son of Hilkiah, son of Meshullam, son of Zadok, son of Meraioth, son of Ahitub, the chief of the Temple of God, 12 and their kinsmen who performed the Temple liturgy: eight hundred and twenty-two; Adaiah son of Jeroham, son of Pelaliah, son of Amzi, son of Zechariah, son of Pashhur, son of Malchijah, 13 and his kinsfolk, heads of families: two hundred and forty-two; and Amashai son of Azarel, son of Ahzai, son of Meshillemoth, son of Immer, 14 and his kinsfolk, outstanding people: one hundred and twenty-eight.

Their chief was Zabdiel son of Haggadol.

15 Of the Levites there were Shemaiah son of Hasshub, son of Azrikam, son of Hashabiah, son of Bunni; 16 Shabbethai and Jozabad, the levitical leaders responsible for work outside the Temple of God; 17 Mattaniah son of Mica, son of Zabdi, son of Asaph, who led the praises and intoned the thanksgiving associated with the prayer, Bakbukiah being his junior colleague; and Obadiah son of Shammua, son of Galal, son of Jeduthun. 18 The total number of Levites in the holy city was two hundred and eighty-four.

19 The gatekeepers: Akkub, Talmon and their kinsmen, who kept watch at the gates: one hundred and seventy-two.e ‡11.20: see below‡

21 The temple slaves lived on Ophel; Ziha and Gishpa were in charge of the temple slaves. 22 The official in charge of the Levites in Jerusalem was Uzzi son of Bani, son of Hashabiah, son of Mattaniah, son of Mica, of the sons of Asaph, who led the singing in the liturgy of the Temple of God; 23 for the singers were under royal orders, with regulations laying down what was required of them day by day. 24 Petahiah son of Meshezabel, of the sons of Zerah son of Judah, was the king's minister for all matters connected with the people.

20 The rest of Israel, including the priests and Levites, made their homes throughout the towns of Judah, each man on his own inheritance, 25 and in the villages near their lands. Some of the sons of Judah made their homes in Kiriath-Arba and its dependencies, Dibon and its dependencies, Jekabzeel and its dependencies, 26 Jeshua, Moladah, Beth-Pelet, 27 Hazar-Shual, Beersheba and its dependencies, 28 Ziklag, Meconah and its dependencies, 29 En-Rimmon, Zorah, Jarmuth, 30 Zanoah, Adullam and their villages, Lachish and its lands, and Azekah and its dependencies; thus, they settled from Beersheba as far as the Valley of Hinnom.

31 And some Benjaminites made their homes in Geba, Michmash, Aija, Bethel and its dependencies, 32 Anathoth, Nob, Ananiah, 33 Hazor, Ramah, Gittaim, 34 Hadid, Zeboim, Neballat, 35 Lod, Ono and the Valley of Craftsmen. 36 Some levitical groups lived in Judah, some in Benjamin.

e 11 v. 20 is transposed to follow v. 24.

12 These are the priests and the Levites who came up with Zerubbabel son of Shealtiel, and Jeshua: Seraiah, Jeremiah, Ezra, 2 Amariah, Malluch, Hattush, 3 Shecaniah, Rehum, Meremoth, 4 Iddo, Ginnethoi, Abijah, 5 Mijamin, Maadiah, Bilgah, 6 Shemaiah, Joiarib, Jedaiah, 7 Sallu, Amok, Hilkiah, Jedaiah. These were the leaders of the priests and of their associates in the days of Jeshua.

8 And the Levites: Jeshua, Binnui, Kadmiel, Sherebiah, Judah, and Mattaniah, who with his associates was in charge of the songs of thanksgiving. 9 And Bakbukiah and Unno their associates stood opposite them in the service. 10 Jeshua was the father of Joiakim, Joiakim the father of Eliashib, Eliashib the father of Joiada, 11 Joiada the father of Jonathan, and Jonathan the father of Jaddua.

12 In the days of Joiakim the priests, heads of ancestral houses, were: of Seraiah, Meraiah; of Jeremiah, Hananiah; 13 of Ezra, Meshullam; of Amariah, Jehohanan; 14 of Malluchi, Jonathan; of Shebaniah, Joseph; 15 of Harim, Adna; of Meraioth, Helkai; 16 of Iddo, Zechariah; of Ginnethon, Meshullam; 17 of Abijah, Zichri; of Miniamin, of Moadiah, Piltai; 18 of Bilgah, Shammua; of Shemaiah, Jehonathan; 19 of Joiarib, Mattenai; of Jedaiah, Uzzi; 20 of Sallai, Kallai; of Amok, Eber; 21 of Hilkiah, Hashabiah; of Jedaiah, Nethanel.

22 As for the Levites, in the days of Eliashib, Joiada, Johanan, and Jaddua, there were recorded the heads of ancestral houses; also the priests until the reign of Darius the Persian. 23 The Levites, heads of ancestral houses, were recorded in the Book of the Annals until the days of Johanan son of Eliashib. 24 And the leaders of the Levites: Hashabiah, Sherebiah, and Jeshua son of Kadmiel, with their associates over against them, to praise and to give thanks, according to the commandment of David the man of God, section opposite to section. 25 Mattaniah, Bakbukiah, Obadiah, Meshullam, Talmon, and Akkub were gatekeepers standing guard at the storehouses of the gates. 26 These were in the days of Joiakim son of Jeshua son of Jozadak, and in the days of the governor Nehemiah and of the priest Ezra, the scribe.

27 Now at the dedication of the wall of Jerusalem they sought out the Levites in all their places, to bring them to Jerusalem to celebrate the dedication with rejoicing, with thanksgivings and with singing, with cymbals, harps, and lyres. 28 The companies of the singers gathered together from the circuit around Jerusalem and from the villages of the Netophathites; 29 also from Beth-gilgal and from the region of Geba and Azmaveth; for the singers had built for themselves villages around Jerusalem. 30 And the priests and the Levites purified themselves; and they purified the people and the gates and the wall.

31 Then I brought the leaders of Judah up onto the wall, and appointed two great companies that gave thanks and went in procession. One went to the right on the wall to the Dung Gate; 32 and after them went Hoshaiah and half the officials of Judah, 33 and Azariah, Ezra, Meshullam, 34 Judah, Benjamin, Shemaiah, and Jeremiah, 35 and some of the young priests with trumpets: Zechariah son of Jonathan son of Shemaiah son of Mattaniah son of Micaiah son of Zaccur son of Asaph, 36 and his kindred, Shemaiah, Azarel, Milalai, Gilalai, Maai, Nethanel, Judah, and Hanani, with the musical instruments of David the man of God; and the scribe Ezra went in front of them. 37 At the Fountain Gate,

12 These are the priests and the Levites who came back with Zerubbabel son of Shealtiel, and with Jeshua: Seraiah, Jeremiah, Ezra, 2 Amariah, Malluch, Hattush, 3 Shecaniah, Rehum, Meremoth, 4 Iddo, Ginnethon, Abiah, 5 Mijamin, Maadiah, Bilgah, 6 Shemaiah, Joiarib, Jedaiah, 7 Sallu, Amok, Hilkiah, Jedaiah. These were the chiefs of the priests and of their brethren in the days of Jeshua.

8 And the Levites: Jeshua, Binnui, Kadmiel, Sherebiah, Judah, and Mattaniah, who with his associates was in charge of the songs of thanksgiving. 9 And Bakbukiah and Unni their brethren stood opposite them in the service. 10 And Jeshua was the father of Joiakim, Joiakim the father of Eliashib, Eliashib of Joiada, 11 Joiada the father of Jonathan, and Jonathan the father of Jaddua. 12 And in the days of Joiakim the priests who were heads of families were: of Seraiah, Meraiah; of Jeremiah, Hananiah; 13 of Ezra, Meshullam; of Amariah, Jehohanan; 14 of Melichu, Jonathan; of Shebaniah, Joseph; 15 of Harim, Adna; of Meraioth, Helkai; 16 of Iddo, Zechariah; of Ginnethon, Meshullam; 17 of Abiah, Zichri; of Miniamin; of Moadiah, Piltai; 18 of Bilgah, Shammua; of Shemaiah, Jehonathan; 19 of Joiarib, Mattenai; of Jedaiah, Uzzi; 20 of Sallu, Kallai; of Amok, Eber; 21 of Hilkiah, Hashabiah; of Jedaiah, Nethanel.

22 The heads of the priestly families in the days of Eliashib, Joiada, Johanan, and Jaddua were recorded down to the reign of Darius the Persian. 23 The heads of the levitical families were recorded in the annals only down to the days of Johanan the grandson of Eliashib. 24 And the chiefs of the Levites: Hashabiah, Sherebiah, Jeshua, Binnui, Kadmiel, with their brethren in the other turn of duty, to praise and to give thanks, according to the commandment of David the man of God, turn by turn. 25 Mattaniah, Bakbukiah, Obadiah, Meshullam, Talmon, and Akkub were gate-keepers standing guard at the gatehouses. 26 This was the arrangement in the days of Joiakim son of Jeshua, son of Jozadak, and in the days of Nehemiah the governor and of Ezra the priest and scribe.

27 At the dedication of the wall of Jerusalem the Levites, wherever they had settled, were sought out and brought to the city to celebrate the dedication with rejoicing, with thanksgiving and song, to the accompaniment of cymbals, harps, and lyres. 28 The Levites, the singers, were assembled from the district round Jerusalem and from the hamlets of the Netophathites, 29 also from Beth-gilgal and the region of Geba and Beth-azmoth; for the singers had built themselves hamlets in the neighbourhood of Jerusalem. 30 When the priests and the Levites had purified themselves, they purified the people, the gates, and the wall.

31 Then I assembled the leading men of Judah on the city wall, and appointed two large choirs to give thanks. One went in procession to the right, going along the wall to the Dung Gate; 32 and after it went Hoshaiah with half the leading men of Judah, 33 and Azariah, Ezra, Meshullam, 34 Judah, Benjamin, Shemaiah, and Jeremiah, 35 and certain of the priests with trumpets: Zechariah son of Jonathan, son of Shemaiah, son of Mattaniah, son of Micaiah, son of Zaccur, son of Asaph, 36 and his kinsmen, Shemaiah, Azarel, Milalai, Gilalai, Maai, Nethanel, Judah, and Hanani, with the musical instruments of David the man of God; and Ezra the scribe led them. 37 They went past the Fountain Gate and

12:11 **Jonathan:** Johanan *in verse 22.* 12:17 **of Miniamin:** *a name is missing here.* 12:20 **Sallu:** *prob. rdg, cp. verse 7; Heb.* Sallai. 12:22 **The heads:** *prob. rdg; Heb. prefixes* The Levites. **heads . . . families:** *prob. rdg; Heb.* heads of the families and the priests. 12:24 **Jeshua, Binnui:** *prob. rdg; Heb.* and Jeshua son of. 12:28 **The Levites:** *prob. rdg; Heb.* The sons of. 12:29 **Beth-azmoth:** *prob. rdg, cp. 7:28; Heb.* Azmoth. 12:31 **One . . . procession:** *prob. rdg; Heb.* Processions.

NEW AMERICAN BIBLE

12 The following are the priests and Levites who returned with Zerubbabel, son of Shealtiel, and Jeshua: Seraiah, Jeremiah, Ezra, 2 Amariah, Malluch, Hattush, 3 Shecaniah, Rehum, Meremoth, 4 Iddo, Ginnethon, Abijah, 5 Mijamin, Maadiah, Bilgah, 6 Shemaiah, and Joiarib, Jedaiah, 7 Sallu, Amok, Hilkiah, Jedaiah. These were the priestly heads and their brethren in the days of Jeshua.

8 The Levites were Jeshua, Binnui, Kadmiel, Sherebiah, Judah, Mattaniah; the last-mentioned, together with his brethren, was in charge of the hymns, 9 while Bakbukiah and Unno and their brethren ministered opposite them by turns.

10 Jeshua became the father of Joiakim, Joiakim became the father of Eliashib, and Eliashib became the father of Joiada. 11 Joiada became the father of Johanan, and Johanan became the father of Jaddua.

12 In the days of Joiakim these were the priestly family heads: for Seraiah, Meraiah; for Jeremiah, Hananiah; 13 for Ezra, Meshullam; for Amariah, Jehohanan; 14 for Malluch, Jonathan; for Shebaniah, Joseph; 15 for Harim, Adna; for Meremoth, Helkai; 16 for Iddo, Zechariah; for Ginnethon, Meshullam; 17 for Abijah, Zichri; for Miamin, . . . ; for Maadiah, Piltai; 18 for Bilgah, Shammua; for Shemaiah, Jehonathan; 19 and for Joiarib, Mattenai; for Jedaiah, Uzzi; 20 for Sallu, Kallai; for Amok, Eber; 21 for Hilkiah, Hashabiah; for Jedaiah, Nethanel.

22 In the time of Eliashib, Joiada, Johanan, and Jaddua, the family heads of the priests were written down in the Book of Chronicles, up until the reign of Darius the Persian. 23 The sons of Levi: the family heads were written down in the Book of Chronicles, up until the time of Johanan, the son of Eliashib.

24 The heads of the Levites were Hashabiah, Sherebiah, Jeshua, Binnui, Kadmiel. Their brethren who stood opposite them to sing praises and thanksgiving in fulfillment of the command of David, the man of God, one section opposite the other, 25 were Mattaniah, Bakbukiah, Obadiah. Meshullam, Talmon, and Akkub were gatekeepers. They kept watch over the storerooms at the gates. 26 All these lived in the time of Joiakim, son of Jeshua, son of Jozadak [and in the time of Nehemiah the governor and of Ezra the priest-scribe].

27 At the dedication of the wall of Jerusalem, the Levites were sought out wherever they lived and were brought to Jerusalem to celebrate a joyful dedication with thanksgiving hymns and the music of cymbals, harps, and lyres. 28 The levitical singers gathered together from the region about Jerusalem, from the villages of the Netophathites, 29 from Beth-gilgal, and from the plains of Geba and Azmaveth (for the singers had built themselves settlements about Jerusalem). 30 The priests and Levites first purified themselves, then they purified the people, the gates, and the wall.

31 I had the princes of Judah mount the wall, and I arranged two great choirs. The first of these proceeded to the right, along the top of the wall, in the direction of the Dung Gate, 32 followed by Hoshaiah and half the princes of Judah, 33 along with Azariah, Ezra, Meshullam, 34 Judah, Benjamin, Shemaiah, and Jeremiah, 35 priests with the trumpets, and also Zechariah, son of Jonathan, son of Shemaiah, son of Mattaniah, son of Micaiah, son of Zaccur, son of Asaph, 36 and his brethren Shemaiah, Azarel, Milalai, Gilalai, Maai, Nethanel, Judah, and Hanani, with the musical instruments of David, the man of God. [Ezra the scribe was at their head.] 37 At the Spring Gate they went

NEW JERUSALEM BIBLE

12 These are the priests and the Levites who came back with Zerubbabel son of Shealtiel, and Jeshua: 2 Seraiah, Jeremiah, Ezra, 3 Amariah, Malluch, Hattush, Shecaniah, Rehum, Meremoth, 4 Iddo, Ginnethoi, Abijah, 5 Mijamin, Maadiah, Bilgah, 6 Shemaiah, and Joiarib, Jedaiah, 7 Sallu, Amok, Hilkiah, Jedaiah — these were the heads of the priests and their kinsmen in the days of Jeshua.

8 The Levites were Jeshua, Binnui, Kadmiel, Sherebiah, Judah, Mattaniah — this last, with his brothers, was in charge of the songs of praise, 9 while Bakbukiah and Unno, their colleagues, formed the alternate choir to theirs.

10 Jeshua fathered Joiakim, Joiakim fathered Eliashib, Eliashib fathered Joiada, 11 Joiada fathered Johanan, and Johanan fathered Jaddua.

12 In the days of Joiakim the heads of the priestly families were: family of Seraiah, Meraiah; of Jeremiah, Hananiah; 13 of Ezra, Meshullam; of Amariah, Jehohanan; 14 of Malluch, Jonathan; of Shebaniah, Joseph; 15 of Harim, Adna; of Meremoth, Helkai; 16 of Iddo, Zechariah; of Ginnethon, Meshullam; 17 of Abijah, Zichri; of Minjamin, . . . ; of Moadiah, Piltai; 18 of Bilgah, Shammua; of Shemaiah, Jehonathan; 19 and of Jojarib, Mattenai; of Jedaiah, Uzzi; 20 of Sallai, Kallai; of Amok, Eber; 21 of Hilkiah, Hashabiah; of Jedaiah, Nethanel.

22 In the time of Eliashib, Joiada, Johanan and Jaddua, the heads of the families of priests were registered in the Book of Chronicles, up to the reign of Darius the Persian.

23 The Levites who were heads of families were registered in the Book of Chronicles up to the time of Johanan, grandson of Eliashib.

24 The heads of the Levites were Hashabiah, Sherebiah, Jeshua, Binnui, Kadmiel, while their brothers who formed an alternate choir for the hymns of praise and thanksgiving, as David, man of God, had prescribed, section corresponding to section, 25 were Mattaniah, Bakbukiah and Obadiah. Meshullam, Talmon and Akkub were the gatekeepers guarding the stores at the gates.

26 These lived in the days of Joiakim son of Jeshua, son of Jozadak, and in the days of Nehemiah the governor and of Ezra the priest-scribe.

27 At the dedication of the wall of Jerusalem the Levites were sent for, wherever they lived, to come to Jerusalem and joyfully perform the dedication with hymns of thanksgiving and songs to the accompaniment of cymbals, lyres and harps. 28 Accordingly, the levitical singers assembled from the district round Jerusalem, from the villages of the Netophathites, 29 from Beth-Gilgal and from their farms at Geba and Azmaveth — for the singers had built themselves villages all round Jerusalem. 30 When the priests and Levites had purified themselves, they then purified the people, the gates and the wall.

31 I then made the leaders of Judah come on to the top of the wall and appointed two large choirs. One made its way along the top of the wall, to the right, towards the Dung Gate; 32 bringing up the rear were Hoshaiah and half the leaders of Judah, 33 and also Azariah, Ezra, Meshullam, 34 Judah, Benjamin, Shemaiah and Jeremiah, 35 of the priests, with trumpets; then Zechariah son of Jonathan, son of Shemaiah, son of Mattaniah, son of Micaiah, son of Zaccur, son of Asaph, 36 with his kinsmen, Shemaiah, Azarel, Milalai, Gilalai, Maai, Nethanel, Juda, Hanani, with the musical instruments of David, man of God. The scribe Ezra walked at their head. 37 At the Fountain Gate they went

in front of them, they went straight up by the stairs of the city of David, at the ascent of the wall, above the house of David, to the Water Gate on the east.

38 The other company of those who gave thanks went to the left, *d* and I followed them with half of the people on the wall, above the Tower of the Ovens, to the Broad Wall, 39 and above the Gate of Ephraim, and by the Old Gate, and by the Fish Gate and the Tower of Hananel and the Tower of the Hundred, as far as the Sheep Gate; and they came to a halt at the Gate of the Guard. 40 So both companies of those who gave thanks stood in the house of God, and I and half of the officials with me; 41 and the priests Eliakim, Maaseiah, Miniamin, Micaiah, Elioenai, Zechariah, and Hananiah, with trumpets; 42 and Maaseiah, Shemaiah, Eleazar, Uzzi, Jehohanan, Malchijah, Elam, and Ezer. And the singers sang with Jezrahiah as their leader. 43 They offered great sacrifices that day and rejoiced, for God had made them rejoice with great joy; the women and children also rejoiced. The joy of Jerusalem was heard far away.

44 On that day men were appointed over the chambers for the stores, the contributions, the first fruits, and the tithes, to gather into them the portions required by the law for the priests and for the Levites from the fields belonging to the towns; for Judah rejoiced over the priests and the Levites who ministered. 45 They performed the service of their God and the service of purification, as did the singers and the gatekeepers, according to the command of David and his son Solomon. 46 For in the days of David and Asaph long ago there was a leader of the singers, and there were songs of praise and thanksgiving to God. 47 In the days of Zerubbabel and in the days of Nehemiah all Israel gave the daily portions for the singers and the gatekeepers. They set apart that which was for the Levites; and the Levites set apart that which was for the descendants of Aaron.

13 On that day they read from the book of Moses in the hearing of the people; and in it was found written that no Ammonite or Moabite should ever enter the assembly of God, 2 because they did not meet the Israelites with bread and water, but hired Balaam against them to curse them — yet our God turned the curse into a blessing. 3 When the people heard the law, they separated from Israel all those of foreign descent.

4 Now before this, the priest Eliashib, who was appointed over the chambers of the house of our God, and who was related to Tobiah, 5 prepared for Tobiah a large room where they had previously put the grain offering, the frankincense, the vessels, and the tithes of grain, wine, and oil, which were given by commandment to the Levites, singers, and gatekeepers, and the contributions for the priests. 6 While this was taking place I was not in Jerusalem, for in the thirty-second year of King Artaxerxes of Babylon I went to the king. After some time I asked leave of the king 7 and returned to Jerusalem. I then discovered the wrong that Eliashib had done on behalf of Tobiah, preparing a room for him in the courts of the house of God. 8 And I was very angry, and I threw all the household furniture of Tobiah out of the room. 9 Then I gave orders and they cleansed the chambers, and I brought back the vessels of the house of God, with the grain offering and the frankincense.

10 I also found out that the portions of the Levites had not been given to them; so that the Levites and the singers, who had conducted the service, had gone back to their fields. 11 So I remonstrated with the officials and said,

thence straight forward by the steps up to the City of David, by the ascent to the city wall, past the house of David, and on to the Water Gate on the east.

38 The other thanksgiving choir went to the left, and I followed it with half the leading men of the people, continuing along the wall, past the Tower of the Ovens to the Broad Wall, 39 and past the Ephraim Gate, and over the Jeshanah Gate, and over the Fish Gate, taking in the Tower of Hananel and the Tower of the Hundred, as far as the Sheep Gate; and they halted at the Guardhouse Gate.

40 Then the two thanksgiving choirs took their place in the house of God, and I and half the magistrates with me; 41 and the priests Eliakim, Maaseiah, Miniamin, Micaiah, Elioenai, Zechariah, and Hananiah, with trumpets; 42 Maaseiah, Shemaiah, Eleazar, Uzzi, Jehohanan, Malchiah, Elam, and Ezer. The singers, led by Izrahiah, raised their voices. 43 A great sacrifice was celebrated that day, and they all rejoiced because God had given them great cause for rejoicing; the women and children rejoiced with them. And the rejoicing in Jerusalem was heard a long way off.

44 Men were appointed at that time to take charge of the storerooms for the contributions, the firstfruits, and the tithes, to gather in the portions required by the law for the priests and Levites according to the extent of the farmlands round the towns; for all Judah was full of rejoicing at the ministry of the priests and Levites, 45 who performed the service of their God and the service of purification, as did the singers and the door-keepers, according to the rules laid down by David and his son Solomon. 46 For it was in the days of David that Asaph took the lead as chief of the singers and director of praise and thanksgiving to God, 47 and in the days of Zerubbabel and of Nehemiah all Israel gave the portions for the singers and the door-keepers as each day required; they set apart the portion for the Levites, and the Levites set apart the portion for the Aaronites.

13 On that day at the public reading from the book of Moses, it was found to be laid down that no Ammonite or Moabite should ever enter the assembly of God, 2 because they did not welcome the Israelites with food and water but hired Balaam to curse them, though our God turned the curse into a blessing. 3 When the people heard the law, they separated off from Israel all who were of mixed blood.

4 But before this, Eliashib the priest, who was appointed over the storerooms of the house of our God, and who was connected by marriage with Tobiah, 5 had provided for his use a large room where formerly they had kept the grain-offering, the frankincense, the temple vessels, the tithes of grain, new wine, and oil prescribed for the Levites, singers, and door-keepers, and the contributions for the priests. 6 All this while I was not in Jerusalem because, in the thirty-second year of King Artaxerxes of Babylon, I had gone to the king. Some time later, however, having asked permission from him, 7 I returned to Jerusalem and there discovered the outrageous thing that Eliashib had done for Tobiah's benefit in providing him with a room in the courts of the house of God. 8 I was greatly displeased and threw all Tobiah's belongings out of the room. 9 I then gave orders that the room should be purified, and that the vessels of the house of God, with the grain-offering and frankincense, should be put back into it.

10 I also learnt that the Levites had not been given their portions; both they and the singers, who were responsible for their respective duties, had made off to their farms. 11 I

12:38 **to the left:** *prob. rdg; Heb.* to the front. **the leading men of:** *prob. rdg; Heb.* omits. 12:39 **Jeshanah Gate:** *or* gate of the Old City. 12:46 **director:** *prob. rdg; Heb.* song.

d Cn: Heb *opposite*

NEW AMERICAN BIBLE

straight up by the steps of the City of David and continued along the top of the wall above the house of David until they came to the Water Gate on the east.

38 The second choir proceeded to the left, followed by myself and the other half of the princes of the people, along the top of the wall past the Oven Tower as far as the Broad Wall, 39 then past the Ephraim Gate [the New City Gate], the Fish Gate, the Tower of Hananel, and the Hundred Tower, as far as the Sheep Gate [and they came to a halt at the Prison Gate].

40 The two choirs took up a position in the house of God; I, too, who had with me half the magistrates, 41 the priests Eliakim, Maaseiah, Minjamin, Micaiah, Elioenai, Zechariah, Hananiah, with the trumpets, 42 and Maaseiah, Shemaiah, Eleazar, Uzzi, Jehohanan, Malchijah, Elam, and Ezer. The singers were heard under the leadership of Jezrahiah. 43 Great sacrifices were offered on that day, and there was rejoicing over the great feast of the LORD in which they shared. The women and the children joined in, and the rejoicing at Jerusalem could be heard from afar off.

44 At that time men were appointed over the chambers set aside for stores, offerings, first fruits, and tithes; in them they were to collect from the fields of the various cities the portions legally assigned to the priests and Levites. For Judah rejoiced in its appointed priests and Levites 45 who carried out the ministry of their God and the ministry of purification (as did the singers and the gatekeepers) in accordance with the prescriptions of David and of Solomon, his son. 46 For the heads of the families of the singers and the hymns of praise and thanksgiving to God came down from the days of David and Asaph in times of old. 47 Thus all Israel, in the days of Zerubbabel [and in the days of Nehemiah], gave the singers and the gatekeepers their portions, according to their daily needs. They made their consecrated offering to the Levites, and the Levites made theirs to the sons of Aaron.

13 At that time, when there was reading from the book of Moses in the hearing of the people, it was found written there that "no Ammonite or Moabite may ever be admitted into the assembly of God; 2 for they would not succor the Israelites with food and water, but they hired Balaam to curse them, though our God turned the curse into a blessing." 3 When they had heard the law, they separated from Israel every foreign element.

4 Before this, the priest Eliashib, who had been placed in charge of the chambers of the house of our God and was an associate of Tobiah, 5 had set aside for the latter's use a large chamber in which had previously been stored the cereal offerings, incense and utensils, the tithes in grain, wine, and oil allotted to the Levites, singers, and gatekeepers, and the offerings due the priests. 6 During all this time I had not been in Jerusalem, for in the thirty-second year of Artaxerxes, king of Babylon, I had gone back to the king. After due time, however, I asked leave of the king 7 and returned to Jerusalem, where I discovered the evil thing that Eliashib had done for Tobiah, in setting aside for him a chamber in the courts of the house of God. 8 This displeased me very much, and I had all of Tobiah's household goods thrown outside the chamber. 9 Then I gave orders to purify the chambers, and I had them replace there the utensils of the house of God, the cereal offerings, and the incense.

10 I learned, too, that the portions due the Levites were no longer being given, so that the Levites and the singers who should have been carrying out the services had deserted, each man to his own field. 11 I took the magistrates to task,

NEW JERUSALEM BIBLE

straight on up the steps of the City of David, along the top of the rampart by the stairway of the wall, above the Palace of David as far as the Water Gate, on the east.

38 The other choir made its way to the left; I and half the leaders of the people followed them along the top of the wall from the Tower of the Furnaces to the Broad Wall, 39 from the Ephraim Gate, the Fish Gate, the Tower of Hananel and the Tower of the Hundred as far as the Sheep Gate, and they came to a halt at the Prison Gate.

40 The two choirs then took their places in the Temple of God. But I had half the magistrates with me 41 as well as the priests, Eliakim, Maaseiah, Miniamin, Micaiah, Elioenai, Zechariah, Hananiah with the trumpets, 42 and Maaseiah, Shemaiah, Eleazar, Uzzi, Jehohanan, Malchijah, Elam and Ezer. The singers sang loudly under the direction of Jezrahiah. 43 There were great sacrifices offered that day and the people rejoiced, God having given them good cause for rejoicing; the women and children rejoiced too, and the joy of Jerusalem could be heard from far away.

44 For the rooms intended for the treasures, contributions, first-fruits and tithes, supervisors were then appointed whose business it was to collect in them those portions from the town lands awarded by the Law to the priests and Levites. For Judah rejoiced in the officiating priests and Levites, 45 since they — with the singers and gatekeepers — performed the liturgy of their God and the rites of purification as ordained by David and his son Solomon. 46 For from ancient times, from the days of David and Asaph, they had been the leaders in rendering hymns of praise and thanksgiving to God. 47 In the days of Zerubbabel and Nehemiah, all Israel supplied regular daily portions for the singers and gatekeepers, and gave the dedicated contributions to the Levites; and the Levites gave the dedicated contributions to the Aaronites.

13 At that time they were reading to the people from the Book of Moses, when they found this written in it, 'No Ammonite or Moabite is to be admitted to the assembly of God, and this is for all time, 2 since they did not come to meet the Israelites with bread and water, and even hired Balaam to oppose them by cursing them; but our God turned the curse into a blessing.' f 3 Having heard the Law, they excluded all foreigners from Israel.

4 Earlier, Eliashib the priest, who was in charge of the rooms of the Temple of our God, and who was close to Tobiah, 5 had provided him with a large room where they previously used to store the meal offerings, incense, utensils, tithes of corn, wine and oil, that is, the part of the Levites, singers and gatekeepers, and the contributions for the priests. 6 While all this was going on I was away from Jerusalem, for in the thirty-second year of Artaxerxes king of Babylon I had gone to see the king. But after some time I asked the king for permission to leave, 7 and returned to Jerusalem, where I learned about the crime which Eliashib had committed for Tobiah's benefit, by providing him with a room in the courts of the Temple of God. 8 I was extremely displeased and threw all Tobiah's household goods out of the room and into the street. 9 I then gave orders for the room to be purified, and had the utensils of the Temple of God, the meal offerings and the incense, all replaced.

10 I also learned that the Levites had not been receiving their allocations, as a result of which the Levites and singers who performed the liturgy had all withdrawn to their farms.

12, 47: The gloss mentioning Nehemiah is not in the ancient Greek version.

f **13** Dt 23:4–6.

"Why is the house of God forsaken?" And I gathered them together and set them in their stations. 12 Then all Judah brought the tithe of the grain, wine, and oil into the storehouses. 13 And I appointed as treasurers over the storehouses the priest Shelemiah, the scribe Zadok, and Pedaiah of the Levites, and as their assistant Hanan son of Zaccur son of Mattaniah, for they were considered faithful; and their duty was to distribute to their associates. 14 Remember me, O my God, concerning this, and do not wipe out my good deeds that I have done for the house of my God and for his service.

15 In those days I saw in Judah people treading wine presses on the sabbath, and bringing in heaps of grain and loading them on donkeys; and also wine, grapes, figs, and all kinds of burdens, which they brought into Jerusalem on the sabbath day; and I warned them at that time against selling food. 16 Tyrians also, who lived in the city, brought in fish and all kinds of merchandise and sold them on the sabbath to the people of Judah, and in Jerusalem. 17 Then I remonstrated with the nobles of Judah and said to them, "What is this evil thing that you are doing, profaning the sabbath day? 18 Did not your ancestors act in this way, and did not our God bring all this disaster on us and on this city? Yet you bring more wrath on Israel by profaning the sabbath."

19 When it began to be dark at the gates of Jerusalem before the sabbath, I commanded that the doors should be shut and gave orders that they should not be opened until after the sabbath. And I set some of my servants over the gates, to prevent any burden from being brought in on the sabbath day. 20 Then the merchants and sellers of all kinds of merchandise spent the night outside Jerusalem once or twice. 21 But I warned them and said to them, "Why do you spend the night in front of the wall? If you do so again, I will lay hands on you." From that time on they did not come on the sabbath. 22 And I commanded the Levites that they should purify themselves and come and guard the gates, to keep the sabbath day holy. Remember this also in my favor, O my God, and spare me according to the greatness of your steadfast love.

23 In those days also I saw Jews who had married women of Ashdod, Ammon, and Moab; 24 and half of their children spoke the language of Ashdod, and they could not speak the language of Judah, but spoke the language of various peoples. 25 And I contended with them and cursed them and beat some of them and pulled out their hair; and I made them take an oath in the name of God, saying, "You shall not give your daughters to their sons, or take their daughters for your sons or for yourselves. 26 Did not King Solomon of Israel sin on account of such women? Among the many nations there was no king like him, and he was beloved by his God, and God made him king over all Israel; nevertheless, foreign women made even him to sin. 27 Shall we then listen to you and do all this great evil and act treacherously against our God by marrying foreign women?"

28 And one of the sons of Jehoiada, son of the high priest Eliashib, was the son-in-law of Sanballat the Horonite; I chased him away from me. 29 Remember them, O my God, because they have defiled the priesthood, the covenant of the priests and the Levites.

30 Thus I cleansed them from everything foreign, and I established the duties of the priests and Levites, each in his work; 31 and I provided for the wood offering, at appointed times, and for the first fruits. Remember me, O my God, for good.

remonstrated with the magistrates: 'Why is the house of God deserted?' I demanded. I recalled the men and restored them to their places. 12 Then all Judah brought the tithes of grain, new wine, and oil into the storehouses. 13 Over the stores I set Shelemiah the priest, Zadok the accountant, and Pedaiah a Levite, with Hanan son of Zaccur, son of Mattaniah, as their assistant, for they were considered trustworthy men; their duty was the distribution of their shares to their brethren.

14 God, remember this to my credit, and do not wipe out of your memory the devotion which I have shown in the house of my God and in his service!

15 In those days I saw men in Judah treading winepresses on the sabbath, collecting quantities of produce and loading it on donkeys — wine, grapes, figs, and every kind of load, which they brought into Jerusalem on the sabbath. I warned them against the selling of food on that day. 16 Tyrians living in Jerusalem were also bringing fish and all kinds of merchandise and selling them on the sabbath to the people of Judah, even in Jerusalem. 17 I complained to the nobles of Judah and said to them, 'How dare you profane the sabbath in this wicked fashion? 18 Is not this just what your forefathers did, so that our God has brought all this evil on us and on this city? Now you are bringing more wrath on Israel by profaning the sabbath.'

19 When the entrances to Jerusalem had been cleared in preparation for the sabbath, I gave orders that the gates should be shut and not opened until after the sabbath; and I posted some of my men at the gates to ensure that no load came in on the sabbath. 20 Then on one or two occasions the merchants and all kinds of traders spent the night just outside Jerusalem, 21 but I warned them: 'Why are you spending the night in front of the city wall? Do it again, and I shall take action against you.' After that they did not come on the sabbath. 22 I instructed the Levites to purify themselves and take up duty as guards at the gates, to ensure that the sabbath was kept holy.

God, remember this also to my credit, and spare me in your great love!

23 In those days also I saw that some Jews had married women from Ashdod, Ammon, and Moab. 24 Half their children spoke the language of Ashdod or of one of the other peoples but could not speak the language of the Jews. 25 I argued with them and reviled them, I beat some of them and tore out their hair; and I made them swear in the name of God: 'We shall not marry our daughters to their sons, or take any of their daughters in marriage for our sons or for ourselves.' 26 'Was it not because of such women', I said, 'that King Solomon of Israel sinned? Among all the nations there was no king like him; he was loved by his God, and God made him king over all Israel; nevertheless even he was led by foreign women into sin. 27 Are we then to follow your example and commit this grave offence, breaking faith with our God by marrying foreign women?' 28 One of the sons of Joiada son of Eliashib the high priest had married a daughter of Sanballat the Horonite; therefore I drove him out of my presence.

29 God, remember to their discredit that they have defiled the priesthood and the covenant of the priests and the Levites.

30 Thus I purified them from everything foreign, and I made the Levites and the priests resume the duties of their office; 31 I also made provision for the delivery of the wood at appointed times, and for the firstfruits.

God, remember me favourably!

demanding, "Why is the house of God abandoned?" Then I brought the Levites together and had them resume their stations. 12 All Judah once more brought in the tithes of grain, wine, and oil to the storerooms; 13 and in charge of the storerooms I appointed the priest Shelemiah, Zadok the scribe, and Pedaiah, one of the Levites, together with Hanan, son of Zaccur, son of Mattaniah, as their assistant; for these men were held to be trustworthy. It was their duty to make the distribution to their brethren. 14 Remember this to my credit, O my God! Let not the devotion which I showed for the house of my God and its services be forgotten!

15 In those days I perceived that men in Judah were treading the winepresses on the sabbath; that they were bringing in sheaves of grain, loading them on their asses, together with wine, grapes, figs, and every other kind of burden, and bringing them to Jerusalem on the sabbath day. I warned them to sell none of these victuals. 16 In Jerusalem itself the Tyrians who were resident there were importing fish and every other kind of merchandise and selling it to the Judahites on the sabbath. 17 I took the nobles of Judah to task, demanding of them: "What is this evil thing that you are doing, profaning the sabbath day? 18 Did not your fathers act in this same way, with the result that our God has brought all this evil upon us and upon this city? Would you add to the wrath against Israel by once more profaning the sabbath?"

19 When the shadows were falling on the gates of Jerusalem before the sabbath, I ordered the doors to be closed and forbade them to be reopened till after the sabbath. I posted some of my own men at the gates so that no burden might enter on the sabbath day. 20 The merchants and sellers of various kinds of merchandise spent the night once or twice outside Jerusalem, 21 but then I warned them, saying to them: "Why do you spend the night alongside the wall? If you keep this up, I will lay hands on you!" From that time on, they did not return on the sabbath. 22 Then I ordered the Levites to purify themselves and to go and watch the gates, so that the sabbath day might be kept holy. This, too, remember in my favor, O my God, and have mercy on me in accordance with your great mercy!

23 Also in those days I saw Jews who had married Ashdodite, Ammonite, or Moabite wives. 24 Of their children, half spoke Ashdodite, and none of them knew how to speak Jewish; and so it was in regard to the languages of the various other peoples. 25 I took them to task and cursed them; I had some of them beaten and their hair pulled out; and I adjured them by God: "You shall not marry your daughters to their sons nor take any of their daughters for your sons or for yourselves! 26 Did not Solomon, the king of Israel, sin because of these? Though among the many nations there was no king like him, and though he was beloved of his God and God had made him king over all Israel, yet even he was made to sin by foreign women. 27 Must it also be heard of you that you have done this same very great evil, betraying our God by marrying foreign women?"

28 One of the sons of Joiada, son of Eliashib the high priest, was the son-in-law of Sanballat the Horonite! I drove him from my presence. 29 Remember against them, O my God, how they defiled the priesthood and the covenant of the priesthood and the Levites!

30 Thus I cleansed them of all foreign contamination. I established the various functions for the priests and Levites, so that each had his appointed task. 31 I also provided for the procurement of wood at stated times and for the first fruits. Remember this in my favor, O my God!

11 I then reprimanded the officials. 'Why is the Temple of God deserted?' I asked. And I collected them together again and brought them back to their posts; 12 and all Judah then delivered the tithe of corn, wine and oil to the storehouses. 13 As supervisors of the storehouses I appointed Shelemiah the priest, Zadok the scribe, Pedaiah one of the Levites and, as their assistant, Hanan son of Zaccur, son of Mattaniah, since they were considered reliable people; their duty was to make the distributions to their kinsmen.

14 Remember me for this, my God, and do not blot out the good deeds which I have done for the Temple of my God and its observances!

15 At the same time I saw people in Judah treading the winepress, bringing in sacks of grain and loading donkeys on the Sabbath; they were also bringing wine, grapes, figs and every kind of merchandise into Jerusalem on the Sabbath day. So I forbade them to sell the food. 16 Tyrians living there were bringing in fish and every kind of merchandise which they were selling to the Judaeans on the Sabbath in Jerusalem itself. 17 So I also reprimanded the leading men of Judah, saying to them, 'What a wicked way to behave, profaning the Sabbath day! 18 Was this not exactly what your ancestors did, with the result that our God brought all this misery down on us and on this city? And now you are adding to the wrath hanging over Israel by profaning the Sabbath yourselves!' 19 So when the gates of Jerusalem were getting dark at the approach of the Sabbath, I gave orders for the doors to be shut and directed that they were not to be opened again until the Sabbath was over. I stationed some of my attendants at the gates to make sure that no merchandise was brought in on the Sabbath day. 20 So the traders and dealers in goods of all kinds spent the night outside Jerusalem once or twice, 21 until I reprimanded them. I said to them, 'Why are you spending the night in front of the wall? Do it again, and I shall use force on you.' After this, they did not come on the Sabbath. 22 I then ordered the Levites to purify themselves and act as guards at the gates, so that the Sabbath day might be kept holy.

Remember this also to my credit, have pity on me in the greatness of your faithful love.

23 At that time too, I saw Jews who had married wives from Ashdod, Ammon and Moab; 24 as regards their children, half of them spoke the language of Ashdod or the language of one of the other peoples, but could no longer speak the language of Judah. 25 I reprimanded them, I cursed them, I struck several of them and tore out their hair and adjured them by God, 'You are not to give your daughters in marriage to their sons or let their daughters marry your sons, or marry them yourselves! 26 Was it not because of women like these that Solomon king of Israel sinned? Although among many nations there was no king like him and he was loved by his God, and God made him king of all Israel, even then foreign women led him into sinning! 27 Were you obedient when you committed this very grave crime: breaking faith with our God by marrying foreign wives?'

28 One of the sons of Jehoiada, son of Eliashib the high priest, was a son-in-law of Sanballat the Horonite; I drove him from my presence.

29 Remember them, my God, for having defiled the priesthood and the covenant of the priests and Levites!

30 And so I purged them of everything foreign; I drew up regulations for the priests and Levites, defining each man's duty, 31 as well as for the deliveries of wood at the proper times, and for the first-fruits.

Remember this, my God, to my credit!

Esther (Hebrew) is included only in the New Revised
Standard and Revised English Bible translations.

Esther (Hebrew) is included only in the New Revised
Standard and Revised English Bible translations.

Esther

Esther

1 This happened in the days of Ahasuerus, the same Ahasuerus who ruled over one hundred twenty-seven provinces from India to Ethiopia.*a* 2 In those days when King Ahasuerus sat on his royal throne in the citadel of Susa, 3 in the third year of his reign, he gave a banquet for all his officials and ministers. The army of Persia and Media and the nobles and governors of the provinces were present, 4 while he displayed the great wealth of his kingdom and the splendor and pomp of his majesty for many days, one hundred eighty days in all.

5 When these days were completed, the king gave for all the people present in the citadel of Susa, both great and small, a banquet lasting for seven days, in the court of the garden of the king's palace. 6 There were white cotton curtains and blue hangings tied with cords of fine linen and purple to silver rings*b* and marble pillars. There were couches of gold and silver on a mosaic pavement of porphyry, marble, mother-of-pearl, and colored stones. 7 Drinks were served in golden goblets, goblets of different kinds, and the royal wine was lavished according to the bounty of the king. 8 Drinking was by flagons, without restraint; for the king had given orders to all the officials of his palace to do as each one desired. 9 Furthermore, Queen Vashti gave a banquet for the women in the palace of King Ahasuerus.

10 On the seventh day, when the king was merry with wine, he commanded Mehuman, Biztha, Harbona, Bigtha and Abagtha, Zethar and Carkas, the seven eunuchs who attended him, 11 to bring Queen Vashti before the king, wearing the royal crown, in order to show the peoples and the officials her beauty; for she was fair to behold. 12 But Queen Vashti refused to come at the king's command conveyed by the eunuchs. At this the king was enraged, and his anger burned within him.

13 Then the king consulted the sages who knew the laws*c* (for this was the king's procedure toward all who were versed in law and custom, 14 and those next to him were Carshena, Shethar, Admatha, Tarshish, Meres, Marsena, and Memucan, the seven officials of Persia and Media, who had access to the king, and sat first in the kingdom): 15 "According to the law, what is to be done to Queen Vashti because she has not performed the command of King Ahasuerus conveyed by the eunuchs?" 16 Then Memucan said in the presence of the king and the officials, "Not only has Queen Vashti done wrong to the king, but also to all the officials and all the peoples who are in all the provinces of King Ahasuerus. 17 For this deed of the queen will be made known to all women, causing them to look with contempt on their husbands, since they will say, 'King Ahasuerus commanded Queen Vashti to be brought before him, and she did not come.' 18 This very day the noble ladies of Persia and Media who have heard of the queen's behavior will rebel against*d* the king's officials, and there will be no end of contempt and wrath! 19 If it pleases the king, let a royal order go out from him, and let it be written among the laws of the Persians and the Medes so that it may not be altered, that Vashti is never again to come before King Ahasuerus; and let the king give her royal position to an-

1 THE events here related happened in the days of Ahasuerus, that Ahasuerus who ruled from India to Ethiopia, a hundred and twenty-seven provinces, 2 at the time when he was settled on the royal throne in Susa, the capital city. 3 In the third year of his reign he gave a banquet for all his officers and his courtiers; the Persians and Medes in full force, along with his nobles and provincial rulers, were in attendance. 4 He put on display for many days, a hundred and eighty in all, the dazzling wealth of his kingdom and the pomp and splendour of his realm. 5 At the end of that time the king gave a banquet for all the people present in Susa the capital city, both high and low; it lasted for seven days and was held in the garden court of the royal pavilion. 6 There were white curtains and violet hangings fastened to silver rings by cords of fine linen with purple thread; the pillars were of marble, and gold and silver couches were placed on a mosaic pavement of malachite, marble, mother-of-pearl, and turquoise. 7 Wine was served in golden goblets, each of a different design: the king's wine flowed in royal style, 8 and the drinking was according to no fixed rule, for the king had laid down that all the palace stewards should respect the wishes of each guest. 9 Queen Vashti too gave a banquet for the women inside the royal palace of King Ahasuerus.

10 On the seventh day, when he was merry with wine, the king ordered Mehuman, Biztha, Harbona, Bigtha, Abagtha, Zethar, and Carcas, the seven eunuchs who were in attendance on the king's person, 11 to bring Queen Vashti into his presence wearing her royal diadem, in order to display her beauty to the people and to the officers; for she was indeed a beautiful woman. 12 But when the royal command was conveyed to her by the eunuchs, Queen Vashti refused to come. This greatly incensed the king, and his wrath flared up. 13 He conferred with wise men versed in precedents, for it was his custom to consult all who were expert in law and usage. 14 Those closest to the king were Carshena, Shethar, Admatha, Tarshish, Meres, Marsena, and Memucan, the seven vicegerents of Persia and Media; they had access to the king and occupied the premier positions in the kingdom. 15 'What', he asked, 'does the law require to be done with Queen Vashti for disobeying my royal command conveyed to her by the eunuchs?'

16 In the presence of the king and the vicegerents, Memucan declared: 'Queen Vashti has done wrong, not to the king alone, but also to all the officers and to all the peoples in every province of King Ahasuerus. 17 The queen's conduct will come to the ears of all women and embolden them to treat their husbands with disrespect; they will say, "King Ahasuerus ordered Queen Vashti to be brought before him, but she would not come!" 18 The great ladies of Persia and Media, who have heard what the queen has said, will quote this day to all the king's officers, and there will be no end to the disrespect and discord!

19 'If it please your majesty, let a royal decree be issued by you, and let it be inscribed among the laws of the Persians and Medes, never to be revoked, that Vashti shall not again appear before King Ahasuerus; and let your majesty give her place as queen to another who is more worthy of it than she. 20 When the edict made by the king is pro-

---

a Or Nubia; Heb *Cush*   *b Or rods*   *c Cn: Heb times*   *d Cn: Heb will tell*

1:1 **Ethiopia:** *Heb*. Cush.   1:6 **thread:** *prob. mng; Heb. omits.*

other who is better than she. 20 So when the decree made by the king is proclaimed throughout all his kingdom, vast as it is, all women will give honor to their husbands, high and low alike."

21 This advice pleased the king and the officials, and the king did as Memucan proposed; 22 he sent letters to all the royal provinces, to every province in its own script and to every people in its own language, declaring that every man should be master in his own house. *e*

2 After these things, when the anger of King Ahasuerus had abated, he remembered Vashti and what she had done and what had been decreed against her. 2 Then the king's servants who attended him said, "Let beautiful young virgins be sought out for the king. 3 And let the king appoint commissioners in all the provinces of his kingdom to gather all the beautiful young virgins to the harem in the citadel of Susa under custody of Hegai, the king's eunuch, who is in charge of the women; let their cosmetic treatments be given them. 4 And let the girl who pleases the king be queen instead of Vashti." This pleased the king, and he did so.

5 Now there was a Jew in the citadel of Susa whose name was Mordecai son of Jair son of Shimei son of Kish, a Benjaminite. 6 Kish *f* had been carried away from Jerusalem among the captives carried away with King Jeconiah of Judah, whom King Nebuchadnezzar of Babylon had carried away. 7 Mordecai *g* had brought up Hadassah, that is Esther, his cousin, for she had neither father nor mother; the girl was fair and beautiful, and when her father and her mother died, Mordecai adopted her as his own daughter. 8 So when the king's order and his edict were proclaimed, and when many young women were gathered in the citadel of Susa in custody of Hegai, Esther also was taken into the king's palace and put in custody of Hegai, who had charge of the women. 9 The girl pleased him and won his favor, and he quickly provided her with her cosmetic treatments and her portion of food, and with seven chosen maids from the king's palace, and advanced her and her maids to the best place in the harem. 10 Esther did not reveal her people or kindred, for Mordecai had charged her not to tell. 11 Every day Mordecai would walk around in front of the court of the harem, to learn how Esther was and how she fared.

12 The turn came for each girl to go in to King Ahasuerus, after being twelve months under the regulations for the women, since this was the regular period of their cosmetic treatment, six months with oil of myrrh and six months with perfumes and cosmetics for women. 13 When the girl went in to the king she was given whatever she asked for to take with her from the harem to the king's palace. 14 In the evening she went in; then in the morning she came back to the second harem in custody of Shaashgaz, the king's eunuch, who was in charge of the concubines; she did not go in to the king again, unless the king delighted in her and she was summoned by name.

15 When the turn came for Esther daughter of Abihail the uncle of Mordecai, who had adopted her as his own daughter, to go in to the king, she asked for nothing except what Hegai the king's eunuch, who had charge of the women, advised. Now Esther was admired by all who saw her. 16 When Esther was taken to King Ahasuerus in his royal palace in the tenth month, which is the month of Tebeth, in the seventh year of his reign, 17 the king loved Esther more than all the other women; of all the virgins she won his favor and devotion, so that he set the royal crown on her head and made her queen instead of Vashti. 18 Then

claimed throughout the length and breadth of the kingdom, all women, high and low alike, will give honour to their husbands.'

21 The advice pleased the king and the vicegerents, and the king did as Memucan had proposed. 22 Dispatches were sent to all the king's provinces, to every province in its own script and to every people in their own language, in order that each man, whatever language he spoke, should be master in his own house.

2 SOME time later, when the anger of King Ahasuerus had died down, he called Vashti to mind, remembering what she had done and what had been decreed against her. 2 The king's attendants said: 'Let there be sought out for your majesty beautiful young virgins; 3 let your majesty appoint commissioners in every province of your kingdom to assemble all these beautiful young virgins and bring them to the women's quarters in the capital Susa. Have them placed under the care of Hegai, the king's eunuch who has charge of the women, and let him provide the cosmetics they need. 4 The girl who is most acceptable to the king shall become queen in place of Vashti.' The advice pleased the king, and he acted on it.

5 In Susa the capital there lived a Jew named Mordecai son of Jair, son of Shimei, son of Kish, a Benjamite; 6 he had been taken into exile from Jerusalem among those whom King Jeconiah of Judah had carried away with King Jeconiah of Judah. 7 He had a foster-child Hadassah, that is, Esther, his uncle's daughter, who had neither father nor mother. She was a beautiful and charming girl, and after the death of her parents, Mordecai had adopted her as his own daughter.

8 When the king's order and decree were proclaimed and many girls were brought to Susa the capital to be committed to the care of Hegai, who had charge of the women, Esther too was taken to the palace to be entrusted to him. 9 He found her pleasing, and she received his special favour: he promptly supplied her with her cosmetics and her allowance of food, and also with seven specially chosen maids from the king's palace. She and her maids were marked out for favourable treatment in the women's quarters.

10 Esther had not disclosed her race or family, because Mordecai had forbidden her to do so. 11 Every day Mordecai would walk past the forecourt of the women's quarters to learn how Esther fared and what was happening to her.

12 The full period of preparation before a girl went to King Ahasuerus was twelve months: six months' treatment with oil of myrrh, and six months' with perfumes and cosmetics. At the end of this each girl's turn came, 13 and, when she went from the women's quarters to the king's palace, she was allowed to take with her whatever she asked. 14 She would enter the palace in the evening and return in the morning to another part of the women's quarters, to be under the care of Shaashgaz, the king's eunuch in charge of the concubines. She would not go again to the king unless he expressed a wish for her and she was summoned by name.

15 When the turn came for Esther, the girl Mordecai had adopted, the daughter of his uncle Abihail, to go in to the king, she asked for nothing to take with her except what was advised by Hegai, the king's eunuch in charge of the women. Esther charmed all who saw her, 16 and when she was brought to King Ahasuerus in the royal palace, in the tenth month, the month of Tebeth, in the seventh year of his reign, 17 the king loved her more than any of his other women. He treated her with greater favour and kindness than all the rest of the virgins, and placed a royal diadem on her head, making her queen in place of Vashti. 18 Then in

e Heb adds *and speak according to the language of his people*
f Heb *a Benjamite* 6 *who* *g* Heb *He*

NEW REVISED STANDARD VERSION

the king gave a great banquet to all his officials and ministers — "Esther's banquet." He also granted a holiday[h] to the provinces, and gave gifts with royal liberality.

19 When the virgins were being gathered together,[i] Mordecai was sitting at the king's gate. 20 Now Esther had not revealed her kindred or her people, as Mordecai had charged her; for Esther obeyed Mordecai just as when she was brought up by him. 21 In those days, while Mordecai was sitting at the king's gate, Bigthan and Teresh, two of the king's eunuchs, who guarded the threshold, became angry and conspired to assassinate[j] King Ahasuerus. 22 But the matter came to the knowledge of Mordecai, and he told it to Queen Esther, and Esther told the king in the name of Mordecai. 23 When the affair was investigated and found to be so, both the men were hanged on the gallows. It was recorded in the book of the annals in the presence of the king.

3 After these things King Ahasuerus promoted Haman son of Hammedatha the Agagite, and advanced him and set his seat above all the officials who were with him. 2 And all the king's servants who were at the king's gate bowed down and did obeisance to Haman; for the king had so commanded concerning him. But Mordecai did not bow down or do obeisance. 3 Then the king's servants who were at the king's gate said to Mordecai, "Why do you disobey the king's command?" 4 When they spoke to him day after day and he would not listen to them, they told Haman, in order to see whether Mordecai's words would avail; for he had told them that he was a Jew. 5 When Haman saw that Mordecai did not bow down or do obeisance to him, Haman was infuriated. 6 But he thought it beneath him to lay hands on Mordecai alone. So, having been told who Mordecai's people were, Haman plotted to destroy all the Jews, the people of Mordecai, throughout the whole kingdom of Ahasuerus.

7 In the first month, which is the month of Nisan, in the twelfth year of King Ahasuerus, they cast Pur — which means "the lot" — before Haman for the day and for the month, and the lot fell on the thirteenth day[k] of the twelfth month, which is the month of Adar. 8 Then Haman said to King Ahasuerus, "There is a certain people scattered and separated among the peoples in all the provinces of your kingdom; their laws are different from those of every other people, and they do not keep the king's laws, so that it is not appropriate for the king to tolerate them. 9 If it pleases the king, let a decree be issued for their destruction, and I will pay ten thousand talents of silver into the hands of those who have charge of the king's business, so that they may put it into the king's treasuries." 10 So the king took his signet ring from his hand and gave it to Haman son of Hammedatha the Agagite, the enemy of the Jews. 11 The king said to Haman, "The money is given to you, and the people as well, to do with them as it seems good to you."

12 Then the king's secretaries were summoned on the thirteenth day of the first month, and an edict, according to all that Haman commanded, was written to the king's satraps and to the governors over all the provinces and to the officials of all the peoples, to every province in its own script and every people in its own language; it was written in the name of King Ahasuerus and sealed with the king's ring. 13 Letters were sent by couriers to all the king's provinces, giving orders to destroy, to kill, and to annihilate all Jews, young and old, women and children, in one day, the thirteenth day of the twelfth month, which is the month of Adar, and to plunder their goods. 14 A copy of the document

REVISED ENGLISH BIBLE

Esther's honour the king gave a great banquet, to which were invited all his officers and courtiers. He also proclaimed a holiday throughout his provinces and distributed gifts worthy of a king.

19 MORDECAI was in attendance in the court. 20 On his instructions Esther had not disclosed her family or her race, obeying Mordecai in this as she used to do when she was his ward. 21 One day when Mordecai was at court, two of the king's eunuchs, Bigthan and Teresh, keepers of the threshold who were disaffected, were plotting to assassinate King Ahasuerus. 22 This became known to Mordecai, who told Queen Esther; and she, on behalf of Mordecai, informed the king. 23 The matter was investigated and, the report being confirmed, the two men were hanged on the gallows. All this was recorded in the court chronicle in the king's presence.

3 IT was after those events that King Ahasuerus promoted Haman son of Hammedatha the Agagite, advancing him and giving him precedence above all his fellow-officers. 2 Everyone in attendance on the king at court bowed down and did obeisance to Haman, for so the king had commanded; but Mordecai would not bow or do obeisance. 3 The courtiers said to him, 'Why do you flout his majesty's command?' 4 They challenged him day after day, and when he refused to listen they informed Haman, in order to discover if Mordecai's conduct would be tolerated, for he had told them that he was a Jew. 5 Haman was furious when he saw that Mordecai was not bowing down or doing obeisance to him; 6 but having learnt who Mordecai's people were, he scorned to lay hands on him alone; he looked for a way to exterminate not only Mordecai but all the Jews throughout the whole kingdom.

7 In the twelfth year of King Ahasuerus, in the first month, Nisan, they cast lots — Pur as it is called — in the presence of Haman, taking the days and months one by one, and the lot fell on the thirteenth day of the twelfth month, the month of Adar.

8 Haman said to King Ahasuerus: 'Dispersed in scattered groups among the peoples throughout the provinces of your realm, there is a certain people whose laws are different from those of every other people. They do not observe the king's laws, and it does not befit your majesty to tolerate them. 9 If it please your majesty, let an order be drawn up for their destruction; and I shall hand over to your majesty's officials the sum of ten thousand talents of silver, to be deposited in the royal treasury.' 10 The king drew off the signet ring from his finger and gave it to Haman son of Hammedatha the Agagite, the enemy of the Jews. 11 'Keep the money,' he said, 'and deal with the people as you think best.'

12 On the thirteenth day of the first month the king's secretaries were summoned and, in accordance with Haman's instructions, a writ was issued to the king's satraps and the governors of every province, and to the rulers over each separate people. It was drawn up in the name of King Ahasuerus and sealed with the king's signet, and transcribed for each province in its own script and for each people in its own language. 13 Dispatches were sent by courier to all the king's provinces with orders to destroy, slay, and exterminate all Jews, young and old, women and children, in one day, the thirteenth day of the twelfth month, the month of Adar; their goods were to be treated as spoil. 14 A copy of the writ was to be issued as a decree in

---

[h] Or an amnesty   [i] Heb adds a second time   [j] Heb to lay hands on   [k] Cn Compare Gk and verse 13 below: Heb the twelfth month

2:18 a holiday: or an amnesty.   2:19 in the court: so Gk; Heb. adds when the virgins were brought together a second time.   3:7 and the lot . . . twelfth month: prob. rdg, cp. Gk and verse 13; Heb. the twelfth.

was to be issued as a decree in every province by proclamation, calling on all the peoples to be ready for that day. 15 The couriers went quickly by order of the king, and the decree was issued in the citadel of Susa. The king and Haman sat down to drink; but the city of Susa was thrown into confusion.

4 When Mordecai learned all that had been done, Mordecai tore his clothes and put on sackcloth and ashes, and went through the city, wailing with a loud and bitter cry; 2 he went up to the entrance of the king's gate, for no one might enter the king's gate clothed with sackcloth. 3 In every province, wherever the king's command and his decree came, there was great mourning among the Jews, with fasting and weeping and lamenting, and most of them lay in sackcloth and ashes.

4 When Esther's maids and her eunuchs came and told her, the queen was deeply distressed; she sent garments to clothe Mordecai, so that he might take off his sackcloth; but he would not accept them. 5 Then Esther called for Hathach, one of the king's eunuchs, who had been appointed to attend her, and ordered him to go to Mordecai to learn what was happening and why. 6 Hathach went out to Mordecai in the open square of the city in front of the king's gate, 7 and Mordecai told him all that had happened to him, and the exact sum of money that Haman had promised to pay into the king's treasuries for the destruction of the Jews. 8 Mordecai also gave him a copy of the written decree issued in Susa for their destruction, that he might show it to Esther, explain it to her, and charge her to go to the king to make supplication to him and entreat him for her people. 9 Hathach went and told Esther what Mordecai had said. 10 Then Esther spoke to Hathach and gave him a message for Mordecai, saying, 11 "All the king's servants and the people of the king's provinces know that if any man or woman goes to the king inside the inner court without being called, there is but one law — all alike are to be put to death. Only if the king holds out the golden scepter to someone, may that person live. I myself have not been called to come in to the king for thirty days." 12 When they told Mordecai what Esther had said, 13 Mordecai told them to reply to Esther, "Do not think that in the king's palace you will escape any more than all the other Jews. 14 For if you keep silence at such a time as this, relief and deliverance will rise for the Jews from another quarter, but you and your father's family will perish. Who knows? Perhaps you have come to royal dignity for just such a time as this." 15 Then Esther said in reply to Mordecai, 16 "Go, gather all the Jews to be found in Susa, and hold a fast on my behalf, and neither eat nor drink for three days, night or day. I and my maids will also fast as you do. After that I will go to the king, though it is against the law; and if I perish, I perish." 17 Mordecai then went away and did everything as Esther had ordered him.

5 On the third day Esther put on her royal robes and stood in the inner court of the king's palace, opposite the king's hall. The king was sitting on his royal throne inside the palace opposite the entrance to the palace. 2 As soon as the king saw Queen Esther standing in the court, she won his favor and he held out to her the golden scepter that was in his hand. Then Esther approached and touched the top of the scepter. 3 The king said to her, "What is it, Queen Esther? What is your request? It shall be given you, even to the half of my kingdom." 4 Then Esther said, "If it pleases the king, let the king and Haman come today to a banquet that I have prepared for the king." 5 Then the king said, "Bring Haman quickly, so that we may do as Esther desires." So the king and Haman came to the banquet that Esther had prepared. 6 While they were drinking wine, the

every province and to be publicly displayed to all the peoples, so that they might be ready for that day. 15 At the king's command the couriers set off post-haste, and the decree was issued in Susa the capital city. The king and Haman sat down to carouse, but in the city of Susa confusion reigned.

4 When Mordecai learnt of all that had been done, he tore his clothes and put on sackcloth and ashes. He went out through the city, lamenting loudly and bitterly, 2 until he came right in front of the palace gate; no one wearing sackcloth was allowed to pass through that gate. 3 In every province reached by the royal command and decree there was great mourning among the Jews, with fasting and weeping and beating of the breast; most of them lay down on beds of sackcloth and ashes. 4 When Queen Esther's maids and eunuchs came in and told her, she was greatly distraught. She sent clothes for Mordecai to wear instead of his sackcloth; but he would not accept them.

5 Esther then summoned Hathach, one of the king's eunuchs appointed to wait on her, and ordered him to find out from Mordecai what was the trouble and the reason for it. 6 Hathach went out to Mordecai in the city square opposite the palace, 7 and Mordecai told him all that had happened to him and how much money Haman had offered to pay into the royal treasury for the destruction of the Jews. 8 He also gave him a copy of the writ for their extermination, which had been issued in Susa, so that he might show it to Esther and tell her about it, directing her to go to the king to implore his favour and intercede for her people. 9 When Hathach came in and informed Esther of what Mordecai had said, 10 she told him to take back this message: 11 'All the courtiers and the people in the king's provinces know that if any person, man or woman, enters the royal presence in the inner court without being summoned, there is but one law: that person shall be put to death, unless the king extends to him the gold sceptre; only then may he live. What is more, I have not been summoned to the king for the last thirty days.'

12 When Esther was told what Mordecai had said, 13 he sent this reply, 'Do not imagine, Esther, that, because you are in the royal palace, you alone of all the Jews will escape. 14 If you remain silent at such a time as this, relief and deliverance for the Jews will appear from another quarter; but you and your father's family will perish. And who knows whether it is not for a time like this that you have become queen?' 15 Esther sent this answer back to Mordecai: 16 'Go and assemble all the Jews that are in Susa, and fast on my behalf; for three days, night and day, take neither food nor drink, and I also will fast with my maids. After that, in defiance of the law, I shall go to the king; if I perish, I perish.' 17 Mordecai then went away and did exactly as Esther had bidden him.

5 On the third day Esther arrayed herself in her royal robes and stood in the inner court, facing the palace itself; the king was seated on his royal throne in the palace, opposite the entrance. 2 When he caught sight of Queen Esther standing in the court, he extended to her the gold sceptre he held, for she had obtained his favour. Esther approached and touched the tip of the sceptre. 3 The king said to her, 'What is it, Queen Esther? Whatever you request, up to half my kingdom, it shall be granted you.' 4 'If it please your majesty,' she answered, 'will you come today, my lord, and Haman with you, to a banquet I have prepared for you?' 5 The king gave orders for Haman to be brought with all speed to meet Esther's wishes; and the king and Haman went to the banquet she had prepared.

NEW REVISED STANDARD VERSION	REVISED ENGLISH BIBLE

king said to Esther, "What is your petition? It shall be granted you. And what is your request? Even to the half of my kingdom, it shall be fulfilled." 7 Then Esther said, "This is my petition and request: 8 If I have won the king's favor, and if it pleases the king to grant my petition and fulfill my request, let the king and Haman come tomorrow to the banquet that I will prepare for them, and then I will do as the king has said."

9 Haman went out that day happy and in good spirits. But when Haman saw Mordecai in the king's gate, and observed that he neither rose nor trembled before him, he was infuriated with Mordecai; 10 nevertheless Haman restrained himself and went home. Then he sent and called for his friends and his wife Zeresh, 11 and Haman recounted to them the splendor of his riches, the number of his sons, all the promotions with which the king had honored him, and how he had advanced him above the officials and the ministers of the king. 12 Haman added, "Even Queen Esther let no one but myself come with the king to the banquet that she prepared. Tomorrow also I am invited by her, together with the king. 13 Yet all this does me no good so long as I see the Jew Mordecai sitting at the king's gate." 14 Then his wife Zeresh and all his friends said to him, "Let a gallows fifty cubits high be made, and in the morning tell the king to have Mordecai hanged on it; then go with the king to the banquet in good spirits." This advice pleased Haman, and he had the gallows made.

6 On that night the king could not sleep, and he gave orders to bring the book of records, the annals, and they were read to the king. 2 It was found written how Mordecai had told about Bigthana and Teresh, two of the king's eunuchs, who guarded the threshold, and who had conspired to assassinate[l] King Ahasuerus. 3 Then the king said, "What honor or distinction has been bestowed on Mordecai for this?" The king's servants who attended him said, "Nothing has been done for him." 4 The king said, "Who is in the court?" Now Haman had just entered the outer court of the king's palace to speak to the king about having Mordecai hanged on the gallows that he had prepared for him. 5 So the king's servants told him, "Haman is there, standing in the court." The king said, "Let him come in." 6 So Haman came in, and the king said to him, "What shall be done for the man whom the king wishes to honor?" Haman said to himself, "Whom would the king wish to honor more than me?" 7 So Haman said to the king, "For the man whom the king wishes to honor, 8 let royal robes be brought, which the king has worn, and a horse that the king has ridden, with a royal crown on its head. 9 Let the robes and the horse be handed over to one of the king's most noble officials; let him[m] robe the man whom the king wishes to honor, and let him[m] conduct him on horseback through the open square of the city, proclaiming before him: 'Thus shall it be done for the man whom the king wishes to honor.' " 10 Then the king said to Haman, "Quickly, take the robes and the horse, as you have said, and do so to the Jew Mordecai who sits at the king's gate. Leave out nothing that you have mentioned." 11 So Haman took the robes and the horse and robed Mordecai and led him riding through the open square of the city, proclaiming, "Thus shall it be done for the man whom the king wishes to honor."

12 Then Mordecai returned to the king's gate, but Haman hurried to his house, mourning and with his head covered. 13 When Haman told his wife Zeresh and all his friends everything that had happened to him, his advisers and his wife Zeresh said to him, "If Mordecai, before whom your downfall has begun, is of the Jewish people, you will not prevail against him, but will surely fall before him."

6 Over the wine the king said to Esther, 'Whatever you ask will be given you; whatever you request, up to half my kingdom, will be granted.' 7 Esther replied, 'What I ask and request is this: 8 If I have found favour with your majesty, and if it please you, my lord, to give me what I ask and to grant my request, will your majesty and Haman come again tomorrow to the banquet that I shall prepare for you both? Tomorrow I shall do as your majesty says.'

9 Haman left the royal presence that day overjoyed and in the best of spirits, but as soon as he saw Mordecai in the king's court and observed that he did not rise or defer to him, he was furious; 10 yet he kept control of himself. When he arrived home, he sent for his friends and for Zeresh his wife 11 and held forth to them about the splendour of his wealth and his many sons, and how the king had promoted him and advanced him above the other officers and courtiers. 12 'Nor is that all,' Haman went on; 'Queen Esther had no one but myself come with the king to the banquet which she had prepared; and I am invited by her again tomorrow with the king. 13 Yet all this gives me no satisfaction so long as I see that Jew Mordecai in attendance at the king's court.' 14 His wife Zeresh and all his friends said to him, 'Have a gallows set up, seventy-five feet high, and in the morning propose to the king that Mordecai be hanged on it. Then you can go with the king to the banquet and enjoy yourself.' This advice seemed good to Haman, and he set up the gallows.

6 That night sleep eluded the king, so he ordered the chronicle of memorable events to be brought, and it was read to him. 2 There it was found recorded how Mordecai had furnished information about Bigthana and Teresh, the two royal eunuchs among the keepers of the threshold who had plotted to assassinate King Ahasuerus. 3 When the king asked what honour or dignity had been conferred on Mordecai for this, his attendants said, 'Nothing has been done for him.' 4 'Who is in the court?' said the king. As Haman had just then entered the outer court of the palace to propose to the king that Mordecai should be hanged on the gallows he had prepared for him, 5 the king's attendants replied, 'Haman is standing there in the court.' 'Let him enter!' commanded the king. 6 When he came in, the king asked him, 'What should be done for the man whom the king wishes to honour?' Haman thought to himself, 'Whom, other than myself, would the king wish to honour?' 7 So he answered, 'For the man whom the king wishes to honour, 8 let there be brought a royal robe which the king himself has worn, and a horse on which the king rides, with a royal diadem on its head. 9 Let the robe and the horse be handed over to one of the king's noble officers, and let him invest the man whom the king wishes to honour and lead him mounted on the horse through the city square, proclaiming as he goes: "This is what is done for the man whom the king wishes to honour." ' 10 The king said to Haman, 'Take the robe and the horse at once, as you have said, and do this for Mordecai the Jew who is present at court. Let nothing be omitted of all you have proposed.' 11 Haman took the robe and the horse, invested Mordecai, and led him on horseback through the city square, proclaiming before him: 'This is what is done for the man whom the king wishes to honour.'

12 Mordecai then returned to court, while Haman in grief hurried off home with his head veiled. 13 When he told his wife Zeresh and all his friends everything that had happened to him, the response he got from his advisers and Zeresh was: 'If you have begun to fall before Mordecai, and he is a Jew, you cannot get the better of him; your downfall before him is certain.'

5:8 **again tomorrow**: *so Gk; Heb. omits.*   5:14 **seventy-five feet**: *lit. fifty cubits.*   6:2 **Bigthana**: *or Bigthan; cp. 2:21.*

[l] Heb *to lay hands on*   [m] Heb *them*

14 While they were still talking with him, the king's eunuchs arrived and hurried Haman off to the banquet that Esther had prepared. 1 So the king and Haman went in to feast with Queen Esther. 2 On the second day, as they were drinking wine, the king again said to Esther, "What is your petition, Queen Esther? It shall be granted you. And what is your request? Even to the half of my kingdom, it shall be fulfilled." 3 Then Queen Esther answered, "If I have won your favor, O king, and if it pleases the king, let my life be given me — that is my petition — and the lives of my people — that is my request. 4 For we have been sold, I and my people, to be destroyed, to be killed, and to be annihilated. If we had been sold merely as slaves, men and women, I would have held my peace; but no enemy can compensate for this damage to the king."[n] 5 Then King Ahasuerus said to Queen Esther, "Who is he, and where is he, who has presumed to do this?" 6 Esther said, "A foe and enemy, this wicked Haman!" Then Haman was terrified before the king and the queen. 7 The king rose from the feast in wrath and went into the palace garden, but Haman stayed to beg his life from Queen Esther, for he saw that the king had determined to destroy him. 8 When the king returned from the palace garden to the banquet hall, Haman had thrown himself on the couch where Esther was reclining; and the king said, "Will he even assault the queen in my presence, in my own house?" As the words left the mouth of the king, they covered Haman's face. 9 Then Harbona, one of the eunuchs in attendance on the king, said, "Look, the very gallows that Haman has prepared for Mordecai, whose word saved the king, stands at Haman's house, fifty cubits high." And the king said, "Hang him on that." 10 So they hanged Haman on the gallows that he had prepared for Mordecai. Then the anger of the king abated.

8 On that day King Ahasuerus gave to Queen Esther the house of Haman, the enemy of the Jews; and Mordecai came before the king, for Esther had told what he was to her. 2 Then the king took off his signet ring, which he had taken from Haman, and gave it to Mordecai. So Esther set Mordecai over the house of Haman.

3 Then Esther spoke again to the king; she fell at his feet, weeping and pleading with him to avert the evil design of Haman the Agagite and the plot that he had devised against the Jews. 4 The king held out the golden scepter to Esther, 5 and Esther rose and stood before the king. She said, "If it pleases the king, and if I have won his favor, and if the thing seems right before the king, and I have his approval, let an order be written to revoke the letters devised by Haman son of Hammedatha the Agagite, which he wrote giving orders to destroy the Jews who are in all the provinces of the king. 6 For how can I bear to see the calamity that is coming on my people? Or how can I bear to see the destruction of my kindred?" 7 Then King Ahasuerus said to Queen Esther and to the Jew Mordecai, "See, I have given Esther the house of Haman, and they have hanged him on the gallows, because he plotted to lay hands on the Jews. 8 You may write as you please with regard to the Jews, in the name of the king, and seal it with the king's ring; for an edict written in the name of the king and sealed with the king's ring cannot be revoked."

9 The king's secretaries were summoned at that time, in the third month, which is the month of Sivan, on the twenty-third day; and an edict was written, according to all that Mordecai commanded, to the Jews and to the satraps

14 While they were still talking with him, the king's eunuchs arrived and Haman was hurried off to the banquet Esther had prepared.

7 So the king and Haman went to Queen Esther's banquet, 2 and again on that second day over the wine the king said, 'Whatever you ask will be given you, Queen Esther. Whatever you request, up to half my kingdom, it will be granted.' 3 She answered, 'If I have found favour with your majesty, and if it please you, my lord, what I ask is that my own life and the lives of my people be spared. 4 For we have been sold, I and my people, to be destroyed, slain, and exterminated. If it had been a matter of selling us, men and women alike, into slavery, I should have kept silence; for then our plight would not have been such as to injure the king's interests.' 5 King Ahasuerus demanded, 'Who is he, and where is he, who has dared to do such a thing?' 6 'A ruthless enemy,' she answered, 'this wicked Haman!' Haman stood aghast before the king and queen. 7 In a rage the king rose from the banquet and went into the garden of the pavilion, while Haman remained where he was to plead for his life with Queen Esther; for he saw that in the king's mind his fate was determined. 8 When the king returned from the pavilion garden to the banqueting hall, Haman had flung himself on the couch where Esther was reclining. The king exclaimed, 'Will he even assault the queen in the palace before my very eyes?' The words had no sooner left the king's lips than Haman's face was covered. 9 Harbona, one of the eunuchs in attendance on the king, said, 'There is a gallows seventy-five feet high standing at Haman's house; he had it erected for Mordecai, whose evidence once saved your majesty.' 'Let Haman be hanged on it!' said the king. 10 So they hanged Haman on the gallows he had prepared for Mordecai. Then the king's anger subsided.

8 That same day King Ahasuerus gave Queen Esther the property of Haman, the enemy of the Jews, and Mordecai came into the king's presence, for Esther had revealed his relationship to her. 2 The king drew off his signet ring, which he had taken back from Haman, and gave it to Mordecai. Esther put Mordecai in charge of Haman's property.

3 ONCE again Esther addressed the king, falling at his feet and imploring him with tears to thwart the wickedness of Haman the Agagite and frustrate his plot against the Jews. 4 The king extended his gold sceptre towards her, and she rose and stood before him. 5 'May it please your majesty,' Esther said; 'if I have found favour with you, and if what I propose seems right to your majesty and I have won your approval, let a writ be issued to recall the dispatches which Haman son of Hammedatha the Agagite wrote in pursuance of his plan to destroy the Jews in all the royal provinces. 6 For how can I bear to witness the disaster which threatens my people? How can I bear to witness the destruction of my kindred?' 7 King Ahasuerus said to Queen Esther and to Mordecai the Jew, 'I have given Haman's property to Esther, and he has been hanged on the gallows because he threatened the lives of the Jews. 8 Now you may issue a writ in my name concerning the Jews, in whatever terms you think fit, and seal it with the royal signet; no order written in the name of the king and sealed with the royal signet can be rescinded.'

9 On the twenty-third day of the third month, the month of Sivan, the king's secretaries were summoned, and a writ exactly as Mordecai directed was issued to the Jews, and to the satraps, the governors, and the rulers of the hundred and

[n] Meaning of Heb uncertain

7:9 **seventy-five feet:** *lit.* fifty cubits.

| NEW REVISED STANDARD VERSION | REVISED ENGLISH BIBLE |

and the governors and the officials of the provinces from India to Ethiopia, *o* one hundred twenty-seven provinces, to every province in its own script and to every people in its own language, and also to the Jews in their script and their language. 10 He wrote letters in the name of King Ahasuerus, sealed them with the king's ring, and sent them by mounted couriers riding on fast steeds bred from the royal herd. *p* 11 By these letters the king allowed the Jews who were in every city to assemble and defend their lives, to destroy, to kill, and to annihilate any armed force of any people or province that might attack them, with their children and women, and to plunder their goods 12 on a single day throughout all the provinces of King Ahasuerus, on the thirteenth day of the twelfth month, which is the month of Adar. 13 A copy of the writ was to be issued as a decree in every province and published to all peoples, and the Jews were to be ready on that day to take revenge on their enemies. 14 So the couriers, mounted on their swift royal steeds, hurried out, urged by the king's command. The decree was issued in the citadel of Susa.

15 Then Mordecai went out from the presence of the king, wearing royal robes of blue and white, with a great golden crown and a mantle of fine linen and purple, while the city of Susa shouted and rejoiced. 16 For the Jews there was light and gladness, joy and honor. 17 In every province and in every city, wherever the king's command and his edict came, there was gladness and joy among the Jews, a festival and a holiday. Furthermore, many of the peoples of the country professed to be Jews, because the fear of the Jews had fallen upon them.

9 Now in the twelfth month, which is the month of Adar, on the thirteenth day, when the king's command and edict were about to be executed, on the very day when the enemies of the Jews hoped to gain power over them, but which had been changed to a day when the Jews would gain power over their foes, 2 the Jews gathered in their cities throughout all the provinces of King Ahasuerus to lay hands on those who had sought their ruin; and no one could withstand them, because the fear of them had fallen upon all peoples. 3 All the officials of the provinces, the satraps and the governors, and the royal officials were supporting the Jews, because the fear of Mordecai had fallen upon them. 4 For Mordecai was powerful in the king's house, and his fame spread throughout all the provinces as the man Mordecai grew more and more powerful. 5 So the Jews struck down all their enemies with the sword, slaughtering, and destroying them, and did as they pleased to those who hated them. 6 In the citadel of Susa the Jews killed and destroyed five hundred people. 7 They killed Parshandatha, Dalphon, Aspatha, 8 Poratha, Adalia, Aridatha, 9 Parmashta, Arisai, Aridai, Vaizatha, 10 the ten sons of Haman son of Hammedatha, the enemy of the Jews; but they did not touch the plunder.

11 That very day the number of those killed in the citadel of Susa was reported to the king. 12 The king said to Queen Esther, "In the citadel of Susa the Jews have killed five hundred people and also the ten sons of Haman. What have they done in the rest of the king's provinces? Now what is your petition? It shall be granted you. And what further is your request? It shall be fulfilled." 13 Esther said, "If it pleases the king, let the Jews who are in Susa be allowed tomorrow also to do according to this day's edict, and let the ten sons of Haman be hanged on the gallows." 14 So the king commanded this to be done; a decree was issued in Susa, and the ten sons of Haman were hanged. 15 The Jews who were in Susa gathered also on the fourteenth day of the month of Adar and they killed three hundred persons in Susa; but they did not touch the plunder.

twenty-seven provinces from India to Ethiopia; it was issued for each province in its own script and for each people in their own language, and also for the Jews in their script and language. 10 The writ was drawn up in the name of King Ahasuerus and sealed with the royal signet, and dispatches were sent by couriers mounted on horses from the royal stables. 11 By these dispatches the king granted permission to the Jews in each and every city to assemble in self-defence, and to destroy, slay, and exterminate every man, woman, and child, of any people or province which might attack them, and to treat their goods as spoil, 12 throughout all the provinces of King Ahasuerus, in one day, the thirteenth day of Adar, the twelfth month. 13 A copy of the writ was to be issued as a decree in every province and published to all peoples, and the Jews were to be ready for that day, the day of vengeance on their enemies. 14 Couriers, mounted on horses from the royal stables, set off post-haste at the king's urgent command; and the decree was proclaimed also in Susa the capital.

15 When Mordecai left the king's presence in a royal robe of violet and white, wearing an imposing gold crown and a cloak of fine linen with purple thread, the city of Susa shouted for joy. 16 All was light and joy, gladness and honour for the Jews; 17 in every province and city reached by the royal command and decree there was joy and gladness for the Jews, feasting and holiday. And many of the peoples of the world professed Judaism, because fear of the Jews had fallen on them.

9 ON the thirteenth day of Adar, the twelfth month, the time came for the king's command and decree to be carried out. That very day on which the enemies of the Jews had hoped to triumph over them was to become the day when the Jews should triumph over those who hated them. 2 Throughout all the provinces of King Ahasuerus, the Jews assembled in their cities to attack those who had sought to bring disaster on them. None could offer resistance, because fear of them had fallen on all the peoples. 3 The rulers of the provinces, the satraps and the governors, and the royal officials all aided the Jews, out of fear of Mordecai, 4 for he had become a person of great power in the royal palace, and as the power of the man increased, his fame spread throughout every province. 5 The Jews put all their enemies to the sword. There was great slaughter and destruction, and they worked their will on those who hated them.

6 In Susa the capital the Jews slaughtered five hundred men; 7 and they also put to death Parshandatha, Dalphon, Aspatha, 8 Poratha, Adalia, Aridatha, 9 Parmashta, Arisai, Aridai, and Vaizatha, 10 the ten sons of Haman son of Hammedatha, the persecutor of the Jews; but they took no plunder.

11 That day when the number of those killed in Susa was reported to the king, 12 he said to Queen Esther, 'In Susa the capital the Jews have slaughtered five hundred men; they have killed the ten sons of Haman; what will they have done in the rest of the provinces of the kingdom? Whatever you ask will be given you; whatever further request you have, it will be granted.' 13 Esther replied, 'If it please your majesty, let the Jews in Susa be permitted tomorrow also to take action according to this day's decree; and let the bodies of Haman's ten sons be hung up on the gallows.' 14 The king gave orders for this to be done; the decree was issued in Susa, and Haman's ten sons were hung up on the gallows. 15 The Jews in Susa assembled again on the fourteenth day of the month of Adar and killed there three hundred men; but they took no plunder.

---

o Or *Nubia*; Heb *Cush*   *p* Meaning of Heb uncertain

8:15 **thread:** *prob. mng; Heb. omits.*

16 Now the other Jews who were in the king's provinces also gathered to defend their lives, and gained relief from their enemies, and killed seventy-five thousand of those who hated them; but they laid no hands on the plunder. 17 This was on the thirteenth day of the month of Adar, and on the fourteenth day they rested and made that a day of feasting and gladness.

18 But the Jews who were in Susa gathered on the thirteenth day and on the fourteenth, and rested on the fifteenth day, making that a day of feasting and gladness. 19 Therefore the Jews of the villages, who live in the open towns, hold the fourteenth day of the month of Adar as a day for gladness and feasting, a holiday on which they send gifts of food to one another.

20 Mordecai recorded these things, and sent letters to all the Jews who were in all the provinces of King Ahasuerus, both near and far, 21 enjoining them that they should keep the fourteenth day of the month Adar and also the fifteenth day of the same month, year by year, 22 as the days on which the Jews gained relief from their enemies, and as the month that had been turned for them from sorrow into gladness and from mourning into a holiday; that they should make them days of feasting and gladness, days for sending gifts of food to one another and presents to the poor. 23 So the Jews adopted as a custom what they had begun to do, as Mordecai had written to them.

24 Haman son of Hammedatha the Agagite, the enemy of all the Jews, had plotted against the Jews to destroy them, and had cast Pur—that is "the lot"—to crush and destroy them; 25 but when Esther came before the king, he gave orders in writing that the wicked plot that he had devised against the Jews should come upon his own head, and that he and his sons should be hanged on the gallows. 26 Therefore these days are called Purim, from the word Pur. Thus because of all that was written in this letter, and of what they had faced in this matter, and of what had happened to them, 27 the Jews established and accepted as a custom for themselves and their descendants and all who joined them, that without fail they would continue to observe these two days every year, as it was written and at the time appointed. 28 These days should be remembered and kept throughout every generation, in every family, province, and city; and these days of Purim should never fall into disuse among the Jews, nor should the commemoration of these days cease among their descendants.

29 Queen Esther daughter of Abihail, along with the Jew Mordecai, gave full written authority, confirming this second letter about Purim. 30 Letters were sent wishing peace and security to all the Jews, to the one hundred twenty-seven provinces of the kingdom of Ahasuerus, 31 and giving orders that these days of Purim should be observed at their appointed seasons, as the Jew Mordecai and Queen Esther enjoined on the Jews, just as they had laid down for themselves and for their descendants regulations concerning their fasts and their lamentations. 32 The command of Queen Esther fixed these practices of Purim, and it was recorded in writing.

10 King Ahasuerus laid tribute on the land and on the islands of the sea. 2 All the acts of his power and might, and the full account of the high honor of Mordecai, to which the king advanced him, are they not written in the annals of the kings of Media and Persia? 3 For Mordecai the Jew was next in rank to King Ahasuerus, and he was powerful among the Jews and popular with his many kindred, for he sought the good of his people and interceded for the welfare of all his descendants.

16 The rest of the Jews throughout the king's provinces rallied in self-defence and so had respite from their enemies; they slaughtered seventy-five thousand of those who hated them, but they took no plunder. 17 That was on the thirteenth day of the month of Adar; on the fourteenth day they rested and made it a day of feasting and joy. 18 The Jews in Susa had assembled on both the thirteenth and fourteenth days of the month; they rested on the fifteenth day and made that a day of feasting and joy. 19 This explains why Jews in the countryside who live in remote villages observe the fourteenth day of Adar with joy and feasting as a holiday, sending presents of food to one another.

20 MORDECAI put these things on record, and he sent letters to all the Jews throughout the provinces of King Ahasuerus, both near and far, 21 requiring them to observe annually the fourteenth and fifteenth days of the month of Adar 22 as the days on which the Jews had respite from their enemies; that was the month which was changed for them from sorrow into joy, from a time of mourning to a holiday. They were to observe them as days of feasting and joy, days for sending presents of food to one another and gifts to the poor. 23 The Jews undertook to continue the practice that they had begun in accordance with Mordecai's letter. 24 This they did because Haman son of Hammedatha the Agagite, the enemy of all the Jews, had plotted to destroy them and had cast lots—Pur as it is called—with intent to crush and destroy them. 25 But when the matter came before the king, he issued written orders that the wicked plot which Haman had devised against the Jews should recoil on his own head, and that he and his sons should be hanged on the gallows. 26 This is why these days were named Purim, from the word Pur. Accordingly, because of all that was written in this letter, because of all they had seen and experienced in this affair, 27 the Jews resolved and undertook, on behalf of themselves, their descendants, and all who might join them, to observe without fail these two days as a yearly festival in the prescribed manner and at the appointed time; 28 further, that these days were to be remembered and celebrated throughout all generations, in every family, province, and city, so that the observance of the days of Purim should never lapse among the Jews, and the commemoration of them should never cease among their descendants.

29 Queen Esther daughter of Abihail gave full authority in writing to Mordecai the Jew, to confirm this second letter about Purim. 30 Letters to ensure peace and security were sent to all the Jews in the one hundred and twenty-seven provinces of King Ahasuerus, 31 requiring the observance of these days of Purim at their appointed time, as Mordecai the Jew and Queen Esther had prescribed for them, and in the same way as regulations for fasts and lamentations were prescribed for themselves and for their descendants. 32 By the command of Esther these regulations for Purim were confirmed and put in writing.

10 King Ahasuerus exacted tribute from the land and the coasts and islands. 2 All his acts of might and power, and the high dignities which he conferred on Mordecai, are recorded in the annals of the kings of Media and Persia. 3 Mordecai the Jew ranked second only to King Ahasuerus himself; he was a great man among the Jews and popular with all his many countrymen, for he sought the good of his people and promoted the welfare of all their descendants.

9:29 **to Mordecai:** *prob. rdg; Heb.* and Mordecai.   10:1 **tribute:** *or* forced labour.

THE BOOK OF

Job

Job

1 There was once a man in the land of Uz whose name was Job. That man was blameless and upright, one who feared God and turned away from evil. 2 There were born to him seven sons and three daughters. 3 He had seven thousand sheep, three thousand camels, five hundred yoke of oxen, and five hundred donkeys, and very many servants; so that this man was the greatest of all the people of the east. 4 His sons used to go and hold feasts in one another's houses in turn; and they would send and invite their three sisters to eat and drink with them. 5 And when the feast days had run their course, Job would send and sanctify them, and he would rise early in the morning and offer burnt offerings according to the number of them all; for Job said, "It may be that my children have sinned, and cursed God in their hearts." This is what Job always did.

6 One day the heavenly beings*a* came to present themselves before the LORD, and Satan*b* also came among them. 7 The LORD said to Satan,*b* "Where have you come from?" Satan*b* answered the LORD, "From going to and fro on the earth, and from walking up and down on it." 8 The LORD said to Satan,*b* "Have you considered my servant Job? There is no one like him on the earth, a blameless and upright man who fears God and turns away from evil." 9 Then Satan*b* answered the LORD, "Does Job fear God for nothing? 10 Have you not put a fence around him and his house and all that he has, on every side? You have blessed the work of his hands, and his possessions have increased in the land. 11 But stretch out your hand now, and touch all that he has, and he will curse you to your face." 12 The LORD said to Satan,*b* "Very well, all that he has is in your power; only do not stretch out your hand against him!" So Satan*b* went out from the presence of the LORD.

13 One day when his sons and daughters were eating and drinking wine in the eldest brother's house, 14 a messenger came to Job and said, "The oxen were plowing and the donkeys were feeding beside them, 15 and the Sabeans fell on them and carried them off, and killed the servants with the edge of the sword; I alone have escaped to tell you." 16 While he was still speaking, another came and said, "The fire of God fell from heaven and burned up the sheep and the servants, and consumed them; I alone have escaped to tell you." 17 While he was still speaking, another came and said, "The Chaldeans formed three columns, made a raid on the camels and carried them off, and killed the servants with the edge of the sword; I alone have escaped to tell you." 18 While he was still speaking, another came and said, "Your sons and daughters were eating and drinking wine in their eldest brother's house, 19 and suddenly a great wind came across the desert, struck the four corners of the house, and it fell on the young people, and they are dead; I alone have escaped to tell you."

20 Then Job arose, tore his robe, shaved his head, and fell on the ground and worshiped. 21 He said, "Naked I came from my mother's womb, and naked shall I return there; the LORD gave, and the LORD has taken away; blessed be the name of the LORD."

22 In all this Job did not sin or charge God with wrongdoing.

1 THERE lived in the land of Uz a man of blameless and upright life named Job, who feared God and set his face against wrongdoing. 2 He had seven sons and three daughters; 3 and he owned seven thousand sheep, three thousand camels, five hundred yoke of oxen, and five hundred she-donkeys, together with a large number of slaves. Thus Job was the greatest man in all the East.

4 His sons used to meet together and give, each in turn, a banquet in his own house, and they would send and invite their three sisters to eat and drink with them. 5 Then, when a round of banquets was over, Job would send for his children and sanctify them, rising early in the morning and sacrificing a whole-offering for each of them; for he thought that they might somehow have sinned against God and committed blasphemy in their hearts. This Job did regularly.

6 The day came when the members of the court of heaven took their places in the presence of the LORD, and the Adversary, Satan, was there among them. 7 The LORD asked him where he had been. 'Ranging over the earth', said the Adversary, 'from end to end.' 8 The LORD asked him, 'Have you considered my servant Job? You will find no one like him on earth, a man of blameless and upright life, who fears God and sets his face against wrongdoing.' 9 'Has not Job good reason to be godfearing?' answered the Adversary. 10 'Have you not hedged him round on every side with your protection, him and his family and all his possessions? Whatever he does you bless, and everywhere his herds have increased beyond measure. 11 But just stretch out your hand and touch all that he has, and see if he will not curse you to your face.' 12 'Very well,' said the LORD. 'All that he has is in your power; only the man himself you must not touch.' With that the Adversary left the LORD's presence.

13 On the day when Job's sons and daughters were eating and drinking in the eldest brother's house, 14 a messenger came to Job and said, 'The oxen were ploughing and the donkeys were grazing near them, 15 when the Sabaeans swooped down and carried them off, after putting the herdsmen to the sword; only I have escaped to bring you the news.' 16 While he was still speaking, another messenger arrived and said, 'God's fire flashed from heaven, striking the sheep and the shepherds and burning them up; only I have escaped to bring you the news.' 17 While he was still speaking, another arrived and said, 'The Chaldaeans, three bands of them, have made a raid on the camels and carried them off, after putting those tending them to the sword; only I have escaped to bring you the news.' 18 While this man was speaking, yet another arrived and said, 'Your sons and daughters were eating and drinking in their eldest brother's house, 19 when suddenly a whirlwind swept across from the desert and struck the four corners of the house, which fell on the young people. They are dead, and only I have escaped to bring you the news.' 20 At this Job stood up, tore his cloak, shaved his head, and threw himself prostrate on the ground, 21 saying:

'Naked I came from the womb,
naked I shall return whence I came.
The LORD gives and the LORD takes away;
blessed be the name of the LORD.'

22 Throughout all this Job did not sin, nor did he ascribe any fault to God.

---

a Heb *sons of God*   *b* Or *the Accuser*; Heb *ha-satan*

1:6 **members . . . heaven:** *lit.* sons of God.

THE BOOK OF
Job

1 In the land of Uz there was a blameless and upright man named Job, who feared God and avoided evil. 2 Seven sons and three daughters were born to him; 3 and he had seven thousand sheep, three thousand camels, five hundred yoke of oxen, five hundred she-asses, and a great number of work animals, so that he was greater than any of the men of the East. 4 His sons used to take turns giving feasts, sending invitations to their three sisters to eat and drink with them. 5 And when each feast had run its course, Job would send for them and sanctify them, rising early and offering holocausts for every one of them. For Job said, "It may be that my sons have sinned and blasphemed God in their hearts." This Job did habitually.

6 One day, when the sons of God came to present themselves before the LORD, Satan also came among them. 7 And the LORD said to Satan, "Whence do you come?" Then Satan answered the LORD and said, "From roaming the earth and patrolling it." 8 And the LORD said to Satan, "Have you noticed my servant Job, and that there is no one on earth like him, blameless and upright, fearing God and avoiding evil?" 9 But Satan answered the LORD and said, "Is it for nothing that Job is God-fearing? 10 Have you not surrounded him and his family and all that he has with your protection? You have blessed the work of his hands, and his livestock are spread over the land. 11 But now put forth your hand and touch anything that he has, and surely he will blaspheme you to your face." 12 And the LORD said to Satan, "Behold, all that he has is in your power; only do not lay a hand upon his person." So Satan went forth from the presence of the LORD.

13 And so one day, while his sons and his daughters were eating and drinking wine in the house of their eldest brother, 14 a messenger came to Job and said, "The oxen were plowing and the asses grazing beside them, 15 and the Sabeans carried them off in a raid. They put the herdsmen to the sword, and I alone have escaped to tell you." 16 While he was yet speaking, another came and said, "Lightning has fallen from heaven and struck the sheep and their shepherds and consumed them; and I alone have escaped to tell you." 17 While he was yet speaking, another came and said, "The Chaldeans formed three columns, seized the camels, carried them off, and put those tending them to the sword, and I alone have escaped to tell you." 18 While he was yet speaking, another came and said, "Your sons and daughters were eating and drinking wine in the house of their eldest brother, 19 when suddenly a great wind came across the desert and smote the four corners of the house. It fell upon the young people and they are dead; and I alone have escaped to tell you." 20 Then Job began to tear his cloak and cut off his hair. He cast himself prostrate upon the ground, 21 and said,

"Naked I came forth from my mother's womb,
and naked shall I go back again.
The LORD gave and the LORD has taken away;
blessed be the name of the LORD!"

22 In all this Job did not sin, nor did he say anything disrespectful of God.

THE BOOK OF
Job

1 There was once a man in the land of Uz called Job: a sound and honest man who feared God and shunned evil. 2 Seven sons and three daughters were born to him. 3 And he owned seven thousand sheep, three thousand camels, five hundred yoke of oxen and five hundred she-donkeys, and many servants besides. This man was the most prosperous of all the Sons of the East. 4 It was the custom of his sons to hold banquets in one another's houses in turn, and to invite their three sisters to eat and drink with them. 5 Once each series of banquets was over, Job would send for them to come and be purified, and at dawn on the following day he would make a burnt offering for each of them. 'Perhaps', Job would say, 'my sons have sinned and in their heart blasphemed.' So that was what Job used to do each time.

6 One day when the sons of God[a] came to attend on Yahweh, among them came Satan. 7 So Yahweh said to Satan, 'Where have you been?' 'Prowling about on earth,' he answered, 'roaming around there.' 8 So Yahweh asked him, 'Did you pay any attention to my servant Job? There is no one like him on the earth: a sound and honest man who fears God and shuns evil.' 9 'Yes,' Satan said, 'but Job is not God-fearing for nothing, is he? 10 Have you not put a wall round him and his house and all his domain? You have blessed all he undertakes, and his flocks throng the countryside. 11 But stretch out your hand and lay a finger on his possessions: then, I warrant you, he will curse you to your face.' 12 'Very well,' Yahweh said to Satan, 'all he has is in your power. But keep your hands off his person.' So Satan left the presence of Yahweh.

13 On the day when Job's sons and daughters were eating and drinking in their eldest brother's house, 14 a messenger came to Job. 'Your oxen', he said, 'were at the plough, with the donkeys grazing at their side, 15 when the Sabaeans swept down on them and carried them off, and put the servants to the sword: I alone have escaped to tell you.' 16 He had not finished speaking when another messenger arrived. 'The fire of God', he said, 'has fallen from heaven and burnt the sheep and shepherds to ashes: I alone have escaped to tell you.' 17 He had not finished speaking when another messenger arrived. 'The Chaldaeans,' he said, 'three bands of them, have raided the camels and made off with them, and put the servants to the sword: I alone have escaped to tell you.' 18 He had not finished speaking when another messenger arrived. 'Your sons and daughters', he said, 'were eating and drinking at their eldest brother's house, 19 when suddenly from the desert a gale sprang up, and it battered all four corners of the house which fell in on the young people. They are dead: I alone have escaped to tell you.'

20 Then Job stood up, tore his robe and shaved his head. Then, falling to the ground, he prostrated himself 21 and said:

Naked I came from my mother's womb,
naked I shall return again.
Yahweh gave, Yahweh has taken back.
Blessed be the name of Yahweh!

22 In all this misfortune Job committed no sin, and he did not reproach God.

---

a 1 God's court and council, the angels. These include Satan, 'the accuser', who is responsible for testing human beings in their faithfulness to God. He is later identified with the spirit of evil.

NEW REVISED STANDARD VERSION

2 One day the heavenly beings*c* came to present themselves before the LORD, and Satan*d* also came among them to present himself before the LORD. 2 The LORD said to Satan,*d* "Where have you come from?" Satan*e* answered the LORD, "From going to and fro on the earth, and from walking up and down on it." 3 The LORD said to Satan,*d* "Have you considered my servant Job? There is no one like him on the earth, a blameless and upright man who fears God and turns away from evil. He still persists in his integrity, although you incited me against him, to destroy him for no reason." 4 Then Satan*d* answered the LORD, "Skin for skin! All that people have they will give to save their lives.*f* 5 But stretch out your hand now and touch his bone and his flesh, and he will curse you to your face." 6 The LORD said to Satan,*d* "Very well, he is in your power; only spare his life."

7 So Satan*d* went out from the presence of the LORD, and inflicted loathsome sores on Job from the sole of his foot to the crown of his head. 8 Job*g* took a potsherd with which to scrape himself, and sat among the ashes.

9 Then his wife said to him, "Do you still persist in your integrity? Curse*h* God, and die." 10 But he said to her, "You speak as any foolish woman would speak. Shall we receive the good at the hand of God, and not receive the bad?" In all this Job did not sin with his lips.

11 Now when Job's three friends heard of all these troubles that had come upon him, each of them set out from his home — Eliphaz the Temanite, Bildad the Shuhite, and Zophar the Naamathite. They met together to go and console and comfort him. 12 When they saw him from a distance, they did not recognize him, and they raised their voices and wept aloud; they tore their robes and threw dust in the air upon their heads. 13 They sat with him on the ground seven days and seven nights, and no one spoke a word to him, for they saw that his suffering was very great.

3 After this Job opened his mouth and cursed the day of his birth. 2 Job said:
3 "Let the day perish in which I was born,
  and the night that said,
  'A man-child is conceived.'
4 Let that day be darkness!
  May God above not seek it,
  or light shine on it.
5 Let gloom and deep darkness claim it.
  Let clouds settle upon it;
  let the blackness of the day terrify it.
6 That night — let thick darkness seize it!
  let it not rejoice among the days of the year;
  let it not come into the number of the months.
7 Yes, let that night be barren;
  let no joyful cry be heard*i* in it.
8 Let those curse it who curse the Sea,*j*
  those who are skilled to rouse up Leviathan.
9 Let the stars of its dawn be dark;
  let it hope for light, but have none;
  may it not see the eyelids of the morning —
10 because it did not shut the doors of my mother's womb,
  and hide trouble from my eyes.

REVISED ENGLISH BIBLE

2 Once again the day came when the members of the court of heaven took their places in the presence of the LORD, and the Adversary was there among them. 2 The LORD enquired where he had been. 'Ranging over the earth', said the Adversary, 'from end to end.' 3 The LORD asked, 'Have you considered my servant Job? You will find no one like him on earth, a man of blameless and upright life, who fears God and sets his face against wrongdoing. You incited me to ruin him without cause, but he still holds fast to his integrity.' 4 The Adversary replied, 'Skin for skin! To save himself there is nothing a man will withhold. 5 But just reach out your hand and touch his bones and his flesh, and see if he will not curse you to your face.' 6 The LORD said to the Adversary, 'So be it. He is in your power; only spare his life.'

7 When the Adversary left the LORD's presence, he afflicted Job with running sores from the soles of his feet to the crown of his head, 8 and Job took a piece of a broken pot to scratch himself as he sat among the ashes. 9 His wife said to him, 'Why do you still hold fast to your integrity? Curse God, and die!' 10 He answered, 'You talk as any impious woman might talk. If we accept good from God, shall we not accept evil?' Throughout all this, Job did not utter one sinful word.

11 When Job's three friends, Eliphaz of Teman, Bildad of Shuah, and Zophar of Naamah, heard of all these calamities which had overtaken him, they set out from their homes, arranging to go and condole with him and comfort him. 12 But when they first saw him from a distance, they did not recognize him; they wept aloud, tore their cloaks, and tossed dust into the air over their heads. 13 For seven days and seven nights they sat beside him on the ground, and none of them spoke a word to him, for they saw that his suffering was very great.

3 1-2 AFTER this Job broke his silence and cursed the day of his birth:
3 Perish the day when I was born,
  and the night which said, 'A boy is conceived'!
4 May that day turn to darkness;
  may God above not look for it,
  nor light of dawn shine on it.
5 May gloom and deep darkness claim it again;
  may cloud smother that day, blackness eclipse its sun.
6 May blind darkness swallow up that night!
  May it not be counted among the days of the year
  or reckoned in the cycle of the months.
7 May that night be barren for ever,
  may no cry of joy be heard in it.
8 Let it be cursed by those whose spells bind the sea monster,
  who have the skill to tame Leviathan.
9 May no star shine out in its twilight;
  may it wait for a dawn that never breaks,
  and never see the eyelids of the morning,
10 because it did not shut the doors of the womb that bore me
  and keep trouble away from my sight.

---

c Heb *sons of God*   *d* Or *the Accuser*; Heb *ha-satan*   *e* Or *The Accuser*; Heb *ha-satan*   *f* Or *All that the man has he will give for his life*   *g* Heb *He*   *h* Heb *Bless*   *i* Heb *come*   *j* Cn: Heb *day*

3:8 **sea monster**: *prob. rdg*; Heb. *day*.

2 Once again the sons of God came to present themselves before the LORD, and Satan also came with them. 2 And the LORD said to Satan, "Whence do you come?" And Satan answered the LORD and said, "From roaming the earth and patrolling it." 3 And the LORD said to Satan, "Have you noticed my servant Job, and that there is no one on earth like him, faultless and upright, fearing God and avoiding evil? He still holds fast to his innocence although you incited me against him to ruin him without cause." 4 And Satan answered the LORD and said, "Skin for skin! All that a man has will he give for his life. 5 But now put forth your hand and touch his bone and his flesh, and surely he will blaspheme you to your face." 6 And the LORD said to Satan, "He is in your power; only spare his life." 7 So Satan went forth from the presence of the LORD and smote Job with severe boils from the soles of his feet to the crown of his head. 8 And he took a potsherd to scrape himself, as he sat among the ashes. 9 Then his wife said to him, "Are you still holding to your innocence? Curse God and die." 10 But he said to her, "Are even you going to speak as senseless women do? We accept good things from God; and should we not accept evil?" Through all this, Job said nothing sinful.

11 Now when three of Job's friends heard of all the misfortune that had come upon him, they set out each one from his own place: Eliphaz from Teman, Bildad from Shuh, and Zophar from Naamath. They met and journeyed together to give him sympathy and comfort. 12 But when, at a distance, they lifted up their eyes and did not recognize him, they began to weep aloud; they tore their cloaks and threw dust upon their heads. 13 Then they sat down upon the ground with him seven days and seven nights, but none of them spoke a word to him; for they saw how great was his suffering.

3 After this, Job opened his mouth and cursed his day. 2 Job spoke out and said:

3 Perish the day on which I was born,
the night when they said, "The child is a boy!"
4 May that day be darkness:
let not God above call for it,
nor light shine upon it!
5 May darkness and gloom claim it,
clouds settle upon it,
the blackness of night affright it!
6 May obscurity seize that day;
let it not occur among the days of the year,
nor enter into the count of the months!
7 May that night be barren;
let no joyful outcry greet it!
8 Let them curse it who curse the sea,
the appointed disturbers of Leviathan!
9 May the stars of its twilight be darkened;
may it look for daylight, but have none,
nor gaze on the eyes of the dawn,
10 Because it kept not shut the doors of the womb
to shield my eyes from trouble!

2 Another day, the sons of God came to attend on Yahweh and Satan came with them too. 2 So Yahweh said to Satan, 'Where have you been?' 'Prowling about on earth,' he answered, 'roaming around there.' 3 So Yahweh asked him, 'Did you pay any attention to my servant Job? There is no one like him on the earth: a sound and honest man who fears God and shuns evil. He persists in his integrity still; you achieved nothing by provoking me to ruin him.' 4 'Skin after skin!'*b* Satan replied. 'Someone will give away all he has to save his life. 5 But stretch out your hand and lay a finger on his bone and flesh; I warrant you, he will curse you to your face.' 6 'Very well,' Yahweh said to Satan, 'he is in your power. But spare his life.' 7 So Satan left the presence of Yahweh.

He struck Job down with malignant ulcers from the sole of his foot to the top of his head. 8 Job took a piece of pot to scrape himself, and went and sat among the ashes. 9 Then his wife said to him, 'Why persist in this integrity of yours? Curse God and die.' 10 'That is how a fool of a woman talks,' Job replied. 'If we take happiness from God's hand, must we not take sorrow too?' And in all this misfortune Job uttered no sinful word.

11 The news of all the disasters that had fallen on Job came to the ears of three of his friends. Each of them set out from home — Eliphaz of Teman, Bildad of Shuah and Zophar of Naamath — and by common consent they decided to go and offer him sympathy and consolation. 12 Looking at him from a distance, they could not recognise him; they wept aloud and tore their robes and threw dust over their heads. 13 They sat there on the ground beside him for seven days and seven nights. To Job they spoke never a word, for they saw how much he was suffering.

3 In the end it was Job who broke the silence and cursed the day of his birth. 2 This is what he said:

3 Perish the day on which I was born
and the night that told of a boy conceived.
4 May that day be darkness,
may God on high have no thought for it,
may no light shine on it.
5 May murk and shadow dark as death claim it for
their own,
clouds hang over it,
eclipse swoop down on it.
6 See! Let obscurity seize on it,
from the days of the year let it be excluded,
into the reckoning of the months not find its
way.
7 And may that night be sterile,
devoid of any cries of joy!
8 Let it be cursed by those who curse certain days*c*
and are ready to rouse Leviathan.
9 Dark be the stars of its morning,
let it wait in vain for light
and never see the opening eyes of dawn.
10 Since it would not shut the doors of the womb on
me
to hide sorrow from my eyes.

---

b 2 Proverb, meaning perhaps that physical hurt is worse than progressive loss of goods. *c* 3 Sorcerers. Leviathan is the monster of primeval chaos, always lurking to engulf order.

NEW REVISED STANDARD VERSION	REVISED ENGLISH BIBLE

NEW REVISED STANDARD VERSION

11 "Why did I not die at birth,
  come forth from the womb and expire?
12 Why were there knees to receive me,
  or breasts for me to suck?
13 Now I would be lying down and quiet;
  I would be asleep; then I would be at rest
14 with kings and counselors of the earth
  who rebuild ruins for themselves,
15 or with princes who have gold,
  who fill their houses with silver.
16 Or why was I not buried like a stillborn child,
  like an infant that never sees the light?
17 There the wicked cease from troubling,
  and there the weary are at rest.
18 There the prisoners are at ease together;
  they do not hear the voice of the taskmaster.
19 The small and the great are there,
  and the slaves are free from their masters.
20 "Why is light given to one in misery,
  and life to the bitter in soul,
21 who long for death, but it does not come,
  and dig for it more than for hidden treasures;
22 who rejoice exceedingly,
  and are glad when they find the grave?
23 Why is light given to one who cannot see the
  way,
  whom God has fenced in?
24 For my sighing comes like^k my bread,
  and my groanings are poured out like water.
25 Truly the thing that I fear comes upon me,
  and what I dread befalls me.
26 I am not at ease, nor am I quiet;
  I have no rest; but trouble comes."

4 Then Eliphaz the Temanite answered:
2 "If one ventures a word with you, will you be
  offended?
  But who can keep from speaking?
3 See, you have instructed many;
  you have strengthened the weak hands.
4 Your words have supported those who were
  stumbling,
  and you have made firm the feeble knees.
5 But now it has come to you, and you are
  impatient;
  it touches you, and you are dismayed.
6 Is not your fear of God your confidence,
  and the integrity of your ways your hope?
7 "Think now, who that was innocent ever
  perished?
  Or where were the upright cut off?
8 As I have seen, those who plow iniquity
  and sow trouble reap the same.
9 By the breath of God they perish,
  and by the blast of his anger they are
  consumed.
10 The roar of the lion, the voice of the fierce lion,
  and the teeth of the young lions are broken.
11 The strong lion perishes for lack of prey,
  and the whelps of the lioness are scattered.
12 "Now a word came stealing to me,
  my ear received the whisper of it.

REVISED ENGLISH BIBLE

11 Why was I not stillborn,
  why did I not perish when I came from the womb?
12 Why was I ever laid on my mother's knees
  or put to suck at her breasts?
16 Or why was I not concealed like an untimely birth,
  like an infant who never saw the light?
13 For now I should be lying in the quiet grave,
  asleep in death, at rest
14 with kings and their earthly counsellors
  who built for themselves cities now laid waste,
15 or with princes rich in gold
  whose houses were replete with silver.
17 There the wicked chafe no more,
  there the tired labourer takes his ease;
18 the captive too finds peace there,
  no slave-driver's voice reaches him;
19 high and low alike are there,
  even the slave, free from his master.
20 Why should the sufferer be born to see the light?
  Why is life given to those who find it so bitter?
21 They long for death but it does not come,
  they seek it more eagerly than hidden treasure.
22 They are glad when they reach the grave;
  when they come to the tomb they exult.
23 Why should a man be born to wander blindly,
  hedged about by God on every side?
24 Sighing is for me all my food;
  groans pour from me in a torrent.
25 Every terror that haunted me has caught up with
  me;
  what I dreaded has overtaken me.
26 There is no peace of mind, no quiet for me;
  trouble comes, and I have no rest.

4 THEN Eliphaz the Temanite spoke up:
2 If one should venture a word with you, would you
  lose patience?
  Yet who could curb his tongue any longer?
3 Think how you once encouraged many,
  how you braced feeble arms,
4 how a word from you upheld those who stumbled
  and put strength into failing knees.
5 But now adversity comes on you, and you are
  impatient;
  it touches you, and you are dismayed.
6 Does your piety give you no assurance?
  Does your blameless life afford you no hope?
7 For consider, has any innocent person ever
  perished?
  Where have the upright ever been destroyed?
8 This is what I have seen:
  those who plough mischief and sow trouble
  reap no other harvest.
9 They perish at the blast of God;
  they are shrivelled by the breath of his nostrils.
10 The roar of the lion, the whimpering of his cubs,
  fall silent;
  the teeth of the young lions are broken;
11 the lion perishes for lack of prey
  and the whelps of the lioness are abandoned.
12 A word came to me stealthily,
  so that my ear caught a mere whisper of it.

^{k}Heb before

3:12–17 *Verse 16 transposed to follow verse 12.*   3:15 **whose . . .**
replete: *or who filled their final resting-places.*

11 Why did I not perish at birth,
come forth from the womb and expire?
16 Or why was I not buried away like an
untimely birth,
like babes that have never seen the light?
12 Wherefore did the knees receive me?
or why did I suck at the breasts?
13 For then I should have lain down and
been tranquil;
had I slept, I should then have been at rest
14 With kings and counselors of the earth
who built where now there are ruins
15 Or with princes who had gold
and filled their houses with silver.
17 There the wicked cease from troubling,
there the weary are at rest.
18 There the captives are at ease together,
and hear not the voice of the slave driver.
19 Small and great are there the same,
and the servant is free from his master.
20 Why is light given to the toilers,
and life to the bitter in spirit?
21 They wait for death and it comes not;
they search for it rather than for
hidden treasures,
22 Rejoice in it exultingly,
and are glad when they reach the grave:
23 Men whose path is hidden from them,
and whom God has hemmed in!
24 For sighing comes more readily to me than food,
and my groans well forth like water.
25 For what I fear overtakes me,
and what I shrink from comes upon me.
26 I have no peace nor ease;
I have no rest, for trouble comes!

4 Then spoke Eliphaz the Temanite, who said:

2 If someone attempts a word with you, will
you mind?
For how can anyone refrain from speaking?
3 Behold, you have instructed many,
and have made firm their feeble hands.
4 Your words have upheld the stumbler;
you have strengthened his faltering knees.
5 But now that it comes to you, you are impatient;
when it touches yourself, you are dismayed.
6 Is not your piety a source of confidence,
and your integrity of life your hope?
7 Reflect now, what innocent person perishes?
Since when are the upright destroyed?
8 As I see it, those who plow for mischief
and sow trouble, reap the same.
9 By the breath of God they perish,
and by the blast of his wrath they are consumed.
10 Though the lion roars, though the king of beasts
cries out,
yet the teeth of the young lions are broken;
11 The old lion perishes for lack of prey,
and the cubs of the lioness are scattered.
12 For a word was stealthily brought to me,
and my ear caught a whisper of it.

11 Why was I not still-born,
or why did I not perish as I left the womb?
12 Why were there knees to receive me,
breasts for me to suck?
13 Now I should be lying in peace,
wrapped in a restful slumber,
14 with the kings and high viziers of earth
who have built their dwellings in desolate
places,
15 or with princes who have quantities of gold
and silver cramming their tombs;
16 or, put away like an abortive child, I should not
have existed,
like little ones that never see the light.
17 Down there, the wicked bustle no more,
there the weary rest.
18 Prisoners, all left in peace,
hear no more the shouts of the oppressor.
19 High and low are there together,
and the slave is free of his master.
20 Why give light to a man of grief?
Why give life to those bitter of heart,
21 who long for a death that never comes,
and hunt for it more than for buried treasure?
22 They would be glad to see the grave-mound
and shout with joy if they reached the tomb.
23 Why give light to one who does not see his way,
whom God shuts in all alone?
24 My only food is sighs,
and my groans pour out like water.
25 Whatever I fear comes true,
whatever I dread befalls me.
26 For me, there is no calm, no peace;
my torments banish rest.

4 Eliphaz of Teman spoke next. He said:

2 If we say something to you, will you bear with us?
Who in any case could refrain from speaking
now?
3 You have schooled many others,
giving strength to feeble hands;
4 your words supported any who wavered
and strengthened every failing knee.
5 And now your turn has come, and you lose
patience,
at the first touch on yourself you are
overwhelmed!
6 Does not your piety give you confidence,
and your integrity of life give you hope?
7 Can you recall anyone guiltless that perished?
Where then have the honest been wiped out?
8 I speak from experience: those who plough iniquity
and sow disaster, reap just that.
9 Under the breath of God, they perish:
a blast of his anger, and they are destroyed;
10 the lion's roars, his savage growls,
like the fangs of a lion cub, are broken off.
11 The lion dies for lack of prey
and the lioness's whelps are dispersed.
12 I have received a secret revelation,
a whisper has come to my ears;

3, 16: This verse has been placed between vv 11 and 12 where it
probably stood originally. There is reason to believe that here, as well
as in several other places in Job, the original order of the poetic lines
was accidentally disturbed in the early transmission of the text; so in
chapters 12-15; 19-21; 24-31; 34; 36; 38-42. The verse numbers
given in such cases are always those of the current Hebrew text,

13 Amid thoughts from visions of the night,
   when deep sleep falls on mortals,
14 dread came upon me, and trembling,
   which made all my bones shake.
15 A spirit glided past my face;
   the hair of my flesh bristled.
16 It stood still,
   but I could not discern its appearance.
   A form was before my eyes;
   there was silence, then I heard a voice:
17 'Can mortals be righteous before^l God?
   Can human beings be pure before^l their
      Maker?
18 Even in his servants he puts no trust,
   and his angels he charges with error;
19 how much more those who live in houses of clay,
   whose foundation is in the dust,
   who are crushed like a moth.
20 Between morning and evening they are destroyed;
   they perish forever without any regarding it.
21 Their tent-cord is plucked up within them,
   and they die devoid of wisdom.'

5 "Call now; is there anyone who will answer you?
   To which of the holy ones will you turn?
2 Surely vexation kills the fool,
   and jealousy slays the simple.
3 I have seen fools taking root,
   but suddenly I cursed their dwelling.
4 Their children are far from safety,
   they are crushed in the gate,
   and there is no one to deliver them.
5 The hungry eat their harvest,
   and they take it even out of the thorns;^{m}
   and the thirsty^n pant after their wealth.
6 For misery does not come from the earth,
   nor does trouble sprout from the ground;
7 but human beings are born to trouble
   just as sparks^o fly upward.

8 "As for me, I would seek God,
   and to God I would commit my cause.
9 He does great things and unsearchable,
   marvelous things without number.
10 He gives rain on the earth
   and sends waters on the fields;
11 he sets on high those who are lowly,
   and those who mourn are lifted to safety.
12 He frustrates the devices of the crafty,
   so that their hands achieve no success.
13 He takes the wise in their own craftiness;
   and the schemes of the wily are brought to a
      quick end.
14 They meet with darkness in the daytime,
   and grope at noonday as in the night.
15 But he saves the needy from the sword of their
      mouth,
   from the hand of the mighty.
16 So the poor have hope,
   and injustice shuts its mouth.

17 "How happy is the one whom God reproves;
   therefore do not despise the discipline of the
      Almighty.^{p}

13 In the anxious visions of the night
   when everyone sinks into deepest sleep,
14 terror seized me and shuddering;
   it made my whole frame tremble with fear.
15 A wind brushed across my face
   and made the hairs of my body stand on end.
16 A figure halted there, whose shape I could not
      discern,
   an apparition loomed before me,
   and I heard a voice murmur:
17 'Can a human being be righteous before God,
   a mere mortal pure before his Maker?
18 If God mistrusts his own servants
   and finds his messengers at fault,
19 how much more those who dwell in houses of
      clay,
   whose foundations are in the dust,
   which can be crushed like a bird's nest,
20 torn down between dawn and dusk.
   How much more shall they perish unheeded for
      ever,
21 die without ever finding wisdom!'

5 Call if you will; is there any to answer you?
   To whom among the holy ones will you turn?
2 Fools are destroyed by their own angry passion,
   and the end of childish resentment is death.
3 I have seen it for myself: fools uprooted,
   their homes in sudden ruin,
4 their children cut off from help,
   browbeaten in court with none to come to their
      defence.
5 Their rich possessions are snatched from them;
   what they have harvested others hungrily devour;
   panting, thirsting for their wealth,
   stronger men seize it from the panniers.
6 Mischief does not grow out of the ground,
   nor does trouble spring from the soil;
7 yet man is born to trouble,
   as surely as birds fly upwards.

8 For my part, I would make my appeal to God;
   I would lay my plea before him
9 who does great and unsearchable things,
   marvels beyond all reckoning.
10 He gives rain to the earth
   and sends water over the fields;
11 he raises the lowly on high,
   and the mourners are lifted to safety;
12 he frustrates the plots of the crafty,
   and they achieve no success;
13 he traps the cunning in their own craftiness,
   and the schemers' plans are thrown into confusion.
14 By day they encounter darkness,
   and grope their way at noon as in the night;
15 he saves the destitute from their greed,
   and the needy from the clutches of the strong.
16 So the poor have hope again,
   to the outrage of the unjust.

17 Happy indeed are they whom God rebukes!
   Therefore do not reject the Almighty's discipline.

4:15 **wind:** or breath.   4:17 **righteous before:** or more righteous
than. **pure before:** or more pure than.   4:19 **bird's nest:** or moth.
4:21 **die . . . wisdom:** prob. rdg, transposing Their rich possessions
are snatched from them to follow 5:4.   5:3 **ruin:** prob. rdg; Heb.
obscure.   5:4 **in court:** lit. in the gate.   5:5 **Their . . . them:**
line transposed from 4:21.   5:7 **birds:** or sparks.   5:15 **greed:**
lit. mouths.

^{l}Or more than ^{m}Meaning of Heb uncertain ^{n}Aquila
Symmachus Syr Vg: Heb snare ^{o}Or birds; Heb sons of Resheph
^{p}Traditional rendering of Heb Shaddai

<table>
<tr><td valign="top">

13 In my thoughts during visions of the night,
   when deep sleep falls on men,
14 Fear came upon me, and shuddering,
   that terrified me to the bones.
15 Then a spirit passed before me,
   and the hair of my flesh stood up.
16 It paused, but its likeness I could not discern;
   a figure was before my eyes, and I heard a
     still voice:
17 "Can a man be righteous as against God?
   Can a mortal be blameless against his Maker?
18 Lo, he puts no trust in his servants,
   and with his angels he can find fault.
19 How much more with those that dwell in houses
    of clay,
   whose foundation is in the dust,
   who are crushed more easily than the moth!
20 Morning or evening they may be shattered;
   with no heed paid to it, they perish forever.
21 The pegs of their tent are plucked up;
   they die without knowing wisdom."

</td><td valign="top">

13 by night when dreams confuse the mind
   and slumber lies heavy on everyone,
14 a shiver of horror ran through me
   and filled all my bones with fright.
15 A breath slid over my face,
   the hairs of my body bristled.
16 Someone stood there — I did not know his face,
   but the form stayed there before my eyes.
   Silence — then I heard a voice,
17 'Can a mortal seem upright to God,
   would anybody seem pure in the presence of his
     Maker?
18 God cannot rely even on his own servants,
   even with his angels he finds fault.
19 What then of those who live in houses of clay,
   who are founded on dust?
20 They are crushed as easily as a moth,
   between morning and evening they are ground to
     powder.
   They vanish for ever, with no one to bring them
     back.
21 Their tent-peg is snatched from them,
   and they die devoid of wisdom.'

</td></tr>
<tr><td valign="top">

5   Call now! Will anyone respond to you?
   To which of the holy ones will you appeal?
2 Nay, impatience kills the fool
   and indignation slays the simpleton.
3 I have seen a fool spreading his roots,
   but his household suddenly decayed.
4 His children shall be far from safety;
   they shall be crushed at the gate without
     a rescuer.
5 What they have reaped the hungry shall eat up;
   [or God shall take it away by blight;]
   and the thirsty shall swallow their substance.
6 For mischief comes not out of the earth,
   nor does trouble spring out of the ground;
7 But man himself begets mischief,
   as sparks fly upward.
8 In your place, I would appeal to God,
   and to God I would state my plea.
10 He gives rain upon the earth
   and sends water upon the fields;
11 He sets up on high the lowly,
   and those who mourn he exalts to safety.
12 He frustrates the plans of the cunning,
   so that their hands achieve no success;
13 He catches the wise in their own ruses,
   and the designs of the crafty are routed.
14 They meet with darkness in the daytime,
   and at noonday they grope as though it
     were night.
15 But the poor from the edge of the sword
   and from the hand of the mighty, he saves.
16 Thus the unfortunate have hope,
   and iniquity closes her mouth.

17 Happy is the man whom God reproves!
   The Almighty's chastening do not reject.

</td><td valign="top">

5   Make your appeal then. Will you find an answer?
   To which of the holy ones will you turn?
2 Resentment kills the senseless,
   and anger brings death to the fool.
3 I have seen the senseless taking root,
   when a curse fell suddenly on his house.
4 His children are deprived of prop and stay,
   ruined at the gate, and no one to defend them;
5 their harvest goes to feed the hungry,
   God snatches it from their mouths,
   and covetous people thirst for their possessions.
6 No, misery does not grow out of the soil,
   nor sorrow spring from the ground.
7 It is people who breed trouble for themselves
   as surely as eagles fly to the height.
8 If I were you, I should appeal to God
   and lay my case before him.
9 His works are great, past all reckoning,
   marvels beyond all counting.
10 He sends down rain to the earth,
   pours down water on the fields.
11 If his will is to raise up the downcast,
   or exalt the afflicted to the heights of prosperity,
12 he frustrates the plans of the artful
   so that they cannot succeed in their intrigues.
13 He traps the crafty in the snare of their own
     trickery,
   throws the plans of the cunning into disarray.
14 In daylight they come up against darkness,
   and grope their way as if at noon were night.
15 He rescues the bankrupt from their jaws,
   and the needy from the grasp of the mighty.
16 Hope springs afresh for the weak,
   and wickedness must shut its mouth.

17 Blessed are those whom God corrects!
   Do not then scorn the lesson of Shaddai![d]

</td></tr>
</table>

---

though the arrangement may differ. The footnotes will advise the
reader of the difficulties and provide him with further indications for
following the progress of thought in the book.
5, 9: Omitted here; it is a duplicate of Jb 9, 10.

[d]5 A name of God in patriarchal times, the dramatic setting of the
dialogues.

18 For he wounds, but he binds up;
  he strikes, but his hands heal.
19 He will deliver you from six troubles;
  in seven no harm shall touch you.
20 In famine he will redeem you from death,
  and in war from the power of the sword.
21 You shall be hidden from the scourge of the
    tongue,
  and shall not fear destruction when it comes.
22 At destruction and famine you shall laugh,
  and shall not fear the wild animals of the earth.
23 For you shall be in league with the stones of the
    field,
  and the wild animals shall be at peace with
    you.
24 You shall know that your tent is safe,
  you shall inspect your fold and miss nothing.
25 You shall know that your descendants will be
    many,
  and your offspring like the grass of the earth.
26 You shall come to your grave in ripe old age,
  as a shock of grain comes up to the threshing
    floor in its season.
27 See, we have searched this out; it is true.
  Hear, and know it for yourself."

6 Then Job answered:
2 "O that my vexation were weighed,
  and all my calamity laid in the balances!
3 For then it would be heavier than the sand of the
    sea;
  therefore my words have been rash.
4 For the arrows of the Almighty*q* are in me;
  my spirit drinks their poison;
  the terrors of God are arrayed against me.
5 Does the wild ass bray over its grass,
  or the ox low over its fodder?
6 Can that which is tasteless be eaten without salt,
  or is there any flavor in the juice of mallows?*r*
7 My appetite refuses to touch them;
  they are like food that is loathsome to me.*r*

8 "O that I might have my request,
  and that God would grant my desire;
9 that it would please God to crush me,
  that he would let loose his hand and cut me
    off!
10 This would be my consolation;
  I would even exult*r* in unrelenting pain;
  for I have not denied the words of the Holy
    One.
11 What is my strength, that I should wait?
  And what is my end, that I should be patient?
12 Is my strength the strength of stones,
  or is my flesh bronze?
13 In truth I have no help in me,
  and any resource is driven from me.

14 "Those who withhold*s* kindness from a friend
  forsake the fear of the Almighty.*q*
15 My companions are treacherous like a
    torrent-bed,
  like freshets that pass away,
16 that run dark with ice,
  turbid with melting snow.
17 In time of heat they disappear;
  when it is hot, they vanish from their place.

18 For, though he wounds, he will bind up;
  the hands that harm will heal.
19 You may meet disaster six times, and he will
    rescue you;
  seven times, and no harm will touch you.
20 In famine he will deliver you from death,
  in battle from the menace of the sword.
21 You will be shielded from the scourge of slander,
  unafraid when violence comes.
22 You will laugh at violence and famine
  and need not fear any beast on earth;
23 for you will be in league with the stones of the
    fields,
  and the wild animals have been constrained to
    leave you at peace.
24 You will know that all is well with your
    household,
  you will look round your home and find nothing
    amiss;
25 you will know that your descendants will be many
  and your offspring like grass, thick on the earth.
26 You will come to the grave in sturdy old age
  as sheaves come in due season to the
    threshing-floor.
27 We have enquired into all this, and so it is;
  this we have heard, and know it to be true for you.

6 Job answered:

2 If only the grounds for my resentment might be
    weighed,
  and my misfortunes placed with them on the
    scales!
3 For they would outweigh the sands of the sea:
  what wonder if my words are frenzied!
4 The arrows of the Almighty find their mark in me,
  and their poison soaks into my spirit;
  God's onslaughts wear me down.
5 Does a wild ass bray when it has grass
  or an ox low when it has fodder?
6 Is tasteless food eaten unseasoned,
  or is there any flavour in the juice of mallows?
7 Such food sticks in my throat,
  and my bowels rumble like an echo.

8 If only I might have my request
  and God would grant what I hope for:
9 that he would be pleased to crush me,
  to sever with his hand and cut me off!
10 That would bring me relief,
  and in the face of unsparing anguish I would leap
    for joy,
  for I have never denied the words of the Holy
    One.
11 Have I the strength to go on waiting?
  What end have I to expect, that I should be
    patient?
12 Is my strength the strength of stone,
  or is my flesh made of bronze?
13 Oh how shall I find help within myself
  now that success has been put beyond my reach?

14 Devotion is due from his friends
  to one who despairs and loses faith in the
    Almighty;
15 but my brothers have been deceptive as a torrent,
  like the watercourses of torrents that run dry.
16 They turn dark with ice
  and are hidden with piled-up snow;
17 but they vanish the moment they are in spate,
  dwindle in the heat and are gone.

q Traditional rendering of Heb *Shaddai*   *r* Meaning of Heb
uncertain   *s* Syr Vg Compare Tg: Meaning of Heb uncertain

18 For he wounds, but he binds up;
    he smites, but his hands give healing.
19 Out of six troubles he will deliver you,
    and at the seventh no evil shall touch you.
20 In famine he will deliver you from death,
    and in war from the threat of the sword;
21 From the scourge of the tongue you shall
        be hidden,
    and shall not fear approaching ruin.
22 At destruction and want you shall laugh;
    the beasts of the earth you need not dread.
23 You shall be in league with the stones of the field,
    and the wild beasts shall be at peace with you.
24 And you shall know that your tent is secure;
    taking stock of your household, you shall
        miss nothing.
25 You shall know that your descendants are many,
    and your offspring as the grass of the earth.
26 You shall approach the grave in full vigor,
    as a shock of grain comes in at its season.
27 Lo, this we have searched out; so it is!
    This we have heard, and you should know.

6 Then Job answered and said:

2 Ah, could my anguish but be measured
    and my calamity laid with it in the scales,
3 They would now outweigh the sands of the sea!
    Because of this I speak without restraint.
4 For the arrows of the Almighty pierce me,
    and my spirit drinks in their poison;
    the terrors of God are arrayed against me.
5 Does the wild ass bray when he has grass?
    Does the ox low over his fodder?
6 Can a thing insipid be eaten without salt?
    Is there flavor in the white of an egg?
7 I refuse to touch them;
    they are loathsome food to me.
8 Oh, that I might have my request,
    and that God would grant what I long for:
9 Even that God would decide to crush me,
    that he would put forth his hand and cut me off!
10 Then I should still have consolation
    and could exult through unremitting pain,
    because I have not transgressed the commands of
        the Holy One.
11 What strength have I that I should endure,
    and what is my limit that I should be patient?
12 Have I the strength of stones,
    or is my flesh of bronze?
13 Have I no helper,
    and has advice deserted me?
14 A friend owes kindness to one in despair,
    though he have forsaken the fear of
        the Almighty.
15 My brethren are undependable as a brook,
    as watercourses that run dry in the wadies;
16 Though they may be black with ice,
    and with snow heaped upon them,
17 Yet once they flow, they cease to be;
    in the heat, they disappear from their place.

18 For he who wounds is he who soothes the sore,
    and the hand that hurts is the hand that heals.
19 Six times he will deliver you from sorrow,
    and the seventh time, evil will not touch you.
20 In time of famine, he will save you from death,
    and in wartime from the stroke of the sword.
21 You will be safe from the lash of the tongue,
    unafraid at the approach of the despoiler.
22 You will laugh at drought and frost,
    and have no fear of the beasts of the earth.
23 You will have a pact with the stones of the field,
    and live in amity with wild beasts.
24 You will know that your tent is secure,
    and your sheepfold unharmed when you inspect
        it.
25 You will see your descendants multiply,
    your offspring grow like the grass in the fields.
26 At a ripe age you will go to the grave,
    like a wheatsheaf stacked in due season.
27 All this we have observed and it is so!
    Heed it, you will be the wiser for it!

6 Job spoke next. He said:

2 If only my misery could be weighed,
    and all my ills be put together on the scales!
3 But they outweigh the sands of the seas:
    what wonder then if my words are wild?
4 The arrows of Shaddai stick fast in me,
    my spirit absorbs their poison,
    God's terrors stand paraded against me.
5 Does a wild donkey bray when it has grass,
    or an ox low when its fodder is within reach?
6 Is not food insipid, eaten without salt,
    is there any taste in egg-white?
7 But the very things my appetite revolts at
    are now my diet in sickness.
8 Will no one hear my prayer,
    will not God himself grant my hope?
9 May it please God to crush me,
    to give his hand free play and do away with me!
10 This thought, at least, would give me comfort
    (a thrill of joy in unrelenting pain),
    that I never rebelled against the Holy One's
        decrees.
11 But have I the strength to go on waiting?
    And why be patient, when doomed to such an
        end?
12 Is mine the strength of stone,
    is my flesh made of bronze?
13 Can I support myself on nothing?
    Has not all help deserted me?
14 Refuse faithful love to your neighbour
    and you forsake the fear of Shaddai.
15 Like the torrent, my brothers have proved
        deceptive,
    as fleeting torrents they flow;
16 the ice makes their waters turgid
    when, above them, the snow melts,
17 but, come the burning summer, they run dry,
    they vanish in the heat of the sun.

NEW REVISED STANDARD VERSION	REVISED ENGLISH BIBLE

NEW REVISED STANDARD VERSION

18 The caravans turn aside from their course;
   they go up into the waste, and perish.
19 The caravans of Tema look,
   the travelers of Sheba hope.
20 They are disappointed because they were
      confident;
   they come there and are confounded.
21 Such you have now become to me;*
   you see my calamity, and are afraid.
22 Have I said, 'Make me a gift'?
   Or, 'From your wealth offer a bribe for me'?
23 Or, 'Save me from an opponent's hand'?
   Or, 'Ransom me from the hand of oppressors'?
24 "Teach me, and I will be silent;
   make me understand how I have gone wrong.
25 How forceful are honest words!
   But your reproof, what does it reprove?
26 Do you think that you can reprove words,
   as if the speech of the desperate were wind?
27 You would even cast lots over the orphan,
   and bargain over your friend.
28 "But now, be pleased to look at me;
   for I will not lie to your face.
29 Turn, I pray, let no wrong be done.
   Turn now, my vindication is at stake.
30 Is there any wrong on my tongue?
   Cannot my taste discern calamity?

7 "Do not human beings have a hard service on
      earth,
   and are not their days like the days of a
      laborer?
2 Like a slave who longs for the shadow,
   and like laborers who look for their wages,
3 so I am allotted months of emptiness,
   and nights of misery are apportioned to me.
4 When I lie down I say, 'When shall I rise?'
   But the night is long,
   and I am full of tossing until dawn.
5 My flesh is clothed with worms and dirt;
   my skin hardens, then breaks out again.
6 My days are swifter than a weaver's shuttle,
   and come to their end without hope.*
7 "Remember that my life is a breath;
   my eye will never again see good.
8 The eye that beholds me will see me no more;
   while your eyes are upon me, I shall be gone.
9 As the cloud fades and vanishes,
   so those who go down to Sheol do not come
      up;
10 they return no more to their houses,
   nor do their places know them any more.
11 "Therefore I will not restrain my mouth;
   I will speak in the anguish of my spirit;
   I will complain in the bitterness of my soul.
12 Am I the Sea, or the Dragon,
   that you set a guard over me?
13 When I say, 'My bed will comfort me,
   my couch will ease my complaint,'
14 then you scare me with dreams
   and terrify me with visions,

REVISED ENGLISH BIBLE

18 Caravans, winding hither and thither,
   go up into the desert and perish.
19 the caravans of Tema look for the water,
   the travelling merchants of Sheba rely on it;
20 but they are disappointed, for all their confidence,
   they arrive, only to be frustrated.
21 Just so unreliable have you now been to me:
   you felt dismay and took fright.
22 Did I ever say, 'Give me this or that,'
   or say, 'Use your wealth to save my life'?
23 Did I say, 'Rescue me from my enemy's grip,'
   or, 'Ransom me from the clutches of ruthless
      people'?
24 Tell me plainly, and I shall listen in silence;
   show me where I have been at fault.
25 How harsh are the words of the upright!
   But what do your arguments prove?
26 Do you mean to argue about mere words?
   Surely such despairing utterance is mere wind.
27 Would you assail an orphan?
   Would you make attacks on your friend?
28 So now, I beg you, turn and look at me:
   am I likely to lie to your faces?
29 Think again, let me have no more injustice;
   think again, for my integrity is in question.
30 Do I ever give voice to injustice?
   Have I not the sense to discern when my words are
      wild?

7 Does not every mortal have hard service on earth,
   and are not his days like those of a hired labourer,
2 like those of a slave longing for the shade
   or a servant kept waiting for his wages?
3 So months of futility are my portion,
   troubled nights are my lot.
4 When I lie down, I think,
   'When will it be day, that I may rise?'
   But the night drags on,
   and I do nothing but toss till dawn.
5 My body is infested with worms,
   and scabs cover my skin;
   it is cracked and discharging.
6 My days pass more swiftly than a weaver's shuttle
   and come to an end as the thread of life runs out.
7 Remember that my life is but a breath of wind;
   I shall never again see good times.
8 The eye that now sees me will behold me no more;
   under your very eyes I shall vanish.
9 As a cloud breaks up and disperses,
   so no one who goes down to Sheol ever comes
      back;
10 he never returns to his house,
   and his abode knows him no more.
11 But I cannot hold my peace;
   I shall speak out in my anguish of spirit
   and complain in my bitterness of soul.
12 Am I the monster of the deep, am I the sea
      serpent,
   that you set a watch over me?
13 When I think that my bed will comfort me,
   that sleep will relieve my complaint,
14 you terrify me with dreams
   and affright me through visions.

---

*Cn Compare Gk Syr: Meaning of Heb uncertain   *Or as the
thread runs out

6:21 **Just . . . to me:** *prob. rdg; Heb. obscure.*   6:27 **orphan:** *or*
blameless person.   7:4 **day, that:** *so Gk; Heb. omits.*   7:6 **as
. . . out:** *or* without hope.   7:9 **Sheol:** *or* the underworld.

18 Caravans turn aside from their routes;
   they go into the desert and perish.
19 The caravans of Tema search,
   the companies of Sheba have hopes;
20 They are disappointed, though they were confident;
   they come there and are frustrated.
21 It is thus that you have now become for me;
   you see a terrifying thing and are afraid.
22 Have I asked you to give me anything,
   to offer a gift for me from your possessions,
23 Or to deliver me from the enemy,
   or to redeem me from oppressors?
24 Teach me, and I will be silent;
   prove to me wherein I have erred.
25 How agreeable are honest words;
   yet how unconvincing is your argument!
26 Do you consider your words as proof,
   but the sayings of a desperate man as wind?
27 You would even cast lots for the orphan,
   and would barter away your friend!
28 Come, now, give me your attention;
   surely I will not lie to your face.
29 Think it over; let there be no injustice.
   Think it over; I still am right.
30 Is there insincerity on my tongue,
   or cannot my taste discern falsehood?

7 Is not man's life on earth a drudgery?
   Are not his days those of a hireling?
2 He is a slave who longs for the shade,
   a hireling who waits for his wages.
3 So I have been assigned months of misery,
   and troubled nights have been told off for me.
4 If in bed I say, "When shall I arise?"
   Then the night drags on;
   I am filled with restlessness until the dawn.
5 My flesh is clothed with worms and scabs;
   my skin cracks and festers;
6 My days are swifter than a weaver's shuttle;
   they come to an end without hope.
7 Remember that my life is like the wind;
   I shall not see happiness again.
8 The eye that now sees me shall no more
   behold me;
   as you look at me, I shall be gone.
9 As a cloud dissolves and vanishes,
   so he who goes down to the nether world shall
   come up no more.
10 He shall not again return to his house;
   his place shall know him no more.
11 My own utterance I will not restrain;
   I will speak in the anguish of my spirit;
   I will complain in the bitterness of my soul.
12 Am I the sea, or a monster of the deep,
   that you place a watch over me?
   Why have you set me up as an object of attack?
   or why should I be a target for you?
13 When I say, "My bed shall comfort me,
   my couch shall ease my complaint,"
14 Then you affright me with dreams
   and with visions terrify me,

18 Caravans leave the trail to find them,
   go deep into wastelands, and are lost.
19 The caravans of Tema look to them,
   and on them Sheba's convoys build their hopes.
20 Their trust brings only embarrassment,
   they reach them only to be thwarted.
21 And this is how you now treat me,
   terrified at the sight of me, you take fright.
22 Have I said to you, 'Give me something,
   make some present for me at your own cost,
23 snatch me from the grasp of an oppressor,
   ransom me from the grip of a violent man'?
24 Put me right, and I shall say no more;
   show me where I have been at fault.
25 Fair comment can be borne without resentment,
   but what are your strictures aimed at?
26 Do you think mere words deserve censure,
   desperate speech that the wind blows away?
27 Soon you will be haggling over the price of an
   orphan,
   and selling your friend at bargain price!
28 Come, I beg you, look at me:
   man to man, I shall not lie.
29 Relent then, no harm is done;
   relent then, since I am upright.
30 Is evil to be found on my lips?
   Can I not recognise misfortune when I taste it?

7 Is not human life on earth just conscript service?
   Do we not live a hireling's life?
2 Like a slave, sighing for the shade,
   or a hireling with no thought but for his wages,
3 I have months of futility assigned to me,
   nights of suffering to be my lot.
4 Lying in bed I wonder, 'When will it be day?'
   No sooner up than, 'When will evening come?'
   And crazy thoughts obsess me till twilight falls.
5 Vermin and loathsome scabs cover my body;
   my skin is cracked and oozes pus.
6 Swifter than a weaver's shuttle my days have
   passed,
   and vanished, leaving no hope behind.
7 Remember that my life is but a breath,
   and that my eyes will never again see joy.
8 The eye that once saw me will look on me no
   more,
   your eyes will turn my way, and I shall not be
   there.
9 A cloud dissolves and is gone,
   so no one who goes down to Sheol ever comes
   up again,
10 ever comes home again,
   and his house knows that person no more.
11 That is why I cannot keep quiet:
   in my anguish of spirit I shall speak,
   in my bitterness of soul I shall complain.
12 Am I the Sea,e or some sea monster,
   that you should keep me under guard?
13 If I say, 'My bed will comfort me,
   my couch will lighten my complaints,'
14 you then frighten me with dreams
   and terrify me with visions,

e 7 In Babylonian myths the Sea was a goddess, held back from
sweeping civilisation away.

NEW REVISED STANDARD VERSION	REVISED ENGLISH BIBLE

NEW REVISED STANDARD VERSION

15 so that I would choose strangling
and death rather than this body.
16 I loathe my life; I would not live forever.
Let me alone, for my days are a breath.
17 What are human beings, that you make so much
of them,
that you set your mind on them,
18 visit them every morning,
test them every moment?
19 Will you not look away from me for a while,
let me alone until I swallow my spittle?
20 If I sin, what do I do to you, you watcher of
humanity?
Why have you made me your target?
Why have I become a burden to you?
21 Why do you not pardon my transgression
and take away my iniquity?
For now I shall lie in the earth;
you will seek me, but I shall not be."

8 Then Bildad the Shuhite answered:
2 "How long will you say these things,
and the words of your mouth be a great wind?
3 Does God pervert justice?
Or does the Almighty*v* pervert the right?
4 If your children sinned against him,
he delivered them into the power of their
transgression.
5 If you will seek God
and make supplication to the Almighty,*v*
6 if you are pure and upright,
surely then he will rouse himself for you
and restore to you your rightful place.
7 Though your beginning was small,
your latter days will be very great.

8 "For inquire now of bygone generations,
and consider what their ancestors have found;
9 for we are but of yesterday, and we know
nothing,
for our days on earth are but a shadow.
10 Will they not teach you and tell you
and utter words out of their understanding?
11 "Can papyrus grow where there is no marsh?
Can reeds flourish where there is no water?
12 While yet in flower and not cut down,
they wither before any other plant.
13 Such are the paths of all who forget God;
the hope of the godless shall perish.
14 Their confidence is gossamer,
a spider's house their trust.
15 If one leans against its house, it will not stand;
if one lays hold of it, it will not endure.
16 The wicked thrive*w* before the sun,
and their shoots spread over the garden.
17 Their roots twine around the stoneheap;
they live among the rocks.*x*
18 If they are destroyed from their place,
then it will deny them, saying, 'I have never
seen you.'
19 See, these are their happy ways,*y*
and out of the earth still others will spring.
20 "See, God will not reject a blameless person,
nor take the hand of evildoers.

REVISED ENGLISH BIBLE

15 I would rather be choked outright;
death would be better than these sufferings of
mine.
16 I am in despair, I have no desire to live;
let me alone, for my days are but a breath.
17 What is man, that you make much of him
and turn your thoughts towards him,
18 only to punish him morning after morning
or to test him every hour of the day?
19 Will you not look away from me for an instant,
leave me long enough to swallow my spittle?
20 If I have sinned, what harm can I do you,
you watcher of the human heart?
Why have you made me your target?
Why have I become a burden to you?
21 Why do you not pardon my offence
and take away my guilt?
For soon I shall lie in the dust of the grave;
you may seek me, but I shall be no more.

8 Then Bildad the Shuhite spoke up:
2 How long will you go on saying such things,
those long-winded ramblings of an old man?
3 Does God pervert justice?
Does the Almighty pervert what is right?
4 If your sons sinned against him,
he has left them to be victims of their own
iniquity.
5 If only you yourself will seek God
and plead for the favour of the Almighty,
6 if you are pure and upright,
then indeed he will watch over you
and see your just intent fulfilled.
7 Then, though your beginnings were humble,
your future will be very great.

8 Enquire now of older generations
and consider the experience of their forefathers;
9 for we are but of yesterday and know nothing;
our days on earth are but a passing shadow.
10 Will they not teach you and tell you
and pour out the wisdom of their minds?
11 Can rushes thrive where there is no marsh?
Can reeds flourish without water?
12 While still in flower and not ready for cutting,
they would wither before any green plant.
13 Such is the fate of all who forget God;
the life-thread of the godless breaks off;
14 his confidence is gossamer,
and the basis of his trust a spider's web.
15 He leans against his house, but it does not stand;
he clutches at it, but it does not hold firm.
16 His is the lush growth of a plant in the sun,
pushing out shoots over the garden;
17 but its roots become entangled in a stony patch
and run against a bed of rock.
18 Then someone uproots it from its place,
which disowns it, saying, 'I have never known
you.'
19 That is how its life withers away,
and other plants spring up from the earth.
20 Be sure, God will not spurn the blameless man,
nor will he clasp the hand of the wrongdoer.

7:15 **sufferings:** *prob. rdg; Heb.* bones.   7:20 **heart:** *so Gk; Heb.*
omits. **to you:** *so Gk; Heb.* to me.   8:6 **see ... fulfilled:** *or*
restore your rightful habitation.   8:13 **life-thread:** *or* hope.
8:18 **which:** *or* and.

v Traditional rendering of Heb *Shaddai*   *w* Heb *He thrives*
x Gk Vg: Meaning of Heb uncertain   *y* Meaning of Heb uncertain

15 So that I should prefer choking
  and death rather than my pains.
16 I waste away: I cannot live forever;
  let me alone, for my days are but a breath.
17 What is man, that you make much of him,
  or pay him any heed?
18 You observe him with each new day
  and try him at every moment!
19 How long will it be before you look away
  from me,
  and let me alone long enough to swallow
  my spittle?
20 Though I have sinned, what can I do to you,
  O watcher of men?
21 Why do you not pardon my offense,
  or take away my guilt?
  For soon I shall lie down in the dust;
  and should you seek me I shall then be gone.

8 Bildad the Shuhite spoke out and said:

2 How long will you utter such things?
  The words from your mouth are like a
  mighty wind!
3 Does God pervert judgment,
  and does the Almighty distort justice?
4 If your children have sinned against him
  and he has left them in the grip of their guilt,
5 Still, if you yourself have recourse to God
  and make supplication to the Almighty,
6 Should you be blameless and upright,
  surely now he will awake for you
  and restore your rightful domain;
7 Your former state will be of little moment,
  for in time to come you will flourish indeed.

8 If you inquire of the former generations,
  and give heed to the experience of the fathers
9 (As we are but of yesterday and have
  no knowledge,
  because our days on earth are but a shadow),
10 Will they not teach you and tell you
  and utter their words of understanding?
11 Can the papyrus grow up without mire?
  Can the reed grass flourish without water?
12 While it is yet green and uncut,
  it withers quicker than any grass.
13 So is the end of everyone who forgets God,
  and so shall the hope of the godless man perish.
14 His confidence is but a gossamer thread
  and his trust is a spider's web.
15 He shall rely upon his family, but it shall not last;
  he shall cling to it, but it shall not endure.
16 He is full of sap before sunrise,
  and beyond his garden his shoots go forth;
17 About a heap of stones are his roots entwined;
  among the rocks he takes hold.
18 Yet if one tears him from his place,
  it will disown him: "I have never seen you!"
19 There he lies rotting beside the road,
  and out of the soil another sprouts.
20 Behold, God will not cast away the upright;
  neither will he take the hand of the wicked.

15 so that strangling would seem welcome in
  comparison,
  yes, death preferable to what I suffer.
16 I am wasting away, my life is not unending;
  leave me then, for my days are but a breath.
17 What are human beings that you should take them
  so seriously,
  subjecting them to your scrutiny,
18 that morning after morning you should examine
  them
  and at every instant test them?
19 Will you never take your eyes off me
  long enough for me to swallow my spittle?
20 Suppose I have sinned, what have I done to you,
  you tireless watcher of humanity?
  Why do you choose me as your target?
  Why should I be a burden to you?
21 Can you not tolerate my sin,
  not overlook my fault?
  For soon I shall be lying in the dust,
  you will look for me and I shall be no more.

8 Bildad of Shuah spoke next. He said:

2 How much longer are you going to talk like this
  and go blustering on in this way?
3 Can God deflect the course of right
  or Shaddai falsify justice?
4 If your sons sinned against him,
  he has punished them for their wrong-doing.
6a For your part, if you are pure and honest,
5   must now seek God, plead with Shaddai
6b Forthwith his light will shine on you and he will
  restore
  an upright man's house to prosperity.
7 Your former state will seem as nothing to you,
  so great will your future be.

8 Question the generation that has passed,
  meditate on the experience of its ancestors —
9 for we children of yesterday, we know nothing,
  our life on earth passes like a shadow —
10 but they will teach you, they will tell you,
  and their thought is expressed in these sayings,
11 'Can papyrus flourish except in marshes?
  Without water can the rushes grow?
12 Even when green and before being cut,
  fastest of all plants they wither.
13 Such is the fate of all who forget God;
  so perishes the hope of the godless.
14 His hope is nothing but gossamer,
  his confidence a spider's web.
15 Let him lean on his house, it will not stand firm;
  cling to it, it will not hold.
16 Like some lush plant in the sunlight,
  he sent his young shoots sprouting over the
  garden;
17 but his roots were twined in a heap of stones,
  he drew his life among the rocks.
18 Snatch him from his bed,
  and it denies it ever saw him.
19 Now he rots on the roadside,
  and others are springing up in the soil.
20 Believe me, God neither spurns anyone of
  integrity,
  nor lends his aid to the evil.

21 He will yet fill your mouth with laughter,
  and your lips with shouts of joy.
22 Those who hate you will be clothed with shame,
  and the tent of the wicked will be no more."

9 Then Job answered:
2 "Indeed I know that this is so;
  but how can a mortal be just before God?
3 If one wished to contend with him,
  one could not answer him once in a thousand.
4 He is wise in heart, and mighty in strength
  —who has resisted him, and succeeded?—
5 he who removes mountains, and they do not
    know it,
  when he overturns them in his anger;
6 who shakes the earth out of its place,
  and its pillars tremble;
7 who commands the sun, and it does not rise;
  who seals up the stars;
8 who alone stretched out the heavens
  and trampled the waves of the Sea;z
9 who made the Bear and Orion,
  the Pleiades and the chambers of the south;
10 who does great things beyond understanding,
  and marvelous things without number.
11 Look, he passes by me, and I do not see him;
  he moves on, but I do not perceive him.
12 He snatches away; who can stop him?
  Who will say to him, 'What are you doing?'

13 "God will not turn back his anger;
  the helpers of Rahab bowed beneath him.
14 How then can I answer him,
  choosing my words with him?
15 Though I am innocent, I cannot answer him;
  I must appeal for mercy to my accuser.a
16 If I summoned him and he answered me,
  I do not believe that he would listen to my
    voice.
17 For he crushes me with a tempest,
  and multiplies my wounds without cause;
18 he will not let me get my breath,
  but fills me with bitterness.
19 If it is a contest of strength, he is the strong one!
  If it is a matter of justice, who can summon
    him?b
20 Though I am innocent, my own mouth would
    condemn me;
  though I am blameless, he would prove me
    perverse.
21 I am blameless; I do not know myself;
  I loathe my life.
22 It is all one; therefore I say,
  he destroys both the blameless and the wicked.
23 When disaster brings sudden death,
  he mocks at the calamityc of the innocent.
24 The earth is given into the hand of the wicked;
  he covers the eyes of its judges—
  if it is not he, who then is it?

25 "My days are swifter than a runner;
  they flee away, they see no good.
26 They go by like skiffs of reed,
  like an eagle swooping on the prey.

21 He will yet fill your mouth with laughter,
  and shouts of joy will be on your lips;
22 your enemies will be wrapped in confusion,
  and the dwellings of the wicked will vanish away.

9 Job answered:

2 Indeed, this I know for the truth:
  that no one can win his case against God.
3 If anyone does choose to argue with him,
  God will not answer one question in a thousand.
4 He is wise, he is all-powerful;
  who has stood up to him and remained unscathed?
5 It is God who moves mountains before they know
    it,
  overturning them in his wrath;
6 who makes the earth start from its place
  so that its pillars are shaken;
7 who commands the sun not to rise
  and shuts up the stars under his seal;
8 who by himself spread out the heavens
  and trod on the back of the sea monster;
9 who made Aldebaran and Orion,
  the Pleiades and the circle of the southern stars;
10 who does great, unsearchable things,
  marvels beyond all reckoning.

11 He goes by me, and I do not see him;
  he moves on his way undiscerned by me.
12 If he hurries on, who can bring him back?
  Who will ask him what he is doing?
13 God does not turn back his wrath;
  the partisans of Rahab lie prostrate at his feet.
14 How much less can I answer him
  or find words to dispute with him?
15 Though I am in the right, I get no answer,
  even if I plead with my accuser for mercy.
16 If I summoned him to court and he responded,
  I do not believe that he would listen to my plea;
17 for he strikes at me for a trifle
  and rains blows on me without cause;
18 he leaves me no respite to recover my breath,
  but sates me with bitter thoughts.
19 If the appeal is to force, see how mighty he is;
  if to justice, who can compel him to give me a
    hearing?
20 Though I am in the right, he condemns me out of
    my own mouth;
  though I am blameless, he makes me out to be
    crooked.
21 Blameless, I say; of myself
  I reck nothing, I hold my life cheap.
22 But it is all one; therefore I declare,
  'He destroys blameless and wicked alike.'
23 When a sudden flood brings death,
  he mocks the plight of the innocent.
24 When a country is delivered into the power of the
    wicked,
  he blindfolds the eyes of its judges.

25 My days have passed more swiftly than a runner,
  they have slipped away without ever seeing
    prosperity;
26 they have glided by like reed-built skiffs,
  swift as an eagle swooping on its prey.

9:3 **If anyone . . . thousand:** or If God is pleased to argue with him,
no one can answer one question in a thousand.   9:8 **on . . .
monster:** or on the crests of the waves.   9:12 **hurries on:** so
some MSS; others seizes.   9:17 **trifle:** lit. hair.   9:19 **him:** so
Gk; Heb. me.   9:24 **blindfolds . . . judges:** prob. rdg; Heb. adds
if not he, then who?

z Or trampled the back of the sea dragon   a Or for my right
b Compare Gk: Heb me   c Meaning of Heb uncertain

21 Once more will he fill your mouth with laughter,
and your lips with rejoicing.
22 They that hate you shall be clothed with shame,
and the tent of the wicked shall be no more.

9 Then Job answered and said:

2 I know well that it is so;
but how can a man be justified before God?
3 Should one wish to contend with him,
he could not answer him once in a
thousand times.
4 God is wise in heart and mighty in strength;
who has withstood him and remained unscathed?
5 He removes the mountains before they know it;
he overturns them in his anger.
6 He shakes the earth out of its place,
and the pillars beneath it tremble.
7 He commands the sun, and it rises not;
he seals up the stars.
8 He alone stretches out the heavens
and treads upon the crests of the sea.
9 He made the Bear and Orion,
the Pleiades and the constellations of the south;
10 He does great things past finding out,
marvelous things beyond reckoning.
11 Should he come near me, I see him not;
should he pass by, I am not aware of him;
12 Should he seize me forcibly, who can say
him nay?
Who can say to him, "What are you doing?"
13 He is God and he does not relent;
the helpers of Rahab bow beneath him.
14 How much less shall I give him any answer,
or choose out arguments against him!
15 Even though I were right, I could not answer him,
but should rather beg for what was due me.
16 If I appealed to him and he answered my call,
I could not believe that he would hearken to
my words;
17 With a tempest he might overwhelm me,
and multiply my wounds without cause;
18 He need not suffer me to draw breath,
but might fill me with bitter griefs.
19 If it be a question of strength, he is mighty;
and if of judgment, who will call him
to account?
20 Though I were right, my own mouth might
condemn me;
were I innocent, he might put me in the wrong.
21 Though I am innocent, I myself cannot know it;
I despise my life.
22 It is all one! therefore I say:
Both the innocent and the wicked he destroys.
23 When the scourge slays suddenly,
he laughs at the despair of the innocent.
24 The earth is given into the hands of the wicked;
he covers the faces of its judges.
If it is not he, who then is it?
25 My days are swifter than a runner,
they flee away; they see no happiness.
26 They shoot by like skiffs of reed,
like an eagle swooping upon its prey.

21 Once again laughter may fill your mouth
and cries of joy break from your lips.
22 Your enemies will be covered with shame
and the tent of the wicked will vanish!'

9 Job spoke next. He said:

2 Indeed, I know it is as you say:
how could anyone claim to be upright before
God?
3 Anyone trying to argue matters with him,
could not give him one answer in a thousand.
4 Among the wisest and the hardiest,
who then can successfully defy him?
5 He moves the mountains, though they do not know
it;
he throws them down when he is angry.
6 He shakes the earth, and moves it from its place,
making all its pillars tremble.
7 The sun, at his command, forbears to rise,
and on the stars he sets a seal.
8 He and no other has stretched out the heavens
and trampled on the back of the Sea.
9 He has made the Bear and Orion,
the Pleiades and the Mansions of the South.
10 The works he does are great and unfathomable,
and his marvels cannot be counted.
11 If he passes me, I do not see him;
he slips by, imperceptible to me.
12 If he snatches his prey, who is going to stop him
or dare to ask, 'What are you doing?'
13 God does not renounce his anger:
beneath him, Rahab's*f* minions still lie
prostrate.
14 And here am I, proposing to defend myself
and select my arguments against him!
15 Even if I am upright, what point is there in
answering him?
I can only plead for mercy with my judge!
16 And if he deigned to answer my citation,
I cannot believe he would listen to what I said,
17 he who crushes me for one hair,
who, for no reason, wounds and wounds again,
18 not even letting me regain my breath,
with so much bitterness he fills me!
19 Shall I try force? Look how strong he is!
Or go to court? But who will summon him?
20 If I prove myself upright, his mouth may condemn
me,
even if I am innocent, he may pronounce me
perverse.
21 But am I innocent? I am no longer sure,
and life itself I despise!
22 It is all one, and hence I boldly say:
he destroys innocent and guilty alike.
23 When a sudden deadly scourge descends,
he laughs at the plight of the innocent.
24 When a country falls into the power of the wicked,
he veils the faces of its judges.
Or if not he, who else?
25 My days pass: more swiftly than a runner
they flee away with never a glimpse of
happiness,
26 they skim past like a reed canoe,
like an eagle swooping on its prey.

f 9 Another name for the Sea as monster of chaos, also used of the
Red Sea.

27 If I say, 'I will forget my complaint;
  I will put off my sad countenance and be of
    good cheer,'
28 I become afraid of all my suffering,
  for I know you will not hold me innocent.
29 I shall be condemned;
  why then do I labor in vain?
30 If I wash myself with soap
  and cleanse my hands with lye,
31 yet you will plunge me into filth,
  and my own clothes will abhor me.
32 For he is not a mortal, as I am, that I might
    answer him,
  that we should come to trial together.
33 There is no umpire*d* between us,
  who might lay his hand on us both.
34 If he would take his rod away from me,
  and not let dread of him terrify me,
35 then I would speak without fear of him,
  for I know I am not what I am thought to be.*e*

10 "I loathe my life;
  I will give free utterance to my complaint;
  I will speak in the bitterness of my soul.
2 I will say to God, Do not condemn me;
  let me know why you contend against me.
3 Does it seem good to you to oppress,
  to despise the work of your hands
  and favor the schemes of the wicked?
4 Do you have eyes of flesh?
  Do you see as humans see?
5 Are your days like the days of mortals,
  or your years like human years,
6 that you seek out my iniquity
  and search for my sin,
7 although you know that I am not guilty,
  and there is no one to deliver out of your
    hand?
8 Your hands fashioned and made me;
  and now you turn and destroy me.*f*
9 Remember that you fashioned me like clay;
  and will you turn me to dust again?
10 Did you not pour me out like milk
  and curdle me like cheese?
11 You clothed me with skin and flesh,
  and knit me together with bones and sinews.
12 You have granted me life and steadfast love,
  and your care has preserved my spirit.
13 Yet these things you hid in your heart;
  I know that this was your purpose.
14 If I sin, you watch me,
  and do not acquit me of my iniquity.
15 If I am wicked, woe to me!
  If I am righteous, I cannot lift up my head,
  for I am filled with disgrace
  and look upon my affliction.
16 Bold as a lion you hunt me;
  you repeat your exploits against me.
17 You renew your witnesses against me,
  and increase your vexation toward me;
  you bring fresh troops against me.*g*
18 "Why did you bring me forth from the womb?
  Would that I had died before any eye had seen
    me,
19 and were as though I had not been,
  carried from the womb to the grave.

27 If I think, 'I shall forget my complaints,
  I shall show a cheerful face and smile,'
28 I still dread all I must suffer;
  I know that you will not acquit me.
29 If I am to be accounted guilty,
  why do I waste my labour?
30 Though I were to wash myself with soap
  and cleanse my hands with lye,
31 you would thrust me into the miry pit
  and my clothes would render me loathsome.
32 God is not as I am, not someone I can challenge,
  and say, 'Let us confront one another in court.'
33 If only there were one to arbitrate between us
  and impose his authority on us both,
34 so that God might take his rod from my back,
  and terror of him might not come on me suddenly.
35 I should then speak out without fear of him,
  for I know I am not what I am thought to be.

10 I am sickened of life;
  I shall give free rein to my complaints,
  speaking out in the bitterness of my soul.
2 I shall say to God, Do not condemn me,
  but let me know the charge against me.
3 Do you find any advantage in oppression,
  in spurning the work of your own hands
  while smiling on the policy of the wicked?
4 Have you the eyes of flesh?
  Do you see as a mortal sees?
5 Are your days as those of a mortal
  or your years as his lifespan?
6 Is that why you look for guilt in me
  and seek in me for sin,
7 though you know that I am guiltless
  and have none to save me from your power?
8 Your hands shaped and fashioned me;
  and will you at once turn and destroy me?
9 Recall that you moulded me like clay;
  and would you reduce me to dust again?
10 Did you not pour me out like milk
  and curdle me like cheese,
11 clothe me with skin and flesh
  and knit me together with bones and sinews?
12 You granted me life and continuing favour,
  and your providence watched over my spirit.
13 Yet this was the secret purpose of your heart,
  and I know what was your intent:
14 that, if I sinned, you would be watching me
  and would not absolve me of my guilt.
15 If indeed I am wicked, all the worse for me!
  If I am upright, I cannot hold up my head;
  I am filled with shame and steeped in my
    affliction.
16 If I am proud as a lion, you hunt me down
  and confront me again with marvellous power;
17 you renew your onslaught on me,
  and with mounting anger against me
  bring fresh forces to the attack.
18 Why did you bring me out of the womb?
  Better if I had expired and no one had set eyes on
    me,
19 if I had been carried from womb to grave
  and were as though I had not been born.

---

*d*Another reading is *Would that there were an umpire*   *e*Cn: Heb
for I am not so in myself   *f*Cn Compare Gk Syr: Heb *made me*
together all around, and you destroy me   *g*Cn Compare Gk: Heb
toward me; changes and a troop are with me

10:16 **If I am:** *so Gk; Heb.* If he is.

27 If I say: I will forget my complaining,
  I will lay aside my sadness and be of
    good cheer,
28 Then I am in dread of all my pains;
  I know that you will not hold me innocent.
29 If I must be accounted guilty,
  why then should I strive in vain?
30 If I should wash myself with snow
  and cleanse my hands with lye,
31 Yet you would plunge me in the ditch,
  so that my garments would abhor me.
32 For he is not a man like myself, that I should
    answer him,
  that we should come together in judgment.
33 Would that there were an arbiter between us,
  who could lay his hand upon us both
34   and withdraw his rod from me.
  Would that his terrors did not frighten me;
35 that I might speak without being afraid of him.
  Since this is not the case with me,

10 ¹ I loathe my life.

  I will give myself up to complaint;
  I will speak from the bitterness of my soul.
2 I will say to God: Do not put me in the wrong!
  Let me know why you oppose me.
3 Is it a pleasure for you to oppress,
  to spurn the work of your hands,
  and smile on the plan of the wicked?
4 Have you eyes of flesh?
  Do you see as man sees?
5 Are your days as the days of a mortal,
  and are your years as a man's lifetime,
6 That you seek for guilt in me
  and search after my sins,
7 Even though you know that I am not wicked,
  and that none can deliver me out of your hand?
8 Your hands have formed me and fashioned me;
  will you then turn and destroy me?
9 Oh, remember that you fashioned me from clay!
  Will you then bring me down to dust again?
10 Did you not pour me out as milk,
  and thicken me like cheese?
11 With skin and flesh you clothed me,
  with bones and sinews knit me together.
12 Grace and favor you granted me,
  and your providence has preserved my spirit.
13 Yet these things you have hidden in your heart;
  I know that they are your purpose:
14 If I should sin, you would keep a watch
    against me,
  and from my guilt you would not absolve me.
15 If I should be wicked, alas for me!
  if righteous, I dare not hold up my head,
  filled with ignominy and sodden with affliction!
16 Should it lift up, you hunt me like a lion:
  repeatedly you show your wondrous power
    against me,
17 You renew your attack upon me
  and multiply your harassment of me;
  in waves your troops come against me.
18 Why then did you bring me forth from the womb?
  I should have died and no eye have seen me.
19 I should be as though I had never lived;
  I should have been taken from the womb to
    the grave.

27 If I decide to stifle my complaining,
  change countenance, and wear a smiling face,
28 fear seizes me at the thought of all my woes,
  for I know you do not regard me as innocent.
29 And if I have done wrong,
  why should I put myself to useless trouble?
30 If I wash myself in melted snow,
  clean my hands with soda,
31 you will only plunge me into the dung,
  till my clothes themselves recoil from me!
32 For he is not human like me: impossible for me to
    answer him
  or appear alongside him in court.
33 There is no arbiter between us,
  to lay his hand on both,
34 to stay his rod from me,
  or keep away his daunting terrors.
35 Nonetheless, unafraid of him, I shall speak:
  since I do not see myself like that at all!

10 Since I have lost all taste for life,
  I shall give free rein to my complaining;
  I shall let my embittered soul speak out.
2 I shall say to God, 'Do not condemn me,
  tell me what your case is against me.
3 Is it right for you to attack me,
  in contempt for what you yourself have made,
  thus abetting the schemes of the wicked?
4 Are your eyes mere human eyes,
  do you see as human beings see?
5 Are you mortal like human beings?
  do your years pass as human days pass?
6 You, who enquire into my faults
  and investigate my sins,
7 you know very well that I am innocent,
  and that no one can rescue me from your grasp.
8 Your hands having shaped and created me,
  now you change your mind and mean to destroy
    me!
9 Having made me, remember, as though of clay,
  now you mean to turn me back into dust!
10 Did you not pour me out like milk,
  and then let me thicken like curds,
11 clothe me with skin and flesh,
  and weave me of bone and sinew?
12 In your love you gave me life,
  and in your care watched over my every breath.
13 Yet, all the while, you had a secret plan:
  I know that you were biding your time
14 to see if I should sin
  and then not acquit me of my faults.
15 Woe to me, if I am guilty;
  even if I am upright, I dare not lift my head,
  so overwhelmed with shame and drunk with pain
    am I!
16 Proud as a lion, you hunt me down,
  multiplying your exploits at my expense,
17 attacking me again and again,
  your fury against me ever increasing,
  your troops assailing me, wave after wave.
18 Why did you bring me out of the womb?
  I should have perished then, unseen by any eye,
19 a being that had never been,
  to be carried from womb to grave.

NEW REVISED STANDARD VERSION	REVISED ENGLISH BIBLE

NEW REVISED STANDARD VERSION

20 Are not the days of my life few?h
    Let me alone, that I may find a little comforti
21 before I go, never to return,
    to the land of gloom and deep darkness,
22 the land of gloomj and chaos,
    where light is like darkness."

11 Then Zophar the Naamathite answered:
2 "Should a multitude of words go unanswered,
    and should one full of talk be vindicated?
3 Should your babble put others to silence,
    and when you mock, shall no one shame you?
4 For you say, 'My conductk is pure,
    and I am clean in God'sl sight.'
5 But oh, that God would speak,
    and open his lips to you,
6 and that he would tell you the secrets of wisdom!
    For wisdom is many-sided.m
    Know then that God exacts of you less than your
    guilt deserves.

7 "Can you find out the deep things of God?
    Can you find out the limit of the Almighty?n
8 It is higher than heaveno — what can you do?
    Deeper than Sheol — what can you know?
9 Its measure is longer than the earth,
    and broader than the sea.
10 If he passes through, and imprisons,
    and assembles for judgment, who can hinder
    him?
11 For he knows those who are worthless;
    when he sees iniquity, will he not consider it?
12 But a stupid person will get understanding,
    when a wild ass is born human.m

13 "If you direct your heart rightly,
    you will stretch out your hands toward him.
14 If iniquity is in your hand, put it far away,
    and do not let wickedness reside in your tents.
15 Surely then you will lift up your face without
    blemish;
    you will be secure, and will not fear.
16 You will forget your misery;
    you will remember it as waters that have
    passed away.
17 And your life will be brighter than the noonday;
    its darkness will be like the morning.
18 And you will have confidence, because there is
    hope;
    you will be protectedp and take your rest in
    safety.
19 You will lie down, and no one will make you
    afraid;
    many will entreat your favor.
20 But the eyes of the wicked will fail;
    all way of escape will be lost to them,
    and their hope is to breathe their last."

12 Then Job answered:
2 "No doubt you are the people,
    and wisdom will die with you.
3 But I have understanding as well as you;
    I am not inferior to you.
    Who does not know such things as these?

REVISED ENGLISH BIBLE

20 Is not my life short and fleeting?
    Let me be, that I may be happy for a moment,
21 before I depart to a land of gloom,
    a land of deepest darkness, never to return,
22 a land of dense darkness and disorder,
    increasing darkness lit by no ray of light.

11 Then Zophar the Naamathite spoke up:

2 Is this spate of words to go unanswered?
    Must the glib of tongue always be right?
3 Is your endless talk to reduce others to silence?
    When you speak irreverently, is no one to take you
    to task?
4 You claim that your opinions are sound;
    you say to God, 'I am spotless in your sight.'
5 But if only God would speak
    and open his lips to reply,
6 to expound to you the secrets of wisdom,
    for wonderful are its achievements!
    Know then that God exacts from you
    less than your sin deserves.
7 Can you fathom the mystery of God,
    or attain to the limits of the Almighty?
8 They are higher than the heavens. What can you
    do?
    They are deeper than Sheol. What can you know?
9 In extent they are longer than the earth
    and broader than the ocean.
10 If he passes by, he may keep secret his passing;
    if he proclaims it, who can turn him back?
11 He surely knows who are false,
    and when he sees iniquity, does he not take note of
    it?
12 A fool will attain to understanding
    when a wild ass's foal is born a human being!

13 If only you had directed your heart rightly
    and spread out your hands in prayer to him!
14 Any wrongdoing you have in hand, thrust it far
    away,
    and do not let iniquity make its home with you.
15 Then you could hold up your head without fault;
    you would be steadfast and fearless.
16 Then you will forget trouble,
    remembering it only as floodwaters that have
    passed.
17 Life will be lasting, radiant as noon,
    and darkness will be turned to morning.
18 You will be confident, because there is hope;
    sure of protection, you will rest in confidence
19 and lie down unafraid.
    The great will court your favour.
20 But blindness will fall on the wicked;
    to them the ways of escape are closed,
    and their only hope is death.

12 Job answered:

2 No doubt you are intelligent people,
    and when you die, wisdom will perish!
3 But I have sense, as well as you;
    in no way do I fall short of you;
    what gifts indeed have you that others have not?

---

h Cn Compare Gk Syr: Heb *Are not my days few? Let him cease!*
i Heb *that I may brighten up a little* j Heb *gloom as darkness, deep
darkness* k Gk: Heb *teaching* l Heb *your* m Meaning of Heb
uncertain n Traditional rendering of Heb *Shaddai* o Heb *The
heights of heaven* p Or *you will look around*

10:22 **increasing . . . light:** *cp. Gk; Heb. obscure.*   11:8 **Sheol:**
or the underworld.   12:2 **intelligent:** *prob. rdg; Heb. omits.*

NEW AMERICAN BIBLE

NEW JERUSALEM BIBLE

20 Are not the days of my life few?
  Let me alone, that I may recover a little
21 Before I go whence I shall not return,
  to the land of darkness and of gloom,
22 The black, disordered land
  where darkness is the only light.

11

And Zophar the Naamathite spoke out and said:

2 Should not the man of many words
    be answered,
  or must the garrulous man necessarily be right?
3 Shall your babblings keep men silent,
  and shall you deride and no one give rebuke?
4 Shall you say: "My teaching is pure,
  and I am clean in your sight"?
5 But oh, that God would speak,
  and open his lips against you,
6 And tell you that the secrets of wisdom
  are twice as effective:
So you might learn that God
  will make you answer for your guilt.
7 Can you penetrate the designs of God?
  Dare you vie with the perfection of
    the Almighty?
8 It is higher than the heavens; what can you do?
  It is deeper than the nether world; what can
    you know?
9 It is longer than the earth in measure,
  and broader than the sea.
10 If he seize and imprison
  or call to judgment, who then can say him nay?
11 For he knows the worthlessness of men
  and sees iniquity; will he then ignore it?
12 Will empty man then gain understanding,
  and the wild jackass be made docile?
13 If you set your heart aright
  and stretch out your hands toward him,
14 If you remove all iniquity from your conduct,
  and let not injustice dwell in your tent,
15 Surely then you may lift up your face in innocence;
  you may stand firm and unafraid.
16 For then you shall forget your misery,
  or recall it like waters that have ebbed away.
17 Then your life shall be brighter than the noonday;
  its gloom shall become as the morning.
18 And you shall be secure, because there is hope;
  you shall look round you and lie down in safety,
19   and you shall take your rest with none
      to disturb.
  Many shall entreat your favor,
20   but the wicked, looking on, shall be consumed
      with envy.
  Escape shall be cut off from them,
    they shall wait to expire.

12

Then Job replied and said:

2 No doubt you are the intelligent folk,
  and with you wisdom shall die!
3 But I have intelligence as well as you;
  for who does not know such things as these?

20 The days of my life are few enough:
  turn your eyes away, leave me a little joy,
21 before I go to the place of no return,
  to the land of darkness and shadow dark as
    death,
22 where dimness and disorder hold sway,
  and light itself is like dead of night.

11

Zophar of Naamath spoke next. He said:

2 Is babbling to go without an answer?
  Is wordiness a proof of uprightness?
3 Do you think your talking strikes people dumb,
  will you jeer with no one to refute you?
4 These were your words, 'My conduct is pure,
  in your eyes I am free of blame!'
5 Will no one let God speak,
  open his lips and give you answer,
6 show you the secrets of wisdom
  which put all cleverness to shame?
  Then you would realise that God is calling you
    to account for your sin.
7 Can you claim to fathom the depth of God,
  can you reach the limit of Shaddai?
8 It is higher than the heavens: what can you do?
  It is deeper than Sheol: what can you know?
9 It would be longer to measure than the earth
  and broader than the sea.
10 If he intervenes to close or convoke the assembly,
  who is to prevent him?
11 He knows how deceptive human beings are,
  and he sees their misdeeds too, and marks them
    well.
12 Hence empty-headed people would do well to
    study sense
  and people who behave like wild donkeys to let
    themselves be tamed.
13 Come, reconsider your attitude,
  stretch out your hands towards him!
14 If you repudiate the sin which you have doubtless
    committed
  and do not allow wickedness to live on in your
    tents,
15 you will be able to raise an unsullied face,
  unwavering and free from fear,
16 for you will forget about your misery,
  thinking of it only as a flood that passed long
    ago.
17 Then begins an existence more radiant than noon,
  and the very darkness will be bright as morning.
18 Confident because there is hope;
  after your troubles, you will sleep secure.
19 When you lie down to rest, no one will trouble
    you,
  and many will seek your favour.
20 But as for the wicked, their eyes are weary,
  there is no refuge for them;
  their only hope is to breathe their last.

12

Job spoke next. He said:

2 Doubtless, you are the voice of the people,
  and when you die, wisdom will die with you!
3 But I have a brain, as well as you,
  I am in no way inferior to you,
  and who, in any case, does not know all that?

NEW REVISED STANDARD VERSION

4 I am a laughingstock to my friends;
   I, who called upon God and he answered me,
   a just and blameless man, I am a
     laughingstock.
5 Those at ease have contempt for misfortune, q
   but it is ready for those whose feet are
     unstable.
6 The tents of robbers are at peace,
   and those who provoke God are secure,
   who bring their god in their hands. r

7 "But ask the animals, and they will teach you;
   the birds of the air, and they will tell you;
8 ask the plants of the earth, s and they will teach
    you;
   and the fish of the sea will declare to you.
9 Who among all these does not know
   that the hand of the LORD has done this?
10 In his hand is the life of every living thing
   and the breath of every human being.
11 Does not the ear test words
   as the palate tastes food?
12 Is wisdom with the aged,
   and understanding in length of days?

13 "With God t are wisdom and strength;
   he has counsel and understanding.
14 If he tears down, no one can rebuild;
   if he shuts someone in, no one can open up.
15 If he withholds the waters, they dry up;
   if he sends them out, they overwhelm the land.
16 With him are strength and wisdom;
   the deceived and the deceiver are his.
17 He leads counselors away stripped,
   and makes fools of judges.
18 He looses the sash of kings,
   and binds a waistcloth on their loins.
19 He leads priests away stripped,
   and overthrows the mighty.
20 He deprives of speech those who are trusted,
   and takes away the discernment of the elders.
21 He pours contempt on princes,
   and looses the belt of the strong.
22 He uncovers the deeps out of darkness,
   and brings deep darkness to light.
23 He makes nations great, then destroys them;
   he enlarges nations, then leads them away.
24 He strips understanding from the leaders u of the
    earth,
   and makes them wander in a pathless waste.
25 They grope in the dark without light;
   he makes them stagger like a drunkard.

13 "Look, my eye has seen all this,
   my ear has heard and understood it.
2 What you know, I also know;
   I am not inferior to you.
3 But I would speak to the Almighty, v
   and I desire to argue my case with God.
4 As for you, you whitewash with lies;
   all of you are worthless physicians.
5 If you would only keep silent,
   that would be your wisdom!

REVISED ENGLISH BIBLE

4 Yet I am a laughing-stock to my friends —
   a laughing-stock, though I am innocent and
    blameless:
   one that called upon God, but he afflicted me.
5 Those at ease look down on misfortune,
   on the blow that fells one who is already reeling,
6 while the marauders' tents are left undisturbed
   and those who provoke God live safe and sound.

7 But ask the beasts, and they will teach you;
   ask the birds of the air to inform you,
8 or tell the creatures that crawl to teach you,
   and the fish of the sea to instruct you.
9 Who does not come to know from all these
   that the hand of the LORD has done this?
10 In his hand are the souls of all that live,
   the spirits of every human being.
11 Does not the ear test words
   as the palate savours food?
12 'Is wisdom with the aged?
   Does long life bring understanding?'

13 'With God are wisdom and power,
   to him belong counsel and understanding.'
14 If he pulls down, there is no rebuilding;
   if he imprisons, there is no release.
15 If he holds back the waters, there is drought;
   if he lets them loose, the earth is overwhelmed.
16 Strength and success belong to him,
   deceived and deceiver are his to use.
17 He makes counsellors behave like madmen
   and turns judges crazy;
18 he looses the bonds imposed by kings
   and removes the girdle of office from their waists;
19 he makes priests behave like idiots
   and overthrows those long in office;
20 trusted counsellors he strikes with dumbness,
   he robs the old of their judgement;
21 he pours scorn on princes
   and abates the arrogance of nobles.
22 He unveils mysteries deep in obscurity
   and into thick darkness he brings light.
23 He leads peoples astray and destroys them,
   he lays them low, and there they lie.
24 He deprives the nations' rulers of their wits
   and leaves them wandering in a trackless desert;
25 without light they grope their way in darkness
   and are left to wander like drunkards.

13 All this I have seen with my own eyes,
   with my own ears I have heard and understood
    it.
2 What you know, I also know;
   in no way do I fall short of you.
3 Nevertheless I would speak with the Almighty;
   I am ready to argue with God,
4 while you go on smearing truth with your
    falsehoods,
   one and all stitching a patchwork of lies.
5 If only you would be silent
   and let silence be your wisdom!

---

q Meaning of Heb uncertain   r Or whom God brought forth by his hand; Meaning of Heb uncertain   s Or speak to the earth t Heb him   u Heb adds of the people   v Traditional rendering of Heb Shaddai

12:4 but ... me: or and he answered me.   12:6 those ... sound: prob. rdg; Heb. adds into whose hands God brings.   12:18 removes ... from: or binds a loincloth on.   12:19 those ... office: or temple servitors.

4 I have become the sport of my neighbors:
"The one whom God answers when he calls
  upon him,
the just, the perfect man," is a laughing-stock;
5 The undisturbed esteem my downfall a disgrace
such as awaits unsteady feet;
6 Yet the tents of robbers are prosperous,
and those who provoke God are secure.
7 But now ask the beasts to teach you,
and the birds of the air to tell you;
8 Or the reptiles on earth to instruct you,
and the fish of the sea to inform you.
9 Which of all these does not know
that the hand of God has done this?
10 In this hand is the soul of every living thing,
and the life breath of all mankind.
11 Does not the ear judge words
as the mouth tastes food?
12 So with old age is wisdom,
and with length of days understanding.
13 With him are wisdom and might;
his are counsel and understanding.
14 If he breaks a thing down, there is no rebuilding;
if he imprisons a man, there is no release.
15 He holds back the waters and there is drought;
he sends them forth and they overwhelm
  the land.
18 He loosens the bonds imposed by kings
and leaves but a waistcloth to bind the king's
  own loins.
21 He breaks down the barriers of the streams
19   and lets their never-failing waters flow away.
16 With him are strength and prudence;
the misled and the misleaders are his.
17 He sends counselors away barefoot,
and of judges he makes fools.
20 He silences the trusted adviser,
and takes discretion from the aged.
22 The recesses of the darkness he discloses,
and brings the gloom forth to the light.
23 He makes nations great and he destroys them;
he spreads peoples abroad and he
  abandons them.
24 He takes understanding from the leaders of
  the land,
25   till they grope in the darkness without light;
he makes them stagger like drunken men.

13 Lo, all this my eye has seen;
my ear has heard and perceived it.
2 What you know, I also know;
I fall not short of you.
3 But I would speak with the Almighty;
I wish to reason with God.
4 You are glossing over falsehoods
and offering vain remedies, every one of you!
5 Oh, that you would be altogether silent!
This for you would be wisdom.

4 Anyone becomes a laughing-stock to his friends
if he cries to God and expects an answer.
People laugh at anyone who has integrity and is
  upright.
5 'Add insult to injury,' think the prosperous,
'strike the fellow now that he is staggering!'
6 And yet the tents of brigands are left in peace:
those who provoke God dwell secure
and so does anyone who makes a god of his fist!
7 You have only to ask the cattle, for them to
  instruct you,
and the birds of the sky, for them to inform you.
8 The creeping things of earth will give you lessons,
and the fish of the sea provide you an
  explanation:
9 there is not one such creature but will know
that the hand of God has arranged things like
  this!
10 In his hand is the soul of every living thing
and the breath of every human being!
11 Can the ear not distinguish the value of what is
  said,
just as the palate can tell one food from another?
12 Wisdom is found in the old,
and discretion comes with great age.
13 But in him there is wisdom, and power too,
and good counsel no less than discretion.
14 What he destroys, no one can rebuild;
whom he imprisons, no one can release.
15 Is there a drought? He has withheld the waters.
Do they play havoc on earth? He has let them
  loose.
16 In him is strength, in him resourcefulness,
beguiler and beguiled alike are his.
17 He robs a country's counsellors of their wits,
turns judges into fools.
18 He undoes the belts of kings
and knots a rope round their waists.
19 He makes priests walk barefoot,
and overthrows the powers that are established.
20 He strikes the most assured of speakers dumb
and robs old people of their discretion.
21 He pours contempt on the nobly born,
and unbuckles the belt of the strong.
22 He unveils the depths of darkness,
brings shadow dark as death to the light.
23 He builds nations up, then ruins them,
he makes peoples expand, then suppresses them.
24 He strips a country's leaders of their judgement,
and leaves them to wander in a trackless waste,
25 to grope about in unlit darkness,
lurching to and fro as though drunk.

13 I have seen all this with my own eyes,
heard with my own ears and understood.
2 Whatever you know, I know too;
I am in no way inferior to you.
3 But my words are intended for Shaddai;
I mean to remonstrate with God.
4 As for you, you are only charlatans,
all worthless as doctors!
5 Will no one teach you to be quiet
— the only wisdom that becomes you!

NEW REVISED STANDARD VERSION	REVISED ENGLISH BIBLE

NEW REVISED STANDARD VERSION

6 Hear now my reasoning,
  and listen to the pleadings of my lips.
7 Will you speak falsely for God,
  and speak deceitfully for him?
8 Will you show partiality toward him,
  will you plead the case for God?
9 Will it be well with you when he searches you
    out?
  Or can you deceive him, as one person
    deceives another?
10 He will surely rebuke you
  if in secret you show partiality.
11 Will not his majesty terrify you,
  and the dread of him fall upon you?
12 Your maxims are proverbs of ashes,
  your defenses are defenses of clay.

13 "Let me have silence, and I will speak,
  and let come on me what may.
14 I will take my flesh in my teeth,
  and put my life in my hand.*w*
15 See, he will kill me; I have no hope;*x*
  but I will defend my ways to his face.
16 This will be my salvation,
  that the godless shall not come before him.
17 Listen carefully to my words,
  and let my declaration be in your ears.
18 I have indeed prepared my case;
  I know that I shall be vindicated.
19 Who is there that will contend with me?
  For then I would be silent and die.
20 Only grant two things to me,
  then I will not hide myself from your face:
21 withdraw your hand far from me,
  and do not let dread of you terrify me.
22 Then call, and I will answer;
  or let me speak, and you reply to me.
23 How many are my iniquities and my sins?
  Make me know my transgression and my sin.
24 Why do you hide your face,
  and count me as your enemy?
25 Will you frighten a windblown leaf
  and pursue dry chaff?
26 For you write bitter things against me,
  and make me reap*y* the iniquities of my youth.
27 You put my feet in the stocks,
  and watch all my paths;
  you set a bound to the soles of my feet.
28 One wastes away like a rotten thing,
  like a garment that is moth-eaten.

14 "A mortal, born of woman, few of days and full
    of trouble,
2 comes up like a flower and withers,
  flees like a shadow and does not last.
3 Do you fix your eyes on such a one?
  Do you bring me into judgment with you?
4 Who can bring a clean thing out of an unclean?
  No one can.
5 Since their days are determined,
  and the number of their months is known to
    you,
  and you have appointed the bounds that they
    cannot pass,

REVISED ENGLISH BIBLE

6 Listen, now, to my arguments;
  attend while I put my case.
7 Is it on God's behalf that you speak so wickedly,
  in his defence that you voice what is false?
8 Must you take God's part,
  putting his case for him?
9 Will all go well when he examines you?
  Can you deceive him as you could a human being?
10 He will most surely expose you
  if you take his part by falsely accusing me.
11 Will not God's majesty strike you with dread,
  and fear of him overcome you?
12 Your moralizing talk is so much dross,
  your arguments crumble like clay.

13 Be silent, leave me to speak my mind,
  and let what may come upon me!
14 Why do I expose myself to danger
  and take my life in my hands?
15 If he wishes to slay me, I have nothing to lose;
  I shall still defend my conduct to his face.
16 This at least assures my deliverance:
  that no godless person may appear before him.
17 Listen closely, then, to my words,
  and give a hearing to my statement.
18 Be sure of this: once I have stated my case
  I know that I shall be acquitted.
19 Who is there that can make a case against me
  so that I should be reduced to silence and death?
20 God, grant me these two conditions only,
  and then I shall not hide out of your sight:
21 remove your hand from upon me
  and let not fear of you strike me with dismay.
22 Then summon me, and I shall respond;
  or let me speak first, and you answer me.
23 How many crimes and sins are laid to my charge?
  Let me know my offence and my sin.
24 Why do you hide your face
  and treat me as your enemy?
25 Will you harass a wind-driven leaf
  and pursue dry chaff,
26 that you draw up bitter charges against me,
  making me heir to the iniquities of my youth,
27 putting my feet in the stocks,
  keeping a close watch on all I do,
  and setting a slave-mark on my instep?

14 Every being born of woman is short-lived and
    full of trouble.
2 He blossoms like a flower and withers away;
  fleeting as a shadow, he does not endure;
  he is like a wineskin that perishes
  or a garment that moths have eaten.
3 It is on such a creature you fix your eyes,
  and bring him into court before you!
5 Truly the days of such a one's life are determined,
  and the number of his months is known to you;
  you have laid down a limit, which cannot be
    exceeded.

13:12 **your arguments . . . clay:** *lit.* the bosses of your shields are bosses of clay.   13:14 **expose . . . danger:** *lit.* take my flesh in my teeth.   13:27 **setting . . . instep:** *prob. rdg; Heb.* adds verse 28, he is like . . . have eaten, *now transposed to follow 14:2.*
14:2 **he is . . . eaten:** *13:28 transposed here.*   14:3 **into . . . you:** so one MS; others add 4Who can produce pure out of unclean? No one.

*w*Gk: Heb *Why should I take . . . in my hand?*   *x*Or *Though he kill me, yet I will trust in him*   *y*Heb *inherit*

6 Hear now the rebuke I shall utter
and listen to the reproof from my lips.
7 Is it for God that you speak falsehood?
Is it for him that you utter deceit?
8 Is it for him that you show partiality?
Do you play advocate on behalf of God?
9 Will it be well when he shall search you out?
Would you impose on him as one does on men?
10 He will openly rebuke you
if even in secret you show partiality.
11 Surely will his majesty affright you
and the dread of him fall upon you.
12 Your reminders are ashy maxims,
your fabrications are mounds of clay.
13 Be silent, let me alone! that I may speak
and give vent to my feelings.
14 I will carry my flesh between my teeth,
and take my life in my hand.
15 Slay me though he might, I will wait for him;
I will defend my conduct before him.
16 And this shall be my salvation,
that no impious man can come into his presence.
17 Pay careful heed to my speech,
and give my statement a hearing.
18 Behold, I have prepared my case,
I know that I am in the right.
19 If anyone can make a case against me,
then I shall be silent and die.
20 These things only do not use against me,
then from your presence I need not hide:
21 Withdraw your hand far from me,
and let not the terror of you frighten me.
22 Then call me, and I will respond;
or let me speak first, and answer me.
23 What are my faults and my sins?
My misdeeds and my sins make known to me!
24 Why do you hide your face
and consider me your enemy?
25 Will you harass a wind-driven leaf,
or pursue a withered straw?
26 For you draw up bitter indictments against me,
and punish in me the faults of my youth.
27 You put my feet in the stocks;
you watch all my paths
and trace out all my footsteps.
‡13.28: see below in ch. 14‡

14 Man born of woman
is short-lived and full of trouble,
2 Like a flower that springs up and fades,
swift as a shadow that does not abide.
3 Upon such a one will you cast your eyes
so as to bring him into judgment before you,
13, 28 Though he wears out like a leather bottle,
like a garment that the moth has consumed?
4 Can a man be found who is clean of defilement?
There is none, 5 however short his days.
You know the number of his months;
you have fixed the limit which he cannot pass.

6 Kindly listen to my accusation
and give your attention to the way I shall plead.
7 Do you mean to defend God by prevarication
and by dishonest argument,
8 and, taking his side like this,
appoint yourselves as his advocates?
9 How would you fare, if he were to scrutinise you?
Can he be duped as mortals are duped?
10 He would inflict a harsh rebuke on you
for your covert partiality.
11 Does his majesty not affright you?
Does his terror not overcome you?
12 Your received ideas are maxims of ash,
your retorts, retorts of clay.
13 Be quiet! Kindly let me do the talking,
happen to me what may.
14 I am putting my flesh between my teeth,
I am taking my life in my hands;
15 let him kill me if he will; I have no other hope
than to justify my conduct in his eyes.
16 And this is what will save me,
for the wicked would not dare to appear before
him.
17 Listen carefully to my words,
and pay attention to what I am going to say.
18 You see, I shall proceed by form of law,
knowing that I am upright.
19 Who wants to contest my case?
In advance, I agree to be silenced and to die!
20 Only grant me two concessions,
and then I shall not hide away from your face:
21 remove your hand, which lies so heavy on me,
no longer make me cower from your terror.
22 Then call me forward and I shall answer,
or rather, I shall speak and you will answer.
23 How many faults and crimes have I committed?
Tell me what my misdeed has been, what my
sin?
24 Why do you hide your face
and look on me as your enemy?
25 Do you want to intimidate a wind-blown leaf,
do you want to pursue a dry straw?
26 You who lay bitter allegations against me
and tax me with the faults of my youth
27 and have put my feet in the stocks;
you examine my every step
and measure my footprints one by one!

28 For his part, he crumbles away like rotten wood,
or like a moth-eaten garment,

14 1 a human being, born of woman,
whose life is short but full of trouble,
2 Like a flower, such a one blossoms and withers,
fleeting as a shadow, transient.
3 And this is the creature on whom you fix your
gaze,
and bring to judgement before you!
4 But will anyone produce the pure from what is
impure?
No one can!
5 Since his days are measured out,
since his tale of months depends on you,
since you assign him bounds he cannot pass,

13, 28: This verse has been transposed from ch 13.

NEW REVISED STANDARD VERSION

6 look away from them, and desist,ᶻ
   that they may enjoy, like laborers, their days.

7 "For there is hope for a tree,
   if it is cut down, that it will sprout again,
   and that its shoots will not cease.
8 Though its root grows old in the earth,
   and its stump dies in the ground,
9 yet at the scent of water it will bud
   and put forth branches like a young plant.
10 But mortals die, and are laid low;
   humans expire, and where are they?
11 As waters fail from a lake,
   and a river wastes away and dries up,
12 so mortals lie down and do not rise again;
   until the heavens are no more, they will not
   awake
   or be roused out of their sleep.
13 Oh that you would hide me in Sheol,
   that you would conceal me until your wrath is
   past,
   that you would appoint me a set time, and
   remember me!
14 If mortals die, will they live again?
   All the days of my service I would wait
   until my release should come.
15 You would call, and I would answer you;
   you would long for the work of your hands.
16 For then you would notᵃ number my steps,
   you would not keep watch over my sin;
17 my transgression would be sealed up in a bag,
   and you would cover over my iniquity.
18 "But the mountain falls and crumbles away,
   and the rock is removed from its place;
19 the waters wear away the stones;
   the torrents wash away the soil of the earth;
   so you destroy the hope of mortals.
20 You prevail forever against them, and they pass
   away;
   you change their countenance, and send them
   away.
21 Their children come to honor, and they do not
   know it;
   they are brought low, and it goes unnoticed.
22 They feel only the pain of their own bodies,
   and mourn only for themselves."

15 Then Eliphaz the Temanite answered:
2 "Should the wise answer with windy
   knowledge,
   and fill themselves with the east wind?
3 Should they argue in unprofitable talk,
   or in words with which they can do no good?
4 But you are doing away with the fear of God,
   and hindering meditation before God.
5 For your iniquity teaches your mouth,
   and you choose the tongue of the crafty.
6 Your own mouth condemns you, and not I;
   your own lips testify against you.

7 "Are you the firstborn of the human race?
   Were you brought forth before the hills?
8 Have you listened in the council of God?
   And do you limit wisdom to yourself?

REVISED ENGLISH BIBLE

6 Look away from him therefore and leave him
   to count off the hours like a hired labourer.

7 If a tree is cut down,
   there is hope that it will sprout again
   and fresh shoots will not fail.
8 Though its root becomes old in the earth,
   its stump dying in the ground,
9 yet when it scents water it may break into bud
   and make new growth like a young plant.
10 But when a human being dies all his power
   vanishes;
   he expires, and where is he then?
11 As the waters of a lake dwindle,
   or as a river shrinks and runs dry,
12 so mortal man lies down, never to rise
   until the very sky splits open.
   If a man dies, can he live again?
   He can never be roused from this sleep.

13 If only you would hide me in Sheol,
   conceal me until your anger is past,
   and only then fix a time to recall me to mind!
14 I would not lose hope, however long my service,
   waiting for my relief to come.
15 You would summon me, and I would answer;
   you would long to see the creature you have made,
16 whereas now you count my every step,
   watching all my errant course.
17 Every offence of mine is stored in your bag,
   where you keep my iniquity under seal.
18 Yet as a falling mountainside is swept away,
   and a rock is dislodged from its place,
19 as water wears away stone,
   and a cloudburst scours the soil from the land,
   so you have wiped out the hope of frail man;
20 finally you overpower him, and he is gone;
   with changed appearance he is banished from your
   sight.
21 His sons may rise to honour, but he is unaware of
   it;
   they may sink into obscurity, but he knows it not.
22 His kinsfolk are grieved for him
   and his slaves mourn his loss.

15 THEN Eliphaz the Temanite answered:
2 Would a sensible person give vent to such hot-air
   arguments
   or puff himself up with an east wind?
3 Would he bandy useless words
   and speeches so unprofitable?
4 Why! You even banish the fear of God from your
   mind,
   cutting off all communication with him.
5 Your iniquity dictates what you say,
   and deceit is your chosen language.
6 You are condemned out of your own mouth, not
   by me;
   your own lips testify against you.

7 Were you the firstborn of mankind,
   brought forth before the hills?
8 Do you listen in God's secret council
   or usurp all wisdom for yourself alone?

14:6 **and leave him:** *so one MS; others that he may cease.*
14:12 **If . . . again:** *line transposed from beginning of verse 14.*
14:13 **Sheol:** *or the underworld.* 14:14 *See note on verse 12.*

ᶻCn: Heb *that they may desist*   ᵃ Syr: Heb lacks *not*

6 Look away from him and let him be,
  while, like a hireling, he completes his day.
7 For a tree there is hope,
  if it be cut down, that it will sprout again
  and that its tender shoots will not cease.
8 Even though its root grow old in the earth,
  and its stump die in the dust,
9 Yet at the first whiff of water it may flourish again
  and put forth branches like a young plant.
10 But when a man dies, all vigor leaves him;
  when man expires, where then is he?
11 As when the waters of a lake fail,
  or a stream grows dry and parches,
12 So men lie down and rise not again.
  Till the heavens are no more, they shall
    not awake,
  nor be roused out of their sleep.
13 Oh, that you would hide me in the nether world
  and keep me sheltered till your wrath is past;
  would fix a time for me, and then remember me!
14 When a man has died, were he to live again,
  all the days of my drudgery I would wait,
  until my relief should come.
15 You would call, and I would answer you;
  you would esteem the work of your hands.
16 Surely then you would count my steps,
  and not keep watch for sin in me.
17 My misdeeds would be sealed up in a pouch,
  and you would cover over my guilt.
18 But as a mountain falls at last
  and its rock is moved from its place,
19 As waters wear away the stones
  and floods wash away the soil of the land,
  so you destroy the hope of man.
20 You prevail once for all against him and he
    passes on;
  with changed appearance you send him away.
21 If his sons are honored, he is not aware of it;
  if they are in disgrace, he does not know
    about them.
22 Only his own flesh pains him, and his soul grieves
  for him.

6 turn your eyes from him, leave him alone,
  like a hired labourer, to finish his day in peace.
7 There is always hope for a tree:
  when felled, it can start its life again;
  its shoots continue to sprout.
8 Its roots may have grown old in the earth,
  its stump rotting in the ground,
9 but let it scent the water, and it buds,
  and puts out branches like a plant newly set.
10 But a human being? He dies, and dead he remains,
  breathes his last, and then where is he?
11 The waters of the sea will vanish,
  the rivers stop flowing and run dry:
12 a human being, once laid to rest, will never rise
    again,
  the heavens will wear out before he wakes up,
  or before he is roused from his sleep.
13 Will no one hide me in Sheol,
  and shelter me there till your anger is past,
  fixing a certain day for calling me to mind —
14   can the dead come back to life? —
  day after day of my service, I should be waiting
  for my relief to come.
15 Then you would call, and I should answer,
  you would want to see once more what you have
    made.
16 Whereas now you count every step I take,
  you would then stop spying on my sin;
17 you would seal up my crime in a bag,
  and put a cover over my fault.
18 Alas! Just as, eventually, the mountain falls down,
  the rock moves from its place,
19 water wears away the stones,
  the cloudburst erodes the soil;
  so you destroy whatever hope a person has.
20 You crush him once for all, and he is gone;
  first you disfigure him, then you dismiss him.
21 His children may rise to honours — he does not
    know it;
  they may come down in the world — he does not
    care.
22 He feels no pangs, except for his own body,
  makes no lament, except for his own self.

15 Then Eliphaz the Temanite spoke and said:

2 Should a wise man answer with airy opinions,
  or puff himself up with wind?
3 Should he argue in speech which does not avail,
  and in words which are to no profit?
4 You in fact do away with piety,
  and you lessen devotion toward God,
5 Because your wickedness instructs your mouth,
  and you choose to speak like the crafty.
6 Your own mouth condemns you, not I;
  your own lips refute you.
7 Are you indeed the first-born of mankind,
  or were you brought forth before the hills?
8 Are you privy to the counsels of God,
  and do you restrict wisdom to yourself?

15 Eliphaz of Teman spoke next. He said:

2 Does anyone wise respond with windy arguments,
  or feed on an east wind?
3 Or make a defence with ineffectual words
  and speeches good for nothing?
4 You do worse: you suppress reverence,
  you discredit discussion before God.
5 Your very fault incites you to speak like this,
  hence you adopt this language of cunning.
6 Your own mouth condemns you, and not I;
  your own lips bear witness against you.
7 Are you the first-born of the human race,
  brought into the world before the hills?
8 Have you been a listener at God's council,
  or established a monopoly of wisdom?

9 What do you know that we do not know?
    What do you understand that is not clear to us?
10 The gray-haired and the aged are on our side,
    those older than your father.
11 Are the consolations of God too small for you,
    or the word that deals gently with you?
12 Why does your heart carry you away,
    and why do your eyes flash,*b*
13 so that you turn your spirit against God,
    and let such words go out of your mouth?
14 What are mortals, that they can be clean?
    Or those born of woman, that they can be
        righteous?
15 God puts no trust even in his holy ones,
    and the heavens are not clean in his sight;
16 how much less one who is abominable and
        corrupt,
    one who drinks iniquity like water!

17 "I will show you; listen to me;
    what I have seen I will declare—
18 what sages have told,
    and their ancestors have not hidden,
19 to whom alone the land was given,
    and no stranger passed among them.
20 The wicked writhe in pain all their days,
    through all the years that are laid up for the
        ruthless.
21 Terrifying sounds are in their ears;
    in prosperity the destroyer will come upon
        them.
22 They despair of returning from darkness,
    and they are destined for the sword.
23 They wander abroad for bread, saying, 'Where is
        it?'
    They know that a day of darkness is ready at
        hand;
24 distress and anguish terrify them;
    they prevail against them, like a king prepared
        for battle.
25 Because they stretched out their hands against
        God,
    and bid defiance to the Almighty,*c*
26 running stubbornly against him
    with a thick-bossed shield;
27 because they have covered their faces with their
        fat,
    and gathered fat upon their loins,
28 they will live in desolate cities,
    in houses that no one should inhabit,
    houses destined to become heaps of ruins;
29 they will not be rich, and their wealth will not
        endure,
    nor will they strike root in the earth;*d*
30 they will not escape from darkness;
    the flame will dry up their shoots,
    and their blossom*e* will be swept away*f* by
        the wind.
31 Let them not trust in emptiness, deceiving
        themselves;
    for emptiness will be their recompense.
32 It will be paid in full before their time,
    and their branch will not be green.
33 They will shake off their unripe grape, like the
        vine,
    and cast off their blossoms, like the olive tree.

9 What do you know that we do not know?
    What insight have you that we do not share?
10 We have age and white hairs in our company,
    men older than your father.
11 Does not consolation from God suffice you,
    a word whispered quietly in your ear?
12 What makes you so bold at heart,
    and why do your eyes flash,
13 that you vent your anger on God
    and pour out such mouthfuls of words?
14 What is any human being, that he should be
        innocent,
    or any child of woman, that he should be justified?
15 If God puts no trust in his holy ones,
    and the heavens are not innocent in his sight,
16 how much less so are human beings, who are
        loathsome and corrupt
    and lap up evil like water!

17 I shall tell you, if only you will listen;
    I shall recount what I have seen—
18 what has been handed down by wise men
    and was not concealed from them by their
        forefathers,
19 to whom alone the land was given,
    and no foreigner moved among them:
20 the wicked through all their days are racked with
        anxiety;
    so it is with the tyrant through all the years allotted
        to him.
21 The noise of the hunter's scare rings in his ears;
    even in time of peace the marauder swoops down
        on him;
22 he cannot hope to escape from dark death;
    he is marked down for the sword.
23 he is flung out as food for vultures;
    he knows that his destruction is certain.
24 Suddenly a black day comes upon him,
    distress and anxiety overwhelm him
    like a king about to fall;
25 for he has lifted his hand against God
    and pits himself against the Almighty,
26 running at him head lowered,
    with the full weight of his bossed shield.

27 Heavy though his jowl is and gross,
    and though his sides bulge with fat,
28 the city where he lives will lie in ruins,
    his house will be deserted,
    destined to crumble in a heap of rubble.
29 He will be rich no longer, his wealth will not
        endure,
    and he will strike no root in the earth;
30 scorching heat will shrivel his shoots,
    and his blossom will be shaken off by the wind.
31 He deceives himself, trusting in his high rank,
    for all his dealings will come to nothing.
32 His palm trees will wither unseasonably,
    and his branches will not be luxuriant;
33 he will be like a vine that sheds its grapes
        unripened,
    like an olive tree that drops its blossom.

---

b Meaning of Heb uncertain   *c* Traditional rendering of Heb
Shaddai   *d* Vg: Meaning of Heb uncertain   *e* Gk: Heb *mouth*
f Cn: Heb *will depart*

15:29 **root:** *prob. rdg., cp. Lat.; Heb. unintelligible.* **in the earth:**
prob. rdg.; Heb. adds he will not escape from darkness.
15:30 **blossom:** *so Gk; Heb.* mouth.   15:32 **His palm trees:**
prob. rdg., cp. Gk; Heb. omits. **wither:** *so Gk; Heb.* be filled.

9 What do you know that we do not know?
   What intelligence have you which we have not?
10 There are gray-haired old men among us
   more advanced in years than your father.
11 Are the consolations of God not enough for you,
   and speech that deals gently with you?
12 Why do your notions carry you away,
   and why do your eyes blink,
13 So that you turn your anger against God
   and let such words escape your mouth!
14 What is a man that he should be blameless,
   one born of woman that he should be righteous?
15 If in his holy ones God places no confidence,
   and if the heavens are not clean in his sight,
16 How much less so is the abominable, the corrupt:
   man, who drinks in iniquity like water!
17 I will show you, if you listen to me;
   what I have seen I will tell —
18 What wise men relate
   and have not contradicted since the days of
   their fathers,
19 To whom alone the land was given,
   when no foreigner moved among them.
20 The wicked man is in torment all his days,
   and limited years are in store for the tyrant;
21 The sound of terrors is in his ears;
   when all is prosperous, the spoiler comes
   upon him.
22 He despairs of escaping the darkness,
   and looks ever for the sword;
23 A wanderer, food for the vultures,
   he knows that his destruction is imminent.
24 By day the darkness fills him with dread;
   distress and anguish overpower him.
25 Because he has stretched out his hand against God
   and bade defiance to the Almighty,
26 One shall rush sternly upon him
   with the stout bosses of his shield,
   like a king prepared for the charge.
27 Because he has blinded himself with his crassness,
   padding his loins with fat,
28 He shall dwell in ruinous cities,
   in houses that are deserted,
   That are crumbling into clay
29   with no shadow to lengthen over the ground.
   He shall not be rich, and his possessions shall
   not endure;
31   for vain shall be his bartering,
30 A flame shall wither him up in his early growth,
   and with the wind his blossoms shall disappear.
32 His stalk shall wither before its time,
   and his branches shall be green no more.
33 He shall be like a vine that sheds its
   grapes unripened,
   and like an olive tree casting off its bloom.

9 What knowledge do you have that we have not,
   what understanding that is not ours too?
10 One of us is an old, grey-headed man
   loaded with more years than your father!
11 Can you ignore these divine consolations
   and the moderate tone of our words?
12 How passion carries you away!
   And how you roll your eyes,
13 when you vent your anger on God
   and speeches come tripping off your tongue!
14 How can anyone be pure,
   anyone born of woman be upright?
15 God cannot rely even on his holy ones,
   to him, even the heavens seem impure.
16 How much more, this hateful, corrupt thing,
   humanity, which soaks up wickedness like
   water!
17 Listen to me, I have a lesson for you:
   I am going to impart my own experience
18 and the tradition of the sages
   who have remained faithful to their ancestors,
19 to whom alone the land was given —
   no foreigner included among them.
20 The life of the wicked is unceasing torment,
   the years allotted to the tyrant are numbered.
21 A cry of panic echoes in his ear;
   when all is peace, his destroyer swoops down on
   him.
22 No one can be count on escaping from the dark,
   but knows that he is destined for the sword,
23 marked down as meat for the vulture.
   He knows that his ruin is at hand.
24 The hour of darkness terrifies him,
   distress and anguish assail him
   as when a king is poised for the assault.
25 He raised his hand against God,
   boldly he defied Shaddai!
26 Head lowered, he charged him,
   with his massively bossed shield.
27 His face had grown full and fat,
   and his thighs too heavy with flesh.
28 He had occupied the towns he had destroyed,
   with their uninhabited houses
   about to fall into ruins;
29 but no great profit to him, his luck will not hold,
   he will cast his shadow over the country no
   longer,
30   (he will not escape the dark).
   A flame will scorch his young shoots,
   the wind will carry off his blossom.
31 Let him not trust in his great height
   or delusion will be his.
32 His palm trees will wither before their time
   and his branches never again be green.
33 Like the vine, he will shake off his unripe fruit,
   like the olive tree, shed his blossom.

NEW REVISED STANDARD VERSION

34 For the company of the godless is barren,
   and fire consumes the tents of bribery.
35 They conceive mischief and bring forth evil
   and their heart prepares deceit."

16 Then Job answered:
2 "I have heard many such things;
   miserable comforters are you all.
3 Have windy words no limit?
   Or what provokes you that you keep on
      talking?
4 I also could talk as you do,
   if you were in my place;
   I could join words together against you,
   and shake my head at you.
5 I could encourage you with my mouth,
   and the solace of my lips would assuage your
      pain.

6 "If I speak, my pain is not assuaged,
   and if I forbear, how much of it leaves me?
7 Surely now God has worn me out;
   he has^g made desolate all my company.
8 And he has^g shriveled me up,
   which is a witness against me;
   my leanness has risen up against me,
   and it testifies to my face.
9 He has torn me in his wrath, and hated me;
   he has gnashed his teeth at me;
   my adversary sharpens his eyes against me.
10 They have gaped at me with their mouths;
   they have struck me insolently on the cheek;
   they mass themselves together against me.
11 God gives me up to the ungodly,
   and casts me into the hands of the wicked.
12 I was at ease, and he broke me in two;
   he seized me by the neck and dashed me to
      pieces;
   he set me up as his target;
13 his archers surround me.
   He slashes open my kidneys, and shows no
      mercy;
   he pours out my gall on the ground.
14 He bursts upon me again and again;
   he rushes at me like a warrior.
15 I have sewed sackcloth upon my skin,
   and have laid my strength in the dust.
16 My face is red with weeping,
   and deep darkness is on my eyelids,
17 though there is no violence in my hands,
   and my prayer is pure.

18 "O earth, do not cover my blood;
   let my outcry find no resting place.
19 Even now, in fact, my witness is in heaven,
   and he that vouches for me is on high.
20 My friends scorn me;
   my eye pours out tears to God,
21 that he would maintain the right of a mortal with
      God,
   as^h one does for a neighbor.
22 For when a few years have come,
   I shall go the way from which I shall not
      return.

17 My spirit is broken, my days are extinct,
   the grave is ready for me.

REVISED ENGLISH BIBLE

34 For the godless, one and all, are barren,
   and their homes, enriched through bribery, are
      destroyed by fire;
35 they conceive mischief and give birth to trouble,
   and the child of their womb is deceit.

16 Job answered:
2 I have heard such things so often before!
   You are trouble-makers one and all!
3 You say, 'Will this windbag never have done?'
   or 'What makes him so stubborn in argument?'
4 If you and I were to change places, I could talk as
      you do;
   how I could harangue you and wag my head at
      you!
5 But no, I would speak words of encouragement,
   and my condolences would be unrestrained.
6 If I speak, my pain is not eased;
   if I am silent, it does not leave me.
7 Meanwhile, my friend wearies me with his
      gloating;
   he and his fellows seize me.
8 He has come forward to give evidence against me;
   the liar testifies against me to my face,
9 in his wrath he tears me and assaults me angrily;
   he gnashes at me with his teeth.

   My enemies look daggers at me,
10 they bare their teeth at me,
   they strike me on the cheek and taunt me;
   they are all in league against me.
11 God has left me at the mercy of malefactors,
   he has cast me into the power of the wicked.
12 I was at ease, but he savaged me,
   seized me by the neck, and worried me.
   He set me up as his target;
13 his arrows rained on me from every side;
   pitiless, he pierced deep into my vitals,
   he spilt my gall on the ground.
14 He made breach after breach in my defences;
   like a warrior he rushed on me.

15 I stitched sackcloth together to cover my body
   and laid my forehead in the dust;
16 my cheeks were inflamed with weeping
   and dark shadows were round my eyes.
17 Yet my hands were free from violence
   and my prayer was sincere.

18 Let not the earth cover my blood,
   and let my cry for justice find no rest!
19 For now my witness is in heaven;
   there is One on high ready to answer for me.
20 My appeal will come before God,
   while my eyes turn anxiously to him.
21 If only there were one to arbitrate between man
      and God,
   as between a man and his neighbour!
22 For there are but few years to come
   before I take the road from which there is no
      return.

17 My mind is distraught, my days are numbered,
   and the grave awaits me.

16:5 **unrestrained:** *so Gk; Heb.* restrained.   16:7 **his fellows:**
prob. rdg; Heb. my fellows.   16:8 **the liar:** *so Lat.; Heb.* my
falsehood.   16:20 **My . . . come:** *so Gk; Heb.* My friends are my
scorners.

^{g} Heb *you have* ^{h} Syr Vg Tg: Heb *and*

NEW AMERICAN BIBLE

NEW JERUSALEM BIBLE

34 For the breed of the impious shall be sterile,
and fire shall consume the tents of extortioners.
35 They conceive malice and bring forth emptiness;
they give birth to failure.

16
Then Job answered and said:

2 I have heard this sort of thing many times.
Wearisome comforters are you all!
3 Is there no end to windy words?
Or what sickness have you that you speak on?
4 I also could talk as you do,
were you in my place.
I could declaim over you,
or wag my head at you;
5 I could strengthen you with talk,
or shake my head with silent lips.
6 If I speak, this pain I have will not be checked;
if I leave off, it will not depart from me.
7 But now that I am exhausted and stunned,
all my company has closed in on me.
8 As a witness there rises up
my traducer, speaking openly against me;
9 I am the prey his wrath assails,
he gnashes his teeth against me.
My enemies lord it over me;
10 their mouths are agape to bite me.
They smite me on the cheek insultingly;
they are all enlisted against me.
11 God has given me over to the impious;
into the clutches of the wicked he has cast me.
12 I was in peace, but he dislodged me;
he seized me by the neck and dashed me
to pieces.
He has set me up for a target;
13 his arrows strike me from all directions,
He pierces my sides without mercy,
he pours out my gall upon the ground.
14 He pierces me with thrust upon thrust;
he attacks me like a warrior.
15 I have fastened sackcloth over my skin,
and have laid my brow in the dust.
16 My face is inflamed with weeping
and there is darkness over my eyes,
17 Although my hands are free from violence,
and my prayer is sincere.
18 O earth, cover not my blood,
nor let my outcry come to rest!
19 Even now, behold, my witness is in heaven,
and my spokesman is on high.
20 My friends it is who wrong me;
before God my eyes drop tears,
21 That he may do justice for a mortal in his presence
and decide between a man and his neighbor.
22 For my years are numbered now,
and I am on a journey from which I shall
not return.

17
My spirit is broken, my lamp of life
extinguished;
my burial is at hand.

34 Yes, sterile is the spawn of the sinner,
and fire consumes the tents of the venal.
35 Whoever conceives malice, breeds disaster,
bears as offspring only a false hope.

16
Job spoke next. He said:

2 How often have I heard all this before!
What sorry comforters you are!
3 'When will these windy arguments be over?'
or again, 'What sickness drives you to defend
yourself?'
4 Oh yes! I too could talk as you do,
if you were in my place;
I could overwhelm you with speeches,
shaking my head over you,
5 and speak words of encouragement,
and then have no more to say.
6 When I speak, my suffering does not stop;
if I say nothing, is it in any way reduced?
7 And now it is driving me to distraction;
you have struck my whole acquaintanceship with
horror,
8 now it rounds on me, my slanderer has now turned
witness,
he appears against me, accusing me face to face;
9 his anger tears and hounds me
with gnashing teeth.
My enemies look daggers at me,
10 and open gaping jaws.
Their sneers strike like slaps in the face;
and they all set on me at once.
11 Yes, God has handed me over to the godless,
and cast me into the hands of the wicked.
12 I was living at peace, until he made me totter,
taking me by the neck to shatter me.
He has set me up as his target:
13 he shoots his arrows at me from all sides,
pitilessly pierces my loins,
and pours my gall out on the ground.
14 Breach after breach he drives through me,
charging on me like a warrior.
15 I have sewn sackcloth over my skin,
thrown my forehead in the dust.
16 My face is red with tears,
and shadow dark as death covers my eyelids.
17 Nonetheless, my hands are free of violence,
and my prayer is pure.
18 Cover not my blood, O earth,
and let my cry mount without cease!
19 Henceforth I have a witness in heaven,
my defender is there on high.
20 Interpreter of my thoughts there with God,
before whom flow my tears,
21 let my anguish plead the cause of a man at grips
with God,
just as a man might defend his fellow.
22 For the years of my life are numbered,
and I am leaving by the road of no return.

17
My breathing is growing weaker
and the gravediggers are gathering for me.

2 Surely there are mockers around me,
   and my eye dwells on their provocation.

3 "Lay down a pledge for me with yourself;
   who is there that will give surety for me?
4 Since you have closed their minds to
     understanding,
   therefore you will not let them triumph.
5 Those who denounce friends for reward —
   the eyes of their children will fail.

6 "He has made me a byword of the peoples,
   and I am one before whom people spit.
7 My eye has grown dim from grief,
   and all my members are like a shadow.
8 The upright are appalled at this,
   and the innocent stir themselves up against the
     godless.
9 Yet the righteous hold to their way,
   and they that have clean hands grow stronger
     and stronger.
10 But you, come back now, all of you,
   and I shall not find a sensible person among
     you.
11 My days are past, my plans are broken off,
   the desires of my heart.
12 They make night into day;
   'The light,' they say, 'is near to the darkness.'*i*
13 If I look for Sheol as my house,
   if I spread my couch in darkness,
14 if I say to the Pit, 'You are my father,'
   and to the worm, 'My mother,' or 'My sister,'
15 where then is my hope?
   Who will see my hope?
16 Will it go down to the bars of Sheol?
   Shall we descend together into the dust?"

18
Then Bildad the Shuhite answered:
2 "How long will you hunt for words?
   Consider, and then we shall speak.
3 Why are we counted as cattle?
   Why are we stupid in your sight?
4 You who tear yourself in your anger —
   shall the earth be forsaken because of you,
   or the rock be removed out of its place?

5 "Surely the light of the wicked is put out,
   and the flame of their fire does not shine.
6 The light is dark in their tent,
   and the lamp above them is put out.
7 Their strong steps are shortened,
   and their own schemes throw them down.
8 For they are thrust into a net by their own feet,
   and they walk into a pitfall.
9 A trap seizes them by the heel;
   a snare lays hold of them.
10 A rope is hid for them in the ground,
   a trap for them in the path.
11 Terrors frighten them on every side,
   and chase them at their heels.
12 Their strength is consumed by hunger,*j*
   and calamity is ready for their stumbling.
13 By disease their skin is consumed,*k*
   the firstborn of Death consumes their limbs.
14 They are torn from the tent in which they trusted,
   and are brought to the king of terrors.

2 Wherever I turn, I am taunted,
   and my eye meets nothing but sneers.
3 Be my surety with yourself,
   for who else will pledge himself for me?
4 You will not let those triumph
   whose minds you have sunk in ignorance;
5 if such a one denounces his friends to their ruin,
   his sons' eyes will fail.

6 I am held up as a byword in every land,
   a marvel for all to see;
7 my eyes are dimmed by grief,
   my limbs wasted to a shadow.
8 The upright are bewildered at this,
   and at my downfall the innocent are indignant.

9 In spite of all, one who is righteous maintains his
     course;
   he goes from strength to strength whose hands are
     clean.
10 But come on, one and all, try again!
   I shall not find one who is wise among you.
11 My days die away like an echo;
   my heart-strings are snapped.
12 Night is turned into day,
   and morning light is darkened before me.
13 If I measure Sheol for my house,
   if I spread my couch in the darkness,
14 if I call the grave my father
   and the worm my mother or my sister,
15 where, then, will my hope be,
   and who will take account of my piety?
16 I cannot take them with me down to Sheol,
   nor shall we descend together to the dust.

18
Then Bildad the Shuhite answered:

2 How soon will you bridle your tongue?
   Show some sense, and then we can talk.
3 What do you mean by treating us as no more than
     cattle?
   Are we nothing but brute beasts to you?
4 Is the earth to be deserted to prove you right,
   or the rocks to be moved from their place?

5 No, it is the evildoer whose light is extinguished,
   from whose fire no flame will rekindle;
6 the light in his tent fades,
   his lamp beside him dies down.
7 His vigorous stride is shortened,
   and he is tripped by his own policy;
8 he rushes headlong into a net
   and his feet are entangled in its meshes;
9 his heel is caught in a snare,
   the thong grips him tightly;
10 a noose lies hidden for him in the ground
   and a trap in his path.
11 Terror of death suddenly besets him
   so that he cannot hold back his urine.
12 For all his vigour he is paralysed with fear;
   strong as he is, disaster awaits him.
13 Disease eats away his skin,
   death's firstborn devours his limbs.
14 He is plucked from the safety of his home,
   and death's terrors escort him to their king.

17:12 **morning:** *prob. rdg; Heb.* near.   17:13 **Sheol:** *or the*
underworld.   17:16 **with . . . Sheol:** *so Gk; Heb.* obscure.
18:2 **bridle:** *prob. rdg; Heb.* unintelligible.   18:3 **Are we . . . to
you?:** *prob. rdg; Heb. adds* (4)rending himself in his anger.

---

*i*Meaning of Heb uncertain   *j*Or *Disaster is hungry for them*
*k*Cn: Heb *It consumes the limbs of his skin*

2 I am indeed mocked,
   and, as their provocation mounts, my eyes
      grow dim.
3 Grant me one to offer you a pledge on my behalf:
   who is there that will give surety for me?
4 You darken their minds to knowledge;
   therefore they do not understand.
5 My lot is described as evil,
6   and I am made a byword of the people;
   their object lesson I have become.
7 My eye has grown blind with anguish,
   and all my frame is shrunken to a shadow.
8 Upright men are astonished at this,
   and the innocent aroused against the wicked.
9 Yet the righteous shall hold to his way,
   and he who has clean hands increase in strength.
10 But turn now, and come on again;
   for I shall not find a wise man among you!
11 My days are passed away, my plans are at an end,
   the cherished purposes of my heart.
12 Such men change the night into day;
   where there is darkness they talk of
      approaching light.
13 If I look for the nether world as my dwelling,
   if I spread my couch in the darkness,
14 If I must call corruption "my father,"
   and the maggot "my mother" and "my sister,"
15 Where then is my hope,
   and my prosperity, who shall see?
16 Will they descend with me into the nether world?
   Shall we go down together into the dust?

18   Then Bildad the Shuhite replied and said:

2 When will you put an end to words?
   Reflect, and then we can have discussion.
3 Why are we accounted like the beasts,
   their equals in your sight?
4 You who tear yourself in your anger,
   shall the earth be neglected on your account
   [or the rock be moved out of its place]?
5 Truly, the light of the wicked is extinguished;
   no flame brightens his hearth.
6 The light is darkened in his tent;
   in spite of him, his lamp goes out.
7 His vigorous steps are hemmed in,
   and his own counsel casts him down.
8 For he rushes headlong into a net,
   and he wanders into a pitfall.
9 A trap seizes him by the heel,
   and a snare lays hold of him.
10 A noose for him is hid on the ground,
   and the toils for him on the way.
11 On every side terrors affright him;
   they harry him at each step.
12 Disaster is ready at his side,
13   the first-born of death consumes his limbs.
14 Fiery destruction lodges in his tent,
   and marches him off to the king of terrors.

2 Scoffers are my only companions,
   their harshness haunts my nights.
3 So you must go bail for me to yourself,
   for which of them cares to clap his hand on
      mine?
4 For you have shut their hearts to reason,
   hence not a hand is lifted.
5 Just so is a man who invites his friends to share
   his property
   while the eyes of his own children languish.
6 I have become a byword among foreigners,
   and a creature on whose face to spit,
7 since I am nearly blind with grief
   and my limbs are reduced to a shadow.
8 Any honest person is appalled at the sight,
   the innocent is indignant at the sinner.
9 Anyone upright grows stronger step by step:
   and anyone whose hands are clean grows ever in
      vigour!
10 Come on then, all of you, back to the attack!
   I shall not find one wise man among you!
11 My days are over, so are my plans,
   my heart-strings are broken;
12 yet they would have me believe that night is day,
   that light to dispel the darkness is at hand,
13 when all I want, in fact, is to dwell in Sheol
   and in that darkness there to make my bed!
14 To the tomb, I cry, 'You are my father!' —
   to the worm, 'You are my mother — you, my
      sister!'
15 Where then is my hope?
   Who can see any happiness for me?
16 unless they come down to Sheol with me,
   all of us sinking into the dust together?

18   Bildad of Shuah spoke next. He said:

2 What prevents you others from saying something?
   Think — for it is our turn to speak!
3 Why do you regard us as animals,
   considering us no more than brutes?
4 Tear yourself to pieces if you will,
   but the world, for all your rage, will not turn to
      desert,
   the rocks will not shift from their places.
5 The light of the wicked must certainly be put out,
   the lamp that gives him light cease to shine.
6 In his tent the light is dimmed,
   the lamp that shone on him is snuffed.
7 His vigorous stride loses its power,
   his own designs falter.
8 For into the net his own feet carry him,
   he walks into the snares.
9 A spring grips him by the heel,
   a trap snaps shut, and he is caught.
10 Hidden in the ground is a snare to catch him,
   pitfalls lie across his path.
11 Terrors threaten him from all sides
   following him step by step.
12 Hunger becomes his companion,
   by his side Disaster stands.
13 Disease devours his skin,
   Death's First-Born gnaws his limbs.
14 He will be torn from the shelter of his tent,
   and you will drag him to the King of Terrors. *g*

g **18** Figures of oriental mythology.

NEW REVISED STANDARD VERSION	REVISED ENGLISH BIBLE

15 In their tents nothing remains;
      sulfur is scattered upon their habitations.
16 Their roots dry up beneath,
      and their branches wither above.
17 Their memory perishes from the earth,
      and they have no name in the street.
18 They are thrust from light into darkness,
      and driven out of the world.
19 They have no offspring or descendant among
      their people,
      and no survivor where they used to live.
20 They of the west are appalled at their fate,
      and horror seizes those of the east.
21 Surely such are the dwellings of the ungodly,
      such is the place of those who do not know
      God."

19 Then Job answered:
2 "How long will you torment me,
      and break me in pieces with words?
3 These ten times you have cast reproach upon me;
      are you not ashamed to wrong me?
4 And even if it is true that I have erred,
      my error remains with me.
5 If indeed you magnify yourselves against me,
      and make my humiliation an argument against
      me,
6 know then that God has put me in the wrong,
      and closed his net around me.
7 Even when I cry out, 'Violence!' I am not
      answered;
      I call aloud, but there is no justice.
8 He has walled up my way so that I cannot pass,
      and he has set darkness upon my paths.
9 He has stripped my glory from me,
      and taken the crown from my head.
10 He breaks me down on every side, and I am
      gone,
      he has uprooted my hope like a tree.
11 He has kindled his wrath against me,
      and counts me as his adversary.
12 His troops come on together;
      they have thrown up siegeworks^l against me,
      and encamp around my tent.

13 "He has put my family far from me,
      and my acquaintances are wholly estranged
      from me.
14 My relatives and my close friends have failed me;
15   the guests in my house have forgotten me;
      my serving girls count me as a stranger;
      I have become an alien in their eyes.
16 I call to my servant, but he gives me no answer;
      I must myself plead with him.
17 My breath is repulsive to my wife;
      I am loathsome to my own family.
18 Even young children despise me;
      when I rise, they talk against me.
19 All my intimate friends abhor me,
      and those whom I loved have turned against
      me.
20 My bones cling to my skin and to my flesh,
      and I have escaped by the skin of my teeth.
21 Have pity on me, have pity on me, O you my
      friends,
      for the hand of God has touched me!
22 Why do you, like God, pursue me,
      never satisfied with my flesh?

15 Fire settles on his tent,
      and brimstone is strewn over his dwelling.
16 His roots beneath dry up,
      and above, his branches wither.
17 All memory of him vanishes from the earth
      and he leaves no name in the inhabited world.
18 He is thrust out from light into darkness
      and banished from the land of the living.
19 He leaves no issue or offspring among his people,
      no survivor where once he lived.
20 In the west people are appalled at his end;
      in the east they shudder with horror.
21 Such is the fate of the dwellings of evildoers,
      of the homes of those who care nothing for God.

19 Job answered:
2 How long will you grieve me
      and crush me with words?
3 You have insulted me now a dozen times
      and shamelessly wronged me.
4 If in fact I had erred,
      the error would still be mine alone.
5 Will you indeed claim to excel me
      and put forward my disgrace as an argument
      against me?
6 I tell you, God himself has put me in the wrong
      and drawn his net about me.
7 If I shout 'Violence!' no one answers;
      if I appeal for help, I get no justice.
8 He has blocked my path so that I cannot go
      forward,
      he has planted a hedge across my way.
9 He has stripped me of all honour
      and taken the crown from my head.
10 On every side he beats me down till I am gone;
      he has uprooted my hope like a tree.
11 His anger is hot against me
      and he regards me as his enemy.
12 His raiders gather in force,
      raising their siege-ramps against me
      and encamping about my tent.

13 My kinsfolk hold aloof,
      my acquaintances are wholly estranged from me;
14-15 my relatives and friends fall away.
      My retainers have forgotten me;
      my slave-girls treat me as a stranger;
      I have become an alien in their eyes.
16 I summon my slave, but he does not answer,
      though I ask him directly as a favour.
17 My breath is offensive to my wife,
      and I stink in the nostrils of my own family.
18 The very children despise me
      and, when I rise, turn their backs on me.
19 All my close companions abhor me,
      and those whom I love have turned against me.
20 My bones stand out under my skin,
      and I gnaw my under-lip with my teeth.
21 Pity me, have pity on me, you that are my friends,
      for the hand of God has touched me.
22 Must you pursue me as God pursues me?
      Have you not had your teeth in me long enough?

---

^{l}Cn: Heb *their way*

18:15 **Fire:** *prob. rdg; Heb. obscure.*   19:3 **wronged me:** *so some MSS; others* are astonished at me.

NEW AMERICAN BIBLE

He is plucked from the security of his tent;
15 over his abode brimstone is scattered.
16 Below, his roots dry up,
and above, his branches wither.
17 His memory perishes from the land,
and he has no name on the earth.
18 He is driven from light into darkness,
and banished out of the world.
19 He has neither son nor grandson among his people,
nor any survivor where once he dwelt.
20 They who come after shall be appalled at his fate;
they who went before are struck with horror.
21 So is it then with the dwelling of the impious man,
and such is the place of him who knows
not God!

19 Then Job answered and said:

2 How long will you vex my soul,
grind me down with words?
3 These ten times you have reviled me,
have assailed me without shame!
4 Be it indeed that I am at fault
and that my fault remains with me.
5 Even so, if you would vaunt yourselves against me
and cast up to me my reproach,
6 Know then that God has dealt unfairly with me,
and compassed me round with his net.
7 If I cry out "Injustice!" I am not heard.
I cry for help, but there is no redress.
8 He has barred my way and I cannot pass;
he has veiled my path in darkness;
9 He has stripped me of my glory,
and taken the diadem from my brow.
10 He breaks me down on every side, and I am gone;
my hope he has uprooted like a tree.
11 His wrath he has kindled against me;
he counts me among his enemies.
12 His troops advance as one man;
they build up their road to attack me,
and they encamp around my tent.
13 My brethren have withdrawn from me,
and my friends are wholly estranged.
14 My kinsfolk and companions neglect me,
and my guests have forgotten me.
15 Even my handmaids treat me as a stranger;
I am an alien in their sight.
16 I call my servant, but he gives no answer,
though in my speech I plead with him.
17 My breath is abhorred by my wife;
I am loathsome to the men of my family.
18 The young children, too, despise me;
when I appear, they speak against me.
19 All my intimate friends hold me in horror;
those whom I loved have turned against me!
20 My bones cleave to my skin,
and I have escaped with my flesh between
my teeth.
21 Pity me, pity me, O you my friends,
for the hand of God has struck me!
22 Why do you hound me as though you were divine,
and insatiably prey upon me?

NEW JERUSALEM BIBLE

15 You can live in the tent, since it is no longer his,
and brimstone will be scattered on his sheepfold.
16 Below, his roots dry out
and his branches are blasted above.
17 His memory fades from the land,
his name is forgotten in the countryside.
18 Driven from the light into the darkness,
he is banished from the world,
19 without issue or posterity among his own people
or a single survivor where he used to live.
20 His end appals the west
and fills the east with terror.
21 Such indeed is the fate of the places where
wickedness dwells —
the home of everyone who knows not God.

19 Job spoke next. He said:

2 How much longer are you going to torment me
and crush me by your speeches?
3 You have insulted me ten times already:
have you no shame at maltreating me?
4 Even if I had gone astray,
my error would still be my own affair.
5 But, whereas you take this superior attitude
and claim that my disgrace is my own fault,
6 I tell you that God has wronged me
and enveloped me in his net.
7 If I protest against such violence, I am not heard,
if I appeal against it, judgement is never given.
8 He has built an impassable wall across my path
and covered my way with darkness.
9 He has deprived me of my glory
and taken the crown from my head.
10 He assails me from all directions to make me
vanish;
he uproots my hope as he might a tree.
11 Inflamed with anger against me,
he regards me as his foe.
12 His troops have come in force,
directing their line of advance towards me,
they are now encamped round my tent.
13 He has alienated my brothers from me,
my relatives take care to avoid me,
14 my intimate friends have gone away
and the guests in my house have forgotten me.
15 My slave-girls regard me as an intruder,
a stranger as far as they are concerned.
16 My servant does not answer when I call him,
I am obliged to beg favours from him!
17 My breath is unbearable to my wife,
my stench to my own brothers.
18 Even the children look down on me,
whenever I stand up, they start jeering at me.
19 All my dearest friends recoil from me in horror:
those I loved best have turned against me.
20 My flesh is rotting under my skin,
my bones are sticking out like teeth.
21 Pity me, pity me, my friends,
since I have been struck by the hand of God.
22 Must you persecute me just as God does,
and give my body no peace?

NEW REVISED STANDARD VERSION	REVISED ENGLISH BIBLE

NEW REVISED STANDARD VERSION

23 "O that my words were written down!
O that they were inscribed in a book!
24 O that with an iron pen and with lead
they were engraved on a rock forever!
25 For I know that my Redeemer[m] lives,
and that at the last he[n] will stand upon the
earth;[o]
26 and after my skin has been thus destroyed,
then in[p] my flesh I shall see God,[q]
27 whom I shall see on my side,[r]
and my eyes shall behold, and not another.
My heart faints within me!
28 If you say, 'How we will persecute him!'
and, 'The root of the matter is found in him';
29 be afraid of the sword,
for wrath brings the punishment of the sword,
so that you may know there is a judgment."

20 Then Zophar the Naamathite answered:
2 "Pay attention! My thoughts urge me to
answer,
because of the agitation within me.
3 I hear censure that insults me,
and a spirit beyond my understanding answers
me.
4 Do you not know this from of old,
ever since mortals were placed on earth,
5 that the exulting of the wicked is short,
and the joy of the godless is but for a moment?
6 Even though they mount up high as the heavens,
and their head reaches to the clouds,
7 they will perish forever like their own dung;
those who have seen them will say, 'Where are
they?'
8 They will fly away like a dream, and not be
found;
they will be chased away like a vision of the
night.
9 The eye that saw them will see them no more,
nor will their place behold them any longer.
10 Their children will seek the favor of the poor,
and their hands will give back their wealth.
11 Their bodies, once full of youth,
will lie down in the dust with them.
12 "Though wickedness is sweet in their mouth,
though they hide it under their tongues,
13 though they are loath to let it go,
and hold it in their mouths,
14 yet their food is turned in their stomachs;
it is the venom of asps within them.
15 They swallow down riches and vomit them up
again;
God casts them out of their bellies.
16 They will suck the poison of asps;
the tongue of a viper will kill them.
17 They will not look on the rivers,
the streams flowing with honey and curds.
18 They will give back the fruit of their toil,
and will not swallow it down;
from the profit of their trading
they will get no enjoyment.
19 For they have crushed and abandoned the poor,
they have seized a house that they did not
build.

REVISED ENGLISH BIBLE

23 Would that my words might be written down,
that they might be engraved in an inscription,
24 incised with an iron tool and filled with lead,
carved in rock as a witness!
25 But I know that my vindicator lives
and that he will rise last to speak in court;
26 I shall discern my witness standing at my side
and see my defending counsel, even God himself,
27 whom I shall see with my own eyes,
I myself and no other.

My heart sank within me 28 when you said,
'What a series of misfortunes befalls him,
and the root of the trouble lies in himself!'
29 Beware of the sword that points at you,
the sword that sweeps away all iniquity;
then you will know that there is a judge.

20 Then Zophar the Naamathite answered:
2 My distress of mind forces me to reply,
and this is why I hasten to speak.
3 I have heard arguments that are an outrage to me,
but a spirit beyond my understanding gives me the
answers.
4 Surely you know that since time began,
since mortals were first set on the earth, this has
been true:
5 the triumph of a wicked person is short-lived,
the glee of one who is godless lasts but a moment!
6 Though in his pride he stands high as the heavens,
and his head touches the clouds,
7 he will be swept utterly away like his own dung,
and those used to seeing him will say, 'Where is
he?'
8 He will fly away like a dream and be found no
more,
gone like a vision of the night;
9 eyes which glimpsed him will do so no more
and never again will they see him in his place.
11 The youthful vigour which filled his bones
will lie with him in the earth.
10 His sons will curry favour with the poor;
his children will give back his wealth.
12 Though evil tastes sweet in his mouth,
and he savours it, rolling it round his tongue,
13 though he lingers over it and will not let it go,
and holds it back on his palate,
14 yet his food turns in his stomach,
changing to asps' venom within him.
15 He gulps down wealth, then spews it up;
God makes him vomit it from his stomach.
16 He sucks the poison of asps,
and the tongue of the viper kills him.
17 Not for him to swill down rivers of cream
or torrents of honey and curds;
18 he must give back his gains unswallowed,
and spew out his profit undigested;
19 for he has oppressed and harassed the poor,
he has seized houses which he did not build.

---

m Or Vindicator   n Or that he the Last   o Heb dust
p Or without   q Meaning of Heb of this verse uncertain   r Or for
myself

19:24 **as a witness:** or for ever.   19:26 **my witness . . . side:**
prob. rdg; Heb. unintelligible.   19:28 **himself:** so many MSS;
others me.   19:29 **judge:** or judgement.   20:2 **this is why:**
prob. rdg; Heb. obscure.   20:10–11 Verses 10 and 11 transposed.
20:10 **children:** prob. rdg; Heb. hands.   20:17 **rivers of cream:**
prob. rdg; Heb. obscure.

23 Oh, would that my words were written down!
    Would that they were inscribed in a record:
24 That with an iron chisel and with lead
    they were cut in the rock forever!
25 But as for me, I know that my Vindicator lives,
    and that he will at last stand forth upon the dust;
27 Whom I myself shall see:
    my own eyes, not another's, shall behold him,
26 And from my flesh I shall see God;
    my inmost being is consumed with longing.
28 But you who say, "How shall we persecute him,
    seeing that the root of the matter is found
        in him?"
29 Be afraid of the sword for yourselves,
    for these crimes deserve the sword;
    that you may know that there is a judgment.

20 Then Zophar the Naamathite spoke and said:

3 A rebuke which puts me to shame I hear,
2   and because of this I am disturbed.
  So now my thoughts provide me with an answer,
    and from my understanding a spirit gives me
      a reply.
4 Do you not know this from olden time,
    since man was placed upon the earth,
5 That the triumph of the wicked is short
    and the joy of the impious but for a moment?
6 Though his pride mount up to the heavens
    and his head reach to the clouds,
7 Yet he perishes forever like the fuel of his fire,
    and the onlookers say, "Where is he?"
8 Like a dream he takes flight and is not
      found again;
    he fades away like a vision of the night.
9 The eye which saw him does so no more;
    nor shall his dwelling again behold him.

‡20.10: see below‡

11 Though his frame is full of youthful vigor,
    this shall lie with him in the dust.
12 Though wickedness is sweet in his mouth,
    and he hides it under his tongue,
13 Though he retains it and will not let it go
    but keeps it still within his mouth,
14 Yet in his stomach the food shall turn;
    it shall be venom of asps inside him.
15 The riches he swallowed he shall disgorge;
    God shall compel his belly to disown them.
16 The poison of asps he shall drink in;
    the viper's fangs shall slay him.
17 He shall see no streams of oil,
    no torrents of honey or milk.
18 Restoring his gains, he shall not enjoy them;
    though his wealth increases, he shall not rejoice.
19 Because he has oppressed the poor,
    and stolen a patrimony he had not built up,

23 Will no one let my words be recorded,
    inscribed on some monument
24 with iron chisel and engraving tool,
    cut into the rock for ever?
25 I know that I have a living Defender[h]
    and that he will rise up last, on the dust of the
      earth.
26 After my awakening, he will set me close to him,
    and from my flesh I shall look on God.
27 He whom I shall see will take my part:
    my eyes will be gazing on no stranger.
    My heart sinks within me.
28 When you say, 'How can we confound him?
    What pretext can we discover against him?'
29 You yourselves had best beware the sword,
    since the wrath bursts into flame at wicked deeds
    and then you will learn that there is indeed a
      judgement!

20 Zophar of Naamath spoke next. He said:

2 My thoughts urge me to reply to this,
    and hence the impatience that grips me.
3 I have put up with prating that outrages me
    and now my mind inspires me with an answer.
4 Do you not know, that since time began
    and human beings were set on the earth,
5 the triumph of the wicked has always been brief,
    and the sinner's gladness has never lasted long?
6 Towering to the sky he may have been,
    his head touching the clouds,
7 but he vanishes, like a phantom, once for all,
    while those who used to see him, ask, 'Where is
      he?'
8 Like a dream that leaves no trace he takes his
      flight,
    like a vision in the night he flies away.
9 The eye accustomed to see him sees him no more,
    his home will never set eyes on him again.
10 His sons will have to reimburse the poor
    and his children pay back his riches.
11 His bones used to be full of youthful vigour:
    and there it lies, in the dust with him, now!
12 Evil was sweet to his mouth,
    he would shelter it under his tongue;
13 cultivating it carefully,
    he would let it linger on his palate.
14 Such food goes bad in his belly,
    working inside him like the poison of a viper.
15 Now he has to vomit up the wealth that he has
      swallowed,
    God makes him disgorge it.
16 He used to suck vipers' venom,
    and the tongue of the adder kills him.
17 No more will he know the streams of oil
    or the torrents of honey and cream.
18 When he gives back his winnings, his cheerfulness
      will fade,
    and the satisfied air he had when business was
      thriving.
19 Since he once destroyed the huts of the poor,
    plundering houses instead of building them up,

h 19 Technical term for the closest relative, the avenger of blood.
Having no belief in life after death, Job yet bursts the bounds of his
belief and asserts that he will somehow see his vindication by God
himself. 'Rise up' is a technical term for the action of defendant or
judge.

NEW REVISED STANDARD VERSION	REVISED ENGLISH BIBLE

20 "They knew no quiet in their bellies;
   in their greed they let nothing escape.
21 There was nothing left after they had eaten;
   therefore their prosperity will not endure.
22 In full sufficiency they will be in distress;
   all the force of misery will come upon them.
23 To fill their belly to the full
   God*s* will send his fierce anger into them,
   and rain it upon them as their food.*t*
24 They will flee from an iron weapon;
   a bronze arrow will strike them through.
25 It is drawn forth and comes out of their body,
   and the glittering point comes out of their gall;
   terrors come upon them.
26 Utter darkness is laid up for their treasures;
   a fire fanned by no one will devour them;
   what is left in their tent will be consumed.
27 The heavens will reveal their iniquity,
   and the earth will rise up against them.
28 The possessions of their house will be carried away,
   dragged off in the day of God's*u* wrath.
29 This is the portion of the wicked from God,
   the heritage decreed for them by God."

21 Then Job answered:
2   "Listen carefully to my words,
   and let this be your consolation.
3 Bear with me, and I will speak;
   then after I have spoken, mock on.
4 As for me, is my complaint addressed to mortals?
   Why should I not be impatient?
5 Look at me, and be appalled,
   and lay your hand upon your mouth.
6 When I think of it I am dismayed,
   and shuddering seizes my flesh.
7 Why do the wicked live on,
   reach old age, and grow mighty in power?
8 Their children are established in their presence,
   and their offspring before their eyes.
9 Their houses are safe from fear,
   and no rod of God is upon them.
10 Their bull breeds without fail;
   their cow calves and never miscarries.
11 They send out their little ones like a flock,
   and their children dance around.
12 They sing to the tambourine and the lyre,
   and rejoice to the sound of the pipe.
13 They spend their days in prosperity,
   and in peace they go down to Sheol.
14 They say to God, 'Leave us alone!
   We do not desire to know your ways.
15 What is the Almighty,*v* that we should serve him?
   And what profit do we get if we pray to him?'
16 Is not their prosperity indeed their own achievement?*w*
   The plans of the wicked are repugnant to me.
17 "How often is the lamp of the wicked put out?
   How often does calamity come upon them?
   How often does God*s* distribute pains in his anger?
18 How often are they like straw before the wind,
   and like chaff that the storm carries away?

20 Because his appetite gave him no rest,
   he let nothing he craved escape him;
21 because nothing survived his greed,
   therefore his wellbeing does not last.
22 With every need satisfied his troubles begin,
   and the full force of hardship strikes him.
23 Let that fill his belly!
   God vents his anger upon him
   and rains on him cruel blows.
24 He is wounded by an iron weapon
   and pierced by a bronze-tipped arrow;
25 the point comes out at his back,
   the gleaming tip from his gall-bladder.
   Terrors threaten him,
26 darkness unrelieved awaits him;
   a fire that needs no fanning will consume him.
   Woe betide any survivor in his tent!
27 The heavens will lay bare his guilt,
   and earth will rise up to condemn him.
28 A flood will sweep away his house,
   rushing waters on the day of wrath.
29 Such is God's reward for the wicked,
   the God-ordained portion for the rebel.

21 Job answered:
2 Give careful heed to my words,
   and let that be the comfort you offer me.
3 Bear with me while I have my say;
   after I have spoken, you may mock.
4 My complaint is not about mortals,
   so have I not cause to be impatient?
5 Look at my plight, and be aghast;
   clap your hand to your mouth.
6 When I stop to think, I am filled with horror,
   and my whole body shudders.
7 Why do the wicked live on,
   hale in old age, and great and powerful?
8 They see their children settled around them,
   their descendants flourishing,
9 their households secure and safe;
   the rod of God's justice does not reach them.
10 Their bull breeds without fail;
   their cow calves and does not cast her calf.
11 Like flocks they produce babes in droves,
   and their little ones skip and dance;
12 they rejoice with tambourine and lyre
   and make merry to the sound of the flute.
13 They live out their days in prosperity,
   and they go down to Sheol in peace.
14 They say to God, 'Leave us alone;
   we do not want to know your ways!
15 What is the Almighty that we should worship him,
   or what should we gain by entreating his favour?'
16 Is not the prosperity of the wicked in their own hands?
   Are not their purposes very different from God's?
17 How often is the lamp of the wicked snuffed out,
   how often does ruin come upon them?
   How often does God in his anger deal out suffering?
18 How often are they like a wisp of straw before the wind,
   like chaff which the storm whirls away?

20:26 **awaits him:** *so Gk; Heb.* awaits his stored things.
20:29 **the rebel:** *prob. rdg; Heb.* his word.   21:12 **with:** *so some*
s Heb *he*   *t* Cn: Meaning of Heb uncertain   *u* Heb *his*   MSS; *others* as to.   21:13 **Sheol:** *or* the underworld.
v Traditional rendering of Heb *Shaddai*   *w* Heb *in their hand*   21:16 **God's:** *prob. rdg; Heb.* mine.

21 Therefore his prosperity shall not endure,
10 and his hands shall yield up his riches.
20 Though he has known no quiet in his greed,
his treasures shall not save him.
22 When he abounds to overflowing, he shall be
brought into straits,
and nought shall be left of his goods.
23 God shall send against him the fury of his wrath
and rain down his missiles of war upon him.
24 Should he escape the iron weapon,
the bow of bronze shall pierce him through;
25 The dart shall come out of his back;
terrors shall fall upon him.
26 Complete darkness is in store for him;
the fire which shall consume him needs not to
be fanned.
27 The heavens shall reveal his guilt,
and the earth shall rise up against him.
28 The flood shall sweep away his house
with the waters that run off in the day of
God's anger.
29 This is the portion of a wicked man,
and the heritage appointed him by God.

21

Then Job said in reply:

2 At least listen to my words,
and let that be the consolation you offer.
3 Bear with me while I speak;
and after I have spoken, you can mock!
4 Is my complaint toward man?
And why should I not be impatient?
5 Look at me and be astonished,
put your hands over your mouths.
6 When I think of it, I am dismayed,
and horror takes hold on my flesh.

7 Why do the wicked survive,
grow old, become mighty in power?
8 Their progeny is secure in their sight;
they see before them their kinsfolk and
their offspring.
9 Their homes are safe and without fear,
nor is the scourge of God upon them.
10 Their bulls gender without fail;
their cows calve and do not miscarry.
11 These folk have infants numerous as lambs,
and their children dance.
12 They sing to the timbrel and harp,
and make merry to the sound of the flute.
13 They live out their days in prosperity,
and tranquilly go down to the nether world.
14 Yet they say to God, "Depart from us,
for we have no wish to learn your ways!
15 What is the Almighty that we should serve him?
And what gain shall we have if we pray
to him?"
16 If their happiness is not in their own hands
and if the counsel of the wicked is repulsive
to God,
17 How often is the lamp of the wicked put out?
How often does destruction come upon them,
the portion he allots in his anger?
18 Let them be like straw before the wind,
and like chaff which the storm snatches away!

20 since his avarice could never be satisfied,
now all his hoarding will not save him;
21 since nothing could escape his greed,
his prosperity will not last.
22 When he has everything he needs, want will seize
him,
and misery will light on him with all its force.
23 On him God looses all his burning wrath,
hurling against his flesh a hail of arrows.
24 If he escapes the weapons of iron,
the bow of bronze will transfix him.
25 Out of his back sticks an arrow,
from his gall a shining point.
The terrors advance on him,
26 all the hidden darknesses are waiting to carry
him off.
A fire unlit by human hand devours him,
and consumes what is left in his tent.
27 The heavens lay bare his iniquity,
and the earth rises up against him.
28 The income of his house pours away,
like the torrents, on the day of retribution.
29 Such is the fate God reserves for the wicked,
the inheritance he assigns to the accursed!

21

Job spoke next. He said:

2 Listen carefully to my words;
let this be the consolation you allow me.
3 Permit me to speak in my turn;
you may jeer when I have spoken.
4 Is my complaint just about a fellow-mortal?
I have good grounds to be perturbed!
5 Give your attention to me; you will be
dumbfounded
and will place your hand over your mouth.
6 I myself am appalled at the very thought,
and my flesh creeps.
7 Why do the wicked still live on,
their power increasing with their age?
8 They see their posterity assured,
and their offspring secure before their eyes.
9 The peace of their houses has nothing to fear,
the rod that God wields is not for them.
10 No mishap with their bull at breeding-time,
nor miscarriage with their cow at calving.
11 They let their infants frisk like lambs,
their children dance like deer.
12 They sing to the tambourine and harp,
and rejoice to the sound of the pipe.
13 They end their lives in happiness
and go down in peace to Sheol.
14 Yet these are the ones who say to God, 'Go away!
We do not want to learn your ways.
15 What is the point of our serving Shaddai?
What should we gain from praying to him?'
16 Surely they have won their own prosperity,
since God is kept so far from their plans?

17 Do we often see the light of the wicked put out,
or disaster overtake him,
or the retribution of God destroy his possessions,
18 or the wind blow him away like a straw,
or a whirlwind carry him off like chaff?

NEW REVISED STANDARD VERSION

19 You say, 'God stores up their iniquity for their
      children.'
   Let it be paid back to them, so that they may
      know it.
20 Let their own eyes see their destruction,
   and let them drink of the wrath of the
      Almighty.*
21 For what do they care for their household after
      them,
   when the number of their months is cut off?
22 Will any teach God knowledge,
   seeing that he judges those that are on high?
23 One dies in full prosperity,
   being wholly at ease and secure,
24 his loins full of milk
   and the marrow of his bones moist.
25 Another dies in bitterness of soul,
   never having tasted of good.
26 They lie down alike in the dust,
   and the worms cover them.
27 "Oh, I know your thoughts,
   and your schemes to wrong me.
28 For you say, 'Where is the house of the prince?
   Where is the tent in which the wicked lived?'
29 Have you not asked those who travel the roads,
   and do you not accept their testimony,
30 that the wicked are spared in the day of calamity,
   and are rescued in the day of wrath?
31 Who declares their way to their face,
   and who repays them for what they have done?
32 When they are carried to the grave,
   a watch is kept over their tomb.
33 The clods of the valley are sweet to them;
   everyone will follow after,
   and those who went before are innumerable.
34 How then will you comfort me with empty
      nothings?
   There is nothing left of your answers but
      falsehood."

22 Then Eliphaz the Temanite answered:
   2 "Can a mortal be of use to God?
   Can even the wisest be of service to him?
3 Is it any pleasure to the Almighty* if you are
      righteous,
   or is it gain to him if you make your ways
      blameless?
4 Is it for your piety that he reproves you,
   and enters into judgment with you?
5 Is not your wickedness great?
   There is no end to your iniquities.
6 For you have exacted pledges from your family
      for no reason,
   and stripped the naked of their clothing.
7 You have given no water to the weary to drink,
   and you have withheld bread from the hungry.
8 The powerful possess the land,
   and the favored live in it.
9 You have sent widows away empty-handed,
   and the arms of the orphans you have
      crushed.*
10 Therefore snares are around you,
   and sudden terror overwhelms you,
11 or darkness so that you cannot see;
   a flood of water covers you.

REVISED ENGLISH BIBLE

19 You say, 'The trouble a man earns, God reserves
      for his sons';
   no, let him be paid for it in full and be punished.
20 Let his own eyes witness the condemnation come
      on him;
   may the wrath of the Almighty be the cup he
      drinks.
21 What joy will he have in his children after him,
   if his months are numbered?
22 Can any human being teach God,
   when it is he who judges even those in heaven
      above?
23 I tell you this: one man dies crowned with success,
   lapped in security and comfort,
24 his loins full of vigour
   and the marrow juicy in his bones;
25 another dies in bitterness of soul,
   never having tasted prosperity.
26 Side by side they are laid in the earth,
   and worms are the shroud of both.
27 I know well what you are thinking
   and the arguments you are marshalling against me;
28 I know you will ask, 'Where now is the great
      man's house,
   what has become of the dwelling of the wicked?'
29 Have you never questioned travellers?
   Do you not accept the evidence they bring:
30 that a wicked person is spared when disaster comes
   and conveyed to safety before the day of wrath?
31 Who will denounce his conduct to his face?
   Who will requite him for what he has done?
32–33 When he is borne to the grave,
   all the world escorts him, before and behind;
   the dust of earth is sweet to him,
   and thousands keep watch at his tomb.
34 How futile, then, is the comfort you offer me!
   How false your answers ring!

22 THEN Eliphaz the Temanite answered:
2 Can anyone be any benefit to God?
   Can he benefit even from the wise?
3 Is it an advantage to the Almighty if you are
      righteous?
   What gain to him if your conduct is perfect?
4 Does he arraign you for your piety —
   is it on this count he brings you to trial?
5 No: it is because your wickedness is so great,
   and your depravity passes all bounds.
6 Without cause you exact pledges from your
      brothers,
   leaving them stripped of their clothes and naked.
7 To the weary you give no water to drink
   and you withhold bread from the starving.
8 Is the earth, then, the preserve of the strong,
   a domain for the favoured few?
9 You have sent widows away empty-handed,
   the fatherless you have left without support.
10 No wonder there are pitfalls in your path,
   scares to fill you with sudden terror!
11 No wonder light is turned to darkness, so that you
      cannot see,
   and a deluge of rain envelops you!

* Traditional rendering of Heb *Shaddai*   y Gk Syr Tg Vg: Heb *were
crushed*

21:27 **you are marshalling:** *so Syriac; Heb.* you do violence.
22:11 **light:** *so Gk; Heb.* or.

NEW AMERICAN BIBLE

NEW JERUSALEM BIBLE

19 May God not store up the man's misery for
    his children;
  let him requite the man himself so that he
    feels it,
20 Let his own eyes see the calamity,
  and the wrath of the Almighty let him drink!
21 For what interest has he in his family after him,
  when the number of his months is finished?
      ‡21.22: see below in ch. 22‡

23 One dies in his full vigor,
  wholly at ease and content;
24 His figure is full and nourished,
  and his bones are rich in marrow.
25 Another dies in bitterness of soul,
  having never tasted happiness.
26 Alike they lie down in the dust,
  and worms cover them both.

27 Behold, I know your thoughts,
  and the arguments you rehearse against me.
28 For you say, "Where is the house of the magnate,
  and where the dwelling place of the wicked?"
29 Have you not asked the wayfarers
  and do you not recognize their monuments?
30 Nay, the evil man is spared calamity when
    it comes;
32 and on the day he is carried to the grave
31 Who will charge him with his conduct to his face,
  and for what he has done who will repay him?
33 Sweet to him are the clods of the valley,
  and over him the funeral mound keeps watch,
  While all the line of mankind follows him,
  and the countless others who have gone before.
34 How then can you offer me vain comfort,
  while in your answers perfidy remains?

22 Then Eliphaz the Temanite answered and said:
2 Can a man be profitable to God?
  Though to himself a wise man be profitable!
21, 22 Can anyone teach God knowledge,
  seeing that he judges those on high?
3 Is it of advantage to the Almighty if you are just?
  Or is it a gain to him if you make your
    ways perfect?
4 Is it because of your piety that he reproves you—
  that he enters with you into judgment?
5 Is not your wickedness manifold?
  Are not your iniquities endless?

6 You have unjustly kept your kinsmen's goods
    in pawn,
  left them stripped naked of their clothing.
7 To the thirsty you have given no water to drink,
  and from the hungry you have withheld bread;
8 As if the land belonged to the man of might,
  and only the privileged were to dwell in it.
9 You have sent widows away empty-handed,
  and the resources of orphans you
    have destroyed.
10 Therefore snares are round about you,
  and a sudden terror causes you dismay,
11 Or darkness, in which you cannot see;
  a deluge of waters covers you.

19 So God is storing up punishment for his children?
  But the wicked himself should be punished, and
    should know it!
20 He himself should witness his own ruin,
  and himself drink the anger of Shaddai.
21 Once he is gone, what joy can he gain from his
    family,
  once the number of his months has been cut off?
22 But who can teach wisdom to God,
  to him who is judge of those on high?
23 And again: one person dies in the fullness of
    strength,
  in all possible happiness and ease,
24 thighs padded with fat
  and the marrow in the bones good and moist.
25 Another dies in bitterness of heart,
  never having tasted happiness.
26 They lie together down in the dust
  and the worms soon cover them both.

27 Oh, I know what is in your minds,
  what you so spitefully think about me!
28 'What has become of the great lord's house,' you
    say,
  'where is the tent where the wicked used to
    live?'
29 Have you never questioned people who travel,
  do you not understand the testimony they give:
30 on the day of disaster, the wicked is spared,
  on the day of retribution, he is kept safe?
31 And who is there then to reproach him for his
    deeds
  and to pay him back for the things he has done?
32 He is carried away to the cemetery,
  and a watch is kept at his tomb.
33 The clods of the ravine lie easy on him,
  and the whole population walk behind.
34 So what sense is there in your empty consolation?
  your answers are the left-overs of infidelity!

22 Eliphaz of Teman spoke next. He said:
2 Can a human being contribute anything to God,
  when even someone intelligent can benefit only
    himself?
3 Does Shaddai derive any benefit from your
    uprightness,
  or profit from your blameless conduct?
4 Do you think he is punishing you for your piety
  and bringing you to justice for that?
5 No, for your great wickedness, more likely,
  for your unlimited sins!
6 You have exacted unearned pledges from your
    brothers,
  stripped people naked of their clothes,
7 failed to give water to the thirsty
  and refused bread to the hungry;
8 handed the land over to a strong man,
  for some favoured person to move in,
9 sent widows away empty-handed
  and crushed the arms of orphans.
10 No wonder, then, if snares are all around you,
  and sudden terrors make you afraid;
11 if light has turned to darkness, so that you cannot
    see,
  and you have been submerged in the flood.

21, 22: This verse has been transposed from ch 21.

12 "Is not God high in the heavens?
    See the highest stars, how lofty they are!
13 Therefore you say, 'What does God know?
    Can he judge through the deep darkness?
14 Thick clouds enwrap him, so that he does not
      see,
    and he walks on the dome of heaven.'
15 Will you keep to the old way
    that the wicked have trod?
16 They were snatched away before their time;
    their foundation was washed away by a flood.
17 They said to God, 'Leave us alone,'
    and 'What can the Almighty*z* do to us?'*a*
18 Yet he filled their houses with good things —
    but the plans of the wicked are repugnant to
      me.
19 The righteous see it and are glad;
    the innocent laugh them to scorn,
20 saying, 'Surely our adversaries are cut off,
    and what they left, the fire has consumed.'
21 "Agree with God,*b* and be at peace;
    in this way good will come to you.
22 Receive instruction from his mouth,
    and lay up his words in your heart.
23 If you return to the Almighty,*z* you will be
      restored,
    if you remove unrighteousness from your tents,
24 if you treat gold like dust,
    and gold of Ophir like the stones of the
      torrent-bed,
25 and if the Almighty*z* is your gold
    and your precious silver,
26 then you will delight yourself in the Almighty,*z*
    and lift up your face to God.
27 You will pray to him, and he will hear you,
    and you will pay your vows.
28 You will decide on a matter, and it will be
      established for you,
    and light will shine on your ways.
29 When others are humiliated, you say it is pride;
    for he saves the humble.
30 He will deliver even those who are guilty;
    they will escape because of the cleanness of
      your hands."*c*

23

Then Job answered:
2 "Today also my complaint is bitter;*d*
    his*e* hand is heavy despite my groaning.
3 Oh, that I knew where I might find him,
    that I might come even to his dwelling!
4 I would lay my case before him,
    and fill my mouth with arguments.
5 I would learn what he would answer me,
    and understand what he would say to me.
6 Would he contend with me in the greatness of his
      power?
    No; but he would give heed to me.
7 There an upright person could reason with him,
    and I should be acquitted forever by my judge.

12 Surely God is at the zenith of the heavens
    and looks down on the topmost stars, high as they
      are.
13 Yet you say, 'What can God know?
    Can he see through thick darkness to judge?
14 His eyes cannot pierce the curtain of the clouds
    as he moves to and fro on the vault of heaven.'
15 Consider the course of the wicked,
    the path the miscreants tread;
16 see how they are snatched off before their time,
    their very foundation flowing away like a river.
17 They said to God, 'Leave us alone.
    What can the Almighty do to us?'
18 Yet it was he who filled their houses with good
      things,
    although their purposes and his were very different.
19 The righteous see and exult,
    the innocent make game of them;
20 for their riches are swept away,
    the profusion of their wealth is consumed by fire.
21 Come to terms with God and you will prosper;
    that is the way to mend your fortune.
22 Accept instruction from his lips
    and take his words to heart.
23 If you come back to the Almighty in sincerity,
    if you banish wrongdoing from your home,
24 if you treat your precious metal as dust
    and the gold of Ophir as stones from the stream,
25 then the Almighty himself will be your precious
      metal;
    he will be your silver in double measure.
26 Then, with sure trust in the Almighty,
    you will raise your face to God;
27 you will pray to him, and he will hear you,
    and you will fulfil your vows.
28 In all your decisions you will have success,
    and on your path light will shine;
29 but God brings down the pride of the haughty
    and keeps safe those who are humble.
30 He will deliver the innocent,
    and you will be delivered, because your hands are
      pure.

23

Job answered:
2 Even today my thoughts are embittered,
    for God's hand is heavy on me in my trouble.
3 If only I knew how to reach him,
    how to enter his court,
4 I should state my case before him
    and set out my arguments in full;
5 then I should learn what answer he would give
    and understand what he had to say to me.
6 Would he exert his great power to browbeat me?
    No; God himself would never set his face against
      me.
7 There in his court the upright are vindicated,
    and I should win from my judge an outright
      acquittal.

22:17 **to us:** *so Gk; Heb.* to them.   22:18 **his:** *so Gk; Heb.* mine.
22:20 **riches:** *so Gk; Heb.* word unknown.   22:24 **If . . . dust:**
prob. rdg.; Heb. if you put your precious metal on dust.
22:26 **with . . . in:** *or* delighting in.   22:29 **but . . . haughty:**
prob. rdg.; Heb. obscure.   22:30 **the innocent:** *prob. rdg.; Heb.*
the not innocent.   23:2 **God's:** *so Gk; Heb.* my.

z Traditional rendering of Heb *Shaddai*   *a* Gk Syr: Heb *them*
b Heb *him*   *c* Meaning of Heb uncertain   *d* Syr Vg Tg: Heb
rebellious   *e* Gk Syr: Heb *my*

12 Does not God, in the heights of the heavens,
  behold the stars, high though they are?
13 Yet you say, "What does God know?
  Can he judge through the thick darkness?
14 Clouds hide him so that he cannot see;
  he walks upon the vault of the heavens!"

15 Do you indeed keep to the ancient way
  trodden by worthless men,
16 Who were snatched away before their time;
  whose foundations a flood swept away?
17 These men said to God, "Depart from us!"
  and, "What can the Almighty do to us?"
18 [Yet he had filled their houses with good things!
  But far be from me the mind of the impious!]
19 The just look on and are gladdened,
  and the innocent deride them:
20 "Truly these have been destroyed where
    they stood,
  and such as were left, fire has consumed!"

21 Come to terms with him to be at peace.
  In this shall good come to you:
22 Receive instruction from his mouth,
  and lay up his words in your heart.
23 If you return to the Almighty, you will be restored;
  if you put iniquity far from your tent,
24 And treat raw gold like dust,
  and the fine gold of Ophir as pebbles from
    the brook,
25 Then the Almighty himself shall be your gold
  and your sparkling silver.

26 For then you shall delight in the Almighty
  and you shall lift up your face toward God.
27 You shall entreat him and he will hear you,
  and your vows you shall fulfill.
28 When you make a decision, it shall succeed
    for you,
  and upon your ways the light shall shine.
29 For he brings down the pride of the haughty,
  but the man of humble mien he saves.
30 God delivers him who is innocent;
  you shall be delivered through cleanness
    of hands.

23

Again Job answered and said:

2 Though I know my complaint is bitter,
  his hand is heavy upon me in my groanings.
3 Oh, that today I might find him,
  that I might come to his judgment seat!
4 I would set out my cause before him,
  and fill my mouth with arguments;
5 I would learn the words with which he
    would answer,
  and understand what he would reply to me.
6 Even should he contend against me with his
    great power,
  yet, would that he himself might heed me!
7 There the upright man might reason with him,
  and I should once and for all preserve my rights.

12 Does not God live high in the heavens,
  does he not see the zenith of the stars?
13 And because he is up there, you have said, 'What
    does God know?
  Can he judge through the dark cloud?
14 The clouds, to him, are an impenetrable veil,
  as he goes his way on the rim of the heavens.'
15 And will you still follow the ancient trail
  trodden by the wicked,
16 those who were borne off before their time,
  whose foundations were swamped by a flood,
17 for having said to God, 'Go away!
  What can Shaddai do to us?'
18 Yet he himself had filled their houses with good
    things,
  although excluded from the plans of the wicked!
19 At such a spectacle, the upright rejoice,
  and the innocent deride them:
20 'See how our enemies have been destroyed!
  See how their wealth has perished in the
    flames!'

21 Well then! Make peace with him, be reconciled,
  and all your happiness will be restored to you.
22 Welcome the teaching from his lips,
  and keep his words close to your heart.
23 If you return, humbled, to Shaddai
  and drive wickedness far from your tent,
24 if you lay your gold down on the dust,
  Ophir down among the pebbles of the torrent,
25 Shaddai will be bars of gold to you
  and silver piled in heaps.
26 Then Shaddai will be all your delight,
  and you will lift your face to God.
27 You will pray, and he will hear;
  and you will be able to fulfil your vows.
28 Whatever you undertake will go well,
  and light will shine on your path;
29 for he casts down the pride of the arrogant,
  but he saves those of downcast eyes.
30 He rescues anyone who is innocent;
  have your hands clean, and you will be saved.

23

Job spoke next. He said:

2 My lament is still rebellious;
  despite my groans, his hand is just as heavy.
3 Will no one help me to know
  how to travel to his dwelling?
4 I should set out my case to him,
  advancing any number of grievances.
5 Then I could learn his defence, every word of it,
  taking note of everything he said to me.
6 Would he put all his strength into this debate with
    me?
  No, he would only have to give his attention to
    me,
7 to recognise his opponent as upright
  and so I should win my case for ever.

22, 18: A gloss, taken partly from Jb 21, 16.

8 "If I go forward, he is not there;
or backward, I cannot perceive him;
9 on the left he hides, and I cannot behold him;
I turn*f* to the right, but I cannot see him.
10 But he knows the way that I take;
when he has tested me, I shall come out like
gold.
11 My foot has held fast to his steps;
I have kept his way and have not turned aside.
12 I have not departed from the commandment of his
lips;
I have treasured in*g* my bosom the words of
his mouth.
13 But he stands alone and who can dissuade him?
What he desires, that he does.
14 For he will complete what he appoints for me;
and many such things are in his mind.
15 Therefore I am terrified at his presence;
when I consider, I am in dread of him.
16 God has made my heart faint;
the Almighty*h* has terrified me;
17 If only I could vanish in darkness,
and thick darkness would cover my face!*i*

24 "Why are times not kept by the Almighty,*h*
and why do those who know him never see his
days?
2 The wicked*j* remove landmarks;
they seize flocks and pasture them.
3 They drive away the donkey of the orphan;
they take the widow's ox for a pledge.
4 They thrust the needy off the road;
the poor of the earth all hide themselves.
5 Like wild asses in the desert
they go out to their toil,
scavenging in the wasteland
food for their young.
6 They reap in a field not their own
and they glean in the vineyard of the wicked.
7 They lie all night naked, without clothing,
and have no covering in the cold.
8 They are wet with the rain of the mountains,
and cling to the rock for want of shelter.

9 "There are those who snatch the orphan child
from the breast,
and take as a pledge the infant of the poor.
10 They go about naked, without clothing;
though hungry, they carry the sheaves;
11 between their terraces*k* they press out oil;
they tread the wine presses, but suffer thirst.

8 If I go to the east, he is not there;
if west, I cannot find him;
9 when I turn north, I do not descry him;
I face south, but he is not to be seen.
10 Yet he knows me in action and at rest;
when he tests me, I shall emerge like gold.
11 My feet have kept to the path he has set me;
without deviating I have kept to his way.
12 I do not neglect the commands he issues,
I have treasured in my heart all he says.
13 When he decides, who can turn him from his
purpose?
What he desires, he does.
14 Whatever he determines for me, that he carries out;
his mind is full of plans like these.
15 That is why I am fearful of meeting him;
when I think about it, I am afraid;
16 it is God who makes me faint-hearted,
the Almighty who fills me with fear,
17 yet I am not reduced to silence by the darkness
or by the mystery which hides him.

24 The day of reckoning is no secret to the
Almighty,
though those who know him have no hint of its
date.
2 The wicked move boundary stones,
and pasture flocks they have stolen.
6 In the field they reap what is not theirs,
and filch the late grapes from the rich man's
vineyard.
3 They drive off the donkey belonging to the
fatherless,
and lead away the widow's ox with a rope.
9 They snatch the fatherless infant from the breast
and take the poor person's child in pledge.
4 They jostle the poor out of the way;
the destitute in the land are forced into hiding
together.
5 The poor rise early like the wild ass,
when it scours the wilderness for food;
but though they work till nightfall,
their children go hungry.
7 Without clothing, they pass the night naked
and with no cover against the cold.
8 Drenched by rainstorms from the hills,
they cling to the rock, their only shelter.
10 Naked and bare they go about their work;
those who carry the sheaves go hungry;
11 they press the oil in the shade where two walls
meet,
they tread the winepress but themselves go thirsty.

23:8 **to the east:** *or* forward. **west:** *or* backward.   23:9 **I turn:**
prob. rdg; Heb. he turns. **north:** *or* left. **I face:** *so Syriac; Heb.* he
faces. **south:** *or* right.   23:10 **me . . . rest:** *so Syriac; Heb.* a way
with me.   23:12 **in my heart:** *so Gk; Heb.* from my allotted
portion.   23:13 **he decides:** *prob. rdg; Heb.* he in one.
23:17 **yet I am not . . . or:** *or* indeed I am . . . and.   24:1 **The
. . . reckoning:** *prob. rdg; Heb.* prefixes Why.   24:2 **The wicked:**
prob. rdg, cp. Gk; Heb. obscure.   24:2–10 *Verses 3–9
rearranged to restore the natural order.*   24:6 **theirs:** *lit.* his.
rich: *or* wicked.   24:3 **with a rope:** *or* in pledge.   24:5 **but
. . . nightfall:** *prob. rdg; Heb.* obscure. **go hungry:** *prob. rdg; Heb.*
to it food.

---

*f*Syr Vg: Heb *he turns*   *g*Gk Vg: Heb *from*   *h*Traditional
rendering of Heb *Shaddai*   *i*Or *But I am not destroyed by the
darkness; he has concealed the thick darkness from me*   *j*Gk: Heb
they   *k*Meaning of Heb uncertain

NEW AMERICAN BIBLE	NEW JERUSALEM BIBLE

8 But if I go to the east, he is not there;
  or to the west, I cannot perceive him;
9 Where the north enfolds him, I behold him not;
  by the south he is veiled, and I see him not.
10 Yet he knows my way;
  if he proved me, I should come forth as gold.
11 My foot has always walked in his steps;
  his way I have kept and have not turned aside.
12 From the commands of his lips I have
  not departed;
  the words of his mouth I have treasured in
  my heart.
13 But he has decided, and who can say him nay?
  What he desires, that he does.
14 For he will carry out what is appointed for me;
  and many such things may yet be in his mind.

15 Therefore am I dismayed before him;
  when I take thought, I fear him.
16 Indeed God has made my courage fail;
  the Almighty has put me in dismay.
17 Yes, would that I had vanished in darkness,
  and that thick gloom were before me to
  conceal me.

24 Why are not times set by the Almighty,
  and why do his friends not see his days?
2 The wicked remove landmarks;
  they steal away herds and pasture them.
3 The asses of orphans they drive away;
  they take the widow's ox for a pledge.
4 They force the needy off the road;
  all the poor of the land are driven into hiding.
5 Like wild asses in the desert, these go forth
  to their task of seeking food;
  The steppe provides food for the young
  among them;
6   they harvest at night in the untilled land.
7 They pass the night naked, without clothing,
  for they have no covering against the cold;
8 They are drenched with the rain of the mountains,
  and for want of shelter they cling to the rock.
11 Between the rows they press out the oil;
  they glean in the vineyard of the wicked.
  They tread the wine presses, yet suffer thirst,
10   and famished are those who carry the sheaves.

8 If I go to the east, he is not there;
  or to the west, I still cannot see him.
9 If I seek him in the north, he is not to be found,
  invisible as ever, if I turn to the south.
10 And yet he knows every step I take!
  Let him test me in the crucible: I shall come out
  pure gold.
11 My footsteps have followed close in his,
  I have walked in his way without swerving;
12 I have not neglected the commandment of his lips,
  in my heart I have cherished the words of his
  mouth.
13 But once he has made up his mind, who can
  change it?
  Whatever he plans, that he carries out.
14 No doubt, then, but he will carry out my sentence,
  like so many other decrees that he has made.
15 That is why I am full of fear before him,
  and the more I think, the greater grows my
  dread of him.
16 God has undermined my courage,
  Shaddai has filled me with fear.
17 The darkness having failed to destroy me,
  I am plunged back into obscurity by him!

24 Why does Shaddai not make known the times he
  has fixed;
  why do his faithful never see his Days?[i]
2 The wicked move boundary-marks away,
  they carry off flock and shepherd.
3 They drive away the orphan's donkey,
  as security, they seize the widow's ox.
4 The needy have to keep out of the way,
  poor country people have to keep out of sight.
5 Like wild desert donkeys, they go out to work,
  searching from dawn for food,
  and at evening for something on which to feed
  their children.
6 They go harvesting in the field of some scoundrel,
  they go pilfering in the vineyards of the wicked.
10 They go about naked, lacking clothes,
  and starving while they carry the sheaves.
11 Two little walls, their shelter at high noon;
  parched with thirst, they have to tread the
  winepress.
7 They spend the night naked, lacking clothes,
  with no covering against the cold.
8 Mountain rainstorms cut them through,
  unsheltered, they hug the rocks.
9 The orphan child is torn from the breast,
  the child of the poor is exacted as security.

24, 1: The text and order of verses in this chapter are not certain;
note the omission of v 9 which duplicates words of vv 2–4.

[i] 24 i.e., his Days of Retribution, as the Day of Yahweh in prophetic
writings.

NEW REVISED STANDARD VERSION

12 From the city the dying groan,
    and the throat of the wounded cries for help;
    yet God pays no attention to their prayer.

13 "There are those who rebel against the light,
    who are not acquainted with its ways,
    and do not stay in its paths.
14 The murderer rises at dusk
    to kill the poor and needy,
    and in the night is like a thief.
15 The eye of the adulterer also waits for the
      twilight,
    saying, 'No eye will see me';
    and he disguises his face.
16 In the dark they dig through houses;
    by day they shut themselves up;
    they do not know the light.
17 For deep darkness is morning to all of them;
    for they are friends with the terrors of deep
      darkness.

18 "Swift are they on the face of the waters;
    their portion in the land is cursed;
    no treader turns toward their vineyards.
19 Drought and heat snatch away the snow waters;
    so does Sheol those who have sinned.
20 The womb forgets them;
    the worm finds them sweet;
    they are no longer remembered;
    so wickedness is broken like a tree.
21 "They harm^l the childless woman,
    and do no good to the widow.
22 Yet God^m prolongs the life of the mighty by his
      power;
    they rise up when they despair of life.
23 He gives them security, and they are supported;
    his eyes are upon their ways.
24 They are exalted a little while, and then are gone;
    they wither and fade like the mallow;^{n}
    they are cut off like the heads of grain.
25 If it is not so, who will prove me a liar,
    and show that there is nothing in what I say?"

25 Then Bildad the Shuhite answered:
2 "Dominion and fear are with God;^{o}
    he makes peace in his high heaven.
3 Is there any number to his armies?
    Upon whom does his light not arise?
4 How then can a mortal be righteous before God?
    How can one born of woman be pure?
5 If even the moon is not bright
    and the stars are not pure in his sight,
6 how much less a mortal, who is a maggot,
    and a human being, who is a worm!"

26 Then Job answered:
2 "How you have helped one who has no power!
    How you have assisted the arm that has no
      strength!
3 How you have counseled one who has no
      wisdom,
    and given much good advice!
4 With whose help have you uttered words,
    and whose spirit has come forth from you?

REVISED ENGLISH BIBLE

12 Far from the city, they groan as if dying,
    and like those mortally wounded they cry out;
    but God remains deaf to their prayer.

13 Some there are who rebel against the light,
    who know nothing of its ways
    and do not stay in its paths.
14–15 Before daylight the murderer rises
    to kill some miserable wretch.
    The seducer watches eagerly for twilight,
    thinking, 'No one will set eyes on me.'
    In the night the thief prowls about,
    his face covered with a mask;
16 in the darkness he breaks into houses
    which he has marked down during the day.
    One and all, they are strangers to the daylight,
17 but dark night is morning to them;
    and amid the terrors of night they are at home.
18 Such men are scum on the surface of the water;
    throughout the land their fields are accursed,
    and no labourer will go near their vineyards.
19 As drought and heat make away with snow,
    so the waters of Sheol make away with sinners.
20 The womb forgets them, the worm sucks them dry;
    they will not be remembered ever after.
    Iniquity is snapped like a stick!
21 They may have wronged the barren childless
      woman
    and been no help to the widow;
22 yet God in his strength carries off the mighty;
    they may rise, but they have no firm hope of life.
23 He lulls them into security and confidence;
    but his eyes are fixed on their ways.
24 For a moment they rise to the heights,
    but they are soon gone.
    Laid low they wilt like a mallow-flower;
    they droop like an ear of grain on the stalk.
25 If this is not so, who will prove me wrong
    and make nonsense of my argument?

25 Then Bildad the Shuhite answered:
2 Authority and awe are with him
    who has established peace in his realm on high.
3 His squadrons are without number;
    at whom will they not spring from ambush?
4 How then can a mere mortal be justified in God's
      sight,
    or one born of woman be regarded as virtuous?
5 If the circling moon is found wanting,
    and the stars are not innocent in his eyes,
6 much more so man, who is but a maggot,
    mortal man, who is a worm.

26 Job answered:
2 What a help you have been to one without
      resource!
    What deliverance you have brought to the
      powerless!
3 What counsel you offer to one bereft of wisdom,
    what sound advice to the simple!
4 Who has prompted you to utter such words,
    and whose spirit is expressed in your speech?

24:14–15 **the thief prowls about:** *prob. rdg; Heb.* let him be like a
thief.   24:16 **he has:** *so Syriac; Heb.* they have. **One and all:**
transposed from after but *in next verse.*   24:19 **snow . . . Sheol:**
prob. rdg; Heb. snow-water, Sheol. **Sheol:** *or* the underworld.
24:21 **They . . . wronged:** *so Aram. (Targ.); Heb.* shepherd.
25:3 **at . . . ambush:** *so Gk; Heb.* on whom does his light not rise?

---

^{l} Gk Tg: Heb *feed on or associate with* ^{m} Heb *he* ^{n} Gk: Heb
like all others ^{o} Heb *him*

NEW AMERICAN BIBLE

12 From the dust the dying groan,
  and the souls of the wounded cry out
  [yet God does not treat it as unseemly].
13 There are those who are rebels against the light;
  they know not its ways;
  they abide not in its paths.
14 When there is no light the murderer rises,
  to kill the poor and needy.
15 The eye of the adulterer watches for the twilight;
  he says, "No eye will see me."
  In the night the thief roams about,
  and he puts a mask over his face;
16 in the dark he breaks into houses.
  By day they shut themselves in;
  none of them know the light,
17 for daylight they regard as darkness.

* * *

18 Their portion in the land is accursed,
20 and wickedness is splintered like wood.
19. 21. . . . .
22 To him who rises without assurance of his life
23 he gives safety and support.
  He sustains the mighty by his strength,
  and his eyes are on their ways.
24 They are exalted for a while, and then they
    are gone;
  they are laid low and, like all others, are
    gathered up;
  like ears of grain they shrivel.

* * *

25 If this be not so, who will confute me,
  and reduce my argument to nought?

NEW JERUSALEM BIBLE

12 From the towns come the groans of the dying
  and the gasp of the wounded crying for help.
  Yet God remains deaf to prayer!
13 In contrast, there are those who reject the light:
  who know nothing of its ways
  and who do not frequent its paths.
14 When all is dark the murderer leaves his bed
  to kill the poor and needy.
  During the night the thief goes on the prowl,
16a breaking into houses while the darkness lasts.
15 The eye of the adulterer watches for twilight,
  'No one will see me,' he mutters
  as he masks his face.
16b In the daytime they keep out of sight,
  these people who do not want to know the light.
17 For all of them, morning is a time of shadow dark
    as death,
  since that is when they know what fear is. *j*

‡24.18–24: see below following ch. 27‡

25 Is this not so? Who can prove me a liar
  or show that my words have no substance?

25 Then Bildad the Shuhite answered and said:

2 Dominion and awesomeness are his
  who brings about harmony in his heavens.
3 Is there any numbering of his troops?
  Yet to which of them does not his light extend?
4 How can a man be just in God's sight,
  or how can any woman's child be innocent?
5 Behold, even the moon is not bright
  and the stars are not clear in his sight.
6 How much less man, who is but a maggot,
  the son of man, who is only a worm?

26 Then Job spoke again and said:

2 What help you give to the powerless,
  what strength to the feeble arm!
3 How you counsel, as though he had no wisdom;
  how profuse is the advice you offer!
4 With whose help have you uttered those words,
  and whose is the breath that comes forth
    from you?

25 Bildad of Shuah spoke next. He said:

2 What sovereignty, what awe, is his
  who creates peace on his heights!
3 Who can count his armies?
  Against whom does his lightning not surge
    forth?
4 Could anyone think God regards him as virtuous,
  the child of woman as pure!
5 Why, the very moon lacks lustre,
  the very stars seem impure to him!
6 How much less a human, this maggot,
  the child of man, this worm! *k*

‡26.1–4: see below‡

24, 17: The asterisks which follow this verse mark off a passage (vv 18–24) which cannot be ascribed to Job with certainty. Vv 17–24 are in general poorly preserved; and much of vv 18–21 has not been translated because these verses are obscure.

j 24 vv. 18–24 are conjecturally placed after 27:23. The text is corrupt. *k* 25 26:1–4 are conjecturally placed after 26:14. They belong to Job's speech.

5 The shades below tremble,
   the waters and their inhabitants.
6 Sheol is naked before God,
   and Abaddon has no covering.
7 He stretches out Zaphon *p* over the void,
   and hangs the earth upon nothing.
8 He binds up the waters in his thick clouds,
   and the cloud is not torn open by them.
9 He covers the face of the full moon,
   and spreads over it his cloud.
10 He has described a circle on the face of the
    waters,
    at the boundary between light and darkness.
11 The pillars of heaven tremble,
    and are astounded at his rebuke.
12 By his power he stilled the Sea;
    by his understanding he struck down Rahab.
13 By his wind the heavens were made fair;
    his hand pierced the fleeing serpent.
14 These are indeed but the outskirts of his ways;
    and how small a whisper do we hear of him!
    But the thunder of his power who can
    understand?"

27 Job again took up his discourse and said:
2 "As God lives, who has taken away my right,
   and the Almighty, *q* who has made my soul
   bitter,
3 as long as my breath is in me
   and the spirit of God is in my nostrils,
4 my lips will not speak falsehood,
   and my tongue will not utter deceit.
5 Far be it from me to say that you are right;
   until I die I will not put away my integrity
   from me.
6 I hold fast my righteousness, and will not let it
   go;
   my heart does not reproach me for any of my
   days.
7 "May my enemy be like the wicked,
   and may my opponent be like the unrighteous.
8 For what is the hope of the godless when God
   cuts them off,
   when God takes away their lives?
9 Will God hear their cry
   when trouble comes upon them?
10 Will they take delight in the Almighty? *q*
    Will they call upon God at all times?
11 I will teach you concerning the hand of God;
    that which is with the Almighty *q* I will not
    conceal.
12 All of you have seen it yourselves;
    why then have you become altogether vain?
13 "This is the portion of the wicked with God,
    and the heritage that oppressors receive from
    the Almighty: *q*

5 The shades below writhe in fear,
   the waters and all that inhabit them are afraid.
6 Sheol is laid bare before him;
   Abaddon lies uncovered.
7 God spreads the canopy of the sky over chaos
   and suspends earth over the void.
8 He keeps the waters penned in dense cloud masses,
   yet no cloud bursts open under their weight.
9 He veils the face of the full moon,
   unrolling his clouds across it.
10 He has fixed the horizon on the surface of the
    waters
    at the boundary between light and darkness.
11 The pillars of heaven quake,
    aghast at the thunder of his voice.
12 With his strong arm he cleft the sea monster;
    he struck down Rahab by his skill.
13 Winds from him clear the skies,
    and his hand slays the twisting sea serpent.
14 These are but the fringes of his power,
    and how faint the whisper that we hear of him!
    Who could comprehend the thunder of his might?

27 Then Job resumed his discourse:
2 I swear by the living God, who has denied me
   justice,
   by the Almighty, who has filled me with
   bitterness,
3 that so long as there is any life left in me
   and the breath of God is in my nostrils,
4 no untrue word will pass my lips,
   nor will my tongue utter any falsehood.
5 Far be it from me to concede that you are right!
   Till I cease to be, I shall not abandon my claim of
   innocence.
6 I maintain and shall never give up the rightness of
   my cause;
   so long as I live, I shall not change.
7 Let my enemy meet the fate of the wicked,
   and my antagonist the doom of the wrongdoer!
8 What hope has a godless man, when he is cut off,
   when God takes away his life?
9 Will God listen to his cry
   when trouble overtakes him?
10 Will he trust himself to the Almighty?
    Will he call upon God at all times?
11 I shall teach you what is in God's power,
    and not conceal the purpose of the Almighty.
12 If all of you have seen these things,
    why then do you talk such empty nonsense?
13 Such is God's reward for the wicked man,
    the Almighty's portion for him who is ruthless.

26:5 **are afraid:** *prob. rdg; Heb. omits.*   26:6 **Sheol:** *or the*
underworld.   26:9 **He veils . . . moon:** *or He overlays the surface*
of his throne.   26:13 **twisting:** *or primeval.*   27:10 **trust . . .**
to: *or delight in.*

p Or the North   *q Traditional rendering of Heb Shaddai*

5 The shades beneath writhe in terror,
  the waters, and their inhabitants.
6 Naked before him is the nether world,
  and Abaddon has no covering.
7 He stretches out the North over empty space,
  and suspends the earth over nothing at all;
8 He binds up the waters in his clouds,
  yet the cloud is not rent by their weight;
9 He holds back the appearance of the full moon
  by spreading his clouds before it.
10 He has marked out a circle on the surface
    of the deep
  as the boundary of light and darkness.
11 The pillars of the heavens tremble
  and are stunned at his thunderous rebuke;
12 By his power he stirs up the sea,
  and by his might he crushes Rahab;
13 With his angry breath he scatters the water,
  and he hurls the lightning against it relentlessly;
  His hand pierces the fugitive dragon
  as from his hand it strives to flee.
14 Lo, these are but the outlines of his ways,
  and how faint is the word we hear!

27 11 I will teach you the manner of God's dealings,
  and the way of the Almighty I will not conceal.
2 As God lives, who withholds my deserts,
  the Almighty, who has made bitter my soul,
3 So long as I still have life in me
  and the breath of God is in my nostrils,
4 My lips shall not speak falsehood,
  nor my tongue utter deceit!
5 Far be it from me to account you right;
  till I die I will not renounce my innocence.
6 My justice I maintain and I will not relinquish it;
  my heart does not reproach me for any of
    my days.
7 Let my enemy be as the wicked
  and my adversary as the unjust!
8 For what can the impious man expect when he is
    cut off,
  when God requires his life?
9 Will God then attend to his cry
  when calamity comes upon him?
10 Will he then delight in the Almighty
  and call upon him constantly?
    ‡27.11: see above‡
12 Behold, you yourselves have all seen it;
  why then do you spend yourselves in idle words!

                    * * *

13 This is the portion of a wicked man from God,
  the inheritance an oppressor receives from
    the Almighty:

26, 13: The last two lines are actually Jb 27, 22.   **27, 2–12:** This
is probably to be read as Job's reply to Zophar's speech of Jb 27,
13–21. In the current Hebrew text the heading for this chapter (Jb
27, 1, here omitted) is identical with Jb 29, 1; we should expect
rather such a heading as is Jb 21, 1; 23, 1; 26, 1.
27, 13–21: This is probably to be read as Zophar's third speech. The
asterisks are present to indicate it is not likely that the sacred writer
intended these words to be ascribed to Job.

26 5 The Shadows¹ tremble underneath the earth,
  the waters and their denizens are afraid.
6 Before his eyes, Sheol is bare,
  Perdition itself is uncovered.
7 He it was who spread the North above the void
  and poised the earth on nothingness.
8 He fastens up the waters in his clouds,
  without the clouds giving way under their
    weight.
9 He covers the face of the full moon,
  spreading his cloud across it.
10 He has traced a ring on the surface of the waters,
  at the boundary between light and dark.
11 The pillars of the heavens tremble,
  awe-struck at his threats.
12 By his power, he has whipped up the Sea,
  by his skill, he has crushed Rahab.
13 His breath has made the heavens luminous,
  his hand transfixed the Fleeing Serpent.
14 This is only a fraction of what he has done
  and all we catch of it is the feeblest echo.
  But who can conceive the thunder of his power?

1 Job spoke next. He said:

2 To one so weak, what a help you are,
  for the arm that is powerless, what a rescuer!
3 What excellent advice you give the unlearned,
  you are never at a loss for a helpful suggestion!
4 For whom are these words of yours intended
  and whence comes that wit you are now
    displaying?

27 And Job continued his solemn discourse. He said:

2 I swear by the living God who denies me justice,
  by Shaddai who has filled me with bitterness,
3 that as long as a shred of life is left in me,
  and the breath of God breathes in my nostrils,
4 my lips will never speak evil
  nor my tongue utter any lie.
5 Far from admitting you to be in the right,
  I shall maintain my integrity to my dying day.
6 I take my stand on my uprightness, I shall not stir:
  in my heart I need not be ashamed of my days.
7 Let my enemy meet the fate of the wicked,
  my adversary, the lot of the evil-doer!
8 For what hope does the godless have when he
    prays
  and raises his soul to God?
9 Is God likely to hear his cries
  when disaster descends on him?
10 Did he make Shaddai all his delight,
  calling on him at every turn?
11 But I am showing you the way that God works,
  making no secret of Shaddai's designs.
12 And if you had all understood them for yourselves,
  you would not have wasted your breath in empty
    words.
13 This is the fate that God assigns to the wicked,
  the inheritance that the violent receive from
    Shaddai.

¹ **26** i.e., the powerless dead.

14 If their children are multiplied, it is for the
      sword;
  and their offspring have not enough to eat.
15 Those who survive them the pestilence buries,
  and their widows make no lamentation.
16 Though they heap up silver like dust,
  and pile up clothing like clay —
17 they may pile it up, but the just will wear it,
  and the innocent will divide the silver.
18 They build their houses like nests,
  like booths made by sentinels of the vineyard.
19 They go to bed with wealth, but will do so no
      more;
  they open their eyes, and it is gone.
20 Terrors overtake them like a flood;
  in the night a whirlwind carries them off.
21 The east wind lifts them up and they are gone;
  it sweeps them out of their place.
22 It*r* hurls at them without pity;
  they flee from its*s* power in headlong flight.
23 It*r* claps its*s* hands at them,
  and hisses at them from its*s* place.

14 Though his sons be many, they will fall by the
      sword,
  and his offspring will never have enough to eat;
15 the survivors will be brought to the grave by
      plague,
  and no widows will weep for them.
16 He may heap up silver like dirt
  and get himself stacks of clothes;
17 he may get them, but the righteous will wear them,
  and his silver will be shared among the innocent.
18 The house he builds is flimsy as a bird's nest
  or a shelter put up by a watchman.
19 He may lie down rich one day, but never again;
  he opens his eyes, to find his wealth is gone.
20 Disaster overtakes him like a flood,
  and a storm snatches him away in the night;
21 an east wind lifts him up and he is gone;
  it sweeps him far from his home;
22 it hurls itself at him without mercy,
  and he is battered and buffeted by its force;
23 it snaps its fingers at him
  and whistles over him wherever he may be.

28 "Surely there is a mine for silver,
      and a place for gold to be refined.
2 Iron is taken out of the earth,
  and copper is smelted from ore.
3 Miners put*t* an end to darkness,
  and search out to the farthest bound
  the ore in gloom and deep darkness.
4 They open shafts in a valley away from human
      habitation;
  they are forgotten by travelers,
  they sway suspended, remote from people.
5 As for the earth, out of it comes bread;
  but underneath it is turned up as by fire.
6 Its stones are the place of sapphires,*u*
  and its dust contains gold.

7 "That path no bird of prey knows,
  and the falcon's eye has not seen it.
8 The proud wild animals have not trodden it;
  the lion has not passed over it.

9 "They put their hand to the flinty rock,
  and overturn mountains by the roots.
10 They cut out channels in the rocks,
  and their eyes see every precious thing.
11 The sources of the rivers they probe;*v*
  hidden things they bring to light.

28 THERE are mines for silver
      and places where gold is refined.
2 Iron is won from the earth
  and copper smelted from the ore.
3 Men master the darkness;
  to the farthest recesses they seek
  ore in gloom and deep darkness.
4 Foreigners cut the shafts;
  forgotten, suspended without foothold,
  they swing to and fro, far away from anyone.
5 While grain is springing from the earth above,
  what lies beneath is turned over like a fire,
6 and out of its rocks comes lapis lazuli,
  dusted with flecks of gold.
7 No bird of prey knows the path there;
  the falcon's keen eye cannot descry it;
8 proud beasts do not set foot on it,
  and no lion passes there.
9 Man sets his hand to the granite rock
  and lays bare the roots of the mountains;
10 he cuts galleries in the rocks,
  and gems of every kind meet his eye;
11 he dams up the sources of the streams
  and brings the hidden riches of the earth to light.

27:19 **but . . . again:** *so Gk; Heb.* but he is not gathered in.
27:22 **and he . . . force:** *or* and he flees headlong from its force.
28:4 **Foreigners . . . shafts:** *prob. rdg; Heb. obscure.*

r Or *He* (that is God)   *s* Or *his*   *t* Heb *He puts*   *u* Or *lapis
lazuli*   *v* Gk Vg: Heb *bind*

14 Though his children be many, the sword is
    their destiny.
    His offspring shall not be filled with bread.
15 His survivors, when they die, shall have no burial,
    and their widows shall not be mourned.
16 Though he heap up silver like dust
    and store away mounds of clothing,
17 What he has stored the just man shall wear,
    and the innocent shall divide the silver.
18 He builds his house as of cobwebs,
    or like a booth put up by the vinekeeper.
19 He lies down a rich man, one last time;
    he opens his eyes and nothing remains to him.
20 Terrors rush upon him by day;
    at night the tempest carries him off.
21 The storm wind seizes him and he disappears;
    it sweeps him out of his place.

* * *

14 Though he have many children, it is but for the
    sword;
    his descendants will never have enough to eat.
15 Plague will bury those he leaves behind him,
    and their widows will have no chance to mourn
    them.
16 Though he amass silver like dust
    and gather fine clothes like clay,
17 let him gather! — some good man will wear them,
    while his silver is shared among the upright.
18 All he has built himself is a spider's web,
    made himself a watchman's shack.
19 He goes to bed rich, but never again:
    he wakes to find it has all gone.
20 Terror assails him in broad daylight,
    and at night a whirlwind sweeps him off.
21 An east wind picks him up and drags him away,
    snatching him up from his homestead.
22 Pitilessly he is turned into a target,
    and forced to flee from the hands that menace
    him.
23 His downfall is greeted with applause,
    he is hissed wherever he goes.

24

18acb He is no more than a straw floating on the
    water,
    his estate is accursed throughout the land,
    nobody goes near his vineyard.
19 As drought and heat make snow disappear,
    so does Sheol anyone who has sinned.
20 The womb that shaped him forgets him
    and his name is recalled no longer.
    Thus wickedness is blasted as a tree is struck.
21 He used to ill-treat the childless woman
    and show no kindness to the widow.
22 But he who lays mighty hold on tyrants
    rises up to take away a life that seemed secure.
23 He let him build his hopes on false security,
    but kept his eyes on every step he took.
24 He had his time of glory, now he vanishes,
    wilting like the saltwort once it is picked,
    and withering like an ear of corn.

28

There is indeed a mine for silver,
    and a place for gold which men refine.
2 Iron is taken from the earth,
    and copper is melted out of stone.

‡28.3: see below‡

4 . . . .

5 The earth, though out of it comes forth bread,
    is in fiery upheaval underneath.
6 Its stones are the source of sapphires,
    and there is gold in its dust.

‡28.7–11: see below‡

28

Silver has its mines,
    and gold a place for refining.
2 Iron is extracted from the earth,
    the smelted rocks yield copper.
3 Man makes an end of darkness,
    to the utmost limit he digs
    the black rock in shadow dark as death.
4 Foreigners bore into ravines
    in unfrequented places,
    swinging suspended far from human beings.
5 That earth from which bread comes
    is ravaged underground by fire.
6 There, the rocks have veins of sapphire
    and their dust contains gold.
7 That is a path unknown to birds of prey,
    unseen by the eye of any vulture;
8 a path not trodden by the lordly beasts,
    where no lion ever walked.
9 Man attacks the flint,
    upturning mountains by their roots.
10 He cuts canals through the rock,
    on the watch for anything precious.
11 He explores the sources of rivers,
    bringing hidden things to light.

27, 21: The Hebrew has two more verses: v 22 (read above with Jb
26, 13); and v 23, which is a variant form of v 21.
28, 1–28: Note the changed order of verses; v 4 is uncertain.

12 "But where shall wisdom be found?
      And where is the place of understanding?
13 Mortals do not know the way to it,[w]
      and it is not found in the land of the living.
14 The deep says, 'It is not in me,'
      and the sea says, 'It is not with me.'
15 It cannot be gotten for gold,
      and silver cannot be weighed out as its price.
16 It cannot be valued in the gold of Ophir,
      in precious onyx or sapphire.[x]
17 Gold and glass cannot equal it,
      nor can it be exchanged for jewels of fine
         gold.
18 No mention shall be made of coral or of crystal;
      the price of wisdom is above pearls.
19 The chrysolite of Ethiopia[y] cannot compare with
         it,
      nor can it be valued in pure gold.

20 "Where then does wisdom come from?
      And where is the place of understanding?
21 It is hidden from the eyes of all living,
      and concealed from the birds of the air.
22 Abaddon and Death say,
      'We have heard a rumor of it with our ears.'

23 "God understands the way to it,
      and he knows its place.
24 For he looks to the ends of the earth,
      and sees everything under the heavens.
25 When he gave to the wind its weight,
      and apportioned out the waters by measure;
26 when he made a decree for the rain,
      and a way for the thunderbolt;
27 then he saw it and declared it;
      he established it, and searched it out.
28 And he said to humankind,
      'Truly, the fear of the Lord, that is wisdom;
      and to depart from evil is understanding.' "

29 Job again took up his discourse and said:
2 "Oh, that I were as in the months of old,
      as in the days when God watched over me;
3 when his lamp shone over my head,
      and by his light I walked through darkness;
4 when I was in my prime,
      when the friendship of God was upon my tent;
5 when the Almighty[z] was still with me,
      when my children were around me;
6 when my steps were washed with milk,
      and the rock poured out for me streams of oil!
7 When I went out to the gate of the city,
      when I took my seat in the square,
8 the young men saw me and withdrew,
      and the aged rose up and stood;
9 the nobles refrained from talking,
      and laid their hands on their mouths;

12 But where can wisdom be found,
      and where is the source of understanding?
13 No one knows the way to it,
      nor is it to be found in the land of the living.
14 'It is not in us,' declare the ocean depths;
      the sea declares, 'It is not with me.'
15 Red gold cannot buy it,
      nor can its price be weighed out in silver;
16 gold of Ophir cannot be set in the scales against it,
      nor precious cornelian or sapphire;
17 gold and crystal are not to be matched with it,
      no work in fine gold can be bartered for it;
18 black coral and alabaster are not worth mention,
      and a parcel of wisdom fetches more than red
         coral;
19 chrysolite from Ethiopia is not to be matched with
         it,
      pure gold cannot be set in the scales against it.
20 Where, then, does wisdom come from?
      Where is the source of understanding?
21 No creature on earth can set eyes on it;
      even from birds of the air it is concealed.
22 Destruction and Death declare,
      'We know of it only by hearsay.'

23 God alone understands the way to it,
      he alone knows its source;
24 for he can see to the ends of the earth
      and observe every place under heaven.
25 When he regulated the force of the wind
      and measured out the waters in proportion,
26 when he laid down a limit for the rain
      and cleared a path for the thunderbolt,
27 it was then he saw wisdom and took stock of it,
      he considered it and fathomed its very depths.
28 And he said to mankind:
      'The fear of the Lord is wisdom,
      and to turn from evil, that is understanding!'

29 THEN Job resumed his discourse:
2 If only I could go back to the old days,
      to the time when God was watching over me,
3 when his lamp shone above my head,
      and by its light I walked through the darkness!
4 If I could be as in the days of my prime,
      when God protected my home,
5 while the Almighty was still there at my side,
      and my servants stood round me,
6 while my path flowed with milk,
      and the rocks poured forth streams of oil for me!
7 When I went out of my gate up to the town
      to take my seat in the public square,
8 young men saw me and kept back out of sight,
      old men rose to their feet,
9 men in authority broke off their talk
      and put their hands to their lips;

28:13 **knows . . . to it:** *so Gk; Heb.* knows its value.
28:16 **sapphire:** *or* lapis lazuli.   28:17 **crystal:** *lit.* glass.
28:22 **Destruction:** *Heb.* Abaddon.   28:27 **considered:** *so some*
MSS; others established.

[w] Gk: Heb *its price*   [x] Or *lapis lazuli*   [y] Or *Nubia*; Heb *Cush*
[z] Traditional rendering of Heb *Shaddai*

12 But whence can wisdom be obtained,
 and where is the place of understanding?
13 Man knows nothing to equal it,
 nor is it to be had in the land of the living.
 ‡28.14: see below‡
15 Solid gold cannot purchase it,
 nor can its price be paid with silver.
16 It cannot be bought with gold of Ophir,
 with the precious onyx or the sapphire.
17 Gold or crystal cannot equal it,
 nor can golden vessels reach its worth.
18 Neither coral nor jasper should be thought of;
 it surpasses pearls and 19 Arabian topaz.

20 Whence, then, comes wisdom,
 and where is the place of understanding?
21 It is hid from the eyes of any beast;
 from the birds of the air it is concealed.
7 The path to it no bird of prey knows,
 nor has the hawk's eye seen that path.
8 The proud beasts have not trodden it,
 nor has the lion gone that way.
14 The abyss declares, "It is not in me";
 and the sea says, "I have it not."
22 Abaddon and Death say,
 "Only by rumor have we heard of it."

23 God knows the way to it;
 it is he who is familiar with its place.
24 For he beholds the ends of the earth
 and sees all that is under the heavens.
3 He has set a boundary for the darkness;
 to the farthest confines he penetrates.
9 He sets his hand to the flinty rock,
 and overturns the mountains at their foundations.
10 He splits channels in the rocks;
 his eyes behold all that is precious.
11 He probes the wellsprings of the streams,
 and brings hidden things to light.
25 He has weighed out the wind,
 and fixed the scope of the waters;
26 When he made rules for the rain
 and a path for the thunderbolts,
27 Then he saw wisdom and appraised it,
 gave it its setting, knew it through and through.
28 And to man he said:
 Behold, the fear of the LORD is wisdom;
 and avoiding evil is understanding.

29

Job took up his theme anew and said:

2 Oh, that I were as in the months past!
 as in the days when God watched over me,
3 While he kept his lamp shining above my head,
 and by his light I walked through darkness;
4 As I was in my flourishing days,
 when God sheltered my tent;
5 When the Almighty was yet with me,
 and my children were round about me;
6 When my footsteps were bathed in milk,
 and the rock flowed with streams of oil;
7 When I went forth to the gate of the city
 and set up my seat in the square —

8 Then the young men saw me and withdrew,
 while the elders rose up and stood;
9 The chief men refrained from speaking
 and covered their mouths with their hands;

12 But where does Wisdom come from?
 Where is Intelligence to be found?

13 No human being knows the way to her,
 she is not to be found on earth where they live.
14 'She is not in me,' says the Abyss;
 'Nor here,' replies the Sea.
15 She cannot be bought with solid gold,
 nor paid for with any weight of silver,
16 nor valued against gold of Ophir,
 precious agate or sapphire.
17 Neither gold nor glass compares with her,
 for her, a vase of fine gold would be no
 exchange,
18 let alone coral or crystal:
 better go fishing for Wisdom than for pearls!
19 Topaz from Cush is worthless in comparison,
 and gold, even refined, is valueless.
20 But where does Wisdom come from?
 Where is Intelligence to be found?

21 She cannot be seen by any living creature,
 she is hidden from the birds of the sky.
22 Perdition and Death both say,
 'We have heard only rumours of her.'
23 God alone understands her path
 and knows where she is to be found.
24 (For he sees to the remotest parts of the earth,
 and observes all that lies under heaven.)
25 When he willed to give weight to the wind
 and measured out the waters with a gauge,
26 when he imposed a law on the rain
 and mapped a route for thunderclaps to follow,
27 then he saw and evaluated her,
 looked her through and through, assessing her.
28 Then he said to human beings,
 'Wisdom? — that is fear of the Lord;
 Intelligence? — avoidance of evil.'

29

And Job continued his solemn discourse. He said:

2 Will no one bring back to me the months that have
 gone,
 and the days when God was my guardian,
3 when his lamp shone over my head,
 and his light was my guide in the darkness?
4 Shall I ever see my days of harvest again
 when God protected my tent;
5 when Shaddai still dwelt with me,
 and my children were around me;
6 when my feet were bathed in milk,
 and streams of oil poured from the rocks?
7 When I went out to the gate of the city,
 when I took my seat in the square,
8 as soon as I appeared, the young men stepped
 aside,
 and the old men rose to their feet.
9 Men of note broke off their speeches,
 and put their hands over their mouths;

10 the voices of princes were hushed,
    and their tongues stuck to the roof of their
        mouths.
11 When the ear heard, it commended me,
    and when the eye saw, it approved;
12 because I delivered the poor who cried,
    and the orphan who had no helper.
13 The blessing of the wretched came upon me,
    and I caused the widow's heart to sing for joy.
14 I put on righteousness, and it clothed me;
    my justice was like a robe and a turban.
15 I was eyes to the blind,
    and feet to the lame.
16 I was a father to the needy,
    and I championed the cause of the stranger.
17 I broke the fangs of the unrighteous,
    and made them drop their prey from their teeth.
18 Then I thought, 'I shall die in my nest,
    and I shall multiply my days like the
        phoenix;[a]
19 my roots spread out to the waters,
    with the dew all night on my branches;
20 my glory was fresh with me,
    and my bow ever new in my hand.'
21 "They listened to me, and waited,
    and kept silence for my counsel.
22 After I spoke they did not speak again,
    and my word dropped upon them like dew.[b]
23 They waited for me as for the rain;
    they opened their mouths as for the spring rain.
24 I smiled on them when they had no confidence;
    and the light of my countenance they did not
        extinguish.[c]
25 I chose their way, and sat as chief,
    and I lived like a king among his troops,
    like one who comforts mourners.

30 "But now they make sport of me,
    those who are younger than I,
whose fathers I would have disdained
    to set with the dogs of my flock.
2 What could I gain from the strength of their
        hands?
    All their vigor is gone.
3 Through want and hard hunger
    they gnaw the dry and desolate ground,
4 they pick mallow and the leaves of bushes,
    and to warm themselves the roots of broom.
5 They are driven out from society;
    people shout after them as after a thief.
6 In the gullies of wadis they must live,
    in holes in the ground, and in the rocks.
7 Among the bushes they bray;
    under the nettles they huddle together.
8 A senseless, disreputable brood,
    they have been whipped out of the land.
9 "And now they mock me in song;
    I am a byword to them.
10 They abhor me, they keep aloof from me;
    they do not hesitate to spit at the sight of me.
11 Because God has loosed my bowstring and
        humbled me,
    they have cast off restraint in my presence.

10 the voices of the nobles died away,
    and every man held his tongue.
    ‡29.11–20: see below‡
21 They listened to me expectantly
    and waited in silence for my counsel.
22 After I had spoken, no one spoke again;
    my words fell gently on them;
23 they waited for me as for rain,
    open-mouthed as for spring showers.
24 When I smiled on them, they took heart;
    when my face lit up, they lost their gloomy looks.
25 I presided over them, planning their course,
    like a king encamped with his troops,
    like one who comforts mourners.
11 Whoever heard of me spoke favourably of me,
    and those who saw me bore witness to my merit,
12 how I saved the poor who appealed for help,
    and the fatherless and him who had no protector.
13 He who was threatened with ruin blessed me,
    and I made the widow's heart sing for joy.
14 I put on righteousness as a garment and it clothed
        me;
    justice, like a cloak and turban, adorned me.
15 I was eyes to the blind
    and feet to the lame;
16 I was a father to the needy,
    and I took up the stranger's cause.
17 I broke the fangs of the miscreant
    and wrested the prey from his teeth.
18 I thought, 'I shall die with my powers unimpaired
    and my days uncounted as the grains of sand,
19 with my roots spreading out to the water
    and the dew lying on my branches,
20 with the bow always new in my grasp
    and the arrow ever ready to my hand.'
    ‡29.21–25: see above‡

30 But now I am laughed to scorn
    by men of a younger generation,
men whose fathers I would have disdained
    to put with the dogs guarding my flock.
2 What use to me was the strength of their arms,
    since their vigour had wasted away?
3 Gaunt with want and hunger,
    they gnawed roots in the desert,
4 they plucked saltwort and wormwood
    and for warmth the root of broom.
5 Driven out from human society,
    pursued like thieves with hue and cry,
6 they made their homes in gullies and ravines,
    in holes in the ground and rocky clefts;
7 they howled like beasts among the bushes,
    huddled together beneath the scrub,
8 vile, disreputable wretches,
    outcasts from the haunts of men.
9 Now I have become the target of their taunts;
    my name is a byword among them.
10 They abhor me, they shun me,
    they dare to spit in my face.
11 They run wild and savage me;
    at sight of me they throw off all restraint.

29:10 *Verses 21–25 transposed to follow this verse.*   29:18 **as . . .
sand:** *or as those of the phoenix.*   29:20 *Verses 21–25 transposed
to follow verse 10.*   30:3 **Gaunt . . . desert:** *prob. rdg; Heb. adds*
yesterday ruin and ruination. **roots:** *prob. rdg; Heb. omits.*
30:4 **warmth:** *or* food.   30:5 **human society:** *prob. rdg; Heb.*
obscure.

[a] Or *like sand*   [b] Heb lacks *like dew*   [c] Meaning of Heb uncertain

NEW AMERICAN BIBLE

10 The voice of the princes was silenced,
and their tongues stuck to the roofs of
their mouths.
‡29.11–20: see below‡

21 For me they listened and waited;
they were silent for my counsel.
22 Once I spoke, they said no more,
but received my pronouncement drop by drop.
23 They waited for me as for the rain;
they drank in my words like the spring rains.

24 When I smiled on them they were reassured;
25 mourners took comfort from my cheerful glance.
I chose out their way and presided;
I took a king's place in the armed forces.
11 Whoever heard of me blessed me;
those who saw me commended me.

12 For I rescued the poor who cried out for help,
the orphans, and the unassisted;
13 The blessing of those in extremity came upon me,
and the heart of the widow I made joyful.
14 I wore my honesty like a garment;
justice was my robe and my turban.
15 I was eyes to the blind,
and feet to the lame was I;
16 I was a father to the needy;
the rights of the stranger I studied,
17 And I broke the jaws of the wicked man;
from his teeth I forced the prey.

18 Then I said: "In my own nest I shall grow old;
I shall multiply years like the phoenix.
19 My root is spread out to the waters;
the dew rests by night on my branches.
20 My glory is fresh within me,
and my bow is renewed in my hand!"
‡29.21–25: see above‡

30 But now they hold me in derision
who are younger in years than I;
Whose fathers I should have disdained
to rank with the dogs of my flock.
2 Such strength as they had, to me meant nought;
they were utterly destitute.

3 In want and hunger was their lot,
they who fled to the parched wastelands:
4 They plucked saltwort and shrubs;
the roots of the broom plant were their food.
5 They were banished from among men,
with an outcry like that against a thief —
6 To dwell on the slopes of the wadies,
in caves of sand and stone;
7 Among the bushes they raised their raucous cry;
under the nettles they huddled together.
8 Irresponsible, nameless men,
they were driven out of the land.

9 Yet now they sing of me in mockery;
I am become a byword among them.
10 They abhor me, they stand aloof from me,
they do not hesitate to spit in my face!
11 Indeed, they have loosed their bonds;
they lord it over me,
and have thrown off restraint in my presence.

NEW JERUSALEM BIBLE

10 the voices of rulers were silenced,
and their tongues stayed still in their mouths.
‡29.11–20: see below‡
21 They[m] waited anxiously to hear me,
and listened in silence to what I had to say.
22 When I had finished, no one contradicted,
my words dropping on them, one by one.
23 They waited for me as though for rain,
open-mouthed as though for a late shower.
24 If I smiled at them, it was too good to be true,
they watched my face for the least sign of
favour.
25 As their chief, I told them which course to take,
like a king living among his troops,
and I led them wherever I chose.

11 On hearing me, people congratulated me,
on seeing me, people deferred to me,
12 because I freed the poor in distress
and the orphan who had no helper.
13 The dying man's blessing rested on me
and I gave the widow's heart cause to rejoice.
14 Uprightness I wore as a garment,
fair judgement was my cloak and my turban.
15 I was eyes for the blind,
and feet for the lame.
16 Who but me was father of the poor?
The stranger's case had a hearing from me.
17 I used to break the fangs of the wicked,
and snatch their prey from their jaws.

18 And I used to say, 'I shall die in honour,
after days as numerous as the sand.
19 My roots can reach the water,
the dews of night settle on my leaves.
20 My glory will be for ever new
and the bow in my hand for ever strong.'
‡29.21–25: see above‡

30 And now I am the laughing-stock
of people who are younger than I am
and whose parents I would have disdained
to put with the dogs guarding my flock.
2 And what use to me was the strength of their
hands? —
enfeebled as they were,
3 worn out by want and hunger,
for they used to gnaw the roots of the thirsty
ground —
that place of gloom, ruin and desolation —
4 they used to pick saltwort among the scrub,
making their meals off roots of broom.
5 Outlawed from human company,
which raised hue and cry against them, as
against thieves,
6 they made their homes in the sides of ravines,
in holes in the earth or in clefts of rock.
7 You could hear them braying from the bushes
as they huddled together in the thistles.
8 Children of scoundrels, worse, nameless people,
the very outcasts of society!
9 And these are the ones who now make up songs
about me
and use me as a byword!
10 Filled with disgust, they keep their distance,
on seeing me, they spit without restraint.
11 And since God has loosened my bow-string and
afflicted me,
they too throw off the bridle in my presence.

m **29** vv. 21–25 are inserted here because they follow on better from
v. 10 and lead up to v. 11.

NEW REVISED STANDARD VERSION	REVISED ENGLISH BIBLE

NEW REVISED STANDARD VERSION

12 On my right hand the rabble rise up;
  they send me sprawling,
  and build roads for my ruin.
13 They break up my path,
  they promote my calamity;
  no one restrains[d] them.
14 As through a wide breach they come;
  amid the crash they roll on.
15 Terrors are turned upon me;
  my honor is pursued as by the wind,
  and my prosperity has passed away like a
    cloud.
16 "And now my soul is poured out within me;
  days of affliction have taken hold of me.
17 The night racks my bones,
  and the pain that gnaws me takes no rest.
18 With violence he seizes my garment;[e]
  he grasps me by[f] the collar of my tunic.
19 He has cast me into the mire,
  and I have become like dust and ashes.
20 I cry to you and you do not answer me;
  I stand, and you merely look at me.
21 You have turned cruel to me;
  with the might of your hand you persecute me.
22 You lift me up on the wind, you make me ride
    on it,
  and you toss me about in the roar of the storm.
23 I know that you will bring me to death,
  and to the house appointed for all living.
24 "Surely one does not turn against the needy,[g]
  when in disaster they cry for help.[h]
25 Did I not weep for those whose day was hard?
  Was not my soul grieved for the poor?
26 But when I looked for good, evil came;
  and when I waited for light, darkness came.
27 My inward parts are in turmoil, and are never
    still;
  days of affliction come to meet me.
28 I go about in sunless gloom;
  I stand up in the assembly and cry for help.
29 I am a brother of jackals,
  and a companion of ostriches.
30 My skin turns black and falls from me,
  and my bones burn with heat.
31 My lyre is turned to mourning,
  and my pipe to the voice of those who weep.

31 "I have made a covenant with my eyes;
  how then could I look upon a virgin?
2 What would be my portion from God above,
  and my heritage from the Almighty[i] on high?
3 Does not calamity befall the unrighteous,
  and disaster the workers of iniquity?
4 Does he not see my ways,
  and number all my steps?
5 "If I have walked with falsehood,
  and my foot has hurried to deceit —
6 let me be weighed in a just balance,
  and let God know my integrity! —
7 if my step has turned aside from the way,
  and my heart has followed my eyes,
  and if any spot has clung to my hands;

REVISED ENGLISH BIBLE

12 On my right flank they attack in a mob;
  they raise their siege-ramps against me;
13 to destroy me they tear down my crumbling
    defences,
  and scramble up against me unhindered;
14 they burst in as through a gaping breach;
  at the moment of the crash they come in waves.
15 Terror after terror overwhelms me;
  my noble designs are swept away as by the wind,
  and my hope of deliverance vanishes like a cloud.
16 So now my life ebbs away;
  misery has me daily in its grip.
17 By night pain pierces my very bones,
  and there is ceaseless throbbing in my veins;
18 my garments are all bespattered with my phlegm,
  which chokes me like the collar of a garment.
19 God himself has flung me down in the mud;
  I have become no better than dust or ashes.
20 I call out to you, God, but you do not answer,
  I stand up to plead, but you keep aloof.
21 You have turned cruelly against me;
  with your strong hand you persecute me.
22 You snatch me up and mount me on the wind;
  the tempest tosses me about.
23 I know that you will hand me over to death,
  to the place appointed for all mortals.
24 Yet no beggar held out his hand to me in vain
  for relief in his distress.
25 Did I not weep for the unfortunate?
  Did not my heart grieve for the destitute?
26 Yet evil has come though I expected good,
  and when I looked for light, darkness came.
27 My bowels are in ferment and know no peace;
  days of misery stretch out in front of me.
28 I go about dejected and comfortless;
  I rise in the assembly, only to appeal for help.
29 The wolf is now my brother,
  the desert-owls have become my companions.
30 My blackened skin peels off,
  and my body is scorched by the heat.
31 My lyre has been tuned for a dirge,
  my flute to the sound of weeping.

31 ‡31.1: see below‡

2 What is the lot prescribed by God above,
  the portion from the Almighty on high?
3 Is not ruin prescribed for the miscreant,
  disaster for the wrongdoer?
4 Yet does not God himself see my ways
  and take account of my every step?
5 I swear I have had no dealings with falsehood
  and have not gone hotfoot after deceit.
1 I have taken an oath
  never to let my eyes linger on a girl.
6 Let God weigh me in the scales of justice,
  and he will know that I am blameless!
7 If my steps have wandered from the way,
  if my heart has followed my eyes,
  or any dirt has stuck to my hands,

[d] Cn: Heb helps   [e] Gk: Heb my garment is disfigured   [f] Heb like
[g] Heb ruin   [h] Cn: Meaning of Heb uncertain   [i] Traditional
rendering of Heb Shaddai

30:12 they . . . mob: prob. rdg; Heb. adds they let loose my feet.
30:24 for relief: prob. rdg; Heb. unintelligible.
30:28 comfortless: prob. rdg; Heb. without heat.   31:2 Verse 1
transposed to follow verse 5.   31:5 Verse 1 transposed to follow
this verse.

NEW AMERICAN BIBLE

12 To subvert my paths they rise up;
  they build their approaches for my ruin.
13 To destroy me, they attack with none to stay them;
14 as through a wide breach they advance.
  Amid the uproar they come on in waves;
15 over me rolls the terror.
  My dignity is borne off on the wind,
    and my welfare vanishes like a cloud.
  ‡30.16–17: see below‡
18 One with great power lays hold of my clothing;
  by the collar of my tunic he seizes me:
19 He has cast me into the mire;
  I am leveled with the dust and ashes.

20 I cry to you, but you do not answer me;
  you stand off and look at me,
21 Then you turn upon me without mercy
  and with your strong hand you buffet me.
22 You raise me up and drive me before the wind;
  I am tossed about by the tempest.
23 Indeed I know you will turn me back in death
  to the destined place of everyone alive.
24 Yet should not a hand be held out
  to help a wretched man in his calamity?
25 Or have I not wept for the hardships of others;
  was not my soul grieved for the destitute?
26 Yet when I looked for good, then evil came;
  when I expected light, then came darkness.

16 My soul ebbs away from me;
27 days of affliction have overtaken me.
17 My frame takes no rest by night;
  my inward parts seethe and will not be stilled.
28 I go about in gloom, without the sun;
  I rise up in public to voice my grief.

29 I have become the brother of jackals,
  companion to the ostrich.
30 My blackened skin falls away from me;
  the heat scorches my very frame.
31 My harp is turned to mourning,
  and my reed pipe to sounds of weeping.

31

‡31.1: see below‡

2 But what is man's lot from God above,
  his inheritance from the Almighty on high?
3 Is it not calamity for the unrighteous,
  and woe for evildoers?
4 Does he not see my ways,
  and number all my steps?
6 Let God weigh me in the scales of justice;
  thus will he know my innocence!

5 If I have walked in falsehood
  and my foot has hastened to deceit;
7 If my steps have turned out of the way,
  and my heart has followed my eyes,
  or any stain clings to my hands,

NEW JERUSALEM BIBLE

12 Their brats surge forward on my right,
  to see when I am having a little peace,
  and advance on me with threatening strides.
13 They cut off all means of escape
  seizing the chance to destroy me, and no one
    stops them.
14 They move in, as if through a wide breach,
  and I go tumbling beneath the rubble.
15 Terror rounds on me,
  my confidence is dispersed as though by the
    wind,
  my hope of safety vanishes like a cloud.

16 And now the life in me trickles away,
  days of grief have gripped me.
17 At night-time sickness saps my bones
  I am gnawed by wounds that never sleep.
18 Violently, he has caught me by my clothes,
  has gripped me by the collar of my coat.
19 He has thrown me into the mud;
  I am no more than dust and ashes.

20 I cry to you, and you give me no answer;
  I stand before you, but you take no notice.
21 You have grown cruel to me,
  and your strong hand torments me unmercifully.
22 You carry me away astride the wind
  and blow me to pieces in a tempest.
23 Yes, I know that you are taking me towards death,
  to the common meeting-place of all the living.

24 Yet have I ever laid a hand on the poor
  when they cried out for justice in calamity?
25 Have I not wept for those whose life is hard,
  felt pity for the penniless?
26 I hoped for happiness, but sorrow came;
  I looked for light, but there was darkness.
27 My stomach seethes, is never still,
  days of suffering have struck me.
28 Sombre I go, yet no one comforts me,
  and if I rise in the council, I rise to weep.
29 I have become brother to the jackal
  and companion to the ostrich.
30 My skin has turned black on me,
  my bones are burnt with fever.
31 My harp is tuned to dirges,
  my pipe to the voice of mourners.

31

I had made an agreement with my eyes
  not to linger on any virgin.
2 Now what portion does God allot from above,
  what fate does Shaddai apportion from his
    heaven —
3 if not the disasters appropriate to the wicked
  and the calamities fit for evil-doers?
4 But surely he sees how I behave,
  does he not count all my steps?
5 Have I been a fellow-traveller with falsehood,
  or hastened my steps towards deceit?
6 Let him weigh me on accurate scales:
  then he, God, will recognise my integrity!
7 If my feet have wandered from the rightful path,
  or if my eyes have led my heart astray,
  or if my hands are smirched with any stain,

NEW REVISED STANDARD VERSION	REVISED ENGLISH BIBLE

8   then let me sow, and another eat;
    and let what grows for me be rooted out.

9   "If my heart has been enticed by a woman,
    and I have lain in wait at my neighbor's door;

10   then let my wife grind for another,
    and let other men kneel over her.

11   For that would be a heinous crime;
    that would be a criminal offense;

12   for that would be a fire consuming down to
    Abaddon,
    and it would burn to the root all my harvest.

13   "If I have rejected the cause of my male or
    female slaves,
    when they brought a complaint against me;

14   what then shall I do when God rises up?
    When he makes inquiry, what shall I answer
    him?

15   Did not he who made me in the womb make
    them?
    And did not one fashion us in the womb?

16   "If I have withheld anything that the poor
    desired,
    or have caused the eyes of the widow to fail,

17   or have eaten my morsel alone,
    and the orphan has not eaten from it—

18   for from my youth I reared the orphan[j] like a
    father,
    and from my mother's womb I guided the
    widow[k]—

19   if I have seen anyone perish for lack of clothing,
    or a poor person without covering,

20   whose loins have not blessed me,
    and who was not warmed with the fleece of
    my sheep;

21   if I have raised my hand against the orphan,
    because I saw I had supporters at the gate;

22   then let my shoulder blade fall from my shoulder,
    and let my arm be broken from its socket.

23   For I was in terror of calamity from God,
    and I could not have faced his majesty.

24   "If I have made gold my trust,
    or called fine gold my confidence;

25   if I have rejoiced because my wealth was great,
    or because my hand had gotten much;

26   if I have looked at the sun[l] when it shone,
    or the moon moving in splendor,

27   and my heart has been secretly enticed,
    and my mouth has kissed my hand;

28   this also would be an iniquity to be punished by
    the judges,
    for I should have been false to God above.

29   "If I have rejoiced at the ruin of those who hated
    me,
    or exulted when evil overtook them—

30   I have not let my mouth sin
    by asking for their lives with a curse—

---

8   then may another eat what I sow,
    and may my crops be uprooted!

9   If my heart has been enticed by a woman
    or I have lurked by my neighbour's door,

10   may my wife be another man's slave,
    and may other men enjoy her.

11   For that would have been a heinous act,
    an offence before the law:

12   it would be a consuming and destructive fire
    raging among my crops.

13   If I ever rejected the plea of my slave or slave-girl
    when they brought a complaint against me,

14   what shall I do if God appears?
    What shall I answer if he intervenes?

15   Did not he who made me in the belly make them?
    Did not the same God create us in the womb?

16   If I have withheld from the poor what they needed
    or made the widow's eye grow dim with tears;

17   if I have eaten my portion of food by myself,
    and the fatherless child has not shared it with
    me—

18   the boy who said, 'From my youth he brought me
    up,'
    or the girl who claimed that from her birth I
    guided her—

19   if I have seen anyone perish for lack of clothing
    or a poor man with nothing to cover him;

20   if his body had no cause to bless me,
    because he was not kept warm with a fleece from
    my flock;

21   if I have raised my hand against the innocent,
    knowing that those who would side with me were
    in court;

22   then may my shoulder-blade be torn from my
    shoulder,
    my arm wrenched out of its socket!

23   But the fear of God was heavy upon me;
    because of his majesty I could do none of these
    things.

24   If I have put my faith in gold
    and my trust in the gold of Nubia;

25   if I have rejoiced in my great wealth
    and in the increase of riches in my possession;

26   if I ever looked on the sun in splendour
    or the moon moving in her glory,

27   and was led astray in my secret heart
    and kissed my hand in homage:

28   this would have been an offence before the law,
    for I should have been unfaithful to God on high.

38   If my land has cried out in reproach at me,
    and its furrows have joined in weeping,

39   If I have eaten its produce without payment
    and left my creditors to languish:

40   may thistles spring up instead of wheat,
    and noxious weeds instead of barley!

29   Have I rejoiced at the ruin of anyone who hated
    me
    or been filled with glee when misfortune overtook
    him,

30   even though I did not allow my tongue to sin
    by laying his life under a curse?

31:10 **be . . . slave:** *lit.* grind corn for another.   31:12 **raging:**
prob. rdg; Heb. uprooting.   31:21 **innocent:** *or* fatherless. **in
court:** *lit.* in the gate.   31:23 **the fear . . . me:** *prob. rdg; Heb.*
fear towards me is a disaster from God.   31:28 *Verses 38, 39,
and part of verse 40 transposed to follow this verse.*
31:39 **creditors:** *or* tenants.

j Heb *him*   *k* Heb *her*   *l* Heb *the light*

NEW AMERICAN BIBLE

8 Then may I sow, but another eat of it,
or may my planting be rooted up!

38 If my land has cried out against me
till its very furrows complained;

39 If I have eaten its produce without payment
and grieved the hearts of its tenants;

40 Then let the thistles grow instead of wheat
and noxious weeds instead of barley!

1 If I have made an agreement with my eyes
and entertained any thoughts against a maiden;

9 If my heart has been enticed toward a woman,
and I have lain in wait at my neighbor's door;

10 Then may my wife grind for another,
and may others cohabit with her!

11 For that would be heinous,
a crime to be condemned;

12 A fire that should burn down to the abyss
till it consumed all my possessions to the roots.

13 Had I refused justice to my manservant
or to my maid, when they had a claim
against me,

14 What then should I do when God rose up;
what could I answer when he demanded
an account?

15 Did not he who made me in the womb make him?
Did not the same One fashion us before
our birth?

16 If I have denied anything to the poor,
or allowed the eyes of the widow to languish

17 While I ate my portion alone,
with no share in it for the fatherless,

18 Though like a father God has reared me from
my youth,
guiding me even from my mother's womb—

19 If I have seen a wanderer without clothing,
or a poor man without covering,

20 Whose limbs have not blessed me
when warmed with the fleece of my sheep;

21 If I have raised my hand against the innocent
because I saw that I had supporters at the gate—

22 Then may my arm fall from the shoulder,
my forearm be broken at the elbow!

23 For the dread of God will be upon me,
and his majesty will overpower me.

24 Had I put my trust in gold
or called fine gold my security;

25 Or had I rejoiced that my wealth was great,
or that my hand had acquired abundance—

26 Had I looked upon the sun as it shone,
or the moon in the splendor of its progress,

27 And had my heart been secretly enticed
to waft them a kiss with my hand;

28 This too would be a crime for condemnation,
for I should have denied God above.

29 Had I rejoiced at the destruction of my enemy
or exulted when evil fell upon him,

30 Even though I had not suffered my mouth to sin
by uttering a curse against his life—

NEW JERUSALEM BIBLE

8 let someone else eat what I have sown
and let my young shoots all be rooted out.

9 If my heart has been seduced by a woman,
or if I have lurked at my neighbour's door,

10 let my wife go and grind for someone else,
let others have intercourse with her!

11 For I would have committed a sin of lust,
a crime punishable by the law,

12 a fire, indeed, burning all to Perdition,
which would have devoured my whole revenue.

13 If I have ever infringed the rights of slave
or slave-girl in legal actions against me—

14 what shall I do, when God stands up?
What shall I say, when he holds his assize?

15 Did he not create them in the womb like me,
the same God forming us in the womb?

38 If my land cries for vengeance against me
and its furrows weep in concert,

39 if I have eaten its produce without paying,
and caused the death of its owners,

40a let brambles grow instead of wheat,
rank weeds instead of barley!

16 Have I been insensible to the needs of the poor,
or let a widow's eyes grow dim?

17 Have I eaten my bit of bread on my own
without sharing it with the orphan?

18 I, whom God has fostered father-like from
childhood,
and guided since I left my mother's womb,

19 have I ever seen a wretch in need of clothing,
or the poor with nothing to wear,

20 without his having cause to bless me from his
heart,
as he felt the warmth of the fleece from my
lambs?

21 Have I raised my hand against an orphan,
presuming on my credit at the gate?

22 If so, let my shoulder fall from its socket,
let my arm break off at the elbow!

23 For the terror of God would fall on me
and I could not then stand my ground before his
majesty.

24 Have I put my faith in gold,
saying to fine gold, 'Ah, my security'?

25 Have I ever gloated over my great wealth,
or the riches that my hands have won?

26 Or has the sight of the sun in its glory,
or the glow of the moon as it walked the sky,

27 secretly stolen my heart,
so that I blew them a kiss?

28 That too would be a criminal offence,
to have denied the supreme God.

29 Have I rejoiced at my enemy's misfortune,
or exulted when disaster overtook him?—

30 I, who would not allow my tongue to sin
or to lay his life under a curse.

NEW REVISED STANDARD VERSION

31 if those of my tent ever said,
   'O that we might be sated with his flesh!' *m* —
32 the stranger has not lodged in the street;
   I have opened my doors to the traveler—
33 if I have concealed my transgressions as others do, *n*
   by hiding my iniquity in my bosom,
34 because I stood in great fear of the multitude,
   and the contempt of families terrified me,
   so that I kept silence, and did not go out of doors—
35 Oh, that I had one to hear me!
   (Here is my signature! let the Almighty *o* answer me!)
   Oh, that I had the indictment written by my adversary!
36 Surely I would carry it on my shoulder;
   I would bind it on me like a crown;
37 I would give him an account of all my steps;
   like a prince I would approach him.
38 "If my land has cried out against me,
   and its furrows have wept together;
39 if I have eaten its yield without payment,
   and caused the death of its owners;
40 let thorns grow instead of wheat,
   and foul weeds instead of barley."

The words of Job are ended.

32 So these three men ceased to answer Job, because he was righteous in his own eyes. 2 Then Elihu son of Barachel the Buzite, of the family of Ram, became angry. He was angry at Job because he justified himself rather than God; 3 he was angry also at Job's three friends because they had found no answer, though they had declared Job to be in the wrong. *p* 4 Now Elihu had waited to speak to Job, because they were older than he. 5 But when Elihu saw that there was no answer in the mouths of these three men, he became angry.

6 Elihu son of Barachel the Buzite answered:
   "I am young in years,
   and you are aged;
   therefore I was timid and afraid
   to declare my opinion to you.
7 I said, 'Let days speak,
   and many years teach wisdom.'
8 But truly it is the spirit in a mortal,
   the breath of the Almighty, *o* that makes for understanding.
9 It is not the old *q* that are wise,
   nor the aged that understand what is right.
10 Therefore I say, 'Listen to me;
   let me also declare my opinion.'

11 "See, I waited for your words,
   I listened for your wise sayings,
   while you searched out what to say.
12 I gave you my attention,
   but there was in fact no one that confuted Job,
   no one among you that answered his words.
13 Yet do not say, 'We have found wisdom;
   God may vanquish him, not a human.'
14 He has not directed his words against me,
   and I will not answer him with your speeches.

REVISED ENGLISH BIBLE

31 The men of my household have indeed said:
   'Who has eaten of his food and not been satisfied?'
32 No stranger has had to spend the night in the street,
   for I have kept open house for the traveller.
33 Have I ever concealed my misdeeds as others do,
   keeping my guilt hidden within my breast,
34–35 because I feared the gossip of the town
   or dreaded the scorn of my fellow-citizens?
   Let me but call a witness in my defence!
   Let the Almighty state his case against me!
   If my accuser had written out his indictment,
   I should not keep silence and remain indoors.
36 No! I should flaunt it on my shoulder
   and wear it like a crown on my head;
37 I should plead the whole record of my life
   and present that in court as my defence.

‡31.38–40a: see above‡

40 Job's speeches are finished.

32 THESE three men gave up answering Job, for he continued to think himself righteous. 2 Then Elihu son of Barakel the Buzite, of the family of Ram, became angry: angry because Job had made himself out to be more righteous than God, 3 and angry with his three friends because they had found no answer to Job and so let God appear wrong. 4 Now Elihu had hung back while they were talking with Job because they were older than he was; 5 but, when he saw that the three had no answer to give, he could no longer contain his anger. 6 So Elihu son of Barakel the Buzite began to speak:

   I am young in years, while you are old;
   that is why I held back and shrank
   from expressing my opinion in front of you.
7 I said to myself, 'Let age speak,
   and length of years expound wisdom.'
8 But it is a spirit in a human being,
   the breath of the Almighty, that gives him understanding;
9 it is not only the old who are wise,
   not only the aged who understand what is right.
10 Therefore I say: Listen to me;
   I too want to express an opinion.

11 Here I have been waiting for what you had to say,
   listening to your reasoning,
   while you picked your words;
12 I have been giving thought to those conclusions,
   but not one of you convicts Job or refutes his arguments.
13 See then that you do not claim to have found wisdom;
   or say 'God will rebut him, not man.'
14 I shall not string words together like you
   or answer him in the way you have done.

31:31 **household:** *lit.* tent.   31:33 **others do:** *or* Adam did.
31:37 *Verses 38, 39, and part of verse 40 transposed to follow verse 28.*   32:2 **had . . . God:** *or* had justified himself with God.
32:3 **and so . . . wrong:** *prob. original rdg; altered in Heb. to* and had not proved Job wrong.   32:14 **I . . . string:** *prob. rdg; Heb.* He has not strung. **like you:** *prob. rdg; Heb.* towards me.

---

m Meaning of Heb uncertain   *n* Or *as Adam did*   *o* Traditional rendering of Heb *Shaddai*   *p* Another ancient tradition reads *answer, and had put God in the wrong*   *q* Gk Syr Vg: Heb *many*

NEW AMERICAN BIBLE

31 Had not the men of my tent exclaimed,
  "Who has not been fed with his meat!"
32 Because no stranger lodged in the street,
  but I opened my door to wayfarers—

33 Had I, out of human weakness, hidden my sins
  and buried my guilt in my bosom
34 Because I feared the noisy multitude
  and the scorn of the tribes terrified me—
  then I should have remained silent, and not
  come out of doors!

35 Oh, that I had one to hear my case,
  and that my accuser would write out
  his indictment!
36 Surely, I should wear it on my shoulder
  or put it on me like a diadem;
37 Of all my steps I should give him an account;
  like a prince I should present myself before him.

This is my final plea; let the Almighty answer me!
The words of Job are ended.

‡31.38–40: see above‡

32 Then the three men ceased to answer Job, because
he was righteous in his own eyes. 2 But the anger of
Elihu, son of Barachel the Buzite, of the family of Ram,
was kindled. He was angry with Job for considering himself
rather than God to be in the right. 3 He was angry also with
the three friends because they had not found a good answer
and had not condemned Job. 4 But since these men were
older than he, Elihu bided his time before addressing Job.
5 When, however, Elihu saw that there was no reply in the
mouths of the three men, his wrath was inflamed. 6 So
Elihu, son of Barachel the Buzite, spoke out and said:

I am young and you are very old;
  therefore I held back and was afraid
  to declare to you my knowledge.
7 Days should speak, I thought,
  and many years teach wisdom!
8 But it is a spirit in man,
  the breath of the Almighty, that gives
  him understanding.
9 It is not those of many days who are wise,
  nor the aged who understand the right.
10 Therefore I say, hearken to me;
  let me too set forth my knowledge!

11 Behold, I have waited for your discourses,
  and have given ear to your arguments.
12 Yes, I followed you attentively
  as you searched out what to say;
And behold, there is none who has convicted Job,
  not one of you who could refute his statements.
13 Yet do not say, "We have met wisdom;
  God may vanquish him but not man!"
14 For had he addressed his words to me,
  I should not then have answered him as you
  have done.

NEW JERUSALEM BIBLE

31 The people of my tent, did they not say,
  'Will anyone name a person whom he has not
  filled with meat?'
32 No stranger ever had to sleep outside,
  my door was always open to the traveller.
33 Have I ever concealed my transgression from
  others
  or kept my fault a secret in my breast?
34 Have I ever stood in fear of common gossip,
  or dreaded any family's contempt,
  and so kept quiet, not venturing out of doors?
35 Will no one give me a hearing?
  I have said my last word; now let Shaddai reply!
When my adversary has drafted his writ against me
36 I shall wear it on my shoulder,
  and bind it round my head like a royal turban.
37 I shall give him an account of my every step
  and go as boldly as a prince to meet him.

‡31.38–40a: see above‡

40b End of the words of Job.

32 These three men stopped arguing with Job, because
he was convinced of his uprightness. 2 But Elihu
son of Barachel the Buzite, of the clan of Ram, became very
angry. He fumed with rage against Job for thinking that he
was right and God was wrong; 3 and he was equally angry
with the three friends for giving up the argument and thus
putting God in the wrong. 4 While they and Job were talking, Elihu had waited, because they were older than he was;
5 but when he saw that the three men had not another word
to say in answer, his anger burst out. 6 And Elihu son of
Barachel the Buzite began to speak. He said:

I am still young,
  and you are old,
so I was shy and hesitant
  to tell you what I know.
7 I thought, 'Age ought to speak,
  advancing years will convey wisdom.'
8 There is, you see, a spirit residing in humanity,
  the breath of God conferring intelligence.
9 Great age does not give wisdom,
  nor seniority fair judgement.
10 And so I ask you for a hearing;
  now it is my turn to tell you what I know.
11 Up to now, I was hanging on your words,
  I paid attention to your arguments
  as each of you chose his words.
12 I paid very close attention;
  and I see that none of you has confounded Job,
  not one of you has refuted what he says.
13 So do not say, 'We have found wisdom;
  our teaching is divine and not human.'
14 I am not going to follow the same line of
  argument;
  my reply to Job will be couched in different
  terms.

31, 37: Final plea: literally, "tau," the last letter of the Hebrew
alphabet; in the current Hebrew text this line is in v 35, while the
following one ends v 40.

NEW REVISED STANDARD VERSION	REVISED ENGLISH BIBLE

NEW REVISED STANDARD VERSION

15 "They are dismayed, they answer no more;
   they have not a word to say.
16 And am I to wait, because they do not speak,
   because they stand there, and answer no more?
17 I also will give my answer;
   I also will declare my opinion.
18 For I am full of words;
   the spirit within me constrains me.
19 My heart is indeed like wine that has no vent;
   like new wineskins, it is ready to burst.
20 I must speak, so that I may find relief;
   I must open my lips and answer.
21 I will not show partiality to any person
   or use flattery toward anyone.
22 For I do not know how to flatter—
   or my Maker would soon put an end to me!

33 "But now, hear my speech, O Job,
   and listen to all my words.
2 See, I open my mouth;
   the tongue in my mouth speaks.
3 My words declare the uprightness of my heart,
   and what my lips know they speak sincerely.
4 The spirit of God has made me,
   and the breath of the Almighty[r] gives me life.
5 Answer me, if you can;
   set your words in order before me; take your
      stand.
6 See, before God I am as you are;
   I too was formed from a piece of clay.
7 No fear of me need terrify you;
   my pressure will not be heavy on you.
8 "Surely, you have spoken in my hearing,
   and I have heard the sound of your words.
9 You say, 'I am clean, without transgression;
   I am pure, and there is no iniquity in me.
10 Look, he finds occasions against me,
   he counts me as his enemy;
11 he puts my feet in the stocks,
   and watches all my paths.'
12 "But in this you are not right. I will answer you:
   God is greater than any mortal.
13 Why do you contend against him,
   saying, 'He will answer none of my[s] words'?
14 For God speaks in one way,
   and in two, though people do not perceive it.
15 In a dream, in a vision of the night,
   when deep sleep falls on mortals,
   while they slumber on their beds,
16 then he opens their ears,
   and terrifies them with warnings,
17 that he may turn them aside from their deeds,
   and keep them from pride,
18 to spare their souls from the Pit,
   their lives from traversing the River.
19 They are also chastened with pain upon their
      beds,
   and with continual strife in their bones,
20 so that their lives loathe bread,
   and their appetites dainty food.
21 Their flesh is so wasted away that it cannot be
      seen;
   and their bones, once invisible, now stick out.
22 Their souls draw near the Pit,
   and their lives to those who bring death.

REVISED ENGLISH BIBLE

15 If these men are confounded and are stuck for an
      answer,
   if words fail them,
16 am I to wait because they do not speak,
   because they stand there, stuck for an answer?
17 I, too, have a furrow to plough;
   I am going to express my opinion,
18 for I am bursting with words,
   as if wind in my belly were griping me.
19 My belly is distended as if with wine,
   about to burst open like a new wineskin;
20 I must speak and find relief,
   I must open my lips and answer;
21 I shall show no favour to anyone;
   I shall flatter no one,
22 for I cannot use flattering titles,
   or my Maker would soon do away with me.

33 But now, Job, listen to my words,
   attend carefully to everything I say.
2 I am ready with my answer as you see;
   the words are on the tip of my tongue.
3 My heart assures me that I speak with knowledge,
   that my lips speak with sincerity.
4 For the spirit of God made me,
   the breath of the Almighty gave me life.
5 Answer me, if you can,
   marshal your arguments and confront me.
6 In God's sight I am just what you are;
   I too am only a handful of clay.
7 Fear of me need not abash you,
   nor any pressure from me overawe you.
8 You have said your say in my hearing;
   I have listened to the words you spoke:
9 'I am innocent', you said, 'and free from offence,
   blameless and without guilt.
10 Yet God finds occasions to put me in the wrong
   and counts me his enemy;
11 he puts my feet in the stocks
   and keeps a close watch on all my conduct.'
12 You are not in the right—that is my answer;
   for God is greater than any mortal.
13 Why then plead your case with him,
   for no one can answer his arguments?
14 Indeed, once God has spoken
   he does not speak a second time to confirm it.
15 In dreams, in visions of the night,
   when deepest slumber falls on mortals,
   while they lie asleep in bed
16 God imparts his message,
   and as a warning strikes them with terror.
17 To turn someone from his evil deeds,
   to check human pride,
18 at the edge of the pit he holds him back alive
   and stops him from crossing the river of death.
19 Or again, someone learns his lesson on a bed of
      pain,
   tormented by a ceaseless ague in his bones;
20 he turns from his food with loathing
   and has no relish for the choicest dishes;
21 his flesh hangs loose on him,
   his bones are loosened and out of joint,
22 his soul draws near the pit,
   his life to the waters of death.

---

[r] Traditional rendering of Heb *Shaddai*   [s] Compare Gk: Heb *his*

33:6 **In God's sight:** *or* In strength.   33:10 **finds ... wrong:** *so Syriac; Heb*. finds ways of thwarting me.   33:17 **pride:** *prob. rdg; Heb*. obscure.   33:22 **waters:** *Heb*. killers.

NEW AMERICAN BIBLE

NEW JERUSALEM BIBLE

15 They are dismayed, they make no more reply;
  words fail them.
16 Must I wait? Now that they speak no more,
  and have ceased to make reply,
17 I too will speak my part;
  I also will show my knowledge!

18 For I am full of matters to utter;
  the spirit within me compels me.
19 Like a new wineskin with wine under pressure,
  my bosom is ready to burst.
20 Let me speak and obtain relief;
  let me open my lips, and make reply.
21 I would not be partial to anyone,
  nor give flattering titles to any.
22 For I know nought of flattery;
  if I did, my Maker would soon take me away.

33 Therefore, O Job, hear my discourse,
  and hearken to all my words.
2 Behold, now I open my mouth;
  my tongue and my voice form words.
3 I will state directly what is in my mind,
  my lips shall utter knowledge sincerely;
4 For the spirit of God has made me,
  the breath of the Almighty keeps me alive.

5 If you are able, refute me;
  draw up your arguments and stand forth.
6 Behold I, like yourself, have been taken
  from the same clay by God.
7 Therefore no fear of me should dismay you,
  nor should my presence weigh heavily upon you.

8 But you have said in my hearing,
  as I listened to the sound of your words:
9 "I am clean and without transgression;
  I am innocent; there is no guilt in me.
10 Yet he invents pretexts against me
  and reckons me as his enemy.
11 He puts my feet in the stocks;
  he watches all my ways!"

12 In this you are not just, let me tell you;
  for God is greater than man.
13 Why, then, do you make complaint against him
  that he gives no account of his doings?
14 For God does speak, perhaps once,
  or even twice, though one perceive it not.

15 In a dream, in a vision of the night,
  [when deep sleep falls upon men]
  as they slumber in their beds,
16 It is then he opens the ears of men
  and as a warning to them, terrifies them;
17 By turning man from evil
  and keeping pride away from him,
18 He withholds his soul from the pit
  and his life from passing to the grave.

19 Or a man is chastened on his bed by pain
  and unceasing suffering within his frame,
20 So that to his appetite food becomes repulsive,
  and his senses reject the choicest nourishment.
21 His flesh is wasted so that it cannot be seen,
  and his bones, once invisible, appear;
22 His soul draws near to the pit,
  his life to the place of the dead.

15 They are nonplussed for an answer,
  words have failed them.
16 I have been waiting. Since they do not speak,
  since they have given up the argument,
17 now I shall have my say,
  my turn has come to say what I know.
18 For I am full of words
  and forced to speak by a spirit within me;
19 within me, it feels like new wine seeking a vent,
  bursting out of new wine-skins.
20 To gain relief, I must speak,
  I must open my lips and reply.
21 I shall not take anyone's side,
  I shall not flatter anyone.
22 I do not know how to flatter—
  or my Creator would make short work of me.

33 So, Job, please listen to my words
  and attend to all I have to say.
2 Now as I open my mouth,
  and my tongue shapes words against my palate,
3 I shall utter words of wisdom from the heart,
  my lips will speak in all sincerity.
5 Refute me, if you can.
  Prepare yourself, take up your position!
6 Look, I am your equal, not some god,
  like you I was moulded out of clay.
4 God's was the spirit that made me,
  Shaddai's the breath that gave me life.
7 No fear of me, therefore, need affright you,
  my hand will not lie heavy over you.
8 How could you say in my hearing—
  for the sound of your words did not escape
    me—
9 'I am clean, and sinless,
  I am pure, without fault.
10 But he keeps inventing excuses against me
  and regards me as his enemy.
11 He puts me in the stocks,
  he watches my every path'?
12 In saying so, I tell you, you are wrong:
  for God is greater than any human being.
13 Why then quarrel with him
  for not replying to you, word for word?
14 God speaks first in one way,
  and then in another, although we do not realise
    it.
15 In dreams and in night-visions,
  when slumber has settled on humanity
  and people are asleep in bed,
16 he speaks in someone's ear,
  frightens him with apparitions
17 to turn him from what he is doing
  and to put an end to his pride.
18 And thus he preserves his soul from the abyss,
  his life from passing down the Canal.
19 Or again, he corrects by the sufferings of the
    sick-bed,
  when someone's bones tremble continuously
20 and the thought of food revolts him,
  however tasty it is,
21 and his flesh rots away while you watch it
  and the bones beneath begin to show,
22 and his soul is drawing nearer to the abyss
  and his life to the dwelling of the dead.

NEW REVISED STANDARD VERSION	REVISED ENGLISH BIBLE

NEW REVISED STANDARD VERSION

23 Then, if there should be for one of them an angel,
a mediator, one of a thousand,
one who declares a person upright,
24 and he is gracious to that person, and says,
'Deliver him from going down into the Pit;
I have found a ransom;
25 let his flesh become fresh with youth;
let him return to the days of his youthful vigor.'
26 Then he prays to God, and is accepted by him,
he comes into his presence with joy,
and God[t] repays him for his righteousness.
27 That person sings to others and says,
'I sinned, and perverted what was right,
and it was not paid back to me.
28 He has redeemed my soul from going down to the Pit,
and my life shall see the light.'
29 "God indeed does all these things,
twice, three times, with mortals,
30 to bring back their souls from the Pit,
so that they may see the light of life.[u]
31 Pay heed, Job, listen to me;
be silent, and I will speak.
32 If you have anything to say, answer me;
speak, for I desire to justify you.
33 If not, listen to me;
be silent, and I will teach you wisdom."

34 Then Elihu continued and said:
2 "Hear my words, you wise men,
and give ear to me, you who know;
3 for the ear tests words
as the palate tastes food.
4 Let us choose what is right;
let us determine among ourselves what is good.
5 For Job has said, 'I am innocent,
and God has taken away my right;
6 in spite of being right I am counted a liar;
my wound is incurable, though I am without transgression.'
7 Who is there like Job,
who drinks up scoffing like water,
8 who goes in company with evildoers
and walks with the wicked?
9 For he has said, 'It profits one nothing
to take delight in God.'
10 "Therefore, hear me, you who have sense,
far be it from God that he should do wickedness,
and from the Almighty[v] that he should do wrong.
11 For according to their deeds he will repay them,
and according to their ways he will make it befall them.
12 Of a truth, God will not do wickedly,
and the Almighty[v] will not pervert justice.
13 Who gave him charge over the earth
and who laid on him[w] the whole world?
14 If he should take back his spirit[x] to himself,
and gather to himself his breath,
15 all flesh would perish together,
and all mortals return to dust.

REVISED ENGLISH BIBLE

23 Yet if an angel, one of a thousand, stands by him,
a mediator between him and God,
to expound God's righteousness to man
and to secure mortal man his due;
24 if he speaks on behalf of him and says,
'Reprieve him from going down to the pit;
I have the price of his release':
25 then his body will grow sturdier than it was in his youth;
he will return to the days of his prime.
26 If he entreats God to show him favour,
to let him enter his presence with joy;
27 if he affirms before everyone, 'I have sinned,
turned right into wrong without a thought':
28 then he saves himself from going down to the pit,
he lives and sees the light.
29 All these things God may do to someone
again and yet again,
30 bringing him back from the pit
to enjoy the full light of life.
31 Listen, Job, and attend to me;
be silent, and let me speak.
32 If you have anything to say, answer me;
speak, for I shall gladly find you proved right.
33 But if you have nothing, then listen to me:
be silent, and I shall teach you wisdom.

34 Then Elihu went on to say:
2 Mark my words, you master-minds!
You that know so much, listen to me!
3 For the ear tests words
as the palate savours food.
4 Let us then examine for ourselves what is right;
let us together establish the true good.
5 Job has said, 'I am innocent,
but God has denied me justice,
6 he has falsified my case;
my state is desperate, yet I have done no wrong.'
7 Was there ever a man like Job
with his thirst for irreverent talk,
8 choosing bad company to share his journeys,
a fellow-traveller with wicked men?
9 For he says that it brings no profit to anyone
to find favour with God.
10 But listen to me, you men of good sense.
Far be it from God to do evil,
from the Almighty to play false!
11 For he requites everyone according to his actions
and sees that each gets the reward his conduct deserves.
12 The truth is, God would never do wrong,
the Almighty does not pervert justice.
13 Who committed the earth to his keeping?
Who but he established the whole world?
14 If he were to turn his thoughts inwards
and withdraw his life-giving spirit,
15 all flesh would perish on the instant,
all mortals would turn again to dust.

---

[t] Heb he   [u] Syr: Heb to be lighted with the light of life
[v] Traditional rendering of Heb Shaddai   [w] Heb lacks on him
[x] Heb his heart his spirit

33:23 **and to . . . due:** line transposed from verse 26.
33:24 **Reprieve:** so some MSS; others have an unknown word.
33:25 **will grow sturdier:** prob. rdg.; Heb. unintelligible.
33:26 See note on verse 23.   34:6 **he has falsified:** so Gk; Heb.
am I falsifying.

23 If then there be for him an angel,
    one out of a thousand, a mediator,
To show him what is right for him
    and bring the man back to justice,
24 He will take pity on him and say,
    "Deliver him from going down to the pit;
    I have found him a ransom."

25 Then his flesh shall become soft as a boy's;
    he shall be again as in the days of his youth.
26 He shall pray and God will favor him;
    he shall see God's face with rejoicing.
27 He shall sing before men and say,
    "I sinned and did wrong,
    yet he has not punished me accordingly.
28 He delivered my soul from passing to the pit,
    and I behold the light of life."

29 Lo, all these things God does,
    twice, or thrice, for a man,
30 Bringing back his soul from the pit
    to the light, in the land of the living.
31 Be attentive, O Job; listen to me!
    Be silent and I will speak.
32 If you have aught to say, then answer me.
    Speak out! I should like to see you justified.
33 If not, then do you listen to me;
    be silent while I teach you wisdom.

34

Then Elihu continued and said:

2 Hear, O wise men, my discourse,
    and you that have knowledge, hear me!
3 For the ear tests words,
    as the taste does food.
4 Let us discern for ourselves what is right;
    let us learn between us what is good.
5 For Job has said, "I am innocent,
    but God has taken what is my due.
6 Notwithstanding my right I am set at nought;
    in my wound the arrow rankles, sinless though I
      am."
7 What man is like Job?
    He drinks in blasphemies like water,
8 Keeps company with evildoers
    and goes along with wicked men,
9 When he says, "It profits a man nought
    that he is pleasing to God."

10 Therefore, men of understanding, hearken to me:
    far be it from God to do wickedness;
    far from the Almighty to do wrong!
11 Rather, he requites men for their conduct,
    and brings home to a man his way of life.
12 Surely, God cannot act wickedly,
    the Almighty cannot violate justice.
13 Who gave him government over the earth,
    or who else set all the land in its place?
14 If he were to take back his spirit to himself,
    withdraw to himself his breath,
15 All flesh would perish together,
    and man would return to the dust.

23 Then, if there is an Angel near him,
    a Mediator, one in a thousand,
    to remind him where his duty lies,
24 to take pity on him and to say,
    'Spare him from going down to the abyss:
    I have found the ransom for his life,'
25 his flesh will recover its childhood freshness,
    he will return to the days of his youth.
26 He will pray to God who has restored him to
      favour,
    and will come into his presence with joy.
He will tell others how he has received saving
      justice
27   and sing this hymn before his companions,
    'I sinned and left the path of right,
    but God has not punished me as my sin
      deserved.
28 He has spared my soul from going down to the
      abyss
    and is making my life see the light.'
29 All this is what God keeps doing
    again and yet again for human beings,
30 to snatch souls back from the abyss
    and to make the light of the living still shine.

31 Pay attention, Job, listen to me:
    keep quiet, I have more to say.
32 If you have anything to say, refute me,
    speak out, for I would gladly accept that you are
      upright.
33 If not, then listen to me:
    keep quiet, and I will teach you wisdom.

34

Elihu continued his speech. He said:

2 And now, you sages, listen to what I say,
    lend me your ears, you learned men.
3 The ear distinguishes the value of what is said,
    just as the palate can tell one food from another.
4 Let us consider together God's ruling
    and decide what we all mean by good.
5 Job has been saying, 'I am upright
    and God denies me fair judgement.
6 My judge is treating me cruelly,
    my wound is incurable, for no fault of mine.'
7 Can anyone else exist like Job,
    who laps up mockery like water,
8 who consorts with evil-doers
    and marches in step with the wicked?
9 Did he not say, 'No one derives any benefit
    from enjoying the society of God'?

10 Listen to me then, like intelligent people.
    Far be evil from God
    or injustice from Shaddai!
11 For he pays people back for what they do,
    treating each as his own conduct deserves.
12 Be sure of it: God never does wrong,
    Shaddai does not pervert what is just.
13 Did someone else entrust the world to his care
    was he given charge of the universe by someone
      else?
14 If he were to recall his spirit,
    to concentrate his breath back in himself,
15 all flesh would instantly perish
    and all people would return to dust.

NEW REVISED STANDARD VERSION	REVISED ENGLISH BIBLE

NEW REVISED STANDARD VERSION

16 "If you have understanding, hear this;
   listen to what I say.
17 Shall one who hates justice govern?
   Will you condemn one who is righteous and
     mighty,
18 who says to a king, 'You scoundrel!'
   and to princes, 'You wicked men!';
19 who shows no partiality to nobles,
   nor regards the rich more than the poor,
   for they are all the work of his hands?
20 In a moment they die;
   at midnight the people are shaken and pass
     away,
   and the mighty are taken away by no human
     hand.
21 "For his eyes are upon the ways of mortals,
   and he sees all their steps.
22 There is no gloom or deep darkness
   where evildoers may hide themselves.
23 For he has not appointed a time^y for anyone
   to go before God in judgment.
24 He shatters the mighty without investigation,
   and sets others in their place.
25 Thus, knowing their works,
   he overturns them in the night, and they are
     crushed.
26 He strikes them for their wickedness
   while others look on,
27 because they turned aside from following him,
   and had no regard for any of his ways,
28 so that they caused the cry of the poor to come to
     him,
   and he heard the cry of the afflicted—
29 When he is quiet, who can condemn?
   When he hides his face, who can behold him,
   whether it be a nation or an individual?—
30 so that the godless should not reign,
   or those who ensnare the people.
31 "For has anyone said to God,
   'I have endured punishment; I will not offend
     any more;
32 teach me what I do not see;
   if I have done iniquity, I will do it no more'?
33 Will he then pay back to suit you,
   because you reject it?
   For you must choose, and not I;
   therefore declare what you know.^z
34 Those who have sense will say to me,
   and the wise who hear me will say,
35 'Job speaks without knowledge,
   his words are without insight.'
36 Would that Job were tried to the limit,
   because his answers are those of the wicked.
37 For he adds rebellion to his sin;
   he claps his hands among us,
   and multiplies his words against God."

35 Elihu continued and said:
2 "Do you think this to be just?
   You say, 'I am in the right before God.'
3 If you ask, 'What advantage have I?
   How am I better off than if I had sinned?'

REVISED ENGLISH BIBLE

16 Now Job, if you have the wit, consider this;
   listen to what I am saying:
17 Can it be that a hater of justice is in control?
   Do you disparage a sovereign whose rule is so fair,
18 who says to a prince, 'You scoundrel,'
   and calls the nobles blackguards to their faces;
19 who shows no special respect to those in office
   and favours the rich no more than the poor?
   All alike are God's creatures,
20 who may die in a moment, in the middle of the
     night;
   at his touch the rich are no more,
   and he removes the mighty without lifting a finger!
21 His eyes are on the ways of everyone,
   and he watches each step they take;
22 there is nowhere so dark, so deep in shadow,
   that wrongdoers may hide themselves.
25 Therefore he repudiates all that they do;
   he turns on them in the night, and they are
     crushed.
23 There are no appointed days for people
   to appear before God for judgement.
24 Without holding an enquiry, he breaks the
     powerful
   and sets others in their place.
26 For their crimes he strikes them down
   as a public spectacle,
27 because they have ceased to obey him,
   and pay no heed to any of his ways,
28 but have caused the cry of the poor to reach his
     ears,
   so that he hears the distressed when they cry.
29-30 Even if he is silent, who can condemn him?
   If he looks away, who can find fault?
   What though he makes a godless man king
   over a stubborn nation and all its people?
31 But suppose you were to say to God,
   'I have overstepped the mark, but shall do no more
     mischief.
32 I am contemptible; grant me guidance;
   whatever wrong I have done, I shall do no more.'
33 Will he, at these words, condone your rejection of
     him?
   It is for you, Job, to decide, not me:
   but what can you answer?
34 Men of good sense will say,
   any intelligent hearer will tell me,
35 'Job is talking without knowledge,
   and there is no sense in his words.
36 If only Job could be put to the test once and for all
   for answering like a mischief-maker!
37 He is a sinner and a rebel as well
   with his endless ranting against God.'

35 Elihu went on to say:
2 Do you reckon this to be a sound plea,
   to maintain that you are in the right against God
3 if you say, 'What would be the advantage to me?
   How much should I gain from sinning'?

34:22–26 *Verse 25 transposed to follow verse 22.*
34:23 **appointed days:** *prob. rdg; Heb.* still.   34:29–30 **a
stubborn:** *so Gk; Heb.* the snares of a.   34:31 **more:** *prob. rdg;
Heb. obscure.*   34:37 **He is . . . well:** *prob. rdg; Heb. adds*
between us it is enough.

^y Cn: Heb *yet*   ^z Meaning of Heb of verses 29-33 uncertain

16 Now, do you, O Job, hear this!
  Hearken to the words I speak!
17 Can an enemy of justice indeed be in control,
  or will you condemn the supreme Just One,
18 Who says to a king, "You are worthless!"
  and to nobles, "You are wicked!"
19 Who neither favors the person of princes,
  nor respects the rich more than the poor?
  For they are all the work of his hands;
20 in a moment they die, even at midnight.
  He brings on nobles, and takes them away,
  removing the powerful without lifting a hand;
21 For his eyes are upon the ways of man,
  and he beholds all his steps.

22 There is no darkness so dense
  that evildoers can hide in it.
25 Therefore he discerns their works;
  he turns at night and crushes them.
23 For he forewarns no man of his time
  to come before God in judgment.
24 Without a trial he breaks the mighty,
  and sets others in their stead,
27 Because they turned away from him
  and heeded none of his ways,
28 But caused the cries of the poor to reach him,
  so that he heard the plea of the afflicted.

29 If he remains tranquil, who then can condemn?
  If he hides his face, who then can behold him?
30 . . . .
31 When anyone says to God,
  "I was misguided; I will offend no more.
32 Teach me wherein I have sinned;
  if I have done wrong, I will do so no more,"
33 Would you then say that God must punish,
  since you reject what he is doing?
  It is you who must choose, not I;
  speak, therefore, what you know.

34 Men of understanding will say to me,
  every wise man who hears my views:
35 "Job speaks without intelligence,
  and his words are without sense."
36 Let Job be tried to the limit,
  since his answers are those of the impious;
37 For he is adding rebellion to his sin
  by brushing off our arguments
  and addressing many words to God.

16 If you have any intelligence, listen to this,
  lend your ear to the sound of my words.
17 Could an enemy of fair judgement ever govern?
  Would you dare condemn the Upright One, the
    Almighty,
18 who says to a king, 'You are a scoundrel!'
  and to nobles, 'You are wicked!',
19 who is unimpressed by princes
  and makes no distinction between rich and poor,
  since all alike have been made by him?
20 They die suddenly, at dead of night,
  they perish — these great ones — and disappear:
  it costs him no effort to remove a tyrant.
21 For his eyes keep watch on human ways,
  and he observes every step.
22 No darkness, no shadow dark as death
  where wrong-doers can hide!
23 He serves no writ on anyone,
  no summons to appear before God's court:
24 he breaks the powerful without enquiry
  and sets up others in their places.
25 He knows the sort of things they do!
  He overthrows them at night, to be trampled on.
26 He beats them like criminals
  chained up for all to see,
27 since they have turned their backs on him,
  having understood so little of his ways
28 as to make the cries of the weak rise to him
  and let him hear the appeal of the afflicted.

29 But if he is still silent and no one can move him,
  if he veils his face, so that no one can see him,
  he is taking pity on nations and individuals,
30 is setting some wrong-doer free from the meshes
    of affliction.
31 When such a one says to God,
  'I was misled, I shall not do wrong any more;
32 although I have sinned, instruct me;
  although I did wrong, I will not do it again,'
33 in your opinion, should he punish such a one —
  you who have rejected his decisions?
  This is for you to decide — not for me! —
  so kindly enlighten us!
34 Ordinary sensible people, however, will say to me,
  and so will any sage who has been listening to
    me,
35 'Job's words are spoken without any knowledge,
  what he says shows no intelligence.
36 Kindly examine him thoroughly,
  since his answers imply that he is a criminal.
37 For to his sin he now adds rebellion,
  bringing law to an end among us
  and heaping abuse on God.'

35

Then Elihu proceeded and said:

2 Do you think it right to say,
  "I am just rather than God"?
3 To say, "What does it profit me;
  what advantage have I more than if
    I had sinned?"

35

Elihu continued his speech. He said:

2 Do you think you can prove yourself upright
  and establish your uprightness before God
3 by daring to say to him, 'What does it matter to
    you,
  or how does it benefit me, whether I have sinned
    or not?'

34, 26. 29f: The extant Hebrew text of these verses contains several
added phrases which either represent duplication or are very obscure.

NEW REVISED STANDARD VERSION	REVISED ENGLISH BIBLE

NEW REVISED STANDARD VERSION

4 I will answer you
  and your friends with you.
5 Look at the heavens and see;
  observe the clouds, which are higher than you.
6 If you have sinned, what do you accomplish
    against him?
  And if your transgressions are multiplied, what
    do you do to him?
7 If you are righteous, what do you give to him;
  or what does he receive from your hand?
8 Your wickedness affects others like you,
  and your righteousness, other human beings.

9 "Because of the multitude of oppressions people
    cry out;
  they call for help because of the arm of the
    mighty.
10 But no one says, 'Where is God my Maker,
  who gives strength in the night,
11 who teaches us more than the animals of the
    earth,
  and makes us wiser than the birds of the air?'
12 There they cry out, but he does not answer,
  because of the pride of evildoers.
13 Surely God does not hear an empty cry,
  nor does the Almighty[a] regard it.
14 How much less when you say that you do not see
    him,
  that the case is before him, and you are
    waiting for him!
15 And now, because his anger does not punish,
  and he does not greatly heed transgression,[b]
16 Job opens his mouth in empty talk,
  he multiplies words without knowledge."

36 Elihu continued and said:
2 "Bear with me a little, and I will show you,
  for I have yet something to say on God's
    behalf.
3 I will bring my knowledge from far away,
  and ascribe righteousness to my Maker.
4 For truly my words are not false;
  one who is perfect in knowledge is with you.

5 "Surely God is mighty and does not despise any;
  he is mighty in strength of understanding.
6 He does not keep the wicked alive,
  but gives the afflicted their right.
7 He does not withdraw his eyes from the
    righteous,
  but with kings on the throne
  he sets them forever, and they are exalted.
8 And if they are bound in fetters
  and caught in the cords of affliction,
9 then he declares to them their work
  and their transgressions, that they are behaving
    arrogantly.
10 He opens their ears to instruction,
  and commands that they return from iniquity.
11 If they listen, and serve him,
  they complete their days in prosperity,
  and their years in pleasantness.
12 But if they do not listen, they shall perish by the
    sword,
  and die without knowledge.

REVISED ENGLISH BIBLE

4 I shall bring arguments myself in reply to you
  and to your three friends as well.
5 Look up at the sky and then consider,
  observe the rain-clouds towering above you.
6 How does it touch God if you have sinned?
  However many your misdeeds, how does it affect
    him?
7 If you do right, what good do you bring him,
  what does he receive at your hand?
8 Your wickedness touches only your
    fellow-creatures;
  any right you do affects none but other mortals.

9 People cry out under the weight of oppression
  and call for help against the power of the great;
10 but none of them asks, 'Where is God, my Maker,
  who gives protection by night,
11 who grants us more knowledge than the beasts of
    the earth
  and makes us wiser than the birds of the air?'
12 So, when they cry out, he does not answer,
  because they are proud and wicked.
13 All to no purpose! God does not listen,
  the Almighty takes no notice.
14 The worse for you when you say you do not see
    him!
  Humble yourself in his presence and wait for his
    word.
15 But now, because God does not grow angry and
    punish,
  because he lets folly pass unheeded,
16 Job gives vent to windy nonsense;
  he babbles a stream of empty words.

36 Then Elihu went on to say:
2 Be patient a little longer, and let me enlighten you;
  there is still more to be said on God's behalf.
3 I shall search far and wide to support my
    conclusions,
  as I ascribe justice to my Maker.
4 There are, I claim, no flaws in my reasoning;
  before you stands one whose conclusions are
    sound.

5 God, I say, repudiates the high and mighty
6 and does not let the wicked prosper,
  but bestows justice on the wronged.
7 He does not deprive sufferers of their due,
  but on the throne with kings
  he seats them in eminence, for ever exalted.
8 Next you may see them loaded with fetters,
  held fast in chains like captives:
9 he denounces their conduct to them,
  showing how, puffed with pride, they lapsed into
    sin.
10 With his warnings sounding in their ears
  he directs them back from their evil courses.
11 If they listen and serve him,
  they will live out their days in prosperity
  and their years in comfort.
12 But, if they do not listen, they cross the river of
    death,
  dying with their lesson unlearnt.

35:4 **three:** *so Gk; Heb. omits.*   35:14 **Humble yourself:** *prob.*
rdg; Heb. Judge.   36:5 **God:** *prob. rdg; Heb. adds* a mighty one
and not. **and:** *prob. rdg; Heb. omits.*   36:7 **deprive . . . due:** *or*
take his eyes off the righteous.

[a] Traditional rendering of Heb *Shaddai*   [b] Theodotion Symmachus
Compare Vg: Meaning of Heb uncertain

4 I have words for a reply to you
   and your three companions as well.
5 Look up to the skies and behold;
   regard the heavens high above you.
6 If you sin, what injury do you do to God?
   Even if your offenses are many, how do you
      hurt him?
7 If you are righteous, what do you give him,
   or what does he receive from your hand?
8 Your wickedness can affect only a man
      like yourself;
   and your justice only a fellow human being.

9 In great oppression men cry out;
   they call for help because of the power of
      the mighty,
10 Saying, "Where is God, my Maker,
   who has given visions in the night,
11 Taught us rather than the beasts of the earth,
   and made us wise rather than the birds of
      the heavens?"
12 Though thus they cry out, he answers not
   against the pride of the wicked.
13 But it is idle to say God does not hear
   or that the Almighty does not take notice.
14 Even though you say that you see him not,
   the case is before him; with trembling should
      you wait upon him.
15 But now that you have done otherwise, God's
      anger punishes,
   nor does he show concern that a man will die.
16 Yet Job to no purpose opens his mouth,
   and without knowledge multiplies words.

36 Elihu proceeded further and said:

2 Wait yet a little and I will instruct you,
   for there are still words to be said on
      God's behalf.
3 I will bring my knowledge from afar,
   and to my Maker I will accord the right.
4 For indeed, my theme cannot fail me:
   the one perfect in knowledge I set before you.

5 Behold, God rejects the obstinate in heart;
   he preserves not the life of the wicked,
6 He withholds not the just man's rights,
   but grants vindication to the oppressed
7 And with kings upon thrones
   he sets them, exalted forever.

8 Or if they are bound with fetters
   and held fast by bonds of affliction,
9 Then he makes known to them what they
      have done
   and their sins of boastful pride.
10 He opens their ears to correction
   and exhorts them to turn back from evil.

11 If they obey and serve him,
   they spend their days in prosperity,
   their years in happiness.
12 But if they obey not, they perish;
   they die for lack of knowledge.

4 Very well, I shall tell you
   and your friends as well.
5 Take a look at the skies and see,
   observe how high the clouds are above you.
6 If you sin, how can you affect him?
   If you heap up crimes, what effect has it on
      him?
7 If you are upright, what do you give him,
   what benefit does he receive at your hands?
8 Your wickedness affects only your fellows,
   your uprightness, other human beings.
9 They too groan under the weight of oppression,
   they cry for help under the tyranny of the
      mighty,
10 but none of them thinks of saying, 'Where is God,
      my Maker,
   who makes glad songs ring out at night,
11 who has made us more intelligent than wild
      animals
   wiser than birds in the sky?'
12 Cry they may, but get no answer,
   to be spared from the arrogance of the wicked.
13 Of course God does not listen to trivialities,
   Shaddai pays no attention to them.
14 And how much less when you say, 'I cannot see
      him,
   my case is open and I am waiting for him.'
15 Or, 'His anger never punishes,
   he does not seem aware of human rebellion.'
16 Hence, when Job speaks, he talks nonsense,
   ignorantly babbling on and on.

36 Elihu went on speaking. He said:

2 Be patient a little longer while I explain,
   for I have more to say on God's behalf.
3 I shall range far afield for my arguments
   to prove my Maker just.
4 I guarantee, nothing I shall say will be untrue:
   you have a man of sound learning here.
5 God does not reject anyone whose heart is pure
6   or let the sinner live on in all his power.
   He does accord fair judgement to the afflicted;
7   he does uphold what the upright deserve.
   When he raises kings to thrones,
   if they grow proud of their unending rule,
8 then he fetters them with chains,
   they are caught in the bonds of affliction.
9 He shows them the import of their deeds,
   of the sins of pride they have committed.
10 In their ears he sounds a warning,
   ordering them to turn back from doing wrong.
11 If they take notice and obey him,
   the rest of their days are prosperous
   and the years pass pleasantly.
12 If not, they go down the Canal
   and perish in their stupidity.

13 "The godless in heart cherish anger;
  they do not cry for help when he binds them.
14 They die in their youth,
  and their life ends in shame.*c*
15 He delivers the afflicted by their affliction,
  and opens their ear by adversity.
16 He also allured you out of distress
  into a broad place where there was no
    constraint,
  and what was set on your table was full of
    fatness.
17 "But you are obsessed with the case of the
    wicked;
  judgment and justice seize you.
18 Beware that wrath does not entice you into
    scoffing,
  and do not let the greatness of the ransom turn
    you aside.
19 Will your cry avail to keep you from distress,
  or will all the force of your strength?
20 Do not long for the night,
  when peoples are cut off in their place.
21 Beware! Do not turn to iniquity;
  because of that you have been tried by
    affliction.
22 See, God is exalted in his power;
  who is a teacher like him?
23 Who has prescribed for him his way,
  or who can say, 'You have done wrong'?
24 "Remember to extol his work,
  of which mortals have sung.
25 All people have looked on it;
  everyone watches it from far away.
26 Surely God is great, and we do not know him;
  the number of his years is unsearchable.
27 For he draws up the drops of water;
  he distills*d* his mist in rain,
28 which the skies pour down
  and drop upon mortals abundantly.
29 Can anyone understand the spreading of the
    clouds,
  the thunderings of his pavilion?
30 See, he scatters his lightning around him
  and covers the roots of the sea.
31 For by these he governs peoples;
  he gives food in abundance.
32 He covers his hands with the lightning,
  and commands it to strike the mark.
33 Its crashing*e* tells about him;
  he is jealous*e* with anger against iniquity.

37 "At this also my heart trembles,
  and leaps out of its place.
2 Listen, listen to the thunder of his voice
  and the rumbling that comes from his mouth.
3 Under the whole heaven he lets it loose,
  and his lightning to the corners of the earth.
4 After it his voice roars;
  he thunders with his majestic voice
  and he does not restrain the lightnings*f* when
    his voice is heard.

13 The proud rage against him
  and do not cry to him for help when caught in his
    toils;
14 so they die in their prime,
  short-lived as male prostitutes.
15 Those who suffer he rescues through suffering
  and teaches them by the discipline of affliction.
16 Beware, if you are tempted to exchange hardship
    for comfort,
  with unlimited plenty spread before you and a
    generous table;
17 if you eat your fill of a rich man's fare
  when you are occupied with the business of the
    law,
18 do not be led astray by lavish gifts of wine
  and do not let bribery warp your judgement.
19 Will that wealth of yours, however great, avail
    you,
  or all the resources of your high position?
21 Take care not to turn to mischief,
  for that is why you are tried by affliction.
20 Have no fear if in the breathless terrors of the
    night
  you see nations vanish where they stand.
22 God is pre-eminent in majesty;
  who wields such sovereign power as he?
23 Who has prescribed his course for him
  or said to him, 'You have done wrong'?
24 Remember, then, to sing the praises of his work,
  as mortals have always sung them.
25 All mankind gazes at him;
  the race of mortals look on from afar.
26 Consider: God is so great that we cannot know
    him;
  the number of his years is past searching out.
27 He draws up drops of water from the sea
  and distils rain from the flood;
28 the rain-clouds pour down in torrents,
  they descend in showers on the ground;
31 thus he sustains the nations
  and provides food in plenty.
29 Can anyone read the secret of the billowing
    clouds,
  spread like a carpet under his pavilion?
30 See how he scatters his light about him,
  and its rays cover the sea.
32 He charges the thunderbolts with flame
  and launches them straight at the mark;
33 in his anger he calls up the tempest,
  and the thunder is the herald of its coming.

37 This too makes my heart beat wildly
  and start from its place.
2 Just listen to the thunder of God's voice,
  the rumbling of his utterance!
3 Under the vault of heaven he lets it roll,
  and his lightning flashes to the ends of the earth.
4 There follows a sound, a roaring
  as he thunders with majestic voice.

36:16 **for comfort:** *prob. rdg; Heb. omits.* **before you:** *so one MS;
others* before her. 36:19–22 *Verses 20 and 21 transposed.*
36:25 **him:** *or it.* 36:27 **from the sea:** *prob. rdg; Heb. omits.*
36:28 **in torrents:** *prob. rdg; Heb.* which. 36:28–32 *Verse 31
transposed to follow verse 28.* 36:29 **spread . . . under:** *prob.
rdg; Heb.* crashing noises. 36:30 **its rays:** *prob. rdg; Heb.* the
roots of. 36:32 **and . . . straight:** *prob. rdg; Heb.* and gives
orders concerning it. 36:33 **in his anger . . . coming:** *prob. rdg;
Heb.* obscure. 37:4 *See note on verse 6.*

c Heb *ends among the temple prostitutes* *d* Cn: Heb *they distill*
e Meaning of Heb uncertain *f* Heb *them*

13 The impious in heart lay up anger for themselves;
　　they cry not for help when he enchains them;
14 Therefore they expire in youth,
　　and perish among the reprobate.
15 But he saves the unfortunate through
　　　their affliction,
　　and instructs them through distress.
16-20 . . . .

21 Take heed, turn not to evil;
　　for you have preferred carousal to affliction.

22 Behold, God is sublime in his power.
　　What teacher is there like him?
23 Who prescribes for him his conduct,
　　or who can say, "You have done wrong"?
24 Remember, you should extol his work,
　　which men have praised in song.
25 All men contemplate it;
　　man beholds it from afar.

26 Lo, God is great beyond our knowledge;
　　the number of his years is past searching
　　　out.
27 He holds in check the waterdrops
　　that filter in rain through his mists,
28 Till the skies run with them
　　and the showers rain down on mankind.
31 For by these he nourishes the nations,
　　and gives them food in abundance.
29. 30 Lo! he spreads the clouds in layers
　　as the carpeting of his tent.
32 In his hands he holds the lightning,
　　and he commands it to strike the mark.
33 His thunder speaks for him
　　and incites the fury of the storm.

37 At this my heart trembles
　　　and leaps out of its place,
2 To hear his angry voice
　　as it rumbles forth from his mouth!
3 Everywhere under the heavens he sends it,
　　with his lightning, to the ends of the earth.
4 Again his voice roars—
　　the majestic sound of his thunder.

13 The stubborn, who cherish their anger
　　and do not cry for help when he chains them,
14 die in the bloom of youth
　　or live among the male prostitutes of the
　　　temple.
15 But God saves the afflicted by his affliction,
　　warning him in his misery.
16 You, too, he would like to snatch from torment.
　　While you were enjoying boundless abundance,
　　with rich food piled high on your table,
17 you did not bring the wicked to trial
　　and did not give fair judgement to the orphan.
18 Beware of being led astray by abundance,
　　of being corrupted by expensive presents.
19 Take the powerful to law, not merely the
　　　penniless,
　　those whose arm is strong, not merely the
　　　weak.
20 Do not crush people you do not know
　　to install your relations in their place.
21 Avoid any tendency to wrong-doing,
　　for this is why affliction is testing you now.

22 See, God is sublime in his strength
　　and who can teach lessons as he does?
23 Who has even told him which course to take,
　　or dared to say to him, 'You have done
　　　wrong'?
24 Consider, rather, how you may praise his work,
　　a theme that many have sung.
25 This is something that everyone can see,
　　gazing, as we do, from afar.
26 Yes, the greatness of God exceeds our
　　　knowledge,
　　the number of his years is past counting.
27 It is he who makes the raindrops small
　　and pulverises the rain into mist.
28 And the clouds then pour this out,
　　sending it streaming down on the human
　　　race.
31 By these means, he sustains the peoples,
　　giving them plenty to eat.
29 And who can fathom how he spreads the
　　　clouds,
　　or why such crashes thunder from his tent?
30 He spreads a mist before him
　　and covers the tops of the mountains.
32 He gathers up the lightning in his hands,
　　assigning it the mark where to strike.
33 His crashing gives warning of its coming,
　　anger flashes out against iniquity.

37 At this, my very heart quakes
　　　and leaps out of its place.
2 Listen, oh listen, to the blast of his voice
　　and the sound that issues from his mouth.
3 His lightning is hurled across the heaven,
　　it strikes to the extremities of earth.
4 After it comes a roaring sound,
　　God thunders with majestic voice.
　　He does not check his thunderbolts
　　until his voice resounds no more.

36, 16–20: The Hebrew text here is in disorder.
36, 29f: Because of the uncertainty of the text, no translation of these
verses has received unanimous approval from exegetes.

5 God thunders wondrously with his voice;
  he does great things that we cannot
    comprehend.
6 For to the snow he says, 'Fall on the earth';
  and the shower of rain, his heavy shower of
    rain,
7 serves as a sign on everyone's hand,
  so that all whom he has made may know it.ᵍ
8 Then the animals go into their lairs
  and remain in their dens.
9 From its chamber comes the whirlwind,
  and cold from the scattering winds.
10 By the breath of God ice is given,
  and the broad waters are frozen fast.
11 He loads the thick cloud with moisture;
  the clouds scatter his lightning.
12 They turn round and round by his guidance,
  to accomplish all that he commands them
  on the face of the habitable world.
13 Whether for correction, or for his land,
  or for love, he causes it to happen.
14 "Hear this, O Job;
  stop and consider the wondrous works of God.
15 Do you know how God lays his command upon
    them,
  and causes the lightning of his cloud to shine?
16 Do you know the balancings of the clouds,
  the wondrous works of the one whose
    knowledge is perfect,
17 you whose garments are hot
  when the earth is still because of the south
    wind?
18 Can you, like him, spread out the skies,
  hard as a molten mirror?
19 Teach us what we shall say to him;
  we cannot draw up our case because of
    darkness.
20 Should he be told that I want to speak?
  Did anyone ever wish to be swallowed up?
21 Now, no one can look on the light
  when it is bright in the skies,
  when the wind has passed and cleared them.
22 Out of the north comes golden splendor;
  around God is awesome majesty.
23 The Almightyʰ — we cannot find him;
  he is great in power and justice,
  and abundant righteousness he will not violate.
24 Therefore mortals fear him;
  he does not regard any who are wise in their
    own conceit."

38 Then the LORD answered Job out of the whirlwind:
2 "Who is this that darkens counsel by words
    without knowledge?
3 Gird up your loins like a man,
  I will question you, and you shall declare to
    me.
4 "Where were you when I laid the foundation of
    the earth?
  Tell me, if you have understanding.
5 Who determined its measurements — surely you
    know!
  Or who stretched the line upon it?

5 At God's command wonderful things come to pass;
  great deeds beyond our knowledge are done by
    him.
6 For he says to the snow, 'Fall over the earth';
  to the rainstorms he says, 'Be violent,'
  and at his voice the rains pour down unchecked.
7 He shuts everyone fast indoors,
  and all whom he has made are quiet;
8 beasts withdraw into their lairs
  and take cover in their dens.
9 The hurricane bursts from its prison,
  and the rain-winds bring bitter cold.
10 By the breath of God the ice is formed,
  and the wide waters are frozen hard.
11 He hurls lightning from the dense clouds,
  and the clouds spread his light,
12 as they travel round in their courses,
  directed by his guiding hand
  to do his bidding
  all over the habitable world;
13 whether for punishment or for love
  he brings them forth.
14 Listen, Job, to this argument;
  stop and consider God's wonderful works.
15 Do you know how God assigns them their tasks,
  how he sends light flashing from his clouds?
16 Do you know how the clouds hang poised
    overhead,
  a wonderful work of his consummate skill?
17 Sweltering there in your stifling clothes,
  when the earth lies sultry under the south wind,
18 can you as he does beat out the vault of the skies,
  hard as a mirror of cast metal?
19 Teach us then what to say to him;
  for all is dark, and we cannot marshal our
    thoughts.
20 Can anyone dictate to God when he is to speak,
  or command him to make proclamation?
21 At one moment the light is not seen,
  being overcast with cloud;
  then the wind passes by and clears it away,
22 and a golden glow comes from the north.
23 But the Almighty we cannot find;
  his power is beyond our ken,
  yet in his great righteousness he does not pervert
    justice.
24 Therefore mortals pay him reverence,
  and all who are wise fear him.

38 THEN the LORD answered Job out of the tempest:
2 Who is this who darkens counsel
  with words devoid of knowledge?
3 Brace yourself and stand up like a man;
  I shall put questions to you, and you must answer.
4 Where were you when I laid the earth's
    foundations?
  Tell me, if you know and understand.
5 Who fixed its dimensions? Surely you know!
  Who stretched a measuring line over it?

37:5 **come to pass:** *prob. rdg; Heb.* he thunders.   37:6 **and . . . unchecked:** *prob. rdg; some words in this line transposed from verse 4.*   37:7 **indoors:** *prob. rdg; Heb.* obscure.
37:13 **punishment:** *prob. rdg; Heb.* adds or for his land.
37:20 **he is:** *prob. rdg; Heb.* I am.   37:22 **golden . . . north:** *prob. rdg; Heb.* adds this refers to God, terrible in majesty.
37:24 **fear him:** *so Gk; Heb.* fear not.

ᵍ Meaning of Heb of verse 7 uncertain   ʰ Traditional rendering of
Heb *Shaddai*

5 He does great things beyond our knowing;
  wonders past our searching out.
6 For he says to the snow, "Fall to the earth";
  likewise to his heavy, drenching rain.
7 He shuts up all mankind indoors;
8   the wild beasts take to cover
  and remain quietly in their dens.

9 Out of its chamber comes forth the tempest;
  from the north winds, the cold.
10 With his breath God brings the frost,
  and the broad waters become congealed.
11 With hail, also, the clouds are laden,
  as they scatter their flashes of light.
12 He it is who changes their rounds, according to
    his plans,
  in their task upon the surface of the earth,
13 whether for punishment or mercy, as
    he commands.

14 Hearken to this, O Job!
  Stand and consider the wondrous works of God!
15 Do you know how God lays his commands
    upon them,
  and makes the light shine forth from his clouds?
16 Do you know how the clouds are banked,
  the wondrous work of him who is perfect
    in knowledge?
17 You, whom the streams of water fail
  when a calm from the south comes over
    the land,
18 Do you spread out with him the firmament of
    the skies,
  hard as a brazen mirror?

19 Teach us then what we shall say to him;
  we cannot, for the darkness, make our plea.
20 Will he be told about it when I speak,
  or when a man says he is being destroyed?
21 Nay, rather, it is as the light which men see not
  while it is obscured among the clouds,
  till the wind comes by and sweeps the
    clouds away.
22 From the North the splendor comes,
  surrounding God's awesome majesty!
23 The Almighty! we cannot discover him,
  pre-eminent in power and judgment;
  his great justice owes no one an accounting.
24 Therefore men revere him,
  though none can see him, however wise
    their hearts.

38 Then the LORD addressed Job out of the storm and
  said:

2 Who is this that obscures divine plans
  with words of ignorance?
3 Gird up your loins now, like a man;
  I will question you, and you tell me the answers!
4 Where were you when I founded the earth?
  Tell me, if you have understanding.
5 Who determined its size; do you know?
  Who stretched out the measuring line for it?

5 Yes, certainly God shows us marvels
  and does great deeds that we cannot understand.
6 When he says to the snow, 'Fall on the earth!'
  to the showers, 'Now rain hard!'
7 he brings all human activity to a standstill,
  for everyone to acknowledge his work.
8 The animals go back to their dens
  and take shelter in their lairs.

9 The storm wind comes from the Mansion of the
    South,
  and the north winds usher in the cold.
10 At the breath of God, ice comes next,
  the surface of the waters hardens over.
11 He weighs the clouds down with moisture,
  and the storm clouds radiate his lightning.
12 He himself guides their wheeling motion
  presiding over their seasonal changes.
  They carry out his orders to the letter
  all over this earthly world.
13 Whether to punish earth's peoples
  or as a work of faithful love, he despatches
    them.

14 Listen to this, Job, without flinching
  and reflect on the marvellous works of God.
15 Do you know how God controls them
  or how his clouds make the lightning flash?
16 Do you know how he balances the clouds —
  a miracle of consummate skill?
17 When your clothes are hot to your body
  and the earth lies still under the south wind,
18 can you, like him, stretch out the sky,
  tempered like a mirror of cast metal?

19 Teach me what we should say to him:
  but better discuss no further, since we are in the
    dark.
20 Does he take note when I speak?
  When human beings give orders, does he take it
    in?
21 There are times when the light vanishes,
  behind darkening clouds;
  then comes the wind, sweeping them away,
22 and brightness spreads from the north.
  God is clothed in fearful splendour:
23 he, Shaddai, is far beyond our reach.
  Supreme in power, in equity,
  excelling in saving justice, yet no oppressor —
24 no wonder then that people fear him:
  everyone thoughtful holds him in awe!

38 Then from the heart of the tempest Yahweh gave
  Job his answer. He said:

2 Who is this, obscuring my intentions
  with his ignorant words?
3 Brace yourself like a fighter;
  I am going to ask the questions, and you are to
    inform me!
4 Where were you when I laid the earth's
    foundations?
  Tell me, since you are so well-informed!
5 Who decided its dimensions, do you know?
  Or who stretched the measuring line across it?

NEW REVISED STANDARD VERSION	REVISED ENGLISH BIBLE

NEW REVISED STANDARD VERSION

6 On what were its bases sunk,
  or who laid its cornerstone

7 when the morning stars sang together
  and all the heavenly beings[i] shouted for joy?

8 "Or who shut in the sea with doors
  when it burst out from the womb?—

9 when I made the clouds its garment,
  and thick darkness its swaddling band,

10 and prescribed bounds for it,
  and set bars and doors,

11 and said, 'Thus far shall you come, and no
  farther,
  and here shall your proud waves be stopped'?

12 "Have you commanded the morning since your
  days began,
  and caused the dawn to know its place,

13 so that it might take hold of the skirts of the
  earth,
  and the wicked be shaken out of it?

14 It is changed like clay under the seal,
  and it is dyed[j] like a garment.

15 Light is withheld from the wicked,
  and their uplifted arm is broken.

16 "Have you entered into the springs of the sea,
  or walked in the recesses of the deep?

17 Have the gates of death been revealed to you,
  or have you seen the gates of deep darkness?

18 Have you comprehended the expanse of the
  earth?
  Declare, if you know all this.

19 "Where is the way to the dwelling of light,
  and where is the place of darkness,

20 that you may take it to its territory
  and that you may discern the paths to its
  home?

21 Surely you know, for you were born then,
  and the number of your days is great!

22 "Have you entered the storehouses of the snow,
  or have you seen the storehouses of the hail,

23 which I have reserved for the time of trouble,
  for the day of battle and war?

24 What is the way to the place where the light is
  distributed,
  or where the east wind is scattered upon the
  earth?

25 "Who has cut a channel for the torrents of rain,
  and a way for the thunderbolt,

26 to bring rain on a land where no one lives,
  on the desert, which is empty of human life,

27 to satisfy the waste and desolate land,
  and to make the ground put forth grass?

28 "Has the rain a father,
  or who has begotten the drops of dew?

29 From whose womb did the ice come forth,
  and who has given birth to the hoarfrost of
  heaven?

30 The waters become hard like stone,
  and the face of the deep is frozen.

31 "Can you bind the chains of the Pleiades,
  or loose the cords of Orion?

32 Can you lead forth the Mazzaroth in their season,
  or can you guide the Bear with its children?

33 Do you know the ordinances of the heavens?
  Can you establish their rule on the earth?

REVISED ENGLISH BIBLE

6 On what do its supporting pillars rest?
  Who set its corner-stone in place,

7 while the morning stars sang in chorus
  and the sons of God all shouted for joy?

8 Who supported the sea at its birth,
  when it burst in flood from the womb—

9 when I wrapped it in a blanket of cloud
  and swaddled it in dense fog,

10 when I established its bounds,
  set its barred doors in place,

11 and said, 'Thus far you come but no farther;
  here your surging waves must halt'?

12 In all your life have you ever called up the dawn
  or assigned the morning its place?

13 Have you taught it to grasp the fringes of the earth
  and shake the Dog-star from the sky;

14 to bring up the horizon in relief as clay under a
  seal,
  until all things stand out like the folds of a cloak,

15 when the light of the Dog-star is dimmed
  and the stars of the Navigator's Line go out one by
  one?

16 Have you gone down to the springs of the sea
  or walked in the unfathomable deep?

17 Have the portals of death been revealed to you?
  Have you seen the door-keepers of the place of
  darkness?

18 Have you comprehended the vast expanse of the
  world?
  Tell me all this, if you know.

19 Which is the way to the home of light,
  and where does darkness dwell?

20 Can you then take each to its appointed boundary
  and escort it on its homeward path?

21 Doubtless you know, for you were already born.
  So long is the span of your life!

22 Have you visited the storehouses of the snow
  or seen the arsenal where hail is stored,

23 which I have kept ready for the day of calamity,
  for war and for the hour of battle?

24 By what paths is the heat spread abroad
  or the east wind dispersed world-wide?

25 Who has cut channels for the downpour
  and cleared a path for the thunderbolt,

26 for rain to fall on land devoid of people,
  on the uninhabited wilderness,

27 clothing waste and derelict lands with green
  and making grass spring up on thirsty ground?

28 Does the rain have a father?
  Who sired the drops of dew?

29 Whose womb gave birth to the ice,
  and who was the mother of the hoar-frost in the
  skies,

30 which lays a stony cover over the waters
  and freezes the surface of the deep?

31 Can you bind the cluster of the Pleiades
  or loose Orion's belt?

32 Can you bring out the signs of the zodiac in their
  season
  or guide Aldebaran and its satellite stars?

33 Did you proclaim the rules that govern the heavens
  or determine the laws of nature on the earth?

38:8 **Who . . . birth:** *prob. rdg; Heb.* And he held back the sea with
two doors.   38:13 **the Dog-star . . . sky:** *lit.* the Dog-stars from
it.   38:27 **thirsty ground:** *prob. rdg; Heb.* source.

[i] Heb *sons of God*   [j] Cn: Heb *and they stand forth*

NEW AMERICAN BIBLE

6 Into what were its pedestals sunk,
  and who laid the cornerstone,
7 While the morning stars sang in chorus
  and all the sons of God shouted for joy?

8 And who shut within doors the sea,
  when it burst forth from the womb;
9 When I made the clouds its garment
  and thick darkness its swaddling bands?
10 When I set limits for it
  and fastened the bar of its door,
11 And said: Thus far shall you come but no farther,
  and here shall your proud waves be stilled!

12 Have you ever in your lifetime commanded
    the morning
  and shown the dawn its place
13 For taking hold of the ends of the earth,
  till the wicked are shaken from its surface?
14 The earth is changed as is clay by the seal,
  and dyed as though it were a garment;
15 But from the wicked the light is withheld,
  and the arm of pride is shattered.

16 Have you entered into the sources of the sea,
  or walked about in the depths of the abyss?
17 Have the gates of death been shown to you,
  or have you seen the gates of darkness?
18 Have you comprehended the breadth of the earth?
  Tell me, if you know all:
19 Which is the way to the dwelling place of light,
  and where is the abode of darkness,
20 That you may take them to their boundaries
  and set them on their homeward paths?
21 You know, because you were born before them,
  and the number of your years is great!

22 Have you entered the storehouse of the snow,
  and seen the treasury of the hail
23 Which I have reserved for times of stress,
  for the days of war and of battle?
24 Which way to the parting of the winds,
  whence the east wind spreads over the earth?

25 Who has laid out a channel for the downpour
  and for the thunderstorm a path
26 To bring rain to no man's land,
  the unpeopled wilderness;
27 To enrich the waste and desolate ground
  till the desert blooms with verdure?
28 Has the rain a father;
  or who has begotten the drops of dew?
29 Out of whose womb comes the ice,
  and who gives the hoarfrost its birth in the skies,
30 When the waters lie covered as though with stone
  that holds captive the surface of the deep?

31 Have you fitted a curb to the Pleiades,
  or loosened the bonds of Orion?
32 Can you bring forth the Mazzaroth in their season,
  or guide the Bear with its train?
33 Do you know the ordinances of the heavens;
  can you put into effect their plan on the earth?

NEW JERUSALEM BIBLE

6 What supports its pillars at their bases?
  Who laid its cornerstone
7 to the joyful concert of the morning stars
  and unanimous acclaim of the sons of God?
8 Who pent up the sea behind closed doors
  when it leapt tumultuous from the womb,
9 when I wrapped it in a robe of mist
  and made black clouds its swaddling bands;
10 when I cut out the place I had decreed for it
  and imposed gates and a bolt?
11 'Come so far,' I said, 'and no further;
  here your proud waves must break!'

12 Have you ever in your life given orders to the
    morning
  or sent the dawn to its post,
13 to grasp the earth by its edges
  and shake the wicked out of it?
14 She turns it as red as a clay seal,
  she tints it as though it were a dress,
15 stealing the light from evil-doers
  and breaking the arm raised to strike.
16 Have you been right down to the sources of the sea
  and walked about at the bottom of the Abyss?
17 Have you been shown the gates of Death,
  have you seen the janitors of the Shadow dark as
    death?
18 Have you an inkling of the extent of the earth?
  Tell me all about it if you have!
19 Which is the way to the home of the Light,
  and where does darkness live? —
20 You could then show them the way to their proper
    places,
  you could put them on the path home again!
21 If you do know, you must have been born when
    they were,
  you must be very old by now!

22 Have you visited the place where the snow is
    stored?
  Have you seen the stores of hail,
23 which I keep for times of distress,
  for days of battle and war?
24 From which direction does the lightning fork,
  where in the world does the east wind blow
    itself out?
25 Who bores a channel for the downpour
  or clears the way for the rolling thunder
26 so that rain may fall on lands where no one lives,
  and the deserts void of human dwelling,
27 to meet the needs of the lonely wastes
  and make grass sprout on the thirsty ground?
28 Has the rain a father?
  Who begets the dewdrops?
29 What womb brings forth the ice,
  who gives birth to the frost of heaven,
30 when the waters grow hard as stone
  and the surface of the deep congeals?

31 Can you fasten the harness of the Pleiades,
  or untie Orion's bands?
32 Can you guide the Crown season by season
  and show the Bear and its cubs which way to
    go?
33 Have you grasped the celestial laws?
  Could you make their writ run on the earth?

NEW REVISED STANDARD VERSION	REVISED ENGLISH BIBLE

NEW REVISED STANDARD VERSION

34 "Can you lift up your voice to the clouds,
so that a flood of waters may cover you?
35 Can you send forth lightnings, so that they may go
and say to you, 'Here we are'?
36 Who has put wisdom in the inward parts,*k*
or given understanding to the mind?*k*
37 Who has the wisdom to number the clouds?
Or who can tilt the waterskins of the heavens,
38 when the dust runs into a mass
and the clods cling together?

39 "Can you hunt the prey for the lion,
or satisfy the appetite of the young lions,
40 when they crouch in their dens,
or lie in wait in their covert?
41 Who provides for the raven its prey,
when its young ones cry to God,
and wander about for lack of food?

39 "Do you know when the mountain goats give birth?
Do you observe the calving of the deer?
2 Can you number the months that they fulfill,
and do you know the time when they give birth,
3 when they crouch to give birth to their offspring,
and are delivered of their young?
4 Their young ones become strong, they grow up in the open;
they go forth, and do not return to them.

5 "Who has let the wild ass go free?
Who has loosed the bonds of the swift ass,
6 to which I have given the steppe for its home,
the salt land for its dwelling place?
7 It scorns the tumult of the city;
it does not hear the shouts of the driver.
8 It ranges the mountains as its pasture,
and it searches after every green thing.

9 "Is the wild ox willing to serve you?
Will it spend the night at your crib?
10 Can you tie it in the furrow with ropes,
or will it harrow the valleys after you?
11 Will you depend on it because its strength is great,
and will you hand over your labor to it?
12 Do you have faith in it that it will return,
and bring your grain to your threshing floor?*l*

13 "The ostrich's wings flap wildly,
though its pinions lack plumage.*k*
14 For it leaves its eggs to the earth,
and lets them be warmed on the ground,
15 forgetting that a foot may crush them,
and that a wild animal may trample them.
16 It deals cruelly with its young, as if they were not its own;
though its labor should be in vain, yet it has no fear;
17 because God has made it forget wisdom,
and given it no share in understanding.
18 When it spreads its plumes aloft,*k*
it laughs at the horse and its rider.

k Meaning of Heb uncertain   *l* Heb *your grain and your threshing floor*

REVISED ENGLISH BIBLE

34 Can you command the clouds
to envelop you in a deluge of rain?
35 If you bid lightning speed on its way,
will it say to you, 'I am ready'?
36 Who put wisdom in depths of darkness
and veiled understanding in secrecy?
37 Who is wise enough to marshal the rain-clouds
and empty the cisterns of heaven,
38 when the dusty soil sets in a dense mass,
and the clods of earth stick fast together?

39 Can you hunt prey for the lioness
and satisfy the appetite of young lions,
40 as they crouch in the lair
or lie in wait in the covert?
41 Who provides the raven with its quarry
when its fledgelings cry aloud,
croaking for lack of food?

39 Do you know when the mountain goats give birth?
Do you attend the wild doe when she is calving?
2 Can you count the months that they carry their young
or know the time of their delivery,
3 when they crouch down to open their wombs
and deliver their offspring,
4 when the fawns growing and thriving in the open country
leave and do not return?

5 Who has let the Syrian wild ass range at will
and given the Arabian wild ass its freedom?
6 I have made its haunts in the wilderness
and its home in the saltings;
7 it disdains the noise of the city
and does not obey a driver's shout;
8 it roams the hills as its pasture
in search of a morsel of green.

9 Is the wild ox willing to serve you
or spend the night in your stall?
10 Can you harness its strength with ropes;
will it harrow the furrows after you?
11 Can you depend on it, strong as it is,
and leave your heavy work to it?
12 Can you rely on it to come,
bringing your grain to the threshing-floor?

13 The wings of the ostrich are stunted;
her pinions and plumage being so scanty,
14 she leaves her eggs on the ground
and lets them be kept warm by the sand.
15 She is unmindful that a foot may crush them,
or a wild animal trample on them;
16 she treats her chicks heartlessly
as if they were not her own,
not caring if her labour is wasted.
17 For God has denied her wisdom
and left her without sense,
18 while like a cock she struts over the uplands,
scorning both horse and rider.

38:36 **secrecy:** *prob. rdg; Heb.* word unknown.   38:37 **empty the cisterns:** *lit.* tilt the water-skins.   38:41 **cry aloud:** *prob. rdg; Heb. adds* to God.   39:10 **its . . . furrows:** *prob. rdg; Heb.* transposes strength *and* furrows.   39:12 **grain to:** *so Gk; Heb.* grain and.   39:13 **ostrich:** *Heb. word of uncertain meaning.* **are stunted:** *prob. rdg; Heb.* unintelligible. **her pinions:** *prob. rdg; Heb.* prefixes if. **scanty:** *prob. rdg; Heb.* obscure.   39:16 **as if they:** *so Lat.; Heb.* those that.   39:18 **while . . . struts:** *lit.* while she plays the male.

NEW AMERICAN BIBLE

NEW AMERICAN BIBLE

34 Can you raise your voice among the clouds,
  or veil yourself in the waters of the storm?
35 Can you send forth the lightnings on their way,
  or will they say to you, "Here we are"?
37 Who counts the clouds in his wisdom?
  Or who tilts the water jars of heaven
38 So that the dust of earth is fused into a mass
  and its clods made solid?
39 Do you hunt the prey for the lioness
  or appease the hunger of her cubs,
40 While they crouch in their dens,
  or lie in wait in the thicket?
36 Who puts wisdom in the heart,
  and gives the cock its understanding?
41 Who provides nourishment for the ravens
  when their young ones cry out to God,
  and they rove abroad without food?

39 Do you know about the birth of the
  mountain goats,
  watch for the birth pangs of the hinds,
2 Number the months that they must fulfill,
  and fix the time of their bringing forth?
3 They crouch down and bear their young;
  they deliver their progeny in the desert.
4 When their offspring thrive and grow,
  they leave and do not return.

5 Who has given the wild ass his freedom,
  and who has loosed him from bonds?
6 I have made the wilderness his home
  and the salt flats his dwelling.
7 He scoffs at the uproar of the city,
  and hears no shouts of a driver.
8 He ranges the mountains for pasture,
  and seeks out every patch of green.

9 Will the wild ox consent to serve you,
  and to pass the nights by your manger?
10 Will a rope bind him in the furrow,
  and will he harrow the valleys after you?
11 Will you trust him for his great strength
  and leave to him the fruits of your toil?
12 Can you rely on him to thresh out your grain
  and gather in the yield of your threshing floor?

13 The wings of the ostrich beat idly;
  her plumage is lacking in pinions.
14 When she leaves her eggs on the ground
  and deposits them in the sand,
15 Unmindful that a foot may crush them,
  that the wild beasts may trample them,
16 She cruelly disowns her young
  and ruthlessly makes nought of her brood;
17 For God has withheld wisdom from her
  and has given her no share in understanding.
18 Yet in her swiftness of foot
  she makes sport of the horse and his rider.

NEW JERUSALEM BIBLE

34 Can your voice carry as far as the clouds
  and make the pent-up waters do your
  bidding?
35 Will lightning flashes come at your command
  and answer, 'Here we are'?
36 Who endowed the ibis with wisdom
  and gave the cock his intelligence?
37 Whose skill details every cloud
  and tilts the water-skins of heaven
38 until the dust solidifies
  and the cracks in the ground close up?

39 Do you go hunting prey for the lioness;
  do you satisfy the hunger of young lions
40 where they crouch in their den,
  waiting eagerly in the bushes?
41 Who makes provision for the raven
  when his little ones cry out to God
  craning their necks in search of food?

39 Do you know when mountain goats give birth?
  Have you ever watched deer in labour?
2 Have you ever counted the months that they carry
  their young?
  Do you know when they give birth?
3 They crouch to drop their young,
  they get rid of their burdens
4 and the calves, having grown big and strong,
  go off into the desert and never come back to
  them.

5 Who has given the wild donkey his freedom,
  who has undone the harness of the brayer?
6 I have given him the wastelands as his home,
  the salt plain as his habitat.
7 He scorns the turmoil of the town,
  obeys no donkey-man's shouts.
8 The mountains are the pastures that he ranges
  in quest of anything green.

9 Is the wild ox willing to serve you
  or spend a night beside your manger?
10 If you tie a rope round his neck
  will he harrow the furrows for you?
11 Can you rely on his massive strength
  and leave him to do your heavy work?
12 Can you depend on him to come home
  and pile your grain on your threshing-floor?

13 Can the wing of the ostrich be compared
  with the plumage of stork or falcon?
14 She leaves her eggs on the ground
  with only earth to warm them;
15 forgetting that a foot may tread on them
  or a wild animal crush them.
16 Cruel to her chicks as if they were not hers,
  little she cares if her labour goes for nothing.
17 God, you see, has deprived her of wisdom
  and given her no share of intelligence.
18 Yet, if she bestirs herself to use her height,
  she can make fools of horse and rider too.

NEW REVISED STANDARD VERSION	REVISED ENGLISH BIBLE

NEW REVISED STANDARD VERSION

19 "Do you give the horse its might?
  Do you clothe its neck with mane?
20 Do you make it leap like the locust?
  Its majestic snorting is terrible.
21 It paws*m* violently, exults mightily;
  it goes out to meet the weapons.
22 It laughs at fear, and is not dismayed;
  it does not turn back from the sword.
23 Upon it rattle the quiver,
  the flashing spear, and the javelin.
24 With fierceness and rage it swallows the ground;
  it cannot stand still at the sound of the trumpet.
25 When the trumpet sounds, it says 'Aha!'
  From a distance it smells the battle,
  the thunder of the captains, and the shouting.

26 "Is it by your wisdom that the hawk soars,
  and spreads its wings toward the south?
27 Is it at your command that the eagle mounts up
  and makes its nest on high?
28 It lives on the rock and makes its home
  in the fastness of the rocky crag.
29 From there it spies the prey;
  its eyes see it from far away.
30 Its young ones suck up blood;
  and where the slain are, there it is."

40 And the LORD said to Job:
2 "Shall a faultfinder contend with the Almighty?*n*
  Anyone who argues with God must respond."

3 Then Job answered the LORD:
4 "See, I am of small account; what shall I answer you?
  I lay my hand on my mouth.
5 I have spoken once, and I will not answer;
  twice, but will proceed no further."

6 Then the LORD answered Job out of the whirlwind:
7 "Gird up your loins like a man;
  I will question you, and you declare to me.
8 Will you even put me in the wrong?
  Will you condemn me that you may be justified?
9 Have you an arm like God,
  and can you thunder with a voice like his?

10 "Deck yourself with majesty and dignity;
  clothe yourself with glory and splendor.
11 Pour out the overflowings of your anger,
  and look on all who are proud, and abase them.
12 Look on all who are proud, and bring them low;
  tread down the wicked where they stand.
13 Hide them all in the dust together;
  bind their faces in the world below.*o*

REVISED ENGLISH BIBLE

19 Do you give the horse his strength?
  Have you clothed his neck with a mane?
20 Do you make him quiver like a locust's wings,
  when his shrill neighing strikes terror?
21 He shows his mettle as he paws and prances;
  in his might he charges the armoured line.
22 He scorns alarms and knows no dismay;
  he does not shy away before the sword.
23 The quiver rattles at his side,
  the spear and sabre flash.
24 Trembling with eagerness, he devours the ground
  and when the trumpet sounds there is no holding him;
25 at the trumpet-call he cries 'Aha!'
  and from afar he scents the battle,
  the shouting of the captains, and the war cries.

26 Does your skill teach the hawk to use its pinions
  and spread its wings towards the south?
27 Do you instruct the eagle to soar aloft
  and build its nest high up?
28 It dwells among the rocks and there it has its nest,
  secure on a rocky crag;
29 from there it searches for food,
  keenly scanning the distance,
30 that its brood may be gorged with blood;
  wherever the slain are, it is there.

41 Can you lift out the whale with a gaff
  or slip a noose round its tongue?
2 Can you pass a rope through its nose
  or pierce its jaw with a hook?
3 Will it take to pleading with you for mercy
  or beg for its life with soft words?
4 Will it enter into an agreement with you
  to become your slave for life?
5 Will you toy with it as with a bird
  or keep it on a leash for your girls?
6 Do partners in the fishing haggle over it
  or merchants share it out?

40 The LORD then said to Job:

2 Is it for a man who disputes with the Almighty to be stubborn?
  Should he who argues with God answer back?

3 Job answered the LORD:

4 What reply can I give you, I who carry no weight?
  I put my finger to my lips.
5 I have spoken once; I shall not answer again;
  twice have I spoken; I shall do so no more.

6 Then the LORD answered Job out of the tempest:

7 Brace yourself and stand up like a man;
  I shall put questions to you, and you must answer.
8 Would you dare deny that I am just,
  or put me in the wrong to prove yourself right?
9 Have you an arm like God's arm;
  can you thunder with a voice like his?
10 Deck yourself out, if you can, in pride and dignity,
  array yourself in pomp and splendour.
11 Unleash the fury of your wrath,
  look on all who are proud, and humble them;
12 look on all who are proud, and bring them low,
  crush the wicked where they stand.
13 bury them in the earth together,
  and shroud them in an unknown grave.

---

m Gk Syr Vg: Heb *they dig*   *n* Traditional rendering of Heb *Shaddai*
o Heb *the hidden place*

39:21 **he paws:** *so Gk; Heb.* they paw.   39:30 41:1–6 (*in Heb.*
40:25–30) *transposed to follow this verse.*

19 Do you give the horse his strength,
  and endow his neck with splendor?
20 Do you make the steed to quiver
  while his thunderous snorting spreads terror?
21 He jubilantly paws the plain
  and rushes in his might against the weapons.
22 He laughs at fear and cannot be deterred;
  he turns not back from the sword.
23 Around him rattles the quiver,
  flashes the spear and the javelin.
24 Frenzied and trembling he devours the ground;
  he holds not back at the sound of the trumpet,
25   but at each blast he cries, "Aha!"
  Even from afar he scents the battle,
  the roar of the chiefs and the shouting.

26 Is it by your discernment that the hawk soars,
  that he spreads his wings toward the south?
27 Does the eagle fly up at your command
  to build his nest aloft?
28 On the cliff he dwells and spends the night,
  on a spur of the cliff or the fortress.
29 From thence he watches for his prey;
  his eyes behold it afar off.
30 His young ones greedily drink blood;
  where the slain are, there is he.

40 The LORD then said to Job:

2 Will we have arguing with the Almighty by
  the critic?
  Let him who would correct God give answer!

3 Then Job answered the LORD and said:

4 Behold, I am of little account; what can I
  answer you?
  I put my hand over my mouth.
5 Though I have spoken once, I will not do so again;
  though twice, I will do so no more.

6 Then the LORD addressed Job out of the storm and said:

7 Gird up your loins now, like a man.
  I will question you, and you tell me the answers!
8 Would you refuse to acknowledge my right?
  Would you condemn me that you may
  be justified?
9 Have you an arm like that of God,
  or can you thunder with a voice like his?
10 Adorn yourself with grandeur and majesty,
  and array yourself with glory and splendor.
11 Let loose the fury of your wrath;
12   tear down the wicked and shatter them.
  Bring down the haughty with a glance;
13   bury them in the dust together;
  in the hidden world imprison them.

19 Are you the one who makes the horse so brave
  and covers his neck with flowing mane?
20 Do you make him leap like a grasshopper?
  His haughty neighing inspires terror.
21 Exultantly he paws the soil of the valley,
  and charges the battle-line in all his strength.
22 He laughs at fear; he is afraid of nothing,
  he recoils before no sword.
23 On his back the quiver rattles,
  the flashing spear and javelin.
24 Trembling with impatience, he eats up the miles;
  when the trumpet sounds, there is no holding
  him.
25 At each trumpet blast he neighs exultantly.
  He scents the battle from afar,
  the thundering of the commanders and the war
  cry.

26 Is it your wisdom that sets the hawk flying
  when he spreads his wings to travel south?
27 Does the eagle soar at your command
  to make her eyrie in the heights?
28 She spends her nights among the crags
  with a needle of rock as her fortress,
29 from which she watches for prey,
  fixing it with her far-ranging eye.
30 Even her young drink blood;
  where anyone has been killed, she is there.

40 Still speaking to Job, Yahweh said:

2 Is Yahweh's opponent going to give way?
  Has God's critic thought up an answer?

3 Job replied to Yahweh:

4 My words have been frivolous: what can I reply?
  I had better lay my hand over my mouth.
5 I have spoken once, I shall not speak again;
  I have spoken twice, I have nothing more to say.

6 Yahweh gave Job his answer from the heart of the
  tempest. He said:

7 Brace yourself like a fighter,
  I am going to ask the questions, and you are to
  inform me!
8 Do you really want to reverse my judgement,
  put me in the wrong and yourself in the right?
9 Has your arm the strength of God's,
  can your voice thunder as loud?
10 Come on, display your majesty and grandeur,
  robe yourself in splendour and glory.
11 Let the fury of your anger burst forth,
  humble the haughty at a glance!
12 At a glance, bring down all the proud,
  strike down the wicked where they stand.
13 Bury the lot of them in the ground,
  shut them, every one, in the Dungeon.

14 Then I will also acknowledge to you
  that your own right hand can give you victory.
15 "Look at Behemoth,
  which I made just as I made you;
  it eats grass like an ox.
16 Its strength is in its loins,
  and its power in the muscles of its belly.
17 It makes its tail stiff like a cedar;
  the sinews of its thighs are knit together.
18 Its bones are tubes of bronze,
  its limbs like bars of iron.
19 "It is the first of the great acts of God —
  only its Maker can approach it with the sword.
20 For the mountains yield food for it
  where all the wild animals play.
21 Under the lotus plants it lies,
  in the covert of the reeds and in the marsh.
22 The lotus trees cover it for shade;
  the willows of the wadi surround it.
23 Even if the river is turbulent, it is not frightened;
  it is confident though Jordan rushes against its
    mouth.
24 Can one take it with hooks*p*
  or pierce its nose with a snare?

41 *q* "Can you draw out Leviathan*r* with a fishhook,
  or press down its tongue with a cord?
2 Can you put a rope in its nose,
  or pierce its jaw with a hook?
3 Will it make many supplications to you?
  Will it speak soft words to you?
4 Will it make a covenant with you
  to be taken as your servant forever?
5 Will you play with it as with a bird,
  or will you put it on leash for your girls?
6 Will traders bargain over it?
  Will they divide it up among the merchants?
7 Can you fill its skin with harpoons,
  or its head with fishing spears?
8 Lay hands on it;
  think of the battle; you will not do it
    again!
9 *s* Any hope of capturing it*t* will be disappointed;
  were not even the gods*u* overwhelmed at the
    sight of it?
10 No one is so fierce as to dare to stir it up.
  Who can stand before it?*v*
11 Who can confront it*v* and be safe?*w*
  —under the whole heaven, who?*x*
12 "I will not keep silence concerning its limbs,
  or its mighty strength, or its splendid frame.
13 Who can strip off its outer garment?
  Who can penetrate its double coat of mail?*y*
14 Who can open the doors of its face?
  There is terror all around its teeth.

14 Then I in turn would acknowledge
  that your own right hand could save you.
15 But consider the chief of beasts, the crocodile,
  who devours cattle as if they were grass:
16 what strength is in his loins!
  What power in the muscles of his belly!
17 His tail is rigid as a cedar,
  the sinews of his flanks are tightly knit;
18 his bones are like tubes of bronze,
  his limbs like iron bars.
19 He is the chief of God's works,
  made to be a tyrant over his fellow-creatures;
20 for he takes the cattle of the hills for his prey
  and in his jaws he crunches all beasts of the
    wild.
21 There under the thorny lotus he lies,
  hidden among the reeds in the swamp;
22 the lotus conceals him in its shade,
  the poplars of the stream surround him.
23 If the river is in spate, that does not perturb him;
  he sprawls at his ease though submerged in the
    torrent.
24 Can anyone blind his eyes and take him
  or pierce his nose with the teeth of a trap?

‡41.1–6: see above following ch. 39‡

41 7 Can you fill his skin with harpoons
  or his head with fishing spears?
8 If ever you lift your hand against him,
  think of the struggle that awaits you, and
    stop!
9 Anyone who tackles him has no hope of success,
  but is overcome at the very sight of him.
10 How fierce he is when roused!
  Who is able to stand up to him?
11 Who has ever attacked him and come out of it
    safely?
  No one under the wide heaven.
12 I shall not pass over in silence his limbs,
  his prowess, and the grace of his proportions.
13 Who has ever stripped off his outer garment
  or penetrated his doublet of hide?
14 Who has ever prised open the portals of his face
  where terror lies in the circuits of his teeth?

40:15 **chief . . . crocodile**: *prob. rdg*; *Heb.* beasts (*behemoth*) which
I have made with you. **cattle . . . grass**: *prob. rdg*; *Heb.* grass like
cattle.   40:19 **fellow-creatures**: *prob. rdg*; *Heb.* sword.
40:24 **Can . . . blind**: *prob. rdg*; *Heb.* obscure.   41:7–8 *In Heb.*
40:31–32; 41:1–6 transposed to follow 39:30.   41:9 *In Heb.*
41:1.   41:10 **him**: *some MSS*; *others* me.   41:11 **him**: *prob.
rdg*; *Heb.* me. **and . . . safely**: *so Gk*; *Heb.* and I am safe. **No one**:
prob. rdg; *Heb.* He is mine.

p Cn: Heb *in his eyes*   *q* Ch 40.25 in Heb   *r* Or *the crocodile*
s Ch 41.1 in Heb   *t* Heb *of it*   *u* Cn Compare Symmachus Syr:
Heb *one is*   *v* Heb *me*   *w* Gk: Heb *that I shall repay*
x Heb *to me*   *y* Gk: Heb *bridle*

14 Then will I too acknowledge
  that your own right hand can save you.

15 See, besides you I made Behemoth,
  that feeds on grass like an ox.
16 Behold the strength in his loins,
  and his vigor in the sinews of his belly.
17 He carries his tail like a cedar;
  the sinews of his thighs are like cables.
18 His bones are like tubes of bronze;
  his frame is like iron rods.

19 He came at the beginning of God's ways,
  and was made the taskmaster of his fellows;
20 For the produce of the mountains is brought
    to him,
  and of all wild animals he makes sport.
21 Under the lotus trees he lies,
  in coverts of the reedy swamp.
22 The lotus trees cover him with their shade;
  all about him are the poplars on the bank.
23 If the river grows violent, he is not disturbed;
  he is tranquil though the torrent surges about
    his mouth.
24 Who can capture him by his eyes,
  or pierce his nose with a trap?

25 Can you lead about Leviathan with a hook,
  or curb his tongue with a bit?
26 Can you put a rope into his nose,
  or pierce through his cheek with a gaff?
27 Will he then plead with you, time after time,
  or address you with tender words?
28 Will he make an agreement with you
  that you may have him as a slave forever?
29 Can you play with him, as with a bird?
  Can you put him in leash for your maidens?
30 Will the traders bargain for him?
  Will the merchants divide him up?

31 Can you fill his hide with barbs,
  or his head with fish spears?
32 Once you but lay a hand upon him,
  no need to recall any other conflict!

41 2 Is he not relentless when aroused;
  who then dares stand before him?
1 Whoever might vainly hope to do so
  need only see him to be overthrown.
3 Who has assailed him and come off safe —
  Who under all the heavens?

4 I need hardly mention his limbs,
  his strength, and the fitness of his armor.
5 Who can strip off his outer garment,
  or penetrate his double corselet?
6 Who can force open the doors of his mouth,
  close to his terrible teeth?

14 And I shall be the first to pay you homage,
  since your own right hand is strong enough to
    save you.

15 But look at Behemoth,[n] my creature, just as you
    are!
  He feeds on greenstuff like the ox,
16 but what strength he has in his loins,
  what power in his stomach muscles!
17 His tail is as stiff as a cedar,
  the sinews of his thighs are tightly knit.
18 His bones are bronze tubes,
  his frame like forged iron.

19 He is the first of the works of God.
  His Maker threatened him with the sword,
20 forbidding him the mountain regions
  and all the wild animals that play there.
21 Under the lotus he lies,
  he hides among the reeds in the swamps.
22 The leaves of the lotus give him shade,
  the willows by the stream shelter him.
23 If the river overflows, he does not worry:
  Jordan might come up to his mouth, but he
    would not care.
24 Who is going to catch him by the eyes
  or put poles through his nose?

25 Leviathan,[o] too! Can you catch him with a
    fish-hook
  or hold his tongue down with a rope?
26 Can you put a cane through his nostrils
  or pierce his jaw with a hook?
27 Will he plead lengthily with you,
  addressing you in diffident tones?
28 Will he strike a bargain with you
  to become your slave for life?
29 Will you make a pet of him, like a bird,
  keep him on a lead to amuse your little girls?
30 Is he to be sold by the fishing guild
  and then retailed by merchants?
31 Riddle his hide with darts?
  Or his head with fishing spears?
32 You have only to lay a finger on him
  never to forget the struggle or risk it again!

41 Any hope you might have would be futile,
  the mere sight of him would overwhelm you.
2 When roused, he grows ferocious,
  who could ever stand up to him?
3 Who has ever attacked him with impunity?
  No one beneath all heaven!
4 Next I will talk of his limbs
  and describe his matchless strength —
5 who can undo the front of his tunic
  or pierce the double armour of his breastplate?
6 Who dare open the gates of his mouth?
  Terror reigns round his teeth!

---

n **40** Lit. 'the Beast', sometimes a mythical buffalo, but here the
hippopotamus.   o **40** Properly the monster of chaos, see 26:13, but
here described as a crocodile.

15 Its backᶻ is made of shields in rows,
 shut up closely as with a seal.
16 One is so near to another
 that no air can come between them.
17 They are joined one to another;
 they clasp each other and cannot be separated.
18 Its sneezes flash forth light,
 and its eyes are like the eyelids of the dawn.
19 From its mouth go flaming torches;
 sparks of fire leap out.
20 Out of its nostrils comes smoke,
 as from a boiling pot and burning rushes.
21 Its breath kindles coals,
 and a flame comes out of its mouth.
22 In its neck abides strength,
 and terror dances before it.
23 The folds of its flesh cling together;
 it is firmly cast and immovable.
24 Its heart is as hard as stone,
 as hard as the lower millstone.
25 When it raises itself up the gods are afraid;
 at the crashing they are beside themselves.
26 Though the sword reaches it, it does not avail,
 nor does the spear, the dart, or the javelin.
27 It counts iron as straw,
 and bronze as rotten wood.
28 The arrow cannot make it flee;
 slingstones, for it, are turned to chaff.
29 Clubs are counted as chaff;
 it laughs at the rattle of javelins.
30 Its underparts are like sharp potsherds;
 it spreads itself like a threshing sledge on the
 mire.
31 It makes the deep boil like a pot;
 it makes the sea like a pot of ointment.
32 It leaves a shining wake behind it;
 one would think the deep to be white-haired.
33 On earth it has no equal,
 a creature without fear.
34 It surveys everything that is lofty;
 it is king over all that are proud."

42 Then Job answered the LORD:
2 "I know that you can do all things,
 and that no purpose of yours can be thwarted.
3 'Who is this that hides counsel without
 knowledge?'
 Therefore I have uttered what I did not
 understand,
 things too wonderful for me, which I did not
 know.
4 'Hear, and I will speak;
 I will question you, and you declare to me.'
5 I had heard of you by the hearing of the ear,
 but now my eye sees you;
6 therefore I despise myself,
 and repent in dust and ashes."

7 After the LORD had spoken these words to Job, the
LORD said to Eliphaz the Temanite: "My wrath is kindled
against you and against your two friends; for you have not
spoken of me what is right, as my servant Job has. 8 Now

15 His back is row upon row of shields,
 enclosed in a wall of flints;
16 one presses so close on the next
 that no air can pass between them,
17 each so firmly clamped to its neighbour
 that they hold and cannot be parted.
18 His sneezing sends out sprays of light,
 and his eyes gleam like the shimmer of dawn.
19 Firebrands shoot from his mouth,
 and sparks come flying out;
20 his nostrils gush forth steam
 like a cauldron on a fire fanned to full heat.
21 His breath sets coals ablaze,
 and flames issue from his mouth.
22 Strength resides in his neck,
 and dismay dances ahead of him.
23 Close-knit is his underbelly,
 no pressure will make it yield.
24 His heart is firm as a rock,
 firm as the nether millstone.

25 When he rears up, strong men are afraid,
 panic-stricken at the lashings of his tail.
26 Sword or spear, dart or javelin
 may touch him, but all without effect.
27 Iron he counts as straw,
 and bronze as rotted wood.
28 No arrow can pierce him,
 and for him sling-stones are so much chaff;
29 to him a cudgel is but a reed,
 and he laughs at the swish of the sabre.
30 Armoured beneath with jagged sherds,
 he sprawls on the mud like a threshing-sledge.
31 He makes the deep water boil like a cauldron,
 he churns up the lake like ointment in a mixing
 bowl.
32 He leaves a shining trail behind him,
 and in his wake the great river is like white hair.
33 He has no equal on earth,
 a creature utterly fearless.
34 He looks down on all, even the highest;
 over all proud beasts he is king.

42 Job answered the LORD:
2 I know that you can do all things
 and that no purpose is beyond you.
3 You ask: Who is this obscuring counsel yet lacking
 knowledge?
 But I have spoken of things
 which I have not understood,
 things too wonderful for me to know.
4 Listen, and let me speak. You said:
 I shall put questions to you, and you must answer.
5 I knew of you then only by report,
 but now I see you with my own eyes.
6 Therefore I yield,
 repenting in dust and ashes.

7 WHEN the LORD had finished speaking to Job, he said to
Eliphaz the Temanite, 'My anger is aroused against you and
your two friends, because, unlike my servant Job, you have
not spoken as you ought about me. 8 Now take seven bulls

41:15 **back:** *prob. rdg; Heb.* pride. **wall:** *prob. rdg; Heb.* seal.
41:18 **shimmer of dawn:** *lit.* eyelids of the morning.   41:20 **full**
heat: *so Syriac; Heb.* rushes.   41:25 **strong men:** *or* leaders *or*
gods.   42:7 **unlike . . . me:** *so some MSS; others* you have not
spoken as you ought about my servant Job.   42:8 **about**
. . . done: *so some MSS; others* to me about him.

ᶻCn Compare Gk Vg: Heb *pride*

NEW AMERICAN BIBLE

⁷ Rows of scales are on his back,
   tightly sealed together;
⁸ They are fitted each so close to the next
   that no space intervenes;
⁹ So joined one to another
   that they hold fast and cannot be parted.

¹⁰ When he sneezes, light flashes forth;
   his eyes are like those of the dawn.
¹¹ Out of his mouth go forth firebrands;
   sparks of fire leap forth.
¹² From his nostrils issues steam,
   as from a seething pot or bowl.
¹³ His breath sets coals afire;
   a flame pours from his mouth.
¹⁴ Strength abides in his neck,
   and terror leaps before him.

15. ¹⁶ His heart is hard as stone:
   his flesh, as the lower millstone.
¹⁷ When he rises up, the mighty are afraid;
   the waves of the sea fall back.
¹⁸ Should the sword reach him, it will not avail;
   nor will the spear, nor the dart, nor the javelin.
¹⁹ He regards iron as straw,
   and bronze as rotten wood.
²⁰ The arrow will not put him to flight;
   slingstones used against him are but straws.
²¹ Clubs he esteems as splinters;
   he laughs at the crash of the spear.

²² His belly is sharp as pottery fragments;
   he spreads like a threshing sledge upon the mire.
²³ He makes the depths boil like a pot;
   the sea he churns like perfume in a kettle.
²⁴ Behind him he leaves a shining path;
   you would think the deep had the hoary head
     of age.
²⁵ Upon the earth there is not his like,
   intrepid he was made.
²⁶ All, however lofty, fear him;
   he is king over all proud beasts.

42 Then Job answered the LORD and said:

² I know that you can do all things,
   and that no purpose of yours can be hindered.
³ I have dealt with great things that I do
   not understand;
   things too wonderful for me, which I
     cannot know.
⁵ I had heard of you by word of mouth,
   but now my eye has seen you.
⁶ Therefore I disown what I have said,
   and repent in dust and ashes.

⁷ And it came to pass after the LORD had spoken these words to Job, that the LORD said to Eliphaz the Temanite, "I am angry with you and with your two friends; for you have not spoken rightly concerning me, as has my servant Job. ⁸ Now, therefore, take seven bullocks and seven rams,

NEW JERUSALEM BIBLE

⁷ His back is like rows of shields,
   sealed with a stone seal,
⁸ touching each other so close
   that no breath could pass between,
⁹ sticking to one another
   making an impervious whole.
¹⁰ His sneezes radiate light,
   his eyes are like the eyelashes of the dawn.
¹¹ From his mouth come fiery torches,
   sparks of fire fly out of it.
¹² His nostrils belch smoke
   like a cauldron boiling on the fire.
¹³ His breath could kindle coals,
   flame issues from his mouth.
¹⁴ His strength resides in his neck,
   violence leaps before him as he goes.
¹⁷ When he stands up, the waves take fright
   and the billows of the sea retreat.
¹⁵ The strips of his flesh are jointed together,
   firmly set in and immovable.
¹⁶ His heart is as hard as rock
   unyielding as the lower millstone.
¹⁸ Sword may strike but will not stick in him,
   no more will spear, javelin or lance.
¹⁹ Iron means no more to him than straw,
   nor bronze than rotten wood.
²⁰ No arrow can make him flee,
   a sling-stone tickles him like hay.
²¹ Club seems to him like straw,
   he laughs at the whirring javelin.
²² He has sharp potsherds underneath,
   and moves across the slime like a harrow.
²³ He makes the depths seethe like a cauldron,
   he makes the sea fume like a scent burner.
²⁴ Behind him he leaves a glittering wake —
   a white fleece seems to float on the deeps.
²⁵ He has no equal on earth,
   being created without fear.
²⁶ He looks the haughtiest in the eye;
   of all the lordly beasts he is king.

42 This was the answer Job gave to Yahweh:

² I know that you are all-powerful:
   what you conceive, you can perform.
³ I was the man who misrepresented your intentions
   with my ignorant words.
   You have told me about great works that I cannot
     understand,
   about marvels which are beyond me, of which I
     know nothing.
⁴ (Listen, please, and let me speak:
   I am going to ask the questions, and you are to
     inform me.)
⁵ Before, I knew you only by hearsay
   but now, having seen you with my own eyes,
⁶ I retract what I have said,
   and repent in dust and ashes.

⁷ When Yahweh had finished saying this to Job, he said to Eliphaz of Teman, 'I burn with anger against you and your two friends, for not having spoken correctly about me as my servant Job has done. ⁸ So now find seven bullocks

NEW REVISED STANDARD VERSION

therefore take seven bulls and seven rams, and go to my servant Job, and offer up for yourselves a burnt offering; and my servant Job shall pray for you, for I will accept his prayer not to deal with you according to your folly; for you have not spoken of me what is right, as my servant Job has done." 9 So Eliphaz the Temanite and Bildad the Shuhite and Zophar the Naamathite went and did what the LORD had told them; and the LORD accepted Job's prayer.

10 And the LORD restored the fortunes of Job when he had prayed for his friends; and the LORD gave Job twice as much as he had before. 11 Then there came to him all his brothers and sisters and all who had known him before, and they ate bread with him in his house; they showed him sympathy and comforted him for all the evil that the LORD had brought upon him; and each of them gave him a piece of money*a* and a gold ring. 12 The LORD blessed the latter days of Job more than his beginning; and he had fourteen thousand sheep, six thousand camels, a thousand yoke of oxen, and a thousand donkeys. 13 He also had seven sons and three daughters. 14 He named the first Jemimah, the second Keziah, and the third Keren-happuch. 15 In all the land there were no women so beautiful as Job's daughters; and their father gave them an inheritance along with their brothers. 16 After this Job lived one hundred and forty years, and saw his children, and his children's children, four generations. 17 And Job died, old and full of days.

a Heb *a qesitah*

REVISED ENGLISH BIBLE

and seven rams, go to my servant Job and offer a whole-offering for yourselves, and he will intercede for you. I shall surely show him favour by not being harsh with you because you have not spoken as you ought about me, as he has done.' 9 Then Eliphaz the Temanite and Bildad the Shuhite and Zophar the Naamathite went and carried out the LORD's command, and the LORD showed favour to Job 10 when he had interceded for his friends.

The LORD restored Job's fortunes, and gave him twice the possessions he had before. 11 All Job's brothers and sisters and his acquaintance of former days came and feasted with him in his home. They consoled and comforted him for all the misfortunes which the LORD had inflicted on him, and each of them gave him a sheep and a gold ring. 12 Thus the LORD blessed the end of Job's life more than the beginning: he had fourteen thousand sheep and six thousand camels, a thousand yoke of oxen, and as many she-donkeys. 13 He also had seven sons and three daughters; 14 he named his eldest daughter Jemimah, the second Keziah, and the third Keren-happuch. 15 There were no women in all the world so beautiful as Job's daughters; and their father gave them an inheritance with their brothers.

16 Thereafter Job lived another hundred and forty years; he saw his sons and his grandsons to four generations, 17 And he died at a very great age.

42:9 **and Zophar:** *so many MSS; others omit* and.   42:11 **sheep:** *or* piece of money.   42:13 **seven:** *or* fourteen.

and go to my servant Job, and offer up a holocaust for yourselves; and let my servant Job pray for you; for his prayer I will accept, not to punish you severely. For you have not spoken rightly concerning me, as has my servant Job." 9 Then Eliphaz the Temanite, and Bildad the Shuhite, and Zophar the Naamathite, went and did as the LORD had commanded them. And the LORD accepted the intercession of Job.

10 Also, the LORD restored the prosperity of Job, after he had prayed for his friends; the LORD even gave to Job twice as much as he had before. 11 Then all his brethren and his sisters came to him, and all his former acquaintances, and they dined with him in his house. They condoled with him and comforted him for all the evil which the LORD had brought upon him; and each one gave him a piece of money and a gold ring.

12 Thus the LORD blessed the latter days of Job more than his earlier ones. For he had fourteen thousand sheep, six thousand camels, a thousand yoke of oxen, and a thousand she-asses. 13 And he had seven sons and three daughters, 14 of whom he called the first Jemimah, the second Keziah, and the third Keren-happuch. 15 In all the land no other women were as beautiful as the daughters of Job; and their father gave them an inheritance among their brethren. 16 After this, Job lived a hundred and forty years; and he saw his children, his grandchildren, and even his great-grandchildren. 17 Then Job died, old and full of years.

and seven rams, and take them back with you to my servant Job and make a burnt offering for yourselves, while Job, my servant, offers prayers for you. I shall show him favour and shall not inflict my displeasure on you for not having spoken about me correctly, as my servant Job has done.' 9 Eliphaz of Teman, Bildad of Shuah and Zophar of Naamath went away to do as Yahweh had ordered, and Yahweh listened to Job with favour.

10 And Yahweh restored Job's condition, while Job was interceding for his friends. More than that, Yahweh gave him double what he had before. 11 And all his brothers and all his sisters and all his friends of former times came to see him. Over dinner in his house, they showed their sympathy and comforted him for all the evils Yahweh had inflicted on him. Each of them gave him a silver coin, and each a gold ring. 12 Yahweh blessed Job's latter condition even more than his former one. He came to own fourteen thousand sheep, six thousand camels, a thousand yoke of oxen and a thousand she-donkeys. 13 He had seven sons and three daughters; 14 his first daughter he called 'Turtledove', the second 'Cassia' and the third 'Mascara'. 15 Throughout the land there were no women as beautiful as the daughters of Job. And their father gave them inheritance rights like their brothers.

16 After this, Job lived for another one hundred and forty years, and saw his children and his children's children to the fourth generation. 17 Then, old and full of days, Job died.

The Psalms

BOOK I

Psalms 1–41

Psalm 1

1 Happy are those
who do not follow the advice of the wicked,
or take the path that sinners tread,
or sit in the seat of scoffers;
2 but their delight is in the law of the LORD,
and on his law they meditate day and night.
3 They are like trees
planted by streams of water,
which yield their fruit in its season,
and their leaves do not wither.
In all that they do, they prosper.

4 The wicked are not so,
but are like chaff that the wind drives away.
5 Therefore the wicked will not stand in the
judgment,
nor sinners in the congregation of the
righteous;
6 for the LORD watches over the way of the
righteous,
but the way of the wicked will perish.

Psalm 2

1 Why do the nations conspire,
and the peoples plot in vain?
2 The kings of the earth set themselves,
and the rulers take counsel together,
against the LORD and his anointed, saying,
3 "Let us burst their bonds asunder,
and cast their cords from us."

4 He who sits in the heavens laughs;
the LORD has them in derision.
5 Then he will speak to them in his wrath,
and terrify them in his fury, saying,
6 "I have set my king on Zion, my holy hill."

7 I will tell of the decree of the LORD:
He said to me, "You are my son;
today I have begotten you.
8 Ask of me, and I will make the nations your
heritage,
and the ends of the earth your possession.
9 You shall break them with a rod of iron,
and dash them in pieces like a potter's vessel."

10 Now therefore, O kings, be wise;
be warned, O rulers of the earth.
11 Serve the LORD with fear,
with trembling 12 kiss his feet,*a*
or he will be angry, and you will perish in the
way;
for his wrath is quickly kindled.

Happy are all who take refuge in him.

a Cn: Meaning of Heb of verses 11b and 12a is uncertain

Psalms

BOOK 1

Psalm 1

1 HAPPY is the one
who does not take the counsel of the wicked for a
guide,
or follow the path that sinners tread,
or take his seat in the company of scoffers.
2 His delight is in the law of the LORD;
it is his meditation day and night.
3 He is like a tree
planted beside water channels;
it yields its fruit in season
and its foliage never fades.
So he too prospers in all he does.

4 The wicked are not like this;
rather they are like chaff driven by the wind.
5 When judgement comes, therefore, they will not
stand firm,
nor will sinners in the assembly of the righteous.

6 The LORD watches over the way of the righteous,
but the way of the wicked is doomed.

Psalm 2

1 WHY are the nations in turmoil?
Why do the peoples hatch their futile plots?
2 Kings of the earth stand ready,
and princes conspire together
against the LORD and his anointed king.
3 'Let us break their fetters,' they cry,
'let us throw off their chains!'

4 He who sits enthroned in the heavens laughs,
the Lord derides them;
5 then angrily he rebukes them,
threatening them in his wrath.
6 'I myself have enthroned my king', he says,
'on Zion, my holy mountain.'

7 I shall announce the decree of the LORD:
'You are my son,' he said to me;
'this day I become your father.
8 Ask of me what you will:
I shall give you nations as your domain,
the earth to its farthest ends as your possession.
9 You will break them with a rod of iron,
shatter them like an earthen pot.'

10 Be mindful, then, you kings;
take warning, you earthly rulers:
11–12 worship the LORD with reverence;
tremble, and pay glad homage to the king,
for fear the LORD may become angry
and you may be struck down in mid-course;
for his anger flares up in a moment.
Happy are all who find refuge in him!

2:11–12 **tremble . . . king:** *poss. mng; Heb.* and rejoice with
trembling; kiss the son.

THE BOOK OF
Psalms

FIRST BOOK
Psalms 1–41

The Psalms

Psalm 1

I
1 Happy those who do not follow
  the counsel of the wicked,
Nor go the way of sinners,
  nor sit in company with scoffers.
2 Rather, the law of the LORD is their joy;
  God's law they study day and night.
3 They are like a tree
  planted near streams of water,
  that yields its fruit in season;
Its leaves never wither;
  whatever they do prospers.
II
4 But not the wicked!
  They are like chaff driven by the wind.
5 Therefore the wicked will not survive judgment,
  nor will sinners in the assembly of the just.
6 The LORD watches over the way of the just,
  but the way of the wicked leads to ruin.

Psalm 1

1 How blessed is anyone who rejects the advice of
    the wicked
  and does not take a stand in the path that sinners
    tread,
  nor a seat in company with cynics,
2 but who delights in the law of Yahweh
  and murmurs his law day and night.

3 Such a one is like a tree planted near streams;
  it bears fruit in season
  and its leaves never wither,
  and every project succeeds.
4 How different the wicked, how different!

Just like chaff blown around by the wind
5 the wicked will not stand firm at the Judgement
  nor sinners in the gathering of the upright.
6 For Yahweh watches over the path of the upright,
  but the path of the wicked is doomed.

Psalm 2

1 Why do the nations protest
  and the peoples grumble in vain?
2 Kings on earth rise up
  and princes plot together
  against the LORD and his anointed:
3 "Let us break their shackles
  and cast off their chains!"
4 The one enthroned in heaven laughs;
  the Lord derides them,
5 Then speaks to them in anger,
  terrifies them in wrath:
6 "I myself have installed my king
  on Zion, my holy mountain."
7 I will proclaim the decree of the LORD,
  who said to me, "You are my son;
  today I am your father.
8 Only ask it of me,
  and I will make your inheritance the nations,
  your possession the ends of the earth.
9 With an iron rod you shall shepherd them,
  like a clay pot you will shatter them."
10 And now, kings, give heed;
  take warning, rulers on earth.
11 Serve the LORD with fear;
  with trembling bow down in homage,
Lest God be angry and you perish from the way
  in a sudden blaze of anger.
Happy are all who take refuge in God!

Psalm 2

1 Why this uproar among the nations,
  this impotent muttering of the peoples?
2 Kings of the earth take up position,
  princes plot together
  against Yahweh and his anointed,
3 'Now let us break their fetters!
  Now let us throw off their bonds!'
4 He who is enthroned in the heavens laughs,
  Yahweh makes a mockery of them,
5 then in his anger rebukes them,
  in his rage he strikes them with terror.
6 'I myself have anointed my king
  on Zion my holy mountain.'

7 I will proclaim the decree of Yahweh:
  He said to me, 'You are my son,
  today have I fathered you.
8 Ask of me, and I shall give you the nations as
    your birthright,
  the whole wide world as your possession.
9 With an iron sceptre you will break them,
  shatter them like so many pots.'

10 So now, you kings, come to your senses,
  you earthly rulers, learn your lesson!
11 In fear be submissive to Yahweh;
12 with trembling kiss his feet,
  lest he be angry and your way come to nothing,
  for his fury flares up in a moment.

How blessed are all who take refuge in him!

NEW REVISED STANDARD VERSION

Psalm 3

A Psalm of David, when he fled from his son Absalom.

1 O LORD, how many are my foes!
   Many are rising against me;
2 many are saying to me,
   "There is no help for you*b* in God."   *Selah*

3 But you, O LORD, are a shield around me,
   my glory, and the one who lifts up my head.
4 I cry aloud to the LORD,
   and he answers me from his holy hill.   *Selah*

5 I lie down and sleep;
   I wake again, for the LORD sustains me.
6 I am not afraid of ten thousands of people
   who have set themselves against me all around.

7 Rise up, O LORD!
   Deliver me, O my God!
   For you strike all my enemies on the cheek;
   you break the teeth of the wicked.

8 Deliverance belongs to the LORD;
   may your blessing be on your people!   *Selah*

Psalm 4

To the leader: with stringed instruments. A Psalm of David.

1 Answer me when I call, O God of my right!
   You gave me room when I was in distress.
   Be gracious to me, and hear my prayer.

2 How long, you people, shall my honor suffer
      shame?
   How long will you love vain words, and seek
      after lies?   *Selah*
3 But know that the LORD has set apart the faithful
      for himself;
   the LORD hears when I call to him.

4 When you are disturbed,*c* do not sin;
   ponder it on your beds, and be silent.   *Selah*
5 Offer right sacrifices,
   and put your trust in the LORD.

6 There are many who say, "O that we might see
      some good!
   Let the light of your face shine on us,
   O LORD!"
7 You have put gladness in my heart
   more than when their grain and wine abound.

8 I will both lie down and sleep in peace;
   for you alone, O LORD, make me lie down in
      safety.

Psalm 5

To the leader: for the flutes. A Psalm of David.

1 Give ear to my words, O LORD;
   give heed to my sighing.
2 Listen to the sound of my cry,
   my King and my God,
   for to you I pray.
3 O LORD, in the morning you hear my voice;
   in the morning I plead my case to you, and
      watch.

REVISED ENGLISH BIBLE

Psalm 3

A psalm: for David (when he fled from his son Absalom)

1 LORD, how numerous are my enemies!
   How many there are who rise against me,
2 how many who say of me,
   'He will not find safety in God!'   [*Selah*

3 But you, LORD, are a shield to cover me:
   you are my glory, you raise my head high.
4 As often as I cry aloud to the LORD,
   he answers from his holy mountain.   [*Selah*
5 I lie down and sleep,
   and I wake again, for the LORD upholds me.
6 I shall not fear their myriad forces
   ranged against me on every side.

7 Arise, LORD; save me, my God!
   You strike all my foes across the face;
   you break the teeth of the wicked.
8 Yours is the victory, LORD;
   may your blessing rest on your people.   [*Selah*

Psalm 4

For the leader: with stringed instruments: a psalm:
for David

1 ANSWER me when I call,
   God, the upholder of my right!
   When I was hard pressed you set me free;
   be gracious to me and hear my prayer.
2 Men of rank, how long will you dishonour my
      glorious one,
   setting your heart on empty idols and resorting to
      false gods?   [*Selah*
3 Know that the LORD has singled out for himself his
      loyal servant;
   the LORD hears when I call to him.
4 Let awe restrain you from sin;
   while you rest, meditate in silence: [*Selah*
5 offer your due of sacrifice,
   and put your trust in the LORD.

6 There are many who say, 'If only we might see
      good times!
   Let the light of your face shine on us, LORD.'
7 But you have put into my heart a greater happiness
   than others had from grain and wine in plenty.
8 Now in peace I shall lie down and sleep;
   for it is you alone, LORD, who let me live in
      safety.

Psalm 5

For the leader: with the flutes: a psalm: for David

1 LISTEN to my words, LORD,
   consider my inmost thoughts;
2 heed my cry for help, my King and God.
3 When I pray to you, LORD,
   in the morning you will hear me.
   I shall prepare a morning sacrifice
   and keep watch.

---

b Syr: Heb *him*   *c* Or *are angry*

NEW AMERICAN BIBLE

Psalm 3

[1] *A psalm of David, when he fled from his son Absalom.*

I

[2] How many are my foes, LORD!
How many rise against me!
[3] How many say of me,
"God will not save that one." *Selah*
[4] But you, LORD, are a shield around me;
my glory, you keep my head high.

II

[5] Whenever I cried out to the LORD,
I was answered from the holy mountain. *Selah*
[6] Whenever I lay down and slept,
the LORD preserved me to rise again.
[7] I do not fear, then, thousands of people
arrayed against me on every side.

III

[8] Arise, LORD! Save me, my God!
You will shatter the jaws of all my foes;
you will break the teeth of the wicked.
[9] Safety comes from the LORD!
Your blessing for your people! *Selah*

Psalm 4

[1] *For the leader; with stringed instruments. A psalm of David.*

I

[2] Answer when I call, my saving God.
In my troubles, you cleared a way;
show me favor; hear my prayer.

II

[3] How long will you people mock my honor,
love what is worthless, chase after lies? *Selah*
[4] Know that the LORD works wonders for the
faithful;
the LORD hears when I call out.
[5] Tremble and do not sin;
upon your beds ponder in silence.
[6] Offer fitting sacrifice
and trust in the LORD.

III

[7] Many say, "May we see better times!
LORD, show us the light of your face!" *Selah*
[8] But you have given my heart more joy
than they have when grain and wine abound.
[9] In peace I shall both lie down and sleep,
for you alone, LORD, make me secure.

Psalm 5

[1] *For the leader; with wind instruments. A psalm of David.*

I

[2] Hear my words, O LORD;
listen to my sighing.
[3] Hear my cry for help,
my king, my God!
To you I pray, O LORD;
[4] at dawn you will hear my cry;
at dawn I will plead before you and wait.

NEW JERUSALEM BIBLE

Psalm 3

*Psalm   Of David   When he was fleeing from
his son Absalom*

[1] Yahweh, how countless are my enemies,
how countless those who rise up against me,
[2] how countless those who say of me,
'No salvation for him from his God!' *Pause*

[3] But you, Yahweh, the shield at my side,
my glory, you hold my head high.
[4] I cry out to Yahweh;
he answers from his holy mountain. *Pause*

[5] As for me, if I lie down and sleep,
I shall awake, for Yahweh sustains me.
[6] I have no fear of people in their thousands upon
thousands,
who range themselves against me wherever I turn.

[7] Arise, Yahweh, rescue me, my God!
You strike all my foes across the face,
you break the teeth of the wicked.
[8] In Yahweh is salvation,
on your people, your blessing! *Pause*

Psalm 4

For the choirmaster   For strings   Psalm   Of David

[1] When I call, answer me, God, upholder of my
right.
In my distress you have set me at large;
take pity on me and hear my prayer!

[2] Children of men, how long will you be heavy of
heart,
why love what is vain and chase after illusions? *Pause*

[3] Realise that Yahweh performs wonders for his
faithful,
Yahweh listens when I call to him.

[4] Be careful not to sin,
speak in your hearts, and on your beds keep
silence. *Pause*

[5] Loyally offer sacrifices, and trust in Yahweh.

[6] Many keep saying, 'Who will put happiness before
our eyes?'
Let the light of your face shine on us.

Yahweh, [7] to my heart you are a richer joy
than all their corn and new wine.

[8] In peace I lie down and at once fall asleep,
for it is you and none other, Yahweh, who make
me rest secure.

Psalm 5

For the choirmaster   For flutes   Psalm   Of David

[1] Give ear to my words, Yahweh,
spare a thought for my sighing.
[2] Listen to my cry for help,
my King and my God!

To you I pray, [3] Yahweh.
At daybreak you hear my voice;
at daybreak I lay my case before you
and fix my eyes on you.

NEW REVISED STANDARD VERSION

4 For you are not a God who delights in
wickedness;
evil will not sojourn with you.
5 The boastful will not stand before your eyes;
you hate all evildoers.
6 You destroy those who speak lies;
the LORD abhors the bloodthirsty and deceitful.

7 But I, through the abundance of your steadfast
love,
will enter your house,
I will bow down toward your holy temple
in awe of you.
8 Lead me, O LORD, in your righteousness
because of my enemies;
make your way straight before me.

9 For there is no truth in their mouths;
their hearts are destruction;
their throats are open graves;
they flatter with their tongues.
10 Make them bear their guilt, O God;
let them fall by their own counsels;
because of their many transgressions cast them
out,
for they have rebelled against you.

11 But let all who take refuge in you rejoice;
let them ever sing for joy.
Spread your protection over them,
so that those who love your name may exult in
you.
12 For you bless the righteous, O LORD;
you cover them with favor as with a shield.

Psalm 6

*To the leader: with stringed instruments; according to The
Sheminith. A Psalm of David.*

1 O LORD, do not rebuke me in your anger,
or discipline me in your wrath.
2 Be gracious to me, O LORD, for I am
languishing;
O LORD, heal me, for my bones are shaking
with terror.
3 My soul also is struck with terror,
while you, O LORD—how long?

4 Turn, O LORD, save my life;
deliver me for the sake of your steadfast love.
5 For in death there is no remembrance of you;
in Sheol who can give you praise?

6 I am weary with my moaning;
every night I flood my bed with tears;
I drench my couch with my weeping.
7 My eyes waste away because of grief;
they grow weak because of all my foes.

8 Depart from me, all you workers of evil,
for the LORD has heard the sound of my
weeping.
9 The LORD has heard my supplication;
the LORD accepts my prayer.
10 All my enemies shall be ashamed and struck with
terror;
they shall turn back, and in a moment be put
to shame.

REVISED ENGLISH BIBLE

4 For you are not a God who welcomes wickedness;
evil can be no guest of yours.
5 The arrogant will not stand in your presence;
you hate all evildoers.
6 you make an end of liars.
The LORD abhors those who are violent and
deceitful.

7 But through your great love I may come into your
house,
and at your holy temple bow down in awe.
8 Lead me and protect me, LORD,
because I am beset by enemies;
give me a straight path to follow.
9 Nothing they say is true;
they are bent on complete destruction.
Their throats are gaping tombs;
smooth talk runs off their tongues.
10 God, bring ruin on them;
let their own devices be their downfall.
Cast them out for their many rebellions,
for they have defied you.

11 But let all who take refuge in you rejoice,
let them for ever shout for joy;
shelter those who love your name,
that they may exult in you.
12 For you, LORD, will bless the righteous;
you will surround them with favour as with a
shield.

Psalm 6

*For the leader: with stringed instruments: according to the
sheminith: a psalm: for David*

1 LORD, do not rebuke me in your anger,
do not punish me in your wrath.
2 Show favour to me, LORD, for my strength fails;
LORD, heal me, for my body is racked with pain;
3 I am utterly distraught.
When will you act, LORD?
4 Return, LORD, deliver me;
save me, for your love is steadfast.
5 Among the dead no one remembers you;
in Sheol who praises you?

6 I am wearied with my moaning;
all night long my pillow is wet with tears,
I drench my bed with weeping.
7 Grief dims my eyes;
they are worn out because of all my adversaries.

8 Leave me alone, you workers of evil,
for the LORD has heard my weeping!
9 The LORD has heard my entreaty;
the LORD will accept my prayer.
10 All my enemies will be confounded, stricken with
terror;
they will turn away in sudden confusion.

6:5 **Sheol:** *or* the underworld.

1136

NEW AMERICAN BIBLE

II

5 You are not a god who delights in evil;
  no wicked person finds refuge with you;
6 the arrogant cannot stand before you.
  You hate all who do evil;
7 you destroy all who speak falsely.
  Murderers and deceivers
    the LORD abhors.

III

8 But I can enter your house
  because of your great love.
  I can worship in your holy temple
  because of my reverence for you, LORD.
9 Guide me in your justice because of my foes;
  make straight your way before me.

IV

10 For there is no sincerity in their mouths;
   their hearts are corrupt.
   Their throats are open graves;
   on their tongues are subtle lies.
11 Declare them guilty, God;
   make them fall by their own devices.
   Drive them out for their many sins;
   they have rebelled against you.

V

12 Then all who take refuge in you will be glad
   and forever shout for joy.
   Protect them that you may be the joy
   of those who love your name.
13 For you, LORD, bless the just;
   you surround them with favor like a shield.

Psalm 6

1 *For the leader; with stringed instruments, "upon the eighth." A psalm of David.*

I

2 Do not reprove me in your anger, LORD,
  nor punish me in your wrath.
3 Have pity on me, LORD, for I am weak;
  heal me, LORD, for my bones are trembling.
4 In utter terror is my soul—
  and you, LORD, how long . . . ?
5 Turn, LORD, save my life;
  in your mercy rescue me.
6 For who among the dead remembers you?
  Who praises you in Sheol?

II

7 I am wearied with sighing;
  all night long tears drench my bed;
  my couch is soaked with weeping.
8 My eyes are dimmed with sorrow,
  worn out because of all my foes.

III

9 Away from me, all who do evil!
  The LORD has heard my weeping.
10 The LORD has heard my prayer;
   the LORD takes up my plea.
11 My foes will be terrified and disgraced;
   all will fall back in sudden shame.

NEW JERUSALEM BIBLE

4 You are not a God who takes pleasure in evil,
  no sinner can be your guest.
5 Boasters cannot stand their ground
  under your gaze.

  You hate evil-doers,
6 liars you destroy;
  the violent and deceitful
  Yahweh detests.

7 But, so great is your faithful love,
  I may come into your house,
  and before your holy temple
  bow down in reverence of you.

8 In your saving justice, Yahweh, lead me,
  because of those who lie in wait for me;
  make your way plain before me.

9 Not a word from their lips can be trusted,
  through and through they are destruction,
  their throats are wide-open graves,
  their tongues seductive.

10 Lay the guilt on them, God,
   make their intrigues their own downfall;
   for their countless offences, thrust them from you,
   since they have rebelled against you.

11 But joy for all who take refuge in you,
   endless songs of gladness!
   You shelter them, they rejoice in you,
   those who love your name.

12 It is you who bless the upright, Yahweh,
   you surround them with favour as with a shield.

Psalm 6[a]

For the choirmaster   For strings
For the octachord   Psalm   Of David

1 Yahweh, let your rebuke to me not be in anger,
  your punishment not in the heat of wrath.
2 Have pity on me, Yahweh, for I am fading away.
  Heal me, Yahweh, my bones are shaken,
3 my spirit is shaken to its very depths.
  But you, Yahweh . . . how long?

4 Yahweh, relent and save my life
  rescue me because of your faithful love,
5 for in death there is no remembrance of you;
  who could sing your praises in Sheol?

6 I am worn out with groaning,
  every night I drench my pillow
  and soak my bed with tears.
7 My eyes waste away with vexation.
  Arrogance from all my foes!
8 Away from me, all evil-doers!

  For Yahweh has heard the sound of my weeping,
9 Yahweh has heard my pleading.
  Yahweh will accept my prayer.
10 Let all my enemies be put to confusion, shaken to
   their depths,
   let them retreat in sudden confusion.

6, 4: *How long?*: elliptical for "How long will it be before you answer my prayer?" Cf Ps 13, 2-3.

a **6** The first of the seven Penitential Psalms (6; 32; 38; 51; 102; 130; 142).

Psalm 7

A Shiggaion of David, which he sang to the LORD
concerning Cush, a Benjaminite.

1 O LORD my God, in you I take refuge;
    save me from all my pursuers, and deliver me,
2 or like a lion they will tear me apart;
    they will drag me away, with no one to rescue.

3 O LORD my God, if I have done this,
    if there is wrong in my hands,
4 if I have repaid my ally with harm
    or plundered my foe without cause,
5 then let the enemy pursue and overtake me,
    trample my life to the ground,
    and lay my soul in the dust.   *Selah*

6 Rise up, O LORD, in your anger;
    lift yourself up against the fury of my enemies;
    awake, O my God;*d* you have appointed a
        judgment.
7 Let the assembly of the peoples be gathered
        around you,
    and over it take your seat*e* on high.
8 The LORD judges the peoples;
    judge me, O LORD, according to my
        righteousness
    and according to the integrity that is in me.

9 O let the evil of the wicked come to an end,
    but establish the righteous,
    you who test the minds and hearts,
    O righteous God.
10 God is my shield,
    who saves the upright in heart.
11 God is a righteous judge,
    and a God who has indignation every day.

12 If one does not repent, God*f* will whet his
        sword;
    he has bent and strung his bow;
13 he has prepared his deadly weapons,
    making his arrows fiery shafts.
14 See how they conceive evil,
    and are pregnant with mischief,
    and bring forth lies.
15 They make a pit, digging it out,
    and fall into the hole that they have made.
16 Their mischief returns upon their own heads,
    and on their own heads their violence
        descends.

17 I will give to the LORD the thanks due to his
        righteousness,
    and sing praise to the name of the LORD, the
        Most High.

Psalm 8

To the leader: according to The Gittith. A Psalm of David.

1 O LORD, our Sovereign,
    how majestic is your name in all the earth!

You have set your glory above the heavens.
2 Out of the mouths of babes and infants
you have founded a bulwark because of your
        foes,
    to silence the enemy and the avenger.

Psalm 7

A shiggaion: for David (which he sang to the LORD because
of Cush, a Benjamite)

1 LORD my God, in you I find refuge;
    rescue me from all my pursuers and save me
2 before they tear at my throat like a lion
    and drag me off beyond hope of rescue.
3 LORD my God, if I have done any of these
        things—
    if I have stained my hands with guilt,
4 if I have repaid a friend evil for good
    or wantonly despoiled an adversary—
5 let an enemy come in pursuit and overtake me,
    let him trample my life to the ground
    and lay my honour in the dust!   *[Selah*

6 Arise, LORD, in your anger,
    rouse yourself in wrath against my adversaries.
    My God who ordered justice to be done, awake.
7 Let the peoples assemble around you;
    take your seat on high above them.
8 The LORD passes sentence on the nations.
    Uphold my cause, LORD, as my righteousness
        deserves,
    for I am clearly innocent.
9 Let the wicked do no more harm,
    but grant support to the righteous,
    you searcher of heart and mind,
    you righteous God.

10 I rely on God to shield me;
    he saves the honest of heart.
11 God is a just judge,
    constant in his righteous anger.

12 The enemy sharpens his sword again,
    strings his bow and makes it ready.
13 It is against himself he has prepared his deadly
        shafts
    and tipped his arrows with fire.
14 He is in labour with iniquity;
    he has conceived mischief and given birth to lies.
15 He has made a pit and dug it deep,
    but he himself will fall into the hole he was
        making.
16 His mischief will recoil upon him,
    and his violence fall on his own head.

17 I shall praise the LORD for his righteousness
    and sing to the name of the LORD Most High.

Psalm 8

For the leader: according to the gittith: a psalm: for David

1 LORD our sovereign,
    how glorious is your name throughout the world!
    Your majesty is praised as high as the heavens,
2 from the mouths of babes and infants at the breast.
    You have established a bulwark against your
        adversaries
    to restrain the enemy and the avenger.

---

d Or awake for me   *e Cn: Heb return*   *f Heb he*

Psalm 7

1 *A plaintive song of David, which he sang to the* Lord *concerning Cush, the Benjaminite.*

I

2 Lord my God, in you I take refuge;
  rescue me; save me from all who pursue me,
3 Lest they maul me like lions,
  tear me to pieces with none to save.

II

4 Lord my God, if I am at fault in this,
  if there is guilt on my hands,
5 If I have repaid my friend with evil —
  I spared even those who hated me without
    cause —
6 Then let my enemy pursue and overtake me,
  trample my life to the ground,
  and leave me dishonored in the dust.   *Selah*

III

7 Rise up, Lord, in your anger;
  rise against the fury of my foes.
  Wake to judge as you have decreed.
8 Have the assembly of the peoples gather about you;
  sit on your throne high above them,
9   O Lord, judge of the nations.
  Grant me justice, Lord, for I am blameless,
    free of any guilt.
10 Bring the malice of the wicked to an end;
  uphold the innocent,
  O God of justice,
    who tries hearts and minds.

IV

11 A shield before me is God
  who saves the honest heart.
12 God is a just judge,
  who rebukes in anger every day.
13 If sinners do not repent,
  God sharpens his sword,
  strings and readies the bow,
14 Prepares his deadly shafts,
  makes arrows blazing thunderbolts.

V

15 Sinners conceive iniquity;
  pregnant with mischief,
  they give birth to failure.
16 They open a hole and dig it deep,
  but fall into the pit they have dug.
17 Their mischief comes back upon themselves;
  their violence falls on their own heads.

VI

18 I praise the justice of the Lord;
  I celebrate the name of the Lord Most High.

Psalm 8

1 *For the leader; "upon the gittith." A psalm of David.*

2 O Lord, our Lord,
  how awesome is your name through all the
    earth!
  You have set your majesty above the heavens!
3 Out of the mouths of babes and infants
  you have drawn a defense against your foes,
  to silence enemy and avenger.

Psalm 7

*Lament   Of David   Which he sang to Yahweh about
    Cush the Benjaminite*

1 Yahweh my God, I take refuge in you,
  save me from all my pursuers and rescue me,
2 or he will savage me like a lion,
  carry me off with no one to rescue me.

3 Yahweh my God, if I have done this:
  if injustice has stained my hands,
4 if I have repaid my ally with treachery
  or spared one who attacked me unprovoked,
5 may an enemy hunt me down and catch me,
  may he trample my life into the ground
  and crush my vital parts into the dust.   *Pause*

6 Arise, Yahweh, in your anger,
  rise up against the arrogance of my foes.
  Awake, my God,
  you demand judgement.
7 Let the assembly of nations gather round you;
  return above it on high!
8 (Yahweh judges the nations.)

  Judge me, Yahweh, as my uprightness
    and my integrity deserve.
9 Put an end to the malice of the wicked,
  make the upright stand firm,
  you who discern hearts and minds,
    God the upright.

10 God is a shield that protects me,
  saving the honest of heart.
11 God is an upright judge,
  slow to anger,
  but a God at all times threatening
12   for those who will not repent.

  Let the enemy whet his sword,
  draw his bow and make ready;
13 but he is making ready instruments of death for
    himself
  and tipping his arrows with fire;
14 look at him: pregnant with malice,
  conceiving spite, he gives birth to treachery.

15 He digs a trap, scoops it out,
  but he falls into the snare he made himself.
16 His spite recoils on his own head,
  his brutality falls back on his own skull.

17 I thank Yahweh for his saving justice.
  I sing to the name of the Most High.

Psalm 8

For the choirmaster   On the . . . of Gath [b]
    Psalm   Of David

1 Yahweh our Lord,
  how majestic is your name throughout the world!

  Whoever keeps singing of your majesty higher than
    the heavens,
2 even through the mouths of children, or of babes in
    arms,
  you make him a fortress, firm against your foes,
  to subdue the enemy and the rebel.

[b] 8 Perhaps on the harp or on a melody of Gath, i.e. Philistine.

3 When I look at your heavens, the work of your
        fingers,
     the moon and the stars that you have
        established;
4 what are human beings that you are mindful of
        them,
     mortals^g that you care for them?

5 Yet you have made them a little lower than
        God,^{h}
     and crowned them with glory and honor.
6 You have given them dominion over the works of
        your hands;
     you have put all things under their feet,
7 all sheep and oxen,
     and also the beasts of the field,
8 the birds of the air, and the fish of the sea,
     whatever passes along the paths of the seas.

9 O LORD, our Sovereign,
     how majestic is your name in all the earth!

Psalm 9

To the leader: according to Muth-labben.
A Psalm of David.

1 I will give thanks to the LORD with my whole
        heart;
     I will tell of all your wonderful deeds.
2 I will be glad and exult in you;
     I will sing praise to your name, O Most High.

3 When my enemies turned back,
     they stumbled and perished before you.
4 For you have maintained my just cause;
     you have sat on the throne giving righteous
        judgment.

5 You have rebuked the nations, you have
        destroyed the wicked;
     you have blotted out their name forever and
        ever.
6 The enemies have vanished in everlasting ruins;
     their cities you have rooted out;
     the very memory of them has perished.

7 But the LORD sits enthroned forever,
     he has established his throne for judgment.
8 He judges the world with righteousness;
     he judges the peoples with equity.

9 The LORD is a stronghold for the oppressed,
     a stronghold in times of trouble.
10 And those who know your name put their trust in
        you,
     for you, O LORD, have not forsaken those who
        seek you.

11 Sing praises to the LORD, who dwells in Zion.
     Declare his deeds among the peoples.
12 For he who avenges blood is mindful of them;
     he does not forget the cry of the afflicted.

13 Be gracious to me, O LORD.
     See what I suffer from those who hate me;
     you are the one who lifts me up from the gates
        of death,
14 so that I may recount all your praises,
     and, in the gates of daughter Zion,
     rejoice in your deliverance.

3 When I look up at your heavens, the work of your
        fingers,
     at the moon and the stars you have set in place,
4 what is a frail mortal, that you should be mindful
        of him,
     a human being, that you should take notice of him?

5 Yet you have made him little less than a god,
     crowning his head with glory and honour.
6 You make him master over all that you have made,
     putting everything in subjection under his feet:
7 all sheep and oxen, all the wild beasts,
8 the birds in the air, the fish in the sea,
     and everything that moves along ocean paths.

9 LORD our sovereign,
     how glorious is your name throughout the world!

Psalms 9–10

For the leader: set to 'Muth labben': a psalm: for David

1 I SHALL give praise to you, LORD, with my whole
        heart,
     I shall recount all your marvellous deeds.
2 I shall rejoice and exult in you, the Most High;
     I shall sing praise to your name
3 because my enemies turn back;
     at your presence they fall headlong and perish.

4 For seated on your throne, a righteous judge,
     you have upheld my right and my cause;
5 you have rebuked the nations and overwhelmed the
        ungodly,
     blotting out their name for all time.
6 The enemy are finished, ruined for evermore.
     You have overthrown their cities; all memory of
        them is lost.

7 The LORD sits enthroned for ever:
     he has established his throne for judgement.
8 He it is who will judge the world with justice,
     who will try the cause of peoples with equity.

9 May the LORD be a tower of strength for the
        oppressed,
     a tower of strength in time of trouble.
10 Those who acknowledge your name will trust in
        you,
     for you, LORD, do not abandon those who seek
        you.

11 Sing to the LORD enthroned in Zion;
     proclaim his deeds among the nations.
12 For the avenger of blood keeps the afflicted in
        mind;
     he does not ignore their cry.

13 Show me favour, LORD; see how my foes afflict
        me;
     you raise me from the gates of death,
14 that I may declare all your praise
     and in the gates of Zion exult at this deliverance.

---

^{g}Heb *ben adam*, lit. *son of man* ^{h}Or *than the divine beings* or
angels: Heb *elohim*

4 When I see your heavens, the work of your
  fingers,
    the moon and stars that you set in place —
5 What are humans that you are mindful of them,
    mere mortals that you care for them?
6 Yet you have made them little less than a god,
    crowned them with glory and honor.
7 You have given them rule over the works of your
  hands,
    put all things at their feet:
8 All sheep and oxen,
    even the beasts of the field,
9 The birds of the air, the fish of the sea,
    and whatever swims the paths of the seas.
10 O Lord, our Lord,
    how awesome is your name through all the
  earth!

Psalms 9–10

1 *For the leader; according to* Muth Labben. *A psalm of*
David.

A

I
2 I will praise you, Lord, with all my heart;
    I will declare all your wondrous deeds.
3 I will delight and rejoice in you,
    I will sing hymns to your name, Most High.
4 For my enemies turn back;
    they stumble and perish before you.
II
5 You upheld my right and my cause,
    seated on your throne, judging justly.
6 You rebuked the nations, you destroyed the
  wicked;
    their name you blotted out for all time.
7 The enemies have been ruined forever;
    you destroyed their cities;
    their memory has perished.
III
8 The Lord rules forever,
    has set up a throne for judgment.
9 It is God who governs the world with justice,
    who judges the peoples with fairness.
10 The Lord is a stronghold for the oppressed,
    a stronghold in times of trouble.
11 Those who honor your name trust in you;
    you never forsake those who seek you, Lord.
IV
12 Sing hymns to the Lord enthroned on Zion;
    proclaim God's deeds among the nations!
13 For the avenger of bloodshed remembers,
    does not forget the cry of the afflicted.
V
14 *Have mercy on me,* Lord;
    see how my foes afflict me!
    You alone can raise me from the gates of death.
15 Then I will declare all your praises,
    sing joyously of your salvation
    in the gates of daughter Zion.

3 I look up at your heavens, shaped by your fingers,
    at the moon and the stars you set firm —
4 what are human beings that you spare a thought for
  them,
    or the child of Adam that you care for him?
5 Yet you have made him little less than a god,
    you have crowned him with glory and beauty,
6 made him lord of the works of your hands,
    put all things under his feet,
7 sheep and cattle, all of them,
    and even the wild beasts,
8 birds in the sky, fish in the sea,
    when he makes his way across the ocean.
9 Yahweh our Lord,
    how majestic your name throughout the world!

Psalms 9–10 c

For the choirmaster   On oboe and harp   Psalm
Of David

Aleph   1 I thank you, Yahweh, with my whole heart,
                I recount all your wonders,
             2 I rejoice and delight in you,
                I sing to your name, Most High.

Bet   3 My enemies are in retreat,
                they stumble and perish at your presence,
             4 for you have given fair judgement in my
                favour,
                seated on your throne as upright judge.

Gimel   5 You have rebuked the nations, destroyed the
                wicked,
                blotted out their name for ever and ever;
             6 the enemy is wiped out — mere ruins for
                ever —
                you have annihilated their cities, their memory
                has perished.

He   See, 7 Yahweh is enthroned for ever,
                keeping his throne firm for judgement;
             8 he will himself judge the world in uprightness,
                will give a true verdict on the nations.

Waw   9 May Yahweh be a stronghold for the
                oppressed,
                a stronghold in times of trouble!
             10 Those who revere your name can rely on you,
                you never desert those who seek you,
                Yahweh.

Zain   11 Sing to Yahweh who dwells in Zion,
                tell the nations his mighty deeds,
             12 for the avenger of blood does not forget them,
                he does not ignore the cry of the afflicted.

Het   13 Have pity on me, Yahweh, see my affliction,
                pull me back from the gates of death,
             14 that I may recount all your praises at the gates
                of the daughter of Zion
                and rejoice in your salvation.

Pss 9-10: Pss 9 and 10 in the Hebrew text have been transmitted as
separate poems but they actually form a single acrostic poem and are
so transmitted in the Greek and Latin tradition.

c **9–10** One poem with initial letters in alphabetical order, though in
our corrupt text some are missing.

15 The nations have sunk in the pit that they made;
    in the net that they hid has their own foot been
        caught.
16 The LORD has made himself known, he has
        executed judgment;
    the wicked are snared in the work of their own
        hands.   *Higgaion. Selah*

17 The wicked shall depart to Sheol,
    all the nations that forget God.

18 For the needy shall not always be forgotten,
    nor the hope of the poor perish forever.

19 Rise up, O LORD! Do not let mortals prevail;
    let the nations be judged before you.
20 Put them in fear, O LORD;
    let the nations know that they are only human.
                                          Selah

Psalm 10

1   Why, O LORD, do you stand far off?
    Why do you hide yourself in times of trouble?
2   In arrogance the wicked persecute the poor—
    let them be caught in the schemes they have
        devised.
3   For the wicked boast of the desires of their heart,
    those greedy for gain curse and renounce the
        LORD.
4   In the pride of their countenance the wicked say,
        "God will not seek it out";
    all their thoughts are, "There is no God."

5   Their ways prosper at all times;
    your judgments are on high, out of their sight;
    as for their foes, they scoff at them.
6   They think in their heart, "We shall not be
        moved;
    throughout all generations we shall not meet
        adversity."

7   Their mouths are filled with cursing and deceit
        and oppression;
    under their tongues are mischief and iniquity.
8   They sit in ambush in the villages;
    in hiding places they murder the innocent.

    Their eyes stealthily watch for the helpless;
9   they lurk in secret like a lion in its covert;
    they lurk that they may seize the poor;
    they seize the poor and drag them off in their
        net.

10 They stoop, they crouch,
    and the helpless fall by their might.
11 They think in their heart, "God has forgotten,
    he has hidden his face, he will never see it."

12 Rise up, O LORD; O God, lift up your hand;
    do not forget the oppressed.
13 Why do the wicked renounce God,
    and say in their hearts, "You will not call us to
        account"?

14 But you do see! Indeed you note trouble and
        grief,
    that you may take it into your hands;
    the helpless commit themselves to you;
    you have been the helper of the orphan.

15 The nations have plunged into a pit of their own
        making;
    their feet are entangled in the net they have hidden.
16 The LORD makes himself known, and justice is
        done:
    the wicked are trapped in their own devices.
                                  [*Higgaion. Selah*

17 The wicked depart to Sheol,
    all the nations who are heedless of God.

18 But the poor will not always be unheeded,
    nor the hope of the destitute be always vain.
19 Arise, LORD, restrain the power of mortals;
    let the nations be judged in your presence.
20 Strike them with fear, LORD;
    let the nations know that they are but human
        beings.   [*Selah*

[10] 1 Why stand far off, LORD?
    Why hide away in times of trouble?
2   The wicked in their arrogance hunt down the
        afflicted:
    may their crafty schemes prove their undoing!
3   The wicked boast of the desires they harbour;
    in their greed they curse and revile the LORD.
4   The wicked in their pride do not seek God;
    there is no place for God in any of their schemes.
5   Their ways are always devious;
    your judgements are beyond their grasp,
    and they scoff at all their adversaries.
6   Because they escape misfortune,
    they think they will never be shaken.

7   The wicked person's mouth is full of cursing,
        deceit, and violence;
    mischief and wickedness are under his tongue.
8   He lurks in ambush near settlements
    and murders the innocent by stealth.
    Ever on the watch for some unfortunate wretch,
9   he seizes him and drags him away in his net.
    He crouches stealthily, like a lion in its lair
    crouching to seize its victim;
10 he strikes and lays him low.
    Unfortunate wretches fall into his toils.
11 He says to himself, 'God has forgotten;
    he has hidden his face and seen nothing.'

12 Arise, LORD, set your hand to the task;
    God, do not forget the afflicted.
13 Why have the wicked rejected you, God,
    and said that you will not call them to account?

14 You see that mischief and grief are their
        companions;
    you take the matter into your own hands.
    The hapless victim commits himself to you;
    in you the fatherless finds a helper.

9:17 **Sheol**: *or* the underworld.

NEW AMERICAN BIBLE

VI

16 The nations fall into the pit they dig;
   in the snare they hide, their own foot is caught.
17 The LORD is revealed in this divine rule:
   by the deeds they do the wicked are trapped.
                                                Higgaion. Selah

VII

18 To Sheol the wicked will depart,
   all the nations that forget God.
19 The needy will never be forgotten,
   nor will the hope of the afflicted ever fade.
20 Arise, LORD, let no mortal prevail;
   let the nations be judged in your presence.
21 Strike them with terror, LORD;
   show the nations they are mere mortals.   *Selah*

B

I

1 Why, LORD, do you stand at a distance
   and pay no heed to these troubled times?
2 Arrogant scoundrels pursue the poor;
   they trap them by their cunning schemes.

II

3 The wicked even boast of their greed;
   these robbers curse and scorn the LORD.
4 In their insolence the wicked boast:
   "God doesn't care, doesn't even exist."
5 Yet their affairs always succeed;
   they ignore your judgment on high;
   they sneer at all who oppose them.
6 They say in their hearts, "We will never fall;
   never will we see misfortune."
7 Their mouths are full of oaths, violence, and lies;
   discord and evil are under their tongues.
8 They wait in ambush near towns;
   their eyes watch for the helpless,
   to murder the innocent in secret.
9 They lurk in ambush like lions in a thicket,
   hide there to trap the poor,
   snare them and close the net.
10 The helpless are crushed, laid low;
    they fall into the power of the wicked,
11 Who say in their hearts, "God pays no attention,
    shows no concern, never bothers to look."

III

12 Rise up, LORD God! Raise your arm!
    Do not forget the poor!
13 Why should the wicked scorn God,
    say in their hearts, "God doesn't care"?
14 But you do see;
    you do observe this misery and sorrow;
    you take the matter in hand.
    To you the helpless can entrust their cause;
    you are the defender of orphans.

NEW JERUSALEM BIBLE

Tet   15 The nations have fallen into the trap they
        made,
        their feet caught in the snare they laid.
        16 Yahweh has made himself known, given
        judgement,
        he has ensnared the wicked in the work of
        their own hands.   *Muted music   Pause*

Yod   17 May the wicked turn away to Sheol,
        all the nations forgetful of God.

Kaph 18 For the needy is not forgotten for ever,
        not for ever does the hope of the poor come
        to nothing.

        19 Arise, Yahweh; human strength shall not
        prevail.
        The nations shall stand trial before you.
        20 Strike them with terror, Yahweh;
        the nations shall know that they are no more
        than human!   *Pause*

10

Lamed 1 Why, Yahweh, do you keep so distant,
         stay hidden in times of trouble?
         2 In his pride the wicked hunts down the weak,
         who is caught in the schemes he devises.

(Mem) 3 The wicked is proud of his inmost desires,
         by his blasphemies the grasping spurns
         Yahweh,

(Nun) 4 the wicked in his arrogance does not look
         very far;
         'There is no God,' is his only thought.

         5 In all circumstances his step is assured;
         your judgements are above his head.
         His rivals? He scoffs at them all.

         6 He says in his heart, 'I shall never be shaken,'
         free of trouble himself, 7 he wishes it on
         others.

(Samek)
Pe   His speech is full of lies and browbeating,
         under his tongue lurk spite and wickedness.
         8 In the undergrowth he lies in ambush,
         in his hiding-place he murders the innocent.

Ain   He watches intently for the downtrodden,
         9 lurking unseen like a lion in his lair,
         lurking to pounce on the poor;
         he pounces on him and drags him off in his
         net.

(Zade) 10 He keeps watch, crouching down low,
         the poor wretch falls into his clutches;
         11 he says in his heart, 'God forgets,
         he has turned away his face to avoid seeing
         the end.'

Qoph   12 Rise, Yahweh! God, raise your hand,
         do not forget the afflicted!
         13 Why should the wicked spurn God,
         assuring himself you will never follow it up?

Resh   14 You have seen for yourself the trouble and
         vexation,
         you watch so as to take it in hand.
         The oppressed relies on you;
         you are the only recourse of the orphan.

NEW REVISED STANDARD VERSION

REVISED ENGLISH BIBLE

15 Break the arm of the wicked and evildoers;
  seek out their wickedness until you find none.
16 The LORD is king forever and ever;
  the nations shall perish from his land.

17 O LORD, you will hear the desire of the meek;
  you will strengthen their heart, you will incline
  your ear
18 to do justice for the orphan and the oppressed,
  so that those from earth may strike terror no
  more. *i*

15 Break the power of the wicked and evil person;
  hunt out his wickedness until you can find no
  more.
16 The LORD is king for ever and ever;
  the nations have vanished from his land.

17 LORD, you have heard the lament of the humble;
  you strengthen their hearts, you give heed to them,
18 bringing redress to the fatherless and the
  oppressed,
  so that no one on earth may ever again inspire
  terror.

Psalm 11

To the leader. Of David.

1 In the LORD I take refuge; how can you say to me,
  "Flee like a bird to the mountains;*j*
2 for look, the wicked bend the bow,
  they have fitted their arrow to the string,
  to shoot in the dark at the upright in heart.
3 If the foundations are destroyed,
  what can the righteous do?"

4 The LORD is in his holy temple;
  the LORD's throne is in heaven.
  His eyes behold, his gaze examines
  humankind.
5 The LORD tests the righteous and the wicked,
  and his soul hates the lover of violence.
6 On the wicked he will rain coals of fire and
  sulfur;
  a scorching wind shall be the portion of their
  cup.
7 For the LORD is righteous;
  he loves righteous deeds;
  the upright shall behold his face.

Psalm 11

For the leader: for David

1 IN the LORD I take refuge. How can you say to
  me,
  'Flee like a bird to the mountains;
2 for see, the wicked string their bows
  and fit the arrow to the bowstring,
  to shoot from the darkness at honest folk'?
3 When foundations are undermined,
  what can the just person do?

4 The LORD is in his holy temple;
  the LORD's throne is in heaven.
  His gaze is upon mankind, his searching eye tests
  them.
5 The LORD weighs just and unjust,
  and he hates all who love violence.
6 He will rain fiery coals and brimstone on the
  wicked;
  scorching winds will be the portion they drink.
7 For the LORD is just and loves just dealing;
  his face is turned towards the upright.

Psalm 12

*To the leader: according to The Sheminith. A Psalm of
David.*

1 Help, O LORD, for there is no longer anyone who
  is godly;
  the faithful have disappeared from humankind.
2 They utter lies to each other;
  with flattering lips and a double heart they
  speak.

3 May the LORD cut off all flattering lips,
  the tongue that makes great boasts,
4 those who say, "With our tongues we will
  prevail;
  our lips are our own—who is our master?"

5 "Because the poor are despoiled, because the
  needy groan,
  I will now rise up," says the LORD;
  "I will place them in the safety for which they
  long."
6 The promises of the LORD are promises that are
  pure,
  silver refined in a furnace on the ground,
  purified seven times.

7 You, O LORD, will protect us;
  you will guard us from this generation forever.

Psalm 12

*For the leader: according to the sheminith: a psalm:
for David*

1 SAVE us, LORD, for no one who is loyal remains;
  good faith between people has vanished.
2 One lies to another:
  both talk with smooth words, but with duplicity in
  their hearts.

3 May the LORD make an end of such smooth words
  and the tongue that talks so boastfully!
4 They say, 'By our tongues we shall prevail.
  With words as our ally, who can master us?'
5 'Now I will arise,' says the LORD,
  'for the poor are plundered, the needy groan;
  I shall place them in the safety for which they
  long.'

6 The words of the LORD are unalloyed:
  silver refined in a crucible,
  gold purified seven times over.
7 LORD, you are our protector
  and will for ever guard us from such people.

---

i Meaning of Heb uncertain   *j* Gk Syr Jerome Tg: Heb *flee to your
mountain, O bird*

12:6 **gold:** *prob. rdg; Heb.* to the earth.   12:7 **our:** *so some MSS;
others* their.

15 Break the arms of the wicked and depraved;
  make them account for their crimes;
  let none of them survive.

IV

16 The Lord is king forever;
  the nations have vanished from God's land.
17 You listen, Lord, to the needs of the poor;
  you encourage them and hear their prayers.
18 You win justice for the orphaned and oppressed;
  no one on earth will cause terror again.

Shin

15 Break the arm of the wicked and evil,
  seek out wickedness till there is none left to
    be found.
16 Yahweh is king for ever and ever,
  the heathen has vanished from his country.

Taw

17 Yahweh, you listen to the laments of the poor,
  you give them courage, you grant them a
    hearing,
18 to give judgement for the orphaned and
    exploited,
  so that earthborn humans may strike terror no
    more.

Psalm 11

1 *For the leader. Of David.*

I

  In the Lord I take refuge;
  how can you say to me,
  "Flee like a bird to the mountains!
2 See how the wicked string their bows,
  fit their arrows to the string
  to shoot from the shadows at the upright.
3 When foundations are being destroyed,
  what can the upright do?"

II

4 The Lord is in his holy temple;
  the Lord's throne is in heaven.
  God's eyes keep careful watch;
  they test all peoples.
5 The Lord tests the good and the bad,
  hates those who love violence,
6 And rains upon the wicked
  fiery coals and brimstone,
  a scorching wind their allotted cup.
7 The Lord is just and loves just deeds;
  the upright shall see his face.

Psalm 11 (V 10)*d*

For the choirmaster   Of David

1 In Yahweh I have found refuge.
  How can you say to me,
  'Bird, flee to your mountain?
2 'For look, the wicked are drawing their bows,
  fitting their arrows to the string
  to shoot honest men from the shadows.
3 If the foundations fall to ruin, what can the upright
    do?'

4 Yahweh in his holy temple!
  Yahweh, his throne is in heaven;
  his eyes watch over the world,
  his gaze scrutinises the children of Adam.
5 Yahweh examines the upright and the wicked,
  the lover of violence he detests.
6 He will rain down red-hot coals,
  fire and sulphur on the wicked,
  a scorching wind will be their lot.
7 For Yahweh is upright and loves uprightness,
  the honest will ever see his face.

Psalm 12

1 *For the leader; "upon the eighth." A psalm of David.*

I

2 Help, Lord, for no one loyal remains;
  the faithful have vanished from the human race.
3 Those who tell lies to one another
  speak with deceiving lips and a double heart.

II

4 May the Lord cut off all deceiving lips,
  and every boastful tongue;
5 Those who say, "By our tongues we prevail;
  when our lips speak, who can lord it over us?"

III

6 "Because they rob the weak, and the needy groan,
  I will now arise," says the Lord;
  "I will grant safety to whoever longs for it."

IV

7 The promises of the Lord are sure,
  silver refined in a crucible,
  silver purified seven times.
8 Lord, protect us always;
  preserve us from this generation.

Psalm 12 (V 11)

*For the choirmaster   On the octachord   Psalm
        Of David*

1 Help, Yahweh! No one loyal is left,
  the faithful have vanished from among the children
    of Adam.
2 Friend tells lies to friend,
  and, smooth-tongued, speaks from an insincere
    heart.
3 May Yahweh cut away every smooth lip,
  every boastful tongue,
4 those who say, 'In our tongue lies our strength,
  our lips are our allies; who can master us?'
5 'For the poor who are plundered, the needy who
    groan,
  now will I act,' says Yahweh,
  'I will grant salvation to those who sigh for it.'
6 Yahweh's promises are promises unalloyed,
  natural silver which comes from the earth seven
    times refined.
7 You, Yahweh, will watch over them,
  you will protect them from that brood for ever.

d 11 In this edition the Hebr. numbering of the Pss is used. From Ps 10 to Ps 147 this is ahead of the Gk and Vulgate numbering, which is given in parentheses.

NEW REVISED STANDARD VERSION

REVISED ENGLISH BIBLE

8 On every side the wicked prowl,
  as vileness is exalted among humankind.

8 The wicked parade about,
  and what is of little worth wins general esteem.

Psalm 13

To the leader. A Psalm of David.

1 How long, O LORD? Will you forget me forever?
  How long will you hide your face from me?
2 How long must I bear pain*k* in my soul,
  and have sorrow in my heart all day long?
  How long shall my enemy be exalted over me?

3 Consider and answer me, O LORD my God!
  Give light to my eyes, or I will sleep the sleep
    of death,
4 and my enemy will say, "I have prevailed";
  my foes will rejoice because I am shaken.

5 But I trusted in your steadfast love;
  my heart shall rejoice in your salvation.
6 I will sing to the LORD,
  because he has dealt bountifully with me.

Psalm 13

For the leader: a psalm: for David

1 How LONG, LORD, will you leave me forgotten,
  how long hide your face from me?
2 How long must I suffer anguish in my soul,
  grief in my heart day after day?
  How long will my enemy lord it over me?

3 Look now, LORD my God, and answer me.
  Give light to my eyes lest I sleep the sleep of
    death,
4 lest my enemy say, 'I have overthrown him,'
  and my adversaries rejoice at my downfall.
5 As for me, I trust in your unfailing love;
  my heart will rejoice when I am brought to safety.
6 I shall sing to the LORD, for he has granted all my
    desire.

Psalm 14

To the leader. Of David.

1 Fools say in their hearts, "There is no God."
  They are corrupt, they do abominable deeds;
  there is no one who does good.

2 The LORD looks down from heaven on
    humankind
  to see if there are any who are wise,
  who seek after God.

3 They have all gone astray, they are all alike
    perverse;
  there is no one who does good,
  no, not one.

4 Have they no knowledge, all the evildoers
  who eat up my people as they eat bread,
  and do not call upon the LORD?

5 There they shall be in great terror,
  for God is with the company of the righteous.
6 You would confound the plans of the poor,
  but the LORD is their refuge.

7 O that deliverance for Israel would come from
    Zion!
  When the LORD restores the fortunes of his
    people,
  Jacob will rejoice; Israel will be glad.

Psalm 14

For the leader: for David

1 THE impious fool says in his heart,
  'There is no God.'
  Everyone is depraved, every deed is vile;
  no one does good!
2 The LORD looks out from heaven
  on all the human race
  to see if any act wisely,
  if any seek God.
3 But all are unfaithful, altogether corrupt;
  no one does good, no, not even one.

4 Have they no understanding,
  all those evildoers who devour my people
  as if eating bread,
  and never call to the LORD?
5 They will be in dire alarm,
  for God is in the assembly of the righteous.
6 Though you would frustrate the counsel of the
    poor,
  the LORD is their refuge.
7 If only deliverance for Israel might come from
    Zion!
  When the LORD restores his people's fortunes,
  let Jacob rejoice, let Israel be glad.

Psalm 15

A Psalm of David.

1 O LORD, who may abide in your tent?
  Who may dwell on your holy hill?

2 Those who walk blamelessly, and do what is
    right,
  and speak the truth from their heart;

Psalm 15

A psalm: for David

1 LORD, who may lodge in your tent?
  Who may dwell on your holy mountain?
2 One of blameless life, who does what is right
  and speaks the truth from his heart;

---

k Syr: Heb *hold counsels*

13:2 **day after day:** *prob. rdg; Heb.* by day.

NEW AMERICAN BIBLE

9 On every side the wicked strut;
the shameless are extolled by all.

Psalm 13

1 For the leader. A psalm of David.

I

2 How long, LORD? Will you utterly forget me?
How long will you hide your face from me?
3 How long must I carry sorrow in my soul,
grief in my heart day after day?
How long will my enemy triumph over me?

II

4 Look upon me, answer me, LORD, my God!
Give light to my eyes lest I sleep in death,
5 Lest my enemy say, "I have prevailed,"
lest my foes rejoice at my downfall.

III

6 I trust in your faithfulness.
Grant my heart joy in your help,
That I may sing of the LORD,
"How good our God has been to me!"

Psalm 14

1 For the leader. Of David.

I

Fools say in their hearts,
"There is no God."
Their deeds are loathsome and corrupt;
not one does what is right.
2 The LORD looks down from heaven
upon the human race,
To see if even one is wise,
if even one seeks God.
3 All have gone astray;
all alike are perverse.
Not one does what is right,
not even one.

II

4 Will these evildoers never learn?
They devour my people as they devour bread;
they do not call upon the LORD.
5 They have good reason, then, to fear;
God is with the company of the just.
6 They would crush the hopes of the poor,
but the poor have the LORD as their refuge.

III

7 Oh, that from Zion might come
the deliverance of Israel,
That Jacob may rejoice, and Israel be glad
when the LORD restores his people!

Psalm 15

1 A psalm of David.

I

LORD, who may abide in your tent?
Who may dwell on your holy mountain?

II

2 Whoever walks without blame,
doing what is right,
speaking truth from the heart;

NEW JERUSALEM BIBLE

8 The wicked will scatter in every direction,
as the height of depravity among the children of
Adam.

Psalm 13 (V 12)

For the choirmaster   Psalm   Of David

1 How long, Yahweh, will you forget me? For ever?
How long will you turn away your face from me?
2 How long must I nurse rebellion in my soul,
sorrow in my heart day and night?
How long is the enemy to domineer over me?
3 Look down, answer me, Yahweh my God!
Give light to my eyes or I shall fall into the sleep
of death.

4 Or my foe will boast, 'I have overpowered him,'
and my enemy have the joy of seeing me stumble.
5 As for me, I trust in your faithful love, Yahweh.
Let my heart delight in your saving help,
let me sing to Yahweh for his generosity to me,
let me sing to the name of Yahweh the Most High!

Psalm 14 (V 13)*e*

For the choirmaster   Of David

1 The fool has said in his heart,
'There is no God.'
Their deeds are corrupt and vile,
not one of them does right.
2 Yahweh looks down from heaven
at the children of Adam.
To see if a single one is wise,
a single one seeks God.
3 All have turned away,
all alike turned sour,
not one of them does right,
not a single one.

4 Are they not aware, all these evil-doers?
They are devouring my people,
this is the bread they eat,
and they never call to Yahweh.
5 They will be gripped with fear,
where there is no need for fear,
for God takes the side of the upright;
6 you may mock the plans of the poor,
but Yahweh is their refuge.
7 Who will bring from Zion salvation for Israel?
When Yahweh brings his people home,
what joy for Jacob, what happiness for Israel!

Psalm 15 (V 14)

Psalm   Of David

1 Yahweh, who can find a home in your tent,
who can dwell on your holy mountain?

2 Whoever lives blamelessly,
who acts uprightly,
who speaks the truth from the heart,

e **14** Almost identical with Ps 53 except that the proper name
'Yahweh' here occurs for 'God'.

NEW REVISED STANDARD VERSION	REVISED ENGLISH BIBLE

3 who do not slander with their tongue,
    and do no evil to their friends,
    nor take up a reproach against their neighbors;
4 in whose eyes the wicked are despised,
    but who honor those who fear the LORD;
    who stand by their oath even to their hurt;
5 who do not lend money at interest,
    and do not take a bribe against the innocent.

Those who do these things shall never be moved.

3 who has no malice on his tongue,
    who never wrongs his fellow,
    and tells no tales against his neighbour;
4 who shows his scorn for those the LORD rejects,
    but honours those who fear the LORD;
    who holds to his oath even to his own hurt,
5 who does not put his money out to usury,
    and never accepts a bribe against the innocent.
He who behaves in this way will remain unshaken.

Psalm 16

A Miktam of David.

1 Protect me, O God, for in you I take refuge.
2 I say to the LORD, "You are my Lord;
    I have no good apart from you."[l]
3 As for the holy ones in the land, they are the
    noble,
    in whom is all my delight.
4 Those who choose another god multiply their
    sorrows;[m]
    their drink offerings of blood I will not pour
    out
    or take their names upon my lips.
5 The LORD is my chosen portion and my cup;
    you hold my lot.
6 The boundary lines have fallen for me in pleasant
    places;
    I have a goodly heritage.
7 I bless the LORD who gives me counsel;
    in the night also my heart instructs me.
8 I keep the LORD always before me;
    because he is at my right hand, I shall not be
    moved.
9 Therefore my heart is glad, and my soul rejoices;
    my body also rests secure.
10 For you do not give me up to Sheol,
    or let your faithful one see the Pit.
11 You show me the path of life.
    In your presence there is fullness of joy;
    in your right hand are pleasures forevermore.

Psalm 16

A miktam: for David

1 KEEP me, God, for in you have I found refuge.
2 I have said to the LORD, 'You are my Lord;
    from you alone comes the good I enjoy.
3 All my delight is in the noble ones,
    the godly in the land.
4 Those who run after other gods find endless
    trouble;
    I shall never offer libations of blood to such gods,
    never take their names on my lips.
5 LORD, you are my allotted portion and my cup;
    you maintain my boundaries;
6 the lines fall for me in pleasant places;
    I am well content with my inheritance.'
7 I shall bless the LORD who has given me counsel:
    in the night he imparts wisdom to my inmost
    being.
8 I have set the LORD before me at all times:
    with him at my right hand I cannot be shaken.
9 Therefore my heart is glad
    and my spirit rejoices,
    my body too rests unafraid;
10 for you will not abandon me to Sheol
    or suffer your faithful servant to see the pit.
11 You will show me the path of life;
    in your presence is the fullness of joy,
    at your right hand are pleasures for evermore.

Psalm 17

A Prayer of David.

1 Hear a just cause, O LORD; attend to my cry;
    give ear to my prayer from lips free of deceit.
2 From you let my vindication come;
    let your eyes see the right.
3 If you try my heart, if you visit me by night,
    if you test me, you will find no wickedness in
    me;
    my mouth does not transgress.
4 As for what others do, by the word of your lips
    I have avoided the ways of the violent.
5 My steps have held fast to your paths;
    my feet have not slipped.

Psalm 17

A prayer: for David

1 LORD, hear my plea for justice,
    give heed to my cry;
    listen to the prayer from my lips,
    for they are innocent of all deceit.
2 Let your judgement be given in my favour;
    let your eyes discern what is right.
3 You have tested my heart and watched me all night
    long;
    you have assayed me and found no malice in me.
4 Guided by the words of your lips,
    I have observed the deeds of mortals, their violent
    ways.
5 My steps have held steadily to your paths;
    my feet have not faltered.

15:4 **even . . . hurt:** *prob. rdg; Heb.* to do evil.   16:10 **Sheol:** *or* the underworld.   17:4–5 **Guided . . . faltered:** *or* I shall not speak of the deeds of men; /I have taken good note of all your sayings. /5I have not strayed from the course you commanded; /I have followed your path and never faltered.

[l] Jerome Tg: Meaning of Heb uncertain   [m] Cn: Meaning of Heb uncertain

3 Who does not slander a neighbor,
  does no harm to another,
  never defames a friend;
4 Who disdains the wicked,
  but honors those who fear the LORD;
Who keeps an oath despite the cost,
5   lends no money at interest,
  accepts no bribe against the innocent.
III
Whoever acts like this
  shall never be shaken.

3 who keeps the tongue under control,

who does not wrong a comrade,
  who casts no discredit on a neighbour,
4 who looks with scorn on the vile,
  but honours those who fear Yahweh,

who stands by an oath at any cost,
5 who asks no interest on loans,
  who takes no bribe to harm the innocent.
No one who so acts can ever be shaken.

Psalm 16

1 A miktam *of David.*

I
Keep me safe, O God;
  in you I take refuge.
2 I say to the LORD,
  you are my Lord,
  you are my only good.
3 Worthless are all the false gods of the land.
  Accursed are all who delight in them.
4 They multiply their sorrows
  who court other gods.
Blood libations to them I will not pour out,
  nor will I take their names upon my lips.
5 LORD, my allotted portion and my cup,
  you have made my destiny secure.
6 Pleasant places were measured out for me;
  fair to me indeed is my inheritance.
II
7 I bless the LORD who counsels me;
  even at night my heart exhorts me.
8 I keep the LORD always before me;
  with the Lord at my right, I shall never be
    shaken.
9 Therefore my heart is glad, my soul rejoices;
  my body also dwells secure,
10 For you will not abandon me to Sheol,
  nor let your faithful servant see the pit.
11 You will show me the path to life,
  abounding joy in your presence,
  the delights at your right hand forever.

Psalm 16 (V 15)

In a quiet voice   Of David

1 Protect me, O God, in you is my refuge.

2 To Yahweh I say, 'You are my Lord,
  my happiness is in none 3 of the sacred spirits of
    the earth.'

They only take advantage of all who love them.
4 People flock to their teeming idols.
Never shall I pour libations to them!
Never take their names on my lips.

5 My birthright, my cup is Yahweh;
  you, you alone, hold my lot secure.
6 The measuring-line marks out for me a delightful
    place,
  my birthright is all I could wish.

7 I bless Yahweh who is my counsellor,
  even at night my heart instructs me.
8 I keep Yahweh before me always,
  for with him at my right hand, nothing can shake
    me.

9 So my heart rejoices, my soul delights,
  my body too will rest secure,
10 for you will not abandon me to Sheol,
  you cannot allow your faithful servant to see the
    abyss.
11 You will teach me the path of life,
  unbounded joy in your presence,
  at your right hand delight for ever.

Psalm 17

1 A prayer of David.

I
Hear, LORD, my plea for justice;
  pay heed to my cry;
Listen to my prayer
  spoken without guile.
2 From you let my vindication come;
  your eyes see what is right.
3 You have tested my heart,
  searched it in the night.
You have tried me by fire,
  but find no malice in me.
My mouth has not transgressed
4   as humans often do.
As your lips have instructed me,
  I have kept the way of the law.
5 My steps have kept to your paths;
  my feet have not faltered.

Psalm 17 (V 16)

Prayer   Of David

1 Listen, Yahweh, to an upright cause,
  pay attention to my cry,
lend an ear to my prayer,
  my lips free from deceit.
2 From your presence will issue my vindication,
  your eyes fixed on what is right.

3 You probe my heart, examine me at night,
  you test me by fire and find no evil.
I have not sinned with my mouth 4 as most people
  do.

I have treasured the word from your lips,
5 my steps never stray from the paths you lay down,
  from your tracks; so my feet never stumble.

NEW REVISED STANDARD VERSION

REVISED ENGLISH BIBLE

6 I call upon you, for you will answer me, O God;
    incline your ear to me, hear my words.
7 Wondrously show your steadfast love,
    O savior of those who seek refuge
    from their adversaries at your right hand.

8 Guard me as the apple of the eye;
    hide me in the shadow of your wings,
9 from the wicked who despoil me,
    my deadly enemies who surround me.
10 They close their hearts to pity;
    with their mouths they speak arrogantly.
11 They track me down;[n] now they surround me;
    they set their eyes to cast me to the ground.
12 They are like a lion eager to tear,
    like a young lion lurking in ambush.

13 Rise up, O LORD, confront them, overthrow them!
    By your sword deliver my life from the
        wicked,
14 from mortals — by your hand, O LORD —
    from mortals whose portion in life is in this
        world.
    May their bellies be filled with what you have
        stored up for them;
    may their children have more than enough;
    may they leave something over to their little
        ones.

15 As for me, I shall behold your face in
        righteousness;
    when I awake I shall be satisfied, beholding
        your likeness.

6 God, I call upon you, for you will answer me.
    Bend down your ear to me, listen to my words.
7 Show me how marvellous is your unfailing love:
    your right hand saves
    those who seek sanctuary from their assailants.
8 Guard me like the apple of your eye;
    hide me in the shadow of your wings
9 from the wicked who do me violence,
    from deadly foes who throng around me.
10 They have stifled all compassion;
    their mouths utter proud words;
11 they press me hard, now they hem me in,
    on the watch to bring me to the ground.
12 The enemy is like a lion hungry for prey,
    like a young lion crouching in ambush.

13 Arise, LORD, confront them and bring them down.
    Save my life from the wicked;
    make an end of them with your sword.
14 With your hand, LORD, make an end of them;
    thrust them out of this world from among the
        living.
    May those whom you cherish have food in plenty,
    may their children be satisfied
    and their little ones inherit their wealth.
15 My plea is just: may I see your face
    and be blest with a vision of you when I awake.

Psalm 18

*To the leader. A Psalm of David the servant of the LORD,
who addressed the words of this song to the LORD on the
day when the LORD delivered him from the hand of all his
enemies, and from the hand of Saul. He said:*

1 I love you, O LORD, my strength.
2 The LORD is my rock, my fortress, and my
        deliverer,
    my God, my rock in whom I take refuge,
    my shield, and the horn of my salvation, my
        stronghold.
3 I call upon the LORD, who is worthy to be
        praised,
    so I shall be saved from my enemies.

4 The cords of death encompassed me;
    the torrents of perdition assailed me;
5 the cords of Sheol entangled me;
    the snares of death confronted me.

6 In my distress I called upon the LORD;
    to my God I cried for help.
    From his temple he heard my voice,
    and my cry to him reached his ears.

7 Then the earth reeled and rocked;
    the foundations also of the mountains trembled
    and quaked, because he was angry.
8 Smoke went up from his nostrils,
    and devouring fire from his mouth;
    glowing coals flamed forth from him.
9 He bowed the heavens, and came down;
    thick darkness was under his feet.
10 He rode on a cherub, and flew;
    he came swiftly upon the wings of the wind.

Psalm 18

*For the leader: for the LORD's servant: for David (who
recited the words of this song to the LORD on the day when
the LORD rescued him from the power of all his enemies
and from the hand of Saul. He said:)*

1 I LOVE you, LORD, my strength.
2 The LORD is my lofty crag, my fortress, my
        champion,
    my God, my rock in whom I find shelter,
    my shield and sure defender, my strong tower.
3 I shall call to the LORD to whom all praise is due;
    then I shall be made safe from my enemies.

4 The bonds of death encompassed me
    and destructive torrents overtook me,
5 the bonds of Sheol tightened about me,
    the snares of death were set to catch me.
6 When in anguish of heart I cried to the LORD
    and called for help to my God,
    he heard me from his temple,
    and my cry reached his ears.

7 The earth shook and quaked,
    the foundations of the mountains trembled,
    shaking because of his anger.
8 Smoke went up from his nostrils,
    devouring fire from his mouth,
    glowing coals and searing heat.
9 He parted the heavens and came down;
    thick darkness lay under his feet.
10 He flew on the back of a cherub,
    he swooped on the wings of the wind.

17:11 **they press me hard:** *prob. rdg; Heb.* our footsteps.
17:14 **make an end of them:** *prob. rdg; Heb.* unintelligible.
18:2–50 *Cp. 2 Sam. 22:2–51.*   18:5 **Sheol:** *or* the underworld.

[n] One Ms Compare Syr: MT *Our steps*

II
6 I call upon you; answer me, O God.
  Turn your ear to me; hear my prayer.
7 Show your wonderful love,
  you who deliver with your right arm
  those who seek refuge from their foes.
8 Keep me as the apple of your eye;
  hide me in the shadow of your wings
9   from the violence of the wicked.

III
  My ravenous enemies press upon me;
10   they close their hearts,
  they fill their mouths with proud roaring.
11 Their steps even now encircle me;
  they watch closely, keeping low to the ground,
12 Like lions eager for prey,
  like young lions lurking in ambush.
13 Rise, O LORD, confront and cast them down;
  rescue me so from the wicked.
14 Slay them with your sword;
  with your hand, LORD, slay them;
  snatch them from the world in their prime.
  Their bellies are being filled with your friends;
  their children are satisfied too,
  for they share what is left with their young.
15 I am just — let me see your face;
  when I awake, let me be filled with your
    presence.

Psalm 18

1 For the leader. Of David, the servant of the LORD, who
sang to the LORD the words of this song after the LORD had
rescued him from the clutches of all his enemies and from the
hand of Saul. 2 He said:

I
  I love you, LORD, my strength,
3   LORD, my rock, my fortress, my deliverer,
  My God, my rock of refuge,
  my shield, my saving horn, my stronghold!
4 Praised be the LORD, I exclaim!
  I have been delivered from my enemies.

II
5 The breakers of death surged round about me;
  the menacing floods terrified me.
6 The cords of Sheol tightened;
  the snares of death lay in wait for me.
7 In my distress I called out: LORD!
  I cried out to my God.
  From his temple he heard my voice;
  my cry to him reached his ears.
8 The earth rocked and shook;
  the foundations of the mountains trembled;
  they shook as his wrath flared up.
9 Smoke rose in his nostrils,
  a devouring fire poured from his mouth;
  it kindled coals into flame.
10 He parted the heavens and came down,
  a dark cloud under his feet.
11 Mounted on a cherub he flew,
  borne along on the wings of the wind.

6 I call upon you, God, for you answer me;
  turn your ear to me, hear what I say.
7 Show the evidence of your faithful love,
  saviour of those who hope in your strength against
    attack.
8 Guard me as the pupil of an eye,
  shelter me in the shadow of your wings
9 from the presence of the wicked who would
    maltreat me;
  deadly enemies are closing in on me.
10 Engrossed in themselves
  they are mouthing arrogant words.
11 They are advancing against me, now they are
    closing in,
  watching for the chance to hurl me to the ground,
12 like a lion preparing to pounce,
  like a young lion crouching in ambush.

13 Arise, Yahweh, confront him and bring him down,
  with your sword save my life from the wicked,
14 Yahweh, from mortals, by your hand,
  from mortals whose part in life is in this world.

  You fill their bellies from your store,
  their children will have all they desire,
  and leave their surplus to their children.
15 But I in my uprightness will see your face,
  and when I awake I shall be filled with the vision
    of you.

Psalm 18 (V 17)f

For the choirmaster   Of David, the servant of Yahweh,
who addressed the words of this song to Yahweh when
Yahweh had delivered him from all his enemies and from
the clutches of Saul. He said:

1 I love you, Yahweh, my strength
  (my Saviour, you have saved me from violence).

2 Yahweh is my rock and my fortress,
  my deliverer is my God.
  I take refuge in him, my rock,
  my shield, my saving strength,
  my stronghold, my place of refuge.

3 I call to Yahweh who is worthy of praise,
  and I am saved from my foes.

4 With Death's breakers closing in on me,
  Belial's torrents ready to swallow me,
5 Sheol's snares every side of me,
  Death's traps lying ahead of me,

6 I called to Yahweh in my anguish,
  I cried for help to my God;
  from his Temple he heard my voice,
  my cry came to his ears.

7 Then the earth quaked and rocked,
  the mountains' foundations shuddered,
  they quaked at his blazing anger.
8 Smoke rose from his nostrils,
  from his mouth devouring fire
  (coals were kindled at it).

9 He parted the heavens and came down,
  a storm-cloud underneath his feet;
10 riding one of the winged creatures, he flew,
  soaring on the wings of the wind.

f 18 // 2 S 22.

NEW REVISED STANDARD VERSION	REVISED ENGLISH BIBLE

11 He made darkness his covering around him,
   his canopy thick clouds dark with water.
12 Out of the brightness before him
   there broke through his clouds
   hailstones and coals of fire.
13 The LORD also thundered in the heavens,
   and the Most High uttered his voice.o
14 And he sent out his arrows, and scattered them;
   he flashed forth lightnings, and routed them.
15 Then the channels of the sea were seen,
   and the foundations of the world were laid bare
   at your rebuke, O LORD,
   at the blast of the breath of your nostrils.

16 He reached down from on high, he took me;
   he drew me out of mighty waters.
17 He delivered me from my strong enemy,
   and from those who hated me;
   for they were too mighty for me.
18 They confronted me in the day of my calamity;
   but the LORD was my support.
19 He brought me out into a broad place;
   he delivered me, because he delighted in me.

20 The LORD rewarded me according to my
   righteousness;
   according to the cleanness of my hands he
   recompensed me.
21 For I have kept the ways of the LORD,
   and have not wickedly departed from my God.
22 For all his ordinances were before me,
   and his statutes I did not put away from me.
23 I was blameless before him,
   and I kept myself from guilt.
24 Therefore the LORD has recompensed me
   according to my righteousness,
   according to the cleanness of my hands in his
   sight.

25 With the loyal you show yourself loyal;
   with the blameless you show yourself
   blameless;
26 with the pure you show yourself pure;
   and with the crooked you show yourself
   perverse.
27 For you deliver a humble people,
   but the haughty eyes you bring down.
28 It is you who light my lamp;
   the LORD, my God, lights up my darkness.
29 By you I can crush a troop,
   and by my God I can leap over a wall.
30 This God—his way is perfect;
   the promise of the LORD proves true;
   he is a shield for all who take refuge in him.

31 For who is God except the LORD?
   And who is a rock besides our God?—
32 the God who girded me with strength,
   and made my way safe.
33 He made my feet like the feet of a deer,
   and set me secure on the heights.
34 He trains my hands for war,
   so that my arms can bend a bow of bronze.
35 You have given me the shield of your salvation,
   and your right hand has supported me;
   your helpp has made me great.
36 You gave me a wide place for my steps under
   me,
   and my feet did not slip.

11 He made darkness around him his covering,
   dense vapour his canopy.
12 Thick clouds came from the radiance before him,
   hail and glowing coals.
13 The LORD thundered from the heavens;
   the Most High raised his voice
   amid hail and glowing coals.
14 He loosed arrows, he sped them far and wide,
   he hurled forth lightning shafts and sent them
   echoing.
15 The channels of the waters were exposed,
   earth's foundations laid bare
   at the LORD's rebuke,
   at the blast of breath from his nostrils.

16 He reached down from on high and took me,
   he drew me out of mighty waters,
17 he delivered me from my enemies, strong as they
   were,
   from my foes when they grew too powerful for
   me.
18 They confronted me in my hour of peril,
   but the LORD was my buttress.
19 He brought me into untrammelled liberty;
   he rescued me because he delighted in me.

20 The LORD repaid me as my righteousness deserved;
   because my conduct was spotless he rewarded me,
21 for I have kept to the ways of the LORD
   and have not turned from my God to wickedness.
22 All his laws I keep before me,
   and have never failed to follow his decrees.
23 In his sight I was blameless
   and kept myself from wrongdoing;
24 because my conduct was spotless in his eyes,
   the LORD rewarded me as my righteousness
   deserved.

25 To the loyal you show yourself loyal
   and blameless to the blameless.
26 To the pure you show yourself pure,
   but skilful in your dealings with the perverse.
27 You bring humble folk to safety,
   but humiliate those who look so high and mighty.
28 LORD, you make my lamp burn bright;
   my God will lighten my darkness.
29 With your help I storm a rampart,
   and by my God's aid I leap over a wall.

30 The way of God is blameless;
   the LORD's word has stood the test;
   he is a shield to all who take refuge in him.
31 What god is there but the LORD?
   What rock but our God?
32 It is God who girds me with strength
   and makes my way free from blame,
33 who makes me swift as a hind
   and sets me secure on the heights,
34 who trains my hands for battle
   so that my arms can aim a bronze-tipped bow.

35 You have given me the shield of your salvation;
   your right hand sustains me;
   you stoop down to make me great.
36 You made room for my steps;
   my feet have not slipped.

o Gk See 2 Sam 22.14: Heb adds *hailstones and coals of fire*
p Or *gentleness*

18:11 **dense:** *prob. rdg, cp. 2 Sam. 22:12; Heb.* dark.
18:29 **rampart:** *prob. rdg; Heb.* troop.   18:33 **the heights:** *so
Gk; Heb.* my heights.

NEW AMERICAN BIBLE

12 He made darkness the cover about him;
   his canopy, heavy thunderheads.
13 Before him scudded his clouds,
   hail and lightning too.
14 The LORD thundered from heaven;
   the Most High made his voice resound.
15 He let fly his arrows and scattered them;
   shot his lightning bolts and dispersed them.
16 Then the bed of the sea appeared;
   the world's foundations lay bare,
   At the roar of the LORD,
   at the storming breath of his nostrils.
17 He reached down from on high and seized me;
   drew me out of the deep waters.
18 He rescued me from my mighty enemy,
   from foes too powerful for me.
19 They attacked me on a day of distress,
   but the LORD came to my support.
20 He set me free in the open;
   he rescued me because he loves me.
   III
21 The LORD acknowledged my righteousness,
   rewarded my clean hands.
22 For I kept the ways of the LORD;
   I was not disloyal to my God.
23 His laws were all before me,
   his decrees I did not cast aside.
24 I was honest toward him;
   I was on guard against sin.
25 So the LORD rewarded my righteousness,
   the cleanness of my hands in his sight.
26 Toward the faithful you are faithful;
   to the honest you are honest;
27 Toward the sincere, sincere;
   but to the perverse you are devious.
28 Humble people you save;
   haughty eyes you bring low.
29 You, LORD, give light to my lamp;
   my God brightens the darkness about me.
30 With you I can rush an armed band,
   with my God to help I can leap a wall.
31 God's way is unerring;
   the LORD's promise is tried and true;
   he is a shield for all who trust in him.
   IV
32 Truly, who is God except the LORD?
   Who but our God is the rock?
33 This God who girded me with might,
   kept my way unerring,
34 Who made my feet swift as a deer's,
   set me safe on the heights,
35 Who trained my hands for war,
   my arms to bend even a bow of bronze.
   V
36 You have given me your protecting shield;
   your right hand has upheld me;
   you stooped to make me great.
37 You gave me room to stride;
   my feet never stumbled.

NEW JERUSALEM BIBLE

11 His covering he made the darkness,
   his pavilion dark waters and dense cloud.
12 A brightness lit up before him,
   hail and blazing fire.
13 Yahweh thundered from the heavens,
   the Most High made his voice heard.
14 He shot his arrows and scattered them,
   he hurled his lightning and routed them.
15 The very springs of ocean were exposed,
   the world's foundations were laid bare,
   at your roaring, Yahweh,
   at the blast of breath from your nostrils!
16 He reached down from on high, snatched me up,
   pulled me from the watery depths,
17 rescued me from my mighty foe,
   from my enemies who were stronger than I.
18 They assailed me on my day of disaster
   but Yahweh was there to support me;
19 he freed me, set me at large,
   he rescued me because he loves me.
20 Yahweh rewards me for my uprightness,
   as my hands are pure, so he repays me,
21 since I have kept the ways of Yahweh,
   and not fallen away from my God.
22 His judgements are all before me,
   his statutes I have not put away from me.
23 I am blameless before him,
   I keep myself clear of evil.
24 So Yahweh repaid me for acting uprightly
   because he could see I was pure.
25 You are faithful to the faithful,
   blameless with the blameless,
26 sincere to the sincere,
   but cunning to the crafty,
27 you save a people that is humble
   and humiliate those with haughty looks.
28 Yahweh, you yourself are my lamp,
   my God lights up my darkness;
29 with you I storm the rampart,
   with my God I can scale any wall.
30 This God, his way is blameless;
   the word of Yahweh is refined in the furnace,
   for he alone is the shield
   of all who take refuge in him.
31 For who is God but Yahweh,
   who is a rock but our God?
32 This God who girds me with strength,
   who makes my way free from blame,
33 who makes me as swift as a deer
   and sets me firmly on the heights,
34 who trains my hands for battle,
   my arms to bend a bow of bronze.
35 You give me your invincible shield
   (your right hand upholds me)
   you never cease to listen to me,
36 you give me the strides of a giant,
   give me ankles that never weaken.

NEW REVISED STANDARD VERSION	REVISED ENGLISH BIBLE

37 I pursued my enemies and overtook them;
    and did not turn back until they were
        consumed.
38 I struck them down, so that they were not able to
    rise;
    they fell under my feet.
39 For you girded me with strength for the battle;
    you made my assailants sink under me.
40 You made my enemies turn their backs to me,
    and those who hated me I destroyed.
41 They cried for help, but there was no one to save
    them;
    they cried to the LORD, but he did not answer
    them.
42 I beat them fine, like dust before the wind;
    I cast them out like the mire of the streets.

43 You delivered me from strife with the peoples;*q*
    you made me head of the nations;
    people whom I had not known served me.
44 As soon as they heard of me they obeyed me;
    foreigners came cringing to me.
45 Foreigners lost heart,
    and came trembling out of their strongholds.

46 The LORD lives! Blessed be my rock,
    and exalted be the God of my salvation,
47 the God who gave me vengeance
    and subdued peoples under me;
48 who delivered me from my enemies;
    indeed, you exalted me above my adversaries;
    you delivered me from the violent.

49 For this I will extol you, O LORD, among the
    nations,
    and sing praises to your name.
50 Great triumphs he gives to his king,
    and shows steadfast love to his anointed,
    to David and his descendants forever.

Psalm 19

To the leader. A Psalm of David.

1 The heavens are telling the glory of God;
    and the firmament*r* proclaims his handiwork.
2 Day to day pours forth speech,
    and night to night declares knowledge.
3 There is no speech, nor are there words;
    their voice is not heard;
4 yet their voice*s* goes out through all the earth,
    and their words to the end of the world.

In the heavens*t* he has set a tent for the sun,
5 which comes out like a bridegroom from his
    wedding canopy,
    and like a strong man runs its course with joy.
6 Its rising is from the end of the heavens,
    and its circuit to the end of them;
    and nothing is hid from its heat.

7 The law of the LORD is perfect,
    reviving the soul;
    the decrees of the LORD are sure,
    making wise the simple;
8 the precepts of the LORD are right,
    rejoicing the heart;
    the commandment of the LORD is clear,
    enlightening the eyes;

37 I pursue and overtake my enemies;
    until I have made an end of them I do not turn
        back.
38 I strike them down and they can rise no more;
    they fall prostrate at my feet.
39 You gird me with strength for the battle
    and subdue my assailants beneath me.
40 You set my foot on my enemies' necks,
    and I wipe out those who hate me.
41 They cry, but there is no one to save them;
    they cry to the LORD, but he does not answer.
42 I shall beat them as fine as dust before the wind,
    like mud in the streets I shall trample them.
43 You set me free from the people who challenge
    me,
    and make me master of nations.
    A people I never knew will be my subjects.
44 Foreigners will come fawning to me;
    as soon as they hear tell of me they will submit.
45 Foreigners will be disheartened
    and come trembling from their strongholds.

46 The LORD lives! Blessed is my rock!
    High above all is God, my safe refuge.

47 You grant me vengeance, God,
    laying nations prostrate at my feet;
48 you free me from my enemies,
    setting me over my assailants;
    you are my deliverer from violent men.
49 Therefore, LORD, I shall praise you among the
    nations
    and sing psalms to your name,
50 to one who gives his king great victories
    and keeps faith with his anointed,
    with David and his descendants for ever.

Psalm 19

For the leader: a psalm: for David

1 THE heavens tell out the glory of God,
    heaven's vault makes known his handiwork.
2 One day speaks to another,
    night to night imparts knowledge,
3 and this without speech or language
    or sound of any voice.
4 Their sign shines forth on all the earth,
    their message to the ends of the world.
    In the heavens an abode is fixed for the sun,
5 which comes out like a bridegroom from the bridal
    chamber,
    rejoicing like a strong man to run his course.
6 Its rising is at one end of the heavens,
    its circuit reaches from one end to the other,
    and nothing is hidden from its heat.

7 The law of the LORD is perfect and revives the
    soul.
    The LORD's instruction never fails;
    it makes the simple wise.
8 The precepts of the LORD are right
    and give joy to the heart.
    The commandment of the LORD is pure
    and gives light to the eyes.

---

q Gk Tg: Heb *people*   *r* Or *dome*   *s* Gk Jerome Compare Syr: Heb
line   *t* Heb *In them*

18:42 **I shall trample them:** *prob. rdg, cp. 2 Sam. 22:43; Heb.* I
shall empty them out.

38 I pursued my enemies and overtook them;
  I did not turn back till I destroyed them.
39 I struck them down; they could not rise;
  they fell dead at my feet.
40 You girded me with strength for war,
  subdued adversaries at my feet.
41 My foes you put to flight before me;
  those who hated me I destroyed.
42 They cried for help, but no one saved them;
  cried to the LORD but got no answer.
43 I ground them fine as dust in the wind;
  like mud in the streets I trampled them down.
44 You rescued me from the strife of peoples;
  you made me head over nations;
  A people I had not known became my slaves;
45   as soon as they heard of me they obeyed.
  Foreigners cringed before me;
46   their courage failed;
  they came trembling from their fortresses.
VI
47 The LORD lives! Blessed be my rock!
  Exalted be God, my savior!
48 O God who granted me vindication,
  made peoples subject to me,
49   and preserved me from my enemies,
  Truly you have exalted me above my adversaries,
  from the violent you have rescued me.
50 Thus I will proclaim you, LORD, among the
    nations;
  I will sing the praises of your name.
51 You have given great victories to your king,
  and shown kindness to your anointed,
  to David and his posterity forever.

Psalm 19

1 *For the leader. A psalm of David.*

I
2 The heavens declare the glory of God;
  the sky proclaims its builder's craft.
3 One day to the next conveys that message;
  one night to the next imparts that knowledge.
4 There is no word or sound;
  no voice is heard;
5 Yet their report goes forth through all the earth,
  their message, to the ends of the world.
  God has pitched there a tent for the sun;
6   it comes forth like a bridegroom from his
    chamber,
  and like an athlete joyfully runs its course.
7 From one end of the heavens it comes forth;
  its course runs through to the other;
  nothing escapes its heat.
II
8 The law of the LORD is perfect,
  refreshing the soul.
  The decree of the LORD is trustworthy,
  giving wisdom to the simple.
9 The precepts of the LORD are right,
  rejoicing the heart.
  The command of the LORD is clear,
  enlightening the eye.

37 I pursue my enemies and overtake them,
  not turning back till they are annihilated;
38 I strike them down and they cannot rise,
  they fall, they are under my feet.
39 You have girded me with strength for the fight,
  bent down my assailants beneath me,
40 made my enemies retreat before me;
  and those who hate me I destroy.
41 They cry out, there is no one to save;
  to Yahweh, but no answer comes.
42 I crumble them like dust before the wind,
  trample them like the mud of the streets.
43 You free me from the quarrels of my people,
  you place me at the head of the nations,
  a people I did not know are now my servants;
44 foreigners come wooing my favour,
  no sooner do they hear than they obey me;
45 foreigners grow faint of heart,
  they come trembling out of their fastnesses.
46 Life to Yahweh! Blessed be my rock!
  Exalted be the God of my salvation,
47 the God who gives me vengeance,
  and subjects whole peoples to me,
48 who rescues me from my raging enemies.
  You lift me high above those who attack me,
  you deliver me from the man of violence.
49 For this I will praise you, Yahweh, among the
    nations,
  and sing praise to your name.
50 He saves his king time after time,
  displays his faithful love for his anointed,
  for David and his heirs for ever.

Psalm 19 (V 18)

For the choirmaster   Psalm   Of David

1 The heavens declare the glory of God,
  the vault of heaven proclaims his handiwork,
2 day discourses of it to day,
  night to night hands on the knowledge.
3 No utterance at all, no speech,
  not a sound to be heard,
4 but from the entire earth the design stands out,
  this message reaches the whole world.

  High above, he pitched a tent for the sun,
5 who comes forth from his pavilion like a
    bridegroom,
  delights like a champion in the course to be run.
6 Rising on the one horizon
  he runs his circuit to the other,
  and nothing can escape his heat.

7   The Law of Yahweh is perfect,
    refreshment to the soul;
  the decree of Yahweh is trustworthy,
    wisdom for the simple.
8   The precepts of Yahweh are honest,
    joy for the heart;
  the commandment of Yahweh is pure,
    light for the eyes.

9 the fear of the LORD is pure,
  enduring forever;
  the ordinances of the LORD are true
  and righteous altogether.
10 More to be desired are they than gold,
  even much fine gold;
  sweeter also than honey,
  and drippings of the honeycomb.
11 Moreover by them is your servant warned;
  in keeping them there is great reward.
12 But who can detect their errors?
  Clear me from hidden faults.
13 Keep back your servant also from the insolent;[u]
  do not let them have dominion over me.
  Then I shall be blameless,
  and innocent of great transgression.
14 Let the words of my mouth and the meditation of
    my heart
  be acceptable to you,
  O LORD, my rock and my redeemer.

Psalm 20

To the leader. A Psalm of David.

1 The LORD answer you in the day of trouble!
  The name of the God of Jacob protect you!
2 May he send you help from the sanctuary,
  and give you support from Zion.
3 May he remember all your offerings,
  and regard with favor your burnt sacrifices.
                                              Selah

4 May he grant you your heart's desire,
  and fulfill all your plans.
5 May we shout for joy over your victory,
  and in the name of our God set up our
    banners.
  May the LORD fulfill all your petitions.

6 Now I know that the LORD will help his anointed;
  he will answer him from his holy heaven
  with mighty victories by his right hand.
7 Some take pride in chariots, and some in horses,
  but our pride is in the name of the LORD our
    God.
8 They will collapse and fall,
  but we shall rise and stand upright.

9 Give victory to the king, O LORD;
  answer us when we call.[v]

Psalm 21

To the leader. A Psalm of David.

1 In your strength the king rejoices, O LORD,
  and in your help how greatly he exults!
2 You have given him his heart's desire,
  and have not withheld the request of his lips.
                                              Selah
3 For you meet him with rich blessings;
  you set a crown of fine gold on his head.
4 He asked you for life; you gave it to him —
  length of days forever and ever.
5 His glory is great through your help;
  splendor and majesty you bestow on him.

9 The fear of the LORD is unsullied; it abides for
    ever.
  The LORD's judgements are true and righteous
    every one,
10 more to be desired than gold, pure gold in plenty,
  sweeter than honey dripping from the comb.
11 It is through them that your servant is warned;
  in obeying them is great reward.

12 Who is aware of his unwitting sins?
  Cleanse me of any secret fault.
13 Hold back your servant also from wilful sins,
  lest they get the better of me.
  Then I shall be blameless,
  innocent of grave offence.

14 May the words of my mouth and the thoughts of
    my mind
  be acceptable to you,
  LORD, my rock and my redeemer!

Psalm 20

For the leader: a psalm: for David

1 MAY the LORD answer you in time of trouble.
  May the name of Jacob's God be your tower of
    strength.
2 May he send you help from the sanctuary,
  and give you support from Zion.
3 May he remember all your offerings
  and look with favour on your sacrifices.   [*Selah*
4 May he give you your heart's desire,
  and grant success to all your plans.
5 Let us sing aloud in praise of your victory,
  let us do homage to the name of our God!
  May the LORD grant your every request!

6 Now I know that the LORD has given victory to his
    anointed one:
  he will answer him from his holy heaven
  with the victorious might of his right hand.
7 Some boast of chariots and some of horses,
  but our boast is the name of the LORD our God.
8 They totter and fall,
  but we rise up and stand firm.
9 LORD, save the king,
  and answer us when we call.

Psalm 21

For the leader: a psalm: for David

1 LORD, the king rejoices in your might:
  well may he exult in your victory.
2 You have granted him his heart's desire
  and have not refused what he requested.   [*Selah*
3 You welcome him with blessings and prosperity
  and place a crown of finest gold on his head.
4 He asked you for life, and you gave it to him,
  length of days for ever and ever.
5 Your victory has brought him great glory;
  you invest him with majesty and honour,

---

[u] Or *from proud thoughts*   [v] Gk: Heb *give victory, O LORD; let the*
King answer us when we call

20:9 **LORD . . . answer us:** *so Gk; Heb.* Save, LORD: let the king
answer us.

10 The fear of the LORD is pure,
  enduring forever.
The statutes of the LORD are true,
  all of them just;
11 More desirable than gold,
  than a hoard of purest gold,
Sweeter also than honey
  or drippings from the comb.
12 By them your servant is instructed;
  obeying them brings much reward.

III
13 Who can detect heedless failings?
  Cleanse me from my unknown faults.
14 But from willful sins keep your servant;
  let them never control me.
Then shall I be blameless,
  innocent of grave sin.
15 Let the words of my mouth meet with your favor,
  keep the thoughts of my heart before you,
  LORD, my rock and my redeemer.

Psalm 20

1 *For the leader. A psalm of David.*

I
2 The LORD answer you in time of distress;
  the name of the God of Jacob defend you!
3 May God send you help from the temple,
  from Zion be your support.
4 May God remember your every offering,
  graciously accept your holocaust,   *Selah*
5 Grant what is in your heart,
  fulfill your every plan.
6 May we shout for joy at your victory,
  raise the banners in the name of our God.
The LORD grant your every prayer!

II
7 Now I know victory is given
  to the anointed of the LORD.
God will answer him from the holy heavens
  with a strong arm that brings victory.
8 Some rely on chariots, others on horses,
  but we on the name of the LORD our God.
9 They collapse and fall,
  but we stand strong and firm.
10 LORD, grant victory to the king;
  answer when we call upon you.

Psalm 21

1 *For the leader. A psalm of David.*

I
2 LORD, the king finds joy in your power;
  in your victory how greatly he rejoices!
3 You have granted him his heart's desire;
  you did not refuse the prayer of his lips.   *Selah*
4 For you welcomed him with goodly blessings;
  you placed on his head a crown of pure gold.
5 He asked life of you;
  you gave it to him,
  length of days forever.
6 Great is his glory in your victory;
  majesty and splendor you confer upon him.

9   The fear of Yahweh is pure,
  lasting for ever;
the judgements of Yahweh are true,
  upright, every one,
10   more desirable than gold,
  even than the finest gold;
his words are sweeter than honey,
  that drips from the comb.
11   Thus your servant is formed by them;
  observing them brings great reward.
12   But who can detect his own failings?
  Wash away my hidden faults.
13   And from pride preserve your servant,
  never let it be my master.
So shall I be above reproach,
  free from grave sin.
14   May the words of my mouth always find favour,
  and the whispering of my heart,
in your presence, Yahweh,
  my rock, my redeemer.

Psalm 20 (V 19)

   For the choirmaster   Psalm   Of David

1 May Yahweh answer you in time of trouble,
  may the name of the God of Jacob protect you!
2 May he send you help from the sanctuary,
  give you support from Zion!
3 May he remember all your sacrifices
  and delight in your burnt offerings!   *Pause*
4 May he grant you your heart's desire
  and crown all your plans with success!
5 So that with joy we can hail your victory
  and draw up our ranks in the name of our God.

May Yahweh grant all your petitions.

6 Now I know that Yahweh
  gives victory to his anointed.
He will respond from his holy heavens
  with great deeds of victory from his right hand.

7 Some call on chariots, some on horses,
  but we on the name of Yahweh our God.
8 They will crumple and fall,
  while we stand upright and firm.

9 Yahweh, save the king,
  answer us when we call.

Psalm 21 (V 20)

   For the choirmaster   Psalm   Of David

1 Yahweh, the king rejoices in your power;
  How your saving help fills him with joy!
2 You have granted him his heart's desire,
  not denied him the prayer of his lips.   *Pause*

3 For you come to meet him with blessings of
    prosperity,
  put a crown of pure gold on his head.
4 He has asked for life, you have given it him,
  length of days for ever and ever.

5 Great his glory through your saving help;
  you invest him with splendour and majesty.

NEW REVISED STANDARD VERSION

6 You bestow on him blessings forever;
  you make him glad with the joy of your
    presence.
7 For the king trusts in the LORD,
  and through the steadfast love of the Most
    High he shall not be moved.

8 Your hand will find out all your enemies;
  your right hand will find out those who hate
    you.
9 You will make them like a fiery furnace
  when you appear.
  The LORD will swallow them up in his wrath,
    and fire will consume them.
10 You will destroy their offspring from the earth,
  and their children from among humankind.
11 If they plan evil against you,
  if they devise mischief, they will not succeed.
12 For you will put them to flight;
  you will aim at their faces with your bows.

13 Be exalted, O LORD, in your strength!
  We will sing and praise your power.

Psalm 22

To the leader: according to The Deer of the Dawn. A
  Psalm of David.

1 My God, my God, why have you forsaken me?
  Why are you so far from helping me, from the
    words of my groaning?
2 O my God, I cry by day, but you do not answer;
  and by night, but find no rest.

3 Yet you are holy,
  enthroned on the praises of Israel.
4 In you our ancestors trusted;
  they trusted, and you delivered them.
5 To you they cried, and were saved;
  in you they trusted, and were not put to shame.

6 But I am a worm, and not human;
  scorned by others, and despised by the people.
7 All who see me mock at me;
  they make mouths at me, they shake their
    heads;
8 "Commit your cause to the LORD; let him
    deliver—
  let him rescue the one in whom he delights!"

9 Yet it was you who took me from the womb;
  you kept me safe on my mother's breast.
10 On you I was cast from my birth,
  and since my mother bore me you have been
    my God.
11 Do not be far from me,
  for trouble is near
  and there is no one to help.

12 Many bulls encircle me,
  strong bulls of Bashan surround me;
13 they open wide their mouths at me,
  like a ravening and roaring lion.

14 I am poured out like water,
  and all my bones are out of joint;
  my heart is like wax;
  it is melted within my breast;
15 my mouth[w] is dried up like a potsherd,
  and my tongue sticks to my jaws;
  you lay me in the dust of death.

[w] Cn: Heb *strength*

REVISED ENGLISH BIBLE

6 for you bestow everlasting blessings on him,
  and make him glad with the joy of your presence,
7 for the king puts his trust in the LORD;
  the loving care of the Most High keeps him
    unshaken.

8 Your hand will reach all your enemies,
  your right hand all who hate you;
9 at your coming you will set them in a fiery
    furnace;
  in his anger the LORD will engulf them,
    and fire will consume them.
10 It will destroy their offspring from the earth
  and rid mankind of their posterity.
11 For they have aimed wicked blows at you;
  in spite of their plots they could not prevail;
12 but you will aim at their faces with your bows
  and force them to turn in flight.

13 Be exalted, LORD, in your might;
  we shall sing a psalm of praise to your power.

Psalm 22

For the leader: set to 'Hind of the Dawn': a psalm:
  for David

1 MY God, my God, why have you forsaken me?
  Why are you so far from saving me,
  so far from heeding my groans?
2 My God, by day I cry to you, but there is no
    answer;
  in the night I cry with no respite.
3 You, the praise of Israel,
  are enthroned in the sanctuary.
4 In you our fathers put their trust;
  they trusted, and you rescued them.
5 To you they cried and were delivered;
  in you they trusted and were not discomfited.

6 But I am a worm, not a man,
  abused by everyone, scorned by the people.
7 All who see me jeer at me,
  grimace at me, and wag their heads:
8 'He threw himself on the LORD for rescue;
  let the LORD deliver him, for he holds him dear!'

9 But you are he who brought me from the womb,
  who laid me at my mother's breast.
10 To your care I was entrusted at birth;
  from my mother's womb you have been my God.
11 Do not remain far from me,
  for trouble is near and I have no helper.
12 A herd of bulls surrounds me,
  great bulls of Bashan beset me.
13 Lions ravening and roaring
  open their mouths wide against me.
14 My strength drains away like water
  and all my bones are racked.
  My heart has turned to wax
  and melts within me.
15 My mouth is dry as a potsherd,
  and my tongue sticks to my gums;
  I am laid low in the dust of death.

21:10 **It:** *or* You.   22:15 **mouth:** *prob. rdg; Heb.* strength. **I am
laid:** *prob. rdg; Heb.* you will lay me.

7 You make him the pattern of blessings forever,
   you gladden him with the joy of your presence.
8 For the king trusts in the LORD,
   stands firm through the love of the Most High.
  II
9 Your hand will reach all your enemies;
   your right hand will reach your foes!
10 At the time of your coming
   you will drive them into a furnace.
Then the LORD's anger will consume them,
   devour them with fire.
11 Even their descendants you will wipe out from the
    earth,
   their offspring from the human race.
12 Though they intend evil against you,
   devising plots, they will not succeed,
13 For you will put them to flight;
   you will aim at them with your bow.
  III
14 Arise, LORD, in your power!
   We will sing and chant the praise of your might.

Psalm 22

1 *For the leader; according to "The deer of the dawn." A
psalm of David.*

  I
2 My God, my God, why have you abandoned me?
   Why so far from my call for help,
   from my cries of anguish?
3 My God, I call by day, but you do not answer;
   by night, but I have no relief.
4 Yet you are enthroned as the Holy One;
   you are the glory of Israel.
5 In you our ancestors trusted;
   they trusted and you rescued them.
6 To you they cried out and they escaped;
   in you they trusted and were not disappointed.
7 But I am a worm, hardly human,
   scorned by everyone, despised by the people.
8 All who see me mock me;
   they curl their lips and jeer;
   they shake their heads at me:
9 "You relied on the LORD—let him deliver you;
   if he loves you, let him rescue you."
10 Yet you drew me forth from the womb,
   made me safe at my mother's breast.
11 Upon you I was thrust from the womb;
   since birth you are my God.
12 Do not stay far from me,
   for trouble is near,
   and there is no one to help.
  II
13 Many bulls surround me;
   fierce bulls of Bashan encircle me.
14 They open their mouths against me,
   lions that rend and roar.
15 Like water my life drains away;
   all my bones grow soft.
My heart has become like wax,
   it melts away within me.
16 As dry as a potsherd is my throat;
   my tongue sticks to my palate;
   you lay me in the dust of death.

6 You confer on him everlasting blessings,
   you gladden him with the joy of your presence.
7 For the king puts his trust in Yahweh;
   the faithful love of the Most High will keep him
    from falling.

8 Your hand will reach all your enemies,
   your right hand all who hate you.
9 You will hurl them into a blazing furnace
   on the day when you appear;
   Yahweh will engulf them in his anger,
   and fire will devour them.
10 You will purge the earth of their descendants,
   the human race of their posterity.

11 They have devised evil against you
   but, plot as they may, they will not succeed,
12 since you will make them turn tail,
   by shooting your arrows in their faces.

13 Rise, Yahweh, in your power!
   We will sing and make music in honour of your
    strength.

Psalm 22 (V 21)

For the choirmaster   To 'the Doe of the Dawn'
      Psalm   Of David

1 My God, my God, why have you forsaken me?
   The words of my groaning do nothing to save me.
2 My God, I call by day but you do not answer,
   at night, but I find no respite.

3 Yet you, the Holy One,
   who make your home in the praises of Israel,
4 in you our ancestors put their trust,
   they trusted and you set them free.
5 To you they called for help and were delivered;
   in you they trusted and were not put to shame.

6 But I am a worm, less than human,
   scorn of mankind, contempt of the people;
7 all who see me jeer at me,
   they sneer and wag their heads,
8 'He trusted himself to Yahweh, let Yahweh set him
    free!
Let him deliver him, as he took such delight in
    him.'

9 It was you who drew me from the womb
   and soothed me on my mother's breast.
10 On you was I cast from my birth,
   from the womb I have belonged to you.
11 Do not hold aloof, for trouble is upon me,
   and no one to help me!

12 Many bulls are encircling me,
   wild bulls of Bashan closing in on me.
13 Lions ravening and roaring
   open their jaws at me.

14 My strength is trickling away,
   my bones are all disjointed,
   my heart has turned to wax,
   melting inside me.
15 My mouth is dry as earthenware,
   my tongue sticks to my jaw.
   You lay me down in the dust of death.

NEW REVISED STANDARD VERSION	REVISED ENGLISH BIBLE

16 For dogs are all around me;
   a company of evildoers encircles me.
   My hands and feet have shriveled;*x*
17 I can count all my bones.
   They stare and gloat over me;
18 they divide my clothes among themselves,
   and for my clothing they cast lots.

19 But you, O LORD, do not be far away!
   O my help, come quickly to my aid!
20 Deliver my soul from the sword,
   my life*y* from the power of the dog!
21 Save me from the mouth of the lion!

From the horns of the wild oxen you have
   rescued*z* me.
22 I will tell of your name to my brothers and
   sisters;*a*
   in the midst of the congregation I will praise
   you:
23 You who fear the LORD, praise him!
   All you offspring of Jacob, glorify him;
   stand in awe of him, all you offspring of
   Israel!
24 For he did not despise or abhor
   the affliction of the afflicted;
   he did not hide his face from me,*b*
   but heard when I*c* cried to him.

25 From you comes my praise in the great
   congregation;
   my vows I will pay before those who fear him.
26 The poor*d* shall eat and be satisfied;
   those who seek him shall praise the LORD.
   May your hearts live forever!

27 All the ends of the earth shall remember
   and turn to the LORD;
   and all the families of the nations
   shall worship before him.*e*
28 For dominion belongs to the LORD,
   and he rules over the nations.

29 To him,*f* indeed, shall all who sleep in*g* the
   earth bow down;
   before him shall bow all who go down to the
   dust,
   and I shall live for him.*h*
30 Posterity will serve him;
   future generations will be told about the Lord,
31 and*i* proclaim his deliverance to a people yet
   unborn,
   saying that he has done it.

16 Hounds are all about me;
   a band of ruffians rings me round,
   and they have bound me hand and foot.
17 I tell my tale of misery,
   while they look on gloating.
18 They share out my clothes among them
   and cast lots for my garments.

19 But do not remain far away, LORD;
   you are my help, come quickly to my aid.
20 Deliver me from the sword,
   my precious life from the axe.
21 Save me from the lion's mouth,
   this poor body from the horns of the wild ox.

22 I shall declare your fame to my associates,
   praising you in the midst of the assembly.
23 You that fear the LORD, praise him;
   hold him in honour, all you descendants of Jacob,
   revere him, you descendants of Israel.
24 For he has not scorned him who is downtrodden,
   nor shrunk in loathing from his plight,
   nor hidden his face from him,
   but he has listened to his cry for help.

25 You inspire my praise in the great assembly;
   I shall fulfil my vows in the sight of those who
   fear you.

26 Let the humble eat and be satisfied.
   Let those who seek the LORD praise him.
   May you always be in good heart!
27 Let all the ends of the earth remember
   and turn again to the LORD;
   let all the families of the nations bow before him.
28 For kingly power belongs to the LORD;
   dominion over the nations is his.

29 How can those who sleep in the earth do him
   homage,
   how can those who go down to the grave do
   obeisance?
   But I shall live for his sake;
30 my descendants will serve him.
   The coming generation will be told of the LORD;
31 they will make known his righteous deeds,
   declaring to a people yet unborn:
   'The LORD has acted.'

Psalm 23

A Psalm of David.

1 The LORD is my shepherd, I shall not want.
2   He makes me lie down in green pastures;
   he leads me beside still waters;*j*
3   he restores my soul.*k*
   He leads me in right paths*l*
   for his name's sake.

Psalm 23

A psalm: for David

1 THE LORD is my shepherd; I lack for nothing.
2 He makes me lie down in green pastures,
   he leads me to water where I may rest;
3 he revives my spirit;
   for his name's sake he guides me in the right
   paths.

---

x Meaning of Heb uncertain   *y* Heb *my only one*   *z* Heb *answered*
a Or *kindred*   *b* Heb *him*   *c* Heb *he*   *d* Or *afflicted*   *e* Gk Syr
Jerome: Heb *you*   *f* Cn: Heb *They have eaten and*   *g* Cn: Heb *all
the fat ones*   *h* Compare Gk Syr Vg: Heb *and he who cannot keep
himself alive*   *i* Compare Gk: Heb *it will be told about the Lord to
the generation,* 31*they will come and*   *j* Heb *waters of rest*
k Or *life*   *l* Or *paths of righteousness*

22:16 **and . . . bound me:** *prob. rdg; Heb.* like a lion.
22:20 **axe:** *or* dog.   22:21 **this poor body:** *prob. rdg; Heb.* you
have answered me.   22:29 **How . . . homage:** *prob. rdg; Heb.* All
the prosperous ones in the land have eaten and worshipped. **I:** *so Gk;
Heb.* he.   22:30 **my:** *so Gk; Heb.* omits.

NEW AMERICAN BIBLE

17 Many dogs surround me;
   a pack of evildoers closes in on me.
So wasted are my hands and feet
18   that I can count all my bones.
They stare at me and gloat;
19   they divide my garments among them;
   for my clothing they cast lots.
20 But you, LORD, do not stay far off;
   my strength, come quickly to help me.
21 Deliver me from the sword,
   my forlorn life from the teeth of the dog.
22 Save me from the lion's mouth,
   my poor life from the horns of wild bulls.

III

23 Then I will proclaim your name to the assembly;
   in the community I will praise you:
24 "You who fear the LORD, give praise!
   All descendants of Jacob, give honor;
   show reverence, all descendants of Israel!
25 For God has not spurned or disdained
   the misery of this poor wretch,
Did not turn away from me,
   but heard me when I cried out.
26 I will offer praise in the great assembly;
   my vows I will fulfill before those who fear
     him.
27 The poor will eat their fill;
   those who seek the LORD will offer praise.
   May your hearts enjoy life forever!"

IV

28 All the ends of the earth
   will worship and turn to the LORD;
All the families of nations
   will bow low before you.
29 For kingship belongs to the LORD,
   the ruler over the nations.
30 All who sleep in the earth
   will bow low before God;
All who have gone down into the dust
   will kneel in homage.
31 And I will live for the LORD;
   my descendants will serve you.
32 The generation to come will be told of the Lord,
   that they may proclaim to a people yet unborn
   the deliverance you have brought.

NEW JERUSALEM BIBLE

16 A pack of dogs surrounds me,
   a gang of villains closing in on me
   as if to hack off my hands and my feet.
17 I can count every one of my bones,
   while they look on and gloat;
18 they divide my garments among them
   and cast lots for my clothing.

19 Yahweh, do not hold aloof!
   My strength, come quickly to my help,
20 rescue my soul from the sword,
   the one life I have from the grasp of the dog!
21 Save me from the lion's mouth,
   my poor life from the wild bulls' horns!

22 I shall proclaim your name to my brothers,
   praise you in full assembly:
23 'You who fear Yahweh, praise him!
   All the race of Jacob, honour him!
   Revere him, all the race of Israel!'
24 For he has not despised
   nor disregarded the poverty of the poor,
   has not turned away his face,
   but has listened to the cry for help.

25 Of you is my praise in the thronged assembly,
   I will perform my vows before all who fear him.
26 The poor will eat and be filled,
   those who seek Yahweh will praise him,
   'May your heart live for ever.'

27 The whole wide world will remember and return to
     Yahweh,
   all the families of nations bow down before him.
28 For to Yahweh, ruler of the nations, belongs kingly
     power!
29 All who prosper on earth will bow before him,
   all who go down to the dust will do reverence
     before him.
And those who are dead, 30 their descendants will
     serve him,
will proclaim his name to generations 31 still to
     come;
and these will tell of his saving justice to a people
     yet unborn:
he has fulfilled it.

Psalm 23

1 *A psalm of David.*

I

The LORD is my shepherd;
   there is nothing I lack.
2 In green pastures you let me graze;
   to safe waters you lead me;
3   you restore my strength.
You guide me along the right path
   for the sake of your name.

Psalm 23 (V 22)

Psalm   Of David

1 Yahweh is my shepherd, I lack nothing.
2 In grassy meadows he lets me lie.

By tranquil streams he leads me
3   to restore my spirit.
He guides me in paths of saving justice
   as befits his name.

4 Even though I walk through the darkest valley,*m*
  I fear no evil;
for you are with me;
  your rod and your staff—
  they comfort me.

5 You prepare a table before me
  in the presence of my enemies;
you anoint my head with oil;
  my cup overflows.
6 Surely*n* goodness and mercy*o* shall follow me
  all the days of my life,
and I shall dwell in the house of the LORD
  my whole life long.*p*

Psalm 24

Of David. A Psalm.

1 The earth is the LORD's and all that is in it,
  the world, and those who live in it;
2 for he has founded it on the seas,
  and established it on the rivers.

3 Who shall ascend the hill of the LORD?
  And who shall stand in his holy place?
4 Those who have clean hands and pure hearts,
  who do not lift up their souls to what is false,
  and do not swear deceitfully.
5 They will receive blessing from the LORD,
  and vindication from the God of their
    salvation.
6 Such is the company of those who seek him,
  who seek the face of the God of Jacob.*q* *Selah*

7 Lift up your heads, O gates!
  and be lifted up, O ancient doors!
  that the King of glory may come in.
8 Who is the King of glory?
  The LORD, strong and mighty,
  the LORD, mighty in battle.
9 Lift up your heads, O gates!
  and be lifted up, O ancient doors!
  that the King of glory may come in.
10 Who is this King of glory?
  The LORD of hosts,
  he is the King of glory.   *Selah*

Psalm 25

Of David.

1 To you, O LORD, I lift up my soul.
2 O my God, in you I trust;
  do not let me be put to shame;
  do not let my enemies exult over me.
3 Do not let those who wait for you be put to
    shame;
  let them be ashamed who are wantonly
    treacherous.

4 Make me to know your ways, O LORD;
  teach me your paths.
5 Lead me in your truth, and teach me,
  for you are the God of my salvation;
  for you I wait all day long.

4 Even were I to walk through a valley of deepest
    darkness
  I should fear no harm, for you are with me;
  your shepherd's staff and crook afford me comfort.

5 You spread a table for me in the presence of my
    enemies;
you have richly anointed my head with oil,
  and my cup brims over.
6 Goodness and love unfailing will follow me
  all the days of my life,
and I shall dwell in the house of the LORD
  throughout the years to come.

Psalm 24

For David: a psalm

1 To THE LORD belong the earth and everything in it,
  the world and all its inhabitants.
2 For it was he who founded it on the seas
  and planted it firm on the waters beneath.

3 Who may go up the mountain of the LORD?
  Who may stand in his holy place?
4 One who has clean hands and a pure heart,
  who has not set his mind on what is false
  or sworn deceitfully.
5 Such a one shall receive blessing from the LORD,
  and be vindicated by God his saviour.
6 Such is the fortune of those who seek him,
  who seek the presence of the God of Jacob. [*Selah*

7 Lift up your heads, you gates,
  lift yourselves up, you everlasting doors,
  that the king of glory may come in.
8 Who is this king of glory?
  The LORD strong and mighty,
  the LORD mighty in battle.

9 Lift up your heads, you gates,
  lift them up, you everlasting doors,
  that the king of glory may come in.
10 Who is he, this king of glory?
  The LORD of Hosts, he is the king of glory. [*Selah*

Psalm 25

For David

1 LORD my God, to you I lift my heart.
2 In you I trust: do not let me be put to shame,
  do not let my enemies exult over me.
3 No one whose hope is in you is put to shame;
  but shame comes to all who break faith without
    cause.
4 Make your paths known to me, LORD;
  teach me your ways.
5 Lead me by your faithfulness and teach me,
  for you are God my saviour;
  in you I put my hope all day long.

---

m Or the valley of the shadow of death   *n Or Only*   *o Or kindness*
p Heb for length of days   *q Gk Syr: Heb your face, O Jacob*   24:6 **the presence . . . Jacob:** *so Gk; Heb.* your face, Jacob.

4Even when I walk through a dark valley,
    I fear no harm for you are at my side;
    your rod and staff give me courage.
II
5You set a table before me
    as my enemies watch;
You anoint my head with oil;
    my cup overflows.
6Only goodness and love will pursue me
    all the days of my life;
I will dwell in the house of the LORD
    for years to come.

Psalm 24

1*A psalm of David.*

I

The earth is the LORD's and all it holds,
    the world and those who live there.
2For God founded it on the seas,
    established it over the rivers.
II
3Who may go up the mountain of the LORD?
    Who can stand in his holy place?
4"The clean of hand and pure of heart,
    who are not devoted to idols,
    who have not sworn falsely.
5They will receive blessings from the LORD,
    and justice from their saving God.
6Such are the people that love the LORD,
    that seek the face of the God of Jacob."   *Selah*
III
7Lift up your heads, O gates;
    rise up, you ancient portals,
    that the king of glory may enter.
8Who is this king of glory?
    The LORD, a mighty warrior,
    the LORD, mighty in battle.
9Lift up your heads, O gates;
    rise up, you ancient portals,
    that the king of glory may enter.
10Who is this king of glory?
    The LORD of hosts is the king of glory.   *Selah*

Psalm 25

1*Of David.*

I

I wait for you, O LORD;
    I lift up my soul 2to my God.
In you I trust; do not let me be disgraced;
    do not let my enemies gloat over me.
3No one is disgraced who waits for you,
    but only those who lightly break faith.
4Make known to me your ways, LORD;
    teach me your paths.
5Guide me in your truth and teach me,
    for you are God my savior.
For you I wait all the long day,
    because of your goodness, LORD.

4Even were I to walk in a ravine as dark as death
I should fear no danger, for you are at my side.
Your staff and your crook are there to soothe me.

5You prepare a table for me
    under the eyes of my enemies;
you anoint my head with oil;
    my cup brims over.
6Kindness and faithful love pursue me
    every day of my life.
I make my home in the house of Yahweh
    for all time to come.

Psalm 24 (V 23)

Psalm   Of David

1To Yahweh belong the earth and all it contains,
    the world and all who live there;
2it is he who laid its foundations on the seas,
    on the flowing waters fixed it firm.

3Who shall go up to the mountain of Yahweh?
    Who shall take a stand in his holy place?

4The clean of hands and pure of heart,
    whose heart is not set on vanities,
    who does not swear an oath in order to deceive.

5Such a one will receive blessing from Yahweh,
    saving justice from the God of his salvation.
6Such is the people that seeks him,
    that seeks your presence, God of Jacob.   *Pause*

7Gates, lift high your heads,
    raise high the ancient gateways,
    and the king of glory shall enter!

8Who is he, this king of glory?
    It is Yahweh, strong and valiant,
    Yahweh valiant in battle.

9Gates, lift high your heads,
    raise high the ancient gateways,
    and the king of glory shall enter!

10Who is he, this king of glory?
    Yahweh Sabaoth,
    he is the king of glory.   *Pause*

Psalm 25 (V 24)

Of David

Aleph	1ADORATION I offer, Yahweh, 2to you, my God.
Bet	BUT in my trust in you do not put me to shame, let not my enemies gloat over me.
Gimel	3CALLING to you, none shall ever be put to shame, but shame is theirs who groundlessly break faith.
Dalet	4DIRECT me in your ways, Yahweh, and teach me your paths.
He	5ENCOURAGE me to walk in your truth and teach me since you are the God who saves me.
(Waw)	FOR my hope is in you all day long— 7csuch is your generosity, Yahweh.

6 Be mindful of your mercy, O LORD, and of your
   steadfast love,
   for they have been from of old.
7 Do not remember the sins of my youth or my
   transgressions;
   according to your steadfast love remember me,
   for your goodness' sake, O LORD!

8 Good and upright is the LORD;
   therefore he instructs sinners in the way.
9 He leads the humble in what is right,
   and teaches the humble his way.
10 All the paths of the LORD are steadfast love and
   faithfulness,
   for those who keep his covenant and his
   decrees.

11 For your name's sake, O LORD,
   pardon my guilt, for it is great.
12 Who are they that fear the LORD?
   He will teach them the way that they should
   choose.

13 They will abide in prosperity,
   and their children shall possess the land.
14 The friendship of the LORD is for those who fear
   him,
   and he makes his covenant known to them.
15 My eyes are ever toward the LORD,
   for he will pluck my feet out of the net.

16 Turn to me and be gracious to me,
   for I am lonely and afflicted.
17 Relieve the troubles of my heart,
   and bring me*r* out of my distress.
18 Consider my affliction and my trouble,
   and forgive all my sins.

19 Consider how many are my foes,
   and with what violent hatred they hate me.
20 O guard my life, and deliver me;
   do not let me be put to shame, for I take
   refuge in you.
21 May integrity and uprightness preserve me,
   for I wait for you.

22 Redeem Israel, O God,
   out of all its troubles.

Psalm 26

Of David.

1 Vindicate me, O LORD,
   for I have walked in my integrity,
   and I have trusted in the LORD without
   wavering.
2 Prove me, O LORD, and try me;
   test my heart and mind.
3 For your steadfast love is before my eyes,
   and I walk in faithfulness to you.*s*

4 I do not sit with the worthless,
   nor do I consort with hypocrites;
5 I hate the company of evildoers,
   and will not sit with the wicked.

6 I wash my hands in innocence,
   and go around your altar, O LORD,
7 singing aloud a song of thanksgiving,
   and telling all your wondrous deeds.

6 Remember, LORD, your tender care and love
   unfailing,
   for they are from of old.
7 Do not remember the sins and offences of my
   youth,
   but remember me in your unfailing love,
   in accordance with your goodness, LORD.

8 The LORD is good and upright;
   therefore he teaches sinners the way they should
   go.
9 He guides the humble in right conduct,
   and teaches them his way.
10 All the paths of the LORD are loving and sure
   to those who keep his covenant and his solemn
   charge.

11 LORD, for the honour of your name
   forgive my wickedness, great though it is.
12 Whoever fears the LORD
   will be shown the path he should choose.
13 He will enjoy lasting prosperity,
   and his descendants will inherit the land.
14 The LORD confides his purposes to those who fear
   him;
   his covenant is for their instruction.
15 My eyes are ever on the LORD,
   who alone can free my feet from the net.

16 Turn to me and show me your favour,
   for I am lonely and oppressed.
17 Relieve the troubles of my heart
   and lead me out of my distress.
18 Look on my affliction and misery
   and forgive me every sin.
19 Look at my enemies, see how many they are,
   how violent their hatred of me.
20 Defend me and deliver me;
   let me not be put to shame, for in you I find
   refuge.
21 Let integrity and uprightness protect me;
   in you, LORD, I put my hope.
22 God, deliver Israel from all their troubles.

Psalm 26

For David

1 LORD, uphold my cause,
   for I have led a blameless life,
   and put unfaltering trust in you.
2 Test me, LORD, and try me,
   putting my heart and mind to the proof;
3 for your constant love is before my eyes,
   and I live by your faithfulness.

4 I have not sat among the worthless,
   nor do I associate with hypocrites;
5 I detest the company of evildoers,
   nor shall I sit among the ungodly.
6 I wash my hands free from guilt
   to go in procession round your altar, LORD,
7 recounting your marvellous deeds,
   making them known with thankful voice.

---

r Or *The troubles of my heart are enlarged; bring me*   *s* Or *in your*
faithfulness

NEW AMERICAN BIBLE

NEW JERUSALEM BIBLE

6 Remember your compassion and love, O LORD;
  for they are ages old.
7 Remember no more the sins of my youth;
  remember me only in light of your love.

II

8 Good and upright is the LORD,
  who shows sinners the way,
9 Guides the humble rightly,
  and teaches the humble the way.
10 All the paths of the LORD are faithful love
  toward those who honor the covenant demands.
11 For the sake of your name, LORD,
  pardon my guilt, though it is great.
12 Who are those who fear the LORD?
  God shows them the way to choose.
13 They live well and prosper,
  and their descendants inherit the land.
14 The counsel of the LORD belongs to the faithful;
  the covenant instructs them.
15 My eyes are ever upon the LORD,
  who frees my feet from the snare.

III

16 Look upon me, have pity on me,
  for I am alone and afflicted.
17 Relieve the troubles of my heart;
  bring me out of my distress.
18 Put an end to my affliction and suffering;
  take away all my sins.
19 See how many are my enemies,
  see how fiercely they hate me.
20 Preserve my life and rescue me;
  do not let me be disgraced, for I trust in you.
21 Let honesty and virtue preserve me;
  I wait for you, O LORD.
22 Redeem Israel, God,
  from all its distress!

Zain   6 GOODNESS and faithful love have been yours
  for ever,
  Yahweh, do not forget them.

Het   7 HOLD not my youthful sins against me,
  but remember me as your faithful love
  dictates.

Tet   8 INTEGRITY and generosity are marks of
  Yahweh
  for he brings sinners back to the path.

Yod   9 JUDICIOUSLY he guides the humble,
  instructing the poor in his way.

Kaph   10 KINDNESS unfailing and constancy mark all
  Yahweh's paths,
  for those who keep his covenant and his
  decrees.

Lamed   11 LET my sin, great though it is, be forgiven,
  Yahweh, for the sake of your name.

Mem   12 MEN who respect Yahweh, what of them?
  He teaches them the way they must choose.

Nun   13 NEIGHBOURS to happiness will they live,
  and their children inherit the land.

Samek   14 ONLY those who fear Yahweh have his secret
  and his covenant, for their understanding.

Ain   15 PERMANENTLY my eyes are on Yahweh,
  for he will free my feet from the snare.

Pe   16 QUICK, turn to me, pity me,
  alone and wretched as I am!

Zade   17 RELIEVE the distress of my heart,
  bring me out of my constraint.

(Qoph)   18 SPARE a glance for my misery and pain,
  take all my sins away.

Resh   19 TAKE note how countless are my enemies,
  how violent their hatred for me.

Shin   20 UNLESS you guard me and rescue me
  I shall be put to shame, for you are my
  refuge.

Taw   21 VIRTUE and integrity be my protection,
  for my hope, Yahweh, is in you.

22 Ransom Israel, O God,
  from all its troubles.

Psalm 26

1 *Of David.*

I

Grant me justice, LORD!
  I have walked without blame.
In the LORD I have trusted;
  I have not faltered.
2 Test me, LORD, and try me;
  search my heart and mind.
3 Your love is before my eyes;
  I walk guided by your faithfulness.

II

4 I do not sit with deceivers,
  nor with hypocrites do I mingle.
5 I hate the company of evildoers;
  with the wicked I do not sit.
6 I will wash my hands in innocence
  and walk round your altar, LORD,
7 Lifting my voice in thanks,
  recounting all your wondrous deeds.

Psalm 26 (V 25)

Of David

1 Yahweh, be my judge!
  I go on my way in innocence,
  my trust in Yahweh never wavers.

2 Probe me, Yahweh, examine me,
  Test my heart and my mind in the fire.
3 For your faithful love is before my eyes,
  and I live my life by your truth.

4 No sitting with wastrels for me,
  no travelling with hypocrites;
5 I hate the company of sinners,
  I refuse to sit down with the wicked.

6 I will wash my hands in innocence
  and join the procession round your altar, Yahweh,
7 to make heard the sound of thanksgiving,
  to proclaim all your wonders.

8 O LORD, I love the house in which you dwell,
and the place where your glory abides.
9 Do not sweep me away with sinners,
nor my life with the bloodthirsty,
10 those in whose hands are evil devices,
and whose right hands are full of bribes.
11 But as for me, I walk in my integrity;
redeem me, and be gracious to me.
12 My foot stands on level ground;
in the great congregation I will bless the LORD.

Psalm 27

Of David.

1 The LORD is my light and my salvation;
whom shall I fear?
The LORD is the stronghold[t] of my life;
of whom shall I be afraid?
2 When evildoers assail me
to devour my flesh —
my adversaries and foes —
they shall stumble and fall.
3 Though an army encamp against me,
my heart shall not fear;
though war rise up against me,
yet I will be confident.
4 One thing I asked of the LORD,
that will I seek after:
to live in the house of the LORD
all the days of my life,
to behold the beauty of the LORD,
and to inquire in his temple.
5 For he will hide me in his shelter
in the day of trouble;
he will conceal me under the cover of his tent;
he will set me high on a rock.
6 Now my head is lifted up
above my enemies all around me,
and I will offer in his tent
sacrifices with shouts of joy;
I will sing and make melody to the LORD.
7 Hear, O LORD, when I cry aloud,
be gracious to me and answer me!
8 "Come," my heart says, "seek his face!"
Your face, LORD, do I seek.
9 Do not hide your face from me.

Do not turn your servant away in anger,
you who have been my help.
Do not cast me off, do not forsake me,
O God of my salvation!
10 If my father and mother forsake me,
the LORD will take me up.
11 Teach me your way, O LORD,
and lead me on a level path
because of my enemies.
12 Do not give me up to the will of my adversaries,
for false witnesses have risen against me,
and they are breathing out violence.
13 I believe that I shall see the goodness of the
LORD
in the land of the living.

8 LORD, I love the house where you dwell,
the place where your glory resides.
9 Do not sweep me away with sinners,
nor cast me out with those who thirst for blood,
10 whose fingers are active in mischief,
whose right hands are full of bribes.
11 But I lead a blameless life;
deliver me and show me your favour.
12 My feet are planted on firm ground;
I shall bless the LORD in the full assembly.

Psalm 27

For David

1 THE LORD is my light and my salvation;
whom should I fear?
The LORD is the stronghold of my life;
of whom then should I go in dread?
2 When evildoers close in on me to devour me,
it is my adversaries, my enemies,
who stumble and fall.
3 Should an army encamp against me,
my heart would have no fear;
if armed men should fall upon me,
even then I would be undismayed.
4 One thing I ask of the LORD,
it is the one thing I seek:
that I may dwell in the house of the LORD
all the days of my life,
to gaze on the beauty of the LORD
and to seek him in his temple.
5 For he will hide me in his shelter
in the day of misfortune;
he will conceal me under cover of his tent,
set me high on a rock.
6 Now my head will be raised high
above the enemy all about me;
so I shall acclaim him in his tent with sacrifice
and sing a psalm of praise to the LORD.
7 Hear, LORD, when I call aloud;
show me favour and answer me.
8 'Come,' my heart has said,
'seek his presence.'
I seek your presence, LORD;
9 do not hide your face from me,
nor in your anger turn away your servant,
whose help you have been;
God my saviour, do not reject me or forsake me.
10 Though my father and my mother forsake me,
the LORD will take me into his care.
11-12 Teach me your way, LORD,
do not give me up to the greed of my enemies;
lead me by a level path
to escape the foes who beset me:
liars breathing malice come forward
to give evidence against me.
13 Well I know that I shall see the goodness of the
LORD
in the land of the living.

27:5 **shelter:** *or* arbour.   27:8 **seek his presence:** *prob. rdg; Heb.*
seek my presence.   27:13 **Well I know:** *so some MSS; others* Had
I not well known.

[t] Or *refuge*

8 LORD, I love the house where you dwell,
the tenting-place of your glory.
III
9 Do not take me away with sinners,
nor my life with the violent.
10 Their hands carry out their schemes;
their right hands are full of bribes.
11 But I walk without blame;
redeem me, be gracious to me!
12 My foot stands on level ground;
in assemblies I will bless the LORD.

Psalm 27

1 *Of David*

A

I
The LORD is my light and my salvation;
whom do I fear?
The LORD is my life's refuge;
of whom am I afraid?
2 When evildoers come at me
to devour my flesh,
These my enemies and foes
themselves stumble and fall.
3 Though an army encamp against me,
my heart does not fear;
Though war be waged against me,
even then do I trust.
II
4 One thing I ask of the LORD;
this I seek:
To dwell in the LORD's house
all the days of my life,
To gaze on the LORD's beauty,
to visit his temple.
5 For God will hide me in his shelter
in time of trouble,
Will conceal me in the cover of his tent;
and set me high upon a rock.
6 Even now my head is held high
above my enemies on every side!
I will offer in his tent
sacrifices with shouts of joy;
I will sing and chant praise to the LORD.

B

I
7 Hear my voice, LORD, when I call;
have mercy on me and answer me.
8 "Come," says my heart, "seek God's face";
your face, LORD, do I seek!
9 Do not hide your face from me;
do not repel your servant in anger.
You are my help; do not cast me off;
do not forsake me, God my savior!
10 Even if my father and mother forsake me,
the LORD will take me in.
II
11 LORD, show me your way;
lead me on a level path
because of my enemies.
12 Do not abandon me to the will of my foes;
malicious and lying witnesses have risen against
me.
13 But I believe I shall enjoy the LORD's goodness
in the land of the living.

8 Yahweh, I love the beauty of your house
and the place where your glory dwells.
9 Do not couple me with sinners,
nor my life with men of violence,
10 whose hands are stained with guilt,
their right hands heavy with bribes.
11 In innocence I will go on my way;
ransom me, take pity on me.
12 I take my stand on the right path;
I will bless you, Yahweh, in the assemblies.

Psalm 27 (V 26)

Of David

1 Yahweh is my light and my salvation,
whom should I fear?
Yahweh is the fortress of my life,
whom should I dread?
2 When the wicked advance against me
to eat me up,
they, my opponents, my enemies,
are the ones who stumble and fall.
3 Though an army pitch camp against me,
my heart will not fear,
though war break out against me,
my trust will never be shaken.
4 One thing I ask of Yahweh,
one thing I seek:
to dwell in Yahweh's house
all the days of my life,
to enjoy the sweetness of Yahweh,
to seek out his temple.
5 For he hides me away under his roof
on the day of evil,
he folds me in the recesses of his tent,
sets me high on a rock.
6 Now my head is held high
above the enemies who surround me;
in his tent I will offer
sacrifices of acclaim.

I will sing, I will make music for Yahweh.

7 Yahweh, hear my voice as I cry,
pity me, answer me!
8 Of you my heart has said,
'Seek his face!'
Your face, Yahweh, I seek;
9 do not turn away from me.

Do not thrust aside your servant in anger,
without you I am helpless.
Never leave me, never forsake me,
God, my Saviour.
10 Though my father and mother forsake me,
Yahweh will gather me up.
11 Yahweh, teach me your way,
lead me on the path of integrity
because of my enemies.
12 do not abandon me to the will of my foes—
false witnesses have risen against me,
and are breathing out violence.
13 This I believe: I shall see the goodness of Yahweh,
in the land of the living.

14 Wait for the LORD;
 be strong, and let your heart take courage;
 wait for the LORD!

Psalm 28

Of David.

1 To you, O LORD, I call;
 my rock, do not refuse to hear me,
for if you are silent to me,
 I shall be like those who go down to the Pit.
2 Hear the voice of my supplication,
 as I cry to you for help,
as I lift up my hands
 toward your most holy sanctuary. *u*

3 Do not drag me away with the wicked,
 with those who are workers of evil,
who speak peace with their neighbors,
 while mischief is in their hearts.
4 Repay them according to their work,
 and according to the evil of their deeds;
repay them according to the work of their hands;
 render them their due reward.
5 Because they do not regard the works of the
  LORD,
 or the work of his hands,
he will break them down and build them up no
  more.

6 Blessed be the LORD,
 for he has heard the sound of my pleadings.
7 The LORD is my strength and my shield;
 in him my heart trusts;
so I am helped, and my heart exults,
 and with my song I give thanks to him.

8 The LORD is the strength of his people;
 he is the saving refuge of his anointed.
9 O save your people, and bless your heritage;
 be their shepherd, and carry them forever.

Psalm 29

A Psalm of David.

1 Ascribe to the LORD, O heavenly beings, *v*
 ascribe to the LORD glory and strength.
2 Ascribe to the LORD the glory of his name;
 worship the LORD in holy splendor.

3 The voice of the LORD is over the waters;
 the God of glory thunders,
 the LORD, over mighty waters.
4 The voice of the LORD is powerful;
 the voice of the LORD is full of majesty.

5 The voice of the LORD breaks the cedars;
 the LORD breaks the cedars of Lebanon.
6 He makes Lebanon skip like a calf,
 and Sirion like a young wild ox.

7 The voice of the LORD flashes forth flames of
  fire.
8 The voice of the LORD shakes the wilderness;
 the LORD shakes the wilderness of Kadesh.

9 The voice of the LORD causes the oaks to whirl, *w*
 and strips the forest bare;
 and in his temple all say, "Glory!"

14 Wait for the LORD; be strong and brave,
 and put your hope in the LORD.

Psalm 28

For David

1 To you, LORD, I call;
 my Rock, do not be deaf to my cry,
lest, if you answer me with silence,
 I become like those who go down to the abyss.
2 Hear my voice as I plead for mercy,
 as I call to you for help
with hands uplifted towards your holy shrine.
3 Do not drag me away with the ungodly,
 with evildoers who speak civilly to their fellows,
 though with malice in their hearts.
4-5 Requite them for their works, their evil deeds;
 repay them for what their hands have done,
because they do not discern the works of the LORD
 or what his hands have done.
May they be given their deserts;
 may he strike them down and never restore them!

6 Blessed be the LORD,
 for he has heard my voice as I plead for mercy.
7 The LORD is my strength and my shield;
 in him my heart trusts.
I am sustained, and my heart leaps for joy,
 and with my song I praise him.
8 The LORD is strength to his people,
 a safe refuge for his anointed one.

9 Save your people and bless those who belong to
  you,
 shepherd them and carry them for ever.

Psalm 29

A psalm: for David

1 Ascribe to the LORD, you angelic powers,
 ascribe to the LORD glory and might.
2 Ascribe to the LORD the glory due to his name;
 in holy attire worship the LORD.

3 The voice of the LORD echoes over the waters;
 the God of glory thunders;
 the LORD thunders over the mighty waters,
4 the voice of the LORD in power,
 the voice of the LORD in majesty.

5 The voice of the LORD breaks the cedar trees,
 the LORD shatters the cedars of Lebanon.
6 He makes Lebanon skip like a calf,
 Sirion like a young wild ox.

7 The voice of the LORD makes flames of fire burst
  forth;
8 the voice of the LORD makes the wilderness writhe
  in travail,
 the LORD makes the wilderness of Kadesh writhe.
9 The voice of the LORD makes the hinds calve;
 he strips the forest bare,
 and in his temple all cry, 'Glory!'

---

u Heb *your innermost sanctuary*   *v* Heb *sons of gods*   *w* Or *causes*
the deer to calve

28:8 **to his people:** *so some MSS; others* to them.   29:9 **strips**
... bare: *or* brings young goats early to birth.

14 Wait for the LORD, take courage;
  be stouthearted, wait for the LORD!

Psalm 28

1 *Of David.*

I

To you, LORD, I call;
  my Rock, do not be deaf to me.
If you fail to answer me,
  I will join those who go down to the pit.
2 Hear the sound of my pleading when I cry to you,
  lifting my hands toward your holy place.
3 Do not drag me off with the wicked,
  with those who do wrong,
Who speak peace to their neighbors
  though evil is in their hearts.
4 Repay them for their deeds,
  for the evil that they do.
For the work of their hands repay them;
  give them what they deserve.
5 They pay no heed to the LORD's works,
  to the deeds of God's hands.
God will tear them down,
  never to be rebuilt.
II
6 Blessed be the LORD,
  who has heard the sound of my pleading.
7 The LORD is my strength and my shield,
  in whom my heart trusted and found help.
So my heart rejoices;
  with my song I praise my God.
III
8 LORD, you are the strength of your people,
  the saving refuge of your anointed king.
9 Save your people, bless your inheritance;
  feed and sustain them forever!

Psalm 29

1 *A psalm of David.*

I

Give to the LORD, you heavenly beings,
  give to the LORD glory and might;
2 Give to the LORD the glory due God's name.
  Bow down before the LORD's holy splendor!
II
3 The voice of the LORD is over the waters;
  the God of glory thunders,
  the LORD, over the mighty waters.
4 The voice of the LORD is power;
  the voice of the LORD is splendor.
5 The voice of the LORD cracks the cedars;
  the LORD splinters the cedars of Lebanon,
6 Makes Lebanon leap like a calf,
  and Sirion like a young bull.
7 The voice of the LORD strikes with fiery flame;
8   the voice of the LORD rocks the desert;
  the LORD rocks the desert of Kadesh.
9 The voice of the LORD twists the oaks
  and strips the forests bare.
  All in his palace say, "Glory!"

14 Put your hope in Yahweh, be strong, let your heart
  be bold,
  put your hope in Yahweh.

Psalm 28 (V 27)

Of David

1 To you, Yahweh, I cry,
  my rock, do not be deaf to me!
If you stay silent
  I shall be like those who sink into oblivion.

2 Hear the sound of my prayer
  when I call upon you,
when I raise my hands, Yahweh,
  towards your Holy of Holies.

3 Do not drag me away with the wicked,
  with evil-doers,
who talk to their partners of peace
  with treachery in their hearts.

4 Repay them as their deeds deserve,
  as befits their treacherous actions;
as befits their handiwork repay them,
  let their deserts fall back on themselves.

5 They do not comprehend the deeds of Yahweh,
  the work of his hands.
May he pull them down and not rebuild them!

6 Blessed be Yahweh
  for he hears the sound of my prayer.

7 Yahweh is my strength and my shield,
  in him my heart trusts.
I have been helped; my body has recovered its
      vigour,
  with all my heart I thank him.

8 Yahweh is the strength of his people,
  a safe refuge for his anointed.
9 Save your people, bless your heritage,
  shepherd them and carry them for ever!

Psalm 29 (V 28)

Psalm   Of David

1 Give Yahweh his due, sons of God,
  give Yahweh his due of glory and strength,
2 give Yahweh the glory due to his name,
  adore Yahweh in the splendour of holiness.

3 Yahweh's voice over the waters, the God of glory
      thunders;
  Yahweh over countless waters.
4 Yahweh's voice in power, Yahweh's voice in
      splendour;

5 Yahweh's voice shatters cedars,
  Yahweh shatters cedars of Lebanon,
6 he makes Lebanon skip like a calf,
  Sirion like a young wild ox.

7 Yahweh's voice carves out lightning-shafts,
8 Yahweh's voice convulses the desert,
  Yahweh convulses the desert of Kadesh,
9 Yahweh's voice convulses terebinths,
  strips forests bare.

In his palace all cry, 'Glory!'

10 The LORD sits enthroned over the flood;
    the LORD sits enthroned as king forever.
11 May the LORD give strength to his people!
    May the LORD bless his people with peace!

Psalm 30

A Psalm. A Song at the dedication of the temple. Of David.

1 I will extol you, O LORD, for you have drawn me
      up,
    and did not let my foes rejoice over me.
2 O LORD my God, I cried to you for help,
    and you have healed me.
3 O LORD, you brought up my soul from Sheol,
    restored me to life from among those gone
      down to the Pit. *x*

4 Sing praises to the LORD, O you his faithful ones,
    and give thanks to his holy name.
5 For his anger is but for a moment;
    his favor is for a lifetime.
    Weeping may linger for the night,
    but joy comes with the morning.

6 As for me, I said in my prosperity,
    "I shall never be moved."
7 By your favor, O LORD,
    you had established me as a strong mountain;
    you hid your face;
    I was dismayed.

8 To you, O LORD, I cried,
    and to the LORD I made supplication:
9 "What profit is there in my death,
    if I go down to the Pit?
    Will the dust praise you?
    Will it tell of your faithfulness?
10 Hear, O LORD, and be gracious to me!
    O LORD, be my helper!"

11 You have turned my mourning into dancing;
    you have taken off my sackcloth
    and clothed me with joy,
12 so that my soul *y* may praise you and not be
      silent.
    O LORD my God, I will give thanks to you
      forever.

Psalm 31

To the leader. A Psalm of David.

1 In you, O LORD, I seek refuge;
    do not let me ever be put to shame;
    in your righteousness deliver me.
2 Incline your ear to me;
    rescue me speedily.
    Be a rock of refuge for me,
    a strong fortress to save me.

3 You are indeed my rock and my fortress;
    for your name's sake lead me and guide me,
4 take me out of the net that is hidden for me,
    for you are my refuge.
5 Into your hand I commit my spirit;
    you have redeemed me, O LORD, faithful God.

10 The LORD is king above the flood,
    the LORD has taken his royal seat as king for ever.
11 The LORD will give strength to his people;
    the LORD will bless his people with peace.

Psalm 30

A psalm (a song for the dedication of the temple):
for David

1 I SHALL exalt you, LORD;
    you have lifted me up
    and have not let my enemies be jubilant over me.
2 LORD my God, I cried to you and you healed me.
3 You have brought me up, LORD, from Sheol,
    and saved my life as I was sinking into the abyss.

4 Sing a psalm to the LORD, all you his loyal
      servants;
    give thanks to his holy name.
5 In his anger is distress, in his favour there is life.
    Tears may linger at nightfall,
    but rejoicing comes in the morning.

6 I felt secure and said,
    'I can never be shaken.'
7 LORD, by your favour you made my mountain
      strong;
    when you hid your face, I was struck with dismay.
8 To you, LORD, I called
    and pleaded with you for mercy:
9 'What profit is there in my death,
    in my going down to the pit?
    Can the dust praise you?
    Can it proclaim your truth?
10 Hear, LORD, and be gracious to me;
    LORD, be my helper.'

11 You have turned my laments into dancing;
    you have stripped off my sackcloth and clothed me
      with joy,
12 that I may sing psalms to you without ceasing.
    LORD my God, I shall praise you for ever.

Psalm 31

For the leader: a psalm: for David

1 IN you, LORD, I have found refuge;
    let me never be put to shame.
    By your saving power deliver me,
2 bend down and hear me,
    come quickly to my rescue.
    Be to me a rock of refuge,
    a stronghold to keep me safe.
3 You are my rock and my stronghold;
    lead and guide me for the honour of your name.
4 Set me free from the net that has been hidden to
      catch me;
    for you are my refuge.
5 Into your hand I commit my spirit.
    You have delivered me, LORD, you God of truth.

30:3 **Sheol:** *or* the underworld. **and saved . . . abyss:** *or* and rescued
me alive from among those who go down to the abyss.   30:5 **In**
his anger . . . life: *or* His anger is for a moment, his favour lifelong.

x Or that I should not go down to the Pit   *y Heb that glory*

III
10 The LORD sits enthroned above the flood!
    The LORD reigns as king forever!
11 May the LORD give might to his people;
    may the LORD bless his people with peace!

Psalm 30

1 *A psalm. A song for the dedication of the temple.*
Of David.

I
2 I praise you, LORD, for you raised me up
    and did not let my enemies rejoice over me.
3 O LORD, my God,
    I cried out to you and you healed me.
4 LORD, you brought me up from Sheol;
    you kept me from going down to the pit.
II
5 Sing praise to the LORD, you faithful;
    give thanks to God's holy name.
6 For divine anger lasts but a moment;
    divine favor lasts a lifetime.
At dusk weeping comes for the night;
    but at dawn there is rejoicing.
III
7 Complacent, I once said,
    "I shall never be shaken."
8 LORD, when you showed me favor
    I stood like the mighty mountains.
But when you hid your face
    I was struck with terror.
9 To you, LORD, I cried out;
    with the Lord I pleaded for mercy:
10 "What gain is there from my lifeblood,
    from my going down to the grave?
Does dust give you thanks
    or declare your faithfulness?
11 Hear, O LORD, have mercy on me;
    LORD, be my helper."
IV
12 You changed my mourning into dancing;
    you took off my sackcloth
    and clothed me with gladness.
13 With my whole being I sing
    endless praise to you.
O LORD, my God,
    forever will I give you thanks.

Psalm 31

1 *For the leader. A psalm of David.*

I
2 In you, LORD, I take refuge;
    let me never be put to shame.
In your justice deliver me;
3   incline your ear to me;
    make haste to rescue me!
Be my rock of refuge,
    a stronghold to save me.
4 You are my rock and my fortress;
    for your name's sake lead and guide me.
5 Free me from the net they have set for me,
    for you are my refuge.
6 Into your hands I commend my spirit;
    you will redeem me, LORD, faithful God.

10 Yahweh was enthroned for the flood,
    Yahweh is enthroned as king for ever.
11 Yahweh will give strength to his people,
    Yahweh blesses his people with peace.

Psalm 30 (V 29)

Psalm   Canticle for the Dedication of the House
Of David

1 I praise you to the heights, Yahweh, for you have
    raised me up,
you have not let my foes make merry over me.
2 Yahweh, my God, I cried to you for help and you
    healed me.
3 Yahweh, you have lifted me out of Sheol,
    from among those who sink into oblivion you have
    given me life.

4 Make music for Yahweh, all you who are faithful
    to him,
praise his unforgettable holiness.
5 His anger lasts but a moment, his favour through
    life;
In the evening come tears, but with dawn cries of
    joy.

6   Carefree, I used to think,
    'Nothing can ever shake me!'
7 Your favour, Yahweh, set me on impregnable
    heights,
but you turned away your face and I was terrified.

8   To you, Yahweh, I call,
    to my God I cry for mercy.
9 What point is there in my death, my going down
    to the abyss?
Can the dust praise you or proclaim your
    faithfulness?

10 Listen, Yahweh, take pity on me,
    Yahweh, be my help!
11 You have turned my mourning into dancing,
    you have stripped off my sackcloth and clothed me
    with joy.
12 So my heart will sing to you unceasingly,
    Yahweh, my God, I shall praise you for ever.

Psalm 31 (V 30)

For the choirmaster   Psalm   Of David

1 In you, Yahweh, I have taken refuge,
    let me never be put to shame,
in your saving justice deliver me, rescue me,
2 turn your ear to me, make haste.

Be for me a rock-fastness,
    a fortified citadel to save me.
3 You are my rock, my rampart;
    true to your name, lead me and guide me!

4 Draw me out of the net they have spread for me,
    for you are my refuge.
5 to your hands I commit my spirit,
    by you have I been redeemed.

6 You hate[z] those who pay regard to worthless
    idols,
    but I trust in the LORD.
7 I will exult and rejoice in your steadfast love,
    because you have seen my affliction;
    you have taken heed of my adversities,
8 and have not delivered me into the hand of the
    enemy;
    you have set my feet in a broad place.

9 Be gracious to me, O LORD, for I am in distress;
    my eye wastes away from grief,
    my soul and body also.
10 For my life is spent with sorrow,
    and my years with sighing;
    my strength fails because of my misery,[a]
    and my bones waste away.

11 I am the scorn of all my adversaries,
    a horror[b] to my neighbors,
    an object of dread to my acquaintances;
    those who see me in the street flee from me.
12 I have passed out of mind like one who is dead;
    I have become like a broken vessel.
13 For I hear the whispering of many—
    terror all around!—
    as they scheme together against me,
    as they plot to take my life.

14 But I trust in you, O LORD;
    I say, "You are my God."
15 My times are in your hand;
    deliver me from the hand of my enemies and
    persecutors.
16 Let your face shine upon your servant;
    save me in your steadfast love.
17 Do not let me be put to shame, O LORD,
    for I call on you;
    let the wicked be put to shame;
    let them go dumbfounded to Sheol.
18 Let the lying lips be stilled
    that speak insolently against the righteous
    with pride and contempt.

19 O how abundant is your goodness
    that you have laid up for those who fear you,
    and accomplished for those who take refuge in
    you,
    in the sight of everyone!
20 In the shelter of your presence you hide them
    from human plots;
    you hold them safe under your shelter
    from contentious tongues.

21 Blessed be the LORD,
    for he has wondrously shown his steadfast love
    to me
    when I was beset as a city under siege.
22 I had said in my alarm,
    "I am driven far[c] from your sight."
    But you heard my supplications
    when I cried out to you for help.

23 Love the LORD, all you his saints.
    The LORD preserves the faithful,
    but abundantly repays the one who acts
    haughtily.
24 Be strong, and let your heart take courage,
    all you who wait for the LORD.

6 I hate all who worship worthless idols;
    I for my part put my trust in the LORD.
7 I shall rejoice and be glad in your unfailing love,
    for you have seen my affliction
    and have cared for me in my distress.
8 You have not abandoned me to the power of the
    enemy,
    but have set me where I have untrammelled liberty.

9 Be gracious to me, LORD, for I am in distress
    and my eyes are dimmed with grief.
10 My life is worn away with sorrow
    and my years with sighing;
    through misery my strength falters
    and my bones waste away.
11 I am scorned by all my enemies,
    my neighbours find me burdensome,
    my friends shudder at me;
    when they see me on the street they turn away
    quickly.
12 Like the dead I have passed out of mind;
    I have become like some article thrown away.
13 For I hear many
    whispering threats from every side,
    conspiring together against me
    and scheming to take my life.

14 But in you, LORD, I put my trust;
    I say, 'You are my God.'
15 My fortunes are in your hand;
    rescue me from the power of my enemies
    and those who persecute me.
16 Let your face shine on your servant;
    save me in your unfailing love.
17 LORD, do not humiliate me when I call to you;
    let humiliation be for the wicked,
    let them sink into Sheol.
18 May lying lips be struck dumb,
    lips speaking with contempt against the righteous
    in pride and arrogance.

19 How great is your goodness,
    stored up for those who fear you,
    made manifest before mortal eyes
    for all who turn to you for shelter.
20 You will hide them under the cover of your
    presence
    from those who conspire together;
    you keep them in your shelter,
    safe from contentious tongues.

21 Blessed be the LORD,
    whose unfailing love for me was wonderful
    when I was in sore straits.
22 In sudden alarm I said,
    'I am shut out from your sight.'
    But you heard my plea
    when I called to you for help.
23 Love the LORD, all you his loyal servants.
    The LORD protects the faithful,
    but the arrogant he repays in full.
24 Be strong and stout-hearted,
    all you whose hope is in the LORD.

---

[z] One Heb Ms Gk Syr Jerome: MT *I hate*   [a] Gk Syr: Heb *my iniquity*
[b] Cn: Heb *exceedingly*   [c] Another reading is *cut off*

31:9 **grief**: *prob. rdg; Heb.* adds my throat and my belly.
31:10 **misery**: *prob. rdg; Heb.* iniquity.   31:17 **Sheol**: *or the*
underworld.   31:21 **when . . . straits**: *lit.* in a city besieged.

7 You hate those who serve worthless idols,
   but I trust in the LORD.
8 I will rejoice and be glad in your love,
   once you have seen my misery,
   observed my distress.
9 You will not abandon me into enemy hands,
   but will set my feet in a free and open space.

II

10 Be gracious to me, LORD, for I am in distress;
   with grief my eyes are wasted,
   my soul and body spent.
11 My life is worn out by sorrow,
   my years by sighing.
   My strength fails in affliction;
   my bones are consumed.
12 To all my foes I am a thing of scorn,
   to my neighbors, a dreaded sight,
   a horror to my friends.
   When they see me in the street,
   they quickly shy away.
13 I am forgotten, out of mind like the dead;
   I am like a shattered dish.
14 I hear the whispers of the crowd;
   terrors are all around me.
   They conspire against me;
   they plot to take my life.
15 But I trust in you, LORD;
   I say, "You are my God."
16 My times are in your hands;
   rescue me from my enemies,
   from the hands of my pursuers.
17 Let your face shine on your servant;
   save me in your kindness.
18 Do not let me be put to shame,
   for I have called to you, LORD.
   Put the wicked to shame;
   reduce them to silence in Sheol.
19 Strike dumb their lying lips,
   proud lips that attack the just
   in contempt and scorn.

III

20 How great is your goodness, LORD,
   stored up for those who fear you.
   You display it for those who trust you,
   in the sight of all the people.
21 You hide them in the shelter of your presence,
   safe from scheming enemies.
   You keep them in your abode,
   safe from plotting tongues.
22 Blessed be the LORD,
   who has shown me wondrous love,
   and been for me a city most secure.
23 Once I said in my anguish,
   "I am shut out from your sight."
   Yet you heard my plea,
   when I cried out to you.
24 Love the LORD, all you faithful.
   The LORD protects the loyal,
   but repays the arrogant in full.
25 Be strong and take heart,
   all you who hope in the LORD.

God of truth, 6 you hate
those who serve useless idols;
   but my trust is in Yahweh:
7 I will delight and rejoice in your faithful love!

You, who have seen my misery,
   and witnessed the miseries of my soul,
8 have not handed me over to the enemy,
   but have given me freedom to roam at large.

9 Take pity on me, Yahweh,
   for I am in trouble.
   Vexation is gnawing away my eyes,
   my soul deep within me.

10 For my life is worn out with sorrow,
   and my years with sighs.
   My strength gives way under my misery,
   and my bones are all wasted away.

11 The sheer number of my enemies
   makes me contemptible,
   loathsome to my neighbours,
   and my friends shrink from me in horror.

When people see me in the street
   they take to their heels.
12 I have no more place in their hearts than a corpse,
   or something lost.

13 All I hear is slander
   —terror wherever I turn—
   as they plot together against me,
   scheming to take my life.

14 But my trust is in you, Yahweh;
   I say, 'You are my God,'
15 every moment of my life is in your hands, rescue
   me
   from the clutches of my foes who pursue me;
16 let your face shine on your servant,
   save me in your faithful love.

17 I call on you, Yahweh, so let disgrace fall not on
   me,
   but on the wicked.
   Let them go down to Sheol in silence,
18   muzzles on their lying mouths,
   which speak arrogantly against the upright
   in pride and contempt.

19 Yahweh, what quantities of good things
   you have in store for those who fear you,
   and bestow on those who make you their refuge,
   for all humanity to see.

20 Safe in your presence you hide them,
   far from human plotting,
   shielding them in your tent,
   far from contentious tongues.

21 Blessed be Yahweh who works for me
   miracles of his faithful love
   (in a fortified city)!
22 In a state of terror I cried,
   'I have been cut off from your sight!'
   Yet you heard my plea for help
   when I cried out to you.

23 Love Yahweh, all his faithful:
   Yahweh protects his loyal servants,
   but he repays the arrogant
   with interest.
24 Be brave, take heart,
   all who put your hope in Yahweh.

Psalm 32

Of David. A Maskil.

1 Happy are those whose transgression is forgiven,
  whose sin is covered.
2 Happy are those to whom the LORD imputes no
    iniquity,
  and in whose spirit there is no deceit.

3 While I kept silence, my body wasted away
  through my groaning all day long.
4 For day and night your hand was heavy upon me;
  my strength was dried up*d* as by the heat of
    summer.   *Selah*

5 Then I acknowledged my sin to you,
  and I did not hide my iniquity;
 I said, "I will confess my transgressions to the
    LORD,"
  and you forgave the guilt of my sin.   *Selah*

6 Therefore let all who are faithful
    offer prayer to you;
 at a time of distress,*e* the rush of mighty waters
  shall not reach them.
7 You are a hiding place for me;
  you preserve me from trouble;
  you surround me with glad cries of
    deliverance.   *Selah*

8 I will instruct you and teach you the way you
    should go;
  I will counsel you with my eye upon you.
9 Do not be like a horse or a mule, without
    understanding,
  whose temper must be curbed with bit and
    bridle,
  else it will not stay near you.

10 Many are the torments of the wicked,
  but steadfast love surrounds those who trust in
    the LORD.
11 Be glad in the LORD and rejoice, O righteous,
  and shout for joy, all you upright in heart.

Psalm 33

1 Rejoice in the LORD, O you righteous.
  Praise befits the upright.
2 Praise the LORD with the lyre;
  make melody to him with the harp of ten
    strings.
3 Sing to him a new song;
  play skillfully on the strings, with loud shouts.

4 For the word of the LORD is upright,
  and all his work is done in faithfulness.
5 He loves righteousness and justice;
  the earth is full of the steadfast love of the
    LORD.

6 By the word of the LORD the heavens were made,
  and all their host by the breath of his mouth.
7 He gathered the waters of the sea as in a bottle;
  he put the deeps in storehouses.

8 Let all the earth fear the LORD;
  let all the inhabitants of the world stand in awe
    of him.
9 For he spoke, and it came to be;
  he commanded, and it stood firm.

d Meaning of Heb uncertain   *e* Cn: Heb *at a time of finding only*

Psalm 32

For David: a maskil

1 HAPPY is he whose offence is forgiven,
  whose sin is blotted out!
2 Happy is he to whom the LORD imputes no fault,
  in whose spirit there is no deceit.

3 While I refused to speak, my body wasted away
  with day-long moaning.
4 For day and night
  your hand was heavy upon me;
  the sap in me dried up as in summer drought.
                                              [*Selah*

5 When I acknowledged my sin to you,
  when I no longer concealed my guilt,
  but said, 'I shall confess my offence to the LORD,'
  then you for your part remitted the penalty of my
    sin.   [*Selah*
6 So let every faithful heart pray to you
  in the hour of anxiety;
  when great floods threaten
  they shall not touch him.
7 You are a hiding-place for me from distress;
  you guard me and enfold me in salvation.   [*Selah*

8 I shall teach you and guide you in the way you
    should go.
  I shall keep you under my eye.
9 Do not behave like a horse or a mule, unreasoning
    creatures
  whose mettle must be curbed with bit and bridle,
  so that they do not come near you.
10 Many are the torments for the ungodly,
  but unfailing love enfolds those who trust in the
    LORD.
11 Rejoice in the LORD and be glad, you righteous
    ones;
  sing aloud, all you of honest heart.

Psalm 33

For David

1 SHOUT for joy in the LORD, you that are righteous;
  praise comes well from the upright.
2 Give thanks to the LORD on the lyre;
  make music to him on the ten-stringed harp.
3 Sing to him a new song;
  strike up with all your skill and shout in triumph,
4 for the word of the LORD holds true,
  and all his work endures.
5 He is a lover of righteousness and justice;
  the earth is filled with the LORD's unfailing love.

6 The word of the LORD created the heavens;
  all the host of heaven was formed at his command.
7 He gathered into a heap the waters of the sea,
  he laid up the deeps in his store-chambers.
8 Let the whole world fear the LORD
  and all earth's inhabitants stand in awe of him.
9 For he spoke, and it was;
  he commanded, and there it stood.

32:6 **of anxiety:** *prob. rdg; Heb.* unintelligible.   32:7 **you guard
me:** *prob. rdg; Heb.* adds an unintelligible word.   33:heading So
Gk; Heb. omits.

NEW AMERICAN BIBLE

Psalm 32

Of David. A maskil.

I

Happy the sinner whose fault is removed,
  whose sin is forgiven.
2 Happy those to whom the LORD imputes no guilt,
  in whose spirit is no deceit.

II

3 As long as I kept silent, my bones wasted away;
  I groaned all the day.
4 For day and night your hand was heavy upon me;
  my strength withered as in dry summer heat.
                                              Selah

5 Then I declared my sin to you;
  my guilt I did not hide.
I said, "I confess my faults to the LORD,"
  and you took away the guilt of my sin.   *Selah*
6 Thus should all your faithful pray
  in time of distress.
Though flood waters threaten,
  they will never reach them.
7 You are my shelter; from distress you keep me;
  with safety you ring me round.   *Selah*

III

8 I will instruct you and show you the way you
    should walk,
  give you counsel and watch over you.
9 Do not be senseless like horses or mules;
  with bit and bridle their temper is curbed,
  else they will not come to you.

IV

10 Many are the sorrows of the wicked,
  but love surrounds those who trust in the LORD.
11 Be glad in the LORD and rejoice, you just;
  exult, all you upright of heart.

Psalm 33

I

1 Rejoice, you just, in the LORD;
  praise from the upright is fitting.
2 Give thanks to the LORD on the harp;
  on the ten-stringed lyre offer praise.
3 Sing to God a new song;
  skillfully play with joyful chant.
4 For the LORD's word is true;
  all his works are trustworthy.
5 The LORD loves justice and right
  and fills the earth with goodness.

II

6 By the LORD's word the heavens were made;
  by the breath of his mouth all their host.
7 The waters of the sea were gathered as in a bowl;
  in cellars the deep was confined.

III

8 Let all the earth fear the LORD;
  let all who dwell in the world show reverence.
9 For he spoke, and it came to be,
  commanded, and it stood in place.

NEW JERUSALEM BIBLE

Psalm 32 (V 31)

Of David   Poem

1 How blessed are those whose offence is forgiven,
  whose sin blotted out.
2 How blessed are those to whom Yahweh imputes
    no guilt,
  whose spirit harbours no deceit.

3 I said not a word, but my bones wasted away
  from groaning all the day;
4 day and night
  your hand lay heavy upon me;
my heart grew parched as stubble
  in summer drought.   *Pause*

5 I made my sin known to you,
  did not conceal my guilt.
I said, 'I shall confess
  my offence to Yahweh.'
And you, for your part, took away my guilt,
  forgave my sin.   *Pause*

6 That is why each of your faithful ones prays to you
  in time of distress.
Even if great floods overflow,
  they will never reach your faithful.
7 You are a refuge for me,
  you guard me in trouble,
  with songs of deliverance you surround me. *Pause*

8 I shall instruct you and teach you the way to go;
  I shall not take my eyes off you.

9 Be not like a horse or a mule;
  that does not understand bridle or bit;
  if you advance to master them,
  there is no means of bringing them near.

10 Countless troubles are in store for the wicked,
  but one who trusts in Yahweh is enfolded in his
    faithful love.

11   Rejoice in Yahweh,
    exult all you upright,
    shout for joy, you honest of heart.

Psalm 33 (V 32)

1 Shout for joy, you upright;
  praise comes well from the honest.
2 Give thanks to Yahweh on the lyre,
  play for him on the ten-stringed lyre.
3 Sing to him a new song,
  make sweet music for your cry of victory.

4 The word of Yahweh is straightforward,
  all he does springs from his constancy.
5 He loves uprightness and justice;
  the faithful love of Yahweh fills the earth.

6 By the word of Yahweh the heavens were made,
  by the breath of his mouth all their array.
7 He collects the waters of the sea like a dam,
  he stores away the abyss in his treasure-house.

8 Let the whole earth fear Yahweh,
  let all who dwell in the world revere him;
9 for, the moment he spoke, it was so,
  no sooner had he commanded, than there it stood!

NEW REVISED STANDARD VERSION

10 The Lord brings the counsel of the nations to
     nothing;
    he frustrates the plans of the peoples.
11 The counsel of the Lord stands forever,
    the thoughts of his heart to all generations.
12 Happy is the nation whose God is the Lord,
    the people whom he has chosen as his heritage.
13 The Lord looks down from heaven;
    he sees all humankind.
14 From where he sits enthroned he watches
    all the inhabitants of the earth—
15 he who fashions the hearts of them all,
    and observes all their deeds.
16 A king is not saved by his great army;
    a warrior is not delivered by his great strength.
17 The war horse is a vain hope for victory,
    and by its great might it cannot save.
18 Truly the eye of the Lord is on those who fear
     him,
    on those who hope in his steadfast love,
19 to deliver their soul from death,
    and to keep them alive in famine.

20 Our soul waits for the Lord;
    he is our help and shield.
21 Our heart is glad in him,
    because we trust in his holy name.
22 Let your steadfast love, O Lord, be upon us,
    even as we hope in you.

Psalm 34

*Of David, when he feigned madness before Abimelech, so
that he drove him out, and he went away.*

1 I will bless the Lord at all times;
    his praise shall continually be in my mouth.
2 My soul makes its boast in the Lord;
    let the humble hear and be glad.
3 O magnify the Lord with me,
    and let us exalt his name together.
4 I sought the Lord, and he answered me,
    and delivered me from all my fears.
5 Look to him, and be radiant;
    so your*f* faces shall never be ashamed.
6 This poor soul cried, and was heard by the Lord,
    and was saved from every trouble.
7 The angel of the Lord encamps
    around those who fear him, and delivers them.
8 O taste and see that the Lord is good;
    happy are those who take refuge in him.
9 O fear the Lord, you his holy ones,
    for those who fear him have no want.
10 The young lions suffer want and hunger,
    but those who seek the Lord lack no good
     thing.

11 Come, O children, listen to me;
    I will teach you the fear of the Lord.
12 Which of you desires life,
    and covets many days to enjoy good?
13 Keep your tongue from evil,
    and your lips from speaking deceit.
14 Depart from evil, and do good;
    seek peace, and pursue it.

REVISED ENGLISH BIBLE

10 The Lord frustrates the purposes of nations;
    he foils the plans of the peoples.
11 But the Lord's own purpose stands for ever,
    and the plans he has in mind endure for all
     generations.
12 Happy is the nation whose God is the Lord,
    the people he has chosen for his own.
13 The Lord looks out from heaven;
    he sees the whole race of mortals,
14 he surveys from his dwelling-place
    all the inhabitants of the earth.
15 It is he who fashions the hearts of them all,
    who discerns everything they do.
16 No king is saved by a great army,
    no warrior delivered by great strength.
17 No one can rely on his horse to save him,
    nor for all its power can it be a means of escape.
18 The Lord's eyes are turned towards those who fear
     him,
    towards those who hope for his unfailing love
19 to deliver them from death,
    and in famine to preserve them alive.

20 We have waited eagerly for the Lord;
    he is our help and our shield.
21 In him our hearts are glad,
    because we have trusted in his holy name.
22 Lord, let your unfailing love rest on us,
    as we have put our hope in you.

Psalm 34

*For David (when he feigned madness in Abimelech's
presence; Abimelech then drove him away, and he
departed)*

1 I shall bless the Lord at all times;
    his praise will be ever on my lips.
2 In the Lord I shall glory;
    the humble will hear and be glad.
3 Glorify the Lord with me;
    let us exalt his name together.
4 I sought the Lord's help; he answered me
    and set me free from all my fears.
5 They who look to him are radiant with joy;
    they will never be put out of countenance.
6 Here is one who cried out in his affliction;
    the Lord heard him and saved him from all his
     troubles.
7 The angel of the Lord is on guard
    round those who fear him, and he rescues them.
8 Taste and see that the Lord is good.
    Happy are they who find refuge in him!
9 Fear the Lord, you his holy people;
    those who fear him lack for nothing.
10 Princes may suffer want and go hungry,
    but those who seek the Lord lack no good thing.

11 Come, children, listen to me;
    I shall teach you the fear of the Lord.
12 Which of you delights in life
    and desires a long life to enjoy prosperity?
13 Then keep your tongue from evil
    and your lips from telling lies;
14 shun evil and do good;
    seek peace and pursue it.

---

f Gk Syr Jerome: Heb *their*

34:10 **Princes:** *or* Unbelievers.

NEW AMERICAN BIBLE

10 The LORD foils the plan of nations,
   frustrates the designs of peoples.
11 But the plan of the LORD stands forever,
   wise designs through all generations.
12 Happy the nation whose God is the LORD,
   the people chosen as his very own.

   IV
13 From heaven the LORD looks down
   and observes the whole human race,
14 Surveying from the royal throne
   all who dwell on earth.
15 The one who fashioned the hearts of them all
   knows all their works.

   V
16 A king is not saved by a mighty army,
   nor a warrior delivered by great strength.
17 Useless is the horse for safety;
   its great strength, no sure escape.
18 But the LORD's eyes are upon the reverent,
   upon those who hope for his gracious help,
19 Delivering them from death,
   keeping them alive in times of famine.

   VI
20 Our soul waits for the LORD,
   who is our help and shield.
21 For in God our hearts rejoice;
   in your holy name we trust.
22 May your kindness, LORD, be upon us;
   we have put our hope in you.

Psalm 34

1 *Of David, when he feigned madness before Abimelech,*
who forced him to depart.

   I
2 I will bless the LORD at all times;
   praise shall be always in my mouth.
3 My soul will glory in the LORD
   that the poor may hear and be glad.
4 Magnify the LORD with me;
   let us exalt his name together.

   II
5 I sought the LORD, who answered me,
   delivered me from all my fears.
6 Look to God that you may be radiant with joy
   and your faces may not blush for shame.
7 In my misfortune I called,
   the LORD heard and saved me from all distress.
8 The angel of the LORD, who encamps with them,
   delivers all who fear God.
9 Learn to savor how good the LORD is;
   happy are those who take refuge in him.
10 Fear the LORD, you holy ones;
   nothing is lacking to those who fear him.
11 The powerful grow poor and hungry,
   but those who seek the LORD lack no good
      thing.

   III
12 Come, children, listen to me;
   I will teach you the fear of the LORD.
13 Who among you loves life,
   takes delight in prosperous days?
14 Keep your tongue from evil,
   your lips from speaking lies.
15 Turn from evil and do good;
   seek peace and pursue it.

NEW JERUSALEM BIBLE

10 Yahweh thwarts the plans of nations,
   frustrates the counsels of peoples;
11 but Yahweh's own plan stands firm for ever,
   his heart's counsel from age to age.
12 How blessed the nation whose God is Yahweh,
   the people he has chosen as his heritage.

13 From heaven Yahweh looks down,
   he sees all the children of Adam,
14 from the place where he sits he watches
   all who dwell on the earth;
15 he alone moulds their hearts,
   he understands all they do.

16 A large army will not keep a king safe,
   nor his strength save a warrior's life;
17 it is delusion to rely on a horse for safety,
   for all its power it cannot save.
18 But see how Yahweh watches over those who fear
      him,
   those who rely on his faithful love,
19 to rescue them from death
   and keep them alive in famine.

20 We are waiting for Yahweh;
   he is our help and our shield,
21 for in him our heart rejoices,
   in his holy name we trust.
22 Yahweh, let your faithful love rest on us,
   as our hope has rested in you.

Psalm 34 (V 33)

Of David, when he had feigned insanity before Abimelech,
and Abimelech sent him away

Aleph	1 I will bless Yahweh at all times, his praise continually on my lips.
Bet	2 I will praise Yahweh from my heart; let the humble hear and rejoice.
Gimel	3 Proclaim with me the greatness of Yahweh, let us acclaim his name together.
Dalet	4 I seek Yahweh and he answers me, frees me from all my fears.
He	5 Fix your gaze on Yahweh and your face will grow bright, you will never hang your head in shame.
Zain	6 A pauper calls out and Yahweh hears, saves him from all his troubles.
Het	7 The angel of Yahweh encamps around those who fear him, and rescues them.
Tet	8 Taste and see that Yahweh is good. How blessed are those who take refuge in him.
Yod	9 Fear Yahweh, you his holy ones; those who fear him lack for nothing.
Kaph	10 Young lions may go needy and hungry, but those who seek Yahweh lack nothing good.
Lamed	11 Come, my children, listen to me, I will teach you the fear of Yahweh.
Mem	12 Who among you delights in life, longs for time to enjoy prosperity?
Nun	13 Guard your tongue from evil, your lips from any breath of deceit.
Samek	14 Turn away from evil and do good, seek peace and pursue it.

NEW REVISED STANDARD VERSION

15 The eyes of the LORD are on the righteous,
and his ears are open to their cry.
16 The face of the LORD is against evildoers,
to cut off the remembrance of them from the
earth.
17 When the righteous cry for help, the LORD hears,
and rescues them from all their troubles.
18 The LORD is near to the brokenhearted,
and saves the crushed in spirit.

19 Many are the afflictions of the righteous,
but the LORD rescues them from them all.
20 He keeps all their bones;
not one of them will be broken.
21 Evil brings death to the wicked,
and those who hate the righteous will be
condemned.
22 The LORD redeems the life of his servants;
none of those who take refuge in him will be
condemned.

Psalm 35

Of David.

1 Contend, O LORD, with those who contend with
me;
fight against those who fight against me!
2 Take hold of shield and buckler,
and rise up to help me!
3 Draw the spear and javelin
against my pursuers;
say to my soul,
"I am your salvation."

4 Let them be put to shame and dishonor
who seek after my life.
Let them be turned back and confounded
who devise evil against me.
5 Let them be like chaff before the wind,
with the angel of the LORD driving them on.
6 Let their way be dark and slippery,
with the angel of the LORD pursuing them.

7 For without cause they hid their net*g* for me;
without cause they dug a pit*h* for my life.
8 Let ruin come on them unawares.
And let the net that they hid ensnare them;
let them fall in it — to their ruin.

9 Then my soul shall rejoice in the LORD,
exulting in his deliverance.
10 All my bones shall say,
"O LORD, who is like you?
You deliver the weak
from those too strong for them,
the weak and needy from those who despoil
them."

11 Malicious witnesses rise up;
they ask me about things I do not know.
12 They repay me evil for good;
my soul is forlorn.
13 But as for me, when they were sick,
I wore sackcloth;
I afflicted myself with fasting.
I prayed with head bowed*i* on my bosom,

g Heb *a pit, their net*   *h* The word *pit* is transposed from the
preceding line   *i* Or *My prayer turned back*

REVISED ENGLISH BIBLE

15 The eyes of the LORD are on the righteous;
his ears are open to their cry.
16 The LORD sets his face against wrongdoers
to cut off all memory of them from the earth.
17 When the righteous cry for help, the LORD hears
and sets them free from all their troubles.
18 The LORD is close to those whose courage is
broken;
he saves those whose spirit is crushed.
19 Though the misfortunes of one who is righteous be
many,
the LORD delivers him out of them all.
20 He guards every bone of his body,
and not one of them will be broken.
21 Misfortune will bring death to the wicked,
and punishment befalls those who hate the
righteous.
22 The LORD delivers the lives of his servants,
and no punishment befalls those who seek refuge
in him.

Psalm 35

For David

1 STRIVE against those who strive against me, LORD;
fight those who fight against me.
2 Grasp shield and buckler,
and rise to my aid.
3 Brandish spear and axe
against my pursuers.
Let me hear you declare,
'I am your salvation.'

4 May shame and disgrace cover those who seek my
life;
may those who plan my downfall retreat in dismay!
5 May they be like chaff before the wind,
driven away by the angel of the LORD!
6 Let their path be dark and slippery
with the angel of the LORD pursuing them!
7 For unprovoked they have hidden a net to catch
me,
unprovoked they have dug a pit to trap me.
8 May destruction unforeseen come upon them;
may the net which they hid catch them;
may they fall into the pit and be destroyed!

9 Then I shall rejoice in the LORD
and delight in his salvation.
10 My whole frame cries out,
'LORD, who is there like you,
saviour of the oppressed from those too strong for
them,
of the oppressed and poor from those who prey on
them?'
11 Malicious witnesses come forward
and question me on matters of which I know
nothing.
12 They return me evil for good,
lying in wait to take my life.
13 Yet when they were ill, I put on sackcloth,
I mortified myself with fasting.
When my prayer came back unanswered,

35:3 **axe:** *so Scroll; Heb.* bar the way.   35:7 **a net:** *prob. rdg,*
transposing a pit *from this line to follow* have dug.   35:12 **lying**
. . . life: *prob. rdg; Heb.* bereavement for me.

NEW AMERICAN BIBLE

16 The LORD has eyes for the just
and ears for their cry.
17 The LORD's face is against evildoers
to wipe out their memory from the earth.
18 When the just cry out, the LORD hears
and rescues them from all distress.
19 The LORD is close to the brokenhearted,
saves those whose spirit is crushed.
20 Many are the troubles of the just,
but the LORD delivers from them all.
21 God watches over all their bones;
not a one shall be broken.
22 Evil will slay the wicked;
those who hate the just are condemned.
23 The LORD redeems loyal servants,
no one is condemned whose refuge is God.

Psalm 35

1 *Of David.*

I

Oppose, LORD, those who oppose me;
war upon those who make war upon me.
2 Take up the shield and buckler;
rise up in my defense.
3 Brandish lance and battle-ax
against my pursuers.
Say to my heart,
"I am your salvation."
4 Let those who seek my life
be put to shame and disgrace.
Let those who plot evil against me
be turned back and confounded.
5 Make them like chaff before the wind,
with the angel of the LORD driving them on.
6 Make their way slippery and dark,
with the angel of the LORD pursuing them.

II

7 Without cause they set their snare for me;
without cause they dug a pit for me.
8 Let ruin overtake them unawares;
let the snare they have set catch them;
let them fall into the pit they have dug.
9 Then I will rejoice in the LORD,
exult in God's salvation.
10 My very bones shall say,
"O LORD, who is like you,
Who rescue the afflicted from the powerful,
the afflicted and needy from the despoiler?"

III

11 Malicious witnesses come forward,
accuse me of things I do not know.
12 They repay me evil for good
and I am all alone.
13 Yet I, when they were ill, put on sackcloth,
afflicted myself with fasting,
sobbed my prayers upon my bosom.

NEW JERUSALEM BIBLE

Ain 15 The eyes of Yahweh are on the upright,
his ear turned to their cry.
Pe 16 But Yahweh's face is set against those who
do evil,
to cut off the memory of them from the earth.
Zade 17 They cry in anguish and Yahweh hears,
and rescues them from all their troubles.
Qoph 18 Yahweh is near to the broken-hearted,
he helps those whose spirit is crushed.
Resh 19 Though hardships without number beset the
upright,
Yahweh brings rescue from them all.
Shin 20 Yahweh takes care of all their bones,
not one of them will be broken.
Taw 21 But to the wicked evil brings death,
those who hate the upright will pay the
penalty.
22 Yahweh ransoms the lives of those who serve
him,
and there will be no penalty for those who
take refuge in him.

Psalm 35 (V 34)

Of David

1 Accuse my accusers, Yahweh,
attack my attackers.
2 Grasp your buckler and shield,
up, and help me.
3 Brandish spear and pike
to confront my pursuers,
give me the assurance, 'I am your Saviour.'

4 Shame and humiliation on those
who are out to kill me!
Defeat and repulse in dismay
on those who plot my downfall.

5 May they be like chaff before the wind,
with the angel of Yahweh to chase them.
6 May their way be dark and slippery,
with the angel of Yahweh to hound them.

7 Unprovoked they laid their snare for me,
unprovoked dug a trap to kill me.
8 Ruin comes upon them unawares;
the snare they have laid will catch them,
and into their own trap they will fall.

9 Then I shall delight in Yahweh,
rejoice that he has saved me.
10 My very bones will all exclaim,
Yahweh, who can compare with you
in rescuing the poor from the oppressor;
the needy from the exploiter?

11 False witnesses come forward against me
asking me questions I cannot answer,
they cross-examine me, 12 repay my kindness with
cruelty,
make my life barren.

13 But I, when they were ill, had worn sackcloth,
and mortified myself with fasting,
praying ever anew in my heart,

NEW REVISED STANDARD VERSION

REVISED ENGLISH BIBLE

14   as though I grieved for a friend or a brother;
I went about as one who laments for a mother,
     bowed down and in mourning.

15 But at my stumbling they gathered in glee,
they gathered together against me;
ruffians whom I did not know
tore at me without ceasing;

16 they impiously mocked more and more, *j*
gnashing at me with their teeth.

17 How long, O LORD, will you look on?
Rescue me from their ravages,
my life from the lions!

18 Then I will thank you in the great congregation;
in the mighty throng I will praise you.

19 Do not let my treacherous enemies rejoice over
     me,
or those who hate me without cause wink the
     eye.

20 For they do not speak peace,
but they conceive deceitful words
against those who are quiet in the land.

21 They open wide their mouths against me;
they say, "Aha, Aha,
our eyes have seen it."

22 You have seen, O LORD; do not be silent!
O Lord, do not be far from me!

23 Wake up! Bestir yourself for my defense,
for my cause, my God and my Lord!

24 Vindicate me, O LORD, my God,
according to your righteousness,
and do not let them rejoice over me.

25 Do not let them say to themselves,
"Aha, we have our heart's desire."
Do not let them say, "We have swallowed you *k*
up."

26 Let all those who rejoice at my calamity
be put to shame and confusion;
let those who exalt themselves against me
be clothed with shame and dishonor.

27 Let those who desire my vindication
shout for joy and be glad,
and say evermore,
"Great is the LORD,
who delights in the welfare of his servant."

28 Then my tongue shall tell of your righteousness
and of your praise all day long.

14 I walked with head bowed in grief as if for a
     brother;
as one in sorrow for his mother I lay prostrate in
     mourning.

15 But when I stumbled, they crowded round
     rejoicing,
they crowded about me;
unknown assailants jeered at me
and nothing would stop them.

16 When I slipped, they mocked and derided me,
grinding their teeth at me.

17 Lord, how long will you look on?
Rescue me from those who would destroy me,
save my precious life from the powerful.

18 Then I shall praise you in the great assembly,
I shall extol you in a large congregation.

19 Let no treacherous enemy gloat over me;
let not those who hate me for no reason leer at me.

20 Their words are hostile
and against the peaceful they hatch intrigues.

21 They open their mouths and shout at me:
'Hurrah! What a sight for us to see!'

22 You have seen all this, LORD; do not keep silence.
Lord, be not far aloof from me.

23 Awake, rouse yourself, my God, my Lord,
to vindicate me and plead my cause.

24 Judge me, LORD my God, as you are righteous;
do not let them gloat over me.

25 Do not let them say to themselves,
'Hurrah! We have got our wish,
we have swallowed him up!'

26 Let all who rejoice at my downfall
be discomfited and dismayed;
let those who glory over me
be covered with shame and dishonour.

27 But let all who want to see me vindicated shout for
     joy,
let them cry continually,
'All glory to the LORD
who wants to see his servant prosper!'

28 And I shall declare your saving power
and your praise all the day long.

Psalm 36

To the leader. Of David, the servant of the LORD.

1 Transgression speaks to the wicked
deep in their hearts;
there is no fear of God
before their eyes.

2 For they flatter themselves in their own eyes
that their iniquity cannot be found out and
hated.

3 The words of their mouths are mischief and
deceit;
they have ceased to act wisely and do good.

4 They plot mischief while on their beds;
they are set on a way that is not good;
they do not reject evil.

Psalm 36

For the leader: for the LORD's servant: for David

1 A WICKED person's talk is prompted by sin in his
     heart;
he sees no need to fear God.

2 For it flatters and deceives him
and, when his iniquity is found out, he does not
change.

3 Everything he says is mischievous and false;
he has lost all understanding of right conduct;

4 he lies in bed planning the mischief he will do.
So set is he on his evil course
that he rejects no wickedness.

---

j Cn Compare Gk: Heb *like the profanest of mockers of a cake*
k Heb *him*

35:15 **unknown assailants:** *or* assailants who give me no rest.
35:16 **and derided me:** *so Gk; Heb. obscure.*   36:1 **his:** *so some
MSS; others* my.   36:2 **he . . . change:** *prob. rdg; Heb.
unintelligible.*

NEW AMERICAN BIBLE

NEW JERUSALEM BIBLE

14 I went about in grief as for my brother,
  bent in mourning as for my mother.
15 Yet when I stumbled they gathered with glee,
  gathered against me like strangers.
  They slandered me without ceasing;
16 without respect they mocked me,
  gnashed their teeth against me.

IV

17 Lord, how long will you look on?
  Save me from roaring beasts,
  my precious life from lions!
18 Then I will thank you in the great assembly;
  I will praise you before the mighty throng.
19 Do not let lying foes smirk at me,
  my undeserved enemies wink knowingly.
20 They speak no words of peace,
  but against the quiet in the land
  they fashion deceitful speech.
21 They open wide their mouths against me.
  They say, "Aha! Good!
  Our eyes relish the sight!"
22 You see this, LORD; do not be silent;
  Lord, do not withdraw from me.
23 Awake, be vigilant in my defense,
  in my cause, my God and my Lord.
24 Defend me because you are just, LORD;
  my God, do not let them gloat over me.
25 Do not let them say in their hearts,
  "Aha! Just what we wanted!"
  Do not let them say,
  "We have devoured that one!"
26 Put to shame and confound
  all who relish my misfortune.
  Clothe with shame and disgrace
  those who lord it over me.
27 But let those who favor my just cause
  shout for joy and be glad.
  May they ever say, "Exalted be the LORD
  who delights in the peace of his loyal servant."
28 Then my tongue shall recount your justice,
  declare your praise, all the day long.

14 as if for a friend or brother; I had wandered
  restless,
  as if mourning a mother,
  so bowed had I been in sorrow.

15 When I stumble they gather in glee,
  gather around me;
  strangers I never even knew
  tear me apart incessantly.
16 If I fall they surround me,
  grinding their teeth at me.

17 How much longer, Lord, will you look on?
  Rescue me from their onslaughts,
  from young lions rescue the one life that I have.
18 I will give you thanks in the great assembly
  praise you where the people gather.

19 Let not my lying enemies
  gloat over me;
  those who hate me unprovoked
  look askance at me.

20 They have no greeting of peace
  to the peace-loving people of the land;
  they think up deceptive speeches.
21 Their mouths wide open to accuse me,
  they say, 'Come on now, we saw you.'

22 You saw it, Yahweh, do not stay silent;
  Lord, do not stand aloof from me.
23 Up, awake, to my defence,
  my God and my Lord, to my cause.
24 In your saving justice give judgement for me,
  Yahweh my God,
  and do not let them gloat over me.

25 Do not let them think, 'Just as we hoped,'
  nor, 'Now we have swallowed him up.'
26 Shame and dismay on them all
  who gloat over my misfortunes.
  Let all who profit at my expense
  be covered with shame and disgrace.

27 But let all who delight in my uprightness
  shout for joy and gladness;
  let them constantly say,
  'Great is Yahweh,
  who delights to see his servant in peace.'
28 And my tongue shall recount your saving justice,
  all day long sing your praise.

Psalm 36

1 For the leader. Of David, the servant of the LORD.

I

2 Sin directs the heart of the wicked;
  their eyes are closed to the fear of God.
3 For they live with the delusion:
  their guilt will not be known and hated.
4 Empty and false are the words of their mouth;
  they have ceased to be wise and do good.
5 In their beds they hatch plots;
  they set out on a wicked way;
  they do not reject evil.

Psalm 36 (V 35)g

For the choirmaster   Of the servant of Yahweh
Of David

1 Sin is the oracle of the wicked
  in the depths of his heart;
  there is no fear of God
  before his eyes.

2 He sees himself with too flattering an eye
  to detect and detest his guilt;
3 all he says is malicious and deceitful,
  he has turned his back on wisdom.

  To get his way 4 he hatches malicious plots
  even in his bed;
  once set on his evil course
  no wickedness is too much for him.

g 36 The two parts of the Ps in different rhythms may have existed
separately.

| NEW REVISED STANDARD VERSION | REVISED ENGLISH BIBLE |

5 Your steadfast love, O LORD, extends to the
heavens,
  your faithfulness to the clouds.
6 Your righteousness is like the mighty mountains,
  your judgments are like the great deep;
  you save humans and animals alike, O LORD.

7 How precious is your steadfast love, O God!
  All people may take refuge in the shadow of
  your wings.
8 They feast on the abundance of your house,
  and you give them drink from the river of your
  delights.
9 For with you is the fountain of life;
  in your light we see light.

10 O continue your steadfast love to those who know
you,
  and your salvation to the upright of heart!
11 Do not let the foot of the arrogant tread on me,
  or the hand of the wicked drive me away.
12 There the evildoers lie prostrate;
  they are thrust down, unable to rise.

Psalm 37

Of David.

1 Do not fret because of the wicked;
  do not be envious of wrongdoers,
2 for they will soon fade like the grass,
  and wither like the green herb.

3 Trust in the LORD, and do good;
  so you will live in the land, and enjoy security.
4 Take delight in the LORD,
  and he will give you the desires of your heart.

5 Commit your way to the LORD;
  trust in him, and he will act.
6 He will make your vindication shine like the
light,
  and the justice of your cause like the noonday.

7 Be still before the LORD, and wait patiently for
him;
  do not fret over those who prosper in their
way,
  over those who carry out evil devices.

8 Refrain from anger, and forsake wrath.
  Do not fret — it leads only to evil.
9 For the wicked shall be cut off,
  but those who wait for the LORD shall inherit
the land.

10 Yet a little while, and the wicked will be no
more;
  though you look diligently for their place, they
will not be there.
11 But the meek shall inherit the land,
  and delight themselves in abundant prosperity.

12 The wicked plot against the righteous,
  and gnash their teeth at them;
13 but the LORD laughs at the wicked,
  for he sees that their day is coming.

14 The wicked draw the sword and bend their bows
  to bring down the poor and needy,
  to kill those who walk uprightly;
15 their sword shall enter their own heart,
  and their bows shall be broken.

5 LORD, your unfailing love reaches to the heavens,
  your faithfulness to the skies.
6 Your righteousness is like the lofty mountains,
  your justice like the great deep;
  LORD who saves man and beast,
7 how precious is your unfailing love!
  Gods and frail mortals seek refuge in the shadow
  of your wings.
8 They are filled with the rich plenty of your house,
  and you give them to drink from the stream of
  your delights;
9 for with you is the fountain of life,
  and by your light we are enlightened.

10 Continue your love unfailing to those who know
you,
  and your saving power towards the honest of heart.
11 Let not the foot of the proud come near me,
  let no wicked hand disturb me.
12 There they lie, the evildoers,
  flung down and not able to rise.

Psalm 37

For David

1 Do NOT fret because of evildoers
  or envy those who do wrong.
2 For like the grass they soon wither,
  and like green pasture they fade away.

3 Trust in the LORD and do good;
  settle in the land and find safe pasture.
4 Delight in the LORD,
  and he will grant you your heart's desire.
5 Commit your way to the LORD;
  trust in him, and he will act.
6 He will make your righteousness shine clear as the
day
  and the justice of your cause like the brightness of
noon.

7 Wait quietly for the LORD, be patient till he comes;
  do not envy those who gain their ends,
  or be vexed at their success.

8 Be angry no more, have done with wrath;
  do not be vexed: that leads to evil.
9 For evildoers will be destroyed,
  while they who hope in the LORD will possess the
land.

10 A little while, and the wicked will be no more;
  however hard you look, you will find their place
empty.
11 But the humble will possess the land
  and enjoy untold prosperity.

12 The wicked plot against the righteous
  and grind their teeth at the sight of them.
13 The Lord will laugh at the wicked,
  for he sees that their day of judgement is coming.

14 They have drawn their swords
  and strung their bows
  to lay low the oppressed and poor,
  and to slaughter those who are honest.
15 Their swords will pierce their own hearts
  and their bows will be shattered.

36:6 **lofty mountains:** *lit.* mountains of God.

NEW AMERICAN BIBLE

NEW JERUSALEM BIBLE

II

6 LORD, your love reaches to heaven;
    your fidelity, to the clouds.
7 Your justice is like the highest mountains;
    your judgments, like the mighty deep;
    all living creatures you sustain, LORD.
8 How precious is your love, O God!
    We take refuge in the shadow of your wings.
9 We feast on the rich food of your house;
    from your delightful stream you give us drink.
10 For with you is the fountain of life,
    and in your light we see light.
11 Continue your kindness toward your friends,
    your just defense of the honest heart.
12 Do not let the foot of the proud overtake me,
    nor the hand of the wicked disturb me.
13 There make the evildoers fall;
    thrust them down, never to rise.

5 Yahweh, your faithful love is in the heavens,
    your constancy reaches to the clouds,
6 your saving justice is like towering mountains,
    your judgements like the mighty deep.

Yahweh, you support both man and beast;
7 how precious, God, is your faithful love.
So the children of Adam
take refuge in the shadow of your wings.

8 They feast on the bounty of your house,
    you let them drink from your delicious streams;
9 in you is the source of life,
    by your light we see the light.

10 Maintain your faithful love to those who
        acknowledge you,
and your saving justice to the honest of heart.
11 Do not let the foot of the arrogant overtake me
or wicked hands drive me away.

12 There they have fallen, the evil-doers,
    flung down, never to rise again.

Psalm 37

1 *Of David.*

Aleph	Do not be provoked by evildoers;
	  do not envy those who do wrong.
	2 Like grass they wither quickly;
	  like green plants they wilt away.

Beth	3 Trust in the LORD and do good
	  that you may dwell in the land and live
	    secure.
	4 Find your delight in the LORD
	  who will give you your heart's desire.

Gimel	5 Commit your way to the LORD;
	  trust that God will act
	6 And make your integrity shine like the dawn,
	  your vindication like noonday.

Daleth	7 Be still before the LORD;
	  wait for God.
	Do not be provoked by the prosperous,
	  nor by malicious schemers.

He	8 Give up your anger, abandon your wrath;
	  do not be provoked; it brings only harm.
	9 Those who do evil will be cut off,
	  but those who wait for the LORD will
	    possess the land.

Waw	10 Wait a little, and the wicked will be no more;
	  look for them and they will not be there.
	11 But the poor will possess the land,
	  will delight in great prosperity.

Zayin	12 The wicked plot against the just
	  and grind their teeth at them;
	13 But the LORD laughs at them,
	  knowing their day is coming.

Heth	14 The wicked draw their swords;
	  they string their bows
	To fell the poor and oppressed,
	  to slaughter those whose way is honest.
	15 Their swords will pierce their own hearts;
	  their bows will be broken.

Psalm 37 (V 36)

Of David

Aleph	1 Do not get heated about the wicked
	  or envy those who do wrong.
	2 Quick as the grass they wither,
	  fading like the green of the fields.

Bet	3 Put your trust in Yahweh and do right,
	  make your home in the land and live secure.
	4 Make Yahweh your joy
	  and he will give you your heart's desires.

Gimel	5 Commit your destiny to Yahweh,
	  be confident in him, and he will act,
	6 making your uprightness clear as daylight,
	  and the justice of your cause as the noon.

Dalet	7 Stay quiet before Yahweh, wait longingly for
	    him,
	do not get heated over someone who is
	    making a fortune,
	succeeding by devious means.

He	8 Refrain from anger, leave rage aside,
	  do not get heated — it can do no good;
	9 for evil-doers will be annihilated,
	  while those who hope in Yahweh shall have
	    the land for their own.

Waw	10 A little while and the wicked will be no more,
	  however well you search for the place, the
	    wicked will not be there;
	11 but the poor will have the land for their own,
	  to enjoy untroubled peace.

Zain	12 The wicked plots against the upright
	  and gnashes his teeth at him,
	13 but Yahweh only laughs at his efforts,
	  knowing that his end is in sight.

Het	14 Though the wicked draw his sword
	  and bend his bow to slaughter the honest
	  and bring down the poor and the needy,
	15 his sword will pierce his own heart,
	  and his bow will be shattered.

NEW REVISED STANDARD VERSION	REVISED ENGLISH BIBLE

NEW REVISED STANDARD VERSION

16 Better is a little that the righteous person has
　　than the abundance of many wicked.
17 For the arms of the wicked shall be broken,
　　but the LORD upholds the righteous.

18 The LORD knows the days of the blameless,
　　and their heritage will abide forever;
19 they are not put to shame in evil times,
　　in the days of famine they have abundance.

20 But the wicked perish,
　　and the enemies of the LORD are like the glory
　　　of the pastures;
　　they vanish — like smoke they vanish away.

21 The wicked borrow, and do not pay back,
　　but the righteous are generous and keep giving;
22 for those blessed by the LORD shall inherit the
　　　land,
　　but those cursed by him shall be cut off.

23 Our steps[l] are made firm by the LORD,
　　when he delights in our[m] way;
24 though we stumble,[n] we[o] shall not fall
　　　headlong,
　　for the LORD holds us[p] by the hand.

25 I have been young, and now am old,
　　yet I have not seen the righteous forsaken
　　　or their children begging bread.
26 They are ever giving liberally and lending,
　　and their children become a blessing.

27 Depart from evil, and do good;
　　so you shall abide forever.
28 For the LORD loves justice;
　　he will not forsake his faithful ones.

　　The righteous shall be kept safe forever,
　　but the children of the wicked shall be cut off.
29 The righteous shall inherit the land,
　　and live in it forever.

30 The mouths of the righteous utter wisdom,
　　and their tongues speak justice.
31 The law of their God is in their hearts;
　　their steps do not slip.

32 The wicked watch for the righteous,
　　and seek to kill them.
33 The LORD will not abandon them to their power,
　　or let them be condemned when they are
　　　brought to trial.

34 Wait for the LORD, and keep to his way,
　　and he will exalt you to inherit the land;
　　you will look on the destruction of the wicked.

35 I have seen the wicked oppressing,
　　and towering like a cedar of Lebanon.[q]
36 Again I[r] passed by, and they were no more;
　　though I sought them, they could not be found.

37 Mark the blameless, and behold the upright,
　　for there is posterity for the peaceable.
38 But transgressors shall be altogether destroyed;
　　the posterity of the wicked shall be cut off.

REVISED ENGLISH BIBLE

16 Better is the little which the righteous person has
　　than all the wealth of the wicked;
17 for the power of the wicked will be broken,
　　but the LORD upholds the righteous.

18 The LORD watches over the upright all their days,
　　and their inheritance will last for ever.
19 When times are bad, they will not be distressed,
　　and in a period of famine they will have enough.
20 But the wicked will perish;
　　the enemies of the LORD, like fuel in a furnace,
　　will go up in smoke.

21 The wicked borrow and do not repay;
　　the righteous give generously.
22 Those whom the LORD has blessed will possess the
　　　land,
　　and those who are cursed by him will be cut off.

23 It is the LORD who directs a person's steps;
　　he holds him firm and approves of his conduct.
24 Though he may fall, he will not go headlong,
　　for the LORD grasps him by the hand.

25 I have been young and now have grown old,
　　but never have I seen the righteous forsaken
　　　or their children begging bread.
26 Day in, day out, such a one lends generously,
　　and his children become a blessing.

27 If you shun evil and do good,
　　you will live at peace for ever;
28 for the LORD is a lover of justice
　　and will not forsake his loyal servants.

　　The lawless are banished for ever
　　and the children of the wicked cut off,
29 while the righteous will possess the land
　　and live there for ever.

30 A righteous person speaks words of wisdom
　　and justice is always on his lips.
31 The law of his God is in his heart;
　　his steps do not falter.

32 The wicked watch out for the righteous
　　and seek to put them to death;
33 but the LORD will not leave them in their power,
　　nor let them be condemned if they are brought to
　　　trial.

34 Wait for the LORD and hold to his way;
　　he will raise you to be master of the land.
　　When the wicked are destroyed, you will be there
　　　to watch.

35 I have seen a wicked man inspiring terror,
　　flourishing as a spreading tree in its native soil.
36 But one day I passed by and he was gone;
　　for all that I searched for him, he was not to be
　　　found.

37 Observe the good man, watch him who is honest,
　　for the man of peace leaves descendants;
38 but transgressors are wiped out one and all,
　　and the descendants of the wicked are cut off.

---

[l] Heb *a man's steps*　　[m] Heb *his*　　[n] Heb *he stumbles*　　[o] Heb *he*
[p] Heb *him*　　[q] Gk: Meaning of Heb uncertain　　[r] Gk Syr Jerome:
Heb *he*

37:20 **like . . . furnace:** *prob. rdg; Heb.* like the worth of rams.
37:28 **The lawless:** *prob. rdg, cp. Gk; Heb.* omits.　　37:36 **I
passed:** *so Gk; Heb.* he passed.

NEW AMERICAN BIBLE	NEW JERUSALEM BIBLE

Teth 16 Better the poverty of the just
than the great wealth of the wicked.
17 The arms of the wicked will be broken;
the LORD will sustain the just.

Yodh 18 The LORD watches over the days of the
blameless;
their heritage lasts forever.
19 They will not be disgraced when times are
hard;
in days of famine they will have plenty.

Kaph 20 The wicked perish,
the enemies of the LORD;
Like the beauty of meadows they vanish;
like smoke they disappear.

Lamedh 21 The wicked borrow but do not repay;
the just are generous in giving.
22 For those blessed by the Lord will possess the
land,
but those accursed will be cut off.

Mem 23 Those whose steps are guided by the LORD;
whose way God approves,
24 May stumble, but they will never fall,
for the LORD holds their hand.

Nun 25 Neither in my youth, nor now in old age
have I ever seen the just abandoned
or their children begging bread.
26 The just always lend generously,
and their children become a blessing.

Samekh 27 Turn from evil and do good,
that you may inhabit the land forever.
28 For the LORD loves justice
and does not abandon the faithful.
When the unjust are destroyed,
and the children of the wicked cut off,

Ayin 29 The just will possess the land
and live in it forever.

Pe 30 The mouths of the just utter wisdom;
their tongues speak what is right.
31 God's teaching is in their hearts;
their steps do not falter.

Sadhe 32 The wicked spy on the just
and seek to kill them.
33 But the LORD does not leave the just in their
power,
nor let them be condemned when tried.

Qoph 34 Wait eagerly for the LORD,
and keep to the way;
God will raise you to possess the land;
you will gloat when the wicked are cut off.

Resh 35 I have seen ruthless scoundrels,
strong as flourishing cedars.
36 When I passed by again, they were gone;
though I searched, they could not be found.

Shin 37 Observe the honest, mark the upright;
those at peace with God have a future.
38 But all sinners will be destroyed;
the future of the wicked will be cut off.

Tet 16 What little the upright possesses
outweighs all the wealth of the wicked;
17 for the weapons of the wicked shall be
shattered,
while Yahweh supports the upright.

Yod 18 The lives of the just are in Yahweh's care,
their birthright will endure for ever;
19 they will not be put to shame when bad times
come,
in time of famine they will have plenty.

Kaph 20 The wicked, enemies of Yahweh, will be
destroyed,
they will vanish like the green of the pasture,
they will vanish in smoke.

Lamed 21 The wicked borrows and will not repay,
but the upright is generous in giving;
22 those he blesses will have the land for their
own,
and those he curses be annihilated.

Mem 23 Yahweh guides a strong man's steps and
keeps them firm;
and takes pleasure in him.
24 When he trips he is not thrown sprawling,
since Yahweh supports him by the hand.

Nun 25 Now I am old, but ever since my youth
I never saw an upright person abandoned,
or the descendants of the upright forced to beg
their bread.
26 The upright is always compassionate, always
lending,
so his descendants reap a blessing.

Samek 27 Turn your back on evil and do good,
you will have a home for ever,
28 for Yahweh loves justice
and will not forsake his faithful.

Ain Evil-doers will perish eternally,
the descendants of the wicked be annihilated,
29 but the upright shall have the land for their
own,
there they shall live for ever.

Pe 30 Wisdom comes from the lips of the upright,
and his tongue speaks what is right;
31 the law of his God is in his heart,
his foot will never slip.

Zade 32 The wicked keeps a close eye on the upright,
looking out for a chance to kill him;
33 Yahweh will never abandon him to the
clutches of the wicked,
nor let him be condemned if he is tried.

Qoph 34 Put your hope in Yahweh, keep to his path,
he will raise you up to make the land your
own;
you will look on while the wicked are
annihilated.

Resh 35 I have seen the wicked exultant,
towering like a cedar of Lebanon.
36 When next I passed he was gone,
I searched for him and he was nowhere to be
found.

Shin 37 Observe the innocent, consider the honest,
for the lover of peace will not lack children.
38 But the wicked will all be destroyed together,
and their children annihilated.

NEW REVISED STANDARD VERSION	REVISED ENGLISH BIBLE

NEW REVISED STANDARD VERSION

39 The salvation of the righteous is from the LORD;
    he is their refuge in the time of trouble.
40 The LORD helps them and rescues them;
    he rescues them from the wicked, and saves
       them,
    because they take refuge in him.

Psalm 38

A Psalm of David, for the memorial offering.

1 O LORD, do not rebuke me in your anger,
    or discipline me in your wrath.
2 For your arrows have sunk into me,
    and your hand has come down on me.

3 There is no soundness in my flesh
    because of your indignation;
there is no health in my bones
    because of my sin.
4 For my iniquities have gone over my head;
    they weigh like a burden too heavy for me.

5 My wounds grow foul and fester
    because of my foolishness;
6 I am utterly bowed down and prostrate;
    all day long I go around mourning.
7 For my loins are filled with burning,
    and there is no soundness in my flesh.
8 I am utterly spent and crushed;
    I groan because of the tumult of my heart.

9 O Lord, all my longing is known to you;
    my sighing is not hidden from you.
10 My heart throbs, my strength fails me;
    as for the light of my eyes—it also has gone
       from me.
11 My friends and companions stand aloof from my
       affliction,
    and my neighbors stand far off.

12 Those who seek my life lay their snares;
    those who seek to hurt me speak of ruin,
    and meditate treachery all day long.

13 But I am like the deaf, I do not hear;
    like the mute, who cannot speak.
14 Truly, I am like one who does not hear,
    and in whose mouth is no retort.

15 But it is for you, O LORD, that I wait;
    it is you, O Lord my God, who will answer.
16 For I pray, "Only do not let them rejoice over
       me,
    those who boast against me when my foot
       slips."

17 For I am ready to fall,
    and my pain is ever with me.
18 I confess my iniquity;
    I am sorry for my sin.
19 Those who are my foes without cause[s] are
       mighty,
    and many are those who hate me wrongfully.
20 Those who render me evil for good
    are my adversaries because I follow after good.

21 Do not forsake me, O LORD;
    O my God, do not be far from me;
22 make haste to help me,
    O Lord, my salvation.

REVISED ENGLISH BIBLE

39 Deliverance for the righteous comes from the
    LORD,
    their refuge in time of trouble.
40 The LORD will help them and deliver them,
    he will keep them safe from the wicked;
    he will save them because they seek shelter in him.

Psalm 38

A psalm: for David: for commemoration

1 LORD, do not rebuke me in anger
    or punish me in your wrath.
2 For your arrows have rained down on me,
    and your hand on me has been heavy.
3 Your indignation has left no part of my body
       unscathed;
because of my sin there is no health in my whole
       frame.
4 For my iniquities tower above my head;
    they are a heavier load than I can bear.
5 My wounds fester and stink because of my folly.
6 I am bowed down and utterly prostrate.
    All day long I go about as if in mourning,
7 for my loins burn with fever,
    and there is no wholesome flesh in me.
8 Faint and badly crushed
    I groan aloud in anguish of heart.

9 All my longing lies open before you, Lord,
    and my sighing is no secret to you.
10 My heart throbs, my strength is spent,
    and the light has faded from my eyes.
11 My friends and companions shun me in my
       sickness,
    and my kinsfolk keep far off.
12 Those who seek my life set their traps,
    those who mean to injure me threaten my
       destruction;
    they plot all the day long.

13 But I am like a deaf man, hearing nothing,
    like a dumb man who cannot open his mouth.
14 I behave like one who does not hear,
    whose tongue offers no defence.
15 On you, LORD, I fix my hope;
    you, LORD my God, will answer.
16 I said, 'Let them never rejoice over me
    who exult when my foot slips.'

17 I am on the brink of disaster,
    and pain is constantly with me.
18 I make no secret of my iniquity;
    I am troubled because of my sin.
19 But many are my enemies, all without cause,
    and numerous are those who hate me without
       reason,
20 who repay good with evil,
    opposing me because my purpose is good.

21 But, LORD, do not forsake me;
    my God, be not far aloof from me.
22 Lord my deliverer, hasten to my aid.

---

[s] Q Ms: MT *my living foes*   38:19 **all . . . cause:** *prob. rdg; Heb.* living.

Taw 39 The salvation of the just is from the LORD,
their refuge in time of distress.
40 The LORD helps and rescues them,
rescues and saves them from the wicked,
because in God they take refuge.

Psalm 38

1 *A psalm of David. For remembrance.*

I

2 LORD, punish me no more in your anger;
in your wrath do not chastise me!
3 Your arrows have sunk deep in me;
your hand has come down upon me.
4 My flesh is afflicted because of your anger;
my frame aches because of my sin.
5 My iniquities overwhelm me,
a burden beyond my strength.

II

6 Foul and festering are my sores
because of my folly.
7 I am stooped and deeply bowed;
all day I go about mourning.
8 My loins burn with fever;
my flesh is afflicted.
9 I am numb and utterly crushed;
I wail with anguish of heart.
10 My Lord, my deepest yearning is before you;
my groaning is not hidden from you.
11 My heart shudders, my strength forsakes me;
the very light of my eyes has failed.
12 Friends and companions shun my pain;
my neighbors stand far off.
13 Those who seek my life lay snares for me;
they seek my misfortune, they speak of ruin;
they plot treachery all the day.

III

14 But I am like the deaf, hearing nothing,
like the dumb, saying nothing,
15 Like someone who does not hear,
who has no answer ready.
16 LORD, I wait for you;
O Lord, my God, answer me.
17 For I fear they will gloat,
exult over me if I stumble.

IV

18 I am very near to falling;
my pain is with me always.
19 I acknowledge my guilt
and grieve over my sin.
20 But many are my foes without cause,
a multitude of enemies without reason,
21 Repaying me evil for good,
harassing me for pursuing good.
22 Forsake me not, O LORD;
my God, be not far from me!
23 Come quickly to help me,
my Lord and my salvation!

Taw 39 The upright have Yahweh for their Saviour,
their refuge in times of trouble;
40 Yahweh helps them and rescues them,
he will rescue them from the wicked,
and save them because they take refuge in
him.

Psalm 38 (V 37)

Psalm   Of David   In commemoration

1 Yahweh, do not correct me in anger,
do not discipline me in wrath.
2 For your arrows have pierced deep into me,
your hand has pressed down upon me.
3 Your indignation has left no part of me unscathed,
my sin has left no health in my bones.
4 My sins stand higher than my head,
they weigh on me as an unbearable weight.
5 I have stinking, festering wounds,
thanks to my folly.
6 I am twisted and bent double,
I spend my days in gloom.
7 My loins burn with fever,
no part of me is unscathed.
8 Numbed and utterly crushed
I groan in distress of heart.
9 Lord, all my longing is known to you,
my sighing no secret from you,
10 my heart is throbbing, my strength has failed,
the light has gone out of my eyes.
11 Friends and companions shun my disease,
even the dearest of them keep their distance.
12 Those with designs on my life lay snares,
those who wish me ill speak of violence
and hatch treachery all day long.
13 But I hear nothing, as though I were deaf,
as though dumb, saying not a word.
14 I am like the one who, hearing nothing,
has no sharp answer to make.
15 For in you, Yahweh, I put my hope,
you, Lord my God, will give answer.
16 I said, 'Never let them gloat over me,
do not let them take advantage of me if my foot
slips.'
17 There is no escape for me from falling,
no relief from my misery.
18 But I make no secret of my guilt,
I am anxious at the thought of my sin.
19 There is no numbering those who oppose me
without cause,
no counting those who hate me unprovoked,
20 repaying me evil for good,
slandering me for trying to do them good.
21 Yahweh, do not desert me,
my God, do not stand aloof from me.
22 Come quickly to my help,
Lord, my Saviour!

Psalm 39

To the leader: to Jeduthun. A Psalm of David.

1 I said, "I will guard my ways
    that I may not sin with my tongue;
I will keep a muzzle on my mouth
    as long as the wicked are in my presence."
2 I was silent and still;
    I held my peace to no avail;
my distress grew worse,
3   my heart became hot within me.
While I mused, the fire burned;
    then I spoke with my tongue:

4 "LORD, let me know my end,
    and what is the measure of my days;
let me know how fleeting my life is.
5 You have made my days a few handbreadths,
    and my lifetime is as nothing in your sight.
Surely everyone stands as a mere breath.   *Selah*
6   Surely everyone goes about like a shadow.
Surely for nothing they are in turmoil;
    they heap up, and do not know who will
        gather.

7 "And now, O Lord, what do I wait for?
    My hope is in you.
8 Deliver me from all my transgressions.
    Do not make me the scorn of the fool.
9 I am silent; I do not open my mouth,
    for it is you who have done it.
10 Remove your stroke from me;
    I am worn down by the blows*t* of your hand.

11 "You chastise mortals
    in punishment for sin,
consuming like a moth what is dear to them;
    surely everyone is a mere breath.   *Selah*

12 "Hear my prayer, O LORD,
    and give ear to my cry;
    do not hold your peace at my tears.
For I am your passing guest,
    an alien, like all my forebears.
13 Turn your gaze away from me, that I may smile
        again,
    before I depart and am no more."

Psalm 40

To the leader. Of David. A Psalm.

1 I waited patiently for the LORD;
    he inclined to me and heard my cry.
2 He drew me up from the desolate pit,*u*
    out of the miry bog,
and set my feet upon a rock,
    making my steps secure.
3 He put a new song in my mouth,
    a song of praise to our God.
Many will see and fear,
    and put their trust in the LORD.

4 Happy are those who make
    the LORD their trust,
who do not turn to the proud,
    to those who go astray after false gods.

Psalm 39

For the leader: for Jeduthun: a psalm: for David

1 I SAID: 'I shall keep watch over my conduct,
    that what I say may be free from sin.
I shall keep a muzzle on my mouth,
    so long as the wicked confront me.'
2 I kept utterly silent,
    I refrained from speech.
My agony was quickened,
3 and my heart burned within me.
As I pondered my mind was inflamed,
    and I began to speak:

4 'LORD, let me know my end and the number of my
        days;
    tell me how short my life is to be.
5 I know you have made my days a mere span long,
    and my whole life is as nothing in your sight.
A human being, however firm he stands, is but a
    puff of wind,   [*Selah*
6 his life but a passing shadow;
    the riches he piles up are no more than vapour,
    and there is no knowing who will enjoy them.'

7 Now, Lord, what do I wait for?
    My hope is in you.
8 Deliver me from all who do me wrong;
    make me no longer the butt of fools.
9 I am dumb, I shall not open my mouth,
    because it is your doing.
10 Rain no more blows on me;
    I am exhausted by your hostility.
11 When you rebuke anyone to punish his sin,
    you make what he desires melt away;
    every mortal being is only a breath of wind. [*Selah*

12 Hear my prayer, LORD;
    listen to my cry,
    do not be deaf to my weeping;
for I find shelter with you;
    I am a passing guest, as all my forefathers were.
13 Frown on me no more; let me look cheerful
    before I depart and cease to be.

Psalm 40

For the leader: for David: a psalm

1 PATIENTLY I waited for the LORD;
    he bent down to me and listened to my cry.
2 He raised me out of the miry pit,
    out of the mud and clay;
he set my feet on rock
    and gave me a firm footing.
3 On my lips he put a new song,
    a song of praise to our God.
Many will look with awe
    and put their trust in the LORD.
4 Happy is he who puts his trust in the LORD
    and does not look to the arrogant and treacherous.

---

*t*Heb *hostility*   *u*Cn: Heb *pit of tumult*   39:6 **the riches:** *prob. rdg; Heb.* they murmur.

Psalm 39

¹ *For the leader, for Jeduthun. A psalm of David.*

I

² I said, "I will watch my ways,
  lest I sin with my tongue;
  I will set a curb on my mouth."
³ Dumb and silent before the wicked,
  I refrained from any speech.
  But my sorrow increased;
⁴   my heart smoldered within me.
  In my thoughts a fire blazed up,
  and I broke into speech:

II

⁵ LORD, let me know my end, the number of my
    days,
  that I may learn how frail I am.
⁶ You have given my days a very short span;
  my life is as nothing before you.
  All mortals are but a breath.   *Selah*
⁷ Mere phantoms, we go our way;
  mere vapor, our restless pursuits;
  we heap up stores without knowing for whom.
⁸ And now, Lord, what future do I have?
  You are my only hope.
⁹ From all my sins deliver me;
  let me not be the taunt of fools.

III

¹⁰ I was silent and did not open my mouth
  because you were the one who did this.
¹¹ Take your plague away from me;
  I am ravaged by the touch of your hand.
¹² You rebuke our guilt and chasten us;
  you dissolve all we prize like a cobweb.
  All mortals are but a breath.   *Selah*
¹³ Listen to my prayer, LORD, hear my cry;
  do not be deaf to my weeping!
  I sojourn with you like a passing stranger,
  a guest, like all my ancestors.
¹⁴ Turn your gaze from me, that I may find peace
  before I depart to be no more.

Psalm 40

¹ *For the leader. A psalm of David.*

A

I

² I waited, waited for the LORD;
  who bent down and heard my cry,
³ Drew me out of the pit of destruction,
  out of the mud of the swamp,
  Set my feet upon rock,
  steadied my steps,
⁴ And put a new song in my mouth,
  a hymn to our God.
  Many shall look on in awe
  and they shall trust in the LORD.

II

⁵ Happy those whose trust is the LORD,
  who turn not to idolatry
  or to those who stray after falsehood.

Psalm 39 (V 38)

For the choirmaster   For Jeduthun   Psalm   Of David

¹ I said, 'I will watch how I behave
  so that I do not sin by my tongue.
  I will keep a muzzle on my mouth
  as long as any sinner is near.'
² I stayed dumb, silent, speechless,
  but the sinner's prosperity redoubled my torment.

³ My heart had been smouldering within me,
  but at the thought of this it flared up
  and the words came bursting out,
⁴ 'Yahweh, let me know my fate,
  how much longer I have to live.
  Show me just how frail I am.

⁵ 'Look, you have given me but a hand's breadth or
    two of life,
  the length of my life is as nothing to you.
  Every human being that stands on earth is a mere
    puff of wind,
⁶ every human being that walks only a shadow;
  a mere puff of wind is the wealth stored away —
  no knowing who will profit from it.'

⁷ So now, Lord, what am I to hope for?
  My hope is in you.
⁸ Save me from all my sins,
  do not make me the butt of fools.
⁹ I keep silence, I speak no more
  since you yourself have been at work.

¹⁰ Take your scourge away from me.
  I am worn out by the blows you deal me.
¹¹ You correct human beings by punishing sin,
  like a moth you eat away all their desires —
  a human being is a mere puff of wind.

¹² Yahweh, hear my prayer,
  listen to my cry for help,
  do not remain deaf to my weeping.
  For I am a stranger in your house,
  a nomad like all my ancestors.
¹³ Turn away your gaze that I may breathe freely
  before I depart and am no more!

Psalm 40 (V 39)

For the choirmaster   Of David   Psalm

¹ I waited, I waited for Yahweh,
  then he stooped to me
  and heard my cry for help.

² He pulled me up from the seething chasm,
  from the mud of the mire.
  He set my feet on rock,
  and made my footsteps firm.

³ He put a fresh song in my mouth,
  praise of our God.
  Many will be awestruck at the sight,
  and will put their trust in Yahweh.

⁴ How blessed are those
  who put their trust in Yahweh,
  who have not sided with rebels
  and those who have gone astray in falsehood.

NEW REVISED STANDARD VERSION	REVISED ENGLISH BIBLE

NEW REVISED STANDARD VERSION

5 You have multiplied, O LORD my God,
  your wondrous deeds and your thoughts toward
    us;
  none can compare with you.
Were I to proclaim and tell of them,
  they would be more than can be counted.

6 Sacrifice and offering you do not desire,
  but you have given me an open ear.*v*
Burnt offering and sin offering
  you have not required.
7 Then I said, "Here I am;
  in the scroll of the book it is written of me.*w*
8 I delight to do your will, O my God;
  your law is within my heart."

9 I have told the glad news of deliverance
  in the great congregation;
see, I have not restrained my lips,
  as you know, O LORD.
10 I have not hidden your saving help within my
    heart,
  I have spoken of your faithfulness and your
    salvation;
I have not concealed your steadfast love and your
    faithfulness
  from the great congregation.

11 Do not, O LORD, withhold
  your mercy from me;
let your steadfast love and your faithfulness
  keep me safe forever.
12 For evils have encompassed me
  without number;
my iniquities have overtaken me,
  until I cannot see;
they are more than the hairs of my head,
  and my heart fails me.

13 Be pleased, O LORD, to deliver me;
  O LORD, make haste to help me.
14 Let all those be put to shame and confusion
  who seek to snatch away my life;
let those be turned back and brought to dishonor
  who desire my hurt.
15 Let those be appalled because of their shame
  who say to me, "Aha, Aha!"

16 But may all who seek you
  rejoice and be glad in you;
may those who love your salvation
  say continually, "Great is the LORD!"
17 As for me, I am poor and needy,
  but the Lord takes thought for me.
You are my help and my deliverer;
  do not delay, O my God.

REVISED ENGLISH BIBLE

5 LORD my God, great things you have done;
  your wonders and your purposes are for our good;
  none can compare with you.
I would proclaim them and speak of them,
  but they are more than I can tell.

6 You have not desired sacrifice or offering,
  you have not demanded whole-offerings or
    purifying offerings;
you have given me receptive ears.
7 Then I said, 'Here I am,'
  as is prescribed for me in a written scroll.
8 God, my desire is to do your will;
  your law is in my heart.
9 In the great assembly I have proclaimed what is
    right;
  I do not hold back my words,
  as you know, LORD.
10 I have not kept your goodness hidden in my heart;
  I have proclaimed your faithfulness and saving
    power,
  and have not concealed your unfailing love and
    truth
  from the great assembly.
11 You, LORD, will not withhold
  your tender care from me;
  may your love and truth for ever guard me.

12 For misfortunes beyond counting
  press on me from all sides;
my iniquities have overtaken me,
  and I cannot see;
they are more in number than the hairs of my
    head;
  my courage fails.
13 Show me favour, LORD, and save me;
  LORD, come quickly to my help.
14 Let all who seek to take my life
  be discomfited and dismayed;
let those who desire my hurt be turned back in
    disgrace;
15 let those who cry 'Hurrah!' at my downfall
  be horrified at their shame.
16 But let all who seek you
  be jubilant and rejoice in you;
and may those who long for your saving aid
  for ever cry, 'All glory to the LORD!'

17 But I am poor and needy;
  may the Lord think of me.
You are my help and my deliverer;
  my God, do not delay.

Psalm 41

To the leader. A Psalm of David.

1 Happy are those who consider the poor;*x*
  the LORD delivers them in the day of trouble.

Psalm 41

For the leader: a psalm: for David

1 HAPPY is anyone who has a concern for the
    helpless!
The LORD will save him in time of trouble;

---

v Heb *ears you have dug for me* *w* Meaning of Heb uncertain
x Or *weak*

40:13–17 *Cp. Ps. 70:1–5.*

NEW AMERICAN BIBLE

6 How numerous, O LORD, my God,
  you have made your wondrous deeds!
And in your plans for us
  there is none to equal you.
Should I wish to declare or tell them,
  too many are they to recount.

III

7 Sacrifice and offering you do not want;
  but ears open to obedience you gave me.
Holocausts and sin-offerings you do not require;
8 so I said, "Here I am;
  your commands for me are written in the scroll.
9 To do your will is my delight;
  my God, your law is in my heart!"
10 I announced your deed to a great assembly;
  I did not restrain my lips;
  you, LORD, are my witness.
11 Your deed I did not hide within my heart,
  your loyal deliverance I have proclaimed.
I made no secret of your enduring kindness
  to a great assembly.

B

I

12 LORD, do not withhold your compassion from me;
  may your enduring kindness ever preserve me.
13 For all about me are evils beyond count;
  my sins so overcome me I cannot see.
They are more than the hairs of my head;
  my courage fails me.

II

14 LORD, graciously rescue me!
  Come quickly to help me, LORD!
15 Put to shame and confound
  all who seek to take my life.
Turn back in disgrace
  those who desire my ruin.
16 Let those who say "Aha!"
  know dismay and shame.
17 But may all who seek you
  rejoice and be glad in you.
May those who long for your help
  always say, "The LORD be glorified."
18 Though I am afflicted and poor,
  the Lord keeps me in mind.
You are my help and deliverer;
  my God, do not delay!

Psalm 41

1 For the leader. A psalm of David.

I

2 Happy those concerned for the lowly and poor;
  when misfortune strikes, the LORD delivers them.

NEW JERUSALEM BIBLE

5 How much you have done,
  Yahweh, my God —
your wonders, your plans for us —
  you have no equal.
I will proclaim and speak of them;
  they are beyond number.

6 You wanted no sacrifice or cereal offering,
  but you gave me an open ear,
you did not ask for burnt offering or sacrifice for
    sin;
7 then I said, 'Here I am, I am coming.'

In the scroll of the book it is written of me,
8 my delight is to do your will;
your law, my God,
  is deep in my heart.

9 I proclaimed the saving justice of Yahweh
  in the great assembly.
See, I will not hold my tongue,
  as you well know.

10 I have not kept your saving justice locked in the
    depths of my heart,
  but have spoken of your constancy and saving
    help.
I have made no secret of your faithful and steadfast
    love,
  in the great assembly.

11 You, Yahweh, have not withheld
  your tenderness from me;
your faithful and steadfast love
  will always guard me.

12 For troubles surround me,
  until they are beyond number;
my sins have overtaken me;
  I cannot see my way.
They outnumber the hairs of my head,
  and my heart fails me.

13 Be pleased, Yahweh, to rescue me,[h]
  Yahweh, come quickly and help me!
14 Shame and dismay to all
  who seek to take my life.

Back with them, let them be humiliated
  who delight in my misfortunes.
15 Let them be aghast with shame,
  those who say to me, 'Aha, aha!'
16 But joy and happiness in you
  to all who seek you!
Let them ceaselessly cry, 'Great is Yahweh'
  who love your saving power.

17 Poor and needy as I am,
  the Lord has me in mind.
You, my helper, my Saviour,
  my God, do not delay.

Psalm 41 (V 40)

For the choirmaster   Psalm   Of David

1 Blessed is anyone who cares for the poor and the
    weak;
in time of trouble Yahweh rescues him.

h 40 vv. 13–17 recur in Ps 70.

1191

NEW REVISED STANDARD VERSION	REVISED ENGLISH BIBLE

NEW REVISED STANDARD VERSION

2 The LORD protects them and keeps them alive;
 they are called happy in the land.
 You do not give them up to the will of their
 enemies.
3 The LORD sustains them on their sickbed;
 in their illness you heal all their infirmities.*y*

4 As for me, I said, "O LORD, be gracious to me;
 heal me, for I have sinned against you."
5 My enemies wonder in malice
 when I will die, and my name perish.
6 And when they come to see me, they utter empty
 words,
 while their hearts gather mischief;
 when they go out, they tell it abroad.
7 All who hate me whisper together about me;
 they imagine the worst for me.
8 They think that a deadly thing has fastened on
 me,
 that I will not rise again from where I lie.
9 Even my bosom friend in whom I trusted,
 who ate of my bread, has lifted the heel
 against me.
10 But you, O LORD, be gracious to me,
 and raise me up, that I may repay them.

11 By this I know that you are pleased with me;
 because my enemy has not triumphed over me.
12 But you have upheld me because of my integrity,
 and set me in your presence forever.

13 Blessed be the LORD, the God of Israel,
 from everlasting to everlasting.
 Amen and Amen.

BOOK II

Psalms 42–72

Psalm 42

To the leader. A Maskil of the Korahites.

1 As a deer longs for flowing streams,
 so my soul longs for you, O God.
2 My soul thirsts for God,
 for the living God.
 When shall I come and behold
 the face of God?
3 My tears have been my food
 day and night,
 while people say to me continually,
 "Where is your God?"
4 These things I remember,
 as I pour out my soul:
 how I went with the throng,*z*
 and led them in procession to the house of
 God,
 with glad shouts and songs of thanksgiving,
 a multitude keeping festival.
5 Why are you cast down, O my soul,
 and why are you disquieted within me?
 Hope in God; for I shall again praise him,
 my help 6and my God.

REVISED ENGLISH BIBLE

2 the LORD protects him and gives him life,
 making him secure in the land;
 the LORD never leaves him to the will of his
 enemies.
3 On his sick-bed he nurses him,
 transforming his every illness to health.

4 I said, 'LORD, be gracious to me!
 Heal me, for I have sinned against you.'
5 'His case is desperate,' my enemies say;
 'when will he die and his name perish?'
6 All who visit me speak from hearts devoid of
 sincerity;
 they are keen to gather bad news
 and go out to spread it abroad.
7 All who hate me whisper together about me,
 imputing the worst to me:
8 'An evil spell is cast on him,' they say;
 'he is laid on his bed, and will never rise again.'
9 Even the friend whom I trusted, who ate at my
 table,
 exults over my misfortune.

10 LORD, be gracious and restore me
 that I may repay them in full.
11 Then shall I know that you delight in me
 and that my enemy will not triumph over me.
12 But I am upheld by you because of my innocence;
 you keep me for ever in your presence.

13 Praise be to the LORD, the God of Israel,
 from everlasting to everlasting.
 Amen and Amen.

BOOK 2

Psalms 42–43

For the leader: a maskil: for the Korahites

1 As a hind longs for the running streams,
 so I long for you, my God.
2 I thirst for God, the living God;
 when shall I come to appear in his presence?
3 Tears are my food day and night,
 while all day long people ask me, 'Where is your
 God?'
4 As I pour out my soul in distress, I call to mind
 how I marched in the ranks of the great to God's
 house,
 among exultant shouts of praise, the clamour of the
 pilgrims.
5 How deep I am sunk in misery, groaning in my
 distress!
 I shall wait for God; I shall yet praise him,
 my deliverer, my God.

41:2 **never leaves him:** *prob. rdg; Heb.* do you not give him up.
41:9 **who ... table:** *or* who slanders me.   41:10 **in full:**
transposed from end of verse 9.   42:4 **of the great:** *so some MSS;
others have an obscure word.*   42:5 **my deliverer:** *so some MSS;
others* his deliverer.

y Heb *you change all his bed*   *z* Meaning of Heb uncertain

1192

NEW AMERICAN BIBLE

NEW JERUSALEM BIBLE

3 The LORD keeps and preserves them,
　makes them happy in the land,
　and does not betray them to their enemies.
4 The LORD sustains them on their sickbed,
　allays the malady when they are ill.

II

5 Once I prayed, "LORD, have mercy on me;
　heal me, I have sinned against you.
6 My enemies say the worst of me:
　'When will that one die and be forgotten?'
7 When people come to visit me,
　they speak without sincerity.
　Their hearts store up malice;
　they leave and spread their vicious lies.
8 My foes all whisper against me;
　they imagine the worst about me:
9 I have a deadly disease, they say;
　I will never rise from my sickbed.
10 Even the friend who had my trust,
　who shared my table, has scorned me.
11 But you, LORD, have mercy and raise me up
　that I may repay them as they deserve."

III

12 By this I know you are pleased with me,
　that my enemy no longer jeers at me.
13 For my integrity you have supported me
　and let me stand in your presence forever.

*　*　*

14 Blessed be the LORD, the God of Israel,
　from all eternity and forever.
　Amen. Amen.

2 Yahweh protects him, gives him life and happiness
　on earth.
　Do not abandon him to his enemies' pleasure!
3 Yahweh sustains him on his bed of sickness;
　you transform altogether the bed where he lies
　sick.

4 For my part I said, 'Yahweh, take pity on me!
　Cure me for I have sinned against you.'
5 My enemies speak to me only of disaster,
　'When will he die and his name disappear?'
6 When people come to see me their talk is hollow,
　when they get out they spread the news with spite
　in their hearts.

7 All who hate me whisper together about me
　and reckon I deserve the misery I suffer.
8 'A fatal sickness has a grip on him;
　now that he is down, he will never get up again.'
9 Even my trusted friend on whom I relied,
　who shared my table, takes advantage of me.

10 But you, Yahweh, take pity on me!
　Put me on my feet and I will give them their due.
11 This will convince me that you delight in me,
　if my enemy no longer exults over me.
12 Then you will keep me unscathed,
　and set me in your presence for ever.

13 Blessed be Yahweh, the God of Israel,
　from eternity to eternity.
　Amen, Amen. *i*

SECOND BOOK

Psalms 42–72

Psalms 42–43

1 *For the leader. A maskil of the Korahites.*

I

2 As the deer longs for streams of water,
　so my soul longs for you, O God.
3 My being thirsts for God, the living God.
　When can I go and see the face of God?
4 My tears have been my food day and night,
　as they ask daily, "Where is your God?"
5 Those times I recall
　as I pour out my soul,
When I went in procession with the crowd,
　I went with them to the house of God,
Amid loud cries of thanksgiving,
　with the multitude keeping festival.
6 Why are you downcast, my soul;
　why do you groan within me?
Wait for God, whom I shall praise again,
　my savior and my God.

Psalms 42–43 (V 41–42)

For the choirmaster　Poem　Of the sons of Korah

1 As a deer yearns
　for running streams,
so I yearn
　for you, my God.

2 I thirst for God,
　the living God;
when shall I go to see
　the face of God?

3 I have no food but tears
　day and night,
as all day long I am taunted,
　'Where is your God?'

4 This I remember
　as I pour out my heart,
how I used to pass under the roof of the Most
　High
　used to go to the house of God,
among cries of joy and praise,
　the sound of the feast.

5 Why be so downcast,
　why all these sighs?
Hope in God! I will praise him still,
　my Saviour, 6 my God.

i 41 A doxology closes each book of the Psalter: Pss 72, 89, 106, 150.

NEW REVISED STANDARD VERSION	REVISED ENGLISH BIBLE

NEW REVISED STANDARD VERSION

My soul is cast down within me;
  therefore I remember you
from the land of Jordan and of Hermon,
  from Mount Mizar.
7 Deep calls to deep
  at the thunder of your cataracts;
all your waves and your billows
  have gone over me.
8 By day the LORD commands his steadfast love,
  and at night his song is with me,
  a prayer to the God of my life.

9 I say to God, my rock,
  "Why have you forgotten me?
Why must I walk about mournfully
  because the enemy oppresses me?"
10 As with a deadly wound in my body,
  my adversaries taunt me,
while they say to me continually,
  "Where is your God?"

11 Why are you cast down, O my soul,
  and why are you disquieted within me?
Hope in God; for I shall again praise him,
  my help and my God.

Psalm 43

1 Vindicate me, O God, and defend my cause
  against an ungodly people;
from those who are deceitful and unjust
  deliver me!
2 For you are the God in whom I take refuge;
  why have you cast me off?
Why must I walk about mournfully
  because of the oppression of the enemy?
3 O send out your light and your truth;
  let them lead me;
let them bring me to your holy hill
  and to your dwelling.
4 Then I will go to the altar of God,
  to God my exceeding joy;
and I will praise you with the harp,
  O God, my God.

5 Why are you cast down, O my soul,
  and why are you disquieted within me?
Hope in God; for I shall again praise him,
  my help and my God.

Psalm 44

To the leader. Of the Korahites. A Maskil.

1 We have heard with our ears, O God,
  our ancestors have told us,
what deeds you performed in their days,
  in the days of old:
2 you with your own hand drove out the nations,
  but them you planted;
you afflicted the peoples,
  but them you set free;

REVISED ENGLISH BIBLE

6 I am sunk in misery, therefore I shall remember
    you
from the springs of Jordan and from the Hermons,
  and from the hill of Mizar.
7 Deep calls to deep in the roar of your cataracts,
  and all your waves, all your breakers, sweep over
    me.
8 By day the LORD grants his unfailing love;
  at night his praise is upon my lips,
  a prayer to the God of my life.

9 I shall say to God, my Rock, 'Why have you
    forgotten me?'
Why must I go like a mourner because my foes
  oppress me?
10 My enemies taunt me with crushing insults:
  the whole day long they ask, 'Where is your God?'
11 How deep I am sunk in misery, groaning in my
    distress!
I shall wait for God; I shall yet praise him,
  my deliverer, my God.

[43] 1 Uphold my cause, God, and give judgement
    for me
against a godless nation;
  rescue me from liars and evil men.
2 For you are my God, my refuge; why have you
    rejected me?
Why must I go like a mourner, oppressed by my
  foes?
3 Send out your light and your truth to be my guide;
  let them lead me to your holy hill, to your
    dwelling-place.
4 Then I shall come to the altar of God,
  the God of my joy and delight,
  and praise you with the lyre, God my God.
5 How deep I am sunk in misery, groaning in my
    distress!
I shall wait for God; I shall yet praise him,
  my deliverer, my God.

Psalm 44

For the leader: for the Korahites: a maskil

1 WE have heard for ourselves, God,
  our forefathers have told us
what deeds you did in their time,
2 all your hand accomplished in days of old.
To plant them in the land, you drove out the
    nations;
to settle them, you laid waste the inhabitants.

42:6 **springs:** *lit.* land.   42:10 **with . . . insults:** *lit.* with a
breaking in my bones.

II
7 My soul is downcast within me;
  therefore I will remember you
From the land of the Jordan and Hermon,
  from the land of Mount Mizar.
8 Here deep calls to deep in the roar of your
    torrents.
  All your waves and breakers sweep over me.
9 At dawn may the LORD bestow faithful love
  that I may sing praise through the night,
  praise to the God of my life.
10 I say to God, "My rock,
  why do you forget me?
Why must I go about mourning
  with the enemy oppressing me?"
11 It shatters my bones, when my adversaries
    reproach me.
  They say to me daily: "Where is your God?"
12 Why are you downcast, my soul,
  why do you groan within me?
Wait for God, whom I shall praise again,
  my savior and my God.

III
1 Grant me justice, God;
  defend me from a faithless people;
  from the deceitful and unjust rescue me.
2 You, God, are my strength.
  Why then do you spurn me?
Why must I go about mourning,
  with the enemy oppressing me?
3 Send your light and fidelity,
  that they may be my guide
And bring me to your holy mountain,
  to the place of your dwelling,
4 That I may come to the altar of God,
  to God, my joy, my delight.
Then I will praise you with the harp,
  O God, my God.
5 Why are you downcast, my soul?
  Why do you groan within me?
Wait for God, whom I shall praise again,
  my savior and my God.

Psalm 44

1 For the leader. A maskil of the Korahites.

I
2 O God, we have heard with our own ears;
  our ancestors have told us
The deeds you did in their days,
  with your own hand in days of old:
3 You rooted out nations to plant them,
  crushed peoples to make room for them.

When I am downcast
  I think of you:
from the land of Jordan and Hermon,
  I think of you, humble mountain.
7 Deep is calling to deep
  by the roar of your cataracts,
all your waves and breakers
  have rolled over me.
8 In the daytime God sends his faithful love,
  and even at night;
the song it inspires in me
  is a prayer to my living God.
9 I shall say to God, my rock,
  'Why have you forgotten me?
Why must I go around in mourning,
  harrassed by the enemy?'
10 With death in my bones,
  my enemies taunt me,
all day long they ask me,
  'Where is your God?'
11 Why so downcast,
  why all these sighs?
Hope in God! I will praise him still,
  my Saviour, my God.

43

1 Judge me, God, defend my cause
  against a people who have no faithful love;
from those who are treacherous and unjust,
  rescue me.
2 For you are the God of my strength;
  why abandon me?
Why must I go around in mourning,
  harrassed by the enemy?
3 Send out your light and your truth;
  they shall be my guide,
to lead me to your holy mountain
  to the place where you dwell.
4 Then I shall go to the altar of God,
  to the God of my joy.
I will rejoice and praise you on the harp,
  O God, my God.
5 Why so downcast,
  why all these sighs?
Hope in God! I will praise him still,
  my Saviour, my God.

Psalm 44 (V 43)

For the choirmaster   Of the sons of Korah   Poem

1 God, we have heard for ourselves,
  our ancestors have told us,
of the deeds you did in their days,
  in days of old, 2 by your hand.

To establish them in the land you drove out
    nations,
  to make room for them you harried peoples.

NEW REVISED STANDARD VERSION	REVISED ENGLISH BIBLE

NEW REVISED STANDARD VERSION

3 for not by their own sword did they win the land,
  nor did their own arm give them victory;
but your right hand, and your arm,
  and the light of your countenance,
  for you delighted in them.

4 You are my King and my God;
  you command[a] victories for Jacob.

5 Through you we push down our foes;
  through your name we tread down our
    assailants.

6 For not in my bow do I trust,
  nor can my sword save me.

7 But you have saved us from our foes,
  and have put to confusion those who hate us.

8 In God we have boasted continually,
  and we will give thanks to your name forever.
                                        Selah

9 Yet you have rejected us and abased us,
  and have not gone out with our armies.

10 You made us turn back from the foe,
  and our enemies have gotten spoil.

11 You have made us like sheep for slaughter,
  and have scattered us among the nations.

12 You have sold your people for a trifle,
  demanding no high price for them.

13 You have made us the taunt of our neighbors,
  the derision and scorn of those around us.

14 You have made us a byword among the nations,
  a laughingstock[b] among the peoples.

15 All day long my disgrace is before me,
  and shame has covered my face

16 at the words of the taunters and revilers,
  at the sight of the enemy and the avenger.

17 All this has come upon us,
  yet we have not forgotten you,
  or been false to your covenant.

18 Our heart has not turned back,
  nor have our steps departed from your way,

19 yet you have broken us in the haunt of jackals,
  and covered us with deep darkness.

20 If we had forgotten the name of our God,
  or spread out our hands to a strange god,

21 would not God discover this?
  For he knows the secrets of the heart.

22 Because of you we are being killed all day long,
  and accounted as sheep for the slaughter.

23 Rouse yourself! Why do you sleep, O Lord?
  Awake, do not cast us off forever!

24 Why do you hide your face?
  Why do you forget our affliction and
    oppression?

25 For we sink down to the dust;
  our bodies cling to the ground.

26 Rise up, come to our help.
  Redeem us for the sake of your steadfast love.

Psalm 45

To the leader: according to Lilies. Of the Korahites.
A Maskil. A love song.

1 My heart overflows with a goodly theme;
  I address my verses to the king;
  my tongue is like the pen of a ready scribe.

REVISED ENGLISH BIBLE

3 It was not our fathers' swords that won them the
    land,
  nor did their strong arm give them victory,
but your right hand and your arm
  and the light of your presence; such was your
    favour to them.

4 God, you are my King;
  command victory for Jacob.

5 By your help we shall throw back our enemies,
  in your name we shall trample down our assailants.

6 My trust is not in my bow,
  nor will my victory be won by my sword;

7 for you deliver us from our foes,
  you put to confusion those hostile to us.

8 In God have we gloried all day long,
  and we shall praise your name for ever.   [*Selah*

9 Yet you have rejected and humbled us
  and no longer lead our armies to battle.

10 You have forced us to retreat before the foe,
  and our enemies have plundered us at will.

11 You have given us up to be slaughtered like sheep
  and scattered us among the nations.

12 You sold your people for next to nothing
  and had no profit from the sale.

13 You have exposed us to the contempt of our
    neighbours,
  to the gibes and mockery of those about us.

14 You have made us a byword among the nations,
  and the peoples toss their heads at us;

15 so all day long my disgrace confronts me,
  and I am covered with shame

16 at the shouts of those who taunt and abuse me
  as the enemy takes his revenge.

17 Though all this has befallen us, we do not forget
    you
  and have not been false to your covenant;

18 our hearts have not been unfaithful,
  nor have our feet strayed from your path.

19 Yet you have crushed us as the sea serpent was
    crushed,
  and covered us with deepest darkness.

20 Had we forgotten the name of our God
  and spread our hands in prayer to alien gods,

21 would not God have found out,
  for he knows the secrets of the heart?

22 For your sake we are being done to death all day
    long,
  treated like sheep for slaughter.

23 Rouse yourself, Lord; why do you sleep?
  Awake! Do not reject us for ever.

24 Why do you hide your face,
  heedless of our misery and our sufferings?

25 For we sink down to the dust
  and lie prone on the ground.

26 Arise and come to our aid;
  for your love's sake deliver us.

Psalm 45

For the leader: set to 'Lilies': for the Korahites: a maskil:
a love song

1 MY heart is astir with a noble theme;
  in honour of a king I recite the song I have
    composed,
  and my tongue runs swiftly like the pen of an
    expert scribe.

---

[a] Gk Syr: Heb *You are my King, O God; command*   [b] Heb *a*
shaking of the head

44:19 **sea serpent:** *so Syriac; Heb.* wolves.

NEW AMERICAN BIBLE

NEW JERUSALEM BIBLE

4 Not with their own swords did they conquer the
    land,
    nor did their own arms bring victory;
  It was your right hand, your own arm,
    the light of your face, for you favored them.
5 You are my king and my God,
    who bestows victories on Jacob.
6 Through you we batter our foes;
    through your name, trample our adversaries.
7 Not in my bow do I trust,
    nor does my sword bring me victory.
8 You have brought us victory over our enemies,
    shamed those who hate us.
9 In God we have boasted all the day long;
    your name we will praise forever.   *Selah*
II
10 But now you have rejected and disgraced us;
    you do not march out with our armies.
11 You make us retreat before the foe;
    those who hate us plunder us at will.
12 You hand us over like sheep to be slaughtered,
    scatter us among the nations.
13 You sell your people for nothing;
    you make no profit from their sale.
14 You make us the reproach of our neighbors,
    the mockery and scorn of those around us.
15 You make us a byword among the nations;
    the peoples shake their heads at us.
16 All day long my disgrace is before me;
    shame has covered my face
17 At the sound of those who taunt and revile,
    at the sight of the spiteful enemy.
III
18 All this has come upon us,
    though we have not forgotten you,
    nor been disloyal to your covenant.
19 Our hearts have not turned back,
    nor have our steps strayed from your path.
20 Yet you have left us crushed,
    desolate in a place of jackals;
    you have covered us with darkness.
21 If we had forgotten the name of our God,
    stretched out our hands to another god,
22 Would not God have discovered this,
    God who knows the secrets of the heart?
23 For you we are slain all the day long,
    considered only as sheep to be slaughtered.
IV
24 Awake! Why do you sleep, O Lord?
    Rise up! Do not reject us forever!
25 Why do you hide your face;
    why forget our pain and misery?
26 We are bowed down to the ground;
    our bodies are pressed to the earth.
27 Rise up, help us!
    Redeem us as your love demands.

3 It was not their own sword that won the land,
    nor their own arms which made them victorious,
  but your hand it was and your arm,
    and the light of your presence, for you loved them.
4 You are my king, my God,
    who decreed Jacob's victories;
5 through you we conquered our opponents,
    in your name we trampled down those who rose up
        against us.
6 For my trust was not in my bow,
    my victory was not won by my sword;
7 it was you who saved us from our opponents,
    you who put to shame those who hate us.
8 Our boast was always of God,
    we praised your name without ceasing.   *Pause*
9 Yet now you have abandoned and humiliated us,
    you no longer take the field with our armies,
10 you leave us to fall back before the enemy,
    those who hate us plunder us at will.
11 You hand us over like sheep for slaughter,
    you scatter us among the nations,
12 you sell your people for a trifle
    and make no profit on the sale.
13 You make us the butt of our neighbours,
    the mockery and scorn of those around us,
14 you make us a by-word among nations,
    other peoples shake their heads over us.
15 All day long I brood on my disgrace,
    the shame written clear on my face,
16 from the sound of insult and abuse,
    from the sight of hatred and vengefulness.
17 All this has befallen us though we had not
        forgotten you,
    nor been disloyal to your covenant.
18 our hearts never turning away,
    our feet never straying from your path.
19 Yet you have crushed us in the place where jackals
        live,
    and immersed us in shadow dark as death.
20 Had we forgotten the name of our God
    and stretched out our hands to a foreign god,
21 would not God have found this out,
    for he knows the secrets of the heart?
22 For your sake we are being massacred all day long,
    treated as sheep to be slaughtered.
23 Wake, Lord! Why are you asleep?
    Awake! Do not abandon us for good.
24 Why do you turn your face away,
    forgetting that we are poor and harrassed?
25 For we are bowed down to the dust,
    and lie prone on the ground.
26 Arise! Come to our help!
    Ransom us, as your faithful love demands.

Psalm 45

1 *For the leader; according to "Lilies." A maskil of the
Korahites. A love song.*

I
2 My heart is stirred by a noble theme,
    as I sing my ode to the king.
  My tongue is the pen of a nimble scribe.

Psalm 45 (V 44)

*For the choirmaster   Tune: 'Lilies . . .'
Of the sons of Korah   Poem   Love song*

1 My heart is stirred by a noble theme,
    I address my poem to the king,
    my tongue the pen of an expert scribe.

| NEW REVISED STANDARD VERSION | REVISED ENGLISH BIBLE |

2 You are the most handsome of men;
　　grace is poured upon your lips;
　　therefore God has blessed you forever.
3 Gird your sword on your thigh, O mighty one,
　　in your glory and majesty.

4 In your majesty ride on victoriously
　　for the cause of truth and to defend*c* the right;
　　let your right hand teach you dread deeds.
5 Your arrows are sharp
　　in the heart of the king's enemies;
　　the peoples fall under you.

6 Your throne, O God,*d* endures forever and ever.
　　Your royal scepter is a scepter of equity;
7 you love righteousness and hate wickedness.
　Therefore God, your God, has anointed you
　　with the oil of gladness beyond your
　　　companions;
8 your robes are all fragrant with myrrh and
　　aloes and cassia.
　From ivory palaces stringed instruments make
　　you glad;
9 daughters of kings are among your ladies of
　　honor;
　　at your right hand stands the queen in gold of
　　Ophir.

10 Hear, O daughter, consider and incline your ear;
　　forget your people and your father's house,
11 and the king will desire your beauty.
　Since he is your lord, bow to him;
12 the people*e* of Tyre will seek your favor with
　　gifts,
　　the richest of the people 13 with all kinds of
　　wealth.

　The princess is decked in her chamber with
　　gold-woven robes;*f*
14 in many-colored robes she is led to the king;
　　behind her the virgins, her companions, follow.
15 With joy and gladness they are led along
　　as they enter the palace of the king.

16 In the place of ancestors you, O king,*g* shall
　　have sons;
　　you will make them princes in all the earth.
17 I will cause your name to be celebrated in all
　　generations;
　　therefore the peoples will praise you forever
　　and ever.

2 You surpass all others in beauty;
　gracious words flow from your lips,
　for you are blessed by God for ever.
3 Gird on your sword at your side, you warrior king,
4 advance in your pomp and splendour,
　ride on in the cause of truth and for justice.
　Your right hand will perform awesome deeds:
5 your arrows are sharp; nations lie beneath your
　　feet.
　The hearts of the king's enemies fail.

6 God has enthroned you for all eternity;
　your royal sceptre is a sceptre of equity.
7 You love right and hate wrong;
　therefore God, your God, has anointed you
　above your fellows with oil, the token of joy.
8 Your robes are all fragrant with myrrh and
　　powdered aloes,
　and you are made glad by string music
　from palaces panelled with ivory.
9 Princesses are among your noble ladies,
　your consort takes her place at your right hand
　in gold of Ophir.

10 Listen, my daughter, hear my words
　and consider them:
　forget your own people and your father's house;
11 let the king desire your beauty,
　for he is your lord.
12 Do him obeisance, daughter of Tyre.
　The richest in the land will court you with gifts.

13 Within the palace the royal bride is adorned,
　arrayed in cloth-of-gold.
14 She will be brought to the king in all her finery.
　Virgins who are her companions
　will be brought to you in her retinue,
15 escorted with the noise of revels and rejoicing
　as they enter the king's palace.

16 You will have sons to succeed your forefathers,
　and you will make them princes throughout the
　　land.
17 I shall declare your fame through all generations;
　therefore nations will praise you for ever and ever.

Psalm 46

To the leader. Of the Korahites. According to Alamoth.
A Song.

1 God is our refuge and strength,
　　a very present*h* help in trouble.
2 Therefore we will not fear, though the earth
　　should change,
　　though the mountains shake in the heart of the
　　sea;
3 though its waters roar and foam,
　　though the mountains tremble with its tumult.
　　　　　　　　　　　　　　　　　　Selah

Psalm 46

For the leader: for the Korahites: according to alamoth:
a song

1 GOD is our refuge and our stronghold,
　a timely help in trouble;
2 so we are not afraid though the earth shakes
　and the mountains move in the depths of the sea,
3 when its waters seethe in tumult
　and the mountains quake before his majesty. [*Selah*

---

*c*Cn: Heb *and the meekness of*　　*d*Or *Your throne is a throne of*
God, it　　*e*Heb *daughter*　　*f*Or *people.* 13*All glorious is the*
princess within, gold embroidery is her clothing　　*g*Heb *lacks*
O king　　*h*Or *well proved*

45:4 **advance:** *or* prosper. **and for:** *prob. rdg; Heb. obscure.*

NEW AMERICAN BIBLE

II

3 You are the most handsome of men;
  fair speech has graced your lips,
  for God has blessed you forever.
4 Gird your sword upon your hip, mighty warrior!
  In splendor and majesty ride on triumphant!
5 In the cause of truth and justice
  may your right hand show you wondrous deeds.
6 Your arrows are sharp;
  peoples will cower at your feet;
  the king's enemies will lose heart.
7 Your throne, O god, stands forever;
  your royal scepter is a scepter for justice.
8 You love justice and hate wrongdoing;
  therefore God, your God, has anointed you
  with the oil of gladness above your fellow kings.
9 With myrrh, aloes, and cassia
  your robes are fragrant.
  From ivory-paneled palaces
  stringed instruments bring you joy.
10 Daughters of kings are your lovely wives;
  a princess arrayed in Ophir's gold
  comes to stand at your right hand.

III

11 Listen, my daughter, and understand;
  pay me careful heed.
  Forget your people and your father's house,
12   that the king might desire your beauty.
  He is your lord;
13   honor him, daughter of Tyre.
  Then the richest of the people
  will seek your favor with gifts.
14 All glorious is the king's daughter as she enters,
  her raiment threaded with gold;
15 In embroidered apparel she is led to the king.
  The maids of her train are presented to the king.
16 They are led in with glad and joyous acclaim;
  they enter the palace of the king.

IV

17 The throne of your fathers your sons will have;
  you shall make them princes through all the
  land.
18 I will make your name renowned through all
  generations;
  thus nations shall praise you forever.

NEW JERUSALEM BIBLE

2 Of all men you are the most handsome,
  gracefulness is a dew upon your lips,
  for God has blessed you for ever.
3 Warrior, strap your sword at your side,
  in your majesty and splendour advance, 4 ride on
  in the cause of truth, gentleness and uprightness.

  Stretch the bowstring tight, lending terror to your
    right hand.
5 Your arrows are sharp, nations lie at your mercy,
  the king's enemies lose heart.
6 Your throne is from God, for ever and ever,
  the sceptre of your kingship a sceptre of justice,
7 you love uprightness and detest evil.

  This is why God, your God, has anointed you
  with oil of gladness, as none of your rivals,
8 your robes all myrrh and aloes.

  From palaces of ivory, harps bring you joy,
9 in your retinue are daughters of kings,
  the consort at your right hand in gold of Ophir.

10 Listen, my daughter, attend to my words and hear;
  forget your own nation and your ancestral home,
11 then the king will fall in love with your beauty;
  he is your lord, bow down before him.
12 The daughter of Tyre will court your favour with
    gifts,
  and the richest of peoples 13 with jewels set in
    gold.

  Clothed 14 in brocade, the king's daughter is led
    within
  to the king with the maidens of her retinue;
  her companions are brought to her,
15 they enter the king's palace with joy and rejoicing.
16 Instead of your ancestors you will have sons;
  you will make them rulers over the whole world.

17 I will make your name endure from generation to
    generation,
  so nations will sing your praise for ever and ever.

Psalm 46

1 *For the leader. A song of the Korahites. According
to alamoth.*

I

2 God is our refuge and our strength,
  an ever-present help in distress.
3 Thus we do not fear, though earth be shaken
  and mountains quake to the depths of the sea,
4 Though its waters rage and foam
  and mountains totter at its surging.
  The LORD of hosts is with us;
  our stronghold is the God of Jacob.   *Selah*

Psalm 46 (V 45)

For the choirmaster   Of the sons of Korah
For oboe   Song

1 God is both refuge and strength for us,
  a help always ready in trouble;
2 so we shall not be afraid though the earth be in
    turmoil,
  though mountains tumble into the depths of the
    sea,
3 and its waters roar and seethe,
  and the mountains totter as it heaves.

  (Yahweh Sabaoth is with us,
  our citadel, the God of Jacob.)   *Pause*

NEW REVISED STANDARD VERSION	REVISED ENGLISH BIBLE

NEW REVISED STANDARD VERSION

4 There is a river whose streams make glad the city
of God,
the holy habitation of the Most High.
5 God is in the midst of the city;*i* it shall not be
moved;
God will help it when the morning dawns.
6 The nations are in an uproar, the kingdoms totter;
he utters his voice, the earth melts.
7 The LORD of hosts is with us;
the God of Jacob is our refuge.*j*   *Selah*

8 Come, behold the works of the LORD;
see what desolations he has brought on the earth.
9 He makes wars cease to the end of the earth;
he breaks the bow, and shatters the spear;
he burns the shields with fire.
10 "Be still, and know that I am God!
I am exalted among the nations,
I am exalted in the earth."
11 The LORD of hosts is with us;
the God of Jacob is our refuge.*j*   *Selah*

Psalm 47

To the leader. Of the Korahites. A Psalm.

1 Clap your hands, all you peoples;
shout to God with loud songs of joy.
2 For the LORD, the Most High, is awesome,
a great king over all the earth.
3 He subdued peoples under us,
and nations under our feet.
4 He chose our heritage for us,
the pride of Jacob whom he loves.   *Selah*

5 God has gone up with a shout,
the LORD with the sound of a trumpet.
6 Sing praises to God, sing praises;
sing praises to our King, sing praises.
7 For God is the king of all the earth;
sing praises with a psalm.*k*

8 God is king over the nations;
God sits on his holy throne.
9 The princes of the peoples gather
as the people of the God of Abraham.
For the shields of the earth belong to God;
he is highly exalted.

Psalm 48

A Song. A Psalm of the Korahites.

1 Great is the LORD and greatly to be praised
in the city of our God.
His holy mountain, 2 beautiful in elevation,
is the joy of all the earth,
Mount Zion, in the far north,
the city of the great King.
3 Within its citadels God
has shown himself a sure defense.

4 Then the kings assembled,
they came on together.
5 As soon as they saw it, they were astounded;
they were in panic, they took to flight;

REVISED ENGLISH BIBLE

4 There is a river whose streams bring joy to the city
of God,
the holy dwelling of the Most High;
5 God is in her midst; she will not be overthrown,
and at the break of day he will help her.
6 Nations are in tumult, kingdoms overturned;
when he thunders, the earth melts.
7 The LORD of Hosts is with us;
the God of Jacob is our fortress.   [*Selah*
8 Come, see what the LORD has done,
the astounding deeds he has wrought on earth;
9 in every part of the wide world he puts an end to
war:
he breaks the bow, he snaps the spear,
he burns the shields in the fire.
10 'Let be then; learn that I am God,
exalted among the nations, exalted in the earth.'
11 The LORD of Hosts is with us;
the God of Jacob is our fortress.   [*Selah*

Psalm 47

For the leader: for the Korahites: a psalm

1 CLAP your hands, all you nations,
acclaim God with shouts of joy.
2 How awesome is the LORD Most High,
great King over all the earth!
3 He subdues nations under us,
peoples under our feet;
4 he chooses for us our heritage,
the pride of Jacob whom he loves.   [*Selah*

5 To the shout of triumph God has gone up,
the LORD has gone up at the sound of the horn.
6 Praise God, praise him with psalms;
praise our King, praise him with psalms,
7 for God is King of all the earth;
sing psalms with all your skill.

8 Seated on his holy throne,
God reigns over the nations.
9 The princes of the nations assemble
with the people of the God of Abraham;
for the mighty ones of earth belong to God,
and he is exalted on high.

Psalm 48

A song: a psalm: for the Korahites

1 GREAT is the LORD and most worthy of praise
in the city of our God.
His holy mountain 2 is fair and lofty,
the joy of the whole earth.
The mountain of Zion, the far recesses of the
north,
is the city of the great King.
3 God in her palaces
is revealed as a tower of strength.

4 See, the kings assemble;
they advance together.
5 They look, and are astounded;
filled with alarm they panic.

46:9 **shields:** *or* wagons.   47:7 **with . . . skill:** *meaning of Heb.
word uncertain.*   47:9 **with:** *prob. rdg; Heb. omits.* **mighty ones:**
lit. shields.   48:2 **the north:** *or* Zaphon.

i Heb *of it*   *j* Or *fortress*   *k* Heb *Maskil*

II

5 Streams of the river gladden the city of God,
   the holy dwelling of the Most High.
6 God is in its midst; it shall not be shaken;
   God will help it at break of day.
7 Though nations rage and kingdoms totter,
   God's voice thunders and the earth trembles.
8 The LORD of hosts is with us;
   our stronghold is the God of Jacob.   Selah

III

9 Come and see the works of the LORD,
   who has done fearsome deeds on earth;
10 Who stops wars to the ends of the earth,
   breaks the bow, splinters the spear,
   and burns the shields with fire;
11 Who says:
   "Be still and confess that I am God!
   I am exalted among the nations,
   exalted on the earth."
12 The LORD of hosts is with us;
   our stronghold is the God of Jacob.   Selah

Psalm 47

1 *For the leader. A psalm of the Korahites.*

I

2 All you peoples, clap your hands;
   shout to God with joyful cries.
3 For the LORD, the Most High, inspires awe,
   the great king over all the earth,
4 Who made people subject to us,
   brought nations under our feet,
5 Who chose a land for our heritage,
   the glory of Jacob, the beloved.   Selah

II

6 God mounts the throne amid shouts of joy;
   the LORD, amid trumpet blasts.
7 Sing praise to God, sing praise;
   sing praise to our king, sing praise.

III

8 God is king over all the earth;
   sing hymns of praise.
9 God rules over the nations;
   God sits upon his holy throne.
10 The princes of the peoples assemble
   with the people of the God of Abraham.
   For the rulers of the earth belong to God,
   who is enthroned on high.

Psalm 48

1 *A psalm of the Korahites. A song.*

I

2 Great is the LORD and highly praised
   in the city of our God:
   The holy mountain, 3 fairest of heights,
   the joy of all the earth,
   Mount Zion, the heights of Zaphon,
   the city of the great king.

II

4 God is its citadel,
   renowned as a stronghold.
5 See! The kings assembled,
   together they invaded.
6 When they looked they were astounded;
   terrified, they were put to flight!

4 There is a river whose streams bring joy to God's
   city,
   it sanctifies the dwelling of the Most High.
5 God is in the city, it cannot fall;
   at break of day God comes to its rescue.
6 Nations are in uproar, kingdoms are tumbling,
   when he raises his voice the earth crumbles away.

7   Yahweh Sabaoth is with us,
     our citadel, the God of Jacob.   *Pause*

8 Come, consider the wonders of Yahweh,
   the astounding deeds he has done on the earth;
9 he puts an end to wars over the whole wide world,
   he breaks the bow, he snaps the spear,
   shields he burns in the fire.
10 'Be still and acknowledge that I am God,
   supreme over nations, supreme over the world.'

11   Yahweh Sabaoth is with us,
     our citadel, the God of Jacob.   *Pause*

Psalm 47 (V 46)

For the choirmaster   Of the sons of Korah   Psalm

1 Clap your hands, all peoples,
   acclaim God with shouts of joy.
2 For Yahweh, the Most High, is glorious,
   the great king over all the earth.
3 He brings peoples under our yoke
   and nations under our feet.

4 He chooses for us our birthright,
   the pride of Jacob whom he loves.   *Pause*

5 God goes up to shouts of acclaim,
   Yahweh to a fanfare on the ram's horn.
6 Let the music sound for our God, let it sound,
   let the music sound for our king, let it sound.
7 For he is king of the whole world;
   learn the music, let it sound for God!
8 God reigns over the nations,
   seated on his holy throne.
9 The leaders of the nations rally
   to the people of the God of Abraham.
   The shields of the earth belong to God,
   who is exalted on high.

Psalm 48 (V 47)

Song   Psalm   Of the sons of Korah

1 Great is Yahweh and most worthy of praise
   in the city of our God,
   the holy mountain, 2 towering in beauty,
   the joy of the whole world:

   Mount Zion in the heart of the north,
   the settlement of the great king;
3 God himself among its palaces
   has proved himself its bulwark.

4 For look, kings made alliance,
   together they advanced;
5 without a second glance, when they saw,
   they panicked and fled away.

|

6 trembling took hold of them there,
  pains as of a woman in labor,
7 as when an east wind shatters
  the ships of Tarshish.
8 As we have heard, so have we seen
  in the city of the LORD of hosts,
  in the city of our God,
  which God establishes forever.   *Selah*

9 We ponder your steadfast love, O God,
  in the midst of your temple.
10 Your name, O God, like your praise,
  reaches to the ends of the earth.
  Your right hand is filled with victory.
11   Let Mount Zion be glad,
  let the towns[l] of Judah rejoice
  because of your judgments.

12 Walk about Zion, go all around it,
  count its towers,
13 consider well its ramparts;
  go through its citadels,
  that you may tell the next generation
14   that this is God,
  our God forever and ever.
  He will be our guide forever.

Psalm 49

To the leader. Of the Korahites. A Psalm.

1 Hear this, all you peoples;
  give ear, all inhabitants of the world,
2 both low and high,
  rich and poor together.
3 My mouth shall speak wisdom;
  the meditation of my heart shall be
  understanding.
4 I will incline my ear to a proverb;
  I will solve my riddle to the music of the harp.

5 Why should I fear in times of trouble,
  when the iniquity of my persecutors surrounds
  me,
6 those who trust in their wealth
  and boast of the abundance of their riches?
7 Truly, no ransom avails for one's life,[m]
  there is no price one can give to God for it.
8 For the ransom of life is costly,
  and can never suffice
9 that one should live on forever
  and never see the grave.[n]

10 When we look at the wise, they die;
  fool and dolt perish together
  and leave their wealth to others.
11 Their graves[o] are their homes forever,
  their dwelling places to all generations,
  though they named lands their own.
12 Mortals cannot abide in their pomp;
  they are like the animals that perish.

13 Such is the fate of the foolhardy,
  the end of those[p] who are pleased with their
  lot.   *Selah*

6 Trembling has seized them there;
  they toss in pain like a woman in labour,
7 like the ships of Tarshish
  when an east wind wrecks them.
8 What we had heard we saw now with our own
  eyes
  in the city of the LORD of Hosts,
  in the city of our God;
  God will establish it for evermore.   [*Selah*
9 God, within your temple
  we meditate on your steadfast love.
10 God, the praise your name deserves
  is heard at earth's farthest bounds.
  Your right hand is full of victory.
11 The hill of Zion rejoices
  and Judah's cities are glad,
  for you redress their wrongs.

12 Go round Zion in procession,
  count the number of her towers,
13 take note of her ramparts,
  pass her palaces in review,
  that you may tell generations yet to come
14 that such is God,
  our God for ever;
  he will be our guide for evermore.

Psalm 49

For the leader: for the Korahites: a psalm

1 HEAR this, all you peoples;
  listen, all you inhabitants of the world,
2 both high and low,
  rich and poor,
3 for the words that I have to speak are wise;
  my thoughts provide understanding.
4 I listen with care to the parable
  and interpret a mystery to the music of the lyre.

5 Why should I be afraid in evil times
  when beset by the wickedness of treacherous foes,
6 trusting in their wealth
  and boasting of their great riches?
7 Alas! No one can ever ransom himself,
  nor pay God the price for his release;
8 the ransom would be too high,
  for ever beyond his power to pay,
9 the ransom that would let him live on for ever
  and not see death's pit.
10 For we see that the wise die,
  as the stupid and senseless all perish,
  leaving their wealth to others.
11 Though they give their names to estates,
  the grave is their eternal home,
  their dwelling for all time to come.
12 For human beings like oxen are short-lived;
  they are like beasts whose lives are cut short.

13 Such is the fate of the foolish
  and of those after them who approve their words.
          [*Selah*

---

[l] Heb *daughters*   [m] Another reading is *no one can ransom a brother*
[n] Heb *the pit*   [o] Gk Syr Compare Tg: Heb *their inward* (thought)
[p] Tg: Heb *after them*

48:14 **evermore:** *poss. meaning; Heb. word uncertain.*
49:7 **Alas! . . . himself:** *or* No one can ever ransom anyone else.
49:11 **the grave:** *so Gk; Heb.* their inward parts.   49:12 **like**
oxen: *prob. rdg; Heb.* in honour.

NEW AMERICAN BIBLE

7 Trembling seized them there,
  anguish, like a woman's labor,
8 As when the east wind wrecks
  the ships of Tarshish!
  III
9 What we had heard we now see
  in the city of the LORD of hosts,
  In the city of our God,
  founded to last forever.   Selah
10 O God, within your temple
  we ponder your steadfast love.
11 Like your name, O God,
  your praise reaches the ends of the earth.
  Your right hand is fully victorious.
12 Mount Zion is glad!
  The cities of Judah rejoice
  because of your saving deeds!
  IV
13 Go about Zion, walk all around it,
  note the number of its towers.
14 Consider the ramparts, examine its citadels,
  that you may tell future generations:
15 "Yes, so mighty is God,
  our God who leads us always!"

Psalm 49

1 *For the leader. A psalm of the Korahites.*

2 Hear this, all you peoples!
  Give ear, all who inhabit the world,
3 You of lowly birth or high estate,
  rich and poor alike.
4 My mouth shall speak wisdom,
  my heart shall offer insight.
5 I will turn my attention to a problem,
  expound my question to the music of a lyre.
  I
6 Why should I fear in evil days,
  when my wicked pursuers ring me round,
7 Those who trust in their wealth
  and boast of their abundant riches?
8 One cannot redeem oneself,
  pay to God a ransom.
9 Too high the price to redeem a life;
  one would never have enough
10 To stay alive forever
  and never see the pit.
11 Anyone can see that the wisest die,
  the fool and the senseless pass away too,
  and must leave their wealth to others.
12 Tombs are their homes forever,
  their dwellings through all generations,
  though they gave their names to their lands.
13 For all their riches
  mortals do not abide;
  they perish like the beasts.
  II
14 This is the destiny of those who trust in folly,
  the end of those so pleased with their wealth.
                                              Selah

NEW JERUSALEM BIBLE

6 Trembling seized them on the spot,
  pains like those of a woman in labour;
7 it was the east wind,
  that wrecker of ships from Tarshish.

8 What we had heard we saw for ourselves
  in the city of our God,
  in the city of Yahweh Sabaoth,
  which God has established for ever.   *Pause*

9 We reflect on your faithful love, God,
  in your temple!
10 Both your name and your praise, God,
  are over the whole wide world.

  Your right hand is full of saving justice,
11 Mount Zion rejoices,
  the daughters of Judah delight
  because of your saving justice.

12 Go round Zion, walk right through her,
  count her bastions,
13 admire her walls,
  examine her palaces,

  to tell future generations
14 that such is God;
  our God for ever and ever,
  he is our guide!

Psalm 49 (V 48)

For the choirmaster   Of the sons of Korah   Psalm

1 Hear this, all nations,
  listen, all who dwell on earth,
2 people high and low,
  rich and poor alike!

3 My lips have wisdom to utter,
  my heart good sense to whisper.
4 I listen carefully to a proverb,
  I set my riddle to the music of the harp.

5 Why should I be afraid in times of trouble?
  Malice dogs me and hems me in.
6 They trust in their wealth,
  and boast of the profusion of their riches.

7 But no one can ever redeem himself
  or pay his own ransom to God,
8 the price for himself is too high;
  it can never be 9 that he will live on for ever
  and avoid the sight of the abyss.

10 For he will see the wise also die
  no less than the fool and the brute,
  and leave their wealth behind for others.

11 For ever no home but their tombs,
  their dwelling-place age after age,
  though they gave their name to whole territories.

12 In prosperity people lose their good sense,
  they become no better than dumb animals.
13 So they go on in their self-assurance,
  right up to the end they are content with their lot.
                                                    Pause

NEW REVISED STANDARD VERSION	REVISED ENGLISH BIBLE

NEW REVISED STANDARD VERSION

14 Like sheep they are appointed for Sheol;
  Death shall be their shepherd;
 straight to the grave they descend,*q*
  and their form shall waste away;
  Sheol shall be their home.*r*

15 But God will ransom my soul from the power of
  Sheol,
  for he will receive me.   *Selah*

16 Do not be afraid when some become rich,
  when the wealth of their houses increases.

17 For when they die they will carry nothing away;
  their wealth will not go down after them.

18 Though in their lifetime they count themselves
  happy
  —for you are praised when you do well for
  yourself—

19 they*s* will go to the company of their ancestors,
  who will never again see the light.

20 Mortals cannot abide in their pomp;
  they are like the animals that perish.

Psalm 50

A Psalm of Asaph.

1 The mighty one, God the LORD,
  speaks and summons the earth
  from the rising of the sun to its setting.

2 Out of Zion, the perfection of beauty,
  God shines forth.

3 Our God comes and does not keep silence,
  before him is a devouring fire,
  and a mighty tempest all around him.

4 He calls to the heavens above
  and to the earth, that he may judge his people:

5 "Gather to me my faithful ones,
  who made a covenant with me by sacrifice!"

6 The heavens declare his righteousness,
  for God himself is judge.   *Selah*

7 "Hear, O my people, and I will speak,
  O Israel, I will testify against you.
  I am God, your God.

8 Not for your sacrifices do I rebuke you;
  your burnt offerings are continually before me.

9 I will not accept a bull from your house,
  or goats from your folds.

10 For every wild animal of the forest is mine,
  the cattle on a thousand hills.

11 I know all the birds of the air,*t*
  and all that moves in the field is mine.

12 "If I were hungry, I would not tell you,
  for the world and all that is in it is mine.

13 Do I eat the flesh of bulls,
  or drink the blood of goats?

14 Offer to God a sacrifice of thanksgiving,*u*
  and pay your vows to the Most High.

15 Call on me in the day of trouble;
  I will deliver you, and you shall glorify me."

16 But to the wicked God says:
  "What right have you to recite my statutes,
  or take my covenant on your lips?

17 For you hate discipline,
  and you cast my words behind you.

REVISED ENGLISH BIBLE

14 Like sheep they head for Sheol;
  with death as their shepherd,
  they go straight down to the grave.
  Their bodies, stripped of all honour,
  waste away in Sheol.

15 But God will ransom my life
  and take me from the power of Sheol.   [*Selah*

16 Do not envy anyone though he grows rich,
  when the wealth of his family increases;

17 at his death he can take nothing,
  for his wealth will not go down with him.

18 Though in his lifetime he counts himself happy
  and he is praised in his prosperity,

19 he will go to join the company of his forefathers
  who will never again see the light.

20 For human beings like oxen are short-lived;
  they are like beasts whose lives are cut short.

Psalm 50

A psalm: for Asaph

1 GOD, the LORD God, has spoken
  and summoned the world
  from the rising of the sun to its setting.

2 God shines out from Zion, perfect in beauty.

3 Our God is coming and will not keep silence;
  consuming fire runs ahead of him
  and round him a great storm rages.

4 The heavens above and the earth
  he summons to the judging of his people:

5 'Gather to me my loyal servants,
  those who by sacrifice made a covenant with me.'

6 The heavens proclaim his justice,
  for God himself is judge.   [*Selah*

7 Listen, my people, and I shall speak;
  I shall bear witness against you, Israel:
  I am God, your God.

8 Not for your sacrifices do I rebuke you,
  your whole-offerings always before me;

9 I need take no young bull from your farmstead,
  no he-goat from your folds;

10 for all the living creatures of the forest are mine
  and the animals in their thousands on my hills.

11 I know every bird on those mountains;
  the teeming life of the plains is my care.

12 If I were hungry, I would not tell you,
  for the world and all that is in it are mine.

13 Do I eat the flesh of bulls
  or drink the blood of he-goats?

14 Offer to God a sacrifice of thanksgiving
  and fulfil your vows to the Most High;

15 then if you call to me in time of trouble,
  I shall come to your rescue, and you will honour
  me.

16 God's word to a wicked person is this:
  What right have you to recite my statutes,
  to take the words of my covenant on your lips?

17 For you hate correction
  and cast my words out of your sight.

---

*q*Cn: Heb *the upright shall have dominion over them in the morning*
*r*Meaning of Heb uncertain   *s*Cn: Heb *you*   *t*Gk Syr Tg: Heb
mountains   *u*Or *make thanksgiving your sacrifice to God*

49:14 **the grave:** *prob. rdg; Heb.* the morning.   49:14,15 **Sheol:**
or the underworld.   49:18 **and he . . . in his:** *prob. rdg; Heb.* and
you are praised in your.   49:19 **he:** *prob. rdg; Heb.* you.
49:20 **like oxen:** *prob. rdg; Heb.* in honour.

NEW AMERICAN BIBLE

15 Like sheep they are herded into Sheol,
  where death will be their shepherd.
Straight to the grave they descend,
  where their form will waste away,
  Sheol will be their palace.
16 But God will redeem my life, *Selah*
  will take me from the power of Sheol.
17 Do not fear when others become rich,
  when the wealth of their houses grows great.
18 When they die they will take nothing with them,
  their wealth will not follow them down.
19 When living, they congratulate themselves and say:
  "All praise you, you do so well."
20 But they will join the company of their forebears,
  never again to see the light.
21 For all their riches,
  if mortals do not have wisdom,
  they perish like the beasts.

Psalm 50

1 *A psalm of Asaph.*

I
The LORD, the God of gods,
  has spoken and summoned the earth
  from the rising of the sun to its setting.
2 From Zion God shines forth,
  perfect in beauty.
3 Our God comes and will not be silent!
  Devouring fire precedes,
  storming fiercely round about.
4 God summons the heavens above
  and the earth to the judgment of his people:
5 "Gather my faithful ones before me,
  those who made a covenant with me by
  sacrifice."
6 The heavens proclaim divine justice,
  for God alone is the judge. *Selah*
II
7 "Listen, my people, I will speak;
  Israel, I will testify against you;
  God, your God, am I.
8 Not for your sacrifices do I rebuke you,
  nor for your holocausts, set before me daily.
9 I need no bullock from your house,
  no goats from your fold.
10 For every animal of the forest is mine,
  beasts by the thousands on my mountains.
11 I know every bird of the heavens;
  the creatures of the field belong to me.
12 Were I hungry, I would not tell you,
  for mine is the world and all that fills it.
13 Do I eat the flesh of bulls
  or drink the blood of goats?
14 Offer praise as your sacrifice to God;
  fulfill your vows to the Most High.
15 Then call on me in time of distress;
  I will rescue you, and you shall honor me."
III
16 But to the wicked God says:
  "Why do you recite my commandments
  and profess my covenant with your lips?
17 You hate discipline;
  you cast my words behind you!

NEW JERUSALEM BIBLE

14 They are penned in Sheol like sheep,
  Death will lead them to pasture,
  and those who are honest will rule over them.

  In the morning all trace of them will be gone,
  Sheol will be their home.
15 But my soul God will ransom
  from the clutches of Sheol, and will snatch me up.
  Pause

16 Do not be overawed when someone gets rich,
  and lives in ever greater splendour;
17 when he dies he will take nothing with him,
  his wealth will not go down with him.
18 Though he pampered himself while he lived
  —and people praise you for looking after
    yourself—
19 he will go to join the ranks of his ancestors,
  who will never again see the light.

20 In prosperity people lose their good sense,
  they become no better than dumb animals.

Psalm 50 (V 49)

Psalm   Of Asaph

1 The God of gods, Yahweh, is speaking,
  from east to west he summons the earth.
2 From Zion, perfection of beauty, he shines forth;
3 he is coming, our God, and will not be silent.

  Devouring fire ahead of him,
  raging tempest around him,
4 he summons the heavens from on high,
  and the earth to judge his people.

5 'Gather to me my faithful,
  who sealed my covenant by sacrifice.'
6 The heavens proclaim his saving justice,
  'God himself is judge.' *Pause*

7 'Listen, my people, I am speaking,
  Israel, I am giving evidence against you,
  I, God, your God.

8 'It is not with your sacrifices that I find fault,
  those burnt offerings constantly before me;
9 I will not accept any bull from your homes,
  nor a single goat from your folds.

10 'For all forest creatures are mine already,
  the animals on the mountains in their thousands.
11 I know every bird in the air,
  whatever moves in the fields is mine.

12 'If I am hungry I shall not tell you,
  since the world and all it holds is mine.
13 Am I to eat the flesh of bulls
  or drink the blood of goats?

14 'Let thanksgiving be your sacrifice to God,
  fulfil the vows you make to the Most High;
15 then if you call to me in time of trouble
  I will rescue you and you will honour me.'

16 But to the wicked, God says:

  'What right have you to recite my statutes,
  to take my covenant on your lips,
17 when you detest my teaching,
  and thrust my words behind you?

NEW REVISED STANDARD VERSION

18 You make friends with a thief when you see one,
   and you keep company with adulterers.
19 "You give your mouth free rein for evil,
   and your tongue frames deceit.
20 You sit and speak against your kin;
   you slander your own mother's child.
21 These things you have done and I have been
      silent;
   you thought that I was one just like yourself.
   But now I rebuke you, and lay the charge before
      you.
22 "Mark this, then, you who forget God,
   or I will tear you apart, and there will be no
      one to deliver.
23 Those who bring thanksgiving as their sacrifice
      honor me;
   to those who go the right way[v]
   I will show the salvation of God."

Psalm 51

*To the leader. A Psalm of David, when the prophet Nathan
came to him, after he had gone in to Bathsheba.*

1 Have mercy on me, O God,
   according to your steadfast love;
   according to your abundant mercy
   blot out my transgressions.
2 Wash me thoroughly from my iniquity,
   and cleanse me from my sin.
3 For I know my transgressions,
   and my sin is ever before me.
4 Against you, you alone, have I sinned,
   and done what is evil in your sight,
   so that you are justified in your sentence
   and blameless when you pass judgment.
5 Indeed, I was born guilty,
   a sinner when my mother conceived me.
6 You desire truth in the inward being;[w]
   therefore teach me wisdom in my secret heart.
7 Purge me with hyssop, and I shall be clean;
   wash me, and I shall be whiter than snow.
8 Let me hear joy and gladness;
   let the bones that you have crushed rejoice.
9 Hide your face from my sins,
   and blot out all my iniquities.
10 Create in me a clean heart, O God,
   and put a new and right[x] spirit within me.
11 Do not cast me away from your presence,
   and do not take your holy spirit from me.
12 Restore to me the joy of your salvation,
   and sustain in me a willing[y] spirit.
13 Then I will teach transgressors your ways,
   and sinners will return to you.
14 Deliver me from bloodshed, O God,
   O God of my salvation,
   and my tongue will sing aloud of your
      deliverance.
15 O Lord, open my lips,
   and my mouth will declare your praise.
16 For you have no delight in sacrifice;
   if I were to give a burnt offering, you would
      not be pleased.

REVISED ENGLISH BIBLE

18 If you meet a thief, you choose him as your friend,
   and you make common cause with adulterers;
19 freely you employ your mouth for evil
   and harness your tongue to deceit.
20 You are forever talking against your brother,
   imputing faults to your own mother's son.
21 When you have done these things, and kept
      silence,
   you thought that I was someone like yourself;
   but I shall rebuke you and indict you to your face.
22 You forget God, but think well on this,
   lest I tear you in pieces and there be no one to
      save you:
23 he honours me who offers a sacrifice of
      thanksgiving,
   and to him who follows my way
   I shall show the salvation of God.

Psalm 51

*For the leader: a psalm: for David (when Nathan the
prophet came to him after he had taken Bathsheba)*

1 GOD, be gracious to me in your faithful love;
   in the fullness of your mercy blot out my
      misdeeds.
2 Wash away all my iniquity
   and cleanse me from my sin.
3 For well I know my misdeeds,
   and my sins confront me all the time.
4 Against you only have I sinned
   and have done what displeases;
   you are right when you accuse me
   and justified in passing sentence.
5 From my birth I have been evil,
   sinful from the time my mother conceived me.
6 You desire faithfulness in the inmost being,
   so teach me wisdom in my heart.
7 Sprinkle me with hyssop, so that I may be
      cleansed;
   wash me, and I shall be whiter than snow.
8 Let me hear the sound of joy and gladness;
   you have crushed me, but make me rejoice again.
9 Turn away your face from my sins
   and wipe out all my iniquity.
10 God, create a pure heart for me,
   and give me a new and steadfast spirit.
11 Do not drive me from your presence
   or take your holy spirit from me.
12 Restore to me the joy of your deliverance
   and grant me a willing spirit to uphold me.
13 I shall teach transgressors your ways,
   and sinners will return to you.
14 My God, God my deliverer, deliver me from
      bloodshed,
   and I shall sing the praises of your saving power.
15 Lord, open my lips,
   that my mouth may proclaim your praise.
16 You have no delight in sacrifice;
   if I were to bring a whole-offering you would not
      accept it.

---

v Heb *who set a way*   w Meaning of Heb uncertain   x Or *steadfast*
y Or *generous*

50:23 **him . . . way:** *prob. rdg; Heb.* him who puts a way.
51:6 **You . . . being:** *or* You have hidden the truth in darkness. **in
my heart:** *or* in secret.   51:7 **hyssop:** *or* marjoram.

NEW AMERICAN BIBLE

18 When you see thieves, you befriend them;
   with adulterers you throw in your lot.
19 You give your mouth free rein for evil;
   you harness your tongue to deceit.
20 You sit maligning your own kin,
   slandering the child of your own mother.
21 When you do these things should I be silent?
   Or do you think that I am like you?
   I accuse you, I lay the charge before you."
   IV
22 "Understand this, you who forget God,
   lest I attack you with no one to rescue.
23 Those who offer praise as a sacrifice honor me;
   to the obedient I will show the salvation of
   God."

NEW JERUSALEM BIBLE

18 'You make friends with a thief as soon as you see
   one,
   you feel at home with adulterers,
19 your conversation is devoted to wickedness,
   and your tongue to inventing lies.
20 'You sit there, slandering your own brother,
   you malign your own mother's son.
21 You do this, and am I to say nothing?
   Do you think that I am really like you?
   I charge you, indict you to your face.
22 'Think it out, you who forget God,
   or I will tear you apart without hope of a rescuer.
23 Honour to me is a sacrifice of thanksgiving;
   to the upright I will show God's salvation.'

Psalm 51

1 *For the leader. A psalm of David,* 2 *when Nathan the*
prophet came to him after his affair with Bathsheba.

   I
3 Have mercy on me, God, in your goodness;
   in your abundant compassion blot out my
      offense.
4 Wash away all my guilt;
   from my sin cleanse me.
5 For I know my offense;
   my sin is always before me.
6 Against you alone have I sinned;
   I have done such evil in your sight
 That you are just in your sentence,
   blameless when you condemn.
7 True, I was born guilty,
   a sinner, even as my mother conceived me.
8 Still, you insist on sincerity of heart;
   in my inmost being teach me wisdom.
9 Cleanse me with hyssop, that I may be pure;
   wash me, make me whiter than snow.
10 Let me hear sounds of joy and gladness;
   let the bones you have crushed rejoice.
   II
11 Turn away your face from my sins;
   blot out all my guilt.
12 A clean heart create for me, God;
   renew in me a steadfast spirit.
13 Do not drive me from your presence,
   nor take from me your holy spirit.
14 Restore my joy in your salvation;
   sustain in me a willing spirit.
15 I will teach the wicked your ways,
   that sinners may return to you.
16 Rescue me from death, God, my saving God,
   that my tongue may praise your healing power.
17 Lord, open my lips;
   my mouth will proclaim your praise.
18 For you do not desire sacrifice;
   a burnt offering you would not accept.

Psalm 51 (V 50)

For the choirmaster   Of David   When the prophet
Nathan had come to him because he had gone to Bathsheba

1 Have mercy on me, O God, in your faithful love,
   in your great tenderness wipe away my offences;
2 wash me clean from my guilt,
   purify me from my sin.
3 For I am well aware of my offences,
   my sin is constantly in mind.
4 Against you, you alone, I have sinned,
   I have done what you see to be wrong,

   that you may show your saving justice when you
      pass sentence,
   and your victory may appear when you give
      judgement,
5 remember, I was born guilty,
   a sinner from the moment of conception.
6 But you delight in sincerity of heart,
   and in secret you teach me wisdom.
7 Purify me with hyssop till I am clean,
   wash me till I am whiter than snow.
8 Let me hear the sound of joy and gladness,
   and the bones you have crushed will dance.
9 Turn away your face from my sins,
   and wipe away all my guilt.
10 God, create in me a clean heart,
   renew within me a resolute spirit,
11 do not thrust me away from your presence,
   do not take away from me your spirit of holiness.
12 Give me back the joy of your salvation,
   sustain in me a generous spirit.
13 I shall teach the wicked your paths,
   and sinners will return to you.
14 Deliver me from bloodshed, God, God of my
      salvation,
   and my tongue will acclaim your saving justice.
15 Lord, open my lips,
   and my mouth will speak out your praise.
16 Sacrifice gives you no pleasure,
   burnt offering you do not desire.

NEW REVISED STANDARD VERSION	REVISED ENGLISH BIBLE

17 The sacrifice acceptable to God[z] is a broken
spirit;
   a broken and contrite heart, O God, you will
   not despise.

18 Do good to Zion in your good pleasure;
   rebuild the walls of Jerusalem,
19 then you will delight in right sacrifices,
   in burnt offerings and whole burnt offerings;
   then bulls will be offered on your altar.

Psalm 52

*To the leader. A Maskil of David, when Doeg the Edomite
came to Saul and said to him, "David has come to the
house of Ahimelech."*

1 Why do you boast, O mighty one,
   of mischief done against the godly?[a]
   All day long 2 you are plotting destruction.
Your tongue is like a sharp razor,
   you worker of treachery.
3 You love evil more than good,
   and lying more than speaking the truth.   *Selah*
4 You love all words that devour,
   O deceitful tongue.

5 But God will break you down forever;
   he will snatch and tear you from your tent;
   he will uproot you from the land of the living.
           Selah
6 The righteous will see, and fear,
   and will laugh at the evildoer,[b] saying,
7 "See the one who would not take
   refuge in God,
but trusted in abundant riches,
   and sought refuge in wealth!"[c]

8 But I am like a green olive tree
   in the house of God.
I trust in the steadfast love of God
   forever and ever.
9 I will thank you forever,
   because of what you have done.
In the presence of the faithful
   I will proclaim[d] your name, for it is good.

Psalm 53

To the leader: according to Mahalath. A Maskil of David.

1 Fools say in their hearts, "There is no God."
   They are corrupt, they commit abominable
      acts;
there is no one who does good.

2 God looks down from heaven on humankind
   to see if there are any who are wise,
   who seek after God.

3 They have all fallen away, they are all alike
   perverse;
there is no one who does good,
   no, not one.

4 Have they no knowledge, those evildoers,
   who eat up my people as they eat bread,
   and do not call upon God?

---

17 God, my sacrifice is a broken spirit;
you, God, will not despise a chastened heart.

18 Show favour to Zion and grant her prosperity;
rebuild the walls of Jerusalem.
19 Then you will delight in the appointed sacrifices;
then young bulls will be offered on your altar.

Psalm 52

*For the leader: a maskil: for David (when Doeg the
Edomite came and told Saul that David had gone to
Abimelech's house)*

1 YOU MIGHTY man, why do you boast all the day
of your infamy against God's loyal servant?
2 You plan destruction;
your slanderous tongue is sharp as a razor.
3 You love evil rather than good,
falsehood rather than truthful speech;   [Selah
4 you love all malicious talk and slander.
5 So may God fling you to the ground,
sweep you away, leave you ruined and homeless,
uprooted from the land of the living.   [Selah
6 The righteous will look on, awestruck,
then laugh at his plight:
7 'This is the man', they say,
'who would not make God his refuge,
but trusted in his great wealth
and took refuge in his riches.'

8 But I am like a spreading olive tree in God's
house,
for I trust in God's faithful love for ever and ever.
9 I shall praise you for ever for what you have done,
and glorify your name among your loyal servants,
for that is good.

Psalm 53

For the leader: set to 'Mahalath': a maskil: for David

1 THE impious fool says in his heart,
'There is no God.'
Everyone is depraved, every deed is vile;
no one does good!
2 God looks out from heaven
on all the human race
to see if any act wisely,
if any seek God.
3 But all are unfaithful, altogether corrupt;
no one does good, no, not even one.

4 Have they no understanding,
those evildoers who devour my people
as if eating bread,
and never call to God?

51:17 **chastened:** *so Syriac; Heb.* broken and wounded.
51:19 **Then . . . sacrifices:** *prob. rdg; Heb.* adds a whole-offering
and one completely consumed.   52:1 **against:** *prob. rdg, cp.*
Syriac; Heb. omits.   52:5 **So may God:** *or* So God will.
52:7 **in his riches:** *so Syriac; Heb.* in his destruction.
53:1–6 *Cp. Ps. 14:1–7.*

---

[z] Or *My sacrifice, O God,*   [a] Cn Compare Syr: Heb *the kindness of*
God   [b] Heb *him*   [c] Syr Tg: Heb *in his destruction*   [d] Cn: Heb
wait for

NEW AMERICAN BIBLE

19 My sacrifice, God, is a broken spirit;
 God, do not spurn a broken, humbled heart.
III
20 Make Zion prosper in your good pleasure;
 rebuild the walls of Jerusalem.
21 Then you will be pleased with proper sacrifice,
 burnt offerings and holocausts;
 then bullocks will be offered on your altar.

Psalm 52

1 *For the leader. A maskil of David,* 2 *when Doeg the Edomite went and told Saul, "David went to the house of Ahimelech."*

I
3 Why do you glory in evil,
 you scandalous liar?
 All day long 4 you plot destruction;
 your tongue is like a sharpened razor,
 you skillful deceiver.
5 You love evil rather than good,
 lies rather than honest speech.   *Selah*
6 You love any word that destroys,
 you deceitful tongue.
II
7 Now God will strike you down,
 leave you crushed forever,
 Pluck you from your tent,
 uproot you from the land of the living.   *Selah*
8 The righteous will look on with awe;
 they will jeer and say:
9 "That one did not take God as a refuge,
 but trusted in great wealth,
 relied on devious plots."
III
10 But I, like an olive tree in the house of God,
 trust in God's faithful love forever.
11 I will praise you always
 for what you have done.
 I will proclaim before the faithful
 that your name is good.

Psalm 53

1 *For the leader; according to* Mahalath. *A maskil of David.*

I
2 Fools say in their hearts,
 "There is no God."
 Their deeds are loathsome and corrupt;
 not one does what is right.
3 God looks down from heaven
 upon the human race,
 To see if even one is wise,
 if even one seeks God.
4 All have gone astray;
 all alike are perverse.
 Not one does what is right, not even one.
II
5 Will these evildoers never learn?
 They devour my people as they devour bread;
 they do not call upon God.

NEW JERUSALEM BIBLE

17 Sacrifice to God is a broken spirit,
 a broken, contrite heart you never scorn.
18 In your graciousness do good to Zion,
 rebuild the walls of Jerusalem.
19 Then you will delight in upright sacrifices,
 — burnt offerings and whole oblations —
 and young bulls will be offered on your altar.

Psalm 52 (V 51)

For the choirmaster   Poem   Of David   When Doeg the Edomite went and warned Saul, 'David has gone to Abimelech's house'

1 Why take pride in being wicked,
 you champion in villainy,
 all day long 2 plotting crime?
 Your tongue is razor-sharp,
 you artist in perfidy.

3 You prefer evil to good,
 lying to uprightness.   *Pause*
4 You revel in destructive talk,
 treacherous tongue!

5 That is why God will crush you,
 destroy you once and for all,
 snatch you from your tent,
 uproot you from the land of the living.   *Pause*

6 The upright will be awestruck as they see it,
 they will mock him,
7 'So much for someone who would not place
 his reliance in God,
 but relied on his own great wealth,
 and made himself strong by crime.'

8 But I, like a flourishing olive tree
 in the house of God,
 put my trust in God's faithful love,
 for ever and ever.

9 I shall praise you for ever
 for what you have done,
 and shall trust in your name, so full of goodness,
 in the presence of your faithful.

Psalm 53 (V 52)*j*

For the choirmaster   In sickness   Poem   Of David

1 The fool has said in his heart,
 'There is no God!'
 They are corrupt, vile and unjust,
 not one of them does right.

2 God looks down from heaven
 at the children of Adam,
 to see if a single one is wise,
 a single one seeks God.

3 All have proved faithless,
 all alike turned sour,
 not one of them does right,
 not a single one.

4 Are they not aware, these evil-doers?
 They are devouring my people;
 this is the bread they eat,
 and they never call upon God.

j 53 Almost identical with Ps 14 except that the name 'Yahweh' is not used.

5 There they shall be in great terror,
   in terror such as has not been.
For God will scatter the bones of the ungodly;*e*
   they will be put to shame,*f* for God has
      rejected them.
6 O that deliverance for Israel would come from
      Zion!
   When God restores the fortunes of his people,
      Jacob will rejoice; Israel will be glad.

Psalm 54

To the leader: with stringed instruments. A Maskil of
David, when the Ziphites went and told Saul, "David is in
hiding among us."

1 Save me, O God, by your name,
   and vindicate me by your might.
2 Hear my prayer, O God;
   give ear to the words of my mouth.
3 For the insolent have risen against me,
   the ruthless seek my life;
   they do not set God before them.   *Selah*
4 But surely, God is my helper;
   the Lord is the upholder of *g* my life.
5 He will repay my enemies for their evil.
   In your faithfulness, put an end to them.
6 With a freewill offering I will sacrifice to you;
   I will give thanks to your name, O LORD, for it
      is good.
7 For he has delivered me from every trouble,
   and my eye has looked in triumph on my
      enemies.

Psalm 55

To the leader: with stringed instruments. A Maskil of David.

1 Give ear to my prayer, O God;
   do not hide yourself from my supplication.
2 Attend to me, and answer me;
   I am troubled in my complaint.
I am distraught 3 by the noise of the enemy,
   because of the clamor of the wicked.
For they bring*h* trouble upon me,
   and in anger they cherish enmity against me.
4 My heart is in anguish within me,
   the terrors of death have fallen upon me.
5 Fear and trembling come upon me,
   and horror overwhelms me.
6 And I say, "O that I had wings like a dove!
   I would fly away and be at rest;
7 truly, I would flee far away;
   I would lodge in the wilderness;   *Selah*
8 I would hurry to find a shelter for myself
   from the raging wind and tempest."

9 Confuse, O Lord, confound their speech;
   for I see violence and strife in the city.
10 Day and night they go around it
   on its walls,
   and iniquity and trouble are within it;

5 They will be in dire alarm
   when God scatters the bones of the godless,
   confounded when God rejects them.
6 If only deliverance for Israel might come from
      Zion!
When God restores his people's fortunes,
   let Jacob rejoice, let Israel be glad.

Psalm 54

For the leader: with stringed instruments: a maskil:
for David (when the Ziphites came and said to Saul, 'David
is in hiding among us.')

1 SAVE me, God, by the power of your name,
   and vindicate me through your might.
2 God, hear my prayer,
   listen to my supplication.
3 Violent men rise to attack me,
   ruthless men seek my life;
   they give no thought to God.   [*Selah*
4 But God is my helper,
   the Lord the sustainer of my life.
5 May their own malice recoil on the foes who beset
      me!
   Show yourself faithful and destroy them.
6 Freely I shall offer you a sacrifice
   and praise your name, LORD, as is most seemly;
7 God has rescued me from every trouble;
   I look with delight on the downfall of my enemies.

Psalm 55

For the leader: on stringed instruments: a maskil: for David

1 LISTEN, God, to my prayer:
   do not hide yourself from my pleading.
2 Hear me and give me an answer,
   for my cares leave me no peace.
3 I am panic-stricken at the hostile shouts,
   at the shrill clamour of the wicked;
   for they heap trouble on me
   and revile me in their fury.
4 My heart is torn with anguish
   and the terrors of death bear down on me.
5 Fear and trembling assail me
   and my whole frame shudders.
6 I say: 'Oh that I had the wings of a dove
   to fly away and find rest!'
7 I would escape far away
   to a refuge in the wilderness.   [*Selah*
8 Soon I would find myself a shelter
   from raging wind and tempest.

9 Frustrate and divide their counsels, Lord!
   I have seen violence and strife in the city;
10 day and night they encircle it,
   all along its walls;
   it is filled with trouble and mischief,

---

e Cn Compare Gk Syr: Heb *him who encamps against you*
f Gk: Heb *you will put to shame*   *g* Gk Syr Jerome: Heb *is of those*
who uphold or *is with those who uphold*   *h* Cn Compare Gk: Heb
they cause to totter

53:5 **They . . . alarm:** *so some MSS; others add* there was no fear.
when God scatters: *or* when God has scattered. **the godless:** *prob.*
rdg, cp. Gk; Heb. one who encamps against you.   54:3 **Violent**
men: *so some MSS; others* Strangers.

6 They have good reason to fear,
　　though now they do not fear.
For God will certainly scatter
　　the bones of the godless.
They will surely be put to shame,
　　for God has rejected them.

III

7 Oh, that from Zion might come
　　the deliverance of Israel,
That Jacob may rejoice and Israel be glad
　　when God restores the people!

Psalm 54

1 *For the leader. On stringed instruments. A maskil of David,* 2 *when the Ziphites came and said to Saul, "David is hiding among us."*

I

3 O God, by your name save me.
　　By your strength defend my cause.
4 O God, hear my prayer.
　　Listen to the words of my mouth.
5 The arrogant have risen against me;
　　the ruthless seek my life;
　　they do not keep God before them.　　*Selah*

II

6 God is present as my helper;
　　the Lord sustains my life.
7 Turn back the evil upon my foes;
　　in your faithfulness, destroy them.
8 Then I will offer you generous sacrifice
　　and praise your gracious name, LORD,
9 Because it has rescued me from every trouble,
　　and my eyes look down on my foes.

Psalm 55

1 *For the leader. On stringed instruments. A maskil of David.*

I

2 Listen, God, to my prayer;
　　do not hide from my pleading;
3 　hear me and give answer.
I rock with grief; I groan
4 　at the uproar of the enemy,
　　the clamor of the wicked.
They heap trouble upon me,
　　savagely accuse me.
5 My heart pounds within me;
　　death's terrors fall upon me.
6 Fear and trembling overwhelm me;
　　shuddering sweeps over me.
7 I say, "If only I had wings like a dove
　　that I might fly away and find rest.
8 Far away I would flee;
　　I would stay in the desert.　　*Selah*
9 I would soon find a shelter
　　from the raging wind and storm."

II

10 Lord, check and confuse their scheming.
　　I see violence and strife in the city,
11 　making rounds on its walls day and night.
Within are mischief and evil;

5 They will be gripped with fear,
　　just where there is no need for fear,
for God scatters the bones of him who besieges you;
　　they are mocked because God rejects them.

6 Who will bring from Zion salvation for Israel?
When God brings his people home,
　　what joy for Jacob, what happiness for Israel!

Psalm 54 (V 53)

For the choirmaster　On stringed instruments　Poem Of David　When the Ziphites went to Saul and said, 'Is not David hiding with us?'

1 God, save me by your name,
　　in your power vindicate me.
2 God, hear my prayer,
　　listen to the words I speak.

Arrogant men are attacking me,
　　llies hounding me to death,
　　room in their thoughts for God.　　*Pause*

4 how God is coming to my help,
5 Md, among those who sustain me.
　　eir wickedness recoil on those who lie in Yahait for me.
6 How in your constancy destroy them.
　　and pra will I offer you sacrifice,
7 for it haur name, for it is good,
　　and my eued me from all my troubles,
　　s feasted on my enemies.

m 55 (V 54)

For the choirmat.　For strings　Poem　Of David

1 God, hear my p.
　　do not hideaw
2 give me a heaingom my plea,
　　my troubles giveer me,
I shudder 3 a the end peace.
　　at the outcy of the houts,
they heap upcharges ai;
　　in their aner bring home,
4 My heart writhes within n cusations against me.
　　the terrors of death com
5 fear and trembling overwheme,
　　and shuddering grips me.

6 And I say,
　　'Who will give me wings like
　　to fly away and find rest?'
7 How far I would escape,
　　and make a nest in the desert.
8 I would soon find a refuge
　　from the storm of abuse,
　　from the 9 destructive tempest, Lord
　　from the flood of their tongues.　　*Pause*

For I see violence
　　and strife in the city,
10 day and night they make their rounds
　　along the city walls.

Inside live malice and mischief,

NEW REVISED STANDARD VERSION

11   ruin is in its midst;
oppression and fraud
   do not depart from its marketplace.

12 It is not enemies who taunt me—
   I could bear that;
it is not adversaries who deal insolently with
   me—
   I could hide from them.

13 But it is you, my equal,
   my companion, my familiar friend,

14 with whom I kept pleasant company;
   we walked in the house of God with the
     throng.

15 Let death come upon them;
   let them go down alive to Sheol;
for evil is in their homes and in their hearts.

16 But I call upon God,
   and the LORD will save me.

17 Evening and morning and at noon
   I utter my complaint and moan,
   and he will hear my voice.

18 He will redeem me unharmed
   from the battle that I wage,
for many are arrayed against me.   *Selah*

19 God, who is enthroned from of old,
   will hear, and will humble them—
because they do not change,
   and do not fear God.

20 My companion laid hands on a f
   and violated a covenant with

21 with speech smoother than but
   but with a heart set on wa
with words that were softer
   but in fact were drawn s

22 Cast your burden *j* on the
   and he will sustain yo
he will never permit
   the righteous to be

23 But you, O God, wil
   into the lowest picheros
the bloodthirsty anf their days.
   shall not live q
But I will trust

Psalm 56

ng to The Dove on Far-off Terebinths.
To the leader, when the Philistines seized him in Gath.
Of David. A to me, O God, for people trample on

1   Be
   long foes oppress me;
   ies trample on me all day long,
2   any fight against me.
   High, 3 when I am afraid,
   t my trust in you.
   d, whose word I praise,
   God I trust; I am not afraid;
   hat can flesh do to me?

  l day long they seek to injure my cause;
  all their thoughts are against me for evil.
They stir up strife, they lurk,
  they watch my steps.
As they hoped to have my life,

o lacks with me   *j Or Cast what he has given you*

REVISED ENGLISH BIBLE

11 destruction is rife within it;
   its public square is never free
   from oppression and deceit.

12 It was no enemy that taunted me,
   or I should have avoided him;
no one that treated me with scorn,
   or should have kept out of his way.

13 was you, a man of my own sort,
   comrade, my own dear friend;
we held pleasant converse together
   walking with the throng in the house of God.

15 May death strike them,
   may they go down alive into Sheol;
   for their homes are haunts of evil!

16 But I appeal to God,
   and the LORD will save me.

17 Evening and morning and at noonday
   I make my complaint and groan.

18 He will hear my cry and deliver me
   and give me security
so that none may attack me,
   for many are hostile to me.

19 God hears, and he humbles them,
   he who is enthroned from of old.   *[Selah*
They have no respect for an oath,
   nor any fear of God.

20 Such men do violence to those at peace with them
   and break their solemn word;

21 their speech is smoother than butter,
   but their thoughts are of war;
their words are softer than oil,
   but they themselves are like drawn swords.

22 Commit your fortunes to the LORD,
   and he will sustain you;
he will never let the righteous be shaken.

23 But you will cast them down, God,
   into the pit of destruction;
bloodthirsty and treacherous,
   they will not live out half their days.
For my part, LORD, I shall put my trust in you.

Psalm 56

For the leader: set to 'The Dove of the Distant Oaks': for
David: a miktam (when the Philistines seized him in Gath)

1 BE gracious to me, God, for I am trampled
     underfoot;
assailants harass me all the day.

2 All day long foes beset and oppress me,
   for numerous are those who assail me.

3 In my day of fear
   I put my trust in you, the Most High,

4 in God, whose promise is my boast,
   in God I trust and shall not be afraid;
   what can mortals do to me?

5 All day long they wound me with words;
   every plan they make is aimed at me.

6 In malice they band together and watch for me,
   they dog my footsteps;
   but, while they lie in wait for me,

55:15 **Sheol:** *or the underworld.*   56:5 **with words:** *prob. rdg;*
Heb. my words.

12 treachery is there as well;
   oppression and fraud never leave its streets.
13 If an enemy had reviled me,
   that I could bear;
   If my foe had viewed me with contempt,
   from that I could hide.
14 But it was you, my other self,
   my comrade and friend,
15 You, whose company I enjoyed,
   at whose side I walked
   in procession in the house of God.
   III
16 Let death take them by surprise;
   let them go down alive to Sheol,
   for evil is in their homes and hearts.
17 But I will call upon God,
   and the LORD will save me.
18 At dusk, dawn, and noon
   I will grieve and complain,
   and my prayer will be heard.
19 God will give me freedom and peace
   from those who war against me,
   though there are many who oppose me.
20 God, who sits enthroned forever,
   will hear me and humble them.
   For they will not mend their ways;
   they have no fear of God.
21 They strike out at friends
   and go back on their promises.
22 Softer than butter is their speech,
   but war is in their hearts.
   Smoother than oil are their words,
   but they are unsheathed swords.
23 Cast your care upon the LORD,
   who will give you support.
   God will never allow
   the righteous to stumble.
24 But you, God, will bring them down
   to the pit of destruction.
   These bloodthirsty liars
   will not live half their days,
   but I put my trust in you.

Psalm 56

1 *For the director. According to* Yonath elem rehoqim. *A*
miktam *of David, when the Philistines seized him at Gath.*

   I
2 Have mercy on me, God,
   for I am treated harshly;
   attackers press me all the day.
3 My foes treat me harshly all the day;
   yes, many are my attackers.
   O Most High, 4 when I am afraid,
   in you I place my trust.
5 God, I praise your promise;
   in you I trust, I do not fear.
   What can mere flesh do to me?
   II
6 All the day they foil my plans;
   their every thought is of evil against me.
7 They hide together in ambush;
   they watch my every step;
   they lie in wait for my life.

11   inside lives destruction,
   tyranny and treachery never absent
      from its central square.
12 Were it an enemy who insulted me,
      that I could bear;
   if an opponent pitted himself against me,
      I could turn away from him.
13 But you, a person of my own rank,
      a comrade and dear friend,
14 to whom I was bound by intimate friendship
      in the house of God!

   May they recoil in disorder,
15   may death descend on them,
   may they go down alive to Sheol,
      since evil shares their home with them.

16 For my part, I appeal to God,
      and Yahweh saves me;
17 evening, morning, noon,
      I complain and I groan.

   He hears my cry,
18 he ransoms me and gives me peace
      from the feud against me,
   for they are taking me to law.

19 But God will listen and will humble them,
   he who has been enthroned from the beginning;
   no change of heart for them,
      for they do not fear God.

20 They attack those at peace with them,
      going back on their oaths;
21 though their mouth is smoother than butter,
      enmity is in their hearts;
   their words more soothing than oil,
      yet sharpened like swords.

22 Unload your burden onto Yahweh
      and he will sustain you;
   never will he allow
      the upright to stumble.

23 You, God, will thrust them down
      to the abyss of destruction,
   men bloodthirsty and deceptive,
      before half their days are spent.

   For my part, I put my trust in you.

Psalm 56 (V 55)

For the choirmaster   Tune: 'The oppression of distant
princes'   Of David   In a quiet voice   When the
Philistines seized him in Gath

1 Take pity on me, God, as they harry me,
   pressing their attacks home all day.
2 Those who harry me lie in wait for me all day,
   countless are those who attack me from the
      heights.

3 When I am afraid, I put my trust in you,
4 in God, whose word I praise,
   in God I put my trust and have no fear,
   what power has human strength over me?

5 All day long they carp at my words,
   their only thought is to harm me,
6 they gather together, lie in wait and spy on my
      movements,
   as though determined to take my life.

7   so repay[k] them for their crime;
     in wrath cast down the peoples, O God!

8 You have kept count of my tossings;
     put my tears in your bottle.
     Are they not in your record?

9 Then my enemies will retreat
     in the day when I call.
     This I know, that[l] God is for me.

10 In God, whose word I praise,
     in the LORD, whose word I praise,

11 in God I trust; I am not afraid.
     What can a mere mortal do to me?

12 My vows to you I must perform, O God;
     I will render thank offerings to you.

13 For you have delivered my soul from death,
     and my feet from falling,
     so that I may walk before God
     in the light of life.

Psalm 57

To the leader: Do Not Destroy. Of David. A Miktam, when
he fled from Saul, in the cave.

1 Be merciful to me, O God, be merciful to me,
     for in you my soul takes refuge;
     in the shadow of your wings I will take refuge,
     until the destroying storms pass by.

2 I cry to God Most High,
     to God who fulfills his purpose for me.

3 He will send from heaven and save me,
     he will put to shame those who trample on me.
                         Selah
  God will send forth his steadfast love and his
     faithfulness.

4 I lie down among lions
     that greedily devour[m] human prey;
     their teeth are spears and arrows,
     their tongues sharp swords.

5 Be exalted, O God, above the heavens.
     Let your glory be over all the earth.

6 They set a net for my steps;
     my soul was bowed down.
     They dug a pit in my path,
     but they have fallen into it themselves.   *Selah*

7 My heart is steadfast, O God,
     my heart is steadfast.
  I will sing and make melody.

8   Awake, my soul!
  Awake, O harp and lyre!
     I will awake the dawn.

9 I will give thanks to you, O Lord, among the
     peoples;
     I will sing praises to you among the nations.

10 For your steadfast love is as high as the heavens;
     your faithfulness extends to the clouds.

11 Be exalted, O God, above the heavens.
     Let your glory be over all the earth.

7 there is no escape for them because of their
     iniquity.
  God, in your anger overthrow the nations.

8 You have noted my grief;
     store my tears in your flask.
     Are they not recorded in your book?

9 Then my enemies will turn back
     on the day when I call to you.
     This I know, that God is on my side.

10 In God, whose promise is my boast,
     in the LORD, whose promise is my boast,

11 in God I trust and shall not be afraid;
     what can mortals do to me?

12 I have bound myself with vows made to you, God,
     and will redeem them with due thank-offerings;

13 for you have rescued me from death
     and my feet from stumbling,
     to walk in the presence of God,
     in the light of life.

Psalm 57

For the leader: set to 'Destroy not': for David: a miktam
(when he was a fugitive from Saul in the cave)

1 GOD, be gracious to me; be gracious,
     for I have made you my refuge.
  I shall seek refuge in the shadow of your wings
     until the storms are past.

2 I shall call to God Most High,
     to the God who will fulfil his purpose for me.

3 He will send from heaven and save me,
     and my persecutors he will put to scorn.   [*Selah*
  May God send his love, unfailing and sure.

4 I lie prostrate among lions, man-eaters
     whose teeth are spears and arrows,
     whose tongues are sharp swords.

5 God, be exalted above the heavens;
     let your glory be over all the earth.

6 Some have prepared a net to catch me as I walk,
     but they themselves were brought low;
  they have dug a pit in my path
     but have themselves fallen into it.   [*Selah*

7 My heart is steadfast, God,
     my heart is steadfast.
  I shall sing and raise a psalm.

8 Awake, my soul,
     awake, harp and lyre;
     I shall awake at dawn.

9 I shall praise you among the peoples, Lord,
     among the nations I shall raise a psalm to you,

10 for your unfailing love is as high as the heavens;
     your faithfulness reaches to the skies.

11 God, be exalted above the heavens;
     let your glory be over all the earth.

---

[k] Cn: Heb *rescue*   [l] Or *because*   [m] Cn: Heb *are aflame for*

56:7 **there is no:** *prob. rdg; cp. Gk.*   56:10 **whose promise:**
prob. rdg; Heb. a promise.   57:6 **they themselves:** *prob. rdg;*
Heb. I myself.   57:7–11 *Cp. Ps. 108:1–5.*

NEW AMERICAN BIBLE

8 They are evil; watch them, God!
    Cast the nations down in your anger!
9 My wanderings you have noted;
    are my tears not stored in your vial,
    recorded in your book?
10 My foes turn back when I call on you.
    This I know: God is on my side.
11 God, I praise your promise;
12   in you I trust, I do not fear.
    What can mere mortals do to me?
    III
13 I have made vows to you, God;
    with offerings I will fulfill them,
14 Once you have snatched me from death,
    kept my feet from stumbling,
    That I may walk before God
    in the light of the living.

Psalm 57

1 *For the director. Do not destroy. A miktam of David,*
when he fled from Saul into a cave.

    I
2 Have mercy on me, God,
    have mercy on me.
    In you I seek shelter.
    In the shadow of your wings I seek shelter
    till harm pass by.
3 I call to God Most High,
    to God who provides for me.
4 May God send help from heaven to save me,
    shame those who trample upon me.
    May God send fidelity and love.   *Selah*
5 I must lie down in the midst of lions
    hungry for human prey.
    Their teeth are spears and arrows,
    their tongue, a sharpened sword.
6 Show yourself over the heavens, God;
    may your glory appear above all the earth.
    II
7 They have set a trap for my feet;
    my soul is bowed down;
    They have dug a pit before me.
    May they fall into it themselves!   *Selah*
8 My heart is steadfast, God,
    my heart is steadfast.
    I will sing and chant praise.
9 Awake, my soul;
    awake, lyre and harp!
    I will wake the dawn.
10 I will praise you among the peoples, Lord;
    I will chant your praise among the nations.
11 For your love towers to the heavens;
    your faithfulness, to the skies.
12 Show yourself over the heavens, God;
    may your glory appear above all the earth.

NEW JERUSALEM BIBLE

7 Because of this crime reject them,
    in your anger, God, strike down the nations.
8 You yourself have counted up my sorrows,
    collect my tears in your wineskin.
9 Then my enemies will turn back
    on the day when I call.

    This I know, that God is on my side.
10 In God whose word I praise,
    in Yahweh whose word I praise,
11 in God I put my trust and have no fear;
    what can mortal man do to me?

12 I am bound by the vows I have made, God,
    I will pay you the debt of thanks,
13 for you have saved my life from death
    to walk in the presence of God,
    in the light of the living.

Psalm 57 (V 56)

For the choirmaster   *Tune: 'Do not destroy'*   *Of David*
In a quiet voice   *When he escaped from Saul in the cave*

1 Take pity on me, God, take pity on me,
    for in you I take refuge,
    in the shadow of your wings I take refuge,
    until the destruction is past.
2 I call to God the Most High,
    to God who has done everything for me;
3 may he send from heaven and save me,
    and check those who harry me;   *Pause*
    may God send his faithful love and his constancy.
4 I lie surrounded by lions,
    greedy for human prey,
    their teeth are spears and arrows,
    their tongue a sharp sword.
5 Be exalted above the heavens, God!
    Your glory over all the earth!
6 They laid a snare in my path
    —I was bowed with care—
    they dug a pit ahead of me,
    but fell in it themselves.   *Pause*
7 My heart is ready, God,
    my heart is ready;
    I will sing, and make music for you.
8   Awake, my glory,
    awake, lyre and harp,
    that I may awake the Dawn.
9 I will praise you among the peoples, Lord,
    I will make music for you among nations,
10 for your faithful love towers to heaven,
    your constancy to the clouds.
11 Be exalted above the heavens, God!
    Your glory over all the earth!

Psalm 58

To the leader: Do Not Destroy. Of David. A Miktam.

1 Do you indeed decree what is right, you gods?[n]
   Do you judge people fairly?
2 No, in your hearts you devise wrongs;
   your hands deal out violence on earth.

3 The wicked go astray from the womb;
   they err from their birth, speaking lies.
4 They have venom like the venom of a serpent,
   like the deaf adder that stops its ear,
5 so that it does not hear the voice of charmers
   or of the cunning enchanter.

6 O God, break the teeth in their mouths;
   tear out the fangs of the young lions, O LORD!
7 Let them vanish like water that runs away;
   like grass let them be trodden down[o] and
   wither.
8 Let them be like the snail that dissolves into
   slime;
   like the untimely birth that never sees the sun.
9 Sooner than your pots can feel the heat of thorns,
   whether green or ablaze, may he sweep them
   away!

10 The righteous will rejoice when they see
   vengeance done;
   they will bathe their feet in the blood of the
   wicked.
11 People will say, "Surely there is a reward for the
   righteous;
   surely there is a God who judges on earth."

Psalm 59

*To the leader: Do Not Destroy. Of David. A Miktam, when
Saul ordered his house to be watched in order to kill him.*

1 Deliver me from my enemies, O my God;
   protect me from those who rise up against me.
2 Deliver me from those who work evil;
   from the bloodthirsty save me.

3 Even now they lie in wait for my life;
   the mighty stir up strife against me.
   For no transgression or sin of mine, O LORD,
4 for no fault of mine, they run and make ready.

   Rouse yourself, come to my help and see!
5 You, LORD God of hosts, are God of Israel.
   Awake to punish all the nations;
   spare none of those who treacherously plot
   evil.   *Selah*

6 Each evening they come back,
   howling like dogs
   and prowling about the city.
7 There they are, bellowing with their mouths,
   with sharp words[p] on their lips—
   for "Who," they think,[q] "will hear us?"

8 But you laugh at them, O LORD;
   you hold all the nations in derision.
9 O my strength, I will watch for you;
   for you, O God, are my fortress.

Psalm 58

For the leader: set to 'Destroy not': for David: a miktam

1 YOU RULERS, are your decisions really just?
   Do you judge your people with equity?
2 No! Your hearts devise wickedness
   and your hands mete out violence in the land.

3 The wicked go astray from birth:
   liars, no sooner born than they take to wrong
   ways.
4 Venomous with the venom of serpents,
   they are like the deaf asp which stops its ears
5 and will not listen to the sound of the charmer,
   however skilfully he may play.

6 God, break the teeth in their mouths;
   LORD, shatter the fangs of the oppressors.
7 May they vanish like water that runs away;
   may he aim his arrows, may they perish by them;
8 may they be like an abortive birth which melts
   away
   or a stillborn child which never sees the sun!
9 Before they know it, may they be rooted up like a
   thorn bush,
   like weeds which a man angrily clears away!

10 The righteous will rejoice at the sight of vengeance
   done;
   they will bathe their feet in the blood of the
   wicked.
11 It will be said,
   'There is after all reward for the righteous;
   there is after all a God who dispenses justice on
   earth.'

Psalm 59

*For the leader: set to 'Destroy not': for David: a miktam
(when Saul sent men to keep watch on David's
house to kill him)*

1 RESCUE me, my God, from my enemies;
   be my strong tower against those who assail me.
2 Rescue me from evildoers;
   deliver me from the bloodthirsty.
3 Violent men lie in wait for me,
   they lie in ambush ready to attack me;
   for no fault or guilt of mine, LORD,
4-5 innocent though I am, they rush to oppose me.
   But you, LORD God of Hosts, Israel's God,
   arouse yourself to come to me and keep watch:
   awake, and punish all the nations.
   Have no mercy on these treacherous evildoers,
                                              [*Selah*
6 who come out at nightfall,
   snarling like dogs as they prowl about the city.
7 From their mouths comes a stream of abuse,
   and words that wound are on their lips;
   for they say, 'Who will hear us?'
8 But you laugh at them, LORD,
   mocking all the nations.

9 My strength, I look to you;
   for God is my strong tower.

58:1 **rulers:** *or* gods.   58:7 **by them:** *prob. rdg; Heb.* like.
58:9 **may . . . up like:** *prob. rdg; Heb.* your pots. **angrily:** *prob.
rdg; Heb.* like anger.   59:4–5 **though I am:** *prob. rdg, cp. Aram.*
(Targ.); *Heb.* omits.   59:9 **My strength:** *so Gk; Heb.* His
strength. **strength:** *or* refuge.

[n]Or *mighty lords*   [o]Cn: Meaning of Heb uncertain   [p]Heb *with
swords*   [q]Heb lacks *they think*

Psalm 58

¹*For the leader. Do not destroy. A miktam of David.*

I

² Do you indeed pronounce justice, O gods;
   do you judge mortals fairly?
³ No, you freely engage in crime;
   your hands dispense violence to the earth.

II

⁴ The wicked have been corrupt since birth;
   liars from the womb, they have gone astray.
⁵ Their poison is like the poison of a snake,
   like that of a serpent stopping its ears,
⁶ So as not to hear the voice of the charmer
   who casts such cunning spells.

III

⁷ O God, smash the teeth in their mouths;
   break the jaw-teeth of these lions, Lord!
⁸ Make them vanish like water flowing away;
   trodden down, let them wither like grass.
⁹ Let them dissolve like a snail that oozes away,
   like an untimely birth that never sees the sun.
¹⁰ Suddenly, like brambles or thistles,
   have the whirlwind snatch them away.
¹¹ Then the just shall rejoice to see the vengeance
   and bathe their feet in the blood of the wicked.
¹² Then it will be said:
   "Truly there is a reward for the just;
   there is a God who is judge on earth!"

Psalm 59

¹*For the director. Do not destroy. A miktam of David,*
when Saul sent people to watch his house and kill him.

I

² Rescue me from my enemies, my God;
   lift me out of reach of my foes.
³ Deliver me from evildoers;
   from the bloodthirsty save me.
⁴ They have set an ambush for my life;
   the powerful conspire against me.
   For no offense or misdeed of mine, Lord,
⁵   for no fault they hurry to take up arms.
   Come near and see my plight!
⁶   You, Lord of hosts, are the God of Israel!
   Awake! Punish all the nations.
   Have no mercy on these worthless traitors. *Selah*
⁷ Each evening they return,
   growling like dogs, prowling the city.
⁸ Their mouths pour out insult;
   sharp words are on their lips.
   They say: "Who is there to hear?"
⁹ You, Lord, laugh at them;
   you deride all the nations.
¹⁰ My strength, for you I watch;
   you, God, are my fortress, ¹¹ my loving God.

Psalm 58 (V 57)

For the choirmaster   Tune: 'Do not destroy'   Of David
In a quiet voice

¹ Divine as you are, do you truly give upright
   verdicts?
   do you judge fairly the children of Adam?
² No! You devise injustice in your hearts,
   and with your hands you administer tyranny on the
   earth.

³ Since the womb they have gone astray, the wicked,
   on the wrong path since their birth, with their
   unjust verdicts.
⁴ They are poisonous as any snake,
   deaf as an adder that blocks its ears
⁵ so as not to hear the magician's music,
   however skilful his spells.

⁶ God, break the teeth in their mouths,
   snap off the fangs of these young lions, Yahweh.
⁷ May they drain away like water running to waste,
   may they wither like trampled grass,
⁸ like the slug that melts as it moves
   or a still-born child that never sees the sun.

⁹ Before they sprout thorns like the bramble,
   green or burnt up, may retribution whirl them
   away.
¹⁰ The upright will rejoice to see vengeance done,
   and will bathe his feet in the blood of the wicked.
¹¹ 'So', people will say, 'the upright does have a
   reward;
   there is a God to dispense justice on earth.'

Psalm 59 (V 58)

For the choirmaster   Tune: 'Do not destroy'   Of David
In a quiet voice   When Saul sent men to watch
David's house in order to have him killed

¹ Rescue me from my enemies, my God,
   be my stronghold from my assailants,
² rescue me from evil-doers,
   from men of violence save me.

³ Look at them, lurking to ambush me,
   violent men are attacking me,
   for no fault, no sin of mine, Yahweh, ⁴ for no
   guilt,
   they come running to take up position.

   Wake up, stand by me and keep watch,
⁵ Yahweh, God of Sabaoth, God of Israel,
   rise up, to punish all the nations,
   show no mercy to all these malicious traitors.
                                              Pause

⁶   Back they come at nightfall,
   snarling like curs,
   prowling through the town.

⁷ Look how they rant in speech
   with swords on their lips,
   'Who is there to hear us?'

⁸ For your part, Yahweh, you laugh at them,
   you make mockery of all nations.
⁹ My strength, I keep my eyes fixed on you.

   For my stronghold is God,

NEW REVISED STANDARD VERSION	REVISED ENGLISH BIBLE

NEW REVISED STANDARD VERSION

10 My God in his steadfast love will meet me;
 my God will let me look in triumph on my
 enemies.
11 Do not kill them, or my people may forget;
 make them totter by your power, and bring
 them down,
 O Lord, our shield.
12 For the sin of their mouths, the words of their
 lips,
 let them be trapped in their pride.
 For the cursing and lies that they utter,
13 consume them in wrath;
 consume them until they are no more.
 Then it will be known to the ends of the earth
 that God rules over Jacob. *Selah*

14 Each evening they come back,
 howling like dogs
 and prowling about the city.
15 They roam about for food,
 and growl if they do not get their fill.

16 But I will sing of your might;
 I will sing aloud of your steadfast love in the
 morning.
 For you have been a fortress for me
 and a refuge in the day of my distress.
17 O my strength, I will sing praises to you,
 for you, O God, are my fortress,
 the God who shows me steadfast love.

REVISED ENGLISH BIBLE

10 My God, in his unfailing love, will go before me;
 with God's help, I shall gloat over the foes who
 beset me.
11 Will you not kill them, lest my people be tempted
 to forget?
 Scatter them by your might and bring them to ruin,
 Lord, my shield.
12 Their every word is a sinful utterance.
 Let them be taken in their pride,
 by the curses and falsehoods they utter.
13 In wrath bring them to an end,
 and they will be no more;
 then it will be known to earth's farthest limits
 that God is ruler in Jacob. *[Selah*
14 They come out at nightfall,
 snarling like dogs as they prowl about the city;
15 they roam here and there in search of food,
 and howl if they are not satisfied.
16 But I shall sing of your strength,
 and acclaim your love when morning comes;
 for you have been my strong tower
 and a refuge in my day of trouble.
17 I shall raise a psalm to you, my strength;
 for God is my strong tower.
 He is my gracious God.

Psalm 60

*To the leader: according to the Lily of the Covenant.
A Miktam of David; for instruction; when he struggled with
Aram-naharaim and with Aram-zobah, and when
Joab on his return killed twelve thousand Edomites
in the Valley of Salt.*

1 O God, you have rejected us, broken our
 defenses;
 you have been angry; now restore us!
2 You have caused the land to quake; you have
 torn it open;
 repair the cracks in it, for it is tottering.
3 You have made your people suffer hard things;
 you have given us wine to drink that made us
 reel.
4 You have set up a banner for those who fear you,
 to rally to it out of bowshot.[r] *Selah*
5 Give victory with your right hand, and answer
 us,[s]
 so that those whom you love may be rescued.

6 God has promised in his sanctuary:[t]
 "With exultation I will divide up Shechem,
 and portion out the Vale of Succoth.
7 Gilead is mine, and Manasseh is mine;
 Ephraim is my helmet;
 Judah is my scepter.
8 Moab is my washbasin;
 on Edom I hurl my shoe;
 over Philistia I shout in triumph."

9 Who will bring me to the fortified city?
 Who will lead me to Edom?
10 Have you not rejected us, O God?
 You do not go out, O God, with our armies.

Psalm 60

*For the leader: set to 'The Lily of Testimony': a miktam:
for David: for instruction (when he fought against
Aram-naharaim and Aram-zobah, and Joab returned and
struck twelve thousand Edomites in the valley of Salt)*

1 YOU HAVE rejected and crushed us, God.
 You have been angry; restore us.
2 You have made the land quake and caused it to
 split open;
 repair its ruins, for it is shattered.
3 You have made your people drunk with a bitter
 draught,
 you have given us wine that makes us stagger.
4 But to those who fear you, you have raised a
 banner
 to which they may escape from the bow. *[Selah*
5 Save with your right hand and respond,
 that those dear to you may be delivered.

6 God has spoken from his sanctuary:
 'I will go up now and divide Shechem;
 I will measure off the valley of Succoth;
7 Gilead and Manasseh are mine;
 Ephraim is my helmet, Judah my sceptre;
8 Moab is my washbowl, on Edom I fling my
 sandals;
 Philistia, shout and acclaim me.'

9 Who will bring me to the fortified city?
 Who will guide me to Edom?
10 Have you rejected us, God,
 and do you no longer lead our armies to battle?

---

[r] Gk Syr Jerome: Heb *because of the truth*   [s] Another reading is *me*
[t] Or *by his holiness*

60:5–12 Cp. Ps. 108:6–13.   60:6 **from his sanctuary:** *or* in his
holiness. **go up now:** *or* exult.

II
May God go before me,
　and show me my fallen foes.
12 Slay them, God,
　lest they deceive my people.
Shake them by your power;
　Lord, our shield, bring them down.
13 For the sinful words of their mouths and lips
　let them be caught in their pride.
For the lies they have told under oath
14　destroy them in anger,
　destroy till they are no more.
Then people will know God rules over Jacob,
　yes, even to the ends of the earth.　　*Selah*
15 Each evening they return,
　growling like dogs, prowling the city.
16 They roam about as scavengers;
　if they are not filled, they howl.
III
17 But I shall sing of your strength,
　extol your love at dawn,
For you are my fortress,
　my refuge in time of trouble.
18 My strength, your praise I will sing;
　you, God, are my fortress, my loving God.

10 the God who loves me faithfully is coming to meet
　　me,
God will let me feast my eyes on those who lie in
　　wait for me.
11 Do not annihilate them, or my people may forget;
　shake them in your power, bring them low,
　　Lord, our shield.
12 Sin is in their mouths, sin on their lips,
　so let them be trapped in their pride
　for the curses and lies that they utter.
13 Destroy them in your anger, destroy them till they
　　are no more,
　and let it be known that God is Master
　in Jacob and the whole wide world.　　*Pause*
14　　Back they come at nightfall,
　　snarling like curs,
　　prowling through the town,
15 scavenging for something to eat,
　growling unless they have their fill.
16 And so I will sing of your strength,
　in the morning acclaim your faithful love;
　you have been a stronghold for me,
　a refuge when I was in trouble.
17 My strength, I will make music for you,
　for my stronghold is God,
　the God who loves me faithfully.

Psalm 60

1 *For the leader; according to "The Lily of ...." A* miktam
of David (for teaching), 2 *when he fought against*
Aram-Naharaim and Aram-Zobah; and Joab, coming back, killed
twelve thousand Edomites in the Valley of Salt.

I
3 O God, you rejected us, broke our defenses;
　you were angry but now revive us.
4 You rocked the earth, split it open;
　repair the cracks for it totters.
5 You made your people go through hardship,
　made us stagger from the wine you gave us.
6 Raise up a flag for those who revere you,
　a refuge for them out of bowshot.　　*Selah*
7 Help with your right hand and answer us
　that your loved ones may escape.
II
8 In the sanctuary God promised:
　"I will exult, will apportion Shechem;
　the valley of Succoth I will measure out.
9 Gilead is mine, mine is Manasseh;
　Ephraim is the helmet for my head,
　Judah, my own scepter.
10 Moab is my washbowl;
　upon Edom I cast my sandal.
I will triumph over Philistia."
III
11 Who will bring me to the fortified city?
　Who will lead me into Edom?
12 Was it not you who rejected us, God?
　Do you no longer march with our armies?

Psalm 60 (V 59)

For the choirmaster　To the tune 'The decree is a lily'
In a quiet voice　Of David　To be learnt
When he was at war with Aram-Naharaim and
Aram-Zobah, and Joab marched back to
destroy twelve thousand Edomites in the Valley of Salt

1 God, you have rejected us, broken us,
　you were angry, come back to us!
2 You made the earth tremble, split it open;
　now mend the rifts, it is tottering still.
3 You have forced your people to drink a bitter
　　draught,
　forced us to drink a wine that made us reel.
4 You gave a signal to those who fear you
　to let them escape out of range of the bow.　　*Pause*
5 To rescue those you love,
　save with your right hand and answer us.
6 God has spoken from his sanctuary,
　'In triumph I will divide up Shechem,
　and share out the Valley of Succoth.
7 'Mine is Gilead, mine Manasseh,
　Ephraim the helmet on my head,
　Judah my commander's baton,
8 'Moab a bowl for me to wash in,
　on Edom I plant my sandal.
　Now try shouting "Victory!" over me, Philistia!'
9 Who will lead me against a fortified city,
　who will guide me into Edom,
10 if not you, the God who has rejected us?
　God, you no longer march with our armies.

11 O grant us help against the foe,
for human help is worthless.
12 With God we shall do valiantly;
it is he who will tread down our foes.

Psalm 61

To the leader: with stringed instruments. Of David.

1 Hear my cry, O God;
listen to my prayer.
2 From the end of the earth I call to you,
when my heart is faint.

Lead me to the rock
that is higher than I;
3 for you are my refuge,
a strong tower against the enemy.

4 Let me abide in your tent forever,
find refuge under the shelter of your wings.
Selah

5 For you, O God, have heard my vows;
you have given me the heritage of those who
fear your name.

6 Prolong the life of the king;
may his years endure to all generations!
7 May he be enthroned forever before God;
appoint steadfast love and faithfulness to watch
over him!

8 So I will always sing praises to your name,
as I pay my vows day after day.

Psalm 62

To the leader: according to Jeduthun. A Psalm of David.

1 For God alone my soul waits in silence;
from him comes my salvation.
2 He alone is my rock and my salvation,
my fortress; I shall never be shaken.

3 How long will you assail a person,
will you batter your victim, all of you,
as you would a leaning wall, a tottering fence?
4 Their only plan is to bring down a person of
prominence.
They take pleasure in falsehood;
they bless with their mouths,
but inwardly they curse.
Selah

5 For God alone my soul waits in silence,
for my hope is from him.
6 He alone is my rock and my salvation,
my fortress; I shall not be shaken.
7 On God rests my deliverance and my honor;
my mighty rock, my refuge is in God.

8 Trust in him at all times, O people;
pour out your heart before him;
God is a refuge for us.
Selah

9 Those of low estate are but a breath,
those of high estate are a delusion;
in the balances they go up;
they are together lighter than a breath.
10 Put no confidence in extortion,
and set no vain hopes on robbery;
if riches increase, do not set your heart on
them.

11 Grant us help against the foe;
in vain we look to any mortal for deliverance.
12 With God's help we shall fight valiantly,
and God himself will tread our foes under foot.

Psalm 61

For the leader: on stringed instruments: for David

1 GOD, hear my cry; listen to my prayer.
2 From the end of the earth I call to you
with fainting heart;
lift me up and set me high on a rock.
3 For you have been my shelter,
a tower of strength against the enemy.
4 In your tent I shall make my home for ever
and find shelter under the cover of your wings.
[*Selah*

5 For you, God, will hear my vows
and grant the wish of those who revere your name.

6 To the king's life add length of days;
prolong his years for many generations.
7 May he abide in God's presence for ever;
may true and constant love preserve him.

8 So I shall ever sing psalms in honour of your name
as I fulfil my vows day after day.

Psalm 62

For the leader: according to Jeduthun: a psalm: for David

1 FOR God alone I wait silently;
my deliverance comes from him.
2 He only is my rock of deliverance,
my strong tower, so that I stand unshaken.
3 How long will you assail with your threats,
all beating against your prey
as if he were a leaning wall, a toppling fence?
4 They aim to topple him from his height.
They take delight in lying;
they bless him with their lips,
but curse him in their hearts.
[*Selah*

5 For God alone I wait silently;
my hope comes from him.
6 He alone is my rock of deliverance,
my strong tower, so that I am unshaken.
7 On God my safety and my honour depend,
God who is my rock of refuge and my shelter.
8 Trust in him at all times, you people;
pour out your hearts before him;
God is our shelter.
[*Selah*

9 The common people are mere empty air,
while people of rank are a sham;
when placed on the scales they rise,
all of them lighter than air.
10 Put no trust in extortion,
no false confidence in robbery;
though wealth increases, do not set your heart on
it.

61:2 **lift me up:** *prob. rdg, cp. Gk; Heb. obscure.*   61:5 **wish:**
prob. rdg; Heb. heritage.   61:7 **preserve:** *so some MSS; others
add an unintelligible word.*

13 Give us aid against the foe;
 worthless is human help.
14 We will triumph with the help of God,
 who will trample down our foes.

Psalm 61

1 *For the leader; with stringed instruments. Of David.*

I
2 Hear my cry, O God,
 listen to my prayer!
3 From the brink of Sheol I call;
 my heart grows faint.
 Raise me up, set me on a rock,
4 for you are my refuge,
 a tower of strength against the foe.
5 Then I will ever dwell in your tent,
 take refuge in the shelter of your wings. Selah
II
6 O God, when you accept my vows
 and hear the plea of those
 who revere your name in prayer:
7 "Add to the days of the king's life;
 may his years be many generations;
8 May he reign before God forever;
 may your love and fidelity preserve him" —
9 Then I will sing your name forever,
 fulfill my vows day after day.

Psalm 62

1 *For the leader; 'al Jeduthun. A psalm of David.*

I
2 My soul rests in God alone,
 from whom comes my salvation.
3 God alone is my rock and salvation,
 my secure height; I shall never fall.
4 How long will you set upon people,
 all of you beating them down,
 As though they were a sagging fence
 or a battered wall?
5 Even from my place on high
 they plot to dislodge me.
 They delight in lies;
 they bless with their mouths,
 but inwardly they curse. Selah
II
6 My soul, be at rest in God alone,
 from whom comes my hope.
7 God alone is my rock and my salvation,
 my secure height; I shall not fall.
8 My safety and glory are with God,
 my strong rock and refuge.
9 Trust God at all times, my people!
 Pour out your hearts to God our refuge! Selah
III
10 Mortals are a mere breath,
 the powerful but an illusion;
 On a balance they rise;
 together they are lighter than air.
11 Do not trust in extortion;
 in plunder put no empty hope.
 Though wealth increase,
 do not set your heart upon it.

11 Bring us help in our time of crisis,
 any human help is worthless.
12 With God we shall do deeds of valour,
 he will trample down our enemies.

Psalm 61 (V 60)

For the choirmaster   For strings   Of David

1 God, hear my cry,
 listen to my prayer.
2 From the end of the earth I call to you
 with fainting heart.
 Lead me to the high rock that stands far out of
 my reach.
3 For you are my refuge,
 a strong tower against the enemy.
4 Let me stay in your tent for ever,
 taking refuge in the shelter of your wings!
5 For you, God, accept my vows,
 you grant me the heritage of those who fear your
 name.
6 Let the king live on and on,
 let his years continue age after age.
7 May his throne be always in God's presence,
 your faithful love and constancy watch over him.

8 Then I shall always sing to your name,
 day after day fulfilling my vows.

Psalm 62 (V 61)

For the choirmaster . . .   Jeduthun   Psalm   Of David

1 In God alone there is rest for my soul,
 from him comes my safety;
2 he alone is my rock, my safety,
 my stronghold so that I stand unshaken.

3 How much longer will you set on a victim,
 all together, intent on murder,
 like a rampart already leaning over,
 a wall already damaged?
4 Trickery is their only plan,
 deception their only pleasure,
 with lies on their lips they pronounce a blessing,
 with a curse in their hearts. Pause
5 Rest in God alone, my soul!
 He is the source of my hope.
6 He alone is my rock, my safety,
 my stronghold, so that I stand unwavering.
7 In God is my safety and my glory,
 the rock of my strength.

 In God is my refuge; 8 trust in him,
 you people, at all times.
 Pour out your hearts to him,
 God is a refuge for us. Pause

9 Ordinary people are a mere puff of wind,
 important people a delusion;
 set both on the scales together,
 and they are lighter than a puff of wind.

10 Put no trust in extortion,
 no empty hopes in robbery;
 however much wealth may multiply,
 do not set your heart on it.

NEW REVISED STANDARD VERSION	REVISED ENGLISH BIBLE

11 Once God has spoken;
  twice have I heard this:
that power belongs to God,
12 and steadfast love belongs to you, O Lord.
For you repay to all
  according to their work.

11 One thing God has spoken,
  two things I have learnt:
'Power belongs to God'
12 and 'Unfailing love is yours, Lord';
  you reward everyone according to what he has
    done.

Psalm 63

*A Psalm of David, when he was in the Wilderness of
Judah.*

1 O God, you are my God, I seek you,
  my soul thirsts for you;
my flesh faints for you,
  as in a dry and weary land where there is no
    water.
2 So I have looked upon you in the sanctuary,
  beholding your power and glory.
3 Because your steadfast love is better than life,
  my lips will praise you.
4 So I will bless you as long as I live;
  I will lift up my hands and call on your name.

5 My soul is satisfied as with a rich feast,[u]
  and my mouth praises you with joyful lips
6 when I think of you on my bed,
  and meditate on you in the watches of the
    night;
7 for you have been my help,
  and in the shadow of your wings I sing for joy.
8 My soul clings to you;
  your right hand upholds me.

9 But those who seek to destroy my life
  shall go down into the depths of the earth;
10 they shall be given over to the power of the
    sword,
  they shall be prey for jackals.
11 But the king shall rejoice in God;
  all who swear by him shall exult,
  for the mouths of liars will be stopped.

Psalm 63

*A psalm: for David (when he was in the wilderness of
Judah)*

1 GOD, you are my God; I seek you eagerly
  with a heart that thirsts for you
and a body wasted with longing for you,
  like a dry land, parched and devoid of water.
2 With such longing I see you in the sanctuary
  and behold your power and glory.

3 Your unfailing love is better than life;
  therefore I shall sing your praises.
4 Thus all my life I bless you;
  in your name I lift my hands in prayer.
5 I am satisfied as with a rich feast
  and there is a shout of praise on my lips.

6 I call you to mind on my bed
  and meditate on you in the night watches,
7 for you have been my help
  and I am safe in the shadow of your wings.
8 I follow you closely
  and your right hand upholds me.

9 May those who seek my life themselves be
    destroyed,
  may they sink into the depths of the earth;
10 may they be given over to the sword,
  and become carrion for jackals.

11 The king will rejoice in God;
  all who swear by God's name will exult,
  while the mouths of liars will be stopped.

Psalm 64

To the leader. A Psalm of David.

1 Hear my voice, O God, in my complaint;
  preserve my life from the dread enemy.
2 Hide me from the secret plots of the wicked,
  from the scheming of evildoers,
3 who whet their tongues like swords,
  who aim bitter words like arrows,
4 shooting from ambush at the blameless;
  they shoot suddenly and without fear.
5 They hold fast to their evil purpose;
  they talk of laying snares secretly,
thinking, "Who can see us?[v]
6 Who can search out our crimes?[w]
We have thought out a cunningly conceived
    plot."
For the human heart and mind are deep.

7 But God will shoot his arrow at them;
  they will be wounded suddenly.
8 Because of their tongue he will bring them to
    ruin;[x]
  all who see them will shake with horror.

Psalm 64

For the leader: a psalm: for David

1 GOD, hear me as I make my lament;
  keep me safe from the terror of the enemy.
2 Protect me from the intrigues of the wicked,
  from the mob of evildoers.
3 They sharpen their tongues like swords
  and aim venomous words like arrows
4 to shoot down the innocent from cover,
  shooting suddenly, themselves unseen.
5 They confirm their wicked resolves;
  they talk of hiding snares
  and say, 'Who will see us?'
6 They hatch their evil plots;
  they conceal the schemes they have devised,
    deep in their inmost heart.

7 But God with his arrow shoots them down,
  and sudden is their overthrow.
8 He will make them fall, using their own words
    against them.
All who see them will flee in horror,

---

[u] Heb with fat and fatness   [v] Syr: Heb *them*   [w] Cn: Heb *They
search out crimes*   [x] Cn: Heb *They will bring him to ruin, their
tongue being against them*

64:5 **us:** *prob. rdg; Heb.* them.

NEW AMERICAN BIBLE | NEW JERUSALEM BIBLE

12 One thing God has said;
  two things I have heard:
  Power belongs to God;
13 so too, Lord, does kindness,
  And you render to each of us
  according to our deeds.

11 Once God has spoken,
  twice have I heard this:
  Strength belongs to God,
12 to you, Lord, faithful love;
  and you repay everyone as their deeds deserve.

Psalm 63

1 *A psalm of David, when he was in the wilderness of
Judah.*

I

2 O God, you are my God—
  for you I long!
For you my body yearns;
  for you my soul thirsts,
Like a land parched, lifeless,
  and without water.
3 So I look to you in the sanctuary
  to see your power and glory.
4 For your love is better than life;
  my lips offer you worship!

II

5 I will bless you as long as I live;
  I will lift up my hands, calling on your name.
6 My soul shall savor the rich banquet of praise,
  with joyous lips my mouth shall honor you!
7 When I think of you upon my bed,
  through the night watches I will recall
8 That you indeed are my help,
  and in the shadow of your wings I shout for joy.
9 My soul clings fast to you;
  your right hand upholds me.

III

10 But those who seek my life will come to ruin;
  they shall go down to the depths of the earth!
11 They shall be handed over to the sword
  and become the prey of jackals!
12 But the king shall rejoice in God;
  all who swear by the Lord shall exult,
  for the mouths of liars will be shut!

Psalm 63 (V 62)

Psalm   Of David   When he was in the desert of Judah

1 God, you are my God, I pine for you;
  my heart thirsts for you,
  my body longs for you,
  as a land parched, dreary and waterless.
2 Thus I have gazed on you in the sanctuary,
  seeing your power and your glory.
3 Better your faithful love than life itself;
  my lips will praise you.
4 Thus I will bless you all my life,
  in your name lift up my hands.
5 All my longings fulfilled as with fat and rich
    foods,
  a song of joy on my lips and praise in my mouth.

6 On my bed when I think of you,
  I muse on you in the watches of the night,
7 for you have always been my help;
  in the shadow of your wings I rejoice;
8 my heart clings to you,
  your right hand supports me.

9 May those who are hounding me to death
  go down to the depths of the earth,
10 given over to the blade of the sword,
  and left as food for jackals.
11 Then the king shall rejoice in God,
  all who swear by him shall gain recognition,
  for the mouths of liars shall be silenced.

Psalm 64

1 *For the leader. A psalm of David.*

I

2 O God, hear my anguished voice;
  from the foes I dread protect my life.
3 Hide me from the malicious crowd,
  the mob of evildoers.
4 They sharpen their tongues like swords,
  ready their bows for arrows of poison words.
5 They shoot at the innocent from ambush,
  shoot without risk, catch them unawares.
6 They resolve on their wicked plan;
  they conspire to set snares;
  they say: "Who will see us?"
7 They devise wicked schemes,
  conceal the schemes they devise;
  the designs of their hearts are hidden.

II

8 But God will shoot arrows at them
  and strike them unawares.
9 They will be brought down by their own tongues;
  all who see them will shake their heads.

Psalm 64 (V 63)

For the choirmaster   Psalm   Of David

1 Listen, God, to my voice as I plead,
  protect my life from fear of the enemy;
2 hide me from the league of the wicked,
  from the gang of evil-doers.

3 They sharpen their tongues like a sword,
  aim their arrows of poisonous abuse,
4 shoot at the innocent from cover,
  shoot suddenly, with nothing to fear.

5 They support each other in their evil designs,
  they discuss how to lay their snares.
  'Who will see us?' they say,
6 'or will penetrate our secrets?'
  He will do that, he who penetrates human nature
    to its depths,
  the depths of the heart.

7 God has shot them with his arrow,
  sudden were their wounds.
8 He brings them down because of their tongue,
  and all who see them shake their heads.

1223

9 Then everyone will fear;
   they will tell what God has brought about,
   and ponder what he has done.

10 Let the righteous rejoice in the LORD
   and take refuge in him.
   Let all the upright in heart glory.

Psalm 65

To the leader. A Psalm of David. A Song.

1 Praise is due to you,
   O God, in Zion;
   and to you shall vows be performed,
2   O you who answer prayer!
   To you all flesh shall come.
3 When deeds of iniquity overwhelm us,
   you forgive our transgressions.
4 Happy are those whom you choose and bring near
   to live in your courts.
   We shall be satisfied with the goodness of your
      house,
      your holy temple.

5 By awesome deeds you answer us with
      deliverance,
   O God of our salvation;
   you are the hope of all the ends of the earth
   and of the farthest seas.
6 By your[y] strength you established the mountains;
   you are girded with might.
7 You silence the roaring of the seas,
   the roaring of their waves,
   the tumult of the peoples.
8 Those who live at earth's farthest bounds are
      awed by your signs;
   you make the gateways of the morning and the
      evening shout for joy.

9 You visit the earth and water it,
   you greatly enrich it;
   the river of God is full of water;
   you provide the people with grain,
   for so you have prepared it.
10 You water its furrows abundantly,
   settling its ridges,
   softening it with showers,
   and blessing its growth.
11 You crown the year with your bounty;
   your wagon tracks overflow with richness.
12 The pastures of the wilderness overflow,
   the hills gird themselves with joy,
13 the meadows clothe themselves with flocks,
   the valleys deck themselves with grain,
   they shout and sing together for joy.

Psalm 66

To the leader. A Song. A Psalm.

1 Make a joyful noise to God, all the earth;
2   sing the glory of his name;
   give to him glorious praise.
3 Say to God, "How awesome are your deeds!
   Because of your great power, your enemies
      cringe before you.
4 All the earth worships you;
   they sing praises to you,
   sing praises to your name."   *Selah*

[y] Gk Jerome: Heb *his*

9 every one terrified.
   'This is God's work,' they declare;
   they understand what he has done.
10 The righteous rejoice and seek refuge in the LORD,
   and all the upright in heart exult.

Psalm 65

For the leader: a psalm: for David: a song

1 IT is fitting to praise you in Zion, God;
   vows should be paid to you.
2 Hearer of prayer,
   to you everyone should come.
3 Evil deeds are too heavy for me;
   only you can wipe out our offences.

4 Happy are those whom you choose
   and bring near to remain in your courts.
   Grant us in abundance the bounty of your house,
   of your holy temple.
5 Through dread deeds you answer us with victory,
   God our deliverer,
   in whom all put their trust
   at the ends of the earth and on distant seas.

6 By your might you fix the mountains in place;
   you are girded with strength;
7 you calm the seas and their raging waves,
   and the tumult of the nations.
8 The dwellers at the ends of the earth
   are overawed by your signs;
   you make east and west sing aloud in triumph.

9 You care for the earth and make it fruitful;
   you enrich it greatly,
   filling its great channels with rain.
   In this way you prepare the earth
   and provide grain for its people.
10 You water its furrows, level its ridges,
   soften it with showers, and bless its growth.
11 You crown the year with your good gifts;
   places where you have passed drip with plenty;
12 the open pastures are lush
   and the hills wreathed in happiness;
13 the meadows are clothed with sheep
   and the valleys decked with grain,
   so that with shouts of joy they break into song.

Psalm 66

For the leader: a song: a psalm

1 LET all the earth acclaim God.
2 Sing to the glory of his name,
   make his praise glorious.
3 Say to God, 'How awesome are your deeds!
   Your foes cower before the greatness of your
      strength.
4 The whole world bows low in your presence;
   they praise your name in song.'   [*Selah*

65:6 **your:** *prob. rdg; Heb.* his.   65:9 **filling . . . rain:** *lit.* the
channel of God is full of water.

NEW AMERICAN BIBLE

NEW JERUSALEM BIBLE

10 Then all will fear and proclaim God's deed,
pondering what has been done.
11 The just will rejoice and take refuge in the LORD;
all the upright will glory in their God.

9 Everyone will be awestruck,
proclaim what God has done,
and understand why he has done it.
10 The upright will rejoice in Yahweh,
will take refuge in him,
and all the honest will praise him.

Psalm 65

1 *For the leader. A psalm of David. A song.*

I

2 To you we owe our hymn of praise,
O God on Zion;
To you our vows must be fulfilled,
3   you who hear our prayers.
To you all flesh must come
4   with its burden of wicked deeds.
We are overcome by our sins;
only you can pardon them.
5 Happy the chosen ones you bring
to dwell in your courts.
May we be filled with the good things of your
house,
the blessings of your holy temple!

II

6 You answer us with awesome deeds of justice,
O God our savior,
The hope of all the ends of the earth
and of far distant islands.
7 You are robed in power,
you set up the mountains by your might.
8 You still the roaring of the seas,
the roaring of their waves,
the tumult of the peoples.
9 Distant peoples stand in awe of your marvels;
east and west you make resound with joy.
10 You visit the earth and water it,
make it abundantly fertile.
God's stream is filled with water;
with it you supply the world with grain.
Thus do you prepare the earth:
11   you drench plowed furrows,
and level their ridges.
With showers you keep the ground soft,
blessing its young sprouts.
12 You adorn the year with your bounty;
your paths drip with fruitful rain.
13 The untilled meadows also drip;
the hills are robed with joy.
14 The pastures are clothed with flocks,
the valleys blanketed with grain;
they cheer and sing for joy.

Psalm 65 (V 64)

For the choirmaster   Psalm   Of David   Song

1 Praise is rightfully yours,
God, in Zion.
Vows to you shall be fulfilled,
2   for you answer prayer.

All humanity must come to you
3   with its sinful deeds.
Our faults overwhelm us,
but you blot them out.

4 How blessed those whom you choose
and invite to dwell in your courts.
We shall be filled with the good things of your
house,
of your holy temple.

5 You respond to us with the marvels of your saving
justice,
God our Saviour,
hope of the whole wide world,
even the distant islands.

6 By your strength you hold the mountains steady,
being clothed in power,
7 you calm the turmoil of the seas,
the turmoil of their waves.

The nations are in uproar,
in panic those who live at the ends of the earth;
8 your miracles bring shouts of joy
to the gateways of morning and evening.

9 You visit the earth and make it fruitful,
you fill it with riches;
the river of God brims over with water,
you provide the grain.

To that end
10 you water its furrows abundantly, level its ridges,
soften it with showers and bless its shoots.

11 You crown the year with your generosity,
richness seeps from your tracks,
12 the pastures of the desert grow moist,
the hillsides are wrapped in joy,
13 the meadows are covered with flocks,
the valleys clothed with wheat;
they shout and sing for joy.

Psalm 66

1 *For the leader. A song; a psalm.*

I

Shout joyfully to God, all you on earth;
2   sing of his glorious name;
give him glorious praise.
3 Say to God: "How awesome your deeds!
Before your great strength your enemies cringe.
4 All on earth fall in worship before you;
they sing of you, sing of your name!"   *Selah*

Psalm 66 (V 65)

For the choirmaster   Song   Psalm

1 Acclaim God, all the earth,
2 sing psalms to the glory of his name,
glorify him with your praises,
3 say to God, 'How awesome you are!

'Your achievements are the measure of your power,
your enemies woo your favour,
4 all the earth bows down before you,
sings psalms to you, sings psalms to your name.'
Pause

NEW REVISED STANDARD VERSION	REVISED ENGLISH BIBLE

NEW REVISED STANDARD VERSION

5 Come and see what God has done:
  he is awesome in his deeds among mortals.
6 He turned the sea into dry land;
  they passed through the river on foot.
  There we rejoiced in him,
7   who rules by his might forever,
  whose eyes keep watch on the nations —
  let the rebellious not exalt themselves.   *Selah*

8 Bless our God, O peoples,
  let the sound of his praise be heard,
9 who has kept us among the living,
  and has not let our feet slip.
10 For you, O God, have tested us;
  you have tried us as silver is tried.
11 You brought us into the net;
  you laid burdens on our backs;
12 you let people ride over our heads;
  we went through fire and through water;
  yet you have brought us out to a spacious
    place.ᶻ

13 I will come into your house with burnt offerings;
  I will pay you my vows,
14 those that my lips uttered
  and my mouth promised when I was in trouble.
15 I will offer to you burnt offerings of fatlings,
  with the smoke of the sacrifice of rams;
  I will make an offering of bulls and goats.   *Selah*

16 Come and hear, all you who fear God,
  and I will tell you what he has done for me.
17 I cried aloud to him,
  and he was extolled with my tongue.
18 If I had cherished iniquity in my heart,
  the Lord would not have listened.
19 But truly God has listened;
  he has given heed to the words of my prayer.

20 Blessed be God,
  because he has not rejected my prayer
  or removed his steadfast love from me.

Psalm 67

To the leader: with stringed instruments. A Psalm. A Song.

1 May God be gracious to us and bless us
  and make his face to shine upon us,   *Selah*
2 that your way may be known upon earth,
  your saving power among all nations.
3 Let the peoples praise you, O God;
  let all the peoples praise you.

4 Let the nations be glad and sing for joy,
  for you judge the peoples with equity
  and guide the nations upon earth.   *Selah*
5 Let the peoples praise you, O God;
  let all the peoples praise you.

6 The earth has yielded its increase;
  God, our God, has blessed us.
7 May God continue to bless us;
  let all the ends of the earth revere him.

REVISED ENGLISH BIBLE

5 Come and see what God has done,
  his awesome dealings with mankind.
6 He changed the sea into dry land;
  his people passed over the river on foot;
  there we rejoiced in him
7 who rules for ever by his power.
  His eyes keep watch on the nations;
  let no rebel rise in defiance.   [*Selah*

8 Bless our God, you nations;
  let the sound of his praise be heard.
9 He preserves us in life;
  he keeps our feet from stumbling.
10 For you, God, have put us to the test
  and refined us like silver.
11 You have brought us into the net,
  you have bound our bodies fast;
12 you have let men ride over our heads.
  We went through fire and water,
  but you have brought us out into a place of plenty.

13 I shall bring whole-offerings into your house
  and fulfil to you vows
14 which my lips have made
  and my mouth promised on oath during my
    distress.
15 I shall offer you fat beasts as whole-offerings
  and burn rams as a soothing offering;
  I shall make ready bulls and he-goats.   [*Selah*

16 Come, listen, all who fear God,
  and I shall tell you what he has done for me;
17 I lifted up my voice in prayer,
  his praise was on my tongue.
18 If I had cherished evil thoughts,
  the Lord would not have listened.
19 but in truth God did listen
  and paid heed to my plea.

20 Blessed is God
  who has not withdrawn from me his love and care.

Psalm 67

For the leader: on stringed instruments: a psalm: a song

1 MAY God be gracious to us and bless us,
  may he cause his face to shine on us,   [*Selah*
2 that your purpose may be known on earth,
  your saving power among all nations.
3 Let the peoples praise you, God;
  let all peoples praise you.

4 Let nations rejoice and shout in triumph;
  for you judge the peoples with equity
  and guide the nations of the earth.   [*Selah*
5 Let the peoples praise you, God;
  let all peoples praise you.

6 The earth has yielded its harvest.
  May God, our God, bless us.
7 God grant us his blessing,
  that all the ends of the earth may fear him.

ᶻCn Compare Gk Syr Jerome Tg: Heb *to a saturation*

66:6 *his people:* Heb. *they.*   66:20 *who . . . withdrawn:* prob.
rdg; Heb. *adds* my prayer and.

NEW AMERICAN BIBLE

II

5 Come and see the works of God,
   awesome in the deeds done for us.
6 He changed the sea to dry land;
   through the river they passed on foot.
   Therefore let us rejoice in him,
7   who rules by might forever,
   Whose eyes are fixed upon the nations.
   Let no rebel rise to challenge!   Selah
8 Bless our God, you peoples;
   loudly sound his praise,
9 Who has kept us alive
   and not allowed our feet to slip.
10 You tested us, O God,
   tried us as silver tried by fire.
11 You led us into a snare;
   you bound us at the waist as captives.
12 You let captors set foot on our neck;
   we went through fire and water;
   then you led us out to freedom.

III

13 I will bring holocausts to your house;
   to you I will fulfill my vows,
14 The vows my lips pronounced
   and my mouth spoke in distress.
15 Holocausts of fatlings I will offer you
   and burnt offerings of rams;
   I will sacrifice oxen and goats.   Selah
16 Come and hear, all you who fear God,
   while I recount what has been done for me.
17 I called to the Lord with my mouth;
   praise was upon my tongue.
18 Had I cherished evil in my heart,
   the Lord would not have heard.
19 But God did hear
   and listened to my voice in prayer.
20 Blessed be God, who did not refuse me
   the kindness I sought in prayer.

Psalm 67

1 For the leader; with stringed instruments. A psalm;
a song.

I

2 May God be gracious to us and bless us;
   may God's face shine upon us.   Selah
3 So shall your rule be known upon the earth,
   your saving power among all the nations.
4 May the peoples praise you, God;
   may all the peoples praise you!

II

5 May the nations be glad and shout for joy;
   for you govern the peoples justly,
   you guide the nations upon the earth.   Selah
6 May the peoples praise you, God;
   may all the peoples praise you!

III

7 The earth has yielded its harvest;
   God, our God, blesses us.
8 May God bless us still;
   that the ends of the earth may revere our God.

NEW JERUSALEM BIBLE

5 Come and see the marvels of God,
   his awesome deeds for the children of Adam:
6 he changed the sea into dry land,
   they crossed the river on foot.

   So let us rejoice in him,
7 who rules for ever by his power;
   his eyes keep watch on the nations
   to forestall rebellion against him.   Pause
8 Nations, bless our God,
   let the sound of his praise be heard;
9 he brings us to life
   and keeps our feet from stumbling.
10 God, you have put us to the test,
   refined us like silver,
11 let us fall into the net;
   you have put a heavy strain on our backs,
12 let men ride over our heads;
   but now the ordeal by fire and water is over,
   you have led us out to breathe again.

13 I bring burnt offerings to your house,
   I fulfil to you my vows,
14 the vows that rose to my lips,
   that I pronounced when I was in trouble.

15 I will offer you rich burnt offerings,
   with the smoke of burning rams.
   I will sacrifice to you bullocks and goats.   Pause

16 Come and listen, all who fear God,
   while I tell what he has done for me.

17 To him I cried aloud,
   high praise was on my tongue.
18 Had I been aware of guilt in my heart,
   the Lord would not have listened,
19 but in fact God did listen,
   attentive to the sound of my prayer.

20   Blessed be God
   who has not turned away my prayer,
   nor his own faithful love from me.

Psalm 67 (V 66)

For the choirmaster   For strings   Psalm   Song

1 May God show kindness and bless us,
   and make his face shine on us.   Pause
2 Then the earth will acknowledge your ways,
   and all nations your power to save.

3 Let the nations praise you, God,
   let all the nations praise you.

4 Let the nations rejoice and sing for joy,
   for you judge the world with justice,
   you judge the peoples with fairness,
   you guide the nations on earth.   Pause

5 Let the nations praise you, God,
   let all the nations praise you.

6 The earth has yielded its produce;
   God, our God, has blessed us.
7 May God continue to bless us,
   and be revered by the whole wide world.

NEW REVISED STANDARD VERSION

REVISED ENGLISH BIBLE

Psalm 68

To the leader. Of David. A Psalm. A Song.

1 Let God rise up, let his enemies be scattered;
  let those who hate him flee before him.
2 As smoke is driven away, so drive them away;
  as wax melts before the fire,
  let the wicked perish before God.
3 But let the righteous be joyful;
  let them exult before God;
  let them be jubilant with joy.

4 Sing to God, sing praises to his name;
  lift up a song to him who rides upon the
    clouds*a* —
  his name is the LORD —
  be exultant before him.
5 Father of orphans and protector of widows
  is God in his holy habitation.
6 God gives the desolate a home to live in;
  he leads out the prisoners to prosperity,
  but the rebellious live in a parched land.

7 O God, when you went out before your people,
  when you marched through the wilderness,
                                        Selah
8 the earth quaked, the heavens poured down rain
  at the presence of God, the God of Sinai,
  at the presence of God, the God of Israel.
9 Rain in abundance, O God, you showered abroad;
  you restored your heritage when it languished;
10 your flock found a dwelling in it;
  in your goodness, O God, you provided for the
    needy.

11 The Lord gives the command;
  great is the company of those*b* who bore the
    tidings:
12 "The kings of the armies, they flee, they flee!"
  The women at home divide the spoil,
13 though they stay among the sheepfolds —
  the wings of a dove covered with silver,
  its pinions with green gold.
14 When the Almighty*c* scattered kings there,
  snow fell on Zalmon.

15 O mighty mountain, mountain of Bashan;
  O many-peaked mountain, mountain of Bashan!
16 Why do you look with envy, O many-peaked
    mountain,
  at the mount that God desired for his abode,
  where the LORD will reside forever?

17 With mighty chariotry, twice ten thousand,
  thousands upon thousands,
  the Lord came from Sinai into the holy place.*d*
18 You ascended the high mount,
  leading captives in your train
  and receiving gifts from people,
  even from those who rebel against the LORD
  God's abiding there.
19 Blessed be the Lord,
  who daily bears us up;
  God is our salvation.   *Selah*
20 Our God is a God of salvation,
  and to GOD, the Lord, belongs escape from
    death.

Psalm 68

For the leader: for David: a psalm: a song

1 MAY God arise and his enemies be scattered,
  and those hostile to him flee at his approach.
2 You disperse them like smoke;
  you melt them like wax near fire.
  The wicked perish at the presence of God,
3 but the righteous are joyful;
  they exult before God
  with gladness and rejoicing.
4 Sing the praises of God, raise a psalm to his name;
  extol him who rides on the clouds.
  The LORD is his name, exult before him,
5 a father to the fatherless, the widow's defender —
  God in his holy dwelling-place.
6 God gives the friendless a home
  and leads the prisoner out in all safety,
  but rebels must remain in the scorching desert.

7 God, when at the head of your people
  you marched out through the barren waste,   [*Selah*
8 earth trembled, rain poured from the heavens
  before God the Lord of Sinai, before God the God
    of Israel.

9 You, God, send plenteous rain;
  when your own land languishes you restore it.
10 There your people settled;
  in your goodness, God, you provide for the poor.
11 The Lord speaks the word;
  the women with the good news are a mighty host.
12 Kings with their armies are in headlong flight,
  while the women at home divide the spoil.
13 Though you linger among the sheepfolds
  the dove's wings are covered with silver
  and its pinions with yellow gold.
14 When the Almighty routs the kings in the land
  snow falls on Zalmon.

15 The hill of Bashan is a lofty hill,
  a hill of many peaks is Bashan's hill.
16 But, you hill of many peaks, why gaze so
    enviously
  at the hill where the LORD delights to dwell,
  where the LORD himself will stay for ever?
17 There were myriads of God's chariots,
  thousands upon thousands,
  when the Lord came in holiness from Sinai.
18 You went up to your dwelling-place on high
  taking captives into captivity;
  everyone brought you tribute;
  no rebel could live in the presence of the LORD
    God.

19 Blessed is the Lord:
  he carries us day by day,
  God our salvation.   [*Selah*
20 Our God is a God who saves;
  to the LORD God belongs all escape from death.

---

a Or *cast up a highway for him who rides through the deserts*
b Or *company of the women*   *c* Traditional rendering of Heb
Shaddai   *d* Cn: Heb *The Lord among them Sinai in the holy* (place)   68:18 **no rebel . . . God:** *so Syriac; Heb. unintelligible.*

NEW AMERICAN BIBLE

Psalm 68

¹ *For the leader. A psalm of David; a song.*

I

² God will arise for battle;
the enemy will be scattered;
those who hate God will flee.
³ The wind will disperse them like smoke;
as wax is melted by fire,
so the wicked will perish before God.
⁴ Then the just will be glad;
they will rejoice before God;
they will celebrate with great joy.

II

⁵ Sing to God, praise the divine name;
exalt the rider of the clouds.
Rejoice before this God
whose name is the LORD.
⁶ Father of the fatherless, defender of widows—
this is the God whose abode is holy,
⁷ Who gives a home to the forsaken,
who leads prisoners out to prosperity,
while rebels live in the desert.

III

⁸ God, when you went forth before your people,
when you marched through the desert,   *Selah*
⁹ The earth quaked, the heavens shook,
before God, the One of Sinai,
before God, the God of Israel.
¹⁰ You claimed a land as your own, O God;
¹¹ your people settled there.
There you poured abundant rains, God,
graciously given to the poor in their need.

IV

¹²ᵃ The Lord announced the news of victory:
¹³ᵃ   "The kings and their armies are in desperate
flight.
¹²ᵇ All you people so numerous,
¹⁴ᵃ   will you stay by the sheepfolds?
¹³ᵇ Every household will share the booty,
¹⁴ᵇ   perhaps a dove sheathed with silver,
¹⁴ᶜ   its wings covered with yellow gold."
¹⁵ When the Almighty routed the kings there,
the spoils were scattered like snow on Zalmon.

V

¹⁶ You high mountains of Bashan,
you rugged mountains of Bashan,
¹⁷ You rugged mountains, why look with envy
at the mountain where God has chosen to dwell,
where the LORD resides forever?
¹⁸ God's chariots were myriad, thousands upon
thousands;
from Sinai the Lord entered the holy place.
¹⁹ You went up to its lofty height;
you took captives, received slaves as tribute.
No rebels can live in the presence of God.

VI

²⁰ Blessed be the Lord day by day,
God, our salvation, who carries us.   *Selah*
²¹ Our God is a God who saves;
escape from death is in the LORD God's hands.

NEW JERUSALEM BIBLE

Psalm 68 (V 67)

For the choirmaster   Of David   Psalm   Song

¹ Let God arise, let his enemies scatter,
let his opponents flee before him.
² You disperse them like smoke;
as wax melts in the presence of a fire,
so the wicked melt at the presence of God.
³ The upright rejoice in the presence of God,
delighted and crying out for joy.
⁴ Sing to God, play music to his name,
build a road for the Rider of the Clouds,
rejoice in Yahweh, dance before him.
⁵ Father of orphans, defender of widows,
such is God in his holy dwelling.
⁶ God gives the lonely a home to live in,
leads prisoners out into prosperity,
but rebels must live in the bare wastelands.
⁷ God, when you set out at the head of your people,
when you strode over the desert, ⁸ the earth rocked,
                                                         Pause
the heavens pelted down rain at the presence of
God,
at the presence of God, the God of Israel.
⁹ God, you rained down a shower of blessings,
when your heritage was weary you gave it
strength.
¹⁰ Your family found a home, which you
in your generosity provided for the humble.
¹¹ The Lord gave a command,
the good news of a countless army.
¹² The chieftains of the army are in flight, in flight,
and the fair one at home is sharing out the spoils.
¹³ While you are at ease in the sheepfolds,
the wings of the Doveᵏ are being covered with
silver,
and her feathers with a sheen of green gold;
¹⁴ when Shaddai scatters the chieftains,
through her it snowsˡ on the Dark Mountain.
¹⁵ A mountain of God, the mountain of Bashan!
a haughty mountain, the mountain of Bashan!
¹⁶ Why be envious, haughty mountains,
of the mountain God has chosen for his dwelling?
There God will dwell for ever.
¹⁷ The chariots of God are thousand upon thousand;
God has come from Sinai to the sanctuary.
¹⁸ You have climbed the heights, taken captives,
you have taken men as tribute, even rebels
that Yahweh God might have a dwelling-place.
¹⁹ Blessed be the Lord day after day,
he carries us along, God our Saviour.   *Pause*
²⁰ This God of ours is a God who saves;
from Lord Yahweh comes escape from death;

68, 12-15: The Hebrew text upon which the translation is based has
apparently suffered dislocation and has been substantially rearranged
for sense.

ᵏ 68 Two obscure vv., referring perhaps to Jg 5; some tribes missed
Israel's glorious victory.   ˡ 68 Perhaps the salt sown on devastated
Shechem after the victory.

NEW REVISED STANDARD VERSION	REVISED ENGLISH BIBLE

NEW REVISED STANDARD VERSION

21 But God will shatter the heads of his enemies,
　　the hairy crown of those who walk in their
　　　guilty ways.
22 The Lord said,
　　"I will bring them back from Bashan,
　I will bring them back from the depths of the sea,
23 so that you may bathe*e* your feet in blood,
　　so that the tongues of your dogs may have
　　　their share from the foe."
24 Your solemn processions are seen, *f* O God,
　　the processions of my God, my King, into the
　　　sanctuary —
25 the singers in front, the musicians last,
　　between them girls playing tambourines:
26 "Bless God in the great congregation,
　　the LORD, O you who are of Israel's fountain!"
27 There is Benjamin, the least of them, in the lead,
　　the princes of Judah in a body,
　　the princes of Zebulun, the princes of Naphtali.
28 Summon your might, O God;
　　show your strength, O God, as you have done
　　　for us before.
29 Because of your temple at Jerusalem
　　kings bear gifts to you.
30 Rebuke the wild animals that live among the
　　　reeds,
　　the herd of bulls with the calves of the
　　　peoples.
　Trample*g* under foot those who lust after tribute;
　　scatter the peoples who delight in war.*h*
31 Let bronze be brought from Egypt;
　　let Ethiopia*i* hasten to stretch out its hands to
　　　God.
32 Sing to God, O kingdoms of the earth;
　　sing praises to the Lord,　　　　　　　　*Selah*
33 O rider in the heavens, the ancient heavens;
　　listen, he sends out his voice, his mighty
　　　voice.
34 Ascribe power to God,
　　whose majesty is over Israel;
　　and whose power is in the skies.
35 Awesome is God in his*j* sanctuary,
　　the God of Israel;
　　he gives power and strength to his people.

　Blessed be God!

Psalm 69

To the leader: according to Lilies. Of David.

1 Save me, O God,
　　for the waters have come up to my neck.
2 I sink in deep mire,
　　where there is no foothold;
　I have come into deep waters,
　　and the flood sweeps over me.
3 I am weary with my crying;
　　my throat is parched.
　My eyes grow dim
　　with waiting for my God.

REVISED ENGLISH BIBLE

21 God himself smites the heads of his enemies,
　　those proud sinners with their flowing locks.
22 The Lord says, 'I shall fetch them back from
　　　Bashan,
　I shall fetch them from the depths of the sea,
23 that you may bathe your feet in blood,
　　while the tongues of your dogs are eager for it.'
24 Your processions, God, come into view,
　　the processions of my God, my King in the
　　　sanctuary:
25 in front the singers, with minstrels following,
　　and in their midst girls beating tambourines.
26 Bless God in the great congregation;
　　let the assembly of Israel bless the LORD.
27 There is the little tribe of Benjamin leading them,
　　there the company of Judah's princes,
　　the princes of Zebulun and of Naphtali.
28 God, set your might to work,
　　the divine might which you have wielded for us.
29 Kings will bring you gifts
　　for the honour of your temple in Jerusalem.
30 Rebuke those wild beasts of the reeds,
　　that herd of bulls, the bull-calf warriors of the
　　　nations,
　who bring bars of silver and prostrate themselves.
　Scatter these nations which delight in war.
31 Envoys will come from Egypt;
　　Nubia will stretch out her hands to God.
32 You kingdoms of the world, sing praises to God,
　　make music to the Lord,　　　　　　　 [*Selah*
33 to him who rides on the heavens, the ancient
　　　heavens.
　Listen! He speaks in the mighty thunder.
34 Ascribe might to God, whose majesty is over
　　　Israel,
　Israel's pride and might throned in the skies.
35 Awesome is God in your sanctuary;
　　he is Israel's God.
　He gives might and power to his people.
　Praise be to God.

Psalm 69

For the leader: set to 'Lilies': for David

1 SAVE me, God,
　　for the water has risen to my neck.
2 I sink in muddy depths where there is no foothold;
　I have come into deep water, and the flood sweeps
　　　me away.
3 I am exhausted with crying, my throat is sore,
　　my eyes are worn out with waiting for God.

---

e Gk Syr Tg: Heb *shatter*　　*f* Or *have been seen*　　*g* Cn: Heb
Trampling　　*h* Meaning of Heb of verse 30 is uncertain
i Or *Nubia*; Heb *Cush*　　*j* Gk: Heb *from your*

68:23 **bathe:** *so Gk; Heb.* smite. **are eager:** *prob. rdg; Heb.*
obscure.　　68:26 **assembly:** *prob. rdg; Heb.* obscure.
68:28 **God . . . your might:** *so Gk; Heb.* Your God has directed.

22 God will crush the skulls of the enemy,
   the hairy heads of those who walk in sin.
23 The Lord has said:
   "Even from Bashan I will fetch them,
   fetch them even from the depths of the sea.
24 You will wash your feet in your enemy's blood;
   the tongues of your dogs will lap it up."
   VII
25 Your procession comes into view, O God,
   your procession into the holy place, my God and
      king.
26 The singers go first, the harpists follow;
   in their midst girls sound the timbrels.
27 In your choirs, bless God;
   bless the LORD, you from Israel's assemblies.
28 In the lead is Benjamin, few in number;
   there the princes of Judah, a large throng,
   the princes of Zebulun, the princes of Naphtali,
      too.
   VIII
29 Summon again, O God, your power,
   the divine power you once showed for us.
30 Show it from your temple on behalf of Jerusalem,
   that kings may bring you tribute.
31 Roar at the wild beast of the reeds,
   the herd of mighty bulls, the lords of nations;
   scatter the nations that delight in war.
32 Exact rich tribute from lower Egypt,
   from upper Egypt, gold and silver;
   make Ethiopia extend its hands to God.
   IX
33 You kingdoms of the earth, sing to God;
   chant the praises of the Lord,   Selah
34 Who rides the heights of the ancient heavens,
   whose voice is thunder, mighty thunder.
35 Confess the power of God,
   whose majesty protects Israel,
   whose power is in the sky.
36 Awesome is God in his holy place,
   the God of Israel,
   who gives power and strength to his people.
   Blessed be God!

21 but God smashes the head of his enemies,
   the long-haired skull of the prowling criminal.
22 The Lord has said, 'I will bring them back from
      Bashan,
   I will bring them back from the depths of the sea,
23 so that you may bathe your feet in blood,
   and the tongues of your dogs feast on your
      enemies.'
24 Your processions, God, are for all to see,
   the processions of my God, of my king, to the
      sanctuary;
25 singers ahead, musicians behind,
   in the middle come girls, beating their drums.
26   In choirs they bless God,
   Yahweh, since the foundation of Israel.
27 Benjamin was there, the youngest in front,
   the princes of Judah in bright-coloured robes,
   the princes of Zebulun, the princes of Naphtali.
28 Take command, my God, as befits your power,
   the power, God, which you have wielded for us,
29 from your temple high above Jerusalem.
   Kings will come to you bearing tribute.
30 Rebuke the Beast of the Reeds,
   that herd of bulls, that people of calves,
   who bow down with ingots of silver.
   Scatter the people who delight in war.
31 From Egypt nobles will come,
   Ethiopia will stretch out its hands to God.
32 Kingdoms of the earth, sing to God,
   play for 33 the Rider of the Heavens, the primeval
      heavens.   Pause
   There he speaks, with a voice of power!
34 Acknowledge the power of God.
   Over Israel his splendour, in the clouds his power.
35 Awesome is God in his sanctuary.
   He, the God of Israel,
   gives strength and power to his people.
   Blessed be God.

Psalm 69

1 *For the leader; according to "Lilies." Of David.*

I
2 Save me, God,
   for the waters have reached my neck.
3 I have sunk into the mire of the deep,
   where there is no foothold.
I have gone down to the watery depths;
   the flood overwhelms me.
4 I am weary with crying out;
   my throat is parched.
My eyes have failed,
   looking for my God.

Psalm 69 (V 68)

For the choirmaster   Tune: 'Lilies . . .'   Of David

1 Save me, God, for the waters
   have closed in on my very being.
2 I am sinking in the deepest swamp
   and there is no firm ground.
I have stepped into deep water
   and the waves are washing over me.
3 I am exhausted with calling out, my throat is
      hoarse,
   my eyes are worn out with searching for my
      God.

4 More in number than the hairs of my head
    are those who hate me without cause;
many are those who would destroy me,
    my enemies who accuse me falsely.
What I did not steal
    must I now restore?
5 O God, you know my folly;
    the wrongs I have done are not hidden from
        you.
6 Do not let those who hope in you be put to
        shame because of me,
    O Lord GOD of hosts;
do not let those who seek you be dishonored
        because of me,
    O God of Israel.
7 It is for your sake that I have borne reproach,
    that shame has covered my face.
8 I have become a stranger to my kindred,
    an alien to my mother's children.
9 It is zeal for your house that has consumed me;
    the insults of those who insult you have fallen
        on me.
10 When I humbled my soul with fasting,*k*
    they insulted me for doing so.
11 When I made sackcloth my clothing,
    I became a byword to them.
12 I am the subject of gossip for those who sit in the
        gate,
    and the drunkards make songs about me.
13 But as for me, my prayer is to you, O LORD.
    At an acceptable time, O God,
    in the abundance of your steadfast love, answer
        me.
With your faithful help 14rescue me
    from sinking in the mire;
let me be delivered from my enemies
    and from the deep waters.
15 Do not let the flood sweep over me,
    or the deep swallow me up,
    or the Pit close its mouth over me.
16 Answer me, O LORD, for your steadfast love is
        good;
    according to your abundant mercy, turn to me.
17 Do not hide your face from your servant,
    for I am in distress — make haste to answer me.
18 Draw near to me, redeem me,
    set me free because of my enemies.
19 You know the insults I receive,
    and my shame and dishonor;
    my foes are all known to you.
20 Insults have broken my heart,
    so that I am in despair.
I looked for pity, but there was none;
    and for comforters, but I found none.
21 They gave me poison for food,
    and for my thirst they gave me vinegar to
        drink.
22 Let their table be a trap for them,
    a snare for their allies.
23 Let their eyes be darkened so that they cannot
        see,
    and make their loins tremble continually.
24 Pour out your indignation upon them,
    and let your burning anger overtake them.

4 Those who hate me without reason
    are more than the hairs of my head;
my persecutors are strong,
    my foes are treacherous.
How can I restore what I have not stolen?
5 God, you know how foolish I am,
    and my guilty deeds are not hidden from you.
6 Lord GOD of Hosts,
    let none of those who hope in you be discouraged
        through me;
God of Israel,
    let none who seek you be humiliated through me.
7 For your sake I have suffered reproach;
    I dare not show my face for shame.
8 I have become a stranger to my brothers,
    an alien to my mother's sons.
9 Zeal for your house has consumed me;
    the insults aimed at you have landed on me.
10 I wept bitterly while I fasted
    and I exposed myself to insults.
11 I have made sackcloth my clothing
    and become a byword among the people.
12 Those who sit by the town gate gossip about me;
    I am the theme of drunken songs.
13 At an acceptable time
    I lift my prayer to you, LORD.
In your great and enduring love
    answer me, God, with sure deliverance.
14 Rescue me from the mire, do not let me sink;
    let me be rescued from my enemies
    and from the watery depths.
15 Let no billows sweep me away,
    no abyss swallow me up,
    no deep close over me.
16 Answer me, LORD, in the goodness of your
        unfailing love,
    in your great compassion turn towards me.
17 Do not hide your face from me, your servant;
    answer me without delay, for I am in dire straits.
18 Come near to me and redeem me;
    deliver me from my enemies.
19 You know what insults I bear,
    my shame and my ignominy;
    all who distress me are well known to you.
20 Insults have broken my heart
    and I am in despair;
I looked for consolation, but received none,
    for comfort, but did not find any.
21 They put poison in my food
    and when I was thirsty they gave me vinegar to
        drink.
22 May their table be a snare to them
    and a trap when they feel secure!
23 May their eyes be darkened so that they do not
        see;
    let a continual ague shake their loins!
24 Vent your indignation on them
    and let your burning anger overtake them.

k Gk Syr: Heb *I wept, with fasting my soul*, or *I made my soul mourn
with fasting*

NEW AMERICAN BIBLE

5 More numerous than the hairs of my head
   are those who hate me without cause.
Too many for my strength
   are my treacherous enemies.
Must I now restore
   what I did not steal?

II

6 God, you know my folly;
   my faults are not hidden from you.
7 Let those who wait for you, LORD of hosts,
   not be shamed through me.
Let those who seek you, God of Israel,
   not be disgraced through me.
8 For your sake I bear insult,
   shame covers my face.
9 I have become an outcast to my kin,
   a stranger to my mother's children.
10 Because zeal for your house consumes me,
   I am scorned by those who scorn you.
11 I have wept and fasted,
   but this led only to scorn.
12 I clothed myself in sackcloth;
   I became a byword for them.
13 They who sit at the gate gossip about me;
   drunkards make me the butt of their songs.

III

14 But I pray to you, LORD,
   for the time of your favor.
God, in your great kindness answer me
   with your constant help.
15 Rescue me from the mire;
   do not let me sink.
Rescue me from my enemies
   and from the watery depths.
16 Do not let the floodwaters overwhelm me,
   nor the deep swallow me,
   nor the mouth of the pit close over me.
17 Answer me, LORD, in your generous love;
   in your great mercy turn to me.
18 Do not hide your face from your servant;
   in my distress hasten to answer me.
19 Come and ransom my life;
   because of my enemies redeem me.
20 You know my reproach, my shame, my disgrace;
   before you stand all my foes.
21 Insult has broken my heart, and I am weak;
   I looked for compassion, but there was none,
   for comforters, but found none.
22 Instead they put gall in my food;
   for my thirst they gave me vinegar.

IV

23 Make their own table a snare for them,
   a trap for their friends.
24 Make their eyes so dim they cannot see;
   keep their backs ever feeble.
25 Pour out your wrath upon them;
   let the fury of your anger overtake them.

NEW JERUSALEM BIBLE

4 More numerous than the hairs of my head
   are those who hate me without reason.
Those who seek to get rid of me are powerful,
   my treacherous enemies.
(Must I give back what I have never stolen?)

5 God, you know how foolish I am,
   my offences are not hidden from you.

6 Those who hope in you must not be made fools of,
   Yahweh Sabaoth, because of me!

Those who seek you must not be disgraced,
   God of Israel, because of me!

7 It is for you I bear insults,
   my face is covered with shame,
8 I am estranged from my brothers,
   alienated from my own mother's sons;
9 for I am eaten up with zeal for your house,
   and insults directed against you fall on me.

10 I mortify myself with fasting,
   and find myself insulted for it,
11 I dress myself in sackcloth
   and become their laughing-stock,
12 the gossip of people sitting at the gate,
   and the theme of drunkards' songs.

13 And so, I pray to you, Yahweh,
   at the time of your favour;
in your faithful love answer me,
   in the constancy of your saving power.

14 Rescue me from the mire before I sink in;
   so I shall be saved from those who hate me,
   from the watery depths.
15 Let not the waves wash over me,
   nor the deep swallow me up,
   nor the pit close its mouth on me.

16 Answer me, Yahweh, for your faithful love is
      generous;
   in your tenderness turn towards me;
17 do not turn away from your servant,
   be quick to answer me, for I am in trouble.
18 Come to my side, redeem me,
   ransom me because of my enemies.

19 You know well the insults,
   the shame and disgrace I endure.
Every one of my oppressors is known to you.
20 Insult has broken my heart past cure.
I hoped for sympathy, but in vain,
   for consolers—not one to be found.
21 To eat they gave me poison,
   to drink, vinegar when I was thirsty.
22 May their own table prove a trap for them,
   and their abundance a snare;
23 may their eyes grow so dim that they cannot see,
   all their muscles lose their strength.

24 Vent your fury on them,
   let your burning anger overtake them.

NEW REVISED STANDARD VERSION	REVISED ENGLISH BIBLE

NEW REVISED STANDARD VERSION

25 May their camp be a desolation;
   let no one live in their tents.
26 For they persecute those whom you have struck
      down,
   and those whom you have wounded, they
      attack still more.[l]
27 Add guilt to their guilt;
   may they have no acquittal from you.
28 Let them be blotted out of the book of the living;
   let them not be enrolled among the righteous.
29 But I am lowly and in pain;
   let your salvation, O God, protect me.

30 I will praise the name of God with a song;
   I will magnify him with thanksgiving.
31 This will please the LORD more than an ox
   or a bull with horns and hoofs.
32 Let the oppressed see it and be glad;
   you who seek God, let your hearts revive.
33 For the LORD hears the needy,
   and does not despise his own that are in bonds.

34 Let heaven and earth praise him,
   the seas and everything that moves in them.
35 For God will save Zion
   and rebuild the cities of Judah;
   and his servants shall live[m] there and possess it;
36   the children of his servants shall inherit it,
   and those who love his name shall live in it.

Psalm 70

To the leader. Of David, for the memorial offering.

1 Be pleased, O God, to deliver me.
   O LORD, make haste to help me!
2 Let those be put to shame and confusion
   who seek my life.
   Let those be turned back and brought to dishonor
   who desire to hurt me.
3 Let those who say, "Aha, Aha!"
   turn back because of their shame.

4 Let all who seek you
   rejoice and be glad in you.
   Let those who love your salvation
   say evermore, "God is great!"
5 But I am poor and needy;
   hasten to me, O God!
   You are my help and my deliverer;
   O LORD, do not delay!

Psalm 71

1 In you, O LORD, I take refuge;
   let me never be put to shame.
2 In your righteousness deliver me and rescue me;
   incline your ear to me and save me.
3 Be to me a rock of refuge,
   a strong fortress,[n] to save me,
   for you are my rock and my fortress.

4 Rescue me, O my God, from the hand of the
      wicked,
   from the grasp of the unjust and cruel.
5 For you, O Lord, are my hope,
   my trust, O LORD, from my youth.

REVISED ENGLISH BIBLE

25 Let their settlements be desolate,
   their tents without inhabitant,
26 for they pursue him whom you have struck down
   and multiply the torments of those whom you have
      wounded.
27 Heap punishment after punishment on them;
   grant them no vindication;
28 let them be blotted out from the book of the living;
   let them not be enrolled among the innocent.
29 I am afflicted and in pain;
   let your saving power, God, set me securely on
      high.

30 I shall praise God's name in song
   and glorify him with thanksgiving;
31 that will please the LORD more than the offering of
      a bull,
   a young bull with horns and cloven hoofs.
32 When the humble see this let them rejoice.
   Take heart, you seekers after God,
33 for the LORD listens to the poor
   and does not despise his captive people.
34 Let sky and earth praise him,
   the seas and all that moves in them,
35 for God will deliver Zion
   and rebuild the cities of Judah;
   his people will settle there and possess it.
36 The children of those who serve him will inherit it,
   and those who love his name will live there.

Psalm 70

For the leader: for David: for commemoration

1 MAKE haste and save me, God;
   LORD, come quickly to my help.
2 Let those who seek my life
   be discomfited and dismayed,
   let those who desire my hurt be turned back in
      disgrace;
3 let those who cry 'Hurrah!'
   withdraw in their shame.
4 But let all who seek you
   be jubilant and rejoice in you;
   and may those who long for your saving aid
   forever cry, 'All glory to God!'
5 But I am oppressed and poor;
   God, come quickly to me.
   You are my help and my deliverer;
   LORD, do not delay.

Psalm 71

1 IN you, LORD, I have found refuge;
   let me never be put to shame.
2 By your saving power rescue and deliver me;
   hear me and save me!
3 Be to me a rock of refuge
   to which at all times I may come;
   you have decreed my deliverance,
   for you are my rock and stronghold.
4 Keep me safe, my God, from the power of the
      wicked,
   from the clutches of the pitiless and unjust.
5 You are my hope, Lord GOD,
   my trust since my childhood.

---

[l]Gk Syr: Heb *recount the pain of*   [m]Syr: Heb *and they shall live*
[n]Gk Compare 31.3: Heb *to come continually you have commanded*

69:26 **multiply:** *so Gk; Heb.* recount.   70:1–5 *Cp. Ps. 40:13–17.*

26 Make their camp desolate,
with none to dwell in their tents.
27 For they pursued the one you struck,
added to the pain of the one you wounded.
28 Add that to their crimes;
let them not attain to your reward.
29 Strike them from the book of the living;
do not count them among the just!

V

30 But I am afflicted and in pain;
let your saving help protect me, God,
31 That I may praise God's name in song
and glorify it with thanksgiving.
32 My song will please the LORD more than oxen,
more than bullocks with horns and hooves:
33 "See, you lowly ones, and be glad;
you who seek God, take heart!
34 For the LORD hears the poor,
does not spurn those in bondage.
35 Let the heavens and the earth sing praise,
the seas and whatever moves in them!"

VI

36 God will rescue Zion,
rebuild the cities of Judah.
God's servants shall dwell in the land and possess
it;
37   it shall be the heritage of their descendants;
those who love God's name shall dwell there.

Psalm 70

1 For the leader; of David. For remembrance.

2 Graciously rescue me, God!
Come quickly to help me, LORD!
3 Confound and put to shame
those who seek my life.
Turn back in disgrace
those who desire my ruin.
4 Let those who say "Aha!"
turn back in their shame.
5 But may all who seek you
rejoice and be glad in you.
May those who long for your help
always say, "God be glorified!"
6 Here I am, afflicted and poor.
God, come quickly!
You are my help and deliverer.
LORD, do not delay!

Psalm 71

I

1 In you, LORD, I take refuge;
let me never be put to shame.
2 In your justice rescue and deliver me;
listen to me and save me!
3 Be my rock and refuge,
my secure stronghold;
for you are my rock and fortress.
4 My God, rescue me from the power of the wicked,
from the clutches of the violent.
5 You are my hope, Lord;
my trust, GOD, from my youth.

25 Reduce their encampment to ruin,
and leave their tents untenanted,
26 for hounding someone you had already stricken,
for redoubling the pain of one you had wounded.

27 Charge them with crime after crime,
exclude them from your saving justice,
28 erase them from the book of life,
do not enrol them among the upright.

29 For myself, wounded wretch that I am,
by your saving power raise me up!
30 I will praise God's name in song,
I will extol him by thanksgiving,
31 for this will please Yahweh more than an ox,
than a bullock horned and hoofed.

32 The humble have seen and are glad.
Let your courage revive, you who seek God.
33 For God listens to the poor,
he has never scorned his captive people.
34 Let heaven and earth and seas,
and all that stirs in them, acclaim him!

35 For God will save Zion,
and rebuild the cities of Judah,
and people will live there on their own land;
36 the descendants of his servants will inherit it,
and those who love his name will dwell there.

Psalm 70 (V 69)[m]

For the choirmaster   Of David   In commemoration

1 Be pleased, God, to rescue me,
Yahweh, come quickly and help me!
2 Shame and dismay to those
who seek my life!

Back with them! Let them be humiliated
who delight in my misfortunes.
3 Let them shrink away covered with shame,
those who say to me, 'Aha, aha!'

4 But joy and happiness in you
to all who seek you.
Let them ceaselessly cry, 'God is great',
who love your saving power.

5 Poor and needy as I am,
God, come quickly to me!
Yahweh, my helper, my Saviour,
do not delay!

Psalm 71 (V 70)

1 In you, Yahweh, I take refuge,
I shall never be put to shame.
2 In your saving justice rescue me, deliver me,
listen to me and save me.

3 Be a sheltering rock for me,
always accessible;
you have determined to save me,
for you are my rock, my fortress.
4 My God, rescue me from the clutches of the
wicked,
from the grasp of the rogue and the ruthless.

5 For you are my hope, Lord,
my trust, Yahweh, since boyhood.

[m] 70 = 40:13–17.

6 Upon you I have leaned from my birth;
    it was you who took me from my mother's
        womb.
My praise is continually of you.

7 I have been like a portent to many,
    but you are my strong refuge.
8 My mouth is filled with your praise,
    and with your glory all day long.
9 Do not cast me off in the time of old age;
    do not forsake me when my strength is spent.
10 For my enemies speak concerning me,
    and those who watch for my life consult
        together.
11 They say, "Pursue and seize that person
    whom God has forsaken,
    for there is no one to deliver."

12 O God, do not be far from me;
    O my God, make haste to help me!
13 Let my accusers be put to shame and consumed;
    let those who seek to hurt me
    be covered with scorn and disgrace.
14 But I will hope continually,
    and will praise you yet more and more.
15 My mouth will tell of your righteous acts,
    of your deeds of salvation all day long,
    though their number is past my knowledge.
16 I will come praising the mighty deeds of the Lord
        GOD,
    I will praise your righteousness, yours alone.

17 O God, from my youth you have taught me,
    and I still proclaim your wondrous deeds.
18 So even to old age and gray hairs,
    O God, do not forsake me,
until I proclaim your might
    to all the generations to come.*o*
Your power 19 and your righteousness, O God,
    reach the high heavens.

You who have done great things,
    O God, who is like you?
20 You who have made me see many troubles and
        calamities
    will revive me again;
from the depths of the earth
    you will bring me up again.
21 You will increase my honor,
    and comfort me once again.

22 I will also praise you with the harp
    for your faithfulness, O my God;
I will sing praises to you with the lyre,
    O Holy One of Israel.
23 My lips will shout for joy
    when I sing praises to you;
    my soul also, which you have rescued.
24 All day long my tongue will talk of your
        righteous help,
for those who tried to do me harm
    have been put to shame, and disgraced.

Psalm 72

Of Solomon.

1 Give the king your justice, O God,
    and your righteousness to a king's son.
2 May he judge your people with righteousness,
    and your poor with justice.

o Gk Compare Syr: Heb *to a generation, to all that come*

6 On you I have leaned from birth;
    you brought me from my mother's womb;
    to you I offer praise at all times.
7 I have become like a portent to many;
    but you are my strong refuge.
8 My mouth will be full of your praises,
    I shall tell of your splendour all day long.
9 Do not cast me off when old age comes
    or forsake me as my strength fails,
10 for my enemies whisper against me
    and those who spy on me intrigue together,
11 saying, 'God has forsaken him;
    harry him and seize him;
    there is no one to come to his rescue.'
12 God, do not stand aloof from me;
    come quickly, my God, to my help.
13 Let my accusers be put to shame and perish;
    let those intent on harming me be covered with
        scorn and dishonour.

14 But as for me, I shall wait in continual hope,
    I shall praise you again and yet again;
15 I shall declare your vindicating power,
    declare all day long your saving acts,
    although I lack the skill to recount them.
16 I shall come declaring your mighty acts, Lord
        GOD,
    and proclaim your sole power to vindicate.
17 You have taught me from childhood, God,
    and all my life I have proclaimed your marvellous
        works.
18 Now that I am old and my hair is grey,
    do not forsake me, God,
    until I have extolled your strength
    to generations yet to come,
19 your might and vindicating power to highest
        heaven;
    for great are the things you have done.
    Who is there like you, my God?
20 You have made me suffer many grievous
        hardships,
    yet you revive me once more
    and lift me again from earth's watery depths.
21 Restore me to honour, and comfort me again;
22 then I shall praise you on the harp
    for your faithfulness, my God;
    on the lyre I shall sing to you,
    the Holy One of Israel.
23 Songs of joy will be on my lips;
    I shall sing to you because you have redeemed me.
24 All day long my tongue will tell of your
        vindicating power,
    for those who seek my hurt are shamed and
        disgraced.

Psalm 72

For Solomon

1 GOD, endow the king with your own justice,
    his royal person with your righteousness,
2 that he may govern your people rightly
    and deal justly with your oppressed ones.

NEW AMERICAN BIBLE

⁶On you I depend since birth;
  from my mother's womb you are my strength;
  my hope in you never wavers.
⁷I have become a portent to many,
  but you are my strong refuge!
⁸My mouth shall be filled with your praise,
  shall sing your glory every day.
  II
⁹Do not cast me aside in my old age;
  as my strength fails, do not forsake me.
¹⁰For my enemies speak against me;
  they watch and plot against me.
¹¹They say, "God has abandoned that one.
  Pursue, seize the wretch!
  No one will come to the rescue!"
¹²God, do not stand far from me;
  my God, hasten to help me.
¹³Bring to a shameful end
  those who attack me;
  Cover with contempt and scorn
  those who seek my ruin.
¹⁴I will always hope in you
  and add to all your praise.
¹⁵My mouth shall proclaim your just deeds,
  day after day your acts of deliverance,
  though I cannot number them all.
¹⁶I will speak of the mighty works of the Lord;
  O GOD, I will tell of your singular justice.
  III
¹⁷God, you have taught me from my youth;
  to this day I proclaim your wondrous deeds.
¹⁸Now that I am old and gray,
  do not forsake me, God,
  That I may proclaim your might
  to all generations yet to come,
  Your power ¹⁹and justice, God,
  to the highest heaven.
  You have done great things;
  O God, who is your equal?
²⁰You have sent me many bitter afflictions,
  but once more revive me.
  From the watery depths of the earth
  once more raise me up.
²¹Restore my honor;
  turn and comfort me,
²²That I may praise you with the lyre
  for your faithfulness, my God,
  And sing to you with the harp,
  O Holy One of Israel!
²³My lips will shout for joy as I sing your praise;
  my soul, too, which you have redeemed.
²⁴Yes, my tongue shall recount
  your justice day by day.
  For those who sought my ruin
  will have been shamed and disgraced.

NEW JERUSALEM BIBLE

⁶On you I have relied since my birth,
  since my mother's womb you have been my
    portion,
  the constant theme of my praise.
⁷Many were bewildered at me,
  but you are my sure refuge.
⁸My mouth is full of your praises,
  filled with your splendour all day long.
⁹Do not reject me in my old age,
  nor desert me when my strength is failing,
¹⁰for my enemies are discussing me,
  those with designs on my life are plotting together.
¹¹'Hound him down, for God has deserted him!
  Seize him, there is no one to rescue him.'
¹²God, do not stand aloof,
  my God, come quickly to help me.
¹³Shame and ruin
  on those who slander me,
  may those intent on harming me
  be covered with insult and infamy.
¹⁴As for me, my hope will never fade,
  I will praise you more and more.
¹⁵My lips shall proclaim your saving justice,
  your saving power all day long.
¹⁶I will come in the power of Yahweh
  to tell of your justice, yours alone.
¹⁷God, you have taught me from boyhood,
  and I am still proclaiming your marvels.
¹⁸ Now that I am old and grey-haired,
    God, do not desert me,
  till I have proclaimed your strength
  to generations still to come,
  your power ¹⁹and justice to the skies.

  You have done great things,
    God, who is like you?
²⁰You have shown me much misery and hardship,
  but you will give me life again,
  You will raise me up again from the depths of the
    earth,
²¹prolong my old age, and comfort me again.
²²For my part, I will thank you on the lyre
  for your constancy, my God.
  I will play the harp in your honour,
    Holy One of Israel.
²³My lips sing for joy as I play to you,
  because you have redeemed me,
²⁴ and all day long my tongue
    muses on your saving justice.
  Shame and disgrace
  on those intent to harm me!

Psalm 72

¹Of Solomon.

I
O God, give your judgment to the king;
  your justice to the son of kings;
²That he may govern your people with justice,
  your oppressed with right judgment,

Psalm 72 (V 71)

Of Solomon

¹God, endow the king with your own fair
    judgement,
  the son of the king with your own saving justice,
²that he may rule your people with justice,
  and your poor with fair judgement.

NEW REVISED STANDARD VERSION

3 May the mountains yield prosperity for the
   people,
   and the hills, in righteousness.
4 May he defend the cause of the poor of the
   people,
   give deliverance to the needy,
   and crush the oppressor.

5 May he live *p* while the sun endures,
   and as long as the moon, throughout all
   generations.
6 May he be like rain that falls on the mown grass,
   like showers that water the earth.
7 In his days may righteousness flourish
   and peace abound, until the moon is no more.

8 May he have dominion from sea to sea,
   and from the River to the ends of the earth.
9 May his foes *q* bow down before him,
   and his enemies lick the dust.
10 May the kings of Tarshish and of the isles
   render him tribute,
   may the kings of Sheba and Seba
   bring gifts.
11 May all kings fall down before him,
   all nations give him service.

12 For he delivers the needy when they call,
   the poor and those who have no helper.
13 He has pity on the weak and the needy,
   and saves the lives of the needy.
14 From oppression and violence he redeems their
   life;
   and precious is their blood in his sight.

15 Long may he live!
   May gold of Sheba be given to him.
   May prayer be made for him continually,
   and blessings invoked for him all day long.
16 May there be abundance of grain in the land;
   may it wave on the tops of the mountains;
   may its fruit be like Lebanon;
   and may people blossom in the cities
   like the grass of the field.
17 May his name endure forever,
   his fame continue as long as the sun.
   May all nations be blessed in him; *r*
   may they pronounce him happy.

18 Blessed be the LORD, the God of Israel,
   who alone does wondrous things.
19 Blessed be his glorious name forever;
   may his glory fill the whole earth.
   Amen and Amen.

20 The prayers of David son of Jesse are ended.

BOOK III

Psalms 73–89

Psalm 73

A Psalm of Asaph.

1 Truly God is good to the upright, *s*
   to those who are pure in heart.
2 But as for me, my feet had almost stumbled;
   my steps had nearly slipped.

REVISED ENGLISH BIBLE

3 May hills and mountains provide your people
   with prosperity in righteousness.
4 May he give judgement for the oppressed among
   the people
   and help to the needy;
   may he crush the oppressor.

5 May he fear you as long as the sun endures,
   and as the moon throughout the ages.
6 May he be like rain falling on early crops,
   like showers watering the earth.
7 In his days may righteousness flourish,
   prosperity abound until the moon is no more.

8 May he hold sway from sea to sea,
   from the Euphrates river to the ends of the earth.
9 May desert tribes bend low before him,
   his enemies lick the dust.
10 May the kings of Tarshish and of the isles bring
   gifts,
   the kings of Sheba and Seba present their tribute.
11 Let all kings pay him homage,
   all nations serve him.

12 For he will rescue the needy who appeal for help,
   the distressed who have no protector.
13 He will have pity on the poor and the needy,
   and deliver the needy from death;
14 he will redeem them from oppression and violence
   and their blood will be precious in his eyes.

15 May the king live long!
   May gifts of gold from Sheba be given him.
   May prayer be made for him continually;
   blessings be his all the day long.
16 May there be grain in plenty throughout the land,
   growing thickly over the heights of the hills;
   may its crops flourish like Lebanon,
   and the sheaves be plenteous as blades of grass.
17 Long may the king's name endure,
   may it remain for ever like the sun;
   then all will pray to be blessed as he was;
   all nations will tell of his happiness.

18 Blessed be the LORD God, the God of Israel,
   who alone does marvellous things;
19 blessed be his glorious name for ever;
   may his glory fill the whole earth.
   Amen and Amen.

20 Here end the prayers of David son of Jesse.

BOOK 3

Psalm 73

A psalm: for Asaph

1 ASSUREDLY God is good to the upright,
   to those who are pure in heart!

2 My feet had almost slipped,
   my foothold had all but given way,

---

p Gk: Heb *may they fear you*   *q* Cn: Heb *those who live in the*
wilderness   *r* Or *bless themselves by him*   *s* Or *good to Israel*

72:7 **righteousness:** *so some MSS; others* a righteous person.
72:15 **gold:** *or* frankincense.   72:16 **the sheaves:** *prob. rdg; Heb.*
from a city.   73:1 **to the upright:** *prob. rdg; Heb.* to Israel.

³ That the mountains may yield their bounty for the
   people,
   and the hills great abundance,
⁴ That he may defend the oppressed among the
   people,
   save the poor and crush the oppressor.

II

⁵ May he live as long as the sun endures,
   like the moon, through all generations.
⁶ May he be like rain coming down upon the fields,
   like showers watering the earth,
⁷ That abundance may flourish in his days,
   great bounty, till the moon be no more.

III

⁸ May he rule from sea to sea,
   from the river to the ends of the earth.
⁹ May his foes kneel before him,
   his enemies lick the dust.
¹⁰ May the kings of Tarshish and the islands bring
   tribute,
   the kings of Arabia and Seba offer gifts.
¹¹ May all kings bow before him,
   all nations serve him.
¹² For he rescues the poor when they cry out,
   the oppressed who have no one to help.
¹³ He shows pity to the needy and the poor
   and saves the lives of the poor.
¹⁴ From extortion and violence he frees them,
   for precious is their blood in his sight.

IV

¹⁵ Long may he live, receiving gold from Arabia,
   prayed for without cease, blessed day by day.
¹⁶ May wheat abound in the land,
   flourish even on the mountain heights.
   May his fruit increase like Lebanon's,
   his wheat like the grasses of the land.
¹⁷ May his name be blessed forever;
   as long as the sun, may his name endure.
   May the tribes of the earth give blessings with his
   name;
   may all the nations regard him as favored.

* * *

¹⁸ Blessed be the LORD, the God of Israel,
   who alone does wonderful deeds.
¹⁹ Blessed be his glorious name forever;
   may all the earth be filled with the LORD's
   glory.
   Amen and amen.

²⁰ The end of the psalms of David, son of Jesse.

³ Mountains and hills,
   bring peace to the people!
   With justice ⁴ he will judge the poor of the people,
   he will save the children of the needy
   and crush their oppressors.

⁵ In the sight of the sun and the moon he will
   endure,
   age after age.
⁶ He will come down like rain on mown grass,
   like showers moistening the land.

⁷ In his days uprightness shall flourish,
   and peace in plenty till the moon is no more.
⁸ His empire shall stretch from sea to sea,
   from the river to the limits of the earth.

⁹ The Beast will cower before him,
   his enemies lick the dust;
¹⁰ the kings of Tarshish and the islands
   will pay him tribute.

   The kings of Sheba and Saba
   will offer gifts;
¹¹ all kings will do him homage,
   all nations become his servants.

¹² For he rescues the needy who calls to him,
   and the poor who has no one to help.
¹³ He has pity on the weak and the needy,
   and saves the needy from death.

¹⁴ From oppression and violence he redeems their
   lives,
   their blood is precious in his sight.
¹⁵ (Long may he live; may the gold of Sheba be
   given him!)
   Prayer will be offered for him constantly,
   and blessings invoked on him all day.

¹⁶ May wheat abound in the land,
   waving on the heights of the hills,
   like Lebanon with its fruits and flowers at their
   best,
   like the grasses of the earth.

¹⁷ May his name be blessed for ever,
   and endure in the sight of the sun.
   In him shall be blessed every race in the world,
   and all nations call him blessed.

¹⁸ Blessed be Yahweh, the God of Israel,
   who alone works wonders;
¹⁹ blessed for ever his glorious name.
   May the whole world be filled with his glory!
   Amen! Amen!

²⁰ End of the prayers of David, son of Jesse.

THIRD BOOK

Psalms 73–89

Psalm 73

¹ *A psalm of Asaph.*

How good God is to the upright,
   the Lord, to those who are clean of heart!

I

² But, as for me, I lost my balance;
   my feet all but slipped,

Psalm 73 (V 72)

Psalm   Of Asaph

¹ Indeed God is good to Israel,
   the Lord to those who are pure of heart.

² My feet were on the point of stumbling,
   a little more and I had slipped,

NEW REVISED STANDARD VERSION	REVISED ENGLISH BIBLE

NEW REVISED STANDARD VERSION

3 For I was envious of the arrogant;
   I saw the prosperity of the wicked.
4 For they have no pain;
   their bodies are sound and sleek.
5 They are not in trouble as others are;
   they are not plagued like other people.
6 Therefore pride is their necklace;
   violence covers them like a garment.
7 Their eyes swell out with fatness;
   their hearts overflow with follies.
8 They scoff and speak with malice;
   loftily they threaten oppression.
9 They set their mouths against heaven,
   and their tongues range over the earth.
10 Therefore the people turn and praise them,[t]
   and find no fault in them.[u]
11 And they say, "How can God know?
   Is there knowledge in the Most High?"
12 Such are the wicked;
   always at ease, they increase in riches.
13 All in vain I have kept my heart clean
   and washed my hands in innocence.
14 For all day long I have been plagued,
   and am punished every morning.
15 If I had said, "I will talk on in this way,"
   I would have been untrue to the circle of your
      children.
16 But when I thought how to understand this,
   it seemed to me a wearisome task,
17 until I went into the sanctuary of God;
   then I perceived their end.
18 Truly you set them in slippery places;
   you make them fall to ruin.
19 How they are destroyed in a moment,
   swept away utterly by terrors!
20 They are[v] like a dream when one awakes;
   on awaking you despise their phantoms.
21 When my soul was embittered,
   when I was pricked in heart,
22 I was stupid and ignorant;
   I was like a brute beast toward you.
23 Nevertheless I am continually with you;
   you hold my right hand.
24 You guide me with your counsel,
   and afterward you will receive me with
      honor.[w]
25 Whom have I in heaven but you?
   And there is nothing on earth that I desire
      other than you.
26 My flesh and my heart may fail,
   but God is the strength[x] of my heart and my
      portion forever.
27 Indeed, those who are far from you will perish;
   you put an end to those who are false to you.
28 But for me it is good to be near God;
   I have made the Lord GOD my refuge,
   to tell of all your works.

REVISED ENGLISH BIBLE

3 because boasters roused my envy
   when I saw how the wicked prosper.
4 No painful suffering for them!
   They are sleek and sound in body;
5 they are not in trouble like ordinary mortals,
   nor are they afflicted like other folk.
6 Therefore they wear pride like a necklace
   and violence like a robe that wraps them round.
7 Their eyes gleam through folds of fat,
   while vain fancies flit through their minds.
8 Their talk is all mockery and malice;
   high-handedly they threaten oppression.
9 Their slanders reach up to heaven,
   while their tongues are never still on earth.
10 So the people follow their lead
   and find in them nothing blameworthy.
11 They say, 'How does God know?
   Does the Most High know or care?'
12 Such are the wicked;
   unshakeably secure, they pile up wealth.
13 Indeed it was all for nothing I kept my heart pure
   and washed my hands free from guilt!
14 For all day long I suffer affliction
   and every morning brings new punishment.
15 Had I thought to speak as they do,
   I should have been false to your people.
16 I set my mind to understand this
   but I found it too hard for me,
17 until I went into God's sanctuary,
   where I saw clearly what their destiny would be.
18 Indeed you place them on slippery ground
   and drive them headlong into utter ruin!
19 In a moment they are destroyed,
   disasters making an end of them,
20 like a dream when one awakes, Lord,
   like images dismissed when one rouses from sleep!
21 My mind was embittered,
   and I was pierced to the heart.
22 I was too brutish to understand,
   in your sight, God, no better than a beast.
23 Yet I am always with you;
   you hold my right hand.
24 You guide me by your counsel
   and afterwards you will receive me with glory.
25 Whom have I in heaven but you?
   And having you, I desire nothing else on earth.
26 Though heart and body fail,
   yet God is the rock of my heart, my portion for
      ever.
27 Those who are far from you will perish;
   you will destroy all who are unfaithful to you.
28 But my chief good is to be near you, God;
   I have chosen you, Lord GOD, to be my refuge,
   and I shall recount all your works.

---

[t] Cn: Heb *his people return here*   [u] Cn: Heb *abundant waters are drained by them*   [v] Cn: Heb *Lord*   [w] Or *to glory*   [x] Heb *rock*   73:10 **and find . . . blameworthy:** *prob. rdg; Heb. obscure.*

3 Because I was envious of the arrogant
  when I saw the prosperity of the wicked.
4 For they suffer no pain;
  their bodies are healthy and sleek.
5 They are free of the burdens of life;
  they are not afflicted like others.
6 Thus pride adorns them as a necklace;
  violence clothes them as a robe.
7 Out of their stupidity comes sin;
  evil thoughts flood their hearts.
8 They scoff and spout their malice;
  from on high they utter threats.
9 They set their mouths against the heavens,
  their tongues roam the earth.
10 So my people turn to them
  and drink deeply of their words.
11 They say, "Does God really know?"
  "Does the Most High have any knowledge?"
12 Such, then, are the wicked,
  always carefree, increasing their wealth.

II
13 Is it in vain that I have kept my heart clean,
  washed my hands in innocence?
14 For I am afflicted day after day,
  chastised every morning.
15 Had I thought, "I will speak as they do,"
  I would have betrayed your people.
16 Though I tried to understand all this,
  it was too difficult for me,
17 Till I entered the sanctuary of God
  and came to understand their end.

III
18 You set them, indeed, on a slippery road;
  you hurl them down to ruin.
19 How suddenly they are devastated;
  undone by disasters forever!
20 They are like a dream after waking, Lord,
  dismissed like shadows when you arise.

IV
21 Since my heart was embittered
  and my soul deeply wounded,
22 I was stupid and could not understand;
  I was like a brute beast in your presence.
23 Yet I am always with you;
  you take hold of my right hand.
24 With your counsel you guide me,
  and at the end receive me with honor.
25 Whom else have I in the heavens?
  None beside you delights me on earth.
26 Though my flesh and my heart fail,
  God is the rock of my heart, my portion forever.
27 But those who are far from you perish;
  you destroy those unfaithful to you.
28 As for me, to be near God is my good,
  to make the Lord GOD my refuge.
  I shall declare all your works
  in the gates of daughter Zion.

3 envying the arrogant as I did,
  and seeing the prosperity of the wicked.
4 For them no such thing as pain,
  untroubled, their comfortable portliness;
5 exempt from the cares which are the human lot,
  they have no part in Adam's afflictions.

6 So pride is a necklace to them,
  violence the garment they wear.
7 From their fat oozes out malice,
  their hearts drip with cunning.

8 Cynically they advocate evil,
  loftily they advocate force.
9 Their mouth claims heaven for themselves,
  and their tongue is never still on earth.

10 That is why my people turn to them,
  and enjoy the waters of plenty,
11 saying, 'How can God know?
  What knowledge can the Most High have?'
12 That is what the wicked are like,
  piling up wealth without any worries.

13 Was it useless, then, to have kept my own heart
    clean,
  to have washed my hands in innocence?
14 When I was under a hail of blows all day long,
  and punished every morning,
15 had I said, 'I shall talk like them,'
  I should have betrayed your children's race.

16 So I set myself to understand this:
  how difficult I found it!
17 Until I went into the sanctuaries of the gods
  and understood what was destined to become of
    them.

18 You place them on a slippery slope
  and drive them down into chaos.

19 How sudden their hideous destruction!
  They are swept away, annihilated by terror!
20 Like a dream upon waking, Lord,
  when you awake, you dismiss their image.

21 My heart grew embittered,
  my affections dried up,
22 I was stupid and uncomprehending,
  a clumsy animal in your presence.

23 Even so, I stayed in your presence,
  you grasped me by the right hand;
24 you will guide me with advice,
  and will draw me in the wake of your glory.

25 Who else is there for me in heaven?
  And, with you, I lack nothing on earth.
26 My heart and my flesh are pining away:
  my heart's rock, my portion, God for ever!

27 Truly, those who abandon you will perish;
  you destroy those who adulterously desert you,
28 whereas my happiness is to be near God.
  I have made the Lord Yahweh my refuge,
  to tell of all your works.

Psalm 74

A Maskil of Asaph.

1 O God, why do you cast us off forever?
  Why does your anger smoke against the sheep
    of your pasture?
2 Remember your congregation, which you
      acquired long ago,
  which you redeemed to be the tribe of your
    heritage.
  Remember Mount Zion, where you came to
    dwell.
3 Direct your steps to the perpetual ruins;
  the enemy has destroyed everything in the
    sanctuary.

4 Your foes have roared within your holy place;
  they set up their emblems there.
5 At the upper entrance they hacked
  the wooden trellis with axes.y
6 And then, with hatchets and hammers,
  they smashed all its carved work.
7 They set your sanctuary on fire;
  they desecrated the dwelling place of your
    name,
  bringing it to the ground.
8 They said to themselves, "We will utterly subdue
    them";
  they burned all the meeting places of God in
    the land.

9 We do not see our emblems;
  there is no longer any prophet,
  and there is no one among us who knows how
    long.
10 How long, O God, is the foe to scoff?
  Is the enemy to revile your name forever?
11 Why do you hold back your hand;
  why do you keep your hand inz your bosom?

12 Yet God my King is from of old,
  working salvation in the earth.
13 You divided the sea by your might;
  you broke the heads of the dragons in the
    waters.
14 You crushed the heads of Leviathan;
  you gave him as fooda for the creatures of the
    wilderness.
15 You cut openings for springs and torrents;
  you dried up ever-flowing streams.
16 Yours is the day, yours also the night;
  you established the luminariesb and the sun.
17 You have fixed all the bounds of the earth;
  you made summer and winter.

18 Remember this, O LORD, how the enemy scoffs,
  and an impious people reviles your name.
19 Do not deliver the soul of your dove to the wild
    animals;
  do not forget the life of your poor forever.

20 Have regard for yourc covenant,
  for the dark places of the land are full of the
    haunts of violence.
21 Do not let the downtrodden be put to shame;
  let the poor and needy praise your name.

Psalm 74

A maskil: for Asaph

1 GOD, why have you cast us off? And is it for ever?
  Why do you fume with anger at the flock you used
    to shepherd?
2 Remember the assembly of your people,
  taken long since for your own,
  redeemed to be your own tribe.
  Remember Mount Zion, which you made your
    dwelling-place.
3 Restore now what has been altogether ruined,
  all the destruction that the foe has brought on your
    sanctuary.

4 The shouts of your enemies filled your temple;
  they planted their standards there as tokens of
    victory.
5 They brought it crashing down,
  like woodmen plying their axes in the forest;
6 they ripped out the carvings,
  they smashed them with hatchet and pick.
7 They set fire to your sanctuary,
  tore down and polluted the abode of your name.
8 They said to themselves, 'Let us together oppress
    them,'
  and they burnt every holy place throughout the
    land.

9 We cannot see any sign for us, we have no prophet
    now;
  no one amongst us knows how long this is to last.
10 How long, God, will the foe utter his taunts?
  Will the enemy pour scorn on your name for ever?
11 Why do you hold back your hand,
  why keep your right hand within your bosom?

12 God, my King from of old,
  whose saving acts are wrought on earth,
13 by your power you cleft the sea monster in two
  and broke the sea serpent's heads in the waters;
14 you crushed the heads of Leviathan
  and threw him to the sharks for food.
15 You opened channels for spring and torrent;
  you dried up streams never known to fail.
16 The day is yours, yours also is the night;
  you ordered the light of moon and sun.
17 You have fixed all the regions of the earth;
  you created both summer and winter.

18 Remember, LORD, the taunts of the enemy,
  the scorn a barbarous nation pours on your name.
19 Do not cast to the beasts the soul that confesses
    you;
  do not forget for ever the sufferings of your
    servants.
20 Look upon your creatures: they are filled with dark
    thoughts,
  and the land is a haunt of violence.
21 Let not the oppressed be shamed and turned away;
  may the poor and the downtrodden praise your
    name.

74:3 **now:** *prob. rdg; Heb.* your steps.   74:5 **They . . . forest:**
prob. rdg; Heb. unintelligible.   74:6 **they ripped out:** *so Gk;
Heb.* and now.   74:14 **to the sharks:** *prob. rdg; Heb.* to a
people, desert-dwellers.   74:19 **that confesses you:** *so Gk; Heb.*
of your turtle-dove.   74:20 **your creatures:** *prob. rdg; Heb.* the
covenant, because.

---

y Cn Compare Gk Syr: Meaning of Heb uncertain   z Cn: Heb *do
you consume your right hand from*   a Heb *food for the people*
b Or *moon*; Heb *light*   c Gk Syr: Heb *the*

Psalm 74

1 *A maskil of Asaph.*

I

Why, God, have you cast us off forever?
  Why does your anger burn against the sheep of
    your pasture?
2 Remember your flock that you gathered of old,
  the tribe you redeemed as your very own.
  Remember Mount Zion where you dwell.
3 Turn your steps toward the utter ruins,
  toward the sanctuary devastated by the enemy.
4 Your foes roared triumphantly in your shrine;
  they set up their own tokens of victory.
5 They hacked away like foresters gathering boughs,
  swinging their axes in a thicket of trees.
6 They smashed all your engraved work,
  pounded it with hammer and pick.
7 They set your sanctuary on fire;
  the abode of your name they razed and profaned.
8 They said in their hearts, "Destroy them all!
  Burn all the shrines of God in the land!"
9 Now we see no signs,
  we have no prophets,
  no one who knows how long.
10 How long, O God, shall the enemy jeer?
  Shall the foe revile your name forever?
11 Why draw back your right hand,
  why keep it idle beneath your cloak?

II

12 Yet you, God, are my king from of old,
  winning victories throughout the earth.
13 You stirred up the sea in your might;
  you smashed the heads of the dragons on the
    waters.
14 You crushed the heads of Leviathan,
  tossed him for food to the sharks.
15 You opened up springs and torrents,
  brought dry land out of the primeval waters.
16 Yours the day and yours the night;
  you set the moon and sun in place.
17 You fixed all the limits of the earth;
  summer and winter you made.
18 Remember how the enemy has jeered, O LORD,
  how a foolish people has reviled your name.
19 Do not surrender to beasts those who praise you;
  do not forget forever the life of your afflicted.
20 Look to your covenant,
  for the land is filled with gloom;
  the pastures, with violence.
21 Let not the oppressed turn back in shame;
  may the poor and needy praise your name.

Psalm 74 (V 73)

Poem   Of Asaph

1 God, why have you finally rejected us,
  your anger blazing against the flock you used to
    pasture?
2 Remember the people you took to yourself long
    ago,
  your own tribe which you redeemed,
  and this Mount Zion where you came to live.
3 Come up to these endless ruins!
  The enemy have sacked everything in the
    sanctuary;
4 your opponents made uproar in the place of
    assemblies,
  they fixed their emblems over the entrance,
  emblems 5 never known before.

Their axes deep in the wood, 6 hacking at the
    panels,
  they battered them down with axe and pick;
7 they set fire to your sanctuary,
  profanely rased to the ground the dwelling-place of
    your name.
8 They said to themselves, 'Let us crush them at one
    stroke!'
  They burned down every sacred shrine in the land.
9 We see no signs, no prophet any more,
  and none of us knows how long it will last.
10 How much longer, God, will the enemy
    blaspheme?
  Is the enemy to insult your name for ever?
11 Why hold back your hand,
  keep your right hand hidden in the folds of your
    robe?

12 Yet, God, my king from the first,
  author of saving acts throughout the earth,
13 by your power you split the sea in two,
  and smashed the heads of the monsters on the
    waters.
14 You crushed Leviathan's[n] heads,
  gave him as food to the wild animals.
15 You released the springs and brooks,
  and turned primordial rivers into dry land.
16 Yours is the day and yours the night,
  you caused sun and light to exist,
17 you fixed all the boundaries of the earth,
  you created summer and winter.
18 Remember, Yahweh, the enemy's blasphemy,
  a foolish people insults your name.
19 Do not surrender your turtledove to the beast;
  do not forget for ever the life of your oppressed
    people.
20 Look to the covenant!
  All the hiding-places of the land are full,
  haunts of violence.
21 Do not let the downtrodden retreat in confusion,
  give the poor and needy cause to praise your name.

[n] **74** Properly a mythical monster of chaos, it stands here for the evil
power of Egypt.

22 Rise up, O God, plead your cause;
 remember how the impious scoff at you all day
  long.
23 Do not forget the clamor of your foes,
 the uproar of your adversaries that goes up
  continually.

Psalm 75

To the leader: Do Not Destroy. A Psalm of Asaph. A Song.

1 We give thanks to you, O God;
 we give thanks; your name is near.
 People tell of your wondrous deeds.
2 At the set time that I appoint
 I will judge with equity.
3 When the earth totters, with all its inhabitants,
 it is I who keep its pillars steady. *Selah*
4 I say to the boastful, "Do not boast,"
 and to the wicked, "Do not lift up your horn;
5 do not lift up your horn on high,
 or speak with insolent neck."

6 For not from the east or from the west
 and not from the wilderness comes lifting up;
7 but it is God who executes judgment,
 putting down one and lifting up another.
8 For in the hand of the LORD there is a cup
 with foaming wine, well mixed;
 he will pour a draught from it,
 and all the wicked of the earth
 shall drain it down to the dregs.
9 But I will rejoice*d* forever;
 I will sing praises to the God of Jacob.

10 All the horns of the wicked I will cut off,
 but the horns of the righteous shall be exalted.

Psalm 76

*To the leader: with stringed instruments. A Psalm of Asaph.
A Song.*

1 In Judah God is known,
 his name is great in Israel.
2 His abode has been established in Salem,
 his dwelling place in Zion.
3 There he broke the flashing arrows,
 the shield, the sword, and the weapons of war.
     Selah

4 Glorious are you, more majestic
 than the everlasting mountains.*e*
5 The stouthearted were stripped of their spoil;
 they sank into sleep;
 none of the troops
 was able to lift a hand.
6 At your rebuke, O God of Jacob,
 both rider and horse lay stunned.

7 But you indeed are awesome!
 Who can stand before you
 when once your anger is roused?
8 From the heavens you uttered judgment,
 the earth feared and was still
9 when God rose up to establish judgment,
 to save all the oppressed of the earth. *Selah*

d Gk: Heb declare   *e Gk: Heb the mountains of prey*

22 Rise up, God, defend your cause;
 remember how fools mock you all day long.
23 Ignore no longer the uproar of your assailants,
 the ever-rising clamour of those who defy you.

Psalm 75

*For the leader: set to 'Destroy not': a psalm: for Asaph:
a song*

1 WE give thanks to you, God, we give you thanks;
 your name is brought very near to us
 in the account of your wonderful deeds.
2 I shall seize the appointed time
 and then judge mankind with equity.
3 When the earth quakes, and all who live on it,
 it is I who hold its pillars firm. [*Selah*
4 To the boastful I say, 'Boast no more,'
 and to the wicked, 'Do not vaunt your strength:
5 do not vaunt yourself against heaven
 or speak arrogantly against the Rock.'

6 No power from the east or from the west,
 no power from the wilderness, can raise anyone
  up.
7 For God is ruler;
 he puts one down, another he raises up.
8 For the LORD holds a cup in his hand,
 and the wine foams in it, richly spiced;
 he pours out this wine,
 and all the wicked on earth must drain it to the
  dregs.
9 But I shall confess him for ever;
 I shall sing praises to the God of Jacob.
10 He will break down the strength of the wicked,
 but the strength of the righteous will be raised
  high.

Psalm 76

*For the leader: on stringed instruments: a psalm: for
Asaph: a song*

1 IN Judah God is known,
 his name is great in Israel;
2 his tent is in Salem,
 his dwelling in Zion.
3 There he has broken the flashing arrows,
 shield and sword and weapons of war. [*Selah*

4 You are awesome, Lord,
 more majestic than the everlasting mountains.
5 The bravest are despoiled,
 they sleep their last sleep,
 and the strongest cannot lift a hand.
6 At your rebuke, God of Jacob,
 rider and horse lie prostrate.

7 You are awesome, Lord;
 when you are angry, who can stand in your
  presence?
8 You gave sentence out of heaven;
 the earth was afraid and kept silence
9 when you rose in judgement, God,
 to deliver all the afflicted in the land. [*Selah*

75:5 **Rock:** *prob. rdg; Heb.* neck.   75:10 **He:** *prob. rdg; Heb.* I.
76:4 **awesome:** *so Gk (Theod.); Heb.* illuminated.

22 Arise, God, defend your cause;
  remember the constant jeers of the fools.
23 Do not ignore the clamor of your foes,
  the unceasing uproar of your enemies.

Psalm 75

1 *For the leader. Do not destroy! A psalm of Asaph; a song.*

I

2 We thank you, God, we give thanks;
  we call upon your name,
  declare your wonderful deeds.
You said:
3 "I will choose the time;
  I will judge fairly.
4 The earth and all its inhabitants will quake,
  but I have firmly set its pillars."   *Selah*
II
5 So I say to the boastful: "Do not boast!"
  to the wicked: "Do not raise your horns!"
6 Do not raise your horns against heaven!
  Do not speak arrogantly against the Rock!"
7 For judgment comes not from east or from west,
  not from the desert or from the mountains,
8 But from God who decides,
  who brings some low and raises others high.
9 Yes, a cup is in the LORD's hand,
  foaming wine, fully spiced.
  When God pours it out,
  they will drain it even to the dregs;
  all the wicked of the earth must drink.
10 But I will rejoice forever;
  I will sing praise to the God of Jacob,
11 Who has said:
  "I will break off all the horns of the wicked,
  but the horns of the just shall be lifted up."

Psalm 76

1 *For the leader; a psalm with stringed instruments. A song of Asaph.*

I

2 Renowned in Judah is God,
  whose name is great in Israel.
3 On Salem is God's tent, a shelter on Zion.
4   There the flashing arrows were shattered,
  shield, sword, and weapons of war.   *Selah*
II
5 Terrible and awesome are you,
  stronger than the ancient mountains.
6 Despoiled are the bold warriors;
  they sleep their final sleep;
  the hands of all the mighty have failed.
7 At your roar, O God of Jacob,
  chariots and steeds lay still.
8 So terrible and awesome are you;
  who can stand before you and your great anger?
9 From the heavens you pronounced sentence;
  the earth was terrified and reduced to silence,
10 When you arose, O God, for judgment
  to deliver the afflicted of the land.   *Selah*

22 Arise, God, champion your own cause,
  remember how fools blaspheme you all day long!
23 Do not forget the shouting of your enemies,
  the ever-mounting uproar of your adversaries.

Psalm 75 (V 74)

*For the choirmaster   Tune: 'Do not destroy'   Psalm
            Of Asaph   Song*

1 We give thanks to you, God, we give thanks to
  you,
  as we call upon your name, as we recount your
  wonders.

2 'At the appointed time
  I myself shall dispense justice.
3 The earth quakes and all its inhabitants;
  it is I who hold its pillars firm.   *Pause*

4 'I said to the boastful, "Do not boast!"
  to the wicked, "Do not flaunt your strength!
5 Do not flaunt your strength so proudly,
  do not talk with that arrogant stance." '

6 No longer from east to west,
  no longer in the mountainous desert,
7 is God judging in uprightness,
  bringing some down, raising others.
8 Yahweh is holding a cup
  filled with a heady blend of wine;
  he will pour it, they will drink it to the dregs,
  all the wicked on earth will drink it.

9 But I shall speak out for ever,
  shall make music for the God of Jacob.
10 I shall break down all the strength of the wicked,
  and the strength of the upright will rise high.

Psalm 76 (V 75)

*For the choirmaster   For strings   Psalm   Of Asaph
                Song*

1 God is acknowledged in Judah,
  his name is great in Israel,
2 his tent is pitched in Salem,
  his dwelling is in Zion;
3 there he has broken the lightning-flashes of the
  bow,
  shield and sword and war.   *Pause*

4 Radiant you are, and renowned
  for the mountains of booty 5 taken from them.
  Heroes are now sleeping their last sleep,
  the warriors' arms have failed them;
6 at your reproof, God of Jacob,
  chariot and horse stand stunned.

7 You, you alone, strike terror! Who can hold his
  ground
  in your presence when your anger strikes?
8 From heaven your verdicts thunder,
  the earth is silent with dread
9 when God takes his stand to give judgement,
  to save all the humble of the earth.   *Pause*

10 Human wrath serves only to praise you,
  when you bind the last bit of your*f* wrath
    around you.
11 Make vows to the LORD your God, and perform
    them;
  let all who are around him bring gifts
    to the one who is awesome,
12 who cuts off the spirit of princes,
  who inspires fear in the kings of the earth.

Psalm 77

To the leader: according to Jeduthun. Of Asaph. A Psalm.

1 I cry aloud to God,
  aloud to God, that he may hear me.
2 In the day of my trouble I seek the Lord;
  in the night my hand is stretched out without
    wearying;
  my soul refuses to be comforted.
3 I think of God, and I moan;
  I meditate, and my spirit faints.   Selah

4 You keep my eyelids from closing;
  I am so troubled that I cannot speak.
5 I consider the days of old,
  and remember the years of long ago.
6 I commune*g* with my heart in the night;
  I meditate and search my spirit:*h*
7 "Will the Lord spurn forever,
  and never again be favorable?
8 Has his steadfast love ceased forever?
  Are his promises at an end for all time?
9 Has God forgotten to be gracious?
  Has he in anger shut up his compassion?"
                                          Selah
10 And I say, "It is my grief
  that the right hand of the Most High has
    changed."

11 I will call to mind the deeds of the LORD;
  I will remember your wonders of old.
12 I will meditate on all your work,
  and muse on your mighty deeds.
13 Your way, O God, is holy.
  What god is so great as our God?
14 You are the God who works wonders;
  you have displayed your might among the
    peoples.
15 With your strong arm you redeemed your people,
  the descendants of Jacob and Joseph.   Selah

16 When the waters saw you, O God,
  when the waters saw you, they were afraid;
  the very deep trembled.
17 The clouds poured out water;
  the skies thundered;
  your arrows flashed on every side.
18 The crash of your thunder was in the whirlwind;
  your lightnings lit up the world;
  the earth trembled and shook.
19 Your way was through the sea,
  your path, through the mighty waters;
  yet your footprints were unseen.
20 You led your people like a flock
  by the hand of Moses and Aaron.

10 Edom, for all his fury, will praise you
  and the remnant left in Hamath will dance in
    worship.
11 Make vows to the LORD your God, and keep them;
  let the peoples all around him bring their tribute;
12 for he curbs the spirit of princes,
  he fills the kings of the earth with awe.

Psalm 77

For the leader: according to Jeduthun: for Asaph: a psalm

1 I CRIED aloud to God,
  I cried to God and he heard me.
2 In the day of my distress I sought the Lord,
  and by night I lifted my hands in prayer.
  My tears ran unceasingly,
  I refused all comfort.
3 When I called God to mind, I groaned;
  as I pondered, faintness overwhelmed me.   [Selah
4 My eyelids were tightly closed;
  I was distraught and could not speak.
5 My thoughts went back to times long past,
  I remembered distant years;
6 all night long I meditated,
  I pondered and examined my heart.

7 Will the Lord always reject me
  and never again show favour?
8 Has his love now failed utterly?
  Will his promise never be fulfilled?
9 Has God forgotten to be gracious?
  Has he in anger withheld his compassion?   [Selah
10 'Has his right hand grown weak?' I said.
  'Has the right hand of the Most High changed?'

11 I call to mind the deeds of the LORD;
  I recall your wonderful acts of old;
12 I reflect on all your works
  and consider what you have done.
13 Your way, God, is holy;
  what god is as great as our God?
14 You are a God who works miracles;
  you have shown the nations your power.
15 With your strong arm you rescued your people,
  the descendants of Jacob and Joseph.   [Selah

16 The waters saw you, God,
  they saw you and writhed in anguish;
  the ocean was troubled to its depths.
17 The clouds poured down water, the skies
    thundered;
  your arrows flashed hither and thither.
18 The sound of your thunder was in the whirlwind,
  lightning-flashes lit up the world,
  the earth shook and quaked.
19 Your path was through the sea,
  your way through mighty waters,
  and none could mark your footsteps.
20 You guided your people like a flock
  shepherded by Moses and Aaron.

76:10 **Edom . . . worship:** *poss. meaning; Heb. obscure.*
76:11 **their tribute:** *prob. rdg; Heb. adds* for the terror.   77:2 **I
lifted:** *prob. rdg; Heb. omits.*   77:6 **I meditated:** *so Gk; Heb.* my
song.   77:8 **his promise:** *so Syriac; Heb. omits* his.
77:10 **grown weak:** *prob. rdg; Heb.* my suffering. **changed:** *prob.
rdg; Heb.* the years of.

f Heb lacks *your*   *g* Gk Syr: Heb *My music*   *h* Syr Jerome: Heb
my spirit searches

NEW AMERICAN BIBLE

11 Even wrathful Edom praises you;
the remnant of Hamath keeps your feast.

III

12 Make and keep vows to the LORD your God.
May all present bring gifts to this awesome God,
13 Who checks the pride of princes,
inspires awe among the kings of earth.

Psalm 77

1 *For the leader;* ʼal Jeduthun. *A psalm of Asaph.*

I

2 I cry aloud to God,
cry to God to hear me.
3 On the day of my distress I seek the Lord;
by night my hands are raised unceasingly;
I refuse to be consoled.
4 When I think of God, I groan;
as I ponder, my spirit grows faint.   *Selah*
5 My eyes cannot close in sleep;
I am troubled and cannot speak.
6 I consider the days of old;
the years long past 7 I remember.
In the night I meditate in my heart;
I ponder and my spirit broods:
8 "Will the Lord reject us forever,
never again show favor?
9 Has God's love ceased forever?
Has the promise failed for all ages?
10 Has God forgotten mercy,
in anger withheld compassion?"   *Selah*
11 I conclude: "My sorrow is this,
the right hand of the Most High has left us."

II

12 I will remember the deeds of the LORD;
yes, your wonders of old I will remember.
13 I will recite all your works;
your exploits I will tell.
14 Your way, O God, is holy;
what god is as great as our God?
15 You alone are the God who did wonders;
among the peoples you revealed your might.
16 With your arm you redeemed your people,
the descendants of Jacob and Joseph.   *Selah*
17 The waters saw you, God;
the waters saw you and lashed about,
trembled even to their depths.
18 The clouds poured down their rains;
the thunderheads rumbled;
your arrows flashed back and forth.
19 The thunder of your chariot wheels resounded;
your lightning lit up the world;
the earth trembled and quaked.
20 Through the sea was your path;
your way, through the mighty waters,
though your footsteps were unseen.
21 You led your people like a flock
under the care of Moses and Aaron.

NEW JERUSALEM BIBLE

10 Human anger serves only to praise you,
the survivors of your anger will huddle round you.
11 Make and fulfil your vows to Yahweh your God,
let those who surround him make offerings to the
Awesome One.
12 He cuts short the breath of princes,
strikes terror in earthly kings.

Psalm 77 (V 76)

For the choirmaster . . . Jeduthun Of Asaph Psalm

1 I cry to God in distress,
I cry to God and he hears me.
2 In the day of my distress I sought the Lord;
all night I tirelessly stretched out my hands,
my heart refused to be consoled.
3 I sigh as I think of God,
my spirit faints away as I ponder on him.   *Pause*
4 You kept me from closing my eyes,
I was too distraught to speak;
5 I thought of former times,
years long past 6 I recalled;
through the night I ponder in my heart,
as I reflect, my spirit asks this question:
7 Is the Lord's rejection final?
Will he never show favour again?
8 Is his faithful love gone for ever?
Has his Word come to an end for all time?
9 Does God forget to show mercy?
In anger does he shut off his tenderness?   *Pause*
10 And I said, 'This is what wounds me,
the right hand of the Most High has lost its
strength.'
11 Remembering Yahweh's great deeds,
remembering your wonders in the past,
12 I reflect on all that you did,
I ponder all your great deeds.
13 God, your ways are holy!
What god is as great as our God?
14 You are the God who does marvellous deeds,
brought nations to acknowledge your power,
15 with your own arm redeeming your people,
the children of Jacob and Joseph.   *Pause*
16 When the waters saw you, God,
when the waters saw you they writhed in anguish,
the very depths shook with fear.
17 The clouds pelted down water,
the sky thundered,
your arrows shot back and forth.
18 The rolling of your thunder was heard,
your lightning-flashes lit up the world,
the earth shuddered and shook.
19 Your way led over the sea,
your path over the countless waters,
and none could trace your footsteps.
20 You guided your people like a flock
by the hand of Moses and Aaron.

NEW REVISED STANDARD VERSION	REVISED ENGLISH BIBLE

Psalm 78

A Maskil of Asaph.

1 Give ear, O my people, to my teaching;
  incline your ears to the words of my mouth.
2 I will open my mouth in a parable;
  I will utter dark sayings from of old,
3 things that we have heard and known,
  that our ancestors have told us.
4 We will not hide them from their children;
  we will tell to the coming generation
  the glorious deeds of the LORD, and his might,
  and the wonders that he has done.

5 He established a decree in Jacob,
  and appointed a law in Israel,
  which he commanded our ancestors
  to teach to their children;
6 that the next generation might know them,
  the children yet unborn,
  and rise up and tell them to their children,
7 so that they should set their hope in God,
  and not forget the works of God,
  but keep his commandments;
8 and that they should not be like their ancestors,
  a stubborn and rebellious generation,
  a generation whose heart was not steadfast,
  whose spirit was not faithful to God.

9 The Ephraimites, armed with[i] the bow,
  turned back on the day of battle.
10 They did not keep God's covenant,
  but refused to walk according to his law.
11 They forgot what he had done,
  and the miracles that he had shown them.
12 In the sight of their ancestors he worked marvels
  in the land of Egypt, in the fields of Zoan.
13 He divided the sea and let them pass through it,
  and made the waters stand like a heap.
14 In the daytime he led them with a cloud,
  and all night long with a fiery light.
15 He split rocks open in the wilderness,
  and gave them drink abundantly as from the deep.
16 He made streams come out of the rock,
  and caused waters to flow down like rivers.

17 Yet they sinned still more against him,
  rebelling against the Most High in the desert.
18 They tested God in their heart
  by demanding the food they craved.
19 They spoke against God, saying,
  "Can God spread a table in the wilderness?
20 Even though he struck the rock so that water gushed out
  and torrents overflowed,
  can he also give bread,
  or provide meat for his people?"

21 Therefore, when the LORD heard, he was full of rage;
  a fire was kindled against Jacob,
  his anger mounted against Israel,
22 because they had no faith in God,
  and did not trust his saving power.
23 Yet he commanded the skies above,
  and opened the doors of heaven;
24 he rained down on them manna to eat,
  and gave them the grain of heaven.

Psalm 78

A maskil: for Asaph

1 MY people, mark my teaching,
  listen to the words I am about to speak.
2 I shall tell you a meaningful story;
  I shall expound the riddle of things past,
3 things that we have heard and know,
  things our forefathers have recounted to us.
4 They were not hidden from their descendants,
  who will repeat them to the next generation:
  the praiseworthy acts of the LORD
  and the wonders he has done.

5 He laid on Jacob a solemn charge
  and established a rule in Israel,
  which he commanded our forefathers
  to teach their descendants;
6 so that it might be known to a future generation,
  to children yet to be born,
  and they in turn would repeat it to their children.
7 They were charged to put their trust in God,
  to hold his great acts ever in mind
  and to keep his commandments,
8 and not to do as their forefathers did,
  a disobedient and rebellious generation,
  a generation with no firm purpose,
  with hearts not fixed steadfastly on God.

9 The Ephraimites, bowmen all and marksmen,
  turned tail in the hour of battle.
10 They had not kept God's covenant;
  they had refused to live by his law;
11 they forgot the things he had done,
  the wonders he had shown them.
12 As their fathers witnessed he performed wonderful deeds
  in Egypt, the region of Zoan:
13 he divided the sea and brought them through;
  he heaped up the waters on either side.
14 He led them with a cloud by day,
  and all night long with a glowing fire.
15 He split the rock in the wilderness
  and gave them water to drink, abundant as the deep;
16 he brought streams out of the crag
  and made water run down like torrents.

17 But they sinned against him yet again:
  in the desert they defied the Most High,
18 trying God's patience wilfully
  by demanding the food they craved.
19 They spoke against God and said,
  'Can God spread a table in the wilderness?'
20 When he struck a rock, water gushed out
  until the wadis overflowed;
  'But can he give bread as well?' they demanded.
  'Can he provide meat for his people?'

21 When the LORD heard this, he was infuriated:
  fire raged against Jacob,
  anger blazed up against Israel,
22 because they put no faith in God,
  no trust in his power to save.
23 Then he gave orders to the skies above
  and threw open heaven's doors;
24 he rained down manna for them to eat
  and gave them the grain of heaven.

[i] Heb *armed with shooting*

NEW AMERICAN BIBLE

Psalm 78

¹*A maskil of Asaph.*

I

Attend, my people, to my teaching;
   listen to the words of my mouth.
²I will open my mouth in story,
   drawing lessons from of old.
³We have heard them, we know them;
   our ancestors have recited them to us.
⁴We do not keep them from our children;
   we recite them to the next generation,
The praiseworthy and mighty deeds of the LORD,
   the wonders that he performed.
⁵God set up a decree in Jacob,
   established a law in Israel:
What he commanded our ancestors,
   they were to teach their children;
⁶That the next generation might come to know,
   children yet to be born.
In turn they were to recite them to their children,
⁷   that they too might put their trust in God,
And not forget the works of God,
   keeping his commandments.
⁸They were not to be like their ancestors,
   a rebellious and defiant generation,
A generation whose heart was not constant,
   whose spirit was not faithful to God,
⁹Like the ranks of Ephraimite archers,
   who retreated on the day of battle.
¹⁰They did not keep God's covenant;
   they refused to walk by his law.
¹¹They forgot his works,
   the wondrous deeds he had shown them.

II

A

¹²In the sight of their ancestors God did wonders,
   in the land of Egypt, the plain of Zoan.
¹³He split the sea and led them across,
   piling up the waters rigid as walls.
¹⁴God led them with a cloud by day,
   all night with the light of fire.
¹⁵He split rock in the desert,
   gave water to drink, abounding as the deep.
¹⁶He made streams flow from crags,
   drew out rivers of water.

B

¹⁷But they went on sinning against him,
   rebelling against the Most High in the desert.
¹⁸They tested God in their hearts,
   demanding the food they craved.
¹⁹They spoke against God, and said,
   "Can God spread a table in the desert?
²⁰True, when he struck the rock,
   water gushed forth,
   the wadis flooded.
But can he also provide bread,
   give meat to his people?"

C

²¹The LORD heard and grew angry;
   fire blazed up against Jacob,
   anger flared up against Israel.
²²For they did not believe in God,
   did not trust in his saving power.
²³So he commanded the skies above;
   the doors of heaven he opened.
²⁴God rained manna upon them for food;
   bread from heaven he gave them.

NEW JERUSALEM BIBLE

Psalm 78 (V 77)

Psalm   Of Asaph

¹My people, listen to my teaching,
   pay attention to what I say.
²I will speak to you in poetry,
   unfold the mysteries of the past.

³What we have heard and know,
   what our ancestors have told us
⁴we shall not conceal from their descendants,
   but will tell to a generation still to come:

the praises of Yahweh, his power,
   the wonderful deeds he has done.
⁵He instituted a witness in Jacob,
   he established a law in Israel,

he commanded our ancestors
   to hand it down to their descendants,
⁶that a generation still to come might know it,
   children yet to be born.

They should be sure to tell their own children,
⁷and should put their trust in God,
   never forgetting God's great deeds,
   always keeping his commands,

⁸and not, like their ancestors,
   be a stubborn and rebellious generation,
   a generation weak of purpose,
   their spirit fickle towards God.

⁹The archer sons of Ephraim
   turned tail when the time came for fighting;
¹⁰they failed to keep God's covenant,
   they refused to follow his Law;

¹¹they had forgotten his great deeds,
   the marvels he had shown them;
¹²he did marvels in the sight of their ancestors
   in Egypt, in the plains of Tanis.

¹³He split the sea and brought them through,
   made the waters stand up like a dam;
¹⁴he led them with a cloud by day,
   and all the night with the light of a fire;

¹⁵he split rocks in the desert,
   let them drink as though from the limitless depths;
¹⁶he brought forth streams from a rock,
   made waters flow down in torrents.

¹⁷But they only sinned against him more than ever,
   defying the Most High in barren country;
¹⁸they deliberately challenged God
   by demanding food to their hearts' content.

¹⁹They insulted God by saying,
   'Can God make a banquet in the desert?
²⁰True, when he struck the rock,
   waters gushed out and flowed in torrents;
   but what of bread? Can he give that,
   can he provide meat for his people?'

²¹When he heard them Yahweh vented his anger,
   fire blazed against Jacob,
   his anger mounted against Israel,
²²because they had no faith in God,
   no trust in his power to save.

²³Even so he gave orders to the skies above,
   he opened the sluice-gates of heaven;
²⁴he rained down manna to feed them,
   he gave them the wheat of heaven;

25 Mortals ate of the bread of angels;
 he sent them food in abundance.
26 He caused the east wind to blow in the heavens,
 and by his power he led out the south wind;
27 he rained flesh upon them like dust,
 winged birds like the sand of the seas;
28 he let them fall within their camp,
 all around their dwellings.
29 And they ate and were well filled,
 for he gave them what they craved.
30 But before they had satisfied their craving,
 while the food was still in their mouths,
31 the anger of God rose against them
 and he killed the strongest of them,
 and laid low the flower of Israel.

32 In spite of all this they still sinned;
 they did not believe in his wonders.
33 So he made their days vanish like a breath,
 and their years in terror.
34 When he killed them, they sought for him;
 they repented and sought God earnestly.
35 They remembered that God was their rock,
 the Most High God their redeemer.
36 But they flattered him with their mouths;
 they lied to him with their tongues.
37 Their heart was not steadfast toward him;
 they were not true to his covenant.
38 Yet he, being compassionate,
 forgave their iniquity,
 and did not destroy them;
often he restrained his anger,
 and did not stir up all his wrath.
39 He remembered that they were but flesh,
 a wind that passes and does not come again.
40 How often they rebelled against him in the
  wilderness
 and grieved him in the desert!
41 They tested God again and again,
 and provoked the Holy One of Israel.
42 They did not keep in mind his power,
 or the day when he redeemed them from the
  foe;
43 when he displayed his signs in Egypt,
 and his miracles in the fields of Zoan.
44 He turned their rivers to blood,
 so that they could not drink of their streams.
45 He sent among them swarms of flies, which
  devoured them,
 and frogs, which destroyed them.
46 He gave their crops to the caterpillar,
 and the fruit of their labor to the locust.
47 He destroyed their vines with hail,
 and their sycamores with frost.
48 He gave over their cattle to the hail,
 and their flocks to thunderbolts.
49 He let loose on them his fierce anger,
 wrath, indignation, and distress,
 a company of destroying angels.
50 He made a path for his anger;
 he did not spare them from death,
 but gave their lives over to the plague.
51 He struck all the firstborn in Egypt,
 the first issue of their strength in the tents of
  Ham.
52 Then he led out his people like sheep,
 and guided them in the wilderness like a flock.

25 So everyone ate the bread of angels;
 he sent them food in plenty.
26 He let loose the east wind from heaven
 and drove the south wind by his power;
27 he rained meat down on them like a dust storm,
 birds flying thick as the sand of the seashore.
28 He made them fall within the camp,
 all around their tents.
29 The people ate and were well filled,
 for he had given them what they wanted.
30 But still they wanted more,
 even while the food was in their mouths.
31 Then the anger of God blazed up against them;
 he spread death among their strongest men
 and laid low the young men of Israel.

32 In spite of all, they persisted in their sin
 and had no faith in his wonders.
33 So he made their days end in emptiness
 and their years in terror.
34 When he brought death among them, they began to
  seek him,
 and look eagerly for God once more;
35 they remembered that God was their rock,
 that God Most High was their redeemer.
36 But still they sought to beguile him with words
 and deceive him with their tongues;
37 but they were not loyal to him in their hearts,
 nor were they faithful to his covenant.
38 Yet he was merciful,
 wiping out guilt and not destroying.
Time and again he restrained his wrath
 and did not give vent to his anger.
39 He remembered that they were but mortal,
 a breath of air which passes by and does not
  return.

40 How often they defied him in the wilderness
 and grieved him in the desert!
41 Again and again they tried God's patience
 and provoked the Holy One of Israel.
42 They did not keep in mind his power
 or the day when he delivered them from the
  enemy,
43 how he displayed his signs in Egypt,
 his portents in the region of Zoan.
44 He turned their streams into blood,
 and they could not drink the running water.
45 He sent swarms of flies which devoured them,
 and frogs which brought devastation;
46 he gave their harvest over to locusts,
 their produce to the grubs;
47 he devastated their vines with hailstones,
 their fig trees with torrents of rain;
48 he abandoned their cattle to the plague,
 their animals to attacks of pestilence.
49 He unleashed his blazing anger on them,
 wrath and enmity and rage,
 launching those messengers of evil.
50 He opened a way for his fury;
 he did not spare them from death,
 but gave them up to the plague.
51 He struck down all the firstborn in Egypt,
 the firstfruits of their manhood in the tents of Ham.
52 He led out his own people like sheep
 and guided them like a flock in the wilderness.

78:48 **plague:** *so one MS; others* hail.

25 All ate a meal fit for heroes;
   food he sent in abundance.
26 He stirred up the east wind in the heavens;
   by his power God brought on the south wind.
27 He rained meat upon them like dust,
   winged fowl like the sands of the sea,
28 Brought them down in the midst of the camp,
   round about their tents.
29 They ate and were well filled;
   he gave them what they had craved.
30 But while they still wanted more,
   and the food was still in their mouths,
31 God's anger attacked them,
   killed their best warriors,
   laid low the youth of Israel.
32 In spite of all this they went on sinning,
   they did not believe in his wonders.

D

33 God ended their days abruptly,
   their years in sudden death.
34 When he slew them, they began to seek him;
   they again inquired of their God.
35 They remembered that God was their rock,
   God Most High, their redeemer.
36 But they deceived him with their mouths,
   lied to him with their tongues.
37 Their hearts were not constant toward him;
   they were not faithful to his covenant.
38 But God is merciful and forgave their sin;
   he did not utterly destroy them.
   Time and again he turned back his anger,
   unwilling to unleash all his rage.
39 He was mindful that they were flesh,
   a breath that passes and does not return.

III

A

40 How often they rebelled against God in the desert,
   grieved him in the wasteland.
41 Again and again they tested God,
   provoked the Holy One of Israel.
42 They did not remember his power,
   the day he redeemed them from the foe,
43 When he displayed his wonders in Egypt,
   his marvels in the plain of Zoan.
44 God changed their rivers to blood;
   their streams they could not drink.
45 He sent insects that devoured them,
   frogs that destroyed them.
46 He gave their harvest to the caterpillar,
   the fruits of their labor to the locust.
47 He killed their vines with hail,
   their sycamores with frost.
48 He exposed their flocks to deadly hail,
   their cattle to lightning.
49 He unleashed against them his fiery breath,
   roar, fury, and distress,
   storming messengers of death.
50 He cleared a path for his anger;
   he did not spare them from death;
   he delivered their beasts to the plague.
51 He struck all the firstborn of Egypt,
   love's first child in the tents of Ham.
52 God led forth his people like sheep;
   he guided them through the desert like a flock.

25 mere mortals ate the bread of the Mighty,
   he sent them as much food as they could want.
26 He roused an east wind in the heavens,
   despatched a south wind by his strength;
27 he rained down meat on them like dust,
   birds thick as sand on the seashore,
28 tumbling into the middle of his camp,
   all around his dwelling-place.
29 They ate as much food as they wanted,
   he satisfied all their cravings;
30 but their cravings were still upon them,
   the food was still in their mouths,
31 when the wrath of God attacked them,
   slaughtering their strongest men,
   laying low the flower of Israel.
32 Despite all this, they went on sinning,
   they put no faith in his marvels.
33 He made their days vanish in mist,
   their years in sudden ruin.
34 Whenever he slaughtered them, they began to seek
      him,
   they turned back and looked eagerly for him,
35 recalling that God was their rock,
   God the Most High, their redeemer.
36 They tried to hoodwink him with their mouths,
   their tongues were deceitful towards him;
37 their hearts were not loyal to him,
   they were not faithful to his covenant.
38 But in his compassion he forgave their guilt
   instead of killing them,
   time and again repressing his anger
   instead of rousing his full wrath,
39 remembering they were creatures of flesh,
   a breath of wind that passes, never to return.

40 How often they defied him in the desert!
   How often they grieved him in the wastelands!
41 Repeatedly they challenged God,
   provoking the Holy One of Israel,
42 not remembering his hand,
   the time when he saved them from the oppressor,
43 he who did his signs in Egypt,
   his miracles in the plains of Tanis,
44 turning their rivers to blood,
   their streams so that they had nothing to drink.
45 He sent horseflies to eat them up,
   and frogs to devastate them,
46 consigning their crops to the caterpillar,
   the fruit of their hard work to the locust;
47 he killed their vines with hail,
   their sycamore trees with frost,
48 delivering up their cattle to hail,
   and their flocks to thunderbolts.

49 He loosed against them the full heat of his anger,
   fury, rage and destruction,
   a detachment of destroying angels;
50 he gave free course to his anger.

   He did not exempt their own selves from death,
   delivering up their lives to the plague.
51 He struck all the first-born in Egypt,
   the flower of the youth in the tents of Ham.

52 He brought out his people like sheep,
   guiding them like a flock in the desert,

53 He led them in safety, so that they were not
        afraid;
    but the sea overwhelmed their enemies.
54 And he brought them to his holy hill,
    to the mountain that his right hand had won.
55 He drove out nations before them;
    he apportioned them for a possession
    and settled the tribes of Israel in their tents.

56 Yet they tested the Most High God,
    and rebelled against him.
    They did not observe his decrees,
57 but turned away and were faithless like their
        ancestors;
    they twisted like a treacherous bow.
58 For they provoked him to anger with their high
        places;
    they moved him to jealousy with their idols.
59 When God heard, he was full of wrath,
    and he utterly rejected Israel.
60 He abandoned his dwelling at Shiloh,
    the tent where he dwelt among mortals,
61 and delivered his power to captivity,
    his glory to the hand of the foe.
62 He gave his people to the sword,
    and vented his wrath on his heritage.
63 Fire devoured their young men,
    and their girls had no marriage song.
64 Their priests fell by the sword,
    and their widows made no lamentation.
65 Then the Lord awoke as from sleep,
    like a warrior shouting because of wine.
66 He put his adversaries to rout;
    he put them to everlasting disgrace.
67 He rejected the tent of Joseph,
    he did not choose the tribe of Ephraim;
68 but he chose the tribe of Judah,
    Mount Zion, which he loves.
69 He built his sanctuary like the high heavens,
    like the earth, which he has founded forever.
70 He chose his servant David,
    and took him from the sheepfolds;
71 from tending the nursing ewes he brought him
    to be the shepherd of his people Jacob,
    of Israel, his inheritance.
72 With upright heart he tended them,
    and guided them with skillful hand.

Psalm 79

A Psalm of Asaph.

1 O God, the nations have come into your
        inheritance;
    they have defiled your holy temple;
    they have laid Jerusalem in ruins.
2 They have given the bodies of your servants
    to the birds of the air for food,
    the flesh of your faithful to the wild animals of
        the earth.
3 They have poured out their blood like water
    all around Jerusalem,
    and there was no one to bury them.
4 We have become a taunt to our neighbors,
    mocked and derided by those around us.

5 How long, O LORD? Will you be angry forever?
    Will your jealous wrath burn like fire?

53 He led them in safety and they were not afraid,
    but their enemies were engulfed by the sea.
54 He brought his people to his holy land,
    to the hill-country which his right hand had won.
55 He drove out nations before them,
    allotting their lands to Israel as a possession
    and settling the tribes in their dwellings.

56 Yet they provoked and defied God Most High,
    refusing to keep his solemn charges;
57 they were renegades, faithless like their fathers,
    unreliable like a bow gone slack.
58 They provoked him to anger with their shrines
    and roused his jealousy with their carved images.
59 God heard and was enraged;
    he utterly rejected Israel.
60 He forsook his dwelling at Shiloh,
    the tabernacle in which he dwelt among mortals;
61 he surrendered his strength to captivity,
    his pride into enemy hands;
62 he gave his people to the sword,
    he was enraged with his own possession.
63 Fire devoured their young men,
    and their maidens could raise no lament for them;
64 their priests fell by the sword,
    and the widows among them could not weep.

65 Then the Lord awoke as a sleeper wakes
    or a warrior flushed with wine;
66 he struck his foes and drove them back,
    bringing perpetual shame upon them.

67 He rejected the clan of Joseph
    and did not choose the tribe of Ephraim;
68 but he chose the tribe of Judah,
    Mount Zion which he loved.
69 He built his sanctuary high as the mountains,
    founded like the earth to last for ever.
70 He chose David to be his servant
    and took him from the sheepfolds;
71 he brought him from minding the ewes
    to be the shepherd of his people Jacob
    and of Israel his possession;
72 he shepherded them in singleness of heart
    and guided them with a skilful hand.

Psalm 79

A psalm: for Asaph

1 THE heathen have invaded your domain, God;
    they have defiled your holy temple
    and laid Jerusalem in ruins.
2 The dead bodies of your servants they have thrown
        out
    as food for the birds;
    everyone loyal to you they have made carrion for
        wild beasts.
3 All round Jerusalem their blood is spilt like water,
    and there is no one to give them burial.
4 We suffer the taunts of our neighbours,
    the gibes and mockery of those about us.

5 How long, LORD, will you be roused to such fury?
    How long will your indignation blaze like a fire?

78:66 **and . . . back:** *or* in the back.

NEW AMERICAN BIBLE

53 He led them on secure and unafraid,
    but the sea enveloped their enemies.
54 He brought them to his holy land,
    the mountain his right hand had won.
55 God drove out the nations before them,
    apportioned them a heritage by lot,
    settled the tribes of Israel in their tents.

B

56 But they tested, rebelled against God Most High,
    his decrees they did not observe.
57 They turned back, deceitful like their ancestors;
    they proved false like a bow with no tension.
58 They enraged him with their high places;
    with their idols they goaded him.

C

59 God heard and grew angry;
    he rejected Israel completely.
60 He forsook the shrine at Shiloh,
    the tent where he dwelt with humans.
61 He gave up his might into captivity,
    his glorious ark into the hands of the foe.
62 God abandoned his people to the sword;
    he was enraged against his heritage.
63 Fire consumed their young men;
    their young women heard no wedding songs.
64 Their priests fell by the sword;
    their widows made no lamentation.

D

65 Then the Lord awoke as from sleep,
    like a warrior from the effects of wine.
66 He put his enemies to flight;
    everlasting shame he dealt them.
67 He rejected the tent of Joseph,
    chose not the tribe of Ephraim.
68 God chose the tribe of Judah,
    Mount Zion which he favored.
69 He built his shrine like the heavens,
    like the earth which he founded forever.
70 He chose David his servant,
    took him from the sheepfold.
71 From tending sheep God brought him,
    to shepherd Jacob, his people,
    Israel, his heritage.
72 He shepherded them with a pure heart;
    with skilled hands he guided them.

Psalm 79

1 *A psalm of Asaph.*

I

O God, the nations have invaded your heritage;
    they have defiled your holy temple,
    have laid Jerusalem in ruins.
2 They have left the corpses of your servants
    as food for the birds of the heavens,
    the flesh of your faithful for the beasts of the
      earth.
3 They have spilled their blood like water
    all around Jerusalem,
    and no one is left to bury them.
4 We have become the reproach of our neighbors,
    the scorn and derision of those around us.

II

5 How long, LORD? Will you be angry forever?
    Will your rage keep burning like fire?

NEW JERUSALEM BIBLE

53 leading them safe and unafraid,
    while the sea engulfed their enemies.
54 He brought them to his holy land,
    the hill-country won by his right hand;
55 he dispossessed nations before them,
    measured out a heritage for each of them,
    and settled the tribes of Israel in their tents.

56 But still they challenged the Most High God and
      defied him,
    refusing to keep his decrees;
57 as perverse and treacherous as their ancestors,
    they gave way like a faulty bow,
58 provoking him with their high places,
    rousing his jealousy with their idols.

59 God listened and vented his wrath,
    he totally rejected Israel;
60 he forsook his dwelling in Shiloh,
    the tent where he used to dwell on the earth.
61 He abandoned his power to captivity,
    his splendour to the enemy's clutches;
62 he gave up his people to the sword,
    he vented his wrath on his own heritage.
63 Fire devoured their young men,
    their young girls had no wedding-song;
64 their priests fell by the sword
    and their widows sang no dirge.

65 The Lord arose as though he had been asleep,
    like a strong man fighting-mad with wine,
66 he struck his enemies on the rump,
    and put them to everlasting shame.
67 Rejecting the tents of Joseph,
    passing over the tribe of Ephraim,
68 he chose the tribe of Judah,
    his well-loved mountain of Zion;
69 he built his sanctuary like high hills,
    like the earth set it firm for ever.
70 He chose David to be his servant,
    took him from the sheepfold,
71 took him from tending ewes
    to pasture his servant Jacob,
    and Israel his heritage.
72 He pastured them with unblemished heart,
    with a sensitive hand he led them.

Psalm 79 (V 78)

Psalm   Of Asaph

1 God, the pagans have invaded your heritage,
    they have defiled your holy temple,
    they have laid Jerusalem in ruins,
2 they have left the corpses of your servants
    as food for the birds of the air,
    the bodies of your faithful for the wild beasts.
3 Around Jerusalem they have shed blood like water,
    leaving no one to bury them.
4 We are the scorn of our neighbours,
    the butt and laughing-stock of those around us.
5 How long will you be angry, Yahweh? For ever?
    Is your jealousy to go on smouldering like a fire?

NEW REVISED STANDARD VERSION

6 Pour out your anger on the nations
   that do not know you,
 and on the kingdoms
   that do not call on your name.
7 For they have devoured Jacob
   and laid waste his habitation.

8 Do not remember against us the iniquities of our
   ancestors;
 let your compassion come speedily to meet us,
   for we are brought very low.
9 Help us, O God of our salvation,
   for the glory of your name;
 deliver us, and forgive our sins,
   for your name's sake.
10 Why should the nations say,
   "Where is their God?"
 Let the avenging of the outpoured blood of your
   servants
 be known among the nations before our eyes.

11 Let the groans of the prisoners come before you;
   according to your great power preserve those
   doomed to die.
12 Return sevenfold into the bosom of our neighbors
   the taunts with which they taunted you,
   O Lord!
13 Then we your people, the flock of your pasture,
   will give thanks to you forever;
   from generation to generation we will recount
   your praise.

Psalm 80

To the leader: on Lilies, a Covenant. Of Asaph. A Psalm.

1 Give ear, O Shepherd of Israel,
   you who lead Joseph like a flock!
 You who are enthroned upon the cherubim, shine
   forth
2   before Ephraim and Benjamin and Manasseh.
 Stir up your might,
   and come to save us!

3 Restore us, O God;
   let your face shine, that we may be saved.

4 O LORD God of hosts,
   how long will you be angry with your people's
   prayers?
5 You have fed them with the bread of tears,
   and given them tears to drink in full measure.
6 You make us the scorn*j* of our neighbors;
   our enemies laugh among themselves.

7 Restore us, O God of hosts;
   let your face shine, that we may be saved.

8 You brought a vine out of Egypt;
   you drove out the nations and planted it.
9 You cleared the ground for it;
   it took deep root and filled the land.
10 The mountains were covered with its shade,
   the mighty cedars with its branches;
11 it sent out its branches to the sea,
   and its shoots to the River.
12 Why then have you broken down its walls,
   so that all who pass along the way pluck its
   fruit?

REVISED ENGLISH BIBLE

6 Pour out your wrath on nations that do not
   acknowledge you,
 on kingdoms that do not call on you by name,
7 for they have devoured Jacob and left his homeland
   a waste.
8 Do not remember against us the guilt of past
   generations;
 rather let your compassion come swiftly to meet
   us,
 for we have been brought so low.
9 Help us, God our saviour, for the honour of your
   name;
 for your name's sake rescue us and wipe out our
   sins.
10 Why should the nations ask, 'Where is their God?'
 Before our very eyes may those nations know
   your vengeance for the slaughter of your servants.

11 Let the groaning of the captives reach your
   presence
 and in your great might save those under sentence
   of death.
12 Turn back sevenfold on their own heads, Lord,
   the contempt our neighbours pour on you.
13 Then we, your people, the flock which you
   shepherd,
 will give you thanks for ever
 and repeat your praise to all generations.

Psalm 80

For the leader: set to 'Lilies': a testimony: for Asaph:
   a psalm

1 HEAR us, Shepherd of Israel,
   leading Joseph like a flock.
 Shine forth, as you sit enthroned on the cherubim.
2 Leading Ephraim, Benjamin, and Manasseh,
   rouse your might and come to our rescue.
3 God, restore us,
   and make your face shine on us, that we may be
   saved.

4 LORD God of Hosts,
   how long will you fume at your people's prayer?
5 You have made sorrow their daily bread
   and copious tears their drink.
6 You have made us an object of contempt to our
   neighbours,
   and a laughing-stock to our enemies.
7 God of Hosts, restore us,
   and make your face shine on us, that we may be
   saved.

8 You brought a vine from Egypt;
   you drove out nations and planted it;
9 you cleared the ground for it,
   so that it struck root and filled the land.
10 The mountains were covered with its shade,
   and its branches were like those of mighty cedars.
11 It put out boughs all the way to the sea,
   its shoots as far as the river.
12 Why have you broken down the vineyard wall
   so that every passer-by can pluck its fruit?

---

j Syr: Heb *strife*   80:5 **copious:** *Heb.* threefold.

NEW AMERICAN BIBLE

6 Pour out your wrath on nations that reject you,
  on kingdoms that do not call on your name,
7 For they have devoured Jacob,
  laid waste his home.
8 Do not hold past iniquities against us;
  may your compassion come quickly,
  for we have been brought very low.

III
9 Help us, God our savior,
  for the glory of your name.
Deliver us, pardon our sins
  for your name's sake.
10 Why should the nations say,
  "Where is their God?"
Before our eyes make clear to the nations
  that you avenge the blood of your servants.

IV
11 Let the groans of prisoners come before you;
  by your great power free those doomed to death.
12 Lord, inflict on our neighbors sevenfold
  the disgrace they inflicted on you.
13 Then we, your people, the sheep of your pasture,
  will give thanks to you forever;
  through all ages we will declare your praise.

Psalm 80

1 *For the leader; according to "Lilies." Eduth. A psalm of Asaph.*

I
2 Shepherd of Israel, listen,
  guide of the flock of Joseph!
From your throne upon the cherubim reveal
    yourself
3   to Ephraim, Benjamin, and Manasseh.
Stir up your power, come to save us.
4   O LORD of hosts, restore us;
Let your face shine upon us,
  that we may be saved.

II
5 LORD of hosts,
  how long will you burn with anger
  while your people pray?
6 You have fed them the bread of tears,
  made them drink tears in abundance.
7 You have left us to be fought over by our
    neighbors;
  our enemies deride us.
8 O LORD of hosts, restore us;
  let your face shine upon us,
  that we may be saved.

III
9 You brought a vine out of Egypt;
  you drove away the nations and planted it.
10 You cleared the ground;
  it took root and filled the land.
11 The mountains were covered by its shadow,
  the cedars of God by its branches.
12 It sent out boughs as far as the sea,
  shoots as far as the river.
13 Why have you broken down the walls,
  so that all who pass by pluck its fruit?

NEW JERUSALEM BIBLE

6 Pour out your anger on the nations
  who do not acknowledge you,
and on the kingdoms
  that do not call on your name;
7 for they have devoured Jacob
  and devastated his home.
8 Do not count against us the guilt of former
    generations,
  in your tenderness come quickly to meet us,
  for we are utterly weakened;
9 help us, God our Saviour,
  for the glory of your name;
Yahweh, wipe away our sins,
  rescue us for the sake of your name.

10 Why should the nations ask,
  'Where is their God?'
Let us see the nations suffer vengeance
  for shedding your servants' blood.
11 May the groans of the captive reach you,
  by your great strength save those who are
    condemned to death!
12 Repay our neighbours sevenfold
  for the insults they have levelled at you, Lord.
13 And we, your people, the flock that you pasture,
  will thank you for ever,
  will recite your praises from age to age.

Psalm 80 (V 79)

For the choirmaster   Tune: 'The decrees are lilies'
          Of Asaph   Psalm

1 Shepherd of Israel, listen,
  you who lead Joseph like a flock,
  enthroned on the winged creatures, shine forth
2 over Ephraim, Benjamin and Manasseh;
  rouse your valour
  and come to our help.

3 God, bring us back,
  let your face shine on us and we shall be safe.

4 Yahweh, God Sabaoth, how long
  will you flare up at your people's prayer?
5 You have made tears their food,
  redoubled tears their drink.
6 You let our neighbours quarrel over us,
  our enemies mock us.

7 God Sabaoth, bring us back,
  let your face shine on us and we shall be safe.

8 You brought a vine out of Egypt,
  to plant it you drove out nations;
9 you cleared a space for it,
  it took root and filled the whole country.

10 The mountains were covered with its shade,
  and the cedars of God with its branches,
11 its boughs stretched as far as the sea,
  its shoots as far as the River.

12 Why have you broken down its fences?
  Every passer-by plucks its grapes,

NEW REVISED STANDARD VERSION	REVISED ENGLISH BIBLE

13 The boar from the forest ravages it,
   and all that move in the field feed on it.

14 Turn again, O God of hosts;
   look down from heaven, and see;
   have regard for this vine,
15   the stock that your right hand planted. *k*
16 They have burned it with fire, they have cut it
      down; *l*
   may they perish at the rebuke of your
      countenance.
17 But let your hand be upon the one at your right
      hand,
   the one whom you made strong for yourself.
18 Then we will never turn back from you;
   give us life, and we will call on your name.

19 Restore us, O LORD God of hosts;
   let your face shine, that we may be saved.

13 The wild boar from the thicket gnaws it,
   and wild creatures of the countryside feed on it.

14 God of Hosts, turn to us, we pray;
   look down from heaven and see.
   Tend this vine,
15 this stock which your right hand has planted.
16 May those who set it on fire and cut it down
   perish before your angry look.
17 Let your hand rest on the one at your right side,
   the one whom you have made strong for your
      service.
18 Then we shall not turn back from you;
   grant us new life, and we shall invoke you by
      name.
19 LORD God of Hosts, restore us,
   and make your face shine on us, that we may be
      saved.

Psalm 81

To the leader: according to The Gittith. Of Asaph.

1 Sing aloud to God our strength;
   shout for joy to the God of Jacob.
2 Raise a song, sound the tambourine,
   the sweet lyre with the harp.
3 Blow the trumpet at the new moon,
   at the full moon, on our festal day.
4 For it is a statute for Israel,
   an ordinance of the God of Jacob.
5 He made it a decree in Joseph,
   when he went out over *m* the land of Egypt.

   I hear a voice I had not known:
6 "I relieved your *n* shoulder of the burden;
   your *n* hands were freed from the basket.
7 In distress you called, and I rescued you;
   I answered you in the secret place of thunder;
   I tested you at the waters of Meribah.   Selah
8 Hear, O my people, while I admonish you;
   O Israel, if you would but listen to me!
9 There shall be no strange god among you;
   you shall not bow down to a foreign god.
10 I am the LORD your God,
   who brought you up out of the land of Egypt.
   Open your mouth wide and I will fill it.

11 "But my people did not listen to my voice;
   Israel would not submit to me.
12 So I gave them over to their stubborn hearts,
   to follow their own counsels.
13 O that my people would listen to me,
   that Israel would walk in my ways!
14 Then I would quickly subdue their enemies,
   and turn my hand against their foes.
15 Those who hate the LORD would cringe before
      him,
   and their doom would last forever.
16 I would feed you *o* with the finest of the wheat,
   and with honey from the rock I would satisfy
      you."

Psalm 81

For the leader: according to the gittith: for Asaph

1 SING out in praise of God our refuge,
   acclaim the God of Jacob.
2 Raise a melody; beat the drum,
   play the tuneful lyre and harp.
3 At the new moon blow the ram's horn,
   and blow it at the full moon on the day of our
      pilgrim-feast.
4 This is a law for Israel,
   an ordinance of the God of Jacob,
5 laid as a solemn charge on Joseph
   at the exodus from Egypt.

   I hear an unfamiliar voice:
6 I lifted the load from his shoulders;
   his hands let go the builder's basket.
7 When you cried to me in distress, I rescued you;
   I answered you from the thunder-cloud.
   I put you to the test at the waters of Meribah.
                                             [Selah
8 Listen, my people, while I give you a solemn
      charge —
   O that you would listen to me, Israel:
9 you shall have no foreign god
   nor bow down to an alien deity;
10 I am the LORD your God
   who brought you up from Egypt.
   Open your mouth, and I shall fill it.

11 But my people did not listen to my voice,
   Israel would have none of me;
12 so I let them go with their stubborn hearts
   to follow their own devices.

13 If my people would but listen to me,
   if Israel would only conform to my ways,
14 I should soon bring their enemies to their knees
   and turn my hand against their foes.
15 Those hostile to the LORD would come cringing to
      him,
   and meet with everlasting punishment,
16 while Israel would be fed with the finest flour
   and satisfied with honey from the rocks.

---

k Heb adds from verse 17 *and upon the one whom you made strong*
for yourself   *l* Cn: Heb *it is cut down*   *m* Or *against*   *n* Heb *his*
o Cn Compare verse 16b: Heb *he would feed him*

80:15 **this stock . . . planted:** *prob. rdg; Heb.* adds *and on the son*
whom you have made strong for your service (*cp. verse 17*).
81:1 **refuge:** *or* strength.

14 The boar from the forest strips the vine;
 the beast of the field feeds upon it.
15 Turn again, LORD of hosts;
 look down from heaven and see;
Attend to this vine,
16 the shoot your right hand has planted.
17 Those who would burn or cut it down —
 may they perish at your rebuke.
18 May your help be with the man at your right hand,
 with the one whom you once made strong.
19 Then we will not withdraw from you;
 revive us, and we will call on your name.
20 LORD of hosts, restore us;
 let your face shine upon us,
 that we may be saved.

Psalm 81

1 *For the leader; "upon the* gittith.*" Of Asaph.*

I
2 Sing joyfully to God our strength;
 shout in triumph to the God of Jacob!
3 Take up a melody, sound the timbrel,
 the sweet-sounding harp and lyre.
4 Blow the trumpet at the new moon,
 at the full moon, on our solemn feast.
5 For this is a law in Israel,
 an edict of the God of Jacob,
6 Who made it a decree for Joseph
 when he came out of the land of Egypt.

II
I hear a new oracle:
7 "I relieved their shoulders of the burden;
 their hands put down the basket.
8 In distress you called and I rescued you;
 unseen, I spoke to you in thunder;
At the waters of Meribah I tested you and said:
         Selah

9 'Listen, my people, I give you warning!
 If only you will obey me, Israel!
10 There must be no foreign god among you;
 you must not worship an alien god.
11 I, the LORD, am your God,
 who brought you up from the land of Egypt.
 Open wide your mouth that I may fill it.'
12 But my people did not listen to my words;
 Israel did not obey me.
13 So I gave them over to hardness of heart;
 they followed their own designs.
14 But even now if my people would listen,
 if Israel would walk in my paths,
15 In a moment I would subdue their foes,
 against their enemies unleash my hand.
16 Those who hate the LORD would tremble,
 their doom sealed forever.
17 But Israel I would feed with the finest wheat,
 satisfy them with honey from the rock."

13 boars from the forest tear at it,
 wild beasts feed on it.

14 God Sabaoth, come back, we pray,
 look down from heaven and see,
 visit this vine;
15 protect what your own hand has planted.
16 They have thrown it on the fire like dung,
 the frown of your rebuke will destroy them.

17 May your hand protect those at your side,
 the child of Adam you have strengthened for
  yourself!
18 Never again will we turn away from you,
 give us life and we will call upon your name.

19 God Sabaoth, bring us back,
 let your face shine on us and we shall be safe.

Psalm 81 (V 80)

For the choirmaster On the . . . of Gath Of Asaph

1 Sing for joy to God our strength,
 shout in triumph to the God of Jacob.

2 Strike up the music, beat the tambourine,
 play the melodious harp and the lyre;
3 blow the trumpet for the new month,
 for the full moon, for our feast day!

4 For Israel has this statute,
 a decision of the God of Jacob,
5 a decree he imposed on Joseph,
 when he went to war against Egypt.

I heard a voice unknown to me,
6 'I freed his shoulder from the burden,
 his hands were able to lay aside the labourer's
  basket.
7 You cried out in your distress, so I rescued you.

'Hidden in the storm, I answered you,
I tested you at the waters of Meribah. *Pause*
8 Listen, my people, while I give you warning;
 Israel, if only you would listen to me!

9 'You shall have no strange gods,
 shall worship no alien god.
10 I, Yahweh, am your God,
 who brought you here from Egypt,
 you have only to open your mouth for me to fill it.

11 'My people would not listen to me,
 Israel would have none of me.
12 So I left them to their stubborn selves,
 to follow their own devices.

13 'If only my people would listen to me,
 if only Israel would walk in my ways,
14 at one stroke I would subdue their enemies,
 turn my hand against their opponents.

15 'Those who hate Yahweh would woo his favour,
 though their doom was sealed for ever,
16 while I would feed him on pure wheat,
 would give you your fill of honey from the rock.'

NEW REVISED STANDARD VERSION

Psalm 82

A Psalm of Asaph.

1 God has taken his place in the divine council;
    in the midst of the gods he holds judgment:
2 "How long will you judge unjustly
    and show partiality to the wicked?   *Selah*
3 Give justice to the weak and the orphan;
    maintain the right of the lowly and the
        destitute.
4 Rescue the weak and the needy;
    deliver them from the hand of the wicked."
5 They have neither knowledge nor understanding,
    they walk around in darkness;
    all the foundations of the earth are shaken.
6 I say, "You are gods,
    children of the Most High, all of you;
7 nevertheless, you shall die like mortals,
    and fall like any prince."*p*

8 Rise up, O God, judge the earth;
    for all the nations belong to you!

Psalm 83

A Song. A Psalm of Asaph.

1 O God, do not keep silence;
    do not hold your peace or be still, O God!
2 Even now your enemies are in tumult;
    those who hate you have raised their heads.
3 They lay crafty plans against your people;
    they consult together against those you protect.
4 They say, "Come, let us wipe them out as a
        nation;
    let the name of Israel be remembered no
        more."
5 They conspire with one accord;
    against you they make a covenant—
6 the tents of Edom and the Ishmaelites,
    Moab and the Hagrites,
7 Gebal and Ammon and Amalek,
    Philistia with the inhabitants of Tyre;
8 Assyria also has joined them;
    they are the strong arm of the children of Lot.
        Selah

9 Do to them as you did to Midian,
    as to Sisera and Jabin at the Wadi Kishon,
10 who were destroyed at En-dor,
    who became dung for the ground.
11 Make their nobles like Oreb and Zeeb,
    all their princes like Zebah and Zalmunna,
12 who said, "Let us take the pastures of God
    for our own possession."

13 O my God, make them like whirling dust,*q*
    like chaff before the wind.
14 As fire consumes the forest,
    as the flame sets the mountains ablaze,
15 so pursue them with your tempest
    and terrify them with your hurricane.
16 Fill their faces with shame,
    so that they may seek your name, O LORD.
17 Let them be put to shame and dismayed forever;
    let them perish in disgrace.
18 Let them know that you alone,
    whose name is the LORD,
    are the Most High over all the earth.

p Or fall as one man, O princes   *q Or a tumbleweed*

REVISED ENGLISH BIBLE

Psalm 82

A psalm: for Asaph

1 GOD takes his place in the court of heaven
    to pronounce judgement among the gods:
2 'How much longer will you judge unjustly
    and favour the wicked?   [*Selah*
3 Uphold the cause of the weak and the fatherless,
    and see right done to the afflicted and destitute.
4 Rescue the weak and the needy,
    and save them from the clutches of the wicked.'
5 But these gods know nothing and understand
        nothing,
    they walk about in darkness;
    meanwhile earth's foundations are all giving way.
6 'This is my sentence: Though you are gods,
    all sons of the Most High,
7 yet you shall die as mortals die,
    and fall as any prince does.'

8 God, arise and judge the earth,
    for all the nations are yours.

Psalm 83

A song: a psalm: for Asaph

1 Do NOT keep silent, God;
    be neither quiet, God, nor still,
2 for your enemies raise an uproar,
    and those who are hostile to you carry their heads
        high.
3 They devise a cunning plot against your people
    and conspire against those whom you treasure:
4 'Let us wipe them out as a nation,' they say;
    'let the name of Israel be remembered no more.'
5 With one mind they have conspired
    to form a league against you:
6 the families of Edom, the Ishmaelites,
    Moabites and Hagar's people,
7 Gebal, Ammon, and Amalek,
    Philistia and the citizens of Tyre.
8 Asshur too is their ally,
    lending aid to the descendants of Lot.   [*Selah*

9 Deal with them as with Sisera,
    as with Jabin by the wadi of Kishon,
10 who were vanquished and fell, as Midian fell at
        En-harod,
    and became manure on the ground.
11 Make their princes like Oreb and Zeeb,
    make all their nobles like Zebah and Zalmunna,
12 who said, 'We will seize for ourselves
    the territory of God's people.'

13 Scatter them, my God, like thistledown,
    like chaff blown before the wind.
14 As a fire raging through the forest,
    as flames which blaze across the hills,
15 so pursue them with your tempest,
    terrify them with your storm-wind.
16 Heap shame on their heads
    until, LORD, they seek your name.
17 Let them be humiliated, and live in constant terror;
    let them suffer disgrace and perish.
18 So let it be known that you, whose name is the
        LORD,
    are alone Most High over all the earth.

83:10 **as Midian:** *transposed from previous verse.* **En-harod:** *prob. rdg; cp. Judg. 7:1; Heb. Endor.*

Psalm 82

1 *A psalm of Asaph.*

I

God rises in the divine council,
  gives judgment in the midst of the gods.
2 "How long will you judge unjustly
  and favor the cause of the wicked?   *Selah*
3 Defend the lowly and fatherless;
  render justice to the afflicted and needy.
4 Rescue the lowly and poor;
  deliver them from the hand of the wicked."

II

5 The gods neither know nor understand,
  wandering about in darkness,
  and all the world's foundations shake.
6 I declare: "Gods though you be,
  offspring of the Most High all of you,
7 Yet like any mortal you shall die;
  like any prince you shall fall."
8 Arise, O God, judge the earth,
  for yours are all the nations.

Psalm 83

1 *A song; a psalm of Asaph.*

I

2 God, do not be silent;
  God, be not still and unmoved!
3 See how your enemies rage;
  your foes proudly raise their heads.
4 They conspire against your people,
  plot against those you protect.
5 They say, "Come, let us wipe out their nation;
  let Israel's name be mentioned no more!"
6 They scheme with one mind,
  in league against you:
7 The tents of Ishmael and Edom,
  the people of Moab and Hagar,
8 Gebal, Ammon, and Amalek,
  Philistia and the inhabitants of Tyre.
9 Assyria, too, in league with them
  gives aid to the descendants of Lot.   *Selah*

II

10 Deal with them as with Midian;
  as with Sisera and Jabin at the torrent Kishon,
11 Those destroyed at Endor,
  who became dung for the ground.
12 Make their nobles like Oreb and Zeeb,
  all their princes like Zebah and Zalmunna,
13 Who made a plan together,
  "Let us seize the pastures of God."
14 My God, turn them into withered grass,
  into chaff flying before the wind.
15 As a fire raging through a forest,
  a flame setting mountains ablaze,
16 Pursue them with your tempest;
  terrify them with your storm.
17 Cover their faces with shame,
  till they pay you homage, LORD.
18 Let them be dismayed and shamed forever;
  let them perish in disgrace.
19 Show them you alone are the LORD,
  the Most High over all the earth.

Psalm 82 (V 81)

Psalm   Of Asaph

1 God takes his stand in the divine assembly,
  surrounded by the gods he gives judgement.
2 'How much longer will you give unjust judgements
  and uphold the prestige of the wicked?
3 Let the weak and the orphan have justice,
  be fair to the wretched and the destitute.   *Pause*
4 'Rescue the weak and the needy,
  save them from the clutches of the wicked.
5 'Ignorant and uncomprehending, they wander in
      darkness,
  while the foundations of the world are tottering.
6 I had thought, "Are you gods,
  are all of you sons of the Most High?"
7 No! you will die as human beings do,
  as one man, princes, you will fall.'
8 Arise, God, judge the world,
  for all nations belong to you.

Psalm 83 (V 82)

Song   Psalm   Of Asaph

1 God, do not remain silent,
  do not stay quiet or unmoved, God!
2 See how your enemies are in uproar,
  how those who hate you are rearing their heads.
3 They are laying plans against your people,
  conspiring against those you cherish;
4 they say, 'Come, let us annihilate them as a
      nation,
  the name of Israel shall be remembered no more!'
5 They conspire with a single mind,
  they conclude an alliance against you,
6 the tents of Edom and the Ishmaelites,
  Moab and the Hagrites,
7 Gebal, Ammon, Amalek,
  Philistia and the Tyrians;
8 even Assyria has joined them
  to reinforce the children of Lot.   *Pause*
9 Treat them like Midian and Sisera,
  like Jabin at the river Kishon;
10 wiped out at En-Dor,
  they served to manure the ground.
11 Treat their leaders like Oreb and Zeeb,
  all their commanders like Zebah and Zalmunna,
12 for they said, 'Let us take for ourselves
  God's settlements.'
13 My God, treat them like thistledown,
  like chaff at the mercy of the wind.
14 As fire devours a forest,
  as a flame sets mountains ablaze,
15 so drive them away with your tempest,
  by your whirlwind fill them with terror.
16 Shame written all over their faces,
  let them seek your name, Yahweh!
17 Dishonour and terror be always theirs,
  death also and destruction.
18 Let them know that you alone bear the name of
      Yahweh,
  Most High over all the earth.

Psalm 84

To the leader: according to The Gittith. Of the Korahites.
A Psalm.

1 How lovely is your dwelling place,
   O LORD of hosts!
2 My soul longs, indeed it faints
   for the courts of the LORD;
   my heart and my flesh sing for joy
   to the living God.

3 Even the sparrow finds a home,
   and the swallow a nest for herself,
   where she may lay her young,
   at your altars, O LORD of hosts,
   my King and my God.
4 Happy are those who live in your house,
   ever singing your praise.   *Selah*

5 Happy are those whose strength is in you,
   in whose heart are the highways to Zion.*r*
6 As they go through the valley of Baca
   they make it a place of springs;
   the early rain also covers it with pools.
7 They go from strength to strength;
   the God of gods will be seen in Zion.

8 O LORD God of hosts, hear my prayer;
   give ear, O God of Jacob!   *Selah*
9 Behold our shield, O God;
   look on the face of your anointed.

10 For a day in your courts is better
    than a thousand elsewhere.
    I would rather be a doorkeeper in the house of
       my God
    than live in the tents of wickedness.
11 For the LORD God is a sun and shield;
    he bestows favor and honor.
    No good thing does the LORD withhold
    from those who walk uprightly.
12 O LORD of hosts,
    happy is everyone who trusts in you.

Psalm 85

To the leader. Of the Korahites. A Psalm.

1 LORD, you were favorable to your land;
   you restored the fortunes of Jacob.
2 You forgave the iniquity of your people;
   you pardoned all their sin.   *Selah*
3 You withdrew all your wrath;
   you turned from your hot anger.

4 Restore us again, O God of our salvation,
   and put away your indignation toward us.
5 Will you be angry with us forever?
   Will you prolong your anger to all generations?
6 Will you not revive us again,
   so that your people may rejoice in you?
7 Show us your steadfast love, O LORD,
   and grant us your salvation.

8 Let me hear what God the LORD will speak,
   for he will speak peace to his people,
   to his faithful, to those who turn to him in
      their hearts.*s*
9 Surely his salvation is at hand for those who fear
      him,
   that his glory may dwell in our land.

Psalm 84

For the leader: according to the gittith: for the Korahites:
a psalm

1 LORD of Hosts,
   how dearly loved is your dwelling-place!
2 I pine and faint with longing
   for the courts of the LORD's temple;
   my whole being cries out with joy
   to the living God.
3 Even the sparrow finds a home,
   and the swallow has her nest
   where she rears her brood beside your altars,
   LORD of Hosts, my King and God.

4 Happy are those who dwell in your house;
   they never cease to praise you!   [*Selah*
5 Happy those whose refuge is in you,
   whose hearts are set on the pilgrim ways!
6 As they pass through the waterless valley
   the LORD fills it with springs,
   and the early rain covers it with pools.
7 So they pass on from outer wall to inner,
   and the God of gods shows himself in Zion.

8 LORD God of hosts, hear my prayer;
   God of Jacob, listen.   [*Selah*
9 God, look upon our shield the king
   and accept your anointed one with favour.

10 Better one day in your courts
    than a thousand days in my home;
    better to linger by the threshold of God's house
    than to live in the dwellings of the wicked.
11 The LORD God is a sun and shield;
    grace and honour are his to bestow.
    The LORD withholds no good thing
    from those whose life is blameless.
12 O LORD of Hosts,
    happy are they who trust in you!

Psalm 85

For the leader: for the Korahites: a psalm

1 LORD, you have been gracious to your land
   and turned the tide of Jacob's fortunes.
2 You have forgiven the guilt of your people
   and put all their sins away.   [*Selah*
3 You have withdrawn all your wrath
   and turned from your hot anger.

4 God our saviour, restore us
   and abandon your displeasure towards us.
5 Will you be angry with us for ever?
   Must your wrath last for all generations?
6 Will you not give us new life
   that your people may rejoice in you?
7 LORD, show us your love
   and grant us your deliverance.

8 Let me hear the words of God the LORD:
   he proclaims peace to his people and loyal
      servants;
   let them not go back to foolish ways.
9 Deliverance is near to those who worship him,
   so that glory may dwell in our land.

---

r Heb lacks *to Zion*   *s* Gk: Heb *but let them not turn back to folly*   84:10 **in my home:** *prob. rdg; Heb. obscure.*

Psalm 84

1 For the leader; "upon the gittith." A psalm of the Korahites.

I

2 How lovely your dwelling,
   O LORD of hosts!
3 My soul yearns and pines
   for the courts of the LORD.
My heart and flesh cry out
   for the living God.
4 As the sparrow finds a home
   and the swallow a nest to settle her young,
My home is by your altars,
   LORD of hosts, my king and my God!
5 Happy are those who dwell in your house!
   They never cease to praise you.   *Selah*

II

6 Happy are those who find refuge in you,
   whose hearts are set on pilgrim roads.
7 As they pass through the Baca valley,
   they find spring water to drink.
Also from pools the Lord provides water
   for those who lose their way.
8 They pass through outer and inner wall
   and see the God of gods on Zion.

III

9 LORD of hosts, hear my prayer;
   listen, God of Jacob.   *Selah*
10 O God, look kindly on our shield;
   look upon the face of your anointed.

IV

11 Better one day in your courts
   than a thousand elsewhere.
Better the threshold of the house of my God
   than a home in the tents of the wicked.
12 For a sun and shield is the LORD God,
   bestowing all grace and glory.
The LORD withholds no good thing
   from those who walk without reproach.
13 O LORD of hosts,
   happy are those who trust in you!

Psalm 85

1 For the leader. A psalm of the Korahites.

I

2 You once favored, LORD, your land,
   restored the good fortune of Jacob.
3 You forgave the guilt of your people,
   pardoned all their sins.   *Selah*
4 You withdrew all your wrath,
   turned back your burning anger.

II

5 Restore us once more, God our savior;
   abandon your wrath against us.
6 Will you be angry with us forever,
   drag out your anger for all generations?
7 Please give us life again,
   that your people may rejoice in you.
8 Show us, LORD, your love;
   grant us your salvation.

III

9 I will listen for the word of God;
   surely the LORD will proclaim peace
To his people, to the faithful,
   to those who trust in him.
10 Near indeed is salvation for the loyal;
   prosperity will fill our land.

Psalm 84 (V 83)

*For the choirmaster   On the . . . of Gath   Of the sons
of Korah   Psalm*

1 How lovely are your dwelling-places,
   Yahweh Sabaoth.
2 My whole being yearns and pines
   for Yahweh's courts,
My heart and my body cry out for joy
   to the living God.
3 Even the sparrow has found a home,
   the swallow a nest to place its young:
your altars, Yahweh Sabaoth,
   my King and my God.
4 How blessed are those who live in your house;
   they shall praise you continually.   *Pause*
5 Blessed those who find their strength in you,
   whose hearts are set on pilgrimage.
6 As they pass through the Valley of the Balsam,
   they make there a water-hole,
and — a further blessing — early rain fills it.
7 They make their way from height to height,
   God shows himself to them in Zion.
8 Yahweh, God Sabaoth, hear my prayer,
   listen, God of Jacob.
9 God, our shield, look,
   and see the face of your anointed.

10 Better one day in your courts
   than a thousand at my own devices,
to stand on the threshold of God's house
   than to live in the tents of the wicked.

11 For Yahweh God is a rampart and shield,
   he gives grace and glory;
Yahweh refuses nothing good
   to those whose life is blameless.

12 Yahweh Sabaoth,
   blessed is he who trusts in you.

Psalm 85 (V 84)

For the choirmaster   Of the sons of Korah   Psalm

1 Yahweh, you are gracious to your land,
   you bring back the captives of Jacob,
2 you take away the guilt of your people,
   you blot out all their sin.   *Pause*
3 You retract all your anger,
   you renounce the heat of your fury.

4 Bring us back, God our Saviour,
   appease your indignation against us!
5 Will you be angry with us for ever?
   Will you prolong your wrath age after age?
6 Will you not give us life again,
   for your people to rejoice in you?
7 Show us, Lord, your faithful love,
   grant us your saving help.

8 I am listening. What is God's message?
   Yahweh's message is peace
for his people, for his faithful,
   if only they renounce their folly.
9 His saving help is near for those who fear him,
   his glory will dwell in our land.

NEW REVISED STANDARD VERSION	REVISED ENGLISH BIBLE

NEW REVISED STANDARD VERSION

10 Steadfast love and faithfulness will meet;
   righteousness and peace will kiss each other.
11 Faithfulness will spring up from the ground,
   and righteousness will look down from the sky.
12 The LORD will give what is good,
   and our land will yield its increase.
13 Righteousness will go before him,
   and will make a path for his steps.

Psalm 86

A Prayer of David.

1 Incline your ear, O LORD, and answer me,
   for I am poor and needy.
2 Preserve my life, for I am devoted to you;
   save your servant who trusts in you.
   You are my God; 3 be gracious to me, O Lord,
   for to you do I cry all day long.
4 Gladden the soul of your servant,
   for to you, O Lord, I lift up my soul.
5 For you, O Lord, are good and forgiving,
   abounding in steadfast love to all who call on
      you.
6 Give ear, O LORD, to my prayer;
   listen to my cry of supplication.
7 In the day of my trouble I call on you,
   for you will answer me.

8 There is none like you among the gods, O Lord,
   nor are there any works like yours.
9 All the nations you have made shall come
   and bow down before you, O Lord,
   and shall glorify your name.
10 For you are great and do wondrous things;
   you alone are God.
11 Teach me your way, O LORD,
   that I may walk in your truth;
   give me an undivided heart to revere your name.
12 I give thanks to you, O Lord my God, with my
      whole heart,
   and I will glorify your name forever.
13 For great is your steadfast love toward me;
   you have delivered my soul from the depths of
      Sheol.

14 O God, the insolent rise up against me;
   a band of ruffians seeks my life,
   and they do not set you before them.
15 But you, O Lord, are a God merciful and
      gracious,
   slow to anger and abounding in steadfast love
      and faithfulness.
16 Turn to me and be gracious to me;
   give your strength to your servant;
   save the child of your serving girl.
17 Show me a sign of your favor,
   so that those who hate me may see it and be
      put to shame,
   because you, LORD, have helped me and
      comforted me.

Psalm 87

Of the Korahites. A Psalm. A Song.

1 On the holy mount stands the city he founded;
2 the LORD loves the gates of Zion

REVISED ENGLISH BIBLE

10 Love and faithfulness have come together;
   justice and peace have embraced.
11 Faithfulness appears from earth
   and justice looks down from heaven.
12 The LORD will grant prosperity,
   and our land will yield its harvest.
13 Justice will go in front of him,
   and peace on the path he treads.

Psalm 86

A prayer: for David

1 LISTEN, LORD, and give me an answer,
   for I am oppressed and poor.
2 Guard me, for I am faithful;
   save your servant who puts his trust in you.
   You are my God. 3 Show me your favour, Lord;
   I call to you all day long.
4 Fill your servant's heart with joy,
   for to you, Lord, I lift up my heart.
5 Lord, you are kind and forgiving,
   full of love towards all who cry to you.
6 LORD, listen to my prayer
   and hear my pleading.
7 In the day of my distress I call to you,
   for you will answer me.

8 Among the gods not one is like you, Lord;
   no deeds compare with yours.
9 All the nations you have made
   will come to bow before you, Lord,
   and honour your name,
10 for you are great, and your works are wonderful;
   you alone are God.

11 LORD, teach me your way,
   that I may walk in your truth.
   Let me worship your name with undivided heart.
12 I shall praise you, Lord my God, with all my heart
   and give honour to your name for ever.
13 For your love towards me is great,
   and you have rescued me from the depths of Sheol.
14 Violent men rise to attack me,
   a band of ruthless men seeks my life;
   they give no thought to you, my God.
15 But you, Lord, are God, compassionate and
      gracious,
   long-suffering, ever faithful and true.
16 Turn to me and show me your favour;
   grant your servant protection
   and rescue your slave-girl's son.
17 Give me a sign of your favour;
   let those who hate me see it and be abashed,
   for you, LORD, have been my help and comfort.

Psalm 87

For the Korahites: a psalm: a song

1 THE city the LORD founded stands on the holy hills.
2 He loves the gates of Zion

85:13 **and peace . . . treads:** *prob. rdg; Heb.* so that he may put his
feet to a way.   86:13 **Sheol:** *or* the underworld.   87:1 **The city
. . . founded:** *lit.* His foundation.

NEW AMERICAN BIBLE

11 Love and truth will meet;
     justice and peace will kiss.
12 Truth will spring from the earth;
     justice will look down from heaven.
13 The LORD will surely grant abundance;
     our land will yield its increase.
14 Prosperity will march before the Lord,
     and good fortune will follow behind.

Psalm 86

1 *A prayer of David.*

I

Hear me, LORD, and answer me,
   for I am poor and oppressed.
2 Preserve my life, for I am loyal;
     save your servant who trusts in you.
3 You are my God; pity me, Lord;
     to you I call all the day.
4 Gladden the soul of your servant;
     to you, Lord, I lift up my soul.
5 Lord, you are kind and forgiving,
     most loving to all who call on you.
6 LORD, hear my prayer;
     listen to my cry for help.
7 In this time of trouble I call,
     for you will answer me.

II

8 None among the gods can equal you, O Lord;
     nor can their deeds compare to yours.
9 All the nations you have made shall come
     to bow before you, Lord,
     and give honor to your name.
10 For you are great and do wondrous deeds;
     and you alone are God.

III

11 Teach me, LORD, your way
     that I may walk in your truth,
     single-hearted and revering your name.
12 I will praise you with all my heart,
     glorify your name forever, Lord my God.
13 Your love for me is great;
     you have rescued me from the depths of Sheol.
14 O God, the arrogant have risen against me;
     a ruthless band has sought my life;
     to you they pay no heed.
15 But you, Lord, are a merciful and gracious God,
     slow to anger, most loving and true.
16 Turn to me, have pity on me;
     give your strength to your servant;
     save this child of your handmaid.
17 Give me a sign of your favor:
     make my enemies see, to their confusion,
     that you, LORD, help and comfort me.

Psalm 87

1 *A psalm of the Korahites. A song.*

I

The LORD loves the city
   founded on holy mountains,
2 Loves the gates of Zion

NEW JERUSALEM BIBLE

10 Faithful Love and Loyalty join together,
     Saving Justice and Peace embrace.
11 Loyalty will spring up from the earth,
     and Justice will lean down from heaven.
12 Yahweh will himself give prosperity,
     and our soil will yield its harvest.
13 Justice will walk before him,
     treading out a path.

Psalm 86 (V 85)

Prayer   Of David

1 Listen to me, Yahweh, answer me,
   for I am poor and needy.
2 Guard me, for I am faithful,
     save your servant who relies on you.

You are my God, 3 take pity on me, Lord,
   for to you I cry all the day.
4 Fill your servant's heart with joy, Lord,
     for to you I raise up my heart.
5 Lord, you are kind and forgiving,
     rich in faithful love for all who call upon you.
6 Yahweh, hear my prayer,
     listen to the sound of my pleading.
7 In my day of distress I call upon you,
     because you answer me, Lord;
8 among the gods there is none to compare with you,
     no great deeds to compare with yours.
9 All nations will come and adore you, Lord,
     and give glory to your name.
10 For you are great and do marvellous deeds,
     you, God, and none other.

11 Teach me, Yahweh, your ways,
     that I may not stray from your loyalty;
     let my heart's one aim be to fear your name.
12 I thank you with all my heart, Lord my God,
     I will glorify your name for ever,
13 for your faithful love for me is so great
     that you have rescued me from the depths of
        Sheol.

14 Arrogant men, God, are rising up against me,
     a brutal gang is after my life,
     in their scheme of things you have no place.
15 But you, Lord, God of tenderness and mercy,
     slow to anger, rich in faithful love and loyalty,
16 turn to me and pity me.

Give to your servant your strength,
   to the child of your servant your saving help,
17 give me a sign of your kindness.
18 My enemies will see to their shame
     that you, Yahweh, help and console me.

Psalm 87 (V 86)

Of the sons of Korah   Psalm   Song

1 With its foundations on the holy mountains,
2 Yahweh loves his city,

NEW REVISED STANDARD VERSION	REVISED ENGLISH BIBLE

NEW REVISED STANDARD VERSION

more than all the dwellings of Jacob.
3 Glorious things are spoken of you,
　O city of God. *Selah*

4 Among those who know me I mention Rahab and
　　Babylon;
　Philistia too, and Tyre, with Ethiopia*ᵗ* —
　"This one was born there," they say.

5 And of Zion it shall be said,
　"This one and that one were born in it";
　for the Most High himself will establish it.
6 The Lᴏʀᴅ records, as he registers the peoples,
　"This one was born there." *Selah*

7 Singers and dancers alike say,
　"All my springs are in you."

Psalm 88

A Song. A Psalm of the Korahites. To the leader: according
to Mahalath Leannoth. A Maskil of Heman the Ezrahite.

1 O Lᴏʀᴅ, God of my salvation,
　when, at night, I cry out in your presence,
2 let my prayer come before you;
　incline your ear to my cry.

3 For my soul is full of troubles,
　and my life draws near to Sheol.
4 I am counted among those who go down to the
　　Pit;
　I am like those who have no help,
5 like those forsaken among the dead,
　like the slain that lie in the grave,
　like those whom you remember no more,
　for they are cut off from your hand.
6 You have put me in the depths of the Pit,
　in the regions dark and deep.
7 Your wrath lies heavy upon me,
　and you overwhelm me with all your waves. *Selah*

8 You have caused my companions to shun me;
　you have made me a thing of horror to them.
　I am shut in so that I cannot escape;
9 　my eye grows dim through sorrow.
　Every day I call on you, O Lᴏʀᴅ;
　I spread out my hands to you.
10 Do you work wonders for the dead?
　Do the shades rise up to praise you? *Selah*
11 Is your steadfast love declared in the grave,
　or your faithfulness in Abaddon?
12 Are your wonders known in the darkness,
　or your saving help in the land of
　　forgetfulness?

13 But I, O Lᴏʀᴅ, cry out to you;
　in the morning my prayer comes before you.
14 O Lᴏʀᴅ, why do you cast me off?
　Why do you hide your face from me?
15 Wretched and close to death from my youth up,
　I suffer your terrors; I am desperate.*ᵘ*
16 Your wrath has swept over me;
　your dread assaults destroy me.
17 They surround me like a flood all day long;
　from all sides they close in on me.

REVISED ENGLISH BIBLE

more than all the dwellings of Jacob.
3 Glorious things are spoken about you,
　city of God. [*Selah*

4 I shall count Rahab and Babylon
　among those who acknowledge me;
　of Philistines, Tyrians, and Nubians
　it will be said, 'Such a one was born there.'
5 Of Zion it will be said,
　'This one and that one were born there.'
　The Most High himself establishes her.
6 The Lᴏʀᴅ will record in the register of the peoples:
　this one was born there. [*Selah*
7 Singers and dancers alike say,
　'The source of all good is in you.'

Psalm 88

A song: a psalm: for the Korahites: for the leader: set to
'Mahalath le-annoth': a maskil: for Heman the Ezrahite

1 Lᴏʀᴅ, my God, by day I call for help,
　by night I cry aloud in your presence.
2 Let my prayer come before you,
　hear my loud entreaty;
3 for I have had my fill of woes,
　which have brought me to the brink of Sheol.
4 I am numbered with those who go down to the
　　abyss;
　I have become like a man beyond help,
5 abandoned among the dead,
　like the slain lying in the grave
　whom you hold in mind no more,
　who are cut off from your care.
6 You have plunged me into the lowest abyss,
　into the darkest regions of the depths.
7 Your wrath bears heavily on me,
　you have brought on me all your fury. [*Selah*
8 You have removed my friends far from me
　and made me utterly loathsome to them.
　I am shut in with no escape;
9 my eyes are dim with anguish.
　Lᴏʀᴅ, every day I have called to you
　and stretched out my hands in prayer.

10 Will it be for the dead you work wonders?
　Or can the shades rise up and praise you? [*Selah*
11 Will they speak in the grave of your love,
　of your faithfulness in the tomb?
12 Will your wonders be known in the region of
　　darkness,
　your victories in the land of oblivion?

13 But as for me, Lᴏʀᴅ, I cry to you,
　my prayer comes before you in the morning.
14 Lᴏʀᴅ, why have you cast me off,
　why do you hide your face from me?
15 From childhood I have suffered and been near to
　　death;
　I have borne your terrors, I am numb.
16 Your burning fury has swept over me,
　your onslaughts have overwhelmed me;
17 all the day long they surge round me like a flood,
　from every side they close in on me.

87:7 **The source . . . good:** *lit.* All my springs.　88:1 **I call for**
help: *prob. rdg; Heb.* my deliverance.　88:3 **Sheol:** *or* the
underworld.　88:7 **fury:** *or* waves.　88:11 **the tomb:** *Heb.*
Abaddon.　88:15 **I am numb:** *prob. rdg; Heb.* unintelligible.

ᵗOr Nubia; Heb Cush　　*ᵘMeaning of Heb uncertain*

NEW AMERICAN BIBLE

more than any dwelling in Jacob.
3 Glorious things are said of you,
O city of God!   *Selah*

II

4 From Babylon and Egypt I count
   those who acknowledge the LORD.
Philistia, Ethiopia, Tyre,
   of them it can be said:
   "This one was born there."
5 But of Zion it must be said:
   "They all were born here."
The Most High confirms this;
6 the LORD notes in the register of the peoples:
   "This one was born here."   *Selah*
7 So all sing in their festive dance:
   "Within you is my true home."

Psalm 88

1 *A song; a psalm of the Korahites. For the leader;*
according to Mahalath. *For singing; a maskil of Heman the*
Ezrahite.

I

2 LORD, my God, I call out by day;
   at night I cry aloud in your presence.
3 Let my prayer come before you;
   incline your ear to my cry.
4 For my soul is filled with troubles;
   my life draws near to Sheol.
5 I am reckoned with those who go down to the pit;
   I am weak, without strength.
6 My couch is among the dead,
   with the slain who lie in the grave.
You remember them no more;
   they are cut off from your care.
7 You plunged me into the bottom of the pit,
   into the darkness of the abyss.
8 Your wrath lies heavy upon me;
   all your waves crash over me.   *Selah*
9 Because of you my friends shun me;
   you make me loathsome to them;
Caged in, I cannot escape;
10 my eyes grow dim from trouble.

II

All day I call on you, LORD;
   I stretch out my hands to you.
11 Do you work wonders for the dead?
   Do the shades arise and praise you?   *Selah*
12 Is your love proclaimed in the grave,
   your fidelity in the tomb?
13 Are your marvels declared in the darkness,
   your righteous deeds in the land of oblivion?

III

14 But I cry out to you, LORD;
   in the morning my prayer comes before you.
15 Why do you reject me, LORD?
   Why hide your face from me?
16 I am mortally afflicted since youth;
   lifeless, I suffer your terrible blows.
17 Your wrath has swept over me;
   your terrors have reduced me to silence.
18 All the day they surge round like a flood;
   from every side they close in on me.

NEW JERUSALEM BIBLE

he prefers the gates of Zion
   to any dwelling-place in Jacob.
3 He speaks of glory for you,
   city of God,   *Pause*
4 'I number Rahab and Babylon
   among those that acknowledge me;
   look at Tyre, Philistia, Ethiopia,
   so and so was born there.'
5 But of Zion it will be said,
   'Every one was born there,'
   her guarantee is the Most High.
6 Yahweh in his register of peoples
   will note against each, 'Born there',   *Pause*
7 princes no less than native-born;
   all make their home in you.

Psalm 88 (V 87)

Song   Psalm   Of the sons of Korah   In sickness
In suffering   Poem   For Heman the native-born

1 Yahweh, God of my salvation,
   when I cry out to you in the night,
2 may my prayer reach your presence,
   hear my cry for help.
3 For I am filled with misery,
   my life is on the brink of Sheol;
4 already numbered among those who sink into
      oblivion,
   I am as one bereft of strength,
5 left alone among the dead,
   like the slaughtered lying in the grave,
   whom you remember no more,
   cut off as they are from your protection.
6 You have plunged me to the bottom of the grave,
   in the darkness, in the depths,
7 weighted down by your anger,
   kept low by your waves.   *Pause*
8 You have deprived me of my friends,
   made me repulsive to them,
   imprisoned, with no escape;
9 my eyes are worn out with suffering.
   I call to you, Yahweh, all day,
   I stretch out my hands to you.
10 Do you work wonders for the dead,
   can shadows rise up to praise you?   *Pause*
11 Do they speak in the grave of your faithful love,
   of your constancy in the place of perdition?
12 Are your wonders known in the darkness,
   your saving justice in the land of oblivion?
13 But, for my part, I cry to you, Yahweh,
   every morning my prayer comes before you;
14 why, Yahweh, do you rebuff me,
   turn your face away from me?
15 Wretched and close to death since childhood,
   I have borne your terrors — I am finished!
16 Your anger has overwhelmed me,
   your terrors annihilated me.
17 They flood around me all day long,
   close in on me all at once.

NEW REVISED STANDARD VERSION	REVISED ENGLISH BIBLE

18 You have caused friend and neighbor to shun me;
   my companions are in darkness.

18 You have taken friend and neighbour far from me;
   darkness is now my only companion.

Psalm 89

A Maskil of Ethan the Ezrahite.

1 I will sing of your steadfast love, O LORD,[v]
   forever;
   with my mouth I will proclaim your
   faithfulness to all generations.
2 I declare that your steadfast love is established
   forever;
   your faithfulness is as firm as the heavens.

3 You said, "I have made a covenant with my
   chosen one,
   I have sworn to my servant David:
4 'I will establish your descendants forever,
   and build your throne for all generations.' "
                                          Selah

5 Let the heavens praise your wonders, O LORD,
   your faithfulness in the assembly of the holy
   ones.
6 For who in the skies can be compared to the
   LORD?
   Who among the heavenly beings is like the
   LORD,
7 a God feared in the council of the holy ones,
   great and awesome[w] above all that are around
   him?
8 O LORD God of hosts,
   who is as mighty as you, O LORD?
   Your faithfulness surrounds you.
9 You rule the raging of the sea;
   when its waves rise, you still them.
10 You crushed Rahab like a carcass;
   you scattered your enemies with your mighty
   arm.
11 The heavens are yours, the earth also is yours;
   the world and all that is in it—you have
   founded them.
12 The north and the south[x]—you created them;
   Tabor and Hermon joyously praise your name.
13 You have a mighty arm;
   strong is your hand, high your right hand.
14 Righteousness and justice are the foundation of
   your throne;
   steadfast love and faithfulness go before you.
15 Happy are the people who know the festal shout,
   who walk, O LORD, in the light of your
   countenance;
16 they exult in your name all day long,
   and extol[y] your righteousness.
17 For you are the glory of their strength;
   by your favor our horn is exalted.
18 For our shield belongs to the LORD,
   our king to the Holy One of Israel.

19 Then you spoke in a vision to your faithful one,
   and said:
   "I have set the crown[z] on one who is mighty,
   I have exalted one chosen from the people.
20 I have found my servant David;
   with my holy oil I have anointed him;
21 my hand shall always remain with him;
   my arm also shall strengthen him.

Psalm 89

A maskil: for Ethan the Ezrahite

1 I SHALL sing always of the loving deeds of the
   LORD;
   throughout every generation I shall proclaim your
   faithfulness.
2 I said: Your love will stand firm for ever;
   in the heavens you have established your
   faithfulness.

3 I have made a covenant with the one I have
   chosen,
   I have sworn on oath to my servant David:
4 'I shall establish your line for ever,
   I shall make your throne endure for all
   generations.'   [*Selah*

5 Let the heavens praise your wonders, LORD;
   let the assembly of the angels exalt your
   faithfulness.
6 In the skies who is there like the LORD,
   who like the LORD in the court of heaven,
7 a God dreaded in the council of the angels,
   great and terrible above all who stand about him?
8 LORD God of Hosts, who is like you?
   Your strength and faithfulness, LORD, are all
   around you.
9 You rule the raging of the sea,
   calming the turmoil of its waves.
10 You crushed and slew the monster Rahab
   and scattered your enemies with your strong arm.

11 The heavens are yours, the earth yours also;
   you founded the world and all that is in it.
12 You created the north and the south;
   Tabor and Hermon echo your name.
13 Strength of arm and valour are yours;
   your hand is mighty, your right hand lifted high;
14 your throne is founded on righteousness and
   justice;
   love and faithfulness are in attendance on you.

15 Happy the people who have learnt to acclaim you,
   who walk in the light of your countenance, LORD!
16 In your name they rejoice all day long;
   your righteousness will lift them up.
17 You are yourself the strength in which they glory;
   through your favour we hold our heads high.
18 To the LORD belongs our shield,
   to the Holy One of Israel our king.

19 A time came when you spoke in a vision,
   declaring to your faithful servant:
   I have granted help to a warrior;
   I have exalted one chosen from the people.
20 I have found David my servant
   and anointed him with my sacred oil.
21 My hand will be ready to help him,
   my arm to give him strength.

[v] Gk: Heb *the steadfast love of the LORD* [w] Gk Syr: Heb *greatly awesome* [x] Or *Zaphon and Yamin* [y] Cn: Heb *are exalted in* [z] Cn: Heb *help*

89:7 **great**: *so Gk; Heb.* greatly. 89:8 **Your strength**: *prob. rdg; Heb. obscure.*

19 Because of you companions shun me;
my only friend is darkness.

Psalm 89

1 A maskil *of Ethan the Ezrahite.*

I

2 The promises of the LORD I will sing forever,
proclaim your loyalty through all ages.
3 For you said, "My love is established forever;
my loyalty will stand as long as the heavens.
4 I have made a covenant with my chosen one,
I have sworn to David my servant:
5 I will make your dynasty stand forever
and establish your throne through all ages."
Selah

II

6 The heavens praise your marvels, LORD,
your loyalty in the assembly of the holy ones.
7 Who in the skies ranks with the LORD?
Who is like the LORD among the gods?
8 A God dreaded in the council of the holy ones,
greater and more awesome than all who sit
there!
9 LORD, God of hosts, who is like you?
Mighty LORD, your loyalty is always present.
10 You rule the raging sea;
you still its swelling waves.
11 You crushed Rahab with a mortal blow;
your strong arm scattered your foes.
12 Yours are the heavens, yours the earth;
you founded the world and everything in it.
13 Zaphon and Amanus you created;
Tabor and Hermon rejoice in your name.
14 Mighty your arm, strong your hand,
your right hand is ever exalted.
15 Justice and judgment are the foundation of your
throne;
love and loyalty march before you.
16 Happy the people who know you, LORD,
who walk in the radiance of your face.
17 In your name they sing joyfully all the day;
at your victory they raise the festal shout.
18 You are their majestic strength;
by your favor our horn is exalted.
19 Truly the LORD is our shield,
the Holy One of Israel, our king!

III

20 Once you spoke in vision;
to your faithful ones you said:
"I have set a leader over the warriors;
I have raised up a hero from the army.
21 I have chosen David, my servant;
with my holy oil I have anointed him.
22 My hand will be with him;
my arm will make him strong.

18 You have deprived me of friends and companions,
and all that I know is the dark.

Psalm 89 (V 88)

Poem   For Ethan the native-born

1 I shall sing the faithful love of Yahweh for ever,
from age to age my lips shall declare your
constancy.
2 for you have said: love is built to last for ever,
you have fixed your constancy firm in the heavens.

3   'I have made a covenant with my Chosen One,
sworn an oath to my servant David:
4   I have made your dynasty firm for ever,
built your throne stable age after age.'   *Pause*

5 The heavens praise your wonders, Yahweh,
your constancy in the gathering of your faithful.
6 Who in the skies can compare with Yahweh?
Who among the sons of god can rival him?

7 God, awesome in the assembly of holy ones,
great and dreaded among all who surround him,
8 Yahweh, God Sabaoth, who is like you?
Mighty Yahweh, your constancy is all round you!

9 You control the pride of the ocean,
when its waves ride high you calm them.
10 You split Rahab*o* in two like a corpse,
scattered your enemies with your mighty arm.

11 Yours are the heavens and yours the earth,
the world and all it holds, you founded them;
12 you created the north and the south,
Tabor and Hermon hail your name with joy.

13 Yours is a strong arm,
mighty your hand, your right hand raised high;
14 Saving Justice and Fair Judgement the foundations
of your throne,
Faithful Love and Constancy march before you.

15 How blessed the nation that learns to acclaim you!
They will live, Yahweh, in the light of your
presence.
16   In your name they rejoice all day long,
by your saving justice they are raised up.

17   You are the flower of their strength,
by your favour our strength is triumphant;
18   for to Yahweh belongs our shield,
to the Holy One of Israel our king.

19   Once you spoke in a vision,
to your faithful you said:
'I have given strength to a warrior,
I have raised up a man chosen from my people.

20   'I have found David my servant,
and anointed him with my holy oil.
21   My hand will always be with him,
my arm will make him strong.

o **89** Usually the sea as a monster of chaos, subdued at creation; or
Egypt subdued at the exodus.

22 The enemy shall not outwit him,
   the wicked shall not humble him.
23 I will crush his foes before him
   and strike down those who hate him.
24 My faithfulness and steadfast love shall be with
      him;
   and in my name his horn shall be exalted.
25 I will set his hand on the sea
   and his right hand on the rivers.
26 He shall cry to me, 'You are my Father,
   my God, and the Rock of my salvation!'
27 I will make him the firstborn,
   the highest of the kings of the earth.
28 Forever I will keep my steadfast love for him,
   and my covenant with him will stand firm.
29 I will establish his line forever,
   and his throne as long as the heavens endure.
30 If his children forsake my law
   and do not walk according to my ordinances,
31 if they violate my statutes
   and do not keep my commandments,
32 then I will punish their transgression with the rod
   and their iniquity with scourges;
33 but I will not remove from him my steadfast
      love,
   or be false to my faithfulness.
34 I will not violate my covenant,
   or alter the word that went forth from my lips.
35 Once and for all I have sworn by my holiness;
   I will not lie to David.
36 His line shall continue forever,
   and his throne endure before me like the sun.
37 It shall be established forever like the moon,
   an enduring witness in the skies."   *Selah*

38 But now you have spurned and rejected him;
   you are full of wrath against your anointed.
39 You have renounced the covenant with your
      servant;
   you have defiled his crown in the dust.
40 You have broken through all his walls;
   you have laid his strongholds in ruins.
41 All who pass by plunder him;
   he has become the scorn of his neighbors.
42 You have exalted the right hand of his foes;
   you have made all his enemies rejoice.
43 Moreover, you have turned back the edge of his
      sword,
   and you have not supported him in battle.
44 You have removed the scepter from his hand,*a*
   and hurled his throne to the ground.
45 You have cut short the days of his youth;
   you have covered him with shame.   *Selah*

46 How long, O LORD? Will you hide yourself
      forever?
   How long will your wrath burn like fire?
47 Remember how short my time is — *b*
   for what vanity you have created all mortals!
48 Who can live and never see death?
   Who can escape the power of Sheol?   *Selah*

22 No enemy will outwit him,
   no wicked person will oppress him;
23 I shall crush his adversaries before him
   and strike down those who are hostile to him.
24 My faithfulness and love will be with him
   and through my name he will hold his head high.
25 I shall establish his rule over the sea,
   his dominion over the rivers.
26 He will call to me, 'You are my father,
   my God, my rock where I find safety.'
27 I shall give him the rank of firstborn,
   highest among the kings of the earth.
28 I shall maintain my love for him for ever
   and be faithful in my covenant with him.
29 I shall establish his line for ever
   and his throne as long as the heavens endure.

30 If his children forsake my law
   and do not conform to my judgements,
31 if they violate my statutes
   and do not observe my commandments,
32 then I shall punish their disobedience with the rod,
   their iniquity with lashes.
33 Yet I shall not deprive him of my love,
   nor swerve from my faithfulness;
34 I shall not violate my covenant,
   nor alter what I have promised.
35 I have sworn by my holiness once and for all,
   I shall not break my word to David:
36 his posterity will continue for ever,
   his throne before me like the sun;
37 like the moon it will endure for ever,
   a faithful witness in the sky.   [*Selah*

38 Yet you have spurned your anointed one,
   you have rejected him and raged against him,
39 you have renounced the covenant with your
      servant,
   defiled his crown and flung it to the ground.
40 You have breached all his walls
   and laid his fortresses in ruins;
41 every passer-by plunders him,
   and he suffers his neighbours' taunts.
42 You have increased the power of his adversaries
   and brought joy to all his foes;
43 you have driven back his drawn sword
   and left him without support in battle.
44 You have put an end to his splendour
   and hurled his throne to the ground;
45 you have cut short the days of his youth
   and covered him as with a cloak of shame.   [*Selah*

46 How long, LORD, will you hide yourself from
      sight?
   How long will your wrath blaze like a fire?
47 Remember how fleeting is our life!
   Have you created all mankind to no purpose?
48 Who can live and not see death?
   Who can save himself from the power of Sheol?
      [*Selah*

---

a Cn: Heb *removed his cleanness*   *b* Meaning of Heb uncertain   89:48 **Sheol:** or the underworld.

23 No enemy shall outwit him,
   nor shall the wicked defeat him.
24 I will crush his foes before him,
   strike down those who hate him.
25 My loyalty and love will be with him;
   through my name his horn will be exalted.
26 I will set his hand upon the sea,
   his right hand upon the rivers.
27 He shall cry to me, 'You are my father,
   my God, the Rock that brings me victory!'
28 I myself make him firstborn,
   Most High over the kings of the earth.
29 Forever I will maintain my love for him;
   my covenant with him stands firm.
30 I will establish his dynasty forever,
   his throne as the days of the heavens.
31 If his descendants forsake my law,
   do not follow my decrees,
32 If they fail to observe my statutes,
   do not keep my commandments,
33 I will punish their crime with a rod
   and their guilt with lashes.
34 But I will not take my love from him,
   nor will I betray my bond of loyalty.
35 I will not violate my covenant;
   the promise of my lips I will not alter.
36 By my holiness I swore once for all:
   I will never be false to David.
37 His dynasty will continue forever,
   his throne, like the sun before me.
38 Like the moon it will stand eternal,
   forever firm like the sky!"   *Selah*

IV

39 But now you have rejected and spurned,
   been enraged at your anointed.
40 You renounced the covenant with your servant,
   defiled his crown in the dust.
41 You broke down all his defenses,
   left his strongholds in ruins.
42 All who pass through seize plunder;
   his neighbors deride him.
43 You have exalted the right hand of his foes,
   have gladdened all his enemies.
44 You turned back his sharp sword,
   did not support him in battle.
45 You brought to an end his splendor,
   hurled his throne to the ground.
46 You cut short the days of his youth,
   covered him with shame.   *Selah*
47 How long, LORD?
   Will you stay hidden forever?
   Must your wrath smolder like fire?
48 Remember how brief is my life,
   how frail the race you created!
49 What mortal can live and not see death?
   Who can escape the power of Sheol?   *Selah*

22   'No enemy will be able to outwit him,
     no wicked man overcome him;
23   I shall crush his enemies before him,
     strike his opponents dead.
24   'My constancy and faithful love will be with
        him,
     in my name his strength will be triumphant.
25   I shall establish his power over the sea,
     his dominion over the rivers.
26   'He will cry to me, "You are my father,
     my God, the rock of my salvation!"
27   So I shall make him my first-born,
     the highest of earthly kings.
28   'I shall maintain my faithful love for him
        always,
     my covenant with him will stay firm.
29   I have established his dynasty for ever,
     his throne to be as lasting as the heavens.
30   'Should his descendants desert my law,
     and not keep to my rulings,
31   should they violate my statutes,
     and not observe my commandments,
32   'then I shall punish their offences with the rod,
     their guilt with the whip,
33   but I shall never withdraw from him my faithful
        love,
     I shall not belie my constancy.
34   'I shall not violate my covenant,
     I shall not withdraw the word once spoken.
35   I have sworn by my holiness, once and for all,
     never will I break faith with David.
36   'His dynasty shall endure for ever,
     his throne like the sun before me,
37   as the moon is established for ever,
     a faithful witness in the skies.'   *Pause*

38   Yet you yourself — you have spurned and
        rejected,
     and have vented your wrath on your anointed,
39   you have repudiated the covenant with your
        servant,
     dishonoured his crown in the dust.
40   You have pierced all his defences,
     and laid his strongholds in ruins,
41   everyone passing by plunders him,
     he has become the butt of his neighbours.
42   You have raised high the right hand of his
        opponents,
     have made all his enemies happy;
43   you have snapped off his sword on a rock,
     and failed to support him in battle.
44   You have stripped him of his splendid sceptre,
     and toppled his throne to the ground.
45   You have aged him before his time,
     enveloped him in shame.   *Pause*

46 How long, Yahweh, will you remain hidden? For
     ever?
   Is your anger to go on smouldering like a fire?
47 Remember me; how long have I left?
   For what pointless end did you create all the
     children of Adam?
48 Who can live and never see death?
   Who can save himself from the clutches of Sheol?
          Pause

NEW REVISED STANDARD VERSION	REVISED ENGLISH BIBLE

NEW REVISED STANDARD VERSION

49 Lord, where is your steadfast love of old,
   which by your faithfulness you swore to
   David?
50 Remember, O Lord, how your servant is taunted;
   how I bear in my bosom the insults of the
   peoples,^c
51 with which your enemies taunt, O LORD,
   with which they taunted the footsteps of your
   anointed.

52 Blessed be the LORD forever.
   Amen and Amen.

BOOK IV

Psalms 90–106

Psalm 90

A Prayer of Moses, the man of God.

1 Lord, you have been our dwelling place^d
   in all generations.
2 Before the mountains were brought forth,
   or ever you had formed the earth and the
   world,
   from everlasting to everlasting you are God.

3 You turn us^e back to dust,
   and say, "Turn back, you mortals."
4 For a thousand years in your sight
   are like yesterday when it is past,
   or like a watch in the night.

5 You sweep them away; they are like a dream,
   like grass that is renewed in the morning;
6 in the morning it flourishes and is renewed;
   in the evening it fades and withers.

7 For we are consumed by your anger;
   by your wrath we are overwhelmed.
8 You have set our iniquities before you,
   our secret sins in the light of your countenance.

9 For all our days pass away under your wrath;
   our years come to an end^f like a sigh.
10 The days of our life are seventy years,
   or perhaps eighty, if we are strong;
   even then their span^g is only toil and trouble;
   they are soon gone, and we fly away.

11 Who considers the power of your anger?
   Your wrath is as great as the fear that is due
   you.
12 So teach us to count our days
   that we may gain a wise heart.

13 Turn, O LORD! How long?
   Have compassion on your servants!
14 Satisfy us in the morning with your steadfast
   love,
   so that we may rejoice and be glad all our
   days.
15 Make us glad as many days as you have afflicted
   us,
   and as many years as we have seen evil.
16 Let your work be manifest to your servants,
   and your glorious power to their children.

REVISED ENGLISH BIBLE

49 Where are your former loving deeds, Lord,
   which you promised faithfully to David?
50 Remember, Lord, the taunts hurled at your servant,
   how I have borne in my heart the calumnies of the
   nations;
51 for your enemies have taunted us, LORD,
   taunted your anointed king at every step.

52 Blessed be the LORD for ever.
   Amen and Amen.

BOOK 4

Psalm 90

A prayer: ascribed to Moses, the man of God

1 LORD, you have been our refuge
   throughout all generations.
2 Before the mountains were brought forth
   or the earth and the world were born,
   from age to age you are God.

3 You turn mortals back to dust,
   saying, 'Turn back, you children of mortals,'
4 for in your sight a thousand years
   are as the passing of one day
   or as a watch in the night.
5 You cut them off;
   they are asleep in death.
   They are like grass which shoots up;
6 though in the morning it flourishes and shoots up,
   by evening it droops and withers.

7 We are brought to an end by your anger,
   terrified by your wrath.
8 You set out our iniquities before you,
   our secret sins in the light of your presence.
9 All our days pass under your wrath;
   our years die away like a murmur.
10 Seventy years is the span of our life,
   eighty if our strength holds;
   at their best they are but toil and sorrow,
   for they pass quickly and we vanish.
11 Who feels the power of your anger,
   who feels your wrath like those who fear you?
12 So make us know how few are our days,
   that our minds may learn wisdom.

13 LORD, how long?
   Turn and show compassion to your servants.
14 Satisfy us at daybreak with your love,
   that we may sing for joy and be glad all our days.
15 Grant us days of gladness for the days you have
   humbled us,
   for the years when we have known misfortune.
16 May your saving acts appear to your servants,
   and your glory to their children.

---

^cCn: Heb *bosom all of many peoples*   ^dAnother reading is *our refuge*   ^eHeb *humankind*   ^fSyr: Heb *we bring our years to an end*   ^gCn Compare Gk Syr Jerome Tg: Heb *pride*

89:50 **the calumnies . . . nations:** *prob. rdg; Heb.* all of many peoples.   90:1 **refuge:** *so some MSS; others* dwelling-place.

NEW AMERICAN BIBLE

50 Where are your promises of old, Lord,
    the loyalty sworn to David?
51 Remember, Lord, the insults to your servants,
    how I bear all the slanders of the nations.
52 Your enemies, LORD, insult your anointed;
    they insult my every endeavor.

* * *

53 Blessed be the LORD forever! Amen and amen!

FOURTH BOOK

Psalms 90–106

Psalm 90

1 *A prayer of Moses, the man of God.*

I
Lord, you have been our refuge
    through all generations.
2 Before the mountains were born,
    the earth and the world brought forth,
    from eternity to eternity you are God.
4 A thousand years in your eyes
    are merely a yesterday;
3 But humans you return to dust,
    saying, "Return, you mortals!"
4c Before a watch passes in the night,
5   you have brought them to their end;
They disappear like sleep at dawn;
    they are like grass that dies.
6 It sprouts green in the morning;
    by evening it is dry and withered.
II
7 Truly we are consumed by your anger,
    filled with terror by your wrath.
8 You have kept our faults before you,
    our hidden sins exposed to your sight.
9 Our life ebbs away under your wrath;
    our years end like a sigh.
10 Seventy is the sum of our years,
    or eighty, if we are strong;
Most of them are sorrow and toil;
    they pass quickly, we are all but gone.
11 Who comprehends your terrible anger?
    Your wrath matches the fear it inspires.
12 Teach us to count our days aright,
    that we may gain wisdom of heart.
13 Relent, O LORD! How long?
    Have pity on your servants!
14 Fill us at daybreak with your love,
    that all our days we may sing for joy.
15 Make us glad as many days as you humbled us,
    for as many years as we have seen trouble.
16 Show your deeds to your servants,
    your glory to their children.

NEW JERUSALEM BIBLE

49 Lord, what of those pledges of your faithful love?
    You made an oath to David by your constancy.
50 Do not forget the insults to your servant;
    I take to heart the taunts of the nations,
51 which your enemies have levelled, Yahweh,
    have levelled at the footsteps of your anointed!

52   Blessed be Yahweh for ever.
    Amen, Amen.

Psalm 90 (V 89)

Prayer   Of Moses, man of God

1 Lord, you have been our refuge
    from age to age.
2 Before the mountains were born,
    before the earth and the world came to birth,
    from eternity to eternity you are God.
3 You bring human beings to the dust,
    by saying, 'Return, children of Adam.'
4 A thousand years are to you
    like a yesterday which has passed,
    like a watch of the night.
5 You flood them with sleep
    —in the morning they will be like growing grass:
6 in the morning it is blossoming and growing,
    by evening it is withered and dry.
7 For we have been destroyed by your wrath,
    dismayed by your anger.
8 You have taken note of our guilty deeds,
    our secrets in the full light of your presence.
9 All our days pass under your wrath,
    our lives are over like a sigh.
10 The span of our life is seventy years—
    eighty for those who are strong—
    but their whole extent is anxiety and trouble,
    they are over in a moment and we are gone.
11 Who feels the power of your anger,
    or who that fears you, your wrath?
12 Teach us to count up the days that are ours,
    and we shall come to the heart of wisdom.
13 Come back, Yahweh! How long must we wait?
    Take pity on your servants.
14 Each morning fill us with your faithful love,
    we shall sing and be happy all our days;
15 let our joy be as long as the time that you afflicted
    us,
    the years when we experienced disaster.
16 Show your servants the deeds you do,
    let their children enjoy your splendour!

90, 4: The translation reverses the order of the difficult Hebrew
verses 3 and 4 to get the probable original order.

17 Let the favor of the Lord our God be upon us,
    and prosper for us the work of our hands—
    O prosper the work of our hands!

Psalm 91

1 You who live in the shelter of the Most High,
    who abide in the shadow of the Almighty,[h]
2 will say to the LORD, "My refuge and my fortress;
    my God, in whom I trust."
3 For he will deliver you from the snare of the
        fowler
    and from the deadly pestilence;
4 he will cover you with his pinions,
    and under his wings you will find refuge;
    his faithfulness is a shield and buckler.
5 You will not fear the terror of the night,
    or the arrow that flies by day,
6 or the pestilence that stalks in darkness,
    or the destruction that wastes at noonday.

7 A thousand may fall at your side,
    ten thousand at your right hand,
    but it will not come near you.
8 You will only look with your eyes
    and see the punishment of the wicked.

9 Because you have made the LORD your refuge,[i]
    the Most High your dwelling place,
10 no evil shall befall you,
    no scourge come near your tent.
11 For he will command his angels concerning you
    to guard you in all your ways.
12 On their hands they will bear you up,
    so that you will not dash your foot against a
        stone.
13 You will tread on the lion and the adder,
    the young lion and the serpent you will trample
        under foot.

14 Those who love me, I will deliver;
    I will protect those who know my name.
15 When they call to me, I will answer them;
    I will be with them in trouble,
    I will rescue them and honor them.
16 With long life I will satisfy them,
    and show them my salvation.

Psalm 92

A Psalm. A Song for the Sabbath Day.

1 It is good to give thanks to the LORD,
    to sing praises to your name, O Most High;
2 to declare your steadfast love in the morning,
    and your faithfulness by night,
3 to the music of the lute and the harp,
    to the melody of the lyre.
4 For you, O LORD, have made me glad by your
        work;
    at the works of your hands I sing for joy.
5 How great are your works, O LORD!
    Your thoughts are very deep!
6 The dullard cannot know,
    the stupid cannot understand this:
7 though the wicked sprout like grass
    and all evildoers flourish,
    they are doomed to destruction forever,

17 May the favour of the Lord our God be on us.
    Establish for us all that we do,
    establish it firmly.

Psalm 91

1 HE who lives in the shelter of the Most High,
    who lodges under the shadow of the Almighty,
2 says of the LORD, 'He is my refuge and fortress,
    my God in whom I put my trust.'

3 He will rescue you
    from the fowler's snare and from deadly pestilence.
4 He will cover you with his wings;
    you will find refuge beneath his pinions.
    His truth will be a shield and buckler.
5 You will not fear the terrors abroad at night
    or the arrow that flies by day,
6 the pestilence that stalks in darkness
    or the plague raging at noonday.
7 A thousand may fall at your side,
    ten thousand close at hand,
    but you it will not touch.
8 With your own eyes you will observe this;
    you will see the retribution on the wicked.
9 Surely you are my refuge, LORD.

    You have made the Most High your
        dwelling-place;
10 no disaster will befall you,
    no calamity touch your home.
11 For he will charge his angels
    to guard you wherever you go,
12 to lift you on their hands
    for fear you strike your foot against a stone.
13 You will tread on asp and cobra,
    you will trample on snake and serpent.

14 Because his love holds fast to me, I shall deliver
        him;
    I shall lift him to safety, for he knows my name.
15 When he calls to me, I shall answer;
    I shall be with him in time of trouble;
    I shall rescue him and bring him to honour.
16 I shall satisfy him with long life
    and show him my salvation.

Psalm 92

A psalm: a song: for the sabbath day

1 IT is good to give thanks to the LORD,
    to sing psalms to your name, Most High,
2 to declare your love in the morning
    and your faithfulness every night
3 to the music of a ten-stringed harp,
    to the sounding chords of the lyre.
4 Your acts, LORD, fill me with exultation;
    I shout in triumph at your mighty deeds.
5 How great are your deeds, LORD,
    how very deep are your thoughts!

6 Anyone who does not grasp this is a stupid person,
    and a fool does not understand it:
7 that though the wicked grow like grass
    and every evildoer prospers,
    they will be finally destroyed,

---

[h] Traditional rendering of Heb *Shaddai* [i] Cn: Heb *Because you,*
LORD, *are my refuge; you have made*

17 May the favor of the Lord our God be ours.
   Prosper the work of our hands!
   Prosper the work of our hands!

Psalm 91

I

1 You who dwell in the shelter of the Most High,
   who abide in the shadow of the Almighty,
2 Say to the LORD, "My refuge and fortress,
   my God in whom I trust."
3 God will rescue you from the fowler's snare,
   from the destroying plague,
4 Will shelter you with pinions,
   spread wings that you may take refuge;
   God's faithfulness is a protecting shield.
5 You shall not fear the terror of the night
   nor the arrow that flies by day,
6 Nor the pestilence that roams in darkness,
   nor the plague that ravages at noon.
7 Though a thousand fall at your side,
   ten thousand at your right hand,
   near you it shall not come.
8 You need simply watch;
   the punishment of the wicked you will see.
9 You have the LORD for your refuge;
   you have made the Most High your stronghold.
10 No evil shall befall you,
   no affliction come near your tent.
11 For God commands the angels
   to guard you in all your ways.
12 With their hands they shall support you,
   lest you strike your foot against a stone.
13 You shall tread upon the asp and the viper,
   trample the lion and the dragon.

II

14 Whoever clings to me I will deliver;
   whoever knows my name I will set on high.
15 All who call upon me I will answer;
   I will be with them in distress;
   I will deliver them and give them honor.
16 With length of days I will satisfy them
   and show them my saving power.

Psalm 92

1 A psalm. A sabbath song.

I

2 It is good to give thanks to the LORD,
   to sing praise to your name, Most High,
3 To proclaim your love in the morning,
   your faithfulness in the night,
4 With the ten-stringed harp,
   with melody upon the lyre.
5 For you make me jubilant, LORD, by your deeds;
   at the works of your hands I shout for joy.

II

6 How great are your works, LORD!
   How profound your purpose!
7 A senseless person cannot know this;
   a fool cannot comprehend.
8 Though the wicked flourish like grass
   and all sinners thrive,
   They are destined for eternal destruction;

17 May the sweetness of the Lord be upon us,
   to confirm the work we have done!

Psalm 91 (V 90)

1 You who live in the secret place of Elyon,
   spend your nights in the shelter of Shaddai,
2 saying to Yahweh, 'My refuge, my fortress,
   my God in whom I trust!'
3 He rescues you from the snare
   of the fowler set on destruction;
4 he covers you with his pinions,
   you find shelter under his wings.
   His constancy is shield and protection.
5 You need not fear the terrors of night,
   the arrow that flies in the daytime,
6 the plague that stalks in the darkness,
   the scourge that wreaks havoc at high noon.
7 Though a thousand fall at your side,
   ten thousand at your right hand,
   you yourself will remain unscathed.
8 You have only to keep your eyes open
   to see how the wicked are repaid,
9 you who say, 'Yahweh my refuge!'
   and make Elyon your fortress.
10 No disaster can overtake you,
   no plague come near your tent;
11 he has given his angels orders about you
   to guard you wherever you go.
12 They will carry you in their arms
   in case you trip over a stone.
13 You will walk upon wild beast and adder,
   you will trample young lions and snakes.
14 'Since he clings to me I rescue him,
   I raise him high, since he acknowledges my name.
15 He calls to me and I answer him:
   in distress I am at his side,
   I rescue him and bring him honour.
16 I shall satisfy him with long life,
   and grant him to see my salvation.'

Psalm 92 (V 91)

Psalm   Song   For the Sabbath

1 It is good to give thanks to Yahweh,
   to make music for your name, Most High,
2 to proclaim your faithful love at daybreak,
   and your constancy all through the night,
3 on the lyre, the ten-stringed lyre,
   to the murmur of the harp.
4 You have brought me joy, Yahweh, by your deeds,
   at the work of your hands I cry out.
5 'How great are your works, Yahweh,
   immensely deep your thoughts!'
6 Stupid people cannot realise this,
   fools do not grasp it.
7 The wicked may sprout like weeds,
   and every evil-doer flourish,
   but only to be eternally destroyed;

NEW REVISED STANDARD VERSION	REVISED ENGLISH BIBLE

8 but you, O LORD, are on high forever.
9 For your enemies, O LORD,
for your enemies shall perish;
all evildoers shall be scattered.

10 But you have exalted my horn like that of the
wild ox;
you have poured over me*j* fresh oil.
11 My eyes have seen the downfall of my enemies;
my ears have heard the doom of my evil
assailants.

12 The righteous flourish like the palm tree,
and grow like a cedar in Lebanon.
13 They are planted in the house of the LORD;
they flourish in the courts of our God.
14 In old age they still produce fruit;
they are always green and full of sap,
15 showing that the LORD is upright;
he is my rock, and there is no unrighteousness
in him.

8 while you, LORD, reign for ever.
9 Your enemies, LORD, your enemies will perish;
all evildoers will be scattered.

10 You have raised my head high
like the horns of a wild ox;
I am anointed richly with oil.
11 I look on my enemies' ruin,
I hear the downfall of my wicked foes.
12 The righteous flourish like a palm tree,
they grow tall as a cedar on Lebanon;
13 planted in the house of the LORD,
and flourishing in the courts of our God,
14 they still bear fruit in old age;
they are luxuriant, wide-spreading trees.
15 They declare that the Lord is just:
my rock, in him there is no unrighteousness.

Psalm 93

1 The LORD is king, he is robed in majesty;
the LORD is robed, he is girded with strength.
He has established the world; it shall never be
moved;
2 your throne is established from of old;
you are from everlasting.

3 The floods have lifted up, O LORD,
the floods have lifted up their voice;
the floods lift up their roaring.
4 More majestic than the thunders of mighty
waters,
more majestic than the waves*k* of the sea,
majestic on high is the LORD!

5 Your decrees are very sure;
holiness befits your house,
O LORD, forevermore.

Psalm 93

1 THE LORD has become King, clothed with majesty;
the LORD is robed, girded with might.

The earth is established immovably;
2 your throne is established from of old;
from all eternity you are God.
3 LORD, the great deep lifts up,
the deep lifts up its voice;
the deep lifts up its crashing waves.
4 Mightier than the sound of great waters,
mightier than the breakers of the sea,
mighty on high is the LORD.

5 Your decrees stand firm,
and holiness befits your house,
LORD, throughout the ages.

Psalm 94

1 O LORD, you God of vengeance,
you God of vengeance, shine forth!
2 Rise up, O judge of the earth;
give to the proud what they deserve!
3 O LORD, how long shall the wicked,
how long shall the wicked exult?

4 They pour out their arrogant words;
all the evildoers boast.
5 They crush your people, O LORD,
and afflict your heritage.
6 They kill the widow and the stranger,
they murder the orphan,
7 and they say, "The LORD does not see;
the God of Jacob does not perceive."

8 Understand, O dullest of the people;
fools, when will you be wise?
9 He who planted the ear, does he not hear?
He who formed the eye, does he not see?
10 He who disciplines the nations,
he who teaches knowledge to humankind,
does he not chastise?

Psalm 94

1 GOD of vengeance, LORD,
God of vengeance, show yourself!
2 Rise, judge of the earth;
repay the arrogant as they deserve.
3 LORD, how long will the wicked,
how long will the wicked exult?
4 Evildoers are all full of bluster,
boasting and bragging.
5 They crush your people, LORD,
and oppress your chosen nation;
6 they murder the widow and the stranger
and put the fatherless to death.
7 They say, 'The LORD does not see,
the God of Jacob pays no heed.'

8 Take heed yourselves, most stupid of people;
you fools, when will you be wise?
9 Can he who implanted the ear not hear,
he who fashioned the eye not see?
10 Will he who instructs the nations not correct them?
The teacher of mankind, has he no knowledge?

---

j Syr: Meaning of Heb uncertain   *k* Cn: Heb *majestic are the waves*   93:2 **God:** *so Aram. (Targ.); Heb. omits.*

NEW AMERICAN BIBLE

NEW JERUSALEM BIBLE

9 for you, LORD, are forever on high.
10 Indeed your enemies, LORD,
    indeed your enemies shall perish;
    all sinners shall be scattered.

III

11 You have given me the strength of a wild bull;
    you have poured rich oil upon me.
12 My eyes look with glee on my wicked enemies;
    my ears delight in the fall of my foes.
13 The just shall flourish like the palm tree,
    shall grow like a cedar of Lebanon.
14 Planted in the house of the LORD,
    they shall flourish in the courts of our God.
15 They shall bear fruit even in old age,
    always vigorous and sturdy,
16 As they proclaim: "The LORD is just;
    our rock, in whom there is no wrong."

8 whereas you are supreme for ever, Yahweh.

9 Look how your enemies perish,
    how all evil-doers are scattered!
10 You give me the strength of the wild ox,
    you anoint me with fresh oil;
11 I caught sight of the ambush against me,
    overheard the plans of the wicked.
12 The upright will flourish like the palm tree,
    will grow like a cedar of Lebanon.
13 Planted in the house of Yahweh,
    they will flourish in the courts of our God.
14 In old age they will still bear fruit,
    will remain fresh and green,
15 to proclaim Yahweh's integrity;
    my rock, in whom no fault can be found.

Psalm 93

1 The LORD is king, robed with majesty;
    the LORD is robed, girded with might.
  The world will surely stand in place,
    never to be moved.
2 Your throne stands firm from of old;
    you are from everlasting, LORD.
3 The flood has raised up, LORD;
    the flood has raised up its roar;
    the flood has raised its pounding waves.
4 More powerful than the roar of many waters,
    more powerful than the breakers of the sea,
    powerful in the heavens is the LORD.
5 Your decrees are firmly established;
    holiness belongs to your house, LORD,
    for all the length of days.

Psalm 93 (V 92)

1 Yahweh is king, robed in majesty,
    robed is Yahweh and girded with power.

2 The world is indeed set firm, it can never be
        shaken;
    your throne is set firm from of old,
    from all eternity you exist.

3 The rivers lift up, Yahweh,
    the rivers lift up their voices,
    the rivers lift up their thunder.

4 Greater than the voice of many waters,
    more majestic than the breakers of the sea,
    Yahweh is majestic in the heights.

5 Your decrees stand firm, unshakeable,
    holiness is the beauty of your house,
    Yahweh, for all time to come.

Psalm 94

I

1 LORD, avenging God,
    avenging God, shine forth!
2 Rise up, judge of the earth;
    give the proud what they deserve.

II

3 How long, LORD, shall the wicked,
    how long shall the wicked glory?
4 How long will they mouth haughty speeches,
    go on boasting, all these evildoers?
5 They crush your people, LORD,
    torment your very own.
6 They kill the widow and alien;
    the fatherless they murder.
7 They say, "The LORD does not see;
    the God of Jacob takes no notice."

III

8 Understand, you stupid people!
    You fools, when will you be wise?
9 Does the one who shaped the ear not hear?
    The one who formed the eye not see?
10 Does the one who guides nations not rebuke?
    The one who teaches humans not have
        knowledge?

Psalm 94 (V 93)

1 God of vengeance, Yahweh,
    God of vengeance, shine forth!
2 Arise, judge of the world,
    give back the proud what they deserve!

3 How long are the wicked, Yahweh,
    how long are the wicked to triumph?
4 They bluster and boast,
    they flaunt themselves, all the evil-doers.

5 They crush your people, Yahweh,
    they oppress your heritage,
6 they murder the widow and the stranger,
    bring the orphan to a violent death.

7 They say, 'Yahweh is not looking,
    the God of Jacob is taking no notice.'
8 Take notice yourselves, you coarsest of people!
    Fools, when will you learn some sense?
9 Shall he who implanted the ear not hear,
    he who fashioned the eye not see?
10 Shall he who instructs nations not punish?
    Yahweh, the teacher of all people,

NEW REVISED STANDARD VERSION	REVISED ENGLISH BIBLE

NEW REVISED STANDARD VERSION

11 The Lord knows our thoughts,*
   that they are but an empty breath.

12 Happy are those whom you discipline, O Lord,
   and whom you teach out of your law,
13 giving them respite from days of trouble,
   until a pit is dug for the wicked.
14 For the Lord will not forsake his people;
   he will not abandon his heritage;
15 for justice will return to the righteous,
   and all the upright in heart will follow it.

16 Who rises up for me against the wicked?
   Who stands up for me against evildoers?
17 If the Lord had not been my help,
   my soul would soon have lived in the land of
   silence.
18 When I thought, "My foot is slipping,"
   your steadfast love, O Lord, held me up.
19 When the cares of my heart are many,
   your consolations cheer my soul.
20 Can wicked rulers be allied with you,
   those who contrive mischief by statute?
21 They band together against the life of the
   righteous,
   and condemn the innocent to death.
22 But the Lord has become my stronghold,
   and my God the rock of my refuge.
23 He will repay them for their iniquity
   and wipe them out for their wickedness;
   the Lord our God will wipe them out.

Psalm 95

1 O come, let us sing to the Lord;
   let us make a joyful noise to the rock of our
   salvation!
2 Let us come into his presence with thanksgiving;
   let us make a joyful noise to him with songs of
   praise!
3 For the Lord is a great God,
   and a great King above all gods.
4 In his hand are the depths of the earth;
   the heights of the mountains are his also.
5 The sea is his, for he made it,
   and the dry land, which his hands have
   formed.

6 O come, let us worship and bow down,
   let us kneel before the Lord, our Maker!
7 For he is our God,
   and we are the people of his pasture,
   and the sheep of his hand.

O that today you would listen to his voice!
8   Do not harden your hearts, as at Meribah,
   as on the day at Massah in the wilderness,
9 when your ancestors tested me,
   and put me to the proof, though they had seen
   my work.
10 For forty years I loathed that generation
   and said, "They are a people whose hearts go
   astray,
   and they do not regard my ways."
11 Therefore in my anger I swore,
   "They shall not enter my rest."

REVISED ENGLISH BIBLE

11 The Lord knows that the thoughts of everyone
   are but a puff of wind.

12 Happy the one whom you, Lord, instruct
   and teach from your law,
13 giving him respite from misfortune
   until a pit is dug for the wicked.
14 The Lord will not abandon his people
   or forsake his chosen nation;
15 for justice will again be joined to right,
   and all who are upright in heart will follow it.

16 Who is on my side against the wicked?
   Who will stand up for me against the evildoers?
17 Had the Lord not been my helper,
   I should soon have dwelt in the silent grave.
18 If I said that my foot was slipping,
   your love, Lord, continued to hold me up.
19 When anxious thoughts filled my heart,
   your comfort brought me joy.
20 Will corrupt justice win you as an ally,
   contriving mischief under cover of law?
21 They conspire to take the life of the righteous
   and condemn the innocent to death.
22 But the Lord has been my strong tower,
   and my God is my rock and refuge.
23 He will repay the wicked for their injustice;
   the Lord our God will destroy them for their
   misdeeds.

Psalm 95

1 Come! Let us raise a joyful song to the Lord,
   a shout of triumph to the rock of our salvation.
2 Let us come into his presence with thanksgiving
   and sing psalms of triumph to him.

3 For the Lord is a great God,
   a great King above all gods.
4 The depths of the earth are in his hands,
   and the peaks of the mountains belong to him;
5 the sea is his, for he made it,
   and the dry land which his hands fashioned.

6 Enter in! Let us bow down in worship,
   let us kneel before the Lord who made us,
7 for he is our God,
   we the people he shepherds, the flock in his care.

If only you would listen to him now!
8 Do not be stubborn, as you were at Meribah,
   as on that day at Massah in the wilderness,
9 when your forefathers made trial of me,
   tested me, though they had seen what I did.
10 For forty years I abhorred that generation
   and said: 'They are a people whose hearts are
   astray,
   who do not discern my ways.'
11 Therefore I vowed in my anger:
   'They shall never enter my rest.'

---

*Heb the thoughts of humankind

95:8 **Meribah:** *that is* Dispute. **Massah:** *that is* Trial.

NEW AMERICAN BIBLE

11 The LORD does know human plans;
   they are only puffs of air.

IV

12 Happy those whom you guide, LORD,
   whom you teach by your instruction.
13 You give them rest from evil days,
   while a pit is being dug for the wicked.
14 You, LORD, will not forsake your people,
   nor abandon your very own.
15 Judgment shall again be just,
   and all the upright of heart will follow it.

V

16 Who will rise up for me against the wicked?
   Who will stand up for me against evildoers?
17 If the LORD were not my help,
   I would long have been silent in the grave.
18 When I say, "My foot is slipping,"
   your love, LORD, holds me up.
19 When cares increase within me,
   your comfort gives me joy.

VI

20 Can unjust judges be your allies,
   those who create burdens in the name of law,
21 Those who conspire against the just
   and condemn the innocent to death?
22 No, the LORD is my secure height,
   my God, the rock where I find refuge,
23 Who will turn back their evil upon them
   and destroy them for their wickedness.
   Surely the LORD our God will destroy them!

Psalm 95

I

1 Come, let us sing joyfully to the LORD;
   cry out to the rock of our salvation.
2 Let us greet him with a song of praise,
   joyfully sing out our psalms.
3 For the LORD is the great God,
   the great king over all gods.
4 Whose hand holds the depths of the earth;
   who owns the tops of the mountains.
5 The sea and dry land belong to God,
   who made them, formed them by hand.

II

6 Enter, let us bow down in worship;
   let us kneel before the LORD who made us.
7 For this is our God,
   whose people we are,
   God's well-tended flock.

III

Oh, that today you would hear his voice:
8   Do not harden your hearts as at Meribah,
   as on the day of Massah in the desert.
9 There your ancestors tested me;
   they tried me though they had seen my works.
10 Forty years I loathed that generation;
   I said: "This people's heart goes astray;
   they do not know my ways."
11 Therefore I swore in my anger:
   "They shall never enter my rest."

NEW JERUSALEM BIBLE

11 knows human plans and how insipid they are.

12 How blessed are those you instruct, Yahweh,
   whom you teach by means of your law,
13 to give them respite in evil times,
   till a pit is dug for the wicked.

14 Yahweh will not abandon his people,
   he will not desert his heritage;
15 for judgement will again become saving justice,
   and in its wake all upright hearts will follow.

16 Who rises up on my side against the wicked?
   Who stands firm on my side against all evil-doers?
17 If Yahweh did not come to my help,
   I should soon find myself dwelling in the silence.

18 I need only say, 'I am slipping,'
   for your faithful love, Yahweh, to support me;
19 however great the anxiety of my heart,
   your consolations soothe me.

20 Are you partner to a destructive court,
   that gives disorder the status of law?
21 They make an attack on the life of the upright,
   and condemn innocent blood.

22 No! Yahweh is a stronghold to me,
   my God is my rock of refuge.
23 He turns back their guilt on themselves,
   annihilates them for their wickedness,
   he annihilates them, Yahweh our God.

Psalm 95 (V 94)

1 Come, let us cry out with joy to Yahweh,
   acclaim the rock of our salvation.
2 Let us come into his presence with thanksgiving,
   acclaim him with music.

3 For Yahweh is a great God,
   a king greater than all the gods.
4 In his power are the depths of the earth,
   the peaks of the mountains are his;
5 the sea belongs to him, for he made it,
   and the dry land, moulded by his hands.

6 Come, let us bow low and do reverence;
   kneel before Yahweh who made us!
7 For he is our God,
   and we the people of his sheepfold,
   the flock of his hand.

If only you would listen to him today!
8 Do not harden your hearts as at Meribah,
   as at the time of Massah in the desert, ᵖ
9 when your ancestors challenged me,
   put me to the test, and saw what I could do!

10 For forty years that generation sickened me,
   and I said, 'Always fickle hearts;
   they cannot grasp my ways.'
11 Then in my anger I swore
   they would never enter my place of rest.

ᵖ 95 Incidents during the desert journey: *Meribah* = dispute, *Massah* = temptation.

NEW REVISED STANDARD VERSION

REVISED ENGLISH BIBLE

Psalm 96

1 O sing to the LORD a new song;
   sing to the LORD, all the earth.
2 Sing to the LORD, bless his name;
   tell of his salvation from day to day.
3 Declare his glory among the nations,
   his marvelous works among all the peoples.
4 For great is the LORD, and greatly to be praised;
   he is to be revered above all gods.
5 For all the gods of the peoples are idols,
   but the LORD made the heavens.
6 Honor and majesty are before him;
   strength and beauty are in his sanctuary.

7 Ascribe to the LORD, O families of the peoples,
   ascribe to the LORD glory and strength.
8 Ascribe to the LORD the glory due his name;
   bring an offering, and come into his courts.
9 Worship the LORD in holy splendor;
   tremble before him, all the earth.

10 Say among the nations, "The LORD is king!
    The world is firmly established; it shall never
      be moved.
    He will judge the peoples with equity."
11 Let the heavens be glad, and let the earth rejoice;
    let the sea roar, and all that fills it;
12 let the field exult, and everything in it.
    Then shall all the trees of the forest sing for joy
13   before the LORD; for he is coming,
    for he is coming to judge the earth.
    He will judge the world with righteousness,
    and the peoples with his truth.

Psalm 96

1 SING a new song to the LORD.
   Sing to the LORD, all the earth.
2 Sing to the LORD and bless his name;
   day by day proclaim his victory.
3 Declare his glory among the nations,
   his marvellous deeds to every people.
4 Great is the LORD and most worthy of praise;
   he is more to be feared than all gods.
5 For the gods of the nations are idols every one;
   but the LORD made the heavens.
6 Majesty and splendour attend him,
   might and beauty are in his sanctuary.

7 Ascribe to the LORD, you families of nations,
   ascribe to the LORD glory and might;
8 ascribe to the LORD the glory due to his name.
   Bring an offering and enter his courts;
9 in holy attire worship the LORD;
   tremble before him, all the earth.

10 Declare among the nations, 'The LORD is King;
    the world is established immovably;
    he will judge the peoples with equity.'
11 Let the heavens rejoice and the earth be glad,
    let the sea resound and everything in it,
12 let the fields exult and all that is in them;
    let all the trees of the forest shout for joy
13 before the LORD when he comes,
    when he comes to judge the earth.
    He will judge the world with justice
    and peoples by his faithfulness.

Psalm 97

1 The LORD is king! Let the earth rejoice;
   let the many coastlands be glad!
2 Clouds and thick darkness are all around him;
   righteousness and justice are the foundation of
     his throne.
3 Fire goes before him,
   and consumes his adversaries on every side.
4 His lightnings light up the world;
   the earth sees and trembles.
5 The mountains melt like wax before the LORD,
   before the Lord of all the earth.
6 The heavens proclaim his righteousness;
   and all the peoples behold his glory.
7 All worshipers of images are put to shame,
   those who make their boast in worthless idols;
   all gods bow down before him.
8 Zion hears and is glad,
   and the towns[m] of Judah rejoice,
   because of your judgments, O God.
9 For you, O LORD, are most high over all the
     earth;
   you are exalted far above all gods.

10 The LORD loves those who hate[n] evil;
    he guards the lives of his faithful;
    he rescues them from the hand of the wicked.
11 Light dawns[o] for the righteous,
    and joy for the upright in heart.

Psalm 97

1 THE LORD has become King; let the earth be glad,
   let coasts and islands all rejoice.
2 Cloud and thick mist enfold him,
   righteousness and justice
   are the foundation of his throne.
3 Fire goes ahead of him
   and consumes his enemies all around.
4 His lightning-flashes light up the world;
   the earth sees and trembles.
5 Mountains melt like wax at the LORD's approach,
   the Lord of all the earth.
6 The heavens proclaim his righteousness,
   and all peoples see his glory.
7 May those who worship images, those who vaunt
     their idols,
   may they all be put to shame.
   Bow down, all you gods, before him!

8 Zion heard and rejoiced, LORD;
   Judah's cities were glad at your judgements.
9 For you, LORD, are Most High over all the earth,
   far exalted above all gods.

10 The LORD loves those who hate evil;
    he keeps his loyal servants safe
    and rescues them from the power of the wicked.
11 A harvest of light has arisen for the righteous,
    and joy for the upright in heart.

---

[m] Heb *daughters*   [n] Cn: Heb *You who love the LORD hate*
[o] Gk Syr Jerome: Heb *is sown*

97:10 **The LORD loves:** *prob. rdg; Heb.* Lovers of the LORD.
97:11 **has arisen:** *so Gk; Heb.* is sown.

NEW AMERICAN BIBLE

Psalm 96

I

1 Sing to the LORD a new song;
  sing to the LORD, all the earth.
2 Sing to the LORD, bless his name;
  announce his salvation day after day.
3 Tell God's glory among the nations;
  among all peoples, God's marvelous deeds.

II

4 For great is the LORD and highly to be praised,
  to be feared above all gods.
5 For the gods of the nations all do nothing,
  but the LORD made the heavens.
6 Splendor and power go before him;
  power and grandeur are in his holy place.

III

7 Give to the LORD, you families of nations,
  give to the LORD glory and might;
8 give to the LORD the glory due his name!
Bring gifts and enter his courts;
9 bow down to the LORD, splendid in holiness.
Tremble before God, all the earth;
10 say among the nations: The LORD is king.
The world will surely stand fast, never to be
    moved.
God rules the peoples with fairness.

IV

11 Let the heavens be glad and the earth rejoice;
  let the sea and what fills it resound;
12 let the plains be joyful and all that is in them.
Then let all the trees of the forest rejoice
13 before the LORD who comes,
  who comes to govern the earth,
To govern the world with justice
  and the peoples with faithfulness.

Psalm 97

I

1 The LORD is king; let the earth rejoice;
  let the many islands be glad.
2 Cloud and darkness surround the Lord;
  justice and right are the foundation of his throne.
3 Fire goes before him;
  everywhere it consumes the foes.
4 Lightning illumines the world;
  the earth sees and trembles.
5 The mountains melt like wax before the LORD,
  before the Lord of all the earth.
6 The heavens proclaim God's justice;
  all peoples see his glory.

II

7 All who serve idols are put to shame,
  who glory in worthless things;
  all gods bow down before you.
8 Zion hears and is glad,
  and the cities of Judah rejoice
  because of your judgments, O LORD.
9 You, LORD, are the Most High over all the earth,
  exalted far above all gods.
10 The LORD loves those who hate evil,
  protects the lives of the faithful,
  rescues them from the hand of the wicked.
11 Light dawns for the just;
  gladness, for the honest of heart.

NEW JERUSALEM BIBLE

Psalm 96 (V 95)

1 Sing a new song to Yahweh!
  Sing to Yahweh, all the earth!
2 Sing to Yahweh, bless his name!

Proclaim his salvation day after day,
3 declare his glory among the nations,
  his marvels to every people!

4 Great is Yahweh, worthy of all praise,
  more awesome than any of the gods.
5 All the gods of the nations are idols!

It was Yahweh who made the heavens;
6 in his presence are splendour and majesty,
  in his sanctuary power and beauty.

7 Give to Yahweh, families of nations,
  give to Yahweh glory and power,
8 give to Yahweh the glory due to his name!

Bring an offering and enter his courts,
9 adore Yahweh in the splendour of his holiness.
Tremble before him, all the earth.

10 Say among the nations, 'Yahweh is king.'
  The world is set firm, it cannot be moved.
He will judge the nations with justice.

11 Let the heavens rejoice and earth be glad!
  Let the sea thunder, and all it holds!
12 Let the countryside exult, and all that is in it,
  and all the trees of the forest cry out for joy,

13 at Yahweh's approach, for he is coming,
  coming to judge the earth;
he will judge the world with saving justice,
  and the nations with constancy.

Psalm 97 (V 96)

1 Yahweh is king! Let earth rejoice,
  the many isles be glad!
2 Cloud, black cloud enfolds him,
  saving justice and judgement the foundations of his
    throne.

3 Fire goes before him,
  sets ablaze his enemies all around;
4 his lightning-flashes light up the world,
  the earth sees it and quakes.
5 The mountains melt like wax,
  before the Lord of all the earth.
6 The heavens proclaim his saving justice,
  all nations see his glory.

7 Shame on all who serve images,
  who pride themselves on their idols;
  bow down to him, all you gods!

8 Zion hears and is glad,
  the daughters of Judah exult,
  because of your judgements, Yahweh.

9 For you are Yahweh,
  Most High over all the earth,
  far transcending all gods.

10 Yahweh loves those who hate evil,
  he keeps safe his faithful,
  rescues them from the clutches of the wicked.

11 Light dawns for the upright,
  and joy for honest hearts.

NEW REVISED STANDARD VERSION

12 Rejoice in the LORD, O you righteous,
   and give thanks to his holy name!

Psalm 98

A Psalm.

1 O sing to the LORD a new song,
    for he has done marvelous things.
  His right hand and his holy arm
    have gotten him victory.
2 The LORD has made known his victory;
    he has revealed his vindication in the sight of
      the nations.
3 He has remembered his steadfast love and
      faithfulness
    to the house of Israel.
  All the ends of the earth have seen
    the victory of our God.

4 Make a joyful noise to the LORD, all the earth;
    break forth into joyous song and sing praises.
5 Sing praises to the LORD with the lyre,
    with the lyre and the sound of melody.
6 With trumpets and the sound of the horn
    make a joyful noise before the King, the LORD.

7 Let the sea roar, and all that fills it;
    the world and those who live in it.
8 Let the floods clap their hands;
    let the hills sing together for joy
9 at the presence of the LORD, for he is coming
    to judge the earth.
  He will judge the world with righteousness,
    and the peoples with equity.

Psalm 99

1 The LORD is king; let the peoples tremble!
    He sits enthroned upon the cherubim; let the
      earth quake!
2 The LORD is great in Zion;
    he is exalted over all the peoples.
3 Let them praise your great and awesome name.
    Holy is he!
4 Mighty King,*p* lover of justice,
    you have established equity;
  you have executed justice
    and righteousness in Jacob.
5 Extol the LORD our God;
    worship at his footstool.
    Holy is he!

6 Moses and Aaron were among his priests,
    Samuel also was among those who called on
      his name.
  They cried to the LORD, and he answered
      them.
7 He spoke to them in the pillar of cloud;
    they kept his decrees,
    and the statutes that he gave them.

8 O LORD our God, you answered them;
    you were a forgiving God to them,
    but an avenger of their wrongdoings.
9 Extol the LORD our God,
    and worship at his holy mountain;
    for the LORD our God is holy.

REVISED ENGLISH BIBLE

12 You that are righteous, rejoice in the LORD
   and praise his holy name.

Psalm 98

A psalm

1 SING a new song to the LORD,
    for he has done marvellous deeds;
  his right hand and his holy arm have won him
      victory.
2 The LORD has made his victory known;
    he has displayed his saving righteousness to all the
      nations.
3 He has remembered his love for Jacob,
    his faithfulness towards the house of Israel.
  All the ends of the earth have seen
    the victory of our God.

4 Acclaim the LORD, all the earth;
    break into songs of joy, sing psalms.
5 Sing psalms in the LORD's honour with the lyre,
    with the lyre and with resounding music,
6 with trumpet and echoing horn
    acclaim the presence of the LORD our King.
7 Let the sea resound and everything in it,
    the world and those who dwell there.
8 Let the rivers clap their hands,
    let the mountains sing aloud together
9 before the LORD; for he comes
    to judge the earth.
  He will judge the world with justice
    and the peoples with equity.

Psalm 99

1 THE LORD has become King; let peoples tremble.
    He is enthroned on the cherubim; let the earth
      shake.
2 The LORD is great in Zion;
    he is exalted above all the peoples.
3 Let them extol your great and terrible name.
    Holy is he.

4 The King in his might loves justice.
    You have established equity;
  you have dealt justly and righteously in Jacob.
5 Exalt the LORD our God
    and bow down at his footstool.
    Holy is he.

6 Moses and Aaron were among his priests,
    and Samuel was among those who invoked his
      name;
  they called to the LORD, and he answered them.
7 He spoke to them in a pillar of cloud;
    they kept his decrees and the statute he gave them.

8 O LORD our God, you answered them;
    you were a God who forgave them,
    yet you called them to account for their misdeeds.
9 Exalt the LORD our God,
    and bow down towards his holy mountain;
    for holy is the LORD our God.

p Cn: Heb *And a king's strength*   98:3 **for Jacob:** *so Gk; Heb. omits.*

12 Rejoice in the LORD, you just,
   and praise his holy name.

Psalm 98

1 *A psalm.*

I

Sing a new song to the LORD,
   who has done marvelous deeds,
Whose right hand and holy arm
   have won the victory.
2 The LORD has made his victory known;
   has revealed his triumph for the nations to see,
3 Has remembered faithful love
   toward the house of Israel.
All the ends of the earth have seen
   the victory of our God.

II

4 Shout with joy to the LORD, all the earth;
   break into song; sing praise.
5 Sing praise to the LORD with the harp,
   with the harp and melodious song.
6 With trumpets and the sound of the horn
   shout with joy to the King, the LORD.

III

7 Let the sea and what fills it resound,
   the world and those who dwell there.
8 Let the rivers clap their hands,
   the mountains shout with them for joy,
9 Before the LORD who comes,
   who comes to govern the earth,
To govern the world with justice
   and the peoples with fairness.

Psalm 99

I

1 The LORD is king, the peoples tremble;
   God is enthroned on the cherubim, the earth
      quakes.
2 The LORD is great on Zion,
   exalted above all the peoples.
3 Let them praise your great and awesome name:
   holy is God!

II

4 O mighty king, lover of justice,
   you alone have established fairness;
   you have created just rule in Jacob.
5 Exalt the LORD, our God;
   bow down before his footstool;
   holy is God!

III

6 Moses and Aaron were among his priests,
   Samuel among those who called on God's name;
   they called on the LORD, who answered them.
7 From the pillar of cloud God spoke to them;
   they kept the decrees, the law they received.
8 O LORD, our God, you answered them;
   you were a forgiving God,
   though you punished their offenses.
9 Exalt the LORD, our God;
   bow down before his holy mountain;
   holy is the LORD, our God.

12 Rejoice in Yahweh, you who are upright,
   praise his unforgettable holiness.

Psalm 98 (V 97)

Psalm

1 Sing a new song to Yahweh,
   for he has performed wonders,
   his saving power is in his right hand
   and his holy arm.
2 Yahweh has made known his saving power,
   revealed his saving justice for the nations to see,
3 mindful of his faithful love and his constancy
   to the House of Israel.

The whole wide world has seen
   the saving power of our God.
4 Acclaim Yahweh, all the earth,
   burst into shouts of joy!
5 Play to Yahweh on the harp,
   to the sound of instruments;
6 to the sound of trumpet and horn,
   acclaim the presence of the King.

7 Let the sea thunder, and all that it holds,
   the world and all who live in it.
8 Let the rivers clap their hands,
   and the mountains shout for joy together,

9 at Yahweh's approach, for he is coming
   to judge the earth;
   he will judge the world with saving justice
   and the nations with fairness.

Psalm 99 (V 98)

1 Yahweh is king, the peoples tremble;
   he is enthroned on the winged creatures, the earth
      shivers;
2 Yahweh is great in Zion.

He is supreme over all nations;
3 let them praise your name, great and awesome;
   holy is he 4 and mighty!

You are a king who loves justice,
   you established honesty, justice and uprightness;
   in Jacob it is you who are active.

5   Exalt Yahweh our God,
   bow down at his footstool;
   holy is he!

6 Moses and Aaron are among his priests, and
      Samuel,
   calling on his name; they called on Yahweh
   and he answered them.
7 He spoke with them in the pillar of fire,
   they obeyed his decrees, the Law he gave them.
8 Yahweh our God, you answered them,
   you were a God of forgiveness to them,
   but punished them for their sins.

9   Exalt Yahweh our God,
   bow down at his holy mountain;
   holy is Yahweh our God!

NEW REVISED STANDARD VERSION	REVISED ENGLISH BIBLE

Psalm 100

A Psalm of thanksgiving.

1 Make a joyful noise to the LORD, all the earth.
2 Worship the LORD with gladness;
  come into his presence with singing.

3 Know that the LORD is God.
  It is he that made us, and we are his;*q*
  we are his people, and the sheep of his
    pasture.

4 Enter his gates with thanksgiving,
  and his courts with praise.
  Give thanks to him, bless his name.

5 For the LORD is good;
  his steadfast love endures forever,
  and his faithfulness to all generations.

Psalm 101

Of David. A Psalm.

1 I will sing of loyalty and of justice;
  to you, O LORD, I will sing.

2 I will study the way that is blameless.
  When shall I attain it?

  I will walk with integrity of heart
    within my house;
3 I will not set before my eyes
    anything that is base.

  I hate the work of those who fall away;
    it shall not cling to me.
4 Perverseness of heart shall be far from me;
    I will know nothing of evil.

5 One who secretly slanders a neighbor
    I will destroy.
  A haughty look and an arrogant heart
    I will not tolerate.

6 I will look with favor on the faithful in the land,
    so that they may live with me;
  whoever walks in the way that is blameless
    shall minister to me.

7 No one who practices deceit
    shall remain in my house;
  no one who utters lies
    shall continue in my presence.

8 Morning by morning I will destroy
    all the wicked in the land,
  cutting off all evildoers
    from the city of the LORD.

Psalm 102

*A prayer of one afflicted, when faint and pleading before
the LORD.*

1 Hear my prayer, O LORD;
  let my cry come to you.
2 Do not hide your face from me
    in the day of my distress.
  Incline your ear to me;
    answer me speedily in the day when I call.

3 For my days pass away like smoke,
  and my bones burn like a furnace.

Psalm 100

A psalm: for thanksgiving

1 LET all the earth acclaim the LORD!
2 Worship the LORD in gladness;
  enter his presence with joyful songs.
3 Acknowledge that the LORD is God;
  he made us and we are his,
  his own people, the flock which he shepherds.
4 Enter his gates with thanksgiving,
  his courts with praise.
  Give thanks to him and bless his name;
5 for the LORD is good and his love is everlasting,
  his faithfulness endures to all generations.

Psalm 101

For David: a psalm

1 I SHALL sing of loyalty and justice,
  as I raise a psalm to you, LORD.

2 I shall lead a wise and blameless life;
  when will you come to me?
  My conduct among my household will be
    blameless.
3 I shall not set before my eyes any shameful thing;
  I hate apostasy, and will have none of it.
4 I shall banish all crooked thoughts,
  and will have no dealings with evil.
5 I shall silence those who whisper slanders;
  I cannot endure the proud and the arrogant.
6 I shall choose for my companions the faithful in
    the land;
  my servants will be those whose lives are
    blameless.
7 No treacherous person will live in my household;
  no liar will establish himself in my presence.
8 Morning after morning I shall reduce all the
    wicked to silence,
  ridding the LORD's city of all evildoers.

Psalm 102

*A prayer: for the afflicted one when he is faint and pours
out his complaint before the LORD*

1 LORD, hear my prayer
  and let my cry for help come to you.
2 Do not hide your face from me
    when I am in dire straits.
  Listen to my prayer
  and, when I call, be swift to reply;
3 for my days vanish like smoke,
  my body is burnt up as in an oven.

q Another reading is and not we ourselves

Psalm 100

¹ A psalm of thanksgiving.

Shout joyfully to the LORD, all you lands;
2   worship the LORD with cries of gladness;
    come before him with joyful song.
³ Know that the LORD is God,
    our maker to whom we belong,
    whose people we are, God's well-tended flock.
⁴ Enter the temple gates with praise,
    its courts with thanksgiving.
    Give thanks to God, bless his name;
5   good indeed is the LORD,
    Whose love endures forever,
    whose faithfulness lasts through every age.

Psalm 101

¹ A psalm of David.

I

I sing of love and justice;
    to you, LORD, I sing praise.
² I follow the way of integrity;
    when will you come to me?
I act with integrity of heart
    within my royal court.
³ I do not allow into my presence
    anyone who speaks perversely.
Whoever acts shamefully I hate;
    no such person can be my friend.
⁴ I shun the devious of heart;
    the wicked I do not tolerate.
⁵ Whoever slanders another in secret
    I reduce to silence.
Haughty eyes and arrogant hearts
    I cannot endure.

II

⁶ I look to the faithful of the land;
    they alone can be my companions.
Those who follow the way of integrity,
    they alone can enter my service.
⁷ No one who practices deceit
    can hold a post in my court.
No one who speaks falsely
    can be among my advisors.
⁸ Each morning I clear the wicked from the land,
    and rid the LORD's city of all evildoers.

Psalm 102

¹ The prayer of one afflicted and wasting away whose anguish is poured out before the LORD.

I

² LORD, hear my prayer;
    let my cry come to you.
³ Do not hide your face from me
    now that I am in distress.
Turn your ear to me;
    when I call, answer me quickly.
⁴ For my days vanish like smoke;
    my bones burn away as in a furnace.

Psalm 100 (V 99)

Psalm   For thanksgiving

¹ Acclaim Yahweh, all the earth,
² serve Yahweh with gladness,
    come into his presence with songs of joy!

³ Be sure that Yahweh is God,
    he made us, we belong to him,
    his people, the flock of his sheepfold.

⁴ Come within his gates giving thanks,
    to his courts singing praise,
    give thanks to him and bless his name!

⁵ For Yahweh is good,
    his faithful love is everlasting,
    his constancy from age to age.

Psalm 101 (V 100)

Of David   Psalm

¹ I will sing of faithful love and judgement;
    to you, Yahweh, will I make music.
² I will go forward in the path of the blameless;
    when will you come to me?

I will live in purity of heart,
    in my house,
³ I will not set before my eyes
    anything sordid.

I hate those who act crookedly;
    this has no attraction for me.
⁴ Let the perverse of heart keep away from me;
    the wicked I disregard.

⁵ One who secretly slanders a comrade,
    I reduce to silence;
haughty looks, proud heart,
    these I cannot abide.

⁶ I look to the faithful of the land
    to be my companions,
only he who walks in the path of the blameless
    shall be my servant.

⁷ There is no room in my house
    for anyone who practises deceit;
no liar will stand his ground
    where I can see him.

⁸ Morning after morning I reduce to silence
    all the wicked in the land,
banishing from the city of Yahweh
    all evil-doers.

Psalm 102 (V 101)q

Prayer of someone afflicted, who in misfortune pours out sorrows before Yahweh

1   Yahweh, hear my prayer,
    let my cry for help reach you.
2   Do not turn away your face from me
    when I am in trouble;
bend down and listen to me,
    when I call, be quick to answer me!

3   For my days are vanishing like smoke,
    my bones burning like an oven;

q **102** Two poems: vv. 1–11 + 23–27 form a personal lament, vv.
12–22 a prayer for pity.

4 My heart is stricken and withered like grass;
   I am too wasted to eat my bread.
5 Because of my loud groaning
   my bones cling to my skin.
6 I am like an owl of the wilderness,
   like a little owl of the waste places.
7 I lie awake;
   I am like a lonely bird on the housetop.
8 All day long my enemies taunt me;
   those who deride me use my name for a curse.
9 For I eat ashes like bread,
   and mingle tears with my drink,
10 because of your indignation and anger;
   for you have lifted me up and thrown me
   aside.
11 My days are like an evening shadow;
   I wither away like grass.

12 But you, O LORD, are enthroned forever;
   your name endures to all generations.
13 You will rise up and have compassion on Zion,
   for it is time to favor it;
   the appointed time has come.
14 For your servants hold its stones dear,
   and have pity on its dust.
15 The nations will fear the name of the LORD,
   and all the kings of the earth your glory.
16 For the LORD will build up Zion;
   he will appear in his glory.
17 He will regard the prayer of the destitute,
   and will not despise their prayer.

18 Let this be recorded for a generation to come,
   so that a people yet unborn may praise the
   LORD:
19 that he looked down from his holy height,
   from heaven the LORD looked at the earth,
20 to hear the groans of the prisoners,
   to set free those who were doomed to die;
21 so that the name of the LORD may be declared in
   Zion,
   and his praise in Jerusalem,
22 when peoples gather together,
   and kingdoms, to worship the LORD.

23 He has broken my strength in midcourse;
   he has shortened my days.
24 "O my God," I say, "do not take me away
   at the mid-point of my life,
   you whose years endure
   throughout all generations."

25 Long ago you laid the foundation of the earth,
   and the heavens are the work of your hands.
26 They will perish, but you endure;
   they will all wear out like a garment.
   You change them like clothing, and they pass
   away;
27 but you are the same, and your years have no
   end.
28 The children of your servants shall live secure;
   their offspring shall be established in your
   presence.

Psalm 103

Of David.

1 Bless the LORD, O my soul,
   and all that is within me,
   bless his holy name.

4 I am stricken, withered like grass;
   I neglect to eat my food.
5 I groan aloud;
   I am just skin and bone.
6 I am like a desert-owl in the wilderness,
   like an owl that lives among ruins.
7 I lie awake and have become like a bird
   solitary on a rooftop.
8 My enemies taunt me the whole day long;
   mad with rage, they conspire against me.
9 I have eaten ashes for bread
   and mingled tears with my drink.
10 In furious anger
   you have taken me up only to fling me aside.
11 My days decline like shadows lengthening;
   I wither away like grass.

12 But you, LORD, are enthroned for ever;
   your fame will endure to all generations.
13 You will arise and have mercy on Zion,
   for it is time to pity her;
   the appointed time has come.
14 Her very stones are dear to your servants,
   and even her dust moves them to pity.
15 The nations will revere your name, LORD,
   and all earthly kings your glory,
16 when the LORD builds Zion again
   and shows himself in his glory,
17 when he turns to hear the prayer of the destitute
   and does not spurn their prayer.

18 This will be written down for future generations,
   that people yet unborn may praise the LORD:
19 'The LORD looks down from his sanctuary on high;
   from heaven he surveys the earth
20 to hear the groaning of the prisoners
   and set free those under sentence of death.'
21 So shall the LORD's name be declared in Zion
   and his praise told in Jerusalem,
22 when peoples are assembled together,
   and kingdoms, to serve the LORD.

23 He has broken my strength before my course is
   run;
   he has cut short the time allotted me.
24 I say, 'Do not carry me off before half my days
   are done,
   for your years extend through all generations.'
25 Long ago you laid earth's foundations,
   and the heavens were your handiwork.
26 They will pass away, but you remain;
   like clothes they will all wear out;
   you will cast them off like a cloak
   and they will vanish.
27 But you are the same and your years will have no
   end.
28 The children of those who serve you will continue,
   and their descendants will be established in your
   presence.

Psalm 103

For David

1 BLESS the LORD, my soul;
   with all my being I bless his holy name.

NEW AMERICAN BIBLE

NEW JERUSALEM BIBLE

5 I am withered, dried up like grass,
   too wasted to eat my food.
6 From my loud groaning
   I become just skin and bones.
7 I am like a desert owl,
   like an owl among the ruins.
8 I lie awake and moan,
   like a lone sparrow on the roof.
9 All day long my enemies taunt me;
   in their rage, they make my name a curse.
10 I eat ashes like bread,
   mingle my drink with tears.
11 Because of your furious wrath,
   you lifted me up just to cast me down.
12 My days are like a lengthening shadow;
   I wither like the grass.
II
13 But you, LORD, are enthroned forever;
   your renown is for all generations.
14 You will again show mercy to Zion;
   now is the time for pity;
   the appointed time has come.
15 Its stones are dear to your servants;
   its dust moves them to pity.
16 The nations shall revere your name, LORD,
   all the kings of the earth, your glory,
17 Once the LORD has rebuilt Zion
   and appeared in glory,
18 Heeding the plea of the lowly,
   not scorning their prayer.
19 Let this be written for the next generation,
   for a people not yet born,
   that they may praise the LORD:
20 "The LORD looked down from the holy heights,
   viewed the earth from heaven,
21 To attend to the groaning of the prisoners,
   to release those doomed to die."
22 Then the LORD's name will be declared on Zion,
   the praise of God in Jerusalem,
23 When all peoples and kingdoms gather
   to worship the LORD.
III
24 God has shattered my strength in mid-course,
   has cut short my days.
25 I plead, O my God,
   do not take me in the midst of my days.
   Your years last through all generations.
26 Of old you laid the earth's foundations;
   the heavens are the work of your hands.
27 They perish, but you remain;
   they all wear out like a garment;
   Like clothing you change them and they are
     changed,
28   but you are the same, your years have no end.
29 May the children of your servants live on;
   may their descendants live in your presence.

4   like grass struck by blight, my heart is
     withering,
   I forget to eat my meals.
5   From the effort of voicing my groans
   my bones stick out through my skin.

6   I am like a desert-owl in the wastes,
   a screech-owl among ruins,
7   I keep vigil and moan
   like a lone bird on a roof.
8   All day long my enemies taunt me,
   those who once praised me now use me as a
     curse.

9   Ashes are the food that I eat,
   my drink is mingled with tears,
10   because of your fury and anger,
   since you have raised me up only to cast me
     away;
11   my days are like a fading shadow,
   I am withering up like grass.

12 But you, Yahweh, are enthroned for ever,
   each generation in turn remembers you.
13 Rise up, take pity on Zion!
   the time has come to have mercy on her,
   the moment has come;
14 for your servants love her very stones,
   are moved to pity by her dust.

15 Then will the nations revere the name of Yahweh,
   and all the kings of the earth your glory;
16 when Yahweh builds Zion anew,
   he will be seen in his glory;
17 he will turn to hear the prayer of the destitute,
   and will not treat their prayer with scorn.

18 This shall be put on record for a future generation,
   and a people yet to be born shall praise God:
19 Yahweh has leaned down from the heights of his
     sanctuary,
   has looked down from heaven to earth,
20 to listen to the sighing of the captive,
   and set free those condemned to death,
21 to proclaim the name of Yahweh in Zion,
   his praise in Jerusalem,
22 nations will gather together,
   and kingdoms to worship Yahweh.

23   In my journeying my strength has failed on the
     way;
24   let me know the short time I have left.
   Do not take me away before half my days are
     done,
   for your years run on from age to age.
25   Long ago you laid earth's foundations,
   the heavens are the work of your hands.
26   They pass away but you remain;
   they all wear out like a garment,
   like outworn clothes you change them;
27   but you never alter, and your years never end.
28   The children of those who serve you will dwell
     secure,
   and their descendants live on in your presence.

Psalm 103

1 *Of David.*

I
Bless the LORD, my soul;
   all my being, bless his holy name!

Psalm 103 (V 102)

Of David

1 Bless Yahweh, my soul,
   from the depths of my being, his holy name;

NEW REVISED STANDARD VERSION

2 Bless the Lord, O my soul,
   and do not forget all his benefits—
3 who forgives all your iniquity,
   who heals all your diseases,
4 who redeems your life from the Pit,
   who crowns you with steadfast love and mercy,
5 who satisfies you with good as long as you live*r*
   so that your youth is renewed like the eagle's.

6 The Lord works vindication
   and justice for all who are oppressed.
7 He made known his ways to Moses,
   his acts to the people of Israel.
8 The Lord is merciful and gracious,
   slow to anger and abounding in steadfast love.
9 He will not always accuse,
   nor will he keep his anger forever.
10 He does not deal with us according to our sins,
   nor repay us according to our iniquities.
11 For as the heavens are high above the earth,
   so great is his steadfast love toward those who
      fear him;
12 as far as the east is from the west,
   so far he removes our transgressions from us.
13 As a father has compassion for his children,
   so the Lord has compassion for those who fear
      him.
14 For he knows how we were made;
   he remembers that we are dust.

15 As for mortals, their days are like grass;
   they flourish like a flower of the field;
16 for the wind passes over it, and it is gone,
   and its place knows it no more.
17 But the steadfast love of the Lord is from
      everlasting to everlasting
   on those who fear him,
   and his righteousness to children's children,
18 to those who keep his covenant
   and remember to do his commandments.

19 The Lord has established his throne in the
      heavens,
   and his kingdom rules over all.
20 Bless the Lord, O you his angels,
   you mighty ones who do his bidding,
   obedient to his spoken word.
21 Bless the Lord, all his hosts,
   his ministers that do his will.
22 Bless the Lord, all his works,
   in all places of his dominion.
   Bless the Lord, O my soul.

Psalm 104

1 Bless the Lord, O my soul.
   O Lord my God, you are very great.
   You are clothed with honor and majesty,
2   wrapped in light as with a garment.
   You stretch out the heavens like a tent,
3   you set the beams of your*s* chambers on the
      waters,
   you make the clouds your*s* chariot,
      you ride on the wings of the wind,
4 you make the winds your*s* messengers,
   fire and flame your*s* ministers.

5 You set the earth on its foundations,
   so that it shall never be shaken.

REVISED ENGLISH BIBLE

2 Bless the Lord, my soul,
   and forget none of his benefits.
3 He pardons all my wrongdoing
   and heals all my ills.
4 He rescues me from death's pit
   and crowns me with love and compassion.
5 He satisfies me with all good in the prime of life,
   and my youth is renewed like an eagle's.

6 The Lord is righteous in all he does;
   he brings justice to all who have been wronged.
7 He revealed his ways to Moses,
   his mighty deeds to the Israelites.
8 The Lord is compassionate and gracious,
   long-suffering and ever faithful;
9 he will not always accuse
   or nurse his anger for ever.
10 He has not treated us as our sins deserve
   or repaid us according to our misdeeds.
11 As the heavens tower high above the earth,
   so outstanding is his love towards those who fear
      him.
12 As far as east is from west,
   so far from us has he put away our offences.
13 As a father has compassion on his children,
   so the Lord has compassion on those who fear
      him;
14 for he knows how we were made,
   he remembers that we are but dust.

15 The days of a mortal are as grass;
   he blossoms like a wild flower in the meadow:
16 a wind passes over him, and he is gone,
   and his place knows him no more.
17 But the Lord's love is for ever on those who fear
      him,
   and his righteousness on their posterity,
18 on those who hold fast to his covenant,
   who keep his commandments in mind.

19 The Lord has established his throne in heaven,
   his kingly power over the whole world.
20 Bless the Lord, you his angels,
   mighty in power, who do his bidding
   and obey his command.
21 Bless the Lord, all you his hosts,
   his ministers who do his will.
22 Bless the Lord, all created things,
   everywhere in his dominion.

   Bless the Lord, my soul.

Psalm 104

1 Bless the Lord, my soul.
   Lord my God, you are very great,
   clothed in majesty and splendour,
2 and enfolded in a robe of light.
   You have spread out the heavens like a tent,
3 and laid the beams of your dwelling on the waters;
   you take the clouds for your chariot,
   riding on the wings of the wind;
4 you make the winds your messengers,
   flames of fire your servants;
5 you fixed the earth on its foundation
   so that it will never be moved.

r Meaning of Heb uncertain   *s* Heb *his*

NEW AMERICAN BIBLE

2 Bless the LORD, my soul;
   do not forget all the gifts of God,
3 Who pardons all your sins,
   heals all your ills,
4 Delivers your life from the pit,
   surrounds you with love and compassion,
5 Fills your days with good things;
   your youth is renewed like the eagle's.
   II
6 The LORD does righteous deeds,
   brings justice to all the oppressed.
7 His ways were revealed to Moses,
   mighty deeds to the people of Israel.
8 Merciful and gracious is the LORD,
   slow to anger, abounding in kindness.
9 God does not always rebuke,
   nurses no lasting anger,
10 Has not dealt with us as our sins merit,
   nor requited us as our deeds deserve.
   III
11 As the heavens tower over the earth,
   so God's love towers over the faithful.
12 As far as the east is from the west,
   so far have our sins been removed from us.
13 As a father has compassion on his children,
   so the LORD has compassion on the faithful.
14 For he knows how we are formed,
   remembers that we are dust.
15 Our days are like the grass;
   like flowers of the field we blossom.
16 The wind sweeps over us and we are gone;
   our place knows us no more.
17 But the LORD's kindness is forever,
   toward the faithful from age to age.
   He favors the children's children
18   of those who keep his covenant,
   who take care to fulfill its precepts.
   IV
19 The LORD's throne is established in heaven;
   God's royal power rules over all.
20 Bless the LORD, all you angels,
   mighty in strength and attentive,
   obedient to every command.
21 Bless the LORD, all you hosts,
   ministers who do God's will.
22 Bless the LORD, all creatures,
   everywhere in God's domain.
   Bless the LORD, my soul!

Psalm 104

   I
1 Bless the LORD, my soul!
   LORD, my God, you are great indeed!
   You are clothed with majesty and glory,
2   robed in light as with a cloak.
   You spread out the heavens like a tent;
3   you raised your palace upon the waters.
   You make the clouds your chariot;
   you travel on the wings of the wind.
4 You make the winds your messengers;
   flaming fire, your ministers.
   II
5 You fixed the earth on its foundation,
   never to be moved.

NEW JERUSALEM BIBLE

2 bless Yahweh, my soul,
   never forget all his acts of kindness.
3 He forgives all your offences,
   cures all your diseases,
4 he redeems your life from the abyss,
   crowns you with faithful love and tenderness;
5 he contents you with good things all your life,
   renews your youth like an eagle's.
6 Yahweh acts with uprightness,
   with justice to all who are oppressed;
7 he revealed to Moses his ways,
   his great deeds to the children of Israel.
8 Yahweh is tenderness and pity,
   slow to anger and rich in faithful love;
9 his indignation does not last for ever,
   nor his resentment remain for all time;
10 he does not treat us as our sins deserve,
   nor repay us as befits our offences.
11 As the height of heaven above earth,
   so strong is his faithful love for those who fear
   him.
12 As the distance of east from west,
   so far from us does he put our faults.
13 As tenderly as a father treats his children,
   so Yahweh treats those who fear him;
14 he knows of what we are made,
   he remembers that we are dust.
15 As for a human person — his days are like grass,
   he blooms like the wild flowers;
16 as soon as the wind blows he is gone,
   never to be seen there again.
17 But Yahweh's faithful love for those who fear him
   is from eternity and for ever;
   and his saving justice to their children's children;
18 as long as they keep his covenant,
   and carefully obey his precepts.
19 Yahweh has fixed his throne in heaven,
   his sovereign power rules over all.
20 Bless Yahweh, all his angels,
   mighty warriors who fulfil his commands,
   attentive to the sound of his words.
21 Bless Yahweh, all his armies,
   servants who fulfil his wishes.
22 Bless Yahweh, all his works,
   in every place where he rules.
   Bless Yahweh, my soul.

Psalm 104 (V 103)

1 Bless Yahweh, my soul,
   Yahweh, my God, how great you are!
   Clothed in majesty and splendour,
2 wearing the light as a robe!

   You stretch out the heavens like a tent,
3 build your palace on the waters above,
   making the clouds your chariot,
   gliding on the wings of the wind,
4 appointing the winds your messengers,
   flames of fire your servants.

5 You fixed the earth on its foundations,
   for ever and ever it shall not be shaken;

6 You cover it with the deep as with a garment;
 the waters stood above the mountains.
7 At your rebuke they flee;
 at the sound of your thunder they take to
 flight.
8 They rose up to the mountains, ran down to the
 valleys
 to the place that you appointed for them.
9 You set a boundary that they may not pass,
 so that they might not again cover the earth.

10 You make springs gush forth in the valleys;
 they flow between the hills,
11 giving drink to every wild animal;
 the wild asses quench their thirst.
12 By the streams*t* the birds of the air have their
 habitation;
 they sing among the branches.
13 From your lofty abode you water the mountains;
 the earth is satisfied with the fruit of your
 work.

14 You cause the grass to grow for the cattle,
 and plants for people to use,*u*
 to bring forth food from the earth,
15 and wine to gladden the human heart,
 oil to make the face shine,
 and bread to strengthen the human heart.
16 The trees of the LORD are watered abundantly,
 the cedars of Lebanon that he planted.
17 In them the birds build their nests;
 the stork has its home in the fir trees.
18 The high mountains are for the wild goats;
 the rocks are a refuge for the coneys.
19 You have made the moon to mark the seasons;
 the sun knows its time for setting.
20 You make darkness, and it is night,
 when all the animals of the forest come
 creeping out.
21 The young lions roar for their prey,
 seeking their food from God.
22 When the sun rises, they withdraw
 and lie down in their dens.
23 People go out to their work
 and to their labor until the evening.

24 O LORD, how manifold are your works!
 In wisdom you have made them all;
 the earth is full of your creatures.
25 Yonder is the sea, great and wide,
 creeping things innumerable are there,
 living things both small and great.
26 There go the ships,
 and Leviathan that you formed to sport in it.

27 These all look to you
 to give them their food in due season;
28 when you give to them, they gather it up;
 when you open your hand, they are filled with
 good things.
29 When you hide your face, they are dismayed;
 when you take away their breath, they die
 and return to their dust.
30 When you send forth your spirit,*v* they are
 created;
 and you renew the face of the ground.

31 May the glory of the LORD endure forever;
 may the LORD rejoice in his works—
32 who looks on the earth and it trembles,
 who touches the mountains and they smoke.

6 The deep covered it like a cloak,
 and the waters stood above the mountains.
7 At your rebuke they fled,
 at the sound of your thunder they rushed away,
8 flowing over the hills,
 pouring down into the valleys
 to the place appointed for them.
9 You fixed a boundary which they were not to pass;
 they were never to cover the earth again.

10 You make springs break out in the wadis,
 so that water from them flows between the hills.
11 The wild beasts all drink from them,
 the wild donkeys quench their thirst;
12 the birds of the air nest on their banks
 and sing among the foliage.

13 From your dwelling you water the hills;
 the earth is enriched by your provision.
14-15 You make grass grow for the cattle
 and plants for the use of mortals,
 producing grain from the earth,
 food to sustain their strength,
 wine to gladden the hearts of the people,
 and oil to make their faces shine.
16 The trees of the LORD flourish,
 the cedars of Lebanon which he planted;
17 birds build their nests in them,
 the stork makes her home in their tops.
18 High hills are the haunt of the mountain goat,
 and crags a cover for the rock-badger.

19 He created the moon to mark the seasons,
 and makes the sun know when to set.
20 You bring darkness, and it is night,
 when all the beasts of the forest go prowling;
21 the young lions roar for prey,
 seeking their food from God;
22 when the sun rises, they slink away
 and seek rest in their lairs.
23 Man goes out to his work
 and his labours until evening.

24 Countless are the things you have made, LORD;
 by your wisdom you have made them all;
 the earth is full of your creatures.
25 Here is the vast immeasurable sea,
 in which move crawling things beyond number,
 living creatures great and small.
26 Here ships sail to and fro;
 here is Leviathan which you have made to sport
 there.

27 All of them look to you in hope
 to give them their food when it is due.
28 What you give them they gather up;
 when you open your hand, they eat their fill of
 good things.
29 When you hide your face, they are dismayed.
 When you take away their spirit, they die
 and return to the dust from which they came.
30 When you send forth your spirit, they are created,
 and you give new life to the earth.

31 May the glory of the LORD stand for ever,
 and may the LORD rejoice in his works!
32 When he looks at the earth, it quakes;
 when he touches the mountains, they pour forth
 smoke.

---

t Heb *By them*   *u* Or *to cultivate*   *v* Or *your breath*   104:17 **in their tops:** *prob. rdg; Heb.* the pine trees.

NEW AMERICAN BIBLE	NEW JERUSALEM BIBLE

6 The ocean covered it like a garment;
    above the mountains stood the waters.
7 At your roar they took flight;
    at the sound of your thunder they fled.
8 They rushed up the mountains, down the valleys
    to the place you had fixed for them.
9 You set a limit they cannot pass;
    never again will they cover the earth.
    III
10 You made springs flow into channels
    that wind among the mountains.
11 They give drink to every beast of the field;
    here wild asses quench their thirst.
12 Beside them the birds of heaven nest;
    among the branches they sing.
13 You water the mountains from your palace;
    by your labor the earth abounds.
14 You raise grass for the cattle
    and plants for our beasts of burden.
    You bring bread from the earth,
15   and wine to gladden our hearts,
    Oil to make our faces gleam,
    food to build our strength.
16 The trees of the LORD drink their fill,
    the cedars of Lebanon, which you planted.
17 There the birds build their nest;
    junipers are the home of the stork.
18 The high mountains are for wild goats;
    the rocky cliffs, a refuge for badgers.
    IV
19 You made the moon to mark the seasons,
    the sun that knows the hour of its setting.
20 You bring darkness and night falls,
    then all the beasts of the forest roam abroad.
21 Young lions roar for prey;
    they seek their food from God.
22 When the sun rises, they steal away
    and rest in their dens.
23 People go forth to their work,
    to their labor till evening falls.
    V
24 How varied are your works, LORD!
    In wisdom you have wrought them all;
    the earth is full of your creatures.
25 Look at the sea, great and wide!
    It teems with countless beings,
    living things both large and small.
26 Here ships ply their course;
    here Leviathan, your creature, plays.
    VI
27 All of these look to you
    to give them food in due time.
28 When you give to them, they gather;
    when you open your hand, they are well filled.
29 When you hide your face, they are lost.
    When you take away their breath, they perish
    and return to the dust from which they came.
30 When you send forth your breath, they are created,
    and you renew the face of the earth.
    VII
31 May the glory of the LORD endure forever;
    may the LORD be glad in these works!
32 If God glares at the earth, it trembles;
    If God touches the mountains, they smoke!

6 you covered it with the deep like a garment,
    the waters overtopping the mountains.
7 At your reproof the waters fled,
    at the voice of your thunder they sped away,
8 flowing over mountains, down valleys,
    to the place you had fixed for them;
9 you made a limit they were not to cross,
    they were not to return and cover the earth.
10 In the ravines you opened up springs,
    running down between the mountains,
11 supplying water for all the wild beasts;
    the wild asses quench their thirst,
12 on their banks the birds of the air make their nests,
    they sing among the leaves.
13 From your high halls you water the mountains,
    satisfying the earth with the fruit of your works:
14 for cattle you make the grass grow,
    and for people the plants they need,
    to bring forth food from the earth,
15 and wine to cheer people's hearts,
    oil to make their faces glow,
    food to make them sturdy of heart.
16 The trees of Yahweh drink their fill,
    the cedars of Lebanon which he sowed;
17 there the birds build their nests,
    on the highest branches the stork makes its home;
18 for the wild goats there are the mountains,
    in the crags the coneys find refuge.
19 He made the moon to mark the seasons,
    the sun knows when to set.
20 You bring on darkness, and night falls,
    when all the forest beasts roam around;
21 young lions roar for their prey,
    asking God for their food.
22 The sun rises and away they steal,
    back to their lairs to lie down,
23 and man goes out to work,
    to labour till evening falls.
24 How countless are your works, Yahweh,
    all of them made so wisely!
    The earth is full of your creatures.
25 Then there is the sea, with its vast expanses
    teeming with countless creatures,
    creatures both great and small;
26 there ships pass to and fro,
    and Leviathan whom you made to sport with.
27 They all depend upon you,
    to feed them when they need it.
28 You provide the food they gather,
    your open hand gives them their fill.
29 Turn away your face and they panic;
    take back their breath and they die
    and revert to dust.
30 Send out your breath and life begins;
    you renew the face of the earth.
31 Glory to Yahweh for ever!
    May Yahweh find joy in his creatures!
32 At his glance the earth trembles,
    at his touch the mountains pour forth smoke.

NEW REVISED STANDARD VERSION	REVISED ENGLISH BIBLE

33 I will sing to the LORD as long as I live;
    I will sing praise to my God while I have
        being.
34 May my meditation be pleasing to him,
    for I rejoice in the LORD.
35 Let sinners be consumed from the earth,
    and let the wicked be no more.
    Bless the LORD, O my soul.
    Praise the LORD!

33 As long as I live I shall sing to the LORD;
    I shall sing psalms to my God all my life long.
34 May my meditation be acceptable to him;
    I shall delight in the LORD.
35 May sinners be banished from the earth
    and may the wicked be no more!

    Bless the LORD, my soul.
    Praise the LORD.

Psalm 105

1 O give thanks to the LORD, call on his name,
    make known his deeds among the peoples.
2 Sing to him, sing praises to him;
    tell of all his wonderful works.
3 Glory in his holy name;
    let the hearts of those who seek the LORD
        rejoice.
4 Seek the LORD and his strength;
    seek his presence continually.
5 Remember the wonderful works he has done,
    his miracles, and the judgments he uttered,
6 O offspring of his servant Abraham,w
    children of Jacob, his chosen ones.

7 He is the LORD our God;
    his judgments are in all the earth.
8 He is mindful of his covenant forever,
    of the word that he commanded, for a thousand
        generations,
9 the covenant that he made with Abraham,
    his sworn promise to Isaac,
10 which he confirmed to Jacob as a statute,
    to Israel as an everlasting covenant,
11 saying, "To you I will give the land of Canaan
    as your portion for an inheritance."

12 When they were few in number,
    of little account, and strangers in it,
13 wandering from nation to nation,
    from one kingdom to another people,
14 he allowed no one to oppress them;
    he rebuked kings on their account,
15 saying, "Do not touch my anointed ones;
    do my prophets no harm."

16 When he summoned famine against the land,
    and broke every staff of bread,
17 he had sent a man ahead of them,
    Joseph, who was sold as a slave.
18 His feet were hurt with fetters,
    his neck was put in a collar of iron;
19 until what he had said came to pass,
    the word of the LORD kept testing him.
20 The king sent and released him;
    the ruler of the peoples set him free.
21 He made him lord of his house,
    and ruler of all his possessions,
22 to instructx his officials at his pleasure,
    and to teach his elders wisdom.

23 Then Israel came to Egypt;
    Jacob lived as an alien in the land of Ham.
24 And the LORD made his people very fruitful,
    and made them stronger than their foes,
25 whose hearts he then turned to hate his people,
    to deal craftily with his servants.

Psalm 105

1 GIVE thanks to the LORD, invoke him by name;
    make known his deeds among the peoples.
2 Pay him honour with song and psalm
    and tell of all his marvellous deeds.
3 Exult in his hallowed name;
    let those who seek the LORD be joyful in heart.
4 Look to the LORD and be strong;
    at all times seek his presence.
5-6 You offspring of Abraham his servant,
    the children of Jacob, his chosen ones,
    remember the marvels he has wrought,
    his portents, and the judgements he has given.

7 He is the LORD our God;
    his judgements cover the whole world.
8 He is ever mindful of his covenant,
    the promise he ordained for a thousand
        generations,
9 the covenant made with Abraham,
    his oath given to Isaac,
10 and confirmed as a statute for Jacob,
    as an everlasting covenant for Israel:
11 'I shall give you the land of Canaan', he said,
    'as your allotted holding.'

12 A small company it was,
    few in number, strangers in that land,
13 roaming from nation to nation,
    from one kingdom to another;
14 but he let no one oppress them,
    on their account he rebuked kings:
15 'Do not touch my anointed servants,' he said;
    'do no harm to my prophets.'

16 He called down famine on the land
    and cut off their daily bread.
17 But he had sent on a man before them,
    Joseph, who was sold into slavery,
18 where they thrust his feet into fetters
    and clamped an iron collar round his neck.
19 He was tested by the LORD's command
    until what he foretold took place.
20 The king sent and had him released,
    the ruler of peoples set him free
21 and made him master of his household,
    ruler over all his possessions,
22 to correct his officers as he saw fit
    and teach his counsellors wisdom.

23 Then Israel too went down into Egypt,
    Jacob came to live in the land of Ham.
24 There God made his people very fruitful,
    too numerous for their enemies,
25 whose hearts he turned to hatred of his people,
    to double-dealing with his servants.

---

w Another reading is *Israel* (compare 1 Chr 16.13)   x Gk Syr
Jerome: Heb *to bind*

105:4 **be strong:** so *Gk; Heb.* his strength.

33 I will sing to the LORD all my life;
 I will sing praise to my God while I live.
34 May my theme be pleasing to God;
 I will rejoice in the LORD.
35 May sinners vanish from the earth,
 and the wicked be no more.
Bless the LORD, my soul! Hallelujah!

Psalm 105

I
1 Give thanks to the LORD, invoke his name;
 make known among the peoples his deeds!
2 Sing praise, play music;
 proclaim all his wondrous deeds!
3 Glory in his holy name;
 rejoice, O hearts that seek the LORD!
4 Rely on the mighty LORD;
 constantly seek his face.
5 Recall the wondrous deeds he has done,
 his signs and his words of judgment,
6 You descendants of Abraham his servant,
 offspring of Jacob the chosen one!
II
7 The LORD is our God,
 who rules the whole earth.
8 He remembers forever his covenant,
 the pact imposed for a thousand generations,
9 Which was made with Abraham,
 confirmed by oath to Isaac,
10 And ratified as binding for Jacob,
 an everlasting covenant for Israel:
11 "To you I give the land of Canaan,
 your own allotted heritage."
III
12 When they were few in number,
 a handful, and strangers there,
13 Wandering from nation to nation,
 from one kingdom to another,
14 He let no one oppress them;
 for their sake he rebuked kings:
15 "Do not touch my anointed,
 to my prophets do no harm."
IV
16 Then he called down a famine on the land,
 destroyed the grain that sustained them.
17 He had sent a man ahead of them,
 Joseph, sold as a slave.
18 They shackled his feet with chains;
 collared his neck in iron,
19 Till his prediction came to pass,
 and the word of the LORD proved him true.
20 The king sent and released him;
 the ruler of peoples set him free.
21 He made him lord over his palace,
 ruler over all his possessions,
22 To instruct his princes by his word,
 to teach his elders wisdom.
V
23 Then Israel entered Egypt;
 Jacob lived in the land of Ham.
24 God greatly increased his people,
 made them too many for their foes.
25 He turned their hearts to hate his people,
 to treat his servants unfairly.

33 I shall sing to Yahweh all my life,
 make music for my God as long as I live.
34 May my musings be pleasing to him,
 for Yahweh gives me joy.
35 May sinners vanish from the earth,
 and the wicked exist no more!

Bless Yahweh, my soul.

Psalm 105 (V 104)

Alleluia!
1 Give thanks to Yahweh, call on his name,
 proclaim his deeds to the peoples!
2 Sing to him, make music for him,
 recount all his wonders!
3 Glory in his holy name,
 let the hearts that seek Yahweh rejoice!
4 Seek Yahweh and his strength,
 tirelessly seek his presence!
5 Remember the marvels he has done,
 his wonders, the judgements he has spoken.
6 Stock of Abraham, his servant,
 children of Jacob whom he chose!
7 He is Yahweh our God,
 his judgements touch the whole world.
8 He remembers his covenant for ever,
 the promise he laid down for a thousand
  generations,
9 which he concluded with Abraham,
 the oath he swore to Isaac.
10 He established it as a statute for Jacob,
 an everlasting covenant with Israel,
11 saying, 'To you I give a land,
 Canaan, your allotted birthright.'
12 When they were insignificant in numbers,
 a handful of strangers in the land,
13 wandering from country to country,
 from one kingdom and nation to another,
14 he allowed no one to oppress them;
 for their sake he instructed kings,
15 'Do not touch my anointed ones,
 to my prophets you may do no harm.'
16 He called down famine on the land,
 he took away their food supply;
17 he sent a man ahead of them,
 Joseph, sold as a slave.
18 So his feet were weighed down with shackles,
 his neck was put in irons.
19 In due time his prophecy was fulfilled,
 the word of Yahweh proved him true.
20 The king sent orders to release him,
 the ruler of nations set him free;
21 he put him in charge of his household,
 the ruler of all he possessed,
22 to instruct his princes as he saw fit,
 to teach his counsellors wisdom.
23 Then Israel migrated to Egypt,
 Jacob settled in the country of Ham.
24 He made his people increase in numbers,
 he gave them more strength than their enemies,
25 whose heart he turned to hate his own people,
 to double-cross his servants.

|

26 He sent his servant Moses,
   and Aaron whom he had chosen.
27 They performed his signs among them,
   and miracles in the land of Ham.
28 He sent darkness, and made the land dark;
   they rebelled *y* against his words.
29 He turned their waters into blood,
   and caused their fish to die.
30 Their land swarmed with frogs,
   even in the chambers of their kings.
31 He spoke, and there came swarms of flies,
   and gnats throughout their country.
32 He gave them hail for rain,
   and lightning that flashed through their land.
33 He struck their vines and fig trees,
   and shattered the trees of their country.
34 He spoke, and the locusts came,
   and young locusts without number;
35 they devoured all the vegetation in their land,
   and ate up the fruit of their ground.
36 He struck down all the firstborn in their land,
   the first issue of all their strength.
37 Then he brought Israel *z* out with silver and gold,
   and there was no one among their tribes who
      stumbled.
38 Egypt was glad when they departed,
   for dread of them had fallen upon it.
39 He spread a cloud for a covering,
   and fire to give light by night.
40 They asked, and he brought quails,
   and gave them food from heaven in abundance.
41 He opened the rock, and water gushed out;
   it flowed through the desert like a river.
42 For he remembered his holy promise,
   and Abraham, his servant.
43 So he brought his people out with joy,
   his chosen ones with singing.
44 He gave them the lands of the nations,
   and they took possession of the wealth of the
      peoples,
45 that they might keep his statutes
   and observe his laws.
   Praise the LORD!

Psalm 106

1 Praise the LORD!
   O give thanks to the LORD, for he is good;
      for his steadfast love endures forever.
2 Who can utter the mighty doings of the LORD,
   or declare all his praise?
3 Happy are those who observe justice,
   who do righteousness at all times.
4 Remember me, O LORD, when you show favor to
      your people;
   help me when you deliver them;
5 that I may see the prosperity of your chosen
      ones,
   that I may rejoice in the gladness of your
      nation,
   that I may glory in your heritage.
6 Both we and our ancestors have sinned;
   we have committed iniquity, have done
      wickedly.

26 He sent his servant Moses
   and Aaron whom he had chosen.
27 They were appointed to announce his signs,
   his portents in the land of Ham.
28 He sent darkness, and all was dark,
   but still the Egyptians resisted his commands.
29 He turned all the water to blood,
   so causing the fish to die.
30 Their land swarmed with frogs,
   even in the royal apartments.
31 At his command there came swarms of flies
   and maggots throughout their land.
32 He sent showers of hail,
   and lightning flashing over their country.
33 He blasted their vines and their fig trees
   and shattered the trees throughout their territory.
34 At his command the locusts came,
   hoppers past all numbering;
35 they devoured every green thing in the land,
   eating up all the produce of the soil.
36 Then he struck down all the firstborn in the land,
   the firstfruits of all their manhood.
37 He led his people out, laden with silver and gold,
   and among all their tribes not one person fell.
38 The Egyptians were glad to see them go,
   for fear of Israel had seized them.
39 He spread a cloud as a screen for them,
   and fire to light up the night.
40 When they asked, he sent them quails;
   he gave them bread of heaven in plenty.
41 He opened a rock and water gushed out,
   flowing in a stream through a parched land;
42 for he was mindful of his solemn promise
   to his servant Abraham.
43 He led out his people rejoicing,
   his chosen ones in triumph.
44 He gave them the lands of heathen nations;
   they took possession where others had toiled,
45 so that they might keep his statutes
   and obey his laws.

   Praise the LORD.

Psalm 106

1 PRAISE the LORD.

   It is good to give thanks to the LORD,
      for his love endures for ever.
2 Who can tell of the LORD's mighty acts
   and make all his praises heard?
3 Happy are they who act justly,
   who do what is right at all times!
4 Remember me, LORD, when you show favour to
      your people;
   look on me when you save them,
5 that I may see the prosperity of your chosen ones,
   that I may rejoice in your nation's joy
   and exult with your own people.
6 Like our forefathers we have sinned,
   we have gone astray and done wrong.

26 He sent his servant Moses,
  Aaron whom he had chosen.
27 They worked his signs in Egypt
  and wonders in the land of Ham.
28 He sent darkness and it grew dark,
  but they rebelled against his word.
29 He turned their waters into blood
  and killed all their fish.
30 Their land swarmed with frogs,
  even the chambers of their kings.
31 He spoke and there came swarms of flies,
  gnats through all their country.
32 For rain he gave them hail,
  flashes of lightning throughout their land.
33 He struck down their vines and fig trees,
  shattered the trees of their country.
34 He spoke and the locusts came,
  grasshoppers without number.
35 They devoured every plant in the land;
  they ravaged the crops of their fields.
36 He struck down every firstborn in the land,
  the first fruits of all their vigor.
37 He brought his people out,
  laden with silver and gold;
  no stragglers among the tribes.
38 Egypt rejoiced when they left,
  for panic had seized them.
VI
39 He spread a cloud as a cover,
  and made a fire to light up the night.
40 They asked and he brought them quail;
  with bread from heaven he filled them.
41 He split the rock and water gushed forth;
  it flowed through the desert like a river.
42 For he remembered his sacred word
  to Abraham his servant.
43 He brought his people out with joy,
  his chosen ones with shouts of triumph.
44 He gave them the lands of the nations,
  the wealth of the peoples to own,
45 That they might keep his laws
  and observe his teachings.
Hallelujah!

Psalm 106

1 Hallelujah!
A
Give thanks to the LORD, who is good,
  whose love endures forever.
2 Who can tell the mighty deeds of the LORD,
  proclaim in full God's praise?
3 Happy those who do what is right,
  whose deeds are always just.
4 Remember me, LORD, as you favor your people;
  come to me with your saving help,
5 That I may see the prosperity of your chosen,
  rejoice in the joy of your people,
  and glory with your heritage.
B
6 We have sinned like our ancestors;
  we have done wrong and are guilty.

26 He sent his servant Moses,
  and Aaron, the man of his choice.
27 They worked there the wonders he commanded,
  marvels in the country of Ham.
28 Darkness he sent, and darkness fell,
  but that nation defied his orders.
29 He turned their rivers to blood,
  and killed all the fish in them.
30 Their country was overrun with frogs,
  even in the royal apartments;
31 at his word came flies,
  and mosquitoes throughout the country.
32 He gave them hail as their rain,
  flames of fire in their land;
33 he blasted their vine and their fig tree,
  and shattered the trees of the country.
34 At his word came locusts,
  hoppers beyond all counting;
35 they devoured every green thing in the land,
  devoured all the produce of the soil.
36 He struck all the first-born in their land,
  the flower of all their manhood;
37 he led Israel out with silver and gold;
  in their tribes there was none who stumbled.
38 Egypt was glad at their leaving,
  for terror of Israel had seized them.
39 He spread out a cloud to cover them,
  and fire to light up the night.
40 They asked and he brought them quails,
  food from heaven to their hearts' content;
41 he opened a rock, the waters gushed out,
  and flowed in dry ground as a river.
42 Faithful to his sacred promise,
  given to his servant Abraham,
43 he led out his people with rejoicing,
  his chosen ones with shouts of joy.
44 He gave them the territories of nations,
  they reaped the fruit of other people's labours,
45 on condition that they kept his statutes,
  and remained obedient to his laws.

Psalm 106 (V 105)

1 Alleluia!
Give thanks to Yahweh, for he is good,
  his faithful love is everlasting!
2 Who can recount all Yahweh's triumphs,
  who can fully voice his praise?
3 How blessed are those who keep to what is just,
  whose conduct is always upright!
4 Remember me, Yahweh,
  in your love for your people.
Come near to me with your saving power,
5 let me share the happiness of your chosen ones,
  let me share the joy of your people,
  the pride of your heritage.
6 Like our ancestors, we have sinned,
  we have acted wickedly, guiltily;

7 Our ancestors, when they were in Egypt,
did not consider your wonderful works;
they did not remember the abundance of your
steadfast love,
but rebelled against the Most High*a* at the Red
Sea.*b*
8 Yet he saved them for his name's sake,
so that he might make known his mighty
power.
9 He rebuked the Red Sea,*b* and it became dry;
he led them through the deep as through a
desert.
10 So he saved them from the hand of the foe,
and delivered them from the hand of the
enemy.
11 The waters covered their adversaries;
not one of them was left.
12 Then they believed his words;
they sang his praise.
13 But they soon forgot his works;
they did not wait for his counsel.
14 But they had a wanton craving in the wilderness,
and put God to the test in the desert;
15 he gave them what they asked,
but sent a wasting disease among them.
16 They were jealous of Moses in the camp,
and of Aaron, the holy one of the LORD.
17 The earth opened and swallowed up Dathan,
and covered the faction of Abiram.
18 Fire also broke out in their company;
the flame burned up the wicked.
19 They made a calf at Horeb
and worshiped a cast image.
20 They exchanged the glory of God*c*
for the image of an ox that eats grass.
21 They forgot God, their Savior,
who had done great things in Egypt,
22 wondrous works in the land of Ham,
and awesome deeds by the Red Sea.*b*
23 Therefore he said he would destroy them —
had not Moses, his chosen one,
stood in the breach before him,
to turn away his wrath from destroying them.
24 Then they despised the pleasant land,
having no faith in his promise.
25 They grumbled in their tents,
and did not obey the voice of the LORD.
26 Therefore he raised his hand and swore to them
that he would make them fall in the wilderness,
27 and would disperse*d* their descendants among the
nations,
scattering them over the lands.
28 Then they attached themselves to the Baal of
Peor,
and ate sacrifices offered to the dead;
29 they provoked the LORD to anger with their
deeds,
and a plague broke out among them.
30 Then Phinehas stood up and interceded,
and the plague was stopped.
31 And that has been reckoned to him as
righteousness
from generation to generation forever.

7 Our forefathers in Egypt disregarded your marvels;
they were not mindful of your many acts of love,
and on their journey they rebelled by the Red Sea.
8 Yet the LORD delivered them for his name's sake
and so made known his mighty power.
9 He rebuked the Red Sea, and it dried up;
he led his people through the deep as through a
desert.
10 He delivered them from those who hated them,
and rescued them from the enemy's hand.
11 The waters closed over their adversaries;
not one of them survived.
12 Then they believed what he had said
and sang his praises.
13 But they soon forgot all he had done
and would not wait to hear his counsel;
14 their greed was insatiable in the wilderness,
there in the desert they tried God's patience.
15 He gave them what they asked,
but followed it with a wasting sickness.
16 In the camp they were envious of Moses,
and of Aaron, who was consecrated to the LORD.
17 The earth opened and swallowed Dathan;
it closed over the company of Abiram.
18 Fire raged through their company;
the wicked perished in flames.
19 At Horeb they made a calf
and worshipped this image;
20 they exchanged their God
for the image of a bull that feeds on grass.
21 They forgot God their deliverer,
who had done great things in Egypt,
22 such marvels in the land of Ham,
awesome deeds at the Red Sea.
23 So he purposed to destroy them,
but Moses, the man he had chosen,
stood before him in the breach
to prevent his wrath from destroying them.
24 Disbelieving his promise,
they rejected the pleasant land.
25 They muttered treason in their tents,
and would not obey the LORD.
26 So with hand uplifted against them he made an
oath
to strike them down in the wilderness,
27 to scatter their descendants among the nations
and disperse them throughout the lands.
28 They joined in worshipping the Baal of Peor
and ate meat sacrificed to lifeless gods.
29 Their deeds provoked the LORD to anger,
and plague broke out amongst them;
30 but Phinehas stood up and intervened,
and the plague was checked.
31 This was counted to him as righteousness
throughout the generations ever afterwards.

---

a Cn Compare 78.17, 56: Heb *rebelled at the sea* *b* Or *Sea of
Reeds* *c* Compare Gk Mss: Heb *exchanged their glory*
d Syr Compare Ezek 20.23: Heb *cause to fall*

106:7 **on their journey:** *so Gk; Heb.* by the sea. **Red Sea:** *or* sea of
Reeds. 106:20 **their God:** *Heb.* their glory. 106:22 **Red Sea:**
or sea of Reeds.

I

7 Our ancestors in Egypt
   did not attend to your wonders.
They did not remember your great love;
   they defied the Most High at the Red Sea.
8 Yet he saved them for his name's sake
   to make his power known.
9 He roared at the Red Sea and it dried up.
   He led them through the deep as through a
      desert.
10 He rescued them from hostile hands,
   freed them from the power of the enemy.
11 The waters covered their oppressors;
   not one of them survived.
12 Then they believed his words
   and sang songs of praise.

II

13 But they soon forgot all he had done;
   they had no patience for his plan.
14 In the desert they gave way to their cravings,
   tempted God in the wasteland.
15 So he gave them what they asked
   and sent among them a wasting disease.

III

16 In the camp they challenged Moses
   and Aaron, the holy one of the Lord.
17 The earth opened and swallowed Dathan,
   it closed on the followers of Abiram.
18 Against that company the fire blazed;
   flames consumed the wicked.

IV

19 At Horeb they fashioned a calf,
   worshiped a metal statue.
20 They exchanged their glorious God
   for the image of a grass-eating bull.
21 They forgot the God who saved them,
   who did great deeds in Egypt,
22 Amazing deeds in the land of Ham,
   fearsome deeds at the Red Sea.
23 He would have decreed their destruction,
   had not Moses, the chosen leader,
Withstood him in the breach
   to turn back his destroying anger.

V

24 Next they despised the beautiful land;
   they did not believe the promise.
25 In their tents they complained;
   they did not obey the Lord.
26 So with raised hand he swore
   to destroy them in the desert,
27 To scatter their descendants among the nations,
   disperse them in foreign lands.

VI

28 They joined in the rites of Baal of Peor,
   ate food sacrificed to dead gods.
29 They provoked him by their actions,
   and a plague broke out among them.
30 Then Phinehas rose to intervene,
   and the plague was brought to a halt.
31 This was counted for him as a righteous deed
   for all generations to come.

7 our ancestors in Egypt never grasped
   the meaning of your wonders.

They did not bear in mind your countless acts of
      love,
   at the Sea of Reeds they defied the Most High;
8 but for the sake of his name he saved them,
   to make known his mighty power.

9 At his rebuke the Sea of Reeds dried up,
   he let them pass through the deep as though it
      were desert,
10 so he saved them from their opponents' clutches,
   rescued them from the clutches of their enemies.

11 The waters enveloped their enemies,
   not one of whom was left.
12 Then they believed what he had said,
   and sang his praises.

13 But they soon forgot his achievements,
   they did not even wait for his plans;
14 they were overwhelmed with greed in the
      wastelands,
   in the solitary wastes they challenged God.

15 He gave them all they asked for,
   but struck them with a deep wasting sickness;
16 in the camp they grew jealous of Moses,
   and of Aaron, Yahweh's holy one.

17 The earth opened and swallowed up Dathan,
   closed in on Abiram's faction;
18 fire flamed out against their faction,
   the renegades were engulfed in flames.

19 At Horeb they made a calf,
   bowed low before cast metal;
20 they exchanged their glory
   for the image of a grass-eating bull.

21 They forgot the God who was saving them,
   who had done great deeds in Egypt,
22 such wonders in the land of Ham,
   such awesome deeds at the Sea of Reeds.

23 He thought of putting an end to them,
   had not Moses, his chosen one,
   taken a stand in the breach and confronted him,
   to turn his anger away from destroying them.

24 They counted a desirable land for nothing,
   they put no trust in his promise;
25 they stayed in their tents and grumbled,
   they would not listen to Yahweh's voice.

26 So he lifted his hand against them,
   to strike them down in the desert,
27 to strike down their descendants among the
      nations,
   to scatter them all over the world.

28 They committed themselves to serve Baal-Peor,
   and ate sacrifices made to lifeless gods.
29 They so provoked him by their actions
   that a plague broke out among them.

30 Then up stood Phinehas to intervene,
   and the plague was checked;
31 for this he is the example of uprightness,
   from age to age for ever.

NEW REVISED STANDARD VERSION	REVISED ENGLISH BIBLE

NEW REVISED STANDARD VERSION

32 They angered the LORD*e* at the waters of
Meribah,
   and it went ill with Moses on their account;
33 for they made his spirit bitter,
   and he spoke words that were rash.

34 They did not destroy the peoples,
   as the LORD commanded them,
35 but they mingled with the nations
   and learned to do as they did.
36 They served their idols,
   which became a snare to them.
37 They sacrificed their sons
   and their daughters to the demons;
38 they poured out innocent blood,
   the blood of their sons and daughters,
   whom they sacrificed to the idols of Canaan;
   and the land was polluted with blood.
39 Thus they became unclean by their acts,
   and prostituted themselves in their doings.

40 Then the anger of the LORD was kindled against
   his people,
   and he abhorred his heritage;
41 he gave them into the hand of the nations,
   so that those who hated them ruled over them.
42 Their enemies oppressed them,
   and they were brought into subjection under
   their power.
43 Many times he delivered them,
   but they were rebellious in their purposes,
   and were brought low through their iniquity.
44 Nevertheless he regarded their distress
   when he heard their cry.
45 For their sake he remembered his covenant,
   and showed compassion according to the
   abundance of his steadfast love.
46 He caused them to be pitied
   by all who held them captive.

47 Save us, O LORD our God,
   and gather us from among the nations,
   that we may give thanks to your holy name
   and glory in your praise.

48 Blessed be the LORD, the God of Israel,
   from everlasting to everlasting.
   And let all the people say, "Amen."
   Praise the LORD!

REVISED ENGLISH BIBLE

32 They roused the LORD's anger at the waters of
Meribah,
   and it went ill with Moses because of them;
33 for when they had embittered his spirit
   he spoke rashly.
34 They did not destroy the nations
   as the LORD had commanded them to do,
35 but they associated with the people
   and learnt their ways;
36 they worshipped their idols
   and were ensnared by them.
37 Their sons and their daughters
   they sacrificed to foreign deities;
38 they shed innocent blood,
   the blood of sons and daughters
   offered to the gods of Canaan,
   and the land was polluted with blood.
39 Thus they defiled themselves by their actions
   and were faithless in their conduct.

40 Then the LORD became angry with his people
   and, though they were his own chosen nation, he
   loathed them;
41 he handed them over to the nations,
   and they were ruled by their foes;
42 their enemies oppressed them
   and kept them in subjection to their power.
43 Time and again he came to their rescue,
   but they were rebellious in their designs,
   and so were brought low by their wrongdoing.
44 Yet when he heard them wail and cry aloud
   he looked with pity on their distress;
45 he called to mind his covenant with them
   and, in his boundless love, relented;
46 he roused compassion for them
   in the hearts of all their captors.

47 Deliver us, LORD our God,
   and gather us in from among the nations,
   that we may give thanks to your holy name
   and make your praise our pride.

48 Blessed be the LORD, the God of Israel,
   from everlasting to everlasting.
   Let all the people say 'Amen.'

Praise the LORD.

BOOK V
Psalms 107–150

Psalm 107

1 O give thanks to the LORD, for he is good;
   for his steadfast love endures forever.
2 Let the redeemed of the LORD say so,
   those he redeemed from trouble
3 and gathered in from the lands,
   from the east and from the west,
   from the north and from the south.*f*

4 Some wandered in desert wastes,
   finding no way to an inhabited town;
5 hungry and thirsty,
   their soul fainted within them.

BOOK 5

Psalm 107

1 IT is good to give thanks to the LORD,
   for his love endures for ever.
2 So let them say who were redeemed by the LORD,
   redeemed by him from the power of the enemy
3 and gathered out of the lands,
   from east and west, from north and south.

4 Some lost their way in desert waste lands;
   they found no path to a city to live in.
5 They were hungry and thirsty,
   and their spirit was faint within them.

---

e Heb *him*   *f* Cn: Heb *sea*   107:3 **and south:** *prob. rdg; cp. Aram. (Targ.); Heb.* and west.

NEW AMERICAN BIBLE

VII
32 At the waters of Meribah they angered God,
and Moses suffered because of them.
33 They so embittered his spirit
that rash words crossed his lips.

VIII
34 They did not destroy the peoples
as the LORD had commanded them,
35 But mingled with the nations
and imitated their ways.
36 They worshiped their idols
and were ensnared by them.
37 They sacrificed to the gods
their own sons and daughters,
38 Shedding innocent blood,
the blood of their own sons and daughters,
Whom they sacrificed to the idols of Canaan,
desecrating the land with bloodshed.
39 They defiled themselves by their actions,
became adulterers by their conduct.
40 So the LORD grew angry with his people,
abhorred his own heritage.
41 He handed them over to the nations,
and their adversaries ruled them.
42 Their enemies oppressed them,
kept them under subjection.
43 Many times did he rescue them,
but they kept rebelling and scheming
and were brought low by their own guilt.
44 Still God had regard for their affliction
when he heard their wailing.
45 For their sake he remembered his covenant
and relented in his abundant love,
46 Winning for them compassion
from all who held them captive.

C
47 Save us, LORD, our God;
gather us from among the nations
That we may give thanks to your holy name
and glory in praising you.

* * *

48 Blessed be the LORD, the God of Israel,
from everlasting to everlasting!
Let all the people say, Amen!
Hallelujah!

FIFTH BOOK
Psalms 107–150

Psalm 107

1 "Give thanks to the LORD who is good,
whose love endures forever!"
2 Let that be the prayer of the LORD's redeemed,
those redeemed from the hand of the foe,
3 Those gathered from foreign lands,
from east and west, from north and south.

I
4 Some had lost their way in a barren desert;
found no path toward a city to live in.
5 They were hungry and thirsty;
their life was ebbing away.

NEW JERUSALEM BIBLE

32 At the waters of Meribah they so angered Yahweh,
that Moses suffered on their account,
33 for they had embittered his spirit,
and he spoke without due thought.

34 They did not destroy the nations,
as Yahweh had told them to do,
35 but intermarried with them,
and adopted their ways.
36 They worshipped those nations' false gods,
till they found themselves entrapped,
37 and sacrificed their own sons
and their daughters to demons.
38 Innocent blood they shed,
the blood of their sons and daughters;
offering them to the idols of Canaan,
they polluted the country with blood.
39 They defiled themselves by such actions,
their behaviour was that of a harlot.
40 Yahweh's anger blazed out at his people,
his own heritage filled him with disgust.
41 He handed them over to the nations,
and their opponents became their masters;
42 their enemies lorded it over them,
crushing them under their rule.
43 Time and again he rescued them,
but they still defied him deliberately,
and sank ever deeper in their guilt;
44 even so he took pity on their distress,
as soon as he heard them cry out.
45 Bearing his covenant with them in mind,
he relented in his boundless and faithful love;
46 he ensured that they received compassion,
in their treatment by all their captors.

47 Save us, Yahweh our God,
gather us from among the nations,
that we may give thanks to your holy name,
and may glory in praising you.

48 Blessed be Yahweh, the God of Israel,
from all eternity and for ever!
Let all the people say, 'Amen'.

Psalm 107 (V 106)

Alleluia!
1 Give thanks to Yahweh for he is good,
his faithful love lasts for ever.

2 So let them say whom Yahweh redeemed,
whom he redeemed from the power of their
enemies,
3 bringing them back from foreign lands,
from east and west, north and south.

4 They were wandering in the desert, in the
wastelands,
could find no way to an inhabited city;
5 they were hungry and thirsty,
their life was ebbing away.

6 Then they cried to the LORD in their trouble,
   and he delivered them from their distress;
7 he led them by a straight way,
   until they reached an inhabited town.
8 Let them thank the LORD for his steadfast love,
   for his wonderful works to humankind.
9 For he satisfies the thirsty,
   and the hungry he fills with good things.

10 Some sat in darkness and in gloom,
   prisoners in misery and in irons,
11 for they had rebelled against the words of God,
   and spurned the counsel of the Most High.
12 Their hearts were bowed down with hard labor;
   they fell down, with no one to help.
13 Then they cried to the LORD in their trouble,
   and he saved them from their distress;
14 he brought them out of darkness and gloom,
   and broke their bonds asunder.
15 Let them thank the LORD for his steadfast love,
   for his wonderful works to humankind.
16 For he shatters the doors of bronze,
   and cuts in two the bars of iron.

17 Some were sick*g* through their sinful ways,
   and because of their iniquities endured
      affliction;
18 they loathed any kind of food,
   and they drew near to the gates of death.
19 Then they cried to the LORD in their trouble,
   and he saved them from their distress;
20 he sent out his word and healed them,
   and delivered them from destruction.
21 Let them thank the LORD for his steadfast love,
   for his wonderful works to humankind.
22 And let them offer thanksgiving sacrifices,
   and tell of his deeds with songs of joy.

23 Some went down to the sea in ships,
   doing business on the mighty waters;
24 they saw the deeds of the LORD,
   his wondrous works in the deep.
25 For he commanded and raised the stormy wind,
   which lifted up the waves of the sea.
26 They mounted up to heaven, they went down to
      the depths;
   their courage melted away in their calamity;
27 they reeled and staggered like drunkards,
   and were at their wits' end.
28 Then they cried to the LORD in their trouble,
   and he brought them out from their distress;
29 he made the storm be still,
   and the waves of the sea were hushed.
30 Then they were glad because they had quiet,
   and he brought them to their desired haven.
31 Let them thank the LORD for his steadfast love,
   for his wonderful works to humankind.
32 Let them extol him in the congregation of the
      people,
   and praise him in the assembly of the elders.

33 He turns rivers into a desert,
   springs of water into thirsty ground,

6 So they cried to the LORD in their trouble,
   and he rescued them from their distress;
7 he led them by a straight and easy path
   until they came to a city where they might live.
8 Let them give thanks to the LORD for his love
   and for the marvellous things he has done for
      mankind;
9 he has satisfied the thirsty
   and filled the hungry with good things.

10 Some sat in the dark, in deepest darkness,
   prisoners bound fast in iron fetters,
11 because they had defied God's commands
   and flouted the purpose of the Most High.
12 Their spirit was subdued by hard labour;
   they stumbled and fell with none to help.
13 So they cried to the LORD in their trouble,
   and he saved them from their distress;
14 he brought them out of the dark, the deepest
      darkness,
   and burst their chains.
15 Let them give thanks to the LORD for his love
   and for the marvellous things he has done for
      mankind;
16 he has shattered bronze gates,
   and cut through iron bars.

17 Some were fools, who took to rebellious ways,
   and for their transgression suffered punishment.
18 Revulsion seized them at the sight of food;
   they were at the very gates of death.
19 So they cried to the LORD in their trouble,
   and he saved them from their distress;
20 he sent his word to heal them
   and snatch them out of the pit of death.
21 Let them give thanks to the LORD for his love
   and for the marvellous things he has done for
      mankind;
22 Let them offer sacrifices of thanksgiving
   and tell of his deeds with joyful shouts.

23 Others there are who go to sea in ships,
   plying their trade on the wide ocean.
24 These have seen what the LORD has done,
   his marvellous actions in the deep.
25 At his command the storm-wind rose
   and lifted the waves high.
26 The seamen were carried up to the skies,
   then plunged down into the depths;
   they were tossed to and fro in peril,
27 they reeled and staggered like drunkards,
   and all their skill was of no avail.
28 So they cried to the LORD in their trouble,
   and he brought them out of their distress.
29 The storm sank to a murmur
   and the waves of the sea were stilled.
30 They rejoiced because it was calm,
   and he guided them to the harbour they were
      making for.
31 Let them give thanks to the LORD for his enduring
      love
   and for the marvellous things he has done for
      mankind;
32 Let them exalt him in the assembly of the people
   and praise him in the elders' council.

33 He turns rivers into desert,
   springs of water into parched ground;

107:20 **out ... death:** *prob. rdg; Heb. obscure.*   107:26 **they were tossed ... peril:** *or their courage melted in the face of peril.*

g Cn: Heb *fools*

NEW AMERICAN BIBLE	NEW JERUSALEM BIBLE

NEW AMERICAN BIBLE

6 In their distress they cried to the LORD,
   who rescued them in their peril,
7 Guided them by a direct path
   so they reached a city to live in.
8 Let them thank the LORD for such kindness,
   such wondrous deeds for mere mortals.
9 For he satisfied the thirsty,
   filled the hungry with good things.

II

10 Some lived in darkness and gloom,
   in prison, bound with chains,
11 Because they rebelled against God's word,
   scorned the counsel of the Most High,
12 Who humbled their hearts through hardship;
   they stumbled with no one to help.
13 In their distress they cried to the LORD,
   who saved them in their peril,
14 Led them forth from darkness and gloom
   and broke their chains asunder.
15 Let them thank the LORD for such kindness,
   such wondrous deeds for mere mortals.
16 For he broke down the gates of bronze
   and snapped the bars of iron.

III

17 Some fell sick from their wicked ways,
   afflicted because of their sins.
18 They loathed all manner of food;
   they were at the gates of death.
19 In their distress they cried to the LORD,
   who saved them in their peril,
20 Sent forth the word to heal them,
   snatched them from the grave.
21 Let them thank the LORD for such kindness,
   such wondrous deeds for mere mortals.
22 Let them offer a sacrifice in thanks,
   declare his works with shouts of joy.

IV

23 Some went off to sea in ships,
   plied their trade on the deep waters.
24 They saw the works of the LORD,
   the wonders of God in the deep.
25 He spoke and roused a storm wind;
   it tossed the waves on high.
26 They rose up to the heavens, sank to the depths;
   their hearts trembled at the danger.
27 They reeled, staggered like drunkards;
   their skill was of no avail.
28 In their distress they cried to the LORD,
   who brought them out of their peril,
29 Hushed the storm to a murmur;
   the waves of the sea were stilled.
30 They rejoiced that the sea grew calm,
   that God brought them to the harbor they longed
   for.
31 Let them thank the LORD for such kindness,
   such wondrous deeds for mere mortal.
32 Let them praise him in the assembly of the people,
   give thanks in the council of the elders.

V

33 God changed rivers into desert,
   springs of water into thirsty ground,

NEW JERUSALEM BIBLE

6 They cried out to Yahweh in their distress,
   he rescued them from their plight,
7 he set them on the road,
   straight to an inhabited city.
8 Let them thank Yahweh for his faithful love,
   for his wonders for the children of Adam!
9 He has fed the hungry to their hearts' content,
   filled the starving with good things.

10 Sojourners in gloom and shadow dark as death,
   fettered in misery and chains,
11 for defying the orders of Yahweh,
   for scorning the plan of the Most High —
12 he subdued their spirit by hard labour;
   if they fell there was no one to help.
13 They cried out to Yahweh in their distress,
   he rescued them from their plight,
14 he brought them out from gloom and shadow dark
   as death,
   and shattered their chains.
15 Let them thank Yahweh for his faithful love,
   for his wonders for the children of Adam!
16 He broke open gates of bronze
   and smashed iron bars.

17 Fools for their rebellious ways,
   wretched because of their sins,
18 finding all food repugnant,
   brought close to the gates of death —
19 they cried out to Yahweh in their distress;
   he rescued them from their plight,
20 he sent out his word and cured them,
   and rescued their life from the abyss.
21 Let them thank Yahweh for his faithful love,
   for his wonders for the children of Adam!
22 Let them offer thanksgiving sacrifices,
   and recount with shouts of joy what he has done!
23 Voyagers on the sea in ships,
   plying their trade on the great ocean,
24 have seen the works of Yahweh,
   his wonders in the deep.
25 By his word he raised a storm-wind,
   lashing up towering waves.
26 Up to the sky then down to the depths!
   Their stomachs were turned to water;
27 they staggered and reeled like drunkards,
   and all their skill went under.
28 They cried out to Yahweh in their distress,
   he rescued them from their plight,
29 he reduced the storm to a calm,
   and all the waters subsided,
30 and he brought them, overjoyed at the stillness,
   to the port where they were bound.
31 Let them thank Yahweh for his faithful love,
   for his wonders for the children of Adam!
32 Let them extol him in the assembly of the people,
   and praise him in the council of elders.

33 He has turned rivers into desert,
   bubbling springs into arid ground,

NEW REVISED STANDARD VERSION	REVISED ENGLISH BIBLE

34 a fruitful land into a salty waste,
  because of the wickedness of its inhabitants.
35 He turns a desert into pools of water,
  a parched land into springs of water.
36 And there he lets the hungry live,
  and they establish a town to live in;
37 they sow fields, and plant vineyards,
  and get a fruitful yield.
38 By his blessing they multiply greatly,
  and he does not let their cattle decrease.

39 When they are diminished and brought low
  through oppression, trouble, and sorrow,
40 he pours contempt on princes
  and makes them wander in trackless wastes;
41 but he raises up the needy out of distress,
  and makes their families like flocks.
42 The upright see it and are glad;
  and all wickedness stops its mouth.
43 Let those who are wise give heed to these things,
  and consider the steadfast love of the LORD.

34 he turns fruitful land into salt-marsh,
  because the people who live there are so wicked.
35 Desert he changes to standing pools,
  arid land into springs of water.
36 There he gives the hungry a home
  and they build themselves a town to live in;
37 they sow fields and plant vineyards
  which yield a good harvest.
38 He blesses them and their numbers grow,
  and he does not let their herds decrease.
39 Tyrants lose their strength and are brought low
  in the grip of misfortune and sorrow;
40 he brings princes into contempt
  and leaves them to wander in a trackless waste.
41 But the poor man he lifts clear of his troubles
  and makes families increase like flocks of sheep.
42 The upright see it and are glad,
  while evildoers are reduced to silence.
43 Whoever is wise, let him lay these things to heart,
  and ponder the loving deeds of the LORD.

Psalm 108

A Song. A Psalm of David.

1 My heart is steadfast, O God, my heart is
    steadfast;*h*
  I will sing and make melody.
  Awake, my soul!*i*
2 Awake, O harp and lyre!
  I will awake the dawn.
3 I will give thanks to you, O LORD, among the
    peoples,
  and I will sing praises to you among the
    nations.
4 For your steadfast love is higher than the
    heavens,
  and your faithfulness reaches to the clouds.
5 Be exalted, O God, above the heavens,
  and let your glory be over all the earth.
6 Give victory with your right hand, and answer
    me,
  so that those whom you love may be rescued.

7 God has promised in his sanctuary:*j*
  "With exultation I will divide up Shechem,
  and portion out the Vale of Succoth.
8 Gilead is mine; Manasseh is mine;
  Ephraim is my helmet;
  Judah is my scepter.
9 Moab is my washbasin;
  on Edom I hurl my shoe;
  over Philistia I shout in triumph."
10 Who will bring me to the fortified city?
  Who will lead me to Edom?
11 Have you not rejected us, O God?
  You do not go out, O God, with our armies.
12 O grant us help against the foe,
  for human help is worthless.
13 With God we shall do valiantly;
  it is he who will tread down our foes.

Psalm 108

A song: a psalm: for David

1 My heart is steadfast, God,
  my heart is steadfast.
  I shall sing and raise a psalm.
  Awake, my soul.
2 Awake, harp and lyre;
  I shall awake at dawn.
3 I shall praise you among the peoples, LORD,
  among the nations I shall raise a psalm to you;
4 for your unfailing love is high above the heavens;
  your faithfulness reaches to the skies.
5 God, be exalted above the heavens;
  let your glory be over all the earth.
6 Save with your right hand and respond,
  that those dear to you may be delivered.

7 God has spoken from his sanctuary:
  'I will go up now and divide Shechem;
  I will measure off the valley of Succoth.
8 Gilead and Manasseh are mine;
  Ephraim is my helmet, Judah my sceptre;
9 Moab is my washbowl, on Edom I fling my
    sandals;
  I shout my war cry against Philistia.'
10 Who will bring me to the impregnable city?
  Who will guide me to Edom?
11 Have you rejected us, God,
  and do you no longer lead our armies to battle?
12 Grant us help against the foe;
  for in vain we look to any mortal for deliverance.
13 With God's help we shall fight valiantly,
  and God himself will tread our foes under foot.

107:39 **Tyrants:** *prob. rdg; Heb. omits.*   108:1–5 *Cp. Ps.*
57:7–11.   108:1 **my heart is steadfast:** *so some MSS; others*
omit. **Awake:** *prob. rdg; Heb. also.*   108:6–13 *Cp. Ps. 60:5–12.*
108:7 **from his sanctuary:** *or in his holiness.* **go up now:** *or exult.*

h Heb Mss Gk Syr: MT lacks *my heart is steadfast*   *i* Compare
57.8: Heb *also my soul*   *j* Or *by his holiness*

34 Fruitful land into a salty waste,
    because of the wickedness of its people.
35 He changed the desert into pools of water,
    arid land into springs of water,
36 And settled the hungry there;
    they built a city to live in.
37 They sowed fields and planted vineyards,
    brought in an abundant harvest.
38 God blessed them, they became very many,
    and their livestock did not decrease.
40 But he poured out contempt on princes,
    made them wander the trackless wastes,
39 Where they were diminished and brought low
    through misery and cruel oppression,
41 While the poor were released from their affliction;
    their families increased like their flocks.
42 The upright saw this and rejoiced;
    all wickedness shut its mouth.
43 Whoever is wise will take note of these things,
    will ponder the merciful deeds of the LORD.

Psalm 108

1 A song; a psalm of David.

I

2 My heart is steadfast, God;
    my heart is steadfast.
    I will sing and chant praise.
3 Awake, my soul; awake, lyre and harp!
    I will wake the dawn.
4 I will praise you among the peoples, LORD;
    I will chant your praise among the nations.
5 For your love towers to the heavens;
    your faithfulness, to the skies.
6 Appear on high over the heavens, God;
    may your glory appear above all the earth.
7 Help with your right hand and answer us
    that your loved ones may escape.

II

8 God promised in the sanctuary:
    "I will exult, I will apportion Shechem;
    the valley of Succoth I will measure out.
9 Gilead is mine, mine is Manasseh;
    Ephraim is the helmet for my head,
    Judah, my own scepter.
10 Moab is my washbowl;
    upon Edom I cast my sandal;
    I will triumph over Philistia."

III

11 Who will bring me to the fortified city?
    Who will lead me into Edom?
12 Was it not you who rejected us, God?
    Do you no longer march with our armies?
13 Give us aid against the foe;
    worthless is human help.
14 We will triumph with the help of God,
    who will trample down our foes.

34 fertile country into salt-flats,
    because the people living there were evil.
35 But he has turned desert into stretches of water,
    arid ground into bubbling springs,
36 and has given the hungry a home,
    where they have built themselves a city.
37 There they sow fields and plant vines,
    and reap a harvest of their produce.
38 He blesses them and their numbers increase,
    he keeps their cattle at full strength.
39 Their numbers had fallen, they had grown weak,
    under pressure of disaster and hardship;
40 he covered princes in contempt,
    left them to wander in trackless wastes.
41 But the needy he raises from their misery,
    makes their families as numerous as sheep.
42 At the sight the honest rejoice,
    and the wicked have nothing to say.
43 Who is wise? Such a one should take this to heart,
    and come to understand Yahweh's faithful love.

Psalm 108 (V 107)r

Song   Psalm   Of David

1 My heart is ready, God,
    I will sing and make music;
    come, my glory!
2 Awake, lyre and harp,
    I will awake the Dawn!

3 I will praise you among the peoples, Yahweh,
    I will play to you among nations,
4 for your faithful love towers to heaven,
    and your constancy to the clouds.

5 Be exalted above the heavens, God.
    Your glory over the whole earth!

6 To rescue those you love,
    save with your right hand and answer us.

7 God has spoken from his sanctuary,
    'In triumph I will divide up Shechem,
    and share out the Valley of Succoth.

8 'Mine is Gilead, mine Manasseh,
    Ephraim the helmet on my head,
    Judah my commander's baton,

9 'Moab a bowl for me to wash in,
    on Edom I plant my sandal,
    over Philistia I cry victory.'

10 Who will lead me against a fortified city,
    who will guide me into Edom,
11 if not you, the God who has rejected us?
    God, you no longer march with our armies.

12 Bring us help in our time of crisis,
    any human assistance is worthless.
13 With God we shall do deeds of valour,
    he will trample down our enemies.

r 108 = 57:7–11 + 60:5–12.

NEW REVISED STANDARD VERSION	REVISED ENGLISH BIBLE

Psalm 109

To the leader. Of David. A Psalm.

1 Do not be silent, O God of my praise.
2 For wicked and deceitful mouths are opened
   against me,
   speaking against me with lying tongues.
3 They beset me with words of hate,
   and attack me without cause.
4 In return for my love they accuse me,
   even while I make prayer for them.[k]
5 So they reward me evil for good,
   and hatred for my love.

6 They say,[l] "Appoint a wicked man against him;
   let an accuser stand on his right.
7 When he is tried, let him be found guilty;
   let his prayer be counted as sin.
8 May his days be few;
   may another seize his position.
9 May his children be orphans,
   and his wife a widow.
10 May his children wander about and beg;
   may they be driven out of[m] the ruins they
   inhabit.
11 May the creditor seize all that he has;
   may strangers plunder the fruits of his toil.
12 May there be no one to do him a kindness,
   nor anyone to pity his orphaned children.
13 May his posterity be cut off;
   may his name be blotted out in the second
   generation.
14 May the iniquity of his father[n] be remembered
   before the LORD,
   and do not let the sin of his mother be blotted
   out.
15 Let them be before the LORD continually,
   and may his[o] memory be cut off from the
   earth.
16 For he did not remember to show kindness,
   but pursued the poor and needy
   and the brokenhearted to their death.
17 He loved to curse; let curses come on him.
   He did not like blessing; may it be far from
   him.
18 He clothed himself with cursing as his coat,
   may it soak into his body like water,
   like oil into his bones.
19 May it be like a garment that he wraps around
   himself,
   like a belt that he wears every day."

20 May that be the reward of my accusers from the
   LORD,
   of those who speak evil against my life.
21 But you, O LORD my Lord,
   act on my behalf for your name's sake;
   because your steadfast love is good, deliver
   me.
22 For I am poor and needy,
   and my heart is pierced within me.
23 I am gone like a shadow at evening;
   I am shaken off like a locust.
24 My knees are weak through fasting;
   my body has become gaunt.
25 I am an object of scorn to my accusers;
   when they see me, they shake their heads.

Psalm 109

For the leader: for David: a psalm

1 GOD to whom I offer praise, do not be silent,
2 for the wicked have heaped calumnies upon me.
   They have lied to my face
3 and encompassed me on every side with words of
   hatred.
   They have assailed me without cause;
4 in return for my love they denounced me,
   though I have done nothing wrong.
5 They have repaid me evil for good,
   hatred in return for my love.
6 They say, 'Put up some rogue to denounce him,
   an accuser to confront him.'
7 But when judgement is given that rogue will be
   exposed
   and his wrongdoing accounted a sin.
8 May his days be few;
   may his hoarded wealth be seized by another!
9 May his children be fatherless,
   his wife a widow!
10 May his children be vagrants and beggars,
   driven from their ruined homes!
11 May the creditor distrain on all his goods
   and strangers run off with his earnings!
12 May none remain loyal to him,
   and none pity his fatherless children!
13 May his line be doomed to extinction,
   may his name be wiped out within a generation!
14 May the sins of his forefathers be remembered
   and his own mother's wickedness never be wiped
   out!
15 May they remain on record before the LORD,
   but may he cut off all memory of them from the
   earth!
16 For that man never set himself
   to be loyal to his friend,
   but persecuted the downtrodden and the poor
   and hounded the broken-hearted to their death.
17 He loved to curse: may the curse recoil on him!
   He took no pleasure in blessing: may no blessing
   be his!
18 He clothed himself in cursing like a garment:
   may it seep into his body like water
   and into his bones like oil!
19 May it wrap him round like the clothes he puts on,
   like the belt which he wears every day!
20 May the LORD so repay my accusers,
   those who speak evil against me!
21 You, LORD my God,
   deal with me as befits your honour;
   in the goodness of your love deliver me,
22 for I am downtrodden and poor,
   and my heart within me is distraught.
23 I fade like a passing shadow,
   I am shaken off like a locust.
24 My knees are weak for want of food
   and my flesh wastes away, so meagre is my fare.
25 I have become the object of their taunts;
   when they see me they wag their heads.

109:4 **though ... wrong:** *prob. rdg; Heb. obscure.* 109:6 **to confront him:** *Heb.* to stand at his right hand. 109:8 **hoarded wealth:** *or* charge, *cp. Acts 1:20.* 109:14 **remembered:** *so Syriac; Heb.* adds before the LORD.

---

[k] Syr: Heb *I prayer*   [l] Heb lacks *They say*   [m] Gk: Heb *and seek*
[n] Cn: Heb *fathers*   [o] Gk: Heb *their*

NEW AMERICAN BIBLE

Psalm 109

¹For the leader. A psalm of David.

I

O God, whom I praise, do not be silent,
2 for wicked and treacherous mouths attack me.
They speak against me with lying tongues;
3 with hateful words they surround me,
   attacking me without cause.
⁴In return for my love they slander me,
   even though I prayed for them.
⁵They repay me evil for good,
   hatred for my love.

II

My enemies say of me:
6 "Find a lying witness,
   an accuser to stand by his right hand,
⁷That he may be judged and found guilty,
   that his plea may be in vain.
⁸May his days be few;
   may another take his office.
⁹May his children be fatherless,
   his wife, a widow.
¹⁰May his children be vagrant beggars,
   driven from their hovels.
¹¹May the usurer snare all he owns,
   strangers plunder all he earns.
¹²May no one treat him kindly
   or pity his fatherless children.
¹³May his posterity be destroyed,
   his name cease in the next generation.
¹⁴May the LORD remember his fathers' guilt;
   his mother's sin not be canceled.
¹⁵May their guilt be always before the LORD,
   till their memory is banished from the earth,
¹⁶For he did not remember to show kindness,
   but hounded the wretched poor
   and brought death to the brokenhearted.
¹⁷He loved cursing; may it come upon him;
   he hated blessing; may none come to him.
¹⁸May cursing clothe him like a robe;
   may it enter his belly like water,
   seep into his bones like oil.
¹⁹May it be near as the clothes he wears,
   as the belt always around him."

III

²⁰May the LORD bring all this upon my accusers,
   upon those who speak evil against me.
²¹But you, LORD, my God,
   deal kindly with me for your name's sake;
   in your great mercy rescue me.
²²For I am sorely in need;
   my heart is pierced within me.
²³Like a lengthening shadow I near my end,
   all but swept away like the locust.
²⁴My knees totter from fasting;
   my flesh has wasted away.
²⁵I have become a mockery to them;
   when they see me, they shake their heads.

NEW JERUSALEM BIBLE

Psalm 109 (V 108)

For the choirmaster   Of David   Psalm

¹God whom I praise, do not be silent!
²Wicked and deceiving words
   are being said about me,
   false accusations are cast in my teeth.
³Words of hate fly all around me,
   though I give no cause for hostility.

⁴In return for my friendship they denounce me,
   and all I can do is pray!
⁵They repay my kindness with evil,
   and friendship with hatred.

6 'Set up a wicked man against him
   as accuser to stand on his right.
⁷At his trial may he emerge as guilty,
   even his prayer construed as a crime!

8 'May his life be cut short,
   someone else take over his office,
⁹his children be orphaned,
   his wife be widowed.

¹⁰ 'May his children wander perpetually,
   beggars, driven from the ruins of their house,
¹¹a creditor seize all his goods,
   and strangers make off with his earnings.

¹² 'May there be none left faithful enough to show
   him love,
   no one take pity on his orphans,
¹³the line of his descendants cut off,
   his name wiped out in one generation.

¹⁴ 'May Yahweh never forget the crimes of his
   ancestors,
   and his mother's sins not be wiped out;
¹⁵may Yahweh keep these constantly in mind,
   to cut off the remembrance of them from the
   earth.'

¹⁶He had no thought of being loyal,
   but hounded the poor and the needy
   and the broken-hearted to their death.
¹⁷He had a taste for cursing; let it recoil on him!
   No taste for blessing; let it never come his way!
¹⁸Cursing has been the uniform he wore;
   let it soak into him like water,
   like oil right into his bones.
¹⁹Let it be as a robe which envelops him completely,
   a sash which he always wears.

²⁰Let this be the salary Yahweh pays
   the accusers who blacken my name.
²¹Yahweh, treat them as your name demands;
   as your faithful love is generous, deliver me.

²²Poor and needy as I am,
   my wounds go right to the heart;
²³I am passing away like a fading shadow,
   they have shaken me off like a locust.

²⁴My knees are weak from lack of food,
   my body lean for lack of fat.
²⁵I have become the butt of their taunts,
   they shake their heads at the sight of me.

26 Help me, O LORD my God!
　　Save me according to your steadfast love.
27 Let them know that this is your hand;
　　you, O LORD, have done it.
28 Let them curse, but you will bless.
　　Let my assailants be put to shame;*p* may your
　　　servant be glad.
29 May my accusers be clothed with dishonor;
　　may they be wrapped in their own shame as in
　　　a mantle.
30 With my mouth I will give great thanks to the
　　LORD;
　　I will praise him in the midst of the throng.
31 For he stands at the right hand of the needy,
　　to save them from those who would condemn
　　　them to death.

Psalm 110

Of David. A Psalm.

1 The LORD says to my lord,
　　"Sit at my right hand
　　until I make your enemies your footstool."

2 The LORD sends out from Zion
　　your mighty scepter.
　　Rule in the midst of your foes.
3 Your people will offer themselves willingly
　　on the day you lead your forces
　　on the holy mountains.*q*
　　From the womb of the morning,
　　like dew, your youth*r* will come to you.
4 The LORD has sworn and will not change his
　　mind,
　　"You are a priest forever according to the order
　　　of Melchizedek."*s*

5 The Lord is at your right hand;
　　he will shatter kings on the day of his wrath.
6 He will execute judgment among the nations,
　　filling them with corpses;
　　he will shatter heads
　　over the wide earth.
7 He will drink from the stream by the path;
　　therefore he will lift up his head.

Psalm 111

1 Praise the LORD!
　　I will give thanks to the LORD with my whole
　　　heart,
　　in the company of the upright, in the
　　　congregation.
2 Great are the works of the LORD,
　　studied by all who delight in them.
3 Full of honor and majesty is his work,
　　and his righteousness endures forever.
4 He has gained renown by his wonderful deeds;
　　the LORD is gracious and merciful.
5 He provides food for those who fear him;
　　he is ever mindful of his covenant.
6 He has shown his people the power of his works,
　　in giving them the heritage of the nations.
7 The works of his hands are faithful and just;
　　all his precepts are trustworthy.

26 Help me, LORD my God;
　　save me by your love,
27 that all may know this is your doing
　　and you alone, LORD, have done it.
28 They may curse, but you will bless;
　　let my opponents be put to shame,
　　but may your servant rejoice!
29 May my accusers be clothed with dishonour,
　　wrapped in their shame as in a cloak!

30 I shall lift up my voice to extol the LORD,
　　before a great company I shall praise him.
31 For he stands at the right hand of the poor
　　to save them from those who bring them to trial.

Psalm 110

For David: a psalm

1 THIS is the LORD's oracle to my lord:
　　'Sit at my right hand,
　　and I shall make your enemies your footstool.'

2 The LORD extends the sway of your powerful
　　　sceptre, saying,
　　'From Zion reign over your enemies.'
3 You gain the homage of your people
　　on the day of your power.
　　Arrayed in holy garments, a child of the dawn,
　　you have the dew of your youth.
4 The LORD has sworn an oath and will not change
　　　his mind:
　　'You are a priest for ever,
　　a Melchizedek in my service.'
5 The Lord is at your right hand;
　　he crushes kings on the day of his wrath.
6 In glorious majesty he judges the nations,
　　shattering heads throughout the wide earth.

7 He will drink from the stream on his way;
　　therefore he will hold his head high.

Psalm 111

1 PRAISE the LORD.

With all my heart I shall give thanks to the LORD
　　in the congregation, in the assembly of the upright.
2 Great are the works of the LORD,
　　pondered over by all who delight in them.
3 His deeds are full of majesty and splendour;
　　his righteousness stands sure for ever.
4 He has won renown for his marvellous deeds;
　　the LORD is gracious and compassionate.
5 He provides food for those who fear him;
　　he keeps his covenant always in mind.
6 He showed his people how powerfully he worked
　　by bestowing on them the lands of the nations.
7 His works are truth and justice;
　　all his precepts are trustworthy,

---

p Gk: Heb *They have risen up and have been put to shame*
q Another reading is *in holy splendor*　　*r* Cn: Heb *the dew of your*
youth　　*s* Or *forever, a rightful king by my edict*

109:28 **let my . . . shame:** *so Gk; Heb.* they rose up and were put to
shame.　　110:4 **a Melchizedek . . . service:** *or* in the succession of
Melchizedek, *cp. Hebrews 5:6.*　　110:6 **In glorious majesty:** *prob.
rdg; Heb.* Full of corpses.

26 Help me, LORD, my God;
   save me in your kindness.
27 Make them know this is your hand,
   that you, LORD, have acted.
28 Though they curse, may you bless;
   shame my foes, that your servant may rejoice.
29 Clothe my accusers with disgrace;
   make them wear shame like a mantle.
30 I will give fervent thanks to the LORD;
   before all I will praise my God.
31 For God stands at the right hand of the poor
   to defend them against unjust accusers.

Psalm 110

1 A psalm of David.

The LORD says to you, my lord:
   "Take your throne at my right hand,
   while I make your enemies your footstool."
2 The scepter of your sovereign might
   the LORD will extend from Zion.
The LORD says: "Rule over your enemies!
3   Yours is princely power from the day of your
      birth.
In holy splendor before the daystar,
   like the dew I begot you."
4 The LORD has sworn and will not waver:
   "Like Melchizedek you are a priest forever."
5 At your right hand is the Lord,
   who crushes kings on the day of wrath,
6 Who, robed in splendor, judges nations,
   crushes heads across the wide earth,
7 Who drinks from the brook by the wayside
   and thus holds high the head.

Psalm 111

1 Hallelujah!

I will praise the LORD with all my heart
   in the assembled congregation of the upright.
2 Great are the works of the LORD,
   to be treasured for all their delights.
3 Majestic and glorious is your work,
   your wise design endures forever.
4 You won renown for your wondrous deeds;
   gracious and merciful is the LORD.
5 You gave food to those who fear you,
   mindful of your covenant forever.
6 You showed powerful deeds to your people,
   giving them the lands of the nations.
7 The works of your hands are right and true,
   reliable all your decrees,

26 Help me, Yahweh my God,
   save me as your faithful love demands.
27 Let them know that yours is the saving hand,
   that this, Yahweh, is your work.
28 Let them curse, provided that you bless;
   let their attacks bring shame to them and joy to
      your servant!
29 Let my accusers be clothed in disgrace,
   enveloped in a cloak of shame.
30 With generous thanks to Yahweh on my lips,
   I shall praise him before all the people,
31 for he stands at the side of the poor,
   to save their lives from those who sit in judgement
      on them.

Psalm 110 (V 109)

Of David   Psalm

1 Yahweh declared to my Lord, 'Take your seat at
      my right hand,
   till I have made your enemies your footstool.'

2 Yahweh will stretch out the sceptre of your power;
   from Zion you will rule your foes all around you.

3 Royal[s] dignity has been yours from the day of
      your birth,
   sacred honour from the womb, from the dawn of
      your youth.

4 Yahweh has sworn an oath he will never retract,
   you are a priest for ever of the order of
      Melchizedek.

5 At your right hand, Lord,
   he shatters kings when his anger breaks out.
6 He judges nations, heaping up corpses,
   he breaks heads over the whole wide world.
7 He drinks from a stream as he goes,
   and therefore he holds his head high.

Psalm 111 (V 110)

1 Alleluia!

Aleph	I give thanks to Yahweh with all my heart,
Bet	in the meeting-place of honest people, in the assembly.
Gimel	2 Great are the deeds of Yahweh,
Dalet	to be pondered by all who delight in them.
He	3 Full of splendour and majesty his work,
Waw	his saving justice stands firm for ever.
Zain	4 He gives us a memorial of his great deeds;
Het	Yahweh is mercy and tenderness.
Tet	5 He gives food to those who fear him,
Yod	he keeps his covenant ever in mind.
Kaph	6 His works show his people his power
Lamed	in giving them the birthright of the nations.
Mem	7 The works of his hands are fidelity and justice,
Nun	all his precepts are trustworthy,

s 110 Conjectural translation of a textually corrupt and obscure v.

8 They are established forever and ever,
  to be performed with faithfulness and
    uprightness.
9 He sent redemption to his people;
  he has commanded his covenant forever.
  Holy and awesome is his name.
10 The fear of the LORD is the beginning of wisdom;
  all those who practice it^r have a good
    understanding.
  His praise endures forever.

8 established to endure for ever,
  enacted in faithfulness and truth.
9 He sent and redeemed his people;
  he decreed that his covenant should endure for
    ever.
  Holy and awe-inspiring is his name.
10 The fear of the LORD is the beginning of wisdom,
  and they who live by it grow in understanding.
  Praise will be his for ever.

Psalm 112

1 Praise the LORD!
  Happy are those who fear the LORD,
    who greatly delight in his commandments.
2 Their descendants will be mighty in the land;
    the generation of the upright will be blessed.
3 Wealth and riches are in their houses,
    and their righteousness endures forever.
4 They rise in the darkness as a light for the
    upright;
  they are gracious, merciful, and righteous.
5 It is well with those who deal generously and
    lend,
  who conduct their affairs with justice.
6 For the righteous will never be moved;
  they will be remembered forever.
7 They are not afraid of evil tidings;
  their hearts are firm, secure in the LORD.
8 Their hearts are steady, they will not be afraid;
  in the end they will look in triumph on their
    foes.
9 They have distributed freely, they have given to
    the poor;
  their righteousness endures forever;
    their horn is exalted in honor.
10 The wicked see it and are angry;
  they gnash their teeth and melt away;
    the desire of the wicked comes to nothing.

Psalm 112

1 PRAISE the LORD.

  Happy is he who fears the LORD,
    who finds deep delight in obeying his
      commandments.
2 His descendants will be powerful in the land,
    a blessed generation of upright people.
3 His house will be full of riches and wealth;
    his righteousness will stand sure for ever.
4 A beacon in darkness for the upright,
    he is gracious, compassionate, good.
5 It is well with one who is gracious in his lending,
    ordering his affairs with equity.
6 Nothing will ever shake him;
    his goodness will be remembered for all time.
7 News of misfortune will have no terrors for him,
    because his heart is steadfast, trusting in the LORD.
8 His confidence is well established, he has no fears,
    and in the end he will see the downfall of his
      enemies.
9 He lavishes his gifts on the needy;
    his righteousness will stand sure for ever;
    in honour he carries his head high.
10 The wicked will see it with rising anger
    and grind their teeth in despair;
    the hopes of the wicked will come to nothing.

Psalm 113

1 Praise the LORD!
  Praise, O servants of the LORD;
    praise the name of the LORD.

2 Blessed be the name of the LORD
  from this time on and forevermore.
3 From the rising of the sun to its setting
  the name of the LORD is to be praised.
4 The LORD is high above all nations,
  and his glory above the heavens.

5 Who is like the LORD our God,
  who is seated on high,
6 who looks far down
  on the heavens and the earth?
7 He raises the poor from the dust,
  and lifts the needy from the ash heap,
8 to make them sit with princes,
  with the princes of his people.
9 He gives the barren woman a home,
  making her the joyous mother of children.
  Praise the LORD!

Psalm 113

1 PRAISE the LORD.

  Praise the LORD, you that are his servants,
    praise the name of the LORD.
2 Blessed be the name of the LORD
  now and evermore.
3 From the rising of the sun to its setting
  may the LORD's name be praised!
4 High is the LORD above all nations,
  high his glory above the heavens.

5-6 There is none like the LORD our God
  in heaven or on earth,
  who sets his throne so high
  but deigns to look down so low;
7 who lifts the weak out of the dust
  and raises the poor from the rubbish heap,
8 giving them a place among princes,
  among the princes of his people;
9 who makes the woman in a childless house
  a happy mother of children.

111:10 **beginning:** or chief part. **it:** so Gk; Heb. them.
113:9 **children:** Heb. adds Praise the LORD, transposed to the
beginning of Ps. 114 as Gk.

^rGk Syr: Heb them

NEW AMERICAN BIBLE | NEW JERUSALEM BIBLE

8 Established forever and ever,
   to be observed with loyalty and care.
9 You sent deliverance to your people,
   ratified your covenant forever;
   holy and awesome is your name.
10 The fear of the LORD is the beginning of wisdom;
   prudent are all who live by it.
   Your praise endures forever.

Samek 8 established for ever and ever,
Ain   accomplished in fidelity and honesty.

Pe 9 Deliverance he sends to his people,
Zade   his covenant he imposes for ever;
Qoph   holy and awesome his name.
Resh 10 The root of wisdom is fear of Yahweh;
Shin   those who attain it are wise.
Taw   His praise will continue for ever.

Psalm 112

1 Hallelujah!

Happy are those who fear the LORD,
   who greatly delight in God's commands.
2 Their descendants shall be mighty in the land,
   a generation upright and blessed.
3 Wealth and riches shall be in their homes;
   their prosperity shall endure forever.
4 They shine through the darkness, a light for the
   upright;
   they are gracious, merciful, and just.
5 All goes well for those gracious in lending,
   who conduct their affairs with justice.
6 They shall never be shaken;
   the just shall be remembered forever.
7 They shall not fear an ill report;
   their hearts are steadfast, trusting the LORD.
8 Their hearts are tranquil, without fear,
   till at last they look down on their foes.
9 Lavishly they give to the poor;
   their prosperity shall endure forever;
   their horn shall be exalted in honor.
10 The wicked shall be angry to see this;
   they will gnash their teeth and waste away;
   the desires of the wicked come to nothing.

Psalm 112 (V 111)

1 Alleluia!

Aleph   How blessed is anyone who fears Yahweh,
Bet   who delights in his commandments!
Gimel 2 His descendants shall be powerful on earth,
Dalet   the race of the honest shall receive blessings:

He 3 Riches and wealth for his family;
Waw   his uprightness stands firm for ever.
Zain 4 For the honest he shines as a lamp in the
   dark,
Het   generous, tender-hearted, and upright.

Tet 5 All goes well for one who lends generously,
Yod   who is honest in all his dealing;
Kaph 6 for all time to come he will not stumble,
Lamed   for all time to come the upright will be
   remembered.

Mem 7 Bad news holds no fears for him,
Nun   firm is his heart, trusting in Yahweh.
Samek 8 His heart held steady, he has no fears,
Ain   till he can gloat over his enemies.

Pe 9 To the needy he gives without stint,
Zade   his uprightness stands firm for ever;
Qoph   his reputation is founded on strength.

Resh 10 The wicked are vexed at the sight,
Shin   they grind their teeth and waste away.
Taw   The desires of the wicked will be frustrated.

Psalm 113

1 Hallelujah!

I
Praise, you servants of the LORD,
   praise the name of the LORD.
2 Blessed be the name of the LORD
   both now and forever.
3 From the rising of the sun to its setting
   let the name of the LORD be praised.
II
4 High above all nations is the LORD;
   above the heavens God's glory.
5 Who is like the LORD,
   our God enthroned on high,
6 looking down on heaven and earth?
7 The LORD raises the needy from the dust,
   lifts the poor from the ash heap,
8 Seats them with princes,
   the princes of the people,
9 Gives the childless wife a home,
   the joyful mother of children.
   Hallelujah!

Psalm 113 (V 112)

1 Alleluia!

Praise, servants of Yahweh,
   praise the name of Yahweh.
2 Blessed be the name of Yahweh,
   henceforth and for ever.
3 From the rising of the sun to its setting,
   praised be the name of Yahweh!

4 Supreme over all nations is Yahweh,
   supreme over the heavens his glory.
5 Who is like Yahweh our God?
   His throne is set on high,
6 but he stoops to look down on heaven and earth.

7 He raises the poor from the dust,
   he lifts the needy from the dunghill,
8 to give them a place among princes,
   among princes of his people.
9 He lets the barren woman be seated at home,
   the happy mother of sons.

NEW REVISED STANDARD VERSION

REVISED ENGLISH BIBLE

Psalm 114

1 When Israel went out from Egypt,
   the house of Jacob from a people of strange
     language,
2 Judah became God's*u* sanctuary,
   Israel his dominion.

3 The sea looked and fled;
   Jordan turned back.
4 The mountains skipped like rams,
   the hills like lambs.

5 Why is it, O sea, that you flee?
   O Jordan, that you turn back?
6 O mountains, that you skip like rams?
   O hills, like lambs?

7 Tremble, O earth, at the presence of the LORD,
   at the presence of the God of Jacob,
8 who turns the rock into a pool of water,
   the flint into a spring of water.

Psalm 115

1 Not to us, O LORD, not to us, but to your name
     give glory,
   for the sake of your steadfast love and your
     faithfulness.
2 Why should the nations say,
   "Where is their God?"

3 Our God is in the heavens;
   he does whatever he pleases.
4 Their idols are silver and gold,
   the work of human hands.
5 They have mouths, but do not speak;
   eyes, but do not see.
6 They have ears, but do not hear;
   noses, but do not smell.
7 They have hands, but do not feel;
   feet, but do not walk;
   they make no sound in their throats.
8 Those who make them are like them;
   so are all who trust in them.

9 O Israel, trust in the LORD!
   He is their help and their shield.
10 O house of Aaron, trust in the LORD!
   He is their help and their shield.
11 You who fear the LORD, trust in the LORD!
   He is their help and their shield.

12 The LORD has been mindful of us; he will bless
     us;
   he will bless the house of Israel;
   he will bless the house of Aaron;
13 he will bless those who fear the LORD,
   both small and great.

14 May the LORD give you increase,
   both you and your children.
15 May you be blessed by the LORD,
   who made heaven and earth.

16 The heavens are the LORD's heavens,
   but the earth he has given to human beings.
17 The dead do not praise the LORD,
   nor do any that go down into silence.

u Heb *his*

Psalm 114

1 PRAISE the LORD.

  When Israel came out of Egypt,
   the house of Jacob from a barbaric people,
2 Judah became God's sanctuary,
   Israel his domain.
3 The sea fled at the sight;
   Jordan turned back.
4 The mountains skipped like rams,
   the hills like lambs of the flock.
5 What made you, the sea, flee away?
   Jordan, what made you turn back?
6 Why did you skip like rams, you mountains,
   and like lambs, you hills?
7 Earth, dance at the presence of the Lord,
   at the presence of the God of Jacob,
8 who turned the rock into a pool of water,
   the flinty cliff into a welling spring.

Psalm 115

1 NOT to us, LORD, not to us,
   but to your name give glory
   for your love, for your faithfulness!
2 Why should the nations ask,
   'Where, then, is their God?'
3 Our God is high in heaven;
   he does whatever he wills.

4 Their idols are silver and gold,
   made by human hands.
5 They have mouths, but cannot speak,
   eyes, but cannot see;
6 they have ears, but cannot hear,
   nostrils, but cannot smell;
7 with their hands they cannot feel,
   with their feet they cannot walk,
   and no sound comes from their throats.
8 Their makers become like them,
   and so do all who put their trust in them.
9 But Israel trusts in the LORD:
   he is their help and their shield.
10 The house of Aaron trusts in the LORD:
   he is their help and their shield.
11 Those who fear the LORD trust in the LORD:
   he is their help and their shield.

12 The LORD who has been mindful of us will bless
     us,
   he will bless the house of Israel,
   he will bless the house of Aaron.
13 The LORD will bless those who fear him,
   both high and low.

14 May the LORD give you increase,
   both you and your children.
15 You are blessed by the LORD,
   the maker of heaven and earth.
16 The heavens belong to the LORD,
   but the earth he has given to mankind.
17 It is not the dead who praise the LORD,
   not those who go down to the silent grave;

114:1 **Praise the LORD:** *transposed from end of Ps. 113; so Gk.*
barbaric people: *or* people of alien speech.   114:7 **dance:** *or*
tremble.

Psalm 114

1 When Israel came forth from Egypt,
   the house of Jacob from an alien people,
2 Judah became God's holy place,
   Israel, God's domain.
3 The sea beheld and fled;
   the Jordan turned back.
4 The mountains skipped like rams;
   the hills, like lambs of the flock.
5 Why was it, sea, that you fled?
   Jordan, that you turned back?
6 You mountains, that you skipped like rams?
   You hills, like lambs of the flock?
7 Tremble, earth, before the Lord,
   before the God of Jacob,
8 Who turned rock into pools of water,
   stone into flowing springs.

Psalm 115

I

1 Not to us, LORD, not to us
   but to your name give glory
   because of your faithfulness and love.
2 Why should the nations say,
   "Where is their God?"
3 Our God is in heaven;
   whatever God wills is done.

II

4 Their idols are silver and gold,
   the work of human hands.
5 They have mouths but do not speak,
   eyes but do not see.
6 They have ears but do not hear,
   noses but do not smell.
7 They have hands but do not feel,
   feet but do not walk,
   and no sound rises from their throats.
8 Their makers shall be like them,
   all who trust in them.

III

9 The house of Israel trusts in the LORD,
   who is their help and shield.
10 The house of Aaron trusts in the LORD,
   who is their help and shield.
11 Those who fear the LORD trust in the LORD,
   who is their help and shield.
12 The LORD remembers us and will bless us,
   will bless the house of Israel,
   will bless the house of Aaron,
13 Will bless those who fear the LORD,
   small and great alike.
14 May the LORD increase your number,
   you and your descendants.
15 May you be blessed by the LORD,
   who made heaven and earth.
16 The heavens belong to the LORD,
   but the earth is given to us.
17 The dead do not praise the LORD,
   all those gone down into silence.

Psalm 114 (V 113A)

Alleluia!

1 When Israel came out of Egypt,
   the House of Jacob from a people of foreign
      speech,
2 Judah became his sanctuary,
   and Israel his domain.

3 The sea fled at the sight,
   the Jordan turned back,
4 the mountains skipped like rams,
   the hills like sheep.

5 Sea, what makes you flee?
   Jordan, why turn back?
6 Why skip like rams, you mountains?
   Why like sheep, you hills?

7 Tremble, earth, at the coming of the Lord,
   at the coming of the God of Jacob,
8 who turns rock into pool,
   flint into fountain.

Psalm 115 (V 113B)

1 Not to us, Yahweh, not to us,
   but to your name give the glory,
   for your faithful love and your constancy!
2 Why should the nations ask, 'Where is their God?'

3 Our God is in heaven,
   he creates whatever he chooses.
4 They have idols of silver and gold,
   made by human hands.

5 These have mouths but say nothing,
   have eyes but see nothing,
6 have ears but hear nothing,
   have noses but smell nothing.

7 They have hands but cannot feel,
   have feet but cannot walk,
   no sound comes from their throats.
8 Their makers will end up like them,
   and all who rely on them.

9 House of Israel, rely on Yahweh;
   he is their help and their shield.
10 House of Aaron, rely on Yahweh;
   he is their help and their shield.
11 You who fear Yahweh, rely on Yahweh;
   he is their help and their shield.

12 Yahweh will keep us in mind, he will bless,
   he will bless the House of Israel,
   he will bless the House of Aaron,
13 he will bless those who fear Yahweh,
   small and great alike.

14 May Yahweh add to your numbers,
   yours and your children's too!
15 May you be blessed by Yahweh,
   who made heaven and earth.

16 Heaven belongs to Yahweh,
   but earth he has given to the children of Adam.
17 The dead cannot praise Yahweh,
   those who sink into silence,

18 But we will bless the LORD
    from this time on and forevermore.
Praise the LORD!

18 but we, the living, shall bless the LORD
    now and for evermore.

Praise the LORD.

Psalm 116

1 I love the LORD, because he has heard
    my voice and my supplications.
2 Because he inclined his ear to me,
    therefore I will call on him as long as I live.
3 The snares of death encompassed me;
    the pangs of Sheol laid hold on me;
    I suffered distress and anguish.
4 Then I called on the name of the LORD:
    "O LORD, I pray, save my life!"

5 Gracious is the LORD, and righteous;
    our God is merciful.
6 The LORD protects the simple;
    when I was brought low, he saved me.
7 Return, O my soul, to your rest,
    for the LORD has dealt bountifully with you.

8 For you have delivered my soul from death,
    my eyes from tears,
    my feet from stumbling.
9 I walk before the LORD
    in the land of the living.
10 I kept my faith, even when I said,
    "I am greatly afflicted";
11 I said in my consternation,
    "Everyone is a liar."

12 What shall I return to the LORD
    for all his bounty to me?
13 I will lift up the cup of salvation
    and call on the name of the LORD,
14 I will pay my vows to the LORD
    in the presence of all his people.
15 Precious in the sight of the LORD
    is the death of his faithful ones.
16 O LORD, I am your servant;
    I am your servant, the child of your serving
      girl.
    You have loosed my bonds.
17 I will offer to you a thanksgiving sacrifice
    and call on the name of the LORD.
18 I will pay my vows to the LORD
    in the presence of all his people,
19 in the courts of the house of the LORD,
    in your midst, O Jerusalem.
Praise the LORD!

Psalm 116

1 I LOVE the LORD, for he has heard me
    and listened to my prayer;
2 he has given me a hearing
    and all my days I shall cry to him.
3 The cords of death bound me,
    Sheol held me in its grip.
    Anguish and torment held me fast;
4 then I invoked the LORD by name,
    'LORD, deliver me, I pray.'

5 Gracious is the LORD and righteous;
    our God is full of compassion.
6 The LORD preserves the simple-hearted;
    when I was brought low, he saved me.
7 My heart, be at peace once more,
    for the LORD has granted you full deliverance.
8 You have rescued me from death,
    my eyes from weeping,
    my feet from stumbling.
9 I shall walk in the presence of the LORD
    in the land of the living.

10 I was sure I should be swept away;
    my distress was bitter.
11 In my alarm I cried,
    'How faithless are all my fellow-creatures!'

12 How can I repay the LORD
    for all his benefits to me?
13 I shall lift up the cup of salvation
    and call on the LORD by name.
14 I shall pay my vows to the LORD
    in the presence of all his people.
15 A precious thing in the LORD's sight
    is the death of those who are loyal to him.
16 Indeed, LORD, I am your slave,
    I am your slave, your slave-girl's son;
    you have loosed my bonds.
17 To you I shall bring a thank-offering
    and call on the LORD by name.
18 I shall pay my vows to the LORD
    in the presence of all his people,
19 in the courts of the LORD's house,
    in the midst of you, Jerusalem.

Praise the LORD.

Psalm 117

1 Praise the LORD, all you nations!
    Extol him, all you peoples!
2 For great is his steadfast love toward us,
    and the faithfulness of the LORD endures
      forever.
Praise the LORD!

Psalm 117

1 PRAISE the LORD, all nations,
2 extol him, all you peoples;
    for his love protecting us is strong,
    the LORD's faithfulness is everlasting.

Praise the LORD.

115:18 **the living:** *so Gk; Heb. omits.*   116:3 **Sheol:** *or the*
underworld.   116:10 **I was . . . away:** *or I believed though I said.*

18 It is we who bless the LORD,
both now and forever.
Hallelujah!

Psalm 116

I

1 I love the LORD, who listened
to my voice in supplication,
2 Who turned an ear to me
on the day I called.
3 I was caught by the cords of death;
the snares of Sheol had seized me;
I felt agony and dread.
4 Then I called on the name of the LORD,
"O LORD, save my life!"

II

5 Gracious is the LORD and just;
yes, our God is merciful.
6 The LORD protects the simple;
I was helpless, but God saved me.
7 Return, my soul, to your rest;
the LORD has been good to you.
8 For my soul has been freed from death,
my eyes from tears, my feet from stumbling.
9 I shall walk before the LORD
in the land of the living.

III

10 I kept faith, even when I said,
"I am greatly afflicted!"
11 I said in my alarm,
"No one can be trusted!"
12 How can I repay the LORD
for all the good done for me?
13 I will raise the cup of salvation
and call on the name of the LORD.
14 I will pay my vows to the LORD
in the presence of all his people.
15 Too costly in the eyes of the LORD
is the death of his faithful.
16 LORD, I am your servant,
your servant, the child of your maidservant;
you have loosed my bonds.
17 I will offer a sacrifice of thanksgiving
and call on the name of the LORD.
18 I will pay my vows to the LORD
in the presence of all his people,
19 In the courts of the house of the LORD,
in your midst, O Jerusalem.
Hallelujah!

Psalm 117

1 Praise the LORD, all you nations!
Give glory, all you peoples!
2 The LORD's love for us is strong;
the LORD is faithful forever.
Hallelujah!

18 but we, the living, shall bless Yahweh,
henceforth and for ever.

Psalm 116 (V 114–115)

Alleluia!

1 I am filled with love when Yahweh listens
to the sound of my prayer,
2 when he bends down to hear me,
as I call.

3 The bonds of death were all round me,
the snares of Sheol held me fast;
distress and anguish held me in their grip,
4 I called on the name of Yahweh.

Deliver me, Yahweh, I beg you.

5 Yahweh is merciful and upright,
our God is tenderness.
6 Yahweh looks after the simple,
when I was brought low he gave me strength.
7 My heart, be at peace once again,
for Yahweh has treated you generously.
8 He has rescued me from death, my eyes from
tears,
and my feet from stumbling.
9 I shall pass my life in the presence of Yahweh,
in the land of the living.

10 My trust does not fail even when I say,
'I am completely wretched.'
11 In my terror I said,
'No human being can be relied on.'
12 What return can I make to Yahweh
for his generosity to me?
13 I shall take up the cup of salvation
and call on the name of Yahweh.

14 I shall fulfil my vows to Yahweh,
witnessed by all his people.

15 Costly in Yahweh's sight
is the death of his faithful.

16 I beg you, Yahweh! I am your servant,
I am your servant and my mother was your
servant;
you have undone my fetters.
17 I shall offer you a sacrifice of thanksgiving
and call on the name of Yahweh.

18 I shall fulfil my vows to Yahweh,
witnessed by all his people,
19 in the courts of the house of Yahweh,
in your very heart, Jerusalem.

Psalm 117 (V 116)

Alleluia!

1 Praise Yahweh, all nations,
extol him, all peoples,
2 for his faithful love is strong
and his constancy never-ending.

NEW REVISED STANDARD VERSION

REVISED ENGLISH BIBLE

Psalm 118

1 O give thanks to the LORD, for he is good;
  his steadfast love endures forever!

2 Let Israel say,
  "His steadfast love endures forever."
3 Let the house of Aaron say,
  "His steadfast love endures forever."
4 Let those who fear the LORD say,
  "His steadfast love endures forever."

5 Out of my distress I called on the LORD;
  the LORD answered me and set me in a broad
    place.
6 With the LORD on my side I do not fear.
  What can mortals do to me?
7 The LORD is on my side to help me;
  I shall look in triumph on those who hate me.

8 It is better to take refuge in the LORD
  than to put confidence in mortals.
9 It is better to take refuge in the LORD
  than to put confidence in princes.

10 All nations surrounded me;
  in the name of the LORD I cut them off!
11 They surrounded me, surrounded me on every
    side;
  in the name of the LORD I cut them off!
12 They surrounded me like bees;
  they blazed^v like a fire of thorns;
  in the name of the LORD I cut them off!
13 I was pushed hard,^w so that I was falling,
  but the LORD helped me.
14 The LORD is my strength and my might;
  he has become my salvation.

15 There are glad songs of victory in the tents of the
    righteous:
  "The right hand of the LORD does valiantly;
16 the right hand of the LORD is exalted;
  the right hand of the LORD does valiantly."

17 I shall not die, but I shall live,
  and recount the deeds of the LORD.
18 The LORD has punished me severely,
  but he did not give me over to death.

19 Open to me the gates of righteousness,
  that I may enter through them
  and give thanks to the LORD.
20 This is the gate of the LORD;
  the righteous shall enter through it.

21 I thank you that you have answered me
  and have become my salvation.
22 The stone that the builders rejected
  has become the chief cornerstone.
23 This is the LORD's doing;
  it is marvelous in our eyes.
24 This is the day that the LORD has made;
  let us rejoice and be glad in it.^x
25 Save us, we beseech you, O LORD!
  O LORD, we beseech you, give us success!
26 Blessed is the one who comes in the name of the
    LORD.^y
  We bless you from the house of the LORD.

Psalm 118

1 IT is good to give thanks to the LORD,
  for his love endures for ever.
2 Let Israel say:
  'His love endures for ever.'
3 Let the house of Aaron say:
  'His love endures for ever.'
4 Let those who fear the LORD say:
  'His love endures for ever.'

5 When in distress I called to the LORD,
  he answered me and gave me relief.
6 With the LORD on my side, I am not afraid;
  what can mortals do to me?
7 With the LORD on my side, as my helper,
  I shall see the downfall of my enemies.
8 It is better to seek refuge in the LORD
  than to trust in any mortal,
9 better to seek refuge in the LORD
  than to trust in princes.

10 The nations all surrounded me,
  but in the LORD's name I drove them off.
11 They surrounded me on every side,
  but in the LORD's name I drove them off.
12 They swarmed round me like bees;
  they attacked me, as fire attacks brushwood,
  but in the LORD's name I drove them off.
13 They thrust hard against me so that I nearly fell,
  but the LORD came to my help.
14 The LORD is my refuge and defence,
  and he has become my deliverer.

15 Listen! Shouts of triumph
  in the camp of the victors:
  'With his right hand the LORD does mighty deeds;
16 the right hand of the LORD raises up,
  with his right hand the LORD does mighty deeds.'
17 I shall not die; I shall live
  to proclaim what the LORD has done.
18 The LORD did indeed chasten me,
  but he did not surrender me to death.

19 Open to me the gates of victory;
  I shall go in by them and praise the LORD.
20 This is the gate of the LORD;
  the victors will enter through it.
21 I shall praise you, for you have answered me
  and have become my deliverer.
22 The stone which the builders rejected
  has become the main corner-stone.
23 This is the LORD's doing;
  it is wonderful in our eyes.
24 This is the day on which the LORD has acted,
  a day for us to exult and rejoice.
25 LORD, deliver us, we pray;
  LORD, grant us prosperity.
26 Blessed is he who enters in the name of the LORD;
  we bless you from the house of the LORD.

---

^vGk: Heb *were extinguished*   ^wGk Syr Jerome: Heb *You pushed
me hard*   ^xOr *in him*   ^yOr *Blessed in the name of the LORD is
the one who comes*

118:13 **They:** *cp. Gk; Heb.* You.   118:15 **victors:** *or* righteous.
118:19 **victory:** *or* righteousness.   118:20 **victors:** *or* righteous.
118:24 **on . . . acted:** *or* the LORD has made.

Psalm 118

I
1 Give thanks to the LORD, who is good,
  whose love endures forever.
2 Let the house of Israel say:
  God's love endures forever.
3 Let the house of Aaron say,
  God's love endures forever.
4 Let those who fear the LORD say,
  God's love endures forever.

II
5 In danger I called on the LORD;
  the LORD answered me and set me free.
6 The LORD is with me; I am not afraid;
  what can mortals do against me?
7 The LORD is with me as my helper;
  I shall look in triumph on my foes.
8 Better to take refuge in the LORD
  than to put one's trust in mortals.
9 Better to take refuge in the LORD
  than to put one's trust in princes.

III
10 All the nations surrounded me;
  in the LORD's name I crushed them.
11 They surrounded me on every side;
  in the LORD's name I crushed them.
12 They surrounded me like bees;
  they blazed like fire among thorns;
  in the LORD's name I crushed them.
13 I was hard pressed and falling,
  but the LORD came to my help.
14 The LORD, my strength and might,
  came to me as savior.

IV
15 The joyful shout of deliverance
  is heard in the tents of the victors:
  "The LORD's right hand strikes with power;
16   the LORD's right hand is raised;
  the LORD's right hand strikes with power."
17 I shall not die but live
  and declare the deeds of the LORD.
18 The LORD chastised me harshly,
  but did not hand me over to death.

V
19 Open the gates of victory;
  I will enter and thank the LORD.
20 This is the LORD's own gate,
  where the victors enter.
21 I thank you for you answered me;
  you have been my savior.
22 The stone the builders rejected
  has become the cornerstone.
23 By the LORD has this been done;
  it is wonderful in our eyes.
24 This is the day the LORD has made;
  let us rejoice in it and be glad.
25 LORD, grant salvation!
  LORD, grant good fortune!

VI
26 Blessed is he
  who comes in the name of the LORD.
  We bless you from the LORD's house.

Psalm 118 (V 117)

Alleluia!
1 Give thanks to Yahweh for he is good,
  for his faithful love endures for ever.

2 Let the House of Israel say,
  'His faithful love endures for ever.'
3 Let the House of Aaron say,
  'His faithful love endures for ever.'
4 Let those who fear Yahweh say,
  'His faithful love endures for ever.'

5 In my distress I called to Yahweh,
  he heard me and brought me relief.
6 With Yahweh on my side I fear nothing;
  what can human beings do to me?
7 With Yahweh on my side as my help,
  I gloat over my enemies.

8 It is better to take refuge in Yahweh
  than to rely on human beings;
9 better to take refuge in Yahweh
  than to rely on princes.

10 Nations were swarming around me,
  in the name of Yahweh I cut them down;
11 they swarmed around me, pressing upon me,
  in the name of Yahweh I cut them down.
12 They swarmed around me like bees,
  they flared up like a brushwood fire,
  in the name of Yahweh I cut them down.
13 I was pushed hard, to make me fall,
  but Yahweh came to my help.
14 Yahweh is my strength and my song,
  he has been my Saviour.

15 Shouts of joy and salvation,
  in the tents of the upright,
  'Yahweh's right hand is triumphant,
16 Yahweh's right hand is victorious,
  Yahweh's right hand is triumphant!'

17 I shall not die, I shall live
  to recount the great deeds of Yahweh.
18 Though Yahweh punished me sternly,
  he has not abandoned me to death.

19 Open for me the gates of saving justice,
  I shall go in and thank Yahweh.
20 This is the gate of Yahweh,
  where the upright go in.
21 I thank you for hearing me,
  and making yourself my Saviour.
22 The stone which the builders rejected
  has become the cornerstone;
23 This is Yahweh's doing,
  and we marvel at it.
24 This is the day which Yahweh has made,
  a day for us to rejoice and be glad.

25 We beg you, Yahweh, save us,
  we beg you, Yahweh, give us victory!
26 Blessed in the name of Yahweh is he who is
      coming!
  We bless you from the house of Yahweh.

NEW REVISED STANDARD VERSION	REVISED ENGLISH BIBLE

27 The LORD is God,
  and he has given us light.
  Bind the festal procession with branches,
  up to the horns of the altar.ᶻ

28 You are my God, and I will give thanks to you;
  you are my God, I will extol you.

29 O give thanks to the LORD, for he is good,
  for his steadfast love endures forever.

27 The LORD is God; he has given us light.
  Link the pilgrims with cords
  as far as the horns of the altar.

28 You are my God and I shall praise you;
  my God, I shall exalt you.

29 It is good to give thanks to the LORD,
  for his love endures for ever.

Psalm 119

1 Happy are those whose way is blameless,
  who walk in the law of the LORD.

2 Happy are those who keep his decrees,
  who seek him with their whole heart,

3 who also do no wrong,
  but walk in his ways.

4 You have commanded your precepts
  to be kept diligently.

5 O that my ways may be steadfast
  in keeping your statutes!

6 Then I shall not be put to shame,
  having my eyes fixed on all your
    commandments.

7 I will praise you with an upright heart,
  when I learn your righteous ordinances.

8 I will observe your statutes;
  do not utterly forsake me.

9 How can young people keep their way pure?
  By guarding it according to your word.

10 With my whole heart I seek you;
  do not let me stray from your commandments.

11 I treasure your word in my heart,
  so that I may not sin against you.

12 Blessed are you, O LORD;
  teach me your statutes.

13 With my lips I declare
  all the ordinances of your mouth.

14 I delight in the way of your decrees
  as much as in all riches.

15 I will meditate on your precepts,
  and fix my eyes on your ways.

16 I will delight in your statutes;
  I will not forget your word.

17 Deal bountifully with your servant,
  so that I may live and observe your word.

18 Open my eyes, so that I may behold
  wondrous things out of your law.

19 I live as an alien in the land;
  do not hide your commandments from me.

20 My soul is consumed with longing
  for your ordinances at all times.

21 You rebuke the insolent, accursed ones,
  who wander from your commandments;

22 take away from me their scorn and contempt,
  for I have kept your decrees.

23 Even though princes sit plotting against me,
  your servant will meditate on your statutes.

24 Your decrees are my delight,
  they are my counselors.

25 My soul clings to the dust;
  revive me according to your word.

Psalm 119

1 HAPPY are they whose way of life is blameless,
  who conform to the law of the LORD.

2 Happy are they who obey his instruction,
  who set their heart on finding him;

3 who have done no wrong,
  but have lived according to his will.

4 You, Lord, have laid down your precepts
  that are to be kept faithfully.

5 If only I might hold a steady course,
  keeping your statutes!

6 Then, if I fixed my eyes on all your
    commandments,
  I should never be put to shame.

7 I shall praise you in sincerity of heart
  as I learn your just decrees.

8 I shall observe your statutes;
  do not leave me forsaken!

9 How may a young man lead a clean life?
  By holding to your words.

10 With all my heart I seek you;
  do not let me stray from your commandments.

11 I treasure your promise in my heart,
  for fear that I might sin against you.

12 Blessed are you, LORD;
  teach me your statutes.

13 I say them over, one by one,
  all the decrees you have announced.

14 I have rejoiced in the path of your instruction
  as one rejoices over wealth of every kind.

15 I shall meditate on your precepts
  and keep your paths before my eyes.

16 In your statutes I find continual delight;
  I shall not forget your word.

17 Grant this to me, your servant: let me live
  so that I may keep your word.

18 Take the veil from my eyes, that I may see
  the wonders to be found in your law.

19 Though I am but a passing stranger here on earth,
  do not hide your commandments from me.

20 My heart pines continually
  with longing for your decrees.

21 The proud have felt your censure;
  cursed are those who turn from your
    commandments.

22 Set me free from scorn and insult,
  for I have obeyed your instruction.

23 Rulers sit scheming together against me;
  but I, your servant, shall study your statutes.

24 Your instruction is my continual delight;
  I turn to it for counsel.

25 I lie prone in the dust;
  revive me according to your word.

ᶻ Meaning of Heb uncertain

118:27 **cords:** or branches.

27 The LORD is God and has given us light.
  Join in procession with leafy branches
    up to the horns of the altar.
VII
28 You are my God, I give you thanks;
    my God, I offer you praise.
29 Give thanks to the LORD, who is good,
    whose love endures forever.

Psalm 119

Aleph 1 Happy those whose way is blameless,
    who walk by the teaching of the LORD.
2 Happy those who observe God's decrees,
    who seek the LORD with all their heart.
3 They do no wrong;
    they walk in God's ways.
4 You have given them the command
    to keep your precepts with care.
5 May my ways be firm
    in the observance of your laws!
6 Then I will not be ashamed
    to ponder all your commands.
7 I will praise you with sincere heart
    as I study your just edicts.
8 I will keep your laws;
    do not leave me all alone.

Beth 9 How can the young walk without fault?
    Only by keeping your words.
10 With all my heart I seek you;
    do not let me stray from your commands.
11 In my heart I treasure your promise,
    that I may not sin against you.
12 Blessed are you, O LORD;
    teach me your laws.
13 With my lips I recite
    all the edicts you have spoken.
14 I find joy in the way of your decrees
    more than in all riches.
15 I will ponder your precepts
    and consider your paths.
16 In your laws I take delight;
    I will never forget your word.

Gimel 17 Be kind to your servant that I may live,
    that I may keep your word.
18 Open my eyes to see clearly
    the wonders of your teachings.
19 I am a sojourner in the land;
    do not hide your commands from me.
20 At all times my soul is stirred
    with longing for your edicts.
21 With a curse you rebuke the proud
    who stray from your commands.
22 Free me from disgrace and contempt,
    for I observe your decrees.
23 Though princes meet and talk against me,
    your servant studies your laws.
24 Your decrees are my delight;
    they are my counselors.

Daleth 25 I lie prostrate in the dust;
    give me life in accord with your word.

27 Yahweh is God,
  he gives us light.

Link your processions, branches in hand,
  up to the horns of the altar.
28 You are my God, I thank you,
    all praise to you, my God.
I thank you for hearing me,
    and making yourself my Saviour.

29 Give thanks to Yahweh for he is good,
  for his faithful love endures for ever.

Psalm 119 (V 118)

Aleph 1 How blessed are those whose way is
    blameless,
    who walk in the Law of Yahweh!
2 Blessed are those who observe his
    instructions,
    who seek him with all their hearts,
3 and, doing no evil,
    who walk in his ways.
4 You lay down your precepts
    to be carefully kept.
5 May my ways be steady
    in doing your will.
6 Then I shall not be shamed,
    if my gaze is fixed on your commandments.
7 I thank you with a sincere heart
    for teaching me your upright judgements.
8 I shall do your will;
    do not ever abandon me wholly.

Bet 9 How can a young man keep his way spotless?
    By keeping your words.
10 With all my heart I seek you,
    do not let me stray from your commandments.
11 In my heart I treasure your promises,
    to avoid sinning against you.
12 Blessed are you, Yahweh,
    teach me your will!
13 With my lips I have repeated
    all the judgements you have given.
14 In the way of your instructions lies my joy,
    a joy beyond all wealth.
15 I will ponder your precepts
    and fix my gaze on your paths.
16 I find my delight in your will,
    I do not forget your words.

Gimel 17 Be generous to your servant and I shall live,
    and shall keep your words.
18 Open my eyes and I shall fix my gaze
    on the wonders of your Law.
19 Wayfarer though I am on the earth,
    do not hide your commandments from me.
20 My heart is pining away with longing
    at all times for your judgements.
21 You have rebuked the arrogant, the accursed,
    who stray from your commandments.
22 Set me free from taunts and contempt
    since I observe your instructions.
23 Though princes sit plotting against me,
    your servant keeps pondering your will.
24 Your instructions are my delight,
    your wishes my counsellors.

Dalet 25 Down in the dust I lie prostrate;
    true to your word, revive me.

NEW REVISED STANDARD VERSION	REVISED ENGLISH BIBLE

NEW REVISED STANDARD VERSION

26 When I told of my ways, you answered me;
    teach me your statutes.
27 Make me understand the way of your precepts,
    and I will meditate on your wondrous works.
28 My soul melts away for sorrow;
    strengthen me according to your word.
29 Put false ways far from me;
    and graciously teach me your law.
30 I have chosen the way of faithfulness;
    I set your ordinances before me.
31 I cling to your decrees, O LORD;
    let me not be put to shame.
32 I run the way of your commandments,
    for you enlarge my understanding.

33 Teach me, O LORD, the way of your statutes,
    and I will observe it to the end.
34 Give me understanding, that I may keep your law
    and observe it with my whole heart.
35 Lead me in the path of your commandments,
    for I delight in it.
36 Turn my heart to your decrees,
    and not to selfish gain.
37 Turn my eyes from looking at vanities;
    give me life in your ways.
38 Confirm to your servant your promise,
    which is for those who fear you.
39 Turn away the disgrace that I dread,
    for your ordinances are good.
40 See, I have longed for your precepts;
    in your righteousness give me life.

41 Let your steadfast love come to me, O LORD,
    your salvation according to your promise.
42 Then I shall have an answer for those who taunt me,
    for I trust in your word.
43 Do not take the word of truth utterly out of my mouth,
    for my hope is in your ordinances.
44 I will keep your law continually,
    forever and ever.
45 I shall walk at liberty,
    for I have sought your precepts.
46 I will also speak of your decrees before kings,
    and shall not be put to shame;
47 I find my delight in your commandments,
    because I love them.
48 I revere your commandments, which I love,
    and I will meditate on your statutes.

49 Remember your word to your servant,
    in which you have made me hope.
50 This is my comfort in my distress,
    that your promise gives me life.
51 The arrogant utterly deride me,
    but I do not turn away from your law.
52 When I think of your ordinances from of old,
    I take comfort, O LORD.
53 Hot indignation seizes me because of the wicked,
    those who forsake your law.
54 Your statutes have been my songs
    wherever I make my home.
55 I remember your name in the night, O LORD,
    and keep your law.

REVISED ENGLISH BIBLE

26 I tell you of my plight and you answer me;
    teach me your statutes.
27 Show me the way set out in your precepts,
    and I shall meditate on your wonders.
28 Because of misery I cannot rest;
    renew my strength in accordance with your promise.
29 Keep falsehood far from me
    and grant me the grace of living by your law.
30 I have chosen the path of faithfulness;
    I have set your decrees before me.
31 I hold fast to your instruction;
    LORD, do not let me be put to shame.
32 I shall run the course made known in your commandments,
    for you set free my heart.

33 Teach me, LORD, the way of your statutes,
    and in keeping them I shall find my reward.
34 Give me the insight to obey your law
    and to keep it wholeheartedly.
35 Make me walk in the path of your commandments,
    for that is my desire.
36 Dispose my heart towards your instruction,
    not towards love of gain;
37 turn my eyes away from all that is futile;
    grant me life by your word.
38 Fulfil your promise for your servant,
    the promise made to those who fear you.
39 Turn away the taunts which I dread,
    for your decrees are good.
40 How I long for your precepts!
    By your righteousness grant me life.

41 Let your love descend on me, LORD,
    your deliverance as you have promised;
42 then I shall have an answer to the taunts aimed at me,
    because I trust in your word.
43 Do not rob me of my power to speak the truth,
    for I put my hope in your decrees.
44 I shall heed your law continually,
    for ever and ever;
45 I walk in freedom wherever I will,
    because I have studied your precepts.
46 I shall speak of your instruction before kings
    and shall not be ashamed;
47 in your commandments I find continuing delight;
    I love them with all my heart.
48 I am devoted to your commandments;
    I love them, and meditate on your statutes.

49 Keep in mind the word spoken to me, your servant,
    on which you have taught me to fix my hope.
50 In my time of trouble my consolation is this:
    your promise has given me life.
51 Proud people treat me with insolent scorn,
    but I do not swerve from your commandments.
52 I have cherished your decrees from of old,
    and in them I find comfort, LORD.
53 Fury seizes me as I think of the wicked
    who forsake your law.
54 Your statutes are the theme of my song
    throughout my earthly life.
55 In the night I remember your name, LORD,
    and dwell upon your instruction.

119:47 **with . . . heart:** *prob. rdg, cp. Gk; Heb. omits.*
119:51 **commandments:** *prob. rdg; Heb. law.*
119:55 **instruction:** *prob. rdg; Heb. law.*

NEW AMERICAN BIBLE

26 I disclosed my ways and you answered me;
   teach me your laws.
27 Make me understand the way of your
     precepts;
   I will ponder your wondrous deeds.
28 I weep in bitter pain;
   in accord with your word to strengthen me.
29 Lead me from the way of deceit;
   favor me with your teaching.
30 The way of loyalty I have chosen;
   I have set your edicts before me.
31 I cling to your decrees, LORD;
   do not let me come to shame.
32 I will run the way of your commands,
   for you open my docile heart.

He   33 LORD, teach me the way of your laws;
   I shall observe them with care.
34 Give me insight to observe your teaching,
   to keep it with all my heart.
35 Lead me in the path of your commands,
   for that is my delight.
36 Direct my heart toward your decrees
   and away from unjust gain.
37 Avert my eyes from what is worthless;
   by your way give me life.
38 For your servant fulfill your promise
   made to those who fear you.
39 Turn away from me the taunts I dread,
   for your edicts bring good.
40 See how I long for your precepts;
   in your justice give me life.

Waw   41 Let your love come to me, LORD,
   salvation in accord with your promise.
42 Let me answer my taunters with a word,
   for I trust in your word.
43 Do not take the word of truth from my mouth,
   for in your edicts is my hope.
44 I will keep your teachings always,
   for all time and forever.
45 I will walk freely in an open space
   because I cherish your precepts.
46 I will speak openly of your decrees
   without fear even before kings.
47 I delight in your commands,
   which I dearly love.
48 I lift up my hands to your commands;
   I study your laws, which I love.

Zayin   49 Remember your word to your servant
   by which you give me hope.
50 This is my comfort in affliction,
   your promise that gives me life.
51 Though the arrogant utterly scorn me,
   I do not turn from your teaching.
52 When I recite your edicts of old
   I am comforted, LORD.
53 Rage seizes me because of the wicked;
   they forsake your teaching.
54 Your laws become my songs
   wherever I make my home.
55 Even at night I remember your name
   in observance of your teaching, LORD.

NEW JERUSALEM BIBLE

26 I tell you my ways and you answer me;
   teach me your wishes.
27 Show me the way of your precepts,
   that I may reflect on your wonders.
28 I am melting away for grief;
   true to your word, raise me up.
29 Keep me far from the way of deceit,
   grant me the grace of your Law.
30 I have chosen the way of constancy,
   I have moulded myself to your judgements.
31 I cling to your instructions,
   Yahweh, do not disappoint me.
32 I run the way of your commandments,
   for you have given me freedom of heart.

He   33 Teach me, Yahweh, the way of your will,
   and I will observe it.
34 Give me understanding and I will observe
     your Law,
   and keep it wholeheartedly.
35 Guide me in the way of your commandments,
   for my delight is there.
36 Bend my heart to your instructions,
   not to selfish gain.
37 Avert my eyes from pointless images,
   by your word give me life.
38 Keep your promise to your servant
   so that all may hold you in awe.
39 Avert the taunts that I dread,
   for your judgements are generous.
40 See how I yearn for your precepts;
   in your saving justice give me life.

Waw   41 Let your faithful love come to me, Yahweh,
   true to your promise, save me!
42 Give me an answer to the taunts against me,
   since I rely on your word.
43 Do not deprive me of that faithful word,
   since my hope lies in your judgements.
44 I shall keep your Law without fail
   for ever and ever.
45 I shall live in all freedom
   because I have sought your precepts.
46 I shall speak of your instructions before kings
   and will not be shamed.
47 Your commandments fill me with delight,
   I love them dearly.
48 I stretch out my hands to your commandments
     that I love,
   and I ponder your judgements.

Zain   49 Keep in mind your promise to your servant
   on which I have built my hope.
50 It is my comfort in distress,
   that your promise gives me life.
51 Endlessly the arrogant have jeered at me,
   but I have not swerved from your Law.
52 I have kept your age-old judgements in mind,
   Yahweh, and I am comforted.
53 Fury grips me when I see the wicked
   who abandon your Law.
54 Your judgements are my song
   where I live in exile.
55 All night, Yahweh, I hold your name in mind,
   I keep your Law.

NEW REVISED STANDARD VERSION	REVISED ENGLISH BIBLE

56 This blessing has fallen to me,
for I have kept your precepts.

57 The LORD is my portion;
I promise to keep your words.

58 I implore your favor with all my heart;
be gracious to me according to your promise.

59 When I think of your ways,
I turn my feet to your decrees;

60 I hurry and do not delay
to keep your commandments.

61 Though the cords of the wicked ensnare me,
I do not forget your law.

62 At midnight I rise to praise you,
because of your righteous ordinances.

63 I am a companion of all who fear you,
of those who keep your precepts.

64 The earth, O LORD, is full of your steadfast love;
teach me your statutes.

65 You have dealt well with your servant,
O LORD, according to your word.

66 Teach me good judgment and knowledge,
for I believe in your commandments.

67 Before I was humbled I went astray,
but now I keep your word.

68 You are good and do good;
teach me your statutes.

69 The arrogant smear me with lies,
but with my whole heart I keep your precepts.

70 Their hearts are fat and gross,
but I delight in your law.

71 It is good for me that I was humbled,
so that I might learn your statutes.

72 The law of your mouth is better to me
than thousands of gold and silver pieces.

73 Your hands have made and fashioned me;
give me understanding that I may learn your
commandments.

74 Those who fear you shall see me and rejoice,
because I have hoped in your word.

75 I know, O LORD, that your judgments are right,
and that in faithfulness you have humbled me.

76 Let your steadfast love become my comfort
according to your promise to your servant.

77 Let your mercy come to me, that I may live;
for your law is my delight.

78 Let the arrogant be put to shame,
because they have subverted me with guile;
as for me, I will meditate on your precepts.

79 Let those who fear you turn to me,
so that they may know your decrees.

80 May my heart be blameless in your statutes,
so that I may not be put to shame.

81 My soul languishes for your salvation;
I hope in your word.

82 My eyes fail with watching for your promise;
I ask, "When will you comfort me?"

83 For I have become like a wineskin in the smoke,
yet I have not forgotten your statutes.

84 How long must your servant endure?
When will you judge those who persecute me?

56 This has been my lot,
for I have kept your precepts.

57 You are my portion, LORD;
I have promised to keep your words.

58 With all my heart I have tried to please you;
fulfil your promise and be gracious to me.

59 I have considered my way of life
and turned back to your instruction;

60 I have never delayed, but always made haste
to keep your commandments.

61 The wicked in crowds close round me,
but I do not forget your law.

62 At midnight I rise to give you thanks
for the justice of your decrees.

63 I keep company with all who fear you,
with all who follow your precepts.

64 LORD, the earth is filled with your unfailing love;
teach me your statutes.

65 You have dealt kindly with your servant,
fulfilling your word, LORD.

66 Give me insight, give me knowledge,
for I put my trust in your commandments.

67 Before I was chastened I went astray,
but now I pay heed to your promise.

68 You are good, and you do what is good;
teach me your statutes.

69 I follow your precepts wholeheartedly,
though those who are proud blacken my name with
lies;

70 they are arrogant and unfeeling,
but I find my delight in your instruction.

71 How good for me to have been chastened,
so that I might be schooled in your statutes!

72 The law you have ordained means more to me
than a fortune in gold and silver.

73 Your hands made me and formed me;
give me insight that I may learn your
commandments.

74 May all who fear you see me and be glad,
because I put my hope in your word.

75 I know, LORD, that your decrees are just
and even in chastening you keep faith with me.

76 Let your love comfort me,
as you have promised me, your servant.

77 Extend your compassion to me, that I may live,
for your law is my delight.

78 Put the proud to shame, for they wrong me with
lies;
but I shall meditate on your precepts.

79 Let those who fear you turn to me,
that they may understand your instruction.

80 Let me give my whole heart to your statutes,
so that I am not put to shame.

81 I long with all my heart for your deliverance;
I have put my hope in your word.

82 My sight grows dim with looking for your promise
and I cry, 'When will you comfort me?'

83 Though I shrivel like a wineskin in the smoke,
I do not forget your statutes.

84 How long must I, your servant, wait?
When will you execute judgement on my
persecutors?

119:70 **instruction:** *prob. rdg; Heb. law.*

NEW AMERICAN BIBLE

NEW JERUSALEM BIBLE

56 This is my good fortune,
for I have observed your precepts.

Heth 57 My portion is the LORD;
I promise to keep your words.

58 I entreat you with all my heart:
have mercy on me in accord with your
promise.

59 I have examined my ways
and turned my steps to your decrees.

60 I am prompt, I do not hesitate
in keeping your commands.

61 Though the snares of the wicked surround me,
your teaching I do not forget.

62 At midnight I rise to praise you
because your edicts are just.

63 I am the friend of all who fear you,
of all who keep your precepts.

64 The earth, LORD, is filled with your love;
teach me your laws.

Teth 65 You have treated your servant well,
according to your word, O LORD.

66 Teach me wisdom and knowledge,
for in your commands I trust.

67 Before I was afflicted I went astray,
but now I hold to your promise.

68 You are good and do what is good;
teach me your laws.

69 The arrogant smear me with lies,
but I observe your precepts with all my
heart.

70 Their hearts are gross and fat;
as for me, your teaching is my delight.

71 It was good for me to be afflicted,
in order to learn your laws.

72 Teaching from your lips is more precious to
me
than heaps of silver and gold.

Yodh 73 Your hands made me and fashioned me;
give me insight to learn your commands.

74 Those who fear you rejoice to see me,
because I hope in your word.

75 I know, LORD, that your edicts are just;
though you afflict me, you are faithful.

76 May your love comfort me
in accord with your promise to your
servant.

77 Show me compassion that I may live,
for your teaching is my delight.

78 Shame the proud for oppressing me unjustly,
that I may study your precepts.

79 Let those who fear you turn to me,
those who acknowledge your decrees.

80 May I be wholehearted toward your laws,
that I may not be put to shame.

Kaph 81 My soul longs for your salvation;
I put my hope in your word.

82 My eyes long to see your promise.
When will you comfort me?

83 I am like a wineskin shriveled by smoke,
but I have not forgotten your laws.

84 How long can your servant survive?
When will your edict doom my foes?

56 This is what it means to me,
observing your precepts.

Het 57 My task, I have said, Yahweh,
is to keep your word.

58 Wholeheartedly I entreat your favour;
true to your promise, take pity on me!

59 I have reflected on my ways,
and I turn my steps to your instructions.

60 I hurry without delay
to keep your commandments.

61 Though caught in the snares of the wicked,
I do not forget your Law.

62 At midnight I rise to praise you
for your upright judgements.

63 I am a friend to all who fear you
and keep your precepts.

64 Your faithful love fills the earth,
Yahweh, teach me your judgements.

Tet 65 You have been generous to your servant,
Yahweh,
true to your promise.

66 Teach me judgement and knowledge,
for I rely on your commandments.

67 Before I was punished I used to go astray,
but now I keep to your promise.

68 You are generous and act generously,
teach me your will.

69 The arrogant blacken me with lies
though I wholeheartedly observe your
precepts.

70 Their hearts are gross like rich fat,
but my delight is in your Law.

71 It was good for me that I had to suffer,
the better to learn your judgements.

72 The Law you have uttered is more precious to
me
than all the wealth in the world.

Yod 73 Your hands have made me and held me firm,
give me understanding and I shall learn your
commandments.

74 Those who fear you rejoice at the sight of me
since I put my hope in your word.

75 I know, Yahweh, that your judgements are
upright,
and in punishing me you show your
constancy.

76 Your faithful love must be my consolation,
as you have promised your servant.

77 Treat me with tenderness and I shall live,
for your Law is my delight.

78 Let the arrogant who tell lies against me be
shamed,
while I ponder your precepts.

79 Let those who fear you rally to me,
those who understand your instructions.

80 My heart shall be faultless towards your will;
then I shall not be ashamed.

Kaph 81 I shall wear myself out for your salvation,
for your word is my hope.

82 My eyes, too, are worn out waiting for your
promise,
when will you have pity on me?

83 For I am like a smoked wineskin,
but I do not forget your will.

84 How long has your servant to live?
When will you bring my persecutors to
judgement?

NEW REVISED STANDARD VERSION	REVISED ENGLISH BIBLE

85 The arrogant have dug pitfalls for me;
    they flout your law.
86 All your commandments are enduring;
    I am persecuted without cause; help me!
87 They have almost made an end of me on earth;
    but I have not forsaken your precepts.
88 In your steadfast love spare my life,
    so that I may keep the decrees of your mouth.
89 The LORD exists forever;
    your word is firmly fixed in heaven.
90 Your faithfulness endures to all generations;
    you have established the earth, and it stands fast.
91 By your appointment they stand today,
    for all things are your servants.
92 If your law had not been my delight,
    I would have perished in my misery.
93 I will never forget your precepts,
    for by them you have given me life.
94 I am yours; save me,
    for I have sought your precepts.
95 The wicked lie in wait to destroy me,
    but I consider your decrees.
96 I have seen a limit to all perfection,
    but your commandment is exceedingly broad.
97 Oh, how I love your law!
    It is my meditation all day long.
98 Your commandment makes me wiser than my enemies,
    for it is always with me.
99 I have more understanding than all my teachers,
    for your decrees are my meditation.
100 I understand more than the aged,
    for I keep your precepts.
101 I hold back my feet from every evil way,
    in order to keep your word.
102 I do not turn away from your ordinances,
    for you have taught me.
103 How sweet are your words to my taste,
    sweeter than honey to my mouth!
104 Through your precepts I get understanding;
    therefore I hate every false way.
105 Your word is a lamp to my feet
    and a light to my path.
106 I have sworn an oath and confirmed it,
    to observe your righteous ordinances.
107 I am severely afflicted;
    give me life, O LORD, according to your word.
108 Accept my offerings of praise, O LORD,
    and teach me your ordinances.
109 I hold my life in my hand continually,
    but I do not forget your law.
110 The wicked have laid a snare for me,
    but I do not stray from your precepts.
111 Your decrees are my heritage forever;
    they are the joy of my heart.
112 I incline my heart to perform your statutes
    forever, to the end.
113 I hate the double-minded,
    but I love your law.
114 You are my hiding place and my shield;
    I hope in your word.
115 Go away from me, you evildoers,
    that I may keep the commandments of my God.

85 The proud who flout your law
    spread tales about me.
86 All your commandments stand sure;
    but the proud hound me with falsehood. Come to my help!
87 They had almost swept me from the earth,
    but I did not forsake your precepts.
88 In your love grant me life,
    that I may follow your instruction.
89 Your word is everlasting, LORD;
    it is firmly fixed in heaven.
90 Your faithfulness endures for all generations,
    and the earth which you have established stands firm.
91 Even to this day your decrees stand fast,
    for all things serve you.
92 Had your law not been my delight,
    I should have perished in my distress;
93 never shall I forget your precepts,
    for through them you have given me life.
94 I am yours; save me,
    for I have sought your precepts.
95 The wicked lie in wait to destroy me;
    but I shall ponder your instruction.
96 I see that all things have an end,
    but your commandment has no limit.
97 How I love your law!
    It is my study all day long.
98 Your commandment makes me wiser than my enemies,
    for it is my possession for ever.
99 I have more insight than all my teachers,
    for your instruction is my study;
100 I have more wisdom than those who are old,
    because I have kept your precepts.
101 I do not set foot on any evil path
    in my obedience to your word;
102 I do not swerve from your decrees,
    for you have been my teacher.
103 How sweet is your promise to my palate,
    sweeter on my tongue than honey!
104 From your precepts I learn wisdom;
    therefore I hate every path of falsehood.
105 Your word is a lamp to my feet,
    a light on my path;
106 I have bound myself by oath and solemn vow
    to keep your just decrees.
107 I am cruelly afflicted;
    LORD, revive me as you have promised.
108 Accept, LORD, the willing tribute of my lips,
    and teach me your decrees.
109 Every day I take my life in my hands,
    yet I never forget your law.
110 The wicked have set a trap for me,
    but I do not stray from your precepts.
111 Your instruction is my everlasting heritage;
    it is the joy of my heart.
112 I am resolved to fulfil your statutes;
    they are a reward that never fails.
113 I hate those who are not single-minded,
    but I love your law.
114 You are my hiding-place and my shield;
    in your word I put my hope.
115 Leave me alone, you evildoers,
    that I may keep the commandments of my God.

NEW AMERICAN BIBLE

85 The arrogant have dug pits for me;
 defying your teaching.
86 All your commands are steadfast.
 Help me! I am pursued without cause.
87 They have almost ended my life on earth,
 but I do not forsake your precepts.
88 In your kindness give me life,
 to keep the decrees you have spoken.

Lamedh 89 Your word, LORD, stands forever;
 it is firm as the heavens.
90 Through all generations your truth endures;
 fixed to stand firm like the earth.
91 By your edicts they stand firm to this day,
 for all things are your servants.
92 Had your teaching not been my delight,
 I would have perished in my affliction.
93 I will never forget your precepts;
 through them you give me life.
94 I am yours; save me,
 for I cherish your precepts.
95 The wicked hope to destroy me,
 but I pay heed to your decrees.
96 I have seen the limits of all perfection,
 but your command is without bounds.

Mem 97 How I love your teaching, LORD!
 I study it all day long.
98 Your command makes me wiser than my foes,
 for it is always with me.
99 I have more understanding than all my
 teachers,
 because I ponder your decrees.
100 I have more insight than my elders,
 because I observe your precepts.
101 I keep my steps from every evil path,
 that I may obey your word.
102 From your edicts I do not turn,
 for you have taught them to me.
103 How sweet to my tongue is your promise,
 sweeter than honey to my mouth!
104 Through your precepts I gain insight;
 therefore I hate all false ways.

Nun 105 Your word is a lamp for my feet,
 a light for my path.
106 I make a solemn vow
 to keep your just edicts.
107 I am very much afflicted, LORD;
 give me life in accord with your word.
108 Accept my freely offered praise;
 LORD, teach me your decrees.
109 My life is always at risk,
 but I do not forget your teaching.
110 The wicked have set snares for me,
 but from your precepts I do not stray.
111 Your decrees are my heritage forever;
 they are the joy of my heart.
112 My heart is set on fulfilling your laws;
 they are my reward forever.

Samekh 113 I hate every hypocrite;
 your teaching I love.
114 You are my refuge and shield;
 in your word I hope.
115 Depart from me, you wicked,
 that I may observe the commands of my
 God.

NEW JERUSALEM BIBLE

85 The arrogant have dug pitfalls for me
 in defiance of your Law.
86 All your commandments show constancy.
 Help me when they pursue me dishonestly.
87 They have almost annihilated me on earth,
 but I have not deserted your precepts.
88 True to your faithful love, give me life,
 and I shall keep the instructions you have laid
 down.

Lamed 89 For ever, Yahweh, your word
 is planted firm in heaven.
90 Your constancy endures from age to age;
 you established the earth and it stands firm.
91 Through your judgements all stands firm to
 this day,
 for all creation is your servant.
92 Had your Law not been my delight,
 I would have perished in my misery.
93 I shall never forget your precepts,
 for by them you have given me life.
94 I am yours, save me,
 for I seek your precepts.
95 The wicked may hope to destroy me,
 but all my thought is of your instructions.
96 I have seen that all perfection is finite,
 but your commandment has no limit.

Mem 97 How I love your Law!
 I ponder it all day long.
98 You make me wiser than my enemies
 by your commandment which is mine for
 ever.
99 I am wiser than all my teachers
 because I ponder your instructions.
100 I have more understanding than the aged
 because I keep your precepts.
101 I restrain my foot from evil paths
 to keep your word.
102 I do not turn aside from your judgements,
 because you yourself have instructed me.
103 How pleasant your promise to my palate,
 sweeter than honey in my mouth!
104 From your precepts I learn wisdom,
 so I hate all deceptive ways.

Nun 105 Your word is a lamp for my feet,
 a light on my path.
106 I have sworn — and shall maintain it —
 to keep your upright judgements.
107 I am utterly wretched, Yahweh;
 true to your promise, give me life.
108 Accept, Yahweh, the tribute from my mouth,
 and teach me your judgements.
109 My life is in your hands perpetually,
 I do not forget your Law.
110 The wicked have laid out a snare for me,
 but I have not strayed from your precepts.
111 Your instructions are my eternal heritage,
 they are the joy of my heart.
112 I devote myself to obeying your statutes,
 their recompense is eternal.

Samek 113 I hate a divided heart,
 I love your Law.
114 You are my refuge and shield,
 I put my hope in your word.
115 Leave me alone, you wicked,
 I shall observe the commandments of my
 God.

116 Uphold me according to your promise, that I may
    live,
    and let me not be put to shame in my hope.
117 Hold me up, that I may be safe
    and have regard for your statutes continually.
118 You spurn all who go astray from your statutes;
    for their cunning is in vain.
119 All the wicked of the earth you count as dross;
    therefore I love your decrees.
120 My flesh trembles for fear of you,
    and I am afraid of your judgments.

121 I have done what is just and right;
    do not leave me to my oppressors.
122 Guarantee your servant's well-being;
    do not let the godless oppress me.
123 My eyes fail from watching for your salvation,
    and for the fulfillment of your righteous
      promise.
124 Deal with your servant according to your
    steadfast love,
    and teach me your statutes.
125 I am your servant; give me understanding,
    so that I may know your decrees.
126 It is time for the LORD to act,
    for your law has been broken.
127 Truly I love your commandments
    more than gold, more than fine gold.
128 Truly I direct my steps by all your precepts;[a]
    I hate every false way.

129 Your decrees are wonderful;
    therefore my soul keeps them.
130 The unfolding of your words gives light;
    it imparts understanding to the simple.
131 With open mouth I pant,
    because I long for your commandments.
132 Turn to me and be gracious to me,
    as is your custom toward those who love your
      name.
133 Keep my steps steady according to your promise,
    and never let iniquity have dominion over me.
134 Redeem me from human oppression,
    that I may keep your precepts.
135 Make your face shine upon your servant,
    and teach me your statutes.
136 My eyes shed streams of tears
    because your law is not kept.

137 You are righteous, O LORD,
    and your judgments are right.
138 You have appointed your decrees in righteousness
    and in all faithfulness.
139 My zeal consumes me
    because my foes forget your words.
140 Your promise is well tried,
    and your servant loves it.
141 I am small and despised,
    yet I do not forget your precepts.
142 Your righteousness is an everlasting
    righteousness,
    and your law is the truth.
143 Trouble and anguish have come upon me,
    but your commandments are my delight.
144 Your decrees are righteous forever;
    give me understanding that I may live.

145 With my whole heart I cry; answer me, O LORD.
    I will keep your statutes.

116 Support me as you have promised, that I may live;
    do not disappoint my hope.
117 Sustain me, that I may see deliverance;
    then I shall always be occupied with your statutes.
118 You reject all who stray from your statutes,
    for their whole talk is malice and lies.
119 In your sight the wicked are all scum of the earth;
    therefore I love your instruction.
120 The dread of you makes my flesh creep;
    I stand in awe of your decrees.

121 I have done what is just and right;
    you will not abandon me to my oppressors.
122 Stand surety for the welfare of your servant;
    do not let the proud oppress me.
123 My eyes grow weary looking for your deliverance,
    with waiting for the victory you have promised.
124 In your dealings with me, LORD, show your love
    and teach me your statutes.
125 I am your servant; give me insight
    to understand your instruction.
126 It is time for you to act, LORD,
    for your law has been broken.
127 Truly I love your commandments
    more than gold, even the finest gold.
128 It is by your precepts that I find the right way;
    I hate the paths of falsehood.

129 Your instruction is wonderful;
    therefore I gladly keep it.
130 Your word is revealed, and all is light;
    it gives understanding even to the untaught.
131 I pant, I thirst,
    longing for your commandments.
132 Turn to me and show me favour,
    just as you have decreed for those who love your
      name.
133 Make my step firm according to your promise,
    and let no wrong have the mastery over me.
134 Deliver me from oppression by my fellows,
    that I may observe your precepts.
135 Let your face shine on your servant
    and teach me your statutes.
136 My eyes stream with tears
    because your law goes unheeded.

137 How just you are, LORD!
    How straight and true are your decrees!
138 How just is the instruction you give!
    It is firm and sure.
139 I am speechless with indignation
    at my enemies' neglect of your words.
140 Your promise has been well tested,
    and I love it, LORD.
141 I may be despised and of little account,
    but I do not forget your precepts.
142 Your justice is an everlasting justice,
    and your law is steadfast.
143 Though I am overtaken by trouble and anxiety,
    your commandments are my delight.
144 Your instruction is ever just;
    give me understanding that I may live.

145 With my whole heart I call; answer me, LORD.
    I shall keep your statutes.

119:119 In . . . earth: so some MSS; others You have made an end
of all the wicked on earth like scum.   119:128 It . . . precepts:
prob. rdg, cp. Gk; Heb. All precepts of all.

a Gk Jerome: Meaning of Heb uncertain

116 Sustain me by your promise that I may live;
 do not disappoint me in my hope.
117 Strengthen me that I may be safe,
 ever to contemplate your laws.
118 You reject all who stray from your laws,
 for vain is their deceit.
119 Like dross you regard all the wicked on earth;
 therefore I love your decrees.
120 My flesh shudders with dread of you;
 I hold your edicts in awe.

Ayin 121 I have fulfilled your just edict;
 do not abandon me to my oppressors.
122 Guarantee your servant's welfare;
 do not let the arrogant oppress me.
123 My eyes long to see your salvation
 and the justice of your promise.
124 Act with kindness toward your servant;
 teach me your laws.
125 I am your servant; give me discernment
 that I may know your decrees.
126 It is time for the LORD to act;
 they have disobeyed your teaching.
127 Truly I love your commands
 more than the finest gold.
128 Thus I follow all your precepts;
 every wrong way I hate.

Pe 129 Wonderful are your decrees;
 therefore I observe them.
130 The revelation of your words sheds light,
 gives understanding to the simple.
131 I sigh with open mouth,
 yearning for your commands.
132 Turn to me and be gracious,
 your edict for lovers of your name.
133 Steady my feet in accord with your promise;
 do not let iniquity lead me.
134 Free me from human oppression,
 that I may keep your precepts.
135 Let your face shine upon your servant;
 teach me your laws.
136 My eyes shed streams of tears
 because your teaching is not followed.

Sadhe 137 You are righteous, LORD,
 and just are your edicts.
138 You have issued your decrees in justice
 and in surpassing faithfulness.
139 I am consumed with rage,
 because my foes forget your words.
140 Your servant loves your promise;
 it has been proved by fire.
141 Though belittled and despised,
 I do not forget your precepts.
142 Your justice is forever right,
 your teaching forever true.
143 Though distress and anguish come upon me,
 your commands are my delight.
144 Your decrees are forever just;
 give me discernment that I may live.

Qoph 145 I call with all my heart, O LORD;
 answer me that I may observe your laws.

116 True to your word, support me and I shall
 live;
 do not disappoint me of my hope.
117 Uphold me and I shall be saved,
 my gaze fixed on your will.
118 You shake off all who stray from your will;
 deceit fills their horizon.
119 In your sight all the wicked of the earth are
 like rust,
 so I love your instructions.
120 My whole body trembles before you,
 your judgements fill me with fear.

Ain 121 All my conduct has been just and upright,
 do not hand me over to my oppressors.
122 Guarantee the well-being of your servant,
 do not let the proud oppress me.
123 My eyes are languishing for your salvation
 and for the saving justice you have promised.
124 Show your faithful love to your servant,
 teach me your judgements.
125 Your servant am I; give me understanding
 and I shall know your instructions.
126 It is time to take action, Yahweh,
 your Law is being broken.
127 So I love your commandments
 more than gold, purest gold.
128 So I rule my life by your precepts,
 I hate all deceptive paths.

Pe 129 Wonderful are your instructions,
 so I observe them.
130 As your word unfolds it gives light,
 and even the simple understand.
131 I open wide my mouth,
 panting eagerly for your commandments.
132 Turn to me, pity me;
 those who love your name deserve it.
133 Keep my steps firm in your promise;
 that no evil may triumph over me.
134 Rescue me from human oppression,
 and I will observe your precepts.
135 Let your face shine on your servant,
 teach me your will.
136 My eyes stream with tears
 because your Law is disregarded.

Zade 137 You are upright, Yahweh,
 and your judgements are honest.
138 You impose uprightness as a witness to
 yourself,
 it is constancy itself.
139 My zeal is burning me up
 because my oppressors forget your word.
140 Your promise is well tested,
 your servant holds it dear.
141 Puny and despised as I am,
 I do not forget your precepts.
142 Your saving justice is for ever just,
 and your Law is trustworthy.
143 Though anguish and distress grip me
 your commandments are my delight.
144 Your instructions are upright for ever,
 give me understanding and I shall live.

Qoph 145 I call with all my heart; answer me, Yahweh,
 and I will observe your judgements.

146 I cry to you; save me,
  that I may observe your decrees.
147 I rise before dawn and cry for help;
  I put my hope in your words.
148 My eyes are awake before each watch of the
    night,
  that I may meditate on your promise.
149 In your steadfast love hear my voice;
  O LORD, in your justice preserve my life.
150 Those who persecute me with evil purpose draw
    near;
  they are far from your law.
151 Yet you are near, O LORD,
  and all your commandments are true.
152 Long ago I learned from your decrees
  that you have established them forever.

153 Look on my misery and rescue me,
  for I do not forget your law.
154 Plead my cause and redeem me;
  give me life according to your promise.
155 Salvation is far from the wicked,
  for they do not seek your statutes.
156 Great is your mercy, O LORD;
  give me life according to your justice.
157 Many are my persecutors and my adversaries,
  yet I do not swerve from your decrees.
158 I look at the faithless with disgust,
  because they do not keep your commands.
159 Consider how I love your precepts;
  preserve my life according to your steadfast
    love.
160 The sum of your word is truth;
  and every one of your righteous ordinances
    endures forever.

161 Princes persecute me without cause,
  but my heart stands in awe of your words.
162 I rejoice at your word
  like one who finds great spoil.
163 I hate and abhor falsehood,
  but I love your law.
164 Seven times a day I praise you
  for your righteous ordinances.
165 Great peace have those who love your law;
  nothing can make them stumble.
166 I hope for your salvation, O LORD,
  and I fulfill your commandments.
167 My soul keeps your decrees;
  I love them exceedingly.
168 I keep your precepts and decrees,
  for all my ways are before you.

169 Let my cry come before you, O LORD;
  give me understanding according to your word.
170 Let my supplication come before you;
  deliver me according to your promise.
171 My lips will pour forth praise,
  because you teach me your statutes.
172 My tongue will sing of your promise,
  for all your commandments are right.
173 Let your hand be ready to help me,
  for I have chosen your precepts.
174 I long for your salvation, O LORD,
  and your law is my delight.
175 Let me live that I may praise you,
  and let your ordinances help me.

146 I call to you; save me
  that I may heed your instruction.
147 Before dawn I rise to cry for help;
  I put my hope in your word.
148 Before the midnight watch my eyes are open
  for meditation on your promise.
149 In your love hear me,
  and give me life, LORD, by your decree.
150 My pursuers in their malice are close behind me,
  but they are far from your law.
151 Yet you are near, LORD,
  and all your commandments are steadfast.
152 I have long known from your instruction
  that you have given it everlasting foundations.

153 See in what trouble I am and set me free,
  for I do not forget your law.
154 Be my advocate and gain my acquittal;
  as you promised, give me life.
155 Such deliverance is beyond the reach of the
    wicked,
  because they do not ponder your statutes.
156 Great is your compassion, LORD;
  by your decree grant me life.
157 Though my persecutors and my foes are many,
  I have not swerved from your instruction.
158 I was cut to the quick when I saw traitors
  who had no regard for your word.
159 See how I love your precepts!
  In your love, LORD, grant me life.
160 Your word is founded in steadfastness,
  and all your just decrees are everlasting.

161 Rulers persecute me without cause,
  but it is your word that fills me with awe.
162 I am jubilant over your promise,
  like someone who finds much booty.
163 Falsehood I abhor and detest,
  but I love your law.
164 Seven times each day I praise you
  for the justice of your decrees.
165 Peace is the reward of those who love your law;
  no pitfalls beset their path.
166 I hope for your deliverance, LORD,
  and I fulfil your commandments;
167 gladly I heed your instruction
  and love it dearly.
168 I heed your precepts and your instruction,
  for all my life lies open before you.

169 Let my cry of joy reach you, LORD;
  give me insight as you have promised.
170 Let my prayers for favour reach you;
  be true to your promise and save me.
171 Let your praise pour from my lips,
  for you teach me your statutes;
172 let the music of your promises be on my tongue,
  for your commandments are justice itself.
173 May your hand be prompt to help me,
  for I have chosen your precepts;
174 I long for your deliverance, LORD,
  and your law is my delight.
175 Let me live to praise you;
  let your decrees be my help.

NEW AMERICAN BIBLE

146 I call to you to save me
    that I may keep your decrees.
147 I rise before dawn and cry out;
    I put my hope in your words.
148 My eyes greet the night watches
    as I meditate on your promise.
149 Hear my voice in your love, O LORD;
    by your edict give me life.
150 Malicious persecutors draw near me;
    they are far from your teaching.
151 You are near, O LORD;
    reliable are all your commands.
152 Long have I known from your decrees
    that you have established them forever.

Resh 153 Look at my affliction and rescue me,
    for I have not forgotten your teaching.
154 Take up my cause and redeem me;
    for the sake of your promise give me life.
155 Salvation is far from sinners
    because they do not cherish your laws.
156 Your compassion is great, O LORD;
    in accord with your edicts give me life.
157 Though my persecutors and foes are many
    I do not turn from your decrees.
158 I view the faithless with loathing,
    because they do not heed your promise.
159 See how I love your precepts, LORD;
    in your kindness give me life.
160 Your every word is enduring;
    all your just edicts are forever.

Shin 161 Princes persecute me without reason,
    but my heart reveres only your word.
162 I rejoice at your promise,
    as one who has found rich spoil.
163 Falsehood I hate and abhor;
    your teaching I love.
164 Seven times a day I praise you
    because your edicts are just.
165 Lovers of your teaching have much peace;
    for them there is no stumbling block.
166 I look for your salvation, LORD,
    and I fulfill your commands.
167 I observe your decrees;
    I love them very much.
168 I observe your precepts and decrees;
    all my ways are before you.

Taw 169 Let my cry come before you, LORD;
    in keeping with your word give me
    discernment.
170 Let my prayer come before you;
    rescue me according to your promise.
171 May my lips pour forth your praise,
    because you teach me your laws.
172 May my tongue sing of your promise,
    for all your commands are just.
173 Keep your hand ready to help me,
    for I have chosen your precepts.
174 I long for your salvation, LORD;
    your teaching is my delight.
175 Let me live to praise you;
    may your edicts give me help.

NEW JERUSALEM BIBLE

146 I call to you; save me,
    and I will keep your instructions.
147 I am awake before dawn to cry for help,
    I put my hope in your word.
148 My eyes are awake before each watch of the
    night,
    to ponder your promise.
149 In your faithful love, Yahweh, listen to my
    voice,
    let your judgements give me life.
150 My pursuers are coming closer to their wicked
    designs,
    and further from your Law.
151 You are close to me, Yahweh,
    and all your commandments are true.
152 Long have I known that your instructions
    were laid down to last for ever.

Resh 153 Look at my suffering and rescue me,
    for I do not forget your Law.
154 Plead my cause and defend me;
    as you promised, give me life.
155 Salvation is far from the wicked,
    for they do not seek your will.
156 Your kindnesses to me are countless, Yahweh;
    true to your judgements, give me life.
157 Though my enemies and oppressors are
    countless,
    I do not turn aside from your instructions.
158 The sight of these renegades appals me;
    they do not observe your promise.
159 See how I love your precepts;
    true to your faithful love, give me life.
160 Faithfulness is the essence of your word,
    your upright judgements hold good for ever.

Shin 161 Though princes hound me unprovoked,
    what fills me with awe is your word.
162 I rejoice in your promise
    like one who finds a vast treasure.
163 Falsehood I hate and detest,
    my love is for your Law.
164 Seven times a day I praise you
    for your upright judgements.
165 Great peace for those who love your Law;
    no stumbling-blocks for them!
166 I am waiting for your salvation, Yahweh,
    I fulfil your commandments.
167 I observe your instructions,
    I love them dearly.
168 I observe your precepts, your judgements,
    for all my ways are before you.

Taw 169 May my cry approach your presence,
    Yahweh;
    by your word give me understanding.
170 May my prayer come into your presence,
    rescue me as you have promised.
171 May my lips proclaim your praise,
    for you teach me your will.
172 May my tongue recite your promise,
    for all your commandments are upright.
173 May your hand be there to help me,
    since I have chosen your precepts.
174 I long for your salvation, Yahweh,
    your Law is my delight.
175 May I live only to praise you,
    may your judgements be my help.

NEW REVISED STANDARD VERSION	REVISED ENGLISH BIBLE

176 I have gone astray like a lost sheep; seek out
your servant,
for I do not forget your commandments.

176 I have strayed like a lost sheep;
come, search for your servant,
for I have not forgotten your commandments.

Psalm 120

A Song of Ascents.

1 In my distress I cry to the LORD,
that he may answer me:
2 "Deliver me, O LORD,
from lying lips,
from a deceitful tongue."

3 What shall be given to you?
And what more shall be done to you,
you deceitful tongue?
4 A warrior's sharp arrows,
with glowing coals of the broom tree!

5 Woe is me, that I am an alien in Meshech,
that I must live among the tents of Kedar.
6 Too long have I had my dwelling
among those who hate peace.
7 I am for peace;
but when I speak,
they are for war.

Psalm 120

A song of the ascents

1 I CALLED to the LORD in my distress,
and he answered me.
2 'LORD,' I cried, 'save me from lying lips
and from the deceitful tongue.'
3 What has he in store for you, deceitful tongue?
What more has he for you?
4 Nothing but a warrior's sharp arrows
and red-hot charcoal.

5 Wretched is my lot, exiled in Meshech,
dwelling by the tents of Kedar.
6 Too long have I lived
among those who hate peace.
7 I am for peace, but whenever I speak of it,
they are for war.

Psalm 121

A Song of Ascents.

1 I lift up my eyes to the hills —
from where will my help come?
2 My help comes from the LORD,
who made heaven and earth.

3 He will not let your foot be moved;
he who keeps you will not slumber.
4 He who keeps Israel
will neither slumber nor sleep.

5 The LORD is your keeper;
the LORD is your shade at your right hand.
6 The sun shall not strike you by day,
nor the moon by night.

7 The LORD will keep you from all evil;
he will keep your life.
8 The LORD will keep
your going out and your coming in
from this time on and forevermore.

Psalm 121

A song of the ascents

1 IF I lift up my eyes to the hills,
where shall I find help?
2 My help comes only from the LORD,
maker of heaven and earth.

3 He will not let your foot stumble;
he who guards you will not sleep.
4 The guardian of Israel
never slumbers, never sleeps.

5 The LORD is your guardian,
your protector at your right hand;
6 the sun will not strike you by day
nor the moon by night.

7 The LORD will guard you against all harm;
he will guard your life.
8 The LORD will guard you as you come and go,
now and for evermore.

Psalm 122

A Song of Ascents. Of David.

1 I was glad when they said to me,
"Let us go to the house of the LORD!"
2 Our feet are standing
within your gates, O Jerusalem.

3 Jerusalem — built as a city
that is bound firmly together.
4 To it the tribes go up,
the tribes of the LORD,
as was decreed for Israel,
to give thanks to the name of the LORD.
5 For there the thrones for judgment were set up,
the thrones of the house of David.

6 Pray for the peace of Jerusalem:
"May they prosper who love you.

Psalm 122

A song of the ascents: for David

1 I REJOICED when they said to me,
'Let us go to the house of the LORD.'
2 Now we are standing
within your gates, Jerusalem:
3 Jerusalem, a city built
compactly and solidly.
4 There the tribes went up, the tribes of the LORD,
to give thanks to the name of the LORD,
the duty laid on Israel.
5 For there the thrones of justice were set,
the thrones of the house of David.

6 Pray for the peace of Jerusalem:
'May those who love you prosper;

120:4 **red-hot charcoal:** *lit.* live coals of desert broom.
122:3 **compactly and solidly:** *or* where people come together in unity.

NEW AMERICAN BIBLE

176 I have wandered like a lost sheep;
 seek out your servant,
 for I do not forget your commands.

Psalm 120

1 A song of ascents.

I

The LORD answered me
 when I called in my distress:
2 LORD, deliver me from lying lips,
 from treacherous tongues.

II

3 What will the Lord inflict on you,
 O treacherous tongue,
 and what more besides?
4 A warrior's sharpened arrows
 and fiery coals of brushwood!

III

5 Alas, I was an alien in Meshech,
 I lived near the tents of Kedar!
6 Too long did I live
 among those who hated peace.
7 When I spoke of peace,
 they were for war.

Psalm 121

1 A song of ascents.

I

I raise my eyes toward the mountains.
 From where will my help come?
2 My help comes from the LORD,
 the maker of heaven and earth.

II

3 God will not allow your foot to slip;
 your guardian does not sleep.
4 Truly, the guardian of Israel
 never slumbers nor sleeps.
5 The LORD is your guardian;
 the LORD is your shade
 at your right hand.
6 By day the sun cannot harm you,
 nor the moon by night.
7 The LORD will guard you from all evil,
 will always guard your life.
8 The LORD will guard your coming and going
 both now and forever.

Psalm 122

1 A song of ascents. Of David.

I

I rejoiced when they said to me,
 "Let us go to the house of the LORD."
2 And now our feet are standing
 within your gates, Jerusalem.
3 Jerusalem, built as a city,
 walled round about.
4 Here the tribes have come,
 the tribes of the LORD,
 As it was decreed for Israel,
 to give thanks to the name of the LORD.
5 Here are the thrones of justice,
 the thrones of the house of David.

II

6 For the peace of Jerusalem pray:
 "May those who love you prosper!

NEW JERUSALEM BIBLE

176 I am wandering like a lost sheep,
 come and look for your servant,

for I have not forgotten your commandments.

Psalm 120 (V 119)

Song of Ascents[1]

1 To Yahweh when I am in trouble
 I call and he answers me.
2 Yahweh, save me from lying lips
 and a treacherous tongue!

3 What will he repay you, what more,
 treacherous tongue?
4 War-arrows made sharp
 over red-hot charcoal.

5 How wretched I am, living in Meshech,
 dwelling in the tents of Kedar!

6 Too long have I lived
 among people who hate peace.
7 When I speak of peace
 they are all for war!

Psalm 121 (V 120)

Song of Ascents

1 I lift up my eyes to the mountains;
 where is my help to come from?
2 My help comes from Yahweh
 who made heaven and earth.

3 May he save your foot from stumbling;
 may he, your guardian, not fall asleep!
4 You see — he neither sleeps nor slumbers,
 the guardian of Israel.

5 Yahweh is your guardian, your shade,
 Yahweh, at your right hand.
6 By day the sun will not strike you,
 nor the moon by night.

7 Yahweh guards you from all harm
 Yahweh guards your life,
8 Yahweh guards your comings and goings,
 henceforth and for ever.

Psalm 122 (V 121)

Song of Ascents   Of David

1 I rejoiced that they said to me,
 'Let us go to the house of Yahweh.'
2 At last our feet are standing
 at your gates, Jerusalem!

3 Jerusalem, built as a city,
 in one united whole,
4 there the tribes go up,
 the tribes of Yahweh,
 a sign for Israel to give thanks
 to the name of Yahweh.
5 For there are set the thrones of judgement,
 the thrones of the house of David.

6 Pray for the peace of Jerusalem,
 prosperity for your homes!

[1] **120** The Songs of Ascents (Pss 120–134) were sung by pilgrims on their way up to Jerusalem.

7 Peace be within your walls,
   and security within your towers."
8 For the sake of my relatives and friends
   I will say, "Peace be within you."
9 For the sake of the house of the LORD our God,
   I will seek your good.

7 peace be within your ramparts
   and prosperity in your palaces.'
8 For the sake of these my brothers and my friends,
   I shall say, 'Peace be within you.'
9 For the sake of the house of the LORD our God
   I shall pray for your wellbeing.

Psalm 123

A Song of Ascents.

1 To you I lift up my eyes,
   O you who are enthroned in the heavens!
2 As the eyes of servants
      look to the hand of their master,
   as the eyes of a maid
      to the hand of her mistress,
   so our eyes look to the LORD our God,
      until he has mercy upon us.

3 Have mercy upon us, O LORD, have mercy upon
      us,
   for we have had more than enough of contempt.
4 Our soul has had more than its fill
      of the scorn of those who are at ease,
      of the contempt of the proud.

Psalm 123

A song of the ascents

1 I LIFT my eyes to you
   whose throne is in heaven.
2 As the eyes of slaves follow their master's hand
   or the eyes of a slave-girl the hand of her mistress,
   so our eyes are turned to the LORD our God,
   awaiting his favour.

3 Show us your favour, LORD, show us favour,
   for we have suffered insult enough.
4 Too long have we had to suffer
   the insults of the arrogant,
   the contempt of the proud.

Psalm 124

A Song of Ascents. Of David.

1 If it had not been the LORD who was on our side
      —let Israel now say—
2 if it had not been the LORD who was on our side,
      when our enemies attacked us,
3 then they would have swallowed us up alive,
      when their anger was kindled against us;
4 then the flood would have swept us away,
      the torrent would have gone over us;
5 then over us would have gone
      the raging waters.

6 Blessed be the LORD,
      who has not given us
      as prey to their teeth.
7 We have escaped like a bird
      from the snare of the fowlers;
   the snare is broken,
      and we have escaped.

8 Our help is in the name of the LORD,
      who made heaven and earth.

Psalm 124

A song of the ascents: for David

1 IF the LORD had not been on our side—
   let Israel now say—
2 if the LORD had not been on our side
   when our foes attacked,
3 then they would have swallowed us alive
   in the heat of their anger against us.
4 Then the waters would have carried us away
   and the torrent swept over us;
5 then over us would have swept
   the raging waters.

6 Blessed be the LORD, who did not leave us
   a prey for their teeth.
7 We have escaped like a bird
   from the fowler's trap;
   the trap is broken, and we have escaped.
8 Our help is in the name of the LORD,
   maker of heaven and earth.

Psalm 125

A Song of Ascents.

1 Those who trust in the LORD are like Mount
      Zion,
   which cannot be moved, but abides forever.
2 As the mountains surround Jerusalem,
      so the LORD surrounds his people,
      from this time on and forevermore.
3 For the scepter of wickedness shall not rest
      on the land allotted to the righteous,
   so that the righteous might not stretch out
      their hands to do wrong.
4 Do good, O LORD, to those who are good,
      and to those who are upright in their hearts.

Psalm 125

A song of the ascents

1 THOSE who trust in the LORD are like Mount Zion:
   it cannot be shaken; it stands fast for ever.
2 As the mountains surround Jerusalem,
   so the LORD surrounds his people both now and
      evermore.
3 Surely wicked rulers will not continue to hold sway
   in the land allotted to the righteous,
   or the righteous may put
   their hands to injustice.
4 Do good, LORD, to the good,
   to those who are upright in heart.

NEW AMERICAN BIBLE

7 May peace be within your ramparts,
 prosperity within your towers."
8 For family and friends I say,
 "May peace be yours."
9 For the house of the LORD, our God, I pray,
 "May blessings be yours."

Psalm 123

1 *A song of ascents.*

 To you I raise my eyes,
  to you enthroned in heaven.
2 Yes, like the eyes of a servant
  on the hand of his master,
 Like the eyes of a maid
  on the hand of her mistress,
 So our eyes are on the LORD our God,
  till we are shown favor.
3 Show us favor, LORD, show us favor,
  for we have our fill of contempt.
4 We have our fill of insult from the insolent,
  of disdain from the arrogant.

Psalm 124

1 *A song of ascents. Of David.*

 I
 Had not the LORD been with us,
  let Israel say,
2 Had not the LORD been with us,
  when people rose against us,
3 They would have swallowed us alive,
  for their fury blazed against us.
4 The waters would have engulfed us,
  the torrent overwhelmed us;
5 seething waters would have drowned us.
 II
6 Blessed be the LORD, who did not leave us
  to be torn by their fangs.
7 We escaped with our lives
  like a bird from the fowler's snare;
  the snare was broken and we escaped.
8 Our help is the name of the LORD,
  the maker of heaven and earth.

Psalm 125

1 *A song of ascents.*

 I
 Like Mount Zion are they
  who trust in the LORD,
  unshakable, forever enduring.
2 As mountains surround Jerusalem,
  the LORD surrounds his people
  both now and forever.
 II
3 The scepter of the wicked will not prevail
  in the land given to the just,
 Lest the just themselves
  turn their hands to evil.
 III
4 Do good, LORD, to the good,
  to those who are upright of heart.

NEW JERUSALEM BIBLE

7 Peace within your walls,
 prosperity in your palaces!
8 For love of my brothers and my friends
 I will say, 'Peace upon you!'
9 For love of the house of Yahweh our God
 I will pray for your well-being.

Psalm 123 (V 122)

Song of Ascents

1 I lift up my eyes to you
  who are enthroned in heaven.
2 Just as the eyes of slaves
  are on their masters' hand,

 or the eyes of a slave-girl
  on the hand of her mistress,
 so our eyes are on Yahweh our God,
  for him to take pity on us.
3 Have pity on us, Yahweh, have pity,
  for we have had our full share of scorn,
4 more than our share
  of jeers from the complacent.

 (Scorn is for the proud.)

Psalm 124 (V 123)

Song of Ascents   Of David

1 If Yahweh had not been on our side
  —let Israel repeat it —
2 if Yahweh had not been on our side
  when people attacked us,
3 they would have swallowed us alive
  in the heat of their anger.
4 Then water was washing us away,
  a torrent running right over us;
5 running right over us then
  were turbulent waters.

6 Blessed be Yahweh for not letting us fall
  a prey to their teeth!
7 We escaped like a bird
  from the fowlers' net.

 The net was broken
  and we escaped;
8 our help is in the name of Yahweh,
  who made heaven and earth.

Psalm 125 (V 124)

Song of Ascents

1 Whoever trusts in Yahweh is like Mount Zion:
  unshakeable, it stands for ever.
2 Jerusalem! The mountains encircle her:
  so Yahweh encircles his people,
  henceforth and for ever.

3 The sceptre of the wicked will not come to rest
  over the heritage of the upright;
 or the upright might set
  their own hands to evil.

4 Do good, Yahweh, to those who are good,
  to the sincere at heart.

NEW REVISED STANDARD VERSION	REVISED ENGLISH BIBLE

5 But those who turn aside to their own crooked
  ways
 the LORD will lead away with evildoers.
 Peace be upon Israel!

Psalm 126

A Song of Ascents.

1 When the LORD restored the fortunes of Zion,*b*
 we were like those who dream.
2 Then our mouth was filled with laughter,
 and our tongue with shouts of joy;
 then it was said among the nations,
  "The LORD has done great things for them."
3 The LORD has done great things for us,
 and we rejoiced.

4 Restore our fortunes, O LORD,
 like the watercourses in the Negeb.
5 May those who sow in tears
 reap with shouts of joy.
6 Those who go out weeping,
 bearing the seed for sowing,
 shall come home with shouts of joy,
 carrying their sheaves.

Psalm 127

A Song of Ascents. Of Solomon.

1 Unless the LORD builds the house,
 those who build it labor in vain.
 Unless the LORD guards the city,
 the guard keeps watch in vain.
2 It is in vain that you rise up early
 and go late to rest,
 eating the bread of anxious toil;
 for he gives sleep to his beloved.*c*

3 Sons are indeed a heritage from the LORD,
 the fruit of the womb a reward.
4 Like arrows in the hand of a warrior
 are the sons of one's youth.
5 Happy is the man who has
 his quiver full of them.
 He shall not be put to shame
 when he speaks with his enemies in the gate.

Psalm 128

A Song of Ascents.

1 Happy is everyone who fears the LORD,
 who walks in his ways.
2 You shall eat the fruit of the labor of your hands;
 you shall be happy, and it shall go well with
  you.

3 Your wife will be like a fruitful vine
 within your house;
 your children will be like olive shoots
 around your table.
4 Thus shall the man be blessed
 who fears the LORD.

---

5 But those who turn aside into crooked ways,
 may the LORD make them go the way of evildoers!

Peace be on Israel!

Psalm 126

A song of the ascents

1 WHEN the LORD restored the fortunes of Zion,
 we were like people renewed in health.
2 Our mouths were full of laughter
 and our tongues sang aloud for joy.
 Then among the nations it was said,
 'The LORD has done great things for them.'
3 Great things indeed the LORD did for us,
 and we rejoiced.

4 Restore our fortunes, LORD,
 as streams return in the Negeb.
5 Those who sow in tears
 will reap with songs of joy.
6 He who goes out weeping,
 carrying his bag of seed,
 will come back with songs of joy,
 carrying home his sheaves.

Psalm 127

A song of the ascents: for Solomon

1 UNLESS the LORD builds the house,
 its builders labour in vain.
 Unless the LORD keeps watch over the city,
 the watchman stands guard in vain.
2 In vain you rise early
 and go late to rest,
 toiling for the bread you eat;
 he supplies the need of those he loves.

3 Sons are a gift from the LORD
 and children a reward from him.
4 Like arrows in the hand of a warrior
 are the sons of one's youth.
5 Happy is he
 who has his quiver full of them;
 someone like that will not have to back down
 when confronted by an enemy in court.

Psalm 128

A song of the ascents

1 HAPPY are all who fear the LORD,
 who conform to his ways.
2 You will enjoy the fruit of your labours,
 you will be happy and prosperous.

3 Within your house
 your wife will be like a fruitful vine;
 your sons round your table
 will be like olive saplings.
4 Such is the blessing in store
 for him who fears the LORD.

---

*b Or brought back those who returned to Zion
for his beloved during sleep* *c Or for he provides* 126:1 **like . . . health:** *or* like dreamers. 127:2 **those he loves:**
prob. rdg; Heb. adds an unintelligible word.

NEW AMERICAN BIBLE

5 But those who turn aside to crooked ways
   may the LORD send down with the wicked.
Peace upon Israel!

Psalm 126

¹ *A song of ascents.*

I
When the LORD restored the fortunes of Zion,
   then we thought we were dreaming.
² Our mouths were filled with laughter;
   our tongues sang for joy.
Then it was said among the nations,
   "The LORD has done great things for them."
³ The LORD had done great things for us;
   Oh, how happy we were!
⁴ Restore again our fortunes, LORD,
   like the dry stream beds of the Negeb.
II
⁵ Those who sow in tears
   will reap with cries of joy.
⁶ Those who go forth weeping,
   carrying sacks of seed,
Will return with cries of joy,
   carrying their bundled sheaves.

Psalm 127

¹ *A song of ascents. Of Solomon.*

I
Unless the LORD build the house,
   they labor in vain who build.
Unless the LORD guard the city,
   in vain does the guard keep watch.
² It is vain for you to rise early
   and put off your rest at night,
To eat bread earned by hard toil—
   all this God gives to his beloved in sleep.
II
³ Children too are a gift from the LORD,
   the fruit of the womb, a reward.
⁴ Like arrows in the hand of a warrior
   are the children born in one's youth.
⁵ Blessed are they whose quivers are full.
They will never be shamed
   contending with foes at the gate.

Psalm 128

¹ *A song of ascents.*

I
Happy are all who fear the LORD,
   who walk in the ways of God.
² What your hands provide you will enjoy;
   you will be happy and prosper:
³ Like a fruitful vine
   your wife within your home,
Like olive plants
   your children around your table.
⁴ Just so will they be blessed
   who fear the LORD.

NEW JERUSALEM BIBLE

⁵ But the crooked, the twisted, turn them away,
   Yahweh, with evil-doers.

Peace to Israel!

Psalm 126 (V 125)

Song of Ascents

¹ When Yahweh brought back Zion's captives
   we lived in a dream;
² then our mouths filled with laughter,
   and our lips with song.

Then the nations kept saying, 'What great deeds
   Yahweh has done for them!'
³ Yes, Yahweh did great deeds for us,
   and we were overjoyed.

⁴ Bring back, Yahweh, our people from captivity
   like torrents in the Negeb!
⁵ Those who sow in tears
   sing as they reap.

⁶ He went off, went off weeping,
   carrying the seed.
He comes back, comes back singing,
   bringing in his sheaves.

Psalm 127 (V 126)

Song of Ascents   Of Solomon

¹ If Yahweh does not build a house
   in vain do its builders toil.
If Yahweh does not guard a city
   in vain does its guard keep watch.

² In vain you get up earlier,
   and put off going to bed,
sweating to make a living,
   since it is he who provides for his beloved as they
      sleep.

³ Sons are a birthright from Yahweh,
   children are a reward from him.
⁴ Like arrows in a warrior's hand
   are the sons you father when young.

⁵ How blessed is the man
   who has filled his quiver with them;
in dispute with his enemies at the city gate
   he will not be worsted.

Psalm 128 (V 127)

Song of Ascents

¹ How blessed are all who fear Yahweh,
   who walk in his ways!

² Your own labours will yield you a living,
   happy and prosperous will you be.
³ Your wife a fruitful vine
   in the inner places of your house.
Your children round your table
   like shoots of an olive tree.

⁴ Such are the blessings that fall
   on those who fear Yahweh.

5 The LORD bless you from Zion.
   May you see the prosperity of Jerusalem
   all the days of your life.
6 May you see your children's children.
   Peace be upon Israel!

Psalm 129

A Song of Ascents.

1 "Often have they attacked me from my youth"
   —let Israel now say—
2 "often have they attacked me from my youth,
   yet they have not prevailed against me.
3 The plowers plowed on my back;
   they made their furrows long."
4 The LORD is righteous;
   he has cut the cords of the wicked.
5 May all who hate Zion
   be put to shame and turned backward.
6 Let them be like the grass on the housetops
   that withers before it grows up,
7 with which reapers do not fill their hands
   or binders of sheaves their arms,
8 while those who pass by do not say,
   "The blessing of the LORD be upon you!
   We bless you in the name of the LORD!"

Psalm 130

A Song of Ascents.

1 Out of the depths I cry to you, O LORD.
2 Lord, hear my voice!
   Let your ears be attentive
   to the voice of my supplications!

3 If you, O LORD, should mark iniquities,
   Lord, who could stand?
4 But there is forgiveness with you,
   so that you may be revered.

5 I wait for the LORD, my soul waits,
   and in his word I hope;
6 my soul waits for the Lord
   more than those who watch for the morning,
   more than those who watch for the morning.

7 O Israel, hope in the LORD!
   For with the LORD there is steadfast love,
   and with him is great power to redeem.
8 It is he who will redeem Israel
   from all its iniquities.

Psalm 131

A Song of Ascents. Of David.

1 O LORD, my heart is not lifted up,
   my eyes are not raised too high;
   I do not occupy myself with things
   too great and too marvelous for me.
2 But I have calmed and quieted my soul,
   like a weaned child with its mother;
   my soul is like the weaned child that is with
   me.*d*

3 O Israel, hope in the LORD
   from this time on and forevermore.

d Or *my soul within me is like a weaned child*

5 May the LORD bless you from Zion;
   may you rejoice in the prosperity of Jerusalem
   all the days of your life.
6 And may you live to see your children's children!

   Peace be on Israel!

Psalm 129

A song of the ascents

1 OFTEN since I was young have I been attacked—
   let Israel now say—
2 often since I was young have I been attacked,
   but never have my attackers prevailed.
3 They scored my back with scourges,
   like ploughmen driving long furrows.
4 The LORD is victorious;
   he has cut me free from the bonds of the wicked.

5 Let all who hate Zion
   be thrown back in confusion;
6 let them be like grass growing on the roof,
   which withers before it can shoot,
7 which will never fill a mower's hand
   nor yield an armful for the harvester,
8 so that passers-by will never say to them,
   'The blessing of the LORD be on you!
   We bless you in the name of the LORD.'

Psalm 130

A song of the ascents

1 LORD, out of the depths I have called to you;
2 hear my cry, Lord;
   let your ears be attentive
   to my supplication.
3 If you, LORD, should keep account of sins,
   who could hold his ground?
4 But with you is forgiveness,
   so that you may be revered.

5 I wait for the LORD with longing;
   I put my hope in his word.
6 My soul waits for the Lord
   more eagerly than watchmen for the morning.
   Like those who watch for the morning,
7 let Israel look for the LORD.
   For in the LORD is love unfailing,
   and great is his power to deliver.
8 He alone will set Israel free
   from all their sins.

Psalm 131

A song of the ascents: for David

1 LORD, my heart is not proud,
   nor are my eyes haughty;
   I do not busy myself with great affairs
   or things too marvellous for me.
2 But I am calm and quiet
   like a weaned child clinging to its mother.

3 Israel, hope in the LORD,
   now and for evermore.

127:5 **in court:** *lit.* in the gate.   131:2 **to its mother:** *prob. rdg; Heb.*
adds as a weaned child clinging to me.

II

5 May the LORD bless you from Zion,
  all the days of your life
That you may share Jerusalem's joy
6   and live to see your children's children.
  Peace upon Israel!

5 May Yahweh bless you from Zion!
May you see Jerusalem prosper
  all the days of your life,
6 and live to see your children's children!

Peace to Israel!

Psalm 129

1 *A song of ascents.*

I

Much have they oppressed me from my youth,
  now let Israel say.
2 Much have they oppressed me from my youth,
  yet they have not prevailed.
3 Upon my back the plowers plowed,
  as they traced their long furrows.
4 But the just LORD cut me free
  from the ropes of the yoke of the wicked.

II

5 May they be scattered in disgrace,
  all who hate Zion.
6 May they be like grass on the rooftops
  withered in early growth,
7 Never to fill the reaper's hands,
  nor the arms of the binders of sheaves,
8 With none passing by to call out:
  "The blessing of the LORD be upon you!
  We bless you in the name of the LORD!"

Psalm 129 (V 128)

Song of Ascents

1 Often as men have attacked me since I was young
  — let Israel repeat it —
2 often as men have attacked me since I was young,
  they have never overcome me.

3 On my back ploughmen have set to work,
  making long furrows,
4 but Yahweh the upright has shattered
  the yoke of the wicked.

5 Let all who hate Zion
  be thrown back in confusion,
6 let them be like grass on a roof,
  dried up before it is cut,
7 never to fill the reaper's arm
  nor the binder's lap,
8 And no passer-by will say,
  'The blessing of Yahweh be on you!

'We bless you in the name of Yahweh.'

Psalm 130

1 *A song of ascents.*

I

Out of the depths I call to you, LORD;
2   Lord, hear my cry!
May your ears be attentive
  to my cry for mercy.
3 If you, LORD, mark our sins,
  Lord, who can stand?
4 But with you is forgiveness
  and so you are revered.

II

5 I wait with longing for the LORD,
  my soul waits for his word.
6 My soul looks for the Lord
  more than sentinels for daybreak.
More than sentinels for daybreak,
7   let Israel look for the LORD,
For with the LORD is kindness,
  with him is full redemption,
8 And God will redeem Israel
  from all their sins.

Psalm 130 (V 129)

Song of Ascents

1 From the depths I call to you, Yahweh:
2   Lord, hear my cry.
Listen attentively
  to the sound of my pleading!

3 If you kept a record of our sins,
  Lord, who could stand their ground?
4 But with you is forgiveness,
  that you may be revered.

5 I rely, my whole being relies,
  Yahweh, on your promise.
6 My whole being hopes in the Lord,
  more than watchmen for daybreak;
more than watchmen for daybreak
7   let Israel hope in Yahweh.

For with Yahweh is faithful love,
  with him generous ransom;
8 and he will ransom Israel
  from all its sins.

Psalm 131

1 *A song of ascents. Of David.*

LORD, my heart is not proud;
  nor are my eyes haughty.
I do not busy myself with great matters,
  with things too sublime for me.
2 Rather, I have stilled my soul,
  hushed it like a weaned child.
Like a weaned child on its mother's lap,
  so is my soul within me.
3 Israel, hope in the LORD,
  now and forever.

Psalm 131 (V 130)

Song of Ascents

1 Yahweh, my heart is not haughty,
  I do not set my sights too high.
I have taken no part in great affairs,
  in wonders beyond my scope.
2 No, I hold myself in quiet and silence,
  like a little child in its mother's arms,
  like a little child, so I keep myself.
3 Let Israel hope in Yahweh
  henceforth and for ever.

NEW REVISED STANDARD VERSION	REVISED ENGLISH BIBLE

Psalm 132

A Song of Ascents.

1 O LORD, remember in David's favor
    all the hardships he endured;
2 how he swore to the LORD
    and vowed to the Mighty One of Jacob,
3 "I will not enter my house
    or get into my bed;
4 I will not give sleep to my eyes
    or slumber to my eyelids,
5 until I find a place for the LORD,
    a dwelling place for the Mighty One of Jacob."

6 We heard of it in Ephrathah;
    we found it in the fields of Jaar.
7 "Let us go to his dwelling place;
    let us worship at his footstool."

8 Rise up, O LORD, and go to your resting place,
    you and the ark of your might.
9 Let your priests be clothed with righteousness,
    and let your faithful shout for joy.
10 For your servant David's sake
    do not turn away the face of your anointed
      one.

11 The LORD swore to David a sure oath
    from which he will not turn back:
    "One of the sons of your body
    I will set on your throne.
12 If your sons keep my covenant
    and my decrees that I shall teach them,
    their sons also, forevermore,
    shall sit on your throne."

13 For the LORD has chosen Zion;
    he has desired it for his habitation:
14 "This is my resting place forever;
    here I will reside, for I have desired it.
15 I will abundantly bless its provisions;
    I will satisfy its poor with bread.
16 Its priests I will clothe with salvation,
    and its faithful will shout for joy.
17 There I will cause a horn to sprout up for David;
    I have prepared a lamp for my anointed one.
18 His enemies I will clothe with disgrace,
    but on him, his crown will gleam."

Psalm 132

A song of the ascents

1 LORD, remember David
    and all the adversity he endured,
2 how he swore an oath to the LORD
    and made this vow to the Mighty One of Jacob:
3 'I will not live in my house
    nor will I go to my bed,
4 I will give myself no rest,
    nor allow myself sleep,
5 until I find a sanctuary for the LORD,
    a dwelling for the Mighty One of Jacob.'

6 We heard of the Ark in Ephrathah;
    we found it in the region of Jaar.
7 Let us enter his dwelling;
    let us bow down at his footstool.

8 Arise, LORD, and come to your resting-place,
    you and your powerful Ark.
9 Let your priests be clothed in righteousness
    and let your loyal servants shout for joy.
10 For your servant David's sake
    do not reject your anointed one.

11 The LORD swore this oath to David,
    an oath which he will not break:
    'A prince of your own line
    I will set on your throne.
12 If your sons keep my covenant
    and heed the teaching that I give them,
    their sons in turn for all time
    will occupy your throne.'
13 For the LORD has chosen Zion,
    desired her for his home:
14 'This is my resting-place for ever;
    here I shall make my home, for that is what I
      want.
15 I shall bless her with food in plenty
    and satisfy her needy with bread.
16 I shall clothe her priests with victory;
    her loyal servants will shout for joy.
17 There I shall make a king of David's line appear
    and prepare a lamp for my anointed one;
18 I shall cover his enemies with shame,
    but on him there will be a shining crown.'

Psalm 133

A Song of Ascents.

1 How very good and pleasant it is
    when kindred live together in unity!
2 It is like the precious oil on the head,
    running down upon the beard,
    on the beard of Aaron,
    running down over the collar of his robes.
3 It is like the dew of Hermon,
    which falls on the mountains of Zion.
    For there the LORD ordained his blessing,
    life forevermore.

Psalm 133

A song of the ascents: for David

1 How GOOD and how pleasant it is
    to live together as brothers in unity!
2 It is like fragrant oil poured on the head
    and falling over the beard,
    Aaron's beard, when the oil runs down
    over the collar of his vestments.
3 It is as if the dew of Hermon were falling
    on the mountains of Zion.
    There the LORD bestows his blessing,
    life for evermore.

132:17 **make ... appear:** *lit.* make a horn shoot for David.

Psalm 132

¹A song of ascents.

I

Lord, remember David
and all his anxious care;
²How he swore an oath to the Lord,
vowed to the Mighty One of Jacob:
³"I will not enter the house where I live,
nor lie on the couch where I sleep;
⁴I will give my eyes no sleep,
my eyelids no rest,
⁵Till I find a home for the Lord,
a dwelling for the Mighty One of Jacob."
⁶"We have heard of it in Ephrathah;
we have found it in the fields of Jaar.
⁷Let us enter God's dwelling;
let us worship at God's footstool."
⁸"Arise, Lord, come to your resting place,
you and your majestic ark.
⁹Your priests will be clothed with justice;
your faithful will shout for joy."
¹⁰For the sake of David your servant,
do not reject your anointed.

II

¹¹The Lord swore an oath to David,
a pledge never to be broken:
"Your own offspring I will set upon your throne.
¹²If your sons observe my covenant,
the laws I shall teach them,
Their sons, in turn,
shall sit forever on your throne."
¹³Yes, the Lord has chosen Zion,
desired it for a dwelling:
¹⁴"This is my resting place forever;
here I will dwell, for I desire it.
¹⁵I will bless Zion with meat;
its poor I will fill with bread.
¹⁶I will clothe its priests with blessing;
its faithful shall shout for joy.
¹⁷There I will make a horn sprout for David's line;
I will set a lamp for my anointed.
¹⁸His foes I will clothe with shame,
but on him my crown shall gleam."

Psalm 133

¹A song of ascents. Of David.

How good it is, how pleasant,
where the people dwell as one!
²Like precious ointment on the head,
running down upon the beard,
Upon the beard of Aaron,
upon the collar of his robe.
³Like dew of Hermon coming down
upon the mountains of Zion.
There the Lord has lavished blessings,
life for evermore!

Psalm 132 (V 131)

Song of Ascents

¹Yahweh, remember David
and all the hardships he endured,
²the oath he swore to Yahweh,
his vow to the Mighty One of Jacob:
³'I will not enter tent or house,
will not climb into bed,
⁴will not allow myself to sleep,
not even to close my eyes,
⁵till I have found a place for Yahweh,
a dwelling for the Mighty One of Jacob!'
⁶Listen, we heard of it in Ephrathah,
we found it at Forest-Fields.
⁷Let us go into his dwelling-place,
and worship at his footstool.
⁸Go up, Yahweh, to your resting-place,
you and the ark of your strength.
⁹Your priests are robed in saving justice,
your faithful are shouting for joy.
¹⁰For the sake of your servant David,
do not reject your anointed.
¹¹Yahweh has sworn to David,
and will always remain true to his word,
'I promise that I will set
a son of yours upon your throne.
¹²If your sons observe my covenant
and the instructions I have taught them,
their sons too for evermore
will occupy your throne.'
¹³For Yahweh has chosen Zion,
he has desired it as a home.
¹⁴'Here shall I rest for evermore,
here shall I make my home as I have wished.
¹⁵'I shall generously bless her produce,
give her needy their fill of food,
¹⁶I shall clothe her priests with salvation,
and her faithful will sing aloud for joy.
¹⁷'There I shall raise up a line of descendants for
David,
light a lamp for my anointed;
¹⁸I shall clothe his enemies with shame,
while his own crown shall flourish.'

Psalm 133 (V 132)

Song of Ascents

¹How good, how delightful it is
to live as brothers all together!
²It is like a fine oil on the head,
running down the beard,
running down Aaron's beard,
onto the collar of his robes.
³It is like the dew of Hermon
falling on the heights of Zion;
for there Yahweh bestows his blessing,
everlasting life.

NEW REVISED STANDARD VERSION

NEW REVISED STANDARD VERSION	REVISED ENGLISH BIBLE

Psalm 134

A Song of Ascents.

1 Come, bless the LORD, all you servants of the
   LORD,
   who stand by night in the house of the LORD!
2 Lift up your hands to the holy place,
   and bless the LORD.

3 May the LORD, maker of heaven and earth,
   bless you from Zion.

Psalm 135

1 Praise the LORD!
   Praise the name of the LORD;
   give praise, O servants of the LORD,
2 you that stand in the house of the LORD,
   in the courts of the house of our God.
3 Praise the LORD, for the LORD is good;
   sing to his name, for he is gracious.
4 For the LORD has chosen Jacob for himself,
   Israel as his own possession.

5 For I know that the LORD is great;
   our Lord is above all gods.
6 Whatever the LORD pleases he does,
   in heaven and on earth,
   in the seas and all deeps.
7 He it is who makes the clouds rise at the end of
   the earth;
   he makes lightnings for the rain
   and brings out the wind from his storehouses.

8 He it was who struck down the firstborn of
   Egypt,
   both human beings and animals;
9 he sent signs and wonders
   into your midst, O Egypt,
   against Pharaoh and all his servants.
10 He struck down many nations
   and killed mighty kings—
11 Sihon, king of the Amorites,
   and Og, king of Bashan,
   and all the kingdoms of Canaan—
12 and gave their land as a heritage,
   a heritage to his people Israel.

13 Your name, O LORD, endures forever,
   your renown, O LORD, throughout all ages.
14 For the LORD will vindicate his people,
   and have compassion on his servants.

15 The idols of the nations are silver and gold,
   the work of human hands.
16 They have mouths, but they do not speak;
   they have eyes, but they do not see;
17 they have ears, but they do not hear,
   and there is no breath in their mouths.
18 Those who make them
   and all who trust them
   shall become like them.

19 O house of Israel, bless the LORD!
   O house of Aaron, bless the LORD!
20 O house of Levi, bless the LORD!
   You that fear the LORD, bless the LORD!
21 Blessed be the LORD from Zion,
   he who resides in Jerusalem.
   Praise the LORD!

Psalm 134

A song of the ascents

1 COME, bless the LORD,
   all you his servants,
   who minister night after night
   in the house of the LORD.
2 Lift up your hands towards the sanctuary
   and bless the LORD.
3 May the LORD, maker of heaven and earth,
   bless you from Zion!

Psalm 135

1 PRAISE the LORD.

Praise the name of the LORD;
   give praise, you servants of the LORD,
2 who minister in the house of the LORD,
   in the temple courts of our God.
3 Praise the LORD, for he is good;
   sing psalms to his name, for that is pleasing.
4 For the LORD has chosen Jacob to be his own,
   Israel as his treasured possession.

5 I know that the LORD is great,
   that our God is above all gods.
6 Whatever the LORD wills,
   that he does, in heaven and on earth,
   in the sea and all the great deep.
7 He brings up the mist from the ends of the earth,
   makes clefts for the rain,
   and brings out the wind out of his storehouses.

8 He struck down all the firstborn in Egypt,
   both of humans and of animals.
9 In Egypt he sent signs and portents
   against Pharaoh and all his subjects.
10 He struck down mighty nations
   and slew powerful kings:
11 Sihon king of the Amorites, King Og of Bashan,
   and all the kingdoms of Canaan.
12 He gave their land as a heritage
   to his people Israel.
13 LORD, your name endures for ever;
   your renown, LORD, will last to all generations,
14 for the LORD will give his people justice;
   he has compassion on his servants.

15 The gods of the nations are idols of silver and
   gold,
   fashioned by human hands.
16 They have mouths that cannot speak
   and eyes that cannot see;
17 they have ears that cannot hear,
   and there is no breath in their mouths.
18 Their makers become like them,
   and so do all who put their trust in them.

19 House of Israel, bless the LORD;
   house of Aaron, bless the LORD.
20 House of Levi, bless the LORD;
   you that fear the LORD, bless the LORD.
21 Blessed from Zion be the LORD,
   he who dwells in Jerusalem.

Praise the LORD.

135:5 **God:** *so Scroll; Heb.* Lord.   135:7 **clefts:** *prob. rdg; Heb.*
lightnings.   135:9 **In Egypt:** *lit.* In your midst, Egypt.

Psalm 134

[1] *A song of ascents.*

Come, bless the LORD,
  all you servants of the LORD
Who stand in the house of the LORD
  through the long hours of night.
[2] Lift up your hands toward the sanctuary,
  and bless the LORD.
[3] May the LORD who made heaven and earth
  bless you from Zion.

Psalm 135

[1] Hallelujah!

I
Praise the name of the LORD!
  Praise, you servants of the LORD,
[2] Who stand in the house of the LORD,
  in the courts of the house of our God!
[3] Praise the LORD; the LORD is good!
  Sing to God's name; it is gracious!
[4] For the LORD has chosen Jacob,
  Israel as a treasured possession.

II
[5] I know that the LORD is great,
  our Lord is greater than all gods.
[6] Whatever the LORD wishes
  he does in heaven and on earth,
  in the seas and in all the deeps.
[7] He raises storm clouds from the end of the earth,
  makes lightning and rain,
  brings forth wind from the storehouse.

III
[8] He struck down Egypt's firstborn,
  human and beast alike,
[9] And sent signs and portents against you, Egypt,
  against Pharaoh and all his servants.
[10] The Lord struck down many nations,
  slew mighty kings —
[11] Sihon, king of the Amorites,
  Og, king of Bashan,
  all the kings of Canaan —
[12] And made their land a heritage,
  a heritage for Israel his people.
[13] O LORD, your name is forever,
  your renown, from age to age!
[14] For the LORD defends his people,
  shows mercy to his servants.

IV
[15] The idols of the nations are silver and gold,
  the work of human hands.
[16] They have mouths but speak not;
  they have eyes but see not;
[17] They have ears but hear not;
  no breath is in their mouths.
[18] Their makers shall be like them,
  all who trust in them.

V
[19] House of Israel, bless the LORD!
  House of Aaron, bless the LORD!
[20] House of Levi, bless the LORD!
  You who fear the LORD, bless the LORD!
[21] Blessed from Zion be the LORD,
  who dwells in Jerusalem!
  Hallelujah!

Psalm 134 (V 133)

Song of Ascents

[1] Come, bless Yahweh,
  all you who serve Yahweh,
  serving in the house of Yahweh,
  in the courts of the house of our God.
  Through the night watches
[2] stretch out your hands towards the sanctuary
  and bless Yahweh.
[3] May Yahweh bless you from Zion,
  he who made heaven and earth!

Psalm 135 (V 134)[u]

[1] Alleluia!

Praise the name of Yahweh,
  you who serve Yahweh, praise him,
[2] serving in the house of Yahweh,
  in the courts of the house of our God.
[3] Praise Yahweh, for Yahweh is good,
  make music for his name — it brings joy —
[4] for Yahweh has chosen Jacob for himself,
  Israel as his own possession.

[5] For I know that Yahweh is great,
  our Lord is above all gods.
[6] Yahweh does whatever he pleases
  in heaven, on earth,
  in the waters and all the depths.
[7] He summons up clouds from the borders of earth,
  sends rain with lightning-flashes,
  and brings the wind out of his storehouse.

[8] He struck the first-born in Egypt,
  man and beast alike,
[9] he sent signs and wonders into the heart of Egypt,
  against Pharaoh and all his officials.
[10] He struck down many nations,
  he slaughtered mighty kings,
[11] Sihon king of the Amorites,
  and Og king of Bashan,
  and all the kingdoms of Canaan.
[12] He gave their land as a birthright,
  a birthright to his people Israel.

[13] Yahweh, your name endures for ever,
  Yahweh, your memory is fresh from age to age.
[14] For Yahweh vindicates his people,
  feels compassion for his servants.

[15] The idols of the nations are silver and gold,
  made by human hands.
[16] These have mouths but say nothing,
  have eyes but see nothing,
[17] have ears but hear nothing,
  and they have no breath in their mouths.
[18] Their makers will end up like them,
  everyone who relies on them.

[19] House of Israel, bless Yahweh,
  House of Aaron, bless Yahweh,
[20] House of Levi, bless Yahweh,
  you who fear Yahweh, bless Yahweh.
[21] Blessed be Yahweh from Zion,
  he who dwells in Jerusalem!

[u] **135** Composed entirely of fragments or reminiscences of other Pss.

NEW REVISED STANDARD VERSION	REVISED ENGLISH BIBLE

Psalm 136   Psalm 136

1 O give thanks to the LORD, for he is good,
   for his steadfast love endures forever.
2 O give thanks to the God of gods,
   for his steadfast love endures forever.
3 O give thanks to the Lord of lords,
   for his steadfast love endures forever;

4 who alone does great wonders,
   for his steadfast love endures forever;
5 who by understanding made the heavens,
   for his steadfast love endures forever;
6 who spread out the earth on the waters,
   for his steadfast love endures forever;
7 who made the great lights,
   for his steadfast love endures forever;
8 the sun to rule over the day,
   for his steadfast love endures forever;
9 the moon and stars to rule over the night,
   for his steadfast love endures forever;

10 who struck Egypt through their firstborn,
   for his steadfast love endures forever;
11 and brought Israel out from among them,
   for his steadfast love endures forever;
12 with a strong hand and an outstretched arm,
   for his steadfast love endures forever;
13 who divided the Red Sea*e* in two,
   for his steadfast love endures forever;
14 and made Israel pass through the midst of it,
   for his steadfast love endures forever;
15 but overthrew Pharaoh and his army in the Red
   Sea,*e*
   for his steadfast love endures forever;
16 who led his people through the wilderness,
   for his steadfast love endures forever;
17 who struck down great kings,
   for his steadfast love endures forever;
18 and killed famous kings,
   for his steadfast love endures forever;
19 Sihon, king of the Amorites,
   for his steadfast love endures forever;
20 and Og, king of Bashan,
   for his steadfast love endures forever;
21 and gave their land as a heritage,
   for his steadfast love endures forever;
22 a heritage to his servant Israel,
   for his steadfast love endures forever.

23 It is he who remembered us in our low estate,
   for his steadfast love endures forever;
24 and rescued us from our foes,
   for his steadfast love endures forever;
25 who gives food to all flesh,
   for his steadfast love endures forever.

26 O give thanks to the God of heaven,
   for his steadfast love endures forever.

---

1 IT is good to give thanks to the LORD,
   for his love endures for ever.
2 Give thanks to the God of gods;
   his love endures for ever.
3 Give thanks to the Lord of lords —
   his love endures for ever;
4 who alone works great marvels —
   his love endures for ever;
5 who made the heavens in wisdom —
   his love endures for ever;
6 who spread out the earth on the waters —
   his love endures for ever.
7 He made the great luminaries —
   his love endures for ever;
8 the sun to rule the day —
   his love endures for ever;
9 the moon and the stars to rule the night —
   his love endures for ever.
10 Give thanks to him
   who struck down the firstborn of the Egyptians —
   his love endures for ever —
11 and brought Israel out from among them;
   his love endures for ever —
12 With strong hand and outstretched arm —
   his love endures for ever —
13 he divided the Red Sea in two —
   his love endures for ever —
14 and made Israel pass through it;
   his love endures for ever.
15 But Pharaoh and his host he swept into the Red
   Sea;
   his love endures for ever.
16 He led his people through the wilderness;
   his love endures for ever.
17 He struck down great kings;
   his love endures for ever.
18 He slew powerful kings;
   his love endures for ever.
19 Sihon king of the Amorites —
   his love endures for ever —
20 and Og the king of Bashan;
   his love endures for ever —
21 He gave their land to Israel —
   his love endures for ever —
22 a heritage to Israel his servant;
   his love endures for ever.
23 He remembered us when our fortunes were low —
   his love endures for ever —
24 and rescued us from our enemies;
   his love endures for ever.
25 He gives food to all mankind;
   his love endures for ever.
26 Give thanks to the God of heaven,
   for his love endures for ever.

Psalm 137   Psalm 137

1 By the rivers of Babylon —
   there we sat down and there we wept
   when we remembered Zion.
2 On the willows*f* there
   we hung up our harps.

---

1 BY the rivers of Babylon we sat down and wept
   as we remembered Zion.
2 On the willow trees there
   we hung up our lyres,

---

e Or Sea of Reeds   *f Or poplars*

136:13,15 **Red Sea:** *or* sea of Reeds.   137:2 **willow trees:** *or* poplars.

Psalm 136

I

1 Praise the LORD, who is so good;
  God's love endures forever;
2 Praise the God of gods;
  God's love endures forever;
3 Praise the Lord of lords;
  God's love endures forever;

II

4 Who alone has done great wonders,
  God's love endures forever;
5 Who skillfully made the heavens,
  God's love endures forever;
6 Who spread the earth upon the waters,
  God's love endures forever;
7 Who made the great lights,
  God's love endures forever;
8 The sun to rule the day,
  God's love endures forever;
9 The moon and stars to rule the night,
  God's love endures forever;

III

10 Who struck down the firstborn of Egypt,
  God's love endures forever;
11 And led Israel from their midst,
  God's love endures forever;
12 With mighty hand and outstretched arm,
  God's love endures forever;
13 Who split in two the Red Sea
  God's love endures forever;
14 And led Israel through,
  God's love endures forever;
15 But swept Pharaoh and his army into the Red Sea,
  God's love endures forever;
16 Who led the people through the desert,
  God's love endures forever;

IV

17 Who struck down great kings,
  God's love endures forever;
18 Slew powerful kings,
  God's love endures forever;
19 Sihon, king of the Amorites,
  God's love endures forever;
20 Og, king of Bashan,
  God's love endures forever;
21 And made their lands a heritage,
  God's love endures forever;
22 A heritage for Israel, God's servant,
  God's love endures forever.

V

23 The LORD remembered us in our misery,
  God's love endures forever;
24 Freed us from our foes,
  God's love endures forever;
25 And gives food to all flesh,
  God's love endures forever.

VI

26 Praise the God of heaven,
  God's love endures forever.

Psalm 137

I

1 By the rivers of Babylon
  we sat mourning and weeping
  when we remembered Zion.
2 On the poplars of that land
  we hung up our harps.

Psalm 136 (V 135)

Alleluia!

1 Give thanks to Yahweh for he is good,
  for his faithful love endures for ever.
2 Give thanks to the God of gods,
  for his faithful love endures for ever.
3 Give thanks to the Lord of lords,
  for his faithful love endures for ever.

4 He alone works wonders,
  for his faithful love endures for ever.
5 In wisdom he made the heavens,
  for his faithful love endures for ever.
6 He set the earth firm on the waters,
  for his faithful love endures for ever.

7 He made the great lights,
  for his faithful love endures for ever.
8 The sun to rule the day,
  for his faithful love endures for ever.
9 Moon and stars to rule the night,
  for his faithful love endures for ever.

10 He struck down the first-born of Egypt,
  for his faithful love endures for ever.
11 He brought Israel out from among them,
  for his faithful love endures for ever.
12 With mighty hand and outstretched arm,
  for his faithful love endures for ever.
13 He split the Sea of Reeds in two,
  for his faithful love endures for ever.
14 Let Israel pass through the middle,
  for his faithful love endures for ever.
15 And drowned Pharaoh and all his army,
  for his faithful love endures for ever.
16 He led his people through the desert,
  for his faithful love endures for ever.

17 He struck down mighty kings,
  for his faithful love endures for ever.
18 Slaughtered famous kings,
  for his faithful love endures for ever.
19 Sihon king of the Amorites,
  for his faithful love endures for ever.
20 And Og king of Bashan,
  for his faithful love endures for ever.
21 He gave their land as a birthright,
  for his faithful love endures for ever.
22 A birthright to his servant Israel,
  for his faithful love endures for ever.
23 He kept us in mind when we were humbled,
  for his faithful love endures for ever.
24 And rescued us from our enemies,
  for his faithful love endures for ever.

25 He provides food for all living creatures,
  for his faithful love endures for ever.
26 Give thanks to the God of heaven,
  for his faithful love endures for ever.

Psalm 137 (V 136)

1 By the rivers of Babylon
  we sat and wept
  at the memory of Zion.
2 On the poplars there
  we had hung up our harps.

NEW REVISED STANDARD VERSION	REVISED ENGLISH BIBLE

NEW REVISED STANDARD VERSION

3 For there our captors
    asked us for songs,
and our tormentors asked for mirth, saying,
    "Sing us one of the songs of Zion!"
4 How could we sing the LORD's song
    in a foreign land?
5 If I forget you, O Jerusalem,
    let my right hand wither!
6 Let my tongue cling to the roof of my mouth,
    if I do not remember you,
if I do not set Jerusalem
    above my highest joy.

7 Remember, O LORD, against the Edomites
    the day of Jerusalem's fall,
how they said, "Tear it down! Tear it down!
    Down to its foundations!"
8 O daughter Babylon, you devastator!g
    Happy shall they be who pay you back
    what you have done to us!
9 Happy shall they be who take your little ones
    and dash them against the rock!

Psalm 138

Of David.

1 I give you thanks, O LORD, with my whole heart;
    before the gods I sing your praise;
2 I bow down toward your holy temple
    and give thanks to your name for your steadfast
        love and your faithfulness;
for you have exalted your name and your word
    above everything.h
3 On the day I called, you answered me,
    you increased my strength of soul.i

4 All the kings of the earth shall praise you,
    O LORD,
for they have heard the words of your mouth.
5 They shall sing of the ways of the LORD,
    for great is the glory of the LORD.
6 For though the LORD is high, he regards the
    lowly;
but the haughty he perceives from far away.

7 Though I walk in the midst of trouble,
    you preserve me against the wrath of my
        enemies;
you stretch out your hand,
    and your right hand delivers me.
8 The LORD will fulfill his purpose for me;
    your steadfast love, O LORD, endures forever.
    Do not forsake the work of your hands.

Psalm 139

To the leader. Of David. A Psalm.

1 O LORD, you have searched me and known me.
2 You know when I sit down and when I rise up;
    you discern my thoughts from far away.
3 You search out my path and my lying down,
    and are acquainted with all my ways.
4 Even before a word is on my tongue,
    O LORD, you know it completely.

REVISED ENGLISH BIBLE

3 for there those who had carried us captive
    asked us to sing them a song,
our captors called on us to be joyful:
    'Sing us one of the songs of Zion.'
4 How could we sing the LORD's song
    in a foreign land?
5 If I forget you, Jerusalem,
    may my right hand wither away;
6 let my tongue cling to the roof of my mouth
    if I do not remember you,
if I do not set Jerusalem
    above my chief joy.

7 Remember, LORD, against the Edomites
    the day when Jerusalem fell,
how they shouted, 'Down with it, down with it,
    down to its very foundations!'
8 Babylon, Babylon the destroyer,
    happy is he who repays you
    for what you did to us!
9 Happy is he who seizes your babes
    and dashes them against a rock.

Psalm 138

For David

1 I SHALL give praise to you, LORD, with my whole
    heart;
in the presence of the gods I shall sing psalms to
    you.
2 I shall bow down towards your holy temple;
    for your love and faithfulness I shall praise your
        name,
for you have exalted your promise above the
        heavens.
3 When I called, you answered me
    and made me bold and strong.

4 Let all the kings of the earth praise you, LORD,
    when they hear the words you have spoken;
5 let them sing of the LORD's ways,
    for great is the glory of the LORD.
6 The LORD is exalted, yet he cares for the lowly
    and from afar he takes note of the proud.

7 Though I am compassed about by trouble,
    you preserve my life,
putting forth your power against the rage of my
        enemies,
and with your right hand you save me.
8 The LORD will accomplish his purpose for me.
    Your love endures for ever, LORD;
    do not abandon what you have made.

Psalm 139

For the leader: for David: a psalm

1 LORD, you have examined me and you know me.
2 You know me at rest and in action;
    you discern my thoughts from afar.
3 You trace my journeying and my resting-places,
    and are familiar with all the paths I take.
4 For there is not a word that I speak
    but you, LORD, know all about it.

---

g Or *you who are devastated*   h Cn: Heb *you have exalted your*
word above all your name   i Syr Compare Gk Tg: Heb *you made*
me arrogant in my soul with strength

NEW AMERICAN BIBLE

³There our captors asked us
  for the words of a song;
Our tormentors, for a joyful song:
  "Sing for us a song of Zion!"
⁴But how could we sing a song of the LORD
  in a foreign land?

II

⁵If I forget you, Jerusalem,
  may my right hand wither.
⁶May my tongue stick to my palate
  if I do not remember you,
If I do not exalt Jerusalem
  beyond all my delights.

III

⁷Remember, LORD, against Edom
  that day at Jerusalem.
They said: "Level it, level it
  down to its foundations!"
⁸Fair Babylon, you destroyer,
  happy those who pay you back
  the evil you have done us!
⁹Happy those who seize your children
  and smash them against a rock.

Psalm 138

¹ *Of David.*

I

I thank you, LORD, with all my heart;
  before the gods to you I sing.
²I bow low toward your holy temple;
  I praise your name for your fidelity and love.
For you have exalted over all
  your name and your promise.
³When I cried out, you answered;
  you strengthened my spirit.

II

⁴All the kings of earth will praise you, LORD,
  when they hear the words of your mouth.
⁵They will sing of the ways of the LORD:
  "How great is the glory of the LORD!"
⁶The LORD is on high, but cares for the lowly
  and knows the proud from afar.
⁷Though I walk in the midst of dangers,
  you guard my life when my enemies rage.
You stretch out your hand;
  your right hand saves me.
⁸The LORD is with me to the end.
  LORD, your love endures forever.
  Never forsake the work of your hands!

Psalm 139

¹ *For the leader. A psalm of David.*

I

LORD, you have probed me, you know me:
² you know when I sit and stand;
  you understand my thoughts from afar.
³My travels and my rest you mark;
  with all my ways you are familiar.
⁴Even before a word is on my tongue,
  LORD, you know it all.

NEW JERUSALEM BIBLE

³For there our gaolers had asked us
  to sing them a song,
our captors to make merry,
  'Sing us one of the songs of Zion.'
⁴How could we sing a song of Yahweh
  on alien soil?
⁵If I forget you, Jerusalem,
  may my right hand wither!
⁶May my tongue remain stuck to my palate
  if I do not keep you in mind,
  if I do not count Jerusalem
  the greatest of my joys.

⁷Remember, Yahweh, to the Edomites' cost,
  the day of Jerusalem,
how they said, 'Down with it! Rase it to the
  ground!'
⁸Daughter of Babel, doomed to destruction,
  a blessing on anyone
who treats you as you treated us,
⁹a blessing on anyone who seizes your babies
  and shatters them against a rock!

Psalm 138 (V 137)

Of David

¹I thank you, Yahweh, with all my heart,
  for you have listened to the cry I uttered.
In the presence of angels I sing to you,
²I bow down before your holy Temple.

I praise your name for your faithful love and your
  constancy;
your promises surpass even your fame.
³You heard me on the day when I called,
  and you gave new strength to my heart.

⁴All the kings of the earth give thanks to you,
  Yahweh,
  when they hear the promises you make;
⁵they sing of Yahweh's ways,
  'Great is the glory of Yahweh!'
⁶Sublime as he is, Yahweh looks on the humble,
  the proud he picks out from afar.

⁷Though I live surrounded by trouble
  you give me life — to my enemies' fury!
You stretch out your right hand and save me,
⁸Yahweh will do all things for me.
Yahweh, your faithful love endures for ever,
  do not abandon what you have made.

Psalm 139 (V 138)

For the choirmaster Of David Psalm

¹Yahweh, you examine me and know me,
²you know when I sit, when I rise,
  you understand my thoughts from afar.
³You watch when I walk or lie down,
  you know every detail of my conduct.
⁴A word is not yet on my tongue
  before you, Yahweh, know all about it.

NEW REVISED STANDARD VERSION | REVISED ENGLISH BIBLE

5 You hem me in, behind and before,
  and lay your hand upon me.
6 Such knowledge is too wonderful for me;
  it is so high that I cannot attain it.

7 Where can I go from your spirit?
  Or where can I flee from your presence?
8 If I ascend to heaven, you are there;
  if I make my bed in Sheol, you are there.
9 If I take the wings of the morning
  and settle at the farthest limits of the sea,
10 even there your hand shall lead me,
  and your right hand shall hold me fast.
11 If I say, "Surely the darkness shall cover me,
  and the light around me become night,"
12 even the darkness is not dark to you;
  the night is as bright as the day,
  for darkness is as light to you.

13 For it was you who formed my inward parts;
  you knit me together in my mother's womb.
14 I praise you, for I am fearfully and wonderfully
    made.
  Wonderful are your works;
  that I know very well.
15   My frame was not hidden from you,
  when I was being made in secret,
  intricately woven in the depths of the earth.
16 Your eyes beheld my unformed substance.
  In your book were written
  all the days that were formed for me,
  when none of them as yet existed.
17 How weighty to me are your thoughts, O God!
  How vast is the sum of them!
18 I try to count them—they are more than the sand;
  I come to the end j—I am still with you.

19 O that you would kill the wicked, O God,
  and that the bloodthirsty would depart from
    me—
20 those who speak of you maliciously,
  and lift themselves up against you for evil! k
21 Do I not hate those who hate you, O LORD?
  And do I not loathe those who rise up against
    you?
22 I hate them with perfect hatred;
  I count them my enemies.
23 Search me, O God, and know my heart;
  test me and know my thoughts.
24 See if there is any wicked l way in me,
  and lead me in the way everlasting. m

5 You keep close guard behind and before me
  and place your hand upon me.
6 Knowledge so wonderful is beyond my grasp;
  it is so lofty I cannot reach it.

7 Where can I escape from your spirit,
  where flee from your presence?
8 If I climb up to heaven, you are there;
  if I make my bed in Sheol, you are there.
9 If I travel to the limits of the east,
  or dwell at the bounds of the western sea,
10 even there your hand will be guiding me,
  your right hand holding me fast.
11 If I say, 'Surely darkness will steal over me,
  and the day around me turn to night,'
12 darkness is not too dark for you
  and night is as light as day;
  to you both dark and light are one.

13 You it was who fashioned my inward parts;
  you knitted me together in my mother's womb.
14 I praise you, for you fill me with awe;
  wonderful you are, and wonderful your works.
  You know me through and through:
15 my body was no mystery to you,
  when I was formed in secret,
  woven in the depths of the earth.
16 Your eyes foresaw my deeds,
  and they were all recorded in your book;
  my life was fashioned
  before it had come into being.
17 How mysterious, God, are your thoughts to me,
  how vast in number they are!
18 Were I to try counting them,
  they would be more than the grains of sand;
  to finish the count, my years must equal yours.

19 If only, God, you would slay the wicked!
  If those murderers would but leave me in peace!
20 They rebel against you with evil intent
  and as your adversaries rise in malice.
21 How I hate those that hate you, LORD!
  I loathe those who defy you;
22 I hate them with undying hatred;
  I reckon them my own enemies.

23 Examine me, God, and know my mind;
  test me, and understand my anxious thoughts.
24 Watch lest I follow any path that grieves you;
  lead me in the everlasting way.

Psalm 140

To the leader. A Psalm of David.

1 Deliver me, O LORD, from evildoers;
  protect me from those who are violent,
2 who plan evil things in their minds
  and stir up wars continually.
3 They make their tongue sharp as a snake's,
  and under their lips is the venom of vipers.
                                          Selah

4 Guard me, O LORD, from the hands of the
    wicked;
  protect me from the violent
  who have planned my downfall.

Psalm 140

For the leader: a psalm: for David

1 RESCUE me, LORD, from evildoers;
  keep me safe from those who use violence,
2 whose hearts are bent on wicked schemes;
  day after day they stir up bitter strife.
3 Their tongues are as deadly as serpents' fangs;
  on their lips is spiders' poison.   [*Selah*

4 Guard me, LORD, from the clutches of the wicked;
  keep me safe from those who use violence,
  who plan to thrust me out of the way.

139:8 **Sheol:** *or* the underworld.   139:11 **and . . . night:** *or, with
Scroll,* night will close around me.   139:14 **you are:** *so Gk; Heb.*
I am. **You . . . and through:** *cp. Gk; Heb.* as I know full well.
139:20 **rebel . . . you:** *so one form of Gk; Heb.* speak of you. **rise:**
so Scroll; Heb. obscure.   140:3 **spiders':** *meaning of Heb. word
uncertain.*

j Or *I awake*   k Cn: Meaning of Heb uncertain   l Heb *hurtful*
m Or *the ancient way.* Compare Jer 6.16

NEW AMERICAN BIBLE

NEW JERUSALEM BIBLE

5 Behind and before you encircle me
  and rest your hand upon me.
6 Such knowledge is beyond me,
  far too lofty for me to reach.
  II
7 Where can I hide from your spirit?
  From your presence, where can I flee?
8 If I ascend to the heavens, you are there;
  if I lie down in Sheol, you are there too.
9 If I fly with the wings of dawn
  and alight beyond the sea,
10 Even there your hand will guide me,
  your right hand hold me fast.
11 If I say, "Surely darkness shall hide me,
  and night shall be my light"—
12 Darkness is not dark for you,
  and night shines as the day.
  Darkness and light are but one.
  III
13 You formed my inmost being;
  you knit me in my mother's womb.
14 I praise you, so wonderfully you made me;
  wonderful are your works!
  My very self you knew;
15   my bones were not hidden from you,
  When I was being made in secret,
  fashioned as in the depths of the earth.
16 Your eyes foresaw my actions;
  in your book all are written down;
  my days were shaped, before one came to be.
  IV
17 How precious to me are your designs, O God;
  how vast the sum of them!
18 Were I to count, they would outnumber the sands;
  to finish, I would need eternity.
19 If only you would destroy the wicked, O God,
  and the bloodthirsty would depart from me!
20 Deceitfully they invoke your name;
  your foes swear faithless oaths.
21 Do I not hate, LORD, those who hate you?
  Those who rise against you, do I not loathe?
22 With fierce hatred I hate them,
  enemies I count as my own.
  V
23 Probe me, God, know my heart;
  try me, know my concerns.
24 See if my way is crooked,
  then lead me in the ancient paths.

5 You fence me in, behind and in front,
  you have laid your hand upon me.
6 Such amazing knowledge is beyond me,
  a height to which I cannot attain.
7 Where shall I go to escape your spirit?
  Where shall I flee from your presence?
8 If I scale the heavens you are there,
  if I lie flat in Sheol, there you are.
9 If I speed away on the wings of the dawn,
  if I dwell beyond the ocean,
10 even there your hand will be guiding me,
  your right hand holding me fast.
11 I will say, 'Let the darkness cover me,
  and the night wrap itself around me,'
12 even darkness to you is not dark,
  and night is as clear as the day.
13 You created my inmost self,
  knit me together in my mother's womb.
14 For so many marvels I thank you;
  a wonder am I, and all your works are wonders.

  You knew me through and through,
15 my being held no secrets from you,
  when I was being formed in secret,
  textured in the depths of the earth.
16 Your eyes could see my embryo.
  In your book all my days were inscribed,
  every one that was fixed is there.
17 How hard for me to grasp your thoughts,
  how many, God, there are!
18 If I count them, they are more than the grains of
    sand;
  if I come to an end, I am still with you.
19 If only, God, you would kill the wicked!—
  Men of violence, keep away from me!—
20 those who speak blasphemously about you,
  and take no account of your thoughts.
21 Yahweh, do I not hate those who hate you,
  and loathe those who defy you?
22 My hate for them has no limits,
  I regard them as my own enemies.
23 God, examine me and know my heart,
  test me and know my concerns.
24 Make sure that I am not on my way to ruin,
  and guide me on the road of eternity.

Psalm 140

1 *For the leader. A psalm of David.*

  I
2 Deliver me, LORD, from the wicked;
  preserve me from the violent,
3 From those who plan evil in their hearts,
  who stir up conflicts every day,
4 Who sharpen their tongues like serpents,
  venom of asps upon their lips.   Selah
  II
5 Keep me, LORD, from the clutches of the wicked;
  preserve me from the violent,
  who plot to trip me up.

Psalm 140 (V 139)

  For the choirmaster   Psalm   Of David

1 Rescue me, Yahweh, from evil men,
  protect me from violent men,
2 whose heart is bent on malice,
  day after day they harbour strife;
3 their tongues as barbed as a serpent's,
  viper's venom behind their lips.   *Pause*

4 Keep me, Yahweh, from the clutches of the
    wicked,
  protect me from violent men,
  who are bent on making me stumble,

NEW REVISED STANDARD VERSION

REVISED ENGLISH BIBLE

5 The arrogant have hidden a trap for me,
   and with cords they have spread a net, *n*
   along the road they have set snares for me.
                                    Selah

6 I say to the LORD, "You are my God;
   give ear, O LORD, to the voice of my
      supplications."
7 O LORD, my Lord, my strong deliverer,
   you have covered my head in the day of battle.
8 Do not grant, O LORD, the desires of the wicked;
   do not further their evil plot. *o*   *Selah*

9 Those who surround me lift up their heads; *p*
   let the mischief of their lips overwhelm them!
10 Let burning coals fall on them!
   Let them be flung into pits, no more to rise!
11 Do not let the slanderer be established in the
      land;
   let evil speedily hunt down the violent!

12 I know that the LORD maintains the cause of the
      needy,
   and executes justice for the poor.
13 Surely the righteous shall give thanks to your
      name;
   the upright shall live in your presence.

Psalm 141

A Psalm of David.

1 I call upon you, O LORD; come quickly to me;
   give ear to my voice when I call to you.
2 Let my prayer be counted as incense before you,
   and the lifting up of my hands as an evening
      sacrifice.

3 Set a guard over my mouth, O LORD;
   keep watch over the door of my lips.
4 Do not turn my heart to any evil,
   to busy myself with wicked deeds
   in company with those who work iniquity;
   do not let me eat of their delicacies.

5 Let the righteous strike me;
   let the faithful correct me.
   Never let the oil of the wicked anoint my head, *q*
   for my prayer is continually *r* against their
      wicked deeds.
6 When they are given over to those who shall
      condemn them,
   then they shall learn that my words were
      pleasant.
7 Like a rock that one breaks apart and shatters on
      the land,
   so shall their bones be strewn at the mouth of
      Sheol. *s*

8 But my eyes are turned toward you, O GOD, my
      Lord;
   in you I seek refuge; do not leave me
      defenseless.
9 Keep me from the trap that they have laid for
      me,
   and from the snares of evildoers.
10 Let the wicked fall into their own nets,
   while I alone escape.

5 The arrogant set hidden traps for me;
   villains spread their nets
   and lay snares for me along my path.   [*Selah*
6 I say to the LORD, 'You are my God;
   LORD, hear my plea for mercy.
7 LORD God, my strong deliverer,
   you shield my head on the day of battle.
8 LORD, frustrate the desires of the wicked;
   do not let their plans succeed.   [*Selah*
9 'When those who beset me raise their heads,
   may their conspiracies engulf them.
10 Let burning coals be rained on them;
   let them be plunged into the miry depths,
   never to rise again.
11 The slanderer will find no home in the land;
   disaster will hound the violent to destruction.'

12 I know that the LORD will give to the needy their
      rights
   and justice to the downtrodden.
13 The righteous will surely give thanks to your name;
   the upright will continue in your presence.

Psalm 141

A psalm: for David

1 LORD, I call to you, come to my aid quickly;
   listen to me when I call.
2 May my prayer be like incense set before you,
   the lifting up of my hands like the evening
      offering.

3 LORD, set a guard on my mouth;
   keep watch at the door of my lips.
4 Let not my thoughts incline to evil,
   to the pursuit of evil courses
   with those who are evildoers;
   let me not partake of their delights.

5 I would rather be beaten by the righteous
   and reproved by those who are good.
   My head will not be anointed with the oil of the
      wicked,
   for while I live my prayer is against their
      wickedness.

6 When they are brought down through the power of
      their rulers
   they will learn how acceptable are my words.
7 As when one ploughs and breaks up the ground,
   our bones are scattered at the mouth of Sheol.

8 But my eyes are fixed on you, LORD God;
   you are my refuge; do not leave me unprotected.
9 Keep me from the trap set for me,
   from the snares of evildoers.
10 Let the wicked fall into their own nets,
   whilst all alone I pass on my way.

---

n Or *they have spread cords as a net*   *o* Heb adds *they are exalted*
p Cn Compare Gk: Heb *those who surround me are uplifted in head*;
Heb divides verses 8 and 9 differently   *q* Gk: Meaning of Heb
uncertain   *r* Cn: Heb *for continually and my prayer*   *s* Meaning
of Heb of verses 5-7 is uncertain

140:9 **When . . . heads:** *prob. rdg; Heb.* obscure.   141:5 **while I
live:** *prob. rdg; Heb.* still and.   141:7 **Sheol:** *or* the underworld.

6 The arrogant have set a trap for me;
  villains have spread a net,
  laid snares for me by the wayside. *Selah*
7 I say to the LORD: You are my God;
  listen, LORD, to the words of my prayer,
8 My revered LORD, my strong helper,
  my helmet on the day of battle.
9 LORD, do not grant the desires of the wicked;
  do not let their plots succeed. *Selah*
10 Around me they raise their proud heads;
  may the mischief they threaten overwhelm them.
11 May God rain burning coals upon them,
  cast them into the grave never more to rise.

III

12 Slanderers will not survive on earth;
  evil will quickly entrap the violent.
13 For I know the LORD will secure
  justice for the needy, their rights for the poor.
14 Then the just will give thanks to your name;
  the upright will dwell in your presence.

Psalm 141

1 *A psalm of David.*

LORD, I call to you;
  come quickly to help me;
  listen to my plea when I call.
2 Let my prayer be incense before you;
  my uplifted hands an evening sacrifice.
3 Set a guard, LORD, before my mouth,
  a gatekeeper at my lips.
4 Do not let my heart incline to evil,
  or yield to any sin.
  I will never feast upon
  the fine food of evildoers.
5 Let the just strike me; that is kindness;
  let them rebuke me; that is oil for my head.
  All this I shall not refuse,
  but will pray despite these trials.
6 When their leaders are cast over the cliff,
  all will learn that my prayers were heard.
7 As when a farmer plows a field into broken clods,
  so their bones will be strewn at the mouth of
  Sheol.
8 My eyes are upon you, O GOD, my Lord;
  in you I take refuge; do not strip me of life.
9 Guard me from the trap they have set for me,
  from the snares of evildoers.
10 Into their own nets let all the wicked fall,
  while I make good my own escape.

5b   laying out snares where I walk,
5a in their arrogance hiding pitfall and noose
5c   to trap me as I pass. *Pause*
6 I said to Yahweh, 'You are my God.'
  Listen, Yahweh, to the sound of my prayer.
7 Yahweh my Lord, my saving strength,
  you shield my head when battle comes.
8 Yahweh, do not grant the wicked their wishes,
  do not let their plots succeed. *Pause*

  Do not let my attackers 9 prevail,
  but let them be overwhelmed by their own
  malice.
10 May red-hot embers rain down on them,
  may they be flung into the mire once and for all.
11 May the slanderer find no rest anywhere,
  may evil hunt down violent men implacably.

12 I know that Yahweh will give judgement for the
  wretched,
  justice for the needy.
13 The upright shall praise your name,
  the honest dwell in your presence.

Psalm 141 (V 140)

Psalm   Of David

1 Yahweh, I am calling, hurry to me,
  listen to my voice when I call to you.
2 May my prayer be like incense in your presence,
  my uplifted hands like the evening sacrifice.
3 Yahweh, mount a guard over my mouth,
  a guard at the door of my lips.
4 Check any impulse to speak evil,
  to share the foul deeds of evil-doers.

  I shall not sample their delights!

5 May the upright correct me with a friend's rebuke;
  but the wicked shall never anoint my head with oil,
  for that would make me party to their crimes.
6 They are delivered into the power of the rock, their
  judge,
  those who took pleasure in hearing me say,
7 'Like a shattered millstone on the ground
  our bones are scattered at the mouth of Sheol.'
8 To you, Yahweh, I turn my eyes,
  in you I take refuge, do not leave me unprotected.
9 Save me from the traps that are set for me,
  the snares of evil-doers.
10 Let the wicked fall each into his own net,
  while I pass on my way.

Psalm 142

A Maskil of David. When he was in the cave. A Prayer.

1 With my voice I cry to the LORD;
  with my voice I make supplication to the
    LORD.
2 I pour out my complaint before him;
  I tell my trouble before him.
3 When my spirit is faint,
  you know my way.

  In the path where I walk
    they have hidden a trap for me.
4 Look on my right hand and see —
    there is no one who takes notice of me;
  no refuge remains to me;
    no one cares for me.

5 I cry to you, O LORD;
  I say, "You are my refuge,
    my portion in the land of the living."
6 Give heed to my cry,
  for I am brought very low.

  Save me from my persecutors,
    for they are too strong for me.
7 Bring me out of prison,
  so that I may give thanks to your name.
  The righteous will surround me,
    for you will deal bountifully with me.

Psalm 143

A Psalm of David.

1 Hear my prayer, O LORD;
  give ear to my supplications in your
    faithfulness;
  answer me in your righteousness.
2 Do not enter into judgment with your servant,
  for no one living is righteous before you.

3 For the enemy has pursued me,
  crushing my life to the ground,
    making me sit in darkness like those long dead.
4 Therefore my spirit faints within me;
  my heart within me is appalled.

5 I remember the days of old,
  I think about all your deeds,
    I meditate on the works of your hands.
6 I stretch out my hands to you;
  my soul thirsts for you like a parched land.
                                               Selah

7 Answer me quickly, O LORD;
  my spirit fails.
  Do not hide your face from me,
    or I shall be like those who go down to the Pit.
8 Let me hear of your steadfast love in the
    morning,
  for in you I put my trust.
  Teach me the way I should go,
    for to you I lift up my soul.

9 Save me, O LORD, from my enemies;
  I have fled to you for refuge.[r]
10 Teach me to do your will,
  for you are my God.
  Let your good spirit lead me
    on a level path.

---

[r] One Heb Ms Gk: MT *to you I have hidden*

Psalm 142

A maskil: for David (when he was in the cave): a prayer

1 I CRY aloud to the LORD;
  to the LORD I plead aloud for mercy.
2 I pour out my complaint before him
  and unfold my troubles in his presence.
3 When my spirit is faint within me,
  you are there to watch over my steps.

  In the path that I should take
    they have hidden a snare for me.
4 I look to my right hand,
  I find no friend by my side;
  no way of escape is in sight,
    no one comes to rescue me.

5 I cry to you, LORD,
  and say, 'You are my refuge;
  you are my portion
    in the land of the living.
6 Give me a hearing when I cry,
  for I am brought very low.
  Save me from those who harass me,
    for they are too strong for me.
7 Set me free from prison
  that I may praise your name.'
  The righteous will place a crown on me,
    when you give me my due reward.

Psalm 143

A psalm: for David

1 LORD, hear my prayer,
  listen to my plea;
  in your faithfulness and righteousness answer me.
2 Do not bring your servant to trial,
  for no person living is innocent before you.
3 An enemy has hunted me down,
  has crushed me underfoot,
  and left me to lie in darkness like those long dead.
4 My spirit fails me
  and my heart is numb with despair.
5 I call to mind times long past;
  I think over all you have done;
  the wonders of your creation fill my mind.
6 Athirst for you like thirsty land,
  I lift my outspread hands to you.   [*Selah*
7 LORD, answer me soon;
  my spirit faints.
  Do not hide your face from me
  or I shall be like those who go down to the abyss.
8 In the morning let me know of your love,
  for I put my trust in you.
  Show me the way that I must take,
  for my heart is set on you.
9 Deliver me, LORD, from my enemies;
  with you I seek refuge.
10 Teach me to do your will, for you are my God;
  by your gracious spirit guide me on level ground.

142:7 **place . . . on:** *or* crowd around.   143:9 **with . . . refuge:**
so one MS; others to you have I hidden.

Psalm 142

1 A maskil *of David, when he was in the cave. A prayer.*

2 With full voice I cry to the LORD;
   with full voice I beseech the LORD.
3 Before God I pour out my complaint,
   lay bare my distress.
4 My spirit is faint within me,
   but you know my path.
  Along the way I walk
   they have hidden a trap for me.
5 I look to my right hand,
   but no friend is there.
  There is no escape for me;
   no one cares for me.
6 I cry out to you, LORD,
   I say, You are my refuge,
   my portion in the land of the living.
7 Listen to my cry for help,
   for I am brought very low.
  Rescue me from my pursuers,
   for they are too strong for me.
8 Lead me out of my prison,
   that I may give thanks to your name.
  Then the just shall gather around me
   because you have been good to me.

Psalm 143

1 A psalm of David.

  LORD, hear my prayer;
   in your faithfulness listen to my pleading;
   answer me in your justice.
2 Do not enter into judgment with your servant;
   before you no living being can be just.
3 The enemy has pursued me;
   they have crushed my life to the ground.
  They have left me in darkness
   like those long dead.
4 My spirit is faint within me;
   my heart is dismayed.
5 I remember the days of old;
   I ponder all your deeds;
   the works of your hands I recall.
6 I stretch out my hands to you;
   I thirst for you like a parched land.   Selah
7 Hasten to answer me, LORD;
   for my spirit fails me.
  Do not hide your face from me,
   lest I become like those descending to the pit.
8 At dawn let me hear of your kindness,
   for in you I trust.
  Show me the path I should walk,
   for to you I entrust my life.
9 Rescue me, LORD, from my foes,
   for in you I hope.
10 Teach me to do your will,
   for you are my God.
  May your kind spirit guide me
   on ground that is level.

Psalm 142 (V 141)

Psalm   Of David   When he was in the cave   Prayer

1 To Yahweh I cry out with my plea.
  To Yahweh I cry out with entreaty.
2 I pour out my worry in his presence,
  in his presence I unfold my troubles.
3 However faint my spirit;
  you are watching over my path.

  On the road I have to travel
  they have hidden a trap for me.
4 Look on my right and see —
  there is no one who recognises me.
  All refuge is denied me,
  no one cares whether I live or die.

5 I cry out to you, Yahweh,
  I affirm, 'You are my refuge,
  my share in the land of the living!'
6 Listen to my calling,
  for I am miserably weak.

  Rescue me from my persecutors,
  for they are too strong for me.
7 Lead me out of prison
  that I may praise your name.
  The upright gather round me
  because of your generosity to me.

Psalm 143 (V 142)

Psalm   Of David

1 Yahweh, hear my prayer,
  listen to my pleading;
  in your constancy answer me,
  in your saving justice;
2 do not put your servant on trial,
  for no one living can be found guiltless at your
   tribunal.

3 An enemy is in deadly pursuit,
  crushing me into the ground,
  forcing me to live in darkness,
  like those long dead.
4 My spirit is faint,
  and within me my heart is numb with fear.

5 I recall the days of old,
  reflecting on all your deeds,
  I ponder the works of your hands.
6 I stretch out my hands to you,
  my heart like a land thirsty for you.   Pause

7 Answer me quickly, Yahweh,
  my spirit is worn out;
  do not turn away your face from me,
  or I shall be like those who sink into oblivion.

8 Let dawn bring news of your faithful love,
  for I place my trust in you;
  show me the road I must travel
  for you to relieve my heart.

9 Rescue me from my enemies, Yahweh,
  since in you I find protection.
10 Teach me to do your will,
  for you are my God.
  May your generous spirit lead me
  on even ground.

NEW REVISED STANDARD VERSION	REVISED ENGLISH BIBLE

NEW REVISED STANDARD VERSION

11 For your name's sake, O LORD, preserve my life.
   In your righteousness bring me out of trouble.
12 In your steadfast love cut off my enemies,
   and destroy all my adversaries,
   for I am your servant.

Psalm 144

Of David.

1 Blessed be the LORD, my rock,
   who trains my hands for war, and my fingers
   for battle;
2 my rock[u] and my fortress,
   my stronghold and my deliverer,
   my shield, in whom I take refuge,
   who subdues the peoples[v] under me.

3 O LORD, what are human beings that you regard
   them,
   or mortals that you think of them?
4 They are like a breath;
   their days are like a passing shadow.

5 Bow your heavens, O LORD, and come down;
   touch the mountains so that they smoke.
6 Make the lightning flash and scatter them;
   send out your arrows and rout them.
7 Stretch out your hand from on high;
   set me free and rescue me from the mighty
   waters,
   from the hand of aliens,
8 whose mouths speak lies,
   and whose right hands are false.

9 I will sing a new song to you, O God;
   upon a ten-stringed harp I will play to you,
10 the one who gives victory to kings,
   who rescues his servant David.
11 Rescue me from the cruel sword,
   and deliver me from the hand of aliens,
   whose mouths speak lies,
   and whose right hands are false.

12 May our sons in their youth
   be like plants full grown,
   our daughters like corner pillars,
   cut for the building of a palace.
13 May our barns be filled,
   with produce of every kind;
   may our sheep increase by thousands,
   by tens of thousands in our fields,
14 and may our cattle be heavy with young.
   May there be no breach in the walls,[w] no exile,
   and no cry of distress in our streets.
15 Happy are the people to whom such blessings fall;
   happy are the people whose God is the LORD.

Psalm 145

Praise. Of David.

1 I will extol you, my God and King,
   and bless your name forever and ever.
2 Every day I will bless you,
   and praise your name forever and ever.
3 Great is the LORD, and greatly to be praised;
   his greatness is unsearchable.

REVISED ENGLISH BIBLE

11 Revive me, LORD, for the honour of your name;
   be my deliverer; release me from distress.
12 In your love for me, destroy my enemies
   and wipe out all who oppress me,
   for I am your servant.

Psalm 144

For David

1 BLESSED be the LORD, my rock,
   who trains my hands for battle,
   my fingers for fighting;
2 my unfailing help, my fortress,
   my strong tower and refuge,
   my shield in whom I trust,
   he who subdues nations under me.

3 LORD, what are human beings that you should care
   for them?
   What are frail mortals that you should take thought
   for them?
4 They are no more than a puff of wind,
   their days like a fleeting shadow.
5 LORD, part the heavens and come down;
   touch the mountains so that they pour forth smoke.
6 Discharge your lightning-flashes far and wide,
   and send your arrows humming.
7 Reach out your hands from on high;
   rescue me and snatch me from mighty waters,
   from the power of aliens
8 whose every word is worthless,
   whose every oath is false.

9 I shall sing a new song to you, my God,
   psalms to the music of a ten-stringed harp.
10 God who gave victory to kings
   and deliverance to your servant David,
   rescue me from the cruel sword;
11 snatch me from the power of aliens
   whose every word is worthless,
   whose every oath is false.

12 Our sons in their youth will be like thriving plants,
   our daughters like sculptured corner pillars of a
   palace.
13 Our barns will be filled with every kind of
   provision;
   our sheep will bear lambs in thousands upon
   thousands;
14 the cattle in our fields will be fat and sleek.
   There will be no miscarriage or untimely birth,
   no cries of distress in our public places.
15 Happy the people who are so blessed!
   Happy the people whose God is the LORD!

Psalm 145

A psalm of praise: for David

1 I SHALL extol you, my God and King,
   and bless your name for ever and ever.
2 Every day I shall bless you
   and praise your name for ever and ever.
3 Great is the LORD and most worthy of praise;
   his greatness is beyond all searching out.

---

[u] With 18.2 and 2 Sam 22.2: Heb *my steadfast love*   [v] Heb Mss Syr
Aquila Jerome: MT *my people*   [w] Heb lacks *in the walls*

144:5 **and come down:** *or* so that they come down.   144:14 **no
. . . birth:** *or* no invasion or exile.

NEW AMERICAN BIBLE

11 For your name's sake, LORD, give me life;
   in your justice lead me out of distress.
12 In your kindness put an end to my foes;
   destroy all who attack me,
   for I am your servant.

Psalm 144

1 *Of David.*

I

Blessed be the LORD, my rock,
   who trains my hands for battle,
   my fingers for war;
2 My safeguard and my fortress,
   my stronghold, my deliverer,
   My shield, in whom I trust,
   who subdues peoples under me.

II

3 LORD, what are mortals that you notice them;
   human beings, that you take thought of them?
4 They are but a breath;
   their days are like a passing shadow.
5 LORD, incline your heavens and come;
   touch the mountains and make them smoke.
6 Flash forth lightning and scatter my foes;
   shoot your arrows and rout them.
7 Reach out your hand from on high;
   deliver me from the many waters;
   rescue me from the hands of foreign foes.
8 Their mouths speak untruth;
   their right hands are raised in lying oaths.
9 O God, a new song I will sing to you;
   on a ten-stringed lyre I will play for you.
10 You give victory to kings;
   you delivered David your servant.
   From the menacing sword 11 deliver me;
   rescue me from the hands of foreign foes.
   Their mouths speak untruth;
   their right hands are raised in lying oaths.

III

12 May our sons be like plants
   well nurtured from their youth,
   Our daughters, like carved columns,
   shapely as those of the temple.
13 May our barns be full
   with every kind of store.
   May our sheep increase by thousands,
   by tens of thousands in our fields;
   may our oxen be well fattened.
14 May there be no breach in the walls,
   no exile, no outcry in our streets.
15 Happy the people so blessed;
   happy the people whose God is the LORD.

Psalm 145

1 *Praise. Of David.*

I will extol you, my God and king;
   I will bless your name forever.
2 Every day I will bless you;
   I will praise your name forever.
3 Great is the LORD and worthy of high praise;
   God's grandeur is beyond understanding.

NEW JERUSALEM BIBLE

11 Yahweh, for the sake of your name,
   in your saving justice give me life,
   rescue me from distress.
12 In your faithful love annihilate my enemies,
   destroy all those who oppress me,
   for I am your servant.

Psalm 144 (V 143)ᵛ

Of David

1 Blessed be Yahweh, my rock,
   who trains my hands for war
   and my fingers for battle,
2 my faithful love, my bastion,
   my citadel, my Saviour;
   I shelter behind him, my shield,
   he makes the peoples submit to me.

3 Yahweh, what is a human being for you to notice,
   a child of Adam for you to think about?
4 Human life, a mere puff of wind,
   days as fleeting as a shadow.

5 Yahweh, part the heavens and come down,
   touch the mountains, make them smoke.
6 Scatter them with continuous lightning-flashes,
   rout them with a volley of your arrows.

7 Stretch down your hand from above,
   save me, rescue me from deep waters,
   from the clutches of foreigners,
8 whose every word is worthless,
   whose right hand is raised in perjury.

9 God, I sing to you a new song,
   I play to you on the ten-stringed lyre,
10 for you give kings their victories,
   you rescue your servant David.

   From the sword of evil 11 save me,
   rescue me from the clutches of foreigners
   whose every word is worthless,
   whose right hand testifies to falsehood.

12 May our sons be like plants
   growing tall from their earliest days,
   our daughters like pillars
   carved fit for a palace,
13 our barns filled to overflowing
   with every kind of crop,
   the sheep in our pastures be numbered
   in thousands and tens of thousands,
14 our cattle well fed,
   free of raids and pillage,
   free of outcry in our streets.

15 How blessed the nation of whom this is true,
   blessed the nation whose God is Yahweh!

Psalm 145 (V 144)

Hymn of Praise   Of David

Aleph	1 I shall praise you to the heights, God my King,
	I shall bless your name for ever and ever.
Bet	2 Day after day I shall bless you,
	I shall praise your name for ever and ever.
Gimel	3 Great is Yahweh and worthy of all praise,
	his greatness beyond all reckoning.

ᵛ **144** After prayers for help (vv. 1–11) drawn from other Pss, vv.
12–15 envisage messianic blessings.

4 One generation shall laud your works to another,
   and shall declare your mighty acts.
5 On the glorious splendor of your majesty,
   and on your wondrous works, I will meditate.
6 The might of your awesome deeds shall be
      proclaimed,
   and I will declare your greatness.
7 They shall celebrate the fame of your abundant
      goodness,
   and shall sing aloud of your righteousness.

8 The LORD is gracious and merciful,
   slow to anger and abounding in steadfast love.
9 The LORD is good to all,
   and his compassion is over all that he has
      made.

10 All your works shall give thanks to you, O LORD,
   and all your faithful shall bless you.
11 They shall speak of the glory of your kingdom,
   and tell of your power,
12 to make known to all people your x mighty
      deeds,
   and the glorious splendor of your y kingdom.
13 Your kingdom is an everlasting kingdom,
   and your dominion endures throughout all
      generations.

   The LORD is faithful in all his words,
      and gracious in all his deeds. z
14 The LORD upholds all who are falling,
   and raises up all who are bowed down.
15 The eyes of all look to you,
   and you give them their food in due season.
16 You open your hand,
   satisfying the desire of every living thing.
17 The LORD is just in all his ways,
   and kind in all his doings.
18 The LORD is near to all who call on him,
   to all who call on him in truth.
19 He fulfills the desire of all who fear him;
   he also hears their cry, and saves them.
20 The LORD watches over all who love him,
   but all the wicked he will destroy.

21 My mouth will speak the praise of the LORD,
   and all flesh will bless his holy name forever
      and ever.

Psalm 146

1 Praise the LORD!
   Praise the LORD, O my soul!
2 I will praise the LORD as long as I live;
   I will sing praises to my God all my life long.

3 Do not put your trust in princes,
   in mortals, in whom there is no help.
4 When their breath departs, they return to the
      earth;
   on that very day their plans perish.

5 Happy are those whose help is the God of Jacob,
   whose hope is in the LORD their God,
6 who made heaven and earth,
   the sea, and all that is in them;
   who keeps faith forever;

4 One generation will commend your works to the
      next
   and set forth your mighty deeds.
5 People will speak of the glorious splendour of your
      majesty;
   I shall meditate on your wonderful deeds.
6 People will declare your mighty and terrible acts,
   and I shall tell of your greatness.
7 They will recite the story of your abounding
      goodness
   and sing with joy of your righteousness.

8 The LORD is gracious and compassionate,
   long-suffering and ever faithful.
9 The LORD is good to all;
   his compassion rests upon all his creatures.
10 All your creatures praise you, LORD,
   and your loyal servants bless you.
11 They talk of the glory of your kingdom
   and tell of your might,
12 to make known to mankind your mighty deeds,
   the glorious majesty of your kingdom.
13 Your kingdom is an everlasting kingdom,
   and your dominion endures throughout all
      generations.

14 In all his promises the LORD keeps faith,
   he is unchanging in all his works;
   the LORD supports all who stumble
   and raises all who are bowed down.
15 All raise their eyes to you in hope,
   and you give them their food when it is due.
16 You open your hand
   and satisfy every living creature with your favour.
17 The LORD is righteous in all his ways,
   faithful in all he does;
18 the LORD is near to all who call to him,
   to all who call to him in sincerity.
19 He fulfils the desire of those who fear him;
   he hears their cry for help and saves them.
20 The LORD watches over all who love him,
   but the wicked he will utterly destroy.
21 My tongue will declare the praises of the LORD,
   and all people will bless his holy name
   for ever and ever.

Psalm 146

1 PRAISE the LORD.

   My soul, praise the LORD.
2 As long as I live I shall praise the LORD;
   I shall sing psalms to my God all my life long.
3 Put no trust in princes
   or in any mortal, for they have no power to save.
4 When they breathe their last breath,
   they return to the dust,
   and on that day their plans come to nothing.

5 Happy is he whose helper is the God of Jacob,
   whose hope is in the LORD his God,
6 maker of heaven and earth,
   the sea, and all that is in them;
   who maintains faithfulness for ever

---

x Gk Jerome Syr: Heb *his*   y Heb *his*   z These two lines supplied
by Q Ms Gk Syr

145:5 **People . . . speak of:** *so Scroll.*   145:14 **In all . . . works:**
so Scroll.   145:16 **and . . . favour:** *or* and satisfy the desire of
every living creature.

4 One generation praises your deeds to the next
   and proclaims your mighty works.
5 They speak of the splendor of your majestic glory,
   tell of your wonderful deeds.
6 They speak of your fearsome power
   and attest to your great deeds.
7 They publish the renown of your abounding
     goodness
   and joyfully sing of your justice.
8 The LORD is gracious and merciful,
   slow to anger and abounding in love.
9 The LORD is good to all,
   compassionate to every creature.
10 All your works give you thanks, O LORD
   and your faithful bless you.
11 They speak of the glory of your reign
   and tell of your great works,
12 Making known to all your power,
   the glorious splendor of your rule.
13 Your reign is a reign for all ages,
   your dominion for all generations.
   The LORD is trustworthy in every word,
   and faithful in every work.
14 The LORD supports all who are falling
   and raises up all who are bowed down.
15 The eyes of all look hopefully to you;
   you give them their food in due season.
16 You open wide your hand
   and satisfy the desire of every living thing.
17 You, LORD, are just in all your ways,
   faithful in all your works.
18 You, LORD, are near to all who call upon you,
   to all who call upon you in truth.
19 You satisfy the desire of those who fear you;
   you hear their cry and save them.
20 You, LORD, watch over all who love you,
   but all the wicked you destroy.
21 My mouth will speak your praises, LORD;
   all flesh will bless your holy name forever.

Dalet   4 Each age will praise your deeds to the next,
   proclaiming your mighty works.
He   5 Your renown is the splendour of your glory,
   I will ponder the story of your wonders.
Waw   6 They will speak of your awesome power,
   and I shall recount your greatness.
Zain   7 They will bring out the memory of your great
     generosity,
   and joyfully acclaim your saving justice.
Het   8 Yahweh is tenderness and pity,
   slow to anger, full of faithful love.
Tet   9 Yahweh is generous to all,
   his tenderness embraces all his creatures.
Yod   10 All your creatures shall thank you, Yahweh,
   and your faithful shall bless you.
Kaph   11 They shall speak of the glory of your kingship
   and tell of your might,
Lamed   12 making known your mighty deeds to the
    children of Adam,
   the glory and majesty of your kingship.
Mem   13 Your kingship is a kingship for ever,
   your reign lasts from age to age.
(Nun)   Yahweh is trustworthy in all his words,
   and upright in all his deeds.
Samek   14 Yahweh supports all who stumble,
   lifts up those who are bowed down.
Ain   15 All look to you in hope
   and you feed them with the food of the
    season.
Pe   16 And, with generous hand,
   you satisfy the desires of every living
    creature.
Zade   17 Upright in all that he does,
   Yahweh acts only in faithful love.
Qoph   18 He is close to all who call upon him,
   all who call on him from the heart.
Resh   19 He fulfils the desires of all who fear him,
   he hears their cry and he saves them.
Shin   20 Yahweh guards all who love him,
   but all the wicked he destroys.
Taw   21 My mouth shall always praise Yahweh,
   let every creature bless his holy name
    for ever and ever.

Psalm 146

1 Hallelujah!

2 Praise the LORD, my soul;
   I shall praise the LORD all my life,
   sing praise to my God while I live.
   I
3 Put no trust in princes,
   in mere mortals powerless to save.
4 When they breathe their last, they return to the
    earth;
   that day all their planning comes to nothing.
   II
5 Happy those whose help is Jacob's God,
   whose hope is in the LORD, their God,
6 The maker of heaven and earth,
   the seas and all that is in them,
Who keeps faith forever,

Psalm 146 (V 145)

1 Alleluia!
   Praise Yahweh, my soul!
2 I will praise Yahweh all my life,
   I will make music to my God as long as I live.

3 Do not put your trust in princes,
   in any child of Adam, who has no power to save.
4 When his spirit goes forth he returns to the earth,
   on that very day all his plans come to nothing.

5 How blessed is he who has Jacob's God to help
    him,
   his hope is in Yahweh his God,
6 who made heaven and earth,
   the sea and all that is in them.

He keeps faith for ever,

7   who executes justice for the oppressed;
      who gives food to the hungry.

    The LORD sets the prisoners free;
8   the LORD opens the eyes of the blind.
    The LORD lifts up those who are bowed down;
      the LORD loves the righteous.
9   The LORD watches over the strangers;
      he upholds the orphan and the widow,
      but the way of the wicked he brings to ruin.

10   The LORD will reign forever,
      your God, O Zion, for all generations.
    Praise the LORD!

Psalm 147

1   Praise the LORD!
    How good it is to sing praises to our God;
      for he is gracious, and a song of praise is
        fitting.
2   The LORD builds up Jerusalem;
      he gathers the outcasts of Israel.
3   He heals the brokenhearted,
      and binds up their wounds.
4   He determines the number of the stars;
      he gives to all of them their names.
5   Great is our Lord, and abundant in power;
      his understanding is beyond measure.
6   The LORD lifts up the downtrodden;
      he casts the wicked to the ground.

7   Sing to the LORD with thanksgiving;
      make melody to our God on the lyre.
8   He covers the heavens with clouds,
      prepares rain for the earth,
      makes grass grow on the hills.
9   He gives to the animals their food,
      and to the young ravens when they cry.
10   His delight is not in the strength of the horse,
      nor his pleasure in the speed of a runner;[a]
11   but the LORD takes pleasure in those who fear
        him,
      in those who hope in his steadfast love.

12   Praise the LORD, O Jerusalem!
      Praise your God, O Zion!
13   For he strengthens the bars of your gates;
      he blesses your children within you.
14   He grants peace[b] within your borders;
      he fills you with the finest of wheat.
15   He sends out his command to the earth;
      his word runs swiftly.
16   He gives snow like wool;
      he scatters frost like ashes.
17   He hurls down hail like crumbs —
      who can stand before his cold?
18   He sends out his word, and melts them;
      he makes his wind blow, and the waters flow.
19   He declares his word to Jacob,
      his statutes and ordinances to Israel.
20   He has not dealt thus with any other nation;
      they do not know his ordinances.
    Praise the LORD!

7   and deals out justice to the oppressed.
    The LORD feeds the hungry
    and sets the prisoner free.
8   The LORD restores sight to the blind
    and raises those who are bowed down;
    the LORD loves the righteous
9   and protects the stranger in the land;
    the LORD gives support to the fatherless and the
      widow,
    but thwarts the course of the wicked.

10   The LORD will reign for ever, Zion,
    your God for all generations.
    Praise the LORD.

Psalm 147

1   PRAISE the LORD.

    How good it is to sing psalms to our God!
    How pleasant and right to praise him!
2   The LORD rebuilds Jerusalem;
    he gathers in the scattered Israelites.
3   It is he who heals the broken in spirit
    and binds up their wounds,
4   who numbers the stars one by one
    and calls each by name.
5   Mighty is our Lord and great his power;
    his wisdom is beyond all telling.
6   The LORD gives support to the humble
    and brings evildoers to the ground.

7   Sing to the LORD a song of thanksgiving,
    sing psalms to the lyre in honour of our God.
8   He veils the sky in clouds
    and provides rain for the earth;
    he clothes the hills with grass.
9   He gives food to the cattle
    and to the ravens when they cry.
10   The LORD does not delight in the strength of a
      horse
    and takes no pleasure in a runner's fleetness;
11   his pleasure is in those who fear him,
    who wait for his steadfast love.

12   Jerusalem, sing to the LORD;
    Zion, praise your God,
13   for he has strengthened your barred gates;
    he has blessed your inhabitants.
14   He has brought peace to your realm
    and given you the best of wheat in plenty.
15   He sends his command over the earth,
    and his word runs swiftly.
16   He showers down snow, white as wool,
    and sprinkles hoar-frost like ashes;
17   he scatters crystals of ice like crumbs;
    he sends the cold, and the water stands frozen;
18   he utters his word, and the ice is melted;
    he makes the wind blow, and the water flows
      again.
19   To Jacob he reveals his word,
    his statutes and decrees to Israel;
20   he has not done this for other nations,
    nor were his decrees made known to them.

    Praise the LORD.

---

[a] Heb *legs of a person*   [b] Or *prosperity*

NEW AMERICAN BIBLE

7 secures justice for the oppressed,
   gives food to the hungry.
 The LORD sets prisoners free;
8 the LORD gives sight to the blind.
 The LORD raises up those who are bowed down;
   the LORD loves the righteous.
9 The LORD protects the stranger,
   sustains the orphan and the widow,
   but thwarts the way of the wicked.
10 The LORD shall reign forever,
   your God, Zion, through all generations!
 Hallelujah!

Psalm 147

1 Hallelujah!
 I
 How good to celebrate our God in song;
   how sweet to give fitting praise.
2 The LORD rebuilds Jerusalem,
   gathers the dispersed of Israel,
3 Heals the brokenhearted,
   binds up their wounds,
4 Numbers all the stars,
   calls each of them by name.
5 Great is our Lord, vast in power,
   with wisdom beyond measure.
6 The LORD sustains the poor,
   but casts the wicked to the ground.
 II
7 Sing to the LORD with thanksgiving;
   with the lyre celebrate our God,
8 Who covers the heavens with clouds,
   provides rain for the earth,
   makes grass sprout on the mountains,
9 Who gives animals their food
   and ravens what they cry for.
10 God takes no delight in the strength of horses,
   no pleasure in the runner's stride.
11 Rather the LORD takes pleasure in the devout,
   those who await his faithful care.
 III
12 Glorify the LORD, Jerusalem;
   Zion, offer praise to your God,
13 Who has strengthened the bars of your gates,
   blessed your children within you,
14 Brought peace to your borders,
   and filled you with finest wheat.
15 The LORD sends a command to earth;
   his word runs swiftly!
16 Thus snow is spread like wool,
   frost is scattered like ash,
17 Hail is dispersed like crumbs;
   before such cold the waters freeze.
18 Again he sends his word and they melt;
   the wind is unleashed and the waters flow.
19 The LORD also proclaims his word to Jacob,
   decrees and laws to Israel.
20 God has not done this for other nations;
   of such laws they know nothing.
 Hallelujah!

NEW JERUSALEM BIBLE

7 gives justice to the oppressed,
   gives food to the hungry;
   Yahweh sets prisoners free.
8 Yahweh gives sight to the blind,
   lifts up those who are bowed down.
9 Yahweh protects the stranger,
   he sustains the orphan and the widow.
8c Yahweh loves the upright,
9c but he frustrates the wicked.
10 Yahweh reigns for ever,
   your God, Zion, from age to age.

Psalm 147 (V 146–147)

Alleluia!
1 Praise Yahweh — it is good to sing psalms
   to our God — how pleasant to praise him.
2 Yahweh, Builder of Jerusalem!
   He gathers together the exiles of Israel,
3 healing the broken-hearted
   and binding up their wounds;
4 he counts out the number of the stars,
   and gives each one of them a name.
5 Our Lord is great, all-powerful,
   his wisdom beyond all telling.
6 Yahweh sustains the poor,
   and humbles the wicked to the ground.
7 Sing to Yahweh in thanksgiving,
   play the harp for our God.
8 He veils the sky with clouds,
   and provides the earth with rain,
   makes grass grow on the hills
   and plants for people to use,
9 gives fodder to cattle
   and to young ravens when they cry.
10 He takes no delight in the power of horses,
   no pleasure in human sturdiness;
11 his pleasure is in those who fear him,
   in those who hope in his faithful love.
12 Praise Yahweh, Jerusalem,
   Zion, praise your God.
13 For he gives strength to the bars of your gates,
   he blesses your children within you,
14 he maintains the peace of your frontiers,
   gives you your fill of finest wheat.
15 He sends his word to the earth,
   his command runs quickly,
16 he spreads the snow like flax,
   strews hoarfrost like ashes,
17 he sends ice-crystals like breadcrumbs,
   and who can withstand that cold?
18 When he sends his word it thaws them,
   when he makes his wind blow, the waters are
      unstopped.
19 He reveals his word to Jacob,
   his statutes and judgements to Israel.
20 For no other nation has he done this,
   no other has known his judgements.

Psalm 148

1 Praise the LORD!
  Praise the LORD from the heavens;
    praise him in the heights!
2 Praise him, all his angels;
    praise him, all his host!
3 Praise him, sun and moon;
    praise him, all you shining stars!
4 Praise him, you highest heavens,
    and you waters above the heavens!

5 Let them praise the name of the LORD,
    for he commanded and they were created.
6 He established them forever and ever;
    he fixed their bounds, which cannot be
      passed.c

7 Praise the LORD from the earth,
    you sea monsters and all deeps,
8 fire and hail, snow and frost,
    stormy wind fulfilling his command!

9 Mountains and all hills,
    fruit trees and all cedars!
10 Wild animals and all cattle,
    creeping things and flying birds!

11 Kings of the earth and all peoples,
    princes and all rulers of the earth!
12 Young men and women alike,
    old and young together!

13 Let them praise the name of the LORD,
    for his name alone is exalted;
    his glory is above earth and heaven.
14 He has raised up a horn for his people,
    praise for all his faithful,
    for the people of Israel who are close to him.
  Praise the LORD!

Psalm 149

1 Praise the LORD!
  Sing to the LORD a new song,
    his praise in the assembly of the faithful.
2 Let Israel be glad in its Maker;
    let the children of Zion rejoice in their King.
3 Let them praise his name with dancing,
    making melody to him with tambourine and
      lyre.
4 For the LORD takes pleasure in his people;
    he adorns the humble with victory.
5 Let the faithful exult in glory;
    let them sing for joy on their couches.
6 Let the high praises of God be in their throats
    and two-edged swords in their hands,
7 to execute vengeance on the nations
    and punishment on the peoples,
8 to bind their kings with fetters
    and their nobles with chains of iron,
9 to execute on them the judgment decreed.
    This is glory for all his faithful ones.
  Praise the LORD!

Psalm 148

1 PRAISE the LORD.

  Praise the LORD from the heavens;
    praise him in the heights above.
2 Praise him, all his angels;
    praise him, all his hosts.
3 Praise him, sun and moon;
    praise him, all you shining stars;
4 praise him, you highest heavens,
    and you waters above the heavens.
5 Let them praise the name of the LORD,
    for by his command they were created;
6 he established them for ever and ever
    by an ordinance which will never pass away.

7 Praise the LORD from the earth,
    you sea monsters and ocean depths;
8 fire and hail, snow and ice,
    gales of wind that obey his voice;
9 all mountains and hills;
    all fruit trees and cedars;
10 wild animals and all cattle,
    creeping creatures and winged birds.
11 Let kings and all commoners,
    princes and rulers over the whole earth,
12 youths and girls,
    old and young together,
13 let them praise the name of the LORD,
    for his name is high above all others,
    and his majesty above earth and heaven.
14 He has exalted his people in the pride of power
    and crowned with praise his loyal servants,
    Israel, a people close to him.

  Praise the LORD.

Psalm 149

1 PRAISE the LORD.

  Sing to the LORD a new song,
    his praise in the assembly of his loyal servants!
2 Let Israel rejoice in their maker;
    let the people of Zion exult in their king.
3 Let them praise his name in the dance,
    and sing to him psalms with tambourine and lyre.
4 For the LORD accepts the service of his people;
    he crowns the lowly with victory.
5 Let his loyal servants exult in triumph;
    let them shout for joy as they prostrate themselves.
6 Let the high praises of God be on their lips
    and a two-edged sword in their hand
7 to wreak vengeance on the nations
    and punishment on the heathen,
8 binding their kings with chains,
    putting their nobles in irons,
9 carrying out the judgement decreed against them—
    this is glory for all his loyal servants.

  Praise the LORD.

---

c Or he set a law that cannot pass away

148:7 **sea monsters:** or waterspouts.

Psalm 148

1 Hallelujah!

I

Praise the LORD from the heavens;
   give praise in the heights.
2 Praise him, all you angels;
   give praise, all you hosts.
3 Praise him, sun and moon;
   give praise, all shining stars.
4 Praise him, highest heavens,
   you waters above the heavens.
5 Let them all praise the LORD's name;
   for the LORD commanded and they were created,
6 Assigned them duties forever,
   gave them tasks that will never change.

II

7 Praise the LORD from the earth,
   you sea monsters and all deep waters;
8 You lightning and hail, snow and clouds,
   storm winds that fulfill his command;
9 You mountains and all hills,
   fruit trees and all cedars;
10 You animals wild and tame,
   you creatures that crawl and fly;
11 You kings of the earth and all peoples,
   princes and all who govern on earth;
12 Young men and women too,
   old and young alike.
13 Let them all praise the LORD's name,
   for his name alone is exalted,
   majestic above earth and heaven.
14 The LORD has lifted high the horn of his people;
   to the glory of all the faithful,
   of Israel, the people near to their God.
Hallelujah!

Psalm 149

1 Hallelujah!

Sing to the LORD a new song,
   a hymn in the assembly of the faithful.
2 Let Israel be glad in their maker,
   the people of Zion rejoice in their king.
3 Let them praise his name in festive dance,
   make music with tambourine and lyre.
4 For the LORD takes delight in his people,
   honors the poor with victory.
5 Let the faithful rejoice in their glory,
   cry out for joy at their banquet,
6 With the praise of God in their mouths,
   and a two-edged sword in their hands,
7 To bring retribution on the nations,
   punishment on the peoples,
8 To bind their kings with chains,
   shackle their nobles with irons,
9 To execute the judgments decreed for them —
   such is the glory of all *God's faithful.*
Hallelujah!

Psalm 148

1 Alleluia!

Praise Yah...
praise him from the heavens,
2 Praise him, heights,
praise him, angels,
3 Praise him, su...
praise him, all
4 praise him, high,
praise him, wa...
5 Let them praise
at whose comm... heavens.
6 he establihed th... hweh
by an unchanging...

7 Praise Yaweh fr...
sea-monsters and ...
8 fire and hail, snow
storm-winds that o...

9 mountains and ever...
orchards and every ...
10 wild animals and all
reptiles and winged b...

11 kings of the earth and ...
princes and all judges ...
12 young men and girls,
old people and children ...

13 Let them praise the nam...
for his name alone is su...
his splendour transcends ...
14 For he heightens the stren...
to the praise of all his fai...
the children of Israel, the ...

Psalm 149

1 Alleluia!

Sing a new song to Yahweh:
   his praise in the assembly of the faithful!
2 Israel shall rejoice in its Maker,
   the children of Zion delight in their king;
3 they shall dance in praise of his name,
   play to him on tambourines and harp!

4 For Yahweh loves his people,
   he will crown the humble with salvation.
5 The faithful exult in glory,
   shout for joy as they worship him,
6 praising God to the heights with their voices,
   a two-edged sword in their hands,

7 to wreak vengeance on the nations,
   punishment on the peoples,
8 to load their kings with chains
   and their nobles with iron fetters,
9 to execute on them the judgement passed —
   to the honour of all his faithful.

Psalm 150

1 Praise the LORD!
Praise God in his sanctuary;d
praise him in his mighty firmament!d

praise him for his mighty deeds surpassing
2 Praise him according to his
greatness
praise him with sound of harp!

3 Praise him with tambourine and dance;
praise him with strings and pipe

Praise him with sounding cymbals;
praise him with loud clashing cymbals!

4 Praise Let everything that breathes praisethe LORD!
Praise the LORD!

Psalm 150

1 PRAISE the LORD.

Praise God in his holy place,
praise him in the mighty vault of heaven;
2 praise him for his acts of power,
praise him for his immeasurable greatness.

3 Praise him with fanfares on the trumpet,
praise him on harp and lyre;
4 praise him with tambourines and dancing,
praise him with flute and strings;
5 praise him with the clash of cymbals;
with triumphant cymbals praise him.

6 Let everything that has breath praise the LORD!
Praise the LORD.

THE BOOK OF
Proverbs

1 The proverbs of Solomon, the son of David,
   king of Israel:
2 That men may appreciate wisdom and discipline,
   may understand words of intelligence;
3 May receive training in wise conduct,
   in what is right, just and honest;
4 That resourcefulness may be imparted to
   the simple,
   to the young man knowledge and discretion.
5 A wise man by hearing them will advance
   in learning,
   an intelligent man will gain sound guidance,
6 That he may comprehend proverb and parable,
   the words of the wise and their riddles.

7 The fear of the LORD is the beginning
   of knowledge;
   wisdom and instruction fools despise.

8 Hear, my son, your father's instruction,
   and reject not your mother's teaching;
9 A graceful diadem will they be for your head;
   a torque for your neck.
10 My son, should sinners entice you, 11 and say,
   "Come along with us!
   Let us lie in wait for the honest man,
   let us, unprovoked, set a trap for the innocent.
12 Let us swallow them up, as the nether world
   does, alive,
   in the prime of life, like those who go down to
   the pit!
13 All kinds of precious wealth shall we gain,
   we shall fill our houses with booty;
14 Cast in your lot with us,
   we shall all have one purse!"—

15 My son, walk not in the way with them,
   hold back your foot from their path!
16 [For their feet run to evil,
   they hasten to shed blood.]
17 It is in vain that a net is spread
   before the eyes of any bird—
18 These men lie in wait for their own blood,
   they set a trap for their own lives.
19 This is the fate of everyone greedy of loot:
   unlawful gain takes away the life of him who
   acquires it.

20 Wisdom cries aloud in the street,
   in the open squares she raises her voice;
21 Down the crowded ways she calls out,
   at the city gates she utters her words:
22 "How long, you simple ones, will you
   love inanity,
23   how long will you turn away at my reproof?
   Lo! I will pour out to you my spirit,
   I will acquaint you with my words.

24 "Because I called and you refused,
   I extended my hand and no one took notice;

The Proverbs

1 The proverbs of Solomon son of David, king of Israel:

2 for learning what wisdom and discipline are,
   for understanding words of deep meaning,
3 for acquiring a disciplined insight,
   uprightness, justice and fair dealing;
4 for teaching sound judgement to the simple,
   and knowledge and reflection to the young;
6 for perceiving the meaning of proverbs and obscure
   sayings,
   the sayings of the sages and their riddles.
5 Let the wise listen and learn yet more,
   and a person of discernment will acquire the art
   of guidance.

7 The fear of Yahweh is the beginning of knowledge;
   fools spurn wisdom and discipline.

8 Listen, my child, to your father's instruction,
   do not reject your mother's teaching:
9 they will be a crown of grace for your head,
   a circlet for your neck.
10 My child, if sinners try to seduce you,
   do not go with them.
11 If they say, 'Come with us:
   let us lie in ambush to shed blood;
   if we plan an ambush for the innocent without
   provocation,
12 we can swallow them alive, like Sheol,
   and whole, like those who sink into oblivion.
13 We shall find treasures of every sort,
   we shall fill our houses with plunder;
14 throw in your lot with us:
   one purse between us all.'
15 My child, do not follow them in their way,
   keep your steps out of their path
16 *for their feet hasten to evil,*
   they are quick to shed blood;[a]
17 for the net is spread in vain
   if any winged creature can see it.
18 It is for their own blood such people lie in wait,
   their ambush is against their own selves!
19 Such are the paths of all who seek dishonest gain:
   which robs of their lives all who take it for their
   own.

20 Wisdom calls aloud in the streets,
   she raises her voice in the public squares;
21 she calls out at the street corners,
   she delivers her message at the city gates.
22 'You simple people, how much longer will you
   cling
   to your simple ways?
   How much longer will mockers revel in their
   mocking
   and fools go on hating knowledge?
23 Pay attention to my warning.
   To you I will pour out my heart
   and tell you what I have to say.
24 Since I have called and you have refused me,
   since I have beckoned and no one has taken
   notice,

---

a **1** A quotation of Is 59:7, absent from the best Gk MSS.

25 and because you have ignored all my counsel
  and would have none of my reproof,
26 I also will laugh at your calamity;
  I will mock when panic strikes you,
27 when panic strikes you like a storm,
  and your calamity comes like a whirlwind,
  when distress and anguish come upon you.
28 Then they will call upon me, but I will not
    answer;
  they will seek me diligently, but will not find
    me.
29 Because they hated knowledge
  and did not choose the fear of the LORD,
30 would have none of my counsel,
  and despised all my reproof,
31 therefore they shall eat the fruit of their way
  and be sated with their own devices.
32 For waywardness kills the simple,
  and the complacency of fools destroys them;
33 but those who listen to me will be secure
  and will live at ease, without dread of
    disaster.”

2 My child, if you accept my words
    and treasure up my commandments within you,
2 making your ear attentive to wisdom
  and inclining your heart to understanding;
3 if you indeed cry out for insight,
  and raise your voice for understanding;
4 if you seek it like silver,
  and search for it as for hidden treasures—
5 then you will understand the fear of the LORD
  and find the knowledge of God.
6 For the LORD gives wisdom;
  from his mouth come knowledge and
    understanding;
7 he stores up sound wisdom for the upright;
  he is a shield to those who walk blamelessly,
8 guarding the paths of justice
  and preserving the way of his faithful ones.
9 Then you will understand righteousness and
    justice
  and equity, every good path;
10 for wisdom will come into your heart,
  and knowledge will be pleasant to your soul;
11 prudence will watch over you;
  and understanding will guard you.
12 It will save you from the way of evil,
  from those who speak perversely,
13 who forsake the paths of uprightness
  to walk in the ways of darkness,
14 who rejoice in doing evil
  and delight in the perverseness of evil;
15 those whose paths are crooked,
  and who are devious in their ways.
16 You will be saved from the loose^b woman,
  from the adulteress with her smooth words,
17 who forsakes the partner of her youth
  and forgets her sacred covenant;
18 for her way^c leads down to death,
  and her paths to the shades;
19 those who go to her never come back,
  nor do they regain the paths of life.

25 because you rejected all my advice
  and would have none of my reproof,
26 I in turn shall laugh at your doom
  and deride you when terror comes,
27 when terror comes like a hurricane
  and your doom approaches like a whirlwind,
  when anguish and distress come upon you.

‘The insolent delight in their insolence;
  the stupid hate knowledge.
28 When they call to me, I shall not answer;
  when they seek, they will not find me.
29 Because they detested knowledge
  and chose not to fear the LORD,
30 because they did not accept my counsel
  and spurned all my reproof,
31 now they will eat the fruits of their conduct
  and have a surfeit of their own devices;
32 for simpletons who turn a deaf ear come to grief,
  and the stupid are ruined by their own
    complacency.
33 But whoever listens to me will live without a care,
  undisturbed by fear of misfortune.’

2 My son, if you take my words to heart
    and treasure my commandments deep within you,
2 giving your attention to wisdom
  and your mind to understanding,
3 if you cry out for discernment
  and invoke understanding,
4 if you seek for her as for silver
  and dig for her as for buried treasure,
5 then you will understand the fear of the LORD
  and attain to knowledge of God.
6 It is the LORD who bestows wisdom
  and teaches knowledge and understanding.
7 Out of his store he endows the upright with ability.
  For those whose conduct is blameless he is a
    shield,
8 guarding the course of justice
  and keeping watch over the way of his loyal
    servants.
9 You will then understand what is right and just
  and keep only to the good man’s path,
10 for wisdom will sink into your mind,
  and knowledge will be your heart’s delight.
11 Discretion will keep watch over you,
  understanding will guard you,
12 to save you from the ways of evildoers,
  from all whose talk is subversive,
13 those who forsake the right road
  to walk in murky ways,
14 who take pleasure in doing evil
  and exult in wicked and subversive acts,
15 whose ways are crooked,
  whose course is devious.
16 It will save you from the adulteress,
  from the loose woman with her smooth words,
17 who has forsaken the partner of her youth
  and forgotten the covenant of her God;
18 for her house is the way down to death,
  and her course leads to the land of the dead.
19 None who resort to her find their way back
  or regain the path to life.

1:27 **The insolent . . . knowledge:** *transposed from end of verse 22.*
2:9 **keep:** *prob. rdg; Heb.* probity.   2:16 **adulteress:** *lit.* strange
woman. **loose woman:** *lit.* alien woman.

b Heb *strange*   *c* Cn: Heb *house*

NEW AMERICAN BIBLE

25 Because you disdained all my counsel,
   and my reproof you ignored—
26 I, in my turn, will laugh at your doom;
   I will mock when terror overtakes you;
27 When terror comes upon you like a storm,
   and your doom approaches like a whirlwind;
   when distress and anguish befall you.

28 "Then they call me, but I answer not;
   they seek me, but find me not;
29 Because they hated knowledge,
   and chose not the fear of the LORD;
30 They ignored my counsel,
   they spurned all my reproof;
   And in their arrogance they preferred arrogance,
   and like fools they hated knowledge:

31 "Now they must eat the fruit of their own way,
   and with their own devices be glutted.
32 For the self-will of the simple kills them,
   the smugness of fools destroys them.
33 But he who obeys me dwells in security,
   in peace, without fear of harm."

2 My son, if you receive my words
   and treasure my commands,
2 Turning your ear to wisdom,
   inclining your heart to understanding;
3 Yes, if you call to intelligence,
   and to understanding raise your voice;
4 If you seek her like silver,
   and like hidden treasures search her out:

5 Then will you understand the fear of the LORD;
   the knowledge of God you will find;
6 For the LORD gives wisdom,
   from his mouth come knowledge
   and understanding;
7 He has counsel in store for the upright,
   he is the shield of those who walk honestly,
8 Guarding the paths of justice,
   protecting the way of his pious ones.

9 Then you will understand rectitude and justice,
   honesty, every good path;
10 For wisdom will enter your heart,
   knowledge will please your soul,
11 Discretion will watch over you,
   understanding will guard you;

12 Saving you from the way of evil men,
   from men of perverse speech,
13 Who leave the straight paths
   to walk in ways of darkness,
14 Who delight in doing evil,
   rejoice in perversity;
15 Whose ways are crooked,
   and devious their paths;

16 Saving you from the wife of another,
   from the adulteress with her smooth words,
17 Who forsakes the companion of her youth
   and forgets the pact with her God;
18 For her path sinks down to death,
   and her footsteps lead to the shades;
19 None who enter thereon come back again,
   or gain the paths of life.

NEW JERUSALEM BIBLE

25 since you have ignored all my advice
   and rejected all my warnings,
26 I, for my part, shall laugh at your distress,
   I shall jeer when terror befalls you,
27 when terror befalls you, like a storm,
   when your distress arrives, like a whirlwind,
   when ordeal and anguish bear down on you.

28 Then they will call me, but I shall not answer,
   they will look eagerly for me and will not find
   me.
29 They have hated knowledge,
   they have not chosen the fear of Yahweh,
30 they have taken no notice of my advice,
   they have spurned all my warnings:
31 so they will have to eat the fruits of their own
   ways of life,
   and choke themselves with their own scheming.
32 For the errors of the simple lead to their death,
   the complacency of fools works their own ruin;
33 but whoever listens to me may live secure,
   will have quiet, fearing no mischance.'

2 My child, if you take my words to heart,
   if you set store by my commandments,
2 tuning your ear to wisdom,
   tuning your heart to understanding,
3 yes, if your plea is for clear perception,
   if you cry out for understanding,
4 if you look for it as though for silver,
   search for it as though for buried treasure,
5 then you will understand what the fear of Yahweh
   is,
   and discover the knowledge of God.
6 For Yahweh himself is giver of wisdom,
   from his mouth issue knowledge and
   understanding.
7 He reserves his advice for the honest,
   a shield to those whose ways are sound;
8 he stands guard over the paths of equity,
   he keeps watch over the way of those faithful to
   him.
9 Then you will understand uprightness, equity and
   fair dealing,
   the paths that lead to happiness.
10 When wisdom comes into your heart
   and knowledge fills your soul with delight,
11 then prudence will be there to watch over you,
   and understanding will be your guardian
12 to keep you from the way that is evil,
   from those whose speech is deceitful,
13 from those who leave the paths of honesty
   to walk the roads of darkness:
14 those who find their joy in doing wrong,
   and their delight in deceitfulness,
15 whose tracks are twisted,
   and the paths that they tread crooked.
16 To keep you, too, from the woman who belongs to
   another,[b]
   from the stranger, with her wheedling words;
17 she has left the partner of her younger days,
   she has forgotten the covenant of her God;
18 her house is tilting towards Death,
   down to the Shades go her paths.
19 Of those who go to her not one returns,
   they never regain the paths of life.

_b_ 2 Adultery, besides its literal meaning, also symbolises desertion of
Yahweh, Israel's spouse.

NEW REVISED STANDARD VERSION

20 Therefore walk in the way of the good,
and keep to the paths of the just.
21 For the upright will abide in the land,
and the innocent will remain in it;
22 but the wicked will be cut off from the land,
and the treacherous will be rooted out of it.

3 My child, do not forget my teaching,
but let your heart keep my commandments;
2 for length of days and years of life
and abundant welfare they will give you.

3 Do not let loyalty and faithfulness forsake you;
bind them around your neck,
write them on the tablet of your heart.
4 So you will find favor and good repute
in the sight of God and of people.

5 Trust in the LORD with all your heart,
and do not rely on your own insight.
6 In all your ways acknowledge him,
and he will make straight your paths.
7 Do not be wise in your own eyes;
fear the LORD, and turn away from evil.
8 It will be a healing for your flesh
and a refreshment for your body.

9 Honor the LORD with your substance
and with the first fruits of all your produce;
10 then your barns will be filled with plenty,
and your vats will be bursting with wine.

11 My child, do not despise the LORD's discipline
or be weary of his reproof,
12 for the LORD reproves the one he loves,
as a father the son in whom he delights.

13 Happy are those who find wisdom,
and those who get understanding,
14 for her income is better than silver,
and her revenue better than gold.
15 She is more precious than jewels,
and nothing you desire can compare with her.
16 Long life is in her right hand;
in her left hand are riches and honor.
17 Her ways are ways of pleasantness,
and all her paths are peace.
18 She is a tree of life to those who lay hold of her;
those who hold her fast are called happy.

19 The LORD by wisdom founded the earth;
by understanding he established the heavens;
20 by his knowledge the deeps broke open,
and the clouds drop down the dew.

21 My child, do not let these escape from your
sight:
keep sound wisdom and prudence,
22 and they will be life for your soul
and adornment for your neck.
23 Then you will walk on your way securely
and your foot will not stumble.
24 If you sit down,*d* you will not be afraid;
when you lie down, your sleep will be sweet.
25 Do not be afraid of sudden panic,
or of the storm that strikes the wicked;
26 for the LORD will be your confidence
and will keep your foot from being caught.

27 Do not withhold good from those to whom it is
due,*e*
when it is in your power to do it.

REVISED ENGLISH BIBLE

20 See then that you follow the footsteps of the good
and keep to the paths of the righteous;
21 for the upright will dwell secure in the land
and the blameless remain there;
22 but the wicked will be cut off from the land,
those who are perfidious uprooted from it.

3 My son, do not forget my teaching,
but treasure my commandments in your heart;
2 for long life and years in plenty
and abundant prosperity will they bring you.
3 Let your loyalty and good faith never fail;
bind them about your neck,
and inscribe them on the tablet of your memory.
4 So will you win favour and success
in the sight of God and man.

5 Put all your trust in the LORD
and do not rely on your own understanding.
6 At every step you take keep him in mind,
and he will direct your path.
7 Do not be wise in your own estimation;
fear the LORD and turn from evil.
8 Let that be medicine to keep you in health,
liniment for your limbs.
9 Honour the LORD with your wealth
and with the firstfruits of all your produce;
10 then your granaries will be filled with grain
and your vats will brim with new wine.
11 My son, do not spurn the LORD's correction
or recoil from his reproof;
12 for those whom the LORD loves he reproves,
and he punishes the son who is dear to him.

13 Happy is he who has found wisdom,
he who has acquired understanding,
14 for wisdom is more profitable than silver,
and the gain she brings is better than gold!
15 She is more precious than red coral,
and none of your jewels can compare with her.
16 In her right hand is long life,
in her left are riches and honour.
17 Her ways are pleasant ways
and her paths all lead to prosperity.
18 She is a tree of life to those who grasp her,
and those who hold fast to her are safe.

19 By wisdom the LORD laid the earth's foundations
and by understanding he set the heavens in place;
20 by his knowledge the springs of the deep burst
forth
and the clouds dropped dew.

21 My son, safeguard sound judgement and discretion;
do not let them out of your sight.
22 They will be a charm hung about your neck,
an ornament to grace your throat.
23 Then you will go on your way without a care,
and your foot will not stumble.
24 When you sit, you need have no fear;
when you lie down, your sleep will be pleasant.
25 Do not be afraid when fools are frightened
or when destruction overtakes the wicked,
26 for the LORD will be at your side,
and he will keep your feet from the trap.
27 Withhold from no one a favour due to him
when you have the power to grant it.

3:10 **with grain:** *or* to overflowing.   3:12 **he punishes:** *prob.
rdg, cp. Gk; Heb.* like a father.   3:22 **charm:** *lit.* life.
3:24 **sit:** *so Gk; Heb.* lie down.

d Gk: Heb lie down   *e Heb from its owners*

20 Thus you may walk in the way of good men,
  and keep to the paths of the just.
21 For the upright will dwell in the land,
  the honest will remain in it;
22 But the wicked will be cut off from the land,
  the faithless will be rooted out of it.

3 My son, forget not my teaching,
  keep in mind my commands;
2 For many days, and years of life,
  and peace, will they bring you.

3 Let not kindness and fidelity leave you;
  bind them around your neck;
4 Then will you win favor and good esteem
  before God and man.

5 Trust in the LORD with all your heart,
  on your own intelligence rely not;
6 In all your ways be mindful of him,
  and he will make straight your paths.

7 Be not wise in your own eyes,
  fear the LORD and turn away from evil;
8 This will mean health for your flesh
  and vigor for your bones.

9 Honor the LORD with your wealth,
  with first fruits of all your produce;
10 Then will your barns be filled with grain,
  with new wine your vats will overflow.
11 The discipline of the LORD, my son, disdain not;
  spurn not his reproof;
12 For whom the LORD loves he reproves,
  and he chastises the son he favors.
13 Happy the man who finds wisdom,
  the man who gains understanding!
14 For her profit is better than profit in silver,
  and better than gold is her revenue;
15 She is more precious than corals,
  and none of your choice possessions can
  compare with her.

16 Long life is in her right hand,
  in her left are riches and honor;
17 Her ways are pleasant ways,
  and all her paths are peace;
18 She is a tree of life to those who grasp her,
  and he is happy who holds her fast.

19 The LORD by wisdom founded the earth,
  established the heavens by understanding;
20 By his knowledge the depths break open,
  and the clouds drop down dew.
21 My son, let not these slip out of your sight:
  keep advice and counsel in view;
22 So will they be life to your soul,
  and an adornment for your neck.
23 Then you may securely go your way;
  your foot will never stumble;
24 When you lie down, you need not be afraid,
  when you rest, your sleep will be sweet.
35 Honor is the possession of wise men,
  but fools inherit shame.
25 Be not afraid of sudden terror,
  of the ruin of the wicked when it comes;
26 For the LORD will be your confidence,
  and will keep your foot from the snare.

27 Refuse no one the good on which he has a claim
  when it is in your power to do it for him.

20 Thus you will tread the way of good people,
  persisting in the paths of the upright.
21 For the land will be for the honest to live in,
  the innocent will have it for their home;
22 while the wicked will be cut off from the land,
  and the faithless rooted out of it.

3 My child, do not forget my teaching,
  let your heart keep my principles;
2 since they will increase your length of days,
  your years of life and your well-being.

3 Let faithful love and constancy never leave you:
  tie them round your neck,
  write them on the tablet of your heart.
4 Thus you will find favour and success
  in the sight of God and of people.
5 Trust wholeheartedly in Yahweh,
  put no faith in your own perception;
6 acknowledge him in every course you take,
  and he will see that your paths are smooth.
7 Do not congratulate yourself on your own wisdom,
  fear Yahweh and turn your back on evil:
8 health-giving, this, to your body,
  relief to your bones.

9 Honour Yahweh with what goods you have
  and with the first-fruits of all your produce;
10 then your barns will be filled with corn,
  your vats overflowing with new wine.
11 My child, do not scorn correction from Yahweh,
  do not resent his reproof;
12 for Yahweh reproves those he loves,
  as a father the child whom he loves.
13 Blessed are those who have discovered wisdom,
  those who have acquired understanding!
14 Gaining her is more rewarding than silver,
  her yield is more valuable than gold.
15 She is beyond the price of pearls,
  nothing you could covet is her equal.
16 In her right hand is length of days;
  in her left hand, riches and honour.
17 Her ways are filled with delight,
  her paths all lead to contentment.
18 She is a tree of life for those who hold her fast,
  those who cling to her live happy lives.
19 In wisdom, Yahweh laid the earth's foundations,
  in understanding he spread out the heavens.
20 Through his knowledge the depths were cleft open,
  and the clouds distil the dew.
21 My child, hold to sound advice and prudence,
  never let them out of sight;
22 they will give life to your soul
  and beauty to your neck.
23 You will go on your way in safety,
  your feet will not stumble.
24 When you go to bed, you will not be afraid;
  once in bed, your sleep will be sweet.
25 Have no fear either of sudden terror
  or of attack mounted by wicked men,
26 since Yahweh will be your guarantor,
  he will keep your steps from the snare.

27 Refuse no kindness to those who have a right to it,
  if it is in your power to perform it.

NEW REVISED STANDARD VERSION	REVISED ENGLISH BIBLE

NEW REVISED STANDARD VERSION

28 Do not say to your neighbor, "Go, and come
  again,
  tomorrow I will give it"—when you have it
  with you.
29 Do not plan harm against your neighbor
  who lives trustingly beside you.
30 Do not quarrel with anyone without cause,
  when no harm has been done to you.
31 Do not envy the violent
  and do not choose any of their ways;
32 for the perverse are an abomination to the LORD,
  but the upright are in his confidence.
33 The LORD's curse is on the house of the wicked,
  but he blesses the abode of the righteous.
34 Toward the scorners he is scornful,
  but to the humble he shows favor.
35 The wise will inherit honor,
  but stubborn fools, disgrace.

4 Listen, children, to a father's instruction,
  and be attentive, that you may gain*f* insight;
2 for I give you good precepts:
  do not forsake my teaching.
3 When I was a son with my father,
  tender, and my mother's favorite,
4 he taught me, and said to me,
  "Let your heart hold fast my words;
  keep my commandments, and live.
5 Get wisdom; get insight: do not forget, nor turn
  away
  from the words of my mouth.
6 Do not forsake her, and she will keep you;
  love her, and she will guard you.
7 The beginning of wisdom is this: Get wisdom,
  and whatever else you get, get insight.
8 Prize her highly, and she will exalt you;
  she will honor you if you embrace her.
9 She will place on your head a fair garland;
  she will bestow on you a beautiful crown."
10 Hear, my child, and accept my words,
  that the years of your life may be many.
11 I have taught you the way of wisdom;
  I have led you in the paths of uprightness.
12 When you walk, your step will not be hampered;
  and if you run, you will not stumble.
13 Keep hold of instruction; do not let go;
  guard her, for she is your life.
14 Do not enter the path of the wicked,
  and do not walk in the way of evildoers.
15 Avoid it; do not go on it;
  turn away from it and pass on.
16 For they cannot sleep unless they have done
  wrong;
  they are robbed of sleep unless they have made
  someone stumble.
17 For they eat the bread of wickedness
  and drink the wine of violence.
18 But the path of the righteous is like the light of
  dawn,
  which shines brighter and brighter until full
  day.
19 The way of the wicked is like deep darkness;
  they do not know what they stumble over.
20 My child, be attentive to my words;
  incline your ear to my sayings.
21 Do not let them escape from your sight;
  keep them within your heart.

REVISED ENGLISH BIBLE

28 Do not say to your neighbour, 'Come back again;
  you can have it tomorrow'—when you could give
  it now.
29 Devise no evil against the neighbour
  living trustingly beside you.
30 Do not pick a quarrel with a man for no reason,
  when he has done you no harm.
31 Do not emulate a violent person
  or choose to follow his example;
32 for one who is not straight is detestable to the
  LORD,
  but those who are upright are in God's confidence.
33 The LORD's curse falls on the house of the wicked,
  but he blesses the home of the righteous.
34 Though God meets the scornful with scorn,
  to the humble he shows favour.
35 The wise win renown,
  but disgrace is the portion of fools.

4 Listen, my sons, to a father's instruction,
  consider attentively how to gain understanding;
2 it is sound learning I give you,
  so do not forsake my teaching.
3 When I was a boy, subject to my father,
  tender in years, my mother's only child,
4 he taught me and said to me:
  'Hold fast to my words with all your heart,
  keep my commandments, and you will have life.
5 'Get wisdom, get understanding;
  do not forget or turn a deaf ear to what I say.
6 Do not forsake her, and she will watch over you;
  love her, and she will safeguard you;
8 cherish her, and she will lift you high;
  if only you embrace her, she will bring you to
  honour.
9 She will set a becoming garland on your head;
  she will bestow on you a glorious crown.
10 'Listen, my son, take my words to heart,
  and the years of your life will be many.
11 I shall guide you in the paths of wisdom;
  I shall lead you in honest ways.
12 When you walk nothing will impede you,
  and when you run nothing will bring you down.
13 Cling to instruction and never let it go;
  guard it well, for it is your life.
14 Do not take to the course of the wicked
  or follow the way of evildoers;
15 do not set foot on it, but avoid it,
  turn from it, and go on your way.
16 For they cannot sleep unless they have done some
  wrong;
  unless they have been someone's downfall they lie
  sleepless.
17 The bread they eat is gained by crime,
  the wine they drink is got by violence.
18 While the course of the righteous is like morning
  light,
  growing ever brighter till it is broad day,
19 the way of the wicked is like deep darkness,
  and they do not know what has been their
  downfall.
20 'My son, attend to my words,
  pay heed to my sayings;
21 do not let them slip from your sight,
  keep them fixed in your mind;

3:34 **humble:** *or* wretched.   4:6 **safeguard you:** *so Gk; Heb.*
adds 7The foundation of wisdom. Get wisdom, get understanding
though it cost all you have.

f Heb *know*

1364

28 Say not to your neighbor, "Go, and come again,
   tomorrow I will give," when you can give
     at once.
29 Plot no evil against your neighbor,
   against him who lives at peace with you.
30 Quarrel not with a man without cause,
   with one who has done you no harm.
31 Envy not the lawless man
   and choose none of his ways:
32 To the LORD the perverse man is an abomination,
   but with the upright is his friendship.
33 The curse of the LORD is on the house of
     the wicked,
   but the dwelling of the just he blesses;
34 When he is dealing with the arrogant, he is stern,
   but to the humble he shows kindness.
   ‡3.35: see above‡

4 Hear, O children, a father's instruction,
   be attentive, that you may gain understanding!
2 Yes, excellent advice I give you;
   my teaching do not forsake.
3 When I was my father's child,
   frail, yet the darling of my mother,
4 He taught me, and said to me:
   "Let your heart hold fast my words:
   keep my commands, that you may live!
5 "Get wisdom, get understanding!
   Do not forget or turn aside from the words
     I utter.
6 Forsake her not, and she will preserve you;
   love her, and she will safeguard you;
7 The beginning of wisdom is: get wisdom;
   at the cost of all you have, get understanding.
8 Extol her, and she will exalt you;
   she will bring you honors if you embrace her;
9 She will put on your head a graceful diadem;
   a glorious crown will she bestow on you."

10 Hear, my son, and receive my words,
   and the years of your life shall be many.
11 On the way of wisdom I direct you,
   I lead you on straightforward paths.
12 When you walk, your step will not be impeded,
   and should you run, you will not stumble.
13 Hold fast to instruction, never let her go;
   keep her, for she is your life.
14 The path of the wicked enter not,
   walk not on the way of evil men;
15 Shun it, cross it not,
   turn aside from it, and pass on.
16 For they cannot rest unless they have done evil;
   to have made no one stumble steals away
     their sleep.
17 For they eat the bread of wickedness
   and drink the wine of violence.
19 The way of the wicked is like darkness;
   they know not on what they stumble.
18 But the path of the just is like shining light,
   that grows in brilliance till perfect day.

20 My son, to my words be attentive,
   to my sayings incline your ear;
21 Let them not slip out of your sight,
   keep them within your heart;

28 Do not say to your neighbour, 'Go away! Come
     another time!
   I will give it you tomorrow,' if you can do it
     now.
29 Do not plot harm against your neighbour
   who is living unsuspecting beside you.
30 Do not pick a groundless quarrel with anyone
   who has done you no harm.
31 Do not envy the man of violence,
   never model your conduct on his;
32 for the wilful wrong-doer is abhorrent to Yahweh,
   who confides only in the honest.
33 Yahweh's curse lies on the house of the wicked,
   but he blesses the home of the upright.
34 He mocks those who mock,
   but accords his favour to the humble.
35 Glory is the portion of the wise,
   all that fools inherit is contempt.

4 Listen, my children, to a father's instruction;
   pay attention, and learn what understanding is.
2 What I am offering you is sound doctrine:
   do not forsake my teaching.
3 I too was once a child with a father,
   in my mother's eyes a tender child, unique.
4 This was what he used to teach me,
   'Let your heart treasure what I have to say,
   keep my principles and you will live;
5 acquire wisdom, acquire understanding,
   never forget her, never deviate from my words.
6 Do not desert her, she will keep you safe;
   love her, she will watch over you.
7 The first principle of wisdom is: acquire wisdom;
   at the cost of all you have, acquire
     understanding!
8 Hold her close, and she will make you great;
   embrace her, and she will be your pride;
9 she will provide a graceful garland for your head,
   bestow a crown of honour on you.'

10 Listen, my child, take my words to heart,
   and the years of your life will be multiplied.
11 I have educated you in the ways of wisdom,
   I have guided you along the path of honesty.
12 When you walk, your going will be unhindered,
   if you run, you will not stumble.
13 Hold fast to discipline, never let her go,
   keep your eyes on her, she is your life.
14 Do not follow the path of the wicked,
   do not walk the way that the evil go.
15 Avoid it, do not take it,
   turn your back on it, pass it by.
16 For they cannot sleep unless they have first done
     wrong,
   they miss their sleep if they have not made
     someone stumble;
17 for the bread of wickedness is what they eat,
   and the wine of violence is what they drink.
18 The path of the upright is like the light of dawn,
   its brightness growing to the fullness of day;
19 the way of the wicked is as dark as night,
   they cannot tell the obstacles they stumble over.

20 My child, pay attention to what I am telling you,
   listen carefully to my words;
21 do not let them out of your sight,
   keep them deep in your heart.

NEW REVISED STANDARD VERSION	REVISED ENGLISH BIBLE

NEW REVISED STANDARD VERSION

22 For they are life to those who find them,
    and healing to all their flesh.
23 Keep your heart with all vigilance,
    for from it flow the springs of life.
24 Put away from you crooked speech,
    and put devious talk far from you.
25 Let your eyes look directly forward,
    and your gaze be straight before you.
26 Keep straight the path of your feet,
    and all your ways will be sure.
27 Do not swerve to the right or to the left;
    turn your foot away from evil.

5 My child, be attentive to my wisdom;
    incline your ear to my understanding,
2 so that you may hold on to prudence,
    and your lips may guard knowledge.
3 For the lips of a loose^g woman drip honey,
    and her speech is smoother than oil;
4 but in the end she is bitter as wormwood,
    sharp as a two-edged sword.
5 Her feet go down to death;
    her steps follow the path to Sheol.
6 She does not keep straight to the path of life;
    her ways wander, and she does not know it.

7 And now, my child,^{h} listen to me,
    and do not depart from the words of my
        mouth.
8 Keep your way far from her,
    and do not go near the door of her house;
9 or you will give your honor to others,
    and your years to the merciless,
10 and strangers will take their fill of your wealth,
    and your labors will go to the house of an
        alien;
11 and at the end of your life you will groan,
    when your flesh and body are consumed,
12 and you say, "Oh, how I hated discipline,
    and my heart despised reproof!
13 I did not listen to the voice of my teachers
    or incline my ear to my instructors.
14 Now I am at the point of utter ruin
    in the public assembly."

15 Drink water from your own cistern,
    flowing water from your own well.
16 Should your springs be scattered abroad,
    streams of water in the streets?
17 Let them be for yourself alone,
    and not for sharing with strangers.
18 Let your fountain be blessed,
    and rejoice in the wife of your youth,
19   a lovely deer, a graceful doe.
    May her breasts satisfy you at all times;
        may you be intoxicated always by her love.
20 Why should you be intoxicated, my son, by
        another woman
    and embrace the bosom of an adulteress?
21 For human ways are under the eyes of the LORD,
    and he examines all their paths.
22 The iniquities of the wicked ensnare them,
    and they are caught in the toils of their sin.
23 They die for lack of discipline,
    and because of their great folly they are lost.

REVISED ENGLISH BIBLE

22 for they are life to those who find them,
    and health to their whole being.
23 Guard your heart more than anything you treasure,
    for it is the source of all life.
24 Keep your mouth from crooked speech
    and banish deceitful talk from your lips.
25 Let your eyes look straight before you,
    fix your gaze on what lies ahead.
26 Mark out the path that your feet must take,
    and your ways will be secure.
27 Deviate to neither right nor left;
    keep clear of evil.

5 'My son, attend to my wisdom
    and listen with care to my counsel,
2 so that you may preserve discretion
    and your lips safeguard knowledge.
3 For though the lips of an adulteress drip honey
    and her tongue is smoother than oil,
4 yet in the end she is as bitter as wormwood,
    as sharp as a two-edged sword.
5 Her feet tread the downward path towards death,
    the road she walks leads straight to Sheol.
6 She does not mark out the path to life;
    her course twists this way and that, but she is
        unconcerned.'

7 Now, my sons, listen to me
    and do not ignore what I say:
8 keep well away from her
    and do not go near the door of her house,
9 or you will surrender your vigour to others,
    the pride of your manhood to the heartless.
10 Strangers will batten on your wealth,
    and your hard-won gains pass to the family of
        another.
11 When you shrink to skin and bone
    you will end by groaning 12 and saying,
'Oh, why did I hate correction
    and set my heart against reproof?
13 Why did I not listen to the voice of my teachers
    and pay heed to my instructors?
14 I was almost brought to ruin
    in the public assembly.'

15 Drink water from your own cistern,
    fresh water from your own spring.
16 Do not let your water overflow into the road,
    your runnels of water pour into the street.
17 Let them be for yourself alone,
    not shared with strangers.
18 Let your fountain, the wife of your youth,
    be blessed; find your joy in her.
19 A lovely doe, a graceful hind, let her be your
        companion;
    her love will satisfy you at all times
    and wrap you round continually.
20 Why, my son, are you wrapped in the love of an
        adulteress?
    Why do you embrace a loose woman?
21 The LORD watches a man's ways,
    marking every course he takes.
22 He who is wicked is caught in his own iniquities,
    held fast in the toils of his own sin;
23 for want of discipline he will perish,
    wrapped in the shroud of his boundless folly.

---

^{g} Heb strange ^{h} Gk Vg: Heb children

5:5 **Sheol:** or the underworld.   5:6 **but . . . unconcerned:** or and she is restless.   5:19 **let . . . companion:** so Gk; Heb. omits.

22 For they are life to those who find them,
to man's whole being they are health.

23 With closest custody, guard your heart,
for in it are the sources of life.
24 Put away from you dishonest talk,
deceitful speech put far from you.
25 Let your eyes look straight ahead
and your glance be directly forward.
26 Survey the path for your feet,
and let all your ways be sure.
27 Turn neither to right nor to left,
keep your foot far from evil.

5 My son, to my wisdom be attentive,
to my knowledge incline your ear,
2 That discretion may watch over you,
and understanding may guard you.
3 The lips of an adulteress drip with honey,
and her mouth is smoother than oil;
4 But in the end she is as bitter as wormwood,
as sharp as a two-edged sword.
5 Her feet go down to death,
to the nether world her steps attain;
6 Lest you see before you the road to life,
her paths will ramble, you know not where.

7 So now, O children, listen to me,
go not astray from the words of my mouth.
8 Keep your way far from her,
approach not the door of her house,
9 Lest you give your honor to others,
and your years to a merciless one;
10 Lest strangers have their fill of your wealth,
your hard-won earnings go to an alien's house;
11 And you groan in the end,
when your flesh and your body are consumed;
12 And you say, "Oh, why did I hate instruction,
and my heart spurn reproof!
13 Why did I not listen to the voice of my teachers,
nor to my instructors incline my ear!
14 I have all but come to utter ruin,
condemned by the public assembly!"

15 Drink water from your own cistern,
running water from your own well.
16 How may your water sources be dispersed abroad,
streams of water in the streets?
17 Let your fountain be yours alone,
not one shared with strangers;
18 And have joy of the wife of your youth,
19   your lovely hind, your graceful doe.
Her love will invigorate you always,
through her love you will flourish continually,
6, 22 When you lie down she will watch over you,
and when you wake, she will share
your concerns;
wherever you turn, she will guide you.
20 Why then, my son, should you go astray for
another's wife
and accept the embraces of an adulteress?

21 For each man's ways are plain to the LORD's sight;
all their paths he surveys;
22 By his own iniquities the wicked man will
be caught,
in the meshes of his own sin he will be
held fast;
23 He will die from lack of discipline,
through the greatness of his folly he will be lost.

6, 22: This is transposed from chapter 6, 22.

22 For they are life to those who find them
and health to all humanity.
23 More than all else, keep watch over your heart,
since here are the wellsprings of life.
24 Turn your back on the mouth that misleads,
keep your distance from lips that deceive.
25 Let your eyes be fixed ahead,
your gaze be straight before you.
26 Let the path you tread be level
and all your ways be firm.
27 Turn neither to right nor to left,
keep your foot clear of evil.

5 My son, pay attention to my wisdom,
listen carefully to what I know;
2 so that you may preserve discretion
and your lips may guard knowledge.
Take no notice of a loose-living woman,
3 for the lips of the adulteress drip with honey,
her palate is more unctuous than oil,
4 but in the end she is bitter as wormwood,
sharp as a two-edged sword.
5 Her feet go down to death,
Sheol the goal of her steps;
6 far from following the path of life,
her course is uncertain and she does not know it.

7 And now, son, listen to me,
never deviate from what I say:
8 set your course as far from her as possible,
go nowhere near the door of her house,
9 or she will hand over your honour to others,
the years of your life to a man without pity,
10 and strangers will batten on your property,
and your produce go to the house of a stranger,
11 and, at your ending,
your body and flesh having been consumed,
you will groan 12 and exclaim,
'Alas, I hated discipline,
my heart spurned all correction;
13 I would not attend to the voice of my masters,
I would not listen to those who tried to teach
me.
14 Now I have come to nearly every kind of misery,
in the assembly and in the community.'

15 Drink the water from your own storage-well,
fresh water from your own spring.
16 Even if your fountains overflow outside,
your streams of water in the public squares:
17 let them be for you alone,
and not for strangers with you.
18 May your fountain-head be blessed!

Find joy with the wife you married in your youth,
19   fair as a hind, graceful as a fawn:
hers the breasts that ever fill you with delight,
hers the love that ever holds you captive.
20 Why be seduced, my son, by someone else's wife,
and fondle the breast of a woman who belongs
to another?
21 For the eyes of Yahweh observe human ways,
and survey all human paths.
22 The wicked is snared in his own misdeeds,
is caught in the meshes of his own sin.
23 For want of discipline, he dies,
led astray by his own excessive folly.

6 My child, if you have given your pledge to your
   neighbor,
   if you have bound yourself to another,[i]
2 you are snared by the utterance of your lips,[j]
   caught by the words of your mouth.
3 So do this, my child, and save yourself,
   for you have come into your neighbor's power:
   go, hurry,[k] and plead with your neighbor.
4 Give your eyes no sleep
   and your eyelids no slumber;
5 save yourself like a gazelle from the hunter,[l]
   like a bird from the hand of the fowler.

6 Go to the ant, you lazybones;
   consider its ways, and be wise.
7 Without having any chief
   or officer or ruler,
8 it prepares its food in summer,
   and gathers its sustenance in harvest.
9 How long will you lie there, O lazybones?
   When will you rise from your sleep?
10 A little sleep, a little slumber,
   a little folding of the hands to rest,
11 and poverty will come upon you like a robber,
   and want, like an armed warrior.

12 A scoundrel and a villain
   goes around with crooked speech,
13 winking the eyes, shuffling the feet,
   pointing the fingers,
14 with perverted mind devising evil,
   continually sowing discord;
15 on such a one calamity will descend suddenly;
   in a moment, damage beyond repair.

16 There are six things that the LORD hates,
   seven that are an abomination to him:
17 haughty eyes, a lying tongue,
   and hands that shed innocent blood,
18 a heart that devises wicked plans,
   feet that hurry to run to evil,
19 a lying witness who testifies falsely,
   and one who sows discord in a family.

20 My child, keep your father's commandment,
   and do not forsake your mother's teaching.
21 Bind them upon your heart always;
   tie them around your neck.
22 When you walk, they[m] will lead you;
   when you lie down, they[m] will watch over
      you;
   and when you awake, they[m] will talk with
      you.
23 For the commandment is a lamp and the teaching
   a light,
   and the reproofs of discipline are the way of
      life,
24 to preserve you from the wife of another,[n]
   from the smooth tongue of the adulteress.
25 Do not desire her beauty in your heart,
   and do not let her capture you with her
      eyelashes;
26 for a prostitute's fee is only a loaf of bread,[o]
   but the wife of another stalks a man's very
      life.
27 Can fire be carried in the bosom
   without burning one's clothes?

[i]Or a stranger   [j]Cn Compare Gk Syr: Heb the words of your
mouth   [k]Or humble yourself   [l]Cn: Heb from the hand
[m]Heb it   [n]Gk: MT the evil woman   [o]Cn Compare Gk Syr Vg
Tg: Heb for because of a harlot to a piece of bread

6 My son, if you give yourself in pledge to another
   person
   and stand surety for a stranger,
2 if you are caught by your promise,
   trapped by some promise you have made,
3 this is what you must do, my son, to save yourself:
   since you have come into the power of another,
   bestir yourself, go and pester the man,
4 give yourself no rest,
   allow yourself no sleep.
5 Free yourself like a gazelle from a net,
   like a bird from the grasp of the fowler.

6 Go to the ant, you sluggard,
   observe her ways and gain wisdom.
7 She has no prince,
   no governor or ruler;
8 but in summer she gathers in her store of food
   and lays in her supplies at harvest.
9 How long, you sluggard, will you lie abed?
   When will you rouse yourself from sleep?
10 A little sleep, a little slumber,
   a little folding of the hands in rest—
11 and poverty will come on you like a footpad,
   want will assail you like a hardened ruffian.

12 A scoundrel and knave is one
   who goes around with crooked talk,
13 a wink of the eye,
   a nudge with the foot,
   a gesture with the fingers.
14 His mind is set on subversion;
   all the time he plots mischief and sows strife.
15 That is why disaster comes upon him suddenly;
   in an instant he is broken beyond all remedy.

16 Six things the LORD hates,
   seven are detestable to him:
17 a proud eye, a false tongue,
   hands that shed innocent blood,
18 a mind given to forging wicked schemes,
   feet that run swiftly to do evil,
19 a false witness telling a pack of lies,
   and one who sows strife between brothers.

20 My son, observe your father's commands
   and do not abandon the teaching of your mother;
21 wear them always next to your heart
   and bind them close about your neck.
22 Wherever you turn, wisdom will guide you;
   when you lie down, she will watch over you,
   and when you wake, she will talk with you.
23 For a commandment is a lamp, and teaching a
   light,
   reproof and correction point the way to life,
24 to keep you from the wife of another man,
   from the seductive tongue of the loose woman.
25 Do not be infatuated by her beauty
   or let her glance captivate you;
26 for a prostitute can be had for the price of a loaf,
   but a married woman is after the prize of a life.
27 Can a man kindle a fire in his bosom
   without setting his clothes alight?

6:5 **net:** so Gk; Heb. hand.   6:22 **wisdom:** lit. she.   6:24 **the
wife . . . man:** prob. rdg; Heb. the evil woman.

6 My son, if you have become surety to
  your neighbor,
  given your hand in pledge to another,
2 You have been snared by the utterance of
  your lips,
  caught by the words of your mouth;
3 So do this, my son, to free yourself,
  since you have fallen into your
  neighbor's power:
  Go, hurry, stir up your neighbor!
4 Give no sleep to your eyes,
  nor slumber to your eyelids;
5 Free yourself as a gazelle from the snare,
  or as a bird from the hand of the fowler.

6 Go to the ant, O sluggard,
  study her ways and learn wisdom;
7 For though she has no chief,
  no commander or ruler,
8 She procures her food in the summer,
  stores up her provisions in the harvest.
9 How long, O sluggard, will you rest?
  when will you rise from your sleep?
10 A little sleep, a little slumber,
  a little folding of the arms to rest—
11 Then will poverty come upon you like
  a highwayman,
  and want like an armed man.

12 A scoundrel, a villain, is he
  who deals in crooked talk.
13 He winks his eyes,
  shuffles his feet,
  makes signs with his fingers;
14 He has perversity in his heart,
  is always plotting evil,
  sows discord.
15 Therefore suddenly ruin comes upon him;
  in an instant he is crushed beyond cure.

16 There are six things the LORD hates,
  yes, seven are an abomination to him;
17 Haughty eyes, a lying tongue,
  and hands that shed innocent blood;
18 A heart that plots wicked schemes,
  feet that run swiftly to evil,
19 The false witness who utters lies,
  and he who sows discord among brothers.

20 Observe, my son, your father's bidding,
  and reject not your mother's teaching;
21 Keep them fastened over your heart always,
  put them around your neck;
    ‡6.22: see above in ch. 5‡
23 For the bidding is a lamp, and the teaching a light,
  and a way to life are the reproofs of discipline;
24 To keep you from your neighbor's wife,
  from the smooth tongue of the adulteress.

25 Lust not in your heart after her beauty,
  let her not captivate you with her glance!
26 For the price of a loose woman
  may be scarcely a loaf of bread,
  But if she is married,
  she is a trap for your precious life.
27 Can a man take fire to his bosom,
  and his garments not be burned?

6 My child, if you have gone surety for your
  neighbour,
  if you have guaranteed the bond of a stranger,
2 if you have committed yourself with your lips,
  if through words of yours you have been
  entrapped,
3 do this, my child, to extricate yourself—
  since you have put yourself in the power of your
  neighbour:
  go, humble yourself, plead with your neighbour,
4 give your eyes no sleep,
  your eyelids no rest,
5 break free like a gazelle from the trap,
  like a bird from the fowler's clutches.

6 Idler, go to the ant;
  ponder her ways and grow wise:
7 no one gives her orders,
  no overseer, no master,
8 yet all through the summer she gets her food
  ready,
  and gathers her supplies at harvest time.
9 How long do you intend to lie there, idler?
  When are you going to rise from your sleep?
10 A little sleep, a little drowsiness,
  a little folding of the arms to lie back,
11 and poverty comes like a vagrant
  and, like a beggar, dearth. c

12 A scoundrel, a vicious man,
  he goes with a leer on his lips,
13 winking his eye, shuffling his foot,
  beckoning with his finger.
14 Trickery in his heart, always scheming evil,
  he sows dissension.
15 Disaster will overtake him sharply for this,
  suddenly, irretrievably, he will be broken.

16 There are six things that Yahweh hates,
  seven that he abhors:
17 a haughty look, a lying tongue,
  hands that shed innocent blood,
18 a heart that weaves wicked plots,
  feet that hurry to do evil,
19 a false witness who lies with every breath,
  and one who sows dissension among brothers.

20 Keep your father's precept, my child,
  do not spurn your mother's teaching.
21 Bind them ever to your heart,
  tie them round your neck.
22 While you are active, they will guide you,
  when you fall asleep, they will watch over you,
  when you wake up, they will converse with you.

23 For the precept is a lamp,
  the teaching is a light;
  correction and discipline are the way to life,
24 preserving you from the woman of bad character,
  from the wheedling talk of a woman who
  belongs to another.
25 Do not covet her beauty in your heart
  or let her captivate you with the play of her
  eyes;
26 a prostitute can be bought for a hunk of bread,
  but a married woman aims to snare a precious
  life.
27 Can a man carry fire inside his shirt
  without setting his clothes alight?

c **6** = 24:33–34.

28 Or can one walk on hot coals
    without scorching the feet?
29 So is he who sleeps with his neighbor's wife;
    no one who touches her will go unpunished.
30 Thieves are not despised who steal only
    to satisfy their appetite when they are hungry.
31 Yet if they are caught, they will pay sevenfold;
    they will forfeit all the goods of their house.
32 But he who commits adultery has no sense;
    he who does it destroys himself.
33 He will get wounds and dishonor,
    and his disgrace will not be wiped away.
34 For jealousy arouses a husband's fury,
    and he shows no restraint when he takes
    revenge.
35 He will accept no compensation,
    and refuses a bribe no matter how great.

7

My child, keep my words
    and store up my commandments with you;
2 keep my commandments and live,
    keep my teachings as the apple of your eye;
3 bind them on your fingers,
    write them on the tablet of your heart.
4 Say to wisdom, "You are my sister,"
    and call insight your intimate friend,
5 that they may keep you from the loose*p* woman,
    from the adulteress with her smooth words.

6 For at the window of my house
    I looked out through my lattice,
7 and I saw among the simple ones,
    I observed among the youths,
    a young man without sense,
8 passing along the street near her corner,
    taking the road to her house
9 in the twilight, in the evening,
    at the time of night and darkness.

10 Then a woman comes toward him,
    decked out like a prostitute, wily of heart.*q*
11 She is loud and wayward;
    her feet do not stay at home;
12 now in the street, now in the squares,
    and at every corner she lies in wait.
13 She seizes him and kisses him,
    and with impudent face she says to him:
14 "I had to offer sacrifices,
    and today I have paid my vows;
15 so now I have come out to meet you,
    to seek you eagerly, and I have found you!
16 I have decked my couch with coverings,
    colored spreads of Egyptian linen;
17 I have perfumed my bed with myrrh,
    aloes, and cinnamon.
18 Come, let us take our fill of love until morning;
    let us delight ourselves with love.
19 For my husband is not at home;
    he has gone on a long journey.
20 He took a bag of money with him;
    he will not come home until full moon."

21 With much seductive speech she persuades him;
    with her smooth talk she compels him.
22 Right away he follows her,
    and goes like an ox to the slaughter,
    or bounds like a stag toward the trap*r*

28 If a man walks on live coals,
    will his feet not be scorched?
29 So is he who commits adultery with his
    neighbour's wife;
    no one can touch such a woman and go free.
30 Is not a thief contemptible if he steals,
    even to satisfy his appetite when he is hungry?
31 And, if he is caught, must he not pay seven times
    over
    and surrender all that his house contains?
32 So one who commits adultery is a senseless fool:
    he dishonours the woman and ruins himself;
33 he will get nothing but blows and contumely
    and can never live down the disgrace;
34 for a husband's anger is rooted in jealousy
    and he will show no mercy when he takes revenge;
35 compensation will not buy his forgiveness,
    nor will a present, however large, purchase his
    connivance.

7

My son, keep my words;
    store up my commands in your mind.
2 Keep my commands if you would live,
    and treasure my teaching as the apple of your eye.
3 Wear them like a ring on your finger;
    inscribe them on the tablet of your memory.
4 Call wisdom your sister,
    greet understanding as a familiar friend;
5 then they will save you from the adulteress,
    from the loose woman with her seductive words.

6 I glanced out of the window of my house,
    I looked down through the lattice,
7 and I saw among the simpletons,
    among the young men there I noticed
    a lad devoid of all sense.
8 He was passing along the street at her corner,
    stepping out in the direction of her house
9 at twilight, as the day faded,
    at dusk as the night grew dark,
10 and there a woman came to meet him.
    She was dressed like a prostitute, full of wiles,
11 flighty and inconstant,
    a woman never content to stay at home,
12 lying in wait by every corner,
    now in the street, now in the public squares.
13 She caught hold of him and kissed him;
    brazenly she accosted him and said,
14 'I had a sacrifice, an offering, to make
    and I have paid my vows today;
15 so I came out to meet you,
    to look for you, and now I have found you.
16 I have spread coverings on my couch,
    coloured linen from Egypt.
17 I have perfumed my bed
    with myrrh, aloes, and cassia.
18 Come! Let us drown ourselves in pleasure,
    let us abandon ourselves to a night of love;
19 for my husband is not at home.
    He has gone away on a long journey,
20 taking a bag of silver with him;
    he will not be home until full moon.'
21 Persuasively she cajoled him,
    coaxing him with seductive words.
22 He followed her, the simple fool,
    like an ox on its way to be slaughtered,
    like an antelope bounding into the noose,

p Heb *strange*   *q* Meaning of Heb uncertain   *r* Cn Compare Gk:
Meaning of Heb uncertain

NEW AMERICAN BIBLE

28 Or can a man walk on live coals,
and his feet not be scorched?
29 So with him who goes in to his neighbor's wife —
none who touches her shall go unpunished.

30 Men despise not the thief if he steals
to satisfy his appetite when he is hungry;
31 Yet if he be caught he must pay back sevenfold;
all the wealth of his house he may yield up.
32 But he who commits adultery is a fool;
he who would destroy himself does it.
33 A degrading beating will he get,
and his disgrace will not be wiped away;
34 For vindictive is the husband's wrath,
he will have no pity on the day of vengeance;
35 He will not consider any restitution,
nor be satisfied with the greatest gifts.

7 My son, keep my words,
and treasure my commands.
2 Keep my commands and live,
my teaching as the apple of your eye;
3 Bind them on your fingers,
write them on the tablet of your heart.
4 Say to Wisdom, "You are my sister!"
call Understanding, "Friend!"
5 That they may keep you from another's wife,
from the adulteress with her smooth words.
6 For at the window of my house,
through my lattice I looked out —

7 And I saw among the simple ones,
I observed among the young men,
a youth with no sense,
8 Going along the street near the corner,
then walking in the direction of her house —
9 In the twilight, at dusk of day,
at the time of the dark of night.
10 And lo! the woman comes to meet him,
robed like a harlot, with secret designs —
11 She is fickle and unruly,
in her home her feet cannot rest;
12 Now she is in the streets, now in the open squares,
and at every corner she lurks in ambush —
13 When she seizes him, she kisses him,
and with an impudent look says to him:

14 "I owed peace offerings,
and today I have fulfilled my vows;
15 So I came out to meet you,
to look for you, and I have found you!
16 With coverlets I have spread my couch,
with brocaded cloths of Egyptian linen;
17 I have sprinkled my bed with myrrh,
with aloes, and with cinnamon.

18 "Come, let us drink our fill of love,
until morning, let us feast on love!
19 For my husband is not at home,
he has gone on a long journey;
20 A bag of money he took with him,
not till the full moon will he return home."

21 She wins him over by her repeated urging,
with her smooth lips she leads him astray;
22 He follows her stupidly,
like an ox that is led to slaughter;
Like a stag that minces toward the net,

NEW JERUSALEM BIBLE

28 Can you walk on red-hot coals
without burning your feet?
29 Just so, the man who makes love to his
neighbour's wife:
no one who touches her will get off unpunished.
30 People attach but little blame to a thief
who steals only to satisfy his hunger;
31 yet even he, if caught, will have to repay sevenfold
and hand over all his family resources.
32 But the adulterer has no sense;
he works his own destruction.
33 All he will get is blows and contempt,
and dishonour never to be blotted out.
34 For jealousy inflames the husband
who will show no mercy when the day comes
for revenge;
35 he will not consider any compensation;
lavish what gifts you may, he will not be
placated.

7 My child, keep my words,
and treasure my precepts,
2 keep my precepts and you will live,
keep my teaching as the apple of your eye.
3 Bind these to your fingers,
write them on the tablet of your heart.
4 Say to Wisdom, 'You are my sister!'
Call Understanding your relation,
5 to save yourself from the woman that belongs to
another,
from the stranger, with her seductive words.

6 While I was at the window of my house,
I was looking out through the lattice
7 and I saw, among the callow youths,
I noticed among the lads,
one boy who had no sense.
8 Going along the lane, near the corner where she
lives,
he reaches the path to her house,
9 at twilight when day is declining,
at dead of night and in the dark.
10 And look, a woman is coming to meet him,
dressed like a prostitute, false of heart.
11 She is loud and brazen;
her feet cannot rest at home.
12 Once in the street, once in the square,
she lurks at every corner.
13 She catches hold of him, she kisses him,
the bold-faced creature says to him,

14 'I had to offer a communion sacrifice,
I have discharged my vows today;
15 that is why I came out to meet you,
to look for you, and now I have found you.
16 I have spread coverlets over my divan,
embroidered stuff, Egyptian material,
17 I have sprinkled my bed with myrrh,
with aloes and cinnamon.

18 Come on, we'll make love as much as we like, till
morning.
Let us enjoy the delights of love!
19 For my husband is not at home,
he has gone on a very long journey,
20 taking his moneybags with him;
he will not be back till the moon is full.'
21 With her persistent coaxing she overcomes him,
lures him on with her wheedling patter.
22 Forthwith he follows her,
like an ox on its way to the slaughterhouse,
like a madman on his way to the stocks,

NEW REVISED STANDARD VERSION	REVISED ENGLISH BIBLE

NEW REVISED STANDARD VERSION

23   until an arrow pierces its entrails.
    He is like a bird rushing into a snare,
      not knowing that it will cost him his life.

24   And now, my children, listen to me,
    and be attentive to the words of my mouth.

25   Do not let your hearts turn aside to her ways;
    do not stray into her paths.

26   for many are those she has laid low,
    and numerous are her victims.

27   Her house is the way to Sheol,
    going down to the chambers of death.

8   Does not wisdom call,
    and does not understanding raise her voice?

2   On the heights, beside the way,
    at the crossroads she takes her stand;

3   beside the gates in front of the town,
    at the entrance of the portals she cries out:

4   "To you, O people, I call,
    and my cry is to all that live.

5   O simple ones, learn prudence;
    acquire intelligence, you who lack it.

6   Hear, for I will speak noble things,
    and from my lips will come what is right;

7   for my mouth will utter truth;
    wickedness is an abomination to my lips.

8   All the words of my mouth are righteous;
    there is nothing twisted or crooked in them.

9   They are all straight to one who understands
    and right to those who find knowledge.

10   Take my instruction instead of silver,
    and knowledge rather than choice gold;

11   for wisdom is better than jewels,
    and all that you may desire cannot compare
      with her.

12   I, wisdom, live with prudence,*s*
    and I attain knowledge and discretion.

13   The fear of the LORD is hatred of evil.
    Pride and arrogance and the way of evil
    and perverted speech I hate.

14   I have good advice and sound wisdom;
    I have insight, I have strength.

15   By me kings reign,
    and rulers decree what is just;

16   by me rulers rule,
    and nobles, all who govern rightly.

17   I love those who love me,
    and those who seek me diligently find me.

18   Riches and honor are with me,
    enduring wealth and prosperity.

19   My fruit is better than gold, even fine gold,
    and my yield than choice silver.

20   I walk in the way of righteousness,
    along the paths of justice,

21   endowing with wealth those who love me,
    and filling their treasuries.

22   The LORD created me at the beginning*t* of his
      work,*u*
    the first of his acts of long ago.

23   Ages ago I was set up,
    at the first, before the beginning of the earth.

24   When there were no depths I was brought forth,
    when there were no springs abounding with
      water.

REVISED ENGLISH BIBLE

23 like a bird hurrying into the trap;
    he did not know he was risking his life
    until the arrow pierced his vitals.

24 But now, my sons, listen to me,
    and attend to what I say.

25 Do not let desire entice you into her ways,
    do not stray down her paths;

26 many has she wounded and laid low,
    and her victims are without number.

27 Her house is the entrance to Sheol,
    leading down to the halls of death.

8 HEAR how wisdom calls
    and understanding lifts her voice.

2 She takes her stand at the crossroads,
    by the wayside, at the top of the hill;

3 beside the gate, at the entrance to the city,
    at the approach by the portals she cries aloud:

4 'It is to you I call,
    to all mankind I appeal:

5 understand, you simpletons, what it is to be
      shrewd;
    you stupid people, understand what it is to have
      sense.

6 Listen! For I shall speak clearly,
    you will have plain speech from me;

7 for I speak nothing but truth,
    and my lips detest wicked talk.

8 All that I say is right,
    not a word is twisted or crooked.

9 All is straightforward to those with understanding,
    all is plain to those who have knowledge.

10 Choose my instruction rather than silver,
    knowledge rather than pure gold;

11 for wisdom is better than red coral,
    and no jewel can match her.

12 'I am wisdom, I bestow shrewdness
    and show the way to knowledge and discretion.

13 To fear the LORD is to hate evil.
    Pride, arrogance, evil ways,
    subversive talk, all those I hate.

14 From me come advice and ability;
    understanding and power are mine.

15 Through me kings hold sway
    and governors enact just laws.

16 Through me princes wield authority,
    from me all rulers on earth derive their rank.

17 Those who love me I love,
    and those who search for me will find me.

18 In my hands are riches and honour,
    boundless wealth and prosperity.

19 My harvest is better even than fine gold,
    and my revenue better than choice silver.

20 I follow the course of justice
    and keep to the path of equity.

21 I endow with riches those who love me;
    I shall fill their treasuries.

22 'The LORD created me the first of his works
    long ago, before all else that he made.

23 I was formed in earliest times,
    at the beginning, before earth itself.

24 I was born when there was yet no ocean,
    when there were no springs brimming with water.

---

s Meaning of Heb uncertain   *t* Or *me as the beginning*
u Heb *way*

7:27 Sheol: *or* the underworld.   8:16 **rulers on earth:** *so some
MSS; others* who rule in righteousness.

23   till an arrow pierces its liver;
    Like a bird that rushes into a snare,
      unaware that its life is at stake.

24 So now, O children, listen to me,
    be attentive to the words of my mouth!
25 Let not your heart turn to her ways,
    go not astray in her paths;
26 For many are those she has struck down dead,
    numerous, those she has slain.
27 Her house is made up of ways to the nether world,
    leading down into the chambers of death.

8   Does not Wisdom call,
    and Understanding raise her voice?
2 On the top of the heights along the road,
    at the crossroads she takes her stand;
3 By the gates at the approaches of the city,
    in the entryways she cries aloud:
4 "To you, O men, I call;
    my appeal is to the children of men.
5 You simple ones, gain resource,
    you fools, gain sense.
6 "Give heed! for noble things I speak;
    honesty opens my lips.
7 Yes, the truth my mouth recounts,
    but wickedness my lips abhor.
8 Sincere are all the words of my mouth,
    no one of them is wily or crooked;
9 All of them are plain to the man of intelligence,
    and right to those who attain knowledge.
10 Receive my instruction in preference to silver,
    and knowledge rather than choice gold.
11 [For Wisdom is better than corals,
    and no choice possession can compare with
      her.]

12 "I, Wisdom, dwell with experience,
    and judicious knowledge I attain.
13 [The fear of the LORD is to hate evil;]
    Pride, arrogance, the evil way,
    and the perverse mouth I hate.
14 Mine are counsel and advice;
    Mine is strength; I am understanding.
15 By me kings reign,
    and lawgivers establish justice;
16 By me princes govern,
    and nobles; all the rulers of earth.

17 "Those who love me I also love,
    and those who seek me find me.
18 With me are riches and honor,
    enduring wealth and prosperity.
19 My fruit is better than gold, yes, than pure gold,
    and my revenue than choice silver.
20 On the way of duty I walk,
    along the paths of justice,
21 Granting wealth to those who love me,
    and filling their treasuries.

22 "The LORD begot me, the firstborn of his ways,
    the forerunner of his prodigies of long ago;
23 From of old I was poured forth,
    at the first, before the earth.
24 When there were no depths I was brought forth,
    when there were no fountains or springs
      of water;

23 until an arrow pierces him to the liver,
    like the bird that dashes into the net
      without realising that its life is at stake.
24 And now, son, listen to me,
    pay attention to the words I have to say:
25 do not let your heart stray into her ways,
    or wander into her paths;
26 she has done so many to death,
    and the strongest have all been her victims.
27 Her house is the way to Sheol,
    the descent to the courts of death.

8   Is not Wisdom calling?
    Is not Understanding raising her voice?
2 On the heights overlooking the road,
    at the crossways, she takes her stand;
3 by the gates, at the entrance to the city,
    on the access-roads, she cries out,
4 'I am calling to you, all people,
    my words are addressed to all humanity.
5 Simpletons, learn how to behave,
    fools, come to your senses.
6 Listen, I have something important to tell you,
    when I speak, my words are right.
7 My mouth proclaims the truth,
    for evil is abhorrent to my lips.
8 All the words from my mouth are upright,
    nothing false there, nothing crooked,
9 everything plain, if you can understand,
    straight, if you have acquired knowledge.
10 Accept my discipline rather than silver,
    and knowledge of me in preference to finest
      gold.
11 For Wisdom is more precious than jewels,
    and nothing else is so worthy of desire.

12 'I, Wisdom, share house with Discretion,
    I am mistress of the art of thought.
13 (Fear of Yahweh means hatred of evil.)
    I hate pride and arrogance,
    wicked behaviour and a lying mouth.
14 To me belong good advice and prudence,
    I am perception: power is mine!
15 By me monarchs rule
    and princes decree what is right;
16 by me rulers govern,
    so do nobles, the lawful authorities.
17 I love those who love me;
    whoever searches eagerly for me finds me.
18 With me are riches and honour,
    lasting wealth and saving justice.
19 The fruit I give is better than gold, even the finest,
    the return I make is better than pure silver.
20 I walk in the way of uprightness
    in the path of justice,
21 to endow my friends with my wealth
    and to fill their treasuries.

22 'Yahweh created me, *d* first-fruits of his
      fashioning,
    before the oldest of his works.
23 From everlasting, I was firmly set,
    from the beginning, before the earth came into
      being.
24 The deep was not, when I was born,
    nor were the springs with their abounding
      waters.

d **8** Wisdom's creation by God was on a different plane to all his other
works. Wisdom almost seems to be a distinct personality, sharing in
God's activity, and his agent in the world. The concept given here
will be used in the NT to express Christ's relationship to his Father.

NEW REVISED STANDARD VERSION	REVISED ENGLISH BIBLE

NEW REVISED STANDARD VERSION

25 Before the mountains had been shaped,
    before the hills, I was brought forth—
26 when he had not yet made earth and fields,[v]
    or the world's first bits of soil.
27 When he established the heavens, I was there,
    when he drew a circle on the face of the deep,
28 when he made firm the skies above,
    when he established the fountains of the deep,
29 when he assigned to the sea its limit,
    so that the waters might not transgress his
      command,
    when he marked out the foundations of the earth,
30   then I was beside him, like a master worker;[w]
    and I was daily his[x] delight,
    rejoicing before him always,
31 rejoicing in his inhabited world
    and delighting in the human race.

32 And now, my children, listen to me:
    happy are those who keep my ways.
33 Hear instruction and be wise,
    and do not neglect it.
34 Happy is the one who listens to me,
    watching daily at my gates,
    waiting beside my doors.
35 For whoever finds me finds life
    and obtains favor from the LORD;
36 but those who miss me injure themselves;
    all who hate me love death."

9 Wisdom has built her house,
    she has hewn her seven pillars.
2 She has slaughtered her animals, she has mixed
      her wine,
    she has also set her table.
3 She has sent out her servant-girls, she calls
    from the highest places in the town,
4 "You that are simple, turn in here!"
    To those without sense she says,
5 "Come, eat of my bread
    and drink of the wine I have mixed.
6 Lay aside immaturity,[y] and live,
    and walk in the way of insight."

7 Whoever corrects a scoffer wins abuse;
    whoever rebukes the wicked gets hurt.
8 A scoffer who is rebuked will only hate you;
    the wise, when rebuked, will love you.
9 Give instruction[z] to the wise, and they will
      become wiser still;
    teach the righteous and they will gain in
      learning.
10 The fear of the LORD is the beginning of wisdom,
    and the knowledge of the Holy One is insight.
11 For by me your days will be multiplied,
    and years will be added to your life.
12 If you are wise, you are wise for yourself;
    if you scoff, you alone will bear it.

13 The foolish woman is loud;
    she is ignorant and knows nothing.
14 She sits at the door of her house,
    on a seat at the high places of the town,
15 calling to those who pass by,
    who are going straight on their way,
16 "You who are simple, turn in here!"
    And to those without sense she says,

REVISED ENGLISH BIBLE

25 Before the mountains were settled in their place,
    before the hills I was born,
26 when as yet he had made neither land nor streams
    nor the mass of the earth's soil.
27 When he set the heavens in place I was there,
    when he girdled the ocean with the horizon,
28 when he fixed the canopy of clouds overhead
    and confined the springs of the deep,
29 when he prescribed limits for the sea
    so that the waters do not transgress his command,
    when he made earth's foundations firm.
30 Then I was at his side each day,
    his darling and delight,
    playing in his presence continually,
31 playing over his whole world,
    while my delight was in mankind.

32 'Now, sons, listen to me;
    happy are those who keep to my ways.
33 Listen to instruction and grow wise;
    do not ignore it.
34 Happy the one who listens to me,
    watching daily at my threshold
    with his eyes on the doorway!
35 For whoever finds me finds life
    and wins favour with the LORD,
36 but whoever fails to find me deprives himself,
    and all who hate me are in love with death.'

9 Wisdom has built her house;
    she has hewn her seven pillars.
2 Now, having slaughtered a beast, spiced her wine,
    and spread her table,
3 she has sent her maidens to proclaim
    from the highest point of the town:
4 'Let the simple turn in here.'
    She says to him who lacks sense,
5 'Come, eat the food I have prepared
    and taste the wine that I have spiced.
6 Abandon the company of simpletons and you will
      live,
    you will advance in understanding.'

7 Correct an insolent person, and you earn abuse;
    reprove a bad one, and you will acquire his faults.
8 Do not reprove the insolent person or he will hate
      you;
    reprove a wise one, and he will be your friend.
9 Lecture a wise person, and he will grow wiser still;
    teach a righteous one, and he will add to his
      learning.
10 The first step to wisdom is the fear of the LORD,
    and knowledge of the Most Holy One is
      understanding;
11 for through me your days will be increased
    and years be added to your life.
12 If you are wise, it will be to your advantage;
    if you are arrogant, you alone must bear the blame.

13 The Lady Stupidity is a flighty creature;
    a fool, she cares for nothing.
14 She sits at the door of her house,
    on a seat in the highest part of the town,
15 to invite the passers-by indoors
    as they hurry on their way:
16 'Turn in here, simpleton,' she says,
    and to him who lacks sense she says,

---

[v] Meaning of Heb uncertain   [w] Another reading is *little child*
[x] Gk: Heb lacks *his*   [y] Or *simpleness*   [z] Heb lacks *instruction*

8:26 **streams:** *or* fields. **the mass:** *or* the first.   8:30 **darling:** *or* craftsman; *Heb. obscure.*

25 Before the mountains were settled into place,
  before the hills, I was brought forth;
26 While as yet the earth and the fields were
    not made,
  nor the first clods of the world.

27 "When he established the heavens I was there,
  when he marked out the vault over the face of
    the deep;
28 When he made firm the skies above,
  when he fixed fast the foundations of the earth;
29 When he set for the sea its limit,
  so that the waters should not transgress
    his command;
30 Then was I beside him as his craftsman,
  and I was his delight day by day,
  Playing before him all the while,
31   playing on the surface of his earth;
  and I found delight in the sons of men.

32 "So now, O children, listen to me;
33   instruction and wisdom do not reject!
  Happy the man who obeys me,
  and happy those who keep my ways,
34 Happy the man watching daily at my gates,
  waiting at my doorposts;
35 For he who finds me finds life,
  and wins favor from the LORD;
36 But he who misses me harms himself;
  all who hate me love death."

9
  Wisdom has built her house,
    she has set up her seven columns;
2 She has dressed her meat, mixed her wine,
  yes, she has spread her table.
3 She has sent out her maidens; she calls
  from the heights out over the city:
4 "Let whoever is simple turn in here;
  to him who lacks understanding, I say,
5 Come, eat of my food,
  and drink of the wine I have mixed!
6 Forsake foolishness that you may live;
  advance in the way of understanding.
11 For by me your days will be multiplied
  and the years of your life increased."

7 He who corrects an arrogant man earns insult;
  and he who reproves a wicked man
    incurs opprobrium.
8 Reprove not an arrogant man, lest he hate you;
  reprove a wise man, and he will love you.
9 Instruct a wise man, and he becomes still wiser;
  teach a just man, and he advances in learning.

10 The beginning of wisdom is the fear of the LORD,
  and knowledge of the Holy One is understanding.
12 If you are wise, it is to your own advantage;
  and if you are arrogant, you alone shall bear it.

13 The woman Folly is fickle,
  she is inane, and knows nothing.
14 She sits at the door of her house
  upon a seat on the city heights,
15 Calling to passers-by
  as they go on their straight way:
16 "Let whoever is simple turn in here,
  or who lacks understanding; for to him I say,

25 Before the mountains were settled,
  before the hills, I came to birth;
26 before he had made the earth, the countryside,
  and the first elements of the world.
27 When he fixed the heavens firm, I was there,
  when he drew a circle on the surface of the
    deep,
28 when he thickened the clouds above,
  when the sources of the deep began to swell,
29 when he assigned the sea its boundaries
  — and the waters will not encroach on the
    shore —
  when he traced the foundations of the earth,
30 I was beside the master craftsman,
  delighting him day after day,
  ever at play in his presence,
31 at play everywhere on his earth,
  delighting to be with the children of men.

32 'And now, my children, listen to me.
  Happy are those who keep my ways.
33 Listen to instruction and become wise,
  do not reject it.
34 Blessed, whoever listens to me,
  who day after day keeps watch at my gates
  to guard my portals.
35 For whoever finds me finds life,
  and obtains the favour of Yahweh;
36 but whoever misses me harms himself,
  all who hate me are in love with death.'

9
  Wisdom has built herself a house,
    she has hewn her seven pillars,
2 she has slaughtered her beasts, drawn her wine,
  she has laid her table.
3 She has despatched her maidservants
  and proclaimed from the heights above the city,
4 'Who is simple? Let him come this way.'
  To the fool she says,
5 'Come and eat my bread,
  drink the wine which I have drawn!
6 Leave foolishness behind and you will live,
  go forwards in the ways of perception.'

7 Reprove a mocker and you attract contempt,
  rebuke the wicked and you attract dishonour.
8 Do not rebuke the mocker, he will hate you.
  Rebuke the wise and he will love you for it.
9 Be open with the wise, he grows wiser still,
  teach the upright, he will gain yet more.
10 The first principle of wisdom is the fear of
    Yahweh,
  What God's holy ones know — this is
    understanding.
11 For by me your days will be multiplied,
  and your years of life increased.
12 Are you wise? You are wise to your own good.
  A mocker? The burden is yours alone.

13 A silly woman acts on impulse,
  is foolish and knows nothing.
14 She sits at the door of her house,
  on a throne high up in the city,
15 calling to the passers-by,
  who are walking straight past on their way,
16 'Who is simple? Turn aside, come over here.'
  To the fool she says,

17 "Stolen water is sweet,
    and bread eaten in secret is pleasant."
18 But they do not know that the dead[a] are there,
    that her guests are in the depths of Sheol.

17 'Stolen water is sweet
    and bread eaten in secret tastes good.'
18 Little does he know that the dead are there,
    that her guests are in the depths of Sheol.

10

The proverbs of Solomon.

A wise child makes a glad father,
    but a foolish child is a mother's grief.
2 Treasures gained by wickedness do not profit,
    but righteousness delivers from death.
3 The LORD does not let the righteous go hungry,
    but he thwarts the craving of the wicked.
4 A slack hand causes poverty,
    but the hand of the diligent makes rich.
5 A child who gathers in summer is prudent,
    but a child who sleeps in harvest brings shame.
6 Blessings are on the head of the righteous,
    but the mouth of the wicked conceals violence.
7 The memory of the righteous is a blessing,
    but the name of the wicked will rot.
8 The wise of heart will heed commandments,
    but a babbling fool will come to ruin.
9 Whoever walks in integrity walks securely,
    but whoever follows perverse ways will be
      found out.
10 Whoever winks the eye causes trouble,
    but the one who rebukes boldly makes peace.[b]
11 The mouth of the righteous is a fountain of life,
    but the mouth of the wicked conceals violence.
12 Hatred stirs up strife,
    but love covers all offenses.
13 On the lips of one who has understanding wisdom
      is found,
    but a rod is for the back of one who lacks
      sense.
14 The wise lay up knowledge,
    but the babbling of a fool brings ruin near.
15 The wealth of the rich is their fortress;
    the poverty of the poor is their ruin.
16 The wage of the righteous leads to life,
    the gain of the wicked to sin.
17 Whoever heeds instruction is on the path to life,
    but one who rejects a rebuke goes astray.
18 Lying lips conceal hatred,
    and whoever utters slander is a fool.
19 When words are many, transgression is not
      lacking,
    but the prudent are restrained in speech.
20 The tongue of the righteous is choice silver;
    the mind of the wicked is of little worth.
21 The lips of the righteous feed many,
    but fools die for lack of sense.
22 The blessing of the LORD makes rich,
    and he adds no sorrow with it.[c]

10

PROVERBS of Solomon:

A wise son is his father's joy,
    but a foolish son is a sorrow to his mother.
2 No good comes of ill-gotten wealth;
    uprightness is a safeguard against death.
3 The LORD will not let the righteous go hungry,
    but he thwarts the desires of the wicked.
4 Idle hands make for penury;
    diligent hands make for riches.
5 A prudent son gathers crops in summer;
    a son who sleeps at harvest is a source of
      disappointment.
6 Blessings are showered on the righteous;
    the speech of the wicked conceals violence.
7 The righteous are remembered in blessings;
    the name of the wicked falls into decay.
8 A person who is wise takes commandments to
      heart,
    but the foolish talker comes to grief.
9 One whose life is pure lives in safety,
    but one whose ways are crooked is brought low.
10 A wink of the eye causes trouble;
    a frank rebuke promotes peace.
11 The words of the righteous are a fountain of life;
    the speech of the wicked conceals violence.
12 Hate is always picking a quarrel,
    but love overlooks every offence.
13 The possessor of understanding has wisdom on his
      lips;
    a rod is in store for the back of the fool.
14 The wise store up knowledge;
    when a fool speaks, ruin is imminent.
15 The wealth of the rich is a strong city,
    but poverty spells disaster for the helpless.
16 The reward of the good leads to life;
    the earnings of the wicked make for a bad end.
17 Heed admonition and you are on the road to life;
    neglect reproof and you miss the way.
18 Lying lips conceal hatred;
    anyone who defames another is foolish.
19 When there is too much talk, offence is never far
      away;
    the prudent hold their tongues.
20 The tongue of the righteous is like pure silver;
    the mind of the wicked is trash.
21 The teaching of the righteous guides many,
    but fools perish through lack of sense.
22 The blessing of the LORD is what brings riches,
    and he sends no sorrow with them.

---

[a] Heb shades   [b] Gk: Heb but a babbling fool will come to ruin
[c] Or and toil adds nothing to it

9:18 **Sheol:** or the underworld.   10:10 **a frank ... peace:** so Gk;
Heb. a foolish talker comes to grief, cp. verse 8.

NEW AMERICAN BIBLE

¹⁷ Stolen water is sweet,
  and bread gotten secretly is pleasing!"
¹⁸ Little he knows that the shades are there,
  that in the depths of the nether world are
  her guests!

10 The Proverbs of Solomon:

A wise son makes his father glad,
  but a foolish son is a grief to his mother.

² Ill-gotten treasures profit nothing,
  but virtue saves from death.

³ The LORD permits not the just to hunger,
  but the craving of the wicked he thwarts.

⁴ The slack hand impoverishes,
  but the hand of the diligent enriches.

⁵ A son who fills the granaries in summer is a credit;
  a son who slumbers during harvest, a disgrace.

⁶ Blessings are for the head of the just,
  but a rod for the back of the fool.

⁷ The memory of the just will be blessed,
  but the name of the wicked will rot.

⁸ A wise man heeds commands,
  but a prating fool will be overthrown.

⁹ He who walks honestly walks securely,
  but he whose ways are crooked will fare badly.

¹⁰ He who winks at a fault causes trouble,
  but he who frankly reproves promotes peace.

¹¹ A fountain of life is the mouth of the just,
  but the mouth of the wicked conceals violence.

¹² Hatred stirs up disputes,
  but love covers all offenses.

¹³ On the lips of the intelligent is found wisdom,
  [but the mouth of the wicked conceals violence].

¹⁴ Wise men store up knowledge,
  but the mouth of a fool is imminent ruin.

¹⁵ The rich man's wealth is his strong city;
  the ruination of the lowly is their poverty.

¹⁶ The just man's recompense leads to life,
  the gains of the wicked, to sin.

¹⁷ A path to life is his who heeds admonition,
  but he who disregards reproof goes astray.

¹⁸ It is the lips of the liar that conceal hostility;
  but he who spreads accusations is a fool.

¹⁹ Where words are many, sin is not wanting;
  but he who restrains his lips does well.

²⁰ Like choice silver is the just man's tongue;
  the heart of the wicked is of little worth.

²¹ The just man's lips nourish many,
  but fools die for want of sense.

²² It is the LORD's blessing that brings wealth,
  and no effort can substitute for it.

NEW JERUSALEM BIBLE

¹⁷ 'Stolen waters are sweet,
  and bread tastes better when eaten in secret.'
¹⁸ But the fool does not know that this is where the
  Shades are
  and that her guests are already in the vales of
  Sheol.

10 The proverbs of Solomon.

A wise child is a father's joy, ᵉ
  a foolish child a mother's grief.

² Treasures wickedly come by give no benefit,
  but uprightness brings delivery from death. ᶠ

³ Yahweh does not let the upright go hungry,
  but he thwarts the greed of the wicked.

⁴ A slack hand brings poverty,
  but the hand of the diligent brings wealth.

⁵ Reaping at harvest-time is the mark of the prudent,
  sleeping at harvest-time is the sign of the
  worthless.

⁶ Blessings are on the head of the upright,
  but the mouth of the godless is a cover for
  violence.

⁷ The upright is remembered with blessings,
  the name of the wicked rots away.

⁸ The wise of heart takes orders,
  but a gabbling fool heads for ruin.

⁹ Anyone whose ways are honourable walks secure,
  but whoever follows crooked ways is soon
  unmasked.

¹⁰ A wink of the eye brings trouble,
  a bold rebuke brings peace.

¹¹ The mouth of the upright is a life-giving fountain,
  but the mouth of the godless is a cover for
  violence.

¹² Hatred provokes disputes,
  but love excuses all offences.

¹³ On the lips of the discerning is found wisdom,
  on the back of a fool, the stick.

¹⁴ Wise people store up knowledge,
  but the mouth of a fool makes ruin imminent.

¹⁵ The wealth of the rich is their stronghold, ᵍ
  poverty is the undoing of the weak.

¹⁶ The wage of the upright affords life,
  but sin is all the wicked earns.

¹⁷ Whoever abides by discipline, walks towards life,
  whoever ignores correction goes astray.

¹⁸ Liars' lips are a cover for hatred,
  whoever utters slander is a fool.

¹⁹ A flood of words is never without fault;
  whoever controls the lips is wise.

²⁰ The tongue of the upright is purest silver,
  the heart of the wicked is of trumpery value.

²¹ The lips of the upright nourish many peoples,
  but fools die for want of sense.

²² The blessing of Yahweh is what brings riches,
  to this, hard toil has nothing to add.

ᵉ **10** = 15:20.   ᶠ **10** = 11:4.   ᵍ **10** = 18:11.

NEW REVISED STANDARD VERSION	REVISED ENGLISH BIBLE

NEW REVISED STANDARD VERSION

23 Doing wrong is like sport to a fool,
  but wise conduct is pleasure to a person of
    understanding.
24 What the wicked dread will come upon them,
  but the desire of the righteous will be granted.
25 When the tempest passes, the wicked are no
    more,
  but the righteous are established forever.
26 Like vinegar to the teeth, and smoke to the eyes,
  so are the lazy to their employers.
27 The fear of the LORD prolongs life,
  but the years of the wicked will be short.
28 The hope of the righteous ends in gladness,
  but the expectation of the wicked comes to
    nothing.
29 The way of the LORD is a stronghold for the
    upright,
  but destruction for evildoers.
30 The righteous will never be removed,
  but the wicked will not remain in the land.
31 The mouth of the righteous brings forth wisdom,
  but the perverse tongue will be cut off.
32 The lips of the righteous know what is
    acceptable,
  but the mouth of the wicked what is perverse.

11 A false balance is an abomination to the LORD,
  but an accurate weight is his delight.
2 When pride comes, then comes disgrace;
  but wisdom is with the humble.
3 The integrity of the upright guides them,
  but the crookedness of the treacherous destroys
    them.
4 Riches do not profit in the day of wrath,
  but righteousness delivers from death.
5 The righteousness of the blameless keeps their
    ways straight,
  but the wicked fall by their own wickedness.
6 The righteousness of the upright saves them,
  but the treacherous are taken captive by their
    schemes.
7 When the wicked die, their hope perishes,
  and the expectation of the godless comes to
    nothing.
8 The righteous are delivered from trouble,
  and the wicked get into it instead.
9 With their mouths the godless would destroy their
    neighbors,
  but by knowledge the righteous are delivered.
10 When it goes well with the righteous, the city
    rejoices;
  and when the wicked perish, there is jubilation.
11 By the blessing of the upright a city is exalted,
  but it is overthrown by the mouth of the
    wicked.
12 Whoever belittles another lacks sense,
  but an intelligent person remains silent.
13 A gossip goes about telling secrets,
  but one who is trustworthy in spirit keeps a
    confidence.
14 Where there is no guidance, a nation*d* falls,
  but in an abundance of counselors there is
    safety.

REVISED ENGLISH BIBLE

23 Lewdness is entertainment for the stupid,
  wisdom a delight to men of understanding.
24 What the wicked dread will overtake them;
  what the righteous desire will be granted.
25 When the whirlwind has swept past, the wicked are
    gone,
  but the righteous are firmly established for ever.
26 Like vinegar to the teeth or smoke to the eyes,
  so is the lazy servant to his master.
27 The fear of the LORD brings length of days;
  the years of the wicked are cut short.
28 The hope of the righteous blossoms;
  the expectation of the wicked withers away.
29 The LORD is a refuge for the blameless,
  but he brings destruction on evildoers.
30 The righteous man will never be shaken;
  the wicked will not remain in the land.
31 Wisdom flows from the mouth of the righteous;
  the subversive tongue will be torn out.
32 The righteous suit words to the occasion;
  the wicked know only subversive talk.

11 False scales are an abomination to the LORD,
  but accurate weights win his favour.
2 When pride comes in, in comes contempt,
  but wisdom goes hand in hand with modesty.
3 Integrity is a guide for the upright;
  the perfidious are ruined by their own duplicity.
4 Wealth avails naught in the day of wrath,
  but uprightness is a safeguard against death.
5 By uprightness the blameless keep their course,
  but the wicked are brought down by their own
    wickedness.
6 Uprightness saves the righteous,
  but the perfidious are trapped by their own lies.
7 When someone wicked dies, all his hopes perish,
  and any expectation of affluence ends.
8 The righteous are rescued from disaster,
  and the wicked plunge into it.
9 By their words the godless try to ruin others,
  but when the righteous plead for them they are
    saved.
10 A city rejoices in the prosperity of the righteous,
  and when the wicked perish there is jubilation.
11 By the blessing of the upright a city is raised to
    greatness,
  but the words of the wicked tear it down.
12 One who belittles others is lacking in sense;
  someone of understanding holds his peace.
13 A tale-bearer gives away secrets,
  but a trustworthy person respects a confidence.
14 For want of skilful strategy an army is lost;
  victory is the fruit of long planning.

d Or an army   11:6 **their own:** so Gk; Heb. omits.

NEW AMERICAN BIBLE	NEW JERUSALEM BIBLE

NEW AMERICAN BIBLE

23 Crime is the entertainment of the fool;
   so is wisdom for the man of sense.

24 What the wicked man fears will befall him,
   but the desire of the just will be granted.

25 When the tempest passes, the wicked man is
   no more;
   but the just man is established forever.

26 As vinegar to the teeth, and smoke to the eyes,
   is the sluggard to those who use him as
   a messenger.

27 The fear of the LORD prolongs life,
   but the years of the wicked are brief.

28 The hope of the just brings them joy,
   but the expectation of the wicked comes to
   nought.

29 The LORD is a stronghold to him who
   walks honestly,
   but to evildoers, their downfall.

30 The just man will never be disturbed,
   but the wicked will not abide in the land.

31 The mouth of the just yields wisdom,
   but the perverse tongue will be cut off.

32 The lips of the just know how to please,
   but the mouth of the wicked, how to pervert.

11 False scales are an abomination to the LORD,
   but a full weight is his delight.

2 When pride comes, disgrace comes;
   but with the humble is wisdom.

3 The honesty of the upright guides them;
   the faithless are ruined by their duplicity.

4 Wealth is useless on the day of wrath,
   but virtue saves from death.

5 The honest man's virtue makes his way straight,
   but by his wickedness the wicked man falls.

6 The virtue of the upright saves them,
   but the faithless are caught in their own intrigue.

7 When a wicked man dies his hope perishes,
   and what is expected from strength comes
   to nought.

8 The just man escapes trouble,
   and the wicked man falls into it in his stead.

9 With his mouth the impious man would ruin
   his neighbor,
   but through their knowledge the just make
   their escape.

10 When the just prosper, the city rejoices;
   and when the wicked perish, there is jubilation.

11 Through the blessing of the righteous the city
   is exalted,
   but through the mouth of the wicked it
   is overthrown.

12 He who reviles his neighbor has no sense,
   but the intelligent man keeps silent.

13 A newsmonger reveals secrets,
   but a trustworthy man keeps a confidence.

14 For lack of guidance a people falls;
   security lies in many counselors.

NEW JERUSALEM BIBLE

23 A fool takes pleasure in doing wrong,
   the intelligent in cultivating wisdom.

24 What the wicked fears overtakes him,
   what the upright desires comes to him as a
   present.

25 When the storm is over, the wicked is no more,
   but the upright stands firm for ever.

26 As vinegar to the teeth, smoke to the eyes,
   so the sluggard to the one who sends him.

27 The fear of Yahweh adds length to life,
   the years of the wicked will be cut short.

28 The hope of the upright is joy,
   the expectations of the wicked come to nothing.

29 The way of Yahweh is a rampart for the honest,
   for evil-doers nothing but ruin.

30 The upright will never have to give way,
   but the land will offer no home for the wicked.

31 The mouth of the upright utters wisdom,
   the tongue that deceives will be cut off.

32 The lips of the upright know about kindness,
   the mouth of the wicked about deceit.

11 A false balance is abhorrent to Yahweh,
   a just weight is pleasing to him.

2 Pride comes first; disgrace soon follows;
   with the humble is wisdom found.

3 The honest have their own honesty for guidance,
   the treacherous are ruined by their own perfidy.

4 In the day of retribution riches will be useless,
   but uprightness delivers from death. *h*

5 The uprightness of the good makes their way
   straight,
   the wicked fall by their own wickedness.

6 Their uprightness sets the honest free,
   the treacherous are imprisoned by their own
   desires.

7 The hope of the wicked perishes with death,
   hope placed in riches comes to nothing.

8 The upright escapes affliction,
   the wicked incurs it instead.

9 Through his mouth the godless is the ruin of his
   neighbour,
   but by knowledge the upright are safeguarded.

10 When the upright prosper the city rejoices,
   when the wicked are ruined there is a shout of
   joy.

11 A city is raised on the blessing of the honest,
   and demolished by the mouth of the wicked.

12 Whoever looks down on a neighbour lacks good
   sense;
   the intelligent keeps a check on the tongue.

13 A tittle-tattler lets secrets out,
   the trustworthy keeps things hidden.

14 For want of leadership a people perishes,
   safety lies in many advisers.

h **11** = 10:2.

| NEW REVISED STANDARD VERSION | REVISED ENGLISH BIBLE |

15 To guarantee loans for a stranger brings trouble,
but there is safety in refusing to do so.
16 A gracious woman gets honor,
but she who hates virtue is covered with
shame.*e*
The timid become destitute,*f*
but the aggressive gain riches.
17 Those who are kind reward themselves,
but the cruel do themselves harm.
18 The wicked earn no real gain,
but those who sow righteousness get a true
reward.
19 Whoever is steadfast in righteousness will live,
but whoever pursues evil will die.
20 Crooked minds are an abomination to the LORD,
but those of blameless ways are his delight.
21 Be assured, the wicked will not go unpunished,
but those who are righteous will escape.
22 Like a gold ring in a pig's snout
is a beautiful woman without good sense.
23 The desire of the righteous ends only in good;
the expectation of the wicked in wrath.
24 Some give freely, yet grow all the richer;
others withhold what is due, and only suffer
want.
25 A generous person will be enriched,
and one who gives water will get water.
26 The people curse those who hold back grain,
but a blessing is on the head of those who sell
it.
27 Whoever diligently seeks good seeks favor,
but evil comes to the one who searches for it.
28 Those who trust in their riches will wither,*g*
but the righteous will flourish like green
leaves.
29 Those who trouble their households will inherit
wind,
and the fool will be servant to the wise.
30 The fruit of the righteous is a tree of life,
but violence*h* takes lives away.
31 If the righteous are repaid on earth,
how much more the wicked and the sinner!

15 Give a pledge for a stranger and you will suffer;
refuse to stand surety and stay safe.
16 A gracious woman gets honour;
a bold man gets only a fortune.
17 Kindness brings its own reward;
cruelty earns trouble for itself.
18 A wicked person earns a delusive profit,
but he who sows goodness reaps a sure reward.
19 Anyone set on righteousness finds life,
but the pursuit of evil leads to death.
20 The LORD detests the crooked heart,
but honesty wins his favour.
21 Depend upon it: an evildoer will not escape
punishment,
but the righteous and all their offspring will go
free.
22 Like a gold ring in a pig's snout
is a beautiful woman without good sense.
23 The righteous desire only what is good;
what the wicked hope for comes to nothing.
24 One may spend freely and yet grow richer;
another is tight-fisted, yet ends in poverty.
25 A generous person enjoys prosperity,
and one who refreshes others will be refreshed.
26 Whoever holds back his grain is cursed by the
people,
but one who sells it earns their blessing.
27 Someone who seeks what is good wins much
favour,
but one who pursues evil finds it recoils upon him.
28 Whoever relies on his wealth is riding for a fall,
but the righteous flourish like leaves sprouting.
29 One who brings trouble on his family inherits the
wind,
and a fool becomes slave to one who is wise.
30 The fruit of the righteous is a tree of life,
but violence results in the taking of life.
31 If the righteous get their deserts on earth,
how much more will the wicked and the sinner!

12 Whoever loves discipline loves knowledge,
but those who hate to be rebuked are stupid.
2 The good obtain favor from the LORD,
but those who devise evil he condemns.
3 No one finds security by wickedness,
but the root of the righteous will never be
moved.
4 A good wife is the crown of her husband,
but she who brings shame is like rottenness in
his bones.
5 The thoughts of the righteous are just;
the advice of the wicked is treacherous.
6 The words of the wicked are a deadly ambush,
but the speech of the upright delivers them.

12 He who loves correction loves knowledge;
he who hates reproof is stupid.
2 The good man wins the LORD's favour,
the schemer his condemnation.
3 No one can be established by wickedness,
but the roots of the righteous will not be
disturbed.
4 A capable wife is her husband's crown;
one who disgraces him is like a canker in his
bones.
5 The purposes of the righteous are just;
the schemes of the wicked are full of deceit.
6 The wicked by their words lay a murderous
ambush,
but the words of the upright save them.

---

e Compare Gk Syr: Heb lacks *but she . . . shame* *f* Gk: Heb lacks
The timid . . . destitute *g* Cn: Heb *fall* *h* Cn Compare Gk Syr:
Heb *a wise man*

11:25 **will be refreshed:** *prob. rdg., cp. Lat.; Heb. obscure.*
11:30 **violence:** *so Gk; Heb. a wise person.*

NEW AMERICAN BIBLE

15 He is in a bad way who becomes surety
for another,
but he who hates giving pledges is safe.

16 A gracious woman wins esteem,
but she who hates virtue is covered with shame.

[The slothful become impoverished,
but the diligent gain wealth.]

17 A kindly man benefits himself,
but a merciless man harms himself.

18 The wicked man makes empty profits,
but he who sows virtue has a sure reward.

19 Virtue directs toward life,
but he who pursues evil does so to his death.

20 The depraved in heart are an abomination to
the LORD,
but those who walk blamelessly are his delight.

21 Truly the evil man shall not go unpunished,
but those who are just shall escape.

22 Like a golden ring in a swine's snout
is a beautiful woman with a
rebellious disposition.

23 The desire of the just ends only in good;
the expectation of the wicked is wrath.

24 One man is lavish yet grows still richer;
another is too sparing, yet is the poorer.

25 He who confers benefits will be amply enriched,
and he who refreshes others will himself
be refreshed.

26 Him who monopolizes grain, the people curse—
but blessings upon the head of him who
distributes it!

27 He who seeks the good commands favor,
but he who pursues evil will have evil
befall him.

28 He who trusts in his riches will fall,
but like green leaves the just flourish.

29 He who upsets his household has empty air for
a heritage;
and the fool will become slave to the wise man.

30 The fruit of virtue is a tree of life,
but violence takes lives away.

31 If the just man is punished on earth,
how much more the wicked and the sinner!

12 He who loves correction loves knowledge,
but he who hates reproof is stupid.

2 The good man wins favor from the LORD,
but the schemer is condemned by him.

3 No man is built up by wickedness,
but the root of the just will never be disturbed.

4 A worthy wife is the crown of her husband,
but a disgraceful one is like rot in his bones.

5 The plans of the just are legitimate;
the designs of the wicked are deceitful.

6 The words of the wicked are a deadly ambush,
but the speech of the upright saves them.

NEW JERUSALEM BIBLE

15 Whoever goes bail for a stranger does himself
harm,
but one who shuns going surety is safe.

16 A gracious woman acquires honour,
violent people acquire wealth.

17 Faithful love brings its own reward,
the inflexible injure their own selves.

18 Disappointment crowns the labours of the wicked,
whoever sows uprightness reaps a solid reward.

19 Whoever establishes uprightness is on the way to
life,
whoever pursues evil, on the way to death.

20 Tortuous hearts are abhorrent to Yahweh,
dear to him, those whose ways are blameless.

21 Be sure of it, the wicked will not go unpunished,
but the race of the upright will come to no
harm.

22 A golden ring in the snout of a pig
is a lovely woman who lacks discretion.

23 The hope of the upright is nothing but good,
the expectation of the wicked is retribution.

24 One scatters money around, yet only adds to his
wealth,
another is excessively mean, but only grows the
poorer.

25 The soul who blesses will prosper,
whoever satisfies others will also be satisfied.

26 The people's curse is on those who hoard the
wheat,
their blessing on the head of those who sell it.

27 Whoever strives for good obtains favour,
whoever looks for evil will get an evil return.

28 Whoever trusts in riches will have a fall,
the upright will flourish like the leaves.

29 Whoever misgoverns a house inherits the wind,
and the fool becomes slave to the wise.

30 The fruit of the upright is a tree of life:
the sage captivates souls.

31 If here on earth the upright gets due reward,
how much more the wicked and the sinner!

12 Whoever loves discipline, loves knowledge,
stupid are those who hate correction.

2 The honest obtains Yahweh's favour,
the schemer incurs his condemnation.

3 No one is made secure by wickedness,
but nothing shakes the roots of the upright.

4 A capable wife, her husband's crown,
a shameless wife, a cancer in his bones.

5 The plans of the upright are honest,
the intrigues of the wicked are full of deceit.

6 The words of the wicked are snares to shed blood,
what the honest say keeps them safe.

NEW REVISED STANDARD VERSION	REVISED ENGLISH BIBLE

NEW REVISED STANDARD VERSION

7 The wicked are overthrown and are no more,
but the house of the righteous will stand.
8 One is commended for good sense,
but a perverse mind is despised.
9 Better to be despised and have a servant,
than to be self-important and lack food.
10 The righteous know the needs of their animals,
but the mercy of the wicked is cruel.
11 Those who till their land will have plenty of
food,
but those who follow worthless pursuits have
no sense.
12 The wicked covet the proceeds of wickedness,*i*
but the root of the righteous bears fruit.
13 The evil are ensnared by the transgression of their
lips,
but the righteous escape from trouble.
14 From the fruit of the mouth one is filled with
good things,
and manual labor has its reward.
15 Fools think their own way is right,
but the wise listen to advice.
16 Fools show their anger at once,
but the prudent ignore an insult.
17 Whoever speaks the truth gives honest evidence,
but a false witness speaks deceitfully.
18 Rash words are like sword thrusts,
but the tongue of the wise brings healing.
19 Truthful lips endure forever,
but a lying tongue lasts only a moment.
20 Deceit is in the mind of those who plan evil,
but those who counsel peace have joy.
21 No harm happens to the righteous,
but the wicked are filled with trouble.
22 Lying lips are an abomination to the LORD,
but those who act faithfully are his delight.
23 One who is clever conceals knowledge,
but the mind of a fool*j* broadcasts folly.
24 The hand of the diligent will rule,
while the lazy will be put to forced labor.
25 Anxiety weighs down the human heart,
but a good word cheers it up.
26 The righteous gives good advice to friends,*k*
but the way of the wicked leads astray.
27 The lazy do not roast*l* their game,
but the diligent obtain precious wealth.*l*
28 In the path of righteousness there is life,
in walking its path there is no death.

13 A wise child loves discipline,*m*
but a scoffer does not listen to rebuke.
2 From the fruit of their words good persons eat
good things,
but the desire of the treacherous is for
wrongdoing.

REVISED ENGLISH BIBLE

7 Once the wicked are down, that is the end of
them,
but the line of the righteous continues.
8 Intelligence is commended,
but a warped mind is despised.
9 It is better to be modest and earn one's living
than to play the grandee on an empty stomach.
10 A right-minded person cares for his beast,
but one who is wicked is cruel at heart.
11 Someone who cultivates his land has plenty to eat,
but one who follows idle pursuits lacks sense.
12 The stronghold of the wicked crumbles like clay,
but the righteous take lasting root.
13 The wicked are ensnared by their own offensive
speech,
but the righteous come safely through trouble.
14 People win success by their words;
they get the reward their work merits.
15 A fool's conduct is right in his own eyes;
to listen to advice shows wisdom.
16 A fool betrays his annoyance at once;
a clever person who is slighted conceals his
feelings.
17 An honest witness comes out with the truth,
but the false one with deceit.
18 Gossip is sharp as a sword,
but the tongue of the wise brings healing.
19 Truthful speech stands firm for ever,
but lies live only for a moment.
20 Those who plot evil delude themselves,
but there is joy for those who seek the common
good.
21 No mischief will befall the righteous,
but the wicked get their fill of adversity.
22 The LORD detests a liar
but delights in honesty.
23 A clever person conceals his knowledge,
but a stupid one blurts out folly.
24 Diligence brings people to power,
but laziness to forced labour.
25 An anxious heart is dispiriting;
a kind word brings cheerfulness.
26 The righteous are freed from evil,
but the wicked take a path that leads astray.
27 The lazy hunter puts up no game;
those who are diligent reap a rich harvest.
28 The way of righteousness leads to life,
but there is a well-worn path to death.

13 A wise son heeds a father's instruction;
the arrogant will not listen to rebuke.
2 The good enjoy the fruit of righteousness,
but violence is meat and drink for the perfidious.

12:12 **The stronghold . . . clay:** *prob. rdg;* Heb. *The wicked covet a
stronghold of crumbling earth.* 12:26 **are. . . evil:** *prob. rdg;
Heb.* let him spy out his friend. 12:27 **those . . . harvest:** *prob.
rdg; Heb. obscure.* 13:1 **heeds:** *prob. rdg, cp. Syriac; Heb.
omits.*

*i Or covet the catch of the wicked j Heb the heart of fools
k Syr: Meaning of Heb uncertain l Meaning of Heb uncertain
m Cn: Heb A wise child the discipline of his father*

NEW AMERICAN BIBLE

NEW JERUSALEM BIBLE

7 The wicked are overthrown and are no more,
   but the house of the just stands firm.

8 According to his good sense a man is praised,
   but one with a warped mind is despised.

9 Better a lowly man who supports himself
   than one of assumed importance who lacks
      bread.

10 The just man takes care of his beast,
    but the heart of the wicked is merciless.

11 He who tills his own land has food in plenty,
    but he who follows idle pursuits is a fool.

12 The stronghold of evil men will be demolished,
    but the root of the just is enduring.

13 In the sin of his lips the evil man is ensnared,
    but the just comes free of trouble.

14 From the fruit of his words a man has his fill of
      good things,
    and the work of his hands comes back to
      reward him.

15 The way of the fool seems right in his own eyes,
    but he who listens to advice is wise.

16 The fool immediately shows his anger,
    but the shrewd man passes over an insult.

17 He tells the truth who states what he is sure of,
    but a lying witness speaks deceitfully.

18 The prating of some men is like sword thrusts,
    but the tongue of the wise is healing.

19 Truthful lips endure forever,
    the lying tongue, for only a moment.

20 Deceit is in the hands of those who plot evil,
    but those who counsel peace have joy.

21 No harm befalls the just,
    but the wicked are overwhelmed
      with misfortune.

22 Lying lips are an abomination to the LORD,
    but those who are truthful are his delight.

23 A shrewd man conceals his knowledge,
    but the hearts of fools gush forth folly.

24 The diligent hand will govern,
    but the slothful will be enslaved.

25 Anxiety in a man's heart depresses it,
    but a kindly word makes it glad.

26 The just man surpasses his neighbor,
    but the way of the wicked leads them astray.

27 The slothful man catches not his prey,
    but the wealth of the diligent man is great.

28 In the path of justice there is life,
    but the abominable way leads to death.

13 A wise son loves correction,
      but the senseless one heeds no rebuke.

2 From the fruit of his words a man eats
      good things,
    but the treacherous one craves violence.

7 Once thrown down, the wicked are no more,
    but the house of the upright stands firm.

8 Prudence wins praise,
    but a tortuous heart incurs only contempt.

9 Better a common fellow who has a slave
    than someone who gives himself airs and has
      nothing to eat.

10 The upright has compassion on his animals,
    but the heart of the wicked is ruthless.

11 Whoever works his land shall have bread and to
      spare,
    but no one who chases fantasies has any sense. *i*

12 The godless delights in the snare of the wicked,
    but the root of the upright bears fruit.

13 In the sin of the lips lies a disastrous trap,
    but the upright finds a way out of misfortune.

14 Abundance of good things is the fruit of the lips;
    labour brings its own return.

15 Fools think the way they go is straight,
    the wise listens to advice.

16 The fool shows anger straightaway,
    the discreet conceals dislike.

17 To tell the truth is to further justice,
    a false witness is nothing but deceit.

18 Thoughtless words can wound like a sword,
    but the tongue of the wise brings healing.

19 Sincere lips endure for ever,
    the lying tongue lasts only a moment.

20 Deceit is in the heart of the schemer,
    joy with those who give counsels of peace.

21 No harm can come to the upright,
    but the wicked are swamped by misfortunes.

22 Lying lips are abhorrent to Yahweh;
    dear to him those who make truth their way of
      life.

23 The discreet keeps knowledge hidden,
    the heart of fools proclaims their folly.

24 For the diligent hand, authority;
    for the slack hand, forced labour.

25 Worry makes a heart heavy,
    a kindly word makes it glad.

26 The upright shows the way to a friend;
    the way of the wicked leads them astray.

27 The idle has no game to roast;
    diligence is anyone's most precious possession.

28 In the way of uprightness is life,
    the ways of the vengeful lead to death.

13 A wise child listens to a father's discipline,
      a cynic will not listen to reproof.

2 The fruit of the mouth provides a good meal,
    but the soul of the treacherous feeds on violence.

i **12** = 28:19.

NEW REVISED STANDARD VERSION

3 Those who guard their mouths preserve their
    lives;
    those who open wide their lips come to ruin.
4 The appetite of the lazy craves, and gets nothing,
    while the appetite of the diligent is richly
      supplied.
5 The righteous hate falsehood,
    but the wicked act shamefully and
      disgracefully.
6 Righteousness guards one whose way is upright,
    but sin overthrows the wicked.
7 Some pretend to be rich, yet have nothing;
    others pretend to be poor, yet have great
      wealth.
8 Wealth is a ransom for a person's life,
    but the poor get no threats.
9 The light of the righteous rejoices,
    but the lamp of the wicked goes out.
10 By insolence the heedless make strife,
    but wisdom is with those who take advice.
11 Wealth hastily gotten[n] will dwindle,
    but those who gather little by little will
      increase it.
12 Hope deferred makes the heart sick,
    but a desire fulfilled is a tree of life.
13 Those who despise the word bring destruction on
      themselves,
    but those who respect the commandment will
      be rewarded.
14 The teaching of the wise is a fountain of life,
    so that one may avoid the snares of death.
15 Good sense wins favor,
    but the way of the faithless is their ruin.[o]
16 The clever do all things intelligently,
    but the fool displays folly.
17 A bad messenger brings trouble,
    but a faithful envoy, healing.
18 Poverty and disgrace are for the one who ignores
      instruction,
    but one who heeds reproof is honored.
19 A desire realized is sweet to the soul,
    but to turn away from evil is an abomination to
      fools.
20 Whoever walks with the wise becomes wise,
    but the companion of fools suffers harm.
21 Misfortune pursues sinners,
    but prosperity rewards the righteous.
22 The good leave an inheritance to their children's
      children,
    but the sinner's wealth is laid up for the
      righteous.
23 The field of the poor may yield much food,
    but it is swept away through injustice.
24 Those who spare the rod hate their children,
    but those who love them are diligent to
      discipline them.
25 The righteous have enough to satisfy their
      appetite,
    but the belly of the wicked is empty.

14 The wise woman[p] builds her house,
    but the foolish tears it down with her own
      hands.

REVISED ENGLISH BIBLE

3 One who minds his words preserves his life;
    one who talks too much faces ruin.
4 Those who are lazy and torn by appetite are
      unsatisfied,
    but the diligent grow prosperous.
5 The righteous hate falsehood;
    the actions of the wicked are base and disgraceful.
6 Right conduct protects the honest,
    but wickedness brings sinners down.
7 One pretends to be rich, although he has nothing;
    another has great wealth but affects poverty.
8 One who is rich has to pay a ransom,
    but one who is poor is immune from threats.
9 The light of the righteous burns brightly;
    the lamp of the wicked will be extinguished.
10 A brainless fool causes strife by his presumption;
    wisdom is found among friends in council.
11 Wealth quickly won dwindles away,
    but if amassed little by little it will grow.
12 Hope deferred makes the heart sick;
    a wish come true is a tree of life.
13 To despise a word of advice is to ask for trouble;
    mind a command, and you will be rewarded.
14 The teaching of the wise is a fountain of life
    offering escape from the snares of death.
15 Good sense wins favour,
    but perfidy leads to disaster.
16 Clever people do everything with understanding,
    but the stupid parade their folly.
17 An evil messenger causes trouble,
    but a trusty envoy brings healing.
18 To refuse correction brings poverty and
      humiliation;
    one who takes reproof to heart comes to honour.
19 Desire fulfilled is sweet to the taste;
    stupid people detest mending their ways.
20 Walk with the wise and learn wisdom;
    mix with the stupid and come to harm.
21 Ill fortune pursues the sinner;
    good fortune rewards the righteous.
22 A good man leaves an inheritance to his
      descendants,
    but the sinner's hoard passes to the righteous.
23 The fallow land of the poor may yield much grain,
    but through injustice it may be stolen.
24 A father who spares the rod hates his son,
    but one who loves his son brings him up strictly.
25 The righteous eat their fill,
    but the bellies of the wicked are empty.

14 Wise women build up their homes,
    but with their own hands the foolish pull theirs
      down.

13:11 **quickly won:** *so Gk; Heb.* because of emptiness.
13:15 **leads to disaster:** *prob. rdg, cp. Gk; Heb.* is enduring.
13:16 **do . . . understanding:** *or* in their understanding conceal
everything.

[n] Gk Vg: Heb *from vanity*   [o] Cn Compare Gk Syr Vg Tg: Heb *is*
enduring   [p] Heb *Wisdom of women*

NEW AMERICAN BIBLE

3 He who guards his mouth protects his life;
   to open wide one's lips brings downfall.

4 The soul of the sluggard craves in vain,
   but the diligent soul is amply satisfied.

5 Anything deceitful the just man hates,
   but the wicked brings shame and disgrace.

6 Virtue guards one who walks honestly,
   but the downfall of the wicked is sin.

7 One man pretends to be rich, yet has nothing;
   another pretends to be poor, yet has
      great wealth.

8 A man's riches serve as ransom for his life,
   but the poor man heeds no rebuke.

9 The light of the just shines gaily,
   but the lamp of the wicked goes out.

10 The stupid man sows discord by his insolence,
   but with those who take counsel is wisdom.

11 Wealth quickly gotten dwindles away,
   but amassed little by little, it grows.

12 Hope deferred makes the heart sick,
   but a wish fulfilled is a tree of life.

13 He who despises the word must pay for it,
   but he who reveres the commandment will
      be rewarded.

14 The teaching of the wise is a fountain of life,
   that a man may avoid the snares of death.

15 Good sense brings favor,
   but the way of the faithless is their ruin.

16 The shrewd man does everything with prudence,
   but the fool peddles folly.

17 A wicked messenger brings on disaster,
   but a trustworthy envoy is a healing remedy.

18 Poverty and shame befall the man who
      disregards correction,
   but he who heeds reproof is honored.

19 Lust indulged starves the soul,
   but fools hate to turn from evil.

20 Walk with wise men and you will become wise,
   but the companion of fools will fare badly.

21 Misfortune pursues sinners,
   but the just shall be recompensed with good.

22 The good man leaves an inheritance to his
      children's children,
   but the wealth of the sinner is stored up for
      the just.

23 A lawsuit devours the tillage of the poor,
   but some men perish for lack of a law court.

24 He who spares his rod hates his son,
   but he who loves him takes care to chastise him.

25 When the just man eats, his hunger is appeased;
   but the belly of the wicked suffers want.

14 Wisdom builds her house,
   but Folly tears hers down with her own hands.

NEW JERUSALEM BIBLE

3 A guard on the mouth makes life secure,
   whoever talks too much is lost.

4 The idler hungers but has no food;
   hard workers get their fill.

5 The upright hates a lying word,
   but the wicked slanders and defames.

6 Uprightness stands guard over one whose way is
      honest,
   sin causes the ruin of the wicked.

7 There are some who, on nothing, pretend to be
      rich,
   some, with great wealth, pretend to be poor.

8 The ransom for life is a person's wealth;
   but the poor will not hear the reproof.

9 The light of the upright is joyful,
   the lamp of the wicked goes out.

10 Insolence breeds only disputes,
   wisdom lies with those who take advice.

11 A sudden fortune will dwindle away,
   accumulation little by little is the way to riches.

12 Hope deferred makes the heart sick,
   desire fulfilled is a tree of life.

13 Contempt for the word is self-destructive,
   respect for the commandment wins salvation.

14 The teaching of the wise is a life-giving fountain
   for eluding the snares of death. *j*

15 Good sense wins favour,
   but the way of the treacherous is hard.

16 Anyone of discretion acts by the light of
      knowledge,
   the fool parades his folly.

17 A bad messenger falls into misfortune,
   a trusty messenger brings healing.

18 Whoever rejects discipline wins poverty and scorn;
   for anyone who accepts correction: honour.

19 Desire fulfilled is sweet to the soul;
   fools are loth to turn — from evil.

20 Whoever walks with the wise becomes wise,
   whoever mixes with fools will be ruined.

21 Evil will pursue the sinner,
   but good will reward the upright.

22 The good bequeaths a heritage to children's
      children,
   the wealth of the sinner is stored away for the
      upright.

23 Though the farms of the poor yield much food,
   some perish for lack of justice.

24 Whoever fails to use the stick hates his child;
   whoever is free with correction loves him.

25 The upright eats to the full,
   the belly of the wicked goes empty.

14 Wisdom builds herself a house;
   with her own hands Folly pulls it down.

j 13 = 14:27.

NEW REVISED STANDARD VERSION	REVISED ENGLISH BIBLE

2 Those who walk uprightly fear the LORD,
but one who is devious in conduct despises
him.
3 The talk of fools is a rod for their backs,*q*
but the lips of the wise preserve them.
4 Where there are no oxen, there is no grain;
abundant crops come by the strength of the ox.
5 A faithful witness does not lie,
but a false witness breathes out lies.
6 A scoffer seeks wisdom in vain,
but knowledge is easy for one who
understands.
7 Leave the presence of a fool,
for there you do not find words of knowledge.
8 It is the wisdom of the clever to understand
where they go,
but the folly of fools misleads.
9 Fools mock at the guilt offering,*r*
but the upright enjoy God's favor.
10 The heart knows its own bitterness,
and no stranger shares its joy.
11 The house of the wicked is destroyed,
but the tent of the upright flourishes.
12 There is a way that seems right to a person,
but its end is the way to death.*s*
13 Even in laughter the heart is sad,
and the end of joy is grief.
14 The perverse get what their ways deserve,
and the good, what their deeds deserve.*t*
15 The simple believe everything,
but the clever consider their steps.
16 The wise are cautious and turn away from evil,
but the fool throws off restraint and is careless.
17 One who is quick-tempered acts foolishly,
and the schemer is hated.
18 The simple are adorned with*u* folly,
but the clever are crowned with knowledge.
19 The evil bow down before the good,
the wicked at the gates of the righteous.
20 The poor are disliked even by their neighbors,
but the rich have many friends.
21 Those who despise their neighbors are sinners,
but happy are those who are kind to the poor.
22 Do they not err that plan evil?
Those who plan good find loyalty and
faithfulness.
23 In all toil there is profit,
but mere talk leads only to poverty.
24 The crown of the wise is their wisdom,*v*
but folly is the garland*w* of fools.
25 A truthful witness saves lives,
but one who utters lies is a betrayer.
26 In the fear of the LORD one has strong
confidence,
and one's children will have a refuge.
27 The fear of the LORD is a fountain of life,
so that one may avoid the snares of death.

2 A person whose conduct is upright fears the LORD;
the double-dealer scorns him.
3 The speech of a fool is a rod for his own back;
the words of the wise are their safeguard.
4 Where there are no oxen, the barn is empty;
the strength of an ox ensures rich crops.
5 A truthful witness does not deceive;
the perjurer produces a pack of lies.
6 The arrogant aspire in vain to wisdom,
while to those with understanding, knowledge
comes readily.
7 Avoid a stupid person;
you will not hear a word of sense from him.
8 Someone who is clever will have the wit to find
the right way;
the folly of the stupid misleads them.
9 Fools are too arrogant to make amends;
the upright know what reconciliation requires.
10 The heart knows its own bitterness,
and in its joy a stranger has no part.
11 The house of the wicked will be torn down,
but the dwelling of the upright will flourish.
12 A road may seem straightforward,
yet end as the way to death.
13 Even in laughter the heart can ache,
and mirth may end in sorrow.
14 Renegades reap the reward of their conduct,
the good the reward of their achievements.
15 A simpleton believes every word he hears;
a clever person watches each step.
16 One who is wise is cautious and avoids trouble,
but one who is stupid is reckless and falls
headlong.
17 Impatience runs into folly;
advancement comes by careful thought.
18 Simpletons wear the trappings of folly;
the clever are crowned with knowledge.
19 Evildoers cringe before the good,
the wicked at the door of the righteous.
20 The poor are not liked even by their friends,
but the rich have friends in plenty.
21 Whoever despises the hungry does wrong,
but happy are they who are generous to the poor.
22 Do not those who intend evil go astray,
while those with good intentions are loyal and
faithful?
23 The pains of toil bring gain;
mere talk yields nothing but need.
24 Their wealth is the crown of the wise,
folly the chief ornament of the stupid.
25 A truthful witness saves lives;
a slanderer utters nothing but lies.
26 One who is strong and trusts in the fear of the
LORD
will be a refuge for his children.
27 The fear of the LORD is a fountain of life
offering escape from the snares of death.

---

q Cn: Heb *a rod of pride*   *r* Meaning of Heb uncertain
s Heb *ways of death*   *t* Cn: Heb *from upon him*   *u* Or *inherit*
v Cn Compare Gk: Heb *riches*   *w* Cn: Heb *is the folly*

14:3 **his . . . back:** *prob. rdg; Heb.* pride.   14:17 **advancement
. . . thought:** *prob. rdg; Heb.* a person of careful thought is hated.
14:21 **the hungry:** *so Gk; Heb.* his friend.

NEW AMERICAN BIBLE

NEW JERUSALEM BIBLE

2 He who walks uprightly fears the LORD,
but he who is devious in his ways spurns him.

3 In the mouth of the fool is a rod for his back,
but the lips of the wise preserve them.

4 Where there are no oxen, the crib remains empty;
but large crops come through the strength of
the bull.

5 A truthful witness does not lie,
but a false witness utters lies.

6 The senseless man seeks in vain for wisdom,
but knowledge is easy to the man of intelligence.

7 To avoid the foolish man, take steps!
But knowing lips one meets with by surprise.

8 The shrewd man's wisdom gives him knowledge of
his way,
but the folly of fools is their deception.

9 Guilt lodges in the tents of the arrogant,
but favor in the house of the just.

10 The heart knows its own bitterness,
and in its joy no one else shares.

11 The house of the wicked will be destroyed,
but the tent of the upright will flourish.

12 Sometimes a way seems right to a man,
but the end of it leads to death!

13 Even in laughter the heart may be sad
and the end of joy may be sorrow.

14 The scoundrel suffers the consequences of
his ways,
and the good man reaps the fruit of his paths.

15 The simpleton believes everything,
but the shrewd man measures his steps.

16 The wise man is cautious and shuns evil;
the fool is reckless and sure of himself.

17 The quick-tempered man makes a fool of himself,
but the prudent man is at peace.

18 The adornment of simpletons is folly,
but shrewd men gain the crown of knowledge.

19 Evil men must bow down before the good,
and the wicked, at the gates of the just.

20 Even by his neighbor the poor man is hated,
but the friends of the rich are many.

21 He sins who despises the hungry;
but happy is he who is kind to the poor!

22 Do not those who plot evil go astray?
But those intent on good gain kindness
and constancy.

23 In all labor there is profit,
but mere talk tends only to penury.

24 The crown of the wise is resourcefulness;
the diadem of fools is folly.

25 The truthful witness saves lives,
but he who utters lies is a betrayer.

26 In the fear of the LORD is a strong defense;
even for one's children he will be a refuge.

27 The fear of the LORD is a fountain of life,
that a man may avoid the snares of death.

2 Whoever keeps to an honest course fears Yahweh,
whoever deserts his paths shows contempt for
him.

3 Pride sprouts in the mouth of the fool,
the lips of the wise keep them safe.

4 No oxen, empty manger;
strong bull, much cash.

5 The truthful witness tells no lies,
the false witness lies with every breath.

6 In vain the mocker looks for wisdom,
knowledge comes easy to the intelligent.

7 Keep well clear of the fool,
you will not find wise lips there.

8 With people of discretion, wisdom keeps a watch
over their conduct,
but the folly of fools leads them astray.

9 Fools mock at the sacrifice for sin,
but favour resides among the honest.

10 The heart knows its own grief best,
nor can a stranger share its joy.

11 The house of the wicked will be destroyed,
the tent of the honest will prosper.

12 There are ways that some think straight,
but they lead in the end to death. *k*

13 Even in laughter the heart finds sadness,
and joy makes way for sorrow.

14 The miscreant will reap the reward of his conduct,
and the good the reward of his deeds.

15 The simpleton believes any message,
a person of discretion treads a careful path.

16 The wise fears evil and avoids it,
the fool is insolent and conceited.

17 A quick-tempered person commits rash acts,
but a schemer is detestable.

18 Simpletons have folly for their portion,
people of discretion knowledge for their crown.

19 The evil bow down before the good,
the wicked, at the gates of the upright.

20 The poor is detestable even to a friend,
but many are they who love someone rich.

21 One who despises the needy is at fault,
one who takes pity on the poor is blessed.

22 Plan evil—isn't this to go astray?
Those who plan for good can earn faithful love
and constancy.

23 Hard work always yields its profit,
idle talk brings only want.

24 The crown of the wise is their riches;
the folly of fools is folly.

25 A truthful witness saves lives,
whoever utters lies is a deceiver.

26 In the fear of Yahweh is powerful security;
for his children he is a refuge.

27 The fear of Yahweh is a life-giving spring
for eluding the snares of death. *l*

k **14** = 16:25.   *l* **14** = 13:14.

28 The glory of a king is a multitude of people;
   without people a prince is ruined.
29 Whoever is slow to anger has great
      understanding,
   but one who has a hasty temper exalts folly.
30 A tranquil mind gives life to the flesh,
   but passion makes the bones rot.
31 Those who oppress the poor insult their Maker,
   but those who are kind to the needy honor
      him.
32 The wicked are overthrown by their evildoing,
   but the righteous find a refuge in their
      integrity. *x*
33 Wisdom is at home in the mind of one who has
      understanding,
   but it is not *y* known in the heart of fools.
34 Righteousness exalts a nation,
   but sin is a reproach to any people.
35 A servant who deals wisely has the king's favor,
   but his wrath falls on one who acts shamefully.

15 A soft answer turns away wrath,
      but a harsh word stirs up anger.
2 The tongue of the wise dispenses knowledge, *z*
   but the mouths of fools pour out folly.
3 The eyes of the LORD are in every place,
   keeping watch on the evil and the good.
4 A gentle tongue is a tree of life,
   but perverseness in it breaks the spirit.
5 A fool despises a parent's instruction,
   but the one who heeds admonition is prudent.
6 In the house of the righteous there is much
      treasure,
   but trouble befalls the income of the wicked.
7 The lips of the wise spread knowledge;
   not so the minds of fools.
8 The sacrifice of the wicked is an abomination to
      the LORD,
   but the prayer of the upright is his delight.
9 The way of the wicked is an abomination to the
      LORD,
   but he loves the one who pursues
      righteousness.
10 There is severe discipline for one who forsakes
      the way,
   but one who hates a rebuke will die.
11 Sheol and Abaddon lie open before the LORD,
   how much more human hearts!
12 Scoffers do not like to be rebuked;
   they will not go to the wise.
13 A glad heart makes a cheerful countenance,
   but by sorrow of heart the spirit is broken.
14 The mind of one who has understanding seeks
      knowledge,
   but the mouths of fools feed on folly.
15 All the days of the poor are hard,
   but a cheerful heart has a continual feast.
16 Better is a little with the fear of the LORD
   than great treasure and trouble with it.
17 Better is a dinner of vegetables where love is
   than a fatted ox and hatred with it.

28 Many subjects make for a king's glory;
   lack of them makes a prince of no account.
29 To be patient shows great understanding;
   quick temper is the height of folly.
30 Peace of mind gives health of body,
   but envy is a canker in the bones.
31 To oppress the poor is to insult the Creator;
   to be generous to the needy is to do him honour.
32 Evildoers are brought down by their wickedness;
   the upright find refuge in their honesty.
33 Wisdom is at home in a discerning mind,
   but in the heart of a fool it is suppressed.
34 Righteousness raises a people to greatness;
   to pursue wrong degrades a nation.
35 A king shows favour to a prudent servant;
   his displeasure falls on those who fail him.

15 A mild answer turns away anger,
      but a sharp word makes tempers rise.
2 The tongues of the wise spread knowledge;
   the stupid talk a lot of nonsense.
3 The eyes of the LORD are everywhere,
   surveying everyone, good and evil.
4 A soothing word is a tree of life,
   but a mischievous tongue breaks the spirit.
5 A fool spurns his father's correction,
   but whoever heeds a reproof shows good sense.
6 In the houses of the righteous there is ample
      wealth;
   the gains of the wicked bring trouble.
7 The lips of the wise promote knowledge;
   the hearts of the stupid are dishonest.
8 The sacrifices of the wicked are abominable to the
      LORD,
   but the prayers of the upright win his favour.
9 The conduct of the wicked is abominable to the
      LORD,
   but he loves the seeker after righteousness.
10 Punishment awaits the one who forsakes the right
      way;
   he who hates reproof will die.
11 Sheol and Abaddon lie open before the LORD;
   how much more does the human heart!
12 The arrogant do not take kindly to reproof;
   they will not consult the wise.
13 A glad heart makes a cheerful face;
   heartache crushes the spirit.
14 A discerning mind seeks knowledge,
   but the stupid feed on folly.
15 To the downtrodden every day is wretched,
   but to have a merry heart is a perpetual feast.
16 Better a pittance with the fear of the LORD
   than wealth with worry in its train.
17 Better a dish of vegetables if love goes with it
   than a fattened ox eaten amid hatred.

---

x Gk Syr: Heb *in their death* *y* Gk Syr: Heb lacks *not* *z* Cn: Heb 14:32 **honesty**: so *Gk*; *Heb*. death. 15:11 **Sheol and Abaddon:**
makes knowledge good or Death and Destruction.

NEW AMERICAN BIBLE

28 In many subjects lies the glory of the king;
   but if his people are few, it is the prince's ruin.

29 The patient man shows much good sense,
   but the quick-tempered man displays folly at its
   height.

30 A tranquil mind gives life to the body,
   but jealousy rots the bones.

31 He who oppresses the poor blasphemes his Maker,
   but he who is kind to the needy glorifies him.

32 The wicked man is overthrown by his wickedness,
   but the just man finds a refuge in his honesty.

33 In the heart of the intelligent wisdom abides,
   but in the bosom of fools it is unknown.

34 Virtue exalts a nation,
   but sin is a people's disgrace.

35 The king favors the intelligent servant,
   but the worthless one incurs his wrath.

15 A mild answer calms wrath,
   but a harsh word stirs up anger.

2 The tongue of the wise pours out knowledge,
   but the mouth of fools spurts forth folly.

3 The eyes of the LORD are in every place,
   keeping watch on the evil and the good.

4 A soothing tongue is a tree of life,
   but a perverse one crushes the spirit.

5 The fool spurns his father's admonition,
   but prudent is he who heeds reproof.

6 In the house of the just there are ample resources,
   but the earnings of the wicked are in turmoil.

7 The lips of the wise disseminate knowledge,
   but the heart of fools is perverted.

8 The sacrifice of the wicked is an abomination to
   the LORD,
   but the prayer of the upright is his delight.

9 The way of the wicked is an abomination to
   the LORD,
   but he loves the man who pursues virtue.

10 Severe punishment is in store for the man who
   goes astray;
   he who hates reproof will die.

11 The nether world and the abyss lie open before
   the LORD;
   how much more the hearts of men!

12 The senseless man loves not to be reproved;
   to wise men he will not go.

13 A glad heart lights up the face,
   but by mental anguish the spirit is broken.

14 The mind of the intelligent man seeks knowledge,
   but the mouth of fools feeds on folly.

15 Every day is miserable for the depressed,
   but a lighthearted man has a continual feast.

16 Better a little with fear of the LORD
   than a great fortune with anxiety.

17 Better a dish of herbs where love is
   than a fatted ox and hatred with it.

NEW JERUSALEM BIBLE

28 Large population, monarch's glory;
   dwindling population, ruler's ruin.

29 Mastery of temper is high proof of intelligence,
   a quick temper makes folly worse than ever.

30 The life of the body is a tranquil heart,
   but envy is a cancer in the bones.

31 To oppress the weak insults the Creator,
   kindness to the needy honours the Creator.

32 For evil-doing, the wicked will be flung headlong,
   but in integrity the upright will find refuge.

33 Wisdom resides in an understanding heart;
   she is not to be found in the hearts of fools.

34 Uprightness makes a nation great,
   by sin whole races are disgraced.

35 A king shows favour to a wise minister,
   but anger to one who shames him.

15 A mild answer turns away wrath,
   sharp words stir up anger.

2 The tongue of the wise makes knowledge
   welcome,
   the mouth of a fool spews folly.

3 The eyes of Yahweh are everywhere:
   observing the wicked and the good.

4 The tongue that soothes is a tree of life;
   the perverse tongue, a breaker of hearts.

5 Only a fool spurns a father's discipline,
   whoever accepts correction is discreet.

6 In the house of the upright there is no lack of
   treasure,
   the earnings of the wicked are fraught with
   anxiety.

7 The lips of the wise spread knowledge,
   not so the hearts of fools.

8 The sacrifice of the wicked is abhorrent to
   Yahweh,
   dear to him is the prayer of the honest.

9 The conduct of the wicked is abhorrent to Yahweh,
   but he loves the person whose goal is
   uprightness.

10 Correction is severe for one who leaves the way;
   whoever hates being reprimanded will die.

11 Sheol and Perdition lie open to Yahweh;
   how much more the human heart!

12 The mocker does not care to be reprimanded,
   and will not choose the wise as companions.

13 Glad heart means happy face,
   where the heart is sad the spirit is broken.

14 The heart of the wise seeks knowledge,
   a fool's mouth feeds on folly.

15 For the poor every day is evil,
   for the joyous heart it is always festival time.

16 Better to have little and with it fear of Yahweh
   than immense wealth and with it anxiety.

17 Better a dish of herbs when love is there
   than a fattened ox and hatred to go with it.

18 Those who are hot-tempered stir up strife,
    but those who are slow to anger calm
        contention.
19 The way of the lazy is overgrown with thorns,
    but the path of the upright is a level highway.
20 A wise child makes a glad father,
    but the foolish despise their mothers.
21 Folly is a joy to one who has no sense,
    but a person of understanding walks straight
        ahead.
22 Without counsel, plans go wrong,
    but with many advisers they succeed.
23 To make an apt answer is a joy to anyone,
    and a word in season, how good it is!
24 For the wise the path of life leads upward,
    in order to avoid Sheol below.
25 The LORD tears down the house of the proud,
    but maintains the widow's boundaries.
26 Evil plans are an abomination to the LORD,
    but gracious words are pure.
27 Those who are greedy for unjust gain make
        trouble for their households,
    but those who hate bribes will live.
28 The mind of the righteous ponders how to
        answer,
    but the mouth of the wicked pours out evil.
29 The LORD is far from the wicked,
    but he hears the prayer of the righteous.
30 The light of the eyes rejoices the heart,
    and good news refreshes the body.
31 The ear that heeds wholesome admonition
    will lodge among the wise.
32 Those who ignore instruction despise themselves,
    but those who heed admonition gain
        understanding.
33 The fear of the LORD is instruction in wisdom,
    and humility goes before honor.

16 The plans of the mind belong to mortals,
    but the answer of the tongue is from the LORD.
2 All one's ways may be pure in one's own eyes,
    but the LORD weighs the spirit.
3 Commit your work to the LORD,
    and your plans will be established.
4 The LORD has made everything for its purpose,
    even the wicked for the day of trouble.
5 All those who are arrogant are an abomination to
        the LORD;
    be assured, they will not go unpunished.
6 By loyalty and faithfulness iniquity is atoned for,
    and by the fear of the LORD one avoids evil.
7 When the ways of people please the LORD,
    he causes even their enemies to be at peace
        with them.
8 Better is a little with righteousness
    than large income with injustice.
9 The human mind plans the way,
    but the LORD directs the steps.

18 Bad temper provokes quarrels,
    but patience heals discord.
19 The path of the sluggard is a tangle of briars,
    but the road of the diligent is a highway.
20 A wise son brings joy to his father;
    a young fool despises his mother.
21 Folly may amuse the empty-headed;
    a person of understanding holds to a straight
        course.
22 Schemes lightly made come to nothing,
    but with detailed planning they succeed.
23 Someone may be pleased with his own retort;
    how much better is a word in season!
24 For the prudent the path of life leads upwards
    and keeps them clear of Sheol below.
25 The LORD will pull down the houses of the proud,
    but maintain the widow's boundary stones.
26 Evil thoughts are an abomination to the LORD,
    but the words of the pure are pleasing.
27 He who is grasping brings trouble on his family,
    but he who spurns a bribe will enjoy long life.
28 The righteous think before they answer;
    but from the mouths of the wicked mischief pours
        out.
29 The LORD stands aloof from the wicked,
    but he listens to the prayer of the righteous.
30 A bright look brings joy to the heart,
    and good news warms the bones to the marrow.
31 Whoever listens to wholesome reproof
    will enjoy the society of the wise.
32 Whoever refuses correction is his own worst
        enemy,
    but one who listens to reproof learns sense.
33 Wisdom's discipline is the fear of the LORD,
    and humility comes before honour.

16 A mortal may order his thoughts,
    but the LORD inspires the words his tongue
        utters.
2 A mortal's whole conduct may seem right to him,
    but the LORD weighs up his motives.
3 Commit to the LORD all that you do,
    and your plans will be successful.
4 The LORD has made each thing for its own end;
    so he has made the wicked for a day of calamity.
5 One and all the proud are abominable to the LORD;
    depend upon it: they will not escape punishment.
6 Guilt is wiped out by loyalty and faith,
    and the fear of the LORD makes mortals turn from
        evil.
7 When the LORD approves someone's conduct,
    he makes even his enemies live at peace with him.
8 Better a pittance honestly earned
    than great gains ill gotten.
9 Someone may plan his journey by his own wit,
    but it is the LORD who guides his steps.

15:19 **diligent:** *so* Gk; Heb. upright.   15:24 **Sheol:** *or the*
underworld.   15:26 **the words . . . pleasing:** *prob. rdg; Heb.*
pleasant words are pure.

NEW AMERICAN BIBLE

18 An ill-tempered man stirs up strife,
but a patient man allays discord.

19 The way of the sluggard is hemmed in as
with thorns,
but the path of the diligent is a highway.

20 A wise son makes his father glad,
but a fool of a man despises his mother.

21 Folly is joy to the senseless man,
but the man of understanding goes the
straight way.

22 Plans fail when there is no counsel,
but they succeed when counselors are many.

23 There is joy for a man in his utterance;
a word in season, how good it is!

24 The path of life leads the prudent man upward,
that he may avoid the nether world below.

25 The Lord overturns the house of the proud,
but he preserves intact the widow's landmark.

26 The wicked man's schemes are an abomination to
the Lord,
but the pure speak what is pleasing to him.

27 He who is greedy of gain brings ruin on his
own house,
but he who hates bribes will live.

28 The just man weighs well his utterance,
but the mouth of the wicked pours out evil.

29 The Lord is far from the wicked,
but the prayer of the just he hears.

30 A cheerful glance brings joy to the heart;
good news invigorates the bones.

31 He who listens to salutary reproof
will abide among the wise.

32 He who rejects admonition despises his own soul,
but he who heeds reproof gains understanding.

33 The fear of the Lord is training for wisdom,
and humility goes before honors.

16 Man may make plans in his heart,
but what the tongue utters is from the Lord.

2 All the ways of a man may be pure in his
own eyes,
but it is the Lord who proves the spirit.

3 Entrust your works to the Lord,
and your plans will succeed.

4 The Lord has made everything for his own ends,
even the wicked for the evil day.

5 Every proud man is an abomination to the Lord;
I assure you that he will not go unpunished.

6 By kindness and piety guilt is expiated,
and by the fear of the Lord man avoids evil.

7 When the Lord is pleased with a man's ways,
he makes even his enemies be at peace
with him.

8 Better a little with virtue,
than a large income with injustice.

9 In his mind a man plans his course,
but the Lord directs his steps.

NEW JERUSALEM BIBLE

18 The hot-headed provokes disputes,
the equable allays dissension.

19 The way of the lazy is like a thorny hedge,
the path of the honest is a broad highway.

20 A wise child is a father's joy; m
only a brute despises his mother.

21 Folly appeals to someone without sense,
a person of understanding goes straight forward.

22 Without deliberation plans come to nothing.
Plans succeed where counsellors are many.

23 Anyone who has a ready answer has joy too:
how satisfying is the apt reply!

24 For the prudent, the path of life leads upwards
thus avoiding Sheol below.

25 Yahweh pulls down the house of the proud,
but he keeps the widow's boundaries intact.

26 Wicked scheming is abhorrent to Yahweh,
but words that are kind are pure.

27 Craving for dishonest gain brings trouble on a
house,
hatred of bribery earns life.

28 The heart of the upright reflects before answering,
the mouth of the wicked spews out wickedness.

29 Yahweh keeps his distance from the wicked,
but he listens to the prayers of the upright.

30 A kindly glance gives joy to the heart,
good news lends strength to the bones.

31 The ear attentive to wholesome correction
finds itself at home in the company of the wise.

32 Whoever rejects correction lacks self-respect,
whoever accepts reproof grows in understanding.

33 The fear of Yahweh is a school of wisdom,
before there can be glory, there must be
humility. n

16 A human heart makes the plans,
Yahweh gives the answer.

2 A person's own acts seem right to the doer,
but Yahweh is the weigher of souls.

3 Commend what you do to Yahweh,
and what you plan will be achieved.

4 Yahweh made everything for its own purpose,
yes, even the wicked for the day of disaster.

5 Every arrogant heart is abhorrent to Yahweh:
be sure this will not go unpunished.

6 By faithful love and constancy sin is expiated;
by fear of Yahweh evil is avoided.

7 Let Yahweh be pleased with someone's way of life
and he makes that person's very enemies into
friends.

8 Better have little and with it uprightness
than great revenues with injustice.

9 The human heart may plan a course,
but it is Yahweh who makes the steps secure.

m **15** = 10:1.   n **15** = 18:12.

10 Inspired decisions are on the lips of a king;
   his mouth does not sin in judgment.
11 Honest balances and scales are the LORD's;
   all the weights in the bag are his work.
12 It is an abomination to kings to do evil,
   for the throne is established by righteousness.
13 Righteous lips are the delight of a king,
   and he loves those who speak what is right.
14 A king's wrath is a messenger of death,
   and whoever is wise will appease it.
15 In the light of a king's face there is life,
   and his favor is like the clouds that bring the
     spring rain.
16 How much better to get wisdom than gold!
   To get understanding is to be chosen rather
     than silver.
17 The highway of the upright avoids evil;
   those who guard their way preserve their lives.
18 Pride goes before destruction,
   and a haughty spirit before a fall.
19 It is better to be of a lowly spirit among the poor
   than to divide the spoil with the proud.
20 Those who are attentive to a matter will prosper,
   and happy are those who trust in the LORD.
21 The wise of heart is called perceptive,
   and pleasant speech increases persuasiveness.
22 Wisdom is a fountain of life to one who has it,
   but folly is the punishment of fools.
23 The mind of the wise makes their speech
     judicious,
   and adds persuasiveness to their lips.
24 Pleasant words are like a honeycomb,
   sweetness to the soul and health to the body.
25 Sometimes there is a way that seems to be right,
   but in the end it is the way to death.
26 The appetite of workers works for them;
   their hunger urges them on.
27 Scoundrels concoct evil,
   and their speech is like a scorching fire.
28 A perverse person spreads strife,
   and a whisperer separates close friends.
29 The violent entice their neighbors,
   and lead them in a way that is not good.
30 One who winks the eyes plans*a* perverse things;
   one who compresses the lips brings evil to
     pass.
31 Gray hair is a crown of glory;
   it is gained in a righteous life.
32 One who is slow to anger is better than the
     mighty,
   and one whose temper is controlled than one
     who captures a city.
33 The lot is cast into the lap,
   but the decision is the LORD's alone.

10 The king's mouth is an oracle;
   he does not err when he passes sentence.
11 Accuracy of scales and balances is the LORD's
     concern;
   all the weights in the bag are his business.
12 Wrongdoing is abhorrent to kings,
   for a throne rests firmly on righteousness.
13 Honest speech is what pleases kings,
   for they hold dear those who speak the truth.
14 A king's anger is a herald of death,
   and the wise will appease it.
15 In the light of the king's countenance is life;
   his favour is like a rain-cloud in the spring.
16 How much better than gold it is to get wisdom,
   and to gain discernment is more desirable than
     silver.
17 The highway of the upright avoids evil;
   he who watches his step preserves his life.
18 Pride goes before disaster,
   and arrogance before a fall.
19 Better live humbly with those in need
   than divide the spoil with the proud.
20 He who is shrewd in business will prosper,
   but happy is he who puts his trust in the LORD.
21 The sensible person seeks advice from the wise;
   persuasive speech increases learning.
22 Good sense is a fountain of life to its possessors,
   but a fool is punished by his own folly.
23 The wise person's mind guides his speech,
   and what his lips impart increases learning.
24 Kind words are like dripping honey:
   sweetness to the palate and health for the body.
25 A road may seem straightforward to the one who is
     on it,
   yet it may end as the way to death.
26 The labourer's appetite impels him to work,
   hunger spurs him on.
27 A scoundrel rakes up evil gossip;
   it is like a scorching fire on his lips.
28 Disaffection sows strife,
   and tale-bearing breaks up the closest friendship.
29 Anyone given to violence will entice others
   and lead them into evil ways.
30 Anyone narrowing his eyes intends dishonesty,
   and one who pinches his lips is bent on mischief.
31 Grey hair is a crown of glory,
   which is won by a virtuous life.
32 Better be slow to anger than a fighter,
   better control one's temper than capture a city.
33 The lots may be cast into the lap,
   but the issue depends wholly on the LORD.

17 Better is a dry morsel with quiet
   than a house full of feasting with strife.
2 A slave who deals wisely will rule over a child
   who acts shamefully,

17 Better a dry crust and amity with it
   than a feast in a house full of strife.
2 Where the son is a wastrel, a prudent slave is
   master,

a Gk Syr Vg Tg: Heb *to plan*

10 The king's lips are an oracle;
   no judgment he pronounces is false.

11 Balance and scales belong to the LORD;
   all the weights used with them are his concern.

12 Kings have a horror of wrongdoing,
   for by righteousness the throne endures.

13 The king takes delight in honest lips,
   and the man who speaks what is right he loves.

14 The king's wrath is like messengers of death,
   but a wise man can pacify it.

15 In the light of the king's countenance is life,
   and his favor is like a rain cloud in spring.

16 How much better to acquire wisdom than gold!
   To acquire understanding is more desirable than
      silver.

17 The path of the upright avoids misfortune;
   he who pays attention to his way safeguards
      his life.

18 Pride goes before disaster,
   and a haughty spirit before a fall.

19 It is better to be humble with the meek
   than to share plunder with the proud.

20 He who plans a thing will be successful;
   happy is he who trusts in the LORD!

21 The wise man is esteemed for his discernment,
   yet pleasing speech increases his persuasiveness.

22 Good sense is a fountain of life to its possessor,
   but folly brings chastisement on fools.

23 The mind of the wise man makes him eloquent,
   and augments the persuasiveness of his lips.

24 Pleasing words are a honeycomb,
   sweet to the taste and healthful to the body.

25 Sometimes a way seems right to a man,
   but the end of it leads to death!

26 The laborer's appetite labors for him,
   for his mouth urges him on.

27 A scoundrel is a furnace of evil,
   and on his lips there is a scorching fire.

28 An intriguer sows discord,
   and a talebearer separates bosom friends.

29 A lawless man allures his neighbor,
   and leads him into a way that is not good.

30 He who winks his eye is plotting trickery;
   he who compresses his lips has mischief ready.

31 Gray hair is a crown of glory;
   it is gained by virtuous living.

32 A patient man is better than a warrior,
   and he who rules his temper, than he who takes
      a city.

33 When the lot is cast into the lap,
   its decision depends entirely on the LORD.

17 Better a dry crust with peace
   than a house full of feasting with strife.

2 An intelligent servant will rule over a
   worthless son,

10 The lips of the king utter prophecies,
   he keeps faith when he speaks in judgement.

11 The balances and scales belong to Yahweh,
   all the weights in the bag are of his making.

12 Evil-doing is abhorrent to kings,
   since uprightness is a throne's foundation.

13 Upright lips are welcome to a king,
   he loves someone of honest words.

14 The king's wrath is the herald of death,
   but the wise will appease it.

15 When the king's face brightens it spells life,
   his favour is like the rain in spring.

16 Better gain wisdom than gold,
   choose understanding in preference to silver.

17 To turn from evil is the way of the honest;
   whoever watches the path keeps life safe.

18 Pride goes before destruction,
   a haughty spirit before a fall.

19 Better be humble with the poor
   than share the booty with the proud.

20 Whoever listens closely to the word finds
      happiness;
   whoever trusts Yahweh is blessed.

21 The wise of heart is acclaimed as intelligent,
   sweetness of speech increases knowledge.

22 Shrewdness is a fountain of life for its possessor,
   the folly of fools is their own punishment.

23 The heart of the wise lends shrewdness to speech
   and makes words more persuasive.

24 Kindly words are a honeycomb,
   sweet to the taste, wholesome to the body.

25 There is a way that some think straight,
   but it leads in the end to death. o

26 A worker's appetite works on his behalf,
   for his hunger urges him on.

27 A worthless person concocts evil,
   such a one's talk is like a scorching fire.

28 A troublemaker sows strife,
   a slanderer divides friend from friend.

29 The violent lures his neighbour astray
   and leads him by a way that is not good.

30 Whoever narrows the eyes to think up tricks
   and purses the lips has already done wrong.

31 White hairs are a crown of honour,
   they are found in the ways of uprightness.

32 Better an equable person than a hero,
   someone with self-mastery than one who takes a
      city.

33 In the fold of the garment the lot is thrown,
   but from Yahweh comes the decision.

17 Better a mouthful of dry bread with peace
   than a house filled with quarrelsome sacrifices.

2 A shrewd servant comes off better than an
   unworthy child,

o 16 = 14:12.

and will share the inheritance as one of the
family.
3 The crucible is for silver, and the furnace is for
gold,
but the LORD tests the heart.
4 An evildoer listens to wicked lips;
and a liar gives heed to a mischievous tongue.
5 Those who mock the poor insult their Maker;
those who are glad at calamity will not go
unpunished.
6 Grandchildren are the crown of the aged,
and the glory of children is their parents.
7 Fine speech is not becoming to a fool;
still less is false speech to a ruler.*b*
8 A bribe is like a magic stone in the eyes of those
who give it;
wherever they turn they prosper.
9 One who forgives an affront fosters friendship,
but one who dwells on disputes will alienate a
friend.
10 A rebuke strikes deeper into a discerning person
than a hundred blows into a fool.
11 Evil people seek only rebellion,
but a cruel messenger will be sent against
them.
12 Better to meet a she-bear robbed of its cubs
than to confront a fool immersed in folly.
13 Evil will not depart from the house
of one who returns evil for good.
14 The beginning of strife is like letting out water;
so stop before the quarrel breaks out.
15 One who justifies the wicked and one who
condemns the righteous
are both alike an abomination to the LORD.
16 Why should fools have a price in hand
to buy wisdom, when they have no mind to
learn?
17 A friend loves at all times,
and kinsfolk are born to share adversity.
18 It is senseless to give a pledge,
to become surety for a neighbor.
19 One who loves transgression loves strife;
one who builds a high threshold invites broken
bones.
20 The crooked of mind do not prosper,
and the perverse of tongue fall into calamity.
21 The one who begets a fool gets trouble;
the parent of a fool has no joy.
22 A cheerful heart is a good medicine,
but a downcast spirit dries up the bones.
23 The wicked accept a concealed bribe
to pervert the ways of justice.
24 The discerning person looks to wisdom,
but the eyes of a fool to the ends of the earth.
25 Foolish children are a grief to their father
and bitterness to her who bore them.
26 To impose a fine on the innocent is not right,
or to flog the noble for their integrity.

and shares the inheritance with the brothers.
3 The smelting pot for silver, the crucible for gold,
but the LORD it is who assays the heart.
4 A rogue gives a ready ear to mischievous talk,
and a liar listens to slander.
5 To sneer at the poor is to insult the Creator,
and whoever gloats over another's misfortune will
answer for it.
6 Grandchildren are the crown of old age,
and parents are the pride of their children.
7 Fine talk is out of place in a boor,
how much more are false words from a noble
character!
8 A bribe works like a charm for him who offers it;
wherever he turns he will prosper.
9 One who covers up another's offence seeks his
goodwill,
but one who betrays a confidence disrupts a
friendship.
10 A reproof makes more impression on a discerning
person
than a hundred blows on one who is stupid.
11 An evil person is set only on rebellion,
so a messenger without mercy will be sent against
him.
12 Better face a she-bear robbed of her cubs
than a fool in his folly.
13 If anyone repays evil for good,
evil will never depart from his house.
14 Stealing water starts a quarrel;
abandon a dispute before you come to blows.
15 To acquit the guilty and to condemn the
innocent—
both are abominable to the LORD.
16 What use is money in the hands of a fool?
Can he buy wisdom if he has no sense?
17 A friend shows his friendship at all times,
and a brother is born to share troubles.
18 Whoever gives a guarantee is without sense;
as surety he surrenders himself to another.
19 One who likes giving offence likes strife.
One who builds a lofty entrance invites disaster.
20 A crooked heart will come to no good,
and a mischievous tongue will end in calamity.
21 Stupid offspring bring sorrow to parents,
and no father has joy of a boorish son.
22 A glad heart makes for good health,
but low spirits sap one's strength.
23 A wicked person produces a bribe from under his
cloak
to pervert the course of justice.
24 Wisdom is never out of sight of those who are
discerning,
but the stupid have their eyes on the ends of the
earth.
25 A stupid son exasperates his father
and is a heartache to the mother who bore him.
26 To punish the innocent is not right,
and it is wrong to inflict blows on those of noble
mind.

_____
b Or *a noble person*

and will share the inheritance with the brothers.

3 The crucible for silver, and the furnace for gold,
 but the tester of hearts is the LORD.

4 The evil man gives heed to wicked lips,
 and listens to falsehood from a
  mischievous tongue.

5 He who mocks the poor blasphemes his Maker;
 he who is glad at calamity will not
  go unpunished.

6 Grandchildren are the crown of old men,
 and the glory of children is their parentage.

7 Fine words are out of place in a fool;
 how much more, lying words in a noble!

8 A man who has a bribe to offer rates it a
  magic stone;
 at every turn it brings him success.

9 He who covers up a misdeed fosters friendship,
 but he who gossips about it separates friends.

10 A single reprimand does more for a man
  of intelligence
 than a hundred lashes for a fool.

11 On rebellion alone is the wicked man bent,
 but a merciless messenger will be sent
  against him.

12 Face a bear robbed of her cubs,
 but never a fool in his folly!

13 If a man returns evil for good,
 from his house evil will not depart.

14 The start of strife is like the opening of a dam;
 therefore, check a quarrel before it begins!

15 He who condones the wicked, he who condemns
  the just,
 are both an abomination to the LORD.

16 Of what use in the fool's hand are the means
 to buy wisdom, since he has no mind for it?

17 He who is a friend is always a friend,
 and a brother is born for the time of stress.

18 Senseless is the man who gives his hand in pledge,
 who becomes surety for his neighbor.

19 He who loves strife loves guilt;
 he who builds his gate high courts disaster.

20 He who is perverse in heart finds no good,
 and a double-tongued man falls into trouble.

21 To be a fool's parent is grief for a man;
 the father of a numskull has no joy.

22 A joyful heart is the health of the body,
 but a depressed spirit dries up the bones.

23 The wicked man accepts a concealed bribe
 to pervert the course of justice.

24 The man of intelligence fixes his gaze on wisdom,
 but the eyes of a fool are on the ends of
  the earth.

25 A foolish son is vexation to his father,
 and bitter sorrow to her who bore him.

26 It is wrong to fine an innocent man,
 but beyond reason to scourge princes.

he will share the inheritance with the brothers.

3 A furnace for silver, a foundry for gold, *p*
 but Yahweh for the testing of hearts!

4 An evil-doer pays heed to malicious talk,
 a liar listens to a slanderous tongue.

5 To mock the poor is to insult the Creator,
 no one who laughs at distress will go
  unpunished.

6 The crown of the aged is their children's children;
 the children's glory is their father.

7 Fine words do not become the foolish,
 false words become a prince still less.

8 A gift works like a talisman for one who holds it:
 it brings prosperity at every turn.

9 Whoever covers an offence promotes love,
 whoever again raises the matter divides friends.

10 A reproof makes more impression on a person of
  understanding
 than a hundred strokes on a fool.

11 The wicked person thinks of nothing but rebellion,
 but a cruel messenger will be sent to such a one.

12 Rather come on a bear robbed of her cubs
 than on a fool in his folly.

13 Disaster will never be far from the house
 of one who returns evil for good.

14 As well unleash a flood as start a dispute;
 desist before the quarrel breaks out.

15 To absolve the guilty and condemn the upright,
 both alike are abhorrent to Yahweh.

16 What good is money in the hand of a fool?
 To buy wisdom with it? The desire is not there.

17 A friend is a friend at all times,
 it is for adversity that a brother is born.

18 Whoever offers guarantees lacks sense
 and goes surety for a neighbour.

19 The double-dealer loves sin,
 the proud courts ruin.

20 The tortuous of heart finds no happiness,
 the perverse of speech falls into misery.

21 He who fathers a stupid child does so to his
  sorrow,
 the father of a fool knows no joy.

22 A glad heart is excellent medicine,
 a depressed spirit wastes the bones away.

23 Under cover of his cloak a bad man takes a gift
 to pervert the course of justice.

24 The intelligent has wisdom there before him,
 but the eyes of a fool range to the ends of the
  earth.

25 A foolish child is a father's sorrow,
 and the grief of her who gave the child birth.

26 To fine the upright is indeed a crime,
 to strike the noble is an injustice.

p 17 = 27:21.

NEW REVISED STANDARD VERSION

27 One who spares words is knowledgeable;
   one who is cool in spirit has understanding.
28 Even fools who keep silent are considered wise;
   when they close their lips, they are deemed
   intelligent.

18 The one who lives alone is self-indulgent,
   showing contempt for all who have sound
   judgment. *c*
2 A fool takes no pleasure in understanding,
   but only in expressing personal opinion.
3 When wickedness comes, contempt comes also;
   and with dishonor comes disgrace.
4 The words of the mouth are deep waters;
   the fountain of wisdom is a gushing stream.
5 It is not right to be partial to the guilty,
   or to subvert the innocent in judgment.
6 A fool's lips bring strife,
   and a fool's mouth invites a flogging.
7 The mouths of fools are their ruin,
   and their lips a snare to themselves.
8 The words of a whisperer are like delicious
      morsels;
   they go down into the inner parts of the body.
9 One who is slack in work
   is close kin to a vandal.
10 The name of the LORD is a strong tower;
   the righteous run into it and are safe.
11 The wealth of the rich is their strong city;
   in their imagination it is like a high wall.
12 Before destruction one's heart is haughty,
   but humility goes before honor.
13 If one gives answer before hearing,
   it is folly and shame.
14 The human spirit will endure sickness;
   but a broken spirit — who can bear?
15 An intelligent mind acquires knowledge,
   and the ear of the wise seeks knowledge.
16 A gift opens doors;
   it gives access to the great.
17 The one who first states a case seems right,
   until the other comes and cross-examines.
18 Casting the lot puts an end to disputes
   and decides between powerful contenders.
19 An ally offended is stronger than a city; *d*
   such quarreling is like the bars of a castle.
20 From the fruit of the mouth one's stomach is
      satisfied;
   the yield of the lips brings satisfaction.
21 Death and life are in the power of the tongue,
   and those who love it will eat its fruits.
22 He who finds a wife finds a good thing,
   and obtains favor from the LORD.
23 The poor use entreaties,
   but the rich answer roughly.

REVISED ENGLISH BIBLE

27 Experience uses few words;
   discernment keeps a cool head.
28 Even a fool, if he keeps his mouth shut, will seem
      wise;
   if he holds his tongue, he will seem intelligent.

18 A solitary person pursues his own desires;
   he quarrels with every sound policy.
2 The foolish have no interest in seeking to
      understand,
   but only in expressing their own opinions.
3 When wickedness comes in, in comes contempt;
   with loss of honour comes reproach.
4 The words of the mouth are a gushing torrent,
   but deep is the water in the well of wisdom.
5 It is wrong to show favour to the wicked,
   to deprive the righteous of justice.
6 When the stupid man talks, contention follows;
   his words provoke blows.
7 The tongue of a stupid person is his undoing;
   his lips put his life in jeopardy.
8 A gossip's whispers are tasty morsels
   swallowed right down.
9 The lazy worker is own brother
   to the man who enjoys destruction.
10 The name of the LORD is a tower of strength,
   where the righteous may run for refuge.
11 The wealth of someone who is rich is his strong
      city;
   he thinks it an unscalable wall.
12 Before disaster comes one may be proud;
   before honour comes one must be humble.
13 To answer a question before you have heard it out
   is both stupid and insulting.
14 A person's spirit sustains in sickness,
   but who can endure if the spirit is crushed?
15 Knowledge comes to the discerning mind;
   the wise ear listens to get knowledge.
16 A gift opens the door to the giver
   and gains access to the great.
17 In a lawsuit the first speaker seems right,
   until another comes forward to cross-examine him.
18 Cast lots, and settle a quarrel,
   and so keep litigants apart.
19 A reluctant brother is more unyielding than a
      fortress,
   and quarrels are as stubborn as the bars of a
      fortress.
20 Someone may live by the fruit of his tongue;
   his lips may earn him a livelihood.
21 The tongue has power of life and death;
   make friends with it and enjoy its fruits.
22 He who finds a wife finds a good thing;
   he has won favour from the LORD.
23 The poor speak in a tone of entreaty;
   the rich give a harsh answer.

---

c Meaning of Heb uncertain   *d* Gk Syr Vg Tg: Meaning of Heb
uncertain

18:4 **The words . . . wisdom:** *prob. rdg, inverting phrases.*

27 He who spares his words is truly wise,
and he who is chary of speech is a man of
intelligence.

28 Even a fool, if he keeps silent, is considered wise;
if he closes his lips, intelligent.

18 In estrangement one seeks pretexts:
with all persistence he picks a quarrel.

2 The fool takes no delight in understanding,
but rather in displaying what he thinks.

3 With wickedness comes contempt,
and with disgrace comes scorn.

4 The words from a man's mouth are deep waters,
but the source of wisdom is a flowing brook.

5 It is not good to be partial to the guilty,
and so to reject a rightful claim.

6 The fool's lips lead him into strife,
and his mouth provokes a beating.

7 The fool's mouth is his ruin;
his lips are a snare to his life.

8 The words of a talebearer are like dainty morsels
that sink into one's inmost being.

9 The man who is slack in his work
is own brother to the man who is destructive.

10 The name of the LORD is a strong tower;
the just man runs to it and is safe.

11 The rich man's wealth is his strong city;
he fancies it a high wall.

12 Before his downfall a man's heart is haughty,
but humility goes before honors.

13 He who answers before he hears —
his is the folly and the shame.

14 A man's spirit sustains him in infirmity —
but a broken spirit who can bear?

15 The mind of the intelligent gains knowledge,
and the ear of the wise seeks knowledge.

16 A man's gift clears the way for him,
and gains him access to great men.

17 The man who pleads his case first seems to be in
the right;
then his opponent comes and puts him to
the test.

18 The lot puts an end to disputes,
and is decisive in a controversy between
the mighty.

19 A brother is a better defense than a strong city,
and a friend is like the bars of a castle.

20 From the fruit of his mouth a man has his fill;
with the yield of his lips he sates himself.

21 Death and life are in the power of the tongue;
those who make it a friend shall eat its fruit.

22 He who finds a wife finds happiness;
it is a favor he receives from the LORD.

23 The poor man implores,
but the rich man answers harshly.

27 Whoever can control the tongue knows what
knowledge is,
someone of understanding keeps a cool temper.

28 If the fool holds his tongue, he may pass for wise;
if he seals his lips, he may pass for intelligent.

18 Whoever lives alone follows private whims,
and is angered by advice of any kind.

2 A fool takes no pleasure in understanding
but only in airing an opinion.

3 When wickedness comes, indignity comes too,
and, with contempt, dishonour.

4 Deep waters, such are human words:
a gushing stream, the utterance of wisdom.

5 It is not good to show partiality for the wicked
and so to deprive the upright when giving
judgement.

6 The lips of a fool go to the law-courts
with a mouth that pleads for a beating.

7 The mouth of the fool works its owner's ruin,
the lips of a fool are a snare for their owner's
life.

8 The words of a slanderer are tasty morsels
that go right down into the belly. *q*

9 Whoever is idle at work
is blood-brother to the destroyer.

10 The name of Yahweh is a strong tower;
the upright runs to it and is secure.

11 The wealth of the rich forms a stronghold, *r*
a high wall, as the rich supposes.

12 The human heart is haughty until destruction
comes,
before there can be glory there must be
humility. *s*

13 To retort without first listening
is both foolish and embarrassing.

14 Sickness the human spirit can endure,
but when the spirit is broken, who can bear this?

15 The heart of the intelligent acquires learning,
the ears of the wise search for knowledge.

16 A present will open all doors
and win access to the great.

17 The first to plead is adjudged to be upright,
until the next comes and cross-examines him.

18 The lot puts an end to disputes
and decides between men of power.

19 A brother offended is worse than a fortified city,
and quarrels are like the locks of a keep.

20 From the fruit of the mouth is a stomach filled,
it is the yield of the lips that gives contentment.

21 Death and life are in the gift of the tongue,
those who indulge it must eat the fruit it yields.

22 He who finds a wife finds happiness,
receiving a mark of favour from Yahweh.

23 The language of the poor is entreaty,
the answer of the rich harshness.

q **18** = 26:22.   *r* **18** = 10:15.   *s* **18** = 15:33.

NEW REVISED STANDARD VERSION | REVISED ENGLISH BIBLE

24 Some[e] friends play at friendship[f]
but a true friend sticks closer than one's nearest kin.

19

Better the poor walking in integrity
than one perverse of speech who is a fool.

2 Desire without knowledge is not good,
and one who moves too hurriedly misses the way.

3 One's own folly leads to ruin,
yet the heart rages against the LORD.

4 Wealth brings many friends,
but the poor are left friendless.

5 A false witness will not go unpunished,
and a liar will not escape.

6 Many seek the favor of the generous,
and everyone is a friend to a giver of gifts.

7 If the poor are hated even by their kin,
how much more are they shunned by their friends!
When they call after them, they are not there.[g]

8 To get wisdom is to love oneself;
to keep understanding is to prosper.

9 A false witness will not go unpunished,
and the liar will perish.

10 It is not fitting for a fool to live in luxury,
much less for a slave to rule over princes.

11 Those with good sense are slow to anger,
and it is their glory to overlook an offense.

12 A king's anger is like the growling of a lion,
but his favor is like dew on the grass.

13 A stupid child is ruin to a father,
and a wife's quarreling is a continual dripping of rain.

14 House and wealth are inherited from parents,
but a prudent wife is from the LORD.

15 Laziness brings on deep sleep;
an idle person will suffer hunger.

16 Those who keep the commandment will live;
those who are heedless of their ways will die.

17 Whoever is kind to the poor lends to the LORD,
and will be repaid in full.

18 Discipline your children while there is hope;
do not set your heart on their destruction.

19 A violent tempered person will pay the penalty;
if you effect a rescue, you will only have to do it again.[g]

20 Listen to advice and accept instruction,
that you may gain wisdom for the future.

21 The human mind may devise many plans,
but it is the purpose of the LORD that will be established.

22 What is desirable in a person is loyalty,
and it is better to be poor than a liar.

23 The fear of the LORD is life indeed;
filled with it one rests secure
and suffers no harm.

---

24 Some companions are good only for idle talk,
but there is a friend who sticks closer than a brother.

19

Better to be poor and above reproach
than rich and double-tongued.

2 It is not good to have zeal without knowledge,
nor to be in too great a hurry and so miss the way.

3 When folly wrecks someone's life,
he rages in his heart against the LORD.

4 Wealth makes many new friends,
but someone without means loses any friend he has.

5 A false witness will not escape punishment;
the perjurer will not go free.

6 Many curry favour with the great;
a lavish giver has the world for his friend.

7 A pauper's brothers all dislike him;
how much more is he shunned by his friends!
The man who picks his words keeps to the point.

8 To learn sense is true self-love;
cherish discernment and make sure of success.

9 A false witness will not escape punishment;
the perjurer will perish.

10 A fool at the helm is out of place,
how much worse a slave in command of men of rank!

11 Forbearance shows intelligence;
to overlook an offence brings glory.

12 A king's rage is like a lion's roar,
but his favour is like dew on the grass.

13 A stupid son is a calamity to his father;
a nagging wife is like water endlessly dripping.

14 Home and wealth may come down from ancestors,
but a sensible wife is a gift from the LORD.

15 Sloth leads to sleep
and negligence to starvation.

16 Keeping the commandments keeps a person safe,
but scorning the way of the LORD brings death.

17 He who is generous to the poor lends to the LORD,
who will recompense him for his deed.

18 Chastise your son while there is hope for him;
only be careful not to flog him to death.

19 Anyone whose temper is violent must bear the consequences;
try to save him, and you make matters worse.

20 Listen to advice and accept instruction,
and in the end you will be wise.

21 The human mind may be full of schemes,
but it is the LORD's purpose that will prevail.

22 Greed is a disgrace to a man;
better be poor than a liar.

23 The fear of the LORD is life;
he who is full of it will rest untouched by evil.

---

e Syr Tg: Heb *A man of*   f Cn Compare Syr Vg Tg: Meaning of Heb uncertain   g Meaning of Heb uncertain

19:1 **rich:** *prob. rdg; so Syriac, cp. 28:6; Heb.* a fool.

NEW AMERICAN BIBLE

24 Some friends bring ruin on us,
  but a true friend is more loyal than a brother.

19 Better a poor man who walks in his integrity
  than he who is crooked in his ways and rich.

2 Without knowledge even zeal is not good;
  and he who acts hastily, blunders.

3 A man's own folly upsets his way,
  but his heart is resentful against the LORD.

4 Wealth adds many friends,
  but the friend of the poor man deserts him.

5 The false witness will not go unpunished,
  and he who utters lies will not escape.

6 Many curry favor with a noble;
  all are friends of the man who has something
  to give.

7 All the poor man's brothers hate him;
  how much more do his friends shun him!

8 He who gains intelligence is his own best friend;
  he who keeps understanding will be successful.

9 The false witness will not go unpunished,
  and he who utters lies will perish.

10 Luxury is not befitting a fool;
  much less should a slave rule over princes.

11 It is good sense in a man to be slow to anger,
  and it is his glory to overlook an offense.

12 The king's wrath is like the roaring of a lion,
  but his favor, like dew on the grass.

13 The foolish son is ruin to his father,
  and the nagging of a wife is a persistent leak.

14 Home and possessions are an inheritance
    from parents,
  but a prudent wife is from the LORD.

15 Laziness plunges a man into deep sleep,
  and the sluggard must go hungry.

16 He who keeps the precept keeps his life,
  but the despiser of the word will die.

17 He who has compassion on the poor lends to
    the LORD,
  and he will repay him for his good deed.

18 Chastise your son, for in this there is hope;
  but do not desire his death.

19 The man of violent temper pays the penalty;
  even if you rescue him, you will have it to
    do again.

20 Listen to counsel and receive instruction,
  that you may eventually become wise.

21 Many are the plans in a man's heart,
  but it is the decision of the LORD that endures.

22 From a man's greed comes his shame;
  rather be a poor man than a liar.

23 The fear of the LORD is an aid to life;
  one eats and sleeps without being visited
    by misfortune.

NEW JERUSALEM BIBLE

24 There are friends who point the way to ruin,
  others are closer than a brother.

19 Better the poor living an honest life
  than the adept at double-talk who is a fool.

2 Where knowledge is wanting, zeal is not good;
  whoever goes too quickly stumbles.

3 Folly leads conduct astray,
  yet it is against Yahweh that the heart rages.

4 Wealth multiplies friends,
  but the one friend the poor has is taken away.

5 The false witness will not go unpunished,[t]
  no one who utters lies will go free.

6 The nobleman has many to court his favour,
  to a giver of gifts, everyone is friend.

7 The poor man's brothers hate him, every one;
  his friends — how much the more do these desert
    him!

  He goes in search of words, but there are none to
    be had.[u]

8 Whoever acquires sense wins profit from it,
  whoever treasures understanding finds happiness.

9 The false witness will not go unpunished,[v]
  whoever utters lies will be destroyed.

10 It is not fitting for a fool to live in luxury,
  still less for a slave to govern princes.

11 Good sense makes for self-control,
  and for pride in overlooking an offence.

12 Like the roaring of a lion, the anger of a king,
  but like dew on the grass his favour.

13 A foolish child is a disaster for the father,
  the bickerings of a wife are like an ever-dripping
    gutter.

14 From fathers comes inheritance of house and
    wealth,
  from Yahweh a wife who is discreet.

15 Idleness lulls to sleep,
  the feckless soul will go hungry.

16 Keeping the commandment is self-preservation,
  but whoever despises these ways will die.

17 Whoever is kind to the poor is lending to Yahweh
  who will repay him the kindness done.

18 While there is hope for him, chastise your child,
  but do not get so angry as to kill him.

19 The violent lays himself open to a penalty;
  spare him, and you aggravate his crime.

20 Listen to advice, accept correction,
  to be the wiser in the time to come.

21 Many are the plans in the human heart,
  but the purpose of Yahweh — that stands firm.

22 Faithful love is what people look for in a person;
  they prefer the poor to a liar.

23 The fear of Yahweh leads to life,
  it brings food and shelter, without fear of evil.

---

t **19** = 19:9.   u **19** A fragment, probably lacking the first line.
v **19** = 19:5.

NEW REVISED STANDARD VERSION

24 The lazy person buries a hand in the dish,
and will not even bring it back to the mouth.
25 Strike a scoffer, and the simple will learn
prudence;
reprove the intelligent, and they will gain
knowledge.
26 Those who do violence to their father and chase
away their mother
are children who cause shame and bring
reproach.
27 Cease straying, my child, from the words of
knowledge,
in order that you may hear instruction.
28 A worthless witness mocks at justice,
and the mouth of the wicked devours iniquity.
29 Condemnation is ready for scoffers,
and flogging for the backs of fools.

20 Wine is a mocker, strong drink a brawler,
and whoever is led astray by it is not wise.
2 The dread anger of a king is like the growling of
a lion;
anyone who provokes him to anger forfeits life
itself.
3 It is honorable to refrain from strife,
but every fool is quick to quarrel.
4 The lazy person does not plow in season;
harvest comes, and there is nothing to be
found.
5 The purposes in the human mind are like deep
water,
but the intelligent will draw them out.
6 Many proclaim themselves loyal,
but who can find one worthy of trust?
7 The righteous walk in integrity —
happy are the children who follow them!
8 A king who sits on the throne of judgment
winnows all evil with his eyes.
9 Who can say, "I have made my heart clean;
I am pure from my sin"?
10 Diverse weights and diverse measures
are both alike an abomination to the LORD.
11 Even children make themselves known by their
acts,
by whether what they do is pure and right.
12 The hearing ear and the seeing eye —
the LORD has made them both.
13 Do not love sleep, or else you will come to
poverty;
open your eyes, and you will have plenty of
bread.
14 "Bad, bad," says the buyer,
then goes away and boasts.
15 There is gold, and abundance of costly stones;
but the lips informed by knowledge are a
precious jewel.
16 Take the garment of one who has given surety for
a stranger;
seize the pledge given as surety for foreigners.
17 Bread gained by deceit is sweet,
but afterward the mouth will be full of gravel.

REVISED ENGLISH BIBLE

24 The sluggard dips his hand into the dish
but will not so much as lift it to his mouth.
25 Strike an arrogant person,
and the simpleton learns prudence;
reprove someone who has understanding,
and he understands what you mean.
26 He who expels his father evicts his mother;
they have a son who brings shame and disgrace on
them.
27 A son who ceases to accept correction
is sure to turn his back on the teachings of
knowledge.
28 A lying witness makes a mockery of justice,
and the talk of the wicked fosters mischief.
29 There is a rod in pickle for the arrogant,
and blows are ready for the fool's back.

20 Wine is an insolent fellow, strong drink a
brawler,
and no one addicted to their company grows wise.
2 A king's threat is like a lion's roar;
one who ignores it puts his life in jeopardy.
3 To draw back from a dispute is honourable,
but every fool comes to blows.
4 The lazy man who does not plough in autumn
looks for a crop at harvest and gets nothing.
5 Counsel in another's heart is like deep water,
but a discerning person will draw it up.
6 Many assert their loyalty,
but where will you find one to keep faith?
7 If someone leads a good and upright life,
happy are his children after him!
8 A king seated on his throne in judgement
has an eye to sift out all that is evil.
9 Who can say, 'I have a clear conscience;
I am purged from my sin'?
10 A double standard in weights and measures
is an abomination to the LORD.
11 By his actions a child reveals himself,
whether or not his conduct is innocent and upright.
12 An attentive ear, an observant eye,
the LORD made them both.
13 Love sleep, and you will know poverty;
keep awake, and you will eat your fill.
14 'A bad bargain!' says the buyer to the seller,
but off he goes to brag about it.
15 There is gold in plenty and a wealth of red coral,
but informed speech is a rarity.
16 Take the garment of anyone who pledges his word
for a stranger;
hold it as security for the unknown person.
17 Bread got by fraud may taste good,
but afterwards it turns to grit in the mouth.

24 The sluggard loses his hand in the dish;
   he will not even lift it to his mouth.

25 If you beat an arrogant man, the simple learn
   a lesson;
   if you rebuke an intelligent man, he gains
   knowledge.

26 He who mistreats his father, or drives away
   his mother,
   is a worthless and disgraceful son.

27 If a son ceases to hear instruction,
   he wanders from words of knowledge.

28 An unprincipled witness perverts justice,
   and the mouth of the wicked pours out iniquity.

29 Rods are prepared for the arrogant,
   and blows for the backs of fools.

20 Wine is arrogant, strong drink is riotous;
   none who goes astray for it is wise.

2 The dread of the king is as when a lion roars;
   he who incurs his anger forfeits his life.

3 It is honorable for a man to shun strife,
   while every fool starts a quarrel.

4 In seedtime the sluggard plows not;
   when he looks for the harvest, it is not there.

5 The intention in the human heart is like water far
   below the surface,
   but the man of intelligence draws it forth.

6 Many are declared to be men of virtue:
   but who can find one worthy of trust?

7 When a man walks in integrity and justice,
   happy are his children after him!

8 A king seated on the throne of judgment
   dispels all evil with his glance.

9 Who can say, "I have made my heart clean,
   I am cleansed of my sin"?

10 Varying weights, varying measures,
   are both an abomination to the LORD.

11 Even by his manners the child betrays
   whether his conduct is innocent and right.

12 The ear that hears, and the eye that sees—
   the LORD has made them both.

13 Love not sleep, lest you be reduced to poverty;
   eyes wide open mean abundant food.

14 "Bad, bad!" says the buyer;
   but once he has gone his way, he boasts.

15 Like gold or a wealth of corals,
   wise lips are a precious ornament.

16 Take his garment who becomes surety for another,
   and for strangers yield it up!

17 The bread of deceit is sweet to a man,
   but afterward his mouth will be filled
   with gravel.

24 Into the dish the idler dips his hand,
   but bring it back to his mouth he cannot. ʷ

25 Strike a cynic, and simpletons will be more wary;
   reprove the intelligent and he will understand
   your meaning.

26 He who ill-treats his father and drives out his
   mother
   is a child both worthless and depraved.

27 Give up listening to instruction, my child,
   if you mean to stray from words of knowledge.

28 A perjured witness holds the law in scorn;
   the mouth of the wicked feasts on evil-doing.

29 Punishments were made for mockers,
   and beating for the backs of fools.

20 Wine is reckless, liquor rowdy;
   unwise is anyone whom it seduces.

2 Like the roaring of a lion is the fury of a king;
   whoever provokes him sins against himself.

3 It is praiseworthy to stop short of a law-suit;
   only a fool flies into a rage.

4 In autumn the idler does not plough,
   at harvest time he looks—nothing there!

5 The resources of the human heart are like deep
   waters:
   an understanding person has only to draw on
   them.

6 Many describe themselves as people of faithful
   love,
   but who can find someone really to be trusted?

7 The upright whose ways are blameless—
   blessed the children who come after!

8 A king enthroned on the judgement seat
   with one look scatters all that is evil.

9 Who can say, 'I have cleansed my heart,
   I am purified of my sin'?

10 One weight here, another there; here one measure,
   there another:
   both alike are abhorrent to Yahweh.

11 A young man's character appears in what he does,
   if his behaviour is pure and straight.

12 Ear that hears, eye that sees,
   Yahweh has made both of these.

13 Do not love sleep or you will know poverty;
   keep your eyes open and have your fill of food.

14 'No good, no good!' says the buyer,
   but he goes off congratulating himself.

15 There are gold and jewels of every type,
   but a priceless ornament is speech informed by
   knowledge.

16 Take the man's clothes! He has gone surety for a
   stranger.
   Take a pledge from him to the profit of persons
   unknown! ˣ

17 Bread is sweet when it is got by fraud,
   but later the mouth is full of grit.

ʷ **19** = 26:15.   ˣ **20** = 27:13.

NEW REVISED STANDARD VERSION

18 Plans are established by taking advice;
   wage war by following wise guidance.
19 A gossip reveals secrets;
   therefore do not associate with a babbler.
20 If you curse father or mother,
   your lamp will go out in utter darkness.
21 An estate quickly acquired in the beginning
   will not be blessed in the end.
22 Do not say, "I will repay evil";
   wait for the LORD, and he will help you.
23 Differing weights are an abomination to the
      LORD,
   and false scales are not good.
24 All our steps are ordered by the LORD;
   how then can we understand our own ways?
25 It is a snare for one to say rashly, "It is holy,"
   and begin to reflect only after making a vow.
26 A wise king winnows the wicked,
   and drives the wheel over them.
27 The human spirit is the lamp of the LORD,
   searching every inmost part.
28 Loyalty and faithfulness preserve the king,
   and his throne is upheld by righteousness. *h*
29 The glory of youths is their strength,
   but the beauty of the aged is their gray hair.
30 Blows that wound cleanse away evil;
   beatings make clean the innermost parts.

21 The king's heart is a stream of water in the hand
      of the LORD;
   he turns it wherever he will.
2 All deeds are right in the sight of the doer,
   but the LORD weighs the heart.
3 To do righteousness and justice
   is more acceptable to the LORD than sacrifice.
4 Haughty eyes and a proud heart—
   the lamp of the wicked—are sin.
5 The plans of the diligent lead surely to
      abundance,
   but everyone who is hasty comes only to want.
6 The getting of treasures by a lying tongue
   is a fleeting vapor and a snare *i* of death.
7 The violence of the wicked will sweep them
      away,
   because they refuse to do what is just.
8 The way of the guilty is crooked,
   but the conduct of the pure is right.
9 It is better to live in a corner of the housetop
   than in a house shared with a contentious wife.
10 The souls of the wicked desire evil;
   their neighbors find no mercy in their eyes.
11 When a scoffer is punished, the simple become
      wiser;
   when the wise are instructed, they increase in
      knowledge.

REVISED ENGLISH BIBLE

18 Counsel is the key to good planning;
   wars are won by statecraft.
19 A gossip will betray secrets,
   so have nothing to do with a tale-bearer.
20 If anyone reviles his father and mother,
   his lamp will fail when darkness is deepest.
21 If you begin by amassing possessions in haste,
   they will bring you no blessing in the end.
22 Do not think to repay evil for evil;
   wait for the LORD to deliver you.
23 A double standard in weights is an abomination to
      the LORD,
   and false scales are unforgivable.
24 It is the LORD who directs a person's steps;
   how can anyone understand the road he travels?
25 It is dangerous to dedicate a gift rashly,
   to make a vow and then have second thoughts.
26 A wise king sifts out the wicked
   and turns the wheel of fortune against them.
27 The LORD shines into a person's soul,
   searching out his inmost being.
28 Loyalty and good faith preserve a king;
   his throne is upheld by justice.
29 The glory of young men is their strength,
   the dignity of old men their grey hairs.
30 A good beating purges the mind of evil,
   and blows chasten the inmost being.

21 The king's heart is in the LORD's hand;
   like runnels of water, he turns it wherever he
      will.
2 A person's whole conduct may be right in his own
      eyes,
   but the LORD weighs up his motives.
3 To do what is right and just
   is more acceptable to the LORD than sacrifice.
4 Haughty looks and a proud heart—
   these sins brand the wicked.
5 Forethought and diligence lead to profit
   as surely as rash haste leads to poverty.
6 He who makes a fortune by telling lies
   runs needlessly into the snares of death.
7 The wicked are caught up in their own violence,
   because they refuse to do what is just.
8 The criminal's conduct is devious;
   straight dealing is a sign of integrity.
9 Better to live on a corner of the housetop
   than share the house with a nagging wife.
10 The wicked are set on evil;
   even friends do not arouse their pity.
11 Simpletons learn wisdom when the insolent are
      punished;
   when the wise prosper they draw a lesson from it.

h Gk: Heb *loyalty*   *i* Gk: Heb *seekers*

20:21 **by . . . haste:** or, *as otherwise read,* by wrongfully
withholding an inheritance.   20:28 **justice:** *so* Gk; *Heb.* loyalty.
21:6 **snares:** *prob. rdg, cp.* Gk; *Heb.* seekers.

NEW AMERICAN BIBLE	NEW JERUSALEM BIBLE

18 Plans made after advice succeed;
   so with wise guidance wage your war.

19 A newsmonger reveals secrets;
   so have nothing to do with a babbler!

20 If one curses his father or mother,
   his lamp will go out at the coming of darkness.

21 Possessions gained hastily at the outset
   will in the end not be blessed.

22 Say not, "I will repay evil!"
   Trust in the LORD and he will help you.

23 Varying weights are an abomination to the LORD,
   and false scales are not good.

24 Man's steps are from the LORD;
   how, then, can a man understand his way?

25 Rashly to pledge a sacred gift is a trap for a man,
   or to regret a vow once made.

26 A wise king winnows the wicked,
   and threshes them under the cartwheel.

27 A lamp from the LORD is the breath of man;
   it searches through all his inmost being.

28 Kindness and piety safeguard the king,
   and he upholds his throne by justice.

29 The glory of young men is their strength,
   and the dignity of old men is gray hair.

30 Evil is cleansed away by bloody lashes,
   and a scourging to the inmost being.

18 Plans are matured by consultation;
   take wise advice when waging war.

19 The bearer of gossip lets out secrets;
   do not mingle with chatterers.

20 Whoever curses father or mother
   will have his lamp put out in the deepest darkness.

21 Property quickly come by at first
   will not be blessed in the end.

22 Do not say, 'I shall repay evil';
   put your hope in Yahweh and he will keep you safe.

23 One weight here, another there: this is abhorrent to Yahweh,
   false scales are not good.

24 Yahweh guides the steps of the powerful:
   but who can comprehend human ways?

25 Anyone is trapped who cries 'Dedicated!'
   and begins to reflect only after the vow.

26 A wise king winnows the wicked
   and makes the wheel pass over them.

27 The human spirit is the lamp of Yahweh —
   searching the deepest self.

28 Faithful love and loyalty mount guard over the king,
   his throne is founded on saving justice.

29 The pride of the young is their strength,
   the ornament of the old, grey hairs.

30 Wounding strokes are good medicine for evil,
   blows have an effect on the inmost self.

21 Like a stream is the king's heart in the hand of the Lord;
   wherever it pleases him, he directs it.

2 All the ways of a man may be right in his own eyes,
   but it is the LORD who proves hearts.

3 To do what is right and just
   is more acceptable to the LORD than sacrifice.

4 Haughty eyes and a proud heart —
   the tillage of the wicked is sin.

5 The plans of the diligent are sure of profit,
   but all rash haste leads certainly to poverty.

6 He who makes a fortune by a lying tongue
   is chasing a bubble over deadly snares.

7 The oppression of the wicked will sweep them away,
   because they refuse to do what is right.

8 The way of the culprit is crooked,
   but the conduct of the innocent is right.

9 It is better to dwell in a corner of the housetop
   than in a roomy house with a quarrelsome woman.

10 The soul of the wicked man desires evil;
   his neighbor finds no pity in his eyes.

11 When the arrogant man is punished, the simple are the wiser;
   when the wise man is instructed, he gains knowledge.

21 Like flowing water is a king's heart in Yahweh's hand;
   he directs it wherever he pleases.

2 All actions are straight in the doer's own eyes,
   but it is Yahweh who weighs hearts.

3 To do what is upright and just
   is more pleasing to Yahweh than sacrifice.

4 Haughty eye, proud heart,
   lamp of the wicked, nothing but sin.

5 The hardworking is thoughtful, and all is gain;
   too much haste, and all that comes of it is want.

6 To make a fortune with the help of a lying tongue:
   such is the idle fantasy of those who look for death.

7 The violence of the wicked proves their ruin,
   for they refuse to do what is right.

8 The way of the felon is devious,
   the conduct of the innocent straight.

9 Better the corner of a roof to live on
   than a house shared with a quarrelsome woman.*y*

10 The soul of the wicked is intent on evil,
   to such a person no neighbour can ever do right.

11 When a cynic is punished, simpletons grow wiser,
   but someone of understanding acquires knowledge by instruction.

y **21** = 25:24.

1403

12 The Righteous One observes the house of the
    wicked;
    he casts the wicked down to ruin.
13 If you close your ear to the cry of the poor,
    you will cry out and not be heard.
14 A gift in secret averts anger;
    and a concealed bribe in the bosom, strong
    wrath.
15 When justice is done, it is a joy to the righteous,
    but dismay to evildoers.
16 Whoever wanders from the way of understanding
    will rest in the assembly of the dead.
17 Whoever loves pleasure will suffer want;
    whoever loves wine and oil will not be rich.
18 The wicked is a ransom for the righteous,
    and the faithless for the upright.
19 It is better to live in a desert land
    than with a contentious and fretful wife.
20 Precious treasure remains *j* in the house of the
    wise,
    but the fool devours it.
21 Whoever pursues righteousness and kindness
    will find life *k* and honor.
22 One wise person went up against a city of
    warriors
    and brought down the stronghold in which they
    trusted.
23 To watch over mouth and tongue
    is to keep out of trouble.
24 The proud, haughty person, named "Scoffer,"
    acts with arrogant pride.
25 The craving of the lazy person is fatal,
    for lazy hands refuse to labor.
26 All day long the wicked covet, *l*
    but the righteous give and do not hold back.
27 The sacrifice of the wicked is an abomination;
    how much more when brought with evil intent.
28 A false witness will perish,
    but a good listener will testify successfully.
29 The wicked put on a bold face,
    but the upright give thought to *m* their ways.
30 No wisdom, no understanding, no counsel,
    can avail against the LORD.
31 The horse is made ready for the day of battle,
    but the victory belongs to the LORD.

22 A good name is to be chosen rather than great
    riches,
    and favor is better than silver or gold.
2 The rich and the poor have this in common:
    the LORD is the maker of them all.
3 The clever see danger and hide;
    but the simple go on, and suffer for it.
4 The reward for humility and fear of the LORD
    is riches and honor and life.
5 Thorns and snares are in the way of the perverse;
    the cautious will keep far from them.
6 Train children in the right way,
    and when old, they will not stray.

12 The Just One deals effectively with the wicked
    household,
    overturning the wicked to their ruin.
13 Whoever stops his ears at the cry of the helpless
    will himself cry for help and not be answered.
14 A gift given privily appeases anger;
    a present in secret allays great wrath.
15 When justice is done, honest folk rejoice,
    but it causes dismay among evildoers.
16 If someone takes leave of common sense
    he will come to rest in the company of the dead.
17 Love pleasure and you will end in want;
    one who loves wine and oil will never grow rich.
18 The wicked serve as a ransom for the righteous,
    so do the perfidious for the upright.
19 Better to live alone in the desert
    than with a nagging and ill-tempered wife!
20 The wise man has a houseful of fine and costly
    treasures;
    the stupid man will fritter them away.
21 He who perseveres in right conduct and loyalty
    finds life, prosperity, and honour.
22 He who is wise can attack a city full of armed men
    and undermine its boasted strength.
23 Keep a guard over your lips and tongue
    and you keep yourself out of trouble.
24 The conceited man is haughty, his name is
    insolence;
    overweening conceit marks all he does.
25 The sluggard's cravings will be the death of him,
    because his hands refuse to work;
26 all day long his cravings go unsatisfied,
    while the righteous give without stint.
27 Sacrifice from a wicked person is an abomination
    to the LORD,
    the more so when it is offered from impure
    motives.
28 A lying witness will be cut short,
    but a truthful witness will speak on.
29 A wicked person puts a bold face on it,
    whereas one who is upright looks to his ways.
30 Face to face with the LORD,
    wisdom, understanding, counsel avail nothing.
31 A horse may be made ready for the day of battle,
    but victory rests with the LORD.

22 A good name is more to be desired than great
    riches;
    esteem is better than silver or gold.
2 Rich and poor have this in common:
    the LORD made them both.
3 A shrewd person sees trouble coming and lies low;
    the simpleton walks straight into it and pays the
    penalty.
4 The fruit of humility is the fear of God
    with riches and honour and life.
5 Snares and pitfalls lie in the path of the crooked;
    the cautious person will steer clear of them.
6 Start a child on the right road,
    and even in old age he will not leave it.

---

j Gk: Heb *and oil*   *k* Gk: Heb *life and righteousness*   *l* Gk: Heb
all day long one covets covetously   *m* Another reading is *establish*

NEW AMERICAN BIBLE

12 The just man appraises the house of the wicked:
     there is one who brings down the wicked
          to ruin.

13 He who shuts his ear to the cry of the poor
     will himself also call and not be heard.

14 A secret gift allays anger,
     and a concealed present, violent wrath.

15 To practice justice is a joy for the just,
     but terror for evildoers.

16 The man who strays from the way of good sense
     will abide in the assembly of the shades.

17 He who loves pleasure will suffer want;
     he who loves wine and perfume will not be rich.

18 The wicked man serves as ransom for the just,
     and the faithless man for the righteous.

19 It is better to dwell in a wilderness
     than with a quarrelsome and vexatious wife.

20 Precious treasure remains in the house of the wise,
     but the fool consumes it.

21 He who pursues justice and kindness
     will find life and honor.

22 The wise man storms a city of the mighty,
     and overthrows the stronghold in which it trusts.

23 He who guards his mouth and his tongue
     keeps himself from trouble.

24 Arrogant is the name for the man of
          overbearing pride
     who acts with scornful effrontery.

25 The sluggard's propensity slays him,
     for his hands refuse to work.

26 Some are consumed with avarice all the day,
     but the just man gives unsparingly.

27 The sacrifice of the wicked is an abomination,
     the more so when they offer it with a bad
          intention.

28 The false witness will perish,
     but he who listens will finally have his say.

29 The wicked man is brazenfaced,
     but the upright man pays heed to his ways.

30 There is no wisdom, no understanding,
     no counsel, against the LORD.

31 The horse is equipped for the day of battle,
     but victory is the LORD's.

22 A good name is more desirable than
          great riches,
     and high esteem, than gold and silver.

2 Rich and poor have a common bond:
     the LORD is the maker of them all.

3 The shrewd man perceives evil and hides,
     while simpletons continue on and suffer the
          penalty.

4 The reward of humility and fear of the LORD
     is riches, honor and life.

5 Thorns and snares are on the path of the crooked;
     he who would safeguard his life will shun them.

6 Train a boy in the way he should go;
     even when he is old, he will not swerve from it.

NEW JERUSALEM BIBLE

12 The Upright One watches the house of the wicked;
     he hurls the wicked to destruction.

13 Whoever refuses to listen to the cry of the weak,
     will in turn plead and not be heard.

14 Anger is mollified by a covert gift,
     raging fury by a present under cover of the
          cloak.

15 Doing what is right fills the upright with joy,
     but evil-doers with terror.

16 Whoever strays far from the way of prudence
     will rest in the assembly of shadows.

17 Pleasure-lovers stay poor,
     no one will grow rich who loves wine and good
          living.

18 The wicked is a ransom for the upright;
     and the law-breaker for the honest.

19 Better to live in a desert land
     than with a quarrelsome and irritable woman.

20 The wise has valuables and oil at home,
     but a fool soon runs through both.

21 Whoever pursues uprightness and faithful love
     will find life, uprightness and honour.

22 A sage can scale a garrisoned city
     and shatter the rampart on which it relied.

23 Watch kept over mouth and tongue
     keeps the watcher safe from disaster.

24 Insolent, haughty — the name is 'Cynic';
     overweening pride marks such behaviour.

25 The idler's desires are the death of him,
     since his hands will do no work.

26 All day long the godless is racked by desire,
     the upright gives without ever refusing.

27 The sacrifice of the wicked is abhorrent,
     above all if it is offered for bad motives.

28 The false witness will perish,
     but no one who knows how to listen will ever be
          silenced.

29 The wicked man's strength shows on his face,
     but the honest it is whose steps are firm.

30 No wisdom, no understanding,
     no advice is worth anything before Yahweh.

31 Fit out the cavalry for the day of battle,
     but the victory is Yahweh's.

22 Fame is preferable to great wealth,
     favour, to silver and gold.

2 Rich and poor rub shoulders,
     Yahweh has made them both.

3 The discreet sees danger and takes shelter,
     simpletons go ahead and pay the penalty. z

4 The reward of humility is the fear of Yahweh,
     and riches, honour and life.

5 Thorns and snares line the path of the wilful,
     whoever values life will stay at a distance.

6 Give a lad a training suitable to his character
     and, even when old, he will not go back on it.

z 22 = 27:12.

NEW REVISED STANDARD VERSION	REVISED ENGLISH BIBLE

NEW REVISED STANDARD VERSION

7 The rich rules over the poor,
  and the borrower is the slave of the lender.
8 Whoever sows injustice will reap calamity,
  and the rod of anger will fail.
9 Those who are generous are blessed,
  for they share their bread with the poor.
10 Drive out a scoffer, and strife goes out;
  quarreling and abuse will cease.
11 Those who love a pure heart and are gracious in
    speech
  will have the king as a friend.
12 The eyes of the LORD keep watch over
    knowledge,
  but he overthrows the words of the faithless.
13 The lazy person says, "There is a lion outside!
  I shall be killed in the streets!"
14 The mouth of a loose[n] woman is a deep pit;
  he with whom the LORD is angry falls into it.
15 Folly is bound up in the heart of a boy,
  but the rod of discipline drives it far away.
16 Oppressing the poor in order to enrich oneself,
  and giving to the rich, will lead only to loss.

17 The words of the wise:

  Incline your ear and hear my words,[o]
  and apply your mind to my teaching;
18 for it will be pleasant if you keep them within
    you,
  if all of them are ready on your lips.
19 So that your trust may be in the LORD,
  I have made them known to you today—yes,
    to you.
20 Have I not written for you thirty sayings
  of admonition and knowledge,
21 to show you what is right and true,
  so that you may give a true answer to those
    who sent you?

22 Do not rob the poor because they are poor,
  or crush the afflicted at the gate;
23 for the LORD pleads their cause
  and despoils of life those who despoil them.
24 Make no friends with those given to anger,
  and do not associate with hotheads,
25 or you may learn their ways
  and entangle yourself in a snare.
26 Do not be one of those who give pledges,
  who become surety for debts.
27 If you have nothing with which to pay,
  why should your bed be taken from under you?
28 Do not remove the ancient landmark
  that your ancestors set up.
29 Do you see those who are skillful in their work?
  they will serve kings;
  they will not serve common people.

REVISED ENGLISH BIBLE

7 The rich lord it over the poor;
  the borrower becomes the lender's slave.
8 Whoever sows injustice will reap trouble;
  the rod of God's wrath will destroy him.
9 One who is kindly will be blessed,
  for he shares his food with the poor.
10 Banish the insolent, and strife goes too;
  discord and disgrace are ended.
11 The LORD loves a person to be sincere;
  by attractive speech a king's friendship is won.
12 The LORD keeps watch over every claim at law,
  and upsets the perjurer's case.
13 The sluggard protests, 'There is a lion outside;
  I shall be killed if I go on the street.'
14 The mouth of an adulteress is like a deep pit;
  he whom the LORD has cursed will fall into it.
15 Folly is deep-rooted in the hearts of children;
  a good beating will drive it out of them.
16 Oppression of the poor brings gain,
  but giving to the rich leads only to penury.

17 PAY heed and listen to the sayings of the wise,
  and apply your mind to the knowledge I impart;
18 to keep them in your heart will give pleasure,
  and then you will always have them ready on your
    lips.
19 I would have you trust in the LORD
  and so I make these things known to you now.
20 Here I have written out for you thirty sayings,
  full of knowledge and wise advice,
21 to impart to you a knowledge of the truth,
  that you may take back a true report to him who
    sent you.

22 Never rob anyone who is helpless because he is
    helpless,
  nor ill-treat a poor wretch in court;
23 for the LORD will take up their cause
  and rob of life those who rob them.
24 Never make friends with someone prone to anger,
  nor keep company with anyone hot-tempered;
25 be careful not to learn his ways
  and find yourself caught in a trap.
26 Never be one to give guarantees,
  or to pledge yourself as surety for another;
27 for if you cannot pay, beware:
  your very bed will be taken from under you.

28 Do not move the ancient boundary stone
  which your ancestors set up.

29 You see an artisan skilful at his craft:
  he will serve kings, not common men.

23 When you sit down to eat with a ruler,
  observe carefully what[p] is before you,
2 and put a knife to your throat
  if you have a big appetite.

23 When you sit down to dine with a ruler,
  give heed to what is before you.
2 Cut down your appetite
  if you are a greedy person.

---

[n] Heb strange [o] Cn Compare Gk: Heb Incline your ear, and hear
the words of the wise [p] Or who

22:8 **destroy him:** prob. rdg; Heb. come to an end.   22:11 **The**
LORD: so Gk; Heb. omits.   22:21 **to impart . . . truth:** prob. rdg;
Heb. adds words of truth.

7 The rich rule over the poor,
and the borrower is the slave of the lender.

8 He who sows iniquity reaps calamity,
and the rod destroys his labors.

9 The kindly man will be blessed,
for he gives of his sustenance to the poor.

10 Expel the arrogant man and discord goes out;
strife and insult cease.

11 The LORD loves the pure of heart;
the man of winning speech has the king for
his friend.

12 The eyes of the LORD safeguard knowledge,
but he defeats the projects of the faithless.

13 The sluggard says, "A lion is outside;
in the streets I might be slain."

14 The mouth of the adulteress is a deep pit;
he with whom the LORD is angry will fall into it.

15 Folly is close to the heart of a child,
but the rod of discipline will drive it far
from him.

16 He who oppresses the poor to enrich himself
will yield up his gains to the rich as sheer loss.

17 The sayings of the wise:

Incline your ear, and hear my words,
and apply your heart to my doctrine;
18 For it will be well if you keep them in
your bosom,
if they all are ready on your lips.
19 That your trust may be in the LORD,
I make known to you the words
of Amen-em-Ope.
20 Have I not written for you the "Thirty,"
with counsels and knowledge,
21 To teach you truly
how to give a dependable report to one who
sends you?

22 Injure not the poor because they are poor,
nor crush the needy at the gate;
23 For the LORD will defend their cause,
and will plunder the lives of those who
plunder them.

24 Be not friendly with a hotheaded man,
nor the companion of a wrathful man,
25 Lest you learn his ways,
and get yourself into a snare.

26 Be not one of those who give their hand in pledge,
of those who become surety for debts;
27 For if you have not the means to pay,
your bed will be taken from under you.

28 Remove not the ancient landmark
which your fathers set up.

29 You see a man skilled at his work?
He will stand in the presence of kings;
he will not stand in the presence of obscure men.

23 When you sit down to dine with a ruler,
keep in mind who is before you;
2 And put a knife to your throat
if you have a ravenous appetite.

7 The rich lords it over the poor,
the borrower is the lender's slave.

8 Whoever sows injustice reaps disaster,
and the rod of such anger will disappear.

9 A kindly eye will earn a blessing,
such a person shares out food with the poor.

10 Expel the mocker and strife goes too,
law-suits and dislike die down.

11 Whoever loves the pure of heart
and is gracious of speech has the king for a
friend.

12 Yahweh's eyes protect knowledge,
but he confounds deceitful speeches.

13 'There is a lion outside,' says the idler,
'I shall be killed in the street!'

14 The mouth of an adulterous woman is a deep pit,
into it falls the man whom Yahweh rebukes.

15 Folly is anchored in the heart of a youth,
the whip of instruction will rid him of it.

16 Harsh treatment enriches the poor,
but a gift impoverishes the rich.

17 Give ear, listen to the sayings of the sages,
and apply your heart to what I know,
18 for it will be a delight to keep them deep within
you
to have them all ready on your lips.
19 So that your trust may be in Yahweh,
it is you whom I wish to instruct today.

20 Have I not written for you thirty chapters
of advice and knowledge,
21 to make you know the certainty of true sayings,
so that you can return with sound answers to
those who sent you?

22 Do not despoil the weak, for he is weak,
and do not oppress the poor at the gate,
23 for Yahweh takes up their cause,
and extorts the life of their extortioners.

24 Do not make friends with one who gives way to
anger,
make no one quick-tempered a companion of
yours,
25 for fear you learn such behaviour
and in it find a snare for yourself.

26 Do not be one of those who go guarantor,
who go surety for debts:
27 if you have no means of paying
your bed will be taken from under you.

28 Do not displace the ancient boundary-stone[a]
set by your ancestors.

29 You see someone alert at his business?
His aim will be to serve kings;
not for him the service of the obscure.

23 If you take your seat at a great man's table,
take careful note of what you have before you;
2 if you have a big appetite
put a knife to your throat.

_a 22 = 23:10._

NEW REVISED STANDARD VERSION	REVISED ENGLISH BIBLE

3 Do not desire the ruler's*q* delicacies,
   for they are deceptive food.
4 Do not wear yourself out to get rich;
   be wise enough to desist.
5 When your eyes light upon it, it is gone;
   for suddenly it takes wings to itself,
   flying like an eagle toward heaven.
6 Do not eat the bread of the stingy;
   do not desire their delicacies;
7 for like a hair in the throat, so are they.*r*
   "Eat and drink!" they say to you;
   but they do not mean it.
8 You will vomit up the little you have eaten,
   and you will waste your pleasant words.
9 Do not speak in the hearing of a fool,
   who will only despise the wisdom of your
     words.
10 Do not remove an ancient landmark
   or encroach on the fields of orphans,
11 for their redeemer is strong;
   he will plead their cause against you.
12 Apply your mind to instruction
   and your ear to words of knowledge.
13 Do not withhold discipline from your children;
   if you beat them with a rod, they will not die.
14 If you beat them with the rod,
   you will save their lives from Sheol.
15 My child, if your heart is wise,
   my heart too will be glad.
16 My soul will rejoice
   when your lips speak what is right.
17 Do not let your heart envy sinners,
   but always continue in the fear of the LORD.
18 Surely there is a future,
   and your hope will not be cut off.
19 Hear, my child, and be wise,
   and direct your mind in the way.
20 Do not be among winebibbers,
   or among gluttonous eaters of meat;
21 for the drunkard and the glutton will come to
     poverty,
   and drowsiness will clothe them with rags.
22 Listen to your father who begot you,
   and do not despise your mother when she is
     old.
23 Buy truth, and do not sell it;
   buy wisdom, instruction, and understanding.
24 The father of the righteous will greatly rejoice;
   he who begets a wise son will be glad in him.
25 Let your father and mother be glad;
   let her who bore you rejoice.
26 My child, give me your heart,
   and let your eyes observe*s* my ways.
27 For a prostitute is a deep pit;
   an adulteress*t* is a narrow well.
28 She lies in wait like a robber
   and increases the number of the faithless.

3 Do not hanker after his dainties,
   for they are not what they seem.
4 Do not slave to get wealth;
   be sensible, and desist.
5 Before you can look around it is gone!
   It will surely grow wings
   like an eagle, like a bird in the sky.
6 Do not go to dine with a miserly person,
   and do not hanker after his dainties;
7 for they will stick in your throat like a hair.
   He will bid you eat and drink,
   but in his heart he does not mean it;
8 you will bring up the morsel you have eaten,
   and your compliments will have been wasted.
9 Do not address yourself to a stupid person,
   for he will disdain your words of wisdom.
10 Do not move an ancient boundary stone
   or encroach on the land of the fatherless:
11 they have a powerful Guardian
   who will take up their cause against you.
12 Apply your mind to instruction
   and your ears to words of knowledge.
13 Do not withhold discipline from a boy;
   take the stick to him, and save him from death.
14 If you take the stick to him yourself,
   you will be preserving him from Sheol.
15 My son, if you are wise at heart,
   my heart in turn will be glad;
16 I shall rejoice with all my soul
   when your lips utter what is right.
17 Do not try to emulate sinners;
   emulate only those who fear the LORD all their
     days;
18 do this, and you may look forward to the future,
   and your hopes will not be cut short.
19 Listen, my son, and become wise;
   set your mind on the right course.
20 Do not keep company with drunkards
   or those who are greedy for the fleshpots.
21 The drunkard and the glutton will end in poverty;
   in a state of stupor they are reduced to rags.
22 Listen to your father, who gave you life,
   and do not despise your mother when she is old.
23 Buy truth, and do not sell it;
   buy wisdom, instruction, and understanding.
24 A good man's father will rejoice
   and he who has a wise son will delight in him.
25 Give your father and mother cause for delight;
   may she who bore you rejoice.
26 My son, pay attention to me
   and accept my guidance willingly.
27 A prostitute is a deep pit,
   a loose woman a narrow well;
28 the one lies in wait like a robber,
   the other is unfaithful with man after man.

---

q Heb *his*   *r* Meaning of Heb uncertain   *s* Another reading is
delight in   *t* Heb *an alien woman*

23:7 **your throat:** *prob. rdg; Heb.* his throat.   23:14 **Sheol:** *or*
the underworld.   23:18 **do this:** *prob. rdg, cp. Gk; Heb.* omits.

3 Do not desire his delicacies;
  they are deceitful food.
4 Toil not to gain wealth,
  cease to be concerned about it;
5 While your glance flits to it, it is gone!
  for assuredly it grows wings,
  like the eagle that flies toward heaven.

6 Do not take food with a grudging man,
  and do not desire his dainties;
7 For in his greed he is like a storm.
  "Eat and drink," he says to you,
  though his heart is not with you;
8 The little you have eaten you will vomit up,
  and you will have wasted your agreeable words.
9 Speak not for the fool's hearing;
  he will despise the wisdom of your words.

10 Remove not the ancient landmark,
  nor invade the fields of orphans;
11 For their redeemer is strong;
  he will defend their cause against you.

12 Apply your heart to instruction,
  and your ears to words of knowledge.

13 Withhold not chastisement from a boy;
  if you beat him with the rod, he will not die.
14 Beat him with the rod,
  and you will save him from the nether world.

15 My son, if your heart be wise,
  my own heart also will rejoice;
16 And my inmost being will exult,
  when your lips speak what is right.

17 Let not your heart emulate sinners,
  but be zealous for the fear of the LORD always;
18 For you will surely have a future,
  and your hope will not be cut off.

19 Hear, my son, and be wise,
  and guide your heart in the right way.
20 Consort not with winebibbers,
  nor with those who eat meat to excess;
21 For the drunkard and the glutton come to poverty,
  and torpor clothes a man in rags.

22 Listen to your father who begot you,
  and despise not your mother when she is old.
23 Get the truth, and sell it not—
  wisdom, instruction and understanding.
24 The father of a just man will exult with glee;
  he who begets a wise son will have joy in him.
25 Let your father and mother have joy;
  let her who bore you exult.

26 My son, give me your heart,
  and let your eyes keep to my ways.
27 For the harlot is a deep ditch,
  and the adulteress a narrow pit;
28 Yes, she lies in wait like a robber,
  and increases the faithless among men.

3 Do not hanker for his delicacies,
  for they are deceptive food.
4 Do not wear yourself out in quest of wealth,
  stop applying your mind to this.
5 Fix your gaze on it, and it is there no longer,
  for it is able to sprout wings
  like an eagle that flies off to the sky.

6 Do not eat the food of anyone whose eye is
    jealous,
  do not hanker for his delicacies.
7 For what he is really thinking about is himself:
  'Eat and drink,' he tells you, but his heart is not
    with you.
8 You will spit out whatever you have eaten
  and find your compliments wasted.

9 Do not waste words on a fool,
  who will not appreciate the shrewdness of your
    remarks.

10 Do not displace the ancient boundary-stone, b
  or encroach on orphans' lands,
11 for they have a powerful avenger,
  and he will take up their cause against you.

12 Apply your heart to discipline,
  and your ears to instructive sayings.

13 Do not be chary of correcting a child,
  a stroke of the cane is not likely to be fatal.
14 Give him a stroke of the cane,
  you will save his soul from Sheol.

15 My child, if your heart is wise,
  then my own heart is glad,
16 and my inmost self rejoices
  when from your lips come honest words.

17 Do not let your heart be envious of sinners
  but remain steady every day in the fear of
    Yahweh;
18 for there is a future,
  and your hope will not come to nothing.

19 Listen, my child, and be wise,
  and guide your heart in the way.
20 Do not be one of those forever tippling wine
  nor one of those who gorge themselves with
    meat;
21 for the drunkard and glutton impoverish
    themselves,
  and sleepiness is clothed in rags.

22 Listen to your father from whom you are sprung,
  do not despise your mother in her old age.
23 Purchase truth—never sell it—
  wisdom, discipline, and discernment.
24 The father of the upright will rejoice indeed,
  he who fathers a wise child will have joy of it.
25 Your father and mother will be happy,
  and she who bore you joyful.

26 My child, pay attention to me,
  let your eyes take pleasure in my way:
27 a prostitute is a deep pit,
  a narrow well, the woman who belongs to
    another.
28 Yes, like a brigand, she lies in wait,
  increasing the number of law-breakers.

b 23 = 22:28.

29 Who has woe? Who has sorrow?
    Who has strife? Who has complaining?
    Who has wounds without cause?
    Who has redness of eyes?
30 Those who linger late over wine,
    those who keep trying mixed wines.
31 Do not look at wine when it is red,
    when it sparkles in the cup
    and goes down smoothly.
32 At the last it bites like a serpent,
    and stings like an adder.
33 Your eyes will see strange things,
    and your mind utter perverse things.
34 You will be like one who lies down in the midst
        of the sea,
    like one who lies on the top of a mast.ᵘ
35 "They struck me," you will say,ᵛ "but I was not
        hurt;
    they beat me, but I did not feel it.
    When shall I awake?
    I will seek another drink."

24 Do not envy the wicked,
    nor desire to be with them;
2 for their minds devise violence,
    and their lips talk of mischief.

3 By wisdom a house is built,
    and by understanding it is established;
4 by knowledge the rooms are filled
    with all precious and pleasant riches.
5 Wise warriors are mightier than strong ones,ʷ
    and those who have knowledge than those who
        have strength;
6 for by wise guidance you can wage your war,
    and in abundance of counselors there is
        victory.
7 Wisdom is too high for fools;
    in the gate they do not open their mouths.

8 Whoever plans to do evil
    will be called a mischief-maker.
9 The devising of folly is sin,
    and the scoffer is an abomination to all.

10 If you faint in the day of adversity,
    your strength being small;
11 if you hold back from rescuing those taken away
        to death,
    those who go staggering to the slaughter;
12 if you say, "Look, we did not know this"—
    does not he who weighs the heart perceive it?
    Does not he who keeps watch over your soul
        know it?
    And will he not repay all according to their
        deeds?

13 My child, eat honey, for it is good,
    and the drippings of the honeycomb are sweet
        to your taste.
14 Know that wisdom is such to your soul;
    if you find it, you will find a future,
    and your hope will not be cut off.

15 Do not lie in wait like an outlaw against the
        home of the righteous;
    do no violence to the place where the righteous
        live;
16 for though they fall seven times, they will rise
        again;
    but the wicked are overthrown by calamity.

29 Whose is the misery? Whose the remorse?
    Whose are the quarrels and the anxiety?
    Who gets the bruises without knowing why?
    Whose eyes are bloodshot?
30 Those who linger late over their wine,
    those always sampling some new spiced liquor.
31 Do not gulp down the wine, the strong red wine,
    when the droplets form on the side of the cup.
32 It may flow smoothly
    but in the end it will bite like a snake
    and poison like a cobra.
33 Then your eyes will see strange sights,
    your wits and your speech will be confused;
34 you become like a man tossing out at sea,
    like one who clings to the top of the rigging;
35 you say, 'If I am struck down, what do I care?
    If I am overcome, what of it?
    As soon as I wake up,
    I shall turn to the wine again.'

24 Do not emulate the wicked
    or desire their friendship;
2 for violence is all they think of,
    and mischief is ever on their lips.

3 Wisdom builds the house,
    good judgement makes it secure,
4 knowledge fills the rooms
    with costly and pleasing furnishings.

5 Wisdom prevails over strength,
    knowledge over brute force;
6 for wars are won by skilful strategy,
    and victory is the fruit of detailed planning.

7 Wisdom is too lofty for a fool to grasp;
    he remains tongue-tied in the public assembly.

8 Whoever is bent on mischief
    gets a name for intrigue;
9 the intrigues of the foolish misfire,
    and the insolent are odious to their fellows.

10 If you have shown yourself weak at a time of
        crisis,
    how limited is your strength!
11 Rescue those being dragged away to death,
    and save those being hauled off to execution.
12 If you say, 'But this person I do not know,'
    God, who fixes a standard for the heart, will take
        note;
    he who watches you will know;
    he will repay everyone according to what he does.

13 Eat honey, my son, for it is good,
    and the honeycomb is sweet to your palate.
14 Seek wisdom for yourself;
    if you find it, you may look forward to the future,
    and your thread of life will not be cut short.

15 Do not lie in wait like a felon at the upright
        person's house,
    or raid his homestead.
16 Though he may fall seven times, he is soon up
        again,
    but the rogue is brought headlong by misfortune.

ᵘMeaning of Heb uncertain   ᵛGk Syr Vg Tg: Heb lacks *you will
say*   ʷGk Compare Syr Tg: Heb *A wise man is strength*

23:34 **clings to:** *prob. rdg; Heb.* lies on.   24:12 **I:** *so Gk; Heb.*
we.   24:14 **thread of life:** *or* hope.

NEW AMERICAN BIBLE

NEW JERUSALEM BIBLE

29 Who scream? Who shriek?
  Who have strife? Who have anxiety?
  Who have wounds for nothing?
  Who have black eyes?
30 Those who linger long over wine,
  those who engage in trials of blended wine.
31 Look not on the wine when it is red,
  when it sparkles in the glass.
  It goes down smoothly;
32 but in the end it bites like a serpent,
  or like a poisonous adder.
33 Your eyes behold strange sights,
  and your heart utters disordered thoughts;
34 You are like one now lying in the depths of
  the sea,
  now sprawled at the top of the mast.
35 "They struck me, but it pained me not;
  they beat me, but I felt it not;
  When shall I awake
  to seek wine once again?"

24 Be not emulous of evil men,
  and desire not to be with them;
2 For their hearts plot violence,
  and their lips speak of foul play.

3 By wisdom is a house built,
  by understanding is it made firm;
4 And by knowledge are its rooms filled
  with every precious and pleasing possession.

5 A wise man is more powerful than a strong man,
  and a man of knowledge than a man of might;
6 For it is by wise guidance that you wage your war,
  and the victory is due to a wealth of counselors.

7 For a fool, to be silent is wisdom;
  not to open his mouth at the gate.
8 He who plots evil doing —
  men call him an intriguer.
9 Beyond intrigue and folly and sin,
  it is arrogance that men find abominable.

10 If you remain indifferent in time of adversity,
  your strength will depart from you.
11 Rescue those who are being dragged to death,
  and from those tottering to execution
  withdraw not.
12 If you say, "I know not this man!"
  does not he who tests hearts perceive it?
  He who guards your life knows it,
  and he will repay each one according to his
  deeds.

13 If you eat honey, my son, because it is good,
  if virgin honey is sweet to your taste;
14 Such, you must know, is wisdom to your soul.
  If you find it, you will have a future,
  and your hope will not be cut off.

15 Lie not in wait against the home of the just man,
  ravage not his dwelling place;
16 For the just man falls seven times and rises again,
  but the wicked stumble to ruin.

29 For whom is pity, for whom contempt,
  for whom is strife, for whom complaint,
  for whom blows struck at random,
  for whom the clouded eye?
30 For those who linger over wine too long,
  ever on the look-out for the blended liquors.
31 Do not gaze at wine, how red it is,
  how it sparkles in the cup!
  How smoothly it slips down the throat!
32 In the end its bite is like a serpent's,
  its sting as sharp as an adder's.
33 Your eyes will see peculiar things,
  you will talk nonsense from your heart.
34 You will be like someone sleeping in mid-ocean,
  like one asleep at the mast-head.
35 'Struck me, have they? But I'm not hurt.
  Beaten me? I don't feel anything.
  When shall I wake up? . . .
  I'll ask for more of it!'

24 Do not be envious of the wicked
  or wish for their company,
2 for their hearts are scheming violence,
  their lips talking mischief.

3 By wisdom a house is built,
  by understanding it is made strong;
4 by knowledge its storerooms are filled
  with riches of every kind, rare and desirable.

5 The wise is mighty in power,
  strength is reinforced by science;
6 for it is by strategy that you wage war,
  and victory depends on having many counsellors.

7 For a fool wisdom is an inaccessible fortress:
  at the city gate he does not open his mouth.

8 Anyone intent on evil-doing
  is known as a master in cunning.

9 Folly dreams of nothing but sin,
  the mocker is abhorrent.

10 If you lose heart when things go wrong,
  your strength is not worth much.
11 Save those being dragged towards death,
  but can you rescue those on their way to
  execution?
12 If you say, 'But look, we did not know,'
  will the Weigher of the heart pay no attention?
  Will not the Guardian of your soul be aware
  and repay you as your deeds deserve?

13 Eat honey, my child, since it is good;
  honey that drips from the comb is sweet to the
  taste:
14 and so, for sure, will wisdom be to your soul:
  find it and you will have a future
  and your hope will not be cut short.

15 Do not lurk, wicked man, round the upright man's
  dwelling,
  do not despoil his house.
16 For though the upright falls seven times, he gets up
  again;
  the wicked are the ones who stumble in
  adversity.

17 Do not rejoice when your enemies fall,
    and do not let your heart be glad when they
        stumble,
18 or else the LORD will see it and be displeased,
    and turn away his anger from them.

19 Do not fret because of evildoers.
    Do not envy the wicked;
20 for the evil have no future;
    the lamp of the wicked will go out.

21 My child, fear the LORD and the king,
    and do not disobey either of them;[x]
22 for disaster comes from them suddenly,
    and who knows the ruin that both can bring?

23 These also are sayings of the wise:

Partiality in judging is not good.
24 Whoever says to the wicked, "You are innocent,"
    will be cursed by peoples, abhorred by nations;
25 but those who rebuke the wicked will have
        delight,
    and a good blessing will come upon them.
26 One who gives an honest answer
    gives a kiss on the lips.

27 Prepare your work outside,
    get everything ready for you in the field;
    and after that build your house.

28 Do not be a witness against your neighbor
        without cause,
    and do not deceive with your lips.
29 Do not say, "I will do to others as they have
        done to me;
    I will pay them back for what they have done."

30 I passed by the field of one who was lazy,
    by the vineyard of a stupid person;
31 and see, it was all overgrown with thorns;
    the ground was covered with nettles,
    and its stone wall was broken down.
32 Then I saw and considered it;
    I looked and received instruction.
33 A little sleep, a little slumber,
    a little folding of the hands to rest,
34 and poverty will come upon you like a robber,
    and want, like an armed warrior.

25 These are other proverbs of Solomon that the offi-
    cials of King Hezekiah of Judah copied.

2 It is the glory of God to conceal things,
    but the glory of kings is to search things out.
3 Like the heavens for height, like the earth for
        depth,
    so the mind of kings is unsearchable.
4 Take away the dross from the silver,
    and the smith has material for a vessel;
5 take away the wicked from the presence of the
        king,
    and his throne will be established in
        righteousness.
6 Do not put yourself forward in the king's
        presence
    or stand in the place of the great;
7 for it is better to be told, "Come up here,"
    than to be put lower in the presence of a noble.

17 Do not rejoice at the fall of your enemy;
    do not gloat when he is brought down,
18 or the LORD will be displeased at the sight,
    and will cease to be angry with him.

19 Do not vie with evildoers
    or emulate the wicked;
20 for those who are evil can expect no future;
    their lamp will be extinguished.

21 My son, fear the LORD and fear the king.
    Have nothing to do with persons of high rank;
22 they will come to sudden disaster,
    and who knows what their ruin will entail?

23 More sayings of the wise:

Partiality in dispensing justice is invidious.
24 A judge who pronounces the guilty innocent
    is cursed by nations, and peoples denounce him;
25 but it will go well with those who convict the
        guilty,
    and they will be blessed with prosperity.
26 A straightforward answer
    is as good as a kiss of friendship.

27 Put in order your work out of doors
    and make everything ready on the land;
    after that build yourself a home.

28 Do not testify against your neighbour without good
        reason
    or misrepresent him in your evidence.
29 Do not say,
    'I shall do to him as he has done to me;
    I am paying off an old score.'

30 I passed by the field of an idle fellow,
    by the vineyard of someone with no sense.
31 I looked, and it was all overgrown with thistles;
    it was covered with weeds,
    and its stone wall was broken down.
32 I saw and I took it to heart,
    I considered and learnt the lesson:
33 a little sleep, a little slumber,
    a little folding of the hands in rest—
34 and poverty will come on you like a footpad,
    want will assail you like a hardened ruffian.

25 MORE proverbs of Solomon, transcribed by the men
    of King Hezekiah of Judah:

2 The glory of God is to keep things hidden,
    but the glory of kings is to fathom them.
3 The heavens for height, the earth for depth:
    unfathomable likewise is the mind of a king.
4 Rid silver of its impurities,
    then it may go to the silversmith;
5 rid the king's presence of the wicked,
    and his throne will rest firmly on righteousness.
6 Do not push yourself forward at court
    or take your stand where the great assemble;
7 for it is better to be told, 'Come up here,'
    than to be moved down to make room for a
        nobleman.

---

[x]Gk: Heb do not associate with those who change

24:22 **they . . . will entail?:** or they will bring about disaster without
warning; who knows what their ruin may cause?

17 Rejoice not when your enemy falls,
  and when he stumbles, let not your heart exult,
18 Lest the LORD see it, be displeased with you,
  and withdraw his wrath from your enemy.

19 Be not provoked with evildoers,
  nor envious of the wicked;
20 For the evil man has no future,
  the lamp of the wicked will be put out.

21 My son, fear the LORD and the king;
  have nothing to do with those who rebel
    against them;
22 For suddenly arises the destruction they send,
  and the ruin from either one, who can measure?

23 These also are sayings of the wise:
  To show partiality in judgment is not good.
24 He who says to the wicked man, "You are just" —
  men will curse him, people will denounce him;
25 But those who convict the evildoer will fare well,
  and on them will come the blessing
    of prosperity.
26 He gives a kiss on the lips
  who makes an honest reply.

27 Complete your outdoor tasks,
  and arrange your work in the field;
  afterward you can establish your house.

28 Be not a witness against your neighbor without
    just cause,
  thus committing folly with your lips.
29 Say not, "As he did to me, so will I do to him;
  I will repay the man according to his deeds."

30 I passed by the field of the sluggard,
  by the vineyard of the man without sense;
31 And behold! it was all overgrown with thistles;
  its surface was covered with nettles,
  and its stone wall broken down.
32 And as I gazed at it, I reflected;
  I saw and learned the lesson:
33 A little sleep, a little slumber,
  a little folding of the arms to rest —
34 Then will poverty come upon you like
    a highwayman,
  and want like an armed man.

25 These also are proverbs of Solomon. The men of
  Hezekiah, king of Judah, transmitted them.

2 God has glory in what he conceals,
  kings have glory in what they fathom.
3 As the heavens in height, and the earth in depth,
  the heart of kings is unfathomable.

4 Remove the dross from silver,
  and it comes forth perfectly purified;
5 Remove the wicked from the presence of the king,
  and his throne is made firm through
    righteousness.

6 Claim no honor in the king's presence,
  nor occupy the place of great men;
7 For it is better that you be told, "Come up closer!"
  than that you be humbled before the prince.

17 Should your enemy fall, do not rejoice,
  when he stumbles do not let your heart exult:
18 for fear that Yahweh will be displeased at the sight
  and turn his anger away from him.

19 Do not be indignant about the wicked,
  do not be envious of the evil,
20 for there is no future for the evil,
  the lamp of the wicked will go out.

21 Fear Yahweh, my child, and fear the king;
  do not ally yourself with innovators;
22 for suddenly disaster will loom for them,
  and who knows what ruin will seize them and
    their friends?

23 The following are also taken from the sages:

  To show partiality in judgement is not good.
24 Whoever tells the wicked, 'You are upright,'
  peoples curse him, nations revile him;
25 but those who correct him, come out of it well,
  on them will come a happy blessing.

26 Whoever returns an honest answer,
  plants a kiss on the lips.

27 Plan what you want on the open ground,
  make your preparation in the field;
  then go and build your house.

28 Do not bear witness lightly against your neighbour,
  nor deceive with your lips.
29 Do not say, 'I will treat my neighbour as my
    neighbour treated me;
  I will repay everyone what each has earned.'

30 By the idler's field I was passing,
  by the vineyard of a man who had no sense,
31 there it all lay, deep in thorns,
  entirely overgrown with weeds,
  and its stone wall broken down.
32 And as I gazed I pondered,
  I drew this lesson from the sight,
33 'A little sleep, a little drowsiness,
  a little folding of the arms to lie back
34 and poverty comes like a vagrant,
  and, like a beggar, dearth.' c

25 Here are some more of Solomon's proverbs, transcribed at the court of Hezekiah king of Judah:

2 To conceal a matter, this is the glory of God,
  to sift it thoroughly, the glory of kings.
3 The heavens for height and the earth for depth,
  unfathomable, as are the hearts of kings.

4 From silver remove the dross
  and it emerges wholly purified;
5 from the king's presence remove the wicked
  and on uprightness his throne is founded.

6 In the presence of the king do not give yourself
    airs,
  do not take a place among the great;
7 better to be invited, 'Come up here',
  than be humiliated in the presence of the prince.

What your eyes have seen
8 do not hastily bring into court;
for *y* what will you do in the end,
when your neighbor puts you to shame?
9 Argue your case with your neighbor directly,
and do not disclose another's secret;
10 or else someone who hears you will bring shame
upon you,
and your ill repute will have no end.

11 A word fitly spoken
is like apples of gold in a setting of silver.
12 Like a gold ring or an ornament of gold
is a wise rebuke to a listening ear.
13 Like the cold of snow in the time of harvest
are faithful messengers to those who send
them;
they refresh the spirit of their masters.
14 Like clouds and wind without rain
is one who boasts of a gift never given.
15 With patience a ruler may be persuaded,
and a soft tongue can break bones.
16 If you have found honey, eat only enough for
you,
or else, having too much, you will vomit it.
17 Let your foot be seldom in your neighbor's
house,
otherwise the neighbor will become weary of
you and hate you.
18 Like a war club, a sword, or a sharp arrow
is one who bears false witness against a
neighbor.
19 Like a bad tooth or a lame foot
is trust in a faithless person in time of trouble.
20 Like vinegar on a wound *z*
is one who sings songs to a heavy heart.
Like a moth in clothing or a worm in wood,
sorrow gnaws at the human heart. *a*
21 If your enemies are hungry, give them bread to
eat;
and if they are thirsty, give them water to
drink;
22 for you will heap coals of fire on their heads,
and the LORD will reward you.
23 The north wind produces rain,
and a backbiting tongue, angry looks.
24 It is better to live in a corner of the housetop
than in a house shared with a contentious wife.
25 Like cold water to a thirsty soul,
so is good news from a far country.
26 Like a muddied spring or a polluted fountain
are the righteous who give way before the
wicked.
27 It is not good to eat much honey,
or to seek honor on top of honor.
28 Like a city breached, without walls,
is one who lacks self-control.

26 Like snow in summer or rain in harvest,
so honor is not fitting for a fool.

What you have witnessed 8 be in no hurry to tell
everyone,
or it will end in reproaches from your friend.
9 Argue your own case with your neighbour,
but do not reveal another's secrets,
10 or he will reproach you when he hears of it
and your indiscretion will then be beyond recall.

11 Like apples of gold set in silver filigree
is a word spoken in season.
12 Like a golden ear-ring or a necklace of Nubian
gold
is a wise person's reproof in an attentive ear.
13 Like the coolness of snow in harvest time
is a trusty messenger to those who send him;
he brings new life to his masters.
14 Like clouds and wind that bring no rain
is he who boasts of gifts he never gives.
15 A prince may be won over by patience,
and a soft tongue may break down authority.
16 If you find honey, eat what you need and no more;
a surfeit will make you sick.
17 Be sparing in visits to your neighbour's house;
if he sees too much of you, he will come to dislike
you.
18 Like a club, a sword, or a sharp arrow
is a false witness who denounces his friend.
19 Like a decaying tooth or a sprained ankle
is a perfidious person relied on in the day of
trouble.
20 Like one who dresses a wound with vinegar,
so is the sweetest of singers to the heavy-hearted.
21 If your enemy is hungry, give him food;
if he is thirsty, give him a drink of water;
22 for so you will heap live coals on his head,
and the LORD will reward you.
23 As the north wind holds back the rain,
so an angry glance holds back slander.
24 Better to live on a corner of the housetop
than share the house with a nagging wife.
25 Like cold water to the throat that is faint with thirst
is good news from a distant land.
26 Like a muddied spring or a polluted well
is a righteous man who gives way to a wicked one.
27 A surfeit of honey is bad for one,
and the quest for glory is onerous.
28 Like a city breached and defenceless
is a man who cannot control his temper.

26 Like snow in summer or rain at harvest,
honour is unseasonable when paid to a fool.

y Cn: Heb *or else* *z* Gk: Heb *Like one who takes off a garment on a cold day, like vinegar on lye* *a* Gk Syr Tg: Heb lacks *Like a moth . . . human heart*

25:20 **one who dresses:** *prob. rdg; Heb. adds* a garment on a cold day.

8 What your eyes have seen
    bring not forth hastily against an opponent;
For what will you do later on
    when your neighbor puts you to shame?
9 Discuss your case with your neighbor,
    but another man's secret do not disclose;
10 Lest, hearing it, he reproach you,
    and your ill repute cease not.

11 Like golden apples in silver settings
    are words spoken at the proper time.

12 Like a golden earring, or a necklace of fine gold,
    is a wise reprover to an obedient ear.

13 Like the coolness of snow in the heat of
      the harvest
    is a faithful messenger for the one who
      sends him.
    [He refreshes the soul of his master.]

14 Like clouds and wind when no rain follows
    is the man who boastfully promises what he
      never gives.

15 By patience is a ruler persuaded,
    and a soft tongue will break a bone.

16 If you find honey, eat only what you need,
    lest you become glutted with it and vomit it up.

17 Let your foot be seldom in your neighbor's house,
    lest he have more than enough of you, and
      hate you.

18 Like a club, or a sword, or a sharp arrow,
    is the man who bears false witness against
      his neighbor.

19 Like an infected tooth or an unsteady foot
    is [dependence on] a faithless man in time
      of trouble.

20 Like a moth in clothing, or a maggot in wood,
    sorrow gnaws at the human heart.

21 If your enemy be hungry, give him food to eat,
    if he be thirsty, give him to drink;

22 For live coals you will heap on his head,
    and the LORD will vindicate you.

23 The north wind brings rain,
    and a backbiting tongue an angry countenance.

24 It is better to dwell in a corner of the housetop
    than in a roomy house with a quarrelsome
      woman.

25 Like cool water to one faint from thirst
    is good news from a far country.

26 Like a troubled fountain or a polluted spring
    is a just man who gives way before the wicked.

27 To eat too much honey is not good;
    nor to seek honor after honor.

28 Like an open city with no defenses
    is the man with no check on his feelings.

26 Like snow in summer, or rain in harvest,
    honor for a fool is out of place.

8 What your eyes have witnessed
    do not produce too quickly at the trial,
for what are you to do at the end
    should your neighbour confute you?
9 Have the quarrel out with your neighbour,
    but do not disclose another's secret,
10 for fear your listener put you to shame,
    and the loss of repute be irremediable.

11 Like apples of gold inlaid with silver
    is a word that is aptly spoken.

12 A golden ring, an ornament of finest gold,
    is a wise rebuke to an attentive ear.

13 The coolness of snow in harvest time,
    such is a trustworthy messenger to those who
      send him:
    he revives the soul of his master.

14 Clouds and wind, but no rain:
    such is anyone whose promises are princely but
      never kept.

15 With patience a judge may be cajoled:
    a soft tongue breaks bones.

16 Eat to your satisfaction what honey you may find,
    but not to excess or you will bring it up again.

17 Do not set foot too often in your neighbour's
      house,
    for fear the neighbour tire of you and come to
      hate you.

18 A mace, a sword, a piercing arrow,
    such is anyone who bears false witness against a
      companion.

19 Decaying tooth, lame foot,
    such is the fickle when trusted in time of trouble:
20   as well take off your coat in bitter weather.

    You are pouring vinegar on a wound
    when you sing songs to a sorrowing heart.

21 If your enemy is hungry, give him something to
      eat;
    if thirsty, something to drink.

22 By this you will be heaping red-hot coals on his
      head,
    and Yahweh will reward you.

23 The north wind begets the rain,
    and a backbiting tongue, black looks.

24 Better the corner of a roof to live on
    than a house shared with a quarrelsome
      woman. _d_

25 Cold water to a thirsty throat;
    such is good news from a distant land.

26 A churned-up spring, a fountain fouled;
    such is the upright person trembling before the
      wicked.

27 It is not good to eat too much honey,
    nor to seek for glory on top of glory.

28 An open town, and without defences:
    such is anyone who lacks self-control.

26 Snow no more befits the summer, nor rain the
      harvest-time,
    than honours befit a fool.

_d_ **25** = 21:9.

2 Like a sparrow in its flitting, like a swallow in its
     flying,
   an undeserved curse goes nowhere.
3 A whip for the horse, a bridle for the donkey,
   and a rod for the back of fools.
4 Do not answer fools according to their folly,
   or you will be a fool yourself.
5 Answer fools according to their folly,
   or they will be wise in their own eyes.
6 It is like cutting off one's foot and drinking down
     violence,
   to send a message by a fool.
7 The legs of a disabled person hang limp;
   so does a proverb in the mouth of a fool.
8 It is like binding a stone in a sling
   to give honor to a fool.
9 Like a thornbush brandished by the hand of a
     drunkard
   is a proverb in the mouth of a fool.
10 Like an archer who wounds everybody
   is one who hires a passing fool or drunkard.b
11 Like a dog that returns to its vomit
   is a fool who reverts to his folly.
12 Do you see persons wise in their own eyes?
   There is more hope for fools than for them.
13 The lazy person says, "There is a lion in the
     road!
   There is a lion in the streets!"
14 As a door turns on its hinges,
   so does a lazy person in bed.
15 The lazy person buries a hand in the dish,
   and is too tired to bring it back to the mouth.
16 The lazy person is wiser in self-esteem
   than seven who can answer discreetly.
17 Like somebody who takes a passing dog by the
     ears
   is one who meddles in the quarrel of another.
18 Like a maniac who shoots deadly firebrands and
     arrows,
19 so is one who deceives a neighbor
   and says, "I am only joking!"
20 For lack of wood the fire goes out,
   and where there is no whisperer, quarreling
     ceases.
21 As charcoal is to hot embers and wood to fire,
   so is a quarrelsome person for kindling strife.
22 The words of a whisperer are like delicious
     morsels;
   they go down into the inner parts of the body.
23 Like the glazec covering an earthen vessel
   are smoothd lips with an evil heart.
24 An enemy dissembles in speaking
   while harboring deceit within;
25 when an enemy speaks graciously, do not believe
     it,
   for there are seven abominations concealed
     within;
26 though hatred is covered with guile,
   the enemy's wickedness will be exposed in the
     assembly.
27 Whoever digs a pit will fall into it,
   and a stone will come back on the one who
     starts it rolling.

2 Like a fluttering sparrow or a darting swallow,
   groundless abuse gets nowhere.
3 The whip for a horse, the bridle for a donkey,
   the rod for the back of a fool!
4 Do not answer a fool as his folly deserves,
   or you will grow like him yourself;
5 answer a fool as his folly deserves,
   or he will think himself wise.
6 Whoever sends a fool on an errand
   cuts his own leg off and displays the stump.
7 A proverb in the mouth of fools
   dangles helpless as the legs of the lame.
8 Like one who ties the stone into his sling
   is he who bestows honour on a fool.
9 Like a thorn-stick brandished by a drunkard
   is a proverb in the mouth of a fool.
10 Like an archer who shoots at any passer-by
   is one who hires a fool or a drunkard.
11 A fool who repeats his folly
   is like a dog returning to its vomit.
12 Do you see that man who thinks himself so wise?
   There is more hope for a fool than for him.
13 The sluggard protests, 'There is a lion in the road,
   a lion at large on the street.'
14 A door turns on its hinges,
   a sluggard on his bed.
15 A sluggard dips his hand into the dish
   but is too lazy to lift it to his mouth.
16 A sluggard is wiser in his own eyes
   than seven who answer sensibly.
17 Like someone who seizes a stray cur by the ears
   is he who meddles in a quarrel not his own.
18 Like a madman shooting at random
   his deadly darts and lethal arrows,
19 so is the man who deceives another
   and then says, 'It was only a joke.'
20 For lack of wood a fire dies down
   and for want of a tale-bearer a quarrel subsides.
21 Like coal for glowing embers and wood for the fire
   is a quarrelsome man for kindling strife.
22 A gossip's whispers are tasty morsels
   swallowed right down.
23 Like glaze spread on earthenware
   is glib speech that covers a spiteful heart.
24 With his lips an enemy may speak you fair
   but in his heart he harbours deceit;
25 when his speech is fair, do not trust him,
   for seven abominations fill his mind;
26 he may cloak his enmity in dissimulation,
   but his wickedness will be exposed before the
     assembly.
27 Whoever digs a pit will fall into it;
   if he rolls a stone, it will roll back upon him.

---

b Meaning of Heb uncertain   c Cn: Heb silver of dross
d Gk: Heb burning

26:10 **passer-by:** transposed from end of verse.   26:17 **meddles:**
so Lat.; Heb. is negligent or becomes enraged.

NEW AMERICAN BIBLE

2 Like the sparrow in its flitting, like the swallow in
  its flight,
  a curse uncalled-for arrives nowhere.

3 The whip for the horse, the bridle for the ass,
  and the rod for the back of fools.

4 Answer not the fool according to his folly,
  lest you too become like him.

5 Answer the fool according to his folly,
  lest he become wise in his own eyes.

6 He cuts off his feet, he drinks down violence,
  who sends messages by a fool.

7 A proverb in the mouth of a fool
  hangs limp, like crippled legs.

8 Like one who entangles the stone in the sling
  is he who gives honor to a fool.

9 Like a thorn stick brandished by the hand of
  a drunkard
  is a proverb in the mouth of fools.

10 Like an archer wounding all who pass by
  is he who hires a drunken fool.

11 As the dog returns to his vomit,
  so the fool repeats his folly.

12 You see a man wise in his own eyes?
  There is more hope for a fool than for him.

13 The sluggard says, "There is a lion in the street,
  a lion in the middle of the square!"

14 The door turns on its hinges,
  the sluggard, on his bed!

15 The sluggard loses his hand in the dish;
  he is too weary to lift it to his mouth.

16 The sluggard imagines himself wiser
  than seven men who answer with good sense.

17 Like the man who seizes a passing dog by the ears
  is he who meddles in a quarrel not his own.

18 Like a crazed archer
  scattering firebrands and deadly arrows

19 Is the man who deceives his neighbor,
  and then says, "I was only joking."

20 For lack of wood, the fire dies out;
  and when there is no talebearer, strife subsides.

21 What a bellows is to live coals, what wood is
  to fire,
  such is a contentious man in enkindling strife.

22 The words of a talebearer are like dainty morsels
  that sink into one's inmost being.

23 Like a glazed finish on earthenware
  are smooth lips with a wicked heart.

24 With his lips an enemy pretends,
  but in his inmost being he maintains deceit;

25 When he speaks graciously, trust him not,
  for seven abominations are in his heart.

26 A man may conceal hatred under dissimulation,
  but his malice will be revealed in the assembly.

27 He who digs a pit falls into it;
  and a stone comes back upon him who rolls it.

NEW JERUSALEM BIBLE

2 As the sparrow escapes, and the swallow flies
  away,
  so the undeserved curse will never hit its mark.

3 A whip for the horse, a bridle for the donkey,
  and for the backs of fools, a stick.

4 Do not answer a fool in the terms of his folly
  for fear you grow like him yourself.

5 Answer a fool in the terms of his folly
  for fear he imagine himself wise.

6 He wounds himself, he takes violence for his
  drink,
  who sends a message by a fool.

7 Unreliable as the legs of the lame,
  so is a proverb in the mouth of fools.

8 As well tie the stone to the sling
  as pay honour to a fool.

9 A thorn branch in a drunkard's hand,
  such is a proverb in the mouth of fools.

10 An archer wounding everyone,
  such is he who hires the passing fool and
  drunkard.

11 As a dog returns to its vomit,
  so a fool reverts to his folly.

12 You see someone who thinks himself wise?
  More to be hoped for from a fool than from
  him!

13 'A wild beast on the road!' says the idler,
  'a lion in the streets!'

14 The door turns on its hinges,
  the idler on his bed.

15 Into the dish the idler dips his hand,
  but is too tired to bring it back to his mouth.*e*

16 The idler thinks himself wiser
  than seven people who answer with discretion.

17 He takes a stray dog by the ears,
  who meddles in someone else's quarrel.

18 Like a madman hurling firebrands,
  arrows and death,

19 so is anyone who lies to a companion
  and then says, 'Aren't I amusing?'

20 No wood, and the fire goes out;
  no slanderer, and quarrelling dies down.

21 Charcoal for live embers, wood for fire,
  and the quarrelsome for kindling strife.

22 The words of a slanderer are tasty morsels
  that go right down into the belly.*f*

23 Base silver-plate on top of clay:
  such are fervent lips and a wicked heart.

24 Whoever hates may hide it in speech,
  but deep within lies treachery;

25 do not trust such a person's pretty speeches,
  since in the heart lurk seven abominations.

26 Hatred may disguise itself with guile,
  to reveal its wickedness later in the assembly.

27 Whoever digs a pit falls into it,
  the stone comes back on him that rolls it.

e 26 = 19:24.   *f* 26 = 18:8.

NEW REVISED STANDARD VERSION	REVISED ENGLISH BIBLE

NEW REVISED STANDARD VERSION

28 A lying tongue hates its victims,
and a flattering mouth works ruin.

27

Do not boast about tomorrow,
for you do not know what a day may bring.

2 Let another praise you, and not your own
mouth —
a stranger, and not your own lips.

3 A stone is heavy, and sand is weighty,
but a fool's provocation is heavier than both.

4 Wrath is cruel, anger is overwhelming,
but who is able to stand before jealousy?

5 Better is open rebuke
than hidden love.

6 Well meant are the wounds a friend inflicts,
but profuse are the kisses of an enemy.

7 The sated appetite spurns honey,
but to a ravenous appetite even the bitter is
sweet.

8 Like a bird that strays from its nest
is one who strays from home.

9 Perfume and incense make the heart glad,
but the soul is torn by trouble. *e*

10 Do not forsake your friend or the friend of your
parent;
do not go to the house of your kindred in the
day of your calamity.
Better is a neighbor who is nearby
than kindred who are far away.

11 Be wise, my child, and make my heart glad,
so that I may answer whoever reproaches me.

12 The clever see danger and hide;
but the simple go on, and suffer for it.

13 Take the garment of one who has given surety for
a stranger;
seize the pledge given as surety for
foreigners. *f*

14 Whoever blesses a neighbor with a loud voice,
rising early in the morning,
will be counted as cursing.

15 A continual dripping on a rainy day
and a contentious wife are alike;

16 to restrain her is to restrain the wind
or to grasp oil in the right hand. *g*

17 Iron sharpens iron,
and one person sharpens the wits *h* of another.

18 Anyone who tends a fig tree will eat its fruit,
and anyone who takes care of a master will be
honored.

19 Just as water reflects the face,
so one human heart reflects another.

20 Sheol and Abaddon are never satisfied,
and human eyes are never satisfied.

21 The crucible is for silver, and the furnace is for
gold,
so a person is tested *i* by being praised.

22 Crush a fool in a mortar with a pestle
along with crushed grain,
but the folly will not be driven out.

23 Know well the condition of your flocks,
and give attention to your herds;

REVISED ENGLISH BIBLE

28 A lying tongue is the enemy of the innocent,
and smooth words bring about their downfall.

27

Do not praise yourself for tomorrow's success;
you never know what a day may bring forth.

2 Let praise come from a stranger, not from yourself,
from the lips of an outsider and not from your
own.

3 Stone is a burden and sand a dead weight,
but to be vexed by a fool is more burdensome than
both.

4 Wrath is cruel and anger is a deluge;
but who can stand up to jealousy?

5 Open reproof is better
than love concealed.

6 The blows a friend gives are well meant,
but the kisses of an enemy are perfidious.

7 Someone who is full may refuse honey from the
comb,
but to the hungry even bitter food tastes sweet.

8 Like a bird that strays from its nest
is a man straying from his home.

9 Oil and incense bring joy to the heart,
but cares torment one's very soul.

10 Do not neglect your own friend or your father's.
Do not run to your brother's house when you are
in trouble.
Better a neighbour near at hand than a brother far
away!

11 Acquire wisdom, my son, and bring joy to my
heart;
I shall have an answer for my critics.

12 A shrewd person sees trouble coming and lies low;
the simpleton walks right into it and pays the
penalty.

13 Take the garment of anyone who pledges his word
for a stranger;
hold it as security for the unknown person.

14 If someone wakes another early with effusive
greetings,
he might as well curse him!

15 A constant dripping on a rainy day —
that is what a woman's nagging is like.

16 As well try to control the wind as to control her!
As well try to pick up oil in one's fingers!

17 As iron sharpens iron,
so one person sharpens the wits of another.

18 He who guards the fig tree will eat its fruit,
and he who watches his master's interests will
come to honour.

19 As someone sees his face reflected in water,
so he sees his own mind reflected in another's.

20 Sheol and Abaddon are insatiable;
so too the human eye is never satisfied.

21 The smelting pot is for silver, the crucible for gold;
so the character is tested by praise.

22 You may pound a fool in a mortar with a pestle,
but his folly will never be knocked out of him.

23 Be careful to know the state of your flock
and take good care of your herds;

---

e Gk: Heb *the sweetness of a friend is better than one's own counsel*
f Vg and 20.16: Heb *for a foreign woman*   *g* Meaning of Heb
uncertain   *h* Heb *face*   *i* Heb lacks *is tested*

26:28 **the innocent:** *prob. rdg; Heb. its crushed ones.*
27:6 **perfidious:** *meaning of Heb. word uncertain.*   27:9 **but**
cares . . . soul: *so Gk; Heb. obscure.*   27:19 **another's:** *or*
himself.   27:20 **Sheol and Abaddon:** *or Death and Destruction.*

NEW AMERICAN BIBLE

28 The lying tongue is its owner's enemy,
and the flattering mouth works ruin.

27 Boast not of tomorrow,
for you know not what any day may bring forth.

2 Let another praise you — not your own mouth;
someone else — not your own lips.

3 Stone is heavy, and sand a burden,
but a fool's provocation is heavier than both.

4 Anger is relentless, and wrath overwhelming —
but before jealousy who can stand?

5 Better is an open rebuke
than a love that remains hidden.

6 Wounds from a friend may be accepted as
well meant,
but the greetings of an enemy one prays against.

7 One who is full, tramples on virgin honey;
but to the man who is hungry, any bitter thing
is sweet.

8 Like a bird that is far from its nest
is a man who is far from his home.

9 Perfume and incense gladden the heart,
but by grief the soul is torn asunder.

10 Your own friend and your father's friend
forsake not;
but if ruin befalls you, enter not a
kinsman's house.
Better is a neighbor near at hand than a brother
far away.

11 If you are wise, my son, you will gladden
my heart,
and I will be able to rebut him who taunts me.

12 The shrewd man perceives evil and hides;
simpletons continue on and suffer the penalty.

13 Take his garment who becomes surety for another,
and for the sake of a stranger, yield it up!

14 When one greets his neighbor with a loud voice in
the early morning,
a curse can be laid to his charge.

15 For a persistent leak on a rainy day
the match is a quarrelsome woman.

16 He who keeps her stores up a stormwind;
he cannot tell north from south.

17 As iron sharpens iron,
so man sharpens his fellow man.

18 He who tends a fig tree eats its fruit,
and he who is attentive to his master will
be enriched.

19 As one face differs from another,
so does one human heart from another.

20 The nether world and the abyss are never satisfied;
so too the eyes of men.

21 As the crucible tests silver and the furnace gold,
so a man is tested by the praise he receives.

22 Though you should pound the fool to bits
with the pestle, amid the grits in a mortar,
his folly would not go out of him.

23 Take good care of your flocks,
give careful attention to your herds;

NEW JERUSALEM BIBLE

28 The lying tongue hates its victims,
the wheedling mouth causes ruin.

27 Do not congratulate yourself about tomorrow,
since you do not know what today will bring
forth.

2 Let someone else sing your praises, but not your
own mouth,
a stranger, but not your own lips.

3 Heavy is the stone, weighty is the sand;
heavier than both — a grudge borne by a fool.

4 Cruel is wrath, overwhelming is anger;
but jealousy, who can withstand that?

5 Better open reproof
than feigned love.

6 Trustworthy are blows from a friend,
deceitful are kisses from a foe.

7 The gorged throat revolts at honey,
the hungry throat finds all bitterness sweet.

8 Like a bird that strays from its nest,
so is anyone who strays away from home.

9 Oil and perfume gladden the heart,
and the sweetness of friendship rather than
self-reliance.

10 Do not give up your friend or your father's friend;
when trouble comes, do not go off to your
brother's house,
better a near neighbour than a distant brother.

11 Learn to be wise, my child, and gladden my heart,
that I may have an answer for anyone who
insults me.

12 The discreet sees danger and takes shelter,
simpletons go ahead and pay the penalty.g

13 Take the man's clothes! He has gone surety for a
stranger.
Take a pledge from him, for persons unknown.h

14 Whoever at dawn loudly blesses his neighbour —
it will be reckoned to him as a curse.

15 The dripping of a gutter on a rainy day
and a quarrelsome woman are alike;

16 whoever can restrain her, can restrain the wind,
and take a firm hold on grease.

17 Iron is sharpened by iron,
one person is sharpened by contact with another.

18 Whoever tends the fig tree eats its figs,
whoever looks after his master will be honoured.

19 As water reflects face back to face,
so one human heart reflects another.

20 Sheol and Perdition are never satisfied,
insatiable, too, are human eyes.

21 A furnace for silver, a foundry for gold:
a person is worth what his reputation is worth.

22 Pound a fool in a mortar,
among grain with a pestle,
his folly will not leave him.

23 Know your flocks' condition well,
take good care of your herds;

g **27** = 22:3.   h **27** = 20:16.

NEW REVISED STANDARD VERSION	REVISED ENGLISH BIBLE

NEW REVISED STANDARD VERSION

24 for riches do not last forever,
  nor a crown for all generations.
25 When the grass is gone, and new growth appears,
  and the herbage of the mountains is gathered,
26 the lambs will provide your clothing,
  and the goats the price of a field;
27 there will be enough goats' milk for your food,
  for the food of your household
  and nourishment for your servant-girls.

28 The wicked flee when no one pursues,
  but the righteous are as bold as a lion.
2 When a land rebels
  it has many rulers;
  but with an intelligent ruler
  there is lasting order.*j*
3 A ruler*k* who oppresses the poor
  is a beating rain that leaves no food.
4 Those who forsake the law praise the wicked,
  but those who keep the law struggle against
  them.
5 The evil do not understand justice,
  but those who seek the LORD understand it
  completely.
6 Better to be poor and walk in integrity
  than to be crooked in one's ways even though
  rich.
7 Those who keep the law are wise children,
  but companions of gluttons shame their
  parents.
8 One who augments wealth by exorbitant interest
  gathers it for another who is kind to the poor.
9 When one will not listen to the law,
  even one's prayers are an abomination.
10 Those who mislead the upright into evil ways
  will fall into pits of their own making,
  but the blameless will have a goodly
  inheritance.
11 The rich is wise in self-esteem,
  but an intelligent poor person sees through the
  pose.
12 When the righteous triumph, there is great glory,
  but when the wicked prevail, people go into
  hiding.
13 No one who conceals transgressions will prosper,
  but one who confesses and forsakes them will
  obtain mercy.
14 Happy is the one who is never without fear,
  but one who is hard-hearted will fall into
  calamity.
15 Like a roaring lion or a charging bear
  is a wicked ruler over a poor people.
16 A ruler who lacks understanding is a cruel
  oppressor;
  but one who hates unjust gain will enjoy a long
  life.
17 If someone is burdened with the blood of another,
  let that killer be a fugitive until death;
  let no one offer assistance.
18 One who walks in integrity will be safe,
  but whoever follows crooked ways will fall
  into the Pit.*l*

REVISED ENGLISH BIBLE

24 for possessions do not last for ever,
  nor will a crown endure to endless generations.
25 The grass is cropped, new shoots are seen,
  and the green growth on the hills is gathered in;
26 the lambs provide you with clothing,
  and the he-goats with the price of a field,
27 while the goats' milk is food enough for your
  household
  and sustenance for your servant-girls.

28 The wicked flee, even though no one pursues,
  but the righteous are as confident as young lions.
2 It is the fault of a violent person that quarrels start,
  but they are settled by one who possesses
  discernment.
3 A tyrant oppressing the poor
  is like driving rain that ruins the crop.
4 Those who abandon God's law applaud the wicked;
  those who keep it contend with them.
5 Evildoers have no understanding of justice,
  but those who seek the LORD understand it well.
6 Better to be poor and above reproach
  than rich and crooked.
7 A discerning son observes God's law,
  but one who keeps profligate company brings
  disgrace on his father.
8 He who grows rich by lending at discount or at
  interest
  is saving for another who will be generous to the
  poor.
9 If anyone turns a deaf ear to God's law,
  even his prayer is an abomination.
10 He who tempts the upright into evil ways
  will himself land in the pit he has dug;
  but the honest will inherit a fortune.
11 The person who is rich may think himself wise,
  but the discerning poor will see through him.
12 When the just triumph, morale is high,
  but when the wicked come to the top, the people
  are downtrodden.
13 Conceal your offences, and you will not prosper;
  confess and renounce them, and you will obtain
  mercy.
14 Happy are those who are scrupulous in conduct,
  but if one hardens his heart he falls into
  misfortune!
15 Like a roaring lion or a prowling bear
  is a wicked ruler governing a helpless people.
16 The leader who is stupid and grasping will perish;
  he who detests ill-gotten gain will live long.
17 Anyone charged with bloodshed
  will jump into a well to escape arrest.
18 Whoever leads an honest life will be safe,
  but a rogue will fall into a pit.

---

j Meaning of Heb uncertain *k* Cn: Heb *A poor person*
l Syr: Heb *fall all at once*

28:2 **a violent person:** *so Gk; Heb.* land. **start:** *prob. rdg., cp. Gk;
Heb.* her officers. **they are settled:** *so Gk; Heb.* a knowing man thus
prolongs. 28:18 **into a pit:** *prob. rdg; Heb.* in one.

24 For wealth lasts not forever,
  nor even a crown from age to age.

25 When the grass is taken away and the
    aftergrowth appears,
  and the mountain greens are gathered in,

26 The lambs will provide you with clothing,
  and the goats will bring the price of a field,

27 And there will be ample goat's milk to supply you,
  to supply your household,
  and maintenance for your maidens.

28 The wicked man flees although no one
      pursues him;
  but the just man, like a lion, feels sure
    of himself.

2 If a land is rebellious, its princes will be many;
  but with a prudent man it knows security.

3 A rich man who oppresses the poor
  is like a devastating rain that leaves no food.

4 Those who abandon the law praise the
    wicked man,
  but those who keep the law war against him.

5 Evil men understand nothing of justice,
  but those who seek the LORD understand all.

6 Better a poor man who walks in his integrity
  than he who is crooked in his ways and rich.

7 He who keeps the law is a wise son,
  but the gluttons' companion disgraces his father.

8 He who increases his wealth by interest
    and overcharge
  gathers it for him who is kind to the poor.

9 When one turns away his ear from hearing the law,
  even his prayer is an abomination.

10 He who seduces the upright into an evil way
  will himself fall into his own pit.
  [And blameless men will gain prosperity.]

11 The rich man is wise in his own eyes,
  but a poor man who is intelligent sees
    through him.

12 When the just are triumphant, there is
    great jubilation;
  but when the wicked gain pre-eminence,
    people hide.

13 He who conceals his sins prospers not,
  but he who confesses and forsakes them
    obtains mercy.

14 Happy the man who is always on his guard;
  but he who hardens his heart will fall into evil.

15 Like a roaring lion or a ravenous bear
  is a wicked ruler over a poor people.

16 The less prudent the prince, the more his
    deeds oppress.
  He who hates ill-gotten gain prolongs his days.

17 Though a man burdened with human blood
  were to flee to the grave, none should
    support him.

18 He who walks uprightly is safe,
  but he whose ways are crooked falls into the pit.

24 for riches do not last for ever,
  crowns do not hand themselves on from age to
    age.

25 The grass once gone, the aftergrowth appearing,
  the hay gathered in from the mountains,

26 you should have lambs to clothe you,
  goats to buy you a field,

27 goat's milk sufficient to feed you,
  to feed your household and provide for your
    serving girls.

28 The wicked flees when no one is pursuing,
  the upright is bold as a lion.

2 A country in revolt throws up many leaders:
  with one person wise and experienced, you have
    stability.

3 The wicked oppresses the weak:
  here is a devastating rain — and farewell, bread!

4 Those who forsake the law sing the praises of the
    wicked,
  those who observe the law are angered by them.

5 The wicked do not know what justice means,
  those who seek Yahweh understand everything.

6 Better someone poor living an honest life
  than someone of devious ways however rich.

7 An intelligent child is one who keeps the Law;
  an associate of profligates brings shame on his
    father.

8 Whoever increases wealth by usury and interest
  amasses it for someone else who will bestow it
    on the poor.

9 Whoever refuses to listen to the Law,
  such a one's very prayer is an abomination.

10 Whoever seduces the honest to evil ways
  will fall into his own pit.
  The blameless are the heirs to happiness.

11 The rich may think himself wise,
  but the intelligent poor will unmask him.

12 When the upright triumph, there is great exultation:
  when the wicked are in the ascendant, people
    take cover. *i*

13 No one who conceals his sins will prosper,
  whoever confesses and renounces them will find
    mercy.

14 Blessed the person who is never without fear,
  whoever hardens his heart will fall into distress.

15 Like a roaring lion or a springing bear
  is a wicked ruler of a powerless people.

16 An unenlightened ruler is rich in rapacity,
  one who hates greed will lengthen his days.

17 A man guilty of murder will flee till he reaches his
    tomb:
  let no one halt him!

18 Whoever lives an honest life will be safe,
  whoever wavers between two ways falls down in
    one of them.

i **28** = 28:28.

NEW REVISED STANDARD VERSION	REVISED ENGLISH BIBLE

19 Anyone who tills the land will have plenty of
    bread,
    but one who follows worthless pursuits will
      have plenty of poverty.
20 The faithful will abound with blessings,
    but one who is in a hurry to be rich will not go
      unpunished.
21 To show partiality is not good —
    yet for a piece of bread a person may do
      wrong.
22 The miser is in a hurry to get rich
    and does not know that loss is sure to come.
23 Whoever rebukes a person will afterward find
      more favor
    than one who flatters with the tongue.
24 Anyone who robs father or mother
    and says, "That is no crime,"
    is partner to a thug.
25 The greedy person stirs up strife,
    but whoever trusts in the LORD will be
      enriched.
26 Those who trust in their own wits are fools;
    but those who walk in wisdom come through
      safely.
27 Whoever gives to the poor will lack nothing,
    but one who turns a blind eye will get many a
      curse.
28 When the wicked prevail, people go into hiding;
    but when they perish, the righteous increase.

19 Those who cultivate their land will have food in
    plenty,
    but those who follow idle pursuits will have
      poverty in plenty.
20 Someone of steady character will enjoy many
    blessings,
    but one in a hurry to get rich will not go
      unpunished.
21 It is invidious to show partiality;
    wrong may be done for a crust of bread.
22 The miser is in a hurry to become rich,
    never dreaming that want may overtake him.
23 Take someone to task and in the end win more
      thanks
    than he who has a flattering tongue.
24 To rob your father or mother and say you do no
      wrong
    is no better than murder.
25 A grasping person provokes quarrels,
    but he who trusts in the LORD will prosper.
26 It is stupid to trust to one's own wits,
    but he whose guide is wisdom will come safely
      through.
27 He who gives to the poor will never want,
    but he who turns a blind eye gets nothing but
      curses.
28 When the wicked come to the top, people go into
    hiding;
    but, when they perish, the righteous come into
      power.

29

One who is often reproved, yet remains stubborn,
    will suddenly be broken beyond healing.
2 When the righteous are in authority, the people
      rejoice;
    but when the wicked rule, the people groan.
3 A child who loves wisdom makes a parent glad,
    but to keep company with prostitutes is to
      squander one's substance.
4 By justice a king gives stability to the land,
    but one who makes heavy exactions ruins it.
5 Whoever flatters a neighbor
    is spreading a net for the neighbor's feet.
6 In the transgression of the evil there is a snare,
    but the righteous sing and rejoice.
7 The righteous know the rights of the poor;
    the wicked have no such understanding.
8 Scoffers set a city aflame,
    but the wise turn away wrath.
9 If the wise go to law with fools,
    there is ranting and ridicule without relief.
10 The bloodthirsty hate the blameless,
    and they seek the life of the upright.
11 A fool gives full vent to anger,
    but the wise quietly holds it back.
12 If a ruler listens to falsehood,
    all his officials will be wicked.
13 The poor and the oppressor have this in common:
    the LORD gives light to the eyes of both.

29

Someone still stubborn after much reproof
    will suddenly be broken past mending.
2 When the righteous are in power the people
      rejoice,
    but they groan when the wicked hold sway.
3 A lover of wisdom brings joy to his father,
    but an associate of harlots squanders wealth.
4 By just government a king maintains a country,
    but by extortion it can be brought to ruin.
5 To flatter a neighbour
    is to spread a net for his feet.
6 An evildoer is ensnared by his sin,
    but the doer of good will live and flourish.
7 The righteous are concerned for the claims of the
      helpless,
    but the wicked cannot understand such concern.
8 Arrogance can inflame a city,
    but wisdom averts the people's anger.
9 If a wise person goes to law with a fool,
    he will meet with unceasing abuse and derision.
10 Bloodthirsty men hate those who are honest,
    but the upright see to their interests.
11 The stupid give free rein to their anger;
    the wise wait for it to cool.
12 If a ruler listens to what liars say,
    all his ministers become wicked.
13 The poor and the oppressors have this in common:
    it is the LORD who gives light to the eyes of both.

28:25 **grasping:** or self-important.   29:6 **will live:** so some MSS;
others obscure.

19 He who cultivates his land will have plenty
 of food,
 but from idle pursuits a man has his fill of
  poverty.

20 The trustworthy man will be richly blessed;
 he who is in haste to grow rich will not go
  unpunished.

21 To show partiality is never good:
 for even a morsel of bread a man may
  do wrong.

22 The avaricious man is perturbed about his wealth,
 and he knows not when want will come
  upon him.

23 He who rebukes a man gets more thanks in the end
 than one with a flattering tongue.

24 He who defrauds father or mother and calls it
 no sin,
 is a partner of the brigand.

25 The greedy man stirs up disputes,
 but he who trusts in the LORD will prosper.

26 He who trusts in himself is a fool,
 but he who walks in wisdom is safe.

27 He who gives to the poor suffers no want,
 but he who ignores them gets many a curse.

28 When the wicked gain pre-eminence, other
 men hide;
 but at their fall the just flourish.

29

The man who remains stiff-necked and
 hates rebuke
will be crushed suddenly beyond cure.

2 When the just prevail, the people rejoice;
 but when the wicked rule, the people groan.

3 He who loves wisdom makes his father glad,
 but he who consorts with harlots squanders his
  wealth.

4 By justice a king gives stability to the land;
 but he who imposes heavy taxes ruins it.

5 The man who flatters his neighbor
 is spreading a net under his feet.

6 The wicked man steps into a snare,
 but the just man runs on joyfully.

7 The just man has a care for the rights of the poor;
 the wicked man has no such concern.

8 Arrogant men set the city ablaze,
 but wise men calm the fury.

9 If a wise man disputes with a fool,
 he may rage or laugh but can have no peace.

10 Bloodthirsty men hate the honest man,
 but the upright show concern for his life.

11 The fool gives vent to all his anger;
 but by biding his time, the wise man calms it.

12 If a ruler listens to lying words,
 his servants all become wicked.

13 The poor and the oppressor have a common bond:
 the LORD gives light to the eyes of both.

19 Whoever works his land shall have bread and to
 spare,
 but no one who chases fantasies has any sense. *j*

20 A trustworthy person will be overwhelmed with
 blessings,
 but no one who tries to get rich quickly will go
  unpunished.

21 It is not good to show partiality,
 but people will do wrong for a mouthful of
  bread.

22 The person of greedy eye chases after wealth,
 not knowing that want will be the result.

23 Anyone who reproves another
 will enjoy more favour in the end than the
  flatterer.

24 Whoever robs father and mother saying, 'Nothing
 wrong in that!'
 is comrade for a brigand.

25 The covetous provokes disputes,
 whoever trusts in Yahweh will prosper.

26 Whoever trusts his own wit is a fool,
 anyone whose ways are wise will be safe.

27 No one who gives to the poor will ever go short,
 but whoever closes his eyes will have curses in
  plenty.

28 When the wicked are in the ascendant, people take
 cover, *k*
 but when they perish, the upright multiply.

29

Whoever is stiff-necked under reproof
 will be suddenly and irremediably broken.

2 When the upright are on the increase, the people
 rejoice;
 when the wicked are in power, the people groan.

3 The lover of Wisdom makes his father glad,
 but the patron of prostitutes fritters his wealth
  away.

4 A king gives a country stability by justice,
 an extortioner brings it to ruin.

5 Whoever flatters his companion
 spreads a net for his feet.

6 In the sin of the wicked lies a snare,
 but the upright exults and rejoices.

7 The upright understands the cause of the weak,
 the wicked has not the wit to understand it.

8 Scoffers set a city in ferment,
 but the wise moderate anger.

9 Let someone wise argue with a fool,
 anger and good humour alike will be wasted.

10 The bloodthirsty hate the honest,
 but the upright seek them out.

11 The fool blurts out every angry feeling,
 but the wise subdues and restrains them.

12 When a ruler listens to false reports,
 all his ministers will be scoundrels.

13 Poor and oppressor are found together,
 Yahweh gives light to the eyes of both.

j **28** = 12:11. *k* **28** = 28:12.

14 If a king judges the poor with equity,
   his throne will be established forever.
15 The rod and reproof give wisdom,
   but a mother is disgraced by a neglected child.
16 When the wicked are in authority, transgression
   increases,
   but the righteous will look upon their downfall.
17 Discipline your children, and they will give you
   rest;
   they will give delight to your heart.
18 Where there is no prophecy, the people cast off
   restraint,
   but happy are those who keep the law.
19 By mere words servants are not disciplined,
   for though they understand, they will not give
   heed.
20 Do you see someone who is hasty in speech?
   There is more hope for a fool than for anyone
   like that.
21 A slave pampered from childhood
   will come to a bad end.*m*
22 One given to anger stirs up strife,
   and the hothead causes much transgression.
23 A person's pride will bring humiliation,
   but one who is lowly in spirit will obtain
   honor.
24 To be a partner of a thief is to hate one's own
   life;
   one hears the victim's curse, but discloses
   nothing.*n*
25 The fear of others*o* lays a snare,
   but one who trusts in the LORD is secure.
26 Many seek the favor of a ruler,
   but it is from the LORD that one gets justice.
27 The unjust are an abomination to the righteous,
   but the upright are an abomination to the
   wicked.

30 The words of Agur son of Jakeh. An oracle.

   Thus says the man: I am weary, O God,
   I am weary, O God. How can I prevail?*p*
2 Surely I am too stupid to be human;
   I do not have human understanding.
3 I have not learned wisdom,
   nor have I knowledge of the holy ones.*q*
4 Who has ascended to heaven and come down?
   Who has gathered the wind in the hollow of
   the hand?
   Who has wrapped up the waters in a garment?
   Who has established all the ends of the earth?
   What is the person's name?
   And what is the name of the person's child?
   Surely you know!
5 Every word of God proves true;
   he is a shield to those who take refuge in him.
6 Do not add to his words,
   or else he will rebuke you, and you will be
   found a liar.
7 Two things I ask of you;
   do not deny them to me before I die:

14 If a king steadfastly deals out justice to the weak
   his throne will be secure for ever.
15 Rod and reprimand impart wisdom,
   but an uncontrolled youth brings shame on his
   mother.
16 When the wicked are in power, sin is in power,
   but the righteous will witness their downfall.
17 Correct your son, and he will be a comfort to you
   and bring you the delights you desire.
18 With no one in authority, the people throw off all
   restraint,
   but he who keeps God's law leads them on a
   straight path.
19 Mere words will not keep a slave in order;
   he may understand, but he will not respond.
20 Do you see someone over-eager to speak?
   There is more hope for a fool than for him.
21 Pamper a slave from childhood,
   and in the end he will prove ungrateful.
22 Someone prone to anger provokes quarrels
   and a hothead is always committing some offence.
23 Pride will bring anyone low,
   but honour awaits the lowly.
24 He who goes shares with a thief is his own enemy:
   he hears himself put on oath but divulges nothing.
25 Fear of men may prove a snare,
   but trust in the LORD is a tower of refuge.
26 Many seek audience of a ruler,
   but it is the LORD who decides each case.
27 The righteous cannot abide the unjust,
   nor can the wicked abide him whose conduct is
   upright.

30 Sayings of Agur son of Jakeh from Massa:

   This is the great man's very word: I am weary,
   God,
   I am weary and worn out;
2 I am a dumb beast, scarcely a man,
   without a man's powers of understanding;
3 I have not learnt wisdom,
   nor have I attained to knowledge of the Most Holy
   One.
4 Who has ever gone up to heaven and come down
   again?
   Who has cupped the wind in the hollow of his
   hands?
   Who has bound up the waters in the fold of his
   garment?
   Who has fixed all the boundaries of the earth?
   What is his name or his son's name? Surely you
   know!
5 God's every promise has stood the test:
   he is a shield to all who take refuge in him.
6 Add nothing to his words,
   or he will convict you and expose you as a liar.
7 Two things I ask of you—
   do not withhold them in my lifetime:

---

m Vg: Meaning of Heb uncertain   *n* Meaning of Heb uncertain
o Or *human fear*   *p* Or *I am spent*. Meaning of Heb uncertain
q Or *Holy One*

29:18 **no one in authority:** *or* no prophecy.   30:1 **from Massa:**
prob. rdg (cp. 31:1); Heb. the oracle.

NEW AMERICAN BIBLE

14 If a king is zealous for the rights of the poor,
  his throne stands firm forever.

15 The rod of correction gives wisdom,
  but a boy left to his whims disgraces his mother.

16 When the wicked prevail, crime increases;
  but their downfall the just will behold.

17 Correct your son, and he will bring you comfort,
  and give delight to your soul.

18 Without prophecy the people become demoralized;
  but happy is he who keeps the law.

19 By words no servant can be trained;
  for he understands what is said, but obeys not.

20 Do you see a man hasty in his words?
  More can be hoped for from a fool!

21 If a man pampers his servant from childhood,
  he will turn out to be stubborn.

22 An ill-tempered man stirs up disputes,
  and a hotheaded man is the cause of many sins.

23 Man's pride causes his humiliation,
  but he who is humble of spirit obtains honor.

24 The accomplice of a thief is his own enemy:
  he hears himself put under a curse, yet
    discloses nothing.

25 The fear of man brings a snare,
  but he who trusts in the LORD is safe.

26 Many curry favor with the ruler,
  but the rights of each are from the LORD.

27 The evildoer is an abomination to the just,
  and he who walks uprightly is an abomination to
    the wicked.

30

The words of Agur, son of Jakeh the Massaite:

The pronouncement of mortal man: "I am not God;
  I am not God, that I should prevail.
2 Why, I am the most stupid of men,
  and have not even human intelligence;
3 Neither have I learned wisdom,
  nor have I the knowledge of the Holy One.
4 Who has gone up to heaven and come
    down again—
  who has cupped the wind in his hands?
Who has bound up the waters in a cloak—
  who has marked out all the ends of the earth?
What is his name, what is his son's name,
  if you know it?"
5 Every word of God is tested;
  he is a shield to those who take refuge in him.
6 Add nothing to his words,
  lest he reprove you, and you be exposed as
    a deceiver.

7 Two things I ask of you,
  deny them not to me before I die:

NEW JERUSALEM BIBLE

14 The king who judges the weak with equity
  sees his throne set firm for ever.

15 The stick and the reprimand bestow wisdom,
  a young man left to himself brings shame on his
    mother.

16 When the wicked are on the increase, sin
    multiplies,
  but the upright will witness their downfall.

17 Correct your child, and he will give you peace of
    mind;
  he will delight your soul.

18 Where there is no vision the people get out of
    hand;
  happy are they who keep the law.

19 Not by words is a slave corrected:
  even if he understands, he will take no notice.

20 You see someone too ready of speech?
  There is more to be hoped for from a fool!

21 If a slave is pampered from childhood,
  he will prove ungrateful in the end.

22 The hot-head provokes disputes,
  someone in a rage commits all sorts of sins.

23 Pride brings humiliation,
  whoever humbles himself will win honour.

24 To hear the curse and disclose nothing
  is to share with the thief and to hate oneself.

25 To be afraid of human beings is a snare,
  whoever trusts in Yahweh is secure.

26 Many people seek a ruler's favour,
  but the rights of each come from Yahweh.

27 Abhorrent to the upright is the sinful,
  abhorrent to the wicked is one whose way is
    straight.

30

The sayings of Agur son of Jakeh, of Massa.[l]
Prophecy of this man for Ithiel, for Ithiel and for
Ucal.

2 I am myself the stupidest of people,
  bereft of human intelligence,
3 I have not learnt wisdom,
  and I lack the knowledge of the holy ones.
4 Who has mounted to the heavens, then come down
    again?
  Who has gathered the wind in the clasp of his
    hand?
Who has wrapped the waters in his cloak?
  Who has set all the ends of the earth firm?
What is his name?
  What is his child's name?
  Do you know?

5 Every word of God is unalloyed,
  a shield to those who take refuge in him.
6 To his words make no addition,
  lest he reprove you
  and account you a liar.

7 Two things I beg of you,
  do not grudge me them before I die:

---

l **30** In northern Arabia, home also of Lemuel (31:1). The wisdom of
eastern sages was proverbial.

8 Remove far from me falsehood and lying;
   give me neither poverty nor riches;
   feed me with the food that I need,
9 or I shall be full, and deny you,
   and say, "Who is the LORD?"
   or I shall be poor, and steal,
   and profane the name of my God.

10 Do not slander a servant to a master,
   or the servant will curse you, and you will be
      held guilty.

11 There are those who curse their fathers
   and do not bless their mothers.
12 There are those who are pure in their own eyes
   yet are not cleansed of their filthiness.
13 There are those — how lofty are their eyes,
   how high their eyelids lift!
14 There are those whose teeth are swords,
   whose teeth are knives,
   to devour the poor from off the earth,
   the needy from among mortals.

15 The leech[r] has two daughters;
   "Give, give," they cry.
   Three things are never satisfied;
   four never say, "Enough":
16 Sheol, the barren womb,
   the earth ever thirsty for water,
   and the fire that never says, "Enough."[r]

17 The eye that mocks a father
   and scorns to obey a mother
   will be pecked out by the ravens of the valley
   and eaten by the vultures.

18 Three things are too wonderful for me;
   four I do not understand:
19 the way of an eagle in the sky,
   the way of a snake on a rock,
   the way of a ship on the high seas,
   and the way of a man with a girl.

20 This is the way of an adulteress:
   she eats, and wipes her mouth,
   and says, "I have done no wrong."

21 Under three things the earth trembles;
   under four it cannot bear up:
22 a slave when he becomes king,
   and a fool when glutted with food;
23 an unloved woman when she gets a husband,
   and a maid when she succeeds her mistress.

24 Four things on earth are small,
   yet they are exceedingly wise:
25 the ants are a people without strength,
   yet they provide their food in the summer;
26 the badgers are a people without power,
   yet they make their homes in the rocks;
27 the locusts have no king,
   yet all of them march in rank;
28 the lizard[s] can be grasped in the hand,
   yet it is found in kings' palaces.

29 Three things are stately in their stride;
   four are stately in their gait:

8 put fraud and lying far from me;
   give me neither poverty nor wealth,
   but provide me with the food I need,
9 for if I have too much I shall deny you
   and say, 'Who is the LORD?'
   and if I am reduced to poverty I shall steal
   and besmirch the name of my God.

10 Never disparage a slave to his master,
   or he will speak ill of you and you will be held
      guilty.
11 There are certain people who defame their fathers
   and speak ill of their own mothers.
12 There are people who are pure in their own
      estimation,
   yet are not cleansed of their filth.
13 There are people — how haughty are their looks,
   how disdainful their glances! —
14 there are people whose teeth are swords,
   whose fangs are knives;
   they devour the wretched from the earth
   and the needy from among mankind.

15 The leech has two daughters;
   'Give,' says one, and 'Give,' says the other.

   Three things there are which will never be
      satisfied,
   four which never say, 'Enough!'
16 Sheol, a barren woman,
   a land thirsty for water,
   and fire that never says, 'Enough!'

17 The eye that mocks a father or scorns a mother's
      old age
   will be plucked out by the ravens of the valley
   or eaten by young vultures.

18 Three things there are which are too wonderful for
      me,
   four which are beyond my understanding:
19 the way of an eagle in the sky,
   the way of a serpent over rock,
   the way of a ship out at sea,
   and the way of a man with a girl.

20 The way of an unfaithful wife is this:
   she eats, then wipes her mouth
   and says, 'I have done nothing wrong.'

21 Under three things the earth shakes,
   four things it cannot bear:
22 a slave becoming king,
   a fool gorging himself,
23 a hateful woman getting wed,
   and a slave supplanting her mistress.

24 Four things there are which are smallest on earth
   yet wise beyond the wisest:
25 ants, a folk with no strength,
   yet they prepare their store of food in the summer;
26 rock-badgers, a feeble folk,
   yet they make their home among the rocks;
27 locusts, which have no king,
   yet they all sally forth in formation;
28 the lizard, which can be grasped in the hand,
   yet is found in the palaces of kings.

29 Three things there are which are stately in their
      stride,
   four which are stately as they move:

30:16 **Sheol:** or The underworld. 30:17 **old age:** prob. rdg; Heb.
unintelligible. 30:22 **fool:** or boor. 30:27 **in formation:**
meaning of Heb. word uncertain.

[r] Meaning of Heb uncertain   [s] Or spider

8 Put falsehood and lying far from me,
  give me neither poverty nor riches;
  [provide me only with the food I need;]
9 Lest, being full, I deny you,
  saying, "Who is the Lord?"
  Or, being in want, I steal,
  and profane the name of my God.

10 Slander not a servant to his master,
  lest he curse you, and you have to pay
    the penalty.

11 There is a group of people that curses its father,
  and blesses not its mother.
12 There is a group that is pure in its own eyes,
  yet is not purged of its filth.
13 There is a group—how haughty their eyes!
  how overbearing their glance!
14 There is a group whose incisors are swords,
  whose teeth are knives,
  Devouring the needy from the earth,
  and the poor from among men.

15 The two daughters of the leech are, "Give, Give."
  Three things are never satisfied,
  four never say, "Enough!"
16 The nether world, and the barren womb;
  the earth, that is never saturated with water,
  and fire, that never says, "Enough!"
17 The eye that mocks a father,
  or scorns an aged mother,
  Will be plucked out by the ravens in the valley;
  the young eagles will devour it.

18 Three things are too wonderful for me,
  yes, four I cannot understand:
19 The way of an eagle in the air,
  the way of a serpent upon a rock,
  The way of a ship on the high seas,
  and the way of a man with a maiden.
20 Such is the way of an adulterous woman:
  she eats, wipes her mouth,
  and says, "I have done no wrong."

21 Under three things the earth trembles,
  yes, under four it cannot bear up:
22 Under a slave when he becomes king,
  and a fool when he is glutted with food;
23 Under an odious woman when she is wed,
  and a maidservant when she displaces
    her mistress.

24 Four things are among the smallest on the earth,
  and yet are exceedingly wise:
25 Ants—a species not strong,
  yet they store up their food in the summer;
26 Rock-badgers—a species not mighty,
  yet they make their home in the crags;
27 Locusts—they have no king,
  yet they migrate all in array;
28 Lizards—you can catch them with your hands,
  yet they find their way into kings' palaces.

29 Three things are stately in their stride,
  yes, four are stately in their carriage:

8 keep falsehood and lies far from me,
  give me neither poverty nor riches,
  grant me only my share of food,
9 for fear that, surrounded by plenty, I should fall
    away
  and say, 'Yahweh—who is Yahweh?'
  or else, in destitution, take to stealing
  and profane the name of my God.

10 Do not blacken a slave's name to his master,
  lest he curse you, and you suffer for it.

11 There is a breed of person that curses his father
  and does not bless his mother;
12 a breed that, laying claim to purity,
  has not yet been cleansed of its filth;
13 a breed haughty of eye,
  with disdain in every glance;
14 a breed with swords for teeth,
  with knives for jaws,
  devouring the oppressed from the earth
  and the needy from the land.

15 The leech has two daughters: 'Give! Give!'
  There are three insatiable things,
  four, indeed, that never say, 'Enough!'
16 Sheol, the barren womb,
  earth which can have its fill of water,
  fire which never says, 'Enough!'
17 The eye which looks jeeringly on a father,
  and scorns the obedience due to a mother,
  will be pecked out by the ravens of the valley,
  and eaten by the vultures.

18 There are three things beyond my comprehension,
  four, indeed, that I do not understand:
19 the way of an eagle through the skies,
  the way of a snake over the rock,
  the way of a ship in mid-ocean,
  the way of a man with a girl.
20 This is how an adulteress behaves:
  she eats, then wipes her mouth and says,
  'I have done nothing wrong!'

21 There are three things at which the earth trembles,
  four, indeed, which it cannot endure:
22 a slave become king,
  a brute gorged with food,
23 a hateful woman wed at last,
  a servant girl inheriting from her mistress.

24 There are four creatures little on the earth,
  though they are wisest of the wise:
25 ants, a race with no strength,
  yet in the summer they make sure of their food;
26 the coneys, a race without defences,
  yet they make their home in the rocks;
27 locusts, which have no king,
  yet they all march in good order;
28 lizards, which you can catch in your hand,
  yet they frequent the palaces of kings.

29 There are three things of stately tread,
  four, indeed, of stately walk:

30 the lion, which is mightiest among wild animals
    and does not turn back before any;
31 the strutting rooster,[t] the he-goat,
    and a king striding before[u] his people.

32 If you have been foolish, exalting yourself,
    or if you have been devising evil,
    put your hand on your mouth.
33 For as pressing milk produces curds,
    and pressing the nose produces blood,
    so pressing anger produces strife.

31 The words of King Lemuel. An oracle that his
mother taught him:

2 No, my son! No, son of my womb!
    No, son of my vows!
3 Do not give your strength to women,
    your ways to those who destroy kings.
4 It is not for kings, O Lemuel,
    it is not for kings to drink wine,
    or for rulers to desire[v] strong drink;
5 or else they will drink and forget what has been
        decreed,
    and will pervert the rights of all the afflicted.
6 Give strong drink to one who is perishing,
    and wine to those in bitter distress;
7 let them drink and forget their poverty,
    and remember their misery no more.
8 Speak out for those who cannot speak,
    for the rights of all the destitute.[w]
9 Speak out, judge righteously,
    defend the rights of the poor and needy.

10 A capable wife who can find?
    She is far more precious than jewels.
11 The heart of her husband trusts in her,
    and he will have no lack of gain.
12 She does him good, and not harm,
    all the days of her life.
13 She seeks wool and flax,
    and works with willing hands.
14 She is like the ships of the merchant,
    she brings her food from far away.
15 She rises while it is still night
    and provides food for her household
    and tasks for her servant-girls.
16 She considers a field and buys it;
    with the fruit of her hands she plants a
        vineyard.
17 She girds herself with strength,
    and makes her arms strong.
18 She perceives that her merchandise is profitable.
    Her lamp does not go out at night.
19 She puts her hands to the distaff,
    and her hands hold the spindle.
20 She opens her hand to the poor,
    and reaches out her hands to the needy.
21 She is not afraid for her household when it
        snows,
    for all her household are clothed in crimson.

30 the lion, mighty among beasts,
    which will not turn tail for anyone;
31 the strutting cock, the he-goat,
    and a king going forth at the head of his army.

32 If you are churlish and arrogant
    and given to scheming, hold your tongue;
33 for as the pressing of milk produces curd,
    and the pressing of the nose produces blood,
    so the pressing of anger leads to strife.

31 Sayings of King Lemuel of Massa, which his mother taught him:

2 What shall I say to you, my son,
    child of my womb and answer to my prayers?
3 Do not give the vigour of your manhood to
        women,
    or consort with women who bring down kings.
4 Lemuel, it is not for kings, not for kings to drink
        wine,
    or for those who govern to crave strong liquor.
5 If they drink, they will forget rights and customs
    and twist the law against all who are defenceless.
6 Give strong drink to the despairing
    and wine to the embittered of heart;
7 let them drink and forget their poverty
    and remember their trouble no more.
8 Speak up for those who cannot speak for
        themselves;
    oppose any that go to law against them;
9 speak out and pronounce just sentence
    and give judgement for the wretched and the poor.

10 WHO can find a good wife?
    Her worth is far beyond red coral.
11 Her husband's whole trust is in her,
    and children are not lacking.
12 She works to bring him good, not evil,
    all the days of her life.
13 She chooses wool and flax
    and with a will she sets about her work.
14 Like a ship laden with merchandise
    she brings home food from far off.
15 She rises while it is still dark
    and apportions food for her household,
    with a due share for her servants.
16 After careful thought she buys a field
    and plants a vineyard out of her earnings.
17 She sets about her duties resolutely
    and tackles her work with vigour.
18 She sees that her business goes well,
    and all night long her lamp does not go out.
19 She holds the distaff in her hand,
    and her fingers grasp the spindle.
20 She is open-handed to the wretched
    and extends help to the poor.
21 When it snows she has no fear for her household,
    for they are wrapped in double cloaks.

[t] Gk Syr Tg Compare Vg: Meaning of Heb uncertain   [u] Meaning of
Heb uncertain   [v] Cn: Heb where   [w] Heb all children of passing
away

30:31 **strutting cock:** or charger; meaning of Heb. uncertain. **going
forth . . . army:** prob. rdg; Heb. unintelligible.   30:33 **anger:** lit.
the nostrils.   31:17 **tackles her work:** so Gk; Heb. omits.

NEW AMERICAN BIBLE

30 The lion, mightiest of beasts,
   who retreats before nothing;
31 The strutting cock, and the he-goat,
   and the king at the head of his people.

32 If you have foolishly been proud
   or presumptuous—put your hand on your mouth;
33 For the stirring of milk brings forth curds,
   and the stirring of anger brings forth blood.

31 The words of Lemuel, king of Massa. The advice
   which his mother gave him:

2 What, my son, my first-born!
   what, O son of my womb;
   what, O son of my vows!
3 Give not your vigor to women,
   nor your strength to those who ruin kings.
4 It is not for kings, O Lemuel,
   not for kings to drink wine;
   strong drink is not for princes!
5 Lest in drinking they forget what the law decrees,
   and violate the rights of all who are in need.
6 Give strong drink to one who is perishing,
   and wine to the sorely depressed;
7 When they drink, they will forget their misery,
   and think no more of their burdens.
8 Open your mouth in behalf of the dumb,
   and for the rights of the destitute;
9 Open your mouth, decree what is just,
   defend the needy and the poor!

10 When one finds a worthy wife,
   her value is far beyond pearls.
11 Her husband, entrusting his heart to her,
   has an unfailing prize.
12 She brings him good, and not evil,
   all the days of her life.
13 She obtains wool and flax
   and makes cloth with skillful hands.
14 Like merchant ships,
   she secures her provisions from afar.
15 She rises while it is still night,
   and distributes food to her household.
16 She picks out a field to purchase;
   out of her earnings she plants a vineyard.
17 She is girt about with strength,
   and sturdy are her arms.
18 She enjoys the success of her dealings;
   at night her lamp is undimmed.
19 She puts her hands to the distaff,
   and her fingers ply the spindle.
20 She reaches out her hands to the poor,
   and extends her arms to the needy.
21 She fears not the snow for her household;
   all her charges are doubly clothed.

NEW JERUSALEM BIBLE

30 the lion, bravest of beasts,
   he will draw back from nothing;
31 a vigorous cock, a he-goat,
   and the king when he harangues his people.

32 If you have been foolish enough to fly into a
   passion
   and now have second thoughts, lay your hand on
   your lips.
33 For by churning the milk you produce butter,
   by wringing the nose you produce blood,
   and by whipping up anger you produce strife.

31 The sayings of Lemuel king of Massa, taught him
   by his mother:

2 What, my son! What, son of my womb!
   What, son of my vows!
3 Do not expend your energy on women
   nor your wealth on those who ruin kings.
4 Not for kings, O Lemuel,
   not for kings the drinking of wine,
   not for princes the love of liquor,
5 for fear that in liquor they forget what they have
   decreed
   and pervert the course of justice against all the
   poor.

6 Procure strong drink for someone about to die,
   wine for him whose heart is heavy:
7 let him drink and forget his misfortune,
   and remember his misery no more.
8 Make your views heard, on behalf of the dumb,
   on behalf of all the unwanted;
9 make your views heard, pronounce an upright
   verdict,
   defend the cause of the poor and the wretched.

Aleph	10 The truly capable woman—who can find her? She is far beyond the price of pearls.
Bet	11 Her husband's heart has confidence in her, from her he will derive no little profit.
Gimel	12 Advantage and not hurt she brings him all the days of her life.
Dalet	13 She selects wool and flax, she does her work with eager hands.
He	14 She is like those merchant vessels, bringing her food from far away.
Waw	15 She gets up while it is still dark giving her household their food, giving orders to her serving girls.
Zain	16 She sets her mind on a field, then she buys it; with what her hands have earned she plants a vineyard.
Het	17 She puts her back into her work and shows how strong her arms can be.
Tet	18 She knows that her affairs are going well; her lamp does not go out at night.
Yod	19 She sets her hands to the distaff, her fingers grasp the spindle.
Kaph	20 She holds out her hands to the poor, she opens her arms to the needy.
Lamed	21 Snow may come, she has no fears for her household, with all her servants warmly clothed.

22 She makes herself coverings;
    her clothing is fine linen and purple.
23 Her husband is known in the city gates,
    taking his seat among the elders of the land.
24 She makes linen garments and sells them;
    she supplies the merchant with sashes.
25 Strength and dignity are her clothing,
    and she laughs at the time to come.
26 She opens her mouth with wisdom,
    and the teaching of kindness is on her tongue.
27 She looks well to the ways of her household,
    and does not eat the bread of idleness.
28 Her children rise up and call her happy;
    her husband too, and he praises her:
29 "Many women have done excellently,
    but you surpass them all."
30 Charm is deceitful, and beauty is vain,
    but a woman who fears the LORD is to be
    praised.
31 Give her a share in the fruit of her hands,
    and let her works praise her in the city gates.

22 She makes her own bed coverings
    and clothing of fine linen and purple.
23 Her husband is well known in the assembly,
    where he takes his seat with the elders of the
    region.
24 She weaves linen and sells it,
    and supplies merchants with sashes.
25 She is clothed in strength and dignity
    and can afford to laugh at tomorrow.
26 When she opens her mouth, it is to speak wisely;
    her teaching is sound.
27 She keeps her eye on the conduct of her household
    and does not eat the bread of idleness.
28 Her sons with one accord extol her virtues;
    her husband too is loud in her praise:
29 'Many a woman shows how gifted she is;
    but you excel them all.'
30 Charm is deceptive and beauty fleeting;
    but the woman who fears the LORD is honoured.
31 Praise her for all she has accomplished;
    let her achievements bring her honour at the city
    gates.

NEW AMERICAN BIBLE

22 She makes her own coverlets;
   fine linen and purple are her clothing.
23 Her husband is prominent at the city gates
   as he sits with the elders of the land.
24 She makes garments and sells them,
   and stocks the merchants with belts.
25 She is clothed with strength and dignity,
   and she laughs at the days to come.
26 She opens her mouth in wisdom,
   and on her tongue is kindly counsel.
27 She watches the conduct of her household,
   and eats not her food in idleness.
28 Her children rise up and praise her;
   her husband, too, extols her:
29 "Many are the women of proven worth,
   but you have excelled them all."
30 Charm is deceptive and beauty fleeting;
   the woman who fears the LORD is to be praised.
31 Give her a reward of her labors,
   and let her works praise her at the city gates.

NEW JERUSALEM BIBLE

Mem	22 She makes her own quilts, she is dressed in fine linen and purple.
Nun	23 Her husband is respected at the city gates, taking his seat among the elders of the land.
Samek	24 She weaves materials and sells them, she supplies the merchant with sashes.
Ain	25 She is clothed in strength and dignity, she can laugh at the day to come.
Pe	26 When she opens her mouth, she does so wisely; on her tongue is kindly instruction.
Zade	27 She keeps good watch on the conduct of her household, no bread of idleness for her.
Qoph	28 Her children stand up and proclaim her blessed, her husband, too, sings her praises:
Resh	29 'Many women have done admirable things, but you surpass them all!'
Shin	30 Charm is deceitful, and beauty empty; the woman who fears Yahweh is the one to praise.
Taw	31 Give her a share in what her hands have worked for, and let her works tell her praises at the city gates.

Ecclesiastes

1 The words of the Teacher,[a] the son of David, king in
Jerusalem.
  2 Vanity of vanities, says the Teacher,[a]
      vanity of vanities! All is vanity.
  3 What do people gain from all the toil
      at which they toil under the sun?
  4 A generation goes, and a generation comes,
      but the earth remains forever.
  5 The sun rises and the sun goes down,
      and hurries to the place where it rises.
  6 The wind blows to the south,
      and goes around to the north;
    round and round goes the wind,
      and on its circuits the wind returns.
  7 All streams run to the sea,
      but the sea is not full;
    to the place where the streams flow,
      there they continue to flow.
  8 All things[b] are wearisome;
      more than one can express;
    the eye is not satisfied with seeing,
      or the ear filled with hearing.
  9 What has been is what will be,
      and what has been done is what will be done;
      there is nothing new under the sun.
  10 Is there a thing of which it is said,
      "See, this is new"?
    It has already been,
      in the ages before us.
  11 The people of long ago are not remembered,
      nor will there be any remembrance
    of people yet to come
      by those who come after them.

12 I, the Teacher,[a] when king over Israel in Jerusalem,
13 applied my mind to seek and to search out by wisdom all
that is done under heaven; it is an unhappy business that
God has given to human beings to be busy with. 14 I saw all
the deeds that are done under the sun; and see, all is vanity
and a chasing after wind.[c]

  15 What is crooked cannot be made straight,
      and what is lacking cannot be counted.

16 I said to myself, "I have acquired great wisdom,
surpassing all who were over Jerusalem before me; and my
mind has had great experience of wisdom and knowledge."
17 And I applied my mind to know wisdom and to know
madness and folly. I perceived that this also is but a chasing
after wind.[c]

  18 For in much wisdom is much vexation,
      and those who increase knowledge increase
          sorrow.

2 I said to myself, "Come now, I will make a test of
pleasure; enjoy yourself." But again, this also was vanity. 2 I said of laughter, "It is mad," and of pleasure, "What
use is it?" 3 I searched with my mind how to cheer my body
with wine — my mind still guiding me with wisdom — and
how to lay hold on folly, until I might see what was good
for mortals to do under heaven during the few days of their
life. 4 I made great works; I built houses and planted vineyards for myself; 5 I made myself gardens and parks, and
planted in them all kinds of fruit trees. 6 I made myself pools

Ecclesiastes

1 THE words of the Speaker, the son of David, king in
Jerusalem.
2 Futility, utter futility, says the Speaker, everything is
futile. 3 What does anyone profit from all his labour and toil
here under the sun? 4 Generations come and generations go,
while the earth endures for ever.

5 The sun rises and the sun goes down; then it speeds to
its place and rises there again. 6 The wind blows to the
south, it veers to the north; round and round it goes and
returns full circle. 7 All streams run to the sea, yet the sea
never overflows; back to the place from which the streams
ran they return to run again.

8 All things are wearisome. No one can describe them all,
no eye can see them all, no ear can hear them all. 9 What has
happened will happen again, and what has been done will
be done again; there is nothing new under the sun. 10 Is there
anything of which it can be said, 'Look, this is new'? No,
it was already in existence, long before our time. 11 Those
who lived in the past are not remembered, and those who
follow will not be remembered by those who follow them.

12 I, the Speaker, ruled as king over Israel in Jerusalem;
13 and I applied my mind to study and explore by means of
wisdom all that is done under heaven. It is a worthless task
that God has given to mortals to keep them occupied. 14 I
have seen everything that has been done here under the sun;
it is all futility and a chasing of the wind. 15 What is crooked
cannot become straight; what is not there cannot be counted. 16 I thought to myself, 'I have amassed great wisdom,
surpassing all my predecessors on the throne at Jerusalem;
I have become familiar with wisdom and knowledge.' 17 So
I applied my mind to understanding wisdom and knowledge, madness and folly, and I came to see that this too is
a chasing of the wind. 18 For in much wisdom is much
vexation; the more knowledge, the more suffering.

2 I said to myself, 'Come, I will test myself with pleasure and get enjoyment'; but that too was futile. 2 Of
laughter I said, 'It is madness!' And of pleasure, 'What is
the good of that?' 3 I sought how to cheer my body with
wine, and, though my mind was still guiding me with wisdom, how to pursue folly; I hoped to find out what was
good for mortals to do under heaven during their brief span
of life.

4 I undertook great works; I built myself palaces and
planted vineyards; 5 I made myself gardens and orchards,
planted with every kind of fruit tree. 6 I constructed ponds

---

[a] Heb Qoheleth, traditionally rendered Preacher   [b] Or words
[c] Or a feeding on wind. See Hos 12.1

1:1 the Speaker: Heb. Koheleth, Gk Ecclesiastes.   1:5 then . . .
place: prob. rdg; Heb. panting to its place.

Ecclesiastes

Ecclesiastes

1 The words of David's son, Qoheleth, king in Jerusalem:

2 Vanity of vanities, says Qoheleth,
vanity of vanities! All things are vanity!
3 What profit has man from all the labor
which he toils at under the sun?
4 One generation passes and another comes,
but the world forever stays.
5 The sun rises and the sun goes down;
then it presses on to the place where it rises.
6 Blowing now toward the south, then toward
the north,
the wind turns again and again, resuming
its rounds.
7 All rivers go to the sea,
yet never does the sea become full.
To the place where they go,
the rivers keep on going.
8 All speech is labored;
there is nothing man can say.
The eye is not satisfied with seeing
nor is the ear filled with hearing.

9 What has been, that will be; what has been done, that will be done. Nothing is new under the sun. 10 Even the thing of which we say, "See, this is new!" has already existed in the ages that preceded us. 11 There is no remembrance of the men of old; nor of those to come will there be any remembrance among those who come after them.

12 I, Qoheleth, was king over Israel in Jerusalem, 13 and I applied my mind to search and investigate in wisdom all things that are done under the sun.

A thankless task God has appointed
for men to be busied about.

14 I have seen all things that are done under the sun, and behold, all is vanity and a chase after wind.

15 What is crooked cannot be made straight,
and what is missing cannot be supplied.

16 Though I said to myself, "Behold, I have become great and stored up wisdom beyond all who were before me in Jerusalem, and my mind has broad experience of wisdom and knowledge"; 17 yet when I applied my mind to know wisdom and knowledge, madness and folly, I learned that this also is a chase after wind.

18 For in much wisdom there is much sorrow,
and he who stores up knowledge stores up grief.

2 I said to myself, "Come, now, let me try you with pleasure and the enjoyment of good things." But behold, this too was vanity. 2 Of laughter I said: "Mad!" and of mirth: "What good does this do?" 3 I thought of beguiling my senses with wine, though my mind was concerned with wisdom, and of taking up folly, until I should understand what is best for men to do under the heavens during the limited days of their life.

4 I undertook great works; I built myself houses and planted vineyards; 5 I made gardens and parks, and set out in them fruit trees of all sorts. 6 And I constructed for myself

1 Composition of Qoheleth son of David, king in Jerusalem.

2 Sheer futility, Qoheleth says. Sheer futility: everything is futile! 3 What profit can we show for all our toil, toiling under the sun? 4 A generation goes, a generation comes, yet the earth stands firm for ever. 5 The sun rises, the sun sets; then to its place it speeds and there it rises. 6 Southward goes the wind, then turns to the north; it turns and turns again; then back to its circling goes the wind. 7 Into the sea go all the rivers, and yet the sea is never filled, and still to their goal the rivers go. 8 All things are wearisome. No one can say that eyes have not had enough of seeing, ears their fill of hearing.

9 What was, will be again,
what has been done, will be done again,
and there is nothing new under the sun!

10 Take anything which people acclaim as being new: it existed in the centuries preceding us. 11 No memory remains of the past, and so it will be for the centuries to come — they will not be remembered by their successors.

12 I, Qoheleth, have reigned over Israel in Jerusalem. 13 Wisely I have applied myself to investigation and exploration of everything that happens under heaven. What a wearisome task God has given humanity to keep us busy! 14 I have seen everything that is done under the sun: how futile it all is, mere chasing after the wind!

15 What is twisted cannot be straightened,
what is not there cannot be counted.

16 I thought to myself: I have acquired a greater stock of wisdom than anyone before me in Jerusalem. I myself have mastered every kind of wisdom and science. 17 I have applied myself to understanding philosophy and science, stupidity and folly, and I now realise that all this too is chasing after the wind.

18 Much wisdom, much grief;
the more knowledge, the more sorrow.

2 I thought to myself, 'Very well, I will try pleasure and see what enjoyment has to offer.' And this was futile too. 2 This laughter, I reflected, is a madness, this pleasure no use at all. 3 I decided to hand my body over to drinking wine, my mind still guiding me in wisdom; I resolved to embrace folly, to discover the best way for people to spend their days under the sun. 4 I worked on a grand scale: built myself palaces, planted vineyards; 5 made myself gardens and orchards, planting every kind of fruit tree in them; 6 had

from which to water the forest of growing trees. 7 I bought male and female slaves, and had slaves who were born in my house; I also had great possessions of herds and flocks, more than any who had been before me in Jerusalem. 8 I also gathered for myself silver and gold and the treasure of kings and of the provinces; I got singers, both men and women, and delights of the flesh, and many concubines. *d*

9 So I became great and surpassed all who were before me in Jerusalem; also my wisdom remained with me. 10 Whatever my eyes desired I did not keep from them; I kept my heart from no pleasure, for my heart found pleasure in all my toil, and this was my reward for all my toil. 11 Then I considered all that my hands had done and the toil I had spent in doing it, and again, all was vanity and a chasing after wind, *e* and there was nothing to be gained under the sun.

12 So I turned to consider wisdom and madness and folly; for what can the one do who comes after the king? Only what has already been done. 13 Then I saw that wisdom excels folly as light excels darkness.

14 The wise have eyes in their head,
   but fools walk in darkness.

Yet I perceived that the same fate befalls all of them. 15 Then I said to myself, "What happens to the fool will happen to me also; why then have I been so very wise?" And I said to myself that this also is vanity. 16 For there is no enduring remembrance of the wise or of fools, seeing that in the days to come all will have been long forgotten. How can the wise die just like fools? 17 So I hated life, because what is done under the sun was grievous to me; for all is vanity and a chasing after wind. *e*

18 I hated all my toil in which I had toiled under the sun, seeing that I must leave it to those who come after me 19 — and who knows whether they will be wise or foolish? Yet they will be master of all for which I toiled and used my wisdom under the sun. This also is vanity. 20 So I turned and gave my heart up to despair concerning all the toil of my labors under the sun, 21 because sometimes one who has toiled with wisdom and knowledge and skill must leave all to be enjoyed by another who did not toil for it. This also is vanity and a great evil. 22 What do mortals get from all the toil and strain with which they toil under the sun? 23 For all their days are full of pain, and their work is a vexation; even at night their minds do not rest. This also is vanity.

24 There is nothing better for mortals than to eat and drink, and find enjoyment in their toil. This also, I saw, is from the hand of God; 25 for apart from him *f* who can eat or who can have enjoyment? 26 For to the one who pleases him God gives wisdom and knowledge and joy; but to the sinner he gives the work of gathering and heaping, only to give to one who pleases God. This also is vanity and a chasing after wind. *e*

3 For everything there is a season, and a time for every matter under heaven:

2 a time to be born, and a time to die;
   a time to plant, and a time to pluck up what is
      planted;
3 a time to kill, and a time to heal;
   a time to break down, and a time to build up;
4 a time to weep, and a time to laugh;
   a time to mourn, and a time to dance;
5 a time to throw away stones, and a time to gather
      stones together;

from which to water a grove of growing trees; 7 I acquired male and female slaves, and I had my home-born slaves as well; I owned possessions, more flocks and herds than any of my predecessors in Jerusalem; 8 I also amassed silver and gold, the treasure of kings and provinces; I got for myself minstrels, male and female, and everything that affords delight. 9 I achieved greatness, surpassing all my predecessors in Jerusalem; and my wisdom stood me in good stead. 10 I did not refuse my eyes anything they coveted; I did not deny myself any pleasure. Indeed I found pleasure in all my labour, and for all my labour this was my reward. 11 I considered my handiwork, all my labour and toil: it was futility, all of it, and a chasing of the wind, of no profit under the sun.

12 Then I considered wisdom and madness and folly. 13 I saw that wisdom is more profitable than folly, as light is more profitable than darkness: 14 the wise person has eyes in his head, but the fool walks in the dark. Yet I realized also that one and the same fate overtakes them both. 15 So I thought, 'I too shall suffer the fate of the fool. To what purpose have I been wise? Where is the profit? Even this', I said to myself, 'is futile. 16 The wise person is remembered no longer than the fool, because in the days to come both will have been forgotten. Alas, both wise and foolish are doomed to die!' 17 So I came to hate life, since everything that was done here under the sun was a trouble to me; for all is futility and a chasing of the wind. 18 I came to hate all my labour and toil here under the sun, since I should have to leave its fruits to my successor. What will the king's successor do? Will he do what has been done before? 19 Who knows whether he will be wise or foolish? Yet he will have in his control all the fruits of my labour and skill here under the sun. This too is futility.

20 Then I turned and gave myself up to despair, as I reflected on all my labour and toil here under the sun. 21 For though someone toils with wisdom, knowledge, and skill he must leave it all to one who has spent no labour on it. This too is futility and a great wrong. 22 What reward does anyone have for all his labour, his planning, and his toil here under the sun? 23 His lifelong activity is pain and vexation to him; even in the night he has no peace of mind. This too is futility.

24 To eat and drink and experience pleasure in return for his labours, this does not come from any good in a person: it comes from God. 25 For without God who can eat with enjoyment? 26 He gives wisdom and knowledge and joy to whosoever is pleasing to him, while to the one who fails to please him is given the task of gathering and amassing wealth only to hand it over to someone else who does please God. This too is futility and a chasing of the wind.

3 FOR everything its season, and for every activity under heaven its time:

2 a time to be born and a time to die;
   a time to plant and a time to uproot;
3 a time to kill and a time to heal;
   a time to break down and a time to build up;
4 a time to weep and a time to laugh;
   a time for mourning and a time for dancing;
5 a time to scatter stones and a time to gather them;

---

d Meaning of Heb uncertain   *e* Or *a feeding on wind*. See Hos 12.1
f Gk Syr: Heb *apart from me*

2:8 **everything . . . delight**: prob. rdg; Heb. adds two unintelligible words.   2:12 **folly**: the rest of verse 12 transposed to follow verse 18.   2:18 **What will . . . done before**: see note on verse 12.

reservoirs to water a flourishing woodland. 7 I acquired male and female slaves, and slaves were born in my house. I also had growing herds of cattle and flocks of sheep, more than all who had been before me in Jerusalem. 8 I amassed for myself silver and gold, and the wealth of kings and provinces. I got for myself male and female singers and all human luxuries. 9 I became great, and I stored up more than all others before me in Jerusalem; my wisdom, too, stayed with me. 10 Nothing that my eyes desired did I deny them, nor did I deprive myself of any joy, but my heart rejoiced in the fruit of all my toil. This was my share for all my toil. 11 But when I turned to all the works that my hands had wrought, and to the toil at which I had taken such pains, behold! all was vanity and a chase after wind, with nothing gained under the sun. 12 For what will the man do who is to come after the king? What men have already done!

I went on to the consideration of wisdom, madness and folly. 13 And I saw that wisdom has the advantage over folly as much as light has the advantage over darkness.

14 The wise man has eyes in his head,
but the fool walks in darkness.

Yet I knew that one lot befalls both of them. 15 So I said to myself, if the fool's lot is to befall me also, why then should I be wise? Where is the profit for me? And I concluded in my heart that this too is vanity. 16 Neither of the wise man nor of the fool will there be an abiding remembrance, for in days to come both will have been forgotten. How is it that the wise man dies as well as the fool! 17 Therefore I loathed life, since for me the work that is done under the sun is evil; for all is vanity and a chase after wind.

18 And I detested all the fruits of my labor under the sun, because I must leave them to a man who is to come after me. 19 And who knows whether he will be a wise man or a fool? Yet he will have control over all the fruits of my wise labor under the sun. This also is vanity. 20 So my feelings turned to despair of all the fruits of my labor under the sun. 21 For there is a man who has labored with wisdom and knowledge and skill, and to another, who has not labored over it, he must leave his property. This also is vanity and a great misfortune. 22 For what profit comes to a man from all the toil and anxiety which he has labored under the sun? 23 All his days sorrow and grief are his occupation; even at night his mind is not at rest. This also is vanity.

24 There is nothing better for man than to eat and drink and provide himself with good things by his labors. Even this, I realized, is from the hand of God. 25 For who can eat or drink apart from him? 26 For to whatever man he sees fit he gives wisdom and knowledge and joy; but to the sinner he gives the task of gathering possessions to be given to whatever man God sees fit. This also is vanity and a chase after wind.

3 There is an appointed time for everything,
  and a time for every affair under the heavens.
  2 A time to be born, and a time to die;
    a time to plant, and a time to uproot the plant.
  3 A time to kill, and a time to heal;
    a time to tear down, and a time to build.
  4 A time to weep, and a time to laugh;
    a time to mourn, and a time to dance.
  5 A time to scatter stones, and a time to gather them;

pools made for watering the young trees of my plantations. 7 I bought slaves, male and female, had home-born slaves as well; herds and flocks I had too, more than anyone in Jerusalem before me. 8 I amassed silver and gold, the treasures of kings and provinces; acquired singers, men and women, and every human luxury, chest upon chest of it. 9 So I grew great, greater than anyone in Jerusalem before me; nor did my wisdom leave me. 10 I denied my eyes nothing that they desired, refused my heart no pleasure, for I found all my hard work a pleasure, such was the return for all my efforts. 11 I then reflected on all that my hands had achieved and all the effort I had put into its achieving. What futility it all was, what chasing after the wind! There is nothing to be gained under the sun.

12 My reflections then turned to wisdom, stupidity and folly. For instance, what can the successor of a king do? What has been done already. 13 More is to be gained from wisdom than from folly, just as one gains more from light than from darkness; this, of course, I see:

14 The wise have their eyes open,
the fool walks in the dark.

No doubt! But I know, too, that one fate awaits them both. 15 'Since the fool's fate', I thought to myself, 'will be my fate too, what is the point of my having been wise?' I realised that this too is futile. 16 For there is no lasting memory for the wise or the fool, and in the days to come both will be forgotten; the wise, no less than the fool, must die. 17 Life I have come to hate, for what is done under the sun disgusts me, since all is futility and chasing after the wind. 18 All I have toiled for under the sun and now bequeath to my successor I have come to hate; 19 who knows whether he will be wise or a fool? Yet he will be master of all the work into which I have put my efforts and wisdom under the sun. That is futile too. 20 I have come to despair of all the efforts I have expended under the sun. 21 For here is one who has laboured wisely, skilfully and successfully and must leave what is his own to someone who has not toiled for it at all. This is futile too, and grossly unjust; 22 for what does he gain for all the toil and strain that he has undergone under the sun — 23 since his days are full of sorrow, his work is full of stress and even at night he has no peace of mind? This is futile too.

24 There is no happiness except in eating and drinking, and in enjoying one's achievements; and I see that this too comes from God's hand; 25 for who would get anything to eat or drink, unless all this came from him? 26 Wisdom, knowledge and joy, God gives to those who please him, but on the sinner he lays the task of gathering and storing up for someone else who is pleasing to him. This too is futility and chasing after the wind.

3 There is a season for everything, a time for every occupation under heaven:
  2 A time for giving birth,
    a time for dying;
    a time for planting,
    a time for uprooting what has been planted.
  3 A time for killing,
    a time for healing;
    a time for knocking down,
    a time for building.
  4 A time for tears,
    a time for laughter;
    a time for mourning,
    a time for dancing.
  5 A time for throwing stones away,
    a time for gathering them;

NEW REVISED STANDARD VERSION	REVISED ENGLISH BIBLE

a time to embrace, and a time to refrain from
embracing;

6 a time to seek, and a time to lose;
a time to keep, and a time to throw away;

7 a time to tear, and a time to sew;
a time to keep silence, and a time to speak;

8 a time to love, and a time to hate;
a time for war, and a time for peace.

9 What gain have the workers from their toil? 10 I have seen the business that God has given to everyone to be busy with. 11 He has made everything suitable for its time; moreover he has put a sense of past and future into their minds, yet they cannot find out what God has done from the beginning to the end. 12 I know that there is nothing better for them than to be happy and enjoy themselves as long as they live; 13 moreover, it is God's gift that all should eat and drink and take pleasure in all their toil. 14 I know that whatever God does endures forever; nothing can be added to it, nor anything taken from it; God has done this, so that all should stand in awe before him. 15 That which is, already has been; that which is to be, already is; and God seeks out what has gone by.g

16 Moreover I saw under the sun that in the place of justice, wickedness was there, and in the place of righteousness, wickedness was there as well. 17 I said in my heart, God will judge the righteous and the wicked, for he has appointed a time for every matter, and for every work. 18 I said in my heart with regard to human beings that God is testing them to show that they are but animals. 19 For the fate of humans and the fate of animals is the same; as one dies, so dies the other. They all have the same breath, and humans have no advantage over the animals; for all is vanity. 20 All go to one place; all are from the dust, and all turn to dust again. 21 Who knows whether the human spirit goes upward and the spirit of animals goes downward to the earth? 22 So I saw that there is nothing better than that all should enjoy their work, for that is their lot; who can bring them to see what will be after them?

a time to embrace and a time to abstain from
embracing;

6 a time to seek and a time to lose;
a time to keep and a time to discard;

7 a time to tear and a time to mend;
a time for silence and a time for speech;

8 a time to love and a time to hate;
a time for war and a time for peace.

9 What profit has the worker from his labour? 10 I have seen the task that God has given to mortals to keep them occupied. 11 He has made everything to suit its time; moreover he has given mankind a sense of past and future, but no comprehension of God's work from beginning to end. 12 I know that there is nothing good for anyone except to be happy and live the best life he can while he is alive. 13 Indeed, that everyone should eat and drink and enjoy himself, in return for all his labours, is a gift of God. 14 I know that whatever God does lasts for ever; there is no adding to it, no taking away. And he has done it all in such a way that everyone must feel awe in his presence. 15 Whatever is has been already, and whatever is to come has been already, with God summoning each event back in its turn.

16 Moreover I saw here under the sun that, where justice ought to be, there was wickedness; and where righteousness ought to be, there was wickedness. 17 I said to myself, 'God will judge the just and the wicked equally; for every activity and every purpose has its proper time.' 18 I said to myself, 'In dealing with human beings it is God's purpose to test them and to see what they truly are. 19 Human beings and beasts share one and the same fate: death comes to both alike. They all draw the same breath. Man has no advantage over beast, for everything is futility. 20 All go to the same place: all came from the dust, and to the dust all return. 21 Who knows whether the spirit of a human being goes upward or whether the spirit of a beast goes downward to the earth?' 22 So I saw that there is nothing better than that all should enjoy their work, since that is their lot. For who will put them in a position to see what will happen afterwards?

4 Again I saw all the oppressions that are practiced under the sun. Look, the tears of the oppressed — with no one to comfort them! On the side of their oppressors there was power — with no one to comfort them. 2 And I thought the dead, who have already died, more fortunate than the living, who are still alive; 3 but better than both is the one who has not yet been, and has not seen the evil deeds that are done under the sun.

4 Then I saw that all toil and all skill in work come from one person's envy of another. This also is vanity and a chasing after wind.h

4 Again, I considered all the acts of oppression perpetrated under the sun; I saw the tears of the oppressed, and there was no one to comfort them. Power was on the side of their oppressors, and there was no one to afford comfort. 2 I accounted the dead happy because they were already dead, happier than the living who still have lives to live; 3 more fortunate than either I reckoned those yet unborn, who have not witnessed the wicked deeds done here under the sun. 4 I considered all toil and all achievement and saw that it springs from rivalry between one person and another. This too is futility and a chasing of the wind. 5 The

3:17 **proper time:** *prob. rdg; Heb.* adds there.   3:18 **what . . . are:** *prob. rdg; Heb.* adds they to them.   4:3 **I reckoned:** *so Lat.;* Heb. *omits.*

g Heb *what is pursued*   h Or *a feeding on wind.* See Hos 12.1

a time to embrace, and a time to be far
from embraces.
6 A time to seek, and a time to lose;
a time to keep, and a time to cast away.
7 A time to rend, and a time to sew;
a time to be silent, and a time to speak.
8 A time to love, and a time to hate;
a time of war, and a time of peace.

9 What advantage has the worker from his toil? 10 I have
considered the task which God has appointed for men to be
busied about. 11 He has made everything appropriate to its
time, and has put the timeless into their hearts, without
men's ever discovering, from beginning to end, the work
which God has done. 12 I recognized that there is nothing
better than to be glad and to do well during life. 13 For every
man, moreover, to eat and drink and enjoy the fruit of all
his labor is a gift of God. 14 I recognized that whatever God
does will endure forever; there is no adding to it, or taking
from it. Thus has God done that he may be revered. 15 What
now is has already been; what is to be, already is; and God
restores what would otherwise be displaced.

16 And still under the sun in the judgment place I saw
wickedness, and in the seat of justice, iniquity. 17 And I said
to myself, both the just and the wicked God will judge,
since there is a time for every affair and on every work a
judgment. 18 I said to myself: As for the children of men, it
is God's way of testing them and of showing that they are
in themselves like beasts. 19 For the lot of man and of beast
is one lot; the one dies as well as the other. Both have the
same life-breath, and man has no advantage over the beast;
but all is vanity. 20 Both go to the same place; both were
made from the dust, and to the dust they both return. 21 Who
knows if the life-breath of the children of men goes upward
and the life-breath of beasts goes earthward? 22 And I saw
that there is nothing better for a man than to rejoice in his
work; for this is his lot. Who will let him see what is to
come after him?

4 Again I considered all the oppressions that take place
under the sun: the tears of the victims with none to
comfort them! From the hand of their oppressors comes
violence, and there is none to comfort them! 2 And those
now dead, I declared more fortunate in death than are the
living to be still alive. 3 And better off than both is the yet
unborn, who has not seen the wicked work that is done
under the sun. 4 Then I saw that all toil and skillful work is
the rivalry of one man for another. This also is vanity and
a chase after wind.

a time for embracing,
a time to refrain from embracing.
6 A time for searching,
a time for losing,
a time for keeping,
a time for discarding.
7 A time for tearing,
a time for sewing;
a time for keeping silent,
a time for speaking.
8 A time for loving,
a time for hating;
a time for war,
a time for peace.

9 What do people gain from the efforts they make? 10 I
contemplate the task that God gives humanity to labour at.
11 All that he does is apt for its time; but although he has
given us an awareness of the passage of time, we can grasp
neither the beginning nor the end of what God does.

12 I know there is no happiness for a human being except
in pleasure and enjoyment through life. 13 And when we eat
and drink and find happiness in all our achievements, this
is a gift from God.

14 I know that whatever God does will be for ever.

To this there is nothing to add,
from this there is nothing to subtract,
and the way God acts inspires dread.

15 What is, has been already,
what will be, is already;
God seeks out anyone who is persecuted.

16 Again I observe under the sun:
crime is where justice should be,
the criminal is where the upright should be.

17 And I think to myself: the upright and the criminal will
both be judged by God, since there is a time for every thing
and every action here.

18 I think to myself: where human beings are concerned,
this is so that God can test them and show them that they are
animals. 19 For the fate of human and the fate of animal is
the same: as the one dies, so the other dies; both have the
selfsame breath. Human is in no way better off than animal
—since all is futile.

20 Everything goes to the same place,
everything comes from the dust,
everything returns to the dust.

21 Who knows if the human spirit mounts upward or if the
animal spirit goes downward to the earth?

22 I see there is no contentment for a human being except
happiness in achievement; such is the lot of a human being.
No one can tell us what will happen after we are gone.

4 Then again, I contemplate all the oppression that is
committed under the sun. Take for instance the tears of
the oppressed. No one to comfort them! The power their
oppressors wield. No one to comfort them! 2 So, rather than
the living who still have lives to live, I congratulate the dead
who have already met death; 3 happier than both of these are
those who are yet unborn and have not seen the evil things
that are done under the sun. 4 I see that all effort and all
achievement spring from mutual jealousy. This too is futility and chasing after the wind.

NEW REVISED STANDARD VERSION

5 Fools fold their hands
and consume their own flesh.
6 Better is a handful with quiet
than two handfuls with toil,
and a chasing after wind.[i]

7 Again, I saw vanity under the sun: 8 the case of solitary individuals, without sons or brothers; yet there is no end to all their toil, and their eyes are never satisfied with riches. "For whom am I toiling," they ask, "and depriving myself of pleasure?" This also is vanity and an unhappy business.

9 Two are better than one, because they have a good reward for their toil. 10 For if they fall, one will lift up the other; but woe to one who is alone and falls and does not have another to help. 11 Again, if two lie together, they keep warm; but how can one keep warm alone? 12 And though one might prevail against another, two will withstand one. A threefold cord is not quickly broken.

13 Better is a poor but wise youth than an old but foolish king, who will no longer take advice. 14 One can indeed come out of prison to reign, even though born poor in the kingdom. 15 I saw all the living who, moving about under the sun, follow that[j] youth who replaced the king;[k] 16 there was no end to all those people whom he led. Yet those who come later will not rejoice in him. Surely this also is vanity and a chasing after wind.[i]

5 1 Guard your steps when you go to the house of God; to draw near to listen is better than the sacrifice offered by fools; for they do not know how to keep from doing evil.[m] 2n Never be rash with your mouth, nor let your heart be quick to utter a word before God, for God is in heaven, and you upon earth; therefore let your words be few.

3 For dreams come with many cares, and a fool's voice with many words.

4 When you make a vow to God, do not delay fulfilling it; for he has no pleasure in fools. Fulfill what you vow. 5 It is better that you should not vow than that you should vow and not fulfill it. 6 Do not let your mouth lead you into sin, and do not say before the messenger that it was a mistake; why should God be angry at your words, and destroy the work of your hands?

7 With many dreams come vanities and a multitude of words;[o] but fear God.

8 If you see in a province the oppression of the poor and the violation of justice and right, do not be amazed at the matter; for the high official is watched by a higher, and there are yet higher ones over them. 9 But all things considered, this is an advantage for a land: a king for a plowed field.[o]

10 The lover of money will not be satisfied with money; nor the lover of wealth, with gain. This also is vanity.

11 When goods increase, those who eat them increase; and what gain has their owner but to see them with his eyes?

12 Sweet is the sleep of laborers, whether they eat little or much; but the surfeit of the rich will not let them sleep.

13 There is a grievous ill that I have seen under the sun: riches were kept by their owners to their hurt, 14 and those riches were lost in a bad venture; though they are parents of children, they have nothing in their hands. 15 As they came

REVISED ENGLISH BIBLE

fool folds his arms and wastes away. 6 Better one hand full, along with peace of mind, than two full, along with toil; that is a chasing of the wind.

7 Here again I saw futility under the sun: 8 someone without a friend, without son or brother, toiling endlessly yet never satisfied with his wealth — 'For whom', he asks, 'am I toiling and denying myself the good things of life?' This too is futile, a worthless task. 9 Two are better than one, for their partnership yields this advantage: 10 if one falls, the other can help his companion up again; but woe betide the solitary person who when down has no partner to help him up. 11 And if two lie side by side they keep each other warm; but how can one keep warm by himself? 12 If anyone is alone, an assailant may overpower him, but two can resist; and a cord of three strands is not quickly snapped.

13 Better a poor and wise youth than an old and foolish king who will listen no longer to advice. 14 One who has been in prison may well rise to be king, though born a pauper in his future kingdom. 15 But I have studied all life here under the sun, and I saw his place taken by yet another young man, 16 and no limit set to the number of people he ruled. He in turn will give no joy to those who come after him. This too is futility and a chasing of the wind.

5 Go circumspectly when you visit the house of God. Better draw near in obedience than offer the sacrifice of fools, who sin without a thought. 2 Do not be impulsive in speech, nor be guilty of hasty utterance in God's presence. God is in heaven and you are on earth, so let your words be few. 3 Dreams come with much business; the voice of the fool comes with much chatter. 4 When you make a vow to God, do not be dilatory in paying it, for he has no use for fools. Whatever you vow, pay! 5 Better not vow at all than vow and fail to pay. 6 Do not let your tongue lead you into sin, and then say before the angel of God that it was unintentional, or God will be angry at your words, and all your achievements will be brought to nothing. 7 A profusion of dreams and a profusion of words are futile. Therefore fear God.

8 If in some province you witness the oppression of the poor and the denial of right and justice, do not be surprised at what goes on, for every official has a higher one set over him, and the highest keeps watch over them all. 9 The best thing for a country is a king whose own lands are well tilled.

10 No one who loves money can ever have enough, and no one who loves wealth enjoys any return from it. This too is futility. 11 When riches increase, so does the number of parasites living off them; and what advantage has the owner, except to feast his eyes on them? 12 Sweet is the sleep of a labourer whether he has little or much to eat, but the rich man who has too much cannot sleep.

13 There is a singular evil here under the sun which I have seen: a man hoards wealth to his own hurt, 14 in that the wealth is lost through an unlucky venture, and the owner's son is left with nothing. 15 As he came from the womb of

---

[i]Or a feeding on wind. See Hos 12.1   [j]Heb the second
[k]Heb him   [l]Ch 4.17 in Heb   [m]Cn: Heb they do not know how to do evil   [n]Ch 5.1 in Heb   [o]Meaning of Heb uncertain

4:10 **if one falls, the other:** prob. rdg; Heb. obscure.   5:1 In Heb. 4:17.   5:2 In Heb. 5:1.   5:9 **whose:** prob. rdg; Heb. for.

NEW AMERICAN BIBLE

5 "The fool folds his arms
    and consumes his own flesh" —
6 Better is one handful with tranquility
    than two with toil and a chase after
    wind!

7 Again I found this vanity under the sun: 8 a solitary man with no companion; with neither son nor brother. Yet there is no end to all his toil, and riches do not satisfy his greed. "For whom do I toil and deprive myself of good things?" This also is vanity and a worthless task. 9 Two are better than one: they get a good wage for their labor. 10 If the one falls, the other will lift up his companion. Woe to the solitary man! For if he should fall, he has no one to lift him up. 11 So also, if two sleep together, they keep each other warm. How can one alone keep warm? 12 Where a lone man may be overcome, two together can resist. A three-ply cord is not easily broken.

13 Better is a poor but wise youth than an old but foolish king who no longer knows caution; 14 for from a prison house one comes forth to rule, since even in his royalty he was poor at birth. 15 Then I saw all those who are to live and move about under the sun with the heir apparent who will succeed to his place. 16 There is no end to all these people, to all over whom he takes precedence; yet the later generations will not applaud him. This also is vanity and a chase after wind.

17 Guard your step when you go to the house of God. Let your approach be obedience, rather than the fools' offering of sacrifice; for they know not how to keep from doing evil.

5 Be not hasty in your utterance and let not your heart be quick to make a promise in God's presence. God is in heaven and you are on earth; therefore let your words be few.

2 For nightmares come with many cares,
    and a fool's utterance with many words.

3 When you make a vow to God, delay not its fulfillment. For God has no pleasure in fools; fulfill what you have vowed. 4 You had better not make a vow than make it and not fulfill it. 5 Let not your utterances make you guilty, and say not before his representative, "It was a mistake," lest God be angered by such words and destroy the works of your hands. 6 Rather, fear God!

7 If you see oppression of the poor, and violation of rights and justice in the realm, do not be shocked by the fact, for the high official has another higher than he watching him and above these are others higher still —. 8 Yet an advantage for a country in every respect is a king for the arable land.

9 The covetous man is never satisfied with money, and the lover of wealth reaps no fruit from it; so this too is vanity. 10 Where there are great riches, there are also many to devour them. Of what use are they to the owner except to feast his eyes upon? 11 Sleep is sweet to the laboring man, whether he eats little or much, but the rich man's abundance allows him no sleep.

12 This is a grievous evil which I have seen under the sun: riches kept by their owner to his hurt. 13 Should the riches be lost through some misfortune, he may have a son when he is without means. 14 As he came forth from his mother's

NEW JERUSALEM BIBLE

5 The fool folds his arms
    and eats his own flesh away.

6 Better one hand full of repose
    than two hands full of achievements
    to chase after the wind.

7 And something else futile I observe under the sun: 8 a person is quite alone — no child, no brother; and yet there is no end to his efforts, his eyes can never have their fill of riches. For whom, then, do I work so hard and grudge myself pleasure? This too is futile, a sorry business.

9 Better two than one alone, since thus their work is really rewarding. 10 If one should fall, the other helps him up; but what of the person with no one to help him up when he falls? 11 Again: if two sleep together they keep warm, but how can anyone keep warm alone? 12 Where one alone would be overcome, two will put up resistance; and a three-fold cord is not quickly broken.

13 Better a youngster poor and wise
    than a monarch old and silly
    who will no longer take advice —
14 even though stepping from prison to the throne,
    even though born a beggar in that kingdom.

15 I observe that all who live and move under the sun support the young newcomer who takes over. 16 He takes his place at the head of innumerable subjects; but his successors will not think the more kindly of him for that. This too is futile and chasing after the wind.

17 Watch your step when you go to the House of God: drawing near to listen is better than the offering of a sacrifice by fools, though they do not know that they are doing wrong.

5 Be in no hurry to speak; do not hastily declare yourself before God; for God is in heaven, you on earth. Be sparing, then, of speech:

2 From too much worrying comes illusion,
    from too much talking, the accents of folly.

3 If you make a vow to God, discharge it without delay, for God has no love for fools. Discharge your vow. 4 Better a vow unmade than made and not discharged. 5 Do not allow your mouth to make a sinner of you, and do not say to the messenger that it was a mistake. Why give God occasion to be angry with you and ruin all the work that you have done?

6 From too many illusions
    come futility and too much talk.

Therefore, fear God.

7 If in a province you see the poor oppressed, fair judgement and justice violated, do not be surprised, for over every official there watches a higher official, and over these, higher officials still. 8 But what the land yields is for the benefit of all, a king is served by the fields.

9 No one who loves money ever has enough,
    no one who loves luxury has any income;

this, too, is futile.

10 Where goods abound, parasites abound:

where is the owner's profit, apart from feasting his eyes?

11 The labourer's sleep is sweet, whether he has eaten little or much, but the surfeit of the rich will not let him sleep at all.

12 Something grossly unjust I observe under the sun: riches stored and turning to loss for their owner. 13 An unlucky venture, and those riches are lost; a son is born to him, and he has nothing to leave him. 14 Naked from his

from their mother's womb, so they shall go again, naked as they came; they shall take nothing for their toil, which they may carry away with their hands. 16 This also is a grievous ill: just as they came, so shall they go; and what gain do they have from toiling for the wind? 17 Besides, all their days they eat in darkness, in much vexation and sickness and resentment.

18 This is what I have seen to be good: it is fitting to eat and drink and find enjoyment in all the toil with which one toils under the sun the few days of the life God gives us; for this is our lot. 19 Likewise all to whom God gives wealth and possessions and whom he enables to enjoy them, and to accept their lot and find enjoyment in their toil—this is the gift of God. 20 For they will scarcely brood over the days of their lives, because God keeps them occupied with the joy of their hearts.

6 There is an evil that I have seen under the sun, and it lies heavy upon humankind: 2 those to whom God gives wealth, possessions, and honor, so that they lack nothing of all that they desire, yet God does not enable them to enjoy these things, but a stranger enjoys them. This is vanity; it is a grievous ill. 3 A man may beget a hundred children, and live many years; but however many are the days of his years, if he does not enjoy life's good things, or has no burial, I say that a stillborn child is better off than he. 4 For it comes into vanity and goes into darkness, and in darkness its name is covered; 5 moreover it has not seen the sun or known anything; yet it finds rest rather than he. 6 Even though he should live a thousand years twice over, yet enjoy no good—do not all go to one place?

7 All human toil is for the mouth, yet the appetite is not satisfied. 8 For what advantage have the wise over fools? And what do the poor have who know how to conduct themselves before the living? 9 Better is the sight of the eyes than the wandering of desire; this also is vanity and a chasing after wind.p

10 Whatever has come to be has already been named, and it is known what human beings are, and that they are not able to dispute with those who are stronger. 11 The more words, the more vanity, so how is one the better? 12 For who knows what is good for mortals while they live the few days of their vain life, which they pass like a shadow? For who can tell them what will be after them under the sun?

7 A good name is better than precious ointment,
  and the day of death, than the day of birth.
2 It is better to go to the house of mourning
  than to go to the house of feasting;
  for this is the end of everyone,
  and the living will lay it to heart.
3 Sorrow is better than laughter,
  for by sadness of countenance the heart is
   made glad.
4 The heart of the wise is in the house of
   mourning;
  but the heart of fools is in the house of mirth.
5 It is better to hear the rebuke of the wise
  than to hear the song of fools.

mother earth, so, naked as he came, must he return; all his toil produces nothing he can take away with him. 16 This too is a singular evil: exactly as he came, so shall he go, and what profit does he get when his labour is all for the wind? 17 What is more, all his days are overshadowed; gnawing anxiety and great vexation are his lot, sickness and resentment.

18 This is what I have seen: that it is good and proper for a man to eat and drink and enjoy himself in return for his labours here under the sun, throughout the brief span of life which God has allotted him. 19 Moreover, it is a gift of God that everyone to whom he has granted wealth and riches and the power to enjoy them should accept his lot and rejoice in his labour. 20 He will not brood overmuch on the passing years, for God fills his time with joy of heart.

6 Here is an evil which I have seen under the sun, and it weighs heavily on the human race. 2 Consider someone to whom God grants wealth, riches, and substance, and who lacks nothing that his heart is set on: if God has not given him the power to enjoy these things, but a stranger enjoys them instead, that is futility and a dire affliction. 3 Or someone may have a hundred children and live to a great age; but however many his days may be, if he does not gain satisfaction from the good things of life and in the end receives no burial, then I maintain that the stillborn child is in better case than he. 4 Its coming is a futile thing, it departs into darkness, and in darkness its name is hidden; 5 it has never seen the sun or known anything, yet its state is better than his. 6 What if the man should live a thousand years twice over, and have no enjoyment? Do not both go to the same place?

7 The end of all man's toil is but to fill his belly, yet his appetite is never satisfied. 8 What advantage then in facing life has the wise man over the fool, or what advantage has the pauper for all his experience? 9 It is better to be satisfied with what is before your eyes than to give rein to desire; this too is futility and a chasing of the wind.

10 Whatever exists has already been given a name; it is known what human beings are and they cannot contend with one who is stronger than they. 11 The more words used the greater is the futility of it all; and where is the advantage to anyone? 12 For who can know what is good for anyone in this life, this brief span of futile existence through which one passes like a shadow? What is to happen afterwards here under the sun, who can tell?

7 A GOOD name smells sweeter than fragrant ointment, and the day of death is better than the day of birth. 2 It is better to visit a house of mourning than a house of feasting; for to be mourned is the lot of everyone, and the living should take this to heart. 3 Grief is better than laughter: a sad face may go with a cheerful heart. 4 The thoughts of the wise are at home in the house of mourning, but a fool's thoughts in the house of mirth. 5 It is better to listen to the rebukes of the wise than to the songs of fools. 6 For the

p Or a feeding on wind. See Hos 12.1

5:17 gnawing anxiety: so Gk; Heb. he eats.   5:20 his: prob. rdg; Heb. omits.

womb, so again shall he depart, naked as he came, having nothing from his labor that he can carry in his hand. 15 This too is a grievous evil, that he goes just as he came. What then does it profit him to toil for wind? 16 All the days of his life are passed in gloom and sorrow, under great vexation, sickness and wrath.

17 Here is what I recognize as good: it is well for a man to eat and drink and enjoy all the fruits of his labor under the sun during the limited days of the life which God gives him; for this is his lot. 18 Any man to whom God gives riches and property, and grants power to partake of them, so that he receives his lot and finds joy in the fruits of his toil, has a gift from God. 19 For he will hardly dwell on the shortness of his life, because God lets him busy himself with the joy of his heart.

6 There is another evil which I have seen under the sun, and it weighs heavily upon man: 2 there is the man to whom God gives riches and property and honor, so that he lacks none of all the things he craves; yet God does not grant him power to partake of them, but a stranger devours them. This is vanity and a dire plague. 3 Should a man have a hundred children and live many years, no matter to what great age, still if he has not the full benefit of his goods, or if he is deprived of burial, of this man I proclaim that the child born dead is more fortunate than he. 4 Though it came in vain and goes into darkness and its name is enveloped in darkness; 5 though it has not seen or known the sun, yet the dead child is at rest rather than such a man. 6 Should he live twice a thousand years and not enjoy his goods, do not both go to the same place?

7 All man's toil is for his mouth, yet his desire is not fulfilled. 8 For what advantage has the wise man over the fool, or what advantage has the poor man in knowing how to conduct himself in life? 9 "What the eyes see is better than what the desires wander after." This also is vanity and a chase after wind.

10 Whatever is, was long ago given its name, and the nature of man is known, and that he cannot contend in judgment with one who is stronger than he. 11 For though there are many sayings that multiply words, what profit is there for a man? 12 For who knows what is good for a man in life, the limited days of his vain life (which God has made like a shadow)? Because — who is there to tell a man what will come after him under the sun?

7 A good name is better than good ointment,
and the day of death than the day of birth.
2 It is better to go to the house of mourning
than to the house of feasting,
For that is the end of every man,
and the living should take it to heart.
3 Sorrow is better than laughter,
because when the face is sad the heart
grows wiser.
4 The heart of the wise is in the house of mourning,
but the heart of fools is in the house of mirth.
5 It is better to hearken to the wise man's rebuke
than to hearken to the song of fools;

mother's womb he came; as naked as he came will he depart; not one of his achievements can he take with him. 15 And something else grossly unjust: that as he came, so must he go; what profit can he show after toiling to earn the wind, 16 as he spends the rest of his days in darkness, mourning, many sorrows, sickness and exasperation.

17 So my conclusion is this: true happiness lies in eating and drinking and enjoying whatever has been achieved under the sun, throughout the life given by God: for this is the lot of humanity. 18 And whenever God gives someone riches and property, with the ability to enjoy them and to find contentment in work, this is a gift from God. 19 For such a person will hardly notice the passing of time, so long as God keeps his heart occupied with joy.

6 I see another evil under the sun, which goes hard with people: 2 suppose someone has received from God riches, property, honours — nothing at all left to wish for; but God does not give the chance to enjoy them, and some stranger enjoys them. This is futile, and grievous suffering too. 3 Or take someone who has had a hundred children and lived for many years, and, having reached old age, has never enjoyed the good things of life and has not even got a tomb; it seems to me, a still-born child is happier.

4 In futility it came, into darkness it departs,
and in darkness will its name be buried.

5 It has never so much as seen or known the sun; all the same, it will rest more easily than that person, 6 who would never have known the good things of life, even by living a thousand years twice over. Do we not all go to the same place in the end?

7 All toil is for the mouth,
yet the appetite is never satisfied.

8 What advantage has the wise over the fool?
And what of the pauper who knows how to behave
in society?

9 Better the object seen than the sting of desire:
for the latter too is futile and chasing after the
wind.

10 What has been is already defined — we know what
people are:
They cannot bring to justice one who is stronger
than themselves.

11 The more we say, the more futile it is: what good can we derive from it? 12 And who knows what is best for someone during life, during the days of futile life which are spent like a shadow? Who can tell anyone what will happen after him under the sun?

7 Better a good name than costly oil,
the day of death than the day of birth.
2 Better go to the house of mourning
than to the house of feasting;
for to this end everyone comes,
let the living take this to heart.
3 Better sadness than laughter:
a joyful heart may be concealed behind sad looks.
4 The heart of the wise is in the house of mourning,
the heart of fools in the house of gaiety.
5 Better attend to the reprimand of the wise
than listen to a song sung by a fool.

| NEW REVISED STANDARD VERSION | REVISED ENGLISH BIBLE |

NEW REVISED STANDARD VERSION

6 For like the crackling of thorns under a pot,
so is the laughter of fools;
this also is vanity.

7 Surely oppression makes the wise foolish,
and a bribe corrupts the heart.

8 Better is the end of a thing than its beginning;
the patient in spirit are better than the proud in
spirit.

9 Do not be quick to anger,
for anger lodges in the bosom of fools.

10 Do not say, "Why were the former days better
than these?"
For it is not from wisdom that you ask this.

11 Wisdom is as good as an inheritance,
an advantage to those who see the sun.

12 For the protection of wisdom is like the
protection of money,
and the advantage of knowledge is that wisdom
gives life to the one who possesses it.

13 Consider the work of God;
who can make straight what he has made
crooked?

14 In the day of prosperity be joyful, and in the day of
adversity consider; God has made the one as well as the
other, so that mortals may not find out anything that will
come after them.

15 In my vain life I have seen everything; there are
righteous people who perish in their righteousness, and
there are wicked people who prolong their life in their evildoing. 16 Do not be too righteous, and do not act too wise;
why should you destroy yourself? 17 Do not be too wicked,
and do not be a fool; why should you die before your time?
18 It is good that you should take hold of the one, without
letting go of the other; for the one who fears God shall
succeed with both.

19 Wisdom gives strength to the wise more than ten
rulers that are in a city.

20 Surely there is no one on earth so righteous as to do
good without ever sinning.

21 Do not give heed to everything that people say, or
you may hear your servant cursing you; 22 your heart knows
that many times you have yourself cursed others.

23 All this I have tested by wisdom; I said, "I will be
wise," but it was far from me. 24 That which is, is far off,
and deep, very deep; who can find it out? 25 I turned my
mind to know and to search out and to seek wisdom and the
sum of things, and to know that wickedness is folly and that
foolishness is madness. 26 I found more bitter than death the
woman who is a trap, whose heart is snares and nets, whose
hands are fetters; one who pleases God escapes her, but the
sinner is taken by her. 27 See, this is what I found, says the
Teacher,q adding one thing to another to find the sum,
28 which my mind has sought repeatedly, but I have not
found. One man among a thousand I found, but a woman
among all these I have not found. 29 See, this alone I found,
that God made human beings straightforward, but they have
devised many schemes.

REVISED ENGLISH BIBLE

laughter of fools is like the crackling of thorns under a pot.
That too is futility. 7 Oppression drives the wise crazy, and
a bribe corrupts the mind. 8 Better the end of anything than
its beginning; better patience than pride! 9 Do not be quick
to take offence, for it is fools who nurse resentment. 10 Do
not ask why the old days were better than the present; for
that is a foolish question. 11 Wisdom is better than possessions and an advantage to all who see the sun. 12 Better have
wisdom behind you than money; wisdom profits by giving
life to those who possess her.

13 Consider God's handiwork; who can straighten what he
has made crooked? 14 When things go well, be glad; but
when they go ill, consider this: God has set the one alongside the other in such a way that no one can find out what
is to happen afterwards. 15 In my futile existence I have seen
it all, from the righteous perishing in their righteousness to
the wicked growing old in wickedness. 16 Do not be over-
righteous and do not be over-wise. Why should you destroy
yourself? 17 Do not be over-wicked and do not be a fool.
Why die before your time? 18 It is good to hold on to the one
thing and not lose hold of the other; for someone who fears
God will succeed both ways. 19 Wisdom makes the possess-
or of wisdom stronger than ten rulers in a city. 20 There is
no one on earth so righteous that he always does right and
never does wrong. 21 Moreover, do not pay attention to
everything folk say, or you may hear your servant speak ill
of you; 22 for you know very well how many times you
yourself have spoken ill of others. 23 All this I have put to
the test of wisdom. I said, 'I am resolved to be wise,' but
wisdom was beyond my reach—24 whatever has happened
lies out of reach, deep down, deeper than anyone can fathom.

25 I went on to reflect how I could know, enquire, and
search for wisdom and for the reason in things, only to
discover that it is folly to be wicked and madness to act like
a fool. 26 I find more bitter than death the woman whose
heart is a net to catch and whose hands are fetters. He who
is pleasing to God may escape her, but the sinner she will
entrap. 27 'See,' says the Speaker, 'this is what I have
found, reasoning things out one by one, 28 after searching
long without success: I have found one man in a thousand
worthy to be called upright, but I have not found one woman among them all. 29 This alone I have found: that God,
when he made man, made him straightforward, but men
invent endless subtleties of their own.'

---

q Qoheleth, traditionally rendered Preacher

NEW AMERICAN BIBLE

NEW JERUSALEM BIBLE

6 For as the crackling of thorns under a pot,
  so is the fool's laughter.

  This also is vanity,
7 For oppression can make a fool of a wise man,
  and a bribe corrupts the heart.
8 Better is the end of speech than its beginning;
  better is the patient spirit than the lofty spirit.
9 Do not in spirit become quickly discontented,
  for discontent lodges in the bosom of a fool.

10 Do not say: How is it that former times were better
than these? For it is not in wisdom that you ask about this.

11 Wisdom and an inheritance are good,
  and an advantage to those that see the sun.

12 For the protection of wisdom is as the protection of
money; and the advantage of knowledge is that wisdom
preserves the life of its owner.
13 Consider the work of God. Who can make straight
what he has made crooked? 14 On a good day enjoy good
things, and on an evil day consider: Both the one and the
other God has made, so that man cannot find fault with him
in anything.
15 I have seen all manner of things in my vain days: a just
man perishing in his justice, and a wicked one surviving in
his wickedness. 16 "Be not just to excess, and be not over-
wise, lest you be ruined. 17 Be not wicked to excess, and be
not foolish. Why should you die before your time?" 18 It is
good to hold to this rule, and not to let that one go; but he
who fears God will win through at all events.
19 Wisdom is a better defense for the wise man than
would be ten princes in the city, 20 yet there is no man on
earth so just as to do good and never sin. 21 Do not give heed
to every word that is spoken lest you hear your servant
speaking ill of you, 22 for you know in your heart that you
have many times spoken ill of others.
23 All these things I probed in wisdom. I said, "I will
acquire wisdom"; but it was beyond me. 24 What exists is
far-reaching; it is deep, very deep: who can find it out? 25 I
turned my thoughts toward knowledge; I sought and pursued wisdom and reason, and I recognized that wickedness
is foolish and folly is madness.
26 More bitter than death I find the woman who is a
hunter's trap, whose heart is a snare and whose hands are
prison bonds. He who is pleasing to God will escape her,
but the sinner will be entrapped by her. 27 Behold, this have
I found, says Qoheleth, adding one thing to another that I
might discover the answer 28 which my soul still seeks and
has not found: One man out of a thousand have I come
upon, but a woman among them all I have not found. 29 Behold, only this have I found out: God made mankind
straight, but men have had recourse to many calculations.

6 For like the crackling of thorns under the cauldron
  is the laughter of fools:
  and that too is futile.
7 But being oppressed drives a sage mad,
  and a present corrupts the heart.
8 Better the end of a matter than its beginning,
  better patience than ambition.

9 Do not be too easily exasperated, for exasperation
dwells in the heart of fools. 10 Do not ask why the past was
better than the present, for this is not a question prompted
by wisdom.

11 Wisdom is as good as a legacy,
  profitable to those who enjoy the light of the sun.
12 For as money protects, so does wisdom,
  and the advantage of knowledge is this:
  that wisdom bestows life on those who possess her.
13 Consider God's creation:
  who, for instance, can straighten what God has
    bent?
14 When things are going well, enjoy yourself,
  and when they are going badly, consider this:
  God has designed the one no less than the other
  so that we should take nothing for granted.
15 In my futile life, I have seen everything:
  the upright person perishing in uprightness
  and the wicked person surviving in wickedness.
16 Do not be upright to excess
  and do not make yourself unduly wise:
  why should you destroy yourself?
17 Do not be wicked to excess,
  and do not be a fool:
  why die before your time?
18 It is wise to hold on to one and not let go of the
    other,
  since the godfearing will find both.

19 Wisdom makes the wise stronger than a dozen governors in a city.
20 No one on earth is sufficiently upright to do good without ever sinning.
21 Again, do not listen to all that people say, then you will
not hear your servant abusing you.
22 For often, as you very well know, you have abused
others.
23 Thanks to wisdom, I have found all this to be true; I
resolved to be wise, but this was beyond my reach!

24 The past is out of reach,
  buried deep—who can discover it?

25 But I have reached the point where, having learnt,
explored and investigated wisdom and reflection, I recognise evil as being a form of madness, and folly as something
stupid.

26 And I find woman more bitter than Death,
  she is a snare,
  her heart is a net, and her arms are chains.
  The man who is pleasing to God eludes her,
  but the sinner is captured by her.
27 This is what I think, says Qoheleth,
  having examined one thing after another to draw
    some conclusion,
28 which I am still looking for, although
    unsuccessfully:
  one man in a thousand, I may find,
  but a woman better than other women—never.
29 This alone is my conclusion:
  God has created man straightforward,
  and human artifices are human inventions.

8 Who is like the wise man?
    And who knows the interpretation of a thing?
Wisdom makes one's face shine,
    and the hardness of one's countenance is
        changed.

2 Keep[r] the king's command because of your sacred oath. 3 Do not be terrified; go from his presence, do not delay when the matter is unpleasant, for he does whatever he pleases. 4 For the word of the king is powerful, and who can say to him, "What are you doing?" 5 Whoever obeys a command will meet no harm, and the wise mind will know the time and way. 6 For every matter has its time and way, although the troubles of mortals lie heavy upon them. 7 Indeed, they do not know what is to be, for who can tell them how it will be? 8 No one has power over the wind[s] to restrain the wind,[s] or power over the day of death; there is no discharge from the battle, nor does wickedness deliver those who practice it. 9 All this I observed, applying my mind to all that is done under the sun, while one person exercises authority over another to the other's hurt.

10 Then I saw the wicked buried; they used to go in and out of the holy place, and were praised in the city where they had done such things.[t] This also is vanity. 11 Because sentence against an evil deed is not executed speedily, the human heart is fully set to do evil. 12 Though sinners do evil a hundred times and prolong their lives, yet I know that it will be well with those who fear God, because they stand in fear before him, 13 but it will not be well with the wicked, neither will they prolong their days like a shadow, because they do not stand in fear before God.

14 There is a vanity that takes place on earth, that there are righteous people who are treated according to the conduct of the wicked, and there are wicked people who are treated according to the conduct of the righteous. I said that this also is vanity. 15 So I commend enjoyment, for there is nothing better for people under the sun than to eat, and drink, and enjoy themselves, for this will go with them in their toil through the days of life that God gives them under the sun.

16 When I applied my mind to know wisdom, and to see the business that is done on earth, how one's eyes see sleep neither day nor night, 17 then I saw all the work of God, that no one can find out what is happening under the sun. However much they may toil in seeking, they will not find it out; even though those who are wise claim to know, they cannot find it out.

9 All this I laid to heart, examining it all, how the righteous and the wise and their deeds are in the hand of God; whether it is love or hate one does not know. Everything that confronts them 2 is vanity,[u] since the same fate

8 Who here is wise enough? Who has insight into the meaning of anything? Wisdom lights up a person's face, and the boldness of his aspect is changed. 2 Do as the king commands you, and if you have to swear by God, 3 do not rush into it. Do not persist in something which displeases the king, and leave his presence, for he can do whatever he likes. 4 His word is sovereign, and who can call in question what he does? 5 Whoever obeys a command will come to no harm. One who is wise knows in his heart the right time and method for action.

6 Every enterprise has its time and method, although man is greatly troubled 7 by ignorance of the future; who can tell him what it will bring? 8 It is not in anyone's power to retain the breath of life, and no one has power over the day of death. In war no one can lay aside his arms, no wealth will save its possessor. 9 All this I have seen, having applied my mind to everything done under the sun, at a time when one person had power over another and could make him suffer.

10 It was then that I saw scoundrels approaching and even entering the holy place; and they went about the city priding themselves on having done right. This too is futility. 11 It is because sentence upon a wicked act is not promptly carried out that evildoers are emboldened to act. 12 A sinner may do wrong and live to old age, yet I know that it will be well with those who fear God: their fear of him ensures this. 13 But it will not be well with the evildoer, nor will his days lengthen like a shadow, because he does not fear God.

14 There is a futile thing found on earth: sometimes the just person gets what is due to the unjust, and the unjust what is due to the just. I maintain that this too is futility. 15 So I commend enjoyment, since there is nothing good for anyone to do here under the sun but to eat and drink and enjoy himself; this is all that will remain with him to reward his toil throughout the span of life which God grants him here under the sun.

16 I applied my mind to acquire wisdom and to observe the tasks undertaken on earth, when mortal eyes are never closed in sleep day or night; 17 and always I perceived that God has so ordered it that no human being should be able to discover what is happening here under the sun. However hard he may try, he will not find out; the wise may think they know, but they cannot find the truth of it.

9 To all this I applied my mind, and I understood—that the righteous and the wise and whatever they do are under God's control; but whether they will earn love or hatred they have no way of knowing. Everything that confronts them, everything is futile, 2 since one and the same

---

[r] Heb I keep   [s] Or breath   [t] Meaning of Heb uncertain
[u] Syr Compare Gk: Heb Everything that confronts them 2 is everything

8:8 **retain . . . life:** or restrain the wind.   8:10 **approaching . . . entering:** prob. rdg; Heb. obscure. **priding themselves on:** so many MSS; others forgotten for.   8:12 **do wrong:** prob. rdg; Heb. adds an unintelligible word.   9:1 **and I understood:** prob. rdg; Heb. and to test. **futile:** so Gk; Heb. all.

NEW AMERICAN BIBLE

NEW JERUSALEM BIBLE

8 Who is like the wise man,
and who knows the explanation of things?
A man's wisdom illumines his face,
but an impudent look is resented.

2 Observe the precept of the king, and in view of your oath to God, 3 be not hasty to withdraw from the king; do not join in with a base plot, for he does whatever he pleases, 4 because his word is sovereign, and who can say to him, "What are you doing?"
5 "He who keeps the commandment experiences no evil, and the wise man's heart knows times and judgments; 6 for there is a time and a judgment for everything." — Yet it is a great affliction for man 7 that he is ignorant of what is to come; for who will make known to him how it will be? 8 There is no man who is master of the breath of life so as to retain it, and none has mastery of the day of death. There is no exemption from the struggle, nor are the wicked saved by their wickedness. 9 All these things I considered and I applied my mind to every work that is done under the sun, while one man tyrannizes over another to his hurt.
10 Meanwhile I saw wicked men approach and enter; and as they left the sacred place, they were praised in the city for what they had done. This also is vanity. 11 Because the sentence against evildoers is not promptly executed, therefore the hearts of men are filled with the desire to commit evil — 12 because the sinner does evil a hundred times and survives. Though indeed I know that it shall be well with those who fear God, for their reverence toward him; 13 and that it shall not be well with the wicked man, and he shall not prolong his shadowy days, for his lack of reverence toward God.
14 This is a vanity which occurs on earth: there are just men treated as though they had done evil and wicked men treated as though they had done justly. This, too, I say is vanity. 15 Therefore I commend mirth, because there is nothing good for man under the sun except eating and drinking and mirth: for this is the accompaniment of his toil during the limited days of the life which God gives him under the sun.
16 When I applied my heart to know wisdom and to observe what is done on earth, 17 I recognized that man is unable to find out all God's work that is done under the sun, even though neither by day nor by night do his eyes find rest in sleep. However much man toils in searching, he does not find it out; and even if the wise man says that he knows, he is unable to find it out.

9 All this I have kept in mind and recognized: the just, the wise, and their deeds are in the hand of God. Love from hatred man cannot tell; both appear equally vain, 2 in

8 Who compares with the sage?
Who else knows how to explain things?
Wisdom lights up the face,
enlivening a grim expression.
2 Obey the king's command and, because of the divine promise,
3 be in no hurry to depart from it;
do not be obstinate in a bad cause,
since the king will do as he likes in any case.
4 Since the word of a king is sovereign,
what is the point of saying, 'Why do that?'
5 One who obeys the command will come to no harm;
the heart of the sage knows the right moment and verdict,
6 for there is a right moment and verdict for everything;
but misfortune lies heavy upon anyone
7 who does not know what the outcome will be,
no one is going to say how things will turn out.
8 No one can control the wind and stop it from blowing,
no one can control the day of death.
From war there is no escape,
no more can wickedness save the person who commits it.

9 I have seen all this to be so, having carefully studied everything taking place under the sun, while one person tyrannises over another to the former's detriment.
10 And again, I have observed the wicked carried to their graves, and people leaving the holy place and, once out in the city, forgetting how the wicked used to behave; how futile this is too!
11 Because the sentence on the evil-doer is not carried out on the instant, people's hearts are full of desire to do wrong. 12 The sinner who does wrong a hundred times lives on. But this too I know, that there is good in store for people who fear God, because they fear him, 13 but there is no good in store for the wicked because he does not fear God, and so, like a shadow, he will not prolong his days. 14 Another futile thing that happens on earth: upright people being treated as though they were wicked and wicked people being treated as though they were upright. To me this is one more example of futility.
15 And therefore I praise joy, since human happiness lies only in eating and drinking and in taking pleasure; this comes from what someone achieves during the days of life that God gives under the sun.
16 Having applied myself to acquiring wisdom and to observing the activity taking place in the world — for day and night our eyes enjoy no rest — 17 I have scrutinised God's whole creation: you cannot get to the bottom of everything taking place under the sun; you may wear yourself out in the search, but you will never find it. Not even a sage can get to the bottom of it, even if he says that he has done so.

9 Yes, I have applied myself to all this and experienced all this to be so: that is to say, that the upright and the wise, with their activities, are in the hands of God.

We do not understand either love or hate,
where we are concerned, both of them are 2 futile.

comes to all, to the righteous and the wicked, to the good and the evil,[v] to the clean and the unclean, to those who sacrifice and those who do not sacrifice. As are the good, so are the sinners; those who swear are like those who shun an oath. 3 This is an evil in all that happens under the sun, that the same fate comes to everyone. Moreover, the hearts of all are full of evil; madness is in their hearts while they live, and after that they go to the dead. 4 But whoever is joined with all the living has hope, for a living dog is better than a dead lion. 5 The living know that they will die, but the dead know nothing; they have no more reward, and even the memory of them is lost. 6 Their love and their hate and their envy have already perished; never again will they have any share in all that happens under the sun.

7 Go, eat your bread with enjoyment, and drink your wine with a merry heart; for God has long ago approved what you do. 8 Let your garments always be white; do not let oil be lacking on your head. 9 Enjoy life with the wife whom you love, all the days of your vain life that are given you under the sun, because that is your portion in life and in your toil at which you toil under the sun. 10 Whatever your hand finds to do, do with your might; for there is no work or thought or knowledge or wisdom in Sheol, to which you are going.

11 Again I saw that under the sun the race is not to the swift, nor the battle to the strong, nor bread to the wise, nor riches to the intelligent, nor favor to the skillful; but time and chance happen to them all. 12 For no one can anticipate the time of disaster. Like fish taken in a cruel net, and like birds caught in a snare, so mortals are snared at a time of calamity, when it suddenly falls upon them.

13 I have also seen this example of wisdom under the sun, and it seemed great to me. 14 There was a little city with few people in it. A great king came against it and besieged it, building great siegeworks against it. 15 Now there was found in it a poor wise man, and he by his wisdom delivered the city. Yet no one remembered that poor man. 16 So I said, "Wisdom is better than might; yet the poor man's wisdom is despised, and his words are not heeded."

17 The quiet words of the wise are more to be
heeded
than the shouting of a ruler among fools.
18 Wisdom is better than weapons of war,
but one bungler destroys much good.

fate comes to all, just and unjust alike, good and bad, ritually clean and unclean, to the one who offers sacrifice and to the one who does not. The good and the sinner fare alike, he who can take an oath and he who dares not. 3 This is what is wrong in all that is done here under the sun: that one and the same fate befalls everyone. The minds of mortals are full of evil; there is madness in their minds throughout their lives, and afterwards they go down to join the dead. 4 But for anyone who is counted among the living there is still hope: remember, a live dog is better than a dead lion. 5 True, the living know that they will die; but the dead know nothing. There is no more reward for them; all memory of them is forgotten. 6 For them love, hate, rivalry, all are now over. Never again will they have any part in what is done here under the sun.

7 Go, then, eat your food and enjoy it, and drink your wine with a cheerful heart; for God has already accepted what you have done. 8 Always be dressed in white, and never fail to anoint your head. 9 Enjoy life with a woman you love all the days of your allotted span here under the sun, futile as they are; for that is your lot while you live and labour here under the sun. 10 Whatever task lies to your hand, do it with might; because in Sheol, for which you are bound, there is neither doing nor thinking, neither understanding nor wisdom.

11 One more thing I have observed here under the sun: swiftness does not win the race nor strength the battle. Food does not belong to the wise, nor wealth to the intelligent, nor success to the skilful; time and chance govern all. 12 Moreover, no one knows when his hour will come; like fish caught in the destroying net, like a bird taken in a snare, so the people are trapped when misfortune comes suddenly on them.

13 This too is an example of wisdom as I have observed it here under the sun, and I find it of great significance. 14 There was once a small town with few inhabitants, which a great king came to attack; he surrounded it and constructed huge siege-works against it. 15 There was in it a poor wise man, and he saved the town by his wisdom. But no one remembered that poor man. 16 I thought, 'Surely wisdom is better than strength'; but a poor man's wisdom is despised, and his words go unheeded. 17 A wise man speaking quietly is more to be heeded than a commander shouting orders among fools. 18 Wisdom is better than weapons of war, but one mistake can undo many things done well.

9:2 **and bad:** *so Gk; Heb. omits.*   9:9 **futile . . . are:** *prob. rdg; Heb. adds* all your days, futile as they are.   9:10 **Sheol:** *or the underworld.*

[v]Gk Syr Vg: Heb lacks *and the evil*

1446

NEW AMERICAN BIBLE

that there is the same lot for all, for the just and the wicked, for the good and the bad, for the clean and the unclean, for him who offers sacrifice and him who does not. As it is for the good man, so it is for the sinner; as it is for him who swears rashly, so it is for him who fears an oath. 3 Among all the things that happen under the sun, this is the worst, that things turn out the same for all. Hence the minds of men are filled with evil, and madness is in their hearts during life; and afterward they go to the dead.

4 Indeed, for any among the living there is hope; a live dog is better off than a dead lion. 5 For the living know that they are to die, but the dead no longer know anything. There is no further recompense for them, because all memory of them is lost. 6 For them, love and hatred and rivalry have long since perished. They will never again have part in anything that is done under the sun.

7 Go, eat your bread with joy and drink your wine with a merry heart, because it is now that God favors your works. 8 At all times let your garments be white, and spare not the perfume for your head. 9 Enjoy life with the wife whom you love, all the days of the fleeting life that is granted you under the sun. This is your lot in life, for the toil of your labors under the sun. 10 Anything you can turn your hand to, do with what power you have; for there will be no work, nor reason, nor knowledge, nor wisdom in the nether world where you are going.

11 Again I saw under the sun that the race is not won by the swift, nor the battle by the valiant, nor a livelihood by the wise, nor riches by the shrewd, nor favor by the experts; for a time of calamity comes to all alike. 12 Man no more knows his own time than fish taken in the fatal net, or birds trapped in the snare; like these the children of men are caught when the evil time falls suddenly upon them.

13 On the other hand I saw this wise deed under the sun, which I thought sublime. 14 Against a small city with few men in it advanced a mighty king, who surrounded it and threw up great siegeworks about it. 15 But in the city lived a man who, though poor, was wise, and he delivered it through his wisdom. Yet no one remembered this poor man. 16 Though I had said, "Wisdom is better than force," yet the wisdom of the poor man is despised and his words go unheeded.

17 "The quiet words of the wise are better heeded
than the shout of a ruler of fools" — !

18 "A fly that dies can spoil the perfumer's ointment,
and a single slip can ruin much that is good."

NEW JERUSALEM BIBLE

And for all of us is reserved a common fate,
for the upright and for the wicked,
for the good and for the bad;
whether we are ritually pure or not,
whether we offer sacrifice or not:
it is the same for the good and for the sinner,
for someone who takes a vow, as for someone who
fears to do so.

3 This is another evil among those occurring under the sun: that there should be the same fate for everyone. The human heart, however, is full of wickedness; folly lurks in our hearts throughout our lives, until we end among the dead.

4 But there is hope for someone still linked to the
rest of the living:
better be a live dog than a dead lion.

5 The living are at least aware that they are going to die, but the dead know nothing whatever. No more wages for them, since their memory is forgotten. 6 Their love, their hate, their jealousy, have perished long since, and they will never have any further part in what goes on under the sun.

7 So, eat your bread in joy,
drink your wine with a glad heart,
since God has already approved your actions.
8 At all times, dress in white
and keep your head well scented.
9 Spend your life with the woman you love,
all the days of futile life God gives you under the
sun,
throughout your futile days,
since this is your lot in life
and in the effort you expend under the sun.
10 Whatever work you find to do,
do it with all your might,
for there is neither achievement, nor planning, nor
science,
nor wisdom in Sheol where you are going.
11 Another thing I have observed under the sun:
that the race is not won by the speediest,
nor the battle by the champions;
it is not the wise who get food,
nor the intelligent wealth,
nor the learned favour:
chance and mischance befall them all.
12 We do not know when our time will come:
like fish caught in the treacherous net,
like birds caught in the snare,
just so are we all trapped by misfortune
when it suddenly overtakes us.

13 Here is another example of the wisdom I have acquired under the sun and it strikes me as important: 14 There was once a small town, with only a few inhabitants; a mighty king made war on it, laying siege to it and building great siege-works round it. 15 But there was in that town a poverty-stricken sage who by his wisdom saved the town. No one remembered this poor man afterwards. 16 So I say:

Wisdom is more effective than brute force,
but the wisdom of a poor man is not valued:
no one listens to what he has to say.

17 The calm words of the wise make themselves heard above the shouts of someone commanding an army of fools.

18 Wisdom is worth more than weapons of war,
but a single sin undoes a deal of good.

10 Dead flies make the perfumer's ointment give off a foul odor;
so a little folly outweighs wisdom and honor.

2 The heart of the wise inclines to the right,
but the heart of a fool to the left.

3 Even when fools walk on the road, they lack sense,
and show to everyone that they are fools.

4 If the anger of the ruler rises against you, do not leave your post,
for calmness will undo great offenses.

5 There is an evil that I have seen under the sun, as great an error as if it proceeded from the ruler: 6 folly is set in many high places, and the rich sit in a low place. 7 I have seen slaves on horseback, and princes walking on foot like slaves.

8 Whoever digs a pit will fall into it;
and whoever breaks through a wall will be bitten by a snake.

9 Whoever quarries stones will be hurt by them;
and whoever splits logs will be endangered by them.

10 If the iron is blunt, and one does not whet the edge,
then more strength must be exerted;
but wisdom helps one to succeed.

11 If the snake bites before it is charmed,
there is no advantage in a charmer.

12 Words spoken by the wise bring them favor,
but the lips of fools consume them.

13 The words of their mouths begin in foolishness,
and their talk ends in wicked madness;

14 yet fools talk on and on.
No one knows what is to happen,
and who can tell anyone what the future holds?

15 The toil of fools wears them out,
for they do not even know the way to town.

16 Alas for you, O land, when your king is a servant,[w]
and your princes feast in the morning!

17 Happy are you, O land, when your king is a nobleman,
and your princes feast at the proper time —
for strength, and not for drunkenness!

18 Through sloth the roof sinks in,
and through indolence the house leaks.

19 Feasts are made for laughter;
wine gladdens life,
and money meets every need.

20 Do not curse the king, even in your thoughts,
or curse the rich, even in your bedroom;
for a bird of the air may carry your voice,
or some winged creature tell the matter.

11 Send out your bread upon the waters,
for after many days you will get it back.

2 Divide your means seven ways, or even eight,
for you do not know what disaster may happen on earth.

3 When clouds are full,
they empty rain on the earth;
whether a tree falls to the south or to the north,
in the place where the tree falls, there it will lie.

10 Dead flies make the sweet ointment of the perfumer turn rancid and ferment; so a little folly can make wisdom lose its worth. 2 The minds of the wise turn to the right, but the mind of a fool to the left. 3 Even when he travels, the fool shows no sense and reveals to everyone how foolish he is.

4 If the anger of the ruler flares up at you, do not leave your post; submission makes amends for grave offences. 5 There is an evil that I have observed here under the sun, an error for which rulers are responsible: 6 fools are given high office, while the rich occupy humble positions. 7 I have seen slaves on horseback and men of high rank going on foot like slaves.

8 He who digs a pit may fall into it, and he who breaks down a wall may be bitten by a snake. 9 He who quarries stones may be hurt by them, and the woodcutter runs a risk of injury. 10 If the axe is blunt for lack of sharpening, then one must use more force; the skilled worker has a better chance of success. 11 If a snake bites before it is charmed, the snake-charmer loses his fee.

12 Wise words win favour, but a fool's tongue is his undoing. 13 He begins by talking nonsense and ends in mischief run mad. 14 A fool talks at great length; but no one knows what is coming, and what will come after that, who can tell? 15 The fool wearies himself to death with his exertions; he does not even know the way to town!

16 Woe betide the land when a slave becomes its king, and its princes begin feasting in the morning. 17 Happy the land when its king is nobly born, and its princes feast at the right time of day, with self-control, and not as drunkards. 18 If the owner is negligent the rafters collapse, and if his hands are idle the house leaks. 19 The table has its pleasures, and wine makes for a cheerful life; but money meets all demands. 20 Do not speak ill of the king when you are at rest, or of a rich man even when you are in your bedroom, for a bird may carry your voice, a winged creature may repeat what you say.

11 Send your grain across the seas, and in time you will get a return. 2 Divide your merchandise among seven or perhaps eight ventures, since you do not know what disasters are in store for the world. 3 If the clouds are heavy with rain, they will shed it on the earth; whether a

w Or *a child*

NEW AMERICAN BIBLE

10 More weighty than wisdom or wealth is a little folly!
2 The wise man's understanding turns him to his right;
the fool's understanding turns him to his left.

3 When the fool walks through the street, in his lack of understanding he calls everything foolish.
4 Should the anger of the ruler burst upon you, forsake not your place; for mildness abates great offenses.
5 I have seen under the sun another evil, like a mistake that proceeds from the ruler: 6 a fool put in lofty position while the rich sit in lowly places. 7 I have seen slaves on horseback, while princes walked on the ground like slaves.

8 He who digs a pit may fall into it,
and he who breaks through a wall may be bitten by a serpent.

9 He who moves stones may be hurt by them,
and he who chops wood is in danger from it.

10 If the iron becomes dull, though at first he made easy progress, he must increase his efforts; but the craftsman has the advantage of his skill.

11 If the serpent bites because it has not been charmed,
then there is no advantage for the charmer.

12 Words from the wise man's mouth win favor,
but the fool's lips consume him.
13 The beginning of his words is folly,
and the end of his talk is utter madness;
14 yet the fool multiplies words.
Man knows not what is to come,
for who can tell him what is to come after him?
15 When will the fool be weary of his labor,
he who knows not the way to the city?

16 Woe to you, O land, whose king was a servant,
and whose princes dine in the morning!
17 Blessed are you, O land, whose king is of noble birth,
and whose princes dine at the right time
(for vigor and not in drinking bouts).
18 When hands are lazy, the rafters sag;
when hands are slack, the house leaks.
19 Bread and oil call forth merriment
and wine makes the living glad,
but money answers for everything.
20 Even in your thoughts do not make light of the king,
nor in the privacy of your bedroom revile the rich.
Because the birds of the air may carry your voice,
a winged creature may tell what you say.

11 Cast your bread upon the waters;
after a long time you may find it again.
2 Make seven or eight portions;
you know not what misfortune may come upon the earth.
3 When the clouds are full,
they pour out rain upon the earth.
Whether a tree falls to the south or to the north,
wherever it falls, there shall it lie.

NEW JERUSALEM BIBLE

10 One dead fly can spoil the scent-maker's oil:
a grain of stupidity outweighs wisdom and glory.

2 The sage's heart leads him aright,
the fool's leads him astray.

3 A fool walks down the road, he has no wit —
and everyone remarks, 'How silly he is!'

4 If the anger of the ruler rises against you, do not leave your post; composure mitigates grave offences.
5 One evil I observe under the sun: the sort of misjudgement to which rulers are prone — 6 folly promoted to the top and the rich taking the lowest place. 7 I see slaves riding on horses and princes on foot like slaves.

8 He who digs a pit falls into it,
he who undermines a wall gets bitten by a snake,
9 he who quarries stones gets hurt by them,
he who chops wood takes a risk from it.

10 If, for want of sharpening, the blade is blunt, you have to work twice as hard; but it is the outcome that makes wisdom rewarding.

11 If, for want of charming, the snake bites,
the snake-charmer gets nothing out of it.

12 The sayings of a sage give pleasure,
what a fool says procures his own ruin:
13 his words have their origin in stupidity
and their ending in treacherous folly.
14 A fool talks a great deal,
but none of us in fact can tell the future;
what will happen after us, who can tell?
15 A fool finds hard work very tiring,
he cannot even find his own way into town.

16 Woe to you, country with a lad for king,
and where princes start feasting in the morning!
17 Happy the land whose king is nobly born,
where princes eat at a respectable hour
to keep themselves strong and not merely to revel!

18 Thanks to idleness, the roof-tree gives way,
thanks to carelessness, the house lets in the rain.

19 We give parties to enjoy ourselves,
wine makes us cheerful
and money has an answer for everything.

20 Do not abuse the king, even in thought,
do not abuse a rich man, even in your bedroom,
for a bird of the air might carry the news,
a winged messenger might repeat what you have said.

11 Cast your bread on the water,
eventually you will recover it.
2 Offer a share to seven or to eight people,
you can never tell what disaster may occur.
3 When clouds are full of rain,
they will shed it on the earth.
If a tree falls, whether south or north,
where it falls, there it will lie.

NEW REVISED STANDARD VERSION

4 Whoever observes the wind will not sow;
   and whoever regards the clouds will not reap.

5 Just as you do not know how the breath comes to the bones in the mother's womb, so you do not know the work of God, who makes everything.

6 In the morning sow your seed, and at evening do not let your hands be idle; for you do not know which will prosper, this or that, or whether both alike will be good.

7 Light is sweet, and it is pleasant for the eyes to see the sun.

8 Even those who live many years should rejoice in them all; yet let them remember that the days of darkness will be many. All that comes is vanity.

9 Rejoice, young man, while you are young, and let your heart cheer you in the days of your youth. Follow the inclination of your heart and the desire of your eyes, but know that for all these things God will bring you into judgment.

10 Banish anxiety from your mind, and put away pain from your body; for youth and the dawn of life are vanity.

12 Remember your creator in the days of your youth, before the days of trouble come, and the years draw near when you will say, "I have no pleasure in them"; 2 before the sun and the light and the moon and the stars are darkened and the clouds return with*x* the rain; 3 in the day when the guards of the house tremble, and the strong men are bent, and the women who grind cease working because they are few, and those who look through the windows see dimly; 4 when the doors on the street are shut, and the sound of the grinding is low, and one rises up at the sound of a bird, and all the daughters of song are brought low; 5 when one is afraid of heights, and terrors are in the road; the almond tree blossoms, the grasshopper drags itself along*y* and desire fails; because all must go to their eternal home, and the mourners will go about the streets; 6 before the silver cord is snapped,*z* and the golden bowl is broken, and the pitcher is broken at the fountain, and the wheel broken at the cistern, 7 and the dust returns to the earth as it was, and the breath*a* returns to God who gave it. 8 Vanity of vanities, says the Teacher;*b* all is vanity.

9 Besides being wise, the Teacher*b* also taught the people knowledge, weighing and studying and arranging many proverbs. 10 The Teacher*b* sought to find pleasing words, and he wrote words of truth plainly.

11 The sayings of the wise are like goads, and like nails firmly fixed are the collected sayings that are given by one shepherd.*c* 12 Of anything beyond these, my child, beware.

REVISED ENGLISH BIBLE

tree falls south or north, it must lie as it falls. 4 He who keeps watching the wind will never sow, and he who keeps his eye on the clouds will never reap. 5 As you do not know how a pregnant woman comes to have a body and a living spirit in her womb, so you do not know the work of God, the maker of all things. 6 In the morning sow your seed in good time, and do not let your hands slack off until evening, for you do not know whether this or that sowing will be successful, or whether both alike will do well.

7 The light of day is sweet, and pleasant to the eye is the sight of the sun. 8 However many years a person may live, he should rejoice in all of them. But let him remember the days of darkness, for they will be many. Everything that is to come will be futility.

9 DELIGHT in your youth, young man, make the most of your early days; let your heart and your eyes show you the way; but remember that for all these things God will call you to account. 10 Banish vexation from your mind, and shake off the troubles of the body, for youth and the prime of life are mere futility.

12 Remember your Creator in the days of your youth, before the bad times come and the years draw near when you will say, 'I have no pleasure in them,' 2 before the sun and the light of day give place to darkness, before the moon and the stars grow dim, and the clouds return with the rain.

3 Remember him in the day when the guardians of the house become unsteady, and the strong men stoop, when the women grinding the meal cease work because they are few, and those who look through the windows can see no longer, 4 when the street doors are shut, when the sound of the mill fades, when the chirping of the sparrow grows faint and the songbirds fall silent; 5 when people are afraid of a steep place and the street is full of terrors, when the blossom whitens on the almond tree and the locust can only crawl and the caper-buds no longer give zest. For mortals depart to their everlasting home, and the mourners go about the street.

6 Remember your Creator before the silver cord is snapped and the golden bowl is broken, before the pitcher is shattered at the spring and the wheel broken at the well, 7 before the dust returns to the earth as it began and the spirit returns to God who gave it.

8 Utter futility, says the Speaker, everything is futile.

9 So the Speaker, in his wisdom, continued to instruct the people. He turned over many maxims in his mind and sought how best to set them out. 10 He chose his words to give pleasure, but what he wrote was straight truth. 11 The sayings of the wise are sharp as goads, like nails driven home; they guide the assembled people, for they come from one shepherd. 12 One further warning, my son: there is no

x Or *after*; Heb *'ahar*   *y* Or *is a burden*   *z* Syr Vg Compare Gk: Heb *is removed*   *a* Or *the spirit*   *b* Qoheleth, traditionally rendered *Preacher*   *c* Meaning of Heb uncertain

12:4 grows faint: *prob. rdg; Heb. obscure.* fall silent: *prob. rdg; Heb. sink low.*   12:7 spirit: *or breath.*

NEW AMERICAN BIBLE

4 One who pays heed to the wind will not sow,
and one who watches the clouds will never reap.
5 Just as you know not how the breath of life
fashions the human frame in the mother's womb,
So you know not the work of God
which he is accomplishing in the universe.
6 In the morning sow your seed,
and at evening let not your hand be idle:
For you know not which of the two will
be successful,
or whether both alike will turn out well.

7 Light is sweet! and it is pleasant for the eyes to see the
sun. 8 However many years a man may live, let him, as he
enjoys them all, remember that the days of darkness will be
many. All that is to come is vanity.

9 Rejoice, O young man, while you are young,
and let your heart be glad in the days of
your youth.
Follow the ways of your heart,
the vision of your eyes;
Yet understand that as regards all this
God will bring you to judgment.
10 Ward off grief from your heart
and put away trouble from your presence,
though the dawn of youth is fleeting.

12 Remember your Creator in the days of
your youth,
before the evil days come
And the years approach of which you will say,
I have no pleasure in them;
2 Before the sun is darkened,
and the light, and the moon, and the stars,
while the clouds return after the rain;
3 When the guardians of the house tremble,
and the strong men are bent,
And the grinders are idle because they are few,
and they who look through the windows
grow blind;
4 When the doors to the street are shut,
and the sound of the mill is low;
When one waits for the chirp of a bird,
but all the daughters of song are suppressed;
5 And one fears heights,
and perils in the street;
When the almond tree blooms,
and the locust grows sluggish
and the caper berry is without effect,
Because man goes to his lasting home,
and mourners go about the streets;
6 Before the silver cord is snapped
and the golden bowl is broken,
And the pitcher is shattered at the spring,
and the broken pulley falls into the well,
7 And the dust returns to the earth as it once was,
and the life breath returns to God who gave it.

8 Vanity of vanities, says Qoheleth,
all things are vanity!

9 Besides being wise, Qoheleth taught the people knowledge, and weighed, scrutinized and arranged many proverbs. 10 Qoheleth sought to find pleasing sayings, and to
write down true sayings with precision. 11 The sayings of
the wise are like goads; like fixed spikes are the topics given
by one collector. 12 As to more than these, my son, beware.

NEW JERUSALEM BIBLE

4 Keep watching the wind and you will never sow,
keep staring at the clouds and you will never reap.
5 You do not understand how the wind blows,
or how the embryo grows in a woman's womb:
no more can you understand the work of God, the
Creator of all.
6 In the morning sow your seed,
until evening, do not cease from labour,
for of any two things you do not know which will
succeed,
or which of the two is the better.

7 How sweet light is,
how delightful it is to see the sun!
8 However many years you live,
enjoy them all,
but remember, the days of darkness will be many:
futility awaits you at the end.

9 Young man, enjoy yourself while you are young,
make the most of the days of your youth,
follow the prompting and desire of heart and eye,
but remember, God will call you to account for
everything.
10 Rid your heart of indignation,
keep your body clear of suffering,
though youth and the age of black hair are both
futile.

12 Remember your Creator while you are still young,
before the bad days come,
before the years come which, you will say, give
you no pleasure;
2 before the sun and the light grow dim
and the moon and stars,
before the clouds return after the rain;
3 the time when your watchmen become shaky,
when strong men are bent double,
when the women, one by one, quit grinding,
and, as they look out of the window, find their
sight growing dim.
4 When the street-door is kept shut,
when the sound of grinding fades away,
when the first cry of a bird wakes you up,
when all the singing has stopped;
5 when going uphill is an ordeal
and you are frightened at every step you take —
yet the almond tree is in flower
and the grasshopper is weighed down
and the caper-bush loses its tang;
while you are on the way to your everlasting home
and the mourners are assembling in the street;
6 before the silver thread snaps,
or the golden bowl is cracked,
or the pitcher shattered at the fountain,
or the pulley broken at the well-head:
7 the dust returns to the earth from which it came,
and the spirit returns to God who gave it.

8 Sheer futility, Qoheleth says, everything is futile.

9 a Besides being a sage, Qoheleth taught the people what
he himself knew, having weighed, studied and emended
many proverbs. 10 Qoheleth took pains to write in an attractive style and by it to convey truths.
11 The sayings of a sage are like goads, like pegs positioned by shepherds: the same shepherd finds a use for both.
12 Furthermore, my child, you must realise that writing

a **12** 12:9 seq. is not by the same hand as the rest. Perhaps by a
disciple with a similar cast of mind.

NEW REVISED STANDARD VERSION

Of making many books there is no end, and much study is a weariness of the flesh.

13 The end of the matter; all has been heard. Fear God, and keep his commandments; for that is the whole duty of everyone. 14 For God will bring every deed into judgment, including[d] every secret thing, whether good or evil.

[d] Or *into the judgment on*

REVISED ENGLISH BIBLE

end to the writing of books, and much study is wearisome.

13 This is the end of the matter: you have heard it all. Fear God and obey his commandments; this sums up the duty of mankind. 14 For God will bring everything we do to judgement, every secret, whether good or bad.

NEW AMERICAN BIBLE

Of the making of many books there is no end, and in much study there is weariness for the flesh.

13 The last word, when all is heard: Fear God and keep his commandments, for this is man's all; 14 because God will bring to judgment every work, with all its hidden qualities, whether good or bad.

NEW JERUSALEM BIBLE

books involves endless hard work, and that much study wearies the body.

13 To sum up the whole matter: fear God and keep his commandments, for that is the duty of everyone. 14 For God will call all our deeds to judgement, all that is hidden, be it good or bad.

The Song of Solomon

1 The Song of Songs, which is Solomon's.

2 Let him kiss me with the kisses of his mouth!
   For your love is better than wine,
3   your anointing oils are fragrant,
   your name is perfume poured out;
      therefore the maidens love you.
4 Draw me after you, let us make haste.
      The king has brought me into his chambers.
   We will exult and rejoice in you;
      we will extol your love more than wine;
      rightly do they love you.

5 I am black and beautiful,
      O daughters of Jerusalem,
   like the tents of Kedar,
      like the curtains of Solomon.
6 Do not gaze at me because I am dark,
      because the sun has gazed on me.
   My mother's sons were angry with me;
      they made me keeper of the vineyards,
      but my own vineyard I have not kept!
7 Tell me, you whom my soul loves,
      where you pasture your flock,
      where you make it lie down at noon;
   for why should I be like one who is veiled
      beside the flocks of your companions?

8 If you do not know,
      O fairest among women,
   follow the tracks of the flock,
      and pasture your kids
      beside the shepherds' tents.

9 I compare you, my love,
      to a mare among Pharaoh's chariots.
10 Your cheeks are comely with ornaments,
      your neck with strings of jewels.
11 We will make you ornaments of gold,
      studded with silver.

12 While the king was on his couch,
      my nard gave forth its fragrance.
13 My beloved is to me a bag of myrrh
      that lies between my breasts.
14 My beloved is to me a cluster of henna blossoms
      in the vineyards of En-gedi.

15 Ah, you are beautiful, my love;
      ah, you are beautiful;
      your eyes are doves.
16 Ah, you are beautiful, my beloved,
      truly lovely.
   Our couch is green;

The Song of Songs

1 SOLOMON's song of songs:

      Bride
2 May he smother me with kisses.

   Your love is more fragrant than wine,
3 fragrant is the scent of your anointing oils,
   and your name is like those oils poured out;
      that is why maidens love you.
4 Take me with you, let us make haste;
   bring me into your chamber, O king.
      Companions
   Let us rejoice and be glad for you;
   let us praise your love more than wine,
      your caresses more than rare wine.
      Bride
5 Daughters of Jerusalem, I am dark and lovely,
      like the tents of Kedar
      or the tent curtains of Shalmah.
6 Do not look down on me; dark of hue I may be
   because I was scorched by the sun,
   when my mother's sons were displeased with me
   and sent me to watch over the vineyards;
   but my own vineyard I did not watch over!
7 Tell me, my true love,
   where you mind your flocks,
   where you rest them at noon,
   that I may not be left picking lice
   as I sit among your companions' herds.
      Bridegroom
8 If you do not know,
   O fairest of women,
   go, follow the tracks of the sheep
   and graze your young goats by the shepherds' huts.

9 I would compare you, my dearest,
      to a chariot-horse of Pharaoh.
10 Your cheeks are lovely between plaited tresses,
      your neck with its jewelled chains.
      Companions
11 We shall make you braided plaits of gold
      set with beads of silver.
      Bride
12 While the king reclines on his couch,
      my spikenard gives forth its scent.
13 My beloved is for me a sachet of myrrh
      lying between my breasts;
14 my beloved is for me a spray of henna blossom
      from the vineyards of En-gedi.
      Bridegroom
15 How beautiful you are, my dearest,
      ah, how beautiful,
      your eyes are like doves!
      Bride
16 How beautiful you are, my love,
      and how handsome!
      Bridegroom
   Our couch is shaded with branches;

The Song of Songs

1 The Song of Songs by Solomon

B ² Let him kiss me with kisses of his mouth!
More delightful is your love than wine!
³ Your name spoken is a spreading perfume —
that is why the maidens love you.
⁴ Draw me! —

D We will follow you eagerly!
B Bring me, O king, to your chambers.

D With you we rejoice and exult,
we extol your love; it is beyond wine:
how rightly you are loved!

B ⁵ I am as dark — but lovely,
O daughters of Jerusalem —
As the tents of Kedar,
as the curtains of Salma.
⁶ Do not stare at me because I am swarthy,
because the sun has burned me.
My brothers have been angry with me;
they charged me with the care of the vineyards:
my own vineyard I have not cared for.

B ⁷ Tell me, you whom my heart loves,
where you pasture your flock,
where you give them rest at midday,
Lest I be found wandering
after the flocks of your companions.

G ⁸ If you do not know,
O most beautiful among women,
Follow the tracks of the flock
and pasture the young ones
near the shepherds' camps.

G ⁹ To the steeds of Pharaoh's chariots
would I liken you, my beloved:
¹⁰ Your cheeks lovely in pendants,
your neck in jewels.
¹¹ We will make pendants of gold for you,
and silver ornaments.

B ¹² For the king's banquet
my nard gives forth its fragrance.
¹³ My lover is for me a sachet of myrrh
to rest in my bosom.
¹⁴ My lover is for me a cluster of henna
from the vineyards of Engedi.

G ¹⁵ Ah, you are beautiful, my beloved,
ah, you are beautiful; your eyes are doves!

B ¹⁶ Ah, you are beautiful, my lover —
yes, you are lovely.
Our couch, too, is verdant;

The Song of Songs

1 Solomon's Song of Songs.

Beloved:
² Let him kiss me with the kisses of his mouth,
for your love-making is sweeter than wine;
³ delicate is the fragrance of your perfume,
your name is an oil poured out,
and that is why girls love you.
⁴ Draw me in your footsteps, let us run.
The king has brought me into his rooms;
you will be our joy and our gladness.
We shall praise your love more than wine;
how right it is to love you.

Beloved:
⁵ I am black but lovely, daughters of Jerusalem,
like the tents of Kedar,
like the pavilions of Salmah.
⁶ Take no notice of my dark colouring,
it is the sun that has burnt me.
My mother's sons turned their anger on me,
they made me look after the vineyards.
My own vineyard I had not looked after!

⁷ Tell me then, sweetheart,
where will you lead your flock to graze,
where will you rest it at noon?
That I may no more wander like a vagabond
beside the flocks of your companions.

Chorus:
⁸ If you do not know this, O loveliest of women,
follow the tracks of the flock,
and take your kids to graze
close by the shepherds' tents.

Lover:
⁹ I compare you, my love,
to my mare harnessed to Pharaoh's chariot.
¹⁰ Your cheeks show fair between their pendants
and your neck within its necklaces.
¹¹ We shall make you golden earrings
and beads of silver.

Duo:
¹² — While the king rests in his own room
my nard yields its perfume.
¹³ My love is a sachet of myrrh
lying between my breasts.
¹⁴ My love is a cluster of henna flowers
among the vines of En-Gedi. ᵃ

¹⁵ — How beautiful you are, my beloved,
how beautiful you are!
Your eyes are doves.

¹⁶ — How beautiful you are, my love,
and how you delight me!
Our bed is the greensward.

1, 1: This title is actually the first verse of chapter 1. **1, 2ff:** The marginal letters indicate the speaker of the verses: B—Bride; D—Daughters of Jerusalem; G—Bridegroom.

ᵃ 1 A fertile oasis of vines and palms on the desolate west shore of the Dead Sea.

17   the beams of our house are cedar,
      our rafters*a* are pine.

2
      I am a rose*b* of Sharon,
         a lily of the valleys.
2   As a lily among brambles,
         so is my love among maidens.
3   As an apple tree among the trees of the wood,
         so is my beloved among young men.
      With great delight I sat in his shadow,
         and his fruit was sweet to my taste.
4   He brought me to the banqueting house,
         and his intention toward me was love.
5   Sustain me with raisins,
         refresh me with apples;
      for I am faint with love.
6   O that his left hand were under my head,
         and that his right hand embraced me!
7   I adjure you, O daughters of Jerusalem,
         by the gazelles or the wild does:
      do not stir up or awaken love
         until it is ready!
8   The voice of my beloved!
         Look, he comes,
      leaping upon the mountains,
         bounding over the hills.
9   My beloved is like a gazelle
         or a young stag.
      Look, there he stands
         behind our wall,
      gazing in at the windows,
         looking through the lattice.
10   My beloved speaks and says to me:
      "Arise, my love, my fair one,
         and come away;
11   for now the winter is past,
         the rain is over and gone.
12   The flowers appear on the earth;
         the time of singing has come,
      and the voice of the turtledove
         is heard in our land.
13   The fig tree puts forth its figs,
         and the vines are in blossom;
         they give forth fragrance.
      Arise, my love, my fair one,
         and come away.
14   O my dove, in the clefts of the rock,
         in the covert of the cliff,
      let me see your face,
         let me hear your voice;
      for your voice is sweet,
         and your face is lovely.
15   Catch us the foxes,
         the little foxes,
      that ruin the vineyards —
         for our vineyards are in blossom."
16   My beloved is mine and I am his;
         he pastures his flock among the lilies.
17   Until the day breathes
         and the shadows flee,
      turn, my beloved, be like a gazelle
         or a young stag on the cleft mountains.*c*

17 the beams of our house are of cedar,
   our rafters are all of pine.
                                    Bride
2
   I am a rose of Sharon,
      a lily growing in the valley.
                              Bridegroom
2 A lily among thorns
   is my dearest among the maidens.
                                    Bride
3 Like an apple tree among the trees of the forest,
   so is my beloved among young men.
   To sit in his shadow is my delight,
      and his fruit is sweet to my taste.
4 He has taken me into the wine-garden
   and given me loving glances.
5 Sustain me with raisins, revive me with apples;
   for I am faint with love.
6 His left arm pillows my head, his right arm is
      round me.
                              Bridegroom
7 I charge you, maidens of Jerusalem,
   by the spirits and the goddesses of the field:
   Do not rouse or awaken love
      until it is ready.
                                    Bride
8 Hark! My beloved! Here he comes,
   bounding over the mountains, leaping over the
      hills.
9 My beloved is like a gazelle
   or a young stag.
   There he stands outside our wall,
      peering in at the windows, gazing through the
      lattice.
10 My beloved spoke, saying to me:
   'Rise up, my darling;
   my fair one, come away.
11 For see, the winter is past!
   The rains are over and gone;
12 the flowers appear in the countryside;
   the season of birdsong is come,
   and the turtle-dove's cooing is heard in our land;
13 the green figs ripen on the fig trees
   and the vine blossoms give forth their fragrance.
   Rise up, my darling;
   my fair one, come away.'
                              Bridegroom
14 My dove, that hides in holes in the cliffs
   or in crannies on the terraced hillside,
   let me see your face and hear your voice;
   for your voice is sweet, your face is lovely.
                              Companions
15 Catch the jackals for us, the little jackals,
   the despoilers of vineyards, for our vineyards are
      full of blossom.
                                    Bride
16 My beloved is mine and I am his;
   he grazes his flock among the lilies.
17 While the day is cool
   and the shadows are dispersing,
   turn, my beloved, and show yourself
   a gazelle or a young stag
   on the hills where aromatic spices grow.

---

a Meaning of Heb uncertain   *b* Heb *crocus*   *c* Or *on the*
mountains of Bether: meaning of Heb uncertain

2:1 **rose:** *or* asphodel.   2:7 **by . . . goddesses:** *or* by the gazelles
and the hinds.   2:15 **jackals:** *or* fruit-bats.   2:17 **on . . . grow:**
or on the rugged hills *or* on the hills of Bether.

17 the beams of our house are cedars,
  our rafters, cypresses.

2 I am a flower of Sharon,
  a lily of the valley.

G ²As a lily among thorns,
  so is my beloved among women.

B ³As an apple tree among the trees of the woods,
  so is my lover among men.
  I delight to rest in his shadow,
  and his fruit is sweet to my mouth.
⁴He brings me into the banquet hall
  and his emblem over me is love.
⁵Strengthen me with raisin cakes,
  refresh me with apples,
  for I am faint with love.
⁶His left hand is under my head
  and his right arm embraces me.
⁷I adjure you, daughters of Jerusalem,
  by the gazelles and hinds of the field,
  Do not arouse, do not stir up love
  before its own time.

B ⁸Hark! my lover—here he comes
  springing across the mountains,
  leaping across the hills.
⁹My lover is like a gazelle
  or a young stag.
  Here he stands behind our wall,
  gazing through the windows,
  peering through the lattices.
¹⁰My lover speaks; he says to me,
  "Arise, my beloved, my beautiful one,
  and come!
¹¹"For see, the winter is past,
  the rains are over and gone.
¹²The flowers appear on the earth,
  the time of pruning the vines has come,
  and the song of the dove is heard in our land.
¹³The fig tree puts forth its figs,
  and the vines, in bloom, give forth fragrance.
  Arise, my beloved, my beautiful one,
  and come!
¹⁴"O my dove in the clefts of the rock,
  in the secret recesses of the cliff,
  Let me see you,
  let me hear your voice,
  For your voice is sweet,
  and you are lovely."

B ¹⁵Catch us the foxes, the little foxes
  that damage the vineyards; for our vineyards are
  in bloom!

¹⁶My lover belongs to me and I to him;
  he browses among the lilies.
¹⁷Until the day breathes cool and the
  shadows lengthen,
  roam, my lover,
  Like a gazelle or a young stag
  upon the mountains of Bether.

17 —The beams of our house are cedar trees,
  its panelling the cypress.

2 —I am the rose of Sharon,
  the lily of the valleys.

² —As a lily among the thistles,
  so is my beloved among girls.

³ —As an apple tree among the trees of the wood,
  so is my love among young men.
  In his delightful shade I sit,
  and his fruit is sweet to my taste.
⁴He has taken me to his cellar,
  and his banner over me is love.
⁵Feed me with raisin cakes,
  restore me with apples,
  for I am sick with love.
⁶His left arm is under my head,
  his right embraces me.
⁷ —I charge you,
  daughters of Jerusalem,
  by all gazelles and wild does,
  do not rouse, do not wake my beloved
  before she pleases.
                    Beloved:
⁸I hear my love.
  See how he comes
  leaping on the mountains,
  bounding over the hills.
⁹My love is like a gazelle,
  like a young stag.

  See where he stands
  behind our wall.
  He looks in at the window,
  he peers through the opening.

¹⁰My love lifts up his voice,
  he says to me,
  'Come then, my beloved,
  my lovely one, come.
¹¹For see, winter is past,
  the rains are over and gone.
¹²'Flowers are appearing on the earth.
  The season of glad songs has come,
  the cooing of the turtledove is heard in our land.
¹³The fig tree is forming its first figs
  and the blossoming vines give out their fragrance.
  Come then, my beloved,
  my lovely one, come.

¹⁴'My dove, hiding in the clefts of the rock,
  in the coverts of the cliff,
  show me your face,
  let me hear your voice;
  for your voice is sweet
  and your face is lovely.'
¹⁵Catch the foxes for us,
  the little foxes
  that make havoc of the vineyards,
  for our vineyards are in fruit.

¹⁶My love is mine and I am his.
  He pastures his flock among the lilies.

¹⁷Before the day-breeze rises,
  before the shadows flee, return!
  Be, my love, like a gazelle, like a young stag,
  on the mountains of Bether.

3 Upon my bed at night
  I sought him whom my soul loves;
I sought him, but found him not;
  I called him, but he gave no answer.[d]
2 "I will rise now and go about the city,
  in the streets and in the squares;
I will seek him whom my soul loves."
  I sought him, but found him not.
3 The sentinels found me,
  as they went about in the city.
"Have you seen him whom my soul loves?"
4 Scarcely had I passed them,
  when I found him whom my soul loves.
I held him, and would not let him go
  until I brought him into my mother's house,
  and into the chamber of her that conceived me.
5 I adjure you, O daughters of Jerusalem,
  by the gazelles or the wild does:
do not stir up or awaken love
  until it is ready!

6 What is that coming up from the wilderness,
  like a column of smoke,
perfumed with myrrh and frankincense,
  with all the fragrant powders of the merchant?
7 Look, it is the litter of Solomon!
  Around it are sixty mighty men
  of the mighty men of Israel,
8 all equipped with swords
  and expert in war,
each with his sword at his thigh
  because of alarms by night.
9 King Solomon made himself a palanquin
  from the wood of Lebanon.
10 He made its posts of silver,
  its back of gold, its seat of purple;
  its interior was inlaid with love.[e]
  Daughters of Jerusalem,
11   come out.
Look, O daughters of Zion,
  at King Solomon,
at the crown with which his mother crowned him
  on the day of his wedding,
  on the day of the gladness of his heart.

4 How beautiful you are, my love,
  how very beautiful!
Your eyes are doves
  behind your veil.
Your hair is like a flock of goats,
  moving down the slopes of Gilead.
2 Your teeth are like a flock of shorn ewes
  that have come up from the washing,
all of which bear twins,
  and not one among them is bereaved.
3 Your lips are like a crimson thread,
  and your mouth is lovely.
Your cheeks are like halves of a pomegranate
  behind your veil.

3 Night after night on my bed
  I have sought my true love;
I have sought him, but I have not found him.
2 I said, 'I will rise and go the rounds of the city
  through streets and squares,
seeking my true love.'
  I sought him, but could not find him.
3 The watchmen came upon me,
  as they made their rounds of the city.
'Have you seen my true love?' I asked them.
4 Scarcely had I left them behind
  when I met my true love.
I held him and would not let him go
  till I had brought him to my mother's house,
  to the room of her who conceived me.
  Bridegroom
5 I charge you, maidens of Jerusalem,
  by the spirits and the goddesses of the field:
Do not rouse or awaken love
  until it is ready.
  Companions
6 Who is this coming up from the wilderness
  like a column of smoke
from the burning of myrrh and frankincense,
  of all the powdered spices that merchants bring?
7 Look! It is Solomon carried in his state litter,
  escorted by sixty of Israel's picked warriors,
8 all of them skilled swordsmen,
  all expert in handling arms,
each with his sword ready at his side
  against the terrors of the night.

9 The palanquin which King Solomon had made for
    himself
  was of wood from Lebanon.
10 Its uprights were made of silver,
  its headrest of gold;
  its seat was of purple stuff,
  its lining of leather.

11 Come out, maidens of Jerusalem,
  you maidens of Zion, welcome King Solomon,
wearing the crown which his mother placed on his
    head
  on his wedding day, his day of joy.

  Bridegroom
4 How beautiful you are, my dearest, how beautiful!
  Your eyes are doves behind your veil,
  your hair like a flock of goats streaming down
    Mount Gilead.
2 Your teeth are like a flock of ewes newly shorn,
  freshly come up from the dipping;
  all of them have twins, and none has lost a lamb.
3 Your lips are like a scarlet thread,
  and your mouth is lovely;
  your parted lips behind your veil
  are like a pomegranate cut open.

---

[d] Gk: Heb lacks this line   [e] Meaning of Heb uncertain   3:5 *by . . . goddesses:* or by the gazelles and the hinds.

3 *B* On my bed at night I sought him
    whom my heart loves —
    I sought him but I did not find him.
2 I will rise then and go about the city;
    in the streets and crossings I will seek
Him whom my heart loves.
    I sought him but I did not find him.
3 The watchmen came upon me,
    as they made their rounds of the city:
Have you seen him whom my heart loves?
4 I had hardly left them
    when I found him whom my heart loves.
I took hold of him and would not let him go
    till I should bring him to the home of
      my mother,
    to the room of my parent.
5 I adjure you, daughters of Jerusalem,
    by the gazelles and hinds of the field,
Do not arouse, do not stir up love
    before its own time.

D 6 What is this coming up from the desert,
    like a column of smoke
Laden with myrrh, with frankincense,
    and with the perfume of every exotic dust?
7 Ah, it is the litter of Solomon;
    sixty valiant men surround it,
    of the valiant men of Israel:
8 All of them expert with the sword,
    skilled in battle,
Each with his sword at his side
    against danger in the watches of the night.

9 King Solomon made himself a carriage
    of wood from Lebanon.
10 He made its columns of silver,
    its roof of gold,
Its seat of purple cloth,
    its framework inlaid with ivory.
11 Daughters of Jerusalem, come forth
    and look upon King Solomon
In the crown with which his mother has
      crowned him
    on the day of his marriage,
    on the day of the joy of his heart.

4 *G* Ah, you are beautiful, my beloved,
    ah, you are beautiful!
Your eyes are doves
    behind your veil.
Your hair is like a flock of goats
    streaming down the mountains of Gilead.
2 Your teeth are like a flock of ewes to be shorn,
    which come up from the washing,
All of them big with twins,
    none of them thin and barren.
3 Your lips are like a scarlet strand;
    your mouth is lovely.
Your cheek is like a half-pomegranate
    behind your veil.

3 On my bed at night I sought
    the man who is my sweetheart:
    I sought but could not find him!
2 So I shall get up and go through the city;
    in the streets and in the squares,
    I shall seek my sweetheart.
    I sought but could not find him!
3 I came upon the watchmen —
    those who go on their rounds in the city:
    'Have you seen my sweetheart?'

4 Barely had I passed them
    when I found my sweetheart.
I caught him, would not let him go,
    not till I had brought him
    to my mother's house,
    to the room where she conceived me!
        Lover:
5 I charge you,
    daughters of Jerusalem,
    by gazelles and wild does,
do not rouse, do not wake my beloved
    before she pleases.
        Poet:
6 What is this coming up from the desert
    like a column of smoke,
    breathing of myrrh and frankincense
    and every exotic perfume?
7 Here comes Solomon's litter.
    Around it are sixty champions,
    the flower of the warriors of Israel;
8 all of them skilled swordsmen,
    expert in war.
Each man has his sword at his side,
    against alarms by night.

9 King Solomon
    has had a palanquin made
    of wood from Lebanon.
10 He has had the posts made of silver,
    the canopy of gold,
    the seat of purple;
    the centre is inlaid with ebony.

11 Daughters of Zion,
    come and see King Solomon,
wearing the diadem with which his mother
      crowned him
    on his wedding day,
    on the day of his heart's joy.

        Lover:
4 How beautiful you are, my beloved,
    how beautiful you are!
Your eyes are doves,
    behind your veil;
your hair is like a flock of goats
    surging down Mount Gilead.
2 Your teeth, a flock of sheep to be shorn
    when they come up from the washing.
Each one has its twin,
    not one unpaired with another.
3 Your lips are a scarlet thread
    and your words enchanting.
Your cheeks, behind your veil,
    are halves of pomegranate.

4 Your neck is like the tower of David,
   built in courses;
on it hang a thousand bucklers,
   all of them shields of warriors.
5 Your two breasts are like two fawns,
   twins of a gazelle,
   that feed among the lilies.
6 Until the day breathes
   and the shadows flee,
I will hasten to the mountain of myrrh
   and the hill of frankincense.
7 You are altogether beautiful, my love;
   there is no flaw in you.

8 Come with me from Lebanon, my bride;
   come with me from Lebanon.
Depart *f* from the peak of Amana,
   from the peak of Senir and Hermon,
from the dens of lions,
   from the mountains of leopards.

9 You have ravished my heart, my sister, my bride,
   you have ravished my heart with a glance of
      your eyes,
   with one jewel of your necklace.
10 How sweet is your love, my sister, my bride!
   how much better is your love than wine,
   and the fragrance of your oils than any spice!
11 Your lips distill nectar, my bride;
   honey and milk are under your tongue;
   the scent of your garments is like the scent of
      Lebanon.
12 A garden locked is my sister, my bride,
   a garden locked, a fountain sealed.
13 Your channel *g* is an orchard of pomegranates
   with all choicest fruits,
   henna with nard,
14 nard and saffron, calamus and cinnamon,
   with all trees of frankincense,
   myrrh and aloes,
   with all chief spices —
15 a garden fountain, a well of living water,
   and flowing streams from Lebanon.

16 Awake, O north wind,
   and come, O south wind!
Blow upon my garden
   that its fragrance may be wafted abroad.
Let my beloved come to his garden,
   and eat its choicest fruits.

4 Your neck is like David's tower,
   which is built with encircling courses;
a thousand bucklers hang upon it,
   and all are warriors' shields.
5 Your two breasts are like two fawns,
   twin fawns of a gazelle
   grazing among the lilies.
6 While the day is cool
   and the shadows are dispersing,
I shall take myself to the mountains of myrrh
   and to the hill of frankincense.
7 You are beautiful, my dearest,
   beautiful without a flaw.

8 Come with me from Lebanon, my bride;
   come with me from Lebanon.
Hurry down from the summit of Amana,
   from the top of Senir and Hermon,
from the lions' lairs, and the leopard-haunted hills.

9 You have stolen my heart, my sister,
   you have stolen it, my bride,
with just one of your eyes, one jewel of your
      necklace.
10 How beautiful are your breasts, my sister and
      bride!
Your love is more fragrant than wine,
   your perfumes sweeter than any spices.
11 Your lips drop sweetness like the honeycomb, my
      bride,
honey and milk are under your tongue,
   and your dress has the scent of Lebanon.
13 Your two cheeks are an orchard of pomegranates,
   an orchard of choice fruits:
14 spikenard and saffron, aromatic cane and cinnamon
   with every frankincense tree,
   myrrh and aloes
   with all the most exquisite spices.
12 My sister, my bride, is a garden close-locked,
   a garden close-locked, a fountain sealed.
         Bride
15 The fountain in my garden is a spring of running
      water
   flowing down from Lebanon.
16 Awake, north wind, and come, south wind!
Blow upon my garden to spread its spices abroad,
   that my beloved may come to his garden
   and enjoy the choice fruit.

4:13 *Verse 12 is transposed to follow verse 14.* **Your two cheeks:**
prob. rdg; Heb. Your shoots. **an orchard . . . fruits:** *prob. rdg;*
Heb. adds henna with spikenard.

---

f Or Look   *g Meaning of Heb uncertain*

4 Your neck is like David's tower
   girt with battlements;
 A thousand bucklers hang upon it,
   all the shields of valiant men.
5 Your breasts are like twin fawns,
   the young of a gazelle
   that browse among the lilies.
6 Until the day breathes cool and the
     shadows lengthen,
   I will go to the mountain of myrrh,
   to the hill of incense.
7 You are all-beautiful, my beloved,
   and there is no blemish in you.

8 Come from Lebanon, my bride,
   come from Lebanon, come!
 Descend from the top of Amana,
   from the top of Senir and Hermon,
 From the haunts of lions,
   from the leopards' mountains.
9 You have ravished my heart, my sister, my bride;
   you have ravished my heart with one glance of
     your eyes,
   with one bead of your necklace.
10 How beautiful is your love, my sister, my bride,
   how much more delightful is your love
     than wine,
   and the fragrance of your ointments than
     all spices!
11 Your lips drip honey, my bride,
   sweetmeats and milk are under your tongue;
 And the fragrance of your garments
   is the fragrance of Lebanon.

G 12 You are an enclosed garden, my sister,
       my bride,
   an enclosed garden, a fountain sealed.
13 You are a park that puts forth pomegranates,
   with all choice fruits;
14 Nard and saffron, calamus and cinnamon,
   with all kinds of incense;
 Myrrh and aloes,
   with all the finest spices.
15 You are a garden fountain, a well of water
   flowing fresh from Lebanon.
16 Arise, north wind! Come, south wind!
   blow upon my garden
   that its perfumes may spread abroad.
B Let my lover come to his garden
   and eat its choice fruits.

4 Your neck is the Tower of David
   built on layers,
   hung round with a thousand bucklers,
   and each the shield of a hero.
5 Your two breasts are two fawns,
   twins of a gazelle,
   that feed among the lilies.
6 Before the day-breeze rises,
   before the shadows flee,
   I shall go to the mountain of myrrh,
   to the hill of frankincense.
7 You are wholly beautiful, my beloved,
   and without a blemish.

8 Come from Lebanon, my promised bride,
   come from Lebanon, come on your way.
 Look down from the heights of Amanus,
   from the crests of Senir and Hermon,
   the haunt of lions,
   the mountains of leopards.
9 You ravish my heart,
   my sister, my promised bride,
   you ravish my heart
   with a single one of your glances,
   with a single link of your necklace.
10 What spells lie in your love,
   my sister, my promised bride!
 How delicious is your love, more delicious than
     wine!
 How fragrant your perfumes,
   more fragrant than all spices!
11 Your lips, my promised bride,
   distil wild honey.
 Honey and milk
   are under your tongue;
   and the scent of your garments
   is like the scent of Lebanon.

12 She is a garden enclosed,
   my sister, my promised bride;
   a garden enclosed,
   a sealed fountain.
13 Your shoots form an orchard of pomegranate trees,
   bearing most exquisite fruit:
14 nard and saffron,
   calamus and cinnamon,
   with all the incense-bearing trees;
   myrrh and aloes,
   with the subtlest odours.
15 Fountain of the garden,
   well of living water,
   streams flowing down from Lebanon!
               Beloved:
16 Awake, north wind,
   come, wind of the south!
 Breathe over my garden,
   to spread its sweet smell around.
 Let my love come into his garden,
   let him taste its most exquisite fruits.

5 I come to my garden, my sister, my bride;
    I gather my myrrh with my spice,
    I eat my honeycomb with my honey,
    I drink my wine with my milk.

Eat, friends, drink,
    and be drunk with love.

2 I slept, but my heart was awake.
Listen! my beloved is knocking.
"Open to me, my sister, my love,
    my dove, my perfect one;
for my head is wet with dew,
    my locks with the drops of the night."
3 I had put off my garment;
    how could I put it on again?
I had bathed my feet;
    how could I soil them?
4 My beloved thrust his hand into the opening,
    and my inmost being yearned for him.
5 I arose to open to my beloved,
    and my hands dripped with myrrh,
my fingers with liquid myrrh,
    upon the handles of the bolt.
6 I opened to my beloved,
    but my beloved had turned and was gone.
My soul failed me when he spoke.
I sought him, but did not find him;
    I called him, but he gave no answer.
7 Making their rounds in the city
    the sentinels found me;
they beat me, they wounded me,
    they took away my mantle,
    those sentinels of the walls.
8 I adjure you, O daughters of Jerusalem,
    if you find my beloved,
tell him this:
    I am faint with love.

9 What is your beloved more than another beloved,
    O fairest among women?
What is your beloved more than another beloved,
    that you thus adjure us?

10 My beloved is all radiant and ruddy,
    distinguished among ten thousand.
11 His head is the finest gold;
    his locks are wavy,
    black as a raven.
12 His eyes are like doves
    beside springs of water,
bathed in milk,
    fitly set.[h]
13 His cheeks are like beds of spices,
    yielding fragrance.
His lips are lilies,
    distilling liquid myrrh.

Bridegroom

5 I have come to my garden, my sister
    and bride;
I have gathered my myrrh and my spices;
I have eaten my honeycomb and my honey,
    and drunk my wine and my milk.
Eat, friends, and drink deep,
    till you are drunk with love.

Bride

2 I sleep, but my heart is awake.
Listen! My beloved is knocking:
'Open to me, my sister, my dearest,
    my dove, my perfect one;
for my head is drenched with dew,
    my locks with the moisture of the night.'

3 'I have put off my robe; must I put it on again?
I have bathed my feet; must I dirty them again?'

4 When my beloved slipped his hand through the
    latch-hole,
    my heart turned over.
5 When I arose to open for my beloved,
    my hands dripped with myrrh;
the liquid myrrh from my fingers
    ran over the handle of the latch.
6 I opened to my love,
    but my love had turned away and was gone;
    my heart sank when he turned his back.
I sought him, but could not find him,
I called, but there was no answer.
7 The watchmen came upon me,
    as they made their rounds of the city.
They beat and wounded me,
    and those on the walls stripped off my cloak.
8 Maidens of Jerusalem, I charge you,
    if you find my beloved, to tell him
that I am faint with love.

Companions

9 What is your beloved more than any other,
    O fairest of women?
What is your beloved more than any other,
    that you should give us this charge?

Bride

10 My beloved is fair and desirable,
    a paragon among ten thousand.
11 His head is gold, finest gold.
His locks are like palm-fronds,
    black as the raven.
12 His eyes are like doves beside pools of water,
    in their setting bathed as it were in milk.
13 His cheeks are like beds of spices, terraces full of
    perfumes;
his lips are lilies, they drop liquid myrrh.

---

[h] Meaning of Heb uncertain

5 G I have come to my garden, my sister,
    my bride;
  I gather my myrrh and my spices,
  I eat my honey and my sweetmeats,
  I drink my wine and my milk.

D Eat, friends; drink! Drink freely of love!

B 2 I was sleeping, but my heart kept vigil;
  I heard my lover knocking:
  "Open to me, my sister, my beloved,
    my dove, my perfect one!
  For my head is wet with dew,
    my locks with the moisture of the night."
  3 I have taken off my robe,
    am I then to put it on?
  I have bathed my feet,
    am I then to soil them?

  4 My lover put his hand through the opening;
    my heart trembled within me,
    and I grew faint when he spoke.
  5 I rose to open to my lover,
    with my hands dripping myrrh:
  With my fingers dripping choice myrrh
    upon the fittings of the lock.
  6 I opened to my lover—
    but my lover had departed, gone.
  I sought him but I did not find him;
    I called to him but he did not answer me.

  7 The watchmen came upon me
    as they made their rounds of the city;
  They struck me, and wounded me,
    and took my mantle from me,
    the guardians of the walls.
  8 I adjure you, daughters of Jerusalem,
    if you find my lover—
  What shall you tell him?—
    that I am faint with love.

D 9 How does your lover differ from any other,
    O most beautiful among women?
  How does your lover differ from any other,
    that you adjure us so?

B 10 My lover is radiant and ruddy;
    he stands out among thousands.
  11 His head is pure gold;
    his locks are palm fronds,
    black as the raven.
  12 His eyes are like doves
    beside running waters,
  His teeth would seem bathed in milk,
    and are set like jewels.
  13 His cheeks are like beds of spice
    with ripening aromatic herbs.
  His lips are red blossoms;
    they drip choice myrrh.

Lover:
5 I come into my garden,
  my sister, my promised bride,
  I pick my myrrh and balsam,
  I eat my honey and my honeycomb,
  I drink my wine and my milk.

Poet:
  Eat, friends, and drink,
  drink deep, my dearest friends.

Beloved:
  2 I sleep, but my heart is awake.
  I hear my love knocking.
  'Open to me, my sister, my beloved,
  my dove, my perfect one,
  for my head is wet with dew,
  my hair with the drops of night.'

  3 —'I have taken off my tunic,
    am I to put it on again?
  I have washed my feet,
    am I to dirty them again?'
  4 My love thrust his hand
    through the hole in the door;
  I trembled to the core of my being.
  5 Then I got up
    to open to my love,
  myrrh ran off my hands,
  pure myrrh off my fingers,
    on to the handle of the bolt.

  6 I opened to my love,
    but he had turned and gone.
  My soul failed at his flight,
  I sought but could not find him,
  I called, but he did not answer.

  7 The watchmen met me,
    those who go on their rounds in the city.
  They beat me, they wounded me,
  they took my cloak away from me:
    those guardians of the ramparts!

  8 I charge you,
    daughters of Jerusalem,
  if you should find my love,
  what are you to tell him?
  —That I am sick with love!

Chorus:
  9 What makes your lover better than other lovers,
    O loveliest of women?
  What makes your lover better than other lovers,
    to put us under such an oath?

Beloved:
  10 My love is fresh and ruddy,
    to be known among ten thousand.
  11 His head is golden, purest gold,
    his locks are palm fronds
    and black as the raven.
  12 His eyes are like doves
    beside the water-courses,
    bathing themselves in milk,
    perching on a fountain-rim.
  13 His cheeks are beds of spices,
    banks sweetly scented.
  His lips are lilies,
    distilling pure myrrh.

NEW REVISED STANDARD VERSION	REVISED ENGLISH BIBLE

NEW REVISED STANDARD VERSION

14 His arms are rounded gold,
　　set with jewels.
　His body is ivory work,*i*
　　encrusted with sapphires.*j*
15 His legs are alabaster columns,
　　set upon bases of gold.
　His appearance is like Lebanon,
　　choice as the cedars.
16 His speech is most sweet,
　　and he is altogether desirable.
　This is my beloved and this is my friend,
　　O daughters of Jerusalem.

6 Where has your beloved gone,
　　O fairest among women?
　Which way has your beloved turned,
　　that we may seek him with you?

2 My beloved has gone down to his garden,
　　to the beds of spices,
　to pasture his flock in the gardens,
　　and to gather lilies.
3 I am my beloved's and my beloved is mine;
　　he pastures his flock among the lilies.

4 You are beautiful as Tirzah, my love,
　　comely as Jerusalem,
　　terrible as an army with banners.
5 Turn away your eyes from me,
　　for they overwhelm me!
　Your hair is like a flock of goats,
　　moving down the slopes of Gilead.
6 Your teeth are like a flock of ewes,
　　that have come up from the washing;
　all of them bear twins,
　　and not one among them is bereaved.
7 Your cheeks are like halves of a pomegranate
　　behind your veil.
8 There are sixty queens and eighty concubines,
　　and maidens without number.
9 My dove, my perfect one, is the only one,
　　the darling of her mother,
　　flawless to her that bore her.
　The maidens saw her and called her happy;
　　the queens and concubines also, and they
　　　praised her.
10 "Who is this that looks forth like the dawn,
　　fair as the moon, bright as the sun,
　　terrible as an army with banners?"

11 I went down to the nut orchard,
　　to look at the blossoms of the valley,
　to see whether the vines had budded,
　　whether the pomegranates were in bloom.
12 Before I was aware, my fancy set me
　　in a chariot beside my prince.*k*

REVISED ENGLISH BIBLE

14 His arms are golden rods set with topaz,
　　his belly a plaque of ivory adorned with sapphires.
15 His legs are pillars of marble set on bases of finest
　　　gold;
　his aspect is like Lebanon, noble as cedars.
16 His mouth is sweetness itself, wholly desirable.
　Such is my beloved, such is my darling,
　　O maidens of Jerusalem.

Companions
6 Where has your beloved gone,
　　O fairest of women?
　Which way did your beloved turn,
　　that we may look for him with you?
Bride
2 My beloved has gone down to his garden,
　　to the beds where balsam grows,
　to delight in the gardens, and to pick the lilies.
3 I am my beloved's, and my beloved is mine;
　　he grazes his flock among the lilies.
Bridegroom
4 You are beautiful as Tirzah, my dearest,
　　lovely as Jerusalem.
5 Turn your eyes away from me;
　　they dazzle me.
　Your hair is like a flock of goats streaming down
　　　Mount Gilead;
6 your teeth are like a flock of ewes
　　newly come up from the dipping,
　all of them have twins, and none has lost a lamb.
7 Your parted lips behind your veil
　　are like a pomegranate cut open.
8 There may be three score princesses,
　　four score concubines, and young women past
　　　counting,
9 but there is one alone, my dove, my perfect one,
　　her mother's only child,
　the favourite of the one who bore her.
　Maidens see her and call her happy,
　　princesses and concubines sing her praises.
10 Who is this that looks out like the dawn,
　　beautiful as the moon, radiant as the sun,
　　majestic as the starry heavens?

11 I went down to a garden of nut trees
　　to look at the green shoots of the palms,
　to see if the vine had budded
　　or the pomegranates were in flower.
12 I did not recognize myself:
　　she made me a prince
　　chosen from myriads of my people.

---

*i*Meaning of Heb uncertain　　*j*Heb *lapis lazuli*　　*k*Cn: Meaning of
Heb uncertain

5:16 **mouth:** *lit.* palate.　6:4 **lovely as Jerusalem:** *prob. rdg;*
Heb. adds majestic as the starry heavens (*see verse 10*).
6:12 **myriads:** *prob. rdg; Heb.* chariots.

NEW AMERICAN BIBLE

NEW JERUSALEM BIBLE

14 His arms are rods of gold
adorned with chrysolites.
His body is a work of ivory
covered with sapphires.
15 His legs are columns of marble
resting on golden bases.
His stature is like the trees on Lebanon,
imposing as the cedars.
16 His mouth is sweetness itself;
he is all delight.
Such is my lover, and such my friend,
O daughters of Jerusalem.

6 D Where has your lover gone,
O most beautiful among women?
Where has your lover gone
that we may seek him with you?
B 2 My lover has come down to his garden,
to the beds of spice,
To browse in the garden
and to gather lilies.
3 My lover belongs to me and I to him;
he browses among the lilies.

G 4 You are as beautiful as Tirzah, my beloved,
as lovely as Jerusalem,
as awe-inspiring as bannered troops.
5 Turn your eyes from me,
for they torment me.
Your hair is like a flock of goats
streaming down from Gilead.
6 Your teeth are like a flock of ewes
which come up from the washing,
All of them big with twins,
none of them thin and barren.
7 Your cheek is like a half-pomegranate
behind your veil.

8 There are sixty queens, eighty concubines,
and maidens without number—
9 One alone is my dove, my perfect one,
her mother's chosen,
the dear one of her parent.
The daughters saw her and declared her fortunate,
the queens and concubines, and they sang
her praises;
D 10 Who is this that comes forth like the dawn,
as beautiful as the moon, as resplendent as
the sun,
as awe-inspiring as bannered troops?

B 11 I came down to the nut garden
to look at the fresh growth of the valley,
To see if the vines were in bloom,
if the pomegranates had blossomed.
12 Before I knew it, my heart had made me
the blessed one of my kinswomen.

14 His hands are golden, rounded,
set with jewels of Tarshish.
His belly a block of ivory
covered with sapphires.
15 His legs are alabaster columns
set in sockets of pure gold.
His appearance is that of Lebanon,
unrivalled as the cedars.
16 His conversation is sweetness itself,
he is altogether lovable.
Such is my love, such is my friend,
O daughters of Jerusalem.

Chorus:

6 Where did your lover go,
O loveliest of women?
Which way did your lover turn
so that we can help you seek him?
Beloved:
2 My love went down to his garden,
to the beds of spices,
to pasture his flock on the grass
and gather lilies.
3 I belong to my love, and my love to me.
He pastures his flock among the lilies.
Lover:
4 You are fair as Tirzah, *b* my beloved,
enchanting as Jerusalem,
formidable as an army!
5 Turn your eyes away from me,
they take me by assault!
Your hair is like a flock of goats
surging down the slopes of Gilead.
6 Your teeth are like a flock of ewes
as they come up from being washed.
Each one has its twin,
not one unpaired with another.
7 Your cheeks, behind your veil,
are halves of pomegranate.

8 There are sixty queens
and eighty concubines
(and countless girls).
9 My dove is my only one,
perfect and mine.
She is the darling of her mother,
the favourite of the one who bore her.
Girls have seen her and proclaimed her blessed,
queens and concubines have sung her praises,
10 'Who is this arising like the dawn,
fair as the moon,
resplendent as the sun,
formidable as an army?'

11 I went down to the nut orchard
to see the fresh shoots in the valley,
to see if the vines were budding
and the pomegranate trees in flower.
12 Before I knew . . . my desire had hurled me
onto the chariots of Amminadib! *c*

b 6 Early capital of the northern kingdom. The name means 'agreeable, pleasant'. *c* 6 Perhaps a mythical figure who rides around on a chariot interfering in love-affairs.

NEW REVISED STANDARD VERSION	REVISED ENGLISH BIBLE

	Companions
13 *l* Return, return, O Shulammite!	13 Come back, O Shulammite, come back;
Return, return, that we may look upon you.	come back, that we may gaze on you.
	Bridegroom
Why should you look upon the Shulammite,	How you love to gaze on the Shulammite,
as upon a dance before two armies?*m*	as she moves between the lines of dancers!

7 How graceful are your feet in sandals,
　　O queenly maiden!
Your rounded thighs are like jewels,
　　the work of a master hand.
2 Your navel is a rounded bowl
　　that never lacks mixed wine.
Your belly is a heap of wheat,
　　encircled with lilies.
3 Your two breasts are like two fawns,
　　twins of a gazelle.
4 Your neck is like an ivory tower.
Your eyes are pools in Heshbon,
　　by the gate of Bath-rabbim.
Your nose is like a tower of Lebanon,
　　overlooking Damascus.
5 Your head crowns you like Carmel,
　　and your flowing locks are like purple;
　　a king is held captive in the tresses.*n*

6 How fair and pleasant you are,
　　O loved one, delectable maiden!*o*
7 You are stately*p* as a palm tree,
　　and your breasts are like its clusters.
8 I say I will climb the palm tree
　　and lay hold of its branches.
Oh, may your breasts be like clusters of the vine,
　　and the scent of your breath like apples,
9 and your kisses*q* like the best wine
　　that goes down*r* smoothly,
　　gliding over lips and teeth.*s*

10 I am my beloved's,
　　and his desire is for me.
11 Come, my beloved,
　　let us go forth into the fields,
　　and lodge in the villages;
12 let us go out early to the vineyards,
　　and see whether the vines have budded,
whether the grape blossoms have opened
　　and the pomegranates are in bloom.
There I will give you my love.
13 The mandrakes give forth fragrance,
　　and over our doors are all choice fruits,
new as well as old,
　　which I have laid up for you, O my beloved.

8 O that you were like a brother to me,
　　who nursed at my mother's breast!
If I met you outside, I would kiss you,
　　and no one would despise me.

7 How beautiful are your sandalled feet, O prince's
　　daughter!
The curves of your thighs are like ornaments
　　devised by a skilled craftsman.
2 Your navel is a rounded goblet
　　that will never lack spiced wine.
Your belly is a heap of wheat
　　encircled by lilies.
3 Your two breasts are like two fawns,
　　twin fawns of a gazelle.
4 Your neck is like a tower of ivory.
Your eyes are the pools in Heshbon,
　　beside the gate of the crowded city.
Your nose is like towering Lebanon
　　that looks towards Damascus.
5 You carry your head like Carmel;
　　your flowing locks are lustrous black,
　　tresses braided with ribbons.
6 How beautiful, how entrancing you are,
　　my loved one, daughter of delights!
7 You are stately as a palm tree,
　　and your breasts are like clusters of fruit.
8 I said, 'Let me climb up into the palm
　　to grasp its fronds.'
May I find your breasts like clusters of grapes on
　　the vine,
　　your breath sweet-scented like apples,
9 Your mouth like fragrant wine
　　flowing smoothly to meet my caresses,
　　gliding over my lips and teeth.

Bride
10 I am my beloved's, his longing is all for me.
11 Come, my beloved, let us go out into the fields
　　to lie among the henna bushes;
12 let us go early to the vineyards
　　and see if the vine has budded or its blossom
　　opened,
　　or if the pomegranates are in flower.
There I shall give you my love,
13 when the mandrakes yield their perfume,
　　and all choice fruits are ready at our door,
fruits new and old
　　which I have in store for you, my love.

8 If only you were to me like a brother
　　nursed at my mother's breast!
Then if I came upon you outside, I could kiss you,
　　and no one would despise me.

---

l Ch 7.1 in Heb　　*m* Or *dance of Mahanaim*　　*n* Meaning of Heb
uncertain　　*o* Syr: Heb *in delights*　　*p* Heb *This your stature is*
q Heb *palate*　　*r* Heb *down for my lover*　　*s* Gk Syr Vg: Heb *lips of*
sleepers

6:13 *In Heb. 7:1.*　　7:9 **mouth:** lit. palate. **over . . . teeth:** so *Gk;
Heb.* lips of sleepers.

NEW AMERICAN BIBLE

7 D Turn, turn, O Shulammite,
  turn, turn, that we may look at you!

B Why would you look at the Shulammite
  as at the dance of the two companies?

D ²How beautiful are your feet in sandals,
  O prince's daughter!
  Your rounded thighs are like jewels,
  the handiwork of an artist.
  ³Your navel is a round bowl
  that should never lack for mixed wine.
  Your body is a heap of wheat
  encircled with lilies.
  ⁴Your breasts are like twin fawns,
  the young of a gazelle.
  ⁵Your neck is like a tower of ivory.
  Your eyes are like the pools in Heshbon
  by the gate of Bath-rabbim.
  Your nose is like the tower on Lebanon
  that looks toward Damascus.
  ⁶Your head rises like Carmel;
  your hair is like draperies of purple;
  a king is held captive in its tresses.

G ⁷How beautiful you are, how pleasing,
  my love, my delight!
  ⁸Your very figure is like a palm tree,
  your breasts are like clusters.
  ⁹I said: I will climb the palm tree,
  I will take hold of its branches.
  Now let your breasts be like clusters of the vine
  and the fragrance of your breath like apples,
  ¹⁰And your mouth like an excellent wine—

B that flows smoothly for my lover,
  spreading over the lips and the teeth.
  ¹¹I belong to my lover
  and for me he yearns.
  ¹²Come, my lover, let us go forth to the fields
  and spend the night among the villages.
  ¹³Let us go early to the vineyards, and see
  if the vines are in bloom,
  If the buds have opened,
  if the pomegranates have blossomed;
  There will I give you my love.
  ¹⁴The mandrakes give forth fragrance,
  and at our doors are all choice fruits;
  Both fresh and mellowed fruits, my lover,
  I have kept in store for you.

8 Oh, that you were my brother,
  nursed at my mother's breasts!
  If I met you out of doors, I would kiss you
  and none would taunt me.

NEW JERUSALEM BIBLE

Chorus:
7 Come back, come back, girl from Shulam,ᵈ
  come back, come back, where we can look
  at you!
  Why are you looking at the girl from Shulam,
  dancing between two lines of dancers?
  Lover:
  ²How beautiful are your feet in their sandals,
  O prince's daughter!
  The curve of your thighs is like the curve of a
  necklace,
  work of a master hand.
  ³Your navel is a bowl well rounded
  with no lack of wine,
  your belly a heap of wheat
  surrounded with lilies.
  ⁴Your two breasts are two fawns,
  twins of a gazelle.
  ⁵Your neck is an ivory tower.
  Your eyes, the pools of Heshbon,
  by the gate of Bath-Rabbim.
  Your nose, the Tower of Lebanon,
  sentinel facing Damascus.
  ⁶Your head is held high like Carmel,
  and its hair is as dark as purple;
  a king is held captive in your tresses.

  ⁷How beautiful you are, how charming,
  my love, my delight!
  ⁸In stature like the palm tree,
  its fruit-clusters your breasts.
  ⁹I have decided, 'I shall climb the palm tree,
  I shall seize its clusters of dates!'
  May your breasts be clusters of grapes,
  your breath sweet-scented as apples,
  ¹⁰and your palate like sweet wine.
  Beloved:
  Flowing down the throat of my love,
  as it runs on the lips of those who sleep.
  ¹¹I belong to my love,
  and his desire is for me.

  ¹²Come, my love,
  let us go to the fields.
  We will spend the night in the villages,
  ¹³and in the early morning we will go to the
  vineyards.
  We will see if the vines are budding,
  if their blossoms are opening,
  if the pomegranate trees are in flower.
  Then I shall give you
  the gift of my love.
  ¹⁴The mandrakes yield their fragrance,
  the most exquisite fruits are at our doors;
  the new as well as the old,
  I have stored them for you, my love.

8 Ah, why are you not my brother,
  nursed at my mother's breast!
  Then if I met you out of doors, I could kiss you
  without people thinking ill of me.

ᵈ**7** Obscure; it may also be a name derived from Solomon, 'she who belongs to Solomon'.

NEW REVISED STANDARD VERSION	REVISED ENGLISH BIBLE

2 I would lead you and bring you
    into the house of my mother,
    and into the chamber of the one who bore
    me.*
I would give you spiced wine to drink,
    the juice of my pomegranates.
3 O that his left hand were under my head,
    and that his right hand embraced me!
4 I adjure you, O daughters of Jerusalem,
    do not stir up or awaken love
    until it is ready!

5 Who is that coming up from the wilderness,
    leaning upon her beloved?

Under the apple tree I awakened you.
There your mother was in labor with you;
    there she who bore you was in labor.

6 Set me as a seal upon your heart,
    as a seal upon your arm;
for love is strong as death,
    passion fierce as the grave.
Its flashes are flashes of fire,
    a raging flame.
7 Many waters cannot quench love,
    neither can floods drown it.
If one offered for love
    all the wealth of his house,
    it would be utterly scorned.

8 We have a little sister,
    and she has no breasts.
What shall we do for our sister,
    on the day when she is spoken for?
9 If she is a wall,
    we will build upon her a battlement of silver;
but if she is a door,
    we will enclose her with boards of cedar.
10 I was a wall,
    and my breasts were like towers;
then I was in his eyes
    as one who brings* peace.
11 Solomon had a vineyard at Baal-hamon;
    he entrusted the vineyard to keepers;
    each one was to bring for its fruit a thousand
        pieces of silver.
12 My vineyard, my very own, is for myself;
    you, O Solomon, may have the thousand,
    and the keepers of the fruit two hundred!

13 O you who dwell in the gardens,
    my companions are listening for your voice;
    let me hear it.

14 Make haste, my beloved,
    and be like a gazelle
or a young stag
    upon the mountains of spices!

---

2 I should lead you to the house of my mother,
    bring you to her who conceived me;
I should give you mulled wine to drink
    and the fresh juice of my pomegranates.
3 His left arm pillows my head, his right arm is
    round me.
          Bridegroom
4 I charge you, maidens of Jerusalem:
Do not rouse or awaken love
until it is ready.
          Companions
5 Who is this coming up from the wilderness
leaning on her beloved?
          Bridegroom
Under the apple tree I roused you.
It was there your mother was in labour with you,
there she who bore you was in labour.

6 Wear me as a seal over your heart,
    as a seal upon your arm;
for love is strong as death,
    passion cruel as the grave;
it blazes up like a blazing fire,
    fiercer than any flame.
7 Many waters cannot quench love,
    no flood can sweep it away;
if someone were to offer for love
    all the wealth in his house,
    it would be laughed to scorn.
          Companions
8 We have a little sister
who as yet has no breasts.
What shall we do with our sister
when she is asked in marriage?
9 If she is a wall,
    we shall build on it a silver parapet;
if she is a door,
    we shall bar it with a plank of cedar-wood.
          Bride
10 I am a wall, and my breasts are like towers;
    so in his eyes I am as one who brings content.
11 Solomon has a vineyard at Baal-hamon;
    he has given his vineyard to others to guard;
each is to bring for its fruit
    a thousand pieces of silver.
12 My vineyard is mine to give;
    keep your thousand pieces, O Solomon;
those who guard the fruit shall have two hundred.
          Bridegroom
13 My bride, you sit in my garden,
    and my friends are listening to your voice.
Let me hear it too.
          Bride
14 Come into the open, my beloved,
    and show yourself like a gazelle or a young stag
on the spice-bearing mountains.

---

*Gk Syr: Heb *my mother; she* (or *you*) *will teach me*   *Or finds*

8:2 **who conceived me:** *prob. rdg based on Gk; Heb.* who taught me.   8:6 **the grave:** *Heb.* Sheol.

2 I would lead you, bring you in
  to the home of my mother.
There you would teach me to give you
  spiced wine to drink, and pomegranate juice.

3 His left hand is under my head
  and his right arm embraces me.
4 I adjure you, daughters of Jerusalem,
  by the gazelles and hinds of the field,
Do not arouse, do not stir up love,
  before its own time.

D 5 Who is this coming up from the desert,
     leaning upon her lover?
G   Under the apple tree I awakened you;
     it was there that your mother conceived you,
     it was there that your parent conceived.

B 6 Set me as a seal on your heart,
     as a seal on your arm;
   For stern as death is love,
     relentless as the nether world is devotion;
     its flames are a blazing fire.
7 Deep waters cannot quench love,
  nor floods sweep it away.
Were one to offer all he owns to purchase love,
  he would be roundly mocked.

8 "Our sister is little
  and she has no breasts as yet.
What shall we do for our sister
  when her courtship begins?
9 If she is a wall,
  we will build upon it a silver parapet;
If she is a door,
  we will reinforce it with a cedar plank."

10 I am a wall,
   and my breasts are like towers.
So now in his eyes I have become
   one to be welcomed.

B 11 Solomon had a vineyard at Baal-hamon;
     he gave over the vineyard to caretakers.
   For its fruit one would have to pay
     a thousand silver pieces.
12 My vineyard is at my own disposal;
   the thousand pieces are for you, O Solomon,
   and two hundred for the caretakers of its fruit.

G 13 O garden-dweller,
     my friends are listening for your voice,
     let me hear it!

B 14 Be swift, my lover,
     like a gazelle or a young stag
     on the mountains of spices!

2 I should lead you, I should take you into my
    mother's house, and you would teach me!
I should give you spiced wine to drink,
  juice of my pomegranates.

3 His left arm is under my head
  and his right embraces me.

  Lover:

4 I charge you,
  daughters of Jerusalem,
do not rouse, do not wake my beloved,
  before she pleases!

5 Who is this coming up from the desert
  leaning on her lover?

I awakened you under the apple tree,
  where your mother conceived you,
  where she who bore you conceived you.

  Beloved:

6 Set me like a seal on your heart,
  like a seal on your arm.
For love is strong as Death,
  passion as relentless as Sheol.
The flash of it is a flash of fire,
  a flame of Yahweh himself.
7 Love no flood can quench,
  no torrents drown.
Were a man to offer all his family wealth
  to buy love,
  contempt is all that he would gain.

8 Our sister is little: her breasts are not yet formed. What
shall we do for our sister on the day she is spoken for? 9 If
she is a rampart, on the crest we shall build a battlement of
silver; if she is a door, we shall board her up with planks of
cedar.

10 I am a wall, and my breasts represent its towers. And
under their eyes I have found true peace.

11 Solomon had a vineyard at Baal-Hamon. He entrusted
it to overseers, and each one was to pay him the value of its
produce, a thousand shekels of silver. 12 But I tend my own
vineyard myself. You, Solomon, may have your thousand
shekels, and those who oversee its produce their two hundred.

13 You who dwell in the gardens, my companions listen
for your voice; let me hear it.

14 Haste away, my love,
  be like a gazelle,
  a young stag,
  on the spice-laden mountains.

Isaiah

1 The vision of Isaiah son of Amoz, which he saw concerning Judah and Jerusalem in the days of Uzziah, Jotham, Ahaz, and Hezekiah, kings of Judah.

2 Hear, O heavens, and listen, O earth;
  for the LORD has spoken:
I reared children and brought them up,
  but they have rebelled against me.
3 The ox knows its owner,
  and the donkey its master's crib;
but Israel does not know,
  my people do not understand.

4 Ah, sinful nation,
  people laden with iniquity,
offspring who do evil,
  children who deal corruptly,
who have forsaken the LORD,
  who have despised the Holy One of Israel,
  who are utterly estranged!

5 Why do you seek further beatings?
  Why do you continue to rebel?
The whole head is sick,
  and the whole heart faint.
6 From the sole of the foot even to the head,
  there is no soundness in it,
but bruises and sores
  and bleeding wounds;
they have not been drained, or bound up,
  or softened with oil.

7 Your country lies desolate,
  your cities are burned with fire;
in your very presence
  aliens devour your land;
  it is desolate, as overthrown by foreigners.
8 And daughter Zion is left
  like a booth in a vineyard,
like a shelter in a cucumber field,
  like a besieged city.
9 If the LORD of hosts
  had not left us a few survivors,
we would have been like Sodom,
  and become like Gomorrah.

10 Hear the word of the LORD,
  you rulers of Sodom!
Listen to the teaching of our God,
  you people of Gomorrah!
11 What to me is the multitude of your sacrifices?
  says the LORD;
I have had enough of burnt offerings of rams
  and the fat of fed beasts;
I do not delight in the blood of bulls,
  or of lambs, or of goats.

12 When you come to appear before me,*a*
  who asked this from your hand?
  Trample my courts no more;

Isaiah

1 THE vision which Isaiah son of Amoz had about Judah and Jerusalem during the reigns of Uzziah, Jotham, Ahaz, and Hezekiah, kings of Judah.

2 Let the heavens and the earth give ear,
  for it is the LORD who speaks:
I reared children and brought them up,
  but they have rebelled against me.
3 An ox knows its owner
  and a donkey its master's stall;
but Israel lacks all knowledge,
  my people has no discernment.
4 You sinful nation, a people weighed down with
    iniquity,
  a race of evildoers, children whose lives are
    depraved,
who have deserted the LORD,
  spurned the Holy One of Israel,
  and turned your backs on him!
5 Why do you invite more punishment,
  why persist in your defection?
Your head is all covered with sores,
  your whole body is bruised;
6 from head to foot there is not a sound spot in
    you—
nothing but weals and welts and raw wounds
which have not felt compress or bandage
  or the soothing touch of oil.
7 Your country is desolate, your cities burnt down.
  Before your eyes strangers devour your land;
  it is as desolate as Sodom after its overthrow.
8 Only Zion is left,
  like a watchman's shelter in a vineyard,
like a hut in a plot of cucumbers,
  like a beleaguered city.
9 Had the LORD of Hosts not left us a few survivors,
  we should have become like Sodom,
  no better than Gomorrah.
10 Listen to the word of the LORD, you rulers of
    Sodom;
  give ear to the teaching of our God, you people of
    Gomorrah:
11 Your countless sacrifices, what are they to me?
  says the LORD.
I am sated with whole-offerings of rams
  and the fat of well-fed cattle;
I have no desire for the blood of bulls,
  of sheep, and of he-goats,
12 when you come into my presence.
  Who has asked you for all this?
  No more shall you tread my courts.

---

a Or *see my face*

1:7 **Sodom:** *prob. rdg; Heb.* strangers.

THE BOOK OF
Isaiah

1 The vision which Isaiah, son of Amoz, had concerning Judah and Jerusalem in the days of Uzziah, Jotham, Ahaz and Hezekiah, kings of Judah.

2 Hear, O heavens, and listen, O earth,
for the Lord speaks:
Sons have I raised and reared,
but they have disowned me!
3 An ox knows its owner,
and an ass, its master's manger;
But Israel does not know,
my people has not understood.
4 Ah! sinful nation, people laden with wickedness,
evil race, corrupt children!
They have forsaken the Lord,
spurned the Holy One of Israel,
apostatized.
5 Where would you yet be struck,
you that rebel again and again?
The whole head is sick,
the whole heart faint.
6 From the sole of the foot to the head
there is no sound spot:
Wound and welt and gaping gash,
not drained, or bandaged,
or eased with salve.
7 Your country is waste,
your cities burnt with fire;
Your land before your eyes
strangers devour
[a waste, like Sodom overthrown]—
8 And daughter Zion is left
like a hut in a vineyard,
Like a shed in a melon patch,
like a city blockaded.

9 Unless the Lord of hosts
had left us a scanty remnant,
We had become as Sodom,
we should be like Gomorrah.
10 Hear the word of the Lord,
princes of Sodom!
Listen to the instruction of our God,
people of Gomorrah!
11 What care I for the number of your sacrifices?
says the Lord.
I have had enough of whole-burnt rams
and fat of fatlings;
In the blood of calves, lambs and goats
I find no pleasure.

12 When you come in to visit me,
who asks these things of you?

Isaiah

1 The vision of Isaiah son of Amoz concerning Judah and Jerusalem, which he received in the reigns of Uzziah, Jotham, Ahaz and Hezekiah kings of Judah.

2 Listen, you heavens; earth, attend, for Yahweh is
speaking,
'I have reared children and brought them up,
but they have rebelled against me.
3 The ox knows its owner and the donkey its
master's crib;
Israel does not know, my people do not
understand.'
4 Disaster, sinful nation, people weighed down with
guilt,
race of wrong-doers, perverted children!
They have abandoned Yahweh, despised the Holy
One of Israel,
they have turned away from him.
5 Where shall I strike you next, if you persist in
treason?
The whole head is sick, the whole heart is
diseased,
6 from the sole of the foot to the head there is
nothing healthy:
only wounds, bruises and open sores
not dressed, not bandaged, not soothed with
ointment,
7 your country a desolation, your towns burnt down,
your soil, foreigners lay it waste before your eyes,
a desolation like devastation by foreigners.
8 The daughter of Zion is left like a shanty in a
vineyard,
like a shed in a cucumber field, like a city
besieged.

9 Had Yahweh Sabaoth not left us a few survivors,
we should be like Sodom, we should be the same
as Gomorrah.

10 Hear what Yahweh says, you rulers of Sodom;
listen to what our God teaches, you people of
Gomorrah.

11 'What are your endless sacrifices to me?' says
Yahweh.
'I am sick of burnt offerings of rams
and the fat of calves.
I take no pleasure in the blood
of bulls and lambs and goats.
12 When you come and present yourselves before me,
who has asked you to trample through my courts?

13 bringing offerings is futile;
        incense is an abomination to me.
    New moon and sabbath and calling of
        convocation—
        I cannot endure solemn assemblies with
            iniquity.
14 Your new moons and your appointed festivals
        my soul hates;
    they have become a burden to me,
        I am weary of bearing them.
15 When you stretch out your hands,
        I will hide my eyes from you;
    even though you make many prayers,
        I will not listen;
        your hands are full of blood.
16 Wash yourselves; make yourselves clean;
        remove the evil of your doings
        from before my eyes;
    cease to do evil,
17   learn to do good;
    seek justice,
        rescue the oppressed,
    defend the orphan,
        plead for the widow.

18 Come now, let us argue it out,
        says the Lord:
    though your sins are like scarlet,
        they shall be like snow;
    though they are red like crimson,
        they shall become like wool.
19 If you are willing and obedient,
        you shall eat the good of the land;
20 but if you refuse and rebel,
        you shall be devoured by the sword;
        for the mouth of the Lord has spoken.

21 How the faithful city
        has become a whore!
    She that was full of justice,
    righteousness lodged in her—
        but now murderers!
22 Your silver has become dross,
        your wine is mixed with water.
23 Your princes are rebels
        and companions of thieves.
    Everyone loves a bribe
        and runs after gifts.
    They do not defend the orphan,
        and the widow's cause does not come before
            them.
24 Therefore says the Sovereign, the Lord of hosts,
        the Mighty One of Israel:
    Ah, I will pour out my wrath on my enemies,
        and avenge myself on my foes!
25 I will turn my hand against you;
        I will smelt away your dross as with lye
        and remove all your alloy.
26 And I will restore your judges as at the first,
        and your counselors as at the beginning.
    Afterward you shall be called the city of
        righteousness,
        the faithful city.

27 Zion shall be redeemed by justice,
        and those in her who repent, by righteousness.
28 But rebels and sinners shall be destroyed
        together,
        and those who forsake the Lord shall be
            consumed.

13 To bring me offerings is futile;
        the reek of sacrifice is abhorrent to me.
    New moons and sabbaths and sacred assemblies—
        such idolatrous ceremonies I cannot endure.
14 I loathe your new moons and your festivals;
        they have become a burden to me,
        and I can tolerate them no longer.
15 When you hold out your hands in prayer,
        I shall turn away my eyes.
    Though you offer countless prayers,
        I shall not listen;
        there is blood on your hands.
16 Wash and be clean;
        put away your evil deeds
        far from my sight;
    cease to do evil, 17 learn to do good.
    Pursue justice, guide the oppressed;
    uphold the rights of the fatherless,
        and plead the widow's cause.

18 Now come, let us argue this out,
        says the Lord.
    Though your sins are scarlet,
        they may yet be white as snow;
    though they are dyed crimson,
        they may become white as wool.
19 If you are willing to obey,
        you will eat the best that earth yields;
20 but if you refuse and rebel,
        the sword will devour you.
    The Lord himself has spoken.

21 How the faithful city has played the whore!
    Once the home of justice where righteousness
        dwelt,
    she is now inhabited by murderers.
22 Your silver has turned to dross
        and your fine liquor is diluted with water.
23 Your rulers are rebels, associates of thieves;
        every one of them loves a bribe
        and chases after gifts;
    they deny the fatherless their rights,
        and the widow's cause is never heard.

24 This therefore is the word of the Lord, the Lord of Hosts,
    the Mighty One of Israel:

    Alas for you! I shall secure a respite from my foes
        and wreak vengeance on my enemies.
25 Once again I shall act against you
        to refine away your dross as if with potash
        and purge all your impurities.
26 I shall make your judges what once they were
        and your counsellors like those of old.
    Then you will be called
        Home of Righteousness, the Faithful City.
27 Zion will be redeemed by justice
        and her returning people by righteousness.
28 Rebels and sinners alike will be broken
        and those who forsake the Lord will cease to be.

1:24 **Alas for you:** *prob. rdg; Heb.* Alas.

NEW AMERICAN BIBLE

NEW JERUSALEM BIBLE

13 Trample my courts no more!
  Bring no more worthless offerings;
    your incense is loathsome to me.
  New moon and sabbath, calling of assemblies,
    octaves with wickedness: these I cannot bear.
14 Your new moons and festivals I detest;
    they weigh me down, I tire of the load.
15 When you spread out your hands,
    I close my eyes to you;
  Though you pray the more,
    I will not listen.
  Your hands are full of blood!
16   Wash yourselves clean!
  Put away your misdeeds from before my eyes;
    cease doing evil; 17 learn to do good.
  Make justice your aim: redress the wronged,
    hear the orphan's plea, defend the widow.

18 Come now, let us set things right,
    says the LORD:
  Though your sins be like scarlet,
    they may become white as snow;
  Though they be crimson red,
    they may become white as wool.
19 If you are willing, and obey,
    you shall eat the good things of the land;
20 But if you refuse and resist,
    the sword shall consume you:
  for the mouth of the LORD has spoken!

21 How has she turned adulteress,
    the faithful city, so upright!
  Justice used to lodge within her,
    but now, murderers.
22 Your silver is turned to dross,
    your wine is mixed with water.
23 Your princes are rebels
    and comrades of thieves;
  Each one of them loves a bribe
    and looks for gifts.
  The fatherless they defend not,
    and the widow's plea does not reach them.
24 Now, therefore, says the Lord,
    the LORD of hosts, the Mighty One of Israel:
  Ah! I will take vengeance on my foes
    and fully repay my enemies!
25 I will turn my hand against you,
    and refine your dross in the furnace,
    removing all your alloy.
26 I will restore your judges as at first,
    and your counselors as in the beginning;
  After that you shall be called
    city of justice, faithful city.
27 Zion shall be redeemed by judgment,
    and her repentant ones by justice.
28 Rebels and sinners alike shall be crushed,
    those who desert the LORD shall be consumed.

13 Bring no more futile cereal offerings,
    the smoke from them fills me with disgust.
  New Moons, Sabbaths, assemblies — I cannot
    endure solemnity combined with guilt.
14 Your New Moons and your meetings I utterly
    detest;
  to me they are a burden I am tired of bearing.
15 When you stretch out your hands I turn my eyes
    away.
  You may multiply your prayers, I shall not be
    listening.
  Your hands are covered in blood,
16 wash, make yourselves clean.
  Take your wrong-doing out of my sight.
  Cease doing evil. 17 Learn to do good,
  search for justice, discipline the violent,
  be just to the orphan, plead for the widow.

18 'Come, let us talk this over,' says Yahweh.
  'Though your sins are like scarlet,
    they shall be white as snow;
  though they are red as crimson, they shall be like
    wool.
19 If you are willing to obey, you shall eat the good
    things of the earth.
20 But if you refuse and rebel, the sword shall eat
    you instead —
  for Yahweh's mouth has spoken.'

21 The faithful city,
  what a harlot*a* she has become!
  Zion, once full of fair judgement,
  where saving justice used to dwell,
  but now assassins!
22 Your silver has turned into dross,
  your wine is watered.
23 Your princes are rebels,
  accomplices of brigands.

  All of them greedy for presents
  and eager for bribes,
  they show no justice to the orphan,
  and the widow's cause never reaches them.

24 Hence, the Lord Yahweh Sabaoth,
  the Mighty One of Israel, says this,
  'Disaster, I shall get the better of my enemies,
  I shall avenge myself on my foes.

25 'I shall turn my hand against you,
  I shall purge your dross as though with potash,
  I shall remove all your alloy.

26 'And I shall restore your judges as at first,
  your counsellors as in bygone days,
  after which you will be called City of Saving
    Justice,
  Faithful City.'

27 Zion will be redeemed by fair judgement,
  and those who return, by saving justice.
28 Rebels and sinners alike will be destroyed,
  and those who abandon Yahweh will perish.

a 1 Prostitution is a frequent figure for unfaithfulness to Yahweh.

NEW REVISED STANDARD VERSION

REVISED ENGLISH BIBLE

29 For you shall be ashamed of the oaks
    in which you delighted;
and you shall blush for the gardens
    that you have chosen.
30 For you shall be like an oak
    whose leaf withers,
    and like a garden without water.
31 The strong shall become like tinder,
    and their work*b* like a spark;
they and their work shall burn together,
    with no one to quench them.

29 The sacred oaks in which you delighted
    will play you false,
    the garden-shrines of your fancy will fail you.
30 You will be like a terebinth with withered leaves,
    like a garden without water.
31 The strongest tree will flare up like tow,
    and what is made from it will go up in sparks;
    both will burn together
    with no one to quench the flames.

2 The word that Isaiah son of Amoz saw concerning Judah and Jerusalem.

2 In days to come
the mountain of the LORD's house
shall be established as the highest of the
    mountains,
    and shall be raised above the hills;
all the nations shall stream to it.
3   Many peoples shall come and say,
"Come, let us go up to the mountain of the
    LORD,
    to the house of the God of Jacob;
that he may teach us his ways
    and that we may walk in his paths."
For out of Zion shall go forth instruction,
    and the word of the LORD from Jerusalem.
4 He shall judge between the nations,
    and shall arbitrate for many peoples;
they shall beat their swords into plowshares,
    and their spears into pruning hooks;
nation shall not lift up sword against nation,
    neither shall they learn war any more.

5 O house of Jacob,
    come, let us walk
    in the light of the LORD!
6 For you have forsaken the ways of*c* your people,
    O house of Jacob.
Indeed they are full of diviners*d* from the east
    and of soothsayers like the Philistines,
    and they clasp hands with foreigners.
7 Their land is filled with silver and gold,
    and there is no end to their treasures;
their land is filled with horses,
    and there is no end to their chariots.
8 Their land is filled with idols;
    they bow down to the work of their hands,
    to what their own fingers have made.
9 And so people are humbled,
    and everyone is brought low—
    do not forgive them!
10 Enter into the rock,
    and hide in the dust
from the terror of the LORD,
    and from the glory of his majesty.
11 The haughty eyes of people shall be brought low,
    and the pride of everyone shall be humbled;
and the LORD alone will be exalted
    in that day.
12 For the LORD of hosts has a day
    against all that is proud and lofty,
    against all that is lifted up and high;*e*
13 against all the cedars of Lebanon,
    lofty and lifted up;
    and against all the oaks of Bashan;

2 This is the message which Isaiah son of Amoz received in a vision about Judah and Jerusalem.

2 In days to come
the mountain of the LORD's house
will be set over all other mountains,
raised high above the hills.
All the nations will stream towards it,
3 and many peoples will go and say,
'Let us go up to the mountain of the LORD,
to the house of the God of Jacob,
that he may teach us his ways
and that we may walk in his paths.'
For instruction comes from Zion,
and the word of the LORD from Jerusalem.
4 He will judge between the nations
as arbiter among many peoples.
They will beat their swords into mattocks
and their spears into pruning-knives;
nation will not lift sword against nation
nor ever again be trained for war.
5 Come, people of Jacob,
let us walk in the light of the LORD.

6 You have abandoned your people, the house of
    Jacob.
Their towns are filled with traders from the east,
and with soothsayers speaking like Philistines;
the children of foreigners are everywhere.
7 Their land is full of silver and gold,
and there is no end to their treasures;
their land is full of horses,
and there is no end to their chariots.
8 Their land is full of idols,
and they bow down to their own handiwork,
to objects their fingers have fashioned.
9 Mankind will be brought low,
everyone will be humbled.
10 Get among the rocks and hide in the ground
from the dread presence of the LORD
and the splendour of his majesty.
11 Haughty looks will be cast down,
loftiness brought low;
the LORD alone will be exalted
on that day.
12 The LORD of Hosts has a day of doom in store
for all that is proud and lofty,
for all that is high and lifted up,
13 for all the cedars of Lebanon, lofty and high,
and all the oaks of Bashan,

---

b Or *its makers*   *c* Heb lacks *the ways of*   *d* Cn: Heb lacks *of*
diviners   *e* Cn Compare Gk: Heb *low*

1:29 **play you false:** *so some MSS; others* play them false.
2:9 **humbled:** *so Scroll; Heb. adds* and do not forgive them.
2:12 **high:** *cp. Gk; Heb.* low.

NEW AMERICAN BIBLE

29 You shall be ashamed of the terebinths which
   you prized,
   and blush for the groves which you chose.
30 You shall become like a tree with falling leaves,
   like a garden that has no water.
31 The strong man shall turn to tow,
   and his work shall become a spark;
   Both shall burn together,
   and there shall be none to quench the flames.

2 This is what Isaiah, son of Amoz, saw concerning
   Judah and Jerusalem.

2   In days to come,
   The mountain of the LORD's house
   shall be established as the highest mountain
   and raised above the hills.
   All nations shall stream toward it;
3   many peoples shall come and say:
   "Come, let us climb the LORD's mountain,
   to the house of the God of Jacob,
   That he may instruct us in his ways,
   and we may walk in his paths."
   For from Zion shall go forth instruction,
   and the word of the LORD from Jerusalem.
4 He shall judge between the nations,
   and impose terms on many peoples.
   They shall beat their swords into plowshares
   and their spears into pruning hooks;
   One nation shall not raise the sword
      against another,
   nor shall they train for war again.

5 O house of Jacob, come,
   let us walk in the light of the LORD!
6 You have abandoned your people,
   the house of Jacob,
   Because they are filled with fortunetellers
   and soothsayers, like the Philistines;
   they covenant with strangers.
7 Their land is full of silver and gold,
   and there is no end to their treasures;
   Their land is full of horses,
   and there is no end to their chariots.
8 Their land is full of idols;
   they worship the works of their hands,
   that which their fingers have made.

9 But man is abased,
   each one brought low.
   [Do not pardon them!]
10 Get behind the rocks,
   hide in the dust,
   From the terror of the LORD
   and the splendor of his majesty!
11 The haughty eyes of man will be lowered,
   the arrogance of men will be abased,
   and the LORD alone will be exalted, on that day.
12 For the LORD of hosts will have his day
   against all that is proud and arrogant,
   all that is high, and it will be brought low;
13 Yes, against all the cedars of Lebanon
   and all the oaks of Bashan,

NEW JERUSALEM BIBLE

29 How ashamed you will be of the terebinths
   which gave you such delight;
   and how you will blush for the gardens which you
   chose!
30 For you will be like a terebinth with faded leaves,
   like a garden without water;
31 the strong will become like tinder, his work like
   the spark;
   both will go up in flames together,
   with no one to put them out.

2 The vision of Isaiah son of Amoz, concerning Judah
   and Jerusalem.

2 It will happen in the final days
   that the mountain of Yahweh's house
   will rise higher than the mountains
   and tower above the heights.
   Then all the nations will stream to it,
3 many peoples will come to it and say,
   'Come, let us go up to the mountain of Yahweh,
   to the house of the God of Jacob
   that he may teach us his ways
   so that we may walk in his paths.'
   For the Law will issue from Zion
   and the word of Yahweh from Jerusalem.
4 Then he will judge between the nations
   and arbitrate between many peoples.
   They will hammer their swords into ploughshares
   and their spears into sickles.
   Nation will not lift sword against nation,
   no longer will they learn how to make war. b

5 House of Jacob, come, let us walk in Yahweh's
   light.
6 You have rejected your people, the House of
   Jacob,
   for it has long been full of sorcerers
   like the Philistines,
   and is overrun with foreigners.
7 The country is full of silver and gold and treasures
   unlimited,
   the country is full of horses, its chariots are
   unlimited,
8 the country is full of idols.
   They bow down before the work of their hands,
   before what their own fingers have made.

9 Human nature has been humbled, humankind
   brought low:
   do not raise them again!
10 Go into the rock, hide in the dust,
   in terror of Yahweh, at the brilliance of his
   majesty,
   when he arises to make the earth quake.
11 Human pride will lower its eyes,
   human arrogance will be humbled,
   and Yahweh alone will be exalted, on that day.
12 That will be a day for Yahweh Sabaoth,
   for all who are majestic and haughty,
   for all who are proud, to be brought low,
13 for all the cedars of Lebanon, high and proud,
   and for all the oaks of Bashan;

b 2 // Mi 4:1–3.

NEW REVISED STANDARD VERSION	REVISED ENGLISH BIBLE

NEW REVISED STANDARD VERSION

14 against all the high mountains,
  and against all the lofty hills;
15 against every high tower,
  and against every fortified wall;
16 against all the ships of Tarshish,
  and against all the beautiful craft. *f*
17 The haughtiness of people shall be humbled,
  and the pride of everyone shall be brought low;
  and the LORD alone will be exalted on that
    day.
18 The idols shall utterly pass away.
19 Enter the caves of the rocks
  and the holes of the ground,
from the terror of the LORD,
  and from the glory of his majesty,
  when he rises to terrify the earth.
20 On that day people will throw away
  to the moles and to the bats
their idols of silver and their idols of gold,
  which they made for themselves to worship,
21 to enter the caverns of the rocks
  and the clefts in the crags,
from the terror of the LORD,
  and from the glory of his majesty,
  when he rises to terrify the earth.
22 Turn away from mortals,
  who have only breath in their nostrils,
  for of what account are they?

3 For now the Sovereign, the LORD of hosts,
  is taking away from Jerusalem and from Judah
support and staff—
  all support of bread,
  and all support of water—
2 warrior and soldier,
  judge and prophet,
  diviner and elder,
3 captain of fifty
  and dignitary,
  counselor and skillful magician
  and expert enchanter.
4 And I will make boys their princes,
  and babes shall rule over them.
5 The people will be oppressed,
  everyone by another
  and everyone by a neighbor;
the youth will be insolent to the elder,
  and the base to the honorable.
6 Someone will even seize a relative,
  a member of the clan, saying,
"You have a cloak;
  you shall be our leader,
and this heap of ruins
  shall be under your rule."
7 But the other will cry out on that day, saying,
"I will not be a healer;
  in my house there is neither bread nor cloak;
you shall not make me
  leader of the people."
8 For Jerusalem has stumbled
  and Judah has fallen,
because their speech and their deeds are against
  the LORD,
  defying his glorious presence.

REVISED ENGLISH BIBLE

14 for all lofty mountains and all high hills,
15 for every tall tower and every towering wall,
16 for all ships of Tarshish and all stately vessels.
17 Then will pride be brought low
  and loftiness humbled;
  the LORD alone will be exalted
  on that day.
18 The idols will utterly pass away.
19 Creep into caves in the rocks
  and openings in the ground
  from the dread presence of the LORD
  and the splendour of his majesty,
  when he arises to strike the world with terror.
20 On that day people will fling away
  the idols of silver and gold
  which they have made and worship,
  fling them to the dung-beetles and bats.
21 They themselves will creep into crevices in rocks
  and crannies in cliffs
  from the dread presence of the LORD
  and the splendour of his majesty,
  when he arises to strike the world with terror.
22 Do not rely on mere mortals. What are they worth?
  No more than the breath in their nostrils.

3 The Lord, the LORD of Hosts,
  is about to strip Jerusalem and Judah
  of every prop and stay,
2 warriors and soldiers,
  judges, prophets, diviners, and elders,
3 captains of companies and men of good standing,
  counsellors, skilled magicians, and expert
    enchanters.
4 I shall appoint youths to positions of authority,
  and they will govern as the whim takes them.
5 The people will deal oppressively with one
    another,
  everyone oppressing his neighbour;
  the young will be arrogant towards their elders,
  mere nobodies towards men of rank.
6 A man will take hold of his brother in his father's
    house,
  saying, 'You have a cloak, you shall be our chief;
  our stricken family shall be in your charge.'
7 But the brother will at once reply,
  'I cannot heal society's wounds
  when in my house there is neither bread nor cloak.
  You shall not put me in authority over the people.'

8 Jerusalem is brought low,
  Judah has come to grief,
  for in word and deed they defied the LORD,
  in open rebellion against his glory.

---

f Compare Gk: Meaning of Heb uncertain

3:1 **prop and stay:** *prob. rdg; Heb. adds* all stay of bread and all
stay of water.

NEW AMERICAN BIBLE	NEW JERUSALEM BIBLE

NEW AMERICAN BIBLE

14 Against all the lofty mountains
  and all the high hills,
15 Against every lofty tower
  and every fortified wall,
16 Against all the ships of Tarshish
  and all stately vessels.
17 Human pride will be abased,
  the arrogance of men brought low,
  And the LORD alone will be exalted, on that day.

18   The idols will perish forever.

19 Men will go into caves in the rocks
  and into holes in the earth,
  From the terror of the LORD
  and the splendor of his majesty,
  when he arises to overawe the earth.

20 On that day men will throw to the moles and the bats
the idols of silver and gold which they made for worship.

21 They go into caverns in the rocks
  and into crevices in the cliffs,
  From the terror of the LORD
  and the splendor of his majesty,
  when he arises to overawe the earth.

22 As for you, let man alone,
  in whose nostrils is but a breath;
  for what is he worth?

3 The Lord, the LORD of hosts,
  shall take away from Jerusalem and from Judah
  support and prop [all supplies of bread
    and water]:
2 Hero and warrior,
  judge and prophet, fortuneteller and elder,
3 The captain of fifty and the nobleman,
  counselor, skilled magician, and expert charmer.
4 I will make striplings their princes;
  the fickle shall govern them,
5 And the people shall oppress one another,
  yes, every man his neighbor.
  The child shall be bold toward the elder,
  and the base toward the honorable.
6 When a man seizes his brother
  in his father's house, saying,
  "You have clothes! Be our ruler,
  and take in hand this ruin!" —
7   Then shall he answer in that day:
  "I will not undertake to cure this,
  when in my own house there is no bread
    or clothing!
  You shall not make me ruler of the people."

8 Jerusalem is crumbling, Judah is falling;
  for their speech and their deeds are before
    the LORD,
  a provocation in the sight of his majesty.

NEW JERUSALEM BIBLE

14 for all the high mountains
  and for all the proud hills;
15 for every lofty tower
  and for every towering wall;
16 for all the ships of Tarshish
  and for everything held precious.

17 Human pride will be humbled,
  human arrogance brought low,
  and Yahweh alone will be exalted, on that day.

18 When the idols all disappear,
19 they will go into the caverns of the rocks
  and into the fissures of the earth
  in terror of Yahweh, at the brilliance of his
    majesty,
  when he arises to make the earth quake.

20 That day, people will fling to moles and bats the silver
idols and golden idols which have been made for them to
worship,

21 and go into the crevices of the rocks
  and the clefts in the cliffs,
  in terror of Yahweh, at the brilliance of his
    majesty,
  when he arises to make the earth quake.

22 Have no more to do with humankind,
  which has only the breath in its nostrils.
  How much is this worth?

3 Now the Lord Yahweh Sabaoth
  is about to deprive Jerusalem and Judah
  of resources and provisions —
  all reserves of food, all reserves of water —
2 of hero, warrior, judge, prophet,
  diviner, elder, 3 captain, dignitary,
  counsellor, architect, soothsayer.
4 'I shall give them boys for princes,
  raw lads to rule over them.'
5 People will be ill-treated by one another,
  each by his neighbour;
  the young will insult the aged,
  and the low, the respected.
6 Yes, a man will catch hold of his brother
  in their father's house, to say,
  'You have a cloak, so you be leader,
  and rule this heap of ruins.'
7 And, that day, the other will protest,
  'I am no healer;
  in my house there is neither food nor clothing;
  do not make me leader of the people.'
8 For Jerusalem has collapsed
  and Judah has fallen,
  because their words and deeds affront Yahweh
  and insult his glorious gaze.

9 The look on their faces bears witness against
  them;
  they proclaim their sin like Sodom,
  they do not hide it.
  Woe to them!
  For they have brought evil on themselves.
10 Tell the innocent how fortunate they are,
  for they shall eat the fruit of their labors.
11 Woe to the guilty! How unfortunate they are,
  for what their hands have done shall be done to
  them.
12 My people—children are their oppressors,
  and women rule over them.
  O my people, your leaders mislead you,
  and confuse the course of your paths.

13 The LORD rises to argue his case;
  he stands to judge the peoples.
14 The LORD enters into judgment
  with the elders and princes of his people:
  It is you who have devoured the vineyard;
  the spoil of the poor is in your houses.
15 What do you mean by crushing my people,
  by grinding the face of the poor? says the Lord
  GOD of hosts.

16 The LORD said:
  Because the daughters of Zion are haughty
  and walk with outstretched necks,
  glancing wantonly with their eyes,
  mincing along as they go,
  tinkling with their feet;
17 the Lord will afflict with scabs
  the heads of the daughters of Zion,
  and the LORD will lay bare their secret parts.

18 In that day the Lord will take away the finery of the
anklets, the headbands, and the crescents; 19 the pendants,
the bracelets, and the scarfs; 20 the headdresses, the armlets,
the sashes, the perfume boxes, and the amulets; 21 the signet
rings and nose rings; 22 the festal robes, the mantles, the
cloaks, and the handbags; 23 the garments of gauze, the
linen garments, the turbans, and the veils.
24 Instead of perfume there will be a stench;
  and instead of a sash, a rope;
  and instead of well-set hair, baldness;
  and instead of a rich robe, a binding of
  sackcloth;
  instead of beauty, shame.*g*
25 Your men shall fall by the sword
  and your warriors in battle.
26 And her gates shall lament and mourn;
  ravaged, she shall sit upon the ground.

4 Seven women shall take hold of one man in that day,
saying,
  "We will eat our own bread and wear our own
  clothes;
  just let us be called by your name;
  take away our disgrace."

2 On that day the branch of the LORD shall be beautiful
and glorious, and the fruit of the land shall be the pride and
glory of the survivors of Israel. 3 Whoever is left in Zion and
remains in Jerusalem will be called holy, everyone who has
been recorded for life in Jerusalem, 4 once the Lord has

9 The look on their faces testifies against them;
  like Sodom they proclaim their sins,
  parading them openly.
  Woe betide them! They have earned the disaster
  that strikes them.
10 Happy the righteous! All goes well with them;
  they enjoy the fruit of their actions.
11 Woe betide the wicked! All goes ill with them;
  they reap the reward they have earned.
12 Moneylenders strip my people bare,
  and usurers lord it over them.
  My people, those who guide you are leading you
  astray
  and putting you on the path to ruin.

13 The LORD comes forward to argue his case,
  standing up to judge his people.
14 The LORD opens the indictment
  against the elders and officers of his people:
  It is you that have ravaged the vineyard;
  in your houses are the spoils taken from the poor.
15 Is it nothing to you that you crush my people
  and grind the faces of the poor?
  This is the word of the LORD of Hosts.

16 The LORD said:
  Because the women of Zion give themselves airs,
  with heads held haughtily, with wanton glances,
  as they move with mincing gait
  and jingling feet,
17 the Lord will smite with baldness the women of
  Zion,
  the LORD will make bare their foreheads.

18 On that day the Lord will take away their finery: anklets,
discs, crescents, 19 pendants, bracelets, coronets, 20 headbands, armlets, necklaces, lockets, charms, 21 signet rings,
nose-rings, 22 fine dresses, mantles, cloaks, flounced skirts,
23 scarves of gauze, kerchiefs of linen, turbans, and flowing
veils.

24 Instead of perfume there will be the stench of
  decay;
  there will be a rope instead of a girdle,
  baldness instead of hair elegantly coiled,
  a loincloth of sacking instead of a fine robe,
  the mark of branding instead of beauty.
25 Zion, your men will fall by the sword,
  your warriors in battle.
26 Zion's gates will mourn and lament,
  and, stripped bare, she will sit on the ground.

4 On that day seven women will take hold of one man
and say, 'We shall provide our own food and clothing
if only we may bear your name. Take away our disgrace!'
2 On that day the plant that the LORD has grown will
become glorious in its beauty, and the fruit of the land will
be the pride and splendour of the survivors of Israel.
3 Then those who are left in Zion, who remain in Jerusalem, every one whose survival in Jerusalem was decreed
will be called holy. 4 When the Lord washes away the filth

3:10 **Happy:** *prob. rdg; Heb.* Say.   3:13 **his people:** *so Gk; Heb.*
peoples.   3:15 **word . . . LORD:** *prob. rdg, cp. Scroll; Heb.* word
of the Lord, the LORD.

g Q Ms: MT lacks *shame*

NEW AMERICAN BIBLE

9 Their very look bears witness against them;
  their sin like Sodom they vaunt,
They hide it not. Woe to them!
  they deal out evil to themselves.
10 Happy the just, for it will be well with them,
  the fruit of their works they will eat.
11 Woe to the wicked man! All goes ill,
  with the work of his hands he will be repaid.
12 My people — a babe in arms will be their tyrant,
  and women will rule them!
  O my people, your leaders mislead,
  they destroy the paths you should follow.

13 The LORD rises to accuse,
  standing to try his people.
14 The Lord enters into judgment
  with his people's elders and princes:
  It is you who have devoured the vineyard;
  the loot wrested from the poor is in your houses.
15 What do you mean by crushing my people,
  and grinding down the poor when they look
    to you?
  says the Lord, the God of hosts.
16 The LORD said:
  Because the daughters of Zion are haughty,
  and walk with necks outstretched
  Ogling and mincing as they go,
  their anklets tinkling with every step,
17 The Lord shall cover the scalps of Zion's daughters
    with scabs,
  and the LORD shall bare their heads.

18 On that day the LORD will do away with the finery of the
anklets, sunbursts, and crescents; 19 the pendants, bracelets,
and veils; 20 the headdresses, bangles, cinctures, perfume
boxes, and amulets; 21 the signet rings, and the nose rings;
22 the court dresses, wraps, cloaks, and purses; 23 the mirrors, linen tunics, turbans, and shawls.

24 Instead of perfume there will be stench,
  instead of the girdle, a rope,
And for the coiffure, baldness;
  for the rich gown, a sackcloth skirt.
    Then, instead of beauty:
25 Your men will fall by the sword,
  and your champions, in war;
26 Her gates will lament and mourn,
  as the city sits desolate on the ground.

4 Seven women will take hold of one man
  on that day, saying:
  "We will eat our own food
  and wear our own clothing;
  Only let your name be given us,
  put an end to our disgrace!"

2   On that day,
  The branch of the LORD will be luster and glory,
  and the fruit of the earth will be honor
    and splendor
  for the survivors of Israel.
3 He who remains in Zion
  and he that is left in Jerusalem
  Will be called holy:
  every one marked down for life in Jerusalem.

NEW JERUSALEM BIBLE

9 Their complacency bears witness against them,
  they parade their sin like Sodom;
  they do not conceal it, all the worse for them,
  for they have hatched their own downfall.
10 Say, 'Blessed the upright,
  for he will feed on the fruit of his deeds;
11 woe to the wicked, it will go ill with him,
  for he will be treated as his actions deserve.'
12 O my people, their oppressors pillage them
  and extortioners rule over them!
  O my people, your rulers mislead you
  and efface the paths you ought to follow!
13 Yahweh has risen to accuse,
  is standing to pass judgement on the people.
14 Yahweh is about to try
  the elders and the princes of his people,
  'You are the ones who have ravaged the vineyard,
  the spoils of the poor are in your houses.
15 By what right do you crush my people
  and grind the faces of the poor?'
  says the Lord Yahweh Sabaoth.

16 Yahweh says:

  Because Zion's daughters are proud
  and walk with heads held high
  and enticing eyes — with mincing steps they go,
  jingling the bangles on their feet —
17 the Lord will give Zion's daughters scabby heads,
  Yahweh will lay their foreheads bare.

18 That day the Lord will take away the ornamental
chains, medallions, crescents, 19 pendants, bracelets, trin-
kets, 20 diadems, ankle-chains, necklaces, scent bottles,
amulets, 21 finger-rings, nose-rings, 22 party dresses,
cloaks, scarves, purses, 23 mirrors, linen clothes, turbans
and mantillas.

24 Then, instead of perfume, a stink;
  instead of belt, a rope,
  instead of hair elaborately dressed, a shaven scalp,
  instead of gorgeous clothes, sacking round the
    waist,
  and brand marks instead of beauty.
25 Your men will fall by the sword,
  your warriors in battle,
26 and her gates will moan and mourn;
  she will sit on the ground, deserted.

4 That day, seven women will catch hold of one man and
  say, 'We will eat our own food, and wear our own
clothing, but just let us bear your name. Take our disgrace
away.'

2 That day, Yahweh's seedling will turn to beauty
    and glory,
  what the earth brings forth will turn to the pride
    and ornament
  of Israel's survivors.
3 Those who are left in Zion and remain in
    Jerusalem
  will be called holy,
  all those in Jerusalem noted down to live.

NEW REVISED STANDARD VERSION	REVISED ENGLISH BIBLE

washed away the filth of the daughters of Zion and cleansed the bloodstains of Jerusalem from its midst by a spirit of judgment and by a spirit of burning. 5 Then the LORD will create over the whole site of Mount Zion and over its places of assembly a cloud by day and smoke and the shining of a flaming fire by night. Indeed over all the glory there will be a canopy. 6 It will serve as a pavilion, a shade by day from the heat, and a refuge and a shelter from the storm and rain.

of the women of Zion and cleanses Jerusalem from bloodstains by a spirit of judgement burning like fire, 5 he will create a cloud of smoke by day and a bright flame of fire by night over the whole building on Mount Zion and over all her assemblies; for his glory will be a canopy over all, 6 a cover giving shade by day from the heat, a refuge and shelter from storm and rain.

5 Let me sing for my beloved
 my love-song concerning his vineyard:
My beloved had a vineyard
 on a very fertile hill.
2 He dug it and cleared it of stones,
 and planted it with choice vines;
he built a watchtower in the midst of it,
 and hewed out a wine vat in it;
he expected it to yield grapes,
 but it yielded wild grapes.

3 And now, inhabitants of Jerusalem
 and people of Judah,
judge between me
 and my vineyard.
4 What more was there to do for my vineyard
 that I have not done in it?
When I expected it to yield grapes,
 why did it yield wild grapes?

5 And now I will tell you
 what I will do to my vineyard.
I will remove its hedge,
 and it shall be devoured;
I will break down its wall,
 and it shall be trampled down.
6 I will make it a waste;
 it shall not be pruned or hoed,
 and it shall be overgrown with briers and
 thorns;
I will also command the clouds
 that they rain no rain upon it.

7 For the vineyard of the LORD of hosts
 is the house of Israel,
and the people of Judah
 are his pleasant planting;
he expected justice,
 but saw bloodshed;
righteousness,
 but heard a cry!

8 Ah, you who join house to house,
 who add field to field,
until there is room for no one but you,
 and you are left to live alone
 in the midst of the land!

9 The LORD of hosts has sworn in my hearing:
Surely many houses shall be desolate,
 large and beautiful houses, without inhabitant.
10 For ten acres of vineyard shall yield but one bath,
 and a homer of seed shall yield a mere
 ephah.ʰ

5 I shall sing for my beloved
 my love song about his vineyard:
My beloved had a vineyard
 high up on a fertile slope.
2 He trenched it, cleared it of stones,
 and planted it with choice red vines;
in the middle he built a watch-tower
 and also hewed out a wine vat.
He expected it to yield choice grapes,
 but all it yielded was a crop of wild grapes.

3 Now, you citizens of Jerusalem
 and people of Judah,
judge between me and my vineyard.
4 What more could have been done for my vineyard
 than I did for it?
Why, when I expected it to yield choice grapes,
 did it yield wild grapes?

5 Now listen while I tell you
 what I am about to do to my vineyard:
I shall take away its hedge
 and let it go to waste,
I shall break down its wall
 and let it be trampled underfoot;
6 I shall leave it derelict.
It will be neither pruned nor hoed,
 but left overgrown with briars and thorns.
I shall command the clouds
 to withhold their rain from it.
7 The vineyard of the LORD of Hosts is Israel,
 Judah the plant he cherished.
He looked for justice but found bloodshed,
 for righteousness but heard cries of distress.

8 Woe betide those who add house to house
 and join field to field,
until everyone else is displaced,
 and you are left as sole inhabitants of the
 countryside.
9 In my hearing the LORD of Hosts made this solemn
 oath:
'Great houses will be brought to ruin,
 fine mansions left uninhabited.
10 Five acres of vineyard will yield only a gallon,
 and ten bushels of seed return only a peck.'

5:9 made . . . oath: *prob. rdg; Heb. omits.*   5:10 Five acres: *lit.*
ten yokes. gallon: *lit.* bath. ten bushels: *lit.* a homer. a peck: *lit.* an
ephah.

ʰThe Heb *bath, homer,* and *ephah* are measures of quantity

4 When the Lord washes away
   the filth of the daughters of Zion,
And purges Jerusalem's blood from her midst
   with a blast of searing judgment,
5 Then will the LORD create,
   over the whole site of Mount Zion
   and over her place of assembly,
A smoking cloud by day
   and a light of flaming fire by night.
6 For over all, his glory will be shelter
   and protection:
   shade from the parching heat of day,
refuge and cover from storm and rain.

5 Let me now sing of my friend,
   my friend's song concerning his vineyard.
My friend had a vineyard
   on a fertile hillside;
2 He spaded it, cleared it of stones,
   and planted the choicest vines;
Within it he built a watchtower,
   and hewed out a wine press.
Then he looked for the crop of grapes,
   but what it yielded was wild grapes.

3 Now, inhabitants of Jerusalem and men of Judah,
   judge between me and my vineyard:
4 What more was there to do for my vineyard
   that I had not done?
Why, when I looked for the crop of grapes,
   did it bring forth wild grapes?
5 Now, I will let you know
   what I mean to do to my vineyard:
Take away its hedge, give it to grazing,
   break through its wall, let it be trampled!
6 Yes, I will make it a ruin:
   it shall not be pruned or hoed,
   but overgrown with thorns and briers;
I will command the clouds
   not to send rain upon it.
7 The vineyard of the LORD of hosts is the house
   of Israel,
   and the men of Judah are his cherished plant;
He looked for judgment, but see, bloodshed!
   for justice, but hark, the outcry!

8 Woe to you who join house to house,
   who connect field with field,
Till no room remains, and you are left to dwell
   alone in the midst of the land!
9 In my hearing the LORD of hosts has sworn:
   Many houses shall be in ruins,
   large ones and fine, with no one to live in them.
10 Ten acres of vineyard
   shall yield but one liquid measure,
And a homer of seed
   shall yield but an ephah.

4 When the Lord has washed away
   the filth of Zion's daughters
and with the wind of judgement and the wind of
   burning cleansed
Jerusalem of the blood shed in her,
5 Yahweh will create,
   over every house on Mount Zion
   and over those who assemble there,
a cloud by day,
   and by night smoke with the brightness of a flaring
   fire.
For over all will be the Glory as canopy 6 and tent
to give shade by day from the heat,
refuge and shelter from the storm and the rain.

5 Let me sing my beloved
   the song of my friend for his vineyard.

My beloved had a vineyard
   on a fertile hillside.
2 He dug it, cleared it of stones,
   and planted it with red grapes.
In the middle he built a tower,
   he hewed a press there too.
He expected it to yield fine grapes:
   wild grapes were all it yielded.

3 And now, citizens of Jerusalem and people of
   Judah,
I ask you to judge between me and my vineyard.
4 What more could I have done for my vineyard
   that I have not done?
Why, when I expected it to yield fine grapes,
   has it yielded wild ones?

5 Very well, I shall tell you what I am going to do
   to my vineyard:
I shall take away its hedge, for it to be grazed on,
   and knock down its wall, for it to be trampled on.
6 I shall let it go to waste, unpruned, undug,
   overgrown by brambles and thorn-bushes,
   and I shall command the clouds to rain no rain on
   it.
7 Now, the vineyard of Yahweh Sabaoth is the
   House of Israel,
   and the people of Judah the plant he cherished.
He expected fair judgement, but found injustice,
   uprightness, but found cries of distress.
8 Woe to those who add house to house
   and join field to field
until there is nowhere left
   and they are the sole inhabitants of the country.
9 Yahweh Sabaoth has sworn this in my hearing,
   'Many houses will be brought to ruin,
   great and fine ones left untenanted;
10 for ten acres of vineyard will yield only one barrel,
   and ten bushel of seed will yield only one bushel.'

NEW REVISED STANDARD VERSION	REVISED ENGLISH BIBLE

NEW REVISED STANDARD VERSION

11 Ah, you who rise early in the morning
in pursuit of strong drink,
who linger in the evening
to be inflamed by wine,
12 whose feasts consist of lyre and harp,
tambourine and flute and wine,
but who do not regard the deeds of the LORD,
or see the work of his hands!
13 Therefore my people go into exile without
knowledge;
their nobles are dying of hunger,
and their multitude is parched with thirst.

14 Therefore Sheol has enlarged its appetite
and opened its mouth beyond measure;
the nobility of Jerusalem*i* and her multitude go
down,
her throng and all who exult in her.
15 People are bowed down, everyone is brought
low,
and the eyes of the haughty are humbled.
16 But the LORD of hosts is exalted by justice,
and the Holy God shows himself holy by
righteousness.
17 Then the lambs shall graze as in their pasture,
fatlings and kids*j* shall feed among the ruins.

18 Ah, you who drag iniquity along with cords of
falsehood,
who drag sin along as with cart ropes,
19 who say, "Let him make haste,
let him speed his work
that we may see it;
let the plan of the Holy One of Israel hasten to
fulfillment,
that we may know it!"
20 Ah, you who call evil good
and good evil,
who put darkness for light
and light for darkness,
who put bitter for sweet
and sweet for bitter!
21 Ah, you who are wise in your own eyes,
and shrewd in your own sight!
22 Ah, you who are heroes in drinking wine
and valiant at mixing drink,
23 who acquit the guilty for a bribe,
and deprive the innocent of their rights!
24 Therefore, as the tongue of fire devours the
stubble,
and as dry grass sinks down in the flame,
so their root will become rotten,
and their blossom go up like dust;
for they have rejected the instruction of the LORD
of hosts,
and have despised the word of the Holy One of
Israel.

25 Therefore the anger of the LORD was kindled
against his people,
and he stretched out his hand against them and
struck them;
the mountains quaked,
and their corpses were like refuse
in the streets.
For all this his anger has not turned away,
and his hand is stretched out still.

REVISED ENGLISH BIBLE

11 Woe betide those who rise early in the morning
to go in pursuit of drink,
who sit late into the night
inflamed with wine,
12 at whose feasts there are harps and lutes,
tabors and pipes and wine;
yet for the work of the LORD they have never a
thought,
no regard for what he has done.
13 Therefore my people shall go into captivity
because they lack all knowledge of me.
The nobles are starving to death,
and the common folk die of thirst.
14 Therefore Sheol gapes with straining throat
and opens her enormous jaws:
down go the nobility and people of Jerusalem,
her noisy throng of revellers.
15 Mankind is brought low, everyone is humbled,
and haughty looks are cast down.
16 But the LORD of Hosts is exalted by judgement,
and by righteousness the Holy God reveals his
holiness.
17 Lambs will feed where fat bullocks once pastured,
young goats will graze broad acres where cattle
grew fat.

18 Woe betide those who drag wickedness and sin
along,
as with a sheep's tether or a heifer's rope,
19 who say, 'Let the LORD make haste:
let him speed up his work that we may see it;
let the purpose of the Holy One of Israel
be soon fulfilled, that we may know it.'
20 Woe betide those who call evil good and good
evil,
who make darkness light and light darkness,
who make bitter sweet and sweet bitter.
21 Woe betide those who are wise in their own sight
and prudent in their own esteem.
22 Woe betide those heroic topers,
those valiant mixers of drink,
23 who for a bribe acquit the guilty
and deny justice to those in the right.

24 As tongues of fire lick up the stubble
and chaff shrivels in the flames,
so their root will moulder away
and their opening buds vanish like fine dust;
for they have spurned the instruction of the LORD
of Hosts
and rejected the word of the Holy One of Israel.
25 So the anger of the LORD is roused against his
people,
and he has stretched out his hand to strike them
down;
the mountains trembled,
and corpses lay like refuse in the streets.
Yet for all this his anger has not abated,
and his hand is still stretched out.

5:14 **Sheol:** *or* the underworld.   5:17 **Lambs . . . grew fat:** *poss.
rdg; Heb.* unintelligible.

i Heb *her nobility*   *j* Cn Compare Gk: Heb *aliens*

17 Lambs shall graze there at pasture,
   and kids shall eat in the ruins of the rich.

11 Woe to those who demand strong drink
   as soon as they rise in the morning,
   And linger into the night
   while wine inflames them!
12 With harp and lyre, timbrel and flute,
   they feast on wine;
   But what the LORD does, they regard not,
   the work of his hands they see not.
13 Therefore my people go into exile,
   because they do not understand;
   Their nobles die of hunger,
   and their masses are parched with thirst.
14 Therefore the nether world enlarges its throat
   and opens its maw without limit;
   Down go their nobility and their masses,
   their throngs and their revelry.
15 Men shall be abased, each one brought low,
   and the eyes of the haughty lowered,
16 But the LORD of hosts shall be exalted by
   his judgment,
   and God the Holy shall be shown holy by
   his justice.
       ‡5.17: see above‡
18 Woe to those who tug at guilt with cords
   of perversity,
   and at sin as if with cart ropes!
19 To those who say, "Let him make haste
   and speed his work, that we may see it;
   On with the plan of the Holy One of Israel!
   let it come to pass, that we may know it!"
20 Woe to those who call evil good, and good evil,
   who change darkness into light, and light
   into darkness,
   who change bitter into sweet, and sweet
   into bitter!
21 Woe to those who are wise in their own sight,
   and prudent in their own esteem!
22 Woe to the champions at drinking wine,
   the valiant at mixing strong drink!
23 To those who acquit the guilty for bribes,
   and deprive the just man of his rights!
24 Therefore, as the tongue of fire licks up stubble,
   as dry grass shrivels in the flame,
   Even so their root shall become rotten
   and their blossom scatter like dust;
   For they have spurned the law of the LORD
   of hosts,
   and scorned the word of the Holy One of Israel.

25 Therefore the wrath of the LORD blazes against
   his people,
   he raises his hand to strike them;
   When the mountains quake,
   their corpses shall be like refuse in the streets.
   For all this, his wrath is not turned back,
   and his hand is still outstretched.

11 Woe to those who get up early to go after strong
   drink,
   and stay up late at night inflamed with wine.
12 Nothing but harp and lyre, tambourine and pipe,
   and wine for their drinking bouts.

   Never a thought for the works of Yahweh,
   never a glance for what his hands have done.
13 That is why my people is in exile, for want of
   perception;
   her dignitaries starving, her populace parched with
   thirst.
14 That is why Sheol opens wide its throat
   and gapes with measureless jaw
   and down go her noblemen and populace
   and her loud revellers merry to the last!
15 Human nature has been humbled, humankind
   brought low,c
   and the eyes of the proud have been humbled.
16 Yahweh Sabaoth is the more respected for his
   judgement,
   God the Holy One has displayed his holiness by
   his justice!
17 Now the lambs will graze in their old pastures,
   and the fields laid waste by fat cattle will feed the
   kids.

18 Woe to those who drag guilt along by the reins of
   duplicity,
   drag along sin as though with a cart rope;
19 to those who say, 'Why doesn't he do his work
   quickly
   so that we can see it;
   why doesn't the Holy One of Israel's design hurry
   up and come true
   so that we can experience it?'
20 Woe to those who call what is bad, good, and
   what is good, bad,
   who substitute darkness for light and light for
   darkness,
   who substitute bitter for sweet and sweet for bitter.
21 Woe to those who think themselves wise
   and believe themselves enlightened.
22 Woe to those whose might lies in wine bibbing,
   their heroism in mixing strong drinks,
23 who acquit the guilty for a bribe
   and deny justice to the upright.
24 Yes, as the flame devours the stubble,
   as the straw flares up and disappears,
   their root will be like decay
   and their shoot be carried off like dust,
   for having rejected the law of Yahweh Sabaoth,
   for having despised the word of the Holy One of
   Israel.

25 This is why Yahweh's anger has blazed out against
   his people;
   and he has raised his hand against them to strike
   them;
   why the mountains have shuddered
   and why corpses are lying like dung in the streets.
   After all this, his anger is not spent.
   No, his hand is still raised!

c 5 The refrain of the poem in 2:6–22; perhaps vv. 14–16 belong
there.

NEW REVISED STANDARD VERSION

26   He will raise a signal for a nation far away,
     and whistle for a people at the ends of the
        earth;
     Here they come, swiftly, speedily!
27   None of them is weary, none stumbles,
     none slumbers or sleeps,
     not a loincloth is loose,
     not a sandal-thong broken;
28   their arrows are sharp,
     all their bows bent,
     their horses' hoofs seem like flint,
     and their wheels like the whirlwind.
29   Their roaring is like a lion,
     like young lions they roar;
     they growl and seize their prey,
     they carry it off, and no one can rescue.
30   They will roar over it on that day,
     like the roaring of the sea.
     And if one look to the land —
     only darkness and distress;
     and the light grows dark with clouds.

6 In the year that King Uzziah died, I saw the Lord sitting on a throne, high and lofty; and the hem of his robe filled the temple. 2 Seraphs were in attendance above him; each had six wings: with two they covered their faces, and with two they covered their feet, and with two they flew. 3 And one called to another and said:

"Holy, holy, holy is the LORD of hosts;
   the whole earth is full of his glory."

4 The pivots[k] on the thresholds shook at the voices of those who called, and the house filled with smoke. 5 And I said: "Woe is me! I am lost, for I am a man of unclean lips, and I live among a people of unclean lips; yet my eyes have seen the King, the LORD of hosts!"

6 Then one of the seraphs flew to me, holding a live coal that had been taken from the altar with a pair of tongs. 7 The seraph[l] touched my mouth with it and said: "Now that this has touched your lips, your guilt has departed and your sin is blotted out." 8 Then I heard the voice of the Lord saying, "Whom shall I send, and who will go for us?" And I said, "Here am I; send me!" 9 And he said, "Go and say to this people:

'Keep listening, but do not comprehend;
   keep looking, but do not understand.'
10   Make the mind of this people dull,
     and stop their ears,
     and shut their eyes,
     so that they may not look with their eyes,
     and listen with their ears,
     and comprehend with their minds,
     and turn and be healed."
11   Then I said, "How long, O Lord?" And he said:
     "Until cities lie waste
     without inhabitant,
     and houses without people,
     and the land is utterly desolate;
12   until the LORD sends everyone far away,
     and vast is the emptiness in the midst of the
        land.

REVISED ENGLISH BIBLE

26 He will hoist a standard as a signal to a nation far
      away,
   he will whistle them up from the ends of the earth,
   and they will come with all speed.
27 None is weary, not one of them stumbles,
   no one slumbers or sleeps.
   None has his belt loose about his waist
   or a broken thong to his sandals.
28 Their arrows are sharpened and all their bows bent,
   their horses' hoofs are like flint,
   their chariot wheels like the whirlwind.
29 Their growling is like that of a lion,
   they growl like young lions;
   they roar as they seize their prey
   and carry it beyond reach of rescue.
30 Their roaring over it on that day
   will be like the roaring of the sea.
   Anyone who looks over the land sees darkness
      closing in,
   and the light overshadowed by the gathering
      clouds.

6 IN the year that King Uzziah died I saw the Lord seated on a throne, high and exalted, and the skirt of his robe filled the temple. 2 Seraphim were in attendance on him. Each had six wings: with one pair of wings they covered their faces and with another their bodies, and with the third pair they flew. 3 They were calling to one another,

'Holy, holy, holy is the LORD of Hosts:
   the whole earth is full of his glory.'

4 As each called, the threshold shook to its foundations at the sound, while the house began to fill with clouds of smoke. 5 Then I said,

'Woe is me! I am doomed,
for my own eyes have seen the King, the LORD of
   Hosts,
I, a man of unclean lips,
I, who dwell among a people of unclean lips.'

6 One of the seraphim flew to me, carrying in his hand a glowing coal which he had taken from the altar with a pair of tongs. 7 He touched my mouth with it and said,

'This has touched your lips;
   now your iniquity is removed
   and your sin is wiped out.'

8 I heard the Lord saying, 'Whom shall I send? Who will go for us?' 9 I said: 'Here am I! Send me.' He replied: 'Go, tell this people:

However hard you listen, you will never
   understand.
However hard you look, you will never perceive.
10 This people's wits are dulled;
   they have stopped their ears and shut their eyes,
   so that they may not see with their eyes,
   nor listen with their ears,
   nor understand with their wits,
   and then turn and be healed.'

11 I asked, 'Lord, how long?' And he answered,

'Until cities fall in ruins and are deserted,
   until houses are left without occupants,
   and the land lies ruined and waste.'
12 The LORD will drive the people far away,
   and the country will be one vast desolation.

5:30 **by . . . clouds:** or on the hilltops.   6:10 **This people's . . .**
shut: or Dull this people's wits, stop their ears, and shut.

---

k Meaning of Heb uncertain   l Heb He

NEW AMERICAN BIBLE

26 He will give a signal to a far-off nation,
and whistle to them from the ends of the earth;
speedily and promptly will they come.
27 None of them will stumble with weariness,
none will slumber and none will sleep.
None will have his waist belt loose,
nor the thong of his sandal broken.
28 Their arrows are sharp,
and all their bows are bent.
The hoofs of their horses seem like flint,
and their chariot wheels like the hurricane.
29 Their roar is that of the lion,
like the lion's whelps they roar;
They growl and seize the prey,
they carry it off and none will rescue it.
30 [They will roar over it, on that day,
with a roaring like that of the sea.]

6 In the year king Uzziah died, I saw the Lord seated on a high and lofty throne, with the train of his garment filling the temple. 2 Seraphim were stationed above; each of them had six wings: with two they veiled their faces, with two they veiled their feet, and with two they hovered aloft. 3 "Holy, holy, holy is the LORD of hosts!" they cried one to the other. "All the earth is filled with his glory!" 4 At the sound of that cry, the frame of the door shook and the house was filled with smoke.

5 Then I said, "Woe is me, I am doomed! For I am a man of unclean lips, living among a people of unclean lips; yet my eyes have seen the King, the LORD of hosts!" 6 Then one of the seraphim flew to me, holding an ember which he had taken with tongs from the altar. 7 He touched my mouth with it. "See," he said, "now that this has touched your lips, your wickedness is removed, your sin purged."

8 Then I heard the voice of the Lord saying, "Whom shall I send? Who will go for us?" "Here I am;" I said; "send me!" 9 And he replied: Go and say to this people:

Listen carefully, but you shall not understand!
Look intently, but you shall know nothing!
10 You are to make the heart of this people sluggish,
to dull their ears and close their eyes;
Else their eyes will see, their ears hear,
their heart understand,
and they will turn and be healed.

11 "How long, O Lord?" I asked. And he replied:

Until the cities are desolate,
without inhabitants,
Houses, without a man,
and the earth is a desolate waste.
12 Until the LORD removes men far away,
and the land is abandoned more and more.

NEW JERUSALEM BIBLE

26 He hoists a signal for a distant nation,
he whistles them up from the ends of the earth;
and see how swift, how fleet they come!
27 None of them tired, none of them stumbling,
none of them asleep or drowsy,
none of them with belt unfastened,
none of them with broken sandal-strap.
28 Their arrows are sharpened,
their bows all strung,
their horses' hoofs you would think were flint
and their wheels, a whirlwind!
29 Their roar is like that of a lioness,
like fierce young lions they roar,
growling they seize their prey
and carry it off, with no one to prevent it,
30 growling at it, that day,
like the growling of the sea.
Only look at the country: darkness and distress,
and the light turned to darkness by the clouds.

6 In the year of King Uzziah's death I saw the Lord seated on a high and lofty throne; his train filled the sanctuary. 2 Above him stood seraphs, each one with six wings: two to cover its face, two to cover its feet and two for flying; 3 and they were shouting these words to each other:

Holy, holy, holy is Yahweh Sabaoth.
His glory fills the whole earth.

4 The door-posts shook at the sound of their shouting, and the Temple was full of smoke. 5 Then I said:

'Woe is me! I am lost,
for I am a man of unclean lips
and I live among a people of unclean lips,
and my eyes have seen the King, Yahweh
Sabaoth.'

6 Then one of the seraphs flew to me, holding in its hand a live coal which it had taken from the altar with a pair of tongs. 7 With this it touched my mouth and said:

'Look, this has touched your lips,
your guilt has been removed
and your sin forgiven.'

8 I then heard the voice of the Lord saying:

'Whom shall I send? Who will go for us?'

And I said, 'Here am I, send me.' 9 He said:

'Go, and say to this people,
"Listen and listen, but never understand!
Look and look, but never perceive!"
10 Make this people's heart coarse,
make their ears dull, shut their eyes tight,
or they will use their eyes to see,
use their ears to hear,
use their heart to understand,
and change their ways and be healed.'

11 I then said, 'Until when, Lord?' He replied, 'Until towns are in ruins and deserted, houses untenanted and a great desolation reigns in the land, 12 and Yahweh has driven the people away and the country is totally aban-

NEW REVISED STANDARD VERSION

13 Even if a tenth part remain in it,
it will be burned again,
like a terebinth or an oak
whose stump remains standing
when it is felled."*m*
The holy seed is its stump.

7 In the days of Ahaz son of Jotham son of Uzziah, king of Judah, King Rezin of Aram and King Pekah son of Remaliah of Israel went up to attack Jerusalem, but could not mount an attack against it. 2 When the house of David heard that Aram had allied itself with Ephraim, the heart of Ahaz*n* and the heart of his people shook as the trees of the forest shake before the wind.

3 Then the LORD said to Isaiah, Go out to meet Ahaz, you and your son Shear-jashub,*o* at the end of the conduit of the upper pool on the highway to the Fuller's Field, 4 and say to him, Take heed, be quiet, do not fear, and do not let your heart be faint because of these two smoldering stumps of firebrands, because of the fierce anger of Rezin and Aram and the son of Remaliah. 5 Because Aram — with Ephraim and the son of Remaliah — has plotted evil against you, saying, 6 Let us go up against Judah and cut off Jerusalem*p* and conquer it for ourselves and make the son of Tabeel king in it; 7 therefore thus says the Lord GOD:

It shall not stand,
    and it shall not come to pass.
8 For the head of Aram is Damascus,
    and the head of Damascus is Rezin.
(Within sixty-five years Ephraim will be shattered, no longer a people.)
9 The head of Ephraim is Samaria,
    and the head of Samaria is the son of
        Remaliah.
If you do not stand firm in faith,
    you shall not stand at all.

10 Again the LORD spoke to Ahaz, saying, 11 Ask a sign of the LORD your God; let it be deep as Sheol or high as heaven. 12 But Ahaz said, I will not ask, and I will not put the LORD to the test. 13 Then Isaiah*q* said: "Hear then, O house of David! Is it too little for you to weary mortals, that you weary my God also? 14 Therefore the Lord himself will give you a sign. Look, the young woman*r* is with child and shall bear a son, and shall name him Immanuel.*s* 15 He shall eat curds and honey by the time he knows how to refuse the evil and choose the good. 16 For before the child knows how to refuse the evil and choose the good, the land before whose two kings you are in dread will be deserted. 17 The LORD will bring on you and on your people and on your ancestral house such days as have not come since the day that Ephraim departed from Judah — the king of Assyria."

REVISED ENGLISH BIBLE

13 Even though a tenth part of the people were to remain,
they too would be destroyed
like an oak or terebinth
when it is felled,
and only a stump remains.
Its stump is a holy seed.

7 WHEN Ahaz son of Jotham and grandson of Uzziah was ruler of Judah, King Rezin of Aram with Pekah son of Remaliah, king of Israel, marched on Jerusalem, but was unable to reduce it. 2 When it was reported to the house of David that the Aramaeans had made an alliance with the Ephraimites, king and people shook like forest trees shaking in the wind. 3 The LORD said to Isaiah, 'Go out with your son Shear-jashub to meet Ahaz at the end of the conduit of the Upper Pool by the causeway leading to the Fuller's Field, 4 and say to him: Remain calm and unafraid; do not let your nerve fail because of the blazing anger of Rezin with his Aramaeans and Remaliah's son, those two smouldering stumps of firewood. 5 The Aramaeans with Ephraim and Remaliah's son have plotted against you: 6 "Let us invade Judah and break her spirit," they said; "let us bring her over to our side, and set Tabeal's son on the throne." 7 The Lord GOD has said:

This shall not happen now or ever,
8-9 that the rule in Aram should belong to Damascus,
    the rule in Damascus to Rezin,
or that the rule in Ephraim should belong to
        Samaria,
and the rule in Samaria to Remaliah's son.
(Within sixty-five years a shattered Ephraim shall
        cease to be a nation.)
Have firm faith, or you will fail to stand firm.'

10 The LORD spoke further to Ahaz. 11 'Ask the LORD your God for a sign,' he said, 'whether from Sheol below or from heaven above.' 12 But Ahaz replied: 'No, I will not put the LORD to the test by asking for a sign.' 13 Then the prophet said: 'Listen, you house of David. Not content with wearing out the patience of men, must you also wear out the patience of my God? 14 Because you do, the Lord of his own accord will give you a sign; it is this: A young woman is with child, and she will give birth to a son and call him Immanuel. 15 By the time he has learnt to reject what is bad and choose what is good, he will be eating curds and honey; 16 before that child has learnt to reject evil and choose good, the territories of those two kings before whom you now cringe in fear will lie desolate. 17 The LORD will bring on you, on your people, and on your father's house, a time the like of which has not been seen since Ephraim broke away from Judah.

---

m Meaning of Heb uncertain   *n* Heb *his heart*   *o* That is *A remnant shall return*   *p* Heb *cut it off*   *q* Heb *he*   *r* Gk *the virgin*   *s* That is *God is with us*

7:3 **Shear-jashub:** *that is* A remnant will return.
7:14 **Immanuel:** *that is* God is with us.   7:17 **Judah:** prob. rdg; Heb. adds the king of Assyria.

13 If there be still a tenth part in it,
    then this in turn shall be laid waste;
As with a terebinth or an oak
    whose trunk remains when its leaves have fallen.
[Holy offspring is the trunk.]

7 In the days of Ahaz, king of Judah, son of Jotham, son of Uzziah, Rezin, king of Aram, and Pekah, king of Israel, son of Remaliah, went up to attack Jerusalem, but they were not able to conquer it. 2 When word came to the house of David that Aram was encamped in Ephraim, the heart of the king and the heart of the people trembled, as the trees of the forest tremble in the wind.

3 Then the LORD said to Isaiah: Go out to meet Ahaz, you and your son Shear-jashub, at the end of the conduit of the upper pool, on the highway of the fuller's field, 4 and say to him: Take care you remain tranquil and do not fear; let not your courage fail before these two stumps of smoldering brands [the blazing anger of Rezin and the Arameans, and of the son of Remaliah], 5 because of the mischief that Aram [Ephraim and the son of Remaliah] plots against you, saying, 6 "Let us go up and tear Judah asunder, make it our own by force, and appoint the son of Tabeel king there."

7 Thus says the LORD:

    This shall not stand, it shall not be!
8 Damascus is the capital of Aram,
    and Rezin the head of Damascus;
Samaria is the capital of Ephraim,
    and Remaliah's son the head of Samaria.
9 But within sixty years and five,
    Ephraim shall be crushed, no longer a nation.
Unless your faith is firm
    you shall not be firm!

10 Again the LORD spoke to Ahaz: 11 Ask for a sign from the LORD, your God; let it be deep as the nether world, or high as the sky! 12 But Ahaz answered, "I will not ask! I will not tempt the LORD!" 13 Then he said: Listen, O house of David! Is it not enough for you to weary men, must you also weary my God? 14 Therefore the Lord himself will give you this sign: the virgin shall be with child, and bear a son, and shall name him Immanuel. 15 He shall be living on curds and honey by the time he learns to reject the bad and choose the good. 16 For before the child learns to reject the bad and choose the good, the land of those two kings whom you dread shall be deserted.

17 The LORD shall bring upon you and your people and your father's house days worse than any since Ephraim seceded from Judah. [This means the king of Assyria.]

doned. 13 And suppose one-tenth of them are left in it, that will be stripped again, like the terebinth, like the oak, cut back to the stock; their stock is a holy seed.'

7 In the reign of Ahaz son of Jotham, son of Uzziah king of Judah, Razon king of Aram advanced on Jerusalem with Pekah son of Remaliah king of Israel, to attack it; but he was unable to attack it. 2 The House of David was informed: 'Aram has halted in Ephraimite territory.' At this, his heart and his people's hearts shook like forest trees shaking in the wind.

3 Yahweh then said to Isaiah, 'Go out with your son Shear-Jashub,*d* and meet Ahaz at the end of the conduit of the upper pool, on the road to the Fuller's Field, 4 and say to him, "Pay attention and keep calm. Do not be frightened or demoralised by these two smouldering sticks of firewood, by the fierce anger of Razon, Aram and the son of Remaliah, 5 or because Aram, Ephraim and the son of Remaliah have been plotting against you and saying: 6 Let us mount an attack on Judah, destroy it, force it onto our side and install the son of Tabeel there as king.

7 "Lord Yahweh says this:

    This will not happen, it will never occur,
8 for the head of Aram is Damascus,
    and the head of Damascus is Razon;
another sixty-five years,
    and Ephraim will cease to be a people.
9 The head of Ephraim is Samaria,
    and the head of Samaria is the son of Remaliah.
If you will not take your stand on me
    you will not stand firm." '

10 Yahweh spoke to Ahaz again and said:

11 Ask Yahweh your God for a sign,
    either in the depths of Sheol or in the heights
      above.

12 But Ahaz said, 'I will not ask. I will not put Yahweh to the test.'

13 He then said:

    Listen now, House of David:
    are you not satisfied with trying human patience
    that you should try my God's patience too?
14 The Lord will give you a sign in any case:
    It is this: the young woman*e* is with child
    and will give birth to a son
    whom she will call Immanuel.
15 On curds and honey will he feed
    until he knows how to refuse the bad
    and choose the good.
16 Before the child knows how to refuse the bad and
      choose the good,
    the lands whose two kings are frightening you will
      be deserted.
17 Yahweh will bring times for you,
    your people and your ancestral House,
    such as have not been seen
    since Ephraim broke away from Judah (the king of
      Assyria).

d 7 The name means 'a remnant will return'.
e 7 Perhaps Ahaz's wife, about to give birth to Hezekiah, but Isaiah sees it as symbolic of the fulfilment of royal messianic prophecies. For 'young woman' Gk reads 'virgin', interpreted by Mt of Mary.

| NEW REVISED STANDARD VERSION | REVISED ENGLISH BIBLE |

18 On that day the LORD will whistle for the fly that is at the sources of the streams of Egypt, and for the bee that is in the land of Assyria. 19 And they will all come and settle in the steep ravines, and in the clefts of the rocks, and on all the thornbushes, and on all the pastures.

20 On that day the Lord will shave with a razor hired beyond the River — with the king of Assyria — the head and the hair of the feet, and it will take off the beard as well.

21 On that day one will keep alive a young cow and two sheep, 22 and will eat curds because of the abundance of milk that they give; for everyone that is left in the land shall eat curds and honey.

23 On that day every place where there used to be a thousand vines, worth a thousand shekels of silver, will become briers and thorns. 24 With bow and arrows one will go there, for all the land will be briers and thorns; 25 and as for all the hills that used to be hoed with a hoe, you will not go there for fear of briers and thorns; but they will become a place where cattle are let loose and where sheep tread.

8 Then the LORD said to me, Take a large tablet and write on it in common characters, "Belonging to Maher-shalal-hash-baz,"*t* 2 and have it attested*u* for me by reliable witnesses, the priest Uriah and Zechariah son of Jeberechiah. 3 And I went to the prophetess, and she conceived and bore a son. Then the LORD said to me, Name him Maher-shalal-hash-baz; 4 for before the child knows how to call "My father" or "My mother," the wealth of Damascus and the spoil of Samaria will be carried away by the king of Assyria.

5 The LORD spoke to me again: 6 Because this people has refused the waters of Shiloah that flow gently, and melt in fear before*v* Rezin and the son of Remaliah; 7 therefore, the Lord is bringing up against it the mighty flood waters of the River, the king of Assyria and all his glory; it will rise above all its channels and overflow all its banks; 8 it will sweep on into Judah as a flood, and, pouring over, it will reach up to the neck; and its outspread wings will fill the breadth of your land, O Immanuel.

9 Band together, you peoples, and be dismayed;
  listen, all you far countries;
  gird yourselves and be dismayed;
  gird yourselves and be dismayed!
10 Take counsel together, but it shall be brought to naught;
  speak a word, but it will not stand,
  for God is with us.*w*

---

18 'On that day the LORD will whistle up flies from the distant streams of Egypt and bees from the land of Assyria. 19 They will all come and settle in the steep wadis and in the clefts of the rock, swarming over the camel-thorn and stinkwort. 20 On that day the Lord will shave the head and body with a razor hired on the banks of the Euphrates, and it will remove the beard as well. 21 On that day a man will keep a young cow and two ewes, 22 and he will get so much milk that he eats curds; all who are left in the land will eat curds and honey. 23 On that day every place where there used to be a thousand vines worth a thousand pieces of silver will be given over to briars and thorns. 24 A man will go there only to hunt with bow and arrows, for briars and thorns will cover the whole land. 25 Daunted by the briars and thorns, no one will set foot on any of those hills once under the hoe. They will become a place where oxen are turned loose and sheep and goats can wander.'

8 The LORD said to me, 'Take a large writing tablet and write on it in common script "Maher-shalal-hash-baz".' 2 I had it witnessed for me by Uriah the priest and Zechariah son of Jeberechiah as reliable witnesses. 3 Then I lay with my wife, and she conceived and gave birth to a son. The LORD said to me, 'Call him Maher-shalal-hash-baz; 4 before the boy can say "Father" or "Mother", the wealth of Damascus and the spoils of Samaria will be carried off and presented to the king of Assyria.'

5 Once again the LORD spoke to me; he said:

6 Because this nation has rejected
  the waters of Shiloah, which flow softly and
    gently,
7 therefore the Lord will bring up against it
  the mighty floodwaters of the Euphrates.
  The river will rise in its channels
  and overflow all its banks.
8 In a raging torrent mounting neck-high
  it will sweep through Judah.
  With his outspread wings
  the whole expanse of the land will be filled,
  for God is with us.
9 Take note, you nations; you will be shattered.
  Listen, all you distant parts of the earth:
  arm yourselves, and be shattered;
  arm yourselves, and be shattered.
10 Devise your plans, but they will be foiled;
  propose what you will, but it will not be carried out;
  for God is with us.

7:20 **Euphrates:** *prob. rdg; Heb. adds* with the king of Assyria. 8:1 **in . . . script:** *lit.* with the pen of a human being. **Maher-shalal-hash-baz:** *that is* Speeding for spoil, hastening for plunder.   8:3 **my wife:** *lit.* the prophetess.   8:6 **gently:** *prob. rdg; Heb. adds* Rezin and the son of Remaliah.   8:7 **Euphrates:** *prob. rdg; Heb. adds* the king of Assyria and all his pomp. 8:8 **God is with us:** *Heb.* Immanuel.   8:9 **Take note:** *so Gk; Heb. unintelligible.*   8:10 **God is with us:** *Heb.* Immanuel.

t That is *The spoil speeds, the prey hastens*   *u* Q Ms Gk Syr: MT and I caused to be attested   *v* Cn: Meaning of Heb uncertain   *w* Heb *immanu el*

NEW AMERICAN BIBLE

NEW JERUSALEM BIBLE

18 On that day

The LORD shall whistle
for the fly that is in the farthest streams
of Egypt,
and for the bee in the land of Assyria.
19 All of them shall come and settle
in the steep ravines and in the rocky clefts,
on all thornbushes and in all pastures.

20 On that day the LORD shall shave with the razor hired
from across the River [with the king of Assyria] the head,
and the hair between the legs. It shall also shave off the
beard.
21 On that day a man shall keep a heifer or a couple of
sheep, 22 and from their abundant yield of milk he shall live
on curds; curds and honey shall be the food of all who
remain in the land. 23 On that day every place where there
used to be a thousand vines, worth a thousand pieces of
silver, shall be turned to briers and thorns. 24 Men shall go
there with bow and arrows; for all the country shall be briers
and thorns. 25 For fear of briers and thorns you shall not go
upon any mountainside which used to be hoed with the
mattock; they shall be grazing land for cattle and shall be
trampled upon by sheep.

8 The LORD said to me: Take a large cylinder-seal, and
inscribe on it in ordinary letters: "Belonging to Maher-
shalal-hash-baz." 2 And I took reliable witnesses, Uriah the
priest, and Zechariah, son of Jeberechiah. 3 Then I went to
the prophetess and she conceived and bore a son. The LORD
said to me: Name him Maher-shalal-hash-baz, 4 for before
the child knows how to call his father or mother by name,
the wealth of Damascus and the spoil of Samaria shall be
carried off by the king of Assyria.
5 Again the LORD spoke to me:

6 Because this people has rejected
the waters of Shiloah that flow gently,
And melts with fear before the loftiness of Rezin
and Remaliah's son,
7 Therefore the LORD raises against them
the waters of the River, great and mighty
[the king of Assyria and all his power].
It shall rise above all its channels,
and overflow all its banks;
8 It shall pass into Judah, and flood it all throughout:
up to the neck it shall reach;
It shall spread its wings
the full width of your land, Immanuel!
9 Know, O peoples, and be appalled!
Give ear, all you distant lands!
Arm, but be crushed! Arm, but be crushed!
10 Form a plan, and it shall be thwarted;
make a resolve, and it shall not be carried out,
for "With us is God!"

18 When that day comes,
Yahweh will whistle up mosquitoes
from the distant streams of Egypt
and bees from the land of Assyria,
19 and they will all come and settle
on the streams in the gullies, in the holes in the
rocks,
on all the thorn-bushes and on all the water-points.
20 That day the Lord will shave,
with a razor hired from the other side of the River
(with the king of Assyria),
the head and the hair of the leg,
and take off the beard, too.
21 When that day comes, each man will raise
one heifer and two sheep,
22 and because of the abundant milk they give
(on curds will he feed)
all who are left in the country
will feed on curds and honey.
23 When that day comes, wherever there used to be a
thousand vines
worth a thousand pieces of silver,
all will be brambles and thorn-bushes;
24 to be ventured into only with arrows and bow,
for the country will be nothing but brambles and
thorn-bushes.
25 No more will you venture
on any hillside formerly under the hoe
for fear of the brambles and thorn-bushes;
it will be fit only for pasturing the cattle,
a tramping-ground for sheep.

8 Yahweh said to me, 'Take a large tablet and on it with
an ordinary stylus write, "Maher-Shalal-Hash-Baz."
2 And take reliable witnesses, the priest Uriah and Zechariah
son of Jeberechiah.'
3 I then had intercourse with the prophetess, who then
conceived and gave birth to a son.f Yahweh said to me,
'Call him Maher-Shalal-Hash-Baz, 4 for before the child
knows how to say "mother" or "father", the wealth of Damascus and the booty of Samaria will be carried away while
the king of Assyria looks on.'
5 Yahweh spoke to me again and said, 6 'Since this people
has rejected the waters of Shiloah which flow smoothly, and
has trembled before Razon and the son of Remaliah, 7 now,
against it, the Lord will bring the mighty, swelling waters
of the River (the king of Assyria and all his glory); the River
will flood up all its channels and overflow all its banks; 8 it
will flow into Judah, flooding everything and passing on; it
will reach right up to the neck, and the spreading of its
wings will cover the whole extent of your country, Immanuel!

9 Realise this, peoples, and be afraid,
listen, all members of far-off nations!
Arm yourselves yet be afraid!
Arm yourselves yet be afraid!
10 Devise plans as you may: they will come to
nothing!
Make what pronouncements you like; it will not
come about!
For God is with us!'

f 8 His name means 'Speedy-spoil-quick-booty', a prediction of the
destruction of Damascus and Samaria in 722 BC.

NEW REVISED STANDARD VERSION

11 For the LORD spoke thus to me while his hand was strong upon me, and warned me not to walk in the way of this people, saying: 12 Do not call conspiracy all that this people calls conspiracy, and do not fear what it fears, or be in dread. 13 But the LORD of hosts, him you shall regard as holy; let him be your fear, and let him be your dread. 14 He will become a sanctuary, a stone one strikes against; for both houses of Israel he will become a rock one stumbles over—a trap and a snare for the inhabitants of Jerusalem. 15 And many among them shall stumble; they shall fall and be broken; they shall be snared and taken.

16 Bind up the testimony, seal the teaching among my disciples. 17 I will wait for the LORD, who is hiding his face from the house of Jacob, and I will hope in him. 18 See, I and the children whom the LORD has given me are signs and portents in Israel from the LORD of hosts, who dwells on Mount Zion. 19 Now if people say to you, "Consult the ghosts and the familiar spirits that chirp and mutter; should not a people consult their gods, the dead on behalf of the living, 20 for teaching and for instruction?" Surely, those who speak like this will have no dawn! 21 They will pass through the land,ˣ greatly distressed and hungry; when they are hungry, they will be enraged and will curseʸ their king and their gods. They will turn their faces upward, 22 or they will look to the earth, but will see only distress and darkness, the gloom of anguish; and they will be thrust into thick darkness.ᶻ

9 ᵃ But there will be no gloom for those who were in anguish. In the former time he brought into contempt the land of Zebulun and the land of Naphtali, but in the latter time he will make glorious the way of the sea, the land beyond the Jordan, Galilee of the nations.
2 ᵇ The people who walked in darkness
   have seen a great light;
 those who lived in a land of deep darkness—
   on them light has shined.
3 You have multiplied the nation,
   you have increased its joy;
 they rejoice before you
   as with joy at the harvest,
   as people exult when dividing plunder.
4 For the yoke of their burden,
   and the bar across their shoulders,
   the rod of their oppressor,
 you have broken as on the day of Midian.
5 For all the boots of the tramping warriors
   and all the garments rolled in blood
   shall be burned as fuel for the fire.

REVISED ENGLISH BIBLE

11 This is what the LORD said to me when he took me by the hand and charged me not to follow the ways of this people: 12 'You are not to call alliance anything that this people calls alliance; you must neither fear nor stand in awe of what they fear. 13 It is the LORD of Hosts whom you should hold sacred; he must be the object of your fear and awe. 14 He will become a snare, an obstacle, and a rock against which the two houses of Israel will strike and stumble, a trap and a snare to the inhabitants of Jerusalem. 15 Over them many will stumble and fall and suffer injury; they will be snared and caught.'

16 I shall tie up the message, I shall seal the
   instruction
   so that it cannot be consulted by my disciples.
17 I shall wait eagerly for the LORD,
   who is hiding his face from the house of
   Jacob;
 I shall watch longingly for him.
18 Here I am with the children the LORD has given
   me
   to be signs and portents in Israel,
   sent by the LORD of Hosts who dwells on Mount
   Zion.
19 People will say to you,
   'Seek guidance from ghosts and familiar spirits
   which squeak and gibber;
 a nation may surely consult its gods,
   consult its dead on behalf of the living
20 for instruction or a message.'
   They will surely say some such thing,
   but what they say has no force.
21 So despondency and fear will come over
   them,
   and when they are afraid and fearful,
   they will rebel against their king and their gods.
   Whether they turn their gaze upwards 22 or look
   down,
   everywhere is distress and darkness inescapable,
   constraint and gloom that cannot be avoided;
9 1 for there is no escape for an oppressed people.

Formerly the lands of Zebulun and Naphtali were lightly regarded, but afterwards honour was bestowed on Galilee of the Nations on the road beyond Jordan to the sea.
2 The people that walked in darkness
   have seen a great light;
 on those who lived in a land as dark as death
   a light has dawned.
3 You have increased their joy
   and given them great gladness;
 they rejoice in your presence
   as those who rejoice at harvest,
   as warriors exult when dividing spoil.
4 For you have broken the yoke that burdened them,
   the rod laid on their shoulders,
   the driver's goad, as on the day of Midian's defeat.
5 The boots of earth-shaking armies on the march,
   the soldiers' cloaks rolled in blood,
   all are destined to be burnt, food for the fire.

8:11 **and . . . follow:** or and he turned me from following.
8:14 **become a snare:** prob. rdg; Heb. become a sanctuary.
8:21–22 Meaning of Heb. uncertain.   9:1 In Heb. 8:23.
9:2 In Heb. 9:1.   9:3 **their joy and:** prob. rdg; Heb. the nation, not.

ˣHeb it   ʸOr curse by   ᶻMeaning of Heb uncertain
ᵃCh 8.23 in Heb   ᵇCh 9.1 in Heb

NEW AMERICAN BIBLE

11 For thus said the Lord to me, taking hold of me and warning me not to walk in the way of this people:

12 Call not alliance what this people calls alliance,
      and fear not, nor stand in awe of what they fear.
13 But with the Lord of hosts make your alliance —
      for him be your fear and your awe.
14 Yet he shall be a snare, an obstacle and a
            stumbling stone
      to both the houses of Israel,
   A trap and a snare
      to those who dwell in Jerusalem;
15 And many among them shall stumble and fall,
      broken, snared, and captured.

16 The record is to be folded and the sealed instruction kept among my disciples. 17 For I will trust in the Lord, who is hiding his face from the house of Jacob; yes, I will wait for him. 18 Look at me and the children whom the Lord has given me: we are signs and portents in Israel from the Lord of hosts who dwells on Mount Zion. 19 And when they say to you, "Inquire of mediums and fortunetellers (who chirp and mutter!); should not a people inquire of their gods, apply to the dead on behalf of the living?" — 20 then this document will furnish its instruction. That kind of thing they will surely say.

‡8.21–22: see below in ch. 14‡

23 First he degraded the land of Zebulun and the land of Naphtali; but in the end he has glorified the seaward road, the land west of the Jordan, the District of the Gentiles.

Anguish has taken wing, dispelled is darkness:
   for there is no gloom where but now there
            was distress.

9   The people who walked in darkness
         have seen a great light;
      Upon those who dwelt in the land of gloom
         a light has shone.
   2 You have brought them abundant joy
         and great rejoicing,
      As they rejoice before you as at the harvest,
         as men make merry when dividing spoils.
   3 For the yoke that burdened them,
         the pole on their shoulder,
      And the rod of their taskmaster
         you have smashed, as on the day of Midian.
   4 For every boot that tramped in battle,
         every cloak rolled in blood,
         will be burned as fuel for flames.

NEW JERUSALEM BIBLE

11 For this was how Yahweh spoke to me when his
            hand seized hold of me
   and he taught me not to follow the path of this
            people, saying,
12 'Do not call conspiracy all that this people calls
            conspiracy;
   do not dread what they dread, have no fear of that.
13 Yahweh Sabaoth is the one you will proclaim holy,
   him you will dread, him you will fear.
14 He will be a sanctuary, a stumbling-stone,
      a rock to trip up the two Houses of Israel;
   a snare and a trap for the inhabitants of Jerusalem,
15 over which many of them will stumble, fall and be
            broken,
      be ensnared and made captive.
16 Bind up the testimony, seal the instruction
      in the heart of my disciples.'
17 My trust is in Yahweh who hides his face from the
            House of Jacob;
   I put my hope in him.
18 Look, I and the children whom Yahweh has given
            me
      shall become signs and portents in Israel on behalf
            of Yahweh Sabaoth who dwells on Mount
            Zion.
19 And should people say to you,
   'Go and consult ghosts and wizards that whisper
            and mutter' —
      a people should certainly consult its gods
      and the dead on behalf of the living!
20 As regards instruction and testimony,
      without doubt this is how they will talk,
      and hence there will be no dawn for them.
21 Oppressed and starving he will wander the country;
   and, once starving, he will become frenzied
      and curse his king and his God; turning his gaze
            upward,
22 then down to earth, there will be only anguish,
      gloom, the confusion of night, swirling darkness.
23 For is not everything dark as night for a country in
            distress?

   As the past humbled the land of Zebulun and the land of Naphtali, so the future will glorify the Way of the Sea, beyond the Jordan, the territory of the nations.

9   The people that walked in darkness have seen a
            great light;
      on the inhabitants of a country in shadow dark as
            death light has blazed forth.
   2 You have enlarged the nation, you have increased
            its joy;
      they rejoice before you as people rejoice at harvest
            time,
      as they exult when they are dividing the spoils.

   3 For the yoke that weighed on it, the bar across its
            shoulders,
      the rod of its oppressor,
      these you have broken as on the day of Midian.

   4 For all the footgear clanking over the ground
      and all the clothing rolled in blood,
      will be burnt, will be food for the flames.

8, 21f: These verses have been transposed and placed within Is 14, 25, which affords the context in which they can be understood.

| NEW REVISED STANDARD VERSION | REVISED ENGLISH BIBLE |

6 For a child has been born for us,
  a son given to us;
authority rests upon his shoulders;
  and he is named
Wonderful Counselor, Mighty God,
  Everlasting Father, Prince of Peace.
7 His authority shall grow continually,
  and there shall be endless peace
for the throne of David and his kingdom.
  He will establish and uphold it
with justice and with righteousness
  from this time onward and forevermore.
The zeal of the Lord of hosts will do this.

8 The Lord sent a word against Jacob,
  and it fell on Israel;
9 and all the people knew it—
  Ephraim and the inhabitants of Samaria—
but in pride and arrogance of heart they said:
10 "The bricks have fallen,
  but we will build with dressed stones;
the sycamores have been cut down,
  but we will put cedars in their place."
11 So the Lord raised adversaries^c against them,
  and stirred up their enemies,
12 the Arameans on the east and the Philistines on
    the west,
  and they devoured Israel with open mouth.
For all this his anger has not turned away;
  his hand is stretched out still.

13 The people did not turn to him who struck them,
  or seek the Lord of hosts.
14 So the Lord cut off from Israel head and tail,
  palm branch and reed in one day—
15 elders and dignitaries are the head,
  and prophets who teach lies are the tail;
16 for those who led this people led them astray,
  and those who were led by them were left in
    confusion.
17 That is why the Lord did not have pity on^d their
    young people,
  or compassion on their orphans and widows;
for everyone was godless and an evildoer,
  and every mouth spoke folly.
For all this his anger has not turned away,
  his hand is stretched out still.

18 For wickedness burned like a fire,
  consuming briers and thorns;
it kindled the thickets of the forest,
  and they swirled upward in a column of
    smoke.
19 Through the wrath of the Lord of hosts
  the land was burned,
and the people became like fuel for the fire;
  no one spared another.
20 They gorged on the right, but still were hungry,
  and they devoured on the left, but were not
    satisfied;
they devoured the flesh of their own kindred;^e
21 Manasseh devoured Ephraim, and Ephraim
    Manasseh,
  and together they were against Judah.
For all this his anger has not turned away;
  his hand is stretched out still.

---

6 For a child has been born to us, a son is given to
    us;
he will bear the symbol of dominion on his
    shoulder,
and his title will be:
Wonderful Counsellor, Mighty Hero,
  Eternal Father, Prince of Peace.
7 Wide will be the dominion
and boundless the peace
bestowed on David's throne and on his kingdom,
to establish and support it
with justice and righteousness
from now on, for evermore.
The zeal of the Lord of Hosts will do this.

8 The Lord has sent forth his word against Jacob
  and it will fall on Israel;
9 all the people will know,
  Ephraim and the inhabitants of Samaria,
though in their pride and arrogance they say,
10 'The bricks have fallen down,
  but we shall rebuild in dressed stone;
the sycomores are cut down,
  but we shall grow cedars in their place.'
11 The Lord has raised their foes against them
  and spurred on their enemies,
12 Aramaeans from the east, Philistines from the
    west,
  and they have swallowed Israel in one mouthful.
For all this his anger has not abated;
  his hand still threatens.

13 Yet the people did not come back to him who
    struck them,
  nor seek guidance from the Lord of Hosts;
14 therefore on one day the Lord cut off from Israel
  head and tail, palm-frond and reed.

(15 The aged and the honoured are the head; the prophets
who give false instruction are the tail.)

16 Those who guide this people have led them astray,
  and those who follow their guidance are engulfed.
17 That is why the Lord showed no mercy to their
    youths,
  no compassion towards the fatherless and widows;
it is a nation of godless evildoers,
  every one speaking impiety.
For all this his anger has not abated;
  his hand still threatens.

18 Wicked men have been set ablaze like a fire
  fed with briars and thorns,
kindled in the thickets of the forest;
  they are wrapped in a pall of smoke.
19 The land is scorched by the fury of the Lord of
    Hosts,
  and the people are like food for the fire.
20 On one side, a man is eating his fill
  but yet remains hungry;
on another, a man is devouring
  but is not satisfied;
each feeds on his own children's flesh,
  and no one spares his own brother.

(Manasseh Ephraim, and Ephraim Manasseh—together
they are against Judah.)

21 For all this his anger has not abated;
  his hand still threatens.

9:7 **Wide:** so Gk; Heb. prefixes two unintelligible letters.
9:11 **their foes:** prob. rdg; Heb. the foes of Rezin.   9:20 **and no
one … brother:** transposed from end of verse 19.

---

^c Cn: Heb the adversaries of Rezin   ^d Q Ms: MT rejoice over
^e Or arm

<table>
<tr><td>

5 For a child is born to us, a son is given us;
  upon his shoulder dominion rests.
They name him Wonder-Counselor, God-Hero,
  Father-Forever, Prince of Peace.
6 His dominion is vast
  and forever peaceful,
From David's throne, and over his kingdom,
  which he confirms and sustains
By judgment and justice,
  both now and forever.
The zeal of the LORD of hosts will do this!

7 The Lord has sent word against Jacob,
  it falls upon Israel;
8 And all the people know it,
  Ephraim and those who dwell in Samaria,
  those who say in arrogance and pride of heart,
9 "Bricks have fallen,
  but we will build with cut stone;
Sycamores are felled,
  but we will replace them with cedars."
10 But the LORD raises up their foes against them
  and stirs up their enemies to action:
11 Aram on the east and the Philistines on the west
  devour Israel with open mouth.
For all this, his wrath is not turned back,
  and his hand is still outstretched!

12 The people do not turn to him who struck them,
  nor seek the LORD of hosts.
13 So the LORD severs from Israel head and tail,
  palm branch and reed in one day.
14 [The elder and the noble are the head,
  the prophet who teaches falsehood is the tail.]
15 The leaders of this people mislead them
  and those to be led are engulfed.
16 For this reason, the Lord does not spare their
    young men,
  and their orphans and widows he does not pity;
They are wholly profaned and sinful,
  and every mouth gives vent to folly.
For all this, his wrath is not turned back,
  his hand is still outstretched!

17 For wickedness burns like fire,
  devouring brier and thorn;
It kindles the forest thickets,
  which go up in columns of smoke.
18 At the wrath of the LORD of hosts the land quakes,
  and the people are like fuel for fire;
No man spares his brother,
  each devours the flesh of his neighbor.
19 Though they hack on the right, they are hungry;
  though they eat on the left, they are not filled.
20 Manasseh devours Ephraim, and
    Ephraim Manasseh;
  together they turn on Judah.
For all this, his wrath is not turned back.
  his hand is still outstretched!

</td><td>

5 For a son has been born for us,
  a son has been given to us,
  and dominion has been laid on his shoulders;
  and this is the name he has been given,
  'Wonder-Counsellor, Mighty-God,
  Eternal-Father, Prince-of-Peace',
6 to extend his dominion in boundless peace,
  over the throne of David and over his kingdom
  to make it secure and sustain it
  in fair judgement and integrity.
From this time onwards and for ever,
  the jealous love of Yahweh Sabaoth will do this.

7 The Lord has launched a word at Jacob
  and it has fallen on Israel;
8 and the people will all soon know it,
  Ephraim and the inhabitants of Samaria,
  who say in the pride of their arrogant hearts,
9 'The bricks have fallen down but we shall rebuild
    with dressed stone;
  the sycamores have been felled but we shall
    replace them with cedars.'
10 But, against them, Yahweh has raised their foe
    Razon,
  he has whipped up their enemies,
11 Aram to the east, Philistines to the west,
  to devour Israel with gaping jaws.
After all this, his anger is not spent.
No, his hand is still raised!

12 But the people would not come back to him who
    struck them,
  they would not seek out Yahweh Sabaoth;
13 hence Yahweh has topped and tailed Israel,
  cutting off palm and reed in a single day.
14 (The 'top' is the elder and the man of rank;
  the 'tail' is the prophet teaching lies.)
15 This people's leaders have led them astray,
  and those who are led by them are swallowed up.
16 Hence the Lord will no longer take delight in their
    young people,
  or pity on their orphans and widows,
  since all of them are godless and evil,
  and everything they say is madness.
After all this, his anger is not spent.
No, his hand is still raised!

17 Yes, wickedness has been burning like a fire,
  devouring bramble and thorn-bush,
  setting the forest thickets ablaze —
  up they go in billowing smoke!
18 The country has been set on fire
  by the fury of Yahweh Sabaoth,
  and the people are like food for the flames.
No one spares a thought for his brother.
19 They have sliced to the right and are still hungry,
  they have eaten to the left and are not satisfied;
  each devours the flesh of his own arm.
20 Manasseh devours Ephraim, Ephraim Manasseh,
  together they turn against Judah.
After all this, his anger is not spent.
No, his hand is still raised!

</td></tr>
</table>

NEW REVISED STANDARD VERSION

10 Ah, you who make iniquitous decrees,
who write oppressive statutes,
2 to turn aside the needy from justice
and to rob the poor of my people of their right,
that widows may be your spoil,
and that you may make the orphans your prey!
3 What will you do on the day of punishment,
in the calamity that will come from far away?
To whom will you flee for help,
and where will you leave your wealth,
4 so as not to crouch among the prisoners
or fall among the slain?
For all this his anger has not turned away;
his hand is stretched out still.

5 Ah, Assyria, the rod of my anger—
the club in their hands is my fury!
6 Against a godless nation I send him,
and against the people of my wrath I command
him,
to take spoil and seize plunder,
and to tread them down like the mire of the
streets.
7 But this is not what he intends,
nor does he have this in mind;
but it is in his heart to destroy,
and to cut off nations not a few.
8 For he says:
"Are not my commanders all kings?
9 Is not Calno like Carchemish?
Is not Hamath like Arpad?
Is not Samaria like Damascus?
10 As my hand has reached to the kingdoms of the
idols
whose images were greater than those of
Jerusalem and Samaria,
11 shall I not do to Jerusalem and her idols
what I have done to Samaria and her images?"

12 When the Lord has finished all his work on Mount
Zion and on Jerusalem, he _f_ will punish the arrogant boasting of the king of Assyria and his haughty pride. 13 For he
says:

"By the strength of my hand I have done it,
and by my wisdom, for I have understanding;
I have removed the boundaries of peoples,
and have plundered their treasures;
like a bull I have brought down those who sat
on thrones.
14 My hand has found, like a nest,
the wealth of the peoples;
and as one gathers eggs that have been forsaken,
so I have gathered all the earth;
and there was none that moved a wing,
or opened its mouth, or chirped."

15 Shall the ax vaunt itself over the one who wields
it,
or the saw magnify itself against the one who
handles it?
As if a rod should raise the one who lifts it up,
or as if a staff should lift the one who is not
wood!
16 Therefore the Sovereign, the LORD of hosts,
will send wasting sickness among his stout
warriors,
and under his glory a burning will be kindled,
like the burning of fire.

_f_ Heb _I_

REVISED ENGLISH BIBLE

10 Woe betide those who enact unjust laws
and draft oppressive edicts,
2 depriving the poor of justice,
robbing the weakest of my people of their rights,
plundering the widow and despoiling the fatherless!
3 What will you do when called to account,
when devastation from afar confronts you?
To whom will you flee for help,
and where will you leave your children
4 so that they do not cower among the prisoners
or fall among the slain?
For all this his anger has not abated;
his hand still threatens.

5 The Assyrian! He is the rod I wield in my anger,
the staff in the hand of my wrath.
6 I send him against a godless nation,
I bid him march against a people who rouse my
fury,
to pillage and plunder at will,
to trample them down like mud in the street.
7 But this man's purpose is lawless,
and lawless are the plans in his mind;
for his thought is only to destroy
and to wipe out nation after nation.
8 'Are not my commanders all kings?' he boasts.
9 'See how Calno has suffered the fate of
Carchemish.
Is not Hamath like Arpad, Samaria like Damascus?
10 Before now I have overcome kingdoms full of
idols,
with more images than have Jerusalem and
Samaria,
11 and now, what I did to Samaria and her worthless
gods,
I shall do also to Jerusalem and her idols.'

12 When the Lord has finished all that he means to do
against Mount Zion and Jerusalem, he will punish the king
of Assyria for the words which spring from his arrogance
and for his high and haughty mien, 13 because he said:

By my own might I have done it,
and in my own far-seeing wisdom
I have swept aside the frontiers of nations
and plundered their treasures;
like a bull I have trampled on their inhabitants.
14 My hand has come on the wealth of nations as on
a nest,
and, as one gathers eggs that have been
abandoned,
so have I taken every land;
not a wing fluttered,
not a beak gaped, no cheep was heard.

15 Will the axe set itself up against the hewer,
or the saw claim mastery over the sawyer,
as if a stick were to brandish him who raises it,
or a wooden staff to wield one who is not wood?

16 Therefore the Lord, the LORD of Hosts,
will inflict a wasting disease on the king's frame,
on his sturdy frame from head to toe,
and in his body a fever like fire will rage.

10:5 **the staff . . . wrath:** _prob. rdg; Heb. obscure._   10:12 **he
will punish:** _so Gk; Heb._ I shall punish.   10:16 **from . . . toe:**
transposed from verse 18; lit. from neck to groin.

10 Woe to those who enact unjust statutes
and who write oppressive decrees,
2 Depriving the needy of judgment
and robbing my people's poor of their rights.
Making widows their plunder,
and orphans their prey!
3 What will you do on the day of punishment,
when ruin comes from afar?
To whom will you flee for help?
Where will you leave your wealth,
4 Lest it sink beneath the captive
or fall beneath the slain?
For all this, his wrath is not turned back,
his hand is still outstretched!

5 Woe to Assyria! My rod in anger,
my staff in wrath.
6 Against an impious nation I send him.
and against a people under my wrath I order him
To seize plunder, carry off loot,
and tread them down like the mud of the streets.
7 But this is not what he intends,
nor does he have this in mind;
Rather, it is in his heart to destroy,
to make an end of nations not a few.
8 "Are not my commanders all kings?" he says,
9 "Is not Calno like Carchemish,
Or Hamath like Arpad,
or Samaria like Damascus?
10 Just as my hand reached out to
idolatrous kingdoms
that had more images than Jerusalem
and Samaria,
11 Just as I treated Samaria and her idols,
shall I not do to Jerusalem and her
graven images?"

12 [But when the Lord has brought to an end all his work
on Mount Zion and in Jerusalem,

I will punish the utterance
of the king of Assyria's proud heart,
13 and the boastfulness of his haughty eyes. For
he says:]

"By my own power I have done it,
and by my wisdom, for I am shrewd.
I have moved the boundaries of peoples,
their treasures I have pillaged,
and, like a giant, I have put down the enthroned.
14 My hand has seized like a nest
the riches of nations;
As one takes eggs left alone,
so I took in all the earth;
No one fluttered a wing,
or opened a mouth, or chirped!"

15 Will the axe boast against him who hews with it?
Will the saw exalt itself above him who
wields it?
As if a rod could sway him who lifts it,
or a staff him who is not wood!
16 Therefore the Lord, the Lord of hosts,
will send among his fat ones leanness,
And instead of his glory there will be kindling
like the kindling of fire.

10 Woe to those who enact unjust decrees,
who compose oppressive legislation
2 to deny justice to the weak
and to cheat the humblest of my people of fair
judgement,
to make widows their prey
and to rob the orphan.
3 What will you do on the day of punishment,
when disaster comes from far away?
To whom will you run for help
and where will you leave your riches,
4 to avoid squatting among the captives
or falling among the slain?
After all this, his anger is not spent.
No, his hand is still raised!

5 Woe to Assyria, rod of my anger,
the club in their hands is my fury!
6 I was sending him against a godless nation,
commissioning him against the people who enraged
me,
to pillage and plunder at will
and trample on them like the mud in the streets.
7 But this was not his intention
nor did his heart plan it so,
for he dreamed of putting an end to them,
of liquidating nations without number!
8 For he thought, 'Are not my officers all kings?
9 Is not Calno like Carchemish,
Hamath like Arpad,
Samaria like Damascus?
10 As my hand has found the kingdoms of the false
gods,
where there were more images than in Jerusalem
and Samaria,
11 as I have treated Samaria and her false gods
shall I not treat Jerusalem and her statues too?'

12 When the Lord has completed all his work on Mount
Zion and in Jerusalem, he will punish the fruit of the king
of Assyria's boastful heart and the insolence of his haughty
looks.
13 For he thinks:

'By the strength of my own arm I have done this
and by my own wisdom: how intelligent I have
been!
I have abolished the frontiers between peoples,
I have plundered their treasures,
like a hero, I have subjugated their inhabitants.
14 My hand has found, as though a bird's nest,
the riches of the peoples.
Like someone collecting deserted eggs,
I have collected the whole world
while no one has fluttered a wing
or opened a beak to squawk.'

15 Does the axe claim more credit than the man who
wields it,
or the saw more strength than the man who handles
it?
As though a staff controlled those who raise it,
or the club could raise what is not made of wood!
16 That is why Yahweh Sabaoth is going to inflict
leanness on his stout men,
and beneath his glory kindle a fever burning like a
fire.

NEW REVISED STANDARD VERSION	REVISED ENGLISH BIBLE

17 The light of Israel will become a fire,
    and his Holy One a flame;
and it will burn and devour
    his thorns and briers in one day.
18 The glory of his forest and his fruitful land
    the LORD will destroy, both soul and body,
and it will be as when an invalid wastes away.
19 The remnant of the trees of his forest will be so
    few
    that a child can write them down.

20 On that day the remnant of Israel and the survivors of the house of Jacob will no more lean on the one who struck them, but will lean on the LORD, the Holy One of Israel, in truth. 21 A remnant will return, the remnant of Jacob, to the mighty God. 22 For though your people Israel were like the sand of the sea, only a remnant of them will return. Destruction is decreed, overflowing with righteousness. 23 For the Lord GOD of hosts will make a full end, as decreed, in all the earth.g

24 Therefore thus says the Lord GOD of hosts: O my people, who live in Zion, do not be afraid of the Assyrians when they beat you with a rod and lift up their staff against you as the Egyptians did. 25 For in a very little while my indignation will come to an end, and my anger will be directed to their destruction. 26 The LORD of hosts will wield a whip against them, as when he struck Midian at the rock of Oreb; his staff will be over the sea, and he will lift it as he did in Egypt. 27 On that day his burden will be removed from your shoulder, and his yoke will be destroyed from your neck.

He has gone up from Rimmon,h
28   he has come to Aiath;
he has passed through Migron,
    at Michmash he stores his baggage;
29 they have crossed over the pass,
    at Geba they lodge for the night;
Ramah trembles,
    Gibeah of Saul has fled.
30 Cry aloud, O daughter Gallim!
    Listen, O Laishah!
    Answer her, O Anathoth!
31 Madmenah is in flight,
    the inhabitants of Gebim flee for safety.
32 This very day he will halt at Nob,
    he will shake his fist
at the mount of daughter Zion,
    the hill of Jerusalem.

33 Look, the Sovereign, the LORD of hosts,
    will lop the boughs with terrifying power;
the tallest trees will be cut down,
    and the lofty will be brought low.
34 He will hack down the thickets of the forest with
    an ax,
and Lebanon with its majestic treesi will fall.

---

17 The Light of Israel will become a fire
    and its Holy One a flame,
which in one day will burn up and consume
    his thorns and his briars;
18 his splendid forest and meadow will be destroyed
    as suddenly as someone falling in a fit;
19 what remain of the trees in his forest will be so
    few
    that a child might record them.

20 On that day the remnant of Israel, the survivors of Jacob, will lean no more on him who scourged them; without wavering they will lean on the LORD, the Holy One of Israel.

21 A remnant will return, a remnant of Jacob,
    to God their strength.
22 Israel, your people may be many as the sands of
    the sea,
but only a remnant will return.
The instrument of final destruction
    will overflow with justice,
23 for the Lord, the LORD of Hosts, will bring final
    destruction
on the whole land.

24 Therefore these are the words of the Lord, the LORD of Hosts: My people, you dwellers in Zion, do not be afraid of the Assyrians, though they beat you with their rod and lift their staff against you as the Egyptians did; 25 for in a very short time my wrath will be over and my anger will be finally spent. 26 Then the LORD of Hosts will brandish his scourge at them as he did when he struck Midian at the Rock of Oreb; he will lift his staff against the Euphrates as he did against Egypt.

27 On that day
    the burden they laid on your shoulder will be
    removed
    and their yoke will be broken from off your neck.

28 An invader from Rimmon has reached Aiath,
    has passed through Migron,
    and left his baggage train at Michmash;
29 he has passed through Maabarah
    and camped for the night at Geba.
Ramah is terrified, Gibeah of Saul is in flight.
30 Bath-gallim, raise a shrill cry.
    Hear it, Laish. Answer her, Anathoth.
31 Madmenah retreats;
    the people of Gebim seek cover.
32 This day he will be at Nob;
    he gives the signal to advance
against the mount of Zion,
    the hill of Jerusalem.

33 The Lord, the LORD of Hosts,
    will shatter the trees with a crash,
the tallest will be hewn down, the lofty laid low,
34 the thickets of the forest will be felled with the
    axe,
and Lebanon with its noble trees will fall.

10.25 **will be finally spent:** *prob. rdg; Heb. obscure.*
10.27–28 **and their . . . Rimmon:** *prob. rdg; Heb.* and their yoke from upon your neck, and a yoke shall be broken because of oil.
(28)He.

g Or *land*   h Cn: Heb *and his yoke from your neck, and a yoke will be destroyed because of fatness*   i Cn Compare Gk Vg: Heb *with a majestic one*

17 The Light of Israel will become a fire,
 Israel's Holy One a flame,
That burns and consumes his briers
 and his thorns in a single day.
18 His splendid forests and orchards
 will be consumed, soul and body;
19 And the remnant of the trees in his forest
 will be so few,
Like poles set up for signals,
 that any boy can record them.
20   On that day
The remnant of Israel,
 the survivors of the house of Jacob,
 will no more lean upon him who struck them;
But they will lean upon the LORD,
 the Holy One of Israel, in truth.
21 A remnant will return, the remnant of Jacob,
 to the mighty God.
22 For though your people, O Israel,
 were like the sand of the sea,
Only a remnant of them will return;
 their destruction is decreed
 as overwhelming justice demands.

23 Yes, the destruction he has decreed, the Lord, the GOD
of hosts, will carry out within the whole land. 24 Therefore
thus says the Lord, the GOD of hosts: O my people, who
dwell in Zion, do not fear the Assyrian, though he strikes
you with a rod, and raises his staff against you. 25 For only
a brief moment more, and my anger shall be over; but them
I will destroy in wrath. 26 Then the LORD of hosts will raise
against them a scourge such as struck Midian at the rock of
Oreb; and he will raise his staff over the sea as he did
against Egypt. 27 On that day,

His burden shall be taken from your shoulder,
 and his yoke shattered from your neck.
He has come up from the direction of Rimmon,
28   he has reached Aiath, passed through Migron,
 at Michmash his supplies are stored.
29 They cross the ravine:
 "We will spend the night at Geba."
Ramah is in terror,
 Gibeah of Saul has fled.
30 Cry and shriek, O daughter of Gallim!
 Hearken, Laishah! Answer her, Anathoth!
31 Madmenah is in flight,
 the inhabitants of Gebim seek refuge.
32 Even today he will halt at Nob,
 he will shake his fist at the mount of
  daughter Zion,
 the hill of Jerusalem!
33 Behold, the Lord, the LORD of hosts,
 lops off the boughs with terrible violence;
The tall of stature are felled,
 and the lofty ones brought low;
34 The forest thickets are felled with the axe,
 and Lebanon in its splendor falls.

17 The light of Israel will become a fire
 and its Holy One a flame
burning and devouring
 his thorn-bushes and brambles in a day.
18 He will consume his luxuriant forest and
  productive ground,
he will ravage body and soul:
 it will be like a consumptive wasting away;
19 and what remain of the trees of his forest
 will be so few that a child could write their
  number.
20 When that day comes,
 the remnant of Israel and the survivors of the
  House of Jacob
will stop relying on the man who strikes them
 and will truly rely on Yahweh,
 the Holy One of Israel.
21 A remnant will return, the remnant of Jacob,
 to the mighty God.
22 Israel, though your people are like the sand of the
  sea,
 only a remnant of them will return:
a destruction has been decreed
 which will make justice overflow,
23 for, throughout the country,
 the Lord Yahweh Sabaoth will enforce the
  destruction now decreed.

24 That is why the Lord Yahweh Sabaoth says this:

My people who live in Zion,
 do not be afraid of Assyria!
He may strike you with the rod,
 he may raise the club against you
 (on the way from Egypt),
25 but in a very short time
 the retribution will come to an end,
 and my anger will destroy them.
26 Yahweh Sabaoth will brandish a whip at him
 as he struck Midian at Oreb's Rock,
 will brandish his rod at the Sea
 as he raised it on the way from Egypt.
27 When that day comes,
 his burden will fall from your shoulder,
 and his yoke from your neck,
 and the yoke will be destroyed . . .
28 He has reached Aiath,
 he has moved on to Migron,
 he has left his baggage train at Michmash.
29 They have passed through the defile,
 they have bivouacked at Geba.
Ramah quaked, Gibeah of Saul has fled.
30 Cry your loudest, Bath-Gallim!
 Pay attention, Laish!
 Answer her, Anathoth!
31 Madmenah has run away,
 the inhabitants of Gebim have taken cover.
32 This very day, as he halts at Nob,
 he will shake his fist at the mountain of the
  daughter of Zion,
 the hill of Jerusalem.
33 See how the Lord Yahweh Sabaoth violently lops
  off the foliage!
 The ones standing highest are cut down, the
  proudest are laid low!
34 The forest thickets fall beneath the axe,
 and the Lebanon falls to the blows of a Mighty
  One.

NEW REVISED STANDARD VERSION

REVISED ENGLISH BIBLE

11 A shoot shall come out from the stump of Jesse,
and a branch shall grow out of his roots.
2 The spirit of the LORD shall rest on him,
the spirit of wisdom and understanding,
the spirit of counsel and might,
the spirit of knowledge and the fear of the
LORD.
3 His delight shall be in the fear of the LORD.

He shall not judge by what his eyes see,
or decide by what his ears hear;
4 but with righteousness he shall judge the poor,
and decide with equity for the meek of the
earth;
he shall strike the earth with the rod of his
mouth,
and with the breath of his lips he shall kill the
wicked.
5 Righteousness shall be the belt around his waist,
and faithfulness the belt around his loins.

6 The wolf shall live with the lamb,
the leopard shall lie down with the kid,
the calf and the lion and the fatling together,
and a little child shall lead them.
7 The cow and the bear shall graze,
their young shall lie down together;
and the lion shall eat straw like the ox.
8 The nursing child shall play over the hole of the
asp,
and the weaned child shall put its hand on the
adder's den.
9 They will not hurt or destroy
on all my holy mountain;
for the earth will be full of the knowledge of the
LORD
as the waters cover the sea.

10 On that day the root of Jesse shall stand as a signal
to the peoples; the nations shall inquire of him, and his
dwelling shall be glorious.
11 On that day the Lord will extend his hand yet a
second time to recover the remnant that is left of his people,
from Assyria, from Egypt, from Pathros, from Ethiopia,^j
from Elam, from Shinar, from Hamath, and from the coastlands of the sea.

12 He will raise a signal for the nations,
and will assemble the outcasts of Israel,
and gather the dispersed of Judah
from the four corners of the earth.
13 The jealousy of Ephraim shall depart,
the hostility of Judah shall be cut off;
Ephraim shall not be jealous of Judah,
and Judah shall not be hostile towards
Ephraim.
14 But they shall swoop down on the backs of the
Philistines in the west,
together they shall plunder the people of the
east.
They shall put forth their hand against Edom and
Moab,
and the Ammonites shall obey them.
15 And the LORD will utterly destroy
the tongue of the sea of Egypt;
and will wave his hand over the River
with his scorching wind;
and will split it into seven channels,
and make a way to cross on foot;

11 Then a branch will grow from the stock of Jesse,
and a shoot will spring from his roots.
2 On him the spirit of the LORD will rest:
a spirit of wisdom and understanding,
a spirit of counsel and power,
a spirit of knowledge and fear of the LORD;
3 and in the fear of the LORD will be his delight.
He will not judge by outward appearances
or decide a case on hearsay;
4 but with justice he will judge the poor
and defend the humble in the land with equity;
like a rod his verdict will strike the ruthless,
and with his word he will slay the wicked.
5 He will wear the belt of justice,
and truth will be his girdle.

6 Then the wolf will live with the lamb,
and the leopard lie down with the kid;
the calf and the young lion will feed together,
with a little child to tend them.
7 The cow and the bear will be friends,
and their young will lie down together;
and the lion will eat straw like cattle.
8 The infant will play over the cobra's hole,
and the young child dance over the viper's nest.
9 There will be neither hurt nor harm in all my holy
mountain;
for the land will be filled with the knowledge of
the LORD,
as the waters cover the sea.

10 On that day a scion from the root of Jesse
will arise like a standard to rally the peoples;
the nations will resort to him,
and his abode will be glorious.

11 On that day the Lord will exert his power a second time
to recover the remnant of his people from Assyria and
Egypt, from Pathros and Cush, from Elam, Shinar, Hamath, and the islands of the sea.

12 He will hoist a standard for the nations
and gather those dispersed from Israel;
he will assemble Judah's scattered people
from the four corners of the earth.
13 Ephraim's jealousy will cease,
and enmity towards Judah will end.
Ephraim will not be jealous of Judah,
nor will Judah be hostile towards Ephraim.
14 They will swoop down on the Philistine flank in
the west
and together plunder the tribes of the east:
Edom and Moab will be in their clutches,
and Ammon will be subject to them.
15 The LORD will divide the tongue of the Egyptian
sea.
He will wave his hand over the Euphrates
to bring a mighty wind,
and will split it into seven wadis
so that it may be crossed dry-shod.

11:4 **ruthless:** *prob. rdg; Heb.* land.   11:6 **will feed:** *so Scroll;*
Heb. and the buffalo.   11:8 **dance over:** *prob. rdg; Heb.* obscure.
11:15 **mighty:** *so Gk; Heb.* glow.

^j Or *Nubia;* Heb *Cush*

11 But a shoot shall sprout from the stump
  of Jesse,
  and from his roots a bud shall blossom.
² The spirit of the LORD shall rest upon him:
  a spirit of wisdom and of understanding,
A spirit of counsel and of strength,
  a spirit of knowledge and of fear of the LORD,
3 and his delight shall be the fear of the LORD.
Not by appearance shall he judge,
  nor by hearsay shall he decide,
⁴ But he shall judge the poor with justice,
  and decide aright for the land's afflicted.
He shall strike the ruthless with the rod of
  his mouth,
  and with the breath of his lips he shall slay
  the wicked.
⁵ Justice shall be the band around his waist,
  and faithfulness a belt upon his hips.

⁶ Then the wolf shall be a guest of the lamb,
  and the leopard shall lie down with the kid;
The calf and the young lion shall browse together,
  with a little child to guide them.
⁷ The cow and the bear shall be neighbors,
  together their young shall rest;
  the lion shall eat hay like the ox.
⁸ The baby shall play by the cobra's den,
  and the child lay his hand on the adder's lair.
⁹ There shall be no harm or ruin on all my
  holy mountain;
  for the earth shall be filled with knowledge of
  the LORD,
  as water covers the sea.

10   On that day,
The root of Jesse,
  set up as a signal for the nations,
The Gentiles shall seek out,
  for his dwelling shall be glorious.
11   On that day,
The Lord shall again take it in hand
  to reclaim the remnant of his people
  that is left from Assyria and Egypt,
Pathros, Ethiopia, and Elam,
  Shinar, Hamath, and the isles of the sea.
¹² He shall raise a signal to the nations
  and gather the outcasts of Israel;
The dispersed of Judah he shall assemble
  from the four corners of the earth.
¹³ The envy of Ephraim shall pass away,
  and the rivalry of Judah be removed;
Ephraim shall not be jealous of Judah,
  and Judah shall not be hostile to Ephraim;
¹⁴ But they shall swoop down on the foothills
  of the Philistines to the west,
  together they shall plunder the Kedemites;
Edom and Moab shall be their possessions,
  and the Ammonites their subjects.
¹⁵ The LORD shall dry up the tongue of the Sea
  of Egypt,
  and wave his hand over the Euphrates in his
  fierce anger
And shatter it into seven streamlets,
  so that it can be crossed in sandals.

11 A shoot will spring from the stock of Jesse,
  a new shoot will grow from his roots.
² On him will rest the spirit of Yahweh,
  the spirit of wisdom and insight,
  the spirit of counsel and power,
  the spirit of knowledge and fear of Yahweh:
³ his inspiration will lie in fearing Yahweh.
His judgement will not be by appearances,
  his verdict not given on hearsay.
⁴ He will judge the weak with integrity
  and give fair sentence for the humblest in the land.
He will strike the country with the rod of his
  mouth
  and with the breath of his lips bring death to the
  wicked.

⁵ Uprightness will be the belt around his waist,
  and constancy the belt about his hips.

⁶ The wolf will live with the lamb,
  the panther lie down with the kid,
  calf, lion and fat-stock beast together,
  with a little boy to lead them.
⁷ The cow and the bear will graze,
  their young will lie down together.
  The lion will eat hay like the ox.
⁸ The infant will play over the den of the adder;
  the baby will put his hand into the viper's lair.
⁹ No hurt, no harm will be done
  on all my holy mountain,
  for the country will be full of knowledge of
  Yahweh
  as the waters cover the sea.

¹⁰ That day, the root of Jesse, standing as a signal for
  the peoples,
  will be sought out by the nations and its home will
  be glorious.
¹¹ When that day comes,
  the Lord will raise his hand a second time
  to ransom the remnant of his people,
  those still left, from Assyria, from Egypt,
  from Pathros, Cush and Elam,
  from Shinar, Hamath and the islands of the Sea.
¹² He will hoist a signal for the nations
  and assemble the outcasts of Israel;
  he will gather the scattered people of Judah
  from the four corners of the earth.
¹³ Then Ephraim's jealousy will cease
  and Judah's enemies be suppressed;
  Ephraim will no longer be jealous of Judah
  nor Judah any longer hostile to Ephraim,
¹⁴ but together they will swoop on the Philistines'
  back, to the west,
  and together pillage the people of the east.
Edom and Moab will be subject to their sway
  and the Ammonites will obey them.
¹⁵ Then Yahweh will dry up the gulf of the Sea of
  Egypt,
  he will raise his hand against the River
  with the heat of his breath.
He will divide it into seven streams
  for them to cross dry-shod.

16 so there shall be a highway from Assyria
for the remnant that is left of his people,
as there was for Israel
when they came up from the land of Egypt.

12

You will say in that day:
I will give thanks to you, O LORD,
for though you were angry with me,
your anger turned away,
and you comforted me.

2 Surely God is my salvation;
I will trust, and will not be afraid,
for the LORD GOD[k] is my strength and my
might;
he has become my salvation.

3 With joy you will draw water from the wells of salvation. 4 And you will say in that day:
Give thanks to the LORD,
call on his name;
make known his deeds among the nations;
proclaim that his name is exalted.

5 Sing praises to the LORD, for he has done
gloriously;
let this be known[l] in all the earth.
6 Shout aloud and sing for joy, O royal[m] Zion,
for great in your midst is the Holy One of
Israel.

13

The oracle concerning Babylon that Isaiah son of
Amoz saw.

2 On a bare hill raise a signal,
cry aloud to them;
wave the hand for them to enter
the gates of the nobles.
3 I myself have commanded my consecrated ones,
have summoned my warriors, my proudly
exulting ones,
to execute my anger.

4 Listen, a tumult on the mountains
as of a great multitude!
Listen, an uproar of kingdoms,
of nations gathering together!
The LORD of hosts is mustering
an army for battle.
5 They come from a distant land,
from the end of the heavens,
the LORD and the weapons of his indignation,
to destroy the whole earth.

6 Wail, for the day of the LORD is near;
it will come like destruction from the
Almighty![n]
7 Therefore all hands will be feeble,
and every human heart will melt,
8 and they will be dismayed.
Pangs and agony will seize them;
they will be in anguish like a woman in labor.
They will look aghast at one another;
their faces will be aflame.
9 See, the day of the LORD comes,
cruel, with wrath and fierce anger,
to make the earth a desolation,
and to destroy its sinners from it.

16 So there will be a causeway for the remnant of his
people,
for the remnant rescued from Assyria,
as there was for the Israelites when they came up
from Egypt.

12

On that day you will say:
'I shall praise you, LORD.
Though you were angry with me,
your anger has abated,
and you have comforted me.
2 God is my deliverer.
I am confident and unafraid,
for the LORD is my refuge and defence
and has shown himself my deliverer.'

3 With joy you will all draw water
from the wells of deliverance.
4 On that day you will say:
'Give thanks to the LORD, invoke him by name,
make known among the peoples what he has done,
proclaim that his name is exalted.
5 Sing psalms to the LORD, for he has triumphed;
let this be known in all the world.
6 Cry out, shout aloud, you dwellers in Zion,
for the Holy One of Israel is among you in
majesty.'

13

BABYLON: an oracle which Isaiah son of Amoz received in a vision.

2 On a wind-swept height hoist the standard,
sound the call to battle,
wave on the advance
towards the Nobles' Gate.
3 I have issued this order to my fighting men,
and summoned my warriors, all eager for my
victory,
to give effect to my anger.

4 A tumult is heard on the mountains,
the sound of a vast multitude;
it is the clamour of kingdoms, of nations
assembling.
The LORD of Hosts is mustering a host for war.
5 They come from a distant land, from beyond the
horizon,
the LORD with the weapons of his wrath,
to lay the whole earth waste.
6 Wail, for the day of the LORD is at hand,
devastation coming from the Almighty!
7 Because of it every hand will hang limp,
every man's courage melt away;
8 they will writhe with terror;
agonizing pangs will grip them,
like a woman in labour.
They will look aghast at each other,
their faces livid with fear.

9 The day of the LORD is coming,
that cruel day of wrath and fierce anger,
to reduce the earth to desolation
and destroy all the wicked there.

---

k Heb for Yah, the LORD   l Or this is made known
m Or O inhabitant of   n Traditional rendering of Heb Shaddai   12:2 **defence:** prob. rdg; Heb. defence of Yah.

NEW AMERICAN BIBLE	NEW JERUSALEM BIBLE

NEW AMERICAN BIBLE

16 There shall be a highway for the remnant of
   his people
      that is left from Assyria,
As there was for Israel
      when he came up from the land of Egypt.

12 On that day, you will say:
   I give you thanks, O LORD;
      though you have been angry with me,
      your anger has abated, and you have
         consoled me.
2 God indeed is my savior;
      I am confident and unafraid.
   My strength and my courage is the LORD,
      and he has been my savior.
3 With joy you will draw water
      at the fountain of salvation, 4 and say on
         that day:
   Give thanks to the LORD, acclaim his name;
      among the nations make known his deeds,
      proclaim how exalted is his name.
5 Sing praise to the LORD for his
      glorious achievement;
      let this be known throughout all the earth.
6 Shout with exultation, O city of Zion,
      for great in your midst
      is the Holy One of Israel!

13 An oracle concerning Babylon; a vision of Isaiah,
   son of Amoz.

2 Upon the bare mountains set up a signal;
      cry out to them,
   Wave for them to enter
      the gates of the volunteers.

3 I have commanded my dedicated soldiers,
      I have summoned my warriors,
      eager and bold to carry out my anger.
4 Listen! the rumble on the mountains:
      that of an immense throng!
   Listen! the noise of kingdoms,
      nations assembled!
   The LORD of hosts is mustering
      an army for battle.
5 They come from a far-off country,
      and from the end of the heavens,
   The LORD and the instruments of his wrath,
      to destroy all the land.

6 Howl, for the day of the LORD is near;
      as destruction from the Almighty it comes.
7 Therefore all hands fall helpless,
      the bows of the young men fall from
         their hands.
   Every man's heart melts 8 in terror.
   Pangs and sorrows take hold of them,
      like a woman in labor they writhe;
   They look aghast at each other,
      their faces aflame.
9 Lo, the day of the LORD comes,
      cruel, with wrath and burning anger;
   To lay waste the land
      and destroy the sinners within it!

NEW JERUSALEM BIBLE

16 And there will be a highway for the remnant of his
   people
      for those still left, from Assyria,
   as there was for Israel
      when he came out of Egypt.

12 And, that day, you will say:

   'I praise you, Yahweh, you have been angry with
      me
   but your anger is now appeased and you have
      comforted me.
2 Look, he is the God of my salvation:
      I shall have faith and not be afraid,
   for Yahweh is my strength and my song,
      he has been my salvation.' *g*

3 Joyfully you will draw water
      from the springs of salvation
4 and, that day, you will say,
      'Praise Yahweh, invoke his name. *h*
   Proclaim his deeds to the people,
      declare his name sublime.
5 Sing of Yahweh, for his works are majestic,
      make them known throughout the world.
6 Cry and shout for joy, you who live in Zion,
   For the Holy One of Israel is among you in his
      greatness.'

13 Proclamation about Babylon, seen by Isaiah son of
   Amoz.

2 On a bare hill hoist a signal,
      shout for them,
   beckon them to come
      to the Nobles' Gate.
3 I have issued orders
      to my sacred warriors,
   I have summoned my heroes to serve my anger,
      my proud champions.
4 The noise of a great crowd in the mountains,
      like an immense people,
   the tumultuous sound of kingdoms,
      of nations mustering:
   it is Yahweh Sabaoth
      marshalling the troops for battle.
5 They come from a distant country, from the far
      horizons,
   Yahweh and the instruments of his fury
      to lay the whole country waste.

6 Howl! For the Day of Yahweh is near,
      coming like devastation from Shaddai.
7 This is why all hands fall limp,
      why all the men are losing heart;
8 they are panic-stricken,
      seized with pains and convulsions;
   they writhe like a woman in labour,
      they look at one another appalled,
      with feverish faces.
9 Look, the Day of Yahweh is coming,
      merciless, with wrath and burning anger,
   to reduce the country to a desert
      and root out the sinners from it.

g 12 // Ex 15:2.   *h* 12 // Ps 105:1.

10 For the stars of the heavens and their
    constellations
  will not give their light;
the sun will be dark at its rising,
  and the moon will not shed its light.

11 I will punish the world for its evil,
  and the wicked for their iniquity;
I will put an end to the pride of the arrogant,
  and lay low the insolence of tyrants.

12 I will make mortals more rare than fine gold,
  and humans than the gold of Ophir.

13 Therefore I will make the heavens tremble,
  and the earth will be shaken out of its place,
at the wrath of the LORD of hosts
  in the day of his fierce anger.

14 Like a hunted gazelle,
  or like sheep with no one to gather them,
all will turn to their own people,
  and all will flee to their own lands.

15 Whoever is found will be thrust through,
  and whoever is caught will fall by the sword.

16 Their infants will be dashed to pieces
  before their eyes;
their houses will be plundered,
  and their wives ravished.

17 See, I am stirring up the Medes against them,
  who have no regard for silver
  and do not delight in gold.

18 Their bows will slaughter the young men;
  they will have no mercy on the fruit of the
    womb;
  their eyes will not pity children.

19 And Babylon, the glory of kingdoms,
  the splendor and pride of the Chaldeans,
will be like Sodom and Gomorrah
  when God overthrew them.

20 It will never be inhabited
  or lived in for all generations;
Arabs will not pitch their tents there,
  shepherds will not make their flocks lie down
    there.

21 But wild animals will lie down there,
  and its houses will be full of howling creatures;
there ostriches will live,
  and there goat-demons will dance.

22 Hyenas will cry in its towers,
  and jackals in the pleasant palaces;
its time is close at hand,
  and its days will not be prolonged.

14 But the LORD will have compassion on Jacob and
will again choose Israel, and will set them in their
own land; and aliens will join them and attach themselves
to the house of Jacob. 2 And the nations will take them and
bring them to their place, and the house of Israel will possess the nations*o* as male and female slaves in the LORD's
land; they will take captive those who were their captors,
and rule over those who oppressed them.

3 When the LORD has given you rest from your pain and
turmoil and the hard service with which you were made to
serve, 4 you will take up this taunt against the king of Babylon:

How the oppressor has ceased!
  How his insolence*p* has ceased!

5 The LORD has broken the staff of the wicked,
  the scepter of rulers,

10 The stars of heaven in their constellations
  will give no light,
the sun will be dark at its rising,
  and the moon will not shed its light.

11 I shall bring disaster on the world
  and due punishment on the wicked.
I shall cut short insolent pride
  and bring down ruthless arrogance.

12 I shall make human beings scarcer than fine gold,
  more rare than gold of Ophir.

13 Then I shall make the heavens shudder,
  and the earth will be shaken to its foundations
at the wrath of the LORD of Hosts,
  on the day of his blazing anger.

14 Like a gazelle pursued by a hunter
  or like a flock with no shepherd to round it up,
every man will head back to his own people,
  each one will flee to his own land.

15 All who are found will fall by the sword,
  all who are taken will be thrust through;

16 their babes will be battered to death before their
    eyes,
their houses looted and their wives raped.

17 I shall stir up the Medes against them;
  they cannot be bought off with silver,
  nor be tempted by gold;

18 they have no pity on little children
  and spare no mother's son.

19 Babylon, fairest of kingdoms,
  proud beauty of the Chaldaeans,
will be like Sodom and Gomorrah
  when overthrown by God.

20 Never again will she be inhabited,
  no one will live in her throughout the ages;
no Arab will pitch his tent there,
  no shepherds fold their flocks.

21 But marmots will have their lairs in her,
  and porcupines will overrun her houses;
desert-owls will dwell there,
  and there he-goats will gambol;

22 jackals will occupy her mansions,
  and wolves her luxurious palaces.
Her time draws very near;
  her days have not long to run.

14 The LORD will show compassion for Jacob and will
once again make Israel his choice. He will resettle
them on their native soil, where aliens will join them and
attach themselves to Jacob's people. 2 Nations will escort
Israel to her homeland, and she will take them over, both
male and female, as slaves in the LORD's land; she will take
her captors captive and lord it over her oppressors.

3 On the day when the LORD gives you relief from your
pain and trouble and from the cruel servitude imposed upon
you, 4 you will take up this taunt-song over the king of
Babylon:

See how still the oppressor has become,
  how still his raging arrogance!

5 The LORD has broken the rod of the wicked,
  the sceptre of rulers

o Heb *them*   *p* Q Ms Compare Gk Syr Vg: Meaning of MT
uncertain

13:18 **they have:** Heb. *prefixes* bows will strike down young men to
the ground.   13:22 **her mansions:** *prob. rdg; Heb.* her widows.
14:4 **his raging arrogance:** *so Scroll; Heb. obscure.*

NEW AMERICAN BIBLE | NEW JERUSALEM BIBLE

10 The stars and constellations of the heavens
  send forth no light;
The sun is dark when it rises,
  and the light of the moon does not shine.
11 Thus I will punish the world for its evil
  and the wicked for their guilt.
I will put an end to the pride of the arrogant,
  the insolence of tyrants I will humble.
12 I will make mortals more rare than pure gold,
  men, than gold of Ophir.
13 For this I will make the heavens tremble
  and the earth shall be shaken from its place,
At the wrath of the LORD of hosts
  on the day of his burning anger.

14 Like a hunted gazelle,
  or a flock that no one gathers,
Every man shall turn to his kindred
  and flee to his own land.
15 Everyone who is caught shall be run through;
  to a man, they shall fall by the sword.
16 Their infants shall be dashed to pieces in
    their sight;
  their houses shall be plundered
  and their wives ravished.

17 I am stirring up against them the Medes,
  who think nothing of silver
  and take no delight in gold.
18 The fruit of the womb they shall not spare,
  nor shall they have eyes of pity for children.
19 And Babylon, the jewel of kingdoms,
  the glory and pride of the Chaldeans,
Shall be overthrown by God
  like Sodom and like Gomorrah.
20 She shall never be inhabited,
  nor dwelt in, from age to age;
The Arab shall not pitch his tent there,
  nor shepherds couch their flocks.
21 But wildcats shall rest there
  and owls shall fill the houses;
There ostriches shall dwell,
  and satyrs shall dance.
22 Desert beasts shall howl in her castles,
  and jackals in her luxurious palaces.
Her time is near at hand
  and her days shall not be prolonged.

10 For in the sky the stars and Orion
  will shed their light no longer,
the sun will be dark when it rises,
  and the moon will no longer give its light.
11 I am going to punish the world for its wickedness
  and the wicked for their guilt,
and put an end to the pride of the arrogant
  and humble the haughtiness of despots.
12 I shall make people scarcer than pure gold,
  human life scarcer than the gold of Ophir.
13 This is why I am going to shake the heavens,
  why the earth will reel on its foundations,
under the wrath of Yahweh Sabaoth,
  the day when his anger ignites.

14 Then like a hunted gazelle, like sheep that nobody
    gathers in,
everyone will head back to his people,
  everyone will flee to his native land.
15 All those who are found will be stabbed,
  all those captured will fall by the sword,
16 their babies dashed to pieces before their eyes,
  their houses plundered, their wives raped.
17 Look, against them I am stirring up the Medes
  who care nothing for silver,
  who set no value by gold.
18 Bows will annihilate the young men,
  they will have no pity for the fruit of the womb,
  or mercy in their eyes for children.
19 And Babylon, that pearl of kingdoms,
  that splendid jewel of the Chaldaeans,
will, like Sodom and Gomorrah,
  be overthrown by God.
20 Never again will anyone live there or reside there
  for all generations to come.
Never again will the Arab pitch his tent there,
  or the shepherds bring their flocks to rest.
21 But beasts of the desert will make their haunt there
  and owls fill their houses,
there ostriches will settle their home,
  there goats will dance.
22 Hyenas will howl in its towers,
  jackals in its delightful palaces,
for its doom is about to come
  and its days will not last long.

14 When the LORD has pity on Jacob and again chooses Israel and settles them on their own soil, the aliens will join them and be counted with the house of Jacob. 2 The house of Israel will take them and bring them along to its place, and possess them as male and female slaves on the Lord's soil, making captives of its captors and ruling over its oppressors. 3 On the day the LORD relieves you of sorrow and unrest and the hard service in which you have been enslaved, 4 you will take up this taunt-song against the king of Babylon:

How the oppressor has reached his end!
  how the turmoil is stilled!
5 The LORD has broken the rod of the wicked,
  the staff of the tyrants

14 Yahweh will have pity on Jacob, he will choose Israel once more and resettle them on their native soil. Foreigners will join them, attaching themselves to the House of Jacob. 2 Peoples will take them and escort them home, and the House of Israel will take them as slaves, men and women on Yahweh's soil. They will enslave those who enslaved them and will master their oppressors.

3 When that day comes, and Yahweh gives you rest from your suffering and torment and the grim servitude to which you have been subjected, 4 you will recite this satire on the king of Babylon and say:

'How did the tyrant end?
  How did his arrogance end?
5 Yahweh has broken the staff of the wicked,
  the sceptre of rulers,

6 that struck down the peoples in wrath
  with unceasing blows,
that ruled the nations in anger
  with unrelenting persecution.
7 The whole earth is at rest and quiet;
  they break forth into singing.
8 The cypresses exult over you,
  the cedars of Lebanon, saying,
"Since you were laid low,
  no one comes to cut us down."
9 Sheol beneath is stirred up
  to meet you when you come;
it rouses the shades to greet you,
  all who were leaders of the earth;
it raises from their thrones
  all who were kings of the nations.
10 All of them will speak
  and say to you:
"You too have become as weak as we!
  You have become like us!"
11 Your pomp is brought down to Sheol,
  and the sound of your harps;
maggots are the bed beneath you,
  and worms are your covering.

12 How you are fallen from heaven,
  O Day Star, son of Dawn!
How you are cut down to the ground,
  you who laid the nations low!
13 You said in your heart,
  "I will ascend to heaven;
I will raise my throne
  above the stars of God;
I will sit on the mount of assembly
  on the heights of Zaphon;q
14 I will ascend to the tops of the clouds,
  I will make myself like the Most High."
15 But you are brought down to Sheol,
  to the depths of the Pit.
16 Those who see you will stare at you,
  and ponder over you:
"Is this the man who made the earth tremble,
  who shook kingdoms,
17 who made the world like a desert
  and overthrew its cities,
  who would not let his prisoners go home?"
18 All the kings of the nations lie in glory,
  each in his own tomb;
19 but you are cast out, away from your grave,
  like loathsome carrion,r
clothed with the dead, those pierced by the
    sword,
  who go down to the stones of the Pit,
  like a corpse trampled underfoot.
20 You will not be joined with them in burial,
  because you have destroyed your land,
  you have killed your people.

May the descendants of evildoers
  nevermore be named!
21 Prepare slaughter for his sons
  because of the guilt of their father.s
Let them never rise to possess the earth
  or cover the face of the world with cities.

22 I will rise up against them, says the LORD of hosts,
and will cut off from Babylon name and remnant, offspring
and posterity, says the LORD. 23 And I will make it a posses-

6 who in anger struck down peoples
  with unerring blows,
who in fury trod nations underfoot
  with relentless persecution.
7 The whole world rests undisturbed;
  it breaks into cries of joy.
8 The very pines and the cedars of Lebanon exult:
  'Since you have been laid low,' they say,
  'no woodman comes to cut us down.'
9 Sheol below was all astir
  to greet you at your coming;
she roused for you the ancient dead,
  all that were leaders on earth;
she had all who had been kings of the nations
  get up from their thrones.
10 All greet you with these words:
  'So you too are impotent as we are,
  and have become like one of us!'
11 Your pride has been brought down to Sheol,
  to the throng of your victims;
maggots are the mattress beneath you,
  and worms your coverlet.

12 Bright morning star, how you have fallen from
    heaven,
thrown to earth, prostrate among the nations!
13 You thought to yourself:
  'I shall scale the heavens
to set my throne high above the mighty stars;
I shall take my seat on the mountain where the
    gods assemble
  in the far recesses of the north.
14 I shall ascend beyond the towering clouds
  and make myself like the Most High!'
15 Instead you are brought down to Sheol,
  into the depths of the abyss.
16 Those who see you stare at you,
  reflecting as they gaze:
'Is this the man who shook the earth,
  who made kingdoms quake,
17 who turned the world into a desert
  and laid its cities in ruins,
  who never set his prisoners free?'
18 All the kings of every nation lie in honour,
  each in his last resting-place.
19 But you have been flung out without burial
  like some loathsome carrion,
a carcass trampled underfoot,
  a companion to the slain pierced by the sword
  who have gone down to the stony abyss.
20 You will not be joined in burial with those kings,
  for you have ruined your land,
  brought death to your people.
  That wicked dynasty will never again be
    mentioned!
21 Prepare the shambles for his children
  butchered for their fathers' sins;
they will not rise and possess the earth
  or cover the world with their cities.

22 I shall rise against them, declares the LORD of Hosts; I
shall destroy what remains of Babylon, her name, her offspring, and her posterity, declares the LORD; 23 I shall make

q Or assembly in the far north r Cn Compare Gk: Heb like a
loathed branch s Syr Compare Gk: Heb fathers

14:9 Sheol: or The underworld.   14:11 the throng of your
victims: so Scroll; Heb. the music of your lutes.   14:19 carrion:
prob. rdg, cp. Gk; Heb. shoot.

NEW AMERICAN BIBLE	NEW JERUSALEM BIBLE

NEW AMERICAN BIBLE

6 That struck the peoples in wrath
  relentless blows;
That beat down the nations in anger,
  with oppression unchecked.
7 The whole earth rests peacefully,
  song breaks forth;
8 The very cypresses rejoice over you,
  and the cedars of Lebanon:
"Now that you are laid to rest,
  there will be none to cut us down."

9 The nether world below is all astir
  preparing for your coming;
It awakens the shades to greet you,
  all the leaders of the earth;
It has the kings of all nations
  rise from their thrones.
10 All of them speak out
  and say to you,
"You too have become weak like us,
  you are the same as we.
11 Down to the nether world your pomp is brought,
  the music of your harps.
The couch beneath you is the maggot,
  your covering, the worm."

12 How have you fallen from the heavens,
  O morning star, son of the dawn!
How are you cut down to the ground,
  you who mowed down the nations!
13 You said in your heart:
  "I will scale the heavens;
Above the stars of God
  I will set up my throne;
I will take my seat on the Mount of Assembly,
  in the recesses of the North.
14 I will ascend above the tops of the clouds;
  I will be like the Most High!"
15 Yet down to the nether world you go
  to the recesses of the pit!
16 When they see you they will stare,
  pondering over you:
"Is this the man who made the earth tremble.
  and kingdoms quake!
17 Who made the world a desert,
  razed its cities,
  and gave his captives no release?
18 All the kings of the nations lie in glory,
  each in his own tomb;
19 But you are cast forth without burial,
  loathsome and corrupt,
Clothed as those slain at sword-point,
  a trampled corpse.
Going down to the pavement of the pit,
20   you will never be one with them in the grave."
For you have ruined your land,
  you have slain your people!

Let him not be named forever,
  that scion of an evil race!
21 Make ready to slaughter his sons
  for the guilt of their fathers;
Lest they rise and possess the earth,
  and fill the breadth of the world with tyrants.

22 I will rise up against them, says the LORD of hosts, and cut off from Babylon name and remnant, progeny and offspring, says the LORD. 23 I will make it a haunt of hoot owls

NEW JERUSALEM BIBLE

6 furiously lashing peoples
  with continual blows,
  angrily hammering nations,
  pursuing without respite.
7 The whole world is at rest and calm,
  shouts of joy resounding,
8 the cypresses, the cedars of Lebanon,
  rejoice aloud at your fate,
"Now that you have been laid low,
  no one comes up to fell us."

9 'On your account, Sheol below
  is astir to greet your arrival.
He has roused the ghosts to greet you,
  all the rulers of the world.
He has made all the kings of the nations
  get up from their thrones.
10 They will all greet you with the words,
"So, you too are now as weak as we are!
  You, too, have become like us.
11 Your pride has been flung down to Sheol
  with the music of your lyres;
under you a mattress of maggots,
  over you a blanket of worms.
12 How did you come to fall from the heavens,
  Daystar, son of Dawn?
How did you come to be thrown to the ground,
  conqueror of nations?
13 You who used to think to yourself:
  I shall scale the heavens;
higher than the stars of God
  I shall set my throne.
I shall sit on the Mount of Assembly
  far away to the north.
14 I shall climb high above the clouds,
  I shall rival the Most High."
15 Now you have been flung down to Sheol,
  into the depths of the abyss!
16 'When they see you, they will scrutinise you
  and consider what you have become,
"Is this the man who made the world tremble,
  who overthrew kingdoms?
17 He made the world a desert,
  he levelled cities
  and never freed his prisoners to go home."
18 All other kings of nations, all of them,
  lie honourably, each in his own tomb;
19 but you have been thrown away, unburied,
  like a loathsome branch,
covered with heaps of the slain pierced by the
  sword
who fall on the rocks of the abyss
  like trampled carrion.
20 'You will not rejoin them in the grave,
  for you have brought your country to ruin
  and destroyed your people.
The offspring of the wicked
  leave no name behind them.
21 Make ready to slaughter his sons
  for the guilt of their father!
Never again must they rise to conquer the world
  and cover the face of the earth with their cities.

22 'I will rise against them, declares Yahweh Sabaoth, and deprive Babylon of name, remnant, offspring and posterity, declares Yahweh. 23 I shall turn it into the haunt of

NEW REVISED STANDARD VERSION	REVISED ENGLISH BIBLE

sion of the hedgehog, and pools of water, and I will sweep it with the broom of destruction, says the LORD of hosts.

24 The LORD of hosts has sworn:
As I have designed,
  so shall it be;
and as I have planned,
  so shall it come to pass:
25 I will break the Assyrian in my land,
  and on my mountains trample him under foot;
his yoke shall be removed from them,
  and his burden from their shoulders.
26 This is the plan that is planned
  concerning the whole earth;
and this is the hand that is stretched out
  over all the nations.
27 For the LORD of hosts has planned,
  and who will annul it?
His hand is stretched out,
  and who will turn it back?

28 In the year that King Ahaz died this oracle came:

29 Do not rejoice, all you Philistines,
  that the rod that struck you is broken,
for from the root of the snake will come forth an adder,
  and its fruit will be a flying fiery serpent.
30 The firstborn of the poor will graze,
  and the needy lie down in safety;
but I will make your root die of famine,
  and your remnant I[t] will kill.
31 Wail, O gate; cry, O city;
  melt in fear, O Philistia, all of you!
For smoke comes out of the north,
  and there is no straggler in its ranks.
32 What will one answer the messengers of the nation?
"The LORD has founded Zion,
  and the needy among his people
  will find refuge in her."

her a haunt of the bustard, a waste of marshland, and sweep her with the besom of destruction. This is the word of the LORD of Hosts.

24 The LORD of Hosts has sworn this oath:
'As I purposed, so most surely it will be;
  as I planned, so it will take place:
25 I shall break the Assyrian in my own land
  and trample him down on my mountains;
his yoke will be lifted from my people,
  his burden taken from their shoulders.'
26 This is the plan prepared for the whole world,
  this the hand stretched out over all the nations.
27 For the LORD of Hosts has prepared his plan:
  who can frustrate it?
His is the hand that is stretched out,
  and who can turn it back?

28 In the year King Ahaz died this oracle came from God:

29 Let none of you Philistines rejoice
  because the rod that chastised you is broken;
for a viper will be born of a snake,
  and its offspring will be a flying serpent.
30 The poor will graze their flocks in my meadows,
  and the destitute will lie down in safety,
but your offspring I shall do to death by famine,
  and your remnant I shall slay.
31 Wail in the gate, cry for help in the city,
  let all Philistia be stricken with panic;
for a formidable foe is coming from the north,
  with not one straggler in his ranks.
32 What answer is there for a nation's envoys?
It is that the LORD has established Zion,
  and in her the afflicted among his people will find refuge.

15 An oracle concerning Moab.

Because Ar is laid waste in a night,
  Moab is undone;
because Kir is laid waste in a night,
  Moab is undone.
2 Dibon[u] has gone up to the temple,
  to the high places to weep;
over Nebo and over Medeba
  Moab wails.
On every head is baldness,
  every beard is shorn;
3 in the streets they bind on sackcloth;
  on the housetops and in the squares
  everyone wails and melts in tears.
4 Heshbon and Elealeh cry out,
  their voices are heard as far as Jahaz;
therefore the loins of Moab quiver;[v]
  his soul trembles.

15 Moab: an oracle.

On the night when Ar is laid waste,
  Moab meets her doom;
on the night when Kir is laid waste,
  Moab meets her doom.
2 The people of Dibon go up to the shrines to weep;
  Moab is wailing over Nebo and over Medeba.
  Every head is shaven, every beard cut off.
3 In their streets they wear sackcloth,
  they cry out on the roofs;
in the public squares every one wails,
  streaming with tears.
4 Heshbon and Elealeh cry out in distress,
  their voices carry to Jahaz.
So Moab's stoutest warriors become alarmed,
  and their courage ebbs away.

---

[t] Q Ms Vg: MT *he*   [u] Cn: Heb *the house and Dibon*
[v] Cn Compare Gk Syr: Heb *the armed men of Moab cry aloud*

14:30 **remnant I:** *so Scroll; Heb.* remnant he.   15:2 **The people . . . go up:** *prob. rdg; Heb.* He has gone up to the house and Dibon.
15:3 **they cry out:** *prob. rdg, cp. Gk; Heb.* omits.

and a marshland; I will sweep it with the broom of destruction, says the LORD of hosts.

24 The LORD of hosts has sworn:
As I have resolved,
so shall it be;
As I have proposed,
so shall it stand:
25 I will break the Assyrian in my land
and trample him on my mountains;
8, 21 He shall pass through it hard-pressed and hungry,
and in his hunger he shall become enraged,
and curse his king and his gods.
He shall look upward,
but there shall be strict darkness
without any dawn;
8, 22 He shall gaze at the earth,
but there shall be distress and darkness,
with the light blacked out by its clouds.
(25) Then his yoke shall be removed from them,
and his burden from their shoulder.
26 This is the plan proposed for the whole earth,
and this the hand outstretched over all nations.
27 The LORD of hosts has planned;
who can thwart him?
His hand is stretched out;
who can turn it back?

28 In the year that King Ahaz died, there came this oracle:

29 Rejoice not, O Philistia, not a man of you,
that the rod which smote you is broken;
For out of the serpent's root shall come an adder,
its fruit shall be a flying saraph.
30 In my pastures the poor shall eat,
and the needy lie down in safety;
But I will kill your root with famine
that shall slay even your remnant.
31 Howl, O gate; cry out, O city!
Philistia, all of you melts away!
For there comes a smoke from the north,
without a straggler in the ranks.
32 What will one answer the messengers of
the nation?
"The LORD has established Zion,
and in her the afflicted of his people
find refuge."

15

Oracle on Moab:
Laid waste in a night,
Ar of Moab is destroyed;
Laid waste in a night,
Kir of Moab is destroyed.
2 Up goes daughter Dibon
to the high places to weep;
Over Nebo and over Medeba
Moab wails.
Every head is shaved,
every beard sheared off.
3 In the streets they wear sackcloth, lamenting
and weeping;
On rooftops and in the squares everyone wails.
4 Heshbon and Elealeh cry out,
they are heard as far as Jahaz.
At this the loins of Moab tremble,
his soul quivers within him;

hedgehogs, a swamp. I shall sweep it with the broom of destruction, declares Yahweh Sabaoth.'

24 Yahweh Sabaoth has sworn it,
'Yes, what I have planned will take place,
what I have decided will be so:
25 'I shall break Assyria in my country,
I shall trample on him on my mountains.
Then his yoke will slip off them,
his burden will slip from their shoulders.'
26 This is the decision taken in defiance of the whole
world;
this, the hand outstretched in defiance of all
nations.
27 Once Yahweh Sabaoth has decided, who will stop
him?
Once he stretches out his hand, who can withdraw
it?

28 In the year Ahaz died came this proclamation:

29 All Philistia, do not rejoice
because the rod which used to beat you is now
broken,
for the serpent stock will produce a viper,
its offspring will be a flying dragon.

30 While the first-born of the poor are grazing
and the destitute are resting in safety,
I shall make your stock die of hunger
and then slaughter what remains of you.

31 Howl, gate! Shriek, city!
Totter, all Philistia!
For a smoke is coming from the north,
and there are no deserters in those battalions.

32 What reply will be given then
to the messengers of that nation? —
That Yahweh founded Zion
and there the poor of his people will find refuge.

15

Proclamation about Moab:[i]

Laid waste in a night,
Ar-Moab lies silent;
Laid waste in a night,
Kir-Moab lies silent.

2 The daughter of Dibon has climbed
to the high places to weep;
on Nebo and in Medeba
Moab laments.

Every head shaven,
every beard cut off,
3 they wear sackcloth in their streets;
on their roofs and in their squares,
everyone is lamenting
and collapsing in tears.

4 Heshbon and Elealeh are crying out in distress,
their voices can be heard as far as Jahaz.
That is why the warriors of Moab are shivering,
his soul trembles at the sound.

8, 21f: He . . . clouds: the two verses have been transposed from chap. 8.

i **15** cf. Jr 48.

5 My heart cries out for Moab;
  his fugitives flee to Zoar,
    to Eglath-shelishiyah.
For at the ascent of Luhith
  they go up weeping;
on the road to Horonaim
  they raise a cry of destruction;
6 the waters of Nimrim
  are a desolation;
the grass is withered, the new growth fails,
  the verdure is no more.
7 Therefore the abundance they have gained
  and what they have laid up
they carry away
  over the Wadi of the Willows.
8 For a cry has gone
  around the land of Moab;
the wailing reaches to Eglaim,
  the wailing reaches to Beer-elim.
9 For the waters of Dibon[w] are full of blood;
  yet I will bring upon Dibon[w] even more —
a lion for those of Moab who escape,
  for the remnant of the land.

16 Send lambs
  to the ruler of the land,
from Sela, by way of the desert,
  to the mount of daughter Zion.
2 Like fluttering birds,
  like scattered nestlings,
so are the daughters of Moab
  at the fords of the Arnon.
3 "Give counsel,
  grant justice;
make your shade like night
  at the height of noon;
hide the outcasts,
  do not betray the fugitive;
4 let the outcasts of Moab
  settle among you;
be a refuge to them
  from the destroyer."

When the oppressor is no more,
  and destruction has ceased,
and marauders have vanished from the land,
5 then a throne shall be established in steadfast love
  in the tent of David,
  and on it shall sit in faithfulness
a ruler who seeks justice
  and is swift to do what is right.

6 We have heard of the pride of Moab
  — how proud he is! —
of his arrogance, his pride, and his insolence;
  his boasts are false.
7 Therefore let Moab wail,
  let everyone wail for Moab.
Mourn, utterly stricken,
  for the raisin cakes of Kir-hareseth.

8 For the fields of Heshbon languish,
  and the vines of Sibmah,
whose clusters once made drunk
  the lords of the nations,
reached to Jazer
  and strayed to the desert;
their shoots once spread abroad
  and crossed over the sea.

5 My heart cries out for Moab,
  whose fugitives have reached Zoar,
  as far as Eglath-shelishiyah.
On the ascent to Luhith they go up weeping;
  on the road to Horonaim there are cries of
    'Disaster!'
6 The waters of Nimrim are desolate;
  the grass is parched, the herbage dead,
  not a green thing is left;
7 the people carry across the wadi Arabim
  their hard-earned wealth and hoarded savings.
8 The cry of distress echoes round the frontiers of
    Moab,
  their wailing reaches Eglaim and Beer-elim.
9 The waters of Dibon run with blood;
  yet I have worse in store for Dibon:
a lion for the survivors of Moab,
  and for the remnant of Admah.

16 The rulers of the land send a present of lambs
  from Sela by the wilderness
to the mount of Zion;
2 the women of Moab at the fords of the Arnon
  are like fluttering birds, like scattered nestlings.
3 'Give us counsel, intervene for us;
  let your shadow shield us at high noon
  as if it were night.
Give the exiles shelter, do not betray the fugitives;
4 let the exiles from Moab find a home with you
  and shelter them from the despoiler.'

When oppression has done its work
  and the despoiling is over,
when the heel of the aggressor has vanished from
    the land,
5 a trusted throne will be set up in David's tent;
  on it there will sit a true judge,
  one who cares for justice and pursues right.

6 We have heard how great is the haughtiness of
    Moab,
  we have heard of his pride, his surpassing pride —
  his boastful talk is groundless!
7 Therefore let Moab wail;
  let all the Moabites wail indeed;
they will mourn for the prosperous farmers of
    Kir-hareseth,
  who face ruin;
8 the vineyards of Heshbon languish,
  the vines of Sibmah,
whose red grapes used to overpower the lords of
    the nations;
they reached as far as Jazer
  and trailed out to the wilderness,
  and their spreading branches crossed the sea.

---

[w] Q Ms Vg Compare Syr: MT *Dimon*

15:5 **there are cries of:** *prob. rdg, cp. Lat.; Heb. unintelligible.*
16:7 **they:** *prob. rdg; Heb. you.*

NEW AMERICAN BIBLE

5 The heart of Moab cries out,
 his fugitives reach Zoar
 [Eglath-shelishiyah].
The ascent of Luhith
 they climb weeping;
On the way to Horonaim
 they utter rending cries.

6 The waters of Nimrim
 have become a waste;
The grass is withered,
 new growth is gone,
 nothing is green.

7 So now whatever they have acquired or
 stored away
 they carry across the Gorge of the Poplars,

8 For the cry has gone round
 the land of Moab;
As far as Eglaim the wailing,
 and to Beer-elim, the wail.

9 The waters of Dimon were filled with blood,
 but I will bring still more upon Dimon:
Lions for those who are fleeing from Moab
 and for those who remain in the land!

16 Send them forth, hugging the earth like reptiles,
 from Sela across the desert,
 to the mount of daughter Zion.

2 Like flushed birds,
 like startled nestlings,
Are the daughters of Moab
 at the fords of the Arnon.

3 Offer counsel, take their part:
 at high noon let your shadow be like the night,
To hide the outcasts,
 to conceal the fugitives.

4 Let the outcasts of Moab live with you,
 be their shelter from the destroyer.
When the struggle is ended, the ruin complete,
 and they have done with trampling the land,

5 A throne shall be set up in mercy,
 and on it shall sit in fidelity
 [in David's tent]
A judge upholding right
 and prompt to do justice.

6 We have heard of the pride of Moab,
 how very proud he is,
With his haughty, arrogant insolence
 that his empty words do not match.

7 Therefore Moab wails for Moab,
 everywhere they wail;
For the raisin cakes of Kir-hareseth
 they sigh, stricken with grief.

8 The terraced slopes of Heshbon languish,
 the vines of Sibmah,
Whose clusters overpowered
 the lords of nations,
While they reached as far as Jazer
 and scattered over the desert,
And whose branches spread forth
 and extended over the sea.

NEW JERUSALEM BIBLE

5 His heart cries out in distress for Moab,
 whose fugitives are already at Zoar,
 nearly at Eglath-Shelishiyah.

They climb the slope of Luhith, *j*
 weeping as they go;
on the road to Horonaim
 they utter heart-rending cries.

6 The Waters of Nimrim
 have become a waste land,
the grass dried up, the plants withered away,
 nothing green any more.

7 That is why they are carrying
 what they could save of their stores
across the Ravine of the Willows.

8 For the cry for help re-echoes
 round the territory of Moab;
their wailing, right to Eglaim,
 to Beer-Elim, their wailing;

9 Dimon's waters are swollen with blood,
 and I have worse in store for Dimon:
a lion for those of Moab who survive,
 for those left on its soil.

16 Send the lamb to the ruler of the land,
 from Sela by the desert,
 to the mountain of the daughter of Zion.

2 for soon, like a fluttered bird,
 like nestlings cast out,
will be the women of Moab at the fords of the
 Arnon.

3 Hold a council, make a decision.
 At noon spread your shadow
 as if it were night.
Hide those who have been driven out,
 do not betray the fugitive,

4 let those who have been driven out of Moab
 come and live with you;
be their refuge in the face of the devastator.
Once the oppression is past,
 and the devastation has stopped
 and those now trampling on the country have gone
 away,

5 the throne will be made secure in faithful love
 and on it will sit in constancy within the tent of
 David,
a judge seeking fair judgement and pursuing
 uprightness.

6 We have heard about Moab's pride,
 about how very proud it is,
about its arrogance, its pride, its rage,
 its bravado, which will come to nothing!

7 And so Moab is wailing for Moab,
 wailing, every one of them.
For the raisin cakes of Kir-Hareseth *k*
 you mourn, stricken with grief.

8 For Heshbon's vineyards are withering,
 the vine of Sibmah
whose red grapes used to overcome
 the overlords of the nations.
It used to reach to Jazer,
 had wound its way into the desert,
 its shoots grew so numerous
 they spread across the sea.

j 15 // Jr 48:5.   *k* 16 // Jr 48:29–30.

NEW REVISED STANDARD VERSION	REVISED ENGLISH BIBLE

NEW REVISED STANDARD VERSION

9 Therefore I weep with the weeping of Jazer
    for the vines of Sibmah;
I drench you with my tears,
    O Heshbon and Elealeh;
for the shout over your fruit harvest
    and your grain harvest has ceased.
10 Joy and gladness are taken away
    from the fruitful field;
and in the vineyards no songs are sung,
    no shouts are raised;
no treader treads out wine in the presses;
    the vintage-shout is hushed. *x*
11 Therefore my heart throbs like a harp for Moab,
    and my very soul for Kir-heres.

12 When Moab presents himself, when he wearies himself upon the high place, when he comes to his sanctuary to pray, he will not prevail. 13 This was the word that the LORD spoke concerning Moab in the past. 14 But now the LORD says, In three years, like the years of a hired worker, the glory of Moab will be brought into contempt, in spite of all its great multitude; and those who survive will be very few and feeble.

17 An oracle concerning Damascus.

See, Damascus will cease to be a city,
    and will become a heap of ruins.
2 Her towns will be deserted forever; *y*
    they will be places for flocks,
    which will lie down, and no one will make
      them afraid.
3 The fortress will disappear from Ephraim,
    and the kingdom from Damascus;
and the remnant of Aram will be
    like the glory of the children of Israel,
            says the LORD of hosts.
4 On that day
    the glory of Jacob will be brought low,
    and the fat of his flesh will grow lean.
5 And it shall be as when reapers gather standing
    grain
    and their arms harvest the ears,
and as when one gleans the ears of grain
    in the Valley of Rephaim.
6 Gleanings will be left in it,
    as when an olive tree is beaten—
two or three berries
    in the top of the highest bough,
four or five
    on the branches of a fruit tree,
            says the LORD God of Israel.

7 On that day people will regard their Maker, and their eyes will look to the Holy One of Israel; 8 they will not have regard for the altars, the work of their hands, and they will not look to what their own fingers have made, either the sacred poles *z* or the altars of incense.

9 On that day their strong cities will be like the deserted places of the Hivites and the Amorites, *a* which they deserted because of the children of Israel, and there will be desolation.

REVISED ENGLISH BIBLE

9 I shall weep for Sibmah's vines as I weep for
    Jazer.
I shall drench you with tears, Heshbon and
    Elealeh;
for the shouts of the enemy have fallen
    on your summer fruits and harvest.
10 Joy and gladness will be banished from the fields,
    no more will they tread wine in the winepresses;
    I have silenced the shouting of the harvesters.
11 Therefore my heart throbs
    like a harp for Moab,
    and my soul for Kir-hareseth.
12 Though the Moabites come to worship
    and weary themselves at the shrines,
though they flock to their sanctuaries to pray,
    it will avail them nothing.

13 Those are the words which the LORD spoke long ago about Moab; 14 and now he says: 'In three years, as a hired labourer counts them off exactly, the vast population in which Moab glories will be brought into contempt; those who are left will be few and feeble and bereft of all honour.'

17 Damascus: an oracle.

Damascus will cease to be a city;
    she will be reduced to a heap of ruins 2 for ever
      desolate.
Flocks will have her for their own
    and lie there undisturbed.
3 No longer will Ephraim boast a fortified city,
    or Damascus a kingdom;
the remnant of Aram will share the fate of Israel's
    glory.
This is the word of the LORD of Hosts.
4 On that day Jacob's glory will wane
    and his prosperity waste away,
5 as when the reaper gathers the standing grain,
    harvesting the ears by armfuls,
or as when one gleans the ears in the vale of
    Rephaim,
6 or as when an olive tree is beaten
    and only gleanings are left on it,
two or three berries on the topmost branch,
    four or five on its fruitful boughs.
This is the word of the LORD the God of Israel.

7 On that day all will look to their Maker, turning their eyes to the Holy One of Israel; 8 they will not look to the altars, their own handiwork, or to objects their fingers have made, sacred poles and incense-altars.

9 On that day your strong cities will be deserted like the deserted cities of the Hivites and the Amorites, which they abandoned at Israel's approach, and they will become desolate.

---

x Gk: Heb *I have hushed*   *y* Cn Compare Gk: Heb *the cities of Aroer are deserted*   *z* Heb *Asherim*   *a* Cn Compare Gk: Heb *places of the wood and the highest bough*

17:2 **for ever . . . own:** *so* Gk; *Heb.* The cities of Aroer will be deserted for flocks.   17:9 **Hivites . . . Amorites:** *prob. rdg, cp. Gk; Heb.* woodland and hill-country.

NEW AMERICAN BIBLE

9 Therefore I weep with Jazer
　for the vines of Sibmah;
I water you with tears,
　Heshbon and Elealeh;
For on your summer fruits and harvests
　the battle cry has fallen.
10 From the orchards are taken away
　joy and gladness,
In the vineyards there is no singing,
　no shout of joy;
In the wine presses no one treads grapes,
　the vintage shout is stilled.
11 Therefore for Moab
　my breast moans like a lyre,
　and my heart for Kir-hareseth.
12 When Moab grows weary on the high places,
　he shall enter his sanctuary to pray,
　but it shall avail him nothing.

13 This is the word the LORD spoke against Moab in times past. 14 But now the LORD has spoken: In three years, like those of a hireling, the glory of Moab shall be degraded despite all its great multitude; there shall be a remnant, very small and weak.

17 　　Oracle on Damascus:
Lo, Damascus shall cease to be a city
　and become a ruin;
2 Her cities shall be forever abandoned,
　given over to flocks to lie in undisturbed.
3 The fortress shall be lost to Ephraim
　and the kingdom to Damascus;
The remnant of Aram shall have the same glory
　as the Israelites,
　says the LORD of hosts.
4 　　On that day
The glory of Jacob shall fade,
　and his full body grow thin,
5 Like the reaper's mere armful of stalks
　when he gathers the standing grain;
Or as when one gleans the ears
　in the Valley of Rephaim.
6 Only a scattering of grapes shall be left!
　As when an olive tree has been beaten,
Two or three olives remain at the very top,
　four or five on its fruitful branches,
　says the LORD, the God of Israel.

7 On that day man shall look to his maker,
　his eyes turned toward the Holy One of Israel.
8 He shall not look to the altars, his handiwork,
　nor shall he regard what his fingers have made:
　the sacred poles or the incense stands.
9 On that day his strong cities shall be
　like those abandoned by the Hivites
　　and Amorites
When faced with the children of Israel:
　they shall be laid waste.

NEW JERUSALEM BIBLE

9 And so I weep, as Jazer weeps,
　for the vine of Sibmah.
I water you with my tears,
　Heshbon and Elealeh.
For over your harvest and vintage
　the cheering has died away;
10 joy and gladness
　have vanished from the orchards.
No more revelry in the vineyards,
　no more happy shouting;
　no more the treader treads wine in the presses,
　the cheering has ceased.
11 That is why my whole being
　quivers like harp strings for Moab,
　my very heart, for Kir-Heres.
12 Moab will be seen,
　wearing itself out on the high places
　and going to its temple to pray,
　but it will accomplish nothing.

13 Such was the word which Yahweh spoke about Moab in the past. 14 And now Yahweh has spoken in these terms, 'Within three years, as a hired worker reckons them, the glory of Moab will be humbled, despite its teeming population. It will be reduced to nothing, an insignificant remnant.'

17 　　Proclamation about Damascus:

Damascus will soon cease to be a city,
　it will become a heap of ruins.
2 Its towns, abandoned for ever,
　will be pastures for flocks;
　there they will rest with no one to disturb them.
3 Ephraim will be stripped of its defences
　and Damascus of its sovereignty;
　and the remnant of Aram will be treated
　like the glory of the Israelites —
　declares Yahweh Sabaoth.

4 When that day comes, Jacob's glory will diminish,
　from being fat he will grow lean;
5 as when a reaper gathers in the standing corn,
　harvesting the ears of corn with his arm,
　or when they glean the ears in the Valley of
　　Rephaim,
6 nothing will remain but pickings,
　as when an olive tree is beaten;
　two or three berries left on the topmost bough,
　four or five berries on the branches of the tree —
　declares Yahweh, God of Israel.

7 That day, a man will look to his Creator and his eyes will turn to the Holy One of Israel. 8 He will no longer look to altars, his own handiwork, or to what his own fingers have made: the sacred poles and incense-altars.

9 That day, its cities of refuge will be abandoned
　as were the woods and heaths
　at the Israelites' advance:
　there will be desolation.

10 For you have forgotten the God of your salvation,
    and have not remembered the Rock of your
        refuge;
therefore, though you plant pleasant plants
    and set out slips of an alien god,
11 though you make them grow on the day that you
        plant them,
    and make them blossom in the morning that
        you sow;
yet the harvest will flee away
    in a day of grief and incurable pain.

12 Ah, the thunder of many peoples,
    they thunder like the thundering of the sea!
Ah, the roar of nations,
    they roar like the roaring of mighty waters!
13 The nations roar like the roaring of many waters,
    but he will rebuke them, and they will flee far
        away,
chased like chaff on the mountains before the
        wind
    and whirling dust before the storm.
14 At evening time, lo, terror!
    Before morning, they are no more.
This is the fate of those who despoil us,
    and the lot of those who plunder us.

18 Ah, land of whirring wings
    beyond the rivers of Ethiopia,*b*
2 sending ambassadors by the Nile
    in vessels of papyrus on the waters!
Go, you swift messengers,
    to a nation tall and smooth,
to a people feared near and far,
    a nation mighty and conquering,
    whose land the rivers divide.

3 All you inhabitants of the world,
    you who live on the earth,
when a signal is raised on the mountains, look!
    When a trumpet is blown, listen!
4 For thus the LORD said to me:
I will quietly look from my dwelling
    like clear heat in sunshine,
    like a cloud of dew in the heat of harvest.
5 For before the harvest, when the blossom is over
    and the flower becomes a ripening grape,
he will cut off the shoots with pruning hooks,
    and the spreading branches he will hew away.
6 They shall all be left
    to the birds of prey of the mountains
    and to the animals of the earth.
And the birds of prey will summer on them,
    and all the animals of the earth will winter on
        them.

7 At that time gifts will be brought to the LORD of hosts
from*c* a people tall and smooth, from a people feared near
and far, a nation mighty and conquering, whose land the
rivers divide, to Mount Zion, the place of the name of the
LORD of hosts.

19 An oracle concerning Egypt.

See, the LORD is riding on a swift cloud
    and comes to Egypt;
the idols of Egypt will tremble at his presence,
    and the heart of the Egyptians will melt within
        them.

b Or Nubia; Heb Cush   c Q Ms Gk Vg: MT of

10 You forgot the God who delivered you,
    and did not keep in mind the rock, your
        stronghold.
Plant then, if you will, your gardens in honour of
        Adonis,
set out your cuttings for a foreign god;
11 though you protect them on the day you plant
        them,
    and though your seeds sprout next morning,
yet the crop will disappear when wasting disease
        comes
    in a day of incurable pain.

12 Listen! It is the thunder of vast forces,
    a thundering like the thunder of the sea.
Listen! It is the roar of nations,
    a roaring like the roar of mighty waters.
13 At his rebuke, they flee far away,
    driven before the wind like chaff on the hills,
    like thistledown before the storm.
14 At evening all is terror;
    before morning it is gone.
Such is the fate of our plunderers,
    the lot of those who despoil us.

18 There is a land of sailing ships
    lying beyond the rivers of Cush;
2 it sends its envoys by the Nile
    in vessels of reed on the waters.
Go, swift messengers,
    to a people tall and smooth-skinned,
to a people dreaded far and near,
    a nation strong and aggressive,
    whose land is scoured by rivers.
3 All you inhabitants of the world, you dwellers on
        earth,
    will see when the standard is hoisted on the
        mountains
    and hear when the trumpet sounds.
4 These were the words of the LORD to me:

From my dwelling-place I shall look on and do
        nothing
    when the heat shimmers in the summer sun,
    when the dew is heavy at harvest time.
5 Before the vintage, when the budding is over
    and the flower ripens into a berry,
the shoots will be cut down with pruning-knives,
    the branches struck off and cleared away.
6 All will be left to birds of prey on the hills
    and to the wild beasts of the earth;
in summer those birds will make their home there,
    in winter those wild beasts.

7 At that time tribute will be brought to the LORD of Hosts
from a people tall and smooth-skinned, dreaded near and
far, a nation strong and aggressive, whose land is scoured
by rivers. They will bring it to the place where the name of
the LORD of Hosts dwells, to Mount Zion.

19 Egypt: an oracle.

The LORD comes riding swiftly on a cloud,
    and he descends on Egypt;
the idols of Egypt quail before him,
    Egypt's courage melts within her.

17:12 **roaring ... waters:** *so some MSS; others add* peoples roar
with the roar of great waters.   18:4 **time:** *so Gk; Heb.* heat.
18:7 **from:** *so Scroll; Heb. omits.*

NEW AMERICAN BIBLE

10 For you have forgotten God, your savior,
and remembered not the Rock, your strength.
Therefore, though you plant your pagan plants
and set out your foreign vine slips,
11 Though you make them grow the day you
plant them
and make your sprouts blossom on the
next morning.
The harvest shall disappear on the day of the
grievous blow,
the incurable blight.

12 Ah! the roaring of many peoples
that roar like the roar of the seas!
The surging of nations
that surge like the surging of mighty waves!
13 But God shall rebuke them,
and they shall flee far away;
Windswept, like chaff on the mountains,
like tumbleweed in a storm.
14 In the evening, they spread terror,
before morning, they are gone!
Such is the portion of those who despoil us,
the lot of those who plunder us.

18 Ah, land of buzzing insects,
beyond the rivers of Ethiopia,
2 Sending ambassadors by sea,
in papyrus boats on the waters!
Go, swift messengers,
to a nation tall and bronzed,
To a people dreaded near and far,
a nation strong and conquering,
whose land is washed by rivers.
3 All you who inhabit the world,
who dwell on earth,
When the signal is raised on the mountain, look!
When the trumpet blows, listen!
4 For thus says the LORD to me:
I will quietly look on from where I dwell,
Like the glowing heat of sunshine,
like a cloud of dew at harvest time.
5 Before the vintage, when the flowering is ended,
and the blooms are succeeded by
ripening grapes,
Then comes the cutting of branches with
pruning hooks
and the discarding of the lopped-off shoots.
6 They shall all be left to the mountain birds of prey,
and to the beasts in the land;
The birds of prey shall summer on them
and on them all the beasts of the earth
shall winter.

7 Then will gifts be brought to the LORD of hosts from a
people tall and bronzed, from a people dreaded near and far,
a nation strong and conquering, whose land is washed by
rivers — to Mount Zion where dwells the name of the LORD
of hosts.

19 Oracle on Egypt:
See, the LORD is riding on a swift cloud
on his way to Egypt;
The idols of Egypt tremble before him,
the hearts of the Egyptians melt within them.

NEW JERUSALEM BIBLE

10 Since you have forgotten the God of your
salvation,
and failed to keep the Rock, your refuge, in mind,
you plant pleasure-gardens,
you sow exotic seeds;
11 the day you plant them, you get them to sprout,
and, next morning, your seedlings are in flower;
but the harvest will vanish on the day of disease
and incurable pain.

12 Disaster! The thunder of vast hordes,
a thunder like the thunder of the seas,
the roar of nations roaring like the roar of mighty
floods,
13 of nations roaring like the roar of ocean!
He rebukes them and far away they flee,
driven like chaff on the mountains before the wind,
like an eddy of dust before the storm.
14 At evening all is terror,
by morning all have disappeared.
Such will be the lot of those who plunder us,
such, the fate of our despoilers.

18 Disaster! Land of the whirring locust
beyond the rivers of Cush,
2 who send ambassadors by sea,
in little reed-boats across the waters!
Go, swift messengers
to a nation tall and bronzed,
to a people feared far and near,
a mighty and masterful nation
whose country is criss-crossed with rivers.
3 All you who inhabit the world,
you who people the earth,
when the signal is hoisted on the mountains, you
will see,
when the ram's-horn is sounded, you will hear.
4 For this is what Yahweh has told me,
'I shall sit here quietly looking down,
like the burning heat in the daytime,
like a dewy mist in the heat of harvest.'
5 For, before the harvest, once the flowering is over
and blossom turns into ripening grape,
the branches will be cut off with pruning knives,
and the shoots taken off, cut away.
6 All has been abandoned
to the mountain birds of prey
and the wild animals:
the birds of prey will summer on them,
and all the wild animals winter on them.

7 Then, an offering will be brought to Yahweh Sabaoth on
behalf of a people tall and bronzed, on behalf of a people
feared far and near, on behalf of a mighty and masterful
nation whose country is criss-crossed with rivers: to the
place where the name of Yahweh Sabaoth resides, Mount
Zion.

19 Proclamation about Egypt:

Look! Yahweh, riding a swift cloud,
is coming to Egypt.
The false gods of Egypt totter before him
and Egypt's heart quails within her.

2 I will stir up Egyptians against Egyptians,
  and they will fight, one against the other,
  neighbor against neighbor,
  city against city, kingdom against kingdom;
3 the spirit of the Egyptians within them will be
    emptied out,
  and I will confound their plans;
they will consult the idols and the spirits of the
    dead
  and the ghosts and the familiar spirits;
4 I will deliver the Egyptians
    into the hand of a hard master;
  a fierce king will rule over them,
    says the Sovereign, the LORD of hosts.

5 The waters of the Nile will be dried up,
  and the river will be parched and dry;
6 its canals will become foul,
    and the branches of Egypt's Nile will diminish
      and dry up,
  reeds and rushes will rot away.
7 There will be bare places by the Nile,
    on the brink of the Nile;
and all that is sown by the Nile will dry up,
  be driven away, and be no more.
8 Those who fish will mourn;
    all who cast hooks in the Nile will lament,
  and those who spread nets on the water will
    languish.
9 The workers in flax will be in despair,
    and the carders and those at the loom will
      grow pale.
10 Its weavers will be dismayed,
    and all who work for wages will be grieved.

11 The princes of Zoan are utterly foolish;
    the wise counselors of Pharaoh give stupid
      counsel.
  How can you say to Pharaoh,
    "I am one of the sages,
    a descendant of ancient kings"?
12 Where now are your sages?
    Let them tell you and make known
  what the LORD of hosts has planned against
    Egypt.
13 The princes of Zoan have become fools,
    and the princes of Memphis are deluded;
  those who are the cornerstones of its tribes
    have led Egypt astray.
14 The LORD has poured into them[d]
    a spirit of confusion;
  and they have made Egypt stagger in all its doings
    as a drunkard staggers around in vomit.
15 Neither head nor tail, palm branch or reed,
    will be able to do anything for Egypt.

16 On that day the Egyptians will be like women, and
tremble with fear before the hand that the LORD of hosts
raises against them. 17 And the land of Judah will become a
terror to the Egyptians; everyone to whom it is mentioned
will fear because of the plan that the LORD of hosts is
planning against them.
18 On that day there will be five cities in the land of
Egypt that speak the language of Canaan and swear allegiance to the LORD of hosts. One of these will be called the
City of the Sun.
19 On that day there will be an altar to the LORD in the
center of the land of Egypt, and a pillar to the LORD at its
border. 20 It will be a sign and a witness to the LORD of hosts
in the land of Egypt; when they cry to the LORD because of

[d] Gk Compare Tg: Heb it

2 I shall incite Egyptian against Egyptian,
  and they will fight one against another,
  neighbour against neighbour,
  city against city, kingdom against kingdom.
3 Egypt's spirit will ebb away within her,
  and I shall throw her counsels into confusion.
  They will resort to idols and oracle-mongers,
  to ghosts and spirits,
4 but I shall hand Egypt over to a hard master,
  and a fierce ruler will be king over them.
  This is the word of the Lord, the LORD of Hosts.

5 The waters of the Nile will disappear,
  the river bed will be parched and dry,
6 and its channels will give off a stench.
  Egypt's canals will fail altogether;
  reeds and rushes will wither away.
7 The lotus beside the Nile
  and everything sown along the river will dry up;
  they will blow away and vanish.
8 The fishermen will groan and lament;
  all who cast their hooks into the Nile
  and those who spread nets on the water will lose
    heart.
9 The flax-dressers will be dejected,
  the women carding and the men weaving grow
    pale.
10 Egypt's spinners will be downcast,
  and all her artisans sick at heart.

11 The princes of Zoan are no better than fools; Pharaoh's
wisest counsellors give stupid advice.

  How can you say to Pharaoh,
    'I am descended from wise men;
    I spring from ancient kings'?
12 Where are your wise men, Pharaoh,
    to teach you and make known to you
  what the LORD of Hosts has planned for Egypt?
13 Zoan's princes are fooled,
    the princes of Noph are dupes;
  the chieftains of her clans have led Egypt astray.
14 The LORD has infused into them
    a spirit that distorts their judgement;
  they make Egypt miss her way in all she does,
    as a vomiting drunkard will miss his footing.
15 There will be nothing in Egypt that anyone can do,
    be they head or tail, palm-frond or reed.

16 When that day comes the Egyptians will become weak as
women; they will be terror-stricken when the LORD of Hosts
raises his hand against them. 17 The land of Judah will throw
the Egyptians into panic; the very mention of its name will
cause dismay, because of the plans that the LORD of Hosts
has laid against them.
18 When that day comes there will be five cities in Egypt
speaking the language of Canaan and swearing allegiance to
the LORD of Hosts, and one of them will be called the City
of the Sun.
19 When that day comes there will be an altar dedicated to
the LORD in the heart of Egypt, and a sacred pillar set up for
the LORD at her frontier. 20 It will stand as a symbol and a
reminder of the LORD of Hosts in Egypt; for they will appeal

19:7 lotus . . . Nile: prob. rdg; Heb. adds the mouth of the Nile.
19:9 grow pale: so Scroll; Heb. white linen.   19:14 them: so Gk;
Heb. her.   19:18 the City of the Sun: or Heliopolis; so some
MSS; others the City of Destruction.

NEW AMERICAN BIBLE

2 I will rouse Egypt against Egypt:
  brother will war against brother,
Neighbor against neighbor,
  city against city, kingdom against kingdom.
3 The courage of the Egyptians ebbs away
    within them,
  and I will bring to nought their counsel;
They shall consult idols and charmers,
  ghosts and spirits.
4 I will deliver Egypt
  into the power of a cruel master,
A harsh king who shall rule over them,
  says the Lord, the LORD of hosts.
5 The waters shall be drained from the sea,
  the river shall shrivel and dry up;
6 Its streams shall become foul,
  and the canals of Egypt shall dwindle and
    dry up.
Reeds and rushes shall wither away,
7   and bulrushes on the bank of the Nile;
All the sown land along the Nile
  shall dry up and blow away, and be no more.
8 The fishermen shall mourn and lament,
  all who cast hook in the Nile;
Those who spread their nets in the water
  shall pine away.
9 The linen-workers shall be disappointed,
  the combers and weavers shall turn pale;
10 The spinners shall be crushed,
  all the hired laborers shall be despondent.
11 Utter fools are the princes of Zoan!
  the wisest of Pharaoh's advisers give
    stupid counsel.
How can you say to Pharaoh,
  "I am a disciple of wise men, of ancient
    kings"?
12 Where then are your wise men?
  Let them tell you and make known
What the LORD of hosts has planned
  against Egypt.
13 The princes of Zoan have become fools,
  the princes of Memphis have been deceived.
The chiefs of her tribes
  have led Egypt astray.
14 The LORD has prepared among them
  a spirit of dizziness,
And they have made Egypt stagger in whatever
    she does,
  as a drunkard staggers in his vomit.
15 Egypt shall have no work to do
  for head or tail, palm branch or reed.

16 On that day the Egyptians shall be like women, trembling with fear, because of the LORD of hosts shaking his fist at them. 17 And the land of Judah shall be a terror to the Egyptians. Every time they remember Judah, they shall stand in dread because of the plan which the LORD of hosts has in mind for them.
18 On that day there shall be five cities in the land of Egypt speaking the language of Canaan and swearing by the LORD of hosts; one shall be called "City of the Sun."
19 On that day there shall be an altar to the LORD in the land of Egypt, and a sacred pillar to the LORD near the boundary. 20 It shall be a sign and a witness to the LORD of hosts in the land of Egypt, when they cry out to the LORD

NEW JERUSALEM BIBLE

2 I shall stir up Egypt against Egypt,
  they will fight one another,
  brother against brother, friend against friend,
  city against city, kingdom against kingdom.
3 Egypt's spirit will fail within her
  and I shall confound her deliberations.
  They will consult false gods and wizards,
  ghosts and sorcerers.
4 And I shall hand Egypt over
  to the clutches of a cruel master,
  a ruthless king will rule them—
  declares Yahweh Sabaoth.
5 The waters will ebb from the sea,
  the river will dry up and run low,
6 the streams will become foul,
  the rivers of Egypt sink and dry up.
  Rush and reed will turn black,
7 the Nile-plants on the banks of the Nile;
  all the vegetation of the Nile,
  will wither, blow away and be no more.
8 The fishermen will groan, it will be mourning
  for all who cast hook in the Nile;
  those who spread nets on the waters will lose
    heart.
9 The workers of carded flax
  and the weavers of white cloth
  will be confounded,
10 the weavers dismayed,
  all the workmen dejected.
11 Yes, the princes of Zoan are fools,
  Pharaoh's wisest councillors make up a stupid
    council.
How dare you say to Pharaoh,
  'I am descended from sages, I am descended from
    bygone kings'?
12 Where are these sages of yours?
  Let them tell you, so that all may know,
  the plans Yahweh Sabaoth has made against Egypt!
13 The princes of Zoan are fools,
  the princes of Noph, self-deceivers,
  the top men of her provinces
  have led Egypt astray.
14 Yahweh has infused them
  with a giddy spirit;
  they have led Egypt astray in all she undertakes
  like a drunkard straying about as he vomits.
15 Nowadays no one does for Egypt
  what top and tail, palm and reed used to do.

16 That day Egypt will be like women, trembling and terrified at the threatening hand of Yahweh Sabaoth, when he raises it against her. 17 The land of Judah will become Egypt's shame; whenever she is reminded of it, she will be terrified, because of the plan which Yahweh Sabaoth has laid against her. 18 That day in Egypt there will be five towns speaking the language of Canaan and pledging themselves to Yahweh Sabaoth; one of them will be called City of the Sun. 19 That day there will be an altar dedicated to Yahweh in the centre of Egypt and, close to the frontier, a pillar dedicated to Yahweh, 20 and this will be a sign and a witness to Yahweh Sabaoth in Egypt. When they cry to

oppressors, he will send them a savior, and will defend and deliver them. 21 The LORD will make himself known to the Egyptians; and the Egyptians will know the LORD on that day, and will worship with sacrifice and burnt offering, and they will make vows to the LORD and perform them. 22 The LORD will strike Egypt, striking and healing; they will return to the LORD, and he will listen to their supplications and heal them.

23 On that day there will be a highway from Egypt to Assyria, and the Assyrian will come into Egypt, and the Egyptian into Assyria, and the Egyptians will worship with the Assyrians.

24 On that day Israel will be the third with Egypt and Assyria, a blessing in the midst of the earth, 25 whom the LORD of hosts has blessed, saying, "Blessed be Egypt my people, and Assyria the work of my hands, and Israel my heritage."

20 In the year that the commander-in-chief, who was sent by King Sargon of Assyria, came to Ashdod and fought against it and took it— 2 at that time the LORD had spoken to Isaiah son of Amoz, saying, "Go, and loose the sackcloth from your loins and take your sandals off your feet," and he had done so, walking naked and barefoot. 3 Then the LORD said, "Just as my servant Isaiah has walked naked and barefoot for three years as a sign and a portent against Egypt and Ethiopia,*e* 4 so shall the king of Assyria lead away the Egyptians as captives and the Ethiopians*f* as exiles, both the young and the old, naked and barefoot, with buttocks uncovered, to the shame of Egypt. 5 And they shall be dismayed and confounded because of Ethiopia*e* their hope and of Egypt their boast. 6 In that day the inhabitants of this coastland will say, 'See, this is what has happened to those in whom we hoped and to whom we fled for help and deliverance from the king of Assyria! And we, how shall we escape?' "

21 The oracle concerning the wilderness of the sea.

As whirlwinds in the Negeb sweep on,
   it comes from the desert,
   from a terrible land.
2 A stern vision is told to me;
   the betrayer betrays,
   and the destroyer destroys.
Go up, O Elam,
   lay siege, O Media;
all the sighing she has caused
   I bring to an end.
3 Therefore my loins are filled with anguish;
   pangs have seized me,
   like the pangs of a woman in labor;
I am bowed down so that I cannot hear,
   I am dismayed so that I cannot see.
4 My mind reels, horror has appalled me;
   the twilight I longed for
   has been turned for me into trembling.
5 They prepare the table,
   they spread the rugs,
   they eat, they drink.
Rise up, commanders,
   oil the shield!
6 For thus the Lord said to me:
   "Go, post a lookout,
   let him announce what he sees.
7 When he sees riders, horsemen in pairs,
   riders on donkeys, riders on camels,
let him listen diligently,
   very diligently."

e Or Nubia; Heb *Cush*   *f Or Nubians*; Heb *Cushites*

to him against their oppressors, and he will send a deliverer to champion their cause and come to their rescue. 21 The LORD will make himself known to the Egyptians. They will acknowledge the LORD when that day comes; they will worship him with sacrifices and grain-offerings, make vows to him, and fulfil them. 22 The LORD will strike down Egypt, and then bring healing; when they turn back to him he will respond to their prayers and heal them.

23 When that day comes there will be a highway between Egypt and Assyria. The Assyrians will link up with Egypt and the Egyptians with Assyria, and Egyptians will worship with Assyrians.

24 When that day comes Israel will rank as a third with Egypt and Assyria and be a blessing in the world. 25 This is the blessing the LORD of Hosts will give: 'Blessed be Egypt my people, Assyria my handiwork, and Israel my possession.'

20 IT was the year that King Sargon of Assyria sent his commander-in-chief to Ashdod, and he took it by storm. 2 Before that time the LORD had said to Isaiah son of Amoz, 'Strip the sackcloth from your waist and take off your sandals.' He had done so, and gone about naked and barefoot. 3 Now the LORD said, 'As my servant Isaiah has gone naked and barefoot for three years, a sign and portent to Egypt and Cush, 4 so will the king of Assyria lead away the captives of Egypt and the exiles of Cush naked and barefoot, young and old alike, with their buttocks shamefully exposed. 5 All will be dismayed; their trust in Cush and their pride in Egypt will be disappointed. 6 On that day those who dwell along this coast will say, "So much for all our hopes on which we relied, our hopes for help and deliverance from the king of Assyria! What escape is there for us?" '

21 'THE wilderness': an oracle.

A day of storms, sweeping through the Negeb,
   coming from the wilderness, from a land of terror!
2 A grim vision is shown to me:
   the traitor betrayed, the spoiler despoiled.
Advance, Elam; up, Media, to the siege!
Throw off all weariness!
3 At this vision my limbs writhe in anguish,
   I am gripped by pangs like a woman in labour.
I am distraught past hearing, disquieted past
   seeing,
4 my mind reels, sudden convulsions assail me.

The evening cool I longed for has become horrible
   to me:
5 the banquet is set, the rugs are spread;
   they are eating and drinking.
Rise, princes, burnish your shields.
6 For these are the words of the Lord to me:
   'Go, post a watchman to report what he sees.
7 If it is a column of horsemen in pairs,
   a column of donkeys, a column of camels,
he must be on the alert, fully on the alert.'

19:23 **will worship with:** *or* will be subject to.   20:2 **to:** *so* Gk; Heb. through.   20:6 **on which we relied:** *so* Scroll; Heb. to which we fled.

NEW AMERICAN BIBLE

NEW JERUSALEM BIBLE

against their oppressors, and he sends them a savior to defend and deliver them. 21 The LORD shall make himself known to Egypt, and the Egyptians shall know the LORD in that day; they shall offer sacrifices and oblations, and fulfill the vows they make to the LORD. 22 Although the LORD shall smite Egypt severely, he shall heal them; they shall turn to the LORD and he shall be won over and heal them.

23 On that day there shall be a highway from Egypt to Assyria; the Assyrians shall enter Egypt, and the Egyptians enter Assyria, and Egypt shall serve Assyria.

24 On that day Israel shall be a third party with Egypt and Assyria, a blessing in the midst of the land, 25 when the LORD of hosts blesses it: "Blessed be my people Egypt, and the work of my hands Assyria, and my inheritance, Israel."

20 In the year the general sent by Sargon, king of Assyria, fought against Ashdod and captured it, 2 the LORD gave a warning through Isaiah, the son of Amoz: Go and take off the sackcloth from your waist, and remove the sandals from your feet. This he did, walking naked and barefoot. 3 Then the LORD said: Just as my servant Isaiah has gone naked and barefoot for three years as a sign and portent against Egypt and Ethiopia, 4 so shall the king of Assyria lead away captives from Egypt, and exiles from Ethiopia, young and old, naked and barefoot, with buttocks uncovered [the shame of Egypt]. 5 They shall be dismayed and ashamed because of Ethiopia, their hope, and because of Egypt, their boast. 6 The inhabitants of this coastland shall say on that day, "Look at our hope! We have fled here for help and deliverance from the king of Assyria; where can we flee now?"

21 Oracle on the wastelands by the sea:
Like whirlwinds sweeping in waves through the Negeb,
   there comes from the desert,
   from the fearful land,
2 A cruel sight, revealed to me:
   the traitor betrays,
   the despoiler spoils.
"Go up, Elam; besiege, O Media;
   I will put an end to all groaning!"
3 Therefore my loins are filled with anguish,
   pangs have seized me like those of a woman in labor;
I am too bewildered to hear,
   too dismayed to look.
4 My mind reels,
   shuddering assails me;
My yearning for twilight
   has turned into dread.
5 They set the table,
   spread out the rugs;
   they eat, they drink.
Rise up, O princes,
   oil the shield!
6 For thus says my Lord to me:
   Go, station a watchman,
   let him tell what he sees.
7 If he sees a chariot,
   a pair of horses,
Someone riding an ass,
   someone riding a camel,
Then let him pay heed,
   very close heed.

Yahweh for help because of oppressors, he will send them a Saviour and leader to deliver them. 21 Yahweh will reveal himself to Egypt, and the Egyptians will acknowledge Yahweh that day and will offer sacrifices and cereal offerings, and will make vows to Yahweh and perform them. 22 And if Yahweh strikes Egypt, having struck he will heal, and they will turn to Yahweh who will hear their prayers and heal them. 23 That day there will be a highway from Egypt to Assyria. Assyria will have access to Egypt and Egypt have access to Assyria. Egypt will serve with Assyria.

24 That day Israel will make a third with Egypt and Assyria, a blessing at the centre of the world, 25 and Yahweh Sabaoth will bless them in the words, 'Blessed be my people Egypt, Assyria my creation, and Israel my heritage.'

20 The year the general-in-chief, sent by Sargon king of Assyria, came to Ashdod and stormed and captured it 2 at that time Yahweh spoke through Isaiah son of Amoz and said, 'Go, undo the sackcloth round your waist and take the sandals off your feet.' And he did so, and walked about, naked and barefoot. 3 Yahweh then said, 'As my servant Isaiah has been walking about naked and barefoot for the last three years as a sign and portent for Egypt and Cush, 4 so the king of Assyria will lead the captives of Egypt and the exiles of Cush, young and old, naked and barefoot, their buttocks bared, to the shame of Egypt. 5 Then they will be afraid and ashamed of Cush their hope and Egypt their pride, 6 and the inhabitants of this coast will say on that day, "Look what has happened to our hope, to those to whom we fled for help, to escape from the king of Assyria. How are we going to escape?" '

21 Proclamation about the coastal desert:
As whirlwinds sweeping over the Negeb,
   he comes from the desert, from a fearsome country.
2 A harsh vision has been shown me,
   'The traitor betrays and the despoiler despoils.
Advance, Elam, lay siege, Media!'
   I have cut short all groaning.
3 This is why my loins are racked with pain,
   why I am seized with pangs like the pangs of a woman in labour;
I am too distressed to hear, too afraid to look.
4 My heart is bewildered, dread overwhelms me,
   the twilight I longed for has become my horror.
5 They lay the table, spread the cloth,
   they eat, they drink.
Up, princes, grease the shield!
6 For this is what the Lord has told me,
   'Go, post a look-out, let him report what he sees.
7 He will see cavalry, horsemen two by two,
   men mounted on donkeys, men mounted on camels;
let him watch alertly, be very alert indeed!'

8 Then the watchers called out:
"Upon a watchtower I stand, O Lord,
    continually by day,
and at my post I am stationed
    throughout the night.
9 Look, there they come, riders,
    horsemen in pairs!"
Then he responded,
    "Fallen, fallen is Babylon;
and all the images of her gods
    lie shattered on the ground."
10 O my threshed and winnowed one,
    what I have heard from the LORD of hosts,
    the God of Israel, I announce to you.

11 The oracle concerning Dumah.

One is calling to me from Seir,
    "Sentinel, what of the night?
    Sentinel, what of the night?"
12 The sentinel says:
    "Morning comes, and also the night.
    If you will inquire, inquire;
    come back again."

13 The oracle concerning the desert plain.

In the scrub of the desert plain you will lodge,
    O caravans of Dedanites.
14 Bring water to the thirsty,
    meet the fugitive with bread,
    O inhabitants of the land of Tema.
15 For they have fled from the swords,
    from the drawn sword,
from the bent bow,
    and from the stress of battle.

16 For thus the Lord said to me: Within a year, according to the years of a hired worker, all the glory of Kedar will come to an end; 17 and the remaining bows of Kedar's warriors will be few; for the LORD, the God of Israel, has spoken.

22 The oracle concerning the valley of vision.

What do you mean that you have gone up,
    all of you, to the housetops,
2 you that are full of shoutings,
    tumultuous city, exultant town?
Your slain are not slain by the sword,
    nor are they dead in battle.
3 Your rulers have all fled together;
    they were captured without the use of a bow.h
All of you who were found were captured,
    though they had fled far away.i
4 Therefore I said:
Look away from me,
    let me weep bitter tears;
do not try to comfort me
    for the destruction of my beloved people.

5 For the Lord GOD of hosts has a day
    of tumult and trampling and confusion
    in the valley of vision,
a battering down of walls
    and a cry for help to the mountains.
6 Elam bore the quiver
    with chariots and cavalry,j
    and Kir uncovered the shield.

g Q Ms: MT *a lion*   h Or *without their bows*   i Gk Syr Vg: Heb
fled from far away   j Meaning of Heb uncertain

8 Then the look-out cried:
    'All day long I stand on the watch-tower, Lord,
    and night after night I am at my post.
9 There they come: a column of horsemen in pairs.'
    A voice called back:
    'Fallen, fallen is Babylon,
    and all the images of her gods
    lie shattered on the ground.'
10 My people, once trodden out on the
        threshing-floor,
    what I have heard from the LORD of Hosts,
    from the God of Israel, I have told you.

11 Dumah: an oracle.

One calls to me from Seir:
    'Watchman, what is left of the night?
    Watchman, what is left of it?'
12 The watchman answered:
    'Morning comes, and so does night.
    Come back again and ask if you will.'

13 'With the Arabs': an oracle.

You caravans of Dedan, that camp in the scrub
        with the Arabs,
14 bring water to meet the thirsty.
    You inhabitants of Tema, meet the fugitives with
        food,
15 for they flee from the sword, the sharp edge of the
        sword,
    from the bent bow, and from the press of battle.

16 For these are the words of the Lord to me: 'Within a year, as a hired labourer counts off years exactly, all Kedar's glory will come to an end; 17 few will be the archers left, the warriors of Kedar.'
The LORD the God of Israel has spoken.

22 'THE Valley of Vision': an oracle.

Tell me, what is amiss with you
    that all of you have climbed up on the roofs?
2 You city full of tumult, you town in ferment
    and filled with uproar,
    your slain did not fall by the sword;
    they did not die in battle.
3 All your commanders are in full flight,
    fleeing in groups from the bow;
    all your stoutest warriors dispersed in groups
    have fled in all directions.
4 That is why I said: Turn your eyes away from me;
    leave me to weep in misery.
    Do not press consolation on me
    for the ruin of my people.

5 For the Lord, the LORD of Hosts, has ordained a day of tumult, a day of trampling and turmoil in the Valley of Vision, clamour and cries among the mountains.

6 Elam took up the quiver,
    horses were harnessed to the chariots of Aram,
    Kir bared the shield.

21:8 **the look-out:** *so Scroll;* Heb. a lion.   22:1 **Vision:** *or* Calamity.   22:3 **your stoutest warriors:** *so Gk;* Heb. those found in you.   22:5 **Vision:** *or* Calamity.   22:6 **Aram:** *prob. rdg;* Heb. man.

NEW AMERICAN BIBLE

8   Then the watchman cried,
"On the watchtower, O my Lord,
  I stand constantly by day;
And I stay at my post
  through all the watches of the night.
9 Here he comes now:
  a single chariot,
  a pair of horses;
He calls out and says,
  'Fallen, fallen is Babylon,
And all the images of her gods
  are smashed to the ground.' "

10 O my people who have been threshed,
  beaten on my threshing floor!
What I have heard
  from the LORD of hosts,
The God of Israel,
  I have announced to you.

11   Oracle on Edom:
They call to me from Seir,
  "Watchman, how much longer the night?
  Watchman, how much longer the night?"
12   The watchman replies,
"Morning has come, and again night.
  If you will ask, ask; come back again."

13   Oracle on Arabia:
In the thicket in the nomad country spend
    the night,
  O caravans of Dedanites.
14 Meet the thirsty, bring them water;
  you who dwell in the land of Tema,
  greet the fugitives with bread.
15 They flee from the sword,
  from the whetted sword;
From the taut bow,
  from the fury of battle.

16 For thus says the Lord to me: In another year, like those
of a hireling, all the glory of Kedar shall come to an end.
17 Few of Kedar's stalwart archers shall remain, for the
LORD, the God of Israel, has spoken.

22   Oracle of the Valley of Vision:
What is the matter with you now, that you have
    gone up,
  all of you, to the housetops,
2 O city full of noise and chaos,
  O wanton town!
Your slain are not slain with the sword,
  nor killed in battle.
3 All your leaders fled away together,
  fled afar off;
All who were in you were captured together,
  captured without the use of a bow.
4 At this I say: Turn away from me,
  let me weep bitterly;
Do not try to comfort me
  for the ruin of the daughter of my people.
5 It is a day of panic, rout and confusion,
  from the Lord, the GOD of hosts, in the Valley
    of Vision.
Walls crash;
  they cry for help to the mountains.
6 Elam takes up the quivers,
  Aram mounts the horses,
  and Kir uncovers the shields.

NEW JERUSALEM BIBLE

8 Then the look-out shouted,
'On the watchtower, Lord,
  I stay all day
  and at my post
  I stand all night.
9 Now the cavalry is coming, horsemen two by two.'
  He shouted again and said,
  'Babylon has fallen, has fallen,
  and all the images of her gods he has shattered to
    the ground!'
10 You whom I have threshed, grain of my
    threshing-floor,
  what I have heard from Yahweh Sabaoth, God of
    Israel,
  I am telling you now.

11 Proclamation about Dumah:

From Seir, someone shouts to me,
  'Watchman, what time of night?
  Watchman, what time of night?'

12 The watchman answers,
  'Morning is coming, then night again.
  If you want to ask, ask!
  Come back! Come here!'

13 Proclamation about the wastelands:

In the thickets, on the wastelands, you spend the
    night,
  you caravans of Dedanites.
14 Bring water for the thirsty!
  The inhabitants of Tema went
  with bread to greet the fugitive.
15 For these have fled before the sword,
  the naked sword and the bent bow,
  the press of battle.

16 For this is what the Lord has told me,
'In one year's time as a hired worker reckons it, all the
glory of Kedar will be finished 17 and, of the valiant archers,
the Kedarites, hardly any will be left, for Yahweh, God of
Israel, has spoken.'

22   Prophecy on the Valley of Vision:

Now what is the matter with you
  for you all to be up on the housetops,
2 full of excitement, boisterous town, joyful city?
  Your slain have not fallen to the sword
  nor died in battle.
3 Your leaders have all fled together,
  captured without a bow between them,
  all who could be found have been captured at a
    blow,
  far though they had fled.
4 That is why I said, 'Turn your eyes away from
    me,
  let me weep bitterly;
  do not try to comfort me
  over the ruin of the daughter of my people.'

5 For this is a day of rout, panic and confusion,
  the work of the Lord Yahweh Sabaoth
  in the Valley of Vision.
  The wall is sapped,
  cries for help ring out to the mountains.
6 Elam has picked up his quiver,
  with manned chariots and horsemen, and Kir has
    bared his shield.

NEW REVISED STANDARD VERSION	REVISED ENGLISH BIBLE

NEW REVISED STANDARD VERSION

7 Your choicest valleys were full of chariots,
and the cavalry took their stand at the gates.
8 He has taken away the covering of Judah.

On that day you looked to the weapons of the House of the Forest, 9 and you saw that there were many breaches in the city of David, and you collected the waters of the lower pool. 10 You counted the houses of Jerusalem, and you broke down the houses to fortify the wall. 11 You made a reservoir between the two walls for the water of the old pool. But you did not look to him who did it, or have regard for him who planned it long ago.

12 In that day the Lord GOD of hosts
called to weeping and mourning,
to baldness and putting on sackcloth;
13 but instead there was joy and festivity,
killing oxen and slaughtering sheep,
eating meat and drinking wine.
"Let us eat and drink,
for tomorrow we die."
14 The LORD of hosts has revealed himself in my ears:
Surely this iniquity will not be forgiven you until you die,
says the Lord GOD of hosts.

15 Thus says the Lord GOD of hosts: Come, go to this steward, to Shebna, who is master of the household, and say to him: 16 What right do you have here? Who are your relatives here, that you have cut out a tomb here for yourself, cutting a tomb on the height, and carving a habitation for yourself in the rock? 17 The LORD is about to hurl you away violently, my fellow. He will seize firm hold on you, 18 whirl you round and round, and throw you like a ball into a wide land; there you shall die, and there your splendid chariots shall lie, O you disgrace to your master's house! 19 I will thrust you from your office, and you will be pulled down from your post.

20 On that day I will call my servant Eliakim son of Hilkiah, 21 and will clothe him with your robe and bind your sash on him. I will commit your authority to his hand, and he shall be a father to the inhabitants of Jerusalem and to the house of Judah. 22 I will place on his shoulder the key of the house of David; he shall open, and no one shall shut; he shall shut, and no one shall open. 23 I will fasten him like a peg in a secure place, and he will become a throne of honor to his ancestral house. 24 And they will hang on him the whole weight of his ancestral house, the offspring and issue, every small vessel, from the cups to all the flagons. 25 On that day, says the LORD of hosts, the peg that was fastened in a secure place will give way; it will be cut down and fall, and the load that was on it will perish, for the LORD has spoken.

REVISED ENGLISH BIBLE

7 Your fairest valleys were overrun by chariots
and the city gates were beset by horsemen;
8 the heart of Judah's defence was laid open.

On that day you checked the weapons stored in the House of the Forest; 9 you filled all the many pools in the City of David, collecting water from the Lower Pool. 10 Then you surveyed the houses in Jerusalem, tearing some down to repair and fortify the wall, 11 and between the two walls you constructed a reservoir for the water of the Old Pool.

You did not look to the Maker of the city
or consider him who fashioned it long ago.

12 On that day the Lord, the LORD of Hosts,
called for weeping and beating the breast in mourning,
for shaving the head and putting on sackcloth.
13 Instead there was joy and merrymaking,
killing of cattle and slaughtering of sheep,
eating of meat and drinking of wine.
'Let us eat and drink,' you said, 'for tomorrow we die!'

14 Here are words revealed to me by the LORD of Hosts:

Assuredly your wickedness will never be wiped out;
you will die for it.
This is the word of the Lord, the LORD of Hosts.

15 These were the words of the Lord, the LORD of Hosts:

Go to the steward,
this Shebna, comptroller of the household, and say:
16 What have you here, or whom have you here,
that you have hewn out a tomb here for yourself?
Why should he hew his tomb in an eminent place,
and carve for himself a resting-place in the rock?
17 The LORD is about to shake you out,
as a garment is shaken to rid it of lice;
18 he will roll you up tightly
and throw you like a ball
into a land of vast expanses.
There you will die,
and there your chariot of honour will remain,
bringing disgrace on your master's household.
19 I shall remove you from office
and pluck you from your post.

20 On that day I shall send for my servant Eliakim son of Hilkiah; 21 I shall invest him with your robe, equip him with your sash of office, and invest him with your authority; he will be a father to the inhabitants of Jerusalem and to the people of Judah. 22 I shall place the key of David's palace on his shoulder; what he opens none will shut, and what he shuts none will open. 23 He will be a seat of honour for his father's family; I shall fasten him firmly in place like a peg. 24 On him will hang the whole glory of the family, even to the meanest members — all the paltriest of vessels, whether bowl or pot. 25 On that day, says the LORD of Hosts, the peg which was firmly fastened in its place will be removed; cut off, it will fall, and the load hanging on it will be destroyed. The LORD has spoken.

22:9 you ... Pool: or you took note of the many breaches in the wall of the City of David, and you collected water from the Lower Pool. 22:17 garment: prob. rdg; Heb. man. 22:19 and pluck: so Syriac; Heb. and he will drive.

NEW AMERICAN BIBLE

7 Your choice valleys are filled with chariots,
    and horses are posted at the gates,
8   and shelter over Judah is removed.

On that day you looked to the weapons in the House of
the Forest; 9 you saw that the breaches in the City of David
were many; you collected the water of the lower pool.
10 You numbered the houses of Jerusalem, tearing some
down to strengthen the wall; 11 you made a reservoir between the two walls for the water of the old pool. But you
did not look to the city's Maker, nor did you consider him
who built it long ago.

12 On that day the Lord,
    the GOD of hosts, called on you
To weep and mourn,
    to shave your head and put on sackcloth.
13 But look! you feast and celebrate,
    you slaughter oxen and butcher sheep,
You eat meat and drink wine:
    "Eat and drink, for tomorrow we die!"
14 This reaches the ears of the LORD of hosts—
    You shall not be pardoned this wickedness till
        you die,
    says the Lord, the GOD of hosts.

15 Thus says the Lord, the GOD of hosts:
    Up, go to that official,
    Shebna, master of the palace,
16 Who has hewn for himself a sepulcher on a height
    and carved his tomb in the rock:
    "What are you doing here, and what people have
        you here,
    that here you have hewn for yourself a tomb?"
17 The LORD shall hurl you down headlong,
        mortal man!
    He shall grip you firmly
18 And roll you up and toss you like a ball
        into an open land
    To perish there, you and the chariots you glory in,
        you disgrace to your master's house!
19 I will thrust you from your office
    and pull you down from your station.
20 On that day I will summon my servant
    Eliakim, son of Hilkiah;
21 I will clothe him with your robe,
    and gird him with your sash,
    and give over to him your authority.
He shall be a father to the inhabitants of Jerusalem,
    and to the house of Judah.
22 I will place the key of the House of David on
        his shoulder;
    when he opens, no one shall shut,
    when he shuts, no one shall open.
23 I will fix him like a peg in a sure spot,
    to be a place of honor for his family;
24 On him shall hang all the glory of his family:
    descendants and offspring,
    all the little dishes, from bowls to jugs.

25 On that day, says the LORD of hosts, the peg fixed in
a sure spot shall give way, break off and fall, and the weight
that hung on it shall be done away with; for the LORD has
spoken.

NEW JERUSALEM BIBLE

7 Your fairest valleys are full of chariots
    and the horsemen take up positions at the gates;
8 thus falls the defence of Judah.

That day you turned your gaze
    to the weapons in the House of the Forest.
9 You saw how many breaches there were in the
        City of David.
    You collected the waters of the lower pool.
10 You surveyed the houses in Jerusalem
    and pulled houses down to strengthen the wall.
11 Between the two walls you made a reservoir
    for the waters of the old pool.
    But you did not look to the Creator of these things,
    you did not look to the One who fashioned them
        long ago.

12 That day the Lord Yahweh Sabaoth called on you
    to weep and mourn,
    to shave your heads, to put on sackcloth.
13 But instead there is joy and merriment,
    killing of oxen, slaughtering of sheep,
    eating of meat, drinking of wine,
    'Let us eat and drink,
    for tomorrow we shall be dead.'
14 Then Yahweh Sabaoth revealed this to my ears,
    'This guilt will never be forgiven you, until you
        are dead,'
    says the Lord Yahweh Sabaoth.

15 The Lord Yahweh Sabaoth says this:

    Go and find that steward,
    Shebna, the master of the palace:
16 'What do you own here, who gave you the right
    for you to hew yourself a tomb here?'
    He is hewing himself a tomb,
    is digging a resting-place for himself in the rock.
17 But Yahweh will throw you away, strong as you
        are,
    will grasp you in his grip,
18 will screw you up into a ball,
    a ball thrown into a vast space.
    There you will die, with your splendid chariots,
    disgrace to your master's palace!
19 I shall hound you from your office,
    I shall snatch you from your post
20 and, when that day comes,
    I shall summon my servant
    Eliakim son of Hilkiah.
21 I shall dress him in your tunic,
    I shall put your sash round his waist,
    I shall invest him with your authority;
    and he will be a father
    to the inhabitants of Jerusalem
    and to the House of Judah.
22 I shall place the key of David's palace on his
        shoulder;
    when he opens, no one will close,
    when he closes, no one will open.
23 I shall drive him like a nail into a firm place;
    and he will become a throne of glory for his
        family.

24 'On him will depend all the glory of his family, the
descendants and offspring, all the vessels of small capacity
too, from cups to pitchers. 25 That day, declares Yahweh
Sabaoth, the nail driven into a firm place will give way, will
be torn out and fall. And the whole load hanging on it will
be lost. For Yahweh has spoken.'

NEW REVISED STANDARD VERSION	REVISED ENGLISH BIBLE

23 The oracle concerning Tyre.

Wail, O ships of Tarshish,
for your fortress is destroyed. *k*
When they came in from Cyprus
they learned of it.
2 Be still, O inhabitants of the coast,
O merchants of Sidon,
your messengers crossed over the sea *l*
3 and were on the mighty waters;
your revenue was the grain of Shihor,
the harvest of the Nile;
you were the merchant of the nations.
4 Be ashamed, O Sidon, for the sea has spoken,
the fortress of the sea, saying:
"I have neither labored nor given birth,
I have neither reared young men
nor brought up young women."
5 When the report comes to Egypt,
they will be in anguish over the report about
Tyre.
6 Cross over to Tarshish—
wail, O inhabitants of the coast!
7 Is this your exultant city
whose origin is from days of old,
whose feet carried her
to settle far away?
8 Who has planned this
against Tyre, the bestower of crowns,
whose merchants were princes,
whose traders were the honored of the earth?
9 The LORD of hosts has planned it—
to defile the pride of all glory,
to shame all the honored of the earth.
10 Cross over to your own land,
O ships of *m* Tarshish;
this is a harbor *n* no more.
11 He has stretched out his hand over the sea,
he has shaken the kingdoms;
the LORD has given command concerning Canaan
to destroy its fortresses.
12 He said:
You will exult no longer,
O oppressed virgin daughter Sidon;
rise, cross over to Cyprus—
even there you will have no rest.

13 Look at the land of the Chaldeans! This is the people;
it was not Assyria. They destined Tyre for wild animals.
They erected their siege towers, they tore down her palaces,
they made her a ruin. *o*
14 Wail, O ships of Tarshish,
for your fortress is destroyed.
15 From that day Tyre will be forgotten for seventy years,
the lifetime of one king. At the end of seventy years, it will
happen to Tyre as in the song about the prostitute:
16 Take a harp,
go about the city,
you forgotten prostitute!
Make sweet melody,
sing many songs,
that you may be remembered.
17 At the end of seventy years, the LORD will visit Tyre, and
she will return to her trade, and will prostitute herself with
all the kingdoms of the world on the face of the earth. 18 Her

23 TYRE: an oracle.

Wail, you ships of Tarshish, for the harbour is
destroyed;
the port of entry from Kittim is swept away.
2 Lament, you people of the sea coast, you
merchants of Sidon,
3 whose envoys cross the great waters,
whose harvest is grain from Shihor,
whose revenue comes from trade between nations.
4 In dismay Sidon, the sea-fortress, says:
'I no longer feel the anguish of labour or bear
children;
I have no young sons to rear, no daughters to bring
up.'
5 When the news reaches Egypt
her people will writhe in anguish at the fate of
Tyre.
6 Make your way to Tarshish;
wail, you dwellers by the sea.
7 Is this your bustling city of ancient foundation,
the founder of colonies in distant parts?

8 Whose was this plan against Tyre,
a city with crowns in its gift,
whose merchants were princes,
whose traders the most honoured men on earth?
9 The LORD of Hosts planned it to prick every
noble's pride
and humiliate all the most honoured men on earth.
10 Take to the tillage of your fields, you people of
Tarshish;
for your market is lost.
11 The LORD has stretched out his hand over the sea
and made kingdoms quake;
he has decreed the destruction of Canaan's marts.
12 He has said, 'You will be busy no more,
you, the sorely oppressed city of Sidon.
Though you make your escape to Kittim,
even there you will find no respite.'

13 Look at this land, the destined home of ships! The Chaldaeans (this was the people; it was not Assyria) erected
siege-towers, tore down its palaces, and laid it in ruins.

14 Wail, you ships of Tarshish;
for your haven is destroyed.

15 From that day Tyre will be forgotten for seventy years,
the span of one king's life. At the end of the seventy years
her plight will be that of the harlot in the song:

16 Take your lyre, walk about the city,
poor, forgotten harlot;
touch the strings sweetly, sing all your songs,
make men remember you once more.

17 At the end of seventy years the LORD will turn again to
Tyre; she will go back to her old trade and hire herself out
to every kingdom on earth. 18 But the profits of her trading

---

k Cn Compare verse 14: Heb *for it is destroyed, without houses*
l Q Ms: MT *crossing over the sea, they replenished you*
m Cn Compare Gk: Heb *like the Nile, daughter*   *n* Cn: Heb *restraint*
o Meaning of Heb uncertain

23:3 **whose envoys**: *prob. rdg, cp. Scroll*; Heb. they have filled you.
whose harvest: *prob. rdg*; Heb. the harvest of the Nile.   23:4 **the
sea-fortress, says**: *prob. rdg*; Heb. for the sea said, the sea-fortress
saying.   23:10 **Take. . . fields**: *so Gk*; Heb. Pass over your fields
like the Nile. **market**: *prob. rdg*; Heb. girdle.

23 Oracle on Tyre:
Wail, O ships of Tarshish,
  for your port is destroyed;
From the land of the Kittim
  the news reaches them.
2 Silence! you who dwell on the coast,
  you merchants of Sidon,
Whose messengers crossed the sea
3   over the deep waters.
The grain of Shihor, the harvest of the Nile, was
  her revenue,
  and she the merchant among nations.
4 Shame, O Sidon, fortress on the sea,
  for the sea has spoken:
"I have not been in labor, nor given birth,
  nor raised young men,
  nor reared virgins."
5 When it is heard in Egypt
  they shall be in anguish at the news of Tyre.
6 Pass over to Tarshish, wailing,
  you who dwell on the coast!
7 Is this your wanton city,
  whose origin is from of old,
Whose feet have taken her
  to dwell in distant lands?
8 Who has planned such a thing
  against Tyre, the bestower of crowns,
Whose merchants are princes,
  whose traders are the earth's honored men?
9 The LORD of hosts has planned it,
  to disgrace all pride of majesty,
  to degrade all the earth's honored men.
10 Cross to your own land,
  O ship of Tarshish;
  the harbor is no more.
11 His hand he stretches out over the sea,
  he shakes kingdoms;
The LORD has ordered the destruction
  of Canaan's strongholds.
12 You shall exult no more, he says,
  you who are now oppressed, virgin
    daughter Sidon.
Arise, pass over to the Kittim,
  even there you shall find no rest.

13 [This people is the land of the Chaldeans, not Assyria.]

  She whom the impious founded,
    setting up towers for her,
  Has had her castles destroyed,
    and has been turned into a ruin.
14 Lament, O ships of Tarshish,
  for your haven is destroyed.

15 On that day, Tyre shall be forgotten for seventy years.
With the days of another king, at the end of seventy years,
it shall be for Tyre as in the song about the harlot:

16 Take a harp, go about the city,
  O forgotten harlot;
Pluck the strings skillfully, sing many songs,
  that they may remember you.

17 At the end of the seventy years the LORD shall visit
Tyre. She shall return to her hire and deal with all the
world's kingdoms on the face of the earth. 18 But her mer-

23 Proclamation about Tyre:

Howl, ships of Tarshish, for all has been
    destroyed—
  no more houses, no way of getting in:
  the news has reached them from Kittim.
2 Be struck dumb, inhabitants of the coast,
  you merchants of Sidon,
  whose messengers cross the sea
3 to the wide ocean.
The grain of the Canal, the harvest of the Nile,
  formed her revenue.
She was the market for the nations.
4 Blush, Sidon (citadel of the seas),
  for this is what the sea has said,
  'I have felt no birth-pangs, never given birth,
  never reared boys nor brought up girls.'
5 When the news reaches Egypt,
  they will tremble to hear Tyre's fate.
6 Cross to Tarshish, howl, inhabitants of the coast.
7 Is this your proud city
  founded far back in the past,
  whose steps led her far afield
  to found her colonies?
8 Who took this decision
  against Tyre, who used to hand out crowns,
  whose traders were princes,
  whose merchants, men honoured in the city?
9 Yahweh Sabaoth took this decision
  to wither the pride of all beauty
  and humiliate those honoured in the city.
10 Cultivate your country like the Delta, daughter of
    Tarshish,
  for your marine docks are no more.
11 He has raised his hand against the sea,
  he has shaken kingdoms,
  Yahweh has ordained the destruction
  of the fortresses of Canaan.

12 He has said, 'Exult no more,
  ill-treated virgin daughter of Sidon!
  Get up, cross to Kittim,
  no respite for you there, either.'
13 Look at the land of the Chaldaeans,
  a people who used not to exist!
Assyria assigned it to the creatures of the wilds;
  they raised their siege-towers against it,
  demolished its bastions,
  reduced it to ruin.
14 Howl, ships of Tarshish, for your fortress has been
    destroyed.

15 When that day comes, Tyre will be forgotten for seventy years, the length of one king's life. But when the
seventy years are over, Tyre will become like the whore in
the song:

16 'Take your harp, walk the town,
  whore whom men have forgotten!
  Play sweetly, song after song,
  to make them remember you.'

17 At the end of the seventy years Yahweh will visit Tyre.
She will receive her pay again and play the whore with all
the kingdoms of the world on the surface of the earth. 18 But

---

23, 13: The gloss here identifies she whom the impious founded with
the land of the Chaldeans.

merchandise and her wages will be dedicated to the LORD; her profits*p* will not be stored or hoarded, but her merchandise will supply abundant food and fine clothing for those who live in the presence of the LORD.

24 Now the LORD is about to lay waste the earth and make it desolate,
and he will twist its surface and scatter its inhabitants.

2 And it shall be, as with the people, so with the priest;
as with the slave, so with his master;
as with the maid, so with her mistress;
as with the buyer, so with the seller;
as with the lender, so with the borrower;
as with the creditor, so with the debtor.

3 The earth shall be utterly laid waste and utterly despoiled;
for the LORD has spoken this word.

4 The earth dries up and withers,
the world languishes and withers;
the heavens languish together with the earth.

5 The earth lies polluted
under its inhabitants;
for they have transgressed laws,
violated the statutes,
broken the everlasting covenant.

6 Therefore a curse devours the earth,
and its inhabitants suffer for their guilt;
therefore the inhabitants of the earth dwindled,
and few people are left.

7 The wine dries up,
the vine languishes,
all the merry-hearted sigh.

8 The mirth of the timbrels is stilled,
the noise of the jubilant has ceased,
the mirth of the lyre is stilled.

9 No longer do they drink wine with singing;
strong drink is bitter to those who drink it.

10 The city of chaos is broken down,
every house is shut up so that no one can enter.

11 There is an outcry in the streets for lack of wine;
all joy has reached its eventide;
the gladness of the earth is banished.

12 Desolation is left in the city,
the gates are battered into ruins.

13 For thus it shall be on the earth
and among the nations,
as when an olive tree is beaten,
as at the gleaning when the grape harvest is ended.

14 They lift up their voices, they sing for joy;
they shout from the west over the majesty of the LORD.

15 Therefore in the east give glory to the LORD;
in the coastlands of the sea glorify the name of the LORD, the God of Israel.

16 From the ends of the earth we hear songs of praise,
of glory to the Righteous One.
But I say, I pine away,
I pine away. Woe is me!
For the treacherous deal treacherously,
the treacherous deal very treacherously.

17 Terror, and the pit, and the snare
are upon you, O inhabitant of the earth!

will be dedicated to the LORD; they will not be stored up or hoarded, but given to those who worship the LORD, to purchase food in plenty and fine apparel.

24 BEWARE, the LORD is about to strip the earth,
split it and turn it upside down,
and scatter its inhabitants!

2 There will be the same fate for priest and people,
for master and slave, mistress and maid,
seller and buyer, borrower and lender, creditor and debtor.

3 The earth is empty and void
and stripped bare.
For this is the word that the LORD has spoken.

4 The earth dries up and withers,
the whole world wilts and withers,
the heights of the earth wilt.

5 The earth itself is desecrated by those who live on it,
for they have broken laws, disobeyed statutes,
and violated the everlasting covenant.

6 That is why a curse consumes the earth
and its inhabitants suffer punishment,
why the inhabitants of the earth dwindle
and only a few are left.

7 The new wine fails, the vines wilt,
and the revellers all groan in sorrow.

8 The merry beat of tambourines is silenced,
the shouts of revelry are hushed,
the joyful lyre is silent.

9 They drink wine but without songs;
liquor tastes bitter to the one who drinks it.

10 The city is shattered and in chaos,
every house barred, that none may enter.

11 In the streets there is a crying out for wine;
all joy has faded,
and merriment is banished from the land.

12 Nothing but desolation is left in the city;
its gates are smashed beyond repair.

13 So it will be throughout the world among the nations,
as when an olive tree is beaten and stripped
at the end of the vintage.

14 People raise their voices and cry aloud,
acclaiming in the west the majesty of the LORD.

15 Therefore let the LORD be glorified in the eastern regions,
and the name of the LORD the God of Israel
in the coasts and islands of the sea.

16 From the ends of the earth we have heard them sing,
ascribing beauty to the righteous nation.

But I said: Depravity, depravity!
Woe betide me! Traitors deal treacherously!
They are double-dyed traitors.

17 The hunter's scare, the pit, and the trap
threaten all you inhabitants of the earth.

23:18 **worship:** *lit.* sit in the presence of.   24:15 **the eastern regions:** *meaning of Heb. uncertain.*

chandise and her hire shall be sacred to the LORD. It shall not be stored up or laid away, but from her merchandise those who dwell before the LORD shall eat their fill and clothe themselves in choice attire.

24 Lo, the LORD empties the land and lays it waste;
　　he turns it upside down,
　　　scattering its inhabitants:
2 Layman and priest alike,
　　servant and master,
　The maid as her mistress,
　　the buyer as the seller,
　The lender as the borrower,
　　the creditor as the debtor.
3 The earth is utterly laid waste, utterly stripped,
　　for the LORD has decreed this thing.
4 The earth mourns and fades,
　　the world languishes and fades;
　　both heaven and earth languish.
5 The earth is polluted because of its inhabitants,
　　who have transgressed laws, violated statutes,
　　broken the ancient covenant.
6 Therefore a curse devours the earth,
　　and its inhabitants pay for their guilt;
　Therefore they who dwell on earth turn pale,
　　and few men are left.
7 The wine mourns, the vine languishes,
　　all the merry-hearted groan.
8 Stilled are the cheerful timbrels,
　　ended the shouts of the jubilant,
　　stilled is the cheerful harp.
9 They cannot sing and drink wine;
　　strong drink is bitter to those who partake of it.
10 Broken down is the city of chaos,
　　shut against entry, every house.
11 In the streets they cry out for lack of wine;
　　all joy has disappeared
　　and cheer has left the land.
12 In the city nothing remains but ruin;
　　its gates are battered and desolate.
13 Thus it is within the land,
　　and among the peoples,
　As with an olive tree after it is beaten,
　　as with a gleaning when the vintage is done.
14 These lift up their voice in acclaim;
　　from the sea they proclaim the majesty of
　　　the LORD:
15 "For this, in the coastlands,
　　give glory to the LORD!
　In the coastlands of the sea,
　　to the name of the LORD, the God of Israel!"
16 From the end of the earth we hear songs:
　　"Splendor to the Just One!"
　But I said, "I am wasted, wasted away.
　　Woe is me! The traitors betray:
　　with treachery have the traitors betrayed!
17 Terror, pit, and trap
　　are upon you, inhabitant of the earth;

her profits and wages will be dedicated to Yahweh. They will not be stored or hoarded, but her profits will go to those who live in Yahweh's presence, for them to have as much food as they want and splendid clothes.

24 See how Yahweh lays the earth waste,
　　makes it a desert, buckles its surface,
　　　scatters its inhabitants,
2 priest and people alike, master and slave,
　　mistress and maid, seller and buyer,
　　lender and borrower, creditor and debtor.
3 Ravaged, ravaged the earth will be,
　　despoiled, despoiled,
　　for Yahweh has uttered this word.
4 The earth is mourning, pining away,
　　the pick of earth's people are withering away.
5 The earth is defiled
　　by the feet of its inhabitants,
　for they have transgressed the laws,
　　violated the decree, broken the everlasting
　　　covenant.
6 That is why the curse has consumed the earth
　　and its inhabitants pay the penalty,
　that is why the inhabitants of the earth have been
　　　burnt up
　　and few people are left.
7 The new wine is mourning, the vine is withering
　　　away,
　　the once merry-hearted are sighing.
8 The cheerful sound of tambourines is silent,
　　the sound of revelling is over,
　　the cheerful sound of the harp is silent.
9 No more will they sing over their wine,
　　liquor will taste bitter to the drinker.
10 The city of nothingness is in ruins,
　　every house is shut, no one can enter.
11 People shout in the streets to try to get wine;
　　all joy has vanished,
　　happiness has been banished from the country.
12 Nothing but rubble in the city,
　　the gate has collapsed in ruins.
13 For at the heart of earth's life, among the peoples,
　　it is as at the beating of the olive trees,
　　as at the gleaning of the grapes
　　　when the grape harvest is over.
14 They raise their voices, shouting for joy,
　　in Yahweh's honour they shout from the west.
15 'Yes, in the east, give glory to Yahweh,
　　in the islands of the sea, to the name of Yahweh,
　　　God of Israel!'
16 We have heard psalms from the remotest parts of
　　　earth,
　　'Glory to the Upright One!'
　But I thought, 'What an ordeal,
　　what an ordeal! What misery for me!'
　The traitors have betrayed,
　　the traitors have acted most treacherously.
17 Fear, the pit and the snare for you,
　　inhabitants of the city!

NEW REVISED STANDARD VERSION

18 Whoever flees at the sound of the terror
    shall fall into the pit;
and whoever climbs out of the pit
    shall be caught in the snare.
For the windows of heaven are opened,
    and the foundations of the earth tremble.
19 The earth is utterly broken,
    the earth is torn asunder,
    the earth is violently shaken.
20 The earth staggers like a drunkard,
    it sways like a hut;
its transgression lies heavy upon it,
    and it falls, and will not rise again.
21 On that day the Lord will punish
    the host of heaven in heaven,
    and on earth the kings of the earth.
22 They will be gathered together
    like prisoners in a pit;
they will be shut up in a prison,
    and after many days they will be punished.
23 Then the moon will be abashed,
    and the sun ashamed;
for the Lord of hosts will reign
    on Mount Zion and in Jerusalem,
and before his elders he will manifest his glory.

25 O Lord, you are my God;
    I will exalt you, I will praise your name;
for you have done wonderful things,
    plans formed of old, faithful and sure.
2 For you have made the city a heap,
    the fortified city a ruin;
the palace of aliens is a city no more,
    it will never be rebuilt.
3 Therefore strong peoples will glorify you;
    cities of ruthless nations will fear you.
4 For you have been a refuge to the poor,
    a refuge to the needy in their distress,
    a shelter from the rainstorm and a shade from
        the heat.
When the blast of the ruthless was like a winter
    rainstorm,
5   the noise of aliens like heat in a dry place,
you subdued the heat with the shade of clouds;
    the song of the ruthless was stilled.
6 On this mountain the Lord of hosts will make for
    all peoples
a feast of rich food, a feast of well-aged wines,
    of rich food filled with marrow, of well-aged
        wines strained clear.
7 And he will destroy on this mountain
    the shroud that is cast over all peoples,
    the sheet that is spread over all nations;
8   he will swallow up death forever.
Then the Lord God will wipe away the tears
    from all faces,
    and the disgrace of his people he will take
        away from all the earth,
for the Lord has spoken.
9 It will be said on that day,
    Lo, this is our God; we have waited for him,
        so that he might save us.
This is the Lord for whom we have waited;
    let us be glad and rejoice in his salvation.
10 For the hand of the Lord will rest on this
    mountain.

The Moabites shall be trodden down in their
    place
as straw is trodden down in a dung-pit.

REVISED ENGLISH BIBLE

18 Whoever runs from the rattle of the scare
    will fall into the pit,
and whoever climbs out of the pit
    will be caught in the trap.
The windows of heaven above are opened
    and earth's foundations shake;
19 the earth is utterly shattered,
    it is convulsed and reels wildly.
20 The earth lurches like a drunkard
    and sways like a watchman's shelter;
the sins of its inhabitants weigh heavy on it,
    and it falls, to rise no more.
21 On that day the Lord will punish
    in heaven the host of heaven,
    and on earth the kings of the earth.
22 They are herded together,
    and packed like prisoners in a dungeon,
shut up in jail, punished over many years.
23 The moon will grow pale
    and the sun hide its face in shame;
for the Lord of Hosts has become king
    on Mount Zion and in Jerusalem,
and is revealed in his glory to the elders of his
      people.

25 Lord, you are my God;
    I shall exalt you, I shall praise your name,
for you have done wonderful things,
    long-planned, certain and sure.
2 You have turned cities into heaps of ruin,
    fortified towns into rubble;
every mansion in the cities is swept away,
    never to be rebuilt.
3 For this many a cruel nation holds you in honour,
    the cities of ruthless peoples treat you with awe.
4 Truly you have been a refuge to the poor,
    a refuge to the needy in their distress,
shelter from tempest, shade from heat.
For the blast of the ruthless is like an icy storm
5 or a scorching drought;
    you subdue the roar of the foe,
    and the song of the ruthless dies away.
6 On this mountain the Lord of Hosts will prepare
    a banquet of rich fare for all the peoples,
    a banquet of wines well matured,
richest fare and well-matured wines strained clear.
7 On this mountain the Lord will destroy
    that veil shrouding all the peoples,
    the pall thrown over all the nations.
8 He will destroy death for ever.
Then the Lord God will wipe away the tears
    from every face,
and throughout the world
    remove the indignities from his people.
The Lord has spoken.
9 On that day the people will say:
    'See, this is our God;
we have waited for him and he will deliver us.
This is the Lord for whom we have waited;
    let us rejoice and exult in his deliverance.'
10 For the hand of the Lord will rest on this
      mountain,
but Moab will be trampled where he stands,
    as straw is trampled in the slush of a midden.

25:5 **foe:** *prob. rdg; Heb. adds* heat in the shadow of a cloud.

| NEW AMERICAN BIBLE | NEW JERUSALEM BIBLE |

18 He who flees at the sound of terror
    will fall into the pit;
He who climbs out of the pit
    will be caught in the trap.
For the windows on high will be opened
    and the foundations of the earth will shake.
19 The earth will burst asunder,
    the earth will be shaken apart,
    the earth will be convulsed.
20 The earth will reel like a drunkard,
    and it will sway like a hut;
Its rebellion will weigh it down,
    until it falls, never to rise again."
21 On that day the LORD will punish
    the host of the heavens in the heavens,
    and the kings of the earth on the earth.
22 They will be gathered together
    like prisoners into a pit;
They will be shut up in a dungeon,
    and after many days they will be punished.
23 Then the moon will blush
    and the sun grow pale,
For the LORD of hosts will reign
    on Mount Zion and in Jerusalem,
    glorious in the sight of his elders.

25 O LORD, you are my God,
    I will extol you and praise your name;
For you have fulfilled your wonderful plans of old,
    faithful and true.
2 For you have made the city a heap,
    the fortified city a ruin;
The castle of the insolent is a city no more,
    nor ever to be rebuilt.
3 Therefore a strong people will honor you,
    fierce nations will fear you.
4 For you are a refuge to the poor,
    a refuge to the needy in distress;
Shelter from the rain,
    shade from the heat.
As with the cold rain,
5   as with the desert heat,
    even so you quell the uproar of the wanton.
6 On this mountain the LORD of hosts
    will provide for all peoples
A feast of rich food and choice wines,
    juicy, rich food and pure, choice wines.
7 On this mountain he will destroy
    the veil that veils all peoples,
The web that is woven over all nations;
8   he will destroy death forever.
The Lord GOD will wipe away
    the tears from all faces;
The reproach of his people he will remove
    from the whole earth; for the LORD has spoken.

9   On that day it will be said:
"Behold our God, to whom we looked to save us!
This is the LORD for whom we looked;
    let us rejoice and be glad that he has saved us!"
10 For the hand of the LORD will rest on
    this mountain,
but Moab will be trodden down
    as a straw is trodden down in the mire.

18 And whoever flees from the cry of fear
    will fall into the pit,
and whoever climbs out of the pit
    will be caught in the snare.*l*
Yes, the sluice-gates above are open,
    the foundations of the earth are quaking.
19 A cracking, the earth cracks open,
    a jolting, the earth gives a jolt,
a lurching, the earth lurches backwards and
        forwards.
20 The earth will reel to and fro like a drunkard,
    it will be shaken like a shanty;
so heavy will be its sin on it,
    it will fall, never to rise again.
21 When that day comes, Yahweh will punish
    the armies of the sky above
    and on earth the kings of the earth;
22 they will be herded together,
    herded together like prisoners in a dungeon
and shut up in gaol,
    and, after long years, punished.
23 The moon will be confused and the sun ashamed,
    for Yahweh Sabaoth is king
on Mount Zion and in Jerusalem,
    and the Glory will radiate on their elders.

25 Yahweh, you are my God,
    I shall praise you to the heights, I shall praise your
        name;
for you have accomplished marvels,
    plans long-conceived, faithfully, firmly.
2 For you have made the town a heap of stones,
    the fortified city a ruin.
The foreigners' citadel is a city no longer,
    it will never be rebuilt.
3 Hence mighty peoples will honour you,
    the city of pitiless nations hold you in awe;
4 For you have been a refuge for the weak,
    a refuge for the needy in distress,
    a shelter from the storm,
    shade from the heat;
for the breath of the pitiless
    is like a winter storm.
5 Like heat in a dry land
    you calm the foreigners' tumult;
as heat under the shadow of a cloud,
    so the song of the pitiless dies away.

6 On this mountain, for all peoples,
    Yahweh Sabaoth is preparing
a banquet of rich food, a banquet of fine wines,
    of succulent food, of well-strained wines.
7 On this mountain, he has destroyed
    the veil which used to veil all peoples,
    the pall enveloping all nations;
8 he has destroyed death for ever.
Lord Yahweh has wiped away the tears from every
        cheek;
he has taken his people's shame away everywhere
        on earth,
for Yahweh has spoken.

9 And on that day, it will be said,
'Look, this is our God,
    in him we put our hope that he should save us,
this is Yahweh, we put our hope in him.
    Let us exult and rejoice since he has saved us.'
10 For Yahweh's hand will rest on this mountain,
    and Moab will be trodden under his feet
    as straw is trodden into the dung-heap.

l **24** // Jr 48:43–44.

NEW REVISED STANDARD VERSION

REVISED ENGLISH BIBLE

11 Though they spread out their hands in the midst
of it,
    as swimmers spread out their hands to swim,
    their pride will be laid low despite the
        struggle*q* of their hands.
12 The high fortifications of his walls will be
        brought down,
    laid low, cast to the ground, even to the dust.

26 On that day this song will be sung in the land of
Judah:
    We have a strong city;
        he sets up victory
        like walls and bulwarks.
2 Open the gates,
    so that the righteous nation that keeps faith
        may enter in.
3 Those of steadfast mind you keep in peace —
    in peace because they trust in you.
4 Trust in the LORD forever,
    for in the LORD GOD*r*
        you have an everlasting rock.
5 For he has brought low
    the inhabitants of the height;
        the lofty city he lays low.
    He lays it low to the ground,
        casts it to the dust.
6 The foot tramples it,
    the feet of the poor,
    the steps of the needy.
7 The way of the righteous is level;
    O Just One, you make smooth the path of the
        righteous.
8 In the path of your judgments,
    O LORD, we wait for you;
    your name and your renown
        are the soul's desire.
9 My soul yearns for you in the night,
    my spirit within me earnestly seeks you.
    For when your judgments are in the earth,
        the inhabitants of the world learn
            righteousness.
10 If favor is shown to the wicked,
    they do not learn righteousness;
    in the land of uprightness they deal perversely
        and do not see the majesty of the LORD.
11 O LORD, your hand is lifted up,
    but they do not see it.
    Let them see your zeal for your people, and be
        ashamed.
    Let the fire for your adversaries consume them.
12 O LORD, you will ordain peace for us,
    for indeed, all that we have done, you have
        done for us.
13 O LORD our God,
    other lords besides you have ruled over us,
    but we acknowledge your name alone.
14 The dead do not live;
    shades do not rise —
    because you have punished and destroyed them,
        and wiped out all memory of them.
15 But you have increased the nation, O LORD,
    you have increased the nation; you are
        glorified;
    you have enlarged all the borders of the land.
16 O LORD, in distress they sought you,
    they poured out a prayer*q*
    when your chastening was on them.

11 In it Moab will spread out his hands
    as a swimmer spreads his hands to swim,
    but his pride will be sunk
        with every stroke of his hands.
12 The LORD will overthrow the high-walled defences,
    level them to the ground,
    and bring them down to the dust.

26 On that day this song will be sung in Judah:
    We have a strong city
        with walls and ramparts built for our safety.
2 Open the gates! Let a righteous nation enter,
    a nation that keeps faith!
3 LORD, you keep those of firm purpose
    untroubled because of their trust in you.
4 Trust in the LORD for ever,
    for he is an eternal rock.
5 He has brought low
    all who dwell high in a towering city;
    he levels it to the ground
        and lays it in the dust,
6 so that the oppressed and the poor
    may tread it underfoot.
7 The path of the righteous is smooth,
    and you, LORD, make level the way for the
        upright.
8 We have had regard to the path prescribed in your
        laws,
    your name and your renown are our heart's desire.
9 With all my heart I long for you in the night,
    at dawn I seek for you;
    for, when your laws prevail on earth,
        the inhabitants of the world learn what justice is.
10 The wicked are destroyed;
    they have never learnt justice.
    Corrupt in a land of honest ways,
        they are blind to the majesty of the LORD.

11 LORD, your hand is lifted high,
    but they do not see your zeal for your people
        (let them see and be ashamed!);
    let the fire reserved for your enemies consume
        them.
12 LORD, you will bestow prosperity on us;
    for in truth all our works are your doing.
13 LORD our God,
    other lords than you have been our masters,
    but you alone do we invoke by name.
14 Those who are dead will not live again,
    those in their graves will not rise:
    you punished and destroyed them,
    and wiped out all memory of them.
15 LORD, you have enlarged the nation,
    enlarged it and won honour for yourself;
    you have extended all the frontiers of the country.
16 In distress, LORD, we sought you out,
    chastened by the whisper of your rebuke.

26:8 **We . . . regard to:** *so Scroll; Heb.* We look to you.
26:11 **your people:** *prob. rdg, cp. Aram. (Targ.); Heb. omits* your.
26:16 **we:** *prob. rdg; Heb.* they.

q Meaning of Heb uncertain   *r* Heb *in Yah, the* LORD

11 He will stretch forth his hands in Moab;
    as a swimmer extends his hands to swim;
He will bring low their pride
    as his hands sweep over them.
12 The high-walled fortress he will raze,
    and strike it down level with the earth, with the
        very dust.

26

On that day they will sing this song in the land of
Judah:

    "A strong city have we;
    he sets up walls and ramparts to protect us.
2 Open up the gates
    to let in a nation that is just,
    one that keeps faith.
3 A nation of firm purpose you keep in peace;
    in peace, for its trust in you."
4 Trust in the LORD forever!
    For the LORD is an eternal Rock.
5 He humbles those in high places,
    and the lofty city he brings down;
He tumbles it to the ground,
    levels it with the dust.
6 It is trampled underfoot by the needy,
    by the footsteps of the poor.
7 The way of the just is smooth;
    the path of the just you make level.
8 Yes, for your way and your judgments, O LORD,
    we look to you;
Your name and your title
    are the desire of our souls.
9 My soul yearns for you in the night,
    yes, my spirit within me keeps vigil for you;
When your judgment dawns upon the earth,
    the world's inhabitants learn justice.
10 The wicked man, spared, does not learn justice;
    in an upright land he acts perversely,
    and sees not the majesty of the LORD.
11 O LORD, your hand is uplifted,
    but they behold it not;
Let them be shamed when they see your zeal for
       your people:
    let the fire prepared for your enemies
       consume them.
12 O LORD, you mete out peace to us,
    for it is you who have accomplished all we
    have done.
13 O LORD, our God, other lords than you have
    ruled us;
    it is from you only that we can call upon your
       name.
14 Dead they are, they have no life,
    shades that cannot rise;
For you have punished and destroyed them,
    and wiped out all memory of them.
15 You have increased the nation, O LORD,
    increased the nation to your own glory,
    and extended far all the borders of the land.
16 O LORD, oppressed by your punishment,
    we cried out in anguish under your chastising.

11 He may stretch his hands wide on the mountain
    like a swimmer stretching out his hands to swim.
But he will humble his pride
    despite what his hands may attempt.
12 And the impregnable fortress of your walls,
    he has overthrown, laid low,
    flung to the ground, in the dust.

26

That day, this song will be sung in Judah:

    'We have a fortress city,
    the walls and ramparts provide safety.
2 Open the gates! Let the upright nation come in,
    the nation that keeps faith!
3 This is the plan decreed: you will guarantee peace,
    the peace entrusted to you.
4 Trust in Yahweh for ever,
    for Yahweh is a rock for ever.
5 He has brought low the dwellers on the heights,
    the lofty citadel;
he lays it low, brings it to the ground,
    flings it down in the dust.
6 It will be trodden under foot,
    by the feet of the needy, the steps of the weak.'
7 The path of the Upright One is honesty;
    you smooth the honest way of the upright.
8 Following the path of your judgements,
    Yahweh, we set our hopes in you,
    your name, your memory are all our soul desires.
9 At night my soul longs for you
    and my spirit within me seeks you out;
for when your judgements appear on earth
    the inhabitants of the world learn what saving
       justice is.
10 If pity is shown to the wicked
    without his learning what saving justice is,
    he will act wrongly in the land of right conduct
    and not see the majesty of Yahweh.
11 Yahweh, your hand is raised but they do not see!
    The antagonists of your people will look and grow
       pale;
with your fiery wrath you will devour your
       enemies.
12 Yahweh, you will grant us peace,
    having completed all our undertakings for us.
13 Yahweh our God, other lords than you have ruled
    us
but, loyal to you alone, we invoke your name.
14 The dead will not come back to life,
    the shadows will not rise again,
    for you have punished them, annihilated them,
    wiping out their very memory.
15 You have made the nation larger, Yahweh,
    made the nation larger and won yourself glory,
    you have rolled back the frontiers of the country.
16 Yahweh, in distress they had recourse to you,
    they expended themselves in prayer,
    since your punishment was on them.

NEW REVISED STANDARD VERSION

REVISED ENGLISH BIBLE

17 Like a woman with child,
  who writhes and cries out in her pangs
  when she is near her time,
so were we because of you, O Lord;
18   we were with child, we writhed,
  but we gave birth only to wind.
We have won no victories on earth,
  and no one is born to inhabit the world.
19 Your dead shall live, their corpses*s* shall rise.
  O dwellers in the dust, awake and sing for joy!
For your dew is a radiant dew,
  and the earth will give birth to those long
    dead.*t*

20 Come, my people, enter your chambers,
  and shut your doors behind you;
hide yourselves for a little while
  until the wrath is past.
21 For the Lord comes out from his place
  to punish the inhabitants of the earth for their
    iniquity;
the earth will disclose the blood shed on it,
  and will no longer cover its slain.

27 On that day the Lord with his cruel and great and
strong sword will punish Leviathan the fleeing serpent, Leviathan the twisting serpent, and he will kill the
dragon that is in the sea.

2 On that day:
A pleasant vineyard, sing about it!
3 I, the Lord, am its keeper;
  every moment I water it.
I guard it night and day
  so that no one can harm it;
4   I have no wrath.
If it gives me thorns and briers,
  I will march to battle against it.
  I will burn it up.
5 Or else let it cling to me for protection,
  let it make peace with me,
  let it make peace with me.

6 In days to come*u* Jacob shall take root,
  Israel shall blossom and put forth shoots,
  and fill the whole world with fruit.

7 Has he struck them down as he struck down
    those who struck them?
  Or have they been killed as their killers were
    killed?
8 By expulsion,*v* by exile you struggled against
    them;
  with his fierce blast he removed them in the
    day of the east wind.
9 Therefore by this the guilt of Jacob will be
    expiated,
  and this will be the full fruit of the removal of
    his sin:
when he makes all the stones of the altars
  like chalkstones crushed to pieces,
  no sacred poles*w* or incense altars will remain
    standing.
10 For the fortified city is solitary,
  a habitation deserted and forsaken, like the
    wilderness;
the calves graze there,
  there they lie down, and strip its branches.

17 As a woman with child cries out in her pains
  when her time is near and she is in labour,
  so were we because of you, Lord.
18 We have been with child, we have been in labour,
  but have given birth to wind.
We have achieved no victories for the land,
  given birth to no one to inhabit the world.
19 But your dead will live,
  their bodies will rise again.
Those who sleep in the earth
  will awake and shout for joy;
for your dew is a dew of sparkling light,
  and the earth will bring those long dead to birth
    again.

20 Go, my people, enter your rooms,
  and shut the doors after you;
withdraw for a little while,
  until the Lord's wrath has passed.
21 The Lord is coming from his dwelling-place
  to punish the inhabitants of the earth for their sins;
then the earth will reveal the blood shed on it
  and hide the slain no more.

27 On that day the Lord with his cruel sword,
  his mighty and powerful sword, will punish
Leviathan that twisting sea serpent,
  that writhing serpent Leviathan;
  he will slay the monster of the deep.
2 On that day sing of the pleasant vineyard.
3 I the Lord am its keeper,
  I water it regularly,
  for fear its leaves should wilt.
Night and day I tend it,
4 but I get no wine.
I would as soon have briars and thorns.
  Then as if in battle I would trample it down,
5 unless it grasps me as its refuge
  and makes peace with me —
  unless it makes its peace with me.

6 In time to come Jacob's posterity will take root
  and Israel will bud and blossom,
  and they will fill the whole earth with fruit.

7 Has the Lord struck them down
  as he struck their enemies?
Have they been slaughtered
  as their attackers were slaughtered?
8 His quarrel with Jerusalem ends
  by driving her into exile,
removing her by a cruel blast
  like that of the east wind.
9 This wipes out Jacob's iniquity,
  and the removal of his sin has this result:
he pounds to chalk all the altar stones,
  and no sacred poles or incense-altars are left
    standing.

10 The fortified city is left solitary,
  a homestead stripped bare, forsaken like a
    wilderness;
the calf grazes and lies down there,
  and eats up every twig.

---

s Cn Compare Syr Tg: Heb *my corpse*   *t* Heb *to the shades*
u Heb *Those to come*   *v* Meaning of Heb uncertain
w Heb *Asherim*

26:18 **in labour:** *prob. rdg, cp. Gk; Heb. adds* like. **given birth to
no . . . world:** *or* the inhabitants of the world have not fallen.
26:19 **their bodies:** *so Syriac; Heb.* my body.   27:1 **twisting:** *or*
primeval.   27:7 **their enemies:** *lit.* those who struck them down.
their attackers: *lit.* those who slew them.

NEW AMERICAN BIBLE

17 As a woman about to give birth
  writhes and cries out in her pains,
  so were we in your presence, O LORD.
18 We conceived and writhed in pain,
    giving birth to wind;
  Salvation we have not achieved for the earth,
    the inhabitants of the world cannot bring it forth.
19 But your dead shall live, their corpses shall rise;
    awake and sing, you who lie in the dust.
  For your dew is a dew of light,
    and the land of shades gives birth.

20 Go, my people, enter your chambers,
    and close your doors behind you;
  Hide yourselves for a brief moment,
    until the wrath is past.
21 See, the LORD goes forth from his place,
    to punish the wickedness of the
      earth's inhabitants;
  The earth will reveal the blood upon her,
    and no longer conceal her slain.

27   On that day,
    The LORD will punish with his sword
      that is cruel, great, and strong,
  Leviathan the fleeing serpent,
    Leviathan the coiled serpent;
    and he will slay the dragon that is in the sea.
2   On that day—
  The pleasant vineyard, sing about it!
3   I, the LORD, am its keeper,
    I water it every moment;
  Lest anyone harm it,
    night and day I guard it.
4 I am not angry,
    but if I were to find briers and thorns,
  In battle I should march against them;
    I should burn them all.
8 Expunging and expelling, I should strive
      against them,
    carrying them off with my cruel wind in time
      of storm.
6 In days to come Jacob shall take root,
    Israel shall sprout and blossom,
    covering all the world with fruit.
7 Is he to be smitten as his smiter was smitten?
    or slain as his slayer was slain?
5 Or shall he cling to me for refuge?
    He must make peace with me;
    peace shall he make with me!
9 This, then, shall be the expiation of Jacob's guilt,
    this the whole fruit of the removal of his sin:
  He shall pulverize all the stones of the altars
    like pieces of chalk;
    no sacred poles or incense altars shall stand.
10 For the fortified city shall be desolate,
    an abandoned pasture, a forsaken wilderness,
    where calves shall browse and lie.
  Its boughs shall be destroyed,

NEW JERUSALEM BIBLE

17 As a pregnant woman near her time of delivery
    writhes and cries out in her pangs,
  so have we been, Yahweh, in your eyes:
18 we have been pregnant, we have writhed,
    but we have given birth only to wind:
  we have not given salvation to the earth,
    no inhabitants for the world have been brought to
      birth.
19 Your dead will come back to life, your corpses
      will rise again.
  Wake up and sing, you dwellers in the dust,
    for your dew will be a radiant dew,
    but the earth will give birth to the shades.

20 Go, my people, go to your private room,
    shut yourselves in.
  Hide yourselves a little while
    until the retribution has passed.
21 For see, Yahweh emerges from his dwelling
    to punish the inhabitants of earth for their guilt;
  and the earth will reveal the blood shed on it
    and no longer hide its slain.

27   That day Yahweh will punish,
    with his unyielding sword, massive and strong,
  Leviathan[m] the fleeing serpent,
  Leviathan the coiling serpent;
    he will kill that dragon that lives in the sea.
2 That day,
    sing of the splendid vineyard!
3 I, Yahweh, am its guardian,
    from time to time I water it;
  so that no harm befall it,
    I guard it night and day.

4 —I do not have a wall.
  Who can reduce me to brambles and thorn-bushes?
  —I shall make war and trample on it
    and at the same time burn it.

5 Or should they beg for my protection,
    let them make their peace with me,
    peace let them make with me.

6 In days to come, Jacob will take root,
    Israel will bud and blossom
    and the surface of the world be one vast harvest.
7 Has he struck him as he was struck by those who
      struck him?
  Has he murdered him as he was murdered by those
      who murdered him?
8 By expelling, by excluding him, you have executed
      a sentence,
  he has blown him away with a breath as rough as
      the east wind.
9 For that is how Jacob's guilt will be forgiven,
    such will be the result of renouncing his sin,
    when all the altar-stones have been smashed to
      pieces
    like lumps of chalk,
    when the sacred poles and incense-altars stand no
      longer.
10 For the fortified city is abandoned now,
    deserted, forsaken as a desert
    where calves browse, where they lie down,
    destroying its branches.

m 27 A mythical monster of primeval chaos.

11 When its boughs are dry, they are broken;
 women come and make a fire of them.
For this is a people without understanding;
 therefore he that made them will not have
  compassion on them,
 he that formed them will show them no favor.

12 On that day the LORD will thresh from the channel of the Euphrates to the Wadi of Egypt, and you will be gathered one by one, O people of Israel. 13 And on that day a great trumpet will be blown, and those who were lost in the land of Assyria and those who were driven out to the land of Egypt will come and worship the LORD on the holy mountain at Jerusalem.

28 Ah, the proud garland of the drunkards of
  Ephraim,
 and the fading flower of its glorious beauty,
 which is on the head of those bloated with rich
  food, of those overcome with wine!
2 See, the Lord has one who is mighty and strong;
 like a storm of hail, a destroying tempest,
 like a storm of mighty, overflowing waters;
 with his hand he will hurl them down to the
  earth.
3 Trampled under foot will be
 the proud garland of the drunkards of Ephraim.
4 And the fading flower of its glorious beauty,
 which is on the head of those bloated with rich
  food,
 will be like a first-ripe fig before the summer;
 whoever sees it, eats it up
 as soon as it comes to hand.

5 In that day the LORD of hosts will be a garland of
  glory,
 and a diadem of beauty, to the remnant of his
  people;
6 and a spirit of justice to the one who sits in
  judgment,
 and strength to those who turn back the battle
  at the gate.

7 These also reel with wine
 and stagger with strong drink;
the priest and the prophet reel with strong drink,
 they are confused with wine,
 they stagger with strong drink;
they err in vision,
 they stumble in giving judgment.
8 All tables are covered with filthy vomit;
 no place is clean.

9 "Whom will he teach knowledge,
 and to whom will he explain the message?
Those who are weaned from milk,
 those taken from the breast?
10 For it is precept upon precept, precept upon
  precept,
 line upon line, line upon line,
 here a little, there a little."x

11 Truly, with stammering lip
 and with alien tongue
he will speak to this people,

11 The boughs grow dry and snap off
 and women come and light their fires with them.
They are a people without sense;
 therefore their Maker will show them no mercy,
 he who formed them will show them no favour.

12 On that day the LORD will beat out the grain,
 from the streams of the Euphrates to the wadi of
  Egypt;
 but you Israelites will be gathered one by one.

13 On that day
 a great trumpet will be sounded,
 and those who are lost in Assyria
 and those dispersed in Egypt will come
 to worship the LORD on Jerusalem's holy
  mountain.

28 ALAS for the proud garlands of Ephraim's
  drunkards,
 fading flowers, lovely in their beauty,
 on the heads of those who drip with perfumes,
 on those who are overcome with wine!
2 The Lord has one at his bidding, mighty and
  strong;
 like a sweeping storm of hail, like a destroying
  tempest,
 like a torrent of water in overwhelming flood
 he will beat down on the land with violence.
3 The proud garlands of Ephraim's drunkards
 will be trampled underfoot.
4 The fading flowers, lovely in their beauty,
 on those who drip with perfumes,
 will be like early figs ripe before summer.
Whoever sees them plucks them,
 and their bloom is gone
 while they lie in the hand.
5 On that day the LORD of Hosts shall be a lovely
  garland,
 a fair diadem for the remnant of his people,
6 a spirit of justice for one who sits as a judge,
 and of valour for those who repel enemy attacks at
  the gate.

7 These also lose their way through wine
 and are set wandering by strong drink:
priest and prophet lose their way through strong
  drink
 and are befuddled with wine;
they are set wandering by strong drink,
 lose their way through tippling,
 and stumble in judgement.
8 Every table is covered with vomit;
 filth is everywhere.

9 Who is there that can be taught?
Who makes sense of what he hears?
They are babes newly weaned,
 just taken from the breast.
10 A babble of meaningless noises,
 mere sounds on every side!
11 So through barbarous speech and a strange tongue
 the Lord will address this people,

x Meaning of Heb of this verse uncertain

28:1,4 those . . . perfumes: *prob. rdg, cp. Scroll; Heb.* a valley of fat things. 28:4 plucks: *prob. rdg; Heb.* sees. 28:6 for those: *prob. rdg; Heb.* omits for.

NEW AMERICAN BIBLE

11   its branches shall wither and be broken off,
    and women shall come to build a fire with them.
This is not an understanding people;
    therefore their maker shall not spare them,
    nor shall he who formed them have mercy
      on them.
12   On that day,
The LORD shall beat out the grain
    between the Euphrates and the Wadi of Egypt,
    and you shall be gleaned one by one, O sons
      of Israel.
13   On that day,
A great trumpet shall blow,
    and the lost in the land of Assyria
    and the outcasts in the land of Egypt
Shall come and worship the LORD
    on the holy mountain, in Jerusalem.

28   Woe to the majestic garland
    of the drunkard Ephraim,
To the fading blooms of his glorious beauty,
    on the head of him who is stupefied with wine.
2 Behold, the LORD has a strong one and a mighty,
    who, like a downpour of hail, a
      destructive storm,
Like a flood of water, great and overflowing,
    levels to the ground with violence;
3 With feet that will trample
    the majestic garland of the drunkard Ephraim.
4 The fading blooms of his glorious beauty
    on the head of the fertile valley
Will be like an early fig before summer:
    when a man sees it,
    he picks and swallows it at once.
5 On that day the LORD of hosts
    will be a glorious crown
And a brilliant diadem
    to the remnant of his people,
6 A spirit of justice
    to him who sits in judgment,
And strength to those
    who turn back the battle at the gate.

7 But these also stagger from wine
    and stumble from strong drink:
Priest and prophet stagger from strong drink,
    overpowered by wine;
Led astray by strong drink,
    staggering in their visions,
    tottering when giving judgment.
8 Yes, all the tables
    are covered with filthy vomit,
    with no place left clean.
9 "To whom would he impart knowledge?
To whom would he convey the message?
To those just weaned from milk,
    those taken from the breast? 10 For he says,
'Command on command, command on command,
    rule on rule, rule on rule,
    here a little, there a little!' "
11 Yes, with stammering lips and in a
      strange language
    he will speak to this people

NEW JERUSALEM BIBLE

11 When boughs go dry, they get burnt,
    women come and use them for firewood.
Now, this is a people that does not understand,
    and so its Maker will not take pity on it,
    he who formed it will not show it any mercy.
12 When that day comes,
    Yahweh will start his threshing
from the course of the River to the Torrent of
      Egypt,
    and you will be gathered one by one, Israelites!
13 When that day comes,
    the great ram's-horn will be sounded,
    and those lost in Assyria will come,
    and those banished to Egypt,
    and they will worship Yahweh
    on the holy mountain, in Jerusalem.

28   Woe to the haughty crown of Ephraim's
      drunkards,
    to the fading flower of its proud splendour
    sited at the head of the lush valley,
    to those prostrated by wine!
2 See, a strong and mighty man in the Lord's
      service,
    like a storm of hail, a destroying tempest,
    like immense flood-waters overflowing,
    with his hand he throws them to the ground.
3 They will be trampled underfoot,
    the haughty crown of Ephraim's drunkards,
4 and the faded flower of its proud splendour
    sited at the head of the lush valley.
Like a fig ripe before summer comes:
    whoever spots it forthwith picks and swallows it.

5 That day Yahweh Sabaoth
    will be a crown of splendour
    and a proud diadem
    for the remnant of his people,
6 a spirit of fair judgement
    for him who sits in judgement,
    and the strength of those who repel the assault on
      the gate.

7 These too have been confused by wine,
    have gone astray owing to liquor.
Priest and prophet have become confused by
      liquor,
    are sodden with wine, have strayed owing to
      liquor,
    have become confused in their visions,
    have strayed in their decisions.
8 Yes, every table is covered in filthy vomit,
    not one is clean!
9 'Whom does he think he is lecturing?
    Whom does he think his message is for?
    Babies just weaned?
    Babies just taken from the breast?
10 With his
    "Sav lasav, sav lasav,
    kav lakav, kav lakav,
    zeer sham, zeer sham!" '
11 Now, with stammering lips
    and in a foreign language,
    he will talk to this nation.

12 to whom he has said,
  "This is rest;
    give rest to the weary;
and this is repose";
    yet they would not hear.
13 Therefore the word of the LORD will be to them,
  "Precept upon precept, precept upon precept,
  line upon line, line upon line,
    here a little, there a little;"*y*
in order that they may go, and fall backward,
  and be broken, and snared, and taken.

14 Therefore hear the word of the LORD, you
    scoffers
  who rule this people in Jerusalem.
15 Because you have said, "We have made a
    covenant with death,
  and with Sheol we have an agreement;
when the overwhelming scourge passes through
  it will not come to us;
for we have made lies our refuge,
  and in falsehood we have taken shelter";
16 therefore thus says the Lord GOD,
See, I am laying in Zion a foundation stone,
  a tested stone,
a precious cornerstone, a sure foundation:
  "One who trusts will not panic."
17 And I will make justice the line,
  and righteousness the plummet;
hail will sweep away the refuge of lies,
  and waters will overwhelm the shelter.
18 Then your covenant with death will be annulled,
  and your agreement with Sheol will not stand;
when the overwhelming scourge passes through
  you will be beaten down by it.
19 As often as it passes through, it will take you;
  for morning by morning it will pass through,
    by day and by night;
and it will be sheer terror to understand the
    message.
20 For the bed is too short to stretch oneself on it,
  and the covering too narrow to wrap oneself in
    it.
21 For the LORD will rise up as on Mount Perazim,
  he will rage as in the valley of Gibeon;
to do his deed—strange is his deed!
  and to work his work—alien is his work!
22 Now therefore do not scoff,
  or your bonds will be made stronger;
for I have heard a decree of destruction
  from the Lord GOD of hosts upon the whole
    land.

23 Listen, and hear my voice;
  Pay attention, and hear my speech.
24 Do those who plow for sowing plow continually?
  Do they continually open and harrow their
    ground?
25 When they have leveled its surface,
  do they not scatter dill, sow cummin,
and plant wheat in rows
  and barley in its proper place,
  and spelt as the border?
26 For they are well instructed;
  their God teaches them.

27 Dill is not threshed with a threshing sledge,
  nor is a cart wheel rolled over cummin;
but dill is beaten out with a stick,
  and cummin with a rod.

y Meaning of Heb of this verse uncertain

12 a people to whom he once said,
  'This is true rest; let the exhausted have rest.
  This is repose,' but they would not listen.
13 Now to them the word of the LORD will be
  a babble of meaningless noises,
  mere sounds on every side.
  And so, as they walk, they will fall backwards,
  they will be injured, trapped, and caught.

14 Therefore listen to the word of the LORD,
  you arrogant rulers of this people in Jerusalem.
15 You say, 'We have made a treaty with Death
  and signed a pact with Sheol:
  when the raging flood sweeps by,
  it will not touch us;
  for we have taken refuge in lies
  and sheltered behind falsehood.'
16 Therefore these are the words of the Lord GOD:
  I am laying a stone in Zion, a block of granite,
  a precious corner-stone well founded;
  he who has faith will not waver.
17 I shall use justice as a plumb-line
  and righteousness as a plummet.
  Then hail will sweep away your refuge of lies
  and floodwaters carry away your shelter.
18 Your treaty with Death will be annulled
  and your pact with Sheol will not stand;
  the raging waters will sweep by,
  and you will be like land overwhelmed by flood.
19 As often as it sweeps by, it will take you;
  daily, morning and night, it will sweep by.
  When you understand what you hear,
  it will mean sheer terror.
20 As the saying goes: 'The bed is too short for a
    person to stretch,
  and the blanket too narrow for a cover.'
21 But the LORD will arise as he rose on Mount
    Perazim
  and storm with rage as he did in the vale of
    Gibeon
  to do what he must do, how strange a deed;
  to perform his task, an alien task!
22 But now have done with your arrogance,
  or your bonds will be tightened;
  for I have heard destruction decreed
  for the whole land by the Lord GOD of Hosts.

23 Listen and hear what I say,
  attend and hear my words.
24 Will the ploughman spend his whole time
    ploughing,
  breaking up his ground and harrowing it?
25 Does he not, once he has levelled it,
  broadcast the dill and scatter the cummin?
  Does he not put in the wheat and barley in rows,
  and vetches along the edge?
26 Does not his God instruct him and train him
    aright?

27 Dill must not be threshed with a threshing-sledge,
  nor the cartwheel rolled over cummin;
  but dill is beaten out with a rod,
  and cummin with a flail.

28:15 **Sheol:** *or* the underworld. 28:16 **a block of granite:** *or* a testing-stone. 28:25 **wheat and barley:** *prob. rdg; Heb. adds an unintelligible word.*

12 to whom he said:
This is the resting place,
   give rest to the weary;
Here is repose —
   but they would not listen.
13 So for them the word of the LORD shall be:
   "Command on command, command
      on command,
Rule on rule, rule on rule,
   here a little, there a little!"
So that when they walk, they stumble backward,
   broken, ensnared, and captured.
14 Therefore, hear the word of the LORD,
   you arrogant,
who rule this people in Jerusalem:
15 Because you say, "We have made a covenant
   with death,
and with the nether world we have made a pact;
When the overwhelming scourge passes,
   it will not reach us;
For we have made lies our refuge,
   and in falsehood we have found a
      hiding place,"—
16   Therefore, thus says the Lord GOD:
   See, I am laying a stone in Zion,
   a stone that has been tested,
A precious cornerstone as a sure
      foundation;
   he who puts his faith in it shall not
      be shaken.
17   I will make of right a measuring line,
   of justice a level. —
Hail shall sweep away the refuge of lies,
   and waters shall flood the hiding place.
18 Your covenant with death shall be canceled
   and your pact with the nether world shall
      not stand.
When the overwhelming scourge passes,
   you shall be trampled down by it.
19 Whenever it passes, it shall take you;
   morning after morning it shall pass,
By day and by night;
   terror alone shall convey the message.
20 For the bed shall be too short to stretch out in,
   and the cover too narrow to wrap in.
21 For the LORD shall rise up as on Mount Perazim,
   bestir himself as in the Valley of Gibeon,
To carry out his work, his singular work,
   to perform his deed, his strange deed.
22 Now, be arrogant no more
   lest your bonds be tightened;
For I have heard from the Lord, the GOD of hosts,
   the destruction decreed for the whole earth.
23 Give ear and hear my voice,
   pay attention and listen to what I say:
24 Is the plowman forever plowing,
   always loosening and harrowing his land
      for planting?
25 When he has leveled the surface,
   does he not scatter gith and sow cumin,
Put in wheat and barley,
   with spelt as its border?
26 He has learned this rule,
   instructed by his God.
27 Gith is not threshed with a sledge,
   nor does a cartwheel roll over cumin.
But gith is beaten out with a staff,
   and cumin crushed for food with a rod.
	12 He used to say to them, 'Here you can rest!
	Here you can let the weary rest!
	Here all is quiet.'
	But they refused to listen.
	13 Now Yahweh is going to say this to them,
	   'Sav lasav, sav lasav,
	   kav lakav, kav lakav,
	   zeer sham, zeer sham.'
	So that when they walk they will fall over
	      backwards
	and so be broken, trapped and taken captive.
	14 Hence listen to Yahweh's word, you insolent men,
	   rulers of this people in Jerusalem.
	15 Because you have said, 'We have made a treaty
	      with Death
	and have struck a pact with Sheol.
	When the scourging flood comes over,
	   it will not touch us,
	for we have made lies our refuge
	   and hidden under falsehood.'
	16 So the Lord Yahweh says this,
	   'Now I shall lay a stone in Zion,
	a granite stone, a precious corner-stone,
	a firm foundation-stone:
	no one who relies on this will stumble.
	17 And I will make fair judgement the measure,
	   and uprightness the plumb-line.'
	
	But hail will sweep away the refuge of lies
	   and floods wash away the hiding-place;
	18 your treaty with Death will be broken
	   and your pact with Sheol will not hold.
	When the scourging flood comes over,
	   you will be trodden down by it;
	19 every time it comes over, it will seize on you,
	   for it will come over, morning after morning,
	   day by day and night by night.
	Nothing but fear will make you understand what
	      you hear.
	20 For the bed is too short to stretch in,
	   the blanket too narrow for covering.
	21 Yes, as on Mount Perazim, Yahweh will rise,
	   as in the Valley of Gibeon, he will storm
	to do his work, his mysterious work,
	to do his deed, his extraordinary deed.
	22 Stop scoffing, then,
	   or your bonds will be tightened further,
	for I have heard it: it has been irrevocably decided
	as regards the whole country
	by the Lord Yahweh Sabaoth.
	23 Listen closely to my words,
	   be attentive, understand what I am saying.
	24 Does the ploughman plough all day to sow,
	   breaking up and harrowing his ground?
	25 Once he has levelled its surface,
	   does he not scatter fennel, sow cummin?
	Then he puts in wheat, millet, barley
	and, round the edges, spelt,
	26 for his God has taught him this rule and instructed
	      him.
	27 Fennel must not be crushed with a sledge,
	   nor cart-wheels driven over cummin;
	fennel must be beaten with a stick,
	   and cummin with a flail.

NEW REVISED STANDARD VERSION

28 Grain is crushed for bread,
  but one does not thresh it forever;
  one drives the cart wheel and horses over it,
  but does not pulverize it.
29 This also comes from the LORD of hosts;
  he is wonderful in counsel,
  and excellent in wisdom.

29

Ah, Ariel, Ariel,
  the city where David encamped!
Add year to year;
  let the festivals run their round.
2 Yet I will distress Ariel,
  and there shall be moaning and lamentation,
  and Jerusalem*z* shall be to me like an Ariel.*a*
3 And like David*b* I will encamp against you;
  I will besiege you with towers
  and raise siegeworks against you.
4 Then deep from the earth you shall speak,
  from low in the dust your words shall come;
  your voice shall come from the ground like the
    voice of a ghost,
  and your speech shall whisper out of the dust.

5 But the multitude of your foes*c* shall be like
    small dust,
  and the multitude of tyrants like flying chaff.
And in an instant, suddenly,
6 you will be visited by the LORD of hosts
  with thunder and earthquake and great noise,
  with whirlwind and tempest, and the flame of a
    devouring fire.
7 And the multitude of all the nations that fight
    against Ariel,
  all that fight against her and her stronghold,
    and who distress her,
  shall be like a dream, a vision of the night.
8 Just as when a hungry person dreams of eating
  and wakes up still hungry,
  or a thirsty person dreams of drinking
  and wakes up faint, still thirsty,
  so shall the multitude of all the nations be
  that fight against Mount Zion.

9 Stupefy yourselves and be in a stupor,
  blind yourselves and be blind!
Be drunk, but not from wine;
  stagger, but not from strong drink!
10 For the LORD has poured out upon you
  a spirit of deep sleep;
  he has closed your eyes, you prophets,
  and covered your heads, you seers.

11 The vision of all this has become for you like the
words of a sealed document. If it is given to those who can
read, with the command, "Read this," they say, "We cannot, for it is sealed." 12 And if it is given to those who
cannot read, saying, "Read this," they say, "We cannot
read."

13 The Lord said:
Because these people draw near with their mouths
  and honor me with their lips,
  while their hearts are far from me,
and their worship of me is a human
  commandment learned by rote;

REVISED ENGLISH BIBLE

28 Grain is crushed, but not too long or too finely;
  cartwheels rumble over it and thresh it,
  but they do not grind it fine.
29 Even this knowledge comes from the LORD of
    Hosts,
  whose counsel is wonderful
  and whose wisdom is great.

29

Woe betide Ariel! Ariel,
  the city where David encamped.
When another year has passed,
  with its full round of pilgrim-feasts,
2 then I shall reduce Ariel to sore straits.
There will be moaning and lamentation
  when I make her my Ariel, my fire-altar.
3 I shall encircle you with my army,
  set a ring of outposts all round you,
  and erect siege-works against you.
4 You will be brought low, you will speak out of the
    ground,
  and your words will issue from the earth;
  your voice will come ghostlike from the ground,
  and your words will squeak out of the earth.

5 Yet the horde of your enemies will crumble into
    dust,
  the horde of ruthless foes will fly like chaff.
Suddenly, all in an instant,
6 punishment will come from the LORD of Hosts
  with thunder and earthquake and a great noise,
  with storm and tempest and a flame of devouring
    fire.
7 The horde of all the nations warring against Ariel,
  all who fight against her with their siege-works,
  all who hem her in,
  will fade as a dream, a vision of the night.
8 Like one who is hungry and dreams that he is
    eating,
  but wakes to find himself empty,
  or like one who is thirsty and dreams that he is
    drinking,
  but wakes to find himself faint with thirst,
  so will it be with the horde of nations
  all warring against Mount Zion.

9 If you confuse yourselves,
  you will stay confused;
  if you blind yourselves,
  you will stay blinded.
Be drunk but not with wine, reel but not with
  strong drink;
10 for the LORD has poured on you a spirit of deep
    stupor;
  he has closed your eyes (that is, the prophets),
  and muffled your heads (they are the seers).

11 The prophetic vision of it all has become for you like the
words in a sealed book. If you hand such a book to one who
can read and say, 'Pray read this,' he will answer, 'I cannot;
it is sealed.' 12 Give it to one who cannot read and say,
'Pray read this'; he will answer, 'I cannot read.'

13 Then the Lord said:

Because this people worship me with empty words
  and pay me lip-service
  while their hearts are far from me,
  and their religion is but a human precept, learnt by
    rote,

---

z Heb *she*   *a* Probable meaning, *altar hearth*; compare Ezek 43.15
b Gk: Meaning of Heb uncertain   *c* Cn: Heb *strangers*

29:7 **siege-works**: *so Scroll; Heb.* strongholds.

28 No, he does not thresh it unendingly,
 nor does he crush it
 with his noisy cartwheels and horses.
29 This too comes from the LORD of hosts;
 wonderful is his counsel and great his wisdom.

29

Woe to Ariel, Ariel,
 the city where David encamped!
Add year to year,
 let the feasts come round.
2 But I will bring distress upon Ariel,
 with mourning and grief.
You shall be to me like Ariel:
3 I will encamp like David against you;
I will encircle you with outposts
 and set up siege works against you.
4 Prostrate you shall speak from the earth,
 and from the base dust your words shall come.
Your voice shall be like a ghost's from the earth,
 and your words like chirping from the dust.
5 The horde of your arrogant shall be like fine dust,
 the horde of the tyrants like flying chaff.
Then suddenly, in an instant,
6 you shall be visited by the LORD of hosts,
With thunder, earthquake, and great noise,
 whirlwind, storm, and the flame of
  consuming fire.

7 Then like a dream,
 a vision in the night,
Shall be the horde of all the nations
 who war against Ariel
with all the earthworks of her besiegers.
8 As when a hungry man dreams he is eating
 and awakens with an empty stomach,
Or when a thirsty man dreams he is drinking
 and awakens faint and dry,
So shall the horde of all the nations be,
 who make war against Zion.

9 Be irresolute, stupefied;
 blind yourselves and stay blind!
Be drunk, but not from wine,
 stagger, but not from strong drink!
10 For the LORD has poured out on you
 a spirit of deep sleep.
He has shut your eyes [the prophets]
 and covered your heads [the seers].

11 For you the revelation of all this has become like the
words of a sealed scroll. When it is handed to one who can
read, with the request, "Read this," he replies, "I cannot; it
is sealed." 12 When it is handed to one who cannot read,
with the request, "Read this," he replies, "I cannot read."

13   The Lord said:
Since this people draws near with words only
 and honors me with their lips alone,
  though their hearts are far from me,
And their reverence for me has become
 routine observance of the precepts of men,

28 When you are threshing wheat,
 you do not waste time crushing it;
 you get the horse and cart-wheel moving,
 but you do not grind it fine.
29 All this is a gift from Yahweh Sabaoth,
 marvellous advice leading to great achievements.

29

Woe, Ariel, [n] Ariel,
 city where David encamped.
Let year after year pass,
 let the feasts make their full round,
2 then I shall inflict trouble on Ariel,
 and there will be sighing and sobbing,
 and I shall make it truly Ariel.
3 I shall encamp all round you,
 I shall lay siege to you
 and mount siege-works against you.
4 You will be laid low, will speak from the
  underworld,
 your words will rise like a murmur from the dust.
Your voice from the earth will be like a ghost's,
 it will whisper as though coming from the dust.

5 The horde of your enemies will be like fine dust,
 the horde of the warriors like flying chaff.
And suddenly, in an instant,
6 you will be visited by Yahweh Sabaoth
 with thunder, earthquake, mighty din,
 hurricane, tempest, flame of devouring fire.
7 It will be like a dream, like a vision at night:
 the horde of all the nations at war with Ariel,
 all those fighting, besieging and troubling it.
8 It will be like the dream of a hungry man:
 he eats, then wakes up with an empty belly;
 or like the dream of a thirsty man:
 he drinks, then wakes up exhausted with a parched
  throat.
So will it be with the horde of all the nations
 making war on Mount Zion.

9 Be stupefied and stunned,
 go blind, unseeing,
drunk but not on wine,
 staggering but not through liquor.
10 For Yahweh has infused you with a spirit of
  lethargy,
 he has closed your eyes (the prophets),
 he has veiled your heads (the seers).

11 For to you every vision has become like the words of
a sealed book. You give it to someone able to read and say,
'Read that.' He replies, 'I cannot, because it is sealed.'
12 You then give the book to someone who cannot read, and
say, 'Read that.' He replies, 'I cannot read.'

13 The Lord then said:

Because this people approaches me only in words,
 honours me only with lip-service
 while their hearts are far from me,
 and reverence for me, as far as they are concerned,
 is nothing but human commandment, a lesson
  memorised,

---

[n] 29 Symbolic name for Jerusalem (= ? lion of God).

NEW REVISED STANDARD VERSION

14 so I will again do
  amazing things with this people,
  shocking and amazing.
The wisdom of their wise shall perish,
  and the discernment of the discerning shall be
    hidden.
15 Ha! You who hide a plan too deep for the LORD,
  whose deeds are in the dark,
  and who say, "Who sees us? Who knows us?"
16 You turn things upside down!
  Shall the potter be regarded as the clay?
Shall the thing made say of its maker,
  "He did not make me";
  or the thing formed say of the one who formed it,
  "He has no understanding"?

17 Shall not Lebanon in a very little while
  become a fruitful field,
  and the fruitful field be regarded as a forest?
18 On that day the deaf shall hear
  the words of a scroll,
  and out of their gloom and darkness
  the eyes of the blind shall see.
19 The meek shall obtain fresh joy in the LORD,
  and the neediest people shall exult in the
    Holy One of Israel.
20 For the tyrant shall be no more,
  and the scoffer shall cease to be;
  all those alert to do evil shall be cut off —
21 those who cause a person to lose a lawsuit,
  who set a trap for the arbiter in the gate,
  and without grounds deny justice to the one in
    the right.

22 Therefore thus says the LORD, who redeemed Abraham, concerning the house of Jacob:
No longer shall Jacob be ashamed,
  no longer shall his face grow pale.
23 For when he sees his children,
  the work of my hands, in his midst,
  they will sanctify my name;
they will sanctify the Holy One of Jacob,
  and will stand in awe of the God of Israel.
24 And those who err in spirit will come to
    understanding,
  and those who grumble will accept instruction.

30 Oh, rebellious children, says the LORD,
  who carry out a plan, but not mine;
  who make an alliance, but against my will,
    adding sin to sin;
2 who set out to go down to Egypt
  without asking for my counsel,
  to take refuge in the protection of Pharaoh,
  and to seek shelter in the shadow of Egypt;
3 Therefore the protection of Pharaoh shall become
    your shame,
  and the shelter in the shadow of Egypt your
    humiliation.
4 For though his officials are at Zoan
  and his envoys reach Hanes,
5 everyone comes to shame
  through a people that cannot profit them,
that brings neither help nor profit,
  but shame and disgrace.

REVISED ENGLISH BIBLE

14 therefore I shall shock this people yet again,
  adding shock to shock:
  the wisdom of their wise men will vanish
  and the discernment of the discerning will be lost.

15 Woe betide those who seek to hide their plans
  too deep for the LORD to see!
  When their deeds are done in the dark
  they say, 'Who sees us? Who knows of us?'
16 How you turn things upside down,
  as if the potter ranked no higher than the clay!
  Will the thing made say of its maker, 'He did not
    make me'?
  Will the pot say of the potter, 'He has no skill'?

17 In but a very short time
  Lebanon will return to garden land
  and the garden land will be reckoned as common
    as scrub.
18 On that day the deaf will hear
  when a book is read,
  and the eyes of the blind will see
  out of impenetrable darkness.
19 The lowly will once again rejoice in the LORD,
  and the poor exult in the Holy One of Israel.
20–21 The ruthless will be no more,
  the arrogant will cease to exist;
  those who are quick to find mischief,
  those who impute sins to others,
  or lay traps for him who brings the wrongdoer into
    court,
  or by falsehood deny justice to the innocent —
  all these will be cut down.

22 Therefore these are the words of the LORD, the deliverer of Abraham, about the house of Jacob:

This is no time for Jacob to be shamed,
  no time for his face to grow pale;
23 for his descendants will hallow my name
  when they see what I have done in their midst.
  They will hold sacred the Holy One of Jacob
  and regard Israel's God with awe;
24 the confused will gain understanding,
  and the obstinate accept instruction.

30 Woe betide the rebellious children! says the
    LORD,
  who make plans, but not of my devising,
  who weave schemes, but not inspired by me,
  so piling sin on sin.
2 Without consulting me they hurry down to Egypt
  to seek shelter under Pharaoh's protection,
  to take refuge under Egypt's shadow.
3 Pharaoh's protection will lead to humiliation
  and refuge under Egypt's shadow will bring you
    disgrace.
4 Though his officers are at Zoan
  and his envoys reach as far as Hanes,
5 that unprofitable nation will leave everyone in
    sorry plight;
  they will find neither help nor profit,
  only humiliation and contempt.

29:23 **they see:** *so Gk; Heb.* he sees.

NEW AMERICAN BIBLE	NEW JERUSALEM BIBLE

NEW AMERICAN BIBLE

14 Therefore I will again deal with this people
  in surprising and wondrous fashion:
 The wisdom of its wise men shall perish
  and the understanding of its prudent men be hid.
15 Woe to those who would hide their plans
  too deep for the LORD!
 Who work in the dark, saying,
  "Who sees us, or who knows us?"
16 Your perversity is as though the potter
  were taken to be the clay:
 As though what is made should say of its maker,
  "He made me not!"
 Or the vessel should say of the potter,
  "He does not understand."

17 But a very little while,
  and Lebanon shall be changed into an orchard,
  and the orchard be regarded as a forest!
18 On that day the deaf shall hear
  the words of a book;
 And out of gloom and darkness,
  the eyes of the blind shall see.
19 The lowly will ever find joy in the LORD,
  and the poor rejoice in the Holy One of Israel.
20 For the tyrant will be no more
  and the arrogant will have gone;
 All who are alert to do evil will be cut off,
21   those whose mere word condemns a man,
 Who ensnare his defender at the gate,
  and leave the just man with an empty claim.
22 Therefore thus says the LORD,
  the God of the house of Jacob,
  who redeemed Abraham:
 Now Jacob shall have nothing to be ashamed of,
  nor shall his face grow pale.
23 When his children see
  the work of my hands in his midst,
 They shall keep my name holy;
  they shall reverence the Holy One of Jacob,
  and be in awe of the God of Israel.
24 Those who err in spirit shall acquire understanding,
  and those who find fault shall
   receive instruction.

30 Woe to the rebellious children,
  says the LORD,
 Who carry out plans that are not mine,
  who weave webs that are not inspired by me,
  adding sin upon sin.
2 They go down to Egypt,
  but my counsel they do not seek.
 They find their strength in Pharaoh's protection
  and take refuge in Egypt's shadow;
3 Pharaoh's protection shall be your shame,
  and refuge in Egypt's shadow your disgrace.
4 When their princes are at Zoan
  and their messengers reach Hanes,
5 All shall be ashamed
  of a people that gain them nothing,
 Neither help nor benefit,
  but only shame and reproach.

NEW JERUSALEM BIBLE

14 very well, I shall have to go on
  astounding this people with prodigies and wonders:
 for the wisdom of its wise men is doomed,
  the understanding of any who understand will
   vanish.

15 Woe to those who burrow down
  to conceal their plans from Yahweh,
 who scheme in the dark
  and say, 'Who can see us? Who knows who we
   are?'
16 How perverse you are!
 Is the potter no better than the clay?
 Something that was made, can it say of its maker,
  'He did not make me'?
 Or a pot say of the potter,
  'He does not know his job'?
17 Is it not true that in a very short time
  the Lebanon will become productive ground,
  so productive you might take it for a forest?
18 That day the deaf
  will hear the words of the book
 and, delivered from shadow and darkness,
  the eyes of the blind will see.
19 The lowly will find ever more joy in Yahweh
  and the poorest of people will delight in the Holy
   One of Israel;
20 for the tyrant will be no more, the scoffer has
   vanished
 and all those on the look-out for evil have been
   destroyed:
21 those who incriminate others by their words,
  those who lay traps for the arbitrator at the gate
 and groundlessly deprive the upright of fair
   judgement.
22 That is why Yahweh, God of the House of Jacob,
  Abraham's redeemer, says this,
 'No longer shall Jacob be disappointed,
  no more shall his face grow pale,
23 for when he sees his children,
  my creatures, home again with him,
 he will acknowledge my name as holy,
 he will acknowledge the Holy One of Jacob to be
   holy
 and will hold the God of Israel in awe.
24 Erring spirits will learn to understand
 and murmurers accept instruction.'

30 Woe to the rebellious children — declares
  Yahweh —
 who make plans which do not come from me
  and make alliances not inspired by me,
  and so add sin to sin!
2 They are leaving for Egypt,
  without consulting me,
 to take refuge in Pharaoh's protection,
  to shelter in Egypt's shadow.
3 Pharaoh's protection will be your shame,
  the shelter of Egypt's shadow your confounding.
4 For his princes have gone to Zoan
  and his messengers have reached Hanes.
5 Everyone has been disappointed
  by a people who cannot help,
 who bring neither aid nor profit,
  only disappointment and confusion.

| NEW REVISED STANDARD VERSION | REVISED ENGLISH BIBLE |

6 An oracle concerning the animals of the Negeb.
   Through a land of trouble and distress,
      of lioness and roaring[d] lion,
      of viper and flying serpent,
   they carry their riches on the backs of donkeys,
      and their treasures on the humps of camels,
   to a people that cannot profit them.
7 For Egypt's help is worthless and empty,
      therefore I have called her,
   "Rahab who sits still."[e]

8 Go now, write it before them on a tablet,
      and inscribe it in a book,
   so that it may be for the time to come
      as a witness forever.
9 For they are a rebellious people,
      faithless children,
   children who will not hear
      the instruction of the LORD;
10 who say to the seers, "Do not see";
      and to the prophets, "Do not prophesy to us
         what is right;
   speak to us smooth things,
      prophesy illusions,
11 leave the way, turn aside from the path,
      let us hear no more about the Holy One of
         Israel."

12 Therefore thus says the Holy One of Israel:
   Because you reject this word,
      and put your trust in oppression and deceit,
      and rely on them;
13 therefore this iniquity shall become for you
      like a break in a high wall, bulging out, and
         about to collapse,
      whose crash comes suddenly, in an instant;
14 its breaking is like that of a potter's vessel
      that is smashed so ruthlessly
   that among its fragments not a sherd is found
      for taking fire from the hearth,
      or dipping water out of the cistern.

15 For thus said the Lord GOD, the Holy One of
      Israel:
   In returning and rest you shall be saved;
      in quietness and in trust shall be your strength.
   But you refused 16 and said,
   "No! We will flee upon horses" —
      therefore you shall flee!
   and, "We will ride upon swift steeds" —
      therefore your pursuers shall be swift!
17 A thousand shall flee at the threat of one,
      at the threat of five you shall flee,
   until you are left
      like a flagstaff on the top of a mountain,
      like a signal on a hill.

18 Therefore the LORD waits to be gracious to you;
      therefore he will rise up to show mercy to you.
   For the LORD is a God of justice;
      blessed are all those who wait for him.

19 Truly, O people in Zion, inhabitants of Jerusalem,
you shall weep no more. He will surely be gracious to you
at the sound of your cry; when he hears it, he will answer
you. 20 Though the Lord may give you the bread of adversity and the water of affliction, yet your Teacher will not
hide himself any more, but your eyes shall see your
Teacher. 21 And when you turn to the right or when you turn

6 'THE Beasts of the South': an oracle.

   Through a land of hardship and distress,
      of lioness and roaring lion,
      of sand-viper and venomous flying serpent,
   they convey their wealth on the backs of donkeys
      and their treasures on camels' humps
   to an unprofitable people.
7 Worthless and futile is the help of Egypt;
      therefore have I given her this name:
   Rahab Subdued.

8 Now in their sight write it on a tablet,
      engrave it as an inscription
   that it may be there in future days,
      a testimony for all time to come.
9 They are a race of rebels, disloyal children,
   children who refuse to listen to the LORD's
      instruction.
10 They say to the seers, 'You are not to see,'
      and to those who have visions,
   'Do not produce true visions for us;
      give us smooth words and illusory visions.
11 Turn aside, leave the straight path,
      and rid us of the Holy One of Israel.'

12 Therefore these are the words of the Holy One of Israel:

   You have rejected this warning
      and put your trust in devious and dishonest
         practices
      on which you lean for support,
13 therefore you shall find this iniquity
      like a crack running down
   a high wall, which bulges out
      and suddenly, all in an instant, comes crashing
         down.
14 It crashes and breaks like an earthen jar
      shattered beyond repair,
   so that among the fragments not a shard is found
      to take an ember from the hearth,
      or to scoop water from a pool.

15 These are the words of the Lord GOD, the Holy One of
Israel:

   In calm detachment lies your safety,
      your strength in quiet trust.
   But you would have none of it; 16 'No,' you said,
      'we shall take horse and flee.'
   Therefore you will be put to flight!
   'We shall ride apace,' you said,
   Therefore swift will be the pace of your pursuers!
17 When a thousand flee at the challenge of one,
      you will flee at the challenge of five,
   until you are left solitary as a mast on a
      mountaintop,
      a signal-post on a hill.
18 Yet the LORD is waiting to show you his favour,
      and he yearns to have pity on you;
   for the LORD is a God of justice.
   Happy are all who wait for him!

19 People of Zion, dwellers in Jerusalem, you will weep no
more. The LORD will show you favour and answer you
when he hears your cry for help. 20 The Lord may give you
bread of adversity and water of affliction, but he who
teaches you will no longer keep himself out of sight, but
with your own eyes you will see him. 21 If you stray from

---

[d] Cn: Heb *from them*   [e] Meaning of Heb uncertain

30:12 **devious**: *prob. rdg; Heb*. oppressive.

NEW AMERICAN BIBLE	NEW JERUSALEM BIBLE

NEW AMERICAN BIBLE

6   [Oracle on the Beasts of the Negeb]

Through the distressed and troubled land
  of the lioness and roaring lion,
  of the viper and flying saraph,
They carry their riches on the backs of asses
  and their treasures on the humps of camels
To a people good for nothing,
7 to Egypt whose help is futile and vain.
Therefore I call her
  "Rahab quelled."
8 Now come, write it on a tablet they can keep,
  inscribe it in a record;
That it may be in future days
  an eternal witness:
9 This is a rebellious people,
  deceitful children,
Children who refuse
  to obey the law of the LORD.
10 They say to the seers, "Have no visions" ;
  to the prophets, "Do not descry for us what
    is right;
speak flatteries to us, conjure up illusions.
11 Out of the way! Out of our path!
  Let us hear no more
  of the Holy One of Israel."
12 Therefore, thus says the Holy One of Israel:
  Because you reject this word,
And put your trust in what is crooked and devious,
  and depend on it,
13 This guilt of yours shall be
  like a descending rift
Bulging out in a high wall
  whose crash comes suddenly, in an instant.
14 It crashes like a potter's jar
  smashed beyond rescue,
And among it fragments cannot be found
  a sherd to scoop fire from the hearth
  or dip water from the cistern.
15 For thus said the Lord GOD,
  the Holy One of Israel:
By waiting and by calm you shall be saved,
  in quiet and in trust your strength lies.
But this you did not wish.
16 "No," you said,
  "Upon horses we will flee."
  — Very well, flee!
"Upon swift steeds we will ride."
  — Not so swift as your pursuers.
17 A thousand shall tremble at the threat of one;
  if five threaten you, you shall flee,
Until you are left like a flagstaff on
    the mountaintop,
  like a flag on the hill.
18 Yet the LORD is waiting to show you favor,
  and he rises to pity you;
For the LORD is a God of justice:
  blessed are all who wait for him!

19 O people of Zion, who dwell in Jerusalem,
  no more will you weep;
He will be gracious to you when you cry out,
  as soon as he hears he will answer you.
20 The Lord will give you the bread you need
  and the water for which you thirst.
No longer will your Teacher hide himself,
  but with your own eyes you shall see
    your Teacher,

NEW JERUSALEM BIBLE

6 Proclamation about the beasts of the Negeb:

Into the land of distress and of anguish,
  of lioness and roaring lion,
  of viper and flying dragon,
they bear their riches on donkeys' backs,
  their treasures on camels' humps,
  to a nation that cannot help:
7 Egypt, whose help is vain and futile;
  and so I call her 'Rahab⁰-the-collapsed'.
8 Now go, inscribe this on a tablet,
  write it on a scroll,
so that it may serve for time to come
  for ever and for ever.
9 This is a rebellious people, they are lying children,
  children who will not listen to Yahweh's Law.
10 To the seers they say, 'See nothing!'
  To the prophets, 'Do not prophesy the truth to us;
  tell us flattering things; have illusory visions;
11 turn aside from the way, leave the path,
  rid us of the Holy One of Israel.'
12 So the Holy One of Israel says this,
  'Since you have rejected this word and put your trust
    in fraud and disloyalty
and rely on these,
13 for you this guilt will prove to be
  a breach opening up,
  a bulge at the top of a wall
which suddenly and all at once comes crashing
    down.
14 He will shatter it like an earthenware pot,
  ruthlessly knocking it to pieces,
so that of the fragments not one shard can be
    found
with which to take up fire from the hearth
  or scoop water from the storage-well.'
15 For Lord Yahweh, the Holy One of Israel, says
    this,
'Your salvation lay in conversion and tranquillity,
  your strength in serenity and trust
  and you would have none of it.
16 "No," you said, "we shall flee on horses."
  And so flee you will!
And again, "We shall ride on swift ones."
  And so your pursuers will be swift!
17 A thousand will quake at the threat of one
  and when five threaten you will flee,
until what is left of you will be
  like a flagstaff on a mountain top,
  like a signal on a hill.'
18 But Yahweh is waiting to be gracious to you,
  the Exalted One, to take pity on you,
for Yahweh is a God of fair judgement;
  blessed are all who hope in him.
19 Yes, people of Zion living in Jerusalem,
  you will weep no more.
He will be gracious to you when your cry for help
    rings out;
as soon as he hears it, he will answer you.
20 When the Lord has given you the bread of
    suffering and the water of distress,
he who is your teacher will hide no longer,
  and you will see your teacher with your own eyes.

to the left, your ears shall hear a word behind you, saying, "This is the way; walk in it." 22 Then you will defile your silver-covered idols and your gold-plated images. You will scatter them like filthy rags; you will say to them, "Away with you!"

23 He will give rain for the seed with which you sow the ground, and grain, the produce of the ground, which will be rich and plenteous. On that day your cattle will graze in broad pastures; 24 and the oxen and donkeys that till the ground will eat silage, which has been winnowed with shovel and fork. 25 On every lofty mountain and every high hill there will be brooks running with water—on a day of the great slaughter, when the towers fall. 26 Moreover the light of the moon will be like the light of the sun, and the light of the sun will be sevenfold, like the light of seven days, on the day when the LORD binds up the injuries of his people, and heals the wounds inflicted by his blow.

27 See, the name of the LORD comes from far away,
     burning with his anger, and in thick rising
          smoke; f
  his lips are full of indignation,
     and his tongue is like a devouring fire;
28 his breath is like an overflowing stream
     that reaches up to the neck—
  to sift the nations with the sieve of destruction,
     and to place on the jaws of the peoples a bridle
          that leads them astray.

29 You shall have a song as in the night when a holy festival is kept; and gladness of heart, as when one sets out to the sound of the flute to go to the mountain of the LORD, to the Rock of Israel. 30 And the LORD will cause his majestic voice to be heard and the descending blow of his arm to be seen, in furious anger and a flame of devouring fire, with a cloudburst and tempest and hailstones. 31 The Assyrian will be terror-stricken at the voice of the LORD, when he strikes with his rod. 32 And every stroke of the staff of punishment that the LORD lays upon him will be to the sound of timbrels and lyres; battling with brandished arm he will fight with him. 33 For his burning place g has long been prepared; truly it is made ready for the king, h its pyre made deep and wide, with fire and wood in abundance; the breath of the LORD, like a stream of sulfur, kindles it.

the path, whether to right or to left, you will hear a voice from behind you sounding in your ears saying, 'This is the way; follow it.' 22 You will treat as things unclean your silver-plated images and your gold-covered idols; you will loathe them like a foul discharge and call them filth.

23 The Lord will give rain for the seed you sow in the ground, and as the produce of your soil he will give you heavy crops. When that day comes your cattle will graze in broad pastures; 24 the oxen and donkeys that plough the land will be fed with well-seasoned fodder, winnowed with shovel and fork. 25 On every high mountain and lofty hill streams of water will flow, on the day of massacre when fortresses fall. 26 The moon will shine as brightly as the sun, and the sun with seven times its wonted brightness, like seven days' light in one, on the day when the LORD binds up the broken limbs of his people and heals the wounds inflicted on them.

27 See, the LORD himself comes from afar,
     his anger blazing and his doom heavy.
  His lips are charged with wrath
     and his tongue is like a devouring fire.
28 His breath is like a torrent in spate,
     to load the nations with an evil yoke.
  He sieves out the nations for destruction;
     he puts a bit in their mouths to lead the peoples
          astray.

29 But for you there will be songs,
     as on a night of a sacred pilgrim-feast,
  and gladness of heart as if one marched to the
          sound of the pipe
  on the way to the mountain of the LORD, to the
          Rock of Israel.
30 Then the LORD will make his voice heard in
          majesty
  and reveal his arm descending in fierce anger
     with devouring flames of fire,
  amid cloudburst and tempests of rain and hail.
31 For at the voice of the LORD Assyria's heart fails
          her,
     as she feels the stroke of his rod;
32 tambourines, lyres, and shaking sistrums will keep
          time
  with every stroke of his rod,
  of the punishment which the LORD inflicts on
          them.
33 Topheth was made ready long ago
  (it, too, was prepared for Molech);
  its fire-pit, made deep and broad,
     is a blazing mass of logs,
  with the breath of the LORD like a stream of
          brimstone
          setting it ablaze.

f Meaning of Heb uncertain   g Or Topheth   h Or Molech

30:27 the LORD himself: lit. the name of the LORD.
30:32 punishment: so some MSS; others foundation.

NEW AMERICAN BIBLE

21 While from behind, a voice shall sound in
     your ears:
  "This is the way; walk in it,"
  when you would turn to the right or to the left.
22 And you shall consider unclean your
     silver-plated idols
  and your gold-covered images;
  You shall throw them away like filthy rags
  to which you say, "Begone!"
23 He will give rain for the seed
  that you sow in the ground,
  And the wheat that the soil produces
  will be rich and abundant.
  On that day your cattle will graze
  in spacious meadows;
24 The oxen and the asses that till the ground
  will eat silage tossed to them
  with shovel and pitchfork.
25 Upon every high mountain and lofty hill
  there will be streams of running water.
  On the day of the great slaughter,
  when the towers fall,
26 The light of the moon will be like that of the sun
  and the light of the sun will be seven
     times greater
  [like the light of seven days].
  On the day the LORD binds up the wounds of
     his people,
  he will heal the bruises left by his blows.

27 See the name of the LORD coming from afar
  in burning wrath, with lowering clouds!
  His lips are filled with fury,
  his tongue is like a consuming fire;
28 His breath, like a flood in a ravine
  that reaches suddenly to the neck,
  Will winnow the nations with a
     destructive winnowing,
  and with repeated winnowings will he battle
     against them
  [and a bridle on the jaws of the peoples to send
     them astray].
30 The LORD will make his glorious voice heard,
  and let it be seen how his arm descends
  In raging fury and flame of consuming fire,
  in driving storm and hail.
31 When the LORD speaks, Assyria will be shattered,
  as he strikes with the rod;
32 While at every sweep of the rod
  which the LORD will bring down on him
     in punishment,
29 You will sing
  as on a night when a feast is observed,
  And be merry of heart,
  as one marching along with a flute
  Toward the mountain of the LORD,
  toward the Rock of Israel,
  accompanied by the timbrels and lyres.
33 For the pyre has long been ready,
  prepared for the king;
  Broad and deep it is piled
  with dry grass and wood in abundance,
  And the breath of the LORD, like a stream
     of sulphur,
  will set it afire.

NEW JERUSALEM BIBLE

21 Your ears will hear these words behind you,
  'This is the way, keep to it,'
  whether you turn to right or left.
22 You will hold unclean the silverplating of your
     idols
  and the goldplating of your images.
  You will throw them away like the polluted things
     they are,
  shouting after them, 'Good riddance!'
23 He will send rain for the seed you sow in the
     ground,
  and the bread that the ground provides will be rich
     and nourishing.
  That day, your cattle will graze in wide pastures.
24 Oxen and donkeys that work the land
  will eat for fodder wild sorrel,
  spread by the shovel-load and fork-load.
25 On every lofty mountain, on every high hill
  there will be streams and water-courses, on the day
     of the great slaughter
  when the strongholds fall.
26 Then moonlight will be bright as sunlight
  and sunlight itself be seven times brighter
  — like the light of seven days in one —
  on the day Yahweh dresses his people's wound
  and heals the scars of the blows they have
     received.

27 See, the name of Yahweh comes from afar,
  blazing his anger, heavy his threat.
  His lips are brimming over with fury,
  his tongue is like a devouring fire.
28 His breath is like a river in spate
  coming up to the neck,
  to sift the nations with the sieve of destruction,
  to harness the peoples in a bridle, that will lead
     them astray.
29 Your song will be like that on a festal night,
  and there will be joy in your hearts
  as when to the sound of the flute people make a
     pilgrimage
  to the mountain of Yahweh, the Rock of Israel.
30 Yahweh will make his majestic voice ring out,
  he will show the weight of his arm
  in the heat of his anger, with a devouring fire,
  with thunderbolt, downpour and hailstones.
31 Yes, at Yahweh's voice Assyria will be terrified,
  he will strike him with his rod;
32 each time he goes by, will fall the punishing rod
  that Yahweh will lay on him,
  to the sound of tambourines and harps,
  in the battles which he will wage against him with
     uplifted hand.
33 Yes, Tophet*p* has been ready for a long time
     now,
  that too is ready for the king,
  deep and wide his pyre,
  fire and wood in plenty.
  Yahweh's breath, like a stream of brimstone,
  will set fire to it.

p 30 The rubbish-dump of Jerusalem.

NEW REVISED STANDARD VERSION	REVISED ENGLISH BIBLE

31 Alas for those who go down to Egypt for help
    and who rely on horses,
who trust in chariots because they are many
    and in horsemen because they are very strong,
but do not look to the Holy One of Israel
    or consult the LORD!
2 Yet he too is wise and brings disaster;
    he does not call back his words,
but will rise against the house of the evildoers,
    and against the helpers of those who work
        iniquity.
3 The Egyptians are human, and not God;
    their horses are flesh, and not spirit.
When the LORD stretches out his hand,
    the helper will stumble, and the one helped
        will fall,
    and they will all perish together.

4 For thus the LORD said to me,
As a lion or a young lion growls over its prey,
    and—when a band of shepherds is called out
        against it—
is not terrified by their shouting
    or daunted at their noise,
so the LORD of hosts will come down
    to fight upon Mount Zion and upon its hill.
5 Like birds hovering overhead, so the LORD of
        hosts
    will protect Jerusalem;
he will protect and deliver it,
    he will spare and rescue it.

6 Turn back to him whom you[i] have deeply betrayed,
O people of Israel. 7 For on that day all of you shall throw
away your idols of silver and idols of gold, which your
hands have sinfully made for you.

8 "Then the Assyrian shall fall by a sword, not of
        mortals;
    and a sword, not of humans, shall devour him;
he shall flee from the sword,
    and his young men shall be put to forced labor.
9 His rock shall pass away in terror,
    and his officers desert the standard in panic,"
says the LORD, whose fire is in Zion,
    and whose furnace is in Jerusalem.

32 See, a king will reign in righteousness,
    and princes will rule with justice.
2 Each will be like a hiding place from the wind,
    a covert from the tempest,
like streams of water in a dry place,
    like the shade of a great rock in a weary land.
3 Then the eyes of those who have sight will not be
        closed,
    and the ears of those who have hearing will
        listen.
4 The minds of the rash will have good judgment,
    and the tongues of stammerers will speak
        readily and distinctly.
5 A fool will no longer be called noble,
    nor a villain said to be honorable.
6 For fools speak folly,
    and their minds plot iniquity:
to practice ungodliness,
    to utter error concerning the LORD,
to leave the craving of the hungry unsatisfied,
    and to deprive the thirsty of drink.

31 Woe betide those who go down to Egypt for help
    and rely upon horses,
who put their trust in chariots because they are
        many,
and in horsemen because of their vast numbers,
    but do not look to the Holy One of Israel
    or seek guidance of the LORD!
2 Yet he too in his wisdom can bring trouble
    and he does not take back his threats;
he will rise up against wrongdoers,
    against all who go to the help of evildoers.
3 The Egyptians are mortals, not gods,
    their horses are flesh, not spirit.
When the LORD stretches out his hand,
    the helper will stumble
and the one who is helped will fall;
    both will perish together.

4 This is what the LORD has said to me:

As a lion or a young lion growls over its prey
    when the shepherds are called out in force,
and it is not scared at their shouting
    or daunted by their clamour,
so the LORD of Hosts will come down to do battle
    on the heights of Mount Zion.
5 Like a hovering bird the LORD of Hosts
    will be a shield over Jerusalem;
he will shield and deliver her,
    sparing and rescuing her.
6 Israel, you have been deeply disloyal,
    yet come back to him,
7 for on that day every one of you will spurn
    the idols of silver and the idols of gold
    which your own sinful hands have made.
8 Assyria will fall, but not by man's sword;
    a sword that no mortal wields will devour him.
He will flee before the sword,
    and his young warriors will be put to forced
        labour;
9 officers will be helpless from terror
    and captains powerless to flee.
This is the word of the LORD
    whose fire blazes in Zion,
    whose furnace burns in Jerusalem.

32 A king will reign in righteousness
    and his ministers rule with justice,
2 each of them a refuge from the wind
    and a shelter from the storm.
They will be like runnels of water in dry ground,
    like the shade of a great rock in a thirsty land.
3 Then those who see will see clearly,
    and those who hear will listen with care;
4 the impetuous mind will understand and know,
    and the stammering tongue will speak fluently and
        plainly.
5 The scoundrel will no longer be thought noble,
    nor the villain considered honourable;
6 for the scoundrel will speak like a scoundrel
    hatching evil in his heart,
godless in all his conduct,
    and a liar to the LORD;
he starves the hungry of their food
    and deprives the thirsty of anything to drink.

_i_ Heb _they_

1544

31
Woe to those who go down to Egypt for help,
 who depend upon horses;
Who put their trust in chariots because of
 their number,
 and in horsemen because of their
 combined power,
But look not to the Holy One of Israel
 nor seek the LORD!
2 Yet he too is wise and will bring disaster;
 he will not turn from what he has threatened
 to do.
He will rise up against the house of the wicked
 and against those who help evildoers.
3 The Egyptians are men, not God,
 their horses are flesh, not spirit;
When the LORD stretches forth his hand,
 the helper shall stumble, the one helped shall fall,
 and both of them shall perish together.

4   Thus says the LORD to me:
As a lion or a lion cub
 growling over its prey,
With a band of shepherds
 assembled against it,
Is neither frightened by their shouts
 nor disturbed by their noise,
So shall the LORD of hosts come down
 to wage war upon the mountain and hill of Zion.
5 Like hovering birds, so the LORD of hosts
 shall shield Jerusalem,
To protect and deliver,
 to spare and rescue it.

6 Return, O children of Israel, to him whom you have
utterly deserted. 7 On that day each one of you shall spurn
his sinful idols of silver and gold, which he made with his
hands.

8 Assyria shall fall by a sword not wielded by man,
 no mortal sword shall devour him;
He shall flee before the sword,
 and his young men shall be impressed
 as laborers.
9 He shall rush past his crag in panic,
 and his princes shall flee in terror from
 his standard,
Says the LORD who has a fire in Zion
 and a furnace in Jerusalem.

32
See, a king will reign justly
 and princes will rule rightly.
2 Each of them will be a shelter from the wind,
 a retreat from the rain.
They will be like streams of water in a
 dry country,
 like the shade of a great rock in a parched land.
3 The eyes of those who see will not be closed;
 the ears of those who hear will be attentive.
4 The flighty will become wise and capable,
 and the stutterers will speak fluently and clearly.
5 No more will the fool be called noble,
 nor the trickster be considered honorable.
6 For the fool speaks foolishly,
 planning evil in his heart:
How to do wickedness,
 to speak perversely against the LORD,
To let the hungry go empty
 and the thirsty be without drink.

31
Woe to those going down to Egypt
 for help,
who put their trust in horses,
who rely on the quantity of chariots,
and on great strength of cavalrymen,
but do not look to the Holy One of Israel
or consult Yahweh.
2 Yet he too is wise and can bring disaster
and he will not go back on his word;
he will rise against the breed of evil-doers
and against those who protect wrong-doers.
3 The Egyptian is human, not divine,
his horses are flesh, not spirit;
Yahweh will stretch out his hand:
the protector will stumble,
the protected will fall
and all will perish together.

4 Yes, this is what Yahweh has said to me:
As a lion or lion cub
growls over its prey,
when scores of shepherds
are summoned to drive it off,
without being frightened by their shouting
or cowed by the noise they make,
just so will Yahweh Sabaoth descend
to fight for Mount Zion and for its hill.
5 Like hovering birds,
so will Yahweh Sabaoth protect Jerusalem;
by protecting it, he will save it,
by supporting it, he will deliver it.
6 Come back to the one whom the Israelites have so
 deeply betrayed!
7 For, that day, each of you will throw away
the false gods of silver and the false gods of gold
which your own sinful hands have made.
8 Assyria will fall by the sword, not that of a man,
will be devoured by the sword, of no human being,
he will flee before the sword
and his young warriors will be enslaved.
9 In his terror he will abandon his rock,
and his panic-stricken officers desert the
 standard —
declares Yahweh, whose fire is in Zion,
whose furnace, in Jerusalem.

32
There will be a king who reigns uprightly
 and princes who rule with fair judgement;
2 each will be like a shelter from the wind,
a refuge from the storm,
like streams on arid ground,
like the shade of a solid rock in a desolate land.
3 The eyes of seers will no longer be closed,
the ears of hearers will be alert,
4 the heart of the hasty will learn to think things
 over,
and the tongue of stammerers will speak promptly
 and clearly.
5 The fool will no longer be called generous,
nor the rascal be styled bountiful.
6 For the fool speaks folly
and his heart is set on villainy;
he is godless in his actions
and his words ascribe error to Yahweh;
he starves the hungry of their food
and refuses drink to the thirsty.

NEW REVISED STANDARD VERSION	REVISED ENGLISH BIBLE

NEW REVISED STANDARD VERSION

7 The villainies of villains are evil;
  they devise wicked devices
to ruin the poor with lying words,
  even when the plea of the needy is right.
8 But those who are noble plan noble things,
  and by noble things they stand.

9 Rise up, you women who are at ease, hear my
    voice;
  you complacent daughters, listen to my speech.
10 In little more than a year
  you will shudder, you complacent ones;
for the vintage will fail,
  the fruit harvest will not come.
11 Tremble, you women who are at ease,
  shudder, you complacent ones;
strip, and make yourselves bare,
  and put sackcloth on your loins.
12 Beat your breasts for the pleasant fields,
  for the fruitful vine,
13 for the soil of my people
  growing up in thorns and briers;
yes, for all the joyous houses
  in the jubilant city.
14 For the palace will be forsaken,
  the populous city deserted;
the hill and the watchtower
  will become dens forever,
the joy of wild asses,
  a pasture for flocks;
15 until a spirit from on high is poured out on us,
  and the wilderness becomes a fruitful field,
  and the fruitful field is deemed a forest.
16 Then justice will dwell in the wilderness,
  and righteousness abide in the fruitful field.
17 The effect of righteousness will be peace,
  and the result of righteousness, quietness and
    trust forever.
18 My people will abide in a peaceful habitation,
  in secure dwellings, and in quiet resting places.
19 The forest will disappear completely,*j*
  and the city will be utterly laid low.
20 Happy will you be who sow beside every stream,
  who let the ox and the donkey range freely.

33 Ah, you destroyer,
  who yourself have not been destroyed;
you treacherous one,
  with whom no one has dealt treacherously!
When you have ceased to destroy,
  you will be destroyed;
and when you have stopped dealing
    treacherously,
  you will be dealt with treacherously.

2 O LORD, be gracious to us; we wait for you.
  Be our arm every morning,
  our salvation in the time of trouble.
3 At the sound of tumult, peoples fled;
  before your majesty, nations scattered.
4 Spoil was gathered as the caterpillar gathers;
  as locusts leap, they leaped*k* upon it.
5 The LORD is exalted, he dwells on high;
  he filled Zion with justice and righteousness;
6 he will be the stability of your times,
  abundance of salvation, wisdom, and
    knowledge;
  the fear of the LORD is Zion's treasure.*l*

REVISED ENGLISH BIBLE

7 The villain's tactics are villainous
  and he devises infamous plans
to bring ruin on the poor with his lies
  and deny justice to the needy.
8 But he who is of noble mind forms noble designs
  and in those designs he stands firm.

9 You women who live at ease,
  listen attentively to what I say;
you daughters without a care, mark my words.
10 You may be carefree now,
  but you will be quaking at the turn of the year,
for the vintage will be a failure,
  with no produce gathered in.
11 You women now at ease, be terrified;
  tremble, you women without a care.
Strip yourselves bare,
  and put on a loincloth of sacking.
12 Beat upon your breasts in mourning
  for the pleasant fields and fruitful vines,
13 for my people's land with its yield of thorns and
    briars,
  for every happy home in the bustling city.
14 Mansions are forsaken and the crowded streets
    deserted;
  citadel and watch-tower are turned into open heath,
  for ever the delight of wild asses and pasture for
    flocks,
15 until a spirit from on high is lavished upon us.

Then the wilderness will become garden land
  and garden land will be reckoned as common as
    scrub.
16 Justice will make its home in the wilderness,
  and righteousness dwell in the grassland;
17 righteousness will yield peace
  and bring about quiet trust for ever.
18 Then my people will live in tranquil country,
  dwelling undisturbed in peace and security;
19 it will be cool on the slopes of the forest then,
  and cities will lie peaceful in the plain.
20 Happy will you be sowing everywhere beside water
  and letting ox and donkey roam freely.

33 Woe betide you, destroyer, yourself undestroyed,
  betrayer still unbetrayed!
After all your destroying, you will be destroyed;
  after all your betrayals, you yourself will be
    betrayed.

2 LORD, show us your favour;
  our hope is in you.
Uphold us every morning,
  save us when troubles come.
3 At the crack of thunder peoples flee,
  nations are scattered at your roar;
4 they are stripped of spoil as if stripped by young
    locusts,
  like a swarm of locusts folk swarm over it.
5 The LORD is supreme, for he dwells on high;
  he has filled Zion with justice and righteousness.
6 Her strength will be in your unchanging stability,
  her deliverance in wisdom and knowledge;
  her treasure is the fear of the LORD.

---

j Cn: Heb *And it will hail when the forest comes down*   *k* Meaning
of Heb uncertain   *l* Heb *his treasure*; meaning of Heb uncertain

33:1 **after all your betrayals:** *so Scroll; Heb.* unintelligible.
33:2 **Uphold us:** *so some MSS; others* Uphold them.   33:6 **her
treasure:** *prob. rdg; Heb.* his treasure.

NEW AMERICAN BIBLE

NEW JERUSALEM BIBLE

7 And the trickster uses wicked trickery,
  planning crimes:
How to ruin the poor with lies,
  and the needy when they plead their case.
8 But the noble man plans noble things,
  and by noble things he stands.

9 O complacent ladies, rise up and hear my voice,
  overconfident women, give heed to my words.
10 In a little more than a year
  you overconfident ones will be shaken;
The vintage will fail,
  there will be no harvest.
11 Tremble, you who are complacent!
  Shudder, you who are overconfident!
Strip yourselves bare,
  with only a loincloth to cover you.
12 Beat your breasts
  for the pleasant fields, the fruitful vine,
13 And the soil of my people,
  overgrown with thorns and briers;
For all the joyful houses,
  the wanton city.
14 Yes, the castle will be forsaken,
  the noisy city deserted;
19 Down it comes, as trees come down in the forest!
  The city will be utterly laid low.
Hill and tower will become wasteland forever
  for wild asses to frolic in, and flocks to pasture,
15 Until the spirit from on high
  is poured out on us.
Then will the desert become an orchard
  and the orchard be regarded as a forest.

16 Right will dwell in the desert
  and justice abide in the orchard.
17 Justice will bring about peace;
  right will produce calm and security.
18 My people will live in peaceful country,
  in secure dwellings and quiet resting places.
‡32.19: see above‡
20 Happy are you who sow beside every stream,
  and let the ox and the ass go freely!

33 Woe, O destroyer never destroyed,
  O traitor never betrayed!
When you finish destroying, you will be destroyed;
  when wearied with betraying, you will
  be betrayed.
2 O LORD, have pity on us, for you we wait.
  Be our strength every morning,
  our salvation in time of trouble!
3 At the roaring sound, peoples flee;
  when you rise in your majesty, nations
  are scattered.
4 Men gather spoil as caterpillars are gathered up;
  they rush upon it like the onrush of locusts.
5 The LORD is exalted, enthroned on high;
  he fills Zion with right and justice.
6 That which makes her seasons lasting,
  the riches that save her, are wisdom
    and knowledge;
  the fear of the LORD is her treasure.

7 Everything to do with the rascal is evil,
  he devises infamous plans
to ruin the poor with lying words
  even when the needy has right on his side;
8 but the noble person plans only noble things,
  noble his every move.

9 Stand up, you haughty women, listen to my words;
  you over-confident daughters, pay attention to what
    I say.
10 Within one year and a few days
  you will tremble, you over-confident women;
grape-harvesting will be finished,
  gathering will never happen again.
11 Shudder, you haughty women,
  tremble, you over-confident women;
  strip, undress, put sackcloth round your waists.
12 Beat your breasts for the pleasant fields,
  for the fruitful vine,
13 for my people's soil where the bramble-bush will
    be growing
  and for all the happy houses, for the rejoicing city.
14 For the citadel will be abandoned
  and the thronged city deserted,
Ophel*q* and the Keep will be denuded for ever,
  the playground of wild donkeys
  and the pasture of flocks,
15 until the spirit is poured out on us from above,
  and the desert becomes an orchard,
  and an orchard that seems like a forest.

16 Fair judgement will fix its home in the desert,
  and uprightness live in this orchard,
17 and the product of uprightness will be peace,
  the effect of uprightness being quiet and security
    for ever.
18 My people will live in a peaceful home,
  in peaceful houses, tranquil dwellings.
19 And should the forest be totally destroyed
  and the city gravely humiliated,
20 you will be happy to sow wherever there is water
  and to let the ox and donkey roam free.

33 Woe to you, destroying though not yourself
    destroyed,
  betraying though not yourself betrayed;
when you have finished destroying, you will be
    destroyed,
  when you have stopped betraying, you will be
    betrayed.
2 Yahweh, show us your mercy,
  we hope in you.
Be our arm every morning
  and our salvation in time of distress.
3 At the sound of tumult the peoples flee,
  when you stand up the nations scatter.
4 Your spoil is gathered in as a grasshopper gathers
    in,
  like a swarm of locusts people descend on it.
5 Yahweh is exalted, for he is enthroned above,
  he has filled Zion with fair judgement and saving
    justice.

6 You can count on this all your days:
  wisdom and knowledge are the riches that save,
  the fear of Yahweh is his treasure.

q **32** The hill of the earliest city of Jerusalem; the keep is presumably a
great tower.

NEW REVISED STANDARD VERSION	REVISED ENGLISH BIBLE

7 Listen! the valiant*m* cry in the streets;
    the envoys of peace weep bitterly.
8 The highways are deserted,
    travelers have quit the road.
  The treaty is broken,
    its oaths*n* are despised,
    its obligation*o* is disregarded.
9 The land mourns and languishes;
    Lebanon is confounded and withers away;
  Sharon is like a desert;
    and Bashan and Carmel shake off their leaves.
10 "Now I will arise," says the LORD,
    "now I will lift myself up;
    now I will be exalted.
11 You conceive chaff, you bring forth stubble;
    your breath is a fire that will consume you.
12 And the peoples will be as if burned to lime,
    like thorns cut down, that are burned in the
      fire."

13 Hear, you who are far away, what I have done;
    and you who are near, acknowledge my might.
14 The sinners in Zion are afraid;
    trembling has seized the godless:
  "Who among us can live with the devouring fire?
  Who among us can live with everlasting
      flames?"
15 Those who walk righteously and speak uprightly,
    who despise the gain of oppression,
  who wave away a bribe instead of accepting it,
  who stop their ears from hearing of bloodshed
    and shut their eyes from looking on evil,
16 they will live on the heights;
    their refuge will be the fortresses of rocks;
    their food will be supplied, their water assured.

17 Your eyes will see the king in his beauty;
    they will behold a land that stretches far away.
18 Your mind will muse on the terror:
  "Where is the one who counted?
  Where is the one who weighed the tribute?
  Where is the one who counted the towers?"
19 No longer will you see the insolent people,
    the people of an obscure speech that you
      cannot comprehend,
    stammering in a language that you cannot
      understand.
20 Look on Zion, the city of our appointed festivals!
    Your eyes will see Jerusalem,
  a quiet habitation, an immovable tent,
    whose stakes will never be pulled up,
    and none of whose ropes will be broken.
21 But there the LORD in majesty will be for us
  a place of broad rivers and streams,
  where no galley with oars can go,
    nor stately ship can pass.
22 For the LORD is our judge, the LORD is our ruler,
    the LORD is our king; he will save us.

23 Your rigging hangs loose;
    it cannot hold the mast firm in its place,
    or keep the sail spread out.

  Then prey and spoil in abundance will be divided;
    even the lame will fall to plundering.
24 And no inhabitant will say, "I am sick";
    the people who live there will be forgiven their
      iniquity.

---

7 Listen, how the valiant cry out aloud for help,
    and envoys sent to sue for peace weep bitterly!
8 The highways are deserted, no one travels the
      roads.
  Covenants are broken, treaties are flouted;
    no one is held of any account.
9 The land is parched and wilting,
    Lebanon is eroded and crumbling;
  Sharon has become like a desert,
    Bashan and Carmel are stripped bare.
10 Now I shall arise, says the LORD;
    now I shall exalt myself, now lift myself up.
11 You will conceive chaff, and bring forth stubble;
    a wind like fire will devour you.
12 Whole nations will be heaps of white ash,
    or like thorns cut down and set on fire.

13 You dwellers afar off, hear what I have done;
    acknowledge my might, you that are near at hand.
14 Sinners in Zion quake with terror,
    the godless are seized with trembling; they ask,
  'Can any of us live with a devouring fire?
  Can any of us live in perpetual flames?'
15 The person who behaves uprightly and speaks the
      truth,
  who scorns to enrich himself by extortion,
  who keeps his hands clean from bribery,
  who stops his ears against talk of murder
  and closes his eyes against looking at evil—
16 he it is who will dwell on the heights,
    his refuge a fastness in the cliffs,
    his food assured and water never failing him.

17 Your eyes will see a king in his splendour
    and look on a land stretching into the distance.
18 You will call to mind what once you feared:
  'Where then is he that reckoned, where is he that
      weighed,
  where is he that counted the treasures?'
19 You will no longer see that barbarous people,
    that people whose language was so obscure,
    whose stuttering speech you could not comprehend.

20 Look to Zion, city of our sacred feasts,
    let your eyes rest on Jerusalem,
  a secure abode, a tent that will never be moved,
    whose pegs will never be pulled up,
    whose ropes will none of them be snapped.
21 There we have the LORD in all his majesty
    in a place of rivers and broad streams;
  but no galleys will be rowed there,
    no stately ships sail by.
22 The LORD is our judge, the LORD our lawgiver,
    the LORD our king—he it is who will save us.
23 (It may be said, 'Your rigging is slack;
    it will not hold the mast firm in its socket,
    nor can it spread the sails.')
  Then the blind will have a full share of the spoil
    and the lame will take part in the pillage.
24 No one dwelling there will say, 'I am sick';
    the sins of the people who live there will be
      pardoned.

---

m Meaning of Heb uncertain   *n* Q Ms: MT *cities*   *o* Or *everyone*

33:8 **treaties:** *so Scroll; Heb.* cities.   33:23 **blind:** *prob. rdg, cp. Aram. (Targ.); Heb. obscure.*

NEW AMERICAN BIBLE

7 See, the men of Ariel cry out in the streets,
    the messengers of Shalem weep bitterly.
8 The highways are desolate,
    travelers have quit the paths,
Covenants are broken, their terms are spurned;
    yet no man gives it a thought.
9 The country languishes in mourning,
    Lebanon withers with shame;
Sharon is like the steppe,
    Bashan and Carmel are stripped bare.
10 Now will I rise up, says the LORD,
    now will I be exalted, now be lifted up.
11 You conceive dry grass, bring forth stubble;
    my spirit shall consume you like fire.
12 The peoples shall be as in a limekiln,
    like brushwood cut down for burning in the fire.
13 Hear, you who are far off, what I have done;
    you who are near, acknowledge my might.
14 On Zion sinners are in dread,
    trembling grips the impious:
"Who of us can live with the consuming fire?
    who of us can live with the everlasting flames?"
15 He who practices virtue and speaks honestly,
    who spurns what is gained by oppression,
Brushing his hands free of contact with a bribe,
    stopping his ears lest he hear of bloodshed,
    closing his eyes lest he look on evil—
16 He shall dwell on the heights,
    his stronghold shall be the rocky fastness,
    his food and drink in steady supply.

17 Your eyes will see a king in his splendor,
    they will look upon a vast land.
18 Your mind will dwell on the terror:
    "Where is he who counted, where is he
      who weighed?
Where is he who counted the towers?"
19 To the people of alien tongue you will look
    no more,
the people of obscure speech,
    stammering in a language not understood.
20 Look to Zion, the city of our festivals;
    let your eyes see Jerusalem
as a quiet abode, a tent not to be struck,
Whose pegs will never be pulled up,
    nor any of its ropes severed.
22 Indeed the LORD will be there with us, majestic;
    yes, the LORD our judge, the LORD our lawgiver,
    the LORD our king, he it is who will save us.
21 In a place of rivers and wide streams
    on which no boat is rowed,
    where no majestic ship passes,
23 The rigging hangs slack;
    it cannot hold the mast in place,
    nor keep the sail spread out.
Then the blind will divide great spoils
    and the lame will carry off the loot.
24 No one who dwells there will say, "I am sick";
    the people who live there will be forgiven
      their guilt.

NEW JERUSALEM BIBLE

7 Look, Ariel is lamenting in the streets,
    the ambassadors of peace are weeping bitterly.
8 The highways are deserted,
    no travellers any more on the roads.
Agreements are broken, witnesses held in
    contempt,
    there is respect for no one.
9 The land pines away in mourning,
    the Lebanon is withering with shame,
Sharon has become like the wasteland,
    Bashan and Carmel are shuddering.
10 'Now I shall stand up,' says Yahweh,
    'now I shall rise, now draw myself up.
11 You conceive chaff, you give birth to straw:
    like fire, my breath will devour you.
12 The peoples will be burnt up as though by
    quicklime,
    like cut thorns they will be burnt on the fire.
13 You who are far away, listen to what I have done,
    and you who are near, realise my strength.'
14 The sinners in Zion are panic-stricken
    and fear seizes on the godless,
'Which of us can survive the devouring fire,
    which of us survive everlasting burning?'
15 The one who acts uprightly and speaks honestly,
    who scorns to get rich by extortion,
    who rejects bribes out of hand,
    who refuses to listen to plans involving bloodshed
    and shuts his eyes rather than countenance crime:
16 such a man will live on the heights,
    the craggy rocks will be his refuge,
    he will be fed, he will not want for water.

17 Your eyes will gaze on the king in his beauty,
    they will look on a country stretching far and wide.
18 Your heart will meditate on past terrors,
    'Where is the man who did the counting?
Where is the man who did the weighing?
Where is the man who counted off the towers?'
19 No more will you see that insolent people,
    that people of unintelligible speech,
    of barbarous and meaningless tongue.
20 Gaze at Zion, city of our feasts;
    your eyes will see Jerusalem
as a home that is secure,
    a tent not to be moved,
none of its tent-pegs ever to be pulled out,
    none of its guy-ropes ever to be broken.

21 There it is that Yahweh shows us his power,
    like a place of rivers and very wide canals
    on which will row no galley,
    over which will pass no majestic ship.
22 (For Yahweh is our judge, Yahweh our lawgiver,
    Yahweh is our king and our Saviour.)
23 Your tackle has given way,
    it cannot support the mast,
    it cannot hoist the pennon.
And so there is much booty to be shared out;
    the lame fall to plundering,
24 and no one living there will say, 'I am sickly';
    the people living there will find their guilt
      forgiven.

NEW REVISED STANDARD VERSION

REVISED ENGLISH BIBLE

34 Draw near, O nations, to hear;
  O peoples, give heed!
Let the earth hear, and all that fills it;
  the world, and all that comes from it.
2 For the LORD is enraged against all the nations,
  and furious against all their hoards;
he has doomed them, has given them over for
    slaughter.
3 Their slain shall be cast out,
  and the stench of their corpses shall rise;
the mountains shall flow with their blood.
4 All the host of heaven shall rot away,
  and the skies roll up like a scroll.
All their host shall wither
  like a leaf withering on a vine,
  or fruit withering on a fig tree.

5 When my sword has drunk its fill in the heavens,
  lo, it will descend upon Edom,
  upon the people I have doomed to judgment.
6 The LORD has a sword; it is sated with blood,
  it is gorged with fat,
  with the blood of lambs and goats,
  with the fat of the kidneys of rams.
For the LORD has a sacrifice in Bozrah,
  a great slaughter in the land of Edom.
7 Wild oxen shall fall with them,
  and young steers with the mighty bulls.
Their land shall be soaked with blood,
  and their soil made rich with fat.

8 For the LORD has a day of vengeance,
  a year of vindication by Zion's cause.*p*
9 And the streams of Edom*q* shall be turned into
    pitch,
  and her soil into sulfur;
  her land shall become burning pitch.
10 Night and day it shall not be quenched;
  its smoke shall go up forever.
From generation to generation it shall lie waste;
  no one shall pass through it forever and ever.
11 But the hawk*r* and the hedgehog*r* shall possess
    it;
  the owl*r* and the raven shall live in it.
He shall stretch the line of confusion over it,
  and the plummet of chaos over*s* its nobles.
12 They shall name it No Kingdom There,
  and all its princes shall be nothing.
13 Thorns shall grow over its strongholds,
  nettles and thistles in its fortresses.
It shall be the haunt of jackals,
  an abode for ostriches.
14 Wildcats shall meet with hyenas,
  goat-demons shall call to each other;
there too Lilith shall repose,
  and find a place to rest.
15 There shall the owl nest
  and lay and hatch and brood in its shadow;
there too the buzzards shall gather,
  each one with its mate.
16 Seek and read from the book of the LORD:
  Not one of these shall be missing;
  none shall be without its mate.
For the mouth of the LORD has commanded,
  and his spirit has gathered them.

34 APPROACH, you nations, and listen;
  attend, you peoples;
let the earth listen and everything in it,
  the world and all that it yields;
2 for the LORD's anger is against all the nations
  and his wrath against all their hordes;
he gives them over to slaughter and destruction.
3 Their slain will be flung out,
  stench will rise from their corpses,
  and the mountains will run with their blood.
4 All the host of heaven will crumble into nothing,
  the heavens will be rolled up like a scroll,
  and all their host fade away,
as the foliage withers from the vine
  and the ripened fruit from the fig tree.

5 For my sword appears in heaven.
See how it descends in judgement on Edom,
  on a people whom I have doomed to destruction.
6 The LORD has a sword sated with blood,
  gorged with fat, the fat of rams' kidneys,
  and with the blood of lambs and goats;
for the LORD has a sacrifice in Bozrah,
  a great slaughter in Edom.
7 Wild oxen will go down also,
  bull and bison together,
and their land will drink deep of blood
  and their soil be enriched with fat.
8 For the LORD has a day of vengeance,
  the champion of Zion has a time of retribution.

9 Edom's torrents will be turned to pitch
  and its soil to brimstone;
  the land will become blazing pitch,
10 never to be quenched night or day;
  smoke will rise from it for ever.
Age after age it will lie waste,
  and no one will ever again pass through it.
11 Horned owl and bustard will make it their home;
  it will be the haunt of screech-owl and raven.
The LORD has stretched over it a measuring line of
    chaos,
  and its boundaries will be a jumble of stones.
12 No king will be acclaimed there,
  and all its princes will come to naught.
13 Its palaces will be overgrown with thorns;
  nettles and briars will cover its strongholds.
It will be the lair of wolves, the haunt of
    desert-owls.
14 Marmots will live alongside jackals,
  and he-goats will congregate there.
There too the nightjar will return to rest
  and find herself a place for repose;
15 there the sand-partridge will make her nest,
  lay her eggs and hatch them,
  and gather her brood under her wings;
there will the kites gather,
  each with its mate.
16 Consult the book of the LORD and read it:
  not one of these will be missing,
  not one will lack its mate,
for with his own mouth he has ordered it
  and by his spirit he has brought them together.

p Or *of recompense by Zion's defender*   *q* Heb *her streams*
r Identification uncertain   *s* Heb lacks *over*

34:5 **appears**: *so Scroll; Heb.* drinks.

34 Come near, O nations, and hear;
   be attentive, O peoples!
Let the earth and what fills it listen,
   the world and all it produces.
2 The LORD is angry with all the nations
   and is wrathful against all their host;
he has doomed them and given them over
      to slaughter.
3 Their slain shall be cast out,
   their corpses shall send up a stench;
The mountains shall run with their blood,
4   and all the hills shall rot;
The heavens shall be rolled up like a scroll,
   and all their host shall wither away,
As the leaf wilts on the vine,
   or as the fig withers on the tree.

5 When my sword has drunk its fill in the heavens,
   lo, it shall come down in judgment
upon Edom, a people I have doomed.
6 The LORD has a sword filled with blood,
   greasy with fat,
With the blood of lambs and goats,
   with the fat of rams' kidneys;
For the LORD has a sacrifice in Bozrah,
   a great slaughter in the land of Edom.
7 Wild oxen shall be struck down with fatlings,
   and bullocks with bulls;
Their land shall be soaked with blood,
   and their earth greasy with fat.
8 For the LORD has a day of vengeance,
   a year of requital by Zion's defender.
9 Edom's streams shall be changed into pitch
   and her earth into sulphur,
   and her land shall become burning pitch;
10 Night and day it shall not be quenched,
   its smoke shall rise forever.
From generation to generation she shall lie waste,
   never again shall anyone pass through her.
11 But the desert owl and hoot owl shall possess her,
   the screech owl and raven shall dwell in her.
The LORD will measure her with line and plummet
   to be an empty waste
   for satyrs to dwell in.

12 Her nobles shall be no more,
   nor shall kings be proclaimed there;
   all her princes are gone.
13 Her castles shall be overgrown with thorns,
   her fortresses with thistles and briers.
She shall become an abode for jackals
   and a haunt for ostriches.
14 Wildcats shall meet with desert beasts,
   satyrs shall call to one another;
There shall the lilith repose,
   and find for herself a place to rest.
15 There the hoot owl shall nest and lay eggs,
   hatch them out and gather them in her shadow;
There shall the kites assemble,
   none shall be missing its mate.

16 Look in the book of the LORD and read:
   No one of these shall be lacking,
For the mouth of the LORD has ordered it,
   and his spirit shall gather them there.

34 Come near and listen, you nations,
   pay attention, you peoples.
Let the earth and its contents listen,
   the world and its entire population.
2 For Yahweh is angry with all the nations,
   enraged with all their hordes.
He has vowed them to destruction,
   handed them over to slaughter.
3 Their dead will be thrown away,
   the stench will rise from their corpses,
   the mountains will run with their blood,
4 the entire array of heaven will fall apart.
The heavens will be rolled up like a scroll
   and all their array will fade away,
as fade the leaves falling from the vine,
   as fade those falling from the fig tree.

5 For my sword has drunk deep in the heavens:
   see how it now falls on Edom,
on the people vowed to destruction,
   to punish them.
6 Yahweh's sword is gorged with blood,
   it is greasy with fat,
with the blood of lambs and goats,
   with the fat of the kidneys of rams.
For Yahweh has a sacrifice in Bozrah,
   a great slaughter in the land of Edom.
7 The wild oxen will fall with them,
   the bullocks with the bulls;
their land will be drenched with blood
   and their dust will be greasy with fat.
8 For this will be Yahweh's day of vengeance,
   the year of retribution in Zion's lawsuit.
9 Its streams will turn into pitch,
   its dust into brimstone,
   its country will turn into blazing pitch.
10 Never quenched night or day,
   its smoke rising for ever,
it will lie waste age after age,
   no one will travel through it for ever and ever.
11 It will be the haunt of pelican and hedgehog,
   the owl and the raven will live there;
over it Yahweh will stretch the measuring line of
      chaos
   and the plumb-line of emptiness.

12 There will be no more nobles
   to proclaim the royal authority;
   there will be an end of all its princes.
13 Brambles will grow in its bastions,
   nettles and thorn-bushes in its fortresses,
it will be the lair of jackals,
   an enclosure for ostriches.
14 Wild cats will meet hyenas there,
   satyr will call to satyr,
there Lilith too will lurk
   and find somewhere to rest.
15 The snake will nest and lay eggs there,
   will hatch and gather its young into the shade;
and there the vultures will assemble,
   each one with its mate.
16 Search in Yahweh's book, and read,
   not one of these will be missing,
   not one of them lacking a mate;
for thus his mouth has ordained it,
   and his spirit has brought them together.

17 He has cast the lot for them,
his hand has portioned it out to them with the
line;
they shall possess it forever,
from generation to generation they shall live in
it.

35 The wilderness and the dry land shall be glad,
the desert shall rejoice and blossom;
like the crocus 2 it shall blossom abundantly,
and rejoice with joy and singing.
The glory of Lebanon shall be given to it,
the majesty of Carmel and Sharon.
They shall see the glory of the LORD,
the majesty of our God.

3 Strengthen the weak hands,
and make firm the feeble knees.
4 Say to those who are of a fearful heart,
"Be strong, do not fear!
Here is your God.
He will come with vengeance,
with terrible recompense.
He will come and save you."

5 Then the eyes of the blind shall be opened,
and the ears of the deaf unstopped;
6 then the lame shall leap like a deer,
and the tongue of the speechless sing for joy.
For waters shall break forth in the wilderness,
and streams in the desert;
7 the burning sand shall become a pool,
and the thirsty ground springs of water;
the haunt of jackals shall become a swamp,*t*
the grass shall become reeds and rushes.

8 A highway shall be there,
and it shall be called the Holy Way;
the unclean shall not travel on it,*u*
but it shall be for God's people;*v*
no traveler, not even fools, shall go astray.
9 No lion shall be there,
nor shall any ravenous beast come up on it;
they shall not be found there,
but the redeemed shall walk there.
10 And the ransomed of the LORD shall return,
and come to Zion with singing;
everlasting joy shall be upon their heads;
they shall obtain joy and gladness,
and sorrow and sighing shall flee away.

36 In the fourteenth year of King Hezekiah, King Sennacherib of Assyria came up against all the fortified
cities of Judah and captured them. 2 The king of Assyria
sent the Rabshakeh from Lachish to King Hezekiah at Jerusalem, with a great army. He stood by the conduit of the
upper pool on the highway to the Fuller's Field. 3 And there
came out to him Eliakim son of Hilkiah, who was in charge
of the palace, and Shebna the secretary, and Joah son of
Asaph, the recorder.

4 The Rabshakeh said to them, "Say to Hezekiah: Thus
says the great king, the king of Assyria: On what do you
base this confidence of yours? 5 Do you think that mere
words are strategy and power for war? On whom do you
now rely, that you have rebelled against me? 6 See, you are

17 He it is who has allotted each its place,
and his hand has measured out their portions;
they will occupy it for all time,
and each succeeding generation will dwell there.

35 Let the wilderness and the parched land be glad,
let the desert rejoice and burst into flower.
2 Let it flower with fields of asphodel,
let it rejoice and shout for joy.
The glory of Lebanon is given to it,
the splendour too of Carmel and Sharon;
these will see the glory of the LORD,
the splendour of our God.

3 Brace the arms that are limp,
steady the knees that give way;
4 say to the anxious, 'Be strong, fear not!
Your God comes to save you
with his vengeance and his retribution.'
5 Then the eyes of the blind will be opened,
and the ears of the deaf unstopped.
6 Then the lame will leap like deer,
and the dumb shout aloud;
for water will spring up in the wilderness
and torrents flow in the desert.
7 The mirage will become a pool,
the thirsty land bubbling springs;
instead of reeds and rushes, grass will grow
in country where wolves have their lairs.

8 And a causeway will appear there;
it will be called the Way of Holiness.
No one unclean will pass along it;
it will become a pilgrim's way,
and no fool will trespass on it.
9 No lion will come there,
no savage beast go by;
not one will be found there.
But by that way those the LORD has redeemed will
return.
10 The LORD's people, set free, will come back
and enter Zion with shouts of triumph,
crowned with everlasting joy.
Gladness and joy will come upon them,
while suffering and weariness flee away.

36 IN the fourteenth year of King Hezekiah's reign,
King Sennacherib of Assyria attacked and captured
all the fortified towns of Judah. 2 From Lachish he sent his
chief officer with a strong force to King Hezekiah at Jerusalem. The officer halted by the conduit of the Upper Pool on
the causeway leading to the Fuller's Field. 3 There Eliakim
son of Hilkiah, the comptroller of the household, came out
to him, with Shebna the adjutant-general and Joah son of
Asaph, the secretary of state.

4 The chief officer said to them, 'Tell Hezekiah that this
is the message of the Great King, the king of Assyria:
"What ground have you for this confidence of yours? 5 Do
you think words can take the place of skill and military
strength? On whom then do you rely for support in your
rebellion against me? 6 On Egypt? Egypt is a splintered cane

35:6 **flow:** *so Scroll; Heb. omits.*   35:8 **causeway:** *so Scroll;
Heb. adds* and a road. **a pilgrim's way:** *prob. rdg; Heb.
unintelligible.*   36:1–22 *Cp.* 2 Kgs. 18:13–37; 2 Chr. 32:1–19.
36:2 **his chief officer:** *or* Rab-shakeh.   36:5 **Do you:** *so Scroll;
Heb.* Do I.

---

t Cn: Heb *in the haunt of jackals is her resting place*   *u* Or *pass it
by*   *v* Cn: Heb *for them*

17 It is he who casts the lot for them,
  and with his hand he marks off their shares
    of her;
  They shall possess her forever,
  and dwell there from generation to generation.

35 The desert and the parched land will exult;
  the steppe will rejoice and bloom.
2 They will bloom with abundant flowers,
  and rejoice with joyful song.
  The glory of Lebanon will be given to them,
  the splendor of Carmel and Sharon;
  They shall see the glory of the LORD,
  the splendor of our God.
3 Strengthen the hands that are feeble,
  make firm the knees that are weak,
4 Say to those whose hearts are frightened:
  Be strong, fear not!
  Here is your God,
  he comes with vindication;
  With divine recompense
  he comes to save you.
5 Then will the eyes of the blind be opened,
  the ears of the deaf be cleared;
6 Then will the lame leap like a stag,
  then the tongue of the dumb will sing.

  Streams will burst forth in the desert,
  and rivers in the steppe.
7 The burning sands will become pools,
  and the thirsty ground, springs of water;
  The abode where jackals lurk
  will be a marsh for the reed and papyrus.
8 A highway will be there,
  called the holy way;
  No one unclean may pass over it,
  nor fools go astray on it.
9 No lion will be there,
  nor beast of prey go up to be met upon it.
  It is for those with a journey to make,
  and on it the redeemed will walk.
10 Those whom the LORD has ransomed will return
  and enter Zion singing,
  crowned with everlasting joy;
  They will meet with joy and gladness,
  sorrow and mourning will flee.

36 In the fourteenth year of King Hezekiah, Sennacherib, king of Assyria, went on an expedition against all the fortified cities of Judah and captured them. 2 From Lachish the king of Assyria sent his commander with a great army to King Hezekiah in Jerusalem. When he stopped at the conduit of the upper pool, on the highway of the fuller's field, 3 there came out to him the master of the palace, Eliakim, son of Hilkiah, and Shebna the scribe, and the herald Joah, son of Asaph. 4 The commander said to them, "Tell King Hezekiah: Thus says the great king, the king of Assyria, 'On what do you base this confidence of yours? 5 Do you think mere words substitute for strategy and might in war? On whom, then, do you rely, that you rebel against me? 6 This Egypt, the staff on which you rely, is in fact a

17 He has thrown the lot for each,
  his hand has measured out their share;
  they will possess it for ever,
  and live there age after age.

35 Let the desert and the dry lands be glad,
  let the wasteland rejoice and bloom;
  like the asphodel, 2 let it burst into flower,
  let it rejoice and sing for joy.
  The glory of Lebanon is bestowed on it,
  the splendour of Carmel and Sharon;
  then they will see the glory of Yahweh,
  the splendour of our God.
3 Strengthen all weary hands,
  steady all trembling knees
4 and say to the faint-hearted,
  'Be strong! Do not be afraid.
  Here is your God,
  vengeance is coming,
  divine retribution;
  he is coming to save you.'
5 Then the eyes of the blind will be opened,
  the ears of the deaf unsealed,
6 then the lame will leap like a deer
  and the tongue of the dumb sing for joy;
  for water will gush in the desert
  and streams in the wastelands,
7 the parched ground will become a marsh
  and the thirsty land springs of water;
  the lairs where the jackals used to live
  will become plots of reed and papyrus.
8 And through it will run a road for them and a
    highway
  which will be called the Sacred Way;
  the unclean will not be allowed to use it;
  He will be the one to use this road,
  the fool will not stray along it.
9 No lion will be there,
  no ferocious beast set foot on it,
  nothing of the sort be found;
  it will be used by the redeemed.
10 For those whom Yahweh has ransomed will return,
  they will come to Zion shouting for joy,
  their heads crowned with joy unending;
  rejoicing and gladness will escort them
  and sorrow and sighing will take flight.

36 r In the fourteenth year of King Hezekiah, Sennacherib king of Assyria advanced on all the fortified towns of Judah and captured them. 2 From Lachish the king of Assyria sent the cupbearer-in-chief with a large force to King Hezekiah in Jerusalem. The cupbearer-in-chief took up position near the conduit of the upper pool on the road to the Fuller's Field. 3 The master of the palace, Eliakim son of Hilkiah, Shebna the secretary and the herald Joah son of Asaph went out to him. 4 The cupbearer-in-chief said to them, 'Say to Hezekiah, "The great king, the king of Assyria, says this: What makes you so confident? 5 Do you think empty words are as good as strategy and military strength? Who are you relying on, to dare to rebel against me? 6 There you are, relying on that broken reed, Egypt,

r 36 chh. 36—39 form a historical appendix, reproducing the story of Isaiah given in 2 K 18:13, 17—20:19.

NEW REVISED STANDARD VERSION

REVISED ENGLISH BIBLE

relying on Egypt, that broken reed of a staff, which will pierce the hand of anyone who leans on it. Such is Pharaoh king of Egypt to all who rely on him. 7 But if you say to me, 'We rely on the LORD our God,' is it not he whose high places and altars Hezekiah has removed, saying to Judah and to Jerusalem, 'You shall worship before this altar'? 8 Come now, make a wager with my master the king of Assyria: I will give you two thousand horses, if you are able on your part to set riders on them. 9 How then can you repulse a single captain among the least of my master's servants, when you rely on Egypt for chariots and for horsemen? 10 Moreover, is it without the LORD that I have come up against this land to destroy it? The LORD said to me, Go up against this land, and destroy it."

11 Then Eliakim, Shebna, and Joah said to the Rabshakeh, "Please speak to your servants in Aramaic, for we understand it; do not speak to us in the language of Judah within the hearing of the people who are on the wall." 12 But the Rabshakeh said, "Has my master sent me to speak these words to your master and to you, and not to the people sitting on the wall, who are doomed with you to eat their own dung and drink their own urine?"

13 Then the Rabshakeh stood and called out in a loud voice in the language of Judah, "Hear the words of the great king, the king of Assyria! 14 Thus says the king: 'Do not let Hezekiah deceive you, for he will not be able to deliver you. 15 Do not let Hezekiah make you rely on the LORD by saying, The LORD will surely deliver us; this city will not be given into the hand of the king of Assyria.' 16 Do not listen to Hezekiah; for thus says the king of Assyria: 'Make your peace with me and come out to me; then everyone of you will eat from your own vine and your own fig tree and drink water from your own cistern, 17 until I come and take you away to a land like your own land, a land of grain and wine, a land of bread and vineyards. 18 Do not let Hezekiah mislead you by saying, The LORD will save us. Has any of the gods of the nations saved their land out of the hand of the king of Assyria? 19 Where are the gods of Hamath and Arpad? Where are the gods of Sepharvaim? Have they delivered Samaria out of my hand? 20 Who among all the gods of these countries have saved their countries out of my hand, that the LORD should save Jerusalem out of my hand?' "

21 But they were silent and answered him not a word, for the king's command was, "Do not answer him." 22 Then Eliakim son of Hilkiah, who was in charge of the palace, and Shebna the secretary, and Joah son of Asaph, the recorder, came to Hezekiah with their clothes torn, and told him the words of the Rabshakeh.

that will run into a man's hand and pierce it if he leans on it. That is what Pharaoh king of Egypt proves to all who rely on him. 7 And if you tell me that you are relying on the LORD your God, is he not the god whose shrines and altars Hezekiah has suppressed, telling Judah and Jerusalem they must worship at this altar?'

8 'Now, make a deal with my master the king of Assyria: I shall give you two thousand horses if you can find riders for them. 9 How then can you reject the authority of even the least of my master's servants and rely on Egypt for chariots and horsemen? 10 Do you think that I have come to attack this land and destroy it without the consent of the LORD? No; the LORD himself said to me, "Go up and destroy this land." '

11 Eliakim, Shebna, and Joah said to the chief officer, 'Please speak to us in Aramaic, for we understand it; do not speak Hebrew to us within earshot of the people on the city wall.' 12 The chief officer answered, 'Is it to your master and to you that my master has sent me to say this? Is it not to the people sitting on the wall who, like you, will have to eat their own dung and drink their own urine?'

13 Then he stood and shouted in Hebrew, 'Hear the message of the Great King, the king of Assyria! 14 These are the king's words: "Do not be taken in by Hezekiah. He is powerless to save you. 15 Do not let him persuade you to rely on the LORD, and tell you that the LORD will surely save you and that this city will never be surrendered to the king of Assyria." 16 Do not listen to Hezekiah, for this is what the king of Assyria says: "Make your peace with me, and surrender. Then every one of you will eat the fruit of his own vine and of his own fig tree, and drink the water of his own cistern, 17 until I come and take you to a land like your own, a land of grain and new wine, of bread and vineyards. 18 Beware that Hezekiah does not mislead you by telling you that the LORD will save you. Did any god of the nations save his land from the king of Assyria's power? 19 Where are the gods of Hamath and Arpad? Where are the gods of Sepharvaim? Where are the gods of Samaria? Did they save Samaria from me? 20 Among all the gods of these nations is there one who saved his land from me? So how is the LORD to save Jerusalem?" '

21 The people remained silent and said not a word in reply, for the king had given orders that no one was to answer him. 22 Eliakim son of Hilkiah, comptroller of the household, Shebna the adjutant-general, and Joah son of Asaph, secretary, came to Hezekiah with their clothes torn and reported the words of the chief officer.

37 When King Hezekiah heard it, he tore his clothes, covered himself with sackcloth, and went into the house of the LORD. 2 And he sent Eliakim, who was in charge of the palace, and Shebna the secretary, and the senior priests, covered with sackcloth, to the prophet Isaiah son of Amoz. 3 They said to him, "Thus says Hezekiah, This day is a day of distress, of rebuke, and of disgrace; children have come to the birth, and there is no strength to bring them forth. 4 It may be that the LORD your God heard the words of the Rabshakeh, whom his master the king of Assyria has sent to mock the living God, and will rebuke the words that the LORD your God has heard; therefore lift up your prayer for the remnant that is left."

5 When the servants of King Hezekiah came to Isaiah,

37 When King Hezekiah heard their report, he tore his clothes, put on sackcloth, and went into the house of the LORD. 2 He sent Eliakim comptroller of the household, Shebna the adjutant-general, and the senior priests, all wearing sackcloth, to the prophet Isaiah son of Amoz, 3 to give him this message from the king: 'Today is a day of trouble for us, a day of reproof and contumely. We are like a woman who lacks the strength to bring to birth the child she is carrying. 4 It may be that the LORD your God will give heed to the words of the chief officer whom his master the king of Assyria sent to taunt the living God, and will confute the words which the LORD your God heard. Offer a prayer for those who still survive.'

5 When King Hezekiah's officials came to Isaiah, 6 they

36:19 **Where are the gods of Samaria?:** *prob. rdg, cp. Gk (Luc.)* at 2 Kgs. 18:34; Heb. omits. 37:1–38 Cp. 2 Kgs. 19:1–37; 2 Chr. 32:20–22.

broken reed which pierces the hand of anyone who leans on it. That is what Pharaoh, king of Egypt, is to all who rely on him. 7 But if you say to me: "We rely on the LORD, our God," is not he the one whose high places and altars Hezekiah removed, commanding Judah and Jerusalem to worship before this altar?'

8 "Now, make a wager with my lord the king of Assyria: 'I will give you two thousand horses, if you can put riders on them.' 9 How then can you repulse even one of the least servants of my lord? And yet you rely on Egypt for chariots and horsemen! 10 'Was it without the LORD's will that I have come up to destroy this land? The LORD said to me, "Go up and destroy that land!"'"

11 Then Eliakim and Shebna and Joah said to the commander, "Please speak to your servants in Aramaic; we understand it. Do not speak to us in Judean within earshot of the people who are on the wall."

12 But the commander replied, "Was it to you and your master that my lord sent me to speak these words? Was it not rather to the men sitting on the wall, who, with you, will have to eat their own excrement and drink their own urine?" 13 Then the commander stepped forward and cried out in a loud voice in Judean, "Listen to the words of the great king, the king of Assyria. 14 Thus says the king: 'Do not let Hezekiah deceive you, since he cannot deliver you. 15 Let not Hezekiah induce you to rely on the LORD, saying, "The LORD will surely save us; this city will not be handed over to the king of Assyria."' 16 Do not listen to Hezekiah, for the king of Assyria says: 'Make peace with me and surrender! Then each of you will eat of his own vine and of his own fig tree, and drink the water of his own cistern, 17 until I come to take you to a land like your own, a land of grain and wine, of bread and vineyards. 18 Do not let Hezekiah seduce you by saying, "The LORD will save us." Has any of the gods of the nations ever rescued his land from the hand of the king of Assyria? 19 Where are the gods of Hamath and Arpad? Where are the gods of Sepharvaim? Where are the gods of Samaria? Have they saved Samaria from my hand? 20 Which of all the gods of these lands ever rescued his land from my hand? Will the LORD then save Jerusalem from my hand?'" 21 But they remained silent and did not answer him one word, for the king had ordered them not to answer him.

22 Then the master of the palace, Eliakim, son of Hilkiah, Shebna the scribe, and the herald Joah, son of Asaph, came to Hezekiah with their garments torn, and reported to him what the commander had said.

37 When King Hezekiah heard this, he tore his garments, wrapped himself in sackcloth, and went into the temple of the LORD. 2 He sent Eliakim, the master of the palace, and Shebna the scribe, and the elders of the priests, wrapped in sackcloth, to tell the prophet Isaiah, son of Amoz: 3 "Thus says Hezekiah: 'This is a day of distress, of rebuke, and of disgrace. Children are at the point of birth, but there is no strength to bring them forth. 4 Perhaps the LORD, your God, will hear the words of the commander, whom his master, the king of Assyria, sent to taunt the living God, and will rebuke him for the words which the LORD, your God, has heard. Send up a prayer for the remnant that is here.'"

5 When the servants of King Hezekiah had come to Isa-

which pricks and pierces the hand of the person who leans on it. That is what Pharaoh king of Egypt is like to all who rely on him. 7 You may say to me: We rely on Yahweh our God. But haven't his high places and altars been suppressed by Hezekiah, who told Judah and Jerusalem: This is the altar before which you must worship? 8 Very well, then, make a wager with my lord the king of Assyria: I will give you two thousand horses if you can find horsemen to ride them. 9 How could you repulse a single one of the least of my master's soldiers? And yet you have relied on Egypt for chariots and horsemen. 10 And lastly, have I marched on this country to lay it waste without warrant from Yahweh? Yahweh himself said to me: March on this country and lay it waste."'

11 Eliakim, Shebna and Joah said to the cupbearer-in-chief, 'Please speak to your servants in Aramaic, for we understand it; do not speak to us in the Judaean language within earshot of the people on the ramparts.' 12 But the cupbearer-in-chief said, 'Do you think my lord sent me here to say these things to your master or to you? On the contrary, it was to the people sitting on the ramparts who, like you, are doomed to eat their own dung and drink their own urine.'

13 The cupbearer-in-chief then drew himself up and shouted loudly in the Judaean language, 'Listen to the words of the great king, the king of Assyria. 14 The king says this, "Do not let Hezekiah delude you! He will be powerless to save you. 15 Do not let Hezekiah persuade you to rely on Yahweh by saying: Yahweh is sure to save us; this city will not fall into the king of Assyria's clutches. 16 Do not listen to Hezekiah, for the king of Assyria says this: Make peace with me, 17 surrender to me, and every one of you will be free to eat the fruit of his own vine and of his own fig tree and to drink the water of his own storage-well until I come and take you away to a country like your own, a land of corn and good wine, a land of bread and vineyards. 18 Do not let Hezekiah delude you by saying: Yahweh will save us. Has any god of any nation been able to save his country from the king of Assyria's clutches? 19 Where are the gods of Hamath and Arpad? Where are the gods of Sepharvaim? Where are the national gods of Samaria? Did they save Samaria from my clutches? 20 Of all the national gods, which ones have saved their countries from my clutches, that Yahweh should be able to save Jerusalem from my clutches?"'

21 They, however, kept quiet and said nothing in reply, since the king had given the order, 'You are not to answer him.' 22 The master of the palace, Eliakim son of Hilkiah, Shebna the secretary and the herald Joah son of Asaph, with their clothes torn, went to Hezekiah and reported what the cupbearer-in-chief had said.

37 On hearing this, King Hezekiah tore his clothes, put on sackcloth and went to the Temple of Yahweh. 2 He sent Eliakim master of the palace, Shebna the secretary and the elders of the priests, wearing sackcloth, to the prophet Isaiah son of Amoz. 3 They said to him, 'This is what Hezekiah says, "Today is a day of suffering, of punishment, of disgrace. Children come to birth and there is no strength to bring them forth. 4 May Yahweh your God hear the words of the cupbearer-in-chief whom his master, the king of Assyria, has sent to insult the living God, and may Yahweh your God punish the words he has heard! Offer your prayer for the remnant still left."'

5 When King Hezekiah's ministers came to Isaiah, 6 he

6 Isaiah said to them, "Say to your master, 'Thus says the LORD: Do not be afraid because of the words that you have heard, with which the servants of the king of Assyria have reviled me. 7 I myself will put a spirit in him, so that he shall hear a rumor, and return to his own land; I will cause him to fall by the sword in his own land.' "

8 The Rabshakeh returned, and found the king of Assyria fighting against Libnah; for he had heard that the king had left Lachish. 9 Now the king^w heard concerning King Tirhakah of Ethiopia,^{x} "He has set out to fight against you." When he heard it, he sent messengers to Hezekiah, saying, 10 "Thus shall you speak to King Hezekiah of Judah: Do not let your God on whom you rely deceive you by promising that Jerusalem will not be given into the hand of the king of Assyria. 11 See, you have heard what the kings of Assyria have done to all lands, destroying them utterly. Shall you be delivered? 12 Have the gods of the nations delivered them, the nations that my predecessors destroyed, Gozan, Haran, Rezeph, and the people of Eden who were in Telassar? 13 Where is the king of Hamath, the king of Arpad, the king of the city of Sepharvaim, the king of Hena, or the king of Ivvah?"

14 Hezekiah received the letter from the hand of the messengers and read it; then Hezekiah went up to the house of the LORD and spread it before the LORD. 15 And Hezekiah prayed to the LORD, saying: 16 "O LORD of hosts, God of Israel, who are enthroned above the cherubim, you are God, you alone, of all the kingdoms of the earth; you have made heaven and earth. 17 Incline your ear, O LORD, and hear; open your eyes, O LORD, and see; hear all the words of Sennacherib, which he has sent to mock the living God. 18 Truly, O LORD, the kings of Assyria have laid waste all the nations and their lands, 19 and have hurled their gods into the fire, though they were no gods, but the work of human hands—wood and stone—and so they were destroyed. 20 So now, O LORD our God, save us from his hand, so that all the kingdoms of the earth may know that you alone are the LORD."

21 Then Isaiah son of Amoz sent to Hezekiah, saying: "Thus says the LORD, the God of Israel: Because you have prayed to me concerning King Sennacherib of Assyria, 22 this is the word that the LORD has spoken concerning him:

> She despises you, she scorns you—
> virgin daughter Zion;
> she tosses her head—behind your back,
> daughter Jerusalem.
>
> 23 Whom have you mocked and reviled?
> Against whom have you raised your voice
> and haughtily lifted your eyes?
> Against the Holy One of Israel!
> 24 By your servants you have mocked the Lord,
> and you have said, 'With my many chariots
> I have gone up the heights of the mountains,
> to the far recesses of Lebanon;
> I felled its tallest cedars,
> its choicest cypresses;
> I came to its remotest height,
> its densest forest.
> 25 I dug wells
> and drank waters,
> I dried up with the sole of my foot
> all the streams of Egypt.'

were given this answer for their master: 'Here is the word of the LORD: Do not be alarmed at what you heard when the Assyrian king's minions blasphemed me. 7 I shall sap his morale till at a mere rumour he will withdraw to his own country; and there I shall make him fall by the sword.'

8 Meanwhile the chief officer went back, and, having heard that the king of Assyria had moved camp from Lachish, he found him attacking Libnah. 9 But when the king learnt that King Tirhakah of Cush was on the way to engage him in battle, he sent messengers again to King Hezekiah of Judah 10 to say to him, 'How can you be deluded by your God on whom you rely when he promises that Jerusalem will not fall into the hands of the king of Assyria? 11 You yourself must have heard what the kings of Assyria have done to all countries: they utterly destroyed them. Can you then hope to escape? 12 Did their gods save the nations which my predecessors wiped out: Gozan, Harran, Rezeph, and the people of Eden living in Telassar? 13 Where are the kings of Hamath, of Arpad, and of Lahir, Sepharvaim, Hena, and Ivvah?'

14 Hezekiah received the letter from the messengers and, having read it, he went up to the temple and spread it out before the LORD 15 with this prayer: 16 'LORD of Hosts, God of Israel, enthroned on the cherubim, you alone are God of all the kingdoms of the world; you made heaven and earth. 17 Incline your ear, LORD, and listen; open your eyes, LORD, and see; hear all the words that Sennacherib has sent to taunt the living God. 18 LORD, it is true that the kings of Assyria have laid waste every country, 19 and have consigned their gods to the flames. They destroyed them, because they were no gods but the work of men's hands, mere wood and stone. 20 Now, LORD our God, save us from his power, so that all the kingdoms of the earth may know that you alone, LORD, are God.'

21 Isaiah son of Amoz sent Hezekiah the following message: 'This is the word of the LORD the God of Israel: I have heard your prayer to me concerning King Sennacherib of Assyria, 22 and this is the word which the LORD has spoken against him:

> The virgin daughter of Zion disdains you,
> she laughs you to scorn;
> the daughter of Jerusalem tosses her head
> as you retreat.
>
> 23 Whom have you taunted and blasphemed?
> Against whom did you raise an outcry,
> casting haughty glances at the Holy One of Israel?
> 24 You sent your servants to taunt the Lord;
> you said: "With my countless chariots
> I have ascended the mountain heights,
> gone to the remote recesses of Lebanon.
> I have felled its tallest cedars,
> the finest of its pines;
> I have reached the highest peak,
> the most luxuriant forest.
> 25 I have dug wells
> and drunk the waters of a foreign land,
> and with the sole of my foot I have dried up
> all the streams of Egypt."

37:9 **again:** *prob. rdg, cp.* 2 Kgs. 19:9; *Heb.* and he heard.
37:18 **every country:** *so Scroll; Heb. adds* and their country.
37:20 **are God:** *so Scroll; Heb. omits* God. 37:21 **I have heard:** *so Gk; Heb. omits.* 37:25 **of a foreign land:** *so Scroll; Heb. omits.*

iah, 6 he said to them: "Tell this to your master: 'Thus says the LORD: Do not be frightened by the words you have heard, with which the servants of the king of Assyria have blasphemed me. 7 I am about to put in him such a spirit that, when he hears a certain report, he will return to his own land, and there I will cause him to fall by the sword.' "

8 When the commander returned to Lachish and heard that the king of Assyria had left there, he found him besieging Libnah. 9 The king of Assyria heard a report that Tirhakah, king of Ethiopia, had come out to fight against him. Again he sent envoys to Hezekiah with this message: "Thus shall you say to Hezekiah, king of Judah: 10 'Do not let your God on whom you rely deceive you by saying that Jerusalem will not be handed over to the king of Assyria. 11 You yourself have heard what the kings of Assyria have done to all the countries: They doomed them! Will you, then, be saved? 12 Did the gods of the nations whom my fathers destroyed save them? Gozen, Haran, Rezeph, and the Edenites in Telassar? 13 Where is the king of Hamath, the king of Arpad, or a king of the cities of Sepharvaim, Hena or Ivvah?' "

14 Hezekiah took the letter from the hand of the messengers and read it; then he went up to the temple of the LORD, and spreading it out before him, 15 he prayed to the LORD: 16 "O LORD of hosts, God of Israel, enthroned upon the cherubim! You alone are God over all the kingdoms of the earth. You have made the heavens and the earth. 17 Incline your ear, O LORD, and listen! Open your eyes, O LORD, and see! Hear all the words of the letter that Sennacherib sent to taunt the living God. 18 Truly, O LORD, the kings of Assyria have laid waste all the nations and their lands, 19 and cast their gods into the fire; they destroyed them because they were not gods but the work of human hands, wood and stone. 20 Therefore, O LORD, our God, save us from his hand, that all the kingdoms of the earth may know that you, O LORD, alone are God."

21 Then Isaiah, son of Amoz, sent this message to Hezekiah: Thus says the LORD, the God of Israel: In answer to your prayer for help against Sennacherib, king of Assyria, 22 this is the word the LORD has spoken concerning him:

> She despises you, laughs you to scorn,
>   the virgin daughter Zion;
> Behind you she wags her head,
>   daughter Jerusalem.
> 23 Whom have you insulted and blasphemed,
>   against whom have you raised your voice
> And lifted up your eyes on high?
>   Against the Holy One of Israel!
> 24 Through your servants you have insulted the LORD:
>   You said, "With my many chariots
> I climbed the mountain heights,
>   the recesses of Lebanon;
> I cut down its lofty cedars,
>   its choice cypresses;
> I reached the remotest heights,
>   its forest park.
> 25 I dug wells and drank water in foreign lands;
>   I dried up with the soles of my feet
>   all the rivers of Egypt."

said to them, 'Say to your master, "Yahweh says this: Do not be afraid of the words which you have heard or the blasphemies which the king of Assyria's minions have uttered against me. 7 Look, I am going to put a spirit in him and, on the strength of a rumour, he will go back to his own country, and in that country I shall make him fall by the sword." '

8 The cupbearer turned about and rejoined the king of Assyria, who was then attacking Libnah, the cupbearer having learnt that the king had already left Lachish 9 on hearing that Tirhakah king of Cush was on his way to attack him.

Sennacherib again sent messengers to Hezekiah, saying, 10 'Tell Hezekiah king of Judah this, "Do not let your God on whom you are relying deceive you with the promise: Jerusalem will not fall into the king of Assyria's clutches. 11 You have learnt by now what the kings of Assyria have done to all the other countries, putting them under the curse of destruction. Are you likely to be saved? 12 Did the gods of the nations whom my ancestors devastated save them — Gozan, Haran, Rezeph and the Edenites who were in Tel Basar? 13 Where is the king of Hamath, the king of Arpad, the king of Lair, of Sepharvaim, of Hena, of Ivvah?" '

14 Hezekiah took the letter from the messengers' hands and read it; he then went up to the Temple of Yahweh and spread it out before Yahweh. 15 Hezekiah said this prayer in the presence of Yahweh, 16 'Yahweh Sabaoth, God of Israel, enthroned on the winged creatures, you alone are God of all the kingdoms of the world, you made heaven and earth. 17 Give ear, Yahweh, and listen; open your eyes, Yahweh, and see! Hear the words of Sennacherib, who has sent to insult the living God. 18 It is true, Yahweh, that the kings of Assyria have destroyed all the nations (and their countries); 19 they have thrown their gods on the fire, for these were not gods but human artefacts — wood and stone — and hence they have destroyed them. 20 But now, Yahweh our God, save us from his clutches, I beg you, and let all the kingdoms of the world know that you alone are God, Yahweh.'

21 Isaiah son of Amoz then sent the following message to Hezekiah, 'Yahweh, God of Israel, says this, "In answer to the prayer which you have addressed to me about Sennacherib king of Assyria. 22 Here is the pronouncement which Yahweh has made about him:

> She despises you, she scorns you,
>   the virgin daughter of Zion;
> she tosses her head at you,
>   the daughter of Jerusalem!
> 23 Whom have you insulted, whom did you
>   blaspheme?
> Against whom raised your voice
>   and lifted your haughty eyes?
>   Against the Holy One of Israel.
> 24 Through your minions you have insulted the Lord,
>   thinking: With my many chariots
> I have climbed the mountain-tops,
>   the utmost peaks of Lebanon.
> I have felled its mighty cedars,
>   its finest cypresses,
> have reached its furthest peak,
>   its forest garden.
> 25 Yes, I have dug and drunk
>   of foreign waters;
> under the soles of my feet
>   I have dried up all Egypt's rivers.

NEW REVISED STANDARD VERSION	REVISED ENGLISH BIBLE

26 Have you not heard
　　that I determined it long ago?
　I planned from days of old
　　what now I bring to pass,
　that you should make fortified cities
　　crash into heaps of ruins,
27 while their inhabitants, shorn of strength,
　　are dismayed and confounded;
　they have become like plants of the field
　　and like tender grass,
　like grass on the housetops,
　　blighted[y] before it is grown.

28 I know your rising up[z] and your sitting down,
　　your going out and coming in,
　　and your raging against me.
29 Because you have raged against me
　　and your arrogance has come to my ears,
　I will put my hook in your nose
　　and my bit in your mouth;
　I will turn you back on the way
　　by which you came.

30 "And this shall be the sign for you: This year eat what grows of itself, and in the second year what springs from that; then in the third year sow, reap, plant vineyards, and eat their fruit. 31 The surviving remnant of the house of Judah shall again take root downward, and bear fruit upward; 32 for from Jerusalem a remnant shall go out, and from Mount Zion a band of survivors. The zeal of the LORD of hosts will do this.

33 "Therefore thus says the LORD concerning the king of Assyria: He shall not come into this city, shoot an arrow there, come before it with a shield, or cast up a siege ramp against it. 34 By the way that he came, by the same he shall return; he shall not come into this city, says the LORD. 35 For I will defend this city to save it, for my own sake and for the sake of my servant David."

36 Then the angel of the LORD set out and struck down one hundred eighty-five thousand in the camp of the Assyrians; when morning dawned, they were all dead bodies. 37 Then King Sennacherib of Assyria left, went home, and lived at Nineveh. 38 As he was worshiping in the house of his god Nisroch, his sons Adrammelech and Sharezer killed him with the sword, and they escaped into the land of Ararat. His son Esar-haddon succeeded him.

26 'Have you not heard?
　Long ago I did it all.
　In days gone by I planned it
　and now I have brought it about,
　till your fortified cities have crashed
　into heaps of rubble.
27 Their inhabitants, shorn of strength,
　disheartened and put to shame,
　were but as plants in the field,
　frail as green herbs,
　as grass on the rooftops blasted by the east wind.
28 I know your rising up and your sitting down,
　your going out and your coming in.
29 The frenzy of your rage against me
　and your arrogance have come to my ears.
　I shall put a ring in your nose
　and a bridle in your mouth,
　and I shall take you back
　by the way on which you came.

30 'This will be the sign for you: this year you will eat the leavings of the grain and in the second year what is self-sown; but in the third year you will sow and reap, plant vineyards and eat their fruit. 31 The survivors left in Judah will strike fresh root below ground and yield fruit above ground, 32 for a remnant will come out of Jerusalem and survivors from Mount Zion. The zeal of the LORD of Hosts will perform this.

33 'Therefore, this is the word of the LORD about the king of Assyria:

　He will not enter this city
　or shoot an arrow there;
　he will not advance against it with his shield
　or cast up a siege-ramp against it.
34 By the way he came he will go back;
　he will not enter this city.
　This is the word of the LORD.
35 I shall shield this city to deliver it
　for my own sake and for the sake of my servant
　　David.'

36 The angel of the LORD went out and struck down a hundred and eighty-five thousand men in the Assyrian camp; when morning dawned, there they all lay dead. 37 King Sennacherib of Assyria broke camp and marched away; he went back to Nineveh and remained there. 38 One day, while he was worshipping in the temple of his god Nisroch, his sons Adrammelech and Sharezer assassinated him and made their escape to the land of Ararat. His son Esarhaddon succeeded him.

38 In those days Hezekiah became sick and was at the point of death. The prophet Isaiah son of Amoz came to him, and said to him, "Thus says the LORD: Set your house in order, for you shall die; you shall not recover." 2 Then Hezekiah turned his face to the wall, and prayed to the LORD: 3 "Remember now, O LORD, I implore you, how I have walked before you in faithfulness with a whole heart, and have done what is good in your sight." And Hezekiah wept bitterly.

4 Then the word of the LORD came to Isaiah: 5 "Go and

38 At this time Hezekiah became mortally ill, and the prophet Isaiah son of Amoz came to him with this message from the LORD: 'Give your last instructions to your household, for you are dying; you will not recover.' 2 Hezekiah turned his face to the wall and offered this prayer to the LORD: 3 'LORD, remember how I have lived before you, faithful and loyal in your service, always doing what was pleasing to you.' And he wept bitterly.

4 Then the word of the LORD came to Isaiah: 5 'Go and say

---

y With 2 Kings 19.26: Heb *field*　　z Q Ms Gk: MT lacks *your rising up*

37:27 **blasted . . . east wind:** *so Scroll; Heb. obscure.*
37:28 **your rising up:** *so Scroll; Heb. omits.*　　37:29 **The frenzy . . . me:** *cp. Scroll; Heb. repeats the frenzy of your rage against me.*
38:1–8,21,22 *Cp. 2 Kgs. 20:1–11.*

NEW AMERICAN BIBLE

NEW JERUSALEM BIBLE

26 Have you not heard?
  Long ago I prepared it,
From days of old I planned it,
  now I have brought it to pass:
That you should reduce fortified cities
  into heaps of ruins,
27 While their inhabitants, shorn of power,
  are dismayed and ashamed,
Becoming like the plants of the field,
  like the green growth,
  like the scorched grass on the housetops.
28 I am aware whether you stand or sit;
  I know whether you come or go,
  and also your rage against me.
29 Because of your rage against me
  and your fury which has reached my ears,
I will put my hook in your nose
  and my bit in your mouth,
  and make you return the way you came.

30 This shall be a sign for you:
  this year you shall eat the aftergrowth,
  next year, what grows of itself;
But in the third year, sow and reap,
  plant vineyards and eat their fruit!
31 The remaining survivors of the house of Judah
  shall again strike root below
  and bear fruit above.
32 For out of Jerusalem shall come a remnant,
  and from Mount Zion, survivors.
  The zeal of the LORD of hosts shall do this.

33 Therefore, thus says the LORD concerning the king of Assyria: He shall not reach this city, nor shoot an arrow at it, nor come before it with a shield, nor cast up siegeworks against it. 34 He shall return by the same way he came, without entering the city, says the LORD. 35 I will shield and save this city for my own sake, and for the sake of my servant David.

36 The angel of the LORD went forth and struck down one hundred and eighty-five thousand in the Assyrian camp. Early the next morning, there they were, all the corpses of the dead. 37 So Sennacherib, the king of Assyria, broke camp and went back home to Nineveh.

38 When he was worshiping in the temple of his god Nisroch, his sons Adrammelech and Sharezer slew him with the sword and fled into the land of Ararat. His son Esarhaddon reigned in his stead.

26 Do you hear? Long ago
  I prepared this,
  from days of old I actually planned it,
  now I carry it out.
You were to lay walled cities
  in heaps of ruins;
27 that was why their inhabitants,
  feeble of hand,
  were dismayed and discomfited,
  were weak as grass,
  were frail as plants,
  were like grass of housetop and meadow
  under the east wind.
28 But whether you stand up or sit down,
  whether you go out or come in, I know it
  (and how you rave against me).
29 Because you have raved against me
  and your arrogance has reached my ears,
I shall put a hook through your nostrils
  and a muzzle on your lips,
  and make you return by the road
  by which you came.

30 And this will be the sign for you:
  This year will be eaten the self-sown grain,
  next year what sprouts in the fallow;
  but in the third year sow and reap,
  plant vineyards and eat their fruit.
31 The surviving remnant of the House of Judah will
  bring forth
  new roots below and fruits above;
32 for a remnant will issue from Jerusalem,
  and survivors from Mount Zion.
  Yahweh Sabaoth's jealous love will accomplish
  this."'

33 'This, then, is what Yahweh says about the king of Assyria:

He will not enter this city,
  will shoot no arrow at it,
  confront it with no shield,
  throw up no earthwork against it.
34 By the road by which he came, by that he will
  return;
  he will not enter this city, declares Yahweh.
35 I shall protect this city and save it
  for my sake and my servant David's sake.'

36 That same night the angel of Yahweh went out and struck down a hundred and eighty-five thousand men in the Assyrian camp. In the early morning when it was time to get up, there they lay, so many corpses. 37 Sennacherib struck camp and left; he returned home and stayed in Nineveh. 38 One day when he was worshipping in the temple of his god Nisroch, his sons Adrammelech and Sharezer struck him down with the sword and escaped into the territory of Ararat. His son Esarhaddon succeeded him.

38 In those days, when Hezekiah was mortally ill, the prophet Isaiah, son of Amoz, came and said to him: "Thus says the LORD: Put your house in order, for you are about to die; you shall not recover." 2 Then Hezekiah turned his face to the wall and prayed to the LORD:

3 "O LORD, remember how faithfully and wholeheartedly I conducted myself in your presence, doing what was pleasing to you!" And Hezekiah wept bitterly.

4 Then the word of the LORD came to Isaiah: 5 "Go, tell

38 About then, Hezekiah fell ill and was at the point of death. The prophet Isaiah son of Amoz came and said to him, 'Yahweh says this, "Put your affairs in order, for you are going to die, you will not live."' 2 Hezekiah turned his face to the wall and addressed this prayer to Yahweh, 3 'Ah, Yahweh, remember, I beg you, that I have behaved faithfully and with sincerity of heart in your presence and done what you regard as right.' And Hezekiah shed many tears.

4 Then the word of Yahweh came to Isaiah, 5 'Go and say

say to Hezekiah, Thus says the LORD, the God of your ancestor David: I have heard your prayer, I have seen your tears; I will add fifteen years to your life. 6 I will deliver you and this city out of the hand of the king of Assyria, and defend this city.

7 "This is the sign to you from the LORD, that the LORD will do this thing that he has promised: 8 See, I will make the shadow cast by the declining sun on the dial of Ahaz turn back ten steps." So the sun turned back on the dial the ten steps by which it had declined.*a*

9 A writing of King Hezekiah of Judah, after he had been sick and had recovered from his sickness:

10 I said: In the noontide of my days
    I must depart;
I am consigned to the gates of Sheol
    for the rest of my years.
11 I said, I shall not see the LORD
    in the land of the living;
I shall look upon mortals no more
    among the inhabitants of the world.
12 My dwelling is plucked up and removed from me
    like a shepherd's tent;
like a weaver I have rolled up my life;
    he cuts me off from the loom;
from day to night you bring me to an end;*a*
13   I cry for help*b* until morning;
like a lion he breaks all my bones;
    from day to night you bring me to an end.*a*

14 Like a swallow or a crane*a* I clamor,
    I moan like a dove.
My eyes are weary with looking upward.
    O Lord, I am oppressed; be my security!
15 But what can I say? For he has spoken to me,
    and he himself has done it.
All my sleep has fled*c*
    because of the bitterness of my soul.

16 O Lord, by these things people live,
    and in all these is the life of my spirit.*a*
    Oh, restore me to health and make me live!
17 Surely it was for my welfare
    that I had great bitterness;
but you have held back*d* my life
    from the pit of destruction,
for you have cast all my sins
    behind your back.
18 For Sheol cannot thank you,
    death cannot praise you;
those who go down to the Pit cannot hope
    for your faithfulness.
19 The living, the living, they thank you,
    as I do this day;
fathers make known to children
    your faithfulness.

20 The LORD will save me,
    and we will sing to stringed instruments*e*
all the days of our lives,
    at the house of the LORD.

21 Now Isaiah had said, "Let them take a lump of figs, and apply it to the boil, so that he may recover." 22 Hezekiah also had said, "What is the sign that I shall go up to the house of the LORD?"

---

a Meaning of Heb uncertain   *b* Cn: Meaning of Heb uncertain
c Cn Compare Syr: Heb *I will walk slowly all my years*
d Cn Compare Gk Vg: Heb *loved*   *e* Heb *my stringed instruments*

to Hezekiah: "This is the word of the LORD the God of your father David: I have heard your prayer and seen your tears; I am going to add fifteen years to your life, 6 and I shall deliver you and this city from the king of Assyria. I shall protect this city." '

21 Isaiah told them to prepare a fig-plaster; when it was made and applied to the inflammation, Hezekiah recovered. 22 He asked Isaiah what proof there was that he would go up to the house of the LORD. 7 Isaiah replied, 'This will be your proof from the LORD that he will do what he has promised: 8 I shall bring back by ten steps the shadow cast by the setting sun on the stairway of Ahaz.' And the sun went back ten steps on the stairway down which it had gone.

9 A poem written by King Hezekiah of Judah on his recovery from his illness:

10 I said, In the prime of life I must pass away;
    for the rest of my days I am consigned to the gates
      of Sheol.
11 I said, I shall no longer see the LORD
    as I did in the land of the living;
I shall no longer see my fellow-men
    as I did when I lived in the world.
12 My dwelling is taken from me,
    pulled up like a shepherd's tent;
you have rolled up my life
    like a weaver when he cuts the web from the
      thrum.
Day and night you torment me;
13 I am racked with pain till the morning.
    All my bones are broken, as if by a lion;
    day and night you torment me.
14 I twitter as if I were a swallow,
    I moan like a dove.
My eyes are raised to heaven:
    'Lord, pay heed; stand surety for me.'
15 How can I complain, what can I say to the LORD
    when he himself has done this?
I shall wander to and fro all my life long
    in bitterness of soul.
16 Yet, Lord, because of you my soul will live.
    Give my spirit rest;
    restore me and give me life.
17 Bitterness, not prosperity, had indeed been my lot,
    but your love saved me from the pit of destruction;
    for you have thrust all my sins behind you.
18 Sheol cannot confess you,
    Death cannot praise you,
nor can those who go down to the abyss
    hope for your truth.
19 The living, only the living can confess you
    as I do this day, my God,
just as a father makes your faithfulness known to
    his sons.
20 The LORD is at hand to save me;
    so let the music of our praises resound
    all our life long in the house of the LORD.

‡38.21–22: see above‡

38:6 *Verses 21,22 transposed to follow this verse; cp. 2 Kgs. 20:7,8.*
38:7 **Isaiah replied:** *prob. rdg, cp. 2 Kgs. 20:9; Heb. omits.*
38:11 **as I did when . . . world:** *so some MSS; others* when I am with those who dwell in the underworld.   38:13 **I . . . pain:** *so Scroll; Heb.* I wait.   38:14 **a swallow:** *so Gk; Heb. adds a* wryneck.   38:15 **what . . . LORD:** *prob. rdg, cp. Aram. (Targ.); Heb.* what can he say to me.   38:16 **Yet . . . rest:** *prob. rdg; Heb. unintelligible.*   38:18 **Sheol:** *or* The underworld.
38:20 *Verses 21,22 transposed to follow verse 6.*

Hezekiah: Thus says the LORD, the God of your father David: I have heard your prayer and seen your tears. I will heal you: in three days you shall go up to the LORD's temple; I will add fifteen years to your life. 6I will rescue you and this city from the hand of the king of Assyria; I will be a shield to this city."

21Isaiah then ordered a poultice of figs to be taken and applied to the boil, that he might recover. 22Then Hezekiah asked, "What is the sign that I shall go up to the temple of the LORD?"

7[Isaiah answered:] "This will be the sign for you from the LORD that he will do what he has promised: 8See, I will make the shadow cast by the sun on the stairway to the terrace of Ahaz go back the ten steps it has advanced." So the sun came back the ten steps it had advanced.

9The song of Hezekiah, king of Judah, after he had been sick and had recovered from his illness:

10Once I said,
　"In the noontime of life I must depart!
　To the gates of the nether world I shall
　　be consigned
　　for the rest of my years."
11I said, "I shall see the LORD no more
　in the land of the living.
　No longer shall I behold my fellow men
　　among those who dwell in the world."
12My dwelling, like a shepherd's tent,
　is struck down and borne away from me;
　You have folded up my life, like a weaver
　　who severs the last thread.
　Day and night you give me over to torment;
13　I cry out until the dawn.
　Like a lion he breaks all my bones;
　[day and night you give me over to torment].
14Like a swallow I utter shrill cries;
　I moan like a dove.
　My eyes grow weak, gazing heavenward:
　　O Lord, I am in straits; be my surety!
15What am I to say or tell him?
　He has done it!
　I shall go on through all my years
　　despite the bitterness of my soul.
16Those live whom the LORD protects;
　yours . . . the life of my spirit.
　You have given me health and life;
17　thus is my bitterness transformed into peace.
　You have preserved my life
　　from the pit of destruction,
　When you cast behind your back
　　all my sins.
18For it is not the nether world that gives
　　you thanks,
　nor death that praises you;
　Neither do those who go down into the pit
　　await your kindness.
19The living, the living give you thanks,
　as I do today.
　Fathers declare to their sons,
　　O God, your faithfulness.
20The LORD is our savior;
　we shall sing to stringed instruments
　In the house of the LORD
　　all the days of our life.

‡38.21–22: see above‡

to Hezekiah, "Yahweh, the God of your ancestor David, says this: I have heard your prayer and seen your tears. I shall cure you: in three days' time you will go up to the Temple of Yahweh. I shall add fifteen years to your life. 6I shall save you and this city from the king of Assyria's clutches and defend this city for my sake and my servant David's sake."

21'Bring a fig poultice,' Isaiah said, 'apply it to the ulcer and he will recover.' 22Hezekiah said, 'What is the sign to tell me that I shall be going up to the Temple of Yahweh?'ˢ 7'Here,' Isaiah replied, 'is the sign from Yahweh that he will do what he has said. 8Look, I shall make the shadow cast by the declining sun on the steps — the steps to Ahaz's roof-room — go back ten steps.' And the sun went back the ten steps by which it had declined.

9Canticle of Hezekiah king of Judah after his illness and recovery.

10I thought: In the noon of my life
　I am to depart.
　At the gates of Sheol I shall be held
　　for the rest of my days.
11I thought: I shall never see Yahweh again
　in the land of the living,
　I shall never see again a single one
　　of those who live on earth.
12My home has been pulled up, and thrown away
　like a shepherd's tent;
　like a weaver, I have rolled up my life,
　　he has cut me from the loom.
　From dawn to dark, you have been making an end
　　of me;
13till daybreak, I cried for help;
　like a lion, he has crushed all my bones,
　from dawn to dark, you have been making an end
　　of me.
14I twitter like a swallow,
　I moan like a dove,
　my eyes have grown dim from looking up.
　Lord, I am overwhelmed, come to my help.
15How can I speak and what can I say to him?
　He is the one to act.
　I must eke out the rest of my years
　　in bitterness of soul.
16The Lord is over them; they live,
　and everything in them lives by his spirit.
　You will cure me. Restore me to life.
17At once, my bitterness turns to well-being.
　For you have preserved my soul
　　from the pit of nothingness,
　you have thrust all my sins behind you.
18For Sheol cannot praise you,
　nor Death celebrate you;
　those who go down to the pit
　　can hope no longer in your constancy.
19The living, the living are the ones who praise you,
　as I do today.
　Fathers tell their sons
　　about your constancy.
20Yahweh, come to my help
　and we will make our harps resound
　all the days of our life
　　in the Temple of Yahweh.

‡38.21–22: see above‡

38, 16: Yours . . . the life of my spirit: the current Hebrew text is corrupt.

ˢ38 vv. 21–22 were misplaced when the canticle of Hezekiah was inserted. They are here restored.

39 At that time King Merodach-baladan son of Baladan of Babylon sent envoys with letters and a present to Hezekiah, for he had heard that he had been sick and had recovered. 2 Hezekiah welcomed them; he showed them his treasure house, the silver, the gold, the spices, the precious oil, his whole armory, all that was found in his storehouses. There was nothing in his house or in all his realm that Hezekiah did not show them. 3 Then the prophet Isaiah came to King Hezekiah and said to him, "What did these men say? From where did they come to you?" Hezekiah answered, "They have come to me from a far country, from Babylon." 4 He said, "What have they seen in your house?" Hezekiah answered, "They have seen all that is in my house; there is nothing in my storehouses that I did not show them."

5 Then Isaiah said to Hezekiah, "Hear the word of the Lord of hosts: 6 Days are coming when all that is in your house, and that which your ancestors have stored up until this day, shall be carried to Babylon; nothing shall be left, says the Lord. 7 Some of your own sons who are born to you shall be taken away; they shall be eunuchs in the palace of the king of Babylon." 8 Then Hezekiah said to Isaiah, "The word of the Lord that you have spoken is good." For he thought, "There will be peace and security in my days."

40 Comfort, O comfort my people,
   says your God.
2 Speak tenderly to Jerusalem,
      and cry to her
   that she has served her term,
      that her penalty is paid,
   that she has received from the Lord's hand
      double for all her sins.

3 A voice cries out:
   "In the wilderness prepare the way of the Lord,
      make straight in the desert a highway for our
         God.
4 Every valley shall be lifted up,
      and every mountain and hill be made low;
   the uneven ground shall become level,
      and the rough places a plain.
5 Then the glory of the Lord shall be revealed,
      and all people shall see it together,
   for the mouth of the Lord has spoken."

6 A voice says, "Cry out!"
      And I said, "What shall I cry?"
   All people are grass,
      their constancy is like the flower of the field.
7 The grass withers, the flower fades,
      when the breath of the Lord blows upon it;
   surely the people are grass.
8 The grass withers, the flower fades;
      but the word of our God will stand forever.
9 Get you up to a high mountain,
      O Zion, herald of good tidings;f
   lift up your voice with strength,
      O Jerusalem, herald of good tidings,g
   lift it up, do not fear;
   say to the cities of Judah,
      "Here is your God!"
10 See, the Lord God comes with might,
      and his arm rules for him;
   his reward is with him,
      and his recompense before him.

39 At that time the king of Babylon, Merodach-baladan son of Baladan, sent envoys with a gift to Hezekiah, for he heard that he had been ill. 2 Hezekiah welcomed them and showed them his treasury, the silver and gold, the spices and fragrant oil, his entire armoury and everything to be found in his storehouses; there was nothing in his palace or in his whole realm that Hezekiah did not show them. 3 The prophet Isaiah came to King Hezekiah and asked, 'What did these men say? Where did they come from?' 'They came to me from a distant country,' Hezekiah answered, 'from Babylon.' 4 'What did they see in your palace?' Isaiah demanded. 'They saw everything,' was the reply; 'there was nothing in my storehouses that I did not show them.' 5 Isaiah said to Hezekiah, 'Hear the word of the Lord of Hosts: 6 The time is coming, says the Lord, when everything in your palace, and all that your forefathers have amassed till the present day, will be carried away to Babylon; not a thing will be left. 7 And some of your sons, your own offspring, will be taken to serve as eunuchs in the palace of the king of Babylon.' 8 Hezekiah answered, 'The word of the Lord which you have spoken is good,' for he was thinking to himself that peace and security would last his lifetime.

40 Comfort my people; bring comfort to them,
   says your God;
2 speak kindly to Jerusalem
   and proclaim to her
   that her term of bondage is served,
   her penalty is paid;
   for she has received at the Lord's hand
   double measure for all her sins.

3 A voice cries:
   'Clear a road through the wilderness for the Lord,
   prepare a highway across the desert for our God.
4 Let every valley be raised,
   every mountain and hill be brought low,
   uneven ground be made smooth,
   and steep places become level.
5 Then will the glory of the Lord be revealed
   and all mankind together will see it.
   The Lord himself has spoken.'

6 A voice says, 'Proclaim!'
   and I asked, 'What shall I proclaim?'
   'All mortals are grass,
   they last no longer than a wild flower of the field.
7 The grass withers, the flower fades,
   when the blast of the Lord blows on them.
   Surely the people are grass!
8 The grass may wither, the flower fade,
   but the word of our God will endure for ever.'

9 Climb to a mountaintop,
   you that bring good news to Zion;
   raise your voice and shout aloud,
   you that carry good news to Jerusalem,
   raise it fearlessly;
   say to the cities of Judah, 'Your God is here!'
10 Here is the Lord God; he is coming in might,
   coming to rule with powerful arm.
   His reward is with him,
   his recompense before him.

39:1–8 Cp. 2 Kgs. 20:12–19.   40:2 speak . . . Jerusalem: or bid Jerusalem be of good heart.   40:9 you . . . to Zion: or Zion, bringer of good news. you that carry . . . Jerusalem: or Jerusalem, bringer of good news.

fOr O herald of good tidings to Zion   gOr O herald of good tidings to Jerusalem

NEW AMERICAN BIBLE

NEW JERUSALEM BIBLE

39 At that time when Merodach-baladan, son of Baladan, king of Babylon, heard that Hezekiah had recovered from his sickness, he sent letters and gifts to him. ²Hezekiah was pleased at this, and therefore showed the messengers his treasury, the silver and gold, the spices and fine oil, his whole armory, and everything that was in his storerooms; there was nothing in his house or in his whole realm that he did not show them.

³Then Isaiah the prophet came to King Hezekiah and asked him, "What did these men say to you? Where did they come from?" Hezekiah answered, "They came to me from a distant land, from Babylon." ⁴"What did they see in your house?" he asked. Hezekiah replied, "They saw everything in my house; there is nothing in my storerooms that I did not show them."

⁵Then Isaiah said to Hezekiah, "Hear the word of the LORD of hosts: ⁶Behold, the days shall come when all that is in your house, and everything that your fathers have stored up until this day, shall be carried off to Babylon; nothing shall be left, says the LORD. ⁷Some of your own bodily descendants shall be taken and made servants in the palace of the king of Babylon." ⁸Hezekiah replied to Isaiah, "The word of the LORD which you have spoken is favorable." For he thought, "There will be peace and security in my lifetime."

40 Comfort, give comfort to my people,
　　says your God.
²Speak tenderly to Jerusalem, and proclaim to her
　　that her service is at an end,
　　her guilt is expiated;
Indeed, she has received from the hand of
　　the LORD
　　double for all her sins.

³　　A voice cries out:
In the desert prepare the way of the LORD!
　　Make straight in the wasteland a highway for
　　our God!
⁴Every valley shall be filled in,
　　every mountain and hill shall be made low;
The rugged land shall be made a plain,
　　the rough country, a broad valley.
⁵Then the glory of the LORD shall be revealed,
　　and all mankind shall see it together;
　　for the mouth of the LORD has spoken.

⁶A voice says, "Cry out!"
　　I answer, "What shall I cry out?"
"All mankind is grass,
　　and all their glory like the flower of the field.
⁷The grass withers, the flower wilts,
　　when the breath of the LORD blows upon it.
　　[So then, the people is the grass.]
⁸Though the grass withers and the flower wilts,
　　the word of our God stands forever."

⁹Go up onto a high mountain,
　　Zion, herald of glad tidings;
Cry out at the top of your voice,
　　Jerusalem, herald of good news!
Fear not to cry out
　　and say to the cities of Judah:
　　Here is your God!
¹⁰Here comes with power
　　the Lord GOD,
　　who rules by his strong arm;
Here is your reward with him,
　　his recompense before him.

39 At that time, the king of Babylon, Merodach-Baladan son of Baladan, sent letters and a gift to Hezekiah, for he had heard of his illness and his recovery. ²Hezekiah was delighted at this and showed the ambassadors his entire treasury, the silver, gold, spices, precious oil, his armoury too, and everything to be seen in his storehouses. There was nothing in his palace or in his whole domain that Hezekiah did not show them.

³The prophet Isaiah then came to King Hezekiah and asked him, 'What have these men said, and where have they come to you from?' Hezekiah answered, 'They have come from a distant country, from Babylon.' ⁴Isaiah said, 'What have they seen in your palace?' 'They have seen everything in my palace,' Hezekiah answered. 'There is nothing in my storehouses that I have not shown them.'

⁵Then Isaiah said to Hezekiah, 'Listen to the word of Yahweh Sabaoth, ⁶"The days are coming when everything in your palace, everything that your ancestors have amassed until now, will be carried off to Babylon. Not a thing will be left," Yahweh says. ⁷"Sons sprung from you, sons begotten by you, will be abducted to be eunuchs in the palace of the king of Babylon." ' ⁸Hezekiah said to Isaiah, 'This word of Yahweh that you announce is reassuring,' for he was thinking, 'There is going to be peace and security during my lifetime.'

40 'Console[t] my people, console them,'
　　says your God.
²'Speak to the heart of Jerusalem
　　and cry to her
　　that her period of service is ended,
　　that her guilt has been atoned for,
　　that, from the hand of Yahweh, she has received
　　double punishment for all her sins.'

³A voice cries, 'Prepare in the desert
　　a way for Yahweh.
Make a straight highway for our God
　　across the wastelands.
⁴Let every valley be filled in,
　　every mountain and hill be levelled,
　　every cliff become a plateau,
　　every escarpment a plain;
⁵then the glory of Yahweh will be revealed
　　and all humanity will see it together,
　　for the mouth of Yahweh has spoken.'

⁶A voice said, 'Cry aloud!' and I said, 'What shall
　　I cry?'
　　—'All humanity is grass
　　and all its beauty like the wild flower's.
⁷The grass withers, the flower fades
　　when the breath of Yahweh blows on them.
　　(The grass is surely the people.)
⁸The grass withers, the flower fades,
　　but the word of our God remains for ever.'

⁹Go up on a high mountain,
　　messenger of Zion.
Shout as loud as you can,
　　messenger of Jerusalem!
Shout fearlessly,
　　say to the towns of Judah,
　　'Here is your God.'
¹⁰Here is Lord Yahweh coming with power,
　　his arm maintains his authority,
　　his reward is with him
　　and his prize precedes him.[u]

---

[t]**40** Hence the title of this second part of Isaiah, 'The Book of the Consolation of Israel'.　[u]**40** = 62:11.

11 He will feed his flock like a shepherd;
   he will gather the lambs in his arms,
   and carry them in his bosom,
   and gently lead the mother sheep.

12 Who has measured the waters in the hollow of
   his hand
   and marked off the heavens with a span,
   enclosed the dust of the earth in a measure,
   and weighed the mountains in scales
   and the hills in a balance?
13 Who has directed the spirit of the LORD,
   or as his counselor has instructed him?
14 Whom did he consult for his enlightenment,
   and who taught him the path of justice?
   Who taught him knowledge,
   and showed him the way of understanding?
15 Even the nations are like a drop from a bucket,
   and are accounted as dust on the scales;
   see, he takes up the isles like fine dust.
16 Lebanon would not provide fuel enough,
   nor are its animals enough for a burnt offering.
17 All the nations are as nothing before him;
   they are accounted by him as less than nothing
   and emptiness.

18 To whom then will you liken God,
   or what likeness compare with him?
19 An idol? —A workman casts it,
   and a goldsmith overlays it with gold,
   and casts for it silver chains.
20 As a gift one chooses mulberry wood*h*
   —wood that will not rot—
   then seeks out a skilled artisan
   to set up an image that will not topple.

21 Have you not known? Have you not heard?
   Has it not been told you from the beginning?
   Have you not understood from the foundations
   of the earth?
22 It is he who sits above the circle of the earth,
   and its inhabitants are like grasshoppers;
   who stretches out the heavens like a curtain,
   and spreads them like a tent to live in;
23 who brings princes to naught.
   and makes the rulers of the earth as nothing.

24 Scarcely are they planted, scarcely sown,
   scarcely has their stem taken root in the earth,
   when he blows upon them, and they wither,
   and the tempest carries them off like stubble.
25 To whom then will you compare me,
   or who is my equal? says the Holy One.
26 Lift up your eyes on high and see:
   Who created these?
   He who brings out their host and numbers them,
   calling them all by name;
   because he is great in strength,
   mighty in power,
   not one is missing.

11 Like a shepherd he will tend his flock
   and with his arm keep them together;
   he will carry the lambs in his bosom
   and lead the ewes to water.

12 WHO has measured the waters of the sea in the
   hollow of his hand,
   or with its span gauged the heavens?
   Who has held all the soil of the earth in a bushel,
   or weighed the mountains on a balance,
   the hills on a pair of scales?
13 Who has directed the spirit of the LORD?
   What counsellor stood at his side to instruct him?
14 With whom did he confer to gain discernment?
   Who taught him this path of justice,
   or taught him knowledge,
   or showed him the way of wisdom?
15 To him nations are but drops from a bucket,
   no more than moisture on the scales;
   to him coasts and islands weigh as light as specks
   of dust!
16 Lebanon does not yield wood enough for fuel,
   beasts enough for a whole-offering.
17 All the nations are as naught in his sight;
   he reckons them as less than nothing.

18 What likeness, then, will you find for God
   or what form to resemble his?
19 An image which a craftsman makes,
   and a goldsmith overlays with gold
   and fits with studs of silver?
20 Or should someone choose mulberry-wood,
   a wood that does not rot,
   and seek out a skilful craftsman for the task
   of setting up an image and making it secure?

[6] Each workman helps his comrade,
   each encourages his fellow.
[7] The craftsman encourages the goldsmith,
   the gilder him who strikes the anvil;
   he declares the soldering to be sound,
   and fastens the image with nails
   so that it will remain secure.

21 Do you not know, have you not heard,
   were you not told long ago,
   have you not perceived ever since the world was
   founded,
22 that God sits enthroned on the vaulted roof of the
   world,
   and its inhabitants appear as grasshoppers?
   He stretches out the skies like a curtain,
   spreads them out like a tent to live in;
23 he reduces the great to naught
   and makes earthly rulers as nothing.
24 Scarcely are they planted, scarcely sown,
   scarcely have they taken root in the ground,
   before he blows on them and they wither,
   and a whirlwind carries them off like chaff.
25 To whom, then, will you liken me,
   whom set up as my equal?
   asks the Holy One.
26 Lift up your eyes to the heavens;
   consider who created these,
   led out their host one by one,
   and summoned each by name.
   Through his great might, his strength and power,
   not one is missing.

---

h Meaning of Heb uncertain

40:20 **mulberry-wood:** *prob. rdg; Heb. adds* a contribution. *Verses
6 and 7 of ch. 41 are transposed to follow this verse.*

NEW AMERICAN BIBLE

11 Like a shepherd he feeds his flock;
   in his arms he gathers the lambs,
Carrying them in his bosom,
   and leading the ewes with care.
12 Who has cupped in his hand the waters of the sea,
   and marked off the heavens with a span?
Who has held in a measure the dust of the earth,
   weighed the mountains in scales
   and the hills in a balance?
13 Who has directed the spirit of the LORD,
   or has instructed him as his counselor?
14 Whom did he consult to gain knowledge?
   Who taught him the path of judgment,
   or showed him the way of understanding?
15 Behold, the nations count as a drop of the bucket,
   as dust on the scales;
   the coastlands weigh no more than powder.
16 Lebanon would not suffice for fuel,
   nor its animals be enough for holocausts.
17 Before him all the nations are as nought,
   as nothing and void he accounts them.
18 To whom can you liken God?
   With what equal can you confront him?
19 An idol, cast by a craftsman,
   which the smith plates with gold
   and fits with silver chains?
20 Mulberry wood, the choice portion
   which a skilled craftsman picks out for himself,
Choosing timber that will not rot,
   to set up an idol that will not be unsteady?
41. 6 One man helps another,
   one says to the other, "Keep on!"
41. 7 The craftsman encourages the goldsmith,
   the one who beats with the hammer, him who
      strikes on the anvil;
He says the soldering is good,
   and he fastens it with nails to steady it.
21 Do you not know? Have you not heard?
   Was it not foretold you from the beginning?
Have you not understood? Since the earth
      was founded
22 He sits enthroned above the vault of the earth,
   and its inhabitants are like grasshoppers;
He stretches out the heavens like a veil,
   spreads them out like a tent to dwell in.
23 He brings princes to nought
   and makes the rulers of the earth as nothing.
24 Scarcely are they planted or sown,
   scarcely is their stem rooted in the earth,
When he breathes upon them and they wither,
   and the stormwind carries them away like straw.
25 To whom can you liken me as an equal?
   says the Holy One.
26 Lift up your eyes on high
   and see who has created these:
He leads out their army and numbers them,
   calling them all by name.
By his great might and the strength of his power
   not one of them is missing!

NEW JERUSALEM BIBLE

11 He is like a shepherd feeding his flock,
   gathering lambs in his arms,
   holding them against his breast
   and leading to their rest the mother ewes.
12 Who was it measured the water of the sea in the
      hollow of his hand
   and calculated the heavens to the nearest inch,
   gauged the dust of the earth to the nearest bushel,
   weighed the mountains in scales,
   the hills in a balance?
13 Who directed the spirit of Yahweh,
   what counsellor could have instructed him?
14 Whom has he consulted to enlighten him,
   to instruct him in the path of judgement,
   to teach him knowledge
   and show him how to understand?
15 See, the nations are like a drop in a bucket,
   they count as a grain of dust on the scales.
See, coasts and islands weigh no more than fine
      powder.
16 The Lebanon is not enough for the burning fires
   nor its animals enough for the burnt offering.
17 All the nations are as nothing before him,
   for him they count as nothingness and emptiness.
18 To whom can you compare God?
   What image can you contrive of him?
19 The craftsman casts an idol,
   a goldsmith overlays it with gold
   and casts silver chains for it.
20 Someone too poor to afford a sacrifice
   chooses a piece of wood that will not rot;
   he then seeks out a skilled craftsman
   to set up an idol that will not totter.

21 Did you not know,
   had you not heard?
Was it not told you from the beginning?
Have you not understood how the earth was set on
      its foundations?
22 He who sits enthroned above the circle of the
      earth,
   the inhabitants of which are like grasshoppers,
   stretches out the heavens like a cloth,
   spreads them out like a tent to live in.
23 He reduces princes to nothing,
   the rulers of the world to mere emptiness.
24 Scarcely are they planted, scarcely sown,
   scarcely has their stem taken root in the soil,
   than he blows on them and they wither
   and the storm carries them away like chaff.
25 'To whom can you compare me,
   or who is my equal?' says the Holy One.
26 Lift your eyes and look:
   he who created these things
   leads out their army in order,
   summoning each of them by name.
So mighty is his power, so great his strength,
   that not one fails to answer.

41, 6–7: These two verses have been transposed from chap. 41.

NEW REVISED STANDARD VERSION	REVISED ENGLISH BIBLE

NEW REVISED STANDARD VERSION

27 Why do you say, O Jacob,
    and speak, O Israel,
"My way is hidden from the LORD,
    and my right is disregarded by my God"?
28 Have you not known? Have you not heard?
The LORD is the everlasting God,
    the Creator of the ends of the earth.
He does not faint or grow weary;
    his understanding is unsearchable.
29 He gives power to the faint,
    and strengthens the powerless.
30 Even youths will faint and be weary,
    and the young will fall exhausted;
31 but those who wait for the LORD shall renew their
    strength,
they shall mount up with wings like eagles,
they shall run and not be weary,
    they shall walk and not faint.

41 Listen to me in silence, O coastlands;
    let the peoples renew their strength;
let them approach, then let them speak;
    let us together draw near for judgment.

2 Who has roused a victor from the east,
    summoned him to his service?
He delivers up nations to him,
    and tramples kings under foot;
he makes them like dust with his sword,
    like driven stubble with his bow.
3 He pursues them and passes on safely,
    scarcely touching the path with his feet.
4 Who has performed and done this,
    calling the generations from the beginning?
I, the LORD, am first,
    and will be with the last.
5 The coastlands have seen and are afraid,
    the ends of the earth tremble;
    they have drawn near and come.
6 Each one helps the other,
    saying to one another, "Take courage!"
7 The artisan encourages the goldsmith,
    and the one who smooths with the hammer
        encourages the one who strikes the anvil,
saying of the soldering, "It is good";
    and they fasten it with nails so that it cannot be
    moved.
8 But you, Israel, my servant,
    Jacob, whom I have chosen,
    the offspring of Abraham, my friend;
9 you whom I took from the ends of the earth,
    and called from its farthest corners,
saying to you, "You are my servant,
    I have chosen you and not cast you off";
10 do not fear, for I am with you,
    do not be afraid, for I am your God;
I will strengthen you, I will help you,
    I will uphold you with my victorious right
    hand.

11 Yes, all who are incensed against you
    shall be ashamed and disgraced;
those who strive against you
    shall be as nothing and shall perish.
12 You shall seek those who contend with you,
    but you shall not find them;
those who war against you
    shall be as nothing at all.

REVISED ENGLISH BIBLE

27 Jacob, why do you complain,
    and you, Israel, why do you say,
'My lot is hidden from the LORD,
    my cause goes unheeded by my God'?
28 Do you not know, have you not heard?
The LORD, the eternal God,
    creator of earth's farthest bounds,
does not weary or grow faint;
    his understanding cannot be fathomed.
29 He gives vigour to the weary,
    new strength to the exhausted.
30 Young men may grow weary and faint,
    even the fittest may stumble and fall;
31 but those who look to the LORD will win new
    strength,
they will soar as on eagles' wings;
they will run and not feel faint,
    march on and not grow weary.

41 Listen in silence to me, all you coasts and
    islands;
let the peoples come to meet me.
Let them draw near, then let them speak up;
together we shall go to the place of judgement.

2 Who has raised up from the east
one greeted by victory wherever he goes,
making nations his subjects
and overthrowing their kings?
He scatters them with his sword like dust
and with his bow like chaff driven before the wind;
3 he puts them to flight and passes on unscathed,
swifter than any traveller on foot.
4 Whose work is this, who has brought it to pass?
Who has summoned the generations from the
    beginning?
I, the LORD, was with the first of them,
    and I am with those who come after.
5 Coasts and islands saw it and were afraid,
the world trembled from end to end.

‡41.6–7: see above in ch. 40‡

8 But you, Israel my servant,
Jacob whom I have chosen,
descendants of my friend Abraham,
9 I have taken you from the ends of the earth,
and summoned you from its farthest corners;
I have called you my servant,
have chosen you and not rejected you:
10 have no fear, for I am with you,
be not afraid, for I am your God.
I shall strengthen you and give you help
and uphold you with my victorious right hand.

11 Now all who defy you
will be confounded and put to shame;
all who set themselves against you
will be as nothing and will vanish.
12 You will look for your assailants
but you will not find them;
those who take up arms against you
will be reduced to nothing.

41:1 **come to meet me:** *prob. rdg, transposed, with slight change,
from end of verse 5; Heb.* win new strength *(repeated from 40:31).*
41:5 *See note on verse 1.*   41:8 *Verses 6 and 7 transposed to
follow 40:20.*

27 Why, O Jacob, do you say,
   and declare, O Israel,
   "My way is hidden from the LORD,
      and my right is disregarded by my God"?
28 Do you not know
      or have you not heard?
   The LORD is the eternal God,
      creator of the ends of the earth.
   He does not faint nor grow weary,
      and his knowledge is beyond scrutiny.
29 He gives strength to the fainting;
      for the weak he makes vigor abound.
30 Though young men faint and grow weary,
      and youths stagger and fall,
31 They that hope in the LORD will renew
      their strength,
   they will soar as with eagles' wings;
   They will run and not grow weary,
      walk and not grow faint.

41 Keep silence before me, O coastlands;
      you peoples, wait for my words!
   Let them draw near and speak;
      let us come together for judgment.

2 Who has stirred up from the East the champion
      of justice,
   and summoned him to be his attendant?
   To him he delivers the nations
      and subdues the kings;
   With his sword he reduces them to dust,
      with his bow, to driven straw.
3 He pursues them, passing on without loss,
      by a path his feet do not even tread.
4 Who has performed these deeds?
   He who has called forth the generations since the
      beginning.

   I, the LORD, am the first,
      and with the last I will also be.
5 The coastlands see, and fear;
      the ends of the earth tremble.
   these things are near, they come to pass.

‡41.6–7: see above in ch. 40‡

8 But you, Israel, my servant,
   Jacob, whom I have chosen,
      offspring of Abraham my friend —
9 You whom I have taken from the ends of the earth
      and summoned from its far-off places,
   You whom I have called my servant,
      whom I have chosen and will not cast off —
10 Fear not, I am with you;
      be not dismayed; I am your God.
   I will strengthen you, and help you,
      and uphold you with my right hand of justice.
11 Yes, all shall be put to shame and disgrace
      who vent their anger against you;
   Those shall perish and come to nought
      who offer resistance.
12 You shall seek out, but shall not find,
      those who strive against you;
   They shall be as nothing at all
      who do battle with you.

27 How can you say, Jacob, how can you repeat,
      Israel,
   'My way is hidden from Yahweh,
      my rights are ignored by my God'?
28 Did you not know? Had you not heard?
   Yahweh is the everlasting God,
   he created the remotest parts of the earth.
   He does not grow tired or weary,
      his understanding is beyond fathoming.
29 He gives strength to the weary,
      he strengthens the powerless.
30 Youths grow tired and weary,
      the young stumble and fall,
31 but those who hope in Yahweh will regain their
      strength,
   they will sprout wings like eagles,
   though they run they will not grow weary,
      though they walk they will never tire.

41 Coasts and islands, fall silent before me,
      and let the peoples renew their strength,
   let them come forward and speak;
      let us assemble for judgement.
2 'Who has raised from the east
   him whom saving justice summons in its train,
   him to whom Yahweh delivers up the nations
      and subjects kings,
   him who reduces them to dust with his sword,
      and to driven stubble with his bow,
3 him who pursues them and advances unhindered,
      his feet scarcely touching the road?
4 Who has acted thus, who has done this?
   He who calls each generation from the beginning:
   I, Yahweh, who am the first
      and till the last I shall still be there.'
5 The coasts and islands have seen and taken fright,
      the remotest parts of earth are trembling:
   they are approaching, they are here!
6 People help one another,
      they say to each other, 'Take heart!'
7 The woodworker encourages the smelter,
      the polisher encourages the hammerer,
   saying of the soldering, 'It is sound';
   and he fastens it with nails
      to keep it steady.

8 But you, Israel, my servant,
   Jacob whom I have chosen,
      descendant of Abraham my friend,
9 whom I have taken to myself, from the remotest
      parts of the earth
   and summoned from countries far away,
   to whom I have said, 'You are my servant,
   I have chosen you, I have not rejected you,'
10 do not be afraid, for I am with you;
      do not be alarmed, for I am your God.
   I give you strength, truly I help you,
      truly I hold you firm with my saving right hand.
11 Look, all those who rage against you
      will be put to shame and humiliated;
   those who picked quarrels with you
      will be reduced to nothing and will perish.
12 You will look for them but will not find them,
      those who used to fight you;
   they will be destroyed and brought to nothing,
      those who made war on you.

13 For I, the LORD your God,
    hold your right hand;
    it is I who say to you, "Do not fear,
    I will help you."

14 Do not fear, you worm Jacob,
        you insect*i* Israel!
    I will help you, says the LORD;
        your Redeemer is the Holy One of Israel.

15 Now, I will make of you a threshing sledge,
        sharp, new, and having teeth;
    you shall thresh the mountains and crush them,
        and you shall make the hills like chaff.

16 You shall winnow them and the wind shall carry
            them away,
        and the tempest shall scatter them.
    Then you shall rejoice in the LORD;
        in the Holy One of Israel you shall glory.

17 When the poor and needy seek water,
        and there is none,
    and their tongue is parched with thirst,
    I the LORD will answer them,
        I the God of Israel will not forsake them.

18 I will open rivers on the bare heights, *j*
        and fountains in the midst of the valleys;
    I will make the wilderness a pool of water,
        and the dry land springs of water.

19 I will put in the wilderness the cedar,
        the acacia, the myrtle, and the olive;
    I will set in the desert the cypress,
        the plane and the pine together,

20 so that all may see and know,
        all may consider and understand,
    that the hand of the LORD has done this,
        the Holy One of Israel has created it.

21 Set forth your case, says the LORD;
        bring your proofs, says the King of Jacob.

22 Let them bring them, and tell us
        what is to happen.
    Tell us the former things, what they are,
        so that we may consider them,
    and that we may know their outcome;
        or declare to us the things to come.

23 Tell us what is to come hereafter,
        that we may know that you are gods;
    do good, or do harm,
        that we may be afraid and terrified.

24 You, indeed, are nothing
        and your work is nothing at all;
    whoever chooses you is an abomination.

25 I stirred up one from the north, and he has come,
        from the rising of the sun he was summoned
            by name. *k*
    He shall trample*l* on rulers as on mortar,
        as the potter treads clay.

26 Who declared it from the beginning, so that we
            might know,
        and beforehand, so that we might say, "He is
            right"?
    There was no one who declared it, none who
            proclaimed,
        none who heard your words.

27 I first have declared it to Zion,*m*
        and I give to Jerusalem a herald of good
            tidings.

13 For I, the LORD your God,
    take you by the right hand
    and say to you, Have no fear;
    it is I who help you.

14 Have no fear, Jacob you worm and Israel you
            maggot.
    It is I who help you, declares the LORD;
        your redeemer is the Holy One of Israel.

15 See, I shall make of you a sharp threshing-sledge,
        new and studded with teeth;
    you will thresh mountains and crush them to dust
        and reduce the hills to chaff;

16 you will winnow them; the wind will carry them
            away
        and a gale will scatter them.
    Then you will rejoice in the LORD
        and glory in the Holy One of Israel.

17 The poor and the needy look for water and find
            none;
        their tongues are parched with thirst.
    But I the LORD shall provide for their wants;
        I, the God of Israel, shall not forsake them.

18 I shall open rivers on the arid heights,
        and wells in the valleys;
    I shall turn the desert into pools
        and dry land into springs of water;

19 I shall plant cedars in the wilderness,
        acacias, myrtles, and wild olives;
    I shall grow pines on the barren heath
        side by side with fir and box tree,

20 that everyone may see and know,
        may once for all observe and understand
    that the LORD himself has done this:
        it is the creation of the Holy One of Israel.

21 Come, open your plea, says the LORD,
        present your case, says Jacob's King;

22 let these idols come forward
        and foretell the future for us.
    Let them declare the meaning of these past events
        that we may reflect on it;
    let them predict the future to us
        that we may know what it holds.

23 Declare what is yet to happen;
        then we shall know you are gods.
    Do something, whether good or bad,
        anything that will strike us with dismay and fear.

24 You cannot! You are sprung from nothing,
        your works are non-existent.
    To choose you is outrageous!

25 I roused one from the north, and he has come;
        I called from the east one summoned in my name;
    he marches over rulers as if they were mud,
        like a potter treading clay.

26 Who has declared this from the beginning,
        that we might know it,
    or told us beforehand
        so that we might say, 'He was right'?
    Not one of you declared, not one foretold,
        no one heard a sound from you.

27 I am the first to appoint a messenger to Zion,
        a bringer of good news to Jerusalem.

---

i Syr: Heb *men of*   *j* Or *trails*   *k* Cn Compare Q Ms Gk: MT *and
he shall call on my name*   *l* Cn: Heb *come*   *m* Cn: Heb *First to
Zion—Behold, behold them*

13 For I am the LORD, your God,
  who grasp your right hand;
It is I who say to you, "Fear not,
  I will help you."
14 Fear not, O worm Jacob,
  O maggot Israel;
I will help you, says the LORD;
  your redeemer is the Holy One of Israel.
15 I will make of you a threshing sledge,
  sharp, new, and double-edged,
To thresh the mountains and crush them,
  to make the hills like chaff.
16 When you winnow them, the wind shall carry
    them off
  and the storm shall scatter them.
But you shall rejoice in the LORD,
  and glory in the Holy One of Israel.
17 The afflicted and the needy seek water in vain,
  their tongues are parched with thirst.
I, the LORD, will answer them;
  I, the God of Israel, will not forsake them.
18 I will open up rivers on the bare heights,
  and fountains in the broad valleys;
I will turn the desert into a marshland,
  and the dry ground into springs of water.
19 I will plant in the desert the cedar,
  acacia, myrtle, and olive;
I will set in the wasteland the cypress,
  together with the plane tree and the pine,
20 That all may see and know,
  observe and understand,
That the hand of the LORD has done this,
  the Holy One of Israel has created it.

21 Present your case, says the LORD;
  bring forward your reasons, says the King
    of Jacob.
22 Let them come near and foretell to us
  what it is that shall happen!
What are the things of long ago?
  Tell us, that we may reflect on them
And know their outcome;
  or declare to us the things to come!
23 Foretell the things that shall come afterward,
  that we may know that you are gods!
Do something, good or evil,
  that will put us in awe and in fear.
24 Why, you are nothing and your work is nought!
  To choose you is an abomination.
25 I have stirred up one from the north, and
    he comes;
  from the east I summon him by name;
He shall trample the rulers down like red earth,
  as the potter treads the clay.
26 Who announced this from the beginning, that we
    might know;
  beforehand, that we might say it is true?
Not one of you foretold it, not one spoke;
  no one heard you say,
27 "The first news for Zion: they are coming now,"
  or, "For Jerusalem I will pick out a bearer of the
    glad tidings."

13 For I, Yahweh, your God,
  I grasp you by your right hand;
I tell you, 'Do not be afraid,
  I shall help you.'
14 Do not be afraid, Jacob, you worm!
  You little handful of Israel!
I shall help you, declares Yahweh;
  your redeemer[v] is the Holy One of Israel.
15 Look, I am making you into a threshing-sledge,
  new, with double teeth;
you will thresh and beat the mountains to dust
  and reduce the hills to straw.
16 You will winnow them and the wind will carry
    them off,
  the gale will scatter them;
whereas you will rejoice in Yahweh,
  will glory in the Holy One of Israel.
17 The oppressed and needy search for water, and
    there is none,
  their tongue is parched with thirst.
I, Yahweh, shall answer them,
  I, the God of Israel, shall not abandon them.
18 I shall open up rivers on barren heights
  and water-holes down in the ravines;
I shall turn the desert into a lake
  and dry ground into springs of water.
19 I shall plant the desert with cedar trees,
  acacias, myrtles and olives;
in the wastelands I shall put cypress trees,
  plane trees and box trees side by side;
20 so that people may see and know,
  so that they may all observe and understand
that the hand of Yahweh has done this,
  that the Holy One of Israel has created it.

21 'Present your case,' says Yahweh,
  'Produce your arguments,' says Jacob's king.
22 'Let them produce and reveal to us
  what is going to happen.
What happened in the past?
  Reveal it so that we can consider it
and know what the outcome will be.
  Or tell us about the future,
23 reveal what is to happen next,
  and then we shall know that you are gods.
At least, do something, be it good or bad,
  so that we may feel alarm and fear.
24 Look, you are less than nothingness,
  and what you do is less than nothing;
to choose you is an outrage.'
25 I have raised him from the north and he has come,
  from the east he has been summoned by name.
He tramples on rulers like mud,
  like a potter treading clay.
26 Who revealed this from the beginning for us to
    know,
  and in the past for us to say, 'That is right'?
No one in fact revealed it, no one proclaimed it,
  no one has heard you speak.
27 First-fruits of Zion, look, here they come!
  I send a messenger to Jerusalem,

―――――――

[v] 41 The go'el, the closest relative, defender and avenger of blood,
often used of Yahweh in the Pss.

NEW REVISED STANDARD VERSION

28 But when I look there is no one;
   among these there is no counselor
   who, when I ask, gives an answer.
29 No, they are all a delusion;
   their works are nothing;
   their images are empty wind.

42

Here is my servant, whom I uphold,
   my chosen, in whom my soul delights;
I have put my spirit upon him;
   he will bring forth justice to the nations.
2 He will not cry or lift up his voice,
   or make it heard in the street;
3 a bruised reed he will not break,
   and a dimly burning wick he will not quench;
   he will faithfully bring forth justice.
4 He will not grow faint or be crushed
   until he has established justice in the earth;
   and the coastlands wait for his teaching.

5 Thus says God, the LORD,
   who created the heavens and stretched them
      out,
   who spread out the earth and what comes from
      it,
who gives breath to the people upon it
   and spirit to those who walk in it:
6 I am the LORD, I have called you in
      righteousness,
   I have taken you by the hand and kept you;
I have given you as a covenant to the people,[n]
   a light to the nations,
7   to open the eyes that are blind,
to bring out the prisoners from the dungeon,
   from the prison those who sit in darkness.
8 I am the LORD, that is my name;
   my glory I give to no other,
   nor my praise to idols.
9 See, the former things have come to pass,
   and new things I now declare;
before they spring forth,
   I tell you of them.

10 Sing to the LORD a new song,
   his praise from the end of the earth!
Let the sea roar[o] and all that fills it,
   the coastlands and their inhabitants.
11 Let the desert and its towns lift up their voice,
   the villages that Kedar inhabits;
let the inhabitants of Sela sing for joy,
   let them shout from the tops of the mountains.
12 Let them give glory to the LORD,
   and declare his praise in the coastlands.
13 The LORD goes forth like a soldier,
   like a warrior he stirs up his fury;
he cries out, he shouts aloud,
   he shows himself mighty against his foes.

14 For a long time I have held my peace,
   I have kept still and restrained myself;
now I will cry out like a woman in labor,
   I will gasp and pant.
15 I will lay waste mountains and hills,
   and dry up all their herbage;
I will turn the rivers into islands,
   and dry up the pools.

REVISED ENGLISH BIBLE

28 When I look round there is no one,
   and among these gods no one to give counsel;
   I ask a question and no one can answer.
29 What empty things they all are!
   Nothing they do amounts to anything,
   their effigies are so much wind, mere nothings.

42

Here is my servant, whom I uphold,
   my chosen one, in whom I take delight!
I have put my spirit on him;
   he will establish justice among the nations.
2 He will not shout or raise his voice,
   or make himself heard in the street.
3 He will not break a crushed reed
   or snuff out a smouldering wick;
   unfailingly he will establish justice.
4 He will never falter or be crushed
   until he sets justice on earth,
   while coasts and islands await his teaching.

5 These are the words of the LORD who is God,
   who created the heavens and stretched them out,
   who fashioned the earth
   and everything that grows in it,
   giving breath to its people
   and life to those who walk on it:
6 I the LORD have called you with righteous purpose
   and taken you by the hand;
   I have formed you, and destined you
   to be a light for peoples,
   a lamp for nations,[a]
7 to open eyes that are blind,
   to bring captives out of prison,
   out of the dungeon where they lie in darkness.
8 I am the LORD; the LORD is my name;
   I shall not yield my glory to another god,
   nor my praise to any idol.
9 The earlier prophecies have come to pass,
   and now I declare new things;
   before they unfold, I announce them to you.

10 Sing a new song to the LORD,
   sing his praise throughout the world,
   you that sail the broad seas,
   and you that inhabit the coasts and islands.
11 Let the wilderness and its settlements rejoice,
   and the encampments where Kedar lives.
   Let the inhabitants of Sela shout for joy,
   let them cry out from the hilltops.
12 Let the coasts and islands ascribe glory to the
      LORD;
   let them sing his praise.
13 The LORD will go forth as a warrior,
   a soldier roused to the fury of battle;
   he will shout, he will raise the battle cry
   and triumph over his foes.

14 Long have I restrained myself,
   I kept silence and held myself in check;
   now I groan like a woman in labour,
   panting and gasping.
15 I shall lay waste mountain and hill
   and shrivel up all their herbage.
   I shall change rivers into desert wastes
   and dry up every pool.

---

[n] Meaning of Heb uncertain   [o] Cn Compare Ps 96.11; 98.7: Heb
Those who go down to the sea

42:6 **a light:** *or* a covenant.   42:15 **desert wastes:** *prob. rdg;*
Heb. coasts and islands.

NEW AMERICAN BIBLE

28 When I look, there is not one,
no one of them to give counsel,
to make an answer when I question them.
29 Ah, all of them are nothing,
their works are nought,
their idols are empty wind!

42 Here is my servant whom I uphold,
my chosen one with whom I am pleased,
Upon whom I have put my spirit;
he shall bring forth justice to the nations,
2 Not crying out, not shouting,
not making his voice heard in the street.
3 A bruised reed he shall not break,
and a smoldering wick he shall not quench,
4 Until he establishes justice on the earth;
the coastlands will wait for his teaching.

5 Thus says God, the LORD,
who created the heavens and stretched them out,
who spreads out the earth with its crops,
Who gives breath to its people
and spirit to those who walk on it:
6 I, the LORD, have called you for the victory
of justice,
I have grasped you by the hand;
I formed you, and set you
as a covenant of the people,
a light for the nations,
7 To open the eyes of the blind,
to bring out prisoners from confinement,
and from the dungeon, those who live
in darkness.
8 I am the LORD, this is my name;
my glory I give to no other,
nor my praise to idols.
9 See, the earlier things have come to pass,
new ones I now foretell;
Before they spring into being,
I announce them to you.

10 Sing to the LORD a new song,
his praise from the end of the earth:
Let the sea and what fills it resound,
the coastlands, and those who dwell in them.
11 Let the steppe and its cities cry out,
the villages where Kedar dwells;
Let the inhabitants of Sela exult,
and shout from the top of the mountains.
12 Let them give glory to the LORD,
and utter his praise in the coastlands.
13 The LORD goes forth like a hero,
like a warrior he stirs up his ardor;
He shouts out his battle cry,
against his enemies he shows his might:
14 I have looked away, and kept silence,
I have said nothing, holding myself in;
But now, I cry out as a woman in labor,
gasping and panting.
15 I will lay waste mountains and hills,
all their herbage I will dry up;
I will turn the rivers into marshes,
and the marshes I will dry up.

NEW JERUSALEM BIBLE

28 and I look — no one,
not a single counsellor among them
who, if I asked, could give an answer.
29 Taken altogether they are nothingness,
what they do is nothing,
their statues, wind and emptiness.

42 Here is my servant[w] whom I uphold,
my chosen one in whom my soul delights.
I have sent my spirit upon him,
he will bring fair judgement to the nations.
2 He does not cry out or raise his voice,
his voice is not heard in the street;
3 he does not break the crushed reed
or snuff the faltering wick.
Faithfully he presents fair judgement;
4 he will not grow faint, he will not be crushed
until he has established fair judgement on earth,
and the coasts and islands are waiting for his
instruction.
5 Thus says God, Yahweh,
who created the heavens and spread them out,
who hammered into shape the earth and what
comes from it,
who gave breath to the people on it,
and spirit to those who walk on it:
6 I, Yahweh, have called you in saving justice,
I have grasped you by the hand and shaped you;
I have made you a covenant of the people
and light to the nations,
7 to open the eyes of the blind,
to free captives from prison,
and those who live in darkness from the dungeon.
8 I am Yahweh, that is my name!
I shall not yield my glory to another,
nor my honour to idols.
9 See how the former predictions have come true.
Fresh things I now reveal;
before they appear I tell you of them.

10 Sing a new song to Yahweh!
Let his praise be sung from remotest parts of the
earth
by those who sail the sea and by everything in it,
by the coasts and islands and those who inhabit
them.
11 Let the desert and its cities raise their voices,
the encampments where Kedar lives.
Let the inhabitants of the Rock cry aloud for joy
and shout from the mountain tops.
12 Let them give glory to Yahweh
and, in the coasts and islands, let them voice his
praise.
13 Yahweh advances like a hero,
like a warrior he rouses his fire.
He shouts, he raises the war cry,
he shows his might against his foes.
14 'From long ago I have been silent,
I have kept quiet, held myself in check,
groaning like a woman in labour,
panting and gasping for air.
15 I shall ravage mountain and hill,
shall wither all their vegetation;
I shall turn the torrents into firm ground
and dry up the marshes.

w **42** The first of the four Songs of the Servant (42:1–9; 49:1–6;
50:4–11; 52:13–53:12).

NEW REVISED STANDARD VERSION	REVISED ENGLISH BIBLE

16 I will lead the blind
　by a road they do not know,
by paths they have not known
　I will guide them.
I will turn the darkness before them into light,
　the rough places into level ground.
These are the things I will do,
　and I will not forsake them.
17 They shall be turned back and utterly put to
　　　shame—
　those who trust in carved images,
who say to cast images,
　"You are our gods."

18 Listen, you that are deaf;
　and you that are blind, look up and see!
19 Who is blind but my servant,
　or deaf like my messenger whom I send?
Who is blind like my dedicated one,
　or blind like the servant of the LORD?
20 He sees many things, but does^p not observe
　　　them;
　his ears are open, but he does not hear.
21 The LORD was pleased, for the sake of his
　　　righteousness,
　to magnify his teaching and make it glorious.
22 But this is a people robbed and plundered,
　all of them are trapped in holes
　and hidden in prisons;
they have become a prey with no one to rescue,
　a spoil with no one to say, "Restore!"
23 Who among you will give heed to this,
　who will attend and listen for the time to
　　　come?
24 Who gave up Jacob to the spoiler,
　and Israel to the robbers?
Was it not the LORD, against whom we have
　　　sinned,
　in whose ways they would not walk,
　and whose law they would not obey?
25 So he poured upon him the heat of his anger
　and the fury of war;
it set him on fire all around, but he did not
　　　understand;
　it burned him, but he did not take it to heart.

43 But now thus says the LORD,
　he who created you, O Jacob,
　he who formed you, O Israel:
Do not fear, for I have redeemed you;
　I have called you by name, you are mine.
2 When you pass through the waters, I will be with
　　　you;
　and through the rivers, they shall not
　　　overwhelm you;
when you walk through fire you shall not be
　　　burned,
　and the flame shall not consume you.
3 For I am the LORD your God,
　the Holy One of Israel, your Savior.
I give Egypt as your ransom,
　Ethiopia^q and Seba in exchange for you.
4 Because you are precious in my sight,
　and honored, and I love you,
I give people in return for you,
　nations in exchange for your life.
5 Do not fear, for I am with you;
　I will bring your offspring from the east,
　and from the west I will gather you;

16 I shall lead the blind on their way
　and guide them along paths they do not know;
I shall turn darkness into light before them
　and make straight their twisting roads.
These things I shall do without fail.
17 Those who put their trust in an image,
　and say to idols, 'You are our gods,'
　will be repulsed in bitter shame.

18 You that are deaf, hear now;
　you that are blind, look and see.
19 Who is blind but my servant,
　who so deaf as the messenger I send?
Who so blind as the one who has my trust,
　so deaf as the servant of the LORD?
20 You have seen much but perceived little,
　your ears are open but you hear nothing.
21 Though it pleased the LORD to further his justice
　by making his law great and glorious,
22 yet here is a people taken as spoil and plundered,
　all of them shut up in holes
　and hidden away in dungeons.
They are carried off as spoil without hope of
　　　rescue,
　as plunder with no one to demand their return.
23 Who among you will pay heed to this?
　Who will give it close attention from now on?
24 Who handed over Jacob for plunder,
　who gave up Israel for spoil?
Was it not the LORD, against whom they sinned?
　They would not follow his ways
　and refused obedience to his law;
25 so on Jacob he poured out his wrath,
　anger and the fury of battle.
It wrapped him in flames, yet he did not learn,
　burnt him, yet he did not lay it to heart.

43 But now, Jacob, this is the word of the LORD,
　the word of your Creator,
of him who fashioned you, Israel:
Have no fear, for I have redeemed you;
　I call you by name; you are mine.
2 When you pass through water I shall be with you;
　when you pass through rivers they will not
　　　overwhelm you;
walk through fire, and you will not be scorched,
　through flames, and they will not burn you.
3 I am the LORD your God,
　the Holy One of Israel, your deliverer;
I give Egypt as ransom for you,
　Nubia and Seba in exchange for you.
4 You are more precious to me than the Assyrians;
　you are honoured, and I love you.
I would give the Edomites in exchange for you,
　and any other people for your life.
5 Have no fear, for I am with you;
　I shall bring your descendants from the east
　and gather you from the west.

42:16 **on their way:** *prob. rdg; Heb.* adds which they do not know.
42:19 **deaf as the servant:** *so some MSS; others* blind as the servant.
42:24 **they sinned:** *so Gk; Heb.* we sinned.

^{p} Heb *You see many things but do*　^{q} Or *Nubia*; Heb *Cush*

NEW AMERICAN BIBLE

16 I will lead the blind on their journey;
  by paths unknown I will guide them.
I will turn darkness into light before them,
  and make crooked ways straight.
These things I do for them,
  and I will not forsake them.
17 They shall be turned back in utter shame
  who trust in idols;
Who say to molten images,
  "You are our gods."
18 You who are deaf, listen,
  you who are blind, look and see!
19 Who is blind but my servant,
  or deaf like the messenger I send?
20 You see many things without taking note;
  your ears are open, but without hearing.
21 Though it pleased the LORD in his justice
  to make his law great and glorious,
22 This is a people despoiled and plundered,
  all of them trapped in holes,
  hidden away in prisons.
They are taken as booty, with no one to
    rescue them,
  as spoil, with no one to demand their return.
23 Who of you gives ear to this?
  Who listens and pays heed for the time to come?
24 Who was it that gave Jacob to be plundered,
  Israel to the despoilers?
Was it not the LORD, against whom we
    have sinned?
In his ways they refused to walk,
  his law they disobeyed.
25 So he poured out wrath upon them,
  his anger, and the fury of battle;
It blazed round about them, yet they did
    not realize,
  it burned them, but they took it not to heart.

43 But now, thus says the LORD,
  who created you, O Jacob, and formed you,
    O Israel:
Fear not, for I have redeemed you;
  I have called you by name: you are mine.
2 When you pass through the water, I will be
    with you;
  in the rivers you shall not drown.
When you walk through fire, you shall not
    be burned;
  the flames shall not consume you.
3 For I am the LORD, your God,
  the Holy One of Israel, your savior.
I give Egypt as your ransom,
  Ethiopia and Seba in return for you.
4 Because you are precious in my eyes
  and glorious, and because I love you.
I give men in return for you
  and peoples in exchange for your life.
5 Fear not, for I am with you;
  from the east I will bring back your descendants,
  from the west I will gather you.

NEW JERUSALEM BIBLE

16 I shall lead the blind by a road they do not know,
  by paths they do not know I shall conduct them.
I shall turn the darkness into light before them
  and the quagmires into solid ground.
This I shall do — without fail.'
17 Those who trust in idols will recoil,
  they will blush for shame, who say to metal
      images,
  'You are our gods.'
18 Listen, you deaf!
  Look and see, you blind!
19 Who so blind as my servant,
  so deaf as the messenger I send?
(Who so blind as the friend I have taken to myself,
  so deaf as Yahweh's servant?)
20 You have seen many things but not observed them;
  your ears are open but you do not hear.
21 Yahweh wished, because of his saving justice,
  to make the Law great and glorious.
22 Yet here is a people pillaged and plundered,
  all of them shut up in caves,
  imprisoned in dungeons.
They have been pillaged, with no one to rescue
      them,
  plundered, with no one to say, 'Give it back!'
23 Which of you will listen to this,
  who pay attention and listen in future?
24 Who surrendered Jacob to the plunderer
  and Israel to the pillagers?
Was it not Yahweh, against whom we had sinned,
  in whose ways they would not walk
  and whose Law they would not obey?
25 On him he poured out his blazing anger
  and the fury of war;
  it enveloped him in flames and yet he did not
      understand;
  it burned him up, but he did not learn a lesson.

43 And now, thus says Yahweh,
  he who created you, Jacob,
  who formed you, Israel:
Do not be afraid, for I have redeemed you;
  I have called you by your name, you are mine.
2 Should you pass through the waters, I shall be with
    you;
  or through rivers, they will not swallow you up.
Should you walk through fire, you will not suffer,
  and the flame will not burn you.
3 For I am Yahweh, your God,
  the Holy One of Israel, your Saviour.
I have given Egypt for your ransom,
  Cush and Seba in exchange for you.
4 Since I regard you as precious,
  since you are honoured and I love you,
  I therefore give people in exchange for you,
  and nations in return for your life.
5 Do not be afraid, for I am with you.
  I shall bring your offspring from the east,
  and gather you from the west.

NEW REVISED STANDARD VERSION	REVISED ENGLISH BIBLE

NEW REVISED STANDARD VERSION

6 I will say to the north, "Give them up,"
  and to the south, "Do not withhold;
bring my sons from far away
  and my daughters from the end of the earth—
7 everyone who is called by my name,
  whom I created for my glory,
  whom I formed and made."

8 Bring forth the people who are blind, yet have
    eyes,
  who are deaf, yet have ears!
9 Let all the nations gather together,
  and let the peoples assemble.
Who among them declared this,
  and foretold to us the former things?
Let them bring their witnesses to justify them,
  and let them hear and say, "It is true."
10 You are my witnesses, says the LORD,
  and my servant whom I have chosen,
so that you may know and believe me
  and understand that I am he.
Before me no god was formed,
  nor shall there be any after me.
11 I, I am the LORD,
  and besides me there is no savior.
12 I declared and saved and proclaimed,
  when there was no strange god among you;
  and you are my witnesses, says the LORD.
13 I am God, and also henceforth I am He;
  there is no one who can deliver from my hand;
  I work and who can hinder it?
14 Thus says the LORD,
  your Redeemer, the Holy One of Israel:
For your sake I will send to Babylon
  and break down all the bars,
  and the shouting of the Chaldeans will be
    turned to lamentation.*r*
15 I am the LORD, your Holy One,
  the Creator of Israel, your King.
16 Thus says the LORD,
  who makes a way in the sea,
  a path in the mighty waters,
17 who brings out chariot and horse,
  army and warrior;
they lie down, they cannot rise,
  they are extinguished, quenched like a wick:
18 Do not remember the former things,
  or consider the things of old.
19 I am about to do a new thing;
  now it springs forth, do you not perceive it?
I will make a way in the wilderness
  and rivers in the desert.
20 The wild animals will honor me,
  the jackals and the ostriches;
for I give water in the wilderness,
  rivers in the desert,
to give drink to my chosen people,
21   the people whom I formed for myself
so that they might declare my praise.

22 Yet you did not call upon me, O Jacob;
  but you have been weary of me, O Israel!

REVISED ENGLISH BIBLE

6 To the north I shall say, 'Give them up,'
  and to the south, 'Do not obstruct them.
Bring my sons and daughters from afar,
  bring them back from the ends of the earth:
7 everyone who bears my name,
  all whom I have created, whom I have formed,
  whom I have made for my glory.'

8 Bring forward this people,
  a people who have eyes but are blind,
  who have ears but are deaf.
9 All the nations are gathered together
  and the peoples assembled.
Who among them can expound what has gone
    before
  or interpret this for us?
Let them produce their witnesses and prove their
    case;
  let people hearing them say, 'That is the truth.'
10 The LORD declares, You are my witnesses,
  you are my servants chosen by me
to know me and put your trust in me
  and understand that I am the Lord.
Before me no god existed,
  nor will there be any after me.
11 I am the LORD,
  and I alone am your deliverer.
12 I have made it known; I declared it,
  I and no alien god among you,
  and you are my witnesses, says the LORD.
I am God; 13 from everlasting I am he.
None can deliver from my hand;
  what I do, none can undo.
14 These are the words of the LORD your Redeemer,
  the Holy One of Israel:
For your sakes I shall send an army to Babylon
  and lay the Chaldaeans prostrate as they flee;
  their cry of triumph will turn to lamentation.
15 Israel, I am the LORD, your Holy One,
  your Creator and your King.
16 This is the word of the LORD,
  who opened a way in the sea,
  a path through mighty waters,
17 who drew on chariot and horse to their destruction,
  an army in all its strength;
they lay down, never to rise again;
  they were extinguished, snuffed out like a wick:
18 Stop dwelling on past events
  and brooding over days gone by.
19 I am about to do something new;
  this moment it will unfold.
Can you not perceive it?
Even through the wilderness I shall make a way,
  and paths in the barren desert.
20 The wild beasts will do me honour,
  the wolf and the desert-owl,
for I shall provide water in the wilderness
  and rivers in the barren desert,
  where my chosen people may drink,
21 this people I have formed for myself,
  and they will proclaim my praises.

22 Yet, Jacob, you did not call upon me;
  much less did you, Israel, weary yourself in my
    service.

---

r Meaning of Heb uncertain

43:12 **I have . . . known:** *prob. rdg; Heb.* adds and I will deliver.
43:19 **paths:** *so Scroll; Heb.* rivers.

6 I will say to the north: Give them up!
and to the south: Hold not back!
Bring back my sons from afar,
and my daughters from the ends of the earth:
7 Everyone who is named as mine,
whom I created for my glory,
whom I formed and made.
8 Lead out the people who are blind though they
have eyes,
who are deaf though they have ears.

9 Let all the nations gather together,
let the peoples assemble!
Who among them could have revealed this,
or foretold to us the earlier things?
Let them produce witnesses to prove
themselves right,
that one may hear and say, "It is true!"
10 You are my witnesses, says the LORD,
my servants whom I have chosen
To know and believe in me
and understand that it is I.
Before me no god was formed,
and after me there shall be none.

11 It is I, I the LORD;
there is no savior but me.
12 It is I who foretold, I who saved;
I made it known, not any strange god
among you;
You are my witnesses, says the LORD.
I am God, 13 yes, from eternity I am He;
There is none who can deliver from my hand:
who can countermand what I do?

14 Thus says the LORD, your redeemer,
the Holy One of Israel:
For your sakes I send to Babylon;
I will lower all the bars,
and the Chaldeans shall cry out in lamentation.
15 I am the LORD, your Holy One,
the creator of Israel, your King.
16 Thus says the LORD,
who opens a way in the sea
and a path in the mighty waters,
17 Who leads out chariots and horsemen,
a powerful army,
Till they lie prostrate together, never to rise,
snuffed out and quenched like a wick.
18 Remember not the events of the past,
the things of long ago consider not;
19 See, I am doing something new!
Now it springs forth, do you not perceive it?
In the desert I make a way,
in the wasteland, rivers.
20 Wild beasts honor me,
jackals and ostriches,
For I put water in the desert
and rivers in the wasteland
for my chosen people to drink.
21 The people whom I formed for myself,
that they might announce my praise.

22 Yet you did not call upon me, O Jacob,
for you grew weary of me, O Israel.

6 To the north I shall say, 'Give them up!'
and to the south, 'Do not hold them back!'
Bring back my sons from far away,
and my daughters from the remotest part of the
earth,
7 everyone who bears my name,
whom I have created for my glory,
whom I have formed, whom I have made.
8 Bring forward the people that is blind, yet has
eyes,
that is deaf and yet has ears.
9 Let all the nations assemble,
let the peoples gather here!
Which of them has proclaimed this
and revealed things to us in the past?
Let them bring their witnesses to justify
themselves,
let others hear and say, 'It is true.'
10 You yourselves are my witnesses, declares
Yahweh,
and the servant whom I have chosen,
so that you may know and believe me
and understand that it is I.
No god was formed before me,
nor will be after me.
11 I, I am Yahweh,
and there is no other Saviour but me.
12 I have revealed, have saved, and have proclaimed,
not some foreigner among you.
You are my witnesses, declares Yahweh,

I am God, 13 yes, from eternity I am.
No one can deliver from my hand;
when I act, who can thwart me?

14 Thus says Yahweh,
your redeemer, the Holy One of Israel:
For your sake I have sent to Babylon,
I shall knock down all the prison bars,
and the Chaldaeans' shouts of joy will change to
lamentations.
15 I am Yahweh, your Holy One,
the Creator of Israel, your king.
16 Thus says Yahweh,
who made a way through the sea,
a path in the raging waters,
17 who led out chariot and horse
together with an army of picked troops:
they lay down never to rise again,
they were snuffed out, put out like a wick.
18 No need to remember past events,
no need to think about what was done before.
19 Look, I am doing something new,
now it emerges; can you not see it?
Yes, I am making a road in the desert
and rivers in wastelands.
20 The wild animals will honour me,
the jackals and the ostriches,
for bestowing water in the desert
and rivers on the wastelands
for my people, my chosen one, to drink.
21 The people I have shaped for myself
will broadcast my praises.

22 But, Jacob, you have not invoked me;
no, Israel, you have grown weary of me.

NEW REVISED STANDARD VERSION	REVISED ENGLISH BIBLE

NEW REVISED STANDARD VERSION

23 You have not brought me your sheep for burnt
offerings,
or honored me with your sacrifices.
I have not burdened you with offerings,
or wearied you with frankincense.
24 You have not bought me sweet cane with money,
or satisfied me with the fat of your sacrifices.
But you have burdened me with your sins;
you have wearied me with your iniquities.

25 I, I am He
who blots out your transgressions for my own
sake,
and I will not remember your sins.
26 Accuse me, let us go to trial;
set forth your case, so that you may be proved
right.
27 Your first ancestor sinned,
and your interpreters transgressed against me.
28 Therefore I profaned the princes of the sanctuary,
I delivered Jacob to utter destruction,
and Israel to reviling.

44 But now hear, O Jacob my servant,
Israel whom I have chosen!
2 Thus says the LORD who made you,
who formed you in the womb and will help
you:
Do not fear, O Jacob my servant,
Jeshurun whom I have chosen.
3 For I will pour water on the thirsty land,
and streams on the dry ground;
I will pour my spirit upon your descendants,
and my blessing on your offspring.
4 They shall spring up like a green tamarisk,
like willows by flowing streams.
5 This one will say, "I am the LORD's,"
another will be called by the name of Jacob,
yet another will write on the hand, "The LORD's,"
and adopt the name of Israel.

6 Thus says the LORD, the King of Israel,
and his Redeemer, the LORD of hosts:
I am the first and I am the last;
besides me there is no god.
7 Who is like me? Let them proclaim it,
let them declare and set it forth before me.
Who has announced from of old the things to
come?[s]
Let them tell us[t] what is yet to be.
8 Do not fear, or be afraid;
have I not told you from of old and declared
it?
You are my witnesses!
Is there any god besides me?
There is no other rock; I know not one.

9 All who make idols are nothing, and the things they
delight in do not profit; their witnesses neither see nor
know. And so they will be put to shame. 10 Who would
fashion a god or cast an image that can do no good? 11 Look,
all its devotees shall be put to shame; the artisans too are
merely human. Let them all assemble, let them stand up;
they shall be terrified, they shall all be put to shame.

REVISED ENGLISH BIBLE

23 You did not bring me whole-offerings from your
flock
or honour me with your sacrifices;
I did not exact grain-offerings from you
or weary you with demands for frankincense.
24 You did not buy me aromatic cane with your
money
or sate me with the fat of your sacrifices.
Rather you burdened me with your sins
and wearied me with your crimes.

25 I am the LORD;
for my own sake I wipe out your transgressions
and remember your sins no more.
26 Cite me to appear, let us argue it out;
set forth your pleading and establish your
innocence.
27 Your first forefather transgressed,
your spokesmen rebelled against me,
28 and your leaders desecrated my sanctuary;
that is why I put Jacob under solemn curse
and left Israel to be reviled.

44 Hear me now, Jacob my servant;
Israel, my chosen one, hear me.
2 Thus says the LORD your maker,
your helper, who fashioned you from birth:
Have no fear, Jacob my servant,
Jeshurun whom I have chosen,
3 for I shall pour down rain on thirsty land,
showers on dry ground.
I shall pour out my spirit on your offspring
and my blessing on your children.
4 They will grow up like a green tamarisk,
like willows by flowing streams.
5 This person will say, 'I am the LORD's';
that one will call himself a son of Jacob;
another will write the LORD's name on his hand
and the name of Israel will be added to his own.

6 Thus says the LORD, Israel's King,
the LORD of Hosts, his Redeemer:
I am the first and I am the last,
and there is no god but me.
7 Who is like me? Let him speak up;
let him declare his proof and set it out for me:
let him announce beforehand things to come,
let him foretell what is yet to be.
8 Take heart, have no fear.
Did I not tell you this long ago?
I foretold it, and you are my witnesses.
Is there any god apart from me,
any other deity? I know none!

9 Those who make idols are all less than nothing;
their cherished images profit nobody;
their worshippers are blind;
their ignorance shows up their foolishness.
10 Whoever makes a god or casts an image,
his labour is wasted.
11 All the votaries are put to shame;
the craftsmen are but mortals.
Let them all assemble and confront me;
they will be afraid and utterly shamed.

43:28 your leaders . . . sanctuary: prob. rdg, cp. Gk; Heb. I have
profaned holy princes.   44:4 willows: or poplars.   44:7 let
him announce beforehand: prob. rdg; Heb. since my appointing an
ancient people and.   44:8 deity: lit. rock.

---

s Cn: Heb from my placing an eternal people and things to come
t Tg: Heb them

NEW AMERICAN BIBLE

²³You did not bring me sheep for your holocausts,
  nor honor me with your sacrifices.
I did not exact from you the service of offerings,
  nor weary you for frankincense.
²⁴You did not buy me sweet cane for money,
  nor fill me with the fat of your sacrifices;
Instead, you burdened me with your sins,
  and wearied me with your crimes.
²⁵It is I, I, who wipe out,
  for my own sake, your offenses;
  your sins I remember no more.
²⁶Would you have me remember, have us come
    to trial?
  Speak up, prove your innocence!
²⁷Your first father sinned,
  your spokesmen rebelled against me
²⁸Till I repudiated the holy gates,
  put Jacob under the ban,
  and exposed Israel to scorn.

44 Hear then, O Jacob, my servant,
      Israel, whom I have chosen.
²Thus says the LORD who made you,
  your help, who formed you from the womb:
Fear not, O Jacob, my servant,
  the darling whom I have chosen.
³I will pour out water upon the thirsty ground,
  and streams upon the dry land;
I will pour out my spirit upon your offspring,
  and my blessing upon your descendants.
⁴They shall spring up amid the verdure
  like poplars beside the flowing waters.
⁵One shall say, "I am the LORD'S,"
  another shall be named after Jacob,
And this one shall write on his hand,
    "The LORD'S,"
  and Israel shall be his surname.

⁶Thus says the LORD, Israel's King
  and redeemer, the LORD of hosts:
I am the first and I am the last;
  there is no God but me.
⁷Who is like me? Let him stand up and speak,
  make it evident, and confront me with it.
Who of old announced future events?
  Let them foretell to us the things to come.
⁸Fear not, be not troubled:
  did I not announce and foretell it long ago?
You are my witnesses! Is there a God
  or any Rock besides me?

⁹Idol makers all amount to nothing, and their precious
works are of no avail, as they themselves give witness. To
their shame, they neither see nor know anything; and they
are more deaf than men are. ¹⁰Indeed, all the associates of
anyone who forms a god, or casts an idol to no purpose, will
be put to shame; ¹¹they will all assemble and stand forth,
to be reduced to fear and shame.

NEW JERUSALEM BIBLE

²³You have not brought me lambs as your burnt
    offerings
  and have not honoured me with your sacrifices.
I have not subjected you to cereal offering,
  I have not wearied you by demanding incense.
²⁴You have not bought expensive reed for me
  or sated me with the fat of your sacrifices.
Instead by your sins you have treated me like a
    slave,
  you have wearied me with your crimes,
²⁵I, it is who blot out your acts of revolt for my
    own sake
  and shall not call your sins to mind.
²⁶Remind me, and we will judge this together;
  state your own case and justify yourself.
²⁷Your first ancestor sinned,
  your interpreters revolted against me.
²⁸That is why I deposed the chief men of my
    sanctuary,
  why I put Jacob under the curse of destruction
  and subjected Israel to insult.

44 And now listen, Jacob my servant,
      Israel whom I have chosen.
²Thus says Yahweh who made you,
  who formed you in the womb; he will help you.
Do not be afraid, Jacob my servant,
  Jeshurunˣ whom I have chosen.
³For I shall pour out water on the thirsty soil
  and streams on the dry ground.
I shall pour out my spirit on your descendants,
  my blessing on your offspring,
⁴and they will spring up among the grass,
  like willows on the banks of a stream.
⁵One person will say, 'I belong to Yahweh,'
  another will call himself by Jacob's name.
On his hand another will write 'Yahweh's'
  and be surnamed 'Israel'.

⁶Thus says Yahweh, Israel's king,
  Yahweh Sabaoth, his redeemer:
I am the first and I am the last;
  there is no God except me.
⁷Who is like me? Let him call out,
  let him affirm it and convince me it is so;
  let him say what has been happening
since I instituted an eternal people,
  and predict to them what will happen next!
⁸Have no fear, do not be afraid:
  have I not told you and revealed it long ago?
You are my witnesses.
  Is there any God except me?
  There is no Rock; I know of none.

⁹The makers of idols are all nothingness; the works they
delight in serve no purpose. And these are the witness
against them: they see nothing, they know nothing; and so
they will be put to shame. ¹⁰Who ever fashioned a god or
cast an image without hope of gain? ¹¹Watch how all its
devotees will be put to shame, and the men who made it
too, who are only human. Let them all assemble, let them
stand forward and feel both fear and shame!

ˣ**44** Rare poetic name of Israel, perhaps meaning 'the upright one'.

12 The ironsmith fashions it*u* and works it over the coals, shaping it with hammers, and forging it with his strong arm; he becomes hungry and his strength fails, he drinks no water and is faint. 13 The carpenter stretches a line, marks it out with a stylus, fashions it with planes, and marks it with a compass; he makes it in human form, with human beauty, to be set up in a shrine. 14 He cuts down cedars or chooses a holm tree or an oak and lets it grow strong among the trees of the forest. He plants a cedar and the rain nourishes it. 15 Then it can be used as fuel. Part of it he takes and warms himself; he kindles a fire and bakes bread. Then he makes a god and worships it, makes it a carved image and bows down before it. 16 Half of it he burns in the fire; over this half he roasts meat, eats it and is satisfied. He also warms himself and says, "Ah, I am warm, I can feel the fire!" 17 The rest of it he makes into a god, his idol, bows down to it and worships it; he prays to it and says, "Save me, for you are my god!"

18 They do not know, nor do they comprehend; for their eyes are shut, so that they cannot see, and their minds as well, so that they cannot understand. 19 No one considers, nor is there knowledge or discernment to say, "Half of it I burned in the fire; I also baked bread on its coals, I roasted meat and have eaten. Now shall I make the rest of it an abomination? Shall I fall down before a block of wood?" 20 He feeds on ashes; a deluded mind has led him astray, and he cannot save himself or say, "Is not this thing in my right hand a fraud?"

21 Remember these things, O Jacob,
    and Israel, for you are my servant;
I formed you, you are my servant;
    O Israel, you will not be forgotten by me.
22 I have swept away your transgressions like a
        cloud,
    and your sins like mist;
return to me, for I have redeemed you.

23 Sing, O heavens, for the LORD has done it;
    shout, O depths of the earth;
break forth into singing, O mountains,
    O forest, and every tree in it!
For the LORD has redeemed Jacob,
    and will be glorified in Israel.

24 Thus says the LORD, your Redeemer,
    who formed you in the womb:
I am the LORD, who made all things,
    who alone stretched out the heavens,
    who by myself spread out the earth;
25 who frustrates the omens of liars,
    and makes fools of diviners;
who turns back the wise,
    and makes their knowledge foolish;
26 who confirms the word of his servant,
    and fulfills the prediction of his messengers;
who says of Jerusalem, "It shall be inhabited,"
    and of the cities of Judah, "They shall be
        rebuilt,
    and I will raise up their ruins";
27 who says to the deep, "Be dry—
    I will dry up your rivers";

12 The blacksmith sharpens a graving tool and hammers out his work hot from the coals and shapes it with his strong arm. Should he go hungry his strength fails; if he has no water to drink he feels exhausted. 13 The woodworker draws his line taut and marks out a figure with a scriber; he planes the wood and measures it with calipers, and he carves it to the shape of a man, comely as the human form, to be set up in a shrine.

14 A man plants a cedar and the rain makes it grow, so that later on he will have a tree to cut down; or he picks out in the forest an ilex or an oak which he will raise into a stout tree for himself. 15 It becomes fuel for his fire: some of it he uses to warm himself, some he kindles and bakes bread on it. Some he even makes into a god, and prostrates himself; he shapes it into an idol and bows down before it. 16 One half of the wood he burns in the fire and on this he roasts meat, so that he may eat this and be satisfied; he also warms himself and he says, 'Good! I can feel the heat as I watch the flames.' 17 Then what is left of the wood he makes into a god, an image to which he bows down and prostrates himself; he prays to it and says, 'Save me; for you are my god.'

18 Such people neither know nor understand, their eyes made too blind to see, their minds too narrow to discern. 19 Such a one will not use his reason; he has neither the wit nor the sense to say, 'Half of it I have burnt, and even used its embers to bake bread; I have roasted meat on them and eaten it; but the rest of it I turn into this abominable object; really I am worshipping a block of wood.' 20 He feeds on ashes indeed! His deluded mind has led him astray, and he cannot recover his senses so far as to say, 'This thing I am holding is a sham.'

21 Jacob, remember all this;
    Israel, remember, for you are my servant:
I have fashioned you, and you are in my service;
    Israel, never forget me.
22 I have swept away your transgressions like mist,
    and your sins are dispersed like clouds;
turn back to me, for I have redeemed you.
23 Shout in triumph, you heavens, for it is the LORD's
        doing;
cry out for joy, you lowest depths of the earth;
break into songs of triumph, you mountains,
    you forest and all your trees;
for the LORD has redeemed Jacob
    and through Israel he wins glory.

24 Thus says the LORD, your Redeemer,
    who formed you from birth:
I am the LORD who made all things,
    by myself I stretched out the heavens,
    alone I fashioned the earth.
25 I frustrate false prophets and their omens,
    and make fools of diviners;
I reverse what wise men say
    and make nonsense of their wisdom.
26 I confirm my servants' prophecies
    and bring about my messengers' plans.
Of Jerusalem I say, 'She will be inhabited once
       more,'
and of the towns of Judah, 'They will be rebuilt;
    I shall restore their ruins.'
27 I say to the deep waters, 'Be dried up;
    I shall make your streams run dry.'

---

u Cn: Heb *an ax*

44:12 **sharpens:** *so Gk; Heb.* omits. **his work:** *prob. rdg; Heb.* he works.   44:13 **shrine:** *or* house.

NEW AMERICAN BIBLE

12 The smith fashions an iron image, works it over the coals, shapes it with hammers, and forges it with his strong arm. He is hungry and weak, drinks no water and becomes exhausted.

13 The carpenter stretches a line and marks with a stylus the outline of an idol. He shapes it with a plane and measures it off with a compass, making it like a man in appearance and dignity, to occupy a shrine. 14 He cuts down cedars, takes a holm or an oak, and lays hold of other trees of the forest, which the Lord had planted and the rain made grow 15 to serve man for fuel. With a part of their wood he warms himself, or makes a fire for baking bread; but with another part he makes a god which he adores, an idol which he worships. 16 Half of it he burns in the fire, and on its embers he roasts his meat; he eats what he has roasted until he is full, and then warms himself and says, "Ah! I am warm, I feel the fire." 17 Of what remains he makes a god, his idol, and prostrate before it in worship, he implores it, "Rescue me, for you are my god."

18 The idols have neither knowledge nor reason; their eyes are coated so that they cannot see, and their hearts so that they cannot understand. 19 Yet he does not reflect, nor have the intelligence and sense to say, "Half of the wood I burned in the fire, and on its embers I baked bread and roasted meat which I ate. Shall I then make an abomination out of the rest, or worship a block of wood?" 20 He is chasing ashes — a thing that cannot save itself when the flame consumes it; yet he does not say, "Is not this thing in my right hand a fraud?"

21 Remember this, O Jacob,
  you, O Israel, who are my servant!
I formed you to be a servant to me;
  O Israel, by me you shall never be forgotten:
22 I have brushed away your offenses like a cloud,
  your sins like a mist;
  return to me, for I have redeemed you.

23 Raise a glad cry, you heavens: the LORD has done this;
  shout, you depths of the earth.
Break forth, you mountains, into song,
  you forest, with all your trees.
For the LORD has redeemed Jacob,
  and shows his glory through Israel.

24 Thus says the LORD, your redeemer,
  who formed you from the womb:
I am the LORD, who made all things,
  who alone stretched out the heavens;
  when I spread out the earth, who was with me?
25 It is I who bring to nought the omens of liars,
  who make fools of diviners;
I turn wise men back
  and make their knowledge foolish.
26 It is I who confirm the words of my servants,
  I carry out the plan announced by
    my messengers;
I say to Jerusalem: Be inhabited;
  to the cities of Judah: Be rebuilt;
  I will raise up their ruins.
27 It is I who said to the deep: Be dry;
  I will dry up your wellsprings.

NEW JERUSALEM BIBLE

12 The blacksmith makes an axe over the charcoal, beats it into shape with a hammer, works on it with his strong arm. Then he feels hungry and his strength deserts him; having drunk no water, he is exhausted.

13 The wood carver takes his measurements, outlines the image with chalk, executes it with the chisel, following the outline with a compass. He makes it look like a human being, with human standards of beauty, so that it can reside in a house. 14 He has cut down cedars, has selected an oak and a terebinth which he has grown for himself among the trees in the forest and has planted a pine tree which the rain has nourished. 15 Once it is suitable to burn, he takes some of it to warm himself; having kindled it, he bakes bread. But he also makes a god and worships it; he makes an idol from it and bows down before it. 16 Half of it he burns on the fire, over this half he roasts meat, eats it and is replete; at the same time he warms himself and says, 'Ah, how warm I am, watching the flames!' 17 With the remainder he makes a god, his idol, bows down before it, worships it and prays to it. 'Save me,' he says, 'for you are my god.'

18 They know nothing, they understand nothing, since their eyes are incapable of seeing and their hearts of reflecting. 19 Not one of them looks into his heart, not one of them has the knowledge and wit to think, 'I burned half of it on the fire and cooked food over the embers. Am I right to make something disgusting out of what is left? Am I right to bow down before a block of wood?'

20 He hankers after ashes, his deluded heart has led him astray; he will not save himself, he will not think, 'What I have in my hand is nothing but a lie!'

21 Remember these things, Jacob,
  and Israel, since you are my servant.
I formed you, you are my servant;
  Israel, I shall not forget you.
22 I have dispelled your acts of revolt like a cloud
  and your sins like a mist.
  Come back to me, for I have redeemed you.
23 Heavens, shout for joy, for Yahweh has acted!
  Underworld, shout aloud!
Shout for joy, you mountains,
  forests and all your trees!
For Yahweh has redeemed Jacob
  and displayed his glory in Israel.

24 Thus says Yahweh, your redeemer,
  he who formed you in the womb:
I, Yahweh, have made all things,
  I alone spread out the heavens.
When I hammered the earth into shape, who was
    with me?
25 I, who foil the omens of soothsayers
  and make fools of diviners,
  who confound sages
  turning their knowledge into folly,
26 who confirm the word of my servant
  and make the plans of my envoys succeed;
  who say to Jerusalem, 'You will be inhabited,'
  and to the towns of Judah, 'You will be rebuilt
  and I shall restore the ruins of Jerusalem';
27 who say to the ocean, 'Dry up!
  I shall make your rivers run dry';

NEW REVISED STANDARD VERSION	REVISED ENGLISH BIBLE

NEW REVISED STANDARD VERSION

28 who says of Cyrus, "He is my shepherd,
  and he shall carry out all my purpose";
and who says of Jerusalem, "It shall be rebuilt,"
  and of the temple, "Your foundation shall be
  laid."

45 Thus says the LORD to his anointed, to Cyrus,
  whose right hand I have grasped
to subdue nations before him
  and strip kings of their robes,
to open doors before him—
  and the gates shall not be closed:
2 I will go before you
  and level the mountains,^{v}
I will break in pieces the doors of bronze
  and cut through the bars of iron,
3 I will give you the treasures of darkness
  and riches hidden in secret places,
so that you may know that it is I, the LORD,
  the God of Israel, who call you by your name.
4 For the sake of my servant Jacob,
  and Israel my chosen,
I call you by your name,
  I surname you, though you do not know me.
5 I am the LORD, and there is no other;
  besides me there is no god.
I arm you, though you do not know me,
6 so that they may know, from the rising of the sun
  and from the west, that there is no one besides
  me;
I am the LORD, and there is no other.
7 I form light and create darkness,
  I make weal and create woe;
I the LORD do all these things.

8 Shower, O heavens, from above,
  and let the skies rain down righteousness;
let the earth open, that salvation may spring up,^{w}
  and let it cause righteousness to sprout up also;
I the LORD have created it.

9 Woe to you who strive with your Maker,
  earthen vessels with the potter!^{x}
Does the clay say to the one who fashions it,
  "What are you making"?
or "Your work has no handles"?
10 Woe to anyone who says to a father, "What are
  you begetting?"
or to a woman, "With what are you in labor?"
11 Thus says the LORD,
  the Holy One of Israel, and its Maker:
Will you question me^y about my children,
  or command me concerning the work of my
  hands?
12 I made the earth,
  and created humankind upon it;
it was my hands that stretched out the heavens,
  and I commanded all their host.
13 I have aroused Cyrus^z in righteousness,
  and I will make all his paths straight;
he shall build my city
  and set my exiles free,
not for price or reward,
  says the LORD of hosts.

REVISED ENGLISH BIBLE

28 I say to Cyrus, 'You will be my shepherd
to fulfil all my purpose,
  so that Jerusalem may be rebuilt
and the foundations of the temple be laid.'

45 Thus says the LORD to Cyrus his anointed,
  whom he has taken by the right hand,
subduing nations before him
  and stripping kings of their strength;
before whom doors will be opened
  and no gates barred:
2 I myself shall go before you
  and level the swelling hills;
I shall break down bronze gates
  and cut through iron bars.
3 I shall give you treasures from dark vaults,
  and hoards from secret places,
so that you may know that I am the LORD,
  Israel's God, who calls you by name.
4 For the sake of Jacob my servant
  and Israel my chosen one
I have called you by name
  and given you a title, though you have not known
  me.
5 I am the LORD, and there is none other;
  apart from me there is no god.
Though you have not known me I shall strengthen
  you,
6 so that from east to west
  all may know there is none besides me:
I am the LORD, and there is none other;
7 I make the light, I create the darkness;
  author alike of wellbeing and woe,
I, the LORD, do all these things.

8 Rain righteousness, you heavens,
  let the skies above pour it down,
let the earth open for it
  that salvation may flourish
with righteousness growing beside it.
I, the LORD, have created this.

9 Will the pot contend with the potter,
  or the earthenware with the hand that shapes it?
Will the clay ask the potter what he is making
  or his handiwork say to him, 'You have no skill'?
10 Will the child say to his father, 'What are you
  begetting?'
or to his mother, 'What are you bringing to birth?'
11 Thus says the LORD, Israel's Holy One, his Maker:
Would you dare question me concerning my
  children,
  or instruct me in my handiwork?
12 I alone made the earth
  and created mankind upon it.
With my own hands I stretched out the heavens
  and directed all their host.
13 With righteous purpose I have roused this man,
  and I shall smooth all his paths;
he it is who will rebuild my city
  and set my exiles free—
not for a price nor for a bribe,
  says the LORD of Hosts.

44:28 **be laid:** *prob. rdg, cp. Scroll; Heb.* you may be laid.
45:9 **Will . . . contend:** *prob. rdg; Heb.* Ho! He has contended. **his
handiwork:** *prob. rdg; Heb.* your handiwork. 45:10 **Will . . .
say:** *prob. rdg; Heb.* Ho! You that say. 45:11 **Would . . .
question me:** *prob. rdg; Heb.* obscure.

^{v}Q Ms Gk: MT *the swellings* ^{w}Q Ms: MT *that they may bring
forth salvation* ^{x}Cn: Heb *with the potsherds,* or *with the potters*
^{y}Cn: Heb *Ask me of things to come* ^{z}Heb *him*

NEW AMERICAN BIBLE

28 I say of Cyrus: My shepherd,
  who fulfills my every wish;
He shall say of Jerusalem, "Let her be rebuilt,"
  and of the temple, "Let its foundations be laid."

45 Thus says the LORD to his anointed, Cyrus,
  whose right hand I grasp,
Subduing nations before him,
  and making kings run in his service,
Opening doors before him
  and leaving the gates unbarred:
2 I will go before you
  and level the mountains;
Bronze doors I will shatter,
  and iron bars I will snap.
3 I will give you treasures out of the darkness,
  and riches that have been hidden away,
That you may know that I am the LORD,
  the God of Israel, who calls you by your name.

4 For the sake of Jacob, my servant,
  of Israel my chosen one,
I have called you by your name,
  giving you a title, though you knew me not.
5 I am the LORD and there is no other,
  there is no God besides me.
It is I who arm you, though you know me not,
6   so that toward the rising and the setting of
    the sun
  men may know that there is none besides me.

I am the LORD, there is no other;
7 I form the light, and create the darkness,
I make well-being and create woe;
  I, the LORD, do all these things.
8 Let justice descend, O heavens, like dew
    from above,
  like gentle rain let the skies drop it down.
Let the earth open and salvation bud forth;
  let justice also spring up!
  I, the LORD, have created this.
9 Woe to him who contends with his Maker;
  a potsherd among potsherds of the earth!
Dare the clay say to its modeler, "What are
    you doing?"
  or, "What you are making has no hands"?
10 Woe to him who asks a father, "What are
    you begetting?"
  or a woman, "What are you giving birth to?"

11 Thus says the LORD,
  the Holy One of Israel, his maker:
You question me about my children,
  or prescribe the work of my hands for me!
12 It was I who made the earth
  and created mankind upon it;
It was my hands that stretched out the heavens;
  I gave the order to all their host.
13 It was I who stirred up one for the triumph
    of justice;
  all his ways I make level.
He shall rebuild my city
  and let my exiles go free
Without price or ransom,
  says the LORD of hosts.

NEW JERUSALEM BIBLE

28 who say to Cyrus, 'My shepherd.'
He will perform my entire will
by saying to Jerusalem, 'You will be rebuilt,'
and to the Temple, 'You will be refounded.'

45 Thus says Yahweh to his anointed one,
  to Cyrus whom, he says, I have grasped by his right
    hand,
to make the nations bow before him
and to disarm kings,
to open gateways before him
so that their gates be closed no more:
2 I myself shall go before you,
I shall level the heights,
I shall shatter the bronze gateways,
I shall smash the iron bars.
3 I shall give you secret treasures
and hidden hoards of wealth,
so that you will know that I am Yahweh,
who call you by your name,
the God of Israel.
4 It is for the sake of my servant Jacob
and of Israel my chosen one,
that I have called you by your name,
have given you a title though you do not know me.
5 I am Yahweh, and there is no other,
there is no other God except me.
Though you do not know me, I have armed you
6 so that it may be known from east to west
that there is no one except me.
I am Yahweh, and there is no other,
7 I form the light and I create the darkness,
I make well-being, and I create disaster,
I, Yahweh, do all these things.

8 Rain down, you heavens, from above,
and let the clouds pour down saving justice,
let the earth open up and blossom with salvation,
and let justice sprout with it;
I, Yahweh, have created it!
9 Woe to anyone who argues with his Maker,
one earthenware pot among many!
Does the clay say to its potter, 'What are you
    doing?
Your work has no hands!'
10 Woe to anyone who asks a father, 'Why are you
    begetting?'
and a woman, 'Why are you giving birth?'
11 Thus says Yahweh,
the Holy One of Israel and his Maker:
I am asked for signs regarding my sons,
I am given orders about the work I do.
12 It was I who made the earth
and I created human beings on it,
mine were the hands that spread out the heavens
and I have given the orders to all their array.
13 I myself have raised him in saving justice
and I shall make all paths level for him.
He will rebuild my city
and bring my exiles home
without ransom or indemnity,
says Yahweh Sabaoth.

14 Thus says the LORD:
  The wealth of Egypt and the merchandise of
    Ethiopia,*a*
    and the Sabeans, tall of stature,
  shall come over to you and be yours,
    they shall follow you;
    they shall come over in chains and bow down
      to you.
  They will make supplication to you, saying,
    "God is with you alone, and there is no other;
      there is no god besides him."
15 Truly, you are a God who hides himself,
    O God of Israel, the Savior.
16 All of them are put to shame and confounded,
    the makers of idols go in confusion together.
17 But Israel is saved by the LORD
    with everlasting salvation;
  you shall not be put to shame or confounded
    to all eternity.

18 For thus says the LORD,
  who created the heavens
    (he is God!),
  who formed the earth and made it
    (he established it;
  he did not create it a chaos,
    he formed it to be inhabited!):
  I am the LORD, and there is no other.
19 I did not speak in secret,
    in a land of darkness;
  I did not say to the offspring of Jacob,
    "Seek me in chaos."
  I the LORD speak the truth,
    I declare what is right.

20 Assemble yourselves and come together,
    draw near, you survivors of the nations!
  They have no knowledge —
    those who carry about their wooden idols,
  and keep on praying to a god
    that cannot save.
21 Declare and present your case;
    let them take counsel together!
  Who told this long ago?
    Who declared it of old?
  Was it not I, the LORD?
    There is no other god besides me,
  a righteous God and a Savior;
    there is no one besides me.
22 Turn to me and be saved,
    all the ends of the earth!
  For I am God, and there is no other.
23 By myself I have sworn,
    from my mouth has gone forth in righteousness
    a word that shall not return:
  "To me every knee shall bow,
    every tongue shall swear."
24 Only in the LORD, it shall be said of me,
    are righteousness and strength;
  all who were incensed against him
    shall come to him and be ashamed.
25 In the LORD all the offspring of Israel
    shall triumph and glory.

14 These are the words of the LORD:
  Toilers of Egypt and Nubian merchants
  and Sabaeans bearing tribute
  will come into your power and be your slaves,
  will come and follow you in chains;
  they will bow in submission before you, and say,
  'Surely God is with you, and there is no other god.
15 How then can you be a God who hides himself,
    God of Israel, the Deliverer?'
16 All the makers of idols are confounded and brought
      to shame,
    they perish in confusion together.
17 But Israel has been delivered by the LORD,
    a deliverance for all time to come;
  they will never be confounded, never put to shame.

18 Thus says the LORD, the Creator of the heavens,
    he who is God,
  who made the earth and fashioned it
    and by himself fixed it firmly,
  who created it not as a formless waste
    but as a place to be lived in:
  I am the LORD, and there is none other.
19 I did not speak in secret, in realms of darkness;
  I did not say to Jacob's people,
    'Look for me in the formless waste.'
  I the LORD speak what is right, I declare what is
    just.

20 Gather together, come, draw near,
    you survivors of the nations,
  who in ignorance carry wooden idols in procession,
    praying to a god that cannot save.
21 Come forward and urge your case, consult
      together:
  who foretold this in days of old,
    who stated it long ago?
  Was it not I, the LORD?
    There is no god but me,
    none other than I, victorious and able to save.
22 From every corner of the earth
    turn to me and be saved;
    for I am God, there is none other.
23 By my life I have sworn,
    I have given a promise of victory,
    a promise that will not be broken;
  to me every knee will bow,
    by me every tongue will swear.
24 saying, 'In the LORD alone
    are victory and might.
  All who defy him
    will stand ashamed in his presence,
25 but all Israel's descendants will be victorious
    and will glory in the LORD.'

---

a Or Nubia; Heb *Cush*

NEW AMERICAN BIBLE

NEW JERUSALEM BIBLE

14 Thus says the LORD:
The earnings of Egypt, the gain of Ethiopia,
   and the Sabeans, tall of stature,
Shall come over to you and belong to you;
   they shall follow you, coming in chains.
Before you they shall fall prostrate,
   saying in prayer:
"With you only is God, and nowhere else;
   the gods are nought.
15 Truly with you God is hidden,
   the God of Israel, the savior!
16 Those are put to shame and disgrace
   who vent their anger against him;
Those go in disgrace
   who carve images.
17 Israel, you are saved by the LORD,
   saved forever!
You shall never be put to shame or disgrace
   in future ages."

18   For thus says the LORD,
The creator of the heavens,
   who is God,
The designer and maker of the earth
   who established it,
Not creating it to be a waste,
   but designing it to be lived in:
I am the LORD, and there is no other.
19 I have not spoken from hiding
   nor from some dark place of the earth,
And I have not said to the descendants of Jacob,
   "Look for me in an empty waste."
I, the LORD, promise justice,
   I foretell what is right.
20 Come and assemble, gather together,
   you fugitives from among the gentiles!
They are without knowledge who bear
      wooden idols
   and pray to gods that cannot save.
21 Come here and declare
   in counsel together;
Who announced this from the beginning
   and foretold it from of old?
Was it not I, the LORD,
   besides whom there is no other God?
There is no just and saving God but me.
22 Turn to me and be safe,
   all you ends of the earth,
   for I am God; there is no other!
23 By myself I swear,
   uttering my just decree
   and my unalterable word:
To me every knee shall bend;
   by me every tongue shall swear,
24 Saying, "Only in the LORD
   are just deeds and power.
Before him in shame shall come
   all who vent their anger against him.
25 In the LORD shall be the vindication and the glory
   of all the descendants of Israel."

14 Thus says Yahweh:
The produce of Egypt, the commerce of Cush
   and the men of Seba, tall of stature,
will come over to you and belong to you.
They will follow you, walking in chains,
   they will bow before you,
   they will pray to you,
'With you alone is God, and there is no other!
The gods do not exist.'
15 Truly, you are a God who conceals himself,
   God of Israel, Saviour!
16 They are shamed and humbled, every one of them,
   humiliated they go, the makers of idols.
17 Israel will be saved by Yahweh,
   saved everlastingly.
You will never be ashamed or humiliated
   for ever and ever.
18 For thus says Yahweh, the Creator of the
      heavens —
he is God, who shaped the earth and made it,
   who set it firm;
he did not create it to be chaos,
he formed it to be lived in:
I am Yahweh, and there is no other.
19 I have not spoken in secret,
   in some dark corner of the underworld.
I did not say, 'Offspring of Jacob,
   search for me in chaos!'
I am Yahweh: I proclaim saving justice,
   I say what is true.
20 Assemble, come, all of you gather round, survivors
      of the nations.
They have no knowledge, those who parade their
      wooden idols
   and pray to a god
   that cannot save.
21 Speak up, present your case,
   let them put their heads together!
Who foretold this in the past,
   who revealed it long ago?
Was it not I, Yahweh?
There is no other god except me,
   no saving God, no Saviour except me!
22 Turn to me and you will be saved,
   all you ends of the earth,
   for I am God, and there is no other.
23 By my own self I swear it;
   what comes from my mouth is saving justice,
   it is an irrevocable word:
All shall bend the knee to me,
   by me every tongue shall swear,
24 saying, 'In Yahweh alone
   are saving justice and strength,'
until all those who used to rage at him
   come to him in shame.
25 In Yahweh the whole race of Israel
   finds justice and glory.

NEW REVISED STANDARD VERSION | REVISED ENGLISH BIBLE

46 Bel bows down, Nebo stoops,
  their idols are on beasts and cattle;
these things you carry are loaded
  as burdens on weary animals.
2 They stoop, they bow down together;
  they cannot save the burden,
  but themselves go into captivity.

3 Listen to me, O house of Jacob,
  all the remnant of the house of Israel,
who have been borne by me from your birth,
  carried from the womb;
4 even to your old age I am he,
  even when you turn gray I will carry you.
I have made, and I will bear;
  I will carry and will save.

5 To whom will you liken me and make me equal,
  and compare me, as though we were alike?
6 Those who lavish gold from the purse,
  and weigh out silver in the scales —
they hire a goldsmith, who makes it into a god;
  then they fall down and worship!
7 They lift it to their shoulders, they carry it,
  they set it in its place, and it stands there;
  it cannot move from its place.
If one cries out to it, it does not answer
  or save anyone from trouble.

8 Remember this and consider,[b]
  recall it to mind, you transgressors,
9   remember the former things of old;
for I am God, and there is no other;
  I am God, and there is no one like me,
10 declaring the end from the beginning
  and from ancient times things not yet done,
saying, "My purpose shall stand,
  and I will fulfill my intention,"
11 calling a bird of prey from the east,
  the man for my purpose from a far country.
I have spoken, and I will bring it to pass;
  I have planned, and I will do it.

12 Listen to me, you stubborn of heart,
  you who are far from deliverance:
13 I bring near my deliverance, it is not far off,
  and my salvation will not tarry;
I will put salvation in Zion,
  for Israel my glory.

47 Come down and sit in the dust,
  virgin daughter Babylon!
Sit on the ground without a throne,
  daughter Chaldea!
For you shall no more be called
  tender and delicate.
2 Take the millstones and grind meal,
  remove your veil,
strip off your robe, uncover your legs,
  pass through the rivers.
3 Your nakedness shall be uncovered,
  and your shame shall be seen.
I will take vengeance,
  and I will spare no one.
4 Our Redeemer — the LORD of hosts is his name —
  is the Holy One of Israel.

5 Sit in silence, and go into darkness,
  daughter Chaldea!
For you shall no more be called

46 Bel has crouched down, Nebo stooped low:
  their images, once carried in your processions,
have been loaded on to beasts and cattle,
  a burden for the weary creatures;
2 though they stoop and crouch,
  they are not able to bring the burden to safety,
  but they themselves go into captivity.

3 Listen to me, house of Jacob
  and all who remain of the house of Israel,
a load on me from your birth,
  upheld by me from the womb:
4 Till you grow old I am the LORD,
  and when white hairs come, I shall carry you still;
I have made you and I shall uphold you,
  I shall carry you away to safety.

5 To whom will you liken me? Who is my equal?
  With whom can you compare me? Where is my
    like?
6 Those who squander their bags of gold
  and weigh out their silver with a balance
hire a goldsmith to fashion it into a god;
  then they prostrate themselves before it in worship;
7 they hoist it shoulder-high and carry it
  and set it down on its place;
there it must stand, it cannot stir from the spot.
  Let a man cry to it as he will, it does not answer;
  it cannot deliver him from his troubles.

8 Remember this and abandon hope;
  consider it well, you rebels.
9 Remember all that happened long ago,
  for I am God, and there is none other;
  I am God, and there is no one like me.
10 From the beginning I reveal the end,
  from ancient times what is yet to be;
I say, 'My purpose stands,
  I shall accomplish all that I please.'
11 I summon a bird of prey from the east —
  from a distant land a man to fulfil my design.
I have spoken and I shall bring it to pass,
  I have planned it, and I shall carry it out.
12 Listen to me, you stubborn of heart,
  for whom victory is far off:
13 I bring my victory near, mine is not far off,
  and my deliverance will not be delayed;
In Zion I shall grant deliverance
  for Israel my glory.

47 Come down and sit in the dust,
  virgin daughter of Babylon.
Descend from your throne and sit on the ground,
  daughter of the Chaldaeans;
never again will you be called
  tender and delicate.
2 Take the handmill, grind meal, remove your veil;
  strip off your skirt, bare your thighs, wade through
    rivers,
3 so that your nakedness may be seen,
  your shame exposed.
I shall take vengeance and show clemency to none,
4 says our Redeemer, the Holy One of Israel,
  whose name is the LORD of Hosts.

5 Daughter of the Chaldaeans,
  go into the darkness and sit in silence;
for never again will you be called

46:13 **for . . . glory:** *or* and give my glory to Israel.   47:4 **says:**
so some Gk MSS; Heb. omits.

[b] Meaning of Heb uncertain

NEW AMERICAN BIBLE

46

Bel bows down, Nebo stoops,
  their idols are upon beasts and cattle;
They must be borne up on shoulders,
  carried as burdens by the weary.
2 They stoop and bow down together;
  unable to save those who bear them,
  they too go into captivity.

3 Hear me, O house of Jacob,
  all who remain of the house of Israel,
My burden since your birth,
  whom I have carried from your infancy.
4 Even to your old age I am the same,
  even when your hair is gray I will bear you;
It is I who have done this, I who will continue,
  and I who will carry you to safety.

5 Whom would you compare me with, as an equal,
  or match me against, as though we were alike?
6 There are those who pour out gold from a purse
  and weigh out silver on the scales;
Then they hire a goldsmith to make it into a god
  before which they fall down in worship.
7 They lift it to their shoulders to carry;
  when they set it in place again, it stays,
  and does not move from the spot.
Although they cry out to it, it cannot answer;
  it delivers no one from distress.

8 Remember this and be firm;
  bear it well in mind, you rebels;
  remember the former things, those long ago:
9 I am God, there is no other;
  I am God, there is none like me.
10 At the beginning I foretell the outcome;
  in advance, things not yet done.
I say that my plan shall stand,
  I accomplish my every purpose.

11 I call from the east a bird of prey,
  from a distant land, one to carry out my plan.
Yes, I have spoken, I will accomplish it;
  I have planned it, and I will do it.
12 Listen to me, you fainthearted,
  you who seem far from the victory of justice:
13 I am bringing on my justice, it is not far off,
  my salvation shall not tarry;
I will put salvation within Zion,
  and give to Israel my glory.

47

Come down, sit in the dust,
  O virgin daughter Babylon;
Sit on the ground, dethroned,
  O daughter of the Chaldeans.
No longer shall you be called
  dainty and delicate.
2 Take the millstone and grind flour,
  remove your veil;
Strip off your train, bare your legs,
  pass through the streams.
3 Your nakedness shall be uncovered
  and your shame be seen;
I will take vengeance,
  I will yield to no entreaty,
  says our redeemer.
4 Whose name is the LORD of hosts,
  the Holy One of Israel.

5 Go into darkness and sit in silence,
  O daughter of the Chaldeans,
No longer shall you be called

NEW JERUSALEM BIBLE

46

Bel is crouching, Nebo cowering,
  their idols are being put on animals, on beasts of
  burden,
the loads you have been carrying
  are a burden to a weary beast.
2 They are cowering and crouching together,
  no one can save this burden,
  they themselves have gone into captivity.

3 Listen to me, House of Jacob,
  all who remain of the House of Israel,
  whom I have carried since the womb,
  whom I have supported since you were conceived.
4 Until your old age I shall be the same,
  until your hair is grey I shall carry you.
As I have done, so I shall support you,
  I myself shall carry and shall save you.

5 With whom can you compare me, equate me,
  to whom can you liken me, making equals of us?
6 They lavish gold from their purses
  and weigh out silver on the scales.
They engage a goldsmith to make a god,
  then bow low and actually adore!
7 They lift it on their shoulders and carry it,
  and put it down where it is meant to stand,
  so that it never moves from the spot.
You may cry out to it in distress, it never replies,
  it never saves anyone in trouble.

8 Remember this and stand firm;
  rebels, look into your hearts.
9 Remember the things that happened long ago,
  for I am God, and there is no other;
  I am God, and there is none like me.
10 From the beginning I revealed the future,
  in advance, what has not yet occurred.
I say: My purpose will come about,
  I shall do whatever I please;
11 I call a bird of prey from the east,
  my man predestined, from a distant land.
What I have said, I shall do,
  what I have planned, I shall perform.
12 Listen to me, you hard-hearted people
  far removed from saving justice:
13 I am bringing my justice nearer,
  it is not far away,
  my salvation will not delay.
I shall place my salvation in Zion
  and my glory in Israel.

47

Step down! Sit in the dust,
  virgin daughter of Babylon.
Sit on the ground, no throne,
  daughter of the Chaldaeans,
for never again will you be called
  tender and delicate.
2 Take the grinding mill, crush up the meal.
Remove your veil,
  tie up your skirt, bare your legs,
  cross the rivers.
3 Let your nakedness be displayed
  and your shame exposed.
I am going to take vengeance
  and no one will stand in my way.

4 Our redeemer, Yahweh Sabaoth is his name,
  the Holy One of Israel, says:
5 Sit in silence, bury yourself in darkness,
  daughter of the Chaldaeans,
for never again will you be called

---

z 46 Bel and Nebo are Babylonian chief gods, of the sky and wisdom
respectively.

NEW REVISED STANDARD VERSION	REVISED ENGLISH BIBLE

NEW REVISED STANDARD VERSION

the mistress of kingdoms.
6 I was angry with my people,
  I profaned my heritage;
I gave them into your hand,
  you showed them no mercy;
on the aged you made your yoke
  exceedingly heavy.
7 You said, "I shall be mistress forever,"
  so that you did not lay these things to heart
  or remember their end.

8 Now therefore hear this, you lover of pleasures,
  who sit securely,
who say in your heart,
  "I am, and there is no one besides me;
I shall not sit as a widow
  or know the loss of children"—
9 both these things shall come upon you
  in a moment, in one day:
the loss of children and widowhood
  shall come upon you in full measure,
in spite of your many sorceries
  and the great power of your enchantments.

10 You felt secure in your wickedness;
  you said, "No one sees me."
Your wisdom and your knowledge
  led you astray,
and you said in your heart,
  "I am, and there is no one besides me."
11 But evil shall come upon you,
  which you cannot charm away;
disaster shall fall upon you,
  which you will not be able to ward off;
and ruin shall come on you suddenly,
  of which you know nothing.

12 Stand fast in your enchantments
  and your many sorceries,
  with which you have labored from your youth;
perhaps you may be able to succeed,
  perhaps you may inspire terror.
13 You are wearied with your many consultations;
  let those who study[c] the heavens
stand up and save you,
  those who gaze at the stars,
  and at each new moon predict
  what[d] shall befall you.

14 See, they are like stubble,
  the fire consumes them;
they cannot deliver themselves
  from the power of the flame.
No coal for warming oneself is this,
  no fire to sit before!
15 Such to you are those with whom you have
    labored,
  who have trafficked with you from your youth;
they all wander about in their own paths;
  there is no one to save you.

48 Hear this, O house of Jacob,
  who are called by the name of Israel,
  and who came forth from the loins[e] of Judah;
who swear by the name of the LORD,
  and invoke the God of Israel,
  but not in truth or right.
2 For they call themselves after the holy city,
  and lean on the God of Israel;
  the LORD of hosts is his name.

REVISED ENGLISH BIBLE

queen of many kingdoms.
6 I was angry with my people;
  I dishonoured my own possession
  and surrendered them into your power.
You showed them no mercy;
  even on the aged you laid a very heavy yoke.
7 You said, 'I shall reign a queen for ever';
  you gave no thought to your actions,
  nor did you consider their outcome.

8 Now listen to this,
  you lover of luxury, carefree on your throne,
  saying to yourself,
  'I am, and there is none other.
I shall never sit in widow's mourning,
  never know the loss of children.'
9 Yet suddenly, in a single day,
  both these things will come upon you;
  they will both come upon you in full measure:
loss of children and widowhood,
  despite your many sorceries, all your countless
    spells.
10 Secure in your wicked ways
  you thought, 'No one can see me.'
It was your wisdom and knowledge
  that led you astray.
You said to yourself,
  'I am, and there is none other.'
11 Therefore evil will overtake you,
  and you will not know how to conjure it away;
disaster will befall you,
  and you will not be able to avert it;
ruin all unforeseen
  will suddenly come upon you.
12 Persist in your spells and your many sorceries,
  in which you have trafficked all your life.
Maybe you can get help from them!
  Maybe you will yet inspire terror!

13 In spite of your many wiles you are powerless.
  Let your astrologers, your star-gazers
who foretell your future month by month,
  persist, and save you!
14 But they are like stubble
  and fire burns them up;
they cannot snatch themselves from the flame.
  It is not a glowing coal to warm them,
  not a fire for them to sit by!
15 So much for your magicians
  with whom you have trafficked all your life:
they have wandered off, each his own way,
  and there is not one to save you.

48 Hear this, you house of Jacob,
  who are called by the name of Israel,
  and have sprung from the seed of Judah;
who swear by the name of the LORD
  and invoke the God of Israel,
  but not with honesty and sincerity,
2 though you call yourselves citizens of the Holy
    City
  and lean for support on the God of Israel,
  whose name is the LORD of Hosts:

---

[c] Meaning of Heb uncertain   [d] Gk Syr Compare Vg: Heb *from what*
[e] Cn: Heb *waters*

47:9 **in full measure:** *or* at random. **despite:** *or* because of.

sovereign mistress of kingdoms.
6 Angry at my people,
I profaned my inheritance,
And I gave them into your hand;
but you showed them no mercy,
And upon old men
you laid a very heavy yoke.
7 You said, "I shall remain always,
a sovereign mistress forever!"
But you did not lay these things to heart,
you disregarded their outcome.
8 Now hear this, voluptuous one,
enthroned securely,
Saying to yourself,
"I, and no one else!
I shall never be a widow,
or suffer the loss of my children"—
9 Both these things shall come to you
suddenly, in a single day:
Complete bereavement and widowhood
shall come upon you
For your many sorceries
and the great number of your spells;
10 Because you felt secure in your wickedness,
and said, "No one sees me."
Your wisdom and your knowledge
led you astray,
And you said to yourself,
"I, and no one else!"
11 But upon you shall come evil
you will not know how to predict;
Disaster shall befall you
which you cannot allay.
Suddenly there shall come upon you
ruin which you will not expect.
12 Keep up, now, your spells
and your many sorceries;
Perhaps you can make them avail,
perhaps you can strike terror!
13 You wearied yourself with many consultations,
at which you toiled from your youth;
Let the astrologers stand forth to save you,
the stargazers who forecast at each new moon
what would happen to you.
14 Lo, they are like stubble,
fire consumes them;
They cannot save themselves
from the spreading flames.
This is no warming ember,
no fire to sit before.
15 Thus do your wizards serve you
with whom you have toiled from your youth;
Each wanders his own way,
with none to save you.

the mistress of kingdoms.
6 Being angry with my people,
I rejected my heritage,
surrendering them into your clutches.
You showed them no mercy,
you made your yoke very heavy on the aged.
7 You thought, 'I shall be a queen for ever.'
You did not reflect on these matters
or think about the future.
8 Now listen to this, voluptuous woman,
lolling at ease
and thinking to yourself,
'I am the only one who matters.
I shall never be widowed,
never know bereavement.'
9 Yet both these things will befall you,
suddenly, in one day.
Bereavement and widowhood
will suddenly befall you
in spite of all your witchcraft
and the potency of your spells.
10 Confident in your wickedness,
you thought, 'No one can see me.'
Your wishes and your knowledge
were what deluded you,
as you thought to yourself,
'I am the only one who matters.'
11 Hence, disaster will befall you
which you will not know how to charm away,
calamity overtake you
which you will not be able to avert,
ruination will suddenly befall you,
such as you have never known.
12 Keep to your spells then,
and all your sorceries,
at which you have worked so hard since you were
young.
Perhaps you will succeed,
perhaps you will strike terror!
13 You have had many tiring consultations:
let the astrologers come forward now and save
you,
the star-gazers
who announce month by month
what will happen to you next.
14 Look, they are like wisps of straw,
the fire will burn them up.
They will not save their lives
from the power of the flame.
No embers these, for keeping warm,
no fire to sit beside!
15 Such will your wizards prove to be for you,
for whom you have worked so hard since you were
young;
each wandering his own way,
none of them can save you.

48 Hear this, O house of Jacob
called by the name Israel,
sprung from the stock of Judah,
You who swear by the name of the LORD
and invoke the God of Israel
without sincerity or justice,
2 Though you are named after the holy city
and rely on the God of Israel,
whose name is the LORD of hosts.

48 Listen to this, House of Jacob,
you who are called by the name of Israel
and issued from the waters of Judah,
who swear by the name of Yahweh
and invoke the God of Israel,
though not in good faith or uprightness;
2 for they call themselves after the holy city
and rely on the God of Israel,
Yahweh Sabaoth is his name.

3 The former things I declared long ago,
    they went out from my mouth and I made them
        known;
    then suddenly I did them and they came to
        pass.
4 Because I know that you are obstinate,
    and your neck is an iron sinew
    and your forehead brass,
5 I declared them to you from long ago,
    before they came to pass I announced them to
        you,
so that you would not say, "My idol did them,
    my carved image and my cast image
        commanded them."

6 You have heard; now see all this;
    and will you not declare it?
From this time forward I make you hear new
        things,
    hidden things that you have not known.
7 They are created now, not long ago;
    before today you have never heard of them,
    so that you could not say, "I already knew
        them."
8 You have never heard, you have never known,
    from of old your ear has not been opened.
For I knew that you would deal very
        treacherously,
    and that from birth you were called a rebel.

9 For my name's sake I defer my anger,
    for the sake of my praise I restrain it for you,
    so that I may not cut you off.
10 See, I have refined you, but not like$f$ silver;
    I have tested you in the furnace of adversity.
11 For my own sake, for my own sake, I do it,
    for why should my name$g$ be profaned?
    My glory I will not give to another.

12 Listen to me, O Jacob,
    and Israel, whom I called:
I am He; I am the first,
    and I am the last.
13 My hand laid the foundation of the earth,
    and my right hand spread out the heavens;
when I summon them,
    they stand at attention.

14 Assemble, all of you, and hear!
    Who among them has declared these things?
The LORD loves him;
    he shall perform his purpose on Babylon,
    and his arm shall be against the Chaldeans.
15 I, even I, have spoken and called him,
    I have brought him, and he will prosper in his
        way.
16 Draw near to me, hear this!
    From the beginning I have not spoken in
        secret,
    from the time it came to be I have been there.
And now the Lord GOD has sent me and his
        spirit.

17 Thus says the LORD,
    your Redeemer, the Holy One of Israel:
I am the LORD your God,
    who teaches you for your own good,
    who leads you in the way you should go.

3 Long ago I announced what would first happen,
    I revealed it with my own mouth;
    suddenly I acted and it came about.
4 Knowing your stubbornness,
    your neck being as stiff as iron, your brow like
        brass,
5 I told you of these things long ago,
    and declared them to you before they happened,
    so that you could not say, 'They were my idol's
        doing;
    my image, the god that I fashioned, ordained
        them.'
6 You have heard what I said; consider it well,
    and admit the truth of it.

From now on I show you new things,
    hidden things you did not know before.
7 They were not created long ago, but in this very
        hour;
    before today you had never heard of them.
    You cannot claim, 'I know them already.'
8 You neither heard nor knew;
    your ears were closed long ago.

I knew that you were treacherous
    and rebellious from your birth.
9 For the sake of my own name I was patient;
    rather than destroy you I held myself in check.
10 I tested you, but not as silver is tested:
    it was in the furnace of affliction I purified you.
11 For my honour's sake, for my own honour I did it;
    I will not let my name be profaned
    or yield my glory to any other god.
12 Listen to me, Jacob,
    and Israel whom I have called:
I am the LORD; I am the first,
    I am the last also.
13 My hand founded the earth,
    my right hand spread the expanse of the heavens;
when I summoned them,
    they came at once into being.
14 Assemble, all of you, and listen;
    which of you has declared what is coming,
    that he whom I love will carry out my purpose
        against Babylon
    and the Chaldaeans will be scattered?
15 I myself have spoken, I have summoned him,
    I have brought him here, and his mission will
        prosper.
16 Draw near to me and hear this:
    from the beginning I have never spoken in secret,
    and at its time of fulfilment I was there.

17 Thus says the LORD your Redeemer, the Holy One
        of Israel:
I am the LORD your God:
    I teach you for your own wellbeing
    and lead you in the way you should go.

48:9 **patient:** *prob. rdg; Heb.* adds my praise.   48:11 **my name:**
so Gk; Heb. omits.   48:14 **which of you:** *so many MSS; others*
which of them. **I:** *prob. rdg, cp. Gk; Heb.* adds the LORD.
48:16 **I was there:** *prob. rdg; Heb.* adds and now the Lord GOD has
sent me, and his spirit.

fCn: Heb *with* gGk Old Latin: Heb *for why should it*

3 Things of the past I foretold long ago,
   they went forth from my mouth, I let you hear
      of them;
   then suddenly I took action and they came to be.
4 Because I know that you are stubborn
   and that your neck is an iron sinew
   and your forehead bronze,
5 I foretold them to you of old;
   before they took place I let you hear of them,
   That you might not say, "My idol did them,
   my statue, my molten image commanded them."
6 Now that you have heard, look at all this;
   must you not admit it?

   From now on I announce new things to you,
   hidden events of which you knew not.
7 Now, not long ago, they are brought into being,
   and beforetime you did not hear of them,
   so that you cannot claim to have known them;
8 You neither heard nor knew,
   they did not reach your ears beforehand.
   Yes, I know you are utterly treacherous,
   a rebel you were called from birth.
9 For the sake of my name I restrain my anger,
   for the sake of my renown I hold it back
      from you,
   lest I should destroy you.
10 See, I have refined you like silver,
   tested you in the furnace of affliction.
11 For my sake, for my own sake, I do this;
   why should I suffer profanation?
   My glory I will not give to another.

12 Listen to me, Jacob,
   Israel, whom I named!
   I, it is I who am the first,
   and also the last am I.
13 Yes, my hand laid the foundations of the earth;
   my right hand spread out the heavens.
   When I call them,
   they stand forth at once.

14 All of you assemble and listen:
   Who among you foretold these things?
   The LORD's friend shall do his will
   against Babylon and the progeny of Chaldea.
15 I myself have spoken, I have called him,
   I have brought him, and his way succeeds!
16 Come near to me and hear this!
   Not from the beginning did I speak it in secret;
   At the time it comes to pass, I am present:
   "Now the Lord GOD has sent me, and his spirit."
17 Thus says the LORD, your redeemer,
   the Holy One of Israel:
   I, the LORD, your God,
   teach you what is for your good,
   and lead you on the way you should go.

3 Things now past I revealed long ago,
   they issued from my mouth, I proclaimed them;
   suddenly I acted and they happened.
4 For I knew you to be obstinate,
   your neck an iron sinew
   and your forehead bronze.
5 As I told you about it long before,
   before it happened I revealed it to you,
   so that you could not say, 'My statue did it,
   my idol, my metal image, ordained this.'
6 You have heard and seen all this,
   why won't you admit it?
   Now I am going to reveal new things to you,
   secrets that you do not know;
7 they have just been created, not long ago,
   and until today you have heard nothing about
      them,
   so that you cannot say, 'Yes, I knew about this.'
8 No, you have not heard, you have not known,
   for a long time your ear has not been attentive,
   for I knew how treacherous you were;
   you have been called a rebel since the womb.
9 For the sake of my name I shall defer my anger,
   for the sake of my honour I shall be patient with
      you, rather than destroy you.
10 Look, I have purchased you, but not for silver,
   I have chosen you out of the cauldron of affliction.
11 For my sake and my sake only shall I act,
   for why should my name be profaned?
   I will not yield my glory to another.

12 Listen to me, Jacob,
   Israel whom I have called:
   I, and none else, am the first,
   I am also the last.
13 My hand laid the foundations of earth
   and my right hand spread out the heavens.
   I summon them
   and they all present themselves together.
14 Assemble, all of you, and listen:
   which of them has revealed this?
   Yahweh loves him; he will do his pleasure
   on Babylon and the race of the Chaldaeans;
15 I, I have spoken, yes, I have summoned him,
   I have brought him, and he will succeed.
16 Come near and listen to this:
   from the first, I never spoke obscurely;
   when it happened, I was there,
   and now Lord Yahweh has sent me with his spirit.
17 Thus says Yahweh, your redeemer, the Holy One
      of Israel:
   I am Yahweh your God and teach you for your
      own good,
   I lead you in the way you ought to go.

NEW REVISED STANDARD VERSION	REVISED ENGLISH BIBLE

NEW REVISED STANDARD VERSION

18 O that you had paid attention to my
   commandments!
   Then your prosperity would have been like a
      river,
   and your success like the waves of the sea;
19 your offspring would have been like the sand,
   and your descendants like its grains;
   their name would never be cut off
   or destroyed from before me.

20 Go out from Babylon, flee from Chaldea,
   declare this with a shout of joy, proclaim it,
   send it forth to the end of the earth;
   say, "The LORD has redeemed his servant
      Jacob!"
21 They did not thirst when he led them through the
      deserts;
   he made water flow for them from the rock;
   he split open the rock and the water gushed
      out.
22 "There is no peace," says the LORD, "for the
      wicked."

49 Listen to me, O coastlands,
   pay attention, you peoples from far away!
The LORD called me before I was born,
   while I was in my mother's womb he named
      me.
2 He made my mouth like a sharp sword,
   in the shadow of his hand he hid me;
he made me a polished arrow,
   in his quiver he hid me away.
3 And he said to me, "You are my servant,
   Israel, in whom I will be glorified."
4 But I said, "I have labored in vain,
   I have spent my strength for nothing and vanity;
yet surely my cause is with the LORD,
   and my reward with my God."

5 And now the LORD says,
   who formed me in the womb to be his servant,
to bring Jacob back to him,
   and that Israel might be gathered to him,
for I am honored in the sight of the LORD,
   and my God has become my strength—
6 he says,
   "It is too light a thing that you should be my
      servant
   to raise up the tribes of Jacob
   and to restore the survivors of Israel;
I will give you as a light to the nations,
   that my salvation may reach to the end of the
      earth."

7 Thus says the LORD,
   the Redeemer of Israel and his Holy One,
to one deeply despised, abhorred by the nations,
   the slave of rulers,
"Kings shall see and stand up,
   princes, and they shall prostrate themselves,
because of the LORD, who is faithful,
   the Holy One of Israel, who has chosen you."

8 Thus says the LORD:
In a time of favor I have answered you,
   on a day of salvation I have helped you;
I have kept you and given you
   as a covenant to the people,[h]
to establish the land,
   to apportion the desolate heritages;

[h] Meaning of Heb uncertain

REVISED ENGLISH BIBLE

18 If only you had listened to my commands,
   your prosperity would have rolled on like a river,
   your success like the waves of the sea;
19 your children would have been like the sand in
      number,
   your descendants countless as its grains;
   their name would never be erased or blotted from
      my sight.

20 Go out from Babylon, hasten away from the
      Chaldaeans;
   proclaim it with joyful song,
   sending out the news to the ends of the earth;
   tell them, 'The LORD has redeemed his servant
      Jacob.'
21 Though he led them through desert places,
   they suffered no thirst;
   he made water flow for them from the rock,
   for them he split the rock and streams gushed
      forth.
22 There is no peace for the wicked,
   says the LORD.

49 LISTEN to me, you coasts and islands,
   pay heed, you peoples far distant:
   the LORD called me before I was born,
   he named me from my mother's womb.
2 He made my tongue a sharp sword
   and hid me under the shelter of his hand;
   he made me into a polished arrow,
   in his quiver he concealed me.
3 He said to me, 'Israel, you are my servant
   through whom I shall win glory.'
4 Once I said, 'I have toiled in vain;
   I have spent my strength for nothing, and to no
      purpose.'
   Yet my cause is with the LORD
   and my reward with my God.
5 The LORD had formed me in the womb to be his
      servant,
   to bring Jacob back to him
   that Israel should be gathered to him,
   so that I might rise to honour in the LORD's sight
   and my God might be my strength.
6 And now the LORD has said to me:
   'It is too slight a task for you, as my servant,
   to restore the tribes of Jacob,
   to bring back the survivors of Israel:
   I shall appoint you a light to the nations
   so that my salvation may reach earth's farthest
      bounds.'

7 These are the words of the Holy One, the LORD
      who redeems Israel,
   to one who is despised,
   and whom people abhor,
   the slave of tyrants:
   Kings will rise when they see you,
   princes will do homage,
   because of the LORD who is faithful,
   because of Israel's Holy One who has chosen you.

8 These are the words of the LORD:
   In the time of my favour I answered you;
   on the day of deliverance I came to your aid.
   I have formed you, and destined you
   to be a light for peoples,
   restoring the land
   and allotting once more its desolate holdings.

49:5 **be gathered to him:** or not be swept away.   49:8 **light:** or
covenant.

18 If you would hearken to my commandments,
   your prosperity would be like a river,
   and your vindication like the waves of the sea;
19 Your descendants would be like the sand,
   and those born of your stock like its grains,
   Their name never cut off
   or blotted out from my presence.
20 Go forth from Babylon, flee from Chaldea!
   With shouts of joy proclaim this, make
     it known;
   Publish it to the ends of the earth, and say,
   "The Lord has redeemed his servant Jacob."
21 They did not thirst
   when he led them through dry lands;
   Water from the rock he set flowing for them;
   he cleft the rock, and waters welled forth."
22 [There is no peace for the wicked,
   says the Lord.]

49 Hear me, O coastlands,
   listen, O distant peoples.
The Lord called me from birth,
   from my mother's womb he gave me my name.
2 He made of me a sharp-edged sword
   and concealed me in the shadow of his arm.
He made me a polished arrow,
   in his quiver he hid me.
3 You are my servant, he said to me,
   Israel, through whom I show my glory.

4 Though I thought I had toiled in vain,
   and for nothing, uselessly, spent my strength,
Yet my reward is with the Lord,
   my recompense is with my God.
5 For now the Lord has spoken
   who formed me as his servant from the womb,
That Jacob may be brought back to him
   and Israel gathered to him;
And I am made glorious in the sight of the Lord,
   and my God is now my strength!
6 It is too little, he says, for you to be my servant,
   to raise up the tribes of Jacob,
   and restore the survivors of Israel;
I will make you a light to the nations,
   that my salvation may reach to the ends of
     the earth.

7 Thus says the Lord,
   the redeemer and the Holy One of Israel,
To the one despised, whom the nations abhor,
   the slave of rulers:
When kings see you, they shall stand up,
   and princes shall prostrate themselves
Because of the Lord who is faithful,
   the Holy One of Israel who has chosen you.

8   Thus says the Lord:
In a time of favor I answer you,
   on the day of salvation I help you,
To restore the land
   and allot the desolate heritages,

18 If only you had listened to my commandments!
   Your prosperity would have been like a river
   and your saving justice like the waves of the sea.
19 Your descendants would have been numbered like
     the sand,
   your offspring as many as its grains.
Their name would never be cancelled or blotted out
   from my presence.

20 Come out from Babylon! Flee from the
     Chaldaeans!
Declare this with cries of joy, proclaim it,
   carry it to the remotest parts of earth,
   say, 'Yahweh has redeemed his servant Jacob.'
21 Those he led through the arid country never went
     thirsty;
   he made water flow for them from the rock,
   he split the rock and out streamed the water.
22 There is no peace, says Yahweh, for the wicked.

49 Coasts and islands, listen to me,
   pay attention, distant peoples.
Yahweh called me when I was in the womb,
   before my birth he had pronounced my name.
2 He made my mouth like a sharp sword,
   he hid me in the shadow of his hand.
He made me into a sharpened arrow
   and concealed me in his quiver.
3 He said to me, 'Israel, you are my servant,
   through whom I shall manifest my glory.'
4 But I said, 'My toil has been futile,
   I have exhausted myself for nothing, to no
     purpose.'
Yet all the while my cause was with Yahweh
   and my reward with my God.
5 And now Yahweh has spoken,
   who formed me in the womb to be his servant,
to bring Jacob back to him
   and to re-unite Israel to him;
—I shall be honoured in Yahweh's eyes,
   and my God has been my strength.—
6 He said, 'It is not enough for you to be my
     servant,
to restore the tribes of Jacob and bring back the
     survivors of Israel;
I shall make you a light to the nations
   so that my salvation may reach the remotest parts
     of earth.'

7 Thus says Yahweh,
   the redeemer, the Holy One of Israel,
to the one who is despised, detested by the nation,
   to the slave of despots:
Kings will stand up when they see,
   princes will see and bow low,
because of Yahweh who is faithful,
   the Holy One of Israel who has chosen you.

8 Thus says Yahweh:
At the time of my favour I have answered you,
   on the day of salvation I have helped you.
I have formed you and have appointed you
   to be the covenant for a people,
   to restore the land,
   to return ravaged properties,

NEW REVISED STANDARD VERSION

9 saying to the prisoners, "Come out,"
   to those who are in darkness, "Show
      yourselves."
They shall feed along the ways,
   on all the bare heights*i* shall be their pasture;
10 they shall not hunger or thirst,
   neither scorching wind nor sun shall strike
      them down,
   for he who has pity on them will lead them,
      and by springs of water will guide them.
11 And I will turn all my mountains into a road,
   and my highways shall be raised up.
12 Lo, these shall come from far away,
   and lo, these from the north and from the west,
      and these from the land of Syene.*j*

13 Sing for joy, O heavens, and exult, O earth;
   break forth, O mountains, into singing!
For the LORD has comforted his people,
   and will have compassion on his suffering
      ones.

14 But Zion said, "The LORD has forsaken me,
   my Lord has forgotten me."
15 Can a woman forget her nursing child,
   or show no compassion for the child of her
      womb?
Even these may forget,
   yet I will not forget you.
16 See, I have inscribed you on the palms of my
      hands;
   your walls are continually before me.
17 Your builders outdo your destroyers,*k*
   and those who laid you waste go away from
      you.
18 Lift up your eyes all around and see;
   they all gather, they come to you.
As I live, says the LORD,
   you shall put all of them on like an ornament,
      and like a bride you shall bind them on.

19 Surely your waste and your desolate places
   and your devastated land —
surely now you will be too crowded for your
      inhabitants,
   and those who swallowed you up will be far
      away.
20 The children born in the time of your
      bereavement
   will yet say in your hearing:
"The place is too crowded for me;
   make room for me to settle."
21 Then you will say in your heart,
   "Who has borne me these?
I was bereaved and barren,
   exiled and put away —
so who has reared these?
I was left all alone —
   where then have these come from?"

22 Thus says the Lord GOD:
   I will soon lift up my hand to the nations,
      and raise my signal to the peoples;
and they shall bring your sons in their bosom,
   and your daughters shall be carried on their
      shoulders.

REVISED ENGLISH BIBLE

9 I said to the prisoners, 'Go free,'
   and to those in darkness, 'Come out into the open.'
Along every path they will find pasture
   and grazing in all the arid places.
10 They will neither hunger nor thirst,
   nor will scorching heat or sun distress them;
for one who loves them will guide them
   and lead them by springs of water.
11 I shall make every hill a path
   and raise up my highways.
12 They are coming: some from far away,
   some from the north and the west,
      and others from the land of Syene.

13 Shout for joy, you heavens; earth, rejoice;
   break into songs of triumph, you mountains,
for the LORD has comforted his people
   and has had pity on them in their distress.

14 But Zion says,
   'The LORD has forsaken me;
      my Lord has forgotten me.'
15 Can a woman forget the infant at her breast,
   or a mother the child of her womb?
But should even these forget,
   I shall never forget you.
16 I have inscribed you on the palms of my hands;
   your walls are always before my eyes.
17 Those who rebuild you make better speed
   than those who pulled you down,
while those who laid you waste leave you and go.
18 Raise your eyes and look around:
   they are all assembling, flocking back to you.
By my life I, the LORD, swear it:
   you will wear them as your jewels,
      and adorn yourself with them like a bride;
19 I did indeed make you waste and desolate,
   I razed you to the ground,
but now the land is too small for its inhabitants,
   while they who made you a ruin are far away.
20 Children born during your bereavement will say,
   'Make room for us to live here,
      the place is too cramped.'
21 Then you will say to yourself,
   'Who bore these children for me,
      bereaved and barren as I was?
Who reared them
   when I was left alone, left by myself;
      where did I get them?'

22 These are the words of the Lord GOD:
   I shall beckon to the nations
      and hoist my signal to the peoples,
and they will bring your sons in their arms
   and your daughters will be carried on their
      shoulders;

---

i Or *the trails*   *j* Q Ms: MT *Sinim*   *k* Or *Your children come
swiftly; your destroyers*

49:19 **I did . . . land:** or your wasted and desolate land, your ruined
countryside.   49:21 **as I was:** *so Gk; Heb. adds* banished and
exiled.

NEW AMERICAN BIBLE

9 Saying to the prisoners: Come out!
To those in darkness: Show yourselves!
Along the ways they shall find pasture,
on every bare height shall their pastures be.
10 They shall not hunger or thirst,
nor shall the scorching wind or the sun
strike them;
For he who pities them leads them
and guides them beside springs of water.
11 I will cut a road through all my mountains,
and make my highways level.
12 See, some shall come from afar,
others from the north and the west,
and some from the land of Syene.

13 Sing out, O heavens, and rejoice, O earth,
break forth into song, you mountains.
For the LORD comforts his people
and shows mercy to his afflicted.

14 But Zion said, "The LORD has forsaken me;
my Lord has forgotten me."
15 Can a mother forget her infant,
be without tenderness for the child of her womb?
Even should she forget,
I will never forget you.
16 See, upon the palms of my hands I have written
your name;
your walls are ever before me.
17 Your rebuilders make haste,
as those who tore you down and laid you waste
go forth from you;
18 Look about and see,
they are all gathering and coming to you.
As I live, says the LORD,
you shall be arrayed with them all as
with adornments,
like a bride you shall fasten them on you.

19 Though you were waste and desolate,
a land of ruins,
Now you shall be too small for your inhabitants,
while those who swallowed you up will be
far away.
20 The children whom you had lost
shall yet say to you,
"This place is too small for me,
make room for me to live in."
21 You shall ask yourself:
"Who has borne me these?
I was bereft and barren
[exiled and repudiated];
who has reared them?
I was left all alone;
where then do these come from?"

22   Thus says the LORD GOD:
See, I will lift up my hand to the nations,
and raise my signal to the peoples;
They shall bring your sons in their arms,
and your daughters shall be carried on
their shoulders.

NEW JERUSALEM BIBLE

9 to say to prisoners, 'Come out,'
to those who are in darkness,
'Show yourselves.'
Along the roadway they will graze,
and any bare height will be their pasture.
10 They will never hunger or thirst,
scorching wind and sun will never plague them;
for he who pities them will lead them,
will guide them to springs of water.
11 I shall turn all my mountains into a road
and my highways will be raised aloft.
12 Look! Here they come from far away,
look, these from the north and the west,
those from the land of Sinim. a

13 Shout for joy, you heavens; earth, exult!
Mountains, break into joyful cries!
For Yahweh has consoled his people,
is taking pity on his afflicted ones.

14 Zion was saying, 'Yahweh has abandoned me,
the Lord has forgotten me.'
15 Can a woman forget her baby at the breast,
feel no pity for the child she has borne?
Even if these were to forget,
I shall not forget you.
16 Look, I have engraved you on the palms of my
hands,
your ramparts are ever before me.
17 Your rebuilders are hurrying,
your destroyers and despoilers will soon go away.
18 Raise your eyes and look around you:
all are assembling, coming to you. b
By my life, declares Yahweh,
you will put them all on like jewels,
like a bride, you will fasten them on.
19 For your desolate places and your ruins
and your devastated country
from now on will be too cramped for your
inhabitants,
and your devourers will be far away.
20 Once more they will say in your hearing,
the children of whom you were bereft,
'The place is too cramped for me,
make room for me to live.'
21 Then you will think to yourself,
'Who has borne me these?
I was bereft and barren,
exiled, turned out of my home;
who has reared these?
I was left all alone,
so where have these come from?'

22 Thus says Lord Yahweh:
Look, I am beckoning to the nations
and hoisting a signal to the peoples:
they will bring your sons in their arms
and your daughters will be carried on their
shoulders.

a 49 Syene in Egypt, modern Aswan, where there was a large Jewish colony.   b 49 = 60:4.

NEW REVISED STANDARD VERSION	REVISED ENGLISH BIBLE

NEW REVISED STANDARD VERSION

23 Kings shall be your foster fathers,
  and their queens your nursing mothers.
  With their faces to the ground they shall bow
    down to you,
  and lick the dust of your feet.
  Then you will know that I am the LORD;
    those who wait for me shall not be put to
      shame.

24 Can the prey be taken from the mighty,
  or the captives of a tyrant[l] be rescued?
25 But thus says the LORD:
  Even the captives of the mighty shall be taken,
  and the prey of the tyrant be rescued;
  for I will contend with those who contend with
    you,
  and I will save your children.
26 I will make your oppressors eat their own flesh,
  and they shall be drunk with their own blood
    as with wine.
  Then all flesh shall know
    that I am the LORD your Savior,
  and your Redeemer, the Mighty One of Jacob.

50 Thus says the LORD:
  Where is your mother's bill of divorce
    with which I put her away?
  Or which of my creditors is it
    to whom I have sold you?
  No, because of your sins you were sold,
    and for your transgressions your mother was
      put away.
2 Why was no one there when I came?
    Why did no one answer when I called?
  Is my hand shortened, that it cannot redeem?
    Or have I no power to deliver?
  By my rebuke I dry up the sea,
    I make the rivers a desert;
  their fish stink for lack of water,
    and die of thirst.[m]
3 I clothe the heavens with blackness,
    and make sackcloth their covering.

4 The Lord GOD has given me
    the tongue of a teacher,[n]
  that I may know how to sustain
    the weary with a word.
  Morning by morning he wakens—
    wakens my ear
  to listen as those who are taught.
5 The Lord GOD has opened my ear,
    and I was not rebellious,
  I did not turn backward.
6 I gave my back to those who struck me,
    and my cheeks to those who pulled out the
      beard;
  I did not hide my face
    from insult and spitting.

7 The Lord GOD helps me;
    therefore I have not been disgraced;
  therefore I have set my face like flint,
    and I know that I shall not be put to shame;
8 he who vindicates me is near.
  Who will contend with me?
  Let us stand up together.
  Who are my adversaries?
  Let them confront me.

REVISED ENGLISH BIBLE

23 kings will be your foster-fathers,
  their princesses serve as your nurses.
  They will bow to the earth before you
  and lick the dust from your feet.
  You will know that I am the LORD;
  none who look to me will be disappointed.

24 Can spoil be snatched from the strong man,
  or a captive liberated from the ruthless?
25 Yes, says the LORD,
  the captive will be taken even from the strong,
  and the spoil of the ruthless will be liberated;
  I shall contend with all who contend against you
  and deliver your children from them.
26 I shall make your oppressors eat their own flesh,
  and they will be drunk with their own blood
    as if with wine,
  and all mankind will know
  that I the LORD am your Deliverer,
  your Redeemer, the Mighty One of Jacob.

50 These are the words of the Lord:
  Is there anywhere a deed of divorce
  by which I put your mother away?
  Which creditor of mine was there
  to whom I sold you?
  No; for your own wickedness you were sold
  and for your misconduct your mother was put
    away.
2 Why did I find no one when I came?
  Why, when I called, did no one answer?
  Can my arm not reach out to deliver?
  Do you think I lacked the power to save?
  Did I not by my rebuke dry up the sea
  and turn rivers into desert,
  the fish in them stinking for lack of water
  and dying of thirst?
3 Did I not clothe the heavens with mourning,
  and cover them with sackcloth?

4 The Lord GOD has given me
  the tongue of one who has been instructed
  to console the weary
  with a timely word;
  he made my hearing sharp every morning,
  that I might listen like one under instruction.
5 The Lord GOD opened my ears
  and I did not disobey or turn back in defiance.
6 I offered my back to the lash,
  and let my beard be plucked from my chin,
  I did not hide my face from insult and spitting.
7 But the Lord GOD is my helper;
  therefore no insult can wound me;
  I know that I shall not be put to shame,
  therefore I have set my face like flint.
8 One who will clear my name is at my side.
  Who dare argue against me? Let us confront one
    another.
  Who will dispute my cause? Let him come
    forward.

---

[l] Q Ms Syr Vg: MT *of a righteous person*   [m] Or *die on the thirsty*
ground   [n] Cn: Heb *of those who are taught*

49:24 **ruthless:** *so Scroll; Heb. righteous.*
prob. rdg, cp. Gk; Heb. adds he aroused.   50:4 **with . . . word:**

NEW AMERICAN BIBLE

23 Kings shall be your foster fathers,
  their princesses your nurses;
Bowing to the ground, they shall worship you
  and lick the dust at your feet.
Then you shall know that I am the LORD,
  and those who hope in me shall never
    be disappointed.

24   Thus says the LORD:
  Can booty be taken from a warrior?
    or captives be rescued from a tyrant?
25 Yes, captives can be taken from a warrior,
    and booty be rescued from a tyrant;
  Those who oppose you I will oppose,
    and your sons I will save.
26 I will make your oppressors eat their own flesh,
    and they shall be drunk with their own blood
      as with the juice of the grape.
  All mankind shall know
    that I, the LORD, am your savior,
    your redeemer, the mighty one of Jacob.

50 Thus says the LORD:
  Where is the bill of divorce
    with which I dismissed your mother?
  Or to which of my creditors
    have I sold you?
  It was for your sins that you were sold,
    for your crimes that your mother was dismissed.

2 Why was no one there when I came?
    Why did no one answer when I called?
  Is my hand too short to ransom?
    Have I not the strength to deliver?
  Lo, with my rebuke I dry up the sea,
    I turn rivers into a desert;
  Their fish rot for lack of water,
    and die of thirst.
3 I clothe the heavens in mourning,
    and make sackcloth their vesture.

4 The Lord GOD has given me
    a well-trained tongue,
  That I might know how to speak to the weary
    a word that will rouse them.
  Morning after morning
    he opens my ear that I may hear;
5 And I have not rebelled,
    have not turned back.
6 I gave my back to those who beat me,
    my cheeks to those who plucked my beard;
  My face I did not shield
    from buffets and spitting.

7 The Lord GOD is my help,
    therefore I am not disgraced;
  I have set my face like flint,
    knowing that I shall not be put to shame.
8 He is near who upholds my right;
    if anyone wishes to oppose me,
    let us appear together.
  Who disputes my right?
    Let him confront me.

NEW JERUSALEM BIBLE

23 Kings will be your foster-fathers
  and their princesses, your foster-mothers.
They will fall prostrate before you, faces to the
    ground,
  and lick the dust at your feet.
And you will know that I am Yahweh;
  those who hope in me will not be disappointed.
24 Can the body be snatched from the warrior,
  can the tyrant's captive be set free?
25 But thus says Yahweh:
  The warrior's captive will indeed be snatched away
  and the tyrant's booty will indeed be set free;
  I myself shall fight those who fight you
  and I myself shall save your children.
26 I shall make your oppressors eat their own flesh,
  they will be as drunk on their own blood as on
    new wine.
And all humanity will know
  that I am Yahweh, your Saviour,
  your redeemer, the Mighty One of Jacob.

50 Thus says Yahweh:
  Where is your mother's writ of divorce
    by which I repudiated her?
  Or to which of my creditors
    have I sold you?
  Look, you have been sold for your own misdeeds,
    your mother was repudiated for your acts of
      rebellion.
2 Why was there no one there when I came?
    Why did no one answer when I called?
  Is my hand too short to redeem?
    Have I not strength to save?
  Look, with a threat I can dry the sea,
    and turn rivers to desert;
  the fish in them go rotten for want of water
    and die of thirst.
3 I dress the heavens in black,
    I cover them in sackcloth.

4 Lord Yahweh has given me a disciple's tongue,
    for me to know how to give a word of comfort to
      the weary.
  Morning by morning he makes my ear alert
    to listen like a disciple.
5 Lord Yahweh has opened my ear
    and I have not resisted,
    I have not turned away.
6 I have offered my back to those who struck me,
    my cheeks to those who plucked my beard;
  I have not turned my face away
    from insult and spitting.

7 Lord Yahweh comes to my help,
    this is why insult has not touched me,
  this is why I have set my face like flint
    and know that I shall not be put to shame.
8 He who grants me saving justice is near!
    Who will bring a case against me?
  Let us appear in court together!
  Who has a case against me?
  Let him approach me!

|

9 It is the Lord God who helps me;
  who will declare me guilty?
All of them will wear out like a garment;
  the moth will eat them up.

10 Who among you fears the Lord
  and obeys the voice of his servant,
who walks in darkness
  and has no light,
yet trusts in the name of the Lord
  and relies upon his God?

11 But all of you are kindlers of fire,
  lighters of firebrands.*o*
Walk in the flame of your fire,
  and among the brands that you have kindled!
This is what you shall have from my hand:
  you shall lie down in torment.

51

Listen to me, you that pursue righteousness,
  you that seek the Lord.
Look to the rock from which you were hewn,
  and to the quarry from which you were dug.
2 Look to Abraham your father
  and to Sarah who bore you;
for he was but one when I called him,
  but I blessed him and made him many.
3 For the Lord will comfort Zion;
  he will comfort all her waste places,
and will make her wilderness like Eden,
  her desert like the garden of the Lord;
joy and gladness will be found in her,
  thanksgiving and the voice of song.

4 Listen to me, my people,
  and give heed to me, my nation;
for a teaching will go out from me,
  and my justice for a light to the peoples.
5 I will bring near my deliverance swiftly,
  my salvation has gone out
and my arms will rule the peoples;
  the coastlands wait for me,
  and for my arm they hope.
6 Lift up your eyes to the heavens,
  and look at the earth beneath;
for the heavens will vanish like smoke,
  the earth will wear out like a garment,
  and those who live on it will die like gnats;*p*
but my salvation will be forever,
  and my deliverance will never be ended.

7 Listen to me, you who know righteousness,
  you people who have my teaching in your
    hearts;
do not fear the reproach of others,
  and do not be dismayed when they revile you.
8 For the moth will eat them up like a garment,
  and the worm will eat them like wool;
but my deliverance will be forever,
  and my salvation to all generations.

9 Awake, awake, put on strength,
  O arm of the Lord!
Awake, as in days of old,
  the generations of long ago!
Was it not you who cut Rahab in pieces,
  who pierced the dragon?

9 The Lord God is my helper;
  who then can declare me guilty?
They will all wear out like a garment;
  the moth will devour them.

10 Whoever among you fears the Lord,
  let him obey his servant's commands.
The one who walks in dark places with no light,
  let him trust in the name of the Lord and rely on
    his God.
11 But all who kindle a fire and set firebrands alight,
  walk by the light of your fire
and the firebrands you have set ablaze.
This is your fate at my hands:
  you shall lie down in torment.

51

Listen to me,
  all who follow after the right, who seek the
    Lord:
consider the rock from which you were hewn,
  the quarry from which you were cut;
2 consider Abraham your father
  and Sarah who gave you birth:
when I called him he was but one;
  I blessed him and made him many.

3 The Lord has comforted Zion,
  comforted all her ruined homes,
turning her wilderness into an Eden,
  her arid plains into a garden of the Lord.
Gladness and joy will be found in her,
  thanksgiving and melody.

4 Pay heed to me, my people,
  and listen to me, my nation,
for instruction will shine forth from me
  and my judgement will be a light to peoples.
5 In an instant I bring near my victory;
  my deliverance will appear
and my arm will rule the peoples;
  coasts and islands will wait for me
  and look to me for protection.

6 Raise your eyes heavenwards;
  look on the earth beneath:
though the heavens be dispersed as smoke
  and the earth wear out like a garment
and its inhabitants die like flies,
  my deliverance will be everlasting
  and my saving power will remain unbroken.

7 Listen to me, my people who know what is right,
  you that lay my instruction to heart:
do not fear the taunts of enemies,
  do not let their reviling dismay you;
8 for they will be like a garment devoured by grubs,
  like wool consumed by moths,
but my saving power will last for ever
  and my deliverance to all generations.

9 Awake, awake! Arm of the Lord, put on strength;
  awake as you did in days of old, in ages long past.
Was it not you who hacked Rahab in pieces
  and ran the dragon through?

50:11 **set . . . alight:** *prob. rdg, cp. Gk; Heb.* gird on firebrands.
51:5 **I bring near:** *prob. rdg; Heb. obscure.*

o Syr: Heb *you gird yourselves with firebrands*   *p* Or *in like manner*

NEW AMERICAN BIBLE

9 See, the Lord GOD is my help;
  who will prove me wrong?
Lo, they will all wear out like cloth,
  the moth will eat them up.
10 Who among you fears the LORD,
  heeds his servant's voice,
And walks in darkness
  without any light,
Trusting in the name of the LORD
  and relying on his God?
11 All of you kindle flames
  and carry about you fiery darts;
Walk by the light of your own fire
  and by the flares you have burnt!
This is your fate from my hand:
  you shall lie down in a place of pain.

51 Listen to me, you who pursue justice,
  who seek the LORD;
Look to the rock from which you were hewn,
  to the pit from which you were quarried;
2 Look to Abraham, your father,
  and to Sarah, who gave you birth;
When he was but one I called him,
  I blessed him and made him many.
3 Yes, the LORD shall comfort Zion
  and have pity on all her ruins;
Her deserts he shall make like Eden,
  her wasteland like the garden of the LORD;
Joy and gladness shall be found in her,
  thanksgiving and the sound of song.

4 Be attentive to me, my people;
  my folk, give ear to me.
For law shall go forth from my presence,
  and my judgment, as the light of the peoples.
5 I will make my justice come speedily;
  my salvation shall go forth
  [and my arm shall judge the nations];
In me shall the coastlands hope,
  and my arm they shall await.

6 Raise your eyes to the heavens,
  and look at the earth below;
Though the heavens grow thin like smoke,
  the earth wears out like a garment
  and its inhabitants die like flies,
My salvation shall remain forever
  and my justice shall never be dismayed.
7 Hear me, you who know justice,
  you people who have my teaching at heart:
Fear not the reproach of men,
  be not dismayed at their revilings.
8 They shall be like a garment eaten by moths,
  like wool consumed by grubs;
But my justice shall remain forever
  and my salvation, for all generations.

9 Awake, awake, put on strength,
  O arm of the LORD!
Awake as in the days of old,
  in ages long ago!
Was it not you who crushed Rahab,
  you who pierced the dragon?

NEW JERUSALEM BIBLE

9 Look, Lord Yahweh is coming to my help!
  Who dares condemn me?
Look at them, all falling apart
  like moth-eaten clothes!
10 Which of you fears Yahweh
  and listens to his servant's voice?
Which of you walks in darkness
  and sees no light?
Let him trust in the name of Yahweh
  and lean on his God!
11 Look, all you who light a fire
  and arm yourselves with firebrands,
walk by the light of your fire
  and the firebrands you have kindled!
This is what you will get from me:
  you will lie down in torment!

51 Listen to me, you who pursue saving justice,
  you who seek Yahweh.
Consider the rock from which you were hewn,
  the quarry from which you were dug.
2 Consider Abraham your father
  and Sarah who gave you birth.
When I called him he was the only one
  but I blessed him and made him numerous.
3 Yes, Yahweh has pity on Zion,
  has pity on all her ruins;
he will turn her desert into an Eden
  and her wastelands into the garden of Yahweh.
Joy and gladness will be found in her,
  thanksgiving and the sound of music.

4 Pay attention to me, my people,
  listen to me, my nation,
for a law will come from me,
  and I shall make my saving justice the light of
    peoples.
5 My justice is suddenly approaching,
  my salvation appears,
  my arm is about to judge the peoples.
The coasts and islands will put their hope in me
  and put their trust in my arm.
6 Raise your eyes to the heavens,
  look down at the earth;
for the heavens will vanish like smoke,
  the earth wear out like clothing
  and its inhabitants die like vermin,
but my salvation will last for ever
  and my saving justice remain inviolable.
7 Listen to me, you who know what saving justice
    means,
  a people who take my laws to heart:
do not fear people's taunts,
  do not be alarmed by their insults,
8 for the moth will eat them like clothing,
  the grub will devour them like wool,
but my saving justice will last for ever
  and my salvation for all generations.

9 Awake, awake! Clothe yourself in strength,
  arm of Yahweh.
Awake, as in the olden days,
  generations long ago!
Was it not you who split Rahab^c in half,
  who pierced the Dragon through?

---

^c **51** Creation is represented as a triumph over the monsters of chaos,
especially the sea.

NEW REVISED STANDARD VERSION	REVISED ENGLISH BIBLE

NEW REVISED STANDARD VERSION

10 Was it not you who dried up the sea,
   the waters of the great deep;
   who made the depths of the sea a way
   for the redeemed to cross over?
11 So the ransomed of the LORD shall return,
   and come to Zion with singing;
   everlasting joy shall be upon their heads;
   they shall obtain joy and gladness,
   and sorrow and sighing shall flee away.
12 I, I am he who comforts you;
   why then are you afraid of a mere mortal who
      must die,
   a human being who fades like grass?
13 You have forgotten the LORD, your Maker,
   who stretched out the heavens
   and laid the foundations of the earth.
   You fear continually all day long
   because of the fury of the oppressor,
   who is bent on destruction.
   But where is the fury of the oppressor?
14 The oppressed shall speedily be released;
   they shall not die and go down to the Pit,
   nor shall they lack bread.
15 For I am the LORD your God,
   who stirs up the sea so that its waves roar—
   the LORD of hosts is his name.
16 I have put my words in your mouth,
   and hidden you in the shadow of my hand,
   stretching out[q] the heavens
   and laying the foundations of the earth,
   and saying to Zion, "You are my people."
17 Rouse yourself, rouse yourself!
   Stand up, O Jerusalem,
   you who have drunk at the hand of the LORD
   the cup of his wrath,
   who have drunk to the dregs
   the bowl of staggering.
18 There is no one to guide her
   among all the children she has borne;
   there is no one to take her by the hand
   among all the children she has brought up.
19 These two things have befallen you
   —who will grieve with you?—
   devastation and destruction, famine and sword—
   who will comfort you?[r]
20 Your children have fainted,
   they lie at the head of every street
   like an antelope in a net;
   they are full of the wrath of the LORD,
   the rebuke of your God.
21 Therefore hear this, you who are wounded,[s]
   who are drunk, but not with wine:
22 Thus says your Sovereign, the LORD,
   your God who pleads the cause of his people:
   See, I have taken from your hand the cup of
      staggering;
   you shall drink no more
   from the bowl of my wrath.
23 And I will put it into the hand of your
      tormentors,
   who have said to you,
   "Bow down, that we may walk on you";
   and you have made your back like the ground
   and like the street for them to walk on.

REVISED ENGLISH BIBLE

10 Was it not you who dried up the sea,
   the waters of the great abyss,
   and made the ocean depths a path for the
      redeemed?
11 The LORD's people, set free, will come back
   and enter Zion with shouts of triumph,
   crowned with everlasting joy.
   Gladness and joy will come upon them,
   while suffering and weariness flee away.
12 I am he who comforts you;
   why then fear man who must die,
   who must perish like grass?
13 Why have you forgotten the LORD your maker,
   who stretched out the heavens and founded the
      earth?
   Why are you in constant fear all the day long?
   Why dread the fury of the oppressors
   bent on your destruction?
   Where is the oppressors' fury?
14 He who cowers under it will soon be set free;
   he will not be consigned to a dungeon
   and die there lacking food.

15 I am the LORD your God, who stirred up the sea so that
its waves roared. The LORD of Hosts is my name. 16 I have
put my words in your mouth and kept you covered under the
shelter of my hand. I who fixed the heavens in place and
established the earth say to Zion, You are my people.

17 Arouse yourself; rise up, Jerusalem.
   From the LORD's hand you have drunk
   the cup of his wrath,
   drained to its dregs the bowl of drunkenness;
18 of all the sons you have borne
   there is not one to guide you,
   of all you have reared
   not one to take you by the hand.
19 This twofold disaster has overtaken you:
   havoc and ruin—who can condole with you?
   Famine and sword—who can comfort you?
20 Your children lie in a stupor at every street corner,
   like antelopes caught in a net.
   They are glutted with the wrath of the LORD,
   with the rebuke of your God.
21 Therefore listen to this in your affliction,
   you that are drunk, but not with wine.
22 Thus says the LORD, your Lord and God,
   who will plead his people's cause:
   I take from your hand
   the cup of drunkenness.
   Never again will you drink from the bowl of my
      wrath;
23 I shall hand it to your tormentors,
   those who said to you, 'Lie down for us to walk
      over you.'
   You flattened your back like ground beneath their
      feet,
   like a road for them to walk over.

---

[q] Syr: Heb *planting*   [r] Q Ms Gk Syr Vg: MT *how may I comfort
you?*   [s] Or *humbled*

51:19 **who can comfort you**: *so Scroll; Heb.* who am I to comfort
you.

10 Was it not you who dried up the sea,
   the waters of the great deep,
Who made the depths of the sea into a way
   for the redeemed to pass over?
11 Those whom the LORD has ransomed will return
   and enter Zion singing,
   crowned with everlasting joy;
They will meet with joy and gladness,
   sorrow and mourning will flee.
12 I, it is I who comfort you.
   Can you then fear mortal man,
   who is human only, to be looked upon as grass,
13 And forget the LORD, your maker,
   who stretched out the heavens
   and laid the foundations of the earth?
All the day you are in constant dread
   of the fury of the oppressor;
But when he sets himself to destroy,
   what is there of the oppressor's fury?

14 The oppressed shall soon be released;
   they shall not die and go down into the pit,
   nor shall they want for bread.
15 For I am the LORD, your God,
   who stirs up the sea so that its waves roar;
   the LORD of hosts by name.
16 I have put my words into your mouth
   and shielded you in the shadow of my hand,
I, who stretched out the heavens,
   who laid the foundations of the earth,
   who say to Zion: You are my people.

17 Awake, awake!
   Arise, O Jerusalem,
You who drank at the LORD's hand
   the cup of his wrath;
Who drained to the dregs
   the bowl of staggering!
18 She has no one to guide her
   of all the sons she bore;
She has no one to grasp her by the hand,
   of all the sons she reared! —
19 Your misfortunes are double;
   who is there to condole with you?
Desolation and destruction, famine and sword!
   Who is there to comfort you?
20 Your sons lie helpless
   at every street corner
   like antelopes in a net.
They are filled with the wrath of the LORD,
   the rebuke of your God.
21 But now, hear this, O afflicted one,
   drunk, but not with wine,
22 Thus says the LORD, your Master,
   your God, who defends his people:
See, I am taking from your hand
   the cup of staggering;
The bowl of my wrath
   you shall no longer drink.
23 I will put it into the hands of your tormentors,
   those who ordered you
to bow down, that they might walk over you,
While you offered your back like the ground,
   like the street for them to walk on.

10 Was it not you who dried up the sea,
   the waters of the great Abyss;
who made the sea-bed into a road
   for the redeemed to go across?
11 This is why those whom Yahweh has ransomed
      will return,
they will enter Zion shouting for joy,
   their heads crowned with a joy unending;
joy and gladness will escort them
   and sorrow and sighing will take flight.
12 I, I am your consoler.
   Why then should you be afraid
of mortal human beings, of a child of man,
   whose fate is that of the grass?
13 You forget about Yahweh your Creator
   who spread out the heavens and laid the earth's
      foundations;
you have never stopped trembling all day long
   before the fury of the oppressor
when he was bent on destruction.
   Where is the oppressor's fury now?
14 The despairing captive is soon to be set free;
   he will not die in the dungeon,
   nor will his food run out.
15 I am Yahweh your God who stirs up the sea,
      making its waves roar—
Yahweh Sabaoth is my name.
16 I put my words into your mouth,
   I hid you in the shadow of my hand,
to spread out the heavens and lay the earth's
      foundations
and say to Zion, 'You are my people.'

17 Awake, awake!
   To your feet, Jerusalem!
You who from Yahweh's hand
   have drunk the cup of his wrath.
The chalice, the stupefying cup,
   you have drained to the dregs.
18 There is no one to guide her
   of all the children she has borne,
no one to grasp her hand
   of all the children she has reared.
19 Double disaster has befallen you—
   who is there to sympathise?
Pillage and ruin, famine and sword—
   who is there to console you?
20 Your children are lying helpless
   at the end of every street
   like an antelope trapped in a net;
they are filled to the brim with Yahweh's wrath,
   with the rebuke of your God.
21 So listen to this, afflicted one,
   drunk, though not with wine.
22 Thus says your Lord Yahweh,
   your God, defender of your people:
Look, I am taking
   the stupefying cup from your hand,
   the chalice, the cup of my wrath,
   you will not have to drink again.
23 I shall hand it to your tormentors
   who used to say to you,
'On the ground! So that we can walk over you!'
And you would flatten your back like the ground,
   like a street for them to walk on.

52

Awake, awake,
    put on your strength, O Zion!
Put on your beautiful garments,
    O Jerusalem, the holy city;
for the uncircumcised and the unclean
    shall enter you no more.
2 Shake yourself from the dust, rise up,
    O captive[t] Jerusalem;
loose the bonds from your neck,
    O captive daughter Zion!

3 For thus says the LORD: You were sold for nothing, and you shall be redeemed without money. 4 For thus says the Lord GOD: Long ago, my people went down into Egypt to reside there as aliens; the Assyrian, too, has oppressed them without cause. 5 Now therefore what am I doing here, says the LORD, seeing that my people are taken away without cause? Their rulers howl, says the LORD, and continually, all day long, my name is despised. 6 Therefore my people shall know my name; therefore in that day they shall know that it is I who speak; here am I.

7   How beautiful upon the mountains
    are the feet of the messenger who announces
        peace,
who brings good news,
    who announces salvation,
    who says to Zion, "Your God reigns."
8   Listen! Your sentinels lift up their voices,
    together they sing for joy;
for in plain sight they see
    the return of the LORD to Zion.
9   Break forth together into singing,
    you ruins of Jerusalem;
for the LORD has comforted his people,
    he has redeemed Jerusalem.
10   The LORD has bared his holy arm
    before the eyes of all the nations;
and all the ends of the earth shall see
    the salvation of our God.

11   Depart, depart, go out from there!
    Touch no unclean thing;
go out from the midst of it, purify yourselves,
    you who carry the vessels of the LORD.
12   For you shall not go out in haste,
    and you shall not go in flight;
for the LORD will go before you,
    and the God of Israel will be your rear guard.

13   See, my servant shall prosper;
    he shall be exalted and lifted up,
    and shall be very high.
14   Just as there were many who were astonished at
        him[u]
    — so marred was his appearance, beyond
        human semblance,
and his form beyond that of mortals —
15   so he shall startle[v] many nations;
    kings shall shut their mouths because of him;
for that which had not been told them they shall
        see,
and that which they had not heard they shall
        contemplate.

52

Awake, awake, Zion, put on your strength;
    Jerusalem, Holy City, put on your splendid
        garments!
For the uncircumcised and the unclean
    will never again come into you.
2 Arise, captive Jerusalem, shake off the dust;
    undo the ropes about your neck,
    you captive daughter of Zion.

3 The LORD says, You were sold but no price was paid, and without payment you will be redeemed. 4 The Lord GOD says: At its beginning my people went down into Egypt to live there, and in the end it was the Assyrians who oppressed them. 5 But now what do I find here? says the LORD. My people carried off and no price paid, their rulers wailing, and my name reviled increasingly all day long, says the LORD. 6 But on that day my people will know my name and know that it is I the LORD who speak; here I am.

7 How beautiful on the mountains are the feet of the
        herald,
    the bringer of good news,
    announcing deliverance,
    proclaiming to Zion, 'Your God has become king.'
8 Your watchmen raise their voices
    and shout together in joy;
for with their own eyes they see
    the LORD return to Zion.
9 Break forth together into shouts of joy,
    you ruins of Jerusalem;
for the LORD has comforted his people,
    he has redeemed Jerusalem.
10 The LORD has bared his holy arm
    in the sight of all nations,
and the whole world from end to end
    shall see the deliverance wrought by our God.

11 Go out, leave Babylon behind,
    touch nothing unclean.
Leave Babylon behind, keep yourselves pure,
    you that carry the vessels of the LORD.
12 But you will not come out in urgent haste
    or leave like fugitives;
for the LORD will go before you,
    your rearguard will be Israel's God.

13 My servant will achieve success,
    he will be raised to honour, high and exalted.
14–15 Time was when many were appalled at you, my
        people;
so now many nations recoil at the sight of him,
    and kings curl their lips in disgust.
His form, disfigured, lost all human likeness;
    his appearance so changed he no longer looked like
        a man.
They see what they had never been told
    and their minds are full of things unheard before.

---

[t] Cn: Heb *rise up, sit*   [u] Syr Tg: Heb *you*   [v] Meaning of Heb uncertain

52 Awake, awake!
Put on your strength, O Zion;
Put on your glorious garments,
O Jerusalem, holy city.
No longer shall the uncircumcised
or the unclean enter you.
2 Shake off the dust,
ascend to the throne, Jerusalem;
Loose the bonds from your neck,
O captive daughter Zion!
3 For thus says the LORD:
You were sold for nothing,
and without money you shall be redeemed.

4 Thus says the Lord GOD:
To Egypt in the beginning my people went down,
to sojourn there;
Assyria, too, oppressed them for nought.
5 But now, what am I to do here?
says the LORD.
My people have been taken away without redress;
their rulers make a boast of it, says the LORD;
all the day my name is constantly reviled.
6 Therefore on that day my people shall know
my renown,
that it is I who have foretold it. Here I am!
7 How beautiful upon the mountains
are the feet of him who brings glad tidings,
Announcing peace, bearing good news,
announcing salvation, and saying to Zion,
"Your God is King!"
8 Hark! Your watchmen raise a cry,
together they shout for joy,
For they see directly, before their eyes,
the LORD restoring Zion.
9 Break out together in song,
O ruins of Jerusalem!
For the LORD comforts his people,
he redeems Jerusalem.
10 The LORD has bared his holy arm
in the sight of all the nations;
All the ends of the earth will behold
the salvation of our God.

11 Depart, depart, come forth from there,
touch nothing unclean!
Out from there! Purify yourselves,
you who carry the vessels of the LORD.
12 Yet not in fearful haste will you come out,
nor leave in headlong flight,
For the LORD comes before you,
and your rear guard is the God of Israel.

13 See, my servant shall prosper,
he shall be raised high and greatly exalted.
14 Even as many were amazed at him—
so marred was his look beyond that of man,
and his appearance beyond that of mortals—
15 So shall he startle many nations,
because of him kings shall stand speechless;
For those who have not been told shall see,
those who have not heard shall ponder it.

52 Awake, awake!
Clothe yourself in strength, Zion.
Put on your finest clothes,
Jerusalem, Holy City;
for the uncircumcised and the unclean
will enter you no more.
2 Shake off your dust; get up,
captive Jerusalem!
The chains have fallen from your neck,
captive daughter of Jerusalem!
3 For Yahweh says this,
'You were sold for nothing;
you will be redeemed without money.'
4 For the Lord Yahweh says this,
'Long ago my people went to Egypt and settled
there as aliens;
finally Assyria oppressed them for no reason.
5 So now what is to be done,'
declares Yahweh,
'since my people have been carried off for nothing,
their masters howl in triumph,'
declares Yahweh,
'and my name is held in contempt all day, every
day?
6 Because of this my people will know my name,
because of this they will know when the day
comes,
that it is I saying, Here I am!'

7 How beautiful on the mountains,
are the feet of the messenger announcing peace,
of the messenger of good news,
who proclaims salvation
and says to Zion,
'Your God is king!'
8 The voices of your watchmen!
Now they raise their voices,
shouting for joy together,
for with their own eyes they have seen
Yahweh returning to Zion.
9 Break into shouts together,
shouts of joy, you ruins of Jerusalem;
for Yahweh has consoled his people,
he has redeemed Jerusalem.
10 Yahweh has bared his holy arm
for all the nations to see,
and all the ends of the earth
have seen the salvation of our God.
11 Go away, go away, leave that place,
do not touch anything unclean.
Get out of her, purify yourselves,
you who carry Yahweh's vessels!
12 For you are not to hurry away,
you are not to leave like fugitives.
No, Yahweh marches at your head
and the God of Israel is your rearguard.

13 Look, my servant will prosper,
will grow great, will rise to great heights.

14 As many people were aghast at him
—he was so inhumanly disfigured
that he no longer looked like a man—
15 so many nations will be astonished
and kings will stay tight-lipped before him,
seeing what had never been told them,
learning what they had not heard before.

53

Who has believed what we have heard?
 And to whom has the arm of the LORD been
 revealed?
2 For he grew up before him like a young plant,
 and like a root out of dry ground;
 he had no form or majesty that we should look at
 him,
 nothing in his appearance that we should desire
 him.
3 He was despised and rejected by others;
 a man of suffering[w] and acquainted with
 infirmity;
 and as one from whom others hide their faces[x]
 he was despised, and we held him of no
 account.

4 Surely he has borne our infirmities
 and carried our diseases;
 yet we accounted him stricken,
 struck down by God, and afflicted.
5 But he was wounded for our transgressions,
 crushed for our iniquities;
 upon him was the punishment that made us
 whole,
 and by his bruises we are healed.
6 All we like sheep have gone astray;
 we have all turned to our own way,
 and the LORD has laid on him
 the iniquity of us all.

7 He was oppressed, and he was afflicted,
 yet he did not open his mouth;
 like a lamb that is led to the slaughter,
 and like a sheep that before its shearers is
 silent,
 so he did not open his mouth.
8 By a perversion of justice he was taken away.
 Who could have imagined his future?
 For he was cut off from the land of the living,
 stricken for the transgression of my people.
9 They made his grave with the wicked
 and his tomb[y] with the rich,[z]
 although he had done no violence,
 and there was no deceit in his mouth.

10 Yet it was the will of the LORD to crush him with
 pain.[a]
 When you make his life an offering for sin,[b]
 he shall see his offspring, and shall prolong his
 days;
 through him the will of the LORD shall prosper.
11 Out of his anguish he shall see light;[c]
 he shall find satisfaction through his knowledge.
 The righteous one,[d] my servant, shall make
 many righteous,
 and he shall bear their iniquities.
12 Therefore I will allot him a portion with the
 great,
 and he shall divide the spoil with the strong;
 because he poured out himself to death,
 and was numbered with the transgressors;
 yet he bore the sin of many,
 and made intercession for the transgressors.

53

Who could have believed what we have heard?
 To whom has the power of the LORD been
 revealed?
2 He grew up before the LORD like a young plant
 whose roots are in parched ground;
 he had no beauty, no majesty to catch our eyes,
 no grace to attract us to him.
3 He was despised, shunned by all,
 pain-racked and afflicted by disease;
 we despised him, we held him of no account,
 an object from which people turn away their eyes.
4 Yet it was our afflictions he was bearing,
 our pain he endured,
 while we thought of him as smitten by God,
 struck down by disease and misery.
5 But he was pierced for our transgressions,
 crushed for our iniquities;
 the chastisement he bore restored us to health
 and by his wounds we are healed.
6 We had all strayed like sheep,
 each of us going his own way,
 but the LORD laid on him
 the guilt of us all.

7 He was maltreated, yet he was submissive
 and did not open his mouth;
 like a sheep led to the slaughter,
 like a ewe that is dumb before the shearers,
 he did not open his mouth.
8 He was arrested and sentenced and taken away,
 and who gave a thought to his fate—
 how he was cut off from the world of the living,
 stricken to death for my people's transgression?
9 He was assigned a grave with the wicked,
 a burial-place among felons,
 though he had done no violence,
 had spoken no word of treachery.

10 Yet the LORD took thought for his oppressed
 servant
 and healed him who had given himself as a
 sacrifice for sin.
 He will enjoy long life and see his children's
 children,
 and in his hand the LORD's purpose will prosper.
11 By his humiliation my servant will justify many;
 after his suffering he will see light and be satisfied;
 it is their guilt he bears.
12 Therefore I shall allot him a portion with the great,
 and he will share the spoil with the mighty,
 because he exposed himself to death
 and was reckoned among transgressors,
 for he bore the sin of many
 and interceded for transgressors.

---

53 Who would believe what we have heard?
To whom has the arm of the LORD
been revealed?
² He grew up like a sapling before him,
like a shoot from the parched earth;
There was in him no stately bearing to make us
look at him,
nor appearance that would attract us to him.
³ He was spurned and avoided by men,
a man of suffering, accustomed to infirmity,
One of those from whom men hide their faces,
spurned, and we held him in no esteem.

⁴ Yet it was our infirmities that he bore,
our sufferings that he endured,
While we thought of him as stricken,
as one smitten by God and afflicted.
⁵ But he was pierced for our offenses,
crushed for our sins,
Upon him was the chastisement that makes
us whole,
by his stripes we were healed.
⁶ We had all gone astray like sheep,
each following his own way;
But the LORD laid upon him
the guilt of us all.
⁷ Though he was harshly treated, he submitted
and opened not his mouth;
Like a lamb led to the slaughter
or a sheep before the shearers,
he was silent and opened not his mouth.
⁸ Oppressed and condemned, he was taken away,
and who would have thought any more of
his destiny?
When he was cut off from the land of the living,
and smitten for the sin of his people,
⁹ A grave was assigned him among the wicked
and a burial place with evildoers,
Though he had done no wrong
nor spoken any falsehood.
¹⁰ [But the LORD was pleased
to crush him in infirmity.]

If he gives his life as an offering for sin,
he shall see his descendants in a long life,
and the will of the LORD shall be accomplished
through him.
¹¹ Because of his affliction
he shall see the light in fullness of days;
Through his suffering, my servant shall
justify many,
and their guilt he shall bear.
¹² Therefore I will give him his portion among
the great,
and he shall divide the spoils with the mighty,
Because he surrendered himself to death
and was counted among the wicked;
And he shall take away the sins of many,
and win pardon for their offenses.

53 Who has given credence to what we have heard?
And who has seen in it a revelation of Yahweh's
arm?
² Like a sapling he grew up before him,
like a root in arid ground.
He had no form or charm to attract us,
no beauty to win our hearts;
³ he was despised, the lowest of men,
a man of sorrows, familiar with suffering,
one from whom, as it were, we averted our gaze,
despised, for whom we had no regard.
⁴ Yet ours were the sufferings he was bearing,
ours the sorrows he was carrying,
while we thought of him as someone being
punished
and struck with affliction by God;
⁵ whereas he was being wounded for our rebellions,
crushed because of our guilt;
the punishment reconciling us fell on him,
and we have been healed by his bruises.
⁶ We had all gone astray like sheep,
each taking his own way,
and Yahweh brought the acts of rebellion
of all of us to bear on him.
⁷ Ill-treated and afflicted,
he never opened his mouth,
like a lamb led to the slaughter-house,
like a sheep dumb before its shearers
he never opened his mouth.

⁸ Forcibly, after sentence, he was taken.
Which of his contemporaries was concerned
at his having been cut off from the land of the
living,
at his having been struck dead for his people's
rebellion?
⁹ He was given a grave with the wicked,
and his tomb is with the rich,
although he had done no violence,
had spoken no deceit.

¹⁰ It was Yahweh's good pleasure to crush him with
pain;
if he gives his life as a sin offering,
he will see his offspring and prolong his life,
and through him Yahweh's good pleasure will be
done.
¹¹ After the ordeal he has endured,
he will see the light and be content.
By his knowledge, the upright one, my servant will
justify many
by taking their guilt on himself.
¹² Hence I shall give him a portion with the many,
and he will share the booty with the mighty,
for having exposed himself to death
and for being counted as one of the rebellious,
whereas he was bearing the sin of many
and interceding for the rebellious.

54 Sing, O barren one who did not bear;
　　burst into song and shout,
　　you who have not been in labor!
For the children of the desolate woman will be
　　more
　　than the children of her that is married, says
　　the LORD.
2　Enlarge the site of your tent,
　　and let the curtains of your habitations be
　　stretched out;
do not hold back; lengthen your cords
　　and strengthen your stakes.
3　For you will spread out to the right and to the
　　left,
　　and your descendants will possess the nations
　　and will settle the desolate towns.

4　Do not fear, for you will not be ashamed;
　　do not be discouraged, for you will not suffer
　　disgrace;
for you will forget the shame of your youth,
　　and the disgrace of your widowhood you will
　　remember no more.
5　For your Maker is your husband,
　　the LORD of hosts is his name;
the Holy One of Israel is your Redeemer,
　　the God of the whole earth he is called.
6　For the LORD has called you
　　like a wife forsaken and grieved in spirit,
like the wife of a man's youth when she is cast
　　off,
　　says your God.
7　For a brief moment I abandoned you,
　　but with great compassion I will gather you.
8　In overflowing wrath for a moment
　　I hid my face from you,
but with everlasting love I will have compassion
　　on you,
　　says the LORD, your Redeemer.

9　This is like the days of Noah to me:
　　Just as I swore that the waters of Noah
　　would never again go over the earth,
so I have sworn that I will not be angry with you
　　and will not rebuke you.
10　For the mountains may depart
　　and the hills be removed,
but my steadfast love shall not depart from you,
　　and my covenant of peace shall not be
　　removed,
　　says the LORD, who has compassion on you.

11　O afflicted one, storm-tossed, and not comforted,
　　I am about to set your stones in antimony,
　　and lay your foundations with sapphires.^{e}
12　I will make your pinnacles of rubies,
　　your gates of jewels,
　　and all your wall of precious stones.
13　All your children shall be taught by the LORD,
　　and great shall be the prosperity of your
　　children.
14　In righteousness you shall be established;
　　you shall be far from oppression, for you shall
　　not fear;
　　and from terror, for it shall not come near you.
15　If anyone stirs up strife,
　　it is not from me;
whoever stirs up strife with you
　　shall fall because of you.

54 Sing, barren woman who never bore a child;
　　break into a shout of joy, you that have never
　　been in labour;
　　for the deserted wife will have more children
　　than she who lives with her husband,
　　says the LORD.
2　Enlarge the space for your dwelling,
　　extend the curtains of your tent to the full;
　　let out its ropes and drive the tent-pegs home;
3　for you will spread from your confines right and
　　left,
　　your descendants will dispossess nations
　　and will people cities now desolate.

4　Fear not, you will not be put to shame;
　　do not be downcast, you will not suffer disgrace.
　　It is time to forget the shame of your younger days
　　and remember no more the reproach of your
　　widowhood;
5　for your husband is your Maker;
　　his name is the LORD of Hosts.
　　He who is called God of all the earth,
　　the Holy One of Israel, is your redeemer.
6　The LORD has acknowledged you a wife again,
　　once deserted and heart-broken;
　　your God regards you as a wife still young,
　　though you were once cast off.
7　For a passing moment I forsook you,
　　but with tender affection I shall bring you home
　　again.
8　In an upsurge of anger I hid my face from you for
　　a moment;
　　but now have I pitied you with never-failing love,
　　says the LORD, your Redeemer.
9　For this to me is like the days of Noah;
　　as I swore that the waters of Noah's flood
　　should never again pour over the earth,
　　so now I swear to you
　　never again to be angry with you or rebuke you.
10　Though the mountains may move and the hills
　　shake,
　　my love will be immovable and never fail,
　　and my covenant promising peace will not be
　　shaken,
　　says the LORD in his pity for you.

11　Storm-battered city, distressed and desolate,
　　now I shall set your stones in the finest mortar
　　and lay your foundations with sapphires;
12　I shall make your battlements of red jasper
　　and your gates of garnet;
　　all your boundary stones will be precious jewels.
13　Your children will all be instructed by the LORD,
　　and they will enjoy great prosperity.
14　You will be restored triumphantly.
　　You will be free from oppression
　　and have nothing to fear;
　　you will be free from terror, for it will not come
　　near you.
15　Should anyone attack you, it will not be my doing;
　　for his attempt the aggressor will perish.

---

^{e} Or lapis lazuli

54:11 **sapphires:** or lapis lazuli.

NEW AMERICAN BIBLE

54 Raise a glad cry, you barren one who did
not bear,
break forth in jubilant song, you who were not
in labor,
For more numerous are the children of the
deserted wife
than the children of her who has a husband,
says the LORD.
2 Enlarge the space for your tent,
spread out your tent cloths unsparingly;
lengthen your ropes and make firm your stakes.
3 For you shall spread abroad to the right and to
the left;
your descendants shall dispossess the nations
and shall people the desolate cities.
4 Fear not, you shall not be put to shame;
you need not blush, for you shall not
be disgraced.
The shame of your youth you shall forget,
the reproach of your widowhood no
longer remember.
5 For he who has become your husband is
your Maker;
his name is the LORD of hosts;
Your redeemer is the Holy One of Israel,
called God of all the earth.
6 The LORD calls you back,
like a wife forsaken and grieved in spirit,
A wife married in youth and then cast off,
says your God.
7 For a brief moment I abandoned you,
but with great tenderness I will take you back.
8 In an outburst of wrath, for a moment
I hid my face from you;
But with enduring love I take pity on you,
says the LORD, your redeemer.

9 This is for me like the days of Noah,
when I swore that the waters of Noah
should never again deluge the earth;
So I have sworn not to be angry with you,
or to rebuke you.
10 Though the mountains leave their place
and the hills be shaken,
My love shall never leave you
nor my covenant of peace be shaken,
says the LORD, who has mercy on you.

11 O afflicted one, storm-battered and unconsoled,
I lay your pavements in carnelians,
and your foundations in sapphires.
12 I will make your battlements of rubies,
your gates of carbuncles,
and all your walls of precious stones.
13 All your sons shall be taught by the LORD,
and great shall be the peace of your children.
14 In justice shall you be established,
far from the fear of oppression,
where destruction cannot come near you.
15 Should there be any attack, it shall not be of
my making;
whoever attacks you shall fall before you.

NEW JERUSALEM BIBLE

54 Shout for joy, barren one who has borne no
children!
Break into cries and shouts of joy, you who were
never in labour!
For the children of the forsaken one are more in
number
than the children of the wedded wife, says
Yahweh.
2 Widen the space of your tent,
extend the curtains of your home, do not hold
back!
Lengthen your ropes, make your tent-pegs firm,
3 for you will burst out to right and to left,
your race will dispossess the nations
and repopulate deserted towns.
4 Do not fear, you will not be put to shame again,
do not worry, you will not be disgraced again;
for you will forget the shame of your youth
and no longer remember the dishonour of your
widowhood.
5 For your Creator is your husband,
Yahweh Sabaoth is his name,
the Holy One of Israel is your redeemer,
he is called God of the whole world.
6 Yes, Yahweh has called you back
like a forsaken, grief-stricken wife,
like the repudiated wife of his youth,
says your God.
7 I did forsake you for a brief moment,
but in great compassion I shall take you back.
8 In a flood of anger, for a moment
I hid my face from you.
But in everlasting love I have taken pity on you,
says Yahweh, your redeemer.
9 For me it will be as in the days of Noah
when I swore that Noah's waters
should never flood the world again.
So now I swear never to be angry with you
and never to rebuke you again.
10 For the mountains may go away
and the hills may totter,
but my faithful love will never leave you,
my covenant of peace will never totter,
says Yahweh who takes pity on you.

11 Unhappy creature, storm-tossed, unpitied,
look, I shall lay your stones on agates
and your foundations on sapphires.
12 I shall make your battlements rubies,
your gateways firestone
and your entire wall precious stones.
13 All your children will be taught by Yahweh
and great will be your children's prosperity.
14 In saving justice you will be made firm,
free from oppression: you will have nothing to
fear;
free from terror: it will not approach you.
15 Should anyone attack you, that will not be my
doing,
and whoever does attack you, for your sake will
fall.

16 See it is I who have created the smith
    who blows the fire of coals,
    and produces a weapon fit for its purpose;
    I have also created the ravager to destroy.
17 No weapon that is fashioned against you shall
      prosper,
    and you shall confute every tongue that rises
      against you in judgment.
This is the heritage of the servants of the LORD
    and their vindication from me, says the LORD.

55

Ho, everyone who thirsts,
    come to the waters;
and you that have no money,
    come, buy and eat!
Come, buy wine and milk
    without money and without price.
2 Why do you spend your money for that which is
      not bread,
    and your labor for that which does not satisfy?
Listen carefully to me, and eat what is good,
    and delight yourselves in rich food.
3 Incline your ear, and come to me;
    listen, so that you may live.
I will make with you an everlasting covenant,
    my steadfast, sure love for David.
4 See, I made him a witness to the peoples,
    a leader and commander for the peoples.
5 See, you shall call nations that you do not know,
    and nations that do not know you shall run to
      you,
because of the LORD your God, the Holy One of
      Israel,
    for he has glorified you.

6 Seek the LORD while he may be found,
    call upon him while he is near;
7 let the wicked forsake their way,
    and the unrighteous their thoughts;
let them return to the LORD, that he may have
      mercy on them,
    and to our God, for he will abundantly pardon.
8 For my thoughts are not your thoughts,
    nor are your ways my ways, says the LORD.
9 For as the heavens are higher than the earth,
    so are my ways higher than your ways
    and my thoughts than your thoughts.

10 For as the rain and the snow come down from
      heaven,
    and do not return there until they have watered
      the earth,
making it bring forth and sprout,
    giving seed to the sower and bread to the eater,
11 so shall my word be that goes out from my
      mouth;
    it shall not return to me empty,
but it shall accomplish that which I purpose,
    and succeed in the thing for which I sent it.

12 For you shall go out in joy,
    and be led back in peace;
the mountains and the hills before you
    shall burst into song,
    and all the trees of the field shall clap their
      hands.
13 Instead of the thorn shall come up the cypress;
    instead of the brier shall come up the myrtle;
and it shall be to the LORD for a memorial,
    for an everlasting sign that shall not be cut off.

16 It was I who created the smith
    to fan the coals in the fire
    and forge weapons for every purpose;
    and I created the destroyer to deal out havoc.
17 But the weapon that will prevail against you has
      not been made,
    and the accuser who rises in court against you will
      be refuted.
These benefits are enjoyed by the servants of the
      LORD;
their victory comes from me.
This is the word of the LORD.

55

Come for water, all who are thirsty;
    though you have no money, come, buy grain and
      eat;
come, buy wine and milk,
    not for money, not for a price.
2 Why spend your money for what is not food,
    your earnings on what fails to satisfy?
Listen to me and you will fare well,
    you will enjoy the fat of the land.
3 Come to me and listen to my words,
    hear me and you will have life:
I shall make an everlasting covenant with you
    to love you faithfully as I loved David.
4 I appointed him a witness to peoples,
    a prince ruling over them;
5 and you in turn will summon nations you do not
      know,
    and nations that do not know you will hasten to
      you,
because the LORD your God,
    Israel's Holy One, has made you glorious.

6 Seek the LORD while he is present,
    call to him while he is close at hand.
7 Let the wicked abandon their ways
    and the evil their thoughts:
let them return to the LORD, who will take pity on
      them,
    and to our God, for he will freely forgive.
8 For my thoughts are not your thoughts,
    nor are your ways my ways.
This is the word of the LORD.
9 But as the heavens are high above the earth,
    so are my ways high above your ways
    and my thoughts above your thoughts.
10 As the rain and snow come down from the heavens
    and do not return there without watering the earth,
    making it produce grain
    to give seed for sowing and bread to eat,
11 so is it with my word issuing from my mouth;
    it will not return to me empty
    without accomplishing my purpose
    and succeeding in the task for which I sent it.

12 You will go out with joy
    and be led forth in peace.
Before you mountains and hills will break into
      cries of joy,
    and all the trees in the countryside will clap their
      hands.
13 Pine trees will grow in place of camel-thorn,
    myrtles instead of briars;
all this will be a memorial for the LORD,
    a sign that for all time will not be cut off.

¹⁶Lo, I have created the craftsman
    who blows on the burning coals
    and forges weapons as his work;
It is I also who have created
    the destroyer to work havoc.
¹⁷No weapon fashioned against you shall prevail;
    every tongue you shall prove false
    that launches an accusation against you.
This is the lot of the servants of the LORD,
    their vindication from me, says the LORD.

55

All you who are thirsty,
    come to the water!
You who have no money,
    come, receive grain and eat;
Come, without paying and without cost,
    drink wine and milk!
²Why spend your money for what is not bread;
    your wages for what fails to satisfy?
Heed me, and you shall eat well,
    you shall delight in rich fare.
³Come to me heedfully,
    listen, that you may have life.
I will renew with you the everlasting covenant,
    the benefits assured to David.
⁴As I made him a witness to the peoples,
    a leader and commander of nations,
⁵So shall you summon a nation you knew not,
    and nations that knew you not shall run to you,
Because of the LORD, your God,
    the Holy One of Israel, who has glorified you.

⁶Seek the LORD while he may be found,
    call him while he is near.
⁷Let the scoundrel forsake his way,
    and the wicked man his thoughts;
Let him turn to the LORD for mercy;
    to our God, who is generous in forgiving.
⁸For my thoughts are not your thoughts,
    nor are your ways my ways, says the LORD.
⁹As high as the heavens are above the earth,
    so high are my ways above your ways
    and my thoughts above your thoughts.
¹⁰For just as from the heavens
    the rain and snow come down
And do not return there
    till they have watered the earth,
    making it fertile and fruitful,
Giving seed to him who sows
    and bread to him who eats,
¹¹So shall my word be
    that goes forth from my mouth;
It shall not return to me void,
    but shall do my will,
    achieving the end for which I sent it.

¹²Yes, in joy you shall depart,
    in peace you shall be brought back;
Mountains and hills shall break out in song
    before you,
    and all the trees of the countryside shall clap
        their hands.
¹³In place of the thornbush, the cypress shall grow,
    instead of nettles, the myrtle.
This shall be to the LORD's renown,
    an everlasting imperishable sign.

¹⁶I created the smith
    who blows on the charcoal-fire
    to produce a weapon for his use;
I also created the destroyer
    to ruin it.
¹⁷No weapon forged against you will succeed.
    Any voice raised against you in court you will
        refute.
Such is the lot of the servants of Yahweh,
    the saving justice I assure them,
    declares Yahweh.

55

Oh, come to the water all you who are thirsty;
    though you have no money, come!
Buy and eat; come, buy wine and milk
    without money, free!
²Why spend money on what cannot nourish
    and your wages on what fails to satisfy?
Listen carefully to me,
    and you will have good things to eat
    and rich food to enjoy.
³Pay attention, come to me;
    listen, and you will live.

I shall make an everlasting covenant with you
    in fulfilment of the favours promised to David.
⁴Look, I have made him a witness to peoples,
    a leader and lawgiver to peoples.
⁵Look, you will summon a nation unknown to you,
    a nation unknown to you will hurry to you
    for the sake of Yahweh your God,
    because the Holy One of Israel has glorified you.

⁶Seek out Yahweh while he is still to be found,
    call to him while he is still near.
⁷Let the wicked abandon his way
    and the evil one his thoughts.
Let him turn back to Yahweh who will take pity
        on him,
    to our God, for he is rich in forgiveness;
⁸for my thoughts are not your thoughts
    and your ways are not my ways,
    declares Yahweh.
⁹For the heavens are as high above earth
    as my ways are above your ways,
    my thoughts above your thoughts.
¹⁰For, as the rain and the snow come down from the
        sky
    and do not return before having watered the earth,
    fertilising it and making it germinate
    to provide seed for the sower and food to eat,
¹¹so it is with the word that goes from my mouth:
    it will not return to me unfulfilled
    or before having carried out my good pleasure
    and having achieved what it was sent to do.

¹²Yes, you will go out with joy
    and be led away in safety.
Mountains and hills will break into joyful cries
        before you
    and all the trees of the countryside clap their
        hands.
¹³Cypress will grow instead of thorns,
    myrtle instead of nettles.
And this will be fame for Yahweh,
    an eternal monument never to be effaced.

NEW REVISED STANDARD VERSION	REVISED ENGLISH BIBLE

NEW REVISED STANDARD VERSION

56 Thus says the LORD:
Maintain justice, and do what is right,
for soon my salvation will come,
and my deliverance be revealed.

2 Happy is the mortal who does this,
the one who holds it fast,
who keeps the sabbath, not profaning it,
and refrains from doing any evil.

3 Do not let the foreigner joined to the LORD say,
"The LORD will surely separate me from his
people";
and do not let the eunuch say,
"I am just a dry tree."

4 For thus says the LORD:
To the eunuchs who keep my sabbaths,
who choose the things that please me
and hold fast my covenant,

5 I will give, in my house and within my walls,
a monument and a name
better than sons and daughters;
I will give them an everlasting name
that shall not be cut off.

6 And the foreigners who join themselves to the
LORD,
to minister to him, to love the name of the
LORD,
and to be his servants,
all who keep the sabbath, and do not profane it,
and hold fast my covenant—

7 these I will bring to my holy mountain,
and make them joyful in my house of prayer;
their burnt offerings and their sacrifices
will be accepted on my altar;
for my house shall be called a house of prayer
for all peoples.

8 Thus says the Lord GOD,
who gathers the outcasts of Israel,
I will gather others to them
besides those already gathered. *f*

9 All you wild animals,
all you wild animals in the forest, come to
devour!

10 Israel's *g* sentinels are blind,
they are all without knowledge;
they are all silent dogs
that cannot bark;
dreaming, lying down,
loving to slumber.

11 The dogs have a mighty appetite;
they never have enough.
The shepherds also have no understanding;
they have all turned to their own way,
to their own gain, one and all.

12 "Come," they say, "let us *h* get wine;
let us fill ourselves with strong drink.
And tomorrow will be like today,
great beyond measure."

57 The righteous perish,
and no one takes it to heart;
the devout are taken away,
while no one understands.
For the righteous are taken away from calamity,

2 and they enter into peace;
those who walk uprightly
will rest on their couches.

REVISED ENGLISH BIBLE

56 THESE are the words of the LORD:
Maintain justice, and do what is right;
for my deliverance is close at hand,
and my victory will soon be revealed.

2 Happy is the person who follows these precepts
and holds fast to them,
who keeps the sabbath unprofaned,
who keeps his hand from all wrongdoing!

3 The foreigner who has given his allegiance to the
LORD must not say,
'The LORD will exclude me from his people.'
The eunuch must not say,
'I am naught but a barren tree.'

4 These are the words of the LORD:
The eunuchs who keep my sabbaths,
who choose to do my will
and hold fast to my covenant,

5 will receive from me something better than sons
and daughters,
a memorial and a name in my own house and
within my walls;
I shall give them everlasting renown,
an imperishable name.

6 So too with the foreigners who give their
allegiance to me,
to minister to me and love my name
and become my servants,
all who keep the sabbath unprofaned
and hold fast to my covenant:

7 these I shall bring to my holy hill
and give them joy in my house of prayer.
Their offerings and sacrifices
will be acceptable on my altar;
for my house will be called
a house of prayer for all nations.

8 This is the word of the Lord GOD,
who gathers those driven out of Israel:
I shall add to those who have already been
gathered.

9 All you beasts of the open country and of the
forest,
come and eat your fill.

10 For all Israel's watchmen are blind, perceiving
nothing;
they are all dumb dogs that cannot bark,
dreaming, as they lie stretched on the ground,
loving their sleep.

11 greedy dogs that can never have enough.
They are shepherds who understand nothing,
all of them going their own way,
one and all intent on their own gain.

12 'Come,' says each of them, 'let me fetch wine,
strong drink, and we shall swill it down;
tomorrow will be like today,
or better still!'

57 The righteous perish,
and no one is concerned;
all who are loyal to their faith are swept away
and no one gives it a thought.
The righteous are swept away by the onset of evil;

2 those who have followed a straight course
shall achieve peace at the last,
as they lie on their deathbeds.

---

f Heb *besides his gathered ones*   *g* Heb *His*   *h* Q Ms Syr Vg Tg:
MT *me*

56

Thus says the LORD:
Observe what is right, do what is just;
for my salvation is about to come,
my justice, about to be revealed.
2 Happy is the man who does this,
the son of man who holds to it;
Who keeps the sabbath free from profanation,
and his hand from any evildoing.
3 Let not the foreigner say,
when he would join himself to the LORD,
"The LORD will surely exclude me from
his people";
Nor let the eunuch say,
"See, I am a dry tree."
4 For thus says the LORD:
To the eunuchs who observe my sabbaths
and choose what pleases me
and hold fast to my covenant,
5 I will give, in my house
and within my walls, a monument and a name
Better than sons and daughters;
an eternal, imperishable name will I give them.

6 And the foreigners who join themselves to
the LORD,
ministering to him,
Loving the name of the LORD,
and becoming his servants —
All who keep the sabbath free from profanation
and hold to my covenant,
7 Them I will bring to my holy mountain
and make joyful in my house of prayer;
Their holocausts and sacrifices
will be acceptable on my altar,
For my house shall be called
a house of prayer for all peoples.
8 Thus says the Lord GOD,
who gathers the dispersed of Israel:
Others will I gather to him
besides those already gathered.

9 All you wild beasts of the field,
come and eat,
all you beasts in the forest!
10 My watchmen are blind,
all of them unaware;
They are all dumb dogs,
they cannot bark;
Dreaming as they lie there,
loving their sleep.
11 They are relentless dogs,
they know not when they have enough.
These are the shepherds
who know no discretion;
Each of them goes his own way,
every one of them to his own gain:
12 "Come, I will fetch some wine;
let us carouse with strong drink,
And tomorrow will be like today,
or even greater."

57

The just man perishes,
but no one takes it to heart;
Devout men are swept away,
with no one giving it a thought.
Though he is taken away from the presence of evil,
the just man 2 enters into peace;
There is rest on his couch
for the sincere, straightforward man.

56

Thus says Yahweh:
Make fair judgement your concern, act with
justice,
for soon my salvation will come
and my saving justice be manifest.
2 Blessed is anyone who does this,
anyone who clings to it,
observing the Sabbath, not profaning it,
and abstaining from every evil deed.
3 No foreigner adhering to Yahweh should say,
'Yahweh will utterly exclude me from his people.'
No eunuch should say,
'Look, I am a dried-up tree.'
4 For Yahweh says this: To the eunuchs who observe
my Sabbaths
and choose to do my good pleasure
and cling to my covenant,
5 I shall give them in my house and within my walls
a monument and a name better than sons and
daughters;
I shall give them an everlasting name
that will never be effaced.

6 As for foreigners who adhere to Yahweh to serve
him,
to love Yahweh's name and become his servants,
all who observe the Sabbath, not profaning it,
and cling to my covenant:
7 these I shall lead to my holy mountain
and make them joyful in my house of prayer.
Their burnt offerings and sacrifices will be
accepted on my altar,
for my house will be called a house of prayer for
all peoples.

8 Lord Yahweh who gathers the exiles of Israel
declares:
There are others I shall gather besides those
already gathered.

9 Come and gorge, all you wild beasts,
all you beasts of the forest!
10 Its watchmen are all blind,
they know nothing.
Dumb watchdogs all, unable to bark,
they dream, lie down, and love to sleep.
11 Greedy dogs, never satisfied, such are the
shepherds,
who understand nothing;
they all go their own way,
each to the last man after his own interest.
12 'Come, let me fetch wine;
we will get drunk on strong drink,
tomorrow will be just as wonderful as today
and even more so!'

57

The upright person perishes
and no one cares.
The faithful is taken off
and no one takes it to heart.
Yes, because of the evil times
the upright is taken off;
2 he will enter peace,
and those who follow the right way
will find rest on their beds.

NEW REVISED STANDARD VERSION	REVISED ENGLISH BIBLE

NEW REVISED STANDARD VERSION

3 But as for you, come here,
  you children of a sorceress,
  you offspring of an adulterer and a whore.*i*
4 Whom are you mocking?
  Against whom do you open your mouth wide
  and stick out your tongue?
  Are you not children of transgression,
  the offspring of deceit —
5 you that burn with lust among the oaks,
  under every green tree;
  you that slaughter your children in the valleys,
  under the clefts of the rocks?
6 Among the smooth stones of the valley is your
  portion;
  they, they, are your lot;
  to them you have poured out a drink offering,
  you have brought a grain offering.
  Shall I be appeased for these things?
7 Upon a high and lofty mountain
  you have set your bed,
  and there you went up to offer sacrifice.
8 Behind the door and the doorpost
  you have set up your symbol;
  for, in deserting me,*j* you have uncovered your
  bed,
  you have gone up to it,
  you have made it wide;
  and you have made a bargain for yourself with
  them,
  you have loved their bed,
  you have gazed on their nakedness.*k*
9 You journeyed to Molech*l* with oil,
  and multiplied your perfumes;
  you sent your envoys far away,
  and sent down even to Sheol.
10 You grew weary from your many wanderings,
  but you did not say, "It is useless."
  You found your desire rekindled,
  and so you did not weaken.
11 Whom did you dread and fear
  so that you lied,
  and did not remember me
  or give me a thought?
  Have I not kept silent and closed my eyes,*m*
  and so you do not fear me?
12 I will concede your righteousness and your
  works,
  but they will not help you.
13 When you cry out, let your collection of idols
  deliver you!
  The wind will carry them off,
  a breath will take them away.
  But whoever takes refuge in me shall possess the
  land
  and inherit my holy mountain.
14 It shall be said,
  "Build up, build up, prepare the way,
  remove every obstruction from my people's
  way."

REVISED ENGLISH BIBLE

3 Come near, you children of a soothsayer.
  You spawn of an adulterer and a harlot,
4 who is the target of your jests?
  Against whom do you open your mouths
  and stick out your tongues?
  Children of sin, spawn of a lie,
5 you are burning with lust under the sacred oaks,
  under every spreading tree,
  and sacrificing children in the wadis,
  under the rocky clefts.
6 And you, woman,
  your place is with the deceitful gods of the wadi;
  that is where you belong.
  To them you have poured a libation
  and presented an offering of grain.
  In spite of this am I to relent?
7 On a high mountaintop
  you have made your bed;
  there too you have gone up to offer sacrifice.
8 Beside door and doorpost you have put up your
  sign.
  Deserting me, you have stripped and lain down
  on the wide bed which you have made;
  you drove bargains with men
  for the pleasure of sleeping together
  and making love.
9 You drenched your tresses with oil,
  were lavish in your use of perfumes;
  you sent out your procurers far and wide
  even down to the confines of Sheol.
10 Though worn out by your unending excesses,
  you never thought your plight desperate.
  You found renewed vigour
  and so had no anxiety.
11 Whom do you fear so much, that you should be
  false,
  that you never remembered me or spared me a
  thought?
  Did I not keep silent and look away
  while you showed no fear of me?
12–13 Now I shall expose your conduct
  that you think so righteous.
  Your idols will not help you when you cry;
  they will not save you.
  The wind will carry them off, one and all,
  a puff of air will take them away;
  but he who makes his refuge will possess the
  land
  and inherit my holy hill.
14 Then the LORD will say:
  Build up a highway, clear the road,
  remove all that blocks my people's path.

i Heb *an adulterer and she plays the whore*   *j* Meaning of Heb
uncertain   *k* Or *their phallus;* Heb *the hand*   *l* Or *the king*
m Gk Vg: Heb *silent even for a long time*

57:3 **and a harlot:** so Gk; Heb. and she played the harlot.

NEW AMERICAN BIBLE	NEW JERUSALEM BIBLE

NEW AMERICAN BIBLE

3 But you, draw near,
  you sons of a sorceress,
  adulterous, wanton race!
4 Of whom do you make sport,
  at whom do you open wide your mouth,
  and put out your tongue?
  Are you not rebellious children,
  a worthless race;
5 You who are in heat among the terebinths,
  under every green tree;
  You who immolate children in the wadies,
  behind the crevices in the cliffs?

6 Among the smooth stones of the wadi is
    your portion,
  these are your lot;
  To these you poured out libations,
  and brought offerings.
  Should I decide not to punish these things?
7 Upon a high and lofty mountain
  you made your bed,
  and there you went up to offer sacrifice.
8 Behind the door and the doorpost
  you placed your indecent symbol.
  Deserting me, you spread out
  your high, wide bed;
  And of those whose embraces you love
  you carved the symbol and gazed upon it
9 While you approached the king with scented oil,
  and multiplied your perfumes;
  While you sent your ambassadors far away,
  down even to the nether world.
10 Though worn out by your many misdeeds,
  you never said, "It is hopeless";
  New strength you found,
  and so you did not weaken.

11 Of whom were you afraid? Whom did you fear,
  that you became false
  And did not remember me
  or give me any thought?
  Was I to remain silent and unseeing,
  so that you would not have me to fear?
12 I will expose your justice
  and your works;
13 They shall not help you when you cry out,
  nor save you in your distress.
  All these the wind shall carry off,
  the breeze shall bear away;
  But he who takes refuge in me shall inherit
    the land,
  and possess my holy mountain.

14 Build up, build up, prepare the way,
  remove the stumbling blocks from my
    people's path.

NEW JERUSALEM BIBLE

3 But you, you children of a witch, come here,
  adulterous race prostituting yourselves!
4 At whom are you jeering,
  at whom are you making faces
  and sticking out your tongue?
  Are you not the spawn of rebellion,
  a lying race?
5 Lusting among the terebinths,
  and under every spreading tree,
  sacrificing children in the ravines,
  below the clefts in the rocks.
6 The smooth stones of the ravines will be your
    portion,
  yes, these will be your lot.
  To these you have poured libations,
  have brought your cereal offering.
  Can all this appease me?
7 On a mountain high and lofty
  you have put your bed.
  Thither, too, you have climbed
  to offer sacrifice.
8 Behind door and doorpost
  you have set your reminder.
  Yes, far from me, you exposed yourself,
  climbed on to your bed,
  and made the most of it.
  You struck a profitable bargain
  with those whose bed you love,
  whoring with them often,
  with your eyes on the sacred symbol.
9 You went to Molech[d] with oil,
  you were prodigal with your perfumes;
  you sent your envoys far afield,
  down to Sheol itself.
10 Though tired by so much travelling,
  you never said, 'It is no use.'
  Finding your strength revive,
  you never gave up.
11 Who was it you dreaded, and feared,
  that you should betray me,
  no longer remember me
  and not spare a thought for me?
  Was I not silent for a long time?
  So you cannot have been afraid of me.
12 Now I shall expose this uprightness of yours,
  and little good it did you.
13 When you cry for help,
  let those thronging round you save you!
  The wind will carry them all away,
  one puff will take them off.
  But whoever trusts in me will inherit the country,
  he will own my holy mountain.

14 Then it will be said:
  Level up, level up, clear the way,
  remove the obstacle from my people's way,

---

[d] 57 'The King', a Semitic deity to whom children were sacrificed.

NRSV	REB

15 For thus says the high and lofty one
   who inhabits eternity, whose name is Holy:
I dwell in the high and holy place,
   and also with those who are contrite and
     humble in spirit,
to revive the spirit of the humble,
   and to revive the heart of the contrite.
16 For I will not continually accuse,
   nor will I always be angry;
for then the spirits would grow faint before me,
   even the souls that I have made.
17 Because of their wicked covetousness I
     was angry;
   I struck them, I hid and was angry;
but they kept turning back to their own ways.
18 I have seen their ways, but I will heal them;
   I will lead them and repay them with comfort,
creating for their mourners the fruit of the
     lips.ⁿ
19 Peace, peace, to the far and the near, says the
     Lord;
   and I will heal them.
20 But the wicked are like the tossing sea
   that cannot keep still;
   its waters toss up mire and mud.
21 There is no peace, says my God, for the wicked.
	15 These are the words of the high and exalted One,
	   who is enthroned for ever, whose name is holy:
	I dwell in a high and holy place
	   and with him who is broken and humble in spirit,
	to revive the spirit of the humble,
	   to revive the courage of the broken.
	16 I shall not be always accusing,
	   I shall not continually nurse my wrath,
	else the spirit of the creatures whom I made
	   would be faint because of me.
	17 For a brief time I was angry at the guilt of Israel.
	   I smote him in my anger and withdrew my favour,
	but he was wayward and went his own way.
	18 I have seen his conduct,
	   yet I shall heal him and give him relief;
	I shall bring him comfort in full measure,
	   and on the lips of those who mourn him
	19 I shall create words of praise.
	Peace, peace, for all, both far and near;
	   I shall heal them, says the Lord.
	20 But the wicked are like a storm-tossed sea,
	   a sea that cannot be still,
	   whose waters cast up mud and dirt.
	21 There is no peace for the wicked,
	   says my God.

58 Shout out, do not hold back!
   Lift up your voice like a trumpet!
Announce to my people their rebellion,
   to the house of Jacob their sins.
2 Yet day after day they seek me
   and delight to know my ways,
as if they were a nation that practiced
     righteousness
   and did not forsake the ordinance of their God;
they ask of me righteous judgments,
   they delight to draw near to God.
3 "Why do we fast, but you do not see?
   Why humble ourselves, but you do not
     notice?"
Look, you serve your own interest on your fast
     day,
   and oppress all your workers.
4 Look, you fast only to quarrel and to fight
   and to strike with a wicked fist.
Such fasting as you do today
   will not make your voice heard on high.
5 Is such the fast that I choose,
   a day to humble oneself?
Is it to bow down the head like a bulrush,
   and to lie in sackcloth and ashes?
Will you call this a fast,
   a day acceptable to the Lord?
6 Is not this the fast that I choose:
   to loose the bonds of injustice,
   to undo the thongs of the yoke,
to let the oppressed go free,
   and to break every yoke?
7 Is it not to share your bread with the hungry,
   and bring the homeless poor into your house;
when you see the naked, to cover them,
   and not to hide yourself from your own kin?
8 Then your light shall break forth like the dawn,
   and your healing shall spring up quickly;
your vindicator^o shall go before you,
   the glory of the Lord shall be your rear guard.

58 Shout aloud without restraint;
   lift up your voice like a trumpet.
Declare to my people their transgression,
   to the house of Jacob their sins,
2 although they ask guidance of me day after day
   and say they delight in knowing my ways.
As if they were a nation which had acted rightly
   and had not abandoned the just laws of their God,
they ask me for righteous laws
   and delight in approaching God.
3 'Why should we fast, if you ignore it?
   Why mortify ourselves, if you pay no heed?'
In fact you serve your own interests on your
     fast-day
   and keep all your men hard at work.
4 Your fasting leads only to wrangling and strife
   and to lashing out with vicious blows.
On such a day the fast you are keeping
   is not one that will carry your voice to heaven.
5 Is this the kind of fast that I require,
   a day of mortification such as this:
that a person should bow his head like a bulrush
   and use sackcloth and ashes for a bed?
Is that what you call a fast,
   a day acceptable to the Lord?
6 Rather, is not this the fast I require:
   to loose the fetters of injustice,
   to untie the knots of the yoke,
   and set free those who are oppressed,
   tearing off every yoke?
7 Is it not sharing your food with the hungry,
   taking the homeless poor into your house,
   clothing the naked when you meet them,
   and never evading a duty to your kinsfolk?
8 Then your light will break forth like the dawn,
   and new skin will speedily grow over your wound;
your righteousness will be your vanguard
   and the glory of the Lord your rearguard.

57:17 **For . . . Israel:** *prob. rdg, cp. Gk; Heb.* I was angry at the guilt of his unjust gain.

ⁿ Meaning of Heb uncertain   ^o Or *vindication*

15 For thus says he who is high and exalted,
    living eternally, whose name is the Holy One:
On high I dwell, and in holiness,
    and with the crushed and dejected in spirit,
To revive the spirits of the dejected,
    to revive the hearts of the crushed.
16 I will not accuse forever,
    nor always be angry;
For their spirits would faint before me,
    the souls that I have made.
17 Because of their wicked avarice I was angry,
    and struck them, hiding myself in wrath,
    as they went their own rebellious way.
18 I saw their ways,
    but I will heal them and lead them;
I will give full comfort
    to them and to those who mourn for them,
19   I, the Creator, who gave them life.

Peace, peace to the far and the near,
    says the Lord; and I will heal them.
20 But the wicked are like the tossing sea
    which cannot be calmed,
And its waters cast up mud and filth.
21   No peace for the wicked! says my God.

58 Cry out full-throated and unsparingly,
    lift up your voice like a trumpet blast;
Tell my people their wickedness,
    and the house of Jacob their sins.
2 They seek me day after day,
    and desire to know my ways,
Like a nation that has done what is just
    and not abandoned the law of their God;
They ask me to declare what is due them,
    pleased to gain access to God.
3 "Why do we fast, and you do not see it?
    afflict ourselves, and you take no note of it?"

Lo, on your fast day you carry out your
    own pursuits,
    and drive all your laborers.
4 Yes, your fast ends in quarreling and fighting,
    striking with wicked claw.
Would that today you might fast
    so as to make your voice heard on high!
5 Is this the manner of fasting I wish,
    of keeping a day of penance:
That a man bow his head like a reed,
    and lie in sackcloth and ashes?
Do you call this a fast,
    a day acceptable to the Lord?
6 This, rather, is the fasting that I wish:
    releasing those bound unjustly,
    untying the thongs of the yoke;
Setting free the oppressed,
    breaking every yoke;
7 Sharing your bread with the hungry,
    sheltering the oppressed and the homeless;
Clothing the naked when you see them,
    and not turning your back on your own.
8 Then your light shall break forth like the dawn,
    and your wound shall quickly be healed;
Your vindication shall go before you,
    and the glory of the Lord shall be your
        rear guard.

15 for thus says the High and Exalted One
who lives eternally
and whose name is holy,
'I live in the holy heights
but I am with the contrite and humble,
to revive the spirit of the humble,
to revive the heart of the contrite.

16 'For I do not want to be forever accusing
nor always to be angry,
or the spirit would fail under my onslaught,
the souls that I myself have made.

17 'Angered by his wicked cupidity,
I hid and struck him in anger,
but he rebelliously went the way of his choice.

18 'I saw how he behaved, but I shall heal him,
I shall lead him, fill him with consolation,
him and those who mourn for him,
19 bringing praise to their lips.
Peace, peace to far and near, Yahweh says,
and I shall heal him.'
20 The wicked, however, are like the restless sea
that cannot be still,
whose waters throw up mud and dirt.
21 'No peace', says Yahweh, 'for the wicked.'

58 Shout for all you are worth, do not hold back,
raise your voice like a trumpet.
To my people proclaim their rebellious acts,
to the House of Jacob, their sins.
2 They seek for me day after day,
they long to know my ways,
like a nation that has acted uprightly
and not forsaken the law of its God.
They ask me for laws that are upright,
they long to be near God:
3 'Why have we fasted, if you do not see,
why mortify ourselves if you never notice?'
Look, you seek your own pleasure on your
        fastdays
and you exploit all your workmen;
4 look, the only purpose of your fasting is to quarrel
        and squabble
and strike viciously with your fist.
Fasting like yours today
will never make your voice heard on high.
5 Is that the sort of fast that pleases me,
a day when a person inflicts pain on himself?
Hanging your head like a reed,
spreading out sackcloth and ashes?
Is that what you call fasting,
a day acceptable to Yahweh?
6 Is not this the sort of fast that pleases me:
to break unjust fetters,
to undo the thongs of the yoke,
to let the oppressed go free,
and to break all yokes?
7 Is it not sharing your food with the hungry,
and sheltering the homeless poor;
if you see someone lacking clothes, to clothe him,
and not to turn away from your own kin?
8 Then your light will blaze out like the dawn
and your wound be quickly healed over.
Saving justice will go ahead of you
and Yahweh's glory come behind you.

NEW REVISED STANDARD VERSION	REVISED ENGLISH BIBLE

NEW REVISED STANDARD VERSION

9 Then you shall call, and the LORD will answer;
  you shall cry for help, and he will say, Here I
  am.

If you remove the yoke from among you,
  the pointing of the finger, the speaking of evil,
10 if you offer your food to the hungry
  and satisfy the needs of the afflicted,
then your light shall rise in the darkness
  and your gloom be like the noonday.
11 The LORD will guide you continually,
  and satisfy your needs in parched places,
  and make your bones strong;
and you shall be like a watered garden,
  like a spring of water,
  whose waters never fail.
12 Your ancient ruins shall be rebuilt;
  you shall raise up the foundations of many
  generations;
you shall be called the repairer of the breach,
  the restorer of streets to live in.

13 If you refrain from trampling the sabbath,
  from pursuing your own interests on my holy
  day;
if you call the sabbath a delight
  and the holy day of the LORD honorable;
if you honor it, not going your own ways,
  serving your own interests, or pursuing your
  own affairs; *p*
14 then you shall take delight in the LORD,
  and I will make you ride upon the heights of
  the earth;
I will feed you with the heritage of your ancestor
  Jacob,
  for the mouth of the LORD has spoken.

59 See, the LORD's hand is not too short to save,
  nor his ear too dull to hear.
2 Rather, your iniquities have been barriers
  between you and your God,
and your sins have hidden his face from you
  so that he does not hear.
3 For your hands are defiled with blood,
  and your fingers with iniquity;
your lips have spoken lies,
  your tongue mutters wickedness.
4 No one brings suit justly,
  no one goes to law honestly;
they rely on empty pleas, they speak lies,
  conceiving mischief and begetting iniquity.
5 They hatch adders' eggs,
  and weave the spider's web;
whoever eats their eggs dies,
  and the crushed egg hatches out a viper.
6 Their webs cannot serve as clothing;
  they cannot cover themselves with what they
  make.
Their works are works of iniquity,
  and deeds of violence are in their hands.
7 Their feet run to evil,
  and they rush to shed innocent blood;
their thoughts are thoughts of iniquity,
  desolation and destruction are in
  their highways.
8 The way of peace they do not know,
  and there is no justice in their paths.
Their roads they have made crooked;
  no one who walks in them knows peace.

REVISED ENGLISH BIBLE

9 Then, when you call, the LORD will answer;
  when you cry to him, he will say, 'Here I am.'
If you cease to pervert justice,
  to point the accusing finger and lay false charges,
10 if you give of your own food to the hungry
  and satisfy the needs of the wretched,
then light will rise for you out of darkness
  and dusk will be for you like noonday;
11 the LORD will be your guide continually
  and will satisfy your needs in the bare desert;
he will give you strength of limb;
  you will be like a well-watered garden,
  like a spring whose waters never fail.
12 Buildings long in ruins will be restored by your
  own kindred
and you will build on ancient foundations;
  you will be called the rebuilder of broken walls,
  the restorer of houses in ruins.

13 If you refrain from sabbath journeys
  and from doing business on my holy day,
if you call the sabbath a day of joy
  and the LORD's holy day worthy of honour,
if you honour it by desisting from work
  and not pursuing your own interests
  or attending to your own affairs,
14 then you will find your joy in the LORD,
  and I shall make you ride on the heights of the
  earth,
and the holding of your father Jacob will be yours
  to enjoy.
The LORD himself has spoken.

59 The LORD's arm is not too short to save
  nor his ear too dull to hear;
2 rather, it is your iniquities that raise a barrier
  between you and your God;
it is your sins that veil his face,
  so that he does not hear.
3 Your hands are stained with blood
  and your fingers with crime;
your lips speak lies
  and your tongues utter injustice.
4 No one sues with just cause,
  no one makes an honest plea in court;
all rely on empty words, they tell lies,
  they conceive mischief and bring forth wickedness.
5 They hatch snakes' eggs; they weave cobwebs.
  Whoever eats those eggs will die,
  for rottenness hatches from rotten eggs.
6 Their webs are useless for making cloth;
  no one can use them for clothing.
Their works breed wickedness
  and their hands are full of acts of violence.
7 They rush headlong into crime
  in furious haste to shed innocent blood;
their schemes are harmful
  and leave a trail of havoc and ruin.
8 They are strangers to the path of peace,
  no justice guides their steps;
all the ways they choose are crooked;
  no one who walks in them feels safe.

p Heb or speaking words

9 Then you shall call, and the LORD will answer,
   you shall cry for help, and he will say: Here
   I am!
If you remove from your midst oppression,
   false accusation and malicious speech;
10 If you bestow your bread on the hungry
   and satisfy the afflicted;
Then light shall rise for you in the darkness,
   and the gloom shall become for you like midday;
11 Then the LORD will guide you always
   and give you plenty even on the parched land.
He will renew your strength,
   and you shall be like a watered garden,
   like a spring whose water never fails.
12 The ancient ruins shall be rebuilt for your sake,
   and the foundations from ages past you shall
   raise up;
"Repairer of the breach," they shall call you,
   "Restorer of ruined homesteads."

13 If you hold back your foot on the sabbath
   from following your own pursuits on my
   holy day;
If you call the sabbath a delight,
   and the LORD's holy day honorable;
If you honor it by not following your ways,
   seeking your own interests, or speaking
   with malice —
14 Then you shall delight in the LORD,
   and I will make you ride on the heights of
   the earth;
I will nourish you with the heritage of Jacob,
   your father,
   for the mouth of the LORD has spoken.

59 Lo, the hand of the LORD is not too short
      to save,
      nor his ear too dull to hear.
2 Rather, it is your crimes
   that separate you from your God,
It is your sins that make him hide his face
   so that he will not hear you.
3 For your hands are stained with blood,
   your fingers with guilt;
Your lips speak falsehood,
   and your tongue utters deceit.
4 No one brings suit justly,
   no one pleads truthfully;
They trust in emptiness and tell lies;
   they conceive mischief and bring forth malice.
5 They hatch adders' eggs,
   and weave spiders' webs:
Whoever eats their eggs will die,
   if one of them is pressed, it will hatch as
   a viper.
6 Their webs cannot serve as clothing,
   nor can they cover themselves with their works.
Their works are evil works,
   and deeds of violence come from their hands.
7 Their feet run to evil,
   and they are quick to shed innocent blood;
Their thoughts are destructive thoughts,
   plunder and ruin are on their highways.
8 The way of peace they know not,
   and there is nothing that is right in their paths;
Their ways they have made crooked,
   whoever threads them knows no peace.

9 Then you will cry for help and Yahweh will
   answer;
you will call and he will say, 'I am here.'
If you do away with the yoke,
   the clenched fist and malicious words,
10 if you deprive yourself for the hungry
   and satisfy the needs of the afflicted,
   your light will rise in the darkness,
   and your darkest hour will be like noon.
11 Yahweh will always guide you,
   will satisfy your needs in the scorched land;
he will give strength to your bones
   and you will be like a watered garden,
   like a flowing spring
   whose waters never run dry.
12 Your ancient ruins will be rebuilt;
   you will build on age-old foundations.
You will be called 'Breach-mender',
   'Restorer of streets to be lived in'.

13 If you refrain from breaking the Sabbath,
   from taking your own pleasure on my holy day,
   if you call the Sabbath 'Delightful',
   and the day sacred to Yahweh 'Honourable',
   if you honour it by abstaining from travel,
   from seeking your own pleasure and from too
   much talk,
14 then you will find true happiness in Yahweh,
   and I shall lead you in triumph over the heights of
   the land.
I shall feed you on the heritage of your father
   Jacob,
for the mouth of Yahweh has spoken.

59 No, the arm of Yahweh is not too short to save,
      nor his ear too dull to hear,
2 but your guilty deeds have made a gulf
   between you and your God.
Your sins have made him hide his face from you
   so as not to hear you,
3 since your hands are stained with blood
   and your fingers with guilt;
   your lips utter lies,
   your tongues murmur wickedness.
4 No one makes upright accusations
   or pleads sincerely.
All rely on empty words, utter falsehood,
   conceive trouble and give birth to evil.

5 They are hatching adders' eggs
   and weaving a spider's web;
eat one of their eggs and you die,
   crush one and a viper emerges.
6 Their webs are useless for clothing,
   their deeds are useless for wearing;
their deeds are deeds of guilt,
   violence fills their hands.
7 Their feet run to do evil;
   they are quick to shed innocent blood.
Their thoughts are thoughts of guilt,
   wherever they go there is havoc and ruin.
8 They do not know the way of peace,
   there is no fair judgement in their course,
they have made their own crooked paths,
   and no one treading them knows any peace.

NEW REVISED STANDARD VERSION	REVISED ENGLISH BIBLE

NEW REVISED STANDARD VERSION

9 Therefore justice is far from us,
 and righteousness does not reach us;
we wait for light, and lo! there is darkness;
 and for brightness, but we walk in gloom.
10 We grope like the blind along a wall,
 groping like those who have no eyes;
we stumble at noon as in the twilight,
 among the vigorous*q* as though we were dead.
11 We all growl like bears;
 like doves we moan mournfully.
We wait for justice, but there is none;
 for salvation, but it is far from us.
12 For our transgressions before you are many,
 and our sins testify against us.
Our transgressions indeed are with us,
 and we know our iniquities:
13 transgressing, and denying the LORD,
 and turning away from following our God,
talking oppression and revolt,
 conceiving lying words and uttering them from
 the heart.
14 Justice is turned back,
 and righteousness stands at a distance;
for truth stumbles in the public square,
 and uprightness cannot enter.
15 Truth is lacking,
 and whoever turns from evil is despoiled.

The LORD saw it, and it displeased him
 that there was no justice.
16 He saw that there was no one,
 and was appalled that there was no one to
 intervene;
so his own arm brought him victory,
 and his righteousness upheld him.
17 He put on righteousness like a breastplate,
 and a helmet of salvation on his head;
he put on garments of vengeance for clothing,
 and wrapped himself in fury as in a mantle.
18 According to their deeds, so will he repay;
 wrath to his adversaries, requital to his
 enemies;
to the coastlands he will render requital.
19 So those in the west shall fear the name of the
 LORD,
 and those in the east, his glory;
for he will come like a pent-up stream
 that the wind of the LORD drives on.
20 And he will come to Zion as Redeemer,
 to those in Jacob who turn from transgression,
 says the LORD.
21 And as for me, this is my covenant with them, says the
LORD: my spirit that is upon you, and my words that I have
put in your mouth, shall not depart out of your mouth, or
out of the mouths of your children, or out of the mouths of
your children's children, says the LORD, from now on and
forever.

60 Arise, shine; for your light has come,
 and the glory of the LORD has risen upon you.
2 For darkness shall cover the earth,
 and thick darkness the peoples;
but the LORD will arise upon you,
 and his glory will appear over you.
3 Nations shall come to your light,
 and kings to the brightness of your dawn.

REVISED ENGLISH BIBLE

9 That is why justice is far removed from us,
 and righteousness is out of our reach.
We look for light, but all is darkness;
 for daybreak, but we must walk in deep gloom.
10 We grope like blind men along a wall,
 feeling our way like those whose sight has gone;
we stumble at noonday as if it were nightfall,
 like the dead in the desolate underworld.
11 All of us growl like bears,
 we keep moaning like doves;
we wait for justice, but there is none,
 for deliverance, but it is far from us.
12 Our transgressions against you are many,
 and our sins bear witness against us;
our transgressions are on our minds,
 and well we know our guilt:
13 we have rebelled and broken faith with the LORD,
 we have relapsed and forsaken our God;
we have conceived lies in our hearts
 and repeated them in slanderous and treacherous
 words.
14 Justice is rebuffed and flouted
 while righteousness stands at a distance;
truth stumbles in court
 and honesty is kept outside,
15 so truth is lost to sight,
 and those who shun evil withdraw.

There was no justice,
 and when the LORD saw it he was displeased.
16 He saw that there was no help forthcoming
 and was outraged that no one intervened;
so his own might brought him the victory
 and his righteousness supported him.
17 He put on righteousness as a breastplate
 and salvation as a helmet on his head;
he put on the garments of vengeance
 and wrapped zeal about him like a cloak.
18 According to their deeds he will repay:
 for his adversaries, anger;
 for his enemies, retribution!
19 So from the west the LORD's name will be feared,
 and his glory revered from the rising of the sun.
His glory will come like a swift river
 on which the wind of the LORD moves.
20 He will come as a redeemer to Zion
 and to those in Jacob who repent of their rebellion.
This is the word of the LORD.

21 This, says the LORD, is my covenant, which I make with
them: My spirit which rests on you and my words which I
have put into your mouth will never fail you from generation to generation or your descendants from now on, for
evermore. The LORD has said it.

60 ARISE, shine, Jerusalem, for your light has come;
 and over you the glory of the LORD has dawned.
2 Though darkness covers the earth
 and dark night the nations,
on you the LORD shines
 and over you his glory will appear;
3 nations will journey towards your light
 and kings to your radiance.

59:18 **retribution:** *so Gk; Heb.* adds he will repay: for the coasts
and islands, retribution. 59:19 **wind:** *or* spirit.
60:1 **Jerusalem:** *so Gk; Heb.* omits.

q Meaning of Heb uncertain

NEW AMERICAN BIBLE

9 That is why right is far from us
    and justice does not reach us.
We look for light, and lo, darkness;
    for brightness, but we walk in gloom!
10 Like blind men we grope along the wall,
    like people without eyes we feel our way.
We stumble at midday as at dusk,
    in Stygian darkness, like the dead.
11 We all growl like bears,
    like doves we moan without ceasing.
We look for right, but it is not there;
    for salvation, and it is far from us.
12 For our offenses before you are many,
    our sins bear witness against us.
Yes, our offenses are present to us,
    and our crimes we know:
13 Transgressing, and denying the LORD,
    turning back from following our God,
Threatening outrage, and apostasy,
    uttering words of falsehood the heart
      has conceived.
14 Right is repelled,
    and justice stands far off;
For truth stumbles in the public square,
    uprightness cannot enter.
15 Honesty is lacking,
    and the man who turns from evil is despoiled.

The LORD saw this, and was aggrieved
    that right did not exist.
16 He saw that there was no one,
    and was appalled that there was none
      to intervene;
So his own arm brought about the victory,
    and his justice lent him its support.
17 He put on justice as his breastplate,
    salvation, as the helmet on his head;
He clothed himself with garments of vengeance,
    wrapped himself in a mantle of zeal.
18 He repays his enemies their deserts,
    and requites his foes with wrath.
19 Those in the west shall fear the name of the LORD,
    and those in the east, his glory;
For it shall come like a pent-up river
    which the breath of the LORD drives on.
20 He shall come to Zion a redeemer
    to those of Jacob who turn from sin, says
      the LORD.
21 This is the covenant with them
    which I myself have made, says the LORD:
My spirit which is upon you
    and my words that I have put into your mouth
Shall never leave your mouth,
    nor the mouths of your children
Nor the mouths of your children's children
    from now on and forever, says the LORD.

60 Rise up in splendor! Your light has come,
    the glory of the Lord shines upon you.
2 See, darkness covers the earth,
    and thick clouds cover the peoples;
But upon you the LORD shines,
    and over you appears his glory.
3 Nations shall walk by your light,
    and kings by your shining radiance.

NEW JERUSALEM BIBLE

9 Thus fair judgement is remote from us
    nor can uprightness overtake us.
We looked for light and all is darkness,
    for brightness and we walk in gloom.
10 Like the blind we feel our way along walls,
    we grope our way like people without eyes.
We stumble as though noon were twilight,
    among the robust we are like the dead.
11 We growl, all of us, like bears,
    like doves we make no sound but moaning,
waiting for the fair judgement that never comes,
    for salvation, but that is far away.
12 How often we have rebelled against you
    and our sins bear witness against us.
Our rebellious acts are indeed with us,
    we are well aware of our guilt:
13 rebellion and denial of Yahweh,
    turning our back on our God,
talking violence and revolt,
    murmuring lies in our heart.
14 Fair judgement is driven away
    and saving justice stands aloof,
for good faith has stumbled in the street
    and sincerity cannot enter.
15 Good faith has vanished;
    anyone abstaining from evil is victimised.

Yahweh saw this and was displeased
    that there was no fair judgement.
16 He saw there was no one
    and wondered there was no one to intervene.
So he made his own arm his mainstay,
    his own saving justice his support.
17 He put on saving justice like a breastplate,
    on his head the helmet of salvation.
He put on the clothes of vengeance like a tunic
    and wrapped himself in jealousy like a cloak.
18 To each he repays his due,
    retribution to his enemies, reprisals on his foes,
to the coasts and islands he will repay their due.
19 From the west, Yahweh's name will be feared,
    and from the east, his glory,
for he will come like a pent-up stream
    impelled by the breath of Yahweh.
20 Then for Zion will come a redeemer,
    for those who stop rebelling in Jacob,
    declares Yahweh.

21 'For my part, this is my covenant with them, says Yahweh. My spirit with which I endowed you, and my words that I have put in your mouth, will not leave your mouth, or the mouths of your children, or the mouths of your children's children, says Yahweh, henceforth and for ever.'

60 Arise, shine out, for your light has come,
    and the glory of Yahweh has risen on you.
2 Look! though night still covers the earth
    and darkness the peoples,
on you Yahweh is rising
    and over you his glory can be seen.
3 The nations will come to your light
    and kings to your dawning brightness.

4 Lift up your eyes and look around;
  they all gather together, they come to you;
your sons shall come from far away,
  and your daughters shall be carried on their
    nurses' arms.
5 Then you shall see and be radiant;
  your heart shall thrill and rejoice,*
because the abundance of the sea shall be brought
    to you,
  the wealth of the nations shall come to you.
6 A multitude of camels shall cover you,
  the young camels of Midian and Ephah;
all those from Sheba shall come.
They shall bring gold and frankincense,
  and shall proclaim the praise of the LORD.
7 All the flocks of Kedar shall be gathered to you,
  the rams of Nebaioth shall minister to you;
they shall be acceptable on my altar,
  and I will glorify my glorious house.

8 Who are these that fly like a cloud,
  and like doves to their windows?
9 For the coastlands shall wait for me,
  the ships of Tarshish first,
to bring your children from far away,
  their silver and gold with them,
for the name of the LORD your God,
  and for the Holy One of Israel,
    because he has glorified you.
10 Foreigners shall build up your walls,
  and their kings shall minister to you;
for in my wrath I struck you down,
  but in my favor I have had mercy on you.
11 Your gates shall always be open;
  day and night they shall not be shut,
so that nations shall bring you their wealth,
  with their kings led in procession.
12 For the nation and kingdom
  that will not serve you shall perish;
  those nations shall be utterly laid waste.
13 The glory of Lebanon shall come to you,
  the cypress, the plane, and the pine,
to beautify the place of my sanctuary;
  and I will glorify where my feet rest.
14 The descendants of those who oppressed you
  shall come bending low to you,
and all who despised you
  shall bow down at your feet;
they shall call you the City of the LORD,
  the Zion of the Holy One of Israel.
15 Whereas you have been forsaken and hated,
  with no one passing through,
I will make you majestic forever,
  a joy from age to age.
16 You shall suck the milk of nations,
  you shall suck the breasts of kings;
and you shall know that I, the LORD, am your
    Savior
  and your Redeemer, the Mighty One of Jacob.

17 Instead of bronze I will bring gold,
  instead of iron I will bring silver;
instead of wood, bronze,
  instead of stones, iron.
I will appoint Peace as your overseer
  and Righteousness as your taskmaster.

4 Raise your eyes and look around:
  they are all assembling, flocking back to you;
  your sons are coming from afar,
  your daughters walking beside them.
5 You will see it, and be radiant with joy,
  and your heart will thrill with gladness;
  sea-borne riches will be lavished on you
  and the wealth of nations will be yours.
6 Camels in droves will cover the land,
  young camels from Midian and Ephah,
  all coming from Sheba
  laden with gold and frankincense,
  heralds of the LORD's praise.
7 Kedar's flocks will all be gathered for you,
  rams of Nebaioth will serve your needs,
  acceptable offerings on my altar;
  I shall enhance the splendour of my temple.

8 Who are these that sail along like clouds,
  that fly like doves to their dovecots?
9 They are vessels assembling from the coasts and
      islands,
  ships of Tarshish leading the convoy;
  they bring your children from far away,
  their silver and gold with them,
  to the honour of the LORD your God,
  the Holy One of Israel;
  for he has made you glorious.

10 Foreigners will rebuild your walls
  and their kings will be your servants;
  though in my wrath I struck you down,
  now in my favour I show you pity.
11 Your gates will stand open at all times;
  day and night they will never be shut,
  so that through them may be brought the wealth of
      nations
  and their kings under escort.

12 For the nation or kingdom which refuses to serve you will
perish; and there will be widespread devastation among
such nations.

13 The glory of Lebanon will come to you,
  pine, fir, and boxwood all together,
  to adorn my holy sanctuary,
  to honour the place where I stand.
14 The sons of your oppressors will come forward to
      do homage,
  all who reviled you will bow low at your feet;
  they will address you as 'City of the LORD,
  Zion of the Holy One of Israel'.
15 No longer will you be deserted,
  like a wife hated and neglected;
  I shall make you an object of everlasting acclaim,
  and a source of never-ending joy.
16 You will suck the milk of nations
  and be suckled at royal breasts.
  Then you will know that I, the LORD, am your
      Deliverer;
  your Redeemer is the Mighty One of Jacob.

17 For copper I shall bring you gold
  and for iron I shall bring silver,
  copper for timber and iron for stone;
  I shall appoint peace to govern you
  and make righteousness rule over you.

Heb be enlarged   60:6 **gold:** *or* golden spice.

NEW AMERICAN BIBLE

NEW JERUSALEM BIBLE

4 Raise your eyes and look about;
    they all gather and come to you:
  Your sons come from afar,
    and your daughters in the arms of their nurses.

5 Then you shall be radiant at what you see,
    your heart shall throb and overflow,
  For the riches of the sea shall be emptied out
      before you,
    the wealth of nations shall be brought to you.
6 Caravans of camels shall fill you,
    dromedaries from Midian and Ephah;
  All from Sheba shall come
    bearing gold and frankincense,
    and proclaiming the praises of the LORD.
7 All the flocks of Kedar shall be gathered for you,
    the rams of Nebaioth shall be your sacrifices;
  They will be acceptable offerings on my altar,
    and I will enhance the splendor of my house.

8 What are these that fly along like clouds,
    like doves to their cotes?
9 All the vessels of the sea are assembled,
    with the ships of Tarshish in the lead,
  To bring your children from afar
    with their silver and gold,
  In the name of the LORD, your God,
    the Holy One of Israel, who has glorified you.

10 Foreigners shall rebuild your walls,
    and their kings shall be your attendants;
  Though I struck you in my wrath,
    yet in my good will I have shown you mercy.
11 Your gates shall stand open constantly;
    day and night they shall not be closed
  But shall admit to you the wealth of nations,
    and their kings, in the vanguard.
12 For the people or kingdom shall perish
    that does not serve you;
    those nations shall be utterly destroyed.
13 The glory of Lebanon shall come to you:
    the cypress, the plane and the pine,
  To bring beauty to my sanctuary,
    and glory to the place where I set my feet.
14 The children of your oppressors shall come,
    bowing low before you;
  All those who despised you
    shall fall prostrate at your feet.
  They shall call you "City of the LORD,"
    "Zion of the Holy One of Israel."

15 Once you were forsaken,
    hated and unvisited,
  Now I will make you the pride of the ages,
    a joy to generation after generation.
16 You shall suck the milk of nations,
    and be nursed at royal breasts;
  You shall know that I, the LORD, am your savior,
    your redeemer, the mighty one of Jacob.
17 In place of bronze I will bring gold,
    instead of iron, silver;
  In place of wood, bronze,
    instead of stones, iron;
  I will appoint peace your governor,
    and justice your ruler.

4 Lift up your eyes and look around:
    all are assembling and coming towards you, e
  your sons coming from far away
    and your daughters being carried on the hip.
5 At this sight you will grow radiant,
    your heart will throb and dilate,
  since the riches of the sea will flow to you,
    the wealth of the nations come to you;
6 camels in throngs will fill your streets,
    the young camels of Midian and Ephah;
  everyone in Saba will come,
    bringing gold and incense
    and proclaiming Yahweh's praises.
7 All the flocks of Kedar will gather inside you,
    the rams of Nebaioth will be at your service
  as acceptable victims on my altar,
    and I shall glorify my glorious house.

8 Who are these flying like a cloud,
    like doves to their dovecote?
9 Why, the coasts and islands put their hope in me
    and the vessels of Tarshish take the lead
  in bringing your children from far away,
    and their silver and gold with them,
  for the sake of the name of Yahweh your God,
    of the Holy One of Israel who has made you
      glorious.
10 Foreigners will rebuild your walls
    and their kings will serve you.
  For though I struck you in anger,
    in mercy I have pitied you.
11 Your gates will always be open,
    never closed, either day or night,
  for the riches of the nations to be brought you
    and their kings to be let in.

12 For the nation and kingdom that will not serve you
      will perish,
    and the nations will be utterly destroyed.

13 The glory of the Lebanon will come to you,
    cypress, plane-tree, box-tree, one and all,
  to adorn the site of my sanctuary,
    for me to honour the place where I stand.
14 Your oppressors' children will humbly approach
      you,
    at your feet all who despised you will fall
  addressing you as 'City of Yahweh',
    'Zion of the Holy One of Israel'.
15 Instead of your being forsaken and hated,
    avoided by everyone,
  I will make you an object of eternal pride,
    a source of joy from age to age.
16 You will suck the milk of nations,
    you will suck the wealth of kings,
  and you will know that I, Yahweh, am your
      Saviour,
    that your redeemer is the Mighty One of Jacob.
17 For bronze I shall bring gold
    and for iron I shall bring silver,
  and for wood, bronze,
    and for stone, iron;
  I shall make Peace your administration
    and Saving Justice your government.

NEW REVISED STANDARD VERSION	REVISED ENGLISH BIBLE

NEW REVISED STANDARD VERSION

18 Violence shall no more be heard in your land,
  devastation or destruction within your borders;
you shall call your walls Salvation,
  and your gates Praise.
19 The sun shall no longer be
  your light by day,
  nor for brightness shall the moon
  give light to you by night;[s]
but the LORD will be your everlasting light,
  and your God will be your glory.
20 Your sun shall no more go down,
  or your moon withdraw itself;
for the LORD will be your everlasting light,
  and your days of mourning shall be ended.
21 Your people shall all be righteous;
  they shall possess the land forever.
They are the shoot that I planted, the work of my
  hands,
  so that I might be glorified.
22 The least of them shall become a clan,
  and the smallest one a mighty nation;
I am the LORD;
  in its time I will accomplish it quickly.

61 The spirit of the Lord GOD is upon me,
  because the LORD has anointed me;
he has sent me to bring good news to the
  oppressed,
  to bind up the brokenhearted,
to proclaim liberty to the captives,
  and release to the prisoners;
2 to proclaim the year of the LORD's favor,
  and the day of vengeance of our God;
  to comfort all who mourn;
3 to provide for those who mourn in Zion—
  to give them a garland instead of ashes,
  the oil of gladness instead of mourning,
  the mantle of praise instead of a faint spirit.
They will be called oaks of righteousness,
  the planting of the LORD, to display his glory.
4 They shall build up the ancient ruins,
  they shall raise up the former devastations;
they shall repair the ruined cities,
  the devastations of many generations.

5 Strangers shall stand and feed your flocks,
  foreigners shall till your land and dress your
  vines;
6 but you shall be called priests of the LORD,
  you shall be named ministers of our God;
you shall enjoy the wealth of the nations,
  and in their riches you shall glory.
7 Because their[t] shame was double,
  and dishonor was proclaimed as their lot,
therefore they shall possess a double portion;
  everlasting joy shall be theirs.
8 For I the LORD love justice,
  I hate robbery and wrongdoing;[u]
I will faithfully give them their recompense,
  and I will make an everlasting covenant with
  them.
9 Their descendants shall be known among the
  nations,
  and their offspring among the peoples;
all who see them shall acknowledge
  that they are a people whom the LORD has
  blessed.

REVISED ENGLISH BIBLE

18 No longer will the sound of violence be heard in
  your land,
  nor havoc and ruin within your borders;
but you will name your walls Deliverance
  and your gates Praise.
19 The sun will no longer be your light by day,
  nor the moon shine on you by night;
the LORD will be your everlasting light,
  your God will be your splendour.
20 Never again will your sun set
  nor your moon withdraw her light;
but the LORD will be your everlasting light
  and your days of mourning will be ended.
21 Your people, all of them righteous,
  will possess the land for ever.
They are a shoot of my own planting,
  a work of my own hands for my adornment.
22 The few will become a thousand;
  the handful, a great nation.
At its appointed time I the LORD shall bring this
  swiftly to pass.

61 The spirit of the Lord GOD is upon me
  because the LORD has anointed me;
he has sent me to announce good news to the
  humble,
  to bind up the broken-hearted,
to proclaim liberty to captives,
  release to those in prison;
2 to proclaim a year of the LORD's favour
  and a day of the vengeance of our God;
  to comfort all who mourn,
3 to give them garlands instead of ashes,
  oil of gladness instead of mourners' tears,
  a garment of splendour for the heavy heart.
They will be called trees of righteousness,
  planted by the LORD for his adornment.
4 Buildings long in ruins will be rebuilt
  and sites long desolate restored;
  they will repair the ruined cities
  which for generations have lain desolate.
5 Foreigners will serve as shepherds of your flocks,
  aliens will till your land and tend your vines,
6 but you will be called priests of the LORD
  and be named ministers of our God.
You will enjoy the wealth of nations
  and succeed to their riches.
7 And so, because shame in double measure
  and insults and abuse have been my people's lot,
  they will receive in their own land a double
  measure of wealth,
  and everlasting joy will be theirs.
8 For I the LORD love justice
  and hate robbery and crime;
I shall grant them a sure reward
  and make an everlasting covenant with them;
9 their posterity will be renowned among the nations
  and their descendants among the peoples;
all who see them will acknowledge
  that they are a race blessed by the LORD.

---

s Q Ms Gk Old Latin Tg: MT lacks *by night*   t Heb *your*
u Or *robbery with a burnt offering*

61:2 **all who mourn:** *prob. rdg; Heb. adds* to appoint to Zion's
mourners.   61:7 **shame:** *prob. rdg; Heb.* your shame. **and abuse:**
prob. rdg; Heb. they shout. **my people's:** *lit.* their.

NEW AMERICAN BIBLE

¹⁸No longer shall violence be heard of in your land,
or plunder and ruin within your boundaries.
You shall call your walls "Salvation"
and your gates "Praise."

¹⁹No longer shall the sun
be your light by day,
Nor the brightness of the moon
shine upon you at night;
The LORD shall be your light forever,
your God shall be your glory.

²⁰No longer shall your sun go down,
or your moon withdraw,
For the LORD will be your light forever,
and the days of your mourning shall be at
an end.

²¹Your people shall all be just,
they shall always possess the land,
They, the bud of my planting,
my handiwork to show my glory.

²²The smallest shall become a thousand,
the youngest, a mighty nation;
I, the LORD, will swiftly accomplish these things
when their time comes.

61 The spirit of the Lord GOD is upon me,
because the LORD has anointed me;
He has sent me to bring glad tidings to the lowly,
to heal the brokenhearted,
To proclaim liberty to the captives
and release to the prisoners,
²To announce a year of favor from the LORD
and a day of vindication by our God,
to comfort all who mourn;
³To place on those who mourn in Zion
a diadem instead of ashes,
To give them oil of gladness in place of mourning,
a glorious mantle instead of a listless spirit.
They will be called oaks of justice,
planted by the LORD to show his glory.

⁴They shall rebuild the ancient ruins,
the former wastes they shall raise up
And restore the ruined cities,
desolate now for generations.
⁵Strangers shall stand ready to pasture your flocks,
foreigners shall be your farmers
and vinedressers.
⁶You yourselves shall be named priests of
the LORD,
ministers of our God you shall be called.
You shall eat the wealth of the nations
and boast of riches from them.

⁷Since their shame was double
and disgrace and spittle were their portion,
They shall have a double inheritance in their land,
everlasting joy shall be theirs.
⁸For I, the LORD, love what is right,
I hate robbery and injustice;
I will give them their recompense faithfully,
a lasting covenant I will make with them.
⁹Their descendants shall be renowned among
the nations,
and their offspring among the peoples;
All who see them shall acknowledge them
as a race the LORD has blessed.

NEW JERUSALEM BIBLE

¹⁸Violence will no longer be heard of in your
country,
nor devastation and ruin within your frontiers.
You will call your walls 'Salvation'
and your gates 'Praise'.

¹⁹No more will the sun give you daylight,
nor moonlight shine on you,
but Yahweh will be your everlasting light,
your God will be your splendour.

²⁰Your sun will set no more
nor will your moon wane,
for Yahweh will be your everlasting light
and your days of mourning will be over.

²¹Your people, all of them upright,
will possess the country for ever,
the shoot I myself have planted,
my handiwork, for my own glory.

²²The smallest will grow into a thousand,
the weakest one into a mighty nation.
When the time is ripe, I, Yahweh,
shall quickly bring it about.

61 The spirit of Lord Yahweh is on me
for Yahweh has anointed me.
He has sent me to bring the news to the afflicted,
to soothe the broken-hearted,
²to proclaim liberty to captives,
release to those in prison,
to proclaim a year of favour from Yahweh
and a day of vengeance for our God,
to comfort all who mourn
³(to give to Zion's mourners),
to give them for ashes a garland,
for mourning-dress, the oil of gladness,
for despondency, festal attire;
and they will be called 'terebinths of saving
justice',
planted by Yahweh to glorify him.

⁴They will rebuild the ancient ruins,
they will raise what has long lain waste,
they will restore the ruined cities,
all that has lain waste for ages past.
⁵Strangers will come forward to feed your flocks,
foreigners be your ploughmen and vinedressers;
⁶but you will be called 'priests of Yahweh'
and be addressed as 'ministers of our God'.
You will feed on the wealth of nations,
you will supplant them in their glory.

⁷To make up for your shame, you will receive
double;
instead of disgrace, shouts of joy will be their lot;
yes, they will have a double portion in their
country
and everlasting joy will be theirs.
⁸For I am Yahweh: I love fair judgement,
I hate robbery and wrong-doing,
and I shall reward them faithfully
and make an everlasting covenant with them.
⁹Their race will be famous throughout the nations
and their offspring throughout the peoples.
All who see them will admit
that they are a race whom Yahweh has blessed.

NEW REVISED STANDARD VERSION

REVISED ENGLISH BIBLE

10 I will greatly rejoice in the LORD,
   my whole being shall exult in my God;
for he has clothed me with the garments of
      salvation,
   he has covered me with the robe of
      righteousness,
as a bridegroom decks himself with a garland,
   and as a bride adorns herself with her jewels.
11 For as the earth brings forth its shoots,
   and as a garden causes what is sown in it to
      spring up,
so the Lord GOD will cause righteousness and
      praise
   to spring up before all the nations.

62 For Zion's sake I will not keep silent,
   and for Jerusalem's sake I will not rest,
until her vindication shines out like the dawn,
   and her salvation like a burning torch.
2 The nations shall see your vindication,
   and all the kings your glory;
and you shall be called by a new name
   that the mouth of the LORD will give.
3 You shall be a crown of beauty in the hand of the
      LORD,
   and a royal diadem in the hand of your God.
4 You shall no more be termed Forsaken,ᵛ
   and your land shall no more be termed
      Desolate;ʷ
but you shall be called My Delight Is in Her,ˣ
   and your land Married;ʸ
for the LORD delights in you,
   and your land shall be married.
5 For as a young man marries a young woman,
   so shall your builderᶻ marry you,
and as the bridegroom rejoices over the bride,
   so shall your God rejoice over you.
6 Upon your walls, O Jerusalem,
   I have posted sentinels;
all day and all night
   they shall never be silent.
You who remind the LORD,
   take no rest,
7 and give him no rest
   until he establishes Jerusalem
and makes it renowned throughout the earth.
8 The LORD has sworn by his right hand
   and by his mighty arm:
I will not again give your grain
   to be food for your enemies,
and foreigners shall not drink the wine
   for which you have labored;
9 but those who garner it shall eat it
   and praise the LORD,
and those who gather it shall drink it
   in my holy courts.

10 Go through, go through the gates,
   prepare the way for the people;
build up, build up the highway,
   clear it of stones,
   lift up an ensign over the peoples.
11 The LORD has proclaimed
   to the end of the earth:
Say to daughter Zion,
   "See, your salvation comes;
his reward is with him,
   and his recompense before him."

10 Let me rejoice in the LORD with all my heart,
   let me exult in my God;
for he has robed me in deliverance
   and arrayed me in victory,
like a bridegroom with his garland,
   or a bride decked in her jewels.
11 As the earth puts forth her blossom
   or plants in the garden burst into flower,
so will the Lord GOD make his victory and renown
   blossom before all the nations.

62 For Zion's sake I shall not keep silent,
   for Jerusalem's sake I shall not be quiet,
until her victory shines forth like the sunrise,
   her deliverance like a blazing torch,
2 and the nations see your victory
   and all their kings your glory.
Then you will be called by a new name
   which the LORD himself will announce;
3 you will be a glorious crown in the LORD's hand,
   a royal diadem held by your God.
4 No more will you be called Forsaken,
   no more will your land be called Desolate,
but you will be named Hephzibah
   and your land Beulah;
for the LORD will take delight in you
   and to him your land will be linked in wedlock.
5 As a young man weds a maiden,
   so will you be wedded to him who rebuilds you,
and as a bridegroom rejoices over the bride,
   so will your God rejoice over you.

6 Jerusalem, on your walls I have posted watchmen,
   who day and night without ceasing will cry:
'You that invoke the LORD's name,
   take no rest, 7 and give no rest to him
until he makes Jerusalem
   a theme of praise throughout the world.'

8 The LORD has sworn with raised right hand and
      mighty arm:
Never again will I give your grain to feed your
      foes,
   never again let foreigners drink the vintage
   for which you have toiled;
9 but those who harvest the grain will eat it
   and give praise to the LORD,
and those who gather the grapes will drink the
      wine
   within my sacred courts.

10 Pass through the gates, go out,
   clear a road for my people;
build a highway, build it up,
   remove the boulders;
   hoist a signal for the peoples.
11 This is the LORD's proclamation
   to earth's farthest bounds:
Tell the daughter of Zion,
   'See, your deliverance comes.
His reward is with him,
   his recompense before him.'

ᵛHeb Azubah   ʷHeb Shemamah   ˣHeb Hephzibah
ʸHeb Beulah   ᶻCn: Heb your sons

62:4 **Hephzibah:** that is My delight is in her. **Beulah:** that is
Wedded.

NEW AMERICAN BIBLE

10 I rejoice heartily in the LORD,
  in my God is the joy of my soul;
For he has clothed me with a robe of salvation,
  and wrapped me in a mantle of justice,
Like a bridegroom adorned with a diadem,
  like a bride bedecked with her jewels.
11 As the earth brings forth its plants,
  and a garden makes its growth spring up,
So will the Lord GOD make justice and praise
  spring up before all the nations.

62 For Zion's sake I will not be silent,
  for Jerusalem's sake I will not be quiet,
Until her vindication shines forth like the dawn
  and her victory like a burning torch.
2 Nations shall behold your vindication,
  and all kings your glory;
You shall be called by a new name
  pronounced by the mouth of the LORD.
3 You shall be a glorious crown in the hand of
  the LORD,
  a royal diadem held by your God.
4 No more shall men call you "Forsaken,"
  or your land "Desolate,"
But you shall be called "My Delight,"
  and your land "Espoused."
For the LORD delights in you,
  and makes your land his spouse.
5 As a young man marries a virgin,
  your Builder shall marry you;
And as a bridegroom rejoices in his bride
  so shall your God rejoice in you.
6 Upon your walls, O Jerusalem,
  I have stationed watchmen;
Never, by day or by night,
  shall they be silent.
O you who are to remind the LORD,
  take no rest
7 And give no rest to him,
  until he re-establishes Jerusalem
And makes of it
  the pride of the earth.
8 The LORD has sworn by his right hand
  and by his mighty arm:
No more will I give your grain
  as food to your enemies;
Nor shall foreigners drink your wine,
  for which you toiled.
9 But you who harvest the grain shall eat it,
  and you shall praise the LORD;
You who gather the grapes shall drink the wine
  in the courts of my sanctuary.
10 Pass through, pass through the gates,
  prepare the way for the people;
Build up, build up the highway,
  clear it of stones,
  raise up a standard over the nations.
11 See, the LORD proclaims
  to the ends of the earth:
Say to daughter Zion,
  your savior comes!
Here is his reward with him,
  his recompense before him.

NEW JERUSALEM BIBLE

10 I exult for joy in Yahweh,
  my soul rejoices in my God,
for he has clothed me in garments of salvation,
  he has wrapped me in a cloak of saving justice,
like a bridegroom wearing his garland,
  like a bride adorned in her jewels.
11 For as the earth sends up its shoots
  and a garden makes seeds sprout,
so Lord Yahweh makes saving justice and praise
  spring up in the sight of all nations.

62 About Zion I will not be silent,
  about Jerusalem I shall not rest
until saving justice dawns for her like a bright light
  and her salvation like a blazing torch.
2 The nations will then see your saving justice,
  and all kings your glory,
and you will be called a new name
  which Yahweh's mouth will reveal.
3 You will be a crown of splendour in Yahweh's
  hand,
  a princely diadem in the hand of your God.
4 No more will you be known as 'Forsaken'
  or your country be known as 'Desolation';
instead, you will be called 'My Delight is in her'
  and your country 'The Wedded';
for Yahweh will take delight in you
  and your country will have its wedding.
5 Like a young man marrying a virgin,
  your rebuilder will wed you,
and as the bridegroom rejoices in his bride,
  so will your God rejoice in you.
6 On your walls, Jerusalem, I have posted
  watchmen;
they will never fall silent, day or night.
No peace for you, as you keep Yahweh's attention!
7 And give him no peace either
  until he restores Jerusalem
and makes her the pride of the world!
8 Yahweh has sworn by his right hand
  and by his mighty arm:
Never again shall I give your grain
  to feed your enemies.
Never again will foreigners drink the wine
  for which you have toiled.
9 No, the reapers will eat it and praise Yahweh,
  the harvesters will drink it in my sacred courts!
10 Pass through, pass through the gates.
  Clear a way for my people!
Level up, level up the highway,
  remove the stones!
Hoist a signal to the peoples!
11 This is what Yahweh has proclaimed
  to the remotest part of earth:
Say to the daughter of Zion, 'Look, your salvation
  is coming;
with him comes his reward, his achievement
  precedes him!'f

f **62** = 40:10.

12 They shall be called, "The Holy People,
   The Redeemed of the LORD";
and you shall be called, "Sought Out,
   A City Not Forsaken."

63

1 "Who is this that comes from Edom,
   from Bozrah in garments stained crimson?
Who is this so splendidly robed,
   marching in his great might?"

"It is I, announcing vindication,
   mighty to save."

2 "Why are your robes red,
   and your garments like theirs who tread the
   wine press?"

3 "I have trodden the wine press alone,
   and from the peoples no one was with me;
I trod them in my anger
   and trampled them in my wrath;
their juice spattered on my garments,
   and stained all my robes.
4 For the day of vengeance was in my heart,
   and the year for my redeeming work had come.
5 I looked, but there was no helper;
   I stared, but there was no one to sustain me;
so my own arm brought me victory,
   and my wrath sustained me.
6 I trampled down peoples in my anger,
   I crushed them in my wrath,
   and I poured out their lifeblood on the earth."

7 I will recount the gracious deeds of the LORD,
   the praiseworthy acts of the LORD,
because of all that the LORD has done for us,
   and the great favor to the house of Israel
that he has shown them according to his mercy,
   according to the abundance of his steadfast
   love.
8 For he said, "Surely they are my people,
   children who will not deal falsely";
and he became their savior
9   in all their distress.
It was no messenger[a] or angel
   but his presence that saved them;[b]
in his love and in his pity he redeemed them;
   he lifted them up and carried them all the days
   of old.

10 But they rebelled
   and grieved his holy spirit;
therefore he became their enemy;
   he himself fought against them.
11 Then they[c] remembered the days of old,
   of Moses his servant.[d]
Where is the one who brought them up out of the
   sea
   with the shepherds of his flock?
Where is the one who put within them
   his holy spirit,
12 who caused his glorious arm
   to march at the right hand of Moses,
who divided the waters before them
   to make for himself an everlasting name,
13   who led them through the depths?
Like a horse in the desert,
   they did not stumble.

12 They will be called the Holy People,
   the Redeemed of the LORD;
and you will be called Sought After,
   City No Longer Forsaken.

63

1 'WHO is this coming from Edom,
   from Bozrah with his garments stained red,
one splendidly attired,
   striding along with mighty power?'

It is I, proclaiming victory,
   I, who am strong to save.

2 'Why are your clothes all red,
   like the garments of one treading grapes in the
   winepress?'

3 I have trodden the press alone,
   for none of my people was with me.
I trod the nations in my anger,
   I trampled them in my fury,
and their blood bespattered my garments
   and all my clothing was stained.
4 I resolved on a day of vengeance;
   the year for redeeming my own had come.
5 I looked for a helper but found none;
   I was outraged that no one upheld me;
yet my own might brought me victory,
   my fury alone upheld me.
6 I stamped on peoples in my anger,
   I shattered them in my fury
   and spilled their blood over the ground.

7 I shall recount the LORD's unfailing love,
   the prowess of the LORD,
according to all he has done for us,
   his great goodness to the house of Israel,
what he has done for them in his tenderness
   and by his many acts of faithful love.
8 He said, 'Surely they are my people,
   children who will not play me false';
and he became their deliverer
9 in all their troubles.
No envoy, no angel, but he himself delivered
   them,
redeemed them in his love and pity;
   he lifted them up and carried them
   through all the days of old.
10 Yet they rebelled and grieved his holy spirit;
   so he turned hostile to them
   and himself fought against them.

11 Then they recalled days long past
   and him who drew out his people:
where is he who brought them up from the Nile
   the shepherd of his flock?
Where is he who put within him
   his holy spirit,
12 who sent his glorious power
   to walk at Moses' right hand?
Where is he who divided the waters before them,
   to win for himself everlasting renown,
13 who brought them through the deep
   sure-footed as horses in open country,

63:1 **striding**: *prob. rdg*; *Heb*. stooping.   63:3 **my people**: *so Scroll*; *Heb*. peoples.   63:11 **him who drew out**: *that is* Moses whose name resembles the Heb. verb meaning 'draw out'; cp. Exod. 2:10 and the note there. **brought up**: *so Scroll*; *Heb*. brought them up.

[a] Gk: Heb *anguish*   [b] Or *savior*. 9In all their distress he was distressed; the angel of his presence saved them;   [c] Heb *he*   [d] Cn: Heb *his people*

12 They shall be called the holy people,
the redeemed of the LORD,
And you shall be called "Frequented,"
a city that is not forsaken.

63

Who is this that comes from Edom,
in crimsoned garments, from Bozrah —
This one arrayed in majesty,
marching in the greatness of his strength?
"It is I, I who announce vindication,
I who am mighty to save."
2 Why is your apparel red,
and your garments like those of the wine
presser?
3 "The wine press I have trodden alone,
and of my people there was no one with me.
I trod them in my anger,
and trampled them down in my wrath;
Their blood spurted on my garments;
all my apparel I stained.
4 For the day of vengeance was in my heart,
my year for redeeming was at hand.
5 I looked about, but there was no one to help,
I was appalled that there was no one to
lend support;
So my own arm brought about the victory
and my own wrath lent me its support.
6 I trampled down the peoples in my anger,
I crushed them in my wrath,
and I let their blood run out upon the ground."

7 The favors of the LORD I will recall,
the glorious deeds of the LORD,
Because of all he has done for us;
for he is good to the house of Israel,
He has favored us according to his mercy
and his great kindness.

8 He said: They are indeed my people,
children who are not disloyal;
So he became their savior
9   in their every affliction.
It was not a messenger or an angel,
but he himself who saved them.
Because of his love and pity
he redeemed them himself,
Lifting them and carrying them
all the days of old.
10 But they rebelled, and grieved
his holy spirit;
So he turned on them like an enemy,
and fought against them.
11 Then they remembered the days of old
and Moses, his servant;
Where is he who brought up out of the sea
the shepherd of his flock?
Where is he who put his holy spirit
in their midst;
12 Whose glorious arm
was the guide at Moses' right;
Who divided the waters before them,
winning for himself eternal renown;
13 Who led them without stumbling through
the depths
like horses in the open country,

12 They will be called 'The Holy People',
'Yahweh's Redeemed',
while you will be called 'Sought-after',
'City-not-forsaken'.

63

Who is this coming from Edom,
from Bozrah in crimson garments,
so magnificently dressed,
marching so full of strength?
— It is I, whose word is saving justice,
whose power is to save.
2 — Why are your garments red,
your clothes like someone treading the winepress?
3 — I have trodden the winepress alone;
of my people, not one was with me.
So I trod them down in my anger,
I trampled on them in my wrath.
Their blood squirted over my garments
and all my clothes are stained.
4 For I have decided on a day of vengeance,
my year of retribution has come.
5 I looked: there was no one to help me;
I was appalled but could find no supporter!
Then my own arm came to my rescue
and my own fury supported me.
6 I crushed the peoples in my anger,
I shattered them in my fury
and sent their blood streaming to the ground.

7 I shall recount Yahweh's acts of faithful love,
Yahweh's praises,
in return for all that Yahweh has done for us,
for his great kindness to the House of Israel,
for all that he has done in his mercy,
for the abundance of his acts of faithful love.

8 For he said, 'Truly they are my people,
children who will not betray me,'
and he became their Saviour.
9 In all their troubles,
it was no messenger or angel
but his presence that saved them.
In his love and pity
he himself redeemed them,
lifted them up and carried them
throughout the days of old.
10 But they rebelled
and vexed his holy Spirit.
Then he became their enemy
and himself waged war on them.
11 But he called the past to mind,
Moses his servant.
Where is he who saved them from the sea,
the Shepherd of his flock?
Where was he who put
his holy Spirit among them,
12 whose glorious arm led the way
by Moses' right hand?
Who divided the waters before them
to win himself everlasting renown,
13 who led them through the depths
as easily as a horse through the desert?
They stumbled as little

14 Like cattle that go down into the valley,
    the spirit of the LORD gave them rest.
Thus you led your people,
    to make for yourself a glorious name.
15 Look down from heaven and see,
    from your holy and glorious habitation.
Where are your zeal and your might?
    The yearning of your heart and your
      compassion?
    They are withheld from me.
16 For you are our father,
    though Abraham does not know us
    and Israel does not acknowledge us;
you, O LORD, are our father;
    our Redeemer from of old is your name.
17 Why, O LORD, do you make us stray from your
    ways
    and harden our heart, so that we do not fear
      you?
Turn back for the sake of your servants,
    for the sake of the tribes that are your heritage.
18 Your holy people took possession for a little
    while;
    but now our adversaries have trampled down
      your sanctuary.
19 We have long been like those whom you do not
    rule,
    like those not called by your name.

64 O that you would tear open the heavens and
    come down,
    so that the mountains would quake at your
      presence —
2 e as when fire kindles brushwood
    and the fire causes water to boil —
to make your name known to your adversaries,
    so that the nations might tremble at your
      presence!
3 When you did awesome deeds that we did not
    expect,
    you came down, the mountains quaked at your
      presence.
4 From ages past no one has heard,
    no ear has perceived,
no eye has seen any God besides you,
    who works for those who wait for him.
5 You meet those who gladly do right,
    those who remember you in your ways.
But you were angry, and we sinned;
    because you hid yourself we transgressed. f
6 We have all become like one who is unclean,
    and all our righteous deeds are like a filthy
      cloth.
We all fade like a leaf,
    and our iniquities, like the wind, take us away.
7 There is no one who calls on your name,
    or attempts to take hold of you;
for you have hidden your face from us,
    and have delivered g us into the hand of our
      iniquity.
8 Yet, O LORD, you are our Father;
    we are the clay, and you are our potter;
    we are all the work of your hand.
9 Do not be exceedingly angry, O LORD,
    and do not remember iniquity forever.
Now consider, we are all your people.

14 like cattle moving down into a valley
    guided by the spirit of the LORD?
Thus you led your people
    to win yourself a glorious name.
15 Look down from heaven and see
    from the heights where you dwell holy and
      glorious.
Where is your zeal, your valour,
    your burning and tender love?
Do not stand aloof, 16 for you are our Father.
Though Abraham were not to know us
    nor Israel to acknowledge us,
you, LORD, are our Father;
    our Redeemer from of old is your name.
17 Why, LORD, do you let us wander from your
    ways
    and harden our hearts until we cease to fear
      you?
Turn again for the sake of your servants,
    the tribes that are your possession.
18 Why have the wicked trespassed on your
    sanctuary,
    why have our enemies trampled on your
      shrine?
19 We have long been reckoned as beyond your
    sway,
    as if we had not been named your own.

64 Why did you not tear asunder the heavens and
    come down,
    that, when you appeared, the mountains might
      shake,
2 that fire might blaze as it blazes in brushwood
    when it makes water boil?
Then would your name be known to your
    adversaries,
    and nations would tremble before you.
3 You surprised us with awesome things;
    the mountains shook when you appeared.
4 Never has ear heard or eye seen
    any other god who acts for those who wait for
      him.
5 You welcome him who rejoices to do what is right,
    who is mindful of your ways.
When you showed your anger, we sinned
    and, in spite of it, we have done evil from of old.
6 We all became like something unclean
    and all our righteous deeds were like a filthy rag;
we have all withered like leaves
    and our iniquities carry us away like the wind.
7 There is no one who invokes you by name
    or rouses himself to hold fast to you;
for you have hidden your face from us
    and left us in the grip of our iniquities.
8 Yet, LORD, you are our Father;
    we are the clay, you the potter,
    and all of us are your handiwork.
9 Do not let your anger pass all bounds, LORD,
    and do not remember iniquity for ever;
    look on us all, look on your people.

63:14 **guided:** *so Gk; Heb.* given rest.   63:15 **Do . . . aloof:**
prob. rdg; Heb. obscure.   63:18 **Why . . . sanctuary:** *prob. rdg;
Heb.* For a little while they possessed your holy people. 64:1 *In
Heb. 63:19b.*   64:2 In Heb. 64:1.   64:5 **in spite . . . old:**
prob. rdg, cp. Gk; Heb. obscure.   64:7 **and left:** *so Gk; Heb.
unintelligible.*

---

e Ch 64.1 in Heb   f Meaning of Heb uncertain   g Gk Syr Old
Latin Tg: Heb melted

NEW AMERICAN BIBLE

14 Like cattle going down into the plain,
    the spirit of the LORD guiding them?
Thus you led your people,
    bringing glory to your name.

15 Look down from heaven and regard us
    from your holy and glorious palace!
Where is your zealous care and your might,
    your surge of pity and your mercy?
O Lord, hold not back,
16   for you are our father.
Were Abraham not to know us,
    nor Israel to acknowledge us,
You, LORD, are our father,
    our redeemer you are named forever.
17 Why do you let us wander, O LORD, from
      your ways,
    and harden our hearts so that we fear
      you not?
Return for the sake of your servants,
    the tribes of your heritage.
18 Why have the wicked invaded your holy
      place,
    why have our enemies trampled your
      sanctuary?
19 Too long have we been like those you do
      not rule,
    who do not bear your name.

Oh, that you would rend the heavens and
    come down,
    with the mountains quaking before
      you,

64 ¹ As when brushwood is set ablaze,
    or fire makes the water boil!
Thus your name would be made known to
    your enemies
    and the nations would tremble before you,
2 While you wrought awesome deeds we could
    not hope for,
3   such as they had not heard of from of old.
No ear has ever heard, no eye ever seen,
    any God but you
    doing such deeds for those who wait for him.
4 Would that you might meet us doing right,
    that we were mindful of you in our ways!
Behold, you are angry, and we are sinful;
5   all of us have become like unclean men,
    all our good deeds are like polluted rags;
We have all withered like leaves,
    and our guilt carries us away like the wind.
6 There is none who calls upon your name,
    who rouses himself to cling to you;
For you have hidden your face from us
    and have delivered us up to our guilt.
7 Yet, O LORD, you are our father;
    we are the clay and you the potter:
    we are all the work of your hands.
8 Be not so very angry, LORD,
    keep not our guilt forever in mind;
    look upon us, who are all your people.

NEW JERUSALEM BIBLE

14 as cattle going down to the plain.
Yahweh's Spirit led them to rest.
This was how you guided your people
    to win yourself glorious renown.

15 Look down from heaven and see
    from your holy and glorious dwelling.
Where is your zeal and your might?
Are your deepest feelings,
    your mercy to me, to be restrained?
16 After all, you are our Father.
If Abraham will not own us,
    if Israel will not acknowledge us,
you, Yahweh, are our Father,
    'Our Redeemer' is your name from of old.
17 Why, Yahweh, do you let us wander from your
      ways
    and let our hearts grow too hard to fear
      you?
Return, for the sake of your servants,
    the tribes of your heritage.
18 Your holy people have owned it for so short a
      time,
    our enemies have trampled on your
      sanctuary.
19 We have long been like those you do
      not rule,
    people who do not bear your name.

Oh, that you would tear the heavens open and
    come down
    — in your presence the mountains would
      quake,

64 ¹ as fire sets brushwood alight,
    as fire makes water boil—
to make your name known to your foes;
    the nations would tremble at your presence,
2 at the unexpected miracles you would do.
(Oh, that you would come down,
    in your presence the mountains would quake!)

3 Never has anyone heard,
    no ear has heard, no eye has seen
    any god but you act like this
    for the sake of those who trust him.
4 You come to meet those
    who are happy to act uprightly;
keeping your ways reminds them of you.
Yes, you have been angry and we have been
      sinners;
now we persist in your ways and we shall be
      saved.
5 We have all been like unclean things
    and our upright deeds like filthy rags.
We wither, all of us, like leaves,
    and all our misdeeds carry us off like the wind.
6 There is no one to invoke your name,
    to rouse himself to hold fast to you,
for you have hidden your face from us
    and given us up to the power of our misdeeds.
7 And yet, Yahweh, you are our Father;
    we the clay and you our potter,
    all of us are the work of your hands.
8 Yahweh, do not let your anger go too far
    and do not remember guilt for ever.
Look, please, we are all your people;

NEW REVISED STANDARD VERSION

REVISED ENGLISH BIBLE

10 Your holy cities have become a wilderness,
    Zion has become a wilderness,
    Jerusalem a desolation.
11 Our holy and beautiful house,
    where our ancestors praised you,
    has been burned by fire,
    and all our pleasant places have become ruins.
12 After all this, will you restrain yourself, O LORD?
    Will you keep silent, and punish us so
      severely?

65 I was ready to be sought out by those who did
      not ask,
    to be found by those who did not seek me.
I said, "Here I am, here I am,"
    to a nation that did not call on my name.
2 I held out my hands all day long
    to a rebellious people,
who walk in a way that is not good,
    following their own devices;
3 a people who provoke me
    to my face continually,
sacrificing in gardens
    and offering incense on bricks;
4 who sit inside tombs,
    and spend the night in secret places;
who eat swine's flesh,
    with broth of abominable things in their
      vessels;
5 who say, "Keep to yourself,
    do not come near me, for I am too holy for
      you."
These are a smoke in my nostrils,
    a fire that burns all day long.
6 See, it is written before me:
    I will not keep silent, but I will repay;
I will indeed repay into their laps
7 their*h* iniquities and their*h* ancestors' iniquities
      together,
                  says the LORD;
because they offered incense on the mountains
    and reviled me on the hills,
I will measure into their laps
    full payment for their actions.
8 Thus says the LORD:
As the wine is found in the cluster,
    and they say, "Do not destroy it,
    for there is a blessing in it,"
so I will do for my servants' sake,
    and not destroy them all.
9 I will bring forth descendants*i* from Jacob,
    and from Judah inheritors*j* of my mountains;
my chosen shall inherit it,
    and my servants shall settle there.
10 Sharon shall become a pasture for flocks,
    and the Valley of Achor a place for herds to lie
      down,
    for my people who have sought me.
11 But you who forsake the LORD,
    who forget my holy mountain,
who set a table for Fortune
    and fill cups of mixed wine for Destiny;
12 I will destine you to the sword,
    and all of you shall bow down to the slaughter;
because, when I called, you did not answer,
    when I spoke, you did not listen,
but you did what was evil in my sight,
    and chose what I did not delight in.

10 Your holy cities are a wilderness,
    Zion a wilderness, Jerusalem desolate;
11 our holy and glorious sanctuary,
    in which our forefathers praised you,
    has been burnt to the ground
    and all that we cherished lies in ruins.
12 Despite this, LORD, will you stand aloof,
    will you keep silent and punish us beyond
      measure?

65 I WAS ready to respond, but no one asked,
    ready to be found, but no one sought me.
I said, 'Here am I! Here am I!'
    to a nation that did not invoke me by name.
2 All day long I held out my hands
    appealing to a rebellious people,
who went their evil way,
    in pursuit of their own devices;
3 they were a people who provoked me
    perpetually to my face,
offering sacrifice in the gardens,
    burning incense on brick altars.
4 They crouch among graves,
    keeping vigil all night long,
eating the flesh of pigs,
    their cauldrons full of a foul brew.
5 'Keep clear!' they cry,
    'Do not touch me, for my holiness will infect you.'
Such people are a smouldering fire,
    smoke in my nostrils all day long.
6 Your record lies before me; I shall not keep silent;
    I shall fully repay 7your iniquities,
both yours and your forefathers', says the LORD,
    for having sacrificed on the mountains
    and shamed me on the hills;
I shall first measure out their reward
    and then repay them in full.
8 These are the words of the LORD:
As there is juice in a cluster of grapes
    and folk say, 'Do not destroy it; there is blessing
      in it,'
so shall I act for the sake of my servants:
    I shall not destroy the whole nation.
9 I shall give descendants to Jacob,
    and to Judah heirs who will possess my mountains;
my chosen ones will take possession of the land,
    and those who serve me will live there.
10 Flocks will range over Sharon,
    and the valley of Achor become a pasture for
      cattle;
they will belong to my people who seek me.
11 But you that forsake the LORD
    and ignore my holy mountain,
who spread a table for the god of Fate,
    and fill bowls of spiced wine in honour of Destiny,
12 I shall destine you for the sword,
    and you will all submit to slaughter,
because, when I called, you did not respond,
    when I spoke, you would not listen.
You did what was wrong in my sight,
    and chose what displeased me.

---

h Gk Syr: Heb *your*   *i* Or *a descendant*   *j* Or *an inheritor*

65:6–7 **I shall fully repay:** *prob. rdg, transposing* and then repay *to follow* reward.

9 Your holy cities have become a desert,
  Zion is a desert, Jerusalem a waste.
10 Our holy and glorious temple
  in which our fathers praised you
  Has been burned with fire;
  all that was dear to us is laid waste.
11 Can you hold back, O LORD, after all this?
  Can you remain silent, and afflict us
  so severely?

65

I was ready to respond to those who asked
  me not,
  to be found by those who sought me not.
  I said: Here I am! Here I am!
  To a nation that did not call upon my name.
2 I have stretched out my hands all the day
  to a rebellious people,
  Who walk in evil paths
  and follow their own thoughts,
3 People who provoke me
  continually, to my face,
  Offering sacrifices in the groves
  and burning incense on bricks,
4 Living among the graves
  and spending the night in caverns,
  Eating swine's flesh,
  with carrion broth in their dishes,
5 Crying out, "Hold back,
  do not touch me; I am too sacred for you!"
  These things enkindle my wrath,
  a fire that burns all the day.
6 Lo, before me it stands written;
  I will not be quiet until I have paid in full
7 Your crimes and the crimes of your fathers as well,
  says the LORD.
  Since they burned incense on the mountains,
  and disgraced me on the hills,
  I will at once pour out in full measure
  their recompense into their laps.

8 Thus says the LORD:
  When the juice is pressed from grapes,
  men say, "Do not discard them,
  for there is still good in them";
  Thus will I do with my servants:
  I will not discard them all;
9 From Jacob I will save offspring,
  from Judah, those who are to inherit
  my mountains;
  My chosen ones shall inherit the land,
  my servants shall dwell there.
10 Sharon shall be a pasture for the flocks
  and the valley of Achor a resting place for
  the cattle
  of my people who have sought me.

11 But you who forsake the LORD,
  forgetting my holy mountain,
  You who spread a table for Fortune
  and fill cups of blended wine for Destiny,
12 You I will destine for the sword;
  you shall all go down in slaughter.
  Since I called and you did not answer,
  I spoke and you did not listen,
  But did what was evil in my sight
  and preferred things which displease me,

9 your holy cities have become a desert,
  Zion has become a desert,
  Jerusalem a wasteland.
10 Our holy and glorious Temple,
  in which our ancestors used to praise you,
  has been burnt to the ground;
  all our delight lies in ruins.
11 Yahweh, can you restrain yourself at all this?
  Will you stay silent and afflict us beyond
  endurance?

65

I have let myself be approached by those who
  did not consult me,
  I have let myself be found by those who did not
  seek me.
  I said, 'Here I am, here I am!'
  to a nation that did not invoke my name.
2 Each day I stretched out my hands
  to a rebellious people
  who follow a way which is not good,
  as the fancy takes them;
3 a people constantly provoking me to my face
  by sacrificing in gardens,
  burning incense on bricks,
4 living in tombs,
  spending the night in dark corners,
  eating the meat of pigs,
  putting unclean foods on their plates.
5 'Keep your distance,' they say,
  'do not touch me, lest my sanctity come near you!'
  Such words are like stifling smoke to me,
  an ever-burning fire.
6 Look, it is inscribed before me:
  I shall not be silent until I have repaid them,
  repaid them in full,
7 punished your guilt and your ancestors' guilt
  together,
  Yahweh declares.
  For having burnt incense on the mountains
  and insulted me on the hills,
  I shall pay them back in full for what they have
  done.

8 Yahweh says this:
  As when a bunch of grapes is found still to have
  juice in it,
  people say, 'Do not destroy it,
  for it contains a blessing,'
  so I shall act for my servants' sake,
  I shall not destroy them all.
9 I shall produce descendants from Jacob
  and heirs to my mountains from Judah,
  my chosen ones will own them
  and my servants will live there.
10 Sharon will be a pasture for flocks,
  the Valley of Achor a feeding ground for cattle,
  for those of my people who have sought me.

11 But as for those of you who abandon Yahweh,
  who forget my holy mountain,
  who lay the table for Gad,g
  who fill cups of mixed wine for Meni,
12 you I shall destine to the sword
  and all of you will stoop to be slaughtered,
  because I called and you would not answer,
  I spoke and you would not listen;
  you have done what I consider evil,
  you chose to do what displeases me.

g **65** Gad is the Aramaean god of luck, Meni an unknown god,
possibly of fate.

NEW REVISED STANDARD VERSION	REVISED ENGLISH BIBLE

NEW REVISED STANDARD VERSION

13 Therefore thus says the Lord GOD:
My servants shall eat,
   but you shall be hungry;
my servants shall drink,
   but you shall be thirsty;
my servants shall rejoice,
   but you shall be put to shame;
14 my servants shall sing for gladness of heart,
   but you shall cry out for pain of heart,
   and shall wail for anguish of spirit.
15 You shall leave your name to my chosen to use
      as a curse,
   and the Lord GOD will put you to death;
   but to his servants he will give a different
      name.
16 Then whoever invokes a blessing in the land
   shall bless by the God of faithfulness,
and whoever takes an oath in the land
   shall swear by the God of faithfulness;
because the former troubles are forgotten
   and are hidden from my sight.

17 For I am about to create new heavens
      and a new earth;
the former things shall not be remembered
   or come to mind.
18 But be glad and rejoice forever
   in what I am creating;
for I am about to create Jerusalem as a joy,
   and its people as a delight.
19 I will rejoice in Jerusalem,
   and delight in my people;
no more shall the sound of weeping be heard in
      it,
   or the cry of distress.
20 No more shall there be in it
   an infant that lives but a few days,
   or an old person who does not live out a
      lifetime;
for one who dies at a hundred years will be
      considered a youth,
   and one who falls short of a hundred will be
      considered accursed.
21 They shall build houses and inhabit them;
   they shall plant vineyards and eat their fruit.
22 They shall not build and another inhabit;
   they shall not plant and another eat;
for like the days of a tree shall the days of my
      people be,
   and my chosen shall long enjoy the work of
      their hands.
23 They shall not labor in vain,
   or bear children for calamity;[k]
for they shall be offspring blessed by the LORD—
   and their descendants as well.
24 Before they call I will answer,
   while they are yet speaking I will hear.
25 The wolf and the lamb shall feed together,
   the lion shall eat straw like the ox;
   but the serpent—its food shall be dust!
They shall not hurt or destroy
   on all my holy mountain,
                              says the LORD.

66 Thus says the LORD:
Heaven is my throne
   and the earth is my footstool;
what is the house that you would build for me,
   and what is my resting place?

REVISED ENGLISH BIBLE

13 Therefore these are the words of the Lord GOD:
My servants will eat, while you go hungry;
my servants will drink, while you go thirsty;
my servants will rejoice, while you are put to
      shame;
14 my servants in the gladness of their hearts
   will shout for joy,
while you cry from an aching heart
   and wail from anguish of spirit.
15 Your name will be used as a curse by my chosen
      ones:
   'May the Lord GOD give you over to death!'
but his servants he will call by another name.
16 Anyone in the land invoking a blessing on himself
   will do so by God whose name is Amen,
and anyone in the land taking an oath
   will do so by God whose name is Amen,
for past troubles are forgotten;
   they have vanished from my sight.

17 See, I am creating new heavens and a new earth!
The past will no more be remembered
   nor will it ever come to mind.
18 Rejoice and be for ever filled with delight
   at what I create;
for I am creating Jerusalem as a delight
   and her people as a joy.
19 I shall take delight in Jerusalem
   and rejoice in my people;
the sound of weeping, the cry of distress
   will be heard in her no more.
20 No child there will ever again die in infancy,
   no old man fail to live out his span of life.
He who dies at a hundred is just a youth,
   and if he does not attain a hundred he is thought
      accursed!
21 My people will build houses and live in them,
   plant vineyards and eat their fruit;
22 they will not build for others to live in
   or plant for others to eat.
They will be as long-lived as a tree,
   and my chosen ones will enjoy the fruit of their
      labour.
23 They will not toil to no purpose
   or raise children for misfortune,
because they and their issue after them
   are a race blessed by the LORD.
24 Even before they call to me, I shall answer,
   and while they are still speaking I shall respond.
25 The wolf and the lamb will feed together
   and the lion will eat straw like the ox,
   and as for the serpent, its food will be dust.
Neither hurt nor harm will be done in all my holy
      mountain,
says the LORD.

66 These are the words of the LORD:
The heavens are my throne and the earth is my
      footstool.
Where will you build a house for me,
   where will my resting-place be?

[k] Or sudden terror

NEW AMERICAN BIBLE

13 therefore thus says the Lord GOD:
 Lo, my servants shall eat,
  but you shall go hungry;
 My servants shall drink,
  but you shall be thirsty;
 My servants shall rejoice,
  but you shall be put to shame;
14 My servants shall shout
  for joy of heart,
 But you shall cry out for grief of heart
  and howl for anguish of spirit.
15 The Lord GOD shall slay you,
  and the name you leave
 Shall be used by my chosen ones for cursing;
  but my servants shall be called by another name
16 By which he will be blessed
  on whom a blessing is invoked in the land;
 He who takes an oath in the land
  shall swear by the God of truth;
 For the hardships of the past shall be forgotten,
  and hidden from my eyes.
17 Lo, I am about to create new heavens
  and a new earth;
 The things of the past shall not be remembered
  or come to mind.
18 Instead, there shall always be rejoicing
  and happiness
 in what I create;
 For I create Jerusalem to be a joy
  and its people to be a delight;
19 I will rejoice in Jerusalem
  and exult in my people.
 No longer shall the sound of weeping be
  heard there,
  or the sound of crying;
20 No longer shall there be in it
 an infant who lives but a few days,
 or an old man who does not round out his
  full lifetime;
 He dies a mere youth who reaches but a
  hundred years,
 and he who fails of a hundred shall be
  thought accursed.
21 They shall live in the houses they build,
  and eat the fruit of the vineyards they plant;
22 They shall not build houses for others to live in,
  or plant for others to eat.
 As the years of a tree, so the years of my people;
  and my chosen ones shall long enjoy
  the produce of their hands.
23 They shall not toil in vain,
  nor beget children for sudden destruction;
 For a race blessed by the LORD
  are they and their offspring.
24 Before they call, I will answer;
  while they are yet speaking, I will hearken
  to them.
25 The wolf and the lamb shall graze alike,
  and the lion shall eat hay like the ox
  [but the serpent's food shall be dust].
 None shall hurt or destroy
  on all my holy mountain, says the LORD.

66 Thus says the LORD:
 The heavens are my throne,
  the earth is my footstool.
 What kind of house can you build for me;
  what is to be my resting place?

NEW JERUSALEM BIBLE

13 Therefore Lord Yahweh says this:
 You will see my servants eating
  while you go hungry;
 you will see my servants drinking
  while you go thirsty;
 you will see my servants rejoicing
  while you are put to shame;
14 you will hear my servants shouting for joy of
  heart,
 while you shriek for sorrow of heart
  and howl with a broken spirit.
15 And you will leave your name behind as a curse
  for my chosen ones,
 'May Lord Yahweh strike you dead!'
 But to his servants he will give another name.
16 Whoever blesses himself on earth will bless
  himself by the God of truth,
 and whoever swears an oath on earth will swear by
  the God of truth,
 for past troubles will be forgotten
  and hidden from my eyes.
17 For look, I am going to create new heavens and a
  new earth,
 and the past will not be remembered
  and will come no more to mind.
18 Rather be joyful, be glad for ever
  at what I am creating,
 for look, I am creating Jerusalem to be 'Joy'
  and my people to be 'Gladness'.
19 I shall be joyful in Jerusalem
  and I shall rejoice in my people.
 No more will the sound of weeping be heard there,
  nor the sound of a shriek;
20 never again will there be an infant there who lives
  only a few days,
 nor an old man who does not run his full course;
  for the youngest will die at a hundred,
 and at a hundred the sinner will be accursed.
21 They will build houses and live in them,
  they will plant vineyards and eat their fruit.
22 They will not build for others to live in,
  or plant for others to eat;
 for the days of my people will be like the days of
  a tree,
 and my chosen ones will themselves use what they
  have made.
23 They will not toil in vain,
  nor bear children destined to disaster,
 for they are the race of Yahweh's blessed ones
  and so are their offspring.
24 Thus, before they call I shall answer,
  before they stop speaking I shall have heard.
25 The wolf and the young lamb will feed together,
  the lion will eat hay like the ox,
 and dust be the serpent's food.
 No hurt, no harm will be done
 on all my holy mountain,[h]
 Yahweh says.

66 Thus says Yahweh:
 With heaven my throne
  and earth my footstool,
 what house could you build me,
  what place for me to rest,

[h] **65** = 11:7, 9.

2 All these things my hand has made,
  and so all these things are mine,[l]
                        says the LORD.
But this is the one to whom I will look,
  to the humble and contrite in spirit,
  who trembles at my word.

3 Whoever slaughters an ox is like one who kills a
      human being;
  whoever sacrifices a lamb, like one who breaks
      a dog's neck;
  whoever presents a grain offering, like one who
      offers swine's blood;[m]
  whoever makes a memorial offering of
      frankincense, like one who blesses an
      idol.
These have chosen their own ways,
  and in their abominations they take delight;
4 I also will choose to mock[n] them,
  and bring upon them what they fear;
because, when I called, no one answered,
  when I spoke, they did not listen;
but they did what was evil in my sight,
  and chose what did not please me.

5 Hear the word of the LORD,
  you who tremble at his word:
Your own people who hate you
  and reject you for my name's sake
have said, "Let the LORD be glorified,
  so that we may see your joy";
but it is they who shall be put to shame.

6 Listen, an uproar from the city!
  A voice from the temple!
The voice of the LORD,
  dealing retribution to his enemies!

7 Before she was in labor
  she gave birth;
before her pain came upon her
  she delivered a son.
8 Who has heard of such a thing?
  Who has seen such things?
Shall a land be born in one day?
  Shall a nation be delivered in one moment?
Yet as soon as Zion was in labor
  she delivered her children.
9 Shall I open the womb and not deliver?
  says the LORD;
shall I, the one who delivers, shut the womb?
  says your God.

10 Rejoice with Jerusalem, and be glad for her,
  all you who love her;
rejoice with her in joy,
  all you who mourn over her—
11 that you may nurse and be satisfied
  from her consoling breast;
that you may drink deeply with delight
  from her glorious bosom.

12 For thus says the LORD:
I will extend prosperity to her like a river,
  and the wealth of the nations like an
      overflowing stream;
and you shall nurse and be carried on her arm,
  and dandled on her knees.
13 As a mother comforts her child,
  so I will comfort you;
  you shall be comforted in Jerusalem.

2 These are all of my own making,
  and all belong to me.
This is the word of the LORD.

The one for whom I have regard
is oppressed and afflicted,
one who reveres my word.

3 Sacrificing an ox is like killing a man,
slaughtering a sheep like breaking a dog's neck,
making an offering of grain like offering pigs'
      blood,
burning frankincense as a token like worshipping
      an idol.
Because people have adopted these practices
and revelled in loathsome rites,
4 I in turn shall adopt a wilful course
and bring on them the very things they dread,
since, when I called, no one responded,
when I spoke, no one listened.
They did what was wrong in my sight
and chose what displeased me.

5 Hear the word of the LORD, you that revere his
      word:
Your fellow-countrymen, who are hostile to you
and spurn you because you bear my name, have
      said,
'Let the LORD show his glory,
that we may see you rejoice!'
But they themselves will be put to shame.

6 That roar from the city, that uproar in the temple,
is the sound of the LORD dealing retribution to his
      foes.

7 Without birth-pains Zion has given birth,
borne a son before the onset of labour.
8 Who has heard of anything like this?
Who has witnessed such a thing?
Can a country be born in a single day,
a nation be brought to birth in a trice?
Yet Zion, at the onset of her pangs, bore her
      children.
9 Shall I bring to the point of birth and not deliver?
says the LORD;
shall I who deliver close the womb?
says your God.

10 Rejoice with Jerusalem and exult in her,
all you that love her;
share her joy with all your heart,
all you that mourned over her.
11 Then you may suck comfort from her and be
      satisfied,
taking with enjoyment her plentiful milk.

12 These are the words of the LORD:
I shall make prosperity flow over her like a river,
and the wealth of nations like a stream in spate;
her babes will be carried in her arms
and dandled on her knees.
13 As a mother comforts her son
so shall I myself comfort you;
in Jerusalem you will find comfort.

---

[l] Gk Syr: Heb *these things came to be*   [m] Meaning of Heb uncertain
[n] Or *to punish*

66:2 **belong to me:** *so Gk; Heb.* omits.   66:12 **her babes:** prob.
rdg; cp. Gk; Heb. you will suck.

2 My hand made all these things
    when all of them came to be, says the LORD.
This is the one whom I approve:
    the lowly and afflicted man who trembles at
      my word.

3 Merely slaughtering an ox is like slaying a man;
    sacrificing a lamb, like breaking a dog's neck;
Bringing a cereal offering, like offering
    swine's blood;
    burning incense, like paying homage to an idol.
Since these have chosen their own ways
    and taken pleasure in their own abominations,
4 I in turn will choose ruthless treatment for them
    and bring upon them what they fear.

Because, when I called, no one answered,
    when I spoke, no one listened;
Because they did what was evil in my sight,
    and chose what gave me displeasure,
5 Hear the word of the LORD,
    you who tremble at his word:
Your brethren who, because of my name,
    hate and reject you, say,
"Let the LORD show his glory
    that we may see your joy";
    but they shall be put to shame.
6 A sound of roaring from the city,
    a sound from the temple,
The sound of the LORD
    repaying his enemies their deserts!

7 Before she comes to labor,
    she gives birth;
Before the pains come upon her,
    she safely delivers a male child.
8 Who ever heard of such a thing,
    or saw the like?
Can a country be brought forth in one day,
    or a nation be born in a single moment?
Yet Zion is scarcely in labor
    when she gives birth to her children.
9 Shall I bring a mother to the point of birth,
    and yet not let her child be born? says the LORD;
Or shall I who allow her to conceive,
    yet close her womb? says your God.

10 Rejoice with Jerusalem and be glad because of her,
    all you who love her;
Exult, exult with her,
    all you who were mourning over her!
11 Oh, that you may suck fully
    of the milk of her comfort,
That you may nurse with delight
    at her abundant breasts!
12   For thus says the LORD:
Lo, I will spread prosperity over her like a river,
    and the wealth of the nations like
    an overflowing torrent.
As nurslings, you shall be carried in her arms,
    and fondled in her lap;
13 As a mother comforts her son,
    so will I comfort you;
    in Jerusalem you shall find your comfort.

2 when all these things were made by me
    and all belong to me? — declares Yahweh.
But my eyes are drawn to the person
    of humbled and contrite spirit,
    who trembles at my word.

3 Some slaughter a bull, some kill a human being,
    some sacrifice a lamb, some strangle a dog,
    some present an offering of pig's blood,
    some burn memorial incense, a revolting blessing;
all these people have chosen their own ways
    and take delight in their disgusting practices.
4 I too take delight in making fools of them,
    I shall bring what they most fear down on them
because I have called and no one would answer,
    I spoke and no one listened.
They have done what I regard as evil,
    have chosen what displeases me.

5 Listen to the word of Yahweh,
    you who tremble at his word.
Your brothers, who hate and reject you
    because of my name, have said,
'Let Yahweh show his glory,
    let us witness your joy!'
    But they will be put to shame.

6 Listen! An uproar from the city!
    A voice from the Temple!
The voice of Yahweh
    bringing retribution on his enemies.

7 Before being in labour she has given birth.
Before the birth pangs came, she has been
    delivered of a child.

8 Who ever heard of such a thing,
    who ever saw anything like this?
Can a country be born in one day?
Can a nation be brought forth all at once?
For Zion, scarcely in labour, has brought forth her
    children!
9 Shall I open the womb and not bring to birth?
    says Yahweh.
Shall I, who bring to birth, close the womb?
    says your God.

10 Rejoice with Jerusalem,
    be glad for her, all you who love her!
Rejoice, rejoice with her,
    all you who mourned her!
11 So that you may be suckled and satisfied
    from her consoling breast,
so that you may drink deep with delight
    from her generous nipple.

12 For Yahweh says this:
Look, I am going to send peace
    flowing over her like a river,
and like a stream in spate
    the glory of the nations.

You will be suckled, carried on her hip
    and fondled in her lap.
13 As a mother comforts a child,
    so I shall comfort you;
    you will be comforted in Jerusalem.

NEW REVISED STANDARD VERSION | REVISED ENGLISH BIBLE

14 You shall see, and your heart shall rejoice;
    your bodies*o* shall flourish like the grass;
and it shall be known that the hand of the LORD
    is with his servants,
    and his indignation is against his enemies.
15 For the LORD will come in fire,
    and his chariots like the whirlwind,
to pay back his anger in fury,
    and his rebuke in flames of fire.
16 For by fire will the LORD execute judgment,
    and by his sword, on all flesh;
    and those slain by the LORD shall be many.

17 Those who sanctify and purify themselves to go into the gardens, following the one in the center, eating the flesh of pigs, vermin, and rodents, shall come to an end together, says the LORD.

18 For I know*p* their works and their thoughts, and I am*q* coming to gather all nations and tongues; and they shall come and shall see my glory, 19 and I will set a sign among them. From them I will send survivors to the nations, to Tarshish, Put,*r* and Lud — which draw the bow — to Tubal and Javan, to the coastlands far away that have not heard of my fame or seen my glory; and they shall declare my glory among the nations. 20 They shall bring all your kindred from all the nations as an offering to the LORD, on horses, and in chariots, and in litters, and on mules, and on dromedaries, to my holy mountain Jerusalem, says the LORD, just as the Israelites bring a grain offering in a clean vessel to the house of the LORD. 21 And I will also take some of them as priests and as Levites, says the LORD.

22 For as the new heavens and the new earth,
    which I will make,
shall remain before me, says the LORD;
    so shall your descendants and your name
      remain.
23 From new moon to new moon,
    and from sabbath to sabbath,
all flesh shall come to worship before me,
    says the LORD.

24 And they shall go out and look at the dead bodies of the people who have rebelled against me; for their worm shall not die, their fire shall not be quenched, and they shall be an abhorrence to all flesh.

14 At the sight your heart will be glad,
    you will flourish like grass in spring;
the LORD will make his power known among his
      servants
and his indignation felt among his foes.
15 See, the LORD is coming in fire,
    his chariots like a whirlwind,
bringing retribution with his furious anger
    and with the flaming fire of his rebukes.
16 The LORD will judge with fire,
    by his sword he will test all mankind,
    and many will be slain by him.
17 Those who consecrate and purify themselves for
      garden-rites,
one after another in a magic ring,
those who eat swine flesh, rats, and vile vermin
    will all meet their end,
    says the LORD,
18 for I know their deeds and their thoughts.

I am coming to gather peoples of every tongue; they will come to see my glory. 19 I shall put a sign on them, and those survivors I shall send to the nations, to Tarshish, Put, and Lud, to Meshech, Rosh, Tubal, and Javan, distant shores which have never yet heard of me or seen my glory; these will declare that glory among the nations. 20 From every nation your countrymen will be brought on horses, in chariots and wagons, on mules and dromedaries, as an offering to the LORD on my holy mountain Jerusalem, says the LORD, just as the Israelites themselves bring grain-offerings in purified vessels to the LORD's house; 21 and some of them I shall take for priests and for Levites, says the LORD.

22 As the new heavens and the new earth
    which I am making will endure before me,
    says the LORD,
so will your posterity and your name endure.
23 Month after month at the new moon,
    week after week on the sabbath,
all mankind will come to bow before me,
    says the LORD.

24 As they go out they will see the corpses of those who rebelled against me, where the devouring worm never dies and the fire is not quenched. All mankind will view them with horror.

66:17 **one . . . ring:** *possible mng; Heb. obscure.*   66:18 **know:** *so Syriac; Heb. omits.* **I am coming:** *so Gk; Heb.* It will come. 66:19 **Put:** *so Gk; Heb. unintelligible.* **Meshech, Rosh:** *prob. rdg; Heb.* those who draw the bow. **Javan:** *or* Greece.

o Heb *bones*   *p* Gk Syr: Heb lacks *know*   *q* Gk Syr Vg Tg: Heb *it is*   *r* Gk: Heb *Pul*

14 When you see this, your heart shall rejoice,
  and your bodies flourish like the grass;
The LORD's power shall be known to his servants,
  but to his enemies, his wrath.

15 Lo, the LORD shall come in fire,
  his chariots like the whirlwind,
To wreak his wrath with burning heat
  and his punishment with fiery flames.
16 For the LORD shall judge all mankind
  by fire and sword,
  and many shall be slain by the LORD.

17 They who sanctify and purify themselves to go to the
groves, as followers of one who stands within, they who eat
swine's flesh, loathsome things and mice, shall all perish
with their deeds and their thoughts, says the LORD.
18 I come to gather nations of every language; they shall
come and see my glory. 19 I will set a sign among them;
from them I will send fugitives to the nations: to Tarshish,
Put and Lud, Mosoch, Tubal and Javan, to the distant coastlands that have never heard of my fame, or seen my glory;
and they shall proclaim my glory among the nations.
20 They shall bring all your brethren from all the nations as
an offering to the LORD, on horses and in chariots, in carts,
upon mules and dromedaries, to Jerusalem, my holy mountain, says the LORD, just as the Israelites bring their offering
to the house of the LORD in clean vessels. 21 Some of these
I will take as priests and Levites, says the LORD.

22 As the new heavens and the new earth
  which I will make
Shall endure before me, says the LORD,
  so shall your race and your name endure.
23 From one new moon to another,
  and from one sabbath to another,
All mankind shall come to worship
  before me, says the LORD.
24 They shall go out and see the corpses
  of the men who rebelled against me;
Their worm shall not die,
  nor their fire be extinguished;
  and they shall be abhorrent to all mankind.

14 At the sight your heart will rejoice,
  and your limbs regain vigour like the grass.
To his servants Yahweh will reveal his hand,
  but to his enemies his fury.

15 For see how Yahweh comes in fire,
  his chariots like the whirlwind,
  to assuage his anger with burning,
  his rebukes with flaming fire.
16 For by fire will Yahweh execute fair judgement,
  and by his sword, on all people;
  and Yahweh's victims will be many.

17 As for those who sanctify themselves
  and purify themselves to enter the gardens,
  following the one in the centre,
  who eat the flesh of pigs, revolting things and rats:
  their deeds and their thoughts will perish together,
  declares Yahweh.

18 I am coming to gather every nation and every language. They will come to witness my glory. 19 I shall give
them a sign and send some of their survivors to the nations:
to Tarshish, Put, Lud, Meshech, Tubal and Javan,[i] to the
distant coasts and islands that have never heard of me or
seen my glory. They will proclaim my glory to the nations,
20 and from all the nations they will bring all your brothers
as an offering to Yahweh, on horses, in chariots, in litters,
on mules and on camels, to my holy mountain, Jerusalem,
Yahweh says, like Israelites bringing offerings in clean vessels to Yahweh's house. 21 And some of them I shall make
into priests and Levites, Yahweh says.
22 For as the new heavens and the new earth I am making
will endure before me, declares Yahweh, so will your race
and your name endure.

23 From New Moon to New Moon,
  from Sabbath to Sabbath,
  all humanity will come and bow
  in my presence, Yahweh says.
24 And on their way out they will see
  the corpses of those
  who rebelled against me;
  for their worm will never die
  nor their fire be put out,
  and they will be held in horror by all humanity.

[i] 66 Possible identifications: Spain, Lybia, Lydia, Phrygia, Cilicia, or
Greece.

Jeremiah

1 The words of Jeremiah son of Hilkiah, of the priests who were in Anathoth in the land of Benjamin, ²to whom the word of the LORD came in the days of King Josiah son of Amon of Judah, in the thirteenth year of his reign. ³It came also in the days of King Jehoiakim son of Josiah of Judah, and until the end of the eleventh year of King Zedekiah son of Josiah of Judah, until the captivity of Jerusalem in the fifth month.

4 Now the word of the LORD came to me saying,

5 "Before I formed you in the womb I knew you,
  and before you were born I consecrated you;
  I appointed you a prophet to the nations."

⁶Then I said, "Ah, Lord GOD! Truly I do not know how to speak, for I am only a boy." ⁷But the LORD said to me,

"Do not say, 'I am only a boy';
for you shall go to all to whom I send you,
and you shall speak whatever I command you.

8 Do not be afraid of them,
  for I am with you to deliver you,
                              says the LORD."

⁹Then the LORD put out his hand and touched my mouth; and the LORD said to me,

"Now I have put my words in your mouth.
10 See, today I appoint you over nations and over
                        kingdoms,
  to pluck up and to pull down,
  to destroy and to overthrow,
  to build and to plant."

11 The word of the LORD came to me, saying, "Jeremiah, what do you see?" And I said, "I see a branch of an almond tree."*a* ¹²Then the LORD said to me, "You have seen well, for I am watching*b* over my word to perform it." ¹³The word of the LORD came to me a second time, saying, "What do you see?" And I said, "I see a boiling pot, tilted away from the north."

14 Then the LORD said to me: Out of the north disaster shall break out on all the inhabitants of the land. ¹⁵For now I am calling all the tribes of the kingdoms of the north, says the LORD; and they shall come and all of them shall set their thrones at the entrance of the gates of Jerusalem, against all its surrounding walls and against all the cities of Judah. ¹⁶And I will utter my judgments against them, for all their wickedness in forsaking me; they have made offerings to other gods, and worshiped the works of their own hands. ¹⁷But you, gird up your loins; stand up and tell them everything that I command you. Do not break down before them, or I will break you before them. ¹⁸And I for my part have made you today a fortified city, an iron pillar, and a bronze

---

THE BOOK OF THE PROPHET

Jeremiah

1 THE words of Jeremiah son of Hilkiah, one of the priests at Anathoth in Benjamin. ²The word of the LORD came to him in the thirteenth year of the reign of Josiah son of Amon, king of Judah. ³It came also during the reign of Jehoiakim son of Josiah, king of Judah, until the end of the eleventh year of Zedekiah son of Josiah, king of Judah. In the fifth month the inhabitants of Jerusalem were carried off into exile.

⁴THIS word of the LORD came to me: ⁵'Before I formed you in the womb I chose you, and before you were born I consecrated you; and I appointed you a prophet to the nations.' ⁶'Ah! Lord GOD,' I answered, 'I am not skilled in speaking; I am too young.' ⁷But the LORD said, 'Do not plead that you are too young; for you are to go to whatever people I send you, and say whatever I tell you to say. ⁸Fear none of them, for I shall be with you to keep you safe.' This was the word of the LORD. ⁹Then the LORD stretched out his hand, and touching my mouth said to me, 'See, I put my words into your mouth. ¹⁰This day I give you authority over nations and kingdoms to uproot and to pull down, to destroy and to demolish, to build and to plant.'

¹¹The word of the LORD came to me: 'What is it that you see, Jeremiah?' 'A branch of an almond tree,' I answered. ¹²'You are right,' said the LORD to me, 'for I am on the watch to carry out my threat.'

¹³The word of the LORD came to me a second time: 'What is it that you see?' 'A cauldron on a fire,' I said; 'it is fanned by the wind and tilted away from the north.' ¹⁴The LORD said:

From the north disaster will be let loose
  against all who live in the land.
15 For now I am summoning all the peoples
  of the kingdoms of the north,
  says the LORD;
  their kings will come
  and each will set his throne in place
  before the gates of Jerusalem;
  they will encircle her walls
  and besiege every town in Judah.
16 I shall state my case against my people
  for all their wickedness in forsaking me,
  in burning sacrifices to other gods,
  and in worshipping the work of their own hands.

17 Brace yourself, Jeremiah;
  stand up and speak to them.
  Tell them everything I bid you;
  when you confront them
  do not let your spirit break,
  or I shall break you before their eyes.
18 This day I make you a fortified city,
  an iron pillar, a bronze wall,

1:11 **almond tree:** *Heb.* shaked.   1:12 **on the watch:** *Heb.* shoked.

a Heb *shaqed*   *b* Heb *shoqed*

THE BOOK OF
Jeremiah

1 The words of Jeremiah, son of Hilkiah, of a priestly family in Anathoth, in the land of Benjamin. ²The word of the LORD first came to him in the days of Josiah, son of Amon, king of Judah, in the thirteenth year of his reign, ³and continued through the reign of Jehoiakim, son of Josiah, king of Judah, and until the downfall and exile of Jerusalem in the fifth month of the eleventh year of Zedekiah, son of Josiah, king of Judah.

⁴The word of the LORD came to me thus:

⁵Before I formed you in the womb I knew you,
    before you were born I dedicated you,
    a prophet to the nations I appointed you.
⁶"Ah, Lord GOD!" I said,
    "I know not how to speak; I am too young."
⁷But the LORD answered me,
    Say not, "I am too young."
    To whomever I send you, you shall go;
    whatever I command you, you shall speak.
⁸Have no fear before them,
    because I am with you to deliver you, says
        the LORD.

⁹Then the LORD extended his hand and touched my mouth, saying,

See, I place my words in your mouth!
¹⁰   This day I set you
    over nations and over kingdoms,
    To root up and to tear down,
        to destroy and to demolish,
        to build and to plant.

¹¹The word of the LORD came to me with the question: What do you see, Jeremiah? "I see a branch of the watching-tree," I replied. ¹²Then the LORD said to me: Well have you seen, for I am watching to fulfill my word. ¹³A second time the word of the LORD came to me with the question: What do you see? "I see a boiling cauldron," I replied, "that appears from the north."

¹⁴And from the north, said the LORD to me, evil will boil over upon all who dwell in the land.

¹⁵Lo, I am summoning
    all the kingdoms of the north, says the LORD;
Each king shall come and set up his throne
    at the gateways of Jerusalem,
Opposite her walls all around
    and opposite all the cities of Judah.
¹⁶I will pronounce my sentence against them
    for all their wickedness in forsaking me,
And in burning incense to strange gods
    and adoring their own handiwork.

¹⁷But do you gird your loins;
    stand up and tell them
    all that I command you.
Be not crushed on their account,
    as though I would leave you crushed
        before them;
¹⁸For it is I this day
    who have made you a fortified city,
A pillar of iron, a wall of brass,

Jeremiah

1 The words of Jeremiah son of Hilkiah, one of the priests living at Anathoth in the territory of Benjamin. ²The word of Yahweh came to him in the days of Josiah son of Amon, king of Judah, in the thirteenth year of his reign; ³then in the days of Jehoiakim son of Josiah, king of Judah, until the end of the eleventh year of Zedekiah son of Josiah, king of Judah, until the deportation of Jerusalem, in the fifth month.

⁴The word of Yahweh came to me, saying:

⁵'Before I formed you in the womb I knew you;
    before you came to birth I consecrated you;
    I appointed you as prophet to the nations.'

⁶I then said, 'Ah, ah, ah, Lord Yahweh; you see, I do not know how to speak: I am only a child!'

⁷But Yahweh replied,
    'Do not say, "I am only a child,"
    for you must go to all to whom I send you
    and say whatever I command you.
⁸Do not be afraid of confronting them,
    for I am with you to rescue you,
    Yahweh declares.'

⁹Then Yahweh stretched out his hand and touched my mouth, and Yahweh said to me:

'There! I have put my words into your mouth.
¹⁰Look, today I have set you
    over the nations and kingdoms,
    to uproot and to knock down,
    to destroy and to overthrow,
    to build and to plant.'

¹¹The word of Yahweh came to me, asking, 'Jeremiah, what do you see?' I answered, 'I see a branch of the Watchful Tree.' ¹²Then Yahweh said, 'Well seen, for I am watching over my word to perform it.'

¹³A second time the word of Yahweh came to me, asking, 'What do you see?' I answered, 'I see a cooking pot on the boil, with its mouth tilting from the north.' ¹⁴Then Yahweh said:

'From the north disaster will come boiling over
    on all who live in the country,
¹⁵for I am now summoning
    all the families of the kingdoms of the north,
    Yahweh declares.
They will come, and each will set his throne
    in front of the gates of Jerusalem,
    all round, against its walls
    and against all the towns of Judah.
¹⁶I shall pronounce my judgements on them
    because of all their wickedness,
    since they have abandoned me,
    offering incense to other gods
    and worshipping what their own hands have made.

¹⁷'As for you, prepare yourself for action.
    Stand up and tell them
    all I command you.
    Have no fear of them
    and in their presence I will make you fearless.
¹⁸For look, today I have made you
    into a fortified city,
    a pillar of iron,
    a wall of bronze

wall, against the whole land—against the kings of Judah, its princes, its priests, and the people of the land. 19 They will fight against you; but they shall not prevail against you, for I am with you, says the LORD, to deliver you.

2 The word of the LORD came to me, saying: 2 Go and proclaim in the hearing of Jerusalem, Thus says the LORD:

I remember the devotion of your youth,
    your love as a bride,
how you followed me in the wilderness,
    in a land not sown.
3 Israel was holy to the LORD,
    the first fruits of his harvest.
All who ate of it were held guilty;
    disaster came upon them,
                            says the LORD.

4 Hear the word of the LORD, O house of Jacob, and all the families of the house of Israel. 5 Thus says the LORD:

What wrong did your ancestors find in me
    that they went far from me,
and went after worthless things, and became
        worthless themselves?
6 They did not say, "Where is the LORD
    who brought us up from the land of Egypt,
who led us in the wilderness,
    in a land of deserts and pits,
in a land of drought and deep darkness,
    in a land that no one passes through,
    where no one lives?"
7 I brought you into a plentiful land
    to eat its fruits and its good things.
But when you entered you defiled my land,
    and made my heritage an abomination.
8 The priests did not say, "Where is the LORD?"
    Those who handle the law did not know me;
the rulers[c] transgressed against me;
    the prophets prophesied by Baal,
    and went after things that do not profit.
9 Therefore once more I accuse you,
                            says the LORD,
    and I accuse your children's children.
10 Cross to the coasts of Cyprus and look,
    send to Kedar and examine with care;
    see if there has ever been such a thing.
11 Has a nation changed its gods,
    even though they are no gods?
But my people have changed their glory
    for something that does not profit.
12 Be appalled, O heavens, at this,
    be shocked, be utterly desolate,
                            says the LORD,
13 for my people have committed two evils:
    they have forsaken me,
the fountain of living water,
    and dug out cisterns for themselves,
cracked cisterns
    that can hold no water.

to withstand the whole land,
    the kings and princes of Judah,
    its priests, and its people.
19 Though they attack you, they will not prevail,
    for I shall be with you to keep you safe.
    This is the word of the LORD.

2 THE word of the LORD came to me: 2 Go, make this proclamation in the hearing of Jerusalem: These are the words of the LORD:

I remember in your favour the loyalty of your
            youth,
    your love during your bridal days,
when you followed me through the wilderness,
    through a land unsown.
3 Israel was holy to the LORD,
    the firstfruits of his harvest;
no one who devoured her went unpunished,
    disaster overtook them.
This is the word of the LORD.

4 Listen to the word of the LORD, people of Jacob, all you families of Israel. 5 These are the words of the LORD:

What fault did your forefathers find in me,
    that they went so far astray from me,
pursuing worthless idols
    and becoming worthless like them;
6 that they did not ask, 'Where is the LORD,
    who brought us up from Egypt
and led us through the wilderness,
    through a barren and broken country,
a country parched and forbidding,
    where no one ever travelled,
    where no one made his home?'
7 I brought you into a fertile land
    to enjoy its fruit and every good thing in it;
but when you entered my land you defiled it
    and made loathsome the home I gave you.
8 The priests no longer asked, 'Where is the LORD?'
    Those who handled the law had no real knowledge
            of me,
the shepherds of the people rebelled against me;
    the prophets prophesied in the name of Baal
    and followed gods who were powerless to help.
9 Therefore I shall bring a charge against you once
            more,
says the LORD,
    against you and against your descendants.
10 Cross to the coasts and islands of Kittim and see,
    send to Kedar and observe closely,
    see whether there has been anything like this:
11 has a nation ever exchanged its gods,
    and these no gods at all?
Yet my people have exchanged their glory
    for a god altogether powerless.
12 Be aghast at this, you heavens,
    shudder in utter horror,
says the LORD.
13 My people have committed two sins:
    they have rejected me,
a source of living water,
    and they have hewn out for themselves cisterns,
cracked cisterns which hold no water.

[c] Heb shepherds

NEW AMERICAN BIBLE

against the whole land;
Against Judah's kings and princes,
   against its priests and people.
19 They will fight against you, but not prevail
      over you,
   for I am with you to deliver you, says the LORD.

2 This word of the LORD came to me: 2 Go, cry out this
message for Jerusalem to hear!

I remember the devotion of your youth,
   how you loved me as a bride,
Following me in the desert,
   in a land unsown.
3 Sacred to the LORD was Israel,
   the first fruits of his harvest;
Should anyone presume to partake of them,
   evil would befall him, says the LORD.

4 Listen to the word of the LORD, O house of Jacob!
   All you clans of the house of Israel,
5   thus says the LORD:
What fault did your fathers find in me
   that they withdrew from me,
Went after empty idols,
   and became empty themselves?
6 They did not ask, "Where is the LORD
   who brought us up from the land of Egypt,
Who led us through the desert,
   through a land of wastes and gullies,
Through a land of drought and darkness,
   through a land which no one crosses, where no
      man dwells?"
7 When I brought you into the garden land
   to eat its goodly fruits,
You entered and defiled my land,
   you made my heritage loathsome.
8 The priests asked not,
   "Where is the LORD?"
Those who dealt with the law knew me not:
   the shepherds rebelled against me.
The prophets prophesied by Baal,
   and went after useless idols.
9 Therefore will I yet accuse you, says the LORD,
   and even your children's children I will accuse.
10 Pass over to the coast of the Kittim and see,
   send to Kedar and carefully inquire:
   Where has the like of this been done?
11 Does any other nation change its gods? —
   yet they are not gods at all!
But my people have changed their glory
   for useless things.
12 Be amazed at this, O heavens,
   and shudder with sheer horror, says the LORD.
13 Two evils have my people done:
   they have forsaken me, the source of
      living waters;
They have dug themselves cisterns,
   broken cisterns, that hold no water.

NEW JERUSALEM BIBLE

to stand against the whole country:
   the kings of Judah, its princes,
   its priests and the people of the country.
19 They will fight against you
   but will not overcome you,
for I am with you,
   Yahweh declares,
      to rescue you.'

2 The word of Yahweh came to me, saying, 2 'Go and
shout this in Jerusalem's ears:

'Yahweh says this:
"I remember your faithful love,
   the affection of your bridal days,
when you followed me through the desert,
   through a land unsown.
3 Israel was sacred to Yahweh;
   the first-fruits of his harvest;
all who ate this incurred guilt,
   disaster befell them,
Yahweh declares." '

4 Listen to Yahweh's word, House of Jacob
   and all the families of the House of Israel.
5 Yahweh says this,
'What did your ancestors find wrong in me
   for them to have deserted me so far
as to follow Futility
   and become futile themselves?
6 They never said, "Where is Yahweh,
   who brought us out of Egypt
and led us through the desert,
   through a land of plains and ravines,
through a land of drought, of shadow dark as
      death,
a land through which no one passes
   and where no human being lives?"
7 I brought you to a country of plenty,
   to enjoy its produce and good things;
but when you entered you defiled my country
   and made my heritage loathsome.
8 The priests never asked, "Where is Yahweh?"
   Those skilled in the Law did not know me,
the shepherds too rebelled against me
   and the prophets prophesied by Baal
   and followed the Useless Ones.
9 So I must state my case against you once more,
   Yahweh declares,
and state my case against your children's children:
10 Cross to the isles of the Kittim[a] and look,
   send to Kedar and carefully observe,
   see if anything like this has happened before!
11 Does a nation change its gods?
   — and these are not gods at all!
Yet my people have exchanged their Glory
   for the Useless One!
12 You heavens, stand aghast at this,
   horrified, utterly appalled,
Yahweh declares.
13 For my people have committed two crimes:
   they have abandoned me,
   the fountain of living water,
and dug water-tanks for themselves,
   cracked water-tanks
   that hold no water.

_a_ **2** i.e. the Greeks. Kedar is a nomadic Arab tribe, so 'Go east or
west'.

NEW REVISED STANDARD VERSION	REVISED ENGLISH BIBLE

NEW REVISED STANDARD VERSION

14 Is Israel a slave? Is he a homeborn servant?
  Why then has he become plunder?
15 The lions have roared against him,
  they have roared loudly.
  They have made his land a waste;
  his cities are in ruins, without inhabitant.
16 Moreover, the people of Memphis and Tahpanhes
  have broken the crown of your head.
17 Have you not brought this upon yourself
  by forsaking the LORD your God,
  while he led you in the way?
18 What then do you gain by going to Egypt,
  to drink the waters of the Nile?
  Or what do you gain by going to Assyria,
  to drink the waters of the Euphrates?
19 Your wickedness will punish you,
  and your apostasies will convict you.
  Know and see that it is evil and bitter
  for you to forsake the LORD your God;
  the fear of me is not in you,
           says the Lord GOD of hosts.

20 For long ago you broke your yoke
  and burst your bonds,
  and you said, "I will not serve!"
  On every high hill
  and under every green tree
  you sprawled and played the whore.
21 Yet I planted you as a choice vine,
  from the purest stock.
  How then did you turn degenerate
  and become a wild vine?
22 Though you wash yourself with lye
  and use much soap,
  the stain of your guilt is still before me,
           says the Lord GOD.
23 How can you say, "I am not defiled,
  I have not gone after the Baals"?
  Look at your way in the valley;
  know what you have done —
  a restive young camel interlacing her tracks,
24   a wild ass at home in the wilderness,
  in her heat sniffing the wind!
  Who can restrain her lust?
  None who seek her need weary themselves;
  in her month they will find her.
25 Keep your feet from going unshod
  and your throat from thirst.
  But you said, "It is hopeless,
  for I have loved strangers,
  and after them I will go."

26 As a thief is shamed when caught,
  so the house of Israel shall be shamed —
  they, their kings, their officials,
  their priests, and their prophets,
27 who say to a tree, "You are my father,"
  and to a stone, "You gave me birth."
  For they have turned their backs to me,
  and not their faces.
  But in the time of their trouble they say,
  "Come and save us!"
28 But where are your gods
  that you made for yourself?
  Let them come, if they can save you,
  in your time of trouble;
  for you have as many gods
  as you have towns, O Judah.

REVISED ENGLISH BIBLE

14 Is Israel a slave? Was he born in slavery?
  If not, why has he become spoil?
15 Lions roar loudly at him;
  his land has been laid waste,
  his towns razed to the ground and abandoned.
16 The people of Noph and Tahpanhes
  will break your heads.
17 Is it not your rejection of the LORD your God
  when he guided you on the way
  that brings all this upon you?
18 And now, why should you make off to Egypt
  to drink the waters of the Nile?
  Or why make off to Assyria
  to drink the waters of the Euphrates?
19 It is your own wickedness that will punish you,
  your own apostasy that will condemn you.
  See for yourselves how bitter a thing it is and how
           evil,
  to reject the LORD your God,
  to hold me in dread no longer.
  This is the word of the Lord GOD of Hosts.
20 Many ages ago you shattered your yoke and
           snapped your traces,
  crying, 'I will not serve you';
  and you sprawled in promiscuous vice
  on all the hilltops, under every spreading tree.
21 I planted you as a choice red vine,
  a wholly pure strain,
  yet now you are turned into a vine
  that has reverted to its wild state!
22 Though you wash with soda and use soap lavishly,
  the stain of your sin is still there for me to see.
  This is the word of the Lord GOD.
23 How can you say, 'I am not defiled;
  I have not followed the baalim'?
  Look at your conduct in the valley;
  recall what you have done:
  you have been like a she-camel,
  twisting and turning as she runs,
24 rushing off into the wilderness,
  snuffing the wind in her lust;
  in her heat who can restrain her?
  None need tire themselves out in pursuit of her;
  she is easily found at mating time.
25 Stop before your feet are bare
  and your throat is parched.
  But you said, 'No; I am desperate.
  I love foreign gods and I must go after them.'
26 As a thief is ashamed when he is found out,
  so the people of Israel feel ashamed,
  they, their kings, their princes,
  their priests, and their prophets,
27 who say to a block of wood, 'You are our father'
  and cry 'Mother' to a stone.
  On me they have turned their backs
  and averted their faces from me.
  Yet in their time of trouble they say,
  'Rise up and save us!'
28 Where are the gods you made for yourselves?
  In your time of trouble let them arise and save
           you.
  For you, Judah, have as many gods as you have
           towns.

2:15 **razed to the ground:** *so some MSS; others* burnt.
2:18 **Nile:** *Heb.* Shihor. 2:24 **rushing off into:** *prob. rdg; Heb.*
a wild ass taught in. 2:28 **towns:** *or* blood-spattered altars.

14 Is Israel a slave, a bondman by birth?
　Why then has he become booty?
15 Against him lions roar
　　full-throated cries.
　They have made his land a waste;
　　his cities are charred ruins, without inhabitant.
16 Yes, the people of Memphis and Tahpanhes
　　shave the crown of your head.
17 Has not the forsaking of the LORD, your God,
　　done this to you?
18 And now, why go to Egypt,
　　to drink the waters of the Nile?
　Why go to Assyria,
　　to drink the waters of the Euphrates?
19 Your own wickedness chastises you,
　　your own infidelities punish you.
　Know then, and see, how evil and bitter
　　is your forsaking the LORD, your God,
　And showing no fear of me,
　　says the Lord, the GOD of hosts.

20 Long ago you broke your yoke,
　　you tore off your bonds.
　"I will not serve," you said.
　On every high hill, under every green tree,
　　you gave yourself to harlotry.
21 I had planted you, a choice vine
　　of fully tested stock;
　How could you turn out obnoxious to me,
　　a spurious vine?
22 Though you scour it with soap,
　　and use much lye,
　The stain of your guilt is still before me,
　　says the Lord GOD.
23 How can you say, "I am not defiled,
　　I have not gone after the Baals"?
　Consider your conduct in the Valley,
　　recall what you have done:
　A frenzied she-camel, coursing near and far,
24　breaking away toward the desert,
　Snuffing the wind in her ardor—
　　who can restrain her lust?
　No beasts need tire themselves seeking her;
　　in her month they will meet her.

25 Stop wearing out your shoes
　　and parching your throat!
　But you say, "No use! no!
　I love these strangers,
　　and after them I must go."
26 As the thief is shamed when caught,
　　so shall the house of Israel be shamed:
　They, their kings and their princes,
　　their priests and their prophets;
27 They who say to a piece of wood, "You are
　　my father,"
　and to a stone, "You gave me birth."
　They turn to me their backs, not their faces;
　　yet, in their time of trouble they cry out,
　　"Rise up and save us!"
28 Where are the gods you made for yourselves?
　Let them rise up!
　Will they save you in your time of trouble?
　For as numerous as your cities
　　are your gods, O Judah!
　And as many as the streets of Jerusalem
　　are the altars you have set up for Baal.

14 'Is Israel a slave?
　Was he born into serfdom,
　　for him to be preyed on like this?
15 Lions have roared at him,
　　they have made their voices heard.
　They have left this country a desert,
　　his towns lie burnt and uninhabited.
16 The people of Noph and Tahpanhes[b]
　　have shaved your skull!
17 Have you not brought this on yourself,
　　by abandoning Yahweh your God,
　　when he was guiding you on your way?
18 What is the good of going to Egypt now
　　to drink the water of the Nile?
　What is the good of going to Assyria
　　to drink the water of the River?
19 Your wickedness will bring its own punishment,
　　your infidelities will bring you to book,
　so give thought and see
　　how evil and bitter it is
　to abandon Yahweh your God
　　and not to stand in awe of me,
　　the Lord Yahweh Sabaoth declares.

20 'It is long ago now since you broke your yoke,
　　burst your bonds
　　and said, "I will not serve!"
　Yet on every high hill
　　and under every green tree
　　you have sprawled and played the whore.
21 Yet I had planted you, a red vine
　　of completely sound stock.
　How is it you have turned into seedlings
　　of a vine that is alien to me?
22 Even though you scrub yourself with soda
　　and put in quantities of soap,
　the stain of your guilt would still be visible to me,
　　the Lord Yahweh declares.
23 How dare you say, "I am not defiled,
　　I have not run after the Baals?"
　Look at your behaviour in the Valley,
　　realise what you have done.
24 A wild she-donkey, at home in the desert,
　　snuffing the breeze in desire;
　　who can control her when she is on heat?
　Males need not trouble to look for her,
　　they will find her in her month.
25 Beware! Your own foot will go unshod,
　　your own throat grow dry!
　But you said, "It is no use! No!
　For I love the Strangers
　　and they are the ones I shall follow."

26 'Like a thief ashamed at being caught,
　　so will the House of Israel be:
　they, their kings, their chief men,
　　their priests and their prophets,
27 who say to a piece of wood, "You are my father,"
　　and to a stone, "You gave birth to me."
　For they turn to me their backs,
　　never their faces;
　yet when trouble comes they shout,
　　"Get up! Save us!"
28 Where are your gods you made for yourself?
　Let them get up if they can save you
　　when trouble comes!
　For you have as many gods
　　as you have towns, Judah![c]

_b_ 2 Noph and Tahpanhes are towns in the Egyptian Delta.
_c_ 2 = 11:13.

NEW REVISED STANDARD VERSION	REVISED ENGLISH BIBLE

29 Why do you complain against me?
　　You have all rebelled against me,
　　　　　　　　　　　　says the LORD.
30 In vain I have struck down your children;
　　they accepted no correction.
　　Your own sword devoured your prophets
　　like a ravening lion.
31 And you, O generation, behold the word of the
　　　　LORD!*d*
　　Have I been a wilderness to Israel,
　　or a land of thick darkness?
　　Why then do my people say, "We are free,
　　we will come to you no more"?
32 Can a girl forget her ornaments,
　　or a bride her attire?
　　Yet my people have forgotten me,
　　days without number.

33 How well you direct your course
　　to seek lovers!
　　So that even to wicked women
　　you have taught your ways.
34 Also on your skirts is found
　　the lifeblood of the innocent poor,
　　though you did not catch them breaking in.
　　Yet in spite of all these things*d*
35 you say, "I am innocent;
　　surely his anger has turned from me."
　　Now I am bringing you to judgment
　　for saying, "I have not sinned."
36 How lightly you gad about,
　　changing your ways!
　　You shall be put to shame by Egypt
　　as you were put to shame by Assyria.
37 From there also you will come away
　　with your hands on your head;
　　for the LORD has rejected those in whom you
　　　　trust,
　　and you will not prosper through them.

3 If*e* a man divorces his wife
　　and she goes from him
　　and becomes another man's wife,
　　will he return to her?
　　Would not such a land be greatly polluted?
　　You have played the whore with many lovers;
　　and would you return to me?
　　　　　　　　　　　says the LORD.
2 Look up to the bare heights,*f* and see!
　　Where have you not been lain with?
　　By the waysides you have sat waiting for lovers,
　　like a nomad in the wilderness.
　　You have polluted the land
　　with your whoring and wickedness.
3 Therefore the showers have been withheld,
　　and the spring rain has not come;
　　yet you have the forehead of a whore,
　　you refuse to be ashamed.
4 Have you not just now called to me,
　　"My Father, you are the friend of my youth —
5 will he be angry forever,
　　will he be indignant to the end?"
　　This is how you have spoken,
　　but you have done all the evil that you could.

29 Why argue your case with me?
　　You are rebels, every one of you.
　　This is the word of the LORD.
30 In vain I punished your people —
　　the lesson was not learnt;
　　your sword devoured your prophets
　　like a ravening lion.
31 Have I shown myself to Israel
　　as some wilderness or waterless land?
　　Why do my people say, 'We have broken away;
　　we shall come to you no more'?

32 Will a girl forget her finery
　　or a bride her wedding ribbons?
　　Yet times without number
　　my people have forgotten me.
33 You pick your way so well in search of lovers;
　　even wanton women can learn from you.
34 Yes, and there is blood on the corners of your
　　　　robe —
　　the life-blood of the innocent poor,
　　though you did not catch them housebreaking.
　　For all these things I shall punish you.
35 You say, 'I am innocent;
　　surely his anger has passed away.'
　　But I shall challenge your claim
　　to have done no sin.
36 Why do you so lightly change your course?
　　You will be let down by Egypt
　　as you were by Assyria;
37 you will go into exile from here
　　with your hands on your heads,
　　for the LORD rejects those on whom you rely,
　　and from them you will gain nothing.

3 If a man divorces his wife and she leaves him, and if
　　she then becomes another's, may he go back to her
again? Is not that woman defiled, a forbidden thing? You
have been unfaithful with many lovers, says the LORD, and
yet you would come back to me?

2 Look up to the bare heights and see:
　　where have you not been lain with?
　　Like an Arab lurking in the desert
　　you sat by the wayside to catch lovers;
　　you defiled the land
　　with your adultery and debauchery.
3 Therefore the showers were withheld
　　and the spring rain failed.
　　But yours was a prostitute's brazenness,
　　and you were resolved to show no shame.
4 Not so long since you called me 'Father,
　　teacher of my youth',
5 thinking, 'Will he keep up his anger for ever?
　　Will he rage to the end?'
　　This is how you spoke, but you have done evil
　　and gone unchallenged.

2:31 **Have . . . Israel:** *prob. rdg; Heb.* prefixes You, O generation, see the word of the LORD.　　2:33 **even . . . from you:** *or* even at wantonness you have made yourself expert.　　2:34 **I shall punish you:** *poss. mng; Heb.* obscure.　　2:37 **those on whom:** *or* the things on which.　　3:1 **If a man:** *so Gk; Heb.* prefixes Saying. **woman:** *so Gk; Heb.* land.　　3:3 **brazenness:** *Heb.* brow.

---

d Meaning of Heb uncertain　　*e* Q Ms Gk Syr: MT *Saying, If*
f Or *the trails*

NEW AMERICAN BIBLE

NEW JERUSALEM BIBLE

29 How dare you still plead with me?
  You have all rebelled against me, says
    the LORD.
30 In vain I struck your children;
  the correction they did not take.
  Your sword devoured your prophets
    like a ravening lion.
31 You, of this generation,
  take note of the word of the Lord:
  Have I been a desert to Israel,
    a land of darkness?
  Why do my people say, "We have moved on,
    we will come to you no more"?
32 Does a virgin forget her jewelry,
    a bride her sash?
  Yet my people have forgotten me
    days without number.

33 How well you pick your way
    when seeking love!
  You who, in your wickedness,
    have gone by ways unclean!
34 You, on whose clothing there is
    the life-blood of the innocent,
  whom you found committing no burglary;
35 Yet withal you say, "I am innocent;
    at least, his anger is turned away from me."
  Behold, I will judge you
    on that word of yours, "I have not sinned."
36 How very base you have become
    in changing your course!
  By Egypt will you be shamed,
    as you were shamed by Assyria.
37 From there also shall you go away
    with hands upon your head;
  For the LORD has rejected those in whom you trust,
    with them you will have no success.

3 If a man sends away his wife
    and, after leaving him,
    she marries another man,
  Does the first husband come back to her?
  Would not the land be wholly defiled?
  But you have sinned with many lovers,
    and yet you would return to me! says the LORD.

2 Lift your eyes to the heights, and see,
    where have men not lain with you?
  By the waysides you waited for them
    like an Arab in the desert.
  You defiled the land
    by your wicked harlotry.
3 Therefore the showers were withheld,
    the spring rain failed.
  But because you have a harlot's brow,
    you refused to blush.

4 Even now do you not call me, "My father,
    you who are the bridegroom of my youth"?
5 "Will he keep his wrath forever,
    will he hold his grudge to the end?"
  This is what you say; yet you do
    all the evil you can.

29 Why make out a case against me?
  You have all rebelled against me,
    Yahweh declares.
30 In vain I have struck your children,
  they have not accepted correction;
  your own sword has devoured your prophets
    like a marauding lion.
31 Now you of this generation, listen to what Yahweh
    says:
  Have I been a desert for Israel,
    or a land of gloom?
  Why do my people say,
    "We are our own masters,
    we will come to you no more"?
32 Does a girl forget her ornaments,
    a bride her sash?
  And yet my people have forgotten me,
    days beyond number.

33 'How well you set your course
    in pursuit of love!
  And so you have schooled your ways
    to wicked deeds.
34 The very skirts of your robe are stained
    with the blood of the poor,
  of innocent men you never caught breaking and
    entering!
  And in spite of all this,
35 you say, "I am innocent,
    let his anger turn from me!"
  Now I pass sentence on you
    for saying, "I have not sinned."

36 'How frivolously you undertake
    a change of course!
  But you will be disappointed by Egypt
    just as you were by Assyria.
37 You will have to leave there too
    with your hands on your head,
  for Yahweh has rejected those that you rely on,
    you will come to no good with them.'

3 'If a man divorces his wife
    and she leaves him
    and becomes someone else's,
  has he the right to go back to her?
  Has not that piece of land
    been totally polluted?
  And you, having played the whore with many
    lovers,
  you claim the right to come back to me!
    Yahweh demands.

2 'Lift your eyes to the bare heights and look!
  Where have you not offered your sex!
  You waited by the roadside for them
    like an Arab in the desert.
  You have polluted the country
    with your prostitution and your vices:
3 this is why the showers have been withheld,
    the late rains have not come.

  'But you maintained a prostitute's bold front,
    with no trace of a blush.
4 From now on, do not cry out at me, "My father!
  My beloved ever since I was young!
5 Will he keep up his anger for ever,
    maintain his wrath to the end?"
  You say this but still go on sinning,
    being so obstinate.'

6 The LORD said to me in the days of King Josiah: Have you seen what she did, that faithless one, Israel, how she went up on every high hill and under every green tree, and played the whore there? 7 And I thought, "After she has done all this she will return to me"; but she did not return, and her false sister Judah saw it. 8 She*g* saw that for all the adulteries of that faithless one, Israel, I had sent her away with a decree of divorce; yet her false sister Judah did not fear, but she too went and played the whore. 9 Because she took her whoredom so lightly, she polluted the land, committing adultery with stone and tree. 10 Yet for all this her false sister Judah did not return to me with her whole heart, but only in pretense, says the LORD.

11 Then the LORD said to me: Faithless Israel has shown herself less guilty than false Judah. 12 Go, and proclaim these words toward the north, and say:

Return, faithless Israel,
says the LORD.
I will not look on you in anger,
 for I am merciful,
says the LORD;
I will not be angry forever.
13 Only acknowledge your guilt,
 that you have rebelled against the LORD your
 God,
and scattered your favors among strangers under
 every green tree,
and have not obeyed my voice,
says the LORD.
14 Return, O faithless children,
says the LORD,
 for I am your master;
I will take you, one from a city and two from a
 family,
 and I will bring you to Zion.

15 I will give you shepherds after my own heart, who will feed you with knowledge and understanding. 16 And when you have multiplied and increased in the land, in those days, says the LORD, they shall no longer say, "The ark of the covenant of the LORD." It shall not come to mind, or be remembered, or missed; nor shall another one be made. 17 At that time Jerusalem shall be called the throne of the LORD, and all nations shall gather to it, to the presence of the LORD in Jerusalem, and they shall no longer stubbornly follow their own evil will. 18 In those days the house of Judah shall join the house of Israel, and together they shall come from the land of the north to the land that I gave your ancestors for a heritage.

19 I thought
 how I would set you among my children,
and give you a pleasant land,
 the most beautiful heritage of all the nations.
And I thought you would call me, My Father,
 and would not turn from following me.
20 Instead, as a faithless wife leaves her husband,
 so you have been faithless to me, O house of
 Israel,
says the LORD.
21 A voice on the bare heights*h* is heard,
 the plaintive weeping of Israel's children,
because they have perverted their way,
 they have forgotten the LORD their God:
22 Return, O faithless children,
 I will heal your faithlessness.

 "Here we come to you;
 for you are the LORD our God.

6 In the reign of King Josiah the LORD said to me: Do you see what apostate Israel has done, how she went to every hilltop and under every spreading tree, and there committed adultery? 7 Even after she had done all this I thought she would come back to me, but she did not. That faithless woman, her sister Judah, saw it; 8 she saw too that I had put apostate Israel away and given her a certificate of divorce because she had committed adultery. Yet that faithless woman, her sister Judah, was not afraid; she too went and committed adultery. 9 She defiled the land with her casual prostitution and her adulterous worship of stone and wood. 10 In spite of all this Judah, that faithless woman, has not come back to me in sincerity, but only in pretence. This is the word of the LORD. 11 The LORD said to me: Apostate Israel is less to blame than that faithless woman Judah.

12 Go and proclaim this message towards the north:

Come back, apostate Israel,
 says the LORD;
I shall no longer frown on you.
For my love is unfailing, says the LORD;
 I shall not keep up my anger for ever.
13 Only acknowledge your wrongdoing,
 your rebellion against the LORD your God,
 your promiscuous traffic with foreign gods
 under every spreading tree,
 and your disobedience to my commands.
 This is the word of the LORD.

14 Come back, apostate people, says the LORD, for I am patient with you, and I shall take you, one from each city and two from each clan, and bring you to Zion. 15 There I shall give you shepherds after my own heart, and they will lead you with knowledge and understanding. 16 In those days, when you have increased and become fruitful in the land, says the LORD, no one will speak any more of the Ark of the Covenant of the LORD; no one will think of it or remember it or resort to it; that will be done no more. 17 At that time Jerusalem will be called the Throne of the LORD, and all nations will gather in Jerusalem to honour the LORD's name; never again will they follow the promptings of their evil and stubborn hearts. 18 In those days Judah will be united with Israel, and together they will come from a northern land into the land I gave their fathers as their holding.

19 I said: How gladly would I treat you as a son,
 giving you a pleasant land,
 a holding fairer than that of any nation!
You would call me 'Father', I thought,
 and never cease to follow me.
20 But like a woman who through illicit love has been
 unfaithful,
so you, Israel, were unfaithful to me.
 This is the word of the LORD.

21 Weeping is heard on the bare places,
 Israel's people pleading for mercy,
because they have taken to crooked ways
 and ignored the LORD their God.
22 Come back, you apostate people;
 I shall heal your apostasy.

 Here we are coming to you,
 for you are the LORD our God.

6 The LORD said to me in the days of King Josiah: See now what rebellious Israel has done! She has gone up every high mountain, and under every green tree she has played the harlot. 7 And I thought, after she has done all this she will return to me. But she did not return. Then, even though her traitor sister Judah saw 8 that for all the adulteries rebellious Israel had committed, I put her away and gave her a bill of divorce, nevertheless her traitor sister Judah was not frightened; she too went off and played the harlot. 9 Eager to sin, she polluted the land, committing adultery with stone and wood. 10 With all this, the traitor sister Judah did not return to me wholeheartedly, but insincerely, says the LORD.

11 Then the LORD said to me: Rebel Israel is inwardly more just than traitorous Judah. 12 Go, proclaim these words toward the north, and say:

> Return, rebel Israel, says the LORD,
> I will not remain angry with you;
> For I am merciful, says the LORD,
> I will not continue my wrath forever.
> 13 Only know your guilt:
> how you rebelled against the LORD, your God,
> How you ran hither and yon to strangers
> [under every green tree]
> and would not listen to my voice, says
> the LORD.
> 14 Return, rebellious children, says the LORD,
> for I am your Master;
> I will take you, one from a city, two from a clan,
> and bring you to Zion.
> 15 I will appoint over you shepherds after my own
> heart,
> who will shepherd you wisely and
> prudently.
> 16 When you multiply and become fruitful in
> the land,
> says the LORD,
> They will in those days no longer say,
> "The ark of the covenant of the LORD!"
> They will no longer think of it, or remember it,
> or miss it, or make another.

17 At that time they will call Jerusalem the LORD's throne; there all nations will be gathered together to honor the name of the LORD at Jerusalem, and they will walk no longer in their hardhearted wickedness. 18 In those days the house of Judah will join the house of Israel; together they will come from the land of the north to the land which I gave to your fathers as a heritage.

> 19 I had thought:
> How I should like to treat you as sons,
> And give you a pleasant land,
> a heritage most beautiful among the nations!
> You would call me, "My Father," I thought,
> and never cease following me.
> 20 But like a woman faithless to her lover,
> even so have you been faithless to me,
> O house of Israel, says the LORD.
> 21 A cry is heard on the heights!
> the plaintive weeping of Israel's children,
> Because they have perverted their ways
> and forgotten the LORD, their God.
> 22 Return, rebellious children,
> and I will cure you of your rebelling.
> "Here we are, we now come to you
> because you are the LORD, our God.

6 In the days of King Josiah, Yahweh said to me, 'Have you seen what disloyal Israel has done? How she has made her way up every high hill and to every green tree, and played the whore there? 7 I thought, "After doing all this she will come back to me." But she did not come back. Her faithless sister Judah saw this. 8 She also saw that I had repudiated disloyal Israel for all her adulteries and given her her divorce papers. Her faithless sister Judah, however, was not afraid: she too went and played the whore. 9 And with her shameless whoring, she polluted the country; she committed adultery with stones and pieces of wood. 10 Worse than all this: Judah, her faithless sister, has come back to me not in sincerity, but only in pretence, Yahweh declares.'

11 And Yahweh said to me, 'Disloyal Israel is upright, compared with faithless Judah. 12 So go and shout words towards the north, and say:

> "Come back, disloyal Israel,
> Yahweh declares,
> I shall frown on you no more,
> since I am merciful,
> Yahweh declares.
> I shall not keep my anger for ever.
> 13 Only acknowledge your guilt:
> how you have rebelled against Yahweh your God,
> how you have prostituted yourself with the
> Strangers
> under every green tree
> and have not listened to my voice,
> Yahweh declares.

14 "Come back, disloyal children, Yahweh declares, for I alone am your Master, and I will take you, one from a town, two from a family, and bring you to Zion. 15 I shall give you shepherds after my own heart, who will pasture you wisely and discreetly. 16 Then, when you have increased and grown numerous in the country, Yahweh declares, no one will ever again say: The ark of the covenant of Yahweh! It will not enter their minds, they will not remember it or miss it, nor will another one be made. 17 When that time comes, Jerusalem will be called: The Throne of Yahweh, and all the nations will converge on her, on Yahweh's name, on Jerusalem, and will no longer follow their own stubborn and wicked inclinations.

18 "When those days come, the House of Judah will join the House of Israel; together they will come from the land of the north to the country I gave your ancestors as their heritage."

> 19 'And I was thinking:
> How am I to rank you as my children?
> I shall give you a country of delights,
> the fairest heritage of all the nations!
> I thought: You will call me Father
> and will never cease to follow me.
> 20 But like a woman betraying her lover,
> House of Israel, you have betrayed me,'
> Yahweh declares.
> 21 A noise is heard on the bare heights:
> the weeping and entreaty of the Israelites,
> for they have gone wildly astray,
> have forgotten Yahweh their God.
> 22 'Come back, disloyal children,
> I want to cure your disloyalty.'
> 'We are here, we are coming to you,
> for you are Yahweh our God.

NEW REVISED STANDARD VERSION

23 Truly the hills are[i] a delusion,
the orgies on the mountains.
Truly in the LORD our God
is the salvation of Israel.

24 "But from our youth the shameful thing has devoured
all for which our ancestors had labored, their flocks and
their herds, their sons and their daughters. 25 Let us lie down
in our shame, and let our dishonor cover us; for we have
sinned against the LORD our God, we and our ancestors,
from our youth even to this day; and we have not obeyed the
voice of the LORD our God."

4 If you return, O Israel,
                                    says the LORD,
if you return to me,
if you remove your abominations from my
presence,
and do not waver,
2 and if you swear, "As the LORD lives!"
in truth, in justice, and in uprightness,
then nations shall be blessed[j] by him,
and by him they shall boast.

3 For thus says the LORD to the people of Judah and to
the inhabitants of Jerusalem:
Break up your fallow ground,
and do not sow among thorns.
4 Circumcise yourselves to the LORD,
remove the foreskin of your hearts,
O people of Judah and inhabitants of
Jerusalem,
or else my wrath will go forth like fire,
and burn with no one to quench it,
because of the evil of your doings.

5 Declare in Judah, and proclaim in Jerusalem, and say:
Blow the trumpet through the land;
shout aloud[k] and say,
"Gather together, and let us go
into the fortified cities!"
6 Raise a standard toward Zion,
flee for safety, do not delay,
for I am bringing evil from the north,
and a great destruction.
7 A lion has gone up from its thicket,
a destroyer of nations has set out;
he has gone out from his place
to make your land a waste;
your cities will be ruins
without inhabitant.
8 Because of this put on sackcloth,
lament and wail:
"The fierce anger of the LORD
has not turned away from us."

9 On that day, says the LORD, courage shall fail the king and
the officials; the priests shall be appalled and the prophets
astounded. 10 Then I said, "Ah, Lord GOD, how utterly you
have deceived this people and Jerusalem, saying, 'It shall
be well with you,' even while the sword is at the throat!"

11 At that time it will be said to this people and to
Jerusalem: A hot wind comes from me out of the bare
heights[l] in the desert toward my poor people, not to win-

REVISED ENGLISH BIBLE

23 There is no help in worship on the hilltops,
no help from clamour on the heights;
truly in the LORD our God
lies Israel's salvation.
24 From our early days
Baal has devoured
the fruits of our fathers' labours,
their flocks and herds, their sons and daughters.
25 Let us lie down in our shame, covered by
dishonour,
for we have sinned against the LORD our God,
both we and our fathers,
from our early days even till now,
and we have not obeyed the LORD our God.

4 Israel, if you will come back,
if you will come back to me, says the LORD,
if you will banish your loathsome idols from my
sight,
and go astray no more,
2 if you swear 'by the life of the LORD'
in truth, justice, and uprightness,
then the nations will pray to be blessed like you
and in you they will boast.

3 These are the words of the LORD to the people of Judah and
Jerusalem:
Break up your ground that lies unploughed,
do not sow among thorns;
4 circumcise yourselves to the service of the LORD,
circumcise your hearts,
you people of Judah, you dwellers in Jerusalem,
or the fire of my fury may blaze up and burn
unquenched,
because of your evil actions.

5 Declare this in Judah,
proclaim it in Jerusalem.
Blow the trumpet throughout the land.
Shout aloud the command: 'Assemble!
Let us move back to the fortified towns.'
6 Raise the signal — to Zion!
Make for safety without delay,
for I am about to bring disaster out of the north
and dire destruction.
7 A lion has risen from his lair,
the destroyer of nations;
he has broken camp and marched out
to devastate your land
and make your cities waste and empty.
8 Therefore put on sackcloth,
beat the breast and wail,
for the fierce anger of the LORD
is not averted from us.
9 On that day, says the LORD,
the courage of the king and his officers will fail,
priests will be aghast and prophets appalled.

10 I said: Ah, Lord GOD, you surely deceived this people
and Jerusalem in promising peace while the sword is at our
throats.

11 At that time this people and Jerusalem will be told:

A scorching wind from the desert heights
sweeps down on my people;
it is no breeze for winnowing or for cleansing.

---

[i] Gk Syr Vg: Heb *Truly from the hills is*   [j] Or *shall bless themselves*
[k] Or *shout, take your weapons*: Heb *shout, fill (your hand)*   [l] Or *the trails*

4:2 **like you and in you:** *prob. rdg; Heb.* like him and in him.

NEW AMERICAN BIBLE

23 Deceptive indeed are the hills,
the thronging mountains;
In the LORD, our God, alone
is the salvation of Israel.
24 The shame-god has devoured
our fathers' toil from our youth,
Their sheep and their cattle,
their sons and their daughters.
25 Let us lie down in our shame,
let our disgrace cover us,
for we have sinned against the LORD, our God,
From our youth to this day, we and our
fathers also;
we listened not to the voice of the LORD,
our God."

4 If you wish to return, O Israel, says the LORD,
return to me.
If you put your detestable things out of my sight,
and do not stray,
2 Then you can swear, "As the LORD lives,"
in truth, in judgment, and in justice;
Then shall the nations use his name in blessing,
and glory in him.

3 For to the men of Judah and to Jerusalem, thus says the
LORD:

Till your untilled ground,
sow not among thorns.
4 For the sake of the LORD, be circumcised,
remove the foreskins of your hearts,
O men of Judah and citizens of Jerusalem:
Lest my anger break out like fire,
and burn till none can quench it,
because of your evil deeds.

5 Proclaim it in Judah,
make it heard in Jerusalem;
Blow the trumpet through the land,
summon the recruits!
Say, "Fall in, let us march
to the fortified cities."
6 Bear the standard to Zion,
seek refuge without delay!
Evil I bring from the north,
and great destruction.
7 Up comes the lion from his lair,
the destroyer of nations has set out,
has left his place,
To turn your land into desolation,
till your cities lie waste and empty.
8 So gird yourselves with sackcloth,
mourn and wail:
"The blazing wrath of the LORD
is not turned away from us."
9   In that day, says the LORD,
The king will lose heart, and the princes;
the priests will be amazed,
and the prophets stunned.
10 "Alas! Lord GOD," they will say,
"You only deceived us
When you said: Peace shall be yours;
for the sword touches our very soul."
11 At that time it will be said
of this people and of Jerusalem,
"From the glaring heights through the desert
a wind comes toward the daughter of
my people."
Not to winnow, not to cleanse,

NEW JERUSALEM BIBLE

23 The hills are a delusion after all,
so is the tumult of the mountains.
Yahweh our God is, after all,
the saving of Israel.
24 Shame has devoured what our ancestors worked for
ever since we were young,
their flocks and herds, their sons and their
daughters.
25 Let us lie down in our shame,
let our confusion cover me,
for we have sinned against Yahweh our God,
we and our ancestors, from our youth until today,
and have not listened to the voice of Yahweh our
God.'

4 'If you come back, Israel,
Yahweh declares,
if you come back to me,
if you take your Horrors out of my sight,
if you go roving no more,
2 if you swear, "As Yahweh lives!"
truthfully, justly, uprightly,
then the nations will bless themselves by him
and glory in him.

3 'For Yahweh says this
to the men of Judah and Jerusalem,
"Clear the ground that lies neglected,
do not sow among thorns.
4 Circumcise yourselves for Yahweh,
apply circumcision to your hearts,
men of Judah and inhabitants of Jerusalem,
or my wrath will leap out like a fire
and burn with no one to quench it,
in return for the wickedness of your deeds." ' d

5 Announce it in Judah,
proclaim it in Jerusalem, say,
'Sound the trumpet in the countryside,
shout the message aloud:
Mobilise!
Take to the fortified towns! e
6 Signpost the way to Zion!
Run! Do not delay!
For I am bringing disaster from the north,
an immense calamity.
7 The lion is up from his thicket,
the destroyer of nations is on his way,
he has come from his home
to reduce your land to a desert;
your towns will be in ruins, uninhabited.
8 So wrap yourselves in sackcloth,
lament and wail,
since Yahweh's burning anger
has not turned away from us.
9 'That day,' Yahweh declares,
'the king's heart will fail him,
the princes' hearts will fail them too,
the priests will stand aghast,
the prophets stupefied.'
10 Then I said, 'Ah, Lord Yahweh,
how sadly you deceived this people and Jerusalem
when you used to say, "You will have peace,"
whereas the sword is now at our throats!
11 When that time comes, this will be said
to this people and to Jerusalem:
The scorching wind from the desert heights
comes towards the daughter of my people
— and not to winnow or to cleanse!

d **4** = 21:12.   e **4** = 8:14.

NEW REVISED STANDARD VERSION	REVISED ENGLISH BIBLE

now or cleanse — 12 a wind too strong for that. Now it is I who speak in judgment against them.

13 Look! He comes up like clouds,
 his chariots like the whirlwind;
his horses are swifter than eagles—
 woe to us, for we are ruined!
14 O Jerusalem, wash your heart clean of
 wickedness
 so that you may be saved.
How long shall your evil schemes
 lodge within you?
15 For a voice declares from Dan
 and proclaims disaster from Mount Ephraim.
16 Tell the nations, "Here they are!"
 Proclaim against Jerusalem,
"Besiegers come from a distant land;
 they shout against the cities of Judah.
17 They have closed in around her like watchers of a
 field,
 because she has rebelled against me,
 says the LORD.
18 Your ways and your doings
 have brought this upon you.
This is your doom; how bitter it is!
 It has reached your very heart."

19 My anguish, my anguish! I writhe in pain!
 Oh, the walls of my heart!
My heart is beating wildly;
 I cannot keep silent;
for I[m] hear the sound of the trumpet,
 the alarm of war.
20 Disaster overtakes disaster,
 the whole land is laid waste.
Suddenly my tents are destroyed,
 my curtains in a moment.
21 How long must I see the standard,
 and hear the sound of the trumpet?
22 "For my people are foolish,
 they do not know me;
they are stupid children,
 they have no understanding.
They are skilled in doing evil,
 but do not know how to do good."

23 I looked on the earth, and lo, it was waste and
 void;
 and to the heavens, and they had no light.
24 I looked on the mountains, and lo, they were
 quaking,
 and all the hills moved to and fro.
25 I looked, and lo, there was no one at all,
 and all the birds of the air had fled.
26 I looked, and lo, the fruitful land was a desert,
 and all its cities were laid in ruins
 before the LORD, before his fierce anger.
27 For thus says the LORD: The whole land shall be a
desolation; yet I will not make a full end.
28 Because of this the earth shall mourn,
 and the heavens above grow black;
for I have spoken, I have purposed;
 I have not relented nor will I turn back.

29 At the noise of horseman and archer
 every town takes to flight;
they enter thickets; they climb among rocks;
 all the towns are forsaken,
 and no one lives in them.

12 A wind too strong for these
 will come at my bidding,
 and now I shall state my case against my people.

13 Like clouds the enemy advances,
 like a whirlwind with his chariots;
 his horses are swifter than eagles:
 'Woe to us, for we are lost!'
14 Jerusalem, cleanse the wrongdoing from your heart
 and you may yet be saved.
How long will you harbour within you
 your evil schemes?
15 News comes from Dan,
 evil tidings from Mount Ephraim.
16 Tell this to the nations,
 proclaim the doom of Jerusalem:
 hordes of invaders are on the way from a distant
 land,
 giving voice against the cities of Judah.
17 As a field surrounded by guards
 she is encircled by them,
 because she has rebelled against me.
 This is the word of the LORD.
18 Your own ways and deeds
 have brought these things on you;
 this is your punishment,
 for your rebellion is seated deep within you.

19 Oh, how I writhe in anguish,
 how my heart throbs!
 I cannot keep silence,
 for I hear the sound of the trumpet,
 the clamour of the battle cry.
20 Crash follows crash,
 for the whole land goes down in ruin.
 Suddenly my tents are thrown down,
 the curtains in an instant.
21 How long must I see the standard raised
 and hear the trumpet-call?
22 My people are foolish, they know nothing of me;
 senseless children, lacking all understanding,
 clever only in wrongdoing,
 but of doing right they know nothing.

23 I looked at the earth, and it was chaos,
 at the heavens, and their light was gone,
24 at the mountains, and they were reeling,
 and all the hills rocked to and fro.
25 I looked: no one was there,
 and all the birds of heaven had taken wing.
26 I looked: the fertile land was wilderness,
 its towns all razed to the ground
 before the LORD, before his fierce anger.
27 These are the words of the LORD:
 The whole land will be desolate,
 and I shall make an end of it.
28 The earth will be in mourning for this
 and the heavens above turn black;
 for I have made known my purpose,
 and I shall not relent or change it.

29 At the sound of the horsemen and archers
 every town is in flight;
 people crawl into the thickets,
 scramble up among the crags.
 Every town is deserted,
 no one lives there.

---

[m] Another reading is *for you, O my soul,*

4:18 **your rebellion:** *prob. rdg; Heb. obscure.* 4:27 **I shall:** *prob. rdg; Heb. adds not.*

NEW AMERICAN BIBLE

12 does this wind from the heights come at my
bidding;
And I myself now pronounce
sentence upon them.

13 See! like storm clouds he advances,
like a hurricane his chariots;
Swifter than eagles are his steeds:
"Woe to us! we are ruined."

14 Cleanse your heart of evil, O Jerusalem,
that you may be saved.
How long must your pernicious thoughts
lodge within you?

15 Listen! They proclaim it from Dan,
from Mount Ephraim they announce destruction:

16 "Make this known to the nations,
announce it to Jerusalem:
The besiegers are coming from the distant land,
shouting their war cry against the cities
of Judah."

17 Like watchmen of the fields they surround her,
for she has rebelled against me, says the LORD.

18 Your conduct, your misdeeds, have done this
to you;
how bitter is this disaster of yours,
how it reaches to your very heart!

19 My breast! my breast! how I suffer!
The walls of my heart!
My heart beats wildly,
I cannot be still;
For I have heard the sound of the trumpet,
the alarm of war.

20 Ruin after ruin is reported;
the whole earth is laid waste.
In an instant my tents are ravaged;
in a flash, my shelters.

21 How long must I see that signal,
hear that trumpet sound!

22 Fools my people are,
they know me not;
Senseless children they are,
having no understanding;
They are wise in evil,
but know not how to do good.

23 I looked at the earth, and it was waste and void;
at the heavens, and their light had gone out!

24 I looked at the mountains, and they
were trembling,
and all the hills were crumbling!

25 I looked and behold, there was no man;
even the birds of the air had flown away!

26 I looked and behold, the garden land was a desert,
with all its cities destroyed
before the LORD, before his blazing wrath.

27 For thus says the LORD:
Waste shall the whole land be;
I will [not] wholly destroy it.

28 Because of this the earth shall mourn,
the heavens above shall darken;
I have spoken, I will not repent,
I have resolved, I will not turn back.

29 At the shout of horseman and bowman
each city takes to flight;
They shrink into the thickets,
they scale the rocks:
All the cities are abandoned,
and no one dwells in them.

NEW JERUSALEM BIBLE

12 A gale of wind comes to me from over there.
Now I myself shall pass sentence on them!'

13 Look, he is advancing like the clouds,
his chariots like a hurricane,
his horses swifter than eagles.
Disaster for us! We are lost!

14 Wash your heart clean of wickedness, Jerusalem,
and so be saved.
How long will you go on harbouring
your pernicious thoughts?

15 For a voice from Dan shouts the news,
proclaims disaster from the highlands of Ephraim.

16 Report it to the nations,
proclaim it to Jerusalem,
'Enemies are coming from a distant country,
shouting their war cry against the towns of Judah;

17 they surround her like watchmen round a field
because she has rebelled against me',
Yahweh declares.

18 'Your own behaviour and actions
have brought this on yourself.
Your wickedness, how bitter,
has stabbed you to the heart!'

19 In the pit of my stomach how great my agony!
Walls of my heart!
My heart is throbbing!
I cannot keep quiet,
for I have heard the trumpet call,
the battle cry.

20 Ruin on ruin is the news:
the whole land is laid waste,
my tents are suddenly destroyed,
in one moment all that sheltered me.

21 How long must I see the standard
and hear the trumpet call?

22 'This is because my people are stupid,
they do not know me,
they are slow-witted children,
they have no understanding,
they are clever enough at doing wrong,
but do not know how to do right.'

23 I looked to the earth — it was a formless waste;
to the heavens, and their light had gone.

24 I looked to the mountains — they were quaking
and all the hills rocking to and fro.

25 I looked — there was no one at all,
the very birds of heaven had all fled.

26 I looked — the fruitful land was a desert,
all its towns in ruins
before Yahweh,
before his burning anger.

27 Yes, Yahweh has said this,
'The whole country will be laid waste,
though I shall not annihilate it completely.

28 For this, the earth will go into mourning
and the heavens above grow dark.
For I have spoken, I have decided,
I shall not change my mind or go back on it.'

29 At the din of horseman and archer
the entire city takes to flight:
some plunge into the thickets,
others scale the rocks;
every town is abandoned,
not a single person is left there.

NEW REVISED STANDARD VERSION	REVISED ENGLISH BIBLE

NEW REVISED STANDARD VERSION

30 And you, O desolate one,
  what do you mean that you dress in crimson,
  that you deck yourself with ornaments of gold,
  that you enlarge your eyes with paint?
  In vain you beautify yourself.
    Your lovers despise you;
    they seek your life.
31 For I heard a cry as of a woman in labor,
    anguish as of one bringing forth her first child,
  the cry of daughter Zion gasping for breath,
    stretching out her hands,
  "Woe is me! I am fainting before killers!"

5 Run to and fro through the streets of Jerusalem,
    look around and take note!
  Search its squares and see
    if you can find one person
  who acts justly
    and seeks truth—
  so that I may pardon Jerusalem.[n]
2 Although they say, "As the LORD lives,"
    yet they swear falsely.
3 O LORD, do your eyes not look for truth?
  You have struck them,
    but they felt no anguish;
  you have consumed them,
    but they refused to take correction.
  They have made their faces harder than rock;
    they have refused to turn back.

4 Then I said, "These are only the poor,
    they have no sense;
  for they do not know the way of the LORD,
    the law of their God.
5 Let me go to the rich[o]
    and speak to them;
  surely they know the way of the LORD,
    the law of their God."
  But they all alike had broken the yoke,
    they had burst the bonds.

6 Therefore a lion from the forest shall kill them,
    a wolf from the desert shall destroy them.
  A leopard is watching against their cities;
    everyone who goes out of them shall be torn in
        pieces—
  because their transgressions are many,
    their apostasies are great.

7 How can I pardon you?
    Your children have forsaken me,
    and have sworn by those who are no gods.
  When I fed them to the full,
    they committed adultery
    and trooped to the houses of prostitutes.
8 They were well-fed lusty stallions,
    each neighing for his neighbor's wife.
9 Shall I not punish them for these things?
                    says the LORD;
    and shall I not bring retribution
    on a nation such as this?

10 Go up through her vine-rows and destroy,
    but do not make a full end;
  strip away her branches,
    for they are not the LORD's.

REVISED ENGLISH BIBLE

30 And you, what are you doing?
  When you dress yourself in scarlet,
  deck yourself out with gold ornaments,
  and enlarge your eyes with antimony,
  you are beautifying yourself to no purpose.
  Your lovers spurn you
  and seek your life.
31 I hear a sound as of a woman in labour,
  the sharp cry of one bearing her first child.
  It is Zion, gasping for breath,
  stretching out her hands.
  'Ah me!' she cries. 'I am weary,
  weary of slaughter.'

5 Go up and down the streets of Jerusalem,
  see, take note;
  search through her wide squares:
  can you find anyone who acts justly,
  anyone who seeks the truth,
  that I may forgive that city?
2 People may swear by the life of the LORD,
  but in fact they perjure themselves.
3 LORD, are your eyes not set upon the truth?
  You punished them,
  but they took no heed;
  you pierced them to the heart,
  but they refused to learn.
  They made their faces harder than flint;
  they refused to repent.
4 I said, 'After all, these are the poor,
  these are folk without understanding,
  who do not know the way of the LORD,
  the ordinances of their God.
5 I shall go to the great ones
  and speak with them;
  for they will know the way of the LORD,
  the ordinances of their God.'
  But they too have broken the yoke
  and snapped their traces.
6 So a lion out of the scrub will strike them down,
  a wolf from the plains will savage them;
  a leopard will prowl about their towns
  and maul any who venture out,
  for their rebellious deeds are many,
  their apostasies past counting.

7 How can I forgive you for all this?
  Your children have forsaken me,
  swearing by gods that are no gods.
  I gave them all they needed,
  yet they committed adultery
  and frequented brothels;
8 each neighs after another man's wife,
  like a well-fed and lusty stallion.
9 Shall I fail to punish them for this,
  says the LORD,
  shall I not exact vengeance on such a people?
10 Go along her rows of vines; destroy them,
  make an end of them.
  Lop off her green branches,
  for they are not the LORD's.

4:30 **And you:** so Gk; Heb. adds overwhelmed.   5:7 **frequented:**
so some MSS; others gashed themselves in.   5:10 **make:** prob.
rdg; Heb. prefixes do not.

[n] Heb it   [o] Or the great

NEW AMERICAN BIBLE

NEW JERUSALEM BIBLE

30 You now who are doomed, what do you mean
   by putting on purple,
   bedecking yourself with gold,
   Shading your eyes with cosmetics,
   beautifying yourself in vain?
   Your lovers spurn you,
   they seek your life.
31 Yes, I hear the moaning, as of a woman in
   travail,
   like the anguish of a mother with her first child—
   The cry of daughter Zion gasping,
   as she stretches forth her hands:
   "Ah, woe is me! I sink exhausted
   before the slayers!"

5 Roam the streets of Jerusalem,
   look about and observe,
   Search through her public places,
   to find even one
   Who lives uprightly
   and seeks to be faithful,
   and I will pardon her!
2 Though they say, "As the LORD lives,"
   they swear falsely.
3 O LORD, do your eyes not look for honesty?
   You struck them, but they did not cringe;
   you laid them low, but they refused correction;
   They set their faces harder than stone,
   and refused to return to you.
4 It is only the lowly, I thought,
   who are foolish;
   For they know not the way of the LORD,
   their duty to their God.
5 I will go to the great ones
   and speak with them;
   For they know the way of the LORD,
   their duty to their God.
   But, one and all, they had broken the yoke,
   torn off the harness.
6 Therefore lions from the forest slay them,
   wolves of the desert ravage them,
   Leopards keep watch round their cities:
   all who come out are torn to pieces
   For their many crimes
   and their numerous rebellions.

7 Why should I pardon you these things?
   Your sons have forsaken me,
   they swear by gods that are not.
   I fed them, but they committed adultery;
   to the harlot's house they throng.
8 Lustful stallions they are,
   each neighs after another's wife.
9 Shall I not punish them for these things?
   says the LORD;
   On a nation such as this shall I not
   take vengeance?
10 Climb to her terraces, and ravage them,
   destroy them [not] wholly.
   Tear away her tendrils,
   they do not belong to the LORD.

30 And, once despoiled, what are you going to do?
   You may dress yourself in scarlet,
   put on ornaments of gold,
   enlarge your eyes with paint
   but you make yourself pretty in vain.
   Your former lovers disdain you,
   your life is what they are seeking.
31 Yes, I hear screams like those of a woman in
   labour,
   anguish like that of a woman giving birth to her
   first child;
   they are the screams of the daughter of Zion,
   gasping,
   hands outstretched,
   'Unhappy me! I am dying,
   the murderers have killed me!'

5 Rove the streets of Jerusalem,
   now look and enquire,
   see in her squares
   if you can find an individual,
   one individual who does right
   and seeks the truth,
   and I will pardon her,
   Yahweh says.
2 Although they say, 'As Yahweh lives,'
   they are, in fact, swearing a false oath.
3 Yahweh, do your eyes not look for truth?
   You have struck them; they have not felt it.
   You have annihilated them, for they ignored the
   lesson.
   They have set their faces harder than rock,
   they have refused to repent.
4 I thought, 'These are only the poor!
   They behave stupidly
   since they do not know Yahweh's way
   or the ruling of their God.
5 I shall approach the great men
   and speak to them,
   for these will know Yahweh's way
   and the ruling of their God.'
   But these, too, have broken the yoke,
   have burst the bonds.
6 And so, a lion from the forest will slaughter them,
   a wolf from the plains will despoil them,
   a leopard will be lurking round their towns:
   anyone who goes out will be torn to pieces—
   because of their many crimes,
   their countless infidelities.

7 'Why should I pardon you?
   Your sons have abandoned me,
   to swear by gods that are not gods at all.
   I fed them full, and they became adulterers,
   they hurried to the brothel,
8 They are well-fed, roving stallions,
   each neighing for his neighbour's wife.
9 Shall I fail to punish this,
   Yahweh demands,
   or on such a nation
   to exact vengeance?f
10 Scale her terraces! Destroy!
   But do not annihilate her completely!
   Strip off her branches,
   for Yahweh does not own them!

f 5 = 5:29; 9:8.

NEW REVISED STANDARD VERSION

11 For the house of Israel and the house of Judah
    have been utterly faithless to me,
                says the LORD.
12 They have spoken falsely of the LORD,
    and have said, "He will do nothing.
No evil will come upon us,
    and we shall not see sword or famine."
13 The prophets are nothing but wind,
    for the word is not in them.
Thus shall it be done to them!

14 Therefore thus says the LORD, the God of hosts:
Because they*p* have spoken this word,
I am now making my words in your mouth a fire,
    and this people wood, and the fire shall devour
    them.
15 I am going to bring upon you
    a nation from far away, O house of Israel,
                says the LORD.
It is an enduring nation,
    it is an ancient nation,
a nation whose language you do not know,
    nor can you understand what they say.
16 Their quiver is like an open tomb;
    all of them are mighty warriors.
17 They shall eat up your harvest and your food;
    they shall eat up your sons and your daughters;
they shall eat up your flocks and your herds;
    they shall eat up your vines and your fig trees;
they shall destroy with the sword
    your fortified cities in which you trust.

18 But even in those days, says the LORD, I will not
make a full end of you. 19 And when your people say, "Why
has the LORD our God done all these things to us?" you shall
say to them, "As you have forsaken me and served foreign
gods in your land, so you shall serve strangers in a land that
is not yours."

20 Declare this in the house of Jacob,
    proclaim it in Judah:
21 Hear this, O foolish and senseless people,
    who have eyes, but do not see,
    who have ears, but do not hear.
22 Do you not fear me? says the LORD;
    Do you not tremble before me?
I placed the sand as a boundary for the sea,
    a perpetual barrier that it cannot pass;
though the waves toss, they cannot prevail,
    though they roar, they cannot pass over it.
23 But this people has a stubborn and rebellious
    heart;
    they have turned aside and gone away.
24 They do not say in their hearts,
    "Let us fear the LORD our God,
who gives the rain in its season,
    the autumn rain and the spring rain,
and keeps for us
    the weeks appointed for the harvest."
25 Your iniquities have turned these away,
    and your sins have deprived you of good.
26 For scoundrels are found among my people;
    they take over the goods of others.
Like fowlers they set a trap;*q*
    they catch human beings.

REVISED ENGLISH BIBLE

11 Faithless are Israel and Judah,
    both faithless to me.
    This is the word of the LORD.
12 They have denied the LORD,
    saying, 'He does not matter.
No harm will come to us;
    we shall see neither sword nor famine.
13 The prophets will prove mere wind;
    the word is not in them.'

14 Therefore, because they talk in this way, these are the
words of the LORD the God of Hosts to me:

I shall make my words a fire in your mouth,
    and it will burn up this people like brushwood.

15 Israel, I am bringing against you a distant nation,
    an ancient people established long ago,
    says the LORD,
    a people whose language you do not know,
    whose speech you will not understand;
16 they are all mighty warriors,
    their jaws are a grave, wide open,
17 to devour your harvest and your food,
    to devour your sons and your daughters,
    to devour your flocks and your herds,
    to devour your vines and your fig trees.
They will beat down with the sword
    the walled cities in which you trust.

18 But in those days, the LORD declares, I shall not make an
end of you. 19 When it is asked, 'Why has the LORD our God
done all this to us?' you are to answer, 'As you have forsak-
en the LORD and served alien gods in your own land, so you
will serve foreigners in a land that is not your own.'

20 Announce this to the people of Jacob,
    proclaim it in Judah:
21 Listen, you foolish and senseless people,
    who have eyes and see nothing,
    ears and hear nothing.
22 Have you no fear of me, says the LORD,
    will you not tremble before me,
    who set the sand as bounds for the sea,
    a limit it never can pass?
Its waves may heave and toss, but they are
        powerless;
    roar as they may, they cannot pass.
23 But this people has a rebellious and defiant heart;
    they have rebelled and gone their own way.
24 They did not say to themselves,
    'Let us fear the LORD our God,
who gives the rains of autumn
    and spring showers in their turn,
who brings us unfailingly
    fixed harvest seasons.'
25 But your wrongdoing has upset nature's order,
    and your sins have kept away her bounty.

26 For among my people there are scoundrels
    who, like fowlers, lay snares and set deadly traps;
    they prey on their fellows.

5:13 **in them**: *prob. rdg; Heb. adds* So may it be done to them.
5:14 **they**: *prob. rdg; Heb.* you.   5:16 **their jaws are**: *so Syriac;*
Heb. their quiver is.   5:19 **foreigners**: *or* foreign gods.
5:26 **who . . . snares**: *prob. rdg; Heb.* unintelligible.

NEW AMERICAN BIBLE

11 For they have openly rebelled against me,
  both the house of Israel and the house of Judah,
  says the LORD,
12 They denied the LORD,
  saying, "Not he —
No evil shall befall us,
  neither sword nor famine shall we see.
13 The prophets have become wind,
  and the word is not in them.
May their threats be carried out
  against themselves!"

14 Now, for this that you have said,
  says the LORD, the God of hosts —
Behold, I make my words
  in your mouth, a fire,
And this people is the wood
  that it shall devour! —
15 Beware, I will bring against you
  a nation from afar,
  O house of Israel, says the LORD;
A long-lived nation, an ancient nation,
  a people whose language you know not,
  whose speech you cannot understand.
16 Their quivers are like open graves;
  all of them are warriors.
17 They will devour your harvest and your bread,
  devour your sons and your daughters,
Devour your sheep and cattle,
  devour your vines and fig trees;
They will beat flat with the sword
  the fortified city in which you trust.

18 Yet even in those days, says the LORD, I will not wholly
destroy you. 19 And when they ask, "Why has the LORD
done all these things to us?" say to them, "As you have
forsaken me to serve strange gods in your own land, so shall
you serve strangers in a land not your own."

20 Announce this to the house of Jacob,
  proclaim it in Judah:
21 Pay attention to this,
  foolish and senseless people
Who have eyes and see not,
  who have ears and hear not.
22 Should you not fear me, says the LORD,
  should you not tremble before me?
I made the sandy shore the sea's limit,
  which by eternal decree it may not overstep.
Toss though it may, it is to no avail;
  though its billows roar, they cannot pass.
23 But this people's heart is stubborn and rebellious;
  they turn and go away,
24 And say not in their hearts,
  "Let us fear the LORD, our God,
Who gives us rain
  early and late, in its time;
Who watches for us
  over the appointed weeks of harvest."
25 Your crimes have prevented these things,
  your sins have turned back these blessings
    from you.
26 For there are among my people criminals;
  like fowlers they set traps,
  but it is men they catch.

NEW JERUSALEM BIBLE

11 How treacherously they have treated me,
  the House of Israel and the House of Judah!
Yahweh declares.
12 'They have denied Yahweh,
  they have said, "He is nothing;
no evil will overtake us,
  we shall not see sword or famine.
13 And the prophets? Nothing but wind;
  the word is not in them;
let those very things happen to them!" '
14 Because of this,
  Yahweh, God Sabaoth, says this,
'Since you have said such things,
  now I shall make my words
a fire in your mouth,
  and make this people wood,
  for the fire to devour.
15 Now I shall bring on you
  a nation from afar, House of Israel,
Yahweh declares,
  an enduring nation,
  an ancient nation,
a nation whose language you do not know,
  nor can you grasp what they say.
16 Their quiver a gaping tomb,
  they are all of them fighters.
17 They will devour your harvest and your food,
  devour your sons and daughters,
devour your flocks and herds,
  devour your vines and fig trees,
and demolish your fortified towns
  in which you trust — with the sword!'

18 'Yet even in those days, Yahweh declares, I shall not
annihilate you completely.
19 'And when you ask, "Why has Yahweh our God done
all this to us?" you will give them this answer, "As you
abandon me to serve alien gods in your own country, so you
must serve aliens in a country not your own."

20 'Announce this in the House of Jacob,
  proclaim it in Judah, and say,
21 "Now listen to this,
  stupid, brainless people
who have eyes and do not see,
  who have ears and do not hear!
22 Have you no fear of me?
  Yahweh demands.
Will you not tremble before me
  who set the sand as limit to the sea,
  as an everlasting barrier it cannot pass?
Its waves may toss but not prevail,
  they may roar but cannot pass beyond.
23 But this people
  has a rebellious, unruly heart;
  they have rebelled and gone!
24 Nor do they say to themselves:
  Now we ought to fear Yahweh our God
who gives the rain, of autumn
  and of spring, at the right season,
and reserves us
  the weeks appointed for harvest.
25 Your misdeeds have upset all this,
  your sins have deprived you of these blessings."
26 Yes, there are wicked men among my people
  who watch like fowlers on the alert;
they set traps
  and they catch human beings.

NEW REVISED STANDARD VERSION	REVISED ENGLISH BIBLE

NEW REVISED STANDARD VERSION

27 Like a cage full of birds,
    their houses are full of treachery;
therefore they have become great and rich,
28   they have grown fat and sleek.
They know no limits in deeds of wickedness;
    they do not judge with justice
the cause of the orphan, to make it prosper,
    and they do not defend the rights of the needy.
29 Shall I not punish them for these things?
                  says the LORD,
  and shall I not bring retribution
    on a nation such as this?

30 An appalling and horrible thing
    has happened in the land:
31 the prophets prophesy falsely,
    and the priests rule as the prophets direct;[r]
my people love to have it so,
    but what will you do when the end comes?

6 Flee for safety, O children of Benjamin,
    from the midst of Jerusalem!
Blow the trumpet in Tekoa,
    and raise a signal on Beth-haccherem;
for evil looms out of the north,
    and great destruction.
2 I have likened daughter Zion
    to the loveliest pasture.[s]
3 Shepherds with their flocks shall come against
    her.
They shall pitch their tents around her;
    they shall pasture, all in their places.
4 "Prepare war against her;
    up, and let us attack at noon!"
"Woe to us, for the day declines,
    the shadows of evening lengthen!"
5 "Up, and let us attack by night,
    and destroy her palaces!"
6 For thus says the LORD of hosts:
Cut down her trees;
    cast up a siege ramp against Jerusalem.
This is the city that must be punished;[t]
    there is nothing but oppression within her.
7 As a well keeps its water fresh,
    so she keeps fresh her wickedness;
violence and destruction are heard within her;
    sickness and wounds are ever before me.
8 Take warning, O Jerusalem,
    or I shall turn from you in disgust,
and make you a desolation,
    an uninhabited land.

9 Thus says the LORD of hosts:
Glean[u] thoroughly as a vine
    the remnant of Israel;
like a grape-gatherer, pass your hand again
    over its branches.

10 To whom shall I speak and give warning,
    that they may hear?
See, their ears are closed,[v]
    they cannot listen.
The word of the LORD is to them an object of
      scorn;
    they take no pleasure in it.

REVISED ENGLISH BIBLE

27 Their houses are full of fraud,
    as a cage is full of birds.
They grow great and rich,
28 sleek and bloated;
    they turn a blind eye to wickedness
and refuse to do justice;
    the claims of the fatherless they do not uphold,
    nor do they defend the poor at law.
29 Shall I fail to punish them for this,
    says the LORD;
    shall I not exact vengeance
    on such a people?

30 An appalling thing, an outrage,
    has appeared in this land:
31 prophets prophesy lies
    and priests are in league with them,
    and my people love to have it so!
How will you fare at the end of it all?

6 People of Benjamin, save yourselves,
    flee from Jerusalem;
sound the trumpet in Tekoa,
light the beacon on Beth-hakkerem,
    for calamity looms from the north
    and great disaster.
2 Zion, delightful and lovely,
    her end is near—
3 she against whom the shepherds will come,
    they and their flocks with them.
They will pitch their tents all around her,
    each grazing his own strip of pasture:
4 'Prepare for battle against her;
    come, let us attack her at noon.'
'Too late! The day declines
    and the shadows lengthen.'
5 'Come then, let us attack by night
    and destroy her palaces.'
6 These are the words of the LORD of Hosts:
Cut down the trees of Jerusalem
    and cast up siege-ramps against her,
a city ripe for punishment;
    oppression is rampant within her.
7 As a well keeps its water fresh,
    so she keeps fresh her wickedness.
Violence and outrage echo in her streets;
    sickness and wounds ever confront me.
8 Learn your lesson, Jerusalem,
    or I shall be estranged from you,
and leave you devastated,
    a land without inhabitants.

9 These are the words of the LORD of Hosts:
Glean like a vine the remnant of Israel;
    one last time, like a vintager,
    pass your hand over the branches.
10 To whom shall I speak,
    to whom give warning? Who will hear me?
Their ears are blocked:
    they are incapable of listening;
they treat the LORD's word as a reproach;
    it has no appeal for them.

---

[r] Or *rule by their own authority*   [s] Or *I will destroy daughter Zion,*
the loveliest pasture   [t] Or *the city of license*   [u] Cn: Heb *They*
shall glean   [v] Heb *are uncircumcised*

5:31 **lies:** *or* by a false god.   6:9 **Glean:** *prob. rdg, cp. Gk; Heb.*
Let them glean.   6:10 **blocked:** *lit.* uncircumcised.

27 Their houses are as full of treachery
    as a bird-cage is of birds;
  Therefore they grow powerful and rich,
28   fat and sleek.
  They go their wicked way;
    justice they do not defend
  By advancing the claim of the fatherless
    or judging the cause of the poor.
29 Shall I not punish these things? says the LORD;
    on a nation such as this shall I not
      take vengeance?
30 A shocking, horrible thing
    has happened in the land:
31 The prophets prophesy falsely,
    and the priests teach as they wish;
  Yet my people will have it so;
    what will you do when the end comes?

6 Flee, sons of Benjamin,
    out of Jerusalem!
  Blow the trumpet in Tekoa,
    raise a signal over Beth-haccherem;
  For evil threatens from the north,
    and mighty destruction.
2 O lovely and delicate
    daughter Zion, you are ruined!
3 Against her, shepherds come with their flocks;
    all around, they pitch their tents,
    each one grazes his portion.
4 "Prepare for war against her,
    Up! let us rush upon her at midday!
  Alas! the day is waning,
    evening shadows lengthen;
5 Up! let us rush upon her by night,
    destroy her palaces!"
6   For thus says the LORD of hosts:
  Hew down her trees,
    throw up a siege mound against Jerusalem.
  Woe to the city marked for punishment;
    nought but oppression within her!
7 As the well gushes out its waters,
    so she gushes out her wickedness.
  Violence and destruction resound in her;
    ever before me are wounds and blows.
8 Be warned, O Jerusalem,
    lest I be estranged from you;
  Lest I turn you into a desert,
    a land where no man dwells.
9   Thus says the LORD of hosts:
  Glean, glean like a vine
    the remnant of Israel;
  Pass your hand, like a vintager,
    repeatedly over the tendrils.
10 To whom shall I speak?
    whom shall I warn, and be heard?
  See! their ears are uncircumcised,
    they cannot give heed;
  See, the word of the LORD has become for them
    an object of scorn, which they will not have.

27 Like a cage full of birds
    so are their houses full of loot;
  they have grown rich and powerful because of it,
28 they are fat, they are sleek,
    in wickedness they go to any lengths:
  they have no respect for rights,
    for orphans' rights, and yet they succeed!
  They have not upheld the cause of the needy.
29 Shall I fail to punish this,
    Yahweh demands,
  or on such a nation
    to exact vengeance?g
30 Horrible, disgusting things
    are happening in the land:
31 the prophets prophesy falsely
    and the priests exploit the people.
  And my people love it!
  But when the end comes, what will you do?

6 Flee in a body, Benjaminites,
    right away from Jerusalem!
  Sound the trumpet in Tekoa!h
  Light the beacon on Beth-ha-Cherem!
  For disaster lowers from the north,
    an immense calamity.
2 Beautiful, delicate as she is,
    I shall destroy the daughter of Zion!
3 Shepherds are advancing on her
    with their flocks.
  They have pitched their tents all round her,
    each grazes his part.
4 Prepare for holy war against her!
    To arms! We shall attack at noon!
  Disaster for us! The light is fading,
    the evening shadows lengthen.
5 To arms! We shall attack at night
    and destroy her palaces.
6 For Yahweh Sabaoth says this,
    'Cut down trees,
  throw up an earthwork outside Jerusalem:
    this is the city to be punished,
    with nothing but oppression in her.
7 As a well keeps its water fresh
    so she keeps her wickedness fresh.
  Violence and ruin are what you hear in her,
    wounds and blows always forced on my attention.
8 Reform, Jerusalem,
    or I shall turn my attention away from you
  and reduce you to a desert,
    a land without people.'
9 Yahweh Sabaoth says this,
    'They will glean, glean what is left of Israel
  like a vine.
  Like a grape-picker, pass your hand again over the
      branches!'
10 To whom should I speak, whom warn,
    for them to hear?
  Look, their ears are uncircumcised,
    they cannot listen.
  Look, for them Yahweh's word is something to
      sneer at,
  they have no taste for it.

g **5** = 5:9; 9:8.   h **6** Both towns are south, but in sight, of Jerusalem.

11 But I am full of the wrath of the LORD;
   I am weary of holding it in.

Pour it out on the children in the street,
   and on the gatherings of young men as well;
both husband and wife shall be taken,
   the old folk and the very aged.
12 Their houses shall be turned over to others,
   their fields and wives together;
for I will stretch out my hand
   against the inhabitants of the land,
                says the LORD.

13 For from the least to the greatest of them,
   everyone is greedy for unjust gain;
and from prophet to priest,
   everyone deals falsely.
14 They have treated the wound of my people
    carelessly,
   saying, "Peace, peace,"
   when there is no peace.
15 They acted shamefully, they committed
    abomination;
   yet they were not ashamed,
   they did not know how to blush.
Therefore they shall fall among those who fall;
   at the time that I punish them, they shall be
    overthrown,
                says the LORD.

16 Thus says the LORD:
Stand at the crossroads, and look,
   and ask for the ancient paths,
where the good way lies; and walk in it,
   and find rest for your souls.
But they said, "We will not walk in it."
17 Also I raised up sentinels for you:
   "Give heed to the sound of the trumpet!"
But they said, "We will not give heed."
18 Therefore hear, O nations,
   and know, O congregation, what will happen
    to them.
19 Hear, O earth; I am going to bring disaster on
    this people,
   the fruit of their schemes,
because they have not given heed to my words;
   and as for my teaching, they have rejected it.
20 Of what use to me is frankincense that comes
    from Sheba,
   or sweet cane from a distant land?
Your burnt offerings are not acceptable,
   nor are your sacrifices pleasing to me.
21 Therefore thus says the LORD:
See, I am laying before this people
   stumbling blocks against which they shall
    stumble;
parents and children together,
   neighbor and friend shall perish.

22 Thus says the LORD:
See, a people is coming from the land of the
    north,
   a great nation is stirring from the farthest parts
    of the earth.
23 They grasp the bow and the javelin,
   they are cruel and have no mercy,
   their sound is like the roaring sea;
they ride on horses,
   equipped like a warrior for battle,
   against you, O daughter Zion!

11 But I am full of the anger of the LORD,
   I cannot hold it back.
I must pour it out on the children in the street,
   on the young men in their gatherings.
Man and wife alike will be caught in it,
   the ageing and the aged.
12 Their houses will be turned over to others,
   fields and women together,
because, says the LORD, I shall raise my hand
   against the inhabitants of the land.
13 For all, high and low,
   are out for ill-gotten gain;
prophets and priests are frauds,
   every one of them;
14 they dress my people's wound,
   but on the surface only,
with their saying, 'All is well.'
   All well? Nothing is well!
15 They ought to be ashamed
   because they practised abominations;
yet they have no sense of shame,
   they could never be put out of countenance.
Therefore they will fall with a great crash,
   and be brought to the ground on the day of my
    reckoning.
The LORD has said it.

16 These are the words of the LORD: Take your stand and
watch at the crossroads; enquire about the ancient paths; ask
which is the way that leads to what is good. Take that way,
and you will find rest for yourselves. But they said, 'We
refuse.' 17 I appointed watchmen to direct them. 'Listen for
the trumpet-call,' I used to say. But they said, 'We refuse.'
18 Therefore hear, you nations, and all who witness it take
note of the plight of this people. 19 Let the earth listen: I am
about to bring ruin on them, the fruit of all their scheming;
for they have given no heed to my words and have spurned
my instruction. 20 What good is it to me if frankincense is
brought from Sheba and fragrant cane from a distant land?
Your whole-offerings are not acceptable to me, your sacrifices do not please me. 21 Therefore these are the words of
the LORD:

I shall set obstacles before this people
   which will bring them to the ground;
fathers and sons, friends and neighbours
   will all perish together.

22 These are the words of the LORD:

See, an army is coming from a northern land,
   a great nation rouses itself from earth's farthest
    corners.
23 Armed with bow and scimitar, they are cruel and
    pitiless;
bestriding their horses, they sound like the thunder
   of the sea;
they are like men arrayed for battle against you,
   Zion.

6:15 **with a great crash:** *or* among the fallen.   6:17 **them:** *so
some MSS; others* you.

<table>
<tr><td>

11 Therefore my wrath brims up within me,
 I am weary of holding it in;
I will pour it out upon the child in the street,
 upon the young men gathered together.
Yes, all will be taken, husband and wife,
 graybeard with ancient.
12 Their houses will fall to strangers,
 their fields and their wives as well;
For I will stretch forth my hand
 against those who dwell in this land, says
 the LORD.
13 Small and great alike, all are greedy for gain;
 prophet and priest, all practice fraud.
14 They would repair, as though it were nought,
 the injury to my people:
"Peace, peace!" they say,
 though there is no peace.
15 They are odious; they have done
 abominable things,
yet they are not at all ashamed,
 they know not how to blush.
Hence they shall be among those who fall;
 in their time of punishment they shall go down,
 says the LORD.

16   Thus says the LORD:
Stand beside the earliest roads,
 ask the pathways of old
Which is the way to good, and walk it;
 thus you will find rest for your souls.
But they said, "We will not walk it."
17 When I raised up watchmen for them:
 "Hearken to the sound of the trumpet!"
 they said, "We will not hearken."
18 Therefore hear, O nations,
 and know, O earth,
what I will do with them:
19 See, I bring evil upon this people,
 the fruit of their own schemes,
Because they heeded not my words,
 because they despised my law.
20 Of what use to me incense that comes from Sheba,
 or sweet cane from far-off lands?
Your holocausts find no favor with me,
 your sacrifices please me not.
21   Therefore, thus says the LORD:
See, I will place before this people
 obstacles to bring them down;
Fathers and sons alike,
 neighbors and friends shall perish.

22   Thus says the LORD:
See, a people comes from the land of the north,
 a great nation, roused from the ends of the earth.
23 Bow and javelin they wield;
 cruel and pitiless are they.
They sound like the roaring sea
 as they ride forth on steeds,
Each in his place, for battle
 against you, daughter Zion.

</td><td>

11 So I am full of Yahweh's wrath,
 I am weary of holding it in.
Then pour it on the children in the streets,
 and on the bands of youths as well,
for husband and wife will both be taken,
 the greybeard and the man weighed down with
 years.
12 Their houses will pass to other men,
 so will their fields and wives.
Yes, I shall stretch my hand
 over those living in this country,
 Yahweh declares.
13 For, from the least to greatest,
 they are all greedy for gain;
prophet no less than priest,
 all of them practise fraud.
14 Without concern they dress my people's wound,
 saying, 'Peace! Peace!'
 whereas there is no peace.
15 They should be ashamed of their loathsome deeds.
 Not they! They feel no shame,
 they do not even know how to blush.
And so as others fall, they too will fall,
 will be thrown down when I come and punish
 them,
 Yahweh says.i

16 Yahweh says this,
 'Stand at the crossroads and look,
 ask for the ancient paths:
which was the good way? Take it
 and you will find rest for yourselves.
But they have said, "We will not take it."
17 I posted look-outs on your behalf:
 Listen to the sound of the trumpet!
 But they said, "We will not listen."
18 Then hear, you nations,
 and know, assembly,
 what is going to happen to them!
19 Listen, earth!
 Watch, I shall bring disaster
 on this people:
 it is the fruit of the way they think,
 since they have not listened to my words
 nor to my law, but have rejected it.
20 What do I care about incense
 imported from Sheba,
 or fragrant cane
 from a distant country?
Your burnt offerings are not acceptable,
 your sacrifices do not please me.'
21 And so, Yahweh says this,
 'In front of this people I shall now lay obstacles
 for them to stumble over;
 father and son alike,
 neighbour and friend will perish.'

22 Yahweh says this,
 'Look, a people is coming from the land of the
 north,
from the far ends of the earth a great nation is
 rising;
23 they are armed with bow and spear,
 they are cruel and pitiless;
 their noise is like the roaring of the sea;
 they are riding horses,
 they are ready to fight against you as one man,
 against you, daughter of Zion.j

</td></tr>
</table>

i 6 = 8:10–12.   *j* 6 = 50:41–43.

NEW REVISED STANDARD VERSION

24 "We have heard news of them,
     our hands fall helpless;
anguish has taken hold of us,
     pain as of a woman in labor.
25 Do not go out into the field,
     or walk on the road;
for the enemy has a sword,
     terror is on every side."

26 O my poor people, put on sackcloth,
     and roll in ashes;
make mourning as for an only child,
     most bitter lamentation:
for suddenly the destroyer
     will come upon us.

27 I have made you a tester and a refiner[w] among
     my people
so that you may know and test their ways.
28 They are all stubbornly rebellious,
     going about with slanders;
they are bronze and iron,
     all of them act corruptly.
29 The bellows blow fiercely,
     the lead is consumed by the fire;
in vain the refining goes on,
     for the wicked are not removed.
30 They are called "rejected silver,"
     for the LORD has rejected them.

7 The word that came to Jeremiah from the LORD:
2 Stand in the gate of the LORD's house, and proclaim
there this word, and say, Hear the word of the LORD, all you
people of Judah, you that enter these gates to worship the
LORD. 3 Thus says the LORD of hosts, the God of Israel:
Amend your ways and your doings, and let me dwell with
you[x] in this place. 4 Do not trust in these deceptive words:
"This is[y] the temple of the LORD, the temple of the LORD,
the temple of the LORD."

5 For if you truly amend your ways and your doings, if
you truly act justly one with another, 6 if you do not oppress
the alien, the orphan, and the widow, or shed innocent
blood in this place, and if you do not go after other gods to
your own hurt, 7 then I will dwell with you in this place, in
the land that I gave of old to your ancestors forever and
ever.

8 Here you are, trusting in deceptive words to no avail.
9 Will you steal, murder, commit adultery, swear falsely,
make offerings to Baal, and go after other gods that you
have not known, 10 and then come and stand before me in
this house, which is called by my name, and say, "We are
safe!"—only to go on doing all these abominations? 11 Has
this house, which is called by my name, become a den of
robbers in your sight? You know, I too am watching, says
the LORD. 12 Go now to my place that was in Shiloh, where
I made my name dwell at first, and see what I did to it for
the wickedness of my people Israel. 13 And now, because
you have done all these things, says the LORD, and when I
spoke to you persistently, you did not listen, and when I
called you, you did not answer, 14 therefore I will do to the
house that is called by my name, in which you trust, and to
the place that I gave to you and to your ancestors, just what
I did to Shiloh. 15 And I will cast you out of my sight, just
as I cast out all your kinsfolk, all the offspring of Ephraim.

16 As for you, do not pray for this people, do not raise
a cry or prayer on their behalf, and do not intercede with
me, for I will not hear you. 17 Do you not see what they are
doing in the towns of Judah and in the streets of Jerusalem?

REVISED ENGLISH BIBLE

24 News of them has reached us
     and our hands hang limp;
agony grips us, pangs as of a woman in labour.
25 Do not go out into the country,
     do not walk by the high road;
for the foe, sword in hand,
     spreads terror all around.
26 Daughter of my people, wrap yourself in sackcloth,
     sprinkle ashes over yourself,
wail bitterly as one who mourns an only son;
     for in an instant the despoiler will be upon us.

27 I have appointed you an assayer and tester of my
     people,
you will know how to assay their conduct:
28 arch-rebels all of them,
     mischief-makers, corrupt to a man.
29 The bellows blow, the fire is ready;
     lead, copper, and iron—in vain the refiner refines;
     the impurities are not removed.
30 Call them reject silver,
     for the LORD has rejected them.

7 THIS word came from the LORD to Jeremiah. 2 Stand at
the gate of the LORD's house and there make this proclamation: Hear the word of the LORD, all you of Judah who
come in through these gates to worship him. 3 These are the
words of the LORD of Hosts the God of Israel: Amend your
ways and your deeds, that I may let you live in this place.
4 You keep saying, 'This place is the temple of the LORD,
the temple of the LORD, the temple of the LORD!' This
slogan of yours is a lie; put no trust in it. 5 If you amend
your ways and your deeds, deal fairly with one another,
6 cease to oppress the alien, the fatherless, and the widow,
if you shed no innocent blood in this place and do not run
after other gods to your own ruin, 7 then I shall let you live
in this place, in the land which long ago I gave to your
forefathers for all time.

8 You gain nothing by putting your trust in this lie. 9 You
steal, you murder, you commit adultery and perjury, you
burn sacrifices to Baal, and you run after other gods whom
you have not known; 10 will you then come and stand before
me in this house which bears my name, and say, 'We are
safe'? Safe, you think, to indulge in all these abominations!
11 Do you regard this house which bears my name as a
bandits' cave? I warn you, I myself have seen all this, says
the LORD.

12 Go to my shrine at Shiloh, which once I made a dwelling for my name, and see what I did to it because of the
wickedness of my people Israel. 13 Now you have done all
these things, says the LORD; though I spoke to you again
and again, you did not listen, and though I called, you did
not respond. 14 Therefore what I did to Shiloh I shall do to
this house which bears my name, the house in which you
put your trust, the place I gave to you and your forefathers;
15 I shall fling you away out of my presence, as I did with
all your kinsfolk, all Ephraim's offspring.

16 Offer up no prayer for this people, Jeremiah, raise no
plea or prayer on their behalf, and do not intercede with me,
for I shall not listen to you. 17 Do you not see what they are
doing in the towns of Judah and in the streets of Jerusalem?

---

[w] Or a fortress   [x] Or and I will let you dwell   [y] Heb They are

6:29 copper, and iron: transposed from after mischief-makers in
verse 28.

1658

24 We hear the report of them;
    helpless fall our hands,
Anguish takes hold of us,
    throes like a mother's in childbirth.
25 Go not forth into the field,
    step not into the street,
Beware of the enemy's sword;
    terror on every side!
26 O daughter of my people, gird on sackcloth,
    roll in the ashes.
Mourn as for an only child
    with bitter wailing,
For sudden upon us
    comes the destroyer.
27 A tester among my people I have appointed you,
    to search and test their way.
28 Arch-rebels are they all,
    dealers in slander,
    all of them corrupt.
29 The bellows roars,
    the lead is consumed by the fire;
In vain has the smelter refined,
    the wicked are not drawn off.
30 "Silver rejected" they shall be called,
    for the LORD has rejected them.

7 The following message came to Jeremiah from the LORD: 2 Stand at the gate of the house of the LORD, and there proclaim this message: Hear the word of the LORD, all you of Judah who enter these gates to worship the LORD! 3 Thus says the LORD of hosts, the God of Israel: Reform your ways and your deeds, so that I may remain with you in this place. 4 Put not your trust in the deceitful words: "This is the temple of the LORD! The temple of the LORD! The temple of the LORD!" 5 Only if you thoroughly reform your ways and your deeds; if each of you deals justly with his neighbor; 6 if you no longer oppress the resident alien, the orphan, and the widow; if you no longer shed innocent blood in this place, or follow strange gods to your own harm, 7 will I remain with you in this place, in the land which I gave your fathers long ago and forever.

8 But here you are, putting your trust in deceitful words to your own loss! 9 Are you to steal and murder, commit adultery and perjury, burn incense to Baal, go after strange gods that you know not, 10 and yet come to stand before me in this house which bears my name, and say: "We are safe; we can commit all these abominations again"? 11 Has this house which bears my name become in your eyes a den of thieves? I too see what is being done, says the LORD. 12 You may go to Shiloh, which I made the dwelling place of my name in the beginning. See what I did to it because of the wickedness of my people Israel. 13 And now, because you have committed all these misdeeds, says the LORD, because you did not listen, though I spoke to you untiringly; because you did not answer, though I called you, 14 I will do to this house named after me, in which you trust, and to this place which I gave to you and your fathers, just as I did to Shiloh. 15 I will cast you away from me, as I cast away all your brethren, all the offspring of Ephraim.

16 You, now, do not intercede for this people; raise not in their behalf a pleading prayer! Do not urge me, for I will not listen to you. 17 Do you not see what they are doing in the cities of Judah, in the streets of Jerusalem? 18 The children

24 We have heard the news,
    our hands fall limp,
anguish has gripped us,
    pain like that of a woman in labour.
25 Do not go out into the countryside,
    do not venture onto the roads,
for the enemy's sword is there,
    terror on every side.
26 Put on sackcloth, daughter of my people,
    roll in ashes;
mourn as for an only son,
    a very bitter dirge.
For on us suddenly
    the destroyer is coming.
27 'I have appointed you as tester of my people,
    to learn and to test how they behave.
28 All of them are total rebels
    peddlers of slander,
hard as bronze and iron,
    all agents of corruption.
29 The bellows blast away
    to make the fire burn away the lead.
In vain does the smelter work,
    for the dross is not purged out.
30 "Silver-reject", men call them,
    and indeed Yahweh has rejected them!'

7 The word that came to Jeremiah from Yahweh, saying, 2 'Stand at the gate of the Temple of Yahweh and there proclaim this message. Say, "Listen to the word of Yahweh, all you of Judah who come in by these gates to worship Yahweh. 3 Yahweh Sabaoth, the God of Israel, says this: Amend your behaviour and your actions and I will let you stay in this place. 4 Do not put your faith in delusive words, such as: This is Yahweh's sanctuary, Yahweh's sanctuary, Yahweh's sanctuary! 5 But if you really amend your behaviour and your actions, if you really treat one another fairly, 6 if you do not exploit the stranger, the orphan and the widow, if you do not shed innocent blood in this place and if you do not follow other gods, to your own ruin, 7 then I shall let you stay in this place, in the country I gave for ever to your ancestors of old. 8 Look, you are putting your faith in delusive, worthless words! 9 Steal, would you, murder, commit adultery, perjure yourselves, burn incense to Baal, follow other gods of whom you know nothing? — 10 and then come and stand before me in this Temple that bears my name, saying: Now we are safe to go on doing all these loathsome things! 11 Do you look on this Temple that bears my name as a den of bandits? I, at any rate, can see straight, Yahweh declares.

12 "Now go to the place which used to be mine at Shiloh, where I once gave my name a home; see what I have done to it because of the wickedness of my people Israel! 13 And now, since you have done all these things, Yahweh declares, and refused to listen when I spoke so urgently, so persistently, or to answer when I called you, 14 I shall treat this Temple that bears my name, and in which you put your heart, the place that I gave you and your ancestors, just as I treated Shiloh. 15 And I shall drive you out of my sight, as I did all your kinsfolk, the whole race of Ephraim."

16 'You, for your part, must not intercede for this people, nor raise either plea or prayer on their behalf; do not plead with me, for I will not listen to you. 17 Can you not see what they are doing in the towns of Judah and in the streets of Jerusalem? 18 The children collect the wood, the fathers

NEW REVISED STANDARD VERSION	REVISED ENGLISH BIBLE

18 The children gather wood, the fathers kindle fire, and the women knead dough, to make cakes for the queen of heaven; and they pour out drink offerings to other gods, to provoke me to anger. 19 Is it I whom they provoke? says the LORD. Is it not themselves, to their own hurt? 20 Therefore thus says the Lord GOD: My anger and my wrath shall be poured out on this place, on human beings and animals, on the trees of the field and the fruit of the ground; it will burn and not be quenched.

21 Thus says the LORD of hosts, the God of Israel: Add your burnt offerings to your sacrifices, and eat the flesh. 22 For in the day that I brought your ancestors out of the land of Egypt, I did not speak to them or command them concerning burnt offerings and sacrifices. 23 But this command I gave them, "Obey my voice, and I will be your God, and you shall be my people; and walk only in the way that I command you, so that it may be well with you." 24 Yet they did not obey or incline their ear, but, in the stubbornness of their evil will, they walked in their own counsels, and looked backward rather than forward. 25 From the day that your ancestors came out of the land of Egypt until this day, I have persistently sent all my servants the prophets to them, day after day; 26 yet they did not listen to me, or pay attention, but they stiffened their necks. They did worse than their ancestors did.

27 So you shall speak all these words to them, but they will not listen to you. You shall call to them, but they will not answer you. 28 You shall say to them: This is the nation that did not obey the voice of the LORD their God, and did not accept discipline; truth has perished; it is cut off from their lips.

29   Cut off your hair and throw it away;
     raise a lamentation on the bare heights,ᶻ
  for the LORD has rejected and forsaken
     the generation that provoked his wrath.

30 For the people of Judah have done evil in my sight, says the LORD; they have set their abominations in the house that is called by my name, defiling it. 31 And they go on building the high placeᵃ of Topheth, which is in the valley of the son of Hinnom, to burn their sons and their daughters in the fire—which I did not command, nor did it come into my mind. 32 Therefore, the days are surely coming, says the LORD, when it will no more be called Topheth, or the valley of the son of Hinnom, but the valley of Slaughter: for they will bury in Topheth until there is no more room. 33 The corpses of this people will be food for the birds of the air, and for the animals of the earth; and no one will frighten them away. 34 And I will bring to an end the sound of mirth and gladness, the voice of the bride and bridegroom in the cities of Judah and in the streets of Jerusalem; for the land shall become a waste.

8 At that time, says the LORD, the bones of the kings of Judah, the bones of its officials, the bones of the priests, the bones of the prophets, and the bones of the inhabitants of Jerusalem shall be brought out of their tombs; 2 and they shall be spread before the sun and the moon and all the host of heaven, which they have loved and served, which they have followed, and which they have inquired of and worshiped; and they shall not be gathered or buried; they shall be like dung on the surface of the ground. 3 Death shall be preferred to life by all the remnant that remains of this evil family in all the places where I have driven them, says the LORD of hosts.

4   You shall say to them, Thus says the LORD:
    When people fall, do they not get up again?
    If they go astray, do they not turn back?

18 Children are gathering wood, fathers lighting the fire, women kneading dough to make crescent-cakes in honour of the queen of heaven; and drink-offerings are poured out to other gods—all to grieve me. 19 But is it I, says the LORD, whom they grieve? No; it is themselves, to their own confusion. 20 Therefore, says the Lord GOD, my anger and my fury will pour out on this place, on man and beast, on trees and crops, and it will burn unquenched.

21 These are the words of the LORD of Hosts the God of Israel: Add your whole-offerings to your sacrifices and eat the flesh yourselves. 22 For when I brought your forefathers out of Egypt, I gave them no instructions or commands about whole-offering or sacrifice. 23 What I did command them was this: Obey me, and I shall be your God and you will be my people. You must conform to all my commands, if you are to prosper.

24 But they did not listen; they paid no heed, and persisted in their own plans with evil and stubborn hearts; they turned their backs and not their faces to me, 25 from the day when your forefathers left Egypt until now. Again and again I sent to them all my servants the prophets; 26 but instead of listening and paying heed to me, they in their stubbornness proved even more wicked than their forefathers. 27 Tell them all this, but they will not listen to you; call them, but they will not respond. 28 Then say to them: This is the nation who did not obey the LORD their God or accept correction. Truth has perished; it is heard no more on their lips.

29 Jerusalem, cut off your hair and throw it away;
    raise a lament on the bare heights.
  For the LORD has spurned and forsaken
    the generation that roused his wrath.

30 The people of Judah have done what is wrong in my eyes, says the LORD. They set up their loathsome idols in the house which bears my name and so defiled it; 31 they have built shrines of Topheth in the valley of Ben-hinnom, at which to burn their sons and daughters. That was no command of mine; indeed it never entered my mind. 32 Therefore the time is coming, says the LORD, when it will no longer be called Topheth or the valley of Ben-hinnom, but the valley of Slaughter; for the dead will be buried in Topheth until there is no room left. 33 So the corpses of this people will become food for the birds of the air and the wild beasts, with none to scare them away. 34 From the towns of Judah and the streets of Jerusalem I shall banish all sounds of joy and gladness, the voices of bridegroom and bride; for the whole land will become desert.

8 At that time, says the LORD, the bones of the kings of Judah, of the officers, priests, and prophets, and of all who have lived in Jerusalem, will be brought out from their graves. 2 They will be exposed to the sun, the moon, and all the host of heaven, which they loved and served and adored, from which they sought guidance and to which they bowed in worship. Those bones will not be gathered up and reburied; they will be dung spread over the ground. 3 All the survivors of this wicked race, wherever I have banished them, would rather die than live. This is the word of the LORD of Hosts.

4 You are to say to them: These are the words of the LORD.

    Does someone fall and not get up,
    or default and not return?

ᶻ Or the trails   ᵃ Gk Tg: Heb high places

7:25 **them:** so one MS; others you.   8:3 **them:** so one MS; others add those who are left.

gather wood, their fathers light the fire, and the women knead dough to make cakes for the queen of heaven, while libations are poured out to strange gods in order to hurt me. 19 Is it I whom they hurt, says the LORD; is it not rather themselves, to their own confusion? 20 See now, says the Lord GOD, my anger and my wrath will pour out upon this place, upon man and beast, upon the trees of the field and the fruits of the earth; it will burn without being quenched.

21 Thus says the LORD of hosts, the God of Israel: Heap your holocausts upon your sacrifices; eat up the flesh! 22 In speaking to your fathers on the day I brought them out of the land of Egypt, I gave them no command concerning holocaust or sacrifice. 23 This rather is what I commanded them: Listen to my voice; then I will be your God and you shall be my people. Walk in all the ways that I command you, so that you may prosper.

24 But they obeyed not, nor did they pay heed. They walked in the hardness of their evil hearts and turned their backs, not their faces, to me. 25 From the day that your fathers left the land of Egypt even to this day, I have sent you untiringly all my servants the prophets. 26 Yet they have not obeyed me nor paid heed; they have stiffened their necks and done worse than their fathers. 27 When you speak all these words to them, they will not listen to you either; when you call to them, they will not answer you. 28 Say to them: This is the nation which does not listen to the voice of the LORD, its God, or take correction. Faithfulness has disappeared; the word itself is banished from their speech.

29 Cut off your dedicated hair and throw it away!
on the heights intone an elegy;
For the LORD has rejected and cast off
the generation that draws down his wrath.

30 The people of Judah have done what is evil in my eyes, says the LORD. They have defiled the house which bears my name by setting up in it their abominable idols. 31 In the Valley of Ben-hinnom they have built the high place of Topheth to immolate in fire their sons and their daughters, such a thing as I never commanded or had in mind. 32 Therefore, beware! days will come, says the LORD, when Topheth and the Valley of Ben-hinnom will no longer be called such, but rather the Valley of Slaughter. For lack of space, Topheth will be a burial place. 33 The corpses of this people will be food for the birds of the sky and for the beasts of the field, which no one will drive away. 34 In the cities of Judah and in the streets of Jerusalem I will silence the cry of joy, the cry of gladness, the voice of the bridegroom and the voice of the bride; for the land will be turned to rubble.

8 At that time, says the LORD, the bones of the kings and princes of Judah, the bones of the priests and the prophets, and the bones of the citizens of Jerusalem will be emptied out of their graves 2 and spread out before the sun and the moon and the whole army of heaven, which they loved and served, which they followed, consulted, and worshiped. They will not be gathered up for burial, but will lie like dung upon the ground. 3 Death will be preferred to life by all the survivors of this wicked race who remain in any of the places to which I banish them, says the LORD of hosts.

4   Tell them: Thus says the LORD:
When someone falls, does he not rise again?
if he goes astray, does he not turn back?

light the fire, the women knead the dough, to make cakes for the Queen of Heaven;[k] and, to spite me, they pour libations to alien gods. 19 Is it really me they spite, Yahweh demands, is it not in fact themselves, to their own confusion? 20 So, Lord Yahweh says this, "My anger, my wrath will be poured down on this place, on man and beast, on the trees of the countryside and the fruits of the soil; it will burn, and not be quenched."

21 'Yahweh Sabaoth, the God of Israel, says this, "Add your burnt offerings to your sacrifices and eat all the meat. 22 For when I brought your ancestors out of Egypt, I said nothing to them, gave them no orders, about burnt offerings or sacrifices. 23 My one command to them was this: Listen to my voice, then I will be your God and you shall be my people. In everything, follow the way that I mark out for you, and you shall prosper. 24 But they did not listen, they did not pay attention; they followed their own devices, their own stubborn and wicked inclinations, and got worse rather than better. 25 From the day your ancestors left Egypt until today, I have sent you all my servants the prophets, persistently sending them day after day. 26 But they have not listened to me, have not paid attention; they have deliberately resisted, behaving worse than their ancestors. 27 So you will tell them all this, but they will not listen to you; you will call them, but they will not answer you." 28 Then you are to say to them, "This is the nation that will neither listen to the voice of Yahweh its God nor take correction. Sincerity is no more, it has vanished from their mouths.

29 "Cut off your tresses, throw them away!
On the bare heights raise a dirge,
for Yahweh has rejected, has abandoned,
a brood that enrages him!"

30 'Yes, the people of Judah have done what displeases me, Yahweh declares. They have set up their Horrors in the Temple that bears my name, to defile it, 31 and have built the high places of Topheth[l] in the Valley of Ben-Hinnom, to burn their sons and daughters: a thing I never ordered, that had never entered my thoughts.[m] 32 So now the days are coming, Yahweh declares, when people will no longer say Topheth or Valley of Ben-Hinnom, but Valley of Slaughter. Topheth will become a burial ground, for lack of other space; 33 the corpses of this people will be food for the birds of the sky and the animals of earth, and there will be no one to drive them off. 34 I shall silence the shouts of rejoicing and mirth and the voices of bridegroom and bride, in the towns of Judah and the streets of Jerusalem, for the country will be reduced to desert.'

8 'When that time comes, Yahweh declares, the bones of the kings of Judah, the bones of its chief men, the bones of the priests, the bones of the prophets and the bones of the inhabitants of Jerusalem, will be taken from their tombs. 2 They will be spread out before the sun, the moon, the whole array of heaven, whom they have loved and served, followed, consulted and worshipped. They will not be gathered or reburied but will be left lying on the surface like dung.[n] 3 And death will seem preferable to life to all the survivors of this wicked race, wherever I have driven them, Yahweh Sabaoth declares.

4 'You are to tell them, "Yahweh says this:
If someone falls, can he not stand up again?
If people stray, can they not turn back?

k 7 Mesopotamian goddess of fertility.   l 7 The
rubbish-dump of Jerusalem, where children were also sacrificed.
m 7 = 32:34–35.   n 8 = 25:33.

NEW REVISED STANDARD VERSION

5 Why then has this people[b] turned away
   in perpetual backsliding?
   They have held fast to deceit,
   they have refused to return.
6 I have given heed and listened,
   but they do not speak honestly;
   no one repents of wickedness,
   saying, "What have I done!"
   All of them turn to their own course,
   like a horse plunging headlong into battle.
7 Even the stork in the heavens
   knows its times;
   and the turtledove, swallow, and crane[c]
   observe the time of their coming;
   but my people do not know
   the ordinance of the LORD.
8 How can you say, "We are wise,
   and the law of the LORD is with us,"
   when, in fact, the false pen of the scribes
   has made it into a lie?
9 The wise shall be put to shame,
   they shall be dismayed and taken;
   since they have rejected the word of the LORD,
   what wisdom is in them?
10 Therefore I will give their wives to others
   and their fields to conquerors,
   because from the least to the greatest
   everyone is greedy for unjust gain;
   from prophet to priest
   everyone deals falsely.
11 They have treated the wound of my people
   carelessly,
   saying, "Peace, peace,"
   when there is no peace.
12 They acted shamefully, they committed
   abomination;
   yet they were not at all ashamed,
   they did not know how to blush.
   Therefore they shall fall among those who fall;
   at the time when I punish them, they shall be
   overthrown,
                          says the LORD.
13 When I wanted to gather them, says the LORD,
   there are[d] no grapes on the vine,
   nor figs on the fig tree;
   even the leaves are withered,
   and what I gave them has passed away from
   them.[c]

14 Why do we sit still?
   Gather together, let us go into the fortified cities
   and perish there;
   for the LORD our God has doomed us to perish,
   and has given us poisoned water to drink,
   because we have sinned against the LORD.
15 We look for peace, but find no good,
   for a time of healing, but there is terror
   instead.

16 The snorting of their horses is heard from Dan;
   at the sound of the neighing of their stallions
   the whole land quakes.
   They come and devour the land and all that fills
   it,
   the city and those who live in it.

REVISED ENGLISH BIBLE

5 Then why are this people so wayward,
   incurable in their waywardness?
   Why have they persisted in their treachery
   and refused to return?
6 I have listened to them
   and heard not one word of truth,
   not one sinner crying remorsefully,
   'What have I done?'
   Each one breaks away in headlong career
   as a war-horse plunges into battle.
7 The stork in the heavens
   knows the time to migrate,
   the dove and the swift and the wryneck
   know the season of return;
   but my people do not know
   the ordinances of the LORD.
8 How can you say, 'We are wise,
   we have the law of the LORD,'
   when scribes with their lying pens
   have falsified it?
9 The wise are put to shame;
   they are dismayed and entrapped.
   They have spurned the word of the LORD,
   so what sort of wisdom is theirs?
10 Therefore I shall give their wives to other men
   and their lands to new owners.
   For all, high and low,
   are out for ill-gotten gain;
   prophets and priests are frauds,
   every one of them;
11 they dress my people's wound,
   but on the surface only,
   with their saying, 'All is well.'
   All well? Nothing is well!
12 They ought to be ashamed
   because they have practised abominations,
   yet they have no sense of shame,
   they could never be put out of countenance.
   Therefore they will fall with a great crash,
   and be brought to the ground on the day of
   reckoning.
   The LORD has said it.
13 I shall gather them all in, says the LORD;
   there will be no grapes on the vine,
   no figs on the fig tree;
   even the foliage will be withered.

14 Why do we sit idle? Assemble!
   Let us move to the fortified towns
   and there meet our doom,
   since the LORD our God has doomed us,
   giving us a draught of bitter poison,
   for we have sinned against him.
15 We hoped to prosper, but nothing went well;
   we hoped for respite, but terror struck.
16 The snorting of their horses is heard from Dan;
   at the neighing of their stallions the whole land
   trembles.
   The enemy come; they devour the land and all its
   store,
   city and citizens alike.

---

[b]One Ms Gk: MT *this people, Jerusalem,*   [c]Meaning of Heb
uncertain   [d]Or *I will make an end of them, says the LORD. There
are*

8:5 **this people:** *so Gk; Heb. adds* Jerusalem.   8:12 **with a great
crash:** *or* among the fallen.   8:13 **withered:** *so Gk; Heb. adds* so
I have allowed men to pass them by.

5 Why do these people rebel
  with obstinate resistance?
Why do they cling to deceptive idols,
  refuse to turn back?
6 I listen closely:
  they speak what is not true;
No one repents of his wickedness,
  saying "What have I done!"
Everyone keeps on running his course,
  like a steed dashing into battle.
7 Even the stork in the air
  knows its seasons;
Turtledove, swallow and thrush
  observe their time of return,
But my people do not know
  the ordinance of the LORD.

8 How can you say, "We are wise,
  we have the law of the LORD"?
Why, that has been changed into falsehood
  by the lying pen of the scribes!
9 The wise are confounded,
  dismayed and ensnared;
Since they have rejected the word of the LORD,
  of what avail is their wisdom?

10 Therefore, I will give their wives to strangers,
  their fields to spoilers.
Small and great alike, all are greedy for gain,
  prophet and priest, all practice fraud.
11 They would repair, as though it were nought,
  the injury to the daughter of my people:
"Peace, peace!" they say,
  though there is no peace.
12 They are odious; they have done
      abominable things,
  yet they are not at all ashamed,
  they know not how to blush.
Hence they shall be among those who fall;
  in their time of punishment they shall go down,
  says the LORD.

13 I will gather them all in, says the LORD:
  no grapes on the vine,
No figs on the fig trees,
  foliage withered!
14 Why do we remain here?
  Let us form ranks and enter the walled cities,
  to perish there;
For the LORD has wrought our destruction,
  he has given us poison to drink,
  because we have sinned against the LORD.
15 We wait for peace to no avail;
  for a time of healing, but terror comes instead.
16 From Dan is heard
  the snorting of his steeds;
The neighing of his stallions
  shakes the whole land.
They come devouring the land and all it contains,
  the city and those who dwell in it.

5 Why does this people persist in acts of infidelity,
  why does Jerusalem persist in continuous
    infidelity?
They cling to illusion,
  they refuse to turn back.
6 I have listened attentively:
  they have never said anything like that.
Not one repents of wickedness
  saying: What have I done?
Each one keeps returning to the course
  like a horse charging into battle.
7 Even the stork in the sky
  knows the appropriate season;
turtledove, swallow and crane
  observe their time of migration.
But my people do not know
  Yahweh's laws!'

8 How can you say, 'We are wise,
  since we have Yahweh's Law?'
Look how it has been falsified
  by the lying pen of the scribes!
9 The wise are put to shame,
  alarmed, caught out
because they have rejected Yahweh's word.
What price their wisdom now?

10 So I shall give their wives to other men,
  their fields to new masters,
for, from the least to greatest,
  they are all greedy for gain;
prophet no less than priest,
  all of them practise fraud.
11 Without concern they dress
  the wound of the daughter of my people,
saying, 'Peace! Peace!'
  whereas there is no peace.
12 They should be ashamed of their loathsome deeds.
Not they! They feel no shame,
  they do not even know how to blush.
And so as others fall, they too will fall,
  will be thrown down when the time for punishing
    them comes,
Yahweh says. o

13 I shall put an end to them, Yahweh declares,
  no more grapes on the vine,
no more figs on the fig tree
  only withered leaves:
I have found them people to trample on them!
14 Why are we sitting still?
  Mobilise!
Take to the fortified towns p
  and there fall silent,
since Yahweh our God means to silence us
  by giving us poisoned water to drink
because we have sinned against him.
15 We are hoping for peace — no good came of it!
  For the time of healing — nothing but terror! q
16 From Dan you can hear
  the snorting of his horses;
at the neighing of his stallions
  the whole country quakes;
they are coming to devour the country and its
    contents,
  the town and those that live in it.

o 8 A duplicate of 6:12–15, absent in the Gk text.   p 8 = 4:5.
q 8 = 14:19.

NEW REVISED STANDARD VERSION

17 See, I am letting snakes loose among you,
    adders that cannot be charmed,
    and they shall bite you,
                    says the LORD.

18 My joy is gone, grief is upon me,
    my heart is sick.
19 Hark, the cry of my poor people
    from far and wide in the land:
    "Is the LORD not in Zion?
    Is her King not in her?"
    ("Why have they provoked me to anger with their
        images,
    with their foreign idols?")
20 "The harvest is past, the summer is ended,
    and we are not saved."
21 For the hurt of my poor people I am hurt,
    I mourn, and dismay has taken hold
        of me.
22 Is there no balm in Gilead?
    Is there no physician there?
    Why then has the health of my poor people
    not been restored?

9 *e* O that my head were a spring of water,
    and my eyes a fountain of tears,
    so that I might weep day and night
    for the slain of my poor people!
2 *f* O that I had in the desert
    a traveler's lodging place,
    that I might leave my people
    and go away from them!
    For they are all adulterers,
    a band of traitors.
3 They bend their tongues like bows;
    they have grown strong in the land for
        falsehood, and not for truth;
    for they proceed from evil to evil,
    and they do not know me, says the LORD.

4 Beware of your neighbors,
    and put no trust in any of your kin;*g*
    for all your kin*h* are supplanters,
    and every neighbor goes around like a
        slanderer.
5 They all deceive their neighbors,
    and no one speaks the truth;
    they have taught their tongues to speak lies;
    they commit iniquity and are too weary to
        repent.*i*
6 Oppression upon oppression, deceit*j* upon deceit!
    They refuse to know me, says the LORD.

7 Therefore thus says the LORD of hosts:
    I will now refine and test them,
    for what else can I do with my sinful people?*k*
8 Their tongue is a deadly arrow;
    it speaks deceit through the mouth.
    They all speak friendly words to their neighbors,
    but inwardly are planning to lay an ambush.
9 Shall I not punish them for these things? says the
        LORD,
    and shall I not bring retribution
    on a nation such as this?

REVISED ENGLISH BIBLE

17 I am sending snakes against you,
    vipers such as no one can charm,
    and they will bite you.
    This is the word of the LORD.

18 There is no cure for my grief;
    I am sick at heart.
19 Hear my people's cry of distress
    from a distant land:
    'Is the LORD not in Zion?
    Is her King no longer there?'
    Why do they provoke me with their
        images
    and with their futile foreign gods?
20 Harvest is past, summer is over,
    and we are not saved.
21 I am wounded by my people's wound;
    I go about in mourning, overcome with
        horror.
22 Is there no balm in Gilead,
    no physician there?
    Why has no new skin grown over their
        wound?

9 Would that my head were a spring of
        water,
    my eyes a fountain of tears,
    that I might weep day and night
    for the slain of my people.
2 Would that I had in the wilderness a wayside shelter,
    that I might leave my people and go away!
    They are all adulterers, a faithless mob.
3 The tongue is their weapon,
    a bow ready bent.
    Lying, not truth, holds sway in the land.
    They proceed from one wrong to another
    and care nothing for me.
    This is the word of the LORD.

4 Be on your guard, each against his friend;
    put no trust even in a brother.
    Brother supplants brother as Jacob did,
    and friend slanders friend.
5 They deceive their friends
    and never speak the truth;
    they have trained their tongues to lying;
    deep in sin, they weary themselves going astray.
6 Wrong follows wrong, deceit follows deceit;
    they refuse to acknowledge me.
    This is the word of the LORD.
7 Therefore these are the words of the LORD of
        Hosts:
    I shall refine and assay them.
    How else should I deal with my people?
8 Their tongues are deadly arrows,
    their mouths speak lies.
    One person talks amicably to another,
    while inwardly planning a trap.
9 Shall I fail to punish them for this,
    says the LORD,
    shall I not exact vengeance
    on such a people?

17 Yes, I will send against you
   poisonous snakes,
Against which no charm will work
   when they bite you, says the LORD.

18 My grief is incurable,
   my heart within me is faint.
19 Listen! the cry of the daughter of my people,
   far and wide in the land!
Is the LORD no longer in Zion,
   is her King no longer in her midst?
[Why do they provoke me with their idols,
   with their foreign nonentities?]
20 "The harvest has passed, the summer is at an
   end,
   and yet we are not safe!"
21 I am broken by the ruin of the daughter of
   my people.
   I am disconsolate; horror has seized me.
22 Is there no balm in Gilead,
   no physician there?
Why grows not new flesh
   over the wound of the daughter of my
   people?
23 Oh, that my head were a spring of water,
   my eyes a fountain of tears,
That I might weep day and night
   over the slain of the daughter of my people!

9 Would that I had in the desert
   a travelers' lodge!
That I might leave my people
   and depart from them.
They are all adulterers,
   a faithless band.
2 They ready their tongues like a drawn bow;
   with lying, and not with truth,
   they hold forth in the land.
They go from evil to evil,
   but me they know not, says the LORD.
3 Be on your guard, everyone against his neighbor;
   put no trust in any brother.
Every brother apes Jacob, the supplanter,
   every friend is guilty of slander.
4 Each one deceives the other,
   no one speaks the truth.
They have accustomed their tongues to lying,
   and are perverse, and cannot repent.
5 Violence upon violence,
   deceit upon deceit:
They refuse to recognize me,
   says the LORD.
6   Therefore, thus says the LORD of hosts:
I will smelt them and test them;
   how else should I deal with their wickedness?
7 A murderous arrow is his tongue,
   his mouth utters deceit;
He speaks cordially with his friends,
   but in his heart he lays an ambush!
8 For these things, says the LORD,
   shall I not punish them?
On a nation such as this
   shall I not take vengeance?

17 Yes, now I am sending you
   poisonous snakes
   against which no charm exists;
   and they will bite you,
   Yahweh declares.

18 Incurable sorrow overtakes me,
   my heart fails me.
19 Hark, from the daughter of my people the cry for
   help,
   ringing far and wide throughout the land!
'Is Yahweh no longer in Zion,
   her King no longer there?'
(Why have they provoked me with their idols,
   with their futile foreign gods?)
20 'Harvest is over, summer at an end,
   and we have not been saved!'
21 The wound of the daughter of my people wounds
   me too,
   all looks dark to me, terror grips me.
22 Is there no balm in Gilead any more?
   Is no doctor there?
Then why is there no progress
   in the cure of the daughter of my people?
23 Who will turn my head into a fountain,
   and my eyes into a spring of tears,
   that I can weep day and night
   over the slain of the daughter of my people?

9 Who will find me a wayfarer's shelter
   in the desert,
   for me to quit my people,
   and leave them far behind?
For all of them are adulterers,
   a conspiracy of traitors.
2 They bend their tongues like a bow;
   not truth but falsehood
   holds sway in the land;
   yes, they go from crime to crime,
   but me they do not know,
   Yahweh declares.
3 Let each be on his guard against his friend;
   do not trust a brother,
   for every brother aims but to supplant,
   and every friend is a peddler of slander.
4 Each one cheats his friend,
   never telling the truth;
   they have trained their tongues to lie
   and devote all their energies to doing wrong.
5 You live in a world of bad faith!
   Out of bad faith, they refuse to know me,
   Yahweh declares.
6 And, so, Yahweh Sabaoth declares,
   now I shall purge them and test them,
   no other way to treat the daughter of my people!
7 Their tongue is a deadly arrow,
   their words are in bad faith;
   with his mouth each wishes his neighbour peace,
   while in his heart plotting a trap for him.
8 Shall I fail to punish them for this,
   Yahweh demands,
   or on such a nation
   fail to exact vengeance?r

r 9 = 5:9, 29.

10 Take up[^l] weeping and wailing for the
          mountains,
    and a lamentation for the pastures of the
          wilderness,
    because they are laid waste so that no one passes
          through,
    and the lowing of cattle is not heard;
    both the birds of the air and the animals
          have fled and are gone.
11 I will make Jerusalem a heap of ruins,
          a lair of jackals;
    and I will make the towns of Judah a desolation,
          without inhabitant.

12 Who is wise enough to understand this? To whom has
the mouth of the LORD spoken, so that they may declare it?
Why is the land ruined and laid waste like a wilderness, so
that no one passes through? 13 And the LORD says: Because
they have forsaken my law that I set before them, and have
not obeyed my voice, or walked in accordance with it, 14 but
have stubbornly followed their own hearts and have gone
after the Baals, as their ancestors taught them. 15 Therefore
thus says the LORD of hosts, the God of Israel: I am feeding
this people with wormwood, and giving them poisonous
water to drink. 16 I will scatter them among nations that
neither they nor their ancestors have known; and I will send
the sword after them, until I have consumed them.

17 Thus says the LORD of hosts:
    Consider, and call for the mourning women to
          come;
    send for the skilled women to come;
18 let them quickly raise a dirge over us,
    so that our eyes may run down with tears,
    and our eyelids flow with water.
19 For a sound of wailing is heard from Zion:
    "How we are ruined!
    We are utterly shamed,
    because we have left the land,
    because they have cast down our dwellings."

20 Hear, O women, the word of the LORD,
    and let your ears receive the word of his
          mouth;
    teach to your daughters a dirge,
    and each to her neighbor a lament.
21 "Death has come up into our windows,
    it has entered our palaces,
    to cut off the children from the streets
    and the young men from the squares."
22 Speak! Thus says the LORD:
    "Human corpses shall fall
    like dung upon the open field,
    like sheaves behind the reaper,
    and no one shall gather them."

23 Thus says the LORD: Do not let the wise boast in their
wisdom, do not let the mighty boast in their might, do not
let the wealthy boast in their wealth; 24 but let those who
boast boast in this, that they understand and know me, that
I am the LORD; I act with steadfast love, justice, and righteousness in the earth, for in these things I delight, says the
LORD.

25 The days are surely coming, says the LORD, when I
will attend to all those who are circumcised only in the
foreskin: 26 Egypt, Judah, Edom, the Ammonites, Moab,
and all those with shaven temples who live in the desert. For
all these nations are uncircumcised, and all the house of
Israel is uncircumcised in heart.

[^l]: Gk Syr: Heb *I will take up*

10 Over the mountains I shall raise weeping and
          wailing,
    and over the open pastures I shall chant a dirge.
    They are scorched and untrodden,
    they hear no lowing of cattle;
    birds of the air and beasts have fled and are gone.
11 I shall make Jerusalem a heap of ruins, a haunt of
          wolves,
    and the towns of Judah waste, without inhabitants.

12 Who is wise enough to understand this, and who has the
LORD's command to proclaim it? Why has the land become
a dead land, scorched like the desert and untrodden? 13 The
LORD said: It is because they rejected my law which I set
before them; they neither obeyed me nor followed it.
14 They followed the promptings of their own stubborn
hearts and followed the baalim as their forefathers had
taught them. 15 Therefore these are the words of the LORD
of Hosts the God of Israel: I shall give this people wormwood to eat and bitter poison to drink. 16 I shall disperse
them among nations whom neither they nor their forefathers
have known; I shall harry them with the sword until I have
made an end of them.

17 These are the words of the LORD of Hosts:

    Summon the wailing women to come,
    send for the women skilled in keening
18 to come quickly and raise a lament for us,
    that our eyes may stream with tears
    and our eyelids be wet with weeping.
19 The sound of lamenting is heard from Zion:
    'How fearful is our ruin! How great our shame!
    We have left our land, our houses have been
          overthrown.'
20 Listen, you women, to the words of the LORD,
    that your ears may catch what he says.
    Teach your daughters the lament;
    teach your neighbours this dirge:
21 'Death has climbed in through our windows
    and entered our palaces,
    cutting off the children in the street
    and the young men in the thoroughfare.'
22 Corpses will fall and lie like dung in the fields,
    like swathes behind the reaper with no one to
          gather them.

23 These are the words of the LORD:

    Let not the wise boast of their wisdom,
    nor the valiant of their valour;
    let not the wealthy boast of their wealth;
24 but if anyone must boast, let him boast of this:
    that he understands and acknowledges me.
    For I am the LORD, I show unfailing love,
    I do justice and right on the earth;
    for in these I take pleasure.
    This is the word of the LORD.

25 The time is coming, says the LORD, when I shall punish
all the circumcised; 26 Egypt and Judah and Edom, Ammon
and Moab, and all who live in the fringes of the desert, for
all alike, the nations and Israel, are uncircumcised in heart.

9:17 **Summon:** *so Gk; Heb. prefixes* Consider and.   9:21 **Death:**
or Plague. **in the thoroughfare:** *so Gk; Heb. adds* (22)Speak, thus the
saying of the LORD.   9:26 **who . . . desert:** *or* the dwellers in the
desert who clip the hair on their temples.

9 Over the mountains, break out in cries
    of lamentation,
  over the pasture lands, intone a dirge:
They are scorched, and no man crosses them,
  unheard is the bleat of the flock;
Birds of the air as well as beasts,
  all have fled, and are gone.
10 I will turn Jerusalem into a heap of ruins,
  a haunt of jackals;
The cities of Judah I will make into a waste,
  where no one dwells.

11 Who is so wise that he can understand this? Let him to
whom the mouth of the LORD has spoken make it known:

  Why is the land ravaged,
    scorched like a wasteland untraversed?

12 The LORD answered: Because they have abandoned my
law, which I set before them, and have not followed it or
listened to my voice, 13 but followed rather the hardness of
their hearts and the Baals, as their fathers had taught them;
14 therefore, thus says the LORD of hosts, the God of Israel:
See now, I will give them wormwood to eat and poison to
drink. 15 I will scatter them among nations whom neither
they nor their fathers have known; I will send the sword to
pursue them until I have completely destroyed them.

16   Thus says the LORD of hosts:
  Attention! tell the wailing women to come,
    summon the best of them;
17 Let them come quickly
    and intone a dirge for us,
  That our eyes may be wet with weeping,
    our cheeks run with tears.
18 The dirge is heard from Zion:
    Ruined we are, and greatly ashamed;
  We must leave the land,
    give up our homes!
19 Hear, you women, the word of the LORD,
    let your ears receive his message.
  Teach your daughters this dirge,
    and each other this lament.
20 Death has come up through our windows,
    has entered our palaces;
  It cuts down the children in the street,
    young people in the squares.
21 The corpses of the slain
    lie like dung on a field,
  Like sheaves behind the harvester,
    with no one to gather them.

22   Thus says the LORD:
  Let not the wise man glory in his wisdom,
    nor the strong man glory in his strength,
    nor the rich man glory in his riches;
23 But rather, let him who glories, glory in this,
    that in his prudence he knows me,
  Knows that I, the LORD, bring about kindness,
    justice and uprightness on the earth;
  For with such am I pleased, says the LORD.

24 See, days are coming, says the LORD, when I will
demand an account of all those circumcised in their flesh:
25 Egypt and Judah, Edom and the Ammonites, Moab and
the desert dwellers who shave their temples. For all these
nations, like the whole house of Israel, are uncircumcised in
heart.

9 I raise the wail and lament for the mountains,
  the dirge for the desert pastures,
for they have been burnt: no one passes there,
  the sound of flocks is heard no more.
Birds of the sky and animals,
  all have fled, all are gone.
10 I shall make Jerusalem a heap of ruins,
  a lair for jackals,
and the towns of Judah
  an uninhabited wasteland.

11 Who is wise enough to understand this? To whom has
Yahweh's mouth spoken to explain it?

  Why is the country annihilated,
    burnt like the desert where no one passes?

12 Yahweh says, 'This is because they have forsaken my
Law which I gave them and have not listened to my voice
or followed it, 13 but have followed their own stubborn
hearts, have followed the Baals as their ancestors taught
them.' 14 So Yahweh Sabaoth, the God of Israel, says this,
'Now I shall give this people wormwood to eat and poisoned water to drink. s 15 I shall scatter them among nations
unknown to their ancestors or to them; and I shall pursue
them with the sword until I have annihilated them.'

16 Yahweh Sabaoth says this,
  'Prepare to call for the mourning women!
    Send for those who are best at it!
17 Let them lose no time in raising the lament over
    us!
  Let our eyes rain tears,
    our eyelids run with weeping!
18 A lament makes itself heard in Zion,
    "What ruin is ours,
  what utter shame!
  For we must leave the country,
    our homes have been knocked down!" '
19 Now listen, you women, to Yahweh's word,
    let your ears take in the word his own mouth
      speaks.
  Teach your daughters how to wail
    and teach one another this dirge,
20 'Death has climbed in at our windows,
    and made its way into our palaces;
  it has cut down the children in the street,
    the young people in the squares —
21 Speak! Yahweh declares this —
    human corpses are strewn
  like dung in the open field,
  like sheaves left by the reaper,
    with no one to gather them.'
22 Yahweh says this,
  'Let the sage not boast of wisdom,
    nor the valiant of valour,
    nor the wealthy of riches!
23 But let anyone who wants to boast, boast of this:
    of understanding and knowing me.
  For I am Yahweh, who acts with faithful love,
    justice, and uprightness on earth;
    yes, these are what please me,'
      Yahweh declares.

24 'Look, the days are coming, Yahweh declares, when I
shall punish all who are circumcised only in the flesh:
25 Egypt, Judah, Edom, the Ammonites, Moab, and all the
men with shaven temples who live in the desert. For all
those nations, and the whole House of Israel too, are uncircumcised at heart.'

s 9 = 23:15.

NEW REVISED STANDARD VERSION

10 Hear the word that the LORD speaks to you, O house of Israel. 2 Thus says the LORD:

Do not learn the way of the nations,
  or be dismayed at the signs of the heavens;
  for the nations are dismayed at them.
3 For the customs of the peoples are false:
a tree from the forest is cut down,
  and worked with an ax by the hands of an
    artisan;
4 people deck it with silver and gold;
  they fasten it with hammer and nails
  so that it cannot move.
5 Their idols*m* are like scarecrows in a cucumber
    field,
  and they cannot speak;
they have to be carried,
  for they cannot walk.
Do not be afraid of them,
  for they cannot do evil,
  nor is it in them to do good.
6 There is none like you, O LORD;
  you are great, and your name is great in might.
7 Who would not fear you, O King of the nations?
  For that is your due;
among all the wise ones of the nations
  and in all their kingdoms
  there is no one like you.
8 They are both stupid and foolish;
  the instruction given by idols
  is no better than wood!*n*
9 Beaten silver is brought from Tarshish,
  and gold from Uphaz.
They are the work of the artisan and of the hands
    of the goldsmith;
  their clothing is blue and purple;
  they are all the product of skilled workers.
10 But the LORD is the true God;
  he is the living God and the everlasting King.
At his wrath the earth quakes,
  and the nations cannot endure his indignation.

11 Thus shall you say to them: The gods who did not make the heavens and the earth shall perish from the earth and from under the heavens.*o*

12 It is he who made the earth by his power,
  who established the world by his wisdom,
  and by his understanding stretched out the
    heavens.
13 When he utters his voice, there is a tumult of
    waters in the heavens,
  and he makes the mist rise from the ends of
    the earth.
He makes lightnings for the rain,
  and he brings out the wind from his
    storehouses.
14 Everyone is stupid and without knowledge;
  goldsmiths are all put to shame by their idols;
for their images are false,
  and there is no breath in them.
15 They are worthless, a work of delusion;
  at the time of their punishment they shall
    perish.

REVISED ENGLISH BIBLE

10 Listen, Israel, to these words that the LORD has spoken against you:

2 Do not fall into the ways of the nations,
  do not be terrified by signs in the heavens.
  It is the nations who go in terror of these.
3 For the carved images of the nations are a sham;
  they are nothing but timber cut from the forest,
  shaped by a craftsman with his chisel
4 and decorated with silver and gold.
  They are made fast with hammer and nails
  to keep them from toppling over.
5 They are as dumb as a scarecrow in a plot of
    cucumbers;
  they have always to be carried,
  for they cannot walk.
Do not be afraid of them: they can do no harm,
  nor have they any power to do good.

6 Where can one be found like you, LORD?
  You are great, and great is the might of your
    name.
7 Who would not fear you, King of the nations,
  for fear is a fitting tribute for you?
Where among the wisest of the nations
  and among all their royalty
  can any be found like you?
8 One and all they are stupid and foolish,
  learning their nonsense from a piece of wood.
9 Beaten silver is brought from Tarshish
  and gold from Ophir;
  they are the work of craftsmen and goldsmiths;
  they are draped in violet and purple,
  all made by skilled workers.
10 But the LORD is God in truth,
  a living God, an everlasting King.
The earth quakes under his fury;
  no nation can endure his wrath.

11 You say this of them: The gods who did not make heaven and earth will perish from the earth and from under these heavens.

12 God made the earth by his power,
  fixed the world in place by his wisdom,
  and by his knowledge unfurled the skies.
13 When he speaks in the thunder
  the waters in the heavens are in tumult;
  he brings up the mist from the ends of the earth,
  he opens rifts for the rain,
  and brings the wind out of his storehouses.
14 Everyone is brutish and ignorant;
  every goldsmith is discredited through his idols;
  for the figures he casts are a sham,
  there is no breath in them.
15 They are worthless, objects of mockery,
  which perish when their day of reckoning comes.

---

m Heb *They* *n* Meaning of Heb uncertain *o* This verse is in Aramaic

10:9 **Ophir:** *so Syriac; Heb.* Uphaz. 10:11 *This verse is in* Aramaic. 10:13 **When . . . thunder:** *prob. rdg; Heb. obscure.* **rifts:** *prob. rdg; Heb.* lightnings.

10 Hear the word which the LORD speaks to you, O house of Israel. ²Thus says the LORD:

Learn not the customs of the nations,
  and have no fear of the signs of the heavens,
  though the nations fear them.
³For the cult idols of the nations are nothing,
  wood cut from the forest,
Wrought by craftsmen with the adze,
⁴ adorned with silver and gold.
With nails and hammers they are fastened,
  that they may not totter.
⁵Like a scarecrow in a cucumber field are they,
  they cannot speak;
They must be carried about,
  for they cannot walk.
Fear them not, they can do no harm,
  neither is it in their power to do good.
⁶No one is like you, O LORD,
  great are you,
  great and mighty is your name.
⁷Who would not fear you,
  King of the nations,
  for it is your due!

Among all the wisest of the nations,
  and in all their domain,
  there is none like you.

⁸One and all they are dumb and senseless,
  these idols they teach about are wooden:
⁹Silver strips brought from Tarshish,
  and gold from Ophir,
The work of the craftsman
  and the handiwork of the smelter,
Clothed with violet and purple—
  all of them the work of artisans.

¹¹Thus shall you say of them: Let the gods that did not make heaven and earth perish from the earth, and from beneath these heavens!

¹⁰The LORD is true God,
  he is the living God, the eternal King,
Before whose anger the earth quakes,
  whose wrath the nations cannot endure:
¹²He who made the earth by his power,
  established the world by his wisdom,
  and stretched out the heavens by his skill.
¹³When he thunders, the waters in the heavens roar,
  and he brings up clouds from the end of
  the earth;
He makes the lightning flash in the rain,
  and releases stormwinds from their chambers.
¹⁴Every man is stupid, ignorant;
  every artisan is put to shame by his idol:
He has molded a fraud,
  without breath of life.
¹⁵Nothingness are they, a ridiculous work;
  they will perish in their time of punishment.

10 Listen, House of Israel, to the word that Yahweh addresses to you. Yahweh says this:

²'Do not learn the ways of the nations
  or take alarm at the heavenly signs,
  alarmed though the nations may be at them.
³Yes, the customs of the peoples are quite futile:
  wood, nothing more, cut out of a forest,
  worked with a blade by a carver's hand,
⁴then embellished with silver and gold,
  then fastened with hammer and nails
  to keep it from moving.
⁵Like scarecrows in a melon patch, they cannot talk,
  they have to be carried, since they cannot walk.
  Have no fear of them: they can do no harm
  —nor any good either!'
⁶Yahweh, there is no one like you,
  so great you are,
  so great your mighty name.
⁷Who would not revere you, King of nations?
  Yes, this is your due.
Since of all the wise among the nations,
  and in all their kingdoms,
  there is not a single one like you.

⁸All of them are brutish and stupid:
  the Futile Ones' teaching is but wood,
⁹silver leaf imported from Tarshish
  and gold from Ophir,
  the work of carver or goldsmith;
  then dressed up in violet and purple,
  all the work of skilled men.
¹⁰But Yahweh is the true God.
  He is the living God,
  the everlasting King.
The earth quakes when he is wrathful,
  the nations cannot endure his fury.

¹¹'Tell them this, "The gods who did not make the heavens and the earth will vanish from the earth and from under these heavens."'

¹²By his power he made the earth,
  by his wisdom set the world firm,
  but his discernment spread out the heavens.
¹³When he thunders
  there is a roaring of waters in heaven;
  he raises clouds from the remotest parts of the earth,
  makes the lightning flash for the downpour,
  and brings the wind from his storehouse.
¹⁴At this all people stand stupefied, uncomprehending,
  every goldsmith blushes for his idols;
  his castings are but delusion,
  with no breath in them.
¹⁵They are futile, a laughable production;
  when the time comes for them to be punished, they will vanish.

NEW REVISED STANDARD VERSION

16 Not like these is the LORD,*p* the portion of
Jacob,
for he is the one who formed all things,
and Israel is the tribe of his inheritance;
the LORD of hosts is his name.

17 Gather up your bundle from the ground,
O you who live under siege!

18 For thus says the LORD:
I am going to sling out the inhabitants of the land
at this time,
and I will bring distress on them,
so that they shall feel it.

19 Woe is me because of my hurt!
My wound is severe.
But I said, "Truly this is my punishment,
and I must bear it."

20 My tent is destroyed,
and all my cords are broken;
my children have gone from me,
and they are no more;
there is no one to spread my tent again,
and to set up my curtains.

21 For the shepherds are stupid,
and do not inquire of the LORD;
therefore they have not prospered,
and all their flock is scattered.

22 Hear, a noise! Listen, it is coming —
a great commotion from the land of the north
to make the cities of Judah a desolation,
a lair of jackals.

23 I know, O LORD, that the way of human beings
is not in their control,
that mortals as they walk cannot direct their
steps.

24 Correct me, O LORD, but in just measure;
not in your anger, or you will bring me to
nothing.

25 Pour out your wrath on the nations that do not
know you,
and on the peoples that do not call on your
name;
for they have devoured Jacob;
they have devoured him and consumed him,
and have laid waste his habitation.

11 The word that came to Jeremiah from the LORD:
2 Hear the words of this covenant, and speak to the
people of Judah and the inhabitants of Jerusalem. 3 You
shall say to them, Thus says the LORD, the God of Israel:
Cursed be anyone who does not heed the words of this
covenant, 4 which I commanded your ancestors when I
brought them out of the land of Egypt, from the iron-
smelter, saying, Listen to my voice, and do all that I command you. So shall you be my people, and I will be your
God, 5 that I may perform the oath that I swore to your
ancestors, to give them a land flowing with milk and honey,
as at this day. Then I answered, "So be it, LORD."

6 And the LORD said to me: Proclaim all these words in
the cities of Judah, and in the streets of Jerusalem: Hear the
words of this covenant and do them. 7 For I solemnly
warned your ancestors when I brought them up out of the
land of Egypt, warning them persistently, even to this day,
saying, Obey my voice. 8 Yet they did not obey or incline

REVISED ENGLISH BIBLE

16 Jacob's chosen God is not like these,
for he is the creator of the universe.
Israel is the people he claims as his own;
the LORD of Hosts is his name.

17 Gather up your goods and flee the country,
for you are living under siege.

18 These are the words of the LORD:
This time I shall throw out
the whole population of the land,
and I shall press them and squeeze them dry.

19 Oh, the pain of my wounds!
The injuries I suffer are cruel.
'I am laid low,' I said, 'and must endure it.'

20 My tent is wrecked, my tent-ropes all severed,
my children have left me and are gone,
there is no one left to pitch my tent again,
no one to put up its curtains.'

21 The shepherds of the people are brutish;
they never consult the LORD,
and so they do not act wisely,
and their entire flock is scattered.

22 Listen, a rumour comes flying,
a great uproar from the land of the north,
an army to make Judah's cities desolate, a haunt of
wolves.

23 I am aware, LORD,
that no one's ways are of his own choosing;
nor is it within his power
to determine his course in life.

24 Correct me, LORD, but with justice, not in anger,
or you will bring me almost to nothing.

25 Pour out your fury on the nations
that have not acknowledged you,
on tribes that have not invoked you by name;
for they have devoured Jacob
and made an end of him
and have left his home a waste.

11 THE word which came to Jeremiah from the LORD:
2 Listen to the terms of this covenant and repeat
them to the inhabitants of Judah and the citizens of Jerusalem, 3 telling them: These are the words of the LORD the
God of Israel: A curse on everyone who does not observe
the terms of this covenant 4 which I enjoined on your forefathers when I brought them out of Egypt, from the smelting
furnace. I said: If you obey me and do all that I command,
you will become my people and I shall become your God.
5 I shall thus make good the oath I swore to your forefathers,
that I would give them a land flowing with milk and honey,
the land you now possess.

I answered, 'Amen, LORD.'

6 Then the LORD said: Proclaim these terms throughout
the towns of Judah and in the streets of Jerusalem. Say:
Listen to the terms of this covenant and carry them out. 7 I
gave solemn warning to your forefathers, from the time
when I brought them out of Egypt till this day; I was at pains
to warn them: Obey me, I said. 8 But they did not obey; they

---

p Heb lacks the LORD

10:25 **for . . . Jacob:** *so some MSS; others add* and they will devour
him.

16 Not like these is the portion of Jacob:
   he is the creator of all things;
Israel is his very own tribe,
   LORD of hosts is his name.

17 Lift your bundle and leave the land,
   O city living in a state of siege!
18   For thus says the LORD:
Behold, this time
   I will sling away the inhabitants of the land;
I will hem them in,
   that they may be taken.
19 Woe is me! I am undone,
   my wound is incurable;
Yet I had thought:
   if I make light of my wound, I can bear it.
20 My tent is ruined,
   all its cords are severed.
My sons have left me, they are no more:
   no one to pitch my tent,
   no one to raise its curtains.
21 Yes, the shepherds were stupid as cattle,
   the LORD they sought not;
Therefore they had no success,
   and all their flocks were scattered.
22 Listen! a noise! it comes closer,
   a great uproar from the northern land:
To turn the cities of Judah
   into a desert haunt of jackals.

23 You know, O LORD,
   that man is not master of his way;
Man's course is not within his choice,
   nor is it for him to direct his step.
24 Punish us, O LORD, but with equity,
   not in anger, lest you have us dwindle away.
25 Pour out your wrath on the nations that know
      you not,
   on the tribes that call not upon your name;
For they have devoured Jacob utterly,
   and laid waste his dwelling.

11 The following message came to Jeremiah from the LORD: 2 Speak to the men of Judah and to the citizens of Jerusalem, 3 saying to them: Thus says the LORD, the God of Israel: Cursed be the man who does not observe the terms of this covenant, 4 which I enjoined upon your fathers the day I brought them up out of the land of Egypt, that iron foundry, saying: Listen to my voice and do all that I command you. Then you shall be my people, and I will be your God. 5 Thus I will fulfill the oath which I swore to your fathers, to give them a land flowing with milk and honey: the one you have today. "Amen, LORD," I answered.
6 Then the LORD said to me: Proclaim all these words in the cities of Judah and in the streets of Jerusalem: Hear the words of this covenant and obey them. 7 Urgently and constantly I warned your fathers to obey my voice, from the day I brought them up out of the land of Egypt even to this day. 8 But they did not listen or give ear. Each one followed

16 The Heritage of Jacob is not like these,
   for he is the maker of everything,
and Israel is the tribe that is his heritage.
   His name is Yahweh Sabaoth. *r*

17 Pick up your pack from the ground,
   you the besieged!
18 For Yahweh says this,
   'Now I shall throw out
   the inhabitants of the country,
   this time,
and bring distress on them,
   so that they may find me!'
19 Disaster is on me! What a wound!
   My injury is incurable!
And I used to think,
   'If this is the worst, I can bear it!'
20 But now my tent is destroyed,
   all my ropes are snapped,
my sons have left me and are no more;
   no one is left to put my tent up again
   or to hang the side-cloths.
21 The shepherds are the ones who have been stupid:
   they have not searched for Yahweh.
This is why they have not prospered
   and why their whole flock has been dispersed.
22 Listen! A terrible noise!
   A mighty uproar from the land of the north
to reduce the towns of Judah
   to desert, to a lair for jackals!

23 I know, Yahweh,
   no one's course is in his control,
nor is it in anyone's power, as he goes his way,
   to guide his own steps.
24 Correct me, Yahweh, but with moderation,
   not in your anger, or you will reduce me to
      nothing.

25 Pour out your anger on the nations
   who do not acknowledge you,
and on the families
   that do not call on your name,
for they have devoured Jacob,
   have devoured and made an end of him
   and reduced his home to desolation.

11 The word that came to Jeremiah from Yahweh, 2 'Hear the terms of this covenant; tell them to the people of Judah and to the inhabitants of Jerusalem. 3 Tell them, "Yahweh, God of Israel, says this: Cursed be anyone who will not listen to the terms of this covenant 4 which I ordained for your ancestors when I brought them out of Egypt, out of that iron-foundry. Listen to my voice, I told them, carry out all my orders, then you will be my people and I shall be your God, 5 so that I may fulfil the oath I swore to your ancestors, that I may give them a country flowing with milk and honey, as is the case today." ' I replied, 'So be it, Yahweh!' 6 Then Yahweh said to me, 'Proclaim all these terms in the towns of Judah and in the streets of Jerusalem, saying, "Listen to the terms of this covenant and obey them. 7 For when I brought your ancestors out of Egypt, I solemnly warned them, and have persistently warned them until today, saying: Listen to my voice. 8 But they did not listen, did not pay attention; instead, each

NEW REVISED STANDARD VERSION

their ear, but everyone walked in the stubbornness of an evil will. So I brought upon them all the words of this covenant, which I commanded them to do, but they did not.

9 And the LORD said to me: Conspiracy exists among the people of Judah and the inhabitants of Jerusalem. 10 They have turned back to the iniquities of their ancestors of old, who refused to heed my words; they have gone after other gods to serve them; the house of Israel and the house of Judah have broken the covenant that I made with their ancestors. 11 Therefore, thus says the LORD, assuredly I am going to bring disaster upon them that they cannot escape; though they cry out to me, I will not listen to them. 12 Then the cities of Judah and the inhabitants of Jerusalem will go and cry out to the gods to whom they make offerings, but they will never save them in the time of their trouble. 13 For your gods have become as many as your towns, O Judah; and as many as the streets of Jerusalem are the altars you have set up to shame, altars to make offerings to Baal.

14 As for you, do not pray for this people, or lift up a cry or prayer on their behalf, for I will not listen when they call to me in the time of their trouble. 15 What right has my beloved in my house, when she has done vile deeds? Can vows*q* and sacrificial flesh avert your doom? Can you then exult? 16 The LORD once called you, "A green olive tree, fair with goodly fruit"; but with the roar of a great tempest he will set fire to it, and its branches will be consumed. 17 The LORD of hosts, who planted you, has pronounced evil against you, because of the evil that the house of Israel and the house of Judah have done, provoking me to anger by making offerings to Baal.

18 It was the LORD who made it known to me, and I knew;
    then you showed me their evil deeds.
19 But I was like a gentle lamb
    led to the slaughter.
And I did not know it was against me
    that they devised schemes, saying,
"Let us destroy the tree with its fruit,
    let us cut him off from the land of the living,
    so that his name will no longer be
      remembered!"
20 But you, O LORD of hosts, who judge
    righteously,
who try the heart and the mind,
let me see your retribution upon them,
    for to you I have committed my cause.

21 Therefore thus says the LORD concerning the people of Anathoth, who seek your life, and say, "You shall not prophesy in the name of the LORD, or you will die by our hand"— 22 therefore thus says the LORD of hosts: I am going to punish them; the young men shall die by the sword; their sons and their daughters shall die by famine; 23 and not even a remnant shall be left of them. For I will bring disaster upon the people of Anathoth, the year of their punishment.

12 You will be in the right, O LORD,
    when I lay charges against you;
    but let me put my case to you.
Why does the way of the guilty prosper?
    Why do all who are treacherous thrive?

REVISED ENGLISH BIBLE

paid no attention to me, and each followed the promptings of his own stubborn and wicked heart. So I brought on them all the penalties laid down in this covenant which I had enjoined upon them, but whose terms they did not observe.

9 The LORD said to me: The inhabitants of Judah and the citizens of Jerusalem have entered into a conspiracy; 10 they have gone back to the sins of their earliest forefathers and refused to listen to me. They have followed other gods and served them; Israel and Judah have broken the covenant which I made with their forefathers. 11 Therefore these are the words of the LORD: I am about to bring on them a disaster from which they cannot escape. They may cry to me for help, but I shall not listen. 12 The inhabitants of the towns of Judah and of Jerusalem may go and cry for help to the gods to whom they have burnt sacrifices, but assuredly they will not save them in the hour of disaster. 13 For you, Judah, have as many gods as you have towns; you have set up as many altars to burn sacrifices to Baal as there are streets in Jerusalem. 14 So, Jeremiah, offer up no prayer for this people; raise no plea or prayer on their behalf, for I shall not listen when they call to me in the hour of their disaster.

15 What right has my beloved in my house
    with her shameless ways?
Can the flesh of fat offerings on the altar
    ward off the disaster that threatens you?
    Now you will feel sharp anguish.
16 Once the LORD called you an olive tree,
    leafy and fair;
with a great roaring noise
    he has set it on fire
    and its branches are consumed.

17 The LORD of Hosts who planted you has threatened you with disaster, because of the evil which Israel and Judah have done, provoking him to anger by burning sacrifices to Baal.

18 It was the LORD who showed me, and so I knew; he opened my eyes to what they were doing. 19 I had been like a pet lamb led trustingly to the slaughter; I did not realize they were hatching plots against me and saying, 'Let us destroy the tree while the sap is in it; let us cut him off from the land of the living, so that his name will be wholly forgotten.'

20 LORD of Hosts, most righteous judge,
    testing the heart and mind,
to you I have committed my cause;
    let me see your vengeance on them.

21 Therefore these are the words of the LORD about the men of Anathoth who seek to take your life, and say, 'Prophesy no more in the name of the LORD or we shall kill you'— 22 these are his words: I am about to punish them: their young men shall die by the sword, their sons and daughters by famine. 23 Not one of them will survive; for in the year of reckoning for them I shall bring disaster on the people of Anathoth.

12 LORD, even if I dispute with you, you remain in the right;
    yet I shall plead my case before you.
Why do the wicked prosper
    and the treacherous all live at ease?

11:13 **altars:** *so Gk; Heb. adds* altars to the shameful thing.
11:15 **fat offerings:** *so Old Latin; Heb.* the many.   11:16 **fair:** *so Gk; Heb. adds* the fruit of.

q Gk: Heb *Can many*

the hardness of his evil heart, till I brought upon them all the threats of this covenant which they had failed to observe as I commanded them.

9 A conspiracy has been found, the LORD said to me, among the men of Judah and the citizens of Jerusalem. 10 They have returned to the crimes of their forefathers who refused to obey my words. They also have followed and served strange gods; the covenant which I had made with their fathers, the house of Israel and the house of Judah have broken. 11 Therefore, thus says the LORD: See, I bring upon them misfortune which they cannot escape. Though they cry out to me, I will not listen to them. 12 Then the cities of Judah and the citizens of Jerusalem will go and cry out to the gods to which they have been offering incense. But these gods will give them no help whatever when misfortune strikes.

13 For as numerous as your cities
    are your gods, O Judah!
And as many as the streets of Jerusalem
    are the altars for offering sacrifice to Baal.

14 Do not intercede on behalf of this people, nor utter a plea for them. I will not listen when they call to me at the time of their misfortune.

15 What right has my beloved in my house,
    while she prepares her plots?
Can vows and sacred meat turn away
    your misfortune from you?
Will you still be jubilant
16   when you hear the great invasion?
A spreading olive tree, goodly to behold,
    the LORD has named you;
Now he sets fire to it,
    its branches burn.

17 The LORD of hosts who planted you has decreed misfortune for you because of the evil done by the house of Israel and by the house of Judah, who provoked me by sacrificing to Baal.

18 I knew it because the LORD informed me; at that time you, O LORD, showed me their doings.

‡11.19–23: see below in ch.12‡

12 You would be in the right, O LORD,
    if I should dispute with you;
    even so, I must discuss the case with you.
Why does the way of the godless prosper,
    why live all the treacherous in contentment?

followed his own stubborn and wicked inclinations. And against them, in consequence, I put into action the words of this covenant which I had ordered them to obey and which they had not obeyed." '

9 Yahweh said to me, 'Plainly there is conspiracy among the people of Judah and the citizens of Jerusalem. 10 They have reverted to the sins of their ancestors who refused to listen to my words: they too are following other gods and serving them. The House of Israel and the House of Judah have broken my covenant which I made with their ancestors. 11 And so, Yahweh says this, "I shall now bring a disaster on them which they cannot escape; they will call to me for help, but I shall not listen to them. 12 The towns of Judah and the citizens of Jerusalem will then go and call for help to the gods to whom they burn incense, but these will be no help at all to them in their time of distress!

13 "For you have as many gods
    as you have towns, Judah![u]
You have built as many altars to Shame,
    as many incense altars to Baal,
    as Jerusalem has streets!

14 "You, for your part, must not intercede for this people, nor raise either plea or prayer on their behalf, for I will not listen when their distress forces them to call to me for help."

15 'What is my beloved doing in my house?
    She has achieved her wicked plans.
Can vows and consecrated meat
    turn disaster from you
    for you to be so happy?
16 "Green olive-tree covered in fine fruit",
    was Yahweh's name for you.
With a shattering noise
    he has set fire to it,
    its branches are broken.'

17 And Yahweh Sabaoth, who planted you, has decreed disaster for you because of the evil the House of Israel and the House of Judah have done, provoking me by burning incense to Baal.

18 Yahweh informed me and I knew it; you then revealed their scheming to me. 19 I for my part was like a trustful lamb being led to the slaughterhouse, not knowing the schemes they were plotting against me, 'Let us destroy the tree in its strength, let us cut him off from the land of the living, so that his name may no longer be remembered!'

20 Yahweh Sabaoth, whose judgement is upright,
    tester of motives and thoughts,
I shall see your vengeance on them,
    for I have revealed my cause to you.[v]

21 Against the people of Anathoth who are determined to kill me and say to me, 'Do not prophesy in the name of Yahweh or you will die at our hands!' 22 Yahweh says this, 'I am about to punish them. Their young people will die by the sword, their sons and daughters by famine. 23 Not one will be left when I bring disaster on the people of Anathoth, when the year for punishing them comes.'

12 Your uprightness is too great, Yahweh,
    for me to dispute with you.
But I should like to discuss some points of justice
    with you:
Why is it that the way of the wicked prospers?
Why do all treacherous people thrive?

_u_ **11** = 2:28.   _v_ **11** = 20:12.

NEW REVISED STANDARD VERSION	REVISED ENGLISH BIBLE

NEW REVISED STANDARD VERSION

2 You plant them, and they take root;
  they grow and bring forth fruit;
you are near in their mouths
  yet far from their hearts.
3 But you, O LORD, know me;
  You see me and test me—my heart is with
    you.
Pull them out like sheep for the slaughter,
  and set them apart for the day of slaughter.
4 How long will the land mourn,
  and the grass of every field wither?
For the wickedness of those who live in it
  the animals and the birds are swept away,
  and because people said, "He is blind to our
    ways."*r*

5 If you have raced with foot-runners and they have
    wearied you,
  how will you compete with horses?
And if in a safe land you fall down,
  how will you fare in the thickets of the Jordan?
6 For even your kinsfolk and your own family,
  even they have dealt treacherously with you;
  they are in full cry after you;
do not believe them,
  though they speak friendly words to you.

7 I have forsaken my house,
  I have abandoned my heritage;
I have given the beloved of my heart
  into the hands of her enemies.
8 My heritage has become to me
  like a lion in the forest;
she has lifted up her voice against me—
  therefore I hate her.
9 Is the hyena greedy*s* for my heritage at my
    command?
  Are the birds of prey all around her?
Go, assemble all the wild animals;
  bring them to devour her.
10 Many shepherds have destroyed my vineyard,
  they have trampled down my portion,
they have made my pleasant portion
  a desolate wilderness.
11 They have made it a desolation;
  desolate, it mourns to me.
The whole land is made desolate,
  but no one lays it to heart.
12 Upon all the bare heights*t* in the desert
  spoilers have come;
for the sword of the LORD devours
  from one end of the land to the other;
  no one shall be safe.
13 They have sown wheat and have reaped thorns,
  they have tired themselves out but profit
    nothing.
They shall be ashamed of their*u* harvests
  because of the fierce anger of the LORD.

REVISED ENGLISH BIBLE

2 You have planted them and their roots strike deep,
  they grow and bear fruit.
You are ever on their lips,
  yet far from their hearts.
3 But you know me, LORD, you see me;
  you test my devotion to you.
Drag them away like sheep to the shambles;
  set them apart for the day of slaughter.

4 How long must the country lie parched
  and all its green grass wither?
No birds and beasts are left, because its people are
    so wicked,
  because they say, 'God does not see what we are
    doing.'

5 If you have raced with men running on foot
  and they have worn you down,
how then can you hope to compete with horses?
If in easy country you fall headlong,
  how will you fare in Jordan's dense thickets?
6 Even your brothers and kinsmen deal treacherously
    with you,
  they are in full cry after you;
do not trust them, for all the fair words they use.

7 I have abandoned the house of Israel,
  I have cast off my own people.
I have given my beloved
  into the power of her foes.
8 My own people have turned on me
  like lions from the jungle;
they roar against me,
  therefore I hate them.
9 Is this land of mine a hyena's lair,
  with birds of prey hovering all around it?
Come, all you wild beasts;
  come, flock to the feast.

10 Many shepherds have ravaged my vineyard
  and trampled down my portion of land,
they have made my pleasant portion a desolate
    wilderness.
11 they have made it a desolation, to my sorrow.
  The whole land is desolate, but no one pays heed.

12 Plunderers have swarmed across the open regions of the
wilderness; a sword of the LORD devours the land from end
to end; there is no peace for any living thing.

13 Men sow wheat and reap thistles;
  they sift but get no grain.
Their harvest is a disappointment to them
  because of the fierce anger of the LORD.

---

r Gk: Heb *to our future*   *s* Cn: Heb *Is the hyena, the bird of prey*
t Or *the trails*   *u* Heb *your*

12:4 **what we are doing:** *so Gk; Heb.* our latter end.   12:9 **come:**
so some MSS; others bring.   12:13 **Their:** *prob. rdg; Heb.* Your.

| NEW AMERICAN BIBLE | NEW JERUSALEM BIBLE |

² You planted them; they have taken root,
  they keep on growing and bearing fruit.
You are upon their lips,
  but far from their inmost thoughts.
³ You, O Lord, know me, you see me,
  you have found that at heart I am with you.
Pick them out like sheep for the slaughter,
  set them apart for the day of carnage.
⁴ How long must the earth mourn,
  the green of the whole countryside wither?
For the wickedness of those who dwell in it
beasts and birds disappear,
  because they say, "God does not see our ways."

⁵ If running against men has wearied you,
  how will you race against horses?
And if in a land of peace you fall headlong,
  what will you do in the thickets of the Jordan?

⁶ For even your own brothers, the members of your father's
house, betray you; they have recruited a force against you.
Do not believe them, even if they are friendly to you in their
words.

¹¹·¹⁹ Yet I, like a trusting lamb led to slaughter, had not
realized that they were hatching plots against me: "Let us
destroy the tree in its vigor; let us cut him off from the land
of the living, so that his name will be spoken no more."
¹¹·²⁰ But, you, O Lord of hosts, O just Judge,
  searcher of mind and heart,
Let me witness the vengeance you take on them,
  for to you I have entrusted my cause!
¹¹·²¹ Therefore, thus says the Lord concerning the men
of Anathoth who seek your life, saying, "Do not prophesy
in the name of the Lord; else you shall die by our hand."
¹¹·²² Therefore, thus says the Lord of hosts: I am going to
punish them. The young men shall die by the sword; their
sons and daughters shall die by famine. ¹¹·²³ None shall
be spared among them, for I will bring misfortune upon
the men of Anathoth, the year of their punishment.

⁷ I abandon my house,
  cast off my heritage;
The beloved of my soul I deliver
  into the hand of her foes.
⁸ My heritage has turned on me
  like a lion in the jungle;
Because she has roared against me,
  I treat her as an enemy.
⁹ My heritage is a prey for hyenas,
  is surrounded by vultures;
Come, gather together, all you beasts of the field,
  come and eat!
¹⁰ Many shepherds have ravaged my vineyard,
  have trodden my heritage underfoot;
The portion that delighted me they have turned
  into a desert waste.
¹¹ They have made it a mournful waste,
  desolate it lies before me,
Desolate, all the land,
  because no one takes it to heart.
¹² Upon every desert height
  brigands have come up.
The Lord has a sword which consumes
  the land, from end to end:
  no peace for all mankind.
¹³ They have sown wheat and reaped thorns,
  they have tired themselves out to no purpose;
They recoil before their harvest,
  the flaming anger of the Lord.

² You plant them, they take root,
  they flourish, yes, and bear fruit.
You are on their lips,
  yet far from their heart.
³ You know me, Yahweh, you see me,
  you probe my heart, which is close to yours.
Drag them off like sheep for the slaughterhouse,
  reserve them for the day of butchery.

⁴ (How long will the land be in mourning, and the grass
wither all over the countryside? The animals and birds are
dying as a result of the wickedness of the inhabitants.)

For they say,
  'God does not see our fate.'
⁵ 'If you find it exhausting to race against me on
    foot,
  how will you compete against horses?
In a country at peace you feel secure,
  but how will you fare in the thickets of the Jordan?

⁶ 'For even your brothers and your own family will betray
you. They will pursue you in full cry. Put no faith in them
when they speak you fair!'

⁷ I have abandoned my house,
  left my heritage,
I have delivered what I dearly loved
  into the clutches of its enemies.
⁸ To me, my heritage has behaved
  like a lion in the forest,
  it roared at me ferociously:
  so I now hate it.
⁹ I see my heritage as a brightly-coloured bird of
    prey
  attacked by birds of prey on every side!
Go, assemble all the wild animals,
  make them come and dine!
¹⁰ Many shepherds have laid my vineyard waste,
  have trampled over my plot of land,
  the plot of land which was my joy,
  reducing my favourite estate
  to a deserted wilderness.
¹¹ They have made it a waste;
  wasted, it mourns before me.
The whole country has been devastated
  and no one takes it to heart.
¹² The devastators have arrived
  on all the bare heights of the desert
  (for Yahweh wields a devouring sword);
  from one end of the country to the other,
  there is no peace for any living thing.
¹³ Wheat they have sown, thorns they reap:
  they have worn themselves out, to no profit.
They are disappointed in their harvests,
  because of Yahweh's burning anger.

11, 19–23: These verses have been transposed from ch 11.

14 Thus says the LORD concerning all my evil neighbors who touch the heritage that I have given my people Israel to inherit: I am about to pluck them up from their land, and I will pluck up the house of Judah from among them. 15 And after I have plucked them up, I will again have compassion on them, and I will bring them again to their heritage and to their land, everyone of them. 16 And then, if they will diligently learn the ways of my people, to swear by my name, "As the LORD lives," as they taught my people to swear by Baal, then they shall be built up in the midst of my people. 17 But if any nation will not listen, then I will completely uproot it and destroy it, says the LORD.

13 Thus said the LORD to me, "Go and buy yourself a linen loincloth, and put it on your loins, but do not dip it in water." 2 So I bought a loincloth according to the word of the LORD, and put it on my loins. 3 And the word of the LORD came to me a second time, saying, 4 "Take the loincloth that you bought and are wearing, and go now to the Euphrates,[v] and hide it there in a cleft of the rock." 5 So I went, and hid it by the Euphrates,[w] as the LORD commanded me. 6 And after many days the LORD said to me, "Go now to the Euphrates,[v] and take from there the loincloth that I commanded you to hide there." 7 Then I went to the Euphrates,[v] and dug, and I took the loincloth from the place where I had hidden it. But now the loincloth was ruined; it was good for nothing.

8 Then the word of the LORD came to me: 9 Thus says the LORD: Just so I will ruin the pride of Judah and the great pride of Jerusalem. 10 This evil people, who refuse to hear my words, who stubbornly follow their own will and have gone after other gods to serve them and worship them, shall be like this loincloth, which is good for nothing. 11 For as the loincloth clings to one's loins, so I made the whole house of Israel and the whole house of Judah cling to me, says the LORD, in order that they might be for me a people, a name, a praise, and a glory. But they would not listen.

12 You shall speak to them this word: Thus says the LORD, the God of Israel: Every wine-jar should be filled with wine. And they will say to you, "Do you think we do not know that every wine-jar should be filled with wine?" 13 Then you shall say to them: Thus says the LORD: I am about to fill all the inhabitants of this land—the kings who sit on David's throne, the priests, the prophets, and all the inhabitants of Jerusalem—with drunkenness. 14 And I will dash them one against another, parents and children together, says the LORD. I will not pity or spare or have compassion when I destroy them.

15 Hear and give ear; do not be haughty,
  for the LORD has spoken.
16 Give glory to the LORD your God
  before he brings darkness,
  and before your feet stumble
    on the mountains at twilight;
  while you look for light,
    he turns it into gloom
    and makes it deep darkness.
17 But if you will not listen,
    my soul will weep in secret for your pride;
  my eyes will weep bitterly and run down with
    tears,
  because the LORD's flock has been taken captive.

18 Say to the king and the queen mother;
    "Take a lowly seat,
  for your beautiful crown
    has come down from your head."[x]

14 These are the words of the LORD about all those evil neighbours who encroach on the land which I allotted to my people Israel as their holding: I shall uproot them from their own soil. Also I shall uproot Judah from among them; 15 but after I have uprooted them, I shall have pity on them again and bring each man back to his holding and land. 16 If they will learn the ways of my people, swearing by my name, 'by the life of the LORD', as they taught my people to swear by the Baal, they will establish families among my people. 17 But the nation that will not listen, I shall uproot and destroy. This is the word of the LORD.

13 These were the words of the LORD to me: Go and buy yourself a linen loincloth and wrap it round your body, but do not put it in water. 2 So I bought one as instructed by the LORD and wrapped it round me. 3 The LORD spoke to me a second time: 4 Take the loincloth which you bought and are wearing and go now to Perath, where you are to hide it in a crevice in the rocks. 5 I went and hid it at Perath, as the LORD had ordered me. 6 A long time afterwards the LORD said to me: Set out now for Perath and fetch the loincloth which I told you to hide there. 7 So I went to Perath and looked for the place where I had hidden it, but when I picked it up, I saw that it was ruined and no good for anything. 8 The LORD spoke to me: 9 Thus shall I ruin the enormous pride of Judah and Jerusalem. 10 This wicked people who refuse to listen to my words, who follow the promptings of their stubborn hearts and go after other gods to serve and worship them, will become like this loincloth, no good for anything. 11 Just as a loincloth is bound close to a man's body, so I bound all Israel and all Judah to myself, says the LORD, so that they should become my people to be a source of renown and praise and glory to me; but they did not listen.

12 You are to say this to them: These are the words of the LORD the God of Israel: Wine jars should be filled with wine. They will answer, 'We are well aware that wine jars should be filled with wine.' 13 Then say to them, These are the words of the LORD: I shall fill all the inhabitants of this land with wine until they are drunk—kings of David's line who sit on his throne, priests, prophets, and all who live in Jerusalem. 14 I shall dash them one against the other, fathers and sons together, says the LORD; I shall show them no compassion or pity or tenderness, nor refrain from destroying them.

15 Pay heed; be not too proud to listen,
  for it is the LORD who speaks.
16 Ascribe glory to the LORD your God
  before the darkness falls,
  before your feet stumble
    against the hillside in the twilight,
  before he turns the light you look for
    to deep gloom and thick darkness.
17 If in those depths you will not listen,
    then for very anguish I can only weep bitterly;
  my eyes must stream with tears,
  for the LORD's flock is carried off into captivity.
18 Say to the king and the queen mother:
    Take a humble seat,
  for your proud crowns are fallen from your heads.

---

[v] Or to Parah; Heb perath [w] Or by Parah; Heb perath [x] Gk Syr Vg: Meaning of Heb uncertain

13:17 **If . . . bitterly:** or If you will not listen to this, for very anguish I must weep in secret. 13:18 **from your heads:** so Gk; Heb. your pillows.

NEW AMERICAN BIBLE

14 Thus says the LORD against all my evil neighbors who plunder the heritage which I gave my people Israel as their own: See, I will pluck them up from their land; the house of Judah I will pluck up in their midst. 15 But after plucking them up, I will pity them again and bring them back, each to his heritage, each to his land. 16 And if they carefully learn my people's custom of swearing by my name, "As the LORD lives," they who formerly taught my people to swear by Baal shall be built up in the midst of my people. 17 But if they do not obey, I will uproot and destroy that nation entirely, says the LORD.

13 The LORD said to me: Go buy yourself a linen loin-cloth; wear it on your loins, but do not put it in water. 2 I bought the loincloth, as the LORD commanded, and put it on. 3 A second time the word of the LORD came to me thus: 4 Take the loincloth which you bought and are wearing, and go now to the Parath; there hide it in a cleft of the rock. 5 Obedient to the LORD's command, I went to the Parath and buried the loincloth. 6 After a long interval, he said to me: Go now to the Parath and fetch the loincloth which I told you to hide there. 7 Again I went to the Parath, sought out and took the loincloth from the place where I had hid it. But it was rotted, good for nothing! 8 Then the message came to me from the LORD: 9 Thus says the LORD: So also I will allow the pride of Judah to rot, the great pride of Jerusalem. 10 This wicked people who refuse to obey my words, who walk in the stubbornness of their hearts, and follow strange gods to serve and adore them, shall be like this loincloth which is good for nothing. 11 For, as close as the loincloth clings to a man's loins, so had I made the whole house of Israel and the whole house of Judah cling to me, says the LORD; to be my people, my renown, my praise, my beauty. But they did not listen.

12 Now speak to them this word: Thus says the LORD, the God of Israel: Every wineflask is meant to be filled with wine. If they reply, "Do we not know that every wineflask is meant to be filled with wine?" 13 say to them: Thus says the LORD: Beware! I am filling with drunkenness all the inhabitants of this land, the kings who succeed to David's throne, the priests and prophets, and all the citizens of Jerusalem. 14 I will dash them against each other, fathers and sons together, says the LORD; I will show no compassion, I will not spare or pity, but will destroy them.

15 Give ear, listen humbly,
  for the LORD speaks.
16 Give glory to the LORD, your God,
  before it grows dark;
Before your feet stumble
  on darkening mountains;
Before the light you look for turns to darkness,
  changes into black clouds.
17 If you do not listen to this in your pride,
  I will weep in secret many tears;
My eyes will run with tears
  for the LORD's flock, led away to exile.

18 Say to the king and to the queen mother:
  come down from your throne;
From your heads fall
  your magnificent crowns.

NEW JERUSALEM BIBLE

14 Yahweh says this, 'As regards all my evil neighbours who have laid hands on the heritage I granted my people Israel, look, I shall uproot them from their soil, (though I shall uproot the House of Judah from among them). 15 But having uprooted them, I shall take pity on them again and bring them back each to its own heritage, each to its own country, 16 and if they carefully learn my people's ways and swear by my name, "As Yahweh lives", as they have taught my people to swear by Baal, then they will be re-established among my people. 17 But if any nation refuses to listen, I shall uproot it for ever and destroy it, Yahweh declares.'

13 Yahweh said this to me, 'Go and buy a linen waist-cloth and put it round your waist. But do not dip it in water.' 2 And so, as Yahweh had ordered, I bought a waistcloth and put it round my waist. 3 A second time the word of Yahweh came to me, 4 'Take the waistcloth that you have bought and are wearing round your waist. Up, go to the Euphratesᵂ and hide it there in a hole in the rock.' 5 So I went and hid it by the Euphrates as Yahweh had ordered me. 6 A long time later, Yahweh said to me, 'Up, go to the Euphrates and fetch the waistcloth I ordered you to hide there.' 7 So I went to the Euphrates, and I searched, and I took the waistcloth from the place where I had hidden it. And there was the waistcloth ruined, no use for anything. 8 Then the word of Yahweh was addressed to me as follows, 9 'Yahweh says this, "In the same way I shall ruin the pride of Judah, the immense pride of Jerusalem. 10 This evil people, these people who refuse to listen to my words, who follow their own stubborn inclinations and run after other gods, serving and worshipping them — this people will become like this waistcloth, no good for anything. 11 For just as a waistcloth clings to a man's waist, so I made the whole House of Israel and the whole House of Judah cling to me, Yahweh declares, to be my people, my glory, my honour and my pride. But they have not listened."

12 'You will also say this to them, "Yahweh, God of Israel, says this: Any jug can be filled with wine." And if they answer you, "Do you think we do not know that any jug can be filled with wine?" 13 you are to say, "Yahweh says this: Look, I shall fill all the inhabitants of this country, the kings who occupy the throne of David, the priests, the prophets and all the citizens of Jerusalem, with drunkenness. 14 Then I shall smash them one against the other, parents and children all together, Yahweh declares. Mercilessly, relentlessly, pitilessly, I shall destroy them." '

15 Listen and pay attention, do not be proud:
  Yahweh is speaking!
16 Give glory to Yahweh your God
  before the darkness comes,
  before your feet stumble
  on the darkened mountains.
You hope for light,
  but he will turn it to shadow dark as death,
  will change it to blackness.
17 If you do not listen to this warning,
  I shall weep in secret for your pride;
  my eyes will weep bitterly
  and stream with tears,
  for Yahweh's flock is being led into captivity.

18 Tell the king and the queen mother,
  'Sit in a lower place,
  since your glorious crown
  has fallen from your head.

w 13 The Euphrates is probably symbolised by the river Parah near Jr's home.

19 The towns of the Negeb are shut up
  with no one to open them;
all Judah is taken into exile,
  wholly taken into exile.

20 Lift up your eyes and see
  those who come from the north.
Where is the flock that was given you,
  your beautiful flock?
21 What will you say when they set as head over
    you
  those whom you have trained
    to be your allies?
Will not pangs take hold of you,
  like those of a woman in labor?
22 And if you say in your heart,
  "Why have these things come upon me?"
it is for the greatness of your iniquity
  that your skirts are lifted up,
  and you are violated.
23 Can Ethiopians*y* change their skin
  or leopards their spots?
Then also you can do good
  who are accustomed to do evil.
24 I will scatter you*z* like chaff
  driven by the wind from the desert.
25 This is your lot,
  the portion I have measured out to you, says
    the LORD,
because you have forgotten me
  and trusted in lies.
26 I myself will lift up your skirts over your face,
  and your shame will be seen.
27 I have seen your abominations,
  your adulteries and neighings, your shameless
    prostitutions
on the hills of the countryside.
Woe to you, O Jerusalem!
  How long will it be
  before you are made clean?

14 The word of the LORD that came to Jeremiah concerning the drought:

2 Judah mourns
  and her gates languish;
they lie in gloom on the ground,
  and the cry of Jerusalem goes up.
3 Her nobles send their servants for water;
  they come to the cisterns,
they find no water,
  they return with their vessels empty.
They are ashamed and dismayed
  and cover their heads,
4 because the ground is cracked.
  Because there has been no rain on the land
the farmers are dismayed;
  they cover their heads.
5 Even the doe in the field forsakes her newborn
    fawn
  because there is no grass.
6 The wild asses stand on the bare heights,*a*
  they pant for air like jackals;
their eyes fail
  because there is no herbage.

7 Although our iniquities testify against us,
  act, O LORD, for your name's sake;
our apostasies indeed are many,
  and we have sinned against you.

19 The towns in the Negeb are besieged,
  and no one can relieve them;
all Judah has been swept into exile,
  swept clean away.
20 Look up and see
  those who are coming from the north.
Where is the flock that was entrusted to you,
  the sheep that were your pride?
21 What will you say when your leaders are missing,
  though trained by you to be your head?
Will not pangs seize you
  like the pangs of a woman in labour,
22 when you wonder,
  'Why has this happened to me'?
For your many sins your skirts are stripped off
    you,
  your limbs uncovered.
23 Can a Nubian change his skin,
  or a leopard its spots?
No more can you do good,
  you who are schooled in evil.
24 I shall scatter you like chaff
  before the desert wind.
25 This is your lot, your portion as a rebel,
  decreed by me, says the LORD,
because you have quite forgotten me
  and trusted in false gods.
26 So I myself have torn off your skirts
  and laid bare your shame:
27 your adulteries, your lustful neighing,
  your wanton lewdness.
On the hills and the open fields
  I have seen your foul deeds.
Woe to you, Jerusalem, in your uncleanness!
  How long will you delay?

14 This came to Jeremiah as the word of the LORD
  concerning the drought:

2 Judah droops, her towns languish,
  the inhabitants sit on the ground in mourning;
  and a crying goes up from Jerusalem.
3 Masters send their servants for water,
  but when they come to the pools they find none
    there,
  and go back with their vessels empty;
  disappointed and shamed, they uncover their heads.
4 Because the ground is cracked
  through lack of rain in the land,
the farmers' hopes are wrecked;
  they uncover their heads in grief.
5 The hind calves in the open country,
  and because there is no grass
  she abandons her young.
6 Wild asses stand on the bare heights
  and snuff the wind as wolves do,
  and their eyes begin to fail for lack of herbage.

7 Though our sins testify against us,
  yet take action, LORD, for your own name's sake.
Our disloyalties indeed are many;
  we have sinned against you.

13:21 **leaders:** *transposed from next line.*   13:24 **you:** *prob. rdg;*
Heb. them.   13:25 **rebel:** *prob. rdg, cp. Gk; Heb.* measures.
13:27 **How . . . delay?:** *prob. rdg; Heb.* unintelligible.
14:4 **Because . . . cracked:** *prob. rdg; Heb.* obscure.

y Or *Nubians;* Heb *Cushites*   *z* Heb *them*   *a* Or *the trails*

NEW AMERICAN BIBLE

19 The cities of the Negeb are besieged,
with no one to relieve them;
All Judah is banished
in universal exile.

20 Lift up your eyes and see
men coming from the north.
Where is the flock entrusted to you,
the sheep that were your glory?
21 What will you say when they place as rulers
over you
those whom you taught to be your lovers?
Will not pangs seize you
like those of a woman giving birth?
22 If you ask in your heart
why these things befall you:
For your great guilt your skirts are stripped away
and you are violated.
23 Can the Ethiopian change his skin?
the leopard his spots?
As easily would you be able to do good,
accustomed to evil as you are.
24 I will scatter them like chaff that flies
when the desert wind blows.
25 This is your lot, the portion measured out to you
from me, says the LORD.
Because you have forgotten me,
and trusted in the lying idol,
26 I now will strip off your skirts from you,
so that your shame will appear.
27 Your adulteries, your neighings,
your shameless prostitutions:
On the hills in the highlands
I see these horrible crimes of yours.
Woe to you, Jerusalem, how long will it yet be
before you become clean!

14 The word of the LORD that came to Jeremiah concerning the drought:

2 Judah mourns,
her gates are lifeless;
Her people sink down in mourning:
from Jerusalem ascends a cry of anguish.
3 The nobles send their servants for water,
but when they come to the cisterns
They find no water
and return with empty jars.
Ashamed, despairing, they cover their heads
4 because of the stricken soil;
Because there is no rain in the land
the farmers are ashamed, they cover their heads.
5 Even the hind in the field deserts her offspring
because there is no grass.
6 The wild asses stand on the bare heights,
gasping for breath like jackals;
Their eyes grow dim,
because there is no vegetation to be seen.
7 Even though our crimes bear witness against us,
take action, O LORD, for the honor of
your name —
Even though our rebellions are many,
though we have sinned against you.

NEW JERUSALEM BIBLE

19 The towns of the Negeb are shut off
with no one to give access to them.
All Judah has been deported,
deported wholesale.'

20 Raise your eyes and look at these
now coming from the north.
Where is the flock once entrusted to you,
the flock which was your pride?
21 What will you say when they come and punish
you,
you yourself having taught them?
Against you, in the lead, will come your friends.
Then will not anguish grip you
as it grips a woman in labour?
22 And should you ask yourself,
'Why is all this happening to me?'
it is because of your great guilt
that your skirts have been pulled up
and you have been manhandled.
23 Can the Ethiopian change his skin,
or the leopard his spots?
And you, can you do right,
being so accustomed to wrong?
24 'I shall scatter you like chaff
on the desert wind.
25 This is your share, the part allotted you,
from me, Yahweh declares,
because you have forgotten me
and put your trust in Delusion.
26 I am the one who pulls your skirts up over your
face
to let your shame be seen.
27 Oh! Your adulteries, your shrieks of pleasure,
your vile prostitution!
On the hills, in the fields,
I have seen your Horrors.
Jerusalem, disaster is coming for you!
How much longer till you are made clean?'

14 The word of Yahweh that came to Jeremiah on the occasion of the drought.

2 'Judah is in mourning,
her towns are pining,
sinking to the ground;
a cry goes up from Jerusalem.
3 The nobles send their servants for water,
they come to the water-tanks,
find no water,
and return with their pitchers empty.
Dismayed and bewildered,
they cover their heads.
4 Because the soil is all cracked
since the country has had no rain;
the farmers are dismayed,
they cover their heads.
5 Even the doe in the countryside
giving birth abandons her young,
for there is no grass;
6 the wild donkeys standing on the bare heights
gasp for air like jackals:
their eyes grow dim
for lack of pasture.'
7 Although our sins witness against us,
Yahweh, for your name's sake, intervene!
Yes, our acts of infidelity have been many,
we have sinned against you!

8 O hope of Israel,
   its savior in time of trouble,
why should you be like a stranger in the land,
   like a traveler turning aside for the night?
9 Why should you be like someone confused,
   like a mighty warrior who cannot give help?
Yet you, O Lord, are in the midst of us,
   and we are called by your name;
   do not forsake us!

10 Thus says the Lord concerning this people:
Truly they have loved to wander,
   they have not restrained their feet;
therefore the Lord does not accept them,
   now he will remember their iniquity
   and punish their sins.

11 The Lord said to me: Do not pray for the welfare of this people. 12 Although they fast, I do not hear their cry, and although they offer burnt offering and grain offering, I do not accept them; but by the sword, by famine, and by pestilence I consume them.

13 Then I said: "Ah, Lord God! Here are the prophets saying to them, 'You shall not see the sword, nor shall you have famine, but I will give you true peace in this place.'" 14 And the Lord said to me: The prophets are prophesying lies in my name; I did not send them, nor did I command them or speak to them. They are prophesying to you a lying vision, worthless divination, and the deceit of their own minds. 15 Therefore thus says the Lord concerning the prophets who prophesy in my name though I did not send them, and who say, "Sword and famine shall not come on this land": By sword and famine those prophets shall be consumed. 16 And the people to whom they prophesy shall be thrown out into the streets of Jerusalem, victims of famine and sword. There shall be no one to bury them — themselves, their wives, their sons, and their daughters. For I will pour out their wickedness upon them.

17 You shall say to them this word:
Let my eyes run down with tears night and day,
   and let them not cease,
for the virgin daughter — my people — is struck
    down with a crushing blow,
   with a very grievous wound.
18 If I go out into the field,
   look — those killed by the sword!
And if I enter the city,
   look — those sick with[b] famine!
For both prophet and priest ply their trade
    throughout the land,
   and have no knowledge.

19 Have you completely rejected Judah?
   Does your heart loathe Zion?
Why have you struck us down
   so that there is no healing for us?
We look for peace, but find no good;
   for a time of healing, but there is terror
    instead.
20 We acknowledge our wickedness, O Lord,
   the iniquity of our ancestors,
   for we have sinned against you.
21 Do not spurn us, for your name's sake;
   do not dishonor your glorious throne;
remember and do not break your covenant with
   us.

8 Hope of Israel, their saviour in time of trouble,
   must you be like a stranger in the land,
   like a traveller breaking his journey to find a
    night's lodging?
9 Must you be like a man suddenly overcome,
   like a warrior powerless to save himself?
You are in our midst, Lord, and we bear your
    name.
Do not forsake us.

10 The Lord says of this people: They love to stray from my ways; they wander where they will. Therefore the Lord has no more pleasure in them; he remembers their guilt now, and punishes their sins.

11 The Lord said to me: Do not pray for the wellbeing of this people. 12 Though they fast, I shall not listen to their cry; though they sacrifice whole-offering and grain-offering, I shall not accept them. I shall make an end of them with sword, famine, and pestilence. 13 But I said: Ah, Lord God, the prophets keep saying to them that they will see no sword and suffer no famine; for you will give them lasting prosperity in this place.

14 The Lord answered me: These are lies the prophets are prophesying in my name. I have not sent them; I have given them no charge; I have not spoken to them. The prophets are offering false visions, worthless augury, and their own day-dreams. 15 Therefore these are the words of the Lord about the prophets who, with no commission from me, prophesy in my name and say that neither sword nor famine will touch this land: By sword and by famine those prophets will meet their end. 16 The people to whom they prophesy will be flung out into the streets of Jerusalem, victims of famine and sword: they, their wives, their sons, and their daughters, and there will be no one to bury them. I shall pour down on them the disaster they deserve.

17 This is what you are to say to them:
Let my eyes stream with tears
   ceaselessly night and day.
For the virgin daughter of my people,
   struck by a cruel blow,
   is grievously wounded.
18 If I go out into the open country,
   I see those slain by the sword;
if I enter the city,
   I see the victims of famine.
Prophet and priest alike
   wander without rest in the land.

19 Have you spurned Judah utterly?
   Do you loathe Zion?
Why have you wounded us past all healing?
We hoped to prosper, but nothing went well.
We hoped for respite, but terror struck.
20 We acknowledge our wickedness,
   the guilt of our forefathers;
Lord, we have sinned against you.
21 Do not despise the place where your name dwells
   or bring contempt on your glorious throne.
Remember your covenant with us and do not make
   it void.

---

[b] Heb look — the sicknesses of

NEW AMERICAN BIBLE

8 O Hope of Israel, O LORD,
   our savior in time of need!
Why should you be a stranger in this land,
   like a traveler who has stopped but for a night?
9 Why are you like a man dumbfounded,
   a champion who cannot save?
You are in our midst, O LORD,
   your name we bear;
   do not forsake us!

10   Thus says the LORD of this people:
They so love to wander
   that they do not spare their feet.
The LORD has no pleasure in them;
   now he remembers their guilt,
   and will punish their sins.

11 Then the LORD said to me: Do not intercede for this people. 12 If they fast, I will not listen to their supplication. If they offer holocausts or cereal offerings, I will not accept them. Rather, I will destroy them with the sword, famine, and pestilence. 13 Ah! Lord GOD, I replied, it is the prophets who say to them, "You shall not see the sword; famine shall not befall you. Indeed, I will give you lasting peace in this place." 14 Lies these prophets utter in my name, the LORD said to me. I did not send them; I gave them no command nor did I speak to them. Lying visions, foolish divination, dreams of their own imagination, they prophesy to you. 15 Therefore, thus says the LORD: Concerning the prophets who prophesy in my name, though I did not send them; who say, "Sword and famine shall not befall this land": by the sword and famine shall these prophets meet their end. 16 The people to whom they prophesy shall be cast out into the streets of Jerusalem by famine and the sword. No one shall bury them, their wives, their sons, or their daughters, for I will pour out upon them their own wickedness. 17 Speak to them this word:

Let my eyes stream with tears
   day and night, without rest,
Over the great destruction which overwhelms
   the virgin daughter of my people,
   over her incurable wound.
18 If I walk out into the field,
   look! those slain by the sword;
If I enter the city,
   look! those consumed by hunger.
Even the prophet and the priest
   forage in a land they know not.

19 Have you cast Judah off completely?
   Is Zion loathsome to you?
Why have you struck us a blow
   that cannot be healed?
We wait for peace, to no avail;
   for a time of healing, but terror comes instead.
20 We recognize, O LORD, our wickedness,
   the guilt of our fathers;
   that we have sinned against you.
21 For your name's sake spurn us not,
   disgrace not the throne of your glory;
   remember your covenant with us, and break
   it not.

NEW JERUSALEM BIBLE

8 Yahweh, hope of Israel,
   its Saviour in time of distress,
why are you like a stranger in this country,
   like a traveller staying only for one night?
9 Why are you like someone bemused,
   like a warrior who has no power to rescue?
And yet, Yahweh, you are among us,
   we are called by your name.
Do not desert us!

10 Yahweh says this about this people, 'They take such pleasure in darting hither and thither, they cannot restrain their feet! But Yahweh takes pleasure in them no longer; now he will keep their guilt in mind and punish their sins.'
11 Yahweh then said to me, 'Do not intercede for this people or their welfare. 12 If they fast, I will not listen to their plea; if they offer burnt offerings and cereal offerings I will not accept them. Rather, I shall make an end of them by sword, famine and plague.'
13 'Ah, Lord Yahweh,' I answered, 'here are the prophets telling them, "You will not see the sword, famine will not touch you; I promise you true peace in this place."'
14 Then Yahweh said to me, 'The prophets are prophesying lies in my name; I have not sent them, I gave them no orders, I never spoke to them. Delusive visions, hollow predictions, daydreams of their own, that is what they prophesy to you. 15 Therefore, Yahweh says this: The prophets who prophesy in my name when I have not sent them, and tell you there will be no sword or famine in this country, these same prophets will meet their end by sword and famine. 16 And as for the people to whom they prophesy, they will be tossed into the streets of Jerusalem, victims of famine and the sword, with not a soul to bury them: neither them nor their wives, nor their sons, nor their daughters. I shall pour their own wickedness down on them.

17 'So say this word to them:
May my eyes shed tears
   night and day, unceasingly,
since the daughter of my people has sustained a
      fearsome wound,
   a crippling injury.
18 If I go into the countryside,
   there lie those killed by the sword;
if I go into the city,
   I see people tortured with hunger;
even prophets and priests
   roam the country at their wits' end.'

19 Have you rejected Judah altogether?
   Does your very soul revolt at Zion?
Why have you struck us down without hope of
      cure?
We were hoping for peace—no good came of it!
For the moment of cure—nothing but terror!ˣ
20 Yahweh, we acknowledge our wickedness
   and our ancestors' guilt:
   we have indeed sinned against you.
21 For your name's sake do not reject us,
   do not dishonour the throne of your glory.
Remember us; do not break your covenant with us.

ˣ 14 = 8:15.

NEW REVISED STANDARD VERSION	REVISED ENGLISH BIBLE

NEW REVISED STANDARD VERSION

22 Can any idols of the nations bring rain?
　Or can the heavens give showers?
Is it not you, O LORD our God?
　We set our hope on you,
　for it is you who do all this.

15 Then the LORD said to me: Though Moses and Samuel stood before me, yet my heart would not turn toward this people. Send them out of my sight, and let them go! 2 And when they say to you, "Where shall we go?" you shall say to them: Thus says the LORD:

　Those destined for pestilence, to pestilence,
　　and those destined for the sword, to the sword;
　those destined for famine, to famine,
　　and those destined for captivity, to captivity.

3 And I will appoint over them four kinds of destroyers, says the LORD: the sword to kill, the dogs to drag away, and the birds of the air and the wild animals of the earth to devour and destroy. 4 I will make them a horror to all the kingdoms of the earth because of what King Manasseh son of Hezekiah of Judah did in Jerusalem.

5 Who will have pity on you, O Jerusalem,
　or who will bemoan you?
Who will turn aside
　to ask about your welfare?
6 You have rejected me, says the LORD,
　you are going backward;
so I have stretched out my hand against you and
　　destroyed you—
　I am weary of relenting.
7 I have winnowed them with a winnowing fork
　in the gates of the land;
I have bereaved them, I have destroyed my
　　people;
　they did not turn from their ways.
8 Their widows became more numerous
　than the sand of the seas;
I have brought against the mothers of youths
　a destroyer at noonday;
I have made anguish and terror
　fall upon her suddenly.
9 She who bore seven has languished;
　she has swooned away;
her sun went down while it was yet day;
　she has been shamed and disgraced.
And the rest of them I will give to the sword
　before their enemies,
　　　　　　　　　　　　　says the LORD.

10 Woe is me, my mother, that you ever bore me, a man of strife and contention to the whole land! I have not lent, nor have I borrowed, yet all of them curse me. 11 The LORD said: Surely I have intervened in your life[c] for good, surely I have imposed enemies on you in a time of trouble and in a time of distress.[d] 12 Can iron and bronze break iron from the north?

13 Your wealth and your treasures I will give as plunder, without price, for all your sins, throughout all your

REVISED ENGLISH BIBLE

22 Can any of the false gods of the nations give rain?
　Or do the heavens of themselves send showers?
Is it not in you, LORD our God,
　that we put our hope?
　You alone made all these things.

15 The LORD said to me: Even if Moses and Samuel stood before me, I would not be moved to pity this people. Banish them from my presence; let them be gone. 2 Should they ask where to go, say to them: These are the words of the LORD:

　Those who are for the plague shall go to the
　　plague,
　and those for the sword to the sword;
　those who are for famine to famine,
　and those for captivity to captivity.

3 Four kinds of doom I ordain for them, says the LORD: the sword to kill, dogs to drag away, birds of prey and wild beasts to devour and destroy. 4 I shall make them abhorrent to all the kingdoms of the earth, because of the crimes committed in Jerusalem by Manasseh son of Hezekiah, king of Judah.

5 Who will take pity on you, Jerusalem,
　who will offer you consolation?
Who will turn aside to ask about your wellbeing?
6 You yourselves cast me off, says the LORD,
　you turned your backs on me,
　so I stretched out my hand to bring you to ruin;
　I was weary of relenting.
7 I winnowed them and scattered them
　in every town in the land;
I brought bereavement on them,
　I destroyed my people;
　they would not abandon their ways.
8 I made widows among them more in number
　than the sands of the seas;
I brought upon the mother of young warriors
　a plunderer at noonday.
I made the terror of invasion fall upon her
　all in a moment.
9 The mother of seven sons grew faint,
　she sank into despair;
her light was quenched while it was yet day;
　she was left humbled and shamed.
The remnant I shall give to the sword,
　to perish at the hand of their enemies.
　This is the word of the LORD.

10 ALAS, my mother, that ever you gave birth to me,
　a man doomed to strife
　with the whole world against me!
I have borrowed from no one,
　I have lent to no one,
　yet everyone abuses me.

11 The LORD said:

　Have I not utterly dismissed you?
　Shall I not bring the enemy against you
　in a time of trouble and distress?
12 Can iron break steel from the north?
13 I shall hand over your wealth as spoil,
　and your treasure for no payment,
　because of all your sin throughout your borders.

---

c Heb *intervened with you*　　d Meaning of Heb uncertain

14:22 **made:** *or* did.　　15:8 **brought:** *so Gk; Heb. adds* to them.
15:12 **Can . . . north:** *prob. rdg; Heb. adds* and bronze.

22 Among the nations' idols is there any that
  gives rain?
Or can the mere heavens send showers?
Is it not you alone, O LORD,
  our God, to whom we look?
You alone have done all these things.

15 The LORD said to me: Even if Moses and Samuel
stood before me, my heart would not turn toward
this people. Send them away from me. 2 If they ask you
where they should go, tell them, Thus says the LORD: Whoever is marked for death, to death; whoever is marked for
the sword, to the sword; whoever is marked for famine, to
famine; whoever is marked for captivity, to captivity. 3 Four
kinds of scourge I have decreed against them, says the
LORD: the sword to slay them; dogs to drag them about; the
birds of the sky and the beasts of the earth to devour and
destroy them. 4 And I will make them an object of horror to
all the kingdoms of the earth because of what Manasseh,
son of Hezekiah, king of Judah, did in Jerusalem.

5 Who will pity you, Jerusalem,
  who will console you?
Who will stop to ask
  about your welfare?
6 You have disowned me, says the LORD,
  turned your back upon me;
And so I stretched out my hand to destroy you,
  I was weary of sparing you.
7 I winnowed them with the fan
  in every city gate.
I destroyed my people through bereavement;
  they returned not from their evil ways.
8 Their widows were more numerous before me
  than the sands of the sea.
I brought against the mother of youths
  the spoiler at midday;
Suddenly I struck her
  with anguish and terror.
9 The mother of seven swoons away,
  gasping out her life;
Her sun sets in full day,
  she is disgraced, despairing.
Their survivors I will give to the sword
  before their enemies, says the LORD.

10 Woe to me, mother, that you gave me birth!
  a man of strife and contention to all the land!
I neither borrow nor lend,
  yet all curse me.
11 Tell me, LORD, have I not served you for
  their good?
Have I not interceded with you
  in the time of misfortune and anguish?

22 Can any of the nations' Futile Ones make it rain?
Can the heavens of their own accord give showers?
Are you not the one, Yahweh our God?
In you is our hope,
  since you make all these things.

15 Yahweh said to me, 'Even if Moses and Samuel
pleaded before me, I could not sympathise with this
people! Drive them out of my sight; away with them! 2 And
if they ask you, "Where shall we go?" tell them this, "Yahweh says this:

Those for the plague, to the plague;
  those for the sword, to the sword;
  those for famine, to famine;
  those for captivity, to captivity!ʸ

3 "I shall consign them to four kinds of thing, Yahweh
declares: the sword to kill, the dogs to drag away, the birds
of heaven and wild animals of earth to devour and to destroy. 4 I shall make them an object of horror to all the
kingdoms of the earth, because of Manasseh son of Hezekiah, king of Judah, and what he did in Jerusalem." '

5 Who is there to pity you, Jerusalem,
  who to grieve for you,
  who to go out of his way
  and ask how you are?
6 'You yourself have rejected me, Yahweh declares,
  you have turned your back on me;
  so I have stretched my hand over you and
    destroyed you.
Tired of relenting,
7 I have winnowed them with a winnow
  at the country's gates.
They have been bereft, I have destroyed my
  people,
  but they refuse to leave their ways.
8 I have made their widows outnumber
  the sand of the sea.
On the mother of young warriors
  I bring the destroyer in broad daylight.
Suddenly I bring
  anguish and terror down on her.
9 The mother of seven sons grows faint
  and gasps for breath.
It is still day, but already her sun has set,
  she is dismayed and distracted;
  and the rest of them I shall consign to the sword,
    to their enemies, Yahweh declares.'

10 ᶻA disaster for me, mother, that you bore me
  to be a man of strife and dissension for the whole
    country.
I neither lend nor borrow,
  yet all of them curse me.
11 Have I not genuinely done my best to serve you,
  Yahweh?
Have I not interceded with you
  in time of disaster and distress!
12 'Can iron break the iron of the north and the
    bronze?
13 Your wealth and your treasures
  I shall hand over to plunder, without repayment,
  because of all your sins, throughout your territory.

15, 12ff: These verses are corruptions of the text and are therefore omitted.

ʸ 15 = 43:11.   ᶻ 15 The 'confessions of Jr' (11:18–12:5; 15:10–21; 17:14–18; 18:18–23; 20:7–18) show Jr in a dialogue of astounding intimacy with Yahweh.

territory. 14 I will make you serve your enemies in a land that you do not know, for in my anger a fire is kindled that shall burn forever.

15 O Lord, you know;
    remember me and visit me,
    and bring down retribution for me on my
        persecutors.
In your forbearance do not take me away;
    know that on your account I suffer insult.
16 Your words were found, and I ate them,
    and your words became to me a joy
    and the delight of my heart;
for I am called by your name,
    O Lord, God of hosts.
17 I did not sit in the company of merrymakers,
    nor did I rejoice;
under the weight of your hand I sat alone,
    for you had filled me with indignation.
18 Why is my pain unceasing,
    my wound incurable,
    refusing to be healed?
Truly, you are to me like a deceitful brook,
    like waters that fail.

19 Therefore thus says the Lord:
If you turn back, I will take you back,
    and you shall stand before me.
If you utter what is precious, and not what is
        worthless,
    you shall serve as my mouth.
It is they who will turn to you,
    not you who will turn to them.
20 And I will make you to this people
    a fortified wall of bronze;
they will fight against you,
    but they shall not prevail over you,
for I am with you
    to save you and deliver you,
                says the Lord.
21 I will deliver you out of the hand of the wicked,
    and redeem you from the grasp of the ruthless.

16 The word of the Lord came to me: 2 You shall not take a wife, nor shall you have sons or daughters in this place. 3 For thus says the Lord concerning the sons and daughters who are born in this place, and concerning the mothers who bear them and the fathers who beget them in this land: 4 They shall die of deadly diseases. They shall not be lamented, nor shall they be buried; they shall become like dung on the surface of the ground. They shall perish by the sword and by famine, and their dead bodies shall become food for the birds of the air and for the wild animals of the earth.

5 For thus says the Lord: Do not enter the house of mourning, or go to lament, or bemoan them; for I have taken away my peace from this people, says the Lord, my steadfast love and mercy. 6 Both great and small shall die in this land; they shall not be buried, and no one shall lament for them; there shall be no gashing, no shaving of the head for them. 7 No one shall break bread*e* for the mourner, to offer comfort for the dead; nor shall anyone give them the cup of consolation to drink for their fathers or their mothers. 8 You shall not go into the house of feasting to sit with them, to eat and drink. 9 For thus says the Lord of hosts, the God of Israel: I am going to banish from this place, in your days and before your eyes, the voice of mirth and the voice of gladness, the voice of the bridegroom and the voice of the bride.

e Two Mss Gk: MT *break for them*

14 I shall make you serve your enemies
    in a land you do not know;
for my anger is a blazing fire
    and it will flare up against you.

15 Lord, you know;
    remember me, and vindicate me,
    avenge me on my persecutors.
Be patient with me and do not put me off,
    see what reproaches I endure for your sake.
16 When I came on your words I devoured them;
    they were joy and happiness to me,
for you, Lord God of Hosts, have named me
        yours.
17 I have never kept company with revellers,
    never made merry with them;
because I felt your hand upon me I have sat alone,
    for you have filled me with indignation.
18 Why then is my pain unending,
    and my wound desperate, past all healing?
You are to me like a brook that fails,
    whose waters are not to be relied on.

19 This was the Lord's answer:

If you turn back to me, I shall take you back
    and you will stand before me.
If you can separate the precious from the base,
    you will be my spokesman.
This people may turn again to you,
    but you are not to turn to them.
20 To withstand them I shall make you strong,
    an unscaled wall of bronze.
Though they attack you, they will not prevail,
    for I am with you to save
    and deliver you, says the Lord;
21 I shall deliver you from the clutches of the wicked,
    I shall rescue you from the grasp of the ruthless.

16 The word of the Lord came to me: 2 You are not to marry or to have sons and daughters in this place. 3 For these are the words of the Lord about any sons and daughters born in this place, about the mothers who bear them and the fathers who beget them in this land: 4 They shall die a horrible death; there must be no wailing for them and no burial; they will be dung spread over the ground. They will perish by sword or famine, and their corpses will be food for birds and beasts.

5 For these are the words of the Lord: Do not enter a house where there is a funeral feast; do not go in to wail or to bring comfort, for, says the Lord, I have withdrawn my peace from this people, my love and compassion. 6 High and low will die in this land, but there must be no burial, no wailing for them; no one is to gash himself or shave his head. 7 No one is to offer the mourner a portion of bread to console him for the dead or give him a cup of consolation for the loss of his father or mother.

8 Nor may you enter a house where there is feasting, to sit eating and drinking there. 9 For these are the words of the Lord of Hosts, the God of Israel: In your own days and in the sight of you all, I shall silence in this place every sound of joy and gladness, the voices of bridegroom and bride.

16:7 **bread:** *so Gk; Heb.* to them. **give him:** *so Gk; Heb.* give them.

NEW AMERICAN BIBLE

15   You know I have.
Remember me, LORD, visit me,
    and avenge me on my persecutors.
Because of your long-suffering banish me not;
    know that for you I have borne insult.
16 When I found your words, I devoured them;
    they became my joy and the happiness of
        my heart,
Because I bore your name,
    O LORD, God of hosts.
17 I did not sit celebrating
    in the circle of merrymakers;
Under the weight of your hand I sat alone
    because you filled me with indignation.
18 Why is my pain continuous,
    my wound incurable, refusing to be healed?
You have indeed become for me a
        treacherous brook,
    whose waters do not abide!
19   Thus the LORD answered me:
If you repent, so that I restore you,
    in my presence you shall stand;
If you bring forth the precious without the vile,
    you shall be my mouthpiece.
Then it shall be they who turn to you,
    and you shall not turn to them;
20 And I will make you toward this people
    a solid wall of brass.
Though they fight against you,
    they shall not prevail,
For I am with you,
    to deliver and rescue you, says the LORD.
21 I will free you from the hand of the wicked,
    and rescue you from the grasp of the violent.

16 This message came to me from the LORD: ²Do not marry any woman; you shall not have sons or daughters in this place, ³for thus says the LORD concerning the sons and daughters who will be born in this place, the mothers who will give them birth, the fathers who will beget them in this land: ⁴Of deadly disease they shall die. Unlamented and unburied they will lie like dung on the ground. Sword and famine will make an end of them, and their corpses will become food for the birds of the sky and the beasts of the field.

⁵Go not into a house of mourning, the LORD continued: go not there to lament or offer sympathy. For I have withdrawn my friendship from this people, says the LORD, my kindness and my pity. ⁶They shall die, the great and the lowly, in this land, and shall go unburied and unlamented. No one will gash himself or shave his head for them. ⁷They will not break bread with the bereaved to console them in their bereavement; they will not give them the cup of consolation to drink over the death of father or mother.

⁸Enter not a house where people are celebrating, to sit with them eating and drinking. ⁹For thus says the LORD of hosts, the God of Israel: Before your very eyes and during your lifetime I will silence from this place the cry of joy and the cry of gladness, the voice of the bridegroom and the voice of the bride.

NEW JERUSALEM BIBLE

14 I shall enslave you to your enemies
    in a country which you do not know,
    for my anger has kindled a fire
    that will burn you up.' ᵃ
15 Yahweh, you know!
    Remember me, take care of me,
    and avenge me on my persecutors.
    However long your anger endures, do not snatch
        me away.
    Realise that I suffer insult for your sake.
16 When your words came, I devoured them:
    your word was my delight
    and the joy of my heart;
    for I was called by your Name,
    Yahweh, God Sabaoth.
17 I never sat in the company of scoffers
    amusing myself;
    with your hands on me I held myself aloof,
    since you had filled me with indignation.
18 Why is my suffering continual,
    my wound incurable, refusing to be healed?
    Truly, for me you are a deceptive stream
    with uncertain waters!
19 To which Yahweh replied,
    'If you repent, I shall restore you
    to plead before me.
    If you distinguish between the precious and the
        base,
    you shall be as my own mouth.
    They will come back to you,
    but you must not go back to them.
20 As far as these people are concerned, I shall make
        you
    a fortified wall of bronze.
    They will fight against you
    but will not overcome you,
    because I am with you
    to save you and rescue you,
    Yahweh declares.
21 I shall rescue you from the clutches of the wicked
    and redeem you from the grasp of the violent.'

16 The word of Yahweh was addressed to me as follows:

²'You are not to marry or have sons and daughters in this place. ³For Yahweh says this regarding the sons and daughters to be born in this place, about the mothers who give birth to them, and about the fathers who beget them in this land, ⁴'They will die of deadly diseases, unlamented and unburied; they will be like dung spread on the ground; they will meet their end by sword and famine, and their corpses will be food for the birds of the sky and the beasts of earth.''

⁵'Yes, Yahweh says this, ''Go into no house where there is mourning, do not go and lament or grieve with them; for I have withdrawn my peace from this people, Yahweh declares, and faithful love and pity too. ⁶High or low, they will die in this country, without burial or lament; there will be no gashing, no shaving of the head for them. ⁷No bread will be broken for the mourner to comfort him for the dead; no cup of consolation will be offered him for his father or his mother.

⁸''And do not enter a house where there is feasting, to sit with them and eat and drink. ⁹For Yahweh Sabaoth, the God of Israel, says this: In this place, before your eyes, in your own days, I will silence the shouts of rejoicing and mirth and the voices of bridegroom and bride.

ᵃ 15 = 17:3–4.

10 And when you tell this people all these words, and they say to you, "Why has the LORD pronounced all this great evil against us? What is our iniquity? What is the sin that we have committed against the LORD our God?" 11 then you shall say to them: It is because your ancestors have forsaken me, says the LORD, and have gone after other gods and have served and worshiped them, and have forsaken me and have not kept my law; 12 and because you have behaved worse than your ancestors, for here you are, every one of you, following your stubborn evil will, refusing to listen to me. 13 Therefore I will hurl you out of this land into a land that neither you nor your ancestors have known, and there you shall serve other gods day and night, for I will show you no favor.

14 Therefore, the days are surely coming, says the LORD, when it shall no longer be said, "As the LORD lives who brought the people of Israel up out of the land of Egypt," 15 but "As the LORD lives who brought the people of Israel up out of the land of the north and out of all the lands where he had driven them." For I will bring them back to their own land that I gave to their ancestors.

16 I am now sending for many fishermen, says the LORD, and they shall catch them; and afterward I will send for many hunters, and they shall hunt them from every mountain and every hill, and out of the clefts of the rocks. 17 For my eyes are on all their ways; they are not hidden from my presence, nor is their iniquity concealed from my sight. 18 And f I will doubly repay their iniquity and their sin, because they have polluted my land with the carcasses of their detestable idols, and have filled my inheritance with their abominations.

19 O LORD, my strength and my stronghold,
   my refuge in the day of trouble,
to you shall the nations come
   from the ends of the earth and say:
Our ancestors have inherited nothing but lies,
   worthless things in which there is no profit.
20 Can mortals make for themselves gods?
   Such are no gods!

21 "Therefore I am surely going to teach them, this time I am going to teach them my power and my might, and they shall know that my name is the LORD."

17 The sin of Judah is written with an iron pen; with a diamond point it is engraved on the tablet of their hearts, and on the horns of their altars, 2 while their children remember their altars and their sacred poles,g beside every green tree, and on the high hills, 3 on the mountains in the open country. Your wealth and all your treasures I will give for spoil as the price of your sin h throughout all your territory. 4 By your own act you shall lose the heritage that I gave you, and I will make you serve your enemies in a land that you do not know, for in my anger a fire is kindled i that shall burn forever.

5 Thus says the LORD:
Cursed are those who trust in mere mortals
   and make mere flesh their strength,
   whose hearts turn away from the LORD.

10 When you tell this people all these things they will ask you, 'Why has the LORD decreed that this great disaster is to come on us? What wrong have we done? What sin have we committed against the LORD our God?' 11 You are to answer: Because your forefathers forsook me, says the LORD, and followed other gods, serving and worshipping them. They forsook me and did not keep my law. 12 And you yourselves have done worse than your forefathers; for each of you follows the promptings of his wicked and stubborn heart instead of obeying me. 13 So I shall fling you headlong out of this land into a country unknown to you and your forefathers; there serve other gods day and night, for I shall show you no favour.

14 Therefore the time is coming, says the LORD, when people will no longer swear 'by the life of the LORD who brought the Israelites up from Egypt'; 15 instead they will swear 'by the life of the LORD who brought the Israelites back from a northern land and from all the lands to which he had dispersed them'; and I shall bring them back to the soil which I gave to their forefathers.

16 I shall send for many fishermen, says the LORD, and they will fish for them. After that I shall send for many hunters, and they will hunt them from every mountain and hill and from the crevices in the rocks. 17 For my eyes are on all their ways; they are not hidden from my sight, nor is their wrongdoing concealed from me. 18 I shall first make them pay double for the wrong they have done and the sin they have committed by defiling the land which belongs to me; they have filled my possession with their lifeless idols and abominations.

19 LORD, my strength and my stronghold,
   my refuge in time of trouble,
to you the nations will come
   from the ends of the earth and say:
Our forefathers inherited only a sham,
   an idol vain and worthless.
20 Can man make gods for himself?
   They would be no gods.
21 Therefore I am teaching them,
   I shall teach them once for all
my power and my might,
   and they will learn that my name is the LORD.

17 The sin of Judah is recorded with an iron stylus,
   engraved with a diamond point on the tablet of
      their hearts,
on the horns of their altars 2 to witness against
      them.
Their altars and their sacred poles stand by every
      spreading tree,
on the heights 3 and the hills in the mountain
      country.
I shall hand over your wealth as spoil,
   and all your treasure for no payment,
because of sin throughout your borders.
4 You will lose possession of the holding
   which I gave you.
I shall make you serve your enemies
   in a land you do not know;
for the fire of my anger is kindled by you
   and it will burn for ever.

5 These are the words of the LORD:
A curse on anyone who trusts in mortals
   and leans for support on human kind,
   while his heart is far from the LORD!

---

f Gk: Heb And first   g Heb Asherim   h Cn: Heb spoil your high places for sin   i Two Mss Theodotion: you kindled

17:2 to witness . . . them: prob. rdg; Heb. as their sons remember.
17:3 for no payment: prob. rdg, cp. 15:13; Heb. your shrines.
17:4 You . . . possession: prob. rdg; Heb. obscure.

10 When you proclaim all these words to this people and they ask you: "Why has the LORD pronounced all these great evils against us? What is our crime? What sin have we committed against the LORD, our God?" — 11 you shall answer them: It is because your fathers have forsaken me, says the LORD, and followed strange gods, which they served and worshiped; but me they have forsaken, and my law they have not observed. 12 And you have done worse than your fathers. Here you are, every one of you, walking in the hardness of his evil heart instead of listening to me. 13 I will cast you out of this land into a land that neither you nor your fathers have known; there you can serve strange gods day and night, because I will not grant you my mercy.

14 However, days will surely come, says the LORD, when it will no longer be said, "As the LORD lives, who brought the Israelites out of Egypt"; 15 but rather, "As the LORD lives, who brought the Israelites out of the land of the north and out of all the countries to which he had banished them." I will bring them back to the land which I gave their fathers.

16 Look! I will send many fishermen, says the LORD, to catch them. After that, I will send many hunters to hunt them out from every mountain and hill and from the clefts of the rocks. 17 For my eyes are upon all their ways; they are not hidden from me, nor does their guilt escape my view. 18 I will at once repay them double for their crime and their sin of profaning my land with their detestable corpses of idols, and filling my heritage with their abominations.

19 O LORD, my strength, my fortress,
    my refuge in the day of distress!
To you will the nations come
    from the ends of the earth, and say,
"Mere frauds are the heritage of our fathers,
    empty idols of no use."
20 Can man make for himself gods?
    These are not gods.
21 Look, then: I will give them knowledge;
    this time I will leave them in no doubt
Of my strength and my power;
    they shall know that my name is LORD.

17 The sin of Judah is written
        with an iron stylus,
Engraved with a diamond point
    upon the tablets of their hearts.

[And the horns of their altars, 2 when their sons remember their altars and their sacred poles, beside the green trees, on the high hills, 3 the peaks in the highland.]

Your wealth and all your treasures
    I will give as spoil.
In recompense for all your sins
    throughout your borders,
4 You will relinquish your hold on your heritage
    which I have given you.
I will enslave you to your enemies
    in a land that you know not:
For a fire has been kindled by my wrath
    that will burn forever.

5   Thus says the LORD:
Cursed is the man who trusts in human beings,
    who seeks his strength in flesh,
    whose heart turns away from the LORD.

10 "When you tell these people this and they ask you: Why has Yahweh decreed such complete and total disaster for us? What have we done wrong? What sin have we committed against Yahweh our God? 11 then you are to answer: It is because your ancestors abandoned me, Yahweh declares, and followed other gods, and served and worshipped them. They abandoned me and did not keep my Law. 12 And you for your part have behaved even worse than your ancestors. Look, each of you follows his own stubborn and wicked inclinations, without listening to me. 13 And so, I shall eject you from this country into a country unknown to you or to your ancestors, and there you can serve other gods, day and night, for I shall show you no more favour."

14 'Look, the days are coming, Yahweh declares, when people will no longer say, "As Yahweh lives who brought the Israelites out of Egypt!" 15 but, "As Yahweh lives who brought the Israelites back from the land of the north and all the countries to which he had driven them." I shall bring them back to the very soil I gave their ancestors.' b

16 'Watch, I shall send for many fishermen, Yahweh declares, and these will fish them up; next, I shall send for many huntsmen, and these will hunt them out of every mountain, every hill, and out of the holes in the rocks. 17 For my eyes watch all their ways, these are not hidden from me, and their guilt does not escape my gaze. 18 I shall requite their guilt and their sin twice over, since they have polluted my country with the carcases of their Horrors, and filled my heritage with their Abominations.' c

19 Yahweh, my strength, my stronghold,
    my refuge in time of distress!
To you the nations will come
    from the remotest parts of the earth and say,
'Our fathers inherited nothing but Delusion,
    Futility of no use whatever.
20 Can human beings make their own gods?
    These are not gods at all!'
21 'Now listen, I will make them acknowledge,
    this time I will make them acknowledge
    my hand and my might;
    and then they will know that Yahweh is my name.'

17 'The sin of Judah is written with an iron pen,
        engraved with a diamond point
    on the tablet of the heart
    and on the horns of their altars,
2 while their children remember
    their altars and their sacred pole
    beside the green trees, on the lofty hills.
3 My mountain on the plain,
    your wealth and all your treasures
    I shall hand over to be plundered,
    because of the sin of your high places
    throughout your territory.
4 You will have to relinquish your heritage
    which I gave you;
I will enslave you to your enemies
    in a country which you do not know,
    for my fiery anger kindled by you
    will burn for ever.' d

5 Yahweh says this,
'Accursed be anyone who trusts in human beings,
    who relies on human strength
    and whose heart turns from Yahweh.

---

b 16 = 23:7–8.   c 16 The Horrors and Abominations are idols.
d 17 = 15:13–14.

6 They shall be like a shrub in the desert,
   and shall not see when relief comes.
They shall live in the parched places of the
      wilderness,
   in an uninhabited salt land.

7 Blessed are those who trust in the LORD,
   whose trust is the LORD.
8 They shall be like a tree planted by water,
   sending out its roots by the stream.
It shall not fear when heat comes,
   and its leaves shall stay green;
in the year of drought it is not anxious,
   and it does not cease to bear fruit.

9 The heart is devious above all else;
   it is perverse —
   who can understand it?
10 I the LORD test the mind
   and search the heart,
to give to all according to their ways,
   according to the fruit of their doings.

11 Like the partridge hatching what it did not lay,
   so are all who amass wealth unjustly;
in mid-life it will leave them,
   and at their end they will prove to be fools.

12 O glorious throne, exalted from the beginning,
   shrine of our sanctuary!
13 O hope of Israel! O LORD!
All who forsake you shall be put to shame;
   those who turn away from you j shall be
      recorded in the underworld, k
   for they have forsaken the fountain of living
      water, the LORD.

14 Heal me, O LORD, and I shall be healed;
   save me, and I shall be saved;
   for you are my praise.
15 See how they say to me,
   "Where is the word of the LORD?
   Let it come!"
16 But I have not run away from being a shepherd l
      in your service,
   nor have I desired the fatal day.
You know what came from my lips;
   it was before your face.
17 Do not become a terror to me;
   you are my refuge in the day of disaster;
18 Let my persecutors be shamed,
   but do not let me be shamed;
let them be dismayed,
   but do not let me be dismayed;
bring on them the day of disaster;
   destroy them with double destruction!

19 Thus said the LORD to me: Go and stand in the People's Gate, by which the kings of Judah enter and by which they go out, and in all the gates of Jerusalem, 20 and say to them: Hear the word of the LORD, you kings of Judah, and all Judah, and all the inhabitants of Jerusalem, who enter by these gates. 21 Thus says the LORD: For the sake of your lives, take care that you do not bear a burden on the sabbath day or bring it in by the gates of Jerusalem. 22 And do not carry a burden out of your houses on the sabbath or do any work, but keep the sabbath day holy, as I commanded your ancestors. 23 Yet they did not listen or incline their ear; they stiffened their necks and would not hear or receive instruction.

6 He will be like a juniper in the steppeland;
   when good comes he is unaware of it.
He will live among the rocks in the wilderness,
   in a salt, uninhabited land.

7 Blessed is anyone who trusts in the LORD,
   and rests his confidence on him.
8 He will be like a tree planted by the waterside,
   that sends out its roots along a stream.
When the heat comes it has nothing to fear;
   its foliage stays green.
Without care in a year of drought,
   it does not fail to bear fruit.

9 The heart is deceitful above any other thing,
   desperately sick; who can fathom it?
10 I, the LORD, search the mind
   and test the heart,
requiting each one for his conduct
   and as his deeds deserve.
11 Like a partridge
   sitting on a clutch of eggs which it has not laid,
   so is he who amasses wealth unjustly.
Before his days are half done it will leave him,
   and he will be a fool at the last.

12 A glorious throne, exalted from the beginning,
   is the site of our sanctuary;
13 LORD, on whom Israel's hope is fixed,
all who reject you will be put to shame;
   those who forsake you will be inscribed in the
      dust,
   for they have rejected the source of living water,
      the LORD.

14 Heal me, LORD, and I shall be healed,
   save me and I shall be saved;
   for you are my praise.
15 They say to me, 'Where is the word of the LORD?
   Let it come, if it can!'
16 It is not the prospect of disaster that makes me
      press after you,
   and I did not desire this day of despair.
You know all that has passed my lips;
   you are fully aware of it.
17 Do not become a terror to me;
   you are my refuge on an evil day.
18 May my persecutors be foiled, not I;
   may they, not I, be terrified.
Bring on them an evil day;
   destroy them, destroy them utterly.

19 These were the words of the LORD to me: Go and stand at the Benjamin Gate, through which the kings of Judah pass in and out, and stand also at all the gates of Jerusalem. 20 Say: Hear the words of the LORD, you kings of Judah, all you people of Judah, and all you citizens of Jerusalem who come in through these gates. 21 These are the words of the LORD: Do not put your lives at risk by carrying any load on the sabbath day or bringing it through the gates of Jerusalem. 22 You are not to bring any load out of your houses or do any work on the sabbath, but you are to keep the sabbath day holy as I commanded your forefathers. 23 They, however, did not obey or pay attention, but stubbornly refused to hear or receive instruction. 24 Now if you will obey me, says

---

17:6 **a juniper:** or one who is a destitute person. 17:13 **who forsake you:** so Lat.; Heb. who forsake me. 17:19 **Benjamin:** prob. rdg.; Heb. sons of the people.

---

j Heb me   k Or in the earth   l Meaning of Heb uncertain

6 He is like a barren bush in the desert
  that enjoys no change of season,
But stands in a lava waste,
  a salt and empty earth.
7 Blessed is the man who trusts in the LORD,
  whose hope is the LORD.
8 He is like a tree planted beside the waters
  that stretches out its roots to the stream:
It fears not the heat when it comes,
  its leaves stay green;
In the year of drought it shows no distress,
  but still bears fruit.
9 More tortuous than all else is the human heart,
  beyond remedy; who can understand it?
10 I, the LORD, alone probe the mind
  and test the heart,
To reward everyone according to his ways,
  according to the merit of his deeds.
11 A partridge that mothers a brood not her own
  is the man who acquires wealth unjustly:
In midlife it will desert him;
  in the end he is only a fool.
12 A throne of glory, exalted from the beginning,
  such is our holy place.
13 O hope of Israel, O LORD!
  all who forsake you shall be in disgrace;
The rebels in the land shall be put to shame;
  they have forsaken the source of living waters
  [the LORD].
14 Heal me, LORD, that I may be healed;
  save me, that I may be saved,
  for it is you whom I praise.
15 See how they say to me,
  "Where is the word of the LORD?
  Let it come to pass!"
16 Yet I did not press you to send calamity;
  the day without remedy I have not desired.
You know what passed my lips;
  it is present before you.
17 Do not be my ruin,
  you, my refuge in the day of misfortune.
18 Let my persecutors, not me, be confounded;
  let them, not me, be broken.
Bring upon them the day of misfortune,
  crush them with repeated destruction.

19 Thus said the LORD to me: Go, stand at the Gate of
Benjamin, where the kings of Judah enter and leave, and at
the other gates of Jerusalem. 20 There say to them: Hear the
word of the LORD, you kings of Judah, and all Judah, and
all you citizens of Jerusalem who enter these gates! 21 Thus
says the LORD: As you love your lives, take care not to carry
burdens on the sabbath day, to bring them in through the
gates of Jerusalem. 22 Bring no burden from your homes on
the sabbath. Do no work whatever, but keep holy the sabbath, as I commanded your fathers, 23 though they did not
listen or give ear, but stiffened their necks so as not to hear
or take correction. 24 If you obey me wholeheartedly, says

6 Such a person is like scrub in the wastelands:
  when good comes, it does not affect him
since he lives in the parched places of the desert,
  uninhabited, salt land.
7 'Blessed is anyone who trusts in Yahweh,
  with Yahweh to rely on.
8 Such a person is like a tree by the waterside
  that thrusts its roots to the stream:
when the heat comes it has nothing to fear,
  its foliage stays green;
untroubled in a year of drought,
  it never stops bearing fruit.
9 'The heart is more devious than any other thing,
  and is depraved; who can pierce its secrets?
10 I, Yahweh, search the heart,
  test the motives,
to give each person what his conduct
  and his actions deserve.
11 'The partridge will hatch eggs it has not laid.
No different is the person who gets riches unjustly:
  his days half done, they will desert him
  and he prove a fool after all.'
12 A glorious throne, sublime from the beginning,
  such is our Holy Place.
13 Yahweh, hope of Israel,
  all who abandon you will be put to shame,
those who turn from you will be registered in the
  underworld,
since they have abandoned Yahweh, the fountain
  of living water.
14 Heal me, Yahweh, and I shall be healed,
  save me, and I shall be saved,
  for you are my praise.
15 Look, they keep saying to me,
  'Where is Yahweh's word? Let it come true then!'
16 Yet I have never urged you to send disaster,
  I never desired the fatal day,
  this you know;
what came from my lips was not concealed from
  you.
17 Do not be a terror to me,
  you, my refuge in time of disaster.
18 Let my persecutors be confounded, not me,
  let them, not me, be terrified.
On them bring the day of disaster,
  destroy them, destroy them twice over!

19 Yahweh said this to me, 'Go and stand at the Gate of
the Sons of the People by which the kings of Judah go in
and out—and at all the gates of Jerusalem. 20 Say to them,
"Listen to the word of Yahweh, you kings of Judah, all you
people of Judah too, and all you inhabitants of Jerusalem
who pass through the gates. 21 Yahweh says this: As you
value your lives, on no account carry a burden on the Sabbath day or bring it in through the gates of Jerusalem.
22 Bring no burden out of your houses on the Sabbath day,
and do no work. Keep the Sabbath day holy, as I ordered
your ancestors. 23 They would not hear, would not pay attention; they deliberately refused to listen or accept instruction. 24 But if you listen carefully to me, Yahweh declares,

| NEW REVISED STANDARD VERSION | REVISED ENGLISH BIBLE |

24 But if you listen to me, says the LORD, and bring in no burden by the gates of this city on the sabbath day, but keep the sabbath day holy and do no work on it, 25 then there shall enter by the gates of this city kings*m* who sit on the throne of David, riding in chariots and on horses, they and their officials, the people of Judah and the inhabitants of Jerusalem; and this city shall be inhabited forever. 26 And people shall come from the towns of Judah and the places around Jerusalem, from the land of Benjamin, from the Shephelah, from the hill country, and from the Negeb, bringing burnt offerings and sacrifices, grain offerings and frankincense, and bringing thank offerings to the house of the LORD. 27 But if you do not listen to me, to keep the sabbath day holy, and to carry in no burden through the gates of Jerusalem on the sabbath day, then I will kindle a fire in its gates; it shall devour the palaces of Jerusalem and shall not be quenched.

18 The word that came to Jeremiah from the LORD: 2 "Come, go down to the potter's house, and there I will let you hear my words." 3 So I went down to the potter's house, and there he was working at his wheel. 4 The vessel he was making of clay was spoiled in the potter's hand, and he reworked it into another vessel, as seemed good to him.

5 Then the word of the LORD came to me: 6 Can I not do with you, O house of Israel, just as this potter has done? says the LORD. Just like the clay in the potter's hand, so are you in my hand, O house of Israel. 7 At one moment I may declare concerning a nation or a kingdom, that I will pluck up and break down and destroy it, 8 but if that nation, concerning which I have spoken, turns from its evil, I will change my mind about the disaster that I intended to bring on it. 9 And at another moment I may declare concerning a nation or a kingdom that I will build and plant it, 10 but if it does evil in my sight, not listening to my voice, then I will change my mind about the good that I had intended to do to it. 11 Now, therefore, say to the people of Judah and the inhabitants of Jerusalem: Thus says the LORD: Look, I am a potter shaping evil against you and devising a plan against you. Turn now, all of you from your evil way, and amend your ways and your doings.

12 But they say, "It is no use! We will follow our own plans, and each of us will act according to the stubbornness of our evil will."

13 Therefore thus says the LORD:
Ask among the nations:
  Who has heard the like of this?
The virgin Israel has done
  a most horrible thing.
14 Does the snow of Lebanon leave
  the crags of Sirion?*n*
Do the mountain*o* waters run dry,*p*
  the cold flowing streams?
15 But my people have forgotten me,
  they burn offerings to a delusion;
they have stumbled*q* in their ways,
  in the ancient roads,
and have gone into bypaths,
  not the highway,
16 making their land a horror,
  a thing to be hissed at forever.
All who pass by it are horrified
  and shake their heads.

the LORD, and refrain from bringing any load through the gates of this city on the sabbath, and keep that day holy by doing no work on it, 25 then kings will come through the gates of this city, kings who will sit on David's throne. They will come riding in chariots or on horseback, escorted by their officers, by the people of Judah, and by the citizens of Jerusalem; and this city will be inhabited for ever. 26 People will come from the towns of Judah, the country round Jerusalem, the territory of Benjamin, the Shephelah, the hill-country, and the Negeb, bringing whole-offerings, sacrifices, grain-offerings, and frankincense, bringing also thank-offerings to the house of the LORD. 27 But if you do not obey me by keeping the sabbath day holy and by carrying no load as you come through the gates of Jerusalem on the sabbath, then I shall set fire to the gates; it will consume the palaces of Jerusalem and will not be put out.

18 THESE are the words which came to Jeremiah from the LORD: 2 Go down now to the potter's house, and there I shall tell you what I have to say. 3 I went down to the potter's house, where I found him working at the wheel. 4 Now and then a vessel he was making from the clay would be spoilt in his hands, and he would remould it into another vessel to his liking.

5 Then the word of the LORD came to me: 6 Israel, can I not deal with you as this potter deals with his clay? says the LORD. House of Israel, you are clay in my hands like the clay in his. 7 At any moment I may threaten to uproot a nation or a kingdom, to pull it down and destroy it. 8 But if the nation which I have threatened turns back from its wicked ways, then I shall think again about the disaster I had in mind for it. 9 At another moment I may announce that I shall build or plant a nation or a kingdom. 10 But if it does evil in my sight by disobeying me, I shall think again about the good I had in mind for it.

11 Go now and tell the people of Judah and the citizens of Jerusalem that these are the words of the LORD: I am framing disaster for you and perfecting my designs against you. Turn back, every one of you, from his evil conduct; mend your ways and your actions. 12 But they will answer, 'Things are past hope. We must stick to our own plans, and each of us follow the promptings of his wicked and stubborn heart.'

13 Therefore these are the words of the LORD:

Enquire among the nations:
  whoever heard the like of this?
The virgin Israel has done a thing most horrible.
14 Does the snow cease to fall from the rocky slopes
  of Lebanon?
Does the cool rain streaming in torrents ever fail?
15 No, but my people have forgotten me:
  they burn sacrifices to idols
which cause them to stumble as they tread the
    ancient ways,
  and they take to byways and unmade roads;
16 their own land they lay waste,
  an object of lasting derision,
at which all passers-by shake their heads in horror.

---

m Cn: Heb *kings and officials*   *n* Cn: Heb *of the field*   *o* Cn: Heb *foreign*   *p* Cn: Heb *Are . . . plucked up?*   *q* Gk Syr Vg: Heb *they made them stumble*

17:25 **city, kings:** *prob. rdg; Heb. adds* and officers.   18:14 **fail:** *prob. rdg; Heb.* become uprooted.

the LORD, and carry no burden through the gates of this city on the sabbath, keeping the sabbath holy and abstaining from all work on it, 25 then, through the gates of this city, kings who sit upon the throne of David will continue to enter, riding in their chariots or upon their horses, along with their princes, and the men of Judah, and the citizens of Jerusalem. This city will remain inhabited forever. 26 To it people will come from the cities of Judah and the neighborhood of Jerusalem, from the land of Benjamin and from the foothills, from the hill country and the Negeb, to bring holocausts and sacrifices, cereal offerings and incense and thank offerings to the house of the LORD. 27 But if you do not obey me and keep holy the sabbath, if you carry burdens and come through the gates of Jerusalem on the sabbath, I will set unquenchable fire to its gates, which will consume the palaces of Jerusalem.

18 This word came to Jeremiah from the LORD: 2 Rise up, be off to the potter's house; there I will give you my message. 3 I went down to the potter's house and there he was, working at the wheel. 4 Whenever the object of clay which he was making turned out badly in his hand, he tried again, making of the clay another object of whatever sort he pleased. 5 Then the word of the Lord came to me: 6 Can I not do to you, house of Israel, as this potter has done? says the LORD. Indeed, like clay in the hand of the potter, so are you in my hand, house of Israel. 7 Sometimes I threaten to uproot and tear down and destroy a nation or a kingdom. 8 But if that nation which I have threatened turns from its evil, I also repent of the evil which I threatened to do. 9 Sometimes, again, I promise to build up and plant a nation or a kingdom. 10 But if that nation does what is evil in my eyes, refusing to obey my voice, I repent of the good with which I promised to bless it.

11 And now, tell this to the men of Judah and the citizens of Jerusalem: Thus says the LORD: Take care! I am fashioning evil against you and making a plan. Return, each of you, from his evil way; reform your ways and your deeds. 12 But they will say, "No use! We will follow our own devices; each one of us will behave according to the stubbornness of his evil heart!"

13   Therefore thus says the LORD:
    Ask among the nations —
        who has ever heard the like?
    Truly horrible things
        has virgin Israel done!
14 Does the snow of Lebanon
        desert the rocky heights?
    Do the gushing waters dry up
        that flow fresh down the mountains?
15 Yet my people have forgotten me:
        they burn incense to a thing that does not exist.
    They stumble out of their ways,
        the paths of old,
    To travel on bypaths,
        not the beaten track.
16 Their land shall be turned into a desert,
        an object of lasting ridicule:
    All passers-by will be amazed,
        will shake their heads.

and bring no burden in through the gates of this city on the Sabbath day, if you keep the Sabbath holy and do no work on that day, 25 then, through the gates of this city, kings and princes occupying the throne of David will continue to make their entry, riding in chariots or on horseback, they, their chief men, the people of Judah and the inhabitants of Jerusalem. And this city will be inhabited for ever. 26 They will come from the towns of Judah, from the districts round Jerusalem, from the territory of Benjamin, from the lowlands, from the highlands, from the Negeb, to offer burnt offering and sacrifice, and cereal offering and incense, to offer thanksgiving sacrifices in the Temple of Yahweh. 27 But if you do not listen to me to keep the Sabbath day holy, and to refrain from entering the gates of Jerusalem with burdens on the Sabbath day, then I shall set fire to its gates; fire will devour the palaces of Jerusalem and not be quenched." '

18 The word that came to Jeremiah from Yahweh as follows, 2 'Get up and make your way down to the potter's house, and there I shall tell you what I have to say.' 3 So I went down to the potter's house; and there he was, working at the wheel. 4 But the vessel he was making came out wrong, as may happen with clay when a potter is at work. So he began again and shaped it into another vessel, as he thought fit. 5 Then the word of Yahweh came to me as follows, 6 'House of Israel, can I not do to you what this potter does? Yahweh demands. Yes, like clay in the potter's hand, so you are in mine, House of Israel. 7 Sometimes I announce that I shall uproot, break down and destroy a certain nation or kingdom, 8 but should the nation I have threatened abandon its wickedness, I then change my mind about the disaster which I had intended to inflict on it. 9 Sometimes I announce that I shall build up and plant a certain nation or kingdom, 10 but should that nation do what displeases me and refuse to listen to my voice, I then change my mind about the good which I was intending to confer on it. 11 So now, say this to the people of Judah and the inhabitants of Jerusalem, "Yahweh says this: Listen, I am preparing a disaster for you, I am working out a plan against you. So now, each one of you, turn back from your evil ways, amend your conduct and actions." 12 They, however, will say, "It is no use! We shall follow our own plans; each of us will act on his own wicked inclinations." '

13 Therefore, Yahweh says this,
    'Ask, please, among the nations
      if anyone has heard anything like this.
    The Virgin of Israel
      has done a very horrible thing.
14 Does the snow of Lebanon
      ever leave the rocks of its slopes?
    Do the rivers of foreign lands,
      their cold flowing waters, ever run dry?
15 And yet my people have forgotten me!
    They burn incense to a Nothing!
    They have been made to stumble in their ways,
      the ancient paths,
    to walk in paths,
      on an unmade road,
16 to make their country an object of horror,
      everlastingly derided:
    every passer-by will be appalled at it
    and shake his head.

17 Like the wind from the east,
    I will scatter them before the enemy.
I will show them my back, not my face,
    in the day of their calamity.

18 Then they said, "Come, let us make plots against Jeremiah—for instruction shall not perish from the priest, nor counsel from the wise, nor the word from the prophet. Come, let us bring charges against him,[r] and let us not heed any of his words."

19 Give heed to me, O LORD,
    and listen to what my adversaries say!
20 Is evil a recompense for good?
    Yet they have dug a pit for my life.
Remember how I stood before you
    to speak good for them,
    to turn away your wrath from them.
21 Therefore give their children over to famine;
    hurl them out to the power of the sword,
let their wives become childless and widowed.
    May their men meet death by pestilence,
    their youths be slain by the sword in battle.
22 May a cry be heard from their houses,
    when you bring the marauder suddenly upon
    them!
For they have dug a pit to catch me,
    and laid snares for my feet.
23 Yet you, O LORD, know
    all their plotting to kill me.
Do not forgive their iniquity,
    do not blot out their sin from your sight.
Let them be tripped up before you;
    deal with them while you are angry.

19 Thus said the LORD: Go and buy a potter's earthenware jug. Take with you[s] some of the elders of the people and some of the senior priests, 2 and go out to the valley of the son of Hinnom at the entry of the Potsherd Gate, and proclaim there the words that I tell you. 3 You shall say: Hear the word of the LORD, O kings of Judah and inhabitants of Jerusalem. Thus says the LORD of hosts, the God of Israel: I am going to bring such disaster upon this place that the ears of everyone who hears of it will tingle. 4 Because the people have forsaken me, and have profaned this place by making offerings in it to other gods whom neither they nor their ancestors nor the kings of Judah have known; and because they have filled this place with the blood of the innocent, 5 and gone on building the high places of Baal to burn their children in the fire as burnt offerings to Baal, which I did not command or decree, nor did it enter my mind. 6 Therefore the days are surely coming, says the LORD, when this place shall no more be called Topheth, or the valley of the son of Hinnom, but the valley of Slaughter. 7 And in this place I will make void the plans of Judah and Jerusalem, and will make them fall by the sword before their enemies, and by the hand of those who seek their life. I will give their dead bodies for food to the birds of the air and to the wild animals of the earth. 8 And I will make this city a horror, a thing to be hissed at; everyone who passes by it will be horrified and will hiss because of all its disasters. 9 And I will make them eat the flesh of their sons and the flesh of their daughters, and all shall eat the flesh of their neighbors in the siege, and in the distress with which their enemies and those who seek their life afflict them.

10 Then you shall break the jug in the sight of those who go with you, 11 and shall say: Thus says the LORD

[r] Heb *strike him with the tongue*   [s] Syr Tg Compare Gk: Heb lacks *take with you*

17 As with a wind from the east
I shall scatter them before their enemies.
In the hour of their downfall
I shall turn my back and not my face towards
    them.

18 The cry was raised: 'Let us consider how to deal with Jeremiah. There will still be priests to guide us, still wise men to give counsel, still prophets to proclaim the word. Let us invent some charges against him; let us pay no heed to anything he says.'

19 But pay heed, LORD,
    and hear what my opponents are saying against
    me.
20 Is good to be repaid with evil,
    that they have dug a pit for me?
Remember how I stood before you,
    interceding on their behalf
    to avert your wrath from them.
21 Therefore give their children over to famine,
    leave them at the mercy of the sword.
Let their women be childless and widowed,
    let their men be slain by pestilence,
    their young men cut down in battle.
22 Bring raiders on them without warning,
    and let screaming be heard from their houses.
They have dug a pit to catch me
    and have laid snares for my feet.
23 Well you know, LORD,
    all their murderous plots against me.
Do not blot out their wrongdoing
    or wipe away their sin from your sight;
when they are brought stumbling before you,
    deal with them on the day of your anger.

19 These are the words of the LORD: Go and buy from the potter an earthenware jar, and taking with you some of the elders of the people and some priests, 2 go out to the valley of Ben-hinnom, on which the Gate of the Potsherds opens, and there proclaim what I tell you. 3 Say: Hear the word of the LORD, you princes of Judah and citizens of Jerusalem. These are the words of the LORD of Hosts the God of Israel: I am about to bring on this place such a disaster as will ring in the ears of all who hear of it, 4 because they have forsaken me, and made this a place of alien worship. They have burnt sacrifices to other gods whom neither they nor their forefathers nor the kings of Judah ever knew, and they have filled this place with the blood of the innocent. 5 They have built shrines to Baal, at which to burn their sons as whole-offerings to Baal. That was no command of mine, a thing I never spoke of, nor did it ever enter my mind.

6 Therefore the time is coming, says the LORD, when it will no longer be called Topheth or the valley of Ben-hinnom, but the valley of Slaughter. 7 In this place I shall make void the plans of Judah and Jerusalem; I shall make the people fall by the sword before their enemies, at the hands of those who seek to kill them; I shall give their corpses to the birds and beasts to devour. 8 I shall make this city a scene of desolation, an object of astonishment, so that every passer-by will be desolated and appalled at the sight of all her wounds. 9 I shall make people eat the flesh of their sons and their daughters; they will devour one another's flesh in the dire straits to which their enemies and those who would kill them will reduce them in the siege.

10 Then you are to smash the jar before the eyes of the men who accompany you 11 and say to them: These are the

17 Like the east wind, I will scatter them
   before their enemies;
I will show them my back, not my face,
   in their day of disaster.

18 "Come," they said, "let us contrive a plot against Jeremiah. It will not mean the loss of instruction from the
priests, nor of counsel from the wise, nor of messages from
the prophets. And so, let us destroy him by his own tongue;
let us carefully note his every word."

19 Heed me, O LORD,
   and listen to what my adversaries say.
20 Must good be repaid with evil
   that they should dig a pit to take my life?
Remember that I stood before you
   to speak in their behalf,
   to turn away your wrath from them.
21 So now, deliver their children to famine,
   do away with them by the sword.
Let their wives be made childless and widows;
   let their men die of pestilence,
   their young men be slain by the sword in battle.
22 May cries be heard from their homes,
   when suddenly you send plunderers
      against them.
For they have dug a pit to capture me,
   they have hid snares for my feet;
23 But you, O LORD, know
   all their plans to slay me.
Forgive not their crime,
   blot not out their sin in your sight!
Let them go down before you,
   proceed against them in the time of your anger.

19 Thus said the LORD: Go, buy a potter's earthen
flask. Take along some of the elders of the people
and of the priests, 2 and go out toward the Valley of Ben-
hinnom, at the entrance of the Potsherd Gate; there proclaim
the words which I will speak to you: 3 Listen to the word of
the LORD, kings of Judah and citizens of Jerusalem: Thus
says the LORD of hosts, the God of Israel: I am going to
bring such evil upon this place that all who hear of it will
feel their ears tingle. 4 This is because they have forsaken
me and alienated this place by burning in it incense to
strange gods which neither they nor their fathers knew; and
the kings of Judah have filled this place with the blood of
the innocent. 5 They have built high places for Baal to immolate their sons in fire as holocausts to Baal: such a thing
as I neither commanded nor spoke of, nor did it ever enter
my mind. 6 Therefore, days will come, says the LORD, when
this place will no longer be called Topheth, or the Valley of
Ben-hinnom, but rather, the Valley of Slaughter. 7 In this
place I will foil the plan of Judah and Jerusalem; I will make
them fall by the sword before their enemies, by the hand of
those that seek their lives. Their corpses I will give as food
to the birds of the sky and the beasts of the field. 8 I will
make this city an object of amazement and derision. Because of all its wounds, every passer-by will be amazed and
will catch his breath. 9 I will have them eat the flesh of their
sons and daughters; they shall eat one another's flesh during
the strict siege by which their enemies and those who seek
their lives will confine them.

10 And you shall break the flask in the sight of the men
who went with you, 11 and say to them: Thus says the LORD

17 Like the east wind, I shall scatter them
   before the enemy.
I shall show them my back, not my face,
   the day they are ruined.'

18 'Come on,' they said, 'let us concoct a plot against
Jeremiah, for the Law will not perish for lack of priests, nor
advice for lack of wise men, nor the word for lack of prophets. Come on, let us slander him and pay no attention to
anything he says.'

19 Pay attention to me, Yahweh,
   hear what my adversaries are saying.
20 Should evil be returned for good?
   Now they are digging a pit for me.
Remember how I pleaded before you
   and spoke good of them,
   to turn your retribution away from them.
21 So, hand their sons over to famine,
   abandon them to the edge of the sword.
Let their wives become
   childless and widowed.
Let their husbands die of plague,
   their young men be cut down by the sword in
      battle.
22 Let cries re-echo from their houses
   as you bring raiders suddenly on them.
For they have dug a pit to catch me,
   they have laid snares to trap my feet.
23 But you, Yahweh, know
   all about their murderous plot against me.
Do not forgive their guilt,
   do not efface their sin from your sight.
Let them be hurled down before you,
   deal with them while you are angry!

19 Then Yahweh said to Jeremiah, 'Go and buy a potter's earthenware jug. Take some of the people's
elders and some of the senior priests with you. 2 Go out
towards the Valley of Ben-Hinnom, just outside the Gate of
the Potsherds. There proclaim the words I shall say to you.
3 You must say, "Kings of Judah, inhabitants of Jerusalem!
Listen to the word of Yahweh! Yahweh Sabaoth, the God
of Israel, says this: I am about to bring a disaster on
this place that the ears of every one who hears of it will ring.
4 For they have abandoned me and have made this place
unrecognisable, and offered incense here to other gods
which neither they nor their ancestors nor the kings of Judah
ever knew before. They have filled this place with the blood
of the innocent; 5 for they have built high places for Baal to
burn their sons as burnt offerings to Baal, a thing I never
ordered, never mentioned, that had never entered my
thoughts. 6 So now the days are coming, Yahweh declares,
when people will no longer call this place Topheth, or Valley of Ben-Hinnom, but Valley of Slaughter. 7 Because of
this place, I shall empty Judah and Jerusalem of sound
advice; I shall make them fall by the sword before their
enemies, by the hand of those determined to kill them; I
shall give their corpses as food to the birds of the sky and
the animals of earth. 8 And I shall make this city an object
of horror and derision; every passer-by will be appalled at
it and whistle at the sight of all the wounds it has sustained.
9 I shall make them eat the flesh of their own sons and
daughters: they will eat one another during the siege, in the
shortage to which their enemies, and those determined to
kill them, will reduce them.

10 'You must break this jug in front of the men who are
with you, 11 and say to them, "Yahweh Sabaoth says this: I

of hosts: So will I break this people and this city, as one breaks a potter's vessel, so that it can never be mended. In Topheth they shall bury until there is no more room to bury. 12 Thus will I do to this place, says the LORD, and to its inhabitants, making this city like Topheth. 13 And the houses of Jerusalem and the houses of the kings of Judah shall be defiled like the place of Topheth—all the houses upon whose roofs offerings have been made to the whole host of heaven, and libations have been poured out to other gods.

14 When Jeremiah came from Topheth, where the LORD had sent him to prophesy, he stood in the court of the LORD's house and said to all the people: 15 Thus says the LORD of hosts, the God of Israel: I am now bringing upon this city and upon all its towns all the disaster that I have pronounced against it, because they have stiffened their necks, refusing to hear my words.

20 Now the priest Pashhur son of Immer, who was chief officer in the house of the LORD, heard Jeremiah prophesying these things. 2 Then Pashhur struck the prophet Jeremiah, and put him in the stocks that were in the upper Benjamin Gate of the house of the LORD. 3 The next morning when Pashhur released Jeremiah from the stocks, Jeremiah said to him, The LORD has named you not Pashhur but "Terror-all-around." 4 For thus says the LORD: I am making you a terror to yourself and to all your friends; and they shall fall by the sword of their enemies while you look on. And I will give all Judah into the hand of the king of Babylon; he shall carry them captive to Babylon, and shall kill them with the sword. 5 I will give all the wealth of this city, all its gains, all its prized belongings, and all the treasures of the kings of Judah into the hand of their enemies, who shall plunder them, and seize them, and carry them to Babylon. 6 And you, Pashhur, and all who live in your house, shall go into captivity, and to Babylon you shall go; there you shall die, and there you shall be buried, you and all your friends, to whom you have prophesied falsely.

7 O LORD, you have enticed me,
    and I was enticed;
  you have overpowered me,
    and you have prevailed.
I have become a laughingstock all day long;
    everyone mocks me.
8 For whenever I speak, I must cry out,
    I must shout, "Violence and destruction!"
For the word of the LORD has become for me
    a reproach and derision all day long.
9 If I say, "I will not mention him,
    or speak any more in his name,"
then within me there is something like a burning
    fire
    shut up in my bones;
I am weary with holding it in,
    and I cannot.
10 For I hear many whispering:
    "Terror is all around!
Denounce him! Let us denounce him!"
    All my close friends
    are watching for me to stumble.
"Perhaps he can be enticed,
    and we can prevail against him,
    and take our revenge on him."
11 But the LORD is with me like a dread warrior;
    therefore my persecutors will stumble,
    and they will not prevail.
They will be greatly shamed,
    for they will not succeed.
Their eternal dishonor
    will never be forgotten.

words of the LORD of Hosts: Thus shall I smash this people and this city as an earthen vessel is smashed beyond all repair, and the dead will be buried in Topheth until there is no room left to bury them. 12 That is how I shall deal with this place and with those who live there, says the LORD: I shall make this city like Topheth. 13 Because of their defilement, the houses of Jerusalem and those of the kings of Judah will be like the site of Topheth, every one of the houses on whose roofs men have burnt sacrifices to all the host of heaven and poured drink-offerings to other gods.

14 When Jeremiah came in from Topheth, where the LORD had sent him to prophesy, he stood in the court of the LORD's house and said to all the people: 15 These are the words of the LORD of Hosts the God of Israel: I am about to bring on this city and on all its dependent towns the whole disaster with which I have threatened it, for its people have remained stubborn and refused to listen to me.

20 The priest Pashhur son of Immer, the chief officer in the house of the LORD, heard Jeremiah prophesying these things, 2 and had him flogged and put him in the stocks at the Upper Benjamin Gate, in the house of the LORD. 3 When next morning Pashhur released him from the stocks, Jeremiah said to him: The LORD has called you not Pashhur but Magor-missabib. 4 For these are the words of the LORD: I shall make you a terror to yourself and to all your friends; they will fall by the sword of the enemy before your very eyes. I shall hand over all Judah to the king of Babylon, and he will deport them to Babylon or put them to the sword. 5 I shall give all this city's store of wealth and riches and all the treasures of the kings of Judah to their enemies; they will seize them as spoil and carry them off to Babylon. 6 You, Pashhur, and all your household will go into captivity. You will come to Babylon; there you will die and there you will be buried, you and all your friends to whom you have been a false prophet.

7 YOU HAVE duped me, LORD,
    and I have been your dupe;
  you have outwitted me and prevailed.
All the day long I have been made a
    laughing-stock;
  everyone ridicules me.
8 Whenever I speak I must needs cry out,
    calling, 'Violence!' and 'Assault!'
I am reproached and derided all the time
    for uttering the word of the LORD.
9 Whenever I said, 'I shall not call it to mind
    or speak in his name again,'
then his word became imprisoned within me
    like a fire burning in my heart.
I was weary with holding it under,
    and could endure no more.
10 For I heard many whispering, 'Terror let loose!
    Denounce him! Let us denounce him.'
All my friends were on the watch for a false step,
    saying, 'Perhaps he may be tricked;
    then we can catch him
    and have our revenge on him.'
11 But the LORD is on my side,
    a powerful champion;
therefore my persecutors will stumble and fall
    powerless.
Their abasement will be bitter when they fail,
    and their dishonour will long be remembered.

20:3 **Magor-missabib:** *that is* Terror let loose.   20:7 **have outwitted me:** *or* were too strong for me.   20:9 **call it:** *or* call him.

NEW AMERICAN BIBLE

NEW JERUSALEM BIBLE

of hosts: Thus will I smash this people and this city, as one smashes a clay pot so that it cannot be repaired. And Topheth shall be a burial place, for lack of place to bury elsewhere. 12 Thus I will do to this place and to its inhabitants, says the LORD; I will make this city like Topheth. 13 And the houses of Jerusalem and the palaces of the kings of Judah shall be defiled like the place of Topheth, all the houses upon whose roofs they burnt incense to the whole host of heaven and poured out libations to strange gods.

14 When Jeremiah returned from Topheth, where the LORD had sent him to prophesy, he stood in the court of the house of God and said to all the people: 15 Thus says the LORD of hosts, the God of Israel: I will surely bring upon this city all the evil with which I threatened it, because they have stiffened their necks and have not obeyed my words.

20 Jeremiah was heard prophesying these things by the priest Pashhur, son of Immer, chief officer in the house of the LORD. 2 So he had the prophet scourged and placed in the stocks at the upper Gate of Benjamin in the house of the LORD. 3 The next morning, after Pashhur had released Jeremiah from the stocks, the prophet said to him: Instead of Pashhur, the LORD will name you "Terror on every side." 4 For thus says the LORD: Indeed, I will deliver you to terror, you and all your friends. Your own eyes shall see them fall by the sword of their enemies. All Judah I will deliver to the king of Babylon, who shall take them captive to Babylon or slay them with the sword. 5 All the wealth of this city, all it has toiled for and holds dear, all the treasures of the kings of Judah, I will give as plunder into the hands of their foes, who shall seize it and carry it away to Babylon. 6 You, Pashhur, and all the members of your household shall go into exile. To Babylon you shall go, you and all your friends; there you shall die and be buried, because you have prophesied lies to them.

7 You duped me, O LORD, and I let myself
    be duped;
  you were too strong for me, and you triumphed.
All the day I am an object of laughter;
  everyone mocks me.
8 Whenever I speak, I must cry out,
  violence and outrage is my message;
The word of the LORD has brought me
  derision and reproach all the day.
9 I say to myself, I will not mention him,
  I will speak in his name no more.
But then it becomes like fire burning in my heart,
  imprisoned in my bones;
I grow weary holding it in,
  I cannot endure it.
10 Yes, I hear the whisperings of many:
  "Terror on every side!
  Denounce! let us denounce him!"
All those who were my friends
  are on the watch for any misstep of mine.
"Perhaps he will be trapped; then we can prevail,
  and take our vengeance on him."
11 But the LORD is with me, like a mighty champion:
  my persecutors will stumble, they will
    not triumph.
In their failure they will be put to utter shame,
  to lasting, unforgettable confusion.

am going to break this people and this city just as one breaks a potter's pot, so that it can never be mended again.

"Topheth will become a burial ground, for lack of other burial space. 12 That is how I shall treat this place, Yahweh declares, and its inhabitants, by making this city like Topheth. 13 The houses of Jerusalem and those of the kings of Judah, all the houses on the roofs of which they offered incense to the whole array of heaven and poured libations to other gods, will be unclean, like this place Topheth." '

14 Jeremiah then came back from Topheth where Yahweh had sent him to prophesy, and stood in the court of the Temple of Yahweh and said to all the people, 15 'Yahweh Sabaoth, the God of Israel, says this, "Yes, on this city, and on all the towns belonging to it, I shall bring all the disaster which I had decreed for it, since they have stubbornly refused to listen to my words." '

20 Now the priest Pashhur son of Immer, who was the chief of police in the Temple of Yahweh, heard Jeremiah making this prophecy. 2 Pashhur struck the prophet Jeremiah and then put him in the stocks, in the Upper Benjamin Gate leading into the Temple of Yahweh. 3 Next day, Pashhur had Jeremiah taken out of the stocks; Jeremiah then said to him, 'Not Pashhur but Terror-on-every-Side is Yahweh's name for you. 4 For Yahweh says this, "I am going to hand you over to terror, you and all your friends; they will fall by the sword of their enemies, your own eyes will see it. The whole of Judah, too, I shall hand over to the king of Babylon; he will carry them off captive to Babylon and put them to the sword. 5 And all the wealth of this city, all its stores, all its valuables, all the treasures of the kings of Judah, I shall hand over to their enemies who will plunder them, round them up and carry them off to Babylon. 6 As for you, Pashhur, and your whole household, you will go into captivity; you will go to Babylon; there you will die, and there be buried, you and all your friends to whom you have prophesied lies." '

7 You have seduced me, Yahweh, and I have let
    myself be seduced;
  you have overpowered me: you were the stronger.
I am a laughing-stock all day long,
  they all make fun of me.
8 For whenever I speak, I have to howl
  and proclaim, 'Violence and ruin!'
For me, Yahweh's word has been the cause
  of insult and derision all day long.
9 I would say to myself, 'I will not think about him,
  I will not speak in his name any more,'
but then there seemed to be a fire burning in my
    heart,
  imprisoned in my bones.
The effort to restrain it wearied me,
  I could not do it.
10 I heard so many disparaging me,
  'Terror on every side!
Denounce him! Let us denounce him!'
All those who were on good terms with me
  watched for my downfall,
  'Perhaps he will be seduced into error.
Then we shall get the better of him
  and take our revenge!'
11 But Yahweh is at my side like a mighty hero;
  my opponents will stumble, vanquished,
  confounded by their failure;
  everlasting, unforgettable disgrace will be theirs.

12 O Lord of hosts, you test the righteous,
    you see the heart and the mind;
let me see your retribution upon them,
    for to you I have committed my cause.

13 Sing to the Lord;
    praise the Lord!
For he has delivered the life of the needy
    from the hands of evildoers.

14 Cursed be the day
    on which I was born!
The day when my mother bore me,
    let it not be blessed!

15 Cursed be the man
    who brought the news to my father, saying,
"A child is born to you, a son,"
    making him very glad.

16 Let that man be like the cities
    that the Lord overthrew without pity;
let him hear a cry in the morning
    and an alarm at noon,

17 because he did not kill me in the womb;
    so my mother would have been my grave,
    and her womb forever great.

18 Why did I come forth from the womb
    to see toil and sorrow,
    and spend my days in shame?

21 This is the word that came to Jeremiah from the Lord, when King Zedekiah sent to him Pashhur son of Malchiah and the priest Zephaniah son of Maaseiah, saying, 2 "Please inquire of the Lord on our behalf, for King Nebuchadrezzar of Babylon is making war against us; perhaps the Lord will perform a wonderful deed for us, as he has often done, and will make him withdraw from us."

3 Then Jeremiah said to them: 4 Thus you shall say to Zedekiah: Thus says the Lord, the God of Israel: I am going to turn back the weapons of war that are in your hands and with which you are fighting against the king of Babylon and against the Chaldeans who are besieging you outside the walls; and I will bring them together into the center of this city. 5 I myself will fight against you with outstretched hand and mighty arm, in anger, in fury, and in great wrath. 6 And I will strike down the inhabitants of this city, both human beings and animals; they shall die of a great pestilence. 7 Afterward, says the Lord, I will give King Zedekiah of Judah, and his servants, and the people in this city—those who survive the pestilence, sword, and famine—into the hands of King Nebuchadrezzar of Babylon, into the hands of their enemies, into the hands of those who seek their lives. He shall strike them down with the edge of the sword; he shall not pity them, or spare them, or have compassion.

8 And to this people you shall say: Thus says the Lord: See, I am setting before you the way of life and the way of death. 9 Those who stay in this city shall die by the sword, by famine, and by pestilence; but those who go out and surrender to the Chaldeans who are besieging you shall live and shall have their lives as a prize of war. 10 For I have set my face against this city for evil and not for good, says the Lord: it shall be given into the hands of the king of Babylon, and he shall burn it with fire.

11 To the house of the king of Judah say: Hear the word of the Lord, 12 O house of David! Thus says the Lord:
    Execute justice in the morning,
        and deliver from the hand of the oppressor
    anyone who has been robbed,
    or else my wrath will go forth like fire,
        and burn, with no one to quench it,
    because of your evil doings.

12 But, Lord of Hosts, you test the righteous
    and search the depths of the heart.
To you I have committed my cause;
    let me see your vengeance on them.

13 Sing to the Lord, praise the Lord;
    for he rescues the poor
    from those who would do them wrong.

14 A curse on the day when I was born!
    The day my mother bore me,
    may it be for ever unblessed!

15 A curse on the man who brought word to my
    father,
    'A child is born to you, a son,'
    and gladdened his heart!

16 May that man fare like the cities
    which the Lord overthrew without mercy.
May he hear cries of alarm in the morning
    and uproar at noon,

17 since death did not claim me before birth,
    and my mother did not become my grave,
    her womb great with me for ever.

18 Why did I come from the womb
    to see only sorrow and toil,
    to end my days in shame?

21 The word which came from the Lord to Jeremiah when King Zedekiah sent to him Pashhur son of Malchiah and the priest Zephaniah son of Maaseiah with this request: 2 'King Nebuchadrezzar of Babylon has declared war on us; enquire of the Lord on our behalf. Perhaps the Lord will perform a miracle as he has done in times past, so that Nebuchadrezzar will raise the siege.'

3 But Jeremiah answered them: Tell Zedekiah 4 that these are the words of the Lord the God of Israel: I shall turn against you your own weapons with which you are fighting the king of Babylon and the Chaldaeans who are besieging you outside the wall; and I shall bring them into the heart of this city. 5 I myself shall fight against you in burning rage and great fury, with an outstretched hand and a strong arm. 6 I shall strike down those who live in this city, men and cattle alike; they will die of a great pestilence. 7 After that, says the Lord, I shall take King Zedekiah of Judah, his courtiers, and the people, all in this city who survive pestilence, sword, and famine, and hand them over to King Nebuchadrezzar of Babylon, to their enemies and those who would kill them. He will put them to the sword and show no pity or mercy or compassion.

8 You are to say further to this people: These are the words of the Lord: I offer you now a choice between the way of life and the way of death. 9 Whoever remains in this city will die by sword, famine, or pestilence; but whoever goes out and surrenders to the Chaldaeans now laying siege to you will survive; he will escape with his life. 10 I have set my face against this city, determined to do them harm, not good, says the Lord. It will be handed over to the king of Babylon, and he will burn it to the ground.

11 To the royal house of Judah:
    Listen to the word of the Lord;

12 house of David, these are the words of the Lord:
    Dispense justice betimes,
    rescue the victim from his oppressor,
    or the fire of my fury may blaze up and burn
        unquenchably
    because of your evil actions.

NEW AMERICAN BIBLE

¹²O Lord of hosts, you who test the just,
  who probe mind and heart,
Let me witness the vengeance you take on them,
  for to you I have entrusted my cause.
¹³Sing to the Lord,
  praise the Lord,
For he has rescued the life of the poor
  from the power of the wicked!

¹⁴Cursed be the day
  on which I was born!
May the day my mother gave me birth
  never be blessed!
¹⁵Cursed be the man who brought the news
  to my father, saying,
  "A child, a son, has been born to you!"
  filling him with great joy.
¹⁶Let that man be like the cities
  which the Lord relentlessly overthrew;
Let him hear war cries in the morning,
  battle alarms at noonday,
¹⁷ because he did not dispatch me in the womb!
Then my mother would have been my grave,
  her womb confining me forever.
¹⁸Why did I come forth from the womb,
  to see sorrow and pain,
  to end my days in shame?

21 The message which came to Jeremiah from the Lord when King Zedekiah sent him Pashhur, son of Malchiah, and the priest Zephaniah, son of Maaseiah, with this request: ²Inquire for us of the Lord, because Nebuchadnezzar, king of Babylon, is attacking us. Perhaps the Lord will deal with us according to all his wonderful works, so that he will withdraw from us. ³But Jeremiah answered them: This is what you shall report to Zedekiah: ⁴Thus says the Lord, the God of Israel: I will turn back in your hands the weapons with which you intend to fight the king of Babylon and the Chaldeans who besiege you outside the walls. These weapons I will pile up in the midst of this city, ⁵and I myself will fight against you with outstretched hand and mighty arm, in anger, and wrath, and great rage! ⁶I will strike the inhabitants of this city, both man and beast; they shall die in a great pestilence. ⁷After that, says the Lord, I will hand over Zedekiah, king of Judah, and his ministers and the people in this city who survive pestilence, sword, and famine, into the hand of Nebuchadnezzar, king of Babylon, into the hands of their enemies and those who seek their lives. He shall strike them with the edge of the sword, without quarter, without pity or mercy. ⁸And to this people you shall say: Thus says the Lord: See, I am giving you a choice between life and death. ⁹Whoever remains in this city shall die by the sword or famine or pestilence. But whoever leaves and surrenders to the besieging Chaldeans shall live and have his life as booty. ¹⁰For I have turned against this city, for its woe and not for its good, says the Lord. It shall be given into the power of the king of Babylon who shall burn it with fire.

¹¹ To the royal house of Judah:
Hear the word of the Lord, ¹²O house of David!
  Thus says the Lord:
Each morning dispense justice,
  rescue the oppressed from the hand of
    the oppressor,
Lest my fury break out like fire
  which burns without being quenched,
  because of the evil of your deeds.

NEW JERUSALEM BIBLE

¹²Yahweh Sabaoth, you*e* who test the upright,
  observer of motives and thoughts, I shall see your
    vengeance on them,
  for I have revealed my cause to you.
¹³Sing to Yahweh,
  praise Yahweh,
for he has delivered the soul of one in need
  from the clutches of evil doers.

¹⁴A curse on the day when I was born!
May the day my mother bore me be unblessed!
¹⁵A curse on the man who brought my father the
    news,
  'A son, a boy has been born to you!'
  making him overjoyed.
¹⁶May this man be like the towns
  that Yahweh overthrew without mercy;
may he hear the warning-cry at dawn
  and the shout of battle at high noon,
¹⁷for not killing me in the womb;
  my mother would have been my grave
  and her womb pregnant for ever.
¹⁸Why ever did I come out of the womb
  to see toil and sorrow
  and end my days in shame?

21 The word that came to Jeremiah from Yahweh when King Zedekiah sent Pashhur*f* son of Malchiah to him, with the priest Zephaniah son of Maaseiah, to say this, ²'Please consult Yahweh for us, since Nebuchadnezzar king of Babylon is making war on us: perhaps Yahweh will work one of his many miracles for us and force him to withdraw.' ³Jeremiah said to them, 'Take this answer to Zedekiah, ⁴"Yahweh, God of Israel, says this: I shall bring back the weapons of war which you are now carrying, and with which you are fighting the king of Babylon and the Chaldaeans now besieging you; from outside the walls, I shall stack them in the centre of this city. ⁵And I shall fight against you myself with outstretched hand and mighty arm, in anger, fury and great wrath. ⁶I shall strike down the inhabitants of this city, human and animal; they will die of a great plague. ⁷Then, Yahweh declares, I shall deliver Zedekiah king of Judah, his officials, the people and those of this city who have escaped the plague, the sword, or the famine, into the clutches of Nebuchadnezzar king of Babylon, into the clutches of their enemies and into the clutches of those determined to kill them; mercilessly, relentlessly, pitilessly, he will put them to the sword."

⁸'And you must say to this people, "Yahweh says this: Look, I offer you a choice between the way of life and the way of death. ⁹Anyone who stays in this city will die by sword, by famine, or by plague; but anyone who leaves it and surrenders to the Chaldaeans now besieging you will live; he will escape with his life.*g* ¹⁰For I am determined on disaster, and not prosperity, for this city, Yahweh declares. It will be handed over to the king of Babylon, and he will burn it down." '

¹¹To the royal House of Judah. Listen to the word of Yahweh, ¹²House of David! Yahweh says this:

Each morning give fair judgement,
  rescue anyone who has been wronged
  from the hands of his oppressor,
  or else my wrath will leap out like a fire,
  it will burn and no one will be able to quench it,
  because of the wickedness of your actions.*h*

e **20** = 11:20.   *f* **21** Not to be confused with the Pashhur of ch. 20, a different person.   *g* **21** = 38:2.   *h* **21** = 4:4.

13 See, I am against you, O inhabitant of the valley,
   O rock of the plain,
                                says the LORD;
   you who say, "Who can come down against us,
      or who can enter our places of refuge?"
14 I will punish you according to the fruit of your
      doings,
                                says the LORD;
   I will kindle a fire in its forest,
      and it shall devour all that is around it.

22 Thus says the LORD: Go down to the house of the
king of Judah, and speak there this word, 2 and say:
Hear the word of the LORD, O King of Judah sitting on the
throne of David—you, and your servants, and your people
who enter these gates. 3 Thus says the LORD: Act with justice and righteousness, and deliver from the hand of the
oppressor anyone who has been robbed. And do no wrong
or violence to the alien, the orphan, and the widow, or shed
innocent blood in this place. 4 For if you will indeed obey
this word, then through the gates of this house shall enter
kings who sit on the throne of David, riding in chariots and
on horses, they, and their servants, and their people. 5 But
if you will not heed these words, I swear by myself, says the
LORD, that this house shall become a desolation. 6 For thus
says the LORD concerning the house of the king of Judah:

   You are like Gilead to me,
      like the summit of Lebanon;
   but I swear that I will make you a desert,
      an uninhabited city.ᶠ
7 I will prepare destroyers against you,
      all with their weapons;
   they shall cut down your choicest cedars
      and cast them into the fire.

8 And many nations will pass by this city, and all of
them will say one to another, "Why has the LORD dealt in
this way with that great city?" 9 And they will answer, "Because they abandoned the covenant of the LORD their God,
and worshiped other gods and served them."

10 Do not weep for him who is dead,
      nor bemoan him;
   weep rather for him who goes away,
      for he shall return no more
      to see his native land.

11 For thus says the LORD concerning Shallum son of
King Josiah of Judah, who succeeded his father Josiah, and
who went away from this place: He shall return here no
more, 12 but in the place where they have carried him captive he shall die, and he shall never see this land again.

13 Woe to him who builds his house by
      unrighteousness,
      and his upper rooms by injustice;
   who makes his neighbors work for nothing,
      and does not give them their wages;
14 who says, "I will build myself a spacious house
      with large upper rooms,"
   and who cuts out windows for it,
      paneling it with cedar,
      and painting it with vermilion.
15 Are you a king
      because you compete in cedar?
   Did not your father eat and drink
      and do justice and righteousness?
   Then it was well with him.
16 He judged the cause of the poor and needy;
      then it was well.
   Is not this to know me?
                                says the LORD.

ᶠCn: Heb uninhabited cities

13 The LORD says: I am against you,
   you inhabitants of the valley,
   the rock in the plain,
   who say, 'Who can come down upon us?
   Who can penetrate our retreats?'
14 I shall punish you as your deeds deserve,
   says the LORD,
   I shall set fire to your heathland,
   and it will devour everything round about.

22 These are the words of the LORD: Go down to the
palace of the king of Judah with this message:
2 King of Judah, occupant of David's throne, listen to the
words of the LORD, you and your courtiers and your people
who come in at these gates.
3 These are the words of the LORD: Deal justly and fairly,
rescue the victim from his oppressor, do not ill-treat or use
violence towards the alien, the fatherless, and the widow,
and do not shed innocent blood in this place. 4 If you obey,
then kings who succeed to David's throne will come riding
through the gates of this palace in chariots and on horses,
with their retinue of courtiers and subjects. 5 But if you do
not obey my words, then by myself I solemnly swear, says
the LORD, this palace will become a ruin. 6 For these are the
words of the LORD about the royal house of Judah:

   Though you are dear to me as Gilead
      or as the crest of Lebanon,
   I swear that I shall turn you into a wilderness,
      a land of towns no longer inhabited.
7 I shall consecrate an armed host to fight against
      you,
   a destructive horde;
   they will cut down your choicest cedars,
      felling them for fuel.

8 People of many nations will pass by this city and say to
one another, 'Why has the LORD done such a thing to this
great city?' 9 The answer will be, 'Because they forsook
their covenant with the LORD their God by worshipping
other gods and serving them.'

10 Weep not for him who is dead nor lament his loss.
   Weep rather for him who is going into exile,
   for he will return no more,
      never again see the land of his birth.

11 For these are the words of the LORD concerning Shallum
son of Josiah, king of Judah, who succeeded his father on
the throne and has gone from this place: He will not
return; 12 he will die in the place of his exile without ever
seeing this land again.

13 Woe betide him who builds his palace on
      unfairness
   and completes its roof-chambers with injustice,
   compelling his countrymen to work without
      payment,
   giving them no wage for their labour!
14 Woe to him who says,
   'I shall build myself a spacious palace
   with airy roof-chambers and windows set in it;
   it will be panelled with cedar
   and painted with vermilion.'
15 Though your cedar is so splendid,
   does that prove you a king?
   Think of your father: he ate and drank,
   dealt justly and fairly; all went well with him.
16 He upheld the cause of the lowly and poor;
   then all was well.
   Did not this show he knew me? says the LORD.

NEW AMERICAN BIBLE	NEW JERUSALEM BIBLE

NEW AMERICAN BIBLE

13 Beware! I am against you, Valley-site,
Rock of the Plain, says the LORD.
You who say, "Who will attack us,
who can penetrate our retreats?"
14 I will punish you, says the LORD,
as your deeds deserve!
I will kindle a fire in its forest
that shall devour all its surroundings.

22 The LORD told me this: Go down to the palace of
the king of Judah and there deliver this message:
2 You shall say: Listen to the word of the LORD, king of
Judah, who sit on the throne of David, you, your ministers,
and your people that enter by these gates! 3 Thus says the
LORD: Do what is right and just. Rescue the victim from the
hand of his oppressor. Do not wrong or oppress the resident
alien, the orphan, or the widow, and do not shed innocent
blood in this place. 4 If you carry out these commands,
kings who succeed to the throne of David will continue to
enter the gates of this palace, riding in chariots or mounted
on horses, with their ministers, and their people. 5 But if
you do not obey these commands, I swear by myself, says
the LORD: this palace shall become rubble. 6 For thus says
the LORD concerning the palace of the king of Judah:

Though you be to me like Gilead,
like the peak of Lebanon,
I will turn you into a waste,
a city uninhabited.
7 Against you I will send destroyers,
each with his axe:
They shall cut down your choice cedars,
and cast them into the fire.

8 Many people will pass by this city and ask one another:
"Why has the LORD done this to so great a city?" 9 And the
answer will be given: "Because they have deserted their
covenant with the LORD, their God, by worshiping and
serving strange gods."

10 Weep not for him who is dead,
mourn not for him!
Weep rather for him who is going away;
never again will he see
the land of his birth.

11 Thus says the LORD concerning Shallum, son of Josiah,
king of Judah, who succeeded his father as king. He has left
this place never to return. 12 Rather, he shall die in the place
where they exiled him; this land he shall not see again.

13 Woe to him who builds his house on wrong,
his terraces on injustice;
Who works his neighbor without pay,
and gives him no wages.
14 Who says, "I will build myself a spacious house,
with airy rooms,"
Who cuts out windows for it,
panels it with cedar,
and paints it with vermillion.
15 Must you prove your rank among kings
by competing with them in cedar?
Did not your father eat and drink?
He did what was right and just,
and it went well with him.
16 Because he dispensed justice to the weak and
the poor,
it went well with him.
Is this not true knowledge of me?
says the LORD.

NEW JERUSALEM BIBLE

13 My quarrel is with you, resident of the valley,
Rock-in-the-Plain,
Yahweh declares,
with you that say, 'Who would dare attack us and
enter our lairs?'
14 I shall punish you as your actions deserve,
Yahweh declares,
I shall set fire to its forest
and it will devour all around it.

22 Yahweh said this, 'Go down to the palace of the
king of Judah and there say this word, 2 "Listen to
the word of Yahweh, king of Judah now occupying the
throne of David, you, your officials and your people who go
through these gates. 3 Yahweh says this: Act uprightly and
justly; rescue from the hands of the oppressor anyone who
has been wronged, do not exploit or ill-treat the stranger,
the orphan, the widow; shed no innocent blood in this place.
4 For if you are scrupulous in obeying this command, then
kings occupying the throne of David will continue to make
their entry through the gates of this palace riding in chariots
or on horseback, they, their officials and their people. 5 But
if you do not listen to these words, then I swear by myself,
Yahweh declares, this palace shall become a ruin!

6 "Yes, this is what Yahweh says about the palace of the
king of Judah:

You are like Gilead to me,
like a peak of Lebanon.
All the same, I will reduce you to a desert,
to uninhabited towns.
7 I dedicate men to destroy you,
each man with his weapons;
they will cut down your finest cedars
and throw them on the fire.

8 "And when many nations pass this city, they will say to
one another: Why has Yahweh treated this great city like
this? 9 And the answer will be: Because they abandoned the
covenant of Yahweh their God to worship other gods and
serve them." '

10 Do not weep for the man who is dead,
do not raise the dirge for him.
Weep rather for the one who has gone away,
since he will never come back,
never see his native land again.

11 For this is what Yahweh has said about Shallum son of
Josiah, king of Judah, who succeeded Josiah his father and
was forced to leave this place, 'He will never come back to
it 12 but will die in the place to which he has been taken
captive; and he will never see this country again.

13 'Disaster for the man who builds his house without
uprightness,
his upstairs rooms without fair judgement,
who makes his fellow-man work for nothing,
without paying him his wages,
14 who says, "I shall build myself a spacious palace
with airy upstairs rooms,"
who makes windows in it,
panels it with cedar, and paints it with vermilion.
15 Are you more of a king
because of your passion for cedar?
Did your father go hungry or thirsty?
But he did what is just and upright,
so all went well for him.
16 He used to examine the cases of poor and needy,
then all went well.
Is not that what it means to know me? Yahweh
demands.

NEW REVISED STANDARD VERSION

17 But your eyes and heart
   are only on your dishonest gain,
for shedding innocent blood,
   and for practicing oppression and violence.

18 Therefore thus says the LORD concerning King Jehoiakim son of Josiah of Judah:
   They shall not lament for him, saying,
      "Alas, my brother!" or "Alas, sister!"
   They shall not lament for him, saying,
      "Alas, lord!" or "Alas, his majesty!"

19 With the burial of a donkey he shall be buried —
   dragged off and thrown out beyond the gates of
      Jerusalem.

20 Go up to Lebanon, and cry out,
   and lift up your voice in Bashan;
cry out from Abarim,
   for all your lovers are crushed.

21 I spoke to you in your prosperity,
   but you said, "I will not listen."
This has been your way from your youth,
   for you have not obeyed my voice.

22 The wind shall shepherd all your shepherds,
   and your lovers shall go into captivity;
then you will be ashamed and dismayed
   because of all your wickedness.

23 O inhabitant of Lebanon,
   nested among the cedars,
how you will groan*u* when pangs come upon
      you,
   pain as of a woman in labor!

24 As I live, says the LORD, even if King Coniah son of Jehoiakim of Judah were the signet ring on my right hand, even from there I would tear you off 25 and give you into the hands of those who seek your life, into the hands of those of whom you are afraid, even into the hands of King Nebuchadrezzar of Babylon and into the hands of the Chaldeans. 26 I will hurl you and the mother who bore you into another country, where you were not born, and there you shall die. 27 But they shall not return to the land to which they long to return.

28 Is this man Coniah a despised broken pot,
   a vessel no one wants?
Why are he and his offspring hurled out
   and cast away in a land that they do not know?

29 O land, land, land,
   hear the word of the LORD!

30 Thus says the LORD:
Record this man as childless,
   a man who shall not succeed in his days;
for none of his offspring shall succeed
   in sitting on the throne of David,
   and ruling again in Judah.

23

Woe to the shepherds who destroy and scatter the sheep of my pasture! says the LORD. 2 Therefore thus says the LORD, the God of Israel, concerning the shepherds who shepherd my people: It is you who have scattered my flock, and have driven them away, and you have not attended to them. So I will attend to you for your evil doings, says the LORD. 3 Then I myself will gather the remnant of my flock out of all the lands where I have driven them, and I will bring them back to their fold, and they shall be fruitful and multiply. 4 I will raise up shepherds over them who will shepherd them, and they shall not fear any longer, or be dismayed, nor shall any be missing, says the LORD.

u Gk Vg Syr: Heb *will be pitied*

REVISED ENGLISH BIBLE

17 But your eyes and your heart are set on naught but
      gain,
   set only on the innocent blood you can shed,
   on the cruel acts of tyranny you perpetrate.

18 Therefore these are the words of the LORD concerning Jehoiakim son of Josiah, king of Judah:

   For him no mourner will say, 'Alas, brother, dear
      brother!'
   no one say, 'Alas, lord and master!'

19 He will be buried like a dead donkey,
   dragged along and flung out
   beyond the gates of Jerusalem.

20 Go up to Lebanon and cry aloud,
   make your voice heard in Bashan,
   cry aloud from Abarim,
   for all who love you are broken.

21 I spoke to you in your days of prosperous ease,
   but you said, 'I shall not listen.'
Since your youth this is how you have behaved;
   you have never obeyed me.

22 A wind will carry away all your friends;
   those who love you will go into captivity.
Then you will be abashed and put to shame
   for all your evil deeds.

23 You dwellers in Lebanon, nestling among the
      cedars,
   how you will groan when pains come on you,
   like the pangs of a woman in labour!

24 By my life, says the LORD, although you, Coniah son of Jehoiakim, king of Judah, are the signet on my right hand, I shall pull you off 25 and hand you over to those who seek your life, to those you fear, to King Nebuchadrezzar of Babylon and to the Chaldaeans. 26 I shall fling you headlong, you and the mother who bore you, into another land, not that of your birth, and there you will both die. 27 You will never come back to your own land, the land for which you long.

28 This man Coniah, then, is he a mere puppet, despised and broken, a thing unwanted? Why else are he and his children flung out headlong and hurled into a country they do not know?

29 Land, land, land! Hear the words of the LORD: 30 These are the words of the LORD: Write this man down as stripped of all honour, one who in his lifetime will not prosper, nor leave descendants to sit in prosperity on David's throne or rule again over Judah.

23

Woe betide the shepherds who let the sheep of my flock scatter and be lost! says the LORD. 2 Therefore these are the words of the LORD the God of Israel to the shepherds who tend my people: You have scattered and dispersed my flock. You have not watched over them; but I am watching you to punish you for your misdeeds, says the LORD. 3 I myself shall gather the remnant of my sheep from all the lands to which I have dispersed them. I shall bring them back to their homes, and they will be fruitful and increase. 4 I shall appoint shepherds who will tend them, so that never again will they know fear or dismay or punishment. This is the word of the LORD.

22:22 **friends:** *or* leaders (*lit.* shepherds).   23:4 **punishment:** *or* be missing.

17 But your eyes and heart are set on nothing
    except on your own gain,
On shedding innocent blood,
    on practicing oppression and extortion.

18 Therefore, thus says the LORD concerning Jehoiakim,
son of Josiah, king of Judah:

They shall not lament him,
    "Alas! my brother"; "Alas! sister."
They shall not lament him,
    "Alas, Lord! alas, Majesty!"
19 The burial of an ass shall he be given,
    dragged forth and cast out
    beyond the gates of Jerusalem.

20 Scale Lebanon and cry out,
    in Bashan lift up your voice;
Cry out from Abarim,
    for all your lovers are crushed.
21 I spoke to you when you were secure,
    but you answered, "I will not listen."
This has been your way from your youth,
    not to listen to my voice.
22 The wind shall shepherd all your shepherds,
    your lovers shall go into exile.
Surely then you shall be ashamed and confounded
    because of all your wickedness.
23 You who dwell on Lebanon,
    who nest in the cedars,
How you shall groan when pains come upon you,
    like the pangs of a woman in travail!

24 As I live, says the LORD, if you, Coniah, son of Jehoiakim, king of Judah, are a signet ring on my right hand, I
will snatch you from it. 25 I will deliver you into the hands
of those who seek your life; the hands of those whom you
fear; the hands of Nebuchadnezzar, king of Babylon, and
the Chaldeans. 26 I will cast you out, you and the mother
who bore you, into a different land from the one you were
born in; and there you shall die. 27 Neither of them shall
come back to the land for which they yearn.

28 Is this man Coniah a vessel despised, to be
    broken up,
    an instrument that no one wants?
Why are he and his descendants cast out?
    why thrown into a land they know not?
29 O land, land, land,
    hear the word of the LORD—
30   Thus says the LORD:
Write this man down as one childless,
    who will never thrive in his lifetime!
No descendant of his shall achieve
    a seat on the throne of David
    as ruler again over Judah.

23 Woe to the shepherds who mislead and scatter the
flock of my pasture, says the LORD. 2 Therefore,
thus says the LORD, the God of Israel, against the shepherds
who shepherd my people: You have scattered my sheep and
driven them away. You have not cared for them, but I will
take care to punish your evil deeds. 3 I myself will gather the
remnant of my flock from all the lands to which I have
driven them and bring them back to their meadow; there
they shall increase and multiply. 4 I will appoint shepherds
for them who will shepherd them so that they need no
longer fear and tremble; and none shall be missing, says the
LORD.

17 You on the other hand have eyes and heart
    for nothing but your own interests,
    for shedding innocent blood
    and perpetrating violence and oppression.'

18 That is why Yahweh says this about Jehoiakim son of
Josiah, king of Judah:

'No lamenting for him,
    "My poor brother! My poor sister!"
No lamenting for him,
    "His poor lordship! His poor majesty!"
19 He will have a donkey's funeral
    —dragged away and thrown
    out of the gates of Jerusalem.'

20 'Climb the Lebanon range and shriek,
    raise your voice in Bashan,
    shriek from the Abarim,
    for all your lovers have been ruined!
21 I spoke to you in your prosperity,
    but you said, "I will not listen!"
From your youth this has been how you behaved,
    refusing to listen to my voice.
22 The wind will shepherd all your shepherds away
    and your lovers will go into captivity.
Then you will blush deep with shame
    at the thought of all your wickedness.
23 You who have made the Lebanon your home
    and made your nest among the cedars,
how you will groan when anguish overtakes you,
    pangs like those of a woman in labour!

24 'As I live, Yahweh declares, even if Coniah[i] son of
Jehoiakim, king of Judah, were the signet ring on my right
hand, I would still wrench you off! 25 I shall hand you over
to those determined to kill you, to those you dread, to
Nebuchadnezzar king of Babylon, to the Chaldaeans. 26 I
shall hurl you and the mother who bore you into another
country; you were not born there but you will both die there.
27 They will not return to the country to which they desperately long to return.'

28 Is he a shoddy broken pot,
    this man Coniah,
    a crock that no one wants?
Why are he and his offspring ejected,
    hurled into a country
    they know nothing of?
29 O land, land, land,
    listen to the word of Yahweh!
30 Yahweh says this,
    'List this man as: Childless;
    a man who made a failure of his life,
since none of his offspring will succeed
    in occupying the throne of David,
    or ruling in Judah again.'

23 'Disaster for the shepherds who lose and scatter the
sheep of my pasture, Yahweh declares. 2 This,
therefore, is what Yahweh, God of Israel, says about the
shepherds who shepherd my people, "You have scattered
my flock, you have driven them away and have not taken
care of them. Right, I shall take care of you for your misdeeds, Yahweh declares! 3 But the remnant of my flock I
myself shall gather from all the countries where I have
driven them, and bring them back to their folds; they will
be fruitful and increase in numbers. 4 For them I shall raise
up shepherds to shepherd them and pasture them. No fear,
no terror for them any more; not one shall be lost, Yahweh
declares!

i 22 Alternative name for Jeconiah.

5 The days are surely coming, says the LORD, when I will raise up for David a righteous Branch, and he shall reign as king and deal wisely, and shall execute justice and righteousness in the land. 6 In his days Judah will be saved and Israel will live in safety. And this is the name by which he will be called: "The LORD is our righteousness."

7 Therefore, the days are surely coming, says the LORD, when it shall no longer be said, "As the LORD lives who brought the people of Israel up out of the land of Egypt," 8 but "As the LORD lives who brought out and led the offspring of the house of Israel out of the land of the north and out of all the lands where he*v* had driven them." Then they shall live in their own land.

9 Concerning the prophets:
My heart is crushed within me,
  all my bones shake;
I have become like a drunkard,
  like one overcome by wine,
because of the LORD
  and because of his holy words.
10 For the land is full of adulterers;
  because of the curse the land mourns,
  and the pastures of the wilderness are dried up.
Their course has been evil,
  and their might is not right.
11 Both prophet and priest are ungodly;
  even in my house I have found their
    wickedness,
                 says the LORD.
12 Therefore their way shall be to them
  like slippery paths in the darkness,
  into which they shall be driven and fall;
for I will bring disaster upon them
  in the year of their punishment,
                 says the LORD.
13 In the prophets of Samaria
  I saw a disgusting thing:
they prophesied by Baal
  and led my people Israel astray.
14 But in the prophets of Jerusalem
  I have seen a more shocking thing:
they commit adultery and walk in lies;
  they strengthen the hands of evildoers,
  so that no one turns from wickedness;
all of them have become like Sodom to me,
  and its inhabitants like Gomorrah.
15 Therefore thus says the LORD of hosts concerning
    the prophets:
"I am going to make them eat wormwood,
  and give them poisoned water to drink;
for from the prophets of Jerusalem
  ungodliness has spread throughout the land."

16 Thus says the LORD of hosts: Do not listen to the words of the prophets who prophesy to you; they are deluding you. They speak visions of their own minds, not from the mouth of the LORD. 17 They keep saying to those who despise the word of the LORD, "It shall be well with you"; and to all who stubbornly follow their own stubborn hearts, they say, "No calamity shall come upon you."

5 The days are coming, says the LORD,
  when I shall make a righteous Branch spring from
    David's line,
a king who will rule wisely,
  maintaining justice and right in the land.
6 In his days Judah will be kept safe,
  and Israel will live undisturbed.
This will be the name to be given to him:
  The LORD our Righteousness.

7 Therefore the time is coming, says the LORD, when people will no longer swear 'by the life of the LORD who brought the Israelites up from Egypt'; 8 instead they will swear 'by the life of the LORD who brought the descendants of the Israelites back from a northern land and from all the lands to which he had dispersed them'; and they will live on their own soil.

9 Of the prophets:
Within my breast my heart gives way,
  there is no strength in my bones;
because of the LORD, because of his holy words,
I have become like a drunken man,
  like one overcome by wine.
10 For the land is full of adulterers,
  and because of them the earth lies parched,
  the open pastures have dried up.
The lives they lead are wicked,
  and the powers they possess are misused.
11 For prophet and priest alike are godless;
  even in my house I have witnessed their evil
    deeds.
This is the word of the LORD.
12 Therefore their path will turn slippery beneath their
    feet;
they will be dispersed in the dark and fall
    headlong,
for I shall bring disaster on them,
  their day of reckoning.
This is the word of the LORD.
13 Among the prophets of Samaria
  I found a lack of sense:
they prophesied in Baal's name
  and led my people Israel astray.
14 Among the prophets of Jerusalem
  I see a thing most horrible:
adulterers and hypocrites.
  They encourage evildoers,
so that no one turns back from sin;
to me all her inhabitants
  are like those of Sodom and Gomorrah.
15 These then are the words of the LORD of Hosts about the
  prophets:
I shall give them wormwood to eat
  and bitter poison to drink;
for from the prophets of Jerusalem
  a godless spirit has spread to the whole country.
16 These are the words of the LORD of Hosts:
Do not listen to what is prophesied to you by the
    prophets,
who buoy you up with false hopes;
  they give voice to their own fancies;
it is not the LORD's words they speak.
17 They say to those who spurn the word of the
    LORD,
'Prosperity will be yours';
  and to all who follow their stubborn hearts they
    say,
'No harm will befall you.'

23:5 **righteous Branch:** *or* legitimate Shoot.   23:8 **he:** *so Gk, cp.* 16:15; Heb. I.   23:10 **adulterers:** *or* idolaters.

v Gk: Heb *I*

5 Behold, the days are coming, says the LORD,
    when I will raise up a righteous shoot to David;
As king he shall reign and govern wisely,
    he shall do what is just and right in the land.
6 In his days Judah shall be saved,
    Israel shall dwell in security.
This is the name they give him:
    "The LORD our justice."

7 Therefore, the days will come, says the LORD, when they shall no longer say, "As the LORD lives, who brought the Israelites out of the land of Egypt"; 8 but rather, "As the LORD lives, who brought the descendants of the house of Israel up from the land of the north"—and from all the lands to which I banished them; they shall again live on their own land.

9   Concerning the prophets:
My heart within me is broken,
    my bones all tremble;
I am like a man who is drunk,
    overcome by wine,
Because of the LORD,
    because of his holy words.
10 With adulterers the land is filled;
    on their account the land mourns,
    the pasture ranges are seared.
Theirs is an evil course,
    theirs is unjust power.
11 Both prophet and priest are godless!
    In my very house I find their wickedness,
    says the LORD.
12 Hence their way shall become for them
    slippery ground.
In the darkness they shall lose their footing,
    and fall headlong;
Evil I will bring upon them:
    the year of their punishment, says the LORD.
13 Among Samaria's prophets
    I saw unseemly deeds:
They prophesied by Baal
    and led my people Israel astray.
14 But among Jerusalem's prophets
    I saw deeds still more shocking:
Adultery, living in lies,
    siding with the wicked,
    so that no one turns from evil;
To me they are all like Sodom,
    its citizens like Gomorrah.

15 Therefore, thus says the LORD of hosts against the prophets:

Behold, I will give them wormwood to eat,
    and poison to drink;
For from Jerusalem's prophets
    ungodliness has gone forth into the whole land.
16   Thus says the LORD of hosts:
Listen not to the words of your prophets,
    who fill you with emptiness;
Visions of their own fancy they speak,
    not from the mouth of the LORD.
17 They say to those who despise the word of
    the LORD,
    "Peace shall be yours";
And to everyone who walks in hardness of heart,
    "No evil shall overtake you."

5 Look, the days are coming, Yahweh declares,
    when I shall raise an upright Branch for David;
he will reign as king and be wise,
    doing what is just and upright in the country.
6 In his days Judah will triumph
    and Israel live in safety.
And this is the name*j* he will be called,
    'Yahweh-is-our-Saving-Justice.' "

7 'So, look, the days are coming, Yahweh declares, when people will no longer say, "As Yahweh lives who brought the Israelites out of Egypt", but, "As Yahweh lives who led back and brought home the offspring of the House of Israel from the land of the north and all the countries to which he had driven them, to live on their own soil." '*k*

9 On the prophets.

My heart is broken within me,
    I tremble in all my bones;
I am like a drunken man,
    like a man overcome with wine,
because of Yahweh and his holy words:

10 'For the country is full of adulterers;
    yes, because of a curse, the country is in mourning
    and the pasturage in the desert has dried up;
they are prompt to do wrong,
    make no effort to do right.
11 Yes, even prophet and priest are godless,
    I have detected their wickedness in my own House,
    Yahweh declares.
12 Because of this, their way will prove
    treacherous going for them;
in the darkness where they are driven,
    there they will fall.
For I shall bring disaster on them,
    when the year for punishing them comes,
    Yahweh declares.

13 'In the prophets of Samaria
    I have seen insanity:
they prophesied in the name of Baal
    and led my people Israel astray.
14 But in the prophets of Jerusalem
    I have seen something horrible:
adultery, persistent lying,
    such abetting of the wicked
    that no one renounces his wickedness.
To me they are all like Sodom
    and its inhabitants are like Gomorrah.

15 So this is what Yahweh Sabaoth says about the prophets,
"Now I shall give them wormwood to eat
    and make them drink poisoned water,*l*
since from the prophets of Jerusalem
    godlessness has spread throughout the land."

16 'Yahweh Sabaoth says this,
"Do not listen to what those prophets prophesy to
    you;
they are deluding you,
they retail visions of their own,
    and not what comes from Yahweh's mouth.
17 To those who despise me, they keep saying:
Yahweh has spoken: you will have peace!
    and to all who follow their own stubborn
       inclinations:
No disaster will touch you."

j 23 This messianic title contrasts with Zedekiah (= Yahweh is my Saving Justice), cf. 33:15–16.   *k* 23 = 16:14–15.   *l* 23 = 9:14.

18 For who has stood in the council of the LORD
   so as to see and to hear his word?
   Who has given heed to his word so as to
      proclaim it?
19 Look, the storm of the LORD!
   Wrath has gone forth,
   a whirling tempest;
   it will burst upon the head of the wicked.
20 The anger of the LORD will not turn back
   until he has executed and accomplished
      the intents of his mind.
   In the latter days you will understand it clearly.
21 I did not send the prophets,
      yet they ran;
   I did not speak to them,
      yet they prophesied.
22 But if they had stood in my council,
   then they would have proclaimed my words to
      my people,
   and they would have turned them from their evil
      way,
   and from the evil of their doings.

23 Am I a God near by, says the LORD, and not a God
far off? 24 Who can hide in secret places so that I cannot see
them? says the LORD. Do I not fill heaven and earth? says
the LORD. 25 I have heard what the prophets have said who
prophesy lies in my name, saying, "I have dreamed, I have
dreamed!" 26 How long? Will the hearts of the prophets ever
turn back — those who prophesy lies, and who prophesy the
deceit of their own heart? 27 They plan to make my people
forget my name by their dreams that they tell one another,
just as their ancestors forgot my name for Baal. 28 Let the
prophet who has a dream tell the dream, but let the one who
has my word speak my word faithfully. What has straw in
common with wheat? says the LORD. 29 Is not my word like
fire, says the LORD, and like a hammer that breaks a rock
in pieces? 30 See, therefore, I am against the prophets, says
the LORD, who steal my words from one another. 31 See, I
am against the prophets, says the LORD, who use their own
tongues and say, "Says the LORD." 32 See, I am against
those who prophesy lying dreams, says the LORD, and who
tell them, and who lead my people astray by their lies and
their recklessness, when I did not send them or appoint
them; so they do not profit this people at all, says the LORD.
33 When this people, or a prophet, or a priest asks you,
"What is the burden of the LORD?" you shall say to them,
"You are the burden,ʷ and I will cast you off, says the
LORD." 34 And as for the prophet, priest, or the people who
say, "The burden of the LORD," I will punish them and their
households. 35 Thus shall you say to one another, among
yourselves, "What has the LORD answered?" or "What has
the LORD spoken?" 36 But "the burden of the LORD" you
shall mention no more, for the burden is everyone's own
word, and so you pervert the words of the living God, the
LORD of hosts, our God. 37 Thus you shall ask the prophet,
"What has the LORD answered you?" or "What has the LORD
spoken?" 38 But if you say, "the burden of the LORD," thus

18 For which of them has stood in the council of the
   LORD,
   has been aware of his word and listened to it?
   Which of them has heeded his word and obeyed?
19 See what a scorching wind has gone out from the
   LORD,
   a furious whirlwind
   which whirls round the heads of the wicked.
20 The LORD's anger is not to be turned aside,
   until he has fully accomplished his purposes.
   In days to come you will truly understand.
21 I did not send these prophets,
   yet they went in haste;
   I did not speak to them,
   yet they prophesied.
22 But if they had stood in my council,
   they would have proclaimed my words to my
      people
   and turned them from their evil ways and their evil
      doings.
23 Am I a God near at hand only, not a God when far
   away?
24 Can anyone hide in some secret place and I not see
   him?
   Do I not fill heaven and earth?
   This is the word of the LORD.

25 I have heard what the prophets say, the prophets who
speak lies in my name; they cry, 'I have had a dream, I have
had a dream!' 26 How much longer will these prophets be
minded to prophesy lies and give voice to their own inventions? 27 By these dreams which they tell one another they
think they will make my people forget my name, just as
their fathers forgot my name for the name of Baal. 28 If a
prophet has a dream, let him tell his dream; if he has my
word, let him speak my word faithfully. Chaff and grain are
quite distinct, says the LORD. 29 Are not my words like fire,
says the LORD; are they not like a hammer that shatters
rock? 30 Therefore I am against those prophets, the impostors who steal my words from the others, says the LORD. 31 I
am against those prophets, says the LORD, who concoct
words of their own and then say, 'This is his word.' 32 I am
against those prophets, says the LORD, who deal in false
dreams and relate them to mislead my people with wild and
reckless falsehoods. It was not I who sent them or commissioned them, and they will do this people no good service.
This is the word of the LORD.
33 When you are asked by this people or by a prophet or
a priest what is the burden of the LORD, you shall answer:
You are the burden, and I shall throw you down, says the
LORD. 34 If anyone, prophet, priest, or layman, mentions
'the LORD's burden', I shall punish that person and his
family. 35 The form of words you shall use in speaking
amongst yourselves is: 'What answer has the LORD given?'
or, 'What has the LORD said?' 36 You must never again
mention 'the burden of the LORD'; for how can his word be
a burden to anyone? But you pervert the words of the living
God, the LORD of Hosts our God. 37 This is the form you are
to use in speaking to a prophet: 'What answer has the LORD
given?' or, 'What has the LORD said?' 38 But to any of you

23:23 **near at hand:** *so Gk; Heb. adds* says the LORD.   23:24 **see
him:** *so Gk; Heb. adds* says the LORD.   23:27 **for the name of:**
or by their worship of.   23:36 **for . . . anyone:** *or* that is reserved
for the man to whom he entrusts his message.

ʷ Gk Vg: Heb *What burden*

18 Now, who has stood in the council of the LORD,
    to see him and to hear his word?
    Who has heeded his word, so as to announce it?
19 See, the storm of the LORD!
    His wrath breaks forth
    In a whirling storm
    that bursts upon the heads of the wicked.
20 The anger of the LORD shall not abate
    until he has done and fulfilled
    what he has determined in his heart.
    When the time comes,
    you shall fully understand.
21 I did not send these prophets,
    yet they ran;
    I did not speak to them,
    yet they prophesied.
22 Had they stood in my council,
    and did they but proclaim to my people
      my words,
    They would have brought them back from
      evil ways
    and from their wicked deeds.
23 Am I a God near at hand only, says the LORD,
    and not a God far off?
24 Can a man hide in secret
    without my seeing him? says the LORD.
    Do I not fill
    both heaven and earth? says the LORD.

25 I have heard the prophets who prophesy lies in my name say, "I had a dream! I had a dream!" 26 How long will this continue? Is my name in the hearts of the prophets who prophesy lies and their own deceitful fancies? 27 By their dreams which they recount to each other, they think to make my people forget my name, just as their fathers forgot my name for Baal. 28 Let the prophet who has a dream recount his dream; let him who has my word speak my word truthfully!

    What has straw to do with the wheat?
      says the LORD.
29 Is not my word like fire, says the LORD,
    like a hammer shattering rocks?

30 Therefore I am against the prophets, says the LORD, who steal my words from each other. 31 Yes, I am against the prophets, says the LORD, who borrow speeches to pronounce oracles. 32 Yes, I am against the prophets who prophesy lying dreams, says the LORD, and who lead my people astray by recounting their lies and by their empty boasting. From me they have no mission or command, and they do this people no good at all, says the LORD.

33 And when this people, or a prophet or a priest asks you, "What is the burden of the LORD?" you shall answer, "You are the burden, and I cast you off, says the LORD." 34 If a prophet or a priest or anyone else mentions "the burden of the LORD," I will punish that man and his house. 35 Thus you shall ask, when speaking to one another, "What answer did the LORD give?" or, "What did the LORD say?" 36 But the burden of the LORD you shall mention no more. For each man his own word becomes the burden so that you pervert the words of the living God, the LORD of hosts, our God. 37 Thus shall you ask the prophet, "What answer did the LORD give?" or, "What did the LORD say?" 38 But if you

18 But who has been present in Yahweh's council and seen, and heard his word? Who has paid attention to his word and listened to it?

19 Look, Yahweh's hurricane, his wrath, bursts out,
    a fearsome hurricane,
    to burst on the heads of the wicked;
20 Yahweh's anger will not withdraw
    until he has performed, has carried out,
    what he has in mind.
    In the final days, you will understand this
      clearly,*m*
21 'I did not send these prophets,
    yet they ran!
    I did not speak to them,
    yet they prophesied!
22 Had they been present in my council,
    they could have proclaimed my words to my
      people
    and turned them from their evil way
    and from the wickedness of their deeds!
23 'Am I a God when near, Yahweh demands,
    and not a God when far away?
24 Can anyone hide somewhere secret
    without my seeing him? Yahweh demands.
    Do I not fill heaven and earth?
    Yahweh demands.

25 'I have heard what the prophets say who make their lying prophecies in my name. "I have had a dream," they say, "I have had a dream!" 26 How long are there to be those among the prophets who prophesy lies and are in fact prophets of their own delusions? 27 They are doing their best, by means of the dreams that they keep telling each other, to make my people forget my name, just as their ancestors forgot my name in favour of Baal. 28 Let the prophet who has had a dream tell it for a dream! And let him who receives a word from me, deliver my word accurately!

    'What have straw and wheat in common?
    Yahweh demands.
29 Is my word not like fire,
    Yahweh demands,
    is it not like a hammer shattering a rock?

30 'So, then, I have a quarrel with the prophets, Yahweh declares, that steal my words from one another. 31 I have a quarrel with the prophets, Yahweh declares, who wag their tongues to utter prophecies. 32 I have a quarrel with the prophets who make prophecies out of lying dreams, Yahweh declares, who recount them, and lead my people astray by their lies and their bragging. I certainly never sent them or commissioned them, and they serve no good purpose for this people, Yahweh declares.

33 'And when this people, or a prophet, or a priest, asks you, "What is Yahweh's burden?" you must answer, "You are the burden, and I shall get rid of you, Yahweh declares!"

34 'As for the prophet, the priest, or anyone else, who says, "Yahweh's burden", I shall punish that man, and his household too. 35 This is what you must say to one another, among yourselves, "What answer has Yahweh given?" or "What has Yahweh said?" 36 But stop using the expression "Yahweh's burden", for what each man says will be his own responsibility. And you twist the words of the living God, of Yahweh Sabaoth, our God. 37 This is the way to speak to a prophet, "What answer has Yahweh given?" or "What has Yahweh said?" 38 But if you say, "Yahweh's

m 23 = 30:23–24.

says the LORD: Because you have said these words, "the burden of the LORD," when I sent to you, saying, You shall not say, "the burden of the LORD," 39 therefore, I will surely lift you up*x* and cast you away from my presence, you and the city that I gave to you and your ancestors. 40 And I will bring upon you everlasting disgrace and perpetual shame, which shall not be forgotten.

24 The LORD showed me two baskets of figs placed before the temple of the LORD. This was after King Nebuchadrezzar of Babylon had taken into exile from Jerusalem King Jeconiah son of Jehoiakim of Judah, together with the officials of Judah, the artisans, and the smiths, and had brought them to Babylon. 2 One basket had very good figs, like first-ripe figs, but the other basket had very bad figs, so bad that they could not be eaten. 3 And the LORD said to me, "What do you see, Jeremiah?" I said, "Figs, the good figs very good, and the bad figs very bad, so bad that they cannot be eaten."

4 Then the word of the LORD came to me: 5 Thus says the LORD, the God of Israel: Like these good figs, so I will regard as good the exiles from Judah, whom I have sent away from this place to the land of the Chaldeans. 6 I will set my eyes upon them for good, and I will bring them back to this land. I will build them up, and not tear them down; I will plant them, and not pluck them up. 7 I will give them a heart to know that I am the LORD; and they shall be my people and I will be their God, for they shall return to me with their whole heart.

8 But thus says the LORD: Like the bad figs that are so bad they cannot be eaten, so will I treat King Zedekiah of Judah, his officials, the remnant of Jerusalem who remain in this land, and those who live in the land of Egypt. 9 I will make them a horror, an evil thing, to all the kingdoms of the earth—a disgrace, a byword, a taunt, and a curse in all the places where I shall drive them. 10 And I will send sword, famine, and pestilence upon them, until they are utterly destroyed from the land that I gave to them and their ancestors.

25 The word that came to Jeremiah concerning all the people of Judah, in the fourth year of King Jehoiakim son of Josiah of Judah (that was the first year of King Nebuchadrezzar of Babylon), 2 which the prophet Jeremiah spoke to all the people of Judah and all the inhabitants of Jerusalem: 3 For twenty-three years, from the thirteenth year of King Josiah son of Amon of Judah, to this day, the word of the LORD has come to me, and I have spoken persistently to you, but you have not listened. 4 And though the LORD persistently sent you all his servants the prophets, you have neither listened nor inclined your ears to hear 5 when they said, "Turn now, everyone of you, from your evil way and wicked doings, and you will remain upon the land that the LORD has given to you and your ancestors from of old and forever; 6 do not go after other gods to serve and worship them, and do not provoke me to anger with the work of your hands. Then I will do you no harm." 7 Yet you did not listen to me, says the LORD, and so you have provoked me to anger with the work of your hands to your own harm.

8 Therefore thus says the LORD of hosts: Because you have not obeyed my words, 9 I am going to send for all the tribes of the north, says the LORD, even for King Nebuchadrezzar of Babylon, my servant, and I will bring them against this land and its inhabitants, and against all these nations around; I will utterly destroy them, and make them an object of horror and of hissing, and an everlasting disgrace.*y*

who do say 'the burden of the LORD', the LORD speaks thus: Because you say 'the burden of the LORD', though I sent to tell you not to say it, 39 therefore I myself shall carry you like a burden and throw you away out of my sight, both you and the city which I gave to you and to your forefathers. 40 I shall inflict on you endless reproach, endless shame which will never be forgotten.

24 THIS is what the LORD showed me: I saw two baskets of figs set out in front of the temple of the LORD. This was after King Nebuchadrezzar of Babylon had deported from Jerusalem Jeconiah son of Jehoiakim, king of Judah, with the officers of Judah, the craftsmen, and the smiths, and taken them to Babylon. 2 In one basket the figs were very good, like those that are first ripe; in the other the figs were very bad, so bad that they were not fit to eat. 3 The LORD said to me, 'What are you looking at, Jeremiah?' 'Figs,' I answered, 'the good very good, and the bad so bad that they are not fit to eat.'

4 Then this word came to me from the LORD: 5 These are the words of the LORD the God of Israel: I count the exiles of Judah whom I sent away from this place to the land of the Chaldaeans as good as these good figs. 6 I shall look to their welfare, and restore them to this land; I shall build them up and not pull them down, plant them and not uproot them. 7 I shall give them the wit to know me, for I am the LORD; they will be my people and I shall be their God, for they will come back to me wholeheartedly.

8 But King Zedekiah of Judah, his officers, and the survivors of Jerusalem, both those who remain in this land and those who have settled in Egypt—all these I shall treat as bad figs, says the LORD, so bad that they are not fit to eat. 9 I shall make them abhorrent to all the kingdoms of the earth, a reproach, a byword, an object of taunting and cursing wherever I banish them. 10 I shall send sword, famine, and pestilence against them until they have vanished from the land which I gave to them and to their forefathers.

25 This came to Jeremiah as the word concerning all the people of Judah in the fourth year of Jehoiakim son of Josiah, king of Judah, which was the first year of King Nebuchadrezzar of Babylon. 2 This is what the prophet Jeremiah said to all Judah and all the inhabitants of Jerusalem: 3 For twenty-three years, from the thirteenth year of Josiah son of Amon, king of Judah, up to the present day, I have been receiving the words of the LORD and speaking to you again and again, but you would not listen. 4 Again and again the LORD has sent you all his servants the prophets, but you would not listen or show any inclination to listen. 5 He promised that if each of you would turn from his wicked ways and evil conduct, then you would live for ever on the soil which the LORD gave to you and to your forefathers. 6 You must not follow other gods, serving and worshipping them, nor must you provoke me to anger with the idols your hands have made; then I shall not harm you. 7 But you would not listen to me, says the LORD; you provoked me to anger with the idols your hands had made and so brought harm upon yourselves.

8 Therefore these are the words of the LORD of Hosts: Because you have not listened to my words, 9 I shall summon all the tribes of the north, says the LORD, and I shall send for my servant King Nebuchadrezzar of Babylon. I shall bring them against this land and all its inhabitants and against all these nations round it; I shall exterminate them and make them an object of horror and astonishment, ruined

---

x Heb Mss Gk Vg: MT *forget you*   *y* Gk Compare Syr: Heb *and everlasting desolations*

23:39 **carry . . . burden:** *or, with some MSS,* forget you.
24:1 **the smiths:** *or* the harem.   24:9 **abhorrent:** *so Gk; Heb. adds* a disaster.

ask about "the burden of the LORD," then thus says the LORD: Because you use this phrase, "the burden of the LORD," though I forbade you to use it, 39 therefore I will lift you on high and cast you from my presence, you and the city which I gave to you and to your fathers. 40 And I will bring upon you eternal reproach, eternal, unforgettable shame.

24 The LORD showed me two baskets of figs placed before the temple of the LORD. — This was after Nebuchadnezzar, king of Babylon, had exiled from Jerusalem Jeconiah, son of Jehoiakim, king of Judah, and the princes of Judah, the artisans and the skilled workers, and brought them to Babylon. — 2 One basket contained excellent figs, the early-ripening kind. But the other basket contained very bad figs, so bad they could not be eaten. 3 Then the LORD said to me: What do you see, Jeremiah? "Figs," I replied; "the good ones are very good, but the bad ones very bad, so bad they cannot be eaten." 4 Thereupon this word of the LORD came to me: 5 Thus says the LORD, the God of Israel: Like these good figs, even so will I regard with favor Judah's exiles whom I sent away from this place into the land of the Chaldeans. 6 I will look after them for their good, and bring them back to this land, to build them up, not to tear them down; to plant them, not to pluck them out. 7 I will give them a heart with which to understand that I am the LORD. They shall be my people and I will be their God, for they shall return to me with their whole heart. 8 And like the figs that are bad, so bad they cannot be eaten — yes, thus says the LORD — even so will I treat Zedekiah, king of Judah, and his princes, the remnant of Jerusalem remaining in this land and those who have settled in the land of Egypt. 9 I will make them an object of horror to all the kingdoms of the earth, a reproach and a byword, a taunt and a curse, in all the places to which I will drive them. 10 I will send upon them the sword, famine, and pestilence, until they have disappeared from the land which I gave them and their fathers.

25 The word that came to Jeremiah concerning all the people of Judah, in the fourth year of Jehoiakim, son of Josiah, king of Judah (the first year of Nebuchadnezzar, king of Babylon). 2 This word the prophet Jeremiah spoke to all the people of Judah and all the citizens of Jerusalem: 3 Since the thirteenth year of Josiah, son of Amon, king of Judah, to this day — these three and twenty years — the word of the LORD has come to me and I spoke to you untiringly, but you would not listen. 4 Though you refused to listen or pay heed, the LORD has sent you without fail all his servants the prophets 5 with this message: Turn back, each of you, from your evil way and from your evil deeds; then you shall remain in the land which the LORD gave you and your fathers, from of old and forever. 6 Do not follow strange gods to serve and adore them, lest you provoke me with your handiwork, and I bring evil upon you. 7 But you would not listen to me, says the LORD, and so you provoked me with your handiwork to your own harm. 8 Hence, thus says the LORD of hosts: Since you would not listen to my words, 9 lo! I will send for and fetch all the tribes of the north, says the LORD (and I will send to Nebuchadnezzar, king of Babylon, my servant); I will bring them against this land, against its inhabitants, and against all these neighboring nations. I will doom them, making them an object of horror, of ridicule, of everlasting reproach.

burden", then Yahweh says this, "Since you use the expression 'Yahweh's burden', when I have warned you to stop saying, 'Yahweh's burden', 39 believe me, I shall pick you up and fling you from my presence, you and the city I gave to you and to your ancestors. 40 I shall bring down everlasting shame on you, everlasting and unforgettable disgrace.' "

24 [n] Yahweh gave me a vision: set out in front of the Temple of Yahweh were two baskets of figs. This was after Nebuchadnezzar king of Babylon had led Jeconiah son of Jehoiakim away into exile from Jerusalem, with the chief men of Judah, the blacksmiths and metalworkers, and had taken them to Babylon. 2 One basket contained excellent figs, like those that ripen first; the other contained very bad figs, so bad they were uneatable. 3 Yahweh said to me, 'What do you see, Jeremiah?' 'Figs,' I answered, 'the good ones excellent, the bad ones very bad, so bad as to be uneatable.' 4 Then the word of Yahweh was addressed to me, 5 'Yahweh, the God of Israel, says this, "As these figs are good, so I mean to concern myself with the welfare of the exiles of Judah whom I have sent from this place to the country of the Chaldaeans. 6 My eyes will watch over them for their good, to bring them back to this country, to build them up and not to break them down, to plant them and not to uproot them. 7 I shall give them a heart to acknowledge that I am Yahweh. They will be my people and I shall be their God, for they will return to me with all their heart. 8 As for the bad figs, the figs so bad as to be uneatable — yes, Yahweh says this — that is how I shall treat Zedekiah king of Judah, his chief men and what is left of Jerusalem, those who remain in this country and those living in Egypt. 9 I shall make them an object of horror, a disaster, to all the kingdoms of the earth, a thing of shame, a byword, a laughing-stock, a curse, wherever I shall drive them. 10 Sword, famine and plague I shall send against them until they have vanished from the soil I gave to them and to their ancestors." '

25 The word that was addressed to Jeremiah about all the people of Judah in the fourth year of Jehoiakim son of Josiah, king of Judah (that is to say the first year of Nebuchadnezzar king of Babylon). 2 The prophet Jeremiah proclaimed it before all the people of Judah and all the inhabitants of Jerusalem:

3 'For twenty-three years, from the thirteenth year of Josiah son of Amon, king of Judah, until today, the word of Yahweh has been addressed to me and I have never tired of speaking to you (but you have not listened). 4 Furthermore, Yahweh has untiringly sent you all his servants the prophets, but you have not listened or paid attention). 5 The message was this, "Turn back, each one of you, from your evil behaviour and your evil actions, and you will go on living on the soil Yahweh long ago gave to you and your ancestors for ever. 6 (And do not follow other gods to serve and worship them, do not provoke me with things you yourselves have made, and then I shall not harm you.) 7 But you have not listened to me (Yahweh declares, so that you have now provoked me with things you yourselves have made, and thus harmed yourselves)."

8 'So — this is what Yahweh Sabaoth says, "Since you have not listened to my words, 9 I shall now send for all the families of the north (Yahweh declares, that is, for Nebuchadnezzar king of Babylon, my servant) and bring them down on this country and its inhabitants (and on all these surrounding nations); I shall curse them with utter destruction and make them an object of horror, of scorn, and ruin them for ever. 10 From them I shall banish the shouts of

n 24 // Ezk 11:14–21.

NEW REVISED STANDARD VERSION	REVISED ENGLISH BIBLE

10 And I will banish from them the sound of mirth and the sound of gladness, the voice of the bridegroom and the voice of the bride, the sound of the millstones and the light of the lamp. 11 This whole land shall become a ruin and a waste, and these nations shall serve the king of Babylon seventy years. 12 Then after seventy years are completed, I will punish the king of Babylon and that nation, the land of the Chaldeans, for their iniquity, says the LORD, making the land an everlasting waste. 13 I will bring upon that land all the words that I have uttered against it, everything written in this book, which Jeremiah prophesied against all the nations. 14 For many nations and great kings shall make slaves of them also; and I will repay them according to their deeds and the work of their hands.

15 For thus the LORD, the God of Israel, said to me: Take from my hand this cup of the wine of wrath, and make all the nations to whom I send you drink it. 16 They shall drink and stagger and go out of their minds because of the sword that I am sending among them.

17 So I took the cup from the LORD's hand, and made all the nations to whom the LORD sent me drink it: 18 Jerusalem and the towns of Judah, its kings and officials, to make them a desolation and a waste, an object of hissing and of cursing, as they are today; 19 Pharaoh king of Egypt, his servants, his officials, and all his people; z all the kings of the land of Uz; all the kings of the land of the Philistines — Ashkelon, Gaza, Ekron, and the remnant of Ashdod; 21 Edom, Moab, and the Ammonites; 22 all the kings of Tyre, all the kings of Sidon, and the kings of the coastland across the sea; 23 Dedan, Tema, Buz, and all who have shaven temples; 24 all the kings of Arabia and all the kings of the mixed peoplesz that live in the desert; 25 all the kings of Zimri, all the kings of Elam, and all the kings of Media; 26 all the kings of the north, far and near, one after another, and all the kingdoms of the world that are on the face of the earth. And after them the king of Sheshacha shall drink.

27 Then you shall say to them, Thus says the LORD of hosts, the God of Israel: Drink, get drunk and vomit, fall and rise no more, because of the sword that I am sending among you.

28 And if they refuse to accept the cup from your hand to drink, then you shall say to them: Thus says the LORD of hosts: You must drink! 29 See, I am beginning to bring disaster on the city that is called by my name, and how can you possibly avoid punishment? You shall not go unpunished, for I am summoning a sword against all the inhabitants of the earth, says the LORD of hosts.

30 You, therefore, shall prophesy against them all these words, and say to them:

> The LORD will roar from on high,
> and from his holy habitation utter his voice;
> he will roar mightily against his fold,
> and shout, like those who tread grapes,
> against all the inhabitants of the earth.
> 31 The clamor will resound to the ends of the earth,
> for the LORD has an indictment against the
> nations;
> he is entering into judgment with all flesh,
> and the guilty he will put to the sword,
> says the LORD.

32 Thus says the LORD of hosts:

> See, disaster is spreading
> from nation to nation,
> and a great tempest is stirring
> from the farthest parts of the earth!

for ever. 10 I shall silence every sound of joy and gladness among them, the voices of bridegroom and bride, and the sound of the handmill; the light of every lamp will be quenched. 11 For seventy years this whole country will be a ruin, an object of horror, and these nations will be in subjection to the king of Babylon. 12 When the seventy years are up, I shall punish the king of Babylon and his people, says the LORD, for all their misdeeds, and make the land of the Chaldaeans a waste for ever. 13 I shall bring on that country all I have pronounced against it, all that is written in this scroll, all that Jeremiah has prophesied against all the nations. 14 Mighty nations and great kings will reduce them to servitude, and thus I shall requite them for their actions and their deeds.

15 These were the words of the LORD the God of Israel to me: Receive from my hand this cup of the wine of wrath, and make all the nations to whom I send you drink from it. 16 When they have drunk they will vomit and become crazed; such is the sword which I am sending among them.

17 I took the cup from the LORD's hand and made all the nations to whom he sent me drink: 18 Jerusalem and the towns of Judah, its kings and officers, turning them into a ruin, an object of horror, derision, and cursing, as they still are; 19 Pharaoh king of Egypt, his courtiers, his officers, all his people, 20 and all his mixed crowd of followers, all the kings of the land of Uz, all the kings of the Philistines, of Ashkelon, Gaza, Ekron, and the remnant of Ashdod; 21 also Edom, Moab, and the Ammonites, 22 all the kings of Tyre, of Sidon, and of the overseas coastlands; 23 also Dedan, Tema, Buz, and all who live in the fringes of the desert, 24 all the kings of Arabia living in the desert, 25 all the kings of Zimri, of Elam, and of the Medes, 26 all the kings of the north, neighbours or distant from each other — all the kingdoms on the face of the earth. Last of all the king of Sheshak will have to drink.

27 Say to them: These are the words of the LORD of Hosts the God of Israel: Drink this, get drunk, and be sick; fall down, never to rise again, because of the sword I am sending among you. 28 If they refuse to accept the cup from you and to drink, say to them: These are the words of the LORD of Hosts: Most certainly you are to drink. 29 I shall first punish the city which bears my name; do you think that you can be exempt? No, you will not be exempt, for I am summoning a sword against all the inhabitants of the earth. This is the word of the LORD of Hosts.

30 Prophesy to them and tell them all I have said:

> The LORD roars from on high,
> he thunders from his holy dwelling-place.
> He roars loudly against his land;
> like those who tread the grapes he utters a shout
> against all the inhabitants of the land.
> 31 The great noise reaches to the ends of the earth,
> for the LORD brings a charge against the nations;
> he arraigns all mankind
> and has handed the wicked over to the sword.
> This is the word of the LORD.

32 These are the words of the LORD of Hosts:

> Ruin spreads from nation to nation,
> a mighty tempest is blowing up
> from the far corners of the earth.

---

z Meaning of Heb uncertain   a Sheshach is a cryptogram for Babel, Babylon

25:23 who live . . . desert: or who clip the hair on their temples.
25:24 kings of Arabia: so Gk; Heb. adds and all the kings of the Arabs.   25:26 Sheshak: a cipher for Babylon.

10 Among them I will bring to an end the song of joy and the song of gladness, the voice of the bridegroom and the voice of the bride, the sound of the millstone and the light of the lamp. 11 This whole land shall be a ruin and a desert. Seventy years these nations shall be enslaved to the king of Babylon: 12 but when the seventy years have elapsed, I will punish the king of Babylon and the nation and the land of the Chaldeans for their guilt, says the LORD. Their land I will turn into everlasting desert. 13 Against that land I will fulfill all the words I have spoken against it [all that is written in this book, which Jeremiah prophesied against all the nations]. 14 They also shall be enslaved to great nations and mighty kings, and thus I will repay them according to their own deeds and according to their own handiwork.

15 For thus said the LORD, the God of Israel, to me: Take this cup of foaming wine from my hand, and have all the nations to whom I will send you drink it. 16 They shall drink, and be convulsed, and go mad, because of the sword I will send among them. 17 I took the cup from the hand of the LORD and gave drink to all the nations to which the LORD sent me: 18 [Jerusalem, the cities of Judah, her kings and her princes, to make them a ruin and a desert, an object of ridicule and cursing, as they are today;] 19 Pharaoh, king of Egypt, and his servants, his princes, all the people under him, native 20 and foreign; all the kings of the land of Uz; all the kings of the land of the Philistines: Ashkelon, Gaza, Ekron, and the remnant of Ashdod; 21 Edom, Moab, and the Ammonites; 22 all the kings of Tyre, of Sidon, and of the shores beyond the sea; 23 Dedan and Tema and Buz, all the desert dwellers who shave their temples; 24 [all the kings of Arabia;] 25 all the kings of Zimri, of Elam, of the Medes; 26 all the kings of the north, near and far, one after the other; all the kingdoms upon the face of the earth [and after them the king of Sheshach shall drink].

27 Tell them: Thus says the LORD of hosts, the God of Israel: Drink! become drunk and vomit; fall, never to rise, before the sword that I will send among you! 28 If they refuse to take the cup from your hand and drink, say to them: Thus says the LORD of hosts: You must drink! 29 For since with this city, which is called by my name, I begin to inflict evil, how can you possibly be spared? You shall not be spared! I will call down the sword upon all who inhabit the earth, says the LORD of hosts.

30 Prophesy against them all these things and say to them:

The LORD roars from on high,
 from his holy dwelling he raises his voice;
Mightily he roars over the range,
 a shout like that of vintagers over the grapes.
31 To all who inhabit the earth to its very ends
 the uproar spreads;
For the LORD has an indictment against the nations,
 he is to pass judgment upon all mankind:
The godless shall be given to the sword,
 says the LORD.
32   Thus says the LORD of hosts:
Lo! calamity stalks
 from nation to nation;
A great storm is unleashed
 from the ends of the earth.

rejoicing and mirth, the voices of bridegroom and bride, the sound of the handmill and the light of the lamp; 11 and this whole country will be reduced to ruin and desolation, and these nations will be enslaved to the king of Babylon for seventy years. 12 (But when the seventy years are over, I shall punish the king of Babylon and that nation, Yahweh declares, for the wrong they have done, that is, the country of the Chaldaeans, and make it desolate for ever), 13 and against that country I shall perform all the words with which I have threatened it, that is, everything written in this book."'

What Jeremiah prophesied against all the nations.

14 ('For these in their turn are to be enslaved to powerful nations and great kings, and I shall pay them back as their deeds and handiwork deserve.')

15 For Yahweh, the God of Israel, said this to me, 'Take this cup of the wine of wrath and make all the nations to whom I send you drink it; 16 they will drink and reel and lose their wits, because of the sword I am sending among them.' 17 I took the cup from Yahweh's hand and made all the nations to whom Yahweh sent me drink it 18 (Jerusalem and the towns of Judah, its kings and its chief men, to make them a ruin, an object of horror and derision and a curse, as is the case today): 19 Pharaoh king of Egypt, his officials, his chief men and all his people, 20 with the whole conglomeration of peoples there (all the kings of the country of Uz); all the kings of the country of the Philistines, Ashkelon, Gaza, Ekron and what is still left of Ashdod; 21 Edom, Moab and the Ammonites; 22 (all) the kings of Tyre, (all) the kings of Sidon, the kings of the island across the sea; 23 Dedan, Tema, Buz, all the people with shaven temples; 24 all the kings of Arabia (and all the kings of the conglomeration of peoples) who live in the desert 25 (all the kings of Zimri), all the kings of Elam, and all the kings of Media; 26 all the kings of the north, near and far, one after another: in short, all the kingdoms on the face of the earth. (As for the king of Sheshak, he will drink last of all.)

27 'You will say to them, "Yahweh Sabaoth, the God of Israel, says this: Drink! Get drunk! Vomit! Fall, never to rise again, before the sword that I am sending among you!" 28 If they refuse to take the cup from your hand and drink, you will say to them, "Yahweh Sabaoth says this: You must drink! 29 Look, for a start, I am bringing disaster on the city that bears my name, so are you likely to go unpunished? You certainly will not go unpunished, for next I shall summon a sword against all the inhabitants of the land, Yahweh declares."

30 'For your part, you are to prophesy all these words to them. Say to them:

"Yahweh roars from on high,
 he thunders from his holy dwelling-place,
loudly he roars at his own fold,
shouts aloud like those who tread the grape
 at all the inhabitants of the land.
31 The noise resounds to the remotest parts of the earth.
For Yahweh is indicting the nations,
arraigning all humanity for judgement;
the wicked he assigns to the sword,
Yahweh declares.
32 Yahweh Sabaoth says this:
Look, disaster is spreading
from nation to nation,
a mighty tempest is rising
from the far ends of the earth.

33 Those slain by the LORD on that day shall extend from one end of the earth to the other. They shall not be lamented, or gathered, or buried; they shall become dung on the surface of the ground.

34 Wail, you shepherds, and cry out;
  roll in ashes, you lords of the flock,
for the days of your slaughter have come — and
    your dispersions,*b*
  and you shall fall like a choice vessel.
35 Flight shall fail the shepherds,
  and there shall be no escape for the lords of
    the flock.
36 Hark! the cry of the shepherds,
  and the wail of the lords of the flock!
For the LORD is despoiling their pasture,
37   and the peaceful folds are devastated,
    because of the fierce anger of the LORD.
38 Like a lion he has left his covert;
  for their land has become a waste
because of the cruel sword,
    and because of his fierce anger.

26 At the beginning of the reign of King Jehoiakim son of Josiah of Judah, this word came from the LORD: 2 Thus says the LORD: Stand in the court of the LORD's house, and speak to all the cities of Judah that come to worship in the house of the LORD; speak to them all the words that I command you; do not hold back a word. 3 It may be that they will listen, all of them, and will turn from their evil way, that I may change my mind about the disaster that I intend to bring on them because of their evil doings. 4 You shall say to them: Thus says the LORD: If you will not listen to me, to walk in my law that I have set before you, 5 and to heed the words of my servants the prophets whom I send to you urgently — though you have not heeded — 6 then I will make this house like Shiloh, and I will make this city a curse for all the nations of the earth.

7 The priests and the prophets and all the people heard Jeremiah speaking these words in the house of the LORD. 8 And when Jeremiah had finished speaking all that the LORD had commanded him to speak to all the people, then the priests and the prophets and all the people laid hold of him, saying, "You shall die! 9 Why have you prophesied in the name of the LORD, saying, 'This house shall be like Shiloh, and this city shall be desolate, without inhabitant'?" And all the people gathered around Jeremiah in the house of the LORD.

10 When the officials of Judah heard these things, they came up from the king's house to the house of the LORD and took their seat in the entry of the New Gate of the house of the LORD. 11 Then the priests and the prophets said to the officials and to all the people, "This man deserves the sentence of death because he has prophesied against this city, as you have heard with your own ears."

12 Then Jeremiah spoke to all the officials and all the people, saying, "It is the LORD who sent me to prophesy against this house and this city all the words you have heard. 13 Now therefore amend your ways and your doings, and obey the voice of the LORD your God, and the LORD will change his mind about the disaster that he has pronounced against you. 14 But as for me, here I am in your hands. Do with me as seems good and right to you. 15 Only know for certain that if you put me to death, you will be bringing innocent blood upon yourselves and upon this city and its inhabitants, for in truth the LORD sent me to you to speak all these words in your ears."

33 Those whom the LORD has slain on that day will lie scattered from one end of the earth to the other; they will not be mourned or taken up for burial; they will be dung spread over the ground.

34 Wail, you shepherds, cry aloud,
  sprinkle yourselves with ashes, you masters of the
    flock.
It is your time to go to the slaughter,
  and you will fall like fine rams.
35 The shepherds will have nowhere to flee,
  the flockmasters no way of escape.
36 The shepherds cry out,
  the flockmasters wail,
  for the LORD is ravaging their pasture,
37 and their peaceful homesteads lie in ruins
  beneath the LORD's fierce anger.
38 They flee like a young lion abandoning his lair,
  for the land has become a waste
  under the sword of the oppressor
  and the fierce anger of the LORD.

26 AT the beginning of the reign of Jehoiakim son of Josiah, king of Judah, this word came from the LORD: 2 These are the words of the LORD: Stand in the court of the LORD's house and speak to the inhabitants of all the towns of Judah who come to worship there. Tell them everything that I charge you to say to them; do not cut it short by one word. 3 Perhaps they may listen, and everyone may turn back from evil ways. If they do, I shall relent, and give up my plan to bring disaster on them for their evil deeds. 4 Say to them: These are the words of the LORD: If you do not obey me, if you do not live according to the law I have set before you, 5 and listen to the words of my servants the prophets, whom again and again I have been sending to you, though you have never listened to them, 6 then I shall do to this house as I did to Shiloh, and make this city an object of cursing to all nations on earth.

7 The priests, the prophets, and all the people heard Jeremiah say this in the LORD's house 8 and, when he came to the end of what the LORD had charged him to say to them, the priests and prophets and all the people seized him and threatened him with death. 9 'Why', they demanded, 'do you prophesy in the LORD's name that this house will become like Shiloh and this city an uninhabited ruin?' The people all crowded round Jeremiah in the LORD's house. 10 When the chief officers of Judah heard what was happening, they went up from the royal palace to the LORD's house and took their places there at the entrance of the New Gate.

11 The priests and the prophets said to the officers and all the people, 'This man deserves to be condemned to death, because he has prophesied against this city, as you yourselves have heard.' 12 Then Jeremiah said to all the officers and people, 'The LORD it was who sent me to prophesy against this house and this city all the things you have heard. 13 Now, if you mend your ways and your actions and obey the LORD your God, he may relent and revoke the disaster which he has pronounced against you. 14 But here I am in your hands; do with me whatever you think right and proper. 15 Only you may be certain that, if you put me to death, you and this city and those who live in it will be guilty of murdering an innocent man; for truly it was the LORD who sent me to you to say all this to you.'

25:34 **slaughter:** *so Gk; Heb. adds an unintelligible word.* **fine rams:** *so Gk; Heb. a fine instrument.* 25:38 **sword:** *so some MSS; others* heat.

b Meaning of Heb uncertain

33 On that day, those whom the LORD has slain will be strewn from one end of the earth to the other. None will mourn them, none will gather them for burial; they shall lie like dung on the field.

34 Howl, you shepherds, and wail!
  roll in the dust, leaders of the flock!
The time for your slaughter has come;
  like choice rams you shall fall.
35 There is no flight for the shepherds,
  no escape for the leaders of the flock.
36 Listen! Wailing from the shepherds,
  howling by the leaders of the flock!
For the LORD lays waste their grazing place,
37   desolate lie the peaceful pastures;
38 The lion leaves his lair,
  and their land is made desolate
By the sweeping sword,
  by the burning wrath of the LORD.

26 In the beginning of the reign of Jehoiakim, son of Josiah, king of Judah, this message came from the LORD: 2 Thus says the LORD: Stand in the court of the house of the LORD and speak to the people of all the cities of Judah who come to worship in the house of the LORD; whatever I command you, tell them, and omit nothing. 3 Perhaps they will listen and turn back, each from his evil way, so that I may repent of the evil I have planned to inflict upon them for their evil deeds. 4 Say to them: Thus says the LORD: If you disobey me, not living according to the law I placed before you 5 and not listening to the words of my servants the prophets, whom I send you constantly though you do not obey them, 6 I will treat this house like Shiloh, and make this the city which all the nations of the earth shall refer to when cursing another.

7 Now the priests, the prophets, and all the people heard Jeremiah speak these words in the house of the LORD. 8 When Jeremiah finished speaking all that the LORD bade him speak to all the people, the priests and prophets laid hold of him, crying, "You must be put to death! 9 Why do you prophesy in the name of the LORD: 'This house shall be like Shiloh,' and 'This city shall be desolate and deserted'?" And all the people gathered about Jeremiah in the house of the LORD.

10 When the princes of Judah were informed of these things, they came up from the king's palace to the house of the LORD and held court at the New Gate of the house of the LORD. 11 The priests and prophets said to the princes and to all the people, "This man deserves death; he has prophesied against this city, as you have heard with your own ears." 12 Jeremiah gave this answer to the princes and all the people: "It was the LORD who sent me to prophesy against this house and city all that you have heard. 13 Now, therefore, reform your ways and your deeds; listen to the voice of the LORD your God, so that the LORD will repent of the evil with which he threatens you. 14 As for me, I am in your hands; do with me what you think good and right. 15 But mark well: if you put me to death, it is innocent blood you bring on yourselves, on this city and its citizens. For in truth it was the LORD who sent me to you, to speak all these things for you to hear."

33 "Those slaughtered by Yahweh that day will be scattered across the world from end to end. No dirge will be raised for them; no one will gather them or bury them; they will stay lying on the surface like dung. *o*

34 "Howl, shepherds, shriek,
  roll on the ground, you lords of the flock,
for your days have come to be slaughtered
  and to be scattered,
and like a choice vase you will fall.
35 No refuge then for the shepherds,
  no escape for the lords of the flock!
36 Listen! A shriek from the shepherds,
  a howl from the lords of the flock!
For Yahweh has laid their pasture waste,
37 the peaceful sheepfolds are reduced to silence
  owing to Yahweh's furious anger,
38 The lion has left his lair
  and their country is a wasteland now,
owing to the devastating fury,
  owing to his furious anger."'

26 At the beginning of the reign of Jehoiakim son of Josiah, king of Judah, this word came to Jeremiah from Yahweh, 2 'Yahweh says this, "Stand in the court of the Temple of Yahweh. To all the people from the towns of Judah who come to worship in the Temple of Yahweh you will say everything I have ordered you to say, not omitting one syllable. 3 Perhaps they will listen and each turn from his evil way: if so, I shall relent and not bring the disaster on them which I intend because of their misdeeds." 4 Say to them, "Yahweh says this: If you will not listen to me and follow my Law which I have given you, 5 and pay attention to the words of my servants the prophets whom I have never tired of sending to you, although you never have paid attention, 6 I shall treat this Temple as I treated Shiloh, and make this city a curse for all the nations of the world." '

7 The priests and prophets and all the people heard Jeremiah say these words in the Temple of Yahweh. 8 When Jeremiah had finished saying everything that Yahweh had ordered him to say to all the people, the priests and prophets and all the people seized hold of him and said, 'You will die for this! 9 Why have you made this prophecy in Yahweh's name, "This Temple will become like Shiloh, and this city become an uninhabited ruin"?' And the people all crowded in on Jeremiah in the Temple of Yahweh. 10 Hearing of this, the chief men of Judah came up from the royal palace to the Temple of Yahweh and took their seats at the entry of the New Gate of the Temple of Yahweh.

11 The priests and prophets then said to the chief men and all the people, 'This man deserves to die, since he has prophesied against this city, as you have heard with your own ears.' 12 Jeremiah, however, replied to all the chief men and all the people as follows, 'Yahweh himself sent me to prophesy against this Temple and this city all the things you have heard. 13 So now amend your behaviour and actions, listen to the voice of Yahweh your God, and Yahweh will relent about the disaster that he has decreed for you. 14 For myself, I am, as you see, in your hands. Do whatever you please or think right with me. 15 But be sure of this, that if you put me to death, you will be bringing innocent blood on yourselves, on this city and on its inhabitants, since Yahweh has truly sent me to you to say all this for you to hear.'

o **25** = 8:2.

| NEW REVISED STANDARD VERSION | REVISED ENGLISH BIBLE |

16 Then the officials and all the people said to the priests and the prophets, "This man does not deserve the sentence of death, for he has spoken to us in the name of the LORD our God." 17 And some of the elders of the land arose and said to all the assembled people, 18 "Micah of Moresheth, who prophesied during the days of King Hezekiah of Judah, said to all the people of Judah: 'Thus says the LORD of hosts,

> Zion shall be plowed as a field;
> Jerusalem shall become a heap of ruins,
> and the mountain of the house a wooded
> height.'

19 Did King Hezekiah of Judah and all Judah actually put him to death? Did he not fear the LORD and entreat the favor of the LORD, and did not the LORD change his mind about the disaster that he had pronounced against them? But we are about to bring great disaster on ourselves."

20 There was another man prophesying in the name of the LORD, Uriah son of Shemaiah from Kiriath-jearim. He prophesied against this city and against this land in words exactly like those of Jeremiah. 21 And when King Jehoiakim, with all his warriors and all the officials, heard his words, the king sought to put him to death; but when Uriah heard of it, he was afraid and fled and escaped to Egypt. 22 Then King Jehoiakim sent*c* Elnathan son of Achbor and men with him to Egypt, 23 and they took Uriah from Egypt and brought him to King Jehoiakim, who struck him down with the sword and threw his dead body into the burial place of the common people.

24 But the hand of Ahikam son of Shaphan was with Jeremiah so that he was not given over into the hands of the people to be put to death.

27 In the beginning of the reign of King Zedekiah*d* son of Josiah of Judah, this word came to Jeremiah from the LORD. 2 Thus the LORD said to me: Make yourself a yoke of straps and bars, and put them on your neck. 3 Send word*e* to the king of Edom, the king of Moab, the king of the Ammonites, the king of Tyre, and the king of Sidon by the hand of the envoys who have come to Jerusalem to King Zedekiah of Judah. 4 Give them this charge for their masters: Thus says the LORD of hosts, the God of Israel: This is what you shall say to your masters: 5 It is I who by my great power and my outstretched arm have made the earth, with the people and animals that are on the earth, and I give it to whomever I please. 6 Now I have given all these lands into the hand of King Nebuchadnezzar of Babylon, my servant, and I have given him even the wild animals of the field to serve him. 7 All the nations shall serve him and his son and his grandson, until the time of his own land comes; then many nations and great kings shall make him their slave.

8 But if any nation or kingdom will not serve this king, Nebuchadnezzar of Babylon, and put its neck under the yoke of the king of Babylon, then I will punish that nation with the sword, with famine, and with pestilence, says the LORD, until I have completed its*f* destruction by his hand. 9 You, therefore, must not listen to your prophets, your diviners, your dreamers,*g* your soothsayers, or your sorcerers, who are saying to you, 'You shall not serve the king of Babylon.' 10 For they are prophesying a lie to you, with the result that you will be removed far from your land; I will drive you out, and you will perish. 11 But any nation that will bring its neck under the yoke of the king of Babylon and serve him, I will leave on its own land, says the LORD, to till it and live there.

16 The officers and all the people then said to the priests and the prophets, 'This man ought not to be condemned to death, for he has spoken to us in the name of the LORD our God.' 17 Some of the elders of the land also stood up and said to the whole assembled people, 18 'In the time of King Hezekiah of Judah, Micah of Moresheth was prophesying and said to all the people of Judah: "These are the words of the LORD of Hosts:

> Zion will become a ploughed field,
> Jerusalem a heap of ruins,
> and the temple hill rough heath."

19 'Did King Hezekiah and all Judah put him to death? Did not the king show reverence for the LORD and seek to placate him, so that the LORD relented and revoked the disaster which he had pronounced on them? But we are on the point of inflicting great disaster on ourselves.'

20 There was another man too who prophesied in the name of the LORD: Uriah son of Shemaiah, from Kiriath-jearim. He prophesied against this city and this land, just as Jeremiah had done. 21 King Jehoiakim with his bodyguard and all his officers heard what he said and sought to put him to death. On hearing of this, Uriah fled in fear to Egypt. 22 King Jehoiakim dispatched Elnathan son of Akbor with some others 23 to fetch Uriah from Egypt. When they brought him to the king, he had him put to the sword and his body flung into the burial-place of the common people. 24 But Ahikam son of Shaphan used his influence on Jeremiah's behalf to save him from death at the hands of the people.

27 At the beginning of the reign of Zedekiah son of Josiah, king of Judah, this word came to Jeremiah from the LORD: 2 These are the words of the LORD to me: Take the cords and crossbars of a yoke and put them on your neck. 3 Then send to the kings of Edom, Moab, Ammon, Tyre, and Sidon by their envoys who have come to King Zedekiah of Judah in Jerusalem, 4 and give them the following message for their masters: These are the words of the LORD of Hosts the God of Israel: Say to your masters: 5 It was I who by my great power and outstretched arm made the earth, along with mankind and the animals all over the earth, and I give it to whom I see fit. 6 Now I have handed over all these lands to my servant King Nebuchadnezzar of Babylon, and I have given him even the creatures of the wild to serve him. 7 All nations will serve him, his son, and his grandson, until the destined hour of his own land comes; mighty nations and great kings will be subject to him. 8 If any nation or kingdom will not serve King Nebuchadnezzar of Babylon or submit to his yoke, I shall punish them with sword, famine, and pestilence, says the LORD, until I have ensured their destruction at his hand.

9 Therefore do not listen to your prophets, your diviners, your women dreamers, your soothsayers, and your sorcerers who keep on saying to you that you will not become subject to the king of Babylon. 10 Their prophecy to you is a lie; you will be carried away far from your native soil, and I shall banish you and you will perish. 11 But the nation which submits to the yoke of the king of Babylon and serves him I shall leave on their own soil, says the LORD; they will cultivate it and live there.

---

c Heb adds *men to Egypt*   *d* Another reading is *Jehoiakim*
e Cn: Heb *send them*   *f* Heb *their*   *g* Gk Syr Vg: Heb *dreams*

27:3 **Then send:** *so Gk (Luc.); Heb. adds* them.

16 Thereupon the princes and all the people said to the priests and prophets, "This man does not deserve death; it is in the name of the LORD, our God, that he speaks to us." 17 At this, some of the elders of the land came forward and said to all the people assembled, 18 "Micah of Moresheth used to prophesy in the days of Hezekiah, king of Judah, and he told all the people of Judah: Thus says the LORD of hosts:

Zion shall become a plowed field,
    Jerusalem a heap of ruins,
    and the temple mount a forest ridge.

19 Did Hezekiah, king of Judah, and all Judah condemn him to death? Did they not rather fear the LORD and entreat the favor of the LORD, so that he repented of the evil with which he had threatened them? But we are on the point of committing this great evil to our own undoing."

20 There was another man who prophesied in the name of the LORD, Uriah, son of Shemaiah, from Kiriath-jearim; he prophesied the same things against this city and land as Jeremiah did. 21 When King Jehoiakim and all his officers and princes were informed of his words, the king sought to kill him. But Uriah heard of it and fled in fear to Egypt. 22 Thereupon King Jehoiakim sent Elnathan, son of Achbor, and others with him into Egypt 23 to bring Uriah back to the king, who had him slain by the sword and his corpse cast into the common grave. 24 But Ahikam, son of Shaphan, protected Jeremiah, so that he was not handed over to the people to be put to death.

27 [In the beginning of the reign of Jehoiakim, son of Josiah, king of Judah,] . . . this message came to Jeremiah from the LORD: 2 Thus said the LORD to me: Make for yourself bands and yoke bars and put them over your shoulders. 3 Send to the kings of Edom, of Moab, of the Ammonites, of Tyre, and of Sidon, through the ambassadors who have come to Jerusalem to Zedekiah, king of Judah, 4 and charge them thus: Tell your masters: Thus says the LORD of hosts, the God of Israel: 5 It was I who made the earth, and man and beast on the face of the earth, by my great power, with my outstretched arm; and I can give them to whomever I think fit. 6 Now I have given all these lands into the hand of Nebuchadnezzar, king of Babylon, my servant; even the beasts of the field I have given him for his use. 7 All nations shall serve him and his son and his grandson, until the time of his land, too, shall come. Then it in turn shall serve great nations and mighty kings. 8 Meanwhile, if any nation or kingdom will not serve Nebuchadnezzar, king of Babylon, or will not bend its neck under the yoke of the king of Babylon, I will punish that nation with sword, famine, and pestilence, says the LORD, until I give them into his hand.

9 You, however, must not listen to your prophets, to your diviners and dreamers, to your soothsayers and sorcerers, who say to you, "You need not serve the king of Babylon." 10 For they prophesy lies to you, in order to drive you far from your land, to make me banish you so that you will perish. 11 The people that submits its neck to the yoke of the king of Babylon to serve him I will leave in peace on its own land, says the LORD, to till it and dwell in it.

16 The chief men and all the people then said to the priests and prophets, 'This man does not deserve to die: he has spoken to us in the name of Yahweh our God.' 17 And some of the country's elders rose to address all the assembled people. 18 'Micah of Moresheth,' they said, 'who prophesied in the days of Hezekiah king of Judah, had this to say to all the people of Judah, "Yahweh Sabaoth says this:

Zion will become ploughland,
Jerusalem a heap of rubble
and the Temple Mount a wooded height." p

19 'Did Hezekiah king of Judah and all Judah put him to death for this? Did they not rather, fearing Yahweh, plead with him, to such effect that Yahweh relented about the disaster which he had decreed for them? Are we now to burden our souls with such a crime?'

20 There was another man, too, who used to prophesy in Yahweh's name, Uriah son of Shemaiah, from Kiriath-Jearim. He prophesied exactly the same things against this city and this country as Jeremiah. 21 When King Jehoiakim with all his officers and all the chief men heard what he said, the king was determined to put him to death. On hearing this, Uriah took fright and, fleeing, escaped to Egypt. 22 King Jehoiakim, however, sent Elnathan son of Achbor to Egypt with others, 23 who brought Uriah back from Egypt and took him to King Jehoiakim, who had him put to the sword and his body thrown into the common burial ground. 24 But Jeremiah had a protector in Ahikam son of Shaphan, so he was not handed over to the people to be put to death.

27 (At the beginning of the reign of Zedekiah son of Josiah, king of Judah, this word came to Jeremiah from Yahweh:) 2 Yahweh said this to me, 'Make yourself thongs and yokes and put them on your neck. 3 Then send them to the king of Edom, the king of Moab, the king of the Ammonites, the king of Tyre, and the king of Sidon, through their envoys accredited to Zedekiah king of Judah in Jerusalem. 4 Give them the following message for their masters, "Yahweh Sabaoth, God of Israel, says this: You must tell your masters this: 5 I by my great power and outstretched arm made the earth, the human beings and the animals that are on earth, and I give them to whom I please. 6 For the present, I have handed all these countries over to Nebuchadnezzar king of Babylon, my servant; I have even put the wild animals at his service. 7 (All the nations will serve him, his son and his grandson, until the time for his own country comes in its turn, when mighty nations and great kings will enslave him.) 8 Any nation or kingdom that will not serve Nebuchadnezzar king of Babylon and will not bow its neck to the yoke of the king of Babylon, I shall punish that nation with sword, famine and plague, Yahweh declares, until I have destroyed it by his hand. 9 For your own part, do not listen to your prophets, your diviners, dreamers, magicians and sorcerers, who tell you: You will not be enslaved by the king of Babylon. 10 They prophesy lies to you, the result of which will be that you will be banished from your soil, that I shall drive you out, and you will perish. 11 The nation, however, that is prepared to bend its neck to the yoke of the king of Babylon and serve him, I shall leave in peace on its own soil, Yahweh declares, to farm it and stay on it."'

27, 1: [In the beginning of the reign of Jehoiakim . . . Judah]: this gloss cannot be correct because according to Jer 28, 1 the time is the fourth year of Zedekiah, 594 B.C., the occasion of an embassy of the neighboring states (v 3), doubtless for the purpose of laying plans against Nebuchadnezzar.

p **26** = Mi 3:12.

12 I spoke to King Zedekiah of Judah in the same way: Bring your necks under the yoke of the king of Babylon, and serve him and his people, and live. 13 Why should you and your people die by the sword, by famine, and by pestilence, as the LORD has spoken concerning any nation that will not serve the king of Babylon? 14 Do not listen to the words of the prophets who are telling you not to serve the king of Babylon, for they are prophesying a lie to you. 15 I have not sent them, says the LORD, but they are prophesying falsely in my name, with the result that I will drive you out and you will perish, you and the prophets who are prophesying to you.

16 Then I spoke to the priests and to all this people, saying, Thus says the LORD: Do not listen to the words of your prophets who are prophesying to you, saying, "The vessels of the LORD's house will soon be brought back from Babylon," for they are prophesying a lie to you. 17 Do not listen to them; serve the king of Babylon and live. Why should this city become a desolation? 18 If indeed they are prophets, and if the word of the LORD is with them, then let them intercede with the LORD of hosts, that the vessels left in the house of the LORD, in the house of the king of Judah, and in Jerusalem may not go to Babylon. 19 For thus says the LORD of hosts concerning the pillars, the sea, the stands, and the rest of the vessels that are left in this city, 20 which King Nebuchadnezzar of Babylon did not take away when he took into exile from Jerusalem to Babylon King Jeconiah son of Jehoiakim of Judah, and all the nobles of Judah and Jerusalem— 21 thus says the LORD of hosts, the God of Israel, concerning the vessels left in the house of the LORD, in the house of the king of Judah, and in Jerusalem: 22 They shall be carried to Babylon, and there they shall stay, until the day when I give attention to them, says the LORD. Then I will bring them up and restore them to this place.

28 In that same year, at the beginning of the reign of King Zedekiah of Judah, in the fifth month of the fourth year, the prophet Hananiah son of Azzur, from Gibeon, spoke to me in the house of the LORD, in the presence of the priests and all the people, saying, 2 "Thus says the LORD of hosts, the God of Israel: I have broken the yoke of the king of Babylon. 3 Within two years I will bring back to this place all the vessels of the LORD's house, which King Nebuchadnezzar of Babylon took away from this place and carried to Babylon. 4 I will also bring back to this place King Jeconiah son of Jehoiakim of Judah, and all the exiles from Judah who went to Babylon, says the LORD, for I will break the yoke of the king of Babylon."

5 Then the prophet Jeremiah spoke to the prophet Hananiah in the presence of the priests and all the people who were standing in the house of the LORD; 6 and the prophet Jeremiah said, "Amen! May the LORD do so; may the LORD fulfill the words that you have prophesied, and bring back to this place from Babylon the vessels of the house of the LORD, and all the exiles. 7 But listen now to this word that I speak in your hearing and in the hearing of all the people. 8 The prophets who preceded you and me from ancient times prophesied war, famine, and pestilence against many countries and great kingdoms. 9 As for the prophet who prophesies peace, when the word of that prophet comes true, then it will be known that the LORD has truly sent the prophet."

10 Then the prophet Hananiah took the yoke from the neck of the prophet Jeremiah, and broke it. 11 And Hananiah spoke in the presence of all the people, saying, "Thus says the LORD: This is how I will break the yoke of King Nebuchadnezzar of Babylon from the neck of all the nations within two years." At this, the prophet Jeremiah went his way.

12 My message to King Zedekiah of Judah is no different: If you will submit to the yoke of the king of Babylon and serve him and his people, then you will save your lives. 13 Why should you and your people die by sword, famine, and pestilence, the fate with which the LORD has threatened any nation which does not serve the king of Babylon? 14 Do not listen to the prophets who say to you that you will not become subject to the king of Babylon. Their prophecy to you is a lie. 15 I have not sent them, says the LORD; they are prophesying falsely in my name; I shall banish you and you will perish, you and the prophets who prophesy to you.

16 I said to the priests and all this people: These are the words of the LORD: Do not listen to your prophets who tell you that very shortly the vessels of the LORD's house will be brought back from Babylon. Their prophecy to you is a lie. 17 Do not listen to them; serve the king of Babylon, and save your lives. Why should this city become a ruin? 18 If they are really prophets and have the word of the LORD, let them intercede with the LORD of Hosts to grant that the things still left in the LORD's house, in the royal palace, and in Jerusalem, may not be carried off to Babylon. 19 For these are the words of the LORD of Hosts about the pillars, the Sea, the trolleys, and all the other furnishings still left in this city, 20 which King Nebuchadnezzar of Babylon did not take when he deported Jeconiah son of Jehoiakim, king of Judah, from Jerusalem to Babylon, together with all the nobles of Judah and Jerusalem. 21 These are the words of the LORD of Hosts the God of Israel about everything still left in the LORD's house, in the royal palace, and in Jerusalem: 22 They will be carried off to Babylon and remain there until I recall them, says the LORD; then I shall bring them back and restore them to this place.

28 That same year, at the beginning of the reign of King Zedekiah of Judah in the fifth month of the first year, Hananiah son of Azzur, the prophet from Gibeon, said to Jeremiah in the house of the LORD before the priests and all the people, 2 'These are the words of the LORD of Hosts the God of Israel: I shall break the yoke of the king of Babylon. 3 Within two years I shall restore to this place everything which King Nebuchadnezzar of Babylon took from the LORD's house and carried off to Babylon. 4 I shall also bring back to this place, says the LORD, Jeconiah son of Jehoiakim, king of Judah, and all the Judaean exiles who went to Babylon; for I shall break the yoke of the king of Babylon.'

5 The prophet Jeremiah gave this reply to Hananiah the prophet in the presence of the priests and all the people standing there in the LORD's house: 6 'May it be so! May the LORD indeed do this: may he fulfil all that you have prophesied, by bringing back the furnishings of the LORD's house together with all the exiles from Babylon to this place! 7 Only hear what I have to say to you and to all the people: 8 The prophets who preceded you and me from earliest times have foretold war, famine, and pestilence for many lands and for great kingdoms. 9 If a prophet foretells prosperity, it will be known that the LORD has sent him only when his words come true.'

10 Then the prophet Hananiah took the yoke from the neck of the prophet Jeremiah and broke it, 11 announcing to all the people, 'These are the words of the LORD: So shall I break the yoke of King Nebuchadnezzar of Babylon; I shall break it off the necks of all nations within two years.' Then the prophet Jeremiah went his way.

28:1 **first**: *prob. rdg; Heb.* fourth.

NEW AMERICAN BIBLE

NEW JERUSALEM BIBLE

12 To Zedekiah, king of Judah, I spoke the same words: Submit your necks to the yoke of the king of Babylon; serve him and his people, so that you may live. 13 Why should you and your people die by sword, famine, and pestilence, with which the LORD has threatened the nation that will not serve the king of Babylon? 14 Do not listen to the words of those prophets who say, "You need not serve the king of Babylon," for they prophesy lies to you. 15 I did not send them, says the LORD, but they prophesy falsely in my name, with the result that I must banish you, and you will perish, you and the prophets who are prophesying to you.

16 To the priests and to all the people I spoke as follows: Thus says the LORD: Do not listen to the words of your prophets who prophesy to you: "The vessels of the house of the LORD will be brought back from Babylon soon now," for they prophesy lies to you. 17 Do not listen to them! Serve the king of Babylon that you may live; else this city will become a heap of ruins. 18 If they were prophets, if the word of the LORD were with them, they would intercede with the LORD of hosts, that the vessels which remain in the house of the LORD and in the palace of the king of Judah and in Jerusalem might not be taken to Babylon. 19 For thus says the LORD of hosts concerning the pillars, the bronze sea, the stands, and the rest of the vessels that remain in this city, 20 which Nebuchadnezzar, king of Babylon, did not take when he exiled Jeconiah, son of Jehoiakim, king of Judah, from Jerusalem to Babylon, along with all the nobles of Judah and Jerusalem — 21 yes, thus says the LORD of hosts, the God of Israel, concerning the vessels that remain in the house of the LORD, in the palace of the king of Judah, and in Jerusalem: 22 To Babylon they shall be brought, and there they shall remain, until the day I look for them, says the LORD; then I will bring them back and restore them to this place.

28 That same year, in [the beginning of] the reign of Zedekiah, king of Judah, in the fifth month of the fourth year, the prophet Hananiah, son of Azzur, from Gibeon, said to me in the house of the LORD in the presence of the priests and all the people: 2 "Thus says the LORD of hosts, the God of Israel: 'I will break the yoke of the king of Babylon. 3 Within two years I will restore to this place all the vessels of the temple of the LORD which Nebuchadnezzar, king of Babylon, took away from this place to Babylon. 4 And I will bring back to this place Jeconiah, son of Jehoiakim, king of Judah, and all the exiles of Judah who went to Babylon,' says the LORD, 'for I will break the yoke of the king of Babylon.' "

5 The prophet Jeremiah answered the prophet Hananiah in the presence of the priests and all the people assembled in house of the LORD, 6 and said: Amen! thus may the LORD do! May he fulfill the things you have prophesied by bringing the vessels of the house of the LORD and all the exiles back from Babylon to this place! 7 But now, listen to what I am about to state in your hearing and the hearing of all the people. 8 From of old, the prophets who were before you and me prophesied war, woe, and pestilence against many lands and mighty kingdoms. 9 But the prophet who prophesies peace is recognized as truly sent by the LORD only when his prophetic prediction is fulfilled.

10 Thereupon the prophet Hananiah took the yoke from the neck of the prophet Jeremiah, broke it, 11 and said in the presence of all the people: "Thus says the LORD: 'Even so, within two years I will break the yoke of Nebuchadnezzar, king of Babylon, from off the neck of all the nations.' " At that, the prophet Jeremiah went away.

12 To Zedekiah king of Judah I spoke in exactly the same terms. 'Bend your necks', I told him, 'to the yoke of the king of Babylon; serve him and his people and you will survive. 13 (Why so anxious to die, you and your people, by sword, famine and plague, with which Yahweh has threatened the nation refusing to serve the king of Babylon?) 14 Do not listen to the words the prophets say to you, "You will not be enslaved by the king of Babylon." They prophesy lies to you. 15 Since I have not sent them, Yahweh declares, they prophesy untruths to you in my name. The result will be that I shall drive you out, you will perish, and so will the prophets who prophesy to you.'

16 I also spoke to the priests and to all this people as follows, 'Yahweh says this, "Do not listen to the words of your prophets who prophesy to you as follows: Look, the vessels of the Temple of Yahweh will very shortly be brought back from Babylon. They prophesy lies to you. 17 (Do not listen to them; serve the king of Babylon and you will survive. Why should this city become a ruin?) 18 If they are real prophets, if Yahweh's word is really with them, they ought now to be pleading with Yahweh Sabaoth that the remaining vessels in the Temple of Yahweh, in the palace of the king of Judah and elsewhere in Jerusalem, do not go to Babylon too! 19 For this is what Yahweh Sabaoth says about (the pillars, the Sea, the stands and) the other vessels still remaining in this city, 20 those not carried off by Nebuchadnezzar king of Babylon when he took Jeconiah son of Jehoiakim, king of Judah, into exile from Jerusalem to Babylon (with all the leading men of Judah and Jerusalem). 21 Yes, this is what Yahweh Sabaoth, God of Israel, says about the vessels still remaining in the Temple of Yahweh, in the palace of the king of Judah and elsewhere in Jerusalem: 22 They will be carried off to Babylon (and stay there until the day I punish them), Yahweh declares. (Then I shall bring them back and restore them to this place.)" '

28 That same year, at the beginning of the reign of Zedekiah king of Judah, in the fifth month of the fourth year, the prophet Hananiah son of Azzur, a Gibeonite, spoke as follows to Jeremiah in the Temple of Yahweh in the presence of the priests and of all the people, 2 'Yahweh Sabaoth, the God of Israel, says this, "I have broken the yoke of the king of Babylon. 3 In exactly two years' time I shall bring back all the vessels of the Temple of Yahweh which Nebuchadnezzar king of Babylon took away from here and carried off to Babylon. 4 And I shall also bring back Jeconiah son of Jehoiakim, king of Judah and all the exiles of Judah who have gone to Babylon, Yahweh declares, for I shall break the yoke of the king of Babylon." '

5 The prophet Jeremiah then replied to the prophet Hananiah in front of the priests and all the people present in the Temple of Yahweh. 6 'So be it!' the prophet Jeremiah said, 'May Yahweh do so! May he fulfil the words that you have prophesied and bring all the vessels of the Temple of Yahweh and all the exiles back to this place from Babylon. 7 Listen carefully, however, to this word that I am now going to say for you and all the people to hear: 8 From remote times, the prophets who preceded you and me prophesied war, disaster and plague for many countries and for great kingdoms; 9 the prophet who prophesies peace can be recognised as one truly sent by Yahweh only when his word comes true.'

10 The prophet Hananiah then snatched the yoke off the neck of the prophet Jeremiah and broke it. 11 In front of all the people Hananiah then said, 'Yahweh says this, "This is how, in exactly two years' time, I shall break the yoke of Nebuchadnezzar king of Babylon and take it off the necks of all the nations." ' At this, the prophet Jeremiah went away.

NEW REVISED STANDARD VERSION

REVISED ENGLISH BIBLE

12 Sometime after the prophet Hananiah had broken the yoke from the neck of the prophet Jeremiah, the word of the LORD came to Jeremiah: 13 Go, tell Hananiah, Thus says the LORD: You have broken wooden bars only to forge iron bars in place of them! 14 For thus says the LORD of hosts, the God of Israel: I have put an iron yoke on the neck of all these nations so that they may serve King Nebuchadnezzar of Babylon, and they shall indeed serve him; I have even given him the wild animals. 15 And the prophet Jeremiah said to the prophet Hananiah, "Listen, Hananiah, the LORD has not sent you, and you made this people trust in a lie. 16 Therefore thus says the LORD: I am going to send you off the face of the earth. Within this year you will be dead, because you have spoken rebellion against the LORD."

17 In that same year, in the seventh month, the prophet Hananiah died.

29 These are the words of the letter that the prophet Jeremiah sent from Jerusalem to the remaining elders among the exiles, and to the priests, the prophets, and all the people, whom Nebuchadnezzar had taken into exile from Jerusalem to Babylon. 2 This was after King Jeconiah, and the queen mother, the court officials, the leaders of Judah and Jerusalem, the artisans, and the smiths had departed from Jerusalem. 3 The letter was sent by the hand of Elasah son of Shaphan and Gemariah son of Hilkiah, whom King Zedekiah of Judah sent to Babylon to King Nebuchadnezzar of Babylon. It said: 4 Thus says the LORD of hosts, the God of Israel, to all the exiles whom I have sent into exile from Jerusalem to Babylon: 5 Build houses and live in them; plant gardens and eat what they produce. 6 Take wives and have sons and daughters; take wives for your sons, and give your daughters in marriage, that they may bear sons and daughters; multiply there, and do not decrease. 7 But seek the welfare of the city where I have sent you into exile, and pray to the LORD on its behalf, for in its welfare you will find your welfare. 8 For thus says the LORD of hosts, the God of Israel: Do not let the prophets and the diviners who are among you deceive you, and do not listen to the dreams that they dream,h 9 for it is a lie that they are prophesying to you in my name; I did not send them, says the LORD.

10 For thus says the LORD: Only when Babylon's seventy years are completed will I visit you, and I will fulfill to you my promise and bring you back to this place. 11 For surely I know the plans I have for you, says the LORD, plans for your welfare and not for harm, to give you a future with hope. 12 Then when you call upon me and come and pray to me, I will hear you. 13 When you search for me, you will find me; if you seek me with all your heart, 14 I will let you find me, says the LORD, and I will restore your fortunes and gather you from all the nations and all the places where I have driven you, says the LORD, and I will bring you back to the place from which I sent you into exile.

15 Because you have said, "The LORD has raised up prophets for us in Babylon," — 16 Thus says the LORD concerning the king who sits on the throne of David, and concerning all the people who live in this city, your kinsfolk who did not go out with you into exile: 17 Thus says the LORD of hosts, I am going to let loose on them sword, famine, and pestilence, and I will make them like rotten figs that are so bad they cannot be eaten. 18 I will pursue them with the sword, with famine, and with pestilence, and will make them a horror to all the kingdoms of the earth, to be an object of cursing, and horror, and hissing, and a derision among all the nations where I have driven them, 19 because

12 After Hananiah had broken the yoke which had been on Jeremiah's neck, the word of the LORD came to Jeremiah: 13 Go and say to Hananiah: These are the words of the LORD: You have broken bars of wood; in their place you will get bars of iron. 14 For these are the words of the LORD of Hosts the God of Israel: I shall lay an iron yoke on the necks of all these nations, making them serve King Nebuchadnezzar of Babylon. They will be enslaved to him. I have given him even the creatures of the wild. 15 Then Jeremiah said to Hananiah, 'Listen, Hananiah. The LORD never sent you, and you have led this nation to trust in false prophecies. 16 Therefore these are the words of the LORD: I shall remove you from the face of the earth; within a year you will die, because you have preached rebellion against the LORD.' 17 The prophet Hananiah died in the seventh month of that same year.

29 Jeremiah sent a letter from Jerusalem to the elders who were left among the exiles, to the priests, prophets, and all the people whom Nebuchadnezzar had deported from Jerusalem to Babylon, 2 after King Jeconiah, with the queen mother and the eunuchs, the officers of Judah and Jerusalem, the craftsmen, and the smiths, had left Jerusalem. 3 The prophet entrusted the letter to Elasah son of Shaphan and Gemariah son of Hilkiah, whom King Zedekiah of Judah had sent to Babylon to King Nebuchadnezzar. This is what he wrote:

4 These are the words of the LORD of Hosts the God of Israel: To all the exiles whom I deported from Jerusalem to Babylon: 5 Build houses and live in them; plant gardens and eat the produce; 6 marry wives and rear families; choose wives for your sons and give your daughters to husbands, so that they may bear sons and daughters. Increase there and do not dwindle away. 7 Seek the welfare of any city to which I have exiled you, and pray to the LORD for it; on its welfare your welfare will depend. 8 For these are the words of the LORD of Hosts the God of Israel: Do not be deceived by the prophets and diviners among you, and pay no attention to the women whom you set to dream dreams. 9 They prophesy falsely to you in my name; I did not send them. This is the word of the LORD.

10 These are the words of the LORD: When a full seventy years have passed over Babylon, I shall take up your cause and make good my promise to bring you back to this place. 11 I alone know my purpose for you, says the LORD: wellbeing and not misfortune, and a long line of descendants after you. 12 If you invoke me and come and pray to me, I shall listen to you: 13 when you seek me, you will find me; if you search wholeheartedly, 14 I shall let you find me, says the LORD. I shall restore your fortunes; I shall gather you from all the nations and all the places to which I have banished you, says the LORD, and restore you to the place from which I carried you into exile.

15 You say that the LORD has raised up prophets for you in Babylon. 16 These are the words of the LORD concerning the king who sits on the throne of David and all the people who live in this city, your fellow-countrymen who have not gone into exile with you: 17 These are the words of the LORD of Hosts: I am bringing sword, famine, and pestilence on them, making them like rotten figs, too bad to eat. 18 I shall pursue them with sword, famine, and pestilence, and make them abhorrent to all the kingdoms of the earth, an object of execration and horror, of derision and reproach among all the nations to which I have banished them. 19 Just as they did not listen to my words,

---

h Cn: Heb your dreams that you cause to dream

29:2 the smiths: or the harem.

12 Some time after the prophet Hananiah had broken the yoke from off the neck of the prophet Jeremiah, the word of the LORD came to Jeremiah: 13 Go tell Hananiah this: Thus says the LORD: By breaking a wooden yoke, you forge an iron yoke! 14 For thus says the LORD of hosts, the God of Israel: A yoke of iron I will place on the necks of all these nations serving Nebuchadnezzar, king of Babylon, and they shall serve him; even the beasts of the field I give him. 15 To the prophet Hananiah the prophet Jeremiah said: Hear this, Hananiah! The LORD has not sent you, and you have raised false confidence in this people. 16 For this, says the LORD, I will dispatch you from the face of the earth; this very year you shall die, because you have preached rebellion against the LORD. 17 That same year, in the seventh month, Hananiah the prophet died.

29 This is the contents of the letter which the prophet Jeremiah sent from Jerusalem to the remaining elders among the exiles, to the priests, the prophets, and all the people who were exiled by Nebuchadnezzar from Jerusalem to Babylon. 2 This was after King Jeconiah and the queen mother, the courtiers, the princes of Judah and Jerusalem, the artisans and the skilled workmen had left Jerusalem. 3 Delivered in Babylon by Elasah, son of Shaphan, and by Gemariah, son of Hilkiah, whom Zedekiah, king of Judah, sent to the king of Babylon, the letter read:

4 Thus says the LORD of hosts, the God of Israel, to all the exiles whom I exiled from Jerusalem to Babylon: 5 Build houses to dwell in; plant gardens, and eat their fruits. 6 Take wives and beget sons and daughters; find wives for your sons and give your daughters husbands, so that they may bear sons and daughters. There you must increase in number, not decrease. 7 Promote the welfare of the city to which I have exiled you; pray for it to the LORD, for upon its welfare depends your own.

‡29.8–9: see below‡

10 Thus says the LORD: Only after seventy years have elapsed for Babylon will I visit you and fulfill for you my promise to bring you back to this place. 11 For I know well the plans I have in mind for you, says the LORD, plans for your welfare, not for woe! plans to give you a future full of hope. 12 When you call me, when you go to pray to me, I will listen to you. 13 When you look for me, you will find me. Yes, when you seek me with all your heart, 14 you will find me with you, says the LORD, and I will change your lot; I will gather you together from all the nations and all the places to which I have banished you, says the LORD, and bring you back to the place from which I have exiled you.

‡29.15: see below‡

16 Thus says the LORD concerning the king who sits on David's throne, and all the people who remain in this city, your brethren who did not go with you into exile; 17 thus says the LORD of hosts: I am sending against them sword, famine and pestilence. I will make them like rotten figs, too bad to be eaten. 18 I will pursue them with sword, famine, and pestilence, and make them an object of horror to all the kingdoms of the earth, of malediction, astonishment, ridicule, and reproach to all the nations among which I will banish them. 19 For they did not listen to my words, says the

12 After the prophet Hananiah had broken the yoke he had snatched off the prophet Jeremiah's neck, the word of Yahweh came to Jeremiah, 13 'Go to Hananiah and tell him this, "Yahweh says this: You have broken the wooden yokes only to make iron yokes to replace them! 14 For Yahweh Sabaoth, the God of Israel, says this: An iron yoke is what I now lay on the necks of all these nations to enslave them to Nebuchadnezzar king of Babylon. (They will be enslaved to him; I have even given him the wild animals.)" ' 15 The prophet Jeremiah said to the prophet Hananiah, 'Listen carefully, Hananiah: Yahweh has not sent you; and thanks to you this people is now relying on what is false. 16 And so, Yahweh says this, "I am going to send you off the face of the earth: you will die this year (since you have preached rebellion against Yahweh)." ' 17 The prophet Hananiah died the same year, in the seventh month.

29 This is the text of the letter that the prophet Jeremiah sent from Jerusalem to those who were left of the elders in exile, to the priests, the prophets and all the people whom Nebuchadnezzar had deported from Jerusalem to Babylon. 2 This was after King Jeconiah had left Jerusalem with the queen mother, the eunuchs, the chief men of Judah and Jerusalem, and the blacksmiths and metalworkers. 3 The letter was entrusted to Elasah son of Shaphan and to Gemariah son of Hilkiah, whom Zedekiah king of Judah had sent to Babylon, to Nebuchadnezzar king of Babylon. The letter said:

4 'Yahweh Sabaoth, the God of Israel, says this to all the exiles deported from Jerusalem to Babylon: 5 Build houses, settle down; plant gardens and eat what they produce; 6 marry and have sons and daughters; choose wives for your sons, find husbands for your daughters so that these can bear sons and daughters in their turn; you must increase there and not decrease. 7 Work for the good of the city to which I have exiled you; pray to Yahweh on its behalf, since on its welfare yours depends. 8 For Yahweh Sabaoth, the God of Israel, says this: Do not be deceived by the prophets who are with you or by your diviners; do not listen to the dreams you have, 9 since they prophesy lies to you in my name. I have not sent them, Yahweh declares. 10 For Yahweh says this: When the seventy years granted to Babylon are over, I shall intervene on your behalf and fulfil my favourable promise to you by bringing you back to this place. 11 Yes, I know what plans I have in mind for you, Yahweh declares, plans for peace, not for disaster, to give you a future and a hope. 12 When you call to me and come and pray to me, I shall listen to you. 13 When you search for me, you will find me; when you search wholeheartedly for me, 14 I shall let you find me (Yahweh declares. I shall restore your fortunes and gather you in from all the nations and wherever I have driven you, Yahweh declares. I shall bring you back to the place from which I exiled you).

15 'Since you say: Yahweh has raised up prophets for us in Babylon — 16 this is what Yahweh says about the king now occupying the throne of David and all the people living in this city, your brothers who did not go with you into exile: 17 Yahweh Sabaoth says this: I am now going to send them sword, famine and plague; I shall make them like rotten figs, so bad as to be uneatable. 18 I shall pursue them with sword, famine and plague. I shall make them an object of terror to all the kingdoms of the earth, a curse, a thing of horror, scorn and derision to all the nations where I have driven them, 19 because they have

NEW REVISED STANDARD VERSION

they did not heed my words, says the LORD, when I persistently sent to you my servants the prophets, but they[i] would not listen, says the LORD. 20 But now, all you exiles whom I sent away from Jerusalem to Babylon, hear the word of the LORD: 21 Thus says the LORD of hosts, the God of Israel, concerning Ahab son of Kolaiah and Zedekiah son of Maaseiah, who are prophesying a lie to you in my name: I am going to deliver them into the hand of King Nebuchadrezzar of Babylon, and he shall kill them before your eyes. 22 And on account of them this curse shall be used by all the exiles from Judah in Babylon: "The LORD make you like Zedekiah and Ahab, whom the king of Babylon roasted in the fire," 23 because they have perpetrated outrage in Israel and have committed adultery with their neighbors' wives, and have spoken in my name lying words that I did not command them; I am the one who knows and bears witness, says the LORD.

24 To Shemaiah of Nehelam you shall say: 25 Thus says the LORD of hosts, the God of Israel: In your own name you sent a letter to all the people who are in Jerusalem, and to the priest Zephaniah son of Maaseiah, and to all the priests, saying, 26 The LORD himself has made you priest instead of the priest Jehoiada, so that there may be officers in the house of the LORD to control any madman who plays the prophet, to put him in the stocks and the collar. 27 So now why have you not rebuked Jeremiah of Anathoth who plays the prophet for you? 28 For he has actually sent to us in Babylon, saying, "It will be a long time; build houses and live in them, and plant gardens and eat what they produce."

29 The priest Zephaniah read this letter in the hearing of the prophet Jeremiah. 30 Then the word of the LORD came to Jeremiah: 31 Send to all the exiles, saying, Thus says the LORD concerning Shemaiah of Nehelam: Because Shemaiah has prophesied to you, though I did not send him, and has led you to trust in a lie, 32 therefore thus says the LORD: I am going to punish Shemaiah of Nehelam and his descendants; he shall not have anyone living among this people to see[j] the good that I am going to do to my people, says the LORD, for he has spoken rebellion against the LORD.

30 The word that came to Jeremiah from the LORD: 2 Thus says the LORD, the God of Israel: Write in a book all the words that I have spoken to you. 3 For the days are surely coming, says the LORD, when I will restore the fortunes of my people, Israel and Judah, says the LORD, and I will bring them back to the land that I gave to their ancestors and they shall take possession of it.

4 These are the words that the LORD spoke concerning Israel and Judah:

5 Thus says the LORD:
We have heard a cry of panic,
of terror, and no peace.
6 Ask now, and see,
can a man bear a child?
Why then do I see every man
with his hands on his loins like a woman in labor?
Why has every face turned pale?
7 Alas! that day is so great
there is none like it;
it is a time of distress for Jacob;
yet he shall be rescued from it.

REVISED ENGLISH BIBLE

says the LORD, when time and again I sent my servants the prophets, so you did not listen, says the LORD.
20 But now listen to the words of the LORD, all you exiles whom I have sent from Jerusalem to Babylon. 21 These are the words of the LORD of Hosts the God of Israel about Ahab son of Kolaiah and Zedekiah son of Maaseiah, who prophesy lies to you in my name. I am handing them over to King Nebuchadrezzar of Babylon, and he will put them to death before your eyes. 22 Their names will be used by all the exiles of Judah in Babylon when they curse anyone; they will say: May the LORD treat you like Zedekiah and Ahab, whom the king of Babylon roasted to death in the fire! 23 For their conduct in Israel was an outrage: they committed adultery with their neighbours' wives, and prophesied in my name without my authority, and what they prophesied was false. I am he who knows and can testify. This is the word of the LORD.

24 To Shemaiah the Nehelamite. 25 These are the words of the LORD of Hosts the God of Israel: You have sent a letter on your own authority to Zephaniah son of Maaseiah the priest, in which you say: 26 'The LORD has appointed you to be priest in place of Jehoiada the priest, and it is your duty, as officer in charge of the LORD's house, to put every crazy person who poses as a prophet into the stocks and the pillory. 27 Why, then, have you not restrained Jeremiah of Anathoth, who acts the prophet among you? 28 On the strength of this he has sent us a message in Babylon to say, "Your exile will be long; build houses and live in them, plant gardens and eat their produce." '

29 When Zephaniah the priest read this letter to Jeremiah the prophet, 30 this word of the LORD came to Jeremiah: 31 Send and tell all the exiles that these are the words of the LORD concerning Shemaiah the Nehelamite: Because Shemaiah has prophesied to you, though I did not send him, and has led you to trust in false prophecies, 32 these are now the words of the LORD: I shall punish Shemaiah and his posterity. He will leave no one to take his place in this nation and witness the wellbeing which I shall bestow on my people, says the LORD, because he has urged rebellion against me.

30 THE word which came to Jeremiah from the LORD. 2 These are the words of the LORD the God of Israel: Write on a scroll all that I have said to you. 3 The time is coming when I shall restore the fortunes of my people, both Israel and Judah, says the LORD, and bring them back to take possession of the land which I gave to their ancestors.

4 This is what the LORD has said to Israel and Judah.
5 These are the words of the LORD:

We have heard a cry of terror, of fear without relief.
6 Enquire and see: can a man bear a child?
Why then do I see every man gripping his sides like a woman in labour?
Why has every face turned deadly pale?
7 How awful is that day:
when has there been its like?
A time of anguish for Jacob,
yet he will come through it safely.

29:25 **authority:** so Gk; Heb. adds to all the people in Jerusalem.
the priest: so Gk; Heb. adds and to all the priests. 29:26 **officer:** so Gk; Heb. officers.

[i] Syr: Heb you   [j] Gk: Heb and he shall not see

NEW AMERICAN BIBLE

NEW JERUSALEM BIBLE

LORD, though I kept sending them my servants the prophets, only to have them go unheeded, says the LORD. ²⁰ You, now, listen to the word of the LORD, all you exiles whom I sent away from Jerusalem to Babylon. ¹⁵ As for your saying, "The LORD has raised up for us prophets here in Babylon" — ⁸ thus says the LORD of hosts, the God of Israel: Do not let yourselves be deceived by the prophets and diviners who are among you; do not listen to those among you who dream dreams. ⁹ For they prophesy lies to you in my name; I did not send them, says the LORD. ²¹ This is what the LORD of hosts, the God of Israel, has to say about those who prophesy lies to you in my name, Ahab, son of Kolaiah, and Zedekiah, son of Maaseiah: I am handing them over to Nebuchadnezzar, king of Babylon, who will slay them before your eyes. ²² All the exiles of Judah in Babylon will pattern a curse after them: "May the LORD make you like Zedekiah and Ahab, whom the king of Babylon roasted in the flames." ²³ For they are criminals in Israel, committing adultery with their neighbors' wives, and alleging in my name things I did not command. I know, I am witness, says the LORD.

²⁴ Say this to Shemaiah, the Nehelamite: ²⁵ Thus says the LORD of hosts, the God of Israel: Because you sent letters on your own authority to all the people of Jerusalem, to all the priests and to Zephaniah, the priest, son of Maaseiah, with this message: ²⁶ "The LORD has appointed you priest in place of the priest Jehoiada, so that there may be police officers in the house of the LORD, to take action against all madmen and those who pose as prophets, by putting them into the stocks or the pillory. ²⁷ Why, then, do you not rebuke Jeremiah of Anathoth who poses as a prophet among you? ²⁸ For he sent us in Babylon this message: It will be a long time; build houses to live in; plant gardens and eat their fruits. . . ."

²⁹ When the priest Zephaniah read this letter to the prophet, ³⁰ the word of the LORD came to Jeremiah: ³¹ Send the message to all the exiles: Thus says the LORD concerning Shemaiah, the Nehelamite: Because Shemaiah prophesies to you without a mission from me, and raises false confidence, ³² says the LORD, I will therefore punish Shemaiah, the Nehelamite, and his offspring. None of them shall survive among this people to see the good I will do to this people, says the LORD, because he preached rebellion against the LORD.

30 The following message came to Jeremiah from the LORD: ² Thus says the LORD, the God of Israel: Write all the words I have spoken to you in a book. ³ For behold, the days will come, says the LORD, when I will change the lot of my people (of Israel and Judah, says the LORD), and bring them back to the land which I gave to their fathers; they shall have it as their possession. ⁴ These are the words which the LORD spoke to Israel and to Judah: ⁵ thus says the LORD:

> A cry of dismay we hear;
>   fear reigns, not peace.
> ⁶ Inquire, and see:
>   since when do men bear children?
> Why, then, do I see all these men,
>   with their hands on their loins
>   like women in childbirth?
> Why have all their faces turned deathly pale?
> ⁷ How mighty is that day —
>   none like it!
> A time of distress for Jacob,
>   though he shall be saved from it.

refused to listen to my words, Yahweh declares, although I have persistently sent them all my servants the prophets; but they would not listen, Yahweh declares. ²⁰ But all you exiles, whom I have sent from Jerusalem to Babylon, listen to Yahweh's word!

²¹ 'This is what Yahweh Sabaoth, God of Israel, says about Ahab son of Kolaiah, and Zedekiah son of Maaseiah, who prophesy lies to you in my name: I shall hand them over now to Nebuchadnezzar king of Babylon who will put them to death before your very eyes. ²² This curse, based on their fate, will be used by all the exiles of Judah in Babylon: May Yahweh treat you like Zedekiah and Ahab, roasted alive by the king of Babylon, ²³ because they have done a scandalous thing in Israel, committing adultery with their neighbour's wives and speaking lying words in my name without orders from me. I know all the same and am witness to it, Yahweh declares.'

²⁴ 'And to Shemaiah of Nehelam you will speak as follows: ²⁵ Yahweh Sabaoth, God of Israel, says this: Since you, on your own initiative, have sent a letter to all the people in Jerusalem, to the priest Zephaniah son of Maaseiah (and to all the priests), saying: ²⁶ Yahweh has appointed you priest in place of the priest Jehoiada to keep order in the Temple of Yahweh, to put any crazy fellow posing as a prophet in the stocks and collar, ²⁷ why then have you not disciplined Jeremiah of Anathoth, now posing as a prophet to you? ²⁸ Why, he has even sent us a message in Babylon, saying: It will be a long time. Build houses, settle down; plant gardens and eat what they produce.' . . .

²⁹ (Now, after the priest Zephaniah had read this letter to the prophet Jeremiah), ³⁰ the word of Yahweh came then to Jeremiah as follows, ³¹ 'Send this message to all the exiles, "This is what Yahweh says about Shemaiah of Nehelam: Since Shemaiah has prophesied to you without my sending him, and since he has caused you to rely on what is false ³² for that reason, Yahweh declares, I shall punish Shemaiah of Nehelam and his descendants; no male member of his family will survive among this people to see the happiness that I will bestow on my people (Yahweh declares, since he has preached rebellion against Yahweh)." '

30 The word which came to Jeremiah from Yahweh, as follows, ² 'Yahweh, God of Israel, says this, "Write for yourself in a book all the words I have spoken to you. ³ For look, the days are coming, Yahweh declares, when I shall bring back the captives of my people Israel (and Judah), Yahweh says. I shall make them come back and take possession of the country I gave to their ancestors." '

⁴ These are the words Yahweh spoke about Israel (and Judah):

> ⁵ Yahweh says this:
> We have heard a cry of panic,
>   of terror, not of peace.
> ⁶ Now ask and see:
>   can a man bear children?
> Then why do I see each man
>   with his hands on his loins like a woman in labour?
> Why has every face grown pale?
> ⁷ Disaster! This is the great day,
>   no other like it:
> a time of distress for Jacob,
>   though he will be saved from it.

29, 26–29: The words of Jeremiah to the false prophet Shemaiah are not fully preserved in the current Hebrew text, as is seen in the incomplete sentence of this translation (vv 25–28).

NEW REVISED STANDARD VERSION	REVISED ENGLISH BIBLE

8 On that day, says the LORD of hosts, I will break the yoke from off his[k] neck, and I will burst his[k] bonds, and strangers shall no more make a servant of him. 9 But they shall serve the LORD their God and David their king, whom I will raise up for them.

10 But as for you, have no fear, my servant Jacob,
　　says the LORD,
　　　and do not be dismayed, O Israel;
　for I am going to save you from far away,
　　and your offspring from the land of their
　　　captivity.
　Jacob shall return and have quiet and ease,
　　and no one shall make him afraid.
11 For I am with you, says the LORD, to save you;
　I will make an end of all the nations
　　among which I scattered you,
　　but of you I will not make an end.
　I will chastise you in just measure,
　　and I will by no means leave you unpunished.

12 For thus says the LORD:
　Your hurt is incurable,
　　your wound is grievous.
13 There is no one to uphold your cause,
　　no medicine for your wound,
　　no healing for you.
14 All your lovers have forgotten you;
　　they care nothing for you;
　for I have dealt you the blow of an enemy,
　　the punishment of a merciless foe,
　because your guilt is great,
　　because your sins are so numerous.
15 Why do you cry out over your hurt?
　　Your pain is incurable.
　Because your guilt is great,
　　because your sins are so numerous,
　　I have done these things to you.
16 Therefore all who devour you shall be devoured,
　　and all your foes, everyone of them, shall go
　　　into captivity;
　those who plunder you shall be plundered,
　　and all who prey on you I will make a prey.
17 For I will restore health to you,
　　and your wounds I will heal,
　　　　　　　　　　　says the LORD,
　because they have called you an outcast:
　　"It is Zion; no one cares for her!"

18 Thus says the LORD:
　I am going to restore the fortunes of the tents of
　　Jacob,
　　and have compassion on his dwellings;
　the city shall be rebuilt upon its mound,
　　and the citadel set on its rightful site.
19 Out of them shall come thanksgiving,
　　and the sound of merrymakers.
　I will make them many, and they shall not be
　　few;
　　I will make them honored, and they shall not
　　　be disdained.
20 Their children shall be as of old,
　　their congregation shall be established before
　　　me;
　and I will punish all who oppress them.
21 Their prince shall be one of their own,
　　their ruler shall come from their midst;
　I will bring him near, and he shall approach me,
　　for who would otherwise dare to approach me?
　　　　　　　　　　　says the LORD.

8 On that day, says the LORD of Hosts, I shall break their yoke off their necks and snap their cords; foreigners will no longer reduce them to servitude; 9 they will serve the LORD their God and David their king, whom I shall raise up for them.

10 But do not be afraid, Jacob my servant;
　Israel, do not despair, says the LORD.
　For I shall bring you back safe from afar,
　　and your posterity from the land where they are
　　　captives.
　Jacob will be at rest once more,
　　secure and untroubled.
11 For I am with you to save you, says the LORD.
　I shall make an end of all the nations
　　among whom I have dispersed you,
　　but I shall not make an end of you.
　I shall discipline you only as you deserve,
　　I shall not leave you wholly unpunished.

12 For these are the words of the LORD to Zion:
　Your wound is past healing;
　　the blow you suffered was cruel.
13 There can be no remedy for your sore;
　　the new skin cannot grow.
14 All your friends have forgotten you;
　　they look for you no longer.
　I have struck you down as an enemy strikes,
　　and have punished you cruelly,
　because of your great wickedness, your flagrant
　　sins.
15 Why complain of your injury,
　　that your sore cannot be healed?
　Because of your great wickedness, your flagrant
　　sins,
　I have done this to you.
16 Yet all who devoured you will themselves be
　　devoured;
　all your oppressors will go into captivity;
　those who plunder you will be plundered,
　　and those who despoil you I shall give up to be
　　　spoiled.
17 I shall cause the new skin to grow
　　and heal your wounds, says the LORD,
　although you are called outcast, Zion,
　　forsaken by all.

18 These are the words of the LORD:
　I shall restore the fortunes of Jacob's clans
　　and show my love for his dwellings.
　Every city will be rebuilt on its own mound,
　　every mansion will occupy its traditional site.
19 From them praise will be heard
　　and sounds of merrymaking.
　I shall increase them, they will not diminish;
　　I shall raise them to honour,
　　no longer to be despised.
20 Their children will be what once they were,
　　and their community will be established in my
　　　sight.
　I shall punish all their oppressors.
21 A ruler will appear, one of themselves;
　a governor will arise from their own number.
　I shall myself bring him near and let him approach
　　me,
　for who dare risk his life by approaching me?
　　says the LORD.

[k] Cn: Heb *your*

30:8 **their necks . . . their cords:** *so Gk; Heb.* your neck . . . your cords. 　30:13 **no:** *prob. rdg; Heb. adds* one judging your case.

NEW AMERICAN BIBLE

8 On that day, says the LORD of hosts, "I will break his yoke from off your necks and snap your bonds." Strangers shall no longer enslave them; 9 instead, they shall serve the LORD, their God, and David, their king, whom I will raise up for them.

10 But you, my servant Jacob, fear not, says
        the LORD,
    be not dismayed, O Israel!
    Behold, I will deliver you from the far-off land,
        your descendants, from their land of exile;
    Jacob shall again find rest,
        shall be tranquil and undisturbed,
11   for I am with you, says the LORD, to
        deliver you.
    I will make an end of all the nations
        among which I have scattered you;
        but of you I will not make an end.
    I will chastise you as you deserve,
        I will not let you go unpunished.

12   For thus says the LORD:
    Incurable is your wound,
        grievous your bruise;
13 There is none to plead your cause,
        no remedy for your running sore,
        no healing for you.
14 All your lovers have forgotten you,
        they do not seek you.
    I struck you as an enemy would strike,
        punished you cruelly;
15 Why cry out over your wound?
        your pain is without relief.
    Because of your great guilt,
        your numerous sins,
    I have done this to you.
16 Yet all who devour you shall be devoured,
        all your enemies shall go into exile.
    All who plunder you shall be plundered,
        all who pillage you I will hand over to pillage.
17 For I will restore you to health;
        of your wounds I will heal you, says the LORD.
    "The outcast" they have called you,
        "with no avenger."

18   Thus says the LORD:
    See! I will restore the tents of Jacob,
        his dwellings I will pity;
    City shall be rebuilt upon hill,
        and palace restored as it was.
19 From them will resound songs of praise,
        the laughter of happy men.
    I will make them not few, but many;
        they will not be tiny, for I will glorify them.
20 His sons shall be as of old,
        his assembly before me shall stand firm;
    I will punish all his oppressors.
21 His leader shall be one of his own,
        and his rulers shall come from his kin.
    When I summon him, he shall approach me;
        how else should one take the deadly risk
        of approaching me? says the LORD.

NEW JERUSALEM BIBLE

8 (That day, Yahweh Sabaoth declares, I shall break the yoke now on your neck and snap your chains; and foreigners will enslave you no more, 9 but Israel and Judah will serve Yahweh their God, and David their king whom I shall raise up for them.)

10 So do not be afraid, my servant Jacob,
        Yahweh declares,
    Israel, do not be alarmed:
    for look, I shall rescue you from distant countries
        and your descendants from the country where they
        are captive.
    Jacob will return and be at peace,
        secure, with no one to trouble him.
11 For I am with you to save you,
        Yahweh declares,
    I shall make an end of all the nations
        where I have driven you,
    but I shall not make an end of you,
        only discipline you in moderation,
        not to let you go quite unpunished. q

12 Yes, Yahweh says this:
    Your wound is incurable,
        your injury past healing.
13 There is no one to plead your cause;
        for an ulcer there are remedies,
        but for you no cure at all.
14 All your lovers have forgotten you,
        they look for you no more.
    Yes, I have struck you as an enemy strikes,
        with cruel punishment
        (because of your great guilt and countless sins).
15 Why cry out because of your wound?
    Your pain is incurable!
    Because of your great guilt and countless sins,
        I have treated you like this.
16 But all those who devoured you will be devoured,
        all your enemies, all, go into captivity,
    those who despoiled you will be despoiled,
        and all who pillaged you be pillaged.
17 For I shall restore you to health
        and heal your wounds, Yahweh declares,
    you who used to be called 'Outcast',
        'Zion for whom no one cares'.

18 Yahweh says this:
    Look, I shall restore the tents of Jacob
        and take pity on his dwellings:
    the town will be rebuilt on its mound,
        the stronghold where it ought to stand.
19 From them will come thanksgiving
        and shouts of joy.
    I shall make them increase, they will not decrease;
        I shall make them honoured, no more to be
        humbled.
20 Their sons will be as once they were,
        their community fixed firmly before me,
        and I shall punish all their oppressors.
21 Their prince will be one of their own,
        their ruler come from their own people,
        and I shall permit him to approach me freely;
    for who, otherwise, would be so bold
        as to approach me, Yahweh demands?

q 30 = 46:27-28.

NEW REVISED STANDARD VERSION	REVISED ENGLISH BIBLE

NEW REVISED STANDARD VERSION

22 And you shall be my people,
    and I will be your God.

23 Look, the storm of the LORD!
    Wrath has gone forth,
a whirling*l* tempest;
    it will burst upon the head of the wicked.

24 The fierce anger of the LORD will not turn back
    until he has executed and accomplished
    the intents of his mind.
In the latter days you will understand this.

31 At that time, says the LORD, I will be the God of all the families of Israel, and they shall be my people.
2 Thus says the LORD:
The people who survived the sword
    found grace in the wilderness;
when Israel sought for rest,
3   the LORD appeared to him*m* from far away.*n*
I have loved you with an everlasting love;
    therefore I have continued my faithfulness to
        you.
4 Again I will build you, and you shall be built,
    O virgin Israel!
Again you shall take*o* your tambourines,
    and go forth in the dance of the merrymakers.
5 Again you shall plant vineyards
    on the mountains of Samaria;
the planters shall plant,
    and shall enjoy the fruit.
6 For there shall be a day when sentinels will call
    in the hill country of Ephraim:
"Come, let us go up to Zion,
    to the LORD our God."

7 For thus says the LORD:
Sing aloud with gladness for Jacob,
    and raise shouts for the chief of the nations;
proclaim, give praise, and say,
    "Save, O LORD, your people,
    the remnant of Israel."
8 See, I am going to bring them from the land of
    the north,
    and gather them from the farthest parts of the
        earth,
among them the blind and the lame,
    those with child and those in labor, together;
    a great company, they shall return here.
9 With weeping they shall come,
    and with consolations*p* I will lead them back,
I will let them walk by brooks of water,
    in a straight path in which they shall not
        stumble;
for I have become a father to Israel,
    and Ephraim is my firstborn.

10 Hear the word of the LORD, O nations,
    and declare it in the coastlands far away;
say, "He who scattered Israel will gather him,
    and will keep him as a shepherd a flock."
11 For the LORD has ransomed Jacob,
    and has redeemed him from hands too strong
        for him.

REVISED ENGLISH BIBLE

22 So you will be my people,
    and I shall be your God.
23 See what a scorching wind has gone out from the
    LORD,
a sweeping whirlwind
    which whirls round the heads of the wicked.
24 The LORD's fierce anger is not to be turned aside
    until he has fully accomplished his purposes.
In days to come you will understand.

31 At that time, says the LORD, I shall be the God of all the families of Israel, and they will be my people. 2 These are the words of the LORD:

A people that escaped the sword
    found favour in the wilderness.
The LORD went to give rest to Israel;
3 from afar he appeared to them:
I have dearly loved you from of old,
    and still I maintain my unfailing care for you.
4 Virgin Israel, I shall build you up again,
    and you will be rebuilt.
Again you will provide yourself with tambourines,
    and go forth with the merry throng of dancers.
5 Again you will plant vineyards on the hills of
        Samaria,
and those who plant them will enjoy the fruit;
6 for a day will come when the watchmen
    cry out on Ephraim's hills,
'Come, let us go up to Zion,
    to the LORD our God.'

7 For these are the words of the LORD:

Break into shouts of joy for Jacob's sake,
    lead the nations, crying loud and clear,
sing out your praises and say:
    'The LORD has saved his people;
    he has preserved a remnant of Israel.'
8 See how I bring them from a northern land;
    I shall gather them from the far ends of the earth,
among them the blind and lame,
    the woman with child and the woman in labour.
A vast company, 9 they come home,
    weeping as they come,
but I shall comfort them and be their escort.
I shall lead them by streams of water;
    their path will be smooth, they will not stumble.
For I have become a father to Israel,
    and Ephraim is my eldest son.
10 Listen to the word of the LORD, you nations,
    announce it, make it known to coastlands far away:
He who scattered Israel will gather them again
    and watch over them as a shepherd watches his
        flock.
11 For the LORD has delivered Jacob
    and redeemed him from a foe too strong for him.

---

l One Ms: Meaning of MT uncertain   *m* Gk: Heb *me*   *n* Or *to him long ago*   *o* Or *adorn yourself with supplications*   *p* Gk Compare Vg Tg: Heb

31:3 **them:** *so Gk; Heb.* me.   31:7 **his:** *so Gk; Heb.* your.
31:9 **I shall comfort them:** *so Gk; Heb.* prayers for favour.

NEW AMERICAN BIBLE

NEW JERUSALEM BIBLE

22 You shall be my people,
　and I will be your God.
23 See, the storm of the LORD!
　His wrath breaks forth
In a whirling storm
　that bursts upon the heads of the wicked.
24 The anger of the LORD will not abate
　until he has done and fulfilled
　what he has determined in his heart.
When the time comes,
　you will fully understand.

31 At that time, says the LORD,
　I will be the God of all the tribes of Israel,
　and they shall be my people.
2　　Thus says the LORD:
The people that escaped the sword
　have found favor in the desert.
As Israel comes forward to be given his rest,
3　the LORD appears to him from afar:
With age-old love I have loved you;
　so I have kept my mercy toward you.
4 Again I will restore you, and you shall be rebuilt,
　O virgin Israel;
Carrying your festive tambourines,
　you shall go forth dancing with
　　the merry-makers.
5 Again you shall plant vineyards
　on the mountains of Samaria;
　those who plant them shall enjoy the fruits.
6 Yes, a day will come when the watchmen
　will call out on Mount Ephraim:
"Rise up, let us go to Zion,
　to the LORD, our God."

7　　For thus says the LORD:
Shout with joy for Jacob,
　exult at the head of the nations;
　proclaim your praise and say:
The LORD has delivered his people,
　the remnant of Israel.
8 Behold, I will bring them back
　from the land of the north;
I will gather them from the ends of the world,
　with the blind and the lame in their midst,
The mothers and those with child;
　they shall return as an immense throng.
9 They departed in tears,
　but I will console them and guide them;
I will lead them to brooks of water,
　on a level road, so that none shall stumble.
For I am a father to Israel,
　Ephraim is my first-born.
10 Hear the word of the LORD, O nations,
　proclaim it on distant coasts, and say:
He who scattered Israel, now gathers
　　them together.
he guards them as a shepherd his flock.
11 The LORD shall ransom Jacob,
　he shall redeem him from the hand of
　　his conqueror.

22 You will be my people and I shall be your God.
23 Look, Yahweh's hurricane, his wrath, bursts out,
　a roaring hurricane,
　to burst on the heads of the wicked;
24 Yahweh's burning anger will not turn aside
　until he has performed, has carried out,
　what he has in mind.
In the final days, you will understand this.r

31 When that time comes, Yahweh declares, I shall be
　the God of all the families of Israel, and they will
be my people.

2 Yahweh says this:
They have found pardon in the desert,
　those who have survived the sword.
Israel is marching to his rest.
3 Yahweh has appeared to me from afar;
I have loved you with an everlasting love
　and so I still maintain my faithful love for you.
4 I shall build you once more, yes, you will be
　　rebuilt,
Virgin of Israel!
Once more in your best attire,
　and with your tambourines,
　you will go out dancing gaily.
5 Once more you will plant vineyards
　on the mountains of Samaria
　(those who plant will themselves enjoy the fruit).
6 Yes, a day will come when the watchmen shout
　on the mountains of Ephraim,
　'Up! Let us go up to Zion,
　to Yahweh our God!'

7 For Yahweh says this:
Shout with joy for Jacob!
Hail the chief of nations!
Proclaim! Praise! Shout,
'Yahweh has saved his people,
　the remnant of Israel!'

8 Watch, I shall bring them back
　from the land of the north
　and gather them in from the far ends of the earth.
With them, the blind and the lame,
　women with child, women in labour,
　all together: a mighty throng will return here!
9 In tears they will return,
　in prayer I shall lead them.
I shall guide them to streams of water,
　by a smooth path where they will not stumble.
For I am a father to Israel,
　and Ephraim is my first-born son.

10 Listen, nations, to the word of Yahweh.
On the farthest coasts and islands proclaim it, say,
'He who scattered Israel is gathering him,
　will guard him as a shepherd guarding his flock.'
11 For Yahweh has ransomed Jacob,
　rescued him from a hand stronger than his own.

r 30 = 23:19–20.

NEW REVISED STANDARD VERSION	REVISED ENGLISH BIBLE

NEW REVISED STANDARD VERSION

12 They shall come and sing aloud on the height of
Zion,
and they shall be radiant over the goodness of
the LORD,
over the grain, the wine, and the oil,
and over the young of the flock and the herd;
their life shall become like a watered garden,
and they shall never languish again.
13 Then shall the young women rejoice in the dance,
and the young men and the old shall be merry.
I will turn their mourning into joy,
I will comfort them, and give them gladness
for sorrow.
14 I will give the priests their fill of fatness,
and my people shall be satisfied with my
bounty,
says the LORD.

15 Thus says the LORD:
A voice is heard in Ramah,
lamentation and bitter weeping.
Rachel is weeping for her children;
she refuses to be comforted for her children,
because they are no more.
16 Thus says the LORD:
Keep your voice from weeping,
and your eyes from tears;
for there is a reward for your work,
says the LORD:
they shall come back from the land of the
enemy;
17 there is hope for your future,
says the LORD:
your children shall come back to their own
country.
18 Indeed I heard Ephraim pleading:
"You disciplined me, and I took the discipline;
I was like a calf untrained.
Bring me back, let me come back,
for you are the LORD my God.
19 For after I had turned away I repented;
and after I was discovered, I struck my thigh;
I was ashamed, and I was dismayed
because I bore the disgrace of my youth."
20 Is Ephraim my dear son?
Is he the child I delight in?
As often as I speak against him,
I still remember him.
Therefore I am deeply moved for him;
I will surely have mercy on him,
says the LORD.

21 Set up road markers for yourself,
make yourself guideposts;
consider well the highway,
the road by which you went.
Return, O virgin Israel,
return to these your cities.
22 How long will you waver,
O faithless daughter?
For the LORD has created a new thing on the
earth:
a woman encompasses^q a man.

23 Thus says the LORD of hosts, the God of Israel: Once
more they shall use these words in the land of Judah and in
its towns when I restore their fortunes:
"The LORD bless you, O abode of righteousness,
O holy hill!"

^{q} Meaning of Heb uncertain

REVISED ENGLISH BIBLE

12 They will come with shouts of joy to Zion's
height,
radiant at the bounty of the LORD:
the grain, the new wine, and the oil,
the young of flock and herd.
They will be like a well-watered garden
and never languish again.
13 Girls will then dance for joy,
and men young and old will rejoice;
I shall turn their grief into gladness,
comfort them, and give them joy after sorrow.
14 I shall satisfy the priests with the fat of the land
and my people will have their fill of my bounty.
This is the word of the LORD.

15 These are the words of the LORD:
Lamentation is heard in Ramah, and bitter
weeping:
Rachel weeping for her children
and refusing to be comforted, because they are no
more.
16 These are the words of the LORD to her:
Cease your weeping,
shed no more tears;
for there will be a reward for your toil,
and they will return from the enemy's land.
17 There will be hope for your posterity;
your children will return within their own borders.
18 I listened intently:
Ephraim was rocking in his grief:
'I was like a calf unbroken to the yoke;
you disciplined me, and I accepted your discipline.
Bring me back and let me return,
for you are the LORD my God.
19 Though I broke away I have repented:
now that I am submissive I beat my breast;
in shame and remorse
I reproach myself for the sins of my youth.'
20 Is Ephraim still so dear a son to me,
a child in whom I so delight
that, as often as I speak against him,
I must think of him again?
Therefore my heart yearns for him;
I am filled with tenderness towards him.
This is the word of the LORD.

21 Build cairns to mark your way,
set up signposts;
make sure of the road,
the path which you will tread.
Come back, virgin Israel,
come back to your cities and towns.
22 How long will you waver, my wayward child?
For the LORD has created a new thing in the earth:
a woman will play a man's part.

23 These are the words of the LORD of Hosts the God of
Israel: Once more will these words be heard in the land of
Judah and in her towns, when I restore their fortunes:
The LORD bless you,
abode of righteousness, holy mountain.

12 Shouting, they shall mount the heights of Zion,
    they shall come streaming to the
        LORD's blessings:
The grain, the wine, and the oil,
    the sheep and the oxen;
They themselves shall be like watered gardens,
    never again shall they languish.
13 Then the virgins shall make merry and dance,
    and young men and old as well.
I will turn their mourning into joy,
    I will console and gladden them after
    their sorrows.
14 I will lavish choice portions upon the priests,
    and my people shall be filled with my blessings,
    says the LORD.

15   Thus says the LORD:
In Ramah is heard the sound of moaning,
    of bitter weeping!
Rachel mourns her children,
    she refuses to be consoled
    because her children are no more.
16   Thus says the LORD:
Cease your cries of mourning,
    wipe the tears from your eyes.
The sorrow you have shown shall have its reward,
    says the LORD,
    they shall return from the enemy's land.
17 There is hope for your future, says the LORD;
    your sons shall return to their own borders.
18 I hear, I hear Ephraim pleading:
    You chastised me, and I am chastened;
    I was an untamed calf.
If you allow me, I will return,
    for you are the LORD, my God.
19 I turn in repentance;
    I have come to myself, I strike my breast;
I blush with shame,
    I bear the disgrace of my youth.
20 Is Ephraim not my favored son,
    the child in whom I delight?
Often as I threaten him,
    I still remember him with favor;
My heart stirs for him,
    I must show him mercy, says the LORD.

21 Set up road markers,
    put up guideposts;
Turn your attention to the highway,
    the road by which you went.
Turn back, O virgin Israel,
    turn back to these your cities.
22 How long will you continue to stray,
    rebellious daughter?
The LORD has created a new thing upon the earth:
    the woman must encompass the man
    with devotion.

23 Thus says the LORD of hosts, the God of Israel: When I change their lot in the land of Judah and her cities, they shall again repeat this greeting: "May the LORD bless you, holy mountain, abode of justice!" 24 Judah and all her cities,

12 They will come, shouting for joy on the heights of
    Zion,
thronging towards Yahweh's lavish gifts,
    for wheat, new wine and oil,
sheep and cattle;
    they will be like a well-watered garden,
    they will sorrow no more.
13 The young girl will then take pleasure in the
    dance,
and young men and old alike;
I shall change their mourning into gladness,
comfort them, give them joy after their troubles;
14 I shall refresh my priests with rich food,
    and my people will gorge themselves on my lavish
    gifts,
Yahweh declares.

15 Yahweh says this:
A voice is heard in Ramah,
    lamenting and weeping bitterly;
it is Rachel[s] weeping for her children,
    refusing to be comforted for her children,
    because they are no more.
16 Yahweh says this:
Stop your lamenting
    dry your eyes,
for your labour will have a reward,
    Yahweh declares,
and they will return from the enemy's country.
17 There is hope for your future after all,
    Yahweh declares,
your children will return to their homeland.
18 I have indeed heard Ephraim's grieving,
    'You flogged me, I took a flogging,
    like a young, untrained bull.
Bring me back, let me come back,
    for you are Yahweh my God!
19 For, since I turned away, I have repented;
    having understood, I beat my breast.
I was deeply ashamed, I blushed,
    aware of the disgrace incurred when I was young.'
20 Is Ephraim, then, so dear a son to me,
    a child so favoured,
that whenever I mention him
    I remember him lovingly still?
That is why I yearn for him,
    why I must take pity on him,
    Yahweh declares.

21 Set up your signposts,
    raise yourself landmarks,
fix your mind on the road,
    the way by which you went.
Come home, Virgin of Israel,
    come home to these towns of yours.
22 How long will you hesitate,
    rebellious daughter?
For Yahweh is creating something new on earth:
    the Woman sets out to find her Husband again.

23 Yahweh Sabaoth, the God of Israel, says this, 'In the country of Judah and in its towns, they will use these words once more, when I bring their captives home:

    "Yahweh bless you,
    home of saving justice,
    holy mountain!"

---

s **31** Ancestor of the deported tribe of Benjamin.

| NEW REVISED STANDARD VERSION | REVISED ENGLISH BIBLE |

24 And Judah and all its towns shall live there together, and the farmers and those who wander*r* with their flocks.

25   I will satisfy the weary,
      and all who are faint I will replenish.

26 Thereupon I awoke and looked, and my sleep was pleasant to me.

27 The days are surely coming, says the LORD, when I will sow the house of Israel and the house of Judah with the seed of humans and the seed of animals. 28 And just as I have watched over them to pluck up and break down, to overthrow, destroy, and bring evil, so I will watch over them to build and to plant, says the LORD. 29 In those days they shall no longer say:

    "The parents have eaten sour grapes,
      and the children's teeth are set on edge."

30 But all shall die for their own sins; the teeth of everyone who eats sour grapes shall be set on edge.

31 The days are surely coming, says the LORD, when I will make a new covenant with the house of Israel and the house of Judah. 32 It will not be like the covenant that I made with their ancestors when I took them by the hand to bring them out of the land of Egypt—a covenant that they broke, though I was their husband,*s* says the LORD. 33 But this is the covenant that I will make with the house of Israel after those days, says the LORD: I will put my law within them, and I will write it on their hearts; and I will be their God, and they shall be my people. 34 No longer shall they teach one another, or say to each other, "Know the LORD," for they shall all know me, from the least of them to the greatest, says the LORD; for I will forgive their iniquity, and remember their sin no more.

35   Thus says the LORD,
    who gives the sun for light by day
      and the fixed order of the moon and the stars
        for light by night,
    who stirs up the sea so that its waves roar—
      the LORD of hosts is his name:
36   If this fixed order were ever to cease
      from my presence, says the LORD,
    then also the offspring of Israel would cease
      to be a nation before me forever.

37   Thus says the LORD:
    If the heavens above can be measured,
      and the foundations of the earth below can be
        explored,
    then I will reject all the offspring of Israel
      because of all they have done,
                says the LORD.

38 The days are surely coming, says the LORD, when the city shall be rebuilt for the LORD from the tower of Hananel to the Corner Gate. 39 And the measuring line shall go out farther, straight to the hill Gareb, and shall then turn to Goah. 40 The whole valley of the dead bodies and the ashes, and all the fields as far as the Wadi Kidron, to the corner of the Horse Gate toward the east, shall be sacred to the LORD. It shall never again be uprooted or overthrown.

32 The word that came to Jeremiah from the LORD in the tenth year of King Zedekiah of Judah, which was the eighteenth year of Nebuchadrezzar. 2 At that time the army of the king of Babylon was besieging Jerusalem, and the prophet Jeremiah was confined in the court of the guard that was in the palace of the king of Judah, 3 where

24 Ploughmen and shepherds with their flocks
    will live together in Judah and all her towns.
25 For I have given deep draughts to the thirsty,
    and satisfied those who were faint with hunger.

26 Thereupon I woke and looked about me, and my sleep had been pleasant.

27 The days are coming, says the LORD, when I shall sow Israel and Judah with the seed of man and the seed of cattle. 28 As I watched over them with intent to pull down and to uproot, to demolish and destroy and inflict disaster, so now I shall watch over them to build and to plant. This is the word of the LORD.

29 In those days it will no longer be said,
    'Parents have eaten sour grapes
    and the children's teeth are set on edge';

30 for everyone will die for his own wrongdoing; he who eats the sour grapes will find his own teeth set on edge.

31 The days are coming, says the LORD, when I shall establish a new covenant with the people of Israel and Judah. 32 It will not be like the covenant I made with their forefathers when I took them by the hand to lead them out of Egypt, a covenant they broke, though I was patient with them, says the LORD. 33 For this is the covenant I shall establish with the Israelites after those days, says the LORD: I shall set my law within them, writing it on their hearts; I shall be their God, and they will be my people. 34 No longer need they teach one another, neighbour or brother, to know the LORD; all of them, high and low alike, will know me, says the LORD, for I shall forgive their wrongdoing, and their sin I shall call to mind no more.

35 These are the words of the LORD,
    who gave the sun for a light by day
    and the moon and stars in their courses
      for a light by night,
    who cleft the sea and its waves roared;
    the LORD of Hosts is his name.

36 Israel could no more cease to be a nation in my sight, says the LORD, than could this fixed order vanish before my eyes.

37 These are the words of the LORD: I could no more spurn the whole of Israel because of what they have done, than anyone could measure the heaven above or fathom the depths of the earth beneath. This is the word of the LORD.

38 The days are coming, says the LORD, when Jerusalem will be rebuilt in the LORD's honour from the Tower of Hananel to the Corner Gate. 39 The measuring line will then be laid straight out over the hill of Gareb and round Goath. 40 All the valley and every field as far as the wadi Kidron to the corner by the Horse Gate eastwards will be holy to the LORD. Never again will it be pulled down or demolished.

32 The word which came to Jeremiah from the LORD in the tenth year of King Zedekiah of Judah, which was the eighteenth year of Nebuchadrezzar. 2 At that time the forces of the Babylonian king were besieging Jerusalem, and the prophet Jeremiah was imprisoned in the court of the guardhouse attached to the royal palace. 3 King Zedekiah

31:32 **I was . . . them:** *or* I had authority over them.
31:39 **Goath:** *or* Goah.   31:40 **the valley:** *prob. rdg; Heb. adds* the corpses and the buried bodies.

r Cn Compare Syr Vg Tg: Heb *and they shall wander*   *s* Or *master*

the farmers and those who lead the flock, shall dwell there together. 25 For I will refresh the weary soul; every soul that languishes I will replenish. 26 Upon this I awoke and opened my eyes; but my sleep was sweet to me.

27 The days are coming, says the LORD, when I will seed the house of Israel and the house of Judah with the seed of man and the seed of beast. 28 As I once watched over them to uproot and pull down, to destroy, to ruin, and to harm, so I will watch over them to build and to plant, says the LORD. 29 In those days they shall no longer say,

> "The fathers ate unripe grapes,
> and the children's teeth are set on edge,"

30 but through his own fault only shall anyone die: the teeth of him who eats the unripe grapes shall be set on edge.

31 The days are coming, says the LORD, when I will make a new covenant with the house of Israel and the house of Judah. 32 It will not be like the covenant I made with their fathers the day I took them by the hand to lead them forth from the land of Egypt; for they broke my covenant and I had to show myself their master, says the LORD. 33 But this is the covenant which I will make with the house of Israel after those days, says the LORD. I will place my law within them, and write it upon their hearts; I will be their God, and they shall be my people. 34 No longer will they have need to teach their friends and kinsmen how to know the LORD. All, from least to greatest, shall know me, says the LORD, for I will forgive their evildoing and remember their sin no more.

35   Thus says the LORD,
He who gives the sun to light the day,
    moon and stars to light the night;
Who stirs up the sea till its waves roar,
    whose name is LORD of hosts:
36 If ever these natural laws give way
    in spite of me, says the LORD,
Then shall the race of Israel cease
    as a nation before me forever.
37   Thus says the LORD:
If the heavens on high can be measured,
    or the foundations below the earth be sounded,
Then will I cast off the whole race of Israel
    because of all they have done, says the LORD.

38 The days are coming, says the LORD, when the city shall be rebuilt as the LORD'S, from the Tower of Hananel to the Corner Gate. 39 The measuring line shall be stretched from there straight to the hill Gareb and then turn to Goah. 40 The whole valley of corpses and ashes, all the slopes toward the Kidron Valley, as far as the corner of the Horse Gate at the east, shall be holy to the LORD. Never again shall the city be rooted up or thrown down.

32 This message came to Jeremiah from the LORD in the tenth year of Zedekiah, king of Judah, the eighteenth year of Nebuchadnezzar. 2 At that time the army of the king of Babylon was besieging Jerusalem, and the prophet Jeremiah was imprisoned in the quarters of the guard, at the king's palace. 3 Zedekiah, king of Judah, had

24 'And in this country, Judah and all its towns, the ploughmen and those who wander with their flocks, will live together, 25 for I shall give the weary all they need and satisfy all those whose strength has gone.'

26 At this, I awoke and saw
    that my sleep had been sweet to me.

27 'Look, the days are coming, Yahweh declares, when I shall sow the House of Israel and the House of Judah with the seed both of people and of cattle. 28 And as I once watched over them to uproot, to knock down, and to overthrow, destroy and bring disaster, so now I shall watch over them to build and to plant, Yahweh declares.

29 'In those days people will no longer say:

> "The fathers have eaten unripe grapes;
> the children's teeth are set on edge."*t*

30 But each will die for his own guilt. Everyone who eats unripe grapes will have his own teeth set on edge.

31 'Look, the days are coming, Yahweh declares, when I shall make a new covenant with the House of Israel (and the House of Judah), 32 but not like the covenant I made with their ancestors the day I took them by the hand to bring them out of Egypt, a covenant which they broke, even though I was their Master, Yahweh declares. 33 No, this is the covenant I shall make with the House of Israel when those days have come, Yahweh declares. Within them I shall plant my Law, writing it on their hearts. Then I shall be their God and they will be my people. 34 There will be no further need for everyone to teach neighbour or brother, saying, "Learn to know Yahweh!" No, they will all know me, from the least to the greatest, Yahweh declares, since I shall forgive their guilt and never more call their sin to mind.'

35 Yahweh who provides the sun to shine by day,
    who regulates moon and stars to shine by night,
    who stirs the sea, making its waves roar,
    he whose name is Yahweh Sabaoth, says this,
36 'Were this established order ever to pass away
    before me, Yahweh declares,
    then the race of Israel would also cease
    being a nation for ever before me!'
37 Yahweh says this,
    'Were the heavens above ever to be measured,
    the foundations of the earth below ever to be
        fathomed,
    then I too would reject the whole race of Israel
    for all that they have done, Yahweh declares.'

38 'Look, the days are coming, Yahweh declares, when the City will be rebuilt for Yahweh, from the Tower of Hananel to the Corner Gate. 39 Then once again the measuring line will stretch straight to the Hill of Gareb, turning then to Goah. 40 And the whole valley, with its corpses and ashes, and all the ground beside the ravine of the Kidron as far as the corner of the Horse Gate, eastwards, will be consecrated to Yahweh. It will never be destroyed or demolished again.

32 The word that came to Jeremiah from Yahweh in the tenth year of Zedekiah king of Judah, which was the eighteenth year of Nebuchadnezzar. 2 The army of the king of Babylon was then besieging Jerusalem, and the prophet Jeremiah was confined in the Court of the Guard in the king of Judah's palace, 3 where Zedekiah king of Judah

t 31 // Ezk 18:2.

King Zedekiah of Judah had confined him. Zedekiah had said, "Why do you prophesy and say: Thus says the LORD: I am going to give this city into the hand of the king of Babylon, and he shall take it; 4 King Zedekiah of Judah shall not escape out of the hands of the Chaldeans, but shall surely be given into the hands of the king of Babylon, and shall speak with him face to face and see him eye to eye; 5 and he shall take Zedekiah to Babylon, and there he shall remain until I attend to him, says the LORD; though you fight against the Chaldeans, you shall not succeed?"

6 Jeremiah said, The word of the LORD came to me: 7 Hanamel son of your uncle Shallum is going to come to you and say, "Buy my field that is at Anathoth, for the right of redemption by purchase is yours." 8 Then my cousin Hanamel came to me in the court of the guard, in accordance with the word of the LORD, and said to me, "Buy my field that is at Anathoth in the land of Benjamin, for the right of possession and redemption is yours; buy it for yourself." Then I knew that this was the word of the LORD.

9 And I bought the field at Anathoth from my cousin Hanamel, and weighed out the money to him, seventeen shekels of silver. 10 I signed the deed, sealed it, got witnesses, and weighed the money on scales. 11 Then I took the sealed deed of purchase, containing the terms and conditions, and the open copy; 12 and I gave the deed of purchase to Baruch son of Neriah son of Mahseiah, in the presence of my cousin Hanamel, in the presence of the witnesses who signed the deed of purchase, and in the presence of all the Judeans who were sitting in the court of the guard. 13 In their presence I charged Baruch, saying, 14 Thus says the LORD of hosts, the God of Israel: Take these deeds, both this sealed deed of purchase and this open deed, and put them in an earthenware jar, in order that they may last for a long time. 15 For thus says the LORD of hosts, the God of Israel: Houses and fields and vineyards shall again be bought in this land.

16 After I had given the deed of purchase to Baruch son of Neriah, I prayed to the LORD, saying: 17 Ah Lord GOD! It is you who made the heavens and the earth by your great power and by your outstretched arm! Nothing is too hard for you. 18 You show steadfast love to the thousandth generation,[t] but repay the guilt of parents into the laps of their children after them, O great and mighty God whose name is the LORD of hosts, 19 great in counsel and mighty in deed; whose eyes are open to all the ways of mortals, rewarding all according to their ways and according to the fruit of their doings. 20 You showed signs and wonders in the land of Egypt, and to this day in Israel and among all humankind, and have made yourself a name that continues to this very day. 21 You brought your people Israel out of the land of Egypt with signs and wonders, with a strong hand and outstretched arm, and with great terror; 22 and you gave them this land, which you swore to their ancestors to give them, a land flowing with milk and honey; 23 and they entered and took possession of it. But they did not obey your voice or follow your law; of all you commanded them to do, they did nothing. Therefore you have made all these disasters come upon them. 24 See, the siege ramps have been cast up against the city to take it, and the city, faced with sword, famine, and pestilence, has been given into the hands of the Chaldeans who are fighting against it. What you spoke has happened, as you yourself can see. 25 Yet you, O Lord GOD, have said to me, "Buy the field for money and get witnesses" — though the city has been given into the hands of the Chaldeans.

26 The word of the LORD came to Jeremiah: 27 See, I am the LORD, the God of all flesh; is anything too hard for me?

had imprisoned him after demanding what he meant by this prophecy: 'These are the words of the LORD: I shall give this city into the power of the king of Babylon, and he will capture it. 4 Nor will King Zedekiah of Judah escape from the Chaldaeans; he will be surrendered to the king of Babylon and will speak with him face to face and see him with his own eyes. 5 Zedekiah will be taken to Babylon and will remain there until the day I visit him, says the LORD. However much you fight against the Chaldaeans you will have no success.'

6 Jeremiah said: This word of the LORD came to me: 7 Hanamel son of your uncle Shallum is coming to you; he will say, 'Buy my field at Anathoth; as next-of-kin you have the right of redemption to buy it.' 8 Just as the LORD had foretold, my cousin Hanamel came to me in the court of the guardhouse and said, 'Buy my field at Anathoth in Benjamin. You have the right of redemption and possession as next-of-kin, so buy it for yourself.'

I recognized that this instruction came from the LORD, 9 so I bought the field at Anathoth from my cousin Hanamel and weighed out the price for him, seventeen shekels of silver. 10 I signed and sealed the deed, had it witnessed, and then weighed the money on the scales. 11 I took my copies of the deed of purchase, both the sealed and the unsealed copies, 12 and handed them over to Baruch son of Neriah, son of Mahseiah, in the presence of Hanamel my cousin and the witnesses whose names were subscribed on the deed of purchase, and of the Judaeans sitting in the court of the guardhouse. 13 In their presence I gave my instructions to Baruch: 14 These are the words of the LORD of Hosts the God of Israel: Take these copies of the deed of purchase, both the sealed and the unsealed copies, and deposit them in an earthenware jar so that they may be preserved for a long time to come. 15 For these are the words of the LORD of Hosts the God of Israel: Houses, fields, and vineyards will again be bought and sold in this land.

16 After I handed over the deed of purchase to Baruch son of Neriah, I offered this prayer to the LORD: 17 Lord GOD, maker of the heavens and the earth by your great power and outstretched arm, nothing is impossible for you. 18 You keep faith with thousands but punish the children for the sins of their fathers. Great and mighty God whose name is the LORD of Hosts, 19 great in purpose and mighty in action, your eyes watch all the ways of mortals, rewarding each according to his conduct and as his deeds deserve. 20 You worked signs and portents in Egypt and have continued them to this day, both in Israel and among all mankind, and have won for yourself renown that lives on to this day. 21 You brought your people Israel out of Egypt amid signs and portents, with a strong hand and an outstretched arm, and with great terror. 22 You gave them this land which you promised with an oath to their forefathers, a land flowing with milk and honey. 23 They came and took possession of it, but they did not obey you or follow your law; they did not perform all you commanded them to do, and so you have brought on them this whole disaster: 24 siege-ramps, and men advancing to take the city; and the city, victim of sword, famine, and pestilence, is given over to the attacking Chaldaeans. What you threatened has come true, as you see. 25 And yet, Lord GOD, you have bidden me buy the field and have the deed witnessed, even though the city is to be given into the power of the Chaldaeans!

26 These are the words of the LORD to Jeremiah: 27 I am the LORD, the God of all mankind; is anything impossible

---

t Or to thousands

32:11 the sealed: so Gk; Heb. adds the command and the statutes.

imprisoned him there, remonstrating: "How dare you prophesy: Thus says the LORD: I am handing over this city to the king of Babylon, who will capture it. 4 Neither shall Zedekiah, king of Judah, escape the hands of the Chaldeans; rather shall he be handed over to the king of Babylon. They shall meet and speak face to face, 5 and Zedekiah shall be taken to Babylon. There he shall remain, until I attend to him, says the LORD; in fighting the Chaldeans, you cannot win!"

6 This message came to me from the LORD, said Jeremiah: 7 Hanamel, son of your uncle Shallum, will come to you with the offer: "Buy for yourself my field in Anathoth, since you, as nearest relative, have the first right of purchase." 8 Then, as the LORD foretold, Hanamel, my uncle's son, came to me to the quarters of the guard and said, "Please buy my field in Anathoth, in the district of Benjamin; as nearest relative, you have the first claim to possess it; make it yours." I knew this was what the LORD meant, 9 so I bought the field in Anathoth from my cousin Hanamel, paying him the money, seventeen silver shekels.

10 When I had written and sealed the deed, called witnesses and weighed out the silver on the scales, 11 I accepted the deed of purchase, both the sealed copy, containing title and conditions, and the open one. 12 This deed of purchase I gave to Baruch, son of Neriah, son of Mahseiah, in the presence of my cousin Hanamel and of the witnesses who had signed the deed, and before all the men of Judah who happened to be in the quarters of the guard.

13 In their presence I gave Baruch this charge: 14 Thus says the LORD of hosts, the God of Israel: Take these deeds, both the sealed and the open deed of purchase, and put them in an earthen jar, so that they can be kept there a long time. 15 For thus says the LORD of hosts, the God of Israel: Houses and fields and vineyards shall again be bought in this land.

16 After giving the deed of purchase to Baruch, son of Neriah, I prayed thus to the LORD: 17 Ah, Lord GOD, you have made heaven and earth by your great might, with your outstretched arm; nothing is impossible to you. 18 You continue your kindness through a thousand generations; and you repay the fathers' guilt, even into the lap of their sons who follow them. O God, great and mighty, whose name is LORD of hosts, 19 great in counsel, mighty in deed, whose eyes are open to all the ways of men, giving to each according to his ways, according to the fruit of his deeds: 20 you have wrought signs and wonders in the land of Egypt and to this day, both in Israel and among all other men, until now you have gained renown. 21 With strong hand and outstretched arm you brought your people Israel out of the land of Egypt amid signs and wonders and great terror. 22 This land you gave them, as you had promised their fathers under oath, a land flowing with milk and honey. 23 They entered and took possession of it, but they did not listen to your voice; by your law they did not live, and what you commanded they failed to do. Hence you let all these evils befall them. 24 See, the siegeworks have arrived at this city to breach it; the city will be handed over to the Chaldeans who are attacking it, amid sword, famine, and pestilence. What you threatened has happened, you see it yourself; 25 and yet you tell me, O Lord GOD: Buy the field with money, call in witnesses. But the city has already been handed over to the Chaldeans!

26 Then this word of the LORD came to Jeremiah: 27 I am the LORD, the God of all mankind! Is anything impossible

had confined him, saying, 'Why do you keep prophesying like this, "Yahweh says this: I am going to hand this city over to the king of Babylon and he will capture it; 4 and Zedekiah king of Judah will not escape the clutches of the Chaldaeans, but will certainly be handed over to the king of Babylon, speak to him personally and see him face to face. 5 He will take Zedekiah away to Babylon and there he will stay (until I attend to him, Yahweh declares. If you fight the Chaldaeans you will not succeed!)" '

6 Jeremiah said, 'The word of Yahweh has been addressed to me as follows, 7 "Look, Hanamel the son of your uncle Shallum will come to you and say: Buy my field at Anathoth, for you have the right of redemption to purchase it." 8 And, as Yahweh had said, my cousin Hanamel came to me, in the Court of the Guard and said, "Buy my field at Anathoth in the territory of Benjamin, for you have the right of inheritance and right of redemption; buy it." I knew then that this was Yahweh's order. 9 Accordingly, I bought the field from my cousin Hanamel of Anathoth and weighed him out the money: seventeen silver shekels. 10 I drew up the deeds and sealed it, called in witnesses and weighed out the money on the scales. 11 I then took both the sealed deed of purchase (with its stipulations and clauses) and its open copy 12 and handed over the deed of purchase to Baruch son of Neriah, son of Mahseiah, in the presence of my cousin Hanamel, of the witnesses who had signed the deed of purchase, and of all the Judaeans who then happened to be in the Court of the Guard. 13 In their presence I gave Baruch this order, 14 "Yahweh Sabaoth, God of Israel, says this: Take these deeds, the sealed deed of purchase and its open copy, and put them in an earthenware pot, so that they may be preserved for a long time. 15 For Yahweh Sabaoth, God of Israel, says this: Houses, fields and vineyards will again be bought in this country."

16 'After I had entrusted the deed of purchase to Baruch son of Neriah, I prayed to Yahweh as follows, 17 "Ah, Lord Yahweh, you made the heavens and the earth by your great power and outstretched arm. To you nothing is impossible. 18 You show faithful love to thousands but repay the fathers' guilt in full to their children after them. Great and mighty God, whose name is Yahweh Sabaoth, 19 great in purpose, mighty in deed, whose eyes are open on all human ways, rewarding every individual as that person's ways and actions deserve! 20 You performed signs and wonders in Egypt, as you still do in Israel and among humanity today. You have won the name for yourself which is yours today. 21 You brought your people Israel out of Egypt with signs and wonders, with mighty hand and outstretched arm and fearsome terror. 22 Then you gave them this country which you had promised on oath to their ancestors, a country flowing with milk and honey. 23 They then entered it, taking possession of it, but they would not listen to your voice nor follow your Law: they would do nothing you ordered them to do; and so you made this total disaster befall them. 24 Look! The earthworks are already in place to take the city and, by means of sword, famine and plague, the city is now within the clutches of the Chaldaeans attacking it. What you said has now come true, as you see. 25 Yet you yourself, Lord Yahweh, told me: Buy the field, pay for it, have it witnessed although the city is already in the Chaldaeans' clutches." '

26 The word of Yahweh was addressed to me as follows, 27 'Look, I am Yahweh, God of all humanity. Is anything impossible to me?

NEW REVISED STANDARD VERSION

28 Therefore, thus says the LORD: I am going to give this city into the hands of the Chaldeans and into the hand of King Nebuchadrezzar of Babylon, and he shall take it. 29 The Chaldeans who are fighting against this city shall come, set it on fire, and burn it, with the houses on whose roofs offerings have been made to Baal and libations have been poured out to other gods, to provoke me to anger. 30 For the people of Israel and the people of Judah have done nothing but evil in my sight from their youth; the people of Israel have done nothing but evil to provoke me to anger by the work of their hands, says the LORD. 31 This city has aroused my anger and wrath, from the day it was built until this day, so that I will remove it from my sight 32 because of all the evil of the people of Israel and the people of Judah that they did to provoke me to anger—they, their kings and their officials, their priests and their prophets, the citizens of Judah and the inhabitants of Jerusalem. 33 They have turned their backs to me, not their faces; though I have taught them persistently, they would not listen and accept correction. 34 They set up their abominations in the house that bears my name, and defiled it. 35 They built the high places of Baal in the valley of the son of Hinnom, to offer up their sons and daughters to Molech, though I did not command them, nor did it enter my mind that they should do this abomination, causing Judah to sin.

36 Now therefore thus says the LORD, the God of Israel, concerning this city of which you say, "It is being given into the hand of the king of Babylon by the sword, by famine, and by pestilence": 37 See, I am going to gather them from all the lands to which I drove them in my anger and my wrath and in great indignation; I will bring them back to this place, and I will settle them in safety. 38 They shall be my people, and I will be their God. 39 I will give them one heart and one way, that they may fear me for all time, for their own good and the good of their children after them. 40 I will make an everlasting covenant with them, never to draw back from doing good to them; and I will put the fear of me in their hearts, so that they may not turn from me. 41 I will rejoice in doing good to them, and I will plant them in this land in faithfulness, with all my heart and all my soul.

42 For thus says the LORD: Just as I have brought all this great disaster upon this people, so I will bring upon them all the good fortune that I now promise them. 43 Fields shall be bought in this land of which you are saying, It is a desolation, without human beings or animals; it has been given into the hands of the Chaldeans. 44 Fields shall be bought for money, and deeds shall be signed and sealed and witnessed, in the land of Benjamin, in the places around Jerusalem, and in the cities of Judah, of the hill country, of the Shephelah, and of the Negeb; for I will restore their fortunes, says the LORD.

33 The word of the LORD came to Jeremiah a second time, while he was still confined in the court of the guard: 2 Thus says the LORD who made the earth,*u* the LORD who formed it to establish it—the LORD is his name: 3 Call to me and I will answer you, and will tell you great and hidden things that you have not known. 4 For thus says the LORD, the God of Israel, concerning the houses of this city and the houses of the kings of Judah that were torn down to make a defense against the siege ramps and before the sword:*v* 5 The Chaldeans are coming in to fight*w* and to fill them with the dead bodies of those whom I shall strike down in my anger and my wrath, for I have hidden my face from this city because of all their wickedness. 6 I am going to bring it recovery and healing; I will heal them and reveal to them abundance*v* of prosperity and security. 7 I will

REVISED ENGLISH BIBLE

for me? 28 Therefore these are the words of the LORD: I am about to give this city into the hands of the Chaldeans and of King Nebuchadrezzar of Babylon, and he will take it. 29 The Chaldaeans assailing this city will enter and set it on fire; they will burn it down, together with the houses on whose roofs sacrifices have been burnt to Baal and drink-offerings poured out to other gods, by which I was provoked to anger.

30 From their earliest days Israel and Judah have been doing what is wrong in my eyes, provoking me to anger by their idolatry, says the LORD. 31 For this city has so roused my anger and my fury, from the time it was built down to this day, that I mean to rid myself of it. 32 Israel and Judah, their kings, officers, priests, prophets, and the people of Judah and the citizens of Jerusalem, have provoked me to anger by their wrongdoing. 33 They have turned their backs on me and averted their faces; though I taught them again and again, they would not hear or learn their lesson. 34 They set up their loathsome idols in the house which bears my name and so defiled it. 35 They built shrines to Baal in the valley of Ben-hinnom, at which to offer up their sons and daughters to Molech. That was no command of mine to them, nor did it ever enter my mind that they should do this abominable thing, so causing Judah to sin.

36 Now, therefore, these are the words of the LORD the God of Israel to this city of which you say, 'It is being given over to the king of Babylon, by sword, famine, and pestilence': 37 I shall gather them from all the lands to which I banished them in my furious anger and great wrath; I shall bring them back to this place and let them dwell there undisturbed. 38 They will be my people and I shall be their God. 39 I shall give them singleness of heart and one way of life so that they will fear me at all times, for their own good and the good of their children after them. 40 I shall enter into an everlasting covenant with them, to follow them unfailingly with my bounty; I shall put fear of me into their hearts, and so they will not turn away from me. 41 It will be a joy to me to do them good, and faithfully with all my heart and soul I shall plant them in this land.

42 For these are the words of the LORD: As I brought upon this people all this great disaster, so shall I bring them all the prosperity which I now promise them. 43 Fields will again be bought and sold in this land of which you now say, 'It is a desolation abandoned by man and beast; it is given over to the Chaldeans.' 44 Fields will be bought and sold, deeds signed, sealed, and witnessed, in Benjamin, in the neighbourhood of Jerusalem, in the towns of Judah, of the hill-country, of the Shephelah, and of the Negeb; for I shall restore their fortunes. This is the word of the LORD.

33 The word of the LORD came to Jeremiah a second time while he was still imprisoned in the court of the guardhouse: 2 These are the words of the LORD who made the earth, who formed and established it; the LORD is his name: 3 If you call to me I shall answer, and tell you great and mysterious things of which you are still unaware. 4 These are the words of the LORD the God of Israel about the houses in this city and the royal palaces of Judah which are razed to the ground, about siege-ramp and sword, 5 and the Chaldaean attackers who leave the houses full of corpses: I struck them down in anger and rage, and hid my face from this city because of all their wicked ways. 6 Now I shall bring healing and care for her; I shall cure Judah and Israel, and let them see lasting peace and security. 7 I shall restore their fortunes and rebuild them as once

---

*u*Gk: Heb *it*   *v*Meaning of Heb uncertain   *w*Cn: Heb *They are coming in to fight against the Chaldeans*

33:2 **the earth:** *so Gk; Heb.* it.

to me? 28 This now is what the LORD says: I will hand over this city to the Chaldeans, for Nebuchadnezzar, king of Babylon, to take. 29 The Chaldeans who are attacking it shall enter this city and set fire to it, burning it and its houses, on the roofs of which incense was burned to Baal and libations were poured out to strange gods as a provocation to me. 30 The Israelites and the Judeans from their youth have done only what is evil in my eyes; the Israelites did nothing but provoke me with the works of their hands, says the LORD. 31 From the day it was built to this day, this city has excited my anger and wrath, 32 so that I must put it out of my sight for all the wickedness the Israelites and Judeans, with their kings and their princes, their priests and their prophets, the men of Judah and the citizens of Jerusalem, have done to provoke me. 33 They turned their backs to me, not their faces; though I kept teaching them, they would not listen to my correction. 34 They defiled the house named after me by the horrid idols they set up in it. 35 They built high places to Baal in the Valley of Ben-hinnom, and immolated their sons and daughters to Molech, bringing sin upon Judah; this I never commanded them, nor did it even enter my mind that they should practice such abominations.

36 Now, therefore, thus says the LORD, the God of Israel, concerning this city, which as you say is handed over to the king of Babylon amid sword, famine, and pestilence: 37 Behold, I will gather them together from all the lands to which in anger, wrath, and great rage I banish them; I will bring them back to this place and settle them here in safety. 38 They shall be my people, and I will be their God. 39 One heart and one way I will give them, that they may fear me always, to their own good and that of their children after them. 40 I will make with them an eternal covenant, never to cease doing good to them; into their hearts I will put the fear of me, that they may never depart from me. 41 I will take delight in doing good to them: I will replant them firmly in this land, with all my heart and soul.

42 For thus says the LORD: Just as I brought upon this people all this great evil, so I will bring upon them all the good I promise them. 43 Fields shall again be bought in this land, which you call a desert, without man or beast, handed over to the Chaldeans. 44 Fields shall be bought with money, deeds written and sealed, and witnesses shall be used in the land of Benjamin, in the suburbs of Jerusalem, in the cities of Judah and of the hill country, in the cities of the foothills and of the Negeb, when I change their lot, says the LORD.

33

The word of the LORD came to Jeremiah a second time while he was still imprisoned in the quarters of the guard: 2 Thus says the LORD who made the earth and gave it form and firmness, whose name is LORD: 3 Call to me, and I will answer you; I will tell to you things great beyond reach of your knowledge. 4 Thus says the LORD, the God of Israel, concerning the houses of this city and the palaces of Judah's kings, which are being destroyed in the face of siegeworks and the sword: 5 men come to battle the Chaldeans, and these houses will be filled with the corpses of those whom I slay in my anger and wrath, when I hide my face from this city for all their wickedness.

6 Behold, I will treat and assuage the city's wounds; I will heal them, and reveal to them an abundance of lasting peace. 7 I will change the lot of Judah and the lot of Israel,

28 'So, Yahweh says this, "I shall hand this city over to the Chaldaeans and to Nebuchadnezzar king of Babylon, and he will capture it; 29 the Chaldaeans attacking this city will enter it, fire it and burn it to the ground, with the houses on whose roofs incense has been offered to Baal and libations poured to other gods, to provoke my anger. 30 For the people of Israel and Judah alike have done nothing but what displeases me since they were young. (The people of Israel in fact have done nothing but provoke my anger by their actions, Yahweh declares.) 31 Yes, from the day when this city was built until today, it has been such cause of anger and wrath to me that I mean to remove it from my sight, 32 on account of all the wickedness the people of Israel and the people of Judah have done to provoke my anger; they, their kings, their chief men, their priests, their prophets, people of Judah and the inhabitants of Jerusalem. 33 They turned to me their backs, never their faces; and though I taught them so urgently, so untiringly, they would not listen and accept correction. 34 Instead, they set up their Horrors in the Temple that bears my name to defile it, 35 and built the high places of Baal in the Valley of Ben-Hinnom, to burn their sons and daughters alive in honour of Molech:^u a thing I have never ordered, that had never entered my thoughts — that they would cause Judah to sin by anything so loathsome!

36 "So now, this is what Yahweh, God of Israel, says about this city of which you now say: By means of sword, famine and plague, it is already within the king of Babylon's clutches: 37 Look, I shall gather them in from all the countries where I have driven them in my anger, my fury and great wrath. I shall bring them back to this place and make them live in safety. 38 Then they will be my people, and I shall be their God. 39 I shall give them singleness of heart and singleness of conduct so that they will always fear me, for their own good and that of their children after them. 40 I shall make an everlasting covenant with them, never to cease in my efforts for their welfare, and I shall put respect for me in their hearts, so that they will never turn away from me again. 41 My joy will lie in them and in doing them good, and I shall plant them firmly in this country, with all my heart and soul. 42 For Yahweh says this: Just as I have brought this complete and total disaster on this people, so I shall bring them all the good things I have promised them. 43 Fields will again be bought in this country of which you now say: It is a wasteland without human or animal, already in the clutches of the Chaldaeans. 44 People will buy fields, pay money, draw up deeds, seal them and have them witnessed in the territory of Benjamin, in the districts round Jerusalem, in the towns of Judah, of the highlands, of the lowlands and of the Negeb. For I shall bring back their captives, Yahweh declares."'

33

Jeremiah was still confined to the Court of the Guard when the word of Yahweh came to him a second time, as follows, 2 'Yahweh who made the earth, who formed it and set it firm — Yahweh is his name — says this, 3 "Call to me and I will answer you; I will tell you great secrets of which you know nothing. 4 For this is what Yahweh, God of Israel, says about the houses of this city and the palaces of the kings of Judah which are about to be destroyed by means of the earthworks and the sword; 5 about those now fighting the Chaldaeans, only to fill the city with corpses, those whom I have slaughtered in my furious anger, those whose wickedness has made me hide my face from this city: 6 Look, I shall bring them remedy and cure; I shall cure them and reveal a new order of peace and loyalty to them. 7 I shall bring back the captives of

u 32 = 7:30–31.

restore the fortunes of Judah and the fortunes of Israel, and rebuild them as they were at first. 8 I will cleanse them from all the guilt of their sin against me, and I will forgive all the guilt of their sin and rebellion against me. 9 And this city*x* shall be to me a name of joy, a praise and a glory before all the nations of the earth who shall hear of all the good that I do for them; they shall fear and tremble because of all the good and all the prosperity I provide for it.

10 Thus says the LORD: In this place of which you say, "It is a waste without human beings or animals," in the towns of Judah and the streets of Jerusalem that are desolate, without inhabitants, human or animal, there shall once more be heard 11 the voice of mirth and the voice of gladness, the voice of the bridegroom and the voice of the bride, the voices of those who sing, as they bring thank offerings to the house of the LORD:

"Give thanks to the LORD of hosts,
    for the LORD is good,
    for his steadfast love endures forever!"

For I will restore the fortunes of the land as at first, says the LORD.

12 Thus says the LORD of hosts: In this place that is waste, without human beings or animals, and in all its towns there shall again be pasture for shepherds resting their flocks. 13 In the towns of the hill country, of the Shephelah, and of the Negeb, in the land of Benjamin, the places around Jerusalem, and in the towns of Judah, flocks shall again pass under the hands of the one who counts them, says the LORD.

14 The days are surely coming, says the LORD, when I will fulfill the promise I made to the house of Israel and the house of Judah. 15 In those days and at that time I will cause a righteous Branch to spring up for David; and he shall execute justice and righteousness in the land. 16 In those days Judah will be saved and Jerusalem will live in safety. And this is the name by which it will be called: "The LORD is our righteousness."

17 For thus says the LORD: David shall never lack a man to sit on the throne of the house of Israel, 18 and the levitical priests shall never lack a man in my presence to offer burnt offerings, to make grain offerings, and to make sacrifices for all time.

19 The word of the LORD came to Jeremiah: 20 Thus says the LORD: If any of you could break my covenant with the day and my covenant with the night, so that day and night would not come at their appointed time, 21 only then could my covenant with my servant David be broken, so that he would not have a son to reign on his throne, and my covenant with my ministers the Levites. 22 Just as the host of heaven cannot be numbered and the sands of the sea cannot be measured, so I will increase the offspring of my servant David, and the Levites who minister to me.

23 The word of the LORD came to Jeremiah: 24 Have you not observed how these people say, "The two families that the LORD chose have been rejected by him," and how they hold my people in such contempt that they no longer regard them as a nation? 25 Thus says the LORD: Only if I had not established my covenant with day and night and the ordinances of heaven and earth, 26 would I reject the offspring of Jacob and of my servant David and not choose any of his descendants as rulers over the offspring of Abraham, Isaac, and Jacob. For I will restore their fortunes, and will have mercy upon them.

they were. 8 I shall cleanse them of all the wickedness and sin that they have committed, and forgive all the evil deeds they have done in rebellion against me. 9 This city will win me renown and praise and glory before all the nations of the world, as they hear of all the blessings I bestow on her; and they will be filled with awe and deeply moved because of all the blessings and the prosperity which I bring on her.

10 These are the words of the LORD: You say of this place, 'It lies in ruins, without people or animals throughout the towns of Judah and the streets of Jerusalem. It is all a waste, inhabited by neither man nor beast.' 11 Yet in this place will be heard once more the sounds of joy and gladness, the voices of bridegroom and bride; here too will be heard voices shouting, 'Praise the LORD of Hosts, for the LORD is good; his love endures for ever,' as they offer praise and thanksgiving in the house of the LORD. For I shall restore the fortunes of the land as once they were. This is the word of the LORD.

12 These are the words of the LORD of Hosts: In this place and in all its towns, now ruined and devoid of both people and animals, there will once more be sheepfolds where shepherds may keep their flocks. 13 In the towns of the hill-country, of the Shephelah, of the Negeb, in Benjamin, in the neighbourhood of Jerusalem and the towns of Judah, flocks will once more pass under the shepherd's hand as he counts them. This is the word of the LORD.

14 The days are coming, says the LORD, when I shall bestow on Israel and Judah all the blessings I have promised them. 15 In those days, at that time, I shall make a righteous Branch spring from David's line; he will maintain law and justice in the land. 16 In those days Judah will be kept safe and Jerusalem will live undisturbed. This will be the name given to him: The LORD our Righteousness.

17 For these are the words of the LORD: David will never lack a successor on the throne of Israel, 18 nor will there ever be lacking a levitical priest to present whole-offerings, to burn grain-offerings, and to make other offerings every day.

19 This word came from the LORD to Jeremiah: 20 These are the words of the LORD: It would be as unthinkable to annul the covenant that I made for the day and the night, so that they should fall out of their proper order, 21 as to annul my covenant with my servant David, so that he would have none of his line to sit on his throne; likewise it would be unthinkable to annul my covenant with the levitical priests who minister to me. 22 Like the innumerable host of heaven or the countless sands of the sea, I shall increase the descendants of my servant David and the Levites who minister to me.

23 The word of the LORD came to Jeremiah: 24 Have you not observed how this people have said, 'It is the two families whom he chose that the LORD has rejected'? So others will despise my people and no longer regard them as a nation. 25 These are the words of the LORD: If there were no covenant for day and night, and if I had not established a fixed order in heaven and earth, 26 then I could spurn the descendants of Jacob and of my servant David, and not take any of David's line to be rulers over the descendants of Abraham, Isaac, and Jacob. But in my compassion I shall restore their fortunes.

---

x Heb *And it*

33:9 **renown**: *prob. rdg; Heb. adds* of joy.

and rebuild them as of old. ⁸I will cleanse them of all the guilt they incurred by sinning against me; all their offenses by which they sinned and rebelled against me, I will forgive. ⁹Then Jerusalem shall be my joy, my praise, my glory, before all the nations of the earth, as they hear of all the good I will do among them. They shall be in fear and trembling over all the peaceful benefits I will give her.

¹⁰Thus says the LORD: In this place of which you say, "How desolate it is, without man, without beast!" and in the cities of Judah, in the streets of Jerusalem that are now deserted, without man, without citizen, without beast, there shall yet be heard ¹¹the cry of joy, the cry of gladness, the voice of the bridegroom, the voice of the bride, the sound of those who bring thank offerings to the house of the LORD, singing, "Give thanks to the LORD of hosts, for the LORD is good; his mercy endures forever." For I will restore this country as of old, says the LORD.

¹²Thus says the LORD of hosts: In this place, now desolate, without man or beast, and in all its cities there shall again be sheepfolds for the shepherds to couch their flocks. ¹³In the cities of the hill country, of the foothills, and of the Negeb, in the land of Benjamin and the suburbs of Jerusalem, and in the cities of Judah, flocks will again pass under the hands of the one who counts them, says the LORD.

¹⁴The days are coming, says the LORD, when I will fulfill the promise I made to the house of Israel and Judah. ¹⁵In those days, in that time, I will raise up for David a just shoot; he shall do what is right and just in the land. ¹⁶In those days Judah shall be safe and Jerusalem shall dwell secure; this is what they shall call her: "The LORD our justice." ¹⁷For thus says the LORD: Never shall David lack a successor on the throne of the house of Israel, ¹⁸nor shall priests of Levi ever be lacking, to offer holocausts before me, to burn cereal offerings, and to sacrifice victims.

This word of the LORD also came to Jeremiah: ¹⁹Thus says the LORD: ²⁰If you can break my covenant with day, and my covenant with night, so that day and night no longer alternate in sequence, ²¹then can my covenant with my servant David also be broken, so that he will not have a son to be king upon his throne, and my covenant with the priests of Levi who minister to me. ²²Like the host of heaven which cannot be numbered, and the sands of the sea which cannot be counted, I will multiply the descendants of my servant David and the Levites who minister to me.

²³This word of the LORD came to Jeremiah: ²⁴Have you not noticed what these people are saying: "The LORD has rejected the two tribes which he had chosen"? They spurn my people as if it were no longer a nation in their eyes. ²⁵Thus says the LORD: When I have no covenant with day and night, and have given no laws to heaven and earth, ²⁶then too will I reject the descendants of Jacob and of my servant David, so as not to take from his descendants rulers for the race of Abraham, Isaac, and Jacob. For I will change their lot and show them mercy.

Judah and the captives of Israel and shall rebuild them as before. ⁸I shall cleanse them of all their guilt, by which they have offended me, I shall forgive all their guilty actions, by which they have offended me and rebelled against me. ⁹And, for me, Jerusalem will become a name of joy and praise and pride for all the nations on earth to see; when they hear of all the prosperity that I shall give, they will be seized with fear and trembling at all the prosperity and the peace that I provide for it."

¹⁰'Yahweh says this, "In this place of which you now say: It is a ruin, without human or animal, in the towns of Judah and desolate streets of Jerusalem where there is neither human nor animal, once more will be heard ¹¹shouts of rejoicing and mirth, the voices of bridegroom and bride, and the singing of those who bring thanksgiving sacrifices to the Temple of Yahweh: Give thanks to Yahweh Sabaoth, for Yahweh is good, for his faithful love is everlasting. For I shall bring back the country's captives, as before, Yahweh says."

¹²'Yahweh Sabaoth says this, "In this ruinous place, without human or animal, in all its towns, once again there will be pastures for the shepherds to rest their flocks. ¹³In the towns of the highlands, of the lowlands and the Negeb, in the territory of Benjamin, in the districts round Jerusalem and in the towns of Judah, once again the flocks shall pass under the hand of someone who counts them, Yahweh says.

¹⁴"Look, the days are coming, Yahweh declares, when I shall fulfil the promise of happiness I made to the House of Israel and the House of Judah:

¹⁵In those days and at that time,
I shall make an upright Branch grow for David,
who will do what is just and upright in the
country.
¹⁶In those days Judah will triumph
and Israel live in safety.
And this is the name the city will be called:
Yahweh-is-our-Saving-Justice."ᵛ

¹⁷'For Yahweh says this, "David will never lack a male descendant to occupy the throne of the House of Israel, ¹⁸nor will the levitical priests ever lack male descendants to stand before me and offer the burnt offering, to burn the cereal offering and offer sacrifice every day."'

¹⁹The word of Yahweh came to Jeremiah as follows, ²⁰'Yahweh says this, "If you could break my covenant with the day and my covenant with the night so that day and night do not come at their due time, ²¹then my covenant with David my servant might also be broken and he would have no son to reign on his throne, and so also might my covenant with the levitical priests, who are my ministers. ²²As surely as the array of heaven cannot be counted, nor the sand of the sea be measured, so surely shall I increase the heirs of David my servant and the Levites who minister to me."'

²³The word of Yahweh came to Jeremiah as follows, ²⁴'Have you not noticed what these people say, "The two families which Yahweh chose he has now rejected"? So they despise my people, whom they no longer think of as a nation. ²⁵Yahweh says this, "If I have not created day and night and fixed the laws governing heaven and earth, ²⁶why, then I shall reject the descendants of Jacob and of David my servant and cease to choose rulers from his descendants for the heirs of Abraham, Isaac and Jacob! For I shall bring back their captives and take pity on them."'

34 The word that came to Jeremiah from the LORD, when King Nebuchadrezzar of Babylon and all his army and all the kingdoms of the earth and all the peoples under his dominion were fighting against Jerusalem and all its cities: 2 "Thus says the LORD, the God of Israel: Go and speak to King Zedekiah of Judah and say to him: Thus says the LORD: I am going to give this city into the hand of the king of Babylon, and he shall burn it with fire. 3 And you yourself shall not escape from his hand, but shall surely be captured and handed over to him; you shall see the king of Babylon eye to eye and speak with him face to face; and you shall go to Babylon. 4 Yet hear the word of the LORD, O King Zedekiah of Judah! Thus says the LORD concerning you: You shall not die by the sword; 5 you shall die in peace. And as spices were burned*y* for your ancestors, the earlier kings who preceded you, so they shall burn spices*z* for you and lament for you, saying, "Alas, lord!" For I have spoken the word, says the LORD.

6 Then the prophet Jeremiah spoke all these words to Zedekiah king of Judah, in Jerusalem, 7 when the army of the king of Babylon was fighting against Jerusalem and against all the cities of Judah that were left, Lachish and Azekah; for these were the only fortified cities of Judah that remained.

8 The word that came to Jeremiah from the LORD, after King Zedekiah had made a covenant with all the people in Jerusalem to make a proclamation of liberty to them, 9 that all should set free their Hebrew slaves, male and female, so that no one should hold another Judean in slavery. 10 And they obeyed, all the officials and all the people who had entered into the covenant that all would set free their slaves, male or female, so that they would not be enslaved again; they obeyed and set them free. 11 But afterward they turned around and took back the male and female slaves they had set free, and brought them again into subjection as slaves. 12 The word of the LORD came to Jeremiah from the LORD: 13 Thus says the LORD, the God of Israel: I myself made a covenant with your ancestors when I brought them out of the land of Egypt, out of the house of slavery, saying, 14 "Every seventh year each of you must set free any Hebrews who have been sold to you and have served you six years; you must set them free from your service." But your ancestors did not listen to me or incline their ears to me. 15 You yourselves recently repented and did what was right in my sight by proclaiming liberty to one another, and you made a covenant before me in the house that is called by my name; 16 but then you turned around and profaned my name when each of you took back your male and female slaves, whom you had set free according to their desire, and you brought them again into subjection to be your slaves. 17 Therefore, thus says the LORD: You have not obeyed me by granting a release to your neighbors and friends; I am going to grant a release to you, says the LORD — a release to the sword, to pestilence, and to famine. I will make you a horror to all the kingdoms of the earth. 18 And those who transgressed my covenant and did not keep the terms of the covenant that they made before me, I will make like*a* the calf when they cut it in two and passed between its parts: 19 the officials of Judah, the officials of Jerusalem, the eunuchs, the priests, and all the people of the land who passed between the parts of the calf 20 shall be handed over to their enemies and to those who seek their lives. Their corpses shall become food for the birds of the air and the wild animals of the earth. 21 And as for King Zedekiah of Judah and his officials, I will hand them over to their enemies and to those who seek their lives, to the army of the king of Babylon, which has withdrawn from you. 22 I am going to

34 THE word which came to Jeremiah from the LORD when King Nebuchadrezzar of Babylon and his whole army, along with all his vassal kingdoms and nations, were attacking Jerusalem and all her towns. 2 These are the words of the LORD the God of Israel: Go and say to King Zedekiah of Judah: These are the words of the LORD: I shall hand over this city to the king of Babylon and he will burn it to the ground. 3 You yourself will not escape; your capture is certain, and you will be delivered into his hands. You will see him with your own eyes, and he will speak to you face to face, and you will go to Babylon. 4 But listen to the LORD's word to you, King Zedekiah of Judah. This is his word: You will not die by the sword; 5 you will die a peaceful death, and they will kindle funeral fires in your honour like the fires kindled in former times for the kings your ancestors who preceded you. 'Alas, my lord!' they will say as they beat their breasts in mourning for you. It is a promise I have made. This is the word of the LORD.

6 The prophet Jeremiah repeated all this to King Zedekiah of Judah in Jerusalem 7 while the army of the king of Babylon was attacking Jerusalem and the remaining towns in Judah, namely Lachish and Azekah, the only fortified towns left there.

8 The word that came to Jeremiah from the LORD after King Zedekiah had entered into an agreement with all the people in Jerusalem to proclaim freedom for their slaves: 9 everyone who had Hebrew slaves, male or female, was to set them free; no one was to keep a fellow-Jew in servitude. 10 All the officers and people, having entered this agreement to set free their slaves, both male and female, and not to keep them in servitude any longer, fulfilled its terms and let them go. 11 Afterwards, however, they changed their minds and forced back again into slavery the men and women whom they had freed.

12 Then this word came from the LORD to Jeremiah: 13 These are the words of the LORD the God of Israel: I made a covenant with your forefathers when I brought them out of Egypt, out of the land of slavery. These were its terms: 14 'Within seven years each of you must liberate any Hebrew who has sold himself to you as a slave and has served you for six years.' Your forefathers did not listen to me or obey me, 15 but recently you proclaimed freedom for the slaves and made an agreement in my presence, in the house that bears my name, and so did what is right in my eyes. 16 Now, however, you have renounced this agreement and profaned my name by taking back the slaves you had set free and forcing them all, both male and female, to become your slaves again.

17 Therefore these are the words of the LORD: After you had proclaimed freedom, a deliverance for your kinsmen and your neighbours, you did not obey me; so I shall proclaim a deliverance for you, says the LORD, a deliverance to sword, pestilence, and famine, and I shall make you abhorrent to all the kingdoms of the earth. 18 You have violated my covenant and have not fulfilled the terms to which you yourselves had agreed before me; so I shall treat you like the calf which was cut in two for all to pass between the pieces, 19 the officers of Judah and Jerusalem, the eunuchs and priests, and all the people of the land. 20 I shall give them up to their enemies who seek their lives; their dead bodies will be food for birds of prey and wild beasts. 21 I shall deliver King Zedekiah of Judah and his officers to their enemies who seek their lives and to the army of the king of Babylon, which is now raising the siege. 22 I shall give the

y Heb *as there was burning like*   *z* Heb *shall burn*   *a* Cn: Heb lacks *like*

34 This word came to Jeremiah from the Lord while Nebuchadnezzar, king of Babylon, and his armies and the earth's kingdoms subject to him, as well as the other peoples, were all attacking Jerusalem and all her cities: 2 Thus says the Lord, the God of Israel: Go to Zedekiah, king of Judah, and tell him: Thus says the Lord: I am handing this city over to the king of Babylon; he will destroy it with fire. 3 Neither shall you escape his hand; rather you will be captured and fall into his hands. You shall see the king of Babylon and speak to him face to face. Then you shall be taken to Babylon.

4 But if you obey the word of the Lord, Zedekiah, king of Judah, then, says the Lord to you, you shall not die by the sword. 5 You shall die in peace, and they will lament you as their lord, and burn spices for your burial as they did for your fathers, the kings who preceded you from the first; it is I who make this promise, says the Lord.

6 The prophet Jeremiah told all these things to Zedekiah, king of Judah, in Jerusalem, 7 while the armies of the king of Babylon were attacking Jerusalem and the remaining cities of Judah, Lachish, and Azekah, since these alone were left of the fortified cities of Judah.

8 This is the word that came to Jeremiah from the Lord after King Zedekiah had made an agreement with all the people in Jerusalem to issue an edict of emancipation. 9 Everyone was to free his Hebrew slaves, male and female, so that no one should hold a man of Judah, his brother, in slavery. 10 All the princes and the others who entered the agreement consented to set free their male and female servants, so that they should be slaves no longer. But though they agreed and freed them, 11 afterward they took back their male and female slaves whom they had set free and again forced them into service.

12 Then this word of the Lord came to Jeremiah: 13 Thus says the Lord, the God of Israel: The day I brought your fathers out of the land of Egypt, out of the place where they were slaves, I made this covenant with them: 14 Every seventh year each of you shall set free his Hebrew brother who has sold himself to you; six years he shall serve you, but then you shall let him go free. Your fathers, however, did not heed me or obey me. 15 Today you indeed repented and did what is right in my eyes by proclaiming the emancipation of your brethren and making an agreement before me in the house that is named after me. 16 But then you changed your mind and profaned my name by taking back your male and female slaves to whom you had given their freedom; you forced them once more into slavery. 17 Therefore, thus says the Lord: You did not obey me by proclaiming your neighbors and kinsmen free. I now proclaim you free, says the Lord, for the sword, famine, and pestilence. I will make you an object of horror to all the kingdoms of the earth. 18 The men who violated my covenant and did not observe the terms of the agreement which they made before me, I will make like the calf which they cut in two, between whose two parts they passed. 19 The princes of Judah and of Jerusalem, the courtiers, the priests, and the common people, who passed between the parts of the calf, 20 I will hand over, all of them, to their enemies, to those who seek their lives; their corpses shall be food for the birds of the air and the beasts of the field.

21 Zedekiah, too, king of Judah, and his princes, I will hand over to their enemies, to those who seek their lives, to the soldiers of the king of Babylon who have at present withdrawn from you. 22 I will give the command, says the

34 The word came to Jeremiah from Yahweh when Nebuchadnezzar king of Babylon and his whole army, with all the kingdoms of the earth under his dominion and all the peoples, were waging war on Jerusalem and all its towns, 2 'Yahweh, God of Israel, says this, "Go and speak to Zedekiah king of Judah and tell him, Yahweh says this: I am going to hand this city over to the power of the king of Babylon, and he will burn it down. 3 And you yourself will not escape his clutches but will certainly be captured and handed over to him. You will see the king of Babylon face to face and speak to him personally. Then you will go to Babylon. 4 Even so, listen to the word of Yahweh, Zedekiah king of Judah! This is what Yahweh says about you: You will not die by the sword; 5 you will die in peace. And as spices were burnt for your ancestors, the kings who in times past preceded you, so spices will be burnt for you and a dirge sung for you: Alas for his highness! I have spoken, Yahweh declares." '

6 The prophet Jeremiah repeated all these words to Zedekiah king of Judah in Jerusalem, 7 while the army of the king of Babylon was attacking Jerusalem and all such towns of Judah as still held out, namely Lachish and Azekah, these being the only fortified towns of Judah remaining.

8 The word came to Jeremiah from Yahweh after King Zedekiah had made a covenant with all the people in Jerusalem to issue a proclamation freeing their slaves: 9 each man was to free his Hebrew slaves, men and women, no one was any longer to keep a brother Judaean in slavery. 10 All the chief men and all the people who had entered into the covenant had agreed that everyone should free his slaves, men or women, and no longer keep them as slaves: they had agreed on this and set them free. 11 Afterwards, however, they changed their minds, recovered the slaves, men and women, whom they had set free, and reduced them to slavery again. 12 The word of Yahweh came then to Jeremiah as follows, 13 'Yahweh, God of Israel, says this, "I made a covenant with your ancestors when I brought them out of Egypt, out of the house of slavery; it said: 14 At the end of seven years each one of you is to free his brother Hebrew who has sold himself to you: he may be your slave for six years, then you must send him away free. But your ancestors did not listen to me and would not pay attention. 15 Now, today you repented and did what pleases me by proclaiming freedom for your neighbour; you made a covenant before me in the Temple that bears my name. 16 And then you changed your minds and, profaning my name, each of you has recovered his slaves, men and women, whom you had sent away free to live their own lives, and has forced them to become your slaves again."

17 'So Yahweh says this: "You have disobeyed me, by failing to grant freedom to brother and neighbour. Very well, I in my turn, Yahweh declares, shall leave sword, famine and plague free to deal with you and I shall make you an object of horror to all the kingdoms of the earth. 18 As for the people who have broken my covenant, who have not observed the terms of the covenant which they made before me, I shall treat them like the calf that people cut in two to pass between its pieces. 19 The chief men of Judah and Jerusalem, the eunuchs, the priests, and all the country people who have passed between the pieces of the calf, 20 I shall hand over to their enemies and those determined to kill them, and their corpses will be food for the birds of the sky and the animals of earth. 21 As for Zedekiah king of Judah and his chief men, I shall hand them over to their enemies, to those determined to kill them, and to the army of the king of Babylon which has just withdrawn. 22 Listen,

command, says the LORD, and will bring them back to this city; and they will fight against it, and take it, and burn it with fire. The towns of Judah I will make a desolation without inhabitant.

35 The word that came to Jeremiah from the LORD in the days of King Jehoiakim son of Josiah of Judah: 2 Go to the house of the Rechabites, and speak with them, and bring them to the house of the LORD, into one of the chambers; then offer them wine to drink. 3 So I took Jaazaniah son of Jeremiah son of Habazziniah, and his brothers, and all his sons, and the whole house of the Rechabites. 4 I brought them to the house of the LORD into the chamber of the sons of Hanan son of Igdaliah, the man of God, which was near the chamber of the officials, above the chamber of Maaseiah son of Shallum, keeper of the threshold. 5 Then I set before the Rechabites pitchers full of wine, and cups; and I said to them, "Have some wine." 6 But they answered, "We will drink no wine, for our ancestor Jonadab son of Rechab commanded us, 'You shall never drink wine, neither you nor your children; 7 nor shall you ever build a house, or sow seed; nor shall you plant a vineyard, or even own one; but you shall live in tents all your days, that you may live many days in the land where you reside.' 8 We have obeyed the charge of our ancestor Jonadab son of Rechab in all that he commanded us, to drink no wine all our days, ourselves, our wives, our sons, or our daughters; 9 and not to build houses to live in. We have no vineyard or field or seed; 10 but we have lived in tents, and have obeyed and done all that our ancestor Jonadab commanded us. 11 But when King Nebuchadrezzar of Babylon came up against the land, we said, 'Come, and let us go to Jerusalem for fear of the army of the Chaldeans and the army of the Arameans.' That is why we are living in Jerusalem."

12 Then the word of the LORD came to Jeremiah: 13 Thus says the LORD of hosts, the God of Israel: Go and say to the people of Judah and the inhabitants of Jerusalem, Can you not learn a lesson and obey my words? says the LORD. 14 The command has been carried out that Jonadab son of Rechab gave to his descendants to drink no wine; and they drink none to this day, for they have obeyed their ancestor's command. But I myself have spoken to you persistently, and you have not obeyed me. 15 I have sent to you all my servants the prophets, sending them persistently, saying, 'Turn now everyone of you from your evil way, and amend your doings, and do not go after other gods to serve them, and then you shall live in the land that I gave to you and your ancestors.' But you did not incline your ear or obey me. 16 The descendants of Jonadab son of Rechab have carried out the command that their ancestor gave them, but this people has not obeyed me. 17 Therefore, thus says the LORD, the God of hosts, the God of Israel: I am going to bring on Judah and on all the inhabitants of Jerusalem every disaster that I have pronounced against them; because I have spoken to them and they have not listened, I have called to them and they have not answered.

18 But to the house of the Rechabites Jeremiah said: Thus says the LORD of hosts, the God of Israel: Because you have obeyed the command of your ancestor Jonadab, and kept all his precepts, and done all that he commanded you, 19 therefore thus says the LORD of hosts, the God of Israel: Jonadab son of Rechab shall not lack a descendant to stand before me for all time.

36 In the fourth year of King Jehoiakim son of Josiah of Judah, this word came to Jeremiah from the LORD: 2 Take a scroll and write on it all the words that I have spoken to you against Israel and all the nations, from the day I spoke to you, from the days of Josiah until today. 3 It may be that when the house of Judah hears of all

command, says the LORD, and bring them back to this city. They will attack it, capture it, and burn it to the ground. I shall make the towns and cities of Judah desolate and unpeopled.

35 This is the word which came to Jeremiah from the LORD in the days of Jehoiakim son of Josiah, king of Judah: 2 Go and speak to the Rechabites; bring them to one of the rooms in the house of the LORD and offer them wine to drink. 3 So I fetched Jaazaniah son of Jeremiah, son of Habazziniah, with his brothers and all his sons, the whole Rechabite family. 4 I brought them into the house of the LORD to the room of the sons of Hanan son of Igdaliah, the man of God; this adjoins the officers' room above that of Maaseiah son of Shallum, the keeper of the threshold. 5 I set bowls full of wine and drinking-cups before the Rechabites and invited them to drink; 6 but they said, 'We never drink wine, for our forefather Jonadab son of Rechab laid this charge on us: "You must never drink wine, neither you nor your children; 7 Do not build houses or sow seed or plant vineyards; you are to have none of these things. Instead, you are to remain tent-dwellers all your days, so that you may live long on the soil where you are sojourners." 8 We have honoured all the commands of our forefather Jonadab son of Rechab and have drunk no wine all our lives, neither we, nor our wives, nor our sons, nor our daughters. 9 We have not built houses to live in, nor have we possessed vineyards or sown fields; 10 we have lived in tents, obeying and observing fully the charge which our forefather Jonadab laid on us. 11 But when King Nebuchadrezzar of Babylon invaded the land we said, "Let us go to Jerusalem to escape the advancing Chaldaean and Aramaean armies." And we have stayed in Jerusalem.'

12 Then the word of the LORD came to Jeremiah: 13 These are the words of the LORD of Hosts the God of Israel: Go and say to the Judaeans and the citizens of Jerusalem: Will you never accept correction and obey my words? says the LORD. 14 The command of Jonadab son of Rechab to his descendants not to drink wine has been honoured; to this day they do not drink wine, for they obey their ancestor's command. But though I have warned you time and again, you have not obeyed me. 15 Time and again I sent all my servants the prophets to say, 'Turn back every one of you from evil conduct, mend your ways, and cease to follow other gods and serve them; then you will remain in the land that I have given to you and to your forefathers.' Yet you did not obey or listen to me. 16 The descendants of Jonadab son of Rechab have honoured the command their forefather laid on them, but this people have not listened to me. 17 Therefore, these are the words of the LORD the God of Hosts, the God of Israel: Because they did not listen when I spoke to them or respond when I called them, I shall bring on Judah and on all the citizens of Jerusalem the full disaster with which I threatened them.

18 To the Rechabites Jeremiah said: These are the words of the LORD of Hosts the God of Israel: Because you have kept the command of Jonadab your forefather, obeying all his instructions and carrying out all that he told you to do, 19 therefore these are the words of the LORD of Hosts the God of Israel: There will never be lacking in my service a man of the line of Jonadab son of Rechab.

36 In the fourth year of Jehoiakim son of Josiah, king of Judah, this word came to Jeremiah from the LORD: 2 Take a scroll and write on it all the words I have spoken to you about Jerusalem, Judah, and all the nations, from the day that I first spoke to you during the reign of Josiah down to the present day. 3 Perhaps the house of Judah

36:2 **Jerusalem**: *so Gk; Heb.* Israel.

LORD, and bring them back to this city. They shall attack and capture it, and destroy it with fire; the cities of Judah I will turn into a desert where no man dwells.

35 This word came to Jeremiah from the LORD in the days of Jehoiakim, son of Josiah, king of Judah: ²Approach the Rechabites and speak to them; bring them into the house of the LORD, to one of the rooms, and give them wine to drink. ³So I went and brought Jaazaniah, son of Jeremiah, son of Habazzaniah, his brothers and all his sons, the whole company of the Rechabites, ⁴into the house of the LORD, to the room of the sons of Hanan, son of Igdaliah, the man of God, next to the princes' room, above the room of Maaseiah, son of Shallum, keeper of the doorway. ⁵I set before these Rechabite men bowls full of wine and offered them cups to drink the wine.

⁶"We do not drink wine," they said to me: "Jonadab, Rechab's son, our father, forbade us in these words: 'Neither you nor your children shall ever drink wine. ⁷Build no house and sow no seed; neither plant nor own a vineyard. You shall dwell in tents all your life, so that you may live long on the earth where you are wayfarers.' ⁸Now we have heeded Jonadab, Rechab's son, our father, in all his prohibitions. All our lives we have not drunk wine, neither we, nor our wives, nor our sons, nor our daughters. ⁹We build no houses to live in; we own no vineyards or fields or crops, ¹⁰and we live in tents; we obediently do everything our father Jonadab commanded us. ¹¹But when Nebuchadnezzar, king of Babylon, invaded this land, we decided to come into Jerusalem to escape the army of the Chaldeans and the army of Aram; that is why we are now living in Jerusalem."

¹²Then this word of the LORD came to Jeremiah: ¹³Thus says the LORD of hosts, the God of Israel: Go, say to the men of Judah and to the citizens of Jerusalem: Will you not take correction and obey my words? says the LORD. ¹⁴The advice of Jonadab, Rechab's son, by which he forbade his children to drink wine, has been followed: to this day they have not drunk it; they obeyed their father's command. Me, however, you have not obeyed, although I spoke to you untiringly and insistently. ¹⁵I kept sending you all my servants the prophets, telling you to turn back, all of you, from your evil way; to reform your conduct, and not follow strange gods or serve them, if you would remain on the land which I gave you and your fathers; but you did not heed me or obey me. ¹⁶Yes, the children of Jonadab, Rechab's son, observed the command which their father laid on them; but this people does not obey me! ¹⁷Now, therefore, says the LORD God of hosts, the God of Israel: I will bring upon Judah and all the citizens of Jerusalem every evil that I threatened; because when I spoke they did not obey, when I called they did not answer.

¹⁸But to the company of the Rechabites Jeremiah said: Thus says the LORD of hosts, the God of Israel: Since you have obeyed the command of Jonadab, your father, kept all his commands and done everything he commanded you, ¹⁹thus therefore says the LORD of hosts, the God of Israel: Never shall there fail to be a descendant of Jonadab, Rechab's son, standing in my service.

36 In the fourth year of Jehoiakim, son of Josiah, king of Judah, this word came to Jeremiah from the LORD: ²Take a scroll and write on it all the words I have spoken to you against Israel, Judah, and all the nations, from the day I first spoke to you, in the days of Josiah, until today. ³Perhaps, when the house of Judah hears all the evil

I shall give the order, Yahweh declares, and bring them back to this city to attack it and capture it and burn it down. And I shall make an uninhabited waste of the towns of Judah."'

35 The word which came to Jeremiah from Yahweh in the days of Jehoiakim son of Josiah, king of Judah, ²'Go to the clan of the Rechabites and speak to them; bring them into one of the rooms of the Temple of Yahweh and offer them wine to drink.' ³So I took Jaazaniah son of Jeremiah, son of Habazziniah, with his brothers and all his sons, the whole Rechabite clan, ⁴and brought them to the Temple of Yahweh into the room of Ben-Johanan son of Igdaliah, a man of God, which was next to that of the chief men, above the room of Maaseiah son of Shallum, guardian of the threshold. ⁵I then set pitchers full of wine, and some cups, before the members of the Rechabite clan and said, 'Drink some wine.'

⁶But they replied, 'We do not drink wine, because our ancestor Jonadab son of Rechab gave us this order, "You must not drink wine, neither you nor your sons for ever; ⁷nor must you build houses, sow seed, plant vineyards or own them, but must live in tents all your lives, so that you may live long on the soil to which you are alien." ⁸We have punctiliously obeyed the orders of our ancestor, Jonadab son of Rechab, never drinking wine ourselves, nor our wives, our sons or our daughters, ⁹not building houses to live in, owning neither vineyard nor field nor seed, ¹⁰living in tents. We have obeyed the orders of our ancestor Jonadab, respecting them in every particular. ¹¹However, when Nebuchadnezzar king of Babylon invaded this country, we decided, "We must get away! We will go to Jerusalem to escape the armies of the Chaldaeans and Aramaeans." So that is why we are living in Jerusalem.'

¹²Then the word of Yahweh came to Jeremiah as follows, ¹³'Yahweh Sabaoth, the God of Israel, says this, "Go and say to the people of Judah and the inhabitants of Jerusalem: Will you never learn the lesson and listen to my words, Yahweh demands? ¹⁴The words of Jonadab son of Rechab, ordering his sons to drink no wine, have been observed; obedient to their ancestor's command, they drink none even today. But to me, who spoke to you so urgently, so untiringly, you have not listened. ¹⁵I have urgently and untiringly sent you all my servants the prophets to say: Turn back, each one of you, from your evil behaviour and amend your actions, do not follow other gods to serve them, and you will go on living on the soil I gave to you and your ancestors. But you have not paid attention or listened to me. ¹⁶Thus the sons of Jonadab son of Rechab have kept the command their ancestor gave them, but this people has not listened to me. ¹⁷And so, Yahweh, God Sabaoth, God of Israel, says this: Look, on Judah and the citizens of Jerusalem I am going to bring all the disaster which I have decreed for them, because I spoke to them and they would not listen, called to them and they would not answer."'

¹⁸Then Jeremiah said to the Rechabite clan, 'Yahweh Sabaoth, the God of Israel, says this, "Because you have obeyed the orders of your ancestor Jonadab and observed all his rules and done everything he ordered you to do, ¹⁹therefore, Yahweh Sabaoth, the God of Israel, says this: Jonadab son of Rechab will never lack a male descendant to stand before me for ever."'

36 In the fourth year of Jehoiakim son of Josiah, king of Judah, this word came to Jeremiah from Yahweh, ²'Take a scroll and on it write all the words I have spoken to you about Israel, Judah and all the nations, from the day I first spoke to you, in the time of Josiah, until today. ³Perhaps when the House of Judah hears about all

NEW REVISED STANDARD VERSION	REVISED ENGLISH BIBLE

the disasters that I intend to do to them, all of them may turn from their evil ways, so that I may forgive their iniquity and their sin.

4 Then Jeremiah called Baruch son of Neriah, and Baruch wrote on a scroll at Jeremiah's dictation all the words of the LORD that he had spoken to him. 5 And Jeremiah ordered Baruch, saying, "I am prevented from entering the house of the LORD; 6 so you go yourself, and on a fast day in the hearing of the people in the LORD's house you shall read the words of the LORD from the scroll that you have written at my dictation. You shall read them also in the hearing of all the people of Judah who come up from their towns. 7 It may be that their plea will come before the LORD, and that all of them will turn from their evil ways, for great is the anger and wrath that the LORD has pronounced against this people." 8 And Baruch son of Neriah did all that the prophet Jeremiah ordered him about reading from the scroll the words of the LORD in the LORD's house.

9 In the fifth year of King Jehoiakim son of Josiah of Judah, in the ninth month, all the people in Jerusalem and all the people who came from the towns of Judah to Jerusalem proclaimed a fast before the LORD. 10 Then, in the hearing of all the people, Baruch read the words of Jeremiah from the scroll, in the house of the LORD, in the chamber of Gemariah son of Shaphan the secretary, which was in the upper court, at the entry of the New Gate of the LORD's house.

11 When Micaiah son of Gemariah son of Shaphan heard all the words of the LORD from the scroll, 12 he went down to the king's house, into the secretary's chamber; and all the officials were sitting there: Elishama the secretary, Delaiah son of Shemaiah, Elnathan son of Achbor, Gemariah son of Shaphan, Zedekiah son of Hananiah, and all the officials. 13 And Micaiah told them all the words that he had heard, when Baruch read the scroll in the hearing of the people. 14 Then all the officials sent Jehudi son of Nethaniah son of Shelemiah son of Cushi to say to Baruch, "Bring the scroll that you read in the hearing of the people, and come." So Baruch son of Neriah took the scroll in his hand and came to them. 15 And they said to him, "Sit down and read it to us." So Baruch read it to them. 16 When they heard all the words, they turned to one another in alarm, and said to Baruch, "We certainly must report all these words to the king." 17 Then they questioned Baruch, "Tell us now, how did you write all these words? Was it at his dictation?" 18 Baruch answered them, "He dictated all these words to me, and I wrote them with ink on the scroll." 19 Then the officials said to Baruch, "Go and hide, you and Jeremiah, and let no one know where you are."

20 Leaving the scroll in the chamber of Elishama the secretary, they went to the court of the king; and they reported all the words to the king. 21 Then the king sent Jehudi to get the scroll, and he took it from the chamber of Elishama the secretary; and Jehudi read it to the king and all the officials who stood beside the king. 22 Now the king was sitting in his winter apartment (it was the ninth month), and there was a fire burning in the brazier before him. 23 As Jehudi read three or four columns, the king[b] would cut them off with a penknife and throw them into the fire in the brazier, until the entire scroll was consumed in the fire that was in the brazier. 24 Yet neither the king, nor any of his servants who heard all these words, was alarmed, nor did they tear their garments. 25 Even when Elnathan and Delaiah and Gemariah urged the king not to burn the scroll, he would not listen to them. 26 And the king commanded Jerahmeel the king's son and Seraiah son of Azriel and Shelemiah son of Abdeel to arrest the secretary Baruch and the prophet Jeremiah. But the LORD hid them.

will be warned of all the disaster I am planning to inflict on them, and everyone will abandon his evil conduct; then I shall forgive their wrongdoing and their sin.

4 Jeremiah summoned Baruch son of Neriah, and Baruch wrote on the scroll at Jeremiah's dictation everything the LORD had said to him. 5 He gave Baruch this instruction: 'As I am debarred from going to the LORD's house, 6 you must go there and on a fast-day read aloud to the people the words of the LORD from the scroll you wrote at my dictation. You are to read them in the hearing of all those who come in from the towns of Judah. 7 Then perhaps they will petition the LORD, and everyone will abandon his evil conduct; for in great anger and wrath the LORD has threatened this people.' 8 Baruch son of Neriah did all that the prophet Jeremiah had told him, about reading from the scroll the words of the LORD in the LORD's house.

9 In the ninth month of the fifth year of the reign of Jehoiakim son of Josiah, king of Judah, all the people in Jerusalem and all who came there from the towns of Judah proclaimed a fast before the LORD. 10 Then in the LORD's house Baruch read aloud Jeremiah's words from the scroll to all the people; he read them from the room of Gemariah son of the adjutant-general Shaphan, which was in the upper court at the entrance to the New Gate of the LORD's house.

11 When Micaiah son of Gemariah, son of Shaphan, heard all the LORD's words from the scroll 12 he went down to the palace, to the chief adviser's room, where he found the officers all in session: Elishama the chief adviser, Delaiah son of Shemaiah, Elnathan son of Akbor, Gemariah son of Shaphan, Zedekiah son of Hananiah, and all the other officers. 13 Micaiah reported to them everything he had heard Baruch read from the scroll in the hearing of the people. 14 Then the officers sent Jehudi son of Nethaniah, son of Shelemiah, son of Cushi, to Baruch with this order: 'Come here and bring the scroll from which you read to the people.' When Baruch son of Neriah appeared before them with the scroll, 15 they said to him, 'Sit down and read it to us,' and he did so. 16 When they had listened to it, they turned to each other in alarm and said, 'We must certainly report this to the king.' 17 They asked Baruch to explain to them how he had come to write all this. 18 He answered, 'Jeremiah dictated every word of it to me, and I wrote it down with ink on the scroll.' 19 The officers said to him, 'You and Jeremiah must go into hiding so that no one may know where you are.' 20 When they had deposited the scroll in the room of Elishama the chief adviser, they went to the court and reported the whole affair to the king.

21 The king sent Jehudi for the scroll and, when he had fetched it from the room of Elishama the chief adviser, Jehudi read it out to the king and to all the officers in attendance on him. 22 Since it was the ninth month of the year, the king was sitting in his winter apartments with a fire burning in a brazier in front of him. 23 Every time Jehudi read three or four columns of the scroll, the king cut them off with a penknife and threw them into the fire in the brazier. He went on doing so until the entire scroll had been destroyed on the fire. 24 Neither the king nor any of his courtiers showed any alarm or tore their clothes as they listened to these words; 25 and though Elnathan, Delaiah, and Gemariah begged the king not to burn the scroll, he refused to listen. 26 but ordered Jerahmeel, a royal prince, Seraiah son of Azriel, and Shelemiah son of Abdeel to arrest Baruch the scribe and the prophet Jeremiah. But the LORD had hidden them.

b Heb *he*

36:17 **all this:** *so Gk; Heb. adds* at his dictation.

I have in mind to do to them, they will turn back each from his evil way, so that I may forgive their wickedness and their sin. 4 So Jeremiah called Baruch, son of Neriah, who wrote down on a scroll, as Jeremiah dictated, all the words which the LORD had spoken to him.

9 In the ninth month, in the fifth year of Jehoiakim, son of Josiah, king of Judah, a fast to placate the LORD was proclaimed for all the people of Jerusalem and all who came from Judah's cities to Jerusalem. 5 Then Jeremiah charged Baruch: I cannot go to the house of the LORD: I am prevented from doing so. 6 Do you go on the fast day and read publicly in the LORD's house the LORD's words from the scroll you wrote at my dictation; read them also to all the men of Judah who come up from their cities. 7 Perhaps they will lay their supplication before the LORD and will all turn back from their evil way; for great is the fury of anger with which the LORD has threatened this people.

8 Baruch, son of Neriah, did everything the prophet Jeremiah commanded; from the bookscroll he read the LORD's words in the LORD's house. ‡36.9: see above‡ 10 It was in the room of Gemariah, son of the scribe Shaphan, in the upper court of the LORD's house, at the entrance of the New Temple-Gate, that Baruch publicly read the words of Jeremiah from his book.

11 Now Micaiah, son of Gemariah, son of Shaphan, heard all the words of the LORD read from the book. 12 So he went down to the king's palace, into the scribe's chamber, where the princes were just then in session: Elishama, the scribe, Delaiah, son of Shemaiah, Elnathan, son of Achbor, Gemariah, son of Shaphan, Zedekiah, son of Hananiah, and the other princes. 13 To them Micaiah reported all that he had heard Baruch read publicly from his book. 14 Thereupon the princes sent Jehudi, son of Nethaniah, son of Shelemiah, son of Cushi, to Baruch with the order: "Come, and bring with you the scroll you read publicly to the people." Scroll in hand, Baruch, son of Neriah, went to them. 15 "Sit down," they said to him, "and read it to us." Baruch read it to them, 16 and when they heard all its words, they were frightened and said to one another, "We must certainly tell the king all these things." 17 Then they asked Baruch: "Tell us, please, how you came to write down all these words." 18 "Jeremiah dictated all these words to me," Baruch answered them, "and I wrote them down with ink in the book." 19 At this the princes said to Baruch, "Go into hiding, you and Jeremiah; let no one know where you are."

20 Leaving the scroll in safekeeping in the room of Elishama the scribe, they entered the room where the king was. When they told him everything that had happened, 21 he sent Jehudi to fetch the scroll. Jehudi brought it from the room of Elishama the scribe, and read it to the king and to all the princes who were in attendance on the king. 22 Now the king was sitting in his winter house, since it was the ninth month, and fire was burning in a brazier before him. 23 Each time Jehudi finished reading three or four columns, the king would cut off the piece with a scribe's knife and cast it into the fire in the brazier, until the entire roll was consumed in the fire. 24 Hearing all these words did not frighten the king and his ministers or cause them to rend their garments. 25 And though Elnathan, Delaiah, and Gemariah urged the king not to burn the scroll, he would not listen to them, 26 but commanded Jerahmeel, a royal prince, and Seraiah, son of Azriel, and Shelemiah, son of Abdeel, to arrest Baruch, the secretary, and the prophet Jeremiah. But the LORD kept them concealed.

the disaster I intend to inflict on them, they will turn, each one of them, from their evil behaviour, so that I can forgive their sinful guilt.' 4 Jeremiah then summoned Baruch son of Neriah, who at his dictation wrote down on the scroll all the words Yahweh had spoken to him.

5 Jeremiah then gave Baruch this order, 'As I am prevented from entering the Temple of Yahweh, 6 you yourself must go and, from the scroll you wrote at my dictation, read all Yahweh's words to the people in his Temple on the day of the fast, and in this way you can read them in the hearing also of all the Judaeans who come in from their towns. 7 Perhaps their prayers will move Yahweh and they will turn one and all from their evil behaviour, for great is the furious anger with which Yahweh has threatened this people.' 8 Baruch son of Neriah duly carried out the order that the prophet Jeremiah had given him, to read all Yahweh's words from the book in his Temple.

9 Now, in the fifth year of Jehoiakim son of Josiah, king of Judah, in the ninth month, all the people of Jerusalem and all the people who could get to Jerusalem from the towns of Judah were summoned to a fast before Yahweh. 10 Baruch then read Jeremiah's words from the book; this happened in the room of Gemariah son of the scribe Shaphan, in the upper court at the entry of the New Gate of the Temple of Yahweh, where all the people could hear.

11 Micaiah son of Gemariah, son of Shaphan, having heard all Yahweh's words read from the book, 12 went down to the royal palace, to the scribe's room. All the chief men were in session: the scribe Elishama, Delaiah son of Shemaiah, Elnathan son of Achbor, Gemariah son of Shaphan, Zedekiah son of Hananiah and all the other chief men; 13 and to them Micaiah reported all the words he heard as Baruch was reading the book aloud to the people. 14 The chief men then by common consent sent Jehudi son of Netaniah to Baruch, with Shelemiah son of Cushi, to say, 'Come, and bring the scroll with you which you have been reading to the people.' 15 Bringing the scroll with him, Baruch son of Neriah appeared before them. 'Sit down,' they said, 'and read it out.' So Baruch read it to them. 16 Having heard all the words they turned to one another in alarm and said to Baruch, 'We must certainly inform the king of this.' 17 They then questioned Baruch, 'Tell us', they said, 'how you came to write all these words.' 18 'Jeremiah dictated them all to me,' Baruch replied, 'and I wrote them down in ink in this book.' 19 The chief men said to Baruch, 'You and Jeremiah had better go into hiding; and do not tell anyone where you are.' 20 Whereupon they went off to the king in the palace court, depositing the scroll in the room of the scribe Elishama. They then informed the king of the whole affair.

21 The king sent Jehudi for the scroll, and he brought it from the room of the scribe Elishama and read it to the king and all the chief men standing round the king. 22 The king was sitting in his winter apartments—it was the ninth month—with a fire burning in a brazier in front of him. 23 Each time Jehudi had read three or four columns, the king cut them off with a scribe's knife and threw them into the fire in the brazier until the whole of the scroll had been burnt in the brazier fire. 24 But in spite of hearing all these words, neither the king nor any of his courtiers took alarm or tore their clothes; 25 and although Elnathan and Delaiah and Gemariah had urged the king not to burn the scroll he would not listen to them, 26 but ordered the king's son Jerahmeel and Seraiah son of Azriel and Shelemiah son of Abdeel to arrest the scribe Baruch and the prophet Jeremiah. But Yahweh had hidden them.

NEW REVISED STANDARD VERSION

27 Now, after the king had burned the scroll with the words that Baruch wrote at Jeremiah's dictation, the word of the LORD came to Jeremiah: 28 Take another scroll and write on it all the former words that were in the first scroll, which King Jehoiakim of Judah has burned. 29 And concerning King Jehoiakim of Judah you shall say: Thus says the LORD, You have dared to burn this scroll, saying, Why have you written in it that the king of Babylon will certainly come and destroy this land, and will cut off from it human beings and animals? 30 Therefore thus says the LORD concerning King Jehoiakim of Judah: He shall have no one to sit upon the throne of David, and his dead body shall be cast out to the heat by day and the frost by night. 31 And I will punish him and his offspring and his servants for their iniquity; I will bring on them, and on the inhabitants of Jerusalem, and on the people of Judah, all the disasters with which I have threatened them — but they would not listen.

32 Then Jeremiah took another scroll and gave it to the secretary Baruch son of Neriah, who wrote on it at Jeremiah's dictation all the words of the scroll that King Jehoiakim of Judah had burned in the fire; and many similar words were added to them.

37 Zedekiah son of Josiah, whom King Nebuchadrezzar of Babylon made king in the land of Judah, succeeded Coniah son of Jehoiakim. 2 But neither he nor his servants nor the people of the land listened to the words of the LORD that he spoke through the prophet Jeremiah.

3 King Zedekiah sent Jehucal son of Shelemiah and the priest Zephaniah son of Maaseiah to the prophet Jeremiah saying, "Please pray for us to the LORD our God." 4 Now Jeremiah was still going in and out among the people, for he had not yet been put in prison. 5 Meanwhile, the army of Pharaoh had come out of Egypt; and when the Chaldeans who were besieging Jerusalem heard news of them, they withdrew from Jerusalem.

6 Then the word of the LORD came to the prophet Jeremiah: 7 Thus says the LORD, God of Israel: This is what the two of you shall say to the king of Judah, who sent you to me to inquire of me, Pharaoh's army, which set out to help you, is going to return to its own land, to Egypt. 8 And the Chaldeans shall return and fight against this city; they shall take it and burn it with fire. 9 Thus says the LORD: Do not deceive yourselves, saying, "The Chaldeans will surely go away from us," for they will not go away. 10 Even if you defeated the whole army of Chaldeans who are fighting against you, and there remained of them only wounded men in their tents, they would rise up and burn this city with fire.

11 Now when the Chaldean army had withdrawn from Jerusalem at the approach of Pharaoh's army, 12 Jeremiah set out from Jerusalem to go to the land of Benjamin to receive his share of property[c] among the people there. 13 When he reached the Benjamin Gate, a sentinel there named Irijah son of Shelemiah son of Hananiah arrested the prophet Jeremiah saying, "You are deserting to the Chaldeans." 14 And Jeremiah said, "That is a lie; I am not deserting to the Chaldeans." But Irijah would not listen to him, and arrested Jeremiah and brought him to the officials. 15 The officials were enraged at Jeremiah, and they beat him and imprisoned him in the house of the secretary Jonathan, for it had been made a prison. 16 Thus Jeremiah was put in the cistern house, in the cells, and remained there many days.

17 Then King Zedekiah sent for him, and received him. The king questioned him secretly in his house, and said, "Is there any word from the LORD?" Jeremiah said, "There is!" Then he said, "You shall be handed over to the king of Babylon." 18 Jeremiah also said to King Zedekiah, "What wrong have I done to you or your servants or this people,

REVISED ENGLISH BIBLE

27 After the king had burnt the scroll with all that Baruch had written on it at Jeremiah's dictation, the word of the LORD came to Jeremiah: 28 Take another scroll and write on it everything that was on the first scroll which King Jehoiakim of Judah burnt. 29 You are to say to the king: These are the words of the LORD: You burnt that scroll and said, 'Why have you written here that the king of Babylon will come and destroy this land and exterminate both man and beast?' 30 Therefore these are the words of the LORD about King Jehoiakim of Judah: He will have no descendant to succeed him on the throne of David, and his dead body will be exposed to scorching heat by day and frost by night. 31 I shall punish him, his offspring, and his courtiers for their wickedness, and I shall bring down on them and on the citizens of Jerusalem and on the people of Judah all the disasters with which I threatened them, for they turned a deaf ear to me.

32 Then Jeremiah took another scroll and gave it to the scribe Baruch son of Neriah, who wrote on it at Jeremiah's dictation all the words of the book which Jehoiakim king of Judah had burnt in the fire; and much else was added to the same effect.

37 Zedekiah son of Josiah was set on the throne of Judah by King Nebuchadrezzar of Babylon, in place of Coniah son of Jehoiakim, 2 but neither he nor his courtiers nor the people of the land heeded the words which the LORD spoke through the prophet Jeremiah. 3 King Zedekiah, however, sent Jehucal son of Shelemiah and the priest Zephaniah son of Maaseiah to Jeremiah to say to him, 'Intercede on our behalf with the LORD our God.' 4 At the time Jeremiah was free to come and go among the people; he had not yet been committed to prison.

5 Meanwhile Pharaoh's army had marched out of Egypt, and when the Chaldaeans who were besieging Jerusalem were apprised of this they raised the siege. 6 Then the word of the LORD came to the prophet Jeremiah: 7 These are the words of the LORD the God of Israel: Take this message to the king of Judah who sent you to consult me: Pharaoh's army which marched out to your aid is on its way back to Egypt, its own land, 8 and the Chaldaeans will return to the attack. They will capture this city and burn it to the ground. 9 These are the words of the LORD: Do not delude yourselves by imagining that the Chaldaeans will go away and leave you alone. They will not; 10 supposing that you were to defeat the whole Chaldaean force now fighting against you, and only the wounded were left lying in their tents, even they would rise and burn down this city.

11 After the Chaldaean army raised the siege of Jerusalem in the face of the advance of Pharaoh's army, 12 Jeremiah was on the way out from Jerusalem to go into Benjamite territory to take possession of his holding among the people there. 13 Irijah son of Shelemiah, son of Hananiah, the officer of the guard, was at the Benjamin Gate when Jeremiah reached it, and he arrested the prophet, accusing him of defecting to the Chaldaeans. 14 'That is not true!' said Jeremiah. 'I am not going over to the Chaldaeans.' Irijah refused to listen but brought him under arrest before the officers. 15 The officers, furious with Jeremiah, had him flogged and imprisoned in the house of Jonathan the scribe, which had been converted into a jail. 16 Jeremiah was put into a vaulted pit beneath the house, and he remained there many days.

17 King Zedekiah had Jeremiah brought to him and questioned him privately in the palace, asking if there was a word from the LORD. 'There is,' said Jeremiah; 'you will fall into the hands of the king of Babylon.' 18 Jeremiah went on, 'What wrong have I done to you or your courtiers or this

c Meaning of Heb uncertain

1740

NEW AMERICAN BIBLE	NEW JERUSALEM BIBLE

NEW AMERICAN BIBLE

27 This word of the LORD came to Jeremiah, after the king burned the scroll with the text Jeremiah had dictated to Baruch: 28 Take another scroll, and write on it everything that the first scroll contained, which Jehoiakim, king of Judah, burned up. 29 And against Jehoiakim, king of Judah, say this: Thus says the LORD: You burned that scroll, saying, "Why did you write on it: Babylon's king shall surely come and lay waste this land and empty it of man and beast?" 30 The LORD now says of Jehoiakim, king of Judah: No descendant of his shall succeed to David's throne; his corpse shall be cast out, exposed to the heat of day, to the cold of night. 31 I will punish him and his descendants and his ministers for their wickedness; against them and the citizens of Jerusalem and the men of Judah I will fulfill all the threats of evil which went unheeded.

32 Jeremiah took another scroll, and gave it to his secretary, Baruch, son of Neriah; he wrote on it at Jeremiah's dictation all the words contained in the book which Jehoiakim, king of Judah, had burned in the fire, and many others of the same kind in addition.

37 Coniah, son of Jehoiakim, was succeeded by King Zedekiah, son of Josiah; he was made king over the land of Judah by Nebuchadnezzar, king of Babylon. 2 Neither he, nor his ministers, nor the people of the land would listen to the words of the LORD spoken by Jeremiah the prophet. 3 Yet King Zedekiah sent Jehucal, son of Shelemiah, and Zephaniah, son of Maaseiah the priest, to the prophet Jeremiah with this request: "Pray to the LORD, our God, for us." 4 At this time Jeremiah had not yet been put into prison; he still came and went freely among the people. 5 Also, Pharaoh's army had set out from Egypt, and when the Chaldeans who were besieging Jerusalem heard this report they marched away from the city.

6 This word of the LORD then came to the prophet Jeremiah: 7 Thus says the LORD, the God of Israel: Give this answer to the king of Judah who sent you to me to consult me: Pharaoh's army which has set out to help you will return to its own land, Egypt. 8 The Chaldeans shall return to the fight against this city; they shall capture it and destroy it with fire. 9 Thus says the LORD: Do not deceive yourselves with the thought that the Chaldeans will leave you for good, because they shall not leave! 10 Even if you were to defeat the whole Chaldean army now attacking you, and only the wounded remained, each in his tent, these would rise up and destroy the city with fire.

11 When the Chaldean army lifted the siege of Jerusalem at the threat of the army of Pharaoh, 12 Jeremiah set out from Jerusalem for the district of Benjamin, to take part with his family in the division of an inheritance. 13 But when he reached the Gate of Benjamin, he met the captain of the guard, a man named Irijah, son of Shelemiah, son of Hananiah; he seized the prophet Jeremiah, saying, "You are deserting to the Chaldeans!" 14 "That is a lie!" Jeremiah answered, "I am not deserting to the Chaldeans." Without listening, Irijah kept Jeremiah in custody and brought him to the princes.

15 The princes were enraged, and had Jeremiah beaten and thrown into prison in the house of Jonathan the scribe, which they were using as a jail. 16 And so Jeremiah entered the vaulted dungeon, where he remained a long time.

17 Once King Zedekiah had him brought to his palace and he asked him secretly whether there was any message from the LORD. Yes! Jeremiah answered: you shall be handed over to the king of Babylon. 18 Jeremiah then asked King Zedekiah: In what have I wronged you, or your ministers,

NEW JERUSALEM BIBLE

27 Then the word of Yahweh came to Jeremiah, after the king had burnt the scroll containing the words Baruch had written at Jeremiah's dictation, 28 'Take another scroll and write down all the words that were written on the first scroll burnt by Jehoiakim king of Judah. 29 And as regards Jehoiakim king of Judah, you are to say, "Yahweh says this: You have burnt that scroll, saying: Why have you written down: The king of Babylon will certainly come and lay this country waste and leave it without human or animal? 30 So, this is what Yahweh says about Jehoiakim king of Judah: He will have no one to occupy the throne of David, and his corpse will be tossed out to the heat of the day and the frost of the night. 31 I shall punish him, his offspring and his courtiers for their guilt; on them, on the citizens of Jerusalem and on the people of Judah I shall bring the total disaster which I had decreed for them but to which they have paid no attention." '

32 Jeremiah then took another scroll and gave it to the scribe Baruch son of Neriah, who in it at Jeremiah's dictation wrote all the words of the book that Jehoiakim king of Judah had burnt, with many similar words in addition.

37 Zedekiah son of Josiah became king, succeeding Coniah son of Jehoiakim. Nebuchadnezzar king of Babylon had made him king of Judah. 2 But neither he nor his courtiers nor the people of the country paid any attention to the words Yahweh spoke through the prophet Jeremiah.

3 King Zedekiah sent Jehucal son of Shelemiah and the priest Zephaniah son of Maaseiah to the prophet Jeremiah with this message, 'Intercede for us with Yahweh our God.' 4 Now Jeremiah was still moving freely among the people: he had not yet been put in prison. 5 Meanwhile Pharaoh's army was on the move from Egypt and the Chaldaeans besieging Jerusalem had raised the siege when they heard the news.

6 Then the word of Yahweh came to the prophet Jeremiah as follows, 7 'Yahweh, God of Israel, says this, "To the king of Judah who sent you to consult me make this reply: Is Pharaoh's army marching to your aid? It will withdraw to its own country, Egypt. 8 The Chaldaeans will return to attack this city; they will capture it and burn it down. 9 Yahweh says this: Do not cheer yourselves up by thinking: The Chaldaeans are leaving us for good. They are not leaving. 10 Even if you cut to pieces the whole Chaldaean army now fighting against you until there were only the wounded left, they would stand up again, each man in his tent, to burn this city down." '

11 At the time when the Chaldaean army, threatened by Pharaoh's army, had raised the siege of Jerusalem, 12 Jeremiah set out from Jerusalem for the territory of Benjamin to see about a piece of his property among the people there. 13 He was at the Benjamin Gate when the guard commander there, a certain Irijah son of Shelemiah, son of Hananiah, arrested the prophet Jeremiah, shouting, 'You are deserting to the Chaldaeans!' 14 Jeremiah answered, 'It is a lie! I am not deserting to the Chaldaeans.' But Irijah would not listen to Jeremiah and took him under arrest to the chief men. 15 And the chief men, furious with Jeremiah, had him beaten and shut up in the house of the scribe Jonathan, which had been turned into a prison. 16 Thus Jeremiah found himself in an underground vault. And there for a long time he stayed.

17 Later, King Zedekiah had him sent for, and the king questioned him privately in his palace. 'Is there any word from Yahweh?' he asked. 'There is,' Jeremiah answered, and added, 'you will be handed over to the king of Babylon.' 18 Jeremiah then said to King Zedekiah, 'What wrong have I done you, or your courtiers or this people, for you to

| NEW REVISED STANDARD VERSION | REVISED ENGLISH BIBLE |

that you have put me in prison? 19 Where are your prophets who prophesied to you, saying, 'The king of Babylon will not come against you and against this land'? 20 Now please hear me, my lord king: be good enough to listen to my plea, and do not send me back to the house of the secretary Jonathan to die there." 21 So King Zedekiah gave orders, and they committed Jeremiah to the court of the guard; and a loaf of bread was given him daily from the bakers' street, until all the bread of the city was gone. So Jeremiah remained in the court of the guard.

38 Now Shephatiah son of Mattan, Gedaliah son of Pashhur, Jucal son of Shelemiah, and Pashhur son of Malchiah heard the words that Jeremiah was saying to all the people, 2 Thus says the LORD, Those who stay in this city shall die by the sword, by famine, and by pestilence; but those who go out to the Chaldeans shall live; they shall have their lives as a prize of war, and live. 3 Thus says the LORD, This city shall surely be handed over to the army of the king of Babylon and be taken. 4 Then the officials said to the king, "This man ought to be put to death, because he is discouraging the soldiers who are left in this city, and all the people, by speaking such words to them. For this man is not seeking the welfare of this people, but their harm." 5 King Zedekiah said, "Here he is; he is in your hands; for the king is powerless against you." 6 So they took Jeremiah and threw him into the cistern of Malchiah, the king's son, which was in the court of the guard, letting Jeremiah down by ropes. Now there was no water in the cistern, but only mud, and Jeremiah sank in the mud.

7 Ebed-melech the Ethiopian,[d] a eunuch in the king's house, heard that they had put Jeremiah into the cistern. The king happened to be sitting at the Benjamin Gate, 8 So Ebed-melech left the king's house and spoke to the king, 9 "My lord king, these men have acted wickedly in all they did to the prophet Jeremiah by throwing him into the cistern to die there of hunger, for there is no bread left in the city." 10 Then the king commanded Ebed-melech the Ethiopian,[d] "Take three men with you from here, and pull the prophet Jeremiah up from the cistern before he dies." 11 So Ebed-melech took the men with him and went to the house of the king, to a wardrobe of[e] the storehouse, and took from there old rags and worn-out clothes, which he let down to Jeremiah in the cistern by ropes. 12 Then Ebed-melech the Ethiopian[d] said to Jeremiah, "Just put the rags and clothes between your armpits and the ropes." Jeremiah did so. 13 Then they drew Jeremiah up by the ropes and pulled him out of the cistern. And Jeremiah remained in the court of the guard.

14 King Zedekiah sent for the prophet Jeremiah and received him at the third entrance of the temple of the LORD. The king said to Jeremiah, "I have something to ask you; do not hide anything from me." 15 Jeremiah said to Zedekiah, "If I tell you, you will put me to death, will you not? And if I give you advice, you will not listen to me." 16 So King Zedekiah swore an oath in secret to Jeremiah, "As the LORD lives, who gave us our lives, I will not put you to death or hand you over to these men who seek your life."

17 Then Jeremiah said to Zedekiah, "Thus says the LORD, the God of hosts, the God of Israel, If you will only surrender to the officials of the king of Babylon, then your life shall be spared, and this city shall not be burned with fire, and you and your house shall live. 18 But if you do not surrender to the officials of the king of Babylon, then this city shall be handed over to the Chaldeans, and they shall burn it with fire, and you yourself shall not escape from their hand." 19 King Zedekiah said to Jeremiah, "I am afraid

people, that you have thrown me into prison? 19 Where are your prophets who prophesied that the king of Babylon would not attack you or this country? 20 I pray you now, my lord king, give me a hearing and let my petition be accepted: do not send me back to the house of Jonathan the scribe, or I shall die there.' 21 Then King Zedekiah gave the order for Jeremiah to be committed to the court of the guard-house, and as long as there was bread in the city he was granted a daily ration of one loaf from the Street of the Bakers. So Jeremiah remained in the court of the guard-house.

38 Shephatiah son of Mattan, Gedaliah son of Pashhur, Jucal son of Shelemiah, and Pashhur son of Malchiah heard how Jeremiah was addressing all the people; he was saying: 2 These are the words of the LORD: Whoever remains in this city will die by sword, famine, or pestilence, but whoever surrenders to the Chaldaeans will survive; he will escape with his life. 3 These are the words of the LORD: This city will assuredly be delivered into the power of the king of Babylon's army, and be captured. 4 The officers said to the king, 'This man ought to be put to death. By talking in this way he is demoralizing the soldiers left in the city and indeed the rest of the people. It is not the people's welfare he seeks but their ruin.' 5 King Zedekiah said, 'He is in your hands; the king is powerless against you.' 6 So they took Jeremiah and put him into the cistern in the court of the guardhouse, letting him down with ropes. There was no water in the cistern, only mud, and Jeremiah sank in the mud.

7-8 Ebed-melech the Cushite, a eunuch, who was in the palace, heard that they had put Jeremiah into a cistern and he went to tell the king, who was seated at the Benjamin Gate. 9 'Your majesty,' he said, 'these men have acted viciously in their treatment of the prophet Jeremiah. They have thrown him into a cistern, and he will die of hunger where he is, for there is no more bread in the city.' 10 The king instructed Ebed-melech the Cushite to take three men with him and hoist Jeremiah out of the cistern before he perished. 11 Ebed-melech went to the palace with the men and took some tattered, cast-off clothes from a storeroom and lowered them with ropes to Jeremiah in the cistern. 12 He called to Jeremiah, 'Put these old clothes under your armpits to pad the ropes.' Jeremiah did so, 13 and they pulled him up out of the cistern with the ropes. Jeremiah remained in the court of the guardhouse.

14 King Zedekiah sent for the prophet Jeremiah and had him brought to the third entrance of the LORD's house. 'I want to ask you something,' he said to him; 'hide nothing from me.' 15 Jeremiah answered, 'If I speak out, you will certainly put me to death; if I offer advice, you will disregard it.' 16 King Zedekiah secretly made this promise on oath to Jeremiah: 'By the life of the LORD who gave us our lives, I shall not put you to death, nor shall I hand you over to these men who are seeking your life.' 17 Jeremiah said to Zedekiah, 'These are the words of the LORD the God of Hosts, the God of Israel: If you go out and surrender to the officers of the king of Babylon, you will live and this city will not be burnt down; you and your family will survive. 18 If, however, you do not surrender to the officers of the king of Babylon, this city will fall into the hands of the Chaldaeans, who will burn it down; you yourself will not escape them.' 19 The king said to Jeremiah, 'I am afraid of

38:6 into the cistern: prob. rdg; Heb. adds Malchiah son of the king.   38:10 three: so one MS; others thirty.   38:11 a storeroom: prob. rdg; Heb. underneath the store.

d Or Nubian; Heb Cushite   e Cn: Heb to under

or this people, that you should put me in prison? 19 And where are your own prophets now, 20 who prophesied to you that the king of Babylon would not attack you or this land? Hear now, my lord king, and grant my petition: do not send me back into the house of Jonathan the scribe, or I shall die there.

21 King Zedekiah ordered that Jeremiah be confined in the quarters of the guard, and given a loaf of bread each day from the bakers' shop until all the bread in the city was eaten up. Thus Jeremiah remained in the quarters of the guard.

38 Shephatiah, son of Mattan, Gedaliah, son of Pashhur, Jucal, son of Shelemiah, and Pashhur, son of Malchiah, heard Jeremiah speaking these words to all the people: 2 Thus says the LORD: He who remains in this city shall die by sword, or famine, or pestilence; but he who goes out to the Chaldeans shall live; his life shall be spared him as booty, and he shall live. 3 Thus says the LORD: This city shall certainly be handed over to the army of the king of Babylon; he shall capture it.

4 "This man ought to be put to death," the princes said to the king; "he demoralizes the soldiers who are left in this city, and all the people, by speaking such things to them; he is not interested in the welfare of our people, but in their ruin." 5 King Zedekiah answered: "He is in your power"; for the king could do nothing with them. 6 And so they took Jeremiah and threw him into the cistern of Prince Malchiah, which was in the quarters of the guard, letting him down with ropes. There was no water in the cistern, only mud, and Jeremiah sank into the mud.

7 Now Ebed-melech, a Cushite, a courtier in the king's palace, heard that they had put Jeremiah into the cistern. The king happened just then to be at the Gate of Benjamin, 8 and Ebed-melech went there from the palace and said to him, 9 "My lord king, these men have been at fault in all they have done to the prophet Jeremiah, casting him into the cistern. He will die of famine on the spot, for there is no more food in the city." 10 Then the king ordered Ebed-melech the Cushite to take three men along with him, and draw the prophet Jeremiah out of the cistern before he should die. 11 Ebed-melech took the men along with him, and went first to the linen closet in the palace, from which he took some old, tattered rags; these he sent down to Jeremiah in the cistern, with ropes. 12 Then he said to Jeremiah, "Put the old, tattered rags between your armpits and the ropes." Jeremiah did so, 13 and they drew him up with the ropes out of the cistern. But Jeremiah remained in the quarters of the guard.

14 Once King Zedekiah summoned the prophet Jeremiah to come to him at the third entrance to the house of the LORD. "I have a question to ask you," the king said to Jeremiah; "hide nothing from me." Jeremiah answered Zedekiah: 15 If I tell you anything, you will have me killed, will you not? If I counsel you, you will not listen to me! 16 But King Zedekiah swore to Jeremiah secretly: "As the LORD lives who gave us the breath of life, I will not kill you; nor will I hand you over to these men who seek your life."

17 Thereupon Jeremiah said to Zedekiah: Thus says the LORD God of hosts, the God of Israel: If you surrender to the princes of Babylon's king, you shall save your life; this city shall not be destroyed with fire, and you and your family shall live. 18 But if you do not surrender to the princes of Babylon's king, this city shall fall into the hands of the Chaldeans, who shall destroy it with fire, and you shall not escape their hands.

19 King Zedekiah, however, said to Jeremiah, "I am

have put me in prison? 19 Where are your prophets now who prophesied, "The king of Babylon will not attack you or this country"? 20 So now I beg you to hear me, my lord king! I beg you to approve my request! Do not have me taken back to the house of the scribe Jonathan, or I shall die there.'

21 King Zedekiah then gave an order, and Jeremiah was confined in the Court of the Guard and given a loaf of bread a day from the Street of the Bakers as long as there was bread left in the city. So Jeremiah stayed in the Court of the Guard.

38 But Shephatiah son of Mattan, Gedaliah son of Pashhur, Jucal son of Shelemiah and Pashhur son of Malchiah heard the words which Jeremiah was saying to all the people, 2 'Yahweh says this, "Anyone who stays in this city will die by sword, famine or plague; but anyone who leaves it and surrenders to the Chaldaeans will live; he will escape with his life. ^{w} 3 Yahweh says this: This city will certainly be handed over to the army of the king of Babylon, and he will capture it." '

4 The chief men then said to the king, 'You must have this man put to death: he is unquestionably disheartening the remaining soldiers in the city, and all the people too, by talking like this. This man is seeking not the welfare of the people but their ruin.' 5 King Zedekiah answered, 'He is in your hands as you know, for the king is powerless to oppose you.' 6 So they took Jeremiah and put him into the storage-well of the king's son Malchiah in the Court of the Guard, letting him down with ropes. There was no water in the storage-well, only mud, and into the mud Jeremiah sank.

7 But Ebed-Melech the Cushite, a eunuch attached to the palace, heard that Jeremiah had been put into the storage-well. As the king was sitting in the Benjamin Gate, 8 Ebed-Melech came out from the palace and spoke to the king. 9 'My lord king,' he said, 'these men have done a wicked thing by treating the prophet Jeremiah like this: they have thrown him into the storage-well. He will starve to death there, since there is no more food in the city.' 10 At this the king gave Ebed-Melech the Cushite the following order: 'Take thirty men with you from here and pull the prophet Jeremiah out of the storage-well before he dies.' 11 Ebed-Melech took the men with him and went into the palace to the Treasury wardrobe; out of it he took some torn, worn-out rags which he lowered on ropes to Jeremiah in the storage-well. 12 Ebed-Melech the Cushite then said to Jeremiah, 'These torn, worn-out rags are for you to put under your armpits to pad the ropes.' Jeremiah did this. 13 Then they hauled Jeremiah up with the ropes and pulled him out of the storage-well. And Jeremiah stayed in the Court of the Guard.

14 King Zedekiah had the prophet Jeremiah summoned to him at the third entrance to the Temple of Yahweh. 'I want to ask you for a word,' the king said to Jeremiah, 'keep nothing back from me.' 15 Jeremiah answered Zedekiah, 'If I do proclaim it to you, are you not sure to have me put to death? And if I give you advice, you will not listen to me.' 16 King Zedekiah then secretly swore this oath to Jeremiah, 'As Yahweh lives, giver of this life of ours, I will have you neither put to death nor handed over to these men who are determined to kill you.' 17 Jeremiah then said to Zedekiah, 'Yahweh, God Sabaoth, God of Israel, says this, "If you go out and surrender to the king of Babylon's generals, your life will be safe and this city will not be burnt down; you and your family will survive. 18 But if you do not go out and surrender to the king of Babylon's generals, this city will be handed over to the Chaldaeans and they will burn it down; nor will you yourself escape their clutches." ' 19 King Zede-

^{w} **38** = 21:9.

NEW REVISED STANDARD VERSION

of the Judeans who have deserted to the Chaldeans, for I might be handed over to them and they would abuse me." 20 Jeremiah said, "That will not happen. Just obey the voice of the LORD in what I say to you, and it shall go well with you, and your life shall be spared. 21 But if you are determined not to surrender, this is what the LORD has shown me — 22 a vision of all the women remaining in the house of the king of Judah being led out to the officials of the king of Babylon and saying,

'Your trusted friends have seduced you
and have overcome you;
Now that your feet are stuck in the mud,
they desert you.'

23 All your wives and your children shall be led out to the Chaldeans, and you yourself shall not escape from their hand, but shall be seized by the king of Babylon; and this city shall be burned with fire."

24 Then Zedekiah said to Jeremiah, "Do not let anyone else know of this conversation, or you will die. 25 If the officials should hear that I have spoken with you, and they should come and say to you, 'Just tell us what you said to the king; do not conceal it from us, or we will put you to death. What did the king say to you?' 26 then you shall say to them, 'I was presenting my plea to the king not to send me back to the house of Jonathan to die there.' " 27 All the officials did come to Jeremiah and questioned him; and he answered them in the very words the king had commanded. So they stopped questioning him, for the conversation had not been overheard. 28 And Jeremiah remained in the court of the guard until the day that Jerusalem was taken.

39 In the ninth year of King Zedekiah of Judah, in the tenth month, King Nebuchadrezzar of Babylon and all his army came against Jerusalem and besieged it; 2 in the eleventh year of Zedekiah, in the fourth month, on the ninth day of the month, a breach was made in the city. 3 When Jerusalem was taken,*f* all the officials of the king of Babylon came and sat in the middle gate: Nergal-sharezer, Samgar-nebo, Sarsechim the Rabsaris, Nergal-sharezer the Rabmag, with all the rest of the officials of the king of Babylon. 4 When King Zedekiah of Judah and all the soldiers saw them, they fled, going out of the city at night by way of the king's garden through the gate between the two walls; and they went toward the Arabah. 5 But the army of the Chaldeans pursued them, and overtook Zedekiah in the plains of Jericho; and when they had taken him, they brought him up to King Nebuchadrezzar of Babylon, at Riblah, in the land of Hamath; and he passed sentence on him. 6 The king of Babylon slaughtered the sons of Zedekiah at Riblah before his eyes; also the king of Babylon slaughtered all the nobles of Judah. 7 He put out the eyes of Zedekiah, and bound him in fetters to take him to Babylon. 8 The Chaldeans burned the king's house and the houses of the people, and broke down the walls of Jerusalem. 9 Then Nebuzaradan the captain of the guard exiled to Babylon the rest of the people who were left in the city, those who had deserted to him, and the people who remained. 10 Nebuzaradan the captain of the guard left in the land of Judah some of the poor people who owned nothing, and gave them vineyards and fields at the same time.

REVISED ENGLISH BIBLE

the Judaeans who have gone over to the enemy. The Chaldaeans may give me up to them, and their treatment of me will be ruthless.' 20 Jeremiah answered, 'You will not be given up. If you obey the LORD in everything I tell you, all will be well with you and your life will be spared. 21 But if you refuse to surrender, this is what the LORD has shown me: 22 all the women left in the king of Judah's palace will be led out to the officers of the king of Babylon. Those women will say to you:

"Your own friends have misled you
and proved too strong for you;
when your feet sank in the mud
they turned and left you."

23 All your women and children will be led out to the Chaldaeans and you yourself will not escape; you will be seized by the king of Babylon, and this city will be burnt down.'

24 Zedekiah said to Jeremiah, 'On pain of death let no one know about this conversation. 25 If the officers hear that I have been speaking with you and they come and say to you, "Tell us what you said to the king and what he said to you; hide nothing from us, and we shall not put you to death," 26 you must reply, "I was petitioning the king not to send me back to the house of Jonathan to die there." ' 27 The officers did all come and question Jeremiah, and he said to them just what the king had told him to say; so they left off questioning him and were none the wiser. 28 Jeremiah remained in the court of the guardhouse till the day Jerusalem fell.

39 In the tenth month of the ninth year of the reign of King Zedekiah of Judah, King Nebuchadrezzar of Babylon advanced with his whole army against Jerusalem, and they laid siege to it. 2 In the fourth month of the eleventh year of Zedekiah, on the ninth day of the month, the city capitulated. 3 All the officers of the king of Babylon came in and took their seats by the middle gate: Nergal-sarezer of Simmagir, Nebusarsekim the chief eunuch, Nergalsarezer the commander of the frontier troops, and all the other officers of the king of Babylon. 4 When King Zedekiah of Judah saw them, he and all his armed escort left the city by night and, fleeing by way of the king's garden through the gate called Between the Two Walls, they made their escape towards the Arabah. 5 The Chaldaean soldiers set off in pursuit and overtook Zedekiah in the lowlands of Jericho. He was seized and brought before King Nebuchadrezzar of Babylon at Riblah in the territory of Hamath, where sentence was passed on him. 6 The king of Babylon had Zedekiah's sons slain before his eyes at Riblah; he also had all the nobles of Judah put to death. 7 Then Zedekiah's eyes were blinded, and he was bound in bronze fetters to be brought to Babylon. 8 The Chaldaeans burnt the royal palace and the house of the LORD and the houses of the people, and demolished Jerusalem's walls. 9 Nebuzaradan captain of the bodyguard deported to Babylon the rest of the people left in the city, those who had defected to him, and any remaining artisans. 10 He left behind only the poorest class of people, those who owned nothing at all; to them he gave vineyards and fields.

38:28 **fell:** *so Gk; Heb.* adds when Jerusalem was captured. 39:3 **the chief eunuch:** *or* Rab-saris. **the commander . . . troops:** *or* Rab-mag. 39:8 **of the LORD and the houses:** *prob. rdg; Heb.* omits. 39:9 **artisans:** *prob. rdg, cp.* 52:15; *Heb.* people who were left.

f This clause has been transposed from 38.28

afraid of the men of Judah who have deserted to the Chaldeans; I may be handed over to them, and they will mistreat me." 20 You will not be handed over, Jeremiah answered. Please obey the voice of the LORD and do as I tell you; then it shall go well with you, and your life will be spared. 21 But if you refuse to surrender, this is what the LORD shows me: 22 All the women left in the house of Judah's king shall be brought out to the princes of Babylon's king, and they shall taunt you thus:

> "They betrayed you, outdid you,
>   your good friends!
> Now that your feet are stuck in the mud,
>   they slink away."

23 All your wives and sons shall be led forth to the Chaldeans, and you shall not escape their hands; you shall be handed over to the king of Babylon, and this city shall be destroyed with fire.

24 Then Zedekiah said to Jeremiah, "Let no one know about this conversation, or you shall die. 25 If the princes hear I spoke to you, if they come and ask you, 'Tell us what you said to the king; do not hide it from us, or we will kill you,' or, 'What did the king say to you?' 26 give them this answer: 'I petitioned the king not to send me back to Jonathan's house to die there.'" 27 When all the princes came to Jeremiah, they questioned him, and he answered them in the very words the king had commanded. They said no more to him, for nothing had been heard of the earlier conversation. 28 Thus Jeremiah stayed in the quarters of the guard till the day Jerusalem was taken.

39

When Jerusalem was taken.... 1 In the tenth month of the ninth year of Zedekiah, king of Judah, Nebuchadnezzar, king of Babylon, and all his army marched against Jerusalem and besieged it. 2 On the ninth day of the fourth month, in the eleventh year of Zedekiah, a breach was made in the city's defenses. 3 All the princes of the king of Babylon came and occupied the middle gate: Nergal-sharezer, of Simmagir, the chief officer, Nebushazban, the high dignitary, and all the other princes of the king of Babylon.... 4 When Zedekiah, king of Judah, saw them, he and all his warriors fled by night, leaving the city on the Royal Garden Road through the gate between the two walls. He went in the direction of the Arabah, 5 but the Chaldean army pursued them, and overtook and captured Zedekiah in the desert near Jericho. He was brought to Riblah, in the land of Hamath, where Nebuchadnezzar, king of Babylon, pronounced sentence upon him. 6 As Zedekiah looked on, his sons were slain at Riblah by order of the king of Babylon, who slew also all the nobles of Judah. 7 He then blinded Zedekiah and bound him in chains to bring him to Babylon.

8 The Chaldeans set fire to the king's palace and the houses of the people, and demolished the walls of Jerusalem. 9 Nebuzaradan, chief of the bodyguard, deported to Babylon the rest of the people left in the city, those who had deserted to him, and the rest of the workmen. 10 But some of the poor who had no property were left in the land of Judah by Nebuzaradan, chief of the bodyguard, and were given at the same time vineyards and farms.

kiah then said to Jeremiah, 'I am afraid of the Judaeans who have already gone over to the Chaldaeans: I might be handed over to them and they would ill-treat me.' 20 'You will not be handed over to them,' Jeremiah replied. 'Please listen to Yahweh's voice as I have relayed it to you, and then all will go well with you and your life will be safe. 21 But if you refuse to surrender, this is what Yahweh has shown me: 22 the sight of all the women left in the king of Judah's palace being led off to the king of Babylon's generals and saying:

> "They have misled you, they have triumphed over
>   you,
> those friends of yours!
> Your feet have sunk in the mud!
> They are up and away!"

23 'Yes, all your wives and children will be led off to the Chaldaeans, and you yourself will not escape their clutches but will be a prisoner in the clutches of the king of Babylon. And as for this city, it will be burnt down.'

24 Zedekiah then said to Jeremiah, 'Do not let anyone else hear these words or you will die. 25 If the chief men hear that I have been talking to you, and come and say, "Tell us what you said to the king and what the king said to you; keep nothing back from us, or we shall put you to death," 26 you must reply, "I presented this request to the king: that he would not have me sent back to Jonathan's house to die."'

27 And in fact all the chief men came to Jeremiah and questioned him. He told them exactly what the king had ordered him to say. They then left him in peace, since the conversation had not been overheard. 28 And Jeremiah stayed in the Court of the Guard until the day Jerusalem was captured. And he was there when Jerusalem actually was captured.

39

In the ninth year of Zedekiah king of Judah, in the tenth month, Nebuchadnezzar king of Babylon advanced on Jerusalem with his entire army, and they laid siege to it. 2 In the eleventh year of Zedekiah, in the fourth month, a breach was made in the city wall.

3 The king of Babylon's officials, all having made their entry, took their seats in the Middle Gate: Nergal-Sharezer, Samgar-Nebo, Sar-Sechim a high dignitary of state, Nergal-Sharezer the chief astrologer, and all the king of Babylon's other officials ...

4 On seeing them, Zedekiah king of Judah and all the fighting men fled, leaving the city under cover of dark, by way of the king's garden through the gate between the two walls, and made their way towards the Arabah. 5 But the Chaldaean troops pursued them and caught up with Zedekiah in the plains of Jericho. They captured him and took him to Nebuchadnezzar king of Babylon at Riblah in the territory of Hamath, where he passed sentence on him. 6 The king of Babylon had Zedekiah's sons slaughtered before his eyes at Riblah; the king of Babylon also had all the leading men of Judah put to death. 7 He then put out Zedekiah's eyes and, loading him with chains, carried him off to Babylon. 8 The Chaldaeans burnt down the royal palace and the private houses, and demolished the walls of Jerusalem. 9 Nebuzaradan commander of the guard deported the remainder of the population left behind in the city, the deserters who had gone over to him, and the rest of the artisans to Babylon. 10 But Nebuzaradan commander of the guard left some of the poor people behind in the country of Judah, those who had nothing, at the same time giving them vineyards and fields.

| NEW REVISED STANDARD VERSION | REVISED ENGLISH BIBLE |

NEW REVISED STANDARD VERSION

11 King Nebuchadrezzar of Babylon gave command concerning Jeremiah through Nebuzaradan, the captain of the guard, saying, 12 "Take him, look after him well and do him no harm, but deal with him as he may ask you." 13 So Nebuzaradan the captain of the guard, Nebushazban the Rabsaris, Nergal-sharezer the Rabmag, and all the chief officers of the king of Babylon sent 14 and took Jeremiah from the court of the guard. They entrusted him to Gedaliah son of Ahikam son of Shaphan to be brought home. So he stayed with his own people.

15 The word of the LORD came to Jeremiah while he was confined in the court of the guard: 16 Go and say to Ebed-melech the Ethiopian:g Thus says the LORD of hosts, the God of Israel: I am going to fulfill my words against this city for evil and not for good, and they shall be accomplished in your presence on that day. 17 But I will save you on that day, says the LORD, and you shall not be handed over to those whom you dread. 18 For I will surely save you, and you shall not fall by the sword; but you shall have your life as a prize of war, because you have trusted in me, says the LORD.

40 The word that came to Jeremiah from the LORD after Nebuzaradan the captain of the guard had let him go from Ramah, when he took him bound in fetters along with all the captives of Jerusalem and Judah who were being exiled to Babylon. 2 The captain of the guard took Jeremiah and said to him, "The LORD your God threatened this place with this disaster; 3 and now the LORD has brought it about, and has done as he said, because all of you sinned against the LORD and did not obey his voice. Therefore this thing has come upon you. 4 Now look, I have just released you today from the fetters on your hands. If you wish to come with me to Babylon, come, and I will take good care of you; but if you do not wish to come with me to Babylon, you need not come. See, the whole land is before you; go wherever you think it good and right to go. 5 If you remain,h then return to Gedaliah son of Ahikam son of Shaphan, whom the king of Babylon appointed governor of the towns of Judah, and stay with him among the people; or go wherever you think it right to go." So the captain of the guard gave him an allowance of food and a present, and let him go. 6 Then Jeremiah went to Gedaliah son of Ahikam at Mizpah, and stayed with him among the people who were left in the land.

7 When all the leaders of the forces in the open country and their troops heard that the king of Babylon had appointed Gedaliah son of Ahikam governor in the land, and had committed to him men, women, and children, those of the poorest of the land who had not been taken into exile to Babylon, 8 they went to Gedaliah at Mizpah — Ishmael son of Nethaniah, Johanan son of Kareah, Seraiah son of Tanhumeth, the sons of Ephai the Netophathite, Jezaniah son of the Maacathite, they and their troops. 9 Gedaliah son of Ahikam son of Shaphan swore to them and their troops, saying, "Do not be afraid to serve the Chaldeans. Stay in the land and serve the king of Babylon, and it shall go well with you. 10 As for me, I am staying at Mizpah to represent you before the Chaldeans who come to us; but as for you, gather wine and summer fruits and oil, and store them in your vessels, and live in the towns that you have taken over." 11 Likewise, when all the Judeans who were in Moab and among the Ammonites and in Edom and in other lands heard that the king of Babylon had left a remnant in Judah and had appointed Gedaliah son of Ahikam son of Shaphan as governor over them, 12 then all the Judeans returned from

REVISED ENGLISH BIBLE

11 King Nebuchadrezzar of Babylon sent orders about Jeremiah to Nebuzaradan captain of the guard. 12 'Hold him,' he said, 'and take good care of him; let him come to no harm, but do for him whatever he asks.' 13 So Nebuzaradan captain of the guard sent Nebushazban the chief eunuch, Nergalsarezer the commander of the frontier troops, and all the chief officers of the king of Babylon, 14 and they fetched Jeremiah from the court of the guardhouse and handed him over to Gedaliah son of Ahikam, son of Shaphan, to take him out to his residence. So he stayed with his own people.

15 While Jeremiah was imprisoned within the word of the LORD had come to him in the court of the guardhouse: 16 Go and say to Ebed-melech the Cushite: These are the words of the LORD of Hosts the God of Israel: I shall make good the words I have spoken against this city, foretelling ruin and not wellbeing, and when that day comes you will recall them. 17 But I shall preserve you on that day, says the LORD, and you will not be handed over to the men you fear. 18 I shall keep you safe, and you will not fall a victim to the sword; because you trusted in me you will escape with your life. This is the word of the LORD.

40 THE word which came from the LORD about Jeremiah: Nebuzaradan captain of the guard had taken him in chains to Ramah along with the other captives from Jerusalem and Judah who were being deported to Babylon. After he set Jeremiah free, 2 he said to him, 'The LORD your God threatened this place with disaster, 3 and has duly carried out his threat that this should happen to the people because they have sinned against the LORD and not obeyed him. 4 But as for you, Jeremiah, I am now removing the fetters from your wrists. If you so wish, come with me to Babylon, and I shall take good care of you; but if you prefer not to come, very well. The whole country lies before you; go wherever you think best.' 5 Before Jeremiah could answer, Nebuzaradan went on, 'Go back to Gedaliah son of Ahikam, son of Shaphan, whom the king of Babylon has appointed governor of the cities and towns of Judah, and stay with him among your people; or go anywhere else you choose.' Then the captain of the guard gave him provisions and a gift, and dismissed him. 6 Jeremiah went to Mizpah to Gedaliah son of Ahikam and stayed with him among the people left in the land.

7 When all the captains of the armed bands in the countryside and their men heard that the king of Babylon had appointed Gedaliah son of Ahikam to be governor of the land, and had put him in charge of the poorer class of the population, the men, women, and children who had not been deported to Babylon, 8 they, together with their men, came to him at Mizpah; they were Ishmael son of Nethaniah, and Johanan and Jonathan sons of Kareah, Seraiah son of Tanhumeth, the sons of Ephai from Netophah, and Jezaniah of Beth-maacah. 9 Gedaliah son of Ahikam, son of Shaphan, gave them this assurance: 'Do not be afraid to serve the Chaldaeans. Settle down in the land, serve the king of Babylon, and all will be well with you. 10 I for my part am to stay in Mizpah and attend on the Chaldaeans whenever they come to us; you can harvest the wine, summer fruits, and oil, store them in jars, and settle in the towns you have taken over.'

11 Likewise when all the Judaeans who were in Moab, Ammon, Edom, and other countries, heard that the king of Babylon had left a remnant in Judah and had set over them Gedaliah son of Ahikam, son of Shaphan, 12 they came back

39:11 to: so Lat.; Heb. by.   40:5 Jeremiah . . . went on: prob. rdg; Heb. unintelligible in context.

g Or Nubian; Heb Cushite   h Syr: Meaning of Heb uncertain

11 Concerning Jeremiah, Nebuchadnezzar, king of Babylon, gave the following orders through Nebuzaradan, chief of the bodyguard: 12 "Take him and look after him; let no harm befall him, but treat him as he himself requests." 13 Thereupon Nebuzaradan, chief of the bodyguard, and Nebushazban, the high dignitary, and Nergal-sharezer, the chief officer, and all the nobles of the king of Babylon, 14 had Jeremiah taken out of the quarters of the guard, and entrusted to Gedaliah, son of Ahikam, son of Shaphan, to be brought home. And so he remained among the people. 15 While Jeremiah was still imprisoned in the quarters of the guard, the word of the LORD came to him: 16 Go, tell this to Ebed-melech the Cushite: Thus says the LORD of hosts, the God of Israel: Behold, I am now fulfilling the words I spoke against this city, for evil and not for good; and this before your very eyes. 17 But on that day I will rescue you, says the LORD; you shall not be handed over to the men of whom you are afraid. 18 I will make certain that you escape and do not fall by the sword. Your life shall be spared as booty, because you trusted in me, says the LORD.

40 This word came to Jeremiah from the LORD, after Nebuzaradan, captain of the bodyguard, had released him in Ramah, where he had found him a prisoner in chains, among the captives of Jerusalem and Judah who were being exiled to Babylon. 2 When the captain of the bodyguard took charge of Jeremiah, he said to him, "The LORD, your God, foretold the ruin of this place. 3 Now he has brought about in deed what he threatened; because you sinned against the LORD and did not obey his voice, this fate has befallen you. 4 And now, I am freeing you today from the fetters that bind your hands; if it seems good to you to come with me to Babylon, you may come: I will look after you well. But if it does not please you to come to Babylon, you need not come. See, the whole land is before you; go wherever you think good and proper"; 5 and then, before he left—"or go to Gedaliah, son of Ahikam, son of Shaphan, whom the king of Babylon has appointed ruler over the cities of Judah; stay with him among the people, or go wherever you please." The captain of the bodyguard gave him food and gifts and let him go. 6 Jeremiah went to Gedaliah, son of Ahikam, in Mizpah, and stayed with him among the people left in the land.

7 When the army leaders who were still in the field with all their men heard that the king of Babylon had given Gedaliah, son of Ahikam, charge of the land, of men, women, and children, and of those poor who had not been led captive to Babylon, 8 they came with their men to Gedaliah in Mizpah: Ishmael, son of Nethaniah; Johanan, son of Kareah; Seraiah, son of Tanhumeth; the sons of Ephai of Netophah; and Jezaniah of Beth-maacah. 9 Gedaliah, son of Ahikam, son of Shaphan, adjured them and their men not to be afraid to serve the Chaldeans: to stay in the land and submit to the king of Babylon, for their own welfare, 10 saying that he himself would remain in Mizpah, as their intermediary with the Chaldeans who should come to them. They were to collect the wine, the fruit, and the oil, to store them in jars, and to settle in the cities they occupied. 11 When the people of Judah in Moab, those among the Ammonites, those in Edom, and those in all other lands heard that the king of Babylon had left a remnant in Judah, and had appointed over them Gedaliah, son of Ahikam, son of Shaphan, 12 they all returned to the land of Judah from

11 With regard to Jeremiah, Nebuchadnezzar king of Babylon had given the following orders to Nebuzaradan, commander of the guard, 12 'Take him, look after him; do him no harm, but treat him as he may ask you.' 13 He entrusted this mission to (Nebuzaradan commander of the guard,) Nebushazban the high dignitary of state, Nergal-Sharezer the chief astrologer and all the king of Babylon's other officials. 14 These despatched men to take Jeremiah from the Court of the Guard and turned him over to Gedaliah son of Ahikam, son of Shaphan for safe conduct home. So he remained among the people. 15 While Jeremiah was confined in the Court of the Guard, the word of Yahweh came to him as follows, 16 'Go and say to Ebed-Melech the Cushite, "Yahweh, God of Israel says this: Look, I am about to perform my words about this city for its ruin and not for its prosperity. That day they will come true before your eyes. 17 But I shall rescue you that day, Yahweh declares, and you will not be handed over to the hands of the men you fear. 18 Yes, I shall certainly rescue you: you will not fall to the sword; you will escape with your life, because you have put your trust in me, Yahweh declares." '

40 The word which came to Jeremiah from Yahweh after Nebuzaradan commander of the guard had released him from Ramah, where he had found him in chains with all the other captives from Jerusalem and Judah who were being deported to Babylon: 2 The commander of the guard took Jeremiah and said to him, 'Yahweh your God foretold calamity for this country, 3 and now he has brought it. He has done what he threatened to do, because you had sinned against Yahweh and would not listen to his voice; so all this has happened to you. 4 Look, today I am having your hands unchained. If you like to come with me to Babylon, come: I shall look after you. If you do not want to come with me to Babylon, do not. Look, you have the whole country before you: go wherever you think it best and most suitable to go.' 5 And before Jeremiah retired, he added, 'You can go back to Gedaliah son of Ahikam, son of Shaphan, whom the king of Babylon has appointed governor of the towns of Judah, and stay with him among the people, or go anywhere else you think suitable.' With that, the commander of the guard gave him provisions and a present, and dismissed him. 6 Jeremiah went to Mizpah, to Gedaliah son of Ahikam and stayed with him, among those people still left in the country.

7 When the military leaders who with their men were still in the field, all heard that the king of Babylon had appointed Gedaliah son of Ahikam as governor of the country, making him responsible for the men, women and children, and those of the poor country people who had not been deported to Babylon, 8 they came to Gedaliah at Mizpah: Ishmael son of Nethaniah, Johanan and Jonathan son of Kareah, Seraiah son of Tanhumeth, the sons of Ephai the Netophathite, Jezaniah son of the Maacathite, they and their men. 9 To them and to their men Gedaliah son of Ahikam, son of Shaphan, swore an oath. 'Do not be afraid', he said, 'of serving the Chaldaeans, stay in the country, serve the king of Babylon, and all will go well with you. 10 I for my part, as the man answerable to the Chaldaeans when they come to us, shall stay here at Mizpah, whereas you can harvest the wine, summer fruit and oil, fill your storage jars and settle in the towns which you have seized.' 11 Similarly, when all the Judaeans living in Moab, with the Ammonites, in Edom and elsewhere, heard that the king of Babylon had left a remnant in Judah and had appointed Gedaliah son of Ahikam, son of Shaphan as their governor,

NEW REVISED STANDARD VERSION

all the places to which they had been scattered and came to the land of Judah, to Gedaliah at Mizpah; and they gathered wine and summer fruits in great abundance.

13 Now Johanan son of Kareah and all the leaders of the forces in the open country came to Gedaliah at Mizpah 14 and said to him, "Are you at all aware that Baalis king of the Ammonites has sent Ishmael son of Nethaniah to take your life?" But Gedaliah son of Ahikam would not believe them. 15 Then Johanan son of Kareah spoke secretly to Gedaliah at Mizpah, "Please let me go and kill Ishmael son of Nethaniah, and no one else will know. Why should he take your life, so that all the Judeans who are gathered around you would be scattered, and the remnant of Judah would perish?" 16 But Gedaliah son of Ahikam said to Johanan son of Kareah, "Do not do such a thing, for you are telling a lie about Ishmael."

41 In the seventh month, Ishmael son of Nethaniah son of Elishama, of the royal family, one of the chief officers of the king, came with ten men to Gedaliah son of Ahikam, at Mizpah. As they ate bread together there at Mizpah, 2 Ishmael son of Nethaniah and the ten men with him got up and struck down Gedaliah son of Ahikam son of Shaphan with the sword and killed him, because the king of Babylon had appointed him governor in the land. 3 Ishmael also killed all the Judeans who were with Gedaliah at Mizpah, and the Chaldean soldiers who happened to be there.

4 On the day after the murder of Gedaliah, before anyone knew of it, 5 eighty men arrived from Shechem and Shiloh and Samaria, with their beards shaved and their clothes torn, and their bodies gashed, bringing grain offerings and incense to present at the temple of the LORD. 6 And Ishmael son of Nethaniah came out from Mizpah to meet them, weeping as he came. As he met them, he said to them, "Come to Gedaliah son of Ahikam." 7 When they reached the middle of the city, Ishmael son of Nethaniah and the men with him slaughtered them, and threw them[i] into a cistern. 8 But there were ten men among them who said to Ishmael, "Do not kill us, for we have stores of wheat, barley, oil, and honey hidden in the fields." So he refrained, and did not kill them along with their companions.

9 Now the cistern into which Ishmael had thrown all the bodies of the men whom he had struck down was the large cistern[j] that King Asa had made for defense against King Baasha of Israel; Ishmael son of Nethaniah filled that cistern with those whom he had killed. 10 Then Ishmael took captive all the rest of the people who were in Mizpah, the king's daughters and all the people who were left at Mizpah, whom Nebuzaradan, the captain of the guard, had committed to Gedaliah son of Ahikam. Ishmael son of Nethaniah took them captive and set out to cross over to the Ammonites.

11 But when Johanan son of Kareah and all the leaders of the forces with him heard of all the crimes that Ishmael son of Nethaniah had done, 12 they took all their men and went to fight against Ishmael son of Nethaniah. They came upon him at the great pool that is in Gibeon. 13 And when all the people who were with Ishmael saw Johanan son of Kareah and all the leaders of the forces with him, they were glad. 14 So all the people whom Ishmael had carried away captive from Mizpah turned around and came back, and went to Johanan son of Kareah. 15 But Ishmael son of Nethaniah escaped from Johanan with eight men, and went to the

REVISED ENGLISH BIBLE

to Judah from all the places where they had scattered and presented themselves before Gedaliah at Mizpah; and they gathered in a good harvest of wine and summer fruit.

13 Johanan son of Kareah and all the captains of the armed bands from the countryside came to Gedaliah at Mizpah 14 and said to him, 'Are you aware that Baalis king of the Ammonites has sent Ishmael son of Nethaniah to assassinate you?' But Gedaliah son of Ahikam would not believe them. 15 Then Johanan son of Kareah spoke privately to Gedaliah: 'Let me go, unknown to anyone else, and kill Ishmael son of Nethaniah. Why let him assassinate you, and so allow all the Judaeans who have rallied round you to be scattered and the remnant of Judah to be lost?' 16 Gedaliah son of Ahikam answered him, 'Do no such thing. What you are saying about Ishmael is not true.'

41 In the seventh month Ishmael son of Nethaniah, son of Elishama, who was a member of the royal house, came with ten men to Gedaliah son of Ahikam at Mizpah. While they were eating together there, 2 Ishmael son of Nethaniah and his ten men rose and assassinated Gedaliah son of Ahikam, son of Shaphan, whom the king of Babylon had appointed governor of the land. 3 Ishmael also murdered all the Judaeans who were with Gedaliah in Mizpah as well as the Chaldaean soldiers stationed there.

4 Next day, while the murder of Gedaliah was not yet common knowledge, 5 eighty men arrived from Shechem, Shiloh, and Samaria. They had shaved off their beards, torn their clothes, and gashed their bodies; they were carrying grain-offerings and frankincense to present to the house of the LORD. 6 Ishmael son of Nethaniah went out from Mizpah to meet them, weeping as he went, and when he met them he said, 'Come to Gedaliah son of Ahikam.' 7 But as soon as they were well inside the town, Ishmael son of Nethaniah and his men murdered them and threw their bodies into a cistern, 8 all except ten of them who said to Ishmael, 'Do not kill us, for we have a secret hoard in the country, wheat and barley, oil and honey.' So he held his hand and did not kill them with the others. 9 The cistern into which he threw all the bodies of those whom he had killed was the large one which King Asa had made when threatened by King Baasha of Israel, and this Ishmael son of Nethaniah filled with the slain. 10 He rounded up the rest of the people in Mizpah, that is the king's daughters and all who had remained in Mizpah when Nebuzaradan captain of the guard appointed Gedaliah son of Ahikam governor; and with these he set out to cross over to the Ammonites.

11 When Johanan son of Kareah and the captains of the armed bands heard of all the crimes committed by Ishmael son of Nethaniah, 12 they mustered their men and set out to attack him. They came up with him by the great pool in Gibeon. 13 The people with Ishmael were glad when they saw Johanan son of Kareah and all the captains of the armed bands with him, 14 while those whom Ishmael had taken prisoner at Mizpah turned and joined Johanan son of Kareah. 15 But Ishmael son of Nethaniah escaped from Johanan with eight men to make his way to the Ammonites.

---

[i] Syr: Heb lacks *and threw them*; compare verse 9 [j] Gk: Heb *whom he had killed by the hand of Gedaliah*

41:1 **royal house:** *so Gk; Heb. adds* and the chief officers of the king. 41:9 **was . . . one:** *so Gk; Heb.* by the hand of Gedaliah.

NEW AMERICAN BIBLE | NEW JERUSALEM BIBLE

the places to which they had scattered. They went to Gedaliah at Mizpah and had a rich harvest of wine and fruit.

13 Now Johanan, son of Kareah, and all the leaders of the armies in the field came to Gedaliah in Mizpah 14 and asked him whether he did not know that Baalis, the king of the Ammonites, had sent Ishmael, son of Nethaniah, to assassinate him. 15 But Gedaliah, son of Ahikam, would not believe them. Then Johanan, son of Kareah, said secretly to Gedaliah in Mizpah: "Let me go and kill Ishmael, son of Nethaniah; no one will know it. Why should he be allowed to kill you? All the Jews who have now rallied to you will be dispersed and the remnant of Judah will perish." 16 Nevertheless, Gedaliah, son of Ahikam, answered Johanan, son of Kareah, "You shall do nothing of the kind; you have lied about Ishmael."

41 In the seventh month Ishmael, son of Nethaniah, son of Elishama, of royal descent, one of the king's nobles, came with ten men to Gedaliah, son of Ahikam, at Mizpah. And while they were together at table in Mizpah, 2 Ishmael, son of Nethaniah, and the ten who were with him, rose up and attacked with swords Gedaliah, son of Ahikam, son of Shaphan, whom the king of Babylon had made ruler over the land; and they killed him. 3 Ishmael also slew all the men of Judah of military age who were with Gedaliah and the Chaldean soldiers who were there.

4 The second day after the murder of Gedaliah, before anyone knew of it, 5 eighty men with beards shaved off, clothes in rags, and with gashes on their bodies came from Shechem, Shiloh, and Samaria, bringing food offerings and incense for the house of the LORD. 6 Ishmael, son of Nethaniah, went out from Mizpah to meet them, weeping as he went. 7 "Come to Gedaliah, son of Ahikam," he said as he met them. When they were once inside the city, Ishmael, son of Nethaniah, and his men slew them and threw them into the cistern. 8 But there were ten among them who pleaded with Ishmael: "Do not kill us; we have stores buried in the field: wheat and barley, oil and honey." And so he spared them and did not kill them, as he had killed their companions. 9 The cistern into which Ishmael threw all the corpses of the men he had killed was the large one made by King Asa to defend himself against Baasha, king of Israel; this cistern Ishmael, son of Nethaniah, filled with the slain.

10 Ishmael, son of Nethaniah, led away the remnant of the people left in Mizpah and the princesses, whom Nebuzaradan, captain of the bodyguard, had confided to Gedaliah, son of Ahikam. With these captives, Ishmael, son of Nethaniah, set out to make his way to the Ammonites.

11 But when Johanan, son of Kareah, and the other army leaders with him heard of the crimes Ishmael, son of Nethaniah, had committed, 12 they took all their men and set out to attack Ishmael, son of Nethaniah. They overtook him at the Great Waters in Gibeon. 13 At the sight of Johanan, son of Kareah, and the other army leaders, the people who were Ishmael's captives rejoiced. 14 All of those whom Ishmael had brought away from Mizpah went over to Johanan, son of Kareah. 15 But Ishmael, son of Nethaniah, escaped from Johanan and fled to the Ammonites with eight men. 16 Then

12 the Judaeans all came back from wherever they had been driven. On their return to the land of Judah, to Gedaliah at Mizpah, they harvested an immense quantity of wine and summer fruit.

13 Now Johanan son of Kareah and all the military leaders still in the field, came to Gedaliah at Mizpah 14 and said to him, 'Are you aware that Baalis king of the Ammonites has sent Ishmael son of Nethaniah to assassinate you?' But Gedaliah son of Ahikam would not believe them. 15 Johanan son of Kareah then spoke in secret to Gedaliah at Mizpah, as follows: 'Please let me go and kill Ishmael son of Nethaniah, and no one will be any the wiser. Why should he assassinate you and cause the dispersal of all the Judaeans who have rallied round you. Why should the remnant of Judah perish?' 16 But Gedaliah son of Ahikam replied to Johanan son of Kareah, 'You will do no such thing, for what you say about Ishmael is false.'

41 In the seventh month, however, Ishmael son of Nethaniah son of Elishama, who was of royal descent, came with officers of the king and ten men to Gedaliah son of Ahikam at Mizpah. And as they were taking their meal together, there at Mizpah, 2 Ishmael son of Nethaniah stood up with his ten men, and attacking Gedaliah son of Ahikam, son of Shaphan, with their swords, they killed the man whom the king of Babylon had made governor of the country. 3 And all the Judaeans who were with him, that is with Gedaliah at Mizpah, and the Chaldaean soldiers who happened to be there, Ishmael killed too.

4 On the day after the murder of Gedaliah, before the news had become known, 5 eighty men arrived from Shechem, Shiloh and Samaria, with their beards shaved off, their clothing torn, and covered in self-inflicted gashes; they were bringing cereal offerings and incense with them to present to the Temple of Yahweh. 6 Ishmael son of Nethaniah went out of Mizpah to meet them, weeping as he went. When he met them he said, 'Come to Gedaliah son of Ahikam.' 7 But once they were well inside the town, Ishmael son of Nethaniah slaughtered them, with the help of his men, and had them thrown into the storage-well. 8 There were ten of them, however, who said to Ishmael, 'Do not kill us: we have stocks of wheat and barley, oil and honey, hidden away in the fields.' So he spared them and did not kill them with their brothers. 9 The storage-well into which Ishmael threw the corpses of all the men he had killed was a large one, the one which King Asa had built as a precaution against Baasha king of Israel. Ishmael son of Nethaniah filled it with the slaughtered men. 10 Ishmael then took all the rest of the people prisoner who were at Mizpah, the king's daughters and all the remaining people in Mizpah, whom Nebuzaradan, commander of the guard, had entrusted to Gedaliah son of Ahikam. Ishmael son of Nethaniah took them prisoner and set out, intending to cross over to the Ammonites.

11 When Johanan son of Kareah and all the military leaders who were with him heard about all the crimes committed by Ishmael son of Nethaniah, 12 they mustered all their men and set out to attack Ishmael son of Nethaniah. They caught up with him at the great Pool of Gibeon. 13 At the sight of Johanan son of Kareah and all the military leaders with him, all the people with Ishmael were delighted. 14 All the people whom Ishmael had taken as prisoners from Mizpah turned about, went back and joined Johanan son of Kareah. 15 Ishmael son of Nethaniah, however, escaped from Johanan with eight of his men and fled to the Ammonites. 16 Johanan

| NEW REVISED STANDARD VERSION | REVISED ENGLISH BIBLE |

Ammonites. 16 Then Johanan son of Kareah and all the leaders of the forces with him took all the rest of the people whom Ishmael son of Nethaniah had carried away captive[k] from Mizpah after he had slain Gedaliah son of Ahikam—soldiers, women, children, and eunuchs, whom Johanan brought back from Gibeon.[l] 17 And they set out, and stopped at Geruth Chimham near Bethlehem, intending to go to Egypt 18 because of the Chaldeans; for they were afraid of them, because Ishmael son of Nethaniah had killed Gedaliah son of Ahikam, whom the king of Babylon had made governor over the land.

42 Then all the commanders of the forces, and Johanan son of Kareah and Azariah[m] son of Hoshaiah, and all the people from the least to the greatest, approached 2 the prophet Jeremiah and said, "Be good enough to listen to our plea, and pray to the LORD your God for us—for all this remnant. For there are only a few of us left out of many, as your eyes can see. 3 Let the LORD your God show us where we should go and what we should do." 4 The prophet Jeremiah said to them, "Very well: I am going to pray to the LORD your God as you request, and whatever the LORD answers you I will tell you; I will keep nothing back from you." 5 They in their turn said to Jeremiah, "May the LORD be a true and faithful witness against us if we do not act according to everything that the LORD your God sends us through you. 6 Whether it is good or bad, we will obey the voice of the LORD our God to whom we are sending you, in order that it may go well with us when we obey the voice of the LORD our God."

7 At the end of ten days the word of the LORD came to Jeremiah. 8 Then he summoned Johanan son of Kareah and all the commanders of the forces who were with him, and all the people from the least to the greatest, 9 and said to them, "Thus says the LORD, the God of Israel, to whom you sent me to present your plea before him: 10 If you will only remain in this land, then I will build you up and not pull you down; I will plant you, and not pluck you up; for I am sorry for the disaster that I have brought upon you. 11 Do not be afraid of the king of Babylon, as you have been; do not be afraid of him, says the LORD, for I am with you, to save you and to rescue you from his hand. 12 I will grant you mercy, and he will have mercy on you and restore you to your native soil. 13 But if you continue to say, 'We will not stay in this land,' thus disobeying the voice of the LORD your God 14 and saying, 'No, we will go to the land of Egypt, where we shall not see war, or hear the sound of the trumpet, or be hungry for bread, and there we will stay,' 15 then hear the word of the LORD, O remnant of Judah. Thus says the LORD of hosts, the God of Israel: If you are determined to enter Egypt and go to settle there, 16 then the sword that you fear shall overtake you there, in the land of Egypt; and the famine that you dread shall follow close after you into Egypt; and there you shall die. 17 All the people who have determined to go to Egypt to settle there shall die by the sword, by famine, and by pestilence; they shall have no remnant or survivor from the disaster that I am bringing upon them.

18 "For thus says the LORD of hosts, the God of Israel: Just as my anger and my wrath were poured out on the inhabitants of Jerusalem, so my wrath will be poured out on you when you go to Egypt. You shall become an object of execration and horror, of cursing and ridicule. You shall see this place no more. 19 The LORD has said to you, O remnant of Judah, Do not go to Egypt. Be well aware that I have warned you today 20 that you have made a fatal mistake. For

16 Johanan son of Kareah and the captains of the armed bands took from Mizpah all the survivors whom he had rescued from Ishmael son of Nethaniah after the murder of Gedaliah son of Ahikam—men, both armed and unarmed, women, children, and eunuchs, whom he had brought back from Gibeon. 17 They started out and broke their journey at Kimham's holding near Bethlehem, on their way into Egypt 18 to escape the Chaldaeans. They were afraid of them because Ishmael son of Nethaniah had assassinated Gedaliah son of Ahikam, whom the king of Babylon had appointed governor of the country.

42 All the captains of the armed bands, including Johanan son of Kareah and Azariah son of Hoshaiah, together with the entire people, high and low, approached 2 the prophet Jeremiah and said, 'May our petition be acceptable to you: Intercede with the LORD your God on our behalf and on behalf of this remnant; as you see for yourself, only a few of us remain out of many. 3 Pray that the LORD your God may tell us which way we are to take and what we ought to do.' 4 Jeremiah answered, 'I have heard your request. I shall pray to the LORD your God as you ask, and whatever answer the LORD gives I shall tell you, keeping nothing back.' 5 They said to Jeremiah, 'May the LORD be a true and faithful witness against us if we do not act exactly as the LORD your God sends you to tell us. 6 Whether it is favourable to us or not, we shall obey the LORD our God to whom we are sending you, in order that it may be well with us through our obedience to him.'

7 When after an interval of ten days the word of the LORD came to Jeremiah, 8 he summoned Johanan son of Kareah, all the captains of the armed bands who were with him, and all the people, both high and low, 9 and addressed them: These are the words of the LORD the God of Israel, to whom you sent me with your petition. 10 If you remain in this land, then I shall build you up and not pull you down, I shall plant you and not uproot you; I grieve for the disaster which I have inflicted on you. 11 Do not be afraid of the king of Babylon whom you now fear. Do not be afraid of him, says the LORD, for I am with you, to save you and deliver you from his power. 12 I shall show you compassion, so that he too has compassion on you, and will let you stay on your own soil. 13 But it may be that you will disobey the LORD your God and insist, 'We are not going to stay in this land. 14 No, we shall go to Egypt, where we shall see no sign of war, never hear the sound of the trumpet, and suffer no lack of food; it is there we shall live.' 15 In that case hear the word of the LORD, you remnant of Judah. These are the words of the LORD of Hosts the God of Israel: If you are determined to go to Egypt, if you do go and settle there, 16 then the sword you fear will overtake you there in Egypt, and the famine you dread will dog you, even in Egypt, and there you will die. 17 All who insist on going to settle in Egypt will die by sword, famine, or pestilence; not one will escape or survive the disaster I shall bring on them.

18 These are the words of the LORD of Hosts the God of Israel: As my anger and my wrath were poured out on the inhabitants of Jerusalem, so will my wrath be poured out on you when you go to Egypt; you will become an object of execration and horror, of cursing and reproach, and you will never see this place again. 19 To you, then, remnant of Judah, the LORD says: Do not go to Egypt. Make no mistake; I give you solemn warning this day. 20 You deceived

---

[k] Cn: Heb *whom he recovered from Ishmael son of Nethaniah*
[l] Meaning of Heb uncertain   [m] Gk: Heb *Jezaniah*

42:1 **Azariah:** *so Gk, cp. 43:2; Heb.* Jezaniah.

NEW AMERICAN BIBLE

Johanan, son of Kareah, and all his army leaders took charge of the remnant of the people, both the soldiers and the women and children with their guardians, whom Ishmael, son of Nethaniah, had brought away from Mizpah after he killed Gedaliah, son of Ahikim. From Gibeon, 17 they retreated to the lodging place of Chimham near Bethlehem, where they stopped, intending to flee into Egypt. 18 They were afraid of the Chaldeans, because Ishmael, son of Nethaniah, had slain Gedaliah, son of Ahikam, whom the king of Babylon had made ruler in the land of Judah.

42 Then all the army leaders, Johanan, son of Kareah, Azariah, son of Hoshaiah, and all the people, high and low, approached the prophet Jeremiah 2 and said, "Grant our petition; pray for us to the LORD, your God, for all this remnant. We are now few who once were many, as you well see. 3 Let the LORD, your God, show us what way we should take and what we should do." 4 Very well! the prophet Jeremiah answered them: I will pray to the LORD, your God, as you desire; whatever the LORD answers you, I will tell you; I will withhold nothing from you. 5 And they said to Jeremiah, "May the LORD be our witness: we will truly and faithfully follow all the instructions the LORD, your God, will send us. 6 Whether it is pleasant or difficult, we will obey the command of the LORD, our God, to whom we are sending you, so that it will go well with us for obeying the command of the LORD, our God."

7 Ten days passed before the word of the LORD came to Jeremiah. 8 Then he called Johanan, son of Kareah, his army leaders, and all the people, high and low, 9 and said to them: Thus says the LORD, the God of Israel, to whom you sent me to offer your prayer: 10 If you remain quietly in this land I will build you up, and not tear you down; I will plant you, not uproot you; for I regret the evil I have done you. 11 Do not fear the king of Babylon, before whom you are now afraid; do not fear him, says the LORD, for I am with you to save you, to rescue you from his power. 12 I will grant you mercy, so that he will be sorry for you and let you return to your land. 13 But if you disobey the voice of the LORD, your God, and decide not to remain in this land, 14 saying, "No, we will go to Egypt, where we will see no more of war, hear the trumpet alarm no longer, nor hunger for bread; there we will live"; 15 then listen to the word of the LORD, remnant of Judah: Thus says the LORD of hosts, the God of Israel: If you are determined to go to Egypt, when you arrive there to stay, 16 the sword you fear shall reach you in the land of Egypt; the hunger you dread shall cling to you no less in Egypt, and there you shall die. 17 All those men who determine to go to Egypt to stay, shall die by the sword, famine, and pestilence; not one shall survive or escape the evil that I will bring upon them. 18 For thus says the LORD of hosts, the God of Israel: Just as my furious anger was poured out upon the citizens of Jerusalem, so shall my anger be poured out on you when you reach Egypt. You shall become an example of malediction and horror, a curse and a reproach, and you shall never see this place again.

19 It is the LORD who has spoken to you, remnant of Judah; do not go to Egypt! You can never say that I did not warn you this day. 20 At the cost of your lives you have

NEW JERUSALEM BIBLE

son of Kareah and all the military leaders with him then rallied all the remaining people whom Ishmael son of Nethaniah had taken as prisoners from Mizpah after killing Gedaliah son of Ahikam: men — fighting men — women, children and eunuchs, whom they brought back from Gibeon. 17 Setting off, they made a halt at Khan Kimham near Bethlehem, intending to go on to Egypt, 18 to get away from the Chaldaeans. They were now terrified of them, since Ishmael son of Nethaniah had killed Gedaliah son of Ahikam whom the king of Babylon had made governor of the country.

42 Then all the military leaders, in particular Johanan son of Kareah and Azariah son of Hoshaiah, and all the people from least to greatest, approached 2 the prophet Jeremiah and said, 'Please hear our petition and intercede with Yahweh your God for us and for all this remnant — and how few of us are left out of many, your own eyes can see — 3 so that Yahweh your God may show us the way we are to go and what we must do.' 4 The prophet Jeremiah replied, 'I hear you; I will indeed pray to Yahweh your God as you ask; and whatever answer Yahweh your God gives you, I will tell you, keeping nothing back from you.' 5 They in their turn said to Jeremiah, 'May Yahweh be a true and faithful witness against us, if we do not follow the instructions that Yahweh your God sends us through you. 6 Whether we like it or not, we shall obey the voice of Yahweh our God to whom we are sending you, so that we may prosper by obeying the voice of Yahweh our God.'

7 Ten days later the word of Yahweh came to Jeremiah. 8 He then summoned Johanan son of Kareah and all the military leaders who were with him, and all the people from least to greatest, 9 and said, 'Yahweh, God of Israel, to whom you deputed me to present your petition says this, 10 "If you will only stay in this country, I shall build you and not overthrow you; I shall plant you and not uproot you, for I am sorry about the disaster I have inflicted on you. 11 Do not be afraid of the king of Babylon, whom you fear now; do not fear him, Yahweh declares, for I am with you to save you and rescue you from his clutches. 12 I shall take pity on you, so that he pities you and lets you return to your native soil. 13 But if you say: We will not stay in this country; if you disobey the voice of Yahweh your God, 14 and say: No, Egypt is where we shall go, where we shall not see war or hear the trumpet-call or go short of food; that is where we want to live; 15 in that case, remnant of Judah, listen to Yahweh's word: Yahweh Sabaoth, God of Israel, says this: If you are determined to go to Egypt, and if you do go and settle there, 16 the sword you fear will overtake you there in Egypt, and there you will die. 17 Yes, all those who are determined to go to Egypt and settle there, will die by sword, famine and plague: not a single one of them will survive or escape the disaster I shall inflict on them. 18 Yes, Yahweh Sabaoth, the God of Israel, says this: Just as my furious anger was poured out on the inhabitants of Jerusalem, so will my fury be poured out on you if you go to Egypt: you will become an object of execration and horror, a curse, a laughing-stock; and you will never see this place again." 19 Remnant of Judah, Yahweh has told you, "Do not go into Egypt." Understand clearly that today I have given you a solemn warning. 20 You were not being sincere when

you yourselves sent me to the LORD your God, saying, 'Pray for us to the LORD our God, and whatever the LORD our God says, tell us and we will do it.' 21 So I have told you today, but you have not obeyed the voice of the LORD your God in anything that he sent me to tell you. 22 Be well aware, then, that you shall die by the sword, by famine, and by pestilence in the place where you desire to go and settle."

43 When Jeremiah finished speaking to all the people all these words of the LORD their God, with which the LORD their God had sent him to them, 2 Azariah son of Hoshaiah and Johanan son of Kareah and all the other insolent men said to Jeremiah, "You are telling a lie. The LORD our God did not send you to say, 'Do not go to Egypt to settle there'; 3 but Baruch son of Neriah is inciting you against us, to hand us over to the Chaldeans, in order that they may kill us or take us into exile in Babylon." 4 So Johanan son of Kareah and all the commanders of the forces and all the people did not obey the voice of the LORD, to stay in the land of Judah. 5 But Johanan son of Kareah and all the commanders of the forces took all the remnant of Judah who had returned to settle in the land of Judah from all the nations to which they had been driven — 6 the men, the women, the children, the princesses, and everyone whom Nebuzaradan the captain of the guard had left with Gedaliah son of Ahikam son of Shaphan; also the prophet Jeremiah and Baruch son of Neriah. 7 And they came into the land of Egypt, for they did not obey the voice of the LORD. And they arrived at Tahpanhes.

8 Then the word of the LORD came to Jeremiah in Tahpanhes: 9 Take some large stones in your hands, and bury them in the clay pavement[n] that is at the entrance to Pharaoh's palace in Tahpanhes. Let the Judeans see you do it, 10 and say to them, Thus says the LORD of hosts, the God of Israel: I am going to send and take my servant King Nebuchadrezzar of Babylon, and he[o] will set his throne above these stones that I have buried, and he will spread his royal canopy over them. 11 He shall come and ravage the land of Egypt, giving

> those who are destined for pestilence, to
> pestilence,
> and those who are destined for captivity, to
> captivity,
> and those who are destined for the sword, to
> the sword.

12 He[p] shall kindle a fire in the temples of the gods of Egypt; and he shall burn them and carry them away captive; and he shall pick clean the land of Egypt, as a shepherd picks his cloak clean of vermin; and he shall depart from there safely. 13 He shall break the obelisks of Heliopolis, which is in the land of Egypt; and the temples of the gods of Egypt he shall burn with fire.

44 The word that came to Jeremiah for all the Judeans living in the land of Egypt, at Migdol, at Tahpanhes, at Memphis, and in the land of Pathros, 2 Thus says the LORD of hosts, the God of Israel: You yourselves have seen all the disaster that I have brought on Jerusalem and on all the towns of Judah. Look at them; today they are a desolation, without an inhabitant in them, 3 because of the wickedness that they committed, provoking me to anger, in that they went to make offerings and serve other gods that they had not known, neither they, nor you, nor your ancestors. 4 Yet I persistently sent to you all my servants the prophets, saying, "I beg you not to do this abominable thing that I hate!" 5 But they did not listen or incline their ear, to turn from their wickedness and make no offerings to other gods.

yourselves when you sent me to the LORD your God and said, 'Intercede for us with the LORD our God; tell us exactly what the LORD our God says and we shall do it.' 21 I have told it all to you today; but you have not obeyed the LORD your God in what he sent me to tell you. 22 So now be sure of this: you will die by sword, famine, and pestilence in the place where you want to go and live.

43 When Jeremiah had finished reporting to the people all that the LORD their God had sent him to say, 2 Azariah son of Hoshaiah and Johanan son of Kareah and their party had the effrontery to say to Jeremiah, 'You are lying! The LORD our God has not sent you to forbid us to go and make our home in Egypt; 3 it is Baruch son of Neriah who is inciting you against us in order to put us in the power of the Chaldaeans, to be killed or deported to Babylon.'

4 Johanan son of Kareah and the captains of the armed bands and all the people refused to obey the LORD's command to stay in Judah. 5 Johanan and the captains collected the remnant of Judah, all who had returned from the countries among which they had been scattered to make their home in Judah — 6 men, women, and children, including the king's daughters, everyone whom Nebuzaradan captain of the guard had left with Gedaliah son of Ahikam, son of Shaphan, as well as the prophet Jeremiah and Baruch son of Neriah; 7 and in defiance of the LORD's command they all went to Egypt and arrived at Tahpanhes.

8 The word of the LORD came to Jeremiah in Tahpanhes: 9 Take some large stones and set them in cement in the pavement at the entrance to Pharaoh's palace in Tahpanhes. Let the Judaeans see you do it, 10 and say to them: These are the words of the LORD of Hosts the God of Israel: I shall send for my servant King Nebuchadrezzar of Babylon, and he will place his throne on these stones that I have set here, and spread his canopy over them. 11 He will come and vanquish Egypt:

> Those who are for the plague shall go to the
> plague,
> those for captivity to captivity,
> and those for the sword to the sword.

12 He will set fire to the temples of the Egyptian gods, burning the buildings and carrying the gods into captivity. He will scour the land of Egypt as a shepherd scours his clothes to rid them of lice. He will come out of Egypt unscathed. 13 He will smash the sacred pillars of Beth-shemesh in Egypt and burn down the temples of the Egyptian gods.

44 The word that came to Jeremiah for all the Judaeans living in Egypt, at Migdol, Tahpanhes, Noph, and in the district of Pathros: 2 These are the words of the LORD of Hosts the God of Israel: You have seen all the disaster I brought on Jerusalem and on all the towns of Judah: today they lie in ruins and are left uninhabited, 3 all because of the wickedness of those who provoked me to anger by going after other gods, gods unknown to them, by burning sacrifices in their service. It was you and your forefathers who did this. 4 Constantly I sent all my servants the prophets to you with this warning: 'Do not do this abominable thing, which I detest.' 5 But your forefathers would not listen or pay any heed. They did not give up their wickedness or cease to burn sacrifices to other gods; 6 so my anger and

---

[n] Meaning of Heb uncertain   [o] Gk Syr: Heb *I*   [p] Gk Syr Vg: Heb *I*

43:10 **he will place:** *so Gk; Heb.* I shall place.   43:12 **He will set fire:** *so Gk; Heb.* I shall set fire.

deceived me, sending me to the LORD, your God, saying, "Pray for us to the LORD, our God; make known to us all that the LORD, our God, shall say, and we will do it." 21 Today I proclaim his message, but you obey the voice of the LORD, your God, in nothing that he has commissioned me to make known to you. 22 Have no doubt of this, you shall die by the sword, famine, and pestilence in the place where you wish to go and settle.

43 When Jeremiah finished speaking to the people all these words of the LORD, their God, with which the LORD had sent him to them, 2 Azariah, son of Hoshaiah, Johanan, son of Kareah, and all the insolent men shouted to Jeremiah: "You lie; it was not the LORD, our God, who sent you to tell us not to go to Egypt to settle. 3 It is Baruch, son of Neriah, who stirs you up against us, to hand us over to the Chaldeans to be killed or exiled to Babylon."

4 Johanan, son of Kareah, and the rest of the leaders and the people did not obey the LORD's command to stay in the land of Judah. 5 Instead, Johanan, son of Kareah, and all the army leaders took along the whole remnant of Judah that had been dispersed among the nations and had returned thence to dwell again in the land of Judah: 6 men, women, and children, the princesses and everyone whom Nebuzaradan, captain of the bodyguard, had entrusted to Gedaliah, son of Ahikam, son of Shaphan; also Jeremiah, the prophet, and Baruch, son of Neriah. 7 Against the LORD's command they went to Egypt, and arrived at Tahpanhes. . . .

8 This word of the LORD came to Jeremiah in Tahpanhes: 9 Take with you large stones and sink them in mortar in the brickyard at the entrance to the royal building in Tahpanhes, while the men of Judah look on, 10 and then say to them: Thus says the LORD of hosts, the God of Israel: I will send for my servant Nebuchadnezzar, king of Babylon, and bring him here. He will set his throne upon these stones which I, Jeremiah, have sunk, and stretch his canopy over them. 11 He shall come and strike the land of Egypt: with death, whoever is marked for death; with exile, everyone destined for exile; with the sword, all who are intended for the sword. 12 He shall set fire to the temples of Egypt's gods, and burn the gods or carry them off. As a shepherd delouses his cloak, he shall delouse the land of Egypt and depart victorious. 13 He shall smash the obelisks of the temple of the sun in the land of Egypt and destroy with fire the temples of the Egyptian gods.

44 This word came to Jeremiah for all the people of Judah who were living in Egypt, at Migdol, Tahpanhes, and Memphis, and in Upper Egypt: 2 Thus says the LORD of hosts, the God of Israel: You have seen all the evil I brought on Jerusalem and the other cities of Judah. Today they are ruins and uninhabited, 3 because of the evil they did to provoke me, going after strange gods, serving them and sacrificing to them, gods which neither they, nor you, nor your fathers knew. 4 Though I kept sending to you all my servants the prophets, with the plea not to commit this horrible deed which I hate, 5 they would not listen or accept the warning to turn away from the evil of sacrificing to strange gods. 6 Therefore the fury of my anger poured forth

you sent me to Yahweh your God and said, "Intercede for us with Yahweh our God; tell us exactly what Yahweh our God says and we will do it." 21 Today I have told you, but you have not obeyed the voice of Yahweh your God or any part of the message he sent you to give you. 22 So understand this clearly: you will die by sword, famine and plague in the place where you want to go and settle.'

43 When Jeremiah had finished telling all the people all the words of Yahweh their God, which Yahweh their God had sent him to tell them—all the words quoted above— 2 Azariah son of Hoshaiah, and Johanan son of Kareah, and all those arrogant men, said to Jeremiah, 'You are lying. Yahweh our God did not send you to say, "Do not go to Egypt and settle there." 3 It was Baruch son of Neriah, who keeps inciting you against us, to hand us over to the Chaldaeans so that they can put us to death or deport us to Babylon.'

4 So neither Johanan nor any of the military leaders nor any of the people obeyed the voice of Yahweh by staying in the country of Judah. 5 Instead, Johanan son of Kareah and all the military leaders led off the entire remnant of Judah, those who had come back from all the nations where they had been driven to live in the country of Judah: 6 men, women, children, the royal princesses too, and every single person that Nebuzaradan commander of the guard had left with Gedaliah son of Ahikam, son of Shaphan, including the prophet Jeremiah and Baruch son of Neriah. 7 And so, in disobedience to the voice of Yahweh, they reached Egypt and arrived at Tahpanhes.

8 At Tahpanhes the word of Yahweh was addressed to Jeremiah as follows, 9 'Take some large stones and bury them in the cement on the terrace outside the entrance of Pharaoh's palace in Tahpanhes, where the Judaeans can see you. 10 Then say to them, "Yahweh, God of Israel, says this: Look, I shall send for my servant Nebuchadnezzar, king of Babylon, and he will place his throne on these stones I have buried, and spread his canopy above them. 11 When he comes, he will defeat Egypt:

Those for the plague, to the plague;
those for captivity, to captivity;
those for the sword, to the sword!^{x}

12 "He will set fire to the temples of the gods of Egypt; he will burn these gods or take them prisoner; like a shepherd wrapping his cloak round him, so he will wrap Egypt round him, and then leave without anyone laying hands on him. 13 He will break the obelisks of the temple of the Sun in Egypt, and burn down the temples of the gods of Egypt."'

44 The word that came to Jeremiah for all the Judaeans living in Egypt, those, that is, living in Migdol, Tahpanhes, Noph and the territory of Pathros.

2 'Yahweh Sabaoth, God of Israel, says this, "You have seen all the disaster I have brought on Jerusalem and all the towns of Judah; today they lie in ruins and uninhabited. 3 This was because of the wicked deeds they committed to provoke my anger, by going and offering incense and serving other gods whom neither they, nor you, nor your ancestors knew anything about, 4 although I urgently and untiringly sent you all my servants the prophets to say: You must not do this loathsome thing, which I hate. 5 But they would not listen or pay attention, and turn from their wickedness and stop offering incense to other gods. 6 And so my furious

^{x} **43** = 15:2.

NEW REVISED STANDARD VERSION

REVISED ENGLISH BIBLE

6 So my wrath and my anger were poured out and kindled in the towns of Judah and in the streets of Jerusalem; and they became a waste and a desolation, as they still are today. 7 And now thus says the LORD God of hosts, the God of Israel: Why are you doing such great harm to yourselves, to cut off man and woman, child and infant, from the midst of Judah, leaving yourselves without a remnant? 8 Why do you provoke me to anger with the works of your hands, making offerings to other gods in the land of Egypt where you have come to settle? Will you be cut off and become an object of cursing and ridicule among all the nations of the earth? 9 Have you forgotten the crimes of your ancestors, of the kings of Judah, of theirq wives, your own crimes and those of your wives, which they committed in the land of Judah and in the streets of Jerusalem? 10 They have shown no contrition or fear to this day, nor have they walked in my law and my statutes that I set before you and before your ancestors.

11 Therefore thus says the LORD of hosts, the God of Israel: I am determined to bring disaster on you, to bring all Judah to an end. 12 I will take the remnant of Judah who are determined to come to the land of Egypt to settle, and they shall perish, everyone; in the land of Egypt they shall fall; by the sword and by famine they shall perish; from the least to the greatest, they shall die by the sword and by famine; and they shall become an object of execration and horror, of cursing and ridicule. 13 I will punish those who live in the land of Egypt, as I have punished Jerusalem, with the sword, with famine, and with pestilence, 14 so that none of the remnant of Judah who have come to settle in the land of Egypt shall escape or survive or return to the land of Judah. Although they long to go back to live there, they shall not go back, except some fugitives.

15 Then all the men who were aware that their wives had been making offerings to other gods, and all the women who stood by, a great assembly, all the people who lived in Pathros in the land of Egypt, answered Jeremiah: 16 "As for the word that you have spoken to us in the name of the LORD, we are not going to listen to you. 17 Instead, we will do everything that we have vowed, make offerings to the queen of heaven and pour out libations to her, just as we and our ancestors, our kings and our officials, used to do in the towns of Judah and in the streets of Jerusalem. We used to have plenty of food, and prospered, and saw no misfortune. 18 But from the time we stopped making offerings to the queen of heaven and pouring out libations to her, we have lacked everything and have perished by the sword and by famine." 19 And the women said,r "Indeed we will go on making offerings to the queen of heaven and pouring out libations to her; do you think that we made cakes for her, marked with her image, and poured out libations to her without our husbands' being involved?"

20 Then Jeremiah said to all the people, men and women, all the people who were giving him this answer: 21 "As for the offerings that you made in the towns of Judah and in the streets of Jerusalem, you and your ancestors, your kings and your officials, and the people of the land, did not the LORD remember them? Did it not come into his mind? 22 The LORD could no longer bear the sight of your evil doings, the abominations that you committed; therefore your land became a desolation and a waste and a curse, without inhabitant, as it is to this day. 23 It is because you burned offerings, and because you sinned against the LORD and did not obey the voice of the LORD or walk in his law and in his statutes and in his decrees, that this disaster has befallen you, as is still evident today."

wrath were poured out, and swept like fire through the towns of Judah and the streets of Jerusalem, until they became the desolate ruin they are today.

7 Now these are the words of the LORD the God of Hosts, the God of Israel: Why bring so great a disaster on yourselves? Why bring destruction on Judaeans, men and women, children and babes, and leave yourselves without a survivor? 8 This is what comes of provoking me by your idol-worship in burning sacrifices to other gods in Egypt where you have made your home. You will destroy yourselves and become an object of cursing and reproach among all the nations on earth. 9 Have you forgotten the wickedness committed by your forefathers, by the kings of Judah and their wives, by yourselves and your wives in the land of Judah and in the streets of Jerusalem? 10 To this day no remorse has been shown, no reverence, no obedience to the law and the statutes which I set before you and your forefathers.

11 These, therefore, are the words of the LORD of Hosts the God of Israel: I have resolved to bring disaster on you and to exterminate all the people of Judah. 12 I shall deal with the remnant of Judah who decided to go to Egypt and make their home there; in Egypt they will all meet their end. Some will fall by the sword, others will meet their end by famine. High and low alike will die by sword or by famine and will be an object of execration and horror, of cursing and reproach. 13 I shall punish those who live in Egypt as I punished those in Jerusalem, by sword, famine, and pestilence. 14 Those who had remained in Judah came to make their home in Egypt, confident that they would return and live once more in Judah. But they will not return; not one of them will survive, not one escape.

15 Then all the men who knew that their wives were burning sacrifices to other gods, and the large crowd of women standing by, indeed all of the people who lived in Pathros in Egypt, answered Jeremiah: 16 'We are not going to listen to what you tell us in the name of the LORD. 17 We intend to fulfil all the vows by which we have bound ourselves: we shall burn sacrifices to the queen of heaven and pour drink-offerings to her as we used to do, we and our forefathers, our kings and leaders, in the towns of Judah and in the streets of Jerusalem. Then we had food in plenty and were content; no disaster touched us. 18 But from the time we left off burning sacrifices to the queen of heaven and pouring drink-offerings to her, we have been in great want, and we have fallen victims to sword and famine.' 19 The women said, 'All the time we burnt sacrifices to the queen of heaven and poured drink-offerings to her, our husbands were fully aware that we were making crescent-cakes marked with her image and pouring drink-offerings to her.'

20 When Jeremiah received this answer from all the people, men and women, he said, 21 'The LORD did not forget those sacrifices which you and your forefathers, your kings and princes, and the people of the land burnt in the towns of Judah and in the streets of Jerusalem, and they mounted up in his mind 22 until he could no longer endure them, so wicked were your deeds, so abominable the things you did. Your land became a desolate waste, an object of horror and cursing, with no inhabitants, as it still is. 23 The disaster you now suffer has come on you because you burnt these sacrifices and sinned against the LORD, refusing to obey the LORD and conform to his law, statutes, and teachings.'

---

q Heb his   r Compare Syr: Heb lacks And the women said

44:14 **But . . . return:** prob. rdg; Heb. adds except fugitives.
44:19 **The women said:** so Gk (Luc.); Heb. omits.

in flame over the cities of Judah and the streets of Jerusalem, so that they became the ruinous waste they are today. 7 Now thus says the LORD God of hosts, the God of Israel: Why do you inflict so great an evil upon yourselves? Will you root out from Judah man and wife, child and nursling, and not leave yourselves even a remnant? 8 Will you go on provoking me by the works of your hands, by sacrificing to strange gods here in the land of Egypt where you have come to live? Will you be rooted out and become a curse and a disgrace among all the nations of the earth? 9 Have you forgotten the evil deeds which your fathers, and the kings of Judah and their wives, and you yourselves and your wives have done in the land of Judah and the streets of Jerusalem? 10 To this day they have not been crushed; they do not fear or follow the law and the statutes which I set before you and your fathers.

11 Hence, thus says the LORD of hosts, the God of Israel: I have determined evil against you; and I will uproot all Judah. 12 I will take away the remnant of Judah who insisted on coming to dwell in Egypt, so that they shall be wholly destroyed. In the land of Egypt they shall fall by the sword or be consumed by hunger. High and low, they shall die by the sword, or by hunger, and become an example of malediction, a horror, a curse and a reproach. 13 Thus will I punish those who live in Egypt, just as I punished Jerusalem with sword, hunger, and pestilence. None of the remnant of Judah that have come to settle in the land of Egypt shall escape or survive. 14 None shall return to the land of Judah, though they yearn to return and live there. Only scattered refugees shall return.

15 From all the men who knew that their wives were burning incense to strange gods, from all the women who were present in the immense crowd, and from all the people who lived in Lower and Upper Egypt, Jeremiah received this answer: 16 "We will not listen to what you say in the name of the LORD. 17 Rather will we continue doing what we had proposed; we will burn incense to the queen of heaven and pour out libations to her, as we and our fathers, our kings and princes have done in the cities of Judah and the streets of Jerusalem. Then we had enough food to eat and we were well off; we suffered no misfortune. 18 But since we stopped burning incense to the queen of heaven and pouring out libations to her, we are in need of everything and are being destroyed by the sword and by hunger. 19 And when we burned incense to the queen of heaven and poured out libations to her, was it without our husbands' consent that we baked for her cakes in her image and poured out libations to her?"

20 To all the people, men and women, who gave him this answer, Jeremiah said: 21 Was it not this that the LORD remembered and brought to mind, that you burned incense in the cities of Judah and the streets of Jerusalem: you, your fathers, your kings and princes, and the people generally? 22 The LORD could no longer bear your evil deeds, the horrible things which you were doing; and so your land became a waste, a desert, a thing accursed and without inhabitants, as it is today. 23 Because you burned incense and sinned against the LORD, not obeying the voice of the LORD, not living by his law, his statutes, and his decrees, this evil has befallen you at the present day.

anger overflowed, burning down the towns of Judah and the streets of Jerusalem, which were reduced to ruins and wasteland, as they still are today. 7 And now, Yahweh, God Sabaoth, God of Israel, says this: Why bring complete disaster on yourselves by cutting yourselves off from Judah — your men, women, children and babes in arms — so as to leave yourselves no remnant, 8 by provoking my wrath by your actions, offering incense to other gods in Egypt where you have come to settle, as though bent on your own destruction and on becoming a curse and a laughing-stock for all the nations of the earth? 9 Have you forgotten the wicked deeds of your ancestors, of the kings of Judah and of your princes, your own wicked deeds and those of your wives, committed in the country of Judah and in the streets of Jerusalem? 10 To this day they have felt neither contrition nor fear; they have not observed my Law or my statutes, which I prescribed for you, as for your ancestors. 11 So, Yahweh Sabaoth, God of Israel, says this: Look, I have determined on disaster and shall destroy Judah completely. 12 I shall take the remnant of Judah who were determined to come to Egypt and settle there, and in Egypt they will perish; they will fall to the sword or perish of famine, from least to greatest; by sword and famine they will die and be an object of execration and horror, a curse, a laughing-stock. 13 I shall punish those who live in Egypt just as I punished Jerusalem: by sword, famine and plague. 14 Of the remnant of Judah which has come to settle in Egypt, not a single one will escape or survive to return to the country of Judah where they long to return and live. For none of them will return, except a few refugees." '

15 At this, all the men who knew that their wives offered incense to other gods, and all the women who were standing there, a great crowd (and all the people living in Egypt, in Pathros), answered Jeremiah as follows, 16 'We have no intention of listening to the word you have just spoken to us in Yahweh's name, 17 but intend to go on doing all we have vowed to do: offering incense to the Queen of Heaven and pouring libations in her honour, as we used to do, we and our ancestors, our kings and our chief men, in the towns of Judah and the streets of Jerusalem: we had food in plenty then, we lived well, we suffered no disasters. 18 But since we gave up offering incense to the Queen of Heaven and pouring libations in her honour, we have been destitute and have perished either by sword or by famine. 19 Besides, when we offer incense to the Queen of Heaven and pour libations in her honour, do you think we make cakes for her with her features on them, and pour libations to her, without our husbands' knowledge?'

20 To all the people, men and women, all those who had made this answer, Jeremiah retorted, 21 'The incense you offered in the towns of Judah and the streets of Jerusalem, you, your ancestors, your kings, your chief men and the people at large — was this not what Yahweh kept remembering, and found so repellent 22 that Yahweh could not endure your misdeeds and your loathsome practices any longer, with the result that your country has become the uninhabited ruin, the object of horror and cursing it is today? 23 Because you offered incense, because you sinned against Yahweh, refusing to listen to the voice of Yahweh, or to observe his Law, his statutes and his decrees — that is why the present disaster has overtaken you.'

NEW REVISED STANDARD VERSION

24 Jeremiah said to all the people and all the women, "Hear the word of the LORD, all you Judeans who are in the land of Egypt, 25 Thus says the LORD of hosts, the God of Israel: You and your wives have accomplished in deeds what you declared in words, saying, 'We are determined to perform the vows that we have made, to make offerings to the queen of heaven and to pour out libations to her.' By all means, keep your vows and make your libations! 26 Therefore hear the word of the LORD, all you Judeans who live in the land of Egypt: Lo, I swear by my great name, says the LORD, that my name shall no longer be pronounced on the lips of any of the people of Judah in all the land of Egypt, saying, 'As the Lord GOD lives.' 27 I am going to watch over them for harm and not for good; all the people of Judah who are in the land of Egypt shall perish by the sword and by famine, until not one is left. 28 And those who escape the sword shall return from the land of Egypt to the land of Judah, few in number; and all the remnant of Judah, who have come to the land of Egypt to settle, shall know whose words will stand, mine or theirs! 29 This shall be the sign to you, says the LORD, that I am going to punish you in this place, in order that you may know that my words against you will surely be carried out: 30 Thus says the LORD, I am going to give Pharaoh Hophra, king of Egypt, into the hands of his enemies, those who seek his life, just as I gave King Zedekiah of Judah into the hand of King Nebuchadrezzar of Babylon, his enemy who sought his life."

45 The word that the prophet Jeremiah spoke to Baruch son of Neriah, when he wrote these words in a scroll at the dictation of Jeremiah, in the fourth year of King Jehoiakim son of Josiah of Judah: 2 Thus says the LORD, the God of Israel, to you, O Baruch: 3 You said, "Woe is me! The LORD has added sorrow to my pain; I am weary with my groaning, and I find no rest." 4 Thus you shall say to him, "Thus says the LORD: I am going to break down what I have built, and pluck up what I have planted—that is, the whole land. 5 And you, do you seek great things for yourself? Do not seek them; for I am going to bring disaster upon all flesh, says the LORD; but I will give you your life as a prize of war in every place to which you may go."

46 The word of the LORD that came to the prophet Jeremiah concerning the nations. 2 Concerning Egypt, about the army of Pharaoh Neco, king of Egypt, which was by the river Euphrates at Carchemish and which King Nebuchadrezzar of Babylon defeated in the fourth year of King Jehoiakim son of Josiah of Judah:

3 Prepare buckler and shield,
    and advance for battle!
4 Harness the horses;
    mount the steeds!
Take your stations with your helmets,
    whet your lances,
    put on your coats of mail!
5 Why do I see them terrified?
    They have fallen back;
their warriors are beaten down,
    and have fled in haste.
They do not look back—
    terror is all around!
                                says the LORD.
6 The swift cannot flee away,
    nor can the warrior escape;

REVISED ENGLISH BIBLE

24 Further, Jeremiah said to all the people, particularly the women: Listen to the word of the LORD, all you from Judah who live in Egypt. 25 These are the words of the LORD of Hosts the God of Israel: You women have made your actions match your words. You said, 'We shall carry out our vows to burn sacrifices to the queen of heaven and to pour drink-offerings to her.' Fulfil your vows by all means; carry them out! 26 But listen to the word of the LORD, all you from Judah who are settled in Egypt. I have sworn by my great name, says the LORD, that my name will never again be invoked by any of the Judaeans, in Egypt they will no longer swear 'by the life of the Lord GOD'. 27 I am on the watch to bring you evil and not good, and all Judaeans who are in Egypt will meet their end by sword and famine until not one is left. 28 It is then that any survivors of Judah who made their home in Egypt will know whose word prevails, mine or theirs.

29 This is the sign I give you, says the LORD, that I intend to punish you in this place, so that you may learn that my threat of disaster against you will prevail. 30 These are the words of the LORD: I shall hand over Pharaoh Hophra king of Egypt to his enemies and to those who seek his life, just as I handed over King Zedekiah of Judah to King Nebuchadrezzar of Babylon, his enemy who sought his life.

45 THE word which the prophet Jeremiah addressed to Baruch son of Neriah when Baruch wrote these words in a scroll at Jeremiah's dictation in the fourth year of Jehoiakim son of Josiah, king of Judah: 2 These are the words of the LORD the God of Israel concerning you, Baruch: 3 You said, 'Woe is me, for the LORD has added grief to my trials. I have worn myself out with my labours and have had no respite.' 4 This is what you shall say to Baruch: These are the words of the LORD: What I have built, I demolish; what I have planted, I uproot. So it will be with the whole earth. 5 You seek great things for yourself; leave off seeking them. I am about to bring disaster on all mankind, says the LORD, but wherever you go I shall let you escape with your life.

46 THIS came to the prophet Jeremiah as the word of the LORD about the nations. 2 OF Egypt: about the army of Pharaoh Necho king of Egypt at Carchemish on the river Euphrates, which King Nebuchadrezzar of Babylon defeated in the fourth year of Jehoiakim son of Josiah, king of Judah.

3 Hold shield and buckler ready
    and advance to battle;
4 harness the horses,
    let the riders mount;
form up with your helmets on,
    your lances burnished;
    on with your coats of mail!
5 But now, what sight is this?
    They are broken and routed,
their warriors defeated;
    they are in headlong flight
    without a backward look.
Terror let loose!
    This is the word of the LORD.

6 Can the swiftest escape,
    the bravest save himself?

NEW AMERICAN BIBLE

NEW JERUSALEM BIBLE

24 Jeremiah said further to all the people, including the women: Hear the word of the LORD, all you Judeans in the land of Egypt: 25 Thus says the LORD of hosts, the God of Israel: You and your wives have stated your intentions, and kept them in fact: "We will continue to fulfill the vows we have made to burn incense to the queen of heaven and to pour out libations to her." Very well! keep your vows, carry out your resolutions! 26 But listen then to the word of the LORD, all you people of Judah who live in Egypt; I swear by my own great name, says the LORD, in the whole land of Egypt no man of Judah shall henceforth pronounce my name, saying, "As the Lord GOD lives." 27 I am watching over them to do evil, not good. All the men of Judah in Egypt shall perish by the sword or famine until they are utterly destroyed. 28 Those who escape the sword to return from the land of Egypt to the land of Judah shall be few in number. The whole remnant of Judah who came to settle in Egypt shall know whose word stands, mine or theirs.

29 That you may know how surely my threats of punishment for you shall be fulfilled, this shall be a sign to you, says the LORD, that I will punish you in this place. 30 Thus says the LORD: See! I will hand over Pharaoh Hophra, king of Egypt, to his enemies, to those who seek his life, just as I handed over Zedekiah, king of Judah, to his enemy and mortal foe, Nebuchadnezzar, king of Babylon.

45 This is the message that the prophet Jeremiah gave to Baruch, son of Neriah, when he wrote in a book the prophecies that Jeremiah dictated in the fourth year of Jehoiakim, son of Josiah, king of Judah: 2 Thus says the LORD, God of Israel, to you, Baruch, 3 because you said, "Alas! the LORD adds grief to my pain; I am weary from groaning, and can find no rest": 4 say this to him, says the LORD: What I have built, I am tearing down; what I have planted, I am uprooting: even the whole land. 5 And do you seek great things for yourself? Seek them not! I am bringing evil on all mankind, says the LORD, but your life I will leave you as booty, wherever you may go.

46 This is the word of the LORD that came to the prophet Jeremiah against the nations.

2 Concerning Egypt. Against the army of Pharaoh Neco, king of Egypt, which was defeated at Carchemish on the Euphrates by Nebuchadnezzar, king of Babylon, in the fourth year of Jehoiakim, son of Josiah, king of Judah:

3 Prepare shield and buckler!
  march to battle!
4 Harness the horses,
  mount, charioteers
Fall in with your helmets;
  polish your spears, put on your breastplates.
5 What do I see?
  With broken ranks
They fall back;
  their heroes are routed,
They flee headlong
  without making a stand.
Terror on every side,
  says the LORD!
6 The swift cannot flee,
  nor the hero escape:

24 Further, Jeremiah said to all the people, and particularly to all the women, 'Listen to the word of Yahweh, all you Judaeans in Egypt, 25 Yahweh Sabaoth, God of Israel, says this, "You and your wives, what your mouths promised, your hands have indeed performed! You said: We shall punctiliously fulfil the vows we have made and offer incense to the Queen of Heaven and pour libations in her honour. Very well, keep your vows, perform them punctiliously! 26 But listen to the word of Yahweh, all you Judaeans living in Egypt: I swear by my great name, Yahweh says, that my name will no longer be uttered by any man of Judah throughout Egypt; no one will say: As Lord Yahweh lives. 27 No, I am going to keep my eye on them for disaster, not for prosperity, and all the Judaeans in Egypt will perish either by the sword or by famine until they are wiped out. 28 Yet, though few in number, those who escape the sword will return to the country of Judah from Egypt. Then the entire remnant of Judah which has come and settled in Egypt will know whose word comes true, mine or theirs.

29 "And here is the sign for you, Yahweh declares, that I shall punish you in this place: so that you will know that the words with which I threaten you will come true: 30 Yahweh says this: Look, I shall hand Pharaoh Hophra, king of Egypt, over to his enemies and to those determined to kill him, just as I handed Zedekiah king of Judah over to his enemy Nebuchadnezzar king of Babylon, who was determined to kill him." '

45 The word that the prophet Jeremiah addressed to Baruch son of Neriah when the latter wrote these words down in a book at Jeremiah's dictation in the fourth year of Jehoiakim son of Josiah, king of Judah, 2 'This is what Yahweh God of Israel says about you, Baruch! 3 "You have been thinking: what disaster for me, and Yahweh has added further grief to my troubles! I am worn out with groaning, and find no relief!" 4 Say to him as follows, "Yahweh says this: Now I am knocking down what I have built, am uprooting what I have planted, over the whole country! 5 And you ask for special treatment? Do not ask, for I am now going to bring disaster on all humanity, Yahweh declares, but you I shall allow to escape with your life, wherever you may go." '

46 y The words of Yahweh that were addressed to the prophet Jeremiah against the nations.

2 On Egypt.

Against the army of Pharaoh Necho king of Egypt, which was at Carchemish on the River Euphrates when Nebuchadnezzar king of Babylon defeated it in the fourth year of Jehoiakim son of Josiah, king of Judah.

3 Buckler and shield at the ready!
  Onward to battle!
4 Harness the horses:
  into the saddle, horsemen!
To your ranks! On with your helmets!
Sharpen your spears,
  put on your breastplates!
5 Why do I see them
  retreating, panic-stricken?
Their heroes, beaten back,
  are fleeing headlong,
  with not a look behind.
Terror on every side,
  Yahweh declares!
6 No flight for the swift,
  no escape for the strong!

y **46** The Hebr. text places the prophecies against the nations at the end of the book, chh. 46–51; in Gk they occur after ch. 25.

in the north by the river Euphrates
    they have stumbled and fallen.
7 Who is this, rising like the Nile,
    like rivers whose waters surge?
8 Egypt rises like the Nile,
    like rivers whose waters surge.
    It said, Let me rise, let me cover the earth,
    let me destroy cities and their inhabitants.
9 Advance, O horses,
    and dash madly, O chariots!
Let the warriors go forth:
    Ethiopia^s and Put who carry the shield,
    the Ludim, who draw^t the bow.
10 That day is the day of the Lord God of hosts,
    a day of retribution,
    to gain vindication from his foes.
The sword shall devour and be sated,
    and drink its fill of their blood.
For the Lord God of hosts holds a sacrifice
    in the land of the north by the river Euphrates.
11 Go up to Gilead, and take balm,
    O virgin daughter Egypt!
In vain you have used many medicines;
    there is no healing for you.
12 The nations have heard of your shame,
    and the earth is full of your cry;
    for warrior has stumbled against warrior;
    both have fallen together.

13 The word that the LORD spoke to the prophet Jeremiah about the coming of King Nebuchadrezzar of Babylon to attack the land of Egypt:
14   Declare in Egypt, and proclaim in Migdol;
    proclaim in Memphis and Tahpanhes;
    Say, "Take your stations and be ready,
    for the sword shall devour those around you."
15   Why has Apis fled?^u
    Why did your bull not stand?
    —because the LORD thrust him down.
16   Your multitude stumbled^v and fell,
    and one said to another,^w
    "Come, let us go back to our own people
    and to the land of our birth,
    because of the destroying sword."
17   Give Pharaoh, king of Egypt, the name
    "Braggart who missed his chance."

18   As I live, says the King,
    whose name is the LORD of hosts,
    one is coming
    like Tabor among the mountains,
    and like Carmel by the sea.
19   Pack your bags for exile,
    sheltered daughter Egypt!
For Memphis shall become a waste,
    a ruin, without inhabitant.

20   A beautiful heifer is Egypt—
    a gadfly from the north lights upon her.
21   Even her mercenaries in her midst
    are like fatted calves;
    they too have turned and fled together,
    they did not stand;
    for the day of their calamity has come upon them,
    the time of their punishment.

In the north, by the river Euphrates,
    they stumble and fall.
7 Who is this rising like the Nile,
    like rivers turbulent in flood?
8 It is Egypt rising like the Nile,
    like rivers turbulent in flood.
I shall arise and cover the earth, says Egypt;
    I shall destroy every city and its people.
9 Let the cavalry charge
    and the chariots drive furiously!
Let the warriors attack,
    Cushites and men of Put bearing shields,
    Lydians with their bows ready strung!
10 That day belongs to the Lord, the GOD of Hosts,
    a day of vengeance, vengeance on his enemies;
    the sword will devour until sated,
    drunk with their blood.
For the GOD of Hosts, the Lord, holds sacrifice
    in a northern land, by the river Euphrates.
11 Virgin daughter of Egypt,
    go up into Gilead and fetch balm.
You have tried many remedies, all in vain;
    no skin will grow over your wounds.
12 The nations have heard your cry,
    and the earth echoes with your screams;
    warrior stumbles against warrior
    and both fall down together.

13 The word which the LORD spoke to the prophet Jeremiah about the advance of King Nebuchadrezzar of Babylon to harry the land of Egypt:
14 Announce it in Egypt, proclaim it in Migdol,
    proclaim it in Noph and Tahpanhes.
Say: Stand to! Be ready!
    For a sword devours all around you.
15 Why does Apis flee? Why does your bull-god not
      stand fast?
Because the LORD has thrust him out.
16 The rabble of Egypt stumbles and falls,
    man against man;
    each says, 'Quick, back to our own people,
    to our native land, far from the oppressor's sword!'
17 Give Pharaoh of Egypt the title King Bombast,
    the man who missed his opportunity.

18 By my life, one will come,
    says the King whose name is the LORD of Hosts,
    one mighty as Tabor among the hills,
    as Carmel by the sea.
19 Get ready your baggage for exile,
    you native people of Egypt;
Noph will become a waste,
    ruined and unpeopled.

20 Egypt was a lovely heifer,
    but a gadfly from the north attacked her.
21 The mercenaries in her land were like stall-fed
      calves;
but they too turned tail and fled,
    not one of them standing his ground.
The day of retribution has come upon them,
    their time of reckoning.

---

^s Or Nubia; Heb Cush   ^t Cn: Heb who grasp, who draw
^u Gk: Heb Why was it swept away   ^v Gk: Meaning of Heb uncertain
^w Gk: Heb and fell one to another and they said

46:12 **your cry:** so Gk; Heb. your shame.   46:15 **Why does Apis
. . . not:** or Why is your bull-god laid low, why does he not.

There in the north, on the Euphrates' bank,
they stumble and fall.
7 Who is this that surges forward like the Nile,
like rivers of billowing waters?
8 Egypt surges like the Nile,
like rivers of billowing waters.
"I will surge forward," he says, "and cover
the earth,
destroying the city and its people.
9 Forward, horses!
drive madly, chariots!
Set out, warriors,
Cush and Put, bearing your shields,
Men of Lud, stretching your bows!"
10 But this is the day of the Lord GOD of hosts,
a day of vengeance, vengeance on his foes!
The sword devours, is sated, drunk with their
blood:
for the Lord GOD of hosts holds a slaughter
feast
in the northland, on the Euphrates.
11 Go up to Gilead, and take balm,
O virgin daughter Egypt!
No use to multiply remedies;
for you there is no cure.
12 The nations hear of your shame,
your cries fill the earth.
Warrior trips over warrior,
both fall together.

13 The message which the LORD gave to the prophet Jeremiah concerning the advance of Nebuchadnezzar, king of
Babylon, to attack the land of Egypt:

14 Announce it in Egypt, publish it in Migdol,
proclaim it in Memphis and Tahpanhes!
Say: Take your stand, prepare yourselves,
the sword has already devoured your neighbors.
15 Why has Apis fled,
your mighty one failed to stand?
The LORD thrust him down;
16 he stumbled repeatedly, and fell.
They said one to another,
"Up! let us return to our own people,
To the land of our birth,
away from the destroying sword."
17 Call Pharaoh, king of Egypt, by the name
"The noise that let its time go by."
18 As I live, says the King
whose name is LORD of hosts,
Like Tabor among the mountains he shall come,
like Carmel above the sea.
19 Pack your baggage for exile,
capital city of daughter Egypt;
Memphis shall become a desert,
an empty ruin.
20 Egypt is a pretty heifer,
from the north a horsefly lights upon her.
21 The mercenaries in her ranks
are like fatted calves;
They too turn and flee together,
stand not their ground,
When the day of their ruin comes upon them,
the time of their punishment.

Up in the north on the River Euphrates,
they have collapsed, have fallen.
7 Who was it rose like the Nile,
his waters foaming like a torrent?
8 Why, Egypt rose like the Nile,
his waters foaming like a torrent.
'I shall rise', he said, 'and drown the earth;
sweep away town and its inhabitants!
9 Charge, horses!
Forward, chariots!
Let the warriors advance,
men from Cush and Put with shield in hand,
men from Lud who bend the bow!'
10 For this is the Day of Lord Yahweh Sabaoth,
a day of vengeance when he takes revenge on his
foes:
the sword will devour until gorged,
until drunk with their blood,
for Lord Yahweh Sabaoth is holding a sacrificial
feast
in the land of the north, on the River Euphrates.
11 Go up to Gilead and fetch balm,
virgin daughter of Egypt!
You multiply remedies in vain,
nothing can cure you!
12 The nations have heard of your shame,
your wailing fills the world,
for warrior has stumbled against warrior,
and both have fallen together.

13 The word that came from Yahweh to the prophet Jeremiah when Nebuchadnezzar king of Babylon advanced to
attack Egypt.

14 Publish it in Egypt,
proclaim it in Migdol,
proclaim it in Noph and Tahpanhes!
Say, 'Stand your ground, be prepared,
for the sword is devouring all round you!'
15 Why has Apis fled?
Why has your Mighty One not stood firm?
Why, Yahweh has overturned him,
16 he has caused many to fall!
Falling over one another,
they say, 'Up, and back to our own people,
to the country where we were born,
away from the devastating sword!'
17 They have given Pharaoh king of Egypt the
nickname,
'Much-noise-but-he-lets-the-chance-slip-by'!
18 As I live, the King declares,
whose name is Yahweh Sabaoth,
he is coming, a very Tabor among mountains,
a Carmel high above the sea!
19 Get your bundle ready for exile,
fair inhabitant of Egypt!
Noph will be reduced to a desert,
desolate, uninhabited.
20 Egypt was a splendid heifer,
but a gadfly from the north has settled on her.
21 The mercenaries she had with her, these too
were like fattened calves:
but they too have taken to their heels,
have all run away, not held their ground,
for their day of disaster has overtaken them,
their time for being punished.

z 46 Cush, Put and Lud are perhaps Ethiopia, Lybia and Lydia
respectively.

NEW REVISED STANDARD VERSION

22 She makes a sound like a snake gliding away;
    for her enemies march in force,
and come against her with axes,
    like those who fell trees.
23 They shall cut down her forest,
                        says the LORD,
    though it is impenetrable,
because they are more numerous
    than locusts;
    they are without number.
24 Daughter Egypt shall be put to shame;
    she shall be handed over to a people from the
        north.

25 The LORD of hosts, the God of Israel, said: See, I am
bringing punishment upon Amon of Thebes, and Pharaoh,
and Egypt and her gods and her kings, upon Pharaoh and
those who trust in him. 26 I will hand them over to those
who seek their life, to King Nebuchadrezzar of Babylon and
his officers. Afterward Egypt shall be inhabited as in the
days of old, says the LORD.

27 But as for you, have no fear, my servant Jacob,
    and do not be dismayed, O Israel;
for I am going to save you from far away,
    and your offspring from the land of their
        captivity.
Jacob shall return and have quiet and ease,
    and no one shall make him afraid.
28 As for you, have no fear, my servant Jacob,
                        says the LORD,
    for I am with you.
I will make an end of all the nations
    among which I have banished you,
    but I will not make an end of you!
I will chastise you in just measure,
    and I will by no means leave you unpunished.

47 The word of the LORD that came to the prophet
    Jeremiah concerning the Philistines, before Pharaoh
attacked Gaza:
2 Thus says the LORD:
See, waters are rising out of the north
    and shall become an overflowing torrent;
they shall overflow the land and all that fills it,
    the city and those who live in it.
People shall cry out,
    and all the inhabitants of the land shall wail.
3 At the noise of the stamping of the hoofs of his
        stallions,
    at the clatter of his chariots, at the rumbling of
        their wheels,
parents do not turn back for children,
    so feeble are their hands,
4 because of the day that is coming
        to destroy all the Philistines,
to cut off from Tyre and Sidon
    every helper that remains.
For the LORD is destroying the Philistines,
    the remnant of the coastland of Caphtor.
5 Baldness has come upon Gaza,
    Ashkelon is silenced.
O remnant of their power!^{x}
    How long will you gash yourselves?
6 Ah, sword of the LORD!
    How long until you are quiet?
Put yourself into your scabbard,
    rest and be still!

REVISED ENGLISH BIBLE

22 Egypt is hissing like a fleeing snake,
    for the enemy has come in force.
They attack her with axes
    like fellers of trees.
23 They cut down her forest, says the LORD,
    for they cannot be numbered;
more numerous than locusts,
    they are past counting.
24 The Egyptians are put to shame,
    enslaved to a northern race.

25 The LORD of Hosts the God of Israel has spoken:
    I am about to punish Amon god of Thebes,
Egypt with her gods and her princes,
    Pharaoh and all who trust in him.
26 I shall deliver them to those bent on their
        destruction,
    to King Nebuchadrezzar of Babylon and his troops;
yet after this the land will be peopled as of old.
    This is the word of the LORD.

27 But, Jacob my servant, do not be afraid;
    Israel, do not be dismayed;
from afar I shall bring you back safe,
    and your children from the land where they are
        captives.
Jacob will be at rest once more,
    secure and untroubled.
28 Do not be afraid, Jacob my servant,
    says the LORD, for I am with you.
I shall make an end of all the nations
    amongst whom I have dispersed you;
but of you I shall not make an end.
I shall discipline you only as you deserve,
    I shall not leave you wholly unpunished.

47 This came to the prophet Jeremiah as the word of
    the LORD concerning the Philistines before Phar-
aoh's attack on Gaza: 2 These are the words of the LORD:

See how waters are rising from the north
    and swelling to a torrent in spate,
flooding the land and all that is in it,
    towns and those who live in them.
People cry out in alarm;
    wailing arises from all the inhabitants of the land.
3 At the noise of the pounding of his chargers'
        hoofs,
    the rattle of his chariots and their rumbling wheels,
fathers have no thought for their children;
    their hands hang powerless,
4 because the day has come
    for all Philistia to be despoiled,
and Tyre and Sidon destroyed to the last defender;
    for the LORD is despoiling the Philistines,
that remnant of the isle of Caphtor.
5 Gaza is shorn bare, Ashkelon ruined,
    the remnant of the Philistine power.
How long will you gash yourselves and cry:
6 'Ah, sword in the hand of the LORD,
    how long will it be before you rest?
Sheathe yourself, cease and be quiet.'

---

^{x} Gk: Heb *their valley*

46:22 **Egypt is hissing:** *cp. Gk; Heb. obscure.*   46:25 **Amon . . .**
Thebes: *prob. rdg; Heb. adds* and Pharaoh.

22 She sounds like a retreating reptile!
  Yes, they come in force;
  like woodchoppers, they attack her with axes.
23 They cut down her forest, says the LORD,
  impenetrable though it be;
  More numerous than locusts,
  they cannot be counted.
24 Disgraced is daughter Egypt,
  handed over to the people of the north.

25 The LORD of hosts, the God of Israel, has said: See! I
will punish Amon of Thebes, and Egypt, her gods and her
kings, Pharaoh, and those who trust in him. 26 I will hand
them over to those who seek their lives, to Nebuchadnezzar,
king of Babylon, and his ministers. But later on Egypt shall
be inhabited again, as in times past, says the LORD.

27 But you, my servant Jacob, fear not;
  be not dismayed, O Israel.
  Behold, I will deliver you from the faroff land,
  your descendants, from their land of exile.
  Jacob shall again find rest,
  shall be tranquil and undisturbed.
28 You, my servant Jacob, never fear, says the LORD,
  for I am with you;
  I will make an end of all the nations
  to which I have driven you,
  But of you I will not make an end:
  I will chastise you as you deserve,
  I will not let you go unpunished.

22 Hear her hissing like a snake
  as they advance in force
  to fall on her with their axes,
  like woodcutters,
23 they will fell her forest, Yahweh declares,
  however impenetrable it was
  for they are more numerous than locusts,
  there is no counting them.
24 The daughter of Egypt is put to shame,
  handed over to a people from the north.

25 Yahweh Sabaoth, God of Israel, has said, 'Look, I
shall punish Amon of No, Pharaoh, Egypt, its gods, its
kings, Pharaoh and those who put their trust in him. 26 I
shall hand him over to those who are determined to kill him,
to Nebuchadnezzar king of Babylon, to his generals. But
afterwards, Egypt will be inhabited again as in the past,
Yahweh declares.

27 But do not be afraid, my servant Jacob,
  Israel, do not be alarmed:
  for look, I shall rescue you from afar
  and your descendants from the country where they
    are captive.
  Jacob will return and be at peace,
  secure, with no one to trouble him.
28 Do not be afraid, my servant Jacob,
  Yahweh declares, for I am with you:
  I shall make an end of all the nations
  where I have driven you,
  but I shall not make an end of you,
  I shall discipline you only as you deserve,
  not leaving you quite unpunished. [a]

47 This is the word that came from the LORD to the
prophet Jeremiah concerning the Philistines, before
Pharaoh attacked Gaza. 2 Thus says the LORD:

  Behold: waters are rising from the north,
  a torrent in flood;
  It shall flood the land and all that is in it,
  the cities and their people.
  All the people of the land
  set up a wailing cry.
3 They hear the stamping hooves of his steeds,
  the rattling chariots, the rumbling wheels.
  Fathers turn not to save their children;
  their hands fall helpless
4 Because of the day which has come
  to ruin all the Philistines,
  And cut off from Tyre and Sidon
  the last of their allies.
  Yes, the LORD is destroying the Philistines,
  the remnant from the coasts of Caphtor.
5 Gaza is shaved bald,
  Ashkelon is reduced to silence;
  Ashdod, the remnant of their strength,
  how long will you gash yourself?
6 Alas, sword of the LORD!
  how long till you find rest?
  Return into your scabbard;
  stop, be still!

47 The word of Yahweh that came to Jeremiah about
the Philistines before Pharaoh attacked Gaza.
2 'Yahweh says this:

  Look, the waters are rising from the north
  to become an overwhelming flood,
  overwhelming the country and all in it,
  the town and its inhabitants!
  People cry for help, and there is wailing
  from all the country's inhabitants
3 at the thunder of his chargers' hoofs,
  the crash of his chariots, the grinding of his
    wheels.
  Fathers forget about their children,
  their hands fall limp
4 because the day has come
  for all the Philistines to be destroyed,
  for Tyre and Sidon to be stripped
  to the last of their allies.
  Yes, Yahweh is destroying the Philistines,
  the remnant from the Isle of Caphtor.
5 Baldness has befallen Gaza,
  Ashkelon has been reduced to silence.
  You who remain in the valley,
  how long will you gash yourselves?
6 Oh, sword of Yahweh,
  how long before you rest?
  Back into your scabbard,
  stop, keep still!

---

[a] **46** = 30:10–11.

NEW REVISED STANDARD VERSION	REVISED ENGLISH BIBLE

NEW REVISED STANDARD VERSION

7 How can it*y* be quiet,
  when the LORD has given it an order?—
Against Ashkelon and against the seashore—
  there he has appointed it.

48 Concerning Moab.

Thus says the LORD of hosts, the God of Israel:
  Alas for Nebo, it is laid waste!
  Kiriathaim is put to shame, it is taken;
  the fortress is put to shame and broken down;
2   the renown of Moab is no more.
In Heshbon they planned evil against her:
  "Come, let us cut her off from being a nation!"
You also, O Madmen, shall be brought to
    silence;*z*
  the sword shall pursue you.

3 Hark! a cry from Horonaim,
  "Desolation and great destruction!"
4 "Moab is destroyed!"
  her little ones cry out.
5 For at the ascent of Luhith
  they go*a* up weeping bitterly;
for at the descent of Horonaim
  they have heard the distressing cry of anguish.
6 Flee! Save yourselves!
  Be like a wild ass*b* in the desert!

7 Surely, because you trusted in your strongholds*c*
    and your treasures,
  you also shall be taken;
Chemosh shall go out into exile,
  with his priests and his attendants.
8 The destroyer shall come upon every town,
  and no town shall escape;
the valley shall perish,
  and the plain shall be destroyed,
  as the LORD has spoken.

9 Set aside salt for Moab,
  for she will surely fall;
her towns shall become a desolation,
  with no inhabitant in them.

10 Accursed is the one who is slack in doing the work
of the LORD; and accursed is the one who keeps back the
sword from bloodshed.

11 Moab has been at ease from his youth,
    settled like wine*d* on its dregs;
he has not been emptied from vessel to vessel,
    nor has he gone into exile;
therefore his flavor has remained
    and his aroma is unspoiled.

12 Therefore, the time is surely coming, says the LORD,
when I shall send to him decanters to decant him, and empty
his vessels, and break his*e* jars in pieces. 13 Then Moab
shall be ashamed of Chemosh, as the house of Israel was
ashamed of Bethel, their confidence.

14 How can you say, "We are heroes
    and mighty warriors"?
15 The destroyer of Moab and his towns has come
    up,
  and the choicest of his young men have gone
    down to slaughter,
  says the King, whose name is the LORD of
    hosts.

REVISED ENGLISH BIBLE

7 How can it rest when the LORD has given it work
    to do
against Ashkelon and the sea coast?
There he has assigned the sword its task.

48 Of Moab. This is what the LORD of Hosts the God
of Israel says:

Woe betide Nebo! It is laid waste;
  Kiriathaim captured and put to shame,
  Misgab reduced to shame and dismay;
2 Moab's glory is no more.
In Heshbon they plot her downfall:
  'Come, put an end to that nation.'
And you, the inhabitants of Madhmen, will also
    perish,
  pursued by the sword.
3 Cries of anguish arise from Horonaim:
  'Havoc and utter destruction!'
4 Moab is broken;
  their cries are heard as far as Zoar.
5 On the ascent to Luhith
  they go up weeping bitterly;
on the descent to Horonaim
  an anguished cry of destruction is heard.
6 Flee, escape with your lives
  and become like one destitute in the wilderness.
7 Because you trust in your defences and arsenals,
  you too will be captured,
and Kemosh will go into exile,
  his priests and those in attendance with him.
8 A despoiler will come against every town;
  no town will escape,
valley and tableland will be laid waste and
    plundered;
  the LORD has spoken.
9 Give a warning signal to Moab,
  for she will be laid in ruins;
and her towns will become waste places
  with no inhabitant in them.
10 A curse on all who are slack in doing the LORD's
    work!
A curse on all who withhold their swords from
    bloodshed!

11 From its earliest days Moab has been undisturbed
  and never gone into exile.
It has been like wine settled on its lees,
  not decanted from vessel to vessel;
  its flavour remains unaltered
  and its aroma stays unchanged.

12 Therefore the days are coming, says the LORD, when I
shall send men to tilt the jars; they will empty the vessels
and smash the jars. 13 Moab will be let down by Kemosh as
Israel was let down by Bethel, a god in whom they trusted.

14 How can you say, 'We are warriors,
    men valiant in battle'?
15 The spoiler of Moab and its towns has launched an
    attack,
  and the flower of its youth goes down to be
    slaughtered.

This is the word of the King whose name is the LORD of
Hosts.

---

y Gk Vg: Heb *you*   *z* The place-name *Madmen* sounds like the
Hebrew verb *to be silent*   *a* Cn: Heb *he goes*   *b* Gk Aquila: Heb
like Aroer   *c* Gk: Heb *works*   *d* Heb lacks *like wine*
e Gk Aquila: Heb *their*

47:7 **can it:** *so Gk; Heb.* can you.   48:6 **one destitute:** *or* a
juniper.   48:9 **Give . . . signal:** *poss. mng; Heb. obscure.* **laid in
ruins:** *prob. rdg; Heb. obscure.*

7 How can it find rest
  when the LORD has commanded it?
Against Ashkelon and the seashore
  he has appointed it.

48 Concerning Moab, thus says the LORD of hosts, the God of Israel:

Woe to Nebo, it is laid waste;
  Kiriathaim is disgraced and captured,
Disgraced and overthrown is the stronghold:
2 Moab's glory is no more.
Evil they plan against Heshbon:
  "Come, let us put an end to her as a people."
You, too, Madmen, shall be reduced to silence;
  behind you stalks the sword.
3 Listen! a cry from Horonaim
  of ruin and great destruction!
4 Moab is crushed,
  their outcry is heard in Zoar.
5 The ascent of Luhith
  they climb weeping;
On the descent to Horonaim
  the cry of destruction is heard.
6 "Flee, save your lives,
  to survive like the wild ass in the desert!"
7 Because you trusted in your works and
      your treasures,
  you also shall be captured.
Chemosh shall go into exile,
  his priests and princes with him.
8 The destroyer comes upon every city,
  not a city escapes;
Ruined is the valley,
  wasted the plain, as the LORD has said.
9 Set up a memorial for Moab,
  for it is an utter wasteland;
Its cities are turned into ruins
  where no one dwells.
10 [Cursed be he who does the LORD's work remissly,
  cursed he who holds back his sword
      from blood.]
11 Moab has been tranquil from his youth,
  has rested upon his lees;
He was not poured from one flask to another,
  he went not into exile.
Thus he kept his taste,
  and his scent was not lost.

12 Hence, the days shall come, says the LORD, when I will send him coopers to turn him over; they shall empty his flasks and break his jars. 13 Chemosh shall disappoint Moab, as Israel was disappointed by Bethel in which they trusted.

14 How can you say, "We are heroes,
  men valiant in war"?
15 The ravager of Moab and his cities advances,
  the flower of his youth goes down to
      be slaughtered,
  says the King, the LORD of hosts by name.

7 Yet how can it rest
  when Yahweh has given it an order,
Ashkelon and the sea coast,
  the targets assigned to it?

48 On Moab. Yahweh, God of Israel, says this:

Wretched Nebo, for it has been ravaged,
  Kiriathaim has been shamed and taken,
  shame and distraction on the citadel,
2 the pride of Moab is no more!
At Heshbon they plotted her downfall,
  'Come, let us put an end to her as a nation!'
And you too, inhabitants of Madmen, will be
      silenced,
  the sword will be after you.

3 A cry of agony goes up from Horonaim,
  'Devastation! Dire calamity.'
4 Moab has been shattered,'
  the agonised cries of her little ones ring out.
5 Up the slope of Luhith,
  weeping they go.
On the road down to Horonaim
  is heard the shriek of disaster,b
6 'Away! Flee for your lives
  like the wild donkey into the desert!'
7 Yes, since you relied on your deeds and your
      wealth,
  you will be captured too.
Chemosh will go into exile,
  with all his priests and princes.
8 The despoiler will descend on every town,
  not one will escape;
  the Valley will be ravaged, the Plain be plundered
      as Yahweh has said.
9 Give Moab wings
  so that she can fly away,
  for her towns will be laid in ruins
  where no one will ever live again.

10 (Accursed be he who does Yahweh's work negligently!
Accursed be he who deprives his sword of blood!)

11 From his youth Moab lived at ease,
  he settled on his lees,
  never having been decanted,
  never having gone into exile:
  and so he kept his own flavour,
  his aroma was unchanged.

12 And so the days are coming, Yahweh declares, when I shall send him decanters to decant him; they will empty his pitchers and break his wine jars to bits. 13 Moab will be shamed by Chemosh then, as the House of Israel was shamed by Bethel in which they put their trust.

14 How can you say, 'We are heroes,
  sturdy fighting men'?
15 Moab has been ravaged, his cities scaled,
  the flower of his youth goes down to the slaughter,
  declares the King, whose name is Yahweh
      Sabaoth.

b 48 // Is 15:5.

NEW REVISED STANDARD VERSION

16 The calamity of Moab is near at hand
  and his doom approaches swiftly.
17 Mourn over him, all you his neighbors,
  and all who know his name;
  say, "How the mighty scepter is broken,
    the glorious staff!"

18 Come down from glory,
  and sit on the parched ground,
  enthroned daughter Dibon!
For the destroyer of Moab has come up against
    you;
  he has destroyed your strongholds.
19 Stand by the road and watch,
  you inhabitant of Aroer!
Ask the man fleeing and the woman escaping;
  say, "What has happened?"
20 Moab is put to shame, for it is broken down;
  wail and cry!
Tell it by the Arnon,
  that Moab is laid waste.

21 Judgment has come upon the tableland, upon Holon, and Jahzah, and Mephaath, 22 and Dibon, and Nebo, and Beth-diblathaim, 23 and Kiriathaim, and Beth-gamul, and Beth-meon, 24 and Kerioth, and Bozrah, and all the towns of the land of Moab, far and near. 25 The horn of Moab is cut off, and his arm is broken, says the LORD.
26 Make him drunk, because he magnified himself against the LORD; let Moab wallow in his vomit; he too shall become a laughingstock. 27 Israel was a laughingstock for you, though he was not caught among thieves; but whenever you spoke of him you shook your head!

28 Leave the towns, and live on the rock,
  O inhabitants of Moab!
Be like the dove that nests
  on the sides of the mouth of a gorge.
29 We have heard of the pride of Moab—
  he is very proud—
of his loftiness, his pride, and his arrogance,
  and the haughtiness of his heart.
30 I myself know his insolence, says the LORD;
  his boasts are false,
  his deeds are false.
31 Therefore I wail for Moab;
  I cry out for all Moab;
  for the people of Kir-heres I mourn.
32 More than for Jazer I weep for you,
  O vine of Sibmah!
Your branches crossed over the sea,
  reached as far as Jazer;f
upon your summer fruits and your vintage
  the destroyer has fallen.
33 Gladness and joy have been taken away
  from the fruitful land of Moab;
I have stopped the wine from the wine presses;
  no one treads them with shouts of joy;
  the shouting is not the shout of joy.

34 Heshbon and Elealeh cry out;g as far as Jahaz they utter their voice, from Zoar to Horonaim and Eglath-shelishiyah. For even the waters of Nimrim have become desolate. 35 And I will bring to an end in Moab, says the LORD, those who offer sacrifice at a high place and make offerings to their gods. 36 Therefore my heart moans for

REVISED ENGLISH BIBLE

16 Retribution on Moab is near at hand,
  disaster rushing swiftly on him.
17 Bewail him, all you his neighbours
  and all who knew his fame;
  and say, 'Alas! The commander's staff is broken,
    that splendid baton.'
18 Come down from your place of honour,
  sit on the parched ground, you natives of Dibon;
  for the spoiler of Moab has come against you
  and destroyed your citadels.
19 You that live in Aroer, stand by the road and
    watch,
  ask the man running away, the woman escaping,
  ask, 'What has happened?'
20 Moab is reduced to shame and dismay:
  wail and cry, proclaim by the Arnon
  that Moab is despoiled.

21 Judgement has come to the tableland, to Holon and Jahaz, Mephaath 22 and Dibon, Nebo and Beth-diblathaim 23 and Kiriathaim, Beth-gamul, Beth-meon, 24 Kerioth and Bozrah, and to all the towns of Moab far and near.

25 Moab's horn is hacked off
  and his strong arm is broken,
  says the LORD.

26 Make Moab drunk—he has defied the LORD.
  Let Moab overflow with his vomit
  and become in turn a butt for derision.
27 Was not Israel your butt?
  Yet was he ever in company with thieves,
  that each time you spoke of him
  you shook your head?
28 Leave your towns, you inhabitants of Moab,
  and find a home among the crags;
  become like a dove which nests
  in the rock-face at the mouth of a cavern.
29 We have heard of Moab's pride, and proud indeed
    he is,
  proud, presumptuous, overbearing, insolent.
30 I know his arrogance, says the LORD;
  his boasting is false, false are his deeds.
31 Therefore I shall wail over Moab,
  cry in anguish for the whole of Moab;
  I shall moan over the men of Kir-heres.
32 More than I wept for Jazer
  I shall weep for you, vine of Sibmah,
  whose branches spread out to the sea
  and reach as far as Jazer.
  The despoiler has fallen on your harvest and
    vintage;
33 gladness and joy are taken away
  from the garden land of Moab;
  I have dried up the flow of wine from the vats,
  and the shouts of those treading the grapes
  will echo no more.

34 Heshbon and Elealeh utter cries of anguish which are heard in Jahaz; the sound carries from Zoar to Horonaim and Eglath-shelishiyah; for the waters of Nimrim have become a desolate waste. 35 In Moab I shall put an end to their sacrificing at shrines and burning of offerings to their gods,

f Two Mss and Isa 16.8: MT the sea of Jazer   g Cn: Heb From the cry of Heshbon to Elealeh

48:32 as far as Jazer: prob. rdg, cp. Isa. 16:8; Heb. the sea of Jazer.   48:34 and Elealeh: prob. rdg, cp. Isa. 15:4; Heb. as far as Elealeh. Horonaim and: so Gk; Heb. omits and.

16 Near at hand is Moab's ruin,
  his disaster hastens apace.
17 Mourn for him, all you his neighbors,
  all you who knew him well!
  Say: How the strong staff is broken,
    the glorious rod!
18 Come down from glory, sit on the ground,
  you that dwell in Dibon;
  Moab's ravager has come up against you,
    he has ruined your strongholds.
19 Stand by the wayside, watch closely,
  you that dwell in Aroer;
  Ask the man who flees, the woman who tries
    to escape:
  say to them, "What has happened?"
20 Moab is disgraced, yes, destroyed,
  howl and cry out;
  Publish it at the Arnon,
    Moab is ruined!

21 For judgment has come on the land of the plateau: on Holon, Jahzah, and Mephaath, 22 on Dibon, Nebo, and Beth-diblathaim, 23 on Kiriathaim, Beth-gamul, and Beth-meon, 24 on Kerioth and on Bozrah: on all the cities of Moab, far and near.

25 Moab's strength is broken,
  his might is shattered, says the LORD.

26 Because he boasted against the LORD, make Moab drunk so that he retches and vomits, and he too becomes a laughingstock. 27 Is Israel a laughingstock to you? Was she caught among thieves, that you shake your head whenever you speak of her?

28 Leave the cities, dwell in the crags,
  you that dwell in Moab.
  Be like a dove that nests
    out of reach on the edge of a chasm.
29 We have heard of the pride of Moab,
  pride beyond bounds:
  His loftiness, his pride, his scorn,
    his insolence of heart.
30 I know, says the LORD, his arrogance;
  liar in boast, liar in deed.
31 And so I wail over Moab,
  over all Moab I cry,
  over the men of Kir-heres I moan.
32 More than for Jazer I weep over you,
  vineyard of Sibmah.
  Your tendrils trailed down to the sea,
    as far as Jazer they stretched.
  Upon your harvest, upon your vintage,
    the ravager has fallen.
33 Joy and jubilation are at an end
  in the fruit gardens of the land of Moab.
  I drain the wine from the wine vats,
    the treader treads no more,
    the vintage shout is stilled.

34 The cry of Heshbon and Elealeh is heard as far as Jahaz; they call from Zoar to Horonaim, and to Eglath-shelishiyah, for even the waters of Nimrim turn into a desert. 35 I will leave no one in Moab, says the LORD, to offer a holocaust on the high place, or to burn incense to his

16 Moab's ruin is coming soon,
  his downfall comes at top speed.
17 Grieve for him, all you living near him,
  all you who knew his name.
  Say, 'How shattered it is, that mighty rod,
    that splendid sceptre!'
18 Come down from your glory, sit on the parched
    ground,
  daughter of Dibon,
  for the despoiler of Moab has advanced on you,
    he has destroyed your strongholds.
19 Stand by the roadside, keep watch,
  daughter of Aroer.
  Question fugitive and runaway,
    ask, 'What has happened?'
20 'Moab has been shattered and shamed.
  Wail and shriek!
  Shout along the Arnon,
    Moab has been laid waste!'

21 Judgement has also come on the Plain, on Holon, Jahzah, Mephaath, 22 Dibon, Nebo, Beth-Diblathaim, 23 Kiriathaim, Beth-Gamul, Beth-Meon, 24 Kerioth, Bozrah, and all the towns of Moab, far and near.

25 Moab's horn has been cut off,
  his arm is broken, Yahweh declares.

26 Make him drunk! He has set himself up against Yahweh; let Moab wallow in his vomit and become a laughingstock in his turn. 27 Was Israel not a laughing-stock to you? Was he caught red-handed with the thieves, for you to shake your head whenever you mention him?

28 Leave the towns, make the rocks your home,
  inhabitants of Moab.
  Learn from the dove that makes its nest
    in the walls of the gaping gorge.

29 We have heard about Moab's pride,
  so very proud!
  What arrogance! What pride! What conceit!
  What a haughty heart!
30 —I know all about his presumption, Yahweh
    declares,
  his empty boasting,
  those empty deeds of his!
31 —and so I lament for Moab,
  for all Moab I raise my cry
  and mourn for the people of Kir-Heres. c
32 More than for Jazer I weep for you,
  vineyard of Sibmah:
  your shoots stretched beyond the sea,
  they reached all the way to Jazer.
  On your harvest and vintage
    the despoiler has descended.
33 Gladness and joy have vanished
  from the orchards of Moab.
  I have dried up the wine in the presses,
    the treader of grapes treads no more,
    the joyful shouting has ceased.

34 The cries of Heshbon and Elealeh can be heard as far as Jahaz. The shrieks resound from Zoar to Horonaim and Eglath-Shelishiyah, for even the Waters of Nimrim have become a wasteland.

35 And in Moab I shall make an end, Yahweh declares, of anyone offering sacrifice on the high places and anyone offering incense to his gods.

c 48 // Is 16:6–7.

NEW REVISED STANDARD VERSION

REVISED ENGLISH BIBLE

Moab like a flute, and my heart moans like a flute for the people of Kir-heres; for the riches they gained have perished.

37 For every head is shaved and every beard cut off; on all the hands there are gashes, and on the loins sackcloth. 38 On all the housetops of Moab and in the squares there is nothing but lamentation; for I have broken Moab like a vessel that no one wants, says the LORD. 39 How it is broken! How they wail! How Moab has turned his back in shame! So Moab has become a derision and a horror to all his neighbors.

40 For thus says the LORD:
Look, he shall swoop down like an eagle,
and spread his wings against Moab;
41 the towns[h] shall be taken
and the strongholds seized.
The hearts of the warriors of Moab, on that day,
shall be like the heart of a woman in labor.
42 Moab shall be destroyed as a people,
because he magnified himself against the
LORD.
43 Terror, pit, and trap
are before you, O inhabitants of Moab!
says the LORD.
44 Everyone who flees from the terror
shall fall into the pit,
and everyone who climbs out of the pit
shall be caught in the trap.
For I will bring these things[i] upon Moab
in the year of their punishment,
says the LORD.

45 In the shadow of Heshbon
fugitives stop exhausted;
for a fire has gone out from Heshbon,
a flame from the house of Sihon;
it has destroyed the forehead of Moab,
the scalp of the people of tumult.[j]
46 Woe to you, O Moab!
The people of Chemosh have perished,
for your sons have been taken captive,
and your daughters into captivity.
47 Yet I will restore the fortunes of Moab
in the latter days, says the LORD.
Thus far is the judgment on Moab.

49 Concerning the Ammonites.

Thus says the LORD:
Has Israel no sons?
Has he no heir?
Why then has Milcom dispossessed Gad,
and his people settled in its towns?
2 Therefore, the time is surely coming,
says the LORD,
when I will sound the battle alarm
against Rabbah of the Ammonites;
it shall become a desolate mound,
and its villages shall be burned with fire;
then Israel shall dispossess those who
dispossessed him,
says the LORD.

3 Wail, O Heshbon, for Ai is laid waste!
Cry out, O daughters[k] of Rabbah!
Put on sackcloth,
lament, and slash yourselves with whips![l]
For Milcom shall go into exile,
with his priests and his attendants.

says the LORD. 36 Therefore I wail for Moab like a reed-pipe, wail like a reed-pipe for the men of Kir-heres. Their accumulated wealth has vanished. 37 Every man's head is shorn in mourning, every beard clipped, every hand gashed, and every waist girded with sackcloth. 38 On all Moab's roofs and in all her broad streets nothing is heard but lamentation, for I have broken Moab like an unwanted pot, says the LORD. 39 Moab is dismayed and has turned away in shame. It has become a butt of derision and a cause of dismay to all round about.

40 For the LORD has spoken:

Like an eagle with outspread wings
he swoops down on Moab.
41 Towns are captured, the strongholds taken;
on that day the spirit of Moab's warriors will fail
like the spirit of a woman in labour.
42 The Moabite nation will be destroyed,
for it vaunted itself against the LORD.
43 The hunter's scare, the pit, and the trap
threaten you dwellers in Moab,
says the LORD.
44 If anyone runs from the scare
he will fall into the pit;
if someone climbs out of the pit
he will be caught in the trap.
All this I shall bring on Moab
in the year of their reckoning.
This is the word of the LORD.
45 In the shadow of Heshbon
the fugitives stand helpless;
for fire has blazed out from Heshbon,
flames from within Sihon
devouring the braggarts of Moab,
both forehead and crown.
46 Woe betide you, Moab!
The people of Kemosh have vanished,
for your sons are taken into captivity,
your daughters led away captive.
47 Yet in days to come I shall restore Moab's
fortunes.
This is the word of the LORD.

Here ends the judgement on Moab.

49 Of the Ammonites. Thus says the LORD:

Has Israel no sons? Has he no heir?
Why then has Milcom inherited the land of Gad,
and why do Milcom's people live in its towns?
2 Therefore a time is coming,
says the LORD,
when I shall make Rabbah of the Ammonites hear
the battle cry,
when it will become a desolate mound
and its villages will be burnt to ashes;
then Israel will disinherit all who disinherited
them,
says the LORD.

3 Wail, Heshbon, for Ai is despoiled;
cry aloud, you villages round Rabbah!
Put on sackcloth and beat your breast,
and score your bodies with gashes,
for Milcom will go into exile,
and with him his priests and attendants.

---

[h] Or Kerioth   [i] Gk Syr: Heb bring upon it   [j] Or of Shaon
[k] Or villages   [l] Cn: Meaning of Heb uncertain

48:39 **dismayed:** so Gk; Heb. adds they howl.   49:3 **gashes:** prob. rdg, cp. Aram. (Targ.); Heb. fences.

gods. 36 Hence the wail of flutes for Moab is in my heart; for the men of Kir-heres the wail of flutes is in my heart: the wealth they acquired has perished. 37 Every head has been made bald, every beard shaved; every hand is gashed, and the loins of all are clothed in sackcloth. 38 On every roof of Moab and in all his squares there is mourning; for I have shattered Moab like a pot that no one wants, says the LORD. 39 How terror seizes Moab, and wailing! How he turns his back in shame! Moab has become a laughingstock and a horror to all his neighbors! 40 For thus says the LORD:

Behold, like an eagle he soars,
   spreads his wings over Moab.
41 Cities are taken,
   strongholds seized:
On that day the hearts of Moab's heroes
   are like the heart of a woman in travail.
42 Moab shall be destroyed, no more a people,
   because he boasted against the LORD.
43 Terror, pit, and trap be upon you,
   people of Moab, says the LORD.
44 He who flees from the terror
   falls into the pit;
He who climbs from the pit
   is caught in the trap;
For I will bring these things upon Moab
   in the year of their punishment, says the LORD.
45 In Heshbon's shadow stop short
   the exhausted refugees;
For fire breaks forth from Heshbon,
   and a blaze from the house of Sihon:
It consumes the brow of Moab,
   the skull of the noisemakers.
46 Woe to you, O Moab,
   you are ruined, O people of Chemosh!
Your sons are taken into exile,
   your daughters into captivity.
47 But I will change the lot of Moab
   in the days to come, says the LORD.
Thus far the judgment of Moab.

49

Concerning the Ammonites, thus says the LORD:

Has Israel no sons?
   has he no heir?
Why then has Milcom disinherited Gad,
   why have his people settled in Gad's cities?
2 But the days are coming, says the LORD,
   when against Rabbah of the Ammonites
   I will sound the battle alarm;
She shall become a mound of ruins,
   and her daughter cities shall be destroyed
      by fire.
Israel shall inherit those who disinherited her,
   says the LORD.
3 Howl, Heshbon, for the ravager approaches,
   shriek, daughters of Rabbah!
Put on sackcloth and mourn,
   run to and fro, gashing yourselves;
For Milcom goes into exile
   along with his priests and captains.

36 That is why my heart sobs like a flute for Moab, sobs like a flute for the people of Kir-Heres, since the wealth he had acquired is lost. 37 Yes, every head is shaved, every beard cut off, gashes are on every hand, sackcloth round every waist. 38 On all the housetops of Moab and in all its squares there is nothing but lamenting, for I have broken Moab like an unwanted pot, Yahweh declares. 39 How shattered he is! Wail! Moab so shamefully in retreat! Moab has become a laughing-stock, a thing of horror to all his neighbours.

40 For Yahweh says this:
(Look, like an eagle, he will hover,
   spreading his wings over Moab.)
41 The towns have been captured,
   the strongholds seized.
(And the heart of Moab's warriors, that day,
   will be like that of a woman in labour pains.)
42 Moab will be destroyed, no longer a people,
   for setting itself up against Yahweh.
43 Terror, the pit and the snare for you,
   inhabitant of Moab,
   Yahweh declares.
44 And anyone who escapes from terror
   will fall into the pit,
and anyone who climbs out of the pit
   will be caught in the snare. d
Yes, I shall bring all this on Moab
   when the year comes for punishing them,
   Yahweh declares.
45 In the shelter of Heshbon the fugitives
   have paused, exhausted.
But fire will burst from Heshbon,
   a flame from the palace of Sihon,
consuming the brows of Moab,
   the head of a turbulent brood.
46 Disaster for you, Moab!
   The people of Chemosh are lost!
For your sons have been taken into exile
   and your daughters into captivity.

47 But I shall bring back Moab's captives
   in the final days, Yahweh declares.

Thus far the judgement on Moab.

49

To the Ammonites.

Yahweh says this:
Has Israel no sons?
Has he no heir?
Why should Milcom have inherited Gad
   and his people have settled in its towns?
2 And so the days are coming,
   Yahweh declares,
when I shall make the war cry ring out
   for Rabbah-of-the-Ammonites.
She will become a desolate mound
   and her daughter towns will be burnt down.
Then Israel will inherit from his heirs,
   Yahweh says.
3 Wail, Heshbon, for Ar has been laid waste!
   Shriek, daughters of Rabbah!
Wrap yourself in sackcloth, raise the dirge,
   run to and fro among the sheep-pens!
For Milcom is going into exile,
   with all his priests and princes.

d 48 // Is 24:17–18.

4 Why do you boast in your strength?
　　Your strength is ebbing,
　O faithless daughter.
　You trusted in your treasures, saying,
　　"Who will attack me?"
5 I am going to bring terror upon you,
　　says the Lord GOD of hosts,
　　from all your neighbors,
　and you will be scattered, each headlong,
　　with no one to gather the fugitives.

6 But afterward I will restore the fortunes of the Ammonites, says the LORD.

7 Concerning Edom.

Thus says the LORD of hosts:
　Is there no longer wisdom in Teman?
　　Has counsel perished from the prudent?
　　Has their wisdom vanished?
8 Flee, turn back, get down low,
　　inhabitants of Dedan!
　For I will bring the calamity of Esau upon him,
　　the time when I punish him.
9 If grape-gatherers came to you,
　　would they not leave gleanings?
　If thieves came by night,
　　even they would pillage only what they
　　　wanted.
10 But as for me, I have stripped Esau bare,
　　I have uncovered his hiding places,
　　and he is not able to conceal himself.
　His offspring are destroyed, his kinsfolk
　　and his neighbors; and he is no more.
11 Leave your orphans, I will keep them alive;
　　and let your widows trust in me.

12 For thus says the LORD: If those who do not deserve to drink the cup still have to drink it, shall you be the one to go unpunished? You shall not go unpunished; you must drink it. 13 For by myself I have sworn, says the LORD, that Bozrah shall become an object of horror and ridicule, a waste, and an object of cursing; and all her towns shall be perpetual wastes.

14 I have heard tidings from the LORD,
　　and a messenger has been sent among the
　　　nations:
　"Gather yourselves together and come against
　　her,
　　and rise up for battle!"
15 For I will make you least among the nations,
　　despised by humankind.
16 The terror you inspire
　　and the pride of your heart have deceived you,
　you who live in the clefts of the rock,[m]
　　who hold the height of the hill.
　Although you make your nest as high as the
　　eagle's,
　　from there I will bring you down,
　　　　　　　　　　　　　　says the LORD.

17 Edom shall become an object of horror; everyone who passes by it will be horrified and will hiss because of all its disasters. 18 As when Sodom and Gomorrah and their neighbors were overthrown, says the LORD, no one shall live there, nor shall anyone settle in it. 19 Like a lion coming

4 Why do you glory in your strength,
　you wayward people who trust in your arsenals
　and say, 'Who will dare attack me?'
5 Beware, I am bringing terror on you from every
　　side,
　says the Lord GOD of Hosts;
　every one of you will be driven headlong
　with no one to rally the fugitives.
6 Yet after this I shall restore the fortunes of
　　Ammon.
　This is the word of the LORD.

7 Of Edom. The LORD of Hosts has said:

　Is wisdom no longer to be found in Teman?
　Have her wise men lost all skill in counsel?
　Has their wisdom been dispersed abroad?
8 Turn and flee, people of Dedan,
　take refuge in remote places;
　for I shall bring retribution on Esau,
　his day of reckoning.
9 If vintagers were to come to you
　they would surely leave gleanings;
　and if thieves were to raid your crops by night,
　they would take only enough for their needs.
10 But I have ransacked Esau's treasure,
　I have uncovered his hiding-places,
　and he has nowhere to conceal himself.
　His children, his kinsfolk, and his neighbours are
　　despoiled;
　there is no one to deliver him.
11 Am I to keep alive your fatherless children?
　Are your widows to depend on me?

12 For these are the words of the LORD: Those who were not doomed to drink the cup must drink it none the less; are you alone to go unpunished? You will not escape; you will have to drink it. 13 For by my life, says the LORD, Bozrah will become an object of horror and reproach, a desolation and a thing of cursing; and all her towns will be desolate for ever.

14 When a herald was sent among the nations crying,
　'Gather and march against her,
　prepare for battle,'
　I heard this message from the LORD:
15 Look, I make you the least of all nations,
　most despised of people.
16 Your overbearing arrogance and your insolent heart
　have led you astray.
　You, whose haunts are in the crannies of the rock,
　you keep your hold on the hilltop.
　Though you nest as high as an eagle,
　even from there I shall bring you down.
　This is the word of the LORD.
17 Edom will become an object of horror,
　all who pass that way will be horror-struck,
　astounded at the sight of all her wounds,
18 overthrown as she is like Sodom and Gomorrah
　　and their neighbours,
　says the LORD.
　No one will live there,
　no human being will make a home in her.

[m] Or of Sela

4 Why do you glory in your strength,
  your ebbing strength, rebellious daughter?
You who trust in your treasures, saying,
  "Who can come against me?"
5 I am bringing terror upon you,
  says the Lord GOD of hosts,
  from all round about you;
You shall be scattered, each man in
  headlong flight,
  with no one to rally the fugitives.
6 But afterward I will change the lot
  of the Ammonites, says the LORD.

7 Concerning Edom, thus says the LORD of hosts:

Is there no more wisdom in Teman,
  has counsel perished from the prudent,
  has their wisdom become corrupt?
8 Flee, retreat, hide in deep holes,
  you who live in Dedan:
For I will bring destruction upon Esau
  when I come to punish him.
9 If vintagers came upon you,
  they would leave no gleanings;
If thieves by night,
  they would destroy as they pleased.
10 So I myself will strip Esau;
  I will uncover his retreats so that he cannot hide.
He is ruined: sons, and brothers,
  and neighbors, so that he is no more.
11 Leave your orphans behind, I will keep them alive;
  your widows, let them trust in me.

12 For thus says the LORD: Even those not sentenced to
drink the cup must drink it! Shall you then go unpunished?
You shall not go unpunished; you shall surely drink it. 13 By
my own self I have sworn, says the LORD: Bozrah shall
become an object of horror and a disgrace, a desolation and
a curse; she and all her cities shall become ruins forever.

14 I have heard a report from the LORD,
  a herald has been sent among the nations:
Gather together, move against her,
  rise up for battle.
15 Small will I make you among the nations,
  despised among men!
16 The terror you spread beguiled you,
  and your presumption of heart;
You that live in rocky crags,
  that hold the heights of the hill:
Though you build your nest high as the eagle,
  from there I will drag you down, says the LORD.

17 Edom shall become an object of horror. Every passer-
by shall be appalled and catch his breath at all her wounds.
18 As when Sodom, Gomorrah, and their neighbors were
overthrown, says the LORD, not a man shall dwell there: no
one shall visit there.

4 How you used to glory in your Valley,
  rebellious daughter,
  confident in your resources,
  'Who will dare to attack me?'
5 Look, I shall bring terror on you,
  Lord Yahweh Sabaoth declares,
  from all directions;
  you shall be driven away, everyone for himself,
  with no one to rally the fugitives.

6 (But later I shall bring back the captive Ammonites, Yahweh declares.)

7 To Edom. e

Yahweh says this:
  Is there no wisdom left in Teman?
  Have the shrewd run out of commonsense,
  has their wisdom vanished?
8 Away! Take to your heels! Go into hiding,
  inhabitants of Dedan,
  for I shall bring ruin on Esau
  when the time comes for me to punish him.
9 If grape-pickers were to come to you,
  would they not leave a few gleanings?
If robbers came during the night,
  would they not steal only as much as they wanted?
10 But I for my part have stripped Esau,
  have laid his hiding places bare:
  he can hide no longer.
His race is destroyed,
  so are his brothers and neighbours; he is no more!
11 Leave your orphans, I shall support them,
  and let your widows rely on me!

12 For Yahweh says this, 'Look, those who would not
have had to drink the cup will have to drink it all the same;
so why should you go unpunished? You will not go unpunished, but will certainly have to drink. 13 For by my own
self I have sworn, Yahweh declares, that Bozrah will become an object of horror, a laughing-stock, a desert, a
curse, and all its towns ruins for ever.'

14 I have received a message from Yahweh,
  a herald has been sent throughout the nations,
  'Muster! March against this people!
  Prepare for battle!'
15 For look, I shall reduce you to the smallest of
  nations,
  to the most despised of people.
16 Your reputation for ferocity,
  your proud heart has misled you.
You whose home is in the crannies of the Rock,
  who cling to the top of the peak!
Though you make your nest as high as the eagle's,
  I shall bring you down from there, Yahweh
  declares.

17 Edom will become an object of horror; everyone going
near will be appalled, and whistle at the sight of all her
wounds. 18 As at the overthrow of Sodom and Gomorrah
and their neighbouring towns, no one will live there any
more, Yahweh says, no human being settle there again. f

e 49 // Ob 1-6.   *f* 49 = 50:40.

| NEW REVISED STANDARD VERSION | REVISED ENGLISH BIBLE |

up from the thickets of the Jordan against a perennial pasture, I will suddenly chase Edom[n] away from it; and I will appoint over it whomever I choose.[o] For who is like me? Who can summon me? Who is the shepherd who can stand before me? 20 Therefore hear the plan that the LORD has made against Edom and the purposes that he has formed against the inhabitants of Teman: Surely the little ones of the flock shall be dragged away; surely their fold shall be appalled at their fate. 21 At the sound of their fall the earth shall tremble; the sound of their cry shall be heard at the Red Sea.[p] 22 Look, he shall mount up and swoop down like an eagle, and spread his wings against Bozrah, and the heart of the warriors of Edom in that day shall be like the heart of a woman in labor.

23 Concerning Damascus.

Hamath and Arpad are confounded,
for they have heard bad news;
they melt in fear, they are troubled like the sea[q]
that cannot be quiet.
24 Damascus has become feeble, she turned to flee,
and panic seized her;
anguish and sorrows have taken hold of her,
as of a woman in labor.
25 How the famous city is forsaken,[r]
the joyful town![s]
26 Therefore her young men shall fall in her squares,
and all her soldiers shall be destroyed in that
day,
says the LORD of hosts.
27 And I will kindle a fire at the wall of Damascus,
and it shall devour the strongholds of
Ben-hadad.

28 Concerning Kedar and the kingdoms of Hazor that King Nebuchadrezzar of Babylon defeated.

Thus says the LORD:
Rise up, advance against Kedar!
Destroy the people of the east!
29 Take their tents and their flocks,
their curtains and all their goods;
carry off their camels for yourselves,
and a cry shall go up: "Terror is all around!"
30 Flee, wander far away, hide in deep places,
O inhabitants of Hazor!
says the LORD.
For King Nebuchadrezzar of Babylon
has made a plan against you
and formed a purpose against you.
31 Rise up, advance against a nation at ease,
that lives secure,
says the LORD,
that has no gates or bars,
that lives alone.
32 Their camels shall become booty,
their herds of cattle a spoil.
I will scatter to every wind
those who have shaven temples,
and I will bring calamity
against them from every side,
says the LORD.

19 Like a lion coming up
from Jordan's dense thickets to the perennial
pastures,
in a moment I shall chase the shepherd away
and round up the choicest of the rams.
For who is like me? Who can arraign me?
What shepherd can stand his ground before me?

20 Therefore listen to the LORD's purpose against Edom and his plans against the people of Teman:

The young of the flock will be dragged off,
and their pasture will be aghast at their fate.
21 At the sound of their downfall the land quakes;
it cries out, and the sound is heard at the Red Sea.
22 Like an eagle with outspread wings
he will soar and swoop down against Bozrah,
and on that day the spirit of Edom's warriors
will be like the spirit of a woman in labour.

23 Of Damascus.

Hamath and Arpad are covered with confusion,
for they have heard news of disaster;
they are tossed up and down in anxiety
like the unresting sea.
24 Damascus has lost heart and turns to flight;
trembling has seized her,
pangs like childbirth have gripped her.
25 How forlorn is the town of joyful song,
the place of gladness!
26 Therefore her young men will fall in her streets
and all her warriors lie still in death that day.
This is the word of the LORD of Hosts.
27 Then I shall kindle a fire within the wall of
Damascus
and it will devour Ben-hadad's palaces.

28 Of Kedar and the kingdoms of Hazor which King Nebuchadrezzar of Babylon subdued. The LORD has said:

Come, attack Kedar,
despoil the eastern desert-dwellers.
29 Carry away their tents and their flocks,
the curtains of their tents and all their goods,
and drive off their camels.
A cry will go up: 'Terror let loose!'
30 Flee and make your escape,
take refuge in remote places, you people of Hazor,
says the LORD;
for King Nebuchadrezzar of Babylon has laid his
plans,
he has formed a design against you:
31 'Come, let us attack a nation at peace,
living in fancied security
with no barred gates,
dwelling in isolation.'
32 Their camels will be carried off as booty,
their vast herds of cattle as plunder;
I shall scatter them to all the winds
to roam the fringes of the desert,
and from every side I shall bring retribution on
them,
says the LORD.

---

n Heb him   o Or and I will single out the choicest of his rams: Meaning of Heb uncertain   p Or Sea of Reeds   q Cn: Heb there is trouble in the sea   r Vg: Heb is not forsaken   s Syr Vg Tg: Heb the town of my joy

49:19 **the choicest of:** prob. rdg; Heb. who is chosen? 49:21 **Red Sea:** or sea of Reeds.   49:23 **like:** so some MSS, others in.   49:25 **of gladness:** so Syriac; Heb. of my gladness. 49:31 **security:** so Gk; Heb. adds says the LORD.   49:32 **them . . . desert:** or to the wind those who clip the hair on their temples.

19 As when a lion comes up from the thicket
  of Jordan
    to the permanent feeding grounds,
So I, in an instant, will drive men off;
  and whom I choose I will establish there!
For who is like me? who can call me to account?
  What shepherd can stand against me?
20 Therefore, hear the counsel of the LORD,
  which he has taken against Edom;
Hear the plans he has made
  against those that live in Teman:
They shall be dragged away, even the smallest
  sheep,
  their own pasture shall be aghast because
    of them.
21 At the noise of their fall the earth quakes,
  to the Red Sea the outcry is heard!
22 See! like an eagle he soars aloft,
  and spreads his wings over Bozrah;
On that day the hearts of Edom's heroes shall be
  like the heart of a woman in travail.

Concerning Damascus:

23 Hamath and Arpad are covered with shame,
  they have heard bad news;
Worried, they toss like the sea
  which cannot rest.
24 Damascus is weakened, she turns to flee,
  panic has seized her.
Distress and pangs take hold of her,
  like those of a woman in travail.
25 How can the city of glory be forsaken,
  the town of delight!
26 But now her young men shall fall in her streets,
  and all her warriors shall be stilled.
On that day, says the LORD of hosts,
27 I will set fire to the wall of Damascus,
  and it shall devour the palaces of Ben-hadad.

28 Of Kedar and the kingdoms of Hazor, defeated by Nebuchadnezzar, king of Babylon, thus says the LORD:

Rise up, attack Kedar,
  ravage the Easterners.
29 Their tents and herds shall be taken away,
  their tent curtains and all their goods;
Their camels they shall carry off for themselves,
  and shout from upon them, "Terror on
    every side!"
30 Flee! leave your homes, hide in deep holes,
  you that live in Hazor, says the LORD;
For counsel has been taken against you,
  a plan has been formed against you
  [Nebuchadnezzar, king of Babylon].
31 Rise up! set out against a nation that is at peace,
  that lives secure, says the LORD,
That has no gates or bars,
  and dwells alone.
32 Their camels shall be your booty,
  their many herds your spoil;
I will scatter to the winds those who shave
  their temples,
  from all sides I will bring ruin upon them,
says the LORD.

19 Look, like a lion he climbs from the thickets of the
  Jordan
    to the perennial pasture!
In a flash, I shall make them run away,
  and there appoint someone I shall choose.
For who is there like me?
Who can hale me into court?
Name me the shepherd
  who can stand up to me.
20 So now hear the plan
  that Yahweh has laid against Edom,
  the schemes he has in mind
  against the inhabitants of Teman:
  they will certainly be dragged away
  like the smallest of the flock!
  Their pastures will certainly be sacked before their
    eyes!
21 The earth quakes at the sound of their downfall,g
  the sound of it echoes to the Sea of Reeds.
22 Look, like an eagle, he will soar and hover,
  spreading his wings over Bozrah.
  And the heart of Edom's warriors, that day,
  will be like that of a woman in labour pains.

23 To Damascus.

Hamath and Arpad are shamed,
  for they have heard bad news.
They are convulsed with anxiety
  like the sea that cannot be calmed.
24 Damascus is aghast, she prepares for flight,
  she is seized with trembling
  (anguish and sorrow have laid hold on her as on a
    woman in labour).
25 What now! That famous town deserted,
  that city of gaiety?

26 And so in her squares her young men will fall, and all
her fighting men will perish, that day, Yahweh Sabaoth
declares.h

27 I shall light a fire inside the walls of Damascus,
  to devour the palaces of Ben-Hadad.

28 To Kedar and the kingdoms of Hazor, which were conquered by Nebuchadnezzar king of Babylon. Yahweh says
this:

Up! March on Kedar,
  destroy the sons of the east!
29 Let their tents and their flocks be captured,
  their tent-cloths and all their gear;
  let their camels be seized
  and the shout go up, 'Terror on every side!'
30 Away! Get into hiding as fast as you can,
  inhabitants of Hazor, Yahweh declares,
  for Nebuchadnezzar king of Babylon has made a
    plan against you,
  he has a scheme in mind against you,
31 Up! March on a nation at its ease,
  living secure, Yahweh declares,
  that has no gates, no bars,
  that lives in a remote place!
32 Their camels will be the plunder,
  their countless sheep the spoil.
I shall scatter them to the winds,
  those Crop-Heads,
  and bring ruin on them from every side,
Yahweh declares.

g **49** = 50:44–46.   h **49** = 50:30.

NEW REVISED STANDARD VERSION	REVISED ENGLISH BIBLE

NEW REVISED STANDARD VERSION

33 Hazor shall become a lair of jackals,
an everlasting waste;
no one shall live there,
nor shall anyone settle in it.

34 The word of the LORD that came to the prophet Jeremiah concerning Elam, at the beginning of the reign of King Zedekiah of Judah.

35 Thus says the LORD of hosts: I am going to break the bow of Elam, the mainstay of their might; 36 and I will bring upon Elam the four winds from the four quarters of heaven; and I will scatter them to all these winds, and there shall be no nation to which the exiles from Elam shall not come. 37 I will terrify Elam before their enemies, and before those who seek their life; I will bring disaster upon them, my fierce anger, says the LORD. I will send the sword after them, until I have consumed them; 38 and I will set my throne in Elam, and destroy their king and officials, says the LORD.

39 But in the latter days I will restore the fortunes of Elam, says the LORD.

50 The word that the LORD spoke concerning Babylon, concerning the land of the Chaldeans, by the prophet Jeremiah:

2 Declare among the nations and proclaim,
set up a banner and proclaim,
do not conceal it, say:
Babylon is taken,
Bel is put to shame,
Merodach is dismayed.
Her images are put to shame,
her idols are dismayed.

3 For out of the north a nation has come up against her; it shall make her land a desolation, and no one shall live in it; both human beings and animals shall flee away.

4 In those days and in that time, says the LORD, the people of Israel shall come, they and the people of Judah together; they shall come weeping as they seek the LORD their God. 5 They shall ask the way to Zion, with faces turned toward it, and they shall come and join[r] themselves to the LORD by an everlasting covenant that will never be forgotten.

6 My people have been lost sheep; their shepherds have led them astray, turning them away on the mountains; from mountain to hill they have gone, they have forgotten their fold. 7 All who found them have devoured them, and their enemies have said, "We are not guilty, because they have sinned against the LORD, the true pasture, the LORD, the hope of their ancestors."

8 Flee from Babylon, and go out of the land of the Chaldeans, and be like male goats leading the flock. 9 For

REVISED ENGLISH BIBLE

33 Hazor will become a haunt of wolves,
for ever desolate,
where no one will live,
no mortal make a home.
This is the word of the LORD.

34 This came to the prophet Jeremiah as the word of the LORD concerning Elam, at the beginning of the reign of King Zedekiah of Judah: 35 Thus says the LORD of Hosts:

I shall break the bow of Elam,
the chief weapon of their might;
36 I shall bring four winds against Elam
from the four quarters of heaven;
I shall scatter them to all these winds,
and there will be no nation
to which the exiles from Elam do not go.
37 I shall break Elam before their foes,
before those who are bent on their destruction;
I shall vent my fierce anger upon them in disaster;
I shall pursue them with the sword
until I make an end of them,
says the LORD.
38 Then I shall set my throne in Elam,
and destroy the king and his officers there.
This is the word of the LORD.
39 Yet in days to come I shall restore the fortunes of
Elam.
This is the word of the LORD.

50 The word which the LORD spoke about Babylon, the land of the Chaldaeans, through the prophet Jeremiah:

2 Declare among the nations, make proclamation;
keep nothing back, spread the news:
Babylon is taken,
Bel put to shame, Marduk dismayed;
the idols of Babylon are put to shame,
her false gods are dismayed.
3 A nation has come out of the north against her;
it will make her land a desolate waste
with no one living there;
man and beast have fled and are gone.

4 In those days and at that time, says the LORD, the people of Israel and the people of Judah will come together, and in tears go in search of the LORD their God; 5 they will ask the way to Zion, turning their faces towards her, and saying, 'Come, let us join ourselves to the LORD in an everlasting covenant which will never be forgotten.'

6 My people were lost sheep, whose shepherds let them stray and run wild on the mountains; they wandered from mountain to hill, forgetful of their fold. 7 All who came on them devoured them; their enemies said, 'We incur no guilt, because they have sinned against the LORD, the LORD who is the true goal and the hope of their forefathers.'

8 Flee from Babylon, from the land of the
Chaldaeans;
go out like he-goats leading the flock.

50:2 **make proclamation:** *so Gk; Heb. adds* and raise a standard, proclaim. 50:5 **let us join ourselves:** *so Syriac; Heb.* they will join themselves.

[r] Gk: Heb *toward it. Come! They shall join*

NEW AMERICAN BIBLE

33 Hazor shall become a haunt of jackals,
   a desert forever,
Where no man lives,
   no human being stays.

34 The following word of the LORD against Elam came to the prophet Jeremiah at the beginning of the reign of Zedekiah, king of Judah: 35 Thus says the LORD of hosts:

Behold, I will break the bow of Elam,
   the mainstay of their might.
36 I will bring upon Elam the four winds
   from the four ends of the heavens;
I will scatter them to all these winds, till there is
      no nation
to which the outcasts of Elam shall not come.
37 I will break Elam before their foes,
   before those who seek their life;
I will bring evil upon them,
   my burning wrath, says the LORD.
I will send the sword to pursue them
   until I have completely made an end of them;
38 My throne I will set up in Elam
   and destroy from there king and princes,
   says the LORD.
39 But in the days to come I will change
   the lot of Elam, says the LORD.

50 The word which the LORD spoke against Babylon, against the land of the Chaldeans, through the prophet Jeremiah:

2 Announce and publish it among the nations;
   publish it, hide it not, but say:
Babylon is taken, Bel confounded,
      Merodach shattered;
   her images are put to shame, her idols shattered.
3 A people from the north advances against her
   to turn her land into a desert,
So that no one shall live there,
   because man and beast have fled away.
4 In those days, at that time, says the LORD,
   the men of Israel and of Judah shall come,
Weeping as they come, to seek the
   LORD, their God;
5   to their goal in Zion they shall ask the way.
"Come, let us join ourselves to the LORD
   with covenant everlasting, never to
      be forgotten."
6 Lost sheep were my people,
   their shepherds misled them,
   straggling on the mountains;
From mountain to hill they wandered,
   losing the way to their fold.
7 Whoever came upon them devoured them,
   and their enemies said, "We incur no guilt,
Because they sinned against the LORD,
   the hope of their fathers, their abode of justice."

8 Flee from Babylon, leave the land of
      the Chaldeans,
   be like the rams at the head of the flock.

NEW JERUSALEM BIBLE

33 Hazor will become the lair of jackals,
   desolate for ever.
No one will live there any more,
   no human being settle there again.

34 The word of Yahweh that came to the prophet Jeremiah about Elam, at the beginning of the reign of Zedekiah king of Judah. 35 'Yahweh Sabaoth says this:

Look, I shall break Elam's bow,
   the source of his might.
36 I shall bring four winds on Elam
   from the four corners of the sky,
and I shall scatter them to all these winds:
   there will not be a single nation
to which people expelled from Elam do not go.
37 I shall make the Elamites tremble before their
      enemies,
   before those determined to kill them.
I shall bring disaster on them,
   my burning anger, Yahweh declares.
I shall pursue them with the sword
   until I have destroyed them all.
38 I shall set up my throne in Elam,
   uprooting its king and princes,
   Yahweh declares.

39 In the final days, I shall bring Elam's captives back,
Yahweh declares.'

50 The word that Yahweh spoke against Babylon, against the country of the Chaldaeans, through the prophet Jeremiah.

2 Announce it to the nations, proclaim it,
   hoist a signal and proclaim it,
making no secret of it, say,
'Babylon is captured, Bel disgraced,
   Marduk[i] shattered.
(Her idols are disgraced,
   her Obscenities shattered.)'
3 For a nation is marching on her from the north,
   to turn her country into a desert:
no one will live there any more;
   human and animal have fled and gone.
4 In those days and at that time
   the people of Israel will return
   (they and the people of Judah);
they will come weeping
   in search of Yahweh their God.
5 They will ask the way to Zion
   and turn their faces towards her,
'Come, let us bind ourselves to Yahweh
   by an everlasting covenant never to be forgotten!'
6 Lost sheep, such were my people;
   their shepherds led them astray, the mountains
      misled them;
from mountain to hill they went,
   forgetful of their fold.
7 Whoever came across them devoured them,
   their enemies said, 'We are not to blame,
since they have sinned against Yahweh, the Home
      of Justice,
against Yahweh, the Hope of their ancestors.'
8 Escape from Babylon,
   leave the country of the Chaldaeans.
Be like he-goats, leading the sheep!

i 50 Bel and Marduk are the chief gods of Babylon.

NEW REVISED STANDARD VERSION

I am going to stir up and bring against Babylon a company of great nations from the land of the north; and they shall array themselves against her; from there she shall be taken. Their arrows are like the arrows of a skilled warrior who does not return empty-handed. 10 Chaldea shall be plundered; all who plunder her shall be sated, says the LORD.

11 Though you rejoice, though you exult,
    O plunderers of my heritage,
  though you frisk about like a heifer on the grass,
    and neigh like stallions,
12 your mother shall be utterly shamed,
    and she who bore you shall be disgraced.
  Lo, she shall be the last of the nations,
    a wilderness, dry land, and a desert.
13 Because of the wrath of the LORD she shall not
    be inhabited,
  but shall be an utter desolation;
  everyone who passes by Babylon shall be
    appalled
    and hiss because of all her wounds.
14 Take up your positions around Babylon,
    all you that bend the bow;
  shoot at her, spare no arrows,
    for she has sinned against the LORD.
15 Raise a shout against her from all sides,
    "She has surrendered;
  her bulwarks have fallen,
    her walls are thrown down."
  For this is the vengeance of the LORD:
    take vengeance on her,
    do to her as she has done.
16 Cut off from Babylon the sower,
    and the wielder of the sickle in time of harvest;
  because of the destroying sword
    all of them shall return to their own people,
    and all of them shall flee to their own land.

17 Israel is a hunted sheep driven away by lions. First the king of Assyria devoured it, and now at the end King Nebuchadrezzar of Babylon has gnawed its bones. 18 Therefore, thus says the LORD of hosts, the God of Israel: I am going to punish the king of Babylon and his land, as I punished the king of Assyria. 19 I will restore Israel to its pasture, and it shall feed on Carmel and in Bashan, and on the hills of Ephraim and in Gilead its hunger shall be satisfied. 20 In those days and at that time, says the LORD, the iniquity of Israel shall be sought, and there shall be none; and the sins of Judah, and none shall be found; for I will pardon the remnant that I have spared.

21 Go up to the land of Merathaim;u
    go up against her,
  and attack the inhabitants of Pekodv
    and utterly destroy the last of them,w
                              says the LORD;
    do all that I have commanded you.
22 The noise of battle is in the land,
    and great destruction!
23 How the hammer of the whole earth
    is cut down and broken!
  How Babylon has become
    a horror among the nations!

REVISED ENGLISH BIBLE

9 I shall stir up a host of mighty nations
    and bring them against Babylon,
  marshalled against her from a northern land;
    and from the north she will be captured.
  Their arrows are like those of a skilled warrior
    who never returns empty-handed;
10 the Chaldaeans will be plundered,
    and all who plunder them will take their fill.
  This is the word of the LORD.
11 You plundered my possession; but though you
      rejoice and exult,
    though you run free like a heifer during the
      threshing,
    though you neigh like a stallion,
12 your mother will be cruelly disgraced,
    she who bore you will be put to shame.
  Look at her, bringing up the rear of the nations,
    a wilderness, parched and barren,
13 uninhabited through the wrath of the LORD,
    an object of horror;
  all who pass by Babylon will be horror-struck
    and astounded at the sight of her many wounds.
14 Marshal your forces and encircle Babylon,
    you whose bows are ready strung;
  shoot at her, spare not your arrows,
    for she has sinned against the LORD.
15 On every side shout in triumph over her;
    she has surrendered,
  her bastions are thrown down, her walls
      demolished.
  This is the vengeance of the LORD;
    be avenged on her;
    as she has done, so do to her.
16 Destroy every sower in Babylon,
    every reaper with his sickle at harvest time.
  To escape the cruel sword
    everyone will turn back to his people,
    everyone flee to his own land.

17 Israel is a scattered flock
    harried and chased by lions:
  the Assyrian king was the first to devour him,
    and now at the last his bones have been gnawed
    by King Nebuchadrezzar of Babylon.

18 Therefore the LORD of Hosts the God of Israel says this:

  I shall punish the king of Babylon and his country
    as once I punished the king of Assyria.
19 But I shall bring Israel back to his own pasture,
    to graze on Carmel and Bashan;
  on Ephraim's hills and in Gilead he will eat his
    fill.

20 In those days, says the LORD, when that time comes, search will be made for the iniquity of Israel, but there will be none, and for the sin of Judah, but it will not be found; for those whom I leave as a remnant I shall pardon.

21 Attack the land of Merathaim;
    attack it and the inhabitants of Pekod;
  put them to the sword and utterly destroy them,
    and do whatever I command you.
  This is the word of the LORD.
22 The sound of war is heard in the land
    and great destruction!
23 See how the hammer of the whole world
    is hacked and broken,
  how Babylon has become
    a thing of horror among the nations!

---

u Or of Double Rebellion   v Or of Punishment   w Tg: Heb destroy
after them

9 See, I am stirring up against Babylon
  a band of great nations from the north;
  from there they advance, and she shall be taken.
  Their arrows are arrows of the skilled warrior;
  none shall return without effect.
10 Chaldea shall be their plunder,
  and all her plunderers shall be enriched,
  says the LORD.
11 Yes, rejoice and exult,
  you that plunder my portion;
  Frisk like calves on the green,
  snort like stallions!
12 Your mother shall be sorely put to shame,
  she that bore you shall be abashed;
  See, the last of the nations,
  a desert, dry and waste.
13 Because of the LORD's wrath she shall be empty,
  and become a total desert;
  Everyone who passes by Babylon will be appalled
  and catch his breath, at all her wounds.
14 Take your posts encircling Babylon,
  you who bend the bow;
  Shoot at her, spare not your arrows,
15   raise the war cry against her on all sides.
  She surrenders, her bastions fall,
  her walls are torn down:
  Vengeance of the LORD is this! Take revenge
    on her,
  as she has done, do to her;
  for she sinned against the LORD.
16 Cut off from Babylon the sower
  and him who wields the sickle in harvest time!
  Before the destroying sword,
  each of them turns to his own people,
  everyone flees to his own land.
17 A stray sheep was Israel
  that lions pursued;
  Formerly the king of Assyria devoured her,
  now Nebuchadnezzar of Babylon gnaws
    her bones.
18 Therefore, thus says the LORD of hosts, the God of
Israel:

  I will punish the king of Babylon and his land,
  as once I punished the king of Assyria;
19 But I will bring back Israel to her fold,
  to feed on Carmel and Bashan,
  And on Mount Ephraim and Gilead,
  till she has her fill.

20 In those days, at that time, says the LORD:

  They shall seek Israel's guilt, but it shall be
    no more,
  and Judah's sins, but these shall no longer
    be found;
  for I will forgive the remnant I preserve.

21 Attack the land of Merathaim,
  and those who live in Pekod;
  Slaughter and doom them, says the LORD,
  do all I have commanded you.
22 Battle alarm in the land,
  dire destruction!
23 How has the hammer of the whole earth
  been broken and shattered!
  What an object of horror
  Babylon has become among the nations.

9 For look, I shall raise a league
  of mighty nations to attack Babylon,
  from the land of the north.
  They will take up position against her;
  by them she will be taken.
  Their arrows, like an experienced soldier's,
  never return in vain.
10 Chaldaea will be plundered,
  all her plunderers will be satisfied, Yahweh
    declares.

11 Rejoice! Have your triumph,
  you plunderers of my heritage!
  Be playful like a heifer let out to grass!
  Neigh like stallions!
12 But your mother is covered with shame,
  disgraced is the woman who bore you;
  she is the least of nations now;
  a desert, a parched land, a wasteland.
13 Because of Yahweh's anger,
  no one will live there any more,
  she will become a total solitude.
  All who pass by Babylon will be appalled
  and whistle at the sight of all her wounds.

14 Take position against Babylon, surround her,
  all you who bend the bow.
  Shoot at her! Do not spare your arrows,
  for she has sinned against Yahweh!
15 Raise the war cry against her from all sides.
  She surrenders! Her bastions fall!
  Her walls collapse!
  This is Yahweh's vengeance! Take revenge on her.
  Treat her as she has treated others.
16 Deprive Babylon of the man who sows,
  of the man who wields the sickle at harvest.
  Away from the devastating sword,
  let everyone return to his own people,
  let everyone flee to his own country!

17 Israel was a straying sheep
  pursued by lions.

First, the king of Assyria devoured him, and latterly Nebuchadnezzar king of Babylon crunched his bones. 18 So
Yahweh Sabaoth, God of Israel, says this: Look, I shall
punish the king of Babylon and his country as I punished the
king of Assyria.

19 I will bring Israel back to his pastures
  to browse on Carmel and in Bashan,
  on the highlands of Ephraim and in Gilead,
  and he will be satisfied.
20 In those days and at that time, Yahweh declares,
  you may look for Israel's guilt, it will not be there,
  for Judah's sins, you will not find them,
  for I shall pardon the remnant that I leave.

21 March on the country of Merathaim,
  march on it
  and on the inhabitants of Pekod;
  slaughter and curse with destruction every last one
    of them,
  Yahweh declares,
  carry out my orders to the letter!
22 The din of battle fills the country,
  immense destruction.

23 How utterly shattered
  that hammer of the whole world!
  What a thing of horror Babylon has become
  throughout the nations!

24 You set a snare for yourself and you were
 caught, O Babylon,
 but you did not know it;
you were discovered and seized,
 because you challenged the LORD.
25 The LORD has opened his armory,
 and brought out the weapons of his wrath,
for the Lord GOD of hosts has a task to do
 in the land of the Chaldeans.
26 Come against her from every quarter;
 open her granaries;
pile her up like heaps of grain, and destroy her
 utterly;
 let nothing be left of her.
27 Kill all her bulls,
 let them go down to the slaughter.
Alas for them, their day has come,
 the time of their punishment!

28 Listen! Fugitives and refugees from the land of Babylon are coming to declare in Zion the vengeance of the
LORD our God, vengeance for his temple.

29 Summon archers against Babylon, all who bend the
bow. Encamp all around her; let no one escape. Repay her
according to her deeds; just as she has done, do to her — for
she has arrogantly defied the LORD, the Holy One of Israel.
30 Therefore her young men shall fall in her squares, and all
her soldiers shall be destroyed on that day, says the LORD.

31 I am against you, O arrogant one,
 says the Lord GOD of hosts;
for your day has come,
 the time when I will punish you.
32 The arrogant one shall stumble and fall,
 with no one to raise him up,
and I will kindle a fire in his cities,
 and it will devour everything around him.

33 Thus says the LORD of hosts: The people of Israel are
oppressed, and so too are the people of Judah; all their
captors have held them fast and refuse to let them go.
34 Their Redeemer is strong; the LORD of hosts is his name.
He will surely plead their cause, that he may give rest to the
earth, but unrest to the inhabitants of Babylon.

35 A sword against the Chaldeans, says the LORD,
 and against the inhabitants of Babylon,
 and against her officials and her sages!
36 A sword against the diviners,
 so that they may become fools!
A sword against her warriors,
 so that they may be destroyed!
37 A sword against her[x] horses and against her[x]
 chariots,
 and against all the foreign troops in her midst,
 so that they may become women!
A sword against all her treasures,
 that they may be plundered!
38 A drought[y] against her waters,
 that they may be dried up!
For it is a land of images,
 and they go mad over idols.

24 Babylon, you have set a snare for yourself
and have been trapped unawares.
There you are, you are caught,
because you have challenged the LORD.
25 The LORD has opened his armoury
and brought out the weapons of his wrath;
for this is work for the Lord the GOD of Hosts to
 do
in the land of the Chaldaeans.
26 Come against her from every quarter;
throw open her granaries,
pile her like heaps of grain;
destroy her completely,
let no survivor be left.
27 Put all her warriors to the sword;
let them be led to the slaughter.
Woe betide them, for their time has come,
their day of reckoning!
28 I hear the fugitives escaping from the land of
 Babylon
to proclaim in Zion the vengeance of the LORD our
 God,
the vengeance he takes for his temple.

29 Let your arrows whistle against Babylon,
all you whose bows are ready strung.
Besiege her on all sides;
let no one escape.
Repay her in full for her misdeeds;
as she has done, so do to her,
for she has insulted the LORD
the Holy One of Israel.
30 Therefore her young men will fall in her streets,
and all her warriors lie still in death that day.
This is the word of the LORD.

31 I am against you, insolent city;
for your time has come, your day of reckoning.
This is the word of the Lord GOD of Hosts.
32 The insolent one will stumble and fall
and no one will lift her up;
I shall kindle fire in her towns
and it will devour everything round about.

33 The LORD of Hosts has said this:

The peoples of Israel and Judah are both
 oppressed;
their captors all hold them fast
and will not let go.
34 But they have a powerful advocate,
whose name is the LORD of Hosts;
he himself will take up their cause,
that he may give distress to the land
and turmoil to the inhabitants of Babylon.

35 A sword hangs over the Chaldaeans,
over the people of Babylon,
her officers and wise men,
says the LORD.
36 A sword hangs over the false prophets,
and they are made fools,
a sword over her warriors, and they despair,
37 a sword over her horses and her chariots
and over all the mixed rabble within her,
and they will become like women;
a sword over her treasures, and they will be
 plundered,
38 a sword over her waters, and they will dry up;
for it is a land of idols
that glories in its dreaded gods.

---

[x] Cn: Heb *his*   [y] Another reading is *A sword*   50:26 **from every quarter:** *prob. rdg; Heb.* at the end.

NEW AMERICAN BIBLE

NEW JERUSALEM BIBLE

24 You ensnared yourself, and were caught,
  O Babylon, before you knew it!
You were discovered and seized,
  because you challenged the LORD.
25 The LORD opens his armory
  and brings forth the weapons of his wrath;
For the Lord GOD of hosts has work to do
  in the land of the Chaldeans.
26 Come upon her from every side,
  open her granaries,
Pile up her goods in heaps and doom it,
  leave not a remnant.
27 Slay all her oxen,
  let them go down to the slaughter;
Woe to them! their day has come,
  the time of their punishment.
28 Listen! the fugitives, the escaped
  from the land of Babylon:
They announce in Zion
  the vengeance of the LORD, our God.
29 Call up against Babylon archers,
  all who bend the bow;
Encamp around her,
  let no one escape.
Repay her for her deeds;
  as she has done, do to her,
For she insulted the LORD,
  the Holy One of Isreal.
30 Therefore her young men shall fall in her streets,
  all her warriors shall perish on that day;
  says the LORD.

31 I am against you, man of insolence,
  says the Lord GOD of hosts;
For your day has come,
  the time for me to punish you.
32 Insolence stumbles and falls;
  there is no one to raise him up.
I will kindle in his cities a fire
  that shall devour everything around him.
33 Thus says the LORD of hosts:
Oppressed are the men of Israel,
  and with them the men of Judah;
All their captors hold them fast
  and refuse to let them go.
34 Strong is their avenger,
  whose name is LORD of hosts;
He will defend their cause with success,
  and give rest to the earth,
  but unrest to those who live in Babylon.

35 A sword upon the Chaldeans, says the LORD,
  upon Babylon's people, her princes and
    wise men!
36 A sword upon the soothsayers,
  that they may become fools!
A sword upon her warriors,
  that they may tremble;
37 A sword upon her motley throng,
  that they may become women!
A sword upon her treasures,
  that they may be plundered;
38 A sword upon her waters,
  that they may dry up!
For it is a land of idols,
  and they shall be made frantic by fearful things.

24 I set a snare for you, Babylon; you were caught
  before you knew it.
You have been found and overpowered
  for having defied Yahweh.
25 Yahweh has opened his armoury
  and taken out the weapons of his fury.
For Lord Yahweh Sabaoth has work to do
  in the country of the Chaldaeans.
26 Fall on her from every side,
  open her granaries,
pile her in heaps, curse her with destruction,
  until nothing is left of her.
27 Slaughter all her bulls,
  down to the slaughterhouse with them!
Disaster on them, their day has come,
  their time for being punished.
28 Listen! Fugitives and runaways
  from the country of Babylon
arrive in Zion and proclaim
  the revenge of Yahweh our God,
  revenge for his Temple!
29 Call up the archers against Babylon!
All you who bend the bow,
  invest her on all sides,
  leave her no way of escape.
Repay her as her deeds deserve;
  treat her as she has treated others,
for she was arrogant to Yahweh,
  to the Holy One of Israel.

30 And so in her squares her young men will fall, and all
her fighting men will perish, that day, Yahweh declares.j

31 My quarrel is with you, 'Arrogance!'
  Lord Yahweh Sabaoth declares,
your day has come,
  the time for me to punish you.
32 'Arrogance' will stumble, she will fall,
  no one will lift her up:
I shall set fire to her towns
  and it will devour all around it.
33 Yahweh Sabaoth says this:
The people of Israel are oppressed
  (and the people of Judah too),
all their captors hold them fast,
  they will not let them go.
34 But their redeemer is strong:
  Yahweh Sabaoth is his name.
He will take up their cause,
  to give our country rest
but make the inhabitants of Babylon tremble.

35 A sword against the Chaldaeans, Yahweh declares,
  against the inhabitants of Babylon,
  against her princes and her sages!
36 A sword against her diviners: may they lose their
    wits!
A sword against her warriors: may they panic!
37 A sword against her horses, her chariots
  and the conglomeration of people inside her:
  may they be like women!
A sword against her treasures: may they be
    plundered!
38 Drought on her waters: may they dry up!
For it is a country of idols,
  and they are mad about those bogeys of theirs!

NEW REVISED STANDARD VERSION	REVISED ENGLISH BIBLE

39 Therefore wild animals shall live with hyenas in Babylon,*z* and ostriches shall inhabit her; she shall never again be peopled, or inhabited for all generations. 40 As when God overthrew Sodom and Gomorrah and their neighbors, says the LORD, so no one shall live there, nor shall anyone settle in her.

41 Look, a people is coming from the north;
a mighty nation and many kings
are stirring from the farthest parts of the earth.
42 They wield bow and spear,
they are cruel and have no mercy.
The sound of them is like the roaring sea;
they ride upon horses,
set in array as a warrior for battle,
against you, O daughter Babylon!

43 The king of Babylon heard news of them,
and his hands fell helpless;
anguish seized him,
pain like that of a woman in labor.

44 Like a lion coming up from the thickets of the Jordan against a perennial pasture, I will suddenly chase them away from her; and I will appoint over her whomever I choose.*a* For who is like me? Who can summon me? Who is the shepherd who can stand before me? 45 Therefore hear the plan that the LORD has made against Babylon, and the purposes that he has formed against the land of the Chaldeans: Surely the little ones of the flock shall be dragged away; surely their*b* fold shall be appalled at their fate. 46 At the sound of the capture of Babylon the earth shall tremble, and her cry shall be heard among the nations.

39 Therefore marmots and jackals will skulk in it, desert-owls will haunt it; never more will it be inhabited and age after age no one will dwell in it. 40 It will be as when God overthrew Sodom and Gomorrah along with their neighbours, says the LORD; no one will live in it, no human being will make a home there.

41 See, an army is coming from the north;
a great nation and mighty kings
rouse themselves from earth's farthest corners.
42 Armed with bow and scimitar,
they are cruel and pitiless;
bestriding their horses,
they sound like the thunder of the sea;
they are like men arrayed
for battle against you, Babylon.
43 News of them has reached the king of Babylon,
and his hands hang limp;
agony grips him,
pangs as of a woman in labour.
44 Like a lion coming up
from Jordan's dense thickets to the perennial
pastures,
in a moment I shall chase the shepherd away
and round up the choicest of the rams.
For who is like me? Who can challenge me?
What shepherd can stand his ground before me?

45 Therefore listen to the LORD's purpose against Babylon and his plans against the land of the Chaldaeans:

The young of the flock will be dragged off,
and their pasture will be aghast at their fate.
46 At the sound of Babylon's capture the land quakes;
it cries out, and the sound is heard throughout the
nations.

51 Thus says the LORD:
I am going to stir up a destructive wind*c*
against Babylon
and against the inhabitants of Leb-qamai;*d*
2 and I will send winnowers to Babylon,
and they shall winnow her.
They shall empty her land
when they come against her from every side
on the day of trouble.
3 Let not the archer bend his bow,
and let him not array himself in his coat of
mail.
Do not spare her young men;
utterly destroy her entire army.
4 They shall fall down slain in the land of the
Chaldeans,
and wounded in her streets.
5 Israel and Judah have not been forsaken
by their God, the LORD of hosts;
though their land is full of guilt
before the Holy One of Israel.

51 For thus says the LORD:

I shall raise a destructive wind
against Babylon and the inhabitants of Leb-kamai.
2 I shall send winnowers to Babylon
who will winnow her land empty;
for they will assail her from all sides
on the day of disaster.
3 How will the archer then string his bow
or put on his coat of mail?

Spare none of her young men, but utterly destroy
her whole army
4 and let them fall dead in the land of the
Chaldaeans,
slain in her streets.
5 Israel and Judah are not left widowed
by their God, by the LORD of Hosts;
but their land is full of guilt,
condemned by the Holy One of Israel.

---

z Heb lacks *in Babylon*   *a* Or *and I will single out the choicest of her rams*: Meaning of Heb uncertain   *b* Syr Gk Tg Compare 49.20: Heb lacks *their*   *c* Or *stir up the spirit of a destroyer*   *d* Leb-qamai is a cryptogram for *Kasdim,* Chaldea

50:44 **the choicest of:** *prob. rdg; Heb.* who is chosen?
51:1 **Leb-kamai:** *a cipher for* Chaldaea.

NEW AMERICAN BIBLE	NEW JERUSALEM BIBLE

NEW AMERICAN BIBLE

39 Hence, wildcats and desert beasts shall dwell there,
  and ostriches shall occupy it;
Never again shall it be peopled, or lived in,
  from age to age.
40 As when God overturned Sodom
  and Gomorrah, with their neighbors, says
    the LORD,
Not a man shall dwell there,
  no human being shall tarry there.
41 See! a people comes from the north,
  a great nation, and mighty kings
    roused from the ends of the earth.
42 Bow and javelin they wield,
  cruel and pitiless are they;
They sound like the roaring sea,
  as they ride forth on steeds,
Each in his place for battle
  against you, daughter Babylon.
43 The king of Babylon hears news of them,
  and helpless fall his hands;
Anguish seizes him,
  throes like a mother's in childbirth.
44 As when a lion comes up from the Jordan's thicket
  to the permanent feeding grounds,
So I, in one instant, will drive them off,
  and whom I choose I will establish there;
For who is like me? who calls me to account?
  what shepherd can stand against me?
45 Therefore hear the counsel of the LORD
  which he has taken against Babylon;
Hear the plans he has made
  against the land of the Chaldeans:
They shall be dragged away, even the
    smallest sheep;
  their own pasture shall be aghast because
    of them.
46 At the cry "Babylon is captured!" the earth quakes;
  the outcry is heard among the nations.

51 Thus says the LORD:
See! I rouse against Babylon,
  and against those who live in Chaldea,
  a destroying wind.
2 Against Babylon I will send winnowers
  to winnow her and lay waste her land;
They shall besiege her from all sides
  on the day of affliction.
3 Let the bowman draw his bow,
  and flaunt his coat of mail;
Spare not her young men,
  doom her entire army.
4 The slain shall fall in the land of Chaldea,
  the transfixed, in her streets;
5 For Israel and Judah are not widowed
  of their God, the LORD of hosts,
And the Chaldean land is full of guilt
  to be punished by the Holy One of Israel.

NEW JERUSALEM BIBLE

39 Hence wild cats and jackals will live there,
  and ostriches make their home there.
She will never again be inhabited, for ever,
  but remain uninhabited age after age.
40 As when God overthrew Sodom and Gomorrah,
  and their neighbouring towns,
  Yahweh declares,
no one will live there any more,
  no human being settle there again. k
41 Look, a people is coming from the north,
  a mighty nation;
from the far ends of the earth
  many kings are stirring.
42 They are armed with bow and spear,
  they are cruel and pitiless;
their noise is like the roaring of the sea;
  they ride horses,
ready as one man to fight you,
  daughter of Babylon!
43 The king of Babylon l has heard the news,
  his hands fall limp,
anguish has seized him,
  pain like that of a woman in labour.
44 Look, like a lion he climbs the thickets of the
    Jordan
  to the perennial pasture!
In a flash I shall make them run away
  and there appoint someone I shall choose.
For who is there like me?
  Who can hale me into court?
Name me the shepherd
  who can stand up to me.
45 So now hear the plan
  that Yahweh has laid against Babylon,
the schemes he has in mind
  against the country of the Chaldaeans:
they will certainly be dragged away
  like the smallest in the flock!
Their pastures will certainly be sacked before their
    eyes!
46 The earth quakes at the sound of Babylon's
    capture, m
  and the shouting echoes through the nations.

51 Yahweh says this:
Against Babylon and the inhabitants of
    Leb-Kamai
I shall rouse a destructive wind.
2 I shall send winnowers to Babylon to winnow her
  and leave her country bare,
for she will be beleaguered on all sides,
  on the day of disaster.
3 Let no archer bend his bow!
Let no man swagger in his breastplate!
  —No quarter for her young men!
Curse her whole army with destruction!
4 In the country of the Chaldaeans the slaughtered
    will fall,
  in the streets of Babylon, those run through by the
    sword.
5 For Israel and Judah have not been bereft
  of their God, Yahweh Sabaoth,
although their country was full of sin
  against the Holy One of Israel.

k 50 = 49:18.   l 50 = 6:22–23.   m 50 = 49:19–21.

NEW REVISED STANDARD VERSION

6 Flee from the midst of Babylon,
      save your lives, each of you!
   Do not perish because of her guilt,
      for this is the time of the LORD's vengeance;
      he is repaying her what is due.
7 Babylon was a golden cup in the LORD's hand,
      making all the earth drunken;
   the nations drank of her wine,
      and so the nations went mad.
8 Suddenly Babylon has fallen and is shattered;
      wail for her!
   Bring balm for her wound;
      perhaps she may be healed.
9 We tried to heal Babylon,
      but she could not be healed.
   Forsake her, and let each of us go
      to our own country;
   for her judgment has reached up to heaven
      and has been lifted up even to the skies.
10 The LORD has brought forth our vindication;
      come, let us declare in Zion
      the work of the LORD our God.

11 Sharpen the arrows!
      Fill the quivers!
The LORD has stirred up the spirit of the kings of the Medes,
because his purpose concerning Babylon is to destroy it, for
that is the vengeance of the LORD, vengeance for his temple.
12 Raise a standard against the walls of Babylon;
      make the watch strong;
   post sentinels;
      prepare the ambushes;
   for the LORD has both planned and done
      what he spoke concerning the inhabitants of
         Babylon.
13 You who live by mighty waters,
      rich in treasures,
   your end has come,
      the thread of your life is cut.
14 The LORD of hosts has sworn by himself:
   Surely I will fill you with troops like a swarm of
      locusts,
   and they shall raise a shout of victory over
      you.

15 It is he who made the earth by his power,
      who established the world by his wisdom,
   and by his understanding stretched out the
      heavens.
16 When he utters his voice there is a tumult of
      waters in the heavens,
   and he makes the mist rise from the ends of
      the earth.
   He makes lightnings for the rain,
      and he brings out the wind from his
         storehouses.
17 Everyone is stupid and without knowledge;
      goldsmiths are all put to shame by their idols;
   for their images are false,
      and there is no breath in them.
18 They are worthless, a work of delusion;
      at the time of their punishment they shall
         perish.
19 Not like these is the LORD,[e] the portion of
      Jacob,
   for he is the one who formed all things,
   and Israel is the tribe of his inheritance;
      the LORD of hosts is his name.

[e] Heb lacks the LORD

REVISED ENGLISH BIBLE

6 Flee out of Babylon, each one for himself,
      or you will perish for her sin;
   for this is the LORD's day of vengeance,
      and he is paying her full recompense.
7 Babylon has been a golden cup in the LORD's hand
      to make all the earth drunk;
   the nations have drunk of her wine,
      and that has made them mad.
8 Suddenly Babylon falls and is broken.
   Wail for her!
   Fetch balm for her wound;
      perhaps she may be healed.
9 We tried to heal Babylon, but she is past healing.
   Leave her and let us be off, each to his own
         country;
   for her doom reaches to heaven
      and mounts up to the skies.
10 The LORD has made our victory plain to see;
      come, let us proclaim in Zion
      what the LORD our God has done.

11 Sharpen the arrows, fill the quivers.
   The LORD has roused the spirit of the king of the
         Medes;
   for the LORD's purpose against Babylon is to
         destroy it,
   and his vengeance is vengeance for his temple.
12 Raise the standard against Babylon's walls,
      mount a strong blockade,
   post sentries, set an ambush;
   for the LORD has both planned and carried out
      his threat against the inhabitants of Babylon.
13 You opulent city, standing beside great waters,
      your end has come, your destiny is certain.
14 The LORD of Hosts has sworn by himself:
   Surely I shall fill you with enemies
      who will swarm like locusts,
   and they will raise a shout of triumph over you.

15 God made the earth by his power,
      fixed the world in place by his wisdom,
   and by his knowledge unfurled the skies.
16 When he speaks in the thunder
      the waters in the heavens are in tumult;
   he brings up the mist from the ends of the earth,
   he opens rifts for the rain,
      and brings the wind out of his storehouses.
17 Everyone is brutish and ignorant,
      every goldsmith is discredited through his idols;
   for the figures he casts are a sham,
      there is no breath in them.
18 They are worthless, mere objects of mockery,
      which perish when their day of reckoning comes.
19 Jacob's chosen God is not like these,
      for he is the creator of the universe.
   Israel is the people he claims as his own;
      the LORD of Hosts is his name.

51:11 **king:** *so Gk; Heb.* kings.   51:13 **destiny:** *lit.* cutting off
(the thread of life).   51:16 **When . . . tumult:** *prob. rdg; Heb.
obscure.* **rifts:** *prob. rdg; Heb.* lightnings.   51:19 **Israel:** *so many
MSS; others omit.*

6 Flee out of Babylon;
  let each one save his life,
  perish not for her guilt;
This is a time of vengeance for the LORD,
  he pays her her due.
7 Babylon was a golden cup in the hand of the LORD
  which made the whole earth drunk;
The nations drank its wine,
  with this they have become mad.
8 Babylon suddenly falls and is crushed:
  howl over her!
Bring balm for her wounds,
  in case she can be healed.
9 "We have tried to heal Babylon,
  but she cannot be healed.
Leave her, let us go, each to his own land."
Her judgment reaches heaven,
  it touches the clouds.
10 The LORD has brought to light our just cause;
  come, let us tell in Zion
what the LORD, our God, has done.

11 Sharpen the arrows,
  fill the quivers;
The LORD has stirred up the spirit of
    Media's kings;
Babylon he is resolved to destroy.
Yes, it is the vengeance of the LORD,
  vengeance for his temple.
12 Against the walls of Babylon raise a signal,
  make strong the watch;
Post sentries,
  arrange ambushes!
For the LORD has planned and he will carry out
  his threat against the inhabitants of Babylon.
13 You who dwell by mighty waters,
  rich in treasure,
Your end has come,
  the term at which you shall be cut off!
14 The LORD of hosts has sworn by himself:
  I will fill you with men as numerous as locusts,
  who shall raise over you the vintage shout!
15 He has sworn who made the earth by his power,
  and established the world by his wisdom,
  and stretched out the heavens by his skill.
16 When he thunders, the waters in the heavens roar,
  and he brings up clouds from the end of
    the earth;
He makes the lightning flash in the rain,
  and releases stormwinds from their chambers.
17 Every man is stupid, ignorant;
  every artisan is put to shame by his idol:
He molded a fraud,
  without breath of life.
18 Nothingness are they, a ridiculous work,
  that will perish in their time of punishment.
19 Not like these is the portion of Jacob,
  he is the creator of all things;
Israel is his very own tribe,
  LORD of hosts is his name.

6 Escape from Babylon
  (save your lives, each one of you);
  do not perish for her guilt,
  for now is the time for Yahweh's vengeance:
  he will pay her her reward!
7 Babylon was a golden cup in Yahweh's hand,
  she made the whole world drunk,
  the nations drank her wine
  and then went mad.
8 Babylon has suddenly fallen, is broken:
  wail for her!
Fetch balm for her wounds,
  perhaps she can be cured!
9 — 'We tried to cure Babylon; she has got no
    better.
Leave her alone and let us each go to his own
    country.'
  —Yes, her sentence reaches to the sky,
  rises to the very clouds.
10 Yahweh has shown the uprightness of our cause.
  Come, let us tell in Zion
  what Yahweh our God has done.

11 Sharpen the arrows,
  fill the quivers!

Yahweh has roused the spirit of the kings of the Medes,
because he has a plan against Babylon to destroy it; this is
Yahweh's revenge, revenge for his Temple.

12 Against the walls of Babylon raise the standard!
  Strengthen the guard!
  Post the sentries!
  Take up concealed positions!

For Yahweh has both planned and done what he promised
he would to the inhabitants of Babylon.

13 Enthroned beside abundant waters,
  rich in treasures,
  you now meet your end,
  the finish of your pillaging.
14 By his own self Yahweh Sabaoth has sworn:
  I shall fill you with men as though with
    grasshoppers,
  and over you they will raise the triumph-shout.

15 By his power he made the earth,
  by his wisdom set the world firm,
  by his discernment spread out the heavens.
16 When he thunders
  there is a roaring of waters in heaven;
  he raises clouds from the furthest limits of the
    earth,
  makes the lightning flash for the downpour,
  and brings the wind from his storehouse.
17 At this everyone stands stupefied,
    uncomprehending,
  every goldsmith blushes for his idols;
  his castings are but delusion,
  with no breath in them.
18 They are futile, a laughable production,
  when the time comes for them to be punished, they
    will vanish.
19 The Heritage of Jacob is not like these,
  for he is the maker of everything,
  and Israel is the tribe that is his heritage;
  His name is Yahweh Sabaoth. [n]

---

[n] 51 = 10:12−16.

NEW REVISED STANDARD VERSION	REVISED ENGLISH BIBLE

NEW REVISED STANDARD VERSION

20 You are my war club, my weapon of battle:
with you I smash nations;
with you I destroy kingdoms;
21 with you I smash the horse and its rider;
with you I smash the chariot and the charioteer;
22 with you I smash man and woman;
with you I smash the old man and the boy;
with you I smash the young man and the girl;
23 with you I smash shepherds and their flocks;
with you I smash farmers and their teams;
with you I smash governors and deputies.

24 I will repay Babylon and all the inhabitants of Chaldea before your very eyes for all the wrong that they have done in Zion, says the LORD.

25 I am against you, O destroying mountain,
says the LORD,
that destroys the whole earth;
I will stretch out my hand against you,
and roll you down from the crags,
and make you a burned-out mountain.
26 No stone shall be taken from you for a corner
and no stone for a foundation,
but you shall be a perpetual waste,
says the LORD.

27 Raise a standard in the land,
blow the trumpet among the nations;
prepare the nations for war against her,
summon against her the kingdoms,
Ararat, Minni, and Ashkenaz;
appoint a marshal against her,
bring up horses like bristling locusts.
28 Prepare the nations for war against her,
the kings of the Medes, with their governors
and deputies,
and every land under their dominion.
29 The land trembles and writhes,
for the LORD's purposes against Babylon stand,
to make the land of Babylon a desolation,
without inhabitant.
30 The warriors of Babylon have given up fighting,
they remain in their strongholds;
their strength has failed,
they have become women;
her buildings are set on fire,
her bars are broken.
31 One runner runs to meet another,
and one messenger to meet another,
to tell the king of Babylon
that his city is taken from end to end:
32 the fords have been seized,
the marshes have been burned with fire,
and the soldiers are in panic.
33 For thus says the LORD of hosts, the God of
Israel:
Daughter Babylon is like a threshing floor
at the time when it is trodden;
yet a little while
and the time of her harvest will come.

34 "King Nebuchadrezzar of Babylon has devoured
me,
he has crushed me;
he has made me an empty vessel,
he has swallowed me like a monster;
he has filled his belly with my delicacies,
he has spewed me out.

REVISED ENGLISH BIBLE

20 You are my battleaxe, my weapon of war;
with you I shall break nations in pieces,
and with you I shall destroy kingdoms.
21 With you I shall break horse and rider,
with you I shall break chariot and charioteer,
22 with you I shall break man and wife,
with you I shall break old and young,
with you I shall break youth and maiden;
23 with you I shall break shepherd and his flock,
with you I shall break ploughman and his team,
with you I shall break viceroys and governors.
24 So shall I repay Babylon and the people of
Chaldaea
for all the wrong which they did in Zion in your
sight.
This is the word of the LORD.

25 I am against you, a destructive mountain
destroying the whole earth, says the LORD.
I shall stretch out my hand against you
and send you tumbling headlong from the rocks
and make you a burnt-out mountain.
26 No stone taken from you will be used as a
corner-stone,
no stone for a foundation;
but you will be for ever desolate.
This is the word of the LORD.

27 Raise a standard on the earth,
blow a trumpet among the nations,
consecrate the nations for war against her,
summon the kingdoms of Ararat, Minni, and
Ashkenaz,
appoint a commander against her,
bring up horses like a dark swarm of locusts.
28 For war against her consecrate the nations,
the king of the Medes, his viceroys and governors,
and all the lands under his sway.
29 The earth quakes and writhes;
for the LORD's designs against Babylon are
fulfilled:
to make the land of Babylon an unpeopled waste.
30 Babylon's warriors have given up the fight;
they skulk in the forts,
their courage has failed,
they have become like women.
The buildings are set on fire,
the bars of the gates broken.
31 Runner speeds to meet runner,
messenger to meet messenger,
reporting to the king of Babylon
that every quarter of his city is taken,
32 the river-crossings are seized,
the guard-towers set on fire,
and the garrison stricken with panic.
33 For these are the words of the LORD of Hosts the God of
Israel:

Babylon is like a threshing-floor when it is
trodden;
very soon harvest time will come for her.
34 'King Nebuchadrezzar of Babylon has devoured me
and sucked me dry;
he has set me aside like an empty jar.
Like a dragon he has gulped me down;
he filled his maw with my delicate flesh
and spewed me up.'

51:27 **on the earth:** or in the land.   51:28 **king:** so Gk (cp. verse 11); Heb. kings.

20 You are my hammer,
  my weapon for war;
With you I shatter nations,
  with you I destroy kingdoms.
21 With you I shatter horse and rider,
  with you I shatter chariot and driver.
22 With you I shatter man and wife,
  with you I shatter old and young,
  with you I shatter youth and maiden.
23 With you I shatter the shepherd and his flock,
  with you I shatter the farmer and his team,
  with you I shatter satraps and prefects.
24 Thus will I repay Babylon,
  and all who live in Chaldea
All the evil they did to Zion,
  as you shall see with your own eyes, says
  the LORD.

25 Beware! I am against you,
  destroying mountain,
  destroyer of the entire earth, says the LORD;
I will stretch forth my hand against you,
  roll you down over the cliffs,
  and make you a burnt mountain:
26 They will not take from you a cornerstone,
  or a foundation stone;
Ruins forever shall you be,
  say the LORD.

27 Raise a signal on the earth,
  blow the trumpet among the nations;
Dedicate peoples to war against her,
  summon against her the kingdoms,
  Ararat, Minni, and Ashkenaz;
Appoint recruiting officers against her,
  send up horses like bristling locusts.
28 Dedicate peoples to war against her:
  the king of Media,
Its governors and all its prefects,
  every land in his domain.
29 The earth quakes and writhes,
  the LORD's plan against Babylon is carried out,
Turning the land of Babylon
  into a desert where no one lives.
30 Babylon's warriors have ceased to fight,
  they remain in their strongholds;
Dried up is their strength,
  they have become women.
Burned are their homes,
  and broken their bars.
31 One runner meets another,
  herald meets herald,
Telling the king of Babylon
  that all his city is taken.
32 The fords have been seized,
  and the fortresses set on fire,
  while warriors are in panic.

33 For thus says the LORD of hosts, the God of Israel:

Daughter Babylon is like a threshing floor
  at the time it is trodden;
Yet a little while,
  and the harvest time will come for her.
34 He has consumed me, routed me,
  [Nebuchadnezzar, king of Babylon,]
  he has left me as an empty vessel;
He has swallowed me like a dragon:
  filled his belly with my delights, and cast
  me out.

20 You were my mace,
  a weapon of war.
With you I crushed nations,
  struck kingdoms down,
21 with you I crushed horse and rider,
  with you I crushed chariot and charioteer,
22 with you I crushed man and woman,
  with you I crushed old man and young,
  with you I crushed young man and girl,

23 with you I crushed shepherd and flock,
  with you I crushed ploughman and team,
  with you I crushed governors and magistrates,

24 and I shall repay Babylon and the inhabitants of Chaldaea, before your eyes, for all the wrongs they have done to Zion, Yahweh declares.

25 I am setting myself against you,
  mountain of destruction,
  Yahweh declares,
  destroyer of the whole world!
I shall reach out my hand for you
  and send you tumbling from the crags
  and make you a burnt-out mountain.
26 No corner-stone will be taken from you again
  and no foundation-stone,
  for you will be a desert for ever,
  Yahweh declares.

27 Raise the standard throughout the world,
  sound the trumpet among the nations!
Consecrate nations to make war on her;
  summon kingdoms against her:
  Ararat, Minni, Ashkenaz;
  appoint a recruiting-officer for her enemies,
  bring up the cavalry, bristling like locusts.
28 Consecrate nations to make war on her: the kings of Media, her governors, all her magistrates and the whole territory under their rule.

29 Then the earth trembled and writhed,
  for Yahweh's plan against Babylon was being
    executed:
  to change the country of Babylon
  into an unpopulated desert.

30 The warriors of Babylon have done with fighting,
  they have stayed inside their fortresses;
  their courage exhausted,
  they are now like women.
  Her houses are on fire,
  her gates are shattered.
31 Courier follows close on courier,
  messenger on messenger,
  to tell the king of Babylon
  that his city has been taken from all sides,
32 the fords occupied,
  the bastions burnt down
  and the fighting men seized with panic.
33 For Yahweh Sabaoth, the God of Israel, says this:
  the daughter of Babylon is like a threshing-floor
  when it is being trodden:
  a little while, and then the time
  for harvesting her will come.

34 He devoured me, consumed me,
  Nebuchadnezzar king of Babylon,
  left me like an empty dish,
  like the Dragon he has swallowed me whole,
  filled his belly with my titbits
  and threw me out.

NEW REVISED STANDARD VERSION	REVISED ENGLISH BIBLE

NEW REVISED STANDARD VERSION

35 May my torn flesh be avenged on Babylon,"
    the inhabitants of Zion shall say.
"May my blood be avenged on the inhabitants of
    Chaldea,"
    Jerusalem shall say.
36 Therefore thus says the LORD:
    I am going to defend your cause
    and take vengeance for you.
I will dry up her sea
    and make her fountain dry;
37 and Babylon shall become a heap of ruins,
    a den of jackals,
an object of horror and of hissing,
    without inhabitant.

38 Like lions they shall roar together;
    they shall growl like lions' whelps.
39 When they are inflamed, I will set out their drink
    and make them drunk, until they become merry
and then sleep a perpetual sleep
    and never wake, says the LORD.
40 I will bring them down like lambs to the
    slaughter,
    like rams and goats.

41 How Sheshach*f* is taken,
    the pride of the whole earth seized!
How Babylon has become
    an object of horror among the nations!
42 The sea has risen over Babylon;
    she has been covered by its tumultuous waves.
43 Her cities have become an object of horror,
    a land of drought and a desert,
a land in which no one lives,
    and through which no mortal passes.
44 I will punish Bel in Babylon,
    and make him disgorge what he has
        swallowed.
The nations shall no longer stream to him;
    the wall of Babylon has fallen.

45 Come out of her, my people!
    Save your lives, each of you,
    from the fierce anger of the LORD!
46 Do not be fainthearted or fearful
    at the rumors heard in the land —
one year one rumor comes,
    the next year another,
rumors of violence in the land
    and of ruler against ruler.

47 Assuredly, the days are coming
    when I will punish the images of Babylon;
her whole land shall be put to shame,
    and all her slain shall fall in her midst.
48 Then the heavens and the earth,
    and all that is in them,
shall shout for joy over Babylon;
    for the destroyers shall come against them out
        of the north,
                         says the LORD.
49 Babylon must fall for the slain of Israel,
    as the slain of all the earth have fallen because
        of Babylon.

50 You survivors of the sword,
    go, do not linger!
Remember the LORD in a distant land,
    and let Jerusalem come into your mind:

REVISED ENGLISH BIBLE

35 Every citizen of Zion will say,
    'On Babylon be the violence done to me,
the vengeance taken on me!'
    Jerusalem will say,
'My blood be on the Chaldaeans!'

36 Therefore the LORD says:
    I shall plead your cause, I shall avenge you;
    I shall dry up her river and make her waters fail.
37 Babylon will become a heap of ruins, a haunt of
        wolves,
    an object of horror and astonishment, with no
        inhabitant.

38 Together they roar like young lions,
    they growl like the whelps of a lioness.
39 I shall cause their drinking bouts to end in fever
    and make them so drunk that they will writhe and
        toss,
then sink into unending sleep, never to wake again.
    This is the word of the LORD.
40 I shall bring them down like lambs to the
        slaughter,
    like rams and he-goats together.

41 Sheshak is captured,
    the pride of the whole world taken.
How Babylon has become
    a thing of horror among the nations!
42 The sea has surged over Babylon,
    she is covered by its roaring waves.
43 Her towns have become waste places,
    a land parched and barren,
a land where no one lives,
    through which no human being travels.
44 I shall punish Bel in Babylon
    and make him disgorge what he has swallowed;
nations will never again come streaming to him.
    Babylon's wall has fallen.

45 My people, come out from her,
    and let every one save himself
from the fierce anger of the LORD.
46 Then beware of losing heart;
    fear no rumours spread abroad in the land,
as rumour follows rumour,
    a new one every year:
of violence on earth,
    of ruler against ruler.

47 Therefore a time is coming
    when I shall punish Babylon's idols;
her whole land will be put to shame,
    and all her slain will lie fallen in her midst.
48 The heavens and the earth
    and all that is in them
will sing in triumph over Babylon;
    for marauders from the north will overrun her.
This is the word of the LORD.
49 Babylon in her turn must fall
    because of Israel's slain,
as the slain of all the world
    have fallen because of Babylon.

50 You that have escaped the sword,
    go, do not linger.
Remember the LORD from afar
    and let Jerusalem come to your minds.

---

f Sheshach is a cryptogram for *Babel,* Babylon

51:41 **Sheshak:** *a cipher for* Babylon.   51:49 **fall because of:**
prob. rdg; Heb. omits because of.

NEW AMERICAN BIBLE

³⁵ My torn flesh be upon Babylon,
  says the city on Zion;
My blood upon the people of Chaldea,
  says Jerusalem.
³⁶ But now, thus says the LORD:
Surely I will defend your cause,
  I will avenge you;
I will dry up her sea,
  and drain her fountain.
³⁷ Babylon shall become a heap of ruins,
  a haunt of jackals;
A place of horror and ridicule,
  where no one lives.
³⁸ They all roar like lions,
  growl like lion cubs.
³⁹ When they are parched, I will set a drink
    before them
  to make them drunk, that they may be overcome
  with perpetual sleep, never to awaken,
    says the LORD.
⁴⁰ I will bring them down like lambs to the slaughter,
  like rams and goats.
⁴¹ How has she been seized, made captive,
  the glory of the whole world!
What a horror has Babylon become among nations:
⁴² against Babylon the sea rises,
  she is overwhelmed by the roaring waves!
⁴³ Her cities have become a desert,
  parched and arid land
Where no man lives,
  and no one passes through.
⁴⁴ I will punish Bel in Babylon,
  and make him disgorge what he swallowed;
  peoples shall stream to him no more.
The wall of Babylon falls!
⁴⁵ Leave her, my people, let each one save himself
  from the burning wrath of the LORD.

⁴⁶ Be not discouraged for fear of rumors spread in the land; this year the rumor comes, then violence in the land, tyrant against tyrant. ⁴⁷ But behold, the days are coming when I will punish the idols of Babylon; her whole land shall be put to shame, and all her slain shall lie fallen within her. ⁴⁸ Then heaven, and earth, and everything in them shall shout over Babylon with joy, when the destroyers come against her from the north, says the LORD. ⁴⁹ Babylon, too, must fall, O slain of Israel, as at the hands of Babylon have fallen the slain of all the earth.

⁵⁰ You who have escaped the sword,
  go on, stand not still;
Remember the LORD from afar,
  let Jerusalem come to your minds.

NEW JERUSALEM BIBLE

³⁵ 'On Babylon be the wounds I suffered!'
  the daughter of Zion will say.
'On the inhabitants of Chaldaea be my blood!'
  Jerusalem will say.
³⁶ So, Yahweh says this:
Look, I am taking up your cause
  to make sure you are avenged.
I shall dry her river up,
  make her springs run dry.
³⁷ Babylon will become a heap of stones,
  the lair of jackals,
a thing of horror and of scorn,
  with no one living in it.
³⁸ Like lions they roar together,
  they growl like lions' whelps.
³⁹ Are they feverish? I will prepare them a drink
  and make them drink until they are tipsy
and fall into an everlasting sleep,
  never to wake again,
  Yahweh declares.
⁴⁰ I will drag them away to the slaughterhouse like
    lambs,
  like rams and goats.

⁴¹ What! Has Sheshak been taken,
  been conquered, the pride of the whole world?
What a thing of horror Babylon has become
  throughout the nations!
⁴² The sea has risen over Babylon,
  she sinks beneath its boisterous waves.
⁴³ Her towns have been turned into wasteland,
  a parched land, a desert,
a country where no one lives
  and where nobody goes.

⁴⁴ I shall punish Bel in Babylon
  and make him disgorge what he has swallowed.
In future the nations
  will stream to him no more.
The very walls of Babylon will fall.
⁴⁵ Get out of her, my people;
  save your lives, each one of you,
  from Yahweh's furious anger.

⁴⁶ But do not be faint-hearted! Do not take fright at rumours hawked round the country: one rumour spreads one year, next year another follows; violence rules on earth and one tyrant succeeds another.

⁴⁷ So look, the days are coming
  when I shall punish the idols of Babylon.
Her entire country will be humbled,
  with all her slaughtered lying on home-soil.
⁴⁸ The heaven and earth and all within them
  will shout for joy over Babylon,
for the destroyers from the north
  are coming to her, Yahweh declares.
⁴⁹ Babylon in her turn must fall,
  you slaughtered ones of Israel,
just as through Babylon there fell
  men slaughtered all over the world.
⁵⁰ You who have escaped her sword,
  leave her, do not wait!
Remember Yahweh from afar,
  let Jerusalem come into your mind.

| NEW REVISED STANDARD VERSION | REVISED ENGLISH BIBLE |

51 We are put to shame, for we have heard insults;
    dishonor has covered our face,
for aliens have come
    into the holy places of the LORD's house.

52 Therefore the time is surely coming, says the
    LORD,
    when I will punish her idols,
and through all her land
    the wounded shall groan.

53 Though Babylon should mount up to heaven,
    and though she should fortify her strong height,
from me destroyers would come upon her,
    says the LORD.

54 Listen!—a cry from Babylon!
    A great crashing from the land of the
        Chaldeans!

55 For the LORD is laying Babylon waste,
    and stilling her loud clamor.
Their waves roar like mighty waters,
    the sound of their clamor resounds;

56 for a destroyer has come against her,
    against Babylon;
her warriors are taken,
    their bows are broken;
for the LORD is a God of recompense,
    he will repay in full.

57 I will make her officials and her sages drunk,
    also her governors, her deputies, and her
        warriors;
they shall sleep a perpetual sleep and never wake,
    says the King, whose name is the LORD of
        hosts.

58 Thus says the LORD of hosts:
The broad wall of Babylon
    shall be leveled to the ground,
and her high gates
    shall be burned with fire.
The peoples exhaust themselves for nothing,
    and the nations weary themselves only for
        fire.g

59 The word that the prophet Jeremiah commanded Seraiah son of Neriah son of Mahseiah, when he went with King Zedekiah of Judah to Babylon, in the fourth year of his reign. Seraiah was the quartermaster. 60 Jeremiah wrote in ah scroll all the disasters that would come on Babylon, all these words that are written concerning Babylon. 61 And Jeremiah said to Seraiah: "When you come to Babylon, see that you read all these words, 62 and say, 'O LORD, you yourself threatened to destroy this place so that neither human beings nor animals shall live in it, and it shall be desolate forever.' 63 When you finish reading this scroll, tie a stone to it, and throw it into the middle of the Euphrates, 64 and say, 'Thus shall Babylon sink, to rise no more, because of the disasters that I am bringing on her.' "i
Thus far are the words of Jeremiah.

52

Zedekiah was twenty-one years old when he began to reign; he reigned eleven years in Jerusalem. His mother's name was Hamutal daughter of Jeremiah of Libnah. 2 He did what was evil in the sight of the LORD, just as Jehoiakim had done. 3 Indeed, Jerusalem and Judah so angered the LORD that he expelled them from his presence.
Zedekiah rebelled against the king of Babylon. 4 And in

51 By the reproaches we have heard we are put to
      shame
and our faces are covered with confusion,
because foreigners have entered
    the sacred courts of the LORD's house.

52 A time is coming therefore, says the LORD,
    when I shall punish her idols,
and throughout her land
    the wounded will groan.

53 Were Babylon to reach the skies
    and make strong her towers in the heights,
I should still send marauders against her.
    This is the word of the LORD.

54 Cries of agony are heard from Babylon,
    sounds of great destruction from Chaldaea.

55 The advancing wave booms and roars
    like mighty waters,
for the LORD is despoiling Babylon
    and will silence the noise of the city.

56 Marauders march on Babylon herself,
    her warriors are captured and their bows broken;
for the LORD, a God of retribution, will repay in
      full.

57 I shall make her princes and her wise men drunk,
    her viceroys and governors and warriors,
and they will sink into unending sleep,
    never to wake again.
This is the word of the King,
    whose name is the LORD of Hosts.

58 The LORD of Hosts says:

The walls of broad Babylon will be razed to the
      ground,
her lofty gates set on fire.
Worthless now is the thing for which peoples
      toiled;
nations wore themselves out for a mere nothing.

59 The instructions given by the prophet Jeremiah to the quartermaster Seraiah son of Neriah and grandson of Mahseiah, when he went to Babylon with King Zedekiah of Judah in the fourth year of his reign. 60 Jeremiah, having written on a scroll a full description of the disaster which would befall Babylon, 61 said to Seraiah, 'When you come to Babylon, see that you read all these words aloud; 62 then say, "LORD, you have declared your purpose to destroy this place and leave it with nothing living in it, man or beast; it will be desolate, for ever waste." 63 When you have finished reading the scroll, tie a stone to it and throw it into the middle of the Euphrates 64 with the words, "So will Babylon sink, never to rise again after the disaster which I am going to bring on her." '

Thus far are the collected sayings of Jeremiah.

52

ZEDEKIAH was twenty-one years old when he came to the throne, and he reigned in Jerusalem for eleven years; his mother was Hamutal daughter of Jeremiah from Libnah. 2 Zedekiah did what was wrong in the eyes of the LORD, as Jehoiakim had done. 3 Jerusalem and Judah so angered the LORD that in the end he banished them from his sight.
Zedekiah rebelled against the king of Babylon. 4 In the

---

g Gk Syr Compare Hab 2.13: Heb and the nations for fire, and they are weary   h Or one   i Gk: Heb on her. And they shall weary themselves

NEW AMERICAN BIBLE

51 We are ashamed because we have heard taunts,
    confusion covers our faces; strangers
        have entered
    the holy places of the house of the LORD.
52 But behold, the days are coming, says the LORD,
    when I will punish her idols,
    and in her whole land the wounded will groan.
53 Though Babylon scale the heavens,
    and make her strong heights inaccessible,
    destroyers from me shall reach her, says
        the LORD.
54 Hear! loud cries from Babylon,
    dire destruction from the land of the Chaldeans;
55 For the LORD lays Babylon waste,
    stills her loud cry,
    Though her waves were roaring like mighty waters,
    and their clamor was heard afar.
56 For the destroyer comes upon her, [Babylon,]
    her heroes are captured, their bows broken;
    The LORD is a God who requites,
    he will surely repay.

57 I will make her princes and her wise men drunk, her
governors, her prefects, and her warriors, so that they sleep
an eternal sleep, never to awaken, says the King, whose
name is the LORD of hosts. 58 Thus says the LORD of hosts:

    The walls of spacious Babylon shall be
        leveled utterly;
    her lofty gates shall be destroyed by fire.
    The toil of the nations is for nothing;
    for the flames the peoples weary themselves.

59 This was the errand given by the prophet Jeremiah to
Seraiah, son of Neriah, son of Mahseiah, when he went to
Babylon for the king in the fourth year of the reign of
Zedekiah; Seraiah was chief quartermaster. 60 Jeremiah had
written all the misfortune that was to befall Babylon in a
single book: all these words that were written against Babylon. 61 And Jeremiah said to Seraiah: When you reach
Babylon, see that you read aloud all these words, 62 and
then say: O LORD, you yourself threatened to destroy this
place, so that neither man nor beast should dwell in it, since
it would remain an everlasting desert. 63 When you have
finished reading this book, tie a stone to it and throw it in
the Euphrates, 64 and say: Thus shall Babylon sink. Never
shall she rise, because of the evil I am bringing upon her.
[To "weary themselves" are the words of Jeremiah.]

52 Zedakiah was twenty-one years old when he became king, and he reigned eleven years in Jerusalem. His mother's name was Hamutal, daughter of Jeremiah
of Libnah. 2 He did what was evil in the eyes of the LORD,
just as Jehoiakim had done. 3 Indeed, what was done in
Jerusalem and in Judah so angered the LORD that he cast
them out from his presence.
    Zedekiah rebelled against the king of Babylon. 4 In the

NEW JERUSALEM BIBLE

51 — 'We were ashamed when we heard of the
        outrage,
    we were covered in confusion
    because foreigners had entered
    the Temple of Yahweh's holy places.'
52 — So look, the days are coming,
    Yahweh declares,
    when I shall punish her idols,
    and the wounded will groan throughout her
        country.
53 Were Babylon to scale the heavens
    or reinforce her towering citadel,
    destroyers would still come to her on my orders,
    Yahweh declares.
54 The din of shouting from Babylon,
    of immense destruction, from the country of the
        Chaldaeans!
55 Yes, Yahweh is laying Babylon waste
    and silencing her monstrous din,
    whose waves used to roar like the ocean
    and their tumultuous voices rang out.
56 For the destroyer has fallen on Babylon,
    her warriors are captured, their bows are broken.
    Yes, Yahweh is a God of retribution,
    he never fails to repay.
57 I shall make her princes and her sages drink,
    her governors, her magistrates, her warriors;
    they will fall into an everlasting sleep,
    never to wake again,
    declares the King,
    whose name is Yahweh Sabaoth.
58 Yahweh Sabaoth says this:
    The walls of Babylon the Great
    will be rased to the ground,
    and her lofty gates
    will be burnt down.
    Thus peoples toil for nothing
    and nations wear themselves out, for the flames.

59 This is the order that the prophet Jeremiah gave to
Seraiah son of Neriah, son of Mahseiah when Seraiah left
for Babylon with Zedekiah king of Judah, in the fourth year
of his reign. Seraiah was lord chamberlain. 60 Now, on one
sheet, Jeremiah had written down the entire disaster that
was to befall Babylon, that is, all these words recorded here
against Babylon. 61 Jeremiah then said to Seraiah, 'When
you reach Babylon, see to it that you read all these words
aloud. 62 Then say, "You, Yahweh, have promised to destroy this place, so that no one will live here ever again,
neither human nor animal, and it will be desolate for ever."
63 Then, when you have finished reading this sheet, tie a
stone to it and throw it into the middle of the Euphrates,
64 with the words, "So shall Babylon sink, never to rise
again from the disaster which I am going to bring on her." '
    Thus far the words of Jeremiah.

52 oZedekiah was twenty-one years old when he came
to the throne, and he reigned for eleven years in
Jerusalem. His mother's name was Hamital daughter of
Jeremiah, of Libnah. 2 He did what is displeasing to Yahweh, just as Jehoiakim had done. 3 That this should happen
to Jerusalem and Judah was due to Yahweh's anger, resulting in his casting them away from his presence.
    Zedekiah rebelled against the king of Babylon. 4 In the

51, 64: To "weary themselves" are the words of Jeremiah: an
editorial remark concerning the end of v 58.

o 52 // 2 K 24:18-25:30.

NEW REVISED STANDARD VERSION	REVISED ENGLISH BIBLE

the ninth year of his reign, in the tenth month, on the tenth day of the month, King Nebuchadrezzar of Babylon came with all his army against Jerusalem, and they laid siege to it; they built siegeworks against it all around. 5 So the city was besieged until the eleventh year of King Zedekiah. 6 On the ninth day of the fourth month the famine became so severe in the city that there was no food for the people of the land. 7 Then a breach was made in the city wall; *j* and all the soldiers fled and went out from the city by night by the way of the gate between the two walls, by the king's garden, though the Chaldeans were all around the city. They went in the direction of the Arabah. 8 But the army of the Chaldeans pursued the king, and overtook Zedekiah in the plains of Jericho; and all his army was scattered, deserting him. 9 Then they captured the king, and brought him up to the king of Babylon at Riblah in the land of Hamath, and he passed sentence on him. 10 The king of Babylon killed the sons of Zedekiah before his eyes, and also killed all the officers of Judah at Riblah. 11 He put out the eyes of Zedekiah, and bound him in fetters, and the king of Babylon took him to Babylon, and put him in prison until the day of his death.

12 In the fifth month, on the tenth day of the month—which was the nineteenth year of King Nebuchadrezzar, king of Babylon—Nebuzaradan the captain of the bodyguard who served the king of Babylon, entered Jerusalem. 13 He burned the house of the LORD, the king's house, and all the houses of Jerusalem; every great house he burned down. 14 All the army of the Chaldeans, who were with the captain of the guard, broke down all the walls around Jerusalem. 15 Nebuzaradan the captain of the guard carried into exile some of the poorest of the people and the rest of the people who were left in the city and the deserters who had defected to the king of Babylon, together with the rest of the artisans. 16 But Nebuzaradan the captain of the guard left some of the poorest people of the land to be vinedressers and tillers of the soil.

17 The pillars of bronze that were in the house of the LORD, and the stands and the bronze sea that were in the house of the LORD, the Chaldeans broke in pieces, and carried all the bronze to Babylon. 18 They took away the pots, the shovels, the snuffers, the basins, the ladles, and all the vessels of bronze used in the temple service. 19 The captain of the guard took away the small bowls also, the firepans, the basins, the pots, the lampstands, the ladles, and the bowls for libation, both those of gold and those of silver. 20 As for the two pillars, the one sea, the twelve bronze bulls that were under the sea, and the stands, *k* which King Solomon had made for the house of the LORD, the bronze of all these vessels was beyond weighing. 21 As for the pillars, the height of the one pillar was eighteen cubits, its circumference was twelve cubits; it was hollow and its thickness was four fingers. 22 Upon it was a capital of bronze; the height of the one capital was five cubits; latticework and pomegranates, all of bronze, encircled the top of the capital. And the second pillar had the same, with pomegranates. 23 There were ninety-six pomegranates on the sides; all the pomegranates encircling the latticework numbered one hundred.

24 The captain of the guard took the chief priest Seraiah, the second priest Zephaniah, and the three guardians of the threshold; 25 and from the city he took an officer who had been in command of the soldiers, and seven men of the king's council who were found in the city; the secretary of the commander of the army who mustered the people of the land; and sixty men of the people of the land who were found inside the city. 26 Then Nebuzaradan the captain of

ninth year of his reign, on the tenth day of the tenth month, King Nebuchadrezzar of Babylon advanced with his whole army against Jerusalem, invested it, and erected siege-towers against it on every side; 5 the siege lasted till the eleventh year of King Zedekiah. 6 In the fourth month of that year, on the ninth day of the month, while famine raged in the city and there was no food for the people, 7 the city capitulated. When King Zedekiah of Judah saw this, he and all his armed escort left the city by night and, fleeing through the gate called Between the Two Walls near the king's garden, they made their way towards the Arabah, although the Chaldaeans were surrounding the city. 8 The Chaldaean soldiers set off in pursuit and overtook King Zedekiah in the lowlands of Jericho; his men had all abandoned him and scattered. 9 Zedekiah, when captured, was brought before the king of Babylon at Riblah in the territory of Hamath, where sentence was passed on him. 10 The king of Babylon had Zedekiah's sons slain before his eyes; he also put to death all the princes of Judah at Riblah. 11 Then Zedekiah's eyes were blinded, and the king of Babylon bound him with bronze fetters and brought him to Babylon, where he committed to prison till the day of his death.

12 On the tenth day of the fifth month, in the nineteenth year of King Nebuchadrezzar of Babylon, Nebuzaradan, captain of the king of Babylon's bodyguard, came to Jerusalem, 13 and set fire to the house of the LORD and the royal palace, indeed all the houses in the city; every notable person's house was burnt down. 14 The whole Chaldaean force under the captain of the guard pulled down all the walls encircling Jerusalem. 15 Nebuzaradan, captain of the guard, deported the rest of the people left in the city, those who had defected to the king of Babylon, and the remaining artisans. 16 He left behind only the poorest class of people, to be vine-dressers and labourers.

17 The Chaldaeans broke up the bronze pillars in the house of the LORD, the trolleys, and the bronze Sea, and carried off all the metal to Babylon. 18 They removed also the pots, shovels, snuffers, tossing-bowls, saucers, and all the bronze vessels used in the service of the temple. 19 The captain of the guard took away the precious metal, whether gold or silver, of which the cups, firepans, tossing-bowls, pots, lampstands, saucers, and flagons were made. 20 The bronze of the two pillars, of the one Sea, and of the twelve oxen supporting it, which King Solomon had made for the house of the LORD, was beyond weighing. 21 One pillar was eighteen cubits high and twelve cubits in circumference; it was hollow, but the metal was four fingers thick. 22 It had a capital of bronze, five cubits high, and a decoration of network and pomegranates ran all round it, wholly of bronze. The other pillar, with its pomegranates, was exactly like it. 23 Ninety-six pomegranates were exposed to view and there were a hundred in all on the network all round.

24 The captain of the guard took Seraiah the chief priest, Zephaniah the deputy chief priest, and the three on duty at the entrance; 25 he took also from the city a eunuch who was in charge of the fighting men, seven of those with right of access to the king who were still in the city, the adjutant-general whose duty was to muster the army for war, and sixty men of the people who were still there. 26 These Nebu-

52:7 **When . . . he and:** *prob. rdg, cp. 39:4; Heb. omits.*
52:15 **Nebuzaradan:** *prob. rdg, cp. 39:9 and 2 Kgs. 25:11; Heb.*
prefixes The poorest class of the people *(cp. verse 16).*
52:20 **supporting it:** *so Gk; Heb.* which were under the trolleys.
52:23 **exposed to view:** *mng of Heb. word uncertain.*

j Heb lacks *wall*   *k* Cn: Heb *that were under the stands*

NEW AMERICAN BIBLE

tenth month of the ninth year of his reign, on the tenth day of the month, Nebuchadnezzar, king of Babylon, and his whole army advanced against Jerusalem, encamped around it, and built siege walls on every side. 5 The siege of the city continued until the eleventh year of King Zedekiah.

6 On the ninth day of the fourth month, when famine had gripped the city and the people had no more bread, 7 the city walls were breached. Then all the soldiers took to flight and left the city by night through the gate between the two walls which was near the king's garden. With the Chaldeans surrounding the city, they went in the direction of the Arabah. 8 But the Chaldean army pursued the king and overtook Zedekiah in the desert near Jericho, while his whole army fled from him.

9 The king, therefore, was arrested and brought to Riblah, in the land of Hamath, to the king of Babylon, who pronounced sentence on him. 10 As Zedekiah looked on, the king of Babylon slew his sons as well as all the princes of Judah at Riblah. 11 Then he blinded Zedekiah, bound him with fetters, and had him brought to Babylon and kept in prison until the day of his death.

12 On the tenth day of the fifth month (this was in the nineteenth year of Nebuchadnezzar, king of Babylon), Nebuzaradan, captain of the bodyguard, came to Jerusalem as the representative of the king of Babylon. 13 He burned the house of the LORD, the palace of the king, and all the houses of Jerusalem; every large building he destroyed with fire. 14 And the Chaldean troops who were with the captain of the guard tore down all the walls that surrounded Jerusalem.

15 Then Nebuzaradan, captain of the guard, led into exile the rest of the people left in the city, and those who had deserted to the king of Babylon, and the rest of the artisans. 16 But some of the country's poor, Nebuzaradan, captain of the guard, left behind as vinedressers and farmers.

17 The bronze pillars that belonged to the house of the LORD, and the wheeled carts and the bronze sea in the house of the LORD, the Chaldeans broke into pieces; they carried away all the bronze to Babylon. 18 They took also the pots, the shovels, the snuffers, the bowls, the pans, and all the bronze vessels used for service. 19 The basins also, the fire holders, the bowls, the pots, the lampstands, the pans, the sacrificial bowls which were of gold or silver, these too the captain of the guard carried off, 20 as well as the two pillars, the one sea, and the twelve oxen of bronze under the sea, and the wheeled carts which King Solomon had made for the house of the LORD. The bronze of all these furnishings could not be weighed.

21 Each of the pillars was eighteen cubits high and twelve cubits in diameter; each was four fingers thick, and hollow inside. 22 A bronze capital five cubits high surmounted the one pillar, and a network with pomegranates encircled the capital, all of brass; and so for the other pillar. The pomegranates . . . 23 there were ninety-six pomegranates. There were a hundred pomegranates, all around the network.

24 The captain of the guard also took Seraiah, the high priest, Zephaniah, the second priest, and the three keepers of the entry. 25 And from the city he took one courtier, a commander of soldiers, and seven men in the personal service of the king who were present in the city, and the scribe of the army commander who mustered the people of the land, and sixty of the common people who were in the city.

NEW JERUSALEM BIBLE

ninth year of his reign, in the tenth month, on the tenth day of the month, Nebuchadnezzar king of Babylon advanced on Jerusalem with his entire army; he pitched camp in front of the city and threw up earthworks round it. 5 The city lay under siege till the eleventh year of King Zedekiah. 6 In the fourth month, on the ninth day of the month, when famine was raging in the city and there was no food for the populace, 7 a breach was made in the city wall. The king and all the fighting men then fled, leaving the city under cover of dark, by way of the gate between the two walls, which is near the king's garden — the Chaldaeans had surrounded the city — and made his way towards the Arabah. 8 The Chaldaean troops pursued the king and caught up with Zedekiah in the plains of Jericho, where all his troops deserted. 9 But the Chaldaeans captured the king and took him to the king of Babylon at Riblah in the territory of Hamath, where he passed sentence on him. 10 He had Zedekiah's sons slaughtered before his eyes; he also had all the chief men of Judah put to death at Riblah. 11 He then put out Zedekiah's eyes and, loading him with chains, the king of Babylon carried him off to Babylon where he kept him prisoner until his dying day.

12 In the fifth month, on the tenth day of the month — it was in the nineteenth year of Nebuchadnezzar king of Babylon — Nebuzaradan commander of the guard, a member of the king of Babylon's staff, entered Jerusalem. 13 He burnt down the Temple of Yahweh, the royal palace and all the houses in Jerusalem. 14 The Chaldaean troops who accompanied the commander of the guard demolished all the walls surrounding Jerusalem.

15 Nebuzaradan commander of the guard deported (some of the poor people and) the remainder of the population left in the city, the deserters who had gone over to the king of Babylon, and the rest of the artisans. 16 But Nebuzaradan commander of the guard left some of the poor country-people behind as vineyard workers and ploughmen.

17 The Chaldaeans broke up the bronze pillars from the Temple of Yahweh, the wheeled stands and the bronze Sea, which were in the Temple of Yahweh, and took all the bronze away to Babylon. 18 They also took the ash containers, the scoops, the knives, the sprinkling bowls, the incense bowls, and all the bronze furnishings used in worship. 19 The commander of the guard also took the bowls, the censers, the sprinkling bowls, the ash containers, the lampstands, the goblets and the saucers: everything that was made of gold and everything made of silver. 20 As regards the two pillars, the one Sea, the twelve bronze oxen supporting the Sea, and the wheeled stands, which King Solomon had made for the Temple of Yahweh, there was no reckoning the weight of bronze in all these objects. 21 As regards the pillars, the height of one pillar was eighteen cubits, its circumference was twelve cubits, it was four fingers thick, and hollow inside; 22 on it stood a capital of bronze, the height of the capital being five cubits; round the capital were filigree and pomegranates, all in bronze. So also for the second pillar. 23 There were ninety-six pomegranates round the sides, making a hundred pomegranates round the filigree in all.

24 The commander of the guard took prisoner Seraiah the chief priest, Zephaniah the priest next in rank, and the three guardians of the threshold. 25 In the city he took prisoner an official who was in command of the fighting men, seven of the king's personal friends who were discovered in the city, the secretary to the army commander responsible for military conscription, and sixty men of distinction discovered in the city. 26 Nebuzaradan commander of the guard took these

NEW REVISED STANDARD VERSION

the guard took them, and brought them to the king of Babylon at Riblah. 27 And the king of Babylon struck them down, and put them to death at Riblah in the land of Hamath. So Judah went into exile out of its land.

28 This is the number of the people whom Nebuchadrezzar took into exile: in the seventh year, three thousand twenty-three Judeans; 29 in the eighteenth year of Nebuchadrezzar he took into exile from Jerusalem eight hundred thirty-two persons; 30 in the twenty-third year of Nebuchadrezzar, Nebuzaradan the captain of the guard took into exile of the Judeans seven hundred forty-five persons; all the persons were four thousand six hundred.

31 In the thirty-seventh year of the exile of King Jehoiachin of Judah, in the twelfth month, on the twenty-fifth day of the month, King Evil-merodach of Babylon, in the year he began to reign, showed favor to King Jehoiachin of Judah and brought him out of prison; 32 he spoke kindly to him, and gave him a seat above the seats of the other kings who were with him in Babylon. 33 So Jehoiachin put aside his prison clothes, and every day of his life he dined regularly at the king's table. 34 For his allowance, a regular daily allowance was given him by the king of Babylon, as long as he lived, up to the day of his death.

REVISED ENGLISH BIBLE

zaradan, captain of the guard, brought to the king of Babylon at Riblah. 27 There, in the land of Hamath, the king had them flogged and put to death. So Judah went into exile from its own land.

28 These were the people deported by Nebuchadrezzar in the seventh year of his reign: three thousand and twenty-three Judaeans. 29 In the eighteenth year, eight hundred and thirty-two people from Jerusalem; 30 in the twenty-third year, seven hundred and forty-five Judaeans were deported by Nebuzaradan the captain of the bodyguard: in all four thousand six hundred people.

31 In the thirty-seventh year of the exile of King Jehoiachin of Judah, on the twenty-fifth day of the twelfth month, King Evil-merodach of Babylon in the year of his accession showed favour to King Jehoiachin of Judah. He released him from prison, 32 treated him kindly, and gave him a seat at table above the kings with him in Babylon. 33 Jehoiachin, discarding his prison clothes, lived as a pensioner of the king for the rest of his life. 34 For his maintenance a regular daily allowance was given him by the king of Babylon to the day of his death.

52:34 **to ... death:** *so Gk; Heb. adds* as long as he lived.

NEW AMERICAN BIBLE

26 The captain of the guard, Nebuzaradan, arrested these and brought them to the king of Babylon at Riblah, 27 who had them struck down and put to death in Riblah, in the land of Hamath.

Thus was Judah exiled from her land. 28 This is the number of the people whom Nebuchadnezzar led away captive: in his seventh year, three thousand and twenty-three people of Judah; 29 in the eighteenth year of Nebuchadnezzar, eight hundred and thirty-two persons from Jerusalem; 30 in the twenty-third year of Nebuchadnezzar, Nebuzaradan, captain of the guard, exiled seven hundred and forty-five people of Judah: four thousand six hundred persons in all.

31 In the thirty-seventh year of the exile of Jehoiachin, king of Judah, on the twenty-fifth day of the twelfth month, Evil-merodach, king of Babylon, in the inaugural year of his reign, took up the case of Jehoiachin, king of Judah, and released him from prison. 32 He spoke kindly to him and gave him a throne higher than that of the other kings who were with him in Babylon. 33 Jehoiachin took off his prison garb and ate at the king's table as long as he lived. 34 The allowance given him by the king of Babylon was a perpetual allowance, in fixed daily amounts, all the days of his life until the day of his death.

NEW JERUSALEM BIBLE

men and brought them to the king of Babylon at Riblah, 27 and at Riblah, in the territory of Hamath, the king of Babylon had them put to death. Thus Judah was deported from its country.

28 The number of people deported by Nebuchadnezzar was as follows. In the seventh year: three thousand and twenty-three Judaeans; 29 in the eighteenth year of Nebuchadnezzar, eight hundred and thirty-two persons were deported from Jerusalem; 30 in the twenty-third year of Nebuchadnezzar, Nebuzaradan commander of the guard deported seven hundred and forty-five Judaeans. In all: four thousand six hundred persons.

31 But in the thirty-seventh year of the exile of Jehoiachin king of Judah, in the twelfth month, on the twenty-fifth day of the month, Evil-Merodach king of Babylon, in the year he came to the throne, pardoned Jehoiachin king of Judah and released him from prison. 32 He treated him kindly and allotted him a seat above those of the other kings who were with him in Babylon. 33 So Jehoiachin laid aside his prisoner's garb and for the rest of his life always ate at the king's table. 34 And his upkeep was permanently ensured by the king, day after day, for the rest of his life until the day he died.

Lamentations

1
How lonely sits the city
 that once was full of people!
How like a widow she has become,
 she that was great among the nations!
She that was a princess among the provinces
 has become a vassal.

2 She weeps bitterly in the night,
 with tears on her cheeks;
among all her lovers
 she has no one to comfort her;
all her friends have dealt treacherously with her,
 they have become her enemies.

3 Judah has gone into exile with suffering
 and hard servitude;
she lives now among the nations,
 and finds no resting place;
her pursuers have all overtaken her
 in the midst of her distress.

4 The roads to Zion mourn,
 for no one comes to the festivals;
all her gates are desolate,
 her priests groan;
her young girls grieve,*a*
 and her lot is bitter.

5 Her foes have become the masters,
 her enemies prosper,
because the LORD has made her suffer
 for the multitude of her transgressions;
her children have gone away,
 captives before the foe.

6 From daughter Zion has departed
 all her majesty.
Her princes have become like stags
 that find no pasture;
they fled without strength
 before the pursuer.

7 Jerusalem remembers,
 in the days of her affliction and wandering,
all the precious things
 that were hers in days of old.
When her people fell into the hand of the foe,
 and there was no one to help her,
the foe looked on mocking
 over her downfall.

8 Jerusalem sinned grievously,
 so she has become a mockery;
all who honored her despise her,
 for they have seen her nakedness;
she herself groans,
 and turns her face away.

9 Her uncleanness was in her skirts;
 she took no thought of her future;
her downfall was appalling,
 with none to comfort her.
"O LORD, look at my affliction,
 for the enemy has triumphed!"

Lamentations

1
How DESERTED lies the city,
 once thronging with people!
Once great among nations,
 now become a widow;
once queen among provinces,
 now put to forced labour!

2 She weeps bitterly in the night;
 tears run down her cheeks.
Among all who loved her
 she has no one to bring her comfort.
Her friends have all betrayed her;
 they have become her enemies.

3 Judah has wasted away through affliction
 and endless servitude.
Living among the nations,
 she has found no resting-place;
her persecutors all fell on her
 in her sore distress.

4 The approaches to Zion mourn,
 for no pilgrims attend her sacred feasts;
all her gates are desolate.
 Her priests groan,
her maidens are made to suffer.
 How bitter is her fate!

5 Her adversaries have become her masters,
 her enemies take their ease,
for the LORD has made her suffer
 because of her countless sins.
Her young children are gone,
 taken captive by an adversary.

6 All splendour has vanished
 from the daughter of Zion.
Her princes have become like deer
 that can find no pasture.
They run on, their strength spent,
 pursued by the hunter.

7 In the days of Jerusalem's misery and restlessness
 she called to mind
all the treasures which were hers
 from days of old,
when her people fell into the power of adversaries
 and she had no one to help her.
The adversaries looked on,
 laughing at her downfall.

8 Jerusalem, greatly sinning,
 was treated like a filthy rag.
All who had honoured her
 held her cheap,
now they had seen her nakedness.
 What could she do but groan
and turn away?

9 Uncleanness afflicted her body,
 and she gave no thought to her fate.
Her fall was beyond belief
 and there was no one to comfort her.
'Look, LORD, on my misery,
 for the enemy has triumphed.'

---

a Meaning of Heb uncertain

1:9 **her fate:** *or* her children after her.

THE BOOK OF
Lamentations

Lamentations

Chapter 1

1

How lonely she is now,
　the once crowded city!
Widowed is she
　who was mistress over nations;
The princess among the provinces
　has been made a toiling slave.

2 Bitterly she weeps at night,
　tears upon her cheeks,
With not one to console her
　of all her dear ones;
Her friends have all betrayed her
　and become her enemies.

3 Judah has fled into exile
　from oppression and cruel slavery;
Yet where she lives among the nations
　she finds no place to rest:
All her persecutors come upon her
　where she is narrowly confined.

4 The roads to Zion mourn
　for lack of pilgrims going to her feasts;
All her gateways are deserted,
　her priests groan,
Her virgins sigh;
　she is in bitter grief.

5 Her foes are uppermost,
　her enemies are at ease;
The LORD has punished her
　for her many sins.
Her little ones have gone away,
　captive before the foe.

6 Gone from daughter Zion
　is all her glory:
Her princes, like rams
　that find no pasture,
Have gone off without strength
　before their captors.

7 Jerusalem is mindful of the days
　of her wretched homelessness,
When her people fell into enemy hands,
　and she had no one to help her;
When her foes gloated over her,
　laughed at her ruin.

8 Through the sin of which she is guilty,
　Jerusalem is defiled;
All who esteemed her think her vile
　now that they see her nakedness;
She herself groans
　and turns away.

9 Her filth is on her skirt;
　she gave no thought how she would end.
Astounding is her downfall,
　with no one to console her.
Look, O LORD, upon her misery,
　for the enemy has triumphed!

Aleph

Bet

Gimel

Dalet

He

Waw

Zain

Het

Tet

1 How deserted she sits,
　the city once thronged with people!
Once the greatest of nations,
　she is now like a widow.
Once the princess of states,
　she is now put to forced labour.

2 All night long she is weeping,
　tears running down her cheeks.
Not one of all her lovers
　remains to comfort her.
Her friends have all betrayed her
　and become her enemies.

3 Judah has gone into exile
　after much pain and toil.
Living among the nations
　she finds no respite;
her persecutors all overtake her
　where there is no way out.

4 The roads to Zion are in mourning;
　no one comes to her festivals now.
Her gateways are all deserted;
　her priests groan;
her young girls are grief-stricken;
　she suffers bitterly.

5 Her foes now have the upper hand,
　her enemies prosper,
for Yahweh has made her suffer
　for her many, many crimes;
her children have gone away into captivity
　driven in front of the oppressor.

6 And from the daughter of Zion
　all her splendour has departed.
Her princes were like stags
　which could find no pasture,
exhausted, as they flee
　before the hunter.

7 Jerusalem remembers
　her days of misery and distress;
when her people fell into the enemy's clutches
　there was no one to help her.
Her enemies looked on
　and laughed at her downfall.

8 Jerusalem has sinned so gravely
　that she has become a thing unclean.
All who used to honour her despise her,
　having seen her nakedness;
she herself groans aloud
　and turns her face away.

9 Her filth befouls her skirts —
　she never thought to end like this,
and hence her astonishing fall
　with no one to comfort her.
Yahweh, look at my misery,
　for the enemy is triumphant!

10 Enemies have stretched out their hands
    over all her precious things;
she has even seen the nations
    invade her sanctuary,
those whom you forbade
    to enter your congregation.

11 All her people groan
    as they search for bread;
they trade their treasures for food
    to revive their strength.
Look, O LORD, and see
    how worthless I have become.

12 Is it nothing to you,[b] all you who pass by?
    Look and see
if there is any sorrow like my sorrow,
    which was brought upon me,
which the LORD inflicted
    on the day of his fierce anger.

13 From on high he sent fire;
    it went deep into my bones;
he spread a net for my feet;
    he turned me back;
he has left me stunned,
    faint all day long.

14 My transgressions were bound[b] into a yoke;
    by his hand they were fastened together;
they weigh on my neck,
    sapping my strength;
the Lord handed me over
    to those whom I cannot withstand.

15 The LORD has rejected
    all my warriors in the midst of me;
he proclaimed a time against me
    to crush my young men;
the Lord has trodden as in a wine press
    the virgin daughter Judah.

16 For these things I weep;
    my eyes flow with tears;
for a comforter is far from me,
    one to revive my courage;
my children are desolate,
    for the enemy has prevailed.

17 Zion stretches out her hands,
    but there is no one to comfort her;
the LORD has commanded against Jacob
    that his neighbors should become his foes;
Jerusalem has become
    a filthy thing among them.

18 The LORD is in the right,
    for I have rebelled against his word;
but hear, all you peoples,
    and behold my suffering;
my young women and young men
    have gone into captivity.

19 I called to my lovers
    but they deceived me;
my priests and elders
    perished in the city
while seeking food
    to revive their strength.

10 The adversary stretched out his hand
    to seize all her treasures.
Indeed she saw Gentiles
    invade her sanctuary,
Gentiles forbidden by you to enter
    the assembly, for it was yours.

11 All her people groaned,
    they begged for bread;
they bartered their treasures for food
    to regain their strength.
'Look, LORD, and see
    how cheap I am accounted.

12 'Is it nothing to you, you passers-by?
    If only you would look and see:
is there any agony like mine,
    like these torments
which the LORD made me suffer
    on the day of his fierce anger?

13 'From heaven he sent down fire,
    which ran through my bones;
he spread out a net to catch my feet,
    and turned me back;
he made me an example of desolation,
    racked with sickness all day long.

14 'My sins were bound like a yoke
    tied fast by his own hand;
set upon my neck,
    it caused my strength to fail.
The LORD abandoned me to my sins,
    and in their grip I could not stand.

15 'The LORD treated with scorn
    all the mighty men within my walls;
he marshalled rank on rank against me
    to crush my young warriors.
The LORD trod down, like grapes in the winepress,
    the virgin daughter of Judah.

16 'This is why I weep over my plight,
    why tears stream from my eyes:
because any who might comfort me and renew my
        strength
    are far away from me;
my children have become desolate,
    for the enemy is victorious.'

17 Zion lifted her hands in prayer,
    but there was no one to comfort her;
the LORD ordered Jacob's enemies
    to beset him on every side.
In their midst Jerusalem became
    an unclean thing to be shunned.

18 'The LORD was in the right,
    for I rebelled against his command.
Listen, all you nations,
    and look on my agony:
my maidens and my young men
    are gone into captivity.

19 'I called to my lovers,
    but they let me down;
my priests and my elders
    perished in the city
while seeking food
    to keep themselves alive.

1:14 **bound:** *prob. mng; Heb. word unknown.*   1:16 **my plight:** *prob. rdg; Heb. my eye.*

[b] Meaning of Heb uncertain

NEW AMERICAN BIBLE

10 The foe stretched out his hand
   to all her treasures;
She has seen those nations
   enter her sanctuary
Whom you forbade to come
   into your assembly.

11 All her people groan,
   searching for bread;
They give their treasures for food,
   to retain the breath of life.
"Look, O LORD, and see
   how worthless I have become!

12 "Come, all you who pass by the way,
   look and see
Whether there is any suffering like my suffering,
   which has been dealt me
When the LORD afflicted me
   on the day of his blazing wrath.

13 "From on high he sent fire
   down into my very frame;
He spread a net for my feet,
   and overthrew me.
He left me desolate,
   in pain all the day.

14 "He has kept watch over my sins;
   by his hand they have been plaited:
They have settled about my neck,
   he has brought my strength to its knees;
The Lord has delivered me into their grip,
   I am unable to rise.

15 "All the mighty ones in my midst
   the Lord has cast away;
He summoned an army against me
   to crush my young men;
The LORD has trodden in the wine press
   virgin daughter Judah.

16 "At this I weep,
   my eyes run with tears:
Far from me are all who could console me,
   any who might revive me;
My sons were reduced to silence
   when the enemy prevailed."

17 Zion stretched out her hands,
   but there was no one to console her;
The LORD gave orders against Jacob
   for his neighbors to be his foes;
Jerusalem has become in their midst
   a thing unclean.

18 "The LORD is just;
   I had defied his command.
Listen, all you peoples,
   and behold my suffering:
My maidens and my youths
   have gone into captivity.

19 "I cried out to my lovers,
   but they failed me.
My priests and my elders
   perished in the city;
Where they sought food for themselves,
   they found it not.

NEW JERUSALEM BIBLE

Yod

10 The enemy stretched out his hand
   for everything she treasured;
she saw the heathen
   enter her sanctuary,
whom you had forbidden
   to enter your Assembly.

Kaph

11 All her people are groaning,
   looking for something to eat;
they have bartered their treasures for food,
   to keep themselves alive.
Look, Yahweh, and consider
   how despised I am!

Lamed

12 All you who pass this way,
   look and see:
is any sorrow like the sorrow
   inflicted on me,
with which Yahweh struck me
   on the day of his burning anger?

Mem

13 He sent fire from on high
   deep into my bones;
he stretched a net for my feet,
   he pulled me back;
he left me shattered,
   sick all day long.

Nun

14 He has watched out for my offences,
   with his hand he enmeshes me,
his yoke is on my neck,
   he has deprived me of strength.
The Lord has put me into clutches
   which I am helpless to resist.

Samek

15 The Lord has rejected
   all my warriors within my walls,
he has summoned a host against me
   to crush my young men;
in the winepress the Lord trampled
   the young daughter of Judah.

Ain

16 And that is why I weep;
   my eyes stream with water,
since a comforter who could revive me
   is far away.
My children are shattered,
   for the enemy has proved too strong.

Pe

17 Zion stretches out her hands,
   with no one to comfort her.
Yahweh has commanded Jacob's enemies
   to surround him;
they treat Jerusalem
   as though she were unclean.

Zade

18 Yahweh is in the right,
   for I rebelled against his command.
Listen, all you peoples,
   and see my sorrow.
My young girls and my young men
   have gone into captivity.

Qoph

19 I called to my lovers;
   they failed me.
My priests and my elders
   expired in the city,
as they searched for food
   to keep themselves alive.

NEW REVISED STANDARD VERSION	REVISED ENGLISH BIBLE

NEW REVISED STANDARD VERSION

20 See, O LORD, how distressed I am;
  my stomach churns,
my heart is wrung within me,
  because I have been very rebellious.
In the street the sword bereaves;
  in the house it is like death.

21 They heard how I was groaning,
  with no one to comfort me.
All my enemies heard of my trouble;
  they are glad that you have done it.
Bring on the day you have announced,
  and let them be as I am.

22 Let all their evil doing come before you;
  and deal with them
as you have dealt with me
  because of all my transgressions;
for my groans are many
  and my heart is faint.

2 How the Lord in his anger
  has humiliated*c* daughter Zion!
He has thrown down from heaven to earth
  the splendor of Israel;
he has not remembered his footstool
  in the day of his anger.

2 The Lord has destroyed without mercy
  all the dwellings of Jacob;
in his wrath he has broken down
  the strongholds of daughter Judah;
he has brought down to the ground in dishonor
  the kingdom and its rulers.

3 He has cut down in fierce anger
  all the might of Israel;
he has withdrawn his right hand from them
  in the face of the enemy;
he has burned like a flaming fire in Jacob,
  consuming all around.

4 He has bent his bow like an enemy,
  with his right hand set like a foe;
he has killed all in whom we took pride
  in the tent of daughter Zion;
he has poured out his fury like fire.

5 The Lord has become like an enemy;
  he has destroyed Israel;
He has destroyed all its palaces,
  laid in ruins its strongholds,
and multiplied in daughter Judah
  mourning and lamentation.

6 He has broken down his booth like a garden,
  he has destroyed his tabernacle;
the LORD has abolished in Zion
  festival and sabbath,
and in his fierce indignation has spurned
  king and priest.

7 The Lord has scorned his altar,
  disowned his sanctuary;
he has delivered into the hand of the enemy
  the walls of her palaces;
a clamor was raised in the house of the LORD
  as on a day of festival.

REVISED ENGLISH BIBLE

20 'LORD, see how sorely distressed I am.
My bowels writhe in anguish
and my heart within me turns over,
  because I wantonly rebelled.
In the street the sword brings bereavement,
  like the plague within the house.

21 'People have heard when I groan
  with no one to comfort me.
My enemies, hearing of my plight,
  all rejoiced at what you had done.
Hasten the day you have promised
  when they will suffer as I do!

22 'Let all their evil deeds come before you;
  torment them in their turn,
as you have tormented me
  on account of all my sins;
for I groan continually
  and I am sick at heart.'

2 WHAT darkness the Lord in his anger
  has brought on the daughter of Zion!
He hurled down from heaven to earth
  the honour of Israel,
with scant regard for Zion his footstool
  on the day of his anger.

2 The Lord overwhelmed without pity
  all the dwellings of Jacob.
In his wrath he overthrew
  the strongholds of the daughter of Judah;
he brought to the ground in dishonour
  the kingdom and its rulers.

3 In his fierce anger he hacked off
  the horn of Israel's pride;
he withdrew his protecting hand
  at the approach of the enemy;
he blazed in Jacob like flaming fire
  that rages far and wide.

4 In enmity he bent his bow;
  like an adversary he took his stand,
and with his strong arm he slew
  all those who had been his delight.
He poured out his fury like fire
  on the tent of the daughter of Zion.

5 The Lord played an enemy's part
  and overwhelmed Israel,
overthrowing all their mansions
  and laying their strongholds in ruins.
To the daughter of Judah he brought
  unending sorrow.

6 He stripped his tabernacle as if it were a garden,
  and made the place of assembly a ruin.
In Zion the LORD blotted out all memory
  of festal assembly and of sabbath;
king and priest alike he spurned
  in the heat of his anger.

7 The Lord rejected his own altar
  and abandoned his sanctuary.
The walls of Zion's mansions
  he delivered into the power of the enemy;
in the LORD's house they raised shouts
  as on a festal day.

c Meaning of Heb uncertain

2:6 **festal assembly:** or appointed seasons.

20 "Look, O LORD, upon my distress:
  all within me is in ferment,
My heart recoils within me
  from my monstrous rebellion.
In the streets the sword bereaves,
  at home death stalks.

21 "Give heed to my groaning;
  there is no one to console me.
All my enemies rejoice at my misfortune:
  it is you who have wrought it.
Bring on the day you have proclaimed,
  that they may be even as I.

22 "Let all their evil come before you;
  deal with them
As you have dealt with me
  for all my sins;
My groans are many,
  and I am sick at heart."

2 How the Lord in his wrath
  has detested daughter Zion!
He has cast down from heaven to earth
  the glory of Israel,
Unmindful of his footstool
  on the day of his wrath.

2 The Lord has consumed without pity
  all the dwellings of Jacob;
He has torn down in his anger
  the fortresses of daughter Judah;
He has brought to the ground in dishonor
  her king and her princes.

3 He broke off, in fiery wrath,
  the horn that was Israel's whole strength;
He withheld the support of his right hand
  when the enemy approached;
He blazed up in Jacob like a flaming fire
  devouring all about it.

4 Like an enemy he made taut his bow;
  with his arrows in his right hand
He took his stand as a foe, and slew
  all on whom the eye doted;
Over the tent of daughter Zion
  he poured out his wrath like fire.

5 The Lord has become an enemy,
  he has consumed Israel:
Consumed all her castles
  and destroyed her fortresses;
For daughter Judah he has multiplied
  moaning and groaning.

6 He has demolished his shelter like a garden booth,
  he has destroyed his dwelling;
In Zion the LORD has made
  feast and sabbath to be forgotten;
He has scorned in fierce wrath
  both king and priest.

7 The Lord has disowned his altar,
  rejected his sanctuary;
The walls of her towers
  he has handed over to the enemy,
Who shout in the house of the LORD
  as on a feast day.

Resh

20 Look, Yahweh. I am in distress!
  My inmost being is in ferment;
my heart turns over inside me—
  how rebellious I have been!
Outside, the sword bereaves;
  inside it is like death.

Shin

21 Listen, for I am groaning,
  with no one to comfort me.
All my enemies have heard of my disaster,
  they are glad about what you have done.
Bring the Day you once foretold,
  so that they may be like me!

Taw

22 Let all their wickedness come before you,
  and treat them
as you have treated me
  for all my crimes;
numberless are my groans,
  and I am sick at heart.

Chapter 2

Aleph

1 In his anger, with what darkness
  has the Lord enveloped the daughter of
    Zion!
He has flung the beauty of Israel
  from heaven to the ground,
without regard for his footstool
  on the day of his anger.

Bet

2 The Lord pitilessly engulfed
  all the homes of Jacob;
in his fury he tore down
  the fortresses of the daughter of Judah;
he threw to the ground, he desecrated
  the kingdom and its princes.

Gimel

3 In his burning anger
  he broke all the might of Israel,
withdrew his protecting right hand
  at the coming of the enemy,
and blazed against Jacob like a fire
  that burns up everything near it.

Dalet

4 Like an enemy he bent his bow,
  and his right hand held firm;
like a foe he slaughtered
  all those who were a delight to see;
on the tent of the daughter of Zion
  he poured out his fury like fire.

He

5 The Lord behaved like an enemy;
  he engulfed Israel,
he engulfed all its citadels,
  he destroyed its fortresses
and for the daughter of Judah
  multiplied weeping on wailing.

Waw

6 He wrecked his domain like a garden,
  destroyed his assembly-points,
Yahweh erased the memory
  of festivals and Sabbaths in Zion;
in the heat of his anger he treated
  king and priest with contempt.

Zain

7 The Lord has rejected his altar,
  he has come to loathe his sanctuary
and has given her palace walls
  into the clutches of the enemy;
from the uproar they made in Yahweh's
    temple
  it might have been a festival day!

NEW REVISED STANDARD VERSION	REVISED ENGLISH BIBLE

8 The LORD determined to lay in ruins
  the wall of daughter Zion;
he stretched the line;
  he did not withhold his hand from destroying;
he caused rampart and wall to lament;
  they languish together.

9 Her gates have sunk into the ground;
  he has ruined and broken her bars;
her king and princes are among the nations;
  guidance is no more,
and her prophets obtain
  no vision from the LORD.

10 The elders of daughter Zion
  sit on the ground in silence;
they have thrown dust on their heads
  and put on sackcloth;
the young girls of Jerusalem
  have bowed their heads to the ground.

11 My eyes are spent with weeping;
  my stomach churns;
my bile is poured out on the ground
  because of the destruction of my people,
because infants and babes faint
  in the streets of the city.

12 They cry to their mothers,
  "Where is bread and wine?"
as they faint like the wounded
  in the streets of the city,
as their life is poured out
  on their mothers' bosom.

13 What can I say for you, to what compare you,
  O daughter Jerusalem?
To what can I liken you, that I may comfort you,
  O virgin daughter Zion?
For vast as the sea is your ruin;
  who can heal you?

14 Your prophets have seen for you
  false and deceptive visions;
they have not exposed your iniquity
  to restore your fortunes,
but have seen oracles for you
  that are false and misleading.

15 All who pass along the way
  clap their hands at you;
they hiss and wag their heads
  at daughter Jerusalem;
"Is this the city that was called
  the perfection of beauty,
  the joy of all the earth?"

16 All your enemies
  open their mouths against you;
they hiss, they gnash their teeth,
  they cry: "We have devoured her!
Ah, this is the day we longed for;
  at last we have seen it!"

17 The LORD has done what he purposed,
  he has carried out his threat;
as he ordained long ago,
  he has demolished without pity;
he has made the enemy rejoice over you,
  and exalted the might of your foes.

18 Cry aloud[d] to the Lord!
  O wall of daughter Zion!

---

8 The LORD was resolved to destroy
  the wall of the daughter of Zion;
he took its measure with his line
  and did not scruple to demolish it.
He made rampart and wall lament,
  and both together lay dejected.

9 He has shattered the bars of her gates,
  and the gates themselves have sunk into the
    ground.
Her king and rulers are exiled among the Gentiles;
  there is no direction from priests,
and her prophets have received
  no vision from the LORD.

10 The elders of Zion
  sit on the ground in silence;
they have cast dust on their heads
  and put on sackcloth.
The maidens of Jerusalem
  bow their heads to the ground.

11 My eyes are blinded with tears,
  my bowels writhe in anguish.
My bile is spilt on the earth
  because of my people's wound,
as children and infants lie fainting
  in the streets of the city.

12 They cry to their mothers,
  'Where is there bread and wine?' —
as they faint like wounded things
  in the streets of the city,
gasping out their lives
  in their mothers' bosoms.

13 How can I cheer you? Whose plight is like yours,
  daughter of Jerusalem?
To what can I compare you for your comfort,
  virgin daughter of Zion?
For your wound gapes as wide as the ocean —
  who can heal you?

14 The visions that your prophets saw for you
  were a false and painted sham.
They did not bring home to you your guilt
  so as to reverse your fortunes.
The visions they saw for you were delusions,
  false and fraudulent.

15 All those who pass by
  snap their fingers at you;
they hiss and wag their heads
  at the daughter of Jerusalem, saying,
'Is this the city once called perfect in beauty,
  the joy of the whole earth?'

16 All your enemies
  jeer at you with open mouths;
they hiss and grind their teeth,
  saying, 'Here we are,
this is the day we have waited for;
  we have lived to see it.'

17 The LORD has done what he planned to do,
  he has fulfilled his threat,
all that he decreed from days of old.
He has demolished without pity
  and let the enemy rejoice over you,
filling your adversaries with pride.

18 Cry to the Lord from the heart
  at the wall of the daughter of Zion;

---

d Cn: Heb *Their heart cried*

2:18 **Cry . . . heart:** *prob. rdg; Heb.* Their heart cried to the Lord.

8 The LORD marked for destruction
the wall of daughter Zion:
He stretched out the measuring line;
his hand brought ruin, yet he did not relent—
He brought grief on wall and rampart
till both succumbed.

9 Sunk into the ground are her gates;
he has removed and broken her bars.
Her king and her princes are among the pagans;
priestly instruction is wanting,
And her prophets have not received
any vision from the LORD.

10 On the ground in silence sit
the old men of daughter Zion;
They strew dust on their heads
and gird themselves with sackcloth;
The maidens of Jerusalem
bow their heads to the ground.

11 Worn out from weeping are my eyes,
within me all is in ferment;
My gall is poured out on the ground
because of the downfall of the daughter of
my people,
As child and infant faint away
in the open spaces of the town.

12 They ask their mothers,
"Where is the cereal?"—in vain,
As they faint away like the wounded
in the streets of the city,
And breathe their last
in their mothers' arms.

13 To what can I liken or compare you,
O daughter Jerusalem?
What example can I show you for your comfort,
virgin daughter Zion?
For great as the sea is your downfall;
who can heal you?

14 Your prophets had for you
false and specious visions;
They did not lay bare your guilt,
to avert your fate;
They beheld for you in vision
false and misleading portents.

15 All who pass by
clap their hands at you;
They hiss and wag their heads
over daughter Jerusalem:
"Is this the all-beautiful city,
the joy of the whole earth?"

16 All your enemies
open their mouths against you;
They hiss and gnash their teeth.
They say, "We have devoured her.
This at last is the day we hoped for;
we have lived to see it!"

17 The LORD has done as he decreed:
he has fulfilled the threat
He set forth from days of old;
he has destroyed and had no pity,
Letting the enemy gloat over you
and exalting the horn of your foes.

18 Cry out to the Lord;
moan, O daughter Zion!

Het
8 Yahweh has resolved to destroy
the walls of the daughter of Zion,
stretching out the line, not staying his hand
until he has engulfed everything,
thus bringing mourning on wall and rampart;
alike they crumbled.

Tet
9 Her gates have sunk into the ground;
he has broken and shattered their bars.
Her king and her princes are among the
gentiles,
there is no instruction,
furthermore her prophets cannot find
any vision from Yahweh.

Yod
10 Mute, they sit on the ground,
the elders of the daughter of Zion;
they have put dust on their heads
and wrapped themselves in sackcloth.
The young girls of Jerusalem bow their heads
to the ground.

Kaph
11 My eyes are worn out with weeping,
my inmost being is in ferment,
my heart plummets
at the destruction of my young people,
as the children and babies grow faint
in the streets of the city.

Lamed
12 They keep saying to their mothers,
'Where is some food?'
as they faint like wounded men
in the streets of the city,
as they breathe their last
on their mothers' breasts.

Mem
13 To what can I compare or liken you,
daughter of Jerusalem?
Who can rescue and comfort you,
young daughter of Zion?
For huge as the sea is your ruin:
who can heal you?

Nun
14 The visions your prophets had for you
were deceptive whitewash;
they did not lay bare your guilt
so as to change your fortunes:
the visions they told you
were deceptive.

Samek
15 All who pass your way
clap their hands at the sight;
they whistle and shake their heads
over the daughter of Jerusalem,
'Is this the city they call Perfection of Beauty,
the joy of the whole world?'

Pe
16 Your enemies open their mouths
in chorus against you;
they whistle and grind their teeth;
they say, 'We have swallowed her up.
This is the day we were waiting for;
at last we have seen it!'

Ain
17 Yahweh has done what he planned,
has carried out his threat,
as he ordained long ago:
he has destroyed without pity,
increasing the might of your foes—
and letting your foes get the credit.

Zade
18 Cry then to the Lord,
rampart of the daughter of Zion;

Let tears stream down like a torrent
    day and night!
Give yourself no rest,
    your eyes no respite!

19 Arise, cry out in the night,
    at the beginning of the watches!
Pour out your heart like water
    before the presence of the Lord!
Lift your hands to him
    for the lives of your children,
who faint for hunger
    at the head of every street.

20 Look, O Lord, and consider!
    To whom have you done this?
Should women eat their offspring,
    the children they have borne?
Should priest and prophet be killed
    in the sanctuary of the Lord?

21 The young and the old are lying
    on the ground in the streets;
my young women and my young men
    have fallen by the sword;
in the day of your anger you have killed them,
    slaughtering without mercy.

22 You invited my enemies from all around
    as if for a day of festival;
and on the day of the anger of the LORD
    no one escaped or survived;
those whom I bore and reared
    my enemy has destroyed.

3 I am one who has seen affliction
    under the rod of God's *e* wrath;
2 he has driven and brought me
    into darkness without any light;
3 against me alone he turns his hand,
    again and again, all day long.

4 He has made my flesh and my skin waste away,
    and broken my bones;
5 he has besieged and enveloped me
    with bitterness and tribulation;
6 he has made me sit in darkness
    like the dead of long ago.

7 He has walled me about so that I cannot escape;
    he has put heavy chains on me;
8 though I call and cry for help,
    he shuts out my prayer;
9 he has blocked my ways with hewn stones,
    he has made my paths crooked.

10 He is a bear lying in wait for me,
    a lion in hiding;
11 he led me off my way and tore me to pieces;
    he has made me desolate;
12 he bent his bow and set me
    as a mark for his arrow.

13 He shot into my vitals
    the arrows of his quiver;
14 I have become the laughingstock of all my
    people,
    the object of their taunt-songs all day long.

let your tears run down like a torrent
    day and night.
Give yourself not a moment's rest,
    let your tears never cease.

19 Arise, cry aloud in the night;
    at the beginning of every watch
pour out your heart like water
    before the presence of the Lord.
Lift up your hands to him
    for the lives of your children,
who are fainting with hunger
    at every street corner.

20 'LORD, look and see:
    who is it you have thus tormented?
Must women eat the fruit of their wombs,
    the children they have held in their arms?
Should priest and prophet be slain
    in the sanctuary of the Lord?

21 'There in the streets both young and old
    lie prostrate on the ground.
My maidens and my young men
    have fallen by the sword;
you have slain them on the day of your anger,
    slaughtered them without pity.

22 'You summoned my enemies from every side,
    like men assembled for a festival;
on the day of the LORD's anger
    no one escaped, not one survived.
All whom I have held in my arms and reared
    my enemies have destroyed.'

3 I am the man who has known affliction
    under the rod of the wrath of the LORD.
2 It was I whom he led away
    and left to walk
    in darkness, where no light is.
3 Against me alone he has turned his hand,
    and so it is all day long.

4 He has wasted away my flesh and my skin
    and broken my bones;
5 he has built up as walls around me
    bitterness and hardship;
6 he has cast me into a place of darkness
    like those long dead.

7 He has hemmed me in so that I cannot escape;
    he has weighed me down with fetters.
8 Even when I cry out and plead for help
    he rejects my prayer.
9 He has barred my road with blocks of stone
    and entangled my way.

10 He lies in wait for me like a bear
    or a lion lurking in a covert.
11 He has forced me aside, thrown me down,
    and left me desolate.
12 He has bent his bow
    and made me the target for his arrows;
13 he has pierced right to my kidneys
    with shafts drawn from his quiver.
14 I have become a laughing-stock to all nations,
    the butt of their mocking songs all day.

e Heb *his*

NEW AMERICAN BIBLE

Let your tears flow like a torrent
  day and night;
Let there be no respite for you,
  no repose for your eyes.

19 Rise up, shrill in the night,
  at the beginning of every watch;
Pour out your heart like water
  in the presence of the Lord;
Lift up your hands to him
  for the lives of your little ones
[Who faint from hunger
  at the corner of every street].

20 "Look, O LORD, and consider:
  whom have you ever treated thus?
Must women eat their offspring,
  their well-formed children?
Are priest and prophet to be slain
  in the sanctuary of the LORD?

21 "Dead in the dust of the streets
  lie young and old;
My maidens and young men
  have fallen by the sword;
You have slain on the day of your wrath,
  slaughtered without pity.

22 "You summoned as for a feast day
  terrors against me from all sides;
There was not, on the day of your wrath,
  either fugitive or survivor;
Those whom I bore and reared
  my enemy has utterly destroyed."

3 I am a man who knows affliction
  from the rod of his anger,
2 One whom he has led and forced to walk
  in darkness, not in the light;
3 Against me alone he brings back his hand
  again and again all the day.

4 He has worn away my flesh and my skin,
  he has broken my bones;
5 He has beset me round about
  with poverty and weariness;
6 He has left me to dwell in the dark
  like those long dead.

7 He has hemmed me in with no escape
  and weighed me down with chains;
8 Even when I cry out for help,
  he stops my prayer;
9 He has blocked my ways with fitted stones,
  and turned my paths aside.

10 A lurking bear he has been to me,
  a lion in ambush!
11 He deranged my ways, set me astray,
  left me desolate.
12 He bent his bow, and set me up
  as the target for his arrow.

13 He pierces my sides
  with shafts from his quiver.
14 I have become a laughingstock for all nations,
  their taunt all the day long;

NEW JERUSALEM BIBLE

let your tears flow like a torrent,
  day and night;
allow yourself no respite,
  give your eyes no rest!

Qoph 19 Up, cry out in the night-time
  as each watch begins!
Pour your heart out like water
  in Yahweh's presence!
Raise your hands to him
  for the lives of your children
(who faint with hunger
  at the end of every street)!

Resh 20 Look, Yahweh, and consider:
  whom have you ever treated like this?
Should women eat their little ones,
  the children they have nursed?
Should priest and prophet be slaughtered
  in the Lord's sanctuary?

Shin 21 Children and old people are lying
  on the ground in the streets;
my young men and young girls
  have fallen by the sword;
you have killed them, on the day of your
    anger,
  you have slaughtered them pitilessly.

Taw 22 As though to a festival you called together
  terrors from all sides,
so that, on the day of Yahweh's anger,
  none escaped and none survived.
Those whom I had nursed and reared,
  my enemy has annihilated them all.

Chapter 3

Aleph 1 I am the man familiar with misery
  under the rod of his fury.
2 He has led and guided me
  into darkness, not light.
3 Against none but me does he turn his hand,
  again and again, all day.

Bet 4 He has wasted my flesh and skin away,
  has broken my bones.
5 He has besieged me and made hardship
  a circlet round my head.
6 He has forced me to dwell where all is dark,
  like those long-dead in their everlasting
    home.

Gimel 7 He has walled me in so that I cannot escape;
  he has weighed me down with chains;
8 even when I shout for help,
  he shuts out my prayer.
9 He has closed my way with blocks of stone,
  he has obstructed my paths.

Dalet 10 For me he is a lurking bear,
  a lion in hiding.
11 Heading me off, he has torn me apart,
  leaving me shattered.
12 He has bent his bow and used me
  as a target for his arrows.

He 13 He has shot deep into me
  with shafts from his quiver.
14 I have become a joke to all my own people,
  their refrain all day long.

NEW REVISED STANDARD VERSION	REVISED ENGLISH BIBLE

NEW REVISED STANDARD VERSION

15 He has filled me with bitterness,
   he has sated me with wormwood.

16 He has made my teeth grind on gravel,
   and made me cower in ashes;

17 my soul is bereft of peace;
   I have forgotten what happiness is;

18 so I say, "Gone is my glory,
   and all that I had hoped for from the LORD."

19 The thought of my affliction and my
   homelessness
   is wormwood and gall!

20 My soul continually thinks of it
   and is bowed down within me.

21 But this I call to mind,
   and therefore I have hope:

22 The steadfast love of the LORD never ceases, *f*
   his mercies never come to an end;

23 they are new every morning;
   great is your faithfulness.

24 "The LORD is my portion," says my soul,
   "therefore I will hope in him."

25 The LORD is good to those who wait for him,
   to the soul that seeks him.

26 It is good that one should wait quietly
   for the salvation of the LORD.

27 It is good for one to bear
   the yoke in youth,

28 to sit alone in silence
   when the Lord has imposed it,

29 to put one's mouth to the dust
   (there may yet be hope),

30 to give one's cheek to the smiter,
   and be filled with insults.

31 For the Lord will not
   reject forever.

32 Although he causes grief, he will have
   compassion
   according to the abundance of his steadfast
   love;

33 for he does not willingly afflict
   or grieve anyone.

34 When all the prisoners of the land
   are crushed under foot,

35 when human rights are perverted
   in the presence of the Most High,

36 when one's case is subverted
   —does the Lord not see it?

37 Who can command and have it done,
   if the Lord has not ordained it?

38 Is it not from the mouth of the Most High
   that good and bad come?

39 Why should any who draw breath complain
   about the punishment of their sins?

40 Let us test and examine our ways,
   and return to the LORD.

41 Let us lift up our hearts as well as our hands
   to God in heaven.

42 We have transgressed and rebelled,
   and you have not forgiven.

43 You have wrapped yourself with anger and
   pursued us,
   killing without pity;

44 you have wrapped yourself with a cloud
   so that no prayer can pass through.

f Syr Tg: Heb LORD, we are not cut off

REVISED ENGLISH BIBLE

15 He has given me my fill of bitter herbs
   and made me drink deep of wormwood.

16 He has broken my teeth on gravel;
   racked with pain, I am fed on ashes.

17 Peace has gone from my life
   and I have forgotten what prosperity is.

18 Then I cry out that my strength has gone
   and so has my hope in the LORD.

19 The memory of my distress and my wanderings
   is wormwood and gall.

20 I remember them indeed
   and am filled with despondency.

21 I shall wait patiently
   because I take this to heart:

22 The LORD's love is surely not exhausted,
   nor has his compassion failed;

23 they are new every morning,
   so great is his constancy.

24 'The LORD', I say, 'is all that I have;
   therefore I shall wait for him patiently.'

25 The LORD is good to those who look to him,
   to anyone who seeks him;

26 it is good to wait in patience
   for deliverance by the LORD.

27 It is good for a man
   to bear the yoke from youth.

28 Let him sit alone in silence
   if it is heavy on him;

29 let him lie face downwards on the ground,
   and there may yet be hope;

30 let him offer his cheek to the smiter
   and endure full measure of abuse.

31 For rejection by the Lord
   does not last for ever.

32 He may punish, yet he will have compassion
   in the fullness of his unfailing love;

33 he does not willingly afflict
   or punish any mortal.

34 To trample underfoot
   prisoners anywhere on earth,

35 to deprive a man of his rights
   in defiance of the Most High,

36 to pervert justice in the courts—
   such things the Lord has never approved.

37 Who can command and have it done
   if the Lord has forbidden it?

38 Do not both bad and good proceed
   from the mouth of the Most High?

39 Why should any man living complain,
   any mortal who has sinned?

40 Let us examine our ways and test them
   and turn back to the LORD;

41 let us lift up our hearts and our hands
   to God in heaven, saying:

42 'We have sinned and rebelled,
   and you have not forgiven.

43 'You have covered us in anger, pursued us,
   and slain without pity;

44 you have covered yourself with cloud
   beyond reach of our prayers;

3:19 **The memory . . . is:** *or* Remember my distress and my
wanderings, the.   3:20 **am filled with despondency:** *prob.
original rdg, altered in Heb. to* I sink down.   3:22 **exhausted:**
prob. rdg; Heb. unintelligible.

NEW AMERICAN BIBLE

15 He has sated me with bitter food,
made me drink my fill of wormwood.

16 He has broken my teeth with gravel,
pressed my face in the dust;

17 My soul is deprived of peace,
I have forgotten what happiness is;

18 I tell myself my future is lost,
all that I hoped for from the LORD.

19 The thought of my homeless poverty
is wormwood and gall;

20 Remembering it over and over
leaves my soul downcast within me.

21 But I will call this to mind,
as my reason to have hope:

22 The favors of the LORD are not exhausted,
his mercies are not spent;

23 They are renewed each morning,
so great is his faithfulness.

24 My portion is the LORD, says my soul;
therefore will I hope in him.

25 Good is the LORD to one who waits for him,
to the soul that seeks him;

26 It is good to hope in silence
for the saving help of the LORD.

27 It is good for a man to bear
the yoke from his youth.

28 Let him sit alone and in silence,
when it is laid upon him.

29 Let him put his mouth to the dust;
there may yet be hope.

30 Let him offer his cheek to be struck,
let him be filled with disgrace.

31 For the Lord's rejection
does not last forever;

32 Though he punishes, he takes pity,
in the abundance of his mercies;

33 He has no joy in afflicting
or grieving the sons of men.

34 When anyone tramples underfoot
all the prisoners in the land,

35 When he distorts men's rights
in the very sight of the Most High,

36 When he presses a crooked claim,
the Lord does not look on unconcerned.

37 Who commands, so that it comes to pass,
except the Lord ordains it;

38 Except it proceeds from the mouth of the
Most High,
whether the thing be good or bad!

39 Why should any living man complain,
any mortal, in the face of his sins?

40 Let us search and examine our ways
that we may return to the LORD!

41 Let us reach out our hearts
toward God in heaven!

42 We have sinned and rebelled;
you have not forgiven us.

43 You veiled yourself in wrath and pursued us,
you slew us and took no pity;

44 You wrapped yourself in a cloud
which prayer could not pierce.

NEW JERUSALEM BIBLE

15 He has given me my fill of bitterness,
he has made me drunk with wormwood.

Waw
16 He has broken my teeth with gravel,
he has fed me on ashes.

17 I have been deprived of peace,
I have forgotten what happiness is

18 and thought, 'My lasting hope
in Yahweh is lost.'

Zain
19 Bring to mind my misery and anguish;
it is wormwood and gall!

20 My heart dwells on this continually
and sinks within me.

21 This is what I shall keep in mind
and so regain some hope:

Het
22 Surely Yahweh's mercies are not over,
his deeds of faithful love not exhausted;

23 every morning they are renewed;
great is his faithfulness!

24 'Yahweh is all I have,' I say to myself,
'and so I shall put my hope in him.'

Tet
25 Yahweh is good to those who trust him,
to all who search for him.

26 It is good to wait in silence
for Yahweh to save.

27 It is good for someone to bear the yoke
from a young age,

Yod
28 to sit in solitude and silence
when it weighs heavy,

29 to lay one's head in the dust—
maybe there is hope—

30 to offer one's cheek to the striker,
to have one's fill of disgrace!

Kaph
31 For the Lord will not reject
anyone for ever.

32 If he brings grief, he will have pity
out of the fullness of his faithful love,

33 for it is not for his own pleasure
that he torments and grieves the human
race.

Lamed
34 When all the prisoners in a country
are crushed underfoot,

35 when human rights are overridden
in defiance of the Most High,

36 when someone is cheated of justice,
does not the Lord see it?

Mem
37 Who has only to speak and it is so done?
Who commands, if not the Lord?

38 From where, if not from the mouth of the
Most High,
do evil and good come?

39 Why then should anyone complain?
Better to be bold against one's sins.

Nun
40 Let us examine our path, let us ponder it
and return to Yahweh.

41 Let us raise our hearts and hands
to God in heaven.

42 We are the ones who have sinned, who have
rebelled,
and you have not forgiven.

Samek
43 You have enveloped us in anger,
pursuing us, slaughtering without pity.

44 You have wrapped yourself in a cloud
too thick for prayer to pierce.

NEW REVISED STANDARD VERSION	REVISED ENGLISH BIBLE

45 You have made us filth and rubbish
    among the peoples.

46 All our enemies
    have opened their mouths against us;
47 panic and pitfall have come upon us,
    devastation and destruction.
48 My eyes flow with rivers of tears
    because of the destruction of my people.

49 My eyes will flow without ceasing,
    without respite,
50 until the LORD from heaven
    looks down and sees.
51 My eyes cause me grief
    at the fate of all the young women in my city.

52 Those who were my enemies without cause
    have hunted me like a bird;
53 they flung me alive into a pit
    and hurled stones on me;
54 water closed over my head;
    I said, "I am lost."

55 I called on your name, O LORD,
    from the depths of the pit;
56 you heard my plea, "Do not close your ear
    to my cry for help, but give me relief!"
57 You came near when I called on you;
    you said, "Do not fear!"

58 You have taken up my cause, O Lord,
    you have redeemed my life.
59 You have seen the wrong done to me, O LORD;
    judge my cause.
60 You have seen all their malice,
    all their plots against me.

61 You have heard their taunts, O LORD,
    all their plots against me.
62 The whispers and murmurs of my assailants
    are against me all day long.
63 Whether they sit or rise — see,
    I am the object of their taunt-songs.

64 Pay them back for their deeds, O LORD,
    according to the work of their hands!
65 Give them anguish of heart;
    your curse be on them!
66 Pursue them in anger and destroy them
    from under the LORD's heavens.

4 How the gold has grown dim,
    how the pure gold is changed!
The sacred stones lie scattered
    at the head of every street.

2 The precious children of Zion,
    worth their weight in fine gold —
how they are reckoned as earthen pots,
    the work of a potter's hands!

3 Even the jackals offer the breast
    and nurse their young,
but my people has become cruel,
    like the ostriches in the wilderness.

---

45 you have treated us as scum and refuse
    among the nations.

46 'Our enemies all jeer at us
    with open mouths.
47 Before us lie hunter's scare and pit,
    devastation and ruin.'
48 My eyes run with streams of water
    because of my people's wound.

49 My eyes stream with unceasing tears
    and refuse all comfort,
50 while the LORD looks down
    and sees from heaven.
51 My eyes ache
    because of the fate of all the women of my city.

52 Those who for no reason were my enemies
    drove me cruelly like a bird;
53 to silence me they thrust me alive into the pit
    and closed the opening with a boulder;
54 waters rose above my head,
    and I said, 'My end has come.'

55 But I called, LORD, on your name
    from the depths of the pit;
56 you heard my plea: 'Do not turn a deaf ear
    when I cry out for relief.'
57 You came near when I called to you;
    you said, 'Have no fear.'

58 Lord, you pleaded my cause;
    you came to my rescue.
59 You saw the injustice done to me, LORD,
    and gave judgement in my favour;
60 you saw all their vindictive behaviour,
    all their plotting against me.

61 You heard their bitter scorn, LORD,
    all their plotting,
62 the whispering and murmuring of my adversaries
    the livelong day.
63 See how, whether they sit or stand,
    I am the object of their taunts.

64 Pay them back for their deeds, LORD,
    pay them as they deserve.
65 Show them how hard your heart can be,
    how little concern you have for them.
66 Pursue them in anger and wipe them out
    from beneath your heavens, LORD.

4 How dulled is the gold,
    how tarnished the fine gold!
The stones of the sanctuary lie strewn
    at every street corner.

2 See Zion's precious sons,
    once worth their weight in finest gold,
now counted as clay jars,
    the work of any potter's hand.

3 Even whales uncover the teat
    and suckle their young;
but the daughters of my people are heartless
    as the ostriches of the desert.

4:1 **The stones of the sanctuary:** *or* Bright gems.   4:3 **whales:**
prob. rdg; Heb. wolves.

NEW AMERICAN BIBLE

NEW JERUSALEM BIBLE

45 You have made us offscourings and refuse
among the nations.

45 You have reduced us to rubbish
and refuse among the nations.

46 All our enemies
have opened their mouths against us;

Pe

46 Our enemies open their mouths
in chorus against us.

47 Terror and the pit have been our lot,
desolation and destruction;

47 Terror and pitfall have been our lot,
ravage and ruin.

48 My eyes run with streams of water
over the downfall of the daughter of my people.

48 My eyes dissolve in torrents of tears
at the ruin of my beloved people.

49 My eyes flow without ceasing,
there is no respite,

Ain

49 My eyes will weep ceaselessly,
without relief,

50 Till the LORD from heaven
looks down and sees.

50 until Yahweh looks down
and sees from heaven.

51 My eyes torment my soul
at the sight of all the daughters of my city.

51 My eyes have grown sore
over all the daughters of my city.

52 Those who were my enemies without cause
hunted me down like a bird;

Zade

52 Unprovoked, my enemies
hunted me down like a bird.

53 They struck me down alive in the pit,
and sealed me in with a stone.

53 They shut me finally in a pit,
they closed me in with a stone.

54 The waters flowed over my head,
and I said, "I am lost!"

54 The waters rose over my head;
I thought, 'I am lost!'

55 I called upon your name, O LORD,
from the bottom of the pit;

Qoph

55 Yahweh, I called on your name
from the deep pit.

56 You heard me call, "Let not your ear
be deaf to my cry for help!"

56 You heard my voice, do not close your ear
to my prayer, to my cry.

57 You came to my aid when I called to you;
you said, "Have no fear!"

57 You are near when I call to you.
You said, 'Do not be afraid!'

58 You defended me in mortal danger,
you redeemed my life.

Resh

58 Lord, you defended my cause,
you have redeemed my life.

59 You see, O LORD, how I am wronged;
do me justice!

59 Yahweh, you have seen the wrong done to
me,
grant me redress.

60 You see all their vindictiveness,
all their plots against me.

60 You have seen their vindictiveness,
all their plots against me.

61 You hear their insults, O LORD,
[all their plots against me],

Shin

61 You have heard their insults, Yahweh,
all their plots against me,

62 The whispered murmurings of my foes,
against me all the day;

62 the whispering and murmuring of my enemies
against me all day long.

63 Whether they sit or stand,
see, I am their taunt song.

63 Look, whether they sit or stand,
I am their refrain.

64 Requite them as they deserve, O LORD,
according to their deeds;

Taw

64 Yahweh, repay them
as their deeds deserve.

65 Give them hardness of heart,
as your curse upon them;

65 Lay hardness of heart
as your curse on them.

66 Pursue them in wrath and destroy them
from under your heavens!

66 Angrily pursue them, root them out
from under your heavens!

Chapter 4

4 How tarnished is the gold,
how changed the noble metal;
How the sacred stones lie strewn
at every street corner!

Aleph

1 How the gold has tarnished,
how the fine gold has changed!
The sacred stones lie scattered
at the corner of every street.

2 Zion's precious sons,
fine gold their counterpart,
Now worth no more than earthen jars
made by the hands of a potter!

Bet

2 The children of Zion,
as precious as finest gold—
to think that they should now be reckoned
like crockery made by a potter!

3 Even the jackals bare their breasts
and suckle their young;
The daughter of my people has become as cruel
as the ostrich in the desert.

Gimel

3 The very jackals give the breast,
and suckle their young:
but the daughter of my people is as cruel
as the ostriches of the desert.

NEW REVISED STANDARD VERSION	REVISED ENGLISH BIBLE

4 The tongue of the infant sticks
   to the roof of its mouth for thirst;
the children beg for food,
   but no one gives them anything.

5 Those who feasted on delicacies
   perish in the streets;
those who were brought up in purple
   cling to ash heaps.

6 For the chastisement*g* of my people has been
      greater
   than the punishment*h* of Sodom,
which was overthrown in a moment,
   though no hand was laid on it.*i*

7 Her princes were purer than snow,
   whiter than milk;
their bodies were more ruddy than coral,
   their hair*i* like sapphire. *j*

8 Now their visage is blacker than soot;
   they are not recognized in the streets.
Their skin has shriveled on their bones;
   it has become as dry as wood.

9 Happier were those pierced by the sword
   than those pierced by hunger,
whose life drains away, deprived
   of the produce of the field.

10 The hands of compassionate women
   have boiled their own children;
they became their food
   in the destruction of my people.

11 The LORD gave full vent to his wrath;
   he poured out his hot anger,
and kindled a fire in Zion
   that consumed its foundations.

12 The kings of the earth did not believe,
   nor did any of the inhabitants of the world,
that foe or enemy could enter
   the gates of Jerusalem.

13 It was for the sins of her prophets
   and the iniquities of her priests,
who shed the blood of the righteous
   in the midst of her.

14 Blindly they wandered through the streets,
   so defiled with blood
that no one was able
   to touch their garments.

15 "Away! Unclean!" people shouted at them;
   "Away! Away! Do not touch!"
So they became fugitives and wanderers;
   it was said among the nations,
   "They shall stay here no longer."

16 The LORD himself has scattered them,
   he will regard them no more;
no honor was shown to the priests,
   no favor to the elders.

17 Our eyes failed, ever watching
   vainly for help;
we were watching eagerly
   for a nation that could not save.

4 With thirst the sucking infant's tongue
   cleaves to the roof of its mouth;
young children beg for bread,
   but no one offers them a crumb.

5 Those who once fed delicately
   are desolate in the streets;
those brought up in purple garments
   now grovel on refuse heaps.

6 The penalty inflicted on my people is worse
   than the punishment of Sodom,
which suffered overthrow in a moment,
   and no hands were wrung.

7 Her crowned princes were once purer than snow,
   whiter than milk;
they were ruddier than branching coral;
   their limbs were lapis lazuli.

8 But their faces turned blacker than soot,
   and no one knew them in the streets;
the skin was shrivelled tight over their bones,
   dry as touchwood.

9 Those who died by the sword were more fortunate
   than those who died of hunger,
who wasted away, deprived
   of the produce of the field.

10 With their own hands tender-hearted women
   boiled their own children;
their children became their food
   on the day of my people's wounding.

11 The LORD glutted his rage
   and poured forth his fierce anger;
he kindled a fire in Zion
   that burnt to the very foundations.

12 No one, neither the kings of the earth
   nor any other inhabitant of the world,
believed that any adversary, any foe
   could penetrate within the gates of Jerusalem.

13 It happened for the sins of her prophets,
   for the crimes of her priests,
who had shed within her walls
   the blood of the righteous.

14 They wandered blindly in the streets;
   they are so stained with blood
that no one would touch
   even their garments.

15 'Go away! Unclean!' people cried to them.
   'Away! Do not come near!'
They hastened away, wandering among the nations,
   unable to find any resting-place.

16 The LORD himself scattered them,
   he thought of them no more;
he showed no favour to priests,
   no pity for elders.

17 Still we strain our eyes,
   looking in vain for help.
We have watched and watched
   for a nation that proved powerless to save.

4:6 **penalty inflicted on:** *or* iniquity of. **punishment:** *or* sin.
4:7 **than branching:** *prob. rdg; Heb.* branch than red.
4:15 **wandering . . . nations:** *prob. rdg; Heb. adds* they said.
4:16 **scattered:** *or* destroyed.

g Or *iniquity*   *h* Or *sin*   *i* Meaning of Heb uncertain   *j* Or *lapis lazuli*

NEW AMERICAN BIBLE

4 The tongue of the suckling cleaves
  to the roof of its mouth in thirst;
The babes cry for food,
  but there is no one to give it to them.

5 Those accustomed to dainty food
  perish in the streets;
Those brought up in purple
  now cling to the ash heaps.

6 The punishment of the daughter of my people
  is greater than the penalty of Sodom,
Which was overthrown in an instant
  without the turning of a hand.

7 Brighter than snow were her princes,
  whiter than milk,
More ruddy than coral,
  more precious than sapphire.

8 Now their appearance is blacker than soot,
  they are unrecognized on the streets;
Their skin shrinks on their bones,
  as dry as wood.

9 Better for those who perish by the sword
  than for those who die of hunger,
Who waste away, as though pierced through,
  lacking the fruits of the field!

10 The hands of compassionate women
  boiled their own children,
To serve them as mourners' food
  in the downfall of the daughter of my people.

11 The LORD has spent his anger,
  poured out his blazing wrath;
He has kindled a fire in Zion
  that has consumed her foundations.

12 The kings of the earth did not believe,
  nor any of the world's inhabitants,
That enemy or foe could enter
  the gates of Jerusalem.

13 Because of the sins of her prophets
  and the crimes of her priests,
Who shed in her midst
  the blood of the just! —

14 They staggered blindly in the streets,
  soiled with blood,
So that people could not touch
  even their garments:

15 "Away, you unclean!" they cried to them,
  "Away, away, do not draw near!"
If they left and wandered among the nations,
  nowhere could they remain.

16 The LORD himself has dispersed them,
  he regards them no more;
He does not receive the priests with favor,
  nor show kindness to the elders.

17 Our eyes ever wasted away,
  looking in vain for aid;
From our watchtower we watched
  for a nation that could not save us.

NEW JERUSALEM BIBLE

Dalet
4 The tongue of the baby at the breast
  sticks to its palate for thirst;
little children ask for bread,
  no one gives them any.

He
5 Those who used to eat only the best,
  now lie dying in the streets;
those who were reared in the purple
  claw at the rubbish heaps,

Waw
6 for the wickedness of the daughter of my
    people
  exceeded the sins of Sodom,
which was overthrown in a moment
  without a hand being laid on it.

Zain
7 Once her young people were brighter than
    snow,
  whiter than milk;
rosier than coral their bodies,
  their hue like sapphire.

Het
8 Now their faces are blacker than soot,
  they are not recognised in the streets,
the skin has shrunk over their bones,
  as dry as a stick.

Tet
9 Happier those killed by the sword
  than those killed by famine:
they waste away, sunken
  for lack of the fruits of the earth.

Yod
10 With their own hands, kindly women
  cooked their children;
this was their food
  when the daughter of my people was
    ruined.

Kaph
11 Yahweh indulged his fury,
  he vented his fierce anger,
he lit a fire in Zion
  which devoured her foundations.

Lamed
12 The kings of the earth never believed,
  nor did any of the inhabitants of the world,
that foe or enemy would ever penetrate
  the gates of Jerusalem.

Mem
13 Owing to the sins of her prophets
  and the crimes of her priests,
who had shed the blood of the upright,
  in the heart of the city,

Nun
14 they wandered blindly through the streets,
  polluted with blood,
so that no one dared
  to touch their clothes.

Samek
15 'Keep away! Unclean!' people shouted,
  'Keep away! Keep away! Don't touch!'
If they left and fled to the nations,
  they were not allowed to stay there either.

Pe
16 The face of Yahweh destroyed them,
  he will look on them no more.
There was no respect for the priests,
  no deference for the elders.

Ain
17 Continually we were wearing out our eyes,
  watching for help — in vain.
From our towers we watched for a nation
  which could not save us anyway.

NEW REVISED STANDARD VERSION	REVISED ENGLISH BIBLE

18 They dogged our steps
    so that we could not walk in our streets;
our end drew near; our days were numbered;
    for our end had come.

19 Our pursuers were swifter
    than the eagles in the heavens;
they chased us on the mountains,
    they lay in wait for us in the wilderness.

20 The LORD's anointed, the breath of our life,
    was taken in their pits—
the one of whom we said, "Under his shadow
    we shall live among the nations."

21 Rejoice and be glad, O daughter Edom,
    you that live in the land of Uz;
but to you also the cup shall pass;
    you shall become drunk and strip yourself bare.

22 The punishment of your iniquity, O daughter
    Zion, is accomplished,
    he will keep you in exile no longer;
but your iniquity, O daughter Edom, he will
    punish,
    he will uncover your sins.

5 Remember, O LORD, what has befallen us;
    look, and see our disgrace!
2 Our inheritance has been turned over to strangers,
    our homes to aliens.
3 We have become orphans, fatherless;
    our mothers are like widows.
4 We must pay for the water we drink;
    the wood we get must be bought.
5 With a yoke*k* on our necks we are hard driven;
    we are weary, we are given no rest.
6 We have made a pact with*l* Egypt and Assyria,
    to get enough bread.
7 Our ancestors sinned; they are no more,
    and we bear their iniquities.
8 Slaves rule over us;
    there is no one to deliver us from their hand.
9 We get our bread at the peril of our lives,
    because of the sword in the wilderness.
10 Our skin is black as an oven
    from the scorching heat of famine.
11 Women are raped in Zion,
    virgins in the towns of Judah.
12 Princes are hung up by their hands;
    no respect is shown to the elders.
13 Young men are compelled to grind,
    and boys stagger under loads of wood.
14 The old men have left the city gate,
    the young men their music.
15 The joy of our hearts has ceased;
    our dancing has been turned to mourning.
16 The crown has fallen from our head;
    woe to us, for we have sinned!
17 Because of this our hearts are sick,
    because of these things our eyes have grown
    dim:

---

18 When we go out, we take to byways
    to avoid the public streets;
our days are all but finished,
    our end has come.

19 Our pursuers have shown themselves swifter
    than eagles in the heavens;
they are hot on our trail over the hills,
    they waylay us in the wilderness.

20 The LORD's anointed, the breath of life to us,
    was caught in their traps;
although we had thought to live among the nations,
    safe under his protection.

21 Rejoice and be glad, daughters of Edom,
    dwellers in the land of Uz.
Yet the cup will pass to you in your turn,
    and when drunk you will expose your nakedness.

22 The punishment for your sin, daughter of Zion, is
    now complete,
and never again will you be carried into exile.
But you, daughter of Edom, your sin will be
    punished,
    and your guilt revealed.

5 REMEMBER, LORD, what has befallen us;
    look, and see how we are scorned.
2 The land we possessed is turned over to strangers,
    our homes to foreigners.
3 We are like orphans, without a father;
    our mothers are like widows.
4 We have to buy water to drink, water which is
    ours;
our own wood can be had only for payment.
5 The yoke is on our necks, we are harassed;
    we are weary, but allowed no rest.
6 We came to terms, now with Egypt,
    now with Assyria, to provide us with food.
7 Our forefathers sinned; now they are no more,
    and we must bear the burden of their guilt.
8 Slaves have become our rulers,
    and there is no one to free us from their power.
9 We must bring in our food from the wilderness
    at the risk of our lives in the scorching heat.
10 Our skins are blackened as in a furnace
    by the ravages of starvation.
11 Women were raped in Zion,
    virgins ravished in the towns of Judah.
12 Princes were hung up by their hands;
    elders received no respect.
13 Young men toil, grinding at the mill;
    boys stagger under loads of wood.
14 Old men have left off their sessions at the city
    gate;
young men no longer pluck the strings.
15 Joy has vanished from our hearts;
    our dancing is turned to mourning.
16 The garlands have fallen from our heads.
    Woe to us, sinners that we are!
17 This is why we are sick at heart;
    all this is why our eyes grow dim:

---

k Symmachus: Heb lacks *With a yoke*   *l* Heb *have given the hand to*

4:18 **our . . . finished:** *prob. rdg; Heb.* our end has drawn near, our days are complete.   5:5 **The yoke:** *so Gk (Symm.); Heb.* omits.

18 Men dogged our steps
so that we could not walk in our streets;
Our end drew near, and came;
our time had expired.

19 Our pursuers were swifter
than eagles in the air,
They harassed us on the mountains
and waylaid us in the desert.

20 The anointed one of the LORD, our breath of life,
was caught in their snares,
He in whose shadow we thought
we could live on among the nations.

21 Though you rejoice and are glad,
O daughter Edom,
you who dwell in the land of Uz,
To you also shall the cup be passed;
you shall become drunk and naked.

22 Your chastisement is completed, O daughter Zion,
he will not prolong your exile;
But your wickedness, O daughter Edom, he
will punish,
he will lay bare your sins.

5 Remember, O LORD, what has befallen us,
look, and see our disgrace:
2 Our inherited lands have been turned over
to strangers,
our homes to foreigners.
3 We have become orphans, fatherless;
widowed are our mothers.
4 The water we drink we must buy,
for our own wood we must pay.
5 On our necks is the yoke of those who drive us;
we are worn out, but allowed no rest.

6 To Egypt we submitted,
and to Assyria, to fill our need of bread.
7 Our fathers, who sinned, are no more;
but we bear their guilt.
8 Slaves rule over us;
there is no one to rescue us from their hands.
9 At the peril of our lives we bring in
our sustenance,
in the face of the desert heat;
10 Our skin is shriveled up, as though by a furnace,
with the searing blasts of famine.

11 The wives in Zion were ravished by the enemy,
the maidens in the cities of Judah;
12 Princes were gibbeted by them,
elders shown no respect.
13 The youths carry the millstones,
boys stagger under their loads of wood.
14 The old men have abandoned the gate,
the young men their music.

15 The joy of our hearts has ceased,
our dance has turned into mourning;
16 The garlands have fallen from our heads:
woe to us, for we have sinned!
17 Over this our hearts are sick,
at this our eyes grow dim:

Zade 18 Men dogged our steps,
to keep us out of our streets.
Our end was near, our days were done,
our end had come.

Qoph 19 Our pursuers were swifter
than eagles in the sky;
they hounded our steps through the mountains,
they lay in ambush for us in the wilds.

Resh 20 The breath of our nostrils, Yahweh's anointed,
was caught in their traps,
he of whom we said, 'In his shadow
we shall live among the nations.'

Shin 21 Rejoice, exult, daughter of Edom,
you who reside in Uz!*a*
To you in turn the cup will pass;
you will get drunk and strip yourself naked!

Taw 22 Your wickedness is atoned for, daughter of
Zion,
he will never banish you again.
But your wickedness, daughter of Edom, will
he punish,
your sins he will lay bare!

Chapter 5

1 Yahweh, remember what has happened to us;
consider, and see our degradation.

2 Our heritage has passed to strangers,
our homes to foreigners.

3 We are orphans, we are fatherless;
our mothers are like widows.

4 We have to buy our own water to drink,
our own wood we can get only at a price.

5 The yoke is on our necks; we are persecuted;
exhausted we are, allowed no rest.

6 We made a pact with Egypt,
with Assyria, to have plenty of food.

7 Our ancestors sinned; they are no more,
and we bear the weight of their guilt.

8 Slaves rule us;
there is no one to rescue us from their clutches.

9 At peril of our lives we earn our bread,
by risking the sword of the desert.

10 Our skin is as hot as an oven,
from the scorch of famine.

11 The women in Zion have been raped,
the young girls in the towns of Judah.

12 Princes have been hanged by their hands;
the face of the old has won no respect.

13 Youths have been put to the mill,
boys stagger under loads of wood.

14 The elders have deserted the gateway;
the young have given up their music.

15 Joy has vanished from our hearts;
our dancing has turned to mourning.

16 The crown has fallen from our heads.
Alas that ever we sinned!

17 This is why our hearts are sick;
this is why our eyes are dim:

a **4** South of Edom. The neighbouring peoples joined in the destruction
of Jerusalem.

18 because of Mount Zion, which lies desolate;
  jackals prowl over it.

19 But you, O LORD, reign forever;
  your throne endures to all generations.
20 Why have you forgotten us completely?
  Why have you forsaken us these many days?
21 Restore us to yourself, O LORD, that we may be
  restored;
  renew our days as of old—
22 unless you have utterly rejected us,
  and are angry with us beyond measure.

18 Mount Zion is desolate
  and overrun with jackals.

19 LORD, your reign is for ever,
  your throne endures from age to age.
20 Why do you forget us so completely
  and forsake us these many days?
21 LORD, turn us back to you, and we shall come
  back;
  renew our days as in times long past.
22 But you have utterly rejected us;
  your anger against us has been great indeed.

18 That Mount Zion should be desolate,
   with jackals roaming there!

19 You, O LORD, are enthroned forever;
   your throne stands from age to age.

20 Why, then, should you forget us,
   abandon us so long a time?

21 Lead us back to you, O LORD, that we may
   be restored:
   give us anew such days as we had of old.

22 For now you have indeed rejected us,
   and in full measure turned your wrath against us.

18 because Mount Zion is desolate;
   jackals roam to and fro on it.

19 Yet you, Yahweh, rule from eternity;
   your throne endures from age to age.

20 Why do you never remember us?
   Why do you abandon us so long?

21 Make us come back to you, Yahweh, and we will
   come back.
   Restore us as we were before!

22 Unless you have utterly rejected us,
   in an anger which knows no limit.

Ezekiel

1 In the thirtieth year, in the fourth month, on the fifth day of the month, as I was among the exiles by the river Chebar, the heavens were opened, and I saw visions of God. 2 On the fifth day of the month (it was the fifth year of the exile of King Jehoiachin), 3 the word of the LORD came to the priest Ezekiel son of Buzi, in the land of the Chaldeans by the river Chebar; and the hand of the LORD was on him there.

4 As I looked, a stormy wind came out of the north: a great cloud with brightness around it and fire flashing forth continually, and in the middle of the fire, something like gleaming amber. 5 In the middle of it was something like four living creatures. This was their appearance: they were of human form. 6 Each had four faces, and each of them had four wings. 7 Their legs were straight, and the soles of their feet were like the sole of a calf's foot; and they sparkled like burnished bronze. 8 Under their wings on their four sides they had human hands. And the four had their faces and their wings thus: 9 their wings touched one another; each of them moved straight ahead, without turning as they moved. 10 As for the appearance of their faces: the four had the face of a human being, the face of a lion on the right side, the face of an ox on the left side, and the face of an eagle; 11 such were their faces. Their wings were spread out above; each creature had two wings, each of which touched the wing of another, while two covered their bodies. 12 Each moved straight ahead; wherever the spirit would go, they went, without turning as they went. 13 In the middle of*a* the living creatures there was something that looked like burning coals of fire, like torches moving to and fro among the living creatures; the fire was bright, and lightning issued from the fire. 14 The living creatures darted to and fro, like a flash of lightning.

15 As I looked at the living creatures, I saw a wheel on the earth beside the living creatures, one for each of the four of them.*b* 16 As for the appearance of the wheels and their construction: their appearance was like the gleaming of beryl; and the four had the same form, their construction being something like a wheel within a wheel. 17 When they moved, they moved in any of the four directions without veering as they moved. 18 Their rims were tall and awesome, for the rims of all four were full of eyes all around. 19 When the living creatures moved, the wheels moved beside them; and when the living creatures rose from the earth, the wheels rose. 20 Wherever the spirit would go, they went, and the wheels rose along with them; for the spirit of the living creatures was in the wheels. 21 When they moved, the others moved; when they stopped, the others stopped; and when they rose from the earth, the wheels rose along with them; for the spirit of the living creatures was in the wheels.

22 Over the heads of the living creatures there was something like a dome, shining like crystal,*c* spread out above their heads. 23 Under the dome their wings were stretched out straight, one toward another; and each of the creatures had two wings covering its body. 24 When they moved, I heard the sound of their wings like the sound of mighty waters, like the thunder of the Almighty,*d* a sound of tumult like the sound of an army; when they stopped, they let down their wings. 25 And there came a voice from

a Gk OL: Heb *And the appearance of*   *b* Heb *of their faces*
c Gk: Heb *like the awesome crystal*   *d* Traditional rendering of Heb *Shaddai*

Ezekiel

1 ON the fifth day of the fourth month in the thirtieth year, while I was among the exiles by the river Kebar, the heavens were opened and I saw visions from God. 2 On the fifth day of the month in the fifth year of the exile of King Jehoiachin, 3 the word of the LORD came to the priest Ezekiel son of Buzi, in Chaldaea by the river Kebar, and there the LORD's hand was upon him.

4 In my vision I saw a storm-wind coming from the north, a vast cloud with flashes of fire and brilliant light about it; and within was a radiance like brass, glowing in the heart of the flames. 5 In the fire was the likeness of four living creatures in human form. 6 Each had four faces and each four wings; 7 their legs were straight, and their hoofs were like the hoofs of a calf, glistening and gleaming like bronze. 8 Under the wings on each of the four sides were human hands; all four creatures had faces and wings, 9 and the wings of one touched those of another. They did not turn as they moved; each creature went straight forward. 10 This is what their faces were like: all four had a human face and a lion's face on the right, on the left the face of an ox and the face of an eagle. 11 Their wings were spread upwards; each living creature had one pair touching those of its neighbour, while one pair covered its body. 12 They moved forward in whatever direction the spirit went; they never swerved from their course. 13 The appearance of the creatures was as if fire from burning coals or torches were darting to and fro among them; the fire was radiant, and out of the fire came lightning.

15 As I looked at the living creatures, I saw wheels on the ground, one beside each of the four. 16 The wheels sparkled like topaz, and they were all alike: in form and working they were like a wheel inside a wheel, 17 and when they moved in any of the four directions they never swerved from their course. 18 I saw that they had rims, and the rims were covered with eyes all around. 19 When the living creatures moved, the wheels moved beside them; when the creatures rose from the ground, the wheels rose; 20 they moved in whichever direction the spirit went; and the wheels rose together with them, for the spirit of the creatures was in the wheels. 21 When one moved, the other moved; when one halted, the other halted; when the creatures rose from the ground, the wheels rose together with them, for the spirit of the creatures was in the wheels.

22 Above the heads of the living creatures was, as it were, a vault glittering like a sheet of ice, awe-inspiring, stretched over their heads above them. 23 Under the vault their wings were spread straight out, touching one another, while one pair covered the body of each. 24 I heard, too, the noise of their wings; when they moved it was like the noise of a mighty torrent or a thunderclap, like the noise of a crowd or an armed camp; when they halted their wings dropped. 25 A

1:4 **brass:** *mng of Heb. word uncertain.*   1:11 **Their wings:** *so Gk; Heb. adds and their faces.* **those . . . neighbour:** *prob. rdg; Heb. unintelligible.*   1:13 **out . . . lightning:** *prob. rdg, cp. Gk; Heb. adds* 14 *and the living creatures went out (prob. rdg; Heb. obscure) and in like rays of light.*   1:15 **one . . . four:** *prob. rdg; Heb. obscure.*   1:16 **The wheels:** *so Gk; Heb. adds and their works.*   1:18 **I saw . . . had rims:** *prob. rdg; Heb. obscure.*   1:23 **while . . . each:** *so some MSS; others repeat* one pair covered the body of each.

THE BOOK OF

Ezekiel

1 In the thirtieth year, on the fifth day of the fourth month, while I was among the exiles by the river Chebar, the heavens opened, and I saw divine visions. — [2] On the fifth day of the month, the fifth year, that is, of King Jehoiachin's exile, [3] the word of the LORD came to the priest Ezekiel, the son of Buzi, in the land of the Chaldeans by the river Chebar. — There the hand of the LORD came upon me.

[4] As I looked, a stormwind came from the North, a huge cloud with flashing fire [enveloped in brightness], from the midst of which [the midst of the fire] something gleamed like electrum. [5] Within it were figures resembling four living creatures that looked like this: their form was human, [6] but each had four faces and four wings, [7] and their legs went straight down; the soles of their feet were round. They sparkled with a gleam like burnished bronze.

‡1.8–9: see below‡

[10] Their faces were like this: each of the four had the face of a man, but on the right side was the face of a lion, and on the left side the face of an ox, and finally each had the face of an eagle. [9] Their faces [and their wings] looked out on all their four sides; they did not turn when they moved, but each went straight forward. ‡1.11: see below‡ [12] [Each went straight forward; wherever the spirit wished to go, there they went; they did not turn when they moved.]

[8] Human hands were under their wings, and the wings of one touched those of another. [11] Each had two wings spread out above so that they touched one another's, while the other two wings of each covered his body. [13] In among the living creatures something like burning coals of fire could be seen; they seemed like torches, moving to and fro among the living creatures. The fire gleamed, and from it came forth flashes of lightning.

[15] As I looked at the living creatures, I saw wheels on the ground, one beside each of the four living creatures. [16] The wheels had the sparkling appearance of chrysolite, and all four of them looked the same: they were constructed as though one wheel were within another. [17] They could move in any of the four directions they faced, without veering as they moved. [18] The four of them had rims, and I saw that their rims were full of eyes all around. [19] When the living creatures moved, the wheels moved with them; and when the living creatures were raised from the ground, the wheels also were raised. [20] Wherever the spirit wished to go, there the wheels went, and they were raised together with the living creatures; for the spirit of the living creatures was in the wheels. [22] Over the heads of the living creatures, something like a firmament could be seen, seeming like glittering crystal, stretched straight out above their heads. [23] Beneath the firmament their wings were stretched out, one toward the other. [Each of them had two covering his body.] [24] Then I heard the sound of their wings, like the roaring of mighty waters, like the voice of the Almighty. When they moved, the sound of the tumult was like the din of an army. [And when they stood still, they lowered their wings.]

Ezekiel

1 In the thirtieth year, on the fifth day of the fourth month, as I was among the exiles by the River Chebar, heaven opened and I saw visions from God. [2] On the fifth of the month — it was the fifth year of exile for King Jehoiachin — [3] the word of Yahweh was addressed to the priest Ezekiel son of Buzi, in Chaldaea by the River Chebar. There the hand of Yahweh came on him.

[4] I looked; a stormy wind blew from the north, a great cloud with flashing fire and brilliant light round it, and in the middle, in the heart of the fire, a brilliance like that of amber, [5] and in the middle what seemed to be four living creatures. They looked like this: They were of human form. [6] Each had four faces, each had four wings. [7] Their legs were straight; they had hooves like calves, glittering like polished brass. [8] Below their wings, they had human hands on all four sides corresponding to their four faces and four wings. [9] They touched one another with their wings; they did not turn as they moved; each one moved straight forward. [10] As to the appearance of their faces, all four had a human face, and a lion's face to the right, and all four had a bull's face to the left, and all four had an eagle's face. [11] Their wings were spread upwards, each had one pair touching its neighbour's, and the other pair covering its body. [12] And each one moved straight forward; they went where the spirit urged them, they did not turn as they moved.

[13] Between these living creatures were what looked like blazing coals, like torches, darting backwards and forwards between the living creatures; the fire gave a brilliant light, and lightning flashed from the fire, [14] and the living creatures kept disappearing and reappearing like flashes of lightning.

[15] Now, as I looked at the living creatures, I saw a wheel touching the ground beside each of the four-faced living creatures. [16] The appearance and structure of the wheels were like glittering chrysolite. All four looked alike, and their appearance and structure were such that each wheel seemed to have another wheel inside it. [17] In whichever of the four directions they moved, they did not need to turn as they moved. [18] Their circumference was of awe-inspiring size, and the rims of all four sparkled all the way round. [19] When the living creatures moved, the wheels moved beside them; and when the living creatures left the ground, the wheels too left the ground. [20] They moved in whichever direction the spirit chose to go, and the wheels rose with them, since the wheels shared the spirit of the animals. [21] When the living creatures moved on, they moved on; when the former halted, the latter halted; when the former left the ground, the wheels too left the ground, since the wheels shared the spirit of the animals. [22] Over the heads of the living creatures was what looked like a solid surface glittering like crystal, spread out over their heads, above them, [23] and under the solid surface, their wings were spread out straight, touching one another, and each had a pair covering its body. [24] I also heard the noise of their wings; when they moved, it was like the noise of floodwaters, like the voice of Shaddai, like the noise of a storm, like the noise of an armed camp; and when they halted, they lowered their wings; [25] there was a noise too.

1, 10–22: Note the changed order of the verses and the omission of the textually uncertain verses 14 and 21. Such changes also occur elsewhere in this book.

NEW REVISED STANDARD VERSION

above the dome over their heads; when they stopped, they let down their wings.

26 And above the dome over their heads there was something like a throne, in appearance like sapphire;*e* and seated above the likeness of a throne was something that seemed like a human form. 27 Upward from what appeared like the loins I saw something like gleaming amber, something that looked like fire enclosed all around; and downward from what looked like the loins I saw something that looked like fire, and there was a splendor all around. 28 Like the bow in a cloud on a rainy day, such was the appearance of the splendor all around. This was the appearance of the likeness of the glory of the LORD.

When I saw it, I fell on my face, and I heard the voice of someone speaking.

2 He said to me: O mortal,*f* stand up on your feet, and I will speak with you. 2 And when he spoke to me, a spirit entered into me and set me on my feet; and I heard him speaking to me. 3 He said to me, Mortal, I am sending you to the people of Israel, to a nation*g* of rebels who have rebelled against me; they and their ancestors have transgressed against me to this very day. 4 The descendants are impudent and stubborn. I am sending you to them, and you shall say to them, "Thus says the Lord GOD." 5 Whether they know or refuse to hear (for they are a rebellious house), they shall know that there has been a prophet among them. 6 And you, O mortal, do not be afraid of them, and do not be afraid of their words, though briers and thorns surround you and you live among scorpions; do not be afraid of their words, and do not be dismayed at their looks, for they are a rebellious house. 7 You shall speak my words to them, whether they hear or refuse to hear; for they are a rebellious house.

8 But you, mortal, hear what I say to you; do not be rebellious like that rebellious house; open your mouth and eat what I give you. 9 I looked, and a hand was stretched out to me, and a written scroll was in it. 10 He spread it before me; it had writing on the front and on the back, and written on it were words of lamentation and mourning and woe.

3 He said to me, O mortal, eat what is offered to you; eat this scroll, and go, speak to the house of Israel. 2 So I opened my mouth, and he gave me the scroll to eat. 3 He said to me, Mortal, eat this scroll that I give you and fill your stomach with it. Then I ate it; and in my mouth it was as sweet as honey.

4 He said to me: Mortal, go to the house of Israel and speak my very words to them. 5 For you are not sent to a people of obscure speech and difficult language, but to the house of Israel— 6 not to many peoples of obscure speech and difficult language, whose words you cannot understand. Surely, if I sent you to them, they would listen to you. 7 But the house of Israel will not listen to you, for they are not willing to listen to me; because all the house of Israel have a hard forehead and a stubborn heart. 8 See, I have made your face hard against their faces, and your forehead hard against their foreheads. 9 Like the hardest stone, harder than flint, I have made your forehead; do not fear them or be dismayed at their looks, for they are a rebellious house. 10 He said to me: Mortal, all my words that I shall speak to you receive in your heart and hear with your ears; 11 then go to the exiles, to your people, and speak to them. Say to them, "Thus says the Lord GOD"; whether they hear or refuse to hear.

12 Then the spirit lifted me up, and as the glory of the LORD rose*h* from its place, I heard behind me the sound of loud rumbling; 13 it was the sound of the wings of the living

REVISED ENGLISH BIBLE

voice was heard from above the vault over their heads, as they halted with drooping wings.

26 Above the vault over their heads there appeared, as it were, a sapphire in the shape of a throne, and exalted on the throne a form in human likeness. 27 From his waist upwards I saw what might have been brass glowing like fire in a furnace; and from his waist downwards I saw what looked like fire. Radiance encircled him. 28 Like a rainbow in the clouds after the rain was the sight of that encircling radiance; it was like the appearance of the glory of the LORD.

When I saw this I prostrated myself, and I heard a voice:

2 1 'Stand up, O man,' he said, 'and let me talk with you.' 2 As he spoke, a spirit came into me and stood me on my feet, and I listened to him speaking. 3 He said to me, 'O man, I am sending you to the Israelites, rebels who have rebelled against me. They and their forefathers have been in revolt against me to this very day, 4 and this generation to which I am sending you is stubborn and obstinate. You are to say to them, "These are the words of the Lord GOD," 5 and they will know that they have a prophet among them, whether they listen or whether in their rebelliousness they refuse to listen.

6 'But you, O man, must not be afraid of them or of what they say, though they resist and reject you and you are sitting on scorpions. There is nothing to fear in their rebellious words, nothing to make you afraid in their rebellious looks. 7 You must speak my words to them, whether they listen or whether in their rebelliousness they refuse to listen. 8 But you, O man, must heed what I say and not be rebellious like them. Open your mouth and eat what I am giving you.'

9 I saw a hand stretched out to me, holding a scroll. 10 He unrolled it before me, and it was written on both sides, back and front, with dirges and laments and words of woe.

3 1 Then he said to me, 'O man, eat what is in front of you; eat this scroll; then go and speak to the Israelites.' 2 I opened my mouth and he gave me the scroll to eat, 3 saying, 'O man, swallow this scroll I give you, and eat your fill.' I ate it, and it tasted as sweet as honey to me.

4 'O man,' he said to me, 'go to the Israelites and declare my message to them. 5 It is not to people whose speech is thick and difficult you are sent, but to Israelites. 6 I am not sending you to great nations whose speech is so thick and so difficult that you cannot make out what they say; had I sent you to them they would have listened to you. 7 But the Israelites will refuse to listen to you, for they refuse to listen to me; all of them are brazen-faced and stubborn-hearted. 8 But I shall make you a match for them. I shall make you as brazen and as stubborn as they are. 9 I shall make your brow like adamant, harder than flint. Do not fear them, do not be terrified by them, rebellious though they are.' 10 He went on: 'Listen carefully, O man, to all that I have to say to you, and take it to heart. 11 Then go to your fellow-countrymen in exile and say to them, "These are the words of the Lord GOD," whether they listen or refuse to listen.'

12 A spirit lifted me up, and I heard behind me a fierce rushing sound as the glory of the LORD rose from his place.

---

e Or *lapis lazuli*   *f* Or *son of man*; Heb *ben adam* (and so throughout the book when Ezekiel is addressed)   *g* Syr: Heb *to nations*   *h* Cn: Heb *and blessed be the glory of the LORD*

1:26 **sapphire**: *or* lapis lazuli.   2:1 **O man:** *lit.* son of man, *and so throughout the book when Ezekiel is addressed.*   3:12 **rose:** *prob. rdg; Heb. obscure.*

26 Above the firmament over their heads something like a throne could be seen, looking like sapphire. Upon it was seated, up above, one who had the appearance of a man. 27 Upward from what resembled his waist I saw what gleamed like electrum; downward from what resembled his waist I saw what looked like fire; he was surrounded with splendor. 28 Like the bow which appears in the clouds on a rainy day was the splendor that surrounded him. Such was the vision of the likeness of the glory of the LORD.

2 When I had seen it, I fell upon my face and heard a voice that said to me: 1 Son of man, stand up! I wish to speak with you. 2 As he spoke to me, spirit entered into me and set me on my feet, and I heard the one who was speaking 3 say to me: Son of man, I am sending you to the Israelites, rebels who have rebelled against me; they and their fathers have revolted against me to this very day. 4 Hard of face and obstinate of heart are they to whom I am sending you. But you shall say to them: Thus says the Lord GOD! 5 And whether they heed or resist—for they are a rebellious house—they shall know that a prophet has been among them. 6 But as for you, son of man, fear neither them nor their words when they contradict you and reject you, and when you sit on scorpions. Neither fear their words nor be dismayed at their looks, for they are a rebellious house. 7 [But speak my words to them, whether they heed or resist, for they are rebellious.] 8 As for you, son of man, obey me when I speak to you: be not rebellious like this house of rebellion, but open your mouth and eat what I shall give you.

9 It was then I saw a hand stretched out to me, in which was a written scroll 10 which he unrolled before me. It was covered with writing front and back, and written on it was: Lamentation and wailing and woe!

3 He said to me: Son of man, eat what is before you; eat this scroll, then go, speak to the house of Israel. 2 So I opened my mouth and he gave me the scroll to eat. 3 Son of man, he then said to me, feed your belly and fill your stomach with this scroll I am giving you. I ate it, and it was as sweet as honey in my mouth. He said: 4 Son of man, go now to the house of Israel, and speak my words to them.

5 Not to a people with difficult speech and barbarous language am I sending you, 6 nor to the many peoples [with difficult speech and barbarous language] whose words you cannot understand. If I were to send you to these, they would listen to you; 7 but the house of Israel will refuse to listen to you, since they will not listen to me. For the whole house of Israel is stubborn of brow and obstinate in heart. 8 But I will make your face as hard as theirs, and your brow as stubborn as theirs, 9 like diamond, harder than flint. Fear them not, nor be dismayed at their looks, for they are a rebellious house.

10 Son of man, he said to me, take into your heart all my words that I speak to you; hear them well. 11 Now go to the exiles, to your countrymen, and say to them: Thus says the Lord GOD!—whether they heed or resist!

12 Then spirit lifted me up, and I heard behind me the noise of a loud rumbling as the glory of the LORD rose from its place: 13 the noise made by the wings of the living crea-

26 Beyond the solid surface above their heads, there was what seemed like a sapphire, in the form of a throne. High above on the form of a throne was a form with the appearance of a human being. 27 I saw a brilliance like amber, like fire, radiating from what appeared to be the waist upwards; and from what appeared to be the waist downwards, I saw what looked like fire, giving a brilliant light all round. 28 The radiance of the encircling light was like the radiance of the bow in the clouds on rainy days. The sight was like the glory of Yahweh. I looked and fell to the ground, and I heard the voice of someone speaking to me.

2 He said, 'Son of man, get to your feet; I will speak to you.' 2 As he said these words the spirit came into me and put me on my feet, and I heard him speaking to me. 3 He said, 'Son of man, I am sending you to the Israelites, to the rebels who have rebelled against me. They and their ancestors have been in revolt against me up to the present day. 4 Because they are stubborn and obstinate children, I am sending you to them, to say, "Lord Yahweh says this." 5 Whether they listen or not, this tribe of rebels will know there is a prophet among them. 6 And you, son of man, do not be afraid of them or of what they say, though you find yourself surrounded with brambles and sitting on scorpions. Do not be afraid of their words or alarmed by their looks, for they are a tribe of rebels. 7 You are to deliver my words to them whether they listen or not, for they are a tribe of rebels. 8 But you, son of man, are to listen to what I say to you; do not be a rebel like that rebellious tribe. Open your mouth and eat what I am about to give you.'

9 When I looked, there was a hand stretching out to me, holding a scroll. 10 He unrolled it in front of me; it was written on, front and back; on it was written 'Lamentations, dirges and cries of grief'.

3 He then said, 'Son of man, eat what you see; eat this scroll, then go and speak to the House of Israel.' 2 I opened my mouth; he gave me the scroll to eat 3 and then said, 'Son of man, feed on this scroll which I am giving you and eat your fill.' So I ate it, and it tasted sweet as honey.

4 He then said, 'Son of man, go to the House of Israel and tell them what I have said. 5 You are not being sent to a nation that speaks a difficult foreign language; you are being sent to the House of Israel. 6 Not to big nations that speak difficult foreign languages, and whose words you would not understand—if I sent you to them, they would listen to you; but the House of Israel will not listen to you because it will not listen to me. The whole House of Israel is defiant and obstinate. 8 But now, I am making you as defiant as they are, and as obstinate as they are; 9 I am making your resolution as hard as a diamond, harder than flint. So do not be afraid of them, do not be overawed by them, for they are a tribe of rebels.'

10 Then he said, 'Son of man, take to heart everything I say to you, listen carefully, 11 then go to your exiled countrymen and talk to them. Say to them, "Lord Yahweh says this," whether they listen or not.'

12 The spirit lifted me up, and behind me I heard a great vibrating sound, 'Blessed be the glory of Yahweh in his dwelling-place!' 13 This was the sound of the living crea-

creatures brushing against one another, and the sound of the wheels beside them, that sounded like a loud rumbling. 14 The spirit lifted me up and bore me away; I went in bitterness in the heat of my spirit, the hand of the LORD being strong upon me. 15 I came to the exiles at Tel-abib, who lived by the river Chebar.[i] And I sat there among them, stunned, for seven days.

16 At the end of seven days, the word of the LORD came to me: 17 Mortal, I have made you a sentinel for the house of Israel; whenever you hear a word from my mouth, you shall give them warning from me. 18 If I say to the wicked, "You shall surely die," and you give them no warning, or speak to warn the wicked from their wicked way, in order to save their life, those wicked persons shall die for their iniquity; but their blood I will require at your hand. 19 But if you warn the wicked, and they do not turn from their wickedness, or from their wicked way, they shall die for their iniquity; but you will have saved your life. 20 Again, if the righteous turn from their righteousness and commit iniquity, and I lay a stumbling block before them, they shall die; because you have not warned them, they shall die for their sin, and their righteous deeds that they have done shall not be remembered; but their blood I will require at your hand. 21 If, however, you warn the righteous not to sin, and they do not sin, they shall surely live, because they took warning; and you will have saved your life.

22 Then the hand of the LORD was upon me there; and he said to me, Rise up, go out into the valley, and there I will speak with you. 23 So I rose up and went out into the valley; and the glory of the LORD stood there, like the glory that I had seen by the river Chebar; and I fell on my face. 24 The spirit entered into me, and set me on my feet; and he spoke with me and said to me: Go, shut yourself inside your house. 25 As for you, mortal, cords shall be placed on you, and you shall be bound with them, so that you cannot go out among the people; 26 and I will make your tongue cling to the roof of your mouth, so that you shall be speechless and unable to reprove them; for they are a rebellious house. 27 But when I speak with you, I will open your mouth, and you shall say to them, "Thus says the Lord GOD"; let those who will hear, hear; and let those who refuse to hear, refuse; for they are a rebellious house.

4 And you, O mortal, take a brick and set it before you. On it portray a city, Jerusalem; 2 and put siegeworks against it, and build a siege wall against it, and cast up a ramp against it; set camps also against it, and plant battering rams against it all around. 3 Then take an iron plate and place it as an iron wall between you and the city; set your face toward it, and let it be in a state of siege, and press the siege against it. This is a sign for the house of Israel.

4 Then lie on your left side, and place the punishment of the house of Israel upon it; you shall bear their punishment for the number of the days that you lie there. 5 For I assign to you a number of days, three hundred ninety days, equal to the number of the years of their punishment; and so you shall bear the punishment of the house of Israel. 6 When you have completed these, you shall lie down a second time, but on your right side, and bear the punishment of the house of Judah; forty days I assign you, one day for each year. 7 You shall set your face toward the siege of Jerusalem, and with your arm bared you shall prophesy against it. 8 See, I am putting cords on you so that you cannot turn from one side to the other until you have completed the days of your siege.

13 I heard the sound of the living creatures' wings brushing against one another, and the sound of the wheels beside them, a fierce rushing sound. 14 A spirit lifted me and carried me along, and I went full of exaltation, the power of the LORD strong upon me. 15 So I came to the exiles at Tel-abib who were settled by the river Kebar. For seven days I stayed there among them in a state of consternation.

16 At the end of seven days this word of the LORD came to me: 17 'I have appointed you, O man, a watchman for the Israelites; you will pass to them the warnings you receive from me. 18 If I pronounce sentence of death on a wicked person and you have not warned him or spoken out to dissuade him from his wicked ways and so save his life, that person will die because of his sin, but I shall hold you answerable for his death. 19 But if you have warned him and he persists in his wicked ways, he will die because of his sin, but you will have discharged your duty. 20 Again, if someone who is righteous goes astray and does wrong, and I cause his downfall, he will die because you have not warned him. He will die for his sin; the righteous deeds he has done will not be taken into account, and I shall hold you responsible for his death. 21 But if you have warned the righteous person not to sin and he does not sin, then he will have saved his life because he heeded the warning, and you will have discharged your duty.'

22 THE LORD's hand was upon me there, and he said to me, 'Rise, go out into the plain, and there I shall speak to you.' 23 I arose, and when I went out into the plain, the glory of the LORD was there, like the glory which I had seen by the river Kebar, and I prostrated myself. 24 Then a spirit came and set me on my feet. The LORD spoke to me: 'Go,' he said, 'and shut yourself up in your house. 25 You will be tied and bound with ropes, O man, so that you cannot go out among the people. 26 I shall make your tongue cleave to the roof of your mouth and you will be unable to speak and so rebuke them, that rebellious people. 27 But when I have something to say to you, I shall give you back the power of speech. Then you will declare to them, "This is what the Lord GOD said." If anyone will listen, he may listen; and if anyone refuses to listen, he may refuse. Rebels indeed they are!'

4 'O man, take a tile and lay it in front of you. Draw a city on it, the city of Jerusalem: 2 portray it under siege, erect towers against it, raise a siege-ramp, put mantelets in position, and bring up battering-rams on every side. 3 Then take a griddle, and put it as if it were an iron wall between you and the city. Keep your eyes fixed on the city; it will be the besieged and you the besieger. This will be a sign to the Israelites.

4 'Next, lie on your left side, putting the weight of Israel's punishment on it; for as many days as you lie on that side you will be bearing their punishment. 5 I ordain that you bear Israel's punishment for three hundred and ninety days, allowing one day for each year of their punishment. 6 When you have completed these days, lie down again, this time on your right side, and bear Judah's punishment; I ordain for you forty days, one day for each year. 7 Then fix your gaze towards the siege of Jerusalem and with bared arm prophesy against it. 8 See how I tie you with ropes so that you cannot turn over from one side to the other until you complete your days of siege.

---

[i] Two Mss Syr: Heb *Chebar, and to where they lived.* Another reading is *Chebar, and I sat where they sat*

3:15 **by ... Kebar:** *so some MSS; others add* and where they were living.

tures striking one another, and by the wheels alongside them, a loud rumbling. 14 The spirit which had lifted me up seized me, and I went off spiritually stirred, while the hand of the LORD rested heavily upon me. 15 Thus I came to the exiles who lived at Tel-abib by the river Chebar, and for seven days I sat among them distraught.

‡3.16: see below in ch. 4‡

17 Thus the word of the LORD came to me: Son of man, I have appointed you a watchman for the house of Israel. When you hear a word from my mouth, you shall warn them for me. 18 If I say to the wicked man, You shall surely die; and you do not warn him or speak out to dissuade him from his wicked conduct so that he may live: that wicked man shall die for his sin, but I will hold you responsible for his death. 19 If, on the other hand, you have warned the wicked man, yet he has not turned away from his evil nor from his wicked conduct, then he shall die for his sin, but you shall save your life.

20 If a virtuous man turns away from virtue and does wrong when I place a stumbling block before him, he shall die. He shall die for his sin, and his virtuous deeds shall not be remembered; but I will hold you responsible for his death if you did not warn him. 21 When, on the other hand, you have warned a virtuous man not to sin, and he has in fact not sinned, he shall surely live because of the warning, and you shall save your own life.

22 The hand of the Lord came upon me, and he said to me: Get up and go out into the plain, where I will speak with you. 23 So I got up and went out into the plain, and I saw that the glory of the LORD was in that place, like the glory I had seen by the river Chebar. I fell prone, 24 but then spirit entered into me and set me on my feet, and he spoke with me.

He said to me: Go shut yourself up in your house. 25 [As for you, son of man, they will put cords upon you and bind you with them, so that you cannot go out among them.] 26 I will make your tongue stick to your palate so that you will be dumb and unable to rebuke them for being a rebellious house. 27 Only when I speak with you and open your mouth, shall you say to them: Thus says the Lord GOD! Let him heed who will, and let him resist who will, for they are a rebellious house.

4 3,16 At the end of seven days . . . : 1 As for you, son of man, take a clay tablet; lay it in front of you, and draw on it a city [Jerusalem]. 2 Raise a siege against it: build a tower, lay out a ramp, pitch camps, and set up battering rams all around. 3 Then take an iron griddle and set it up as an iron wall between you and the city. Fix your gaze on it: it shall be in the state of siege, and you shall besiege it. This shall be a sign for the house of Israel. 4 Then you shall lie on your left side, while I place the sins of the house of Israel upon you. As many days as you lie thus, you shall bear their sins. 5 For the years of their sins I allot you the same number of days, three hundred and ninety, during which you will bear the sins of the house of Israel. 6 When you finish this, you are to lie down again, but on your right side, and bear the sins of the house of Judah forty days; one day for each year I have allotted you. 7 Fixing your gaze on the siege of Jerusalem, with bared arm you shall prophesy against it. 8 See, I will bind you with cords so that you cannot turn from one side to the other until you have completed the days of your siege.

tures' wings beating against each other, and the sound of the wheels beside them: a great vibrating sound. 14 The spirit lifted me up and took me, and I went, bitter and angry, and the hand of Yahweh lay heavy on me. 15 I came to Tel Abib, to the exiles beside the River Chebar where they were living, and there I stayed with them in a stupor for seven days.

16 After seven days the word of Yahweh was addressed to me as follows,a 17 'Son of man, I have appointed you as watchman for the House of Israel. When you hear a word from my mouth, warn them from me. 18 If I say to someone wicked, "You will die," and you do not warn this person; if you do not speak to warn someone wicked to renounce evil and so save his life, it is the wicked person who will die for the guilt, but I shall hold you responsible for that death. 19 If, however, you do warn someone wicked who then fails to renounce wickedness and evil ways, the wicked person will die for the guilt, but you yourself will have saved your life. 20 When someone upright renounces uprightness to do evil and I set a trap for him, it is he who will die; since you failed to warn him, he will die for his guilt, and the uprightness he practised will no longer be remembered; but I shall hold you responsible for his death. 21 If, however, you warn someone upright not to sin and this person does not sin, such a one will live, thanks to your warning, and you too will have saved your life.'

22 While I was there the hand of Yahweh came on me; he said, 'Get up, go out into the valley, and there I shall speak to you.' 23 I got up and went out into the valley; the glory of Yahweh was resting there, like the glory I had seen by the River Chebar, and I fell to the ground. 24 The spirit of Yahweh then entered me and put me on my feet and spoke to me.

He said, 'Go and shut yourself in your house. 25 Son of man, you are about to be tied and bound, and unable to mix with other people. 26 I am going to make your tongue stick to the roof of your mouth; you will be dumb, and no longer able to reprove them, for they are a tribe of rebels. 27 When I speak to you, however, I shall open your mouth and then you will say to them, "Lord Yahweh says this: Let anyone prepared to listen, listen; let anyone who refuses, refuse!" — for they are a tribe of rebels.'

4 'For your part, son of man, take a brick and lay it in front of you; on it scratch a city, Jerusalem. 2 You are then to besiege it, trench round it, build earthworks, pitch camps and bring up battering-rams all round. 3 Then take an iron pan and place it as though it were an iron wall between you and the city. Then fix your gaze on it; it is being besieged and you are besieging it. This is a sign for the House of Israel.

4 'Lie down on your left side and take the guilt of the House of Israel on yourself. You will bear their guilt for as many days as you lie on that side. 5 Allowing one day for every year of their guilt, I ordain that you bear it for three hundred and ninety days; this is how you will bear the House of Israel's guilt. 6 And when you have finished doing this, you are to lie down again, on your right side, and bear the guilt of the House of Judah for forty days. I have set the length for you as one day for one year. 7 Then fix your gaze on the siege of Jerusalem, raise your bared arm and prophesy against her. 8 Look, I am going to tie you up and you will not be able to turn over from one side to the other until the period of your seclusion is over.

3, 16: At the end of seven days . . . : the incomplete sentence probably contained some such words as "the word of the Lord came to me." This verse has been transposed from ch 3.

a 3 A summary of the fuller version in 33:1–9.

NEW REVISED STANDARD VERSION

9 And you, take wheat and barley, beans and lentils, millet and spelt; put them into one vessel, and make bread for yourself. During the number of days that you lie on your side, three hundred ninety days, you shall eat it. 10 The food that you eat shall be twenty shekels a day by weight; at fixed times you shall eat it. 11 And you shall drink water by measure, one-sixth of a hin; at fixed times you shall drink. 12 You shall eat it as a barley-cake, baking it in their sight on human dung. 13 The LORD said, "Thus shall the people of Israel eat their bread, unclean, among the nations to which I will drive them." 14 Then I said, "Ah Lord GOD! I have never defiled myself; from my youth up until now I have never eaten what died of itself or was torn by animals, nor has carrion flesh come into my mouth." 15 Then he said to me, "See, I will let you have cow's dung instead of human dung, on which you may prepare your bread."

16 Then he said to me, Mortal, I am going to break the staff of bread in Jerusalem; they shall eat bread by weight and with fearfulness; and they shall drink water by measure and in dismay. 17 Lacking bread and water, they will look at one another in dismay, and waste away under their punishment.

5 And you, O mortal, take a sharp sword; use it as a barber's razor and run it over your head and your beard; then take balances for weighing, and divide the hair. 2 One third of the hair you shall burn in the fire inside the city, when the days of the siege are completed; one third you shall take and strike with the sword all around the city;*j* and one third you shall scatter to the wind, and I will unsheathe the sword after them. 3 Then you shall take from these a small number, and bind them in the skirts of your robe. 4 From these, again, you shall take some, throw them into the fire and burn them up; from there a fire will come out against all the house of Israel.

5 Thus says the Lord GOD: This is Jerusalem; I have set her in the center of the nations, with countries all around her. 6 But she has rebelled against my ordinances and my statutes, becoming more wicked than the nations and the countries all around her, rejecting my ordinances and not following my statutes. 7 Therefore thus says the Lord GOD: Because you are more turbulent than the nations that are all around you, and have not followed my statutes or kept my ordinances, but have acted according to the ordinances of the nations that are all around you; 8 therefore thus says the Lord GOD: I, I myself, am coming against you; I will execute judgments among you in the sight of the nations. 9 And because of all your abominations, I will do to you what I have never yet done, and the like of which I will never do again. 10 Surely, parents shall eat their children in your midst, and children shall eat their parents; I will execute judgments on you, and any of you who survive I will scatter to every wind. 11 Therefore, as I live, says the Lord GOD, surely, because you have defiled my sanctuary with all your detestable things and with all your abominations — therefore I will cut you down;*k* my eye will not spare, and I will have no pity. 12 One third of you shall die of pestilence or be consumed by famine among you; one third shall fall by the sword around you; and one third I will scatter to every wind and will unsheathe the sword after them.

13 My anger shall spend itself, and I will vent my fury on them and satisfy myself; and they shall know that I, the LORD, have spoken in my jealousy, when I spend my fury on them. 14 Moreover I will make you a desolation and an

REVISED ENGLISH BIBLE

9 'Take wheat, barley, beans, lentils, millet, and vetches, and mixing them all in one bowl make your bread from them. You are to eat it during the three hundred and ninety days you spend lying on your side. 10 Twenty shekels' weight is your ration for a day, eaten at a set time each day. 11 You are to measure out your drinking water; you may drink a sixth of a hin at a set time each day. 12 The bread you are to eat is to be baked like barley cakes, with human dung as fuel, and you must bake it where people can see you.' 13 The LORD said, 'This is the unclean bread that the Israelites will eat among the peoples where I shall banish them.' 14 I protested: 'Lord GOD, I have never been made unclean. Never in my whole life have I eaten what has died a natural death or been mauled by wild beasts; no tainted meat has ever passed my lips.' 15 He answered, 'Very well; I shall allow you to use cow dung instead of human dung to bake your bread.'

16 He then said, 'O man, I am cutting short their daily bread in Jerusalem; people will weigh out anxiously the bread they eat, and measure with dismay the water they drink. 17 So their food and their water will run short until dismay spreads from one to another and they waste away because of their iniquity.

5 'O man, take a sharp sword, and use it like a razor to shave your head and your chin. Then take scales and divide the hair into three lots. 2 When the siege comes to an end, burn one third of the hair in a fire in the centre of the city; cut up one third with the sword round about the city; scatter the last third to the wind, and I shall follow it with drawn sword. 3 Take a few of these hairs and tie them up in a fold of your robe. 4 Then take others, throw them into the fire and burn them.

'Say to all Israel: 5 These are the words of the Lord GOD: This city of Jerusalem I have set among the nations, with lands all around her, 6 but she has rebelled against my laws and my statutes more wickedly than those nations and lands; for her people have rejected my laws and refused to conform to my statutes.

7 'The Lord GOD says: Since you have been more insubordinate than the nations around you and have not conformed to my statutes and have not kept my laws or even the laws of the nations around you, 8 therefore, says the Lord GOD, I in turn shall be against you; in the sight of the nations I shall execute judgements in your midst, 9 such judgements as I have never executed before, nor ever shall again, so abominable have all your offences been. 10 Parents will eat their children and children their parents in your midst, Jerusalem; I shall execute judgements on you, and any who survive in you I shall scatter to the four winds. 11 As I live, says the Lord GOD, because you have defiled my holy place with all your vile and abominable rites, I in turn shall destroy you and show no pity; I shall spare no one. 12 One third of your people will die by pestilence or perish by famine in your midst; one third will fall by the sword in the country round about; and one third I shall scatter to the four winds and follow with drawn sword. 13 When my anger is spent and my fury is abated I shall be appeased; when my fury against them is spent they will know that I, the LORD, have spoken in my jealousy. 14 I

---

j Heb *it*   *k* Another reading is *I will withdraw*   5:4 **Say:** *so Gk; Heb. obscure.*   5:7 **or even:** *some MSS* but.

9 Again, take wheat and barley, and beans and lentils, and millet and spelt; put them in a single vessel and make bread out of them. Eat it for as many days as you lie upon your side, three hundred and ninety. 10 The food you eat shall be twenty shekels a day by weight; each day the same. 11 And the water you drink shall be the sixth of a hin by measure; each day the same. 16 Then he said to me: Son of man, I am breaking the staff of bread in Jerusalem. They shall eat bread which they have weighed out anxiously, and they shall drink water which they have measured out fearfully, 17 so that, owing to the scarcity of bread and water, everyone shall be filled with terror and waste away because of his sins.

12 For your food you must bake barley loaves over human excrement in their sight, said the LORD. 13 Thus the Israelites shall eat their food unclean among the nations where I scatter them. 14 "Oh no, Lord GOD!" I protested. "Never have I been made unclean, and from my youth till now, never have I eaten carrion flesh or that torn by wild beasts: never has any unclean meat entered my mouth." 15 Very well, he replied, I allow you cow's dung in place of human excrement; bake your bread on that.

‡4.16–17: see above‡

5 As for you, son of man, take a sharp sword and use it like a barber's razor, passing it over your head and beard. Then take a set of scales and divide the hair you have cut. 2 Burn a third in the fire, within the city, when the days of your siege are completed; place another third around the city and strike it with the sword; the final third strew in the wind, and pursue it with the sword. 3 [But of the last take a small number and tie them in the hem of your garment. 4 Then take some of these and throw them in the midst of the fire and burn them.]

Say to the whole house of Israel: 5 Thus says the Lord GOD: This is Jerusalem! In the midst of the nations I placed her, surrounded by foreign countries. 6 But she rebelled against my ordinances more wickedly than the nations, and against my statutes more than the foreign countries surrounding her; she has spurned my ordinances and has not lived by my statutes. 7 Therefore thus says the Lord GOD: Because you have been more rebellious than the nations surrounding you, not living by my statutes nor fulfilling my ordinances, but acting according to the ordinances of the surrounding nations; 8 therefore thus says the Lord GOD: see, I am coming at you! I will inflict punishments in your midst while the nations look on. 9 Because of all your abominations I will do with you what I have never done before, the like of which I will never do again. 10 This means that fathers within you shall eat sons, and sons shall eat fathers. I will inflict punishments upon you and scatter all that remain of your people in every direction.

11 Therefore, as I live, says the Lord GOD, because you have defiled my sanctuary with all your detestable abominations, I swear to cut you down. I will not look upon you with pity nor have mercy. 12 A third of your people shall die of pestilence and perish of hunger within you; another third shall fall by the sword all around you; and a third I will scatter in every direction, and I will pursue them with the sword. 16 When I loose against you the cruel, destructive arrows of hunger, I will break your staff of bread; 17 I will send famine against you, and wild beasts that shall rob you of your children. Pestilence and bloodshed shall stalk through you, and I will bring the sword upon you. I, the LORD, have spoken!

13 Thus shall my anger spend itself, and I will wreak my fury upon them till I am appeased; they shall know that I, the LORD, have spoken in my jealousy when I spend my fury upon them. 14 I will make you a waste and a reproach

9 'Now take wheat, barley, beans, lentils, millet and spelt; put them all in the same pot and make them into bread for yourself. You are to eat it for as many days as you are lying on your side — three hundred and ninety. 10 Of this food, you are to weigh out a daily portion of twenty shekels and eat it a little piece at a time. 11 And you are to ration the water you drink — a sixth of a hin — drinking that a little at a time. 12 You are to eat this in the form of a barley cake baked where they can see you, on human dung.' 13 And Yahweh said, 'This is how the Israelites will have to eat their defiled food, wherever I disperse them among the nations.' 14 I then said, 'Lord Yahweh, my soul is not defiled. From my childhood until now, I have never eaten an animal that has died a natural death or been savaged; no tainted meat has ever entered my mouth.' 15 'Very well,' he said, 'I grant you cow-dung instead of human dung; you are to bake your bread on that.' 16 He then said, 'Son of man, I am going to cut off Jerusalem's food supply; in their extremity, the food they eat will be weighed out; to their horror, the water they drink will be rationed, 17 until there is no food or water left, and they fall into a stupor and waste away because of their guilt.'

5 'Son of man, take a sharp sword, use it like a barber's razor and run it over your head and beard. Then take scales and divide the hair you have cut off. 2 Burn one-third inside the city, while the days of the siege are working themselves out. Then take another third and chop it up with the sword all round the city. The last third you are to scatter to the wind, while I unsheathe the sword behind them. 3 Also take a few hairs and tie them up in the folds of your cloak; 4 and of these again take a few, and throw them on the fire and burn them. From them fire will come on the whole House of Israel.

5 'The Lord Yahweh says this, "This is Jerusalem, which I have placed in the middle of the nations, surrounded with foreign countries. 6 She has rebelled more perversely against my observances than the nations have, and against my laws than the surrounding countries have; for they have rejected my observances and not kept my laws."

7 'Therefore, the Lord Yahweh says this, "Because your disorders are worse than those of the nations round you, since you do not keep my laws or respect my observances, and since you do not respect even the observances of the surrounding nations, 8 very well, the Lord Yahweh says this: I, too, am against you and shall execute my judgements on you for the nations to see. 9 Because of all your loathsome practices I shall do such things as I have never done before, nor shall ever do again. 10 Those of you who are parents will eat their children, and children will eat their parents. I shall execute judgement on you and disperse what remains of you to the winds. 11 For, as I live — declares Lord Yahweh — as sure as you have defiled my sanctuary with all your horrors and all your loathsome practices, so I too shall reject you without a glance of pity, I shall not spare you. 12 A third of your citizens will die of plague or starve to death inside you; a third will fall by the sword round you; and a third I shall scatter to the winds, unsheathing the sword behind them. 13 I shall sate my anger and bring my fury to rest on them until I am avenged; and when I have sated my fury on them, then they will know that I, Yahweh, spoke out of jealousy for you. 14 Yes, I shall reduce you to

NEW REVISED STANDARD VERSION	REVISED ENGLISH BIBLE

object of mocking among the nations around you, in the sight of all that pass by. 15 You shall be[l] a mockery and a taunt, a warning and a horror, to the nations around you, when I execute judgments on you in anger and fury, and with furious punishments—I, the LORD, have spoken— 16 when I loose against you[m] my deadly arrows of famine, arrows for destruction, which I will let loose to destroy you, and when I bring more and more famine upon you, and break your staff of bread. 17 I will send famine and wild animals against you, and they will rob you of your children; pestilence and bloodshed shall pass through you; and I will bring the sword upon you. I, the LORD, have spoken.

6 The word of the LORD came to me: 2 O mortal, set your face toward the mountains of Israel, and prophesy against them, 3 and say, You mountains of Israel, hear the word of the Lord GOD! Thus says the Lord GOD to the mountains and the hills, to the ravines and the valleys: I, I myself will bring a sword upon you, and I will destroy your high places. 4 Your altars shall become desolate, and your incense stands shall be broken; and I will throw down your slain in front of your idols. 5 I will lay the corpses of the people of Israel in front of their idols; and I will scatter your bones around your altars. 6 Wherever you live, your towns shall be waste and your high places ruined, so that your altars will be waste and ruined,[n] your idols broken and destroyed, your incense stands cut down, and your works wiped out. 7 The slain shall fall in your midst; then you shall know that I am the LORD.

8 But I will spare some. Some of you shall escape the sword among the nations and be scattered through the countries. 9 Those of you who escape shall remember me among the nations where they are carried captive, how I was crushed by their wanton heart that turned away from me, and their wanton eyes that turned after their idols. Then they will be loathsome in their own sight for the evils that they have committed, for all their abominations. 10 And they shall know that I am the LORD; I did not threaten in vain to bring this disaster upon them.

11 Thus says the Lord GOD: Clap your hands and stamp your foot, and say, Alas for all the vile abominations of the house of Israel! For they shall fall by the sword, by famine, and by pestilence. 12 Those far off shall die of pestilence; those nearby shall fall by the sword; and any who are left and are spared shall die of famine. Thus I will spend my fury upon them. 13 And you shall know that I am the LORD, when their slain lie among their idols around their altars, on every high hill, on all the mountain tops, under every green tree, and under every leafy oak, wherever they offered pleasing odor to all their idols. 14 I will stretch out my hand against them, and make the land desolate and waste, throughout all their settlements, from the wilderness to Riblah.[o] Then they shall know that I am the LORD.

7 The word of the LORD came to me: 2 You, O mortal, thus says the Lord GOD to the land of Israel:
An end! The end has come
  upon the four corners of the land.
3 Now the end is upon you,
  I will let loose my anger upon you;
  I will judge you according to your ways,
  I will punish you for all your abominations.
4 My eye will not spare you, I will have no pity.
  I will punish you for your ways,
  while your abominations are among you.
Then you shall know that I am the LORD.

have reduced you to a ruin, an object of mockery to the nations around you, and all who pass by will see it. 15 You will be an object of mockery and abuse, an appalling lesson to the nations round about, when I pass sentence on you and execute judgement in anger and fury. I, the LORD, have spoken.

16 'When I loose the deadly arrows of famine against you, arrows of destruction, I shall shoot them to destroy you. I shall send one famine after another on you and cut off your daily bread; 17 I shall unleash famine and savage beasts on you, and they will leave you childless. Pestilence and bloodshed will sweep through you, and I shall bring the sword against you. I, the LORD, have spoken.'

6 THIS word of the LORD came to me: 2 'O man, face towards the mountains of Israel and prophesy against them 3 and say: Mountains of Israel, listen to the word of the Lord GOD. He says this to the mountains and hills, the ravines and valleys: I am bringing a sword against you, and I shall destroy your shrines. 4 Your altars will be devastated, your incense-altars shattered, and I shall throw down your slain in front of your idols. 5 I shall lay the corpses of the Israelites before their idols and scatter your bones around your altars. 6 In all your settlements the blood-spattered altars will be laid waste and the shrines devastated. Your altars will be laid waste and devastated, your idols shattered and brought to an end, your incense-altars hewn down, and the gods you have made will be wiped out. 7 As the slain fall all about you, you will know that I am the LORD. 8 But among the nations there will be some of you that have survived the sword, and are scattered in foreign lands. 9 They will remember me in exile among the nations, when I destroy their wanton and wayward hearts and their eyes which rove wantonly after their idols. Then they will loathe themselves for the evil they have done with all their abominations. 10 Then they will know that I, the LORD, was uttering no vain threat when I said that I would inflict this evil on them.

11 'The Lord GOD says: Beat your hands together, stamp your feet, bemoan all your vile abominations, people of Israel, who will fall by sword, famine, and pestilence. 12 Those far away will die by pestilence; those nearer home will fall by the sword; any who survive or are spared will die by famine, and so at last my anger at them will be spent. 13 You will know that I am the LORD when their slain fall among the idols round their altars, on every high hill or mountaintop, under every spreading tree or leafy terebinth, wherever they have offered sweet-smelling sacrifices to appease all their idols. 14 I shall stretch out my hand over them and reduce the land in all their settlements to a desolate waste, more desolate than the desert of Riblah. Then they will know that I am the LORD.'

7 This word of the LORD came to me: 2 'O man, the Lord GOD says to the land of Israel: The end is coming on the four corners of the earth. 3 Now the end is upon you; I shall unleash my anger against you; I shall call you to account for your conduct and bring all your abominations on your own heads. 4 I shall neither show pity, nor spare you; I shall make you suffer for your conduct and the abominations that are in your midst. Then you will know that I am the LORD.

---

[l] Gk Syr Vg Tg: Heb *It shall be* [m] Heb *them* [n] Syr Vg Tg: Heb *and be made guilty* [o] Another reading is *Diblah*

5:16 **against you:** *prob. rdg; Heb.* against them.   6:6 **blood-spattered altars:** *or* cities.   6:8 **But among:** *so Gk; Heb.* prefixes and I will leave.   6:9 **I destroy:** *so Lat.; Heb.* I am grieved with.   6:14 **Riblah:** *prob. rdg; Heb.* Diblah.

among the nations that surround you, which every passer-by may see. 15 When I execute judgment upon you in anger and fury and with furious chastisements, you shall be a reproach and an object of scorn, a terrible warning to the nations that surround you. I, the LORD, have spoken!

‡5.16–17: see above‡

6 Thus the word of the LORD came to me: 2 Son of man, turn toward the mountains of Israel, and prophesy against them: 3 Mountains of Israel, hear the word of the Lord GOD. Thus says the Lord GOD [to the mountains and hills, the ravines and valleys]: See, I am bringing a sword against you, and I will destroy your high places. 4 Your altars shall be laid waste, your incense stands shall be broken, and I will cast down your slain ones before your idols; 5 I will scatter their bones all around your altars. 6 In all your dwelling places cities shall be made desolate and high places laid waste, so that your altars shall be made desolate and laid waste, your idols broken and removed, and your incense stands smashed to bits. 7 [The slain shall fall in your midst, and you shall know that I am the LORD. 8 I have warned you.]

When some of your people have escaped to other nations from the sword, and have been scattered over the foreign lands, 9 then those who have escaped will remember me among the nations to which they have been exiled, after I have broken their adulterous hearts that turned away from me [and their eyes which lusted after idols]. They shall loathe themselves because of their evil deeds, all their abominations. 10 Then they shall know that it was not in vain that I, the LORD, threatened to inflict this calamity upon them.

11 Thus says the Lord GOD: Clap your hands, stamp your feet, and cry "Alas!" because of all the abominations of the house of Israel, for which they shall fall by the sword, by famine, and by pestilence. 12 He that is far off shall die of pestilence, he that is near shall fall by the sword, and he that is besieged shall perish by famine; so will I spend my fury upon them. 13 Then shall they know that I am the LORD, when their slain shall lie amid their idols, all about their altars, on every high hill and mountaintop, beneath every green tree and leafy oak, wherever they offered appeasing odors to any of their gods. 14 I will stretch out my hand against them, and wherever they live I will make the land a desolate waste, from the desert to Riblah; thus shall they know that I am the LORD.

7 Thus the word of the LORD came to me: 2 Son of man, now say: Thus says the Lord GOD to the land of Israel: An end! The end has come upon the four corners of the land! 3 Now the end is upon you; I will unleash my anger against you and judge you according to your conduct and lay upon you the consequences of all your abominations. 4 I will not look upon you with pity nor have mercy; I will bring your conduct down upon you, and the consequences of your abominations shall be in your midst; then shall you know that I am the LORD.

a ruin, an object of derision to the surrounding nations, in the eyes of all who pass by. 15 You will be an object of derision and insults, an example, an object of amazement to the surrounding nations, when I execute judgement on you in furious anger and furious punishments. I, Yahweh, have spoken. 16 On them I shall send the deadly arrows of famine, which will destroy you — for I shall send them to destroy you; then I shall make the famine worse and cut off your food supply. 17 I shall send famine and wild animals on you to rob you of your children; plague and bloodshed will sweep through you, and I shall bring the sword down on you. I, Yahweh, have spoken." '

6 The word of Yahweh was addressed to me as follows, 2 'Son of man, turn towards the mountains of Israel and prophesy against them. 3 Say, "Mountains of Israel, hear the word of the Lord Yahweh. The Lord Yahweh says this to mountains and hills and ravines and valleys: Look, I am going to summon the sword against you and destroy your high places. 4 Your altars will be wrecked, and your incense burners smashed; I shall fling your butchered inhabitants down in front of your foul idols; 5 I shall lay the corpses of the Israelites in front of their foul idols and scatter their bones all round your altars. 6 Wherever you live, the towns will be destroyed and the high places wrecked, to the ruin and wrecking of your altars, the shattering and abolition of your foul idols, the smashing of your incense burners and the utter destruction of all your works. 7 As the butchered fall about you, you will know that I am Yahweh.

8 "But I shall spare some of you to escape the sword among the nations, when you have been dispersed in their lands; 9 and your survivors will remember me among the nations where they are held captive, since I shall have broken their adulterous hearts for having deserted me, and destroyed their eyes for having turned adulterously towards their foul idols. They will loathe themselves for all the wrong they have caused by their loathsome practices. 10 Then they will know that I am Yahweh and that I was not talking lightly when I said that I would inflict these disasters on them."

11 'The Lord Yahweh says this, "Clap your hands, stamp your feet, and say: Alas for all the loathsome sins of the House of Israel, which is about to fall by sword, famine and plague! 12 Far off, they will die by plague; near at hand they will fall by the sword; and any who survive or are spared will die of famine. This is how I shall sate my fury on them. 13 Then you will know that I am Yahweh, when their butchered corpses lie among their foul idols, all round their altars, on every high hill, on every mountain top, under every green tree, under every leafy oak, wherever they offer a smell pleasing to all their idols. 14 I shall point my finger at them and reduce the country to an empty wasteland from the desert to Riblah, everywhere they live, and they will know that I am Yahweh." '

7 The word of Yahweh was addressed to me as follows, 2 'Son of man, say, "Lord Yahweh says this to the land of Israel: Finished! The end is coming for the four corners of the country. 3 This is the end for you; I shall unleash my anger on you, and judge you as your conduct deserves and call you to account for all your loathsome practices. 4 I shall show you no pity, I shall not spare you; I shall repay you for your conduct and for the loathsome practices in which you persist. Then you will know that I am Yahweh.

5 Thus says the Lord GOD:
     Disaster after disaster! See, it comes.
6   An end has come, the end has come.
     It has awakened against you; see, it comes!
7   Your doom*p* has come to you,
          O inhabitant of the land.
     The time has come, the day is near—
          of tumult, not of reveling on the mountains.
8   Soon now I will pour out my wrath upon you;
          I will spend my anger against you.
     I will judge you according to your ways,
          and punish you for all your abominations.
9   My eye will not spare; I will have no pity.
     I will punish you according to your ways,
          while your abominations are among you.
Then you shall know that it is I the LORD who strike.
10   See, the day! See, it comes!
     Your doom*p* has gone out.
     The rod has blossomed, pride has budded.
11   Violence has grown into a rod of wickedness.
     None of them shall remain,
          not their abundance, not their wealth;
          no pre-eminence among them.*p*
12   The time has come, the day draws near;
          let not the buyer rejoice, nor the seller mourn,
          for wrath is upon all their multitude.
13 For the sellers shall not return to what has been sold as
long as they remain alive. For the vision concerns all their
multitude; it shall not be revoked. Because of their iniquity,
they cannot maintain their lives.*p*
14   They have blown the horn and made everything
               ready;
          but no one goes to battle,
          for my wrath is upon all their multitude.
15   The sword is outside, pestilence and famine are
               inside;
          those in the field die by the sword;
          those in the city—famine and pestilence devour
               them.
16   If any survivors escape,
          they shall be found on the mountains
          like doves of the valleys,
          all of them moaning over their iniquity.
17   All hands shall grow feeble,
          all knees turn to water.
18   They shall put on sackcloth,
          horror shall cover them.
     Shame shall be on all faces,
          baldness on all their heads.
19   They shall fling their silver into the streets,
          their gold shall be treated as unclean.
Their silver and gold cannot save them on the day of the
wrath of the LORD. They shall not satisfy their hunger or fill
their stomachs with it. For it was the stumbling block of
their iniquity. 20 From their*q* beautiful ornament, in which
they took pride, they made their abominable images, their
detestable things; therefore I will make of it an unclean
thing to them.
21   I will hand it over to strangers as booty,
          to the wicked of the earth as plunder;
          they shall profane it.
22   I will avert my face from them,
          so that they may profane my treasured*r* place;
     the violent shall enter it,
          they shall profane it.
23   Make a chain!*s*

5 'The Lord GOD says: Disasters are coming, one after
another. 6 The end is coming; it is roused against you.
7 Doom is coming upon you, dweller in the land; the time
is coming, the day is near, a day of panic and not of rejoicing. 8 Very soon I shall vent my wrath on you and let my
anger spend itself. I shall call you to account for your conduct and bring all your abominations on your own heads. 9 I
shall neither show pity nor spare you; I shall make you
suffer for your conduct and the abominations that are in
your midst. Then you will know that it is I, the LORD, who
struck you.
10 'The day is coming, doom is here; it has burst upon
them. Injustice buds, insolence blossoms. 11 Violence leads
to flagrant injustice. Is it not their fault, the fault of their
turbulence and tumult? There is nothing but turmoil in
them. 12 The time has come, the day has arrived; there is no
joy for the buyer, no sorrow for the seller, for their turmoil
has called forth my wrath. 13 The seller will not recover
what he has sold in their lifetime, for because of all the
turmoil the agreement will never be revoked, and because
of their sin none will have a sure hold on life. 14 The trumpet
has sounded and all are ready, but no one goes to war, for
their turmoil has called forth my wrath.
15 'Outside is the sword, inside are pestilence and famine;
those in the country will die by the sword, those in the city
will be devoured by famine and pestilence. 16 If any escape
like moaning doves and take to the mountains, there I shall
slay them, each for his iniquity, 17 while every hand hangs
limp and every knee turns to water. 18 They will go in sackcloth, shuddering from head to foot, with faces downcast
and heads close shaved. 19 They will fling their silver into
the street and treat their gold like so much filth; their silver
and gold will not avail to save them on the day of the
LORD's fury. Their hunger will not be satisfied, nor their
bellies filled; for their iniquity will be the cause of their
downfall. 20 Their beautiful jewellery, which was their pride
and delight, they have made into vile, abominable images.
Therefore I shall treat their jewellery as so much filth, 21 I
shall hand it over as plunder to foreigners and as booty to
earth's most evil nations, who will defile it. 22 I shall turn
my face from them, while brigands encroach on my treasured land to defile it 23 and create confusion, for the land

---

p Meaning of Heb uncertain   *q* Syr Symmachus: Heb *its*
r Or *secret*   *s* Meaning of Heb uncertain

7:7 **a day . . . rejoicing:** *prob. rdg; Heb. obscure.*   7:23 **and
create confusion:** *so Gk; Heb. obscure.*

NEW AMERICAN BIBLE

5 Thus says the Lord GOD: Disaster upon disaster! See it coming! 6 An end is coming, the end is coming upon you! See it coming! 7 The climax has come for you who dwell in the land! The time has come, near is the day: a time of consternation, not of rejoicing. 8 Soon now I will pour out my fury upon you and spend my anger upon you; I will judge you according to your conduct and lay upon you the consequences of all your abominations. 9 I will not look upon you with pity nor have mercy; I will deal with you according to your conduct, and the consequences of your abominations shall be in your midst; then shall you know that it is I, the LORD, who strike.

10 See, the day of the LORD! See, the end is coming! Lawlessness is in full bloom, insolence flourishes, 11 violence has risen to support wickedness. It shall not be long in coming, nor shall it delay. 12 The time has come, the day dawns. Let not the buyer rejoice nor the seller mourn, for wrath shall be upon all the throng. 13 The seller shall not regain what he sold as long as he lives, for wrath shall be upon all the throng. Because of his sins, no one shall preserve his life. 14 They shall sound the trumpet and make everything ready, yet no one shall go to war, for my wrath is upon all the throng.

15 The sword is outside; pestilence and hunger are within. He that is in the country shall die by the sword; pestilence and famine shall devour those in the city. 16 Even those who escape and flee to the mountains like the doves of the valleys—I will put them all to death, each one for his own sins. 17 All their hands shall be limp, and all their knees shall run with water. 18 They shall put on sackcloth, and horror shall cover them; shame shall be on all their faces and baldness on all their heads. 19 They shall fling their silver into the streets, and their gold shall be considered refuse. Their silver and gold cannot save them on the day of the LORD's wrath. They shall not be allowed to satisfy their craving or fill their bellies, for this has been the occasion of their sin. 20 In the beauty of their ornaments they put their pride: they made of them their abominable images [their idols]. For this reason I make them refuse. 21 I will hand them over as booty to foreigners, to be spoiled and defiled by the wicked of the earth. 22 I will turn away my face from them, and my treasure shall be profaned: robbers shall enter and profane it.

23 They shall wreak slaughter, for the land is filled with

NEW JERUSALEM BIBLE

5 "The Lord Yahweh says this: Disaster, a unique disaster, is coming. 6 The end is coming, the end is coming, it is on the move towards you, it is coming now. 7 Now it is your turn, you who dwell in this country. Doom is coming, the day is near; no joy now, only tumult, on the mountains. 8 Now I shall soon vent my fury on you and sate my anger on you: I shall judge you as your conduct deserves and repay you for all your loathsome practices. 9 I shall show neither pity nor mercy, but shall repay you for your conduct and the loathsome practices in which you persist. Then you will know that I am Yahweh and that I strike.

10 "Now is the day, your turn has come, it has come, it appears, the sceptre has blossomed, pride is at its peak. 11 Violence has risen to become the scourge of wickedness . . . 12 Doom is coming, the day is near. Neither should buyer rejoice, nor seller regret, for the fury rests on everyone alike. 13 The seller will not be able to go back on his bargain; each persists in his sins; they take no defensive measures. 14 The trumpet sounds, all is ready, but no one goes into battle, since my fury rests on all alike.

15 "Outside, the sword; inside, plague and famine. Whoever is living in the countryside will die by the sword; whoever is living in the city will be devoured by famine and plague. 16 And those who escape will escape to the mountains and there, like doves of the valleys, I shall slaughter them all, each one for his sin. 17 Every hand will grow limp, every knee turn to water. 18 They will put on sackcloth, each one trembling. Every face will be ashamed and every head be shaved. 19 They will throw their silver away in the streets and their gold they will regard as a pollution; neither their silver nor their gold will be able to save them on the day of Yahweh's fury. Never again will they have enough to eat, never again will they fill their bellies, since that was the occasion for their guilt. 20 They used to pride themselves on the beauty of their jewellery, out of which they made their loathsome images, their horrors; so now I have made it pollute them. 21 I shall hand it over as plunder to foreigners, as loot to the most evil people on earth. They will profane it. 22 I shall turn my face away from them, while my treasure-house is profaned and robbers will force their way in and profane it.

23 "Forge yourself a chain; for the country is full of

For the land is full of bloody crimes;
    the city is full of violence.
24 I will bring the worst of the nations
    to take possession of their houses.
I will put an end to the arrogance of the strong,
    and their holy places shall be profaned.
25 When anguish comes, they will seek peace,
    but there shall be none.
26 Disaster comes upon disaster,
    rumor follows rumor;
they shall keep seeking a vision from the prophet;
    instruction shall perish from the priest,
    and counsel from the elders.
27 The king shall mourn,
    the prince shall be wrapped in despair,
    and the hands of the people of the land shall
      tremble.
According to their way I will deal with them;
    according to their own judgments I will judge
      them.
And they shall know that I am the LORD.

8 In the sixth year, in the sixth month, on the fifth day of the month, as I sat in my house, with the elders of Judah sitting before me, the hand of the Lord GOD fell upon me there. 2 I looked, and there was a figure that looked like a human being;[t] below what appeared to be its loins it was fire, and above the loins it was like the appearance of brightness, like gleaming amber. 3 It stretched out the form of a hand, and took me by a lock of my head; and the spirit lifted me up between earth and heaven, and brought me in visions of God to Jerusalem, to the entrance of the gateway of the inner court that faces north, to the seat of the image of jealousy, which provokes to jealousy. 4 And the glory of the God of Israel was there, like the vision that I had seen in the valley.

5 Then God[u] said to me, "O mortal, lift up your eyes now in the direction of the north." So I lifted up my eyes toward the north, and there, north of the altar gate, in the entrance, was this image of jealousy. 6 He said to me, "Mortal, do you see what they are doing, the great abominations that the house of Israel are committing here, to drive me far from my sanctuary? Yet you will see still greater abominations."

7 And he brought me to the entrance of the court; I looked, and there was a hole in the wall. 8 Then he said to me, "Mortal, dig through the wall"; and when I dug through the wall, there was an entrance. 9 He said to me, "Go in, and see the vile abominations that they are committing here." 10 So I went in and looked; there, portrayed on the wall all around, were all kinds of creeping things, and loathsome animals, and all the idols of the house of Israel. 11 Before them stood seventy of the elders of the house of Israel, with Jaazaniah son of Shaphan standing among them. Each had his censer in his hand, and the fragrant cloud of incense was ascending. 12 Then he said to me, "Mortal, have you seen what the elders of the house of Israel are doing in the dark, each in his room of images? For they say, 'The LORD does not see us, the LORD has forsaken the land.'" 13 He said also to me, "You will see still greater abominations that they are committing."

14 Then he brought me to the entrance of the north gate of the house of the LORD; women were sitting there weeping for Tammuz. 15 Then he said to me, "Have you seen this, O mortal? You will see still greater abominations than these."

16 And he brought me into the inner court of the house of the LORD; there, at the entrance of the temple of the LORD, between the porch and the altar, were about twenty-

is full of bloodshed and the city full of violence. 24 I shall let in the most ruthless of nations to take possession of the houses; I shall quell the pride of the strong, and their sanctuaries will be profaned. 25 Shuddering will come over my people, and they will look in vain for peace. 26 Tempest will follow upon tempest and rumour upon rumour. People will pester a prophet for a vision; there will be no more guidance from a priest, no counsel from elders. 27 The king will go mourning, the ruler will be clothed with terror, the hands of the people will shake with fright. I shall deal with them as they deserve, and call them to account for their conduct. Then they will know that I am the LORD.'

8 ON the fifth day of the sixth month in the sixth year, as I was sitting at home and the elders of Judah were sitting with me, suddenly I felt the power of the Lord GOD come upon me. 2 I saw what looked like a man; from the waist down he seemed to be all fire and from the waist up to shine and glitter like brass. 3 He stretched out what appeared to be a hand and took me by the forelock. In a vision from God a spirit lifted me up between earth and heaven, carried me to Jerusalem, and put me down at the entrance to the inner gate facing north, where stands the idolatrous image which arouses God's indignation. 4 The glory of the God of Israel was there, like the vision I had seen in the plain. 5 The LORD said to me, 'O man, look northwards.' I did so, and there to the north of the Altar Gate, at the entrance, was that idolatrous image. 6 'O man,' he said, 'do you see what they are doing? The monstrous abominations which the Israelites practise here are making me abandon my sanctuary, and you will see even greater abominations.'

7 Then he brought me to the entrance of the court, where I saw that there was a hole in the wall. 8 'O man,' he said to me, 'dig through the wall.' I did so, and made an opening. 9 'Go in,' he said, 'and see the vile abominations they practise here.' 10 I went in and saw figures of creeping things, beasts, and vermin, and all the idols of the Israelites, carved round the walls. 11 Standing in front of them were seventy elders of Israel, with Jaazaniah son of Shaphan in the middle, and each held a censer from which rose the fragrant smoke of incense. 12 He said to me, 'O man, do you see what the elders of Israel are doing in darkness, each at the shrine of his own carved image? They think that the LORD does not see them, that he has forsaken the land. 13 You will see even greater abominations practised by them,' he said.

14 Next he brought me to the gateway of the LORD's house which faces north; and there sat women wailing for Tammuz. 15 'O man, do you see that?' he asked me. 'But you will see greater abominations than these.'

16 So he brought me to the inner court of the LORD's house, and there, by the entrance to the sanctuary of the LORD, between porch and altar, were some twenty-five men

---

[t] Gk: Heb like fire   [u] Heb he

7:23 **bloodshed:** *prob. rdg; Heb.* the judgement of bloodshed.

bloodshed and the city full of violence. 24 I will bring in the worst of the nations, who shall take possession of their houses. I will put an end to their proud strength, and their sanctuaries shall be profaned. 25 When anguish comes they shall seek peace, but there will be none. 26 There shall be disaster after disaster, rumor after rumor. Prophetic vision shall fade; instruction shall be lacking to the priest, and counsel to the elders, 27 while the prince shall be enveloped in terror, and the hands of the common people shall tremble. I will deal with them according to their conduct, and according to their judgments I will judge them; thus they shall know that I am the LORD.

‡8,1–2: see below‡

8 3 Spirit lifted me up in the air and brought me in divine visions to Jerusalem, to the entrance of the north gate, where stood the statue of jealousy which stirs up jealousy.
‡8.4: see below in ch. 10‡
5 He said to me: Son of man, look toward the north! I looked toward the north and saw northward of the gate the altar of the statue of jealousy. 6 Son of man, he asked me, do you see what they are doing? Do you see the great abominations that the house of Israel is practicing here, so that I must depart from my sanctuary? But you shall see still greater abominations!
7 Then he brought me to the entrance of the court, where I saw there was a hole in the wall. 8 Son of man, he ordered, dig through the wall. I dug through the wall and saw a door. 9 Enter, he said to me, and see the abominable evils which they are doing here. 10 I entered and saw that all around upon the wall were pictured the figures of all kinds of creeping things and loathsome beasts [all the idols of the house of Israel]. 11 Before these stood seventy of the elders of the house of Israel, among whom stood Jaazaniah, son of Shaphan, each of them with his censer in his hand, and the fragrance of the incense was rising upward. 12 Then he said to me: Do you see, son of man, what each of these elders of the house of Israel is doing in his idol room? They think: "The LORD cannot see us; the LORD has forsaken the land." 13 He continued: You shall see still greater abominations that they are practicing.
14 Then he brought me to the entrance of the north gate of the temple, and I saw sitting there the women who were weeping for Tammuz. 15 Then he said to me: Do you see this, son of man? You shall see other abominations, greater than these!
16 Then he brought me into the inner court of the LORD's house, and there at the door of the LORD's temple, between the vestibule and the altar, were about twenty-five men with

bloody executions and the city full of deeds of violence, 24 so I shall bring the cruellest of the nations to seize their houses. I shall put an end to the pride of their élite, and their sanctuary will be profaned. 25 Terror is on the way: they will look for peace and there will be none. 26 Disaster will follow on disaster, rumour on rumour; they will pester the prophet for a vision; the priest will be at a loss over the law and the elders on how to advise. 27 The king will go into mourning, the prince be plunged in grief, the hands of the country people tremble. I shall treat them as their conduct deserves, and judge them as their own verdicts merit. Then they will know that I am Yahweh!" '

8 b In the sixth year, on the fifth day of the sixth month, I was sitting at home and the elders of Judah were sitting with me, when suddenly the hand of the Lord Yahweh fell on me there.
2 I looked, and there was a form with the appearance of a human being. Downwards from what seemed to be the waist there was fire; and upwards from the waist there was a brilliance like the glitter of amber. 3 Something like a hand was stretched out and it took me by a lock of my hair; and the spirit lifted me between heaven and earth and, in visions from God, took me to Jerusalem, to the entrance of the inner north gate, where stands the idol that provokes jealousy. 4 There was the glory of the God of Israel; it looked like what I had seen in the valley. 5 He said, 'Son of man, raise your eyes to the north.' I raised my eyes to the north, and there, to the north of the altar gate, stood this statue of jealousy at the entrance. 6 He said, 'Son of man, do you see what they are doing, the monstrous, loathsome things that the House of Israel is practising here, to drive me out of my sanctuary? And you will see practices more loathsome still.'
7 He next took me to the entrance to the court. I looked; there was a hole in the wall. 8 He said, 'Son of man, bore through the wall.' I bored through the wall, until I had made an opening. 9 He said, 'Go in and look at the loathsome things they are doing inside.' 10 I went in and looked and there was every kind of reptile and repulsive animal, and all the foul idols of the House of Israel, carved all round the walls. 11 Seventy elders of the House of Israel were worshipping the idols — among them Jaazaniah son of Shaphan — each one with his censer in his hand, from which rose a fragrant cloud of incense. 12 He said, 'Son of man, have you seen what the elders of the House of Israel do in the dark, each in his personal image-shrine? They say, "Yahweh cannot see us; Yahweh has abandoned the country." ' 13 He said, 'You will see them at practices more loathsome still.'
14 He next took me to the entrance of the north gate of the Temple of Yahweh where women were sitting, weeping for Tammuz. c 15 He said, 'Son of man, do you see that? You will see even more loathsome things than that.'
16 He then led me to the inner court of the Temple of Yahweh. And there, at the entrance to Yahweh's sanctuary, between the portico and the altar, there were about twenty-

b 8 chh. 8-11 are a vision four years before the final siege.   c 8 A vegetation god whose annual death and rebirth were mourned and greeted.

five men, with their backs to the temple of the LORD, and their faces toward the east, prostrating themselves to the sun toward the east. 17 Then he said to me, "Have you seen this, O mortal? Is it not bad enough that the house of Judah commits the abominations done here? Must they fill the land with violence, and provoke my anger still further? See, they are putting the branch to their nose! 18 Therefore I will act in wrath; my eye will not spare, nor will I have pity; and though they cry in my hearing with a loud voice, I will not listen to them."

9 Then he cried in my hearing with a loud voice, saying, "Draw near, you executioners of the city, each with his destroying weapon in his hand." 2 And six men came from the direction of the upper gate, which faces north, each with his weapon for slaughter in his hand; among them was a man clothed in linen, with a writing case at his side. They went in and stood beside the bronze altar.

3 Now the glory of the God of Israel had gone up from the cherub on which it rested to the threshold of the house. The LORD called to the man clothed in linen, who had the writing case at his side; 4 and said to him, "Go through the city, through Jerusalem, and put a mark on the foreheads of those who sigh and groan over all the abominations that are committed in it." 5 To the others he said in my hearing, "Pass through the city after him, and kill; your eye shall not spare, and you shall show no pity. 6 Cut down old men, young men and young women, little children and women, but touch no one who has the mark. And begin at my sanctuary." So they began with the elders who were in front of the house. 7 Then he said to them, "Defile the house, and fill the courts with the slain. Go!" So they went out and killed in the city. 8 While they were killing, and I was left alone, I fell prostrate on my face and cried out, "Ah Lord GOD! will you destroy all who remain of Israel as you pour out your wrath upon Jerusalem?" 9 He said to me, "The guilt of the house of Israel and Judah is exceedingly great; the land is full of bloodshed and the city full of perversity; for they say, 'The LORD has forsaken the land, and the LORD does not see.' 10 As for me, my eye will not spare, nor will I have pity, but I will bring down their deeds upon their heads."

11 Then the man clothed in linen, with the writing case at his side, brought back word, saying, "I have done as you commanded me."

with their backs to the sanctuary and their faces to the east, prostrating themselves to the rising sun. 17 He said to me, 'O man, do you see that? Do you think it a trifling matter for Judah to practise these abominations here? They have filled the land with violence and have provoked me to anger again and again. Look at them at their worship, holding twigs to their noses. 18 I shall turn on them in my rage and show them no pity, nor spare them. Loudly though they cry to me, I shall not listen.'

9 A loud voice rang in my ears: 'Here they come, those appointed to punish the city, each carrying his weapon of destruction.' 2 I saw six men approaching from the road that leads to the upper gate which faces north, each carrying a battle-club, and among them one was dressed in linen, with a writer's pen and ink at his waist; they advanced until they stood by the bronze altar. 3 The glory of the God of Israel had risen from above the cherubim where it rested, and had come to the terrace of the temple. He called to the man dressed in linen, with pen and ink at his waist. 4 'Go through the city of Jerusalem,' said the LORD, 'and mark with a cross the foreheads of those who groan and lament over all the abominations practised there.' 5 To the others I heard him say, 'Follow him through the city and deal out death; show no pity; spare no one. 6 Kill and destroy men old and young, girls, little children, and women, but touch no one who bears the mark. Begin at my sanctuary.' So they began with the elders in front of the temple. 7 'Defile the temple,' he said, 'and fill the courts with dead bodies; then go out and spread death in the city.'

8 While the killing went on, I was left alone, and I threw myself on the ground, crying out, 'Lord GOD, are you going to destroy all the Israelites who are left, in this outpouring of your anger on Jerusalem?' 9 He answered, 'The iniquity of Israel and Judah is very great indeed; the land is full of bloodshed, the city is filled with injustice. They are saying, "The LORD has forsaken the land and does not see." 10 But I shall show no pity, nor spare them; I shall make their conduct recoil on their own heads.' 11 When the man dressed in linen, with pen and ink at his waist, returned he reported: 'I have carried out your orders.'

9:3 **cherubim:** *so Gk; Heb.* cherub.   9:7 **go out:** *so Gk; Heb.* adds and they will go out.

their backs to the LORD's temple and their faces toward the east; they were bowing down to the sun. 17 Do you see, son of man? he asked me. Is it such a trivial matter for the house of Judah to do the abominable things they have done here — for they have filled the land with violence, and again and again they have provoked me — that now they must also put the branch to my nose? 18 Therefore I in turn will act furiously: I will not look upon them with pity nor will I show mercy.

9 Then he cried loud for me to hear: Come, you scourges of the city! 2 With that I saw six men coming from the direction of the upper gate which faces the north, each with a destroying weapon in his hand. In their midst was a man dressed in linen, with a writer's case at his waist. They entered and stood beside the bronze altar. 3 Then he called to the man dressed in linen with the writer's case at his waist, 4 saying to him: Pass through the city [through Jerusalem] and mark an X on the foreheads of those who moan and groan over all the abominations that are practiced within it. 5 To the others I heard him say: Pass through the city after him and strike! Do not look on them with pity nor show any mercy! 6 Old men, youths and maidens, women and children — wipe them out! But do not touch any marked with the X; begin at my sanctuary. So they began with the men [the elders] who were in front of the temple. 7 Defile the temple, he said to them, and fill the courts with the slain; then go out and strike in the city.

8 As they began to strike, I was left alone. I fell prone, crying out, "Alas, Lord GOD! Will you destroy all that is left of Israel when you pour out your fury on Jerusalem?" 9 He answered me: The sins of the house of Israel are great beyond measure; the land is filled with bloodshed, the city with lawlessness. They think that the LORD has forsaken the land, that he does not see them. 10 I, however, will not look upon them with pity, nor show any mercy. I will bring down their conduct upon their heads.

11 Then I saw the man dressed in linen with the writing case at his waist make his report: "I have done as you ordered."

11,24 Spirit lifted me up and brought me back to the exiles in Chaldea [in a vision, by God's spirit]. Then the vision I had seen left me, 11,25 and I told the exiles everything the LORD had shown me.

10 8,1 On the fifth day of the sixth month, in the sixth year, as I was sitting in my house, and the elders of Judah sat before me, the hand of the Lord GOD fell upon me there. 8,2 I looked up and saw a form that looked like a man. Downward from what seemed to be his waist, there was fire; from his waist upward there seemed to be a brightness like the sheen of electrum. He stretched out what appeared to be a hand and seized me by the hair of my head. . . .

8,4 I saw there the glory of the God of Israel, like the vision I had seen in the plain. The cherubim were stationed to the right of the temple; 20 these were the living creatures I had seen beneath the God of Israel by the river Chebar, whom I now recognized to be cherubim. 21 Each had four faces and four wings; something like human hands were under their wings. 22 Their faces looked just like those I had seen by the river Chebar; each one went straight forward. 14 Each had four faces: the first face was that of an ox, the second that of a man, the third that of a lion, and the fourth

five men, with their backs to Yahweh's sanctuary and their faces turned towards the east. They were prostrating themselves to the east, before the rising sun. 17 He said to me, 'Son of man, do you see that? Is it not bad enough for the House of Judah to be doing the loathsome things they are doing here? But they fill the country with violence and provoke my anger further; look at them now putting that branch to their nostrils. 18 And so I shall react in fury; I shall show neither pity nor mercy. They may cry as loudly as they like to me; I will not listen.'

9 Then he shouted loudly for me to hear, 'The scourges of the city are approaching, each carrying his weapon of destruction!' 2 Immediately six men advanced from the upper north gate, each holding a deadly weapon. Among them was a man dressed in linen, with a scribe's ink-horn in his belt. They came in and halted in front of the bronze altar. 3 The glory of the God of Israel rose from above the winged creature where it had been, towards the threshold of the Temple. He called to the man dressed in linen with a scribe's ink-horn in his belt 4 and Yahweh said to him, 'Go all through the city, all through Jerusalem, and mark a cross on the foreheads of all who grieve and lament over all the loathsome practices in it.' 5 I heard him say to the others, 'Follow him through the city and strike. Not one glance of pity; show no mercy; 6 old men, young men, girls, children, women, kill and exterminate them all. But do not touch anyone with a cross on his forehead. Begin at my sanctuary.' So they began with the old men who were in the Temple. 7 He said to them, 'Defile the Temple; fill the courts with corpses; then go out!' They went out and hacked their way through the city.

8 While they were hacking them down, I was left alone; I fell on my face, crying out, 'Ah, Lord Yahweh, are you going to annihilate all that is left of Israel by venting your fury on Jerusalem?' 9 He said, 'The guilt of the House of Israel and Judah is immense; the country is full of bloodshed, the city full of perversity, for they say, "Yahweh has abandoned the country, Yahweh cannot see." 10 Then, I too shall neither give one glance of pity nor show any mercy. I shall repay them for what they have done.' 11 The man dressed in linen with the scribe's ink-horn in his belt then came back and made his report, 'I have carried out your orders.'

11, 24f: These verses have been transposed from ch 11. **10, 1:** In chapters 8, 1–11, 25 of the current Hebrew text, several visions involving the temple of Jerusalem were combined to form a single continuous vision. The redistribution of verses in this translation is an attempt to separate the original visions. (8, 1. 2. 4. have been transposed from ch 8) **8, 2:** The dots suppose the omission of some words describing the prophet's being transported in his visions to the court of the temple.

10 Then I looked, and above the dome that was over the heads of the cherubim there appeared above them something like a sapphire,[v] in form resembling a throne. 2 He said to the man clothed in linen, "Go within the wheelwork underneath the cherubim; fill your hands with burning coals from among the cherubim, and scatter them over the city." He went in as I looked on. 3 Now the cherubim were standing on the south side of the house when the man went in; and a cloud filled the inner court. 4 Then the glory of the LORD rose up from the cherub to the threshold of the house; the house was filled with the cloud, and the court was full of the brightness of the glory of the LORD. 5 The sound of the wings of the cherubim was heard as far as the outer court, like the voice of God Almighty[w] when he speaks.

6 When he commanded the man clothed in linen, "Take fire from within the wheelwork, from among the cherubim," he went in and stood beside a wheel. 7 And a cherub stretched out his hand from among the cherubim to the fire that was among the cherubim, took some of it and put it into the hands of the man clothed in linen, who took it and went out. 8 The cherubim appeared to have the form of a human hand under their wings.

9 I looked, and there were four wheels beside the cherubim, one beside each cherub; and the appearance of the wheels was like gleaming beryl. 10 And as for their appearance, the four looked alike, something like a wheel within a wheel. 11 When they moved, they moved in any of the four directions without veering as they moved; but in whatever direction the front wheel faced, the others followed without veering as they moved. 12 Their entire body, their rims, their spokes, their wings, and the wheels — the wheels of the four of them — were full of eyes all around. 13 As for the wheels, they were called in my hearing "the wheelwork." 14 Each one had four faces: the first face was that of the cherub, the second face was that of a human being, the third that of a lion, and the fourth that of an eagle.

15 The cherubim rose up. These were the living creatures that I saw by the river Chebar. 16 When the cherubim moved, the wheels moved beside them; and when the cherubim lifted up their wings to rise up from the earth, the wheels at their side did not veer. 17 When they stopped, the others stopped, and when they rose up, the others rose up with them; for the spirit of the living creatures was in them.

18 Then the glory of the LORD went out from the threshold of the house and stopped above the cherubim. 19 The cherubim lifted up their wings and rose up from the earth in my sight as they went out with the wheels beside them. They stopped at the entrance of the east gate of the house of the LORD; and the glory of the God of Israel was above them.

10 Then in my vision I saw, above the vault over the heads of the cherubim, as it were a sapphire in the shape of a throne. 2 The LORD said to the man dressed in linen, 'Come in between the circling wheels under the cherubim, and take a handful of the burning embers lying among the cherubim; then throw it over the city.' As I watched he went in.

3 The cherubim stood on the right side of the temple as the man entered, and a cloud filled the inner court. 4 The glory of the LORD rose high above the cherubim and moved to the terrace of the temple; and the temple was filled with the cloud, while the radiance of the glory of the LORD filled the court. 5 The sound of the wings of the cherubim could be heard as far as the outer court; it was as if God Almighty were speaking.

6 When the man dressed in linen was told by the LORD to take fire from between the circling wheels and from among the cherubim, he went and stood by a wheel, 7 and one of the cherubim reached out to the fire that was in their midst and, taking some fire, handed it to the man dressed in linen, who received it and went away. 8 Under the wings of the cherubim there could be seen what looked like a human hand.

9 I saw four wheels beside the cherubim, one wheel beside each cherub. In appearance they were like sparkling topaz, 10 and all four were alike, like a wheel inside a wheel. 11 When the cherubim moved in any of the four directions, they never swerved from their course; they went straight on in the direction in which their heads were turned, never swerving. 12 Their whole bodies, the backs, hands, and wings of all four of them, as well as the wheels, were covered all over with eyes, 13 and I could hear the whirring of the wheels. 14 Each had four faces: the first was a cherub's face, the second a human face, the third a lion's face, and the fourth an eagle's face.

15 The cherubim raised themselves from the ground, those same living creatures I had seen by the river Kebar. 16 When they moved, the wheels moved beside them; when they lifted their wings and rose from the ground, the wheels did not move from their side. 17 When one halted, the other halted; when one rose, the other rose, for the spirit of the creatures was in the wheels.

18 The glory of the LORD left the temple terrace and halted above the cherubim. 19 They spread their wings and raised themselves from the ground; I watched them go with the wheels beside them. They halted at the eastern gateway of the LORD's house, with the glory of the God of Israel over

10:1 **sapphire:** *or* lapis lazuli.   10:2 **under the cherubim:** *so Gk;* Heb. under the cherub.   10:4 **cherubim:** Heb. cherub.
10:12 **four of them:** *prob. rdg; Heb. adds* their wheels.

[v] Or *lapis lazuli*   [w] Traditional rendering of Heb *El Shaddai*

that of an eagle. 15 Such were the living creatures I had seen by the river Chebar.

9 I also saw four wheels beside them, one wheel beside each cherub; the wheels appeared to have the luster of chrysolite stone. 10 All four of them seemed to be made the same, as though there were a wheel within a wheel. 11 When they moved, they went in any one of their four directions without veering as they moved; for in whichever direction they were faced, they went straight towards it without veering as they moved. 12 The rims of the four wheels were full of eyes all around. 13 I heard the wheels given the name "wheelwork." 16 When the cherubim moved, the wheels went beside them; when the cherubim lifted their wings to rise from the earth, even then the wheels did not leave their sides. 17 When they stood still, the wheels stood still; when they rose, the wheels rose with them; for the living creatures' spirit was in them.

1 I looked and saw in the firmament above the cherubim what appeared to be sapphire stone; something like a throne could be seen upon it. 2 He said to the man dressed in linen: Go within the wheelwork under the cherubim; fill both your hands with burning coals from among the cherubim, then scatter them over the city. As I looked on, he entered.

The glory of the God of Israel had gone up from the cherubim, upon which it had been, to the threshold of the temple. 3 As the man entered, the cloud filled the inner court, 4 and the glory of the LORD rose from over the cherubim to the threshold of the temple; the temple was filled with the cloud, and all the court was bright with the glory of the LORD. 5 The noise of the wings of the cherubim could be heard as far as the outer court; it was like the voice of God the Almighty when he speaks.

6 When he had commanded the man dressed in linen to take fire from within the wheelwork, among the cherubim, the man entered and stood by one of the wheels. 7 Thereupon its cherub stretched out his hand toward the fire that was among the cherubim. He took up some of it and put it in the hands of the one dressed in linen, who took it and came out. 8 [Something like human hands could be seen under the wings of the cherubim.]

‡10.9–17: see above‡

18 Then the glory of the LORD left the threshold of the temple and rested upon the cherubim. 19 These lifted their wings, and I saw them rise from the earth, the wheels rising along with them. They stood at the entrance of the eastern gate of the LORD's house, and the glory of the God of Israel was up above them.

10 Then, in vision I saw that above the solid surface over the heads of the winged creatures there was above them something like sapphire, which seemed to be like a throne. 2 He then said to the man dressed in linen, 'Go in between the wheels below the winged creatures; take a handful of burning coal from between the winged creatures and scatter it over the city.' He went in as I watched.

3 The winged creatures were on the right of the Temple as the man went in, and the cloud filled the inner court. 4 The glory of Yahweh rose from above the winged creatures, towards the threshold of the Temple; the Temple was filled by the cloud and the court was full of the brightness of the glory of Yahweh. 5 The noise of the winged creatures' wings could be heard even in the outer court, like the voice of God Almighty when he speaks.

6 When he had given the order to the man dressed in linen, 'Take the fire from between the wheels, between the winged creatures,' the man went in and stood by one of the wheels. 7 One of the winged creatures then reached his hand out towards the fire between the winged creatures, took some of it and put it into the hands of the man dressed in linen, who took it and came out again.

8 There appeared to be what looked like a human hand under the winged creatures' wings. 9 And I looked, and there were four wheels beside the winged creatures, one wheel beside each winged creature, and the appearance of the wheels was like the sparkle of chrysolite. 10 In appearance, all four looked alike, as though each wheel had another wheel inside it.

11 In whichever of the four directions they moved, they did not need to turn as they moved, but whichever way the head was facing there they followed; they did not turn as they moved, 12 and their entire bodies, their backs, their hands, their wings, as well as the wheels, had eyes all the way round (the wheels of all four). 13 In my hearing, these wheels were called 'galgal'. 14 Each had four faces; the first was a winged creature's face, the second a human face, the third a lion's face and the fourth an eagle's face. 15 The winged creatures rose; this was the being I had seen by the River Chebar. 16 When the winged creatures moved, the wheels moved beside them; and when the winged creatures raised their wings to leave the ground, the wheels did not turn beside them. 17 When the former halted the latter halted; when the former rose, the latter rose with them, since they shared the same living spirit.

18 The glory of Yahweh then came out over the Temple threshold and paused over the winged creatures. 19 These raised their wings and rose from the ground as I watched, and the wheels were beside them. They paused at the entrance to the east gate of the Temple of Yahweh, with the

20 These were the living creatures that I saw underneath the God of Israel by the river Chebar; and I knew that they were cherubim. 21 Each had four faces, each four wings, and underneath their wings something like human hands. 22 As for what their faces were like, they were the same faces whose appearance I had seen by the river Chebar. Each one moved straight ahead.

11 The spirit lifted me up and brought me to the east gate of the house of the LORD, which faces east. There, at the entrance of the gateway, were twenty-five men; among them I saw Jaazaniah son of Azzur, and Pelatiah son of Benaiah, officials of the people. 2 He said to me, "Mortal, these are the men who devise iniquity and who give wicked counsel in this city; 3 they say, 'The time is not near to build houses; this city is the pot, and we are the meat.' 4 Therefore prophesy against them; prophesy, O mortal."

5 Then the spirit of the LORD fell upon me, and he said to me, "Say, Thus says the LORD: This is what you think, O house of Israel; I know the things that come into your mind. 6 You have killed many in this city, and have filled its streets with the slain. 7 Therefore thus says the Lord GOD: The slain whom you have placed within it are the meat, and this city is the pot; but you shall be taken out of it. 8 You have feared the sword; and I will bring the sword upon you, says the Lord GOD. 9 I will take you out of it and give you over to the hands of foreigners, and execute judgments upon you. 10 You shall fall by the sword; I will judge you at the border of Israel. And you shall know that I am the LORD. 11 This city shall not be your pot, and you shall not be the meat inside it; I will judge you at the border of Israel. 12 Then you shall know that I am the LORD, whose statutes you have not followed, and whose ordinances you have not kept, but you have acted according to the ordinances of the nations that are around you."

13 Now, while I was prophesying, Pelatiah son of Benaiah died. Then I fell down on my face, cried with a loud voice, and said, "Ah Lord GOD! will you make a full end of the remnant of Israel?"

14 Then the word of the LORD came to me: 15 Mortal, your kinsfolk, your own kin, your fellow exiles,ˣ the whole house of Israel, all of them, are those of whom the inhabitants of Jerusalem have said, "They have gone far from the LORD; to us this land is given for a possession." 16 Therefore say: Thus says the Lord GOD: Though I removed them far away among the nations, and though I scattered them among the countries, yet I have been a sanctuary to them for a little whileʸ in the countries where they have gone. 17 Therefore say: Thus says the Lord GOD: I will gather you from the peoples, and assemble you out of the countries where you have been scattered, and I will give you the land of Israel. 18 When they come there, they will remove from it all its detestable things and all its abominations. 19 I will give them oneᶻ heart, and put a new spirit within them; I will remove the heart of stone from their flesh and give them a heart of flesh, 20 so that they may follow my statutes and keep my ordinances and obey them. Then they shall be my people, and I will be their God. 21 But as for those whose heart goes after their detestable things and their abominations,ᵃ I will bring their deeds upon their own heads, says the Lord GOD.

22 Then the cherubim lifted up their wings, with the wheels beside them; and the glory of the God of Israel was above them. 23 And the glory of the LORD ascended from the middle of the city, and stopped on the mountain east of the city. 24 The spirit lifted me up and brought me in a vision by

them. 20 These were the living creatures I had seen beneath the God of Israel at the river Kebar, and so I knew that they were cherubim. 21 Each had four faces and four wings and what looked like human hands under their wings. 22 Their faces were like those I had seen in my vision by the river Kebar. They all moved straight forward.

11 A spirit lifted me up and brought me to the east-ward-facing gate of the LORD's house. There by the gateway I saw twenty-five men, among them two of high office, Jaazaniah son of Azzur and Pelatiah son of Benaiah. 2 The LORD said to me, 'O man, these are the men who are planning mischief and offering bad advice in this city, 3 saying, "The time has not yet come to build; the city is a cooking pot and we are the meat in it." 4 Therefore', he said, 'prophesy against them, O man, prophesy.'

5 The spirit of the LORD came upon me, and he told me to say, 'These are the words of the LORD: This is what you are saying to yourselves, you men of Israel; well do I know the thoughts that rise in your mind. 6 You have caused the death of many in this city, heaping the streets with the dead. 7 Therefore, this is what the Lord GOD says: The bodies of your victims, they are the meat, and the city is the cooking pot. But I shall drive you out of the city. 8 You fear the sword, and it is a sword I shall bring on you, says the Lord GOD. 9 I shall drive you out of the city and hand you over to a foreign power; I shall bring you to justice. 10 You will fall by the sword when I bring you to judgement on the frontier of Israel; thus you will know that I am the LORD. 11 So the city will no longer be your cooking pot, nor you the meat in it; on the frontier of Israel I shall bring you to judgement. 12 Then you will know that I am the LORD. You have not conformed to my statutes, nor kept my laws, but have followed the laws of the nations round about you.'

13 While I was prophesying, Pelatiah son of Benaiah fell dead; and I threw myself on the ground, crying aloud, 'Lord GOD, are you going to make an end of all the Israelites who are left?'

14 This word of the LORD came to me: 15 'O man, they are your brothers and your kinsmen, this whole people of Israel, to whom the inhabitants now in Jerusalem have said, "They are separated far from the LORD; the land has been made over to us to possess." 16 Say therefore: These are the words of the Lord GOD: When I sent them far away among the nations and dispersed them over the earth, for a little time I became their sanctuary in the countries to which they had gone. 17 Say therefore: These are the words of the Lord GOD: I shall gather you from among the nations and bring you together from the countries where you have been dispersed, and I shall give the land of Israel to you. 18 When they come there, they will abolish all the vile and abominable practices. 19 I shall give them singleness of heart and put a new spirit in them; I shall remove the heart of stone from their bodies and give them a heart of flesh, 20 so that they will conform to my statutes and keep my laws. They will be my people, and I shall be their God. 21 But those whose hearts are set on vile and abominable practices will be made to answer for all they have done. This is the word of the Lord GOD.'

22 Then the cherubim lifted their wings, with the wheels beside them and the glory of the God of Israel above them. 23 The glory of the LORD rose up and left the city, and halted on the mountain to the east of it. 24 In a vision sent by the

ˣGk Syr: Heb *people of your kindred*   ʸOr *to some extent*
ᶻAnother reading is *a new*   ᵃCn: Heb *And to the heart of their detestable things and their abominations their heart goes*

10:22 **by . . . Kebar:** *prob. rdg; Heb.* adds *and them.*   11:16 **for . . . time:** *or* in a limited way.   11:19 **in them:** *so Gk; Heb.* in you.   11:21 **those . . . set on:** *prob. mng; Heb.* obscure.

‡10.20–22: see above‡

11,22 Then the cherubim lifted their wings, and the wheels went along with them, while up above them was the glory of the God of Israel. 11,23 And the glory of the LORD rose from the city and took a stand on the mountain which is to the east of the city.

11 Spirit lifted me up and brought me to the east gate of the temple. At the entrance of the gate I saw twenty-five men, among whom were Jaazaniah, son of Azzur, and Pelatiah, son of Benaiah, princes of the people. 2 The LORD said to me: Son of man, these are the men who are planning evil and giving wicked counsel in this city. 3 "Shall we not," they say, "be building houses soon? The city is the kettle, and we are the meat." 4 Therefore prophesy against them, son of man, prophesy! 5 Then the spirit of the LORD fell upon me, and he told me to say: Thus says the LORD: This is the way you talk, house of Israel, and what you are plotting I well know. 6 You have slain many in this city and have filled its streets with your slain. 7 Therefore thus says the Lord GOD: Your slain whom you have placed within it, they are the meat, and the city is the kettle; but you I will take out of it. 8 You fear the sword, but the sword I will bring upon you, says the Lord GOD. 9 I will bring you out of the city, and hand you over to foreigners, and inflict punishments upon you. 10 By the sword you shall fall; at the boundaries of Israel I will judge you; thus you shall know that I am the LORD. 11 The city shall not be a kettle for you, nor shall you be the meat within it. At the boundaries of Israel I will judge you, 12 and you shall know that I am the LORD, by whose statutes you have not lived, and whose ordinances you have not kept; rather, you have acted according to the ordinances of the nations around you.

13 While I was prophesying, Pelatiah, the son of Benaiah, died. I fell prone and cried out in a loud voice: "Alas, Lord GOD! will you utterly wipe out what remains of Israel?"

14 Thus the word of the LORD came to me: 15 Son of man, it is about your kinsmen, your fellow exiles, and the whole house of Israel that the inhabitants of Jerusalem say, "They are far away from the LORD; to us the land of Israel has been given as our possession." 16 Therefore say: Thus says the Lord GOD: Though I have removed them far among the nations and scattered them over foreign countries — and was for a while their only sanctuary in the countries to which they had gone — 17 I will gather you from the nations and assemble you from the countries over which you have been scattered, and I will restore to you the land of Israel. 18 They shall return to it and remove from it all its detestable abominations. 19 I will give them a new heart and put a new spirit within them; I will remove the stony heart from their bodies, and replace it with a natural heart, 20 so that they will live according to my statutes, and observe and carry out my ordinances; thus they shall be my people and I will be their God. 21 But as for those whose hearts are devoted to their detestable abominations, I will bring down their conduct upon their heads, says the Lord GOD.

‡11.22–23: see above in ch. 10‡

glory of the God of Israel over them, above. 20 This was the winged creature I had seen beneath the God of Israel by the River Chebar; I knew that they were winged creatures. 21 Each had four faces and four wings and what seemed to be human hands under their wings. 22 Their faces were like those I had seen by the River Chebar. Each one moved straight forward.

11 The spirit lifted me up and brought me to the east gate of the Temple of Yahweh, the gate that looks eastwards. There at the entrance to the gate stood twenty-five men, among whom I saw Jaazaniah son of Azzur and Pelatiah son of Benaiah, leaders of the people.

2 He said to me, 'Son of man, these are the wicked schemers who are spreading their bad advice through this city. 3 They say, "There will be no house-building yet awhile. The city is the cooking pot and we are the meat." 4 So prophesy against them, prophesy, son of man!' 5 The spirit of Yahweh fell on me, and he said to me, 'Say, "Yahweh says this: I know what you are saying, House of Israel, I know how insolent you are. 6 You have filled this city with more and more of your victims; you have strewn its streets with victims. 7 And so the Lord Yahweh says this: Your victims, whom you have put in it, are the meat, and the city is the cooking pot; but I shall take you out of it. 8 You are afraid of the sword, and I shall bring the sword down on you — declares the Lord Yahweh — 9 and I shall take you out of it and hand you over to foreigners and bring you to justice; 10 you will fall by the sword on the soil of Israel; I shall execute justice on you, and you will know that I am Yahweh. 11 This city will be no cooking pot for you, nor will you be the meat inside; I shall execute justice on you on the soil of Israel; 12 and you will know that I am Yahweh, whose laws you have not obeyed and whose judgements you have not kept; instead, you have adopted the customs of the nations round you." '

13 Now as I was prophesying, Pelatiah son of Benaiah dropped dead. I fell to the ground and cried out, 'Ah, Lord Yahweh, are you going to annihilate the remnant of Israel?'

14 The word of Yahweh was then addressed to me as follows, 15 'Son of man, to your brothers one and all, to your kinsfolk and to the whole House of Israel, the inhabitants of Jerusalem have said, "Keep well away from Yahweh. This country has now been made over to us!" 16 So say, "The Lord Yahweh says this: Yes, I have sent them far away among the nations and I have dispersed them to foreign countries; and for a while I have been a sanctuary for them in the country to which they have gone." 17 So say, "The Lord Yahweh says this: I shall gather you back from the peoples, I shall collect you in from the countries where you have been scattered and give you the land of Israel. 18 When they come back, they will purge it of all its horrors and loathsome practices. 19 I shall give them a single heart and I shall put a new spirit in them; I shall remove the heart of stone from their bodies and give them a heart of flesh, 20 so that they can keep my laws and respect my judgements and put them into practice. Then they will be my people and I shall be their God. 21 But those whose hearts are set on their horrors and loathsome practices I shall repay for their conduct — declares the Lord Yahweh." '

22 The winged creatures then raised their wings and the wheels moved with them, with the glory of the God of Israel over them, above. 23 And the glory of Yahweh rose from the centre of the city and halted on the mountain to the east of the city.

11, 22f: These verses have been transposed from ch 11.

the spirit of God into Chaldea, to the exiles. Then the vision that I had seen left me. 25 And I told the exiles all the things that the LORD had shown me.

12 The word of the LORD came to me: 2 Mortal, you are living in the midst of a rebellious house, who have eyes to see but do not see, who have ears to hear but do not hear; 3 for they are a rebellious house. Therefore, mortal, prepare for yourself an exile's baggage, and go into exile by day in their sight; you shall go like an exile from your place to another place in their sight. Perhaps they will understand, though they are a rebellious house. 4 You shall bring out your baggage by day in their sight, as baggage for exile; and you shall go out yourself at evening in their sight, as those do who go into exile. 5 Dig through the wall in their sight, and carry the baggage through it. 6 In their sight you shall lift the baggage on your shoulder, and carry it out in the dark; you shall cover your face, so that you may not see the land; for I have made you a sign for the house of Israel.

7 I did just as I was commanded. I brought out my baggage by day, as baggage for exile, and in the evening I dug through the wall with my own hands; I brought it out in the dark, carrying it on my shoulder in their sight.

8 In the morning the word of the LORD came to me: 9 Mortal, has not the house of Israel, the rebellious house, said to you, "What are you doing?" 10 Say to them, "Thus says the Lord GOD: This oracle concerns the prince in Jerusalem and all the house of Israel in it." 11 Say, "I am a sign for you: as I have done, so shall it be done to them; they shall go into exile, into captivity." 12 And the prince who is among them shall lift his baggage on his shoulder in the dark, and shall go out; he*b* shall dig through the wall and carry it through; he shall cover his face, so that he may not see the land with his eyes. 13 I will spread my net over him, and he shall be caught in my snare; and I will bring him to Babylon, the land of the Chaldeans, yet he shall not see it; and he shall die there. 14 I will scatter to every wind all who are around him, his helpers and all his troops; and I will unsheathe the sword behind them. 15 And they shall know that I am the LORD, when I disperse them among the nations and scatter them through the countries. 16 But I will let a few of them escape from the sword, from famine and pestilence, so that they may tell of all their abominations among the nations where they go; then they shall know that I am the LORD.

17 The word of the LORD came to me: 18 Mortal, eat your bread with quaking, and drink your water with trembling and with fearfulness; 19 and say to the people of the land, Thus says the Lord GOD concerning the inhabitants of Jerusalem in the land of Israel: They shall eat their bread with fearfulness, and drink their water in dismay, because their land shall be stripped of all it contains, on account of the violence of all those who live in it. 20 The inhabited cities shall be laid waste, and the land shall become a desolation; and you shall know that I am the LORD.

21 The word of the LORD came to me: 22 Mortal, what is this proverb of yours about the land of Israel, which says, "The days are prolonged, and every vision comes to nothing"? 23 Tell them therefore, "Thus says the Lord GOD: I will put an end to this proverb, and they shall use it no more as a proverb in Israel." But say to them, The days are near, and the fulfillment of every vision. 24 For there shall no longer be any false vision or flattering divination within the house of Israel. 25 But I the LORD will speak the word that I speak, and it will be fulfilled. It will no longer be delayed; but in your days, O rebellious house, I will speak the word and fulfill it, says the Lord GOD.

26 The word of the LORD came to me: 27 Mortal, the

b Gk Syr: Heb *they*

spirit of God, a spirit lifted me up and brought me back to the exiles in Chaldaea. After the vision left me, 25 I told the exiles all that the LORD had revealed to me.

12 THIS word of the LORD came to me: 2 'O man, you are living among a rebellious people. They have eyes and see nothing; they have ears and hear nothing, because they are rebellious. 3 You must pack what you need, O man, for going into exile, and set off by day while they look on. When they see you leave for exile, it may be they will realize that they are rebellious. 4 Bring out your belongings, packed as if for exile; do it in the daytime in their presence, and then again at evening, still before them, leave home as if for exile; 5 break a hole through the wall, and carry your belongings out through it. 6 Shoulder your pack in their presence, and set off when dusk falls, with your face covered so that you cannot see the land, for I am making you a warning sign for the Israelites.'

7 I did exactly as I had been told. In the daytime I brought out my belongings, packed for exile; at evening with my own hands I broke through the wall, and when dusk fell I shouldered my pack and carried it out before their eyes.

8 Next morning this word of the LORD came to me: 9 'O man, the Israelites, that rebellious people, have asked you what you are doing. 10 Tell them that these are the words of the Lord GOD: This oracle concerns the ruler and all the people of Jerusalem. 11 Tell them that you are a sign to warn them; what you have done will be done to them; they will go as captives into exile. 12 In the dusk their ruler will shoulder his pack and go through a hole made to let him out, with his face covered so that he cannot see the land. 13 But I shall throw my net over him, and he will be caught in the meshes. I shall take him to Babylon, to the land of the Chaldaeans, where he will die without ever seeing it. 14 I shall scatter his bodyguard and drive all his squadrons to the four winds; I shall pursue them with drawn sword. 15 Then they will know that I am the LORD, when I disperse them among the nations and scatter them over the earth. 16 But I shall leave a few of them, survivors of the sword, famine, and pestilence, to describe all their abominations to the peoples among whom they go. They will know that I am the LORD.'

17 THIS word of the LORD came to me: 18 'O man, as you eat your bread you are to tremble, and as you drink the water you are to shudder with fear. 19 Say to the people: This is what the Lord GOD says concerning the inhabitants of Jerusalem in the land of Israel: They will eat bread with fear and be filled with horror as they drink water; the land will be waste and empty because of the violence of all who live there. 20 Inhabited towns will be deserted, and the land will become a waste. Thus you will know that I am the LORD.'

21 This word of the LORD came to me: 22 'O man, what is this proverb current in the land of Israel: "Days pass and visions perish"? 23 Very well! Say to them: This is what the Lord GOD says: I have put an end to this proverb; it will never again be quoted in Israel. Rather say to them: The days are near when every vision will be fulfilled. 24 There will be no more false visions, no misleading divination among the Israelites, 25 for I, the LORD, shall say what I will, and it will be done. It will be put off no longer: you rebellious people, in your lifetime I shall do what I have said. This is the word of the Lord GOD.'

26 This word of the LORD came to me: 27 'O man, the

12:6 **set off:** *so Gk; Heb.* bring out.

NEW AMERICAN BIBLE

NEW JERUSALEM BIBLE

‡11.24–25: see above in ch. 9‡

24 Then the spirit lifted me up and took me, in vision, in the spirit of God, to the exiles in Chaldaea, and the vision which I had seen faded. 25 I then told the exiles everything that Yahweh had shown me.

12 Thus the word of the LORD came to me: 2 Son of man, you live in the midst of a rebellious house; they have eyes to see but do not see, and ears to hear but do not hear, for they are a rebellious house. 3 Now, son of man, during the day while they are looking on, prepare your baggage as though for exile, and again while they are looking on, migrate from where you live to another place; perhaps they will see that they are a rebellious house. 4 You shall bring out your baggage like an exile in the daytime while they are looking on; in the evening, again while they are looking on, you shall go out like one of those driven into exile; 5 while they look on, dig a hole in the wall and pass through it; 6 while they look on, shoulder the burden and set out in the darkness; cover your face that you may not see the land, for I have made you a sign for the house of Israel.

7 I did as I was told. During the day I brought out my baggage as though it were that of an exile, and at evening I dug a hole through the wall with my hand and, while they looked on, set out in the darkness, shouldering my burden.

8 Then, in the morning, the word of the LORD came to me: 9 Son of man, did not the house of Israel, that rebellious house, ask you what you were doing? 10 Tell them: Thus says the Lord GOD: This oracle concerns Jerusalem and the whole house of Israel within it. 11 I am a sign for you: as I have done, so shall it be done to them; as captives they shall go into exile. 12 The prince who is among them shall shoulder his burden and set out in darkness, going through a hole that he has dug in the wall, and covering his face lest he be seen by anyone. 13 But I will spread my net over him, and he shall be taken in my snare. I will bring him to Babylon, into the land of the Chaldeans — but he shall not see it — and there he shall die. 14 All his retinue, his aides, and his troops I will scatter in every direction, and pursue them with the sword. 15 Then shall they know that I am the LORD, when I disperse them among the nations and scatter them over foreign lands. 16 Yet I will leave a few of them to escape the sword, famine and pestilence, so that they may tell of all their abominations among the nations to which they will come; thus they shall know that I am the LORD.

17 Thus the word of the LORD came to me: 18 Son of man, eat your bread trembling, and drink your water shaking with anxiety. 19 Then say to the people of the land: Thus says the Lord GOD of the inhabitants of Jerusalem [to the land of Israel]: They shall eat their bread in anxiety and drink their water in horror, that their land may be emptied of the violence of all its inhabitants that now fills it. 20 Inhabited cities shall be in ruins, and the land shall be a waste; thus you shall know that I am the LORD.

21 Thus the word of the LORD came to me: 22 Son of man, what is this proverb that you have in the land of Israel: "The days drag on, and no vision ever comes to anything"? 23 Say to them therefore: Thus says the Lord GOD: I will put an end to this proverb; they shall never quote it again in Israel. Rather, say to them: The days are at hand, and also the fulfillment of every vision. 25 Whatever I speak is final, and it shall be done without further delay. In your days, rebellious house, whatever I speak I will bring about, says the Lord GOD.

24 There shall no longer be any false visions or deceitful divinations within the house of Israel, because it is I, the LORD, who will speak.

26 Thus the word of the LORD came to me: 27 Son of man,

12 The word of Yahweh was addressed to me as follows, 2 'Son of man, you are living among a tribe of rebels who have eyes and never see, they have ears and never hear, because they are a tribe of rebels. 3 So, son of man, pack an exile's bundle and set off for exile by daylight while they watch. You will leave your home and go somewhere else while they watch. Then perhaps they will see that they are a tribe of rebels. 4 You will pack your baggage like an exile's bundle, by daylight, while they watch, and leave like an exile in the evening, while they watch. 5 While they watch, make a hole in the wall, and go out through it. 6 While they watch, you will shoulder your pack and go out into the dark; you will cover your face so that you cannot see the ground, since I have made you an omen for the House of Israel.'

7 I did as I had been told. I packed my baggage like an exile's bundle, by daylight; and in the evening I made a hole through the wall with my hands; then I went out into the dark and shouldered my pack while they watched.

8 Next morning the word of Yahweh was addressed to me as follows, 9 'Son of man, did not the House of Israel, did not that tribe of rebels, ask you, "What are you doing?" 10 Say, "The Lord Yahweh says this: This prophecy concerns Jerusalem and the whole House of Israel who live there." 11 Say, "I am an omen for you; as I have done, so will be done to them; they will be deported into exile. 12 Their prince will shoulder his pack in the dark and go out through the wall; a hole will be made to let him out; he will cover his face, so that he cannot see the country. 13 I shall throw my net over him and catch him in my mesh; I shall take him to Babylon,*d* to the land of the Chaldaeans, though he will not see it; and there he will die. 14 And all those in attendance on him, his army and all his troops, I shall scatter to all the winds and unsheathe the sword behind them. 15 Then they will know that I am Yahweh, when I scatter them throughout the nations and disperse them in foreign countries. 16 But I shall let a few of them escape the sword, famine and plague, to describe all their loathsome practices to the peoples among whom they will go, so that these too may know that I am Yahweh." '

17 The word of Yahweh was addressed to me as follows, 18 'Son of man, you are to tremble as you eat your food and shudder apprehensively as you drink your water, 19 and you are to say to the people of the country, "The Lord Yahweh says this to the inhabitants of Jerusalem. They will shudder apprehensively as they eat their food, and drink their water in fear, so that the country and its population may be freed from the violence of its inhabitants. 20 When the populous cities have been destroyed and the country has been reduced to desert, then you will know that I am Yahweh." '

21 The word of Yahweh was addressed to me as follows, 22 'Son of man, what do you understand by the saying pronounced over the land of Israel, "Days go by and visions fade"?

23 'Very well, tell them, "The Lord Yahweh says this: I shall put an end to this saying; it will never be used in Israel again." Instead, tell them:

"The days are coming when every vision will come true, 24 for there will be no more futile visions or deceptive prophecy in the House of Israel, 25 since I, Yahweh, shall speak. And what I shall say will come true without delay; for what I shall say, I shall perform in your own lifetime, you tribe of rebels — declares the Lord Yahweh." '

26 The word of Yahweh was addressed to me as follows,

d 12 = 17:20.

house of Israel is saying, "The vision that he sees is for many years ahead; he prophesies for distant times." 28 Therefore say to them, Thus says the Lord GOD: None of my words will be delayed any longer, but the word that I speak will be fulfilled, says the Lord GOD.

13 The word of the LORD came to me: 2 Mortal, prophesy against the prophets of Israel who are prophesying; say to those who prophesy out of their own imagination: "Hear the word of the LORD!" 3 Thus says the Lord GOD, Alas for the senseless prophets who follow their own spirit, and have seen nothing! 4 Your prophets have been like jackals among ruins, O Israel. 5 You have not gone up into the breaches, or repaired a wall for the house of Israel, so that it might stand in battle on the day of the LORD. 6 They have envisioned falsehood and lying divination; they say, "Says the LORD," when the LORD has not sent them, and yet they wait for the fulfillment of their word! 7 Have you not seen a false vision or uttered a lying divination, when you have said, "Says the LORD," even though I did not speak?

8 Therefore thus says the Lord GOD: Because you have uttered falsehood and envisioned lies, I am against you, says the Lord GOD. 9 My hand will be against the prophets who see false visions and utter lying divinations; they shall not be in the council of my people, nor be enrolled in the register of the house of Israel, nor shall they enter the land of Israel; and you shall know that I am the Lord GOD. 10 Because, in truth, because they have misled my people, saying, "Peace," when there is no peace; and because, when the people build a wall, these prophets^c smear whitewash on it. 11 Say to those who smear whitewash on it that it shall fall. There will be a deluge of rain, ^d great hailstones will fall, and a stormy wind will break out. 12 When the wall falls, will it not be said to you, "Where is the whitewash you smeared on it?" 13 Therefore thus says the Lord GOD: In my wrath I will make a stormy wind break out, and in my anger there shall be a deluge of rain, and hailstones in wrath to destroy it. 14 I will break down the wall that you have smeared with whitewash, and bring it to the ground, so that its foundation will be laid bare; when it falls, you shall perish within it; and you shall know that I am the LORD. 15 Thus I will spend my wrath upon the wall, and upon those who have smeared it with whitewash; and I will say to you, The wall is no more, nor those who smeared it— 16 the prophets of Israel who prophesied concerning Jerusalem and saw visions of peace for it, when there was no peace, says the Lord GOD.

17 As for you, mortal, set your face against the daughters of your people, who prophesy out of their own imagination; prophesy against them 18 and say, Thus says the Lord GOD: Woe to the women who sew bands on all wrists, and make veils for the heads of persons of every height, in the hunt for human lives! Will you hunt down lives among my people, and maintain your own lives? 19 You have profaned me among my people for handfuls of barley and for pieces of bread, putting to death persons who should not die and keeping alive persons who should not live, by your lies to my people, who listen to lies.

20 Therefore thus says the Lord GOD: I am against your bands with which you hunt lives;^e I will tear them from your arms, and let the lives go free, the lives that you hunt down like birds. 21 I will tear off your veils, and save my

Israelites say, "The visions which prophets now see are not to be fulfilled for many years: they are prophesying of a time far off." 28 Very well! Say to them: This is what the Lord GOD said: No word of mine will be delayed; whatever I say will be done. This is the word of the Lord GOD.'

13 This word of the LORD came to me: 2 'O man, prophesy against the prophets of Israel who are prophesying; say to those whose prophecies come from their own minds: Hear what the LORD says: 3 These are the words of the Lord GOD: Woe betide the prophets bent on wickedness, who follow their own enthusiasms, for they have seen no vision! 4 Your prophets, Israel, have been like jackals among ruins. 5 They have not stepped into the breach to repair the broken wall for the Israelites, so that they might stand firm in battle on the day of the LORD. 6 The vision is false, the divination a lie! They claim, "It is the word of the LORD," when it is not the LORD who has sent them, yet they expect him to confirm their prophecies! 7 Is it not a false vision that you prophets have seen? Is not your divination a lie? You call it the word of the LORD, but it is not I who have spoken.

8 'The Lord GOD says: Because what you say is false and your visions are a lie, therefore I have set myself against you, says the Lord GOD. 9 I shall raise my hand against the prophets whose visions are false, whose divinations are a lie. They will have no place in the assembly of my people; their names will not be entered in the roll of Israel, nor will they set foot on her soil. Thus you will know that I am the Lord GOD.

10 'This they deserve, for they have misled my people by saying that all is well when nothing is well. It is as if my people were building a wall and the prophets used whitewash for the daubing. 11 Tell these daubers that it will fall, for rain will pour down in torrents, and I shall send hailstones streaming down and unleash a storm-wind. 12 When the wall collapses, it will be said, "Where is the plaster you used?" 13 So this is what the Lord GOD says: In my rage I shall unleash a storm-wind; rain will come in torrents in my anger, hailstones in my fury, until all is destroyed. 14 I shall overthrow the wall which you have daubed with whitewash and level it to the ground, laying bare its foundations. It will fall, and you will be destroyed with it: thus you will know that I am the LORD. 15 I shall vent my rage on the wall and on those who daubed it with whitewash; and I shall say, "Gone is the wall and gone those who daubed it, 16 those prophets of Israel who prophesied to Jerusalem, who saw visions of well-being for her when there was no well-being." This is the word of the Lord GOD.

17 'Now set your face, O man, against the women of your people whose prophecies come from their own minds; prophesy against them 18 and say: This is the word of the Lord GOD: Woe betide you women who hunt men's lives by sewing magic bands on the wrists and putting veils over the heads of persons of every age! Are you to hunt the lives of my people and keep your own lives safe? 19 You have dishonoured me in front of my people for some handfuls of barley and scraps of bread. By telling my people lies they wish to hear, you bring death to those who should not die, and keep alive those who should not live. 20 So this is what the Lord GOD says: I have set my face against your magic bands with which you hunt men's lives for the excitement of it. I shall tear them from your arms and set free those lives that you hunt just for excitement. 21 I shall tear up your

---

^c Heb *they*   ^d Heb *rain and you*   ^e Gk Syr: Heb *lives for birds*   13:18 **the wrists:** *so some MSS; others* my wrists.

listen to the house of Israel saying, "The vision he sees is a long way off; he prophesies of the distant future!" 28 Say to them therefore: Thus says the Lord GOD: None of my words shall be delayed any longer; whatever I speak is final, and it shall be done, says the Lord GOD.

13 Thus the word of the LORD came to me: 2 Son of man, prophesy against the prophets of Israel, prophesy! Say to those who prophesy their own thought: Hear the word of the LORD: ‡13.3–4: see below‡ 5 You did not step into the breach, nor did you build a wall about the house of Israel that would stand firm against attack on the day of the LORD. ‡13.6: see below‡ 7 Was not the vision you saw false, and your divination lying? 8 Therefore thus says the Lord GOD: Because you have spoken falsehood and have seen lying visions, therefore see! I am coming at you, says the Lord GOD. ‡13.9: see below‡

10 For the very reason that they led my people astray, saying, "Peace!" when there was no peace, and that, as one built a wall, they would cover it with whitewash, 11 say then to the whitewashers: I will bring down a flooding rain; hailstones shall fall, and a stormwind shall break out. 12 And when the wall has fallen, will you not be asked: Where is the whitewash you spread on?

13 Therefore thus says the Lord GOD: In my fury I will let loose stormwinds; because of my anger there shall be a flooding rain, and hailstones shall fall with destructive wrath. 14 I will tear down the wall that you have whitewashed and level it to the ground, laying bare its foundations. When it falls, you shall be crushed beneath it; thus you shall know that I am the LORD. 15 When I have spent my fury on the wall and its whitewashers, I tell you there shall be no wall, nor shall there be whitewashers — 16 those prophets of Israel who prophesied to Jerusalem and saw for it visions of peace when there was no peace, says the Lord GOD.

3 Thus says the Lord GOD: Woe to those prophets who are fools, who follow their own spirit and have seen no vision. 4 Like foxes among ruins are your prophets, O Israel! 6 Their visions are false and their divination lying. They say, "Thus says the LORD!" though the LORD did not send them; then they wait for him to fulfill their word! 9 But I will stretch out my hand against the prophets who have false visions and who foretell lies. They shall not belong to the community of my people, nor be recorded in the register of the house of Israel, nor enter the land of Israel; thus you shall know that I am the LORD.

17 Now, son of man, turn toward the daughters of your people who prophesy their own thoughts; against these, prophesy: Thus says the Lord GOD: ‡13.18–21: see below‡ 22 Because you have disheartened the upright man with lies when I did not wish him grieved, and have encouraged the wicked man not to turn from his evil conduct and save his life; 23 therefore you shall no longer see false visions and practice divination, but I will rescue my people from your power. Thus you shall know that I am the LORD.

18 Woe to those who sew bands for everyone's wrists and make veils for every size of head so as to entrap their owners. Do you think to entrap the lives of my people, yet keep yourselves alive? 19 You dishonor me before my people with handfuls of barley and crumbs of bread, killing those who should not die and keeping alive those who should not live, lying to my people who willingly hear lies. 20 Therefore thus says the Lord GOD: See! I am coming at those bands of yours in which you entrap men's lives: I will tear them from their arms and set free those you have caught. 21 I will tear off your veils and rescue my people

27 'Son of man, the House of Israel is now saying, "The vision that this man sees concerns the distant future; he is prophesying for times far ahead." 28 Very well, tell them, "The Lord Yahweh says this: There will be no further delay in the fulfilling of any of my words. What I have said shall be done now — declares the Lord Yahweh." '

13 The word of Yahweh was addressed to me as follows, 2 'Son of man, prophesy against the prophets of Israel; prophesy, and say to those who make up prophecies out of their own heads, "Hear what Yahweh says: 3 The Lord Yahweh says this: Disaster is in store for the foolish prophets who follow their own spirit and have seen nothing! 4 Your prophets, Israel, are like ruin-haunting jackals!

5 "You have not ventured into the breach; you have not built up the wall round the House of Israel, to hold fast in battle on the Day of Yahweh. 6 Theirs are futile visions and false predictions, who say: A prophecy from Yahweh, when Yahweh has not sent them; yet they expect their words to come true. 7 Have not the visions you saw been futile, have not the predictions you make been false, although you say: A prophecy of Yahweh, when I have not spoken?

8 "Very well, the Lord Yahweh says this: Because of your futile words and false predictions, I am now against you — declares Lord Yahweh. 9 My hand will be against the prophets who have futile visions and give false predictions; they will not be admitted to the council of my people, their names will not be entered in the roll of the House of Israel, they will not set foot on the soil of Israel; and they will know that I am the Lord Yahweh. 10 This is because they have misled my people by saying Peace! when there is no peace. When my people were repairing a wall, these men came and plastered it over! 11 Tell these plasterers: It will rain hard, it will hail, it will blow a gale, 12 and down will come the wall! Will not people ask you: What has become of the plaster you slapped on it? 13 Well then, the Lord Yahweh says this: I am going to unleash a stormy wind in my fury, torrential rain in my anger, hailstones in my destructive fury, 14 and I shall shatter the wall you plastered and knock it down and lay its foundations bare. It will fall and you will perish under it; then you will know that I am Yahweh."

15 'When I have sated my anger on the wall and those who plastered it, I shall say to you, "The wall is gone, and so are those who plastered over it, 16 the prophets of Israel who prophesy about Jerusalem and have visions of peace for her when there is no peace — declares the Lord Yahweh."

17 'Also, son of man, turn to the women of your people who make up prophecies out of their own heads; prophesy against them. 18 Say, "The Lord Yahweh says this: Disaster is in store for women who sew ribbons round each wrist and make head-cloths for people of all sizes, in their hunt for souls! Are you to hunt the souls of my people and keep your own souls safe? 19 You dishonour me in front of my people for a few handfuls of barley, a few bits of bread, killing those who ought not to die and sparing those who ought not to live, lying to my people who love listening to lies.

20 "Very well, the Lord Yahweh says this: Look, I am now against your ribbons, with which you hunt souls like birds, and I shall tear them off your arms and free those souls whom you hunt like birds. 21 I shall tear your head-

---

13, 3–23: These verses have been transposed according to the following order: 7–8. 10–16. 3–4. 6.9.17. 22–23. 18–21.

people from your hands; they shall no longer be prey in your hands; and you shall know that I am the LORD. 22 Because you have disheartened the righteous falsely, although I have not disheartened them, and you have encouraged the wicked not to turn from their wicked way and save their lives; 23 therefore you shall no longer see false visions or practice divination; I will save my people from your hand. Then you will know that I am the LORD.

14 Certain elders of Israel came to me and sat down before me. 2 And the word of the LORD came to me: 3 Mortal, these men have taken their idols into their hearts, and placed their iniquity as a stumbling block before them; shall I let myself be consulted by them? 4 Therefore speak to them, and say to them, Thus says the Lord GOD: Any of those of the house of Israel who take their idols into their hearts and place their iniquity as a stumbling block before them, and yet come to the prophet — I the LORD will answer those who come with the multitude of their idols, 5 in order that I may take hold of the hearts of the house of Israel, all of whom are estranged from me through their idols.

6 Therefore say to the house of Israel, Thus says the Lord GOD: Repent and turn away from your idols; and turn away your faces from all your abominations. 7 For any of those of the house of Israel, or of the aliens who reside in Israel, who separate themselves from me, taking their idols into their hearts and placing their iniquity as a stumbling block before them, and yet come to a prophet to inquire of me by him, I the LORD will answer them myself. 8 I will set my face against them; I will make them a sign and a byword and cut them off from the midst of my people; and you shall know that I am the LORD.

9 If a prophet is deceived and speaks a word, I, the LORD, have deceived that prophet, and I will stretch out my hand against him, and will destroy him from the midst of my people Israel. 10 And they shall bear their punishment — the punishment of the inquirer and the punishment of the prophet shall be the same — 11 so that the house of Israel may no longer go astray from me, nor defile themselves any more with all their transgressions. Then they shall be my people, and I will be their God, says the Lord GOD.

12 The word of the LORD came to me: 13 Mortal, when a land sins against me by acting faithlessly, and I stretch out my hand against it, and break its staff of bread and send famine upon it, and cut off from it human beings and animals, 14 even if Noah, Daniel,f and Job, these three, were in it, they would save only their own lives by their righteousness, says the Lord GOD. 15 If I send wild animals through the land to ravage it, so that it is made desolate, and no one may pass through because of the animals; 16 even if these three men were in it, as I live, says the Lord GOD, they would save neither sons nor daughters; they alone would be saved, but the land would be desolate. 17 Or if I bring a sword upon that land and say, 'Let a sword pass through the land,' and I cut off human beings and animals from it; 18 though these three men were in it, as I live, says the Lord GOD, they would save neither sons nor daughters, but they alone would be saved. 19 Or if I send a pestilence into that land, and pour out my wrath upon it with blood, to cut off humans and animals from it; 20 even if Noah, Daniel,f and Job were in it, as I live, says the Lord GOD, they would save neither son nor daughter; they would save only their own lives by their righteousness.

veils; I shall rescue my people from your clutches, and you will no longer have it in your power to hunt them. Thus you will know that I am the LORD. 22 With your lying you undermined the righteous, when I meant no hurt; you so strengthened the wicked that they would not abandon their evil ways and save themselves. 23 So never again will you see your false visions or practise divination. I shall rescue my people from your clutches; and thus you will know that I am the LORD.'

14 Some of the elders of Israel visited me, and while they were sitting in my presence 2 this word of the LORD came to me, 3 'O man, these people have set their hearts on their idols and keep their eyes fixed on the sinful things that cause their downfall. Am I to be consulted by such men? 4 Speak to them, therefore, and tell them that this is what the Lord GOD says: If any Israelite, with his heart set on his idols and his eyes fixed on the sinful things that cause his downfall, comes to a prophet, I, the LORD, give him his answer, despite his gross idolatry. 5 My answer will grip the hearts of the Israelites, who through their idols are all estranged from me.

6 'So tell the Israelites that this is what the Lord GOD says: Repent, turn from your idols, turn your backs on all your abominations. 7 If anyone, Israelite or resident alien, renounces me, setting his heart on idols and fixing his eyes on the sinful things that cause his downfall — if such a one comes to consult me through a prophet, I, the LORD, shall give him his answer directly. 8 I shall set my face against him; I shall make him an example and a byword; I shall root him out from among my people. Thus you will know that I am the LORD.

9 'If a prophet is deceived into making a prophecy, it is I, the LORD, who have deceived him; I shall stretch out my hand to destroy him and rid my people Israel of him. 10 Both will be punished; the prophet and the person who consults him alike are guilty. 11 Never again will the Israelites stray from their allegiance, never again defile themselves by their sins; they will be my people, and I shall be their God. This is the word of the Lord GOD.'

12 THIS word of the LORD came to me: 13 'O man, when a country sins by breaking faith with me, I stretch out my hand and cut short its daily bread. I send famine on it and destroy all the inhabitants along with their cattle. 14 Even if these three men, Noah, Daniel, and Job, were there, they would by their righteousness save none but themselves. This is the word of the Lord GOD. 15 If I were to turn wild beasts loose in a country to destroy the population, until it became a waste through which no one would pass for fear of the beasts, 16 and if those three men were there, as I live, says the Lord GOD, they would not be able to save even their own sons and daughters; they would save themselves alone, and the country would become a waste. 17 Or if I were to bring the sword upon that country, commanding it to pass through the land, so that I might destroy people and cattle, 18 and if those three men were there, as I live, says the Lord GOD, they could save neither son nor daughter; they would save themselves alone. 19 Or if I were to send pestilence on that land and pour out my fury on it in bloodshed, destroying people and cattle, 20 and if Noah, Daniel, and Job were there, as I live, says the Lord GOD, they would save neither son nor daughter; they would by their righteousness save none but themselves.

---

f Or, as otherwise read, Danel

from your power, so that they shall no longer be prey to your hands. Thus you shall know that I am the LORD.

‡13.22–23: see above‡

14 When certain elders of Israel came and sat down before me, ²the word of the LORD came to me: ³Son of man, these men have the memory of their idols fresh in their hearts, and they keep the occasion of their sin before them. Why should I allow myself to be consulted by them? ⁴Therefore speak with them, and say to them: Thus says the Lord GOD: If anyone of the house of Israel, holding the memory of his idols in his heart and keeping the occasion of his sin before him, has recourse to a prophet, I, the LORD, will be his answer in person because of his many idols. ⁵Thus would I bring back to their senses the house of Israel, who have become estranged from me through all their idols.

⁶Therefore say to the house of Israel: Thus says the Lord GOD: Return and be converted from your idols; turn yourselves away from all your abominations. ⁷For if anyone of the house of Israel or any alien resident in Israel is estranged from me, and holds the memory of his idols in his heart and keeps the occasion of his sin before him, yet asks a prophet to consult me for him, I, the LORD, will be his answer in person. ⁸I will turn against that man, and make of him an example and a byword. I will cut him off from the midst of my people. Thus you shall know that I am the LORD.

⁹As for the prophet, if he is beguiled into speaking a word, I, the LORD, shall have beguiled that prophet; I will stretch out my hand against him and root him out of my people Israel. ¹⁰Each shall receive punishment for his sin, the inquirer and the prophet shall be punished alike, ¹¹so that the house of Israel may no longer stray from me and may no longer be defiled by all their sins. Thus they shall be my people, and I will be their God, says the Lord GOD.

¹²Thus the word of the LORD came to me: ¹³Son of man, when a land sins against me by breaking faith, I stretch out my hand against it and break its staff of bread, I let famine loose upon it and cut off from it both man and beast; ¹⁴and even if these three men were in it, Noah, Daniel, and Job, they could save only themselves by their virtue, says the Lord GOD. ¹⁵If I were to cause wild beasts to prowl the land, depopulating it so that it became a waste, traversed by none because of the wild beasts, ¹⁶and these three men were in it, as I live, says the Lord GOD, I swear they could save neither sons nor daughters; they alone would be saved, and the land would be a waste. ¹⁷Or if I brought the sword upon this country, commanding the sword to pass through the land cutting off from it man and beast, ¹⁸and these three men were in it, as I live, says the Lord GOD, they would be unable to save either sons or daughters; they alone would be saved. ¹⁹Or if I were to send pestilence into this land, pouring out upon it my bloodthirsty fury, cutting off from it man and beast, ²⁰even if Noah, Daniel, and Job were in it, as I live, says the Lord GOD, I swear that they could save neither son nor daughter; they would save only themselves by their virtue.

cloths to pieces and rescue my people from your clutches; no longer will they be fair game for you to ensnare. Then you will know that I am Yahweh.

²²"For having intimidated with lies the heart of the upright whom I had done nothing to alarm, and for having encouraged the wicked not to give up wicked ways and so be saved, ²³very well, you will have no more futile visions and make no more predictions, for I shall rescue my people from your clutches, and you will know that I am Yahweh." '

14 Next, some elders of Israel visited me and while they were sitting with me, ²the word of Yahweh was addressed to me as follows, ³'Son of man, these men have enshrined their foul idols in their hearts and placed the cause of their sinning right before their eyes. Why should I let myself be consulted by them? ⁴So speak to them; tell them this, "Lord Yahweh says this: Every member of the House of Israel who enshrines his foul idols in his heart and places the cause of his sinning right before his eyes, and who then approaches the prophet, will get this answer from me, Yahweh, as the multiplicity of his idols deserves, ⁵and in this way I hope to win back the hearts of the House of Israel who have all been estranged from me by their foul idols."

⁶'So say to the House of Israel, "The Lord Yahweh says this: Come back, turn away from your foul idols, turn your backs on all your loathsome practices; ⁷for if any member of the House of Israel — or any foreigner living in Israel — deserts me to enshrine his foul idols in his heart and places the cause of his sinning right before his eyes and then approaches a prophet to consult me through him, he will get his answer from me, Yahweh. ⁸I shall set my face against that person; I shall make him an example and a byword; I shall rid my people of him, and you will know that I am Yahweh. ⁹And if the prophet is seduced into saying something, I, Yahweh, shall have seduced that prophet; I shall point my finger at him and rid my people Israel of him. ¹⁰Both will be punished for their guilt; the prophet's punishment will be the same as that of the person who consults him, ¹¹so that the House of Israel will never stray from me again or defile themselves again with these crimes, but be my people and I their God — declares the Lord Yahweh." '

¹²The word of Yahweh was addressed to me:ᵉ ¹³'Son of man, when a country sins against me by being unfaithful and I point my finger at it and destroy its supply of food, inflicting famine on it and denuding it of human and animal, ¹⁴even if the three men, Noah, Danel and Job,ᶠ were living in it, they would save no one but themselves by their uprightness — declares the Lord Yahweh. ¹⁵Were I to unleash wild beasts on that country to rob it of its children and reduce it to a desert which no one would dare to cross because of the animals, ¹⁶even if these three men were living there, as I live — declares the Lord Yahweh — they would not be able to save either son or daughter; they alone would be saved, and the country would become a desert. ¹⁷Were I to bring the sword down on that country and say, "Sword, cross the country!" so as to denude it of human and animal, ¹⁸even if these three men were living there, as I live — declares the Lord Yahweh — they would not be able to save either son or daughter; they alone would be saved. ¹⁹If I were to send the plague on that country and vent my fury on it by bloodshed, so as to denude it of human and animal, ²⁰even if Noah and Danel and Job were living there, as I live — declares the Lord Yahweh — they would be able to save neither son nor daughter, only themselves by their uprightness.

ᵉ**14** cf. 18; 33:10–20, and Dt 24; Jr 31 on individual responsibility.
ᶠ**14** Three celebrated heroes of uprightness. Danel is known from other Near Eastern ancient poetry.

21 For thus says the Lord GOD: How much more when I send upon Jerusalem my four deadly acts of judgment, sword, famine, wild animals, and pestilence, to cut off humans and animals from it! 22 Yet, survivors shall be left in it, sons and daughters who will be brought out; they will come out to you. When you see their ways and their deeds, you will be consoled for the evil that I have brought upon Jerusalem, for all that I have brought upon it. 23 They shall console you, when you see their ways and their deeds; and you shall know that it was not without cause that I did all that I have done in it, says the Lord GOD.

15

The word of the LORD came to me: 2 O mortal, how does the wood of the vine surpass all other wood —
the vine branch that is among the trees of the forest?
3 Is wood taken from it to make anything?
Does one take a peg from it on which to hang any object?
4 It is put in the fire for fuel;
when the fire has consumed both ends of it
and the middle of it is charred,
is it good for anything?
5 When it was whole it was used for nothing;
how much less — when the fire has consumed it,
and it is charred —
can it ever be used for anything!

6 Therefore thus says the Lord GOD: Like the wood of the vine among the trees of the forest, which I have given to the fire for fuel, so I will give up the inhabitants of Jerusalem. 7 I will set my face against them; although they escape from the fire, the fire shall still consume them; and you shall know that I am the LORD, when I set my face against them. 8 And I will make the land desolate, because they have acted faithlessly, says the Lord GOD.

16

The word of the LORD came to me: 2 Mortal, make known to Jerusalem her abominations, 3 and say, Thus says the Lord GOD to Jerusalem: Your origin and your birth were in the land of the Canaanites; your father was an Amorite, and your mother a Hittite. 4 As for your birth, on the day you were born your navel cord was not cut, nor were you washed with water to cleanse you, nor rubbed with salt, nor wrapped in cloths. 5 No eye pitied you, to do any of these things for you out of compassion for you; but you were thrown out in the open field, for you were abhorred on the day you were born.

6 I passed by you, and saw you flailing about in your blood. As you lay in your blood, I said to you, "Live! 7 and grow up*g* like a plant of the field." You grew up and became tall and arrived at full womanhood;*h* your breasts were formed, and your hair had grown; yet you were naked and bare.

8 I passed by you again and looked on you; you were at the age for love. I spread the edge of my cloak over you, and covered your nakedness: I pledged myself to you and entered into a covenant with you, says the Lord GOD, and you became mine. 9 Then I bathed you with water and washed off the blood from you, and anointed you with oil. 10 I clothed you with embroidered cloth and with sandals of fine leather; I bound you in fine linen and covered you with rich fabric.*i* 11 I adorned you with ornaments: I put bracelets on your arms, a chain on your neck, 12 a ring on your nose, earrings in your ears, and a beautiful crown upon your head. 13 You were adorned with gold and silver, while your

21 'The Lord GOD says: How much less hope is there for Jerusalem when I inflict on her these four terrible punishments of mine, sword, famine, wild beasts, and pestilence, to destroy both people and cattle! 22 Yet some will be left in her, some survivors to be brought out, both men and women. Look at them as they come out to you, and see how they have behaved and what they have done. This will be consolation to you for the disaster I have brought on Jerusalem, for all I have inflicted on her. 23 It will bring you consolation when you consider how they have behaved and what they have done; for you will know that it was not without good reason that I dealt thus with her. This is the word of the Lord GOD.'

15

THIS word of the LORD came to me:

2 'O man, how is the vine better than any other tree, than a branch from a tree in the forest?
3 Is wood got from it
useful for making anything?
Can one make it into a peg
and hang something on it?
4 If it is put on the fire for fuel,
if its two ends are burnt by the fire
and the middle is charred,
is it fit for anything useful?
5 Nothing useful could be made from it, even when whole;
how much less is it useful for making anything
when burnt and charred by fire!

6 'The Lord GOD says: As the wood of the vine among all kinds of wood from the forest is useful only for burning, even so I treat the inhabitants of Jerusalem. 7 I have set my face against them. They have escaped from the fire, but fire will burn them up. Thus you will know that I am the LORD when I set my face against them, 8 and make the land a waste because they have broken faith. This is the word of the Lord GOD.'

16

This word of the LORD came to me: 2 'O man, make Jerusalem see her abominable conduct. 3 Tell her that these are the words of the Lord GOD to her: Canaan is the land of your ancestry and your birthplace; your father was an Amorite, your mother a Hittite. 4 This is how you were treated when you were born: at birth your navel-string was not tied, you were not bathed in water and rubbed with oil; no salt was put on you, nor were you wrapped in swaddling clothes. 5 No one cared enough for you to do any of these things, or felt enough compassion; you were thrown out on the bare ground in your own filth on the day you were born. 6 I came by and saw you kicking helplessly as you lay in your blood; I decreed that you should continue to live in your blood. 7 I tended you like an evergreen plant growing in the fields; you throve and grew. You came to full womanhood; your breasts became firm and your hair grew, but you were still quite naked and exposed.

8 'I came by again and saw that you were ripe for love. I spread the skirt of my robe over you and covered your naked body. I plighted my troth and entered into a covenant with you, says the Lord GOD, and you became mine. 9 Then I bathed you with water to wash off the blood; I anointed you with oil. 10 I gave you robes of brocade and sandals of dugong-hide; I fastened a linen girdle round you and dressed you in fine linen. 11 I adorned you with jewellery: bracelets on your wrists, a chain round your neck, 12 a ring in your nose, pendants in your ears, and a splendid crown on your head. 13 You were adorned with gold and silver,

g Gk Syr: Heb *Live! I made you a myriad ornaments*   *h* Cn: Heb *ornament of*   *i* Meaning of Heb uncertain

16:4 **tied:** *prob. rdg, cp. one MS; others* cut.

NEW AMERICAN BIBLE

NEW JERUSALEM BIBLE

21 Thus says the Lord GOD: Even though I send Jerusalem my four cruel punishments, the sword, famine, wild beasts, and pestilence, to cut off from it man and beast, 22 still some survivors shall be left in it who will bring out sons and daughters; when they come out to you, you shall see their conduct and their actions and be consoled regarding the evil I have brought on Jerusalem [all that I have brought upon it]. 23 They shall console you when you see their conduct and actions, for you shall then know that it was not without reason that I did to it what I did, says the Lord GOD.

21 'The Lord Yahweh says this, "Even if I send my four dreadful scourges on Jerusalem — sword, famine, wild beasts and plague — to denude it of human and animal, 22 even so, there will be a remnant left, a few men and women who come through; when they come to you and you see their conduct and actions, you will take comfort in spite of the disaster which I have brought on Jerusalem, in spite of all I have brought on her. 23 They will comfort you, when you see their conduct and actions, and so you will know that I have not done in vain all I have done to her — declares the Lord Yahweh." '

15

Thus the word of the LORD came to me: 2 Son of man, what makes the wood of the vine better than any other wood? That branch among the trees of the forest! 3 Can you use its wood to make anything worthwhile? Can you make even a peg from it, to hang on it any kind of vessel? 4 If you throw it on the fire as fuel and the fire devours both ends and even the middle is scorched, is it still good for anything? 5 Why, even when it was whole it was good for nothing; how much less, when the fire has devoured and scorched it, can it be used for anything! 6 Therefore, thus says the Lord GOD: Like the wood of the vine among the trees of the forest, which I have destined as fuel for the fire, do I make the inhabitants of Jerusalem. 7 I will set my face against them; they have escaped from the fire, but the fire shall devour them. Thus you shall know that I am the LORD, when I turn my face against them. 8 I will make the land a waste, because they have broken faith, says the Lord God.

15

The word of Yahweh was addressed to me as follows:

2 Son of man, how is the wood of the vine better than wood from the branch of a forest tree?
3 Is its wood used for making anything?
Are pegs on which to hang things made from it?
4 There it is, thrown on the fire for fuel.
The fire burns off both ends;
the middle is charred; can it be kept for anything now?
5 While it was intact, you could make nothing with it;
burned and charred, is it any more useful now?
6 So, the Lord Yahweh says this:
As the wood of the vine among the forest trees,
which I have thrown on the fire for fuel,
so shall I treat the inhabitants of Jerusalem.
7 I shall set my face against them.
They have escaped one fire, but fire will devour them yet.
And you will know that I am Yahweh, when I set my face against them.
8 I shall reduce the country to a desert, because of their infidelity —
declares the Lord Yahweh.

16

Thus the word of the LORD came to me: 2 Son of man, make known to Jerusalem her abominations. 3 Thus says the Lord GOD to Jerusalem: By origin and birth you are of the land of Canaan; your father was an Amorite and your mother a Hittite. 4 As for your birth, the day you were born your navel cord was not cut; you were neither washed with water nor anointed, nor were you rubbed with salt, nor swathed in swaddling clothes. 5 No one looked on you with pity or compassion to do any of these things for you. Rather, you were thrown out on the ground as something loathsome, the day you were born.

6 Then I passed by and saw you weltering in your blood. I said to you: Live in your blood 7 and grow like a plant in the field. You grew and developed, you came to the age of puberty; your breasts were formed, your hair had grown, but you were still stark naked. 8 Again I passed by you and saw that you were now old enough for love. So I spread the corner of my cloak over you to cover your nakedness; I swore an oath to you and entered into a covenant with you; you became mine, says the Lord GOD. 9 Then I bathed you with water, washed away your blood, and anointed you with oil. 10 I clothed you with an embroidered gown, put sandals of fine leather on your feet; I gave you a fine linen sash and robes to wear. 11 I adorned you with jewelry: I put bracelets on your arms, a necklace about your neck, 12 a ring in your nose, pendants in your ears, and a glorious diadem upon your head. 13 Thus you were adorned with

16

8 The word of Yahweh was addressed to me as follows, 2 'Son of man, confront Jerusalem with her loathsome practices! 3 Say, "The Lord Yahweh says this: By origin and birth you belong to the land of Canaan. Your father was an Amorite and your mother a Hittite. 4 At birth, the very day you were born, there was no one to cut your navel-string, or wash you in water to clean you, or rub you with salt, or wrap you in swaddling clothes. 5 No one looked at you with pity enough to do any of these things out of sympathy for you. You were exposed in the open fields in your own dirt on the day you were born.

6 "I saw you kicking on the ground in your blood as I was passing, and I said to you as you lay in your blood: Live! 7 and I made you grow like the grass of the fields. You developed, you grew, you reached marriageable age. Your breasts became firm and your hair grew richly, but you were stark naked. 8 Then I saw you as I was passing. Your time had come, the time for love. I spread my cloak over you and covered your nakedness; I gave you my oath, I made a covenant with you — declares the Lord Yahweh — and you became mine. 9 I bathed you in water, I washed the blood off you, I anointed you with oil. 10 I gave you embroidered dresses, fine leather shoes, a linen headband and a cloak of silk. 11 I loaded you with jewels, gave you bracelets for your wrists and a necklace for your throat. 12 I gave you nose-ring and earrings; I put a beautiful diadem on your head. 13 You were loaded with gold and silver and dressed in linen

clothing was of fine linen, rich fabric,*j* and embroidered cloth. You had choice flour and honey and oil for food. You grew exceedingly beautiful, fit to be a queen. 14 Your fame spread among the nations on account of your beauty, for it was perfect because of my splendor that I had bestowed on you, says the Lord GOD.

15 But you trusted in your beauty, and played the whore because of your fame, and lavished your whorings on any passer-by.*k* 16 You took some of your garments, and made for yourself colorful shrines, and on them played the whore; nothing like this has ever been or ever shall be.*j* 17 You also took your beautiful jewels of my gold and my silver that I had given you, and made for yourself male images, and with them played the whore; 18 and you took your embroidered garments to cover them, and set my oil and my incense before them. 19 Also my bread that I gave you — I fed you with choice flour and oil and honey — you set it before them as a pleasing odor; and so it was, says the Lord GOD. 20 You took your sons and your daughters, whom you had borne to me, and these you sacrificed to them to be devoured. As if your whorings were not enough! 21 You slaughtered my children and delivered them up as an offering to them. 22 And in all your abominations and your whorings you did not remember the days of your youth, when you were naked and bare, flailing about in your blood.

23 After all your wickedness (woe, woe to you! says the Lord GOD), 24 you built yourself a platform and made yourself a lofty place in every square; 25 at the head of every street you built your lofty place and prostituted your beauty, offering yourself to every passer-by, and multiplying your whoring. 26 You played the whore with the Egyptians, your lustful neighbors, multiplying your whoring, to provoke me to anger. 27 Therefore I stretched out my hand against you, reduced your rations, and gave you up to the will of your enemies, the daughters of the Philistines, who were ashamed of your lewd behavior. 28 You played the whore with the Assyrians, because you were insatiable; you played the whore with them, and still you were not satisfied. 29 You multiplied your whoring with Chaldea, the land of merchants; and even with this you were not satisfied.

30 How sick is your heart, says the Lord GOD, that you did all these things, the deeds of a brazen whore; 31 building your platform at the head of every street, and making your lofty place in every square! Yet you were not like a whore, because you scorned payment. 32 Adulterous wife, who receives strangers instead of her husband! 33 Gifts are given to all whores; but you gave your gifts to all your lovers, bribing them to come to you from all around for your whorings. 34 So you were different from other women in your whorings: no one solicited you to play the whore; and you gave payment, while no payment was given to you; you were different.

35 Therefore, O whore, hear the word of the LORD: 36 Thus says the Lord GOD, Because your lust was poured out and your nakedness uncovered in your whoring with your lovers, and because of all your abominable idols, and because of the blood of your children that you gave to them, 37 therefore, I will gather all your lovers, with whom you took pleasure, all those you loved and all those you hated; I will gather them against you from all around, and will uncover your nakedness to them, so that they may see all your nakedness. 38 I will judge you as women who commit adultery and shed blood are judged, and bring blood upon you in wrath and jealousy. 39 I will deliver you into their hands, and they shall throw down your platform and break down your lofty places; they shall strip you of your clothes and take your beautiful objects and leave you naked and bare. 40 They shall bring up a mob against you, and they

and clothed with linen, fine linen and brocade. Fine flour and honey and olive oil were your food; you became a great beauty and rose to be a queen. 14 Your beauty was famed throughout the world; it was perfect because of the splendour I bestowed on you. This is the word of the Lord GOD.

15 'Relying on your beauty and exploiting your fame, you played the harlot and offered yourself freely to every passer-by. 16 You used some of your clothes to deck shrines in gay colours and there you committed fornication. 17 You took the splendid gold and silver jewellery that I had given you, and made for yourself male images with which you committed fornication. 18 You covered them with your robes of brocade, and you offered up my oil and my incense to them. 19 The food I had provided for you, the fine flour, the oil, and the honey, you set before them as an offering of soothing odour. This is the word of the Lord GOD.

20-21 'The sons and daughters whom you had borne to me you took and sacrificed to these images as their food. Was this slaughtering of my children, this handing them over and surrendering them to your images, any less a sin than your fornication? 22 With all your abominable fornication you never recalled those early days when you lay quite naked, kicking helplessly in your blood.

23 'Woe betide you! says the Lord GOD. After all the evil you had done 24 you set up a couch for yourself and erected a shrine in every open place. 25 You built your shrines at the top of every street and debased your beauty, offering your body to every passer-by in countless acts of harlotry. 26 You committed fornication with your lustful neighbours, the Egyptians, and provoked me to anger by your repeated harlotry.

27 'I stretched out my hand against you and reduced your territory. I gave you up to the will of your enemies, the Philistine women, who were disgusted by your lewd conduct. 28 Still unsatisfied, you committed fornication with the Assyrians, and still were not satisfied. 29 You committed many acts of fornication in Chaldaea, a land of traders, and even with this you were not satisfied.

30 'How you anger me! says the Lord GOD. You have done all this like the headstrong harlot you are. 31 You have set up your couches at the top of every street and erected your shrines in every open place, but, unlike the common prostitute, you have scorned a fee. 32 You adulterous wife who receives strangers rather than her husband! 33 All prostitutes receive presents; but you give presents to all your lovers, bribing them to come from far and wide to commit fornication with you. 34 When you are so engaged you are the very opposite of those other women: no one runs after you, and you do not receive a fee; you give one!

35 'Listen, you harlot, to the word of the LORD. 36 The Lord GOD says: Because of your brazen excesses, exposing your naked body in fornication with your lovers, because of your abominable idols and the slaughter of the children you have offered to them, 37 I shall assemble all those lovers whom you charmed, all whom you loved and all whom you turned against. I shall gather them in from all around against you; I shall strip you before them, and they will see you altogether naked. 38 I shall bring you to trial for adultery and murder, and I shall give you over to blood spilt in fury and jealousy. 39 When I hand you over to them, they will demolish your couch and pull down your shrine; they will strip off your clothes, take away your splendid jewellery, and leave you stark naked. 40 They will bring up a mob to punish you;

---

j Meaning of Heb uncertain   *k* Heb adds *let it be his*

16:15 **passer-by:** *Heb. has obscure addition.*   16:16 **fornication:** *Heb. has obscure addition.*   16:19 **soothing odour:** *so Syriac; Heb. adds and it was.*

gold and silver; your garments were of fine linen, silk, and embroidered cloth. Fine flour, honey, and oil were your food. You were exceedingly beautiful, with the dignity of a queen. 14 You were renowned among the nations for your beauty, perfect as it was, because of my splendor which I had bestowed on you, says the Lord God.

15 But you were captivated by your own beauty, you used your renown to make yourself a harlot, and you lavished your harlotry on every passer-by, whose own you became. 16 You took some of your gowns and made for yourself gaudy high places, where you played the harlot. . . . 17 You took the splendid gold and silver ornaments that I had given you and made for yourself male images, with which also you played the harlot. 18 You took your embroidered gowns to cover them; my oil and my incense you set before them; 19 the food that I had given you, the fine flour, the oil, and the honey with which I fed you, you set before them as an appeasing odor, says the Lord GOD. 20 The sons and daughters you had borne me you took and offered as sacrifices to be devoured by them! Was it not enough that you had become a harlot? 21 You slaughtered and immolated my children to them, making them pass through fire. 22 And through all your abominations and harlotries you remembered nothing of when you were a girl, stark naked and weltering in your blood.

23 Then after all your evildoing — woe, woe to you! says the Lord GOD — 24 you raised for yourself a platform and a dais in every public place. 25 At every street corner you built a dais for yourself to use your beauty obscenely, spreading your legs for every passer-by, playing the harlot countless times. 26 You played the harlot with the Egyptians, your lustful neighbors, so many times that I was provoked to anger. 27 Therefore I stretched out my hand against you, I diminished your allowance and delivered you over to the will of your enemies, the Philistines, who revolted at your lewd conduct. 28 You also played the harlot with the Assyrians, because you were not satisfied; and after playing the harlot with them, you were still not satisfied. 29 Again and again you played the harlot, now going to Chaldea, the land of the traders; but despite this, you were still not satisfied.

30 How wild your lust! says the Lord GOD, that you did all these things, acting like a shameless prostitute, 31 building your platform at every street corner and erecting your dais in every public place! Yet you were unlike a prostitute, since you disdained payment. 32 The adulterous wife receives, instead of her husband, payment. 33 All harlots receive gifts. But you rather bestowed your gifts on all your lovers, bribing them to come to you from all sides for your harlotry. 34 Thus in your harlotry you were different from all other women. No one sought you out for prostitution. Since you gave payment instead of receiving it, how different you were!

35 Therefore, harlot, hear the word of the LORD! 36 Thus says the Lord GOD: Because you poured out your lust and revealed your nakedness in your harlotry with your lovers and abominable idols, and because you sacrificed the life-blood of your children to them, 37 I will now gather together all your lovers whom you tried to please, whether you loved them or loved them not; I will gather them against you from all sides and expose you naked for them to see. 38 I will inflict on you the sentence of adulteresses and murderesses; I will wreak fury and jealousy upon you. 39 I will hand you over to them to tear down your platform and demolish your dais; they shall strip you of your garments and take away your splendid ornaments, leaving you stark naked. 40 They

and silk and brocade. Your food was the finest flour, honey and oil. You grew more and more beautiful; and you rose to be queen. 14 The fame of your beauty spread through the nations, since it was perfect, because I had clothed you with my own splendour — declares the Lord Yahweh.

15 "But you became infatuated with your own beauty and used your fame to play the whore, lavishing your debauchery on all comers. 16 You took some of your clothes to make for yourself high places bright with colours and there you played the whore. 17 You also took your jewellery, made with my gold and silver which I had given you, and made yourself male images to serve your whorings. 18 You took your embroidered clothes and used these to dress them up, and you offered them my oil and my incense. 19 And the bread I gave you, the finest flour, the oil and honey with which I fed you, you offered them as a pleasing smell.

"What is more — declares the Lord Yahweh — 20 you took the sons and daughters you had borne me and sacrificed them as food to the images. Was not your whoring enough in itself, 21 for you to slaughter my children and hand them over to be burnt in their honour? 22 And in all your loathsome practices and your whorings you never called your early days to mind, when you were stark naked, kicking on the ground in your own blood.

23 "To crown your wickedness — disaster upon you, disaster! declares the Lord Yahweh — 24 you built yourself a mound and made yourself a high place in every open space. 25 At the entry to every alley you made yourself a high place, defiling your beauty and opening your legs to all comers in countless acts of fornication. 26 You have also fornicated with your big-membered neighbours, the Egyptians, provoking my anger with further acts of fornication. 27 So now I have raised my hand against you, I have cut down on your food, I have put you at the mercy of your enemies, the Philistine women, who blush at your lewd behaviour. 28 Still unsatisfied, you prostituted yourself to the Assyrians; you played the whore with them, but were not satisfied even then. 29 You committed further acts of fornication in the country of merchants, with the Chaldaeans, and these did not satisfy you either.

30 "How simple-minded you are! — declares the Lord Yahweh — for although you do all the things that a professional prostitute would, 31 in building a mound and making yourself a high place in every street, you do not act like a proper prostitute because you disdain to take a fee. 32 An adulteress welcomes strangers instead of her husband. 33 All prostitutes accept presents, but you give presents to all your lovers, you bribe them to come from all over the place to fornicate with you! 34 In fornicating, you are the opposite of other women, since no one runs after you to fornicate with you; since you give the fee and do not get one, you are the very opposite!

35 "Very well, whore, hear the word of Yahweh! 36 The Lord Yahweh says this: For having squandered your money and let yourself be seen naked while whoring with your lovers and all the foul idols of your loathsome practices and for giving them your children's blood — 37 for all this, I shall assemble all the lovers to whom you have given pleasure, all the ones you liked and also all the ones you disliked; yes, I shall assemble them round you and strip you naked in front of them, and let them see you naked from head to foot. 38 I shall pass on you the sentence that adulteresses and murderesses receive; I shall hand you over to their jealous fury; 39 I shall hand you over to them; they will destroy your mound and pull down your high place; they will tear off your clothes, take away your jewels and leave you stark naked. 40 Then they will call an assembly of citi-

shall stone you and cut you to pieces with their swords. 41 They shall burn your houses and execute judgments on you in the sight of many women; I will stop you from playing the whore, and you shall also make no more payments. 42 So I will satisfy my fury on you, and my jealousy shall turn away from you; I will be calm, and will be angry no longer. 43 Because you have not remembered the days of your youth, but have enraged me with all these things; therefore, I have returned your deeds upon your head, says the Lord GOD.

Have you not committed lewdness beyond all your abominations? 44 See, everyone who uses proverbs will use this proverb about you, "Like mother, like daughter." 45 You are the daughter of your mother, who loathed her husband and her children; and you are the sister of your sisters, who loathed their husbands and their children. Your mother was a Hittite and your father an Amorite. 46 Your elder sister is Samaria, who lived with her daughters to the north of you; and your younger sister, who lived to the south of you, is Sodom with her daughters. 47 You not only followed their ways, and acted according to their abominations; within a very little time you were more corrupt than they in all your ways. 48 As I live, says the Lord GOD, your sister Sodom and her daughters have not done as you and your daughters have done. 49 This was the guilt of your sister Sodom: she and her daughters had pride, excess of food, and prosperous ease, but did not aid the poor and needy. 50 They were haughty, and did abominable things before me; therefore I removed them when I saw it. 51 Samaria has not committed half your sins; you have committed more abominations than they, and have made your sisters appear righteous by all the abominations that you have committed. 52 Bear your disgrace, you also, for you have brought about for your sisters a more favorable judgment; because of your sins in which you acted more abominably than they, they are more in the right than you. So be ashamed, you also, and bear your disgrace, for you have made your sisters appear righteous.

53 I will restore their fortunes, the fortunes of Sodom and her daughters and the fortunes of Samaria and her daughters, and I will restore your own fortunes along with theirs, 54 in order that you may bear your disgrace and be ashamed of all that you have done, becoming a consolation to them. 55 As for your sisters, Sodom and her daughters shall return to their former state, Samaria and her daughters shall return to their former state, and you and your daughters shall return to your former state. 56 Was not your sister Sodom a byword in your mouth in the day of your pride, 57 before your wickedness was uncovered? Now you are a mockery to the daughters of Aram[l] and all her neighbors, and to the daughters of the Philistines, those all around who despise you. 58 You must bear the penalty of your lewdness and your abominations, says the LORD.

59 Yes, thus says the Lord GOD: I will deal with you as you have done, you who have despised the oath, breaking the covenant; 60 yet I will remember my covenant with you in the days of your youth, and I will establish with you an everlasting covenant. 61 Then you will remember your ways, and be ashamed when I[m] take your sisters, both your elder and your younger, and give them to you as daughters, but not on account of my[n] covenant with you. 62 I will establish my covenant with you, and you shall know that I am the LORD, 63 in order that you may remember and be confounded, and never open your mouth again because of your shame, when I forgive you all that you have done, says the Lord GOD.

they will stone you and hack you to pieces with their swords. 41 They will burn down your houses and execute judgement on you in the sight of many women. I shall put a stop to your harlotry, and never again will you pay a fee to your lovers. 42 Then I shall abate my fury, and my jealousy will turn away from you. I shall be calm and no longer be provoked to anger. 43 You never called to mind the days of your youth, but enraged me with all your doings; I in turn brought retribution on you for your conduct. This is the word of the Lord GOD.

'Did you not commit these obscenities, as well as all your other abominations? 44 Everyone who quotes proverbs will quote this one about you, "Like mother, like daughter." 45 You are a true daughter of a mother who rejected her husband and children. You are a true sister of your sisters who rejected their husbands and children. You are daughters of a Hittite mother and an Amorite father. 46 Your elder sister was Samaria, who lived with her daughters to the north of you; your younger sister was Sodom, who lived with her daughters to the south. 47 Did you not behave as they did and commit the same abominations? Indeed you surpassed them in depraved conduct. 48 As I live, says the Lord GOD, your sister Sodom and her daughters never behaved as you and your daughters have done! 49 This was the iniquity of your sister Sodom: she and her daughters had the pride that goes with food in plenty, comfort, and ease, yet she never helped the poor in their need. 50 They grew haughty and committed what was abominable in my sight, and I swept them away, as you are aware. 51 Nor did Samaria commit half the sins of which you have been guilty; you have committed more abominations than she. All the abominations you have committed have made your sister look innocent. 52 It is you that must bear the humiliation, for your sins have pleaded your sisters' cause; your conduct is so much more abominable than theirs that they appear innocent in comparison. Now you must bear your shame and humiliation and make your sisters look innocent.

53 'I shall restore the fortunes of Sodom and her daughters and of Samaria and her daughters (and I shall restore yours at the same time). 54 When you bring them comfort, you will bear your shame and be disgraced for all you have done. 55 After your sister Sodom and her daughters become what they were of old, and when your sister Samaria and her daughters become what they were of old, then you and your daughters will be restored likewise. 56 Did you not speak contemptuously of your sister Sodom in the days of your pride, 57 before your wickedness was exposed? Even so now you are despised by the daughters of Aram and all those nations around them, and the daughters of Philistia round about who also despise you. 58 You must bear the consequences of your lewd and abominable conduct. This is the word of the LORD.

59 'The Lord GOD says: I shall treat you as you have deserved, because you violated an oath and made light of a covenant. 60 But I shall call to mind the covenant I made with you when you were young, and I shall establish with you a covenant which will last for ever. 61 You will remember your past conduct and feel ashamed when you receive your sisters, the elder and the younger. I shall give them to you as daughters, though they are not included in my covenant with you. 62 Thus I shall establish my covenant with you, and you will know that I am the LORD. 63 You will remember, and will be so ashamed and humiliated that you will never open your mouth again, once I have pardoned you for all you have done. This is the word of the Lord GOD.'

16:47 **Indeed . . . conduct:** *prob. mng; Heb. obscure.*
16:57 **Aram:** *so some MSS; others* Edom.

---

[l] Another reading is *Edom*   [m] Syr: Heb *you*   [n] Heb lacks *my*

shall lead an assembly against you to stone you and hack you with their swords. 41 They shall burn your apartments with fire and inflict punishments on you while many women look on. Thus I will put an end to your harlotry, and you shall never again give payment. 42 When I have wreaked my fury upon you I will cease to be jealous of you, I will be quiet and no longer vexed. 43 Because you did not remember what happened when you were a girl, but enraged me with all these things, therefore in return I am bringing down your conduct upon your head, says the Lord GOD. For did you not add lewdness to the rest of your abominable deeds?

44 See, everyone who is fond of proverbs will say of you, 'Like mother, like daughter.' 45 Yes, you are the true daughter of the mother who spurned her husband and children, and you are a true sister to those who spurned their husbands and children — your mother was a Hittite and your father an Amorite. 46 Your elder sister was Samaria with her daughters, living to the north of you; and your younger sister, living to the south of you, was Sodom with her daughters. 47 Yet not only in their ways did you walk, and act as abominably as they did; in a very short time you became more corrupt in all your ways than they. 48 As I live, says the Lord GOD, I swear that your sister Sodom, with her daughters, has not done as you and your daughters have done! 49 And look at the guilt of your sister Sodom: she and her daughters were proud, sated with food, complacent in their prosperity, and they gave no help to the poor and needy. 50 Rather, they became haughty and committed abominable crimes in my presence; then, as you have seen, I removed them. 51 Samaria did not commit half your sins! You have done more abominable things than they, and have even made your sisters appear just, with all the abominable deeds you have done. 52 You, then, bear your shame; you are an argument in favor of your sisters! In view of your sinful deeds, more abominable than theirs, they appear just in comparison with you. Blush for shame, and bear the shame of having made your sisters appear just.

53 I will restore their fortunes, the fortune of Sodom and her daughters and of Samaria and her daughters [and I will restore your fortune along with them], 54 that you may bear your shame and be disgraced for all the comfort you brought them. 55 Yes, your sisters, Sodom and her daughters, Samaria and her daughters, shall return to their former state [you and your daughters shall return to your former state]. 56 Was not your sister Sodom kept in bad repute by you while you felt proud of yourself, 57 before your wickedness became evident? Now you are like her, reproached by the Edomites and all your neighbors, despised on all sides by the Philistines. 58 The penalty of your lewdness and your abominations — you must bear it all, says the LORD.

59 For thus speaks the Lord GOD: I will deal with you according to what you have done, you who despised your oath, breaking a covenant. 60 Yet I will remember the covenant I made with you when you were a girl, and I will set up an everlasting covenant with you. 61 Then you shall remember your conduct and be ashamed when I take your sisters, those older and younger than you, and give them to you as daughters, even though I am not bound by my covenant with you. 62 For I will re-establish my covenant with you, that you may know that I am the LORD, 63 that you may remember and be covered with confusion, and that you may be utterly silenced for shame when I pardon you for all you have done, says the Lord GOD.

zens to deal with you, who will stone you to death and hack you to pieces with their swords, 41 and burn down your premises and execute justice on you, while many other women look on; and I shall put an end to your whoring: no more paid lovers for you! 42 Once my fury is exhausted with you, then my jealousy will leave you; I shall be calm and not angry any more. 43 Since you never called to mind your early days and have done nothing but provoke me, now I in my turn shall bring your conduct down on your own head — declares the Lord Yahweh!

"Have you not added this lewd behaviour to your other loathsome practices? 44 So now all dealers in proverbs will apply this one to you: Like mother, like daughter. 45 Yes; you are a true daughter of your mother, who hated her husband and her children; you are a true sister of your sisters, who hated their husbands and their children. Your mother was a Hittite and your father an Amorite. 46 Your elder sister is Samaria, who lives to the north of you with her daughters. Your younger sister is Sodom, who lives to the south of you with her daughters. 47 You never failed to imitate their behaviour and copy their loathsome practices, and soon your behaviour was more corrupt than theirs was. 48 As I live — declares the Lord Yahweh — your sister Sodom and her daughters never did what you and your daughters have done. 49 The crime of your sister Sodom was pride, gluttony, calm complacency; such were hers and her daughters' crimes. They never helped the poor and needy; 50 they were proud, and engaged in loathsome practices before me, and so I swept them away as you have seen. 51 And yet Samaria never committed half the crimes that you have.

"You have done more loathsome things than they have. By all your loathsome practices you have made your sisters seem innocent, 52 and now you bear the shame of which you have freed your sisters; since the sins which you have committed are more revolting than theirs, they are more upright than you are. So now, bear the disgrace and shame of having put your sisters in the right.

53 "I shall restore their fortunes, I shall restore Sodom and her daughters, I shall restore Samaria and her daughters, and then I shall restore your fortune with theirs, 54 so that you can bear your shame and disgrace for all you have done, and so console them. 55 When your sisters, Sodom and her daughters, are restored to what they were, and Samaria and her daughters are restored to what they were, then you too and your daughters will be restored to what you were. 56 Did you not gloat over your sister Sodom when you were so proud, 57 before you were stripped naked? Like her, you are now the laughing-stock of the women of Edom, of all the women round, of the women of Philistia, who pour out their contempt on you. 58 You have brought this on yourself, with your lewdness and your loathsome practices — declares the Lord Yahweh.

59 "For the Lord Yahweh says this: I shall treat you as you have deserved for making light of an oath and breaking a covenant, 60 but I shall remember my covenant with you when you were a girl and shall conclude a covenant with you that will last for ever. 61 And you for your part will remember your behaviour and feel ashamed of it when you receive your elder and younger sisters and I make them your daughters, although this is not included in my covenant with you. 62 I shall renew my covenant with you; and you will know that I am Yahweh, 63 and so remember and feel ashamed and in your confusion be reduced to silence, when I forgive you for everything you have done — declares the Lord Yahweh."'

NEW REVISED STANDARD VERSION

17 The word of the LORD came to me: 2 O mortal, propound a riddle, and speak an allegory to the house of Israel. 3 Say: Thus says the Lord GOD:

A great eagle, with great wings and long pinions,
  rich in plumage of many colors,
    came to the Lebanon.
He took the top of the cedar,
4 broke off its topmost shoot;
He carried it to a land of trade,
  set it in a city of merchants.
5 Then he took a seed from the land,
  placed it in fertile soil;
A plant*o* by abundant waters,
  he set it like a willow twig.
6 It sprouted and became a vine
  spreading out, but low;
Its branches turned toward him,
  its roots remained where it stood.
So it became a vine;
  it brought forth branches,
  put forth foliage.

7 There was another great eagle,
  with great wings and much plumage.
And see! This vine stretched out
  its roots toward him;
It shot out its branches toward him,
  so that he might water it.
From the bed where it was planted
8 it was transplanted
to good soil by abundant waters,
  so that it might produce branches
  and bear fruit
  and become a noble vine.
9 Say: Thus says the Lord GOD:
  Will it prosper?
Will he not pull up its roots,
  cause its fruit to rot*o* and wither,
  its fresh sprouting leaves to fade?
No strong arm or mighty army will be needed
  to pull it from its roots.
10 When it is transplanted, will it thrive?
When the east wind strikes it,
  will it not utterly wither,
  wither on the bed where it grew?

11 Then the word of the LORD came to me: 12 Say now to the rebellious house: Do you not know what these things mean? Tell them: The king of Babylon came to Jerusalem, took its king and its officials, and brought them back with him to Babylon. 13 He took one of the royal offspring and made a covenant with him, putting him under oath (he had taken away the chief men of the land), 14 so that the kingdom might be humble and not lift itself up, and that by keeping his covenant it might stand. 15 But he rebelled against him by sending ambassadors to Egypt, in order that they might give him horses and a large army. Will he succeed? Can one escape who does such things? Can he break the covenant and yet escape? 16 As I live, says the Lord GOD, surely in the place where the king resides who made him king, whose oath he despised, and whose covenant with him he broke—in Babylon he shall die. 17 Pharaoh with his mighty army and great company will not help him in war, when ramps are cast up and siege walls built to cut off many lives. 18 Because he despised the oath and broke the covenant, because he gave his hand and yet did all these things, he shall not escape. 19 Therefore thus says the Lord

*o*Meaning of Heb uncertain

REVISED ENGLISH BIBLE

17 This word of the LORD came to me: 2 'O man, pose this riddle, expound this parable to the Israelites. 3 Tell them that these are the words of the Lord GOD:

A great eagle
with broad wings and long pinions,
in full plumage, richly patterned,
came to Lebanon.
He took the very top of a cedar tree,
4 plucked its highest twig;
he carried it off to a land of traders,
and planted it in a city of merchants.
5 Then he took a native seed
and put it in a prepared plot;
he set it like a willow,
a shoot beside abundant water.
6 It sprouted and became a vine,
sprawling low along the ground
and bending its boughs towards him
with its roots growing beneath him.
So it became a vine; it branched out
and sent forth shoots.

7 'But there was another great eagle
with broad wings and thick plumage;
and this vine gave its roots
a twist towards him;
from the bed where it was planted, seeking drink,
it pushed out its trailing boughs towards him,
8 though it had been set
in good ground beside abundant water
that it might branch out and be fruitful,
and become a noble vine.

9 'Tell them that the Lord GOD says:

Will such a vine flourish?
Will not its roots be torn up
and its fruit stripped off,
and all its freshly sprouted leaves wither,
until it is uprooted and carried away
with little effort and a small force?
10 If it is transplanted, will it flourish?
Will it not be utterly shrivelled,
as though by the touch of the east wind,
on the bed where it ought to sprout?'

11 This word of the LORD came to me: 12 'Say to that rebellious people: Have you no idea what all this means? The king of Babylon came to Jerusalem, took its king and those in high office, and brought them back with him to Babylon. 13 He chose a prince of the royal line and made a treaty with him, putting him on his oath. He carried away the chief men of the country, 14 so that it should become a humble kingdom, submissive, ready to observe the treaty and keep it in force. 15 But the prince rebelled against him and sent envoys to Egypt with a request for horses and a large force of troops. Will such a man be successful? Will he escape destruction if he acts in this way? Can he violate a treaty and escape unpunished? 16 As I live, says the Lord GOD, I swear that he will die in Babylon, in the land of the king who put him on the throne, the king whose oath he disregarded, whose treaty he violated. 17 No large army will come from Pharaoh, no great force to be a protection for him in battle, when siege-ramps are thrown up and towers are built for the destruction of many. 18 Because he violated a treaty and disregarded his oath, because he submitted, and yet did all these things, he will not escape.

17:7 **another:** *so Gk; Heb.* one.

17 Thus the word of the LORD came to me: 2 Son of man, propose a riddle, and speak this proverb to the house of Israel: 3 Thus speaks the Lord GOD:

The great eagle, with great wings, with
long pinions,
with thick plumage, many-hued, came
to Lebanon.
He took the crest of the cedar,
4 tearing off its topmost branch,
And brought it to a land of tradesmen,
set it in a city of merchants.
5 Then he took some seed of the land,
and planted it in a seedbed;
A shoot by plentiful waters,
like a willow he placed it,
6 To sprout and grow up a vine,
dense and low-lying,
Its branches turned toward him,
its roots lying under him.
Thus it became a vine, produced branches
and put forth shoots.
7 But there was another great eagle,
great of wing, rich in plumage;
To him this vine bent its roots,
sent out its branches,
That he might water it more freely
than the bed where it was planted.
8 In a fertile field by plentiful waters it was planted,
to grow branches, bear fruit,
and become a majestic vine.

9 Say: Thus says the Lord GOD: Can it prosper? Will he not rather tear it out by the roots and strip off its fruit, so that all its green growth will wither when he pulls it up by the roots? [No need of a mighty arm or many people to do this.] 10 True, it is planted, but will it prosper? Will it not rather wither, when touched by the east wind, in the bed where it grew?

11 Thus the word of the LORD came to me: 12 Son of man, say now to the rebellious house: Do you not understand what this means? It is this: The king of Babylon came to Jerusalem and took away its king and princes with him to Babylon. 13 Then he selected a man of the royal line with whom he made a covenant, binding him under oath, while removing the nobles of the land, 14 so that the kingdom would remain a modest one, without aspirations, and would keep his covenant and obey him. 15 But this man rebelled against him, sending envoys to Egypt to obtain horses and a great army. Can he prosper? Can he who does such things escape? Can he break a covenant and still go free? 16 As I live, says the Lord GOD, in the home of the king who set him up to rule, whose oath he spurned, whose covenant with him he broke, there in Babylon I swear he shall die! 17 When ramps are cast up and siege towers are built for the destruction of many lives, he shall not be saved in the conflict by Pharaoh with a great army and numerous troops. 18 He spurned his oath, breaking his covenant. Though he gave his hand in pledge, he did all these things. He shall not escape!

17 The word of Yahweh was addressed to me as follows, 2 'Son of man, put a riddle, propound a parable to the House of Israel. 3 Say, "The Lord Yahweh says this:

A great eagle with great wings,
long-pinioned,
rich with many-coloured plumage,
came to the Lebanon.
4 He took the top of the cedar tree,
he plucked off the top branch,
he carried it off to the country of merchants
and set it down in a city of shopkeepers.
5 Next, he took one of the country's seeds
and put it in a fertile field;
by the side of a generous stream,
like a willow tree, he placed it.
6 It grew and became a fruitful vine
of modest size,
grew up towards the eagle,
its roots grew downwards.
So it became a vine,
branching out and sprouting new shoots.
7 But there was another great eagle
with great wings and thick plumage.
And now the vine twisted its roots towards him
and stretched its branches towards him,
for him to water it
away from the bed where it was planted.
8 It was in a fertile field,
by the side of a wide stream
that the vine had been planted,
to branch out and bear fruit
and become a noble vine."

9 Say, "The Lord Yahweh says this:
Will it succeed?
Will the eagle not tear out its roots
and strip off its fruit,
so that all the new leaves it puts out will wither,
and no great strength is needed nor many people
to pull it up by the roots?
10 Planted it may be — will it succeed?
Will it not shrivel up when the east wind blows?
It will wither in the bed where it was growing!" '

11 The word of Yahweh was addressed to me as follows: 12 'Say to that tribe of rebels, "Do you not know what this means?" Say this, 'Look, the king of Babylon came to Jerusalem; he carried away the king and the princes, and took them to his home in Babylon. 13 He took a member of the royal family and made a treaty with him, forcing him to swear loyalty, having already deported the leading men of the country, 14 so that the kingdom would remain modest and without ambitions, and would keep and honour his treaty. 15 But the prince rebelled against him and sent envoys to Egypt to procure himself horses and a large number of troops. Will he succeed? Will a man who has done this go unpunished? Can he break a treaty and go unpunished? 16 As I live, I swear it — declares the Lord Yahweh — in Babylon, in the country of the king who put him on the throne, whose oath he has disregarded and whose treaty he has broken, there he will die. 17 Despite the pharaoh's great army and hordes of men, he will not be able to save him by fighting, however many earthworks are raised, however many trenches dug to the loss of many lives. 18 He has disregarded the oath by breaking the treaty to which he had pledged himself and, having done all this, will not go unpunished.

GOD: As I live, I will surely return upon his head my oath that he despised, and my covenant that he broke. 20 I will spread my net over him, and he shall be caught in my snare; I will bring him to Babylon and enter into judgment with him there for the treason he has committed against me. 21 All the pick*p* of his troops shall fall by the sword, and the survivors shall be scattered to every wind; and you shall know that I, the LORD, have spoken.

22 Thus says the Lord GOD:

I myself will take a sprig
from the lofty top of a cedar;
I will set it out.
I will break off a tender one
from the topmost of its young twigs;
I myself will plant it
on a high and lofty mountain.
23 On the mountain height of Israel
I will plant it,
in order that it may produce boughs and bear
fruit,
and become a noble cedar.
Under it every kind of bird will live;
in the shade of its branches will nest
winged creatures of every kind.
24 All the trees of the field shall know
that I am the LORD.
I bring low the high tree,
I make high the low tree;
I dry up the green tree
and make the dry tree flourish.
I the LORD have spoken;
I will accomplish it.

18 The word of the LORD came to me: 2 What do you mean by repeating this proverb concerning the land of Israel, "The parents have eaten sour grapes, and the children's teeth are set on edge"? 3 As I live, says the Lord GOD, this proverb shall no more be used by you in Israel. 4 Know that all lives are mine; the life of the parent as well as the life of the child is mine: it is only the person who sins that shall die.

5 If a man is righteous and does what is lawful and right — 6 if he does not eat upon the mountains or lift up his eyes to the idols of the house of Israel, does not defile his neighbor's wife or approach a woman during her menstrual period, 7 does not oppress anyone, but restores to the debtor his pledge, commits no robbery, gives his bread to the hungry and covers the naked with a garment, 8 does not take advance or accrued interest, withholds his hand from iniquity, executes true justice between contending parties, 9 follows my statutes, and is careful to observe my ordinances, acting faithfully — such a one is righteous; he shall surely live, says the Lord GOD.

10 If he has a son who is violent, a shedder of blood, 11 who does any of these things (though his father*q* does none of them), who eats upon the mountains, defiles his neighbor's wife, 12 oppresses the poor and needy, commits robbery, does not restore the pledge, lifts up his eyes to the idols, commits abomination, 13 takes advance or accrued interest; shall he then live? He shall not. He has done all these abominable things; he shall surely die; his blood shall be upon himself.

14 But if this man has a son who sees all the sins that his father has done, considers, and does not do likewise, 15 who does not eat upon the mountains or lift up his eyes to the idols of the house of Israel, does not defile his neighbor's wife, 16 does not wrong anyone, exacts no pledge,

19 'The Lord GOD says: As I live, he has made light of the oath sworn in my name and has violated the covenant he made with me. For this I shall bring retribution upon him. 20 Because he has broken faith with me I shall throw my net over him, and he will be caught in the meshes; I shall carry him to Babylon and bring him to judgement there. 21 The picked troops in all his squadrons will fall by the sword; those who are left will be scattered to all the winds. Thus you will know that it is I, the LORD, who have spoken.

22 'The Lord GOD says:

I, too, shall take a slip
from the lofty crown of the cedar
and set it in the soil;
I shall pluck a tender shoot from the topmost
branch
and plant it on a high and lofty mountain,
23 the highest mountain in Israel.
It will put out branches, bear its fruit,
and become a noble cedar.
Birds of every kind will roost under it,
perching in the shelter of its boughs.
24 All the trees of the countryside will know
that it is I, the LORD,
who bring low the tall tree
and raise the lowly tree high,
who shrivel up the green tree
and make the shrivelled tree put forth buds.
I, the LORD, have spoken; I shall do it.'

18 THIS word of the LORD came to me: 2 'What do you all mean by repeating this proverb in the land of Israel:

Parents eat sour grapes,
and their children's teeth are set on edge?

3 'As I live, says the Lord GOD, this proverb will never again be used by you in Israel. 4 Every living soul belongs to me; parent and child alike are mine. It is the person who sins that will die.

5 'Consider the man who is righteous and does what is just and right. 6 He never feasts at mountain shrines, never looks up to idols worshipped in Israel, never dishonours another man's wife, never approaches a menstruous woman; 7 he oppresses no one, he returns the debtor's pledge, he never commits robbery; he gives his food to the hungry and clothes to those who have none. 8 He never lends either at discount or at interest, but shuns injustice and deals fairly between one person and another. 9 He conforms to my statutes and loyally observes my laws. Such a one is righteous: he will live, says the Lord GOD.

10 'He may have a son who is given to violence and bloodshed, one who turns his back on these commandments; 11 obeying none of them, he feasts at mountain shrines, dishonours another man's wife, 12 oppresses the poor in their need; he commits robbery, he does not return the debtor's pledge, he looks up to idols, and joins in abominable rites; 13 he lends both at discount and at interest. Such a one will not live; because he has committed all these abominations he must die. His blood be on his own head!

14 'This person in turn may have a son who sees all his father's sins, but in spite of seeing them commits none of them. 15 He never feasts at mountain shrines, never looks up to the idols worshipped in Israel, never dishonours another man's wife, 16 oppresses no one, takes no pledge, does not

18:7 **the debtor's pledge:** *so Gk; Heb. unintelligible.* 18:10 **who turns . . . commandments:** *prob. rdg; Heb. unintelligible.*

---

p Another reading is *fugitives*   *q* Heb *he*

NEW AMERICAN BIBLE

19 Therefore say: Thus says the Lord GOD: As I live, my oath which he spurned, my covenant which he broke, I swear to bring down upon his head. 20 I will spread my net over him, and he shall be taken in my snare. I will bring him to Babylon and enter into judgment with him there over his breaking faith with me. 21 All the crack troops among his forces shall fall by the sword, and the survivors shall be scattered in every direction. Thus you shall know that I, the LORD, have spoken.

22 Therefore say: Thus says the Lord GOD:

I, too, will take from the crest of the cedar,
from its topmost branches tear off a
tender shoot,
And plant it on a high and lofty mountain;
23 on the mountain heights of Israel I will plant it.
It shall put forth branches and bear fruit,
and become a majestic cedar.
Birds of every kind shall dwell beneath it,
every winged thing in the shade of its boughs.
24 And all the trees of the field shall know
that I, the LORD,
Bring low the high tree,
lift high the lowly tree,
Wither up the green tree,
and make the withered tree bloom.

As I, the LORD, have spoken, so will I do.

18 Thus the word of the LORD came to me: Son of man, 2 what is the meaning of this proverb that you recite in the land of Israel:

"Fathers have eaten green grapes,
thus their children's teeth are on edge"?

3 As I live, says the Lord GOD: I swear that there shall no longer be anyone among you who will repeat this proverb in Israel. 4 For all lives are mine; the life of the father is like the life of the son, both are mine; only the one who sins shall die.

5 If a man is virtuous — if he does what is right and just, 6 if he does not eat on the mountains, nor raise his eyes to the idols of the house of Israel; if he does not defile his neighbor's wife, nor have relations with a woman in her menstrual period; 7 if he oppresses no one, gives back the pledge received for a debt, commits no robbery; if he gives food to the hungry and clothes the naked; 8 if he does not lend at interest nor exact usury; if he holds off from evildoing, judges fairly between a man and his opponent; 9 if he lives by my statutes and is careful to observe my ordinances, that man is virtuous — he shall surely live, says the Lord GOD.

10 But if he begets a son who is a thief, a murderer, or who does any of these things 11 (though the father does none of them), a son who eats on the mountains, defiles the wife of his neighbor, 12 oppresses the poor and needy, commits robbery, does not give back a pledge, raises his eyes to idols, does abominable things, 13 lends at interest and exacts usury — this son certainly shall not live. Because he practiced all these abominations, he shall surely die; his death shall be his own fault.

14 On the other hand, if a man begets a son who, seeing all the sins his father commits, yet fears and does not imitate him; 15 a son who does not eat on the mountains, or raise his eyes to the idols of the house of Israel, or defile his neighbor's wife; 16 who does not oppress anyone, or exact a

NEW JERUSALEM BIBLE

19 "So, the Lord Yahweh says this: As I live, I swear it: my oath which he has disregarded, my treaty which he has broken, I shall make them both recoil on his own head. 20 I shall throw my net over him, he will be caught in my mesh; I shall take him to Babylon[h] and punish him there for being unfaithful to me. 21 All the pick of all his troops will fall by the sword, and the survivors be scattered to all the winds. And you will know that I, Yahweh, have spoken.

22 "The Lord Yahweh says this:

From the top of the tall cedar tree,
from the highest branch I shall take a shoot
and plant it myself on a high and lofty mountain.
23 I shall plant it on the highest mountain in Israel.
It will put out branches and bear fruit
and grow into a noble cedar tree.
Every kind of bird will live beneath it,
every kind of winged creature will rest in the shade
of its branches.
24 And all the trees of the countryside will know that
I, Yahweh, am the one
who lays the tall tree low and raises the low tree
high,
who makes the green tree wither and makes the
withered bear fruit.
I, Yahweh, have spoken, and I will do it.'"

18 The word of Yahweh was addressed to me as follows, 2 'Why do you keep repeating this proverb in the land of Israel:

The parents have eaten unripe grapes;
and the children's teeth are set on edge?[i]

3 'As I live — declares the Lord Yahweh — you will have no further cause to repeat this proverb in Israel. 4 Look, all life belongs to me; the father's life and the son's life, both alike belong to me. The one who has sinned is the one to die.

5 'But if a man is upright, his actions law-abiding and upright, 6 and he does not eat on the mountains or raise his eyes to the foul idols of the House of Israel, does not defile his neighbour's wife or touch a woman during her periods, 7 oppresses no one, returns the pledge on a debt, does not rob, gives his own food to the hungry, his clothes to those who lack clothing, 8 does not lend for profit, does not charge interest, abstains from evil, gives honest judgement between one person and another, 9 keeps my laws and sincerely respects my judgements — someone like this is truly upright and will live — declares the Lord Yahweh.

10 'But if he has a son prone to violence and bloodshed, who commits one of these misdeeds — 11 even though the father never has — a son who dares to eat on the mountains, who defiles his neighbour's wife, 12 who oppresses the poor and needy, robs, fails to return pledges, raises his eyes to foul idols, engages in loathsome practices, 13 lends for profit, or charges interest, such a person will by no means live; having committed all these appalling crimes he will die, and his blood be on his own head.

14 'But if he in turn has a son who, in spite of seeing all the sins that his father has committed, does not imitate him, 15 does not eat on the mountains or raise his eyes to the foul idols of the House of Israel, does not defile his neighbour's wife, 16 oppresses no one, takes no pledges, does not rob,

h **17** = 12:13.   *i* **18** // Jr 31:29, cf. Ezk 14:12.

NEW REVISED STANDARD VERSION	REVISED ENGLISH BIBLE

commits no robbery, but gives his bread to the hungry and covers the naked with a garment, 17 withholds his hand from iniquity,r takes no advance or accrued interest, observes my ordinances, and follows my statutes; he shall not die for his father's iniquity; he shall surely live. 18 As for his father, because he practiced extortion, robbed his brother, and did what is not good among his people, he dies for his iniquity.

19 Yet you say, "Why should not the son suffer for the iniquity of the father?" When the son has done what is lawful and right, and has been careful to observe all my statutes, he shall surely live. 20 The person who sins shall die. A child shall not suffer for the iniquity of a parent, nor a parent suffer for the iniquity of a child; the righteousness of the righteous shall be his own, and the wickedness of the wicked shall be his own.

21 But if the wicked turn away from all their sins that they have committed and keep all my statutes and do what is lawful and right, they shall surely live; they shall not die. 22 None of the transgressions that they have committed shall be remembered against them; for the righteousness that they have done they shall live. 23 Have I any pleasure in the death of the wicked, says the Lord GOD, and not rather that they should turn from their ways and live? 24 But when the righteous turn away from their righteousness and commit iniquity and do the same abominable things that the wicked do, shall they live? None of the righteous deeds that they have done shall be remembered; for the treachery of which they are guilty and the sin they have committed, they shall die.

25 Yet you say, "The way of the Lord is unfair." Hear now, O house of Israel: Is my way unfair? Is it not your ways that are unfair? 26 When the righteous turn away from their righteousness and commit iniquity, they shall die for it; for the iniquity that they have committed they shall die. 27 Again, when the wicked turn away from the wickedness they have committed and do what is lawful and right, they shall save their life. 28 Because they considered and turned away from all the transgressions that they had committed, they shall surely live; they shall not die. 29 Yet the house of Israel says, "The way of the Lord is unfair." O house of Israel, are my ways unfair? Is it not your ways that are unfair?

30 Therefore I will judge you, O house of Israel, all of you according to your ways, says the Lord GOD. Repent and turn from all your transgressions; otherwise iniquity will be your ruin.s 31 Cast away from you all the transgressions that you have committed against me, and get yourselves a new heart and a new spirit! Why will you die, O house of Israel? 32 For I have no pleasure in the death of anyone, says the Lord GOD. Turn, then, and live.

19 As for you, raise up a lamentation for the princes of Israel, 2 and say:

What a lioness was your mother
   among lions!
She lay down among young lions,
   rearing her cubs.
3 She raised up one of her cubs;
   he became a young lion,
and he learned to catch prey;
   he devoured humans.
4 The nations sounded an alarm against him;
   he was caught in their pit;
and they brought him with hooks
   to the land of Egypt.

---

rob; he gives his food to the hungry and clothes to those who have none; 17 he shuns injustice and never lends either at discount or at interest. He keeps my laws and conforms to my statutes. Such a one is not to die for his father's wrongdoing; he will live.

18 'If his father has been guilty of oppression and robbery and lived an evil life in the community, and died because of his iniquity, 19 you may ask, "Why is the son not punished for his father's iniquity?" Because he has always done what is just and right and has been careful to obey all my laws, he will live. 20 It is the person who sins that will die; a son will not bear responsibility for his father's guilt, nor a father for his son's. The righteous person will have his own righteousness placed to his account, and the wicked person his own wickedness.

21 'If someone who is wicked renounces all his sinful ways and keeps all my laws, doing what is just and right, he will live; he will not die. 22 None of the offences he has committed will be remembered against him; because of his righteous conduct he will live. 23 Have I any desire for the death of a wicked person? says the Lord GOD. Is not my desire rather that he should mend his ways and live?

24 'If someone who is righteous turns from his righteous ways and commits every kind of abomination that the wicked practise, is he to do this and live? No, none of his former righteousness will be remembered in his favour; because he has been faithless and has sinned, he must die.

25 'You say that the Lord acts without principle? Listen, you Israelites! It is not I who act without principle; it is you. 26 If a righteous man turns from his righteousness, takes to evil ways, and dies, it is because of these evil ways that he dies. 27 Again, if a wicked man gives up his wicked ways and does what is just and right, he preserves his life; 28 he has seen his offences and turned his back on them all, and so he will not die; he will live. 29 "The Lord acts without principle," say the Israelites. No, it is you, Israel, that acts without principle, not I.

30 'Therefore I shall judge every one of you Israelites on his record, says the Lord GOD. Repent, renounce all your offences, or your iniquity will be your downfall. 31 Throw off the load of your past misdeeds; get yourselves a new heart and a new spirit. Why should you Israelites die? 32 I have no desire for the death of anyone. This is the word of the Lord GOD.

19 'Raise a dirge over the rulers of Israel 2 and say:

What a lioness was your mother
   among the lions!
She made her lair among the young lions
   and reared her cubs.
3 One of her cubs she singled out;
   he grew into a young lion,
he learnt to tear his prey,
   he devoured men.
4 Then the nations raised a shout at him;
   he was caught in their pit,
and they dragged him off
   with hooks to Egypt.

---

r Gk: Heb *the poor*   s Or *so that they shall not be a stumbling block of iniquity to you*

18:17 **injustice:** *so Gk; Heb.* the unfortunate.   18:18 **robbery:** *so Gk; Heb.* robbery of a brother.   18:32 **the Lord GOD:** *so Gk; Heb. adds* and bring back and live.

pledge, or commit robbery; who gives his food to the hungry and clothes the naked; 17 who holds off from evildoing, accepts no interest or usury, but keeps my ordinances and lives by my statutes — this one shall not die for the sins of his father, but shall surely live. 18 Only the father, since he violated rights, and robbed, and did what was not good among his people, shall in truth die for his sins. 19 You ask: "Why is not the son charged with the guilt of his father?" Because the son has done what is right and just, and has been careful to observe all my statutes, he shall surely live. 20 Only the one who sins shall die. The son shall not be charged with the guilt of his father, nor shall the father be charged with the guilt of his son. The virtuous man's virtue shall be his own, as the wicked man's wickedness shall be his.

21 But if the wicked man turns away from all the sins he committed, if he keeps all my statutes and does what is right and just, he shall surely live, he shall not die. 22 None of the crimes he committed shall be remembered against him; he shall live because of the virtue he has practiced. 23 Do I indeed derive any pleasure from the death of the wicked? says the Lord God. Do I not rather rejoice when he turns from his evil way that he may live?

24 And if the virtuous man turns from the path of virtue to do evil, the same kind of abominable things that the wicked man does, can he do this and still live? None of his virtuous deeds shall be remembered, because he has broken faith and committed sin; because of this, he shall die. 25 You say, "The LORD'S way is not fair!" Hear now, house of Israel: Is it my way that is unfair, or rather, are not your ways unfair? 26 When a virtuous man turns away from virtue to commit iniquity, and dies, it is because of the iniquity he committed that he must die. 27 But if a wicked man, turning from the wickedness he has committed, does what is right and just, he shall preserve his life; 28 since he has turned away from all the sins which he committed, he shall surely live, he shall not die. 29 And yet the house of Israel says, "The LORD'S way is not fair!" Is it my way that is not fair, house of Israel, or rather, is it not that your ways are not fair?

30 Therefore I will judge you, house of Israel, each one according to his ways, says the Lord God. Turn and be converted from all your crimes, that they may be no cause of guilt for you. 31 Cast away from you all the crimes you have committed, and make for yourselves a new heart and a new spirit. Why should you die, O house of Israel? 32 For I have no pleasure in the death of anyone who dies, says the Lord God. Return and live!

19

As for you, son of man, raise a lamentation over the prince of Israel:

2 What a lioness was your mother,
  a lion of lions!
 Among young lions she couched
  to rear her whelps.
3 One whelp she raised up,
  a young lion he became;
 He learned to seize prey,
  men he devoured.
4 Then nations raised cries against him,
  in their pit he was caught;
 They took him away with hooks
  to the land of Egypt.

gives his own food to the hungry, his clothes to those who lack clothing, 17 abstains from evil, does not lend for profit or charge interest, respects my judgements and keeps my laws, he will not die for his father's sins: he will most certainly live. 18 But his father, because he was violent, robbed others and never did good among his people, will most certainly die in his guilt.

19 'Now, you say, "Why doesn't the son bear his father's guilt?" If the son has been law-abiding and upright, has kept all my laws and followed them, most certainly live. 20 The one who has sinned is the one who must die; a son is not to bear his father's guilt, nor a father his son's guilt. The upright will be credited with his uprightness, and the wicked with his wickedness.

21 'If the wicked, however, renounces all the sins he has committed, respects my laws and is law-abiding and upright, he will most certainly live; he will not die. 22 None of the crimes he committed will be remembered against him from then on; he will most certainly live *j* because of his upright actions. 23 Would I take pleasure in the death of the wicked — declares the Lord Yahweh — and not prefer to see him renounce his wickedness and live?

24 'But if the upright abandons uprightness and does wrong by copying all the loathsome practices of the wicked, is he to live? All his upright actions will be forgotten from then on; for the infidelity of which he is guilty and the sin which he has committed, he will most certainly die.

25 'Now, you say, "What the Lord does is unjust." Now listen, House of Israel: is what I do unjust? Is it not what you do that is unjust? 26 When the upright abandons uprightness and does wrong and dies, he dies because of the wrong which he himself has done. 27 Similarly, when the wicked abandons wickedness to become law-abiding and upright, he saves his own life. 28 Having chosen to renounce all his previous crimes, he will most certainly live: he will not die. 29 And yet the House of Israel says, "What the Lord does is unjust." Is what I do unjust, House of Israel? Is it not what you do that is unjust? 30 So in future, House of Israel, I shall judge each of you by what that person does — declares the Lord Yahweh. *k* Repent, renounce all your crimes, avoid all occasions for guilt. 31 Shake off all the crimes you have committed, and make yourselves a new heart and a new spirit! Why die, House of Israel? 32 I take no pleasure in the death of anyone — declares the Lord Yahweh — so repent and live!'

19

'Now, raise a lament for the princes of Israel. 2 Say:

What was your mother?
 A lioness among lions;
 lying among the cubs
 she nursed her whelps.
3 She reared one of her whelps:
 he grew into a young lion;
 he learnt to tear his prey;
 he became a man-eater.
4 The nations came to hear of him;
 he was caught in their pit;
 they dragged him away with hooks
 to Egypt. *l*

---

j 18 = 33:16.   *k* 18 = 33:20.   *l* 19 King Jehoahaz, the whelp of Israel, was deposed and taken to Egypt.

| NEW REVISED STANDARD VERSION | REVISED ENGLISH BIBLE |

5 When she saw that she was thwarted,
   that her hope was lost,
  she took another of her cubs
   and made him a young lion.
6 He prowled among the lions;
  he became a young lion,
  and he learned to catch prey;
  he devoured people.
7 And he ravaged their strongholds,[t]
  and laid waste their towns;
  the land was appalled, and all in it,
   at the sound of his roaring.
8 The nations set upon him
   from the provinces all around;
  they spread their net over him;
   he was caught in their pit.
9 With hooks they put him in a cage,
   and brought him to the king of Babylon;
  they brought him into custody,
  so that his voice should be heard no more
   on the mountains of Israel.

10 Your mother was like a vine in a vineyard[u]
   transplanted by the water,
  fruitful and full of branches
   from abundant water.
11 Its strongest stem became
   a ruler's scepter;[v]
  it towered aloft
   among the thick boughs;
  it stood out in its height
   with its mass of branches.
12 But it was plucked up in fury,
   cast down to the ground;
  the east wind dried it up;
   its fruit was stripped off,
  its strong stem was withered;
   the fire consumed it.
13 Now it is transplanted into the wilderness,
   into a dry and thirsty land.
14 And fire has gone out from its stem,
   has consumed its branches and fruit,
  so that there remains in it no strong stem,
   no scepter for ruling.

This is a lamentation, and it is used as a lamentation.

20 In the seventh year, in the fifth month, on the tenth day of the month, certain elders of Israel came to consult the LORD, and sat down before me. 2 And the word of the LORD came to me: 3 Mortal, speak to the elders of Israel, and say to them: Thus says the Lord GOD: Why are you coming? To consult me? As I live, says the Lord GOD, I will not be consulted by you. 4 Will you judge them, mortal, will you judge them? Then let them know the abominations of their ancestors, 5 and say to them: Thus says the Lord GOD: On the day when I chose Israel, I swore to the offspring of the house of Jacob — making myself known to them in the land of Egypt — I swore to them, saying, I am the LORD your God. 6 On that day I swore to them that I would bring them out of the land of Egypt into a land that I had searched out for them, a land flowing with milk and honey, the most glorious of all lands. 7 And I said to them, Cast away the detestable things your eyes feast on, every one of you, and do not defile yourselves with the idols of Egypt; I am the LORD your God. 8 But they rebelled against

5 When she saw that her hope in him
   was disappointed and dashed,
  she took another of her cubs
   and made a young lion of him.
6 He prowled among the lions
   and acted like a young lion.
  He learnt to tear his prey,
   he devoured men;
7 he broke down their palaces,
   laid their cities in ruins.
  The land and all in it were aghast
   at the sound of his roaring.
8 From the regions all around
   the nations raised a hue and cry;
  they cast their net over him
   and he was caught in their pit.
9 With hooks they drew him into a cage
   and brought him to the king of Babylon;
  he was put in prison
  that his roar might never again be heard
   on the mountains of Israel.

10 'Your mother was a vine
   planted by the waterside.
  It grew fruitful and luxuriant,
   for there was water in plenty.
11 It had stout branches,
   sceptres for those who bear rule.
  It grew tall, finding its way through the foliage;
  it was conspicuous for its height and many boughs.
12 But it was torn up in anger
   and thrown to the ground;
  the east wind blighted it,
   its fruit was blown off,
  its strong branches were blighted,
   and fire burnt it.
13 Now it is transplanted in the wilderness,
   in a dry and thirsty land;
14 fire bursts forth from its own branches
   and burns up its shoots.
  It has no strong branch any more,
   no sceptre for those who bear rule.'

This is a lament and it has passed into use as such.

20 On the tenth day of the fifth month in the seventh year, some of the elders of Israel came to consult the LORD and were sitting with me. 2 Then this word of the LORD came to me: 3 'O man, say to the elders of Israel: The Lord GOD says: Do you come to consult me? As I live, I refuse to be consulted by you. This is the word of the Lord GOD.

4 'Bring a charge against them, O man! Tell them of the abominations of their forefathers 5 and say to them: The Lord GOD says: On the day I chose Israel, with uplifted hand I bound myself by oath to the descendants of Jacob and revealed myself to them in Egypt, declaring: I am the LORD your God. 6 That day I swore with hand uplifted that I would bring them out of Egypt into the land I had sought out for them, a land flowing with milk and honey, the fairest of all lands. 7 I told every one of them to cast away the loathsome things to which they looked up, and not to defile themselves with the idols of Egypt. I am the LORD your God, I said.

---

t Heb *his widows* u Cn: Heb *in your blood* v Heb *Its strongest stems became rulers' scepters*

19:5 **another:** *so Gk; Heb.* one. 19:7 **he broke . . . palaces:** *so Aram. (Targ.); Heb.* he knew his widows. 19:10 **vine:** *prob. rdg; Heb.* obscure. 19:14 **burns . . . shoots:** *prob. rdg; Heb. adds* its fruit.

NEW AMERICAN BIBLE

5 Then she saw that in vain she had waited,
  her hope was destroyed.
She took another of her whelps,
  him she made a young lion.
6 He prowled among the lions,
  a young lion he became;
He learned to seize prey,
  men he devoured;
7 He ravaged their strongholds,
  their cities he wasted.
The land and all in it were appalled
  at the noise of his roar.
8 Nations laid out against him
  snares all about him;
They spread their net to take him,
  in their pit he was caught.
9 They put him in a cage and took him away
  to the king of Babylon,
So that his voice would not be heard
  on the mountains of Israel.

10 Your mother was like a vine
  planted by the water;
Fruitful and branchy was she
  because of the abundant water.
11 One strong branch she put out
  as a royal scepter.
Stately was her height
  amid the dense foliage;
Notably tall was she
  with her many clusters.
12 But she was torn up in fury
  and flung to the ground;
The east wind withered her up,
  her fruit was torn off;
Then her strong branch withered up,
  fire devoured it.
13 So now she is planted in the desert,
  in a land dry and parched,
14 For fire came out of the branch
  and devoured her shoots;
She is now without a strong branch,
  a ruler's scepter.

This is a lamentation and serves as a lamentation.

20 In the seventh year, on the tenth day of the fifth month, some of the elders of Israel came to consult the LORD and sat down before me. 2 Then the word of the LORD came to me: 3 Son of man, speak with the elders of Israel and say to them: Thus says the Lord GOD: Have you come to consult me? As I live! I swear I will not allow myself to be consulted by you, says the Lord GOD.

4 Will you judge them? Will you judge, son of man? Make known to them the abominations of their ancestors 5 in these words: Thus speaks the Lord GOD: The day I chose Israel, I swore to the decendants of the house of Jacob; in the land of Egypt I revealed myself to them and swore: I am the LORD, your God. 6 That day I swore to bring them out of the land of Egypt to the land I had scouted for them, a land flowing with milk and honey, a jewel among all lands. 7 Then I said to them: Throw away, each of you, the detestable things that have held your eyes; do not defile yourselves with the idols of Egypt: I am the LORD, your God.

NEW JERUSALEM BIBLE

5 Her expectation thwarted,
  and seeing her hope dashed,
she took another of her whelps
  and made a young lion of him.
6 He prowled among the lions,
  he grew into a young lion,
he learnt to tear his prey;
  he became a man-eater.
7 He tore down their palaces,
  he destroyed their cities;
the land and all its inhabitants were appalled
  by the sound of his roars.
8 The nations marched out against him
  from the surrounding provinces;
they spread their net over him;
  he was caught in their pit.
9 They shackled him with hooks,
  they took him to the king of Babylon
and threw him into a fortress,
  so that his voice could never again be heard
  on the mountains of Israel.

10 Your mother was like a vine
  planted beside the water,
fruitful and leafy,
  because the water flowed so full.
11 She had stout stems
  which became kingly sceptres;
she grew higher and higher,
  up into the clouds;
she was admired for her height
  and the number of her branches.
12 But she was furiously uprooted
  and thrown on the ground;
the east wind dried up her fruit,
  she was broken to pieces;
her stout stem dried up,
  the fire devoured it.
13 Now she has been transplanted to the desert,
  to a dry and thirsty land.
14 Fire burst out of her stem
  devouring her branches and fruit.
No more stout stem for her,
  no more kingly sceptre.'

This is a lament; it was used as such.

20 In the seventh year, on the tenth day of the fifth month, some of the elders of Israel came to consult Yahweh and were sitting with me, 2 when the word of Yahweh was addressed to me as follows, 3 'Son of man, speak to the elders of Israel. Say, "The Lord Yahweh says this: Have you come to consult me? As I live, I will not be consulted by you—declares the Lord Yahweh."

4 'Are you ready to judge them? Are you ready to judge them, son of man? Confront them with the loathsome practices of their ancestors. 5 Say, "The Lord Yahweh says this: On the day when I chose Israel, when I pledged my word to the House of Jacob, I made myself known to them in Egypt; I pledged my word to them and said: I am Yahweh your God. 6 That day I pledged them my word that I would bring them out of Egypt to a country which I had reconnoitred for them, a country flowing with milk and honey, and the loveliest of them all. 7 And I said to them: Each of you must reject the horrors which attract you; do not pollute yourselves with the foul idols of Egypt; I am Yahweh your

NEW REVISED STANDARD VERSION

me and would not listen to me; not one of them cast away the detestable things their eyes feasted on, nor did they forsake the idols of Egypt.

Then I thought I would pour out my wrath upon them and spend my anger against them in the midst of the land of Egypt. 9 But I acted for the sake of my name, that it should not be profaned in the sight of the nations among whom they lived, in whose sight I made myself known to them in bringing them out of the land of Egypt. 10 So I led them out of the land of Egypt and brought them into the wilderness. 11 I gave them my statutes and showed them my ordinances, by whose observance everyone shall live. 12 Moreover I gave them my sabbaths, as a sign between me and them, so that they might know that I the LORD sanctify them. 13 But the house of Israel rebelled against me in the wilderness; they did not observe my statutes but rejected my ordinances, by whose observance everyone shall live; and my sabbaths they greatly profaned.

Then I thought I would pour out my wrath upon them in the wilderness, to make an end of them. 14 But I acted for the sake of my name, so that it should not be profaned in the sight of the nations, in whose sight I had brought them out. 15 Moreover I swore to them in the wilderness that I would not bring them into the land that I had given them, a land flowing with milk and honey, the most glorious of all lands, 16 because they rejected my ordinances and did not observe my statutes, and profaned my sabbaths; for their heart went after their idols. 17 Nevertheless my eye spared them, and I did not destroy them or make an end of them in the wilderness.

18 I said to their children in the wilderness, Do not follow the statutes of your parents, nor observe their ordinances, nor defile yourselves with their idols. 19 I the LORD am your God; follow my statutes, and be careful to observe my ordinances, 20 and hallow my sabbaths that they may be a sign between me and you, so that you may know that I the LORD am your God. 21 But the children rebelled against me; they did not follow my statutes, and were not careful to observe my ordinances, by whose observance everyone shall live; they profaned my sabbaths.

Then I thought I would pour out my wrath upon them and spend my anger against them in the wilderness. 22 But I withheld my hand, and acted for the sake of my name, so that it should not be profaned in the sight of the nations, in whose sight I had brought them out. 23 Moreover I swore to them in the wilderness that I would scatter them among the nations and disperse them through the countries, 24 because they had not executed my ordinances, but had rejected my statutes and profaned my sabbaths, and their eyes were set on their ancestors' idols. 25 Moreover I gave them statutes that were not good and ordinances by which they could not live. 26 I defiled them through their very gifts, in their offering up all their firstborn, in order that I might horrify them, so that they might know that I am the LORD.

27 Therefore, mortal, speak to the house of Israel and say to them, Thus says the Lord GOD: In this again your ancestors blasphemed me, by dealing treacherously with me. 28 For when I had brought them into the land that I swore to give them, then wherever they saw any high hill or any leafy tree, there they offered their sacrifices and presented the provocation of their offering; there they sent up their pleasing odors, and there they poured out their drink offerings. 29 (I said to them, What is the high place to which you go? So it is called Bamah^w to this day.) 30 Therefore say to the house of Israel, Thus says the Lord GOD: Will you defile yourselves after the manner of your ancestors and go astray after their detestable things? 31 When you

REVISED ENGLISH BIBLE

8 'But in rebellion against me they refused to listen, and not one of them cast away the loathsome things to which he looked up or forsook the idols of Egypt. I resolved to pour out my wrath and exhaust my anger on them in Egypt. 9 But then I acted for the honour of my name, that it might not be profaned in the sight of the nations among whom Israel was living: I revealed myself to them by bringing Israel out of Egypt.

10 'I brought them out of Egypt and led them into the wilderness. 11 There I gave my statutes to them and taught them my laws; it is by keeping them that mortals have life. 12 Further, I gave them my sabbaths to serve as a sign between us, so that they would know that I am the LORD who sanctified them. 13 But the Israelites rebelled against me in the wilderness; they did not conform to my statutes, they rejected my laws, though it is by keeping them that mortals have life, and they totally desecrated my sabbaths. I resolved to pour out my wrath on them in the wilderness to destroy them. 14 But then I acted for the honour of my name, that it might not be profaned in the sight of the nations who had seen me bring them out.

15 'However, in the wilderness I swore to them with uplifted hand that I would not bring them into the land I had given them, that land flowing with milk and honey, the fairest of all lands. 16 They loved to follow idols of their own, so they rejected my laws, they would not conform to my statutes, and they desecrated my sabbaths. 17 Yet I pitied them too much to destroy them and did not make an end of them in the wilderness. 18 I warned their children in the wilderness not to conform to the rules and usages of their fathers, nor to defile themselves with their idols. 19 I am the LORD your God, I said; you must conform to my statutes, you must observe my laws and act according to them. 20 You must keep my sabbaths holy, and they will become a sign between us; so you will know that I am the LORD your God.

21 'But those children rebelled against me; they did not conform to my statutes or observe my laws, though obedience to them would have given life. Moreover they desecrated my sabbaths. Again I resolved to pour out my wrath and vent my anger on them in the wilderness. 22 But I stayed my hand. I acted for the honour of my name, so that it might not be profaned in the sight of the nations who had seen me bring them out of Egypt. 23 However, in the wilderness I swore to them with uplifted hand that I would disperse them among the nations and scatter them over the earth, 24 because they had disobeyed my laws, rejected my statutes, desecrated my sabbaths, and had regard only for the idols of their forefathers. 25 I even imposed on them statutes that were malign and laws which would not lead to life. 26 I let them defile themselves with gifts to idols; I made them surrender their eldest sons to them so that I might fill them with revulsion. Thus they would know that I am the LORD.

27 'Speak therefore, O man, to the Israelites; say to them: The Lord GOD says: Once again your forefathers reviled me and broke faith with me: 28 when I brought them into the land which I had sworn with uplifted hand to give them, they noted every hilltop and every leafy tree, and there they offered their sacrifices, there they presented the gifts which roused my anger, there they set out their offerings of soothing odour and poured out their drink-offerings. 29 I asked them: What is this bamah to which you go? And 'bamah' has been the name for a shrine ever since.

30 'So tell the Israelites: The Lord GOD says: Are you defiling yourselves as your forefathers did, and lusting after their loathsome gods? 31 You are defiling yourselves to this

---

w That is High Place

8 But they rebelled against me and refused to listen to me; none of them threw away the detestable things that had held their eyes, they did not abandon the idols of Egypt. Then I thought of pouring out my fury on them and spending my anger on them there in the land of Egypt; 9 but I acted for my name's sake, that it should not be profaned in the sight of the nations among whom they were, in whose presence I had made myself known to them, revealing that I would bring them out of the land of Egypt. 10 Therefore I led them out of the land of Egypt and brought them into the desert. 11 Then I gave them my statutes and made known to them my ordinances, which everyone must keep, to have life through them. 12 I also gave them my sabbaths to be a sign between me and them, to show that it was I, the LORD, who made them holy.

13 But the house of Israel rebelled against me in the desert. They did not observe my statutes, and they despised my ordinances that bring life to those who keep them. My sabbaths, too, they desecrated grievously. Then I thought of pouring out my fury on them in the desert to put an end to them, 14 but I acted for my name's sake, that it should not be profaned in the sight of the nations in whose presence I had brought them out. 15 Nevertheless I swore to them in the desert not to bring them to the land I had given them, a land flowing with milk and honey, a jewel among all lands. 16 So much were their hearts devoted to their idols, they had not lived by my statutes, but despised my ordinances and desecrated my sabbaths. 17 But I looked on them with pity, not wanting to destroy them, so I did not put an end to them in the desert.

18 Then I said to their children in the desert: Do not observe the statutes of your parents or keep their ordinances; do not defile yourselves with their idols. 19 I am the LORD, your God: observe my statutes and be careful to keep my ordinances; 20 keep holy my sabbaths, as a sign between me and you to show that I am the LORD, your God. 21 But their children rebelled against me: they did not observe my statutes or keep my ordinances that bring life to those who observe them, and my sabbaths they desecrated. Then I thought of pouring out my fury on them, of spending my anger on them in the desert; 22 but I stayed my hand, acting for my name's sake, lest it be profaned in the sight of the nations in whose presence I brought them out. 23 Nevertheless I swore to them in the desert that I would disperse them among the nations and scatter them over foreign lands; 24 for they did not keep my ordinances, but despised my statutes and desecrated my sabbaths with eyes only for the idols of their fathers. 25 Therefore I gave them statutes that were not good, and ordinances through which they could not live. 26 I let them become defiled by their gifts, by their immolation of every first-born, so as to make them an object of horror.

27 Therefore speak to the house of Israel, son of man, and tell them: Thus says the Lord GOD: In this way also your fathers blasphemed me, breaking faith with me: 28 when I had brought them to the land I had sworn to give them, and they saw all its high hills and leafy trees, there they offered their sacrifices [there they brought their offensive offerings], there they sent up appeasing odors, and there they poured out their libations. 29 I asked them: To what sort of high place do you betake yourselves? — and so they call it a high place even to the present day. 30 Therefore say to the house of Israel: Thus says the Lord GOD: Will you defile yourselves like your fathers? Will you lust after their detestable idols? 31 By offering your gifts, by making your chil-

God. 8 But they rebelled against me and would not listen to me. Not one of them rejected the horrors which attracted them; they did not give up the foul idols of Egypt. I then resolved to vent my fury on them, to sate my anger on them in Egypt. 9 But respect for my own name kept me from letting it be profaned in the eyes of the nations among whom they were living, and before whom I had made myself known to them and promised to bring them out of Egypt. 10 So I brought them out of Egypt and led them into the desert. 11 I gave them my laws and taught them my judgements, in whose observance people find life. 12 And I also gave them my Sabbaths as a sign between me and them, so that they might know that I, Yahweh, am the one who sanctifies them. 13 The House of Israel, however, rebelled against me in the desert; they refused to keep my laws, they scorned my judgements, in whose observance people find life, and they grossly profaned my Sabbaths. I then resolved to vent my fury on them in the desert and destroy them. 14 But respect for my own name kept me from letting it be profaned in the eyes of the nations, before whom I had brought them out. 15 Even so, I pledged them my word in the desert that I would not lead them to the country which I had given them, a country flowing with milk and honey, and the loveliest of them all, 16 since they had scorned my judgements, had refused to keep my laws and had profaned my Sabbaths, their hearts being attached to foul idols. 17 In spite of this, I took pity on them; I refrained from destroying them and did not make an end of them in the desert.

18 "I said to their children in the desert: Do not follow the laws of your ancestors, do not practise their judgements, do not defile yourselves with their foul idols. 19 I am Yahweh your God. Keep my laws, respect my judgements and practise them. 20 Keep my Sabbaths holy; let them be a sign between me and you, so that people may know that I am Yahweh your God. 21 Their children, however, rebelled against me; they refused to keep my laws, they did not respect or practise my judgements, which must be practised by all who want to live; they profaned my Sabbaths. I then resolved to vent my fury on them, to sate my anger on them in the desert. 22 But I restrained my hand; respect for my own name kept me from letting it be profaned in the eyes of the nations, before whom I had brought them out. 23 Once again, however, I pledged them my word that I would scatter them throughout the nations and disperse them in foreign countries, 24 because they had not followed my judgements but had rejected my laws and profaned my Sabbaths, their eyes being fastened on the foul idols of their ancestors. 25 And for this reason I gave them laws that were not good and judgements by which they could never live; 26 and I polluted them with their own offerings, making them sacrifice every first-born son in order to fill them with revulsion, so that they would know that I am Yahweh."

27 'For this reason, son of man, speak to the House of Israel. Say to them, "The Lord Yahweh says this: Here is another way by which your ancestors outraged me by their infidelity. 28 Once I had brought them into the country which I had pledged my word to give them, they then saw all sorts of high hills, all kinds of leafy trees, and there they performed their sacrifices and made offerings that provoked my anger; there they set out their pleasing smell and poured their libations. 29 I then said to them: What is this high place where you go? And they gave, and still give it, the name of Bamah."

30 'So, say to the House of Israel, "The Lord Yahweh says this: If you are polluting yourselves as your ancestors did by fornicating with their horrors — 31 for by offering

offer your gifts and make your children pass through the fire, you defile yourselves with all your idols to this day. And shall I be consulted by you, O house of Israel? As I live, says the Lord GOD, I will not be consulted by you.

32 What is in your mind shall never happen—the thought, "Let us be like the nations, like the tribes of the countries, and worship wood and stone."

33 As I live, says the Lord GOD, surely with a mighty hand and an outstretched arm, and with wrath poured out, I will be king over you. 34 I will bring you out from the peoples and gather you out of the countries where you are scattered, with a mighty hand and an outstretched arm, and with wrath poured out; 35 and I will bring you into the wilderness of the peoples, and there I will enter into judgment with you face to face. 36 As I entered into judgment with your ancestors in the wilderness of the land of Egypt, so I will enter into judgment with you, says the Lord GOD. 37 I will make you pass under the staff, and will bring you within the bond of the covenant. 38 I will purge out the rebels among you, and those who transgress against me; I will bring them out of the land where they reside as aliens, but they shall not enter the land of Israel. Then you shall know that I am the LORD.

39 As for you, O house of Israel, thus says the Lord GOD: Go serve your idols, everyone of you now and hereafter, if you will not listen to me; but my holy name you shall no more profane with your gifts and your idols.

40 For on my holy mountain, the mountain height of Israel, says the Lord GOD, there all the house of Israel, all of them, shall serve me in the land; there I will accept them, and there I will require your contributions and the choicest of your gifts, with all your sacred things. 41 As a pleasing odor I will accept you, when I bring you out from the peoples, and gather you out of the countries where you have been scattered; and I will manifest my holiness among you in the sight of the nations. 42 You shall know that I am the LORD, when I bring you into the land of Israel, the country that I swore to give to your ancestors. 43 There you shall remember your ways and all the deeds by which you have polluted yourselves; and you shall loathe yourselves for all the evils that you have committed. 44 And you shall know that I am the LORD, when I deal with you for my name's sake, not according to your evil ways, or corrupt deeds, O house of Israel, says the Lord GOD.

45ˣ The word of the LORD came to me: 46 Mortal, set your face toward the south, preach against the south, and prophesy against the forest land in the Negeb; 47 say to the forest of the Negeb, Hear the word of the LORD: Thus says the Lord GOD, I will kindle a fire in you, and it shall devour every green tree in you and every dry tree; the blazing flame shall not be quenched, and all faces from south to north shall be scorched by it. 48 All flesh shall see that I the LORD have kindled it; it shall not be quenched. 49 Then I said, "Ah Lord GOD! they are saying of me, 'Is he not a maker of allegories?'"

21 ʸ The word of the LORD came to me: 2 Mortal, set your face toward Jerusalem and preach against the sanctuaries; prophesy against the land of Israel 3 and say to the land of Israel, Thus says the LORD: I am coming against you, and will draw my sword out of its sheath, and will cut off from you both righteous and wicked. 4 Because I will cut off from you both righteous and wicked, therefore my sword shall go out of its sheath against all flesh from south to north; 5 and all flesh shall know that I the LORD have drawn my sword out of its sheath; it shall not be sheathed again. 6 Moan therefore, mortal; moan with breaking heart

very day with all your idols when you bring your gifts and pass your children through the fire. How then can I let you consult me, men of Israel? As I live, says the Lord GOD, I refuse to be consulted by you. 32 When you say to yourselves, "Let us become like the nations and tribes of other lands and worship wood and stone," you are thinking of something that can never be. 33 As I live, says the Lord GOD, I shall reign over you with a strong hand, with arm outstretched and wrath outpoured. 34 By my strong hand, an outstretched arm, and outpoured wrath I shall bring you out from the peoples and gather you from the lands where you have been dispersed. 35 I shall bring you into the Wilderness of the Peoples; there I shall confront you and bring you to judgement. 36 Even as I did in the wilderness of Egypt against your forefathers, so against you I shall state my case. This is the word of the Lord GOD.

37 'I shall make you pass under the rod, counting you as you enter. 38 I shall purge you of those who revolt and rebel against me. I shall take them out of the land where they now live, but they will not set foot on the soil of Israel. Thus you will know that I am the LORD.

39 'Now, you Israelites, the Lord GOD says: Go, each one of you, and serve your idols! But in days to come I shall punish you for your disobedience to me, and no more will you desecrate my holy name with your gifts and your idolatries. 40 But on my holy mountain, the lofty mountain of Israel, says the Lord GOD, there in the land all the Israelites will serve me. There I shall accept them; there I shall require your gifts and your choicest offerings, with all else that you consecrate to me. 41 I shall accept you when you make offerings with their soothing odour, after I have brought you out from the peoples and gathered you from the lands where you have been dispersed. I alone shall have your worship, and the nations will witness it.

42 'You will know that I am the LORD, when I bring you home to the soil of Israel, to the land which I swore with uplifted hand to give your forefathers. 43 There you will remember your past conduct and all the acts by which you defiled yourselves, and you will loathe yourselves for all the wickedness you have committed. 44 You will know that I am the LORD, when I deal with you Israelites, not as your wicked ways and your vicious deeds deserve, but as the honour of my name demands. This is the word of the Lord GOD.'

45 This word of the LORD came to me: 46 'O man, turn and face towards the south and utter your words towards it; prophesy to the scrubland of the Negeb. 47 Say to it: Listen to the word of the LORD. The Lord GOD says: I am about to kindle a fire in you, and it will consume all the wood, green and dry alike. Its fiery flame will not be put out, but from the Negeb northwards everyone will be scorched by it. 48 Everyone will see that it is I, the LORD, who have set it ablaze; it will not be put out.' 49 'Ah Lord GOD,' I cried; 'they are always saying of me, "He deals only in figures of speech."'

21 THIS word of the LORD came to me: 2 'O man, turn and face towards Jerusalem, and utter your words against her sanctuary; prophesy against the land of Israel. 3 Say to that land: The LORD says: I am against you; I shall draw my sword from the scabbard and make away with both righteous and wicked from among you. 4 It is because I intend to make away with righteous and wicked alike that my sword will be drawn from the scabbard against everyone, from the Negeb northwards. 5 All shall know that I, the LORD, have drawn my sword; it will never again be sheathed. 6 Groan while they look on, O man, groan bitterly

20:37 **counting . . . enter:** *prob. rdg; Heb. obscure.*   20:45 *In Heb. 21:1.*

ˣ Ch 21.1 in Heb   ʸ Ch 21.6 in Heb

dren pass through the fire, you defile yourselves with all your idols even to this day. Shall I let myself be consulted by you, house of Israel? As I live! says the Lord GOD: I swear I will not let myself be consulted by you.

32 What you are thinking of shall never happen: "We shall be like the nations, like the peoples of foreign lands, serving wood and stone." 33 As I live, says the Lord GOD, with a mighty hand and outstretched arm, with poured-out wrath, I swear I will be king over you! 34 With a mighty hand and outstretched arm, with poured-out wrath, I will bring you out from the nations and gather you from the countries over which you are scattered; 35 then I will lead you to the desert of the peoples, where I will enter into judgment with you face to face. 36 Just as I entered into judgment with your fathers in the desert of the land of Egypt, so will I enter into judgment with you, says the Lord GOD. 37 I will count you with the staff and bring back but a small number. 38 I will separate from you those who have rebelled and transgressed against me; from the land where they sojourned as aliens I will bring them out, but they shall not return to the land of Israel. Thus you shall know that I am the LORD.

39 As for you, house of Israel, thus says the Lord GOD: Come, each one of you, destroy your idols! Then listen to me, and never again profane my holy name with your gifts and your idols. 40 For on my holy mountain, on the mountain height of Israel, says the Lord GOD, there the whole house of Israel without exception shall worship me; there I will accept them, and there I will claim your tributes and the first fruits of your offerings, and all that you dedicate. 41 As a pleasing odor I will accept you, when I have brought you from among the nations and gathered you out of the countries over which you were scattered; and by means of you I will manifest my holiness in the sight of the nations. 42 Thus you shall know that I am the LORD, when I bring you back to the land of Israel, the land which I swore to give to your fathers. 43 There you shall recall your conduct and all the deeds by which you defiled yourselves; and you shall loathe yourselves because of all the evil things you did. 44 And you shall know that I am the LORD when I deal with you thus, for my name's sake, and not according to your evil conduct and corrupt actions, O house of Israel, says the Lord GOD.

21 Thus the word of the LORD came to me: 2 Son of man, look southward, preach toward the south, and prophesy against the forest of the southern land. 3 Hear the word of the LORD! you shall say to the southern forest. Thus says the Lord GOD: See! I am kindling a fire in you that shall devour all trees, the green as well as the dry. The blazing flame shall not be quenched, but from south to north every face shall be scorched by it. 4 Everyone shall see that I, the LORD, have kindled it, and it shall not be quenched.

5 But I said, 'Alas! Lord GOD, they say to me, 'Is not this the one who is forever spinning parables?' " 6 Then the word of the LORD came to me: 7 Son of man, look toward Jerusalem, preach against their sanctuary, and prophesy against the land of Israel, 8 saying to the land of Israel: Thus says the LORD: See! I am coming at you; I will draw my sword from its sheath and cut off from you the virtuous and the wicked. 9 Thus my sword shall leave its sheath against everyone from south to north, 10 and everyone shall know that I, the LORD, have drawn my sword from its sheath, and it shall not be sheathed again.

your gifts and by burning your children as sacrifices, you have been polluting yourselves with all your foul idols to this very day — shall I let myself be consulted by you, House of Israel? As I live — declares Lord Yahweh — I shall not let myself be consulted by you. 32 And what you sometimes imagine will never be so, when you say: We shall be like the peoples, the tribes of foreign lands, worshipping wood and stone. 33 As I live I swear it — declares the Lord Yahweh — I am the one who will reign over you, with a strong hand and outstretched arm, once my fury is sated. 34 With a strong hand and outstretched arm, once my fury is sated, I shall bring you back from the peoples and gather you again from the countries throughout which you have been scattered. 35 I shall lead you into the desert of the nations and there I shall judge you face to face. 36 As I judged your ancestors in the desert of Egypt, so will I judge you — declares the Lord Yahweh. 37 I shall make you pass under the crook, bring you to respect the covenant 38 and rid you of the rebels who have revolted against me; I shall bring them out of the country where they are staying, but they will not enter the country of Israel, and you will know that I am Yahweh. 39 House of Israel, Lord Yahweh says this: Go on, all of you, worship your foul idols, but later we shall see if you don't listen to me! Then you will stop profaning my holy name with your offerings and your foul idols. 40 For on my holy mountain, on the high mountain of Israel — declares the Lord Yahweh — is where the whole House of Israel, everyone in the country, will worship me. There I shall accept and there expect your presents, your choicest offering and all your consecrated gifts. 41 I shall welcome you like a pleasing smell when I bring you back from the peoples and gather you from the countries throughout which you have been scattered, and through you I shall display my holiness for all the nations to see; 42 and you will know that I am Yahweh, when I bring you back to the soil of Israel, to the country which I pledged my word to give to your ancestors. 43 There you will remember your past behaviour and all the actions by which you have defiled yourselves, and you will loathe yourselves for all the wrongs which you have committed. 44 And you will know that I am Yahweh, when I treat you as respect for my own name requires, and not as your wicked behaviour and corrupt actions deserve, House of Israel — declares the Lord Yahweh." '

21 *m*The word of Yahweh was addressed to me as follows, 2 'Son of man, turn to the right; utter your word towards the south, prophesy against the forest land of the Negeb. 3 Say to the forest of Negeb, "Hear the word of Yahweh! The Lord Yahweh says this: Listen; I am about to kindle a fire in you which will burn up every green tree in you as well as every dry one; it will be an unquenchable blaze and every face will be scorched by it from the Negeb to the north. 4 All humanity will see that it was I, Yahweh, who kindled it, and it will not be extinguished." ' 5 I said, 'Lord Yahweh, they say of me, "He does nothing but speak in riddles!" '

6 Then the word of Yahweh was addressed to me as follows, 7 'Son of man, turn towards Jerusalem, utter your word towards the sanctuary and prophesy against the land of Israel. 8 Say to the land of Israel, "Yahweh says this: Now I am against you; I am about to unsheathe my sword and rid you of the upright and the wicked alike. 9 Since I am going to rid you of upright and wicked alike, I shall unsheathe my sword against everyone alive, from the Negeb to the north, 10 so that everyone alive will know that I, Yahweh, am the one who has unsheathed my sword; it will not go back again."

m 21 Four separate sayings (1–12; 13–22; 23–32; 33–37) linked only by the word 'sword'.

and bitter grief before their eyes. 7 And when they say to you, "Why do you moan?" you shall say, "Because of the news that has come. Every heart will melt and all hands will be feeble, every spirit will faint and all knees will turn to water. See, it comes and it will be fulfilled," says the Lord God.

8 And the word of the LORD came to me: 9 Mortal, prophesy and say: Thus says the Lord; Say:

A sword, a sword is sharpened,
    it is also polished;
10 It is sharpened for slaughter,
    honed to flash like lightning!
How can we make merry?
    You have despised the rod,
    and all discipline.z
11 The sworda is given to be polished,
    to be grasped in the hand;
It is sharpened, the sword is polished,
    to be placed in the slayer's hand.
12 Cry and wail, O mortal,
    for it is against my people;
    it is against all Israel's princes,
    they are thrown to the sword,
    together with my people.
    Ah! Strike the thigh!
13 For consider: What! If you despise the rod, will it not happen?z says the Lord GOD.
14 And you, mortal, prophesy;
    Strike hand to hand.
    Let the sword fall twice, thrice;
    it is a sword for killing.
    A sword for great slaughter—
    it surrounds them;
15 therefore hearts melt
    and many stumble.
    At all their gates I have set
    the pointz of the sword.
    Ah! It is made for flashing,
    it is polishedb for slaughter!
16 Attack to the right!
    Engage to the left!
    Wherever your edge is directed.
17 I too will strike hand to hand,
    I will satisfy my fury;
    I the LORD have spoken.

18 The word of the LORD came to me: 19 Mortal, mark out two roads for the sword of the king of Babylon to come; both of them shall issue from the same land. And make a signpost, make it for a fork in the road leading to a city; 20 mark out the road for the sword to come to Rabbah of the Ammonites or to Judah and toc Jerusalem the fortified. 21 For the king of Babylon stands at the parting of the way, at the fork in the two roads, to use divination; he shakes the arrows, he consults the teraphim,d he inspects the liver. 22 Into his right hand comes the lot for Jerusalem, to set battering rams, to call out for slaughter, for raising the battle cry, to set battering rams against the gates, to cast up ramps, to build siege towers. 23 But to them it will seem like a false divination; they have sworn solemn oaths; but he brings their guilt to remembrance, bringing about their capture.

24 Therefore thus says the Lord GOD: Because you have brought your guilt to remembrance, in that your transgressions are uncovered, so that in all your deeds your sins appear—because you have come to remembrance, you shall be taken in hand.e

until you collapse. 7 When they ask why you are groaning, say, "Because what I have heard is about to come. All hearts will melt, all hands will hang limp, all courage will fail, all knees will turn to water. See, it is coming; it is here!" This is the word of the Lord GOD.'

8 The LORD said to me: 9 'Prophesy, O man, and say: This is the word of the LORD:

A sword, a sword is sharpened and burnished,
10 sharpened to kill and kill again,
    burnished to flash like lightning.
    (Look, the rod is brandished, my son,
    to defy all wooden idols!)
11 The sword is given to be burnished
    ready for the hand to grasp.
    The sword is sharpened,
    it is burnished,
    ready to be given into the slayer's hand.

12 'Cry aloud and wail, O man; for it falls on my people, and on all Israel's rulers who are delivered over to the sword and are slain with my people. Therefore slap your thigh in remorse. 13 (When the test comes, what if the rod does not in truth defy?) This is the word of the Lord GOD.

14 'But you, O man, prophesy and strike your hands together;
    swing the sword twice, thrice:
    it is the sword of slaughter,
    the great sword of slaughter whirling about them.
15 That their hearts may be fearful and many may stumble and fall,
    I have set the threat of the sword at all their gates,
    the threat of the sword flashing like lightning
    and drawn to kill.
16 Be sharpened, turn right; be unsheathed, turn left,
    wherever your point is aimed.

17 'I, too, shall strike my hands together and abate my anger. I, the LORD, have spoken.'

18 This word of the LORD came to me: 19 'O man, trace out two roads by which the sword of the king of Babylon may come, both starting from the same land. Then make a signpost for the point where the highway forks. 20 Mark a road for the sword to come to the Ammonite city of Rabbah, and a road to Judah, with Jerusalem at its heart. 21 At the parting of the ways where the road divides, the king of Babylon will halt to take the omens. He will cast lots with arrows, consult household gods, and inspect the livers of beasts. 22 The arrow marked "Jerusalem" will fall at his right hand: here, then, he will give the command for slaughter and sound the battle cry, set battering-rams against the gates, cast up siege-ramps, and build watch-towers. 23 The people will think that the auguries are groundless, the king of Babylon will remind me of their wrongdoing, and they will fall into his hand. 24 Therefore the Lord GOD says: Because you have kept me mindful of your wrongdoing by your open rebellion, and your sins have been revealed in everything you do, because you have kept yourselves in my mind, you will fall into the enemy's hand.

21:10 to flash: prob. rdg; Heb. unintelligible. the rod ... idols: or the rod is waved, my son, defying all wooden defences.
21:13 When ... defy: Heb. obscure.   21:15 the threat of the sword [flashing]: prob. rdg; Heb. obscure.   21:16 Be sharpened: so Aram. (Targ.); Heb. Unify yourself.   21:20 come to: so Gk; Heb. come with.   21:22 here, then: prob. rdg; Heb. adds he must set battering-rams.   21:23 groundless: so Gk; Heb. adds an unintelligible phrase.

z Meaning of Heb uncertain   a Heb It   b Tg: Heb wrapped up   c Gk Syr: Heb Judah in   d Or the household gods   e Or be taken captive

11 As for you, son of man, groan! with shattered strength groan bitterly while they look on. 12 And when they ask you, "Why are you groaning?", you shall say: Because of a report; when it comes every heart shall fail, every hand shall fall helpless, every spirit shall be daunted, and every knee shall run with water. See, it is coming, it is here! says the Lord GOD.

13 Thus the word of the LORD came to me: 14 Son of man, prophesy! say: Thus says the LORD:

A sword, a sword has been sharpened,
    a sword, a sword has been burnished:
15 To work slaughter has it been sharpened,
    to flash lightning has it been burnished.
Why should I now withdraw it?
    You have spurned the rod and every judgment!
16 I have given it over to the burnisher
    that he might hold it in his hand,
A sword sharpened and burnished
    to be put in the hand of a slayer.
17 Cry out and wail, son of man,
    for it is destined for my people;
It is for all the princes of Israel,
    victims of the sword with my people.

Therefore, slap your thigh, 18 for the sword has been tested; and why should it not be so? says the Lord GOD, since you have spurned the rod.

19 As for you, son of man, prophesy,
    brushing one hand against the other:
While the sword is doubled and tripled,
    this sword of slaughter,
This great sword of slaughter
    which threatens all around,
20 That every heart may tremble;
    for many will be the fallen.
At all their gates
    I have appointed the sword for slaughter,
Fashioned to flash lightning,
    burnished for slaughter.
21 Cleave to the right! destroy!
    to the left! wherever your edge is turned.

22 Then I, too, shall brush one hand against the other and wreak my fury. I, the LORD, have spoken.

23 Thus the word of the LORD came to me: 24 Son of man, make for yourself two roads over which the sword of the king of Babylon can come. Both roads shall lead out from the same land. Then put a signpost at the head of each road, 25 so that the sword can come to Rabbah of the Ammonites or to Judah's capital, Jerusalem. 26 For at the fork where the two roads divide stands the king of Babylon, divining; he has shaken the arrows, inquired of the teraphim, inspected the liver. 27 In his right hand is the divining arrow marked "Jerusalem," bidding him to give the order for slaying, to raise his voice in the battle cry, to post battering rams at the gates, to cast up a ramp, to build a siege tower. 28 In their eyes this is but a lying oracle; yet they are bound by the oaths they have sworn, and the arrow taken in hand marks their guilt.

29 Therefore thus says the Lord GOD: Because you have drawn attention to your guilt, with your crimes laid bare and your sinfulness in all your wicked deeds revealed (because attention has been drawn to you), you shall be taken in

11 'Son of man, groan as though your heart were breaking. Utter your bitter groans where they can see you. 12 And if they say, "Why these groans?" reply, "Because of the news which is about to come, all hearts will sink, all hands grow weak, all spirits grow faint and all knees turn to water. It is coming now, it is here! —declares Lord Yahweh." '

13 The word of Yahweh was addressed to me as follows, 14 'Son of man, prophesy. Say, "The Lord says this. Say:

The sword, the sword
    has been sharpened and polished,
15 sharpened for slaughter,
    polished to flash like lightning . . .
16 He has had it polished to be wielded,
    this sword sharpened and polished
    to put in the slaughterer's hand!
17 Shout and wail, son of man,
    for it will come on my people,
    on all the chief men of Israel doomed like my
        people to the sword!
So beat your breast, 18 for this will be an
        ordeal . . .
declares the Lord Yahweh.
19 So prophesy, son of man, and clap your hands!
Let the sword pass three times,
    that sword for victims,
    that sword for a great victim,
    threatening them from every side!
20 To make hearts sink and make sure many fall,
    I have posted the slaughtering sword at every gate
    to flash like lightning, polished for slaughter.
21 Be sharp, on the right, be ready on the left,
    whichever way your blade is needed!
22 I too shall clap my hands
    and sate my fury!
I, Yahweh, have spoken." '

23 The word of Yahweh was addressed to me as follows, 24 'Son of man, mark out two roads for the sword of the king of Babylon to come along, making both of them begin from the same country. Then put up a signpost, put it where the road leaves for the city, 25 trace the route which the sword should take for Rabbah-of-the-Ammonites, and for Judah, to the fortress of Jerusalem. 26 For the king of Babylon has halted at the fork where these two roads diverge, to take the omens. He has shaken the arrows, questioned the household gods, inspected the liver. 27 The lot marked 'Jerusalem' is in his right hand: there to set up battering-rams, give the word for slaughter, raise the war cry, level battering-rams against the gates, cast up earthworks, build entrenchments. 28 The inhabitants will believe that these omens are idle, for they have received sworn guarantees, but he will bring their guilt to mind and capture them. 29 And so the Lord Yahweh says this, "Since you have brought your guilt to mind by parading your misdeeds and flaunting your sins in everything you do: because you have drawn attention to your-

25 As for you, vile, wicked prince of Israel,
    you whose day has come,
    the time of final punishment,
26 thus says the Lord GOD:
Remove the turban, take off the crown;
    things shall not remain as they are.
Exalt that which is low,
    abase that which is high.
27 A ruin, a ruin, a ruin —
    I will make it!
    (Such has never occurred.)
Until he comes whose right it is;
    to him I will give it.

28 As for you, mortal, prophesy, and say, Thus says the Lord GOD concerning the Ammonites, and concerning their reproach; say:
A sword, a sword! Drawn for slaughter
Polished to consume, f to flash like lightning!
29 Offering false visions for you,
    divining lies for you,
they place you over the necks
    of the vile, wicked ones —
those whose day has come,
    the time of final punishment.
30 Return it to its sheath!
In the place where you were created,
    in the land of your origin,
    I will judge you.
31 I will pour out my indignation upon you,
    with the fire of my wrath
    I will blow upon you.
I will deliver you into brutish hands,
    those skillful to destroy.
32 You shall be fuel for the fire,
    your blood shall enter the earth;
You shall be remembered no more,
    for I the LORD have spoken.

22 The word of the LORD came to me: 2 You, mortal, will you judge, will you judge the bloody city? Then declare to it all its abominable deeds. 3 You shall say, Thus says the Lord GOD: A city! Shedding blood within itself; its time has come; making its idols, defiling itself. 4 You have become guilty by the blood that you have shed, and defiled by the idols that you have made; you have brought your day near, the appointed time of your years has come. Therefore I have made you a disgrace before the nations, and a mockery to all the countries. 5 Those who are near and those who are far from you will mock you, you infamous one, full of tumult.

6 The princes of Israel in you, everyone according to his power, have been bent on shedding blood. 7 Father and mother are treated with contempt in you; the alien residing within you suffers extortion; the orphan and the widow are wronged in you. 8 You have despised my holy things, and profaned my sabbaths. 9 In you are those who slander to shed blood, those in you who eat upon the mountains, who commit lewdness in your midst. 10 In you they uncover their fathers' nakedness; in you they violate women in their menstrual periods. 11 One commits abomination with his neighbor's wife; another lewdly defiles his daughter-in-law; another in you defiles his sister, his father's daughter. 12 In you, they take bribes to shed blood; you take both advance interest and accrued interest, and make gain of your neighbors by extortion; and you have forgotten me, says the Lord GOD.

25 'And you, impious and wicked ruler of Israel, your fate has come upon you in the hour of final punishment. 26 The Lord GOD says: Off with the diadem! Away with the crown! All is overturned; raise the low and bring down the high. 27 Ruin! Ruin! I shall bring about such ruin as never was, until one comes who is the rightful ruler; and I shall install him.

28 'O MAN, prophesy and say: The Lord GOD says to the Ammonites and to their shameful god:

A sword, a sword drawn for slaughter,
burnished for destruction
    to flash like lightning!
29 Your visions are false, your auguries a lie,
    which bid you bring it down
upon the necks of the impious and the wicked;
    their fate will come upon them
    in the hour of final punishment.
30 Return the sword to the sheath.
I shall judge you in the place where you were
    born,
    the land of your origin.
31 I shall pour out my wrath on you;
    I shall fan my blazing anger over you.
I shall hand you over to barbarous men,
    skilled in destruction.
32 You will become fuel for fire,
    your blood will be shed within the land
    and you will leave no memory behind.

'I, the LORD, have spoken.'

22 THIS word of the LORD came to me: 2 'O man, will you bring a charge against her? Will you charge the murderous city and bring home to her all her abominable deeds? 3 Say to her: The Lord GOD has said: Woe betide the city that sheds blood within her walls and brings her fate on herself, the city that makes idols for herself and is defiled by them! 4 You are guilty because of the blood you have shed, you are defiled because of the idols you have made. You have shortened your days by this and hastened your end. This is why I exposed you to the contempt of the nations and the mockery of every country. 5 Lands both far and near will taunt you with your infamy and monstrous disorder. 6 In you all the rulers of Israel have used their power to shed blood; 7 in you fathers and mothers have been treated contemptuously, aliens have been oppressed, the fatherless and the widow have been wronged. 8 You have despised what I hold sacred, and desecrated my sabbaths. 9 In you, Jerusalem, perjurers have worked to procure bloodshed; in you are men who have feasted at mountain shrines and have committed lewdness. 10 In you men have exposed their fathers' nakedness; they have violated women who were menstruating; 11 they have committed an outrage with their neighbours' wives and have lewdly defiled their own daughters-in-law; they have ravished their sisters, their own fathers' daughters. 12 In you people have accepted bribes to shed blood. You have exacted discount and interest, and have oppressed your fellows for gain. You have committed apostasy. This is the word of the Lord GOD.

f Cn: Heb *to contain*

21:26 **diadem:** *lit.* turban.   21:28 **for destruction:** *prob. rdg;* Heb. *obscure.*   21:29 **it:** *prob. rdg; Heb. you.*

hand. 30 And as for you, depraved and wicked prince of Israel, whose day is coming when your life of crime will be ended, 31 thus says the Lord GOD: Off with the turban and away with the crown! Nothing shall be as it was! Up with the low and down with the high! 32 Twisted, twisted, twisted will I leave it; it shall not be the same until he comes who has the claim against the city; and to him I will hand it over.

33 As for you, son of man, prophesy: Thus says the Lord GOD against the Ammonites and their insults: A sword, a sword is drawn for slaughter, burnished to consume and to flash lightning, 34 because you planned with false visions and lying divinations to lay it on the necks of depraved and wicked men whose day has come when their crimes are at an end. 35 Return it to its sheath! In the place where you were created, in the land of your origin, I will judge you. 36 I will pour out my indignation upon you, breathing my fiery wrath upon you; I will hand you over to ravaging men, artisans of destruction. 37 You shall be fuel for the fire, your blood shall flow throughout the land. You shall not be remembered, for I, the LORD, have spoken.

selves, you will be captured. 30 As for you, impious and wicked prince of Israel, whose doom is approaching to put an end to your crimes, 31 the Lord Yahweh says this: They will take away your diadem and remove your crown. Everything will be changed; the low will be raised and the high brought low. 32 Ruin, ruin, I shall bring such ruin as never was before, until the rightful ruler comes, on whom I shall bestow it."

33 'Son of man, prophesy and say, "The Lord Yahweh says this: In reply to the Ammonites and their jeers, say: The sword, the sword is drawn for slaughter, polished to devour, to flash like lightning — 34 while you have empty visions and consult lying omens — to cut the throats of the wicked, whose doom is approaching to put an end to their crimes. 35 Put it back in the scabbard. The place where you were created, the land of your origin, will be where I judge you. 36 I shall vent my fury on you, breathe the fire of my rage against you and hand you over to barbarous men whose trade is destruction. 37 You will be fuel for the fire, your blood will flow through the country, you will leave no memory behind you; for I, Yahweh, have spoken!" '

22 Thus the word of the LORD came to me: 2 You, son of man, would you judge, would you judge the bloody city? Then make known all her abominations, 3 and say: Thus says the Lord GOD: Woe to the city which sheds blood within herself so that her time has come, and which has made known all her idols for her own defilement. 4 By the blood which you shed you have been made guilty, and with the idols you made you have become defiled; you have brought on your day, so that the end of your years has come. Therefore I make you an object of scorn to the nations and a laughingstock to all foreign lands. 5 Those near you and those far off shall deride you because of your foul reputation and your great perversity. 6 See! the princes of Israel, family by family, are in you only for bloodshed. 7 Within you, father and mother are despised; in your midst, they extort from the resident alien; within you, they oppress orphans and widows. 8 What is holy to me you have spurned, and my sabbaths you have desecrated. 9 There are those in you who slander to cause bloodshed; within you are those who feast on the mountains; in your midst are those who do lewd things. 10 In you are those who uncover the nakedness of their fathers, and in you those who coerce women in their menstrual period. 11 There are those in you who do abominable things with the wives of their neighbors, men who defile their daughters-in-law by incest, men who coerce their sisters, the daughters of their own fathers. 12 There are those in you who take bribes to shed blood. You exact interest and usury; you despoil your neighbors violently; and me you have forgotten, says the Lord GOD.

22 The word of Yahweh was addressed to me as follows, 2 'Son of man, are you ready to judge? Are you ready to judge the blood-stained city? Confront her with all her loathsome practices! 3 Say, "The Lord Yahweh says this: City shedding blood inside yourself to hasten your doom, making foul idols on your soil to defile yourself, 4 you have incurred guilt by the blood you have shed, you have defiled yourself with the foul idols you have made, you have shortened your days, you have come to the end of your years. This is why I have made you an object of scorn to the nations and a laughing-stock to every country. 5 From far and near they will taunt you with your infamous disorders.

6 "Look! In you the princes of Israel, one and all, have furthered their own interests at the cost of bloodshed; 7 in you people have despised their fathers and mothers; in you they have ill-treated the settler; in you they have oppressed the widow and orphan. 8 You have treated my sanctuary with contempt, you have profaned my Sabbaths. 9 In you informers incite to bloodshed; in you people eat on the mountains and act licentiously; 10 in you they have sexual intercourse with their fathers; in you they force themselves on women in their periods; 11 in you one man engages in loathsome practices with his neighbour's wife, another lewdly defiles his daughter-in-law, another violates his sister, his own father's daughter. 12 In you people take bribes for shedding blood; you lend for profit and charge interest, you profit from your fellow by extortion and have forgotten about me — declares the Lord Yahweh.

21, 33–37: The present oracle against Ammon is inserted here, rather than in chapters 25–32, in order to complement the oracle against Jerusalem.

NEW REVISED STANDARD VERSION

13 See, I strike my hands together at the dishonest gain you have made, and at the blood that has been shed within you. 14 Can your courage endure, or can your hands remain strong in the days when I shall deal with you? I the LORD have spoken, and I will do it. 15 I will scatter you among the nations and disperse you through the countries, and I will purge your filthiness out of you. 16 And I *g* shall be profaned through you in the sight of the nations; and you shall know that I am the LORD.

17 The word of the LORD came to me: 18 Mortal, the house of Israel has become dross to me; all of them, silver, *h* bronze, tin, iron, and lead. In the smelter they have become dross. 19 Therefore thus says the Lord GOD: Because you have all become dross, I will gather you into the midst of Jerusalem. 20 As one gathers silver, bronze, iron, lead, and tin into a smelter, to blow the fire upon them in order to melt them; so I will gather you in my anger and in my wrath, and I will put you in and melt you. 21 I will gather you and blow upon you with the fire of my wrath, and you shall be melted within it. 22 As silver is melted in a smelter, so you shall be melted in it; and you shall know that I the LORD have poured out my wrath upon you.

23 The word of the LORD came to me: 24 Mortal, say to it: You are a land that is not cleansed, not rained upon in the day of indignation. 25 Its princes *i* within it are like a roaring lion tearing the prey; they have devoured human lives; they have taken treasure and precious things; they have made many widows within it. 26 Its priests have done violence to my teaching and have profaned my holy things; they have made no distinction between the holy and the common, neither have they taught the difference between the unclean and the clean, and they have disregarded my sabbaths, so that I am profaned among them. 27 Its officials within it are like wolves tearing the prey, shedding blood, destroying lives to get dishonest gain. 28 Its prophets have smeared whitewash on their behalf, seeing false visions and divining lies for them, saying, "Thus says the Lord GOD," when the LORD has not spoken. 29 The people of the land have practiced extortion and committed robbery; they have oppressed the poor and needy, and have extorted from the alien without redress. 30 And I sought for anyone among them who would repair the wall and stand in the breach before me on behalf of the land, so that I would not destroy it; but I found no one. 31 Therefore I have poured out my indignation upon them; I have consumed them with the fire of my wrath; I have returned their conduct upon their heads, says the Lord GOD.

23 The word of the LORD came to me: 2 Mortal, there were two women, the daughters of one mother; 3 they played the whore in Egypt; they played the whore in their youth; their breasts were caressed there, and their virgin bosoms were fondled. 4 Oholah was the name of the elder and Oholibah the name of her sister. They became mine, and they bore sons and daughters. As for their names, Oholah is Samaria, and Oholibah is Jerusalem.

5 Oholah played the whore while she was mine; she lusted after her lovers the Assyrians, warriors *j* 6 clothed in blue, governors and commanders, all of them handsome young men, mounted horsemen. 7 She bestowed her favors upon them, the choicest men of Assyria all of them; and she defiled herself with all the idols of everyone for whom she lusted. 8 She did not give up her whorings that she had practiced since Egypt; for in her youth men had lain with her and fondled her virgin bosom and poured out their lust

---

REVISED ENGLISH BIBLE

13 'See, I strike with my clenched fist at your ill-gotten gains and at the bloodshed within your walls. 14 Will your courage and strength endure when I deal with you? I, the LORD, have spoken and I shall act. 15 I shall disperse you among the nations and scatter you over the earth to rid you of your defilement. 16 I shall sift you in the sight of the nations, and you will know that I am the LORD.'

17 THIS word of the LORD came to me: 18 'O man, to me all Israelites are but an alloy, their silver debased with copper, tin, iron, and lead. 19 Therefore, these are the words of the Lord GOD: Because you are all alloyed, I shall gather you into Jerusalem, 20 as silver, copper, iron, lead, and tin are gathered into a crucible, where fire is blown to full heat to melt them. So shall I gather you in my anger and wrath, put you in it, and melt you; 21 I shall gather you in Jerusalem and fan the fire of my anger until you are melted. 22 As silver is melted in a crucible so will you be melted, and you will know that I, the LORD, have poured out my anger on you.'

23 THIS word of the LORD came to me: 24 'O man, say to Jerusalem: You are like a land on which no rain has fallen, no shower has come in the time of my wrath. 25 The princes within her are like lions growling as they tear their prey. They devour the people, and seize their wealth and valuables; they make widows of many women within her. 26 Her priests give rulings which violate my law, and profane what is sacred to me. They do not distinguish between sacred and profane, and enforce no distinction between clean and unclean. They disregard my sabbaths, and I am dishonoured among them. 27 The city's leaders are like wolves tearing their prey, shedding blood and destroying people's lives to obtain ill-gotten gain. 28 Her prophets whitewash over the cracks, their vision is false and their divination a lie. They say, "This is the word of the Lord GOD," when the LORD has not spoken. 29 The common people resort to oppression and robbery; they ill-treat the unfortunate and the poor, they oppress the alien and deny him justice.

30 'I looked among them for a man who would build a barricade in the breach and withstand me, to avert the destruction of the land; but I found no such person. 31 I poured out my wrath on them and utterly consumed them in my blazing anger. Thus I brought on them the punishment they had deserved. This is the word of the Lord GOD.'

23 This word of the LORD came to me: 2 'O man, there were once two women, daughters of the same mother, 3 who while they were still girls played the whore in Egypt. There they let their breasts be fondled and their virgin bosoms be pressed. 4 The elder was named Oholah, her sister Oholibah. They became mine and gave birth to sons and daughters. Oholah is Samaria, Oholibah Jerusalem.

5 'Though Oholah owed me obedience she played the whore and was infatuated with her Assyrian lovers, officers 6 in blue, viceroys and governors, all of them handsome young men riding on horseback. 7 She played the whore with all of them, the flower of Assyrian manhood; and because of her lust for all their idols she was defiled. 8 She never gave up the ways she had learnt in Egypt, where men had lain with her while she was still young, had pressed her virgin bosom and overwhelmed her with their fornication.

---

g Gk Syr Vg: Heb *you*   *h* Transposed from the end of the verse; compare verse 20   *i* Gk: Heb *indignation*. 25 *A conspiracy of its prophets*   *j* Meaning of Heb uncertain

22:18 **their silver . . . lead:** *prob. rdg; Heb.* copper, tin, iron, and lead inside a crucible; they are an alloy, silver.   22:24 **on which . . . fallen:** *so Gk; Heb.* which has not been cleansed.   22:25 **The princes . . . are:** *so Gk; Heb.* The conspiracy of her prophets within her is.

13 See, I am brushing one hand against the other because of the unjust profits you have made and because of the bloodshed in your midst. 14 Can your heart remain firm, will your hands be strong, in the days when I deal with you? I, the LORD, have spoken, and I will act. 15 I will disperse you among the nations and scatter you over foreign lands, so that I may purge your uncleanness. 16 In you I will allow myself to be profaned in the eyes of the nations; thus you shall know that I am the LORD.

17 Thus the word of the LORD came to me: 18 Son of man, the house of Israel has become dross for me. All of them are bronze and tin, iron and lead [in the midst of a furnace]: dross from silver have they become. 19 Therefore thus says the Lord GOD: Because all of you have become dross, therefore I must gather you together within Jerusalem. 20 Just as silver, bronze, iron, lead, and tin are gathered into a furnace and smelted in the roaring flames, so I will gather you together in my furious wrath, put you in, and smelt you. 21 When I have assembled you, I will blast you with the fire of my anger and smelt you with it. 22 You shall be smelted by it just as silver is smelted in a furnace. Thus you shall know that I, the Lord, have poured out my fury on you.

23 Thus the word of the LORD came to me: 24 Son of man, say to her: You are a land unrained on [that is, not rained on] at the time of my fury. 25 Her princes are like roaring lions that tear prey; they devour people, seizing their wealth and precious things, and make widows of many within her. 26 Her priests violate my law and profane what is holy to me; they do not distinguish between the sacred and the profane, nor teach the difference between the unclean and the clean; they pay no attention to my sabbaths, so that I have been profaned in their midst. 27 Her nobles within her are like wolves that tear prey, shedding blood and destroying lives to get unjust gain. 28 Her prophets cover them with whitewash, pretending to visions that are false and performing lying divinations, saying, "Thus says the Lord GOD," although the LORD has not spoken. 29 The people of the land practice extortion and commit robbery; they afflict the poor and the needy, and oppress the resident alien without justice. 30 Thus I have searched among them for someone who could build a wall or stand in the breach before me to keep me from destroying the land; but I found no one. 31 Therefore I have poured out my fury upon them; with my fiery wrath I have consumed them; I have brought down their conduct upon their heads, says the Lord GOD.

23 Thus the word of the LORD came to me: 2 Son of man, there were two women, daughters of the same mother, 3 who even as young girls played the harlot in Egypt. There the Egyptians caressed their bosoms and fondled their virginal breasts. 4 Oholah was the name of the elder, and the name of her sister was Oholibah. They became mine and bore sons and daughters. [As for their names: Samaria is Oholah, and Jerusalem is Oholibah.] 5 Oholah became a harlot faithless to me; she lusted after her lovers, the Assyrians, warriors 6 dressed in purple, governors and officers, all of them attractive young men, knights mounted on horses. 7 Thus she gave herself as a harlot to them, to all the elite of the Assyrians, and she defiled herself with all those for whom she lusted [with all their idols]. 8 She did not give up the harlotry which she had begun in Egypt, when they had lain with her as a young girl, fondling her virginal breasts and pouring out their impurities on her.

13 "Now I shall clap my hands at your acts of banditry and the blood that flows in you. 14 Will your heart be able to resist, will your hands be steady, the day when I call you to account? I, Yahweh, have spoken and shall act. 15 I shall scatter you among the nations and disperse you in foreign countries, and so put an end to the filthiness now inside you; 16 through your own fault, you will be profaned in the eyes of the nations, and you will know that I am Yahweh!" '

17 The word of Yahweh was addressed to me as follows, 18 'Son of man, for me, the House of Israel has become dross: copper, tin, iron, lead, all mixed up together in the melting-pot; they are dross. 19 And so, Lord Yahweh says this, "Since you have all become dross, right! I shall collect you inside Jerusalem. 20 As silver, copper, iron, lead and tin are collected in the melting-pot, and the fire is blown underneath to melt them down, so I shall collect you in my furious anger and have you melted down; 21 I shall collect you and blow up the fire of my rage for you and have you melted down inside the city. 22 As silver is melted in the melting-pot, so you will be melted down inside the city, and you will know that I, Yahweh, have vented my fury on you." '

23 The word of Yahweh was addressed to me as follows, 24 'Son of man, say to her, "You are a land that has not received rain or shower on the day of anger. 25 In you, the princes are like a roaring lion tearing its prey. They have eaten the people, seized wealth and jewels and widowed many inside her. 26 Her priests have violated my law and desecrated my sanctuary; they have made no distinction between sacred and profane, they have not taught people the difference between clean and unclean; they have turned their eyes away from my Sabbaths and I have been dishonoured by them. 27 In her the leaders are wolves tearing their prey, shedding blood and killing people to steal their possessions. 28 Her prophets have plastered these things over with their empty visions and lying prophecies, saying: Yahweh says this, although Yahweh has not spoken. 29 The people of the country have taken to extortion and banditry; they have oppressed the poor and needy and ill-treated the settler in a way that is unjustifiable. 30 I have been looking for someone among them to build a barricade and oppose me in the breach, to defend the country and prevent me from destroying it; but I have found no one. 31 Hence I have vented my fury on them; I have put an end to them in the fire of my rage. I have made their conduct recoil on their own heads—declares the Lord Yahweh." '

23 n The word of Yahweh was addressed to me as follows, 2 'Son of man, there were once two women, daughters of the same mother. 3 They played the whore in Egypt; they played the whore when they were still girls. There their nipples were handled, there their virgin breasts were first fondled. 4 Their names were: Oholah the elder, Oholibah her sister. They belonged to me and bore sons and daughters. As regards their names, Samaria is Oholah, Jerusalem Oholibah. 5 Now Oholah played the whore, although she belonged to me; she lusted after her lovers, her neighbours the Assyrians, 6 dressed in purple, governors and magistrates, all of them young and desirable, and skilful horsemen. 7 She played the whore with all of them, the pick of Assyria, and defiled herself with all the foul idols of all those with whom she was in love, 8 nor did she give up the whoring begun in Egypt, where men had slept with her from her girlhood, fondling her virgin breasts, debauching her over and over again.

---

n 23 = 16.

NEW REVISED STANDARD VERSION

upon her. 9 Therefore I delivered her into the hands of her lovers, into the hands of the Assyrians, for whom she lusted. 10 These uncovered her nakedness; they seized her sons and her daughters; and they killed her with the sword. Judgment was executed upon her, and she became a byword among women.

11 Her sister Oholibah saw this, yet she was more corrupt than she in her lusting and in her whorings, which were worse than those of her sister. 12 She lusted after the Assyrians, governors and commanders, warriors[k] clothed in full armor, mounted horsemen, all of them handsome young men. 13 And I saw that she was defiled; they both took the same way. 14 But she carried her whorings further; she saw male figures carved on the wall, images of the Chaldeans portrayed in vermilion, 15 with belts around their waists, with flowing turbans on their heads, all of them looking like officers — a picture of Babylonians whose native land was Chaldea. 16 When she saw them she lusted after them, and sent messengers to them in Chaldea. 17 And the Babylonians came to her into the bed of love, and they defiled her with their lust; and after she defiled herself with them, she turned from them in disgust. 18 When she carried on her whorings so openly and flaunted her nakedness, I turned in disgust from her, as I had turned from her sister. 19 Yet she increased her whorings, remembering the days of her youth, when she played the whore in the land of Egypt 20 and lusted after her paramours there, whose members were like those of donkeys, and whose emission was like that of stallions. 21 Thus you longed for the lewdness of your youth, when the Egyptians[l] fondled your bosom and caressed[m] your young breasts.

22 Therefore, O Oholibah, thus says the Lord GOD: I will rouse against you your lovers from whom you turned in disgust, and I will bring them against you from every side: 23 the Babylonians and all the Chaldeans, Pekod and Shoa and Koa, and all the Assyrians with them, handsome young men, governors and commanders all of them, officers and warriors,[n] all of them riding on horses. 24 They shall come against you from the north[o] with chariots and wagons and a host of peoples; they shall set themselves against you on every side with buckler, shield, and helmet, and I will commit the judgment to them, and they shall judge you according to their ordinances. 25 I will direct my indignation against you, in order that they may deal with you in fury. They shall cut off your nose and your ears, and your survivors shall fall by the sword. They shall seize your sons and your daughters, and your survivors shall be devoured by fire. 26 They shall also strip you of your clothes and take away your fine jewels. 27 So I will put an end to your lewdness and your whoring brought from the land of Egypt; you shall not long for them, or remember Egypt any more. 28 For thus says the Lord GOD: I will deliver you into the hands of those whom you hate, into the hands of those from whom you turned in disgust; 29 and they shall deal with you in hatred, and take away all the fruit of your labor, and leave you naked and bare, and the nakedness of your whorings shall be exposed. Your lewdness and your whorings 30 have brought this upon you, because you played the whore with the nations, and polluted yourself with their idols. 31 You have gone the way of your sister; therefore I will give her cup into your hand. 32 Thus says the Lord GOD:

> You shall drink your sister's cup,
> deep and wide;
> you shall be scorned and derided,
> it holds so much.

REVISED ENGLISH BIBLE

9 So I abandoned her to her lovers, the Assyrians, with whom she was infatuated. 10 They ravished her, they took away her sons and daughters, and they put her to the sword. She became notorious among women, and judgement was executed on her.

11 'Oholibah, her sister, saw it, but she surpassed her sister in lust and outdid her in playing the whore. 12 She too was infatuated with Assyrians, viceroys and governors, all handsome officers in full dress and riding on horseback. 13 I saw that she too had let herself be defiled. Both had gone the same way, 14 but she carried her fornication to greater lengths: she saw male figures carved on the wall, sculptured forms of Chaldaeans picked out in vermilion, 15 with belts round their waists and flowing turbans on their heads. All had the appearance of high Babylonian officers, natives of Chaldaea. 16 When she set eyes on them she was infatuated, and sent messengers to Chaldaea for them. 17 The Babylonians came to her to share her bed, and defiled her with fornication; she was defiled by them until her love turned to revulsion. 18 When she made no secret that she was a whore and let herself be ravished, I recoiled with revulsion from her as I recoiled from her sister. 19 Remembering how in her youth she had played the whore in Egypt, she played the whore over and over again. 20 She was infatuated with their male prostitutes, whose members were like those of donkeys and whose seed came in floods like that of stallions. 21 So, Oholibah, you relived the lewdness of your girlhood in Egypt when you let your bosom be pressed and your breasts fondled.

22 'The Lord GOD has said: I shall rouse against you, Oholibah, those lovers of yours who have filled you with revulsion, and bring them against you from every side: 23 the Babylonians, all the Chaldaeans from Pekod, Shoa, and Koa, and with them all the Assyrians, handsome young men, viceroys and governors, commanders and officers, all on horseback. 24 They will advance against you with war-horses, with chariots and wagons, with a host drawn from the nations, armed with shield, buckler, and helmet; they will beset you on every side. I shall give them authority to judge, and they will use that authority to execute judgement on you. 25 I shall turn my jealous wrath against you, and they will bring their fury to bear on you. They will cut off your nose and ears, and those of you left will fall by the sword. They will take your sons and daughters, and those of you left will end in flames. 26 They will strip you of your clothes and take away your finery. 27 So I shall put a stop to your lewdness and the harlotry which you first learnt in Egypt. You will never cast longing eyes on such things again, never remember Egypt any more.

28 'The Lord GOD says: I am handing you over to those whom you hate, those who have filled you with revulsion; 29 and they will bring their fury to bear on you. They will take all you have earned and leave you stark naked; the body with which you have played the whore will be ravished. It is your lewdness and your fornication 30 that have brought this on you; it is because you adopted heathen ways, played the whore, and became defiled with idols. 31 As you have followed in your sister's footsteps, I shall put her cup into your hand.

32 'The Lord GOD says:

> You will drink from your sister's cup,
> a cup deep and wide,
> charged to the very brim
> with mockery and scorn.

---

k Meaning of Heb uncertain   l Two Mss: MT from Egypt
m Cn: Heb for the sake of   n Compare verses 6 and 12: Heb officers
and called ones   o Gk: Meaning of Heb uncertain

23:21 fondled: prob. rdg; Heb. unintelligible.   23:23 officers:
prob. rdg, cp. verses 5 and 12; Heb. obscure.   23:25 those . . .
left: or your successors.

9 Therefore I handed her over to her lovers, the Assyrians for whom she had lusted. 10 They exposed her nakedness, her sons and daughters they took away, and herself they slew with the sword. Thus she became a byword for women, for they punished her grievously.

11 Though her sister Oholibah saw all this, her lust was more depraved than her sister's, and she outdid her in harlotry. 12 She too lusted after the Assyrians, governors and officers, warriors impeccably clothed, knights mounted on horses, all of them attractive young men. 13 I saw that she had defiled herself. Both had gone down the same path, 14 yet she went further in her harlotry. When she saw men drawn on the wall, the images of Chaldeans drawn with vermillion, 15 with sashes girded about their waists, flowing turbans on their heads, all looking like chariot warriors, the portraits of Babylonians, natives of Chaldea, 16 she lusted for them; no sooner had she set eyes on them than she sent messengers to them in Chaldea. 17 Then the Babylonians came to her, to the love couch, and defiled her with their intercourse. As soon as she was defiled by them, she became disgusted with them. 18 Her harlotry was discovered and her shame was revealed, and I became disgusted with her as I had become disgusted with her sister. 19 But she played the harlot all the more, recalling the days of her girlhood, when she had been a harlot in the land of Egypt. 20 She lusted for the lechers of Egypt, whose members are like that of an ass, and whose heat is like those of stallions. 21 You yearned for the lewdness of your girlhood, when the Egyptians fondled your breasts, caressing your bosom. 22 Therefore, Oholibah, thus says the Lord GOD: I will now stir up your lovers against you, those with whom you are disgusted, and I will bring them against you from every side: 23 the men of Babylon and all of Chaldea, Pekod, Shoa and Koa, along with all those of Assyria, attractive young men, all of them governors and officers, charioteers and warriors, all of them horsemen. 24 They shall come against you from the north with chariots and wagons and many peoples. Shields, bucklers, and helmets they shall array against you everywhere. 25 I will leave it to them to judge, and they will judge you by their own ordinances. I will let loose my jealousy against you, so that they shall deal with you in fury, cutting off your nose and ears; and what is left of you shall fall by the sword. They shall take away your sons and daughters, and what is left of you shall be devoured by fire. 26 They shall strip off your clothes and seize your splendid ornaments. 27 I will put an end to your lewdness and to the harlotry you began in Egypt; you shall no longer look toward it, nor shall you remember Egypt again. 28 For thus says the Lord GOD: I am now handing you over to those whom you hate, to those who fill you with disgust. 29 They shall deal with you in hatred, seizing all that you have worked for and leaving you stark naked, so that your indecent nakedness is exposed. Your lewdness and harlotry 30 have brought these things upon you, because you played the harlot with the nations by defiling yourself with their idols. 31 Because you followed in the path of your sister, I will hand you her cup. 32 Thus says the Lord GOD:

The cup of your sister you shall drink,
  so wide and deep, which holds so much,

9 'That is why I have handed her over to her lovers, to the Assyrians with whom she was in love. 10 They stripped her naked, seized her sons and daughters and put her to the sword. She became notorious among women for the justice done on her.

11 'Her sister Oholibah saw all this, but she was even more depraved, and her whorings were worse than her sister's. 12 She fell in love with her neighbours the Assyrians, governors and magistrates, dressed in sumptuous clothes, skilful horsemen, all young and desirable. 13 Then I saw that she had defiled herself, that both sisters were equally bad. 14 She began whoring worse than ever; no sooner had she seen wall-carvings of men, pictures of Chaldaeans coloured vermilion, 15 men with sashes round their waists and elaborate turbans on their heads, all so lordly of bearing, depicting the Babylonians, natives of Chaldaea, 16 than she fell in love with them at first sight and sent messengers to them in Chaldaea. 17 The Babylonians came to her, shared her love-bed and defiled her with their whoring. Once defiled by them, she withdrew her affection from them. 18 Thus she flaunted her whoring, exposing her body, until I withdrew my affection from her as I had withdrawn it from her sister. 19 But she began whoring worse than ever, remembering her girlhood, when she had played the whore in Egypt, 20 when she had been in love with her profligates, big-membered as donkeys, ejaculating as violently as stallions. 21 'You were hankering for the debauchery of your girlhood, when they used to handle your nipples in Egypt and fondle your young breasts. 22 And so, Oholibah, Lord Yahweh says this, "I shall set all your lovers against you, from whom you have withdrawn your affection, and bring them to assault you from all directions: 23 the Babylonians and all the Chaldaeans, the men of Pekod and Shoa and Koa, and all the Assyrians with them, young and desirable, all governors and magistrates, all famous lords and skilful horsemen. 24 From the north, they will advance on you with chariots and wagons and an international army and beset you with shield, buckler and helmet on all sides. I shall charge them to pass sentence on you and they will pass sentence on you as they think fit. 25 I shall direct my jealousy against you; they will treat you with fury; they will cut off your nose and ears, and what is left of your family will fall by the sword; they will seize your sons and daughters, and what is left will be burnt. 26 They will strip off your garments and rob you of your jewels. 27 I shall put an end to your debauchery and to the whorings you began in Egypt; you will not look to the Egyptians any more, you will never think of them again. 28 For the Lord Yahweh says this: Now, I shall hand you over to those you hate, to those for whom you no longer feel affection. 29 They will treat you with hatred, they will rob you of the entire fruit of your labours and leave you stark naked. And thus your shameful whorings will be exposed, your debauchery and your whorings. 30 This will happen to you because you have played the whore with the nations and have defiled yourself with their foul idols. 31 Since you have copied your sister's behaviour, I shall put her cup in your hand." 32 The Lord Yahweh says this:

You will drink your sister's cup,
  a cup both deep and wide,
  leading to laughter and mockery,
  so ample the draught it holds.

NEW REVISED STANDARD VERSION

33 You shall be filled with drunkenness and sorrow.
A cup of horror and desolation
is the cup of your sister Samaria;

34 you shall drink it and drain it out,
and gnaw its sherds,
and tear out your breasts;

for I have spoken, says the Lord GOD. 35 Therefore thus says the Lord GOD: Because you have forgotten me and cast me behind your back, therefore bear the consequences of your lewdness and whorings.

36 The LORD said to me: Mortal, will you judge Oholah and Oholibah? Then declare to them their abominable deeds. 37 For they have committed adultery, and blood is on their hands; with their idols they have committed adultery; and they have even offered up to them for food the children whom they had borne to me. 38 Moreover this they have done to me: they have defiled my sanctuary on the same day and profaned my sabbaths. 39 For when they had slaughtered their children for their idols, on the same day they came into my sanctuary to profane it. This is what they did in my house.

40 They even sent for men to come from far away, to whom a messenger was sent, and they came. For them you bathed yourself, painted your eyes, and decked yourself with ornaments; 41 you sat on a stately couch, with a table spread before it on which you had placed my incense and my oil. 42 The sound of a raucous multitude was around her, with many of the rabble brought in drunken from the wilderness; and they put bracelets on the arms[p] of the women, and beautiful crowns upon their heads.

43 Then I said, Ah, she is worn out with adulteries, but they carry on their sexual acts with her. 44 For they have gone in to her, as one goes in to a whore. Thus they went in to Oholah and to Oholibah, wanton women. 45 But righteous judges shall declare them guilty of adultery and of bloodshed; because they are adulteresses and blood is on their hands.

46 For thus says the Lord GOD: Bring up an assembly against them, and make them an object of terror and of plunder. 47 The assembly shall stone them and with their swords they shall cut them down; they shall kill their sons and their daughters, and burn up their houses. 48 Thus will I put an end to lewdness in the land, so that all women may take warning and not commit lewdness as you have done. 49 They shall repay you for your lewdness, and you shall bear the penalty for your sinful idolatry; and you shall know that I am the Lord GOD.

24 In the ninth year, in the tenth month, on the tenth day of the month, the word of the LORD came to me: 2 Mortal, write down the name of this day, this very day. The king of Babylon has laid siege to Jerusalem this very day. 3 And utter an allegory to the rebellious house and say to them, Thus says the Lord GOD:

Set on the pot, set it on,
pour in water also;

4 put in it the pieces,
all the good pieces, the thigh and the shoulder;
fill it with choice bones.

5 Take the choicest one of the flock,
pile the logs[q] under it;
boil its pieces,[r]
seethe[s] also its bones in it.

REVISED ENGLISH BIBLE

33 It will be full of drunkenness and grief,
a cup of uttermost ruin,
the cup of your sister Samaria;

34 you will drink it to the dregs,
and then gnaw it into shreds
while you tear your breasts.

'This is my sentence, says the Lord GOD.

35 'The Lord GOD says: Because you have forsaken me and cast me behind your back, you will have to bear the guilt of your lewdness and fornication.'

36 The LORD said to me, 'O man, will you bring a charge against Oholah and Oholibah? Then tax them with their vile offences. 37 They have committed adultery, and there is blood on their hands. They have committed adultery with their idols and offered to them as food the children they had borne me. 38 Here is another thing they have done to me: they have polluted my sanctuary and desecrated my sabbaths. 39 They came into my sanctuary and desecrated it by slaughtering their sons as an offering to their idols; this they did in my house.

40 'Then also they would send for men from a far-off country, who would come at the messenger's bidding. For them you bathed your body, painted your eyes, decked yourself in your finery, 41 sat yourself on a splendid couch, and had a table placed before it on which you laid my incense and oil. 42 There was loud shouting from a carefree crowd. Besides ordinary folk, Sabaeans were there, brought in from the desert; they put bracelets on the harlots' arms and beautiful garlands on their heads. 43 I thought: Ah, that woman, grown old in adultery! Now they will commit fornication with her—her of all women! 44 They resorted to her as to a prostitute; they resorted to Oholah and Oholibah, those lewd women. 45 Upright men will condemn them for their adultery and bloodshed; they are adulterous, and have blood on their hands.

46 'The Lord GOD says: Bring up a mob to punish them; give them over to terror and pillage. 47 Let the mob stone them and hack them to pieces with their swords, kill their sons and daughters, and burn down their houses. 48 In this way I shall put an end to lewdness in the land, and all the women will take warning not to follow their lewd example. 49 When they punish you for your lewd conduct and you pay the penalty for your idolatries, you will know that I am the Lord GOD.'

24 THIS word of the LORD came to me on the tenth day of the tenth month in the ninth year: 2 'O man, write down as the name for this special day: This day the king of Babylon besieged Jerusalem. 3 Sing a song of derision to this body of rebels; say to them: These are the words of the Lord GOD:

Set a cauldron on the fire,
set it on and pour in water.

4 Into it collect the pieces,
every choice piece,
fill it with leg and shoulder, the best of the bones;

5 take the pick of the flock.
Pile the wood underneath;
seethe the stew
and boil the bones in it.

23:38 **sanctuary:** *so* Gk; *Heb. adds* on that day.
23:39 **desecrated it:** *so* Gk; *Heb. adds* on that day.   23:43 **her of all women:** *lit. and* her.   23:44 **They resorted to her:** *so one* MS; *others* He resorted to her.   23:48 **their:** *so* Gk; *Heb.* your.
24:5 **wood:** *prob. rdg, cp. verse* 10; *Heb.* bones.

p Heb *hands*   *q* Compare verse 10: Heb *the bones*   *r* Two Mss: Heb *its boilings*   *s* Cn: Heb *its bones seethe*

33 Filled with destruction and grief,
a cup of dismay, the cup of your sister.

34 You shall drain it dry, and gnaw at the very sherds of the cup, and you shall tear out your breasts; for I have spoken, says the Lord GOD. 35 Therefore thus says the Lord GOD: Because you have forgotten me and cast me behind your back, it is for you to bear the penalty of your lewdness and harlotry.

36 Then the LORD said to me: Son of man, would you judge Oholah and Oholibah? Then make known to them their abominations. 37 For they committed adultery, and blood is on their hands. They committed adultery with their idols; to feed them they immolated the children they had borne me. 38 [This, too, they did to me: they defiled my sanctuary and desecrated my sabbaths. 39 On the very day they slew their children for their idols, they entered my sanctuary to desecrate it. Thus they acted within my house.] 40 Moreover, they sent for men who had to come from afar, to whom messengers were sent. And so they came — and for them you bathed yourself, painted your eyes, and put on ornaments. 41 You sat on a couch prepared for them, with a table spread before it, on which you had set my incense and oil. 42 Then was heard the shout of a carefree mob in the city, and these were men brought in from the desert, who put bracelets on the women's arms and splendid diadems on their heads. 43 So I said: "Oh, this woman jaded with adulteries! Now they will commit whoredom with her, and as for her. . . ." 44 And indeed they did come to her as men come to a harlot. Thus they came to Oholah and Oholibah, the lewd women. 45 But just men shall punish them with the sentence meted out to adulteresses and murderesses, for they have committed adultery, and blood is on their hands.

46 Thus says the Lord GOD: Summon an assembly against them, and deliver them over to terror and plunder. 47 The assembly shall stone them and hack them to pieces with their swords. They shall slay their sons and daughters, and burn their houses with fire. 48 Thus I will put an end to lewdness in the land, and all the women will be warned not to imitate your lewdness. 49 They shall inflict on you the penalty of your lewdness, and you shall pay for your sins of idolatry. Thus you shall know that I am the LORD.

24 On the tenth day of the tenth month, in the ninth year, the word of the LORD came to me: 2 Son of man, write down this date today, for this very day the king of Babylon has invested Jerusalem. 3 Propose this parable to the rebellious house: Thus says the Lord GOD:

Set up the pot, set it up,
then pour in some water.
4 Put in it pieces of meat,
all good pieces: thigh and shoulder;
Fill it with the choicest joints
5 taken from the pick of the flock.
Then pile the wood beneath it;
bring to a boil these pieces
and the joints that are in it.

33 You will be filled with drunkenness and sorrow.
Cup of affliction and devastation,
the cup of your sister Samaria,
34 you will drink it, you will drain it;
then you will break it in pieces
and lacerate your own breasts.

For I have spoken — declared the Lord Yahweh.

35 "And so, the Lord Yahweh says this: Since you have forgotten me and have turned your back on me, you too will have to bear the weight of your debauchery and whorings." ' 36 And Yahweh said to me, 'Son of man, are you ready to judge Oholah and Oholibah and charge them with their loathsome practices? 37 They have been adulteresses, their hands are dripping with blood, they have committed adultery with their foul idols. As for the children they had borne me, they have offered them as burnt sacrifices to feed them. 38 And here is something else they have done to me: they have defiled my sanctuary today and have profaned my Sabbaths. 39 The same day as sacrificing their children to their idols, they have been to my sanctuary and profaned it. Yes, this is what they have done in my own house.

40 'Worse still, they summoned men from far away, invited by messenger, and they came. For them you bathed, you painted your eyes, put on your jewels 41 and sat on a sumptuous bed, by which a table was laid out. On this you had put my incense and my oil. 42 The noise of the carefree company resounded, made by the crowd of men brought in from the desert; they put bracelets on the women's arms and magnificent crowns on their heads. 43 I thought, "That woman, worn out with adultery! Are they going to fornicate with her too?" 44 Yet they visit her like any common prostitute, just as they visited those profligate women Oholah and Oholibah. 45 All the same, there are upright men who will judge them as adulteresses and murderesses are judged, since they are adulteresses and their hands are dripping with blood."

46 'The Lord Yahweh says this, "Summon an assembly to deal with them, and hand them over to terror and pillage; 47 let the assembly stone them and dispatch them with their swords; let their sons and daughters be slaughtered and their houses set on fire. 48 This is how I shall purge the country of debauchery, so that all women will be taught the lesson never to ape your debauchery again. 49 Your debauchery will recoil on yourselves, and you will bear the weight of the sins committed with your foul idols and you will know that I am the Lord Yahweh." '

24 In the ninth year, on the tenth day of the tenth month, the word of Yahweh was addressed to me as follows, 2 'Son of man, write down today's date, yes, today's, for this very day the king of Babylon began his attack on Jerusalem. 3 So pronounce a parable for this tribe of rebels. Say, "The Lord Yahweh says this:

Put the pot on the fire;
put it on; pour the water in!
4 Now put the cuts of meat all in together,
all the best cuts, leg and shoulder.
Fill it with the best bones.
5 Take the best of the flock,
then heap wood underneath;
boil it thoroughly
until even the bones are cooked.

NEW REVISED STANDARD VERSION

6 Therefore thus says the Lord GOD:
 Woe to the bloody city,
  the pot whose rust is in it,
  whose rust has not gone out of it!
 Empty it piece by piece,
  making no choice at all.*t*

7 For the blood she shed is inside it;
  she placed it on a bare rock;
 she did not pour it out on the ground,
  to cover it with earth.

8 To rouse my wrath, to take vengeance,
 I have placed the blood she shed
  on a bare rock,
 so that it may not be covered.

9 Therefore thus says the Lord GOD:
 Woe to the bloody city!
  I will even make the pile great.

10 Heap up the logs, kindle the fire;
 boil the meat well, mix in the spices,
  let the bones be burned.

11 Stand it empty upon the coals,
 so that it may become hot, its copper glow,
  its filth melt in it, its rust be consumed.

12 In vain I have wearied myself;*u*
 its thick rust does not depart.
  To the fire with its rust!*v*

13 Yet, when I cleansed you in your filthy lewdness,
  you did not become clean from your filth;
 you shall not again be cleansed
  until I have satisfied my fury upon you.

14 I the LORD have spoken; the time is coming, I will act. I will not refrain, I will not spare, I will not relent. According to your ways and your doings I will judge you, says the Lord GOD.

15 The word of the LORD came to me: 16 Mortal, with one blow I am about to take away from you the delight of your eyes; yet you shall not mourn or weep, nor shall your tears run down. 17 Sigh, but not aloud; make no mourning for the dead. Bind on your turban, and put your sandals on your feet; do not cover your upper lip or eat the bread of mourners.*w* 18 So I spoke to the people in the morning, and at evening my wife died. And on the next morning I did as I was commanded.

19 Then the people said to me, "Will you not tell us what these things mean for us, that you are acting this way?" 20 Then I said to them: The word of the LORD came to me: 21 Say to the house of Israel, Thus says the Lord GOD: I will profane my sanctuary, the pride of your power, the delight of your eyes, and your heart's desire; and your sons and your daughters whom you left behind shall fall by the sword. 22 And you shall do as I have done; you shall not cover your upper lip or eat the bread of mourners.*w* 23 Your turbans shall be on your heads and your sandals on your feet; you shall not mourn or weep, but you shall pine away in your iniquities and groan to one another. 24 Thus Ezekiel shall be a sign to you; you shall do just as he has done. When this comes, then you shall know that I am the Lord GOD.

25 And you, mortal, on the day when I take from them their stronghold, their joy and glory, the delight of their eyes and their heart's affection, and also*x* their sons and their daughters, 26 on that day, one who has escaped will come to you to report to you the news. 27 On that day your

REVISED ENGLISH BIBLE

6 'The Lord GOD says:

 Woe betide the city running with blood,
  woe to the pot green with corrosion
 which will never come off!
 Empty it, piece after piece,
  with no lot cast for any of them.

7 The city had blood in her midst
 and she poured it on the bare rock;
 it was not shed on the ground
  for the dust to cover it.

8 I have spilt her blood on the bare rock
 so that it cannot be covered;
 it will arouse anger
  and call out for vengeance.

9 'The Lord GOD says:

 Woe betide the city running with blood!
  I myself shall make a great fire-pit.

10 Fill it with logs, kindle the fire;
 make an end of the meat,
  pour out all the broth and the bones with it.

11 Then set the pot empty on the coals
 so that its copper may be heated red-hot,
 that the impurities in it may be melted
  and the corrosion burnt off.

12 Though you exhaust yourself with your efforts
 the corrosion is so deep it will not come off;
  only fire will rid it of corrosion.

13 When in your filthy lewdness I wished to cleanse you,
  you did not become clean,
 nor will you ever be clean again
  until I have spent my anger against you.

14 'I, the LORD, have spoken: The time is coming and I shall act. I shall not condone or pity or relent. You will be judged by your conduct and by what you have done. This is the word of the Lord GOD.'

15 THIS word of the LORD came to me: 16 'O man, I am taking from you at one stroke the dearest thing you have, but you are not to wail or weep or give way to tears. 17 Suppress your grief, and observe no mourning for the dead. Wrap your turban on your head and put on your sandals. You are not to veil your beard in mourning or eat the bread of sorrow.'

18 I spoke to the people in the morning. That evening my wife died, and next morning I did as I had been commanded. 19 The people asked me what meaning my actions had for them. 20 I answered, 'This word of the LORD came to me: 21 Tell the Israelites: The Lord GOD has said: I am about to desecrate my sanctuary, which has been your strong boast, the delight of your eyes, and your heart's desire, and the sons and daughters you have left behind will fall by the sword. 22 You are to do as I have done,' I said: 'you are not to cover your beard in mourning or eat the bread of sorrow. 23 Your turbans are to be on your heads and your sandals on your feet; you are not to wail or weep. Because of your wickedness you will pine away, groaning to each other. 24 Ezekiel will be a sign to warn you, says the LORD, and you are to do as he has done. When judgement befalls you, you will know that I am the Lord GOD.'

25 'Now, O man, I am taking from them at that time the stronghold whose beauty so gladdened them, the delight of their eyes, their heart's desire, and I am taking their sons and daughters. 26 When a fugitive then comes and brings the news to you, 27 you will recover the power of speech and,

---

t Heb *piece, no lot has fallen on it* *u* Cn: Meaning of Heb uncertain
v Meaning of Heb uncertain *w* Vg Tg: Heb *of men* *x* Heb lacks *and also*

24:10 **pour . . . broth:** *prob. rdg; Heb.* mix ointment. **with it:** *prob. rdg; Heb.* will be scorched. 24:12 **Though. . . efforts:** *prob. rdg; Heb.* obscure.

NEW AMERICAN BIBLE

⁶Take out its pieces, one by one,
without casting lots for it.

Therefore, thus says the Lord GOD: Woe to the bloody city, a pot containing rust, whose rust has not been removed. ⁷For the blood she shed is in her midst; she poured it on the bare rock; she did not pour it out on the earth, to be covered with dust. ⁸To work up my wrath, to excite my vengeance, she put her blood on the bare rock, not to be covered. ⁹Therefore, thus says the Lord GOD:

I, too, will heap up a great bonfire,
10   piling on wood and kindling the fire,
Till the meat has been cooked,
    till the broth has boiled.

¹¹Then I will set the pot empty on the coals till its metal glows red hot, till the impurities in it melt, and its rust disappears. ¹²Yet not even with fire will its great rust be removed. ¹³Because you have sullied yourself with lewdness when I would have purified you, and you refused to be purified of your uncleanness, therefore you shall not be purified until I wreak my fury on you. ¹⁴I, the LORD, have spoken; it is coming, for I will bring it about without fail. I will not have pity nor repent. By your conduct and your deeds you shall be judged, says the Lord GOD.

¹⁵Thus the word of the LORD came to me: ¹⁶Son of man, by a sudden blow I am taking away from you the delight of your eyes, but do not mourn or weep or shed any tears. ¹⁷Groan in silence, make no lament for the dead, bind on your turban, put your sandals on your feet, do not cover your beard, and do not eat the customary bread. ¹⁸That evening my wife died, and the next morning I did as I had been commanded. ¹⁹Then the people asked me, "Will you not tell us what all these things that you are doing mean for us?" I therefore spoke to the people that morning, ²⁰saying to them: Thus the word of the LORD came to me: ²¹Say to the house of Israel: Thus says the Lord GOD: I will now desecrate my sanctuary, the stronghold of your pride, the delight of your eyes, the desire of your soul. The sons and daughters you left behind shall fall by the sword. ²⁴Ezekiel shall be a sign for you: all that he did you shall do when it happens. Thus you shall know that I am the LORD. ²²You shall do as I have done, not covering your beards nor eating the customary bread. ²³Your turbans shall remain on your heads, your sandals on your feet. You shall not mourn or weep, but you shall rot away because of your sins and groan one to another.

²⁵As for you, son of man, truly, on the day I take away from them their bulwark, their glorious joy, the delight of their eyes, the desire of their soul, and the pride of their hearts, their sons and daughters, ²⁶that day the fugitive will come to you, that you may hear it for yourself; ²⁷that day

NEW JERUSALEM BIBLE

⁶"For the Lord Yahweh says this:

Disaster is in store for the bloody city,
for that rusty cooking pot
whose rust will not come off!
Empty it, bit by bit,
not bothering to draw lots;
⁷for she is still full of bloodshed,
she has put blood on the naked rock;
she did not pour it on the ground
so as to cover it with dust.
⁸To make anger rise, to exact vengeance,
I have put her blood on the naked rock,
so that it should not be covered:

⁹"So, the Lord Yahweh says this:

Disaster is in store for the bloody city!
I too plan to build a great fire.
10Heap on the wood, light it,
cook the meat, prepare the seasoning
let the bones burn!
11Put the empty pot on the coals
to make it hot,
until the bronze glows,
the filth inside melts
and the rust is burnt away!

¹²"But all that rust would not come off in the fire. ¹³Your filth is infamous. Since I have tried to purge you and you would not let yourself be purged of your filth, so now you will never be purged of your filth until I have sated my anger on you. ¹⁴I, Yahweh, have spoken; this will happen; I shall act and not relent; I shall show no pity, no compassion. You will be judged as your conduct and actions deserve—declares the Lord Yahweh." '

¹⁵The word of Yahweh was addressed to me as follows, ¹⁶'Son of man, at a blow I am about to deprive you of the delight of your eyes. But you are not to lament, not to weep, not to let your tears run down. ¹⁷Groan in silence, do not go into mourning for the dead, knot your turban round your head, put your sandals on your feet, do not cover your beard, do not eat the usual food.' ¹⁸I told this to the people in the morning, and my wife died in the evening, and the next morning I did as I had been ordered. ¹⁹The people then said to me, 'Will you not explain what meaning these actions have for us?' ²⁰I replied, 'The word of Yahweh has been addressed to me as follows, ²¹'Say to the House of Israel, the Lord Yahweh says this: I am about to profane my sanctuary, the pride of your strength, the delight of your eyes, the joy of your hearts. Your sons and daughters whom you have left behind will fall by the sword. ²²Then you will do as I have done: you will not cover your beards or eat the usual food; ²³you will keep your turbans on your heads and your sandals on your feet; you will not lament or weep but will waste away for your crimes, groaning among yourselves. ²⁴Thus Ezekiel is a sign for you. You will do exactly what he has done. And when this happens, you will know that I am Lord Yahweh!" '

²⁵'And, son of man, the day that I deprive them of their strength, their crowning joy, the delight of their eyes, the joy of their hearts, their sons and daughters, ²⁶that day a survivor will bring you the news. ²⁷That day your mouth

mouth shall be opened to the one who has escaped, and you shall speak and no longer be silent. So you shall be a sign to them; and they shall know that I am the LORD.

25 The word of the LORD came to me: 2 Mortal, set your face toward the Ammonites and prophesy against them. 3 Say to the Ammonites, Hear the word of the Lord GOD: Thus says the Lord GOD, Because you said, "Aha!" over my sanctuary when it was profaned, and over the land of Israel when it was made desolate, and over the house of Judah when it went into exile; 4 therefore I am handing you over to the people of the east for a possession. They shall set their encampments among you and pitch their tents in your midst; they shall eat your fruit, and they shall drink your milk. 5 I will make Rabbah a pasture for camels and Ammon a fold for flocks. Then you shall know that I am the LORD. 6 For thus says the Lord GOD: Because you have clapped your hands and stamped your feet and rejoiced with all the malice within you against the land of Israel, 7 therefore I have stretched out my hand against you, and will hand you over as plunder to the nations. I will cut you off from the peoples and will make you perish out of the countries; I will destroy you. Then you shall know that I am the LORD.

8 Thus says the Lord GOD: Because Moab ʸ said, The house of Judah is like all the other nations, 9 therefore I will lay open the flank of Moab from the towns ᶻ on its frontier, the glory of the country, Beth-jeshimoth, Baal-meon, and Kiriathaim. 10 I will give it along with Ammon to the people of the east as a possession. Thus Ammon shall be remembered no more among the nations, 11 and I will execute judgments upon Moab. Then they shall know that I am the LORD.

12 Thus says the Lord GOD: Because Edom acted revengefully against the house of Judah and has grievously offended in taking vengeance upon them, 13 therefore thus says the Lord GOD, I will stretch out my hand against Edom, and cut off from it humans and animals, and I will make it desolate; from Teman even to Dedan they shall fall by the sword. 14 I will lay my vengeance upon Edom by the hand of my people Israel; and they shall act in Edom according to my anger and according to my wrath; and they shall know my vengeance, says the Lord GOD.

15 Thus says the Lord GOD: Because with unending hostilities the Philistines acted in vengeance, and with malice of heart took revenge in destruction; 16 therefore thus says the Lord GOD, I will stretch out my hand against the Philistines, cut off the Cherethites, and destroy the rest of the seacoast. 17 I will execute great vengeance on them with wrathful punishments. Then they shall know that I am the LORD, when I lay my vengeance on them.

26 In the eleventh year, on the first day of the month, the word of the LORD came to me: 2 Mortal, because Tyre said concerning Jerusalem,

"Aha, broken is the gateway of the peoples;
    it has swung open to me;
I shall be replenished,
    now that it is wasted."

3 Therefore, thus says the Lord GOD:
    See, I am against you, O Tyre!
    I will hurl many nations against you,
        as the sea hurls its waves.
4   They shall destroy the walls of Tyre
        and break down its towers.

no longer dumb, you will speak with the fugitive. So you will be a warning to the people, and they will know that I am the LORD.'

25 THIS word of the LORD came to me: 2 'O man, face towards the Ammonites and prophesy against them. 3 Say this to them: Listen to the word of the Lord GOD. He says: Because you cried "Hurrah!" when my holy place was desecrated, when Israel's land was laid waste, and the people of Judah sent into exile, 4 I am giving you into the possession of tribes from the east. They will pitch their tents and establish their camps among you; they will eat your crops and drink your milk. 5 I shall turn Rabbah into a camel pasture and Ammon into a sheep-walk. Thus you will know that I am the LORD.

6 'These are the words of the Lord GOD: Because you clapped your hands and stamped your feet and exulted over the land of Israel with spiteful contempt, 7 I shall stretch out my hand over you and give you up to be plundered by the nations. I shall cut you off from other peoples, destroy you in every land, and bring you to ruin. Thus you will know that I am the LORD.

8 'The Lord GOD says: Because Moab said, "Judah is like all other nations," 9 I shall expose the flank of Moab and from one end to the other lay open its towns, the glory of the land: Beth-jeshimoth, Baal-meon, and Kiriathaim. 10 I shall give Moab and Ammon into the possession of tribes from the east, so that all memory of the Ammonites will be blotted out among the nations, 11 and so that I may execute judgement upon Moab. Thus they will know that I am the LORD.

12 'The Lord GOD says: Because Edom exacted harsh revenge on Judah and by so doing incurred lasting guilt, 13 I shall stretch my hand out over Edom, says the Lord GOD, and destroy both people and animals in it, laying waste the land from Teman as far as Dedan; they will fall by the sword. 14 I shall wreak my vengeance on Edom through my people Israel. They will deal with Edom as my anger and fury demand, and it will feel my vengeance. This is the word of the Lord GOD.

15 'The Lord GOD says: Because the Philistines have resorted to revenge, avenging themselves with spiteful contempt, and destroying to satisfy an age-long enmity, 16 I shall stretch out my hand over the Philistines, says the Lord GOD. I shall wipe out the Kerethites and destroy the other dwellers by the sea. 17 I shall take mighty vengeance upon them and punish them in my fury. When I exact my vengeance, they will know that I am the LORD.'

26 This word of the LORD came to me on the first day of the first month in the eleventh year: 2 'O man, since Tyre has said of Jerusalem,

"Aha! She who was the gateway of the nations is
        broken,
    her gates lie open before me;
    I prosper, she lies in ruin,"

3 the Lord GOD says:

    I am against you, Tyre!
    As the sea raises up its waves,
    so shall I raise up many nations against you.
    4 They will destroy the walls of Tyre
        and overthrow her towers.

ʸ Gk Old Latin: Heb *Moab and Seir*   ᶻ Heb *towns from its towns*

25:8 **Moab:** *so Gk; Heb. adds* and Seir.   26:1 **first month:** *so Gk; Heb. omits* first.

your mouth shall be opened and you shall be dumb no longer. Thus you shall be a sign to them, and they shall know that I am the LORD.

25 Thus the word of the LORD came to me: ²Son of man, turn toward the Ammonites and prophesy against them. ³Say to the Ammonites: Hear the word of the LORD! Thus says the Lord GOD: Because you cried out your joy over the desecration of my sanctuary, the devastation of the land of Israel, and the exile of the house of Judah, ⁴therefore I will deliver you into the possession of the Easterners. They shall set up their encampments among you and pitch their tents; they shall eat your fruits and drink your milk. ⁵I will make Rabbah a pasture for camels, and the villages of the Ammonites a resting place for flocks. Thus you shall know that I am the LORD.

⁶For thus says the Lord GOD: Because you clapped your hands and stamped your feet, rejoicing most maliciously in your heart over the land of Israel, ⁷therefore I will stretch out my hand against you. I will make you plunder for the nations, I will cut you off from the peoples, and remove you from the lands. I will destroy you, and thus you shall know that I am the LORD.

⁸Thus says the Lord GOD: Because Moab said, "See! the house of Judah is like all other nations," ⁹therefore I will clear the shoulder of Moab totally of its cities, the jewels of the land: Beth-jesimoth, Baal-meon, and Kiriathaim. ¹⁰I will hand her over, along with the Ammonites, into the possession of the Easterners, that she may not be remembered among the peoples. ¹¹Thus I will execute judgment upon Moab, that they may know that I am the LORD.

¹²Thus says the Lord GOD: Because Edom has taken vengeance on the house of Judah and has made itself grievously guilty by taking vengeance on them, ¹³therefore thus says the Lord GOD: I will stretch out my hand against Edom and cut off from it man and beast. I will make it a waste from Teman to Dedan; they shall fall by the sword. ¹⁴My vengeance upon Edom I will entrust to my people Israel, who will deal with Edom in accordance with my anger and my fury; thus they shall know my vengeance, says the Lord GOD.

¹⁵Thus says the Lord GOD: Because the Philistines have acted revengefully, and have taken vengeance with destructive malice in their hearts, with an undying enmity, ¹⁶therefore thus says the Lord GOD: See! I am stretching out my hand against the Philistines; I will cut off the Cherethites and wipe out the remnant on the seacoast. ¹⁷I will execute great acts of vengeance on them, punishing them furiously. Thus they shall know that I am the LORD, when I wreak my vengeance on them.

26 On the first day of the . . . month in the eleventh year, the word of the LORD came to me: ²Son of man, because of what Tyre said of Jerusalem:

"Aha! it is broken, the gateway to the peoples;
    now that it is ruined, its wealth reverts to me!"
³   therefore thus says the Lord GOD:
See! I am coming at you, Tyre;
    I will churn up against you many nations,
    even as the sea churns up its waves;
⁴They shall destroy the walls of Tyre
    and raze her towers.

will be opened to speak to the survivor; you will speak and no longer be dumb; you will be a sign for them, and they will know that I am Yahweh.'

25 The word of Yahweh was addressed to me as follows, ²'Son of man, turn towards the Ammonites and prophesy against them. ³Say to the Ammonites, "Hear the word of the Lord Yahweh. The Lord Yahweh says this:

"Since you gloated over my sanctuary when it was profaned, and over the land of Israel when it was ravaged, and over the House of Judah when it went into exile, ⁴I shall let the sons of the East take possession of you; they will pitch their camps inside you, they will make their home in you. They will be the ones to eat your produce and drink your milk. ⁵I shall turn Rabbah into a camel yard and the towns of Ammon into sheepfolds. And so you will know that I am Yahweh.

⁶"The Lord Yahweh says this: Since you have clapped your hands and danced for joy, full of malicious delight at Israel's fate, ⁷my hand will be against you for this; I shall hand you over to be looted by the peoples, obliterate you as a nation and wipe you out as a country. I shall reduce you to nothing, and you will know that I am Yahweh.

⁸"The Lord Yahweh says this:

"Since Moab and Seir have said: Look at the House of Judah; it is no different from any other nation; ⁹very well, I shall expose Moab's heights; its cities will no longer be cities throughout the land — the jewels of the country, Beth-Jeshimoth, Baal-Meon and Kiriathaim. ¹⁰I shall let the sons of the East and the Ammonites take possession of them, so that they will no longer be remembered by the nations. ¹¹I shall bring Moab to justice, and they will know that I am Yahweh.

¹²"The Lord Yahweh says this:

"Since Edom has taken revenge on the House of Judah and committed great crimes in doing so, ¹³very well, the Lord Yahweh says this: My hand will be against Edom and denude it of human and animal. I shall lay it waste, from Teman as far as Dedan they will be put to the sword. ¹⁴I shall take vengeance on Edom by means of my people Israel. They will treat Edom as my anger and fury dictate, and they will know this is my vengeance — declares the Lord Yahweh.

¹⁵"The Lord Yahweh says this,

"Since the Philistines have acted in revenge and, motivated by malice, have taken revenge, doing their best to destroy because of their long-standing hatred, ¹⁶very well, the Lord Yahweh says this: My hand will be against the Philistines; I shall exterminate the Cherethites and destroy the rest of the coastal peoples. ¹⁷I shall perform frightful acts of vengeance and inflict furious punishments on them; and they will know that I am Yahweh, when I exact my vengeance on them." '

26 In the eleventh year, on the first of the month, the word of Yahweh was addressed to me as follows, ²'Son of man, since Tyre has said of Jerusalem:

"Aha! She is shattered, the Gateway to the Nations;
    she now gives way to me.
    Her riches are ruined!"
³Very well, the Lord Yahweh says this,
    "Now, Tyre, I am against you,
⁴I shall raise many nations against you
    as the sea raises its waves.
They will destroy the walls of Tyre,
    they will demolish her towers;

I will scrape its soil from it
and make it a bare rock.
5 It shall become, in the midst of the sea,
a place for spreading nets.
I have spoken, says the Lord GOD.
It shall become plunder for the nations,
6 and its daughter-towns in the country
shall be killed by the sword.
Then they shall know that I am the LORD.
7 For thus says the Lord GOD: I will bring against Tyre
from the north King Nebuchadrezzar of Babylon, king of
kings, together with horses, chariots, cavalry, and a great
and powerful army.
8 Your daughter-towns in the country
he shall put to the sword.
He shall set up a siege wall against you,
cast up a ramp against you,
and raise a roof of shields against you.
9 He shall direct the shock of his battering rams
against your walls
and break down your towers with his axes.
10 His horses shall be so many
that their dust shall cover you.
At the noise of cavalry, wheels, and chariots
your very walls shall shake,
when he enters your gates
like those entering a breached city.
11 With the hoofs of his horses
he shall trample all your streets.
He shall put your people to the sword,
and your strong pillars shall fall to the ground.
12 They will plunder your riches
and loot your merchandise;
they shall break down your walls
and destroy your fine houses.
Your stones and timber and soil
they shall cast into the water.
13 I will silence the music of your songs;
the sound of your lyres shall be heard no more.
14 I will make you a bare rock;
you shall be a place for spreading nets.
You shall never again be rebuilt,
for I the LORD have spoken,
says the Lord GOD.

15 Thus says the Lord GOD to Tyre: Shall not the coastlands shake at the sound of your fall, when the wounded
groan, when slaughter goes on within you? 16 Then all the
princes of the sea shall step down from their thrones; they
shall remove their robes and strip off their embroidered
garments. They shall clothe themselves with trembling, and
shall sit on the ground; they shall tremble every moment,
and be appalled at you. 17 And they shall raise a lamentation
over you, and say to you:
How you have vanished*a* from the seas,
O city renowned,
once mighty on the sea,
you and your inhabitants,*b*
who imposed your*c* terror
on all the mainland!*d*
18 Now the coastlands tremble
on the day of your fall;
the coastlands by the sea
are dismayed at your passing.

19 For thus says the Lord GOD: When I make you a city
laid waste, like cities that are not inhabited, when I bring up
the deep over you, and the great waters cover you, 20 then

I shall scrape the soil off her
and leave her only bare rock;
5 she will be an island
where nets are spread to dry.
This is my word, says the Lord GOD.
She will become the prey of nations,
6 and her daughters on the mainland will be slain.
Then they will know that I am the LORD.

7 'The Lord GOD says: From the north I am bringing against
Tyre King Nebuchadrezzar of Babylon, king of kings. He
will come with horses and chariots, cavalry, and a great
force of infantry.

8 'He will put to the sword
your daughters on the mainland.
He will set up siege-towers
and cast up siege-ramps against you,
and raise a screen of shields facing you.
9 He will launch his battering-rams on your walls
and break down your towers with his axes.
10 Dust will cover you
from his innumerable cavalry.
At the thunder of the horses
and of the chariot wheels
your walls will shake
when he enters your gates
as though entering a city that is breached.
11 All your streets will be trampled
by the hoofs of his horses.
He will put your people to the sword,
and bring your strong pillars to the ground.
12 Your wealth will become spoil,
your merchandise will be plundered.
Your walls will be levelled,
and your fine houses pulled down;
the stones, timber, and rubble
will be dumped in the sea.
13 I shall silence the chorus of your songs,
and the sound of your harps will be heard no
more.
14 I shall make you a bare rock,
a place where nets are spread to dry.
You will never be rebuilt.

'I, the LORD, have spoken. This is the word of the Lord
GOD.

15 'THE Lord GOD says to Tyre: How the coasts and islands will shake at the sound of your downfall, while the
wounded groan and slaughter prevails in your midst!
16 Then the sea-kings will descend from their thrones, lay
aside their cloaks, and strip off their brocaded robes. They
will put on loincloths and sit on the ground, shuddering
incessantly, aghast at your fate. 17 They will raise this dirge
over you:

"How you are undone, swept from the seas,
you city of renown!
You whose strength lay in the sea,
you and your inhabitants,
who spread your terror throughout the world.
18 Now the coastlands shudder
on the day of your downfall,
and the isles are appalled at your passing."

19 'For the Lord GOD says: When I make you a desolate city,
like cities where no one lives, when I bring the primeval
ocean up over you and the great waters cover you, 20 I shall

---

*a*Gk OL Aquila: Heb *have vanished, O inhabited one,*   *b*Heb *it*
and its inhabitants   *c*Heb *their*   *d*Cn: Heb *its inhabitants*

26:14 **You will:** *so Gk; Heb.* She will.   26:17 **swept:** *so Gk;
Heb.* inhabited.

I will scrape the ground from her
and leave her a bare rock;
⁵She shall be a drying place for nets
in the midst of the sea.

I have spoken, says the Lord GOD: and she shall be booty
for the nations. ⁶And her daughters on the mainland shall be
slaughtered by the sword; thus they shall know that I am the
LORD.

⁷For thus says the Lord GOD: I am now bringing up
against Tyre from the north Nebuchadnezzar the king of
Babylon, the king of kings, with horses and chariots, with
cavalry and a great and mighty army.

⁸Your daughters on the mainland
he shall slay with the sword;
He shall place a siege tower against you,
cast up a ramp about you,
and raise his shields against you.
⁹He shall pound your walls with battering-rams
and break down your towers with his weapons.
¹⁰The surge of his horses shall cover you with dust,
amid the noise of steeds, of wheels and
of chariots.
Your walls shall shake as he enters your gates,
even as one enters a city that is breached.
¹¹With the hoofs of his horses
he shall trample all your streets;
Your people he shall slay by the sword;
your mighty pillars he shall pull to the ground.
¹²Your wealth shall be plundered,
your merchandise pillaged;
Your walls shall be torn down,
your precious houses demolished;
Your stones, your timber, and your clay
shall be cast into the sea.
¹³I will put an end to the noise of your songs,
and the sound of your lyres shall be heard
no more.
¹⁴I will make you a bare rock;
a drying place for nets shall you be.

Never shall you be rebuilt, for I have spoken, says the Lord
GOD.

¹⁵Thus says the Lord GOD to Tyre: At the noise of your
fall, at the groaning of the wounded, when the sword slays
in your midst, shall not the isles quake? ¹⁶All the princes of
the sea shall step down from their thrones, lay aside their
robes, and strip off their embroidered garments. They shall
be clothed in mourning and, sitting on the ground, they
shall tremble at every moment and be horrified at you.
¹⁷Then they shall utter a lament over you:

How have you perished, gone from the seas,
city most prized!
Once she was mighty on the sea,
she and her dwellers,
Who spread terror into all
that dwelt by the sea.
¹⁸On this, the day of your fall,
the islands quake!

The isles in the sea are terrified at your passing.

¹⁹For thus says the Lord GOD: When I make you a city
desolate like cities that are no longer inhabited, when I
churn up the abyss against you, and its mighty waters cover

I shall sweep the dust of her away
and reduce her to a naked rock.
⁵She will be a drying-ground out to sea for
fishing-nets.
For I have spoken — declares Lord Yahweh.
She will be the prey of the nations.
⁶As for her daughters on the mainland,
these will be put to the sword,
and they will know that I am Yahweh."

⁷'For the Lord Yahweh says this, "From the north, I shall
bring Nebuchadnezzar, king of Babylon, king of kings,
down on Tyre with horses, chariots, cavalry and an enormous army.

⁸He will put your daughters
on the mainland to the sword.
He will build siege-works against you,
cast up a siege-ramp against you,
raise a screen against you;
⁹he will pound your walls with his battering-rams,
and demolish your towers with his siege-engines.
¹⁰His horses are so many that their dust will hide
you.
The noise of his horsemen and his chariot-wheels
will make your walls tremble as he enters your
gates
as though storming into a city through the breach.
¹¹With his horses' hoofs he will trample through all
your streets;
he will put your people to the sword,
and throw your massive pillars to the ground.
¹²Your wealth will be seized, your merchandise
looted,
your walls rased, your luxurious houses shattered,
your stones, your timbers, your very dust, thrown
into the sea.
¹³I shall put an end to the sound of your songs;
the sound of your harps will not be heard again.
¹⁴I shall reduce you to a naked rock,
and make you into a drying-ground for
fishing-nets,
never to be rebuilt;
for I, Yahweh, have spoken
— declares the Lord Yahweh."

¹⁵'The Lord Yahweh says this to Tyre, "Will not the
islands quake at the sound of your fall, while the wounded
groan and the slaughter takes place inside you? ¹⁶All the
princes of the sea will leave their thrones, lay aside their
cloaks, take off their embroidered robes. Dressed in terror
they will sit on the ground trembling incessantly, stunned at
your fate.

¹⁷"They will raise the lament for you as follows:

You are destroyed then, vanished from the seas,
famous city, former sea-power,
who with your citizens,
used to spread terror
all over the mainland!
¹⁸Now the islands are trembling
on the day of your fall;
the islands of the sea are terrified by your end.

¹⁹"For the Lord Yahweh says this:
"When I make you a ruined city like other deserted cities,
when I raise the deep against you and the ocean covers you,

NEW REVISED STANDARD VERSION	REVISED ENGLISH BIBLE

I will thrust you down with those who descend into the Pit, to the people of long ago, and I will make you live in the world below, among primeval ruins, with those who go down to the Pit, so that you will not be inhabited or have a place[e] in the land of the living. 21 I will bring you to a dreadful end, and you shall be no more; though sought for, you will never be found again, says the Lord GOD.

27 The word of the LORD came to me: 2 Now you, mortal, raise a lamentation over Tyre, 3 and say to Tyre, which sits at the entrance to the sea, merchant of the peoples on many coastlands, Thus says the Lord GOD:

O Tyre, you have said,
"I am perfect in beauty."
4 Your borders are in the heart of the seas;
your builders made perfect your beauty.
5 They made all your planks
of fir trees from Senir;
they took a cedar from Lebanon
to make a mast for you.
6 From oaks of Bashan
they made your oars;
they made your deck of pines[f]
from the coasts of Cyprus,
inlaid with ivory.
7 Of fine embroidered linen from Egypt
was your sail,
serving as your ensign;
blue and purple from the coasts of Elishah
was your awning.
8 The inhabitants of Sidon and Arvad
were your rowers;
skilled men of Zemer[g] were within you,
they were your pilots.
9 The elders of Gebal and its artisans were within
you,
caulking your seams;
all the ships of the sea with their mariners were
within you,
to barter for your wares.
10 Paras[h] and Lud and Put
were in your army,
your mighty warriors;
they hung shield and helmet in you;
they gave you splendor.
11 Men of Arvad and Helech[i]
were on your walls all around;
men of Gamad were at your towers.
They hung their quivers all around your walls;
they made perfect your beauty.

12 Tarshish did business with you out of the abundance of your great wealth; silver, iron, tin, and lead they exchanged for your wares. 13 Javan, Tubal, and Meshech traded with you; they exchanged human beings and vessels of bronze for your merchandise. 14 Beth-togarmah exchanged for your wares horses, war horses, and mules. 15 The Rhodians[j] traded with you; many coastlands were your own special markets; they brought you in payment ivory tusks and ebony. 16 Edom[k] did business with you because of your abundant goods; they exchanged for your wares turquoise, purple, embroidered work, fine linen, coral, and rubies. 17 Judah and the land of Israel traded with you; they exchanged for your merchandise wheat from Minnith, millet,[l] honey, oil, and balm. 18 Damascus traded with you for your abundant goods — because of your great

thrust you down with those who go down to the abyss, to the dead of all the ages; I shall make you dwell in the underworld as in places long desolate, with those that go down to the abyss. So you will never again be inhabited or take your place in the land of the living. 21 I shall bring destruction on you, and you will be no more; people may look for you but will never find you again. This is the word of the Lord GOD.'

27 This word of the LORD came to me: 2 'O man, raise a dirge over Tyre 3 and say to her who is enthroned at the gateway to the sea, who carries the trade of the nations to many coasts and islands: These are the words of the Lord GOD:

Tyre, you declared,
"I am perfect in beauty."
4 Your frontiers were on the high seas,
your builders made your beauty perfect;
5 they used pine from Senir
to fashion all your ribs;
they took a cedar from Lebanon
to set up a mast for you.
6 They made your oars of oaks from Bashan;
for your deck they used cypress
from the coasts of Kittim.
7 Your canvas was linen,
patterned linen from Egypt
to serve you for sails;
your awnings were violet and purple
from the coasts of Elishah.
8 Men from Sidon and Arvad served as your
oarsmen;
you had skilled men among you, Tyre,
acting as your helmsmen.
9 You had skilled veterans from Gebal
to caulk your seams.

'Every fully manned seagoing ship visited your
harbour
to traffic in your wares;
10 Persia, Lydia, and Put
supplied mercenaries for your army;
they arrayed shield and helmet in you,
and it was they who gave you your splendour.
11 Men of Arvad and Cilicia manned your walls on
every side,
men of Gammad were posted on your towers;
they arrayed their bucklers around your
battlements,
making your beauty perfect.

12 'Tarshish was a source of your commerce, from its abundant resources offering silver, iron, tin, and lead as your staple wares. 13 Javan, Tubal, and Meshech dealt with you, offering slaves and bronze utensils as your imports. 14 Men from Togarmah offered horses, cavalry steeds, and mules as your wares. 15 Rhodians dealt with you; many islands were a source of your commerce, paying their dues to you in ivory tusks and ebony. 16 Edom was a source of your commerce, so many were your undertakings, and offered purple garnets, brocade and fine linen, black coral and red jasper, for your wares. 17 Judah and Israel traded with you, offering wheat from Minnith and meal, grape-syrup, oil, and balm as your imports. 18 Damascus was a source of your commerce, so many were your undertakings, from its abundant

---

[e] Gk: Heb I will give beauty   [f] Or boxwood   [g] Cn Compare Gen 10.18: Heb your skilled men, O Tyre   [h] Or Persia   [i] Or and your army   [j] Gk: Heb The Dedanites   [k] Another reading is Aram   [l] Meaning of Heb uncertain

26:20 **or . . . place:** so Gk; Heb. I shall give beauty.   27:6 **used:** prob. rdg; Heb. adds ivory.   27:13 **Javan:** or Greece.   27:15 **Rhodians:** so Gk; Heb. Dedanites.

NEW AMERICAN BIBLE

NEW JERUSALEM BIBLE

you, 20 then I will thrust you down with those who descend into the pit, those of the bygone age; and I will make you dwell in the nether lands, in the everlasting ruins, with those who go down to the pit, so that you may never return to take your place in the land of the living. 21 I will make you a devastation, and you shall be no more; you shall be sought, but never again found, says the Lord GOD.

20 when I fling you down with those who go down into the abyss, with the people of long ago, and put you deep in the underworld, in the ruins of long ago with those who sink into oblivion, so that you can never come back or be restored to the land of the living, 21 I will make you an object of terror; you will not exist. People will look for you but never find you again—declares the Lord Yahweh!" '

27 Thus the word of the LORD came to me: 2 As for you, son of man, utter a lament over Tyre, 3 and say to Tyre that is situated at the approaches of the sea, that brought the trade of the peoples to many a coastland: Thus says the Lord GOD:

27 The word of Yahweh was addressed to me as follows, 2 'Son of man, raise the lament for Tyre. 3 Say to Tyre, "City enthroned at the gateway of the sea, agent between the peoples and the many islands, Lord Yahweh says this:

Tyre, you said, "I am a ship,
perfect in beauty."
4 In the midst of the sea your builders placed you,
perfected your beauty.
5 With cypress from Senir they built for you
all of your decks;
Cedar from Lebanon they took
to make you a mast;
6 From the highest oaks of Bashan
they made your oars;
Your bridge they made of cypress wood
from the coasts of Kittim.
7 Fine embroidered linen from Egypt
became your sail [to serve you as a banner].
Purple and scarlet from the coasts of Elishah
covered your cabin.
8 Citizens of Sidon and Arvad
served as your oarsmen;
Skilled men of Zemer were in you
to be your mariners;
9 The elders and experts of Gebal were in you
to caulk your seams.

Tyre, you used to say: I am a ship
perfect in beauty.
4 Your frontiers were far out to sea;
those who built you
made you perfect in beauty.
5 Cypress from Senir they used
for all your planking.
They took a cedar from Lebanon
to make a mast above you.
6 From oaks of Bashan
they made your oars.
They built you a deck of cedar inlaid with ivory
from the Kittim isles.
7 Embroidered linen from Egypt was used for your
sail
and for your flag.
Purple and scarlet from the Elishah islands
formed your deck-tent.
8 The people of Sidon and Arvad
were your oarsmen.
The sages of Tyre were aboard,
serving as sailors.
9 The elders and craftsmen of Gebal were there
to caulk your seams.

Every ship and sailor on the sea came to you to carry trade. 10 Persia and Lud and Put were in your army as warriors; shield and helmet they hung upon you, increasing your splendor. 11 The men of Arvad were all about your walls, and the Gamadites were in your towers; they hung their bucklers all around on your walls, and made perfect your beauty. 12 Tarshish traded with you, so great was your wealth, exchanging silver, iron, tin, and lead for your wares. 13 Javan, Tubal, and Meshech were also traders with you, exchanging slaves and articles of bronze for your goods. 14 From Beth-togarmah horses, steeds, and mules were exchanged for your wares. 15 The Rhodanites trafficked with you; many coastlands traded with you; ivory tusks and ebony wood they gave you for payment. 16 Edom traded with you, so many were your products, exchanging garnets, purple, embroidered cloth, fine linen, coral, and rubies for your wares. 17 Judah and the land of Israel trafficked with you, exchanging Minnith wheat, figs, honey, oil, and balm for your goods. 18 Damascus traded with you, so great was your wealth, exchanging Helbon wine and

"Every sea-going ship and crew frequented you to guarantee your trade. 10 Men from Persia, Lud and Put served as warriors in your army; hanging up shield and helmet in you, they displayed your splendour. 11 The sons of Arvad with their army manned your walls all round, while the Gammadians manned your towers; hanging their shields all round your walls, they completed your beauty. 12 Tarshish traded with you because of your abundant resources and exchanged your merchandise for silver, iron, tin and lead. 13 Javan, Tubal and Meshech traded with you. For your merchandise they traded slaves and bronze artefacts. 14 The people of Beth-Togarmah traded your horses, chargers, mules. 15 The people of Dedan traded with you; many islands were your customers and paid you in ivory tusks and ebony. 16 Edom traded with you for the sake of your many manufactured goods, exchanging garnets, purple, embroideries, fine linen, coral and rubies for your goods. 17 Judah and the land of Israel also traded with you, bringing corn from Minnith, *pannag*, honey, oil and balm. 18 Damascus traded with you, for quantities of your manufactured goods

wealth of every kind — wine of Helbon, and white wool. 19 Vedan and Javan from Uzal*m* entered into trade for your wares; wrought iron, cassia, and sweet cane were bartered for your merchandise. 20 Dedan traded with you in saddle-cloths for riding. 21 Arabia and all the princes of Kedar were your favored dealers in lambs, rams, and goats; in these they did business with you. 22 The merchants of Sheba and Raamah traded with you; they exchanged for your wares the best of all kinds of spices, and all precious stones, and gold. 23 Haran, Canneh, Eden, the merchants of Sheba, Asshur, and Chilmad traded with you. 24 These traded with you in choice garments, in clothes of blue and embroidered work, and in carpets of colored material, bound with cords and made secure; in these they traded with you.*n* 25 The ships of Tarshish traveled for you in your trade.

So you were filled and heavily laden
    in the heart of the seas.
26 Your rowers have brought you
    into the high seas.
The east wind has wrecked you
    in the heart of the seas.
27 Your riches, your wares, your merchandise,
    your mariners and your pilots,
your caulkers, your dealers in merchandise,
    and all your warriors within you,
with all the company
    that is with you,
sink into the heart of the seas
    on the day of your ruin.
28 At the sound of the cry of your pilots
    the countryside shakes,
29 and down from their ships
    come all that handle the oar.
The mariners and all the pilots of the sea
    stand on the shore
30 and wail aloud over you,
    and cry bitterly.
They throw dust on their heads
    and wallow in ashes;
31 they make themselves bald for you,
    and put on sackcloth,
and they weep over you in bitterness of soul,
    with bitter mourning.
32 In their wailing they raise a lamentation for you,
    and lament over you:
"Who was ever destroyed*o* like Tyre
    in the midst of the sea?
33 When your wares came from the seas,
    you satisfied many peoples;
with your abundant wealth and merchandise
    you enriched the kings of the earth.
34 Now you are wrecked by the seas,
    in the depths of the waters;
your merchandise and all your crew
    have sunk with you.
35 All the inhabitants of the coastlands
    are appalled at you;
and their kings are horribly afraid,
    their faces are convulsed.
36 The merchants among the peoples hiss at you;
    you have come to a dreadful end
    and shall be no more forever."

28 The word of the LORD came to me: 2 Mortal, say to the prince of Tyre, Thus says the Lord GOD:

resources offering Helbon wine and Suhar wool, 19 and casks of wine from Izalla, in exchange for your wares; wrought iron, cassia, and sweet cane were among your imports. 20 Dedan traded with you in coarse woollens for saddle-cloths. 21 Arabia and all the rulers of Kedar traded with you; they were the source of your commerce in lambs, rams, and goats. 22 Merchants from Sheba and Raamah traded with you, offering all the choicest spices, every kind of precious stone, and gold as your wares. 23 Harran, Kanneh, and Eden, merchants from Asshur and all Media, traded with you; 24 they were your dealers in choice stuffs: violet cloths and brocades, in stores of coloured fabric rolled up and tied with cords.

25 'Ships of Tarshish were the caravans for your imports;
    you were deeply laden with full cargoes
    on the high seas.
26 Your oarsmen brought you into many waters,
    but an east wind wrecked you on the high seas.
27 Your wealth, your wares, your imports,
    your sailors and your helmsmen,
your caulkers, your merchants, and all your warriors,
    all who were in the ship with you
    were flung into the sea when it sank.
28 Amid the cries of your helmsmen
    the troubled waters tossed.
29 When rowers disembark from their ships,
    when sailors and the helmsmen, all together, go ashore,
30 they mourn aloud over your fate
    and cry out bitterly;
they throw dust on their heads
    and sprinkle themselves with ashes.
31 At your plight they cut off their hair
    and put on sackcloth;
they weep bitterly over you
    with most bitter wailing.
32 In their lamentation they raise a dirge
    and bewail you, saying:
"Who was like Tyre,
    set in the midst of the sea?
33 When your wares were unloaded off the seas
    you met the needs of many nations;
with your vast resources and your imports
    you enriched the kings of the earth.
34 Now you are wrecked at sea,
    sunk in deep water;
your wares and all your crew have gone down with you.
35 All who dwell on the coasts and islands
    are aghast at your fate;
horror is written on the faces of their kings
    and their hair stands on end.
36 Among the nations the merchants gasp at the sight of you;
    destruction has come on you, and you shall be no more."'

28 This word of the LORD came to me: 2 'O man, say to the ruler of Tyre: This is what the Lord GOD says:

---

m Meaning of Heb uncertain   *n* Cn: Heb *in your market*
o Tg Vg: Heb *like silence*

27:19 **casks . . . Izalla:** *prob. rdg; Heb. obscure.*
27:23 **merchants from:** *so Gk; Heb. adds* Sheba. **all Media:** *prob. rdg, cp. Aram. (Targ.); Heb.* Kilmad.   27:32 **set:** *prob. rdg; Heb. obscure.*

NEW AMERICAN BIBLE

NEW JERUSALEM BIBLE

Zahar wool. 19 Javan exchanged wrought iron, cassia, and aromatic cane from Uzal for your wares. 20 Dedan traded with you for riding gear. 21 The trade of Arabia and of all the sheikhs of Kedar belonged to you; they dealt in lambs, rams, and goats. 22 The merchants of Sheba and Raamah also traded with you, exchanging for your wares the very choicest spices, all kinds of precious stones, and gold. 23 Haran, Canneh, and Eden, the merchants of Sheba, Asshur, and Chilmad 24 traded with you, marketing with you rich garments, violet mantles, embroidered cloth, varicolored carpets, and firmly woven cords. 25 Ships of Tarshish journeyed for you in your merchandising.

You were full and heavily laden
   in the heart of the sea.
26 Through the deep waters your oarsmen
      brought you home,
But the east wind smashed you
   in the heart of the sea.
27 Your wealth, your goods, your wares,
   your sailors, and your crew,

[the caulkers of your seams, those who traded for your goods, all your warriors who were in you, and all the great crowd within you]

Sank into the heart of the sea
   on the day of your shipwreck.
28 Hearing the shouts of your mariners,
   the shores begin to quake.
29 Down from their ships
   come all who ply the oar;
The sailors, all the mariners of the sea,
   stand on the shore,
30 Making their voice heard on your behalf,
   shouting bitter cries,
Strewing dust on their heads,
   rolling in the ashes.
31 For you they shave their heads
   and put on sackcloth,
For you they weep in anguish,
   with bitter lament.
32 In their mourning they utter a lament over you;
   thus they wail over you:
Who was ever destroyed like Tyre
   in the midst of the sea?
33 With your goods which you drew from the seas
   you filled many peoples;
With your great wealth and merchandise
   you enriched the kings of the earth.
34 Now you are wrecked in the sea,
   in the watery depths;
Your wares and all your crew
   have gone down with you.
35 All who dwell on the coastlands
   are aghast over you,
Their kings are terrified,
   their faces convulsed.
36 The traders among the peoples
   now hiss at you;
You have become a horror,
   and you shall be no more.

and other goods of all kinds, furnishing you with wine from Helbon and wool from Zahar. 19 Dan and Javan, from Uzal onwards, supplied you with wrought iron, cassia and reeds in exchange for your goods. 20 Dedan traded with you in saddle-cloths. 21 Arabia and all the sheikhs of Kedar were your customers; they paid in lambs, rams and he-goats. 22 The merchants of Sheba and Raamah traded with you; they supplied you with the finest spices, precious stones and gold for your merchandise. 23 Haran, Canneh and Eden, the merchants of Sheba, Asshur and Chilmad traded with you. 24 They traded rich clothes, embroidered and purple cloaks, multi-coloured materials and strong plaited cords for your markets.

25 Ships of Tarshish sailed on your business;
   you were full and heavily loaded
   far out to sea.
26 Out to the open sea
   your oarsmen rowed you.
The east wind has wrecked you
   far out to sea.
27 Your riches, your goods, your cargo,
   your seamen, your sailors,
   your caulkers, your commercial agents,
   all the warriors you carry,
   and all the passengers who are aboard
   will founder far out to sea
   on the day of your shipwreck.
28 When they hear the cries of your sailors
   the coasts will tremble.
29 Then the oarsmen will all desert
      their ships.
The sailors and seafaring people
   will stay ashore.
30 They will raise their voices for you
   and weep bitterly.
They will throw dust on their heads
   and roll in ashes;
31 they will shave their heads for you
   and put sackcloth round their waists.
With heartfelt bitterness they will weep for you,
   bitterly wail.
32 Wailing, they will raise the lament for you,
   they will lament over you:
Who is like Tyre,
   far out to sea?
33 When you unloaded your goods
   to satisfy so many peoples,
you enriched the kings of the earth
   with your excess of wealth and goods.
34 Now you have been wrecked by the waves,
   by the depths of the sea.
Your cargo and all your passengers
   have foundered with you.
35 All those who live in the islands
   will be stunned at your fate.
Their kings will quake with horror,
   with downcast expressions.
36 The merchants of the nations
   will whistle at your fate.
You will be an object of terror,
   gone for ever." '

28 Thus the word of the LORD came to me: 2 Son of man, say to the prince of Tyre: Thus says the Lord GOD:

28 The word of Yahweh was addressed to me as follows, 2 'Son of man, say to the ruler of Tyre, "The Lord Yahweh says this:

| NEW REVISED STANDARD VERSION | REVISED ENGLISH BIBLE |

Because your heart is proud
    and you have said, "I am a god;
I sit in the seat of the gods,
    in the heart of the seas,"
yet you are but a mortal, and no god,
    though you compare your mind
      with the mind of a god.
3 You are indeed wiser than Daniel; *p*
    no secret is hidden from you;
4 by your wisdom and your understanding
    you have amassed wealth for yourself,
and have gathered gold and silver
    into your treasuries.
5 By your great wisdom in trade
    you have increased your wealth,
    and your heart has become proud in your
      wealth.
6 Therefore thus says the Lord GOD:
Because you compare your mind
    with the mind of a god,
7 therefore, I will bring strangers against you,
    the most terrible of the nations;
they shall draw their swords against the beauty of
      your wisdom
    and defile your splendor.
8 They shall thrust you down to the Pit,
    and you shall die a violent death
    in the heart of the seas.
9 Will you still say, "I am a god,"
    in the presence of those who kill you,
though you are but a mortal, and no god,
    in the hands of those who wound you?
10 You shall die the death of the uncircumcised
    by the hand of foreigners;
    for I have spoken, says the Lord GOD.

11 Moreover the word of the LORD came to me: 12 Mortal, raise a lamentation over the king of Tyre, and say to him, Thus says the Lord GOD:
You were the signet of perfection, *q*
    full of wisdom and perfect in beauty.
13 You were in Eden, the garden of God;
    every precious stone was your covering,
    carnelian, chrysolite, and moonstone,
    beryl, onyx, and jasper,
    sapphire, *r* turquoise, and emerald;
    and worked in gold were your settings
    and your engravings. *q*
On the day that you were created
    they were prepared.
14 With an anointed cherub as guardian I placed
    you; *q*
you were on the holy mountain of God;
    you walked among the stones of fire.
15 You were blameless in your ways
    from the day that you were created,
    until iniquity was found in you.
16 In the abundance of your trade
    you were filled with violence, and you sinned;
so I cast you as a profane thing from the
      mountain of God,
    and the guardian cherub drove you out
    from among the stones of fire.

In your arrogance you say,
"I am a god;
I sit enthroned like a god on the high seas."
Though you are a man and no god,
you give yourself godlike airs.
3 What, are you wiser than Daniel?
Is no secret beyond your grasp?
4 By your skill and shrewdness
you have amassed wealth,
gold and silver in your treasuries.
5 By great skill in commerce
you have heaped up riches,
and with your riches your arrogance has grown.

6 'The Lord GOD says:

Because you give yourself godlike airs,
7 I am about to bring foreigners against you,
the most ruthless of nations;
they will draw their swords against your fine
    wisdom
and defile your splendour;
8 they will thrust you down to destruction,
to a violent death on the high seas.
9 When you face your attackers,
will you still say, "I am a god"?
You are a man and no god
in the hands of those who lay you low.
10 You will die the death of the uncircumcised
at the hands of foreigners.

'I have spoken. This is the word of the Lord GOD.'

11 THIS word of the LORD came to me: 12 'O man, raise this dirge over the king of Tyre, and say to him: This is what the Lord GOD says:

You set the seal on perfection;
you were full of wisdom and flawless in beauty.
13 In an Eden, a garden of God, you dwelt,
adorned with gems of every kind:
sardin and chrysolite and jade,
topaz, cornelian, and green jasper,
sapphire, purple garnet, and green feldspar.
Your jingling beads were of gold,
and the spangles you wore were made for you
on the day of your birth.
14 I appointed a towering cherub as your guardian;
you were on God's holy mountain
and you walked proudly among stones of fire.
15 You were blameless in your ways
from the day of your birth
until iniquity came to light in you.
16 Your commerce grew so great
that lawlessness filled your heart
and led to wrongdoing.
I brought you down in disgrace
from the mountain of God,
and the guardian cherub banished you
from among the stones that flashed like fire.

---

p Or, as otherwise read, *Danel*   *q* Meaning of Heb uncertain
r Or *lapis lazuli*

Because you are haughty of heart,
    you say, "A god am I!
I occupy a godly throne
    in the heart of the sea!" —
And yet you are a man, and not a god,
    however you may think yourself like a god.
3 Oh yes, you are wiser than Daniel,
    there is no secret that is beyond you.
4 By your wisdom and your intelligence
    you have made riches for yourself;
You have put gold and silver
    into your treasuries.
5 By your great wisdom applied to your trading
    you have heaped up your riches;
your heart has grown haughty from
      your riches —
6   therefore thus says the Lord GOD:
Because you have thought yourself
    to have the mind of a god,
7 Therefore I will bring against you
    foreigners, the most barbarous of nations.
They shall draw their swords
    against your beauteous wisdom,
    they shall run them through your
      splendid apparel.
8 They shall thrust you down to the pit, there to die
    a bloodied corpse, in the heart of the sea.
9 Will you then say, "I am a god!"
    when you face your murderers?
No, you are a man, not a god,
    handed over to those who will slay you.
10 You shall die the death of the uncircumcised
    at the hands of foreigners,
    for I have spoken, says the Lord GOD.
 	
11 Thus the word of the LORD came to me: 12 Son of man,
utter a lament over the king of Tyre, saying to him: Thus
says the Lord GOD:
 	
You were stamped with the seal of perfection,
    of complete wisdom and perfect beauty.
13 In Eden, the garden of God, you were,
    and every precious stone was your covering
 	
[carnelian, topaz, and beryl, chrysolite, onyx, and jasper,
sapphire, garnet, and emerald];
 	
Of gold your pendants and jewels
    were made, on the day you were created.
14 With the Cherub I placed you;
    you were on the holy mountain of God,
    walking among the fiery stones.
15 Blameless you were in your conduct
    from the day you were created,
Until evil was found in you,
16   the result of your far-flung trade;
    violence was your business, and you sinned.
Then I banned you from the mountain of God;
    the Cherub drove you from among the
      fiery stones.
	Because your heart has grown proud,
	    you thought: I am a god;
	I am divinely enthroned
	    far out to sea.
	Though you are human, not divine,
	    you have allowed yourself to think like God. *o*
	3 So, you are wiser than Danel;
	    no sage as wise as you!
	4 By your wisdom and your intelligence
	    you have made yourself a fortune,
	    you have put gold and silver
	    into your treasuries.
	5 Such is your skill in trading,
	    your fortune has continued to increase,
	    and your fortune has made your heart grow
	      prouder.
	6 "And so, the Lord Yahweh says this:
	
	Since you have allowed yourself to think like God,
	7 very well, I am going to bring foreigners against
	      you,
	    the most barbarous of the nations.
	They will draw sword against your fine wisdom,
	    they will desecrate your splendour,
	8 they will throw you down into the grave
	    and you will die a violent death
	    far out to sea.
	9 Will you still think: I am a god,
	    when your slaughterers confront you?
	But you will be human, not divine,
	    in the clutches of the ones who strike you down!
	10 You will die like the uncircumcised
	    at the hand of foreigners.
	
	"For I have spoken — declares the Lord Yahweh." '
	
	11 The word of Yahweh was addressed to me as follows,
	12 'Son of man, raise a lament for the king of Tyre. Say to
	him, "The Lord Yahweh says this:
	
	You used to be a model of perfection,
	    full of wisdom,
	    perfect in beauty;
	13 you were in Eden, in the garden of God.
	All kinds of gem formed your mantle:
	    sard, topaz, diamond, chrysolite, onyx,
	    jasper, sapphire, garnet, emerald,
	    and your ear-pendants and spangles were made of
	      gold;
	    all was ready on the day you were created.
	14 I made you a living creature with outstretched
	      wings, as guardian,
	    you were on the holy mountain of God;
	    you walked amid red-hot coals.
	15 Your behaviour was exemplary from the day you
	      were created
	    until guilt first appeared in you,
	16 because your busy trading
	    has filled you with violence and sin.
	I have thrown you down from the mountain of God
	    and destroyed you, guardian winged creature, amid
	      the coals.

o **28** Some features of the story of Adam's fall in Eden recur here.

17 Your heart was proud because of your beauty;
   you corrupted your wisdom for the sake of
      your splendor.
I cast you to the ground;
   I exposed you before kings,
      to feast their eyes on you.
18 By the multitude of your iniquities,
   in the unrighteousness of your trade,
      you profaned your sanctuaries.
So I brought out fire from within you;
   it consumed you,
and I turned you to ashes on the earth
   in the sight of all who saw you.
19 All who know you among the peoples
   are appalled at you;
you have come to a dreadful end
   and shall be no more forever.

20 The word of the LORD came to me: 21 Mortal, set your face toward Sidon, and prophesy against it, 22 and say, Thus says the Lord GOD:

I am against you, O Sidon,
   and I will gain glory in your midst.
They shall know that I am the LORD
   when I execute judgments in it,
   and manifest my holiness in it;
23 for I will send pestilence into it,
   and bloodshed into its streets;
and the dead shall fall in its midst,
   by the sword that is against it on every side.
And they shall know that I am the LORD.

24 The house of Israel shall no longer find a pricking brier or a piercing thorn among all their neighbors who have treated them with contempt. And they shall know that I am the Lord GOD.

25 Thus says the Lord GOD: When I gather the house of Israel from the peoples among whom they are scattered, and manifest my holiness in them in the sight of the nations, then they shall settle on their own soil that I gave to my servant Jacob. 26 They shall live in safety in it, and shall build houses and plant vineyards. They shall live in safety, when I execute judgments upon all their neighbors who have treated them with contempt. And they shall know that I am the LORD their God.

29 In the tenth year, in the tenth month, on the twelfth day of the month, the word of the LORD came to me: 2 Mortal, set your face against Pharaoh king of Egypt, and prophesy against him and against all Egypt; 3 speak, and say, Thus says the Lord GOD:

I am against you,
   Pharaoh king of Egypt,
the great dragon sprawling
   in the midst of its channels,
saying, "My Nile is my own;
   I made it for myself."
4 I will put hooks in your jaws,
   and make the fish of your channels stick to
      your scales.
I will draw you up from your channels,
   with all the fish of your channels
      sticking to your scales.
5 I will fling you into the wilderness,
   you and all the fish of your channels;
you shall fall in the open field,
   and not be gathered and buried.
To the animals of the earth and to the birds of the
      air
   I have given you as food.

17 Your beauty made you arrogant;
   you debased your wisdom to enhance your
      splendour.
I flung you to the ground,
   I left you exposed to the gaze of kings.
18 So great was the sin in your dishonest trading
   that you desecrated your sanctuaries.
I kindled a fire within you,
   and it devoured you.
I reduced you to ashes on the ground
   for everyone to see.
19 Among the nations all who knew you were aghast:
   destruction has come on you, and you will be no
      more.'

20 This word of the LORD came to me: 21 'O man, face towards Sidon and prophesy against her. 22 The Lord GOD says:

Sidon, I am against you
   and I shall show my glory in your midst.

'People will know that I am the LORD
   when I execute judgement on her
   and show my holiness in her.
23 I shall let loose pestilence on her
   and bloodshed in her streets;
beset on all sides by the sword
   the slain will fall within her walls.
Then people will know that I am the LORD.

24 'No longer will the Israelites suffer from the scorn of their neighbours, the pricking of briars and scratching of thorns, and they will know that I am the Lord GOD.

25 'The Lord GOD says: When I gather the Israelites from the peoples among whom they are dispersed, I shall show my holiness in them for all the nations to see. They will live on their own soil, which I gave to my servant Jacob. 26 They will live there undisturbed, build houses, and plant vineyards. When I execute judgement on all their scornful neighbours, they will live undisturbed. Thus they will know that I am the LORD their God.'

29 This word of the LORD came to me on the twelfth day of the tenth month in the tenth year: 2 'O man, face towards Pharaoh king of Egypt and prophesy against him and the whole of Egypt. 3 Say to them: The Lord GOD says:

I am against you,
   Pharaoh king of Egypt,
you great monster,
   lurking in the streams of the Nile.
You have said, "My Nile is my own;
   it was I who made it."
4 But I shall put hooks in your jaws
   and they will cling to your scales.
I shall haul you up out of its streams
   with all its fish clinging to your scales.
5 I shall fling you into the desert,
   you and all the fish in your streams;
you will fall on the ground
   with none to give you burial;
I shall give you as food
   to beasts and birds.

29:3 it was . . . it: so Syriac, cp. verse 9; Heb. I even made myself.
29:4 they will cling: prob. rdg; Heb. make the fish of your streams cling.

NEW AMERICAN BIBLE	NEW JERUSALEM BIBLE

NEW AMERICAN BIBLE

17 You became haughty of heart because of
    your beauty;
for the sake of splendor you debased
    your wisdom.
I cast you to the earth, so great was your guilt;
    I made you a spectacle in the sight of kings.
18 Because of your guilt, your sinful trade,
    I have profaned your sanctuaries,
And I have brought out fire from your midst
    which will devour you.
I have reduced you to dust on the earth
    in the sight of all who should see you.
19 Among the peoples, all who knew you
    stand aghast at you;
You have become a horror,
    you shall be no more.

20 Thus the word of the LORD came to me: Son of man,
look toward Sidon, 21 and prophesy against it: 22 Thus says
the Lord GOD: See! I am coming at you, Sidon; I will be
glorified in your midst. Then they shall know that I am the
LORD, when I inflict punishments upon it and use it to
manifest my holiness.

23 Into it I will send pestilence,
    and blood shall flow in its streets.
Within it shall fall those slain
    by the sword that comes against it from
      every side.

Thus they shall know that I am the LORD. 24 Sidon shall no
longer be a tearing thorn for the house of Israel, a brier that
scratches them more than all the others about them who
despise them; thus they shall know that I am the LORD.
25 Thus says the Lord GOD: When I gather the house of
Israel from the peoples among whom they are scattered,
then I will manifest my holiness through them in the sight
of the nations. Then they shall live on their land which I
gave to my servant Jacob; 26 they shall live on it in security,
building houses and planting vineyards. They shall dwell
secure while I inflict punishments on all their neighbors
who despised them; thus they shall know that I, the LORD,
am their God.

29 On the twelfth day of the tenth month in the tenth
year, the word of the LORD came to me: 2 Son of
man, set your face against Pharaoh, king of Egypt, and
prophesy against him and against all Egypt. 3 Say this to
him: Thus says the Lord GOD:

See! I am coming at you, Pharaoh,
    king of Egypt,
Great crouching monster
    amidst your Niles:
Who say, "The Niles are mine;
    it is I who made them!"

4 I will put hooks in your jaws and make the fish of your
Niles stick to your scales, then draw you up from the midst
of your Niles along with all the fish of your Niles sticking
to your scales.

5 I will cast you into the desert,
    you and all the fish of your Niles;
You shall fall upon the open field,
    you shall not be taken up or buried;
To the beasts of the earth and the birds of the air
    I give you as food,

NEW JERUSALEM BIBLE

17 Your heart has grown proud because of your
    beauty,
your wisdom has been corrupted by your
    splendour.
I have thrown you to the ground;
I have made you a spectacle for kings.
18 By the immense number of your crimes,
by the dishonesty of your trading,
you have defiled your sanctuary.
So I have brought fire out of you to devour you;
I have reduced you to ashes on the ground
before the eyes of all who saw you.
19 Of the nations, all who know you
are stunned at your fate.
You are an object of terror;
    gone for ever." '

20 The word of Yahweh was addressed to me as follows,
21 'Son of man, turn towards Sidon and prophesy against
her. 22 Say, "The Lord Yahweh says this:

I am against you, Sidon,
I will show my glory in you!
They will know I am Yahweh,
once I execute sentence on her
and display my holiness in her.
23 For I shall send her the plague,
and there will be blood in her streets,
and in her the dead will fall
under the sword raised against her from all sides,
and they will know that I am Yahweh.

24 "No more, for the House of Israel, shall any of the
hostile nations surrounding them be a thorn that wounds or
a briar that tears; and they will know that I am Yahweh.
25 "The Lord Yahweh says this: When I gather the House
of Israel back from the peoples where they are dispersed, I
shall display my glory in them for the nations to see. They
will live on the soil which I gave to my servant Jacob.
26 They will live there in confidence, build houses, plant
vineyards. They will live in safety, once I inflict punishments on all the hostile nations surrounding them, and they
will know that I am Yahweh their God." '

29 In the twelfth day of the tenth
month, the word of Yahweh was addressed to me as
follows, 2 'Son of man, turn towards Pharaoh king of Egypt
and prophesy against him and against the whole of Egypt.
3 Speak and say, "The Lord Yahweh says this:

Look, I am against you, Pharaoh king of Egypt—
the great crocodile wallowing in his Niles
who thought: My Nile is mine, I made it.
4 I shall put hooks through your jaws,
make your Nile fish stick to your scales,
and pull you out of your Niles
with all your Nile fish sticking to your scales.
5 I shall drop you in the desert, with all your Nile
    fish.
You will fall in the wilds
and not be taken up or buried.
I shall give you as food
to the wild animals and the birds of heaven,

NEW REVISED STANDARD VERSION

6 Then all the inhabitants of Egypt shall know
    that I am the Lord
because you[s] were a staff of reed
    to the house of Israel;
7 when they grasped you with the hand, you broke,
    and tore all their shoulders;
and when they leaned on you, you broke,
    and made all their legs unsteady.[t]

8 Therefore, thus says the Lord God: I will bring a sword upon you, and will cut off from you human being and animal; 9 and the land of Egypt shall be a desolation and a waste. Then they shall know that I am the Lord.
Because you[u] said, "The Nile is mine, and I made it," 10 therefore, I am against you, and against your channels, and I will make the land of Egypt an utter waste and desolation, from Migdol to Syene, as far as the border of Ethiopia.[v] 11 No human foot shall pass through it, and no animal foot shall pass through it; it shall be uninhabited forty years. 12 I will make the land of Egypt a desolation among desolated countries; and her cities shall be a desolation forty years among cities that are laid waste. I will scatter the Egyptians among the nations, and disperse them among the countries.

13 Further, thus says the Lord God: At the end of forty years I will gather the Egyptians from the peoples among whom they were scattered; 14 and I will restore the fortunes of Egypt, and bring them back to the land of Pathros, the land of their origin; and there they shall be a lowly kingdom. 15 It shall be the most lowly of the kingdoms, and never again exalt itself above the nations; and I will make them so small that they will never again rule over the nations. 16 The Egyptians[w] shall never again be the reliance of the house of Israel; they will recall their iniquity, when they turned to them for aid. Then they shall know that I am the Lord God.

17 In the twenty-seventh year, in the first month, on the first day of the month, the word of the Lord came to me: 18 Mortal, King Nebuchadrezzar of Babylon made his army labor hard against Tyre; every head was made bald and every shoulder was rubbed bare; yet neither he nor his army got anything from Tyre to pay for the labor that he had expended against it. 19 Therefore thus says the Lord God: I will give the land of Egypt to King Nebuchadrezzar of Babylon; and he shall carry off its wealth and despoil it and plunder it; and it shall be the wages for his army. 20 I have given him the land of Egypt as his payment for which he labored, because they worked for me, says the Lord God.

21 On that day I will cause a horn to sprout up for the house of Israel, and I will open your lips among them. Then they shall know that I am the Lord.

30 The word of the Lord came to me: 2 Mortal, prophesy, and say, Thus says the Lord God:
    Wail, "Alas for the day!"
3   For a day is near,
        the day of the Lord is near;
    it will be a day of clouds,
        a time of doom[x] for the nations.
4 A sword shall come upon Egypt,
    and anguish shall be in Ethiopia,[v]
  when the slain fall in Egypt,
    and its wealth is carried away,
    and its foundations are torn down.
5 Ethiopia,[v] and Put, and Lud, and all Arabia, and Libya,[y] and the people of the allied land[z] shall fall with them by the sword.

REVISED ENGLISH BIBLE

6 Then all who live in Egypt will know
    that I am the Lord.
The support you gave the Israelites
    was no better than a reed.
7 When they grasped you, you splintered in their hands
    and tore their armpits;
  when they leaned on you, you broke
    and their limbs gave way.

8 'The Lord God says: I am bringing a sword on you to destroy both people and animals. 9 Egypt will become a desolate waste land, and they will know that I am the Lord. Because you said, "The Nile is mine; it was I who made it," 10 I am against you and your Nile. I shall make Egypt desolate, wasted by drought, from Migdol to Syene and as far as the frontier of Cush. 11 Untrodden by people or animals, it will lie uninhabited for forty years. 12 I shall make Egypt the most desolate of desolate lands, her cities the most derelict of derelict cities. For forty years they will lie derelict, and I shall scatter the Egyptians among the nations, dispersing them throughout the earth.

13 'The Lord God says: At the end of forty years I shall gather the Egyptians from the peoples among whom they are scattered. 14 I shall restore the fortunes of Egypt and bring her people back to Pathros, the land of their origin, where they will be a petty kingdom. 15 It will become the most paltry of kingdoms and never again lord it over the nations, for I shall make the Egyptians too few to rule over them. 16 The Israelites, always mindful of their sin in turning to Egypt for help, will never trust Egypt again. They will know that I am the Lord God.'

17 This word of the Lord came to me on the first day of the first month in the twenty-seventh year: 18 'O man, King Nebuchadrezzar of Babylon kept his army in the field against Tyre so long that everyone's head was rubbed bare and everyone's shoulder chafed. But no gain from Tyre accrued to him or to his army from their campaign. 19 This, therefore, is the word of the Lord God. I am now giving Egypt to King Nebuchadrezzar of Babylon. He will carry off its wealth, he will despoil and plunder it, and so his army will receive their wages. 20 I have given him Egypt in payment for his service because they have spurned my authority. This is the word of the Lord God.

21 'At that time I shall make Israel renew her strength, and give you back the power to speak among them, and they will know that I am the Lord.'

30 This word of the Lord came to me: 2 'O man, prophesy and say: The Lord God says:
    Wail! Alas for the day!
3 A day is near,
    a day of the Lord is near,
    a day of cloud, a day of reckoning for the nations!
4 A sword will come on Egypt,
    and there will be anguish in Cush,
  when the slain fall in Egypt,
  when her wealth is seized,
    her foundations are demolished.
5 Cush and Put and Lydia,
    all the Arabs, Libyans, and peoples of allied lands
  will fall by the sword along with Egypt.

---

[s] Gk Syr Vg: Heb *they*   [t] Syr: Heb *stand*   [u] Gk Syr Vg: Heb *he*
[v] Or *Nubia*; Heb *Cush*   [w] Heb *It*   [x] Heb lacks *of doom*
[y] Compare Gk Syr Vg: Heb *Cub*   [z] Meaning of Heb uncertain

29:6 **you:** *so Gk; Heb.* they.   29:9 **you:** *so Gk; Heb.* he.
30:5 **Libyans:** *so Gk; Heb.* Kub.

NEW AMERICAN BIBLE

NEW JERUSALEM BIBLE

6 That all who dwell in Egypt may know
that I am the LORD.
Because you have been a reed staff
for the house of Israel:
7 When they held you in hand, you splintered,
throwing every shoulder out of joint;
When they leaned on you, you broke,
bringing each one of them down headlong;

8 therefore thus says the Lord GOD: See! I will bring the sword against you, and cut off from you both man and beast. 9 The land of Egypt shall become a desolate waste; thus they shall know that I am the LORD.
Because you said, "The Niles are mine; it is I who made them," 10 therefore see! I am coming at you and against your Niles; I will make the land of Egypt a waste and a desolation from Migdol to Syene, and even to the frontier of Ethiopia. 11 No foot of man or beast shall pass through it; they shall not pass through it, and it will be uninhabited for forty years. 12 I will make the land of Egypt the most desolate of lands, and its cities shall be the most deserted of cities for forty years; and I will scatter the Egyptians among the nations and strew them over foreign lands. 13 Yet thus says the Lord GOD: At the end of forty years I will gather the Egyptians from the peoples among whom they are scattered, 14 and I will restore Egypt's fortune, bringing them back to the land of Pathros, the land of their origin, where it will be the lowliest 15 of kingdoms, never more to set itself above the nations. I will make them few, that they may not dominate the nations. 16 No longer shall they be for the house of Israel to trust in, but the living reminder of its guilt for having turned to follow after them. Thus they shall know that I am the LORD.

17 On the first day of the first month in the twenty-seventh year, the word of the LORD came to me: 18 Son of man, Nebuchadnezzar, the king of Babylon, has led his army in an exhausting campaign against Tyre. Their heads became bald and their shoulders were galled; but neither he nor his army received any wages from Tyre for the campaign he led against it. 19 Therefore thus says the Lord GOD: I am now giving the land of Egypt to Nebuchadnezzar, king of Babylon. He shall carry off its riches, plundering and pillaging it for the wages of his soldiers, who did it for me; 20 as payment for his toil I have given him the land of Egypt, says the Lord GOD.

21 On that day I will make a horn sprout for the house of Israel, and I will cause you to speak out in their midst; thus they shall know that I am the LORD.

30 Thus the word of the LORD came to me: 2 Son of man, speak this prophecy: Thus says the Lord GOD: Cry, Oh, the day! 3 for near is the day, near is the day of the Lord; a day of clouds, doomsday for the nations shall it be. 4 Then a sword shall come upon Egypt, and anguish shall be in Ethiopia, when the slain fall in Egypt, when her riches are seized and her foundations are overthrown. 5 Ethiopia, Put, Lud, all Arabia, Libya, and people of the allied territory shall fall by the sword with them. 6 Those who support

6 and all the inhabitants of Egypt will know that I
am Yahweh,
for they have given no more support than a reed to
the House of Israel.
7 Wherever they grasped you, you broke in their
hands
and cut their hands all over.
Whenever they leaned on you, you broke,
making all their limbs give way.

8 "So, the Lord Yahweh says this: I shall send the sword against you to denude you of human and animal. 9 Egypt will become a desolate waste, and they will know that I am Yahweh. Because he thought: The Nile is mine, I made it, 10 very well, I am against you and your Niles. I shall make Egypt a waste and a desolation, from Migdol to Syene and beyond to the frontiers of Ethiopia. 11 No human foot will pass through it, no animal foot will pass through it. For forty years it will remain uninhabited. 12 I shall make Egypt the most desolate of countries; for forty years its cities will be the most desolate of wasted cities. And I shall scatter the Egyptians among the nations and disperse them among the countries. 13 The Lord Yahweh, however, says this: After forty years have passed, I shall gather the Egyptians back from the nations where they were dispersed. 14 I shall bring the Egyptian captives back and re-install them in the land of Pathros, in the country of their origin. There they will constitute a modest kingdom. 15 Egypt will be the most modest of kingdoms and no longer dominate other nations; for I shall reduce it, so that it will not rule other nations ever again. 16 It will no longer be anything for the House of Israel to trust in, but will be a reminder of the guilt which lay in turning to it for help. And they will know that I am Lord Yahweh." '

17 In the twenty-seventh year, on the first day of the first month, the word of Yahweh was addressed to me as follows:

18 'Son of man, Nebuchadnezzar king of Babylon has taken his army in a great expedition against Tyre. Their heads have all gone bald, their shoulders are all chafed, but even so he has derived no profit, either for himself or for his army, from the expedition mounted against Tyre. 19 Since this is so, the Lord Yahweh says this, "Look, I shall hand Egypt over to Nebuchadnezzar king of Babylon. He will carry off its riches, loot it, put it to the sack; that will be the wages for his army. 20 As wages for the trouble he has taken, I am giving him Egypt instead (for they have been working for me) — declares the Lord Yahweh.

21 "That day, I shall raise up a new stock for the House of Israel and allow you to open your mouth among them. And they will know that I am Yahweh." '

30 The word of Yahweh was addressed to me as follows, 2 'Son of man, prophesy and say, "The Lord Yahweh says this: Howl: Disaster day! 3 For the day is near, the day of Yahweh is near; it will be a day dark with cloud, a time of doom for the nations.

4 "The sword will come on Egypt, and anguish on the country of Cush when the slaughtered fall in Egypt, when her riches are carried away and her foundations are destroyed. 5 Cush, Put and Lud, all Arabia, Cub and the children of the country of the covenant will fall by the sword with them.

6 Thus says the LORD:
Those who support Egypt shall fall,
    and its proud might shall come down;
from Migdol to Syene
they shall fall within it by the sword,
says the Lord GOD.
7 They shall be desolated among other desolated
        countries,
    and their cities shall lie among cities laid
        waste.
8 Then they shall know that I am the LORD,
    when I have set fire to Egypt,
    and all who help it are broken.

9 On that day, messengers shall go out from me in ships
to terrify the unsuspecting Ethiopians;[a] and anguish shall
come upon them on the day of Egypt's doom;[b] for it is
coming!

10 Thus says the Lord GOD:
    I will put an end to the hordes of Egypt,
        by the hand of King Nebuchadrezzar of
            Babylon.
11 He and his people with him, the most terrible of
        the nations,
    shall be brought in to destroy the land;
    and they shall draw their swords against Egypt,
        and fill the land with the slain.
12 I will dry up the channels,
    and will sell the land into the hand of
        evildoers;
    I will bring desolation upon the land and
        everything in it
    by the hand of foreigners;
    I the LORD have spoken.

13 Thus says the Lord GOD:
    I will destroy the idols
        and put an end to the images in Memphis;
    there shall no longer be a prince in the land of
        Egypt;
    so I will put fear in the land of Egypt.
14 I will make Pathros a desolation,
    and will set fire to Zoan,
    and will execute acts of judgment on Thebes.
15 I will pour my wrath upon Pelusium,
    the stronghold of Egypt,
    and cut off the hordes of Thebes.
16 I will set fire to Egypt;
    Pelusium shall be in great agony;
    Thebes shall be breached,
    and Memphis face adversaries by day.
17 The young men of On and of Pi-beseth shall fall
    by the sword;
    and the cities themselves[c] shall go into
        captivity.
18 At Tehaphnehes the day shall be dark,
    when I break there the dominion of Egypt,
    and its proud might shall come to an end;
    the city[d] shall be covered by a cloud,
    and its daughter-towns shall go into captivity.
19 Thus I will execute acts of judgment on Egypt.
    Then they shall know that I am the LORD.

20 In the eleventh year, in the first month, on the seventh day of the month, the word of the LORD came to me:
21 Mortal, I have broken the arm of Pharaoh king of Egypt;
it has not been bound up for healing or wrapped with a
bandage, so that it may become strong to wield the sword.

6 'The LORD says:
Those who support Egypt will fall
and her boasted might will be brought low;
from Migdol to Syene they will fall by the sword.
This is the word of the Lord GOD.

7 'They will be the most desolate of desolate lands, their
cities the most derelict of derelict cities. 8 When I set Egypt
on fire and all her helpers are shattered, they will know that
I am the LORD. 9 When that day comes messengers will go
out in ships from my presence to strike terror into Cush, still
undisturbed, and anguish shall come on her in Egypt's hour.
Now it is near.

10 'The Lord GOD says:
I shall make an end of Egypt's hordes
at the hand of King Nebuchadrezzar of Babylon.
11 He and his people with him, the most ruthless of
        nations,
will be brought to ravage the land.
They will draw their swords against Egypt
and fill the land with the slain.
12 I shall turn the streams of the Nile into dry land
and sell Egypt into the power of evil men.
'By the hands of foreigners I shall lay waste the land and
everything in it. I, the LORD, have spoken.

13 'The Lord GOD says:
I shall make an end of the petty rulers
and wipe out the chieftains of Noph;
never again will a prince arise in Egypt.
I shall instil terror into that land:
14 I shall lay Pathros waste and set fire to Zoan
and execute judgement on No.
15 I shall vent my wrath on Sin,
the bastion of Egypt,
and destroy the hordes of Noph.
16 I shall set Egypt on fire,
and Syene will writhe in anguish;
the walls of No will be breached
and floodwaters will burst into it.
17 The young men of On and Pi-beseth will fall by
        the sword
and the cities themselves will go into captivity.
18 Daylight will fail in Tahpanhes
when I break the power of Egypt there;
there her boasted might will be brought to an end.
A cloud will cover her,
and her daughters will go into captivity.
19 I shall execute judgement on Egypt,
and they will know that I am the LORD.'

20 This word of the LORD came to me on the seventh day of
the first month in the eleventh year: 21 'O man, I have broken the arm of Pharaoh king of Egypt, and it has not been
bound up with dressings or bandaged to make it strong
enough to wield a sword. 22 The Lord GOD says: I am

---

a Or Nubians; Heb Cush   b Heb the day of Egypt   c Heb and they
d Heb she

30:7 **their:** prob. rdg, cp. Gk; Heb. his.   30:15 **Noph:** so Gk;
Heb. No.   30:16 **Syene:** so Gk; Heb. Sin. **floodwaters . . . it:**
prob. rdg, cp. Gk; Heb. obscure.

Egypt shall fall, and down shall come her proud strength; from Migdol to Syene they shall fall there by the sword, says the Lord GOD. 7 She shall be the most devastated of lands, and her cities shall be the most desolate of all. 8 Then they shall know that I am the LORD, when I set fire to Egypt and when all who help her are broken. 9 On that day messengers shall hasten forth at my command to terrify the unsuspecting Ethiopia; they shall be in anguish on the day of Egypt, which is surely coming.

10 Thus says the Lord GOD: I will put an end to the throngs of Egypt by the hand of Nebuchadnezzar, king of Babylon. 11 He and his people with him, the most ruthless of nations, shall be brought in to devastate the land. They shall draw their swords against Egypt, and fill the land with the slain. 12 I will turn the Niles into dry land and sell the land over to the power of the wicked. The land and everything in it I will hand over to foreigners to devastate. I, the LORD, have spoken.

13 Thus says the Lord GOD: I will put an end to the great ones of Memphis and the princes of the land of Egypt, that they may be no more. I will cast fear into the land of Egypt, and devastate Pathros. 14 I will set fire to Zoan, and inflict punishments on Thebes. 15 I will pour out my wrath on Pelusium, Egypt's stronghold, and cut down the crowds in Memphis. 16 I will set fire to Egypt; Syene shall writhe in anguish; Thebes shall be breached and its walls shall be demolished. 17 The young men of On and of Pibeseth shall fall by the sword, and the cities themselves shall go into captivity. 18 In Tehaphnehes the day shall be darkened when I break the scepter of Egypt. Her haughty pride shall cease from her, clouds shall cover her, and her daughters shall go into captivity. 19 Thus will I inflict punishments on Egypt, that they may know that I am the LORD.

20 On the seventh day of the first month in the eleventh year, the word of the LORD came to me: 21 Son of man, I have broken the arm of Pharaoh, the king of Egypt, and see, it has not been bound up with bandages and healing remedies that it may be strong enough to hold the sword.

6 "Yahweh says this:

"The supports of Egypt will fall; the pride of her strength will crumble; they will fall by the sword from Migdol to Syene — declares the Lord Yahweh.

7 "They will be the most desolate of desolate countries, and its cities the most ruined of cities. 8 And they will know that I am Yahweh when I set fire to Egypt and all its supports are shattered.

9 "That day, I shall send messengers by ship to terrify the carefree Cushites, and anguish will overtake them on the day of Egypt — it is coming now! 10 The Lord Yahweh says this: I shall destroy the huge population of Egypt at the hand of Nebuchadnezzar king of Babylon. 11 He and his people, the most barbarous of nations, will be brought to ravage the country. They will draw the sword against Egypt and fill the country with corpses. 12 I shall dry up the courses of the Nile and sell the country to the wicked. I shall lay the whole country waste and everything in it, at the hand of foreigners. I, Yahweh, have spoken.

13 "The Lord Yahweh says this: I shall destroy the foul idols and take the false gods away from Noph. Egypt will be left without a ruler. I shall spread fear through Egypt. 14 I shall lay Pathros waste, set Zoan on fire, inflict my punishments on No. 15 I shall vent my fury on Sin, the bastion of Egypt; I shall wipe out the throngs of No. 16 I shall set fire to Egypt; Sin will be seized with convulsions; a breach will be opened at No and the waters flood out. 17 The young men of On and Pi-Beseth will fall by the sword and the cities themselves go into captivity. 18 At Tahpanhes day will turn to darkness when I shatter the sceptres of Egypt there, when the pride of her strength ceases. A cloud will cover Egypt itself, and its daughters will go into captivity. 19 Such will be the punishments I inflict on Egypt. And they will know that I am Yahweh." '

20 In the eleventh year, on the seventh day of the first month, the word of Yahweh was addressed to me as follows, 21 'Son of man, I have broken the arm of Pharaoh king of Egypt; you can see that no one has dressed his wound by applying remedies to it, by bandaging it and by dressing it, to make it strong enough to wield the sword. 22 This being

22 Therefore thus says the Lord GOD: I am against Pharaoh king of Egypt, and will break his arms, both the strong arm and the one that was broken; and I will make the sword fall from his hand. 23 I will scatter the Egyptians among the nations, and disperse them throughout the lands. 24 I will strengthen the arms of the king of Babylon, and put my sword in his hand; but I will break the arms of Pharaoh, and he will groan before him with the groans of one mortally wounded. 25 I will strengthen the arms of the king of Babylon, but the arms of Pharaoh shall fall. And they shall know that I am the LORD, when I put my sword into the hand of the king of Babylon. He shall stretch it out against the land of Egypt, 26 and I will scatter the Egyptians among the nations and disperse them throughout the countries. Then they shall know that I am the LORD.

31 In the eleventh year, in the third month, on the first day of the month, the word of the LORD came to me: 2 Mortal, say to Pharaoh king of Egypt and to his hordes:

Whom are you like in your greatness?
3   Consider Assyria, a cedar of Lebanon,
    with fair branches and forest shade,
        and of great height,
        its top among the clouds. e
4   The waters nourished it,
        the deep made it grow tall,
    making its rivers flow f
        around the place it was planted,
    sending forth its streams
        to all the trees of the field.
5   So it towered high
        above all the trees of the field;
    its boughs grew large
        and its branches long,
        from abundant water in its shoots.
6   All the birds of the air
        made their nests in its boughs;
    under its branches all the animals of the field
        gave birth to their young;
    and in its shade
        all great nations lived.
7   It was beautiful in its greatness,
        in the length of its branches;
    for its roots went down
        to abundant water.
8   The cedars in the garden of God could not rival
        it,
        nor the fir trees equal its boughs;
    the plane trees were as nothing
        compared with its branches;
    no tree in the garden of God
        was like it in beauty.
9   I made it beautiful
        with its mass of branches,
    the envy of all the trees of Eden
        that were in the garden of God.

10   Therefore thus says the Lord GOD: Because it g towered high and set its top among the clouds, e and its heart was proud of its height, 11 I gave it into the hand of the prince of the nations; he has dealt with it as its wickedness deserves. I have cast it out. 12 Foreigners from the most terrible of the nations have cut it down and left it. On the mountains and in all the valleys its branches have fallen, and its boughs lie broken in all the watercourses of the land; and all the peoples of the earth went away from its shade and left it.

against Pharaoh king of Egypt; I shall break both his arms, the sound and the broken, and make the sword fall from his hand. 23 I shall scatter the Egyptians among the nations and disperse them throughout the earth. 24 I shall strengthen the arms of the king of Babylon and put my sword in his hand; I shall break Pharaoh's arms, and he will lie wounded and groaning before him. 25 I shall give strength to the arms of the king of Babylon, but Pharaoh's arms will fall. All will know that I am the LORD, when I put my sword into the hand of the king of Babylon, and he stretches it out over the land of Egypt. 26 I shall scatter the Egyptians among the nations and disperse them throughout the earth, and they will know that I am the LORD.'

31 On the first day of the third month in the eleventh year this word of the LORD came to me: 2 'O man, say to Pharaoh king of Egypt and to his hordes:

In your greatness, what are you like?
3 Look at Assyria: it was a cedar in Lebanon,
    towering high with its crown pushing through the
        foliage
    and its fair branches overshadowing the forest.
4 Springs nourished it, the underground waters made
        it lofty,
    their streams washed the soil all round it
    and sent channels of water to every tree in the
        country.
5 So it grew taller than every other tree.
    Its boughs were many, its branches far-spreading;
        for water was abundant in the channels.
6 In its boughs all the birds of the air had their nests,
    under its branches all wild creatures bore their
        young,
    and in its shade all great nations made their home.
7 A splendid, great tree it was, with its far-spreading
        boughs,
    for its roots were beside abundant waters.
8 No cedar in God's garden eclipsed it,
    no juniper could compare with its boughs,
    and no plane tree had such branches;
    not a tree in God's garden
    could rival its beauty.
9 I, the LORD, made it beautiful
    with its mass of spreading boughs,
    the envy of every tree in Eden,
    the garden of God.

10 'The Lord GOD says: Because it grew so high, raising its crown through the foliage, and its pride mounted as it grew, 11 I handed it over to a prince of the nations to deal with it; I made an example of it as its wickedness deserved. 12 Foreigners, the most ruthless of nations, cut it down and left it lying. Its sweeping boughs fell on the mountains and in all the valleys, and its branches lay broken in every water-channel on earth. All the peoples of the earth came out from under its shade and left it. 13 On its fallen trunk the birds all

---

e Gk: Heb *thick boughs*   f Gk: Heb *rivers going*   g Syr Vg: Heb *you*

31:10 **Because it grew:** *so Syriac; Heb.* Because you grew.

22 Therefore thus says the Lord GOD: See! I am coming at Pharaoh, the king of Egypt. I will break his strong arm, so that the sword drops from his hand. 23 I will scatter the Egyptians among the nations and strew them over foreign lands. 24 But I will strengthen the arms of the king of Babylon, and put my sword in his hand, which he will bring against Egypt so as to plunder and pillage it. 25 [I will make the arms of the king of Babylon strong, but the arms of Pharaoh shall drop.] Then they shall know that I am the LORD, when I put my sword in the hand of the king of Babylon for him to wield against the land of Egypt. 26 [I will scatter the Egyptians among the nations and strew them over foreign lands.] Thus they shall know that I am the LORD.

31 On the first day of the third month in the eleventh year, the word of the LORD came to me: 2 Son of man, say to Pharaoh, the king of Egypt, and to his hordes: What are you like in your greatness?

3 Behold, a cypress [cedar] in Lebanon,
    beautiful of branch, lofty of stature,
    amid the very clouds lifted its crest.
4 Waters made it grow, the abyss made it flourish,
    sending its rivers round where it was planted,
    turning its streams to all the trees of the field.
5 Thus it grew taller than every other tree of
        the field,
    and longer of branch because of the
        abundant water.
6 In its boughs nested all the birds of the air,
    under its branches all beasts of the field
        gave birth,
    in its shade dwelt numerous peoples of
        every race.
7 It became beautiful and stately in its spread
        of foliage,
    for its roots were turned toward abundant water.
8 The cedars in the garden of God were not
        its equal,
    nor could the fir trees match its boughs,
    Neither were the plane trees like it for branches;
    no tree in the garden of God matched its beauty.
9 I made it beautiful, with much foliage,
    the envy of all Eden's trees in the garden
        of God.

10 Therefore thus says the Lord GOD: Because it became lofty in stature, raising its crest among the clouds, and because it became proud in heart at its height, 11 I have handed it over to the mightiest of the nations, which has dealt with it in keeping with its wickedness. I humiliated it. 12 Foreigners, the most ruthless of nations, cut it down and left it on the mountains. Its foliage was brought low in all the valleys, its branches lay broken in all the ravines of the land, and all the peoples of the land withdrew from its shade, abandoning it.

so, the Lord Yahweh says this, "Look, I am against Pharaoh king of Egypt; I shall break his arms, the sound one and the broken one, and make the sword drop from his hand. 23 I shall scatter Egypt among the nations and disperse it among the countries. 24 I shall strengthen the arms of the king of Babylon and put my sword in his hand. I shall break Pharaoh's arms and, confronted with his enemy, he will groan like a dying man. 25 I shall strengthen the arms of the king of Babylon, and the arms of Pharaoh will fall. And they will know that I am Yahweh, when I put my sword into the hands of the king of Babylon and he wields it against Egypt. 26 I shall scatter Egypt among the nations and disperse it among the countries; and they will know that I am Yahweh." '

31 In the eleventh year, on the first day of the third month, the word of Yahweh was addressed to me as follows, 2 'Son of man, say to Pharaoh king of Egypt and his throng of subjects:

"What can compare with you for greatness?
3 I know: a cedar tree in the Lebanon
    with noble branches, dense foliage, lofty height.
    Its top pierces the clouds.
4 The waters have made it grow, the deep has made
        it tall,
    pouring its rivers round the place where it is
        planted,
    sending rivulets to all the wild trees.
5 This is why its height was greater than that of
        other wild trees,
    its branches increased in number, its boughs
        stretched wide,
    because of the plentiful waters making it grow.
6 All the birds of heaven nested in its branches;
    under its boughs all wild animals dropped their
        young;
    in its shade sat many, many people.
7 It was beautiful in its size, in the span of its
        boughs;
    for its roots were in plentiful waters.
8 There was no cedar like it in the garden of God,
    no cypress had branches such as these,
    no plane tree could match its boughs,
    no tree in the garden of God could rival its beauty.
9 I had made it so lovely with its many branches
    that it was the envy of every tree in Eden, in the
        garden of God.

10 "Very well, the Lord Yahweh says this:
"Since it has raised itself to its full height, has lifted its top into the clouds, and has grown arrogant about its height, 11 I have handed it over to the prince of the nations, for him to treat as its wickedness deserves; I have rejected it. 12 Foreigners, the most barbarous of nations, have cut it down and deserted it. On the mountains, in all the valleys, lie its branches; its broken boughs are in every ravine throughout the country; everybody in the country has fled its shade and

13 On its fallen trunk settle
    all the birds of the air,
    and among its boughs lodge
      all the wild animals.
14 All this is in order that no trees by the waters may grow
to lofty height or set their tops among the clouds,*h* and that
no trees that drink water may reach up to them in height.
  For all of them are handed over to death,
    to the world below;
  along with all mortals,
    with those who go down to the Pit.

15 Thus says the Lord GOD: On the day it went down to
Sheol I closed the deep over it and covered it; I restrained
its rivers, and its mighty waters were checked. I clothed
Lebanon in gloom for it, and all the trees of the field fainted
because of it. 16 I made the nations quake at the sound of its
fall, when I cast it down to Sheol with those who go down
to the Pit; and all the trees of Eden, the choice and best of
Lebanon, all that were well watered, were consoled in the
world below. 17 They also went down to Sheol with it, to
those killed by the sword, along with its allies,*i* those who
lived in its shade among the nations.

18 Which among the trees of Eden was like you in glory
and in greatness? Now you shall be brought down with the
trees of Eden to the world below; you shall lie among the
uncircumcised, with those who are killed by the sword.
This is Pharaoh and all his horde, says the Lord GOD.

32 In the twelfth year, in the twelfth month, on the first
day of the month, the word of the LORD came to
me: 2 Mortal, raise a lamentation over Pharaoh king of
Egypt, and say to him:
  You consider yourself a lion among the nations,
    but you are like a dragon in the seas;
  you thrash about in your streams,
    trouble the water with your feet,
    and foul your*j* streams.
3 Thus says the Lord GOD:
  In an assembly of many peoples
  I will throw my net over you;
    and I*k* will haul you up in my dragnet.
4 I will throw you on the ground,
    on the open field I will fling you,
  and will cause all the birds of the air to settle on
    you,
  and I will let the wild animals of the whole
    earth gorge themselves with you.
5 I will strew your flesh on the mountains,
    and fill the valleys with your carcass.*l*
6 I will drench the land with your flowing blood
    up to the mountains,
  and the watercourses will be filled with you.
7 When I blot you out, I will cover the heavens,
    and make their stars dark;
  I will cover the sun with a cloud,
    and the moon shall not give its light.
8 All the shining lights of the heavens
    I will darken above you,
    and put darkness on your land,
              says the Lord GOD.
9 I will trouble the hearts of many peoples,
    as I carry you captive*m* among the nations,
    into countries you have not known.

settled, the wild creatures all sought shelter among its
branches. 14 Never again will the well-watered trees grow so
high or push their crowns up through the foliage. Nor will
the strongest of them, though well-watered, attain their full
height; for all have been given over to death, to the world
below, to share the fate of mortals and go down to the
abyss.

15 'The Lord GOD says: When he went down to Sheol, I
dried up the deep, I dammed its rivers, the great waters
were held back. I brought mourning on Lebanon for him,
and all the trees of the countryside wilted. 16 I made nations
shake at the sound of his downfall, when I brought him
down to Sheol with those who go down to the abyss. From
this all the trees of Eden, the choicest and best of Lebanon,
all the well-watered trees, drew comfort in the world below.
17 They too like him had gone down to Sheol, to those slain
by the sword, and those among the nations who had lived
in his shade.

18 'Which among the trees of Eden was like you in glory
and greatness? Yet you will be brought down with the trees
of Eden to the world below; you will lie with those who
have been slain by the sword, in the company of the uncircumcised dead. So it will be with Pharaoh and all his
hordes. This is the word of the Lord GOD.'

32 On the first day of the twelfth month in the twelfth
year this word of the LORD came to me: 2 'O man,
raise a dirge over Pharaoh king of Egypt and say to him:
  Young lion of the nations, your end has come.
  You were like a monster in the waters of the Nile
  scattering the water with its snout,
  churning up the water with its feet
  and muddying the streams.

3 'The Lord GOD says: When many nations are assembled I
shall spread my net over you, and you will be hauled ashore
in its meshes. 4 I shall fling you on land, dashing you on the
ground. I shall let all the birds of the air settle upon you and
all the wild beasts gorge themselves on you. 5 I shall leave
your carcass on the mountains, and fill the valleys with the
worms that feed on it. 6 I shall drench the land with your
blood as it pours out on the mountains, and the ravines will
be filled with it. 7 When your light is quenched I shall veil
the sky and darken its stars; I shall veil the sun with clouds,
and the moon will give no light. 8 I shall darken all the
shining lights of the sky above you and bring darkness over
your land. This is the word of the Lord GOD.

9 'I shall cause disquiet to many peoples when I bring
your broken army among the nations, into lands you have

---

h Gk: Heb *thick boughs*   *i* Heb *its arms*   *j* Heb *their*   *k* Gk Vg:
Heb *they*   *l* Symmachus Syr Vg: Heb *your height*   *m* Gk: Heb
bring your destruction

31:15 **Sheol:** *or* the underworld.   32:2 **snout:** *prob. rdg; Heb.*
streams.

13 On its fallen trunk rested all the birds of the air,
    and by its branches were all the beasts of
        the field.

14 Thus no tree may grow lofty in stature or raise its crest
among the clouds; no tree fed by water may stand by itself
in its loftiness.

> For all of them are destined for death,
>   for the land below,
> For the company of mortals,
>   those who go down into the pit.

15 Thus says the Lord GOD: On the day he went down to
the nether world I made the abyss close up over him; I
stopped its streams so that the deep waters were held back.
I cast gloom over Lebanon because of him, so that all the
trees in the land drooped on his account. 16 At the crash of
his fall I made the nations rock, when I cast him down to
the nether world with those who go down into the pit. In the
land below, all Eden's trees were consoled, Lebanon's
choice and best, all that were fed by water. 17 They too have
come down with him to the nether world, to those slain by
the sword; those who dwelt in his shade are dispersed
among the nations. 18 Which was your equal in glory or size
among the trees of Eden? Yet you have been brought down
with the trees of Eden to the land below. You shall lie with
the uncircumcised, with those slain by the sword. Such are
Pharaoh and all his hordes, says the Lord GOD.

32 On the first day of the twelfth month in the twelfth
year, the word of the LORD came to me: 2 Son of
man, utter a lament over Pharaoh, the king of Egypt, saying
to him: Lion of the nations, you are destroyed.

> You were like a monster in the sea,
>   spouting in your streams,
> Stirring the water with your feet
>   and churning its streams.

3 Thus says the Lord GOD:
I will spread my net over you
    [with a host of many nations],
    and draw you up in my seine.
4 I will leave you on the land;
    on the open field I will cast you.
I will have all the birds of the air alight on you,
    and all the beasts of the earth eat their fill
        of you.
5 I will leave your flesh on the mountains,
    and fill the valleys with your carcass.
6 I will water the land with what flows from you,
    and the river beds shall be filled with
        your blood.
7 When I snuff you out I will cover the heavens,
    and all their stars I will darken;
The sun I will cover with clouds,
    and the moon shall not give its light.
8 All the shining lights in the heavens
    I will darken on your account,
And I will spread darkness over your land,
    say the Lord GOD.

9 I will grieve the hearts of many peoples when I lead you
captive among the nations, to lands which you do not know.

deserted it. 13 On its wreckage perch all the birds of heaven;
all the wild animals have advanced on its branches.

14 "So in future let no tree rear its height beside the waters, none push its top into the clouds, no watered tree
stretch its height towards them. For all of them are doomed
to death, to the depths of the underworld, with the common
run of humanity, with those who sink into oblivion.

15 "The Lord Yahweh says this: The day it went down to
Sheol, I imposed mourning, I closed the deep over it. I
stopped its rivers and the plentiful waters dried up; I made
Lebanon dark because of it, and all the wild trees wilted
because of it. 16 With the noise when it fell I made the
nations quake, as I hurled it down to Sheol, with those who
sink into oblivion. In the depths of the underworld all the
trees of Eden took comfort, the pick of the loveliest trees of
the Lebanon, all irrigated by the waters. 17 And its offspring
among the nations, once living in its shade, went down to
Sheol with it, to those who have been slaughtered by the
sword.

18 "Which of the trees of Eden compares with you for
glory and greatness? Yet you have been hurled down with
the trees of Eden, to the depths of the underworld, among
the uncircumcised, and there you lie with those who have
been slaughtered by the sword. So much for Pharaoh and all
his throng — declares the Lord Yahweh." '

32 In the twelfth year, on the first day of the twelfth
month, the word of Yahweh was addressed to me as
follows, 2 'Son of man, raise a lament for Pharaoh king of
Egypt. Say to him:

> "Young lion of nations, you are destroyed!
> Once you were like a crocodile in the lagoons;
> emerging from your rivers,
> you churned up the water with your trampling
> and fouled their streams.

3 "The Lord Yahweh says this:

> I shall throw my net over you in a great concourse
>   of nations;
> and they will trawl you up in my net.
> Then I shall leave you high and dry,
4 I shall throw you out into the wilds
> and make all the birds of heaven settle on you,
> and glut all the beasts of the earth with you.
5 I shall strew your flesh on your mountains
> and fill the valleys with your corruption;
6 I shall water the country with what flows from
>   you,
> with your blood, on the mountainsides,
> and you will fill the ravines.
7 When I extinguish you I shall cover the skies
> and darken the stars.
> I shall cover the sun with clouds
> and the moon will not give its light.
8 I shall dim every luminary in heaven because of
>   you
> and cover your country in darkness
> — declares the Lord Yahweh.

9 "I shall grieve the heart of many peoples when I bring
about your destruction among the nations, in countries un-

10 I will make many peoples appalled at you;
    their kings shall shudder because of you.
When I brandish my sword before them,
    they shall tremble every moment
for their lives, each one of them,
    on the day of your downfall.

11 For thus says the Lord GOD:
The sword of the king of Babylon shall come
    against you.
12 I will cause your hordes to fall
    by the swords of mighty ones,
all of them most terrible among the nations.
They shall bring to ruin the pride of Egypt,
    and all its hordes shall perish.
13 I will destroy all its livestock
    from beside abundant waters;
and no human foot shall trouble them any more,
    nor shall the hoofs of cattle trouble them.
14 Then I will make their waters clear,
    and cause their streams to run like oil, says the
    Lord GOD.
15 When I make the land of Egypt desolate
    and when the land is stripped of all that fills it,
when I strike down all who live in it,
    then they shall know that I am the LORD.
16 This is a lamentation; it shall be chanted.
    The women of the nations shall chant it.
Over Egypt and all its hordes they shall chant it,
    says the Lord GOD.

17 In the twelfth year, in the first month,*n* on the fifteenth day of the month, the word of the LORD came to me:
18 Mortal, wail over the hordes of Egypt,
    and send them down,
with Egypt*o* and the daughters of majestic
    nations,
    to the world below,
    with those who go down to the Pit.
19 "Whom do you surpass in beauty?
    Go down! Be laid to rest with the
    uncircumcised!"
20 They shall fall among those who are killed by the sword. Egypt*p* has been handed over to the sword; carry away both it and its hordes. 21 The mighty chiefs shall speak of them, with their helpers, out of the midst of Sheol: "They have come down, they lie still, the uncircumcised, killed by the sword."
22 Assyria is there, and all its company, their graves all around it, all of them killed, fallen by the sword. 23 Their graves are set in the uttermost parts of the Pit. Its company is all around its grave, all of them killed, fallen by the sword, who spread terror in the land of the living.
24 Elam is there, and all its hordes around its grave; all of them killed, fallen by the sword, who went down uncircumcised into the world below, who spread terror in the land of the living. They bear their shame with those who go down to the Pit. 25 They have made Elam*o* a bed among the slain with all its hordes, their graves all around it, all of them uncircumcised, killed by the sword; for terror of them was spread in the land of the living, and they bear their shame with those who go down to the Pit; they are placed among the slain.
26 Meshech and Tubal are there, and all their multitude, their graves all around them, all of them uncircumcised, killed by the sword; for they spread terror in the land of the living. 27 And they do not lie with the fallen warriors of long

never known. 10 I shall appal many peoples with your fate; when I brandish my sword in the presence of their kings, their hair will stand on end. On the day of your downfall not a moment will pass without each trembling for his own fate. 11 For the Lord GOD has said: The king of Babylon's sword will come upon you. 12 I shall make your hordes of people fall by the sword of warriors who are of all men the most ruthless. They will shatter the pride of Egypt, and all her hordes will be wiped out. 13 I shall destroy all their cattle beside abundant waters. No foot or hoof will ever churn them up again. 14 Then I shall let their waters settle and their streams glide smooth as oil. This is the word of the Lord GOD. 15 When I have laid Egypt waste, and the whole land lies empty, when I strike down all who live there, they will know that I am the LORD.

16 'The women of the nations will raise this dirge, singing it as a dirge over Egypt and all her hordes. This is the word of the Lord GOD.'

17 On the fifteenth day of the first month in the twelfth year, this word of the LORD came to me:

18 'O man, raise a lament, you and the daughters of
    the nations,
    over Egypt's hordes and her nobility.
I shall consign them to the world below,
    in company with those who go down to the abyss.
19 Are you better favoured than others?
    Go down and lie with the uncircumcised dead.

20 'A sword is drawn. Those who marched with her, together with all her hordes, will descend into the company of those slain by the sword. 21 Warrior chieftains in Sheol speak to Pharaoh and his allies.

' "The uncircumcised dead, slain by the sword, have come down and lie there. 22 Assyria is there with all her company buried around her, all of them slain, victims of the sword. 23 Their graves are set in the farthest depths of the abyss, with her slain buried round about her, all victims of the sword, who once spread terror in the land of the living. 24 Elam is there with all her people buried around her, all of them slain, victims of the sword. They have gone down uncircumcised to the world below, who spread terror in the land of the living, but now bear disgrace with those who go down to the abyss. 25 A bed has been made for her in the midst of the slain. All her peoples are buried around her, all of them uncircumcised, victims of the sword. Those, who once spread terror in the land of the living, now bear disgrace with those who go down to the abyss, and are assigned a place in the midst of the slain. 26 Meshech and Tubal are there with all their hordes buried around them, all of them uncircumcised, slain by the sword, who once spread terror in the land of the living. 27 Do they not rest

---

n Gk: Heb lacks *in the first month*   *o* Heb *it*   *p* Heb *It*

32:17 **first:** *so Gk; Heb. omits.*   32:18 **her nobility . . . them:** *prob. rdg; Heb. obscure.*

10 Many peoples shall be appalled at you, and their kings shall shudder over you in horror when they see me brandish my sword, and on the day of your downfall every one of them shall continuously tremble for his own life. 11 For thus says the Lord GOD: The sword of the king of Babylon shall come upon you.

12 I will cut down your horde with the blades
of warriors,
all of them the most ruthless of the nations;
They shall lay waste the glory of Egypt,
and all her hordes shall be destroyed.
13 I will have all of her animals perish
beside her abundant waters;
The foot of man shall stir them no longer,
nor shall the hoof of beast disturb them.
14 Then will I make their waters clear,
and their streams flow like oil,
says the Lord GOD.

15 When I turn Egypt into a waste, the land shall be devastated of all that is in it; when I strike all who live there, they shall know that I am the LORD. 16 This is a dirge, and it shall be sung: the daughters of the nations shall chant it; over Egypt and all its hordes shall they chant it, says the Lord GOD.

17 On the fifteenth day of the first month in the twelfth year, the word of the LORD came to me: 18 Son of man, lament over the throngs of Egypt, for the mighty nations have thrust them down to the bottom of the earth, with those who go down into the pit. 20 In the midst of those slain by the sword shall they fall, and place shall be made with them for all their hordes. Then from the midst of the nether world, the mighty warriors shall speak to Egypt: 19 "Whom do you excel in beauty? 21 Come down, you and your allies, lie with the uncircumcised, with those slain by the sword."

22 There is Assyria with all her company, all of them slain, 23 whose graves have been made in the recesses of the pit; her company is around Egypt's grave, all of them slain, fallen by the sword, who spread terror in the land of the living. 24 There is Elam with all her throng about Egypt's grave, all of them slain, fallen by the sword: they have gone down uncircumcised to the bottom of the earth, who spread their terror in the land of the living, and they bear their disgrace with those who go down into the pit; 25 in the midst of the slain they are placed. 26 There are Meshech and Tubal and all their throng about her grave, all of them uncircumcised, slain by the sword, for they spread their terror in the land of the living.

27 They do not lie with the mighty men fallen of old, who

known to you. 10 I shall stun many peoples with shock at your fate; their kings will tremble with horror at your fate, when I brandish my sword before their eyes. The day you fall, each will tremble in terror for his life. 11 For the Lord Yahweh says this: The sword of the king of Babylon will overtake you. 12 I shall make your throngs of subjects fall at the swords of my warriors. They are the most barbarous of nations. They will annihilate the pride of Egypt, and all its throngs will be destroyed. 13 I shall also destroy all its cattle beside the plentiful waters. No human foot will churn them, no animal foot will churn them up again; 14 then I shall let their waters settle and make their rivers glide like oil — declares the Lord Yahweh.

15 "When I reduce Egypt to a ruin and the country is stripped of its contents, when I strike all those who live there, they will know that I am Yahweh.

16 "Such is the lament which the daughters of the nations will raise. They will raise it over Egypt and all its throng. This is the lament they will raise — declares the Lord Yahweh." '

17 In the twelfth year, on the fifteenth day of the first month, the word of Yahweh was addressed to me as follows, 18 'Son of man, lament over the throng of Egypt, for down she must go with the daughters of majestic nations to the depths of the underworld with those who sink into oblivion.

19 'Whom do you surpass in beauty? Down with you, make your bed with the uncircumcised, 20 with those who have been slaughtered by the sword. (The sword has been given, it has been drawn.) She and all her throngs have fallen. 21 From the depths of Sheol, the mightiest heroes, her allies, will say to her, "They have come down, they have lain down, uncircumcised, slaughtered by the sword."

22 'Assyria is there and all her hordes, with their graves all round her; all of them slaughtered, fallen by the sword; 23 their graves have been made in the deepest part of the abyss, and her hordes, with their graves all round her; all of them slaughtered, killed by the sword, who once spread terror through the world of the living.

24 'Elam is there and all her throng round her grave, all of them slaughtered, fallen by the sword; they have gone down uncircumcised to the depths of the underworld, who once spread terror throughout the world of the living. They have borne their shame with those who sink into oblivion. 25 Among the slaughtered, they have put a bed for her, among her throng with their tombs round her, all of them uncircumcised, slaughtered by the sword for having spread terror throughout the world of the living. They have borne their shame with those who sink into oblivion. They have been put among the slaughtered.

26 'Meshech, Tubal are there and all her throng, with their graves round her, all of them uncircumcised, slaughtered by the sword for having spread terror through the world of the living. 27 They do not lie with the heroes who fell long ago,

NEW REVISED STANDARD VERSION	REVISED ENGLISH BIBLE

ago*q* who went down to Sheol with their weapons of war, whose swords were laid under their heads, and whose shields*r* are upon their bones; for the terror of the warriors was in the land of the living. 28 So you shall be broken and lie among the uncircumcised, with those who are killed by the sword.

29 Edom is there, its kings and all its princes, who for all their might are laid with those who are killed by the sword; they lie with the uncircumcised, with those who go down to the Pit.

30 The princes of the north are there, all of them, and all the Sidonians, who have gone down in shame with the slain, for all the terror that they caused by their might; they lie uncircumcised with those who are killed by the sword, and bear their shame with those who go down to the Pit.

31 When Pharaoh sees them, he will be consoled for all his hordes—Pharaoh and all his army, killed by the sword, says the Lord God. 32 For he*s* spread terror in the land of the living; therefore he shall be laid to rest among the uncircumcised, with those who are slain by the sword—Pharaoh and all his multitude, says the Lord God.

33 The word of the Lord came to me: 2 O Mortal, speak to your people and say to them, If I bring the sword upon a land, and the people of the land take one of their number as their sentinel; 3 and if the sentinel sees the sword coming upon the land and blows the trumpet and warns the people; 4 then if any who hear the sound of the trumpet do not take warning, and the sword comes and takes them away, their blood shall be upon their own heads. 5 They heard the sound of the trumpet and did not take warning; their blood shall be upon themselves. But if they had taken warning, they would have saved their lives. 6 But if the sentinel sees the sword coming and does not blow the trumpet, so that the people are not warned, and the sword comes and takes any of them, they are taken away in their iniquity, but their blood I will require at the sentinel's hand.

7 So you, mortal, I have made a sentinel for the house of Israel; whenever you hear a word from my mouth, you shall give them warning from me. 8 If I say to the wicked, "O wicked ones, you shall surely die," and you do not speak to warn the wicked to turn from their ways, the wicked shall die in their iniquity, but their blood I will require at your hand. 9 But if you warn the wicked to turn from their ways, and they do not turn from their ways, the wicked shall die in their iniquity, but you will have saved your life.

10 Now you, mortal, say to the house of Israel, Thus you have said: "Our transgressions and our sins weigh upon us, and we waste away because of them; how then can we live?" 11 Say to them, As I live, says the Lord God, I have no pleasure in the death of the wicked, but that the wicked turn from their ways and live; turn back, turn back from your evil ways; for why will you die, O house of Israel? 12 And you, mortal, say to your people, The righteousness of the righteous shall not save them when they transgress; and as for the wickedness of the wicked, it shall not make them stumble when they turn from their wickedness; and the righteous shall not be able to live by their righteousness*r* when they sin. 13 Though I say to the righteous that they shall surely live, yet if they trust in their righteousness and commit iniquity, none of their righteous deeds shall be remembered; but in the iniquity that they have committed they shall die. 14 Again, though I say to the wicked, "You shall surely die," yet if they turn from their sin and do what is lawful and right— 15 if the wicked restore the pledge, give

---

with warriors fallen uncircumcised, who have gone down to Sheol with their weapons, their swords laid under their heads and their shields over their bones, though the terror of the warriors once weighed heavily on the land of the living? 28 Pharaoh, you also will lie broken in the company of the uncircumcised dead, lying with those slain by the sword. 29 Edom is there, with her kings and all her princes, who, despite their might, have been laid with those slain by the sword. They will lie with the uncircumcised dead and with those who go down to the abyss. 30 All the princes of the north and the Sidonians are there, who, despite the terror inspired by their might, have gone down in shame with the slain. They lie uncircumcised with those slain by the sword, and they bear disgrace with those who go down to the abyss."

31 'Pharaoh will see them and be consoled for his lost hordes—Pharaoh who, with all his army, is slain by the sword, says the Lord God. 32 Though he spread terror throughout the land of the living, yet he with all his hordes is laid with those slain by the sword, in the company of the uncircumcised dead. This is the word of the Lord God.'

33 This word of the Lord came to me: 2 'O man, say to your fellow-countrymen: When I bring a sword against a land, its people choose one of themselves to be their watchman, 3 and if he sees the enemy approach, he blows his trumpet to warn the people. 4 If anyone does not heed the warning and is overtaken by the sword, his fate be on his own head! 5 He ignored the alarm when he heard it. Had he taken heed, he would have escaped with his life. 6 But if the watchman does not blow his trumpet to give warning when he sees the approach of the enemy, and if anyone who is killed is caught with his sins on him, I shall hold the watchman answerable for his death.

7 'I have appointed you, O man, a watchman for the Israelites, and you must pass to them any warnings you receive from me. 8 If I pronounce sentence of death on a person because he is wicked and you do not speak out to dissuade him from his ways, that person will die because of his sin, but I shall hold you answerable for his death. 9 However, if you have warned him to give up his ways, and he persists in them, he will die because of his sin, but you will have saved yourself.

10 'O man, say to the Israelites: You complain, "We are burdened by our sins and offences; we are pining away because of them, and despair of life." 11 Tell them: As I live, says the Lord God, I have no desire for the death of the wicked. I would rather that the wicked should mend their ways and live. Give them up, give up your evil ways, Israelites, why should you die?

12 'O man, say to your fellow-countrymen: When a righteous person transgresses, his righteousness will not save him. When a wicked person mends his ways, his former wickedness will not bring him down. When a righteous person sins, all his righteousness cannot save his life. 13 When I tell the righteous person that he will save his life, then if he presumes on his righteousness and does wrong, none of his righteous deeds will be remembered: but for the wrong he has done he will die. 14 When I pronounce sentence of death on the wicked, then if he mends his ways and does what is just and right— 15 if he restores the pledges he

---

q Gk Old Latin: Heb *of the uncircumcised*   *r* Cn: Heb *iniquities*
s Cn: Heb *I*   *t* Heb *by it*

32:27 **and their shields:** *prob. rdg; Heb. unintelligible.*   32:32 **he spread:** *prob. rdg; Heb.* I have spread.

went down to the nether world with their weapons of war, whose swords were placed under their heads and whose shields were laid over their bones, though the mighty men caused terror in the land of the living. 28 But in the midst of the uncircumcised shall you lie, with those slain by the sword.

29 There are Edom, her kings, and all her princes, who despite their might have been placed with those slain by the sword; with the uncircumcised they lie, and with those who go down into the pit. 30 There are all the princes of the north and all the Sidonians, who have gone down with the slain, because of the terror their might inspired; they lie uncircumcised with those slain by the sword and bear their disgrace with those who go down to the pit. 31 When Pharaoh sees these, he shall be comforted for all his hordes slain by the sword—Pharaoh and all his army, says the Lord GOD. 32 Since he spread his terror in the land of the living, therefore is he laid to rest among the uncircumcised, with those slain by the sword—Pharaoh and all his hordes, says the Lord GOD.

33 Thus the word of the LORD came to me: 2 Son of man, speak thus to your countrymen: When I bring the sword against a country, and the people of this country select one of their number to be their watchman, 3 and the watchman, seeing the sword coming against the country, blows the trumpet to warn the people, 4 anyone hearing but not heeding the warning of the trumpet and therefore slain by the sword that comes against him, shall be responsible for his own death. 5 He heard the trumpet blast yet refused to take warning; he is responsible for his own death, for had he taken warning he would have escaped with his life. 6 But if the watchman sees the sword coming and fails to blow the warning trumpet, so that the sword comes and takes anyone, I will hold the watchman responsible for that person's death, even though that person is taken because of his own sin.

7 You, son of man, I have appointed watchman for the house of Israel; when you hear me say anything, you shall warn them for me. 8 If I tell the wicked man that he shall surely die, and you do not speak out to dissuade the wicked man from his way, he [the wicked man] shall die for his guilt, but I will hold you responsible for his death. 9 But if you warn the wicked man, trying to turn him from his way, and he refuses to turn from his way, he shall die for his guilt, but you shall save yourself.

10 As for you, son of man, speak to the house of Israel: You people say, "Our crimes and our sins weigh us down; we are rotting away because of them. How can we survive?" 11 Answer them: As I live, says the Lord GOD, I swear I take no pleasure in the death of the wicked man, but rather in the wicked man's conversion, that he may live. Turn, turn from your evil ways! Why should you die, O house of Israel?

12 As for you, son of man, tell your countrymen: The virtue which a man has practiced will not save him on the day that he sins; neither will the wickedness that a man has done bring about his downfall on the day that he turns from his wickedness [nor can the virtuous man, when he sins, remain alive]. 13 Though I say to the virtuous man that he shall surely live, if he then presumes on his virtue and does wrong, none of his virtuous deeds shall be remembered; because of the wrong he has done, he shall die. 14 And though I say to the wicked man that he shall surely die, if he turns away from his sin and does what is right and just,

those who went down to Sheol fully armed, who had their swords laid under their heads and their shields put under their bones, since the heroes inspired the world of the living with terror. 28 But you will be broken with the uncircumcised and lie with those slaughtered by the sword.

29 'Edom is there, her kings and all her princes who, despite their valour, have been laid with those slaughtered by the sword. They lie with the uncircumcised, with those who sink into oblivion.

30 'All the princes of the north and all the Sidonians are there, who have gone down with the slaughtered, because of the terror which their power inspired. Ashamed, uncircumcised, they lie among those slaughtered by the sword and bear their shame with those who sink into oblivion.

31 'Pharaoh will see them and take comfort at the sight of all this throng slaughtered by the sword—Pharaoh and all his throng—declares the Lord Yahweh. 32 For having spread terror through the world of the living, he will be laid with the uncircumcised, with those slaughtered by the sword, Pharaoh and all his throng—declares the Lord Yahweh.'

33 The word of Yahweh was addressed to me as follows, 2 'Son of man, speak to the people of your country. Say to them, "When I send the sword against the people of that country, take one of their number and post him as a watchman; 3 if he sees the sword coming against the country, he must sound his horn to warn the people. 4 If someone hears the sound of the horn but pays no attention and the sword overtakes him and destroys him, he will have been responsible for his own death. 5 He has heard the sound of the horn and paid no attention; his death will be his own responsibility. But the life of someone who pays attention will be secure.

6 "If, however, the watchman has seen the sword coming but has not blown his horn, and so the people are not alerted and the sword overtakes them and destroys a single one of them, that person will indeed die for his guilt, but I shall hold the watchman responsible for his death."

7 'Son of man I have appointed you as watchman for the House of Israel. When you hear a word from my mouth, warn them from me. 8 If I say to someone wicked, "Evildoer, you are to die," and you do not speak to warn the wicked person to renounce such ways, the wicked person will die for this guilt, but I shall hold you responsible for the death. 9 If, however, you do warn someone wicked to renounce such ways and repent, and that person does not repent, then the culprit will die for this guilt, but you yourself will have saved your life.

10 'Son of man, say to the House of Israel, "You are continually saying: Our crimes and sins weigh heavily on us; we are wasting away because of them. How are we to go on living?" 11 Say to them, "As I live—declares the Lord Yahweh—I do not take pleasure in the death of the wicked but in the conversion of the wicked who changes his ways and saves his life. Repent, turn back from your evil ways. Why die, House of Israel?"

12 'Son of man, say to the members of your nation, "The uprightness of an upright person will not save him once he takes to wrong-doing; the wickedness of a wicked person will not ruin him once he renounces his wickedness. No one upright will be able to live on the strength of uprightness, having once taken to sinning. 13 If I say to someone upright: You are to live, and then, trusting in this uprightness, he does wrong, none of the uprightness will be remembered; because of the wrong-doing, he will die. 14 If, however, I say to someone wicked: You are to die, and he turns back from sin and does what is lawful and upright, 15 if he returns

NEW REVISED STANDARD VERSION

back what they have taken by robbery, and walk in the statutes of life, committing no iniquity — they shall surely live, they shall not die. 16 None of the sins that they have committed shall be remembered against them; they have done what is lawful and right, they shall surely live.

17 Yet your people say, "The way of the Lord is not just," when it is their own way that is not just. 18 When the righteous turn from their righteousness, and commit iniquity, they shall die for it.*u* 19 And when the wicked turn from their wickedness, and do what is lawful and right, they shall live by it.*u* 20 Yet you say, "The way of the Lord is not just." O house of Israel, I will judge all of you according to your ways!

21 In the twelfth year of our exile, in the tenth month, on the fifth day of the month, someone who had escaped from Jerusalem came to me and said, "The city has fallen." 22 Now the hand of the LORD had been upon me the evening before the fugitive came; but he had opened my mouth by the time the fugitive came to me in the morning; so my mouth was opened, and I was no longer unable to speak.

23 The word of the LORD came to me: 24 Mortal, the inhabitants of these waste places in the land of Israel keep saying, "Abraham was only one man, yet he got possession of the land; but we are many; the land is surely given us to possess." 25 Therefore say to them, Thus says the Lord GOD: You eat flesh with the blood, and lift up your eyes to your idols, and shed blood; shall you then possess the land? 26 You depend on your swords, you commit abominations, and each of you defiles his neighbor's wife; shall you then possess the land? 27 Say this to them, Thus says the Lord GOD: As I live, surely those who are in the waste places shall fall by the sword; and those who are in the open field I will give to the wild animals to be devoured; and those who are in strongholds and in caves shall die by pestilence. 28 I will make the land a desolation and a waste, and its proud might shall come to an end; and the mountains of Israel shall be so desolate that no one will pass through. 29 Then they shall know that I am the LORD, when I have made the land a desolation and a waste because of all their abominations that they have committed.

30 As for you, mortal, your people who talk together about you by the walls, and at the doors of the houses, say to one another, each to a neighbor, "Come and hear what the word is that comes from the LORD." 31 They come to you as people come, and they sit before you as my people, and they hear your words, but they will not obey them. For flattery is on their lips, but their heart is set on their gain. 32 To them you are like a singer of love songs,*v* one who has a beautiful voice and plays well on an instrument; they hear what you say, but they will not do it. 33 When this comes — and come it will! — then they shall know that a prophet has been among them.

34 The word of the LORD came to me: 2 Mortal, prophesy against the shepherds of Israel: prophesy, and say to them — to the shepherds: Thus says the Lord GOD: Ah, you shepherds of Israel who have been feeding yourselves! Should not shepherds feed the sheep? 3 You eat the fat, you clothe yourselves with the wool, you slaughter the fatlings; but you do not feed the sheep. 4 You have not strengthened the weak, you have not healed the sick, you have not bound up the injured, you have not brought back the strayed, you have not sought the lost, but with force and harshness you have ruled them. 5 So they were scattered, because there was no shepherd; and scattered, they became food for all the wild animals. My sheep were scattered, 6 My sheep were scattered,

REVISED ENGLISH BIBLE

has taken, makes good what he has stolen, and, doing no more wrong, follows the rules that ensure life — he will live and not die. 16 None of the sins he has committed will be remembered against him; because he does what is just and right, he will live.

17 'Yet your fellow-countrymen say, "The Lord acts without principle," but in fact it is their ways which are unprincipled. 18 If a righteous man gives up his righteousness and does wrong, he will die because of it; 19 if a wicked man gives up his wickedness and does what is just and right, he will live. 20 Israel, how can you say that the Lord acts without principle, when I judge each one of you according to his deeds?'

21 In the twelfth year of our captivity, on the fifth day of the tenth month, a fugitive came from Jerusalem and reported that the city had fallen. 22 The evening before he arrived, the hand of the LORD had come upon me, but by the time the fugitive reached me in the morning the LORD had given me back the power of speech. My speech was restored and I was no longer dumb.

23 The word of the LORD came to me: 24 'O man, the inhabitants of these ruins on Israel's soil say, "When Abraham took possession of the land he was but one man; we are many, and surely the land has been granted to us." 25 Tell them, therefore, that the Lord GOD says: You eat meat with the blood still in it, you worship idols, you shed blood; and yet you expect to possess the land! 26 You resort to the sword, you commit abominations, you defile one another's wives, and yet you expect to keep possession of the land! 27 Tell them that the Lord GOD says: As I live, those among the ruins will fall by the sword; those in the open country I shall give to wild beasts for food; those in dens and caves will die by pestilence. 28 I shall make the land a desolate waste; her boasted might will be brought to an end, and the mountains of Israel will be an untrodden desert. 29 When I make the land a desolate waste because of all the abominations they have committed, then they will know that I am the LORD.

30 'O man, your fellow-countrymen gather in groups and talk of you by the walls and in doorways, saying to one another, "Let us go and see what message there is from the LORD." 31 So my people will come in to you, as people are wont to do. They will sit down in front of you, and hear what you have to say, but they will not act on it. "Fine words!" they will say with insincerity, for their hearts are set on selfish gain. 32 To them you are no more than a singer of fine songs with a lovely voice and skill as a harpist. They will listen to what you say, but none of them will act on it. 33 When it comes, as come it will, they will know that there has been a prophet in their midst.'

34 This word of the LORD came to me: 2 'Prophesy, O man, against the rulers of Israel. Prophesy and say to them: You shepherds, these are the words of the Lord GOD: Woe betide Israel's shepherds who care only for themselves! Should not the shepherd care for the flock? 3 You consume the milk, wear the wool, and slaughter the fat beasts, but you do not feed the sheep. 4 You have not restored the weak, tended the sick, bandaged the injured, recovered the straggler, or searched for the lost; you have driven them with ruthless severity. 5 They are scattered abroad for want of a shepherd, and have become the prey of every wild beast. Scattered, 6 my sheep go straying over

u Heb *them* *v* Cn: Heb *like a love song*

|

15 giving back pledges, restoring stolen goods, living by the statutes that bring life, and doing no wrong, he shall surely live, he shall not die. 16 None of the sins he committed shall be held against him; he has done what is right and just, he shall surely live.

17 Yet your countrymen say, "The way of the LORD is not fair!"; but it is their way that is not fair. 18 When a virtuous man turns away from what is right and does wrong, he shall die for it. 19 But when a wicked man turns away from wickedness and does what is right and just, because of this he shall live. 20 And still you say, "The way of the LORD is not fair!"? I will judge every one of you according to his ways, O house of Israel.

21 On the fifth day of the tenth month, in the twelfth year of our exile, the fugitive came to me from Jerusalem and said, "The city is taken!" 22 The hand of the LORD had come upon me the evening before the fugitive arrived, and he opened my mouth when the fugitive reached me in the morning. My mouth was opened, and I was dumb no longer.

23 Thus the word of the Lord came to me: 24 Son of man, they who live in the ruins on the land of Israel reason thus: "Abraham, though but a single individual, received possession of the land; we, therefore, being many, have as permanent possession the land that has been given to us." 25 Give them this answer: Thus says the Lord GOD: You eat on the mountains, you raise your eyes to your idols, you shed blood — yet you would keep possession of the land? 26 You rely on your sword, you do abominable things, each one of you defiles his neighbor's wife — yet you would keep possession of the land? 27 Tell them this: Thus says the Lord GOD: As I live, those who are in the ruins I swear shall fall by the sword; those who are in the open field I have given to the wild beasts for food; and those who are in fastnesses and in caves shall die by the plague. 28 I will make the land a desolate waste, so that its proud strength will come to an end, and the mountains of Israel shall be so desolate that no one will cross them. 29 Thus they shall know that I am the LORD, when I make the land a desolate waste because of all the abominable things they have done.

30 As for you, son of man, your countrymen are talking about you along the walls and in the doorways of houses. They say to one another, "Come and hear the latest word that comes from the LORD." 31 My people come to you as people always do; they sit down before you and hear your words, but they will not obey them, for lies are on their lips and their desires are fixed on dishonest gain. 32 For them you are only a ballad singer, with a pleasant voice and a clever touch. They listen to your words, but they will not obey them. 33 But when it comes — and it is surely coming! — they shall know that there was a prophet among them.

34 Thus the word of the LORD came to me: 2 Son of man, prophesy against the shepherds of Israel, in these words prophesy to them [to the shepherds]: Thus says the Lord GOD: Woe to the shepherds of Israel who have been pasturing themselves! Should not shepherds, rather, pasture sheep? 3 You have fed off their milk, worn their wool, and slaughtered the fatlings, but the sheep you have not pastured. 4 You did not strengthen the weak nor heal the sick nor bind up the injured. You did not bring back the strayed nor seek the lost, but you lorded it over them harshly and brutally. 5 So they were scattered for lack of a shepherd, and became food for all the wild beasts. My sheep were scattered 6 and wandered over all the mountains

pledges, restores what he has stolen, keeps the laws that give life and no longer does wrong, he will live and will not die. 16 None of his previous sins will be remembered against him; having done what is lawful and upright, he will live. *p*

17 "But the members of your nation say: What the Lord does is unjust. But it is what you do that is unjust. 18 When an upright person gives up being upright and does wrong, he dies for it. 19 And when a wicked person gives up being wicked and does what is lawful and upright, because of this he lives. 20 But you say: What the Lord does is unjust! I shall judge each of you by what you do, House of Israel." *q*

21 In the twelfth year of our captivity, on the fifth day of the tenth month, a fugitive arrived from Jerusalem and said to me, 'The city has been taken.' 22 Now the hand of the Lord had been on me the evening before the fugitive arrived; he had opened my mouth before the fugitive came to me the next morning; my mouth had been opened and I was dumb no longer.

23 The word of Yahweh was then addressed to me as follows, 24 'Son of man, the people living in those ruins on the soil of Israel say this, "Abraham was alone when he was given possession of this country. But we are many; the country has been given us as our heritage."

25 'Very well, tell them, "The Lord Yahweh says this: You eat blood, you raise your eyes to your foul idols, you shed blood; are you to own the country? 26 You rely on your swords, you engage in loathsome practices, each of you defiles his neighbour's wife; are you to own the country?" 27 Tell them this, "The Lord Yahweh says this: As I live, I swear it, those in the ruins will fall to the sword, those in the countryside I shall give to the wild animals for them to eat, and those among the crags and in caves will die of plague. 28 I shall make the country a desolate waste, and the pride of its strength will be at an end. The mountains of Israel will be deserted and no one will pass that way again. 29 Then they will know that I am Yahweh, when I make the country a desolate waste because of all the filthy things they have done."

30 'Son of man, the members of your nation are talking about you on the ramparts and in doorways. They keep saying to one another, "Come and hear the word that has come from Yahweh." 31 They throng towards you; my people sit down in front of you and listen to your words, but they do not act on them. What they act on is the lie in their mouths, and their hearts are set on dishonest gain. 32 As far as they are concerned, you are like a love song pleasantly sung to a good musical accompaniment. They listen to your words, but no one acts on them. 33 When the thing takes place — and it is beginning now — they will know that there has been a prophet among them.'

34 The word of Yahweh was addressed to me as follows, 2 'Son of man, prophesy against the shepherds of Israel; prophesy and say to them, "Shepherds, the Lord Yahweh says this: Disaster is in store for the shepherds of Israel who feed themselves! Are not shepherds meant to feed a flock? 3 Yet you have fed on milk, you have dressed yourselves in wool, you have sacrificed the fattest sheep, but failed to feed the flock. 4 You have failed to make weak sheep strong, or to care for the sick ones, or bandage the injured ones. You have failed to bring back strays or look for the lost. On the contrary, you have ruled them cruelly and harshly. 5 For lack of a shepherd they have been scattered, to become the prey of all the wild animals; they have been scattered. 6 My flock is astray on every mountain and

NEW REVISED STANDARD VERSION	REVISED ENGLISH BIBLE

they wandered over all the mountains and on every high hill; my sheep were scattered over all the face of the earth, with no one to search or seek for them.

7 Therefore, you shepherds, hear the word of the LORD: 8 As I live, says the Lord GOD, because my sheep have become a prey, and my sheep have become food for all the wild animals, since there was no shepherd; and because my shepherds have not searched for my sheep, but the shepherds have fed themselves, and have not fed my sheep; 9 therefore, you shepherds, hear the word of the LORD: 10 Thus says the Lord GOD, I am against the shepherds; and I will demand my sheep at their hand, and put a stop to their feeding the sheep; no longer shall the shepherds feed themselves. I will rescue my sheep from their mouths, so that they may not be food for them.

11 For thus says the Lord GOD: I myself will search for my sheep, and will seek them out. 12 As shepherds seek out their flocks when they are among their scattered sheep, so I will seek out my sheep. I will rescue them from all the places to which they have been scattered on a day of clouds and thick darkness. 13 I will bring them out from the peoples and gather them from the countries, and will bring them into their own land; and I will feed them on the mountains of Israel, by the watercourses, and in all the inhabited parts of the land. 14 I will feed them with good pasture, and the mountain heights of Israel shall be their pasture; there they shall lie down in good grazing land, and they shall feed on rich pasture on the mountains of Israel. 15 I myself will be the shepherd of my sheep, and I will make them lie down, says the Lord GOD. 16 I will seek the lost, and I will bring back the strayed, and I will bind up the injured, and I will strengthen the weak, but the fat and the strong I will destroy. I will feed them with justice.

17 As for you, my flock, thus says the Lord GOD: I shall judge between sheep and sheep, between rams and goats: 18 Is it not enough for you to feed on the good pasture, but you must tread down with your feet the rest of your pasture? When you drink of clear water, must you foul the rest with your feet? 19 And must my sheep eat what you have trodden with your feet, and drink what you have fouled with your feet?

20 Therefore, thus says the Lord GOD to them: I myself will judge between the fat sheep and the lean sheep. 21 Because you pushed with flank and shoulder, and butted at all the weak animals with your horns until you scattered them far and wide, 22 I will save my flock, and they shall no longer be ravaged; and I will judge between sheep and sheep.

23 I will set up over them one shepherd, my servant David, and he shall feed them: he shall feed them and be their shepherd. 24 And I, the LORD, will be their God, and my servant David shall be prince among them; I, the LORD, have spoken.

25 I will make with them a covenant of peace and banish wild animals from the land, so that they may live in the wild and sleep in the woods securely. 26 I will make them and the region around my hill a blessing; and I will send down the showers in their season; they shall be showers of blessing. 27 The trees of the field shall yield their fruit, and the earth shall yield its increase. They shall be secure on their soil; and they shall know that I am the LORD, when I break the bars of their yoke, and save them from the hands of those who enslaved them. 28 They shall no more be plunder for the nations, nor shall the animals of the land devour them; they shall live in safety, and no one shall make them afraid. 29 I will provide for them a splendid vegetation so that they shall no more be consumed with hunger in the land, and no longer suffer the insults of the nations. 30 They

all the mountains and on every high hill; my flock is dispersed over the whole earth, with no one to enquire after them or search for them.

7 'Therefore, you shepherds, hear the word of the LORD. 8 As surely as I live, says the Lord GOD, because for lack of a shepherd my sheep are ravaged by all the wild beasts and have become their prey, because my shepherds have not taken thought for the sheep, but have cared only for themselves and not for the sheep—9 therefore, you shepherds, hear the word of the LORD. 10 The Lord GOD says: I am against the shepherds and shall demand from them an account of my sheep. I shall dismiss those shepherds from tending my flock: no longer will they care only for themselves; I shall rescue my sheep from their mouths, and they will feed on them no more.

11 'For the Lord GOD says: Now I myself shall take thought for my sheep and search for them. 12 As a shepherd goes in search of his sheep when his flock is scattered from him in every direction, so I shall go in search of my sheep and rescue them, no matter where they were scattered in a day of cloud and darkness. 13 I shall lead them out from the nations, gather them in from different lands, and bring them home to their own country. I shall shepherd them on the mountains of Israel and by her streams, wherever there is a settlement. 14 I shall feed them on good grazing-ground, and their pasture will be Israel's high mountains. There they will rest in good pasture, and find rich grazing on the mountains of Israel. 15 I myself shall tend my flock, and find them a place to rest, says the Lord GOD. 16 I shall search for the lost, recover the straggler, bandage the injured, strengthen the sick, leave the healthy and strong to play, and give my flock their proper food.

17 'The Lord GOD says to you, my flock: I shall judge between one sheep and another. As for you rams and he-goats, 18 are you not satisfied with grazing on the best pastures, that you must also trample down the rest with your feet? Or with drinking clear water, that you must also muddy the rest with your feet? 19 My flock has to graze on what you have trampled underfoot and drink what you have muddied. 20 Therefore, the Lord GOD says to them: Now I myself shall judge between the fat sheep and the lean. 21 You push aside the weak with flank and shoulder, you butt them with your horns until you have scattered them in every direction. 22 Therefore I shall save my flock, and they will be ravaged no more; I shall judge between one sheep and another.

23 'I shall set over them one shepherd to take care of them, my servant David; he will care for them and be their shepherd. 24 I, the LORD, shall be their God, and my servant David will be prince among them. I, the LORD, have spoken. 25 I shall make a covenant with them to ensure peace and prosperity; I shall rid the land of wild beasts, and people will live on the open pastures and sleep in the woods free from danger. 26 I shall settle them in the neighbourhood of my hill and bless them with rain in due season. 27 Trees in the countryside will bear their fruit, the ground will yield its produce, and my people will live in security on their own soil. When I break the bars of their yokes and rescue them from the power of those who have enslaved them they will know that I am the LORD. 28 They will never again be ravaged by the nations, nor will wild beasts devour them; they will live in security, free from terror. 29 I shall make their crops renowned, and they will never again be victims of famine in the land, nor bear any longer the taunts of the

and high hills; my sheep were scattered over the whole earth, with no one to look after them or to search for them. ⁷Therefore, shepherds, hear the word of the LORD: ⁸As I live, says the Lord GOD, because my sheep have been given over to pillage, and because my sheep have become food for every wild beast, for lack of a shepherd; because my shepherds did not look after my sheep, but pastured themselves and did not pasture my sheep; ⁹because of this, shepherds, hear the word of the LORD: ¹⁰Thus says the Lord GOD: I swear I am coming against these shepherds. I will claim my sheep from them and put a stop to their shepherding my sheep so that they may no longer pasture themselves. I will save my sheep, that they may no longer be food for their mouths.

¹¹For thus says the Lord GOD: I myself will look after and tend my sheep. ¹²As a shepherd tends his flock when he finds himself among his scattered sheep, so will I tend my sheep. I will rescue them from every place where they were scattered when it was cloudy and dark. ¹³I will lead them out from among the peoples and gather them from the foreign lands; I will bring them back to their own country and pasture them upon the mountains of Israel [in the land's ravines and all its inhabited places]. ¹⁴In good pastures will I pasture them, and on the mountain heights of Israel shall be their grazing ground. There they shall lie down on good grazing ground, and in rich pastures shall they be pastured on the mountains of Israel. ¹⁵I myself will pasture my sheep; I myself will give them rest, says the Lord GOD. ¹⁶The lost I will seek out, the strayed I will bring back, the injured I will bind up, the sick I will heal [but the sleek and the strong I will destroy], shepherding them rightly.

¹⁷As for you, my sheep, says the Lord GOD, I will judge between one sheep and another, between rams and goats. ¹⁸Was it not enough for you to graze on the best pasture, that you had to trample the rest of your pastures with your feet? Was it not enough for you to drink the clearest water, that you had to foul the remainder with your feet? ¹⁹Thus my sheep had to graze on what your feet had trampled and drink what your feet had fouled. ²⁰Therefore thus says the Lord GOD: Now will I judge between the fat and the lean sheep. ²¹Because you push with side and shoulder, and butt all the weak sheep with your horns until you have driven them out, ²²I will save my sheep so that they may no longer be despoiled, and I will judge between one sheep and another. ²³I will appoint one shepherd over them to pasture them, my servant David; he shall pasture them and be their shepherd. ²⁴I, the Lord, will be their God, and my servant David shall be prince among them. I, the LORD, have spoken.

²⁵I will make a covenant of peace with them, and rid the country of ravenous beasts, that they may dwell securely in the desert and sleep in the forests. ²⁶I will place them about my hill, sending rain in due season, rains that shall be a blessing to them. ²⁷The trees of the field shall bear their fruits, and the land its crops, and they shall dwell securely on their own soil. Thus they shall know that I am the LORD when I break the bonds of their yoke and free them from the power of those who enslaved them. ²⁸They shall no longer be despoiled by the nations or devoured by beasts of the earth, but shall dwell secure, with no one to frighten them. ²⁹I will prepare for them peaceful fields for planting; they shall no longer be carried off by famine in the land, or bear the reproaches of the nations. ³⁰Thus they shall know that

on every high hill; my flock has been scattered all over the world; no one bothers about them and no one looks for them.

⁷"Very well, shepherds, hear the word of Yahweh: ⁸As I live, I swear it—declares the Lord Yahweh—since my flock has been pillaged and for lack of a shepherd is now the prey of every wild animal, since my shepherds have ceased to bother about my flock, since my shepherds feed themselves rather than my flock, ⁹very well, shepherds, hear the word of Yahweh: ¹⁰The Lord Yahweh says this: Look, I am against the shepherds. I shall take my flock out of their charge and henceforth not allow them to feed my flock. And the shepherds will stop feeding themselves, because I shall rescue my sheep from their mouths to stop them from being food for them.

¹¹"For the Lord Yahweh says this: Look, I myself shall take care of my flock and look after it. ¹²As a shepherd looks after his flock when he is with his scattered sheep, so shall I look after my sheep. I shall rescue them from wherever they have been scattered on the day of clouds and darkness. ¹³I shall bring them back from the peoples where they are; I shall gather them back from the countries and bring them back to their own land. I shall pasture them on the mountains of Israel, in the ravines and in all the inhabited parts of the country. ¹⁴I shall feed them in good pasturage; the highest mountains of Israel will be their grazing ground. There they will rest in good grazing grounds; they will browse in rich pastures on the mountains of Israel. ¹⁵I myself shall pasture my sheep, I myself shall give them rest—declares the Lord Yahweh. ¹⁶I shall look for the lost one, bring back the stray, bandage the injured and make the sick strong. I shall watch over the fat and healthy. I shall be a true shepherd to them.

¹⁷"As for you, my sheep, the Lord Yahweh says this: I shall judge between sheep and sheep, between rams and he-goats. ¹⁸Not content to drink the clearest of the water, you foul the rest with your feet. ¹⁹And my sheep must graze on what your feet have trampled and drink what your feet have fouled. ²⁰Very well, the Lord Yahweh says this: I myself shall judge between the fat sheep and the thin sheep. ²¹Since you have jostled with flank and shoulder and butted all the ailing sheep with your horns, until you have scattered them outside, ²²I shall come and save my sheep and stop them from being victimised. I shall judge between sheep and sheep.

²³"I shall raise up one shepherd, my servant David, and put him in charge of them to pasture them; he will pasture them and be their shepherd. ²⁴I, Yahweh, shall be their God, and my servant David will be ruler among them. I, Yahweh, have spoken. ²⁵I shall make a covenant of peace with them; I shall rid the country of wild animals. They will be able to live secure in the desert and go to sleep in the woods. ²⁶I shall settle them round my hill; I shall send rain at the proper time; it will be a rain of blessings. ²⁷The trees of the countryside will yield their fruit and the soil will yield its produce; they will be secure on their own soil. And they will know that I am Yahweh when I break the bars of their yoke and rescue them from the clutches of their slave-masters. ²⁸No more will they be a prey to the nations, no more will the wild animals of the country devour them. They will live secure, with no one to frighten them. ²⁹I shall make splendid vegetation grow for them; no more will they suffer from famine in the country; no more will they have to bear the insults of other nations. ³⁰So they will know that I, their

NEW REVISED STANDARD VERSION

shall know that I, the LORD their God, am with them, and that they, the house of Israel, are my people, says the Lord GOD. ³¹ You are my sheep, the sheep of my pasture[w] and I am your God, says the Lord GOD.

35 The word of the LORD came to me: ²Mortal, set your face against Mount Seir, and prophesy against it, ³ and say to it, Thus says the Lord GOD:

I am against you, Mount Seir;
    I stretch out my hand against you
    to make you a desolation and a waste.
⁴   I lay your towns in ruins;
    you shall become a desolation,
    and you shall know that I am the LORD.

⁵ Because you cherished an ancient enmity, and gave over the people of Israel to the power of the sword at the time of their calamity, at the time of their final punishment; ⁶ therefore, as I live, says the Lord GOD, I will prepare you for blood, and blood shall pursue you; since you did not hate bloodshed, bloodshed shall pursue you. ⁷ I will make Mount Seir a waste and a desolation; and I will cut off from it all who come and go. ⁸ I will fill its mountains with the slain; on your hills and in your valleys and in all your watercourses those killed with the sword shall fall. ⁹ I will make you a perpetual desolation, and your cities shall never be inhabited. Then you shall know that I am the LORD.

10 Because you said, "These two nations and these two countries shall be mine, and we will take possession of them," — although the LORD was there — ¹¹ therefore, as I live, says the Lord GOD, I will deal with you according to the anger and envy that you showed because of your hatred against them; and I will make myself known among you,[x] when I judge you. ¹² You shall know that I, the LORD, have heard all the abusive speech that you uttered against the mountains of Israel, saying, "They are laid desolate, they are given us to devour." ¹³ And you magnified yourselves against me with your mouth, and multiplied your words against me; I heard it. ¹⁴ Thus says the Lord GOD: As the whole earth rejoices, I will make you desolate. ¹⁵ As you rejoiced over the inheritance of the house of Israel, because it was desolate, so I will deal with you; you shall be desolate, Mount Seir, and all Edom, all of it. Then they shall know that I am the LORD.

36 And you, mortal, prophesy to the mountains of Israel, and say: O mountains of Israel, hear the word of the LORD. ² Thus says the Lord GOD: Because the enemy said of you, "Aha!" and, "The ancient heights have become our possession," ³ therefore prophesy, and say: Thus says the Lord GOD: Because they made you desolate indeed, and crushed you from all sides, so that you became the possession of the rest of the nations, and you became an object of gossip and slander among the people; ⁴ therefore, O mountains of Israel, hear the word of the Lord GOD: Thus says the Lord GOD to the mountains and the hills, the watercourses and the valleys, the desolate wastes and the deserted towns, which have become a source of plunder and an object of derision to the rest of the nations all around; ⁵ therefore thus says the Lord GOD: I am speaking in my hot jealousy against the rest of the nations, and against all Edom, who, with wholehearted joy and utter contempt, took my land as their possession, because of its pasture, to plunder it. ⁶ Therefore prophesy concerning the land of Is-

REVISED ENGLISH BIBLE

nations. ³⁰ Then they will know that I, the LORD their God, am with them, and that they are my people Israel, says the Lord GOD. ³¹ You are my flock, the flock I feed, and I am your God. It is the word of the Lord GOD.'

35 This word of the LORD came to me: ²'O man, face towards the hill-country of Seir and prophesy against it. ³ Say: These are the words of the Lord GOD:

Hill-country of Seir, I am against you:
    I shall stretch out my hand to strike you
    and reduce you to a desolate waste.
⁴ I shall lay your towns in ruins
    and you will become a desolation.
    Then you will know that I am the LORD;
⁵ for you have kept up an ancient feud
    and handed over the Israelites to the sword
    in the hour of their doom,
    the hour of their final punishment.

⁶ 'Therefore, as I live, says the Lord GOD,
    I shall make blood your destiny, and it will pursue you;
    you are most surely guilty of blood,
    and it will pursue you.
⁷ I shall make the hill-country of Seir a desolate waste
    and prevent anyone travelling to and fro in it;
⁸ I shall cover your hills and valleys with the slain,
    and those slain by the sword will fall into your streams.
⁹ I shall make you desolate for ever,
    and your cities will not be inhabited.
    Then you will know that I am the LORD.

10 'You say, "The two nations and the two countries will be mine and I shall take possession of them, though the LORD has been there." ¹¹ Therefore, as I live, says the Lord GOD, your anger and jealousy will be repaid, for I shall do to you what you have done in your hatred towards them. I shall be known among you by the way I judge you; ¹² you will know that I am the LORD. I have heard all your blasphemous talk about the mountains of Israel. You have said, "They are desolate and have been given to us to devour." ¹³ You have boasted against me and spoken wildly. I myself have heard you. ¹⁴ The Lord GOD says: I shall make you so desolate that the whole world will gloat over you. ¹⁵ I shall treat you as you treated Israel my own possession when you gloated over its desolation. Hill-country of Seir, the whole of Edom, you will be desolate. Then all will know that I am the LORD.

36 'O man, prophesy to the mountains of Israel and say: Mountains of Israel, hear the word of the LORD. ² The Lord GOD says: The enemy has boasted over you, "Aha! Now the ancient heights are ours." ³⁻⁴ Therefore prophesy and say: These are the words of the Lord GOD: You mountains of Israel, all round you men gloated over you and trampled you down when you were seized and occupied by the rest of the nations; your name was bandied about in common gossip. Therefore, listen to the words of the Lord GOD when he speaks to the mountains and hills, to the streams and valleys, to ruined places and deserted cities, all plundered and despised by the rest of the surrounding nations. ⁵ The Lord GOD says: In the heat of my jealousy I have spoken out against the rest of the nations, and against Edom above all, for with hearts full of glee and feelings of contempt they seized my land as spoil. ⁶ Therefore prophesy

---

[w] Gk OL: Heb *pasture, you are people*   [x] Gk: Heb *them*

35:6 **are . . . guilty of:** *so Gk; Heb.* most surely hate.
35:11 **among you:** *so Gk; Heb.* among them.

NEW AMERICAN BIBLE

NEW JERUSALEM BIBLE

I, the LORD, am their God, and they are my people, the house of Israel, says the Lord GOD. 31 [You, my sheep, you are the sheep of my pasture, and I am your God, says the Lord GOD.]

35 Thus the word of the LORD came to me: 2 Son of man, set your face against Mount Seir, and prophesy against it. 3 Say to it: Thus says the Lord GOD: See! I am coming at you, Mount Seir. I will stretch out my hand against you and make you a desolate waste. 4 Your cities I will turn into ruins, and you shall be a waste; thus you shall know that I am the LORD.

5 Because you never let die your hatred for the Israelites, whom you delivered over to the power of the sword at the time of their trouble, when their crimes came to an end, 6 therefore, as I live, says the Lord GOD, you have been guilty of blood, and blood, I swear, shall pursue you. 7 I will make Mount Seir a desolate waste, and cut off from it any traveler. 8 With the slain I will fill your hills, your valleys, and all your ravines [in them the slain shall fall by the sword]: 9 desolate will I make you forever, and leave your cities without inhabitants; thus you shall know that I am the LORD.

10 Because you said: The two nations and the two lands have become mine; we shall possess them—although the LORD was there— 11 therefore, as I live, says the Lord GOD, I will deal with you according to your anger and your envy which you have exercised [in your hatred] against them. I will make myself known among you when I judge you, 12 and you shall know that I am the LORD.

I have heard all the contemptuous things you have uttered against the mountains of Israel: "They are desolate, they have been given us to devour." 13 I have heard the insolent and wild words you have spoken against me. 14 Thus says the Lord GOD: Just as you rejoiced over my land because it was desolate, so will I do to you. 15 In keeping with your glee over the devastation of the inheritance of the house of Israel, so will I treat you. A waste shall you be, Mount Seir, you and the whole of Edom. Thus they shall know that I am the LORD.

36 As for you, son of man, prophesy to the mountains of Israel: Mountains of Israel, hear the word of the LORD! 2 Thus says the Lord GOD: Because the enemy has said of you, "Ha! the everlasting heights have become our possession" 3 [therefore prophesy in these words: Thus says the Lord GOD:]; because you have been ridiculed and despised on all sides for having become a possession for the rest of the nations, and have become a byword and a popular jeer; 4 therefore, mountains of Israel, hear the word of the LORD: [Thus says the Lord GOD to the mountains and hills, the ravines and valleys, the desolate ruins and abandoned cities, which have been given over to the pillage and mockery of the remaining nations round about; 5 therefore thus says the Lord GOD:] Truly, with burning jealousy I speak against the rest of the nations [and against all of Edom] who with wholehearted joy and utter contempt have considered my land their possession to be delivered over to plunder. 6 [Therefore, prophesy concerning the land of Is-

God, am with them and that they, the House of Israel, are my people—declares the Lord Yahweh. 31 And you, my sheep, are the flock of my human pasture, and I am your God—declares the Lord Yahweh.'"

35 The word of Yahweh was addressed to me as follows, 2 'Son of man, turn towards Mount Seir and prophesy against it. 3 Say to it, "The Lord Yahweh says this: Look, I am against you, Mount Seir; I shall stretch out my hand against you; I shall make you a desolate waste. 4 I shall lay your towns in ruins. You will become a waste and you will know that I am Yahweh. 5 Since, following a long-standing hatred, you betrayed the Israelites to the sword on the day of their distress, on the day when an end came for their guilt, 6 very well, as I live—declares the Lord Yahweh—I destine you to bloodshed, and bloodshed will pursue you. I swear it; you have incurred guilt by shedding blood, and bloodshed will pursue you. 7 I shall make Mount Seir a desolate waste and denude it of anyone travelling to and fro. 8 I shall fill its mountains with its slaughtered; on your hills, in your valleys and in all your ravines, those slaughtered by the sword will fall. 9 I shall make you a perpetual waste, your towns will never be inhabited again, and you will know that I am Yahweh.

10 "Since you said: The two nations and the two countries will be mine; we are going to take possession of it, although Yahweh was there, 11 very well, as I live—declares the Lord Yahweh—I shall act with the same anger and jealousy as you acted in your hatred for them. I shall make myself known for their sake, when I punish you, 12 and you will know that I, Yahweh, have heard all the blasphemies which you have uttered against the mountains of Israel, such as: They have been laid waste, they have been given to us for us to devour. 13 Great was your insolence towards me, many your speeches against me; I have heard! 14 Lord Yahweh says this: To the joy of the whole world, I shall make you a waste. 15 Since you rejoiced because the heritage of the House of Israel had been laid waste, I shall do the same to you, Mount Seir; and you will become a waste, and so will the whole of Edom; and they will know that I am Yahweh.'"

36 'Son of man, prophesy to the mountains of Israel. Say, "Mountains of Israel, hear the word of Yahweh. 2 The Lord Yahweh says this: Since the enemy has gloated over you by saying: Aha! These eternal heights are owned by us now, 3 very well, prophesy! Say: The Lord Yahweh says this: Since you have been ravaged and seized on from all sides, and have become the property of the rest of the nations, and become the subject of people's talk and gossip, 4 very well, mountains of Israel, hear the word of the Lord Yahweh! The Lord Yahweh says this to the mountains and hills, to the ravines and valleys, to the devastated ruins and abandoned cities which have been put to the sack and have become a laughing-stock to the rest of the nations all round; 5 very well, the Lord Yahweh says this: I swear it in the heat of my jealousy; I am speaking to the rest of the nations and to the whole of Edom who so exultantly and contemptuously took possession of my country to despoil its pastureland."

rael, and say to the mountains and hills, to the watercourses and valleys, Thus says the Lord GOD: I am speaking in my jealous wrath, because you have suffered the insults of the nations," 7 therefore thus says the Lord GOD: I swear that the nations that are all around you shall themselves suffer insults.

8 But you, O mountains of Israel, shall shoot out your branches, and yield your fruit to my people Israel; for they shall soon come home. 9 See now, I am for you; I will turn to you, and you shall be tilled and sown; 10 and I will multiply your population, the whole house of Israel, all of it; the towns shall be inhabited and the waste places rebuilt; 11 and I will multiply human beings and animals upon you. They shall increase and be fruitful; and I will cause you to be inhabited as in your former times, and will do more good to you than ever before. Then you shall know that I am the LORD. 12 I will lead people upon you — my people Israel — and they shall possess you, and you shall be their inheritance. No longer shall you bereave them of children.

13 Thus says the Lord GOD: Because they say to you, "You devour people, and you bereave your nation of children," 14 therefore you shall no longer devour people and no longer bereave your nation of children, says the Lord GOD; 15 and no longer will I let you hear the insults of the nations, no longer shall you bear the disgrace of the peoples; and no longer shall you cause your nation to stumble, says the Lord GOD.

16 The word of the LORD came to me: 17 Mortal, when the house of Israel lived on their own soil, they defiled it with their ways and their deeds; their conduct in my sight was like the uncleanness of a woman in her menstrual period. 18 So I poured out my wrath upon them for the blood that they had shed upon the land, and for the idols with which they had defiled it. 19 I scattered them among the nations, and they were dispersed through the countries; in accordance with their conduct and their deeds I judged them. 20 But when they came to the nations, wherever they came, they profaned my holy name, in that it was said of them, "These are the people of the LORD, and yet they had to go out of his land." 21 But I had concern for my holy name, which the house of Israel had profaned among the nations to which they came.

22 Therefore say to the house of Israel, Thus says the Lord GOD: It is not for your sake, O house of Israel, that I am about to act, but for the sake of my holy name, which you have profaned among the nations to which you came. 23 I will sanctify my great name, which has been profaned among the nations, and which you have profaned among them; and the nations shall know that I am the LORD, says the Lord GOD, when through you I display my holiness before their eyes. 24 I will take you from the nations, and gather you from all the countries, and bring you into your own land. 25 I will sprinkle clean water upon you, and you shall be clean from all your uncleannesses, and from all your idols I will cleanse you. 26 A new heart I will give you, and a new spirit I will put within you; and I will remove from your body the heart of stone and give you a heart of flesh. 27 I will put my spirit within you, and make you follow my statutes and be careful to observe my ordinances. 28 Then you shall live in the land that I gave to your ancestors; and you shall be my people, and I will be your God. 29 I will save you from all your uncleannesses, and I will summon the grain and make it abundant and lay no famine upon you. 30 I will make the fruit of the tree and the produce of the field abundant, so that you may never again suffer the disgrace of famine among the nations. 31 Then you shall remember your evil ways, and your dealings that were not good; and you shall loathe yourselves for your iniquities and your abominable deeds. 32 It is not for your sake that I will

over the soil of Israel; say to the mountains and hills, the streams and valleys: The Lord GOD has said: I have spoken my mind in jealous anger because you have had to endure the taunts of the nations. 7 Therefore, says the Lord GOD, I swear with uplifted hand that the nations round about you will in turn endure taunting. 8 But you, mountains of Israel, will put forth your branches and yield your fruit for my people Israel, for their homecoming is near. 9 See now, I am for you, I shall turn to you, and you will be tilled and sown. 10 I shall settle on you many people — the whole house of Israel. The towns will again be inhabited and the ruined places rebuilt. 11 I shall settle in you many people and beasts; they will increase and be fruitful. I shall make you populous as in days of old, and more prosperous than you were in your earliest times. Thus you will know that I am the LORD. 12 I shall make my people Israel tread your paths again. They will settle in you, and you will be their possession. Never again will you leave them childless.

13 'The Lord GOD says: It is said that you are a land that devours human beings and leaves your nation childless. 14 But never again will you devour them or leave your nation childless, says the Lord GOD. 15 I shall never let you hear again the taunts of the surrounding nations, nor will you have to suffer the scorn of foreigners. This is the word of the Lord GOD.'

16 This word of the LORD came to me: 17 'O man, when the Israelites were living on their own soil they defiled it with their ways and deeds; their ways were loathsome and unclean in my sight. 18 I poured out my fury on them for the blood they had poured out on the land, and for the idols with which they had defiled it. 19 I scattered them among the nations, and they were dispersed in many lands. I passed a sentence on them which their ways and deeds deserved. 20 But whenever they came among the nations, they caused my holy name to be profaned. It was said of them, "These are the LORD's people, and it is from his land they have gone into exile." 21 So I spared them for the sake of my holy name which the Israelites had profaned among the nations to whom they had gone.

22 'Therefore tell the Israelites that the Lord GOD says: It is not for the sake of you Israelites that I am acting, but for the sake of my holy name, which you have profaned among the peoples where you have gone. 23 I shall hallow my great name, which you have profaned among those nations. When they see that I reveal my holiness through you, they will know that I am the LORD, says the Lord GOD. 24 I shall take you from among the nations, and gather you from every land, and bring you to your homeland. 25 I shall sprinkle pure water over you, and you will be purified from everything that defiles you; I shall purify you from the taint of all your idols. 26 I shall give you a new heart and put a new spirit within you; I shall remove the heart of stone from your body and give you a heart of flesh. 27 I shall put my spirit within you and make you conform to my statutes; you will observe my laws faithfully. 28 Then you will live in the land I gave to your forefathers; you will be my people, and I shall be your God.

29 'Having saved you from all that defiles you, I shall command the grain to be plentiful; I shall bring no more famine upon you. 30 I shall make the trees bear abundant fruit and the ground yield heavy crops, so that you will never again have to bear among the nations the reproach of famine. 31 You will recall your wicked conduct and evil deeds, and you will loathe yourselves because of your wrongdoing and your abominations. 32 I assure you it is not

36:15 foreigners: so Gk; Heb. adds and you will no more cause your tribes to fall.

rael, and say to the mountains and hills, the ravines and valleys: Thus says the Lord GOD:] With jealous fury I speak, because you have borne the reproach of the nations. 7 Therefore do I solemnly swear that your neighboring nations shall bear their own reproach.

8 As for you, mountains of Israel, you shall grow branches and bear fruit for my people Israel, for they shall soon return. 9 See, I come to you, it is to you that I turn; you will be tilled and sown, 10 and I will settle crowds of men upon you, the whole house of Israel; cities shall be repeopled, and ruins rebuilt. 11 I will settle crowds of men and beasts upon you, to multiply and be fruitful. I will repeople you as in the past, and be more generous to you than in the beginning; thus you shall know that I am the LORD. 12 [My people Israel are the ones whom I will have walk upon you; they shall take possession of you, and you shall be their heritage. Never again shall you rob them of their children.]

13 Thus says the Lord GOD: Because they have said of you, "You are a land that devours men, and you rob your people of their children"; 14 therefore, never again shall you devour men or rob your people of their children, says the Lord GOD. 15 No more will I permit you to hear the reproach of nations, or bear insults from peoples, or rob your people of their children, says the Lord GOD.

16 Thus the word of the LORD came to me: 17 Son of man, when the house of Israel lived in their land, they defiled it by their conduct and deeds. In my sight their conduct was like the defilement of a menstruous woman. 18 Therefore I poured out my fury upon them [because of the blood which they poured out on the ground, and because they defiled it with idols]. 19 I scattered them among the nations, dispersing them over foreign lands; according to their conduct and deeds I judged them. 20 But when they came among the nations [wherever they came], they served to profane my holy name, because it was said of them: "These are the people of the LORD, yet they had to leave their land." 21 So I have relented because of my holy name which the house of Israel profaned among the nations where they came. 22 Therefore say to the house of Israel: Thus says the Lord GOD: Not for your sakes do I act, house of Israel, but for the sake of my holy name, which you profaned among the nations to which you came. 23 I will prove the holiness of my great name, profaned among the nations, in whose midst you have profaned it. Thus the nations shall know that I am the LORD, says the Lord GOD, when in their sight I prove my holiness through you. 24 For I will take you away from among the nations, gather you from all the foreign lands, and bring you back to your own land. 25 I will sprinkle clean water upon you to cleanse you from all your impurities, and from all your idols I will cleanse you. 26 I will give you a new heart and place a new spirit within you, taking from your bodies your stony hearts and giving you natural hearts. 27 I will put my spirit within you and make you live by my statutes, careful to observe my decrees. 28 You shall live in the land I gave your fathers; you shall be my people, and I will be your God. 29 I will save you from all your impurities; I will order the grain to be abundant, and I will not send famine against you. 30 I will increase the fruit on your trees and the crops in your fields; thus you shall no longer bear among the nations the reproach of famine. 31 Then you shall remember your evil conduct, and that your deeds were not good; you shall loathe yourselves for your sins and your abominations.

6 'Because of this, prophesy about the land of Israel. Say to the mountains and hills, to the ravines and valleys, "The Lord Yahweh says this: I am speaking in my jealousy and rage; because you are enduring the insults of the nations, 7 very well, the Lord Yahweh says this: I raise my hand and I swear that the nations all around you shall have their own insults to bear.

8 "Mountains of Israel, you will grow branches and bear fruit for my people Israel, who will soon return. 9 Yes, I am coming to you, I shall turn to you; you will be tilled and sown. 10 I shall increase your population, the whole House of Israel, yes, all. The cities will be inhabited and the ruins rebuilt. 11 I shall increase your population, both human and animal; they will be fertile and reproduce. I shall repopulate you as you were before; I shall make you more prosperous than you were before, and you will know that I am Yahweh. 12 Thanks to me, men will tread your soil again, my people Israel; they will own you and you will be their heritage, and never again will you rob them of their children.

13 "The Lord Yahweh says this: Since people have said of you: You are a man-eater, you have robbed your nation of its children, 14 very well, you will eat no more men, never rob your nation of its children again — declares the Lord Yahweh. 15 I shall never again let you hear the insults of the nations, you will never again have to bear the taunts of the peoples, you will never again rob the nation of its children — declares the Lord Yahweh." '

16 The word of Yahweh was addressed to me as follows, 17 'Son of man, the members of the House of Israel used to live in their own territory, but they defiled it by their conduct and actions; to me their conduct was as unclean as a woman's menstruation. 18 I then vented my fury on them because of the blood they shed in the country and the foul idols with which they defiled it. 19 I scattered them among the nations and they were dispersed throughout the countries. I sentenced them as their conduct and actions deserved. 20 They have profaned my holy name among the nations where they have gone, so that people say of them, "These are the people of Yahweh; they have been exiled from his land." 21 But I have been concerned about my holy name, which the House of Israel has profaned among the nations where they have gone. 22 And so, say to the House of Israel, "The Lord Yahweh says this: I am acting not for your sake, House of Israel, but for the sake of my holy name, which you have profaned among the nations where you have gone. 23 I am going to display the holiness of my great name, which has been profaned among the nations, which you have profaned among them. And the nations will know that I am Yahweh — declares the Lord Yahweh — when in you I display my holiness before their eyes. 24 For I shall take you from among the nations and gather you back from all the countries, and bring you home to your own country. 25 I shall pour clean water over you and you will be cleansed; I shall cleanse you of all your filth and of all your foul idols. 26 I shall give you a new heart, and put a new spirit in you; I shall remove the heart of stone from your bodies and give you a heart of flesh instead. 27 I shall put my spirit in you, and make you keep my laws, and respect and practise my judgements. 28 You will live in the country which I gave to your ancestors. You will be my people and I shall be your God. 29 I shall save you from everything that defiles you, I shall summon the wheat and make it plentiful and impose no more famines on you. 30 I shall increase the yield of tree and field, so that you will never again bear the ignominy of famine among the nations. 31 Then you will remember your evil conduct and actions. You will loathe yourselves for your guilt and your loathsome practices. 32 I

NEW REVISED STANDARD VERSION	REVISED ENGLISH BIBLE

act, says the Lord GOD; let that be known to you. Be ashamed and dismayed for your ways, O house of Israel.

33 Thus says the Lord GOD: On the day that I cleanse you from all your iniquities, I will cause the towns to be inhabited, and the waste places shall be rebuilt. 34 The land that was desolate shall be tilled, instead of being the desolation that it was in the sight of all who passed by. 35 And they will say, "This land that was desolate has become like the garden of Eden; and the waste and desolate and ruined towns are now inhabited and fortified." 36 Then the nations that are left all around you shall know that I, the LORD, have rebuilt the ruined places, and replanted that which was desolate; I, the LORD, have spoken, and I will do it.

37 Thus says the Lord GOD: I will also let the house of Israel ask me to do this for them: to increase their population like a flock. 38 Like the flock for sacrifices,*y* like the flock at Jerusalem during her appointed festivals, so shall the ruined towns be filled with flocks of people. Then they shall know that I am the LORD.

37 The hand of the LORD came upon me, and he brought me out by the spirit of the LORD and set me down in the middle of a valley; it was full of bones. 2 He led me all around them; there were very many lying in the valley, and they were very dry. 3 He said to me, "Mortal, can these bones live?" I answered, "O Lord GOD, you know." 4 Then he said to me, "Prophesy to these bones, and say to them: O dry bones, hear the word of the LORD. 5 Thus says the Lord GOD to these bones: I will cause breath*z* to enter you, and you shall live. 6 I will lay sinews on you, and will cause flesh to come upon you, and cover you with skin, and put breath*z* in you, and you shall live; and you shall know that I am the LORD."

7 So I prophesied as I had been commanded; and as I prophesied, suddenly there was a noise, a rattling, and the bones came together, bone to its bone. 8 I looked, and there were sinews on them, and flesh had come upon them, and skin had covered them; but there was no breath in them. 9 Then he said to me, "Prophesy to the breath, prophesy, mortal, and say to the breath:*a* Thus says the Lord GOD: Come from the four winds, O breath,*a* and breathe upon these slain, that they may live." 10 I prophesied as he commanded me, and the breath came into them, and they lived, and stood on their feet, a vast multitude.

11 Then he said to me, "Mortal, these bones are the whole house of Israel. They say, 'Our bones are dried up, and our hope is lost; we are cut off completely.' 12 Therefore prophesy, and say to them, Thus says the Lord GOD: I am going to open your graves, and bring you up from your graves, O my people; and I will bring you back to the land of Israel. 13 And you shall know that I am the LORD, when I open your graves, and bring you up from your graves, O my people. 14 I will put my spirit within you, and you shall live, and I will place you on your own soil; then you shall know that I, the LORD, have spoken and will act," says the LORD.

15 The word of the LORD came to me: 16 Mortal, take a stick and write on it, "For Judah, and the Israelites associated with it"; then take another stick and write on it, "For Joseph (the stick of Ephraim) and all the house of Israel associated with it"; 17 and join them together into one stick, so that they may become one in your hand. 18 And when your people say to you, "Will you not show us what you mean by these?" 19 say to them, Thus says the Lord GOD: I

for your sake that I am acting, says the Lord GOD, so feel the shame and disgrace of your ways, people of Israel.

33 'The Lord GOD says: When I have cleansed you of all your wrongdoing, I shall resettle the towns, and the ruined places will be rebuilt. 34 The land now desolate will be tilled, instead of lying waste for every passer-by to see. 35 Everyone will say that this land which was waste has become like a garden of Eden, and the towns once ruined, wasted, and shattered will now be fortified and inhabited. 36 The nations still left around you will know that it is I, the LORD, who have rebuilt the shattered towns and replanted the land laid waste; I, the LORD, have spoken and I shall do it.

37 'The Lord GOD says: Once again I shall let the Israelites pray to me for help. I shall make their people as numerous as a flock of sheep. 38 As Jerusalem is filled with sheep offered as holy-gifts at times of festival, so will their ruined cities be filled with flocks of people. Then they will know that I am the LORD.'

37 The LORD's hand was upon me, and he carried me out by his spirit and set me down in a plain that was full of bones. 2 He made me pass among them in every direction. Countless in number and very dry, they covered the plain. 3 He said to me, 'O man, can these bones live?' I answered, 'Only you, Lord GOD, know that.' 4 He said, 'Prophesy over these bones; say: Dry bones, hear the word of the LORD. 5 The Lord GOD says to these bones: I am going to put breath into you, and you will live. 6 I shall fasten sinews on you, clothe you with flesh, cover you with skin, and give you breath, and you will live. Then you will know that I am the LORD.'

7 I began to prophesy as I had been told, and as I prophesied there was a rattling sound and the bones all fitted themselves together. 8 As I watched, sinews appeared upon them, flesh clothed them, and they were covered with skin, but there was no breath in them. 9 Then he said to me, 'Prophesy to the wind, prophesy, O man, and say to it: These are the words of the Lord GOD: Let winds come from every quarter and breathe into these slain, that they may come to life.' 10 I prophesied as I had been told; breath entered them, and they came to life and rose to their feet, a mighty company.

11 He said to me, 'O man, these bones are the whole people of Israel. They say, "Our bones are dry, our hope is gone, and we are cut off." 12 Prophesy, therefore, and say to them: The Lord GOD has said: My people, I shall open your graves and bring you up from them, and restore you to the land of Israel. 13 You, my people, will know that I am the LORD when I open your graves and bring you up from them. 14 Then I shall put my spirit into you and you will come to life, and I shall settle you on your own soil, and you will know that I the LORD have spoken and I shall act. This is the word of the LORD.'

15 THIS word of the LORD came to me: 16 'O man, take one leaf of a wooden tablet and write on it, "Judah and the Israelites associated with him". Then take another leaf and write on it, "Joseph, the leaf of Ephraim and all the Israelite tribes". 17 Now bring the two together to form one tablet; then they will be a folding tablet in your hand. 18 When your fellow-countrymen ask you to tell them what you mean by this, 19 say to them: The Lord GOD has said: I am taking the

---

y Heb *flock of holy things*   *z* Or *spirit*   *a* Or *wind* or *spirit*   37:5 **breath:** or wind or spirit.   37:14 **spirit:** or breath.

32 Not for your sakes do I act, says the Lord GOD — let this be known to you! Be ashamed and abashed because of your conduct, O house of Israel.

33 Thus says the Lord GOD: When I purify you from all your crimes, I will repeople the cities, and the ruins shall be rebuilt; **34** the desolate land shall be tilled, which was formerly a wasteland exposed to the gaze of every passer-by. **35** "This desolate land has been made into a garden of Eden," they shall say. "The cities that were in ruins, laid waste, and destroyed are now repeopled and fortified." **36** Thus the neighboring nations that remain shall know that I, the LORD, have rebuilt what was destroyed and replanted what was desolate. I, the LORD, have promised, and I will do it.

37 Thus says the Lord GOD: This also I will be persuaded to do for the house of Israel: to multiply them like sheep. **38** As with sacrificial sheep, the sheep of Jerusalem on its feast days, the cities which were in ruins shall be filled with flocks of men; thus they shall know that I am the LORD.

37 The hand of the LORD came upon me, and he led me out in the spirit of the LORD and set me in the center of the plain, which was now filled with bones. **2** He made me walk among them in every direction so that I saw how many they were on the surface of the plain. How dry they were! **3** He asked me: Son of man, can these bones come to life? "Lord GOD," I answered, "you alone know that." **4** Then he said to me: Prophesy over these bones, and say to them: Dry bones, hear the word of the LORD! **5** Thus says the Lord GOD to these bones: See! I will bring spirit into you, that you may come to life. **6** I will put sinews upon you, make flesh grow over you, cover you with skin, and put spirit in you so that you may come to life and know that I am the LORD. **7** I prophesied as I had been told, and even as I was prophesying I heard a noise; it was a rattling as the bones came together, bone joining bone. **8** I saw the sinews and the flesh come upon them, and the skin cover them, but there was no spirit in them. **9** Then he said to me: Prophesy to the spirit, prophesy, son of man, and say to the spirit: Thus says the Lord GOD: From the four winds come, O spirit, and breathe into these slain that they may come to life. **10** I prophesied as he told me, and the spirit came into them; they came alive and stood upright, a vast army. **11** Then he said to me: Son of man, these bones are the whole house of Israel. They have been saying, "Our bones are dried up, our hope is lost, and we are cut off." **12** Therefore, prophesy and say to them: Thus says the Lord GOD: O my people, I will open your graves and have you rise from them, and bring you back to the land of Israel. **13** Then you shall know that I am the LORD, when I open your graves and have you rise from them, O my people! **14** I will put my spirit in you that you may live, and I will settle you upon your land; thus you shall know that I am the LORD. I have promised, and I will do it, says the LORD.

15 Thus the word of the LORD came to me: **16** Now, son of man, take a single stick, and write on it: Judah and those Israelites who are associated with him. Then take another stick and write on it: Joseph [the stick of Ephraim] and all the house of Israel associated with him. **17** Then join the two sticks together, so that they form one stick in your hand. **18** When your countrymen ask you, "Will you not tell us what you mean by all this?", **19** answer them: Thus says the

assure you that I am not doing this for your sake — declares the Lord Yahweh. Be ashamed and blush for your conduct, House of Israel.

33 "The Lord Yahweh says this: On the day I cleanse you from all your guilt, I shall repopulate the cities and cause the ruins to be rebuilt. **34** Waste land, once desolate for every passer-by to see, will now be farmed again. **35** And people will say: This land, so recently a waste, is now like a garden of Eden, and the ruined cities once abandoned and levelled to the ground are now strongholds with people living in them. **36** And the nations left round you will know that I, Yahweh, have rebuilt what was levelled and replanted what was ruined. I, Yahweh, have spoken and shall do it.

37 "The Lord Yahweh says this: As a further mark of favour, I shall let myself be consulted by the House of Israel; I shall increase their numbers like a human flock, **38** like a flock of sacrificial animals, like the flock in Jerusalem on her solemn feasts. So your ruined cities will be filled with human flocks, and they will know that I am Yahweh." '

37 The hand of Yahweh was on me; he carried me away by the spirit of Yahweh and set me down in the middle of the valley, a valley full of bones. **2** He made me walk up and down and all around among them. There were vast quantities of these bones on the floor of the valley; and they were completely dry. **3** He said to me, 'Son of man, can these bones live?' I said, 'You know, Lord Yahweh.' **4** He said, 'Prophesy over these bones. Say, "Dry bones, hear the word of Yahweh. **5** The Lord Yahweh says this to these bones: I am now going to make breath enter you, and you will live. **6** I shall put sinews on you, I shall make flesh grow on you, I shall cover you with skin and give you breath, and you will live; and you will know that I am Yahweh." ' **7** I prophesied as I had been ordered. While I was prophesying, there was a noise, a clattering sound; it was the bones coming together. **8** And as I looked, they were covered with sinews; flesh was growing on them and skin was covering them, yet there was no breath in them. **9** He said to me, 'Prophesy to the breath; prophesy, son of man. Say to the breath, "The Lord Yahweh says this: Come from the four winds, breath; breathe on these dead, so that they come to life!" ' **10** I prophesied as he had ordered me, and the breath entered them; they came to life and stood up on their feet, a great, an immense army.

11 Then he said, 'Son of man, these bones are the whole House of Israel. They keep saying, "Our bones are dry, our hope has gone; we are done for." **12** So, prophesy. Say to them, "The Lord Yahweh says this: I am now going to open your graves; I shall raise you from your graves, my people, and lead you back to the soil of Israel. **13** And you will know that I am Yahweh, when I open your graves and raise you from your graves, my people, **14** and put my spirit in you, and you revive, and I resettle you on your own soil. Then you will know that I, Yahweh, have spoken and done this — declares the Lord Yahweh." '

15 The word of Yahweh was addressed to me as follows, **16** 'Son of man, take a stick and write on it, "Judah and those Israelites loyal to him." Take another stick and write on it, "Joseph (Ephraim's wood) and all the House of Israel loyal to him."

17 'Join one to the other to make a single piece of wood, a single stick in your hand. **18** And when the members of your nation say, "Will you not tell us what you mean?"

am about to take the stick of Joseph (which is in the hand of Ephraim) and the tribes of Israel associated with it; and I will put the stick of Judah upon it,*b* and make them one stick, in order that they may be one in my hand. 20 When the sticks on which you write are in your hand before their eyes, 21 then say to them, Thus says the Lord GOD: I will take the people of Israel from the nations among which they have gone, and will gather them from every quarter, and bring them to their own land. 22 I will make them one nation in the land, on the mountains of Israel; and one king shall be king over them all. Never again shall they be two nations, and never again shall they be divided into two kingdoms. 23 They shall never again defile themselves with their idols and their detestable things, or with any of their transgressions. I will save them from all the apostasies into which they have fallen,*c* and will cleanse them. Then they shall be my people, and I will be their God.

24 My servant David shall be king over them; and they shall all have one shepherd. They shall follow my ordinances and be careful to observe my statutes. 25 They shall live in the land that I gave to my servant Jacob, in which your ancestors lived; they and their children and their children's children shall live there forever; and my servant David shall be their prince forever. 26 I will make a covenant of peace with them; it shall be an everlasting covenant with them; and I will bless*d* them and multiply them, and will set my sanctuary among them forevermore. 27 My dwelling place shall be with them; and I will be their God, and they shall be my people. 28 Then the nations shall know that I the LORD sanctify Israel, when my sanctuary is among them forevermore.

38 The word of the LORD came to me: 2 Mortal, set your face toward Gog, of the land of Magog, the chief prince of Meshech and Tubal. Prophesy against him 3 and say: Thus says the Lord GOD: I am against you, O Gog, chief prince of Meshech and Tubal; 4 I will turn you around and put hooks into your jaws, and I will lead you out with all your army, horses and horsemen, all of them clothed in full armor, a great company, all of them with shield and buckler, wielding swords. 5 Persia, Ethiopia,*e* and Put are with them, all of them with buckler and helmet; 6 Gomer and all its troops; Beth-togarmah from the remotest parts of the north with all its troops — many peoples are with you.

7 Be ready and keep ready, you and all the companies that are assembled around you, and hold yourselves in reserve for them. 8 After many days you shall be mustered; in the latter years you shall go against a land restored from war, a land where people were gathered from many nations on the mountains of Israel, which had long lain waste; its people were brought out from the nations and now are living in safety, all of them. 9 You shall advance, coming on like a storm; you shall be like a cloud covering the land, you and all your troops, and many peoples with you.

10 Thus says the Lord GOD: On that day thoughts will come into your mind, and you will devise an evil scheme. 11 You will say, "I will go up against the land of unwalled villages; I will fall upon the quiet people who live in safety, all of them living without walls, and having no bars or gates"; 12 to seize spoil and carry off plunder; to assail the waste places that are now inhabited, and the people who were gathered from the nations, who are acquiring cattle and goods, who live at the center*f* of the earth. 13 Sheba

leaf of Joseph, which belongs to Ephraim and the other tribes of Israel, and joining to it the leaf of Judah. Thus I shall make them one tablet, and they will be one in my hand. 20 When the leaves on which you write are there in your hand for all to see, 21 say to them: The Lord GOD has said: I am going to take the Israelites from their places of exile among the nations; I shall assemble them from every quarter and restore them to their own soil. 22 I shall make them a single nation in the land, on the mountains of Israel, and one king will be over them all. No longer will they be two nations, no longer divided into two kingdoms. 23 They will never again be defiled with their idols, their loathsome ways, and all their acts of disloyalty. I shall save them from all their sinful backsliding and purify them. Thus they will be my people, and I shall be their God. 24 My servant David will be king over them; they will all have one shepherd. They will conform to my laws and my statutes and observe them faithfully. 25 They will live in the land which I gave to my servant Jacob, the land where your forefathers lived. They and their descendants will live there for ever, and my servant David is to be their prince for ever. 26 I shall make an everlasting covenant with them to ensure peace and prosperity. I shall greatly increase their numbers, and I shall put my sanctuary in their midst for all time. 27 They will live under the shelter of my dwelling; I shall be their God and they will be my people. 28 The nations will know that I the LORD am keeping Israel sacred to myself, because my sanctuary is in their midst for ever.'

38 THIS word of the LORD came to me: 2 'O man, face towards Gog in the land of Magog, the prince of Rosh, Meshech, and Tubal, and prophesy against him. 3 Say: These are the words of the Lord GOD: I am against you, Gog, prince of Rosh, Meshech, and Tubal. 4 I shall put hooks in your jaws and turn you round. I shall lead you out, you and your whole army, horses and horsemen, all fully equipped, a great host with bucklers and shields, every man wielding a sword. 5 With them will march the men of Persia, Cush, and Put, all with shields and helmets, 6 Gomer and all its squadrons, Beth-togarmah with all its squadrons from the far recesses of the north — a great concourse of peoples with you. 7 Be prepared; make ready, you and all the host which has rallied to you, and hold yourselves at my disposal. 8 After a long time has passed you will be summoned; in years to come you will invade a land restored from ruin, whose people are gathered from many nations on the mountains of Israel that have been so long desolate. The Israelites, brought out from the nations, will all be living undisturbed; 9 and you will come up, advancing like a hurricane; you will be like a cloud covering the land, you and all your squadrons, a great concourse of peoples.

10 'The Lord GOD says: At that time a thought will enter your head and you will hatch an evil plan. 11 You will say, "I shall attack a land of open villages and fall upon a people living quiet and undisturbed, undefended by walls or barred gates." 12 You will expect to come plundering, spoiling, and stripping bare the settlements which once lay in ruins, but are now inhabited by a people gathered out of the nations, a people acquiring livestock and goods, and making their home at the very centre of the world. 13 Sheba and Dedan,

---

b Heb *I will put them upon it*   *c* Another reading is *from all the settlements in which they have sinned*   *d* Tg: Heb *give*   *e* Or *Nubia*; Heb *Cush*   *f* Heb *navel*

37:19 **joining**: *prob. rdg; Heb. adds* them.   37:23 **backsliding**: *so Gk (Symm.); Heb.* dwellings.   37:26 **an everlasting . . . prosperity**: *prob. rdg; Heb. adds* and I shall put them.   38:7 **my**: *so Gk; Heb.* their.

Lord God: [I will take the stick of Joseph, which is in the hand of Ephraim, and of the tribes of Israel associated with him, and I will join to it the stick of Judah, making them a single stick; they shall be one in my hand. 20 The sticks on which you write you shall hold up before them to see. 21 Tell them: Thus speaks the Lord God:] I will take the Israelites from among the nations to which they have come, and gather them from all sides to bring them back to their land. 22 I will make them one nation upon the land, in the mountains of Israel, and there shall be one prince for them all. Never again shall they be two nations, and never again shall they be divided into two kingdoms.

23 No longer shall they defile themselves with their idols, their abominations, and all their transgressions. I will deliver them from all their sins of apostasy, and cleanse them so that they may be my people and I may be their God. 24 My servant David shall be prince over them, and there shall be one shepherd for them all; they shall live by my statutes and carefully observe my decrees. 25 They shall live on the land which I gave to my servant Jacob, the land where their fathers lived; they shall live on it forever, they, and their children, and their children's children, with my servant David their prince forever. 26 I will make with them a covenant of peace; it shall be an everlasting covenant with them, and I will multiply them, and put my sanctuary among them forever. 27 My dwelling shall be with them; I will be their God, and they shall be my people. 28 Thus the nations shall know that it is I, the Lord, who make Israel holy, when my sanctuary shall be set up among them forever.

38 Thus the word of the Lord came to me: 2 Son of man, turn toward Gog [the land of Magog], the chief prince of Meshech and Tubal, and prophesy against him: 3 Thus says the Lord God: See! I am coming at you, Gog, chief prince of Meshech and Tubal. 4 I will lead you forth with all your army, horses and riders all handsomely outfitted, a great horde with bucklers and shields, all of them carrying swords: 5 Persia, Cush, and Put with them [all with shields and helmets], 6 Gomer with all its troops, Beth-togarmah from the recesses of the north with all its troops, many peoples with you. 7 Prepare yourself, be ready, you and all your horde assembled about you, and be at my disposal. 8 After many days you will be mustered [in the last years you will come] against a nation which has survived the sword, which has been assembled from many peoples [on the mountains of Israel which were long a ruin], which has been brought forth from among the peoples and all of whom now dwell in security. 9 You shall come up like a sudden storm, advancing like a cloud to cover the earth, you and all your troops and the many peoples with you.

10 Thus says the Lord God: At that time thoughts shall arise in your mind, and you shall devise an evil scheme: 11 "I will go up against a land of open villages and attack the peaceful people who are living in security, all of them living without walls, having neither bars nor gates, 12 to plunder and pillage, turning my hand against the ruins that were repeopled and against a people gathered from the nations, a people concerned with cattle and goods, who dwell at the navel of the earth." 13 Sheba and Dedan, the merchants of

19 say, "The Lord Yahweh says this: I am taking the stick of Joseph (now in Ephraim's hand) and those tribes of Israel loyal to him and shall join them to the stick of Judah. I shall make one stick out of the two, a single stick in my hand."

20 'When the pieces of wood you have written on are in your hand in full sight of them, 21 say, "The Lord Yahweh says this: I shall take the Israelites from the nations where they have gone. I shall gather them together from everywhere and bring them home to their own soil. 22 I shall make them into one nation in the country, on the mountains of Israel, and one king is to be king of them all; they will no longer form two nations, nor be two separate kingdoms. 23 They will no longer defile themselves with their foul idols, their horrors and any of their crimes. I shall save them from the acts of infidelity which they have committed and shall cleanse them; they will be my people and I shall be their God. 24 My servant David will reign over them, one shepherd for all; they will follow my judgements, respect my laws and practise them. 25 They will live in the country which I gave to my servant Jacob, the country in which your ancestors lived. They will live in it, they, their children, their children's children, for ever. David my servant is to be their prince for ever. 26 I shall make a covenant of peace with them, an eternal covenant with them. I shall resettle them and make them grow; I shall set my sanctuary among them for ever. 27 I shall make my home above them; I shall be their God, and they will be my people. 28 And the nations will know that I am Yahweh the sanctifier of Israel, when my sanctuary is with them for ever." '

38 The word of Yahweh was addressed to me as follows, 2 'Son of man, turn towards Gog, to the country of Magog, towards the paramount prince of Meshech and Tubal, and prophesy against him. 3 Say, "The Lord Yahweh says this: I am against you, Gog, paramount prince of Meshech and Tubal. 4 I shall turn you about, I shall fix hooks in your jaws and bring you out with your entire army, horses and horsemen, all perfectly equipped, a huge array armed with shields and bucklers, and all wielding swords. 5 Persia and Cush and Put are with them, all with buckler and helmet; 6 Gomer and all its troops, Beth-Togarmah in the far north and all its troops, and many nations with you. 7 Be ready, be well prepared, you and all your troops and the others rallying to you, and hold yourself at my service.

8 "Many days will pass before you are given orders; in the final years you will march on this country, whose inhabitants will have been living in confidence, remote from other peoples, since they escaped the sword and were gathered in from various nations, here in the long-deserted mountains of Israel. 9 Like a storm you will approach, you will advance and cover the country like a cloud, you, all your troops and many nations with you.

10 "The Lord Yahweh says this: That day, a thought will enter your mind and you will form a sinister plan. 11 You will think: I shall attack this undefended country and march on this peaceful nation living secure, all living in towns without walls or bars or gates. 12 You will come to plunder and loot and turn your might against the ruins they live in, against this people gathered back from the nations, these stock-breeders and traders who live at the Navel of the World. 13 Sheba and Dedan, the merchants and all the mag-

NEW REVISED STANDARD VERSION

and Dedan and the merchants of Tarshish and all its young warriors*g* will say to you, "Have you come to seize spoil? Have you assembled your horde to carry off plunder, to carry away silver and gold, to take away cattle and goods, to seize a great amount of booty?"

14 Therefore, mortal, prophesy, and say to Gog: Thus says the Lord GOD: On that day when my people Israel are living securely, you will rouse yourself*h* 15 and come from your place out of the remotest parts of the north, you and many peoples with you, all of them riding on horses, a great horde, a mighty army; 16 you will come up against my people Israel, like a cloud covering the earth. In the latter days I will bring you against my land, so that the nations may know me, when through you, O Gog, I display my holiness before their eyes.

17 Thus says the Lord GOD: Are you he of whom I spoke in former days by my servants the prophets of Israel, who in those days prophesied for years that I would bring you against them? 18 On that day, when Gog comes against the land of Israel, says the Lord GOD, my wrath shall be aroused. 19 For in my jealousy and in my blazing wrath I declare: On that day there shall be a great shaking in the land of Israel; 20 the fish of the sea, and the birds of the air, and the animals of the field, and all creeping things that creep on the ground, and all human beings that are on the face of the earth, shall quake at my presence, and the mountains shall be thrown down, and the cliffs shall fall, and every wall shall tumble to the ground. 21 I will summon the sword against Gog*i* in*j* all my mountains, says the Lord GOD; the swords of all will be against their comrades. 22 With pestilence and bloodshed I will enter into judgment with him; and I will pour down torrential rains and hailstones, fire and sulfur, upon him and his troops and the many peoples that are with him. 23 So I will display my greatness and my holiness and make myself known in the eyes of many nations. Then they shall know that I am the LORD.

39 And you, mortal, prophesy against Gog, and say: Thus says the Lord GOD: I am against you, O Gog, chief prince of Meshech and Tubal! 2 I will turn you around and drive you forward, and bring you up from the remotest parts of the north, and lead you against the mountains of Israel. 3 I will strike your bow from your left hand, and will make your arrows drop out of your right hand. 4 You shall fall upon the mountains of Israel, you and all your troops and the peoples that are with you; I will give you to birds of prey of every kind and to the wild animals to be devoured. 5 You shall fall in the open field; for I have spoken, says the Lord GOD. 6 I will send fire on Magog and on those who live securely in the coastlands; and they shall know that I am the LORD.

7 My holy name I will make known among my people Israel; and I will not let my holy name be profaned any more; and the nations shall know that I am the LORD, the Holy One in Israel. 8 It has come! It has happened, says the Lord GOD. This is the day of which I have spoken.

9 Then those who live in the towns of Israel will go out and make fires of the weapons and burn them—bucklers and shields, bows and arrows, handpikes and spears—and they will make fires of them for seven years. 10 They will not need to take wood out of the field or cut down any trees in the forests, for they will make their fires of the weapons; they will despoil those who despoiled them, and plunder those who plundered them, says the Lord GOD.

REVISED ENGLISH BIBLE

the traders of Tarshish and her leading merchants, will say to you, "Is it for plunder that you have come? Have you mustered your host to get spoil, to carry off silver and gold, to take livestock and goods, to seize much booty?"

14 'Therefore, O man, prophesy and say to Gog: The Lord GOD says: On that day when my people Israel are living undisturbed, will you not bestir yourself 15 and come with many nations from your home in the far recesses of the north, all riding on horses, a large host, a mighty army? 16 You will advance against my people Israel like a cloud that covers the earth. In the last days I shall bring you against my land, that the nations may know me, when they see me prove my holiness at Gog's expense.

17 'The Lord GOD says: When I spoke in days of old through my servants the prophets, who prophesied in those days unceasingly, it was you whom I threatened to bring against Israel. 18 On that day, when at length Gog invades Israel, says the Lord GOD, my wrath will boil over. 19 In my jealousy and in the heat of my anger I swear that there will be a great earthquake throughout the land of Israel on that day, 20 and the fish in the sea and the birds in the air, the wild animals and all creatures that move on the ground, and every human being on the face of the earth will quake before me. Mountains will be overthrown, the terraced hills collapse, and every wall crash to the ground. 21 I shall summon universal terror against Gog, says the Lord GOD, and his men will turn their swords against one another. 22 I shall bring him to judgement with pestilence and bloodshed; I shall pour torrential rain and hailstones as well as fire and brimstone on him and his squadrons and the whole concourse of peoples with him. 23 I shall show myself great and holy and make myself known to many nations. Then they will know that I am the LORD.

39 'O man, prophesy against Gog and say: The Lord GOD says: I am against you, Gog, prince of Rosh, Meshech, and Tubal. 2 I shall turn you round and drive you on. I shall lead you from the far recesses of the north and bring you to the mountains of Israel. 3 I shall strike the bow from your left hand and dash the arrows from your right hand. 4 On the mountains of Israel you will fall, you and all your squadrons and allies. I shall give you as food to every kind of bird of prey and to the wild beasts. 5 You will fall on the ground, for it is I who have spoken. This is the word of the Lord GOD. 6 I shall send fire on Magog and on those who live undisturbed in the coasts and islands. Then they will know that I am the LORD. 7 My holy name I shall make known in the midst of my people Israel and no longer let it be profaned; the nations will know that I, the LORD, am holy in Israel.

8 'See, it is coming; it is here! says the Lord GOD; it is the day of which I have spoken. 9 Those who live in Israel's towns will go out and gather weapons for fuel, bucklers and shields, bows and arrows, throwing-sticks and lances; for seven years they will kindle fires with them. 10 They will take no wood from the fields, nor cut it from the forests, but will use the weapons to light their fires. Thus they will plunder those who plundered them and spoil their despoilers. This is the word of the Lord GOD.

---

g Heb *young lions*   *h* Gk: Heb *will you not know?*   *i* Heb *him*
j Heb *to* or *for*

38:14 **bestir yourself:** *so Gk; Heb.* know.   38:21 **universal terror:** *so Gk; Heb.* for all my mountains a sword.

NEW AMERICAN BIBLE

NEW JERUSALEM BIBLE

Tarshish and all her young lions shall ask you: "Is it for plunder that you have come? Is it for pillage that you have summoned your horde, to carry off silver and gold, to take away cattle and goods, to seize much plunder?"

‡38.14–16: see below‡

17 Thus says the Lord GOD: It is of you that I spoke in ancient times through my servants, the prophets of Israel, who prophesied in those days that I would bring you against them. 18 But on that day, the day when Gog invades the land of Israel, says the Lord GOD, my fury shall be aroused. In my anger 19 and in my jealousy, in my fiery wrath, I swear: On that day there shall be a great shaking upon the land of Israel. 20 Before me shall tremble the fish of the sea and the birds of the air, the beasts of the field and all the reptiles that crawl upon the ground, and all men who are on the land. Mountains shall be overturned, and cliffs shall tumble, and every wall shall fall to the ground. 21 Against him I will summon every terror, says the Lord GOD, every man's sword against his brother. I will hold judgment with him in pestilence and bloodshed; 22 flooding rain and hailstones, fire and brimstone, I will rain upon him, upon his troops, and upon the many peoples with him. 23 I will prove my greatness and holiness and make myself known in the sight of many nations; thus they shall know that I am the LORD.

14 Therefore prophesy, son of man, and say to Gog: Thus says the Lord GOD: When my people Israel are dwelling in security, will you not bestir yourself 15 and come from your home in the recesses of the north, you and many peoples with you, all mounted on horses, a great horde and a mighty army? 16 You shall come up against my people Israel like a cloud covering the land. In the last days I will bring you against my land, that the nations may know of me, when in their sight I prove my holiness through you, O Gog.

39 Now, son of man, prophesy against Gog in these words: Thus says the Lord GOD: See! I am coming at you, Gog, chief prince of Meshech and Tubal. 2 I will turn you about, I will urge you on, and I will make you come up from the recesses of the north; I will lead you against the mountains of Israel. 3 Then I will strike the bow from your left hand, and make the arrows drop from your right. 4 Upon the mountains of Israel you shall fall, you and all your troops and the peoples who are with you. To birds of prey of every kind and to the wild beasts I am giving you to be eaten. 5 On the open field you shall fall, for I have decreed it, says the Lord GOD.

6 I will send fire upon Magog and upon those who live securely in the coastlands; thus they shall know that I am the LORD. 7 I will make my holy name known among my people Israel; I will no longer allow my holy name to be profaned. Thus the nations shall know that I am the LORD, the Holy One in Israel. 8 Yes, it is coming and shall be fulfilled, says the Lord GOD. This is the day I have decreed.

9 Then shall those who live in the cities of Israel go out and burn weapons: [shields and bucklers,] bows and arrows, clubs and lances; for seven years they shall make fires with them. 10 They shall not have to bring in wood from the fields or cut it down in the forests, for they shall make fires with the weapons. Thus they shall plunder those who plundered them and pillage those who pillaged them, says the Lord GOD.

nates of Tarshish will ask you: Have you come for plunder? Are you massing your troops with a view to looting? To make off with gold and silver, seize cattle and goods, and come away with unlimited spoil?"

14 'So, son of man, prophesy. Say to Gog, "The Lord Yahweh says this: Is it not true that you will set out at a time when my people Israel is living secure? 15 You will leave your home in the far north, you and many nations with you, a great army of countless troops all mounted. 16 You will invade Israel, my people. You will be like a cloud covering the country. In the final days, I myself shall bring you to attack my country, so that the nations will know who I am, when I display my holiness to them, by means of you, Gog.

17 "The Lord Yahweh says this: It was of you that I spoke in the past through my servants the prophets of Israel, who prophesied in those days, foretelling your invasion. 18 The day Gog attacks the land of Israel — declares the Lord Yahweh — my furious wrath will boil up. In my anger, 19 in my jealousy, in the heat of my fury I say it: That day, I swear, there will be such a huge earthquake in the land of Israel, 20 that the fish in the sea and the birds of heaven, the wild beasts, all the reptiles creeping along the ground, and all people on the surface of the earth will quake before me. Mountains will fall, cliffs crumble, all walls collapse, and 21 I shall summon every kind of sword against him — declares the Lord Yahweh — and each will turn his sword against his comrade. 22 I shall punish him with plague and bloodshed, and rain down torrential rain, hailstones, fire and brimstone on him, on his troops and on the many nations with him. 23 I shall display my greatness and holiness and bring the many nations to acknowledge me; and they will know that I am Yahweh." '

39 'So, son of man, prophesy against Gog. Say, "The Lord Yahweh says this: Look, I am against you, Gog, paramount prince of Meshech and Tubal. 2 I shall turn you about, lead you on, and bring you from the farthest north against the mountains of Israel. 3 I shall break the bow in your left hand and dash the arrows out of your right. 4 You will fall on the mountains of Israel, you, all your troops and the nations with you. I shall make you food for every kind of bird of prey and wild animals. 5 You will fall in the wilds, for I have spoken — declares the Lord Yahweh. 6 I shall send down fire on Magog and on those living undisturbed in the islands, and they will know that I am Yahweh. 7 I shall see that my holy name is acknowledged by my people Israel, and no longer allow my holy name to be profaned; and the nations will know that I am Yahweh, holy in Israel.

8 "All this is to happen, all this is to take place — declares the Lord Yahweh. This is the day I predicted.

9 "The inhabitants of the towns of Israel will go out and set fire to and burn the weapons, the shields and bucklers, bows and arrows, javelins and spears. They will burn these for seven years 10 and not fetch wood from the countryside or cut it in the forests, since they will be burning the weapons. They will plunder those who plundered them, and despoil those who despoiled them — declares the Lord Yahweh.

11 On that day I will give to Gog a place for burial in Israel, the Valley of the Travelers[k] east of the sea; it shall block the path of the travelers, for there Gog and all his horde will be buried; it shall be called the Valley of Hamongog.[l] 12 Seven months the house of Israel shall spend burying them, in order to cleanse the land. 13 All the people of the land shall bury them; and it will bring them honor on the day that I show my glory, says the Lord GOD. 14 They will set apart men to pass through the land regularly and bury any invaders[m] who remain on the face of the land, so as to cleanse it; for seven months they shall make their search. 15 As the searchers[m] pass through the land, anyone who sees a human bone shall set up a sign by it, until the buriers have buried it in the Valley of Hamon-gog.[l] 16 (A city Hamonah[n] is there also.) Thus they shall cleanse the land.

17 As for you, mortal, thus says the Lord GOD: Speak to the birds of every kind and to all the wild animals: Assemble and come, gather from all around to the sacrificial feast that I am preparing for you, a great sacrificial feast on the mountains of Israel, and you shall eat flesh and drink blood. 18 You shall eat the flesh of the mighty, and drink the blood of the princes of the earth — of rams, of lambs, and of goats, of bulls, all of them fatlings of Bashan. 19 You shall eat fat until you are filled, and drink blood until you are drunk, at the sacrificial feast that I am preparing for you. 20 And you shall be filled at my table with horses and charioteers,[o] with warriors and all kinds of soldiers, says the Lord GOD.

21 I will display my glory among the nations; and all the nations shall see my judgment that I have executed, and my hand that I have laid on them. 22 The house of Israel shall know that I am the LORD their God, from that day forward. 23 And the nations shall know that the house of Israel went into captivity for their iniquity, because they dealt treacherously with me. So I hid my face from them and gave them into the hand of their adversaries, and they all fell by the sword. 24 I dealt with them according to their uncleanness and their transgressions, and hid my face from them.

25 Therefore thus says the Lord GOD: Now I will restore the fortunes of Jacob, and have mercy on the whole house of Israel; and I will be jealous for my holy name. 26 They shall forget[p] their shame, and all the treachery they have practiced against me, when they live securely in their land with no one to make them afraid, 27 when I have brought them back from the peoples and gathered them from their enemies' lands, and through them have displayed my holiness in the sight of many nations. 28 Then they shall know that I am the LORD their God because I sent them into exile among the nations, and then gathered them into their own land. I will leave none of them behind; 29 and I will never again hide my face from them, when I pour out my spirit upon the house of Israel, says the Lord GOD.

40 In the twenty-fifth year of our exile, at the beginning of the year, on the tenth day of the month, in the fourteenth year after the city was struck down, on that very day, the hand of the LORD was upon me, and he brought me there. 2 He brought me, in visions of God, to the land of Israel, and set me down upon a very high mountain, on which was a structure like a city to the south. 3 When he brought me there, a man was there, whose appearance shone like bronze, with a linen cord and a measuring reed in his hand; and he was standing in the gateway. 4 The man said to me, "Mortal, look closely and listen attentively, and set your mind upon all that I shall show you, for you were brought here in order that I might show it to you; declare all that you see to the house of Israel."

11 'On that day, instead of a burial-ground in Israel, I shall assign to Gog the valley of Abarim east of the Dead Sea. There Gog with all his horde will be buried, and Abarim will be entirely blocked. It will be called the Valley of Gog's Horde. 12 It will take the Israelites seven months to bury them and to purify the land, 13 and all the people will share in the task. The day that I win myself honour will be a memorable day for them. This is the word of the Lord GOD. 14 Men will be picked for the regular duty of going through the country to bury any left above ground, and so purify the land. They will begin their search at the end of the seven months: 15 they will go up and down the country, and whenever one of them sees a human bone he is to put a marker beside it, until it has been buried in the Valley of Gog's Horde. 16 So no more will be heard of that great horde, and the land will be purified.

17 'O man, the Lord GOD says: Cry to every bird that flies and to all the wild beasts: Assemble and come, gather from every side to my sacrifice, the great sacrifice I am preparing for you on the mountains of Israel. Eat flesh and drink blood, 18 eat the flesh of warriors and drink the blood of the rulers of the earth; all these are your rams, sheep, he-goats, and bulls, and buffaloes of Bashan. 19 You will sate yourselves with fat and drink yourselves drunk on blood at the sacrifice which I am preparing for you. 20 At my table you will eat your fill of horses and riders, of warriors and fighting men of every kind. This is the word of the Lord GOD.

21 'I shall display my glory among the nations; all will see the judgement that I execute and the hand I lay upon them. 22 From that day forward the Israelites will know that I am the LORD their God, 23 and the nations will know that the Israelites went into exile for their iniquity in being unfaithful to me. I hid my face from them and handed them over to their enemies, and they fell, every one of them, by the sword. 24 I dealt out to them what their defilement and rebelliousness deserved, and I hid my face from them.

25 'The Lord GOD says: Now I shall restore the fortunes of Jacob and show my compassion for all Israel, and I shall be jealous for my holy name. 26 They will forget their shame and all their unfaithfulness to me, when they live once more in their homeland undisturbed and free from terror. 27 When I bring them back from the nations and gather them from the lands of their enemies, I shall make them exemplify my holiness for many nations to see. 28 They will know that I am the LORD their God, because, having sent them into exile among the nations, I bring them together again in their homeland and leave none of them behind. 29 No longer shall I hide my face from them, I who have poured out my spirit on Israel. This is the word of the Lord GOD.'

40 AT the beginning of the year, on the tenth day of the month, in the twenty-fifth year of our exile, that is fourteen years after the city had fallen, on that very day the hand of the LORD came upon me and he brought me there. 2 In a vision from God I was brought to the land of Israel and set on a very high mountain, on which were what seemed to be the buildings of a city to the south. 3 He led me towards it, and I saw a man like a figure of bronze standing at the gate and holding a cord of linen thread and a measuring rod. 4 'O man,' he said to me, 'look closely and listen carefully; note well all that I show you, for this is why you have been brought here. Tell the Israelites everything you see.'

---

[k] Or of the Abarim   [l] That is, the Horde of Gog   [m] Heb travelers   [n] That is The Horde   [o] Heb chariots   [p] Another reading is They shall bear

39:11 instead of: prob. rdg; Heb. there.   39:16 So . . . horde: prob. rdg; Heb. obscure.   Chs. 40—43 In chapters 40—43 there are several Hebrew technical terms whose meaning is not certain and has to be determined, as well as may be, from the context.

11 On that day I will give Gog for his tomb a well-known place in Israel, the Valley of Abarim east of the sea [it is blocked to travelers]. Gog shall be buried there with all his horde, and it shall be named "Valley of Hamon-gog." 12 To purify the land, the house of Israel shall need seven months to bury them. 13 All the people of the land shall bury them and gain renown for it, when I reveal my glory, says the Lord God. 14 Men shall be permanently employed to pass through the land burying those who lie unburied, so as to purify the land. For seven months they shall keep searching. 15 When they pass through, should they see a human bone, let them put up a marker beside it, until others have buried it in the Valley of Hamon-gog. 16 [Also the name of the city shall be Hamonah.] Thus the land shall be purified.

17 As for you, son of man, says the Lord God, say to birds of every kind and to all the wild beasts: Come together, from all sides gather for the slaughter I am about to provide for you, a great slaughter on the mountains of Israel: you shall have flesh to eat and blood to drink. 18 You shall eat the flesh of warriors and drink the blood of the princes of the land [rams, lambs, and goats, bullocks, fatlings of Bashan, all of them]. 19 From the slaughter which I will provide for you, you shall eat fat until you are filled and drink blood until you are drunk. 20 You shall be filled at my table with horses and riders, with warriors and soldiers of every kind, says the Lord God.

21 Thus I will display my glory among the nations, and all the nations shall see the judgment I have executed and the hand I have laid upon them. 22 From that day forward the house of Israel shall know that I am the Lord, their God. 23 The nations shall know that because of its sins the house of Israel went into exile; for they transgressed against me, and I hid my face from them and handed them over to their foes, so that all of them fell by the sword. 24 According to their uncleanness and their transgressions I dealt with them, hiding my face from them.

25 Therefore, thus says the Lord God: Now I will restore the fortunes of Jacob and have pity on the whole house of Israel, and I will be jealous for my holy name. 26 They shall forget their disgrace and all the times they broke faith with me, when they live in security on their land with no one to frighten them. 27 When I bring them back from among the peoples, I will gather them from the lands of their enemies, and will prove my holiness through them in the sight of many nations. 28 Thus they shall know that I, the Lord, am their God, since I who exiled them among the nations, will gather them back on their land, not leaving any of them behind. 29 No longer will I hide my face from them, for I have poured out my spirit upon the house of Israel, says the Lord God.

40 On the tenth day of the month beginning the twenty-fifth year of our exile, fourteen years after the city was taken, that very day the hand of the Lord came upon me and brought me 2 in divine visions to the land of Israel, where he set me down on a very high mountain. On it there seemed to be a city being built before me. 3 When he had brought me there, all at once I saw a man whose appearance was that of bronze; he was standing in the gate, holding a linen cord and a measuring rod. 4 The man said to me, "Son of man, look carefully and listen intently, and pay strict attention to all that I will show you, for you have been brought here so that I might show it to you. Tell the house of Israel all that you see." 5 [Then I saw an outer wall that

11 "That day, I shall give Gog a famous spot in Israel for his grave, the valley of the Obarim, east of the Sea — the valley that halts the traveller — and there Gog and his whole throng will be buried, and it will be called the Valley of Hamon-Gog. 12 The House of Israel will take seven months to bury them and cleanse the country. 13 All the people of the country will dig their graves, thus winning themselves renown, the day when I display my glory — declares the Lord Yahweh. 14 And men will be detailed to the permanent duty of going through the country and burying those left above ground and cleansing it. They will begin their search once the seven months are over, 15 and as they go through the country, if one of them sees any human bones, he will set up a marker beside them until the gravediggers have buried them in the valley of Hamon-Gog 16 (and Hamonah is also the name of a town) and have cleansed the country."

17 'Son of man, the Lord Yahweh says this, "Say to the birds of every kind and to all the wild animals: Muster, come, gather from everywhere around for the sacrifice I am making for you, a great sacrifice on the mountains of Israel, so that you can eat flesh and drink blood. 18 You will eat the flesh of heroes, you will drink the blood of the princes of the world. They are all rams and lambs, goats and fat bulls of Bashan. 19 You will glut yourselves on fat and drink yourselves drunk on blood at this sacrifice I am making for you. 20 You will glut yourselves at my table on horses and chargers, on heroes and every kind of warrior — declares the Lord Yahweh."

21 'I shall display my glory to the nations, and all nations will see my sentence when I inflict it and my hand when I strike them. 22 The House of Israel will know that I am Yahweh their God, from that day forward for ever. 23 The nations too will know that the House of Israel were exiled for their guilt; because they were unfaithful to me, I hid my face from them and put them into the clutches of their enemies, so that they all fell by the sword. 24 I treated them as their loathsome acts of infidelity deserved and hid my face from them.

25 'So, the Lord Yahweh says this, "Now I shall bring Jacob's captives back and take pity on the whole House of Israel and show myself jealous for my holy name. 26 They will forget their disgrace and all the acts of infidelity which they committed against me when they were living safely in their own country, with no one to disturb them. 27 When I bring them home from the peoples, when I gather them back from the countries of their enemies, when I display my holiness in them for many nations to see, 28 they will know that I am Yahweh their God who, having sent them into exile among the nations, have reunited them in their own country, not leaving a single one behind. 29 I shall never hide my face from them again, since I shall pour out my spirit on the House of Israel — declares the Lord Yahweh."'

40 r In the twenty-fifth year of our captivity, at the beginning of the year, on the tenth day of the month, fourteen years to the day from the capture of the city, the hand of Yahweh was on me. He carried me away: 2 in divine visions, he carried me away to the land of Israel and put me down on a very high mountain, on the south of which there seemed to be built a city. 3 He took me to it, and there I saw a man, whose appearance was like brass. He had a flax cord and a measuring rod in his hand and was standing in the gateway. 4 The man said to me, 'Son of man, look carefully, listen closely and pay attention to everything I show you, since you have been brought here only for me to show it to you. Tell the House of Israel everything that you see.'

r 40 This last section, chh. 40–48, is a blueprint for the restored community, alive to the presence of God in his spirit and inspired by the ideal of holiness.

NEW REVISED STANDARD VERSION

5 Now there was a wall all around the outside of the temple area. The length of the measuring reed in the man's hand was six long cubits, each being a cubit and a handbreadth in length; so he measured the thickness of the wall, one reed; and the height, one reed. 6 Then he went into the gateway facing east, going up its steps, and measured the threshold of the gate, one reed deep.q There were 7 recesses, and each recess was one reed wide and one reed deep; and the space between the recesses, five cubits; and the threshold of the gate by the vestibule of the gate at the inner end was one reed deep. 8 Then he measured the inner vestibule of the gateway, one cubit. 9 Then he measured the vestibule of the gateway, eight cubits; and its pilasters, two cubits; and the vestibule of the gate was at the inner end. 10 There were three recesses on either side of the east gate; the three were of the same size, and the pilasters on either side were of the same size. 11 Then he measured the width of the opening of the gateway, ten cubits; and the width of the gateway, thirteen cubits. 12 There was a barrier before the recesses, one cubit on either side; and the recesses were six cubits on either side. 13 Then he measured the gate from the backr of the one recess to the backr of the other, a width of twenty-five cubits, from wall to wall.s 14 He measuredt also the vestibule, twenty cubits; and the gate next to the pilaster on every side of the court.u 15 From the front of the gate at the entrance to the end of the inner vestibule of the gate was fifty cubits. 16 The recesses and their pilasters had windows, with shuttersu on the inside of the gateway all around, and the vestibules also had windows on the inside all around; and on the pilasters were palm trees.

17 Then he brought me into the outer court; there were chambers there, and a pavement, all around the court; thirty chambers fronted on the pavement. 18 The pavement ran along the side of the gates, corresponding to the length of the gates; this was the lower pavement. 19 Then he measured the distance from the inner front ofv the lower gate to the outer front of the inner court, one hundred cubits.w

20 Then he measured the gate of the outer court that faced north — its depth and width. 21 Its recesses, three on either side, and its pilasters and its vestibule were of the same size as those of the first gate; its depth was fifty cubits, and its width twenty-five cubits. 22 Its windows, its vestibule, and its palm trees were of the same size as those of the gate that faced toward the east. Seven steps led up to it; and its vestibule was on the inside.x 23 Opposite the gate on the north, as on the east, was a gate to the inner court; he measured from gate to gate, one hundred cubits.

24 Then he led me toward the south, and there was a gate on the south; and he measured its pilasters and its vestibule; they had the same dimensions as the others. 25 There were windows all around in it and in its vestibule, like the windows of the others; its depth was fifty cubits, and its width twenty-five cubits. 26 There were seven steps leading up to it; its vestibule was on the inside.x It had palm trees on its pilasters, one on either side. 27 There was a gate on the south of the inner court; and he measured from gate to gate toward the south, one hundred cubits.

REVISED ENGLISH BIBLE

5 Right round the outside of the temple ran a wall. The length of the rod which the man was holding was six cubits, reckoning by the long cubit which was one cubit and a hand's breadth. He measured the thickness and the height of the wall; each was one rod. 6 The man went to the gate which faced eastwards, and mounting its steps he measured the threshold of the gateway; its depth was one rod. 7 Each cell was one rod long and one rod wide; and there was a space of five cubits between the cells. The threshold of the gateway at the end of the vestibule on the side facing the temple was one rod. 8 He measured the vestibule of the gateway 9 and it was eight cubits, with pilasters two cubits thick; the vestibule of the gateway lay at the end nearer the temple. 10 Now the cells of the gateway, looking back eastwards, were three in number on each side, all of the same size, and their pilasters on either side were also identical in size. 11 He measured the entrance to the gateway; it was ten cubits wide, and the width of the gateway itself throughout its length was thirteen cubits. 12 In front of the cells on each side lay a kerb, one cubit wide; each cell was six cubits by six. 13 He measured the width of the gateway through the cell doors which faced one another, from the back of one cell to the back of the opposite cell; he made it twenty-five cubits, 14 and the vestibule twenty cubits across; the gateway on every side projected into the court. 15 From the front of the entrance gate to the outer face of the vestibule of the inner gate the distance was fifty cubits. 16 Both cells and pilasters had embrasures all round inside the gateway, and the vestibule had windows all round within, and each pilaster was decorated with carved palm trees.

17 The man brought me to the outer court, and I saw rooms and a pavement all round the court: there were thirty rooms along the pavement. 18 The pavement ran up to the side of the gateways, as wide as they were long; this was the lower pavement. 19 He measured the width of the court from the front of the lower gateway to the outside of the inner gateway; it was a hundred cubits.

The man led me round to the north 20 and I saw a gateway facing north belonging to the outer court, and he measured its length and its breadth. 21 Its cells, three on each side, together with its pilasters and its vestibule, were the same size as those of the first gateway, fifty cubits long by twenty-five wide. 22 So too its windows, and those of its vestibule, and its palm trees, were the same size as those of the gateway which faced east; it was approached by seven steps with its vestibule facing them. 23 A gate like that on the east side led to the inner court opposite the north gateway; he measured from gateway to gateway, and it was a hundred cubits.

24 Then the man led me round to the south, where I saw a gateway facing south. He measured its cells, its pilasters, and its vestibule, and found it the same size as the others, 25 fifty cubits long by twenty-five wide. Both gateway and vestibule had windows all round like the others. 26 It was approached by seven steps with a vestibule facing them and palms carved on each pilaster. 27 The inner court had a gateway facing south, and when he measured from gateway to gateway it was a hundred cubits.

40:6 **one rod:** *so Gk; Heb. adds* and one threshold, one rod in width. 40:13 **back:** *so Gk; Heb.* roof. 40:14 **vestibule:** *prob. rdg, cp. Gk; Heb.* the pilasters. **twenty cubits:** *so Gk; Heb.* sixty cubits. **projected into:** *prob. rdg; Heb. adds* pilaster. 40:19 **inner gateway:** *so Gk; Heb.* inner court. 40:19–20 **cubits . . . gateway:** *so Gk; Heb.* cubits, east and north, 20and the gate. 40:22 **and those of:** *prob. rdg; Heb. omits* those of. 40:23 **like . . . side:** *so Gk; Heb.* and to the east. 40:24 **its cells:** *so Gk; Heb. omits.*

q Heb *deep, and one threshold, one reed deep*   r Gk: Heb roof
s Heb *opening facing opening*   t Heb *made*   u Meaning of Heb
uncertain   v Compare Gk: Heb *from before*   w Heb adds *the east*
and the north   x Gk: Heb *before them*

completely surrounded the temple. The man was holding a measuring rod six cubits long, each cubit being a cubit and a handbreadth; he measured the width and the height of the structure, each of which was found to be one rod.]

6 Then he went to the gate which faced the east, climbed its steps, and measured the gate's threshold, which was found to be a rod wide. 7 The cells were a rod long and a rod wide, and the pilasters between the cells measured five cubits. The threshold of the gate adjoining the vestibule of the gate toward the inside measured one rod. 8 He measured the vestibule of the gate, 9 which was eight cubits, and its pilasters, which were two cubits. The vestibule of the gate was toward the inside. 10 The cells of the east gate were three on either side, of equal size, and the pilasters on either side were also of equal size. 11 He measured the gate's entrance, which was ten cubits wide, while the width of the gate's passage itself was thirteen cubits. 12 The border before each of the cells on both sides was one cubit; the cells themselves were six cubits on either side, from opening to opening. 13 He measured the gate from the back wall of one cell to the back wall of the cell on the opposite side: the width was twenty-five cubits. 14 He measured the vestibule, which was twenty-five cubits. The pilasters adjoining the court on either side were six cubits. 15 The length of the gate from the front entrance to the front of the vestibule on the inside was fifty cubits. 16 Within the gateway on both sides there were splayed windows let into the cells [and into their pilasters]; likewise, within the vestibule on both sides there were windows. The pilasters were decorated with palms.

17 Then he brought me to the outer court, where there were chambers and a pavement. The pavement was laid all around the court, and the chambers, which were on the pavement, were thirty in number. 18 The pavement lay alongside the gates, as wide as the gates were long; this was the lower pavement. 19 He measured the width of the court from the front of the lower gate to the front of the inner gate; it was one hundred cubits between them.

Then he proceeded north, 20 where, on the outer court, there was a gate facing north, whose length and width he measured. 21 Its cells, three on either side, its pilasters, and its vestibule had the same measurements as those of the first gate; it was fifty cubits long and twenty-five cubits wide. 22 Its windows, the windows of its vestibule, and its palm decorations were of the same proportions as those of the gate facing the east. Seven steps led up to it, and its vestibule was toward the inside. 23 The inner court had a gate opposite the north gate, just as at the east gate; he measured one hundred cubits from one gate to the other.

24 Then he led me south, to where there was a southern gate, whose cells, pilasters, and vestibule he measured; they were the same size as the others. 25 The gate and its vestibule had windows on both sides, like the other windows. It was fifty cubits long and twenty-five cubits wide. 26 It was ascended by seven steps; its vestibule was toward the inside; and it was decorated with palms here and there on its pilasters. 27 The inner court also had a southern gate; from gate to gate he measured one hundred cubits.

5 Now, the Temple was surrounded on all sides by an outer wall. The man was holding a measuring rod six cubits long, each cubit a forearm and a handsbreadth. He measured the thickness of this construction — one rod; and its height — one rod.

6 He went to the east gate, climbed the steps and measured its threshold: one rod deep. 7 Each guardroom one rod by one rod; and the piers between the guardrooms five cubits thick, and the threshold of the gate inwards from the porch of the gate: one rod.s 9 He measured the porch of the gate: eight cubits; its piers: two cubits; the porch of the gate was at the inner end. 10 There were three guardrooms on each side of the east gate, all three of the same size; the piers between them all of the same thickness each side. 11 He measured the width of the entrance: ten cubits; and the width all down the gateway: thirteen cubits. 12 There was a rail in front of the guardrooms; each rail on either side was one cubit. And the guardrooms on either side were six cubits square. 13 He measured the width of the gate from the back wall of one guardroom to the back wall of the other; it was twenty-five cubits across, the openings being opposite each other. 14 He measured the porch: twenty cubits; the court surrounded the gate on all sides. 15 From the front of the entrance gate, to the far end of the porch of the inner gate: fifty cubits. 16 All round inside the gate there were trellised windows in the guardrooms and in their piers; similarly, in the porch there were windows all round and palm trees on the piers.

17 He then took me to the outer court, which had rooms and a paved terrace going all the way round; there were thirty rooms on this terrace. 18 This terrace, which came up to the sides of the gates and matched their depth, was the Lower Terrace. He measured the width of the court, 19 from the front of the lower gate to the facade of the inner court, outside: a hundred cubits (on the east and on the north).

20 He measured the length and breadth of the north gate of the outer court. 21 It had three guardrooms on each side; its piers and porch were of the same size as those of the first gate: fifty cubits long and twenty-five cubits wide. 22 Its windows, its porch and its palm trees were of the same size as those of the east gate. There were seven steps up to it, and its porch was at the inner end. 23 In the inner court there was, opposite the north gate, a gate like the one opposite the east gate. He measured the distance from one gate to the other: a hundred cubits.

24 He took me to the south side where there was a south gate; he measured its guardrooms, piers and porch; they were of the same size as the others. 25 The gateway, as well as its porch, had windows all round, like the windows of the others; it was fifty cubits long and twenty-five cubits wide, 26 and it had seven steps up to it; its porch was at the inner end and had palm trees on its piers, one on either side. 27 The inner court had a south gate; he measured the distance southwards from one gate to the other: a hundred cubits.

---

s **40** v. 8 is omitted: it doubles v. 7.

NEW REVISED STANDARD VERSION

28 Then he brought me to the inner court by the south gate, and he measured the south gate; it was of the same dimensions as the others. 29 Its recesses, its pilasters, and its vestibule were of the same size as the others; and there were windows all around in it and in its vestibule; its depth was fifty cubits, and its width twenty-five cubits. 30 There were vestibules all around, twenty-five cubits deep and five cubits wide. 31 Its vestibule faced the outer court, and palm trees were on its pilasters, and its stairway had eight steps.

32 Then he brought me to the inner court on the east side, and he measured the gate; it was of the same size as the others. 33 Its recesses, its pilasters, and its vestibule were of the same dimensions as the others; and there were windows all around in it and in its vestibule; its depth was fifty cubits, and its width twenty-five cubits. 34 Its vestibule faced the outer court, and it had palm trees on its pilasters, on either side; and its stairway had eight steps.

35 Then he brought me to the north gate, and he measured it; it had the same dimensions as the others. 36 Its recesses, its pilasters, and its vestibule were of the same size as the others;[y] and it had windows all around. Its depth was fifty cubits, and its width twenty-five cubits. 37 Its vestibule[z] faced the outer court, and it had palm trees on its pilasters, on either side; and its stairway had eight steps.

38 There was a chamber with its door in the vestibule of the gate,[a] where the burnt offering was to be washed. 39 And in the vestibule of the gate were two tables on either side, on which the burnt offering and the sin offering and the guilt offering were to be slaughtered. 40 On the outside of the vestibule[b] at the entrance of the north gate were two tables; and on the other side of the vestibule of the gate were two tables. 41 Four tables were on the inside, and four tables on the outside of the side of the gate, eight tables, on which the sacrifices were to be slaughtered. 42 There were also four tables of hewn stone for the burnt offering, a cubit and a half long, and one cubit and a half wide, and one cubit high, on which the instruments were to be laid with which the burnt offerings and the sacrifices were slaughtered. 43 There were pegs, one handbreadth long, fastened all around the inside. And on the tables the flesh of the offering was to be laid.

44 On the outside of the inner gateway there were chambers for the singers in the inner court, one[c] at the side of the north gate facing south, the other at the side of the east gate facing north. 45 He said to me, "This chamber that faces south is for the priests who have charge of the temple, 46 and the chamber that faces north is for the priests who have charge of the altar; these are the descendants of Zadok, who alone among the descendants of Levi may come near to the LORD to minister to him." 47 He measured the court, one hundred cubits deep, and one hundred cubits wide, a square; and the altar was in front of the temple.

48 Then he brought me to the vestibule of the temple and measured the pilasters of the vestibule, five cubits on either side; and the width of the gate was fourteen cubits; and the sidewalls of the gate were three cubits[d] on either side. 49 The depth of the vestibule was twenty cubits, and the width twelve[e] cubits; ten steps led up[f] to it; and there were pillars beside the pilasters on either side.

41
Then he brought me to the nave, and measured the pilasters; on each side six cubits was the width of the pilasters.[g] 2 The width of the entrance was ten cubits;

REVISED ENGLISH BIBLE

28 The man brought me into the inner court through the south gateway, measured it, and found it the same size as the others. 29 So were its cells, pilasters, and vestibule, fifty cubits long by twenty-five wide. The court and its vestibule had windows all round. 31 Its vestibule faced the outer court; it had palm trees carved on its pilasters, and eight steps led up to it.

32 The man brought me to the inner court on the east side and measured the gateway, and he found it the same size as the others. 33 So too were its cells, pilasters, and vestibule; it and its vestibule had windows all round, and it was fifty cubits long by twenty-five wide. 34 Its vestibule gave on to the outer court and had a palm tree carved on each pilaster; eight steps led up to it.

35 Then the man brought me to the north gateway and measured it and found it the same size as the others. 36 So were its cells, pilasters, and vestibule, and it had windows all round; it was fifty cubits long by twenty-five wide. 37 Its vestibule faced the outer court and had palm trees carved on the pilaster at each side; eight steps led up to it.

38 Opening off the vestibule of the gateway was a room in which the whole-offerings were to be washed. 39 On each side at the vestibule were two tables where the whole-offering, the purification-offering, and the reparation-offering were to be slaughtered. 40 At the corner on the outside, on the way up to the entrance of the north gateway, stood two tables, and two more at the other corner of the vestibule of the gateway; 41 another four stood on each side at the corner of the gateway—eight tables in all, at which the slaughtering was to be done. 42 Four tables used for the whole-offering were of hewn stone, each one and a half cubits long by one and a half cubits wide and a cubit high; and on them they put the instruments used for the whole-offering and other sacrifices. 43 The flesh of the offerings was on the tables, and rims a hand's breadth in width were fixed all round facing inwards.

44 Then the man brought me right into the inner court, where there were two rooms, one at the corner of the north gateway, facing south, and one at the corner of the south gateway, facing north. 45 This room facing south, the man told me, is for the priests in charge of the temple buildings. 46 The room facing north is for the priests in charge of the altar: that is, the descendants of Zadok, who alone of the Levites may come near to serve the LORD. 47 He measured the court; it was square, a hundred cubits each way, and the altar stood in front of the temple.

48 The man brought me into the vestibule of the temple, and measured a pilaster of the vestibule; it was five cubits on each side. The width of the gateway was fourteen cubits, and that of the corners of the gateway three cubits in each direction. 49 The vestibule was twenty cubits long by twelve wide; ten steps led up to it, and by the pilasters rose pillars, one on either side.

41
He brought me into the sanctuary and measured the pilasters; they were six cubits wide on each side.

40:29 **all round:** so some MSS; others add 30 It had vestibules all round, and it was twenty-five cubits long by five wide.   40:37 **Its vestibule:** so Gk; Heb. Its pilasters.   40:38 **the vestibule of the gateway:** prob. rdg; Heb. pilasters, the gates.   40:44 **Then . . . rooms:** so Gk; Heb. And outside the inner gate singers' rooms in the inner court. **south gateway:** so Gk; Heb. east gateway.   40:48 **fourteen . . . gateway:** so Gk; Heb. omits.   40:49 **twelve:** so Gk; Heb. eleven.   41:1 **side:** so Gk; Heb. adds the width of the tent.

---

[y] One Ms: Compare verses 29 and 33: MT lacks were of the same size as the others   [z] Gk Vg Compare verses 26, 31, 34: Heb pilasters   [a] Cn: Heb at the pilasters of the gates   [b] Cn: Heb to him who goes up   [c] Heb lacks one   [d] Gk: Heb and the width of the gate was three cubits   [e] Gk: Heb eleven   [f] Gk: Heb and by steps that went up   [g] Compare Gk: Heb tent

NEW AMERICAN BIBLE	NEW JERUSALEM BIBLE

NEW AMERICAN BIBLE

28 Then he brought me to the inner court by the south gate, where he measured the south gate. Its dimensions were the same as the others; 29 its cells, its pilasters, and its vestibule were the same size as the others. The gate and its vestibule had windows on both sides; and it was fifty cubits long and twenty-five cubits wide. 31 But its vestibule was toward the outer court; palms were on its pilasters, and it had a stairway of eight steps. 32 Then he brought me to the gate facing the east, where he measured the gate, whose dimensions were found to be the same. 33 Its cells, its pilasters, and its vestibule were the same size as the others; the gate and its vestibule had windows on both sides; it was fifty cubits long and twenty-five cubits wide. 34 But its vestibule was toward the outer court; palms were on its pilasters here and there, and it had a stairway of eight steps. 35 Then he brought me to the north gate, where he measured the dimensions 36 of its cells, its pilasters, and its vestibule, and found them the same. The gate and its vestibule had windows on both sides; it was fifty cubits long and twenty-five cubits wide. 37 Its vestibule was toward the outer court; palms were on its pilasters here and there, and it had a stairway of eight steps.

38 There was a chamber opening off the vestibule of the gate, where the holocausts were rinsed. 39 In the vestibule of the gate there were two tables on either side, on which were slaughtered the sin offerings and guilt offerings. 40 Along the wall of the vestibule, but outside, near the entrance of the north gate, were two tables, and on the other side of the vestibule of the gate there were two tables. 41 There were four tables on either side of the gate [eight tables], on which the sacrifices were slaughtered. 42 There were four tables for holocausts, made of cut stone, one and a half cubits long, one and a half cubits wide, and one cubit high. 43 The ledges, a handbreadth wide, were set on the inside all around, and on them were laid the instruments with which the holocausts were slaughtered. On the tables themselves the flesh was laid. 44 He then led me to the inner court where there were two chambers, one beside the north gate, facing south, and the other beside the south gate, facing north. 45 He said to me, "This chamber which faces south is for the priests who have charge of the temple, 46 and the chamber which faces north is for the priests who have charge of the altar. These are the Zadokites, the only Levites who may come near to minister to the LORD." 47 Then he measured the court, which was a hundred cubits long and a hundred cubits wide, a perfect square. The altar stood in front of the temple.

48 Then he brought me into the vestibule of the temple and measured the pilasters on each side, which were five cubits. The width of the doorway was fourteen cubits, and the side walls on either side of the door measured three cubits. 49 The vestibule was twenty cubits wide and twelve cubits deep; ten steps led up to it, and there were columns by the pilasters, one on either side.

41 Then he brought me to the nave and measured the pilasters, which were six cubits thick on either side.

NEW JERUSALEM BIBLE

28 He then took me into the inner court by the south gate; he measured the south gate which was of the same size as the others. 29 Its guardrooms, piers and porch were of the same size as the others. 30 The gateway, as well as its porch, had windows all round; it was fifty cubits long and twenty-five cubits wide. 31 The porch gave on to the outer court. It had palm trees on its piers and eight steps leading up to it.

32 He took me to the eastern part of the inner court and measured the gate. It was of the same size as the others. 33 Its guardrooms, piers and porch were of the same size as the others. The gateway, as well as its porch, had windows all round; it was fifty cubits long and twenty-five cubits wide. 34 Its porch gave on to the outer court. There were palm trees on its piers on either side and eight steps leading up to it.

35 He then took me to the north gate and measured it. 36 Its guardrooms, piers and porch were of the same size as the others. The gateway had windows all round; it was fifty cubits long and twenty-five cubits wide. 37 Its porch gave on to the outer court. There were palm trees on its piers on either side and eight steps leading up to it.

38 There was a room, the entrance to which was in the porch of the gateway, where they washed the burnt offerings. 39 And inside the porch of the gateway were slabs, two on either side, for slaughtering the burnt offerings, the sacrifice for sin and the sacrifice of reparation. 40 Outside, at the approach to the entrance of the north gate, were two slabs, and on the other side, at the porch end of the gate were two slabs. 41 There were four slabs on one side and four slabs on the other side of the gateway, eight slabs in all, on which the slaughtering was done. 42 There were also four slabs of dressed stone for the burnt offerings, a cubit and a half long, a cubit and a half wide and a cubit high, on which the instruments for slaughtering the burnt offerings and sacrifice were placed; 43 runnels a handsbreadth wide went all round the top, and on these slabs was put the sacrificial flesh.

44 Then he took me into the inner court; there were two rooms in the inner court, one on the side of the north gate, facing south, the other on the side of the south gate, facing north. 45 He told me, 'The room looking south is for the priests responsible for the service of the Temple, 46 and the room looking north is for the priests responsible for the service of the altar. These are the sons of Zadok, those of the sons of Levi who approach Yahweh to serve him.'

47 He measured the court; it was a hundred cubits long and a hundred cubits wide, a square with the altar standing in front of the Temple.

48 He took me to the Ulam of the Temple and measured the piers of the Ulam: five cubits either side; and the width of the entrance was three cubits either side. 49 The length of the Ulam was twenty cubits and its width twelve cubits. There were ten steps leading up to it, and there were columns by the piers, one on either side.

41 He took me to the Hekal and measured its piers: six cubits wide on the one side, six cubits wide on the

40, 29: Verse 30, a dittography of v 29, is omitted.

and the sidewalls of the entrance were five cubits on either side. He measured the length of the nave, forty cubits, and its width, twenty cubits. 3 Then he went into the inner room and measured the pilasters of the entrance, two cubits; and the width of the entrance, six cubits; and the sidewalls[h] of the entrance, seven cubits. 4 He measured the depth of the room, twenty cubits, and its width, twenty cubits, beyond the nave. And he said to me, This is the most holy place.

5 Then he measured the wall of the temple, six cubits thick; and the width of the side chambers, four cubits, all around the temple. 6 The side chambers were in three stories, one over another, thirty in each story. There were offsets[i] all around the wall of the temple to serve as supports for the side chambers, so that they should not be supported by the wall of the temple. 7 The passageway[j] of the side chambers widened from story to story; for the structure was supplied with a stairway all around the temple. For this reason the structure became wider from story to story. One ascended from the bottom story to the uppermost story by way of the middle one. 8 I saw also that the temple had a raised platform all around; the foundations of the side chambers measured a full reed of six long cubits. 9 The thickness of the outer wall of the side chambers was five cubits; and the free space between the side chambers of the temple 10 and the chambers of the court was a width of twenty cubits all around the temple on every side. 11 The side chambers opened onto the area left free, one door toward the north, and another door toward the south; and the width of the part that was left free was five cubits all around.

12 The building that was facing the temple yard on the west side was seventy cubits wide; and the wall of the building was five cubits thick all around, and its depth ninety cubits.

13 Then he measured the temple, one hundred cubits deep; and the yard and the building with its walls, one hundred cubits deep; 14 also the width of the east front of the temple and the yard, one hundred cubits.

15 Then he measured the depth of the building facing the yard at the west, together with its galleries[k] on either side, one hundred cubits.

The nave of the temple and the inner room and the outer[l] vestibule 16 were paneled,[m] and, all around, all three had windows with recessed[n] frames. Facing the threshold the temple was paneled with wood all around, from the floor up to the windows (now the windows were covered), 17 to the space above the door, even to the inner room, and on the outside. And on all the walls all around in the inner room and the nave there was a pattern.[o] 18 It was formed of cherubim and palm trees, a palm tree between cherub and cherub. Each cherub had two faces: 19 a human face turned toward the palm tree on the one side, and the face of a young lion turned toward the palm tree on the other side. They were carved on the whole temple all around; 20 from the floor to the area above the door, cherubim and palm trees were carved on the wall.[p]

21 The doorposts of the nave were square. In front of the holy place was something resembling 22 an altar of wood, three cubits high, two cubits long, and two cubits wide;[q] its corners, its base,[r] and its walls were of wood. He said to me, "This is the table that stands before the LORD." 23 The nave and the holy place had each a double door. 24 The doors had two leaves apiece, two swinging

2 The entrance was ten cubits wide and its corners five cubits wide in each direction. He measured the length of the sanctuary; it was forty cubits, and its width twenty. 3 He went into the inner sanctuary and measured the pilasters at the entrance: they were two cubits; the entrance itself was six cubits, and the corners of the entrance were seven cubits in each direction. 4 Then he measured the room at the far end of the sanctuary; its length and its breadth were each twenty cubits. He said to me, 'This is the Holy of Holies.'

5 The man measured the wall of the temple; it was six cubits high, and each arcade all round the temple was four cubits wide. 6 The arcades were arranged in three tiers, each tier in thirty sections. In the wall all round the temple there were rebatements for the arcades, so that they could be supported without being fastened into the wall of the temple. 7 The higher up the arcades were, the broader they were all round by the addition of the rebatements, one above the other all round the temple; the temple itself had a ramp running upwards on a base, and in this way there was access from the lowest to the highest tier by way of the middle tier.

8 I saw the temple had a raised pavement all round it, and the foundations of the arcades were flush with it and measured a full rod, six cubits high. 9 The outer wall of the arcades was five cubits thick. There was an unoccupied area beside the terrace which was adjacent to the temple, 11 and the arcades opened on to this area, one opening facing north and one south; the unoccupied area was five cubits wide on all sides. 10 There was a free space twenty cubits wide all round the temple. 12 On the western side, at the far end of the free space, stood a building seventy cubits wide; its wall was five cubits thick all round, and its length ninety cubits.

13 The man measured the temple; it was a hundred cubits long; the free space, the building, and its walls came to a hundred cubits in all. 14 The east front of the temple along with the free space was a hundred cubits wide. 15 He measured the length of the building at the far end of the free space to the west of the temple, and its corridors on each side: a hundred cubits.

The sanctuary, the inner shrine, and the outer vestibule were panelled; 16 the embrasures around the three of them were framed with wood all round. From the ground up to the windows 17 and above the door, in both the inner and outer chambers, round all the walls, inside and out, 18 were carved figures, cherubim and palm trees, one palm tree between every pair of cherubim. Each cherub had two faces: 19 one the face of a man, looking towards one palm tree, and the other the face of a lion, looking towards the palm tree on its other side. Such was the carving round the whole of the temple. 20 The cherubim and the palm trees were carved on the walls from the ground up to the top of the doorway. 21 The doorposts of the sanctuary were square.

In front of the Holy Place was what seemed 22 an altar of wood, three cubits high and two cubits long; it was fitted with corner-posts, and its base and sides also were of wood. He told me that this was the table which stands before the LORD. 23 The sanctuary had a double door, as also had the Holy Place: 24 the double doors had hinged leaves, a pair for

h Gk: Heb width   i Gk Compare 1 Kings 6.6: Heb they entered   j Cn: Heb it was surrounded   k Cn: Meaning of Heb uncertain   l Gk: Heb of the court   m Gk: Heb the thresholds   n Cn Compare Gk 1 Kings 6.4: Meaning of Heb uncertain   o Heb measures   p Cn Compare verse 25: Heb and the wall   q Gk: Heb lacks two cubits wide   r Gk: Heb length

41:3 **corners:** so Gk; Heb. width.   41:7 **by . . . rebatements:** so Gk; Heb. for the surrounding of the house.   41:9 **beside the terrace:** prob. rdg; Heb. between the arcades.   41:11 Verses 10 and 11 transposed.   41:10 **There . . . space:** prob. rdg; Heb. Between the rooms.   41:15–17 **the inner shrine . . . the door:** prob. rdg, cp. Gk; Heb. unintelligible.   41:18 **were . . . figures:** prob. rdg; Heb. measures 18 and carving.   41:21 **The doorposts . . . square:** prob. rdg; Heb. unintelligible.   41:22 **base:** so Gk; Heb. length.

2 The width of the entrance was ten cubits, and the walls at either side of it measured five cubits each. He measured the length of the nave, which was found to be forty cubits, while its width was twenty.

3 Then he went in beyond and measured the pilasters flanking that entrance, which were two cubits; the width of the entrance was six cubits, and the walls at either side of it extended seven cubits each. 4 He measured the space beyond the nave, twenty cubits long and twenty cubits wide, and said to me, "This is the holy of holies."

5 Then he measured the wall of the temple, which was six cubits thick; the side chambers, which extended all the way around the temple, had a width of four cubits. 6 There were thirty side chambers built one above the other in three stories, and there were offsets in the outside wall of the temple that enclosed the side chambers; these served as supports, so that there were no supports in the temple wall proper. 7 There was a broad circular passageway that led upward to the side chambers, for the temple was enclosed all the way around and all the way upward; therefore the temple had a broad way running upward so that one could pass from the lowest to the middle and the highest story. 8 About the temple was a raised pavement completely enclosing it — the foundations of the side chambers — a full rod of six cubits in extent. 9 The width of the outside wall which enclosed the side chambers was five cubits. Between the side chambers of the temple 10 and the chambers of the court was an open space twenty cubits wide going all around the temple. 11 The side chambers had entrances to the open space, one entrance on the north and another on the south. The width of the wall surrounding the open space was five cubits. 12 The building fronting the free area on the west side was seventy cubits front to back; the wall of the building was five cubits thick all around, and it measured ninety cubits from side to side. 13 He measured the temple, which was one hundred cubits long. The free area, together with the building and its walls, was a hundred cubits in length. 14 The façade of the temple, along with the free area, on the east side, was one hundred cubits wide. 15 He measured the building which lay the length of the free area and behind it, and together with its walls on both sides it was one hundred cubits.

The inner nave and the outer vestibule 16 were paneled with precious wood all around, covered from the ground to the windows. There were splayed windows with trellises about them [facing the threshold]. 17 As high as the lintel of the door, even into the interior part of the temple as well as outside, on every wall on every side in both the inner and outer rooms were carved 18 the figures of cherubim and palmtrees: a palmtree between every two cherubim. Each cherub had two faces: 19 a man's face looking at a palmtree on one side, and a lion's face looking at a palmtree on the other; thus they were figured on every side throughout the whole temple. 20 From the ground to the lintel of the door the cherubim and palmtrees were carved on the walls. 21 The way into the nave was a square doorframe. In front of the holy place was something that looked like 22 a wooden altar, three cubits in height, two cubits long, and two cubits wide. It had corners, and its base and sides were of wood. He said to me, "This is the table which is before the LORD." 23 The nave had a double door, and also the holy place had 24 a double door. Each door had two movable

other. 2 The width of the entrance was ten cubits, and the returns of the entrance were five cubits on the one side and five cubits on the other. He measured its length: forty cubits; and its width: twenty cubits.

3 He then went inside and measured the pier at the entrance: two cubits; then the entrance: six cubits; and the returns of the entrance: seven cubits. 4 He measured its length; twenty cubits; and its width against the Hekal: twenty cubits. He then said to me, 'This is the Holy of Holies.'

5 He then measured the wall of the Temple: six cubits. The width of the lateral structure was four cubits, all round the Temple. 6 The cells were one above the other in three tiers of thirty cells each. The cells were recessed into the wall, the wall of the structure comprising the cells, all round, forming offsets; but there were no offsets in the wall of the Temple itself. 7 The width of the cells increased, storey by storey, corresponding to the amount taken in from the wall from one storey to the next, all round the Temple. 8 Then I saw that there was a paved terrace all round the Temple. The height of this, which formed the base of the side cells, was one complete rod of six cubits. 9 The outer wall of the side cells was five cubits thick. There was a passage between the cells of the Temple 10 and the rooms, twenty cubits wide, all round the Temple. 11 As a way in to the lateral cells on the passage there was one entrance on the north side and one entrance on the south side. The width of the passage was five cubits right round.

12 The building on the west side of the court was seventy cubits wide, the wall of the building was five cubits thick all round and its length was ninety cubits. 13 He measured the length of the Temple: a hundred cubits. 14 The length of the court plus the building and its walls: a hundred cubits. 15 He measured the length of the building, along the court, at the back, and its galleries on either side: a hundred cubits.

The inside of the Hekal and the porches of the court, 16 the thresholds, the windows, the galleries on three sides, facing the threshold, were panelled with wood all round from floor to windows, and the windows were screened with latticework. 17 From the door to the inner part of the Temple, as well as outside, and on the wall all round, both inside and out, 18 were carved great winged creatures and palm trees, one palm tree between two winged creatures; each winged creature had two faces: 19 a human face turned towards the palm tree on one side and the face of a lion towards the palm tree on the other side, throughout the Temple, all round. 20 Winged creatures and palm trees were carved on the wall from the floor to above the entrance. 21 The doorposts of the Temple were square.

In front of the sanctuary there was something like 22 a wooden altar, three cubits high and two cubits square. Its corners, base and sides were of wood. He said to me, 'This is the table in the presence of Yahweh.'

23 The Hekal had double doors and the sanctuary 24 double doors. These doors had two hinged leaves, two leaves

NEW REVISED STANDARD VERSION

leaves for each door. 25 On the doors of the nave were carved cherubim and palm trees, such as were carved on the walls; and there was a canopy of wood in front of the vestibule outside. 26 And there were recessed windows and palm trees on either side, on the sidewalls of the vestibule.s

42

Then he led me out into the outer court, toward the north, and he brought me to the chambers that were opposite the temple yard and opposite the building on the north. 2 The lengtht of the building that was on the north sidet wasu one hundred cubits, and the width fifty cubits. 3 Across the twenty cubits that belonged to the inner court, and facing the pavement that belonged to the outer court, the chambers rosev galleryw by galleryw in three stories. 4 In front of the chambers was a passage on the inner side, ten cubits wide and one hundred cubits deep,x and itsy entrances were on the north. 5 Now the upper chambers were narrower, for the galleriesw took more away from them than from the lower and middle chambers in the building. 6 For they were in three stories, and they had no pillars like the pillars of the outerz court; for this reason the upper chambers were set back from the ground more than the lower and the middle ones. 7 There was a wall outside parallel to the chambers, toward the outer court, opposite the chambers, fifty cubits long. 8 For the chambers on the outer court were fifty cubits long, while those opposite the temple were one hundred cubits long. 9 At the foot of these chambers ran a passage that one entered from the east in order to enter them from the outer court. 10 The width of the passagea is fixed by the wall of the court.

On the southb also, opposite the vacant area and opposite the building, there were chambers 11 with a passage in front of them; they were similar to the chambers on the north, of the same length and width, with the same exitsc and arrangements and doors. 12 So the entrances of the chambers to the south were entered through the entrance at the head of the corresponding passage, from the east, along the matching wall.w

13 Then he said to me, "The north chambers and the south chambers opposite the vacant area are the holy chambers, where the priests who approach the LORD shall eat the most holy offerings; there they shall deposit the most holy offerings — the grain offering, the sin offering, and the guilt offering, for the place is holy. 14 When the priests enter the holy place, they shall not go out of it into the outer court without laying there the vestments in which they minister, for these are holy; they shall put on other garments before they go near to the area open to the people."

15 When he had finished measuring the interior of the temple area, he led me out by the gate that faces east, and measured the temple area all around. 16 He measured the east side with the measuring reed, five hundred cubits by the measuring reed. 17 Then he turned and measuredd the north side, five hundred cubits by the measuring reed. 18 Then he turned and measuredd the south side, five hundred cubits by the measuring reed. 19 Then he turned to the west side and measured, five hundred cubits by the measuring reed. 20 He measured it on the four sides. It had a wall around it, five hundred cubits long and five hundred cubits wide, to make a separation between the holy and the common.

each door. 25 Carved on them were cherubim and palm trees like those on the walls. Outside there was a wooden cornice over the vestibule; 26 on both sides of the vestibule were embrasures, with palm trees carved at the corners.

42

Then the man took me to the outer court round by the north and brought me to the rooms facing the free space and facing the buildings to the north. 2 The length along the northern side was a hundred cubits, and the breadth fifty. 3 Facing the twenty cubits of free space which adjoined the inner court, and facing the pavement of the outer court, were corridors at three levels corresponding to each other. 4 In front of the rooms a passage, ten cubits wide and a hundred cubits long, ran towards the inner court; the entrances to the rooms faced north. 5 The upper rooms were narrower than the lower and middle rooms, because the corridors took building space from them. 6 For they were all at three levels and had no pillars such as the courts had, so that the lower and middle levels were recessed from the ground upwards. 7 An outside wall, fifty cubits long, ran parallel to the rooms and in front of them, on the side of the outer court, 8 and while the rooms adjacent to the outer court were fifty cubits long, those facing the sanctuary were a hundred cubits. 9 Below these rooms was an entry from the east on the way in from the outer court 10 where the wall of the court began.

On the south side, adjacent to the free space and the building, 11 were other rooms with a passage in front of them. These rooms corresponded, in length and breadth and in general character, to those facing north, 12 whose exits and entrances were the same as those of the rooms on the south. On the eastern approach, where the passages began, there was an entrance in the face of the inner wall.

13 The man said to me, 'The north and south rooms facing the free space are the consecrated rooms where the priests who approach the LORD are to eat the most sacred offerings. There they are to put these offerings as well as the grain-offering, the purification-offering, and the reparation-offering; for the place is holy. 14 When the priests have entered the Holy Place they must not go into the outer court again without leaving there the vestments they have worn while performing their duties. Those are holy vestments and they are to put on other garments before going to the place assigned to the people.'

15 When the man had finished measuring the inner temple, he brought me out through the gateway which faces east and measured the whole area. 16 He measured the east side with the measuring rod, and it was five hundred cubits. He turned 17 and measured the north side with his rod, and it was five hundred cubits. He turned to 18 the south side and measured it with his rod; it was five hundred cubits. 19 He turned to the west and measured it with his rod; it was five hundred cubits. 20 So he measured all four sides of the enclosing wall; in each direction it measured five hundred cubits. This marked off the sacred area from the secular.

---

s Cn: Heb vestibule. And the side chambers of the temple and the canopies   t Gk: Heb door   u Gk: Heb before the length   v Heb lacks the chambers rose   w Meaning of Heb uncertain   x Gk Syr: Heb a way of one cubit   y Heb their   z Gk: Heb lacks outer   a Heb lacks of the passage   b Gk: Heb east   c Heb and all their exits   d Gk: Heb measuring reed all around. He measured

41:26 corners: prob. rdg; Heb. adds and the arcades of the temple and the cornices.   42:2 The length . . . cubits: prob. rdg, cp. Gk; Heb. unintelligible.   42:4 and . . . long: so Gk; Heb. unintelligible.   42:10 began: prob. rdg; Heb. breadth. south: so Gk; Heb. east.   42:16,17,18,19,20 cubits: prob. rdg; Heb. rods.   42:17 He turned to: so Gk; Heb. round about.   42:18–19 Some MSS place verse 18 after verse 19.

leaves; two leaves were on one doorjamb and two on the other. 25 Carved upon them [on the doors of the nave] were cherubim and palmtrees, like those carved on the walls. Before the vestibule outside was a wooden lattice. 26 There were splayed windows [and palmtrees] on both side walls of the vestibule, and the side chambers of the temple. . . .

42 Then he led me north to the outer court, bringing me to some chambers on the north that lay across the free area and which were also across from the building. 2 Their length was a hundred cubits on the north side, and they were fifty cubits wide. 3 Across the twenty cubits of the inner court and the pavement of the outer court, there were three parallel rows of them on different levels. 4 In front of the chambers, to the inside, was a walk ten cubits broad and a wall of one cubit; but the entrances of the chambers were on the north. 5 The outermost chambers were the lowest, for the system of levels set them at a level lower than the closest chambers and those in between; 6 for they were in three rows and had no foundations to conform with the foundations of the courts, therefore they were on a lower terrace of the ground than the closest and the middle chambers. 7 On the far side there was a wall running parallel to the chambers along the outer court; its length before these chambers was fifty cubits, 8 for the length of the chambers belonging to the outer court was fifty cubits, but along its entire length the wall measured one hundred cubits. 9 Below these chambers there was the way in from the east, so that one could enter from the outer court 10 where the wall of the court began.

To the south along the side of the free area and the building there were also chambers, 11 before which was a passage. These looked like the chambers to the north, just as long and just as wide, with the same exits and plan and entrances. 12 Below the chambers to the south there was an entrance at the beginning of the way which led to the back wall, by which one could enter from the east. 13 He said to me, "The north and south chambers which border on the free area are the sanctuary chambers; here the priests who draw near to the LORD shall eat the most sacred meals, and here they shall keep the most sacred offerings: cereal offerings, sin offerings, and guilt offerings; for it is a holy place. 14 When the priests have once entered, they shall not leave the holy place for the outer court until they have left here the clothing in which they ministered, for it is holy. They shall put on other garments, and then approach the place destined for the people."

15 When he had finished measuring the inner temple area, he brought me out by way of the gate which faces east and measured all the limits of the court. 16 He measured the east side: five hundred cubits by his measuring rod. Then he turned 17 and measured the north side: five hundred cubits by the measuring rod. He turned 18 to the south and measured five hundred cubits by the measuring rod. 19 Then he turned to the west and measured five hundred cubits by the measuring rod. 20 Thus he measured it in the four directions, five hundred cubits long and five hundred cubits wide. It was surrounded by a wall, to separate the sacred from the profane.

for the one door, two leaves for the other. 25 On them (on the doors of the Hekal), were carved great winged creatures and palm trees like those carved on the walls. There was a wooden porch roof on the front of the Ulam on the outside, 26 and windows with flanking palm trees on the sides of the Ulam, the cells to the side of the Temple and the porch-roofs.

42 He then took me out into the outer court on the north side and led me to the room facing the court, that is to say, to the front of the building on the north side. 2 Along the front, it was a hundred cubits long on the north side and fifty cubits wide. 3 Facing the gateways of the inner court and facing the paving of the outer court was a gallery in front of the triple gallery, 4 and in front of the rooms was a walk, ten cubits measured inwards and a hundred cubits long; their doors looked north. 5 The top-floor rooms were narrow because the galleries took up part of the width, being narrower than those on the ground floor or those on the middle floor of the building; 6 these were divided into three storeys and had no columns such as the court had. Hence they were narrower than the ground floor ones or the middle-floor ones (below them). 7 The outer wall parallel to the rooms, facing them and giving onto the outer court, was fifty cubits long, 8 the length of the rooms facing the outer court being fifty cubits, while for those facing the hall of the Temple it was a hundred cubits. 9 Beneath the rooms there was an entrance from the east, leading in from the outer court.

10 In the thickness of the wall of the court, on the south side fronting the court and the building, were rooms. 11 A walk ran in front of them, as with the rooms built on the north side; they were of the same length and breadth, and were of similar design with similar doors in and out. 12 Before the rooms on the south side there was an entrance at the end of each walk, opposite the corresponding wall on the east side, at their entries. 13 He said to me, 'The northern and southern rooms giving onto the court are the rooms of the sanctuary, in which the priests who approach Yahweh will eat the most holy things. In them will be placed the most holy things: the oblation, the sacrifice for sin and the sacrifice of reparation, since this is a holy place. 14 Once the priests have entered, they will not go out of the holy place into the outer court without leaving their liturgical vestments there, since these vestments are holy; they will put on other clothes before going near places assigned to the people.'

15 When he had finished measuring the inside of the Temple, he took me out to the east gate and measured it right round the sides. 16 He measured the east side with his measuring rod: a total of five hundred cubits by the measuring rod. 17 He then measured the north side: a total of five hundred cubits by the measuring rod. 18 He then measured the south side: five hundred cubits by the measuring rod 19 was the total. On the west side he measured five hundred cubits by the measuring rod. 20 He measured the entire enclosing wall on all four sides: length five hundred, breadth five hundred, separating the sacred from the profane.

43

Then he brought me to the gate, the gate facing east. 2 And there, the glory of the God of Israel was coming from the east; the sound was like the sound of mighty waters; and the earth shone with his glory. 3 The*e* vision I saw was like the vision that I had seen when he came to destroy the city, and *f* like the vision that I had seen by the river Chebar; and I fell upon my face. 4 As the glory of the LORD entered the temple by the gate facing east, 5 the spirit lifted me up, and brought me into the inner court; and the glory of the LORD filled the temple.

6 While the man was standing beside me, I heard someone speaking to me out of the temple. 7 He said to me: Mortal, this is the place of my throne and the place for the soles of my feet, where I will reside among the people of Israel forever. The house of Israel shall no more defile my holy name, neither they nor their kings, by their whoring, and by the corpses of their kings at their death. *g* 8 When they placed their threshold by my threshold and their doorposts beside my doorposts, with only a wall between me and them, they were defiling my holy name by their abominations that they committed; therefore I have consumed them in my anger. 9 Now let them put away their idolatry and the corpses of their kings far from me, and I will reside among them forever.

10 As for you, mortal, describe the temple to the house of Israel, and let them measure the pattern; and let them be ashamed of their iniquities. 11 When they are ashamed of all that they have done, make known to them the plan of the temple, its arrangement, its exits and its entrances, and its whole form — all its ordinances and its entire plan and all its laws; and write it down in their sight, so that they may observe and follow the entire plan and all its ordinances. 12 This is the law of the temple: the whole territory on the top of the mountain all around shall be most holy. This is the law of the temple.

13 These are the dimensions of the altar by cubits (the cubit being one cubit and a handbreadth): its base shall be one cubit high, *h* and one cubit wide, with a rim of one span around its edge. This shall be the height of the altar: 14 From the base on the ground to the lower ledge, two cubits, with a width of one cubit; and from the smaller ledge to the larger ledge, four cubits, with a width of one cubit; 15 and the altar hearth, four cubits; and from the altar hearth projecting upward, four horns. 16 The altar hearth shall be square, twelve cubits long by twelve wide. 17 The ledge also shall be square, fourteen cubits long by fourteen wide, with a rim around it half a cubit wide, and its surrounding base, one cubit. Its steps shall face east.

18 Then he said to me: Mortal, thus says the Lord GOD: These are the ordinances for the altar: On the day when it is erected for offering burnt offerings upon it and for dashing blood against it, 19 you shall give to the levitical priests of the family of Zadok, who draw near to me to minister to me, says the Lord GOD, a bull for a sin offering. 20 And you shall take some of its blood, and put it on the four horns of the altar, and on the four corners of the ledge, and upon the rim all around; thus you shall purify it and make atonement for it. 21 You shall also take the bull of the sin offering, and it shall be burnt in the appointed place belonging to the temple, outside the sacred area.

22 On the second day you shall offer a male goat without blemish for a sin offering; and the altar shall be purified, as it was purified with the bull. 23 When you have finished purifying it, you shall offer a bull without blemish and a ram from the flock without blemish. 24 You shall present them before the LORD, and the priests shall throw salt on them and offer them up as a burnt offering to the LORD.

43

The man led me to the gate which faced east, 2 and there, coming from the east, was the glory of the God of Israel. The sound of his coming was like that of a mighty torrent, and the earth was bright with his glory. 3 The form that I saw was the same as I had seen when he came to destroy the city, the same I had seen by the river Kebar, and I prostrated myself.

4 As the glory of the LORD came to the temple by the east gate, 5 a spirit lifted me up and brought me into the inner court, and I saw the glory of the LORD fill the temple. 6 With the man standing beside me I heard someone speak to me from the temple 7 and say, 'O man, do you see the place of my throne, the place where I set my feet, and where I shall dwell among the Israelites for ever? Neither they nor their kings must ever defile my holy name again with their wanton idolatry, and with the monuments raised to dead kings. 8 They set their threshold beside mine and their doorpost beside mine, with only a wall between me and them. They defiled my holy name with the abominations they committed; so I destroyed them in my anger. 9 But now they must put away their wanton idolatry and remove the monuments to their kings far from me, and I shall dwell among them for ever.

10 'Tell the Israelites, O man, about this temple, that they may be ashamed of their iniquities. 11 If they are ashamed of all they have done, you are to describe to them the temple and its fittings, its exits and entrances, all the details and particulars of its elevation and plan. Make a sketch for them to look at, so that they may keep them in mind and carry them out. 12 This is the plan of the temple to be built on the top of the mountain: all its precincts on every side shall be most holy.'

13 These were the dimensions of the altar in cubits (the cubit that is a cubit and a hand's breadth). This was the height of the altar: the base was a cubit high and projected a cubit; on its edge was a rim one span deep. 14 From the base to the cubit-wide ridge of the lower pedestal-block was two cubits, and from this smaller pedestal-block to the cubit-wide ridge of the larger pedestal-block was four cubits. 15 The altar-hearth was four cubits high and was surmounted by four horns a cubit high. 16 The hearth was square, twelve cubits long and twelve cubits wide. 17 The upper pedestal-block was fourteen cubits long and fourteen cubits wide on its four sides, and the rim round it was half a cubit deep. The base of the altar projected a cubit, and there were steps facing east.

18 He said to me, 'O man, the Lord GOD says: Here are the regulations for the altar when it has been made, for sacrificing whole-offerings on it and for flinging the blood against it. 19 Only the levitical priests of the family of Zadok may come near to serve me, says the Lord GOD. You are to assign them a young bull for a purification-offering; 20 you must take some of the blood and apply it to the four horns of the altar, on the four corners of the upper pedestal, and all round the rim, and so purify and make expiation for the altar. 21 Then take the bull chosen as the purification-offering, and let the priests destroy it by fire in the proper place within the precincts, but outside the Holy Place.

22 'On the following day you are to present a he-goat without blemish as a purification-offering, and with it they are to purify the altar as they did with the bull. 23 When you have completed the purifying of the altar, you are to present a young bull without blemish and a ram without blemish. 24 Present them before the LORD, and have the priests throw salt on them and sacrifice them as a whole-offering to the LORD. 25 For seven days you are to offer a goat as a daily

---

e Gk: Heb *Like the vision*   *f* Syr: Heb *and the visions*   *g* Or on *their high places*   *h* Gk: Heb lacks *high*

43:7 **do you see:** *so* Gk; *Heb. omits.*   43:10 **iniquities:** *prob. rdg;* Heb. adds *and they shall measure the proportions.*   43:13 **the base . . . high:** *prob. rdg;* Heb. *unintelligible.*   43:15 **a cubit high:** *Heb. omits.*

NEW AMERICAN BIBLE

43 Then he led me to the gate which faces the east, 2and there I saw the glory of the God of Israel coming from the east. I heard a sound like the roaring of many waters, and the earth shone with his glory. 3The vision was like that which I had seen when he came to destroy the city, and like that which I had seen by the river Chebar. I fell prone 4as the glory of the LORD entered the temple by way of the gate which faces the east, 5but spirit lifted me up and brought me to the inner court. And I saw that the temple was filled with the glory of the LORD. 6Then I heard someone speaking to me from the temple, while the man stood beside me. 7The voice said to me: Son of man, this is where my throne shall be, this is where I will set the soles of my feet; here I will dwell among the Israelites forever. Never again shall they and their kings profane my holy name with their harlotries and with the corpses of their kings [their high places]. 8When they placed their threshold against my threshold and their doorpost next to mine, so that only a wall was between us, they profaned my holy name by their abominable deeds; therefore I consumed them in my wrath. 9From now on they shall put far from me their harlotry and the corpses of their kings, and I will dwell in their midst forever.

10As for you, son of man, describe the temple to the house of Israel [that they may be ashamed of their sins], both its measurements and its design; 11[and if they are ashamed of all that they have done,] make known to them the form and design of the temple, its exits and entrances, all its statutes and laws; write these down for them to see, that they may carefully observe all its laws and statutes. 12This is the law of the temple: its whole surrounding area on the mountain top shall be most sacred.

13These were the measurements of the altar in cubits of one cubit plus a handbreadth. Its base was one cubit high and one cubit deep, with a rim around its edge of one span. The height of the altar itself was as follows: 14from its base at the bottom up to the lower ledge it was two cubits high, and this ledge was one cubit deep; from the lower to the upper ledge it was four cubits high, and this ledge also was one cubit deep; 15the hearth of the altar was four cubits high, and extending from the top of the hearth were the four horns of the altar. 16The hearth was a square: twelve cubits long and twelve cubits wide. 17The upper ledge was also a square: fourteen cubits long and fourteen cubits wide. The lower ledge, likewise a square, was sixteen cubits long and sixteen cubits wide, with a half-cubit rim surrounding it. And there was a base of one cubit all around. The steps of the altar face the east.

18Then he said to me: Son of man, thus says the Lord GOD: These are the statutes for the altar when it is set up for the offering of holocausts upon it and for the sprinkling of blood against it. 19Give a young bull as a sin offering to the priests, the Levites who are of the line of Zadok, who draw near me to minister to me, says the Lord GOD. 20Take some of its blood and put it on the four horns of the altar, and on the four corners of the ledge, and on the rim all around. Thus you shall purify it and make atonement for it. 21Then take the bull of the sin offering, which is to be burnt in a designated part of the temple, outside the sanctuary. 22On the second day present an unblemished he-goat as a sin offering, to purify the altar as was done with the bull. 23When you have finished the purification, bring an unblemished young bull and an unblemished ram from the flock, 24and present them before the LORD; the priests shall strew salt on them and offer them to the LORD as holocausts.

NEW JERUSALEM BIBLE

43 He took me to the gate, the one facing east. 2I saw the glory of the God of Israel approaching from the east. A sound came with him like the sound of the ocean, and the earth shone with his glory. 3This vision was like the one I had seen when I had come for the destruction of the city, and like the one I had seen by the River Chebar. Then I fell to the ground.

4The glory of Yahweh arrived at the Temple by the east gate. 5The Spirit lifted me up and brought me into the inner court; I saw the glory of Yahweh fill the Temple. 6And I heard someone speaking to me from the Temple while the man stood beside me. 7He said, 'Son of man, this is the dais of my throne, the step on which I rest my feet. I shall live here among the Israelites for ever; and the House of Israel, they and their kings, will never again defile my holy name with their whorings and the corpses of their kings, 8by putting their threshold beside my threshold and their doorposts beside my doorposts, with a party wall shared by them and me. They used to defile my holy name by their loathsome practices, and this is why I put an end to them in my anger. 9From now on they will banish their whorings and the corpses of their kings from my presence and I shall live among them for ever.

10'Son of man, describe this Temple to the House of Israel, to shame them out of their loathsome practices. (Let them draw up the plan of it.) 11And, if they are ashamed of their behaviour, show them the design and plan of the Temple, its exits and entrances, its shape, how all of it is arranged, the entire design and all its principles. Give them all this in writing so that they can see and take note of its design and the way it is all arranged and carry it out. 12This is the charter of the Temple: all the surrounding space on the mountain top is an especially holy area. (Such is the charter of the Temple.)'

13These were the dimensions of the altar, in cubits each of a cubit plus a handsbreadth. The base: one cubit high and one cubit wide; the space by the runnel, all round the edge of the altar, one handsbreadth. 14From the ground level of the base up to the lower plinth, two cubits high and one cubit wide; from the lesser plinth to the greater plinth, four cubits high and one cubit wide. 15The altar hearth: four cubits high, with four horns projecting from the hearth, 16the hearth was four-square: twelve cubits by twelve cubits; 17and the square plinth: fourteen cubits by fourteen cubits; and the ledge all round: half a cubit; and the base: one cubit all round. The steps were on the east side.

18He said to me, 'Son of man, the Lord Yahweh says this, "As regards the altar, this is how things must be done when it has been built for the sacrifice of the burnt offering and for the pouring of blood. 19To the levitical priests — those of the race of Zadok — who approach me to serve me — declares the Lord Yahweh — you must give a young bull as a sacrifice for sin. 20You must take some of its blood and put it on the four horns, on the four corners of the plinth and on the surrounding ledge. In this way you will purify it and make expiation on it. 21Then take the bull of the sacrifice for sin and burn it in that part of the Temple which is cut off from the sanctuary. 22On the second day, you must offer an unblemished he-goat as the sacrifice for sin, and the altar must be purified again as was done with the bull. 23When you have finished the purification, you must offer a young, unblemished bull and an unblemished ram from the flock. 24You must present them before Yahweh, and the priests will sprinkle salt on them and offer them as burnt offerings to Yahweh. 25As a sacrifice for sin, every day for

25 For seven days you shall provide daily a goat for a sin offering; also a bull and a ram from the flock, without blemish, shall be provided. 26 Seven days they shall make atonement for the altar and cleanse it, and so consecrate it. 27 When these days are over, then from the eighth day onward the priests shall offer upon the altar your burnt offerings and your offerings of well-being; and I will accept you, says the Lord GOD.

44 Then he brought me back to the outer gate of the sanctuary, which faces east; and it was shut. 2 The LORD said to me: This gate shall remain shut; it shall not be opened, and no one shall enter by it; for the LORD, the God of Israel, has entered by it; therefore it shall remain shut. 3 Only the prince, because he is a prince, may sit in it to eat food before the LORD; he shall enter by way of the vestibule of the gate, and shall go out by the same way.

4 Then he brought me by way of the north gate to the front of the temple; and I looked, and lo! the glory of the LORD filled the temple of the LORD; and I fell upon my face. 5 The LORD said to me: Mortal, mark well, look closely, and listen attentively to all that I shall tell you concerning all the ordinances of the temple of the LORD and all its laws; and mark well those who may be admitted to[i] the temple and all those who are to be excluded from the sanctuary. 6 Say to the rebellious house,[j] to the house of Israel, Thus says the Lord GOD: O house of Israel, let there be an end to all your abominations 7 in admitting foreigners, uncircumcised in heart and flesh, to be in my sanctuary, profaning my temple when you offer to me my food, the fat and the blood. You[k] have broken my covenant with all your abominations. 8 And you have not kept charge of my sacred offerings; but you have appointed foreigners[l] to act for you in keeping my charge in my sanctuary.

9 Thus says the Lord GOD: No foreigner, uncircumcised in heart and flesh, of all the foreigners who are among the people of Israel, shall enter my sanctuary. 10 But the Levites who went far from me, going astray from me after their idols when Israel went astray, shall bear their punishment. 11 They shall be ministers in my sanctuary, having oversight at the gates of the temple, and serving in the temple; they shall slaughter the burnt offering and the sacrifice for the people, and they shall attend on them and serve them. 12 Because they ministered to them before their idols and made the house of Israel stumble into iniquity, therefore I have sworn concerning them, says the Lord GOD, that they shall bear their punishment. 13 They shall not come near to me, to serve me as priest, nor come near any of my sacred offerings, the things that are most sacred; but they shall bear their shame, and the consequences of the abominations that they have committed. 14 Yet I will appoint them to keep charge of the temple, to do all its chores, all that is to be done in it.

15 But the levitical priests, the descendants of Zadok, who kept the charge of my sanctuary when the people of Israel went astray from me, shall come near to me to minister to me; and they shall attend me to offer me the fat and the blood, says the Lord GOD. 16 It is they who shall enter my sanctuary, it is they who shall approach my table, to minister to me, and they shall keep my charge. 17 When they enter the gates of the inner court, they shall wear linen vestments; they shall have nothing of wool on them, while they minister at the gates of the inner court, and within. 18 They shall have linen turbans on their heads, and linen undergarments on their loins; they shall not bind themselves with anything that causes sweat. 19 When they go out into

purification-offering, as well as a young bull, and a ram without blemish from the flock. 26 For seven days they are to make expiation for the altar, and, having pronounced it ritually clean, they are to consecrate it. 27 At the end of that time, on the eighth day and onwards, the priests will sacrifice on the altar your whole-offerings and your shared-offerings, and I shall accept you. This is the word of the Lord GOD.'

44 The man again brought me round to the outer gate of the sanctuary facing east. It was shut, and 2 he said to me, 'This gate is to be kept closed and is not to be opened. No one may enter by it, for the LORD the God of Israel has entered by it. It must be kept shut. 3 Only the ruling prince himself may sit there to eat the sacrificial meal in the presence of the LORD. He is to come in and go out by the vestibule of the gate.'

4 The man brought me round by the north gate to the front of the temple, and I saw the glory of the LORD filling the LORD's house, and I prostrated myself. 5 He said to me, 'Note carefully, O man, look closely, and listen attentively to all I say to you, to all the rules and the regulations for the LORD's house. Take note of the entrance to the house and all the exits from the sanctuary. 6 Say to Israel: The Lord GOD says: Enough of all those abominations of yours, you Israelites! 7 You admit foreigners, uncircumcised in mind and body, into my sanctuary, so defiling my house, when you present to me the fat and blood which are my food. They have made my covenant void with your abominations. 8 Instead of keeping charge of my holy things yourselves, you have put these men in charge of my sanctuary.

9 'The Lord GOD says: No foreigner, uncircumcised in mind and body, who may be living among the Israelites is to enter my sanctuary. 10 But the Levites, though they deserted me when the Israelites went astray after their idols and had to bear the punishment of their iniquity, 11 may yet be servants in my sanctuary, having charge of the gates of the temple and serving in it. They are to slaughter the whole-offering and the sacrifice for the people and be in attendance to serve them. 12 Because they served the Israelites in the presence of their idols and caused the people to fall into sin, I have sworn with uplifted hand, says the Lord GOD, that they shall bear the punishment of their iniquity. 13 They shall not have access to me, to serve me as priests; nor shall they approach any of my holy or most holy things. They shall bear the shame of the abominable deeds they have committed. 14 I shall put them in charge of all the work which has to be done in the temple.

15 'But the levitical priests of the family of Zadok who remained in charge of my sanctuary when the Israelites went astray from me, they shall approach and serve me. They shall stand before me, to present the fat and the blood, says the Lord GOD. 16 It is they who are to enter my sanctuary and approach my table to serve me and keep my charge.

17 'When they come to the gates of the inner court they must put on linen garments; they must wear no wool when serving me at the gates of the inner court and inside it. 18 They are to wear linen turbans, and have linen drawers on their loins; they must not fasten their clothes with a belt, which might cause sweating. 19 Before going out to the

---

i Cn: Heb the entrance of   j Gk: Heb lacks house   k Gk Syr Vg:
Heb They   l Heb lacks foreigners

44:2 he: prob. rdg; Heb. the LORD.   44:5 He: prob. rdg; Heb.
The LORD. the entrance to: or those who may enter. the exits: or
those to be excluded.   44:7 with: so Gk; Heb. in addition to.

25 Daily for seven days you shall offer a he-goat as a sin offering, and a young bull and a ram from the flock, all unblemished, shall be offered 26 for seven days. Thus atonement shall be made for the altar, and it shall be purified and dedicated. 27 And when these days are over, from the eighth day on, the priests shall offer your holocausts and peace offerings on the altar. Then I will accept you, says the Lord God.

44 Then he brought me back to the outer gate of the sanctuary, facing the east; but it was closed. 2 He said to me: This gate is to remain closed; it is not to be opened for anyone to enter by it; since the Lord, the God of Israel, has entered by it, it shall remain closed. 3 Only the prince may sit down in it to eat his meal in the presence of the Lord. He must enter by way of the vestibule of the gate, and leave by the same way.

4 Then he brought me by way of the north gate to the façade of the temple, and when I looked I saw the glory of the Lord filling the Lord's temple, and I fell prone. 5 Then he said to me: Son of man, pay strict attention, look carefully, and listen intently to all that I will tell you about the statutes and laws of the Lord's temple; be attentive in regard to those who are to be admitted to the temple and all those who are to be excluded from the sanctuary. 6 Say to that rebellious house, the house of Israel: Thus says the Lord God: Enough of all these abominations of yours, O house of Israel! 7 You have admitted foreigners, uncircumcised both in heart and flesh, to my sanctuary to profane it when you offered me food, fat, and blood; thus you have broken my covenant by all your abominations. 8 Instead of caring for the service of my temple, you have appointed such as these to serve me in my sanctuary in your stead. 9 Thus says the Lord God: No foreigners, uncircumcised in heart and in flesh, shall ever enter my sanctuary; none of the foreigners who live among the Israelites.

10 But as for the Levites who departed from me when Israel strayed from me to pursue their idols, they shall bear the consequences of their sin. 11 They shall serve in my sanctuary as gatekeepers and temple servants; they shall slaughter the holocausts and the sacrifices for the people, and they shall stand before the people to minister for them. 12 Because they used to minister for them before their idols, and became an occasion of sin to the house of Israel, therefore I have sworn an oath against them, says the Lord God: they shall bear the consequences of their sin. 13 They shall no longer draw near me to serve as my priests, nor shall they touch any of my sacred things, or the most sacred things. Thus they shall bear their disgrace because of all their abominable deeds. 14 But I will set them to the service of the temple, for all its work and for everything that is to be done in it.

15 As for the levitical priests, however, the Zadokites who cared for my sanctuary when the Israelites strayed from me, they shall draw near me to minister to me, and they shall stand before me to offer me fat and blood, says the Lord God. 16 It is they who shall enter my sanctuary, they who shall approach my table to minister to me, and they who shall carry out my service. 17 Whenever they enter the gates of the inner court, they shall wear linen garments; they shall not put on anything woolen when they minister at the gates of the inner court or within the temple. 18 They shall have linen turbans on their heads and linen drawers on their loins; they shall not gird themselves with anything that causes sweat. 19 When they are to go out to the people in the outer

seven days you must offer a he-goat, a bull and an unblemished ram from the flock. 26 In this way the altar will be expiated and will be purified and inaugurated. 27 At the end of that time, on the eighth day and afterwards, the priest will offer your burnt offerings and your communion sacrifices on the altar, and I shall look favourably on you—declares the Lord Yahweh." '

44 He brought me back to the outer east gate of the sanctuary. It was shut. 2 Yahweh said to me, 'This gate will be kept shut. No one may open it or go through it, since Yahweh, God of Israel, has been through it. And so it must be kept shut. 3 The prince himself, however, may sit there to take his meal in the presence of Yahweh. He must enter and leave through the porch of the gate.'

4 He led me through the north gate to the front of the Temple. And then I looked; I saw the glory of Yahweh filling the Temple of Yahweh; and I fell to the ground. 5 Yahweh said to me, 'Son of man, pay attention, look carefully and listen closely to everything I explain; these are all the arrangements of the Temple of Yahweh and all its laws. Be careful about who is admitted to the Temple and who is excluded from the sanctuary. 6 And say to the rebels of the House of Israel, "The Lord Yahweh says this: You have gone beyond all bounds with all your loathsome practices, House of Israel, 7 by admitting aliens, uncircumcised in heart and body, to frequent my sanctuary and profane my Temple, while offering my food, the fat and the blood, and breaking my covenant with all your loathsome practices. 8 Instead of maintaining the service of my holy things, you have deputed someone else to maintain my service in my sanctuary. 9 The Lord Yahweh says this: No alien, uncircumcised in heart and body, may enter my sanctuary, none of the aliens living among the Israelites.

10 "As regards the Levites who abandoned me when Israel strayed far from me by following its idols, they must bear the weight of their own sin. 11 They must be servants in my sanctuary, responsible for guarding the Temple gates and serving the Temple. They will kill the burnt offerings and the sacrifice for the people, and hold themselves at the service of the people. 12 Since they used to be at their service in front of their idols and were an occasion of guilt for the House of Israel, very well, I stretch out my hand against them—declares the Lord Yahweh—they will bear the weight of their guilt. 13 They may never approach me again to perform the priestly office in my presence, nor touch my holy things and my most holy things; they must bear the disgrace of their loathsome practices. 14 I shall give them the responsibility of serving the Temple; I shall make them responsible for serving it and for everything to be done in it.

15 "As regards the levitical priests, the sons of Zadok, who maintained the service of my sanctuary when the Israelites strayed far from me, they will approach me to serve me; they will stand in my presence to offer me the fat and blood—declares the Lord Yahweh. 16 They will enter my sanctuary and approach my table to serve me; they will maintain my service. 17 Once they enter the gates of the inner court, they must wear linen vestments; they must wear no wool when they serve inside the gates of the inner court and in the Temple. 18 They must wear linen caps on their heads and linen breeches on their loins; they may not wear anything round their waists that makes them sweat. 19 When

the outer court to the people, they shall remove the vestments in which they have been ministering, and lay them in the holy chambers; and they shall put on other garments, so that they may not communicate holiness to the people with their vestments. 20 They shall not shave their heads or let their locks grow long; they shall only trim the hair of their heads. 21 No priest shall drink wine when he enters the inner court. 22 They shall not marry a widow, or a divorced woman, but only a virgin of the stock of the house of Israel, or a widow who is the widow of a priest. 23 They shall teach my people the difference between the holy and the common, and show them how to distinguish between the unclean and the clean. 24 In a controversy they shall act as judges, and they shall decide it according to my judgments. They shall keep my laws and my statutes regarding all my appointed festivals, and they shall keep my sabbaths holy. 25 They shall not defile themselves by going near to a dead person; for father or mother, however, and for son or daughter, and for brother or unmarried sister they may defile themselves. 26 After he has become clean, they shall count seven days for him. 27 On the day that he goes into the holy place, into the inner court, to minister in the holy place, he shall offer his sin offering, says the Lord God.

28 This shall be their inheritance: I am their inheritance; and you shall give them no holding in Israel; I am their holding. 29 They shall eat the grain offering, the sin offering, and the guilt offering; and every devoted thing in Israel shall be theirs. 30 The first of all the first fruits of all kinds, and every offering of all kinds from all your offerings, shall belong to the priests; you shall also give to the priests the first of your dough, in order that a blessing may rest on your house. 31 The priests shall not eat of anything, whether bird or animal, that died of itself or was torn by animals.

45 When you allot the land as an inheritance, you shall set aside for the Lord a portion of the land as a holy district, twenty-five thousand cubits long and twenty[m] thousand cubits wide; it shall be holy throughout its entire extent. 2 Of this, a square plot of five hundred by five hundred cubits shall be for the sanctuary, with fifty cubits for an open space around it. 3 In the holy district you shall measure off a section twenty-five thousand cubits long and ten thousand wide, in which shall be the sanctuary, the most holy place. 4 It shall be a holy portion of the land; it shall be for the priests, who minister in the sanctuary and approach the Lord to minister to him; and it shall be both a place for their houses and a holy place for the sanctuary. 5 Another section, twenty-five thousand cubits long and ten thousand cubits wide, shall be for the Levites who minister at the temple, as their holding for cities to live in.[n]

6 Alongside the portion set apart as the holy district you shall assign as a holding for the city an area five thousand cubits wide, and twenty-five thousand cubits long; it shall belong to the whole house of Israel.

7 And to the prince shall belong the land on both sides of the holy district and the holding of the city, alongside the holy district and the holding of the city, on the west and on the east, corresponding in length to one of the tribal portions, and extending from the western to the eastern boundary 8 of the land. It is to be his property in Israel. And my princes shall no longer oppress my people; but they shall let the house of Israel have the land according to their tribes.

9 Thus says the Lord God: Enough, O princes of Israel! Put away violence and oppression, and do what is just and right. Cease your evictions of my people, says the Lord God.

people in the outer court, they are to remove the clothes they have worn while serving; leaving them in the sacred rooms, they are to put on other clothes, so that they do not by means of their clothing transmit holiness to the people.

20 'They must neither shave their heads nor let their hair grow long; they must keep their hair trimmed. 21 No priest may drink wine when he is to enter the inner court. 22 He may not marry a widow or a divorced woman, but only a virgin of Israelite birth. He may, however, marry the widow of a priest.

23 'They are to teach my people to distinguish the sacred from the profane, and show them the difference between unclean and clean. 24 When disputes arise, let them take their place in court and decide each case according to my laws. At all my appointed seasons they must observe my rules and statutes, and they are to keep my sabbaths holy.

25 'They must not defile themselves by contact with any dead person, except father or mother, son or daughter, brother or unmarried sister. 26 After purification, they are to count off seven days and then they will be clean, 27 and when they re-enter the inner court to serve in the Holy Place, they are to present their purification-offering, says the Lord God.

28 'They are to own no holding in Israel; I am their holding. No possession is to be granted them in Israel; I am their possession. 29 The grain-offering, the purification-offering, and the reparation-offering are to be eaten by them. Everything in Israel devoted to God will be theirs. 30 The first of all the firstfruits and all your contributions of every kind are to belong wholly to the priests. You must give the first lump of your dough to the priests, so that a blessing may rest on your house.

31 'The priests must eat nothing, whether bird or beast, which has died a natural death or been killed by a wild animal.

45 'When you divide the land by lot among the tribes, you are to set apart for the Lord a sacred reserve, twenty-five thousand cubits in length and twenty thousand in width; the whole area is to be sacred. 2 Of this a square plot, five hundred cubits each way, must be devoted to the sanctuary, with fifty cubits of open land round it. 3 From the area set apart, measure off a space twenty-five thousand cubits by ten thousand cubits, within which the sanctuary, the holiest place of all, will stand. 4 This part is sacred and is for the priests who serve in the sanctuary and who come near to serve the Lord. It will include room for their houses and a sacred plot for the sanctuary. 5 An area of twenty-five thousand by ten thousand cubits is to be for the Levites, the temple servants, and on it will stand the places in which they live. 6 You are to allot to the city an area of five thousand by twenty-five thousand cubits alongside the sacred reserve; this will belong to all Israel.

7 'On either side of the sacred reserve and of the city's share the ruler is to have land facing the sacred reserve and the city's share, running westwards and eastwards. It is to run alongside one of the tribal portions, and extend from the western to the eastern borders 8 of the land; it will be his share in Israel. The rulers of Israel will never oppress my people again, but they will assign the land to Israel, tribe by tribe.

9 'The Lord God says: Enough, you rulers of Israel! Have done with lawlessness and robbery; do what is right and just. Give up evicting my people from their land, says the

---

44:26 **and then . . . clean:** *so Syriac; Heb. omits.* 44:28 **no holding:** *so Lat.; Heb. omits* no. 45:1 **twenty thousand:** *so Gk; Heb.* ten thousand. 45:5 **on it . . . live:** *so Gk; Heb.* twenty rooms.

---

[m] Gk: Heb *ten* [n] Gk: Heb *as their holding, twenty chambers*

court, they shall take off the garments in which they ministered and leave them in the chambers of the sanctuary, putting on other garments; thus they will not transmit holiness to the people with their garments.

20 They shall not shave their heads nor let their hair hang loose, but they shall keep their hair carefully trimmed. 21 No priest shall drink wine when he is to enter the inner court. 22 They shall not take for their wives either widows or divorced women, but only virgins of the race of Israel; however, they may marry women who are the widows of priests. 23 They shall teach my people to distinguish between the sacred and the profane, and make known to them the difference between the clean and the unclean. 24 In capital cases they shall stand as judges, judging them according to my decrees. They shall observe my laws and statutes on all my festivals, and keep my sabbaths holy.

25 They shall not make themselves unclean by coming near any dead person, unless it be their father, mother, son, daughter, brother, or maiden sister; for these they may make themselves unclean. 26 After a priest has been cleansed, he must wait an additional seven days, 27 and on the day he enters the inner court to minister in the sanctuary, he shall present his sin offering, says the Lord GOD. 28 They shall have no inheritance, for I am their inheritance; you shall give them no property in Israel, for I am their property. 29 They shall eat the cereal offering, the sin offering, and the guilt offering; whatever is under the ban in Israel shall be theirs. 30 All the choicest first fruits of every kind, and all the best of your offerings of every kind, shall belong to the priests; likewise the best of your dough you shall give to the priests to bring a blessing down upon your house. 31 The priests shall not eat anything, whether flesh or fowl, that has died of itself or has been killed by wild beasts.

45 When you apportion the land into inheritances, you shall set apart a sacred tract of land for the LORD, twenty-five thousand cubits long and twenty thousand wide; its whole area shall be sacred. 2 Of this land a square plot, five hundred by five hundred cubits, surrounded by a free space of fifty cubits, shall be assigned to the sanctuary. 3 Also from this sector measure off a strip, twenty-five thousand cubits long and ten thousand wide, within which shall be the sanctuary, the holy of holies. 4 This shall be the sacred part of the land belonging to the priests, the ministers of the sanctuary, who draw near to minister to the LORD; it shall be a place for their homes and pasture land for their cattle. 5 Also there shall be a strip twenty-five thousand cubits long and ten thousand wide as property for the Levites, the ministers of the temple, that they may have cities to live in. 6 As property of the City you shall designate a strip five thousand cubits wide and twenty-five thousand long, parallel to the sacred tract; this shall belong to the whole house of Israel. 7 The prince shall have a section bordering on both sides of the combined sacred tract and City property, extending westward on the western side and eastward on the eastern side, corresponding in length to one of the tribal portions from the western boundary 8 of the land. This shall be his property in Israel, so that the princes of Israel will no longer oppress my people, but will leave the land to the house of Israel according to their tribes.

9 Thus says the Lord GOD: Enough, you princes of Israel! Put away violence and oppression, and do what is right and just! Stop evicting my people! says the Lord GOD. 10 You

they go out to the people in the outer court, they must remove the vestments in which they have performed the liturgy and leave them in the rooms of the Holy Place, and put on other clothes, so as not to hallow the people with their vestments. 20 They may neither shave their heads nor let their hair grow long, but must cut their hair carefully. 21 No priest may drink wine on the day he enters the inner court. 22 They may not marry widows or divorced women, but only virgins of the race of Israel; they may, however, marry a widow, if she is the widow of a priest. 23 They must teach my people the difference between what is sacred and what is profane and make them understand the difference between what is clean and what is unclean. 24 They must be judges in law-suits; they must judge in the spirit of my judgements; they must follow my laws and ordinances at all my feasts and keep my Sabbaths holy. 25 They may not go near a dead person, in case they become unclean, except in these permissible cases, that is, for father, mother, daughter, son, brother or unmarried sister. 26 After one of them has been purified, seven days must elapse; 27 then, the day he enters the Holy Place in the inner court to minister in the Holy Place, he must offer his sacrifice for sin — declares the Lord Yahweh. 28 They may have no heritage; I myself shall be their heritage. You may give them no patrimony in Israel; I myself shall be their patrimony. 29 Their food must be the oblation, the sacrifice for sin and the sacrifice of reparation. Everything dedicated by vow in Israel shall be for them. 30 The best of all your first-fruits and of all the dues and of everything you offer, must go to the priests; and the best of your dough you must also give to the priests, so that a blessing may rest on your house. 31 Priests must not eat the flesh of anything that has died a natural death or been savaged, be it bird or animal."

45 ' "When you draw lots to divide the country by heritage, you must set a sacred portion of the country aside for Yahweh: twenty-five thousand cubits long and twenty thousand wide. The whole of this land must be sacred, 2 and of this an area five hundred by five hundred cubits must be for the sanctuary, with a boundary fifty cubits wide right round. 3 Out of this area you must also measure a section twenty-five thousand by ten thousand cubits, in which will be the sanctuary, the Holy of Holies. 4 This will be the sacred portion of the country, belonging to the priests who officiate in the sanctuary and approach Yahweh to serve him. It will contain room for their houses and room for the sanctuary. 5 A portion twenty-five thousand by ten thousand cubits will be owned by the Levites serving the Temple, with towns for them to live in. 6 You must give the city possession of an area five thousand by twenty-five thousand cubits, near the land belonging to the sanctuary; this must be for the whole House of Israel.

7 "The prince must have a territory either side of the sacred portion and of the property of the city, adjacent to the sacred portion and the property of the city, stretching westwards from the west and eastwards from the east, its size equal to one of the portions between the west and the east frontiers 8 of the country. This will be his property in Israel. Then my princes will no longer oppress my people; they must leave the rest of the country for the House of Israel, for its tribes.

9 "The Lord Yahweh says this: Enough, princes of Israel! Give up your violence and plundering, do what is upright and just, stop crushing my people with taxation — declares

10 You shall have honest balances, an honest ephah, and an honest bath.*o* 11 The ephah and the bath shall be of the same measure, the bath containing one-tenth of a homer, and the ephah one-tenth of a homer; the homer shall be the standard measure. 12 The shekel shall be twenty gerahs. Twenty shekels, twenty-five shekels, and fifteen shekels shall make a mina for you.

13 This is the offering that you shall make: one-sixth of an ephah from each homer of wheat, and one-sixth of an ephah from each homer of barley, 14 and as the fixed portion of oil,*p* one-tenth of a bath from each cor (the cor,*q* like the homer, contains ten baths); 15 and one sheep from every flock of two hundred, from the pastures of Israel. This is the offering for grain offerings, burnt offerings, and offerings of well-being, to make atonement for them, says the Lord GOD. 16 All the people of the land shall join with the prince in Israel in making this offering. 17 But this shall be the obligation of the prince regarding the burnt offerings, grain offerings, and drink offerings, at the festivals, the new moons, and the sabbaths, all the appointed festivals of the house of Israel: he shall provide the sin offerings, grain offerings, the burnt offerings, and the offerings of well-being, to make atonement for the house of Israel.

18 Thus says the Lord GOD: In the first month, on the first day of the month, you shall take a young bull without blemish, and purify the sanctuary. 19 The priest shall take some of the blood of the sin offering and put it on the doorposts of the temple, the four corners of the ledge of the altar, and the posts of the gate of the inner court. 20 You shall do the same on the seventh day of the month for anyone who has sinned through error or ignorance; so you shall make atonement for the temple.

21 In the first month, on the fourteenth day of the month, you shall celebrate the festival of the passover, and for seven days unleavened bread shall be eaten. 22 On that day the prince shall provide for himself and all the people of the land a young bull for a sin offering. 23 And during the seven days of the festival he shall provide as a burnt offering to the LORD seven young bulls and seven rams without blemish, on each of the seven days; and a male goat daily for a sin offering. 24 He shall provide as a grain offering an ephah for each bull, an ephah for each ram, and a hin of oil to each ephah. 25 In the seventh month, on the fifteenth day of the month and for the seven days of the festival, he shall make the same provision for sin offerings, burnt offerings, and grain offerings, and for the oil.

46 Thus says the Lord GOD: The gate of the inner court that faces east shall remain closed on the six working days; but on the sabbath day it shall be opened and on the day of the new moon it shall be opened. 2 The prince shall enter by the vestibule of the gate from outside, and shall take his stand by the post of the gate. The priests shall offer his burnt offering and his offerings of well-being, and he shall bow down at the threshold of the gate. Then he shall go out, but the gate shall not be closed until evening. 3 The people of the land shall bow down at the entrance of that gate before the LORD on the sabbaths and on the new moons. 4 The burnt offering that the prince offers to the LORD on the sabbath day shall be six lambs without blemish and a ram without blemish; 5 and the grain offering with the ram shall be an ephah, and the grain offering with the lambs shall be as much as he wishes to give, together with a hin of oil to each ephah. 6 On the day of the new moon he shall offer a young bull without blemish, and six lambs and a ram, which shall be without blemish; 7 as a grain offering he

Lord GOD. 10 Your scales must be honest, as must your ephah and your bath. 11 There must be one standard for each, taking each as the tenth of a homer, and the homer must have its fixed standard. 12 Your shekel weight must contain twenty gerahs, and your mina be the sum of twenty and twenty-five and fifteen shekels.

13 'These are the contributions you are to set aside: out of every homer of wheat or of barley, one sixth of an ephah. 14 For oil the rule is one tenth of a bath from every kor, at ten bath to the kor; 15 one sheep in every flock of two hundred is to be reserved by every Israelite clan. For a grain-offering, a whole-offering, and a shared-offering, to make expiation for them, says the Lord GOD, 16 all the people of the land must bring this contribution to the ruler in Israel. 17 He is to be responsible for the whole-offering, the grain-offering, and the drink-offering, at pilgrim-feasts, new moons, sabbaths, and every sacred season observed by Israel. He himself is to provide the purification-offering and the grain-offering, the whole-offering and the shared-offering, needed to make expiation for Israel.

18 The Lord GOD says: On the first day of the first month you are to take a young bull without blemish and purify the sanctuary. 19 The priest must take some of the blood from the purification-offering and put it on the doorposts of the temple, on the four corners of the altar pedestal, and on the gateposts of the inner court. 20 You are to do the same on the seventh day of the month for the man who has sinned through inadvertence or ignorance. So you are to purify the temple.

21 'On the fourteenth day of the first month you are to celebrate the pilgrim-feast of Passover, and for the seven days of the feast you must eat bread made without yeast. 22 On that day the ruler is to provide a bull as a purification-offering for himself and for all the people. 23 During the seven days of the feast he is to offer daily as a whole-offering to the LORD seven bulls and seven rams, all without blemish, and one he-goat daily as a purification-offering. 24 With every bull and ram he is to provide a grain-offering of one ephah, together with a hin of oil for each ephah. 25 'He is to do the same thing also for the pilgrim-feast which falls on the fifteenth day of the seventh month; this also will last seven days, and he must provide the same purification-offering and whole-offering and the same quantity of grain and oil.

46 'The Lord GOD says: The east gate of the inner court must remain closed during the six working days; it is to be opened only on the sabbath and at new moon. 2 When the ruler comes through the porch of the gate from the outside, he is to take his stand by the gatepost, while the priests sacrifice his whole-offering and shared-offerings. At the threshold of the gate he is to bow down in worship and then go out, but the gate is not to be closed until evening. 3 On sabbaths and at new moons the people also must bow down before the LORD at the entrance to that gate.

4 'On the sabbath the whole-offering which the prince brings to the LORD is to be six lambs without blemish and a ram without blemish. 5 The grain-offering is to be an ephah with the ram and whatever he can give with the lambs, together with a hin of oil to every ephah. 6 At the new moon it is to be a young bull without blemish, six lambs and a ram, all without blemish; 7 he is to provide as

---

45:14 **the rule is:** *prob. rdg; Heb.* adds the bath, the oil. **every kor:** *so Gk; Heb.* adds the homer is ten bath. **to the kor:** *so Lat.; Heb.* to the homer. 45:15 **clan:** *so Gk; Heb.* unintelligible. 45:16 **all . . . bring:** *prob. rdg; Heb.* unintelligible.

---

o A Heb measure of volume   *p* Cn: Heb *oil, the bath the oil*
q Vg: Heb *homer*

shall have honest scales, an honest ephah, and an honest liquid measure. 11 The ephah and the liquid measure shall be of the same size: the liquid measure equal to a tenth of a homer, and the ephah equal to a tenth of a homer; by the homer they shall be determined. 12 The shekel shall be twenty gerahs. Twenty shekels, twenty-five shekels, plus fifteen shekels shall be your mina.

13 These are the offerings you shall make: one sixth of an ephah from each homer of wheat, and one sixth of an ephah from each homer of barley. 14 The regulation for oil: for every measure of oil, a tenth of a measure, computed by the kor of ten liquid measures [or a homer, for ten liquid measures make a homer]. 15 One sheep from the flock for every two hundred from the pasturage of Israel, for sacrifice — holocausts and peace offerings and atonement sacrifices, says the Lord GOD. 16 All the people of the land shall be bound to this offering [for the prince in Israel]. 17 It shall be the duty of the prince to provide the holocausts, cereal offerings, and libations on the feasts, new moons, and sabbaths, on all the festivals of the house of Israel. He shall offer the sin offerings, cereal offerings, holocausts, and peace offerings, to make atonement on behalf of the house of Israel.

18 Thus says the Lord GOD: On the first day of the first month you shall use an unblemished young bull as a sacrifice to purify the sanctuary. 19 Then the priest shall take some of the blood from the sin offering and put it on the doorposts of the temple, on the four corners of the ledge of the altar, and on the doorposts of the gates of the inner court. 20 You shall repeat this on the first day of the seventh month for those who have sinned through inadvertence or ignorance; thus you shall make atonement for the temple. 21 On the fourteenth day of the first month you shall observe the feast of the Passover; for seven days unleavened bread is to be eaten. 22 On that day the prince shall offer on his own behalf, and on behalf of all the people of the land, a bull as a sin offering. 23 On each of the seven days of the feast he shall offer as a holocaust to the Lord seven bulls and seven rams without blemish, and as a sin offering he shall offer one male goat each day. 24 As a cereal offering he shall offer one ephah for each bull and one ephah for each ram; and he shall offer one hin of oil for each ephah.

25 On the fifteenth day of the seventh month, the feast day, and for seven days, he shall perform the same rites, making the same sin offerings, the same holocausts, the same cereal offerings and offerings of oil.

46 Thus says the Lord GOD: The gate toward the east of the inner court shall remain closed throughout the six working days, but on the sabbath and on the day of the new moon it shall be open. 2 The prince shall enter from outside by way of the vestibule of the gate and remain standing at the doorpost of the gate; then while the priests offer his holocausts and peace offerings, he shall worship at the threshold of the gate and then leave; the gate shall not be closed until evening. 3 The people of the land shall worship before the LORD at the door of this gate on the sabbaths and new moons. 4 The holocausts which the prince presents to the LORD on the sabbath shall consist of six unblemished lambs and an unblemished ram, 5 together with a cereal offering of one ephah for the ram, whatever he pleases for the lambs, and a hin of oil for each ephah. 6 On the day of the new moon he shall provide an unblemished young bull, also six lambs and a ram without blemish, 7 with a cereal

the Lord Yahweh. 10 Have fair scales, a fair *ephah*, a fair *bat*. 11 Let the *ephah* and *bat* be equal, let the *bat* hold one-tenth of a *homer* and the *ephah* one-tenth of a *homer*. Let the measures be based on the *homer*. 12 The shekel must be twenty *gerah*. Twenty shekels, twenty-five shekels and fifteen shekels must make one *mina*.

13 "This is the offering that you must levy: the sixth of an *ephah* for every *homer* of wheat, and the sixth of an *ephah* for every *homer* of barley. 14 The dues on oil: one *bat* of oil out of every ten *bat* or out of every *kor* (which is equal to ten *bat* or one *homer*, since ten *bat* equal one *homer*). 15 You must levy one sheep on every flock of two hundred from the pastures of Israel for the oblation, the burnt offerings and the communion sacrifice. This must form your expiation — declares the Lord Yahweh. 16 Let all the people of the country be subject to this due for the prince of Israel. 17 The prince must make himself responsible for providing the burnt offerings, the oblation and the libations for feasts, New Moons, Sabbaths and all the solemn festivals of the House of Israel. He must provide the sacrifice for sin, the oblation, the burnt offerings and the communion sacrifices to make expiation for the House of Israel.

18 "The Lord Yahweh says this: On the first day of the first month, you must take a young bull without blemish, to purify the sanctuary. 19 The priest must take blood from the sacrifice for sin and put it on the doorposts of the Temple, on the four corners of the altar plinth and on the doorposts of the gates of the inner court. 20 You must do the same on the seventh of the month, on behalf of anyone who has sinned through inadvertence or ignorance. This is how you must make expiation for the Temple. 21 On the fourteenth day of the first month, you must celebrate the feast of the Passover. For seven days everyone must eat unleavened loaves. 22 On that day, the prince must offer a bull as a sacrifice for sin, for himself and all the people of the country. 23 For the seven days of the feast, he must offer Yahweh burnt offerings of seven bulls and seven rams without blemish, daily for a week, and one he-goat daily as a sacrifice for sin, 24 and as an oblation, one *ephah* for each bull and one *ephah* for each ram, and a *hin* of oil for every *ephah*.

25 "For the feast that falls on the fifteenth day of the seventh month, he must do the same for seven days, offering the sacrifice for sin, the burnt offerings, the oblation and the oil." '

46 ' "The Lord Yahweh says this: The east gate of the inner court must be kept shut for the six working days. On the Sabbath day, however, it must be opened, as also on the day of the New Moon; 2 and the prince must go in through the porch of the outer gate and take his position by the doorposts of the gate. The priests must then offer his burnt offerings and his communion sacrifice. He must prostrate himself on the threshold of the gate and go out, and the gate must not be shut again until the evening. 3 The people of the country must prostrate themselves in the presence of Yahweh at the entrance to the gate on Sabbaths and days of the New Moon. 4 The burnt offering offered to Yahweh by the prince on the Sabbath day must consist of six unblemished lambs and one unblemished ram, 5 with an oblation of one *ephah* for the ram, and such oblation as he pleases for the lambs, and a *hin* of oil for every *ephah*. 6 On the day of the New Moon it must consist of an unblemished young bull, six unblemished lambs and one unblemished ram,

NEW REVISED STANDARD VERSION	REVISED ENGLISH BIBLE

shall provide an ephah with the bull and an ephah with the ram, and with the lambs as much as he wishes, together with a hin of oil to each ephah. 8 When the prince enters, he shall come in by the vestibule of the gate, and he shall go out by the same way.

9 When the people of the land come before the LORD at the appointed festivals, whoever enters by the north gate to worship shall go out by the south gate; and whoever enters by the south gate shall go out by the north gate: they shall not return by way of the gate by which they entered, but shall go out straight ahead. 10 When they come in, the prince shall come in with them; and when they go out, he shall go out.

11 At the festivals and the appointed seasons the grain offering with a young bull shall be an ephah, and with a ram an ephah, and with the lambs as much as one wishes to give, together with a hin of oil to an ephah. 12 When the prince provides a freewill offering, either a burnt offering or offerings of well-being as a freewill offering to the LORD, the gate facing east shall be opened for him; and he shall offer his burnt offering or his offerings of well-being as he does on the sabbath day. Then he shall go out, and after he has gone out the gate shall be closed.

13 He shall provide a lamb, a yearling, without blemish, for a burnt offering to the LORD daily; morning by morning he shall provide it. 14 And he shall provide a grain offering with it morning by morning regularly, one-sixth of an ephah, and one-third of a hin of oil to moisten the choice flour, as a grain offering to the LORD; this is the ordinance for all time. 15 Thus the lamb and the grain offering and the oil shall be provided, morning by morning, as a regular burnt offering.

16 Thus says the Lord GOD: If the prince makes a gift to any of his sons out of his inheritance,ʳ it shall belong to his sons, it is their holding by inheritance. 17 But if he makes a gift out of his inheritance to one of his servants, it shall be his to the year of liberty; then it shall revert to the prince; only his sons may keep a gift from his inheritance. 18 The prince shall not take any of the inheritance of the people, thrusting them out of their holding; he shall give his sons their inheritance out of his own holding, so that none of my people shall be dispossessed of their holding.

19 Then he brought me through the entrance, which was at the side of the gate, to the north row of the holy chambers for the priests; and there I saw a place at the extreme western end of them. 20 He said to me, "This is the place where the priests shall boil the guilt offering and the sin offering, and where they shall bake the grain offering, in order not to bring them out into the outer court and so communicate holiness to the people."

21 Then he brought me out to the outer court, and led me past the four corners of the court; and in each corner of the court there was a court — 22 in the four corners of the court were smallˢ courts, forty cubits long and thirty wide; the four were of the same size. 23 On the inside, around each of the four courtsᵗ was a row of masonry, with hearths made at the bottom of the rows all around. 24 Then he said to me, "These are the kitchens where those who serve at the temple shall boil the sacrifices of the people."

47 Then he brought me back to the entrance of the temple; there, water was flowing from below the threshold of the temple toward the east (for the temple faced east); and the water was flowing down from below the south end of the threshold of the temple, south of the altar. 2 Then he brought me out by way of the north gate, and led me around on the outside to the outer gate that faces toward the east;ᵘ and the water was coming out on the south side.

the grain-offering one ephah with the bull and one ephah with the ram, with the lambs whatever he can afford, adding a hin of oil for every ephah.

8 'Whenever the ruler comes in, he is to enter through the porch of the gate and go out by the same way. 9 When the people come to worship before the LORD on festal days, anyone who enters by the north gate to worship must leave by the south gate, and anyone who enters by the south gate must leave by the north gate. He is not to turn back and go out through the gate by which he came in but to continue in the same direction. 10 The ruler will then be among them, going in when they go in and coming out when they come out.

11 'At pilgrim-feasts and on festal days the grain-offering is to be an ephah with a bull, an ephah with a ram, and as much as he can afford with a lamb, together with a hin of oil for every ephah.

12 'When the ruler provides a whole-offering or shared-offerings as a voluntary sacrifice to the LORD, the east gate is to be opened for him, and he will make his whole-offering and his shared-offerings as he does on the sabbath. When he goes out, the gate must be closed behind him.

13 'You must provide a yearling lamb without blemish daily as a whole-offering to the LORD; you are to provide it every morning. 14 With it every morning you must provide as a grain-offering one sixth of an ephah with a third of a hin of oil to moisten the flour. The LORD's grain-offering is an observance prescribed for all time. 15 Every morning, as a regular whole-offering, a lamb is to be offered with the grain-offering and the oil.

16 'The Lord GOD says: If the ruler makes a gift out of his property to any of his sons, it will belong to his sons, since it is part of the family property. 17 But when he makes such a gift to one of his slaves, it will belong to the slave only until the year of manumission, when it will revert to the ruler; it is the property of his sons and will belong to them.

18 'The ruler must not oppress the people by taking any part of their holdings of land; he is to endow his sons from his own property, so that my people may not be deprived of their holdings.'

19 Then the man brought me through the entrance by the side of the gate to the rooms which face north, the rooms set apart for the priests, and, pointing to a place on their west side, 20 he said to me, 'This is the place where the priests boil the reparation-offering and the purification-offering and bake the grain-offering; they may not take it into the outer court, for fear of transmitting holiness to the people.'

21 The man then brought me out into the outer court and led me across to the four corners of the court, at each of which there was a further court. 22 These four courts were vaulted and were the same size, forty cubits long by thirty cubits wide. 23 Round each of the four was a course of stonework, with fire-places constructed close up against the stones. 24 'These are the kitchens', he said, 'where the attendants boil the people's sacrifices.'

47 The man brought me back to the entrance of the temple, and I saw a spring of water issuing towards the east from under the threshold of the temple; for the temple faced east. The water was running down along the south side, to the right of the altar. 2 He took me out through the north gate and led me round by an outside path to the east gate of the court, and I saw water was trickling from the south side. 3 With a line in his hand the man went out

---

ʳ Gk: Heb it is his inheritance   ˢ Gk Syr Vg: Meaning of Heb uncertain   ᵗ Heb the four of them   ᵘ Meaning of Heb uncertain

47:2 the court: so Gk; Heb. unintelligible.

offering of one ephah for the bull and one for the ram, for the lambs as much as he has at hand, and for each ephah a hin of oil.

8 The prince shall always enter and depart by the vestibule of the gate. 9 When the people of the land enter the presence of the LORD to worship on the festivals, if they enter by the north gate they shall leave by the south gate, and if they enter by the south gate they shall leave by the north gate; no one shall return by the gate through which he has entered, but he shall leave by the opposite gate. 10 The prince shall be in their midst when they enter, and he shall also leave with them. 11 On the feasts and festivals the cereal offering shall be an ephah for a bull, an ephah for a ram, but for the lambs as much as one pleases, and a hin of oil with each ephah. 12 When the prince makes a freewill offering to the LORD, whether holocausts or peace offerings, the eastern gate shall be opened for him, and he shall offer his holocausts or his peace offerings as on the sabbath; then he shall leave, and the gate shall be closed after his departure. 13 He shall offer as a daily holocaust to the LORD an unblemished yearling lamb; this he shall offer every morning. 14 With it every morning he shall provide as a cereal offering one sixth of an ephah, with a third of a hin of oil to moisten the fine flour. This cereal offering to the LORD is mandatory with the established holocaust. 15 The lamb, the cereal offering, and the oil are to be offered every morning as an established holocaust.

16 Thus says the Lord GOD: If the prince makes a gift of part of his inheritance to any of his sons, it shall belong to his sons; that property is theirs by inheritance. 17 But if he makes a gift of part of his inheritance to one of his servants, it shall belong to the latter only until the year of release, when it shall revert to the prince. Only the inheritance given to his sons is permanent. 18 The prince shall not seize any part of the inheritance of the people by evicting them from their property. He shall provide an inheritance for his sons from his own property, so that none of my people will be driven from their property.

19 Then he brought me by the entrance which is on the side of the gate to the chambers [of the sanctuary, reserved to the priests] which face the north. There, at their west end, I saw a place, 20 concerning which he said to me, "Here the priests cook the guilt offerings and the sin offerings, and bake the cereal offerings, so that they do not have to take them into the outer court at the risk of transmitting holiness to the people." 21 Then he led me into the outer court and had me pass around the four corners of the court, and I saw that in each corner there was another court: 22 in the four corners of the court, minor courts, forty cubits long and thirty wide, all four of them the same size. 23 A wall of stones surrounded each of the four, and hearths were built beneath the stones all the way around. 24 He said to me, "These are the kitchens where the temple ministers cook the sacrifices of the people."

47 Then he brought me back to the entrance of the temple, and I saw water flowing out from beneath the threshold of the temple toward the east, for the façade of the temple was toward the east; the water flowed down from the southern side of the temple, south of the altar. 2 He led me outside by the north gate, and around to the outer gate facing the east, where I saw water trickling from the southern side. 3 Then when he had walked off to the east

7 when he must make an oblation of one *ephah* for the bull and one *ephah* for the ram, and what he pleases for the lambs, and a *hin* of oil for every *ephah*.

8 "When the prince goes in, he must enter by the porch of the gate, and he must leave by the same way. 9 When the people of the country come into the presence of Yahweh at the solemn festivals, those who have come in by the north gate to prostrate themselves must go out by the south gate, and those who have come in by the south gate must go out by the north gate; no one must turn back to leave through the gate by which he entered but must go out on the opposite side. 10 The prince will be with them, coming in like them and going out like them.

11 "On feast days and solemn festivals the oblation must be one *ephah* for every bull, one *ephah* for every ram, what he pleases for the lambs, and a *hin* of oil for every *ephah*. 12 When the prince offers Yahweh voluntary burnt offerings or a voluntary communion sacrifice, the east gate must be opened for him, and he must offer his burnt offerings and his communion sacrifice as he does on the Sabbath day; when he has gone out, the gate must be shut after him. 13 Every day he must offer an unblemished lamb one year old as a burnt offering to Yahweh; he must offer this every morning. 14 Every morning in addition he must offer an oblation of one-sixth of an *ephah* and one-third of a *hin* of oil, for mixing with the flour. This is the oblation to Yahweh, a perpetual decree, fixed for ever. 15 The lamb, the oblation and the oil must be offered morning after morning for ever.

16 "Lord Yahweh says this: If the prince presents part of his hereditary portion to one of his sons, the gift must pass into the ownership of his sons and become their hereditary property. 17 If, however, he presents part of his hereditary portion to one of his slaves, it will belong to the man only until the year of liberation and then must revert to the prince. Only his sons may retain his hereditary portion. 18 The prince may not take any part of the people's hereditary portion, thus robbing them of what is theirs; he must provide the patrimony of his sons out of his own property, so that no member of my people is robbed of what is his!" '

19 He took me through the entrance at the side of the north gate that leads to the rooms of the Holy Place set apart for the priests. And there before us, to the west, was a space at the end. 20 He said to me, 'This is where the priests must boil the slaughtered animals for the sacrifice for sin and the sacrifice of reparation, and where they must bake the oblation, without having to carry them into the outer court and so run the risk of hallowing the people.' 21 He then took me into the outer court and led me to each of its four corners; in each corner of the outer court was a compound; 22 in other words, the four corners of the court contained four small compounds, forty cubits by thirty, all four being the same size. 23 All four were enclosed by a wall, with hearths all round the bottom of the wall. 24 He said, 'These are the kitchens where the Temple servants must boil the sacrifices offered by the people.'

47 He brought me back to the entrance of the Temple, where a stream flowed eastwards from under the Temple threshold, for the Temple faced east. The water flowed from under the right side of the Temple, south of the altar. 2 He took me out by the north gate and led me right round outside as far as the outer east gate where the water flowed out on the right-hand side. 3 The man went off to the

3 Going on eastward with a cord in his hand, the man measured one thousand cubits, and then led me through the water; and it was ankle-deep. 4 Again he measured one thousand, and led me through the water; and it was knee-deep. Again he measured one thousand, and led me through the water; and it was up to the waist. 5 Again he measured one thousand, and it was a river that I could not cross, for the water had risen; it was deep enough to swim in, a river that could not be crossed. 6 He said to me, "Mortal, have you seen this?"

Then he led me back along the bank of the river. 7 As I came back, I saw on the bank of the river a great many trees on the one side and on the other. 8 He said to me, "This water flows toward the eastern region and goes down into the Arabah; and when it enters the sea, the sea of stagnant waters, the water will become fresh. 9 Wherever the river goes,^{v} every living creature that swarms will live, and there will be very many fish, once these waters reach there. It will become fresh; and everything will live where the river goes. 10 People will stand fishing beside the sea^w from En-gedi to En-eglaim; it will be a place for the spreading of nets; its fish will be of a great many kinds, like the fish of the Great Sea. 11 But its swamps and marshes will not become fresh; they are to be left for salt. 12 On the banks, on both sides of the river, there will grow all kinds of trees for food. Their leaves will not wither nor their fruit fail, but they will bear fresh fruit every month, because the water for them flows from the sanctuary. Their fruit will be for food, and their leaves for healing."

13 Thus says the Lord GOD: These are the boundaries by which you shall divide the land for inheritance among the twelve tribes of Israel. Joseph shall have two portions. 14 You shall divide it equally; I swore to give it to your ancestors, and this land shall fall to you as your inheritance.

15 This shall be the boundary of the land: On the north side, from the Great Sea by way of Hethlon to Lebo-hamath, and on to Zedad,^{x} 16 Berothah, Sibraim (which lies between the border of Damascus and the border of Hamath), as far as Hazer-hatticon, which is on the border of Hauran. 17 So the boundary shall run from the sea to Hazar-enon, which is north of the border of Damascus, with the border of Hamath to the north.^{y} This shall be the north side.

18 On the east side, between Hauran and Damascus; along the Jordan between Gilead and the land of Israel; to the eastern sea and as far as Tamar.^{z} This shall be the east side.

19 On the south side, it shall run from Tamar as far as the waters of Meribath-kadesh, from there along the Wadi of Egypt^a to the Great Sea. This shall be the south side.

20 On the west side, the Great Sea shall be the boundary to a point opposite Lebo-hamath. This shall be the west side.

21 So you shall divide this land among you according to the tribes of Israel. 22 You shall allot it as an inheritance for yourselves and for the aliens who reside among you and have begotten children among you. They shall be to you as citizens of Israel; with you they shall be allotted an inheritance among the tribes of Israel. 23 In whatever tribe aliens reside, there you shall assign them their inheritance, says the Lord GOD.

eastwards, and he measured off a thousand cubits and made me walk through the water; it came up to my ankles. 4 Again he measured a thousand cubits and made me walk through the water; it came up to my knees. He measured another thousand and made me walk through the water; it was up to my waist. 5 He measured another thousand, and it was a torrent I could not cross; the water had risen and was deep enough to swim in, a torrent impossible to cross. 6 'Take note of this, O man,' he said, and led me back to the bank. 7 When I got to the bank I saw a great number of trees on each side. 8 He said to me, 'This water flows out to the region lying east, and down to the Arabah; it will run into the sea whose waters are noxious, and they will be made fresh. 9 When any one of the living creatures that swarm upon the earth comes where the torrent flows, it will draw life from it. Fish will be plentiful, for wherever these waters come the sea will be made fresh, and where the torrent flows everything will live. 10 From En-gedi as far as En-eglaim fishermen will stand on its shores and spread their nets. All kinds of fish will be there in shoals, like the fish of the Great Sea. 11 Its swamps and pools will not have their waters made fresh; they will be left to serve as salt-pans. 12 Beside the torrent on either bank fruitful trees of every kind will grow. Their leaves will not wither, nor will their fruit fail; they will bear fruit early every month, for the water then flows from the sanctuary; their fruit is for food and their leaves for healing.

13 'THE Lord GOD says: Here are the boundaries within which the twelve tribes of Israel will enter into possession of the land, Joseph receiving two portions. 14 The land which I swore with hand uplifted to give to your forefathers you are to divide with each other; it must be assigned to you by lot as your holding. 15 This is the frontier: on its northern side, from the Great Sea through Hethlon, Lebo-hamath, 16 Zedad, Berothah, and Sibraim, located between the frontiers of Damascus and Hamath, to Hazar-enan, near the frontier of Hauran. 17 The frontier will extend from the sea to Hazar-enan on the frontier of Damascus and northwards; this is its northern side. 18 The eastern side runs alongside the territories of Hauran, Damascus, and Gilead, and alongside the territory of Israel; Jordan forms the boundary to the eastern sea, to Tamar. This is the eastern boundary. 19 The southern side runs from Tamar to the waters of Meribah-by-Kadesh; the region assigned to you reaches the Great Sea. This is the southern side towards the Negeb. 20 The western side is the Great Sea, which forms a boundary as far as a point opposite Lebo-hamath. This is the western side.

21 'You are to distribute this land among the tribes of Israel 22 and assign it by lot as a share for yourselves and for any aliens who are living in your midst and have children among you. They are to be treated like native-born Israelites and receive with you a share by lot among the tribes of Israel. 23 You are to give the alien his share in whatever tribe he is resident. This is the word of the Lord GOD.

---

^{v} Gk Syr Vg Tg: Heb *the two rivers go* ^{w} Heb *it* ^{x} Gk: Heb *Lebo-zedad*, ^{16}*Hamath* ^{y} Meaning of Heb uncertain ^{z} Compare Syr: Heb *you shall measure* ^{a} Heb lacks *of Egypt*

47:9 **torrent**: *so* Gk; Heb. two torrents.   47:15–16 **Lebo-hamath, Zedad**: *prob. rdg, cp.* Gk; Heb. Lebo, Zedad, Hamath.
47:16 **Hazar-enan**: *prob. rdg, cp.* 48:1; Heb. Hazer-hattikon.
47:17 **northwards**: *so* Gk; Heb. adds northwards and the frontier of Hamath.

with a measuring cord in his hand, he measured off a thousand cubits and had me wade through the water, which was ankle-deep. 4 He measured off another thousand and once more had me wade through the water, which was now knee-deep. Again he measured off a thousand and had me wade; the water was up to my waist. 5 Once more he measured off a thousand, but there was now a river through which I could not wade; for the water had risen so high it had become a river that could not be crossed except by swimming. 6 He asked me, "Have you seen this, son of man?" Then he brought me to the bank of the river, where he had me sit. 7 Along the bank of the river I saw very many trees on both sides. 8 He said to me, "This water flows into the eastern district down upon the Arabah, and empties into the sea, the salt waters, which it makes fresh. 9 Wherever the river flows, every sort of living creature that can multiply shall live, and there shall be abundant fish, for wherever this water comes the sea shall be made fresh. 10 Fishermen shall be standing along it from En-gedi to En-eglaim, spreading their nets there. Its kinds of fish shall be like those of the Great Sea, very numerous. 11 Only its marshes and swamps shall not be made fresh; they shall be left for salt. 12 Along both banks of the river, fruit trees of every kind shall grow; their leaves shall not fade, nor their fruit fail. Every month they shall bear fresh fruit, for they shall be watered by the flow from the sanctuary. Their fruit shall serve for food, and their leaves for medicine."

13 Thus says the Lord God: These are the boundaries within which you shall apportion the land among the twelve tribes of Israel [Joseph having two portions]. 14 All of you shall have a like portion in this land which I swore to give to your fathers, that it might fall to you as your inheritance. 15 This is the boundary of the land on the north side: from the Great Sea in the direction of Hethlon, past Labo of Hamath, to Zedad, 16 Berothah, and Sibraim, along the frontiers of Hamath and Damascus, to Hazar-enon which is on the border of the Hauran. 17 Thus the border shall extend from the sea to Hazar-enon, with the frontier of Hamath and Damascus to the north. This is the northern boundary. 18 The eastern boundary: between the Hauran — toward Damascus — and Gilead on the one side, and the land of Israel on the other side, the Jordan shall form the boundary down to the eastern sea as far as Tamar. This is the eastern boundary. 19 The southern boundary: from Tamar to the waters of Meribath-kadesh, thence to the Wadi of Egypt, and on to the Great Sea. This is the southern boundary. 20 The western boundary: the Great Sea forms the boundary up to a point parallel to Labo of Hamath. This is the western boundary.

21 You shall distribute this land among yourselves according to the tribes of Israel. 22 You shall allot it as inheritances for yourselves and for the aliens resident in your midst who have bred children among you. The latter shall be to you like native Israelites; along with you they shall receive inheritances among the tribes of Israel. 23 In whatever tribe the alien may be resident, there you shall assign him his inheritance, says the Lord God.

east holding his measuring line and measured off a thousand cubits; he then made me wade across the stream; the water reached my ankles. 4 He measured off another thousand and made me wade across the stream again; the water reached my knees. He measured off another thousand and made me wade across the stream again; the water reached my waist. 5 He measured off another thousand; it was now a river which I could not cross; the stream had swollen and was now deep water, a river impossible to cross. 6 He then said, 'Do you see, son of man?' He then took me and brought me back to the bank on the river. 7 Now, when I reached it, I saw an enormous number of trees on each bank of the river. 8 He said, 'This water flows east down to the Arabah and to the sea; and flowing into the sea it makes its waters wholesome. 9 Wherever the river flows, all living creatures teeming in it will live. Fish will be very plentiful, for wherever the water goes it brings health, and life teems wherever the river flows. 10 There will be fishermen on its banks. Fishing nets will be spread from En-Gedi to En-Eglaim. The species of fish will be the same as the fish of the Great Sea. 11 The marshes and lagoons, however, will not become wholesome, but will remain salt. 12 Along the river, on either bank, will grow every kind of fruit tree with leaves that never wither and fruit that never fails; they will bear new fruit every month, because this water comes from the sanctuary. And their fruit will be good to eat and the leaves medicinal.'

13 'The Lord Yahweh says this, "This will be the territory which you must distribute among the twelve tribes of Israel, with two portions for Joseph. 14 You will each have a fair share of it, since I swore to your fathers that I would give it to them, and this country now falls to you as your heritage. 15 These will be the frontiers of the country. On the north, from the Great Sea, the road from Hethlon to the Pass of Hamath, Zedad, 16 Berothah, Sibraim lying between the territories of Damascus and Hamath, to Hazer-ha-Tikon on the borders of Hauran; 17 the frontier will extend from the sea to Hazer-Enon, with the territory of Damascus and the territory of Hamath to the north; that will be the northern frontier. 18 On the east, the Jordan will serve as frontier between Hauran and Damascus, between Gilead and Israel, down to the Eastern Sea as far as Tamar; that will be the eastern frontier. 19 On the south, from Tamar southward to the Waters of Meribah in Kadesh, to the Wadi and the Great Sea; that will be the southern frontier. 20 And to the west, the Great Sea will serve as frontier up to the point opposite the Pass of Hamath; that will be the western frontier. 21 You must distribute this country among yourselves, among the tribes of Israel. 22 You must distribute it as a heritage for yourselves and the aliens settled among you who have fathered children among you, since you must treat them as citizens of Israel. They must draw lots for their heritage with you, among the tribes of Israel. 23 You will give the alien his heritage in the tribe where he has settled — declares the Lord Yahweh."'

NEW REVISED STANDARD VERSION

48 These are the names of the tribes: Beginning at the northern border, on the Hethlon road,[b] from Lebo-hamath, as far as Hazar-enon (which is on the border of Damascus, with Hamath to the north), and[c] extending from the east side to the west,[d] Dan, one portion. 2 Adjoining the territory of Dan, from the east side to the west, Asher, one portion. 3 Adjoining the territory of Asher, from the east side to the west, Naphtali, one portion. 4 Adjoining the territory of Naphtali, from the east side to the west, Manasseh, one portion. 5 Adjoining the territory of Manasseh, from the east side to the west, Ephraim, one portion. 6 Adjoining the territory of Ephraim, from the east side to the west, Reuben, one portion. 7 Adjoining the territory of Reuben, from the east side to the west, Judah, one portion.

8 Adjoining the territory of Judah, from the east side to the west, shall be the portion that you shall set apart, twenty-five thousand cubits in width, and in length equal to one of the tribal portions, from the east side to the west, with the sanctuary in the middle of it. 9 The portion that you shall set apart for the LORD shall be twenty-five thousand cubits in length, and twenty[e] thousand in width. 10 These shall be the allotments of the holy portion: the priests shall have an allotment measuring twenty-five thousand cubits on the northern side, ten thousand cubits in width on the western side, ten thousand in width on the eastern side, and twenty-five thousand in length on the southern side, with the sanctuary of the LORD in the middle of it. 11 This shall be for the consecrated priests, the descendants[f] of Zadok, who kept my charge, who did not go astray when the people of Israel went astray, as the Levites did. 12 It shall belong to them as a special portion from the holy portion of the land, a most holy place, adjoining the territory of the Levites. 13 Alongside the territory of the priests, the Levites shall have an allotment twenty-five thousand cubits in length and ten thousand in width. The whole length shall be twenty-five thousand cubits and the width twenty[g] thousand. 14 They shall not sell or exchange any of it; they shall not transfer this choice portion of the land, for it is holy to the LORD.

15 The remainder, five thousand cubits in width and twenty-five thousand in length, shall be for ordinary use for the city, for dwellings and for open country. In the middle of it shall be the city; 16 and these shall be its dimensions: the north side four thousand five hundred cubits, the south side four thousand five hundred, the east side four thousand five hundred, and the west side four thousand five hundred. 17 The city shall have open land: on the north two hundred fifty cubits, on the south two hundred fifty, on the east two hundred fifty, on the west two hundred fifty. 18 The remainder of the length alongside the holy portion shall be ten thousand cubits to the east, and ten thousand to the west, and it shall be alongside the holy portion. Its produce shall be food for the workers of the city. 19 The workers of the city, from all the tribes of Israel, shall cultivate it. 20 The whole portion that you shall set apart shall be twenty-five thousand cubits square, that is, the holy portion together with the property of the city.

REVISED ENGLISH BIBLE

48 'These are the names of the tribes: In the extreme north, in the direction of Hethlon, to Lebo-hamath and Hazar-enan, with Damascus on the northern frontier in the direction of Hamath, and so from the eastern boundary to the western, will be Dan: one portion.

2 'Bordering on Dan, from the eastern boundary to the western, will be Asher: one portion.

3 'Bordering on Asher, from the eastern boundary to the western, will be Naphtali: one portion.

4 'Bordering on Naphtali, from the eastern boundary to the western, will be Manasseh: one portion.

5 'Bordering on Manasseh, from the eastern boundary to the western, will be Ephraim: one portion.

6 'Bordering on Ephraim, from the eastern boundary to the western, will be Reuben: one portion.

7 'Bordering on Reuben, from the eastern boundary to the western, will be Judah: one portion.

8 'Bordering on Judah, from the eastern boundary to the western, will be the sacred reserve which you must set apart. Its breadth will be twenty-five thousand cubits and its length the same as that of the tribal portions, from the eastern boundary to the western, and the sanctuary is to be in the centre of it.

9 'The reserve which you must set apart for the LORD is to measure twenty-five thousand cubits by twenty thousand. 10 The reserve is to be apportioned thus: the priests will have an area measuring twenty-five thousand cubits on the north side, ten thousand on the west, ten thousand on the east, and twenty-five thousand in length on the south side; the sanctuary of the LORD is to be in the centre of it. 11 It is to be for the consecrated priests of the family of Zadok, who kept my charge and did not follow the Israelites when they went astray, as the Levites did. 12 The area set apart for the priests from the reserved territory will be most sacred, adjoining the territory of the Levites.

13 'The Levites are to have a portion running parallel to the border of the priests. It is to be twenty-five thousand cubits long by ten thousand wide; altogether, the length is to be twenty-five thousand cubits and the breadth ten thousand.

14 'They must neither sell nor exchange any part of it; it is the best of the land and must not be alienated, for it is holy to the LORD.

15 'The remaining strip, five thousand cubits in width by twenty-five thousand, is the city's secular land for dwellings and common land. The city will be in the middle, 16 and these are to be its dimensions: on the northern side four thousand five hundred cubits, on the southern side four thousand five hundred cubits, on the eastern side four thousand five hundred cubits, on the western side four thousand five hundred cubits. 17 The common land belonging to the city is to be two hundred and fifty cubits to the north, two hundred and fifty to the south, two hundred and fifty to the east, and two hundred and fifty to the west. 18 What is left parallel to the reserve, ten thousand cubits to the east and ten thousand to the west, will provide food for those who work in the city. 19 Those who work in the city are to cultivate it; they may be drawn from any of the tribes of Israel. 20 You are to set apart as sacred the whole reserve, twenty-five thousand cubits square, as far as the holding of the city.

---

[b] Compare 47.15: Heb *by the side of the way*   [c] Cn: Heb *and they shall be his*   [d] Gk Compare verses 2-8: Heb *the east side the west*   [e] Compare 45.1: Heb *ten*   [f] One Ms Gk: Heb *of the descendants*   [g] Gk: Heb *ten*

48:1 **from . . . western:** *so Gk; Heb.* the eastern corner is the sea.   48:9 **twenty thousand:** *prob. rdg; Heb.* ten thousand.   48:18 **to the west:** *prob. rdg; Heb.* adds and it will be parallel to the sacred reserve.

48 This is the list of the tribes. Dan: at the northern extremity, adjoining Hamath, all along from the approaches to Hethlon through Labo of Hamath to Hazarenon, on the northerly border with Damascus, with his possession reaching from the eastern to the western boundary. 2 Asher: on the frontier of Dan, from the eastern to the western boundary. 3 Naphtali: on the frontier of Asher, from the eastern to the western boundary. 4 Manasseh: on the frontier of Naphtali, from the eastern to the western boundary. 5 Ephraim: on the frontier of Manasseh, from the eastern to the western boundary. 6 Reuben: on the frontier of Ephraim, from the eastern to the western boundary. 7 Judah: on the frontier of Reuben, from the eastern to the western boundary.

8 On the frontier of Judah, from the eastern to the western boundary there shall be the tract which you shall set apart, twenty-five thousand cubits from north to south, and as wide as one of the tribal portions from the eastern to the western boundary. In the center of the tract shall be the sanctuary. 9 The tract that you set aside for the LORD shall be twenty-five thousand cubits across by twenty thousand north and south. 10 In this sacred tract the priests shall have twenty-five thousand cubits on the north, ten thousand on the west, ten thousand on the east, and twenty-five thousand on the south; and the sanctuary of the LORD shall be in its center. 11 The consecrated priests, the Zadokites, who fulfilled my service and did not stray along with the Israelites as the Levites did, 12 shall have within this tract of land their own most sacred domain, next to the territory of the Levites. 13 The Levites shall have a territory corresponding to that of the priests, twenty-five thousand cubits by ten thousand. The whole tract shall be twenty-five thousand cubits across and twenty thousand north and south. 14 They may not sell or exchange or alienate this, the best part of the land, for it is sacred to the LORD. 15 The remaining five thousand cubits along the twenty-five-thousand-cubit line are profane land, assigned to the City for dwellings and pasture; the City shall be at their center. 16 These are the dimensions of the City: the north side, forty-five hundred cubits; the south side, forty-five hundred cubits; the east side, forty-five hundred cubits; and the west side, forty-five hundred cubits. 17 The pasture lands of the City shall extend north two hundred and fifty cubits, south two hundred and fifty cubits, east two hundred and fifty cubits, and west two hundred and fifty cubits. 18 There shall remain an area along the sacred tract, ten thousand cubits to the east and ten thousand to the west, whose produce shall provide food for the workers of the City. 19 The workers in the City shall be taken from all the tribes of Israel. 20 The entire tract shall be twenty-five thousand by twenty-five thousand cubits; as a perfect square you shall set apart the sacred tract together with the City property.

48 ' "This is the list of the tribes. One portion in the far north by way of Hethlon to the Pass of Hamath, to Hazer-Enon, with the territory of Damascus to the north, and marching with Hamath, from the eastern limit to the western limit: Dan. 2 One portion bordering Dan, from the eastern limit to the western limit: Asher. 3 One portion bordering Asher, from the eastern limit to the western limit: Naphtali. 4 One portion bordering Naphtali, from the eastern limit to the western limit: Manasseh. 5 One portion bordering Manasseh, from the eastern limit to the western limit: Ephraim. 6 One portion bordering Ephraim, from the eastern limit to the western limit: Reuben. 7 One portion bordering Reuben, from the eastern limit to the western limit: Judah. 8 One portion bordering Judah, from the eastern limit to the western limit, is the portion which you must set aside, twenty-five thousand cubits wide, and as long as each of the other portions from the eastern limit to the western limit. The sanctuary will be in the centre of it.

9 "The portion which you must set aside for Yahweh must be twenty-five thousand cubits long and ten thousand cubits wide. 10 This sacred portion must belong to the priests, being, on the north side, twenty-five thousand cubits; on the west side ten thousand cubits wide, on the east side ten thousand cubits wide and on the south side twenty-five thousand cubits long; the sanctuary of Yahweh will be in the centre of it. 11 This will be for the consecrated priests, those of the sons of Zadok who maintained my liturgy and did not go astray with the straying Israelites, as the Levites went astray. 12 And so their portion must be taken out of the especially holy portion of the land, near the territory of the Levites. 13 The territory of the Levites, like the territory of the priests, must be twenty-five thousand cubits long and ten thousand cubits wide—the whole length being twenty-five thousand and the width ten thousand. 14 It will be illegal for them to sell or exchange any part of it, and the domain can never be alienated, since it is consecrated to Yahweh. 15 As regards the remainder, an area of five thousand cubits by twenty-five thousand, this must be for the common use of the city, for houses and pastures. In the middle will be the city. 16 These will be its dimensions: on the north side, four thousand five hundred cubits; on the south side, four thousand five hundred cubits; on the east side, four thousand five hundred cubits; on the west side, four thousand five hundred cubits. 17 The pasture land of the city must extend two hundred and fifty cubits to the north, two hundred and fifty to the south, two hundred and fifty to the east, two hundred and fifty to the west. 18 One strip, contiguous to the sacred portion, must be left over, consisting of ten thousand cubits to eastward and ten thousand to westward, marching with the sacred portion; this will bring in a revenue for feeding the municipal workmen. 19 And the municipal workmen, drawn from all the tribes of Israel, will farm it. 20 The portion must have a total area of twenty-five thousand cubits by twenty-five thousand. You must allocate a square area from the sacred portion to constitute the city.

NEW REVISED STANDARD VERSION

21 What remains on both sides of the holy portion and of the property of the city shall belong to the prince. Extending from the twenty-five thousand cubits of the holy portion to the east border, and westward from the twenty-five thousand cubits to the west border, parallel to the tribal portions, it shall belong to the prince. The holy portion with the sanctuary of the temple in the middle of it, 22 and the property of the Levites and of the city, shall be in the middle of that which belongs to the prince. The portion of the prince shall lie between the territory of Judah and the territory of Benjamin.

23 As for the rest of the tribes: from the east side to the west, Benjamin, one portion. 24 Adjoining the territory of Benjamin, from the east side to the west, Simeon, one portion. 25 Adjoining the territory of Simeon, from the east side to the west, Issachar, one portion. 26 Adjoining the territory of Issachar, from the east side to the west, Zebulun, one portion. 27 Adjoining the territory of Zebulun, from the east side to the west, Gad, one portion. 28 And adjoining the territory of Gad to the south, the boundary shall run from Tamar to the waters of Meribath-kadesh, from there along the Wadi of Egypt[h] to the Great Sea. 29 This is the land that you shall allot as an inheritance among the tribes of Israel, and these are their portions, says the Lord GOD.

30 These shall be the exits of the city: On the north side, which is to be four thousand five hundred cubits by measure, 31 three gates, the gate of Reuben, the gate of Judah, and the gate of Levi, the gates of the city being named after the tribes of Israel. 32 On the east side, which is to be four thousand five hundred cubits, three gates, the gate of Joseph, the gate of Benjamin, and the gate of Dan. 33 On the south side, which is to be four thousand five hundred cubits by measure, three gates, the gate of Simeon, the gate of Issachar, and the gate of Zebulun. 34 On the west side, which is to be four thousand five hundred cubits, three gates,[i] the gate of Gad, the gate of Asher, and the gate of Naphtali. 35 The circumference of the city shall be eighteen thousand cubits. And the name of the city from that time on shall be, The LORD is There.

[h] Heb lacks *of Egypt*   [i] One Ms Gk Syr: MT *their gates three*

REVISED ENGLISH BIBLE

21 'What is left over on either side of the sacred reserve and the city holding is to be assigned to the ruler. Eastwards, what lies over against the reserved twenty-five thousand cubits, as far as the eastern side, and westwards, what lies over against the twenty-five thousand cubits to the western side, parallel to the tribal portions, is to be assigned to the ruler; the sacred reserve and the sanctuary itself will be in the centre. 22 The holding of the Levites and the holding of the city will be in the middle of that which is assigned to the ruler; it will be between the frontiers of Judah and Benjamin.

23 'The rest of the tribes: from the eastern boundary to the western will be Benjamin: one portion.

24 'Bordering on Benjamin, from the eastern boundary to the western, will be Simeon: one portion.

25 'Bordering on Simeon, from the eastern boundary to the western, will be Issachar: one portion.

26 'Bordering on Issachar, from the eastern boundary to the western, will be Zebulun: one portion.

27 'Bordering on Zebulun, from the eastern boundary to the western, will be Gad: one portion.

28 'Bordering on Gad, on the side of the Negeb, the frontier on the south stretches from Tamar to the waters of Meribah-by-Kadesh, to the wadi of Egypt as far as the Great Sea.

29 'That is the land which you are to allot as a holding to the tribes of Israel, and those will be their allotted portions. This is the word of the Lord GOD.

30–31 'These are to be the ways out of the city, the gates being named after the tribes of Israel. The northern side, four thousand five hundred cubits long, is to have three gates, those of Reuben, Judah, and Levi; 32 the eastern side, four thousand five hundred cubits long, three gates, those of Joseph, Benjamin, and Dan; 33 the southern side, four thousand five hundred cubits long, three gates, those of Simeon, Issachar, and Zebulun; 34 the western side, four thousand five hundred cubits long, three gates, those of Gad, Asher, and Naphtali. 35 The perimeter of the city will be eighteen thousand cubits, and for all time to come the city's name will be "The LORD is there".'

21 The remainder shall belong to the prince: the land on both sides of the sacred tract and the City property, extending along the twenty-five-thousand-cubit line eastward to the eastern boundary, and westward along the twenty-five-thousand-cubit line to the western boundary, a territory parallel with the tribal portions for the prince. The sacred tract and the sanctuary of the temple shall be in the middle. 22 Thus, except for the property of the Levites and the City property, which lie in the midst of the prince's property, the territory between the portions of Judah and of Benjamin shall belong to the prince.

23 These are the remaining tribes. Benjamin: from the eastern to the western boundary. 24 Simeon: on the frontier of Benjamin, from the eastern to the western boundary. 25 Issachar: on the frontier of Simeon, from the eastern to the western boundary. 26 Zebulun: on the frontier of Issachar, from the eastern to the western boundary. 27 Gad: on the frontier of Zebulun, from the eastern to the western boundary. 28 Along the frontier of Gad shall be the southern boundary, which shall extend from Tamar to the waters of Meribath-kadesh, and from there to the Wadi of Egypt, and on to the Great Sea. 29 Such is the land which you shall apportion as inheritances among the tribes of Israel, and these are their portions, says the Lord GOD.

30 These are the exits of the City, the gates of which are named after the tribes of Israel. On the north side, measuring forty-five hundred cubits, 31 there shall be three gates: the gate of Reuben, the gate of Judah, and the gate of Levi. 32 On the east side, measuring forty-five hundred cubits, there shall be three gates: the gate of Joseph, the gate of Benjamin, and the gate of Dan. 33 On the south side, measuring forty-five hundred cubits, there shall be three gates: the gate of Simeon, the gate of Issachar, and the gate of Zebulun. 34 On the west side, measuring forty-five hundred cubits, there shall be three gates: the gate of Gad, the gate of Asher, and the gate of Naphtali. 35 The perimeter of the City is eighteen thousand cubits. The name of the City shall henceforth be "The LORD is here."

21 What is left over will be for the prince, on either side of the sacred portion and of the property of the city, marching with the twenty-five thousand cubits to eastward to the eastern frontier, and marching with the twenty-five thousand cubits to westward to the western frontier — running parallel with the other portions and belonging to the prince. In the centre will be the sacred portion and the sanctuary of the Temple. 22 Thus, apart from the property of the Levites and the property of the city which lie in the middle of the prince's portion, everything between the borders of Judah and the borders of Benjamin must belong to the prince.

23 "As regards the rest of the tribes: One portion from the eastern limit to the western limit: Benjamin. 24 One portion bordering Benjamin, from the eastern limit to the western limit: Simeon. 25 One portion bordering Simeon, from the eastern limit to the western limit: Issachar. 26 One portion bordering Issachar, from the eastern limit to the western limit: Zebulun. 27 One portion bordering Zebulun, from the eastern limit to the western limit: Gad. 28 On the southern border of Gad, on the south side, the border will run from Tamar to the Waters of Meribah in Kadesh, to the Wadi and the Great Sea. 29 This is how you must distribute the country to the tribes of Israel as their heritage, and these must be their portions — declares the Lord Yahweh.

30 "Here are the exits from the city. On the north side, four thousand five hundred cubits are to be measured off. 31 The gates of the city are to be named after the tribes of Israel. Three gates to the north: one the gate of Reuben; one the gate of Judah; one the gate of Levi. 32 On the east side, there will be four thousand five hundred cubits and three gates: one the gate of Joseph; one the gate of Benjamin; one the gate of Dan. 33 On the south side, four thousand five hundred cubits are to be measured off, and there are to be three gates: one the gate of Simeon; one the gate of Issachar; one the gate of Zebulun. 34 On the west side, there will be four thousand five hundred cubits and three gates: one the gate of Gad; one the gate of Asher; one the gate of Naphtali. 35 Total perimeter: eighteen thousand cubits.

"The name of the city in future must be: Yahweh-is-there." [r]

[r] 48 Hebr. *yahweh-sham* suggests 'Jerusalem'.

THE BOOK OF
Daniel

Daniel

1 In the third year of the reign of King Jehoiakim of Judah, King Nebuchadnezzar of Babylon came to Jerusalem and besieged it. 2 The Lord let King Jehoiakim of Judah fall into his power, as well as some of the vessels of the house of God. These he brought to the land of Shinar,ª and placed the vessels in the treasury of his gods.

3 Then the king commanded his palace master Ashpenaz to bring some of the Israelites of the royal family and of the nobility, 4 young men without physical defect and handsome, versed in every branch of wisdom, endowed with knowledge and insight, and competent to serve in the king's palace; they were to be taught the literature and language of the Chaldeans. 5 The king assigned them a daily portion of the royal rations of food and wine. They were to be educated for three years, so that at the end of that time they could be stationed in the king's court. 6 Among them were Daniel, Hananiah, Mishael, and Azariah, from the tribe of Judah. 7 The palace master gave them other names: Daniel he called Belteshazzar, Hananiah he called Shadrach, Mishael he called Meshach, and Azariah he called Abednego.

8 But Daniel resolved that he would not defile himself with the royal rations of food and wine; so he asked the palace master to allow him not to defile himself. 9 Now God allowed Daniel to receive favor and compassion from the palace master. 10 The palace master said to Daniel, "I am afraid of my lord the king; he has appointed your food and your drink. If he should see you in poorer condition than the other young men of your own age, you would endanger my head with the king." 11 Then Daniel asked the guard whom the palace master had appointed over Daniel, Hananiah, Mishael, and Azariah: 12 "Please test your servants for ten days. Let us be given vegetables to eat and water to drink. 13 You can then compare our appearance with the appearance of the young men who eat the royal rations, and deal with your servants according to what you observe." 14 So he agreed to this proposal and tested them for ten days. 15 At the end of ten days it was observed that they appeared better and fatter than all the young men who had been eating the royal rations. 16 So the guard continued to withdraw their royal rations and the wine they were to drink, and gave them vegetables. 17 To these four young men God gave knowledge and skill in every aspect of literature and wisdom; Daniel also had insight into all visions and dreams.

18 At the end of the time that the king had set for them to be brought in, the palace master brought them into the presence of Nebuchadnezzar, 19 and the king spoke with them. And among them all, no one was found to compare with Daniel, Hananiah, Mishael, and Azariah; therefore they were stationed in the king's court. 20 In every matter of wisdom and understanding concerning which the king inquired of them, he found them ten times better than all the magicians and enchanters in his whole kingdom. 21 And Daniel continued there until the first year of King Cyrus.

ª Gk Theodotion: Heb adds *to the house of his own gods*

1 IN the third year of the reign of King Jehoiakim of Judah, Nebuchadnezzar, the Babylonian king, came and laid siege to Jerusalem. 2 The Lord handed King Jehoiakim over to him, together with all that was left of the vessels from the house of God; and he carried them off to the land of Shinar, to the temple of his god, where he placed the vessels in the temple treasury.

3 The king ordered Ashpenaz, his chief eunuch, to bring into the palace some of the Israelite exiles, members of their royal house and of the nobility. 4 They were to be young men free from physical defect, handsome in appearance, at home in all branches of knowledge, well-informed, intelligent, and so fitted for service in the royal court; and he was to instruct them in the writings and language of the Chaldaeans. 5 The king assigned them a daily allowance of fine food and wine from the royal table, and their training was to last for three years; at the end of that time they would enter his service. 6 Among them were certain Jews: Daniel, Hananiah, Mishael, and Azariah. 7 To them the master of the eunuchs gave new names: Daniel he called Belteshazzar, Hananiah Shadrach, Mishael Meshach, and Azariah Abed-nego.

8 Daniel determined not to become contaminated with the food and wine from the royal table, and begged the master of the eunuchs to excuse him from touching it. 9 God caused the master to look on Daniel with kindness and goodwill, 10 and to Daniel's request he replied, 'I am afraid of my lord the king: he has assigned you food and drink, and if he were to see you and your companions looking miserable compared with the other young men of your own age, my head would be forfeit.' 11 Then Daniel said to the attendant whom the master of the eunuchs had put in charge of Hananiah, Mishael, Azariah, and himself, 12 'Submit us to this test for ten days: give us only vegetables to eat and water to drink; 13 then compare our appearance with that of the young men who have lived on the king's food, and be guided in your treatment of us by what you see for yourself.' 14 He agreed to the proposal and submitted them to this test. 15 At the end of the ten days they looked healthier and better nourished than any of the young men who had lived on the food from the king. 16 So the attendant took away the food assigned to them and the wine they were to drink, and gave them vegetables only.

17 To all four of these young men God gave knowledge, understanding of books, and learning of every kind, and Daniel had a gift for interpreting visions and dreams of every kind. 18 At the time appointed by the king for introducing the young men to court, the master of the eunuchs brought them into the presence of Nebuchadnezzar. 19 The king talked with them all, but found none of them to compare with Daniel, Hananiah, Mishael, and Azariah; so they entered the royal service. 20 Whenever the king consulted them on any matter calling for insight and judgement, he found them ten times superior to all the magicians and exorcists in his whole kingdom.

21 Daniel remained there until the accession of King Cyrus.

The version of Daniel included here omits the Greek additions at Dan 3.24–90 (The Prayer of Azariah and The Song of the Three Young Men); Dan ch 13 (Susanna); and Dan ch 14 (Bel and the Dragon). These will be found among the Apocryphal/Deuterocanonical books beginning on p. 2421.

The version of Daniel included here omits the Greek additions at Dan 3.24–90 (The Prayer of Azariah and The Song of the Three Young Men); Dan ch 13 (Susanna); and Dan ch 14 (Bel and the Dragon). These will be found among the Apocryphal/Deuterocanonical books beginning on p. 2421.

THE BOOK OF
Daniel

1 In the third year of the reign of Jehoiakim, king of Judah, King Nebuchadnezzar of Babylon came and laid siege to Jerusalem. 2 The Lord handed over to him Jehoiakim, king of Judah, and some of the vessels of the temple of God, which he carried off to the land of Shinar, and placed in the temple treasury of his god.

3 The king told Ashpenaz, his chief chamberlain, to bring in some of the Israelites of royal blood and of the nobility, 4 young men without any defect, handsome, intelligent and wise, quick to learn, and prudent in judgment, such as could take their place in the king's palace; they were to be taught the language and literature of the Chaldeans; 5 after three years' training they were to enter the king's service. The king allotted them a daily portion of food and wine from the royal table. 6 Among these were men of Judah: Daniel, Hananiah, Mishael, and Azariah. 7 The chief chamberlain changed their names: Daniel to Belteshazzar, Hananiah to Shadrach, Mishael to Meshach, and Azariah to Abednego.

8 But Daniel was resolved not to defile himself with the king's food or wine; so he begged the chief chamberlain to spare him this defilement. 9 Though God had given Daniel the favor and sympathy of the chief chamberlain, 10 he nevertheless said to Daniel, "I am afraid of my lord the king; it is he who allotted your food and drink. If he sees that you look wretched by comparison with the other young men of your age, you will endanger my life with the king." 11 Then Daniel said to the steward whom the chief chamberlain had put in charge of Daniel, Hananiah, Mishael, and Azariah, 12 "Please test your servants for ten days. Give us vegetables to eat and water to drink. 13 Then see how we look in comparison with the other young men who eat from the royal table, and treat your servants according to what you see." 14 He acceded to this request, and tested them for ten days; 15 after ten days they looked healthier and better fed than any of the young men who ate from the royal table. 16 So the steward continued to take away the food and wine they were to receive, and gave them vegetables.

17 To these four young men God gave knowledge and proficiency in all literature and science, and to Daniel the understanding of all visions and dreams. 18 At the end of the time the king had specified for their preparation, the chief chamberlain brought them before Nebuchadnezzar. 19 When the king had spoken with all of them, none was found equal to Daniel, Hananiah, Mishael, and Azariah; and so they entered the king's service. 20 In any question of wisdom or prudence which the king put to them, he found them ten times better than all the magicians and enchanters in his kingdom. 21 Daniel remained there until the first year of King Cyrus.

Daniel

1 In the third year of the reign of Jehoiakim king of Judah, Nebuchadnezzar king of Babylon marched on Jerusalem and besieged it. 2 The Lord let Jehoiakim king of Judah fall into his power, as well as some of the vessels belonging to the Temple of God. These he took away to Shinar, putting the vessels into the treasury of his own gods.

3 From the Israelites, the king ordered Ashpenaz, his chief eunuch, to bring a certain number of boys of royal or noble descent; 4 they had to be without any physical defect, of good appearance, versed in every branch of wisdom, well-informed, discerning, suitable for service at the royal court. Ashpenaz was to teach them to speak and write the language of the Chaldaeans. 5 The king assigned them a daily allowance of food and wine from the royal table. They were to receive an education lasting for three years, after which they would enter the royal service. 6 Among these were the Judaeans Daniel, Hananiah, Mishael and Azariah. 7 The chief eunuch gave them other names, calling Daniel Belteshazzar, Hananiah Shadrach, Mishael Meshach, and Azariah Abed-Nego.

8 Daniel, who was determined not to incur pollution by food and wine from the royal table, begged the chief eunuch to spare him this defilement. 9 God allowed Daniel to receive faithful love and sympathy from the chief eunuch. 10 But the eunuch warned Daniel, 'I am afraid of my lord the king: he has assigned you food and drink, and if he sees you looking thinner in the face than the other boys of your age, my head will be in danger with the king because of you.' 11 To the guard assigned to Daniel, Hananiah, Mishael and Azariah by the chief eunuch, Daniel then said, 12 'Please allow your servants a ten days' trial, during which we are given only vegetables to eat and water to drink. 13 You can then compare our looks with those of the boys who eat the king's food; go by what you see, and treat your servants accordingly.' 14 The man agreed to do what they asked and put them on ten days' trial. 15 When the ten days were over, they looked better and fatter than any of the boys who had eaten their allowance from the royal table; 16 so the guard withdrew their allowance of food and the wine they were to drink, and gave them vegetables. 17 To these four boys God gave knowledge and skill in every aspect of literature and learning; Daniel also had the gift of interpreting every kind of vision and dream.

18 When the time stipulated by the king for the boys to be presented to him came round, the chief eunuch presented them to Nebuchadnezzar. 19 The king conversed with them, and among all the boys found none to equal Daniel, Hananiah, Mishael and Azariah. So they became members of the king's court, 20 and on whatever point of wisdom or understanding he might question them, he found them ten times better than all the magicians and soothsayers in his entire kingdom. Daniel remained there until the first year of King Cyrus.

NEW REVISED STANDARD VERSION	REVISED ENGLISH BIBLE

2 In the second year of Nebuchadnezzar's reign, Nebuchadnezzar dreamed such dreams that his spirit was troubled and his sleep left him. 2 So the king commanded that the magicians, the enchanters, the sorcerers, and the Chaldeans be summoned to tell the king his dreams. When they came in and stood before the king, 3 he said to them, "I have had such a dream that my spirit is troubled by the desire to understand it." 4 The Chaldeans said to the king (in Aramaic),*b* "O king, live forever! Tell your servants the dream, and we will reveal the interpretation." 5 The king answered the Chaldeans, "This is a public decree: if you do not tell me both the dream and its interpretation, you shall be torn limb from limb, and your houses shall be laid in ruins. 6 But if you do tell me the dream and its interpretation, you shall receive from me gifts and rewards and great honor. Therefore tell me the dream and its interpretation." 7 They answered a second time, "Let the king first tell his servants the dream, then we can give its interpretation." 8 The king answered, "I know with certainty that you are trying to gain time, because you see I have firmly decreed: 9 if you do not tell me the dream, there is but one verdict for you. You have agreed to speak lying and misleading words to me until things take a turn. Therefore, tell me the dream, and I shall know that you can give me its interpretation." 10 The Chaldeans answered the king, "There is no one on earth who can reveal what the king demands! In fact no king, however great and powerful, has ever asked such a thing of any magician or enchanter or Chaldean. 11 The thing that the king is asking is too difficult, and no one can reveal it to the king except the gods, whose dwelling is not with mortals."

12 Because of this the king flew into a violent rage and commanded that all the wise men of Babylon be destroyed. 13 The decree was issued, and the wise men were about to be executed; and they looked for Daniel and his companions, to execute them. 14 Then Daniel responded with prudence and discretion to Arioch, the king's chief executioner, who had gone out to execute the wise men of Babylon; 15 he asked Arioch, the royal official, "Why is the decree of the king so urgent?" Arioch then explained the matter to Daniel. 16 So Daniel went in and requested that the king give him time and he would tell the king the interpretation.

17 Then Daniel went to his home and informed his companions, Hananiah, Mishael, and Azariah, 18 and told them to seek mercy from the God of heaven concerning this mystery, so that Daniel and his companions with the rest of the wise men of Babylon might not perish. 19 Then the mystery was revealed to Daniel in a vision of the night, and Daniel blessed the God of heaven.

20 Daniel said:
"Blessed be the name of God from age to age,
    for wisdom and power are his.
21 He changes times and seasons,
    deposes kings and sets up kings;
he gives wisdom to the wise
    and knowledge to those who have
        understanding.
22 He reveals deep and hidden things;
    he knows what is in the darkness,
    and light dwells with him.
23 To you, O God of my ancestors,
    I give thanks and praise,
for you have given me wisdom and power,
    and have now revealed to us what we asked of
        you,
    for you have revealed to us what the king
        ordered."

b The text from this point to the end of chapter 7 is in Aramaic

2 IN the second year of his reign Nebuchadnezzar was troubled by dreams he had, so much so that he could not sleep. 2 He gave orders for the magicians, exorcists, sorcerers, and Chaldaeans to be summoned to expound to him what he had been dreaming. When they presented themselves before the king, 3 he said to them, 'I have had a dream, and my mind has been troubled to know what the dream was.' 4 The Chaldaeans, speaking in Aramaic, said, 'Long live the king! Relate the dream to us, your servants, and we shall give you the interpretation.' 5 The king answered, 'This is my firm decision: if you do not make both dream and interpretation known to me, you will be hacked limb from limb and your houses will be reduced to rubble. 6 But if you tell me the dream and its interpretation, you will be richly rewarded by me and loaded with honours. Tell me, then, the dream and its interpretation.' 7 They said again, 'Let the king relate the dream to his servants, and we shall tell him the interpretation.' 8 The king rejoined, 'It is clear to me that you are trying to gain time, because you see that I have come to this firm decision: 9 if you do not make the dream known to me, there is but one verdict for you, and one only. What is more, you have conspired to tell me mischievous lies to my face in the hope that with time things may alter. Relate the dream to me, therefore, and then I shall know that you can give me its interpretation.' 10 The Chaldaeans answered, 'No one on earth can tell your majesty what you wish to know. No king, however great and powerful, has ever made such a demand of a magician, exorcist, or Chaldaean. 11 What your majesty asks is too hard; none but the gods can tell you, and they dwell remote from mortals.' 12 At this the king became furious, and in great rage he ordered all the wise men of Babylon to be put to death. 13 A decree was issued for the execution of the wise men, and search was made for Daniel and his companions.

14 As Arioch, captain of the royal bodyguard, set out to execute the wise men of Babylon, Daniel made a discreet and tactful approach to him. 15 He said, 'May I ask you, sir, as the king's representative, why his majesty has issued so peremptory a decree?' Arioch explained the matter, 16 and Daniel went to the king and begged to be allowed a certain time by which he would give the king the interpretation. 17 He then went home and made the matter known to Hananiah, Mishael, and Azariah, his companions, saying 18 they should implore the God of heaven to disclose this secret in his mercy, so that they should not be put to death along with the rest of the wise men of Babylon. 19 The secret was then revealed to Daniel in a vision by night, and he blessed the God of heaven 20 in these words:

'Blessed be God's name from age to age,
    for to him belong wisdom and power.
21 He changes seasons and times;
    he deposes kings and sets up kings;
    he gives wisdom to the wise
    and knowledge to those who have discernment;
22 he reveals deep mysteries;
    he knows what lies in darkness;
    with him light has its dwelling.
23 God of my fathers, to you I give thanks and
        praise,
    for you have given me wisdom and power.
Now you have made known to me what we asked;
    you have given us the answer for the king.'

2:4 **Long live:** *from here to the end of ch. 7 the text is in Aramaic.*
2:5 **reduced to rubble:** *or* forfeit.

NEW AMERICAN BIBLE

2 In the second year of his reign, King Nebuchadnezzar
had a dream which left his spirit no rest and robbed
him of his sleep. 2 So he ordered that the magicians, enchanters, sorcerers, and Chaldeans be summoned to interpret the dream for him. When they came and presented
themselves to the king, 3 he said to them, "I had a dream
which will allow my spirit no rest until I know what it
means." 4 The Chaldeans answered the king [Aramaic]:
"O king, live forever! Tell your servants the dream and we
will give its meaning." 5 The king answered the Chaldeans,
"This is what I have decided: unless you tell me the dream
and its meaning, you shall be cut to pieces and your houses
destroyed. 6 But if you tell me the dream and its meaning,
you shall receive from me gifts and presents and great honors. Now tell me the dream and its meaning."

7 Again they answered, "Let the king tell his servants the
dream and we will give its meaning." 8 But the king replied:
"I know for certain that you are bargaining for time, since
you know what I have decided. 9 If you do not tell me the
dream, there can be but one decree for you. You have
framed a false and deceitful interpretation to present me
with till the crisis is past. Tell me the dream, therefore, that
I may be sure that you can also give its correct interpretation."

10 The Chaldeans answered the king: "There is not a man
on earth who can do what you ask, O king; never has any
king, however great and mighty, asked such a thing of any
magician, enchanter, or Chaldean. 11 What you demand,
O king, is too difficult; there is no one who can tell it to the
king except the gods who do not dwell among men." 12 At
this the king became violently angry and ordered all the
wise men of Babylon to be put to death. 13 When the decree
was issued that the wise men should be slain, Daniel and his
companions were also sought out.

14 Then Daniel prudently took counsel with Arioch, the
captain of the king's guard, who had set out to kill the wise
men of Babylon: 15 "O officer of the king," he asked, "what
is the reason for this harsh order from the king?" When
Arioch told him, 16 Daniel went and asked for time from the
king, that he might give him the interpretation.

17 Daniel went home and informed his companions Hananiah, Mishael, and Azariah, 18 that they might implore the
mercy of the God of heaven in regard to this mystery, so
that Daniel and his companions might not perish with the
rest of the wise men of Babylon. 19 During the night the
mystery was revealed to Daniel in a vision, and he blessed
the God of heaven:

20 "Blessed be the name of God forever and ever,
for wisdom and power are his.
21 He causes the changes of the times and seasons,
makes kings and unmakes them.
He gives wisdom to the wise
and knowledge to those who understand.
22 He reveals deep and hidden things
and knows what is in the darkness,
for the light dwells with him.
23 To you, O God of my fathers,
I give thanks and praise,
because you have given me wisdom and power.
Now you have shown me what we asked of you,
you have made known to us the king's dream."

2, 4: Aramaic: from Dn 2, 4 to 7, 28 the text of Daniel is in
Aramaic, not Hebrew, as indicated by this gloss.

NEW JERUSALEM BIBLE

2 In the second year of his reign, Nebuchadnezzar had a
series of dreams; he was perturbed by this and sleep
deserted him. 2 The king then had magicians and soothsayers, sorcerers and Chaldaeans summoned to tell him what
his dreams meant. They arrived and stood in the king's
presence. 3 The king said to them, 'I have had a dream, and
my mind is troubled by a wish to understand it.' 4 The
Chaldaeans answered the king:

'May your majesty live for ever! Tell your servants the
dream, and we shall reveal its meaning for you.' 5 The king
answered the Chaldaeans, 'This is my firm resolve: if you
cannot tell me what I dreamt and what it means, I shall have
you torn limb from limb and your houses turned into dunghills. 6 If, on the other hand, you can tell me what I dreamt
and what it means, I shall give you presents, rewards and
high honour. So tell me what I dreamt and what it means.'
7 A second time they said, 'Let the king tell his dream to his
servants, and we shall reveal its meaning.' 8 But the king
retorted, 'It is plain to me that you are trying to gain time,
knowing my proclaimed resolve. 9 If you do not interpret
my dream for me, there will be but one sentence passed on
you all; you have agreed among yourselves to make me
misleading and tortuous speeches while the time goes by.
So tell me what my dream was, and then I shall know
whether you can interpret it.' 10 The Chaldaeans answered
the king, 'Nobody in the world could explain the king's
problem; what is more, no other king, governor or chief
would think of putting such a question to any magician,
soothsayer or Chaldaean. 11 The question the king asks is
difficult, and no one can find the king an answer to it,
except the gods, whose dwelling is not with mortals.' 12 At
this the king flew into a rage and ordered all the Babylonian
sages to be put to death. 13 On publication of the decree to
have the sages killed, search was made for Daniel and his
companions to have them put to death.

14 Then, with shrewd and cautious words, Daniel approached Arioch, the king's chief executioner, when he was
on his way to kill the Babylonian sages. 15 To this royal
official Arioch he said, 'Why has the king issued such a
harsh decree?' Arioch explained matters to Daniel, 16 and
Daniel went off to ask the king for a stay of execution to
give him the opportunity of revealing his interpretation to
the king. 17 Daniel then went home and told his friends
Hananiah, Mishael and Azariah what had happened,
18 urging them to beg the God of heaven to show his mercy
and explain the mysterious secret, so that Daniel and his
friends might be spared the fate of the other Babylonian
sages. 19 The mystery was then revealed to Daniel in a
night-vision, and Daniel blessed the God of heaven. 20 This
is what Daniel said:

May the name of God
be blessed for ever and ever,
since wisdom and power are his alone.
21 It is he who controls the procession of times and
seasons,
who makes and unmakes kings,
who confers wisdom on the wise,
and knowledge on those with discernment,
22 who uncovers depths and mysteries,
who knows what lies in darkness;
and light dwells with him.
23 To you, God of my fathers, I give thanks and
praise
for having given me wisdom and strength:
to me you have explained what we asked you,
to us you have explained the king's problem.

NEW REVISED STANDARD VERSION	REVISED ENGLISH BIBLE

NEW REVISED STANDARD VERSION

24 Therefore Daniel went to Arioch, whom the king had appointed to destroy the wise men of Babylon, and said to him, "Do not destroy the wise men of Babylon; bring me in before the king, and I will give the king the interpretation." 25 Then Arioch quickly brought Daniel before the king and said to him: "I have found among the exiles from Judah a man who can tell the king the interpretation." 26 The king said to Daniel, whose name was Belteshazzar, "Are you able to tell me the dream that I have seen and its interpretation?" 27 Daniel answered the king, "No wise men, enchanters, magicians, or diviners can show to the king the mystery that the king is asking, 28 but there is a God in heaven who reveals mysteries, and he has disclosed to King Nebuchadnezzar what will happen at the end of days. Your dream and the visions of your head as you lay in bed were these: 29 To you, O king, as you lay in bed, came thoughts of what would be hereafter, and the revealer of mysteries disclosed to you what is to be. 30 But as for me, this mystery has not been revealed to me because of any wisdom that I have more than any other living being, but in order that the interpretation may be known to the king and that you may understand the thoughts of your mind.

31 "You were looking, O king, and lo! there was a great statue. This statue was huge, its brilliance extraordinary; it was standing before you, and its appearance was frightening. 32 The head of that statue was of fine gold, its chest and arms of silver, its middle and thighs of bronze, 33 its legs of iron, its feet partly of iron and partly of clay. 34 As you looked on, a stone was cut out, not by human hands, and it struck the statue on its feet of iron and clay and broke them in pieces. 35 Then the iron, the clay, the bronze, the silver, and the gold, were all broken in pieces and became like the chaff of the summer threshing floors; and the wind carried them away, so that not a trace of them could be found. But the stone that struck the statue became a great mountain and filled the whole earth.

36 "This was the dream; now we will tell the king its interpretation. 37 You, O king, the king of kings — to whom the God of heaven has given the kingdom, the power, the might, and the glory, 38 into whose hand he has given human beings, wherever they live, the wild animals of the field, and the birds of the air, and whom he has established as ruler over them all — you are the head of gold. 39 After you shall arise another kingdom inferior to yours, and yet a third kingdom of bronze, which shall rule over the whole earth. 40 And there shall be a fourth kingdom, strong as iron; just as iron crushes and smashes everything,^{c} it shall crush and shatter all these. 41 As you saw the feet and toes partly of potter's clay and partly of iron, it shall be a divided kingdom; but some of the strength of iron shall be in it, as you saw the iron mixed with the clay. 42 As the toes of the feet were part iron and part clay, so the kingdom shall be partly strong and partly brittle. 43 As you saw the iron mixed with clay, so will they mix with one another in marriage,^{d} but they will not hold together, just as iron does not mix with clay. 44 And in the days of those kings the God of heaven will set up a kingdom that shall never be destroyed, nor shall this kingdom be left to another people. It shall crush all these kingdoms and bring them to an end, and it shall stand forever; 45 just as you saw that a stone was cut

REVISED ENGLISH BIBLE

24 Daniel therefore went to Arioch, whom the king had charged with the execution of the wise men of Babylon. He approached him and said, 'Do not put the wise men to death; bring me before the king and I shall tell him the interpretation of his dream.' 25 Greatly agitated, Arioch brought Daniel before the king. 'I have found among the Jewish exiles', he said, 'a man who will make known to your majesty the interpretation of your dream.' 26 The king asked Daniel (who was also called Belteshazzar), 'Are you able to make known to me what I saw in my dream and to interpret it?' 27 Daniel answered: 'No wise man, exorcist, magician, or diviner can tell your majesty the secret about which you ask. 28 But there is in heaven a God who reveals secrets, and he has made known to King Nebuchadnezzar what is to be at the end of this age. This is the dream and these are the visions that came into your head: 29 the thoughts that came to you, your majesty, as you lay on your bed, concerned the future, and he who reveals secrets has made known to you what is to be. 30 This secret has been revealed to me, not because I am wiser than anyone alive, but in order that your majesty may know the interpretation and understand the thoughts which have entered your mind.

31 'As you watched, there appeared to your majesty a great image. Huge and dazzling, it stood before you, fearsome to behold. 32 The head of the image was of fine gold, its chest and arms of silver, its belly and thighs of bronze, 33 its legs of iron, its feet part iron and part clay. 34 While you watched, you saw a stone hewn from a mountain by no human hand; it struck the image on its feet of iron and clay and shattered them. 35 Then the iron, the clay, the bronze, the silver, and the gold were all shattered into fragments, and as if they were chaff from a summer threshing-floor the wind swept them away until no trace of them remained. But the stone which struck the image grew and became a huge mountain and filled the whole earth.

36 'That was the dream; now we shall relate to your majesty its interpretation. 37 Your majesty, the king of kings, to whom the God of heaven has given the kingdom with its power, its might, and its honour, 38 in whose hands he has placed mankind wherever they live, the wild animals, and the birds of the air, granting you sovereignty over them all: you yourself are that head of gold. 39 After you there will arise another kingdom, inferior to yours, then a third kingdom, of bronze, which will have sovereignty over the whole world. 40 There will be a fourth kingdom, strong as iron; just as iron shatters and breaks all things, it will shatter and crush all the others. 41 As in your vision the feet and toes were part potter's clay and part iron, so it will be a divided kingdom, and just as you saw iron mixed with clay from the ground, so it will have in it something of the strength of iron. 42 The toes being part iron and part clay means that the kingdom will be partly strong and partly brittle. 43 As in your vision the iron was mixed with the clay, so there will be a mixing of families by intermarriage, but such alliances will not be stable: iron does not mix with clay. 44 In the times of those kings the God of heaven will establish a kingdom which will never be destroyed, nor will it ever pass to another people; it will shatter all these kingdoms and make an end of them, while it will itself endure for ever. 45 This is the meaning of your vision of the stone being

^{c} Gk Theodotion Syr Vg: Aram adds *and like iron that crushes*
^{d} Aram *by human seed*

2:34 **from a mountain:** *so Gk; Aram. omits.*

24 So Daniel went to Arioch, whom the king had appointed to destroy the wise men of Babylon, and said to him, "Do not put the wise men of Babylon to death. Bring me before the king, and I will tell him the interpretation of the dream." Arioch quickly brought Daniel to the king and said, 25 "I have found a man among the Judean captives who can give the interpretation to the king." 26 The king asked Daniel, whose name was Belteshazzar, "Can you tell me the dream that I had, and its meaning?" 27 In the king's presence Daniel made this reply:

"The mystery about which the king has inquired, the wise men, enchanters, magicians, and astrologers could not explain to the king. 28 But there is a God in heaven who reveals mysteries, and he has shown King Nebuchadnezzar what is to happen in days to come; this was the dream you saw as you lay in bed. 29 To you in your bed there came thoughts about what should happen in the future, and he who reveals mysteries showed you what is to be. 30 To me also this mystery has been revealed; not that I am wiser than any other living person, but in order that its meaning may be made known to the king, that you may understand the thoughts in your own mind.

31 "In your vision, O king, you saw a statue, very large and exceedingly bright, terrifying in appearance as it stood before you. 32 The head of the statue was pure gold, its chest and arms were silver, its belly and thighs bronze, 33 the legs iron, its feet partly iron and partly tile. 34 While you looked at the statue, a stone which was hewn from a mountain without a hand being put to it, struck its iron and tile feet, breaking them in pieces. 35 The iron, tile, bronze, silver, and gold all crumbled at once, fine as the chaff on the threshing floor in summer, and the wind blew them away without leaving a trace. But the stone that struck the statue became a great mountain and filled the whole earth.

36 "This was the dream; the interpretation we shall also give in the king's presence. 37 You, O king, are the king of kings; to you the God of heaven has given dominion and strength, power and glory; 38 men, wild beasts, and birds of the air, wherever they may dwell, he has handed over to you, making you ruler over them all; you are the head of gold. 39 Another kingdom shall take your place, inferior to yours, then a third kingdom, of bronze, which shall rule over the whole earth. 40 There shall be a fourth kingdom, strong as iron; it shall break in pieces and subdue all these others, just as iron breaks in pieces and crushes everything else. 41 The feet and toes you saw, partly of potter's tile and partly of iron, mean that it shall be a divided kingdom, but yet have some of the hardness of iron. As you saw the iron mixed with clay tile, 42 and the toes partly iron and partly tile, the kingdom shall be partly strong and partly fragile. 43 The iron mixed with clay tile means that they shall seal their alliances by intermarriage, but they shall not stay united, any more than iron mixes with clay. 44 In the lifetime of those kings the God of heaven will set up a kingdom that shall never be destroyed or delivered up to another people; rather, it shall break in pieces all these kingdoms and put an end to them, and it shall stand forever. 45 That

24 So Daniel went to see Arioch, whom the king had made responsible for putting the Babylonian sages to death. Going in, he said, 'Do not put the Babylonian sages to death. Take me into the king's presence and I will reveal the meaning to the king.' 25 Arioch lost no time in bringing Daniel to the king. 'Among the exiles from Judah,' he said, 'I have discovered a man who can reveal the meaning to the king.' 26 The king said to Daniel (who had been given the name Belteshazzar), 'Can you tell me what I dreamt and what it means?' 27 Facing the king, Daniel replied, 'None of the sages, soothsayers, magicians or exorcists has been able to tell the king the truth of the mystery which the king has propounded; 28 but there is a God in heaven who reveals mysteries and who has shown King Nebuchadnezzar what is to take place in the final days. These, then, are the dream and the visions that passed through your head as you lay in bed: a

29 'Your Majesty, on your bed your thoughts turned to what would happen in the future, and the Revealer of Mysteries disclosed to you what is to take place. 30 This mystery has been revealed to me, not that I am wiser than anyone else, but for this sole purpose: that the king should learn what it means, and that you should understand your inmost thoughts.

31 'You have had a vision, Your Majesty; this is what you saw: a statue, a great statue of extreme brightness, stood before you, terrible to see. 32 The head of this statue was of fine gold, its chest and arms were of silver, its belly and thighs of bronze, 33 its legs of iron, its feet part iron, part clay. 34 While you were gazing, a stone broke away, untouched by any hand, and struck the statue, struck its feet of iron and clay and shattered them. 35 Then, iron and clay, bronze, silver and gold, all broke into pieces as fine as chaff on the threshing-floor in summer. The wind blew them away, leaving not a trace behind. And the stone that had struck the statue grew into a great mountain, filling the whole world. 36 This was the dream; we shall now explain to the king what it means.

37 'You, Your Majesty, king of kings, to whom the God of heaven has given sovereignty, power, strength and honour— 38 human beings, wild animals, birds of the air, wherever they live, he has entrusted to your rule, making you king of them all—you are the golden head. 39 And, after you, another kingdom will rise, not as great as yours, and then a third, of bronze, which will rule the whole world. 40 There will be a fourth kingdom, hard as iron, as iron that pulverises and crushes all. Like iron that breaks everything to pieces, it will crush and break all the earlier kingdoms. 41 The feet you saw, part earthenware, part iron, are a kingdom which will be split in two, but which will retain something of the strength of iron, just as you saw the iron and the clay of the earthenware mixed together. 42 The feet were part iron, part potter's clay: the kingdom will be partly strong and partly brittle. 43 And just as you saw the iron and the clay of the earthenware mixed together, so the two will be mixed together in human seed; b but they will not hold together any more than iron will blend with clay. 44 In the days of those kings, the God of heaven will set up a kingdom which will never be destroyed, and this kingdom will not pass into the hands of another race: it will shatter and absorb all the previous kingdoms and itself last for ever— 45 just as you saw a stone, untouched by hand, break

a 2 Under the image of metals these allegories describe successive empires, Babylonian, Median, Persian, Greek, which finally give way to the messianic kingdom. b 2 The short-lived marriage alliance between the Seleucids of Syria and the Ptolemies of Egypt.

NEW REVISED STANDARD VERSION	REVISED ENGLISH BIBLE

from the mountain not by hands, and that it crushed the iron, the bronze, the clay, the silver, and the gold. The great God has informed the king what shall be hereafter. The dream is certain, and its interpretation trustworthy."

46 Then King Nebuchadnezzar fell on his face, worshiped Daniel, and commanded that a grain offering and incense be offered to him. 47 The king said to Daniel, "Truly, your God is God of gods and Lord of kings and a revealer of mysteries, for you have been able to reveal this mystery!" 48 Then the king promoted Daniel, gave him many great gifts, and made him ruler over the whole province of Babylon and chief prefect over all the wise men of Babylon. 49 Daniel made a request of the king, and he appointed Shadrach, Meshach, and Abednego over the affairs of the province of Babylon. But Daniel remained at the king's court.

3 King Nebuchadnezzar made a golden statue whose height was sixty cubits and whose width was six cubits; he set it up on the plain of Dura in the province of Babylon. 2 Then King Nebuchadnezzar sent for the satraps, the prefects, and the governors, the counselors, the treasurers, the justices, the magistrates, and all the officials of the provinces to assemble and come to the dedication of the statue that King Nebuchadnezzar had set up. 3 So the satraps, the prefects, and the governors, the counselors, the treasurers, the justices, the magistrates, and all the officials of the provinces, assembled for the dedication of the statue that King Nebuchadnezzar had set up. When they were standing before the statue that Nebuchadnezzar had set up, 4 the herald proclaimed aloud, "You are commanded, O peoples, nations, and languages, 5 that when you hear the sound of the horn, pipe, lyre, trigon, harp, drum, and entire musical ensemble, you are to fall down and worship the golden statue that King Nebuchadnezzar has set up. 6 Whoever does not fall down and worship shall immediately be thrown into a furnace of blazing fire." 7 Therefore, as soon as all the peoples heard the sound of the horn, pipe, lyre, trigon, harp, drum, and entire musical ensemble, all the peoples, nations, and languages fell down and worshiped the golden statue that King Nebuchadnezzar had set up.

8 Accordingly, at this time certain Chaldeans came forward and denounced the Jews. 9 They said to King Nebuchadnezzar, "O king, live forever! 10 You, O king, have made a decree, that everyone who hears the sound of the horn, pipe, lyre, trigon, harp, drum, and entire musical ensemble, shall fall down and worship the golden statue, 11 and whoever does not fall down and worship shall be thrown into a furnace of blazing fire. 12 There are certain Jews whom you have appointed over the affairs of the province of Babylon: Shadrach, Meshach, and Abednego. These pay no heed to you, O King. They do not serve your gods and they do not worship the golden statue that you have set up."

13 Then Nebuchadnezzar in furious rage commanded that Shadrach, Meshach, and Abednego be brought in; so they brought those men before the king. 14 Nebuchadnezzar said to them, "Is it true, O Shadrach, Meshach, and Abednego, that you do not serve my gods and you do not worship the golden statue that I have set up? 15 Now if you are ready when you hear the sound of the horn, pipe, lyre, trigon, harp, drum, and entire musical ensemble to fall down and worship the statue that I have made, well and good.e But if you do not worship, you shall immediately be thrown into a furnace of blazing fire, and who is the god that will deliver you out of my hands?"

---

hewn from a mountain by no human hand, and then shattering the iron, the bronze, the clay, the silver, and the gold. A mighty God has made known to your majesty what is to be hereafter. The dream and its interpretation are true and trustworthy.

46 At this King Nebuchadnezzar prostrated himself and did homage to Daniel, and he gave orders that there should be presented to him a tribute of grain and soothing offerings. 47 'Truly,' he said, 'your God is indeed God of gods and Lord over kings, and a revealer of secrets, since you have been able to reveal this secret.' 48 The king then promoted Daniel to high position and bestowed on him many rich gifts. He gave him authority over the whole province of Babylon and put him in charge of all Babylon's wise men. 49 At Daniel's request the king appointed Shadrach, Meshach, and Abed-nego to administer the province of Babylon, while Daniel himself remained at court.

3 KING Nebuchadnezzar made a gold image, ninety feet high and nine feet broad, and had it set up on the plain of Dura in the province of Babylon. 2 The king then summoned the satraps, prefects, governors, counsellors, treasurers, judges, magistrates, and all the provincial officials to assemble and attend the dedication of the image he had set up. 3 The satraps, prefects, governors, counsellors, treasurers, judges, magistrates, and all governors of provinces assembled for the dedication of the image King Nebuchadnezzar had set up, and they took their places in front of the image. 4 A herald proclaimed in a loud voice, 'Peoples and nations of every language, you are commanded, 5 when you hear the sound of horn, pipe, zither, triangle, dulcimer, a full consort of music, to prostrate yourselves and worship the gold image which King Nebuchadnezzar has set up. 6 Whosoever does not prostrate himself and worship will be thrown forthwith into a blazing furnace.' 7 Accordingly, no sooner did the sound of horn, pipe, zither, triangle, dulcimer, a full consort of music, reach them than all the peoples and nations of every language prostrated themselves and worshipped the gold image set up by King Nebuchadnezzar.

8 Some Chaldaeans seized the opportunity to approach the king with a malicious accusation against the Jews. 9 They said, 'Long live the king! 10 Your majesty has issued a decree that everyone who hears the sound of horn, pipe, zither, triangle, dulcimer, a full consort of music, must fall down and worship the gold image; 11 and whoever does not do so will be thrown into a blazing furnace. 12 There are certain Jews whom you have put in charge of the administration of the province of Babylon. These men, Shadrach, Meshach, and Abed-nego, have disregarded your royal command; they do not serve your gods, nor do they worship the gold image you set up.' 13 In furious rage Nebuchadnezzar ordered Shadrach, Meshach, and Abed-nego to be fetched, and when they were brought into his presence, 14 he asked them, 'Is it true, Shadrach, Meshach, and Abed-nego, that you do not serve my gods or worship the gold image which I have set up? 15 Now if you are ready to prostrate yourselves as soon as you hear the sound of horn, pipe, zither, triangle, dulcimer, a full consort of music, and to worship the image that I have made, well and good. But if you do not worship it, you will be thrown forthwith into the blazing furnace; and what god is there that can deliver you from my power?' 16 Their reply to the king was: 'Your

---

e Aram lacks *well and good*

3:1 **ninety . . . broad:** *lit.* sixty cubits high and six cubits broad.

is the meaning of the stone you saw hewn from the mountain without a hand being put to it, which broke in pieces the tile, iron, bronze, silver, and gold. The great God has revealed to the king what shall be in the future; this is exactly what you dreamed, and its meaning is sure."

46 Then King Nebuchadnezzar fell down and worshiped Daniel and ordered sacrifice and incense offered to him. 47 To Daniel the king said, "Truly your God is the God of gods and Lord of kings and a revealer of mysteries; that is why you were able to reveal this mystery." 48 He advanced Daniel to a high post, gave him many generous presents, made him ruler of the whole province of Babylon and chief prefect over all the wise men of Babylon. 49 At Daniel's request the king made Shadrach, Meshach, and Abednego administrators of the province of Babylon, while Daniel himself remained at the king's court.

3 King Nebuchadnezzar had a golden statue made, sixty cubits high and six cubits wide, which he set up in the plain of Dura in the province of Babylon. 2 He then ordered the satraps, prefects, and governors, the counselors, treasurers, judges, magistrates and all the officials of the provinces to be summoned to the dedication of the statue which he had set up. 3 The satraps, prefects, and governors, the counselors, treasurers, judges, and magistrates and all the officials of the provinces, all these came together for the dedication and stood before the statue which King Nebuchadnezzar had set up. 4 A herald cried out: "Nations and peoples of every language, when you hear the sound of the trumpet, flute, lyre, harp, psaltery, bagpipe, and all the other musical instruments, 5 you are ordered to fall down and worship the golden statue which King Nebuchadnezzar has set up. 6 Whoever does not fall down and worship shall be instantly cast into a white-hot furnace." 7 Therefore, as soon as they heard the sound of the trumpet, flute, lyre, harp, psaltery, bagpipe, and all the other musical instruments, the nations and peoples of every language all fell down and worshiped the golden statue which King Nebuchadnezzar had set up.

8 At that point, some of the Chaldeans came and accused the Jews 9 to King Nebuchadnezzar: "O king, live forever! 10 O king, you issued a decree that everyone who heard the sound of the trumpet, flute, lyre, harp, psaltery, bagpipe, and all the other musical instruments should fall down and worship the golden statue; 11 whoever did not was to be cast into a white-hot furnace. 12 There are certain Jews whom you have made administrators of the province of Babylon: Shadrach, Meshach, Abednego; these men, O king, have paid no attention to you; they will not serve your god or worship the golden statue which you set up."

13 Nebuchadnezzar flew into a rage and sent for Shadrach, Meshach, and Abednego, who were promptly brought before the king. 14 King Nebuchadnezzar questioned them: "Is it true, Shadrach, Meshach, and Abednego, that you will not serve my god, or worship the golden statue that I set up? 15 Be ready now to fall down and worship the statue I had made, whenever you hear the sound of the trumpet, flute, lyre, harp, psaltery, bagpipe, and all the other musical instruments; otherwise, you shall be instantly cast into the white-hot furnace; and who is the God that can deliver you out of my hands?" 16 Shadrach, Meshach, and

away from the mountain and reduce iron, bronze, earthenware, silver and gold to powder. The Great God has shown the king what is to take place. The dream is true, the interpretation exact.'

46 At this, King Nebuchadnezzar fell prostrate before Daniel; he gave orders for Daniel to be offered an oblation and a fragrant sacrifice. 47 The king said to Daniel, 'Your god is indeed the God of gods, the Master of kings, and the Revealer of Mysteries, since you have been able to reveal this mystery.' 48 The king then conferred high rank on Daniel and gave him many handsome presents. He also made him governor of the whole province of Babylon and head of all the sages of Babylon. 49 At Daniel's request, the king entrusted the affairs of the province of Babylon to Shadrach, Meshach and Abed-Nego; Daniel himself remained in attendance on the king.

3 King Nebuchadnezzar had a golden statue made, sixty cubits high and six cubits wide, which he set up on the plain of Dura, in the province of Babylon. 2 King Nebuchadnezzar then summoned the satraps, magistrates, governors, counsellors, treasurers, judges, lawyers, and all the provincial authorities to assemble and attend the dedication of the statue set up by King Nebuchadnezzar. 3 Satraps, magistrates, governors, counsellors, treasurers, judges, lawyers and all the provincial authorities then assembled for the dedication of the statue set up by King Nebuchadnezzar and stood in front of the statue which King Nebuchadnezzar had set up. 4 A herald then loudly proclaimed: 'Peoples, nations, languages! Thus are you commanded: 5 the moment you hear the sound of horn, pipe, lyre, zither, harp, bagpipe and every other kind of instrument, you will prostrate yourselves and worship the golden statue set up by King Nebuchadnezzar. 6 Anyone who does not prostrate himself and worship will immediately be thrown into the burning fiery furnace.' 7 And so, the instant all the peoples heard the sound of horn, pipe, lyre, zither, harp, bagpipe and all the other instruments, all the peoples, nations and languages prostrated themselves and worshipped the statue set up by King Nebuchadnezzar.

8 Some Chaldaeans then came forward and maliciously accused the Jews. 9 They said to King Nebuchadnezzar, 'May Your Majesty live for ever! 10 You have issued a decree, Your Majesty, to the effect that everyone on hearing the sound of horn, pipe, lyre, zither, harp, bagpipe and every other kind of instrument is to prostrate himself and worship the golden statue; 11 and that anyone who does not prostrate himself and worship is to be thrown into the burning fiery furnace. 12 Now, there are certain Jews to whom you have entrusted the affairs of the province of Babylon: Shadrach, Meshach and Abed-Nego; these men have ignored your command, Your Majesty; they do not serve your gods, and refuse to worship the golden statue you have set up.' 13 Shaking with fury, Nebuchadnezzar sent for Shadrach, Meshach and Abed-Nego. The men were immediately brought before the king. 14 Nebuchadnezzar addressed them, 'Shadrach, Meshach and Abed-Nego, is it true that you do not serve my gods, and that you refuse to worship the golden statue I have set up? 15 When you hear the sound of horn, pipe, lyre, zither, harp, bagpipe and every other kind of instrument, are you prepared to prostrate yourselves and worship the statue I have made? If you refuse to worship it, you will be thrown forthwith into the burning fiery furnace; then which of the gods could save you from my power?' 16 Shadrach, Meshach and Abed-Nego replied to

16 Shadrach, Meshach, and Abednego answered the king, "O Nebuchadnezzar, we have no need to present a defense to you in this matter. 17 If our God whom we serve is able to deliver us from the furnace of blazing fire and out of your hand, O king, let him deliver us. *f* 18 But if not, be it known to you, O king, that we will not serve your gods and we will not worship the golden statue that you have set up."

19 Then Nebuchadnezzar was so filled with rage against Shadrach, Meshach, and Abednego that his face was distorted. He ordered the furnace heated up seven times more than was customary, 20 and ordered some of the strongest guards in his army to bind Shadrach, Meshach, and Abednego and to throw them into the furnace of blazing fire. 21 So the men were bound, still wearing their tunics, *g* their trousers, *g* their hats, and their other garments, and they were thrown into the furnace of blazing fire. 22 Because the king's command was urgent and the furnace was so overheated, the raging flames killed the men who lifted Shadrach, Meshach, and Abednego. 23 But the three men, Shadrach, Meshach, and Abednego, fell down, bound, into the furnace of blazing fire.

24 Then King Nebuchadnezzar was astonished and rose up quickly. He said to his counselors, "Was it not three men that we threw bound into the fire?" They answered the king, "True, O king." 25 He replied, "But I see four men unbound, walking in the middle of the fire, and they are not hurt; and the fourth has the appearance of a god." *h* 26 Nebuchadnezzar then approached the door of the furnace of blazing fire and said, "Shadrach, Meshach, and Abednego, servants of the Most High God, come out! Come here!" So Shadrach, Meshach, and Abednego came out from the fire. 27 And the satraps, the prefects, the governors, and the king's counselors gathered together and saw that the fire had not had any power over the bodies of those men; the hair of their heads was not singed, their tunics *g* were not harmed, and not even the smell of fire came from them. 28 Nebuchadnezzar said, "Blessed be the God of Shadrach, Meshach, and Abednego, who has sent his angel and delivered his servants who trusted in him. They disobeyed the king's command and yielded up their bodies rather than serve and worship any god except their own God. 29 Therefore I make a decree: Any people, nation, or language that utters blasphemy against the God of Shadrach, Meshach, and Abednego shall be torn limb from limb, and their houses laid in ruins; for there is no other god who is able to deliver in this way." 30 Then the king promoted Shadrach, Meshach, and Abednego in the province of Babylon.

4 *i* King Nebuchadnezzar to all peoples, nations, and languages that live throughout the earth: May you have abundant prosperity! 2 The signs and wonders that the Most High God has worked for me I am pleased to recount.

3 How great are his signs,
   how mighty his wonders!
His kingdom is an everlasting kingdom,
   and his sovereignty is from generation to
      generation.

4 *j* I, Nebuchadnezzar, was living at ease in my home and prospering in my palace. 5 I saw a dream that frightened me; my fantasies in bed and the visions of my head terrified me. 6 So I made a decree that all the wise men of Babylon should be brought before me, in order that they might tell me the interpretation of the dream. 7 Then the magicians, the en-

majesty, we have no need to answer you on this matter. 17 If there is a god who is able to save us from the blazing furnace, it is our God whom we serve; he will deliver us from your majesty's power. 18 But if not, be it known to your majesty that we shall neither serve your gods nor worship the gold image you have set up.'

19 At this Nebuchadnezzar was furious with them, and his face became distorted with anger. He ordered that the furnace should be heated to seven times its usual heat, 20 and commanded some of the strongest men in his army to bind Shadrach, Meshach, and Abed-nego and throw them into the blazing furnace. 21 Then, just as they were, in trousers, shirts, headdresses, and their other clothes, they were bound and thrown into the furnace. 22 Because the king's order was peremptory and the furnace exceedingly hot, those who were carrying the three men were killed by the flames; 23 and Shadrach, Meshach, and Abed-nego fell bound into the blazing furnace.

24 Then King Nebuchadnezzar, greatly agitated, sprang to his feet, saying to his courtiers, 'Was it not three men whom we threw bound into the fire?' They answered, 'Yes, certainly, your majesty.' 25 'Yet', he insisted, 'I can see four men walking about in the fire, free and unharmed; and the fourth looks like a god.' 26 Nebuchadnezzar approached the furnace door and called, 'Shadrach, Meshach, and Abed-nego, servants of the Most High God, come out!' When Shadrach, Meshach, and Abed-nego emerged from the fire, 27 the satraps, prefects, governors, and the king's courtiers gathered round them and saw how the fire had had no power to harm their bodies. The hair of their heads had not been singed, their trousers were untouched, and no smell of fire lingered about them.

28 Nebuchadnezzar declared: 'Blessed be the God of Shadrach, Meshach, and Abed-nego! He has sent his angel to save his servants who, trusting in him, disobeyed the royal command; they were willing to submit themselves to the fire rather than to serve or worship any god other than their own God. 29 I therefore issue this decree: anyone, whatever his people, nation, or language, if he speaks blasphemy against the God of Shadrach, Meshach, and Abed-nego, is to be hacked limb from limb and his house is to be reduced to rubble; for there is no other god who can save in such a manner.' 30 Then the king advanced the fortunes of Shadrach, Meshach, and Abed-nego in the province of Babylon.

4 King Nebuchadnezzar to all peoples and nations of every language throughout the whole world: May your prosperity increase! 2 It is my pleasure to recount the signs and wonders which the Most High God has worked for me:

3 How great are his signs,
   how mighty his wonders!
His kingdom is an everlasting kingdom,
   his sovereignty endures through all generations.

4 I, Nebuchadnezzar, was living contentedly at home in the luxury of my palace, 5 but as I lay on my bed, I had a dream which filled me with fear, and the fantasies and visions which came into my head caused me dismay. 6 I issued an order summoning to my presence all the wise men of Babylon to make known to me the interpretation of the dream. 7 When the magicians, exorcists, Chaldaeans, and diviners

f Or If our God whom we serve is able to deliver us, he will deliver us from the furnace of blazing fire and out of your hand, O king.
g Meaning of Aram word uncertain   h Aram a son of the gods
i Ch 3.31 in Aram   j Ch 4.1 in Aram

3:23 The Prayer of Azariah and The Song of the Three (printed in the Revised English Bible Apocrypha) follow this verse in some translations of the Bible.   3:28 to the fire: so Gk; Aram. omits. 4:1 In Aram. 3:31.   4:4 In Aram. 4:1.

Abednego answered King Nebuchadnezzar, "There is no need for us to defend ourselves before you in this matter. 17 If our God, whom we serve, can save us from the white-hot furnace and from your hands, O king, may he save us! 18 But even if he will not, know, O king, that we will not serve your god or worship the golden statue which you set up."

19 Nebuchadnezzar's face became livid with utter rage against Shadrach, Meshach, and Abednego. He ordered the furnace to be heated seven times more than usual 20 and had some of the strongest men in his army bind Shadrach, Meshach, and Abednego and cast them into the white-hot furnace. 21 They were bound and cast into the white-hot furnace with their coats, hats, shoes and other garments, 22 for the king's order was urgent. So huge a fire was kindled in the furnace that the flames devoured the men who threw Shadrach, Meshach, and Abednego into it. 23 But these three fell, bound, into the midst of the white-hot furnace.

‡3.24–90 (the Greek addition): see p. 2421‡

Hearing them sing, and astonished at seeing them alive, 91 King Nebuchadnezzar rose in haste and asked his nobles, "Did we not cast three men bound into the fire?" "Assuredly, O king," they answered. 92 "But," he replied, "I see four men unfettered and unhurt, walking in the fire, and the fourth looks like a son of God." 93 Then Nebuchadnezzar came to the opening of the white-hot furnace and called to Shadrach, Meshach, and Abednego: "Servants of the most high God, come out." Thereupon Shadrach, Meshach, and Abednego came out of the fire. 94 When the satraps, prefects, governors, and nobles of the king came together, they saw that the fire had had no power over the bodies of these men; not a hair of their heads had been singed, nor were their garments altered; there was not even a smell of fire about them. 95 Nebuchadnezzar exclaimed, "Blessed be the God of Shadrach, Meshach, and Abednego, who sent his angel to deliver the servants that trusted in him; they disobeyed the royal command and yielded their bodies rather than serve or worship any god except their own God. 96 Therefore I decree for nations and peoples of every language that whoever blasphemes the God of Shadrach, Meshach, and Abednego shall be cut to pieces and his house destroyed. For there is no other God who can rescue like this." 97 Then the king promoted Shadrach, Meshach, and Abednego in the province of Babylon.

98 King Nebuchadnezzar to the nations and peoples of every language, wherever they dwell on earth: abundant peace! 99 It has seemed good to me to publish the signs and wonders which the most high God has accomplished in my regard.

100 How great are his signs, how mighty his wonders;
his kingdom is an everlasting kingdom,
and his dominion endures through
all generations.

4 I, Nebuchadnezzar, was at home in my palace, content and prosperous. 2 I had a terrifying dream as I lay in bed, and the images and the visions of my mind frightened me. 3 So I issued a decree that all the wise men of Babylon should be brought before me to give the interpretation of the dream. 4 When the magicians, enchanters, Chaldeans, and

King Nebuchadnezzar, 'Your question needs no answer from us: 17 if our God, the one we serve, is able to save us from the burning fiery furnace and from your power, Your Majesty, he will save us; 18 and even if he does not, then you must know, Your Majesty, that we will not serve your god or worship the statue you have set up.' 19 This infuriated King Nebuchadnezzar; his expression was changed now as he looked at Shadrach, Meshach and Abed-Nego. He gave orders for the furnace to be made seven times hotter than usual 20 and commanded certain stalwarts from his army to bind Shadrach, Meshach and Abed-Nego and throw them into the burning fiery furnace. 21 They were then bound in their cloaks, trousers, headgear and other garments, and thrown into the burning fiery furnace. 22 The king's command was so urgent and the heat of the furnace was so fierce, that the men carrying Shadrach, Meshach and Abed-Nego were burnt to death by the flames from the fire; 23 the three men, Shadrach, Meshach and Abed-Nego fell, bound, into the burning fiery furnace.

‡3.24–90 (the Greek addition): see p. 2421‡

24/91 c King Nebuchadnezzar sprang to his feet in amazement. He said to his advisers, 'Did we not have these three men thrown bound into the fire?' They answered the king, 'Certainly, Your Majesty'. 25/92 'But', he went on, 'I can see four men walking free in the heart of the fire and quite unharmed! And the fourth looks like a child of the gods!' 26/93 Nebuchadnezzar approached the mouth of the burning fiery furnace and said, 'Shadrach, Meshach and Abed-Nego, servants of God Most High, come out, come here!' And from the heart of the fire out came Shadrach, Meshach and Abed-Nego. 27/94 The satraps, magistrates, governors, and advisers of the king crowded round the three men to examine them: the fire had had no effect on their bodies: not a hair of their heads had been singed, their cloaks were not scorched, no smell of burning hung about them. Nebuchadnezzar said, 28/95 'Blessed be the God of Shadrach, Meshach and Abed-Nego: he has sent his angel to rescue his servants who, putting their trust in him, defied the order of the king, and preferred to forfeit their bodies rather than serve or worship any god but their God. 29/96 I therefore decree as follows, "Peoples, nations, and languages! Let any of you speak disrespectfully of the God of Shadrach, Meshach and Abed-Nego, and I shall have him torn limb from limb and his house turned into a dunghill; for there is no other god who can save like this." '

30/97 The king then showered favours on Shadrach, Meshach and Abed-Nego in the province of Babylon.

31/98 'King Nebuchadnezzar, to all peoples, nations and languages dwelling throughout the world: may you prosper more and more!

32/99 'It is my pleasure to make known the signs and wonders with which the Most High God has favoured me.

33/100 How great his signs,
how mighty his wonders!
His kingdom is an everlasting kingdom,
his empire endures age after age!'

4 'I, Nebuchadnezzar, was living comfortably in my house, prosperously in my palace. 2 I had a dream; it appalled me. Dread assailed me as I lay in bed; the visions that passed through my head tormented me. 3 So I decreed that all the sages of Babylon be summoned to explain to me what the dream meant. 4 Magicians, soothsayers, Chaldae-

c 3 At this point the Hebr. resumes. The verse numbering is therefore given according to both Hebr. and Gk.

chanters, the Chaldeans, and the diviners came in, and I told them the dream, but they could not tell me its interpretation. 8 At last Daniel came in before me — he who was named Belteshazzar after the name of my god, and who is endowed with a spirit of the holy gods[k] — and I told him the dream: 9 "O Belteshazzar, chief of the magicians, I know that you are endowed with a spirit of the holy gods[k] and that no mystery is too difficult for you. Hear[l] the dream that I saw; tell me its interpretation.

10 [m] Upon my bed this is what I saw;
    there was a tree at the center of the earth,
    and its height was great.
11 The tree grew great and strong,
    its top reached to heaven,
    and it was visible to the ends of the whole earth.
12 Its foliage was beautiful,
    its fruit abundant,
    and it provided food for all.
The animals of the field found shade under it,
    the birds of the air nested in its branches,
    and from it all living beings were fed.

13 I continued looking, in the visions of my head as I lay in bed, and there was a holy watcher, coming down from heaven. 14 He cried aloud and said:

'Cut down the tree and chop off its branches,
    strip off its foliage and scatter its fruit.
Let the animals flee from beneath it
    and the birds from its branches.
15 But leave its stump and roots in the ground,
    with a band of iron and bronze,
    in the tender grass of the field.
Let him be bathed with the dew of heaven,
    and let his lot be with the animals of the field
    in the grass of the earth.
16 Let his mind be changed from that of a human,
    and let the mind of an animal be given to him.
    And let seven times pass over him.
17 The sentence is rendered by decree of the watchers,
    the decision is given by order of the holy ones,
    in order that all who live may know
    that the Most High is sovereign over the kingdom of mortals;
    he gives it to whom he will
    and sets over it the lowliest of human beings.'

18 This is the dream that I, King Nebuchadnezzar, saw. Now you, Belteshazzar, declare the interpretation, since all the wise men of my kingdom are unable to tell me the interpretation. You are able, however, for you are endowed with a spirit of the holy gods."[k]

19 Then Daniel, who was called Belteshazzar, was severely distressed for a while. His thoughts terrified him. The king said, "Belteshazzar, do not let the dream or the interpretation terrify you." Belteshazzar answered, "My lord, may the dream be for those who hate you, and its interpretation for your enemies! 20 The tree that you saw, which grew great and strong, so that its top reached to heaven and was visible to the end of the whole earth, 21 whose foliage was beautiful and its fruit abundant, and which provided food for all, under which animals of the field lived, and in whose branches the birds of the air had nests — 22 it is you, O king! You have grown great and strong. Your greatness has increased and reaches to heaven, and your sovereignty to the ends of the earth. 23 And

came in, I related my dream to them, but they were unable to interpret it for me. 8 Finally there came before me Daniel, who is called Belteshazzar after the name of my god, a man in whom resides the spirit of the holy gods. To him also I related the dream: 9 'Belteshazzar, chief of the magicians, you have in you, as I know, the spirit of the holy gods, and no secret baffles you; listen to what I saw in my dream, and tell me its interpretation.

10 'This is the vision which came to me while I lay on my bed:

As I was looking,
    there appeared a very lofty tree at the centre of the earth;
11 the tree grew great and became strong;
    its top reached to the sky,
    and it was visible to earth's farthest bounds.
12 Its foliage was beautiful
    and its fruit abundant,
    and it yielded food for all.
Beneath it the wild beasts found shelter,
    the birds lodged in the branches,
    and from it all living creatures fed.

13 'This is what I saw in the vision which came to me while I lay on my bed:

There appeared a watcher,
    a holy one coming down from heaven.
14 In a mighty voice he cried,
    "Hew down the tree, lop off the branches,
    strip away its foliage and scatter the fruit;
    let the wild beasts flee from beneath it
    and the birds from its branches;
15 but leave the stump with its roots in the ground.

' "So, bound with iron and bronze among the lush grass,
    let him be drenched with the dew of heaven
    and share the lot of the beasts in their pasture —
16 his mind will cease to be human,
    and he will be given the mind of a beast.
    Seven times will pass over him.
17 The issue has been determined by the watchers
    and the sentence pronounced by the holy ones.

' "Thereby the living will know that the Most High is sovereign in the kingdom of men: he gives the kingdom to whom he wills, and may appoint over it the lowliest of mankind."

18 'This is the dream which I, King Nebuchadnezzar, dreamt; now, Belteshazzar, tell me its interpretation, for, though not one of the wise men in all my kingdom is able to make its meaning known to me, you can do it, because in you is the spirit of the holy gods.'

19 Daniel, who was called Belteshazzar, was dumbfounded for a moment, dismayed by his thoughts; but the king said, 'Do not let the dream and its interpretation dismay you.' Belteshazzar answered, 'My lord, if only the dream applied to those who hate you and its interpretation to your enemies! 20 The tree which you saw grow great and become strong, reaching with its top to the sky and visible to earth's farthest bounds, 21 its foliage beautiful and its fruit abundant, a tree which yielded food for all, beneath which the wild beasts dwelt and in whose branches the birds lodged: 22 that tree, your majesty, is you. You have become great and strong; your power has grown and reaches the sky; your sovereignty extends to the ends of the earth. 23 Also, your

---

k Or a holy, divine spirit   l Theodotion: Aram The visions of
m Theodotion Syr Compare Gk: Aram adds The visions of my head

4:9 listen to: so Gk (Theod.); Aram. visions of.

astrologers had come in, I related the dream before them; but none of them could tell me its meaning. 5 Finally there came before me Daniel, whose name is Belteshazzar after the name of my god, and in whom is the spirit of the holy God. I repeated the dream to him: 6 "Belteshazzar, chief of the magicians, I know that the spirit of the holy God is in you and no mystery is too difficult for you; tell me the meaning of the visions that I saw in my dream.

7 "These were the visions I saw while in bed: I saw a tree of great height at the center of the world. 8 It was large and strong, with its top touching the heavens, and it could be seen to the ends of the earth. 9 Its leaves were beautiful and its fruit abundant, providing food for all. Under it the wild beasts found shade, in its branches the birds of the air nested; all men ate of it. 10 In the vision I saw while in bed, a holy sentinel came down from heaven, 11 and cried out:

" 'Cut down the tree and lop off its branches,
    strip off its leaves and scatter its fruit;
let the beasts flee its shade, and the birds
    its branches.
12 But leave in the earth its stump and roots,
    fettered with iron and bronze, in the grass of
        the field.
Let him be bathed with the dew of heaven;
    his lot be to eat, among beasts, the grass of
        the earth.
13 Let his mind be changed from the human;
    let him be given the sense of a beast,
    till seven years pass over him.
14 By decree of the sentinels is this decided,
    by order of the holy ones, this sentence;
That all who live may know
    that the Most High rules over the kingdom
        of men:
He can give it to whom he will,
    or set over it the lowliest of men.'

15 "This is the dream that I, King Nebuchadnezzar, had. Now, Belteshazzar, tell me its meaning. Although none of the wise men in my kingdom can tell me the meaning, you can, because the spirit of the holy God is in you."

16 Then Daniel, whose name was Belteshazzar, was appalled for a while, terrified by his thoughts. "Belteshazzar," the king said to him, "let not the dream or its meaning terrify you." 17 "My lord," Belteshazzar replied, "this dream should be for your enemies, and its meaning for your foes. The large, strong tree that you saw, with its top touching the heavens, that could be seen by the whole earth, 18 which had beautiful foliage and abundant fruit, providing food for all, under which the wild beasts lived, and in whose branches the birds of the air dwelt— 19 you are that tree, O king, large and strong! Your majesty has become so great as to touch the heavens, and your rule extends over the whole earth. 20 As for the king's vision of a holy sentinel

ans and exorcists came, and I told them what I had dreamt, but they could not interpret it for me. 5 Daniel, renamed Belteshazzar after my own god, and in whom the spirit of the holy gods resides, then came into my presence. I told him my dream:

6 ' "Belteshazzar, chief of magicians," I said, "I know that the spirit of the holy gods resides in you and that no mystery puts you at a loss. This is the dream I have had; tell me what it means.

7 ' "The visions that passed through my head as I lay in bed were these:

I saw a tree
    in the middle of the world;
    it was very tall.
8 The tree grew taller and stronger,
    until its top reached the sky
    and it could be seen from the very ends of the
        earth.
9 Its foliage was beautiful, its fruit abundant,
    in it was food for all.
For the wild animals it provided shade,
    the birds of heaven nested in its branches,
    all living creatures found their food on it.

10 ' "I watched the visions passing through my head as I lay in bed:

Next, a Watchful One, d a holy one, came down
        from heaven.
11 At the top of his voice he shouted:
Cut the tree down, lop off its branches,
    strip off its leaves, throw away its fruit;
let the animals flee from its shelter
    and the birds from its branches.
12 But leave the stump with its roots in the ground,
    bound with hoops of iron and bronze,
    in the grass of the countryside.
Let it be drenched by the dew of heaven
    and have its lot with the animals, eating grass!
13 Let it cease to have a human heart,
    and be given the heart of a beast,
    and seven times shall pass over him!
14 Such is the sentence proclaimed by the Watchers,
    the verdict announced by the holy ones—
so that every living thing may learn
    that the Most High rules over human sovereignty;
    he confers it on whom he pleases,
    and raises the lowest of humankind.

15 ' "This was the dream I had—I, Nebuchadnezzar the king. Now it is for you, Belteshazzar, to pronounce on its meaning, since not one of the sages in my kingdom has been able to interpret it for me; you, however, can do so, since the spirit of the holy gods resides in you." '

16 Daniel, known as Belteshazzar, was confused for a time and upset.

The king said, 'Belteshazzar, do not be upset at the dream and its meaning.' Belteshazzar answered, 'My lord, may the dream apply to those who hate you, and its meaning to your foes! 17 The tree you saw, so large and strong and tall that it reached the sky and could be seen throughout the world, 18 the tree with beautiful foliage and abundant fruit, with food for all in it, providing shade for the wild animals, with the birds of heaven nesting in its branches: 19 that tree is yourself, Your Majesty, for you have grown great and strong; your stature is now so great that it reaches the sky, and your empire extends to the ends of the earth.

d 4 An angel, one of God's attendants, a term common in extra-biblical contemporary works.

NEW REVISED STANDARD VERSION

whereas the king saw a holy watcher coming down from heaven and saying, 'Cut down the tree and destroy it, but leave its stump and roots in the ground, with a band of iron and bronze, in the grass of the field; and let him be bathed with the dew of heaven, and let his lot be with the animals of the field, until seven times pass over him' — 24 this is the interpretation, O king, and it is a decree of the Most High that has come upon my lord the king: 25 You shall be driven away from human society, and your dwelling shall be with the wild animals. You shall be made to eat grass like oxen, you shall be bathed with the dew of heaven, and seven times shall pass over you, until you have learned that the Most High has sovereignty over the kingdom of mortals, and gives it to whom he will. 26 As it was commanded to leave the stump and roots of the tree, your kingdom shall be re-established for you from the time that you learn that Heaven is sovereign. 27 Therefore, O king, may my counsel be acceptable to you: atone for[n] your sins with righteousness, and your iniquities with mercy to the oppressed, so that your prosperity may be prolonged."

28 All this came upon King Nebuchadnezzar. 29 At the end of twelve months he was walking on the roof of the royal palace of Babylon, 30 and the king said, "Is this not magnificent Babylon, which I have built as a royal capital by my mighty power and for my glorious majesty?" 31 While the words were still in the king's mouth, a voice came from heaven: "O King Nebuchadnezzar, to you it is declared: The kingdom has departed from you! 32 You shall be driven away from human society, and your dwelling shall be with the animals of the field. You shall be made to eat grass like oxen, and seven times shall pass over you, until you have learned that the Most High has sovereignty over the kingdom of mortals and gives it to whom he will." 33 Immediately the sentence was fulfilled against Nebuchadnezzar. He was driven away from human society, ate grass like oxen, and his body was bathed with the dew of heaven, until his hair grew as long as eagles' feathers and his nails became like birds' claws.

34 When that period was over, I, Nebuchadnezzar, lifted my eyes to heaven, and my reason returned to me.

I blessed the Most High,
and praised and honored the one who lives
forever.
For his sovereignty is an everlasting sovereignty,
and his kingdom endures from generation to
generation.
35 All the inhabitants of the earth are accounted as
nothing,
and he does what he wills with the host of
heaven
and the inhabitants of the earth.
There is no one who can stay his hand
or say to him, "What are you doing?"

36 At that time my reason returned to me; and my majesty and splendor were restored to me for the glory of my kingdom. My counselors and my lords sought me out, I was re-established over my kingdom, and still more greatness was added to me. 37 Now I, Nebuchadnezzar, praise and extol and honor the King of heaven,

for all his works are truth,
and his ways are justice;
and he is able to bring low
those who walk in pride.

5 King Belshazzar made a great festival for a thousand of his lords, and he was drinking wine in the presence of the thousand.

REVISED ENGLISH BIBLE

majesty, you saw a watcher, a holy one, coming down from heaven and saying, "Hew down the tree and destroy it, but leave the stump with its roots in the ground. So, bound with iron and bronze among the lush grass, let him be drenched with the dew of heaven and share the lot of the beasts until seven times pass over him."

24 'This is the interpretation, your majesty: it is a decree of the Most High which affects my lord the king. 25 You will be banished from human society; you will be made to live with the wild beasts; like oxen you will feed on grass, and you will be drenched with the dew of heaven. Seven times will pass over you until you have acknowledged that the Most High is sovereign over the realm of humanity and gives it to whom he wills. 26 As the command was given to leave the stump of the tree with its roots, by this you may know that from the time you acknowledge the sovereignty of Heaven your rule will endure. 27 Your majesty, be advised by me: let charitable deeds replace your sins, generosity to the poor your wrongdoing. It may be that you will long enjoy contentment.'

28 All this befell King Nebuchadnezzar. 29 At the end of twelve months the king was walking on the roof of the royal palace at Babylon, 30 and he exclaimed, 'Is not this Babylon the great which I have built as a royal residence by my mighty power and for the honour of my own majesty?' 31 The words were still on his lips, when there came a voice from heaven: 'To you, King Nebuchadnezzar, the word is spoken: the kingdom has passed from you. 32 You are banished from human society; you are to live with the wild beasts and feed on grass like oxen. Seven times will pass over you until you have acknowledged that the Most High is sovereign over the realm of humanity and gives it to whom he will.' 33 At that very moment this judgement came upon Nebuchadnezzar: he was banished from human society to eat grass like oxen, and his body was drenched with the dew of heaven, until his hair became shaggy like an eagle and his nails grew like birds' claws.

34 At the end of the appointed time, I, Nebuchadnezzar, looked up towards heaven and I was restored to my right mind. I blessed the Most High, praising and glorifying the Ever-living One:

His sovereignty is everlasting
and his kingdom endures through all generations.
35 All who dwell on earth count for nothing;
he does as he pleases with the host of heaven
and with those who dwell on earth.
No one can oppose his power
or question what he does.

36 At that very time I was restored to my right mind and, for the glory of my kingdom, my majesty and royal splendour returned to me. My courtiers and my nobles sought audience of me, and I was re-established in my kingdom and my power was greatly increased. 37 Now I, Nebuchadnezzar, praise and exalt and glorify the King of heaven; for all his acts are right and his ways are just, and he can bring low those whose conduct is arrogant.

5 KING Belshazzar gave a grand banquet for a thousand of his nobles and he was drinking wine in their presence. 2 Under the influence of the wine, Belshazzar gave

[n] Aram break off

that came down from heaven and proclaimed: 'Cut down the tree and destroy it, but leave in the earth its stump and roots, fettered with iron and bronze in the grass of the field; let him be bathed with the dew of heaven, and let his lot be among wild beasts till seven years pass over him' — 21 this is its meaning, O king; this is the sentence which the Most High has passed upon my lord king: 22 You shall be cast out from among men and dwell with wild beasts; you shall be given grass to eat like an ox and be bathed with the dew of heaven; seven years shall pass over you, until you know that the Most High rules over the kingdom of men and gives it to whom he will. 23 The command that the stump and roots of the tree are to be left means that your kingdom shall be preserved for you, once you have learned it in heaven that rules. 24 Therefore, O king, take my advice; atone for your sins by good deeds, and for your misdeeds by kindness to the poor; then your prosperity will be long."

25 All this happened to King Nebuchadnezzar. 26 Twelve months later, as he was walking on the roof of the royal palace in Babylon, 27 the king said, "Babylon the great! Was it not I, with my great strength, who built it as a royal residence for my splendor and majesty?" 28 While these words were still on the king's lips, a voice spoke from heaven, "It has been decreed for you, King Nebuchadnezzar, that your kingdom is taken from you! 29 You shall be cast out from among men, and shall dwell with wild beasts; you shall be given grass to eat like an ox, and seven years shall pass over you, until you learn that the Most High rules over the kingdom of men and gives it to whom he will." 30 At once this was fulfilled. Nebuchadnezzar was cast out from among men, he ate grass like an ox, and his body was bathed with the dew of heaven, until his hair grew like the feathers of an eagle, and his nails like the claws of a bird.

31 When this period was over, I, Nebuchadnezzar, raised my eyes to heaven; my reason was restored to me, and I blessed the Most High, I praised and glorified him who lives forever:

His dominion is an everlasting dominion,
and his kingdom endures through all generations.
32 All who live on the earth are counted as nothing;
he does as he pleases with the powers of heaven
as well as with those who live on the earth.
There is no one who can stay his hand
or say to him, "What have you done?"

33 At the same time my reason returned to me, and for the glory of my kingdom, my majesty and my splendor returned to me. My nobles and lords sought me out; I was restored to my kingdom, and became much greater than before. 34 Therefore, I, Nebuchadnezzar, now praise and exalt and glorify the King of heaven, because all his works are right and his ways just; and those who walk in pride he is able to humble.

5 King Belshazzar gave a great banquet for a thousand of his lords, with whom he drank. 2 Under the influence

20 'And the Watchful One seen by the king, the holy one coming down from heaven and saying, "Cut the tree down and destroy it, but leave stump and roots in the ground, bound with hoops of iron and bronze in the grass of the countryside; let it be drenched by the dew and have its lot with the wild animals until seven times have passed over it": 21 the meaning of this, Your Majesty, the verdict of the Most High passed on my lord the king, is this:

22 You will be driven from human society
and will make your home with the wild animals,
you will feed on grass, as oxen do,
you will be drenched by the dew of heaven;
seven times will pass over you
until you have learnt
that the Most High rules over human sovereignty
and confers it on whom he pleases.

23 'And the order, "Leave the stump and roots of the tree", means that your kingdom will be kept for you until you come to understand that Heaven rules all. 24 May it please the king to accept my advice: by upright actions break with your sins, break with your crimes by showing mercy to the poor, and so live long and peacefully.'

25 This all happened to King Nebuchadnezzar. 26 At the end of twelve months, while strolling on the roof of the royal palace in Babylon, 27 the king was saying, 'Great Babylon! Was it not built by me as a royal residence, by the force of my might and for the majesty of my glory?' 28 The words were not out of his mouth when a voice came down from heaven:

'Of you, King Nebuchadnezzar, it is decreed:
the empire has been taken from you,
29 you will be driven from human society
and will make your home with the wild animals;
you will feed on grass, as oxen do,
and seven times will pass over you
until you have learnt
that the Most High rules over human sovereignty
and gives it to whom he pleases.'

30 The words were immediately fulfilled: Nebuchadnezzar was driven from human society and ate grass as oxen do; he was drenched by the dew of heaven; his hair grew like an eagle's feathers, and his nails became like a bird's talons.

31 'When the time was over, I, Nebuchadnezzar, raised my eyes to heaven: my reason returned. And I blessed the Most High,

praising and glorifying him who lives for ever,
for his empire is an everlasting empire,
his kingship endures, age after age.
32 All who dwell on earth count for nothing;
as he thinks fit, he disposes the army of heaven
and those who dwell on earth.
No one can arrest his hand
or ask him, "What have you done?"

33 'At that moment my reason returned and, for the honour of my royal state, my glory and splendour returned too. My counsellors and noblemen acclaimed me; I was restored to my throne, and to my past greatness even more was added. 34 And now I, Nebuchadnezzar,

praise, extol and glorify the King of heaven,
all of whose deeds are true,
all of whose ways are right,
and who can humble those who walk in pride.'

5 King Belshazzar gave a great banquet for his noblemen, a thousand of them, and, in the presence of this thousand, he drank his wine. 2 Having tasted the wine, Bel-

NEW REVISED STANDARD VERSION

2 Under the influence of the wine, Belshazzar commanded that they bring in the vessels of gold and silver that his father Nebuchadnezzar had taken out of the temple in Jerusalem, so that the king and his lords, his wives, and his concubines might drink from them. 3 So they brought in the vessels of gold and silver*o* that had been taken out of the temple, the house of God in Jerusalem, and the king and his lords, his wives, and his concubines drank from them. 4 They drank the wine and praised the gods of gold and silver, bronze, iron, wood, and stone.

5 Immediately the fingers of a human hand appeared and began writing on the plaster of the wall of the royal palace, next to the lampstand. The king was watching the hand as it wrote. 6 Then the king's face turned pale, and his thoughts terrified him. His limbs gave way, and his knees knocked together. 7 The king cried aloud to bring in the enchanters, the Chaldeans, and the diviners; and the king said to the wise men of Babylon, "Whoever can read this writing and tell me its interpretation shall be clothed in purple, have a chain of gold around his neck, and rank third in the kingdom." 8 Then all the king's wise men came in, but they could not read the writing or tell the king the interpretation. 9 Then King Belshazzar became greatly terrified and his face turned pale, and his lords were perplexed.

10 The queen, when she heard the discussion of the king and his lords, came into the banqueting hall. The queen said, "O king, live forever! Do not let your thoughts terrify you or your face grow pale. 11 There is a man in your kingdom who is endowed with a spirit of the holy gods.*p* In the days of your father he was found to have enlightenment, understanding, and wisdom like the wisdom of the gods. Your father, King Nebuchadnezzar, made him chief of the magicians, enchanters, Chaldeans, and diviners,*q* 12 because an excellent spirit, knowledge, and understanding to interpret dreams, explain riddles, and solve problems were found in this Daniel, whom the king named Belteshazzar. Now let Daniel be called, and he will give the interpretation."

13 Then Daniel was brought in before the king. The king said to Daniel, "So you are Daniel, one of the exiles of Judah, whom my father the king brought from Judah? 14 I have heard of you that a spirit of the gods*r* is in you, and that enlightenment, understanding, and excellent wisdom are found in you. 15 Now the wise men, the enchanters, have been brought in before me to read this writing and tell me its interpretation, but they were not able to give the interpretation of the matter. 16 But I have heard that you can give interpretations and solve problems. Now if you are able to read the writing and tell me its interpretation, you shall be clothed in purple, have a chain of gold around your neck, and rank third in the kingdom."

17 Then Daniel answered in the presence of the king, "Let your gifts be for yourself, or give your rewards to someone else! Nevertheless I will read the writing to the king and let him know the interpretation. 18 O king, the Most High God gave your father Nebuchadnezzar kingship, greatness, glory, and majesty. 19 And because of the greatness that he gave him, all peoples, nations, and languages trembled and feared before him. He killed those he wanted to kill, kept alive those he wanted to keep alive, honored those he wanted to honor, and degraded those he wanted to degrade. 20 But when his heart was lifted up and his spirit was hardened so that he acted proudly, he was deposed from his kingly throne, and his glory was stripped from him. 21 He was driven from human society, and his mind

REVISED ENGLISH BIBLE

orders for the vessels of gold and silver which his father Nebuchadnezzar had taken from the temple at Jerusalem to be fetched, so that he and his nobles, along with his concubines and courtesans, might drink from them. 3 So those vessels belonging to the house of God, the temple at Jerusalem, were brought, and the king, the nobles, and the concubines and courtesans drank from them. 4 They drank their wine and they praised their gods of gold, silver, bronze, iron, wood, and stone.

5 Suddenly there appeared the fingers of a human hand writing on the plaster of the palace wall opposite the lamp, and the king saw the palm of the hand as it wrote. 6 At this the king turned pale; dismay filled his mind, the strength went from his legs, and his knees knocked together. 7 He called in a loud voice for the exorcists, Chaldaeans, and diviners to be brought in; then, addressing Babylon's wise men, he said, 'Whoever reads this writing and tells me its interpretation shall be robed in purple and have a gold chain hung round his neck, and he shall rank third in the kingdom.' 8 All the king's wise men came, but they could neither read the writing nor make known to the king its interpretation. 9 Then his deep dismay drove all colour from King Belshazzar's cheeks, and his nobles were in a state of confusion.

10 Drawn by what the king and his nobles were saying, the queen entered the banqueting hall: 'Long live the king!' she said. 'Why this dismay, and why do you look so pale? 11 There is a man in your kingdom who has the spirit of the holy gods in him; he was known in your father's time to possess clear insight and godlike wisdom, so that King Nebuchadnezzar, your father, appointed him chief of the magicians, exorcists, Chaldaeans, and diviners. 12 This Daniel, whom the king named Belteshazzar, is known to have exceptional ability, with knowledge and insight, and the gift of interpreting dreams, explaining riddles, and unravelling problems; let him be summoned now and he will give the interpretation.'

13 Daniel was then brought into the royal presence, and the king addressed him: 'So you are Daniel, one of the Jewish exiles whom my royal father brought from Judah. 14 I am informed that the spirit of the gods resides in you and that you are known as a man of clear insight and exceptional wisdom. 15 The wise men, the exorcists, have just been brought before me to read this writing and make known its interpretation to me, but they have been unable to give its meaning. 16 I am told that you are able to furnish interpretations and unravel problems. Now, if you can read the writing and make known the interpretation, you shall be robed in purple and have a gold chain hung round your neck, and you shall rank third in the kingdom.' 17 Daniel replied, 'Your majesty, I do not look for gifts from you; give your rewards to another. Nevertheless I shall read your majesty the writing and make known to you its interpretation.

18 'My lord king, the Most High God gave a kingdom with power, glory, and majesty to your father Nebuchadnezzar; 19 and, because of the power he bestowed on him, all peoples and nations of every language trembled with fear before him. He put to death whom he would and spared whom he would, he promoted them at will and at will abased them. 20 But, when he became haughty and stubborn and presumptuous, he was deposed from his royal throne and stripped of his glory. 21 He was banished from human

---

o Theodotion Vg: Aram lacks *and silver*   *p* Or *a holy, divine spirit*
q Aram adds *the king your father*   *r* Or *a divine spirit*

5:10 **queen:** *or* queen mother.   5:12 **unravelling problems:** *or* unbinding spells.   5:16 **unravel problems:** *or* unbind spells.

of the wine, he ordered the gold and silver vessels which Nebuchadnezzar, his father, had taken from the temple in Jerusalem, to be brought in so that the king, his lords, his wives and his entertainers might drink from them. 3 When the gold and silver vessels taken from the house of God in Jerusalem had been brought in, and while the king, his lords, his wives and his entertainers were drinking 4 wine from them, they praised their gods of gold and silver, bronze and iron, wood and stone.

5 Suddenly, opposite the lampstand, the fingers of a human hand appeared, writing on the plaster of the wall in the king's palace. When the king saw the wrist and hand that wrote, 6 his face blanched; his thoughts terrified him, his hip joints shook, and his knees knocked. 7 The king shouted for the enchanters, Chaldeans, and astrologers to be brought in. "Whoever reads this writing and tells me what it means," he said to the wise men of Babylon, "shall be clothed in purple, wear a golden collar about his neck, and be third in the government of the kingdom." 8 But though all the king's wise men came in, none of them could either read the writing or tell the king what it meant. 9 Then King Belshazzar was greatly terrified; his face went ashen, and his lords were thrown into confusion.

10 When the queen heard of the discussion between the king and his lords, she entered the banquet hall and said, "O king, live forever! Be not troubled in mind, nor look so pale! 11 There is a man in your kingdom in whom is the spirit of the holy God; during the lifetime of your father he was seen to have brilliant knowledge and god-like wisdom. In fact, King Nebuchadnezzar, your father, made him chief of the magicians, enchanters, Chaldeans, and astrologers, 12 because of the extraordinary mind possessed by this Daniel, whom the king named Belteshazzar. He knew and understood how to interpret dreams, explain enigmas, and solve difficulties. Now therefore, summon Daniel to tell you what this means."

13 Then Daniel was brought into the presence of the king. The king asked him, "Are you the Daniel, the Jewish exile, whom my father, the king, brought from Judah? 14 I have heard that the spirit of God is in you, that you possess brilliant knowledge and extraordinary wisdom. 15 Now, the wise men and enchanters were brought in to me to read this writing and tell me its meaning, but they could not say what the words meant. 16 But I have heard that you can interpret dreams and solve difficulties; if you are able to read the writing and tell me what it means, you shall be clothed in purple, wear a gold collar about your neck, and be third in the government of the kingdom."

17 Daniel answered the king: "You may keep your gifts, or give your presents to someone else; but the writing I will read for you, O king, and tell you what it means. 18 The Most High God gave your father Nebuchadnezzar a great kingdom and glorious majesty. 19 Because he made him so great, the nations and peoples of every language dreaded and feared him. Whomever he wished, he killed or let live; whomever he wished, he exalted or humbled. 20 But when his heart became proud and his spirit hardened by insolence, he was put down from his royal throne and deprived of his glory; 21 he was cast out from among men and was made

shazzar gave orders for the gold and silver vessels to be brought which his father Nebuchadnezzar had taken from the sanctuary in Jerusalem, so that the king, his noblemen, his wives and the women who sang for him might drink out of them. 3 The gold and silver vessels taken from the sanctuary of the Temple of God in Jerusalem were brought in, and the king, his noblemen, his wives and the women who sang for him drank out of them. 4 They drank their wine and praised their idols of gold and silver, of bronze and iron, of wood and stone. 5 Suddenly, the fingers of a human hand appeared and began to write on the plaster of the palace wall, directly behind the lamp-stand; and the king could see the hand as it wrote. 6 The king turned pale with alarm: his hip-joints went slack and his knees began to knock. 7 He shouted for his soothsayers, Chaldaeans, and exorcists. And the king said to the Babylonian sages, 'Anyone who can read this writing and tell me what it means shall be dressed in purple, and have a chain of gold put round his neck, and be one of the three men who govern the kingdom.' 8 The king's sages all crowded forward, but they could neither read the writing nor explain to the king what it meant. 9 Greatly alarmed, King Belshazzar turned even paler, and his noblemen were equally disturbed. 10 Then the queen, attracted by the noise made by the king and his noblemen, came into the banqueting hall. 'May Your Majesty live for ever!' said the queen. 'Do not be alarmed, do not look so pale. 11 In your kingdom there is a man in whom lives the spirit of the holy gods. In your father's days he was known for a perception, intelligence and wisdom comparable to that of the gods. King Nebuchadnezzar, your father, made him head of the magicians, soothsayers, Chaldaeans and exorcists. 12 Since this man Daniel, whom the king had renamed Belteshazzar, is filled with such a marvellous spirit and such knowledge and intelligence in interpreting dreams, solving enigmas and unravelling difficult problems, send for him; he will be able to tell you what this means.'

13 Daniel was brought into the king's presence; the king said to Daniel, 'Are you the Daniel who was one of the Judaean exiles brought by my father the king from Judah? 14 I am told that the spirit of the gods lives in you, and that you are known for your perception, intelligence and marvellous wisdom. 15 The sages and soothsayers have already been brought to me to read this writing and tell me what it means, but they have been unable to reveal its meaning. 16 I am told that you are able to give interpretations and to unravel difficult problems, so if you can read the writing and tell me what it means, you shall be dressed in purple, and have a chain of gold put round your neck, and be one of the three men who govern the kingdom.'

17 Then Daniel spoke up in the presence of the king. 'Keep your gifts for yourself,' he said, 'and give your rewards to others! I can certainly read the writing to the king and tell him what it means. 18 Your Majesty, the Most High God gave Nebuchadnezzar your father sovereignty, greatness, majesty and glory. 19 He made him so great that all peoples, nations and languages shook with dread before him: he killed whom he pleased, spared whom he pleased, promoted whom he pleased, degraded whom he pleased. 20 But because his heart grew swollen with pride, and his spirit stiff with arrogance, he was deposed from his sovereign throne and stripped of his glory. 21 He was driven from

was made like that of an animal. His dwelling was with the wild asses, he was fed grass like oxen, and his body was bathed with the dew of heaven, until he learned that the Most High God has sovereignty over the kingdom of mortals, and sets over it whomever he will. 22 And you, Belshazzar his son, have not humbled your heart, even though you knew all this! 23 You have exalted yourself against the Lord of heaven! The vessels of his temple have been brought in before you, and you and your lords, your wives and your concubines have been drinking wine from them. You have praised the gods of silver and gold, of bronze, iron, wood, and stone, which do not see or hear or know; but the God in whose power is your very breath, and to whom belong all your ways, you have not honored.

24 "So from his presence the hand was sent and this writing was inscribed. 25 And this is the writing that was inscribed: MENE, MENE, TEKEL, and PARSIN. 26 This is the interpretation of the matter: MENE, God has numbered the days of*s* your kingdom and brought it to an end; 27 TEKEL, you have been weighed on the scales and found wanting; 28 PERES,*t* your kingdom is divided and given to the Medes and Persians."

29 Then Belshazzar gave the command, and Daniel was clothed in purple, a chain of gold was put around his neck, and a proclamation was made concerning him that he should rank third in the kingdom.

30 That very night Belshazzar, the Chaldean king, was killed. 31 *u* And Darius the Mede received the kingdom, being about sixty-two years old.

6 It pleased Darius to set over the kingdom one hundred twenty satraps, stationed throughout the whole kingdom, 2 and over them three presidents, including Daniel; to these the satraps gave account, so that the king might suffer no loss. 3 Soon Daniel distinguished himself above all the other presidents and satraps because an excellent spirit was in him, and the king planned to appoint him over the whole kingdom. 4 So the presidents and the satraps tried to find grounds for complaint against Daniel in connection with the kingdom. But they could find no grounds for complaint or any corruption, because he was faithful, and no negligence or corruption could be found in him. 5 The men said, "We shall not find any ground for complaint against this Daniel unless we find it in connection with the law of his God."

6 So the presidents and satraps conspired and came to the king and said to him, "O King Darius, live forever! 7 All the presidents of the kingdom, the prefects and the satraps, the counselors and the governors are agreed that the king should establish an ordinance and enforce an interdict, that whoever prays to anyone, divine or human, for thirty days, except to you, O king, shall be thrown into a den of lions. 8 Now, O king, establish the interdict and sign the document, so that it cannot be changed, according to the law of the Medes and the Persians, which cannot be revoked." 9 Therefore King Darius signed the document and interdict.

10 Although Daniel knew that the document had been signed, he continued to go to his house, which had windows in its upper room open toward Jerusalem, and to get down on his knees three times a day to pray to his God and praise him, just as he had done previously. 11 The conspirators came and found Daniel praying and seeking mercy before his God. 12 Then they approached the king and said con-

society, and his mind became like that of an animal; he had to live with the wild asses and to feed on grass like oxen, and his body was drenched with the dew of heaven, until he came to acknowledge that the Most High God is sovereign over the realm of humanity and appoints over it whom he will. 22 But although you knew all this, you, his son Belshazzar, did not humble your heart. 23 You have set yourself up against the Lord of heaven; his temple vessels have been fetched for you and your nobles, your concubines and courtesans to drink from them. You have praised gods fashioned from silver, gold, bronze, iron, wood, and stone, which cannot see or hear or know, and you have not given glory to God, from whom comes your every breath, and in whose charge are all your ways. 24 That is why he sent the hand and why he wrote this inscription.

25 'The words inscribed were: "Mene mene tekel u-pharsin." 26 Their interpretation is this: mene, God has numbered the days of your kingdom and brought it to an end; 27 tekel, you have been weighed in the balance and found wanting; 28 u-pharsin, your kingdom has been divided and given to the Medes and Persians.' 29 Then at Belshazzar's command Daniel was robed in purple and a gold chain was hung round his neck, and proclamation was made that he should rank third in the kingdom.

30 That very night Belshazzar king of the Chaldaeans was slain, 31 and Darius the Mede took the kingdom, being then about sixty-two years old.

6 IT pleased Darius to appoint a hundred and twenty satraps to be in charge throughout his kingdom, 2 and over them three chief ministers, to whom the satraps were to submit their reports so that the king's interests might not suffer; of these three ministers, Daniel was one. 3 Daniel outshone the other ministers and the satraps because of his exceptional ability, and it was the king's intention to appoint him over the whole kingdom. 4 The ministers and satraps began to look round for some pretext to attack Daniel's administration of the kingdom, but they failed to find any malpractice on his part, for he was faithful to his trust. Since they could discover neither negligence nor malpractice, 5 they said, 'We shall not find any ground for bringing a charge against this Daniel unless it is connected with his religion.' 6 These ministers and satraps, having watched for an opportunity to approach the king, said to him, 'Long live King Darius! 7 We, the ministers of the kingdom, prefects, satraps, courtiers, and governors, have taken counsel and all are agreed that the king should issue a decree and bring into force a binding edict to the effect that whoever presents a petition to any god or human being other than the king during the next thirty days is to be thrown into the lion-pit. 8 Now let your majesty issue the edict and have it put in writing so that it becomes unalterable, for the law of the Medes and Persians may never be revoked.' 9 Accordingly the edict was signed by King Darius.

10 When Daniel learnt that this decree had been issued, he went into his house. It had in the roof-chamber windows open towards Jerusalem; and there he knelt down three times a day and offered prayers and praises to his God as was his custom. 11 His enemies, on the watch for an opportunity to catch him, found Daniel at his prayers making supplication to his God. 12 They then went into the king's

---

5:26 **mene:** *that is* numbered.   *5:27* **tekel:** *that is* shekel *or* weight.   *5:28* **u-pharsin:** *prob. rdg; Aram.* peres. *There is a play on three possible meanings:* half-mina *or* divisions *or* Persians.   *5:31* *In Aram.* 6:1.

---

s Aram lacks *the days of*   *t* The singular of *Parsin*   *u* Ch 6.1 in
Aram

NEW AMERICAN BIBLE | NEW JERUSALEM BIBLE

insensate as a beast; he lived with wild asses, and ate grass like an ox; his body was bathed with the dew of heaven, until he learned that the Most High God rules over the kingdom of men and appoints over it whom he will. 22 You, his son, Belshazzar, have not humbled your heart, though you knew all this; 23 you have rebelled against the Lord of heaven. You had the vessels of his temple brought before you, so that you and your nobles, your wives and your entertainers, might drink wine from them; and you praised the gods of silver and gold, bronze and iron, wood and stone, that neither see nor hear nor have intelligence. But the God in whose hand is your life breath and the whole course of your life, you did not glorify. 24 By him were the wrist and hand sent, and the writing set down.

25 "This is the writing that was inscribed: MENE, TEKEL, and PERES. These words mean: 26 MENE, God has numbered your kingdom and put an end to it; 27 TEKEL, you have been weighed on the scales and found wanting; 28 PERES, your kingdom has been divided and given to the Medes and Persians."

29 Then by order of Belshazzar they clothed Daniel in purple, with a gold collar about his neck, and proclaimed him third in the government of the kingdom. 30 The same night Belshazzar, the Chaldean king, was slain:

6 1 And Darius the Mede succeeded to the kingdom at the age of sixty-two.

2 Darius decided to appoint over his entire kingdom one hundred and twenty satraps, to safeguard his interests; 3 these were accountable to three supervisors, one of whom was Daniel. 4 Daniel outshone all the supervisors and satraps because an extraordinary spirit was in him, and the king thought of giving him authority over the entire kingdom. 5 Therefore the supervisors and satraps tried to find grounds for accusation against Daniel as regards the administration. But they could accuse him of no wrongdoing; because he was trustworthy, no fault of neglect or misconduct was to be found in him. 6 Then these men said to themselves, "We shall find no grounds for accusation against this Daniel unless by way of the law of his God." 7 So these supervisors and satraps went thronging to the king and said to him, "King Darius, live forever! 8 All the supervisors of the kingdom, the prefects, satraps, nobles, and governors are agreed that the following prohibition ought to be put in force by royal decree: no one is to address any petition to god or man for thirty days, except to you, O king; otherwise he shall be cast into a den of lions. 9 Now, O king, issue the prohibition over your signature, immutable and irrevocable under Mede and Persian law." 10 So King Darius signed the prohibition and made it law.

11 Even after Daniel heard that this law had been signed, he continued his custom of going home to kneel in prayer and give thanks to his God in the upper chamber three times a day, with the windows open toward Jerusalem. 12 So these men rushed in and found Daniel praying and pleading before his God. 13 Then they went to remind the king about the

human society, his heart was more like an animal's than a man's; he lived with the wild donkeys; he fed on grass like oxen; his body was drenched by the dew of heaven, until he had learnt that the Most High rules over human sovereignty and appoints whom he pleases to rule it. 22 But you, Belshazzar, who are his son, you have not humbled your heart, in spite of knowing all this. 23 You have defied the Lord of heaven, you have had the vessels from his Temple brought to you, and you, your noblemen, your wives and the women singing for you have drunk your wine out of them. You have praised gods of gold and silver, of bronze and iron, of wood and stone, which can neither see, hear nor understand; but you have given no glory to the God in whose hands are your breath itself and all your fortunes. 24 That is why he has sent the hand which has written these words. 25 The writing reads: *mene, mene, teqel* and *parsin.* 26 The meaning of the words is this:*e mene*: God has *measured* your sovereignty and put an end to it; 27 *teqel*: you have been *weighed* in the balance and found wanting; 28 *parsin*: your kingdom has been *divided* and given to the Medes and the *Persians*.'

29 At Belshazzar's order Daniel was dressed in purple, a chain of gold was put round his neck and he was proclaimed as one of the three men who governed the kingdom.

30 That same night, the Chaldaean king Belshazzar was murdered, 1 and Darius the Mede received the kingdom, at the age of sixty-two.

6 2 It pleased Darius to appoint a hundred and twenty satraps over his kingdom for the various parts, 3 and over them three presidents — of whom Daniel was one — to whom the satraps were to be responsible. This was to safeguard the king's interests. 4 This Daniel, by virtue of the marvellous spirit residing in him, was so evidently superior to the other presidents and satraps that the king considered appointing him to rule the whole kingdom. 5 The presidents and satraps, in consequence, started hunting for some affair of state by which they could discredit Daniel; but they could find nothing to his discredit, and no case of negligence; he was so punctilious that they could not find a single instance of maladministration or neglect. 6 These men then thought, 'We shall never find a way of discrediting Daniel unless we try something to do with the law of his God.' 7 The presidents and satraps then went in a body to the king. 'King Darius,' they said, 'live for ever! 8 We are all agreed, presidents of the realm, magistrates, satraps, councillors and governors, that the king should issue an edict enforcing the following regulation: Whoever within the next thirty days prays to anyone, divine or human, other than to yourself, Your Majesty, is to be thrown into the lions' den. 9 Your Majesty, ratify the edict at once by signing this document, making it unalterable, as befits the law of the Medes and the Persians, which cannot be revoked.' 10 King Darius accordingly signed the document embodying the edict.

11 When Daniel heard that the document had been signed, he retired to his house. The windows of his upstairs room faced towards Jerusalem. Three times each day, he went down on his knees, praying and giving praise to God as he had always done. 12 These men came along in a body and found Daniel praying and pleading with God. 13 They then

---

e 5 The untranslatable play on Aramaic words is shown in the text by italics.

NEW REVISED STANDARD VERSION

cerning the interdict, "O king! Did you not sign an interdict, that anyone who prays to anyone, divine or human, within thirty days except to you, O king, shall be thrown into a den of lions?" The king answered, "The thing stands fast, according to the law of the Medes and Persians, which cannot be revoked." 13 Then they responded to the king, "Daniel, one of the exiles from Judah, pays no attention to you, O king, or to the interdict you have signed, but he is saying his prayers three times a day."

14 When the king heard the charge, he was very much distressed. He was determined to save Daniel, and until the sun went down he made every effort to rescue him. 15 Then the conspirators came to the king and said to him, "Know, O king, that it is a law of the Medes and Persians that no interdict or ordinance that the king establishes can be changed."

16 Then the king gave the command, and Daniel was brought and thrown into the den of lions. The king said to Daniel, "May your God, whom you faithfully serve, deliver you!" 17 A stone was brought and laid on the mouth of the den, and the king sealed it with his own signet and with the signet of his lords, so that nothing might be changed concerning Daniel. 18 Then the king went to his palace and spent the night fasting; no food was brought to him, and sleep fled from him.

19 Then, at break of day, the king got up and hurried to the den of lions. 20 When he came near the den where Daniel was, he cried out anxiously to Daniel, "O Daniel, servant of the living God, has your God whom you faithfully serve been able to deliver you from the lions?" 21 Daniel then said to the king, "O king, live forever! 22 My God sent his angel and shut the lions' mouths so that they would not hurt me, because I was found blameless before him; and also before you, O king, I have done no wrong." 23 Then the king was exceedingly glad and commanded that Daniel be taken up out of the den. So Daniel was taken up out of the den, and no kind of harm was found on him, because he had trusted in his God. 24 The king gave a command, and those who had accused Daniel were brought and thrown into the den of lions—they, their children, and their wives. Before they reached the bottom of the den the lions overpowered them and broke all their bones in pieces.

25 Then King Darius wrote to all peoples and nations of every language throughout the whole world: "May you have abundant prosperity! 26 I make a decree, that in all my royal dominion people should tremble and fear before the God of Daniel:

For he is the living God,
    enduring forever.
His kingdom shall never be destroyed,
    and his dominion has no end.
27 He delivers and rescues,
    he works signs and wonders in heaven and on
        earth;
for he has saved Daniel
    from the power of the lions."

28 So this Daniel prospered during the reign of Darius and the reign of Cyrus the Persian.

7 In the first year of King Belshazzar of Babylon, Daniel had a dream and visions of his head as he lay in bed. Then he wrote down the dream:v 2 I,w Daniel, saw in my vision by night the four winds of heaven stirring up the great sea, 3 and four great beasts came up out of the sea, different from one another. 4 The first was like a lion and had eagles'

REVISED ENGLISH BIBLE

presence and reminded him of the edict. 'Your majesty,' they said, 'have you not issued an edict that any person who, within the next thirty days, presents a petition to any god or human being other than your majesty is to be thrown into the lion-pit?' The king answered, 'The matter has been determined in accordance with the law of the Medes and Persians, which may not be revoked.' 13 So they said to the king, 'Daniel, one of the Jewish exiles, has disregarded both your majesty and the edict, and is making petition to his God three times a day.' 14 When the king heard this, he was greatly distressed; he tried to think of a way to save Daniel, and continued his efforts till sunset. 15 The men watched for an opportunity to approach the king, and said to him, 'Your majesty must know that by the law of the Medes and Persians no edict or decree issued by the king may be altered.' 16 Then the king gave the order for Daniel to be brought and thrown into the lion-pit; but he said to Daniel, 'Your God whom you serve at all times, may he save you.' 17 A stone was brought and put over the mouth of the pit, and the king sealed it with his signet and with the signets of his nobles, so that no attempt could be made to rescue Daniel.

18 The king went to his palace and spent the night fasting; no woman was brought to him, and sleep eluded him. 19 He was greatly agitated and, at the first light of dawn, he rose and went to the lion-pit. 20 When he came near he called anxiously, 'Daniel, servant of the living God, has your God whom you serve continually been able to save you from the lions?' 21 Daniel answered, 'Long live the king! 22 My God sent his angel to shut the lions' mouths and they have not injured me; he judged me innocent, and moreover I had done your majesty no injury.' 23 The king was overjoyed and gave orders that Daniel should be taken up out of the pit. When this was done no trace of injury was found on him, because he had put his faith in his God. 24 By order of the king those who out of malice had accused Daniel were brought and flung into the lion-pit along with their children and their wives, and before they reached the bottom the lions were upon them and devoured them, bones and all.

25 King Darius wrote to all peoples and nations of every language throughout the whole world: 'May your prosperity increase! 26 I have issued a decree that in all my royal domains everyone is to fear and reverence the God of Daniel,

for he is the living God, the everlasting,
    whose kingly power will never be destroyed;
    whose sovereignty will have no end—
27 a saviour, a deliverer, a worker of signs and
        wonders
in heaven and on earth,
who has delivered Daniel from the power of the
        lions.'

28 Prosperity attended Daniel during the reigns of Darius and Cyrus the Persian.

7 In the first year that Belshazzar was king of Babylon, a dream and visions came to Daniel as he lay on his bed. Then he wrote down the dream, and here his account begins.

2 In my vision during the night while I, Daniel, was gazing intently I saw the Great Sea churned up by the four winds of heaven, 3 and four great beasts rising out of the sea, each one different from the others. 4 The first was like

---

v Q Ms Theodotion: MT adds *the beginning of the words; he said*
w Theodotion: Aram *Daniel answered and said, "I*

prohibition: "Did you not decree, O king, that no one is to address a petition to god or man for thirty days, except to you, O king; otherwise he shall be cast into a den of lions?" The king answered them, "The decree is absolute, irrevocable under the Mede and Persian law." 14 To this they replied, "Daniel, the Jewish exile, has paid no attention to you, O king, or to the decree you issued; three times a day he offers his prayer." 15 The king was deeply grieved at this news and he made up his mind to save Daniel; he worked till sunset to rescue him. 16 But these men insisted. "Keep in mind, O king," they said, "that under the Mede and Persian law every royal prohibition or decree is irrevocable." 17 So the king ordered Daniel to be brought and cast into the lions' den. To Daniel he said, "May your God, whom you serve so constantly, save you." 18 To forestall any tampering, the king sealed with his own ring and the rings of the lords the stone that had been brought to block the opening of the den.

19 Then the king returned to his palace for the night; he refused to eat and he dismissed the entertainers. Since sleep was impossible for him, 20 the king rose very early the next morning and hastened to the lions' den. 21 As he drew near, he cried out to Daniel sorrowfully, "O Daniel, servant of the living God, has the God whom you serve so constantly been able to save you from the lions?" 22 Daniel answered the king: "O king, live forever! 23 My God has sent his angel and closed the lions' mouths so that they have not hurt me. For I have been found innocent before him; neither to you have I done any harm, O king!" 24 This gave the king great joy. At his order Daniel was removed from the den, unhurt because he trusted in his God. 25 The king then ordered the men who had accused Daniel, along with their children and their wives, to be cast into the lions' den. Before they reached the bottom of the den, the lions overpowered them and crushed all their bones.

26 Then King Darius wrote to the nations and peoples of every language, wherever they dwell on the earth: "All peace to you! 27 I decree that throughout my royal domain the God of Daniel is to be reverenced and feared:

"For he is the living God, enduring forever;
   his kingdom shall not be destroyed,
   and his dominion shall be without end.
28 He is a deliverer and savior,
   working signs and wonders in heaven and
      on earth,
   and he delivered Daniel from the lions' power."

29 So Daniel fared well during the reign of Darius and the reign of Cyrus the Persian.

went to the king and reminded him of the royal edict, 'Have you not signed an edict forbidding anyone for the next thirty days to pray to anyone, divine or human, other than to yourself, Your Majesty, on pain of being thrown into the lions' den?' 'The decision stands', the king replied, 'as befits the law of the Medes and the Persians, which cannot be revoked.' 14 They then said to the king, 'Your Majesty, this man Daniel, one of the exiles from Judah, disregards both you and the edict which you have signed: he is at his prayers three times each day.' 15 When the king heard these words he was deeply distressed and determined to save Daniel; he racked his brains until sunset to find some way to save him. 16 But the men kept pressing the king, 'Your Majesty, remember that in conformity with the law of the Medes and the Persians, no edict or decree can be altered when once issued by the king.'

17 The king then ordered Daniel to be brought and thrown into the lion pit. The king said to Daniel, 'Your God, whom you have served so faithfully, will have to save you.' 18 A stone was then brought and laid over the mouth of the pit; and the king sealed it with his own signet and with that of his noblemen, so that there could be no going back on the original decision about Daniel. 19 The king returned to his palace, spent the night in fasting and refused to receive any of his concubines. Sleep eluded him, 20 and at the first sign of dawn he got up and hurried to the lion pit. 21 As he approached the pit he called in anguished tones to Daniel, 'Daniel, servant of the living God! Has your God, whom you serve so faithfully, been able to save you from the lions?' 22 Daniel answered the king, 'May Your Majesty live for ever! 23 My God sent his angel who sealed the lions' jaws; they did me no harm, since in his sight I am blameless; neither have I ever done you any wrong, Your Majesty.' 24 The king was overjoyed and ordered Daniel to be released from the pit. Daniel was released from the pit and found to be quite unhurt, because he had trusted in his God. 25 The king then sent for the men who had accused Daniel and had them thrown into the lion pit, and their wives and children too; and before they reached the floor of the pit the lions had seized them and crushed their bones to pieces.

26 King Darius then wrote to all nations, peoples and languages dwelling throughout the world:

'May you prosper more and more! 27 This is my decree: Throughout every dominion of my realm, let all tremble with fear before the God of Daniel:

He is the living God, he endures for ever,
   his kingdom will never be destroyed
   and his empire never come to an end.
28 He saves, sets free, and works signs and wonders
   in the heavens and on earth;
   he has saved Daniel from the power of the lions.'

29 This Daniel flourished in the reign of Darius and the reign of Cyrus the Persian.

7 In the first year of King Belshazzar of Babylon, Daniel had a dream as he lay in bed, and was terrified by the visions of his mind. Then he wrote down the dream; the account began: 2 In the vision I saw during the night, suddenly the four winds of heaven stirred up the great sea, 3 from which emerged four immense beasts, each different from the others. 4 The first was like a lion, but with eagle's

7 In the first year of Belshazzar king of Babylon, Daniel had a dream and visions that passed through his head as he lay in bed. He wrote the dream down, and this is how the narrative began: 2 Daniel said, 'I have been seeing visions in the night. I saw that the four winds of heaven were stirring up the Great Sea; 3 four great beasts emerged from the sea, each different from the others. 4 The first was like

NEW REVISED STANDARD VERSION

wings. Then, as I watched, its wings were plucked off, and it was lifted up from the ground and made to stand on two feet like a human being; and a human mind was given to it. 5 Another beast appeared, a second one, that looked like a bear. It was raised up on one side, had three tusks*x* in its mouth among its teeth and was told, "Arise, devour many bodies!" 6 After this, as I watched, another appeared, like a leopard. The beast had four wings of a bird on its back and four heads; and dominion was given to it. 7 After this I saw in the visions by night a fourth beast, terrifying and dreadful and exceedingly strong. It had great iron teeth and was devouring, breaking in pieces, and stamping what was left with its feet. It was different from all the beasts that preceded it, and it had ten horns. 8 I was considering the horns, when another horn appeared, a little one coming up among them; to make room for it, three of the earlier horns were plucked up by the roots. There were eyes like human eyes in this horn, and a mouth speaking arrogantly.

   9 As I watched,
     thrones were set in place,
      and an Ancient One*y* took his throne,
     his clothing was white as snow,
      and the hair of his head like pure wool;
     his throne was fiery flames,
      and its wheels were burning fire.
10 A stream of fire issued
     and flowed out from his presence.
     A thousand thousands served him,
      and ten thousand times ten thousand stood
       attending him.
     The court sat in judgment,
      and the books were opened.

11 I watched then because of the noise of the arrogant words that the horn was speaking. And as I watched, the beast was put to death, and its body destroyed and given over to be burned with fire. 12 As for the rest of the beasts, their dominion was taken away, but their lives were prolonged for a season and a time. 13 As I watched in the night visions,

    I saw one like a human being*z*
     coming with the clouds of heaven.
    And he came to the Ancient One*a*
     and was presented before him.
  14 To him was given dominion
     and glory and kingship,
     that all peoples, nations, and languages
      should serve him.
    His dominion is an everlasting dominion
     that shall not pass away,
    and his kingship is one
     that shall never be destroyed.

15 As for me, Daniel, my spirit was troubled within me,*b* and the visions of my head terrified me. 16 I approached one of the attendants to ask him the truth concerning all this. So he said that he would disclose to me the interpretation of the matter: 17 "As for these four great beasts, four kings shall arise out of the earth. 18 But the holy ones of the Most High shall receive the kingdom and possess the kingdom forever — forever and ever."

19 Then I desired to know the truth concerning the fourth beast, which was different from all the rest, exceedingly terrifying, with its teeth of iron and claws of bronze, and which devoured and broke in pieces, and stamped what was left with its feet; 20 and concerning the ten horns that were on its head, and concerning the other horn, which came up and to make room for which three of them fell out — the horn that had eyes and a mouth that spoke arrogantly, and that seemed greater than the others. 21 As I

REVISED ENGLISH BIBLE

a lion, but it had an eagle's wings. I watched until its wings were plucked off and it was lifted from the ground and made to stand on two feet as if it were a human being; it was also given the mind of a human being. 5 Then I saw another, a second beast, like a bear. It had raised itself on one side, and it had three ribs in its mouth between its teeth. The command was given to it: 'Get up and gorge yourself with flesh.' 6 After this as I gazed I saw another, a beast like a leopard with four wings like those of a bird on its back; this creature had four heads, and it was invested with sovereign power. 7 Next in the night visions I saw a fourth beast, fearsome and grisly and exceedingly strong, with great iron teeth. It devoured and crunched, and it trampled underfoot what was left. It was different from all the beasts which went before it, and had ten horns. 8 While I was considering the horns there appeared another horn, a little one, springing up among them, and three of the first horns were uprooted to make room for it. In this horn were eyes like human eyes, and a mouth that uttered bombast. 9 As I was looking,

    thrones were set in place
    and the Ancient in Years took his seat;
    his robe was white as snow,
    his hair like lamb's wool.
    His throne was flames of fire
    and its wheels were blazing fire;
10 a river of fire flowed from his presence.
    Thousands upon thousands served him
    and myriads upon myriads were in attendance.
    The court sat, and the books were opened.

11 Then because of the bombast the horn was mouthing, I went on watching until the beast was killed; its carcass was destroyed and consigned to the flames. 12 The rest of the beasts, though deprived of their sovereignty, were allowed to remain alive until an appointed time and season. 13 I was still watching in visions of the night and I saw one like a human being coming with the clouds of heaven; he approached the Ancient in Years and was presented to him. 14 Sovereignty and glory and kingly power were given to him, so that all peoples and nations of every language should serve him; his sovereignty was to be an everlasting sovereignty which was not to pass away, and his kingly power was never to be destroyed.

15 My spirit within me was troubled; and, dismayed by the visions which came into my head, I, Daniel, 16 approached one of those who were standing there and enquired what all this really signified; and he made known to me its interpretation. 17 'These great beasts, four in number,' he said, 'are four kingdoms which will arise from the earth. 18 But the holy ones of the Most High will receive the kingly power and retain possession of it always, for ever and ever.'

19 Then I wished to know what the fourth beast really signified, the beast that was different from all the others, exceedingly fearsome with its iron teeth and bronze claws, devouring and crunching, then trampling underfoot what was left. 20 I wished also to know about the ten horns on its head and about the other horn which sprang up and at whose coming three of them fell, the horn which had eyes and a mouth uttering bombast and which in its appearance was more imposing than the others. 21 As I still watched, this

---

x Or ribs   *y* Aram *an Ancient of Days*   *z* Aram *one like a son of man*   *a* Aram *the Ancient of Days*   *b* Aram *troubled in its sheath*

7:13 **human being:** lit. son of man.

wings. While I watched, the wings were plucked; it was raised from the ground to stand on two feet like a man, and given a human mind. 5 The second was like a bear; it was raised up on one side, and among the teeth in its mouth were three tusks. It was given the order, "Up, devour much flesh." 6 After this I looked and saw another beast, like a leopard; on its back were four wings like those of a bird, and it had four heads. To this beast dominion was given. 7 After this, in the visions of the night I saw the fourth beast, different from all the others, terrifying, horrible, and of extraordinary strength; it had great iron teeth with which it devoured and crushed, and what was left it trampled with its feet. 8 I was considering the ten horns it had, when suddenly another, a little horn, sprang out of their midst, and three of the previous horns were torn away to make room for it. This horn had eyes like a man, and a mouth that spoke arrogantly. 9 As I watched,

> Thrones were set up
> and the Ancient One took his throne.
> His clothing was snow bright,
> and the hair on his head as white as wool;
> His throne was flames of fire,
> with wheels of burning fire.
> 10 A surging stream of fire
> flowed out from where he sat;
> Thousands upon thousands were ministering
> to him,
> and myriads upon myriads attended him.

The court was convened, and the books were opened. 11 I watched, then, from the first of the arrogant words which the horn spoke, until the beast was slain and its body thrown into the fire to be burnt up. 12 The other beasts, which also lost their dominion, were granted a prolongation of life for a time and a season. 13 As the visions during the night continued, I saw

> One like a son of man coming,
> on the clouds of heaven;
> When he reached the Ancient One
> and was presented before him,
> 14 He received dominion, glory, and kingship;
> nations and peoples of every language
> serve him.
> His dominion is an everlasting dominion
> that shall not be taken away,
> his kingship shall not be destroyed.

15 I, Daniel, found my spirit anguished within its sheath of flesh, and I was terrified by the visions of my mind. 16 I approached one of those present and asked him what all this meant in truth; in answer, he made known to me the meaning of the things: 17 "These four great beasts stand for four kingdoms which shall arise on the earth. 18 But the holy ones of the Most High shall receive the kingship, to possess it forever and ever."

19 But I wished to make certain about the fourth beast, so very terrible and different from the others, devouring and crushing with its iron teeth and bronze claws, and trampling with its feet what was left; 20 about the ten horns on its head, and the other one that sprang up, before which three horns fell; about the horn with the eyes and the mouth that spoke arrogantly, which appeared greater than its fellows. 21 For,

a lion with eagle's wings and, as I looked, its wings were torn off, and it was lifted off the ground and set standing on its feet like a human; and it was given a human heart. 5 And there before me was a second beast, like a bear, rearing up on one side, with three ribs in its mouth, between its teeth. "Up!" came the command. "Eat quantities of flesh!" 6 After this I looked; and there before me was another beast, like a leopard, and with four bird's wings on its flanks; it had four heads and was granted authority. 7 Next, in the visions of the night, I saw another vision: there before me was a fourth beast, fearful, terrifying, very strong; it had great iron teeth, and it ate its victims, crushed them, and trampled their remains underfoot. It was different from the previous beasts and had ten horns. *f*

8 'While I was looking at these horns, I saw another horn sprouting among them, a little one; three of the original horns were pulled out by the roots to make way for it; and in this horn I saw eyes like human eyes, and a mouth full of boasting.

> 9 While I was watching,
> thrones were set in place
> and one most venerable took his seat.
> His robe was white as snow,
> the hair of his head as pure as wool.
> His throne was a blaze of flames,
> its wheels were a burning fire.
> 10 A stream of fire poured out,
> issuing from his presence.
> A thousand thousand waited on him,
> ten thousand times ten thousand stood before him.
> The court was in session
> and the books lay open.

11 'I went on watching: then, because of the noise made by the boastings of the horn, as I watched, the beast was put to death, and its body destroyed and committed to the flames. 12 The other beasts were deprived of their empire, but received a lease of life for a season and a time.

> 13 I was gazing into the visions of the night,
> when I saw, coming on the clouds of heaven,
> as it were a son of man. *g*
> He came to the One most venerable
> and was led into his presence.
> 14 On him was conferred rule,
> honour and kingship,
> and all peoples, nations and languages became his
> servants.
> His rule is an everlasting rule
> which will never pass away,
> and his kingship will never come to an end.

15 'I, Daniel, was deeply disturbed and the visions that passed through my head alarmed me. 16 So I approached one of those who were standing by and asked him about all this. And in reply he revealed to me what these things meant. 17 "These four great beasts are four kings who will rise up from the earth. 18 Those who receive royal power are the holy ones of the Most High, and kingship will be theirs for ever, for ever and ever." 19 Then I asked about the fourth beast, different from all the rest, very terrifying, with iron teeth and bronze claws; it ate its victims, crushed them, and trampled their remains underfoot; 20 and about the ten horns on its head — and why the other one sprouted and the three original horns fell, and why this horn had eyes and a mouth full of boasting, and why it looked more impressive than its fellows. 21 This was the horn I had watched making war on

f 7 The ten Seleucid kings. The little horn (v. 8) will be Antiochus Epiphanes the persecutor.   *g* 7 This human figure represents the people of God, but may well bear an individual sense too, as their leader and representative.

looked, this horn made war with the holy ones and was prevailing over them, 22 until the Ancient One[c] came; then judgment was given for the holy ones of the Most High, and the time arrived when the holy ones gained possession of the kingdom.

23 This is what he said: "As for the fourth beast,
  there shall be a fourth kingdom on earth
  that shall be different from all the other
    kingdoms;
  it shall devour the whole earth,
  and trample it down, and break it to pieces.
24 As for the ten horns,
  out of this kingdom ten kings shall arise,
  and another shall arise after them.
This one shall be different from the former ones,
  and shall put down three kings.
25 He shall speak words against the Most High,
  shall wear out the holy ones of the Most High,
  and shall attempt to change the sacred seasons
    and the law;
  and they shall be given into his power
  for a time, two times,[d] and half a time.
26 Then the court shall sit in judgment,
  and his dominion shall be taken away,
  to be consumed and totally destroyed.
27 The kingship and dominion
  and the greatness of the kingdoms under the
    whole heaven
  shall be given to the people of the holy ones of
    the Most High;
  their kingdom shall be an everlasting kingdom,
  and all dominions shall serve and obey them."

28 Here the account ends. As for me, Daniel, my thoughts greatly terrified me, and my face turned pale; but I kept the matter in my mind.

8 In the third year of the reign of King Belshazzar a vision appeared to me, Daniel, after the one that had appeared to me at first. 2 In the vision I was looking and saw myself in Susa the capital, in the province of Elam,[e] and I was by the river Ulai.[f] 3 I looked up and saw a ram standing beside the river.[g] It had two horns. Both horns were long, but one was longer than the other, and the longer one came up second. 4 I saw the ram charging westward and northward and southward. All beasts were powerless to withstand it, and no one could rescue from its power; it did as it pleased and became strong.

5 As I was watching, a male goat appeared from the west, coming across the face of the whole earth without touching the ground. The goat had a horn[h] between its eyes. 6 It came toward the ram with the two horns that I had seen standing beside the river,[g] and it ran at it with savage force. 7 I saw it approaching the ram. It was enraged against it and struck the ram, breaking its two horns. The ram did not have power to withstand it; it threw the ram down to the ground and trampled upon it, and there was no one who could rescue the ram from its power. 8 Then the male goat grew exceedingly great; but at the height of its power, the great horn was broken, and in its place there came up four prominent horns toward the four winds of heaven.

9 Out of one of them came another[i] horn, a little one, which grew exceedingly great toward the south, toward the east, and toward the beautiful land. 10 It grew as high as the host of heaven. It threw down to the earth some of the host and some of the stars, and trampled on them. 11 Even

horn was waging war on the holy ones and proving too strong for them 22 until the Ancient in Years came. Then judgement was pronounced in favour of the holy ones of the Most High, and the time came when the holy ones gained possession of the kingly power.

23 The explanation he gave was this: 'The fourth beast signifies a fourth kingdom which will appear on earth. It will differ from the other kingdoms; it will devour the whole earth, treading it down and crushing it. 24 The ten horns signify ten kings who will rise from this kingdom; after them will arise another king, who will be different from his predecessors; and he will bring low three kings. 25 He will hurl defiance at the Most High and wear down the holy ones of the Most High. He will have it in mind to alter the festival seasons and religious laws; and the holy ones will be delivered into his power for a time, and times, and half a time. 26 But when the court sits, he will be deprived of his sovereignty, so that it may be destroyed and abolished for ever. 27 The kingly power, sovereignty, and greatness of all the kingdoms under heaven will be given to the holy people of the Most High. Their kingly power will last for ever, and every realm will serve and obey them.'

28 Here the account ends. As for me, Daniel, my thoughts dismayed me greatly and I turned pale; but I kept these things to myself.

8 In the third year of the reign of King Belshazzar, a vision appeared to me, Daniel, following my earlier vision. 2 In this vision I was in Susa, the capital of the province of Elam, watching beside the Ulai canal. 3 I looked up and saw a ram with two horns standing by the canal. The two horns were long, with the longer of the two coming up after the other. 4 I watched the ram butting towards the west, the north, and the south. No beast could stand against it, and from its power there was no escape. It did as it pleased, and made a great display of strength.

5 While I pondered this, suddenly a he-goat came from the west skimming over the whole earth without touching the ground; it had a prominent horn between its eyes. 6 It approached the two-horned ram which I had seen standing by the canal, and charged it with impetuous force. 7 I saw it advance on the ram, working itself into a fury against it. Then it struck the ram and shattered both its horns; the ram was powerless to resist. The he-goat threw it to the ground and stamped on it, and there was no one to rescue the ram.

8 The he-goat in turn made a great display of its strength, but when it was at the height of its power its great horn broke, and in place of this there came up four prominent horns pointing towards the four quarters of heaven. 9 Out of one of them there emerged a little horn, which as it grew put forth its strength towards the south and the east and towards the fairest of all lands. 10 It aspired to be as great as the host of heaven, and it flung down to the earth some of the host, even some of the stars, and stamped on them. 11 It aspired

---

c Aram the Ancient of Days   d Aram a time, times
e Gk Theodotion: MT Q Ms repeat in the vision I was looking
f Or the Ulai Gate   g Or gate   h Theodotion: Gk one horn; Heb a horn of vision   i Cn Compare 7.8: Heb one

7:25 a time . . . half a time: or three and a half years.   8:1 Here the Hebrew text resumes (see note at 2:4).

as I watched, that horn made war against the holy ones and was victorious 22 until the Ancient One arrived; judgment was pronounced in favor of the holy ones of the Most High, and the time came when the holy ones possessed the kingdom. 23 He answered me thus:

"The fourth beast shall be a fourth kingdom
on earth,
different from all the others;
It shall devour the whole earth,
beat it down, and crush it.
24 The ten horns shall be ten kings
rising out of that kingdom;
another shall rise up after them,
Different from those before him,
who shall lay low three kings.
25 He shall speak against the Most High
and oppress the holy ones of the Most High,
thinking to change the feast days and the
law.
They shall be handed over to him
for a year, two years, and a half-year.
26 But when the court is convened,
and his power is taken away
by final and absolute destruction,
27 Then the kingship and dominion and majesty
of all the kingdoms under the heavens
shall be given to the holy people of the
Most High,
Whose kingdom shall be everlasting:
all dominions shall serve and obey him."

28 The report concluded: I, Daniel, was greatly terrified by my thoughts, and my face blanched, but I kept the matter to myself.

8 After this first vision, I, Daniel, had another, in the third year of the reign of King Belshazzar. 2 In my vision I saw myself in the fortress of Susa in the province of Elam; I was beside the river Ulai. 3 I looked up and saw standing by the river a ram with two great horns, the one larger and newer than the other. 4 I saw the ram butting toward the west, north, and south. No beast could withstand it or be rescued from its power; it did what it pleased and became very powerful.

5 As I was reflecting, a he-goat with a prominent horn on its forehead suddenly came from the west across the whole earth without touching the ground. 6 It approached the two-horned ram I had seen standing by the river, and rushed toward it with savage force. 7 I saw it attack the ram with furious blows when they met, and break both its horns. It threw the ram, which had not the force to withstand it, to the ground, and trampled upon it; and no one could rescue it from its power.

8 The he-goat became very powerful, but at the height of its power the great horn was shattered, and in its place came up four others, facing the four winds of heaven. 9 Out of one of them came a little horn which kept growing toward the south, the east, and the glorious country. 10 Its power extended to the host of heaven, so that it cast down to earth some of the host and some of the stars and trampled on them. 11 It boasted even against the prince of the host, from

the holy ones and proving the stronger, 22 until the coming of the One most venerable who gave judgement in favour of the holy ones of the Most High, when the time came for the holy ones to assume kingship. 23 This is what he said:

"The fourth beast
is to be a fourth kingdom on earth,
different from all other kingdoms.
It will devour the whole world,
trample it underfoot and crush it.
24 As for the ten horns: from this kingdom
will rise ten kings, and another after them;
this one will be different from the previous ones
and will bring down three kings;
25 he will insult the Most High,
and torment the holy ones of the Most High.
He will plan to alter the seasons and the Law,
and the Saints will be handed over to him
for a time, two times, and half a time.
26 But the court will sit, and he will be stripped of
his royal authority
which will be finally destroyed and reduced to
nothing.
27 And kingship and rule
and the splendours of all the kingdoms under
heaven
will be given to the people of the holy ones of the
Most High,
whose royal power is an eternal power,
whom every empire will serve and obey."

28 'Here the narrative ends.
'I, Daniel, was greatly disturbed in mind, and I grew pale; but I kept these things to myself.'

8 In the third year of King Belshazzar a vision appeared to me, Daniel, after the one that had originally appeared to me. 2 I gazed at the vision, and as I gazed I found myself in Susa, the citadel in the province of Elam; gazing at the vision, I found myself at the Ulai Gate. 3 I raised my eyes to look, and I saw a ram standing in front of the gate. It had two horns; both were tall, but one taller than the other, and the one that rose the higher was the second. 4 I saw the ram butting westwards, northwards and southwards. No animal could stand up to it, nothing could escape its power. It did as it pleased and became strong.

5 This is what I observed: a he-goat from the west, encroaching over the entire surface of the world though never touching the ground, and between its eyes the goat had one majestic horn. 6 It advanced on the two-horned ram, which I had seen standing in front of the gate, and charged at it in the full force of its fury. 7 I saw it reach the ram; it was enraged with the ram and struck it, breaking both its horns, so that the ram was not strong enough to hold its ground; it threw it to the ground and trampled it underfoot; no one was there to rescue the ram. 8 The he-goat then grew more powerful than ever; but at the height of its strength the great horn snapped, and in its place sprouted four majestic horns, pointing to the four winds of heaven.

9 From one of these, the small one, sprang a horn which grew to great size towards south and east and towards the Land of Splendour. 10 It grew right up to the armies of heaven and flung armies and stars to the ground, and trampled them underfoot. 11 It even challenged the power of the

against the prince of the host it acted arrogantly; it took the regular burnt offering away from him and overthrew the place of his sanctuary. 12 Because of wickedness, the host was given over to it together with the regular burnt offering;^{j} it cast truth to the ground, and kept prospering in what it did. 13 Then I heard a holy one speaking, and another holy one said to the one that spoke, "For how long is this vision concerning the regular burnt offering, the transgression that makes desolate, and the giving over of the sanctuary and host to be trampled?"^{j} 14 And he answered him,^{k} "For two thousand three hundred evenings and mornings; then the sanctuary shall be restored to its rightful state."

15 When I, Daniel, had seen the vision, I tried to understand it. Then someone appeared standing before me, having the appearance of a man, 16 and I heard a human voice by the Ulai, calling, "Gabriel, help this man understand the vision." 17 So he came near where I stood; and when he came, I became frightened and fell prostrate. But he said to me, "Understand, O mortal,^{l} that the vision is for the time of the end."

18 As he was speaking to me, I fell into a trance, face to the ground; then he touched me and set me on my feet. 19 He said, "Listen, and I will tell you what will take place later in the period of wrath; for it refers to the appointed time of the end. 20 As for the ram that you saw with the two horns, these are the kings of Media and Persia. 21 The male goat^m is the king of Greece, and the great horn between its eyes is the first king. 22 As for the horn that was broken, in place of which four others arose, four kingdoms shall arise from his^n nation, but not with his power.

23 At the end of their rule,
when the transgressions have reached their full
measure,
a king of bold countenance shall arise,
skilled in intrigue.
24 He shall grow strong in power,^{o}
shall cause fearful destruction,
and shall succeed in what he does.
He shall destroy the powerful
and the people of the holy ones.
25 By his cunning
he shall make deceit prosper under his hand,
and in his own mind he shall be great.
Without warning he shall destroy many
and shall even rise up against the Prince of
princes.
But he shall be broken, and not by human hands.
26 The vision of the evenings and the mornings that has been told is true. As for you, seal up the vision, for it refers to many days from now."

27 So I, Daniel, was overcome and lay sick for some days; then I arose and went about the king's business. But I was dismayed by the vision and did not understand it.

9 In the first year of Darius son of Ahasuerus, by birth a Mede, who became king over the realm of the Chaldeans — 2 in the first year of his reign, I, Daniel, perceived in the books the number of years that, according to the word of the LORD to the prophet Jeremiah, must be fulfilled for the devastation of Jerusalem, namely, seventy years.

to be as great as the Prince of the host, suppressed his regular offering, and even threw down his sanctuary. 12 The heavenly host was delivered up, and the little horn raised itself impiously against the regular offering and cast true religion to the ground; it succeeded in all that it did.

13 I heard a holy one speaking and another holy one answering. The one speaker said, 'How long will the period of this vision last? How long will the regular offering be suppressed and impiety cause desolation? How long will the Holy Place and the fairest of all lands be given over to be trodden down?' 14 The answer came, 'For two thousand three hundred evenings and mornings; then the Holy Place will be restored.'

15 All the while that I, Daniel, was seeing the vision, I was trying to understand it. Suddenly I saw standing before me one with the appearance of a man; 16 at the same time I heard a human voice calling to him across the bend of the Ulai, 'Gabriel, explain the vision to this man.' 17 He came to where I was standing; and at his approach I prostrated myself in terror. But he said to me, 'Understand, O man: the vision points to the time of the end.' 18 While he spoke to me, I lay face downwards in a trance, but at his touch I was made to stand up where I was. 19 'I shall make known to you', he said, 'what is to happen at the end of the period of wrath; for there is an end at the appointed time. 20 The two-horned ram which you saw signifies the kings of Media and Persia, 21 the he-goat is the king of Greece, the great horn on its forehead being its first king. 22 As for the horn which was broken off and replaced by four other horns: four kingdoms will rise out of that nation, but they will lack its power.

23 'In the last days of those kingdoms,
when their sin is at its height,
a king of grim aspect will appear, a master of
stratagem.
24 His power will be great, and he will work havoc
untold;
he will succeed in whatever he does.
He will work havoc on the mighty nations and the
holy people.
25 By cunning and deceit
he will succeed in his designs;
he will devise great schemes
and wreak havoc on many when they least expect
it.
He will challenge even the Prince of princes
and be broken, but by no human hand.
26 This revelation which has been given
of the evenings and the mornings is true;
but you must keep the vision secret,
for it points to days far ahead.'

27 As for me, Daniel, my strength failed and I lay sick for some days. Then I rose and attended to the king's business. But I was perplexed by the revelation and no one could explain it.

9 IN the first year of the reign of Darius son of Ahasuerus (a Mede by birth, who was appointed ruler over the kingdom of the Chaldeans) 2 I, Daniel, was reading the scriptures and reflecting on the seventy years which, according to the word of the LORD to the prophet Jeremiah, were to pass while Jerusalem lay in ruins. 3 Then I turned to

---

^{j} Meaning of Heb uncertain ^{k} Gk Theodotion Syr Vg: Heb me
^{l} Heb son of man ^{m} Or shaggy male goat ^{n} Gk Theodotion Vg:
Heb the ^{o} Theodotion and one Gk Ms: Heb repeats (from 8.22)
but not with his power

8:12 **and the . . . itself:** prob. rdg; Heb. omits.   8:13 **be
suppressed:** so Gk; Heb. omits. **and impiety cause desolation:** prob.
rdg; Heb. obscure. **fairest . . . lands:** prob. rdg, cp. verse 9; Heb.
host.   8:21 **Greece:** Heb. Javan.   8:24 **His power . . . great:**
so Gk (Theod.); Heb. adds and not with his power.

whom it removed the daily sacrifice, and whose sanctuary it cast down, 12 as well as the host, while sin replaced the daily sacrifice. It cast truth to the ground, and was succeeding in its undertaking.

13 I heard a holy one speaking, and another said to whichever one it was that spoke, "How long shall the events of this vision last concerning the daily sacrifice, the desolating sin which is placed there, the sanctuary, and the trampled host?" 14 He answered him, "For two thousand three hundred evenings and mornings; then the sanctuary shall be purified."

15 While I, Daniel, sought the meaning of the vision I had seen, a manlike figure stood before me, 16 and on the Ulai I heard a human voice that cried out, "Gabriel, explain the vision to this man." 17 When he came near where I was standing, I fell prostrate in terror. But he said to me, "Understand, son of man, that the vision refers to the end time." 18 As he spoke to me, I fell forward in a faint; he touched me and made me stand up. 19 "I will show you," he said, "what is to happen later in the period of wrath; for at the appointed time, there will be an end.

20 "The two-horned ram you saw represents the kings of the Medes and Persians. 21 The he-goat is the king of the Greeks, and the great horn on its forehead is the first king. 22 The four that rose in its place when it was broken are four kingdoms that will issue from his nation, but without its strength.

23 "After their reign,
when sinners have reached their measure,
There shall arise a king, impudent
and skilled in intrigue.
24 He shall be strong and powerful,
bring about fearful ruin,
and succeed in his undertaking.
He shall destroy powerful peoples;
25   his cunning shall be against the holy ones,
his treacherous conduct shall succeed.
He shall be proud of heart
and destroy many by stealth.
But when he rises against the prince of princes,
he shall be broken without a hand being raised.
26 The vision of the evenings and the mornings
is true, as spoken;
Do you, however, keep this vision undisclosed,
because the days are to be many."

27 I, Daniel, was weak and ill for some days; then I arose and took care of the king's affairs. But I was appalled at the vision, which I could not understand.

9 It was the first year that Darius, son of Ahasuerus, of the race of the Medes, reigned over the kingdom of the Chaldeans; 2 in the first year of his reign I, Daniel, tried to understand in the Scriptures the counting of the years of which the LORD spoke to the prophet Jeremiah: that for the ruins of Jerusalem seventy years must be fulfilled.

Prince of the army; it abolished the perpetual sacrifice and overthrew the foundation of his sanctuary, 12 and the army too; over the sacrifice it installed iniquity and flung truth to the ground; the horn was active and successful.

13 I heard a holy one speaking, and another holy one say to the speaker, 'How long is this vision to be — of perpetual sacrifice, of horrifying iniquity, of sanctuary and army trampled underfoot?' 14 The first replied, 'Until two thousand three hundred evenings and mornings have gone by: then the sanctuary will have its rights restored.'

15 As I, Daniel, gazed at the vision and tried to understand it, I saw someone standing in front of me who looked like a man. 16 I heard a human voice cry over the Ulai, 'Gabriel, tell him the meaning of the vision!' 17 He approached the place where I was standing; as he approached, I was seized with terror and fell prostrate on the ground. 'Son of man,' he said to me, 'understand this: the vision shows the time of the End.' 18 He was still speaking, when I fainted, face downwards on the ground. He touched me, however, and raised me to my feet. 19 'Come,' he said, 'I shall tell you what is going to happen when the Retribution is over, about the final times. 20 As for the ram which you saw, its two horns are the kings of Media and of Persia. 21 The hairy he-goat is the king of Greece, the large horn between its eyes is the first king. 22 The horn which snapped and the four horns which sprouted in its place are four kingdoms rising from his nation but not having his strength.

23 'And at the end of their reign, when the measure
of their sins is full,
a king will arise, a proud-faced, ingenious-minded
man.
24 His power will grow greater and greater,
though not through any power of his own;
he will plot incredible schemes,
he will succeed in whatever he undertakes,
he will destroy powerful men
and the holy ones, God's people.
25 Such will be his resourcefulness of mind
that all his treacherous activities will succeed.
He will grow arrogant of heart
and destroy many people by taking them unawares.
He will challenge the power of the Prince of
princes
but, without any human intervention, he will be
broken.
26 The vision of the evenings and the mornings which
has been revealed is true,
but you must keep the vision secret, for there are
still many days to go.'

27 At this I, Daniel, lost consciousness; I was ill for several days. Then I got up to discharge my duties in the king's service, keeping the vision a secret and still not understanding what it meant.

9 It was the first year of Darius son of Artaxerxes, a Mede by race who assumed the throne of Chaldaea. 2 In the first year of his reign I, Daniel, was studying the scriptures, counting over the number of years — as revealed by Yahweh to the prophet Jeremiah — that were to pass before the desolation of Jerusalem would come to an end, namely seventy years. 3 I turned my face to the Lord God

3 Then I turned to the Lord God, to seek an answer by prayer and supplication with fasting and sackcloth and ashes. 4 I prayed to the LORD my God and made confession, saying,

"Ah, Lord, great and awesome God, keeping covenant and steadfast love with those who love you and keep your commandments, 5 we have sinned and done wrong, acted wickedly and rebelled, turning aside from your commandments and ordinances. 6 We have not listened to your servants the prophets, who spoke in your name to our kings, our princes, and our ancestors, and to all the people of the land.

7 "Righteousness is on your side, O Lord, but open shame, as at this day, falls on us, the people of Judah, the inhabitants of Jerusalem, and all Israel, those who are near and those who are far away, in all the lands to which you have driven them, because of the treachery that they have committed against you. 8 Open shame, O LORD, falls on us, our kings, our officials, and our ancestors, because we have sinned against you. 9 To the Lord our God belong mercy and forgiveness, for we have rebelled against him, 10 and have not obeyed the voice of the LORD our God by following his laws, which he set before us by his servants the prophets.

11 "All Israel has transgressed your law and turned aside, refusing to obey your voice. So the curse and the oath written in the law of Moses, the servant of God, have been poured out upon us, because we have sinned against you. 12 He has confirmed his words, which he spoke against us and against our rulers, by bringing upon us a calamity so great that what has been done against Jerusalem has never before been done under the whole heaven. 13 Just as it is written in the law of Moses, all this calamity has come upon us. We did not entreat the favor of the LORD our God, turning from our iniquities and reflecting on his *p* fidelity. 14 So the LORD kept watch over this calamity until he brought it upon us. Indeed, the LORD our God is right in all that he has done; for we have disobeyed his voice.

15 "And now, O Lord our God, who brought your people out of the land of Egypt with a mighty hand and made your name renowned even to this day — we have sinned, we have done wickedly. 16 O Lord, in view of all your righteous acts, let your anger and wrath, we pray, turn away from your city Jerusalem, your holy mountain; because of our sins and the iniquities of our ancestors, Jerusalem and your people have become a disgrace among all our neighbors. 17 Now therefore, O our God, listen to the prayer of your servant and to his supplication, and for your own sake, Lord,*q* let your face shine upon your desolated sanctuary. 18 Incline your ear, O my God, and hear. Open your eyes and look at our desolation and the city that bears your name. We do not present our supplication before you on the ground of our righteousness, but on the ground of your great mercies. 19 O Lord, hear; O Lord, forgive; O Lord, listen and act and do not delay! For your own sake, O my God, because your city and your people bear your name!"

20 While I was speaking, and was praying and confessing my sin and the sin of my people Israel, and presenting my supplication before the LORD my God on behalf of the holy mountain of my God — 21 while I was speaking in prayer, the man Gabriel, whom I had seen before in a vision, came to me in swift flight at the time of the evening sacrifice. 22 He came*r* and said to me, "Daniel, I have now come out to give you wisdom and understanding. 23 At the beginning of your supplications a word went out, and I have come to declare it, for you are greatly beloved. So consider the word and understand the vision:

the Lord God in earnest prayer and supplication with fasting and with sackcloth and ashes. 4 I prayed and made this confession to the LORD my God:

'Lord, great and terrible God, keeping covenant and faith with those who love you and observe your commandments, 5 we have sinned, doing what was wrong and wicked; we have rebelled and rejected your commandments and your decrees. 6 We have turned a deaf ear to your servants the prophets, who spoke in your name to our kings and princes, to our forefathers, and to all the people of the land. 7 Lord, the right is on your side; the shame, now as ever, belongs to us, the people of Judah and the citizens of Jerusalem, and to all the Israelites near and far in every land to which you have banished them for their disloyal behaviour towards you. 8 LORD, the shame falls on us, on our kings, our princes, and our forefathers. We have sinned against you. 9 Compassion and forgiveness belong to the Lord our God, because we have rebelled against him. 10 We have not obeyed the LORD our God, in that we have not conformed to the laws which he laid down for our guidance through his servants the prophets. 11 All Israel has broken your law and refused to obey your command, so that the oath and curses recorded in the law of Moses, the servant of God, have rained down upon us; for we have sinned against God. 12 He has made good the warning he gave about us and our rulers, by bringing on us and on Jerusalem a disaster greater than has ever happened in all the world; 13 and this whole disaster which has come upon us was foretold in the law of Moses. Yet we have done nothing to appease the LORD our God; we have neither repented of our wrongful deeds, nor remembered that you are true to your word. 14 The LORD has kept strict watch and has now brought the disaster upon us. In all that he has done the LORD our God has been just; yet we have not obeyed him.

15 'Now, Lord our God who brought your people out of Egypt by a strong hand, winning for yourself a name that lives on to this day, we have sinned, we have done wrong. 16 Lord, by all your saving deeds we beg that your wrath and anger may depart from Jerusalem, your own city, your holy hill; on account of our sins and our fathers' crimes, Jerusalem and your people have become a byword among all our neighbours. 17 Listen, our God, to your servant's prayer and supplication; for your own sake, Lord, look favourably on your sanctuary which lies desolate. 18 God, incline your ear to us and hear; open your eyes and look upon our desolation and upon the city that bears your name. It is not because of any righteous deeds of ours, but because of your great mercy that we lay our supplications before you. 19 Lord, hear; Lord, forgive; Lord, listen and act; God, for your own sake do not delay, because your city and your people bear your name.'

20 I was speaking and praying, confessing my own sin and the sin of my people Israel, and laying my supplication before the LORD my God on behalf of his holy hill; 21 indeed I was still praying, when the man Gabriel, whom I had already seen in the vision, flew close to me at the hour of the evening offering. 22 He explained to me: 'Daniel, I have now come to enlighten your understanding. 23 As you began your supplications a decree went forth, and I have come to make it known, for you are greatly beloved. Consider well the word, consider the vision: 24 seventy times seven years

3 I turned to the Lord God, pleading in earnest prayer, with fasting, sackcloth, and ashes. 4 I prayed to the LORD, my God, and confessed, "Ah, Lord, great and awesome God, you who keep your merciful covenant toward those who love you and observe your commandments! 5 We have sinned, been wicked and done evil; we have rebelled and departed from your commandments and your laws. 6 We have not obeyed your servants the prophets, who spoke in your name to our kings, our princes, our fathers, and all the people of the land. 7 Justice, O Lord, is on your side; we are shamefaced even to this day: the men of Judah, the residents of Jerusalem, and all Israel, near and far, in all the countries to which you have scattered them because of their treachery toward you. 8 O LORD, we are shamefaced, like our kings, our princes, and our fathers, for having sinned against you. 9 But yours, O Lord, our God, are compassion and forgiveness! Yet we rebelled against you 10 and paid no heed to your command, O LORD, our God, to live by the law you gave us through your servants the prophets. 11 Because all Israel transgressed your law and went astray, not heeding your voice, the sworn malediction, recorded in the law of Moses, the servant of God, was poured out over us for our sins. 12 You carried out the threats you spoke against us and against those who governed us, by bringing upon us in Jerusalem the greatest calamity that has ever occurred under heaven. 13 As it is written in the law of Moses, this calamity came full upon us. As we did not appease the LORD, our God, by turning back from our wickedness and recognizing his constancy, 14 so the Lord kept watch over the calamity and brought it upon us. You, O LORD, our God, are just in all that you have done, for we did not listen to your voice.

15 "Now, O Lord, our God, who led your people out of the land of Egypt with a strong hand, and made a name for yourself even to this day, we have sinned, we are guilty. 16 O Lord, in keeping with all your just deeds, let your anger and your wrath be turned away from your city Jerusalem, your holy mountain. On account of our sins and the crimes of our fathers, Jerusalem and your people have become the reproach of all our neighbors. 17 Hear, therefore, O God, the prayer and petition of your servant; and for your own sake, O Lord, let your face shine upon your desolate sanctuary. 18 Give ear, O my God, and listen; open your eyes and see our ruins and the city which bears your name. When we present our petition before you, we rely not on our just deeds, but on your great mercy. 19 O Lord, hear! O Lord, pardon! O Lord, be attentive and act without delay, for your own sake, O my God, because this city and your people bear your name!"

20 I was still occupied with my prayer, confessing my sin and the sin of my people Israel, presenting my petition to the LORD, my God, on behalf of his holy mountain— 21 I was still occupied with this prayer, when Gabriel, the one whom I had seen before in vision, came to me in rapid flight at the time of the evening sacrifice. 22 He instructed me in these words: "Daniel, I have now come to give you understanding. 23 When you began your petition, an answer was given which I have come to announce, because you are beloved. Therefore, mark the answer and understand the vision.

begging for time to pray and to plead, with fasting, sackcloth and ashes. 4 I pleaded with Yahweh my God and made this confession:

'O my Lord, God great and to be feared, you keep the covenant and show faithful love towards those who love you and who observe your commandments: 5 we have sinned, we have done wrong, we have acted wickedly, we have betrayed your commandments and rulings and turned away from them. 6 We have not listened to your servants the prophets, who spoke in your name to our kings, our chief men, our ancestors and all people of the country. 7 Saving justice, Lord, is yours; we have only the look of shame we wear today, we, the people of Judah, the inhabitants of Jerusalem, the whole of Israel, near and far away, in every country to which you have dispersed us because of the treachery we have committed against you. 8 To us, our kings, our chief men and our ancestors, belongs the look of shame, O Yahweh, since we have sinned against you. 9 And it is for the Lord our God to have mercy and to pardon, since we have betrayed him, 10 and have not listened to the voice of Yahweh our God nor followed the laws he has given us through his servants the prophets. 11 The whole of Israel has flouted your Law and turned away, unwilling to listen to your voice; and the curse and imprecation written in the Law of Moses, the servant of God, have come pouring down on us, because we have sinned against him. 12 He has carried out the threats which he made against us and the chief men who governed us — that he would bring so great a disaster down on us that the fate of Jerusalem would find no parallel under all heaven. 13 And now, as written in the Law of Moses, this whole calamity has befallen us; even so, we have not appeased Yahweh our God by renouncing our crimes and learning your truth. 14 Yahweh has watched for the right moment to bring disaster on us, since Yahweh our God is just in all his dealings with us, and we have not listened to his voice. 15 And now, Lord our God, who by your mighty hand brought us out of Egypt — the renown you won then endures to this day — we have sinned, we have done wrong. 16 Lord, by all your acts of saving justice, turn away your anger and your fury from Jerusalem, your city, your holy mountain, for as a result of our sins and the crimes of our ancestors, Jerusalem and your people are objects of scorn to all who surround us. 17 And now, our God, listen to the prayer and pleading of your servant. For your own sake, Lord, let your face smile again on your desolate sanctuary. 18 Listen, my God, listen to us; open your eyes and look at our plight and at the city that bears your name. Relying not on our upright deeds but on your great mercy, we pour out our plea to you. 19 Listen, Lord! Forgive, Lord! Hear, Lord, and act! For your own sake, my God, do not delay — since your city and your people alike bear your name.'

20 I was still speaking, still at prayer, confessing my own sins and the sins of my people Israel, and placing my plea before Yahweh my God for the holy mountain of my God, 21 still speaking, still at prayer, when Gabriel, the being I had originally seen in vision, swooped on me in full flight at the hour of the evening sacrifice. 22 He came, he spoke, he said to me, 'Now, Daniel; I have come down to teach you how to understand. 23 When your pleading began, a word was uttered, and I have come to tell you. You are a man specially chosen. Grasp the meaning of the word, understand the vision:

NEW REVISED STANDARD VERSION

REVISED ENGLISH BIBLE

24 "Seventy weeks are decreed for your people and your holy city: to finish the transgression, to put an end to sin, and to atone for iniquity, to bring in everlasting righteousness, to seal both vision and prophet, and to anoint a most holy place.s 25 Know therefore and understand: from the time that the word went out to restore and rebuild Jerusalem until the time of an anointed prince, there shall be seven weeks; and for sixty-two weeks it shall be built again with streets and moat, but in a troubled time. 26 After the sixty-two weeks, an anointed one shall be cut off and shall have nothing, and the troops of the prince who is to come shall destroy the city and the sanctuary. Itst end shall come with a flood, and to the end there shall be war. Desolations are decreed. 27 He shall make a strong covenant with many for one week, and for half of the week he shall make sacrifice and offering cease; and in their placeu shall be an abomination that desolates, until the decreed end is poured out upon the desolator."

are marked out for your people and your holy city; then rebellion will be stopped, sin brought to an end, iniquity expiated, everlasting right ushered in, vision and prophecy ratified, and the Most Holy Place anointed.

25 'Know, then, and understand: from the time that the decree went forth that Jerusalem should be restored and rebuilt, seven of those seventy will pass till the appearance of one anointed, a prince; then for sixty-two it will remain restored, rebuilt with streets and conduits. At the critical time, 26 after the sixty-two have passed, the anointed prince will be removed, and no one will take his part. The horde of an invading prince will work havoc on city and sanctuary. The end of it will be a cataclysm, inevitable war with all its horrors. 27 The prince will make a firm league with the many for one of the seventy; and, with that one half spent, he will put a stop to sacrifice and offering. And in the train of these abominations will come the perpetrator of desolation; then, in the end, what has been decreed concerning the desolation will be poured out.'

10 In the third year of King Cyrus of Persia a word was revealed to Daniel, who was named Belteshazzar. The word was true, and it concerned a great conflict. He understood the word, having received understanding in the vision.

2 At that time I, Daniel, had been mourning for three weeks. 3 I had eaten no rich food, no meat or wine had entered my mouth, and I had not anointed myself at all, for the full three weeks. 4 On the twenty-fourth day of the first month, as I was standing on the bank of the great river (that is, the Tigris), 5 I looked up and saw a man clothed in linen, with a belt of gold from Uphaz around his waist. 6 His body was like beryl, his face like lightning, his eyes like flaming torches, his arms and legs like the gleam of burnished bronze, and the sound of his words like the roar of a multitude. 7 I, Daniel, alone saw the vision; the people who were with me did not see the vision, though a great trembling fell upon them, and they fled and hid themselves. 8 So I was left alone to see this great vision. My strength left me, and my complexion grew deathly pale, and I retained no strength. 9 Then I heard the sound of his words; and when I heard the sound of his words, I fell into a trance, face to the ground.

10 But then a hand touched me and roused me to my hands and knees. 11 He said to me, "Daniel, greatly beloved, pay attention to the words that I am going to speak to you. Stand on your feet, for I have now been sent to you." So while he was speaking this word to me, I stood up trembling. 12 He said to me, "Do not fear, Daniel, for from the first day that you set your mind to gain understanding and to humble yourself before your God, your words have

10 IN the third year that Cyrus was king of Persia a revelation came to Daniel, who had been given the name Belteshazzar. The word was true, yet only after much struggle did understanding come to him in the course of the vision.

2 At that time I, Daniel, mourned for three whole weeks. 3 I refrained from all choice food; no meat or wine passed my lips, and I did not anoint myself until the three weeks had passed. 4 On the twenty-fourth day of the first month, I found myself on the bank of the great river, the Tigris, 5 and when I looked up I saw a man robed in linen with a belt of Ophir gold round his waist. 6 His body glowed like topaz, his face shone like lightning, his eyes flamed like torches, his arms and feet glittered like burnished bronze, and when he spoke his voice sounded like the voice of a multitude. 7 I, Daniel, alone saw the vision; those who were near me did not see it, but such great trepidation fell upon them that they crept away into hiding. 8 I was left by myself gazing at this great vision, and my strength drained away; and sapped of all strength I became a sorry figure of a man. 9 I heard the sound of his words and, as I did so, I lay prone on the ground in a trance.

10 Suddenly, at the touch of a hand, I was set, all trembling, on my hands and knees. 11 'Daniel, man greatly beloved,' he said to me, 'attend to the words I am about to speak to you and stand upright where you are, for I am now sent to you.' When he spoke to me, I stood up trembling with apprehension. 12 He went on, 'Do not be afraid, Daniel, for from the very first day that you applied your mind to understanding, and to mortify yourself before your God, your prayers have been heard, and I have come in answer

9:27 **many:** or mighty.   10:5 **Ophir:** so some MSS; others Uphaz.

sOr thing or one   tOr His   uCn: Meaning of Heb uncertain

NEW AMERICAN BIBLE

24 "Seventy weeks are decreed
　　for your people and for your holy city:
Then transgression will stop and sin will end,
　　guilt will be expiated,
Everlasting justice will be introduced,
　　vision and prophecy ratified,
　　and a most holy will be anointed.
25 　　　　Know and understand this:
From the utterance of the word
　　that Jerusalem was to be rebuilt
Until one who is anointed and a leader,
　　there shall be seven weeks.
During sixty-two weeks
　　it shall be rebuilt,
With streets and trenches,
　　in time of affliction.
26 After the sixty-two weeks
　　an anointed shall be cut down
　　when he does not possess the city;
And the people of a leader who will come
　　shall destroy the sanctuary.
Then the end shall come like a torrent;
　　until the end there shall be war,
　　the desolation that is decreed.
27 For one week he shall make
　　a firm compact with the many;
Half the week
　　he shall abolish sacrifice and oblation;
On the temple wing shall be the
　　horrible abomination
　　until the ruin that is decreed
　　is poured out upon the horror."

10 In the third year of Cyrus, king of Persia, a revelation was given to Daniel, who had been named Belteshazzar. The revelation was certain: a great war; he understood it from the vision. 2 In those days, I, Daniel, mourned three full weeks. 3 I ate no savory food, I took no meat or wine, and I did not anoint myself at all until the end of the three weeks.

4 On the twenty-fourth day of the first month I was on the bank of the great river, the Tigris. 5 As I looked up, I saw a man dressed in linen with a belt of fine gold around his waist. 6 His body was like chrysolite, his face shone like lightning, his eyes were like fiery torches, his arms and feet looked like burnished bronze, and his voice sounded like the roar of a multitude. 7 I alone, Daniel, saw the vision; but great fear seized the men who were with me; they fled and hid themselves, although they did not see the vision. 8 So I was left alone, seeing this great vision. No strength remained in me; I turned the color of death and was powerless. 9 When I heard the sound of his voice, I fell face forward in a faint.

10 But then a hand touched me, raising me to my hands and knees. 11 "Daniel, beloved," he said to me, "understand the words which I am speaking to you; stand up, for my mission now is to you." When he said this to me, I stood up trembling. 12 "Fear not, Daniel," he continued; "from the first day you made up your mind to acquire understanding and humble yourself before God, your prayer was heard.

NEW JERUSALEM BIBLE

24 'Seventy weeks are decreed
　　for your people and your holy city,
　　for putting an end to transgression,
　　for placing the seal on sin,
　　for expiating crime,
　　for introducing everlasting uprightness,
　　for setting the seal on vision and on prophecy,
　　for anointing the holy of holies.
25 Know this, then, and understand:
From the time there went out this message:
　　"Return and rebuild Jerusalem"
to the coming of an Anointed Prince, seven weeks
　　and sixty-two weeks,
with squares and ramparts restored and rebuilt,
　　but in a time of trouble.
26 And after the sixty-two weeks
an Anointed One put to death without his . . .
city and sanctuary ruined
by a prince who is to come.
The end of that prince will be catastrophe
and, until the end, there will be war
and all the devastation decreed.
27 He will strike a firm alliance with many people
　　for the space of a week;
and for the space of one half-week
he will put a stop to sacrifice and oblation,
and on the wing of the Temple will be the
　　appalling abomination *h*
until the end, until the doom assigned to the
　　devastator.'

10 In the third year of Cyrus king of Persia, a revelation was made to Daniel known as Belteshazzar, a true revelation of a great conflict. He grasped the meaning of the revelation; what it meant was disclosed to him in a vision.

2 At that time, I, Daniel, was doing a three-week penance; 3 I ate no agreeable food, touched no meat or wine, and did not anoint myself, until these three weeks were over. 4 On the twenty-fourth day of the first month, as I stood on the bank of that great river, the Tigris, 5 I raised my eyes to look about me, and this is what I saw:
A man dressed in linen, with a belt of pure gold
　　round his waist:
　6 his body was like beryl,
　his face looked like lightning,
　his eyes were like fiery torches,
　his arms and his face had the gleam of burnished
　　bronze,
　the sound of his voice was like the roar of a
　　multitude.

7 I, Daniel, alone saw the apparition; the men who were with me did not see the vision, but so great a trembling overtook them that they fled to hide. 8 I was left alone, gazing on this great vision; I was powerless, my appearance was changed and contorted; my strength deserted me.

9 I heard a voice speaking, and at the sound of the voice I fell fainting, face downwards on the ground. 10 I felt a hand touching me, setting my knees and my hands trembling. 11 He said, 'Daniel, you are a man specially chosen; understand the words that I am about to say; stand up; I have been sent to you now.' He said this, and I stood up trembling. 12 He then said, 'Daniel, do not be afraid: from that first day when, the better to understand, you resolved to mortify yourself before God, your words have been heard;

h 9 The Hebr. evokes idols of Baal. Antiochus set up a statue of Zeus in the Temple.

been heard, and I have come because of your words. 13 But the prince of the kingdom of Persia opposed me twenty-one days. So Michael, one of the chief princes, came to help me, and I left him there with the prince of the kingdom of Persia,ᵛ 14 and have come to help you understand what is to happen to your people at the end of days. For there is a further vision for those days."

15 While he was speaking these words to me, I turned my face toward the ground and was speechless. 16 Then one in human form touched my lips, and I opened my mouth to speak, and said to the one who stood before me, "My lord, because of the vision such pains have come upon me that I retain no strength. 17 How can my lord's servant talk with my lord? For I am shaking,ʷ no strength remains in me, and no breath is left in me."

18 Again one in human form touched me and strengthened me. 19 He said, "Do not fear, greatly beloved, you are safe. Be strong and courageous!" When he spoke to me, I was strengthened and said, "Let my lord speak, for you have strengthened me." 20 Then he said, "Do you know why I have come to you? Now I must return to fight against the prince of Persia, and when I am through with him, the prince of Greece will come. 21 But I am to tell you what is inscribed in the book of truth. There is no one with me who contends against these princes except Michael, your prince.

11 ¹ As for me, in the first year of Darius the Mede, I stood up to support and strengthen him.

2 "Now I will announce the truth to you. Three more kings shall arise in Persia. The fourth shall be far richer than all of them, and when he has become strong through his riches, he shall stir up all against the kingdom of Greece. 3 Then a warrior king shall arise, who shall rule with great dominion and take action as he pleases. 4 And while still rising in power, his kingdom shall be broken and divided toward the four winds of heaven, but not to his posterity, nor according to the dominion with which he ruled; for his kingdom shall be uprooted and go to others besides these.

5 "Then the king of the south shall grow strong, but one of his officers shall grow stronger than he and shall rule a realm greater than his own realm. 6 After some years they shall make an alliance, and the daughter of the king of the south shall come to the king of the north to ratify the agreement. But she shall not retain her power, and her offspring shall not endure. She shall be given up, she and her attendants and her child and the one who supported her.

"In those times 7 a branch from her roots shall rise up in his place. He shall come against the army and enter the fortress of the king of the north, and he shall take action against them and prevail. 8 Even their gods, with their idols and with their precious vessels of silver and gold, he shall carry off to Egypt as spoils of war. For some years he shall refrain from attacking the king of the north; 9 then the latter shall invade the realm of the king of the south, but will return to his own land.

10 "His sons shall wage war and assemble a multitude of great forces, which shall advance like a flood and pass through, and again shall carry the war as far as his fortress. 11 Moved with rage, the king of the south shall go out and do battle against the king of the north, who shall muster a great multitude, which shall, however, be defeated by his enemy. 12 When the multitude has been carried off, his heart shall be exalted, and he shall overthrow tens of thousands, but he shall not prevail. 13 For the king of the north shall again raise a multitude, larger than the former, and after some yearsˣ he shall advance with a great army and abundant supplies.

to them. 13 But the guardian angel of the kingdom of Persia resisted me for twenty-one days, and then, seeing that I had held out there, Michael, one of the chief princes, came to help me against the prince of the kingdom of Persia. 14 I have come to explain to you what will happen to your people at the end of this age; for this too is a vision for those days.'

15 While he spoke in this fashion to me, I fixed my eyes on the ground and was unable to speak. 16 Suddenly one with a human appearance touched my lips; then I broke my silence and addressed him as he stood before me: 'Sir,' I said, 'at this vision anguish has gripped me, and I am sapped of all my strength. 17 How can I, my lord's servant, presume to talk with such as my lord, since my strength has now failed me and there is no more spirit left in me?'

18 Again the figure touched me and put strength into me, 19 saying, 'Do not be afraid, man greatly beloved; all will be well with you. Take heart, and be strong.' As he spoke, my strength returned, and I said, 'Speak, sir, for you have given me strength.' 20 He said, 'Do you know why I have come to you? I am first going back to fight with the prince of Persia, and, as soon as I have left, the prince of Greece will appear: 21 I have no ally on my side for support and help, except Michael your prince. However I shall expound to you what is written in the Book of Truth; 2 here

11 and now I shall tell you what is true.

'Three more kings will appear in Persia, followed by a fourth who will far surpass all the others in wealth; and when by his wealth he has extended his power, he will mobilize the whole empire against the kingdom of Greece. 3 Then there will appear a warrior king, who will rule a vast kingdom and do whatever he pleases. 4 But once he is established, his kingdom will be broken up and divided to the four quarters of heaven. It will not pass to his descendants; nor will its power be comparable to his, for his kingdom will be uprooted and given to others besides his posterity.

5 'The king of the south will become strong; but one of his generals will surpass him in strength and win a greater dominion. 6 In the course of time the two will enter into an alliance, and to seal the agreement the daughter of the king of the south will be given in marriage to the king of the north, but she will not maintain her influence and their line will not last. She and those who escorted her, along with her child, and also her lord and master, will all be the victims of foul play. 7 Then another shoot from the same stock as hers will appear in her father's place. He will penetrate the defences of the king of the north, invade his fortress, and win a decisive victory. 8 He will carry away as booty to Egypt even the images of their gods cast in metal and their valuable vessels of silver and gold. Then for some years he will refrain from attacking the king of the north. 9 After that the king of the north will invade the southern kingdom and then retire to his own land.

10 'His sons will press on with the assembling of a large force of armed men. One of them will sweep on like an irresistible flood. In a second campaign he will press as far as the enemy stronghold. 11 The king of the south, working himself up into a fury, will set out to do battle with the king of the north. He in turn will muster a large army, but it will be delivered into the hands of his enemy. 12 At the capture of this force, the victor will be elated and will slaughter tens of thousands; yet he will not maintain his advantage. 13 The king of the north will once more raise an army, one even greater than the last, and after a number of years he will advance with his huge force and a great baggage train.

ᵛ Gk Theodotion: Heb *I was left there with the kings of Persia*

ʷ Gk: Heb *from now* ˣ Heb *and at the end of the times years*

10:13 **prince:** *so Gk; Heb. omits.* Ch. 11: *Heb. adds* ¹and as for me, in the first year of Darius the Mede, I stood to support and help him.

NEW AMERICAN BIBLE

NEW JERUSALEM BIBLE

Because of it I started out, 13 but the prince of the kingdom of Persia stood in my way for twenty-one days, until finally Michael, one of the chief princes, came to help me. I left him there with the prince of the kings of Persia, 14 and came to make you understand what shall happen to your people in the days to come; for there is yet a vision concerning those days."

15 While he was speaking thus to me, I fell forward and kept silent. 16 Then something like a man's hand touched my lips; I opened my mouth and said to the one facing me, "My lord, I was seized with pangs at the vision and I was powerless. 17 How can my lord's servant speak with you, my lord? For now no strength or even breath is left in me." 18 The one who looked like a man touched me again and strengthened me, saying, 19 "Fear not, beloved, you are safe; take courage and be strong." 20 When he spoke to me, I grew strong and said, "Speak, my lord, for you have strengthened me." "Do you know," he asked, "why I have come to you? Soon I must fight the prince of Persia again. When I leave, the prince of Greece will come; 21 but I shall tell you what is written in the truthful book. No one supports me against all these except Michael, your prince,

11 1 standing as a reinforcement and a bulwark for me. 2 Now I shall tell you the truth.

"Three kings of Persia are yet to come; and a fourth shall acquire the greatest riches of all. Strengthened by his riches, he shall rouse all the kingdom of Greece. 3 But a powerful king shall appear and rule with great might, doing as he pleases. 4 No sooner shall he appear than his kingdom shall be broken and divided in the four directions under heaven; but not among his descendants or in keeping with his mighty rule, for his kingdom shall be torn to pieces and belong to others than they.

5 "The king of the south shall grow strong, but one of his princes shall grow stronger still and govern a domain greater than his. 6 After some years they shall become allies: the daughter of the king of the south shall come to the king of the north in the interest of peace. But her bid for power shall fail: and her line shall not be recognized, and she shall be given up, together with those who brought her, her son and her husband. But later 7 a descendant of her line shall succeed to his rank, and shall come against the rampart and enter the stronghold of the king of the north, and conquer them. 8 Even their gods, with their molten images and their precious vessels of silver and gold, he shall carry away as booty into Egypt. For years he shall have nothing to do with the king of the north. 9 Then the latter shall invade the land of the king of the south, and return to his own country.

10 "But his sons shall prepare and assemble a great armed host, which shall advance like a flood, then withdraw. When it returns and surges around the stronghold, 11 the king of the south, provoked, shall go out to fight against the king of the north, whose great host shall make a stand but shall be given into his hand 12 and be carried off. In the pride of his heart, he shall lay low tens of thousands, but he shall not triumph. 13 For the king of the north shall raise another army, greater than before; after some years he shall attack with this large army and great resources. 14 In those

and your words are the reason why I have come. 13 The Prince of the kingdom of Persia has been resisting me for twenty-one days, but Michael, one of the Chief Princes, came to my assistance. I have left him confronting the kings of Persia 14 and have come to tell you what will happen to your people in the final days. For here is a new vision about those days.'

15 When he had said these things to me, I prostrated myself on the ground, without saying a word; 16 then someone looking like a man touched my lips. I opened my mouth to speak, and I said to the person standing in front of me, 'My lord, anguish overcomes me at this vision, and my strength deserts me. 17 How can your servant speak to my lord now that I have no strength left and my breath fails me?' 18 Once again, the person like a man touched me; he gave me strength. 19 'Do not be afraid,' he said, 'you are a man specially chosen; peace be with you; play the man, be strong!' And as he spoke to me I felt strong again and said, 'Let my lord speak, you have given me strength.'

20a He then said, 'Do you know why I have come to you? 21a It is to tell you what is written in the Book of Truth. 20b I must go back to fight the Prince of Persia; when I have overcome him, the Prince of Javan will come next. 21b In all this, there is no one to lend me support except Michael your

11 Prince, 1 on whom I rely to give me support and to reinforce me. 2 And now I shall tell you the truth about these things.

'Three more kings are going to rise in Persia; a fourth will come and be richer than all the others, and when, thanks to his wealth, he has grown powerful, he will make war on all the kingdoms of Greece. 3 A mighty king will rise and govern a vast empire and do whatever he pleases. 4 But once he has come to power, his empire will be broken up and parcelled out to the four winds of heaven, though not to his descendants: it will not be ruled as he ruled it, for his sovereignty will be uprooted and will pass to others than his own descendants.

5 'The king of the south will grow powerful, but one of his princes will grow more powerful still, with an empire greater than his own. 6 Some years later, these will conclude a treaty and, to ratify the agreement, the daughter of the king of the south will go to the king of the north. Her arm will not, however, retain its strength, nor his posterity endure: she will be handed over, she, her escorts and her child, and he who has had authority over her. In due time 7 a sprig from her roots will rise in his place, will march on the defences, force the stronghold of the king of the north, and succeed in overcoming them. 8 He will even carry off all their gods, their statues, their precious gold and silver vessels as booty to Egypt. For some years he will leave the king of the north in peace, 9 but the latter will invade the kingdom of the king of the south, then retire to his own country. 10 His sons will next be on the march, mustering a host of powerful forces; and he will advance, deploy, break through and march on the southern stronghold once again. 11 The king of the south will fly into a rage and set out to give battle to the king of the north, who will have an immense army on his side, but this army will be defeated by him. 12 The army will be annihilated; he will be triumphant; he will overthrow tens of thousands; yet he will have no enduring strength. 13 The king of the north will come back, having recruited an even larger army than before, and finally, after some years, he will advance a second time with a great army and plentiful supplies. 14 At that time, many

NEW REVISED STANDARD VERSION

14 "In those times many shall rise against the king of the south. The lawless among your own people shall lift themselves up in order to fulfill the vision, but they shall fail. 15 Then the king of the north shall come and throw up siege-works, and take a well-fortified city. And the forces of the south shall not stand, not even his picked troops, for there shall be no strength to resist. 16 But he who comes against him shall take the actions he pleases, and no one shall withstand him. He shall take a position in the beautiful land, and all of it shall be in his power. 17 He shall set his mind to come with the strength of his whole kingdom, and he shall bring terms of peace y and perform them. In order to destroy the kingdom, z he shall give him a woman in marriage; but it shall not succeed or be to his advantage. 18 Afterward he shall turn to the coastlands, and shall capture many. But a commander shall put an end to his insolence; indeed, a he shall turn his insolence back upon him. 19 Then he shall turn back toward the fortresses of his own land, but he shall stumble and fall, and shall not be found.

20 "Then shall arise in his place one who shall send an official for the glory of the kingdom; but within a few days he shall be broken, though not in anger or in battle. 21 In his place shall arise a contemptible person on whom royal majesty had not been conferred; he shall come in without warning and obtain the kingdom through intrigue. 22 Armies shall be utterly swept away and broken before him, and the prince of the covenant as well. 23 And after an alliance is made with him, he shall act deceitfully and become strong with a small party. 24 Without warning he shall come into the richest parts b of the province and do what none of his predecessors had ever done, lavishing plunder, spoil, and wealth on them. He shall devise plans against strongholds, but only for a time. 25 He shall stir up his power and determination against the king of the south with a great army, and the king of the south shall wage war with a much greater and stronger army. But he shall not succeed, for plots shall be devised against him 26 by those who eat of the royal rations. They shall break him, his army shall be swept away, and many shall fall slain. 27 The two kings, their minds bent on evil, shall sit at one table and exchange lies. But it shall not succeed, for there remains an end at the time appointed. 28 He shall return to his land with great wealth, but his heart shall be set against the holy covenant. He shall work his will, and return to his own land.

29 "At the time appointed he shall return and come into the south, but this time it shall not be as it was before. 30 For ships of Kittim shall come against him, and he shall lose heart and withdraw. He shall be enraged and take action against the holy covenant. He shall turn back and pay heed to those who forsake the holy covenant. 31 Forces sent by him shall occupy and profane the temple and fortress. They shall abolish the regular burnt offering and set up the abomination that makes desolate. 32 He shall seduce with intrigue those who violate the covenant; but the people who are loyal to their God shall stand firm and take action. 33 The wise among the people shall give understanding to many; for some days, however, they shall fall by sword and flame, and suffer captivity and plunder. 34 When they fall victim, they shall receive a little help, and many shall join them insincerely. 35 Some of the wise shall fall, so that they may

REVISED ENGLISH BIBLE

14 'During these times many will resist the king of the south, but some renegades among your own people will rashly attempt to give substance to a vision and will be brought to disaster. 15 The king of the north will then come and cast up siege-ramps and capture a well-fortified city. The forces of the south will not stand up to him; even the flower of the army will not be able to hold their ground. 16 The invader will do as he pleases and meet with no opposition. He will establish himself in the fairest of all lands, and it will come wholly into his power. 17 He will resolve to advance with the full might of his kingdom; and, when he has agreed terms with the king of the south, he will give his young daughter in marriage to him, with a view to the destruction of the kingdom; but the treaty will not last nor will it be his purpose which is served. 18 Then he will turn to the coasts and islands and take many prisoners, but a foreign commander will wear him down and put an end to his challenge; thus he will throw his challenge back at him. 19 He will retreat to strongholds in his own country; there he will meet with disaster and be overthrown, and he will be seen no more.

20 'His successor will be one who will send out an officer with a royal escort to exact tribute; after but a brief time this king too will meet his end, yet neither openly nor in battle.

21 'His place will be taken by a despicable creature, one who had not been given recognition as king; he will come when he is least expected and seize the kingdom by smooth dissimulation. 22 As he advances, he will sweep away all forces of opposition, and even the Prince of the Covenant will be broken. 23 He will enter into alliances but dishonour them and, although only a few people are behind him, he will rise to power and establish himself 24 against all expectation. He will overrun the richest districts of the province, and succeed where all his ancestors failed, and distribute spoil, booty, and goods among his followers. He will frame stratagems against fortresses, but only for a time.

25 'He will rouse himself in all his strength and courage to lead a great army against the king of the south, who will fight back with a very large and powerful army; yet, hampered by treachery, the king of the south will not persist. 26 Those who eat at his board will be his undoing; his army will be swept away, and many will fall slain in battle. 27 The two kings, bent on mischief though seated at the same table, will lie to each other but with advantage to neither, for an end is yet to be at the appointed time. 28 Then the king of the north will return home with spoils in plenty, and with hostility in his heart against the Holy Covenant; he will work his will and return to his own country.

29 'At the appointed time he will once again invade the south, but he will have less success than he had before. 30 Ships of Kittim will sail against him, and he will suffer a rebuff. As he retreats he will vent his fury against the Holy Covenant, and on his return home will single out those who have forsaken it. 31 Soldiers in his command will desecrate the sanctuary and citadel; they will abolish the regular offering, and will set up "the abominable thing that causes desolation". 32 By plausible promises he will win over those who are ready to violate the covenant, but the people who are faithful to their God will be resolute and take action. 33 Wise leaders of the nation will give guidance to the people at large, who for a while will fall victims to sword and fire, to captivity and pillage. 34 But these victims will have some help, though only a little, even if many who join them are insincere. 35 Some of these leaders will themselves fall vic-

---

y Gk: Heb kingdom, and upright ones with him   z Heb it
a Meaning of Heb uncertain   b Or among the richest men

11:17 when . . . south: prob. rdg; Heb. obscure.   11:18 will wear him down: prob. rdg; Heb. obscure.

times many shall resist the king of the south, and outlaws of your people shall rise up in fulfillment of vision, but they shall fail. 15 When the king of the north comes, he shall set up siegeworks and take the fortified city by storm. The power of the south shall not withstand him, and not even his picked troops shall have the strength to resist. 16 He shall attack him and do as he pleases, with no one to withstand him. He shall stop in the glorious land, dealing destruction. 17 He shall set himself to penetrate the entire strength of his kingdom. He shall conclude an agreement with him and give him a daughter in marriage in order to destroy the kingdom, but this shall not succeed in his favor. 18 He shall turn to the coastland and take many, but a leader shall put an end to his shameful conduct, so that he cannot renew it against him. 19 He shall turn to the strongholds of his own land, but shall stumble and fall, to be found no more. 20 In his stead one shall arise who will send a tax collector through the glorious kingdom, but he shall soon be destroyed, though not in conflict or in battle.

21 "There shall rise in his place a despicable person, to whom the royal insignia shall not be given. By stealth and fraud he shall seize the kingdom. 22 Armed might shall be completely overwhelmed by him and crushed, and even the prince of the covenant. 23 After allying with him, he shall treacherously rise to power with a small party. 24 By stealth he shall enter prosperous provinces and do that which his fathers or grandfathers never did; he shall distribute spoil, booty, and riches among them and devise plots against their strongholds; but only for a time. 25 He shall call on his strength and cleverness to meet the king of the south with a great army; the king of the south shall prepare for battle with a very large and strong army, but he shall not succeed because of the plots devised against him. 26 Even his table companions shall seek to destroy him, his army shall be overwhelmed, and many shall fall slain. 27 The two kings, resolved on evil, shall sit at table together and exchange lies, but they shall have no success, because the appointed end is not yet.

28 "He shall turn back toward his land with great riches, his mind set against the holy covenant; he shall arrange matters and return to his land. 29 At the time appointed he shall come again to the south, but this time it shall not be as before. 30 When ships of the Kittim confront him, he shall lose heart and retreat. Then he shall direct his rage and energy against the holy covenant; those who forsake it he shall once more single out. 31 Armed forces shall move at his command and defile the sanctuary stronghold, abolishing the daily sacrifice and setting up the horrible abomination. 32 By his deceit he shall make some who were disloyal to the covenant apostatize; but those who remain loyal to their God shall take strong action. 33 The nation's wise men shall instruct the many; though for a time they will become victims of the sword, of flames, exile, and plunder. 34 When they fall, few people shall help them, but many shall join them out of treachery. 35 Of the wise men, some shall fall,

will take up arms against the king of the south, and the more violent of your own people will rebel in the hope of realising the vision; but they will fail. 15 The king of the north will then come and throw up siege-works to capture a strongly fortified city. The forces of the south will not stand their ground; the pick of the people will not be strong enough to resist. 16 The invader will do as he pleases, no one will be able to resist him: he will take his stand in the Land of Splendour, destruction in his hands. 17 He will set about conquering his entire kingdom, but will then make a treaty with him and, to overthrow the kingdom, give him a woman's hand; but this will not last or be to his advantage. 18 He will next turn to the coasts and islands and conquer many of them, but a magistrate will put a stop to his outrages in such a way that he will be unable to repay outrage for outrage.

19 He will then turn on the strongholds of his own country, but will stumble, fall, and never be seen again. 20 In his place there will rise a man who will send an extortioner to despoil the royal splendour; in a few days he will be shattered, though neither publicly nor in battle.

21 'In his place will rise a wretch: royal honours will not be given to him, but rather he will insinuate himself into them at his pleasure and will gain possession of the kingdom by intrigue. 22 Armies will be utterly routed and crushed by him, the Prince of the covenant too. 23 Through his alliances he will act treacherously and, despite the smallness of his following, grow ever stronger. 24 At his pleasure, he will invade rich provinces, acting as his fathers or his fathers' fathers never acted, distributing among them plunder, spoil and wealth, plotting his stratagems against the fortresses — for a time. 25 'He will summon up his might and courage against the king of the south with a great army. The king of the south will march to war with a huge and powerful army but will not succeed, since he will be outwitted by trickery. 26 Those who shared his food will ruin him; his army will be swept away, many will fall in the slaughter.

27 'The two kings, seated at one table, hearts bent on evil, will tell their lies; but they will not have their way, for the appointed time is still to come. 28 Then the wretch will return greatly enriched to his own country, his heart set against the holy covenant; he will take action and then return to his own country. 29 In due time, he will make his way southwards again, but this time the outcome will not be as before. 30 The ships of the Kittim will oppose him, and he will be worsted. He will retire and take furious action against the holy covenant and, as before, will favour those who forsake that holy covenant.

31 'Forces of his will come and profane the Citadel-Sanctuary; they will abolish the perpetual sacrifice and install the appalling abomination there. 32 Those who break the covenant he will seduce by his blandishments, but the people who know their God will stand firm and take action. 33 Those of the people who are wise leaders will instruct many; for some days, however, they will stumble from sword and flame, captivity and pillage. 34 And thus stumbling, little help will they receive, though many will be scheming in their support. 35 Of the wise leaders some will

NEW REVISED STANDARD VERSION

be refined, purified, and cleansed,c until the time of the end, for there is still an interval until the time appointed. 36 "The king shall act as he pleases. He shall exalt himself and consider himself greater than any god, and shall speak horrendous things against the God of gods. He shall prosper until the period of wrath is completed, for what is determined shall be done. 37 He shall pay no respect to the gods of his ancestors, or to the one beloved by women; he shall pay no respect to any other god, for he shall consider himself greater than all. 38 He shall honor the god of fortresses instead of these; a god whom his ancestors did not know he shall honor with gold and silver, with precious stones and costly gifts. 39 He shall deal with the strongest fortresses by the help of a foreign god. Those who acknowledge him he shall make more wealthy, and shall appoint them as rulers over many, and shall distribute the land for a price.

40 "At the time of the end the king of the south shall attack him. But the king of the north shall rush upon him like a whirlwind, with chariots and horsemen, and with many ships. He shall advance against countries and pass through like a flood. 41 He shall come into the beautiful land, and tens of thousands shall fall victim, but Edom and Moab and the main part of the Ammonites shall escape from his power. 42 He shall stretch out his hand against the countries, and the land of Egypt shall not escape. 43 He shall become ruler of the treasures of gold and of silver, and all the riches of Egypt; and the Libyans and the Ethiopiansd shall follow in his train. 44 But reports from the east and the north shall alarm him, and he shall go out with great fury to bring ruin and complete destruction to many. 45 He shall pitch his palatial tents between the sea and the beautiful holy mountain. Yet he shall come to his end, with no one to help him.

12 "At that time Michael, the great prince, the protector of your people, shall arise. There shall be a time of anguish, such as has never occurred since nations first came into existence. But at that time your people shall be delivered, everyone who is found written in the book. 2 Many of those who sleep in the dust of the earthe shall awake, some to everlasting life, and some to shame and everlasting contempt. 3 Those who are wise shall shine like the brightness of the sky,f and those who lead many to righteousness, like the stars forever and ever. 4 But you, Daniel, keep the words secret and the book sealed until the time of the end. Many shall be running back and forth, and evilg shall increase."

5 Then I, Daniel, looked, and two others appeared, one standing on this bank of the stream and one on the other. 6 One of them said to the man clothed in linen, who was upstream, "How long shall it be until the end of these wonders?" 7 The man clothed in linen, who was upstream, raised his right hand and his left hand toward heaven. And I heard him swear by the one who lives forever that it would be for a time, two times, and half a time,h and that when the shattering of the power of the holy people comes to an end, all these things would be accomplished. 8 I heard but

REVISED ENGLISH BIBLE

tims for a time, so that they may be tested, refined, and made shining white; for an end is yet to be at the appointed time.

36 'The king will do as he pleases; he will exalt and magnify himself above every god, and against the God of gods he will utter monstrous blasphemies. Things will go well for him until the divine wrath is spent, for what is determined must be done. 37 Heedless of his ancestral gods and the god beloved of women, indeed heedless of all gods, for he will magnify himself above them all, 38 he will honour the god of fortresses, a god unknown to his ancestors, with gold and silver, gems and costly gifts. 39 He will garrison his strongest fortresses with aliens, the people of a foreign god. Those whom he favours he will load with honour, putting them into authority over the people and distributing land as a reward.

40 'At the time of the end, the king of the south will make a feint at the king of the north, but the king of the north will come storming against him with chariots and cavalry and a fleet of ships. He will pass through country after country, sweeping over them like a flood, 41 among them the fairest of all lands, and tens of thousands will fall victim; but these lands, Edom and Moab and the chief part of the Ammonites, will escape his clutches. 42 As he gets country after country into his grasp, not even Egypt will escape; 43 he will seize control of her hidden stores of gold and silver and of all her treasures; Libyans and Cushites will follow in subjection to him. 44 Then, alarmed by rumours from east and north, he will depart in a great rage to destroy and to exterminate many. 45 He will pitch his royal pavilion between the sea and the holy hill, the fairest of all hills; and he will meet his end with no one to help him.

12 'At that time there will appear
   Michael the great captain,
who stands guarding your fellow-countrymen;
   and there will be a period of anguish
   such as has never been known
   ever since they became a nation till that moment.
But at that time your people will be delivered,
   everyone whose name is entered in the book:
2 many of those who sleep in the dust of the earth
   will awake,
   some to everlasting life
   and some to the reproach of eternal abhorrence.
3 The wise leaders will shine like the bright vault of
   heaven,
   and those who have guided the people in the true
      path
   will be like the stars for ever and ever.

4 'But you, Daniel, keep the words secret and seal the book until the time of the end. Many will rush to and fro, trying to gain such knowledge.'

5 I, Daniel, looked and saw two others standing, one on this bank of the river and the other on the farther bank. 6 To the man robed in linen who was above the waters of the river I said, 'How long will it be until the end of these portents?' 7 The man robed in linen who was above the waters raised his right hand and his left heavenwards, and I heard him swear by him who lives for ever: 'It shall be for a time and times and half a time. When the power of the holy people is no longer being shattered, all these things will cease.'

---

c Heb made them white   d Or Nubians; Heb Cushites   e Or the land of dust   f Or dome   g Cn Compare Gk: Heb knowledge   h Heb a time, times, and a half

11:35 for an end . . . time: prob. rdg; Heb. has different word order. 12:6 I: so Gk; Heb. he.

so that the rest may be tested, refined, and purified, until the end time which is still appointed to come.

36 "The king shall do as he pleases, exalting himself and making himself greater than any god; he shall utter dreadful blasphemies against the God of gods. He shall prosper only till divine wrath is ready, for what is determined must take place. 37 He shall have no regard for the gods of his ancestors or for the one in whom women delight; for no god shall he have regard, because he shall make himself greater than all. 38 Instead, he shall give glory to the god of strongholds; a god unknown to his fathers he shall glorify with gold, silver, precious stones, and other treasures. 39 To defend the strongholds he shall station a people of a foreign god. Whoever acknowledges him he shall provide with abundant honor; he shall make them rule over the many and distribute the land as a reward.

40 "At the appointed time the king of the south shall come to grips with him, but the king of the north shall overwhelm him with chariots and horsemen and a great fleet, passing through the countries like a flood. 41 He shall enter the glorious land and many shall fall, except Edom, Moab, and the chief part of Ammon, which shall escape from his power. 42 He shall extend his power over the countries, and not even the land of Egypt shall escape. 43 He shall control the riches of gold and silver and all the treasures of Egypt; Libya and Ethiopia shall be in his train. 44 When news from the east and the north terrifies him, he shall set out with great fury to slay and to doom many. 45 He shall pitch the tents of his royal pavilion between the sea and the glorious holy mountain, but he shall come to his end with none to help him.

12 "At that time there shall arise
Michael, the great prince,
    guardian of your people;
It shall be a time unsurpassed in distress
    since nations began until that time.
At that time your people shall escape,
    everyone who is found written in the book.
2 Many of those who sleep
    in the dust of the earth shall awake;
Some shall live forever,
    others shall be an everlasting horror
      and disgrace.
3 But the wise shall shine brightly
    like the splendor of the firmament,
And those who lead the many to justice
    shall be like the stars forever.

4 "As for you, Daniel, keep secret the message and seal the book until the end time; many shall fall away and evil shall increase."

5 I, Daniel, looked and saw two others, one standing on either bank of the river. 6 One of them said to the man clothed in linen, who was upstream, "How long shall it be to the end of these appalling things?" 7 The man clothed in linen, who was upstream, lifted his right and left hands to heaven; and I heard him swear by him who lives forever that it should be for a year, two years, a half-year; and that, when the power of the destroyer of the holy people was brought to an end, all these things should end. 8 I heard, but

stumble, and so a number of them will be purged, purified and made clean — until the time of the End, for the appointed time is still to come.

36 'The king will do as he pleases, growing more and more arrogant, considering himself greater than all the gods; he will utter incredible blasphemies against the God of gods, and he will thrive until the wrath reaches bursting point; for what has been decreed will certainly be fulfilled. 37 Heedless of his fathers' gods, heedless of the god whom women love, heedless of any god whatever, he will consider himself greatest of all. 38 Instead of them, he will honour the god of fortresses, will honour a god unknown to his ancestors with gold and silver, precious stones and valuable presents. 39 He will use the people of an alien god to defend the fortresses; he will confer great honours on those whom he acknowledges, by giving them wide authority and by parcelling the country out for rent.

40 'When the time comes for the End, the king of the south will try conclusions with him; but the king of the north will come storming down on him with chariots, cavalry, and a large fleet. He will invade countries, overrun them and drive on. 41 He will invade the Land of Splendour, and many will fall; but Edom, Moab, and what remains of the sons of Ammon will escape him. 42 'He will reach out to attack countries: Egypt will not escape him. 43 The gold and silver treasures and all the valuables of Egypt will lie in his power. Libyans and Cushites will be at his feet: 44 but reports coming from the East and the north will worry him, and in great fury he will set out to bring ruin and complete destruction to many. 45 He will pitch the tents of his royal headquarters between the sea and the mountains of the Holy Splendour. Yet he will come to his end — there will be no help for him.'

12 'At that time Michael will arise — the great Prince, defender of your people. That will be a time of great distress, unparalleled since nations first came into existence. When that time comes, your own people will be spared — all those whose names are found written in the Book.

2 'Of those who are sleeping in the Land of Dust, many will awaken, some to everlasting life, some to shame and everlasting disgrace. 3 Those who are wise will shine as brightly as the expanse of the heavens, and those who have instructed many in uprightness, as bright as stars for all eternity.

4 'But you, Daniel, must keep these words secret and keep the book sealed until the time of the End. Many will roam about, this way and that, and wickedness will continue to increase.'

5 I, Daniel, then looked and saw two other people standing, one on the near bank of the river, the other on the far. 6 One of them said to the man dressed in linen who was standing further up the stream, 'How long until these wonders take place?' 7 I heard the man speak who was dressed in linen, standing further up the stream: he raised his right hand and his left to heaven and swore by him who lives for ever, 'A time and two times, and half a time; and all these things will come true, once the crushing of the holy peo-

NEW REVISED STANDARD VERSION

could not understand; so I said, "My lord, what shall be the outcome of these things?" ⁹ He said, "Go your way, Daniel, for the words are to remain secret and sealed until the time of the end. ¹⁰ Many shall be purified, cleansed, and refined, but the wicked shall continue to act wickedly. None of the wicked shall understand, but those who are wise shall understand. ¹¹ From the time that the regular burnt offering is taken away and the abomination that desolates is set up, there shall be one thousand two hundred ninety days. ¹² Happy are those who persevere and attain the thousand three hundred thirty-five days. ¹³ But you, go your way,ⁱ and rest; you shall rise for your reward at the end of the days."

ⁱ Gk Theodotion: Heb adds *to the end*

REVISED ENGLISH BIBLE

⁸ I heard, but I did not understand; so I said, 'Sir, what will be the outcome of these things?' ⁹ He replied, 'Go your way, Daniel, for the words are to be kept secret and sealed till the time of the end. ¹⁰ Many will purify themselves and be refined, making themselves shining white, but the wicked will continue in wickedness and none of them will understand; only the wise leaders will understand. ¹¹ From the time when the regular offering is abolished and "the abomination of desolation" is set up, one thousand two hundred and ninety days will elapse. ¹² Happy are those who wait and live to see the completion of one thousand three hundred and thirty-five days! ¹³ But you, Daniel, go your way till the end; you will rest, and then, at the end of the age, you will arise to your destiny.'

NEW AMERICAN BIBLE

I did not understand; so I asked, "My lord, what follows this?" 9 "Go, Daniel," he said, "because the words are to be kept secret and sealed until the end time. 10 Many shall be refined, purified, and tested, but the wicked shall prove wicked; none of them shall have understanding, but the wise shall have it. 11 From the time that the daily sacrifice is abolished and the horrible abomination is set up, there shall be one thousand two hundred and ninety days. 12 Blessed is the man who has patience and perseveres until the one thousand three hundred and thirty-five days. 13 Go, take your rest, you shall rise for your reward at the end of days."

‡Chs. 13, 14: see pp. 2429–2437‡

NEW JERUSALEM BIBLE

ple's power is over.' 8 I listened but did not understand. I then said, 'My lord, what is to be the outcome?' 9 'Go, Daniel,' he said. 'These words are to remain secret and sealed until the time of the End. 10 Many will be cleansed, made white and purged; the wicked will persist in doing wrong; the wicked will never understand; those who are wise will understand. 11 From the moment that the perpetual sacrifice is abolished and the appalling abomination set up: a thousand two hundred and ninety days. 12 Blessed is he who perseveres and attains a thousand three hundred and thirty-five days. 13 But you, go away and rest; and you will rise for your reward at the end of time.'

‡Chs. 13, 14: see pp. 2429–2437‡

Hosea

1 The word of the LORD that came to Hosea son of Beeri, in the days of Kings Uzziah, Jotham, Ahaz, and Hezekiah of Judah, and in the days of King Jeroboam son of Joash of Israel.

2 When the LORD first spoke through Hosea, the LORD said to Hosea, "Go, take for yourself a wife of whoredom and have children of whoredom, for the land commits great whoredom by forsaking the LORD." 3 So he went and took Gomer daughter of Diblaim, and she conceived and bore him a son.

4 And the LORD said to him, "Name him Jezreel;[a] for in a little while I will punish the house of Jehu for the blood of Jezreel, and I will put an end to the kingdom of the house of Israel. 5 On that day I will break the bow of Israel in the valley of Jezreel."

6 She conceived again and bore a daughter. Then the LORD said to him, "Name her Lo-ruhamah,[b] for I will no longer have pity on the house of Israel or forgive them. 7 But I will have pity on the house of Judah, and I will save them by the LORD their God; I will not save them by bow, or by sword, or by war, or by horses, or by horsemen."

8 When she had weaned Lo-ruhamah, she conceived and bore a son. 9 Then the LORD said, "Name him Lo-ammi,[c] for you are not my people and I am not your God."[d]

10[e] Yet the number of the people of Israel shall be like the sand of the sea, which can be neither measured nor numbered; and in the place where it was said to them, "You are not my people," it shall be said to them, "Children of the living God." 11 The people of Judah and the people of Israel shall be gathered together, and they shall appoint for themselves one head; and they shall take possession of[f] the land, for great shall be the day of Jezreel.

2 [g] Say to your brother,[h] Ammi,[i] and to your sister,[j] Ruhamah.[k]

2 Plead with your mother, plead—
    for she is not my wife,
    and I am not her husband—
that she put away her whoring from her face,
    and her adultery from between her breasts,
3 or I will strip her naked
    and expose her as in the day she was born,
and make her like a wilderness,
    and turn her into a parched land,
    and kill her with thirst.
4 Upon her children also I will have no pity,
    because they are children of whoredom.

Hosea

1 THE word of the LORD which came to Hosea son of Beeri during the reigns of Uzziah, Jotham, Ahaz, and Hezekiah, kings of Judah, and during the reign of Jeroboam son of Joash king of Israel.

2 THIS is the beginning of the LORD's message given by Hosea. He said, 'Go and take an unchaste woman as your wife, and with this woman have children; for like an unchaste woman this land is guilty of unfaithfulness to the LORD.' 3 So he married Gomer daughter of Diblaim, and she conceived and bore him a son. 4 The LORD said to Hosea, 'Call him Jezreel, for in a little while I am going to punish the dynasty of Jehu for the blood shed in the valley of Jezreel, and bring the kingdom of Israel to an end. 5 On that day I shall break Israel's bow in the vale of Jezreel.' 6 Gomer conceived again and bore a daughter, and the LORD said to Hosea,

Call her Lo-ruhamah;
    for I shall never again show love to Israel,
    never again forgive them.

7 But Judah I shall love and save.
    I shall save them not by bow or sword or weapon
        of war,
    not by horses and horsemen,
    but I shall save them by the LORD their God.

8 After weaning Lo-ruhamah, Gomer conceived and bore a son; 9 and the LORD said,

Call him Lo-ammi;
    for you are not my people,
    and I shall not be your God.

10 The Israelites will be as countless as the sands of
        the sea,
    which can neither be measured nor numbered;
    it will no longer be said to them, 'You are not my
        people';
    they will be called Children of the Living God.
11 The people of Judah and of Israel will be reunited
    and will choose for themselves one leader;
    they will spring up from the land,
    for great will be the day of Jezreel.

2 You are to say to your brothers, 'You are my
        people,'
    and to your sisters, 'You are loved.'

2 Call your mother to account,
    for she is no longer my wife
    nor am I her husband.
Let her put an end to her infidelity
    and banish the lovers from her bosom,
3 or else I shall strip her bare
    and parade her naked as the day she was born.
I shall make her bare as the wilderness,
    parched as the desert,
    and leave her to die of thirst.
4 I shall show no love towards her children,
    for they are the offspring of adultery.

---

a That is God sows   b That is Not pitied   c That is Not my
people   d Heb I am not yours   e Ch 2.1 in Heb   f Heb rise up
from   g Ch 2.3 in Heb   h Gk: Heb brothers   i That is My
People   j Gk Vg: Heb sisters   k That is Pitied

1:6 Lo-ruhamah: that is Not loved. never again forgive: or I shall
totally remove.   1:9 Lo-ammi: that is Not my people. your God:
lit. to you.   1:10 In Heb. 2:1.   1:11 Jezreel: that is God
sows.

THE BOOK OF

Hosea

1 The word of the LORD that came to Hosea, the son of Beeri, in the days of Uzziah, Jotham, Ahaz, Hezekiah, kings of Judah, and in the days of Jeroboam, son of Joash, king of Israel. ²In the beginning of the LORD's speaking to Hosea, the LORD said to Hosea:

Go, take a harlot wife and harlot's children,
for the land gives itself to harlotry,
turning away from the LORD.

³So he went and took Gomer, the daughter of Diblaim; and she conceived and bore him a son. ⁴Then the LORD said to him:

Give him the name Jezreel,
for in a little while
I will punish the house of Jehu
for the bloodshed at Jezreel
And bring to an end the kingdom
of the house of Israel;
⁵On that day I will break the bow of Israel
in the valley of Jezreel.

⁶When she conceived again and bore a daughter, the LORD said to him:

Give her the name Lo-ruhama;
I no longer feel pity for the house of Israel:
rather, I abhor them utterly.
⁷Yet for the house of Judah I feel pity;
I will save them by the LORD, their God;
But I will not save them by war,
by sword or bow, by horses or horsemen.

⁸After she weaned Lo-ruhama, she conceived and bore a son. ⁹Then the LORD said:

Give him the name Lo-ammi,
for you are not my people,
and I will not be your God.

‡2.1–3: see below in ch.3‡

2 ⁴Protest against your mother, protest!
for she is not my wife,
and I am not her husband.
Let her remove her harlotry from before her,
her adultery from between her breasts,
⁵Or I will strip her naked,
leaving her as on the day of her birth;
I will make her like the desert,
reduce her to an arid land,
and slay her with thirst.
⁶I will have no pity on her children,
for they are the children of harlotry.

1, 7: The terrible punishments announced by the prophets were so fully realized that later generations made a point of recalling the same prophets' messages of consolation also, even though it meant taking these from another context. Thus, an editor placed the words of Hos 2, 1ff after the repudiation of Israel in Hos 1, 9; here the more natural order has been restored. The present verse is another example of the same thing.

Hosea

1 The word of Yahweh which came to Hosea son of Beeri during the reigns of Uzziah, Jotham, Ahaz and Hezekiah kings of Judah, and of Jeroboam son of Joash, king of Israel.

²The beginning of what Yahweh said through Hosea: Yahweh said to Hosea, 'Go, marry a whore, and get children with a whore; for the country itself has become nothing but a whore by abandoning Yahweh.'

³So he went and married Gomer daughter of Diblaim, who conceived and bore him a son. ⁴Yahweh then said to him, 'Call him Jezreel, for in a little while I shall punish the House of Jehu for the bloodshed at Jezreel[a] and put an end to the sovereignty of the House of Israel. ⁵When that day comes, I shall break the bow of Israel in the Valley of Jezreel.'

⁶She conceived a second time and gave birth to a daughter. Yahweh then said to him, 'Call her Lo-Ruhamah, for I shall show no more pity for the House of Israel, I shall never forgive them again. ⁷(Instead, I shall take pity on the House of Judah and shall save them, not by bow or sword or force of arms, not by horses or horsemen, but by Yahweh their God.)'

⁸After weaning Lo-Ruhamah, she conceived and gave birth to a son. ⁹Yahweh said, 'Call him Lo-Ammi, for you are not my people and I do not exist for you.'

2 But the Israelites will become as numerous as the sands of the sea, which cannot be measured or counted. In the very place where they were told, 'You are not my people,'

they will be told they are 'Children of the living
God'.
²The Judaeans and Israelites will be reunited
and will choose themselves a single head,
and will spread far beyond their country,
for great will be the Day of Jezreel!
³Then call your brothers, 'My people',
and your sisters, 'You have been pitied'.
⁴To court, take your mother to court!
For she is no longer my wife
nor am I her husband.
She must either remove her whoring ways from her
face
and her adulteries from between her breasts,
⁵or I shall strip her and expose her
naked as the day she was born;
I shall make her as bare as the desert,
I shall make her as dry as arid country,
and let her die of thirst.
⁶And I shall feel no pity for her children
since they are the children of her whorings.

a 1 2 K 9:15-10:14.

5 For their mother has played the whore;
  she who conceived them has acted shamefully.
For she said, "I will go after my lovers;
  they give me my bread and my water,
  my wool and my flax, my oil and my drink."
6 Therefore I will hedge up her[l] way with thorns;
  and I will build a wall against her,
  so that she cannot find her paths.
7 She shall pursue her lovers,
  but not overtake them;
and she shall seek them,
  but shall not find them.
Then she shall say, "I will go
  and return to my first husband,
  for it was better with me then than now."
8 She did not know
  that it was I who gave her
  the grain, the wine, and the oil,
and who lavished upon her silver
  and gold that they used for Baal.
9 Therefore I will take back
  my grain in its time,
  and my wine in its season;
and I will take away my wool and my flax,
  which were to cover her nakedness.
10 Now I will uncover her shame
  in the sight of her lovers,
  and no one shall rescue her out of my hand.
11 I will put an end to all her mirth,
  her festivals, her new moons, her sabbaths,
  and all her appointed festivals.
12 I will lay waste her vines and her fig trees,
  of which she said,
"These are my pay,
  which my lovers have given me."
I will make them a forest,
  and the wild animals shall devour them.
13 I will punish her for the festival days of the
    Baals,
  when she offered incense to them
and decked herself with her ring and jewelry,
  and went after her lovers,
  and forgot me, says the Lord.

14 Therefore, I will now allure her,
  and bring her into the wilderness,
  and speak tenderly to her.
15 From there I will give her her vineyards,
  and make the Valley of Achor a door of hope.
There she shall respond as in the days of her
    youth,
  as at the time when she came out of the land
    of Egypt.
16 On that day, says the Lord, you will call me, "My hus-band," and no longer will you call me, "My Baal."[m] 17 For I will remove the names of the Baals from her mouth, and they shall be mentioned by name no more. 18 I will make for you[n] a covenant on that day with the wild animals, the birds of the air, and the creeping things of the ground; and I will abolish[o] the bow, the sword, and war from the land; and I will make you lie down in safety. 19 And I will take you for my wife forever; I will take you for my wife in righteousness and in justice, in steadfast love, and in mercy. 20 I will take you for my wife in faithfulness; and you shall know the Lord.

5 Their mother has been promiscuous;
  she who conceived them is shameless.
She says, 'I will go after my lovers,
  who supply me with food and drink,
  with my wool and flax, my oil and perfumes.'
6 That is why I shall close her road with thorn
    bushes
  and obstruct her path with a wall,
  so that she can no longer find a way through.
7 Though she pursues her lovers
  she will not overtake them,
though she looks for them
  she will not find them.
At last she will say,
  'I shall go back to my husband again,
  for I was better off then than I am now.'
8 She does not know that it was I who gave her
  the grain, the new wine, and fresh oil,
I who lavished on her silver and gold
  which they used for the Baal.

9 That is why I am going to take back
  my grain at the harvest and my new wine at the
    vintage,
take away the wool and the flax
  which I provided to cover her naked body.
10 Now I shall reveal her shame to her lovers,
  and no one will rescue her from me.
11 I shall put a stop to all her merrymaking,
  her pilgrimages, new moons, and sabbaths,
  all her festivals.
12 I shall ravage the vines and the fig trees,
  of which she says, 'These are the fees
  which my lovers have paid me,'
  and I shall leave them to grow wild
  so that beasts may eat them.
13 I shall punish her for the holy days
  when she burnt sacrifices to the baalim,
  when she decked herself with her rings and
    necklaces,
  when, forgetful of me, she ran after her lovers.
  This is the word of the Lord.

14 But now I shall woo her,
  lead her into the wilderness,
  and speak words of encouragement to her.
15 There I shall restore her vineyards to her,
  turning the valley of Achor into a gate of hope;
  there she will respond as in her youth,
  as when she came up from Egypt.
16–17 On that day she will call me 'My husband'
  and will no more call me 'My Baal';
  I shall banish from her lips the very names of the
    baalim;
  never again will their names be invoked.
  This is the word of the Lord.

18 Then I shall make a covenant on Israel's behalf with the wild beasts, the birds of the air, and the creatures that creep on the ground, and I shall break bow and sword and weapon of war and sweep them off the earth, so that my people may lie down without fear. 19 I shall betroth you to myself for ever, bestowing righteousness and justice, loyalty and love; 20 I shall betroth you to myself, making you faithful, and you will know the Lord. 21 At that time I shall answer, says

l Gk Syr: Heb your   m That is, "My master"   n Heb them
o Heb break

2:6 her road: so Gk; Heb. your road.   2:16–17 she: so Gk; Heb. you. My Baal: also means My husband.

NEW AMERICAN BIBLE

7 Yes, their mother has played the harlot;
  she that conceived them has acted shamefully.
"I will go after my lovers," she said,
  "who give me my bread and my water,
  my wool and my flax, my oil and my drink."
‡2.8–9: see below‡

10 Since she has not known
  that it was I who gave her
  the grain, the wine, and the oil,
And her abundance of silver,
  and of gold, which they used for Baal,
11 Therefore I will take back my grain in its time,
  and my wine in its season;
I will snatch away my wool and my flax,
  with which she covers her nakedness.
12 So now I will lay bare her shame
  before the eyes of her lovers,
  and no one can deliver her out of my hand.
13 I will bring an end to all her joy,
  her feasts, her new moons, her sabbaths,
  and all her solemnities.
14 I will lay waste her vines and fig trees,
  of which she said, "These are the hire
  my lovers have given me";
I will turn them into rank growth
  and wild beasts shall devour them.
15 I will punish her for the days of the Baals,
  for whom she burnt incense
While she decked herself out with her rings and her
    jewels,
  and, in going after her lovers,
  forgot me, says the LORD.
8 Therefore, I will hedge in her way with thorns
  and erect a wall against her,
  so that she cannot find her paths.
9 If she runs after her lovers, she shall not
    overtake them;
  if she looks for them she shall not find them.
Then she shall say,
  "I will go back to my first husband,
  for it was better with me then than now."

16 So I will allure her;
  I will lead her into the desert
  and speak to her heart.
17 From there I will give her the vineyards she had,
  and the valley of Achor as a door of hope.
She shall respond there as in the days of her youth,
  when she came up from the land of Egypt.

18   On that day, says the LORD,
She shall call me "My husband,"
  and never again "My baal."
19 Then will I remove from her mouth the names of
    the Baals,
  so that they shall no longer be invoked.
20 I will make a covenant for them on that day,
  with the beasts of the field,
With the birds of the air,
  and with the things that crawl on the ground.
Bow and sword and war
  I will destroy from the land,
  and I will let them take their rest in security.

21 I will espouse you to me forever:
  I will espouse you in right and in justice,
  in love and in mercy;
22 I will espouse you in fidelity,
  and you shall know the LORD.

NEW JERUSALEM BIBLE

7 Yes, their mother has played the whore,
  she who conceived them has disgraced herself
by saying, 'I shall chase after my lovers;
  they will assure me my keep,
  my wool, my flax, my oil and my drinks.'

8 This is why I shall block her way with thorns,
  and wall her in to stop her in her tracks;
9 then if she chases her lovers she will not catch
    them,
  if she looks for them she will not find them,
  and then she will say, 'I shall go back to my first
    husband,
  I was better off then than I am now;'
10 she had never realised before
  that I was the one who was giving her
  the grain, new wine and oil,
  giving her more and more silver and gold
  which they have spent on Baal!
11 This is why I shall take back my grain when it is
    due
  and my new wine, when the season for it comes.
  I shall withdraw my wool and my flax
  which were to cover her naked body,
12 and then display her infamy before her lovers'
    eyes—
  no one will take her from me then!
13 I shall put an end to all her merrymaking,
  her festivals, her New Moons and her Sabbaths
  and all her solemn feasts.
14 I shall make her vines and fig trees derelict
  of which she used to say,
  'These are the pay my lovers gave me.'
I shall turn them into a jungle:
  wild animals will feed on them.
15 I mean to make her pay for the feast-days
  on which she burnt incense to the Baals,
  when she tricked herself out in her earrings and
    necklaces
to chase after her lovers,
  and forget me!
  —declares Yahweh.

16 But look, I am going to seduce her
  and lead her into the desert
  and speak to her heart.
17 There I shall give her back her vineyards,
  and make the Vale of Achorᵇ a gateway of hope.
There she will respond as when she was young,
  as on the day when she came up from Egypt.

18 When that day comes—declares Yahweh—
  you will call me, 'My husband',
  no more will you call me, 'My Baal'.
19 I shall banish the names of the Baals from her lips
  and their name will be mentioned no more.
20 When that day comes I shall make a treaty for
    them with the wild animals,
  with the birds of heaven and the creeping things of
    the earth;
  I shall break the bow and the sword
  and warfare, and banish them from the country,
  and I will let them sleep secure.
21 I shall betroth you to myself for ever,
  I shall betroth you in uprightness and justice,
  and faithful love and tenderness.
22 Yes, I shall betroth you to myself in loyalty
  and in the knowledge of Yahweh.

ᵇ 2 The scene of Achan's sin, Jos 7:24.

NEW REVISED STANDARD VERSION	REVISED ENGLISH BIBLE

NEW REVISED STANDARD VERSION

21 On that day I will answer, says the LORD,
    I will answer the heavens
    and they shall answer the earth;
22 and the earth shall answer the grain, the wine,
    and the oil,
    and they shall answer Jezreel;*p*
23 and I will sow him*q* for myself in the land.
    And I will have pity on Lo-ruhamah,*r*
    and I will say to Lo-ammi,*s* "You are my
    people";
    and he shall say, "You are my God."

3 The LORD said to me again, "Go, love a woman who has a lover and is an adulteress, just as the LORD loves the people of Israel, though they turn to other gods and love raisin cakes." 2 So I bought her for fifteen shekels of silver and a homer of barley and a measure of wine.*t* 3 And I said to her, "You must remain as mine for many days; you shall not play the whore, you shall not have intercourse with a man, nor I with you." 4 For the Israelites shall remain many days without king or prince, without sacrifice or pillar, without ephod or teraphim. 5 Afterward the Israelites shall return and seek the LORD their God, and David their king; they shall come in awe to the LORD and to his goodness in the latter days.

4 Hear the word of the LORD, O people of Israel;
    for the LORD has an indictment against the
        inhabitants of the land.
    There is no faithfulness or loyalty,
        and no knowledge of God in the land.
2 Swearing, lying, and murder,
    and stealing and adultery break out;
    bloodshed follows bloodshed.
3 Therefore the land mourns,
    and all who live in it languish;
    together with the wild animals
    and the birds of the air,
    even the fish of the sea are perishing.

4 Yet let no one contend,
    and let none accuse,
    for with you is my contention, O priest.*u*

REVISED ENGLISH BIBLE

the LORD; I shall answer the heavens and they will answer the earth, 22 and the earth will answer the grain, the new wine, and fresh oil, and they will answer Jezreel. 23 Israel will be my new sowing in the land, and I shall show love to Lo-ruhamah and say to Lo-ammi, 'You are my people,' and he will say, 'You are my God.'

3 The LORD said to me,

    Go again and bestow your love on a woman
    loved by another man, an adulteress;
    love her as I, the LORD, love the Israelites,
    although they resort to other gods
    and love the cakes of raisins offered to idols.

2 So I bought her for fifteen pieces of silver, a homer of barley, and a measure of wine; 3 and I said to her,

    You will live in my house for a long time
    and you will not lead an immoral life.
    You must have relations with no one else,
    indeed not even with me.
4 So the Israelites will live for a long time
    without king or leader,
    without sacrifice or sacred pillar,
    without ephod or teraphim.
5 After that they will again seek
    the LORD their God and David their king,
    and turn with reverence to the LORD
    and seek his bounty for the days to come.

4 ISRAEL, hear the word of the LORD;
    for the LORD has a charge to bring
        against the inhabitants of the land:
    There is no good faith or loyalty,
        no acknowledgement of God in the land.
2 People swear oaths and break them;
    they kill and rob and commit adultery;
    there is violence, one deed of blood after another.
3 Therefore the land will be desolate
    and all who live in it will languish,
    with the wild beasts and the birds of the air;
    even the fish will vanish from the sea.
4 But it is not for mankind to bring charges,
    not for them to prove a case;
    it is my quarrel, and it is with you, the priest.

---

p That is *God sows*   *q* Cn: Heb *her*   *r* That is *Not pitied*
s That is *Not my people*   *t* Gk: Heb *a homer of barley and a lethech of barley*   *u* Cn: Meaning of Heb uncertain

2:22 **Jezreel:** *that is* God sows.   3:2 **wine:** *so Gk; Heb.* barley.
4:4 **my quarrel:** *prob. rdg; Heb.* like my quarrel.

NEW AMERICAN BIBLE

23 On that day I will respond, says the LORD;
    I will respond to the heavens,
    and they shall respond to the earth;
24 The earth shall respond to the grain, and wine,
    and oil,
    and these shall respond to Jezreel.
25 I will sow him for myself in the land,
    and I will have pity on Lo-ruhama.
    I will say to Lo-ammi, "You are my people,"
    and he shall say, "My God!"

3 Again the LORD said to me:
    Give your love to a woman
    beloved of a paramour, an adulteress;
    Even as the LORD loves the people of Israel,
    though they turn to other gods
    and are fond of raisin cakes.

2 So I bought her for fifteen pieces of silver and a homer and a lethech of barley. 3 Then I said to her:

"Many days you shall wait for me;
    you shall not play the harlot
Or belong to any man;
    I in turn will wait for you."
4 For the people of Israel shall remain many days
    without king or prince,
Without sacrifice or sacred pillar,
    without ephod or household idols.
5 Then the people of Israel shall turn back
    and seek the LORD, their God,
    and David, their king;
They shall come trembling to the LORD
    and to his bounty, in the last days.
2,1 The number of the Israelites
    shall be like the sand of the sea,
    which can be neither measured nor counted.
Whereas they were called,
    "Lo-ammi,"
They shall be called,
    "Children of the living God."
2,2 Then the people of Judah and of Israel
    shall be gathered together;
They shall appoint for themselves one head
    and come up from other lands,
    for great shall be the day of Jezreel.
2,3 Say to your brothers, "Ammi,"
    and to your sisters, "Ruhama."

4 Hear the word of the LORD, O people of Israel,
    for the LORD has a grievance
    against the inhabitants of the land:
There is no fidelity, no mercy,
    no knowledge of God in the land.
2 False swearing, lying, murder, stealing
    and adultery!
    in their lawlessness, bloodshed
    follows bloodshed.
3 Therefore the land mourns,
    and everything that dwells in it languishes:
The beasts of the field,
    the birds of the air,
    and even the fish of the sea perish.

4 But let no one protest, let no one complain;
    with you is my grievance, O priests!

NEW JERUSALEM BIBLE

23 When that day comes, I shall respond
    — declares Yahweh —
    I shall respond to the heavens
    and they will respond to the earth
24 and the earth will respond to the grain, the new
    wine and oil,
    and they will respond to Jezreel.
25 I shall sow her in the country to be mine,
    I shall take pity on Lo-Ruhamah,
    I shall tell Lo-Ammi, 'You are my people,'
    and he will say, 'You are my God.'

3 Yahweh said to me, 'Go again, love a woman who
    loves another man, an adulteress, and love her as Yahweh loves the Israelites although they turn to other gods and love raisin cakes.' 2 So I bought her for fifteen shekels of silver, a homer of barley and a skin of wine, 3 and I said to her, 'You will have to spend a long time waiting for me without playing the whore and without giving yourself to any man, and I will behave in the same way towards you.'

4 For the Israelites will have to spend a long time without king or leader, without sacrifice or sacred pillar, without ephod or domestic images; 5 but after that, the Israelites will return and again seek Yahweh their God and David their king, and turn trembling to Yahweh for his bounty in the final days.

4 Israelites, hear what Yahweh says,
    for Yahweh indicts the citizens of the country:
    there is no loyalty, no faithful love,
    no knowledge of God in the country,
2 only perjury and lying, murder, theft,
    adultery and violence,
    bloodshed after bloodshed.
3 This is why the country is in mourning
    and all its citizens pining away,
    the wild animals also and birds of the sky,
    even the fish in the sea will disappear.

4 But let no one denounce, no one rebuke;
    it is you, priest, that I denounce.

2, 1–3: These verses (The number . . . Ruhama) (transposed from ch
2) continue the conditional promise of restoration made in Hos 3,
1–5, reversing the dire predictions of chapter 1.

NEW REVISED STANDARD VERSION	REVISED ENGLISH BIBLE

NEW REVISED STANDARD VERSION

5 You shall stumble by day;
   the prophet also shall stumble with you by
      night,
   and I will destroy your mother.
6 My people are destroyed for lack of knowledge;
   because you have rejected knowledge,
   I reject you from being a priest to me.
   And since you have forgotten the law of your
      God,
   I also will forget your children.

7 The more they increased,
   the more they sinned against me;
   they changed[v] their glory into shame.
8 They feed on the sin of my people;
   they are greedy for their iniquity.
9 And it shall be like people, like priest;
   I will punish them for their ways,
   and repay them for their deeds.
10 They shall eat, but not be satisfied;
   they shall play the whore, but not multiply;
   because they have forsaken the LORD
   to devote themselves to 11 whoredom.

   Wine and new wine
   take away the understanding.
12 My people consult a piece of wood,
   and their divining rod gives them oracles.
   For a spirit of whoredom has led them astray,
   and they have played the whore, forsaking their
      God.
13 They sacrifice on the tops of the mountains,
   and make offerings upon the hills,
   under oak, poplar, and terebinth,
   because their shade is good.

   Therefore your daughters play the whore,
   and your daughters-in-law commit adultery.
14 I will not punish your daughters when they play
      the whore,
   nor your daughters-in-law when they commit
      adultery;
   for the men themselves go aside with whores,
   and sacrifice with temple prostitutes;
   thus a people without understanding comes to
      ruin.

15 Though you play the whore, O Israel,
   do not let Judah become guilty.
   Do not enter into Gilgal,
   or go up to Beth-aven,
   and do not swear, "As the LORD lives."
16 Like a stubborn heifer,
   Israel is stubborn;
   can the LORD now feed them
   like a lamb in a broad pasture?

17 Ephraim is joined to idols —
   let him alone.
18 When their drinking is ended, they indulge in
      sexual orgies;
   they love lewdness more than their glory.[w]
19 A wind has wrapped them[x] in its wings,
   and they shall be ashamed because of their
      altars.[y]

REVISED ENGLISH BIBLE

5 By day and by night you blunder on,
   you and the prophet with you.
   Your nation is brought to ruin;
6 want of knowledge has been the ruin of my people.
   As you have rejected knowledge,
   so will I reject you as a priest to me.
   As you have forsaken the teaching of God,
   so will I, your God, forsake your children.

7 The more priests there are,
   the more they sin against me;
   their dignity I shall turn into dishonour.
8 They feed on the sin of my people
   and batten on their iniquity.
9 But people and priest will fare alike.
   I shall punish them for their conduct
   and repay them for their deeds.
10 They will eat but never be satisfied,
   resort to prostitutes and never have children,
   for they have abandoned the LORD
11 to give themselves to immorality.
   Wine, old and new, steals my people's wits;
12 they ask advice from a piece of wood
   and accept the guidance of the diviner's wand;
   for a spirit of promiscuity has led them astray
   and they are unfaithful to their God.
13 They sacrifice on mountaintops
   and burn offerings on the hills,
   under oak and poplar
   and the terebinth's pleasant shade.
   That is why your daughters turn to prostitution
   and your sons' brides commit adultery.
14 I shall not punish your daughters for becoming
      prostitutes
   or your sons' brides for their adultery,
   because your men resort to whores
   and sacrifice with temple-prostitutes.
   A people so devoid of understanding comes to
      grief.
15 Israel, though you are adulterous,
   let not Judah incur such guilt;
   let her not come to Gilgal
   or go up to Beth-aven
   to swear by the life of the LORD.
16 Like a heifer, Israel has turned stubborn;
   will the LORD now feed them
   like lambs in a broad meadow?
17-18 Ephraim has associated with idols;
   a drunken rabble,
   they have devoted their lives to immorality,
   preferring dishonour to glory.
19 The wind with its wings will carry them off,
   and they will find their sacrifices a delusion.

4:10 **have children:** or be wealthy.   4:17–18 **a drunken rabble:** prob. rdg; Heb. unintelligible. **to glory:** prob. rdg, cp. Gk; Heb. her shields.

[v] Ancient Heb tradition: MT *I will change*   [w] Cn Compare Gk:
Meaning of Heb uncertain   [x] Heb *her*   [y] Gk Syr: Heb *sacrifices*

NEW AMERICAN BIBLE

⁵You shall stumble in the day,
  and the prophets shall stumble with you at night;
  I will destroy your mother.
⁶My people perish for want of knowledge!
  Since you have rejected knowledge,
  I will reject you from my priesthood;
  Since you have ignored the law of your God,
  I will also ignore your sons.
⁷One and all they sin against me,
  exchanging their glory for shame.
⁸They feed on the sin of my people,
  and are greedy for their guilt.
⁹The priests shall fare no better than the people:
  I will punish them for their ways,
  and repay them for their deeds.
¹⁰They shall eat but not be satisfied,
  they shall play the harlot but not increase.
  Because they have abandoned the LORD
¹¹ to practice harlotry.
  Old wine and new
  deprive my people of understanding.
¹²They consult their piece of wood,
  and their wand makes pronouncements for them,
  For the spirit of harlotry has led them astray;
  they commit harlotry, forsaking their God.
¹³On the mountaintops they offer sacrifice
  and on the hills they burn incense,
  Beneath oak and poplar and terebinth,
  because of their pleasant shade.
  That is why your daughters play the harlot,
  and your daughters-in-law are adulteresses.
¹⁴Am I then to punish your daughters for
      their harlotry,
  your daughters-in-law for their adultery?
  You yourselves consort with harlots,
  and with prostitutes you offer sacrifice!
  So must a people without understanding come
      to ruin.
¹⁵Though you play the harlot, O Israel,
  let not Judah become guilty!
  Come not to Gilgal,
  nor up to Beth-aven,
  to swear, "As the Lord lives!"
¹⁶For Israel is as stubborn as a heifer;
  will the LORD now give them broad pastures
  as though they were lambs?
¹⁷Ephraim is an associate of idols,
  let him alone!
¹⁸When their carousing is over,
  they give themselves to harlotry;
  in their arrogance they love shame.
¹⁹The wind has bound them up in its pinions;
  they shall have only shame from their altars.

NEW JERUSALEM BIBLE

⁵Priest, you will stumble in broad daylight,
  and the prophet will stumble with you in the dark,
  and I will make your mother perish.
⁶My people perish for want of knowledge.
  Since you yourself have rejected knowledge,
  so I shall reject you from my priesthood;
  since you have forgotten the teaching of your God,
  I in my turn shall forget your children.
⁷The more of them there have been,
  the more they have sinned against me;
  they have bartered their Glory for Shame.ᶜ
⁸They feed on the sin of my people,
  they are greedy for their iniquity.
⁹But as with the people, so with the priest,
  I shall punish them for their conduct,
  I shall pay them back for their deeds.
¹⁰They will eat but never be satisfied,
  they will play the whore but not grow more
      prolific,
  since they have deserted Yahweh
  to give themselves up ¹¹to whoring.

  Old wine and new wine addle my people's wits,
¹²they consult their block of wood,
  and their stick explains what they should do.
  For an urge to go whoring has led them astray
  and whoring they go and desert their God;
¹³they offer sacrifice on the mountain tops,
  they burn incense on the hills,
  under oak and poplar and terebinth,
  for pleasant is their shade.
  So, although your daughters play the whore
  and your daughters-in-law commit adultery,
¹⁴I shall not punish your daughters for playing the
      whore
  nor your daughters-in-law for committing adultery,
  when the men themselves are wandering off with
      whores
  and offering sacrifice with sacred prostitutes,
  for a people with no understanding is doomed.
¹⁵Though you, Israel, play the whore,
  there is no need for Judah to sin too.
  Do not go to Gilgal,
  do not go up to Beth-Aven,ᵈ
  do not swear oaths 'by Yahweh's life',
¹⁶for Israel is as stubborn
  as a stubborn heifer;
  so is Yahweh likely to pasture him
  like a lamb in a broad meadow?
¹⁷Ephraim has made a pact with idols — let him
      alone!
¹⁸Their drunken orgy over,
  they do nothing but play the whore,
  preferring Shame to their Pride;
¹⁹the wind with its wings will carry them off
  and their sacrifices will bring them nothing but
      disgrace.

ᶜ4 A contemptuous name for Baal.   ᵈ4 A nickname (= House of Evil) for the northern national sanctuary at Bethel (= House of God).

NEW REVISED STANDARD VERSION	REVISED ENGLISH BIBLE

5 Hear this, O priests!
  Give heed, O house of Israel!
Listen, O house of the king!
  For the judgment pertains to you;
for you have been a snare at Mizpah,
  and a net spread upon Tabor,
2 and a pit dug deep in Shittim;z
  but I will punish all of them.

3 I know Ephraim,
  and Israel is not hidden from me;
for now, O Ephraim, you have played the whore;
  Israel is defiled.
4 Their deeds do not permit them
  to return to their God.
For the spirit of whoredom is within them,
  and they do not know the LORD.

5 Israel's pride testifies against him;
  Ephraima stumbles in his guilt;
Judah also stumbles with them.
6 With their flocks and herds they shall go
  to seek the LORD,
but they will not find him;
  he has withdrawn from them.
7 They have dealt faithlessly with the LORD,
  for they have borne illegitimate children.
Now the new moon shall devour them along
  with their fields.

8 Blow the horn in Gibeah,
  the trumpet in Ramah.
Sound the alarm at Beth-aven;
  look behind you, Benjamin!
9 Ephraim shall become a desolation
  in the day of punishment;
among the tribes of Israel
  I declare what is sure.
10 The princes of Judah have become
  like those who remove the landmark;
on them I will pour out
  my wrath like water.
11 Ephraim is oppressed, crushed in judgment,
  because he was determined to go after vanity.b
12 Therefore I am like maggots to Ephraim,
  and like rottenness to the house of Judah.
13 When Ephraim saw his sickness,
  and Judah his wound,
then Ephraim went to Assyria,
  and sent to the great king.c
But he is not able to cure you
  or heal your wound.
14 For I will be like a lion to Ephraim,
  and like a young lion to the house of Judah.
I myself will tear and go away;
  I will carry off, and no one shall rescue.
15 I will return again to my place
  until they acknowledge their guilt and seek my
    face.
  In their distress they will beg my favor:

6 "Come, let us return to the LORD;
  for it is he who has torn, and he will heal us;
he has struck down, and he will bind us up.
2 After two days he will revive us;
  on the third day he will raise us up,
that we may live before him.

---

5 Hear this, you priests, and listen, Israel;
  let the royal house mark my words.
Sentence is passed on you,
  for you have been a snare at Mizpah,
  a net spread out on Tabor,
2 and a deep pit at Shittim.
  I shall punish them all.
3 I have cared for Ephraim
  and not neglected Israel;
but now Ephraim has become promiscuous
  and Israel has brought defilement on himself.
4 Their misdeeds have barred the way back to their
    God,
for the spirit of immorality which is in them
  prevents them from knowing the LORD.
5 Israel's arrogance cries out against him;
  Ephraim's guilt is his downfall,
  and Judah in turn is brought down.
6 They go with sacrifices of sheep and cattle
  to seek the LORD, but do not find him,
  for he has withdrawn from them.
7 They have deceived the LORD,
  for their children are bastards.
Now an invader is set to devour their fields.

8 Blow the trumpet in Gibeah,
  the horn in Ramah,
raise the battle cry in Beth-aven:
  'We are with you, Benjamin!'
9 On the day of punishment
  Ephraim will be laid waste.
This is the certain doom
  I have decreed for Israel's tribes.
10 Judah's rulers act like men
  who move their neighbour's boundary;
on them I shall pour out
  my wrath like a flood.
11 Ephraim is an oppressor trampling on justice,
  obstinately pursuing what is worthless.
12 But I am going to be a festering sore to Ephraim,
  a canker to the house of Judah.

13 When Ephraim found that he was sick,
  and Judah found that he was covered with sores,
Ephraim turned to Assyria
  and sent envoys to the Great King.
But he had no power to cure you
  or heal your sores.
14 I shall be fierce as a panther to Ephraim,
  fierce as a lion to Judah;
I shall maul the prey and go,
  carry it off beyond hope of rescue.
15 I shall return to my dwelling-place,
  until in remorse they seek me
and search diligently for me in their distress.

6 Come, let us return to the LORD.
  He has torn us, but he will heal us,
he has wounded us, but he will bind up our
    wounds;
2 after two days he will revive us,
  on the third day he will raise us
to live in his presence.

---

z Cn: Meaning of Heb uncertain   a Heb *Israel and Ephraim*
b Gk: Meaning of Heb uncertain   c Cn: Heb *to a king who will*
contend

5:2 **deep . . . Shittim:** *prob. rdg; Heb. obscure.*   5:5 **Ephraim's:**
prob. rdg; Heb. prefixes Israel.

NEW AMERICAN BIBLE

5 Hear this, O priests,
Pay attention, O house of Israel,
O household of the king, give ear!
It is you who are called to judgment.
For you have become a snare at Mizpah,
and a net spread upon Tabor.
2 In their perversity they have sunk into wickedness,
and I am rejected by them all.
3 I know Ephraim,
and Israel is not hidden from me;
Now Ephraim has played the harlot,
Israel is defiled.
4 Their deeds do not allow them
to return to their God;
For the spirit of harlotry is in them,
and they do not recognize the LORD.

5 The arrogance of Israel bears witness against him;
Ephraim stumbles in his guilt,
and Judah stumbles with them.
6 With their flocks and their herds they shall go
to seek the LORD, but they shall not find him:
he has withdrawn himself from them.
7 They have been untrue to the LORD,
for they have begotten illegitimate children;
Now shall the new moon devour them
together with their fields.

8 Blow the horn in Gibeah,
the trumpet in Ramah!
Sound the alarm in Beth-aven:
"Look behind you, O Benjamin!"
9 Ephraim shall become a waste
on the day of chastisement
Against the tribes of Israel
I announce what is sure to be.
10 The princes of Judah have become
like those that move a boundary line;
Upon them I will pour out
my wrath like water.
11 Is Ephraim maltreated, his rights violated?
No, he has willingly gone after filth!
12 I am like a moth for Ephraim,
like maggots for the house of Judah.
13 When Ephraim saw his infirmity,
and Judah his sore,
Ephraim went to Assyria,
and Judah sent to the great king.
But he cannot heal you
nor take away your sore.
14 For I am like a lion to Ephraim,
like a young lion to the house of Judah;
It is I who rend the prey and depart,
I carry it away and no one can save it from me.

15 I will go back to my place
until they pay for their guilt
and seek my presence.
In their affliction, they shall look for me:
6 1 "Come, let us return to the LORD,
For it is he who has rent, but he will heal us;
he has struck us, but he will bind our wounds.
2 He will revive us after two days;
on the third day he will raise us up,
to live in his presence.

NEW JERUSALEM BIBLE

5 Hear this, you priests,
listen, House of Israel,
pay attention, royal House,
for it is you who have justice in your care,
but you have been a snare at Mizpah
and a net outspread on Tabor.
2 They have dug the ditch deep at Shittim
and so I am going to punish them all.
3 Ephraim have I known,
Israel is not hidden from me;
and yet, Ephraim, you have played the whore,
Israel is befouled.
4 Their deeds do not allow them to return to their
God,
since an urge to play the whore possesses them
and they no longer know Yahweh.
5 Israel's arrogance is his accuser,
the guilt of Israel and Ephraim is their undoing,
Judah too will be undone with them.
6 Though they go in search of Yahweh with their
sheep and cattle,
they will not find him;
he has withdrawn from them.
7 They have betrayed Yahweh
because they have fathered bastards;
now the new moon will devour them and their
fields.

8 Sound the horn in Gibeah,
the trumpet in Ramah,
raise the war cry in Beth-Aven,
'We are behind you, Benjamin!'
9 When the day of punishment comes, Ephraim will
be a wasteland;
on the tribes of Israel I have pronounced certain
doom.
10 The rulers of Judah act like men who move the
boundary stone;
I shall pour my wrath out on them like a flood.
11 Ephraim is oppressed, crushed by the sentence,
for having deliberately followed a Lie.
12 Because of this, I shall be like ringworm for
Ephraim
and like gangrene for the House of Judah.
13 Once Ephraim realised that he was sick
and Judah that he had an ulcer,
Ephraim then went to Assyria,
he sent messengers to the Great King;
but he has no power to cure you
or to heal you of your sore;
14 for I shall be like a lion to Ephraim,
like a young lion to the House of Judah;
I myself shall rend them, then go my way,
shall carry them off, beyond hope of rescue.

15 I shall go back to my place
until they confess their guilt and seek me,
seek me eagerly in their distress.
6 Come, let us return to Yahweh.
He has rent us and he will heal us;
he has struck us and he will bind up our wounds;
2 after two days he will revive us,
on the third day he will raise us up
and we shall live in his presence.

NEW REVISED STANDARD VERSION	REVISED ENGLISH BIBLE

NEW REVISED STANDARD VERSION

3 Let us know, let us press on to know the LORD;
  his appearing is as sure as the dawn;
he will come to us like the showers,
  like the spring rains that water the earth."
4 What shall I do with you, O Ephraim?
  What shall I do with you, O Judah?
Your love is like a morning cloud,
  like the dew that goes away early.
5 Therefore I have hewn them by the prophets,
  I have killed them by the words of my mouth,
  and my[d] judgment goes forth as the light.
6 For I desire steadfast love and not sacrifice,
  the knowledge of God rather than burnt
    offerings.

7 But at[e] Adam they transgressed the covenant;
  there they dealt faithlessly with me.
8 Gilead is a city of evildoers,
  tracked with blood.
9 As robbers lie in wait[f] for someone,
  so the priests are banded together;[g]
they murder on the road to Shechem,
  they commit a monstrous crime.
10 In the house of Israel I have seen a horrible
    thing;
  Ephraim's whoredom is there, Israel is defiled.

11 For you also, O Judah, a harvest is appointed.

7 1 When I would restore the fortunes of my people,
  when I would heal Israel,
  the corruption of Ephraim is revealed,
  and the wicked deeds of Samaria;
for they deal falsely,
  the thief breaks in,
  and the bandits raid outside.
2 But they do not consider
  that I remember all their wickedness.
Now their deeds surround them,
  they are before my face.
3 By their wickedness they make the king glad,
  and the officials by their treachery.
4 They are all adulterers;
  they are like a heated oven,
whose baker does not need to stir the fire,
  from the kneading of the dough until it is
    leavened.
5 On the day of our king the officials
  became sick with the heat of wine;
  he stretched out his hand with mockers.
6 For they are kindled[h] like an oven, their heart
    burns within them;
  all night their anger smolders;
  in the morning it blazes like a flaming fire.
7 All of them are hot as an oven,
  and they devour their rulers.
All their kings have fallen;
  none of them calls upon me.

8 Ephraim mixes himself with the peoples;
  Ephraim is a cake not turned.
9 Foreigners devour his strength,
  but he does not know it;
gray hairs are sprinkled upon him,
  but he does not know it.

REVISED ENGLISH BIBLE

3 Let us strive to know the LORD,
  whose coming is as sure as the sunrise.
He will come to us like the rain,
  like spring rains that water the earth.
4 How shall I deal with you, Ephraim?
  How shall I deal with you, Judah?
Your loyalty to me is like the morning mist,
  like dew that vanishes early.
5 That is why I have cut them to pieces by the
    prophets
  and slaughtered them with my words:
  my judgement goes forth like light.
6 For I require loyalty, not sacrifice,
  acknowledgement of God rather than
    whole-offerings.

7 At Admah they violated my covenant,
  there they played me false.
8 Gilead is a haunt of evildoers,
  marked by a trail of blood.
9 Like marauders lying in wait,
  priests are banded together
to do murder on the road to Shechem;
  their behaviour is an outrage.
10 At Bethel I have seen a horrible thing:
  there Ephraim became promiscuous
  and Israel brought defilement on himself.

11 And for you, too, Judah, a harvest of reckoning
    will come.

When I am minded to restore the fortunes of my
    people,
7 1 when I am minded to heal Israel,
  the guilt of Ephraim stands revealed,
  the wickedness of Samaria.
They have not kept faith;
  they are thieves breaking into houses,
  bandits raiding in the countryside,
2 unaware that I have their wickedness ever in mind.
Now their misdeeds encircle them;
  they are ever before my eyes.
3 They divert the king with their wickedness
  and princes with their treachery.
4 All of them are adulterers;
  they are like an oven fire
  which the baker does not have to stir
  from the kneading of the dough until it has risen.
5 On their king's festal day the courtiers
  become inflamed with wine,
  and he himself joins with arrogant men;
6 their hearts are heated like an oven by their
    intrigues.
During the night their passion slumbers,
  but in the morning it flares up
  like a blazing fire;
7 they are all as heated as an oven
  and devour their rulers.
King after king falls from power,
  but not one of them calls to me.

8 Ephraim is mixed up with aliens;
  he is like a cake half done.
9 Foreigners feed on his strength,
  but he is unaware;
grey hairs may come on him,
  but he is unaware.

---

[d] Gk Syr: Heb *your*   [e] Cn: Heb *like*   [f] Cn: Meaning of Heb
uncertain   [g] Syr: Heb *are a company*   [h] Gk Syr: Heb *brought
near*

6:7 **At Admah:** *prob. rdg; Heb.* Like Adam.   6:10 **At Bethel:**
prob. rdg; Heb. In the house of Israel.   7:5 **their:** *so Aram.*
(*Targ.*); *Heb.* our.   7:6 **are heated:** *so Gk; Heb.* draw near.

NEW AMERICAN BIBLE

³Let us know, let us strive to know the LORD;
as certain as the dawn is his coming,
and his judgment shines forth like the light
of day!
He will come to us like the rain,
like spring rain that waters the earth."
⁴What can I do with you, Ephraim?
What can I do with you, Judah?
Your piety is like a morning cloud,
like the dew that early passes away.
⁵For this reason I smote them through the prophets,
I slew them by the words of my mouth;
⁶For it is love that I desire, not sacrifice,
and knowledge of God rather than holocausts.
⁷But they, in their land, violated the covenant;
there they were untrue to me.
⁸Gilead is a city of evildoers,
tracked with blood.
⁹As brigands ambush a man,
a band of priests slay on the way to Shechem,
committing monstrous crime.
¹⁰In the house of Israel I have seen a horrible thing:
there harlotry is found in Ephraim,
Israel is defiled.
¹¹For you also, O Judah,
a harvest has been appointed.

7 When I would bring about the restoration of
my people,
when I would heal Israel,
The guilt of Ephraim stands out,
the wickedness of Samaria;
They practice falsehood,
thieves break in, bandits plunder abroad.
²Yet they do not remind themselves
that I remember all their wickedness.
Even now their crimes surround them,
present to my sight.
³In their wickedness they regale the king,
the princes too, with their deceits.
⁴They are all kindled to wrath
like a blazing oven,
Whose fire the baker desists from stirring
once the dough is kneaded until it has risen.
⁵On the day of our king,
the princes are overcome with the heat of wine.
He extends his hand among dissemblers;
6 the plotters approach with hearts like ovens.
All the night their anger sleeps;
in the morning it flares like a blazing fire.
⁷They are all heated like ovens,
and consume their rulers.
All their kings have fallen;
none of them calls upon me.

⁸Ephraim mingles with the nations.
Ephraim is a hearth cake unturned.
⁹Strangers have sapped his strength,
but he takes no notice of it;
Of gray hairs, too, there is a sprinkling,
but he takes no notice of it.

NEW JERUSALEM BIBLE

³Let us know, let us strive to know Yahweh;
that he will come is as certain as the dawn.
He will come to us like a shower,
like the rain of springtime to the earth.
⁴What am I to do with you, Ephraim?
What am I to do with you, Judah?
For your love is like morning mist,
like the dew that quickly disappears.
⁵This is why I have hacked them to pieces by
means of the prophets,
why I have killed them with words from my
mouth,
why my sentence will blaze forth like the dawn—
⁶for faithful love is what pleases me, not sacrifice;
knowledge of God, not burnt offerings.
⁷But they have broken the covenant at Adam,
there they have betrayed me.
⁸Gilead is a city of evil-doers,
full of bloody footprints.
⁹Like so many robbers in ambush,
a gang of priests commits murder on the road to
Shechem—
what infamous behaviour!
¹⁰At Bethel I have seen a horrible thing;
there Ephraim plays the whore,
Israel is befouled.
¹¹For you too, Judah, a harvest is in store,
when I restore my people's fortunes.

7 Whenever I would heal Israel,
I am confronted by the guilt of Ephraim
and the evil-doings of Samaria;
for deceit is their principle of behaviour;
the thief breaks into the house,
marauders raid in the open;
²and they never pause to consider
that I remember all their wicked deeds;
and now their own deeds hem them in
and stare me in the face.
³They amuse the king with their wickedness
and the chief men with their lies.
⁴They are all adulterers, hot as an oven
which the baker need not stoke
from the time he has kneaded the dough until it
rises.
⁵At the holiday for our king,
the ministers become inflamed with wine,
while he accepts the homage of people ⁶who laugh
at him.
Their hearts are like an oven as they plot,
all night their passion slumbers,
then in the morning it bursts into flame;
⁷yes, all of them as hot as ovens,
they consume their rulers.
All their kings have fallen thus,
not one of them has ever called on me.

⁸Ephraim mixes with the nations.
Ephraim is a half-baked cake.
⁹Foreigners have eaten his strength away
but he is unconscious of it;
even his hair is turning grey
but he is unconscious of it.

NEW REVISED STANDARD VERSION	REVISED ENGLISH BIBLE

NEW REVISED STANDARD VERSION

10 Israel's pride testifies against*i* him;
　yet they do not return to the Lord their God,
　or seek him, for all this.

11 Ephraim has become like a dove,
　silly and without sense;
　they call upon Egypt, they go to Assyria.

12 As they go, I will cast my net over them;
　I will bring them down like birds of the air;
　I will discipline them according to the report
　　made to their assembly. *j*

13 Woe to them, for they have strayed from me!
　Destruction to them, for they have rebelled
　　against me!
　I would redeem them,
　but they speak lies against me.

14 They do not cry to me from the heart,
　but they wail upon their beds;
　they gash themselves for grain and wine;
　they rebel against me.

15 It was I who trained and strengthened their arms,
　yet they plot evil against me.

16 They turn to that which does not profit;*k*
　they have become like a defective bow;
　their officials shall fall by the sword
　because of the rage of their tongue.
　So much for their babbling in the land of Egypt.

8 Set the trumpet to your lips!
　One like a vulture*j* is over the house of the
　　Lord,
　because they have broken my covenant,
　and transgressed my law.

2 Israel cries to me,
　"My God, we — Israel — know you!"

3 Israel has spurned the good;
　the enemy shall pursue him.

4 They made kings, but not through me;
　they set up princes, but without my knowledge.
　With their silver and gold they made idols
　for their own destruction.

5 Your calf is rejected, O Samaria.
　My anger burns against them.
　How long will they be incapable of innocence?

6 For it is from Israel,
　an artisan made it;
　it is not God.
　The calf of Samaria
　shall be broken to pieces.*l*

7 For they sow the wind,
　and they shall reap the whirlwind.
　The standing grain has no heads,
　it shall yield no meal;
　if it were to yield,
　foreigners would devour it.

8 Israel is swallowed up;
　now they are among the nations
　as a useless vessel.

9 For they have gone up to Assyria,
　a wild ass wandering alone;
　Ephraim has bargained for lovers.

10 Though they bargain with the nations,
　I will now gather them up.
　They shall soon writhe
　under the burden of kings and princes.

11 When Ephraim multiplied altars to expiate sin,
　they became to him altars for sinning.

REVISED ENGLISH BIBLE

10 Israel's arrogance openly indicts them;
　but they do not return to the Lord their God
　nor, in spite of everything, do they seek him.

11 Ephraim is like a silly, senseless pigeon,
　now calling to Egypt,
　now turning to Assyria for help.

12 Wherever they turn, I shall cast my net over them
　and bring them down like birds;
　I shall take them captive when I hear them
　　gathering.

13 Woe betide them, for they have strayed from me!
　May disaster befall them for rebelling against me!
　I long to deliver them,
　but they tell lies about me.

14 There is no sincerity in their cry to me;
　for all their wailing on their beds
　and gashing of themselves over grain and new
　　wine,
　they are turning away from me.

15 Though I support and strengthen them,
　they plot evil against me.

16 Like a bow gone slack,
　they relapse into useless worship;
　their leaders will fall by the sword
　because of their angry talk.
　There will be derision at them in Egypt.

8 Put the trumpets to your lips!
　An eagle circles over the sanctuary of the Lord;
　they have violated my covenant
　and rebelled against my instruction.

2 Israel cries to me for help:
　'We acknowledge you as our God.'

3 But Israel rejects what is good,
　and an enemy pursues him.

4 They make kings, but not on my authority;
　they set up rulers, but without my knowledge;
　from their silver and gold they have made for
　　themselves
　idols for their own destruction.

5 Samaria, your calf-god is loathsome!
　My anger burns against them!
　How long must they remain guilty?

6 The calf was made in Israel;
　a craftsman fashioned it and it is no god;
　it will be reduced to splinters.

7 Israel sows the wind and reaps the whirlwind;
　there are no heads on the standing grain,
　it yields no flour;
　and, if it did yield any,
　strangers would swallow it up.

8 Israel is swallowed up;
　now among the nations
　they are like a thing of no value.

9 Like a wild ass that goes its own way,
　they have gone up to Assyria.
　Ephraim has bargained for lovers.

10 because they have so bargained among the nations
　I will now round them up.
　Soon they will have to abandon
　the setting up of kings and rulers.

11 Ephraim has built altars everywhere
　and they have become occasions for sin.

7:14 **gashing of themselves:** *so many MSS; others* rolling about.
7:16 **useless worship:** *prob. rdg, cp. Gk; Heb.* obscure.　8:1 **An eagle:** *prob. rdg; Heb.* As an eagle.　8:3 **Israel . . . good:** *or* Israel is utterly loathsome.

i Or *humbles*　*j* Meaning of Heb uncertain　*k* Cn: Meaning of Heb uncertain　*l* Or *shall go up in flames*

10 The arrogance of Israel bears witness against him;
  yet they do not return to the LORD, their God,
  nor seek him, for all that.
11 Ephraim is like a dove,
  silly and senseless;
  They call upon Egypt,
  they go to Assyria.
12 Even as they go I will spread my net around them,
  like birds in the air I will bring them down.
  In an instant I will send them captive from
  their land.

13 Woe to them, they have strayed from me!
  Ruin to them, they have sinned against me!
  Though I wished to redeem them,
  they spoke lies against me.
14 They have not cried to me from their hearts
  when they wailed upon their beds;
  For wheat and wine they lacerated themselves,
  while they rebelled against me.
15 Though I trained and strengthened their arms,
  yet they devised evil against me.
16 They have again become useless,
  like a treacherous bow.
  Their princes shall fall by the sword
  because of the insolence of their tongues;
  thus they shall be mocked in the land of Egypt.

8 A trumpet to your lips,
  You who watch over the house of the LORD!
  Since they have violated my covenant,
  and sinned against my law,
2 While to me they cry out,
  "O God of Israel, we know you!"
3 The men of Israel have thrown away what is good;
  the enemy shall pursue them.
4 They made kings, but not by my authority;
  they established princes, but without
  my approval.
  With their silver and gold they made
  idols for themselves, to their own destruction.
5 Cast away your calf, O Samaria!
  my wrath is kindled against them;
  How long will they be unable to attain
  innocence in Israel?
6 The work of an artisan,
  no god at all,
  Destined for the flames—
  such is the calf of Samaria!

7 When they sow the wind,
  they shall reap the whirlwind;
  The stalk of grain that forms no ear
  can yield no flour;
  Even if it could,
  strangers would swallow it.
8 Israel is swallowed up;
  he is now among the nations
  a thing of no value.
9 They went up to Assyria—
  a wild ass off on its own—
  Ephraim bargained for lovers.
10 Even though they bargain with the nations,
  I will now gather an army;
  King and princes shall shortly
  succumb under the burden.

11 When Ephraim made many altars to expiate sin,
  his altars became occasions of sin.

10 (Israel's arrogance is his own accuser;
  but they do not come back to Yahweh their God
  or seek him, despite all this.)
11 Ephraim is like a silly, witless pigeon
  calling on Egypt, turning to Assyria.
12 Wherever they turn, I shall spread my net over
  them,
  I shall bring them down like the birds of the sky,
  I shall punish them for their perversity.
13 Woe to them for having fled from me!
  Ruin seize them for having wronged me!
  I have rescued them again and again
  and they have only told lies about me.
14 Theirs is no heartfelt cry to me
  when they lament on their beds;
  when they gash themselves over the grain and new
  wine,
  they are still rebelling against me.
15 Though I supported and gave strength to their
  arms,
  they plan how to hurt me.
16 They turn to what does not exist,
  they are like a faulty bow.
  Their leaders will fall by the sword
  because of their arrogant talk;
  how they will be laughed at in Egypt!

8 Put the trumpet to your lips!
  Like an eagle, disaster is swooping on Yahweh's
  home!
  Because they have violated my covenant
  and been unfaithful to my Law,
2 in vain will they cry, 'My God!'
  In vain, 'We, Israel, know you!'
3 Israel has rejected the good,
  the enemy will pursue them.
4 They have set up kings, but without my consent,
  and appointed princes, but without my knowledge.
  With their silver and gold, they have made
  themselves idols,
  but only to be destroyed.
5 I spurn your calf,ᵉ Samaria!
  My anger blazes against them!
  How long will it be before they recover their
  innocence?
6 For it is the product of Israel—
  a craftsman made the thing,
  it is no god at all!
  The calf of Samaria will be broken to pieces!
7 Since they sow the wind, they will reap the
  whirlwind;
  stalk without ear, it will never yield flour—
  or if it does, foreigners will swallow it.
8 Israel has himself been swallowed;
  now they are lost among the nations
  like something no one wants,
9 for having made approaches to Assyria—
  like a wild donkey, all alone.
  Ephraim has rented lovers
10 and because he has rented them from the nations
  I am now going to round them up;
  soon they will feel the weight of the king of
  princes!

11 Ephraim keeps building altars for his sins,
  these very altars are themselves a sin.

ᵉ 8 The golden bull on which the sanctuary at Bethel was centred.

NEW REVISED STANDARD VERSION	REVISED ENGLISH BIBLE

NEW REVISED STANDARD VERSION

12 Though I write for him the multitude of my
　　instructions,
　　they are regarded as a strange thing.
13 Though they offer choice sacrifices, *m*
　　though they eat flesh,
　　the LORD does not accept them.
　Now he will remember their iniquity,
　　and punish their sins;
　　they shall return to Egypt.
14 Israel has forgotten his Maker,
　　and built palaces;
　and Judah has multiplied fortified cities;
　　but I will send a fire upon his cities,
　　and it shall devour his strongholds.

9

　Do not rejoice, O Israel!
　　Do not exult *n* as other nations do;
　for you have played the whore, departing from
　　your God.
　　You have loved a prostitute's pay
　　on all threshing floors.
2 Threshing floor and wine vat shall not feed them,
　　and the new wine shall fail them.
3 They shall not remain in the land of the LORD;
　　but Ephraim shall return to Egypt,
　　and in Assyria they shall eat unclean food.
4 They shall not pour drink offerings of wine to the
　　LORD,
　　and their sacrifices shall not please him.
　Such sacrifices shall be like mourners' bread;
　　all who eat of it shall be defiled;
　for their bread shall be for their hunger only;
　　it shall not come to the house of the LORD.
5 What will you do on the day of appointed
　　festival,
　　and on the day of the festival of the LORD?
6 For even if they escape destruction,
　　Egypt shall gather them,
　　Memphis shall bury them.
　Nettles shall possess their precious things of
　　silver; *o*
　　thorns shall be in their tents.
7 The days of punishment have come,
　　the days of recompense have come;
　　Israel cries, *p*
　"The prophet is a fool,
　　the man of the spirit is mad!"
　Because of your great iniquity,
　　your hostility is great.
8 The prophet is a sentinel for my God over
　　Ephraim,
　　yet a fowler's snare is on all his ways,
　　and hostility in the house of his God.
9 They have deeply corrupted themselves
　　as in the days of Gibeah;
　he will remember their iniquity,
　　he will punish their sins.

REVISED ENGLISH BIBLE

12 Though I give him many written laws,
　　they are treated as irrelevant;
13 though they sacrifice offerings of flesh and eat
　　them,
　　the LORD will not accept them.
　Their guilt will be remembered
　　and their sins punished.
　Let them go back to Egypt!
14 Israel has forgotten his Maker
　　and built palaces;
　Judah has many walled cities,
　　but I shall burn his cities,
　　and fire will devour his citadels.

9

　Do not rejoice, Israel, or exult like other peoples;
　　for you have been unfaithful to your God,
　you have been attracted by a prostitute's fee
　　on every threshing-floor heaped with grain.
2 Threshing-floor and winepress will see them no
　　more,
　　there will be no new wine for them.
3 They will not dwell in the LORD's land:
　　Ephraim will go back to Egypt,
　　or eat unclean food in Assyria.
4 They are not to pour out wine to the LORD;
　　their sacrifices will not be pleasing to him;
　it would be like mourners' fare for them,
　　and all who ate it would be polluted.
　Their food must serve only to stay their hunger;
　　it must not be offered in the house of the LORD.
5 What will you do on the festal day,
　　the day of the LORD's pilgrim-feast?
6 For look, the people have fled from a scene of
　　devastation:
　　Egypt will receive them,
　　Memphis will be their grave.
　Weeds will engulf their silver treasures,
　　and thorns their dwellings.
7 The days of punishment have come,
　　the days of vengeance are here
　　and Israel knows it.
　The prophet has become a fool,
　　the inspired seer a madman,
　　because of your great guilt and enmity.
8 God appointed the prophet as a watchman for
　　Ephraim,
　　but he has become a fowler's trap on all their
　　ways.
　There is enmity in the very temple of God.
9 They are deep in sin
　　as at the time of Gibeah.
　Their guilt will be remembered
　　and their sins punished.

m Cn: Meaning of Heb uncertain　　*n* Gk: Heb *To exultation*
o Meaning of Heb uncertain　　*p* Cn Compare Gk: Heb *shall know*

9:1 **or exult:** *so Gk; Heb.* to exultation.　　9:2 **see:** *so Gk; Heb.*
pasture.

NEW AMERICAN BIBLE

NEW JERUSALEM BIBLE

12 Though I write for him my many ordinances,
    they are considered as a stranger's.
13 Though they offer sacrifice,
    immolate flesh and eat it,
    the LORD is not pleased with them.
He shall still remember their guilt
    and punish their sins;
    they shall return to Egypt.
14 Israel has forgotten his maker
    and built palaces.
Judah, too, has fortified many cities;
    but I will send fire upon his cities,
    to devour their castles.

9 Rejoice not, O Israel,
    exult not like the nations!
For you have been unfaithful to your God,
    loving a harlot's hire
    upon every threshing floor.
2 Threshing floor and wine press shall not
        nourish them,
    the new wine shall fail them.

3 They shall not dwell in the LORD's land;
    Ephraim shall return to Egypt,
    and in Assyria they shall eat unclean food.
4 They shall not pour libations of wine to the LORD,
    or proffer their sacrifices before him.
Theirs will be like mourners' bread,
    that makes unclean all who eat of it;
Such food as they have shall be for themselves;
    it cannot enter the house of the LORD.

5 What will you do on the festival day,
    the day of the LORD's feast?
6 When they go from the ruins,
    Egypt shall gather them in, Memphis shall
        bury them.
Weeds shall overgrow their silver treasures,
    and thorns invade their tents.

7 They have come, the days of punishment!
    they have come, the days of recompense!
Let Israel know it!
    "The prophet is a fool,
    the man of the spirit is mad!"
Because your iniquity is great,
    great, too, is your hostility.
8 A prophet is Ephraim's watchman with God,
    yet a fowler's snare is on all his ways,
    hostility in the house of his God.
9 They have sunk to the depths of corruption,
    as in the days of Gibeah;
He shall remember their iniquity
    and punish their sins.

12 However much of my Law I write for him,
    Ephraim regards it as alien to him.
13 They offer sacrifices to me and eat the meat,
    they do not win Yahweh's favour.
On the contrary, he will remember their guilt
    and punish their sins;
    they will have to go back to Egypt.
14 Israel has forgotten his Maker
    and has built palaces,
    while Judah keeps on building fortified towns;
    but I shall send fire down on his cities
    to devour their citadels.

9 No merrymaking, Israel, for you,
    no rejoicing like other peoples,
    for you have deserted your God to play the whore,
    you have loved the fee of prostitution on every
        threshing-floor.
2 The threshing-floor and wine-press will not feed
        them;
    they will be disappointed of new wine.

3 No more will they live in Yahweh's country;
    Ephraim will have to go back to Egypt,
    and eat polluted food in Assyria.
4 No more will they pour libations of wine to
        Yahweh,
    and their sacrifices will not win his favour
    but will be like funeral fare for them:
    whoever eats them will be polluted;
    for their food will be for themselves alone,
    not being offered in Yahweh's home.

5 What will you do on the solemn feast-day,
    on the day of Yahweh's festival?
6 What a scene of devastation they have left!
    Egypt will round them up, Memphis will bury
        them,
    nettles will inherit their fields
    and thorn-bushes invade their homesteads.

7 The days of punishment have come,
    the days of retribution are here;
    Israel knows it!
    'The prophet is mad and the inspired man a fool!'
    Great has been your guilt —
    all the greater then the hostility!
8 The watchman of Ephraim is with my God:
    it is the prophet —
    and a fowler's trap is placed on all his paths;
    and in the shrine of his God there is enmity
        towards him.
9 They have become deeply corrupt
    as in the days of Gibeah;
    he will remember their guilt,
    he will punish their sins.

NEW REVISED STANDARD VERSION	REVISED ENGLISH BIBLE

NEW REVISED STANDARD VERSION

10 Like grapes in the wilderness,
  I found Israel.
Like the first fruit on the fig tree,
  in its first season,
  I saw your ancestors.
But they came to Baal-peor,
  and consecrated themselves to a thing of
    shame,
  and became detestable like the thing they
    loved.

11 Ephraim's glory shall fly away like a bird—
  no birth, no pregnancy, no conception!

12 Even if they bring up children,
  I will bereave them until no one is left.
Woe to them indeed
  when I depart from them!

13 Once I saw Ephraim as a young palm planted in
    a lovely meadow, *q*
  but now Ephraim must lead out his children for
    slaughter.

14 Give them, O LORD—
  what will you give?
Give them a miscarrying womb
  and dry breasts.

15 Every evil of theirs began at Gilgal;
  there I came to hate them.
Because of the wickedness of their deeds
  I will drive them out of my house.
I will love them no more;
  all their officials are rebels.

16 Ephraim is stricken,
  their root is dried up,
  they shall bear no fruit.
Even though they give birth,
  I will kill the cherished offspring of their
    womb.

17 Because they have not listened to him,
  my God will reject them;
  they shall become wanderers among the
    nations.

10 Israel is a luxuriant vine
  that yields its fruit.
The more his fruit increased
  the more altars he built;
as his country improved,
  he improved his pillars.

2 Their heart is false;
  now they must bear their guilt.
The LORD *r* will break down their altars,
  and destroy their pillars.

3 For now they will say:
  "We have no king,
for we do not fear the LORD,
  and a king—what could he do for us?"

4 They utter mere words;
  with empty oaths they make covenants;
so litigation springs up like poisonous weeds
  in the furrows of the field.

5 The inhabitants of Samaria tremble
  for the calf *s* of Beth-aven.
Its people shall mourn for it,
  and its idolatrous priests shall wail *t* over it,
  over its glory that has departed from it.

REVISED ENGLISH BIBLE

10 I came upon Israel like grapes in the wilderness;
  as at the first ripe figs
I looked on their forefathers with joy,
  but they resorted to Baal-peor
  and consecrated themselves to a thing of shame.
Ephraim became as loathsome as the thing they
    loved.

11 Their honour will fly away like a bird:
  no childbirth, no fruitful womb, no conceiving!

12 Even if they rear their children,
  I will make them childless, without posterity.
Woe betide them when I turn away from them!

13 As lions lead out their cubs, just to be hunted,
  so must Ephraim bring out his children for
    slaughter.

14 Give them whatever you, LORD, are going to give.
  Give them wombs that miscarry and dry breasts.

15 All their wickedness at Gilgal aroused my hatred.
  I shall drive them from my house because of their
    evil deeds,
  I shall love them no more, for all their rulers are in
    revolt.

16 Ephraim is struck down:
  their root is withered, and they yield no fruit;
if ever they give birth,
  I shall slay the cherished offspring of their womb.

17 My God will reject them,
  because they have not listened to him,
  and they will become wanderers among the
    nations.

10 ISRAEL is like a spreading vine with ripening
    fruit:
  the more his fruit, the more his altars;
  the more beautiful his land, the more beautiful his
    pillars.

2 They are false at heart;
  now they must pay the penalty.
God himself will break down their altars
  and demolish their sacred pillars.

3 Well may they say, 'We have no king,
  because we do not fear the LORD;
  and what could the king do for us?'

4 There is nothing but talk;
  they swear false oaths and draw up treaties,
  and litigation spreads like a poisonous weed
  along the furrows of the fields.

5 The inhabitants of Samaria tremble
  for the calf-god of Beth-aven;
  the people mourn over it
  and its priests lament,
  distressed for the image of their god
  which is carried away into exile.

---

q Meaning of Heb uncertain   *r* Heb *he*   *s* Gk Syr: Heb *calves*
t Cn: Heb *exult*

9:13 **As lions . . . hunted:** *prob. rdg; Heb. unintelligible.*
10:2 **God himself:** *lit.* He.   10:5 **the image of their god:** *lit.*
their glory.

NEW AMERICAN BIBLE

¹⁰Like grapes in the desert,
  I found Israel;
Like the first fruits of the fig tree in its prime,
  I considered your fathers.
When they came to Baal-peor
  and consecrated themselves to the Shame,
  they became as abhorrent as the thing
    they loved.
¹¹The glory of Ephraim flies away like a bird:
  no birth, no carrying in the womb,
    no conception.
Were they to bear children,
  I would slay the darlings of their womb.
¹²Even though they bring up their children,
  I will make them childless, till not one is left.
Woe to them
  when I turn away from them!
¹³Ephraim, as I saw, was like Tyre,
  planted in a beauteous spot;
But Ephraim shall bring out
  his children to the slayer.
¹⁴Give them, O LORD!
  give them what?
Give them an unfruitful womb,
  and dry breasts!

¹⁵All their wickedness is in Gilgal;
  yes, there they incurred my hatred.
Because of their wicked deeds
  I will drive them out of my house.
I will love them no longer;
  all their princes are rebels.
¹⁶Ephraim is stricken,
  their root is dried up;
  they shall bear no fruit.

¹⁷My God will disown them
  because they have not listened to him;
  they shall be wanderers among the nations.

10 Israel is a luxuriant vine
  whose fruit matches its growth.
The more abundant his fruit,
  the more altars he built;
The more productive his land,
  the more sacred pillars he set up.
²Their heart is false,
  now they pay for their guilt;
God shall break down their altars
  and destroy their sacred pillars.
³If they would say,
  "We have no king" —
Since they do not fear the LORD,
  what can the king do for them?
⁴Nothing but make promises,
  swear false oaths, and make alliances,
While justice grows wild
  like wormwood in a plowed field!
⁵The inhabitants of Samaria fear
  for the calf of Beth-aven;
The people mourn for it
  and its priests wail over it,
  because the glory has departed from it.

NEW JERUSALEM BIBLE

¹⁰It was like finding grapes in the desert when I
    found Israel,
  like seeing early fruit on a fig tree when I saw
    your ancestors;
  but when they reached Baal-Peor they devoted
    themselves to Shame*f*
  and became as loathsome as the thing they loved.
¹¹The glory of Ephraim will fly away like a bird:
  no giving birth, no pregnancy, no conceiving.
¹²If they rear their children, I shall take them away
  before they grow up!
  Woe to them indeed when I leave them!
¹³Ephraim looked to me like Tyre, planted in a
    meadow,
  so Ephraim will present his children to the
    slaughterer.
¹⁴Give them, Yahweh — what are you to give? —
  give them wombs that miscarry and dried-up
    breasts.

¹⁵Their wickedness appeared in full at Gilgal,
  there I came to hate them.
  Because of the wickedness of their deeds
  I shall drive them from my home,
  I shall love them no longer;
  all their princes are rebels.
¹⁶Ephraim is blasted,
  their root has dried out,
  they will bear no more fruit.
  And even if they do bear children
  I shall slaughter the darlings of their womb.
¹⁷Because they have not listened to him, my God
    will cast them off
  and they will become wanderers among the
    nations.

10 Israel was a luxuriant vine yielding plenty of fruit.
  The more his fruit increased,
  the more altars he built;
  the richer his land became,
  the richer he made the sacred pillars.
²Theirs is a divided heart;
  now they will have to pay for it.
  He himself will hack down their altars
  and wreck their sacred pillars.
³Then they will say,
  'We have no king
  because we have not feared Yahweh,
  but what could the king do for us?'
⁴Speeches are made, oaths sworn to no purpose,
  agreements concluded,
  and so-called justice spreads like a poisonous weed
  along the furrows of the fields!
⁵Samaria's citizens will tremble
  for the calf of Beth-Aven;
  the people there will mourn for it,
  so will its idol-priests,
  as they exult in its glory
  once it has been carried away!

f 9 A nickname for Baal, worshipped at Baal-Peor, Nb 25.

NEW REVISED STANDARD VERSION	REVISED ENGLISH BIBLE

NEW REVISED STANDARD VERSION

6 The thing itself shall be carried to Assyria
 as tribute to the great king.[u]
 Ephraim shall be put to shame,
 and Israel shall be ashamed of his idol.[v]

7 Samaria's king shall perish
 like a chip on the face of the waters.

8 The high places of Aven, the sin of Israel,
 shall be destroyed.
 Thorn and thistle shall grow up
 on their altars.
 They shall say to the mountains, Cover us,
 and to the hills, Fall on us.

9 Since the days of Gibeah you have sinned,
 O Israel;
 there they have continued.
 Shall not war overtake them in Gibeah?

10 I will come[w] against the wayward people to
 punish them;
 and nations shall be gathered against them
 when they are punished[x] for their double
 iniquity.

11 Ephraim was a trained heifer
 that loved to thresh,
 and I spared her fair neck;
 but I will make Ephraim break the ground;
 Judah must plow;
 Jacob must harrow for himself.

12 Sow for yourselves righteousness;
 reap steadfast love;
 break up your fallow ground;
 for it is time to seek the LORD,
 that he may come and rain righteousness upon
 you.

13 You have plowed wickedness,
 you have reaped injustice,
 you have eaten the fruit of lies.
 Because you have trusted in your power
 and in the multitude of your warriors,

14 therefore the tumult of war shall rise against your
 people,
 and all your fortresses shall be destroyed,
 as Shalman destroyed Beth-arbel on the day of
 battle
 when mothers were dashed in pieces with their
 children.

15 Thus it shall be done to you, O Bethel,
 because of your great wickedness.
 At dawn the king of Israel
 shall be utterly cut off.

11 When Israel was a child, I loved him,
 and out of Egypt I called my son.

2 The more I[y] called them,
 the more they went from me;[z]
 they kept sacrificing to the Baals,
 and offering incense to idols.

3 Yet it was I who taught Ephraim to walk,
 I took them up in my[a] arms;
 but they did not know that I healed them.

4 I led them with cords of human kindness,
 with bands of love.
 I was to them like those
 who lift infants to their cheeks.[b]
 I bent down to them and fed them.

REVISED ENGLISH BIBLE

6 It will be carried to Assyria
 as tribute to the Great King;
 disgrace will overtake Ephraim,
 and Israel, lacking counsel, will be put to shame.

7 Samaria and her king are swept away
 like flotsam on the water;

8 the shrines of Aven are destroyed,
 the shrines where Israel sinned;
 the altars are overgrown with thorns and thistles.
 They will say to the mountains, 'Cover us,'
 and to the hills, 'Fall upon us.'

9 Since the time of Gibeah Israel has sinned;
 there they took their stand in rebellion.
 Will not war overtake them in Gibeah?

10 I have come against the rebels to chastise them,
 and the peoples will mass against them
 to chastise them for their two shameful deeds.

11 Ephraim is like a heifer broken in,
 which loves to thresh grain;
 across that fair neck of hers I have laid a yoke.
 I have harnessed Ephraim to the pole to plough,
 that Jacob may harrow the land.

12 Sow justice, and reap loyalty.
 Break up your fallow ground;
 it is time to seek the LORD,
 till he comes and rains justice on you.

13 You have ploughed wickedness
 and reaped depravity;
 you have eaten the fruit of treachery.

 Because you have trusted in your chariots,
 in the number of your warriors,

14 the tumult of war will arise against your people,
 and all your fortresses will be overthrown
 as Shalman overthrew Beth-arbel in the day of
 battle,
 dashing mothers and babes to the ground.

15 So it is to be done to you, Bethel,
 because of your great wickedness;
 as swiftly as the passing of dawn,
 the king of Israel will be swept away.

11 When Israel was a youth, I loved him;
 out of Egypt I called my son;

2 but the more I called, the farther they went from
 me;
 they must needs sacrifice to the baalim
 and burn offerings to images.

3 It was I who taught Ephraim to walk,
 I who took them in my arms;
 but they did not know that [4]I secured them with
 reins
 and led them with bonds of love,
 that I lifted them like a little child to my cheek,
 that I bent down to feed them.

---

[u] Cn: Heb *to a king who will contend* [v] Cn: Heb *counsel*
[w] Cn Compare Gk: Heb *In my desire* [x] Gk: Heb *bound*
[y] Gk: Heb *they* [z] Gk: Heb *them* [a] Gk Syr Vg: Heb *his*
[b] Or *who ease the yoke on their jaws*

10:10 **I have come:** *prob. rdg, cp. Gk; Heb.* By my desire.
10:11 **a yoke:** *prob. rdg; Heb.* omits. **to plough:** *prob. rdg; Heb.*
that Judah may plough.   10:13 **chariots:** *so Gk; Heb.* way.
11:2 **I:** *so Gk; Heb.* they. **me:** *so Gk; Heb.* them.   11:3 **I who
took:** *so Gk; Heb.* unintelligible. **my:** *so Gk; Heb.* his.

NEW AMERICAN BIBLE

6 It too shall be carried to Assyria,
   as an offering to the great king.
Ephraim shall be taken into captivity,
   Israel be shamed by his schemes.

7 The king of Samaria shall disappear,
   like foam upon the waters.
8 The high places of Aven shall be destroyed,
   the sin of Israel;
   thorns and thistles shall overgrow their altars.
Then they shall cry out to the mountains,
      "Cover us!"
   and to the hills, "Fall upon us!"

9 Since the days of Gibeah
   you have sinned, O Israel.
There they took their stand;
   war was not to reach them in Gibeah.
10 Against the wanton people I came
   and I chastised them;
I gathered troops against them
   when I chastised them for their two crimes.
11 Ephraim was a trained heifer,
   willing to thresh;
I myself laid a yoke
   upon her fair neck;
Ephraim was to be harnessed, Judah was to plow,
   Jacob was to break his furrows:
12 "Sow for yourselves justice,
   reap the fruit of piety;
Break up for yourselves a new field,
   for it is time to seek the LORD,
   till he come and rain down justice upon you."
13 But you have cultivated wickedness,
   reaped perversity,
   and eaten the fruit of falsehood.

Because you have trusted in your chariots,
   and in your many warriors,
14 Turmoil shall break out among your tribes
   and all your fortresses shall be ravaged
As Salman ravaged Beth-arbel in time of war,
   smashing mothers and their children.
15 So shall it be done to you, Bethel,
   because of your utter wickedness:
At dawn the king of Israel
   shall perish utterly.

11 When Israel was a child I loved him,
   out of Egypt I called my son.
2 The more I called them,
   the farther they went from me,
Sacrificing to the Baals
   and burning incense to idols.
3 Yet it was I who taught Ephraim to walk,
   who took them in my arms;
4 I drew them with human cords,
   with bands of love;
I fostered them like one
   who raises an infant to his cheeks;
Yet, though I stooped to feed my child,
   they did not know that I was their healer.

NEW JERUSALEM BIBLE

6 It will be carried off to Assyria
   as tribute to the Great King.
Ephraim will reap the shame,
   and Israel blush for his intentions.

7 Samaria has had her day.
   Her king is like a straw drifting on the water.
8 The high places of Aven, the sin of Israel,
   will be destroyed;
   thorns and thistles will grow over their altars.
Then they will say to the mountains, 'Cover us!'
   and to the hills, 'Fall on us!'

9 Since the days of Gibeah, Israel, you have sinned.
   There they have taken their stand,
   and will not war overtake the guilty at Gibeah?
10 I am coming to punish them;
   nations will muster against them
   to punish them for their two crimes.

11 Ephraim is a well-trained heifer
   that loves to tread the grain.
But I have laid a yoke on her fine neck,
   I shall put Ephraim into harness,
   Judah will have to plough,
   Jacob must draw the harrow.

12 Sow saving justice for yourselves,
   reap a harvest of faithful love;
break up your fallow ground:
   it is time to seek out Yahweh
   until he comes to rain saving justice down on you.

13 You have ploughed wickedness,
   you have reaped iniquity,
   you have eaten the fruit of falsehood.
Because you have trusted in your chariots,
   in your great numbers of warriors,
14 turmoil is going to break out among your people,
   and all your fortresses will be laid waste.
As Shalman laid Beth-Arbel waste
   on the day of battle,
   dashing mothers to pieces on their children,
15 so it shall be done to you, Bethel,
   because of your great wickedness;
   at dawn, the king of Israel will be no more.

11 When Israel was a child I loved him,
   and I called my son out of Egypt.
2 But the more I called, the further they went away
      from me;
they offered sacrifice to Baal
   and burnt incense to idols.
3 I myself taught Ephraim to walk,
   I myself took them by the arm,
   but they did not know that I was the one caring for
      them,
4 that I was leading them with human ties,
   with leading-strings of love,
that, with them, I was like someone lifting an
      infant to his cheek,
   and that I bent down to feed him.

NEW REVISED STANDARD VERSION

5 They shall return to the land of Egypt,
   and Assyria shall be their king,
   because they have refused to return to me.
6 The sword rages in their cities,
   it consumes their oracle-priests,
   and devours because of their schemes.
7 My people are bent on turning away from me.
   To the Most High they call,
   but he does not raise them up at all.[c]

8 How can I give you up, Ephraim?
   How can I hand you over, O Israel?
   How can I make you like Admah?
   How can I treat you like Zeboiim?
   My heart recoils within me;
   my compassion grows warm and tender.
9 I will not execute my fierce anger,
   I will not again destroy Ephraim;
   for I am God and no mortal,
   the Holy One in your midst,
   and I will not come in wrath.[c]

10 They shall go after the LORD,
   who roars like a lion;
   when he roars,
   his children shall come trembling from the
      west.
11 They shall come trembling like birds from Egypt,
   and like doves from the land of Assyria;
   and I will return them to their homes, says the
      LORD.

12d Ephraim has surrounded me with lies,
   and the house of Israel with deceit;
   but Judah still walks[e] with God,
   and is faithful to the Holy One.

12 Ephraim herds the wind,
   and pursues the east wind all day long;
   they multiply falsehood and violence;
   they make a treaty with Assyria,
   and oil is carried to Egypt.

2 The LORD has an indictment against Judah,
   and will punish Jacob according to his ways,
   and repay him according to his deeds.
3 In the womb he tried to supplant his brother,
   and in his manhood he strove with God.
4 He strove with the angel and prevailed,
   he wept and sought his favor;
   he met him at Bethel,
   and there he spoke with him.[f]
5 The LORD the God of hosts,
   the LORD is his name!
6 But as for you, return to your God,
   hold fast to love and justice,
   and wait continually for your God.

7 A trader, in whose hands are false balances,
   he loves to oppress.
8 Ephraim has said, "Ah, I am rich,
   I have gained wealth for myself;
   in all of my gain
   no offense has been found in me
   that would be sin."[c]
9 I am the LORD your God
   from the land of Egypt;
   I will make you live in tents again,
   as in the days of the appointed festival.

REVISED ENGLISH BIBLE

5 Back they will go to Egypt,
   the Assyrian will be their king;
   for they have refused to return to me.
6 The sword will be brandished in their cities
   and it will make an end of their priests
   and devour them because of their scheming.
7 My people are bent on rebellion,
   but though they call in unison to Baal
   he will not lift them up.

8 How can I hand you over, Ephraim,
   how can I surrender you, Israel?
   How can I make you like Admah
   or treat you as Zeboyim?
   A change of heart moves me,
   tenderness kindles within me.
9 I am not going to let loose my fury,
   I shall not turn and destroy Ephraim,
   for I am God, not a mortal;
   I am the Holy One in your midst.
   I shall not come with threats.

10 They will follow the LORD
   who roars like a lion, and when he roars,
   his sons will speed out of the west.
11 They will come speedily like birds out of Egypt,
   like pigeons from Assyria,
   and I shall settle them in their own homes.
   This is the word of the LORD.
12 The treachery of Ephraim encompasses me,
   as does the deceit of the house of Israel;
   and Judah is still restive under God,
   still loyal to the idols he counts holy.

12 Ephraim feeds on wind,
   he pursues the east wind all day,
   he piles up treachery and havoc;
   he makes a treaty with Assyria
   and carries tribute of oil to Egypt.

2 The LORD has a charge to bring against Judah
   and is resolved to punish Jacob for his conduct;
   he will requite him for his misdeeds.
3 Even in the womb Jacob supplanted his brother,
   and in manhood he strove with God.
4 He strove with the angel and prevailed;
   he wept and entreated his favour.
   God met him at Bethel
   and spoke with him there.
5 The LORD the God of Hosts, the LORD is his name!

6 Turn back by God's help;
   maintain loyalty and justice
   and wait continually for your God.
7 False scales are in merchants' hands,
   and they love to cheat.
8 Ephraim says,
   'Surely I have become rich,
   I have made my fortune,
   but despite all my gains
   the guilt of sin will not be found in me.'
9 Yet I have been the LORD your God
   since your days in Egypt;
   I shall make you live in tents yet again,
   as in the days of the Tent of Meeting.

---

c Meaning of Heb uncertain   d Ch 12.1 in Heb   e Heb roams or rules   f Gk Syr: Heb us   11:7 though . . . Baal: prob. rdg; Heb. obscure.   11:12 In Heb. 12:1.   12:4 with him: so Gk; Heb. with us.

NEW AMERICAN BIBLE

NEW JERUSALEM BIBLE

<table>
<tr><td>

5 He shall return to the land of Egypt,
  and Assyria shall be his king;
6 The sword shall begin with his cities
  and end by consuming his solitudes.
Because they refused to repent,
  their own counsels shall devour them.
7 His people are in suspense about returning to him;
  and God, though in unison they cry out to him,
  shall not raise them up.

8 How could I give you up, O Ephraim,
  or deliver you up, O Israel?
How could I treat you as Admah,
  or make you like Zeboiim?
My heart is overwhelmed,
  my pity is stirred.
9 I will not give vent to my blazing anger,
  I will not destroy Ephraim again;
For I am God and not man,
  the Holy One present among you;
I will not let the flames consume you.

10 They shall follow the LORD,
  who roars like a lion;
When he roars,
  his sons shall come frightened from the west,
11 Out of Egypt they shall come trembling,
  like sparrows,
  from the land of Assyria, like doves;
And I will resettle them in their homes,
  says the LORD.

12 Ephraim has surrounded me with lies,
  the house of Israel, with deceit;
Judah is still rebellious against God,
  against the Holy One, who is faithful.
2 Ephraim chases the wind,
  ever pursuing the gale.
His lies and falsehoods are many:
  he comes to terms with Assyria,
  and carries oil to Egypt.
3 The LORD has a grievance against Israel:
  he shall punish Jacob for his conduct,
  for his deeds he shall repay him.
4 In the womb he supplanted his brother,
  and as a man he contended with God;
5 He contended with the angel and triumphed,
  entreating him with tears.
At Bethel he met God
  and there he spoke with him:
6 The LORD, the God of hosts,
  the LORD is his name!
7 You shall return by the help of your God,
  if you remain loyal and do right
  and always hope in your God.

8 A merchant who holds a false balance,
  who loves to defraud!
9 Though Ephraim says,
  "How rich I have become;
  I have made a fortune!"
All his gain shall not suffice him
  for the guilt of his sin.
10 I am the LORD, your God,
  since the land of Egypt;
I will again have you live in tents,
  as in that appointed time.

</td><td>

5 He will not have to go back to Egypt,
  Assyria will be his king instead!
Since he has refused to come back to me,
6 the sword will rage through his cities,
  destroying the bars of his gates,
  devouring them because of their plots.
7 My people are bent on disregarding me;
  if they are summoned to come up,
  not one of them makes a move.

8 Ephraim, how could I part with you?
Israel, how could I give you up?
How could I make you like Admah
  or treat you like Zeboiim?
My heart within me is overwhelmed,
  fever grips my inmost being.
9 I will not give rein to my fierce anger,
  I will not destroy Ephraim again,
for I am God, not man,
  the Holy One in your midst,
  and I shall not come to you in anger.

10 They will follow Yahweh;
  he will roar like a lion,
  and when he roars,
  his children will come fluttering from the west,
11 fluttering like sparrows from Egypt,
  like pigeons from Assyria,
  and I shall settle them in their homes
  —declares Yahweh.

12 Ephraim besieges me with lying,
  the House of Israel with duplicity.
(But Judah still is on God's side,
  he is faithful to the Holy One.)
2 Ephraim feeds himself on wind,
  all day he chases the wind from the East,
  he heaps up cheating and violence;
  they make a treaty with Assyria,
  at the same time sending oil to Egypt.
3 Yahweh has a case against Judah,
  he will punish Jacob as his conduct merits,
  he will repay him as his deeds deserve.
4 In the very womb he overreached his brother,
  in maturity he wrestled against God.
5 He wrestled with the angel and beat him,
  he wept and pleaded with him.
He met him at Bethel
  and there God spoke to us—
6 yes, Yahweh, God Sabaoth, Yahweh is his title!
7 So turn back with God's help,
  maintain faithful love and loyalty
  and always put your trust in your God.
8 Merchants use fraudulent scales.
To defraud is his delight.
9 'How rich I have become!' says Ephraim,
  'I have made a fortune.'
But of all his gains he will keep nothing
  because of the sin of which he is guilty.

10 But I have been Yahweh your God since your days
  in Egypt
  and will make you live in tents again
  as in the days of Meeting.

</td></tr>
</table>

NEW REVISED STANDARD VERSION

10 I spoke to the prophets;
    it was I who multiplied visions,
and through the prophets I will bring
    destruction.
11 In Gilead*g* there is iniquity,
    they shall surely come to nothing.
In Gilgal they sacrifice bulls,
    so their altars shall be like stone heaps
    on the furrows of the field.
12 Jacob fled to the land of Aram,
    there Israel served for a wife,
and for a wife he guarded sheep.*h*
13 By a prophet the LORD brought Israel up from
    Egypt,
    and by a prophet he was guarded.
14 Ephraim has given bitter offense,
    so his Lord will bring his crimes down on him
    and pay him back for his insults.

13 When Ephraim spoke, there was trembling;
    he was exalted in Israel;
    but he incurred guilt through Baal and died.
2 And now they keep on sinning
    and make a cast image for themselves,
idols of silver made according to their
    understanding,
    all of them the work of artisans.
"Sacrifice to these," they say.*i*
    People are kissing calves!
3 Therefore they shall be like the morning mist
    or like the dew that goes away early,
like chaff that swirls from the threshing floor
    or like smoke from a window.
4 Yet I have been the LORD your God
    ever since the land of Egypt;
you know no God but me,
    and besides me there is no savior.
5 It was I who fed*j* you in the wilderness,
    in the land of drought.
6 When I fed*k* them, they were satisfied;
    they were satisfied, and their heart was proud;
    therefore they forgot me.
7 So I will become like a lion to them,
    like a leopard I will lurk beside the way.
8 I will fall upon them like a bear robbed of her
    cubs,
    and will tear open the covering of their heart;
there I will devour them like a lion,
    as a wild animal would mangle them.
9 I will destroy you, O Israel;
    who can help you?*l*
10 Where now is*m* your king, that he may save you?
    Where in all your cities are your rulers,
of whom you said,
    "Give me a king and rulers"?
11 I gave you a king in my anger,
    and I took him away in my wrath.

12 Ephraim's iniquity is bound up;
    his sin is kept in store.
13 The pangs of childbirth come for him,
    but he is an unwise son;
for at the proper time he does not present himself
    at the mouth of the womb.

REVISED ENGLISH BIBLE

10 I spoke to the prophets;
    it was I who gave vision after vision:
    I declared my mind through them.
11 In Gilead there was idolatry,
    the people were worthless
and sacrificed to bull-gods in Gilgal;
    their altars were like heaps of stones
    beside a ploughed field.
12 Jacob fled to the land of Aram;
    Israel did service to win a wife,
    to win her he tended sheep.
13 By a prophet the LORD brought Israel up from
    Egypt
    and by a prophet Israel was tended.
14 Ephraim gave bitter provocation;
    he will be left to suffer for the blood he has shed;
    his Lord will punish him for all his blasphemy.

13 Ephraim was a prince and a leader
    and he was exalted in Israel,
but, guilty of Baal-worship, he suffered death.
2 Yet now they sin more and more;
    they cast for themselves images,
they use their silver to make idols,
    all fashioned by craftsmen.
It is said of Ephraim:
    'They offer human sacrifice and kiss calf-images.'
3 Therefore they will be like the morning mist,
    like dew that vanishes early,
like chaff blown from the threshing-floor
    or smoke from a chimney.
4 But since your days in Egypt
    I have been the LORD your God;
you do not know any god but me,
    any saviour other than me.
5 I cared for you in the wilderness,
    in a land of burning heat.
6 They were fed and satisfied,
    and, once satisfied, they grew proud,
    and so they deserted me.
7 Now I shall be like a panther to them,
    I shall prowl like a leopard by the wayside;
8 I shall come on them like a she-bear robbed of her
    cubs
and tear their ribs apart,
    like a lioness I shall devour them on the spot,
    like a wild beast I shall rip them up.

9 I have destroyed you, Israel;
    who is there to help you?
10 Where now is your king that he may save you,
    in all your cities where are your rulers?
    'Give me a king and princes,' you said.
11 I gave you a king in my anger,
    and in my wrath I took him away.

12 Ephraim's guilt is tied up in a scroll,
    his sins are kept on record.
13 When the pangs of his birth came over his mother,
    he showed himself a senseless child;
for at the proper time he could not present himself
    at the mouth of the womb.

---

g Compare Syr: Heb *Gilead*   *h* Heb lacks *sheep*   *i* Cn Compare
Gk: Heb *To these they say sacrifices of people*
knew   *k* Cn: Heb *according to their pasture*   *l* Gk Syr: Heb *for in
me is your help*   *m* Gk Syr Vg: Heb *I will be*   *j* Gk Syr: Heb

13:1 **Ephraim . . . prince:** *meaning of Heb. uncertain.*   13:7 **I
shall be:** *so Gk; Heb.* I was.   13:9 **who:** *so Gk; Heb.* in me.

NEW AMERICAN BIBLE

11 I granted many visions
    and spoke to the prophets,
    through whom I set forth examples.
12 In Gilead is falsehood, they have come to nought,
    in Gilgal they sacrifice to bullocks;
    Their altars are like heaps of stones
    in the furrows of the field.
13 When Jacob fled to the land of Aram,
    he served for a wife;
    for a wife Israel tended sheep.
14 By a prophet the LORD brought Israel out of Egypt,
    and by a prophet they were protected.
15 Ephraim has exasperated his lord;
    therefore he shall cast his bloodguilt upon him
    and repay him for his outrage.

13

Ephraim's word caused fear,
    for he was exalted in Israel;
    but he sinned through Baal and died.

2 Now they continue to sin,
    making for themselves molten images,
    Silver idols according to their fancy,
    all of them the work of artisans.
    "To these," they say, "offer sacrifice."
    Men kiss calves!
3 Therefore, they shall be like a morning cloud
    or like the dew that early passes away,
    Like chaff storm-driven from the threshing floor
    or like smoke out of the window.
4 I am the LORD, your God,
    since the land of Egypt;
    You know no God besides me,
    and there is no savior but me.
5 I fed you in the desert,
    in the torrid land.
6 They ate their fill;
    when filled, they became proud of heart
    and forgot me.
7 Therefore, I will be like a lion to them,
    like a panther by the road I will keep watch.
8 I will attack them like a bear robbed of its young,
    and tear their hearts from their breasts;
    I will devour them on the spot like a lion,
    as though a wild beast were to rend them.
9 Your destruction, O Israel!
    who is there to help you?
10 Where now is your king,
    that he may rescue you in all your cities?
    And your rulers, of whom you said,
    "Give me a king and princes"?
11 I give you a king in my anger,
    and I take him away in my wrath.
12 The guilt of Israel is wrapped up,
    his sin is stored away.
13 The birth pangs shall come for him,
    but he shall be an unwise child;
    For when it is time he shall not present himself
    where children break forth.

NEW JERUSALEM BIBLE

11 I will speak through prophets,
    I will give vision after vision
    and through the ministry of prophets
    will speak in parables.
12 Is Gilead a sink of iniquity?
    Yes, they are a worthless lot!
    At Gilgal they sacrifice to bulls,
    that is why their altars are like heaps of stones
    in a ploughed field.
13 Jacob fled to the countryside of Aram,
    Israel slaved to win a wife,
    to win a wife he looked after sheep.
14 By a prophet Yahweh brought Israel out of Egypt
    and by a prophet Israel was preserved.
15 Ephraim gave bitter provocation—
    Yahweh will bring his bloodshed down on him,
    his Lord will repay him for his insult.

13

When Ephraim used to speak, all trembled;
    he was a power in Israel;
    but once he had incurred guilt with Baal, he died.

2 And now they compound their sins
    by casting images for themselves out of their
        silver,
    idols of their own invention,
    the work of craftsmen, all of it!
    'Sacrifice to them,' they say!
    Men bestow kisses to calves!
3 That is why they will be like morning mist,
    like the dew that quickly disappears,
    like the chaff whirled from the threshing-floor,
    like smoke escaping through the window.
4 But I have been Yahweh your God since your days
        in Egypt
    when you knew no god but me,
    since you had no one else to save you.
5 I cared for you in the desert,
    in the land of dreadful drought.
6 I pastured them, and they were satisfied;
    once satisfied, their hearts grew proud,
    and therefore they forgot me.
7 So now I shall be like a lion to them,
    like a leopard I shall lurk beside the road,
8 like a bear robbed of her cubs I shall meet them
    and rend the membrane of their heart,
    and there like a lioness I shall eat them,
    like a wild beast tear them to shreds.
9 Israel, you have destroyed yourself
    though in me lies your help.
10 Your king, where is he now, to save you,
    or the governors in all your cities?—
    whom you once pleaded for, saying,
    'Give me a king and princes!'
11 In my anger I gave you a king
    and in my wrath I have taken him away.
12 Ephraim's guilt is packed away,
    his sin is locked up.
13 Pangs as of childbirth overtake him,
    and a stupid child he is;
    his time is due, but he does not leave the womb.

NEW REVISED STANDARD VERSION	REVISED ENGLISH BIBLE

NEW REVISED STANDARD VERSION

14 Shall I ransom them from the power of Sheol?
   Shall I redeem them from Death?
 O Death, where are[n] your plagues?
   O Sheol, where is[n] your destruction?
   Compassion is hidden from my eyes.

15 Although he may flourish among rushes,[o]
   the east wind shall come, a blast from the
     LORD,
   rising from the wilderness;
 and his fountain shall dry up,
   his spring shall be parched.
 It shall strip his treasury
   of every precious thing.
16[p] Samaria shall bear her guilt,
   because she has rebelled against her God;
 they shall fall by the sword,
   their little ones shall be dashed in pieces,
   and their pregnant women ripped open.

14 Return, O Israel, to the LORD your God,
     for you have stumbled because of your
       iniquity.
 2 Take words with you
     and return to the LORD;
   say to him,
     "Take away all guilt;
   accept that which is good,
     and we will offer
     the fruit[q] of our lips.
 3 Assyria shall not save us;
     we will not ride upon horses;
   we will say no more, 'Our God,'
     to the work of our hands.
   In you the orphan finds mercy."

 4 I will heal their disloyalty;
     I will love them freely,
     for my anger has turned from them.
 5 I will be like the dew to Israel;
     he shall blossom like the lily,
     he shall strike root like the forests of
       Lebanon.[r]
 6 His shoots shall spread out;
     his beauty shall be like the olive tree,
     and his fragrance like that of Lebanon.
 7 They shall again live beneath my[s] shadow,
     they shall flourish as a garden;[t]
   they shall blossom like the vine,
     their fragrance shall be like the wine of
       Lebanon.
 8 O Ephraim, what have I[u] to do with idols?
     It is I who answer and look after you.[v]
   I am like an evergreen cypress;
     your faithfulness[w] comes from me.
 9 Those who are wise understand these things;
     those who are discerning know them.
   For the ways of the LORD are right,
     and the upright walk in them,
     but transgressors stumble in them.

REVISED ENGLISH BIBLE

14 Shall I deliver him from the grave?
   Shall I redeem him from death?
   Where are your plagues, death?
   Grave, where is your sting?
   I shall put compassion out of my sight.
15 Though he flourishes among his
     brothers,
   an east wind will come, a blast from the
     LORD
   rising over the desert,
   causing springs to fail and fountains to run
     dry.
   The enemy will plunder his wealth,
   all his costly treasures.
16 Samaria will become desolate
   because she has rebelled against her God;
   her babes will fall by the sword
   and be dashed to the ground,
   and pregnant women will be ripped up.

14 RETURN, Israel, to the LORD your God;
     for your iniquity has been your downfall.
 2 Come back to the LORD
   with your words of confession;
   say to him, 'You will surely take away iniquity.
   Accept our wealth;
   we shall pay our vows with cattle from our pens.
 3 Assyria will not save us, nor shall we rely on
     horses;
   what we have made with our own hands
   we shall never again call gods;
   for in you the fatherless find compassion.'
 4 I shall heal my people's apostasy;
   I shall love them freely,
   for my anger is turned away from them.
 5 I shall be as dew to Israel
   that they may flower like the lily,
   strike root like the poplar,
 6 and put out fresh shoots,
   that they may be as fair as the olive
   and fragrant as Lebanon.
 7 Israel will again dwell in my shadow;
   they will grow vigorously like grain,
   they will flourish like a vine,
   and be as famous as the wine of Lebanon.
 8 What further dealings has Ephraim with idols?
   I declare it and affirm it:
   I am the pine tree that shelters you;
   your prosperity comes from me.

9 Let the wise consider these things and let the prudent
acknowledge them: the LORD's ways are straight and the
righteous walk in them, while sinners stumble.

---

[n] Gk Syr: Heb *I will be*   [o] Or *among brothers*   [p] Ch 14.1 in Heb
[q] Gk Syr: Heb *bulls*   [r] Cn: Heb *like Lebanon*   [s] Heb *his*
[t] Cn: Heb *they shall grow grain*   [u] Or *What more has Ephraim*
[v] Heb *him*   [w] Heb *your fruit*

13:14 **the grave:** *Heb.* Sheol.   13:16 *In Heb. 14:1.*
14:2 **surely:** *prob. rdg, cp. Gk; Heb.* all.   14:5 **poplar:** *prob.*
rdg; Heb. Lebanon.   14:7 **my:** *prob. rdg; Heb.* its.
14:8 **What . . . Ephraim:** *prob. rdg, cp. Gk.*

NEW AMERICAN BIBLE

14 Shall I deliver them from the power of the
        nether world?
    shall I redeem them from death?
    Where are your plagues, O death!
        where is your sting, O nether world!
    My eyes are closed to compassion.

15 Though he be fruitful among his fellows,
        an east wind shall come, a wind from the LORD,
        rising from the desert,
    That shall dry up his spring,
        and leave his fountain dry.
    It shall loot his land
        of every precious thing.

14 Samaria shall expiate her guilt,
        for she has rebelled against her God.
    They shall fall by the sword,
        their little ones shall be dashed to pieces,
        their expectant mothers shall be ripped open.

2 Return, O Israel, to the LORD, your God;
        you have collapsed through your guilt.
3 Take with you words,
        and return to the LORD;
    Say to him, "Forgive all iniquity,
        and receive what is good, that we may render
        as offerings the bullocks from our stalls.
4 Assyria will not save us,
        nor shall we have horses to mount;
    We shall say no more, 'Our god,'
        to the work of our hands;
        for in you the orphan finds compassion."

5 I will heal their defection,
        I will love them freely;
        for my wrath is turned away from them.
6 I will be like the dew for Israel:
        he shall blossom like the lily;
    He shall strike root like the Lebanon cedar,
7   and put forth his shoots.
    His splendor shall be like the olive tree
        and his fragrance like the Lebanon cedar.
8 Again they shall dwell in his shade
        and raise grain;
    They shall blossom like the vine,
        and his fame shall be like the wine of Lebanon.

9 Ephraim! What more has he to do with idols?
        I have humbled him, but I will prosper him.
    "I am like a verdant cypress tree" —
        Because of me you bear fruit!

                        * * *

10 Let him who is wise understand these things;
        let him who is prudent know them.
    Straight are the paths of the LORD,
        in them the just walk,
        but sinners stumble in them.

NEW JERUSALEM BIBLE

14 Shall I save them from the clutches of Sheol?
    Shall I buy them back from Death?
    Where are your plagues, Death?
    Where are your scourges, Sheol?
    Compassion will be banished from my sight!
15 Though Ephraim bears more fruit than his brothers,
    the wind from the East will come,
    Yahweh's breath blowing up from the desert
    to dry his spring, to dry up his fountain,
    to strip his treasury
    of everything worth having.

14 Samaria will pay the penalty
        for having rebelled against her God.
    They will fall by the sword,
        their little children will be dashed to pieces
        and their pregnant women disembowelled.

2 Israel, come back to Yahweh your God
        your guilt was the cause of your downfall.
3 Provide yourself with words
        and come back to Yahweh.
    Say to him, 'Take all guilt away
        and give us what is good,
        instead of bulls we will dedicate to you our lips.
4 Assyria cannot save us,
        we will not ride horses any more,
        or say, "Our God!" to our own handiwork,
        for you are the one in whom orphans find
            compassion.'

5 I shall cure them of their disloyalty,
        I shall love them with all my heart,
        for my anger has turned away from them.
6 I shall fall like dew on Israel,
        he will bloom like the lily
        and thrust out roots like the cedar of Lebanon;
7 he will put out new shoots,
        he will have the beauty of the olive tree
        and the fragrance of Lebanon.
8 They will come back to live in my shade;
        they will grow wheat again,
        they will make the vine flourish,
        their wine will be as famous as Lebanon's.

9 What has Ephraim to do with idols any more
        when I hear him and watch over him?
    I am like an evergreen cypress,
        you owe your fruitfulness to me.

10 Let the wise understand these words,
        let the intelligent grasp their meaning,
        for Yahweh's ways are straight
        and the upright will walk in them,
        but sinners will stumble.

Joel

1

The word of the LORD that came to Joel son of Pethuel:

2 Hear this, O elders,
　　give ear, all inhabitants of the land!
Has such a thing happened in your days,
　　or in the days of your ancestors?
3 Tell your children of it,
　　and let your children tell their children,
　　and their children another generation.

4 What the cutting locust left,
　　the swarming locust has eaten.
What the swarming locust left,
　　the hopping locust has eaten,
and what the hopping locust left,
　　the destroying locust has eaten.

5 Wake up, you drunkards, and weep;
　　and wail, all you wine-drinkers,
over the sweet wine,
　　for it is cut off from your mouth.
6 For a nation has invaded my land,
　　powerful and innumerable;
its teeth are lions' teeth,
　　and it has the fangs of a lioness.
7 It has laid waste my vines,
　　and splintered my fig trees;
it has stripped off their bark and thrown it down;
　　their branches have turned white.

8 Lament like a virgin dressed in sackcloth
　　for the husband of her youth.
9 The grain offering and the drink offering are cut
　　off
　　from the house of the LORD.
The priests mourn,
　　the ministers of the LORD.
10 The fields are devastated,
　　the ground mourns;
for the grain is destroyed,
　　the wine dries up,
　　the oil fails.

11 Be dismayed, you farmers,
　　wail, you vinedressers,
over the wheat and the barley;
　　for the crops of the field are ruined.
12 The vine withers,
　　the fig tree droops.
Pomegranate, palm, and apple —
　　all the trees of the field are dried up;
surely, joy withers away
　　among the people.

13 Put on sackcloth and lament, you priests;
　　wail, you ministers of the altar.
Come, pass the night in sackcloth,
　　you ministers of my God!
Grain offering and drink offering
　　are withheld from the house of your God.

Joel

1

THE word of the LORD which came to Joel son of
Pethuel.

2 HEAR this, you elders;
　　listen to me, all you inhabitants of the land!
Has the like of this happened in your days
　　or in the days of your forefathers?
3 Tell it to your children and let them tell it to theirs;
　　let one generation pass it on to another.
4 What the locust has left,
　　the swarmer devours;
what the swarmer has left,
　　the hopper devours;
and what the hopper has left,
　　the grub devours.

5 Wake up, you drunkards, and weep!
　　Mourn for the new wine,
all you wine-drinkers,
　　for it is denied to you.
6 A horde, vast and past counting,
　　has invaded my land;
they have teeth like a lion's teeth,
　　they have the fangs of a lioness.
7 They have laid waste my vines
　　and left my fig trees broken;
they have plucked them bare
　　and stripped them of their bark,
leaving the branches white.
8 Wail like a virgin in sackcloth,
　　wailing over the betrothed of her youth:
9 the grain-offering and drink-offering are cut off
　　from the house of the LORD.
Mourn, you priests, who minister to the LORD!
10 The fields are ruined, the ground mourns;
　　for the grain is ruined, the new wine has come to
　　　　naught,
　　the oil has failed.
11 Despair, you farmers, and lament, you
　　　　vine-dressers,
　　over the wheat and the barley;
　　the harvest of the fields is lost.
12 The vines have come to naught,
　　and the fig trees have failed;
pomegranate, palm, and apple,
　　every tree of the countryside is dried up,
and all the people's joy
　　has come to an end.

13 Put on sackcloth, you priests, and mourn;
　　lament, you ministers of the altar;
come, lie in sackcloth all night long,
　　you ministers of my God;
for grain-offerings and drink-offerings
　　are withheld from the house of your God.

THE BOOK OF
Joel

Joel

1 The word of the LORD which came to Joel, the son of Pethuel.

2 Hear this, you elders!
  Pay attention, all you who dwell in the land!
  Has the like of this happened in your days,
  or in the days of your fathers?
3 Tell it to your children,
  and your children to their children,
  and their children to the next generation.
4 What the cutter left,
  the locust swarm has eaten;
  What the locust swarm left,
  the grasshopper has eaten;
  And what the grasshopper left,
  the devourer has eaten.

5 Wake up, you drunkards, and weep;
  wail, all you drinkers of wine,
  Because the juice of the grape
  will be withheld from your mouths.
6 For a people has invaded my land,
  mighty and without number;
  His teeth are the teeth of a lion,
  and his molars those of a lioness.
7 He has laid waste my vine,
  and blighted my fig tree;
  He has stripped it, sheared off its bark;
  its branches are made white.
8 Lament like a virgin girt with sackcloth
  for the spouse of her youth.
9 Abolished are offering and libation
  from the house of the LORD;
  In mourning are the priests,
  the ministers of the LORD.
10 The field is ravaged,
  the earth mourns,
  Because the grain is ravaged,
  the must has failed,
  the oil languishes.

11 Be appalled, you husbandmen!
  wail, you vinedressers!
  Over the wheat and the barley,
  because the harvest of the field has perished.
12 The vine has dried up,
  the fig tree is withered;
  The pomegranate, the date palm also, and
    the apple,
  all the trees of the field are dried up;
  Yes, joy has withered away
  from among mankind.

13 Gird yourselves and weep, O priests!
  wail, O ministers of the altar!
  Come, spend the night in sackcloth,
    O ministers of my God!
  The house of your God is deprived
  of offering and libation.

1 The word of Yahweh that was addressed to Joel son of Pethuel.

2 Listen to this, you elders;
  everybody in the country, attend!
  Has anything like this ever happened in your day,
  or in your ancestors' days?
3 Tell your children about it
  and let your children tell their children,
  and their children the next generation!
4 What the nibbler has left, the grown locust has
    eaten,
  what the grown locust has left, the hopper has
    eaten,
  and what the hopper has left, the shearer has eaten.

5 Wake up, you drunkards, and weep!
  All you wine-bibbers, lament
  for the new wine: it has been snatched from your
    lips.
6 For a nation has invaded my country,
  mighty and innumerable,
  with teeth like a lion's teeth,
  with the fangs of a lioness.
7 It has reduced my vines to a desolation
  and my fig trees to splinters,
  stripped them and broken them down,
  leaving their branches white.
8 Mourn, as a virgin-bride in sackcloth
  for the bridegroom of her youth!
9 Cereal offering and libation
  are lost to Yahweh's Temple.
  The priests, the ministers of Yahweh,
  are in mourning.
10 The fields are ruined,
  the land is in mourning,
  for the grain has been ruined,
  the new wine has failed,
  of olive oil only a trickle.

11 Stand dismayed, you farmers,
  wail, you vinedressers,
  for the wheat, for the barley!
  The harvest of the fields has been lost!
12 The vine has withered,
  the fig tree wilts away;
  pomegranate, palm tree, apple tree,
  every tree in the countryside is dry,
  and for human beings
  joy has run dry too.

13 Priests, put on sackcloth and lament!
  You ministers of the altar, wail!
  Come here, lie in sackcloth all night long,
  you ministers of my God!
  For the Temple of your God has been deprived
  of cereal offering and libation.

14 Sanctify a fast,
  call a solemn assembly.
Gather the elders
  and all the inhabitants of the land
to the house of the LORD your God,
  and cry out to the LORD.

15 Alas for the day!
For the day of the LORD is near,
  and as destruction from the Almighty*a* it
    comes.

16 Is not the food cut off
    before our eyes,
joy and gladness
  from the house of our God?

17 The seed shrivels under the clods,*b*
  the storehouses are desolate;
the granaries are ruined
  because the grain has failed.

18 How the animals groan!
  The herds of cattle wander about
because there is no pasture for them;
  even the flocks of sheep are dazed.*c*

19 To you, O LORD, I cry.
For fire has devoured
  the pastures of the wilderness,
and flames have burned
  all the trees of the field.

20 Even the wild animals cry to you
  because the watercourses are dried up,
and fire has devoured
  the pastures of the wilderness.

2 Blow the trumpet in Zion;
  sound the alarm on my holy mountain!
Let all the inhabitants of the land tremble,
  for the day of the LORD is coming, it is near—

2 a day of darkness and gloom,
  a day of clouds and thick darkness!
Like blackness spread upon the mountains
  a great and powerful army comes;
their like has never been from of old,
  nor will be again after them
  in ages to come.

3 Fire devours in front of them,
  and behind them a flame burns.
Before them the land is like the garden of Eden,
  but after them a desolate wilderness,
  and nothing escapes them.

4 They have the appearance of horses,
  and like war-horses they charge.

5 As with the rumbling of chariots,
  they leap on the tops of the mountains,
like the crackling of a flame of fire
  devouring the stubble,
like a powerful army
  drawn up for battle.

6 Before them peoples are in anguish,
  all faces grow pale.*b*

7 Like warriors they charge,
  like soldiers they scale the wall.
Each keeps to its own course,
  they do not swerve from*d* their paths.

14 Appoint a solemn fast, proclaim a day of
    abstinence.
You elders, gather all who live in the land
  to the house of the LORD your God,
  and cry out to him:

15 'The day is near,
  the day of the LORD: it comes
  as a mighty destruction from the Almighty.'

16 It is already before our eyes:
  food is cut off from the house of our God
  and there is neither joy nor gladness.

17 Under the clods the seeds have shrivelled,
  the water-channels are dry,
  the barns lie in ruins;
  for the harvests have come to naught.

18 How the cattle moan!
  The herds of oxen are distraught
because they have no pasture;
  even the flocks of sheep waste away.

19 To you, LORD, I cry out;
  for fire has consumed the open pastures,
  flames have burnt up every tree in the countryside.

20 Even the beasts in the field look to you;
  for the streams are dried up,
  and fire has consumed the open pastures.

2 Blow the trumpet in Zion,
  sound the alarm on my holy mountain!
Let all the inhabitants of the land tremble,
  for the day of the LORD is coming,
a day of darkness and gloom is at hand,
  a day of cloud and dense fog.
Like blackness spread over the mountains
  a vast and countless host appears;
their like has never been known,
  nor will be in all the ages to come.

3 Their vanguard is a devouring fire,
  their rearguard a leaping flame;
before them the land is a garden of Eden,
  but behind them it is a desolate waste;
  nothing survives their passing.

4 In appearance like horses,
  like cavalry they charge;

5 they bound over the peaks
  with a din like chariots,
like crackling flames burning up stubble,
  like a vast host in battle array.

6 Nations tremble at their onset,
  every face is drained of colour.

7 Like warriors they charge,
  like soldiers they scale the walls;
each keeps in line
  with no confusion in the ranks,

---

a Traditional rendering of Heb *Shaddai*   *b* Meaning of Heb
uncertain   *c* Compare Gk Syr Vg: Meaning of Heb uncertain
d Gk Syr Vg: Heb *they do not take a pledge along*

2:6 **drained of colour:** *meaning of Heb. uncertain.*

NEW AMERICAN BIBLE	NEW JERUSALEM BIBLE

NEW AMERICAN BIBLE

14 Proclaim a fast,
    call an assembly;
Gather the elders,
    all who dwell in the land,
Into the house of the LORD, your God,
    and cry to the LORD!

15 Alas, the day!
    for near is the day of the LORD,
    and it comes as ruin from the Almighty.

16 From before our very eyes
    has not the food been cut off;
And from the house of our God,
    joy and gladness?

17 The seed lies shriveled under its clods;
    the stores are destroyed,
The barns are broken down,
    for the grain has failed.

18 How the beasts groan!
    The herds of cattle are bewildered!
Because they have no pasturage,
    even the flocks of sheep have perished.

19 To you, O LORD, I cry!
    for fire has devoured the pastures of the plain,
    and flame has enkindled all the trees of the field.

20 Even the beasts of the field
    cry out to you;
For the streams of water are dried up,
    and fire has devoured the pastures of the plain.

2 Blow the trumpet in Zion,
    sound the alarm on my holy mountain!
Let all who dwell in the land tremble,
    for the day of the LORD is coming;

2 Yes, it is near, a day of darkness and of gloom,
    a day of clouds and somberness!
Like dawn spreading over the mountains,
    a people numerous and mighty!
Their like has not been from of old,
    nor will it be after them,
    even to the years of distant generations.

3 Before them a fire devours,
    and after them a flame enkindles;
Like the garden of Eden is the land before them,
    and after them a desert waste;
    from them there is no escape.

4 Their appearance is that of horses;
    like steeds they run.

5 As with the rumble of chariots
    they leap on the mountaintops;
As with the crackling of a fiery flame
    devouring stubble;
Like a mighty people
    arrayed for battle.

6 Before them peoples are in torment,
    every face blanches.

7 Like warriors they run,
    like soldiers they scale the wall;
They advance, each in his own lane,
    without swerving from their paths.

NEW JERUSALEM BIBLE

14 Order a fast,
    proclaim a solemn assembly;
you elders,
    summon everybody in the country
    to the Temple of Yahweh your God.
Cry out to Yahweh:

15 'Alas for the day!
For the Day of Yahweh is near,
    coming as destruction from Shaddai.'

16 Has not the food disappeared
    before our very eyes?
Have not joy and gladness vanished
    from the Temple of our God?

17 The seeds shrivel
    under their clods;
the granaries are deserted,
    the barns are in ruins,
because the harvest has dried out.

18 Loudly the cattle groan!
The herds of oxen are bewildered
because they have no pasture.
The flocks of sheep bear the punishment too.

19 Yahweh, to you I cry:
    for fire has devoured the desert pastures,
    flame has burnt up all the trees in the countryside.

20 Even the wild animals pant loudly for you,
    for the watercourses have run dry,
    and fire has devoured the desert pastures.

2 Blow the ram's-horn in Zion,
    sound the alarm on my holy mountain!
Let everybody in the country tremble,
    for the Day of Yahweh is coming,
    yes, it is near.

2 Day of darkness and gloom,[a]
Day of cloud and blackness.
Like the dawn, across the mountains
    spreads a vast and mighty people,
such as has never been before,
such as will never be again
    to the remotest ages.

3 In their van a fire devours,
    in their rear a flame consumes.
The country is like a garden of Eden ahead of
    them
and a desert waste behind them.
Nothing escapes them.

4 They look like horses,
    like chargers they gallop on,

5 with a racket like that of chariots
    they spring over the mountain tops,
with a crackling like a blazing fire
    devouring the stubble,
a mighty army in battle array.

6 At the sight of them, people are appalled
    and every face grows pale.

7 Like fighting men they press forward,
    like warriors they scale the walls,
each marching straight ahead,
    not turning from his path;

NEW REVISED STANDARD VERSION

8 They do not jostle one another,
 each keeps to its own track;
they burst through the weapons
 and are not halted.
9 They leap upon the city,
 they run upon the walls;
they climb up into the houses,
 they enter through the windows like a thief.
10 The earth quakes before them,
 the heavens tremble.
The sun and the moon are darkened,
 and the stars withdraw their shining.
11 The LORD utters his voice
 at the head of his army;
how vast is his host!
 Numberless are those who obey his command.
Truly the day of the LORD is great;
 terrible indeed — who can endure it?

12 Yet even now, says the LORD,
 return to me with all your heart,
with fasting, with weeping, and with mourning;
13 rend your hearts and not your clothing.
Return to the LORD, your God,
 for he is gracious and merciful,
slow to anger, and abounding in steadfast love,
 and relents from punishing.
14 Who knows whether he will not turn and relent,
 and leave a blessing behind him,
a grain offering and a drink offering
 for the LORD, your God?

15 Blow the trumpet in Zion;
 sanctify a fast;
call a solemn assembly;
16 gather the people.
Sanctify the congregation;
 assemble the aged;
gather the children,
 even infants at the breast.
Let the bridegroom leave his room,
 and the bride her canopy.

17 Between the vestibule and the altar
 let the priests, the ministers of the LORD,
 weep.
Let them say, "Spare your people, O LORD,
 and do not make your heritage a mockery,
 a byword among the nations.
Why should it be said among the peoples,
 'Where is their God?' "

18 Then the LORD became jealous for his land,
 and had pity on his people.
19 In response to his people the LORD said:
I am sending you
 grain, wine, and oil,
 and you will be satisfied;
and I will no more make you
 a mockery among the nations.

20 I will remove the northern army far from you,
 and drive it into a parched and desolate land,
its front into the eastern sea,
 and its rear into the western sea;
its stench and foul smell will rise up.
 Surely he has done great things!

21 Do not fear, O soil;
 be glad and rejoice,
for the LORD has done great things!

REVISED ENGLISH BIBLE

8 none jostling his neighbour;
 each keeps to his course.
Weapons cannot halt their attack;
9 they burst into the city,
 race along the wall,
climb into the houses,
 entering like thieves through the windows.
10 At their onset the earth shakes,
 the heavens shudder,
sun and moon are darkened,
 and the stars withhold their light.
11 The LORD thunders as he leads his host;
 his is a mighty army,
countless are those who do his bidding.
Great is the day of the LORD and most terrible;
 who can endure it?

12 Yet even now, says the LORD,
 turn back to me wholeheartedly
with fasting, weeping, and mourning.
13 Rend your hearts and not your garments,
 and turn back to the LORD your God,
for he is gracious and compassionate,
 long-suffering and ever constant,
ready always to relent when he threatens disaster.
14 It may be he will turn back and relent
 and leave a blessing behind him,
blessing enough for grain-offerings and
  drink-offerings
to be presented to the LORD your God.
15 Blow the trumpet in Zion,
 appoint a solemn fast, proclaim a day of
  abstinence.
16 Gather the people together, appoint a solemn
  assembly;
 summon the elders,
gather the children, even babes at the breast;
 bid the bridegroom leave his wedding-chamber
 and the bride her bower.
17 Let the priests, the ministers of the LORD,
 stand weeping between the porch and the altar
and say, 'Spare your people, LORD;
 do not expose your own people to insult,
to be made a byword by other nations.
Why should the peoples say,
 "Where is their God?" '

18 THEN the LORD showed his ardent love for his
  land,
 and was moved with compassion for his people.
19 He answered their appeal and said:
I shall send you corn, new wine, and oil,
 and you will have them in plenty.
I shall expose you no longer
 to the reproach of other nations.
20 I shall remove the northern peril far from you
 and banish it into a land arid and waste,
the vanguard into the eastern sea,
 the rearguard into the western sea;
the stench and foul smell of it will go up.
 He has done great things!
21 Earth, fear not, but rejoice and be glad;
 for the LORD has done great things.

NEW AMERICAN BIBLE

⁸No one crowds another,
  each advances in his own track;
Though they fall into the ditches,
  they are not checked.

⁹They assault the city,
  they run upon the wall,
  they climb into the houses;
In at the windows
  they come like thieves.

¹⁰Before them the earth trembles,
  the heavens shake;
The sun and the moon are darkened,
  and the stars withhold their brightness.

¹¹The LORD raises his voice
  at the head of his army;
For immense indeed is his camp,
  yes, mighty, and it does his bidding.
For great is the day of the LORD,
  and exceedingly terrible; who can bear it?

¹²Yet even now, says the LORD,
  return to me with your whole heart,
  with fasting, and weeping, and mourning;

¹³Rend your hearts, not your garments,
  and return to the LORD, your God.
For gracious and merciful is he,
  slow to anger, rich in kindness,
  and relenting in punishment.

¹⁴Perhaps he will again relent
  and leave behind him a blessing,
Offerings and libations
  for the LORD, your God.

¹⁵Blow the trumpet Zion!
  proclaim a fast,
  call an assembly;

¹⁶Gather the people,
  notify the congregation;
Assemble the elders,
  gather the children
  and the infants at the breast;
Let the bridegroom quit his room,
  and the bride her chamber.

¹⁷Between the porch and the altar
  let the priests, the ministers of the LORD, weep,
And say, "Spare, O LORD, your people,
  and make not your heritage a reproach,
  with the nations ruling over them!
Why should they say among the peoples,
  'Where is their God?' "

¹⁸Then the LORD was stirred to concern for his land and took pity on his people. ¹⁹The LORD answered and said to his people:

See, I will send you
  grain, and wine, and oil,
  and you shall be filled with them;
No more will I make you
  a reproach among the nations.

²⁰No, the northerner I will remove far from you,
  and drive him out into a land arid and waste,
With his van toward the eastern sea,
  and his rear toward the western sea;
And his foulness shall go up,
  and his stench shall go up.

²¹Fear not, O land!
  exult and rejoice!
  for the LORD has done great things.

NEW JERUSALEM BIBLE

⁸they never jostle each other,
  each marches straight ahead:
  arrows fly, they still press forward,
  never breaking ranks.

⁹They hurl themselves at the city,
  they leap onto the walls,
  swarm up the houses,
  getting in through the windows
  like thieves.

¹⁰As they come on, the earth quakes,
  the skies tremble,
  sun and moon grow dark,
  the stars lose their brilliance.ᵇ

¹¹Yahweh's voice rings out
  at the head of his troops!
For mighty indeed is his army,
  strong, the enforcer of his orders,
  for great is the Day of Yahweh,
  and very terrible — who can face it?

¹²'But now — declares Yahweh —
  come back to me with all your heart,
  fasting, weeping, mourning.'

¹³Tear your hearts and not your clothes,
  and come back to Yahweh your God,
  for he is gracious and compassionate,
  slow to anger, rich in faithful love,
  and he relents about inflicting disaster.

¹⁴Who knows if he will not come back, relent
  and leave a blessing behind him,
  a cereal offering and a libation
  to be presented to Yahweh your God?

¹⁵Blow the ram's-horn in Zion!
  Order a fast,
  proclaim a solemn assembly,

¹⁶call the people together,
  summon the community,
  assemble the elders,
  gather the children,
  even infants at the breast!
Call the bridegroom from his bedroom
  and the bride from her bower!

¹⁷Let the priests, the ministers of Yahweh,
  stand weeping between portico and altar,
  saying, 'Spare your people, Yahweh!
Do not expose your heritage to the contempt,
  to the sarcasm of the nations!
Why give the peoples cause to say,
  "Where is their God?" '

¹⁸Then, becoming jealous over his country,
  Yahweh took pity on his people.
¹⁹Yahweh said in answer to his people,
  'Now I shall send you
  wheat, wine and olive oil
  until you have enough.
Never again will I expose you
  to the contempt of the nations.

²⁰I shall take the northerner far away from you
  and drive him into an arid, desolate land,
  his vanguard to the eastern sea,
  his rearguard to the western sea.
He will give off a stench,
  he will give off a foul stink
  (for what he made bold to do).'

²¹Land, do not be afraid;
  be glad, rejoice,
  for Yahweh has done great things.

ᵇ 2 = 4:15.

22 Do not fear, you animals of the field,
    for the pastures of the wilderness are green;
the tree bears its fruit,
    the fig tree and vine give their full yield.
23 O children of Zion, be glad
    and rejoice in the LORD your God;
for he has given the early rain*e* for your
        vindication,
he has poured down for you abundant rain,
    the early and the later rain, as before.
24 The threshing floors shall be full of grain,
    the vats shall overflow with wine and oil.

25 I will repay you for the years
    that the swarming locust has eaten,
the hopper, the destroyer, and the cutter,
    my great army, which I sent against you.

26 You shall eat in plenty and be satisfied,
    and praise the name of the LORD your God,
    who has dealt wondrously with you.
And my people shall never again
        be put to shame.
27 You shall know that I am in the midst of Israel,
    and that I, the LORD, am your God and there is
        no other.
And my people shall never again be put to shame.

28*f* Then afterward
    I will pour out my spirit on all flesh;
your sons and your daughters shall
        prophesy,
    your old men shall dream dreams,
    and your young men shall see
        visions.
29 Even on the male and female slaves,
    in those days, I will pour out my
        spirit.

30 I will show portents in the heavens and on the earth,
blood and fire and columns of smoke. 31 The sun shall be
turned to darkness, and the moon to blood, before the great
and terrible day of the LORD comes. 32 Then everyone who
calls on the name of the LORD shall be saved; for in Mount
Zion and in Jerusalem there shall be those who escape, as
the LORD has said, and among the survivors shall be those
whom the LORD calls.

3*g* For then, in those days and at that time, when I restore
the fortunes of Judah and Jerusalem, 2 I will gather all
the nations and bring them down to the valley of Jehoshaphat, and I will enter into judgment with them there, on
account of my people and my heritage Israel, because they
have scattered them among the nations. They have divided
my land, 3 and cast lots for my people, and traded boys for
prostitutes, and sold girls for wine, and drunk it down.

22 Fear not, you beasts in the field;
    for the open pastures will be green,
    the trees will bear fruit,
    the fig and the vine yield their harvest.
23 People of Zion, rejoice,
    be glad in the LORD your God,
    who gives you food in due measure
    by sending you rain,
    the autumn and spring rains as of old.
24 The threshing-floors will be heaped with
        grain,
    the vats will overflow with new wine
        and oil.
25 I shall recompense you for the years
    that the swarmer has eaten,
    hopper and grub and locust,
    my great army which I sent against you.
26 You will eat until you are satisfied,
    and praise the name of the LORD your
        God
    who has done wonderful things for you,
    and my people will never again be put to
        shame.
27 You will know that I am present in Israel,
    that I and no other am the LORD your God;
    and my people will never again be put to
        shame.
28 After this I shall pour out my spirit on all
        mankind;
    your sons and daughters will prophesy,
    your old men will dream dreams
    and your young men see visions;
29 I shall pour out my spirit in those days
    even on slaves and slave-girls.
30 I shall set portents in the sky and on earth,
    blood and fire and columns of smoke.
31 The sun will be turned to darkness
    and the moon to blood
    before the coming of the great and terrible day of
        the LORD.
32 Then everyone who invokes the LORD's name will
        be saved:
    on Mount Zion and in Jerusalem there will be a
        remnant
    as the LORD has promised,
    survivors whom the LORD calls.

3 When that time comes, on that day
    when I reverse the fortunes of Judah and
        Jerusalem,
    2 I shall gather all the nations together
    and lead them down to the valley of Jehoshaphat.
    There I shall bring them to judgement
    on behalf of Israel, my own people,
    whom they have scattered among the nations;
    they have shared out my land
    3 and divided my people by lot,
    bartering a boy for a whore
    and selling a girl for a drink of wine.

---

e Meaning of Heb uncertain   *f* Ch 3.1 in Heb   *g* Ch 4.1 in Heb

2:28 *In Heb. 3:1.*   3:1 *In Heb. 4:1.*   3:2 **Jehoshaphat:** *that is*
The LORD has judged.

NEW AMERICAN BIBLE	NEW JERUSALEM BIBLE

NEW AMERICAN BIBLE

22 Fear not, beasts of the field!
  for the pastures of the plain are green;
The tree bears its fruit,
  the fig tree and the vine give their yield.
23 And do you, O children of Zion, exult
  and rejoice in the LORD, your God!
He has given you the teacher of justice:
  he has made the rain come down for you,
  the early and the late rain as before.
24 The threshing floors shall be full of grain
  and the vats shall overflow with wine and oil.
25 And I will repay you for the years
  which the locust has eaten,
The grasshopper, the devourer, and the cutter,
  my great army which I sent among you.
26 You shall eat and be filled,
  and shall praise the name of the LORD,
    your God,
Because he has dealt wondrously with you;
  my people shall nevermore be put to shame.
27 And you shall know that I am in the midst
    of Israel;
  I am the LORD, your God, and there is no other;
  my people shall nevermore be put to shame.

3

Then afterward I will pour out
  my spirit upon all mankind.
Your sons and daughters shall prophesy,
  your old men shall dream dreams,
  your young men shall see visions;
2 Even upon the servants and the handmaids,
  in those days, I will pour out my spirit.
3 And I will work wonders in the heavens and on
    the earth,
  blood, fire, and columns of smoke;
4 The sun will be turned to darkness,
  and the moon to blood,
At the coming of the day of the LORD,
  the great and terrible day.
5 Then everyone shall be rescued
  who calls on the name of the LORD;
For on Mount Zion there shall be a remnant,
  as the LORD has said,
And in Jerusalem survivors
  whom the LORD shall call.

4

Yes, in those days, and at that time,
  when I would restore the fortunes
    of Judah and Jerusalem,
2 I will assemble all the nations
  and bring them down to the Valley
    of Jehoshaphat,
And I will enter into judgment with them there
  on behalf of my people and my
    inheritance, Israel;
Because they have scattered them among
    the nations,
  and divided my land.
3 Over my people they have cast lots;
  they gave a boy for a harlot,
  and sold a girl for the wine they drank.

NEW JERUSALEM BIBLE

22 Wild animals, do not be afraid;
  the desert pastures are green again,
  the trees bear fruit,
  vine and fig tree yield their richness.
23 Sons of Zion, be glad,
  rejoice in Yahweh your God;
for he has given you
  autumn rain as justice demands,
  and he will send the rains down for you,
  the autumn and spring rain as of old.
24 The threshing-floors will be full of grain,
  the vats overflow with wine and oil.
25 'I will make up to you for the years
  devoured by grown locust and hopper,
  by shearer and young locust,
  my great army
  which I sent to invade you.
26 'You will eat to your heart's content,
  and praise the name of Yahweh your God
  who has treated you so wonderfully.
  (My people will never be humiliated again!)
27 'And you will know that I am among you in Israel,
  I, Yahweh your God, and no one else.
  My people will never be humiliated again!'

3

'After this
  I shall pour out my spirit on all humanity.
Your sons and daughters shall prophesy,
  your old people shall dream dreams,
  and your young people see visions.
2 Even on the slaves, men and women,
  shall I pour out my spirit in those days.
3 I shall show portents in the sky and on earth,
  blood and fire and columns of smoke.'
4 The sun will be turned into darkness,
  and the moon into blood,
  before the Day comes,
  that great and terrible Day.
5 All who call on the name of Yahweh will be
    saved,
  for *on Mount Zion will be those who have
    escaped*,c
  as Yahweh has said,
  and in Jerusalem a remnant whom Yahweh is
    calling.

4

'For in those days and at that time,
  when I restore the fortunes of Judah and
    Jerusalem,
2 I shall gather all the nations together
  and take them down to the Valley of
    Jehoshaphat;d
  there I shall put them on trial
  because of Israel, my people and my heritage,
  for having scattered them among the nations
  and having divided my land among themselves.
3 They drew lots for my people,
  bartering a boy for a whore
  and selling a girl for wine to drink.

c **3** Ob 17.   d **4** A symbolic name (= Yahweh judges).

NEW REVISED STANDARD VERSION

4 What are you to me, O Tyre and Sidon, and all the regions of Philistia? Are you paying me back for something? If you are paying me back, I will turn your deeds back upon your own heads swiftly and speedily. 5 For you have taken my silver and my gold, and have carried my rich treasures into your temples.ʰ 6 You have sold the people of Judah and Jerusalem to the Greeks, removing them far from their own border. 7 But now I will rouse them to leave the places to which you have sold them, and I will turn your deeds back upon your own heads. 8 I will sell your sons and your daughters into the hand of the people of Judah, and they will sell them to the Sabeans, to a nation far away; for the LORD has spoken.

9 Proclaim this among the nations:
Prepare war,ⁱ
    stir up the warriors.
Let all the soldiers draw near,
    let them come up.
10 Beat your plowshares into swords,
    and your pruning hooks into spears;
let the weakling say, "I am a warrior."

11 Come quickly,ʲ
    all you nations all around,
    gather yourselves there.
Bring down your warriors, O LORD.
12 Let the nations rouse themselves,
    and come up to the valley of Jehoshaphat;
for there I will sit to judge
    all the neighboring nations.

13 Put in the sickle,
    for the harvest is ripe.
Go in, tread,
    for the wine press is full.
The vats overflow,
    for their wickedness is great.

14 Multitudes, multitudes,
    in the valley of decision!
For the day of the LORD is near
    in the valley of decision.
15 The sun and the moon are darkened,
    and the stars withdraw their shining.

16 The LORD roars from Zion,
    and utters his voice from Jerusalem,
    and the heavens and the earth shake.
But the LORD is a refuge for his people,
    a stronghold for the people of Israel.

17 So you shall know that I, the LORD your God,
    dwell in Zion, my holy mountain.
And Jerusalem shall be holy,
    and strangers shall never again pass through it.

18 In that day
the mountains shall drip sweet wine,
    the hills shall flow with milk,
and all the stream beds of Judah
    shall flow with water;
a fountain shall come forth from the house of the
        LORD
    and water the Wadi Shittim.

REVISED ENGLISH BIBLE

4 What are you to me, Tyre and Sidon and all the districts of Philistia? Are you bent on taking vengeance on me? If you were to take vengeance, I should make your deeds recoil swiftly and speedily on your own heads. 5 You have taken my silver and gold and carried off my costly treasures to your temples; 6 you have sold the people of Judah and Jerusalem to the Greeks, and removed them far beyond their own frontiers. 7 But I shall rouse them to leave the places to which they have been sold. I shall make your deeds recoil on your own heads, 8 by selling your sons and your daughters to the people of Judah, who will then sell them to the Sabaeans, a distant nation. Those are the LORD's words.

9 Proclaim this amongst the nations:
Declare war, call your troops to arms!
Let all the fighting men advance to the attack.
10 Beat your mattocks into swords
and your pruning-knives into spears.
Let even the weakling say, 'I am strong.'
11 Muster, all you nations round about;
let them gather together there.
LORD, send down your champions!
12 Let the nations hear the call to arms
and march up to the valley of Jehoshaphat.
There I shall sit in judgement
on all the nations round about.
13 Wield the knife, for the harvest is ripe;
come, tread the grapes,
for the winepress is full;
empty the vats, for they are full to the brim.
14 A noisy throng in the valley of Decision!
The day of the LORD is at hand
in the valley of Decision:
15 sun and moon are darkened
and the stars withhold their light.
16 The LORD roars from Zion
and thunders from Jerusalem
so that heaven and earth shudder;
but the LORD is a refuge for his people,
a defence for Israel.
17 Thus you will know that I am the LORD your God,
dwelling in Zion, my holy mountain;
Jerusalem will be holy,
and foreigners will never again set foot in it.

18 When that day comes,
the mountains will run with the new wine
and the hills flow with milk.
Every channel in Judah will be full of water;
a fountain will spring from the LORD's house
and water the wadi of Shittim.

ʰ Or palaces   ⁱ Heb sanctify war   ʲ Meaning of Heb uncertain

NEW AMERICAN BIBLE

4 Moreover, what are you to me, Tyre and Sidon, and all the regions of Philistia? Would you take vengeance upon me by some action? But if you do take action against me, swiftly, speedily, I will return your deed upon your own head. 5 You took my silver and my gold, and brought my precious treasures into your temples! 6 You sold the people of Judah and Jerusalem to the Greeks, removing them far from their own country! 7 See, I will rouse them from the place into which you have sold them, and I will return your deed upon your own head. 8 I will sell your sons and your daughters to the people of Judah, who shall sell them to the Sabeans, a nation far off. Indeed, the LORD has spoken.

9 Declare this among the nations:
proclaim a war,
rouse the warriors to arms!
Let all the soldiers
report and march!
10 Beat your plowshares into swords,
and your pruning hooks into spears;
let the weak man say, "I am a warrior!"

11 Hasten and come, all you neighboring peoples,
assemble there!
[Bring down, O Lord, your warriors!]
12 Let the nations bestir themselves and come up
to the Valley of Jehoshaphat;
For there will I sit in judgment
upon all the neighboring nations.

13 Apply the sickle,
for the harvest is ripe;
Come and tread,
for the wine press is full;
The vats overflow,
for great is their malice.
14 Crowd upon crowd
in the valley of decision;
For near is the day of the LORD
in the valley of decision.
15 Sun and moon are darkened,
and the stars withhold their brightness.
16 The LORD roars from Zion,
and from Jerusalem raises his voice;
The heavens and the earth quake,
but the LORD is a refuge to his people,
a stronghold to the men of Israel.

17 Then shall you know that I, the LORD, am
your God,
dwelling on Zion, my holy mountain;
Jerusalem shall be holy,
and strangers shall pass through her no more.
18 And then, on that day,
the mountains shall drip new wine,
and the hills shall flow with milk;
And the channels of Judah
shall flow with water:
A fountain shall issue from the house of the LORD,
to water the Valley of Shittim.

NEW JERUSALEM BIBLE

4 'And what are you to me, Tyre and Sidon
and all you regions of Philistia?
Can you take revenge on me?
If you take revenge on me,
I shall quickly, instantly, make your revenge recoil
on your own heads
5 for having taken my silver and gold away
and carried off my valuable treasures to your
temples,
6 and for having sold
the children of Judah and Jerusalem to the Ionians,
to be taken far away from their own frontiers.
7 Look, I shall rouse them from the places to which
you have sold them;
I shall make your actions recoil on your own heads
8 by selling your sons and daughters
to the sons of Judah,
who in turn will sell them to the Sabaeans,
to a nation far away —
Yahweh has spoken!'

9 Proclaim this among the nations.
Prepare for war!
Rouse the champions!
All you troops, advance,
march!
10 Hammer your ploughshares into swords,
your bill-hooks into spears;
let the weakling say, 'I am tough!'
11 Hurry and come,
all the nations around,
and assemble there!
(Yahweh, send down your champions!)
12 'Let the nations rouse themselves and march
to the Valley of Jehoshaphat,
for there I shall sit in judgement
on all the nations around.
13 Ply the sickle,
for the harvest is ripe;
come and tread,
for the winepress is full;
the vats are overflowing,
so great is their wickedness!'

14 Multitude on multitude
in the Valley of Decision!
For the Day of Yahweh is near
in the Valley of the Verdict!
15 Sun and moon grow dark,
the stars lose their brilliance.e
16 Yahweh roars from Zion,
he thunders from Jerusalem;f
heaven and earth tremble.

But Yahweh will be a shelter for his people,
a stronghold for the Israelites.

17 'Then you will know that I am Yahweh your God
residing on Zion, my holy mountain.
Jerusalem will then be a sanctuary,
no foreigners will overrun it ever again.'

18 When that Day comes,
the mountains will run with new wine
and the hills will flow with milk,
and all the stream-beds of Judah
will run with water.
A fountain will spring from Yahweh's Temple
and water the Gorge of the Acacias.

e4 // 2:10.   f4 // Am 1:2.

NEW REVISED STANDARD VERSION

19 Egypt shall become a desolation
and Edom a desolate wilderness,
because of the violence done to the people of
Judah,
in whose land they have shed innocent blood.
20 But Judah shall be inhabited forever,
and Jerusalem to all generations.
21 I will avenge their blood, and I will not clear the
guilty,[k]
for the LORD dwells in Zion.

[k] Gk Syr: Heb *I will hold innocent their blood that I have not held
innocent*

REVISED ENGLISH BIBLE

19 Egypt will become a desolation
and Edom a desolate waste,
because of the violence done to Judah
and the innocent blood shed in her land.
20 But Judah will be inhabited for ever,
Jerusalem for generation after generation.
21 I shall avenge their blood,
the blood I have not yet avenged,
and the LORD will dwell in Zion.

NEW AMERICAN BIBLE

19 Egypt shall be a waste,
   and Edom a desert waste,
   Because of violence done to the people of Judah,
   because they shed innocent blood in their land.
20 But Judah shall abide forever,
   and Jerusalem for all generations.
21 I will avenge their blood,
   and not leave it unpunished.
   The LORD dwells in Zion.

NEW JERUSALEM BIBLE

19 Egypt will become a desolation,
   and Edom a desert waste
   on account of the violence done to the children of
      Judah
   whose innocent blood they shed in their country.
20 But Judah will be inhabited for ever,
   and Jerusalem from generation to generation!
21 'I shall avenge their blood and let none go
      unpunished,'
   and Yahweh will dwell in Zion.

Amos

1 The words of Amos, who was among the shepherds of Tekoa, which he saw concerning Israel in the days of King Uzziah of Judah and in the days of King Jeroboam son of Joash of Israel, two years*a* before the earthquake. 2 And he said:

The LORD roars from Zion,
and utters his voice from Jerusalem;
the pastures of the shepherds wither,
and the top of Carmel dries up.

3 Thus says the LORD:
For three transgressions of Damascus,
and for four, I will not revoke the
punishment;*b*
because they have threshed Gilead
with threshing sledges of iron.
4 So I will send a fire on the house of Hazael,
and it shall devour the strongholds of
Ben-hadad.
5 I will break the gate bars of Damascus,
and cut off the inhabitants from the Valley of
Aven,
and the one who holds the scepter from
Beth-eden;
and the people of Aram shall go into exile to
Kir,
says the LORD.

6 Thus says the LORD:
For three transgressions of Gaza,
and for four, I will not revoke the
punishment;*b*
because they carried into exile entire
communities,
to hand them over to Edom.
7 So I will send a fire on the wall of Gaza,
fire that shall devour its strongholds.
8 I will cut off the inhabitants from Ashdod,
and the one who holds the scepter from
Ashkelon;
I will turn my hand against Ekron,
and the remnant of the Philistines shall perish,
says the Lord GOD.

9 Thus says the LORD:
For three transgressions of Tyre,
and for four, I will not revoke the
punishment;*b*
because they delivered entire communities over to
Edom,
and did not remember the covenant of kinship.
10 So I will send a fire on the wall of Tyre,
fire that shall devour its strongholds.

11 Thus says the LORD:
For three transgressions of Edom,
and for four, I will not revoke the
punishment;*b*
because he pursued his brother with the sword
and cast off all pity;
he maintained his anger perpetually,*c*
and kept his wrath*d* forever.

Amos

1 THE words of Amos, one of the sheep-farmers of Tekoa. He received these words in visions about Israel during the reigns of Uzziah king of Judah and Jeroboam son of Jehoash king of Israel, two years before the earthquake. 2 He said,

The LORD roars from Zion
and thunders from Jerusalem;
the shepherds' pastures are dried up
and the choicest farmland is parched.

3 THESE are the words of the LORD:

For crime after crime of Damascus
I shall grant them no reprieve,
because they threshed Gilead
under threshing-sledges spiked with basalt.
4 Therefore I shall send fire on Hazael's house,
fire to consume Ben-hadad's palaces;
5 I shall crush the nobles of Damascus
and wipe out those who live in the vale of Aven
and the sceptred ruler of Beth-eden;
the people of Aram will be carried to exile in Kir.
It is the word of the LORD.

6 These are the words of the LORD:

For crime after crime of Gaza
I shall grant them no reprieve,
because they deported a whole community into
exile
and delivered them to Edom.
7 Therefore I shall send fire on the walls of Gaza,
fire to consume its palaces.
8 I shall wipe out those who live in Ashdod
and the sceptred ruler of Ashkelon;
I shall turn my hand against Ekron,
and the Philistines who are left will perish.
It is the word of the Lord GOD.

9 These are the words of the LORD:

For crime after crime of Tyre
I shall grant them no reprieve,
because, ignoring the brotherly alliance,
they handed over a whole community to exile in
Edom.
10 Therefore I shall send fire on the walls of Tyre,
fire to consume its palaces.

11 These are the words of the LORD:

For crime after crime of Edom
I shall grant them no reprieve,
because, sword in hand and stifling their natural
affections,
they hunted down their kinsmen.
Their anger raged unceasingly,
their fury stormed unchecked.

---

a Or *during two years*   *b* Heb *cause it to return*   *c* Syr Vg: Heb *and his anger tore perpetually*   *d* Gk Syr Vg: Heb *and his wrath kept*

1:2 **choicest farmland:** *or* summit of Carmel.   1:3 **basalt:** *or* iron.   1:5 **nobles:** *or* barred gates.

THE BOOK OF

Amos

1 The words of Amos, a shepherd from Tekoa, which he received in vision concerning Israel, in the days of Uzziah, king of Judah, and in the days of Jeroboam, son of Joash, king of Israel, two years before the earthquake:

2 The Lord will roar from Zion,
and from Jerusalem raise his voice:
The pastures of the shepherds will languish,
and the summit of Carmel wither.

3   Thus says the Lord:
For three crimes of Damascus, and for four,
I will not revoke my word;
Because they threshed Gilead
with sledges of iron,
4 I will send fire upon the house of Hazael,
to devour the castles of Ben-hadad.
5 I will break the bar of Damascus;
I will root out those who live in the Valley
of Aven,
And the sceptered ruler of Beth-eden;
the people of Aram shall be exiled to Kir,
says the Lord.

6   Thus says the Lord:
For three crimes of Gaza, and for four,
I will not revoke my word;
Because they took captive whole groups
to hand over to Edom,
7 I will send fire upon the wall of Gaza,
to devour her castles;
8 I will root out those who live in Ashdod,
and the sceptered ruler of Ashkelon;
I will turn my hand against Ekron,
and the last of the Philistines shall perish,
says the Lord God.

9   Thus says the Lord:
For three crimes of Tyre, and for four,
I will not revoke my word;
Because they delivered whole groups captive
to Edom,
and did not remember the pact of brotherhood,
10 I will send fire upon the wall of Tyre,
to devour her castles.

11   Thus says the Lord:
For three crimes of Edom, and for four,
I will not revoke my word;
Because he pursued his brother with the sword,
choking up all pity;
Because he persisted in his anger
and kept his wrath to the end,

Amos

1 Words of Amos one of the shepherds of Tekoa. The visions he had about Israel, in the time of Uzziah king of Judah and Jeroboam son of Joash, king of Israel, two years before the earthquake.
2 He said:

Yahweh roars from Zion,
and makes himself heard from Jerusalem;[a]
the shepherds' pastures mourn,
and the crown of Carmel dries up.

3 Yahweh says this:

For the three crimes, the four crimes of Damascus,
I have made my decree and will not relent:
because they have threshed Gilead with iron
threshing-sledges,
4 I shall send fire down on the House of Hazael
to devour the palaces of Ben-Hadad;
5 I shall break the gate-bar of Damascus,
I shall destroy the inhabitant of Bikath-Aven,
the holder of the sceptre in Beth-Eden,
and the people of Aram will be deported to Kir,
Yahweh says.

6 Yahweh says this:

For the three crimes, the four crimes of Gaza,
I have made my decree and will not relent:
because they have deported entire nations as slaves
to Edom,
7 I shall send fire down on the walls of Gaza
to devour its palaces;
8 I shall destroy the inhabitant of Ashdod,
the holder of the sceptre in Ashkelon;
I shall turn my hand against Ekron
and the remnant of the Philistines will perish,
says the Lord Yahweh.

9 Yahweh says this:

For the three crimes, the four crimes of Tyre,
I have made my decree and will not relent:
because they have handed hosts of captives over to
Edom,
heedless of a covenant of brotherhood,
10 I shall send fire down on the walls of Tyre
to devour its palaces.

11 Yahweh says this:

For the three crimes, the four crimes of Edom,
I have made my decree and will not relent:
because he has pursued his brother with the sword,
because he has stifled any sense of pity,
and perpetually nursed his anger
and constantly cherished his rage,

NEW REVISED STANDARD VERSION

12 So I will send a fire on Teman,
  and it shall devour the strongholds of Bozrah.

13 Thus says the LORD:
  For three transgressions of the Ammonites,
    and for four, I will not revoke the
      punishment;*e*
  because they have ripped open pregnant women
    in Gilead
    in order to enlarge their territory.
14 So I will kindle a fire against the wall of Rabbah,
  fire that shall devour its strongholds,
  with shouting on the day of battle,
    with a storm on the day of the whirlwind;
15 then their king shall go into exile,
  he and his officials together,
                                     says the LORD.

2 Thus says the LORD:
  For three transgressions of Moab,
    and for four, I will not revoke the
      punishment;*e*
  because he burned to lime
    the bones of the king of Edom.
2 So I will send a fire on Moab,
  and it shall devour the strongholds of Kerioth,
  and Moab shall die amid uproar,
    amid shouting and the sound of the trumpet;
3 I will cut off the ruler from its midst,
  and will kill all its officials with him,
                                     says the LORD.

4 Thus says the LORD:
  For three transgressions of Judah,
    and for four, I will not revoke the
      punishment;*e*
  because they have rejected the law of the LORD,
    and have not kept his statutes,
  but they have been led astray by the same lies
    after which their ancestors walked.
5 So I will send a fire on Judah,
  and it shall devour the strongholds of
    Jerusalem.

6 Thus says the LORD:
  For three transgressions of Israel,
    and for four, I will not revoke the
      punishment;*e*
  because they sell the righteous for silver,
    and the needy for a pair of sandals—
7 they who trample the head of the poor into the
    dust of the earth,
    and push the afflicted out of the way;
  father and son go in to the same girl,
    so that my holy name is profaned;
8 they lay themselves down beside every altar
    on garments taken in pledge;
  and in the house of their God they drink
    wine bought with fines they imposed.

9 Yet I destroyed the Amorite before them,
  whose height was like the height of cedars,
  and who was as strong as oaks;
  I destroyed his fruit above,
    and his roots beneath.
10 Also I brought you up out of the land of Egypt,
  and led you forty years in the wilderness,
  to possess the land of the Amorite.

REVISED ENGLISH BIBLE

12 Therefore I shall send fire on Teman,
  fire to consume the palaces of Bozrah.

13 These are the words of the LORD:

  For crime after crime of the Ammonites
  I shall grant them no reprieve,
  because in their greed for land
  they ripped open the pregnant women in Gilead.
14 Therefore I shall set fire to the walls of Rabbah,
  fire to consume its palaces
  amid war cries on the day of battle,
  with a whirlwind on the day of sweeping tempest;
15 then their king will go into exile,
  he and his officers with him.
  It is the word of the LORD.

2 These are the words of the LORD:

  For crime after crime of Moab
  I shall grant them no reprieve,
  because they burnt to lime
  the bones of the king of Edom.
2 Therefore I shall send fire on Moab,
  fire to consume the palaces of Kerioth;
  Moab will perish in uproar,
  amid war cries and the sound of trumpets,
3 and I shall make away with its ruler
  and with him slay all the officers.
  It is the word of the LORD.

4 These are the words of the LORD:

  For crime after crime of Judah
  I shall grant them no reprieve,
  because they have spurned the law of the LORD
  and have not observed his decrees;
  they have been led astray by the same false gods
  their fathers followed.
5 Therefore I shall send fire on Judah,
  fire to consume the palaces of Jerusalem.

6 These are the words of the LORD:

  For crime after crime of Israel
  I shall grant them no reprieve,
  because they sell honest folk for silver
  and the poor for a pair of sandals.
7 They grind the heads of the helpless into the dust
  and push the humble out of their way.
  Father and son resort to the temple girls,
  so profaning my holy name.
8 Men lie down beside every altar
  on garments held in pledge,
  and in the house of their God they drink wine
  on the proceeds of fines.

9 It was I who destroyed the Amorite before them;
  he was as tall as the cedars,
  as sturdy as the oak;
  I destroyed his fruit above
  and his root below.
10 It was I who brought you up out of Egypt,
  and for forty years led you in the wilderness,
  to take possession of the country of the Amorite;

1:13 **ripped . . . Gilead:** *or* invaded the plains of Gilead.
2:1 **lime:** *or* ash.   2:7 **They grind:** *prob. rdg; Heb. obscure.* **the
temple girls:** *lit.* the girl.   2:8 **God:** *or* gods.

e Heb *cause it to return*

NEW AMERICAN BIBLE

12 I will send fire upon Teman,
and it will devour the castles of Bozrah.

13 Thus says the LORD:
For three crimes of the Ammonites, and for four,
I will not revoke my word;
Because they ripped open expectant mothers
in Gilead,
while extending their territory,
14 I will kindle a fire upon the wall of Rabbah,
and it will devour her castles
Amid clamor on the day of battle
and stormwind in a time of tempest.
15 Their king shall go into captivity,
he and his princes with him, says the LORD.

2 Thus says the LORD:
For three crimes of Moab, and for four,
I will not revoke my word;
Because he burned to ashes
the bones of Edom's king,
2 I will send fire upon Moab,
to devour the castles of Kerioth;
Moab shall meet death amid uproar
and shouts and trumpet blasts.
3 I will root out the judge from her midst,
and her princes I will slay with him, says
the LORD.

4 Thus says the LORD:
For three crimes of Judah, and for four,
I will not revoke my word;
Because they spurned the law of the LORD,
and did not keep his statutes;
Because the lies which their fathers followed
have led them astray,
5 I will send fire upon Judah,
to devour the castles of Jerusalem.

6 Thus says the LORD:
For three crimes of Israel, and for four,
I will not revoke my word;
Because they sell the just man for silver,
and the poor man for a pair of sandals.
7 They trample the heads of the weak
into the dust of the earth,
and force the lowly out of the way.
Son and father go to the same prostitute,
profaning my holy name.
8 Upon garments taken in pledge
they recline beside any altar;
And the wine of those who have been fined
they drink in the house of their god.

9 Yet it was I who destroyed the Amorites
before them,
who were as tall as the cedars,
and as strong as the oak trees.
I destroyed their fruit above,
and their roots beneath.
10 It was I who brought you up from the land
of Egypt,
and who led you through the desert for
forty years,
to occupy the land of the Amorites:

NEW JERUSALEM BIBLE

12 I shall send fire down on Teman
to devour the palaces of Bozrah.

13 Yahweh says this:
For the three crimes, the four crimes of the
Ammonites,
I have made my decree and will not relent:
because they have disembowelled the pregnant
women of Gilead
in order to extend their own frontiers,
14 I shall light a fire against the walls of Rabbah
to devour its palaces
amid war cries on the day of battle,
in a whirlwind on the day of storm,
15 and their king shall go into captivity,
he and his chief men with him,
says Yahweh.

2 Yahweh says this:
For the three crimes, the four crimes of Moab,
I have made my decree and will not relent:
because they have burnt the bones of the king of
Edom to ash,
2 I shall send fire down into Moab
to devour the palaces of Kerioth,
and Moab will die in the tumult,
amid war cries and the blare of trumpets;
3 I shall destroy the ruler there
and slaughter all the chief men there with him,
says Yahweh.

4 Yahweh says this:
For the three crimes, the four crimes of Judah,
I have made my decree and will not relent:
because they have despised Yahweh's law
and not kept his commandments,
since their Falsehoods, which their ancestors
followed,
have led them astray,
5 I shall send fire down on Judah
to devour the palaces of Jerusalem.

6 Yahweh says this:
For the three crimes, the four crimes of Israel,
I have made my decree and will not relent:
because they have sold the upright for silver
and the poor for a pair of sandals,b
7 because they have crushed the heads of the weak
into the dust
and thrust the rights of the oppressed to one side,
father and son sleeping with the same girl
and thus profaning my holy name,
8 lying down beside every altar
on clothes acquired as pledges,
and drinking the wine of the people they have
fined
in the house of their god.

9 Yet it was I who destroyed the Amorite before
them,
he who was as tall as the cedars,
as strong as the oaks;
I who destroyed his fruit above ground
and his roots below.
10 It was I who brought you up from Egypt
and for forty years led you through the desert
to take possession of the Amorite's country;

b 2 = 8:6.

NEW REVISED STANDARD VERSION	REVISED ENGLISH BIBLE

NEW REVISED STANDARD VERSION

11 And I raised up some of your children to be
   prophets
   and some of your youths to be nazirites. *f*
   Is it not indeed so, O people of Israel?
                                    says the LORD.

12 But you made the nazirites *f* drink wine,
   and commanded the prophets,
   saying, "You shall not prophesy."

13 So, I will press you down in your place,
   just as a cart presses down
   when it is full of sheaves. *g*

14 Flight shall perish from the swift,
   and the strong shall not retain their strength,
   nor shall the mighty save their lives;

15 those who handle the bow shall not stand,
   and those who are swift of foot shall not save
   themselves,
   nor shall those who ride horses save their lives;

16 and those who are stout of heart among the
   mighty
   shall flee away naked in that day,
                                    says the LORD.

3 Hear this word that the LORD has spoken against you,
O people of Israel, against the whole family that I
brought up out of the land of Egypt:

2 You only have I known
   of all the families of the earth;
   therefore I will punish you
   for all your iniquities.

3 Do two walk together
   unless they have made an appointment?

4 Does a lion roar in the forest,
   when it has no prey?
   Does a young lion cry out from its den,
   if it has caught nothing?

5 Does a bird fall into a snare on the earth,
   when there is no trap for it?
   Does a snare spring up from the ground,
   when it has taken nothing?

6 Is a trumpet blown in a city,
   and the people are not afraid?
   Does disaster befall a city,
   unless the LORD has done it?

7 Surely the Lord GOD does nothing,
   without revealing his secret
   to his servants the prophets.

8 The lion has roared;
   who will not fear?
   The Lord GOD has spoken;
   who can but prophesy?

9 Proclaim to the strongholds in Ashdod,
   and to the strongholds in the land of Egypt,
   and say, "Assemble yourselves on Mount *h*
   Samaria,
   and see what great tumults are within it,
   and what oppressions are in its midst."

10 They do not know how to do right, says the
   LORD,
   those who store up violence and robbery in
   their strongholds.

11 Therefore thus says the Lord GOD:
   An adversary shall surround the land,
   and strip you of your defense;
   and your strongholds shall be plundered.

REVISED ENGLISH BIBLE

11 I raised up prophets from among your sons,
   Nazirites from among your young men.
   Israelites, is this not true?
   says the LORD.

12 But you have made the Nazirites drink wine,
   and said to the prophets, 'You are not to
   prophesy.'

13 Listen, I groan under the burden of you,
   as a wagon creaks under a full load.

14 Flight will be cut off for the swift,
   the strong will not recover strength.
   The warrior will not save himself,

15 the archer will not stand his ground;
   the swift of foot will not escape,
   nor the horseman save himself.

16 On that day the bravest of warriors
   will throw away his weapons and flee.
   It is the word of the LORD.

3 LISTEN, Israelites, to these words that the LORD addresses to you, to the whole nation which he brought
up from Egypt:

2 You alone I have cared for
   among all the nations of the world;
   that is why I shall punish you
   for all your wrongdoing.

3 Do two people travel together
   unless they have so agreed?

4 Does a lion roar in the thicket
   if he has no prey?
   Does a young lion growl in his den
   unless he has caught something?

5 Does a bird fall into a trap on the ground
   if no bait is set for it?
   Does a trap spring from the ground
   and take nothing?

6 If a trumpet sounds in the city,
   are not the people alarmed?
   If disaster strikes a city,
   is it not the work of the LORD?

7 Indeed, the Lord GOD does nothing without revealing his
plan to his servants the prophets.

8 The lion has roared; who is not frightened?
   The Lord GOD has spoken; who will not prophesy?

9 Upon the palaces of Ashdod
   and upon the palaces of Egypt,
   make this proclamation:
   'Assemble on the hills of Samaria,
   look at the tumult seething among her people,
   at the oppression in her midst;

10 what do they care for straight dealing
   who hoard in their palaces
   the gains of violence and plundering?'
   This is the word of the LORD.

11 Therefore these are the words of the Lord GOD:

   An enemy will encompass the land;
   your stronghold will be thrown down
   and your palaces sacked.

---

f That is, *those separated* or *those consecrated*   *g* Meaning of Heb
uncertain   *h* Gk Syr: Heb *the mountains of*

3:11 **will encompass:** *prob. rdg; Heb.* and round.

NEW AMERICAN BIBLE

11 I who raised up prophets among your sons,
and nazirites among your young men.
Is this not so, O men of Israel?
says the LORD.
12 But you gave the nazirites wine to drink,
and commanded the prophets not to prophesy.
13 Beware, I will crush you into the ground
as a wagon crushes when laden with sheaves.
14 Flight shall perish from the swift,
and the strong man shall not retain his strength;
The warrior shall not save his life,
15 nor the bowman stand his ground;
The swift of foot shall not escape,
nor the horseman save his life.
16 And the most stouthearted of warriors
shall flee naked on that day, says the LORD.

3 Hear this word, O men of Israel, that the LORD pronounces over you, over the whole family that I brought
up from the land of Egypt:

2 You alone have I favored,
more than all the families of the earth;
Therefore I will punish you
for all your crimes.

3 Do two walk together
unless they have agreed?
4 Does a lion roar in the forest
when it has no prey?
Does a young lion cry out from its den
unless it has seized something?
5 Is a bird brought to earth by a snare
when there is no lure for it?
Does a snare spring up from the ground
without catching anything?
6 If the trumpet sounds in a city,
will the people not be frightened?
If evil befalls a city,
has not the LORD caused it?
7 Indeed, the Lord GOD does nothing
without revealing his plan
to his servants, the prophets.

8 The lion roars —
who will not be afraid!
The Lord GOD speaks —
who will not prophesy!

9 Proclaim this in the castles of Ashdod,
in the castles of the land of Egypt:
"Gather about the mountain of Samaria,
and see the great disorders within her,
the oppression in her midst."
10 For they know not how to do what is right,
says the LORD,
Storing up in their castles
what they have extorted and robbed.
11 Therefore, thus says the Lord GOD:
An enemy shall surround the land,
and strip you of your strength,
and pillage your castles.

NEW JERUSALEM BIBLE

11 I who raised up prophets from your sons
and Nazirites from your young men.
Israelites, is this not true?
—declares Yahweh!
12 But you have made the Nazirite drink wine
and given orders to the prophets,
'Do not prophesy.'
13 Very well! Like a cart overloaded with sheaves
I shall crush you where you stand;
14 flight will be cut off for the swift,
the strong will have no chance to exert his strength
nor the warrior be able to save his life;
15 the archer will not stand his ground,
the swift of foot will not escape,
nor will the horseman save his life;
16 even the bravest of warriors
will jettison his arms and run away, that day!
—declares Yahweh!

3 Listen, Israelites, to this prophecy which Yahweh pronounces against you, against the whole family which I
brought up from Egypt:

2 You alone have I intimately known of all the
families of earth,
that is why I shall punish you for all your
wrong-doings.

3 Do two people travel together
unless they have agreed to do so?
4 Does the lion roar in the forest
if it has no prey?
Does the young lion growl in his lair
if it has caught nothing?
5 Does a bird fall on the ground in a net
unless a trap has been set for it?
Will the net spring up from the ground
without catching something?
6 Does the trumpet sound in the city
without the people being alarmed?
Does misfortune come to a city
if Yahweh has not caused it?
7 No indeed, Lord Yahweh does nothing
without revealing his secret to his servants the
prophets.
8 The lion roars: who is not afraid?
Lord Yahweh has spoken: who will not prophesy?

9 From the palace roofs of Assyria
and from the palace roofs of Egypt,
proclaim aloud,
'Assemble on the hills of Samaria
and observe the grave disorders inside her
and the acts of oppression there!'
10 Little they know of right conduct
—declares Yahweh—
who cram their palaces with violence and
extortion.
11 This is why—Lord Yahweh says this—
an enemy will soon besiege the land,
he will bring down your strength
and your palaces will be looted.

12 Thus says the LORD: As the shepherd rescues from the mouth of the lion two legs, or a piece of an ear, so shall the people of Israel who live in Samaria be rescued, with the corner of a couch and part*i* of a bed.

13 Hear, and testify against the house of Jacob,
    says the Lord GOD, the God of hosts:
14 On the day I punish Israel for its transgressions,
    I will punish the altars of Bethel,
and the horns of the altar shall be cut off
    and fall to the ground.
15 I will tear down the winter house as well as the
    summer house;
and the houses of ivory shall perish,
and the great houses*j* shall come to an end,
        says the LORD.

4 Hear this word, you cows of Bashan
    who are on Mount Samaria,
who oppress the poor, who crush the needy,
    who say to their husbands, "Bring something to
    drink!"
2 The Lord GOD has sworn by his holiness:
    The time is surely coming upon you,
when they shall take you away with hooks,
    even the last of you with fishhooks.
3 Through breaches in the wall you shall leave,
    each one straight ahead;
and you shall be flung out into Harmon,*i*
        says the LORD.
4 Come to Bethel—and transgress;
    to Gilgal—and multiply transgression;
bring your sacrifices every morning,
    your tithes every three days;
5 bring a thank offering of leavened bread,
    and proclaim freewill offerings, publish them;
for so you love to do, O people of Israel!
        says the Lord GOD.

6 I gave you cleanness of teeth in all your cities,
    and lack of bread in all your places,
yet you did not return to me,
        says the LORD.

7 And I also withheld the rain from you
    when there were still three months to the
    harvest;
I would send rain on one city,
    and send no rain on another city;
one field would be rained upon,
    and the field on which it did not rain withered;
8 so two or three towns wandered to one town
    to drink water, and were not satisfied;
yet you did not return to me,
        says the LORD.

9 I struck you with blight and mildew;
    I laid waste*k* your gardens and your vineyards;
the locust devoured your fig trees and your
    olive trees;
yet you did not return to me,
        says the LORD.

*i*Meaning of Heb uncertain   *j*Or *many houses*   *k*Cn: Heb *the multitude of*

12 These are the words of the LORD:

As a shepherd rescues from the jaws of a lion
    a pair of shin-bones or the tip of an ear,
so will the Israelites who live in Samaria be
    rescued,
who repose on the finest beds and on divans from
    Damascus.
13 Listen and testify against the descendants of Jacob.
    This is the word of the Lord GOD, the God of
    Hosts.
14 On the day when I deal with Israel for their
    crimes,
I shall deal with the altars of Bethel:
    the horns of the altar will be hacked off
    and fall to the ground.
15 I shall break down both winter houses and summer
    residences;
the houses adorned with ivory will perish,
    and great houses will be no more.
This is the word of the LORD.

4 Listen to this word,
    you Bashan cows on the hill of Samaria,
who oppress the helpless and grind down the poor,
    who say to your lords, 'Bring us drink':
2 the Lord GOD has sworn by his holiness
    that your time is coming
when men will carry you away on shields
    and your children in fish-baskets.
3 You will each be carried straight out
    through the breaches in the wall
    and thrown on a dunghill.
This is the word of the LORD.
4 Come to Bethel—and infringe my law!
    Come to Gilgal—and infringe it yet more!
Bring your sacrifices for the morning,
    your tithes within three days.
5 Burn your thank-offering without leaven;
    announce publicly your freewill-offerings;
for that is what you Israelites love to do!
    This is the word of the Lord GOD.

6 It was I who brought starvation to all your towns,
    who spread famine through all your settlements;
yet you did not come back to me.
    This is the word of the LORD.

7 It was I who withheld the heavy showers from you
    while there were still three months to the harvest.
I would send rain on one town
    and no rain on another;
rain would fall on one field,
    another would be parched for lack of it.
8 From this town and that, people would stagger to
    another
for water to drink, but would not find enough;
    yet you did not come back to me.
This is the word of the LORD.

9 I struck you with black blight and red;
    I dried up your gardens and vineyards;
the locust devoured your fig trees and your olives;
    yet you did not come back to me.
This is the word of the LORD.

3:12 **who repose . . . Damascus:** *prob. rdg; Heb. obscure.*
4:2 **on shields:** *or* with hooks. **in fish-baskets:** *or* with fish-hooks.
4:3 **a dunghill:** *prob. rdg; Heb.* the Harmon.   4:4 **within:** *or* on.
4:6 **starvation:** *lit.* cleanness of teeth.   4:9 **I dried up:** *prob. rdg;*
Heb. to increase.

·

NEW AMERICAN BIBLE

12 Thus says the LORD:
As the shepherd snatches from the mouth of
the lion
a pair of legs or the tip of an ear of his sheep,
So the Israelites who dwell in Samaria shall escape
with the corner of a couch or a piece of a cot.

13 Hear and bear witness against the house of Jacob, says
the Lord GOD, the God of hosts:

14 On the day when I punish Israel for his crimes,
I will visit also the altars of Bethel:
The horns of the altar shall be broken off
and fall to the ground.

15 Then will I strike the winter house
and the summer house;
The ivory apartments shall be ruined,
and their many rooms shall be no more,
says the LORD.

4 Hear this word, women of the mountain
of Samaria,
you cows of Bashan,
You who oppress the weak
and abuse the needy;
Who say to your lords,
"Bring drink for us!"

2 The Lord GOD has sworn by his holiness:
Truly the days are coming upon you
When they shall drag you away with hooks,
the last of you with fishhooks;

3 You shall go out through the breached walls
each by the most direct way,
And you shall be cast into the mire,
says the LORD.

4 Come to Bethel and sin,
to Gilgal, and sin the more;
Each morning bring your sacrifices,
every third day, your tithes;

5 Burn leavened food as a thanksgiving sacrifice,
proclaim publicly your freewill offerings,
For so you love to do, O men of Israel, says the
Lord GOD.

6 Though I have made your teeth
clean of food in all your cities,
and have made bread scarce in all
your dwellings,
Yet you returned not to me,
says the LORD.

7 Though I also withheld the rain from you
when the harvest was still three months away;
I sent rain upon one city
but not upon another;
One field was watered by rain,
but another without rain dried up;

8 Though two or three cities staggered to one city
for water that did not quench their thirst;
Yet you returned not to me,
says the LORD.

9 I struck you with blight and searing wind;
your many gardens and vineyards,
your fig trees and olive trees the
locust devoured;
Yet you returned not to me,
says the LORD.

NEW JERUSALEM BIBLE

12 Yahweh says this:
As the shepherd rescues two legs or the tip of an
ear
from the lion's mouth,
so will the children of Israel be salvaged
who now loll in Samaria in the corners of their
beds, on their divans of Damascus.

13 Listen and testify against the House of Jacob
—declares the Lord Yahweh, God Sabaoth—

14 the day when I punish Israel for his crimes
I shall also punish the altars of Bethel;
the horns of the altar will be hacked off
and will fall to the ground.

15 I shall blast winter house with summer house,
ivory houses will be destroyed
and many mansions cease to be
—declares Yahweh.

4 Listen to this saying, you cows of Bashan
living on the hill of Samaria,
exploiting the weak and ill-treating the poor,
saying to your husbands, 'Bring us something to
drink!'

2 The Lord God has sworn by his holiness:
Look, the days will soon be on you
when he will use hooks to drag you away
and fish-hooks for the very last of you;

3 through the breaches in the wall you will leave,
each one straight ahead,
and be herded away towards Hermon
—declares Yahweh.

4 Go to Bethel, and sin,
to Gilgal, and sin even harder!
Bring your sacrifices each morning,
your tithes every third day,

5 burn your thank-offering of leaven
and widely publicise your free-will offerings,
for this, children of Israel, is what makes you
happy
—declares the Lord Yahweh.

6 I even gave you clean teeth in all your towns
and a shortage of food in all your villages
and still you would not come back to me
—declares Yahweh.

7 I even withheld the rain from you
full three months before harvest-time;
I caused rain to fall in one town
and caused no rain to fall in another;
one field was rained on
and the next for want of rain dried up;

8 two towns, three towns went tottering
to one town for water to drink
but went unsatisfied,
and still you would not come back to me
—declares Yahweh.

9 I struck you with blight and mildew,
I dried up your gardens and vineyards;
the locust devoured your fig trees and olive trees
and still you would not come back to me
—declares Yahweh.

NEW REVISED STANDARD VERSION	REVISED ENGLISH BIBLE

NEW REVISED STANDARD VERSION

10 I sent among you a pestilence after the manner of
   Egypt;
   I killed your young men with the sword;
   I carried away your horses;[l]
      and I made the stench of your camp go up into
         your nostrils;
   yet you did not return to me,
                                              says the LORD.

11 I overthrew some of you,
      as when God overthrew Sodom and Gomorrah,
      and you were like a brand snatched from the
         fire;
   yet you did not return to me,
                                              says the LORD.

12 Therefore thus I will do to you, O Israel;
      because I will do this to you,
      prepare to meet your God, O Israel!

13 For lo, the one who forms the mountains, creates
      the wind,
      reveals his thoughts to mortals,
   makes the morning darkness,
      and treads on the heights of the earth—
   the LORD, the God of hosts, is his name!

5 Hear this word that I take up over you in lamentation,
   O house of Israel:
2 Fallen, no more to rise,
      is maiden Israel;
   forsaken on her land,
      with no one to raise her up.

3 For thus says the Lord GOD:
   The city that marched out a thousand
      shall have a hundred left,
   and that which marched out a hundred
      shall have ten left.[m]

4 For thus says the LORD to the house of Israel:
   Seek me and live;
5   but do not seek Bethel,
   and do not enter into Gilgal
      or cross over to Beer-sheba;
   for Gilgal shall surely go into exile,
      and Bethel shall come to nothing.

6 Seek the LORD and live,
      or he will break out against the house of
         Joseph like fire,
      and it will devour Bethel, with no one to
         quench it.

7 Ah, you that turn justice to wormwood,
      and bring righteousness to the ground!

8 The one who made the Pleiades and Orion,
      and turns deep darkness into the morning,
      and darkens the day into night,
   who calls for the waters of the sea,
      and pours them out on the surface of the earth,
   the LORD is his name,

9 who makes destruction flash out against the
      strong,
      so that destruction comes upon the fortress.

10 They hate the one who reproves in the gate,
      and they abhor the one who speaks the truth.

REVISED ENGLISH BIBLE

10 I sent plague among you like the plagues of Egypt;
   with the sword I slew
      your young men and your troops of horses.
   I made your camps stink in your nostrils;
   yet you did not come back to me.
   This is the word of the LORD.

11 I brought destruction among you
      like the terrible destruction that befell Sodom and
         Gomorrah;
   you were like a brand snatched from the burning;
   yet you did not come back to me.
   This is the word of the LORD.

12 Therefore, Israel, this is what I shall do to you;
   and, because this is what I shall do,
   Israel, prepare to meet your God.
13 It is he who fashions the mountains,
   who creates the wind,
      and declares his thoughts to mankind;
   it is he who darkens the dawn with thick clouds
   and marches over the heights of the earth—
   his name is the LORD, the God of Hosts.

5 Listen, Israel, to these words, the dirge I raise over you:

2 She has fallen, to rise no more,
      the virgin Israel,
   prostrate on her own soil,
      with no one to lift her up.

3 These are the words of the Lord GOD:

   The city that marched out to war a thousand strong
      will have but a hundred left,
   and that which marched out a hundred strong
      will have but ten left for Israel.

4 These are the words of the LORD to the people of Israel:

   If you would live, make your way to me, 5 not to
      Bethel;
   do not go to Gilgal or pass on to Beersheba;
   for Gilgal will surely go into exile
      and Bethel come to nothing.
6 If you would live, make your way to the LORD,
      or he will break out against Joseph's descendants
         like fire,
   fire which will devour Bethel with no one to
      quench it.

8 He who made the Pleiades and Orion,
   who turns deep darkness into dawn
      and darkens day into night,
   who summons the waters of the sea
      and pours them over the earth—
   the LORD is his name—
9 who makes destruction flash forth against the
      mighty
   so that destruction comes upon the stronghold.

7 You that turn justice to poison
      and thrust righteousness to the ground,
10 you that hate a man who brings the wrongdoer to
      court
   and abominate him who speaks nothing less than
      truth:

[l] Heb *with the captivity of your horses*   [m] Heb adds *to the house of Israel*

4:10 **troops of:** *or* captured.   4:11 **the terrible:** *or* God's.
5:8 *Verse 7 transposed to follow verse 9.*   5:9 **who makes . . .
stronghold:** *or* who makes Taurus rise after Capella, and Taurus set
hard on the rising of the Vintager.

NEW AMERICAN BIBLE

10 I sent upon you a pestilence like that of Egypt,
    and with the sword I slew your young men;
Your horses I let be captured,
    to your nostrils I brought the stench of
        your camps;
Yet you returned not to me,
    says the LORD.

11 I brought upon you such upheaval
    as when God overthrew Sodom and Gomorrah:
    you were like a brand plucked from the fire;
Yet you returned not to me,
    says the LORD.

12 So now I will deal with you in my own way,
    O Israel!
    and since I will deal thus with you,
    prepare to meet your God, O Israel:
13 Him who formed the mountains, and created
        the wind,
    and declares to man his thoughts;
Who made the dawn and the darkness,
    and strides upon the heights of the earth:
The LORD, the God of hosts by name.

5 Hear this word which I utter over you,
    a lament, O house of Israel:
2 She is fallen, to rise no more,
    the virgin Israel;
She lies abandoned upon her land,
    with no one to raise her up.

3   For thus says the Lord GOD:
The city that marched out with a thousand
    shall be left with a hundred,
Another that marched out with a hundred
    shall be left with ten,
    of the house of Israel.

4 For thus says the LORD
    to the house of Israel:
Seek me, that you may live,
5   but do not seek Bethel;
Do not come to Gilgal,
    and do not cross to Beer-sheba.
For Gilgal shall be led into exile,
    and Bethel shall become nought.
6 Seek the LORD, that you may live,
    lest he come upon the house of Joseph like a fire
That shall consume, with none to quench it
    for the house of Israel:
8 He who made the Pleiades and Orion,
    who turns darkness into dawn,
    and darkens day into night;
Who summons the waters of the sea,
    and pours them out upon the surface of
        the earth;
9 Who flashes destruction upon the strong,
    and brings ruin upon the fortress;
    whose name is LORD.

7 Woe to those who turn judgment to wormwood
    and cast justice to the ground!
10 They hate him who reproves at the gate
    and abhor him who speaks the truth.

NEW JERUSALEM BIBLE

10 I sent plague on you like Egypt's plague,
I slaughtered your young men with the sword
and at the same time your horses were captured;
I filled your nostrils with the stench of your camps
and still you would not come back to me
—declares Yahweh.

11 I overturned you as God overturned Sodom and
        Gomorrah;
you were like a brand snatched from the blaze
and still you would not come back to me
—declares Yahweh.

12 So this, Israel, is what I plan to do to you.
Because I am going to do this to you,
Israel, prepare to meet your God!

13 cFor look, he it is who forges the mountains,
        creates the wind,
who reveals his mind to humankind,
changes the dawn into darkness
and strides on the heights of the world:
Yahweh, God Sabaoth, is his name.

5 Listen to this word which I utter against you,
it is a dirge, House of Israel:
2 She has fallen down, never to rise again,
the virgin Israel.
There she lies on her own soil,
with no one to lift her up.

3 For Lord Yahweh says this:
The town which used to put a thousand in the field
will be left with a hundred,
and the one which used to put a hundred
will be left with ten, to fight for the House of
        Israel.

4 For Yahweh says this to the House of Israel:
Seek me out and you will survive,
5 but do not seek out Bethel,
do not go to Gilgal,
do not journey to Beersheba,
for Gilgal is going into captivity
and Bethel will be brought to nothing.
6 Seek out Yahweh and you will survive
or else he will sweep like fire upon the House of
        Joseph
and burn it down, with no one at Bethel able to
        quench the flames.
7 They turn justice into wormwood
and throw uprightness to the ground.

8 He it is who makes the Pleiades and Orion,
who turns shadow dark as death into morning
and day to darkest night,
who summons the waters of the sea
and pours them over the surface of the land.
Yahweh is his name.d
9 He brings destruction on the strong
and ruin comes on the fortress.

10 They hate the man who teaches justice at the city
        gate
and detest anyone who declares the truth.

---

c4 A hymnic fragment, probably added later, as 5:8–9 and 9:5–6.
d5 = 9:6.

11 Therefore because you trample on the poor
    and take from them levies of grain,
  you have built houses of hewn stone,
    but you shall not live in them;
  you have planted pleasant vineyards,
    but you shall not drink their wine.
12 For I know how many are your transgressions,
    and how great are your sins—
  you who afflict the righteous, who take a bribe,
    and push aside the needy in the gate.
13 Therefore the prudent will keep silent in such a
        time;
    for it is an evil time.

14 Seek good and not evil,
    that you may live;
  and so the Lord, the God of hosts, will be with
        you,
    just as you have said.
15 Hate evil and love good,
    and establish justice in the gate;
  it may be that the Lord, the God of hosts,
    will be gracious to the remnant of Joseph.

16 Therefore thus says the Lord, the God of hosts,
        the Lord:
  In all the squares there shall be wailing;
    and in all the streets they shall say, "Alas!
        alas!"
  They shall call the farmers to mourning,
    and those skilled in lamentation, to wailing;
17 in all the vineyards there shall be wailing,
    for I will pass through the midst of you,
                        says the Lord.

18 Alas for you who desire the day of the Lord!
    Why do you want the day of the Lord?
  It is darkness, not light;
19 as if someone fled from a lion,
    and was met by a bear;
  or went into the house and rested a hand against
        the wall,
    and was bitten by a snake.
20 Is not the day of the Lord darkness, not light,
    and gloom with no brightness in it?

21 I hate, I despise your festivals,
    and I take no delight in your solemn
        assemblies.
22 Even though you offer me your burnt offerings
        and grain offerings,
    I will not accept them;
  and the offerings of well-being of your fatted
        animals
    I will not look upon.
23 Take away from me the noise of your songs;
    I will not listen to the melody of your harps.
24 But let justice roll down like waters,
    and righteousness like an ever-flowing stream.

25 Did you bring to me sacrifices and offerings the forty
years in the wilderness, O house of Israel? 26 You shall take
up Sakkuth your king, and Kaiwan your star-god, your
images,[n] which you made for yourselves; 27 therefore I will
take you into exile beyond Damascus, says the Lord,
whose name is the God of hosts.

11 for all this, because you levy taxes on the poor
    and extort a tribute of grain from them,
  though you have built houses of hewn stone,
    you will not live in them;
  though you have planted pleasant vineyards,
    you will not drink wine from them.
12 For I know how many are your crimes,
    how monstrous your sins:
  you bully the innocent, extort ransoms,
    and in court push the destitute out of the way.
13 In such a time, therefore, it is prudent to stay
        quiet,
    for it is an evil time.

14 Seek good, and not evil,
    that you may live,
  that the Lord, the God of Hosts, may be with you,
    as you claim he is.
15 Hate evil, and love good;
    establish justice in the courts;
  it may be that the Lord, the God of Hosts,
    will show favour to the survivors of Joseph.

16 Therefore these are the words of the Lord, the God of
Hosts.

  In all the public squares, there will be wailing,
    the sound of grief in every street.
  The farmer will be called to mourning,
    and wailing proclaimed to those skilled in the
        dirge;
17 there will be wailing in every vineyard;
    for I shall pass through your midst,
    says the Lord.

18 Woe betide those who long for the day of the
        Lord!
  What will the day of the Lord mean for you?
    It will be darkness, not light;
19 it will be as when someone runs from a lion,
    only to be confronted by a bear,
  or as when he enters his house
    and leans with his hand on the wall,
    only to be bitten by a snake.
20 The day of the Lord is indeed darkness, not light,
    a day of gloom without a ray of brightness.

21 I spurn with loathing your pilgrim-feasts;
    I take no pleasure in your sacred ceremonies.
22 When you bring me your whole-offerings and your
        grain-offerings
  I shall not accept them,
    nor pay heed to your shared-offerings of stall-fed
        beasts.
23 Spare me the sound of your songs;
    I shall not listen to the strumming of your lutes.
24 Instead let justice flow on like a river
    and righteousness like a never-failing torrent.
25 Did you, people of Israel, bring me sacrifices and
        offerings
    those forty years in the wilderness?
26 No! But now you will take up
    the shrine of your idol-king
  and the pedestals of your images,
    which you have made for yourselves,
27 and I shall drive you into exile beyond Damascus.

So says the Lord; the God of Hosts is his name.

5:22 **stall-fed beasts:** *or* buffaloes.   5:26 **the shrine . . . images:**
prob. rdg; Heb. adds the star of your gods; *or* Sakkuth your king and
Kaiwan your star-god, the images.

[n] Heb *your images, your star-god*

11 Therefore, because you have trampled upon
the weak
and exacted of them levies of grain,
Though you have built houses of hewn stone,
you shall not live in them!
Though you have planted choice vineyards,
you shall not drink their wine!
12 Yes, I know how many are your crimes,
how grievous your sins:
Oppressing the just, accepting bribes,
repelling the needy at the gate!
13 Therefore the prudent man is silent at this time,
for it is an evil time.
14 Seek good and not evil,
that you may live;
Then truly will the LORD, the God of hosts,
be with you as you claim!
15 Hate evil and love good,
and let justice prevail at the gate;
Then it may be that the LORD, the God of hosts,
will have pity on the remnant of Joseph.

16 Therefore, thus says the LORD,
the God of hosts, the Lord:
In every square there shall be lamentation,
and in every street they shall cry, Alas! Alas!
They shall summon the farmers to wail
and professional mourners to lament,
17 And in every vineyard there shall be lamentation
when I pass through your midst, says the LORD.

18 Woe to those who yearn for the day of the LORD!
What will this day of the LORD mean for you?
Darkness and not light!
19 As if a man were to flee from a lion,
and a bear should meet him;
Or as if on entering his house
he were to rest his hand against the wall,
and a snake should bite him.
20 Will not the day of the LORD be darkness and
not light,
gloom without any brightness?

21 I hate, I spurn your feasts,
I take no pleasure in your solemnities;
22 Your cereal offerings I will not accept,
nor consider your stall-fed peace offerings.
23 Away with your noisy songs!
I will not listen to the melodies of your harps.
But if you would offer me holocausts,
24   then let justice surge like water,
and goodness like an unfailing stream.
25 Did you bring me sacrifices and offerings
for forty years in the desert, O house of Israel?
26 You will carry away Sakkuth, your king,
and Kaiwan, your star god,
the images that you have made for yourselves;
27 For I will exile you beyond Damascus,
say I, the LORD, the God of hosts by name.

11 For trampling on the poor man
and for extorting levies on his wheat:
although you have built houses of dressed stone,
you will not live in them;
although you have planted pleasant vineyards,
you will not drink wine from them:
12 for I know how many your crimes are
and how outrageous your sins,
you oppressors of the upright, who hold people to
ransom
and thrust the poor aside at the gates.
13 That is why anyone prudent keeps silent now,
since the time is evil.
14 Seek good and not evil
so that you may survive,
and Yahweh, God Sabaoth, be with you
as you claim he is.
15 Hate evil, love good,
let justice reign at the city gate:
it may be that Yahweh, God Sabaoth,
will take pity on the remnant of Joseph.

16 Therefore Yahweh Sabaoth, the Lord, says this:
In every public square there will be lamentation,
in every street they will cry out, 'Alas! Alas!'
The farmer will be called on to mourn,
the professional mourners to lament,
17 and there will be wailing in every vineyard,
for I mean to pass through among you,
Yahweh says.

18 Disaster for you who long for the Day^e of
Yahweh!
What will the Day of Yahweh mean for you?
It will mean darkness, not light,
19 as when someone runs away from a lion,
only to meet a bear;
he goes into his house and puts his hand on the
wall,
only for a snake to bite him.
20 Will not the Day of Yahweh be darkness, not light,
totally dark, without a ray of light?

21 I hate, I scorn your festivals,
I take no pleasure in your solemn assemblies.
22 When you bring me burnt offerings . . .^f
your oblations, I do not accept them
and I do not look at your communion sacrifices of
fat cattle.
23 Spare me the din of your chanting,
let me hear none of your strumming on lyres,
24 but let justice flow like water,
and uprightness like a never-failing stream!
25 Did you bring me sacrifices and oblations
those forty years in the desert, House of Israel?
26 Now you must shoulder Sakkuth your king
and the star of your God, Kaiwan,
those idols you made for yourselves;
27 for I am about to drive you into captivity beyond
Damascus,
Yahweh says — God Sabaoth is his name.

e 5 A day of retribution, punishment of the wicked and vindication of
God's faithful people. It figures prominently in all the prophets.
f 5 A line seems to be missing here.

NEW REVISED STANDARD VERSION

6 Alas for those who are at ease in Zion,
and for those who feel secure on Mount
Samaria,
the notables of the first of the nations,
to whom the house of Israel resorts!
2 Cross over to Calneh, and see;
from there go to Hamath the great;
then go down to Gath of the Philistines.
Are you better*o* than these kingdoms?
Or is your*p* territory greater than their *q*
territory,
3 O you that put far away the evil day,
and bring near a reign of violence?

4 Alas for those who lie on beds of ivory,
and lounge on their couches,
and eat lambs from the flock,
and calves from the stall;
5 who sing idle songs to the sound of the harp,
and like David improvise on instruments of
music;
6 who drink wine from bowls,
and anoint themselves with the finest oils,
but are not grieved over the ruin of Joseph!
7 Therefore they shall now be the first to go into
exile,
and the revelry of the loungers shall pass away.

8 The Lord GOD has sworn by himself
(says the LORD, the God of hosts):
I abhor the pride of Jacob
and hate his strongholds;
and I will deliver up the city and all that is in
it.

9 If ten people remain in one house, they shall die.
10 And if a relative, one who burns the dead,*r* shall take up
the body to bring it out of the house, and shall say to
someone in the innermost parts of the house, "Is anyone
else with you?" the answer will come, "No." Then the
relative*s* shall say, "Hush! We must not mention the name
of the LORD."

11 See, the LORD commands,
and the great house shall be shattered to bits,
and the little house to pieces.
12 Do horses run on rocks?
Does one plow the sea with oxen?*t*
But you have turned justice into poison
and the fruit of righteousness into
wormwood —
13 you who rejoice in Lo-debar,*u*
who say, "Have we not by our own strength
taken Karnaim*v* for ourselves?"
14 Indeed, I am raising up against you a nation,
O house of Israel, says the LORD, the God of
hosts,
and they shall oppress you from Lebo-hamath
to the Wadi Arabah.

7 This is what the Lord GOD showed me: he was forming
locusts at the time the latter growth began to sprout (it
was the latter growth after the king's mowings). 2 When
they had finished eating the grass of the land, I said,
"O Lord GOD, forgive, I beg you!
How can Jacob stand?
He is so small!"
3 The LORD relented concerning this;
"It shall not be," said the LORD.

REVISED ENGLISH BIBLE

6 Woe betide those living at ease in Zion,
and those complacent on the hill of Samaria,
men of mark in the first of nations,
those to whom the people of Israel have recourse!
2 Go over and look at Calneh,
travel on to great Hamath,
then go down to Gath of the Philistines —
are they better than these kingdoms,
or is their territory greater than yours?
3 You thrust aside all thought of the evil day
and hasten the reign of violence.
4 You loll on beds inlaid with ivory
and lounge on your couches;
you feast on lambs from the flock
and stall-fed calves;
5 you improvise on the lute
and like David invent musical instruments,
6 you drink wine by the bowlful
and anoint yourselves with the richest of oils;
but at the ruin of Joseph you feel no grief.
7 Now, therefore, you will head the column of
exiles;
lounging and laughter will be at an end.

8 The Lord GOD has sworn by himself:
I abhor the arrogance of Jacob,
I detest his palaces;
I shall abandon the city and its people to their fate.

9 If ten are left in one house, they will die. 10 If a relative and
an embalmer take up a body to carry it out of the house for
burial, they will call to someone in a corner of the house,
'Any more there?' and he will answer, 'No'; then he will
add, 'Hush!' — for the name of the LORD must not be mentioned.

11 When the LORD commands,
great houses will be reduced to rubble
and the small houses shattered.

12 Can horses gallop over rocks?
Can the sea be ploughed with oxen?
Yet you have turned into venom the process of
law,
justice itself you have turned into poison.
13 Jubilant over a nothing, you boast,
'Have we not won power by our own strength?'
14 Israel, I am raising a nation against you,
and they will harry your land
from Lebo-hamath to the wadi of the Arabah.
This is the word of the LORD the God of Hosts.

7 THIS was what the Lord GOD showed me: it was a
swarm of locusts hatching when the later corn, which
comes after the king's early crop, was beginning to sprout.
2 As they devoured every trace of vegetation in the land, I
said, 'Lord GOD, forgive, I pray you. How can Jacob survive? He is so small.' 3 The LORD relented. 'This will not
happen,' he said.

---

o Or *Are they better* *p* Heb *their* *q* Heb *your* *r* Or *who makes
a burning for him* *s* Heb *he* *t* Or *Does one plow them with oxen*
u Or *in a thing of nothingness* *v* Or *horns*

6:8 **by himself:** *so Gk; Heb.* adds This is the word of the LORD the
God of Hosts.   6:13 **nothing . . . power:** *Heb.* Lo-debar . . .
Karnaim, *making a word-play on the two placenames.*

NEW AMERICAN BIBLE

NEW JERUSALEM BIBLE

6 Woe to the complacent in Zion,
To the overconfident on the mount of Samaria,
Leaders of a nation favored from the first,
to whom the people of Israel have recourse!
2 Pass over to Calneh and see,
go from there to Hamath the great,
and down to Gath of the Philistines!
Are you better than these kingdoms,
or is your territory wider than theirs?
3 You would put off the evil day,
yet you hasten the reign of violence!

4 Lying upon beds of ivory,
stretched comfortably on their couches,
They eat lambs taken from the flock,
and calves from the stall!
5 Improvising to the music of the harp,
like David, they devise their
own accompaniment.
6 They drink wine from bowls
and anoint themselves with the best oils;
yet they are not made ill by the collapse
of Joseph!
7 Therefore, now they shall be the first to go
into exile,
and their wanton revelry shall be done
away with.

8 The Lord GOD has sworn by his very self,
say I, the LORD, the God of hosts:
I abhor the pride of Jacob,
I hate his castles,
and I give over the city with everything in it;
9 Should there remain ten men
in a single house, these shall die.
10 Only a few shall be left
to carry the dead out of the houses;
If one says to a man inside a house,
"Is anyone with you?" and he answers,
"No one,"
Then he shall say, "Silence!"
for no one must mention the name of the LORD.
11 Indeed, the LORD has given the command
to shatter the great house to bits,
and reduce the small house to rubble.

12 Can horses run across a cliff?
or can one plow the sea with oxen?
Yet you have turned judgment into gall,
and the fruit of justice into wormwood.
13 You rejoice in Lodebar,
and say, "Have we not, by our own strength,
seized for ourselves Karnaim?"
14 Beware, I am raising up against you, O house
of Israel,
say I, the LORD, the God of hosts,
A nation that shall oppress you
from Labo of Hamath even to the Wadi Arabah.

7 This is what the Lord GOD showed me: He was forming a locust swarm when the late growth began to come
up (the late growth after the king's mowing). 2 While they
were eating all the grass in the land, I said:

Forgive, O Lord GOD!
How can Jacob stand?
He is so small!

3 And the LORD repented of this. "It shall not be," said the
Lord GOD.

6 Disaster for those so comfortable in Zion
and for those so confident on the hill of Samaria,
the notables of this first of nations,
those to whom the House of Israel has recourse!
2 Travel to Calneh and look,
go on from there to Hamath the great,
then go down to Gath⁸ in Philistia.
Are they more powerful than these kingdoms?
Is their territory larger than yours?
3 Thinking to defer the evil day,
you are hastening the reign of violence.

4 Lying on ivory beds
and sprawling on their divans,
they dine on lambs from the flock,
and stall-fattened veal;
5 they bawl to the sound of the lyre
and, like David, they invent musical instruments;
6 they drink wine by the bowlful,
and lard themselves with the finest oils,
but for the ruin of Joseph they care nothing.
7 That is why they will now go into captivity,
heading the column of captives.
The sprawlers' revelry is over.

8 Lord Yahweh has sworn by his own self
—declares Yahweh, God Sabaoth:
I detest the pride of Jacob,
I hate his palaces,
I shall hand over the city and all in it.
9 If ten people are left in a single house,
they will die
10 and a few will be left to carry
the bones from the house,
and they will say to anyone deep inside the house,
'Any more there?' and he will answer, 'No.'
Then he will say, 'Hush! —
Yahweh's name must not be mentioned.'
11 For look, Yahweh gives the command:
as he strikes, the great house falls to pieces
and the small house is in fragments.

12 Can horses gallop over rocks?
Can the sea be ploughed with oxen?
Yet you have changed justice into poison,
and the fruit of uprightness into wormwood,
13 while rejoicing over Lo-Debar
and saying, 'Wasn't it by our own strength
that we captured Karnaim?'
14 But look, House of Israel, against you
—declares Yahweh, God Sabaoth—
I am raising a nation to oppress you
from the Pass of Hamath to the Gorge of the
Arabah.

7 This is what Lord Yahweh showed me:
there was a swarm of locusts
when the second crop was sprouting,
full-grown locusts, after the king's hay had been
cut.
2 When they had eaten all the grass in the land,
I said, 'Lord Yahweh, forgive, I beg you.
How can Jacob survive, being so small?'
3 Then Yahweh relented;
'It will not happen,' said Yahweh.

⁸ 6 Calneh, Hamath and Gath were taken by Assyria in 738, 720,
711 BC respectively.

4 This is what the Lord GOD showed me: the Lord GOD was calling for a shower of fire, [w] and it devoured the great deep and was eating up the land. 5 Then I said,

"O Lord GOD, cease, I beg you!
How can Jacob stand?
He is so small!"

6 The LORD relented concerning this;
"This also shall not be," said the Lord GOD.

7 This is what he showed me: the Lord was standing beside a wall built with a plumb line, with a plumb line in his hand. 8 And the LORD said to me, "Amos, what do you see?" And I said, "A plumb line." Then the Lord said,

"See, I am setting a plumb line
in the midst of my people Israel;
I will never again pass them by;
9 the high places of Isaac shall be made desolate,
and the sanctuaries of Israel shall be laid
waste,
and I will rise against the house of Jeroboam
with the sword."

10 Then Amaziah, the priest of Bethel, sent to King Jeroboam of Israel, saying, "Amos has conspired against you in the very center of the house of Israel; the land is not able to bear all his words. 11 For thus Amos has said,

'Jeroboam shall die by the sword,
and Israel must go into exile
away from his land.' "

12 And Amaziah said to Amos, "O seer, go, flee away to the land of Judah, earn your bread there, and prophesy there; 13 but never again prophesy at Bethel, for it is the king's sanctuary, and it is a temple of the kingdom."

14 Then Amos answered Amaziah, "I am [x] no prophet, nor a prophet's son; but I am [x] a herdsman, and a dresser of sycamore trees, 15 and the LORD took me from following the flock, and the LORD said to me, 'Go, prophesy to my people Israel.'

16 "Now therefore hear the word of the LORD.
You say, 'Do not prophesy against Israel,
and do not preach against the house of Isaac.'
17 Therefore thus says the LORD:
'Your wife shall become a prostitute in the city,
and your sons and your daughters shall fall by
the sword,
and your land shall be parceled out by line;
you yourself shall die in an unclean land,
and Israel shall surely go into exile away from
its land.' "

8 This is what the Lord GOD showed me — a basket of summer fruit.[y] 2 He said, "Amos, what do you see?" And I said, "A basket of summer fruit."[y] Then the LORD said to me,

"The end [z] has come upon my people Israel;
I will never again pass them by.
3 The songs of the temple[a] shall become wailings
in that day,"
says the Lord GOD;
"the dead bodies shall be many,
cast out in every place. Be silent!"

4 Hear this, you that trample on the needy,
and bring to ruin the poor of the land,

4 This was what the Lord GOD showed me: the Lord GOD was summoning a flame of fire to devour the great abyss, and to devour the land. 5 I said, 'Lord GOD, cease, I pray you. How can Jacob survive? He is so small.' 6 The LORD relented. 'This also will not happen,' he said.

7 This was what the Lord showed me: there he was standing by a wall built with the aid of a plumb-line, and he had a plumb-line in his hand. 8 The LORD asked me, 'What do you see, Amos?' 'A plumb-line', I answered. Then the LORD said, 'I am setting a plumb-line in the midst of my people Israel; never again shall I pardon them. 9 The shrines of Isaac will be desolated and the sanctuaries of Israel laid waste; and sword in hand I shall rise against the house of Jeroboam.'

10 AMAZIAH, the priest of Bethel, reported to King Jeroboam of Israel: 'Amos has conspired against you here in the heart of Israel; the country cannot tolerate all his words. 11 This is what he is saying: "Jeroboam will die by the sword, and the Israelites will assuredly be deported from their native land." ' 12 To Amos himself Amaziah said, 'Seer, go away! Off with you to Judah! Earn your living and do your prophesying there. 13 But never prophesy again at Bethel, for this is the king's sanctuary, a royal shrine.' 14 'I was no prophet,' Amos replied to Amaziah, 'nor was I a prophet's son; I was a herdsman and fig-grower. 15 But the LORD took me as I followed the flock and it was the LORD who said to me, "Go and prophesy to my people Israel." 16 So now listen to the word of the LORD. You tell me I am not to prophesy against Israel or speak out against the people of Isaac. 17 Now these are the words of the LORD: Your wife will become a prostitute in the city, and your sons and daughters will fall by the sword. Your land will be parcelled out with a measuring line, you yourself will die in a heathen country, and Israel will be deported from their native land.'

8 THIS was what the Lord GOD showed me: it was a basket of summer fruit. 2 'What is that you are looking at, Amos?' he said. I answered, 'A basket of ripe summer fruit.' Then the LORD said to me, 'The time is ripe for my people Israel. Never again shall I pardon them. 3 On that day, says the Lord GOD, the palace songs will give way to lamentation: "So many corpses, flung out everywhere! Silence!" '

4 Listen to this, you that grind the poor and suppress the humble in the land 5 while you say, 'When will the new

---

7:4 **a flame of fire:** *prob. rdg; Heb.* to contend with fire.   7:14 **I was no:** *or* I am no. **nor was I:** *or* nor am I. **son:** *or* disciple. **I was a:** *or* I am a. **fig-grower:** *lit.* pricker of sycamore-figs.   8:2 **ripe summer . . . ripe for my people:** *a play on the Heb.* qais ('summer') *and* qes ('end').

[w] Or *for a judgment by fire*   [x] Or *was*   [y] Heb *qayits*   [z] Heb *qets*
[a] Or *palace*

NEW AMERICAN BIBLE

4 Then the Lord GOD showed me this: he called for a judgment by fire. It had devoured the great abyss, and was consuming the land, 5 when I said:

Cease, O Lord GOD!
How can Jacob stand?
He is so small!

6 The LORD repented of this. "This also shall not be," said the Lord GOD.

7 Then the Lord GOD showed me this: he was standing by a wall, plummet in hand. 8 The LORD asked me, "What do you see, Amos?" And when I answered, "A plummet," the LORD said:

See, I will lay the plummet
in the midst of my people Israel;
I will forgive them no longer.
9 The high places of Isaac shall be laid waste,
and the sanctuaries of Israel made desolate;
I will attack the house of Jeroboam with
the sword.

10 Amaziah, the priest of Bethel, sent word to Jeroboam, king of Israel: "Amos has conspired against you here within Israel; the country cannot endure all his words. 11 For this is what Amos says:

Jeroboam shall die by the sword,
and Israel shall surely be exiled from its land."

12 To Amos, Amaziah said: "Off with you, visionary, flee to the land of Judah! There earn your bread by prophesying, 13 but never again prophesy in Bethel; for it is the king's sanctuary and a royal temple." 14 Amos answered Amaziah, "I was no prophet, nor have I belonged to a company of prophets; I was a shepherd and a dresser of sycamores. 15 The LORD took me from following the flock, and said to me, Go, prophesy to my people Israel. 16 Now hear the word of the LORD!"

You say: prophesy not against Israel,
preach not against the house of Isaac.
17   Now thus says the LORD:
Your wife shall be made a harlot in the city,
and your sons and daughters shall fall by
the sword;
Your land shall be divided by measuring line,
and you yourself shall die in an unclean land;
Israel shall be exiled far from its land.

8 This is what the Lord GOD showed me: a basket of ripe fruit. 2 "What do you see, Amos?" he asked. I answered, "A basket of ripe fruit." Then the LORD said to me:

The time is ripe to have done with my
people Israel;
I will forgive them no longer.
3 The temple songs shall become wailings on
that day,
says the Lord GOD.
Many shall be the corpses,
strewn everywhere. — Silence!

4 Hear this, you who trample upon the needy
and destroy the poor of the land!

NEW JERUSALEM BIBLE

4 This is what Lord Yahweh showed me:
Lord Yahweh summoning fire in punishment;
it had devoured the great Abyss
and was encroaching on the land,
5 when I said, 'Lord Yahweh, stop, I beg you.
How can Jacob survive, being so small?'
6 Then Yahweh relented.
'This will not happen either,' said the Lord
Yahweh.

7 This is what he showed me:
the Lord standing by a wall,
with a plumb-line in his hand.
8 'What do you see, Amos?' Yahweh asked me.
'A plumb-line,' I said.
Then the Lord said,
'Look, I am going to put a plumb-line
in among my people Israel;
never again will I overlook their offences.
9 The high places of Isaac will be ruined
and the sanctuaries of Israel laid waste,
and, sword in hand, I will attack the House of
Jeroboam.'

10 Amaziah the priest of Bethel then sent word to Jeroboam king of Israel as follows, 'Amos is plotting against you in the heart of the House of Israel; the country cannot tolerate his speeches. 11 For this is what Amos says, "Jeroboam is going to die by the sword, and Israel will go into captivity far from its native land." ' 12 To Amos himself Amaziah said, 'Go away, seer, take yourself off to Judah, earn your living there, and there you can prophesy! 13 But never again will you prophesy at Bethel, for this is a royal sanctuary, a national temple.' 14 'I am not a prophet,' Amos replied to Amaziah, 'nor do I belong to a prophetic brotherhood. I am merely a herdsman and dresser of sycamore-figs. 15 But Yahweh took me as I followed the flock, and Yahweh said to me, "Go and prophesy to my people Israel." 16 So now listen to what Yahweh says:

"You say: Do not prophesy against Israel,
do not foretell doom on the House of Isaac!"
17 Very well, this is what Yahweh says,
"Your wife will become a prostitute in the streets,
your sons and daughters will fall by the sword,
your land will be parcelled out by measuring line,
and you yourself will die on polluted soil
and Israel will go into captivity far from its own
land!" '

8 This is what Lord Yahweh showed me:
A basket of ripe fruit.
2 'What do you see, Amos?' he asked.
'A basket of ripe fruit,' I said.
Then Yahweh said,
'The time is ripe for my people Israel;
I will not continue to overlook their offences.
3 That day, the palace songs will turn to howls,
—declares the Lord Yahweh—
the corpses will be many that are thrown down
everywhere.
Keep silent!'

4 Listen to this, you who crush the needy
and reduce the oppressed to nothing,

5 saying, "When will the new moon be over
     so that we may sell grain;
and the sabbath,
     so that we may offer wheat for sale?
We will make the ephah small and the shekel
          great,
     and practice deceit with false balances,
6 buying the poor for silver
     and the needy for a pair of sandals,
     and selling the sweepings of the wheat."

7 The Lord has sworn by the pride of Jacob:
     Surely I will never forget any of their deeds.
8 Shall not the land tremble on this account,
     and everyone mourn who lives in it,
and all of it rise like the Nile,
     and be tossed about and sink again, like the
          Nile of Egypt?

9 On that day, says the Lord God,
     I will make the sun go down at noon,
     and darken the earth in broad daylight.
10 I will turn your feasts into mourning,
     and all your songs into lamentation;
I will bring sackcloth on all loins,
     and baldness on every head;
I will make it like the mourning for an only son,
     and the end of it like a bitter day.

11 The time is surely coming, says the Lord God,
     when I will send a famine on the land;
not a famine of bread, or a thirst for water,
     but of hearing the words of the Lord.
12 They shall wander from sea to sea,
     and from north to east;
they shall run to and fro, seeking the word of the
          Lord,
     but they shall not find it.

13 In that day the beautiful young women and the
          young men
     shall faint for thirst.
14 Those who swear by Ashimah of Samaria,
     and say, "As your god lives, O Dan,"
and, "As the way of Beer-sheba lives" —
     they shall fall, and never rise again.

9 I saw the Lord standing beside[b] the altar, and he said:
     Strike the capitals until the thresholds shake,
          and shatter them on the heads of all the
               people;[c]
and those who are left I will kill with the sword;
     not one of them shall flee away,
     not one of them shall escape.

2 Though they dig into Sheol,
     from there shall my hand take them;
though they climb up to heaven,
     from there I will bring them down.
3 Though they hide themselves on the top of
          Carmel,
     from there I will search out and take them;
and though they hide from my sight at the bottom
          of the sea,
     there I will command the sea-serpent, and it
          shall bite them.

moon be over so that we may sell grain? When will the
sabbath be past so that we may expose our wheat for sale,
giving short measure in the bushel and taking overweight in
the silver, tilting the scales fraudulently, 6 and selling the
refuse of the wheat; that we may buy the weak for silver and
the poor for a pair of sandals?' 7 The Lord has sworn by the
arrogance of Jacob: I shall never forget any of those activities of theirs.

8 Will not the earth quake on account of this?
     Will not all who live on it mourn?
     The whole earth will surge and seethe like the Nile
          and subside like the river of Egypt.

9 On that day, says the Lord God,
     I shall make the sun go down at noon
          and darken the earth in broad daylight.
10 I shall turn your pilgrim-feasts into mourning
          and all your songs into lamentation.
I shall make you all put sackcloth round your
          waists
     and have everyone's head shaved.
I shall make it like mourning for an only son
     and the end of it like a bitter day.

11 The time is coming, says the Lord God,
     when I shall send famine on the land,
     not hunger for bread or thirst for water,
     but for hearing the word of the Lord.
12 People will stagger from sea to sea,
     they will range from north to east,
     in search of the word of the Lord,
     but they will not find it.
13 On that day fair maidens and young men
     will faint from thirst;
14 all who take their oath by Ashimah, goddess of
          Samaria,
     all who swear, 'As your god lives, Dan',
     and, 'By the sacred way to Beersheba',
     they all will fall to rise no more.

9 I saw the Lord standing by the altar, and he said:

Strike the capitals so that the whole porch is
          shaken;
     smash them down on the heads of the people,
and those who are left I shall put to the sword.
     No fugitive will escape,
     no survivor find safety.
2 Though they dig down to Sheol,
     from there my hand will take them;
though they climb up to the heavens,
     from there I shall bring them down.
3 If they hide on the summit of Carmel,
     there I shall hunt them out and take them;
if they conceal themselves from my sight in the
          depths of the sea,
     there at my command the sea serpent will bite
          them.

8:5 **bushel:** *Heb.* ephah.   8:14 **the sacred way to Beersheba:** or,
with Gk, the life of your god, Beersheba.   9:1 **those who are left:** or
their children.   9:2 **Sheol:** or the underworld.

[b] Or on   [c] Heb all of them

NEW AMERICAN BIBLE

5 "When will the new moon be over," you ask,
  "that we may sell our grain,
  and the sabbath, that we may display the wheat?
We will diminish the ephah,
  add to the shekel,
  and fix our scales for cheating!
6 We will buy the lowly man for silver,
  and the poor man for a pair of sandals;
  even the refuse of the wheat we will sell!"
7 The LORD has sworn by the pride of Jacob:
  Never will I forget a thing they have done!
8 Shall not the land tremble because of this,
  and all who dwell in it mourn,
While it rises up and tosses like the Nile,
  and settles back like the river of Egypt?

9 On that day, says the Lord GOD,
  I will make the sun set at midday
  and cover the earth with darkness in
    broad daylight.
10 I will turn your feasts into mourning
  and all your songs into lamentations.
I will cover the loins of all with sackcloth
  and make every head bald.
I will make them mourn as for an only son,
  and bring their day to bitter end.

11 Yes, days are coming, says the Lord GOD,
  when I will send famine upon the land:
Not a famine of bread, or thirst for water,
  but for hearing the word of the LORD.
12 Then shall they wander from sea to sea
  and rove from the north to the east
In search of the word of the LORD,
  but they shall not find it.

13 On that day, fair virgins and young men
  shall faint from thirst;
14 Those who swear by the shameful idol of Samaria,
  "By the life of your god, O Dan!"
"By the life of your love, O Beer-sheba!"
  those shall fall, never to rise again.

9 I saw the Lord standing beside the altar, and he said:

  Strike the bases, so that the doorjambs totter
    till you break them off on the heads of them all!
  Those who are left I will slay with the sword;
    not one shall flee,
    no survivor shall escape.
2 Though they break through to the nether world,
    even from there my hand shall bring them out;
  Though they climb to the heavens,
    I will bring them down;
3 Though they hide on the summit of Carmel,
    there too I will hunt them out and take
      them away;
  Though they hide from my gaze
    in the bottom of the sea,
    I will command the serpent there to bite them;

NEW JERUSALEM BIBLE

5 you who say, 'When will New Moon be over
  so that we can sell our corn,
  and Sabbath, so that we can market our wheat?
Then, we can make the bushel-measure smaller
  and the shekel-weight bigger,
  by fraudulently tampering with the scales.
6 We can buy up the weak for silver
  and the poor for a pair of sandals,h
  and even get a price for the sweepings of the
    wheat.'
7 Yahweh has sworn by the pride of Jacob,
  'Never will I forget anything they have done.'
8 Will not the earth tremble for this
  and all who live on it lament,
  as it all rises together like the Nile in Egypt,
  it swells and then subsides like the Egyptian
    Nile?i

9 'On that Day — declares the Lord Yahweh —
  I shall make the sun go down at noon
  and darken the earth in broad daylight.
10 I shall turn your festivals into mourning
  and all your singing into lamentation;
  I shall make you all wear sacking round your
    waists
  and have all your heads shaved.
I shall make it like the mourning for an only child,
  and it will end like the bitterest of days.

11 'The days are coming — declares the Lord
    Yahweh —
  when I shall send a famine on the country,
  not hunger for food, not thirst for water,
  but famine for hearing Yahweh's word.
12 People will stagger from sea to sea,
  will wander from the north to the east,
  searching for Yahweh's word,
  but will not find it.

13 'That Day, fine girls and stalwart youths
  will faint from thirst.
14 The people who swear by the Sinj of Samaria,
  who say, "Long live your god, Dan!"
  and "Hurrah for the pilgrimage to Beersheba!"
  will all fall, never to rise again.'

9 I saw the Lord standing by the altar, and he said,
  'Strike the top of the pillar so that the thresholds
    shake!
  Smash their heads in, one and all!
  And I shall put any survivors to the sword;
    whoever runs away will not run far,
    whoever escapes will not make good his escape.
2 Should they burrow into Sheol,
    my hand will haul them out;
  should they climb to heaven,
    I shall bring them down.
3 Should they hide on the top of Carmel,
    I shall track them down and catch them;
  should they hide from me on the sea bed,
    I shall order the Serpent there to bite them;

h8 = 2:6.   i8 = 9:5.   j8 The Hebr. word is 'ashemah, a pun on the name of the goddess Ashimah.

4 And though they go into captivity in front of their
enemies,
there I will command the sword, and it shall
kill them;
and I will fix my eyes on them
for harm and not for good.

5 The Lord, GOD of hosts,
he who touches the earth and it melts,
and all who live in it mourn,
and all of it rises like the Nile,
and sinks again, like the Nile of Egypt;
6 who builds his upper chambers in the heavens,
and founds his vault upon the earth;
who calls for the waters of the sea,
and pours them out upon the surface of the
earth—
the LORD is his name.

7 Are you not like the Ethiopians[d] to me,
O people of Israel? says the LORD.
Did I not bring Israel up from the land of Egypt,
and the Philistines from Caphtor and the
Arameans from Kir?
8 The eyes of the Lord GOD are upon the sinful
kingdom,
and I will destroy it from the face of the earth
—except that I will not utterly destroy the
house of Jacob,
says the LORD.

9 For lo, I will command,
and shake the house of Israel among all the
nations
as one shakes with a sieve,
but no pebble shall fall to the ground.
10 All the sinners of my people shall die by the
sword,
who say, "Evil shall not overtake or meet us."

11 On that day I will raise up
the booth of David that is fallen,
and repair its[e] breaches,
and raise up its[f] ruins,
and rebuild it as in the days of old;
12 in order that they may possess the remnant of
Edom
and all the nations who are called by my name,
says the LORD who does this.

13 The time is surely coming, says the LORD,
when the one who plows shall overtake the one
who reaps,
and the treader of grapes the one who sows the
seed;
the mountains shall drip sweet wine,
and all the hills shall flow with it.
14 I will restore the fortunes of my people Israel,
and they shall rebuild the ruined cities and
inhabit them;
they shall plant vineyards and drink their wine,
and they shall make gardens and eat their fruit.
15 I will plant them upon their land,
and they shall never again be plucked up
out of the land that I have given them,
says the LORD your God.

[d] Or Nubians; Heb Cushites   [e] Gk: Heb their   [f] Gk: Heb his

4 If they are herded off into captivity by their
enemies,
there I shall command the sword to slay them;
I shall fix my eye on them
for evil, and not for good.

5 The LORD the God of Hosts—
at his touch the earth heaves,
and all who live on it mourn,
while the whole earth surges like the Nile
and subsides like the river of Egypt;
6 he builds his upper chambers in the heavens
and arches the vault of the sky over the earth;
he summons the waters of the sea
and pours them over the earth—
his name is the LORD.

7 Are not you Israelites like the Cushites to me?
says the LORD.
Did I not bring Israel up from Egypt,
and the Philistines from Caphtor, the Aramaeans
from Kir?
8 Behold, I, the Lord GOD,
have my eyes on this sinful kingdom,
and I shall destroy it from the face of the earth.

YET I shall not totally destroy Jacob's posterity,
says the LORD.
9 No; I shall give the command,
and shake Israel among all the nations,
as a sieve is shaken to and fro
without one pebble falling to the ground.
10 They will die by the sword, all the sinners of my
people,
who say, 'You will not let disaster approach
or overtake us.'
11 On that day I shall restore
David's fallen house;
I shall repair its gaping walls and restore its ruins;
I shall rebuild it as it was long ago,
12 so that Israel may possess what is left of Edom
and of all the nations who were once named as
mine.

This is the word of the LORD, who will do this.

13 A time is coming, says the LORD,
when the ploughman will follow hard on the
reaper,
and he who treads the grapes after him who sows
the seed.
The mountains will run with fresh wine,
and every hill will flow with it.

14 I shall restore the fortunes of my people Israel;
they will rebuild their devastated cities and live in
them,
plant vineyards and drink the wine,
cultivate gardens and eat the fruit.
15 Once more I shall plant them on their own soil,
and never again will they be uprooted
from the soil I have given them.
It is the word of the LORD your God.

9:5 **mourn:** *or* wither.   9:6 **upper chambers in:** *prob. rdg; Heb.*
stair up to.   9:11 **house:** *lit.* booth.

NEW AMERICAN BIBLE

4 Though they are led into captivity by
their enemies,
there will I command the sword to slay them.
I will fix my gaze upon them
for evil, and not for good,
5 I, the Lord GOD of hosts.
I melt the earth with my touch,
so that all who dwell on it mourn,
While it all rises up like the Nile,
and settles back like the river of Egypt;
6 I have built heaven, my upper chamber,
and established my vault over the earth;
I summon the waters of the sea
and pour them out upon the surface of the earth,
I, the LORD by name.

7 Are you not like the Ethiopians to me,
O men of Israel, says the LORD?
Did I not bring the Israelites from the land
of Egypt
As I brought the Philistines from Caphtor
and the Arameans from Kir?
8 The eyes of the Lord GOD are on this
sinful kingdom:
I will destroy it from off the face of the earth.

But I will not destroy the house of
Jacob completely,
says the LORD.
9 For see, I have given the command
to sift the house of Israel among all the nations,
As one sifts with a sieve,
letting no pebble fall to the ground.
10 By the sword shall all sinners among my
people die,
those who say, "Evil will not reach or
overtake us."
11 On that day I will raise up
the fallen hut of David;
I will wall up its breaches,
raise up its ruins,
and rebuild it as in the days of old,
12 That they may conquer what is left of Edom
and all the nations that shall bear my name,
say I, the LORD, who will do this.
13 Yes, days are coming,
says the LORD,
When the plowman shall overtake the reaper,
and the vintager, him who sows the seed;
The juice of grapes shall drip down the mountains,
and all the hills shall run with it.
14 I will bring about the restoration of my
people Israel;
they shall rebuild and inhabit their ruined cities,
Plant vineyards and drink the wine,
set out gardens and eat the fruits.
15 I will plant them upon their own ground;
never again shall they be plucked
From the land I have given them,
say I, the LORD, your God.

NEW JERUSALEM BIBLE

4 if their enemies herd them into captivity,
I shall order the sword to kill them there,
and I shall fix my eyes on them
for evil and not for good.'
5 Lord Yahweh Sabaoth —
he touches the earth and it melts,
and all living things on it lament,
as all rises together like the Nile in Egypt
and then subsides like the Egyptian Nile. k
6 He who builds his mansions in the heavens,
supporting his vault on the earth;
who summons the waters of the sea
and pours them over the surface of the land:
Yahweh is his name. l

7 Are not you and the Cushites all the same to me,
children of Israel? — declares Yahweh.
Did I not bring Israel up from Egypt
and the Philistines from Caphtor, and the
Aramaeans from Kir?
8 Look, Lord Yahweh's eyes are on the sinful
kingdom,
I shall wipe it off the face of the earth,
although I shall not destroy the House of Jacob
completely
— declares Yahweh.
9 For look, I shall give the command
and shall shake out the House of Israel among all
nations
as a sieve is shaken out
without one grain falling on the ground.
10 All the sinners of my people will perish by the
sword, who say,
'Disaster will never approach or overtake us.'
11 m On that Day, I shall rebuild the tottering hut of
David,
make good the gaps in it, restore its ruins
and rebuild it as it was in the days of old,
12 for them to be master of what is left of Edom
and of all the nations once called mine
— Yahweh declares, and he will perform it.

13 The days are coming — declares Yahweh —
when the ploughman will tread on the heels of the
reaper,
and the treader of grapes on the heels of the sower
of seed,
and the mountains will run with new wine
and the hills all flow with it.
14 I shall restore the fortunes of my people Israel;
they will rebuild the ruined cities and live in them,
they will plant vineyards and drink their wine,
they will lay out gardens and eat their produce.
15 And I shall plant them in their own soil
and they will never be uprooted again
from the country which I have given them,
declares Yahweh, your God.

k 9 = 8:8.   l 9 = 5:8.   m 9 Vv. 11-15, the only hopeful passage in
Amos, were perhaps added later.

Obadiah

Obadiah

1 The vision of Obadiah.

Thus says the Lord GOD concerning Edom:
We have heard a report from the LORD,
and a messenger has been sent among the
nations:
"Rise up! Let us rise against it for battle!"
2 I will surely make you least among the nations;
you shall be utterly despised.
3 Your proud heart has deceived you,
you that live in the clefts of the rock,^a
whose dwelling is in the heights.
You say in your heart,
"Who will bring me down to the ground?"
4 Though you soar aloft like the eagle,
though your nest is set among the stars,
from there I will bring you down,
says the LORD.

5 If thieves came to you,
if plunderers by night
—how you have been destroyed!—
would they not steal only what they wanted?
If grape-gatherers came to you,
would they not leave gleanings?
6 How Esau has been pillaged,
his treasures searched out!
7 All your allies have deceived you,
they have driven you to the border;
your confederates have prevailed against you;
those who ate^b your bread have set a trap for
you—
there is no understanding of it.
8 On that day, says the LORD,
I will destroy the wise out of Edom,
and understanding out of Mount Esau.
9 Your warriors shall be shattered, O Teman,
so that everyone from Mount Esau will be cut
off.
10 For the slaughter and violence done to your
brother Jacob,
shame shall cover you,
and you shall be cut off forever.
11 On the day that you stood aside,
on the day that strangers carried off his wealth,
and foreigners entered his gates
and cast lots for Jerusalem,
you too were like one of them.
12 But you should not have gloated^c over^d your
brother
on the day of his misfortune;
you should not have rejoiced over the people of
Judah
on the day of their ruin;
you should not have boasted
on the day of distress.

THE vision of Obadiah: the words of the Lord GOD about
Edom.

While envoys were being dispatched among the
nations, saying,
'Up! Let us attack Edom,'
I heard this message from the LORD:
2 I shall make you the least of all nations,
an object of utter contempt.
3 The pride in your heart has led you astray,
you that haunt the crannies among the rocks
and make your home on the heights,
saying to yourself, 'Who can bring me to the
ground?'
4 Though you soar as high as an eagle
and your nest is set among the stars,
even from there I shall bring you down.
This is the word of the LORD.

5 If thieves or robbers were to come to you by night,
though your loss might be heavy,
they would take only enough for their needs;
if vintagers were to come to you,
would they not leave gleanings?
6 But see how Esau is ransacked,
their secret wealth hunted out!
7 All your former allies have pushed you to the
frontier,
your confederates have misled and subjugated you,
those who eat at your table lay a snare for your
feet.
Where is his wisdom now?
8 This is the word of the LORD: On that day
I shall destroy all the wise men of Edom
and leave no wisdom on the mountains of Esau.
9 Then your warriors, Teman, will be so
terror-stricken
that no survivors will be left on the mountains of
Esau.
10 For the violence done to your brother Jacob
you will be covered with shame and cut off for
ever.
11 On the day when you stood aloof,
while strangers carried off his wealth,
while foreigners passed through his gates
and shared out Jerusalem by lot,
you were at one with them.
12 Do not gloat over your brother when disaster
strikes him,
or rejoice over Judah on the day of his ruin.
Do not boast when he suffers distress,

---

^a Or clefts of Sela   ^b Cn: Heb lacks those who ate   ^c Heb But do
not gloat (and similarly through verse 14)   ^d Heb on the day of

1 **I heard:** prob. rdg, so Gk; Heb. we heard.

THE BOOK OF
Obadiah

Obadiah

¹ The vision of Obadiah.

[Thus says the LORD God:]
Of Edom we have heard a message from the LORD,
   and a herald has been sent among the nations:
   "Up! let us go to war against him!"

² See, I make you small among the nations;
   you are held in dire contempt.
³ The pride of your heart has deceived you:
   you who dwell in the clefts of the rock,
   whose abode is in the heights,
Who say in your heart,
   "Who will bring me down to earth?"
⁴ Though you go as high as the eagle,
   and your nest be set among the stars,
From there will I bring you down,
   says the LORD.
⁵ If thieves came to you, if robbers by night,
   how could you be thus destroyed:
   would they not steal merely till they
      had enough?
If vintagers came to you,
   would they not leave some gleanings?
⁶ How they search Esau,
   seek out his hiding places!
⁷ To the border they drive you —
   all your allies;
They deceive you, they overpower you —
   those at peace with you;
Those who eat your bread
   lay snares beneath you:
There is no understanding in him!
⁸ Shall I not, says the LORD, on that day
   make the wise men disappear from Edom,
   and understanding from the mount of Esau?
⁹ Your warriors, O Teman, shall be crushed,
   till all on Mount Esau are destroyed.

¹⁰ Because of violence to your brother Jacob,
   disgrace shall cover you
   and you shall be destroyed forever.
¹¹ On the day when you stood by,
   on the day when aliens carried off
      his possessions,
And strangers entered his gates
   and cast lots over Jerusalem,
   you too were one of them.
¹² Gaze not upon the day of your brother,
   the day of his disaster;
Exult not over the children of Judah
   on the day of their ruin;
Speak not haughtily
   on the day of distress!

Vision of Obadiah: about Edom.

^{1c} I have received a message from Yahweh,
   a herald has been sent throughout the nations:
   'Up! Let us march against this people.
   Into battle!'

^{1b} The Lord Yahweh says this:
² Look, I have reduced you to the smallest of
      nations,
   you are now beneath contempt.

³ Your proud heart has misled you,
   you whose home is in the crannies of the Rock,
   who make the heights your dwelling,
   who think to yourself,
   'Who can bring me down to earth?'
⁴ Though you soar like an eagle,
   though you set your nest among the stars,
   I shall bring you down from there! — declares
      Yahweh.^a

⁵ If thieves were to come to you
   (or robbers during the night)
   surely they would steal only as much as they
      wanted?
If grape-pickers were to come to you,
   surely they would leave a few gleanings?

But how you have been pillaged!
⁶ How Esau has been looted,
   his hidden treasures routed out!^b
⁷ Your allies all pursued you right to the frontier,
   your confederates kept you in suspense, then got
      the better of you,
   your own guests laid a trap for you,
   'He has quite lost his wits.'

⁸ When that day comes — declares Yahweh —
   shall I not eliminate sages from Edom
   and intelligence from Mount Esau?
⁹ Your warriors, Teman, will be so demoralised
   that the people of Mount Esau will be massacred
   to the last one.
For the slaughter, ¹⁰ for the violence
   done to your brother Jacob,
   shame will cover you
   and you will be annihilated for ever.

¹¹ On the day, when you stood aloof
   while strangers carried off his riches,
   while foreigners passed through his gate
   and cast lots for Jerusalem,
   you were as bad as the rest of them.

¹² Do not feast your eyes on your brother
   on the day of his misfortune.
Do not gloat over the children of Judah
   on the day of their ruin.
Do not play the braggart
   on the day of distress.

a // Jr 49:14–16.   *b* // Jr 49:9–10.

13 You should not have entered the gate of my
    people
  on the day of their calamity;
you should not have joined in the gloating over
    Judah's*e* disaster
  on the day of his calamity;
you should not have looted his goods
  on the day of his calamity.
14 You should not have stood at the crossings
    to cut off his fugitives;
you should not have handed over his survivors
  on the day of distress.

15 For the day of the LORD is near against all the
    nations.
  As you have done, it shall be done to you;
    your deeds shall return on your own head.
16 For as you have drunk on my holy mountain,
    all the nations around you shall drink;
  they shall drink and gulp down,*f*
    and shall be as though they had never been.
17 But on Mount Zion there shall be those that
    escape,
  and it shall be holy;
and the house of Jacob shall take possession of
    those who dispossessed them.
18 The house of Jacob shall be a fire,
    the house of Joseph a flame,
    and the house of Esau stubble;
  they shall burn them and consume them,
    and there shall be no survivor of the house of
    Esau;
                          for the LORD has spoken.
19 Those of the Negeb shall possess Mount Esau,
    and those of the Shephelah the land of the
    Philistines;
  they shall possess the land of Ephraim and the
    land of Samaria,
    and Benjamin shall possess Gilead.
20 The exiles of the Israelites who are in Halah*g*
    shall possess*h* Phoenicia as far as Zarephath;
  and the exiles of Jerusalem who are in Sepharad
    shall possess the towns of the Negeb.
21 Those who have been saved*i* shall go up to
    Mount Zion
  to rule Mount Esau;
    and the kingdom shall be the LORD's.

e Heb *his*   *f* Meaning of Heb uncertain   *g* Cn: Heb *in this army*
h Cn: Meaning of Heb uncertain   *i* Or *Saviors*

13 or enter my people's gates on the day of their
    calamity.
  Do not join in the gloating when calamity
    overtakes them,
  or seize their treasure on the day of their calamity.
14 Do not stand at the crossroads to cut down his
    fugitives,
  or betray the survivors on the day of distress.
15 The day of the LORD is at hand for all the nations.
  You will be treated as you have treated others:
    your deeds will recoil on your own head.

16 The draught you, my people, have drunk on my
    holy mountain
  all the nations will drink in turn;
    they will drink and gulp it down
    and be as though they had never been.

17 But on Mount Zion there will be a remnant
    which will be holy,
  and Jacob will dispossess those that dispossessed
    them.
18 Then the house of Jacob will be a fire,
    the house of Joseph a flame,
    and the house of Esau will be stubble;
  they will set it alight and burn it up,
    and the house of Esau will have no survivors.
  Those are the LORD's words.

19 My people will possess the Negeb, the mountains of
Esau, and the Shephelah of the Philistines; they will possess
the countryside of Ephraim and Samaria, and Benjamin will
possess Gilead. 20 Exiles from Israel will possess Canaan as
far as Zarephath, while exiles from Jerusalem who are in
Sepharad will possess the towns of the Negeb. 21 Those who
wield authority on Mount Zion will go up to hold sway over
the mountains of Esau, and dominion will belong to the
LORD.

20 **Exiles from:** *prob. rdg; Heb. adds* this army. **will possess
Canaan:** *prob. rdg; Heb.* which Canaan.

13 Enter not the gate of my people
on the day of their calamity;
Gaze not, you at least, upon his misfortune
on the day of his calamity;
Lay not hands upon his possessions
on the day of his calamity!
14 Stand not at the crossroads
to slay his refugees;
Betray not his fugitives
on the day of distress!
15 For near is the day of the LORD
for all the nations!
As you have done, so shall it be done to you,
your deed shall come back upon your own head:
16 As you have drunk upon my holy mountain,
so shall all the nations drink continually.
Yes, they shall drink and swallow,
and shall become as though they had not been.

17 But on Mount Zion there shall be a portion saved;
the mountain shall be holy,
And the house of Jacob shall take possession
of those that dispossessed them.
18 The house of Jacob shall be a fire,
and the house of Joseph a flame;
The house of Esau shall be stubble,
and they shall set them ablaze and devour them;
Then none shall survive of the house of Esau,
for the LORD has spoken.
19 They shall occupy the Negeb, the mount of Esau,
and the foothills of the Philistines;
And they shall occupy the lands of Ephraim
and the lands of Samaria,
and Benjamin shall occupy Gilead.
20 The captives of this host of the children of Israel
shall occupy the Canaanite land as far
as Zarephath,
And the captives of Jerusalem who are in Sepharad
shall occupy the cities of the Negeb.
21 And saviors shall ascent Mount Zion
to rule the mount of Esau,
and the kingship shall be the LORD's.

13 Do not enter my people's gate
on their day of calamity.
Do not, you especially, feast your eyes on their
suffering
on their day of calamity.
Do not touch their possessions
on their day of calamity.
14 Do not wait at the crossroads
to annihilate their fugitives.
Do not hand over their survivors
on the day of distress.
15 For the Day of Yahweh is near
for all the nations.
As you have done, so will it be done to you:
your deeds will recoil on your own head.
16 Just as you have drunk on my holy mountain,
so will all the nations drink continually,
they will drink, will drink greedily,
but they will be as though they had never been!

17 But on Mount Zion will be those who have
escaped
— it will be a sanctuary —
and the House of Jacob will recover
what is rightfully theirs.
18 Then the House of Jacob will be a fire,
the House of Joseph a flame,
and the House of Esau like stubble.
They will set it alight and burn it up,
and no one of the House of Esau will survive.
Yahweh has spoken.
19 People from the Negeb will occupy the Mount of
Esau,
people from the lowlands the country of the
Philistines;
they will occupy Ephraim and Samaria,
and Benjamin will occupy Gilead.
20 The exiles of this army, the sons of Israel,
will have the Canaanites' land as far as
Zarephthah,
while the exiles from Jerusalem now in Sepharad
will have the cities of the Negeb.
21 Victorious, they will climb Mount Zion
to rule over Mount Esau,
and sovereignty will be Yahweh's!

Jonah

1 Now the word of the LORD came to Jonah son of Amittai, saying, 2 "Go at once to Nineveh, that great city, and cry out against it; for their wickedness has come up before me." 3 But Jonah set out to flee to Tarshish from the presence of the LORD. He went down to Joppa and found a ship going to Tarshish; so he paid his fare and went on board, to go with them to Tarshish, away from the presence of the LORD.

4 But the LORD hurled a great wind upon the sea, and such a mighty storm came upon the sea that the ship threatened to break up. 5 Then the mariners were afraid, and each cried to his god. They threw the cargo that was in the ship into the sea, to lighten it for them. Jonah, meanwhile, had gone down into the hold of the ship and had lain down, and was fast asleep. 6 The captain came and said to him, "What are you doing sound asleep? Get up, call on your god! Perhaps the god will spare us a thought so that we do not perish."

7 The sailors*a* said to one another, "Come, let us cast lots, so that we may know on whose account this calamity has come upon us." So they cast lots, and the lot fell on Jonah. 8 Then they said to him, "Tell us why this calamity has come upon us. What is your occupation? Where do you come from? What is your country? And of what people are you?" 9 "I am a Hebrew," he replied. "I worship the LORD, the God of heaven, who made the sea and the dry land." 10 Then the men were even more afraid, and said to him, "What is this that you have done!" For the men knew that he was fleeing from the presence of the LORD, because he had told them so.

11 Then they said to him, "What shall we do to you, that the sea may quiet down for us?" For the sea was growing more and more tempestuous. 12 He said to them, "Pick me up and throw me into the sea; then the sea will quiet down for you; for I know it is because of me that this great storm has come upon you." 13 Nevertheless the men rowed hard to bring the ship back to land, but they could not, for the sea grew more and more stormy against them. 14 Then they cried out to the LORD, "Please, O LORD, we pray, do not let us perish on account of this man's life. Do not make us guilty of innocent blood; for you, O LORD, have done as it pleased you." 15 So they picked Jonah up and threw him into the sea; and the sea ceased from its raging. 16 Then the men feared the LORD even more, and they offered a sacrifice to the LORD and made vows.

17*b* But the LORD provided a large fish to swallow up Jonah; and Jonah was in the belly of the fish three days and three nights.

2 Then Jonah prayed to the LORD his God from the belly of the fish, 2 saying,

"I called to the LORD out of my distress,
  and he answered me;
out of the belly of Sheol I cried,
  and you heard my voice.
3 You cast me into the deep,
  into the heart of the seas,
  and the flood surrounded me;
all your waves and your billows
  passed over me.

Jonah

1 THE word of the LORD came to Jonah son of Amittai: 2 'Go to the great city of Nineveh; go and denounce it, for I am confronted by its wickedness.' 3 But to escape from the LORD Jonah set out for Tarshish. He went down to Joppa, where he found a ship bound for Tarshish. He paid the fare and went on board to travel with it to Tarshish out of the reach of the LORD.

4 The LORD let loose a hurricane on the sea, which rose so high that the ship threatened to break up in the storm. 5 The sailors were terror-stricken; everyone cried out to his own god for help, and they threw things overboard to lighten the ship. Meanwhile Jonah, who had gone below deck, was lying there fast asleep. 6 When the captain came upon him he said, 'What, fast asleep? Get up and call to your god! Perhaps he will spare a thought for us, and we shall not perish.'

7 The sailors said among themselves, 'Let us cast lots to find who is to blame for our misfortune.' They cast lots, and when Jonah was singled out 8 they wanted to be told how he was to blame. They questioned him: 'What is your business? Where do you come from? Which is your country? What is your nationality?' 9 'I am a Hebrew,' he answered, 'and I worship the LORD the God of heaven, who made both sea and dry land.' 10 At this the sailors were even more afraid. 'What is this you have done?' they said, because they knew he was trying to escape from the LORD, for he had told them. 11 'What must we do with you to make the sea calm for us?' they asked; for it was getting worse. 12 'Pick me up and throw me overboard,' he replied; 'then the sea will go down. I know it is my fault that this great storm has struck you.' 13 Though the crew rowed hard to put back to land it was no use, for the sea was running higher and higher. 14 At last they called to the LORD, 'Do not let us perish, LORD, for this man's life; do not hold us responsible for the death of an innocent man, for all this, LORD, is what you yourself have brought about.' 15 Then they took Jonah and threw him overboard, and the raging of the sea subsided. 16 Seized by a great fear of the LORD, the men offered a sacrifice and made vows to him.

17 The LORD ordained that a great fish should swallow Jonah, and he remained in its belly for three days and three nights.

2 From the fish's belly Jonah offered this prayer to the LORD his God:

2 'In my distress I called to the LORD,
  and he answered me;
from deep within Sheol I cried for help,
  and you heard my voice.
3 You cast me into the depths,
  into the heart of the ocean,
  and the flood closed around me;
all your surging waves swept over me.

a Heb *They*   *b* Ch 2.1 in Heb

THE BOOK OF

Jonah

1 This is the word of the LORD that came to Jonah, son of Amittai: 2 "Set out for the great city of Nineveh, and preach against it; their wickedness has come up before me." 3 But Jonah made ready to flee to Tarshish away from the LORD. He went down to Joppa, found a ship going to Tarshish, paid the fare, and went aboard to journey with them to Tarshish, away from the LORD.

4 The LORD, however, hurled a violent wind upon the sea, and in the furious tempest that arose the ship was on the point of breaking up. 5 Then the mariners became frightened and each one cried to his god. To lighten the ship for themselves, they threw its cargo into the sea. Meanwhile, Jonah had gone down into the hold of the ship, and lay there fast asleep. 6 The captain came to him and said, "What are you doing asleep? Rise up, call upon your God! Perhaps God will be mindful of us so that we may not perish."

7 Then they said to one another, "Come, let us cast lots to find out on whose account we have met with this misfortune." So they cast lots, and thus singled out Jonah. 8 "Tell us," they said, "what is your business? Where do you come from? What is your country, and to what people do you belong?" 9 "I am a Hebrew," Jonah answered them; "I worship the LORD, the God of heaven, who made the sea and the dry land."

10 Now the men were seized with great fear and said to him, "How could you do such a thing!" — They knew that he was fleeing from the LORD, because he had told them. — 11 "What shall we do with you," they asked, "that the sea may quiet down for us?" For the sea was growing more and more turbulent. 12 Jonah said to them, "Pick me up and throw me into the sea, that it may quiet down for you; since I know it is because of me that this violent storm has come upon you."

13 Still the men rowed hard to regain the land, but they could not, for the sea grew ever more turbulent. 14 Then they cried to the LORD: "We beseech you, O LORD, let us not perish for taking this man's life; do not charge us with shedding innocent blood, for you, LORD, have done as you saw fit." 15 Then they took Jonah and threw him into the sea, and the sea's raging abated. 16 Struck with great fear of the LORD, the men offered sacrifice and made vows to him.

2 But the LORD sent a large fish, that swallowed Jonah; and he remained in the belly of the fish three days and three nights. 2 From the belly of the fish Jonah said this prayer to the LORD, his God:

3 Out of my distress I called to the LORD,
  and he answered me;
From the midst of the nether world I cried
    for help,
  and you heard my voice.
4 For you cast me into the deep, into the heart of
    the sea,
  and the flood enveloped me;
All your breakers and your billows passed
    over me.

Jonah

1 The word of Yahweh was addressed to Jonah son of Amittai: 2 'Up!' he said, 'Go to Nineveh, the great city, and proclaim to them that their wickedness has forced itself upon me.' 3 Jonah set about running away from Yahweh, and going to Tarshish. He went down to Jaffa and found a ship bound for Tarshish; he paid his fare and boarded it, to go with them to Tarshish, to get away from Yahweh. 4 But Yahweh threw a hurricane at the sea, and there was such a great storm at sea that the ship threatened to break up. 5 The sailors took fright, and each of them called on his own god, and to lighten the ship they threw the cargo overboard. Jonah, however, had gone below, had lain down in the hold and was fast asleep, 6 when the boatswain went up to him and said, 'What do you mean by sleeping? Get up! Call on your god! Perhaps he will spare us a thought and not leave us to die.' 7 Then they said to each other, 'Come on, let us draw lots to find out who is to blame for bringing us this bad luck.' So they cast lots, and the lot pointed to Jonah. 8 Then they said to him, 'Tell us, what is your business? Where do you come from? What is your country? What is your nationality?' 9 He replied, 'I am a Hebrew, and I worship Yahweh, God of Heaven, who made both sea and dry land.' 10 The sailors were seized with terror at this and said, 'Why ever did you do this?' since they knew that he was trying to escape from Yahweh, because he had told them so. 11 They then said, 'What are we to do with you, to make the sea calm down for us?' For the sea was growing rougher and rougher. 12 He replied, 'Take me and throw me into the sea, and then it will calm down for you. I know it is my fault that this great storm has struck you.' 13 The sailors rowed hard in an effort to reach the shore, but in vain, since the sea was growing rougher and rougher. 14 So at last they called on Yahweh and said, 'O, Yahweh, do not let us perish for the sake of this man's life, and do not hold us responsible for causing an innocent man's death; for you, Yahweh, have acted as you saw fit.' 15 And taking hold of Jonah they threw him into the sea; and the sea stopped raging. 16 At this, the men were seized with dread of Yahweh; they offered a sacrifice to Yahweh and made vows to him.

2 Now Yahweh ordained that a great fish should swallow Jonah; and Jonah remained in the belly of the fish for three days and three nights. 2 From the belly of the fish, Jonah prayed*a* to Yahweh, his God; he said:

3 Out of my distress I cried to Yahweh
  and he answered me,
  from the belly of Sheol I cried out;
  you heard my voice!

4 For you threw me into the deep,
  into the heart of the seas,
  and the floods closed round me.
All your waves and billows passed over me;

---

a 2 The prayer is a later mosaic of psalms.

NEW REVISED STANDARD VERSION

4 Then I said, 'I am driven away
  from your sight;
 how^c shall I look again
  upon your holy temple?'
5 The waters closed in over me;
  the deep surrounded me;
 weeds were wrapped around my head
6 at the roots of the mountains.
I went down to the land
 whose bars closed upon me forever;
yet you brought up my life from the Pit,
 O Lord my God.
7 As my life was ebbing away,
 I remembered the Lord;
and my prayer came to you,
 into your holy temple.
8 Those who worship vain idols
 forsake their true loyalty.
9 But I with the voice of thanksgiving
 will sacrifice to you;
what I have vowed I will pay.
 Deliverance belongs to the Lord!"

10 Then the Lord spoke to the fish, and it spewed Jonah out upon the dry land.

3 The word of the Lord came to Jonah a second time, saying, 2"Get up, go to Nineveh, that great city, and proclaim to it the message that I tell you." 3 So Jonah set out and went to Nineveh, according to the word of the Lord. Now Nineveh was an exceedingly large city, a three days' walk across. 4 Jonah began to go into the city, going a day's walk. And he cried out, "Forty days more, and Nineveh shall be overthrown!" 5 And the people of Nineveh believed God; they proclaimed a fast, and everyone, great and small, put on sackcloth.

6 When the news reached the king of Nineveh, he rose from his throne, removed his robe, covered himself with sackcloth, and sat in ashes. 7 Then he had a proclamation made in Nineveh: "By the decree of the king and his nobles: No human being or animal, no herd or flock, shall taste anything. They shall not feed, nor shall they drink water. 8 Human beings and animals shall be covered with sackcloth, and they shall cry mightily to God. All shall turn from their evil ways and from the violence that is in their hands. 9 Who knows? God may relent and change his mind; he may turn from his fierce anger, so that we do not perish." 10 When God saw what they did, how they turned from their evil ways, God changed his mind about the calamity that he had said he would bring upon them; and he did not do it.

4 But this was very displeasing to Jonah, and he became angry. 2 He prayed to the Lord and said, "O Lord! Is not this what I said while I was still in my own country? That is why I fled to Tarshish at the beginning; for I knew that you are a gracious God and merciful, slow to anger, and abounding in steadfast love, and ready to relent from punishing. 3 And now, O Lord, please take my life from me, for it is better for me to die than to live." 4 And the Lord said, "Is it right for you to be angry?" 5 Then Jonah went out of the city and sat down east of the city, and made a booth for himself there. He sat under it in the shade, waiting to see what would become of the city.

6 The Lord God appointed a bush,^d and made it come up over Jonah, to give shade over his head, to save him from his discomfort; so Jonah was very happy about the bush. 7 But when dawn came up the next day, God appointed a worm that attacked the bush, so that it withered.

REVISED ENGLISH BIBLE

4 I thought I was banished from your sight
 and should never again look towards your holy
  temple.
5 'The water about me rose to my neck,
 for the deep was closing over me;
 seaweed twined about my head
6 at the roots of the mountains;
 I was sinking into a world
 whose bars would hold me fast for ever.
But you brought me up, Lord my God, alive from
 the pit.
7 As my senses failed I remembered the Lord,
 and my prayer reached you in your holy temple.
8 'Those who cling to false gods
 may abandon their loyalty,
9 but I with hymns of praise
 shall offer sacrifice to you;
what I have vowed I shall fulfil.
 Victory is the Lord's!'

10 The Lord commanded the fish, and it spewed Jonah out on the dry land.

3 A second time the word of the Lord came to Jonah: 2 'Go to the great city of Nineveh; go and denounce it in the words I give you.' 3 Jonah obeyed and went at once to Nineveh. It was a vast city, three days' journey across, 4 and Jonah began by going a day's journey into it. Then he proclaimed: 'In forty days Nineveh will be overthrown!'

5 The people of Nineveh took to heart this warning from God; they declared a public fast, and high and low alike put on sackcloth. 6 When the news reached the king of Nineveh he rose from his throne, laid aside his robes of state, covered himself with sackcloth, and sat in ashes. 7 He had this proclamation made in Nineveh: 'By decree of the king and his nobles, neither man nor beast is to touch any food; neither herd nor flock may eat or drink. 8 Every person and every animal is to be covered with sackcloth. Let all pray with fervour to God, and let them abandon their wicked ways and the injustice they practise. 9 It may be that God will relent and turn from his fierce anger: and so we shall not perish.' 10 When God saw what they did and how they gave up their wicked ways, he relented and did not inflict on them the punishment he had threatened.

4 This greatly displeased Jonah. In anger 2 he prayed to the Lord: 'It is just as I feared, Lord, when I was still in my own country, and it was to forestall this that I tried to escape to Tarshish. I knew that you are a gracious and compassionate God, long-suffering, ever constant, always ready to relent and not inflict punishment. 3 Now take away my life, Lord; I should be better dead than alive.' 4 'Are you right to be angry?' said the Lord.

5 Jonah went out and sat down to the east of Nineveh, where he made himself a shelter and sat in its shade, waiting to see what would happen in the city. 6 The Lord God ordained that a climbing gourd should grow up above Jonah's head to throw its shade over him and relieve his discomfort, and he was very glad of it. 7 But at dawn the next day God ordained that a worm should attack the gourd, and it withered; 8 and when the sun came up God ordained

---

^cTheodotion: Heb *surely*   ^dHeb *qiqayon*, possibly *the castor bean plant*

4:6 **a climbing gourd:** *or* a castor-oil plant.

NEW AMERICAN BIBLE

NEW JERUSALEM BIBLE

5 Then I said, "I am banished from your sight!
    yet would I again look upon your holy temple."
6 The waters swirled about me, threatening my life;
    the abyss enveloped me;
    seaweed clung about my head.
7 Down I went to the roots of the mountains;
    the bars of the nether world
    were closing behind me forever,
But you brought up my life from the pit,
    O LORD, my God.
8 When my soul fainted within me,
    I remembered the LORD;
My prayer reached you
    in your holy temple.
9 Those who worship vain idols
    forsake their source of mercy.
10 But I, with resounding praise,
    will sacrifice to you;
What I have vowed I will pay:
    deliverance is from the LORD.

11 Then the LORD commanded the fish to spew Jonah upon the shore.

3 The word of the LORD came to Jonah a second time: 2 "Set out for the great city of Nineveh, and announce to it the message that I will tell you." 3 So Jonah made ready and went to Nineveh, according to the LORD's bidding. Now Nineveh was an enormously large city; it took three days to go through it. 4 Jonah began his journey through the city, and had gone but a single day's walk announcing, "Forty days more and Nineveh shall be destroyed," 5 when the people of Nineveh believed God; they proclaimed a fast and all of them, great and small, put on sackcloth.

6 When the news reached the king of Nineveh, he rose from his throne, laid aside his robe, covered himself with sackcloth, and sat in the ashes. 7 Then he had this proclaimed throughout Nineveh, by decree of the king and his nobles: "Neither man nor beast, neither cattle nor sheep, shall taste anything; they shall not eat, nor shall they drink water. 8 Man and beast shall be covered with sackcloth and call loudly to God; every man shall turn from his evil way and from the violence he has in hand. 9 Who knows, God may relent and forgive, and withold his blazing wrath, so that we shall not perish." 10 When God saw by their actions how they turned from their evil way, he repented of the evil that he had threatened to do to them; he did not carry it out.

4 But this was greatly displeasing to Jonah, and he became angry. 2 "I beseech you, LORD," he prayed, "is not this what I said while I was still in my own country? This is why I fled at first to Tarshish. I knew that you are a gracious and merciful God, slow to anger, rich in clemency, loathe to punish. 3 And now, LORD, please take my life from me; for it is better for me to die than to live." 4 But the LORD asked, "Have you reason to be angry?"

5 Jonah then left the city for a place to the east of it, where he built himself a hut and waited under it in the shade, to see what would happen to the city. 6 And when the LORD God provided a gourd plant, that grew up over Jonah's head, giving shade that relieved him of any discomfort, Jonah was very happy over the plant. 7 But the next morning at dawn God sent a worm which attacked the plant, so that it withered. 8 And when the sun arose, God sent a burning

5 then I thought, 'I am banished from your sight;
    how shall I ever see your holy Temple again?'
6 The waters round me rose to my neck,
    the deep was closing round me,
    seaweed twining round my head.
7 To the roots of the mountains,
    I sank into the underworld,
    and its bars closed round me for ever.

But you raised my life from the Pit,
    Yahweh my God!
8 When my soul was growing ever weaker,
    Yahweh, I remembered you,
and my prayer reached you
    in your holy Temple.

9 Some abandon their faithful love
    by worshipping false gods,
10 but I shall sacrifice to you
    with songs of praise.
The vow I have made I shall fulfil!
    Salvation comes from Yahweh!

11 Yahweh spoke to the fish, which then vomited Jonah onto the dry land.

3 The word of Yahweh was addressed to Jonah a second time. 2 'Up!' he said, 'Go to Nineveh, the great city, and preach to it as I shall tell you.' 3 Jonah set out and went to Nineveh in obedience to the word of Yahweh. Now Nineveh was a city great beyond compare; to cross it took three days. 4 Jonah began by going a day's journey into the city and then proclaimed, 'Only forty days more and Nineveh will be overthrown.' 5 And the people of Nineveh believed in God; they proclaimed a fast and put on sackcloth, from the greatest to the least. 6 When the news reached the king of Nineveh, he rose from his throne, took off his robe, put on sackcloth and sat down in ashes. 7 He then had it proclaimed throughout Nineveh, by decree of the king and his nobles, as follows: 'No person or animal, herd or flock, may eat anything; they may not graze, they may not drink any water. 8 All must put on sackcloth and call on God with all their might; and let everyone renounce his evil ways and violent behaviour. 9 Who knows? Perhaps God will change his mind and relent and renounce his burning wrath, so that we shall not perish.' 10 God saw their efforts to renounce their evil ways. And God relented about the disaster which he had threatened to bring on them, and did not bring it.

4 This made Jonah very indignant; he fell into a rage. 2 He prayed to Yahweh and said, 'Please, Yahweh, isn't this what I said would happen when I was still in my own country? That was why I first tried to flee to Tarshish, since I knew you were a tender, compassionate God, slow to anger, rich in faithful love, who relents about inflicting disaster. 3 So now, Yahweh, please take my life, for I might as well be dead as go on living.' 4 Yahweh replied, 'Are you right to be angry?'

5 Jonah then left the city and sat down to the east of the city. There he made himself a shelter and sat under it in the shade, to see what would happen to the city. 6 Yahweh God then ordained that a castor-oil plant should grow up over Jonah to give shade for his head and soothe his ill-humour; Jonah was delighted with the castor-oil plant. 7 But at dawn the next day, God ordained that a worm should attack the castor-oil plant — and it withered. 8 Next, when the sun

NEW REVISED STANDARD VERSION

8 When the sun rose, God prepared a sultry east wind, and the sun beat down on the head of Jonah so that he was faint and asked that he might die. He said, "It is better for me to die than to live."

9 But God said to Jonah, "Is it right for you to be angry about the bush?" And he said, "Yes, angry enough to die." 10 Then the LORD said, "You are concerned about the bush, for which you did not labor and which you did not grow; it came into being in a night and perished in a night. 11 And should I not be concerned about Nineveh, that great city, in which there are more than a hundred and twenty thousand persons who do not know their right hand from their left, and also many animals?"

REVISED ENGLISH BIBLE

that a scorching wind should blow from the east. The sun beat down on Jonah's head till he grew faint, and he prayed for death; 'I should be better dead than alive,' he said. 9 At this God asked, 'Are you right to be angry over the gourd?' 'Yes,' Jonah replied, 'mortally angry!' 10 But the LORD said, 'You are sorry about the gourd, though you did not have the trouble of growing it, a plant which came up one night and died the next. 11 And should not I be sorry about the great city of Nineveh, with its hundred and twenty thousand people who cannot tell their right hand from their left, as well as cattle without number?'

east wind; and the sun beat upon Jonah's head till he became faint. Then he asked for death, saying, "I would be better off dead than alive."

⁹But God said to Jonah, "Have you reason to be angry over the plant?" "I have reason to be angry," Jonah answered, "angry enough to die." ¹⁰Then the LORD said, "You are concerned over the plant which cost you no labor and which you did not raise; it came up in one night and in one night it perished. ¹¹And should I not be concerned over Nineveh, the great city, in which there are more than a hundred and twenty thousand persons who cannot distinguish their right hand from their left, not to mention the many cattle?"

rose, God ordained that there should be a scorching east wind; the sun beat down so hard on Jonah's head that he was overcome and begged for death, saying, 'I might as well be dead as go on living.' ⁹God said to Jonah, 'Are you right to be angry about the castor-oil plant?' He replied, 'I have every right to be angry, mortally angry!' ¹⁰Yahweh replied, 'You are concerned for the castor-oil plant which has not cost you any effort and which you did not grow, which came up in a night and has perished in a night. ¹¹So why should I not be concerned for Nineveh, the great city, in which there are more than a hundred and twenty thousand people who cannot tell their right hand from their left, to say nothing of all the animals?'

Micah

1 The word of the LORD that came to Micah of Moresheth in the days of Kings Jotham, Ahaz, and Hezekiah
of Judah, which he saw concerning Samaria and Jerusalem.

2 Hear, you peoples, all of you;
    listen, O earth, and all that is in it;
and let the Lord GOD be a witness against you,
    the Lord from his holy temple.
3 For lo, the LORD is coming out of his place,
    and will come down and tread upon the high
        places of the earth.
4 Then the mountains will melt under him
    and the valleys will burst open,
like wax near the fire,
    like waters poured down a steep place.
5 All this is for the transgression of Jacob
    and for the sins of the house of Israel.
What is the transgression of Jacob?
    Is it not Samaria?
And what is the high place*a* of Judah?
    Is it not Jerusalem?
6 Therefore I will make Samaria a heap in the open
       country,
    a place for planting vineyards.
I will pour down her stones into the valley,
    and uncover her foundations.
7 All her images shall be beaten to pieces,
    all her wages shall be burned with fire,
    and all her idols I will lay waste;
for as the wages of a prostitute she gathered
       them,
    and as the wages of a prostitute they shall
       again be used.

8 For this I will lament and wail;
    I will go barefoot and naked;
I will make lamentation like the jackals,
    and mourning like the ostriches.
9 For her wound*b* is incurable.
    It has come to Judah;
it has reached to the gate of my people,
    to Jerusalem.

10 Tell it not in Gath,
    weep not at all;
in Beth-leaphrah
    roll yourselves in the dust.
11 Pass on your way,
    inhabitants of Shaphir,
    in nakedness and shame;
the inhabitants of Zaanan
    do not come forth;
Beth-ezel is wailing
    and shall remove its support from you.
12 For the inhabitants of Maroth
    wait anxiously for good,
yet disaster has come down from the LORD
    to the gate of Jerusalem.

Micah

1 THE word of the LORD which came to Micah of Moresheth during the reigns of Jotham, Ahaz, and Hezekiah, kings of Judah; he received it in visions about Samaria
and Jerusalem.

2 LISTEN, all you peoples;
    let the earth and all who are in it give heed,
    so that the Lord GOD, the Lord from his holy
       temple,
    may bear witness among you.
3 Even now, the LORD is leaving his dwelling-place;
    he comes down and walks on the heights of the
       earth.
4 At his touch mountains dissolve
    like wax before fire;
valleys are torn open
    as when torrents pour down a hillside:
5 all this for Jacob's crime and Israel's sin.
    What is the crime of Jacob? Is it not Samaria?
    What is the sin of Judah? Is it not Jerusalem?
6 I shall reduce Samaria to a ruin in the open
       country,
    a place for planting vines;
I shall hurl her stones into the valley
    and lay bare her foundations.
7 All her carved figures will be smashed,
    all her images burnt with fire;
I shall reduce all her idols to rubble.
    She amassed them out of earnings for prostitution,
    and a prostitute's hire will they become once more.

8 That is why I lament and wail,
    despoiled and naked;
I howl like a wolf, mourn like a desert-owl.
9 Israel has suffered a deadly blow,
    and now it has fallen on Judah;
it has reached the very gate of my people,
    even Jerusalem itself.
10 Will you not tell it in Gath?
    Will you not weep bitterly?
    In Beth-aphrah sprinkle yourselves with dust.
11 Take to the road, you that dwell in Shaphir!
    Have not the people of Zaanan gone out
    in shame from their city?
Beth-ezel is a place of lamentation;
    she can lend you support no longer.
12 The people of Maroth are in the depths of despair,
    for disaster from the LORD has come down
    to the very gate of Jerusalem.

1:5 **sin of Judah:** *prob. rdg, so Gk; Heb.* shrines of Judah.
1:10 **Beth-aphrah:** *so Lat.; Heb.* Beth-le-aphrah.   1:11 **from
their city:** *prob. rdg, cp. Gk; Heb.* nakedness.

a Heb *what are the high places*   *b* Gk Syr Vg: Heb *wounds*

THE BOOK OF
Micah

1 The word of the LORD which came to Micah of Moresheth in the days of Jotham, Ahaz, and Hezekiah, kings of Judah: that is, the vision he received concerning Samaria and Jerusalem.

2 Hear, O peoples, all of you,
　　give heed, O earth, and all that fills you!
Let the LORD GOD be witness against you,
　　the LORD from his holy temple!
3 For see, the LORD comes forth from his place,
　　he descends and treads upon the heights of
　　　　the earth.
4 The mountains melt under him
　　and the valleys split open,
Like wax before the fire,
　　like water poured down a slope.

5 For the crime of Jacob all this comes to pass,
　　and for the sins of the house of Israel.
What is the crime of Jacob?
　　Is it not Samaria?
And what is the sin of the house of Judah?
　　Is it not Jerusalem?
6 I will make Samaria a stone heap in the field,
　　a place to plant for vineyards;
I will throw down into the valley her stones,
　　and lay bare her foundations.
7 All her idols shall be broken to pieces,
　　all her wages shall be burned in the fire,
　　and all her statues I will destroy.
As the wages of a harlot they were gathered,
　　and to the wages of a harlot shall they return.

8 For this reason I lament and wail,
　　I go barefoot and naked;
I utter lamentation like the jackals,
　　and mourning like the ostriches.
9 There is no remedy for the blow she has
　　　　been struck;
　　rather, it has come even to Judah,
It reaches to the gate of my people,
　　even to Jerusalem.
10 Publish it not in Gath,
　　weep not at all;
In Beth-leaphrah
　　roll in the dust.
11 Pass by,
　　you who dwell in Shaphir!
The inhabitants of Zaanan
　　come not forth from their city.
The lamentation of Beth-ezel
　　finds in you its grounds.
12 How can the inhabitants of Maroth
　　hope for good?
For evil has come down from the LORD
　　to the gate of Jerusalem.

Micah

1 The word of Yahweh which came to Micah of Moresheth during the reigns of Jotham, Ahaz and Hezekiah kings of Judah. His visions about Samaria and Jerusalem.

2 Listen, all you peoples,
　　attend, earth and everyone on it!
Yahweh intends to give evidence against you,
　　the Lord, from his holy temple.
3 For look, Yahweh is leaving his home,
　　down he comes, he treads the heights of earth.
4 Beneath him, the mountains melt,
　　and valleys are torn open,
like wax near a fire,
　　like water pouring down a slope.

5 All this is because of the crime of Jacob,
　　the sin of the House of Israel.
What is the crime of Jacob?
　　Is it not Samaria?
What is the sin of the House of Judah?
　　Is it not Jerusalem?
6 So I shall make Samaria a ruin in the open
　　　　country,
　　a place for planting vines.
I shall send her stones rolling into the valley,
　　until I have laid her foundations bare.
7 All her images will be shattered,
　　all her earnings consumed by fire.
I shall leave all her idols derelict—
　　they were amassed out of prostitutes' earnings
　　and prostitutes' earnings once more they will be.

8 This is why I shall howl and wail,
　　why I shall go barefoot and naked,
why I shall howl like the jackals,
　　why I shall shriek like the owls;
9 for there is no cure for the wounds that Yahweh
　　　　inflicts:
　　the blow falls on Judah,
it falls on the gateway of my people,
　　on Jerusalem itself.
10 *Do not announce it in Gath,*[a]
　　in . . .[b] shed no tears!
In Beth-Leaphrah
　　roll in the dust!
11 Sound the horn,
　　inhabitant of Shaphir!
She has not left her city,
　　she who lives in Zaanan.
Beth-Ezel is torn from its foundations,
　　from its strong supports.
12 What hope has she of happiness,
　　she who lives in Maroth?
Instead Yahweh sent down disaster
　　on the gateway of Jerusalem itself!

---

[a] 1 2 S 1:20. The predictions pun on the names of the towns, e.g. Shaphir and *shophar* = horn.   [b] 1 Only one letter is left of this place-name.

13 Harness the steeds to the chariots,
    inhabitants of Lachish;
it was the beginning of sin
    to daughter Zion,
for in you were found
    the transgressions of Israel.
14 Therefore you shall give parting gifts
    to Moresheth-gath;
the houses of Achzib shall be a deception
    to the kings of Israel.
15 I will again bring a conqueror upon you,
    inhabitants of Mareshah;
the glory of Israel
    shall come to Adullam.
16 Make yourselves bald and cut off your hair
    for your pampered children;
make yourselves as bald as the eagle,
    for they have gone from you into exile.

2   Alas for those who devise wickedness
    and evil deeds[c] on their beds!
When the morning dawns, they perform it,
    because it is in their power.
2 They covet fields, and seize them;
    houses, and take them away;
they oppress householder and house,
    people and their inheritance.
3 Therefore thus says the LORD:
Now, I am devising against this family an evil
    from which you cannot remove your necks;
and you shall not walk haughtily,
    for it will be an evil time.
4 On that day they shall take up a taunt song
    against you,
and wail with bitter lamentation,
and say, "We are utterly ruined;
    the LORD[d] alters the inheritance of my people;
how he removes it from me!
    Among our captors[e] he parcels out our fields."
5 Therefore you will have no one to cast the line
    by lot
    in the assembly of the LORD.

6 "Do not preach"—thus they preach—
    "one should not preach of such things;
    disgrace will not overtake us."
7 Should this be said, O house of Jacob?
    Is the LORD's patience exhausted?
    Are these his doings?
Do not my words do good
    to one who walks uprightly?
8 But you rise up against my people[f] as an enemy;
    you strip the robe from the peaceful,[g]
from those who pass by trustingly
    with no thought of war.
9 The women of my people you drive out
    from their pleasant houses;
from their young children you take away
    my glory forever.
10 Arise and go;
    for this is no place to rest,
because of uncleanness that destroys
    with a grievous destruction.[h]

13 You people of Lachish,
    who first led the daughter of Zion into sin,
harness the steeds to the chariots;
    in you the crimes of Israel are to be found.
14 Therefore you must give parting gifts to
    Moresheth-gath.
Beth-achzib has betrayed the kings of Israel.
15 And you too, people of Mareshah,
    I shall send others to take your place;
    and the glory of Israel will be hidden in Adullam.
16 Shave the hair from your head in mourning
    for the children who were your delight;
make yourself bald as a vulture,
    for they have gone away from you into exile.

2   Woe betide those who lie in bed
    planning evil and wicked deeds,
and rise at daybreak to do them,
    knowing that they have the power to do evil!
2 They covet fields and take them by force;
    if they want a house they seize it;
they lay hands on both householder and house,
    on a man and all he possesses.
3 Therefore these are the words of the LORD:

I am planning disaster for this nation,
    a yoke which you cannot remove from your necks;
you will not walk haughtily,
    for the hour of disaster will have come.

4 On that day there will be heard this verse about
    you,
this sorrowful lamentation:
'We are utterly despoiled,
    for our people's land changes hands.
It is taken away from us;
    our fields are parcelled out to renegades.'
5 Therefore there will be no one to allot you
    any share in the LORD's assembly.

6 'Do not hold forth,' they say, holding forth
    themselves.
But do not they hold forth about these things?
Do not they spin words?

7 House of Jacob, can one ask,
    'Is the LORD's patience truly at an end?
    Are these his deeds?
Does good not come of his words?
    Is he not with those who are upright?'
8 But you are not my people;
    you rise up as my enemy to my face,
to strip the cloaks from travellers who felt safe
    or from men returning from the battle,
9 to drive the women of my people from their
    pleasant homes,
and rob their children of my glory for ever.
10 Up and be gone! This is no resting-place for you;
    to defile yourselves you would commit any
    mischief however cruel.

---

[c] Cn: Heb *work evil*   [d] Heb *he*   [e] Cn: Heb *the rebellious*
[f] Cn: Heb *But yesterday my people rose*   [g] Cn: Heb *from before a garment*   [h] Meaning of Heb uncertain

1:14 **Beth-achzib has:** *prob. rdg; Heb.* The houses of Achzib have.
2:7 **his words:** *so Gk; Heb.* my words.   2:8 **But you are not:**
prob. rdg; Heb. But yesterday. **my face:** *prob. rdg; Heb.* omits my.

13 Harness steeds to the chariots,
  O inhabitants of Lachish;
Lachish, the beginning of sin
  for daughter Zion,
Because there were in you
  the crimes of Israel.
14 Therefore you shall give parting gifts
  to Moresheth-gath;
Beth-achzib is a deception
  to the kings of Israel.
15 Yet must I bring to you the conqueror,
  O inhabitants of Mareshah;
Even to Adullam shall go
  the glory of Israel.

16 Make yourself bald, pluck out your hair,
  for the children whom you cherish;
Let your baldness be as the eagle's,
  because they are exiled from you.

2 Woe to those who plan iniquity,
  and work out evil on their couches;
In the morning light they accomplish it
  when it lies within their power.
2 They covet fields, and seize them;
  houses, and they take them;
They cheat an owner of his house,
  a man of his inheritance.
3   Therefore thus says the LORD:
Behold, I am planning against this race an evil
  from which you shall not withdraw your necks;
Nor shall you walk with head high,
  for it will be a time of evil.

4 On that day a satire shall be sung over you,
  and there shall be a plaintive chant:
"Our ruin is complete,
  our fields are portioned out among our captors,
The fields of my people are measured out,
  and no one can get them back!"
5 Thus you shall have no one
  to mark out boundaries by lot
  in the assembly of the LORD.

6 "Preach not," they preach,
  "let them not preach of these things!"
The shame will not withdraw.
7 How can it be said, O house of Jacob,
  "Is the LORD short of patience,
  or are such his deeds?"
Do not my words promise good
  to him who walks uprightly?

8 But of late my people has risen up as an enemy:
  you have stripped off the mantle covering
    the tunic
Of those who go their way in confidence,
  as though it were spoils of war.
9 The women of my people you drive out
  from their pleasant houses;
From their children you take away
  forever the honor I gave them.
10 "Up! Be off,
  this is no place to rest";
For any trifle you exact
  a crippling pledge.

13 Harness the horse to the chariot,
  you inhabitant of Lachish!
That is where the sin of the daughter of Zion
    began;
  the crimes of Israel can be traced to you!
14 And so you must provide a dowry
  for Moresheth-Gath.
Beth-Achzib will prove a disappointment
  for the kings of Israel.
15 The plunderer will come to you again,
  you citizen of Mareshah!
And into Adullam will vanish
  the glory of Israel.

16 Off with your hair, shave your head,
  for the children that were your joy.
Make yourselves bald like the vulture,
  for they have left you for exile.

2 Disaster for those who plot evil,
  who lie in bed planning mischief!
No sooner is it dawn than they do it,
  since they have the power to do so.
2 Seizing the fields that they covet,
  they take over houses as well,
  owner and house they seize alike,
  the man himself as well as his inheritance.
3 So Yahweh says this:
Look, I am now plotting
  a disaster for this breed
from which you will not extricate your necks;
  you will not hold your heads up then,
  for the times will be disastrous indeed.
4 That day they will make a satire on you,
  they will strike up a dirge and say,
'We have been stripped of everything;
  my people's land has been divided up,
  no one else can restore it to them,
  our fields have been awarded to our despoiler.'
5 Because of this, you will have no one
  to measure out a share
  in Yahweh's community.

6 'Do not drivel,' they drivel,
  'do not drivel like this!
Disgrace will not overtake us!
7 'Can the House of Jacob be accursed?
Has Yahweh grown short-tempered?
Is that his way of going to work?
His prophecies can only be favourable
  for his people Israel!'
8 But you are the ones who play the enemy
  to my people.
From the inoffensive man you snatch his cloak,
  on those who feel safe you inflict the damage of
    war.
9 My people's women you evict
  from the homes they love,
  and deprive the children
  of my glory for ever,
10 saying, 'Up and off with you! You can't stay
    here!'
For a worthless thing you exact
  an extortionate pledge.

2, 6f: The words in quotation marks are the protestations of the
people against the prophet's predictions of doom.

NEW REVISED STANDARD VERSION

11 If someone were to go about uttering empty
     falsehoods,
   saying, "I will preach to you of wine and
     strong drink,"
   such a one would be the preacher for this
     people!

12 I will surely gather all of you, O Jacob,
   I will gather the survivors of Israel;
   I will set them together
     like sheep in a fold,
   like a flock in its pasture;
     it will resound with people.

13 The one who breaks out will go up before them;
   they will break through and pass the gate,
     going out by it.
   Their king will pass on before them,
     the LORD at their head.

3 And I said:
   Listen, you heads of Jacob
     and rulers of the house of Israel!
   Should you not know justice? —
2   you who hate the good and love the evil,
   who tear the skin off my people,[i]
     and the flesh off their bones;
3 who eat the flesh of my people,
     flay their skin off them,
   break their bones in pieces,
     and chop them up like meat[j] in a kettle,
     like flesh in a caldron.

4 Then they will cry to the LORD,
     but he will not answer them;
   he will hide his face from them at that time,
     because they have acted wickedly.

5 Thus says the LORD concerning the prophets
     who lead my people astray,
   who cry "Peace"
     when they have something to eat,
   but declare war against those
     who put nothing into their mouths.
6 Therefore it shall be night to you, without vision,
     and darkness to you, without revelation.
   The sun shall go down upon the prophets,
     and the day shall be black over them;
7 the seers shall be disgraced,
     and the diviners put to shame;
   they shall all cover their lips,
     for there is no answer from God.
8 But as for me, I am filled with power,
     with the spirit of the LORD,
     and with justice and might,
   to declare to Jacob his transgression
     and to Israel his sin.

9 Hear this, you rulers of the house of Jacob
     and chiefs of the house of Israel,
   who abhor justice
     and pervert all equity,
10 who build Zion with blood
     and Jerusalem with wrong!
11 Its rulers give judgment for a bribe,
     its priests teach for a price,
     its prophets give oracles for money;
   yet they lean upon the LORD and say,
   "Surely the LORD is with us!
     No harm shall come upon us."

REVISED ENGLISH BIBLE

11 If anyone had gone about uttering falsehood and lies,
saying: 'I shall hold forth to you about wine and strong
drink,' his holding forth would be just what this people
likes.
12 I shall assemble you, the whole house of Jacob;
   I shall gather together those that are left in Israel.
   I shall herd them like sheep into a fold,
   like a flock in the pasture, moved away by men.
13 Their leader breaks out before them,
   and they all break through the gate and go out
   with their King going before them,
   the LORD leading the way.

3 I said:
   'Listen, you leaders of Jacob, rulers of Israel,
   surely it is for you to know what is right,
2 and yet you hate good and love evil;
   you flay the skin of my people
   and tear the flesh from their bones.'
3 They devour the flesh of my people,
   strip off their skin,
   lay bare their bones;
   they cut them up like flesh for the pot,
   like meat for the cauldron.

4 Then they will call to the LORD, but he will not
     answer.
   When that time comes he will hide his face from
     them,
   so wicked are their deeds.

5 These are the words of the LORD about the prophets who
lead my people astray, who promise prosperity in return for
food, but declare open war against those who give them
nothing to eat:
6 For you night will bring no vision,
   darkness no divination;
   the sun will go down on the prophets,
   daytime will be blackness over them.
7 Seers and diviners alike will be overcome with
     shame;
   they will all put their hands over their mouths,
   for there is no answer from God.
8 But I am full of strength, of justice and power,
   to declare to Jacob his crime,
   to Israel his sin.
9 Listen to this, leaders of Jacob,
   you rulers of Israel,
   who abhor what is right
   and pervert what is straight,
10 building Zion with bloodshed,
   Jerusalem with iniquity.
11 Her leaders sell verdicts for a bribe,
   her priests give rulings for payment,
   her prophets practise divination for money,
   yet claim the LORD's authority.
   'Is not the LORD in our midst?' they say.
   'No disaster can befall us.'

3:3 **like flesh:** *so Gk; Heb.* as.   3:8 **full of strength:** *prob. rdg;*
Heb. adds the spirit of the LORD.

[i] Heb *from them*   [j] Gk: Heb *as*

NEW AMERICAN BIBLE

11 If one, acting on impulse, should make the
    futile claim:
"I pour you wine and strong drink as
    my prophecy,"
then he would be the prophet of this people.
12 I will gather you, O Jacob, each and every one,
    I will assemble all the remnant of Israel;
I will group them like a flock in the fold,
    like a herd in the midst of its corral;
they shall not be thrown into panic by men.
13 With a leader to break the path
    they shall burst open the gate and go out
        through it;
Their king shall go through before them,
    and the LORD at their head.

3   And I said:
Hear, you leaders of Jacob,
    rulers of the house of Israel!
Is it not your duty to know what is right,
2   you who hate what is good, and love evil?
You who tear their skin from them,
    and their flesh from their bones!
3 They eat the flesh of my people,
    and flay their skin from them,
    and break their bones.
They chop them in pieces like flesh in a kettle,
    and like meat in a caldron.
4 When they cry to the LORD,
    he shall not answer them;
Rather shall he hide his face from them at
        that time,
because of the evil they have done.

5 Thus says the LORD regarding the prophets
    who lead my people astray;
Who, when their teeth have something to bite,
    announce peace,
But when one fails to put something in
       their mouth,
proclaim war against him.
6 Therefore you shall have night, not vision,
    darkness, not divination;
The sun shall go down upon the prophets,
    and the day shall be dark for them.
7 Then shall the seers be put to shame,
    and the diviners confounded;
They shall cover their lips, all of them,
    because there is no answer from God.
8 But as for me, I am filled with power,
    with the spirit of the LORD,
    with authority and with might;
To declare to Jacob his crimes
    and to Israel his sins.
9 Hear this, you leaders of the house of Jacob,
    you rulers of the house of Israel!
You who abhor what is just,
    and pervert all that is right;
10 Who build up Zion with bloodshed,
    and Jerusalem with wickedness!
11 Her leaders render judgment for a bribe,
    her priests give decisions for a salary,
    her prophets divine for money,
While they rely on the LORD, saying,
    "Is not the LORD in the midst of us?
No evil can come upon us!"

NEW JERUSALEM BIBLE

11 If a man of the spirit came and invented this lie,
    'I prophesy wine and liquor for you,'
he would be the prophet for a people like this.
12 I shall assemble the whole of Jacob,
    I shall gather the remnant of Israel,
I shall gather them together like sheep in an
        enclosure.
And like a flock within their fold,
    they will bleat far away from anyone,
13 their leader will break out first,
    then all break out through the gate and escape,
with their king leading the way
    and with Yahweh at their head.

3   Then I said,
'Kindly listen, you leaders of the House of Jacob,
    you princes of the House of Israel.
Surely you are the ones who ought to know what
        is right,
2 and yet you hate what is good and love what is
        evil,
skinning people alive, pulling the flesh off their
        bones,
3 eating my people's flesh, stripping off their skin,
breaking up their bones, chopping them up small
like flesh for the pot, like meat in the stew-pan?'
4 Then they will call to Yahweh,
    but he will not answer them.
When the time comes he will hide his face from
        them
because of the crimes they have committed.

5 Yahweh says this against the prophets
    who lead my people astray:
So long as they have something to eat
    they cry 'Peace'.
But on anyone who puts nothing into their mouths
    they declare war.
6 And so, for you, night will be without vision
    and for you the darkness without divination.
The sun will set for the prophets,
    the daylight will go black above them.
7 Then the seers will be covered with shame,
    the diviners with confusion;
they will all put their hands over their mouths
because there is no answer from God.
8 Not so with me, I am full of strength
    (full of Yahweh's spirit),
of the sense of right, of energy
to accuse Jacob of his crime
    and Israel of his sin.
9 Kindly listen to this, you leaders of the House of
        Jacob,
you princes of the House of Israel,
    who detest justice,
wresting it from its honest course,
10 who build Zion with blood,
    and Jerusalem with iniquity!
11 Her leaders give verdicts for presents,
    her priests take a fee for their rulings,
    her prophets divine for money
and yet they rely on Yahweh!
'Isn't Yahweh among us?' they say,
'No disaster is going to overtake us.'

NEW REVISED STANDARD VERSION

12 Therefore because of you
  Zion shall be plowed as a field;
Jerusalem shall become a heap of ruins,
  and the mountain of the house a wooded
    height.

4 In days to come
  the mountain of the LORD's house
shall be established as the highest of the
    mountains,
  and shall be raised up above the hills.
Peoples shall stream to it,
2   and many nations shall come and say:
"Come, let us go up to the mountain of the
    LORD,
  to the house of the God of Jacob;
that he may teach us his ways
  and that we may walk in his paths."
For out of Zion shall go forth instruction,
  and the word of the LORD from Jerusalem.
3 He shall judge between many peoples,
  and shall arbitrate between strong nations far
    away;
they shall beat their swords into plowshares,
  and their spears into pruning hooks;
nation shall not lift up sword against nation,
  neither shall they learn war any more;
4 but they shall all sit under their own vines and
    under their own fig trees,
  and no one shall make them afraid;
  for the mouth of the LORD of hosts has spoken.

5 For all the peoples walk,
  each in the name of its god,
but we will walk in the name of the LORD our
    God
  forever and ever.

6 In that day, says the LORD,
  I will assemble the lame
and gather those who have been driven away,
  and those whom I have afflicted.
7 The lame I will make the remnant,
  and those who were cast off, a strong nation;
and the LORD will reign over them in Mount Zion
  now and forevermore.

8 And you, O tower of the flock,
  hill of daughter Zion,
to you it shall come,
  the former dominion shall come,
  the sovereignty of daughter Jerusalem.

9 Now why do you cry aloud?
  Is there no king in you?
Has your counselor perished,
  that pangs have seized you like a woman in
    labor?
10 Writhe and groan,k O daughter Zion,
  like a woman in labor;
for now you shall go forth from the city
  and camp in the open country;
  you shall go to Babylon.
There you shall be rescued,
  there the LORD will redeem you
  from the hands of your enemies.

11 Now many nations
  are assembled against you,
saying, "Let her be profaned,
  and let our eyes gaze upon Zion."

k Meaning of Heb uncertain

REVISED ENGLISH BIBLE

12 Therefore, because of you
  Zion will become a ploughed field,
Jerusalem a heap of ruins,
  and the temple mount rough moorland.

4 IN days to come
  the mountain of the LORD's house
will be established higher than all other mountains,
  towering above other hills.
Peoples will stream towards it;
2 many nations will go, saying,
'Let us go up to the mountain of the LORD,
  to the house of Jacob's God,
that he may teach us his ways
  and we may walk in his paths.'
For instruction issues from Zion,
  the word of the LORD from Jerusalem.
3 He will be judge between many peoples
  and arbiter among great and distant nations.
They will hammer their swords into mattocks
  and their spears into pruning-knives.
Nation will not take up sword against nation;
  they will never again be trained for war.
4 Each man will sit under his own vine
  or his own fig tree, with none to cause alarm.
The LORD of Hosts himself has spoken.

5 Other peoples may be loyal to their own deities,
  but our loyalty will be for ever to the LORD our
    God.

6 On that day, says the LORD,
  I shall gather those who are lost;
I shall assemble the dispersed and those I have
    afflicted.
7 I shall restore the lost as a remnant
  and turn the outcasts into a mighty nation.
The LORD will be their king on Mount Zion
  for ever from that time forward.
8 And you, watch-tower of the flock, hill of Zion,
  the promises made to you will be fulfilled,
  and your former sovereignty will come again,
  the dominion of Jerusalem.

9 Why are you now crying out in distress?
Have you no king,
  no counsellor left,
that you are seized with writhing like a woman in
    labour?
10 Zion, writhe and shout like a woman in childbirth,
  for now you must leave the city
  and camp in the open country.
You must go to Babylon;
  there you will be saved;
  there the LORD will deliver you from your enemies.
11 But now many nations are massed against you;
  they say, 'Let her suffer outrage;
  let us gloat over Zion.'

NEW AMERICAN BIBLE

¹²Therefore, because of you,
Zion shall be plowed like a field,
and Jerusalem reduced to rubble,
And the mount of the temple
to a forest ridge.

4 In days to come
the mount of the LORD's house
Shall be established higher than the mountains;
it shall rise high above the hills,
And peoples shall stream to it:
² Many nations shall come, and say,
"Come, let us climb the mount of the LORD,
to the house of the God of Jacob,
That he may instruct us in his ways,
that we may walk in his paths."
For from Zion shall go forth instruction,
and the word of the LORD from Jerusalem.
³He shall judge between many peoples
and impose terms on strong and distant nations;
They shall beat their swords into plowshares,
and their spears into pruning hooks;
One nation shall not raise the sword
against another,
nor shall they train for war again.
⁴Every man shall sit under his own vine
or under his own fig tree, undisturbed;
for the mouth of the LORD of hosts has spoken.
⁵For all the peoples walk
each in the name of its god,
But we will walk in the name of the LORD,
our God, forever and ever.
⁶On that day, says the LORD,
I will gather the lame,
And I will assemble the outcasts,
and those whom I have afflicted.
⁷I will make of the lame a remnant,
and of those driven far off a strong nation;
And the LORD shall be king over them on
Mount Zion,
from now on forever.
⁸And you, O Magdal-eder,
hillock of daughter Zion!
Unto you shall it come:
the former dominion shall be restored,
the kingdom of daughter Jerusalem.

⁹Now why do you cry out so?
Are you without a king?
Or has your counselor perished,
That you are seized with pains
like a woman in travail?
¹⁰Writhe in pain, grow faint,
O daughter Zion,
like a woman in travail;
For now shall you go forth from the city
and dwell in the fields;
To Babylon shall you go,
there shall you be rescued.
There shall the LORD redeem you
from the hand of your enemies.
¹¹How many nations are gathered against you!
They say, "Let her be profaned,
let our eyes see Zion's downfall!"

NEW JERUSALEM BIBLE

¹²That is why, thanks to you,
Zion will become ploughland,
Jerusalem a heap of rubble
and the Temple Mount a wooded height.

4 But in days to come^c
Yahweh's Temple Mountain
will tower above the mountains,
rise higher than the hills.
²Then the peoples will stream to it,
then many nations will come and say,
'Come, we will go up to Yahweh's mountain,
to the Temple of the God of Jacob,
so that he may teach us his ways
and we may walk in his paths;
for the Law issues from Zion
and Yahweh's word from Jerusalem.'
³He will judge between many peoples
and arbitrate between mighty nations.
They will hammer their swords into ploughshares
and their spears into bill-hooks.
Nation will not lift sword against nation
or ever again be trained to make war.
⁴But each man will sit under his vine and fig tree
with no one to trouble him.
The mouth of Yahweh Sabaoth has spoken.

⁵For all peoples go forward, each in the name of its
god,
while we go forward in the name of Yahweh our
God
for ever and ever.

⁶That day —declares Yahweh—
I shall gather in the lame
and bring together the strays
and those whom I have treated harshly.
⁷From the footsore I shall make a remnant,
and from the far-flung a mighty nation.
And Yahweh will reign over them on Mount Zion
thenceforth and for ever.

⁸And to you, Tower of the Flock,
Ophel of the daughter of Zion,
to you your former sovereignty will return,
the royal power of the daughter of Jerusalem.

⁹Why are you crying out now?
Have you no king?
Has your counsellor perished,
for pangs to grip you like those of a woman in
labour?
¹⁰Writhe in pain and cry aloud,
daughter of Zion, like a woman in labour,
for now you must leave the city
and camp in the open country;
to Babylon you must go,
and there you will be rescued;
there Yahweh will ransom you
from the clutches of your enemies.

¹¹Now many nations
have mustered against you.
They say, 'Let us desecrate her,
let us gloat over Zion!'

^c4 vv. 1–3 = Is 2:2–4. The universalist theme fits better in Isaiah.

NEW REVISED STANDARD VERSION

12 But they do not know
the thoughts of the LORD;
they do not understand his plan,
that he has gathered them as sheaves to the
threshing floor.
13 Arise and thresh,
O daughter Zion,
for I will make your horn iron
and your hoofs bronze;
you shall beat in pieces many peoples,
and shall*l* devote their gain to the LORD,
their wealth to the Lord of the whole earth.

5*m* Now you are walled around with a wall;*n*
siege is laid against us;
with a rod they strike the ruler of Israel
upon the cheek.

2 *o* But you, O Bethlehem of Ephrathah,
who are one of the little clans of Judah,
from you shall come forth for me
one who is to rule in Israel,
whose origin is from of old,
from ancient days.
3 Therefore he shall give them up until the time
when she who is in labor has brought forth;
then the rest of his kindred shall return
to the people of Israel.
4 And he shall stand and feed his flock in the
strength of the LORD,
in the majesty of the name of the LORD his
God.
And they shall live secure, for now he shall be
great
to the ends of the earth;
5 and he shall be the one of peace.

If the Assyrians come into our land
and tread upon our soil,*p*
we will raise against them seven shepherds
and eight installed as rulers.
6 They shall rule the land of Assyria with the
sword,
and the land of Nimrod with the drawn
sword;*q*
they*r* shall rescue us from the Assyrians
if they come into our land
or tread within our border.

7 Then the remnant of Jacob,
surrounded by many peoples,
shall be like dew from the LORD,
like showers on the grass,
which do not depend upon people
or wait for any mortal.
8 And among the nations the remnant of Jacob,
surrounded by many peoples,
shall be like a lion among the animals of the
forest,
like a young lion among the flocks of sheep,
which, when it goes through, treads down
and tears in pieces, with no one to deliver.
9 Your hand shall be lifted up over your
adversaries,
and all your enemies shall be cut off.

10 In that day, says the LORD,
I will cut off your horses from among you
and will destroy your chariots;

REVISED ENGLISH BIBLE

12 They do not know the LORD's thoughts
or understand his purpose;
for he has gathered them
like sheaves to the threshing-floor.
13 Start your threshing, you people of Zion;
for I shall make your horns iron,
your hoofs bronze,
and you will crush many peoples.
You are to devote their ill-gotten gain to the LORD,
their wealth to the LORD of all the earth.

5 Now withdraw behind your walls,
you people of a walled city;
the siege is pressed home against you:
Israel's ruler is struck on the cheek with a
rod.

2 But from you, Bethlehem in Ephrathah,
small as you are among Judah's clans,
from you will come a king for me over Israel,
one whose origins are far back in the past, in
ancient times.
3 Therefore only until she who is pregnant has given
birth
will he give up Israel;
and then those of the people that survive
will rejoin their brethren.
4 He will rise up to lead them
in the strength of the LORD,
in the majesty of the name of the LORD his God.
They will enjoy security, for then his greatness will
reach
to the ends of the earth.
5 Then there will be peace.

Should the Assyrians invade our land,
should they overrun our strongholds,
we shall raise against them some seven or eight
men
to be rulers and princes.
6 They will rule Assyria with the sword
and the land of Nimrod with drawn blades.
They will deliver us from the Assyrians,
should they invade our land,
should they encroach on our frontiers.
7 All that are left of Jacob,
dispersed among many peoples,
will be like dew from the LORD,
like copious rain on the grass,
which does not wait for mortal command
or linger for any mortal's bidding.
8 All that are left of Jacob among the nations,
dispersed among many peoples,
will be like a lion among the beasts of the forest,
like a young lion at large in a flock of sheep;
running through he will trample and tear,
with no rescuer in sight.
9 Your hand will be raised high over your foes,
and all your enemies will be destroyed!

10 On that day, says the LORD,
I shall slaughter your horses
and destroy your chariots.

l Gk Syr Tg: Heb *and I will*   *m* Ch 4.14 in Heb   *n* Cn Compare
Gk: Meaning of Heb uncertain   *o* Ch 5.1 in Heb   *p* Gk: Heb *in
our palaces*   *q* Cn: Heb *in its entrances*   *r* Heb *he*

5:1 *In Heb. 4:14.* **Now . . . city:** *prob. rdg, cp. Gk; Heb.* Gash
yourself, daughter of a band. **against you:** *so Gk; Heb.* against us.
5:2 *In Heb. 5:1.*   5:5 **Then . . . peace:** *or* And he shall be a man
of peace.

NEW AMERICAN BIBLE

12 But they know not the thoughts of the LORD,
    nor understand his counsel,
    When he has gathered them
      like sheaves on the threshing-floor.
13 Arise and thresh, O daughter Zion;
    your horn I will make iron
    And your hoofs bronze,
      that you may crush many peoples;
    You shall devote their spoils to the LORD,
      and their riches to the Lord of the whole earth.

14 Now fence yourself in, Bat-gader!
    "They have laid siege against us!"
    With the rod they strike on the cheek
      the ruler of Israel.

5 But you, Bethlehem-Ephrathah,
    too small to be among the clans of Judah,
    From you shall come forth for me
      one who is to be ruler in Israel;
    Whose origin is from of old,
      from ancient times.
2 (Therefore the Lord will give them up, until
      the time
    when she who is to give birth has borne,
    And the rest of his brethren shall return
      to the children of Israel.)
3 He shall stand firm and shepherd his flock
    by the strength of the LORD,
    in the majestic name of the LORD, his God;
    And they shall remain, for now his greatness
      shall reach to the ends of the earth;
4   he shall be peace.

If Assyria invades our country
    and treads upon our land,
    We shall raise against it seven shepherds,
      eight men of royal rank;
5 And they shall tend the land of Assyria with
      the sword,
    and the land of Nimrod with the drawn sword;
    And we shall be delivered from Assyria,
      if it invades our land
      and treads upon our borders.

6 The remnant of Jacob shall be
    in the midst of many peoples,
    Like dew coming from the LORD,
      like raindrops on the grass,
    Which wait for no man,
      nor tarry for the sons of men.
7 And the remnant of Jacob shall be among
      the nations,
    in the midst of many peoples,
    Like a lion among beasts of the forest,
      like a young lion among flocks of sheep;
    When it passes through, it tramples
      and tears, and there is none to deliver.
8 Your hand shall be lifted above your foes,
    and all your enemies shall be destroyed.
9   On that day, says the LORD,
    I will destroy the horses from your midst
      and ruin your chariots;

NEW JERUSALEM BIBLE

12 But they do not know Yahweh's thoughts,
    they do not understand his design:
    he has collected them like sheaves on the
      threshing-floor.
13 Start your threshing, daughter of Zion,
    for I shall make your horn like iron,
    I shall make your hooves like bronze,
    so that you can crush many peoples.
    And you will devote what they have stolen to
      Yahweh,
    their wealth to the Lord of the whole earth.

14 Now look to your fortifications, Fortress!
    They have laid siege to us;
    the ruler of Israel will be struck
      on the cheek with a rod.

5 But you (Bethlehem) Ephrathah,
    the least of the clans of Judah,
    from you will come for me
    a future ruler of Israel
    whose origins go back to the distant past,
    to the days of old.
2 Hence Yahweh will abandon them
    only until she who is in labour gives birth,
    and then those who survive of his race
    will be reunited to the Israelites.
3 He will take his stand and he will shepherd them
    with the power of Yahweh,
    with the majesty of the name of his God,
    and they will be secure, for his greatness will
      extend
    henceforth to the most distant parts of the country.

4 He himself will be peace!
    Should the Assyrian invade our country,
    should he set foot in our land,
    we shall raise seven shepherds against him,
    eight leaders of men;
5 they will shepherd Assyria with the sword,
    the country of Nimrod with naked blade.
    He will save us from the Assyrian,
    should he invade our country,
    should he set foot inside our frontiers.

6 Then what is left of Jacob,
    surrounded by many peoples,
    will be like a dew from Yahweh,
    like showers on the grass,
    which do not depend on human agency
    and are beyond human control.

7 Then what is left of Jacob,
    surrounded by many peoples,
    will be like a lion among the forest beasts,
    like a fierce lion among flocks of sheep
    trampling as he goes,
    mangling his prey which no one takes from him.

8 You will be victorious over your foes
    and all your enemies will be torn to pieces.
9 When that day comes — declares Yahweh —
    I shall tear your horses away from you,
    I shall destroy your chariots;

NEW REVISED STANDARD VERSION	REVISED ENGLISH BIBLE

NEW REVISED STANDARD VERSION

11 and I will cut off the cities of your land
  and throw down all your strongholds;
12 and I will cut off sorceries from your hand,
  and you shall have no more soothsayers;
13 and I will cut off your images
  and your pillars from among you,
  and you shall bow down no more
  to the work of your hands;
14 and I will uproot your sacred poles[s] from among
  you
  and destroy your towns.
15 And in anger and wrath I will execute vengeance
  on the nations that did not obey.

6 Hear what the LORD says:
  Rise, plead your case before the mountains,
  and let the hills hear your voice.
2 Hear, you mountains, the controversy of the
  LORD,
  and you enduring foundations of the earth;
  for the LORD has a controversy with his people,
  and he will contend with Israel.

3 "O my people, what have I done to you?
  In what have I wearied you? Answer me!
4 For I brought you up from the land of Egypt,
  and redeemed you from the house of slavery;
  and I sent before you Moses,
  Aaron, and Miriam.
5 O my people, remember now what King Balak of
  Moab devised,
  what Balaam son of Beor answered him,
  and what happened from Shittim to Gilgal,
  that you may know the saving acts of the
  LORD."

6 "With what shall I come before the LORD,
  and bow myself before God on high?
  Shall I come before him with burnt offerings,
  with calves a year old?
7 Will the LORD be pleased with thousands of rams,
  with ten thousands of rivers of oil?
  Shall I give my firstborn for my transgression,
  the fruit of my body for the sin of my soul?"
8 He has told you, O mortal, what is good;
  and what does the LORD require of you
  but to do justice, and to love kindness,
  and to walk humbly with your God?

9 The voice of the LORD cries to the city
  (it is sound wisdom to fear your name):
  Hear, O tribe and assembly of the city![t]
10 Can I forget[u] the treasures of wickedness in
  the house of the wicked,
  and the scant measure that is accursed?
11 Can I tolerate wicked scales
  and a bag of dishonest weights?
12 Your[v] wealthy are full of violence;
  your[w] inhabitants speak lies,
  with tongues of deceit in their mouths.
13 Therefore I have begun[x] to strike you down,
  making you desolate because of your sins.

REVISED ENGLISH BIBLE

11 I shall devastate the cities of your land
  and raze your fortresses to the ground.
12 I shall destroy your sorcerers,
  and there will be no more soothsayers among you.
13 I shall cut down your images and your sacred
  pillars;
  you will no longer bow before things your hands
  have made.
14 I shall pull up your sacred poles
  and demolish your blood-spattered altars.
15 In anger and fury I shall wreak vengeance
  on the nations who disobey me.

6 HEAR what the LORD is saying:

  Stand up and state your case before the mountains;
  let the hills hear your plea.
2 Hear the LORD's case, you mountains;
  listen, you pillars that support the earth,
  for the LORD has a case against his people,
  and will argue it with Israel.

3 My people, what have I done to you?
  How have I wearied you? Bring your charges!
4 I brought you up from Egypt,
  I set you free from the land of slavery,
  I sent Moses, Aaron, and Miriam to lead you.
5 My people, remember the plans
  devised by King Balak of Moab,
  and how Balaam son of Beor answered him;
  consider the crossing from Shittim to Gilgal,
  so that you may know the victories of the LORD.

6 What shall I bring when I come before the LORD,
  when I bow before God on high?
  Am I to come before him with whole-offerings,
  with yearling calves?
7 Will the LORD be pleased with thousands of rams
  or ten thousand rivers of oil?
  Shall I offer my eldest son for my wrongdoing,
  my child for the sin I have committed?

8 The LORD has told you mortals what is good,
  and what it is that the LORD requires of you:
  only to act justly, to love loyalty,
  to walk humbly with your God.

9 The LORD calls to the city
  (the fear of his name brings success):
  Listen, you tribe and assembled citizens,
10 can I forgive the false measure,
  the accursed short bushel?
11 Can I connive at misleading scales
  or a bag of fraudulent weights?
12 The rich men of the city are steeped in violence;
  her citizens are all liars,
  their tongues utter deceit.
13 But now I inflict severe punishment on you,
  bringing you to ruin for your sins:

6:2 **listen:** *prob. rdg; Heb. obscure.* 6:5 **consider the crossing:** *prob. rdg; Heb. omits.* 6:9 **his name:** *so Gk; Heb. your name.* **assembled citizens:** *prob. rdg; Heb. unintelligible.* 6:10 **can I forgive:** *prob. rdg; Heb. obscure.* **false measure:** *prob. rdg; Heb. adds treasures of wickedness.* **bushel:** *Heb. ephah.*

[s] Heb *Asherim* [t] Cn Compare Gk: Heb *tribe, and who has appointed it yet?* [u] Cn: Meaning of Heb uncertain [v] Heb *Whose* [w] Heb *whose* [x] Gk Syr Vg: Heb *have made sick*

NEW AMERICAN BIBLE	NEW JERUSALEM BIBLE

NEW AMERICAN BIBLE

10 I will demolish the cities of your land
and tear down all your fortresses.
11 I will abolish the means of divination from
your use,
and there shall no longer be soothsayers
among you.
12 I will abolish your carved images
and the sacred pillars from your midst;
And you shall no longer adore
the works of your hands.
13 I will tear out the sacred poles from your midst,
and destroy your cities.
14 I will wreak vengeance in anger and wrath
upon the nations that have not hearkened.

6 Hear, then, what the LORD says:
Arise, present your plea before the mountains,
and let the hills hear your voice!
2 Hear, O mountains, the plea of the LORD,
pay attention, O foundations of the earth!
For the LORD has a plea against his people,
and he enters into trial with Israel.
3 O my people, what have I done to you,
or how have I wearied you? Answer me!
4 For I brought you up from the land of Egypt,
from the place of slavery I released you;
And I sent before you Moses,
Aaron, and Miriam.
5 My people, remember what Moab's King
Balak planned,
and how Balaam, the son of Beor, answered him
. . . from Shittim to Gilgal,
that you may know the just deeds of the LORD.
6 With what shall I come before the LORD,
and bow before God most high?
Shall I come before him with holocausts,
with calves a year old?
7 Will the LORD be pleased with thousands of rams,
with myriad streams of oil?
Shall I give my first-born for my crime,
the fruit of my body for the sin of my soul?
8 You have been told, O man, what is good,
and what the LORD requires of you:
Only to do the right and to love goodness,
and to walk humbly with your God.

9 Hark! the LORD cries to the city.
[It is wisdom to fear your name!]
Hear, O tribe and city council,
12 You whose rich men are full of violence,
whose inhabitants speak falsehood
with deceitful tongues in their heads!
10 Am I to bear any longer criminal hoarding
and the meager ephah that is accursed?
11 Shall I acquit criminal balances,
bags of false weights?
13 Rather I will begin to strike you
with devastation because of your sins.

NEW JERUSALEM BIBLE

10 I shall tear the cities from your country,
I shall overthrow all your fortresses;
11 I shall tear the spells out of your hands
and you will have no more soothsayers;
12 I shall tear away your images
and your sacred pillars from among you,
and no longer will you worship
things which your own hands have made!
13 I shall uproot your sacred poles
and shall destroy your cities!
14 In furious anger I shall wreak vengeance
on the nations who have disobeyed me!

6 Now listen to what Yahweh says:
'Stand up, state your case to the mountains
and let the hills hear what you have to say!'
2 Listen, mountains, to the case as Yahweh puts it,
give ear, you foundations of the earth,
for Yahweh has a case against his people
and he will argue it with Israel.
3 'My people, what have I done to you,
how have I made you tired of me? Answer me!
4 For I brought you up from Egypt,
I ransomed you from the place of slave-labour
and sent Moses, Aaron and Miriam
to lead you.
5 My people, please remember:
what was Balak king of Moab's plan
and how did Balaam son of Beor answer him?
. . .d from Shittim to Gilgal,
for you to know Yahweh's saving justice.
6 'With what shall I enter Yahweh's presence
and bow down before God All-high?
Shall I enter with burnt offerings,
with calves one year old?
7 Will he be pleased with rams by the thousand,
with ten thousand streams of oil?
Shall I offer my eldest son for my wrong-doing,
the child of my own body for my sin?
8 'You have already been told what is right
and what Yahweh wants of you.
Only this, to do what is right,
to love loyalty
and to walk humbly with your God.'

9 Yahweh's voice! He thunders to the city,
'Listen, tribe of assembled citizens!
10 Can I overlook the false measure,
that abomination, the short bushel?
11 Can I connive at rigged scales
and at the bag of fraudulent weights?
12 For the rich there are steeped in violence,
and the citizens there are habitual liars.
13 'I myself have therefore begun to strike you down,
to bring you to ruin for your sins.

6, 5: The text is defective; however, it is evident that this verse
continues the remembrance of God's deeds of mercy to Israel,
beginning with the Exodus (v 4) and extending to the conquest, deeds
which have provoked so little response from his people.

d 6 Some words are missing in the Hebrew text.

NEW REVISED STANDARD VERSION	REVISED ENGLISH BIBLE

NEW REVISED STANDARD VERSION

14 You shall eat, but not be satisfied,
  and there shall be a gnawing hunger within
    you;
  you shall put away, but not save,
  and what you save, I will hand over to the
    sword.
15 You shall sow, but not reap;
  you shall tread olives, but not anoint
    yourselves with oil;
  you shall tread grapes, but not drink wine.
16 For you have kept the statutes of Omri*y*
  and all the works of the house of Ahab,
  and you have followed their counsels.
  Therefore I will make you a desolation, and
    your*z* inhabitants an object of hissing;
  so you shall bear the scorn of my people.

7 Woe is me! For I have become like one who,
  after the summer fruit has been gathered,
  after the vintage has been gleaned,
  finds no cluster to eat;
  there is no first-ripe fig for which I hunger.
2 The faithful have disappeared from the land,
  and there is no one left who is upright;
  they all lie in wait for blood,
  and they hunt each other with nets.
3 Their hands are skilled to do evil;
  the official and the judge ask for a bribe,
  and the powerful dictate what they desire;
  thus they pervert justice.*a*
4 The best of them is like a brier,
  the most upright of them a thorn hedge.
  The day of their*b* sentinels, of their*b*
    punishment, has come;
  now their confusion is at hand.
5 Put no trust in a friend,
  have no confidence in a loved one;
  guard the doors of your mouth
  from her who lies in your embrace;
6 for the son treats the father with contempt,
  the daughter rises up against her mother,
  the daughter-in-law against her mother-in-law;
  your enemies are members of your own
    household.
7 But as for me, I will look to the Lord,
  I will wait for the God of my salvation;
  my God will hear me.

8 Do not rejoice over me, O my enemy;
  when I fall, I shall rise;
  when I sit in darkness,
  the Lord will be a light to me.
9 I must bear the indignation of the Lord,
  because I have sinned against him,
  until he takes my side
  and executes judgment for me.
  He will bring me out to the light;
  I shall see his vindication.
10 Then my enemy will see,
  and shame will cover her who said to me,
  "Where is the Lord your God?"
  My eyes will see her downfall;*c*
  now she will be trodden down
  like the mire of the streets.
11 A day for the building of your walls!
  In that day the boundary shall be far extended.

REVISED ENGLISH BIBLE

14 you will eat, but not be satisfied;
  your food will lie heavy in your stomach;
  you will come to labour, but not bring forth;
  even if you bear a child
  I shall give it to the sword;
15 you will sow, but not reap;
  you will press the olives, but not use the oil;
  you will tread the grapes, but not drink the wine.
16 You have kept the precepts of Omri
  and all the practices of Ahab;
  you have adopted all their policies.
  So I shall lay you utterly waste;
  your citizens will be an object of horror,
  and you will endure the insults aimed at my
    people.

7 ALAS! I am now like the last gatherings of summer
    fruit,
  the last gleanings of the vintage,
  when there are no grapes left to eat,
  none of those early figs I love so much.
2 The faithful have vanished from the land;
  not one honest person is to be found.
  All who remain lie in wait to do murder;
  each one hunts his kinsman with a net.
3 They are bent on devising wrong—
  the grasping officer, the venal judge,
  and the powerful man who follows his own
    desires.
4 Their goodness is twisted like rank weeds
  and their honesty like briars.
  The day of their punishment has come;
  now confusion seizes them.
5 Put no trust in a neighbour,
  no confidence in a close friend.
  Seal your lips even from your wife whom you
    love.
6 Son maligns father,
  daughter rebels against mother,
  daughter-in-law against mother-in-law,
  and a person's enemies are found under his own
    roof.
7 But I shall watch for the Lord,
  I shall wait for God my saviour;
  my God will hear me.

8 My enemies, do not exult over me.
  Though I have fallen, I shall rise again;
  though I live in darkness, the Lord is my light.
9 Because I have sinned against the Lord,
  I must bear his anger, until he champions my cause
  and gives judgement for me,
  until he brings me into the light,
  and with gladness I see his justice.
10 When my enemies see it, they are confounded,
  those who said to me, 'Where is the Lord your
    God?'
  I shall gloat over them;
  let them be trampled like mud in the streets.
11 That will be a day for rebuilding your walls,
  a day when your boundaries will be extended,

---

y Gk Syr Vg Tg: Heb *the statutes of Omri are kept*   *z* Heb *its*
a Cn: Heb *they weave it*   *b* Heb *your*   *c* Heb lacks *downfall*

6:16 **You have kept:** *so Gk; Heb.* He has kept.   7:4 **Their . . .
briars:** *prob. rdg; Heb. obscure.* **their punishment:** *prob. rdg; Heb.*
your watchmen, your punishment.

NEW AMERICAN BIBLE

15 You shall sow, yet not reap,
 tread out the olive, yet pour no oil,
 and the grapes, yet drink no wine.
14 You shall eat, without being satisfied,
 food that will leave you empty;
 What you acquire, you cannot save;
 what you do save, I will deliver up to
 the sword.
16 You have kept the decrees of Omri,
 and all the works of the house of Ahab,
 and you have walked in their counsels;
 Therefore I will deliver you up to ruin,
 and your citizens to derision;
 and you shall bear the reproach of the nations.

7 Alas! I am as when the fruit is gathered,
 as when the vines have been gleaned;
 There is no cluster to eat,
 no early fig that I crave.
2 The faithful are gone from the earth,
 among men the upright are no more!
 They all lie in wait to shed blood,
 each one ensnares the other.
3 Their hands succeed at evil;
 the prince makes demands,
 The judge is had for a price,
 the great man speaks as he pleases,
4 The best of them is like a brier,
 the most upright like a thorn hedge.
 The day announced by your watchmen!
 your punishment has come;
 now is the time of your confusion.
5 Put no trust in a friend,
 have no confidence in a companion;
 Against her who lies in your bosom
 guard the portals of your mouth.
6 For the son dishonors his father,
 the daughter rises up against her mother,
 The daughter-in-law against her mother-in-law,
 and a man's enemies are those of his household.
7 But as for me, I will look to the LORD,
 I will put my trust in God my savior;
 my God will hear me!
8 Rejoice not over me, O my enemy!
 though I have fallen, I will arise;
 though I sit in darkness, the LORD is my light.
9 The wrath of the LORD I will endure
 because I have sinned against him,
 Until he takes up my cause,
 and establishes my right.
 He will bring me forth to the light;
 I will see his justice.
10 When my enemy sees this,
 shame shall cover her:
 She who said to me,
 "Where is the LORD, thy God?"
 My eyes shall see her downfall;
 now shall she be trampled underfoot,
 like the mire in the streets.
11 It is the day for building your walls;
 on that day the boundary shall be taken away.

NEW JERUSALEM BIBLE

14 You will eat but not be satisfied;
 you will store up but never keep safe;
 what you do keep safe I shall hand over to the
 sword;
15 you will sow but will not reap,
 press the olive but will not rub yourself with oil,
 tread the grape but will not drink the wine.
16 'For you keep the laws of Omri;
 what the House of Ahab did, you have done;
 by modelling yourselves on their standards,
 you force me to make an appalling example of you
 and reduce your citizens to a laughing-stock;
 hence you will endure the scorn of other peoples.'

7 How wretched I am,
 a harvester in summer time,
 like a gleaner at the vintage:
 not a single cluster to eat,
 none of those early figs I love!
2 The faithful have vanished from the land:
 there is no one honest left.
 All of them are on the alert for blood,
 every man hunting his brother with a net.
3 Their hands are adept at wrong-doing:
 the official makes his demands,
 the judge gives judgement for a bribe,
 the man in power pronounces as he pleases.
4 The best of them is like a briar,
 the most honest of them like a thorn-hedge.
 Now from the north their punishment approaches!
 That will be when they are confounded!
5 Trust no neighbour,
 put no confidence in a friend;
 do not open your mouth
 to the wife who shares your bed.
6 For son insults father,
 daughter rebels against mother,
 daughter-in-law against mother-in-law;
 a person's enemies come from within the
 household itself.
7 But I shall look to Yahweh,
 my hope is in the God who will save me;
 my God will hear me. e
8 Do not gloat over me, my enemy:
 though I have fallen, I shall rise;
 though I live in darkness,
 Yahweh is my light.
9 I must endure Yahweh's anger
 for I have sinned against him,
 until he takes up my cause
 and rights my wrongs;
 he will bring me out into the light,
 and then I shall contemplate his saving justice.
10 When my enemy sees this,
 she will be covered with shame,
 having sneered, 'Where is Yahweh your God?'
 This time, I shall be watching
 as she is trampled underfoot
 like mud in the streets.
11 That will be the day for rebuilding your walls!
 The day for expanding your frontiers!

e 7 Originally the end of the book. vv. 8–11 are exilic, vv. 14–17
even later, and vv. 18–20 a final psalm.

12 In that day they will come to you
   from Assyria to[d] Egypt,
and from Egypt to the River,
   from sea to sea and from mountain to
      mountain.
13 But the earth will be desolate
   because of its inhabitants,
   for the fruit of their doings.

14 Shepherd your people with your staff,
   the flock that belongs to you,
which lives alone in a forest
   in the midst of a garden land;
let them feed in Bashan and Gilead
   as in the days of old.
15 As in the days when you came out of the land of
      Egypt,
   show us[e] marvelous things.
16 The nations shall see and be ashamed
   of all their might;
they shall lay their hands on their mouths;
   their ears shall be deaf;
17 they shall lick dust like a snake,
   like the crawling things of the earth;
they shall come trembling out of their fortresses;
   they shall turn in dread to the LORD our God,
   and they shall stand in fear of you.

18 Who is a God like you, pardoning iniquity
   and passing over the transgression
   of the remnant of your[f] possession?
He does not retain his anger forever,
   because he delights in showing clemency.
19 He will again have compassion upon us;
   he will tread our iniquities under foot.
You will cast all our[g] sins
   into the depths of the sea.
20 You will show faithfulness to Jacob
   and unswerving loyalty to Abraham,
   as you have sworn to our ancestors
      from the days of old.

d One Ms: MT *Assyria and cities of*   e Cn: Heb *I will show him*
f Heb *his*   g Gk Syr Vg Tg: Heb *their*

12 a day when your people will return to you,
   from Assyria to Egypt,
from Egypt to the Euphrates,
   from every sea and every mountain.
13 The earth will be a waste because of its
      inhabitants;
   this will be as their deeds deserve.

14 Shepherd your people with your crook,
   the flock that is your own,
that lives apart on a moor with meadows all
      around;
   let them graze in Bashan and Gilead, as in days
      gone by.
15 Show us miracles as in the days when you came
      out of Egypt.
16 Let nations see and be confounded by their
      impotence,
   let them keep their mouths shut tight,
   let their ears be stopped.
17 May they lick the dust like snakes,
   like creatures that crawl on the ground.
Let them come trembling from their strongholds
   to the LORD our God;
   let them approach with awe and fear.

18 Who is a god like you? You take away guilt,
   you forgive the sins of the remnant of your people.
You do not let your anger rage for ever,
   for to be merciful is your true delight.
19 Once more you will show us compassion
   and wash away our guilt,
   casting all our sins into the depths of the sea.
20 You will show faithfulness to Jacob,
   unfailing mercy to Abraham,
   as you swore to our forefathers in days gone by.

7:12 **Assyria to:** *so one MS; others* Assyria and the cities of.
7:15 **Show us:** *prob. rdg; Heb.* I shall show him.   7:19 **our sins:**
so Gk; Heb. their sins.

12 It is the day; and they shall come to you
   from Assyria and from Egypt,
From Tyre even to the River,
   from sea to sea, and from mountain to mountain;
13 And the land shall be a waste
   because of its citizens,
   as a result of their deeds.

14 Shepherd your people with your staff,
   the flock of your inheritance,
That dwells apart in a woodland,
   in the midst of Carmel.
Let them feed in Bashan and Gilead,
   as in the days of old;
15 As in the days when you came from the land
   of Egypt,
   show us wonderful signs.

16 The nations shall behold and be put to shame,
   in spite of all their strength;
They shall put their hands over their mouths;
   their ears shall become deaf.
17 They shall lick the dust like the serpent,
   like reptiles on the ground;
They shall come quaking from their fastnesses,
   trembling in fear of you [the Lord, our God].

18 Who is there like you, the God who removes guilt
   and pardons sin for the remnant of
   his inheritance;
Who does not persist in anger forever,
   but delights rather in clemency,
19 And will again have compassion on us,
   treading underfoot our guilt?
You will cast into the depths of the sea all
   our sins;
20 You will show faithfulness to Jacob,
   and grace to Abraham,
As you have sworn to our fathers
   from days of old.

12 The day when others come to you
   all the way from Assyria, from Egypt,
   from Tyre and all the way from the Euphrates,
   from sea to sea, from the mountains to the
      mountains!
13 The earth will become a desert
   by reason of its inhabitants, in return for what they
      have done.

14 With shepherd's crook lead your people to pasture,
   the flock that is your heritage,
   living confined in a forest
   with meadow land all round.
Let them graze in Bashan and Gilead
   as in the days of old!
15 As in the days when you came out of Egypt,
   grant us to see wonders!
16 The nations will see and be confounded
   in spite of all their power;
   they will put their hands over their mouths,
   their ears will be deafened.
17 They will lick the dust like snakes,
   like reptiles that crawl on the earth.
They will creep trembling out of their lairs,
   in terror before you.

18 What god can compare with you
   for pardoning guilt
   and for overlooking crime?
He does not harbour anger for ever,
   since he delights in showing faithful love.
19 Once more have pity on us,
   tread down our faults;
   throw all our sins
   to the bottom of the sea.
20 Grant Jacob your faithfulness,
   and Abraham your faithful love,
   as you swore to our ancestors
   from the days of long ago.

Nahum

1 An oracle concerning Nineveh. The book of the vision of Nahum of Elkosh.

2 A jealous and avenging God is the LORD,
 the LORD is avenging and wrathful;
 the LORD takes vengeance on his adversaries
 and rages against his enemies.
3 The LORD is slow to anger but great in power,
 and the LORD will by no means clear the
 guilty.

His way is in whirlwind and storm,
 and the clouds are the dust of his feet.
4 He rebukes the sea and makes it dry,
 and he dries up all the rivers;
Bashan and Carmel wither,
 and the bloom of Lebanon fades.
5 The mountains quake before him,
 and the hills melt;
the earth heaves before him,
 the world and all who live in it.
6 Who can stand before his indignation?
 Who can endure the heat of his anger?
His wrath is poured out like fire,
 and by him the rocks are broken in pieces.
7 The LORD is good,
 a stronghold in a day of trouble;
he protects those who take refuge in him,
8 even in a rushing flood.
He will make a full end of his adversaries,[a]
 and will pursue his enemies into darkness.
9 Why do you plot against the LORD?
 He will make an end;
no adversary will rise up twice.
10 Like thorns they are entangled,
 like drunkards they are drunk;
 they are consumed like dry straw.
11 From you one has gone out
 who plots evil against the LORD,
 who counsels wickedness.

12 Thus says the LORD,
 "Though they are at full strength and many,[b]
 they will be cut off and pass away.
Though I have afflicted you,
 I will afflict you no more.
13 And now I will break off his yoke from you
 and snap the bonds that bind you."

14 The LORD has commanded concerning you:
 "Your name shall be perpetuated no longer;
from the house of your gods I will cut off
 the carved image and the cast image.
I will make your grave, for you are worthless."

Nahum

1 AN oracle about Nineveh: the book of the vision of Nahum from Elkosh.

2 THE LORD is a jealous God, a God of vengeance;
 the LORD takes vengeance and is quick to anger.
The LORD takes vengeance on his adversaries
 and directs his wrath against his enemies.
3 The LORD is long-suffering and of great might,
 but he will not let the guilty escape punishment.
His path is in the whirlwind and storm,
 and the clouds are the fine dust beneath his feet.
4 He rebukes the sea and dries it up
 and makes all the rivers fail.
Bashan and Carmel languish,
 and on Lebanon the young shoots wither.
5 The mountains quake before him,
 and the hills dissolve;
the earth is in tumult at his presence,
 the world and all who live in it.
6 Who can stand before his wrath?
 Who can resist the fury of his anger?
His rage is poured out like fire,
 and the rocks are dislodged before him.
7 The LORD is a sure protection in time of trouble,
 and cares for all who make him their refuge.
8 With a raging flood he makes an end of those who
 oppose him,
 and pursues his enemies into darkness.

9 Why do you make plots against the LORD?
 He will make an end of you,
 and you will suffer affliction once and for all.
10 Like a thicket of tangled briars,
 like dry stubble, they are utterly consumed.
11 From you, Nineveh, has come forth a wicked
 counsellor,
 one who plots evil against the LORD.

12 THESE are the words of the LORD:

Judah, though your punishment has been great,
 yet it will pass away and be gone.
I have afflicted you, but I shall not afflict you
 again.
13 Now I shall break his yoke from your necks
 and snap the cords that bind you.

14 Nineveh, this is what the LORD has ordained for
 you:
No more children will be born to you;
I shall hew down image and idol
 in the temples of your gods;
I shall prepare your grave,
 for you are of no account.

1:8 **those . . . him:** *prob. rdg, cp. Gk; Heb.* her place.
1:10 **tangled briars:** *prob. rdg; Heb.* adds two unintelligible words.
they . . . consumed: *prob. rdg; Heb.* for unto.

a Gk: Heb *of her place*   *b* Meaning of Heb uncertain

THE BOOK OF

Nahum

Nahum

1 Oracle about Nineveh. The book of the vision of Nahum of Elkosh.

2 A jealous and avenging God is the LORD,
  an avenger is the LORD, and angry;
The LORD brings vengeance on his adversaries,
  and lays up wrath for his enemies;
3 The LORD is slow to anger, yet great in power,
  and the LORD never leaves the guilty unpunished.
In hurricane and tempest is his path,
  and clouds are the dust at his feet;
4 He rebukes the sea and leaves it dry,
  and all the rivers he dries up.
Withered are Bashan and Carmel,
  and the bloom of Lebanon fades;
5 The mountains quake before him,
  and the hills dissolve;
The earth is laid waste before him,
  the world and all who dwell in it.
6 Before his wrath, who can stand firm,
  and who can face his blazing anger?
His fury is poured out like fire,
  and the rocks are rent asunder before him.
7 The LORD is good,
  a refuge on the day of distress;
He takes care of those who have recourse to him,
8   when the flood rages;
He makes an end of his opponents,
  and his enemies he pursues with darkness.
9 What are you imputing to the LORD?
  It is he who will make an end!
The enemy shall not rise a second time;
10 As when a tangle of thornbushes is set aflame,
  like dry stubble, they shall be utterly consumed.
12 For, says the LORD,
  be they ever so many and so vigorous,
  still they shall be mown down and disappear.
Though I have humbled you,
  I will humble you no more.
13 Now will I break his yoke from off you,
  and burst asunder your bonds.
11 From you he came
  who devised evil against the LORD,
  the scoundrel planner.
14 The LORD has commanded regarding you:
  no descendant shall come to bear your name;
From your temple I will abolish
  the carved and the molten image;
  I will make your grave a mockery.

1 Prophecy about Nineveh. Book of the vision of Nahum of Elkosh.

Aleph
2 Yahweh is a jealous and vengeful God,
  Yahweh takes vengeance, he is rich in wrath;
Yahweh takes vengeance on his foes,
  he stores up fury for his enemies.
3 Yahweh is slow to anger but great in power,
  Yahweh never lets evil go unpunished.
Bet
In storm and whirlwind he takes his way,
  the clouds are the dust stirred up by his feet.
Gimel
4 He rebukes the sea, dries it up,
  and makes all the rivers run dry.
Dalet
. . . Bashan and Carmel wither,
  the greenery of the Lebanon withers too.
He
5 The mountains tremble before him,
  the hills reel;
Waw
the earth collapses before him,
  the world and all who live in it.
Zain
6 His fury — who can withstand it?
  Who can endure his burning wrath?
Het
His anger pours out like fire
  and the rocks break apart before him.
Tet
7 Yahweh is better than a fortress
  in time of distress;
Yod
8 he recognizes those who trust in him even
  when the flood rushes on;
Kaph
he will make an end once and for all of those
  who defy him,
  and pursue his foes into darkness.
9 What are your thoughts about Yahweh?
He it is who makes a final end:
  his adversaries will not rise up a second time;
10 like a thicket of tangled brambles,
  like dry straw, they will be burnt up completely.

To Assyria
11 From you has emerged
someone plotting evil against Yahweh,
one of Belial's counsellors.*a*

To Judah
12 Yahweh says this:
Unopposed and many though they be,
  they will be cut down and pass away.
Though I have made you suffer,
  I shall make you suffer no more,
13 for now I shall break his yoke which presses hard
    on you
  and snap your chains.

To the king of Nineveh
14 As for you, this is Yahweh's decree:
You will have no heirs to your name,
  from the temple of your gods I shall remove
carved image and cast image,
  and I shall devastate your tomb, for you are
    accursed!

---

a **1** Belial (= useless) stands for the power of evil.

15c Look! On the mountains the feet of one
        who brings good tidings,
        who proclaims peace!
   Celebrate your festivals, O Judah,
        fulfill your vows,
   for never again shall the wicked invade you;
        they are utterly cut off.

2 A shatterer[d] has come up against you.
        Guard the ramparts;
        watch the road;
   gird your loins;
        collect all your strength.

2 (For the LORD is restoring the majesty of Jacob,
        as well as the majesty of Israel,
   though ravagers have ravaged them
        and ruined their branches.)

3 The shields of his warriors are red;
        his soldiers are clothed in crimson.
   The metal on the chariots flashes
        on the day when he musters them;
        the chargers[e] prance.

4 The chariots race madly through the streets,
        they rush to and fro through the squares;
   their appearance is like torches,
        they dart like lightning.

5 He calls his officers;
        they stumble as they come forward;
   they hasten to the wall,
        and the mantelet[f] is set up.

6 The river gates are opened,
        the palace trembles.

7 It is decreed[f] that the city[g] be exiled,
        its slave women led away,
   moaning like doves
        and beating their breasts.

8 Nineveh is like a pool
        whose waters[h] run away.
   "Halt! Halt!" —
        but no one turns back.

9 "Plunder the silver,
        plunder the gold!
   There is no end of treasure!
        An abundance of every precious thing!"

10 Devastation, desolation, and destruction!
        Hearts faint and knees tremble,
   all loins quake,
        all faces grow pale!

11 What became of the lions' den,
        the cave[i] of the young lions,
   where the lion goes,
        and the lion's cubs, with no one to disturb
        them?

12 The lion has torn enough for his whelps
        and strangled prey for his lionesses;
   he has filled his caves with prey
        and his dens with torn flesh.

13 See, I am against you, says the LORD of hosts, and I
will burn your[j] chariots in smoke, and the sword shall
devour your young lions; I will cut off your prey from the
earth, and the voice of your messengers shall be heard no
more.

---

[c]Ch 2.1 in Heb   [d]Cn: Heb scatterer   [e]Cn Compare Gk Syr:
Heb cypresses   [f]Meaning of Heb uncertain   [g]Heb it
[h]Cn Compare Gk: Heb a pool, from the days that she has become,
and they   [i]Cn: Heb pasture   [j]Heb her

15 There on the mountains are the feet of the
        herald
   who proclaims good news!
   Keep your pilgrim-feasts, Judah,
        and fulfil your vows.
   The wicked will never again overrun you;
        they are totally destroyed.

2 2 The LORD will restore the pride of Jacob and
        Israel alike,
   for pillagers have despoiled them
        and ravaged their vines.

1 THE aggressor is coming against you.
   Man the ramparts, keep a watch on the road,
        brace yourselves, exert your strength!

3 The shields of their warriors are gleaming red,
        their fighting men are all in scarlet;
   their chariots in battle line flash like fire.
        The squadrons of horse advance;

4 they charge madly on the city,
        they storm through the outskirts,
   like torches, like the zigzag of lightning.

5 The leaders display their prowess,
        rushing in headlong career;
   they dash to the city wall,
        and mantelets are set in position.

6 The floodgates of the rivers are opened,
        the palace topples down;

7 the train of captives goes into exile,
        their slave-girls are carried off,
   moaning like doves and beating their breasts.

8 Nineveh is like a pool of water ebbing away.
   The cry goes up, 'Stop! Stop!' but none turn back.

9 Spoil is taken, spoil of silver and gold;
        there is no end to its store,
   treasure costly beyond all desire.

10 Plundered, pillaged, despoiled!
   Courage failing and knees giving way,
   limbs in turmoil, and every face drained of colour!

11 Where now is the lion's den,
        the cave in which the lion cubs lived,
   to which lion, lioness, and cubs made their way
        with none to scare them?

12 The lion tore prey for its cubs,
        for its lionesses it broke its victim's neck;
   it filled its lairs with prey,
        its dens with flesh it had torn.

13 As you see, I am against you, says the LORD of
        Hosts;
   I shall smoke out your den,
        and the sword will devour your young lions.
   I shall cut off the prey you have taken on the
        earth,
   and the voices of your envoys will no more be
        heard.

1:15 In Heb. 2:1.   2:1–2 Verses 1 and 2 transposed.
2:3 **flash:** prob. rdg; Heb. obscure. **squadrons of horse:** so Gk;
Heb. fir trees. **advance:** prob. rdg; Heb. are made to quiver.
2:7 **the train . . . carried off:** prob. rdg; Heb. obscure.
2:10 **drained of colour:** meaning of Heb. uncertain.   2:11 **cave:**
prob. rdg; Heb. pasture.   2:13 **your den:** prob. rdg; Heb. her
chariot.

NEW AMERICAN BIBLE

2 See, upon the mountains there advances
    the bearer of good news, announcing peace!
Celebrate your feasts, O Judah,
    fulfill your vows!
For nevermore shall you be invaded
    by the scoundrel; he is completely destroyed.
3 The LORD will restore the vine of Jacob,
    the pride of Israel,
Though ravagers have ravaged them
    and ruined the tendrils.

2 The hammer comes up against you;
    guard the rampart,
Keep watch on the road, gird your loins,
    marshal all your strength!
4 The shields of his warriors are crimsoned,
    the soldiers colored in scarlet;
Fiery steel are the chariots
    on the day of his mustering.
The horses are frenzied;
5   the chariots dash madly through the streets
And wheel in the squares,
    looking like firebrands,
    flashing like lightning bolts.
6 His picked troops are called,
    ranks break at their charge;
To the wall they rush,
    the mantelet is set up.
7 The river gates are opened,
    the palace shudders,
8 Its mistress is led forth captive,
    and her handmaids, under guard,
Moaning like doves,
    beating their breasts.
9 Nineveh is like a pool
    whose waters escape;
"Stop! Stop!"
    but none turns back.
10 "Plunder the silver, plunder the gold!"
    There is no end to the treasure,
    to their wealth in precious things of every kind!

11 Emptiness, desolation, waste;
    melting hearts and trembling knees,
Writhing in every frame,
    every face blanched!
12 Where is the lions' cave,
    the young lions' den,
Where the lion went in and out,
    and the cub, with no one to disturb them?
13 The lion snatched enough for his cubs,
    and strangled for his lionesses;
He filled his dens with prey,
    and his caves with plunder.
14 I come against you,
    says the LORD of hosts;
I will consume in smoke your chariots,
    and the sword shall devour your young lions;
Your preying on the land I will bring to an end,
    the cry of your lionesses shall be heard no more.

NEW JERUSALEM BIBLE

2 *To Judah*
See on the mountains the feet of the herald!
    'Peace!' he proclaims.
Judah, celebrate your feasts,
    carry out your vows,
for Belial will never pass through you again;
    he has been utterly destroyed.

2 The destroyer has advanced on you,
    guarding the siege-works, watching the road,
    bracing himself, mustering great strength!
3 (For Yahweh has restored the vine of Jacob,
    yes, the vine of Israel,
although the plunderers had plundered them,
    although they had snapped off their vine-shoots!)
4 The shields of his fighting men show red,
    his warriors are dressed in scarlet;
the metal of the chariots sparkles
    as he prepares for battle;
the horsemen are impatient for action;
5 the chariots storm through the streets,
    jostling one another in the squares;
they look like blazing flames,
    like lightning they dash to and fro.
6 His captains are called out;
    stumbling as they go,
they speed towards the wall,
    and the mantelet is put in position.
7 The sluices of the River are opened,
    and the palace melts in terror.
8 Beauty[b] is taken captive, carried away,
    her slave-girls moaning like doves
9 and beating their breasts.
Nineveh is like a lake,
    whose waters are draining away.
'Stop! Stop!'
    But no one turns back.
10 'Plunder the silver! Plunder the gold!'
    There is no end to the treasure,
    a mass of everything you could desire!
11 Ravaged, wrecked, ruined!
    Heart fails and knees give way,
anguish is in the loins of all,
    and every face grows pale!
12 Where is the lions' den now,
    the cave of the lion's whelps,
where the lion and lioness walked with their cubs
    and no one molested them,
13 where the lion would tear up food for his whelps
    and strangle the kill for his mates,
where he filled his caverns with prey
    and his lairs with spoil?
14 Look, I am against you! —declares Yahweh
        Sabaoth—
I shall send your chariots up in smoke,
    and the sword will devour your whelps;
I shall cut short your depredations on earth,
    and the voices of your envoys will be heard no
        more.

b 2 The statue of the goddess Ishtar, a fertility deity.

NEW REVISED STANDARD VERSION	REVISED ENGLISH BIBLE

3 Ah! City of bloodshed,
  utterly deceitful, full of booty—
  no end to the plunder!
2 The crack of whip and rumble of wheel,
  galloping horse and bounding chariot!
3 Horsemen charging,
  flashing sword and glittering spear,
  piles of dead,
  heaps of corpses,
  dead bodies without end—
  they stumble over the bodies!
4 Because of the countless debaucheries of
    the prostitute,
  gracefully alluring, mistress of sorcery,
  who enslaves[k] nations through her debaucheries,
  and peoples through her sorcery,
5 I am against you,
  says the LORD of hosts,
  and will lift up your skirts over your face;
  and I will let nations look on your nakedness
  and kingdoms on your shame.
6 I will throw filth at you
  and treat you with contempt,
  and make you a spectacle.
7 Then all who see you will shrink from you and
    say,
  "Nineveh is devastated; who will bemoan her?"
  Where shall I seek comforters for you?
8 Are you better than Thebes[l]
  that sat by the Nile,
  with water around her,
  her rampart a sea,
  water her wall?
9 Ethiopia[m] was her strength,
  Egypt too, and that without limit;
  Put and the Libyans were her[n] helpers.
10 Yet she became an exile,
  she went into captivity;
  even her infants were dashed in pieces
  at the head of every street;
  lots were cast for her nobles,
  all her dignitaries were bound in fetters.
11 You also will be drunken,
  you will go into hiding;[o]
  you will seek
  a refuge from the enemy.
12 All your fortresses are like fig trees
  with first-ripe figs—
  if shaken they fall
  into the mouth of the eater.
13 Look at your troops:
  they are women in your midst.
  The gates of your land
  are wide open to your foes;
  fire has devoured the bars of your gates.
14 Draw water for the siege,
  strengthen your forts;
  trample the clay,
  tread the mortar,
  take hold of the brick mold!
15 There the fire will devour you,
  the sword will cut you off.
  It will devour you like the locust.

  Multiply yourselves like the locust,
  multiply like the grasshopper!

3 Woe betide the blood-stained city, steeped in
    deceit,
  full of pillage, never empty of prey!
2 The crack of the whip, the rattle of wheels,
  the stamping of horses, swaying chariots, 3 rearing
    chargers,
  the gleam of swords, the flash of spears!
  Myriads of slain, heaps of corpses,
  bodies innumerable, and men stumbling over
    them—
4 all for the persistent harlotry of a harlot,
  the alluring mistress of sorcery,
  who by her harlotry and sorceries
  beguiled nations and peoples.
5 I am against you, says the LORD of Hosts,
  I shall tear off your skirts to your disgrace
  and expose your naked body to every nation,
  your shame to every kingdom.
6 I shall pelt you with loathsome filth;
  I shall hold you in contempt and make a spectacle
    of you.
7 Then all who see you will shrink from you and
    say,
  'Nineveh is laid waste!' Who will console her?
  Where shall I look for anyone to comfort you?
8 Will you fare better than No-amon,
  situated by the streams of the Nile
  and encompassed by water,
  whose rampart was the Nile, whose wall was
    water?
9 Cush and Egypt were a source of endless strength
    to her,
  Put and the Libyans were her allies.
10 Even she became an exile and went into captivity,
  even her infants were dashed to the ground at
    every street corner,
  her nobles were shared out by lot,
  all her great men were thrown into chains.
11 You also will drink the cup of wrath until you are
    overcome;
  you also will flee for refuge from the enemy.
12 All your fortifications are like the first ripe figs:
  shaken, they fall into the mouth of the eater.
13 Your troops behave like women.
  The gates of your country stand open to the enemy;
  fire has consumed the barred gates.
14 Draw yourselves water for the siege,
  strengthen your fortifications;
  go down into the clay, trample the mortar,
  repair the brickwork of the fort.
15 Even there the fire will consume you,
  and the sword will cut you off.

  Make yourselves as many as the locusts,
  make yourselves as many as the hoppers.

---

[k] Heb sells [l] Heb No-amon [m] Or Nubia; Heb Cush
[n] Gk: Heb your [o] Meaning of Heb uncertain

3:6 **make . . . you:** or treat you like dung.   3:9 **her allies:** so Gk;
Heb. your allies.   3:15 **cut you off:** prob. rdg; Heb. adds and
consume you like locusts.

3 Woe to the bloody city, all lies,
  full of plunder, whose looting never stops!
2 The crack of the whip, the rumbling sounds
    of wheels;
  horses a-gallop, chariots bounding,
3 Cavalry charging,
  The flame of the sword, the flash of the spear,
  the many slain, the heaping corpses,
  the endless bodies to stumble upon!
4 For the many debaucheries of the harlot,
  fair and charming, a mistress of witchcraft,
  Who enslaved nations with her harlotries,
  and peoples by her witchcraft:
5 I am come against you,
  and I will strip your skirt from you;
  I will show your nakedness to the nations,
  to the kingdoms your shame!
6 I will cast filth upon you,
  disgrace you and put you to shame;
7 Till everyone who sees you runs from you, saying,
  "Nineveh is destroyed; who can pity her?
  Where can one find any to console her?"

8 Are you better than No-amon
  that was set among the streams,
  Surrounded by waters,
  with the flood for her rampart
  and water her wall?
9 Ethiopia was her strength, and Egypt,
  and others without end;
  Put and the Libyans were her auxiliaries.
10 Yet even she went captive into exile,
  even her little ones were dashed to pieces
  at the corner of every street;
  For her nobles they cast lots,
  and all her great men were put into chains.
11 You, too, shall drink of this till you faint away;
  you, too, shall seek a refuge from the foe.
12 All your fortresses are but fig trees,
  bearing early figs
  That fall, when shaken,
  into the hungry mouth.
13 See, the troops are women in your midst;
  to your foes the gates of your land are
    open wide,
  fire has consumed their bars.
14 Draw water for the siege,
  strengthen your fortresses;
  Go down into the mud and tread the clay,
  take hold of the brick mold!
15 There the fire shall consume you,
  the sword shall cut you down.
  Multiply like the grasshoppers,
  multiply like the locusts!

3 Disaster to the city of blood,
  packed throughout with lies,
  stuffed with booty,
  where plundering has no end!
2 The crack of the whip!
  The rumble of wheels!
  Galloping horse,
  jolting chariot,
3 charging cavalry,
  flashing swords,
  gleaming spears,
  a mass of wounded,
  hosts of dead,
  countless corpses;
  they stumble over corpses —
4 because of the countless whorings of the harlot,
  the graceful beauty, the cunning witch,
  who enslaved nations by her harlotries
  and tribes by her spells.

5 Look, I am against you! — declares Yahweh
    Sabaoth —
  I shall lift your skirts as high as your face
  and show your nakedness to the nations,
  your shame to the kingdoms.
6 I shall pelt you with filth,
  I shall shame you and put you in the pillory.
7 Then all who look at you
  will shrink from you and say,
  'Nineveh has been ruined!'
  Who will mourn for her?
  Where would I find people to comfort you?

8 Are you better off than No-Amon[c]
  situated among rivers,
  her defences the seas,
  her rampart the waters?
9 In Ethiopia and Egypt
  lay her strength, and it was boundless;
  Put and the Libyans served in her army.
10 But she too went into exile,
  into captivity;
  her little ones too were dashed to pieces
  at every crossroad;
  lots were drawn for her nobles,
  all her great men were put in chains.

11 You too will become drunk,
  you will go into hiding;
  you too will have to search
  for a refuge from the enemy.
12 Your fortifications are all fig trees,
  with early ripening figs:
  as soon as they are shaken,
  they fall into the mouth of the eater.
13 Look at your people:
  you are a nation of women!
  The gates of your country
  gape open to your enemies;
  fire has devoured their bars!
14 Draw yourselves water for the siege,
  strengthen your fortifications!
  Into the mud with you, puddle the clay,
  repair the brick-kiln!
15 There the fire will burn you up,
  the sword will cut you down.

  Make yourselves as numerous as locusts,
  make yourselves as numerous as the hoppers,

---

[c] **3** Thebes in Upper Egypt, taken by Assyria in 633 BC.

16 You increased your merchants
    more than the stars of the heavens.
    The locust sheds its skin and flies away.
17 Your guards are like grasshoppers,
    your scribes like swarms*p* of locusts
settling on the fences
    on a cold day—
when the sun rises, they fly away;
    no one knows where they have gone.
18 Your shepherds are asleep,
    O king of Assyria;
    your nobles slumber.
Your people are scattered on the mountains
    with no one to gather them.
19 There is no assuaging your hurt,
    your wound is mortal.
All who hear the news about you
    clap their hands over you.
For who has ever escaped
    your endless cruelty?

p Meaning of Heb uncertain

16 You have spies as numerous as the stars in the
    sky,
    like hoppers which raid and then fly away.
17 Your agents are like locusts,
    your commanders like the hoppers
    which lie dormant in the walls on a cold day;
    but when the sun rises, they make off,
    no one knows where.
18 Your rulers slumber, king of Assyria,
    your leaders are asleep;
    your people are scattered over the mountains,
    with no one to round them up.
19 Your wounds cannot be relieved, your injury is
    mortal;
all who hear of your fate clap their hands in joy.
Who has not suffered your relentless cruelty?

3:18 **are asleep:** *prob. rdg; Heb.* dwell.

NEW AMERICAN BIBLE

16 Make your couriers more numerous than the stars,
17 your garrisons as many as grasshoppers,
And your scribes as locust swarms
    gathered on the rubble fences on a cold day!
Yet when the sun warms them,
    the grasshoppers will spread their wings and fly,
    and vanish, no one knows where.
18 Alas! how your shepherds slumber, O king
        of Assyria,
    your nobles have gone to rest;
Your people are scattered upon the mountains,
    with none to gather them.

19 There is no healing for your hurt,
    your wound is mortal.
All who hear this news of you
    clap their hands over you;
For who has not been overwhelmed,
    steadily, by your malice?

NEW JERUSALEM BIBLE

16a let your commercial agents
    outnumber the stars of heaven,
17a your garrisons, like locusts,
    and your marshals, like swarms of hoppers!
They settle on the walls
    when the day is cold.
The sun appears,
16b the locusts spread their wings, they fly away,
17b away they fly, no one knows where.

    Alas, 18 your shepherds are asleep,
    king of Assyria,
    your bravest men slumber;
    your people are scattered on the mountains
    with no one to gather them.
19 There is no remedy for your wound,
    your injury is past healing.
All who hear the news of you
    clap their hands at your downfall.
For who has not felt
    your unrelenting cruelty?

Habakkuk

1 The oracle that the prophet Habakkuk saw.

2 O Lord, how long shall I cry for help,
    and you will not listen?
Or cry to you "Violence!"
    and you will not save?
3 Why do you make me see wrongdoing
    and look at trouble?
Destruction and violence are before me;
    strife and contention arise.
4 So the law becomes slack
    and justice never prevails.
The wicked surround the righteous—
    therefore judgment comes forth perverted.

5 Look at the nations, and see!
    Be astonished! Be astounded!
For a work is being done in your days
    that you would not believe if you were told.
6 For I am rousing the Chaldeans,
    that fierce and impetuous nation,
who march through the breadth of the earth
    to seize dwellings not their own.
7 Dread and fearsome are they;
    their justice and dignity proceed from
        themselves.
8 Their horses are swifter than leopards,
    more menacing than wolves at dusk;
    their horses charge.
Their horsemen come from far away;
    they fly like an eagle swift to devour.
9 They all come for violence,
    with faces pressing[a] forward;
    they gather captives like sand.
10 At kings they scoff,
    and of rulers they make sport.
They laugh at every fortress,
    and heap up earth to take it.
11 Then they sweep by like the wind;
    they transgress and become guilty;
    their own might is their god!

12 Are you not from of old,
    O Lord my God, my Holy One?
You[b] shall not die.
O Lord, you have marked them for judgment;
    and you, O Rock, have established them for
        punishment.
13 Your eyes are too pure to behold evil,
    and you cannot look on wrongdoing;
why do you look on the treacherous,
    and are silent when the wicked swallow
those more righteous than they?
14 You have made people like the fish of the sea,
    like crawling things that have no ruler.

15 The enemy[c] brings all of them up with a hook;
    he drags them out with his net,
he gathers them in his seine;
    so he rejoices and exults.

Habakkuk

1 AN oracle which the prophet Habakkuk received in a vision.

2 How long, Lord, will you be deaf to my plea?
'Violence!' I cry out to you,
    but you do not come to the rescue.
3 Why do you let me look on such wickedness,
    why let me see such wrongdoing?
Havoc and violence confront me,
    strife breaks out, discord arises.
4 Therefore law becomes ineffective,
    and justice is defeated;
the wicked hem in the righteous,
    so that justice is perverted.

5 Look around among the nations;
    see there a sight which will utterly astound you;
you will not believe it when you are told
    what is being done in your days:
6 I am raising up the Chaldaeans,
    that savage and impetuous nation,
who march far and wide over the earth
    to seize and occupy what is not theirs.
7 Fear and terror go with them;
    they impose their own justice and judgements.
8 Their horses are swifter than leopards,
    keener than the wolves of the plain;
their cavalry prance and gallop,
    swooping from afar like vultures to devour the
        prey.
9 Bent on violence, their whole army advances,
    a horde moving onward like an east wind;
they round up captives countless as the sand.
10 They hold kings in derision,
    they make light of rulers;
they laugh at every fortress
    and raise siege-works to capture them.
11 Then they sweep on like the wind and are gone;
    they ascribe their strength to their gods.

12 Lord, are you not from ancient times
    my God and Holy One, who is immortal?
Lord, you have appointed them to execute
        judgement;
my Rock, you have commissioned them to punish.
13 Your eyes are too pure to look on evil;
    you cannot countenance wrongdoing.
Why then do you countenance the treachery of the
        wicked?
Why keep silent when they devour those who are
        more righteous?
14 You have made people like the fish of the sea,
    like creeping creatures with no ruler over them.
15 The wicked haul them up with hooks
    or catch them in their nets
or drag them in their trawls.
    So they make merry and rejoice,

---

a Meaning of Heb uncertain   b Ancient Heb tradition: MT We
c Heb He

1:8 **plain:** or evening. **and gallop:** so Scroll; Heb. their cavalry.
1:11 **ascribe:** so Scroll; Heb. are guilty.   1:12 **who is immortal:**
prob. original rdg; altered in Heb. to we shall not die.

THE BOOK OF

Habakkuk

1 The oracle which Habakkuk the prophet received in vision.

2 How long, O LORD? I cry for help
but you do not listen!
I cry out to you, "Violence!"
but you do not intervene.
3 Why do you let me see ruin;
why must I look at misery?
Destruction and violence are before me;
there is strife, and clamorous discord.
4 This is why the law is benumbed,
and judgment is never rendered.
Because the wicked circumvent the just;
this is why judgment comes forth perverted.

5 Look over the nations and see,
and be utterly amazed!
For a work is being done in your days
that you would not have believed, were it told.
6 For see, I am raising up Chaldea,
that bitter and unruly people,
That marches the breadth of the land
to take dwellings not his own.
7 Terrible and dreadful is he,
from himself derive his law and his majesty.
8 Swifter than leopards are his horses,
and keener than wolves at evening.
His horses prance,
his horsemen come from afar;
They fly like the eagle hastening to devour;
9   each comes for the rapine,
Their combined onset is that of a stormwind
that heaps up captives like sand.
10 He scoffs at kings,
and princes are his laughingstock;
He laughs at any fortress,
heaps up a ramp, and conquers it.
11 Then he veers like the wind and is gone—
this culprit who makes his own strength his god!

12 Are you not from eternity, O LORD,
my holy God, immortal?
O LORD, you have marked him for judgment,
O Rock, you have readied him for punishment!
13 Too pure are your eyes to look upon evil,
and the sight of misery you cannot endure.
Why, then, do you gaze on the faithless in silence
while the wicked man devours
one more just than himself?
14 You have made man like the fish of the sea,
like creeping things without a ruler.
15 He brings them all up with his hook,
he hauls them away with his net,
He gathers them in his seine;
and so he rejoices and exults.

Habakkuk

1 The charge that Habakkuk the prophet received in a vision.

2 How long, Yahweh, am I to cry for help
while you will not listen;
to cry, 'Violence!' in your ear
while you will not save?

3 Why do you make me see wrong-doing,
why do you countenance oppression?
Plundering and violence confront me,
contention and discord flourish.

4 And so the law loses its grip
and justice never emerges,
since the wicked outwits the upright
and so justice comes out perverted.

5 Cast your eyes over the nations, look,
and be amazed, astounded.
For I am doing something in your own days
which you will not believe if you are told of it.
6 For look, I am stirring up the Chaldaeans,
that fierce and fiery nation
who march miles across country
to seize the homes of others.
7 They are dreadful and awesome,
a law and authority to themselves.

8 Their horses are swifter than leopards,
fiercer than wolves at night;
their horsemen gallop on,
their horsemen advance from afar,
swooping like an eagle anxious to feed.

9 They are all bent on violence,
their faces scorching like an east wind;
they scoop up prisoners like sand.

10 They scoff at kings,
they despise princes.
They make light of all fortresses:
they heap up earth and take them.

11 Then the wind changes and is gone . . .
Guilty is he who makes his strength his god.

12 Surely you, Yahweh, are from ancient times,
my holy God, who never dies!
Yahweh, you have appointed him to execute
judgement;
O Rock, you have set him firm to punish.

13 Your eyes are too pure to rest on evil,
you cannot look on at oppression.
Why do you look on at those who play the traitor,
why say nothing while the wicked swallows
someone more upright than himself?
14 Why treat people like fish of the sea,
like gliding creatures who have no leader?
15 They haul them all up on their hook,
they catch them in their net,
they sweep them up in their dragnet
and then make merry and rejoice.

NEW REVISED STANDARD VERSION	REVISED ENGLISH BIBLE

NEW REVISED STANDARD VERSION

16 Therefore he sacrifices to his net
  and makes offerings to his seine;
for by them his portion is lavish,
  and his food is rich.
17 Is he then to keep on emptying his net,
  and destroying nations without mercy?

2 I will stand at my watchpost,
  and station myself on the rampart;
I will keep watch to see what he will say to me,
  and what he[d] will answer concerning my
    complaint.
2 Then the LORD answered me and said:
Write the vision;
  make it plain on tablets,
  so that a runner may read it.
3 For there is still a vision for the appointed time;
  it speaks of the end, and does not lie.
If it seems to tarry, wait for it;
  it will surely come, it will not delay.
4 Look at the proud!
  Their spirit is not right in them,
  but the righteous live by their faith.[e]
5 Moreover, wealth[f] is treacherous;
  the arrogant do not endure.
They open their throats wide as Sheol;
  like Death they never have enough.
They gather all nations for themselves,
  and collect all peoples as their own.

6 Shall not everyone taunt such people and, with mocking riddles, say about them,
  "Alas for you who heap up what is not your
    own!"
  How long will you load yourselves with goods
    taken in pledge?
7 Will not your own creditors suddenly rise,
  and those who make you tremble wake up?
  Then you will be booty for them.
8 Because you have plundered many nations,
  all that survive of the peoples shall plunder
    you—
because of human bloodshed, and violence to the
    earth,
  to cities and all who live in them.

9 "Alas for you who get evil gain for your houses,
  setting your nest on high
  to be safe from the reach of harm!"
10 You have devised shame for your house
  by cutting off many peoples;
  you have forfeited your life.
11 The very stones will cry out from the wall,
  and the plaster[g] will respond from the
    woodwork.

12 "Alas for you who build a town by bloodshed,
  and found a city on iniquity!"
13 Is it not from the LORD of hosts
  that peoples labor only to feed the flames,
  and nations weary themselves for nothing?

REVISED ENGLISH BIBLE

16 offering sacrifices to their nets
  and burning offerings to their trawls,
for it is thanks to them that they live sumptuously
  and enjoy rich fare.
17 Are they to draw the sword every day
  to slaughter the nations pitilessly?

2 I shall stand at my post,
  I shall take up my position on the watch-tower,
keeping a look-out to learn what he says to me,
  how he responds to my complaint.
2 The LORD gives me this answer:
Write down a vision, inscribe it clearly on tablets,
  so that it may be read at a glance.
3 There is still a vision for the appointed time;
  it will testify to the destined hour and will not
    prove false.
Though it delays, wait for it,
  for it will surely come before too long.
4 The reckless will lack an assured future,
  while the righteous will live by being faithful.
5 As for one who is conceited, treacherous, and
    arrogant,
  still less will he reach his goal;
his throat gapes as wide as Sheol
  and he is insatiable as Death,
rounding up every nation,
  gathering in all peoples to himself.
6 Surely with veiled taunts and insults
  they will all turn on him and say,
'Woe betide the person who amasses wealth that is
    not his
  and enriches himself with goods taken in pledge!'

7 Will not your debtors suddenly start up?
  Will not those be roused who will shake you till
    you are empty?
  Will you not fall a victim to them?
8 Because you yourself have plundered many
    nations,
because of the bloodshed and violence you inflicted
  on cities and all their inhabitants over the earth,
  now the rest of the world will plunder you.

9 Woe betide the person who seeks unjust gain for
    his house,
  building his nest on a height
  to save himself from the onset of disaster!
10 Your schemes to overthrow many nations
  will bring dishonour to your house
  and put your own life in jeopardy.
11 The stones will cry out from the wall,
  and from the timbers a beam will answer them.

12 Woe betide the person who has built a city with
    bloodshed
  and founded a town on injustice,
13 so that nations toil for a pittance,
  peoples weary themselves for a mere nothing!
  Is not all this the doing of the LORD of Hosts?

1:17 **the sword:** *so Scroll; Heb.* the net. 2:1 **he responds:** *prob. rdg; Heb.* I respond. 2:2 **so that . . . glance:** *or* ready for a messenger to carry it with speed. 2:5 **conceited:** *cp. Gk; Heb.* wine. **Sheol:** *or* the underworld. 2:6 **his:** *prob. rdg; Heb. adds* till when.

d Syr: Heb I   e Or *faithfulness*   f Other Heb Mss read *wine*
g Or *beam*

NEW AMERICAN BIBLE

NEW JERUSALEM BIBLE

16 Therefore he sacrifices to his net,
and burns incense to his seine;
For thanks to them his portion is generous,
and his repast sumptuous.
17 Shall he, then, keep on brandishing his sword
to slay peoples without mercy?

2 I will stand at my guard post,
and station myself upon the rampart,
And keep watch to see what he will say to me,
and what answer he will give to my complaint.

2 Then the LORD answered me and said:
Write down the vision
Clearly upon the tablets,
so that one can read it readily.
3 For the vision still has its time,
presses on to fulfillment, and will not disappoint;
If it delays, wait for it,
it will surely come, it will not be late.
4 The rash man has no integrity;
but the just man, because of his faith, shall live.
Wealth, too, is treacherous:
the proud, unstable man—
5 He who opens wide his throat like the
nether world,
and is insatiable as death,
Who gathers to himself all the nations,
and rallies to himself all the peoples—
6 Shall not all these take up a taunt against him,
satire and epigrams about him, to say:

Woe to him who stores up what is not his:
how long can it last!
he loads himself down with debts.
7 Shall not your creditors rise suddenly?
Shall not they who make you tremble awake?
You shall become their spoil!
8 Because you despoiled many peoples
all the rest of the nations shall despoil you;
Because of men's blood shed,
and violence done to the land,
to the city and to all who dwell in it.

9 Woe to him who pursues evil gain for
his household,
setting his nest on high
to escape the reach of misfortune!
10 You have devised shame for your household,
cutting off many peoples, forfeiting your
own life:
11 For the stone in the wall shall cry out,
and the beam in the woodwork shall answer it!

12 Woe to him who builds a city by bloodshed,
and establishes a town by wickedness!

13 Is not this from the LORD of hosts:
peoples toil for the flames,
and nations grow weary for nought!

16 And so they offer a sacrifice to their net,
and burn incense to their dragnet,
for by these they get a rich living
and live off the fat of the land.
17 Are they to go on emptying their net unceasingly,
slaughtering the nations without pity?

2 I shall stand at my post,
I shall station myself on my watch-tower,
watching to see what he will say to me,
what answer he will make to my complaints.

2 Then Yahweh answered me and said,
'Write the vision down,
inscribe it on tablets
to be easily read.
3 For the vision is for its appointed time,
it hastens towards its end and it will not lie;
although it may take some time, wait for it,
for come it certainly will before too long.
4 'You see, anyone whose heart is not upright will
succumb,
but the upright will live through faithfulness.'*a*
5 Now, surely, wealth is treacherous!
He is arrogant, for ever on the move,
with appetite as large as Sheol
and as insatiable as Death,
gathering in all the nations,
and making a harvest of all peoples.
6 Are not the peoples all bound to satirise
and make up cryptic riddles about him?
As for instance:

Disaster to anyone who amasses goods not his
(for how long?)
and to anyone who weighs himself down with
goods taken in pledge!
7 Will not your creditors suddenly stand up,
will not those who make you shiver wake up,
and you will fall a prey to them?
8 Since you have plundered many nations,
all the nations that remain will plunder you,
because of the bloodshed and violence done to the
country,
to the city and to all who live in it.

9 Disaster to anyone who amasses ill-gotten gains for
his house,
so as to fix his nest on high
and so evade the reach of misfortune!
10 You have conspired to bring shame on your house:
by overthrowing many peoples
you have worked your own ruin.
11 For the very stone will protest from the wall,
and the beam will respond from the framework.

12 Disaster to anyone who builds a town with
bloodshed
and founds a city on wrong-doing!

13 Is it not thanks to Yahweh Sabaoth
that the peoples' toil is fuel for the fire,
and the nations' labour came to nothing?

a 2 Paul uses the Gk version 'faith' for the doctrine of justification by
faith in Rm 1:17.

NEW REVISED STANDARD VERSION	REVISED ENGLISH BIBLE

14 But the earth will be filled
  with the knowledge of the glory of the LORD,
  as the waters cover the sea.

15 "Alas for you who make your neighbors drink,
  pouring out your wrath[h] until they are drunk,
  in order to gaze on their nakedness!"

16 You will be sated with contempt instead of glory.
  Drink, you yourself, and stagger![i]
  The cup in the LORD's right hand
  will come around to you,
  and shame will come upon your glory!

17 For the violence done to Lebanon will overwhelm
    you;
  the destruction of the animals will terrify
    you—[j]
  because of human bloodshed and violence to the
    earth,
  to cities and all who live in them.

18 What use is an idol
  once its maker has shaped it—
  a cast image, a teacher of lies?
  For its maker trusts in what has been made,
  though the product is only an idol that cannot
    speak!

19 Alas for you who say to the wood, "Wake up!"
  to silent stone, "Rouse yourself!"
  Can it teach?
  See, it is gold and silver plated,
  and there is no breath in it at all.

20 But the LORD is in his holy temple;
  let all the earth keep silence before him!

3 A prayer of the prophet Habakkuk according to Shigionoth.

2 O LORD, I have heard of your renown,
  and I stand in awe, O LORD, of your work.
  In our own time revive it;
  in our own time make it known;
  in wrath may you remember mercy.

3 God came from Teman,
  the Holy One from Mount Paran.   Selah
  His glory covered the heavens,
  and the earth was full of his praise.

4 The brightness was like the sun;
  rays came forth from his hand,
  where his power lay hidden.

5 Before him went pestilence,
  and plague followed close behind.

6 He stopped and shook the earth;
  he looked and made the nations tremble.
  The eternal mountains were shattered;
  along his ancient pathways
  the everlasting hills sank low.

7 I saw the tents of Cushan under affliction;
  the tent-curtains of the land of Midian
    trembled.

8 Was your wrath against the rivers,[k] O LORD?
  Or your anger against the rivers,[k]
  or your rage against the sea,[l]
  when you drove your horses,
  your chariots to victory?

---

14 The earth will be full of the knowledge of the
    LORD's glory
  as the waters fill the sea.

15 Woe betide the person who makes his companions
    drink
  the outpouring of God's wrath,
  making them drunk to watch their naked orgies!

16 You will drink deep draughts,
  not of glory but of shame,
  drinking in your turn until you stagger.
  The cup in the LORD's right hand is passed to you,
  and your shame will exceed your glory.

17 The violence done to Lebanon will overwhelm
    you,
  the havoc wrought on its beasts will shatter you,
  because of the bloodshed and violence you inflicted
  on cities and all their inhabitants over the earth.

18 What use is an idol after its maker has shaped it?
  It is only an image, a source of lies!
  What use is it when the maker trusts what he has
    made?
  He is only making dumb idols!

19 Woe betide the person who says to a block of
    wood, 'Wake up,'
  to a lifeless stone, 'Bestir yourself'!
  Overlaid with gold and silver it may be,
  but there is no breath in it.

20 The LORD is in his holy temple;
  let all the earth be silent in his presence.

3 [1] A prayer of the prophet Habakkuk: according
to shigionoth

2 LORD, I have heard of your fame;
  LORD, I am in awe of what you have done.
  Through all generations you have made yourself
    known,
  and in your wrath you did not forget mercy.

3 God comes from Teman,
  the Holy One from Mount Paran;   [Selah
  his radiance covers the sky,
  and his splendour fills the earth.

4 His brightness is like the dawn,
  rays of light flash from his hand,
  and thereby his might is veiled.

5 Pestilence stalks before him,
  and plague follows close behind.

6 When he stands, the earth shakes;
  at his glance the nations panic;
  the everlasting mountains are riven,
  the ancient hills sink down.
  He journeys as he did of old.

7 The tents of Cushan are wrecked,
  the tent curtains of Midian flutter.

8 LORD, are you angry with the streams?
  Is your rage against the rivers,
  your wrath against the sea,
  that your steeds are mounted
  and you ride your chariots to victory?

2:16 **until you stagger:** so Scroll; Heb. obscure.   2:19 **Bestir
yourself:** prob. rdg; Heb. adds he will teach.   3:2 **what you have
done:** prob. rdg; Heb. adds in the midst of the years quicken it.
3:7 **are wrecked:** prob. rdg; Heb. under wickedness I have seen.

---

[h] Or poison   [i] Q Ms Gk: MT be uncircumcised   [j] Gk Syr:
Meaning of Heb uncertain   [k] Or against River   [l] Or against Sea

NEW AMERICAN BIBLE

14 But the earth shall be filled
  with the knowledge of the LORD's glory
  as water covers the sea.
15 Woe to you who give your neighbors
  a flood of your wrath to drink,
  and make them drunk, till their nakedness
    is seen!
16 You are filled with shame instead of glory;
  drink, you too, and stagger!
  On you shall revert the cup from the LORD's
    right hand,
  and utter shame on your glory.
17 For the violence done to Lebanon shall cover you,
  and the destruction of the beasts shall
    terrify you;
  Because of men's blood shed,
  and violence done to the land,
  to the city and to all who dwell in it.
19 Woe to him who says to wood, "Awake!"
  to dumb stone, "Arise!"
  Can such a thing give oracles?
  See, it is overlaid with gold and silver,
  but there is no life breath in it.
18 Of what avail is the carved image,
  that its maker should carve it?
  Or the molten image and lying oracle,
  that its very maker should trust in it,
  and make dumb idols?
20 But the LORD is in his holy temple;
  silence before him, all the earth!

3 Prayer of Habakkuk, the prophet. To a plaintive tune.

2 O LORD, I have heard your renown,
  and feared, O LORD, your work.
  In the course of the years revive it,
  in the course of the years make it known;
  in your wrath remember compassion!
3 God comes from Teman,
  the Holy One from Mount Paran.
  Covered are the heavens with his glory,
  and with his praise the earth is filled.
4 His splendor spreads like the light;
  rays shine forth from beside him,
  where his power is concealed.
5 Before him goes pestilence,
  and the plague follows in his steps.
6 He pauses to survey the earth;
  his look makes the nations tremble.
  The eternal mountains are shattered,
  the age-old hills bow low
  along his ancient ways.
7 I see the tents of Cushan collapse;
  trembling are the pavilions of the land
    of Midian.
8 Is your anger against the streams, O LORD?
  Is your wrath against the streams,
  your rage against the sea,
  That you drive the steeds
  of your victorious chariot?

NEW JERUSALEM BIBLE

14 *But the earth will be full of the knowledge of the*
  glory of Yahweh
  as the waters cover the depths of the sea. b
15 Disaster to anyone who makes his neighbours
    drink,
  pouring out his poison until they are drunk,
  so that he can see them naked!
16 You are full of shame, not glory!
  Your turn now to drink and show your foreskin.
  The cup in Yahweh's right hand comes round to
    you,
  and disgrace will overshadow your glory.
17 For the violence done to the Lebanon will
    overwhelm you
  and the massacre of animals will terrify you,
  because of the bloodshed and violence done to the
    country,
  to the city and to all who live in it.
19c Disaster to anyone who says to the log, 'Wake
    up!',
  to the dumb stone, 'On your feet!'
  (This is the prophecy!)
  Look, he is encased in gold and silver,
  —but not a breath of life inside it!
18 What use is a sculpted image that a sculptor should
    make it?
  —a metal image, a lying instructor!
  And why does the image-maker put his trust in it,
  that he should make dumb idols?
20 But Yahweh is in his holy Temple:
  let the whole earth be silent before him.

3 A prayer of the prophet Habakkuk; tone as for dirges.

2 Yahweh, I have heard of your renown;
  your work, Yahweh, inspires me with dread.
  Make it live again in our time,
  make it known in our time;
  in wrath remember mercy.
3 Eloah d comes from Teman,
  and the Holy One from Mount Paran.   *Pause*
  His majesty covers the heavens,
  and his glory fills the earth.
4 His brightness is like the day,
  rays flash from his hands,
  that is where his power lies hidden.
5 Pestilence goes before him
  and Plague follows close behind.
6 When he stands up, he makes the earth tremble,
  with his glance he makes the nations quake.
  And the eternal mountains are dislodged,
  the everlasting hills sink down,
  his pathway from of old.
7 I saw the tents of Cushan in trouble,
  the tent-curtains of Midian shuddering.
8 Yahweh, are you enraged with the rivers,
  are you angry with the sea,
  that you should mount your chargers,
  your rescuing chariots?

b 2 Is 11:9.   c 2 vv. 18 and 19 have been transposed.
d 3 An ancient name for God. Teman is a district, Paran a mountain in
Edom.

NEW REVISED STANDARD VERSION	REVISED ENGLISH BIBLE

NEW REVISED STANDARD VERSION

9 You brandished your naked bow,
  sated[m] were the arrows at your command.[n]
                                              Selah
  You split the earth with rivers.
10 The mountains saw you, and writhed;
  a torrent of water swept by;
  the deep gave forth its voice.
  The sun[o] raised high its hands;
11 the moon[p] stood still in its exalted place,
  at the light of your arrows speeding by,
  at the gleam of your flashing spear.
12 In fury you trod the earth,
  in anger you trampled nations.
13 You came forth to save your people,
  to save your anointed.
  You crushed the head of the wicked house,
  laying it bare from foundation to roof.[q]   *Selah*
14 You pierced with his own arrows the head[q] of
      his warriors,[r]
  who came like a whirlwind to scatter us,[s]
  gloating as if ready to devour the poor who
      were in hiding.
15 You trampled the sea with your horses,
  churning the mighty waters.

16 I hear, and I tremble within;
  my lips quiver at the sound.
  Rottenness enters into my bones,
  and my steps tremble[t] beneath me.
  I wait quietly for the day of calamity
  to come upon the people who attack us.

17 Though the fig tree does not blossom,
  and no fruit is on the vines;
  though the produce of the olive fails
  and the fields yield no food;
  though the flock is cut off from the fold
  and there is no herd in the stalls,
18 yet I will rejoice in the LORD;
  I will exult in the God of my salvation.
19 GOD, the Lord, is my strength;
  he makes my feet like the feet of a deer,
  and makes me tread upon the heights.[u]

  To the leader: with stringed[v] instruments.

[m] Cn: Heb *oaths*   [n] Meaning of Heb uncertain   [o] Heb *It*
[p] Heb *sun, moon*   [q] Or *leader*   [r] Vg Compare Gk Syr: Meaning
of Heb uncertain   [s] Heb *me*   [t] Cn Compare Gk: Meaning of Heb
uncertain   [u] Heb *my heights*   [v] Heb *my stringed*

REVISED ENGLISH BIBLE

9 You draw your bow from its case
  and charge your quiver with arrows.   [*Selah*]
  You cleave the earth with streams;
10 the mountains see you and writhe with fear.
  The torrent of water rushes by
  and the deep thunders aloud.
11 At the gleam of your speeding arrows
  and the glint of your flashing spear,
  the sun forgets to turn in its course
  and the moon stands still at its zenith.
12 Furiously you traverse the earth;
  in anger you trample down the nations.
13 You go forth to save your people,
  to save your anointed one.
  You shatter the house of the wicked,
  laying bare its foundations to the bedrock.   [*Selah*]
14 You pierce their chiefs with your arrows;
  their leaders are swept away by a whirlwind,
  as they open their jaws
  to devour their wretched victims in secret.
15 When you tread the sea with your steeds
  the mighty waters foam.

16 I hear, and my body quakes;
  my lips quiver at the sound;
  weakness overcomes my limbs,
  and my feet totter in their tracks;
  I long for the day of disaster
  to dawn over our assailants.

17 The fig tree has no buds,
  the vines bear no harvest,
  the olive crop fails,
  the orchards yield no food,
  the fold is bereft of its flock,
  and there are no cattle in the stalls.
18 Even so I shall exult in the LORD
  and rejoice in the God who saves me.
19 The LORD God is my strength;
  he makes me as sure-footed as a hind
  and sets my feet on the heights.

For the leader: with stringed instruments

3:9 **and charge . . . arrows:** *prob. rdg, cp. Gk (Luc.); Heb.*
obscure.   3:10 **aloud:** *prob. rdg; Heb. adds* raised its hands on
high.   3:13 **shatter:** *prob. rdg; Heb. adds* a head from. **laying**
bare: *so Lat.; Heb.* bare places. **bedrock:** *prob. rdg; Heb.* neck.
3:14 **your arrows:** *prob. rdg; Heb.* his arrows.   3:16 **my feet:**
prob. rdg, cp. Gk; Heb. which.

9 Bared and ready is your bow,
  filled with arrows is your quiver.
Into streams you split the earth;
10 at sight of you the mountains tremble.
A torrent of rain descends;
  the ocean gives forth its roar.
The sun forgets to rise,
11 the moon remains in its shelter,
At the light of your flying arrows,
  at the gleam of your flashing spear.
12 In wrath you bestride the earth,
  in fury you trample the nations.
13 You come forth to save your people,
  to save your anointed one.
You crush the heads of the wicked,
  you lay bare their bases at the neck.
14 You pierce with your shafts the heads of
    their princes
  whose boast would be of devouring
  the wretched in their lair.
15 You tread the sea with your steeds
  amid the churning of the deep waters.

16 I hear, and my body trembles;
  at the sound, my lips quiver.
Decay invades my bones,
  my legs tremble beneath me.
I await the day of distress
  that will come upon the people who attack us.
17 For though the fig tree blossom not
  nor fruit be on the vines,
Though the yield of the olive fail
  and the terraces produce no nourishment,
Though the flocks disappear from the fold
  and there be no herd in the stalls,
18 Yet will I rejoice in the LORD
  and exult in my saving God.
19 GOD, my Lord, is my strength;
  he makes my feet swift as those of hinds
  and enables me to go upon the heights.

For the leader; with stringed instruments.

9 You uncover your bow,
  and give the string its fill of arrows.   *Pause*

You drench the soil with torrents;
10 the mountains see you and tremble,
  great floods sweep by,
  the abyss roars aloud,
  lifting high its waves.

11 Sun and moon stay inside their dwellings,
  they flee at the light of your arrows,
  at the flash of your lightning-spear.

12 In rage you stride across the land,
  in anger you trample the nations.

13 You marched to save your people,
  to save your anointed one;
  you wounded the head of the house of the wicked,
  laid bare the foundation to the rock.   *Pause*

14 With your shafts you pierced the leader of his
    warriors
  who stormed out with shouts of joy to scatter us,
  as if they meant to devour some poor wretch in
    their lair.

15 With your horses you trampled through the sea,
  through the surging abyss!

16 When I heard, I trembled to the core,
  my lips quivered at the sound;
  my bones became disjointed
  and my legs gave way beneath me.

Calmly I await the day of anguish
  which is dawning on the people now attacking us.

17 (For the fig tree is not to blossom,
  nor will the vines bear fruit,
  the olive crop will disappoint
  and the fields will yield no food;
  the sheep will vanish from the fold;
  no cattle in the stalls.)

18 But I shall rejoice in Yahweh,
  I shall exult in God my Saviour.

19 Yahweh my Lord is my strength,
  he will make my feet as light as a doe's,
  and set my steps on the heights.

For the choirmaster; on stringed instruments.

Zephaniah

1 The word of the LORD that came to Zephaniah son of Cushi son of Gedaliah son of Amariah son of Hezekiah, in the days of King Josiah son of Amon of Judah.

2 I will utterly sweep away everything
    from the face of the earth, says the LORD.
3 I will sweep away humans and animals;
    I will sweep away the birds of the air
    and the fish of the sea.
I will make the wicked stumble.*a*
    I will cut off humanity
    from the face of the earth, says the LORD.
4 I will stretch out my hand against Judah,
    and against all the inhabitants of Jerusalem;
and I will cut off from this place every remnant
    of Baal
and the name of the idolatrous priests;*b*
5 those who bow down on the roofs
    to the host of the heavens;
those who bow down and swear to the LORD,
    but also swear by Milcom;*c*
6 those who have turned back from following the
    LORD,
    who have not sought the LORD or inquired of
    him.

7 Be silent before the Lord GOD!
    For the day of the LORD is at hand;
the LORD has prepared a sacrifice,
    he has consecrated his guests.
8 And on the day of the LORD's sacrifice
I will punish the officials and the king's sons
    and all who dress themselves in foreign attire.
9 On that day I will punish
    all who leap over the threshold,
who fill their master's house
    with violence and fraud.

10 On that day, says the LORD,
    a cry will be heard from the Fish Gate,
a wail from the Second Quarter,
    a loud crash from the hills.
11 The inhabitants of the Mortar wail,
    for all the traders have perished;
all who weigh out silver are cut off.
12 At that time I will search Jerusalem with lamps,
    and I will punish the people
who rest complacently*d* on their dregs,
    those who say in their hearts,
"The LORD will not do good,
    nor will he do harm."
13 Their wealth shall be plundered,
    and their houses laid waste.
Though they build houses,
    they shall not inhabit them;
though they plant vineyards,
    they shall not drink wine from them.

---

a Cn: Heb *sea, and those who cause the wicked to stumble*
b Compare Gk: Heb *the idolatrous priests with the priests*
c Gk Mss Syr Vg: Heb *Malcam* (or, *their king*)   *d* Heb *who thicken*

Zephaniah

1 THIS is the word of the LORD which came to Zephaniah son of Cushi, son of Gedaliah, son of Amariah, son of Hezekiah, when Josiah son of Amon was king of Judah.

2 I SHALL utterly destroy everything
    from the face of the earth,
    says the LORD.
3 I shall destroy human beings and animals,
    the birds of the air and the fish in the sea.
I shall bring the wicked to their knees
    and wipe out all people from the earth.
    This is the word of the LORD.

4 I shall stretch my hand over Judah,
    over all who live in Jerusalem.
I shall wipe out from that place the last remnant of
    Baal,
    every memory of the heathen priests,
5 those who bow down on the housetops
    to the host of heaven,
    those who swear by Milcom,
6 who have turned their backs on the LORD,
    who have neither sought the LORD nor consulted
    him.

7 Keep silent in the presence of the Lord GOD,
    for the day of the LORD is near.
The LORD has prepared a sacrifice
    and set apart those he has invited.

8 On the day of the LORD's sacrifice
I shall punish the royal house and its chief officers
    and all who appear in foreign apparel.
9 On that day I shall punish
    all who dance on the temple terrace,
who fill their Lord's house
    with crimes of violence and fraud.
10 On that day, says the LORD,
    a sound of crying will be heard from the Fish
      Gate,
    wailing from the Second Quarter of the city;
    there will be a loud crash from the hills.
11 Those who live in the Lower Town will wail,
    for all the merchants are destroyed,
    and the dealers in silver are all wiped out.

12 At that time
    I shall search Jerusalem by lantern-light
    and punish all who are ruined by complacency
    like wine left on its lees,
    who say to themselves,
    'The LORD will do nothing, neither good nor bad.'
13 Their wealth will be plundered,
    their houses laid in ruins;
they will build houses but not live in them,
    they will plant vineyards but not drink the wine.

1:3 **I shall bring . . . knees:** *prob. rdg; Heb.* the ruins with the
wicked.   1:4 **heathen priests:** *so Gk; Heb. adds* together with the
(*legitimate*) priests.   1:5 **those . . . heaven:** *prob. rdg, cp. Gk;
Heb. adds* those who worship, who swear by the LORD.   1:9 **who
dance . . . terrace:** *or* who leap over the threshold. **Lord's:** *or*
master's.   1:11 **Lower Town:** *lit.* Quarry.

THE BOOK OF

Zephaniah

1 The word of the Lord which came to Zephaniah, the son of Cushi, the son of Gedaliah, the son of Amariah, the son of Hezekiah, in the days of Josiah, the son of Amon, king of Judah.

2 I will completely sweep away all things
   from the face of the earth, says the Lord.
3 I will sweep away man and beast,
   I will sweep away the birds of the sky,
   and the fishes of the sea.
I will overthrow the wicked;
   I will destroy mankind
   from the face of the earth, says the Lord.
4 I will stretch out my hand against Judah,
   and against all the inhabitants of Jerusalem;
I will destroy from this place the last vestige
   of Baal,
   the very names of his priests,
5 And those who adore the host of heaven on
   the roofs,
   with those who adore the Lord
   but swear by Milcom;
6 And those who have fallen away from the Lord,
   and those who do not seek the Lord.
7 Silence in the presence of the Lord God!
   for near is the day of the Lord,
Yes, the Lord has prepared a slaughter feast,
   he has consecrated his guests.
8   On the day of the Lord's slaughter feast
I will punish the princes, and the king's sons,
   and all that dress in foreign apparel.
9 I will punish, on that day,
   all who leap over the threshold,
Who fill the house of their master
   with violence and deceit.
10   On that day, says the Lord,
A cry will be heard from the Fish Gate,
   a wail from the New Quarter,
   loud crashing from the hills.
11 Wail, O inhabitants of the Mortar!
   for all the merchants will be destroyed,
   all who weigh out silver, done away with.
12 At that time I will explore Jerusalem with lamps;
   I will punish the men who thicken on their lees,
Who say in their hearts,
   "Neither good nor evil can the Lord do."
13 Their wealth shall be given to pillage
   and their houses to devastation;
They will build houses, but shall not dwell
   in them,
   plant vineyards, but not drink their wine.

Zephaniah

1 The word of Yahweh which was addressed to Zephaniah son of Cushi, son of Gedaliah, son of Amariah, son of Hezekiah, in the days of Josiah son of Amon king of Judah.

2 I shall sweep away everything
   off the face of the earth,
   declares Yahweh.
3 I shall sweep away humans and animals,
   the birds of the air and the fish of the sea,
   I shall topple the wicked
   and wipe all people off the face of the earth
   —declares Yahweh.
4 I shall raise my hand against Judah
   and against all who live in Jerusalem,
   and from this place I will wipe out Baal's remnant,
   the very name of his priests,
5 and those who prostrate themselves on the roofs
   before the array of heaven,
   and those who prostrate themselves before Yahweh
   but swear by Milcom,[a]
6 and those who have turned their back on Yahweh,
   who do not seek Yahweh
   and do not consult him.
7 Silence before Lord Yahweh,
   for the Day of Yahweh is near!
Yahweh has prepared a sacrifice,
   he has consecrated his guests.
8 On the Day of Yahweh's sacrifice,
   I shall punish the courtiers,
   the royal princes
   and all who dress
   in outlandish clothes.
9 On that day I shall punish
   all who go up the Step
   and fill the Temple of their lords,
   with violence and deceit.
10 On that Day—declares Yahweh—
   uproar will be heard from the Fish Gate,
   wailing from the New Quarter
   and a great crash from the hills.
11 Wail, you who live in the Hollow,
   for it is all over with the merchants,
   all the money-bags have been wiped out!
12 When that time comes
   I shall search Jerusalem by lamplight
   and punish the men
   stagnating over the remains of their wine,
   who say in their hearts,
   'Yahweh can do nothing,
   either good or bad.'
13 For this, their wealth will be looted
   and their houses laid in ruins;
   they will build houses but not live in them,
   they will plant vineyards but not drink their wine.

---

a 1 A god of Ammon.

NEW REVISED STANDARD VERSION	REVISED ENGLISH BIBLE

NEW REVISED STANDARD VERSION

14 The great day of the LORD is near,
  near and hastening fast;
the sound of the day of the LORD is bitter,
  the warrior cries aloud there.
15 That day will be a day of wrath,
  a day of distress and anguish,
a day of ruin and devastation,
  a day of darkness and gloom,
a day of clouds and thick darkness,
16   a day of trumpet blast and battle cry
against the fortified cities
  and against the lofty battlements.

17 I will bring such distress upon people
  that they shall walk like the blind;
because they have sinned against the LORD,
  their blood shall be poured out like dust,
  and their flesh like dung.
18 Neither their silver nor their gold
  will be able to save them
  on the day of the LORD's wrath;
in the fire of his passion
  the whole earth shall be consumed;
for a full, a terrible end
  he will make of all the inhabitants of the earth.

2 Gather together, gather,
  O shameless nation,
2 before you are driven away
  like the drifting chaff,^e
before there comes upon you
  the fierce anger of the LORD,
before there comes upon you
  the day of the LORD's wrath.
3 Seek the LORD, all you humble of the land,
  who do his commands;
seek righteousness, seek humility;
  perhaps you may be hidden
  on the day of the LORD's wrath.
4 For Gaza shall be deserted,
  and Ashkelon shall become a desolation;
Ashdod's people shall be driven out at noon,
  and Ekron shall be uprooted.
5 Ah, inhabitants of the seacoast,
  you nation of the Cherethites!
The word of the LORD is against you,
  O Canaan, land of the Philistines;
and I will destroy you until no inhabitant is
    left.
6 And you, O seacoast, shall be pastures,
  meadows for shepherds
  and folds for flocks.
7 The seacoast shall become the possession
  of the remnant of the house of Judah,
  on which they shall pasture,
and in the houses of Ashkelon
  they shall lie down at evening.
For the LORD their God will be mindful of them
  and restore their fortunes.

8 I have heard the taunts of Moab
  and the revilings of the Ammonites,
how they have taunted my people
  and made boasts against their territory.

REVISED ENGLISH BIBLE

14 The great day of the LORD is near,
  near and coming fast;
no runner is so swift as that day,
  no warrior so fleet.
15 That day is a day of wrath,
  a day of anguish and torment,
a day of destruction and devastation,
  a day of darkness and gloom,
a day of cloud and dense fog,
16 a day of trumpet-blasts and battle cries
against the fortified cities and lofty bastions.
17 I shall bring dire distress on the people;
  they will walk like the blind
because of their sin against the LORD.
  Their blood will be poured out like dust
  and their bowels like dung;
18 neither their silver nor their gold
  will avail to save them.
On the day of the LORD's wrath
  by the fire of his jealousy
the whole land will be consumed;
  for he will make a sudden and terrible end
of all who live in the land.

2 Humble yourself, unruly nation; be humble,
2 before you are driven away to disappear like
    chaff,
before the burning anger of the LORD comes upon
    you,
before the day of the LORD's anger comes upon
    you.
3 Seek the LORD,
  all in the land who live humbly, obeying his laws;
seek righteousness, seek humility;
  it may be that you will find shelter
  on the day of the LORD's anger.

4 Gaza will be deserted,
  Ashkelon left a waste;
the people of Ashdod will be driven out at
    noonday,
  and Ekron will be uprooted.
5 Woe betide you Kerethites who live by the coast!
This word of the LORD is spoken against you:
Land of the Philistines, I shall crush you,
  I shall lay you in ruins, bereft of inhabitants.
6 Kereth will become pastures and sheepfolds,
7 and the coastland will belong to the survivors of
    Judah.
They will pasture their flocks by the sea
and lie down at evening in the houses at Ashkelon,
  for the LORD their God will turn to them
  and restore their fortunes.

8 I have heard the insults of Moab,
  the taunts of the Ammonites,
how they reviled my people
  and encroached on their frontiers.

1:14 **no runner . . . fleet:** *prob. rdg; Heb.* hark, the day of the LORD
is bitter; there the warrior cries aloud.   2:1 **Humble . . . humble:**
prob. meaning; Heb. obscure.   2:2 **you are . . . disappear:** *prob.
rdg; Heb. obscure.*   2:5 **I shall crush you:** *prob. rdg; Heb.*
Canaan.   2:6 **Kereth:** *so Gk; Heb.* adds the region of the sea.
2:7 **by the sea:** *prob. rdg; Heb.* upon them.

---

^e Cn Compare Gk Syr: Heb *before a decree is born; like chaff a day
has passed away*

NEW AMERICAN BIBLE

NEW JERUSALEM BIBLE

NEW AMERICAN BIBLE

14 Near is the great day of the LORD,
   near and very swiftly coming;
   Hark, the day of the LORD!
   bitter, then, the warrior's cry.
15 A day of wrath is that day,
   a day of anguish and distress,
   A day of destruction and desolation,
   a day of darkness and gloom,
   A day of thick black clouds,
16   a day of trumpet blasts and battle alarm
   Against fortified cities,
   against battlements on high.
17 I will hem men in
   till they walk like the blind,
   because they have sinned against the LORD;
   And their blood shall be poured out like dust,
   and their brains like dung.
18 Neither their silver nor their gold
   shall be able to save them
   on the day of the LORD's wrath,
   When in the fire of his jealousy
   all the earth shall be consumed.
   For he shall make an end, yes, a sudden end,
   of all who live on the earth.

2 Gather, gather yourselves together,
   O nation without shame!
2 Before you are driven away,
   like chaff that passes on;
   Before there comes upon you
   the blazing anger of the LORD;
   Before there comes upon you
   the day of the LORD's anger.
3 Seek the LORD, all you humble of the earth,
   who have observed his law;
   Seek justice, seek humility;
   perhaps you may be sheltered
   on the day of the LORD's anger.
4 For Gaza shall be forsaken,
   and Ashkelon shall be a waste,
   Ashdod they shall drive out at midday,
   and Ekron shall be uprooted.
5 Woe to you who dwell by the seacoast,
   to the Cretan folk!
   The word of the LORD is against you,
   I will humble you, land of the Philistines,
   and leave you to perish without an inhabitant!
6 The coastland of the Cretans shall become
   fields for shepherds, and folds for flocks.
7 The coast shall belong
   to the remnant of the house of Judah;
   by the sea they shall pasture.
   In the houses of Ashkelon at evening
   they shall couch their flocks,
   For the LORD their God shall visit them,
   and bring about their restoration.

8 I have heard the revilings uttered by Moab,
   and the insults of the Ammonites,
   When they reviled my people
   and made boasts against their territory.

NEW JERUSALEM BIBLE

14 The great Day of Yahweh is near,
   near, and coming with great speed.
   How bitter the sound of the Day of Yahweh,
   the Day when the warrior shouts his cry of war.
15 That Day is a day of retribution,
   a day of distress and tribulation,
   a day of ruin and of devastation,
   a day of darkness and gloom,
   a day of cloud and thick fog,
16 a day of trumpet blast and battle cry
   against fortified town
   and high corner-tower.
17 I shall bring such distress on humanity
   that they will grope their way like the blind
   for having sinned against Yahweh.
   Their blood will be poured out like mud,
   yes, their corpses like dung;
18 nor will their silver or gold
   be able to save them.
   On the Day of Yahweh's anger,
   by the fire of his jealousy,
   the whole earth will be consumed.
   For he will destroy, yes, annihilate
   everyone living on earth.

2 Gather together, gather together,
   nations without shame,
2 before you are dispersed like chaff
   which disappears in a day;
   before Yahweh's burning anger overtakes you
   (before the Day of Yahweh's anger overtakes you).
3 Seek Yahweh,
   all you humble of the earth,
   who obey his commands.
   Seek uprightness,
   seek humility:
   you may perhaps find shelter
   on the Day of Yahweh's anger.
4 For Gaza will be abandoned
   and Ashkelon reduced to ruins;
   Ashdod will be driven out in broad daylight
   and Ekron[b] uprooted.
5 Disaster to the members of the coastal league,
   to the nation of the Cherethites!
   This is the word of Yahweh against you:
   I shall subdue you, land of the Philistines,
   I shall destroy you till there are no inhabitants left;
6 and the coastal league will be reduced to pasture
      land,
   to grazing grounds for shepherds
   and folds for sheep;
7 and the league will belong
   to the remnant of the House of Judah;
   they will pasture their flocks there,
   at night they will rest in the houses of Ashkelon;
   for, when Yahweh their God has punished them,
   he will restore their fortunes.

8 I have heard the taunt of Moab
   and the insults of the Ammonites,
   as they taunted my people
   and boasted of their own domains.

b 2 Four of the five Philistine coastal cities. Gath was already in ruins.

9 Therefore, as I live, says the LORD of hosts,
the God of Israel,
Moab shall become like Sodom
and the Ammonites like Gomorrah,
a land possessed by nettles and salt pits,
and a waste forever.
The remnant of my people shall plunder them,
and the survivors of my nation shall possess
them.

10 This shall be their lot in return for their pride,
because they scoffed and boasted
against the people of the LORD of hosts.

11 The LORD will be terrible against them;
he will shrivel all the gods of the earth,
and to him shall bow down,
each in its place,
all the coasts and islands of the nations.

12 You also, O Ethiopians,*f*
shall be killed by my sword.

13 And he will stretch out his hand against the
north,
and destroy Assyria;
and he will make Nineveh a desolation,
a dry waste like the desert.

14 Herds shall lie down in it,
every wild animal;*g*
the desert owl*h* and the screech owl*h*
shall lodge on its capitals;
the owl*i* shall hoot at the window,
the raven*j* croak on the threshold;
for its cedar work will be laid bare.

15 Is this the exultant city
that lived secure,
that said to itself,
"I am, and there is no one else"?
What a desolation it has become,
a lair for wild animals!
Everyone who passes by it
hisses and shakes the fist.

3 Ah, soiled, defiled,
oppressing city!

2 It has listened to no voice;
it has accepted no correction.
It has not trusted in the LORD;
it has not drawn near to its God.

3 The officials within it
are roaring lions;
its judges are evening wolves
that leave nothing until the morning.

4 Its prophets are reckless,
faithless persons;
its priests have profaned what is sacred,
they have done violence to the law.

5 The LORD within it is righteous;
he does no wrong.
Every morning he renders his judgment,
each dawn without fail;
but the unjust knows no shame.

6 I have cut off nations;
their battlements are in ruins;
I have laid waste their streets
so that no one walks in them;
their cities have been made desolate,
without people, without inhabitants.

9 For this, by my life,
says the LORD of Hosts, the God of Israel,
Moab shall become like Sodom,
Ammon like Gomorrah,
a mass of weeds, a heap of saltwort,
waste land for evermore.
Those of my people who survive will plunder
them,
the remnant of my nation will dispossess them.

10 This will be retribution for their pride, because they have
insulted the people of the LORD of Hosts and encroached
upon their land. 11 The LORD will bring terror on them; he
will reduce to beggary all the gods of the earth. Then the
nations in all the coasts and islands will worship him, each
in its own land.

12 You Cushites also will be slain
by the sword of the LORD.

13 He will stretch out his hand against the north
and destroy Assyria,
making Nineveh a waste,
arid as the desert.

14 Flocks will couch there,
and every kind of wild animal.
The horned owl and the bustard
will roost on her capitals;
the tawny owl will screech in the window,
and the raven in the doorway.

15 This is the city that exulted in her security,
saying to herself, 'I and I alone am supreme.'
And what is she now? A waste, a haunt of wild
animals,
at which every passer-by may jeer and gesture!

3 Woe betide the tyrant city,
filthy and foul!

2 She heeded no warning voice,
took no rebuke to heart;
she did not put her trust in the LORD,
nor did she draw near to her God.

3 The leaders within her were roaring lions,
her rulers wolves of the plain
that left nothing over till morning.

4 Her prophets were reckless and perfidious;
her priests profaned the sanctuary
and did violence to the law.

5 But the LORD in her midst is just;
he does no wrong;
morning after morning he gives his judgement,
every day without fail;
yet the wrongdoer knows no shame.

6 I have wiped out this arrogant people;
their bastions are demolished.
I have destroyed their streets;
no one walks along them.
Their cities are laid waste,
abandoned and unpeopled.

f Or *Nubians*; Heb *Cushites* *g* Tg Compare Gk: Heb *nation* *h* Meaning of Heb uncertain *i* Cn: Heb *a voice* *j* Gk Vg: Heb *desolation*

2:12 **the sword of the LORD:** *prob. rdg*; Heb. my sword.
2:14 **tawny owl:** *prob. rdg*; Heb. voice. **in the doorway:** *prob. rdg*;
Heb. *adds an unintelligible phrase.* 3:3 **plain:** *or* evening.
3:6 **this . . . people:** *so* Gk; Heb. nations.

2074

9 Therefore, as I live, says the LORD of hosts,
   the God of Israel,
Moab shall become like Sodom,
   the land of Ammon like Gomorrah:
A field of nettles and a salt pit
   and a waste forever.
The remnant of my people shall plunder them,
   the survivors of my nation dispossess them.
10 Such shall be the requital of their pride,
   because they reviled and boasted against
    the people of the LORD of hosts.
11 The LORD shall inspire them with fear
   when he makes all the gods of earth to
    waste away;
Then, each from its own place,
   all the coastlands of the nations shall adore him.

12 You too, O Cushites,
   shall be slain by the sword of the LORD.
13 He will stretch out his hand against the north,
   to destroy Assyria;
He will make Nineveh a waste,
   dry as the desert.
14 In her midst shall settle in droves
   all the wild life of the hollows;
The screech owl and the desert owl
   shall roost in her columns;
Their call shall resound from the window,
   the raven's croak from the doorway.
15 Is this the exultant city
   that dwelt secure;
That told herself,
   "There is no other than I!"
How has she become a waste,
   a lair for wild beasts?
Whoever passes by her
   hisses, and shakes his fist!

3   Woe to the city, rebellious and polluted,
   to the tyrannical city!
2 She hears no voice,
   accepts no correction;
In the LORD she has not trusted,
   to her God she has not drawn near.
3 Her princes in her midst
   are roaring lions;
Her judges are wolves of the night
   that have had no bones to gnaw by morning.
4 Her prophets are insolent,
   treacherous men;
Her priests profane what is holy,
   and do violence to the law.
5 The LORD within her is just,
   who does no wrong;
Morning after morning he renders judgment
   unfailingly, at dawn.

6 I have destroyed nations,
   their battlements are laid waste;
I have made their streets deserted,
   with no one passing through;
Their cities are devastated,
   with no man dwelling in them.

9 For this, as I live — declares Yahweh Sabaoth,
God of Israel —
Moab will become like Sodom
   and the Ammonites like Gomorrah:
a realm of nettles, a heap of salt,
   a desolation for ever.
What is left of my people will plunder them,
   the survivors of my nation will take their heritage.
10 This will be the price of their pride
   for having taunted and boasted
   over the people of Yahweh Sabaoth.
11 Yahweh will be fearsome to them,
   for he will scatter all the gods of the earth,
   and they will bow down to him,
   each from his own place —
   all the islands of the nations.

12 You Ethiopians too
   will be run through by my sword.
13 He will raise his hand against the north
   and bring Assyria down in ruins;
he will make Nineveh a waste,
   as dry as a desert.
14 Flocks will rest inside there,
   so will wild animals;
pelican and porcupine
   will nest round her cornices at night;
the owl will hoot at the window
   and the raven croak on the doorstep —
   for the cedar has been torn down.
15 This is what the city will be like,
   once living happy and carefree
and thinking to itself,
   'I have no rival — not I!'
And what will it be now? A ruin,
   a lair for wild beasts to rest in,
and everyone who passes by
   will whistle and throw up his hands.

3   Disaster to the rebellious, the befouled,
   the tyrannical city!
2 She has not listened to the call,
   she has not bowed to correction,
she has not trusted in Yahweh,
   she has not drawn near to her God.
3 The rulers she has
   are roaring lions,
her judges are wolves of the wastelands
   which leave nothing over for the morning,
4 her prophets are braggarts,
   impostors,
her priests have profaned what is holy
   and violated the Law.

5 Yahweh the Upright is in her,
   he does no wrong;
morning by morning he gives judgement,
   each dawn unfailingly
   (but the wrong-doer knows no shame).

6 I have exterminated the nations,
   their corner-towers lie in ruins;
I have emptied their streets,
   no one walks through them;
their cities have been destroyed
   and are now deserted and unpeopled.

7 I said, "Surely the city*k* will fear me,
    it will accept correction;
it will not lose sight*l*
    of all that I have brought upon it."
But they were the more eager
    to make all their deeds corrupt.

8 Therefore wait for me, says the LORD,
    for the day when I arise as a witness.
For my decision is to gather nations,
    to assemble kingdoms,
to pour out upon them my indignation,
    all the heat of my anger;
for in the fire of my passion
    all the earth shall be consumed.

9 At that time I will change the speech of the
      peoples
    to a pure speech,
that all of them may call on the name of the
    LORD
    and serve him with one accord.

10 From beyond the rivers of Ethiopia*m*
    my suppliants, my scattered ones,
    shall bring my offering.

11 On that day you shall not be put to shame
    because of all the deeds by which you have
      rebelled against me;
for then I will remove from your midst
    your proudly exultant ones,
and you shall no longer be haughty
    in my holy mountain.

12 For I will leave in the midst of you
    a people humble and lowly.
They shall seek refuge in the name of the
    LORD—

13   the remnant of Israel;
they shall do no wrong
    and utter no lies,
nor shall a deceitful tongue
    be found in their mouths.
Then they will pasture and lie down,
    and no one shall make them afraid.

14 Sing aloud, O daughter Zion;
    shout, O Israel!
Rejoice and exult with all your heart,
    O daughter Jerusalem!

15 The LORD has taken away the judgments against
      you,
    he has turned away your enemies.
The king of Israel, the LORD, is in your midst;
    you shall fear disaster no more.

16 On that day it shall be said to Jerusalem:
Do not fear, O Zion;
    do not let your hands grow weak.

17 The LORD, your God, is in your midst,
    a warrior who gives victory;
he will rejoice over you with gladness,
    he will renew you*n* in his love;
he will exult over you with loud singing

18   as on a day of festival.*o*
I will remove disaster from you,*p*
    so that you will not bear reproach for it.

7 I said, 'Surely she will fear me;
    she will take my instruction to heart,
all the commands I laid on her
    that her dwelling-place might escape destruction.'
But they hastened all the more
    to perform their evil deeds.

8 Therefore wait for me, says the LORD,
    wait for the day when I stand up to accuse you;
I have decided to gather nations
    and assemble kingdoms,
in order to pour my wrath on them,
    all my burning anger;
the whole earth will be consumed
    by the fire of my jealousy.

9 Then I shall restore pure lips to all peoples,
    that they may invoke the LORD by name
    and serve him with one accord.

10 My worshippers, dispersed beyond the rivers of
      Cush,
    will bring offerings to me.

11 On that day, Jerusalem,
    you will not be put to shame for any of the deeds
    by which you have rebelled against me,
because I shall rid you then
    of your proud and arrogant citizens,
and never again will you flaunt your pride
    on my holy mountain.

12 I shall leave a remnant in you,
    lowly and poor people.
The survivors in Israel will find refuge in the
    LORD's name.

13 They will do no wrong, nor speak lies;
    no words of deceit will pass their lips;
they will feed and lie down
    with no one to terrify them.

14 Zion, cry out for joy;
    raise the shout of triumph, Israel;
be glad, rejoice with all your heart,
    daughter of Jerusalem!

15 The LORD has averted your punishment,
    he has swept away your foes.
Israel, the LORD is among you as king;
    never again need you fear disaster.

16 On that day this must be the message to Jerusalem:
Fear not, Zion, let not your hands hang limp.

17 The LORD your God is in your midst,
    a warrior who will keep you safe.
He will rejoice over you and be glad;
    he will show you his love once more;
    he will exult over you with a shout of joy

18 as on a festal day.

I shall take away your cries of woe
and you will no longer endure reproach.

---

k Heb *it*   *l* Gk Syr: Heb *its dwelling will not be cut off*
m Or *Nubia*; Heb *Cush*   *n* Gk Syr: Heb *he will be silent*
o Gk Syr: Meaning of Heb uncertain   *p* Cn: Heb *I will remove from
you; they were*

3:17 **he will show . . . more:** *prob. rdg, cp. Gk; Heb.* he will be
silent in his love.   3:18 **as . . . day:** *so Gk; Heb. obscure.* **cries
of woe:** *prob. rdg; Heb. obscure.* **endure reproach:** *prob. rdg; Heb.
adds* because of her.

7 I said, "Surely now you will fear me,
   you will accept correction";
She should not fail to see
   all I have visited upon her.
Yet all the more eagerly have they done
   all their corrupt deeds.
8 Therefore, wait for me, says the LORD,
   against the day when I arise as accuser;
For it is my decision to gather together the nations,
   to assemble the kingdoms,
In order to pour out upon them my wrath,
   all my blazing anger;
For in the fire of my jealousy
   shall all the earth be consumed.
9 For then I will change and purify
   the lips of the peoples,
That they all may call upon the name of the LORD,
   to serve him with one accord;
10 From beyond the rivers of Ethiopia
   and as far as the recesses of the North,
   they shall bring me offerings.

11   On that day
You need not be ashamed
   of all your deeds,
   your rebellious actions against me;
For then will I remove from your midst
   the proud braggarts,
And you shall no longer exalt yourself
   on my holy mountain.
12 But I will leave as a remnant in your midst
   a people humble and lowly,
Who shall take refuge in the name of the Lord:
13   the remnant of Israel.
They shall do no wrong
   and speak no lies;
Nor shall there be found in their mouths
   a deceitful tongue;
They shall pasture and couch their flocks
   with none to disturb them.

14 Shout for joy, O daughter Zion!
   sing joyfully, O Israel!
Be glad and exult with all your heart,
   O daughter Jerusalem!
15 The LORD has removed the judgment against you,
   he has turned away your enemies;
The King of Israel, the LORD, is in your midst,
   you have no further misfortune to fear.
16 On that day, it shall be said to Jerusalem:
   Fear not, O Zion, be not discouraged!
17 The LORD, your God, is in your midst,
   a mighty savior;
He will rejoice over you with gladness,
   and renew you in his love,
He will sing joyfully because of you,
18   as one sings at festivals.
I will remove disaster from among you,
   so that none may recount your disgrace.

7 I thought, 'At least you will fear me,
   at least you will bow to correction,'
and none of the punishments I brought on them
   will disappear from their view.
But no, it only made them more anxious
   to do whatever was corrupt.

8 So wait for me — declares Yahweh —
   for the day when I rise as accuser,
for I am determined to gather the nations,
   to assemble the kingdoms,
and on you to vent my fury,
   the whole heat of my anger
(for the whole earth will be devoured
   by the fire of my jealousy).

9 Yes, then I shall purge
   the lips of the peoples,
so that all may invoke the name of Yahweh
   and serve him shoulder to shoulder.
10 From beyond the rivers of Ethiopia,
   my suppliants will bring me tribute.

11 When that Day comes
   you will never again be ashamed of all the deeds
   with which you once rebelled against me,
for I shall rid you
   of those who exult in your pride;
never again will you strut
   on my holy mountain.
12 But in you I shall leave surviving
   a humble^c and lowly people,
13 and those who are left in Israel
   will take refuge in the name of Yahweh.
They will do no wrong,
   will tell no lies;
nor will a deceitful tongue
   be found in their mouths.
But they will be able to graze and rest
   with no one to alarm them.

14 ^d Shout for joy, daughter of Zion,
   Israel, shout aloud!
Rejoice, exult with all your heart,
   daughter of Jerusalem!
15 Yahweh has repealed your sentence;
   he has turned your enemy away.
Yahweh is king among you, Israel,
   you have nothing more to fear.

16 When that Day comes, the message for Jerusalem
      will be:
Zion, have no fear,
   do not let your hands fall limp.
17 Yahweh your God is there with you,
   the warrior-Saviour.
He will rejoice over you with happy song,
   he will renew you by his love,
he will dance with shouts of joy for you,
18 as on a day of festival.
I have taken away your misfortune,
   no longer need you bear the disgrace of it.

---

c 3 In the prophets the humble and oppressed, specially dependent on
Yahweh, are the object of his special care. Here and in the Pss
poverty is a spiritual quality, openness to God's love.
d 3 These two final psalms (vv. 14-18) were probably added later.

NEW REVISED STANDARD VERSION

19 I will deal with all your oppressors
    at that time.
And I will save the lame
    and gather the outcast,
and I will change their shame into praise
    and renown in all the earth.
20 At that time I will bring you home,
    at the time when I gather you;
for I will make you renowned and praised
    among all the peoples of the earth,
when I restore your fortunes
    before your eyes, says the LORD.

REVISED ENGLISH BIBLE

19 When that time comes;
    I shall deal with all who oppress you;
    I shall rescue the lost and gather the dispersed.
    I shall win for my people praise and renown
    throughout the whole world.
20 When that time comes I shall gather you
    and bring you home.
    I shall win you renown and praise
    among all the peoples of the earth,
    when I restore your fortunes before your eyes.
    It is the LORD who speaks.

3:19 **throughout . . . world:** *prob. rdg; Heb. adds* their shame.

NEW AMERICAN BIBLE

19 Yes, at that time I will deal
    with all who oppress you:
I will save the lame,
    and assemble the outcasts;
I will give them praise and renown
    in all the earth, when I bring about
        their restoration.
20 At that time I will bring you home,
    and at that time I will gather you;
For I will give you renown and praise,
    among all the peoples of the earth,
When I bring about your restoration
    before your very eyes, says the LORD.

NEW JERUSALEM BIBLE

19 I am taking action here and now
    against your oppressors.
When that time comes I will rescue the lame,
    and gather the strays,
    and I will win them praise and renown
when I restore their fortunes.

20 At that time I shall be your guide,
    at the time when I gather you in,
I shall give you praise and renown
    among all the peoples of the earth
    when I restore your fortunes under your own eyes,
        declares Yahweh.

Haggai

1 In the second year of King Darius, in the sixth month, on the first day of the month, the word of the Lord came by the prophet Haggai to Zerubbabel son of Shealtiel, governor of Judah, and to Joshua son of Jehozadak, the high priest: 2 Thus says the Lord of hosts: These people say the time has not yet come to rebuild the Lord's house. 3 Then the word of the Lord came by the prophet Haggai, saying: 4 Is it a time for you yourselves to live in your paneled houses, while this house lies in ruins? 5 Now therefore thus says the Lord of hosts: Consider how you have fared. 6 You have sown much, and harvested little; you eat, but you never have enough; you drink, but you never have your fill; you clothe yourselves, but no one is warm; and you that earn wages earn wages to put them into a bag with holes.

7 Thus says the Lord of hosts: Consider how you have fared. 8 Go up to the hills and bring wood and build the house, so that I may take pleasure in it and be honored, says the Lord. 9 You have looked for much, and, lo, it came to little; and when you brought it home, I blew it away. Why? says the Lord of hosts. Because my house lies in ruins, while all of you hurry off to your own houses. 10 Therefore the heavens above you have withheld the dew, and the earth has withheld its produce. 11 And I have called for a drought on the land and the hills, on the grain, the new wine, the oil, on what the soil produces, on human beings and animals, and on all their labors.

12 Then Zerubbabel son of Shealtiel, and Joshua son of Jehozadak, the high priest, with all the remnant of the people, obeyed the voice of the Lord their God, and the words of the prophet Haggai, as the Lord their God had sent him; and the people feared the Lord. 13 Then Haggai, the messenger of the Lord, spoke to the people with the Lord's message, saying, I am with you, says the Lord. 14 And the Lord stirred up the spirit of Zerubbabel son of Shealtiel, governor of Judah, and the spirit of Joshua son of Jehozadak, the high priest, and the spirit of all the remnant of the people; and they came and worked on the house of the Lord of hosts, their God, 15 on the twenty-fourth day of the month, in the sixth month.

2 In the second year of King Darius, 1 in the seventh month, on the twenty-first day of the month, the word of the Lord came by the prophet Haggai, saying: 2 Speak

Haggai

1 In the second year of King Darius, on the first day of the sixth month, the word of the Lord, spoken through the prophet Haggai, came to the governor of Judah Zerubbabel son of Shealtiel, and to the high priest Joshua son of Jehozadak. 2 'These are the words of the Lord of Hosts: This nation says that the time has not yet come for the house of the Lord to be rebuilt.' 3 Then this word came through Haggai the prophet: 4 'Is it a time for you yourselves to live in your well-roofed houses, while this house lies in ruins? 5 Now these are the words of the Lord of Hosts: Consider your way of life; 6 you have sown much but reaped little, you eat but never enough to satisfy, you drink but never enough to cheer you, you are clothed but never warm, and he who earns wages puts them into a purse with a hole in it.

7 'These are the words of the Lord of Hosts: Consider your way of life. 8 Go up into the hill-country, fetch timber, and build a house acceptable to me, where I can reveal my glory, says the Lord. 9 You look for much and get little and when you bring home the harvest I blast it away. And why? says the Lord of Hosts. Because my house lies in ruins, while each of you has a house he can hurry to. 10 It is your fault that the heavens withhold their moisture and the earth its produce. 11 So I have proclaimed a drought against land and mountain, against grain, new wine, and oil, and everything that the ground yields, against human beings and cattle and all the products of your labour.'

12 Zerubbabel son of Shealtiel, Joshua son of Jehozadak, the high priest, and all the rest of the people listened to the words of the Lord their God and to what the prophet Haggai said when the Lord their God sent him, and they were filled with fear because of the Lord. 13 So Haggai the Lord's messenger, as the Lord had commissioned him, said to the people: 'I am with you, says the Lord.' 14 Then the Lord stirred up the spirit of the governor of Judah Zerubbabel son of Shealtiel, of the high priest Joshua son of Jehozadak, and of the rest of the people, so that they went and set to work on the house of the Lord of Hosts their God 15 on the twenty-fourth day of the sixth month.

2 In the second year of King Darius, 1 on the twenty-first day of the seventh month, these words came from the Lord through the prophet Haggai: 2 'Say to the governor of Judah Zerubbabel son of Shealtiel, to the high

1:4 **well-roofed:** *or* well-panelled.

2080

THE BOOK OF
Haggai

Haggai

1 On the first day of the sixth month in the second year of King Darius, the word of the LORD came through the prophet Haggai to the governor of Judah, Zerubbabel, son of Shealtiel, and to the high priest Joshua, son of Jehozadak:

2 Thus says the LORD of hosts: This people says: "Not now has the time come to rebuild the house of the LORD." 3 (Then this word of the LORD came through Haggai, the prophet:) 4 Is it time for you to dwell in your own paneled houses, while this house lies in ruins?

5 Now thus says the LORD of hosts:
  Consider your ways!
6 You have sown much, but have brought in little;
    you have eaten, but have not been satisfied;
You have drunk, but have not been exhilarated;
    have clothed yourselves, but not been warmed;
And he who earned wages
    earned them for a bag with holes in it.

7   Thus says the LORD of hosts:
  Consider your ways!
8   Go up into the hill country;
    bring timber, and build the house
That I may take pleasure in it
    and receive my glory, says the LORD.
9 You expected much, but it came to little;
    and what you brought home, I blew away.
For what cause? says the LORD of hosts.
    Because my house lies in ruins,
    while each of you hurries to his own house.
10 Therefore the heavens withheld from you
    their dew,
    and the earth her crops.
11 And I called for a drought
    upon the land and upon the mountains;
Upon the grain, and upon the wine, and upon
    the oil,
    and upon all that the ground brings forth;
Upon men and upon beasts,
    and upon all that is produced by hand.

12 Then Zerubbabel, son of Shealtiel, and the high priest Joshua, son of Jehozadak, and all the remnant of the people listened to the voice of the LORD, their God, and to the words of the prophet Haggai, because the LORD, their God, had sent him, and the people feared because of the LORD. 13 And the LORD's messenger, Haggai, proclaimed to the people as the message of the LORD: I am with you, says the LORD.

14 Then the LORD stirred up the spirit of the governor of Judah, Zerubbabel, son of Shealtiel, and the spirit of the high priest Joshua, son of Jehozadak, and the spirit of all the remnant of the people, so that they came and set to work on the house of the LORD of hosts, their God, 15 on the twenty-fourth day of the sixth month.

2 In the second year of King Darius, on the twenty-first day of the seventh month, the word of the LORD came through the prophet Haggai: 2 Tell this to the governor of

1 In the second year of King Darius, on the first day of the sixth month, the word of Yahweh was addressed through the prophet Haggai to Zerubbabel son of Shealtiel governor of Judah and to Joshua son of Jehozadak the high priest as follows, 2 'Yahweh Sabaoth says this, "This people says: The time has not yet come to rebuild the Temple of Yahweh." ' 3 (And the word of Yahweh was addressed through the prophet Haggai, as follows,) 4 'Is this a time for you to live in your panelled houses, when this House lies in ruins? 5 So now, Yahweh Sabaoth says this, "Think carefully about your behaviour. 6 You have sown much and harvested little; you eat but never have enough, drink but never have your fill, put on clothes but feel no warmth. The wage-earner gets his wages only to put them in a bag with a hole in it." 7 Yahweh Sabaoth says this, "Think carefully about your behaviour. 8 Go up into the hills, fetch timber and rebuild the House; and I shall take pleasure in it and manifest my glory there — Yahweh says. 9 The abundance you expected proved to be little. When you brought the harvest in, I blasted it. And why? — Yahweh Sabaoth declares. Because while my House lies in ruins, each of you is busy with his own house. 10 That is why the sky has withheld the rain and the earth withheld its yield. 11 I have called down drought on land and hills, on grain, on new wine, on olive oil and on all the produce of the ground, on humans and animals and all your labours." '

12 Zerubbabel son of Shealtiel, Joshua son of Jehozadak the high priest and the entire remnant of the people, paid attention to the voice of Yahweh their God and to the words of the prophet Haggai, which Yahweh their God had sent him to deliver. And the people were filled with fear before Yahweh. 13 Haggai, the messenger of Yahweh, then passed on Yahweh's message to the people, 'I am with you — declares Yahweh.' 14 And Yahweh roused the spirit of Zerubbabel son of Shealtiel governor of Judah, the spirit of Joshua son of Jehozadak the high priest and the spirit of the entire remnant of the people; they came and set to work in the Temple of Yahweh Sabaoth, their God. 15 This was on the twenty-fourth day of the sixth month.

2 In the second year of King Darius, 1 on the twenty-first day of the seventh month, the word of Yahweh was addressed through the prophet Haggai, as follows, 2 'You are to speak to Zerubbabel son of Shealtiel governor

now to Zerubbabel son of Shealtiel, governor of Judah, and to Joshua son of Jehozadak, the high priest, and to the remnant of the people, and say, 3 Who is left among you that saw this house in its former glory? How does it look to you now? Is it not in your sight as nothing? 4 Yet now take courage, O Zerubbabel, says the LORD; take courage, O Joshua, son of Jehozadak, the high priest; take courage, all you people of the land, says the LORD; work, for I am with you, says the LORD of hosts, 5 according to the promise that I made you when you came out of Egypt. My spirit abides among you; do not fear. 6 For thus says the LORD of hosts: Once again, in a little while, I will shake the heavens and the earth and the sea and the dry land; 7 and I will shake all the nations, so that the treasure of all nations shall come, and I will fill this house with splendor, says the LORD of hosts. 8 The silver is mine, and the gold is mine, says the LORD of hosts. 9 The latter splendor of this house shall be greater than the former, says the LORD of hosts; and in this place I will give prosperity, says the LORD of hosts.

10 On the twenty-fourth day of the ninth month, in the second year of Darius, the word of the LORD came by the prophet Haggai, saying: 11 Thus says the LORD of hosts: Ask the priests for a ruling: 12 If one carries consecrated meat in the fold of one's garment, and with the fold touches bread, or stew, or wine, or oil, or any kind of food, does it become holy? The priests answered, "No." 13 Then Haggai said, "If one who is unclean by contact with a dead body touches any of these, does it become unclean?" The priests answered, "Yes, it becomes unclean." 14 Haggai then said, So is it with this people, and with this nation before me, says the LORD; and so with every work of their hands; and what they offer there is unclean. 15 But now, consider what will come to pass from this day on. Before a stone was placed upon a stone in the LORD's temple, 16 how did you fare?*a* When one came to a heap of twenty measures, there were but ten; when one came to the wine vat to draw fifty measures, there were but twenty. 17 I struck you and all the products of your toil with blight and mildew and hail; yet you did not return to me, says the LORD. 18 Consider from this day on, from the twenty-fourth day of the ninth month. Since the day that the foundation of the LORD's temple was laid, consider: 19 Is there any seed left in the barn? Do the vine, the fig tree, the pomegranate, and the olive tree still yield nothing? From this day on I will bless you.

priest Joshua son of Jehozadak, and to the rest of the people: 3 Is there anyone still among you who saw this house in its former glory? How does it appear to you now? To you does it not seem as if it were not there? 4 But now, Zerubbabel, take heart, says the LORD; take heart, Joshua son of Jehozadak, high priest; take heart, all you people, says the LORD. Begin the work, for I am with you, says the LORD of Hosts, 5 and my spirit remains among you. Do not be afraid.

6 'For these are the words of the LORD of Hosts: In a little while from now I shall shake the heavens and the earth, the sea and the dry land. 7 I shall shake all the nations, and the treasure of all nations will come here; and I shall fill this house with splendour, says the LORD of Hosts. 8 Mine is the silver and mine the gold, says the LORD of Hosts, 9 and the splendour of this latter house will surpass the splendour of the former, says the LORD of Hosts. In this place I shall grant prosperity and peace. This is the word of the LORD of Hosts.'

10 In the second year of Darius, on the twenty-fourth day of the ninth month, this word came from the LORD to the prophet Haggai: 11 'These are the words of the LORD of Hosts: Ask the priests to give a ruling on this. 12 If someone who is carrying consecrated flesh in a fold of his robe lets the fold touch bread or broth or wine or oil or any food, will that also become consecrated?' The priests answered, 'No.' 13 Haggai went on, 'But if a person defiled by contact with a corpse touches any one of these things, will that become defiled?' 'It will,' answered the priests. 14 Haggai replied, 'In my view, so it is with this people and nation and all that they do, says the LORD; whatever offering they make here is defiled.

15 'Now look back over recent times down to this day: before one stone was laid on another in the LORD's temple, 16 how were you then? If someone came to a heap of grain expecting twenty measures, he found only ten; if he came to a wine vat to draw fifty measures, he found only twenty. 17 I blasted you and all your harvest with black blight and red and with hail, yet you had no mind to return to me, says the LORD. 18 Consider, from this day onwards, from this twenty-fourth day of the ninth month, the day when the foundations of the temple of the LORD are laid, consider: 19 will the seed still be diminished in the barn? Will the vine and the fig, the pomegranate and the olive still bear no fruit? Not so; from this day I shall bless you.'

2:4 **the LORD of Hosts:** *so Gk; Heb. adds* (5)the thing I covenanted with you when you came out of Egypt.   2:6 **In . . . while:** *prob. rdg; Heb. obscure.*   2:16 **fifty measures:** *so Syriac; Heb. adds* winepress.   2:19 **diminished:** *prob. rdg; Heb. omits.*

*a*Gk: Heb *since they were*

NEW AMERICAN BIBLE

Judah, Zerubbabel, son of Shealtiel, and to the high priest Joshua, son of Jehozadak, and to the remnant of the people:

3 Who is left among you
   that saw this house in its former glory?
And how do you see it now?
   Does it not seem like nothing in your eyes?
4 But now take courage, Zerubbabel, says the LORD,
   and take courage, Joshua, high priest, son
      of Jehozadak,
And take courage, all you people of the land,
   says the LORD, and work!
For I am with you, says the LORD of hosts.
5 This is the pact that I made with you
   when you came out of Egypt,
And my spirit continues in your midst;
   do not fear!

6   For thus says the LORD of hosts:
One moment yet, a little while,
   and I will shake the heavens and the earth,
   the sea and the dry land.
7 I will shake all the nations,
   and the treasures of all the nations will come in,
And I will fill this house with glory,
   says the LORD of hosts.
8 Mine is the silver and mine the gold,
   says the LORD of hosts.
9 Greater will be the future glory of this house
   than the former, says the LORD of hosts;
And in this place I will give peace,
   says the LORD of hosts!

10 On the twenty-fourth day of the ninth month, in the second year of King Darius, the word of the LORD came to the prophet Haggai: 11 Thus says the LORD of hosts: Ask the priests for a decision: 12 If a man carries sanctified flesh in the fold of his garment and the fold touches bread, or pottage, or wine, or oil, or any other food, do they become sanctified? "No," the priests answered. 13 Then Haggai said: If a person unclean from contact with a corpse touches any of these, do they become unclean? The priests answered, "They become unclean." 14 Then Haggai continued:

So is this people, and so is this nation
   in my sight, says the LORD:
And so are all the works of their hands;
   and what they offer there is unclean.

15 But now, consider from this day forward. Before there was a stone laid upon a stone in the temple of the LORD, 16 how did you fare?

When one went to a heap of grain for
      twenty measures,
   it would yield but ten;
When another went to the vat to draw
      fifty measures,
   there would be but twenty.
17 I struck you in all the works of your hands
   with blight, searing wind, and hail,
   yet you did not return to me, says the LORD.

18 [Consider from this day forward: from the twenty-fourth day of the ninth month. From the day on which the temple of the LORD was founded, consider!]

19 Indeed, the seed has not sprouted,
   nor have the vine, the fig, the pomegranate
   and the olive tree yet borne.
From this day, I will bless!

NEW JERUSALEM BIBLE

of Judah, to Joshua son of Jehozadak the high priest and to the remnant of the people. Say this, 3 "Is there anyone left among you who saw this Temple in its former glory? And how does it look to you now? Does it not seem as though there is nothing there? 4 But take courage now, Zerubbabel! — Yahweh declares. Courage, Joshua son of Jehozadak high priest! Courage, all you people of the country! — Yahweh declares. To work! I am with you — Yahweh Sabaoth declares — 5 and my spirit is present among you. Do not be afraid! 6 For Yahweh Sabaoth says this: A little while now, and I shall shake the heavens and the earth, the sea and the dry land. 7 I shall shake all the nations, and the treasures of all the nations will flow in, and I shall fill this Temple with glory, says Yahweh Sabaoth. 8 Mine is the silver, mine the gold! — Yahweh Sabaoth declares. 9 The glory of this new Temple will surpass that of the old, says Yahweh Sabaoth, and in this place I shall give peace — Yahweh Sabaoth declares." '

10 On the twenty-fourth day of the ninth month, in the second year of Darius, the word of Yahweh was addressed to the prophet Haggai as follows, 11 'Yahweh Sabaoth says this, "Ask the priests to give a ruling on this: 12 If someone is carrying consecrated meat in the fold of his gown and allows the fold to touch bread, broth, wine, oil or food of any kind, will that become holy?" ' The priests replied, 'No.' 13 Haggai then said, 'If anyone rendered unclean by contact with a corpse touches any of these things, will that become unclean?' The priests replied, 'It will become unclean.' 14 Haggai then spoke out. 'It is the same with this people,' he said, 'the same with this nation, in my view — Yahweh declares — the same with everything they turn their hands to; and whatever they offer here is unclean.

15 'So now think carefully, today and henceforth: before one stone had been laid on another in the sanctuary of Yahweh, 16 what state were you in? You would come to a twenty-measure heap and find only ten; you would come to a vat to draw fifty measures and find only twenty. 17 Everything you turned your hands to, I struck with wind-blast, mildew and hail, and still you would not return to me — Yahweh declares. 18 So think carefully, today and henceforth (from the twenty-fourth day of the ninth month, from the day the foundation of the sanctuary of Yahweh was laid, think carefully) 19 if seed-corn is still short in the barn, and if vine and fig tree, pomegranate and olive tree still bear no fruit.

'From today onwards I intend to bless you.'

NEW REVISED STANDARD VERSION

20 The word of the LORD came a second time to Haggai on the twenty-fourth day of the month: 21 Speak to Zerubbabel, governor of Judah, saying, I am about to shake the heavens and the earth, 22 and to overthrow the throne of kingdoms; I am about to destroy the strength of the kingdoms of the nations, and overthrow the chariots and their riders; and the horses and their riders shall fall, every one by the sword of a comrade. 23 On that day, says the LORD of hosts, I will take you, O Zerubbabel my servant, son of Shealtiel, says the LORD, and make you like a signet ring; for I have chosen you, says the LORD of hosts.

REVISED ENGLISH BIBLE

20 On that day, the twenty-fourth day of the month, the word of the LORD came to Haggai a second time: 21 'Tell Zerubbabel, governor of Judah, I shall shake the heavens and the earth; 22 I shall overthrow the thrones of kings, break the power of heathen realms, overturn chariots and their riders; horses and riders will fall by the sword of their comrades. 23 On that day, says the LORD of Hosts, I shall take you, Zerubbabel son of Shealtiel, my servant, and shall wear you as a signet ring; for it is you whom I have chosen. This is the word of the LORD of Hosts.'

NEW AMERICAN BIBLE

20 The message of the LORD came a second time to Haggai on the twenty-fourth day of the month: 21 Tell this to Zerubbabel, the governor of Judah:

I will shake the heavens and the earth;
22   I will overthrow the thrones of kingdoms,
   destroy the power of the kingdoms of
     the nations.
I will overthrow the chariots and their riders,
   and the riders with their horses
     shall go down by one another's sword.
23   On that day, says the LORD of hosts,
I will take you, Zerubbabel,
   son of Shealtiel, my servant, says the LORD,
And I will set you as a signet ring;
   for I have chosen you, says the LORD of hosts.

NEW JERUSALEM BIBLE

20 On the twenty-fourth day of the month the word of Yahweh was addressed a second time to Haggai, as follows, 21 'Speak to Zerubbabel governor of Judah. Say this, "I am going to shake the heavens and the earth. 22 I shall overturn the thrones of kingdoms and destroy the power of the kings of the nations. I shall overthrow the chariots and their crews; horses and their riders will fall, every one to the sword of his comrade. 23 When that day comes — Yahweh Sabaoth declares — I shall take you, Zerubbabel son of Shealtiel my servant — Yahweh declares — and make you like a signet ring. For I have chosen you — Yahweh Sabaoth declares." '

Zechariah

Zechariah

1 In the eighth month, in the second year of Darius, the word of the LORD came to the prophet Zechariah son of Berechiah son of Iddo, saying: 2 The LORD was very angry with your ancestors. 3 Therefore say to them, Thus says the LORD of hosts: Return to me, says the LORD of hosts, and I will return to you, says the LORD of hosts. 4 Do not be like your ancestors, to whom the former prophets proclaimed, "Thus says the LORD of hosts, Return from your evil ways and from your evil deeds." But they did not hear or heed me, says the LORD. 5 Your ancestors, where are they? And the prophets, do they live forever? 6 But my words and my statutes, which I commanded my servants the prophets, did they not overtake your ancestors? So they repented and said, "The LORD of hosts has dealt with us according to our ways and deeds, just as he planned to do."

7 On the twenty-fourth day of the eleventh month, the month of Shebat, in the second year of Darius, the word of the LORD came to the prophet Zechariah son of Berechiah son of Iddo; and Zechariah*a* said, 8 In the night I saw a man riding on a red horse! He was standing among the myrtle trees in the glen; and behind him were red, sorrel, and white horses. 9 Then I said, "What are these, my lord?" The angel who talked with me said to me, "I will show you what they are." 10 So the man who was standing among the myrtle trees answered, "They are those whom the LORD has sent to patrol the earth." 11 Then they spoke to the angel of the LORD who was standing among the myrtle trees, "We have patrolled the earth, and lo, the whole earth remains at peace." 12 Then the angel of the LORD said, "O LORD of hosts, how long will you withhold mercy from Jerusalem and the cities of Judah, with which you have been angry these seventy years?" 13 Then the LORD replied with gracious and comforting words to the angel who talked with me. 14 So the angel who talked with me said to me, Proclaim this message: Thus says the LORD of hosts; I am very jealous for Jerusalem and for Zion. 15 And I am extremely angry with the nations that are at ease; for while I was only a little angry, they made the disaster worse. 16 Therefore, thus says the LORD, I have returned to Jerusalem with compassion; my house shall be built in it, says the LORD of hosts, and the measuring line shall be stretched out over Jerusalem. 17 Proclaim further: Thus says the LORD of hosts: My cities shall again overflow with prosperity; the LORD will again comfort Zion and again choose Jerusalem.

18*b* And I looked up and saw four horns. 19 I asked the angel who talked with me, "What are these?" And he answered me, "These are the horns that have scattered Judah, Israel, and Jerusalem." 20 Then the LORD showed me four blacksmiths. 21 And I asked, "What are they coming to do?" He answered, "These are the horns that scattered Judah, so that no head could be raised; but these have come to terrify them, to strike down the horns of the nations that lifted up their horns against the land of Judah to scatter its people."*c*

2 *d* I looked up and saw a man with a measuring line in his hand. 2 Then I asked, "Where are you going?" He

1 IN the eighth month of the second year of Darius, this word of the LORD came to the prophet Zechariah son of Berechiah, son of Iddo: 2 The LORD was exceedingly angry with your forefathers. 3 Say therefore to the people: These are the words of the LORD of Hosts: If you return to me, I shall turn back to you, says the LORD of Hosts. 4 Do not be like your forefathers, who heard the prophets of old proclaim, 'These are the words of the LORD of Hosts: Turn back from your evil ways and your evil deeds.' They refused to listen and pay heed to me, says the LORD. 5 Your forefathers, where are they now? And the prophets, do they live for ever? 6 But did not the warnings and the decrees with which I charged my servants the prophets overtake your forefathers? They repented and said, 'The LORD of Hosts has fulfilled his intention, and has dealt with us as our lives and as our deeds deserved.'

7 ON the twenty-fourth day of the eleventh month, the month of Shebat, in the second year of Darius, the word of the LORD came to the prophet Zechariah son of Berechiah, son of Iddo.

8 In the night I had a vision in which I saw a man among the myrtles in a hollow; he was on a bay horse and behind him were other horses, bay, sorrel, and white. 9 'What are these, sir?' I asked, and the angel who was talking with me answered, 'I shall show you what they are.' 10 Then the man standing among the myrtles said, 'They are those whom the LORD has sent to range throughout the world.'

11 They reported to the angel of the LORD who was standing among the myrtles: 'We have ranged through the world, and the whole world is quiet and at peace.' 12 The angel of the LORD then said, 'LORD of Hosts, how long will you withhold your compassion from Jerusalem and the towns of Judah, on which you have vented your wrath these seventy years?' 13 In answer the LORD spoke kind and comforting words to the angel who was talking with me. 14 This angel then said to me: Announce that these are the words of the LORD of Hosts: I am very jealous for Jerusalem and Zion, 15 but I am deeply angry with the nations that are enjoying their ease, because, although my anger was only mild, they aggravated the suffering. 16 Therefore these are the words of the LORD: I have returned to Jerusalem with compassion; my house is to be rebuilt there, says the LORD of Hosts, and the measuring line will be stretched over Jerusalem. 17 Proclaim once more: These are the words of the LORD of Hosts: My cities will again brim with prosperity; once again the LORD will comfort Zion, once again he will make Jerusalem the city of his choice.

18 I looked up and saw four horns. 19 I asked the angel who talked with me what they were, and he answered, 'These are the horns which scattered Judah, Israel, and Jerusalem.' 20 The LORD then showed me four smiths. 21 I asked what they were coming to do, and he said, 'Those horns scattered Judah so completely that no one could hold up his head; but these smiths have come to rout them, overthrowing the horns which the nations had raised against the land of Judah to scatter its people.'

2 I looked up and saw a man carrying a measuring line. 2 I asked him where he was going. 'To measure Jerusa-

---

a Heb *and he*   *b* Ch 2.1 in Heb   *c* Heb *it*   *d* Ch 2.5 in Heb   1:18 *In Heb.* 2:1.

THE BOOK OF
Zechariah

1 In the second year of Darius, in the eighth month, the word of the LORD came to the prophet Zechariah, son of Berechiah, son of Iddo: 2 The LORD was indeed angry with your fathers. . . . 3 and say to them: Thus says the LORD of hosts: Return to me, says the LORD of hosts, and I will return to you, says the LORD of hosts. 4 Be not like your fathers whom the former prophets warned: Thus says the LORD of hosts: Turn from your evil ways and from your wicked deeds. But they would not listen or pay attention to me, says the LORD. 5 Your fathers, where are they? And the prophets, can they live forever? 6 But my words and my decrees, which I entrusted to my servants the prophets, did not these overtake your fathers? Then they repented and admitted: "The LORD of hosts has treated us according to our ways and deeds, just as he had determined he would."

7 In the second year of Darius, on the twenty-fourth day of Shebat, the eleventh month, the word of the LORD came to the prophet Zechariah, son of Berechiah, son of Iddo, in the following way: 8 I had a vision during the night. There appeared the driver of a red horse, standing among myrtle trees in a shady place, and behind him were red, sorrel, and white horses. 9 Then I asked, "What are these, my lord?"; and the angel who spoke with me answered me, "I will show you what these are." 10 The man who was standing among the myrtle trees spoke up and said, "These are they whom the LORD has sent to patrol the earth." 11 And they answered the angel of the LORD who was standing among the myrtle trees and said, "We have patrolled the earth; see, the whole earth is tranquil and at rest!"

12 Then the angel of the Lord spoke out and said, "O LORD of hosts, how long will you be without mercy for Jerusalem and the cities of Judah that have felt your anger these seventy years?" 13 To the angel who spoke with me, the LORD replied with comforting words.

14 And the angel who spoke with me said to me, Proclaim: Thus says the LORD of hosts: I am deeply moved for the sake of Jerusalem and Zion, 15 and I am exceedingly angry with the complacent nations; whereas I was but a little angry, they added to the harm. 16 Therefore, says the LORD: I will turn to Jerusalem in mercy; my house shall be built in it, says the LORD of hosts, and a measuring line shall be stretched over Jerusalem. 17 Proclaim further: Thus says the LORD of hosts: My cities shall again overflow with prosperity; the LORD will again comfort Zion, and again choose Jerusalem.

2 I raised my eyes and looked: there were four horns. 2 Then I asked the angel who spoke with me what these were. He answered me, "These are the horns that scattered Judah and Israel and Jerusalem."

3 Then the LORD showed me four blacksmiths. And I asked, "What are these coming to do?" 4 And he said, "Here are the horns that scattered Judah, so that no man raised his head any more; but these have come to terrify them: to cast down the horns of the nations that raised their horns to scatter the land of Judah."

5 Again I raised my eyes and looked: there was a man with a measuring line in his hand. 6 "Where are you going?"

Zechariah

1 In the second year of Darius, in the eighth month, the word of Yahweh was addressed to the prophet Zechariah (son of Berechiah), son of Iddo, as follows, 2 'Yahweh was deeply angry with your ancestors. 3 So say this to them, "Yahweh Sabaoth[a] says this: Return to me — Yahweh Sabaoth declares — and I will return to you, says Yahweh Sabaoth. 4 Do not be like your ancestors when the prophets in the past cried to them: Yahweh Sabaoth says this: Turn back from your evil ways and evil deeds — they would not listen or pay attention to me — Yahweh declares. 5 Where are your ancestors now? And the prophets, do they live for ever? 6 But did not my words and statutes, with which I had charged my servants the prophets, overtake your ancestors just the same?" '

So they repented and said, 'Yahweh Sabaoth has treated us as he resolved to do, and as our ways and deeds deserved.'

7 On the twenty-fourth day of the eleventh month (the month of Shebat), in the second year of Darius, the word of Yahweh was addressed to the prophet Zechariah (son of Berechiah), son of Iddo, as follows, 8 'I had a vision during the night. There was a man riding a red horse standing among the deep-rooted myrtles; behind him were other horses — red, chestnut and white. 9 I said, "What are these, my lord?" And the angel who was talking to me said, "I will show you what they are." 10 The man standing among the myrtles then replied, "Those are they whom Yahweh has sent to patrol the world." 11 They reported to the angel of Yahweh as he stood among the myrtles, "We have been patrolling the world, and indeed the whole world is still and at peace." 12 The angel of Yahweh then spoke and said, "Yahweh Sabaoth, how long will you wait before taking pity on Jerusalem and the cities of Judah, on which you have inflicted your anger for the past seventy years?" 13 Yahweh then replied with kind and comforting words to the angel who was talking to me. 14 The angel who was talking to me then said to me, "Make this proclamation: Yahweh Sabaoth says this: I am burning with jealousy for Jerusalem and Zion 15 but am deeply angry with the nations now at ease; before, I was only mildly angry, but they contributed to the disaster. 16 So now Yahweh says this: In compassion I have returned to Jerusalem; my Temple will be rebuilt there — Yahweh Sabaoth declares — and the measuring line will be stretched over Jerusalem. 17 Make this proclamation too: Yahweh Sabaoth says this: My cities are once more to be very prosperous. Yahweh will comfort Zion once again, and again make Jerusalem his choice." '

2 Then, raising my eyes, I had a vision. It was this: There were four horns. 2 I said to the angel who was talking to me, 'What are these?' He said to me, 'These are the horns which scattered Judah (Israel) and Jerusalem.' 3 Yahweh then showed me four smiths. 4 And I said, 'What are these coming to do?' He said to me, '(Those horns scattered Judah so completely that no one dared to raise his head; but) these have come to terrify them, to throw down the horns of the nations who raised their horns over the land of Judah to scatter it.'

5 Then, raising my eyes, I had a vision. There was a man with a measuring line in his hand. 6 I asked him, 'Where are

answered me, "To measure Jerusalem, to see what is its width and what is its length." 3 Then the angel who talked with me came forward, and another angel came forward to meet him, 4 and said to him, "Run, say to that young man: Jerusalem shall be inhabited like villages without walls, because of the multitude of people and animals in it. 5 For I will be a wall of fire all around it, says the LORD, and I will be the glory within it."

6 Up, up! Flee from the land of the north, says the LORD; for I have spread you abroad like the four winds of heaven, says the LORD. 7 Up! Escape to Zion, you that live with daughter Babylon. 8 For thus said the LORD of hosts (after his glory*e* sent me) regarding the nations that plundered you: Truly, one who touches you touches the apple of my eye.*f* 9 See now, I am going to raise*g* my hand against them, and they shall become plunder for their own slaves. Then you will know that the LORD of hosts has sent me. 10 Sing and rejoice, O daughter Zion! For lo, I will come and dwell in your midst, says the LORD. 11 Many nations shall join themselves to the LORD on that day, and shall be my people; and I will dwell in your midst. And you shall know that the LORD of hosts has sent me to you. 12 The LORD will inherit Judah as his portion in the holy land, and will again choose Jerusalem.

13 Be silent, all people, before the LORD; for he has roused himself from his holy dwelling.

3 Then he showed me the high priest Joshua standing before the angel of the LORD, and Satan*h* standing at his right hand to accuse him. 2 And the LORD said to Satan,*h* "The LORD rebuke you, O Satan!*h* The LORD who has chosen Jerusalem rebuke you! Is not this man a brand plucked from the fire?" 3 Now Joshua was dressed with filthy clothes as he stood before the angel. 4 The angel said to those who were standing before him, "Take off his filthy clothes." And to him he said, "See, I have taken your guilt away from you, and I will clothe you with festal apparel." 5 And I said, "Let them put a clean turban on his head." So they put a clean turban on his head and clothed him with the apparel; and the angel of the LORD was standing by.

6 Then the angel of the LORD assured Joshua, saying 7 "Thus says the LORD of hosts: If you will walk in my ways and keep my requirements, then you shall rule my house and have charge of my courts, and I will give you the right of access among those who are standing here. 8 Now listen, Joshua, high priest, you and your colleagues who sit before you! For they are an omen of things to come: I am going to bring my servant the Branch. 9 For on the stone that I have

lem and discover its breadth and length,' he replied. 3 Then, as the angel who talked with me was going away, another angel came out to meet him 4 and said, 'Run to the young man there and tell him that Jerusalem will be without walls, so numerous will be the people and cattle in it. 5 I myself shall be a wall of fire all round it, says the LORD, and a glorious presence within it.'

6 Away, away! Flee from the land of the north, says the LORD, for I have dispersed you to the four winds of heaven, says the LORD. 7 Away! Escape, you people of Zion who live in Babylon.

8 These are the words of the LORD of Hosts, spoken when he sent me on a glorious mission*a* to the nations who have plundered you, for whoever touches you touches the apple of his eye: 9 I shall brandish my hand against them, and they will be plunder for those they enslaved. You will then know that the LORD of Hosts has sent me.

10 Shout aloud and rejoice, daughter of Zion! I am coming, I shall make my dwelling among you, says the LORD. 11 Many nations will give their allegiance to the LORD on that day and become his people, and he will dwell in your midst. Then you will know that the LORD of Hosts has sent me to you. 12 The LORD will claim Judah as his own portion in the holy land, and once again make Jerusalem the city of his choice.

13 Let all mortals be silent in the presence of the LORD! For he has bestirred himself and come out from his holy dwelling-place.

3 Then he showed me Joshua the high priest standing before the angel of the LORD, with Satan standing at his right hand to accuse him. 2 The angel said to Satan, 'The LORD silence you, Satan! May the LORD, who has chosen Jerusalem, silence you! Is not this man a brand snatched from the fire?' 3 Joshua was wearing filthy clothes as he stood before the angel, 4 who now said to those in attendance on him, 'Take off his filthy clothes.' Then to Joshua he said, 'See how I have taken away your guilt from you; and I shall clothe you in fine vestments. 5 Let a clean turban be put on his head,' he ordered. So while the angel of the LORD stood by, they put a clean turban on his head and clothed him in clean garments.

6 The angel gave Joshua this solemn charge: 7 'These are the words of the LORD of Hosts: If you conform to my ways and carry out your duties towards me, you are to administer my house and be in control of my courts, and I shall grant you the right to come and go amongst those in attendance here. 8 Listen, High Priest Joshua, you and your colleagues seated here before you, for they are an omen of good things to come: I shall now bring my servant, the Branch. 9-10 In

---

e Cn: Heb *after glory he*   *f* Heb *his eye*   *g* Or *wave*   *h* Or *the Accuser*; Heb *the Adversary*

2:8 **on a glorious mission**: *prob. rdg; Heb*. after glory.
3:2 **angel**: *prob. rdg, so Syriac; Heb*. LORD.

NEW AMERICAN BIBLE

I asked. "To measure Jerusalem," he answered; "to see how great is its width and how great its length."

7 Then the angel who spoke with me advanced, and another angel came out to meet him 8 and said to him, "Run, tell this to that young man: People will live in Jerusalem as though in open country, because of the multitude of men and beasts in her midst. 9 But I will be for her an encircling wall of fire, says the LORD, and I will be the glory in her midst."

10 Up, up! Flee from the land of the north, says the LORD; for I scatter you to the four winds of heaven, says the LORD. 11 Up, escape to Zion! you who dwell in daughter Babylon. 12 For thus said the LORD of hosts (after he had already sent me) concerning the nations that have plundered you: Whoever touches you touches the apple of my eye. 13 See, I wave my hand over them; they become plunder for their slaves. Thus you shall know that the LORD of hosts has sent me.

14 Sing and rejoice, O daughter Zion! See, I am coming to dwell among you, says the LORD. 15 Many nations shall join themselves to the LORD on that day, and they shall be his people, and he will dwell among you, and you shall know that the LORD of hosts has sent me to you. 16 The LORD will possess Judah as his portion in the holy land, and he will again choose Jerusalem. 17 Silence, all mankind, in the presence of the LORD! for he stirs forth from his holy dwelling.

3 Then he showed me Joshua the high priest standing before the angel of the LORD, while Satan stood at his right hand to accuse him. 2 And the angel of the LORD said to Satan, "May the LORD rebuke you, Satan; may the LORD who has chosen Jerusalem rebuke you! Is not this man a brand snatched from the fire?"

3 Now Joshua was standing before the angel, clad in filthy garments. 4 He spoke and said to those who were standing before him, "Take off his filthy garments, and clothe him in festal garments." 5 He also said, "Put a clean miter on his head." And they put a clean miter on his head and clothed him with the garments. Then the angel of the LORD, standing, said, "See, I have taken away your guilt."

6 The angel of the LORD then gave Joshua this assurance: 7 "Thus says the LORD of hosts: If you walk in my ways and heed my charge, you shall judge my house and keep my courts, and I will give you access among these standing here. 8 Listen, O Joshua, high priest! You and your associates who sit before you are men of good omen. Yes, I will bring my servant the Shoot. 9 Look at the stone that I have

NEW JERUSALEM BIBLE

you going?' He said, 'To measure Jerusalem, to calculate her width and length.' 7 And then, while the angel who was talking to me walked away, another angel came out to meet him. 8 He said to him, 'Run, and tell that young man this, "Jerusalem is to remain unwalled, because of the great number of men and cattle inside. 9 For I — Yahweh declares — shall be a wall of fire all round her and I shall be the Glory within her." '

10 Look out! Look out! Flee from the land of the
   north
— Yahweh declares —
for I have scattered you to the four winds of
   heaven
— Yahweh declares.
11 Look out! Make your escape, Zion,
   now living with the daughter of Babylon!
12 For Yahweh Sabaoth says this,
   since the Glory commissioned me,
   about the nations who plundered you,
'Whoever touches you touches the apple of my
   eye.
13 Now look, I shall wave my hand over them
   and they will be plundered by those whom they
      have enslaved.'
Then you will know that Yahweh Sabaoth has sent
   me!

14 Sing, rejoice, daughter of Zion,
   for now I am coming
   to live among you
— Yahweh declares!

15 And on that day many nations
   will be converted to Yahweh.
   Yes, they will become his people,
   and they will live among you.
   Then you will know that Yahweh Sabaoth has sent
      me to you!
16 Yahweh will take possession of Judah,
   his portion in the Holy Land,
   and again make Jerusalem his choice.
17 Let all people be silent before Yahweh,
   now that he is stirring from his holy Dwelling!

3 He then showed me the high priest Joshua, standing before the angel of Yahweh, with Satan standing on his right to accuse him. 2 The angel of Yahweh said to Satan, 'May Yahweh rebuke you, Satan! May Yahweh rebuke you, since he has made Jerusalem his choice. Is not this man a brand snatched from the fire?' 3 Now Joshua was dressed in dirty clothes as he stood before the angel. 4a The latter then spoke as follows to those who were standing before him, 'Take off his dirty clothes 4c and dress him in splendid robes 5 and put a clean turban on his head.' So they put a clean turban on his head and dressed him in clean clothes, while the angel of Yahweh stood by 4b and said, 'You see, I have taken your guilt away.' 6 The angel of Yahweh then made this declaration to Joshua, 7 'Yahweh Sabaoth says this, "If you walk in my ways and keep my ordinances, you shall govern my house, you shall watch over my courts, and I will give you free access among those in attendance here. 9a For this is the stone which I have put before Joshua, a stone on which are seven eyes; and I myself shall cut the inscription on it — Yahweh Sabaoth declares."

8 'So listen, High Priest Joshua, you and the colleagues over whom you preside — for they are an omen of things to come — for now I shall bring in my servant the Branch, *b*

---

b 3 A messianic title (*see* Jr 23:5) later applied to Zerubbabel (6:12).

set before Joshua, on a single stone with seven facets, I will engrave its inscription, says the LORD of hosts, and I will remove the guilt of this land in a single day. 10 On that day, says the LORD of hosts, you shall invite each other to come under your vine and fig tree."

4 The angel who talked with me came again, and wakened me, as one is wakened from sleep. 2 He said to me, "What do you see?" And I said, "I see a lampstand all of gold, with a bowl on the top of it; there are seven lamps on it, with seven lips on each of the lamps that are on the top of it. 3 And by it there are two olive trees, one on the right of the bowl and the other on its left." 4 I said to the angel who talked with me, "What are these, my lord?" 5 Then the angel who talked with me answered me, "Do you not know what these are?" I said, "No, my lord." 6 He said to me, "This is the word of the LORD to Zerubbabel: Not by might, nor by power, but by my spirit, says the LORD of hosts. 7 What are you, O great mountain? Before Zerubbabel you shall become a plain; and he shall bring out the top stone amid shouts of 'Grace, grace to it!' "

8 Moreover the word of the LORD came to me, saying, 9 "The hands of Zerubbabel have laid the foundation of this house; his hands shall also complete it. Then you will know that the LORD of hosts has sent me to you. 10 For whoever has despised the day of small things shall rejoice, and shall see the plummet in the hand of Zerubbabel.

"These seven are the eyes of the LORD, which range through the whole earth." 11 Then I said to him, "What are these two olive trees on the right and the left of the lampstand?" 12 And a second time I said to him, "What are these two branches of the olive trees, which pour out the oil^i through the two golden pipes?" 13 He said to me, "Do you not know what these are?" I said, "No, my lord." 14 Then he said, "These are the two anointed ones who stand by the Lord of the whole earth."

5 Again I looked up and saw a flying scroll. 2 And he said to me, "What do you see?" I answered, "I see a flying scroll; its length is twenty cubits, and its width ten cubits." 3 Then he said to me, "This is the curse that goes out over the face of the whole land; for everyone who steals shall be cut off according to the writing on one side, and everyone who swears falsely^j shall be cut off according to the writing on the other side. 4 I have sent it out, says the LORD of hosts, and it shall enter the house of the thief, and the house of anyone who swears falsely by my name; and it shall abide in that house and consume it, both timber and stones."

5 Then the angel who talked with me came forward and said to me, "Look up and see what this is that is coming out." 6 I said, "What is it?" He said, "This is a basket^k coming out." And he said, "This is their iniquity^l in all the land." 7 Then a leaden cover was lifted, and there was a woman sitting in the basket!^{k} 8 And he said, "This is Wickedness." So he thrust her back into the basket,^{k} and pressed the leaden weight down on its mouth. 9 Then I looked up and saw two women coming forward. The wind was in their wings; they had wings like the wings of a stork, and they lifted up the basket^k between earth and sky. 10 Then I said to the angel who talked with me, "Where are they taking the basket?"^{k} 11 He said to me, "To the land of Shinar, to build

a single day I shall wipe away the guilt of this land. On that day, says the LORD of Hosts, you are to invite each other to come and sit under your vines and fig trees.

'Here is the stone that I set before Joshua, a stone on which are seven eyes. I shall reveal its meaning to you, says the LORD of Hosts.'

4 ‡4.1–3: see below‡
4 I asked the angel of the LORD who talked with me, 'Sir, what are these?' 5 He answered, 'Do you not know what they are?' 'No, sir,' I answered. 'These seven', he said, 'are the eyes of the LORD which range over the whole earth.'

6 Then he said to me, 'This is the word of the LORD concerning Zerubbabel: Neither by force nor by strength, but by my spirit! says the LORD of Hosts. 7 How does a mountain, the greatest mountain, compare with Zerubbabel? It is no higher than a plain. He will bring out the stone called Foundation while the people shout, "All blessing be upon it!" ' 8 There came this word from the LORD to me: 9 Zerubbabel with his own hands laid the foundation of this house; with his own hands he will finish it. So you will know that the LORD of Hosts has sent me to you. 10 Who has despised the day of small things? The people will rejoice when they see Zerubbabel holding the stone called Separation. ‡4.11–14: see below‡ 1 The angel who talked with me came back and roused me as someone is roused from sleep. 2 He asked me what I saw, and I answered, 'A lampstand entirely of gold, with a bowl on it. It holds seven lamps, and there are seven pipes for the lamps on top of it. 3 There are also two olive trees standing by it, one on the right and the other on the left. 11 What are these two olive trees on the right and on the left of the lampstand?' 12 I put a further question to him, 'What are the two sprays of olive beside the golden pipes which discharge the golden oil?' 13 He said, 'Do you not know what they mean?' 'No, sir,' I answered. 14 'These', he said, 'are the two consecrated with oil who attend the Lord of all the earth.'

5 I looked up again and saw a flying scroll. 2 He asked me what I saw, and I answered, 'I see a flying scroll, twenty cubits long and ten cubits wide.' 3 He told me: 'This is the curse which goes out over the whole land; for according to the writing on one side every thief will be swept away, and according to the writing on the other every perjurer will be swept away. 4 I have sent it out, says the LORD of Hosts, and it will enter the house of the thief and the house of the man who has committed perjury in my name; it will stay inside the house and demolish it, both timber and stone.'

5 The angel who talked with me came out and said, 'Look at this thing that is coming.' 6 I asked what it was, and he said, 'The thing that is coming is a barrel for measuring'; and he added, 'it is a symbol of the people's guilt throughout the land.' 7 Then its round, leaden cover was raised, and there was a woman sitting inside the barrel. 8 He said, 'This is Wickedness,' and he thrust her down into the barrel and pressed the leaden weight down on the opening.

9 I looked up again and saw two women coming forth with the wind in their wings (for they had wings like those of a stork), and they lifted up the barrel midway between earth and sky. 10 I asked the angel who talked with me where they were taking the barrel, 11 and he answered, 'To

---

4:4–11 *The verses traditionally numbered 4:1–3 are transposed to follow 4:10.* 4:5 **These seven . . . earth:** *transposed from verse 10.* 4:2 **seven pipes:** *so Gk; Heb.* seven pipes each. 4:14 **two . . . oil:** *lit.* two sons of oil. 5:6 **a barrel for measuring:** *Heb.* an ephah. **guilt:** *so Gk; Heb.* eye.

^{i} Cn: Heb *gold* ^{j} The word *falsely* added from verse 4
^{k} Heb *ephah* ^{l} Gk Compare Syr: Heb *their eye*

NEW AMERICAN BIBLE

placed before Joshua, one stone with seven facets. I will engrave its inscription, says the LORD of hosts, and I will take away the guilt of the land in one day. 10 On that day, says the LORD of hosts, you will invite one another under your vines and fig trees."

‡4.1–3: see below‡

4 4 Then I said to the angel who spoke with me, "What are these things, my lord?" 5 And the angel who spoke with me replied, "Do you not know what these things are?" "No, my lord," I answered. 6 Then he said to me, "This is the LORD'S message to Zerubbabel: Not by an army, nor by might, but by my spirit, says the LORD of hosts. 7 What are you, O great mountain? Before Zerubbabel you are but a plain. He shall bring out the capstone amid exclamations of 'Hail, Hail' to it."

8 This word of the LORD then came to me: 9 The hands of Zerubbabel have laid the foundations of this house, and his hands shall finish it; then you shall know that the LORD of hosts has sent me to you. 10 For even they who were scornful on that day of small beginnings shall rejoice to see the select stone in the hands of Zerubbabel. These seven facets are the eyes of the LORD that range over the whole earth.

‡4.11–14: see below‡

1 Then the angel who spoke with me returned and awakened me, like a man awakened from his sleep. 2 "What do you see?" he asked me. "I see a lampstand all of gold, with a bowl at the top," I replied; "on it are seven lamps with their tubes, 3 and beside it are two olive trees, one on the right and the other on the left." 11 I then asked him, "What are these two olive trees at each side of the lampstand?" 12 And again I asked, "What are the two olive tufts which freely pour out fresh oil through the two golden channels?" 13 "Do you not know what these are?" he said to me. "No, my lord," I answered him. 14 He said, "These are the two anointed who stand by the LORD of the whole earth."

5 Then I raised my eyes again and saw a scroll flying. 2 "What do you see?" he asked me. I answered, "I see a scroll flying; it is twenty cubits long and ten cubits wide." 3 Then he said to me: "This is the curse which is to go forth over the whole earth; in accordance with it shall every thief be swept away, and in accordance with it shall every perjurer be expelled from here. 4 I will send it forth, says the LORD of hosts, and it shall come into the house of the thief, or into the house of him who perjures himself with my name; it shall lodge within his house, consuming it, timber and stones."

5 Then the angel who spoke with me came forward and said to me, "Raise your eyes and see what this is that comes forth." 6 "What is it?" I asked. And he answered, "This is a bushel container coming. This is their guilt in all the land." 7 Then a leaden cover was lifted, and there was a woman sitting inside the bushel. 8 "This is Wickedness," he said; and he thrust her inside the bushel, pushing the leaden cover into the opening. 9 Then I raised my eyes and saw two women coming forth with a wind ruffling their wings, for they had wings like the wings of a stork. As they lifted up the bushel into the air, 10 I said to the angel who spoke with me, "Where are they taking the bushel?" 11 He replied, "To

9b and I shall remove this country's guilt in a single day. 10 On that day—Yahweh Sabaoth declares—invite each other to come under your vine and your fig tree." '

4 The angel who was talking to me came back and roused me as though rousing someone who was asleep. 2 And he asked me, 'What do you see?' I replied, 'As I look, there is a lamp-stand entirely of gold with a bowl at the top of it; it holds seven lamps, with seven openings for the lamps on it. 3 By it are two olive trees, one to the right and the other to the left.' 4 I then said to the angel who was talking to me, 'What are those things, my lord?' 5 The angel who was talking to me replied, 'Do you not know what they are?' I said, 'No, my lord.' 6a He then gave me this answer, ‡4.6b–10a: see below‡ 10b 'These seven are the eyes of Yahweh, which range over the whole world.' 11 Then I went on to ask him, 'What is the meaning of these two olive trees, to right and left of the lamp-stand?' 12 (And I went on to ask him further, 'What is the meaning of the two olive branches discharging oil through the two golden openings?') 13 He replied, 'Do you not know what they are?' I said, 'No, my lord.' 14 He said, 'These are the two anointed ones in attendance on the Lord of the whole world.

6b This is the word of Yahweh with regard to Zerubbabel, 'Not by might and not by power, but by my spirit'—says Yahweh Sabaoth.

7 'What are you, great mountain? Beside Zerubbabel you shall become a plain! He will bring out the keystone while it is cheered with Hurrah! Hurrah!'

8 The word of Yahweh was addressed to me as follows, 9 'The hands of Zerubbabel have laid the foundation of this Temple; his hands will finish it. (Then you will know that Yahweh Sabaoth has sent me to you.) 10a A day of little things, no doubt, but who would dare despise it? How they will rejoice when they see the chosen stone in the hands of Zerubbabel!'

5 Again raising my eyes, I had a vision. There was a flying scroll. 2 The angel who was talking to me said, 'What do you see?' I replied, 'I see a flying scroll; it is twenty cubits long and ten cubits wide.' 3 He then said to me, 'This is God's curse sweeping across the face of the whole country; for, according to what it says on one side, every thief will be banished and, according to what it says on the other, everyone who commits perjury in my name will be banished from it. 4 I am going to release it—Yahweh Sabaoth declares—for it to enter the house of the thief and of anyone who commits perjury in my name, for it to settle deep within his house and consume it, timber, stone and all.'

5 The angel who was talking to me appeared and said to me, 'Raise your eyes, and see what this is, going along.' 6 I said, 'What is it?' He said, 'It is a bushel measure going along.' He went on, 'This is their guilt throughout the country.' 7 At this, a disc of lead was raised, and I saw a woman sitting inside the barrel. 8 He said, 'This is Wickedness.' And he rammed her back into the barrel and jammed its mouth shut with the mass of lead. 9 I raised my eyes, and there were two women appearing. The wind caught their wings—they had wings like a stork's; they raised the barrel midway between earth and heaven. 10 I then said to the angel who was talking to me, 'Where are they taking the

a house for it; and when this is prepared, they will set the basket[m] down there on its base."

6 And again I looked up and saw four chariots coming out from between two mountains—mountains of bronze. 2 The first chariot had red horses, the second chariot black horses, 3 the third white horses, and the fourth chariot dappled gray[n] horses. 4 Then I said to the angel who talked with me, "What are these, my lord?" 5 The angel answered me, "These are the four winds[o] of heaven going out, after presenting themselves before the LORD of all the earth. 6 The chariot with the black horses goes toward the north country, the white ones go toward the west country,[p] and the dappled ones go toward the south country." 7 When the steeds came out, they were impatient to get off and patrol the earth. And he said, "Go, patrol the earth." So they patrolled the earth. 8 Then he cried out to me, "Lo, those who go toward the north country have set my spirit at rest in the north country."

9 The word of the LORD came to me: 10 Collect silver and gold[q] from the exiles—from Heldai, Tobijah, and Jedaiah—who have arrived from Babylon; and go the same day to the house of Josiah son of Zephaniah. 11 Take the silver and gold and make a crown,[r] and set it on the head of the high priest Joshua son of Jehozadak; 12 say to him: Thus says the LORD of hosts: Here is a man whose name is Branch: for he shall branch out in his place, and he shall build the temple of the LORD. 13 It is he that shall build the temple of the LORD; he shall bear royal honor, and shall sit and rule on his throne. There shall be a priest by his throne, with peaceful understanding between the two of them. 14 And the crown[s] shall be in the care of Heldai,[t] Tobijah, Jedaiah, and Josiah[u] son of Zephaniah, as a memorial in the temple of the LORD.

15 Those who are far off shall come and help to build the temple of the LORD; and you shall know that the LORD of hosts has sent me to you. This will happen if you diligently obey the voice of the LORD your God.

7 In the fourth year of King Darius, the word of the LORD came to Zechariah on the fourth day of the ninth month, which is Chislev. 2 Now the people of Bethel had sent Sharezer and Regem-melech and their men, to entreat the favor of the LORD, 3 and to ask the priests of the house of the LORD of hosts and the prophets, "Should I mourn and practice abstinence in the fifth month, as I have done for so many years?" 4 Then the word of the LORD of hosts came to me: 5 Say to all the people of the land and the priests: When you fasted and lamented in the fifth month and in the seventh, for these seventy years, was it for me that you fasted? 6 And when you eat and when you drink, do you not eat and drink only for yourselves? 7 Were not these the words that the LORD proclaimed by the former prophets, when Jerusalem was inhabited and in prosperity, along with the towns around it, and when the Negeb and the Shephelah were inhabited?

8 The word of the LORD came to Zechariah, saying: 9 Thus says the LORD of hosts: Render true judgments, show kindness and mercy to one another; 10 do not oppress the widow, the orphan, the alien, or the poor; and do not devise evil in your hearts against one another. 11 But they refused to listen, and turned a stubborn shoulder, and stopped their ears in order not to hear. 12 They made their hearts adamant

build a house for it in the land of Shinar; once the house is ready, the barrel will be set there on the place prepared for it.'

6 I looked up again and saw four chariots coming out between two mountains, which were mountains of copper. 2 The first chariot had bay horses, the second black, 3 the third white, and the fourth dappled. 4 I asked the angel who talked with me, 'Sir, what are these?' 5 He answered, 'These are the four winds of heaven; after attending the Lord of the whole earth, they are now going forth. 6 The chariot with the black horses is going to the land of the north, that with the white to the far west, that with the dappled to the south, 7 and that with the roan to the land of the east.' They were eager to set off and range over the whole earth. 'Go,' he said, 'range over the earth,' and they did so. 8 Then he called me to look and said, 'Those going to the land of the north have made my spirit rest on that land.'

9 THE word of the LORD came to me: 10 Receive the gifts from the exiles Heldai, Tobiah, and Jedaiah who have returned from Babylon, and go the same day to the house of Josiah son of Zephaniah. 11 Take the silver and gold and make a crown; place it on the head of the high priest, Joshua son of Jehozadak, 12 and say to him: These are the words of the LORD of Hosts: Here is a man whose name is Branch; he will branch out from where he is and rebuild the temple of the LORD. 13 It is he who will rebuild the temple, he who will assume royal dignity, who will sit on his throne as ruler. There will be a priest beside his throne, and there will be harmony between them. 14 The crown will serve as a memorial for Heldai, Tobiah, Jedaiah, and Josiah son of Zephaniah in the temple of the LORD.

15 Men from far away will come and work on the rebuilding of the temple of the LORD; so you will know that the LORD of Hosts has sent me to you. This will come about if you hearken with diligence to the LORD your God!

7 THE word of the LORD came to Zechariah in the fourth year of King Darius, on the fourth day of Kislev, the ninth month. 2 Bethel-sharezer sent Regem-melech together with his men to entreat the favour of the LORD. 3 They were to say to the priests in the house of the LORD of Hosts and to the prophets, 'Am I to lament and fast in the fifth month as I have done these many years?' 4 Then the word of the LORD of Hosts came to me: 5 Say to all the people of the land and to the priests: When you fasted and lamented in the fifth and seventh months these past seventy years, was it indeed with me in mind that you fasted? 6 And when you ate and drank, was it not to please yourselves? 7 Was it not this that the LORD proclaimed through the prophets of old, while Jerusalem was populous and peaceful, as were the towns round about, and there were people settled in the Negeb and the Shephelah?

8 The word of the LORD came to Zechariah: 9 These are the words of the LORD of Hosts: Administer true justice, show kindness and compassion to each other, 10 do not oppress the widow or the fatherless, the resident alien or the poor, and do not plot evil against one another. 11 But they refused to listen; they turned their backs defiantly on me, they stopped their ears so as not to hear. 12 They were ada-

---

build a temple for it in the land of Shinar; when the temple is ready, they will deposit it there in its place."

6 Again I raised my eyes and saw four chariots coming out from between two mountains; and the mountains were of bronze. 2 The first chariot had red horses, the second chariot black horses, 3 the third chariot white horses, and the fourth chariot spotted horses — all of them strong horses. 4 I asked the angel who spoke with me, "What are these, my lord?" 5 The angel said to me in reply, "These are the four winds of the heavens, which are coming forth after being reviewed by the LORD of all the earth." 6 The chariot with the black horses was turning toward the land of the north, the red and the white horses went after them, and the spotted ones went toward the land of the south. 7 As these strong horses emerged, eager to set about patrolling the earth, he said, "Go, patrol the earth!" Then, as they patrolled the earth, 8 he called out to me and said, "See, they that go forth to the land of the north will make my spirit rest in the land of the north."

9 This word of the LORD then came to me: 10 Take from the returned captives Heldai, Tobijah, Jedaiah; and go the same day to the house of Josiah, son of Zephaniah (these had come from Babylon). 11 Silver and gold you shall take, and make a crown; place it on the head of [Joshua, son of Jehozadak, the high priest] Zerubbabel. 12 And say to him: Thus says the LORD of hosts: Here is a man whose name is Shoot, and where he is he shall sprout, and he shall build the temple of the LORD. 13 Yes, he shall build the temple of the LORD, and taking up the royal insignia, he shall sit as ruler upon his throne. The priest shall be at his right hand, and between the two of them there shall be friendly understanding. 14 The crown itself shall be a memorial offering in the temple of the LORD in favor of Heldai, Tobijah, Jedaiah, and the son of Zephaniah. 15 And they who are from afar shall come and build the temple of the LORD, and you shall know that the LORD of hosts has sent me to you. And if you heed carefully the voice of the LORD your God. . . .

7 In the fourth year of Darius the king [the word of the LORD came to Zechariah], on the fourth day of Chislev, the ninth month, 2 Bethel-sarezer sent Regemmelech and his men to implore favor of the LORD 3 and to ask the priests of the house of the LORD of hosts, and the prophets, "Must I mourn and abstain in the fifth month as I have been doing these many years?" 4 Thereupon this word of the LORD of hosts came to me: 5 Say to all the people of the land and to the priests: When you fasted and mourned in the fifth and in the seventh month these seventy years, was it really for me that you fasted? 6 And when you were eating and drinking, was it not for yourselves that you ate, and for yourselves that you drank? 7 Were not these the words which the LORD spoke through the former prophets, when Jerusalem and the surrounding cities were inhabited and at peace, when the Negeb and the foothills were inhabited? 8 [This word of the LORD came to Zechariah: 9 Thus says the LORD of hosts:] Render true judgment, and show kindness and compassion toward each other. 10 Do not oppress the widow or the orphan, the alien or the poor; do not plot evil against one another in your hearts. 11 But they refused to listen; they stubbornly turned their backs and stopped their ears so as not to hear. 12 And they made their hearts diamond-hard so

barrel?' 11 He replied, 'To build a temple for it in the land of Shinar^c and make a pedestal on which to put it.'

6 Again I raised my eyes, and this is what I saw: four chariots coming out between two mountains, and the mountains were mountains of bronze. 2 The first chariot had red horses, the second chariot had black horses, 3 the third chariot had white horses and the fourth chariot had vigorous, piebald horses. 4 I asked the angel who was talking to me, 'What are these, my lord?' 5 The angel replied, 'They are the four winds of heaven now leaving, after attending the Lord of the whole world. 6 The black horses are leaving for the land of the north; the white are following them, and the piebald are leaving for the land of the south.' 7 They came out vigorously, eager to patrol the world. He said to them, 'Go and patrol the world.' And they patrolled the world. 8 He called to me and said, 'Look, the ones going to the land of the north brought my spirit to rest on the land of the north.'

9 Then the word of Yahweh was addressed to me as follows, 10 'Collect silver and gold from the exiles, from Heldai, Tobijah and Jedaiah, then (you yourself go the same day) go to the house of Josiah son of Zephaniah, who has arrived from Babylon. 11 Then, taking the silver and gold, make a crown and place it on the head of the high priest Joshua^d son of Jehozadak. 12 And say this to him, "Yahweh Sabaoth says this: Here is a man whose name is Branch; where he is, there will be a branching out (and he will rebuild Yahweh's sanctuary). 13 Yes, he is the one who will rebuild Yahweh's sanctuary; he will wear the royal insignia and sit on his throne and govern, with a priest on his right. Perfect peace will reign between these two. 14 And the crown will serve Heldai, Tobijah, Jedaiah and the son of Zephaniah as a memorial of favour in Yahweh's sanctuary. 15 And those now far away will come and work on the building of Yahweh's sanctuary."

'Then you will know that Yahweh Sabaoth has sent me to you. It will happen if you diligently obey the voice of Yahweh your God.'

7 In the fourth year of King Darius, the word of Yahweh was addressed to Zechariah on the fourth day of the ninth month, the month of Chislev. 2 Bethel sent Sharezer with a deputation to entreat Yahweh's favour 3 and to ask the priests in the Temple of Yahweh Sabaoth and the prophets, 'Ought I to go on mourning and fasting in the fifth month as I have been doing for so many years past?'

4 Then the word of Yahweh Sabaoth was addressed to me as follows, 5 'Say to all the people of the country and to the priests, "While you have been fasting and mourning in the fifth and seventh months for the past seventy years, have you really been fasting for my sake? 6 And when you were eating and drinking, were you not eating and drinking for your own sake? 7 Do you not know the words which Yahweh proclaimed through the prophets in the past, when Jerusalem was inhabited and secure, as were her surrounding towns, and when the Negeb and the lowlands were inhabited?" ' (8 The word of Yahweh was addressed to Zechariah as follows, 9 'Yahweh Sabaoth says this.) He said, "Apply the law fairly, and show faithful love and compassion towards one another. 10 Do not oppress the widow and the orphan, the foreigner and the poor, and do not secretly plan evil against one another." 11 But they would not listen; they turned a rebellious shoulder; they stopped their ears rather than hear; 12 they made their hearts

---

6, 11: Make a crown; place it on the head of [Joshua, son of Jehozadak, the high priest] Zerubbabel: according to the current Hebrew text, Joshua the high priest is to be crowned. However, since the crown is a sign of royalty, the original text must have had the name of Zerubbabel here, not that of Joshua.

^c 5 Babylon, where Wickedness has its temple, leaving the Holy Land pure.   ^d 6 The original reading must have been 'Zerubbabel'; 'Joshua' was later substituted, when the high priest became the unique head of the community after the disappearance of the royal house.

in order not to hear the law and the words that the LORD of hosts had sent by his spirit through the former prophets. Therefore great wrath came from the LORD of hosts. 13 Just as, when I[v] called, they would not hear, so, when they called, I would not hear, says the LORD of hosts, 14 and I scattered them with a whirlwind among all the nations that they had not known. Thus the land they left was desolate, so that no one went to and fro, and a pleasant land was made desolate.

8 The word of the LORD of hosts came to me, saying: 2 Thus says the LORD of hosts: I am jealous for Zion with great jealousy, and I am jealous for her with great wrath. 3 Thus says the LORD: I will return to Zion, and will dwell in the midst of Jerusalem; Jerusalem shall be called the faithful city, and the mountain of the LORD of hosts shall be called the holy mountain. 4 Thus says the LORD of hosts: Old men and old women shall again sit in the streets of Jerusalem, each with staff in hand because of their great age. 5 And the streets of the city shall be full of boys and girls playing in its streets. 6 Thus says the LORD of hosts: Even though it seems impossible to the remnant of this people in these days, should it also seem impossible to me, says the LORD of hosts? 7 Thus says the LORD of hosts: I will save my people from the east country and from the west country; 8 and I will bring them to live in Jerusalem. They shall be my people and I will be their God, in faithfulness and in righteousness.

9 Thus says the LORD of hosts: Let your hands be strong — you that have recently been hearing these words from the mouths of the prophets who were present when the foundation was laid for the rebuilding of the temple, the house of the LORD of hosts. 10 For before those days there were no wages for people or for animals, nor was there any safety from the foe for those who went out or came in, and I set them all against one other. 11 But now I will not deal with the remnant of this people as in the former days, says the LORD of hosts. 12 For there shall be a sowing of peace; the vine shall yield its fruit, the ground shall give its produce, and the skies shall give their dew; and I will cause the remnant of this people to possess all these things. 13 Just as you have been a cursing among the nations, O house of Judah and house of Israel, so I will save you and you shall be a blessing. Do not be afraid, but let your hands be strong.

14 For thus says the LORD of hosts: Just as I purposed to bring disaster upon you, when your ancestors provoked me to wrath, and I did not relent, says the LORD of hosts, 15 so again I have purposed in these days to do good to Jerusalem and to the house of Judah; do not be afraid. 16 These are the things that you shall do: Speak the truth to one another, render in your gates judgments that are true and make for peace, 17 do not devise evil in your hearts against one another, and love no false oath; for all these are things that I hate, says the LORD.

mant in their refusal to accept the law and the teaching which the LORD of Hosts had sent by his spirit through the prophets of old; and in great anger the LORD of Hosts said: 13 As they did not listen when I called, so I would not listen when they called. 14 I drove them out among all the nations where they were strangers, leaving their land deserted behind them, so that no one came and went. Thus their pleasant land was turned into a desert.

8 The word of the LORD of Hosts came to me: 2 These are the words of the LORD of Hosts: I have been very jealous for Zion, fiercely jealous for her. 3 Now, says the LORD, I shall come back to Zion and dwell in Jerusalem. Jerusalem will be called the City of Faithfulness, and the mountain of the LORD of Hosts will be called the Holy Mountain. 4 These are the words of the LORD of Hosts: Once again old men and women will sit in the streets of Jerusalem, each leaning on a stick because of great age; 5 and the streets of the city will be full of boys and girls at play. 6 These are the words of the LORD of Hosts: Even if this may seem impossible to the remnant of this nation in those days, will it also seem impossible to me? This is the word of the LORD of Hosts. 7 These are the words of the LORD of Hosts: I am about to rescue my people from the countries in the east and the west, 8 and bring them back to live in Jerusalem. They will be my people, and I shall be their God, in faithfulness and justice.

9 These are the words of the LORD of Hosts: Take heart, all who now hear the promise that the temple is to be rebuilt; you hear it from the prophets who were present when foundations for the house of the LORD of Hosts were laid. 10 Before that time there was no hiring of people or animals; because of enemies, no one could go about his business in safety, for I had set everyone at odds with everyone else. 11 But I do not feel the same now towards the remnant of this people as I did in former days, says the LORD of Hosts. 12 For they will sow in safety; the vine will yield its fruit and the soil its produce, and the heavens will give their moisture; with all these things I shall endow the remnant of this people. 13 To the nations you, house of Judah and house of Israel, have become proverbial as a curse; now I shall save you, and you will become proverbial as a blessing. Courage! Do not lose heart.

14 For these are the words of the LORD of Hosts: Whereas I resolved to bring disaster on you when your forefathers provoked my wrath, says the LORD of Hosts, and I did not relent, 15 so I have resolved to do good again in these days to Jerusalem and to the house of Judah. Do not be afraid. 16 This is what you must do: speak the truth to each other, administer true and sound justice in your courts. 17 Do not plot evil against one another, and do not love perjury, for all these are things I hate. This is the word of the LORD.

as not to hear the teaching and the message that the LORD of hosts had sent by his spirit through the former prophets. 13 Then the LORD of hosts in his great anger said that, as they had not listened when he called, so he would not listen when they called, 14 but would scatter them with a whirlwind among all the nations that they did not know. Thus the land was left desolate after them with no one traveling to and fro; they made the pleasant land into a desert.

8 This word of the LORD of hosts came: Thus says the LORD of hosts:

2 I am intensely jealous for Zion,
   stirred to jealous wrath for her.
3   Thus says the LORD:
I will return to Zion,
   and I will dwell within Jerusalem;
Jerusalem shall be called the faithful city,
   and the mountain of the LORD of hosts,
   the holy mountain.

4 Thus says the LORD of hosts: Old men and old women, each with staff in hand because of old age, shall again sit in the streets of Jerusalem. 5 The city shall be filled with boys and girls playing in her streets. 6 Thus says the LORD of hosts: Even if this should seem impossible in the eyes of the remnant of this people, shall it in those days be impossible in my eyes also, says the LORD of hosts? 7 Thus says the LORD of hosts: Lo, I will rescue my people from the land of the rising sun, and from the land of the setting sun. 8 I will bring them back to dwell within Jerusalem. They shall be my people, and I will be their God, with faithfulness and justice.

9 Thus says the LORD of hosts: Let your hands be strong, you who in these days hear these words spoken by the prophets on the day when the foundation of the house of the LORD of hosts was laid for the building of the temple. 10 For before those days there were no wages for men, or hire for beasts; those who came and went had no security from the enemy, for I set every man against his neighbor. 11 But now I will not deal with the remnant of this people as in former days, says the LORD of hosts, 12 for it is the seedtime of peace: the vine shall yield its fruit, the land shall bear its crops, and the heavens shall give their dew; all these things I will have the remnant of the people possess. 13 Just as you were a curse among the nations, O house of Judah and house of Israel, so will I save you that you may be a blessing; do not fear, but let your hands be strong.

14 Thus says the LORD of hosts: As I determined to harm you when your fathers provoked me to wrath, says the LORD of hosts, and I did not relent, 15 so again in these days I have determined to favor Jerusalem and the house of Judah; do not fear! 16 These then are the things you should do: Speak the truth to one another; let there be honesty and peace in the judgments at your gates, 17 and let none of you plot evil against another in his heart, nor love a false oath. For all these things I hate, says the LORD.

---

adamant rather than listen to the teaching and the words that Yahweh Sabaoth had sent — by his spirit — through the prophets in the past; and consequently the fury of Yahweh Sabaoth overtook them. 13 And so, since when he called they would not listen, "I would not listen when they called", says Yahweh Sabaoth, 14 "but scattered them among all the nations unknown to them. Hence, after they had gone, the country was deserted, and no one came or went. They had turned a land of delights into a desert." '

8 The word of Yahweh Sabaoth came as follows:

2 Yahweh Sabaoth says this:
   I have been burning with jealousy for Zion,
   with furious jealousy for her sake.

3 Yahweh says this:
   I am coming back to Zion
   and shall live in the heart of Jerusalem.
   Jerusalem will be called Faithful City
   and the mountain of Yahweh Sabaoth, the Holy
      Mountain.

4 Yahweh Sabaoth says this:
   Aged men and women once again will sit
   in the squares of Jerusalem,
   each with a stick to lean on
   because of their great age.
5 And the squares of the city will be full
   of boys and girls
   playing there.

6 Yahweh Sabaoth says this:
   If this seems a miracle
   to the remnant of this people (in those days),
   will it seem one to me?
   declares Yahweh.

7 Yahweh Sabaoth says this:
   Look, I shall rescue my people
   from the countries of the east
   and from the countries of the west.
8 I shall bring them back
   to live in the heart of Jerusalem,
   and they will be my people
   and I shall be their God,
   faithful and just.

9 'Yahweh Sabaoth says this, "Take heart, you who today hear these promises uttered by the prophets since the day when the foundations of the Temple of Yahweh Sabaoth were laid, that the sanctuary would indeed be rebuilt. 10 For up to now, men were not paid their wages and nothing was paid for the animals either; and it has not been safe for anyone to come and go, because of the enemy, since I had set each one against everyone else. 11 But from now on, I shall not treat the remnant of this people as I have treated them in time past — declares Yahweh Sabaoth. 12 Now they will sow in peace; the vine will give its fruit, the soil will give its produce and heaven will give its dew. I shall bestow all these on the remnant of this people. 13 Just as once you were a curse among the nations, House of Judah and House of Israel, so now I shall save you, and you will be a blessing. Do not be afraid. Take heart!"

14 'For Yahweh Sabaoth says this, "Just as I resolved to ill-treat you when your ancestors provoked me to anger and did not relent — says Yahweh Sabaoth — 15 so now I have changed my mind and intend to treat Jerusalem and the House of Judah well. Do not be afraid!

16 "These are the things that you must do. Speak the truth to one another; at your gates, administer fair judgement conducive to peace; 17 do not secretly plot evil against one another; do not love perjury; since I hate all this — Yahweh declares." '

NEW REVISED STANDARD VERSION

18 The word of the LORD of hosts came to me, saying:
19 Thus says the LORD of hosts: The fast of the fourth month, and the fast of the fifth, and the fast of the seventh, and the fast of the tenth, shall be seasons of joy and gladness, and cheerful festivals for the house of Judah: therefore love truth and peace.

20 Thus says the LORD of hosts: Peoples shall yet come, the inhabitants of many cities; 21 the inhabitants of one city shall go to another, saying, "Come, let us go to entreat the favor of the LORD, and to seek the LORD of hosts; I myself am going." 22 Many peoples and strong nations shall come to seek the LORD of hosts in Jerusalem, and to entreat the favor of the LORD. 23 Thus says the LORD of hosts: In those days ten men from nations of every language shall take hold of a Jew, grasping his garment and saying, "Let us go with you, for we have heard that God is with you."

9 An Oracle.

The word of the LORD is against the land of
    Hadrach
    and will rest upon Damascus.
For to the LORD belongs the capital ^{w} of Aram, ^{x}
    as do all the tribes of Israel;
2 Hamath also, which borders on it,
    Tyre and Sidon, though they are very wise.
3 Tyre has built itself a rampart,
    and heaped up silver like dust,
    and gold like the dirt of the streets.
4 But now, the Lord will strip it of its possessions
    and hurl its wealth into the sea,
    and it shall be devoured by fire.

5 Ashkelon shall see it and be afraid;
    Gaza too, and shall writhe in anguish;
    Ekron also, because its hopes are withered.
The king shall perish from Gaza;
    Ashkelon shall be uninhabited;
6 a mongrel people shall settle in Ashdod,
    and I will make an end of the pride of
    Philistia.
7 I will take away its blood from its mouth,
    and its abominations from between its teeth;
it too shall be a remnant for our God;
    it shall be like a clan in Judah,
    and Ekron shall be like the Jebusites.
8 Then I will encamp at my house as a guard,
    so that no one shall march to and fro;
no oppressor shall again overrun them,
    for now I have seen with my own eyes.

9 Rejoice greatly, O daughter Zion!
    Shout aloud, O daughter Jerusalem!
Lo, your king comes to you;
    triumphant and victorious is he,
humble and riding on a donkey,
    on a colt, the foal of a donkey.
10 He ^{y} will cut off the chariot from Ephraim
    and the war horse from Jerusalem;
and the battle bow shall be cut off,
    and he shall command peace to the nations;
his dominion shall be from sea to sea,
    and from the River to the ends of the earth.

REVISED ENGLISH BIBLE

18 The word of the LORD of Hosts came to me: 19 These are the words of the LORD of Hosts: The fasts of the fourth month, and of the fifth, seventh, and tenth months, are to become festivals of joy and gladness for the house of Judah. So love truth and peace.

20 These are the words of the LORD of Hosts: Nations and dwellers in many cities will come in the future; 21 people of one city will approach those of another and say, 'Let us go to entreat the favour of the LORD; let us resort to the LORD of Hosts; and I too shall go.' 22 Many peoples and mighty nations will resort to the LORD of Hosts in Jerusalem and entreat his favour. 23 These are the words of the LORD of Hosts: In those days, ten people from nations of every language will take hold of the robe of one Jew and say, 'Let us accompany you, for we have heard that God is with you.'

9 AN oracle:

The word of the LORD is in the land of Hadrach;
    it alights on Damascus,
for, no less than all the tribes of Israel,
    the capital of Aram belongs to the LORD.
2 It alights also on Hamath which borders on
    Damascus,
    and for all their wisdom it alights on Tyre and
    Sidon.
3 Tyre, who built herself a rampart,
    has amassed silver like dust
    and gold like the dirt on the streets.
4 But the Lord will take from her all she possesses;
    he will break her power at sea,
    and the city itself will be destroyed by fire.

5 Let Ashkelon see and be afraid;
    Gaza will writhe in terror,
    and Ekron's hope will come to naught.
Kings will vanish from Gaza,
    and Ashkelon will be empty of people.
6 A mixed race will settle in Ashdod,
    and I shall cut down the pride of the Philistines.
7 I shall stop them eating flesh with the blood still in
    it
    and feeding on detestable things.
Those who survive will belong to our God;
    they will be like a clan in Judah,
    and Ekron will become like the Jebusites.
8 I shall post a garrison for my house
    so that none may pass to and fro that way,
    and no oppressor may ever again overrun them,
    for now I am taking note of their suffering.

9 Daughter of Zion, rejoice with all your heart;
    shout in triumph, daughter of Jerusalem!
See, your king is coming to you,
    his cause won, his victory gained,
    humble and mounted on a donkey,
    on a colt, the foal of a donkey.
10 He will banish the chariot from Ephraim,
    the war-horse from Jerusalem;
    the warrior's bow will be banished,
    and he will proclaim peace to the nations.
His rule will extend from sea to sea,
    from the River to the ends of the earth.

9:1 **capital:** *prob. rdg; Heb.* eye. **Aram:** *so one MS; others* Adam.
9:4 **power:** *or* wealth.   9:8 **of their suffering:** *prob. rdg; Heb.*
with my eyes.   9:10 **He will banish:** *so Gk; Heb.* I shall banish.

^{w} Heb *eye* ^{x} Cn: Heb *of Adam* (or *of humankind*) ^{y} Gk: Heb *I*

18 This word of the LORD of hosts came to me: 19 Thus says the LORD of hosts: The fast days of the fourth, the fifth, the seventh, and the tenth months shall become occasions of joy and gladness, cheerful festivals for the house of Judah; only love faithfulness and peace. 20 Thus says the LORD of hosts: There shall yet come peoples, the inhabitants of many cities; 21 and the inhabitants of one city shall approach those of another, and say, "Come! let us go to implore the favor of the LORD"; and, "I too will go to seek the LORD." 22 Many peoples and strong nations shall come to seek the LORD of hosts in Jerusalem and to implore the favor of the LORD. 23 Thus says the LORD of hosts: In those days ten men of every nationality, speaking different tongues, shall take hold, yes, take hold of every Jew by the edge of his garment and say, "Let us go with you, for we have heard that God is with you."

9 An oracle:

The word of the LORD is upon the land of Hadrach,
  and Damascus is its resting place,
For the cities of Aram are the LORD's,
  as are all the tribes of Israel,
2 Hamath also, on its border,
  Tyre, too, and Sidon, however wise they be.
3 Tyre built herself a stronghold,
  and heaped up silver like dust,
  and gold like the mire of the streets.
4 Lo, the LORD will strip her of her possessions,
  and smite her power on the sea,
  and she shall be devoured by fire.
5 Ashkelon shall see it and be afraid;
  Gaza also: she shall be in great anguish;
  Ekron, too, for her hope shall come to nought.
The king shall disappear from Gaza,
  and Ashkelon shall not be inhabited,
6   and the baseborn shall occupy Ashdod.
I will destroy the pride of the Philistine
7   and take from his mouth his bloody meat,
  and his abominations from between his teeth:
He also shall become a remnant for our God,
  and shall be like a family in Judah,
  and Ekron shall be like the Jebusites.
8 I will encamp by my house as a guard
  that none may pass to and fro;
No oppressor shall pass over them again,
  for now I have regard for their affliction.

9 Rejoice heartily, O daughter Zion,
  shout for joy, O daughter Jerusalem!
See, your king shall come to you;
  a just savior is he,
Meek, and riding on an ass,
  on a colt, the foal of an ass.
10 He shall banish the chariot from Ephraim,
  and the horse from Jerusalem;
The warrior's bow shall be banished,
  and he shall proclaim peace to the nations.
His dominion shall be from sea to sea,
  and from the River to the ends of the earth.

18 The word of Yahweh Sabaoth was addressed to me as follows:
19 'Yahweh Sabaoth says this, "The fast of the fourth month, the fast of the fifth, the fast of the seventh and the fast of the tenth are to become glad, joyful, happy festivals for the House of Judah. So love truth and peace!" '
20 'Yahweh Sabaoth says this, "In the future, peoples and citizens of many cities will come; 21 and citizens of one city will go to the next and say: We must certainly go to entreat Yahweh's favour and seek out Yahweh Sabaoth; I am going myself. 22 Yes, many peoples and great nations will seek out Yahweh Sabaoth in Jerusalem and entreat Yahweh's favour."
23 'Yahweh Sabaoth says this, "In those days, ten men from nations of every language will take a Jew by the sleeve and say: We want to go with you, since we have learnt that God is with you." '

9 A proclamation.

The word of Yahweh is against Hadrach,
  it has come to rest on Damascus,
  for the source of Aram belongs to Yahweh
  no less than all the tribes of Israel;
2 on Hamath too, which borders on it,
  and on (Tyre and) Sidon, despite her acumen.
3 Tyre has built herself a fortress,
  has heaped up silver like dust
  and gold like the dirt of the streets.
4 And now the Lord is going to dispossess her;
  at sea he will break her power,
  and she herself will go up in flames.
5 Seeing this, Ashkelon will be terrified,
  Gaza too, and writhe with grief,
  Ekron too, at the ruin of her prospects;
  the king will vanish from Gaza
  and Ashkelon be unpeopled,
6 while a half-breed will live in Ashdod!
  Yes, I shall destroy the pride of the Philistine;
7 I shall snatch his blood from his mouth,
  his abominations from between his teeth.
But his remnant too will belong to our God,
  becoming like a clan in Judah,
  and Ekron will become like a Jebusite.
8 I shall stand guard before my home
  to defend it against all comers,
  and no oppressor will overrun them ever again,
  for now I am on the alert.

9 Rejoice heart and soul, daughter of Zion!
  Shout for joy, daughter of Jerusalem!
Look, your king is approaching,
  he is vindicated and victorious,
  humble and riding on a donkey,
  on a colt, the foal of a donkey.
10 He will banish chariots from Ephraim
  and horses from Jerusalem;
  the bow of war will be banished.
He will proclaim peace to the nations,
  his empire will stretch from sea to sea,
  from the River to the limits of the earth.

NEW REVISED STANDARD VERSION	REVISED ENGLISH BIBLE

NEW REVISED STANDARD VERSION

11 As for you also, because of the blood of my
   covenant with you,
      I will set your prisoners free from the waterless
         pit.
12 Return to your stronghold, O prisoners of hope;
      today I declare that I will restore to you
         double.
13 For I have bent Judah as my bow;
      I have made Ephraim its arrow.
   I will arouse your sons, O Zion,
      against your sons, O Greece,
      and wield you like a warrior's sword.

14 Then the LORD will appear over them,
      and his arrow go forth like lightning;
   the Lord GOD will sound the trumpet
      and march forth in the whirlwinds of the south.
15 The LORD of hosts will protect them,
      and they shall devour and tread down the
         slingers;[z]
   they shall drink their blood[a] like wine,
      and be full like a bowl,
      drenched like the corners of the altar.

16 On that day the LORD their God will save them
      for they are the flock of his people;
   for like the jewels of a crown
      they shall shine on his land.
17 For what goodness and beauty are his!
      Grain shall make the young men flourish,
      and new wine the young women.

10 Ask rain from the LORD
         in the season of the spring rain,
      from the LORD who makes the storm clouds,
         who gives showers of rain to you,[b]
         the vegetation in the field to everyone.
2 For the teraphim[c] utter nonsense,
      and the diviners see lies;
   the dreamers tell false dreams,
      and give empty consolation.
   Therefore the people wander like sheep;
      they suffer for lack of a shepherd.

3 My anger is hot against the shepherds,
      and I will punish the leaders;[d]
   for the LORD of hosts cares for his flock, the
         house of Judah,
      and will make them like his proud war horse.
4 Out of them shall come the cornerstone,
      out of them the tent peg,
   out of them the battle bow,
      out of them every commander.
5 Together they shall be like warriors in battle,
      trampling the foe in the mud of the streets;
   they shall fight, for the LORD is with them,
      and they shall put to shame the riders on
         horses.

6 I will strengthen the house of Judah,
      and I will save the house of Joseph.
   I will bring them back because I have compassion
         on them,
      and they shall be as though I had not rejected
         them;
   for I am the LORD their God and I will answer
         them.

REVISED ENGLISH BIBLE

11 As for you, because of your blood covenant with
   me
      I shall release your people imprisoned in a
         waterless dungeon.
12 Come back to the Citadel, you captives waiting in
   hope.
   Now is the day announced
      when I shall grant you twofold reparation.
13 For my bow is strung, Judah;
      I have laid the arrow to it, Ephraim;
   I have roused your sons, Zion,
      and made you into a warrior's sword
      against the sons of Javan.

14 The LORD will appear over them,
      and his arrow will flash forth like lightning;
   the Lord GOD will sound the trumpet
      and advance with the storm-winds of the south.
15 The LORD of Hosts will protect them;
      they will prevail, trampling underfoot the
         sling-stones;
   they will be roaring drunk as if with wine,
      brimful as a bowl, drenched like the corners of the
         altar.

16 On that day the LORD their God
      will save them, his own people, like a flock.
   For they are the precious stones in a crown
      which sparkle all about his land.
17 What wealth is theirs, what beauty!
      Grain to strengthen young men,
      and new wine for maidens!

10 Ask the LORD for rain at the time of the spring
         rain,
      the LORD who makes the storm-clouds,
      and he will give the heavy rains
      and grass in the fields for everyone;
2 for the household gods utter empty promises;
      diviners see false signs,
   they produce lies as dreams,
      and the comfort they offer is illusory.
   So the people are left to wander about
      like sheep in distress for lack of a shepherd.
3 My anger burns against the shepherds,
      and I shall punish the leaders of the flock.

   The LORD of Hosts will care for his flock,
      the people of Judah,
      and transform them into his royal war-horses.
4 From Judah will come corner-stone and tent-peg,
      the bow ready for battle, and all the commanders.
5 Together they will be like warriors
      trampling the muddy tracks of the battlefield;
   they will fight because the LORD is with them,
      and they will put to rout even those on horseback.
6 I shall give triumph to the house of Judah
      and victory to the house of Joseph;
   I shall restore them in my compassion for them,
      and they will be as though I had never cast them
         off;
   for I am the LORD their God and I shall answer
         them.

---

[z] Cn: Heb *the slingstones*   [a] Gk: Heb *shall drink*   [b] Heb *them*
[c] Or *household gods*   [d] Or *male goats*

|

11 As for you, for the blood of your covenant
with me,
I will bring forth your prisoners from the
dungeon.
12 In the return to the fortress
of the waiting prisoners,
This very day, I will return you
double for your exile.
13 For I will bend Judah as my bow,
I will arm myself with Ephraim;
I will arouse your sons, O Zion,
[against your sons, O Yavan,]
and I will use you as a warrior's sword.
14 The LORD shall appear over them,
and his arrow shall shoot forth as lightning;
The LORD God shall sound the trumpet,
and come in a storm from the south.
15 The LORD of hosts shall be a shield over them,
they shall overcome sling stones
and trample them underfoot;
They shall drink blood like wine,
till they are filled with it like libation bowls,
like the corners of the altar.
16 And the LORD, their God, shall save them on
that day,
his people, like a flock.
For they are the jewels in a crown
raised aloft over his land.
17 For what wealth is theirs, and what beauty!
grain that makes the youths flourish,
and new wine, the maidens!

10 Ask of the LORD rain in the spring season!
It is the LORD who makes the storm clouds,
And sends men the pouring rain;
for everyone, grassy fields.
2 For the teraphim speak nonsense,
the diviners have false visions:
Deceitful dreams they tell,
empty comfort they offer.
This is why they wander like sheep,
wretched: they have no shepherd.
3 My wrath is kindled against the shepherds,
and I will punish the leaders;
For the LORD of hosts will visit his flock,
the house of Judah,
and make them his stately war horse.

4 From him shall come leader and chief,
from him warrior's bow and every officer.
5 They shall all be warriors,
trampling the mire of the streets in battle;
They shall wage war because the LORD is
with them,
and shall put the horsemen to rout.
6 I will strengthen the house of Judah,
the house of Joseph I will save;
I will bring them back, because I have mercy
on them,
they shall be as though I had never cast
them off,
for I am the LORD, their God, and I will
hear them.

11 As for you, because of the blood of your covenant
I have released your prisoners from the pit
in which there is no water.
12 Come back to the fortress,
you prisoners waiting in hope.
This very day, I vow,
I shall make it up to you twice over.
13 For I have strung Judah as a bow for myself,
laid Ephraim on the string as an arrow,
have roused your sons, Zion,
against your sons, Javan,e
and have made you like a warrior's sword.
14 Then Yahweh will appear above them
and his arrow will flash out like lightning.
(The Lord) Yahweh will sound the trumpet
and advance in the storm-winds of the south.
15 Yahweh Sabaoth will protect them!
They will devour, will trample on the sling-stones,
they will drink blood like wine,
awash like bowls, like the corners of the altar,
16 Yahweh their God will give them victory
when that day comes,
like the sheep who are his people;
yes, the stones of a diadem
will sparkle over his country.
17 How fine, how splendid that will be,
with wheat to make the young men flourish,
and new wine the maidens!

10 Ask Yahweh for rain in autumn
and at the time of the spring rains.
Yahweh is the one to make the storm-clouds.
He will give them showers of rain;
to each, grass in his field.
2 Since the domestic idols have talked nonsense,
and the diviners have seen false signs,
and dreams have purveyed delusions,
affording empty comfort,
that is why they have strayed like sheep,
in distress for want of a shepherd.

3 My anger has been roused by the shepherds,
and I shall vent it on the he-goats.

When Yahweh Sabaoth comes to visit his flock,
the House of Judah,
he will make it his royal war-horse.
4 From it will emerge Cornerstone and Tent-peg,
from it, Bow-ready-for-Battle,
from it, every type of leader.
Together 5 they will be like warriors
trampling the dirt of the streets in battle;
when they fight, because Yahweh is with them,
they will put mounted men to rout.

6 Then I shall make the House of Judah mighty
and the House of Joseph victorious.
I shall restore them, because I have taken pity on
them,
and they will be as though I had never cast them
off,
for I am Yahweh their God and shall answer their
prayer.

e 9 Greece, now conquering the East under Alexander the Great.

NEW REVISED STANDARD VERSION

7 Then the people of Ephraim shall become like
warriors,
and their hearts shall be glad as with wine.
Their children shall see it and rejoice,
their hearts shall exult in the LORD.

8 I will signal for them and gather them in,
for I have redeemed them,
and they shall be as numerous as they were
before.

9 Though I scattered them among the nations,
yet in far countries they shall remember me,
and they shall rear their children and return.

10 I will bring them home from the land of Egypt,
and gather them from Assyria;
I will bring them to the land of Gilead and to
Lebanon,
until there is no room for them.

11 They[e] shall pass through the sea of distress,
and the waves of the sea shall be struck down,
and all the depths of the Nile dried up.
The pride of Assyria shall be laid low,
and the scepter of Egypt shall depart.

12 I will make them strong in the LORD,
and they shall walk in his name,
says the LORD.

11 Open your doors, O Lebanon,
so that fire may devour your cedars!
2 Wail, O cypress, for the cedar has fallen,
for the glorious trees are ruined!
Wail, oaks of Bashan,
for the thick forest has been felled!
3 Listen, the wail of the shepherds,
for their glory is despoiled!
Listen, the roar of the lions,
for the thickets of the Jordan are destroyed!

4 Thus said the LORD my God: Be a shepherd of the
flock doomed to slaughter. 5 Those who buy them kill them
and go unpunished; and those who sell them say, "Blessed
be the LORD, for I have become rich"; and their own shepherds have no pity on them. 6 For I will no longer have pity
on the inhabitants of the earth, says the LORD. I will cause
them, every one, to fall each into the hand of a neighbor,
and each into the hand of the king; and they shall devastate
the earth, and I will deliver no one from their hand.

7 So, on behalf of the sheep merchants, I became the
shepherd of the flock doomed to slaughter. I took two staffs;
one I named Favor, the other I named Unity, and I tended
the sheep. 8 In one month I disposed of the three shepherds,
for I had become impatient with them, and they also detested me. 9 So I said, "I will not be your shepherd. What
is to die, let it die; what is to be destroyed, let it be destroyed; and let those that are left devour the flesh of one
another!" 10 I took my staff Favor and broke it, annulling the
covenant that I had made with all the peoples. 11 So it was
annulled on that day, and the sheep merchants, who were
watching me, knew that it was the word of the LORD. 12 I
then said to them, "If it seems right to you, give me my
wages; but if not, keep them." So they weighed out as my
wages thirty shekels of silver. 13 Then the LORD said to me,
"Throw it into the treasury"[f]—this lordly price at which I
was valued by them. So I took the thirty shekels of silver
and threw them into the treasury[f] in the house of the LORD.
14 Then I broke my second staff Unity, annulling the family
ties between Judah and Israel.

REVISED ENGLISH BIBLE

7 So the Ephraimites will be like warriors,
with hearts gladdened as if by wine;
their children will see and be glad;
their hearts will rejoice in the LORD.
8 I shall whistle to call them in,
for I have delivered them,
and they will be as many as they used to be.
9 Though dispersed among the nations,
yet in far-off lands they will remember me;
they will rear their children and return.
10 I shall bring them home from Egypt
and gather them from Assyria;
I shall lead them into Gilead and Lebanon
until there is no more room for them.
11 They will pass through the sea of Egypt
and strike its waves;
all the depths of the Nile will become dry.
The pride of Assyria will be brought down,
and the sceptre of Egypt will be no more.
12 But Israel's strength will be in the LORD;
they will march proudly in his name.
This is the word of the LORD.

11 Lebanon, throw open your gates
so that fire may devour your cedars.
2 Wail, every pine tree, for the cedars have fallen,
the mighty trees are ravaged.
Wail, every oak of Bashan,
for the impenetrable forest is laid low.
3 Hark to the wailing of the shepherds!
Their rich pastures are ravaged.
Hark to the roar of the lions!
Jordan's dense thickets are ravaged.

4 These were the words of the LORD my God: Be a shepherd
to the flock destined for slaughter. 5 Those who buy will
slaughter them and incur no guilt; those who sell will then
say, 'Praise the LORD, I have become rich!' Even their
shepherds feel no pity for them. 6 For I shall no longer have
pity on the land's inhabitants, says the LORD. I am about to
put everyone into the power of his shepherd and his king,
and when the land is crushed I shall not rescue them from
their hands.

7 So I became a shepherd to the flock destined to be
slaughtered by the dealers. I took two staffs: one I called
Favour and the other Union, and so I looked after the flock.
8 In a single month I got rid of the three shepherds; I had lost
patience with the flock and they had come to abhor me.
9 Then I said to them, 'I shall not be a shepherd to you any
more. Any that are to die, let them die; any that are missing,
let them stay missing; and the rest can devour one another.'
10 I took my staff called Favour and snapped it in two,
annulling the covenant which the LORD had made with all
nations. 11 So it was annulled that day, and the dealers who
were watching me knew that this was a word from the
LORD. 12 I said to them, 'If it suits you, give me my wages;
otherwise keep them.' Then they weighed out my wages,
thirty silver pieces. 13 The LORD said to me, 'Throw it into
the treasury.' I took the thirty pieces of silver—the princely
sum at which I was paid off by them!—and threw them into
the house of the LORD, into the treasury. 14 Then I broke in
two my second staff called Union, annulling the brotherhood between Judah and Israel.

10:11 **They:** so Gk; Heb. He. **sea of Egypt:** prob. rdg; Heb. sea of
distress.   11:6 **shepherd:** or neighbour.   11:10 **the LORD:**
prob. rdg; Heb. I.   11:13 **into the treasury:** so Syriac; Heb. to
the potter.

e Gk: Heb He   f Syr: Heb it to the potter

7 Then Ephraim shall be valiant men,
and their hearts shall be cheered as by wine.
Their children shall see it and be glad,
their hearts shall rejoice in the LORD.

8 I will whistle for them to come together,
and when I redeem them
they will be as numerous as before.
9 I sowed them among the nations,
yet in distant lands they remember me;
they shall rear their children and return.
10 I will bring them back from the land of Egypt,
and gather them from Assyria.
I will bring them into Gilead and into Lebanon,
but these shall not suffice them;
11 I will cross over to Egypt
and smite the waves of the sea
and all the depths of the Nile shall be dried up.
The pride of Assyria shall be cast down,
and the scepter of Egypt taken away.
12 I will strengthen them in the LORD,
and they shall walk in his name, says the LORD.

11 Open your doors, O Lebanon,
that the fire may devour your cedars!
2 Wail, you cypress trees,
for the cedars are fallen,
the mighty have been despoiled.
Wail, you oaks of Bashan,
for the impenetrable forest is cut down!
3 Hark! the wailing of the shepherds,
their glory has been ruined.
Hark! the roaring of the young lions,
the jungle of the Jordan is laid waste.

4 Thus said the LORD, my God: Shepherd the flock to be slaughtered. 5 For they who buy them slay them with impunity; while those who sell them say, "Blessed be the LORD, I have become rich!" Even their own shepherds do not feel for them. 6 (Nor shall I spare the inhabitants of the earth any more, says the LORD. Yes, I will deliver each of them into the power of his neighbor, or into the power of his king; they shall crush the earth, and I will not deliver it out of their power.)
7 So I became the shepherd of the flock to be slaughtered for the sheep merchants. I took two staffs, one of which I called "Favor," and the other, "Bonds," and I fed the flock. 8 In a single month I did away with the three shepherds. I wearied of them, and they behaved badly toward me. 9 "I will not feed you," I said. "What is to die, let it die; what is to perish, let it perish, and let those that are left devour one another's flesh."
10 Then I took my staff "Favor" and snapped it asunder, breaking off the covenant which I had made with all peoples; 11 that day it was broken off. The sheep merchants who were watching me understood that this was the word of the LORD. 12 I said to them, "If it seems good to you, give me my wages; but if not, let it go." And they counted out my wages, thirty pieces of silver. 13 But the LORD said to me, "Throw it in the treasury, the handsome price at which they valued me." So I took the thirty pieces of silver and threw them into the treasury in the house of the LORD.
14 Then I snapped asunder my other staff, "Bonds," breaking off the brotherhood between Judah and Israel.

7 Ephraim will be like a warrior.
Their hearts will be cheered as though by wine.
Their children will see this and rejoice,
their hearts will exult in Yahweh.

8 I shall whistle to them and gather them in,
for I have redeemed them;
they will be as numerous as they used to be.
9 I shall scatter them among the peoples
but in distant countries they will remember me,
they will instruct their children and then return.
10 I shall bring them home from Egypt
and gather them back from Assyria;
I shall lead them into Gilead and the Lebanon,
and even that will not be large enough for them.
11 They will cross the sea of Egypt
(and the waves of the sea will be struck);
all the depths of the River will be dried up.
The arrogance of Assyria will be cast down
and the sceptre of Egypt taken away.
12 I shall make them mighty in Yahweh,
and they will march in my name
— Yahweh declares.

11 Open your gateways, Lebanon,
and the fire shall burn down your cedar trees!
2 Wail, juniper,
for the cedar tree has fallen,
the majestic ones have been ravaged!
Wail, oaks of Bashan,
for the impenetrable forest has been felled!
3 The sound of the wailing of shepherds!
Their majesty has been ravaged.
The sound of the roaring of young lions!
The pride of the Jordan has been ravaged.

4 Yahweh my God says this, 'Pasture the sheep for slaughter, 5 whose buyers kill them and go unpunished, whose sellers say of them, "Blessed be Yahweh; now I am rich!" and whose own shepherds show them no pity. 6 For I shall show no further pity for the inhabitants of the country — Yahweh declares! Instead, I shall put everyone into the clutches of a neighbour, into the clutches of the king. They will crush the country and I shall not rescue anyone from their clutches.'
7 Then I pastured for slaughter the sheep belonging to the sheep-dealers. I took two staves: the one I called 'Goodwill', the other 'Couplers'; and I pastured the sheep myself, 8 getting rid of three shepherds in one month. But I lost patience with them, and they equally detested me. 9 I then said, 'I am not going to pasture you any more; the one doomed to die can die; the one doomed to perish can perish; and the rest can devour one another.' 10 I then took my staff, 'Goodwill', and broke it in half, to break my covenant, which I had made with all the peoples. 11 When it was broken, that day the sheep-dealers, who were watching me, realised that this had been a word of Yahweh. 12 I then said to them, 'If you see fit, give me my wages; if not, never mind.' So they weighed out my wages: thirty shekels of silver. 13 Yahweh said to me, 'Throw it to the smelter, this princely sum at which they have valued me!' Taking the thirty shekels of silver, I threw them into the Temple of Yahweh, for the smelter. 14 I then broke my second staff, 'Couplers,' in half, to rupture the brotherly relationship between Judah and Israel.

NEW REVISED STANDARD VERSION	REVISED ENGLISH BIBLE

15 Then the LORD said to me: Take once more the implements of a worthless shepherd. 16 For I am now raising up in the land a shepherd who does not care for the perishing, or seek the wandering,*g* or heal the maimed, or nourish the healthy,*h* but devours the flesh of the fat ones, tearing off even their hoofs.

17 Oh, my worthless shepherd,
      who deserts the flock!
   May the sword strike his arm
      and his right eye!
   Let his arm be completely withered,
      his right eye utterly blinded!

12 An Oracle.

The word of the LORD concerning Israel: Thus says the LORD, who stretched out the heavens and founded the earth and formed the human spirit within: 2 See, I am about to make Jerusalem a cup of reeling for all the surrounding peoples; it will be against Judah also in the siege against Jerusalem. 3 On that day I will make Jerusalem a heavy stone for all the peoples; all who lift it shall grievously hurt themselves. And all the nations of the earth shall come together against it. 4 On that day, says the LORD, I will strike every horse with panic, and its rider with madness. But on the house of Judah I will keep a watchful eye, when I strike every horse of the peoples with blindness. 5 Then the clans of Judah shall say to themselves, "The inhabitants of Jerusalem have strength through the LORD of hosts, their God."

6 On that day I will make the clans of Judah like a blazing pot on a pile of wood, like a flaming torch among sheaves; and they shall devour to the right and to the left all the surrounding peoples, while Jerusalem shall again be inhabited in its place, in Jerusalem.

7 And the LORD will give victory to the tents of Judah first, that the glory of the house of David and the glory of the inhabitants of Jerusalem may not be exalted over that of Judah. 8 On that day the LORD will shield the inhabitants of Jerusalem so that the feeblest among them on that day shall be like David, and the house of David shall be like God, like the angel of the LORD, at their head. 9 And on that day I will seek to destroy all the nations that come against Jerusalem.

10 And I will pour out a spirit of compassion and supplication on the house of David and the inhabitants of Jerusalem, so that, when they look on the one*i* whom they have pierced, they shall mourn for him, as one mourns for an only child, and weep bitterly over him, as one weeps over a firstborn. 11 On that day the mourning in Jerusalem will be as great as the mourning for Hadad-rimmon in the plain of Megiddo. 12 The land shall mourn, each family by itself; the family of the house of David by itself, and their wives by themselves; the family of the house of Nathan by itself, and their wives by themselves; 13 the family of the house of Levi by itself, and their wives by themselves; the family of the Shimeites by itself, and their wives by themselves; 14 and all the families that are left, each by itself, and their wives by themselves.

13 On that day a fountain shall be opened for the house of David and the inhabitants of Jerusalem, to cleanse them from sin and impurity.

---

15 The LORD said to me, 'Equip yourself again as a shepherd, a worthless one; 16 for I am about to install a shepherd in the land who will neither care about any that are gone missing, nor search for those that have strayed, nor heal the injured, nor nurse the sickly, but will eat the flesh of the fat beasts and throw away the broken bones.

17 'Woe betide the worthless shepherd who abandons
      the sheep!
   May a sword fall on his arm and on his right eye!
   May his arm be all shrivelled,
      and his right eye be totally blind!'

12 AN oracle.

This is the word of the LORD about Israel, the word of the LORD who spread out the heavens and founded the earth, and who formed the spirit in mortals. 2 I am about to make Jerusalem an intoxicating cup for all the nations pressing round her; and Judah will be caught up in the siege of Jerusalem. 3 On that day, when all the nations of the earth are gathered to attack her, I shall make Jerusalem a rock too heavy for any people to remove, and all who try to carry it will be torn by it. 4 On that day, says the LORD, I shall strike all their horses with panic and the riders with madness; I shall keep watch over Judah, while I strike with blindness all the horses of the other nations. 5 Then the families of Judah will say in their hearts, 'The inhabitants of Jerusalem find their strength in the LORD of Hosts, their God.'

6 On that day I shall make the families of Judah like a burning brazier in woodland, like a burning torch among sheaves. They will consume all the surrounding nations, right and left, while the people of Jerusalem remain safe in their city. 7 The LORD will set free all the families of Judah first, so that the glory of David's line and of the citizens of Jerusalem may not surpass that of Judah.

8 On that day the LORD will shield the inhabitants of Jerusalem; on that day the weakest of them will be like David, and the line of David godlike, like the angel of the LORD going before them.

9 On that day I shall set about the destruction of every nation that attacks Jerusalem, 10 but I shall pour a spirit of pity and compassion on the house of David and the inhabitants of Jerusalem. Then they will look on me, on him whom they have pierced, and will lament over him as over an only child, and will grieve for him bitterly as for a firstborn son.

11 On that day the mourning in Jerusalem will be as great as the mourning over Hadad-rimmon in the vale of Megiddo. 12 The land will mourn, each family by itself: the family of David by itself and its women by themselves; the family of Nathan by itself and its women by themselves; 13 the family of Levi by itself and its women by themselves; the family of Shimei by itself and its women by themselves; 14 all the remaining families by themselves and their women by themselves.

13 On that day a fountain will be opened for the line of David and for the inhabitants of Jerusalem, to remove their sin and impurity.

---

g Syr Compare Gk Vg: Heb *the youth* *h* Meaning of Heb uncertain *i* Heb *on me*

12:2 **and:** *so Lat.; Heb.* adds against. 12:5 **The inhabitants . . . strength:** *prob. rdg; one Heb. MS* Inhabitants of Jerusalem, I am strong.

NEW AMERICAN BIBLE

15 The LORD said to me: This time take the gear of a foolish shepherd. 16 For I will raise up a shepherd in the land who will take no note of those that perish, nor seek the strays, nor heal the injured, nor feed what survives — he will eat the flesh of the fat ones and tear off their hoofs!

17 Woe to my foolish shepherd
    who forsakes the flock!
May the sword fall upon his arm
    and upon his right eye;
Let his arm wither away entirely,
    and his right eye be blind forever!

12 An oracle: the word of the LORD concerning Israel. Thus says the LORD, who spreads out the heavens, lays the foundations of the earth, and forms the spirit of man within him: 2 See, I will make Jerusalem a bowl to stupefy all peoples round about. [Judah will be besieged, even Jerusalem.] 3 On that day I will make Jerusalem a weighty stone for all peoples. All who attempt to lift it shall injure themselves badly, and all the nations of the earth shall be gathered against her. 4 On that day, says the LORD, I will strike every horse with fright, and its rider with madness. I will strike blind all the horses of the peoples, but upon the house of Judah I will open my eyes, 5 and the princes of Judah shall say to themselves, "The inhabitants of Jerusalem have their strength in the LORD of hosts, their God." 6 On that day I will make the princes of Judah like a brazier of fire in the woodland, and like a burning torch among sheaves, and they shall devour right and left all the surrounding peoples; but Jerusalem shall still abide on its own site. 7 The LORD shall save the tents of Judah first, that the glory of the house of David and the glory of the inhabitants of Jerusalem may not be exalted over Judah. 8 On that day, the LORD will shield the inhabitants of Jerusalem, and the weakling among them shall be like David on that day, and the house of David godlike, like an angel of the Lord before them. 9 On that day I will seek the destruction of all nations that come against Jerusalem.

10 I will pour out on the house of David and on the inhabitants of Jerusalem a spirit of grace and petition; and they shall look on him whom they have thrust through, and they shall mourn for him as one mourns for an only son, and they shall grieve over him as one grieves over a first-born. 11 On that day the mourning in Jerusalem shall be as great as the mourning of Hadadrimmon in the plain of Megiddo. 12 And the land shall mourn, each family apart: the family of the house of David, and their wives; the family of the house of Nathan, and their wives; 13 the family of the house of Levi, and their wives; the family of Shemei, and their wives; 14 and all the rest of the families, each family apart, and the wives apart.

13 On that day there shall be open to the house of David and to the inhabitants of Jerusalem, a fountain to purify from sin and uncleanness. 2 On that day, says

NEW JERUSALEM BIBLE

15 Next, Yahweh said to me, 'This time, take the gear of a good-for-nothing shepherd. 16 For I am now going to raise a shepherd in this country, who will not bother about the lost, who will not go in search of the stray, who will not heal the injured, who will not support the swollen, but who will eat the meat of the fat ones, tearing off their very hoofs.

17 Disaster to the shepherd
    who deserts his flock!
May the sword attack his arm
    and his right eye!
May his arm shrivel completely
    and his right eye be totally blinded!'

12 A proclamation. The word of Yahweh about Israel (2b and also about Judah). Yahweh, who spread out the heaven and founded the earth and formed the human spirit within, declares: 2a 'Look, I shall make Jerusalem a cup to set all the surrounding peoples reeling. (That will be at the time of the siege of Jerusalem.) 3 'When that day comes, I shall make Jerusalem a stone too heavy for all the peoples to lift; all those who try to lift it will hurt themselves severely, although all the nations of the world will be massed against her. 4 When that day comes — declares Yahweh — I shall strike all the horses with panic and their riders with madness. And I shall strike all the peoples with blindness. (But I shall keep watch over Judah.) 5 Then the rulers of Judah will say to themselves, "The strength of the inhabitants of Jerusalem lies in Yahweh Sabaoth their God." 6 When that day comes, I shall make the rulers of Judah like a brazier burning in a pile of wood, like a torch flaming in a sheaf; and they will devour all the peoples round them to right and left. And Jerusalem will be full of people as before, where she stands (in Jerusalem). 7 Yahweh will first save the tents of Judah, so that the glory of the House of David and the glory of the inhabitants of Jerusalem do not increase at Judah's expense. 8 When that day comes, Yahweh will protect the inhabitants of Jerusalem; and the frailest of them will be like David when that day comes, and the House of David will be like God, like the angel of Yahweh, at their head.

9 'When that day comes, I shall set about destroying all the nations who advance against Jerusalem. 10 But over the House of David and the inhabitants of Jerusalem I shall pour out a spirit of grace and prayer, and they will look to me. They will mourn for the one whom they have pierced as though for an only child, and weep for him as people weep for a first-born child. 11 When that day comes, the mourning in Jerusalem will be as great as the mourning for Hadad Rimmon in the Plain of Megiddo. 12 And the country will mourn clan by clan:

The clan of the House of David by itself,
    and their women by themselves;
the clan of the House of Nathan by itself,
    and their women by themselves;
13 the clan of the House of Levi by itself,
    and their women by themselves;
the clan of the House of Shimei by itself,
    and their women by themselves;
14 all the rest of the clans, every clan by itself,
    and their women by themselves.'

13 'When that day comes, a fountain will be opened for the House of David and the inhabitants of Jerusalem, to wash sin and impurity away.

2 On that day, says the LORD of hosts, I will cut off the names of the idols from the land, so that they shall be remembered no more; and also I will remove from the land the prophets and the unclean spirit. 3 And if any prophets appear again, their fathers and mothers who bore them will say to them, "You shall not live, for you speak lies in the name of the LORD"; and their fathers and their mothers who bore them shall pierce them through when they prophesy. 4 On that day the prophets will be ashamed, every one, of their visions when they prophesy; they will not put on a hairy mantle in order to deceive, 5 but each of them will say, "I am no prophet, I am a tiller of the soil; for the land has been my possession *j* since my youth." 6 And if anyone asks them, "What are these wounds on your chest?" *k* the answer will be "The wounds I received in the house of my friends."

7 "Awake, O sword, against my shepherd,
  against the man who is my associate,"
                    says the LORD of hosts.
  Strike the shepherd, that the sheep may be
      scattered;
  I will turn my hand against the little ones.
8 In the whole land, says the LORD,
  two-thirds shall be cut off and perish,
  and one-third shall be left alive.
9 And I will put this third into the fire,
  refine them as one refines silver,
  and test them as gold is tested.
  They will call on my name,
  and I will answer them.
  I will say, "They are my people";
  and they will say, "The LORD is our God."

14 See, a day is coming for the LORD, when the plunder taken from you will be divided in your midst. 2 For I will gather all the nations against Jerusalem to battle, and the city shall be taken and the houses looted and the women raped; half the city shall go into exile, but the rest of the people shall not be cut off from the city. 3 Then the LORD will go forth and fight against those nations as when he fights on a day of battle. 4 On that day his feet shall stand on the Mount of Olives, which lies before Jerusalem on the east; and the Mount of Olives shall be split in two from east to west by a very wide valley; so that one half of the Mount shall withdraw northward, and the other half southward. 5 And you shall flee by the valley of the LORD's mountain, *l* for the valley between the mountains shall reach to Azal; *m* and you shall flee as you fled from the earthquake in the days of King Uzziah of Judah. Then the LORD my God will come, and all the holy ones with him.

6 On that day there shall not be *n* either cold or frost. *o* 7 And there shall be continuous day (it is known to the LORD), not day and not night, for at evening time there shall be light.

8 On that day living waters shall flow out from Jerusalem, half of them to the eastern sea and half of them to the western sea; it shall continue in summer as in winter.

9 And the LORD will become king over all the earth; on that day the LORD will be one and his name one.

10 The whole land shall be turned into a plain from Geba to Rimmon south of Jerusalem. But Jerusalem shall remain aloft on its site from the Gate of Benjamin to the place of the former gate, to the Corner Gate, and from the Tower of Hananel to the king's wine presses. 11 And it shall

2 On that day, says the LORD of Hosts, I shall expunge the names of the idols from the land, and they shall be remembered no more; I shall also expel the prophets and the spirit of uncleanness from the land. 3 Thereafter, if anyone continues to prophesy, his parents, his own father and mother, will say to him, 'You are not to remain alive, for you have uttered lies in the LORD's name.' His own father and mother will run him through because he has prophesied. 4 On that day every prophet will be ashamed of his prophetic vision, and he will not wear a robe of coarse hair in order to deceive. 5 He will say, 'I am not a prophet, I am a worker on the land, for the land has been my possession from my early days.' 6 If someone asks, 'What are these scars on your chest?' he will answer, 'I got them in the house of my friends.'

7 This is the word of the LORD of Hosts:
  Sword, awake against my shepherd,
  against him who works with me.
  Strike the shepherd, and the sheep will be
      scattered;
  and I shall turn my hand against the lambs.
8 This also is the word of the LORD:
  It will happen throughout the land
  that two thirds of the people will be struck down
      and die,
  while one third of them will be left there.
9 Then I shall pass this third through the fire;
  I shall refine them as silver is refined
  and assay them as gold is assayed.
  They will invoke me by my name,
  and I myself shall answer them;
  I shall say, 'These are my people';
  they will say, 'The LORD is my God.'

14 A day is coming for the LORD to act, and the plunder taken from you will be shared out while you stand by. 2 I shall gather all the nations to make war on Jerusalem; the city will be taken, the houses ransacked, and the women raped. Half of the city will go into exile, but the rest of the population will not be taken away from the city. 3 Then the LORD will go out and fight against the nations, fighting as on a day of battle. 4 On that day his feet will stand on the mount of Olives, which lies to the east of Jerusalem, and the mount will be cleft in two by an immense valley running east and west; half the mount will move northwards and half southwards. 5 The valley between the hills will be blocked, for the new valley between them will reach as far as Asal. It will be blocked as it was by the earthquake in the time of King Uzziah of Judah. Then the LORD my God will appear attended by all the holy ones.

6 On that day there will be neither heat nor cold nor frost. 7 It will be one continuous day, whose coming is known only to the LORD; there will be no distinction between day and night; even in the evening there will be light.

8 On that day, whether in summer or in winter, running water will issue from Jerusalem, half flowing to the eastern sea and half to the western sea. 9 The LORD will become king over all the earth; on that day he will be the only LORD and his name the only name. 10 The whole land will become like the Arabah from Geba to Rimmon south of Jerusalem. But Jerusalem will stand high in her place, and be full of people from the Benjamin Gate to the point where the former gate stood, to the Corner Gate, and from the Tower of Hananel to the king's winepresses. 11 Jerusalem will be in-

---

j Cn: Heb *for humankind has caused me to possess* *k* Heb *wounds between your hands* *l* Heb *my mountains* *m* Meaning of Heb uncertain *n* Cn: Heb *there shall not be light* *o* Compare Gk Syr Vg Tg: Meaning of Heb uncertain

13:5 **for the land . . . possession:** *prob. rdg; Heb.* for a man has made his possession. 14:5 **the hills:** *prob. rdg, so Syriac; Heb.* my hills. **It will . . . was by:** *or* You shall flee just as you fled before. 14:6 **cold:** *so Gk; Heb.* precious things.

NEW AMERICAN BIBLE

the LORD of hosts, I will destroy the names of the idols from the land, so that they shall be mentioned no more; I will also take away the prophets and the spirit of uncleanness from the land. 3 If a man still prophesies, his parents, father and mother, shall say to him, "You shall not live, because you have spoken a lie in the name of the LORD." When he prophesies, his parents, father and mother, shall thrust him through.

4 On that day, every prophet shall be ashamed to prophesy his vision, neither shall he assume the hairy mantle to mislead, 5 but he shall say, "I am no prophet, I am a tiller of the soil, for I have owned land since my youth." 6 And if anyone asks him, "What are these wounds on your chest?" he shall answer, "With these I was wounded in the house of my dear ones."

7 Awake, O sword, against my shepherd,
   against the man who is my associate,
   says the LORD of hosts.
Strike the shepherd
   that the sheep may be dispersed,
   and I will turn my hand against the little ones.
8 In all the land, says the LORD,
   two thirds of them shall be cut off and perish,
   and one third shall be left.
9 I will bring the one third through fire,
   and I will refine them as silver is refined,
   and I will test them as gold is tested.
   They shall call upon my name, and I will
      hear them.
   I will say, "They are my people,"
   and they shall say, "The LORD is my God."

14 Lo, a day shall come for the LORD when the spoils shall be divided in your midst. 2 And I will gather all the nations against Jerusalem for battle: the city shall be taken, houses plundered, women ravished; half of the city shall go into exile, but the rest of the people shall not be removed from the city. 3 Then the LORD shall go forth and fight against those nations, fighting as on a day of battle. 4 That day his feet shall rest upon the Mount of Olives, which is opposite Jerusalem to the east. The Mount of Olives shall be cleft in two from east to west by a very deep valley, and half of the mountain shall move to the north and half of it to the south. 5 And the valley of the LORD's mountain shall be filled up when the valley of those two mountains reaches its edge; it shall be filled up as it was filled up by the earthquake in the days of King Uzziah of Judah. Then the LORD, my God, shall come, and all his holy ones with him.

6 On that day there shall no longer be cold or frost. 7 There shall be one continuous day, known to the LORD, not day and night, for in the evening time there shall be light.

8 On that day, living waters shall flow from Jerusalem, half to the eastern sea, and half to the western sea, and it shall be so in summer and in winter. 9 The LORD shall become king over the whole earth; on that day the LORD shall be the only one, and his name the only one.

10 And from Geba to Rimmon in the Negeb, all the land shall turn into a plain; but Jerusalem shall remain exalted in its place. From the Gate of Benjamin to the place of the First Gate, to the Corner Gate; and from the Tower of Hananel to the king's wine presses, 11 they shall occupy her.

NEW JERUSALEM BIBLE

2 'When that day comes — Yahweh declares — I shall cut off the names of the idols from the country, and they will never be remembered again; I shall also rid the country of the prophets, and of the spirit of impurity. 3 Then, if anyone still goes on prophesying, his parents, his own father and mother will say to him, "You shall not live, since you utter lies in Yahweh's name." And even while he is prophesying, his parents, his own father and mother will pierce him through. 4 When that day comes, the prophets will all be ashamed to relate their visions when they prophesy and no longer put on their hair cloaks with intent to deceive. 5 Instead, they will say, "I am no prophet. I am a man who tills the soil, for the land has been my living since I was a boy." 6 And if anyone asks him, "What are those gashes on your chest?" *f* he will reply, "I got them when I was with my friends." '

7 Awake, sword, against my shepherd,
   against the man who is close to me —
   declares Yahweh Sabaoth!
Strike the shepherd, scatter the sheep!
And I shall turn my hand against the young!
8 So it will be, throughout the country —
   declares Yahweh Sabaoth —
   two-thirds in it will be cut off (be killed)
   and the other third will be left.
9 I shall pass this third through the fire,
   refine them as silver is refined,
   test them as gold is tested.
   He will call on my name
   and I shall answer him;
   I shall say, 'He is my people,'
   and he will say, 'Yahweh is my God!'

14 Look, the Day of Yahweh is coming, when the spoils taken from you will be shared out among you. 2 For I shall gather all the nations to Jerusalem to battle. The city will be taken, the houses plundered, the women ravished. Half the city will go into exile, but the rest of the people will not be ejected from the city. 3 Then Yahweh will sally out and fight those nations as once he fought on the day of battle. 4 When that day comes, his feet will rest on the Mount of Olives, which faces Jerusalem on the east, and the Mount of Olives will be split in half from east to west, forming a huge valley; half the Mount will recede northwards, the other half southwards. 5 The valley between the hills will be filled in, yes, it will be blocked as far as Jasol, it will be filled in as it was by the earthquake in the days of Uzziah king of Judah. And Yahweh my God will come, and all the holy ones with him.

6 That Day, there will be no light, but only cold and frost. 7 And it will be one continuous day — Yahweh knows — there will be no more day and night, and it will remain light right into the time of evening. 8 When that Day comes, living waters will issue from Jerusalem, half towards the eastern sea, half towards the western sea; they will flow summer and winter. 9 Then Yahweh will become king of the whole world. When that Day comes, Yahweh will be the one and only and his name the one name. 10 The entire country will be transformed into plain, from Geba to Rimmon in the Negeb, but Jerusalem will stand high in her place and be full of people from the Benjamin Gate to the site of the earlier gate, to the Corner Gate, and from the Tower of Hananel to the king's wine-presses. 11 People will

---

f 13 Such scars were once the hallmark of a prophet (1 K 18:28).

| NEW REVISED STANDARD VERSION | REVISED ENGLISH BIBLE |

be inhabited, for never again shall it be doomed to destruction; Jerusalem shall abide in security.

12 This shall be the plague with which the LORD will strike all the peoples that wage war against Jerusalem: their flesh shall rot while they are still on their feet; their eyes shall rot in their sockets, and their tongues shall rot in their mouths. 13 On that day a great panic from the LORD shall fall on them, so that each will seize the hand of a neighbor, and the hand of the one will be raised against the hand of the other; 14 even Judah will fight at Jerusalem. And the wealth of all the surrounding nations shall be collected — gold, silver, and garments in great abundance. 15 And a plague like this plague shall fall on the horses, the mules, the camels, the donkeys, and whatever animals may be in those camps.

16 Then all who survive of the nations that have come against Jerusalem shall go up year after year to worship the King, the LORD of hosts, and to keep the festival of booths.p 17 If any of the families of the earth do not go up to Jerusalem to worship the King, the LORD of hosts, there will be no rain upon them. 18 And if the family of Egypt do not go up and present themselves, then on them shallq come the plague that the LORD inflicts on the nations that do not go up to keep the festival of booths.p 19 Such shall be the punishment of Egypt and the punishment of all the nations that do not go up to keep the festival of booths.p

20 On that day there shall be inscribed on the bells of the horses, "Holy to the LORD." And the cooking pots in the house of the LORD shall be as holy asr the bowls in front of the altar; 21 and every cooking pot in Jerusalem and Judah shall be sacred to the LORD of hosts, so that all who sacrifice may come and use them to boil the flesh of the sacrifice. And there shall no longer be traderss in the house of the LORD of hosts on that day.

p Or tabernacles; Heb succoth   q Gk Syr: Heb shall not
r Heb shall be like   s Or Canaanites

habited, and never again will a ban for her destruction be laid on her; all will live there in security.

12 The LORD will strike with this plague all the nations who warred against Jerusalem: their flesh will rot while they are still standing on their feet, their eyes will rot in their sockets, and their tongues will rot in their mouths. 13 On that day a great panic sent by the LORD will fall on them, with everyone laying hands on his neighbour and attacking him. 14 Judah too will fight at Jerusalem, and the wealth of the surrounding nations will be gathered up— gold and silver and clothing in great quantities. 15 Plague will also be the fate of horse and mule, camel and donkey, the fate of every animal in those armies.

16 Any survivors among the nations which fought against Jerusalem are to go up year by year to worship the King, the LORD of Hosts, and to keep the pilgrim-feast of Tabernacles. 17 Should any of the families of the earth not go up to Jerusalem to worship the King, the LORD of Hosts, no rain will fall on them. 18 If any family of Egypt does not go up and enter the city, then the same disaster will overtake it as that which the LORD will inflict on any nation which does not go up to keep the feast. 19 This will be the punishment which befalls Egypt and any nation which does not go up to keep the feast of Tabernacles.

20 On that day 'Holy to the LORD' will be inscribed on the horses' bells, and the pots in the house of the LORD will be like the sacred bowls before the altar. 21 Every pot in Jerusalem and Judah will be holy to the LORD of Hosts, and all who come to sacrifice will use them for boiling the flesh of the sacrifice. When that time comes, no longer will any trader be seen in the house of the LORD of Hosts.

14:18 will overtake: so Gk; Heb. adds not.

Never again shall she be doomed; Jerusalem shall abide in security.

12 And this shall be the plague with which the LORD shall strike all the nations that have fought against Jerusalem: their flesh shall rot while they stand upon their feet, and their eyes shall rot in their sockets, and their tongues shall rot in their mouths.

13 On that day there shall be among them a great tumult from the LORD: every man shall seize the hand of his neighbor, and the hand of each shall be raised against that of his neighbor. 14 Judah also shall fight against Jerusalem. The riches of all the surrounding nations shall be gathered together, gold, silver, and garments, in great abundance.

15 Similar to this plague shall be the plague upon the horses, mules, camels, asses, and upon all the beasts that are in those camps.

16 All who are left of all the nations that came against Jerusalem shall come up year after year to worship the King, the LORD of hosts, and to celebrate the feast of Booths. 17 If any of the families of the earth does not come up to Jerusalem to worship the King, the LORD of hosts, no rain shall fall upon them. 18 And if the family of Egypt does not come up, or enter, upon them shall fall the plague which the LORD will inflict upon all the nations that do not come up to celebrate the feast of Booths. 19 This shall be the punishment of Egypt, and the punishment of all the nations that do not come up to celebrate the feast of Booths.

20 On that day there shall be upon the bells of the horses, "Holy to the LORD." The pots in the house of the LORD shall be as the libation bowls before the altar. 21 And every pot in Jerusalem and in Judah shall be holy to the LORD of hosts; and all who come to sacrifice shall take them and cook in them. On that day there shall no longer be any merchant in the house of the LORD of hosts.

make their homes there. The curse of destruction will be lifted; Jerusalem will be safe to live in.

12 And this is the plague with which Yahweh will strike all the nations who have fought against Jerusalem; their flesh will rot while they are still standing on their feet; their eyes will rot in their sockets; their tongues will rot in their mouths. 15 And the plague afflicting the horses, mules, camels, donkeys and all the other animals in those armies will be the same. 13 When that Day comes, a great terror will fall on them from Yahweh; each man will grab his neighbour's hand and they will fall to fighting among themselves. 14 Even Judah will fight against Jerusalem. The wealth of all the surrounding nations will be heaped together: gold, silver, clothing, in vast quantity.

16 After this, all the survivors of all the nations which have attacked Jerusalem will come up year after year to worship the King, Yahweh Sabaoth, and to keep the feast of Shelters. 17 Should one of the races of the world fail to come up to Jerusalem to worship the King, Yahweh Sabaoth, there will be no rain for that one. 18 Should the race of Egypt fail to come up and pay its visit, on it will fall the plague which Yahweh will inflict on each of those nations which fail to come up to keep the feast of Shelters. 19 Such will be the punishment for Egypt and the punishment for all the nations which fail to come up to keep the feast of Shelters.

20 When that Day comes, the very bells on the horses will be inscribed with the words, 'Sacred to Yahweh', and the cooking pots of the house of Yahweh will be as holy as the sprinkling bowls before the altar. 21 Yes, every cooking pot in Jerusalem and in Judah shall be sacred to Yahweh Sabaoth, and all who come to offer sacrifice will help themselves and do their cooking in them, and there will be no more traders in the Temple of Yahweh Sabaoth, when that Day comes.

Malachi

1 An oracle. The word of the LORD to Israel by Malachi.*a*

2 I have loved you, says the LORD. But you say, "How
have you loved us?" Is not Esau Jacob's brother? says the
LORD. Yet I have loved Jacob 3 but I have hated Esau; I have
made his hill country a desolation and his heritage a desert
for jackals. 4 If Edom says, "We are shattered but we will
rebuild the ruins," the LORD of hosts says: They may build,
but I will tear down, until they are called the wicked country, the people with whom the LORD is angry forever. 5 Your
own eyes shall see this, and you shall say, "Great is the
LORD beyond the borders of Israel!"

6 A son honors his father, and servants their master. If
then I am a father, where is the honor due me? And if I am
a master, where is the respect due me? says the LORD of
hosts to you, O priests, who despise my name. You say,
"How have we despised your name?" 7 By offering polluted
food on my altar. And you say, "How have we polluted
it?"*b* By thinking that the LORD's table may be despised.
8 When you offer blind animals in sacrifice, is that not
wrong? And when you offer those that are lame or sick, is
that not wrong? Try presenting that to your governor; will
he be pleased with you or show you favor? says the LORD
of hosts. 9 And now implore the favor of God, that he may
be gracious to us. The fault is yours. Will he show favor to
any of you? says the LORD of hosts. 10 Oh, that someone
among you would shut the temple*c* doors, so that you
would not kindle fire on my altar in vain! I have no pleasure
in you, says the LORD, and I will not accept an
offering from your hands. 11 For from the rising of the sun
to its setting my name is great among the nations, and in
every place incense is offered to my name, and a pure
offering; for my name is great among the nations, says the
LORD of hosts. 12 But you profane it when you say that the
Lord's table is polluted, and the food for it*d* may be de-

Malachi

1 AN oracle. The word of the LORD to Israel through
Malachi.

2 I HAVE shown you love, says the LORD. But you ask,
'How have you shown love to us?' Is not Esau Jacob's
brother? the LORD answers. Jacob I love, 3 but Esau I hate,
and I have reduced his hill-country to a waste, and his
ancestral land to desert pastures. 4 When Edom says, 'We
are beaten down, but let us rebuild our ruined homes,' these
are the words of the LORD of Hosts: If they rebuild, I shall
pull down. They will be called a country of wickedness, a
people with whom the LORD is angry for ever. 5 Your own
eyes will see it, and you yourselves will say, 'The LORD's
greatness reaches beyond the confines of Israel.'

6 A son honours his father and a slave his master. If I am
a father, where is the honour due to me? If I am a master,
where is the fear due to me? So says the LORD of Hosts to
you, priests who despise my name. You ask, 'How have we
despised your name?' 7 By offering defiled food on my
altar. You ask, 'How have we defiled you?' By saying that
the table of the LORD may be despised, 8 that if you offer a
blind victim, there is nothing wrong, and if you offer a
victim which is lame or sickly, there is nothing wrong. If
you brought such a gift to your governor, would he receive
you or show you favour? says the LORD of Hosts. 9 But
now, if you placate God, he may show you mercy! If you
do this, will he withhold his favour from you? So the LORD
of Hosts has spoken. 10 Better far that one of you should
close the great door altogether, to keep fire from being lit
on my altar to no purpose! I have no pleasure in you, says
the LORD of Hosts, nor will I accept any offering from you.
11 From farthest east to farthest west my name is great
among the nations, and everywhere incense and pure offerings are presented to my name; for my name is great among
the nations, says the LORD of Hosts. 12 But you profane me
by thinking that the table of the LORD may be defiled, and
you can offer on it food that you hold in no esteem. 13 You

a Or *by my messenger*   *b* Gk: Heb *you*   *c* Heb lacks *temple*
d Compare Syr Tg: Heb *its fruit, its food*

1:1 **Malachi:** *or my messenger.*   1:3 **desert pastures:** *prob. rdg,
cp. Gk; Heb. obscure.*   1:12 **food:** *prob. rdg, cp. Aram. (Targ.);
Heb. adds* its produce.

THE BOOK OF
Malachi

Malachi

1 An oracle. The word of the LORD to Israel through Malachi.

2 I have loved you, says the LORD;
but you say, "How have you loved us?"
3 Was not Esau Jacob's brother? says the LORD:
yet I loved Jacob, but hated Esau;
I made his mountains a waste,
his heritage a desert for jackals.
4 If Edom says, "We have been crushed
but we will rebuild the ruins,"
Thus says the LORD of hosts:
They indeed may build, but I will tear down,
And they shall be called the land of guilt,
the people with whom the LORD is
angry forever.
5 Your own eyes shall see it, and you will say,
"Great is the LORD, even beyond the land
of Israel."

6 A son honors his father,
and a servant fears his master;
If then I am a father,
where is the honor due to me?
And if I am a master,
where is the reverence due to me? —
So says the LORD of hosts to you, O priests,
who despise his name.
But you ask, "How have we despised your name?"
7 By offering polluted food on my altar!
Then you ask, "How have we polluted it?"
By saying the table of the LORD may
be slighted!
8 When you offer a blind animal for sacrifice,
is this not evil?
When you offer the lame or the sick,
is it not evil?
Present it to your governor; see if he will accept it,
or welcome you, says the LORD of hosts.
9 So now if you implore God for mercy on us,
when you have done the like
Will he welcome any of you?
says the LORD of hosts.
10 Oh, that one among you would shut the
temple gates
to keep you from kindling fire on my altar
in vain!
I have no pleasure in you, says the LORD of hosts;
neither will I accept any sacrifice from
your hands,
11 For from the rising of the sun, even to its setting,
my name is great among the nations;
And everywhere they bring sacrifice to my name,
and a pure offering;
For great is my name among the nations,
says the LORD of hosts.
12 But you behave profanely toward me by thinking
the LORD's table and its offering may
be polluted,
and its food slighted.

1 A message.
The word of Yahweh to Israel through Malachi.

2 'I have loved you, says Yahweh. But you ask, "How have you shown your love?" Was not Esau[a] Jacob's brother? declares Yahweh; even so, I loved Jacob 3 but I hated Esau. I turned his mountains into a desert and his heritage into dwellings in the wastelands. 4 If Edom says, "We have been struck down but we shall rebuild our ruins," Yahweh Sabaoth says this, "Let them build, but I shall pull down! They will be known as Land of Wickedness and Nation-with-which-Yahweh-is-angry-for-ever. 5 You will see this yourselves and you will say: Yahweh is mighty beyond the borders of Israel."

6 'The son honours his father, the slave stands in awe of his master. But if I am indeed father, where is the honour due to me? And if I am indeed master, where is the awe due to me? says Yahweh Sabaoth to you priests who despise my name. You ask, "How have we despised your name?" 7 By putting polluted food on my altar. You ask, "How have we polluted you?" By saying, "The table of Yahweh deserves no respect." 8 When you bring blind animals for sacrifice, is this not wrong? When you bring the lame and the diseased, is this not wrong? If you offer them to your governor, see if he is pleased with them or receives you graciously, says Yahweh Sabaoth. 9 In that case, try pleading with God to take pity on us (that is what you have done), and will he take any notice? says Yahweh Sabaoth. 10 Why does one of you not close the doors and so stop the pointless lighting of fires on my altar? I am not pleased with you, says Yahweh Sabaoth; from your hands I find no offerings acceptable. 11 But from farthest east to farthest west my name is great among the nations, and everywhere incense and a pure gift are offered to my name, since my name is great among the nations, says Yahweh Sabaoth.

12 'But you have profaned it by saying, "The table of the Lord is polluted, hence the food offered on it deserves no

a 1 Considered the ancestor of Edom, which is often also called Esau.

NEW REVISED STANDARD VERSION	REVISED ENGLISH BIBLE

spised. 13 "What a weariness this is," you say, and you sniff at me,e says the LORD of hosts. You bring what has been taken by violence or is lame or sick, and this you bring as your offering! Shall I accept that from your hand? says the LORD. 14 Cursed be the cheat who has a male in the flock and vows to give it, and yet sacrifices to the Lord what is blemished; for I am a great King, says the LORD of hosts, and my name is reverenced among the nations.

2 And now, O priests, this command is for you. 2 If you will not listen, if you will not lay it to heart to give glory to my name, says the LORD of hosts, then I will send the curse on you and I will curse your blessings; indeed I have already cursed them,f because you do not lay it to heart. 3 I will rebuke your offspring, and spread dung on your faces, the dung of your offerings, and I will put you out of my presence.g

4 Know, then, that I have sent this command to you, that my covenant with Levi may hold, says the LORD of hosts. 5 My covenant with him was a covenant of life and well-being, which I gave him; this called for reverence, and he revered me and stood in awe of my name. 6 True instruction was in his mouth, and no wrong was found on his lips. He walked with me in integrity and uprightness, and he turned many from iniquity. 7 For the lips of a priest should guard knowledge, and people should seek instruction from his mouth, for he is the messenger of the LORD of hosts. 8 But you have turned aside from the way; you have caused many to stumble by your instruction; you have corrupted the covenant of Levi, says the LORD of hosts, 9 and so I make you despised and abased before all the people, inasmuch as you have not kept my ways but have shown partiality in your instruction.

10 Have we not all one father? Has not one God created us? Why then are we faithless to one another, profaning the covenant of our ancestors? 11 Judah has been faithless, and abomination has been committed in Israel and in Jerusalem; for Judah has profaned the sanctuary of the LORD, which he loves, and has married the daughter of a foreign god. 12 May the LORD cut off from the tents of Jacob anyone who does this — any to witness$h$ or answer, or to bring an offering to the LORD of hosts.

sniff scornfully at it, says the LORD of Hosts, and exclaim, 'How tiresome!' If you bring as your offering victims that are mutilated, lame, or sickly, am I to accept them from you? says the LORD. 14 A curse on the cheat who pays his vows by sacrificing a damaged victim to the Lord, though he has a sound ram in his flock! I am a great king, says the LORD of Hosts, and my name is held in awe among the nations.

2 And now, you priests, this decree is for you: 2 unless you listen to me and pay heed to the honouring of my name, says the LORD of Hosts, I shall lay a curse on you. I shall turn your blessings into a curse; yes, into a curse, because you pay no heed. 3 I shall cut off your arms, fling offal in your faces, the offal from your pilgrim-feasts, and I shall banish you from my presence. 4 Then you will know that I have issued this decree against you: my covenant with Levi falls, says the LORD of Hosts. 5 My covenant was with him: I bestowed life and welfare on him, and laid on him the duty of reverence; he revered me and lived in awe of my name. 6 The instruction he gave was true, and no word of injustice fell from his lips; he walked in harmony with me and in uprightness, and he turned many back from sin. 7 For men hang on the words of the priest and seek knowledge and instruction from him, because he is the messenger of the LORD of Hosts. 8 But you have turned aside from that course; you have caused many to stumble with your instruction; you have set at naught the covenant with the Levites, says the LORD of Hosts. 9 So I in my turn shall make you despicable and degraded in the eyes of all the people, inasmuch as you disregard my ways and show partiality in your interpretation of the law.

10 Have we not all one father? Did not one God create us? Why then are we faithless to one another by violating the covenant of our forefathers? 11 Judah is faithless, and abominable things are done in Israel and in Jerusalem; in marrying the daughter of a foreign god, Judah has violated the sacred place loved by the LORD. 12 May the LORD banish from the dwellings of Jacob any who do this, whether nomads or settlers, even though they bring offerings to the LORD of Hosts.

---

e Another reading is *at it* f Heb *it* g Cn Compare Gk Syr: Heb *and he shall bear you to it* h Cn Compare Gk: Heb *arouse*

2:3 **cut off:** *so Gk; Heb.* rebuke. **and I . . . presence:** *prob. rdg, cp. Gk; Heb.* and he will take you away to him.

13 You also say, "What a burden!"
and you scorn it, says the LORD of hosts;
You bring in what you seize, or the lame, or
the sick;
yes, you bring it as a sacrifice.
Shall I accept it from your hands?
says the LORD.
14 Cursed is the deceiver, who has in his flock
a male,
but under his vow sacrifices to the LORD
a gelding;
For a great King am I, says the LORD of hosts,
and my name will be feared among the nations.

2 And now, O priests, this commandment is
for you:
If you do not listen,
2 And if you do not lay it to heart,
to give glory to my name, says the LORD
of hosts,
I will send a curse upon you
and of your blessing I will make a curse.
Yes, I have already cursed it,
because you do not lay it to heart.
3 Lo, I will deprive you of the shoulder
and I will strew dung in your faces,
The dung of your feasts,
and you will be carried off with it.
4 Then you will know that I sent you
this commandment
because I have a covenant with Levi,
says the LORD of hosts.
5 My covenant with him was one of life and peace;
fear I put in him, and he feared me,
and stood in awe of my name.
6 True doctrine was in his mouth,
and no dishonesty was found upon his lips;
He walked with me in integrity and uprightness,
and turned many away from evil.
7 For the lips of the priest are to keep knowledge,
and instruction is to be sought from his mouth,
because he is the messenger of the LORD
of hosts.
8 But you have turned aside from the way,
and have caused many to falter by
your instruction;
You have made void the covenant of Levi,
says the LORD of hosts.
9 I, therefore, have made you contemptible
and base before all the people,
Since you do not keep my ways,
but show partiality in your decisions.
10 Have we not all the one Father?
Has not the one God created us?
Why then do we break faith with each other,
violating the covenant of our fathers?
11 Judah has broken faith; an abominable thing
has been done in Israel and in Jerusalem.
Judah has profaned the temple which the
LORD loves,
and has married an idolatrous woman.
12 May the LORD cut off from the man who does this
both witness and advocate out of the tents
of Jacob,
and anyone to offer sacrifice to the LORD
of hosts!

respect." 13 You say, "How tiresome it all is!" and sniff
disdainfully at me, says Yahweh Sabaoth. You bring a stolen, lame or diseased animal, you bring that as an offering!
Am I to accept this from you? says Yahweh Sabaoth.
14 Cursed be the rogue who has a male in his flock but pays
his vow by sacrificing a blemished animal to me! For I am
a great king, says Yahweh Sabaoth, and among the nations
my name inspires awe.'

2 'And now, priests, this commandment is for you. 2 If
you will not listen, if you will not sincerely resolve to
glorify my name, says Yahweh Sabaoth, I shall certainly
lay a curse on you and I shall curse your blessing. Indeed
I will lay a curse, for none of you makes this resolve.
3 Now, I am going to break your arm and throw offal in your
faces — the offal of your solemn feasts — and sweep you
away with it. 4 Then you will know that I sent this commandment to you, to affirm my intention to maintain my
covenant with Levi, says Yahweh Sabaoth. 5 My covenant
was with him — a covenant of life and peace, and these were
what I gave him — a covenant of respect, and he respected
me and held my name in awe. 6 The law of truth was in his
mouth and guilt was not found on his lips; he walked in
peace and justice with me and he converted many from
sinning. 7 The priest's lips ought to safeguard knowledge;
his mouth is where the law should be sought, since he is
Yahweh Sabaoth's messenger. 8 But you yourselves have
turned aside from the way; you have caused many to lapse
by your teaching. Since you have destroyed the covenant of
Levi, says Yahweh Sabaoth, 9 so I in my turn have made
you contemptible and vile to the whole people, for not
having kept my ways and for being partial in applying the
law.

10 'Is there not one Father of us all? Did not one God
create us? Why, then, do we break faith with one another,
profaning the covenant of our ancestors? 11 Judah has broken faith; a detestable thing has been done in Israel and in
Jerusalem. For Judah has profaned Yahweh's beloved sanctuary; he has married the daughter of an alien god. 12 May
Yahweh deprive such an offender of witness and advocate
in the tents of Jacob among those who present offerings to
Yahweh Sabaoth!

| NEW REVISED STANDARD VERSION | REVISED ENGLISH BIBLE |

13 And this you do as well: You cover the LORD's altar with tears, with weeping and groaning because he no longer regards the offering or accepts it with favor at your hand. 14 You ask, "Why does he not?" Because the LORD was a witness between you and the wife of your youth, to whom you have been faithless, though she is your companion and your wife by covenant. 15 Did not one God make her?*i* Both flesh and spirit are his.*j* And what does the one God*k* desire? Godly offspring. So look to yourselves, and do not let anyone be faithless to the wife of his youth. 16 For I hate*l* divorce, says the LORD, the God of Israel, and covering one's garment with violence, says the LORD of hosts. So take heed to yourselves and do not be faithless.

17 You have wearied the LORD with your words. Yet you say, "How have we wearied him?" By saying, "All who do evil are good in the sight of the LORD, and he delights in them." Or by asking, "Where is the God of justice?"

13 Here is another thing you do: you weep and moan, drowning the LORD's altar with tears, but he still refuses to look at the offering or receive favourably a gift from you. 14 You ask why. It is because the LORD has borne witness against you on behalf of the wife of your youth. You have broken faith with her, though she is your partner, your wife by solemn covenant. 15 Did not the one God make her, both flesh and spirit? And what does the one God require but godly children? Keep watch on your spirit, and let none of you be unfaithful to the wife of your youth. 16 If a man divorces or puts away his wife, says the LORD God of Israel, he overwhelms her with cruelty, says the LORD of Hosts. Keep watch on your spirit, and do not be unfaithful.

17 You have wearied the LORD with your talk. You ask, 'How have we wearied him?' By saying that all evildoers are good in the eyes of the LORD, that he is pleased with them, or by asking, 'Where is the God of justice?'

3 See, I am sending my messenger to prepare the way before me, and the Lord whom you seek will come to his temple. The messenger of the covenant in whom you delight—indeed, he is coming, says the LORD of hosts. 2 But who can endure the day of his coming, and who can stand when he appears?

For he is like a refiner's fire and like fullers' soap; 3 he will sit as a refiner and purifier of silver, and he will purify the descendants of Levi and refine them like gold and silver, until they present offerings to the LORD in righteousness.*m* 4 Then the offering of Judah and Jerusalem will be pleasing to the LORD as in the days of old and as in former years.

5 Then I will draw near to you for judgment; I will be swift to bear witness against the sorcerers, against the adulterers, against those who swear falsely, against those who oppress the hired workers in their wages, the widow and the orphan, against those who thrust aside the alien, and do not fear me, says the LORD of hosts.

6 For I the LORD do not change; therefore you, O children of Jacob, have not perished. 7 Ever since the days of your ancestors you have turned aside from my statutes and have not kept them. Return to me, and I will return to you, says the LORD of hosts. But you say, "How shall we return?"

8 Will anyone rob God? Yet you are robbing me! But you say, "How are we robbing you?" In your tithes and offerings! 9 You are cursed with a curse, for you are robbing me—the whole nation of you! 10 Bring the full tithe into the

3 1 I am about to send my messenger to clear a path before me. Suddenly the Lord whom you seek will come to his temple; the messenger of the covenant in whom you delight is here, here already, says the LORD of Hosts. 2 Who can endure the day of his coming? Who can stand firm when he appears? He is like a refiner's fire, like a fuller's soap; 3 he will take his seat, testing and purifying; he will purify the Levites and refine them like gold and silver, and so they will be fit to bring offerings to the LORD. 4 Thus the offerings of Judah and Jerusalem will be pleasing to the LORD as they were in former days, in years long past. 5 I shall appear before you in court, quick to testify against sorcerers, adulterers, and perjurers; against those who cheat the hired labourer of his wages, who wrong the widow and the fatherless, who thrust the alien aside and do not fear me, says the LORD of Hosts.

6 I, the LORD, do not change, and you have not ceased to be children of Jacob. 7 Ever since the days of your forefathers you have been wayward and have not kept my laws. If you return to me, I shall turn back to you, says the LORD of Hosts. You ask, 'How can we return?' 8 Can a human being defraud God? Yet you defraud me. You ask, 'How have we defrauded you?' Why, over tithes and contributions. 9 There is a curse on you all, your entire nation, because you defraud me. 10 Bring the whole tithe into the

---

i Or *Has he not made one?*   *j* Cn: Heb *and a remnant of spirit was his*   *k* Heb *he*   *l* Cn: Heb *he hates*   *m* Or *right offerings to the LORD*

3:1 **my messenger:** Heb. malachi.   3:3 **purifying:** *prob. rdg*; Heb. adds silver.

NEW AMERICAN BIBLE

13 This also you do: the altar of the LORD you cover
 with tears, weeping and groaning,
 Because he no longer regards your sacrifice
 nor accepts it favorably from your hand;
14 And you say, "Why is it?" —
 Because the LORD is witness
 between you and the wife of your youth,
 With whom you have broken faith
 though she is your companion, your
 betrothed wife.
15 Did he not make one being, with flesh and spirit:
 and what does that one require but
 godly offspring?
 You must then safeguard life that is your own,
 and not break faith with the wife of your youth.
16 For I hate divorce,
 says the LORD, the God of Israel,
 And covering one's garment with injustice,
 says the LORD of hosts;
 You must then safeguard life that is your own,
 and not break faith.

17 You have wearied the LORD with your words,
 yet you say, "How have we wearied him?"
 By your saying, "Every evildoer
 is good in the sight of the LORD,
 And he is pleased with him";
 or else, "Where is the just God?"

3 Lo, I am sending my messenger
 to prepare the way before me;
 And suddenly there will come to the temple
 the LORD whom you seek,
 And the messenger of the covenant whom
 you desire.
 Yes, he is coming, says the LORD of hosts.
2 But who will endure the day of his coming?
 And who can stand when he appears?
 For he is like the refiner's fire,
 or like the fuller's lye.
3 He will sit refining and purifying [silver],
 and he will purify the sons of Levi,
 Refining them like gold or like silver
 that they may offer due sacrifice to the LORD.
4 Then the sacrifice of Judah and Jerusalem
 will please the LORD,
 as in the days of old, as in years gone by.
5 I will draw near to you for judgment,
 and I will be swift to bear witness
 Against the sorcerers, adulterers, and perjurers,
 those who defraud the hired man of his wages,
 Against those who defraud widows and orphans;
 those who turn aside the stranger,
 and those who do not fear me, says the LORD
 of hosts.
6 Surely I, the LORD, do not change,
 nor do you cease to be sons of Jacob.
7 Since the days of your fathers you have turned aside
 from my statutes, and have not kept them.
 Return to me, and I will return to you,
 says the LORD of hosts.
 Yet you say, "How must we return?"
8 Dare a man rob God? Yet you are robbing me!
 And you say, "How do we rob you?"
 In tithes and in offerings!
9 You are indeed accursed,
 for you, the whole nation, rob me.
10 Bring the whole tithe
 into the storehouse,
 That there may be food in my house,

NEW JERUSALEM BIBLE

13 'And here is something else you do: you cover the altar
 of Yahweh with tears, with weeping and wailing, because
 he now refuses to consider the offering or to accept it from
 you. 14 And you ask, "Why?" Because Yahweh stands as
 witness between you and the wife of your youth, with
 whom you have broken faith, even though she was your
 partner and your wife by covenant. 15 Did he not create a
 single being, having flesh and the breath of life? And what
 does this single being seek? God-given offspring! Have
 respect for your own life then, and do not break faith with
 the wife of your youth. 16 For I hate divorce, says Yahweh,
 God of Israel, and people concealing their cruelty under a
 cloak, says Yahweh Sabaoth. Have respect for your own
 life then, and do not break faith.

17 'You have wearied Yahweh with your talk. You ask,
 "How have we wearied him?" When you say, "Any evildoer is good as far as Yahweh is concerned; indeed he is
 delighted with them"; or when you say, "Where is the God
 of fair judgement now?"

3 'Look, I shall send my messenger to clear a way before
 me. And suddenly the Lord whom you seek will come
 to his Temple; yes, the angel of the covenant, for whom you
 long, is on his way, says Yahweh Sabaoth. 2 Who will be
 able to resist the day of his coming? Who will remain standing when he appears? For he will be like a refiner's fire, like
 fullers' alkali. 3 He will take his seat as refiner and purifier;
 he will purify the sons of Levi and refine them like gold and
 silver, so that they can make the offering to Yahweh with
 uprightness. 4 The offering of Judah and Jerusalem will then
 be acceptable to Yahweh as in former days, as in the years
 of old. 5 I am coming to put you on trial and I shall be a
 ready witness against sorcerers, adulterers, perjurers, and
 against those who oppress the wage-earner, the widow and
 the orphan, and who rob the foreigner of his rights and do
 not respect me, says Yahweh Sabaoth.

6 'No; I, Yahweh, do not change; and you have not
 ceased to be children of Jacob! 7 Ever since the days of your
 ancestors, you have evaded my statutes and not observed
 them. Return to me and I will return to you, says Yahweh
 Sabaoth. b You ask, "How are we to return? 8 Can a human
 being cheat God?" Yet you try to cheat me! You ask, "How
 do we try to cheat you?" Over tithes and contributions. 9 A
 curse lies on you because you, this whole nation, try to
 cheat me. 10 Bring the tithes in full to the treasury, so that

b 3 // Zc 1:3.

storehouse, so that there may be food in my house, and thus put me to the test, says the LORD of hosts; see if I will not open the windows of heaven for you and pour down for you an overflowing blessing. 11 I will rebuke the locust[n] for you, so that it will not destroy the produce of your soil; and your vine in the field shall not be barren, says the LORD of hosts. 12 Then all nations will count you happy, for you will be a land of delight, says the LORD of hosts.

13 You have spoken harsh words against me, says the LORD. Yet you say, "How have we spoken against you?" 14 You have said, "It is vain to serve God. What do we profit by keeping his command or by going about as mourners before the LORD of hosts? 15 Now we count the arrogant happy; evildoers not only prosper, but when they put God to the test they escape."

16 Then those who revered the LORD spoke with one another. The LORD took note and listened, and a book of remembrance was written before him of those who revered the LORD and thought on his name. 17 They shall be mine, says the LORD of hosts, my special possession on the day when I act, and I will spare them as parents spare their children who serve them. 18 Then once more you shall see the difference between the righteous and the wicked, between one who serves God and one who does not serve him.

4 ⁰ See, the day is coming, burning like an oven, when all the arrogant and all evildoers will be stubble; the day that comes shall burn them up, says the LORD of hosts, so that it will leave them neither root nor branch. 2 But for you who revere my name the sun of righteousness shall rise, with healing in its wings. You shall go out leaping like calves from the stall. 3 And you shall tread down the wicked, for they will be ashes under the soles of your feet, on the day when I act, says the LORD of hosts.

4 Remember the teaching of my servant Moses, the statutes and ordinances that I commanded him at Horeb for all Israel.

5 Lo, I will send you the prophet Elijah before the great and terrible day of the LORD comes. 6 He will turn the hearts of parents to their children and the hearts of children to their parents, so that I will not come and strike the land with a curse.[p]

[n] Heb devourer   [o] Ch 4.1-6 are Ch 3.19-24 in Heb   [p] Or a ban of utter destruction

treasury; let there be food in my house. Put me to the proof, says the LORD of Hosts, and see if I do not open windows in the sky and pour a blessing on you as long as there is need. 11 I shall forbid pests to destroy the produce of your soil, and your vines will not shed their fruit, says the LORD of Hosts. 12 All nations will count you happy, for yours will be a favoured land, says the LORD of Hosts.

13 YOU HAVE used hard words about me, says the LORD. Yet you ask, 'How have we spoken against you?' 14 You have said, 'To serve God is futile. What do we gain from the LORD of Hosts by observing his rules and behaving with humble submission? 15 We for our part count the arrogant happy; it is evildoers who prosper; they have put God to the proof and come to no harm.'

16 Then those who feared the LORD talked together, and the LORD paid heed and listened. A record was written before him of those who feared him and had respect for his name. 17 They will be mine, says the LORD of Hosts, my own possession against the day that I appoint, and I shall spare them as a man spares the son who serves him. 18 Once more you will tell the good from the wicked, the servant of God from the person who does not serve him.

4 The day comes, burning like a furnace; all the arrogant and all evildoers will be stubble, and that day when it comes will set them ablaze, leaving them neither root nor branch, says the LORD of Hosts. 2 But for you who fear my name, the sun of righteousness will rise with healing in its wings, and you will break loose like calves released from the stall. 3 On the day I take action, you will tread down the wicked, for they will be as ashes under the soles of your feet, says the LORD of Hosts.

4 Remember the law of Moses my servant, the rules and precepts which I told him to deliver to all Israel at Horeb.

5 Look, I shall send you the prophet Elijah before the great and terrible day of the LORD comes. 6 He will reconcile parents to their children and children to their parents, lest I come and put the land under a ban to destroy it.

4:1 In Heb. 3:19.

and try me in this, says the LORD of hosts:
Shall I not open for you the floodgates of heaven,
    to pour down blessing upon you without
        measure?
11 For your sake I will forbid the locust
    to destroy your crops;
And the vine in the field will not be barren,
    says the LORD of hosts.
12 Then all nations will call you blessed,
    for you will be a delightful land,
    says the LORD of hosts.
13 You have defied me in word, says the LORD,
    yet you ask, "What have we spoken
        against you?"
14 You have said, "It is vain to serve God,
    and what do we profit by keeping his command,
And going about in penitential dress
    in awe of the LORD of hosts?
15 Rather must we call the proud blessed;
    for indeed evildoers prosper,
    and even tempt God with impunity."
16 Then they who fear the LORD spoke with
        one another,
    and the LORD listened attentively;
And a record book was written before him
    of those who fear the LORD and trust in
        his name.
17 And they shall be mine, says the LORD of hosts,
    my own special possession, on the day I
        take action.
And I will have compassion on them,
    as a man has compassion on his son who
        serves him.
18 Then you will again see the distinction
    between the just and the wicked;
Between him who serves God,
    and him who does not serve him.
19 For lo, the day is coming, blazing like an oven,
    when all the proud and all evildoers will
        be stubble,
And the day that is coming will set them on fire,
    leaving them neither root nor branch,
    says the LORD of hosts.
20 But for you who fear my name, there will arise
    the sun of justice with its healing rays;
And you will gambol like calves out of the stall
21   and tread down the wicked;
They will become ashes under the soles of
        your feet,
    on the day I take action, says the LORD of hosts.

22 Remember the law of Moses my servant,
    which I enjoined upon him on Horeb,
The statutes and ordinances
    for all Israel.
23 Lo, I will send you
    Elijah, the prophet,
Before the day of the LORD comes,
    the great and terrible day,
24 To turn the hearts of the fathers to their children,
    and the hearts of the children to their fathers,
Lest I come and strike
    the land with doom.
Lo, I will send you
Elijah, the prophet,
Before the day of the LORD comes,
the great and terrible day.

3, 24: The words in fine print, a repetition of v 23a-d, have been
added by the scribes so that the collection of the twelve minor
prophets will not end with the threat of doom.

there is food in my house; put me to the test now like this,
says Yahweh Sabaoth, and see if I do not open the floodgates of heaven for you and pour out an abundant blessing
for you. 11 For your sakes, I shall forbid the locust to destroy the produce of your soil or prevent the vine from
bearing fruit in your field, says Yahweh Sabaoth, 12 and all
the nations will call you blessed, for you will be a land of
delights, says Yahweh Sabaoth.
13 'You have said harsh things about me, says Yahweh.
And yet you say, "What have we said against you?" 14 You
have said, "It is useless to serve God; what is the good of
keeping his commands or of walking mournfully before
Yahweh Sabaoth? 15 In fact, we now call the proud the
happy ones; the evil-doers are the ones who prosper; they
put God to the test, yet come to no harm!" '
16 Then those who feared Yahweh talked to one another
about this, and Yahweh took note and listened; and a book
of remembrance was written in his presence recording those
who feared him and kept his name in mind. 17 'On the day
when I act, says Yahweh Sabaoth, they will be my most
prized possession, and I shall spare them in the way a man
spares the son who serves him. 18 Then once again you will
see the difference between the upright person and the
wicked one, between the one who serves God and the one
who does not serve him.

19 'For look, the Day is coming, glowing like a furnace.
All the proud and all the evil-doers will be the stubble, and
the Day, when it comes, will set them ablaze, says Yahweh
Sabaoth, leaving them neither root nor branch. 20 But for
you who fear my name, the Sun of justice will rise with
healing in his rays, and you will come out leaping like
calves from the stall, 21 and trample on the wicked, who will
be like ashes under the soles of your feet on the day when
I act, says Yahweh Sabaoth.
22 'Remember the Law of my servant Moses to whom at
Horeb I prescribed decrees and rulings for all Israel.
23 'Look, I shall send you the prophet Elijah before the
great and awesome Day of Yahweh comes. 24 He will reconcile parents to their children and children to their parents,
to forestall my putting the country under the curse of destruction.'

THE APOCRYPHAL/DEUTEROCANONICAL BOOKS

of the Old Testament

THE APOCRYPHAL / DEUTEROCANONICAL BOOKS

The arrangement of books in this section follows that in the New Revised Standard Version translation, which places them in groups according to their differing canonical status in the various Christian communities. This differing status means that some books are not represented in all four translations.

The books and parts of books from Tobit through 2 Maccabees are included in all four translations.

First Esdras, the Prayer of Manasseh, and 2 Esdras are included only in the New Revised Standard Version and Revised English Bible translations.

Third Maccabees, 4 Maccabees, and Psalm 151 are included only in the New Revised Standard Version translation.

Tobit

Tobit

1 This book tells the story of Tobit son of Tobiel son of Hananiel son of Aduel son of Gabael son of Raphael son of Raguel of the descendants*a* of Asiel, of the tribe of Naphtali, ²who in the days of King Shalmaneser*b* of the Assyrians was taken into captivity from Thisbe, which is to the south of Kedesh Naphtali in Upper Galilee, above Asher toward the west, and north of Phogor.

3 I, Tobit, walked in the ways of truth and righteousness all the days of my life. I performed many acts of charity for my kindred and my people who had gone with me in exile to Nineveh in the land of the Assyrians. ⁴When I was in my own country, in the land of Israel, while I was still a young man, the whole tribe of my ancestor Naphtali deserted the house of David and Jerusalem. This city had been chosen from among all the tribes of Israel, where all the tribes of Israel should offer sacrifice and where the temple, the dwelling of God, had been consecrated and established for all generations forever.

5 All my kindred and our ancestral house of Naphtali sacrificed to the calf*c* that King Jeroboam of Israel had erected in Dan and on all the mountains of Galilee. ⁶But I alone went often to Jerusalem for the festivals, as it is prescribed for all Israel by an everlasting decree. I would hurry off to Jerusalem with the first fruits of the crops and the firstlings of the flock, the tithes of the cattle, and the first shearings of the sheep. ⁷I would give these to the priests, the sons of Aaron, at the altar; likewise the tenth of the grain, wine, olive oil, pomegranates, figs, and the rest of the fruits to the sons of Levi who ministered at Jerusalem. Also for six years I would save up a second tenth in money and go and distribute it in Jerusalem. ⁸A third tenth*d* I would give to the orphans and widows and to the converts who had attached themselves to Israel. I would bring it and give it to them in the third year, and we would eat it according to the ordinance decreed concerning it in the law of Moses and according to the instructions of Deborah, the mother of my father Tobiel,*e* for my father had died and left me an orphan. ⁹When I became a man I married a woman,*f* a member of our own family, and by her I became the father of a son whom I named Tobias.

10 After I was carried away captive to Assyria and came as a captive to Nineveh, everyone of my kindred and my people ate the food of the Gentiles, ¹¹but I kept myself from eating the food of the Gentiles. ¹²Because I was mindful of God with all my heart, ¹³the Most High gave me favor and good standing with Shalmaneser,*b* and I used to buy everything he needed. ¹⁴Until his death I used to go into Media, and buy for him there. While in the country of Media I left bags of silver worth ten talents in trust with Gabael, the brother of Gabri. ¹⁵But when Shalmaneser*b* died, and his son Sennacherib reigned in his place, the highways into Media became unsafe and I could no longer go there.

16 In the days of Shalmaneser*b* I performed many acts of charity to my kindred, those of my tribe. ¹⁷I would give

1 THIS is the story of Tobit son of Tobiel, son of Hananiel, son of Aduel, son of Gabael, son of Raphael, son of Raguel, of the family of Asiel, of the tribe of Naphtali. ²In the time of King Shalmaneser of Assyria he was taken captive from Thisbe which is south of Kedesh-naphtali in Upper Galilee above Hazor, beyond the road to the west, north of Peor.

³I, TOBIT, have made truth and righteousness my lifelong guide. I did many acts of charity to my kinsmen, those of my nation who had gone with me into captivity at Nineveh in Assyria. ⁴While I was quite young in my own country, Israel, the whole tribe of Naphtali my ancestor broke away from the dynasty of David and from Jerusalem, the city chosen out of all the tribes of Israel as the one place of sacrifice; it was there that God's dwelling-place, the temple, had been consecrated, built to last for all generations. ⁵My kinsmen, the whole house of my ancestor Naphtali, sacrificed on the mountains of Galilee to the image of a bull-calf which King Jeroboam of Israel had set up in Dan.

6At the festivals I, and I alone, made the frequent journey to Jerusalem prescribed as an eternal commandment for all Israel. I would hurry off to Jerusalem with the firstfruits of crops and herds, the tithes of the cattle, and the first shearings of the sheep; these I gave to the priests of Aaron's line for the altar, 7while the tithe of wine, grain, olive oil, pomegranates, and other fruits I gave to the Levites ministering at Jerusalem. The second tithe for the six years I turned into money and brought it year by year to Jerusalem for distribution 8among the orphans and widows and among the converts who had attached themselves to Israel. Every third year when I brought it and gave it to them, we held a feast in accordance with the command prescribed in the law of Moses and the instructions enjoined by Deborah the mother of Hananiel our grandfather; for on the death of my father I had been left an orphan.

9When I grew up, I took a wife from our kindred and had by her a son whom I called Tobias. 10After the deportation to Assyria in which I was taken captive and came to Nineveh, everyone of my family and nation ate gentile food; 11but I myself scrupulously avoided doing so. 12And since I was wholeheartedly mindful of my God, 13the Most High endowed me with a presence which won me the favour of Shalmaneser, and I became his buyer of supplies. 14During his lifetime I used to travel to Media and buy for him there, and I deposited bags of money to the value of ten talents of silver with my kinsman Gabael son of Gabri in Media. 15When Shalmaneser died and was succeeded by his son Sennacherib, the roads to Media passed out of Assyrian control and I could no longer make the journey.

16In the days of Shalmaneser, I had done many acts of charity to my fellow-countrymen: I would share my food with the hungry 17and provide clothing for those who had

---

*a*Other ancient authorities lack *of Raphael son of Raguel of the descendants*   *b*Gk *Enemessaros*   *c*Other ancient authorities read *heifer*   *d*A *third tenth* added from other ancient authorities
*e*Lat: Gk *Hananiel*   *f*Other ancient authorities add *Anna*

1:2 **Shalmaneser:** *Gk* Enemessaros.

THE BOOK OF

Tobit

1 This book tells the story of Tobit, son of Tobiel, son of Hananiel, son of Aduel, son of Gabael of the family of Asiel, of the tribe of Naphtali, ²who during the reign of Shalmaneser, king of Assyria, was taken captive from Thisbe, which is south of Kedesh Naphtali in upper Galilee, above and to the west of Asser, north of Phogor.

³I, Tobit, have walked all the days of my life on the paths of truth and righteousness. I performed many charitable works for my kinsmen and my people who had been deported with me to Nineveh, in Assyria. ⁴When I lived as a young man in my own country, Israel, the entire tribe of my forefather Naphtali had broken away from the house of David and from Jerusalem. This city had been singled out of all Israel's tribes, so that they all might offer sacrifice in the place where the temple, God's dwelling, had been built and consecrated for all generations to come. ⁵All my kinsmen, like the rest of the tribe of my forefather Naphtali, used to offer sacrifice on all the mountains of Galilee as well as to the young bull which Jeroboam, king of Israel, had made in Dan.

⁶I, for my part, would often make the pilgrimage alone to Jerusalem for the festivals, as is prescribed for all Israel by perpetual decree. Bringing with me the first fruits of the field and the firstlings of the flock, together with a tenth of my income and the first shearings of the sheep, I would hasten to Jerusalem ⁷and present them to the priests, Aaron's sons, at the altar. To the Levites who were doing service in Jerusalem I would give the tithe of grain, wine, olive oil, pomegranates, figs, and other fruits. And except for sabbatical years, I used to give a second tithe in money, which each year I would go and disburse in Jerusalem. ⁸The third tithe I gave to orphans and widows, and to converts who were living with the Israelites. Every third year I would bring them this offering, and we ate it in keeping with the decree of the Mosaic law and the commands of Deborah, the mother of my father Tobiel; for when my father died, he left me an orphan.

⁹When I reached manhood, I married Anna, a woman of our own lineage. By her I had a son whom I named Tobiah. ¹⁰Now after I had been deported to Nineveh, all my brothers and relatives ate the food of heathens, ¹¹but I refrained from eating that kind of food. ¹²Because of this wholehearted service of God, ¹³the Most High granted me favor and status with Shalmaneser, so that I became purchasing agent for all his needs. ¹⁴Every now and then until his death I would go to Media to buy goods for him. I also deposited several pouches containing a great sum of money with my kinsman Gabael, son of Gabri, who lived at Rages, in Media. ¹⁵But when Shalmaneser died and his son Sennacherib succeeded him as king, the roads to Media became unsafe, so I could no longer go there.

¹⁶During Shalmaneser's reign I performed many charitable works for my kinsmen and my people. ¹⁷I would give

Tobit

1 The tale of Tobit son of Tobiel, son of Ananiel, son of Aduel, son of Gabael, of the lineage of Asiel and tribe of Naphtali. ²In the days of Shalmaneser king of Assyria, he was exiled from Thisbe, which is south of Kedesh-Naphtali in Upper Galilee, above Hazor, some distance to the west, north of Shephat.

³I, Tobit, have walked in paths of truth and in good works all the days of my life. I have given much in alms to my brothers and fellow country-folk, exiled like me to Nineveh in the country of Assyria. ⁴In my young days, when I was still at home in the land of Israel, the whole tribe of Naphtali my ancestor broke away from the House of David and from Jerusalem, though this was the city chosen out of all the tribes of Israel for their sacrifices; here, the Temple —God's dwelling-place—had been built and hallowed for all generations to come. ⁵All my brothers and the House of Naphtali sacrificed on every hill-top in Galilee to the calf that Jeroboam king of Israel had made at Dan.

⁶Often I was quite alone in making the pilgrimage to Jerusalem, fulfilling the Law that binds all Israel perpetually. I would hurry to Jerusalem with the first yield of fruits and beasts, the tithe of cattle and the sheep's first shearings. ⁷I would give these to the priests, the sons of Aaron, for the altar. To the Levites ministering at Jerusalem I would give my tithe of wine and corn, olives, pomegranates and other fruits. Six years in succession I took the second tithe in money and went and paid it annually at Jerusalem. ⁸I gave the third to orphans and widows and to the strangers who live among the Israelites; I brought it them as a gift every three years. When we ate, we obeyed both the ordinances of the law of Moses and the exhortations of Deborah the mother of our ancestor Ananiel; for my father had died and left me an orphan. ⁹When I came to man's estate, I married a woman from our kinsfolk whose name was Anna; she bore me a son whom I called Tobias.

¹⁰When the banishment into Assyria came, I was taken away and went to Nineveh. All my brothers and the people of my race ate the food of the heathen, ¹¹but for my part I was careful not to eat the food of the heathen. ¹²And because I had kept faith with my God with my whole heart, ¹³the Most High granted me the favour of Shalmaneser, and I became the king's purveyor. ¹⁴Until his death I used to travel to Media, where I transacted business on his behalf, and I deposited sacks of silver worth ten talents with Gabael the brother of Gabrias at Rhages in Media.

¹⁵On the death of Shalmaneser his son Sennacherib succeeded; the roads into Media were barred, and I could no longer go there. ¹⁶In the days of Shalmaneser I had often given alms to the people of my race; ¹⁷I gave my bread to

my food to the hungry and my clothing to the naked; and if I saw the dead body of any of my people thrown out behind the wall of Nineveh, I would bury it. 18 I also buried any whom King Sennacherib put to death when he came fleeing from Judea in those days of judgment that the king of heaven executed upon him because of his blasphemies. For in his anger he put to death many Israelites; but I would secretly remove the bodies and bury them. So when Sennacherib looked for them he could not find them. 19 Then one of the Ninevites went and informed the king about me, that I was burying them; so I hid myself. But when I realized that the king knew about me and that I was being searched for to be put to death, I was afraid and ran away. 20 Then all my property was confiscated; nothing was left to me that was not taken into the royal treasury except my wife Anna and my son Tobias.

21 But not forty*g* days passed before two of Sennacherib's*h* sons killed him, and they fled to the mountains of Ararat, and his son Esar-haddon*i* reigned after him. He appointed Ahikar, the son of my brother Hanael,*j* over all the accounts of his kingdom, and he had authority over the entire administration. 22 Ahikar interceded for me, and I returned to Nineveh. Now Ahikar was chief cupbearer, keeper of the signet, and in charge of administrations of the accounts under King Sennacherib of Assyria; so Esar-haddon*i* reappointed him. He was my nephew and so a close relative.

2 Then during the reign of Esar-haddon*i* I returned home, and my wife Anna and my son Tobias were restored to me. At our festival of Pentecost, which is the sacred festival of weeks, a good dinner was prepared for me and I reclined to eat. 2 When the table was set for me and an abundance of food placed before me, I said to my son Tobias, "Go, my child, and bring whatever poor person you may find of our people among the exiles in Nineveh, who is wholeheartedly mindful of God,*k* and he shall eat together with me. I will wait for you, until you come back." 3 So Tobias went to look for some poor person of our people. When he had returned he said, "Father!" And I replied, "Here I am, my child." Then he went on to say, "Look, father, one of our own people has been murdered and thrown into the market place, and now he lies there strangled." 4 Then I sprang up, left the dinner before even tasting it, and removed the body*l* from the square*m* and laid it*l* in one of the rooms until sunset when I might bury it.*l* 5 When I returned, I washed myself and ate my food in sorrow. 6 Then I remembered the prophecy of Amos, how he said against Bethel,*n*

"Your festivals shall be turned into mourning,
    and all your songs into lamentation."
And I wept.

7 When the sun had set, I went and dug a grave and buried him. 8 And my neighbors laughed and said, "Is he still not afraid? He has already been hunted down to be put to death for doing this, and he ran away; yet here he is again burying the dead!" 9 That same night I washed myself and went into my courtyard and slept by the wall of the courtyard; and my face was uncovered because of the heat. 10 I

none, and if I saw the dead body of anyone of my people thrown outside the wall of Nineveh, I gave it burial.

18 I buried all those who fell victim to Sennacherib after his headlong retreat from Judaea, when the King of heaven brought judgement on him for his blasphemies. In his rage Sennacherib killed many of the Israelites, but I stole their bodies away and buried them, and when search was made for them by Sennacherib they were not to be found. 19 One of the Ninevites disclosed to the king that it was I who had been giving burial to his victims and that I had gone into hiding. When I learnt that the king knew about me and was seeking my life, I was alarmed and made my escape. 20 All that I possessed was seized and confiscated for the royal treasury; I was left with nothing but Anna my wife and my son Tobias.

21 However, less than forty days afterwards the king was murdered by two of his sons, and when they sought refuge in the mountains of Ararat, his son Esarhaddon succeeded to the throne. He appointed Ahikar, my brother Anael's son, to oversee all the revenues of his kingdom, with control of the entire administration. 22 Then Ahikar interceded on my behalf and I came back to Nineveh; he had been chief cupbearer, keeper of the signet, comptroller, and treasurer when Sennacherib was king of Assyria, and Esarhaddon confirmed him in office. Ahikar was a relative of mine; he was my nephew.

2 DURING the reign of Esarhaddon, I returned to my house, and my wife Anna and my son Tobias were restored to me. At our festival of Pentecost, that is the feast of Weeks, a fine meal was prepared for me and I took my place. 2 The table being laid and food in plenty put before me, I said to Tobias: 'My son, go out and, if you find among our people captive here in Nineveh some poor man who is wholeheartedly mindful of God, bring him back to share my meal. I shall wait for you, son, till you return.' 3 Tobias went to look for a poor man of our people, but came straight back and cried, 'Father!' 'Yes, my son?' I replied. 'Father,' he answered, 'one of our nation has been murdered! His body is lying in the market-place; he has just been strangled.' 4 I jumped up and left my meal untasted. I took the body from the square and put it in one of the outbuildings until sunset when I could bury it; 5 then I went indoors, duly bathed myself, and ate my food in sorrow. 6 I recalled the words of the prophet Amos in the passage about Bethel:

Your festivals shall be turned into mourning,
    and all your songs into lamentation,

and I wept. 7 When the sun had gone down, I went and dug a grave and buried the body. 8 My neighbours jeered. 'Is he no longer afraid?' they said. 'He ran away last time, when they were hunting for him to put him to death for this very offence; and here he is again burying the dead!' 9 That night, after bathing myself, I went into my courtyard and lay down to sleep by the courtyard wall, leaving my face uncovered because of the heat. 10 I did not know

---

g Other ancient authorities read either *forty-five* or *fifty*   *h* Gk *his*
i Gk *Sacherdonos*   *j* Other authorities read *Hananael*   *k* Lat: Gk
wholeheartedly mindful   *l* Gk *him*   *m* Other ancient authorities
lack *from the square*   *n* Other ancient authorities read *against*
Bethlehem

2:6 **songs:** *so one* Vs. (*cp. Amos 8:10*); Gk *ways.*

NEW AMERICAN BIBLE

NEW JERUSALEM BIBLE

my bread to the hungry and my clothing to the naked. If I saw one of my people who had died and been thrown outside the walls of Nineveh, I would bury him. 18 I also buried anyone whom Sennacherib slew when he returned as a fugitive from Judea during the days of judgment decreed against him by the heavenly King because of the blasphemies he had uttered. In his rage he killed many Israelites, but I used to take their bodies by stealth and bury them; so when Sennacherib looked for them, he could not find them. 19 But a certain citizen of Nineveh informed the king that it was I who buried the dead. When I found out that the king knew all about me and wanted to put me to death, I went into hiding; then in my fear I took to flight. 20 Afterward, all my property was confiscated; I was left with nothing. All that I had was taken to the king's palace, except for my wife Anna and my son Tobiah.

21 But less than forty days later the king was assassinated by two of his sons, who then escaped into the mountains of Ararat. His son Esarhaddon, who succeeded him as king, placed Ahiqar, my brother Anael's son, in charge of all the accounts of his kingdom, so that he took control over the entire administration. 22 Then Ahiqar interceded on my behalf, and I was able to return to Nineveh. For under Sennacherib, king of Assyria, Ahiqar had been chief cupbearer, keeper of the seal, administrator, and treasurer; and Esarhaddon reappointed him. He was a close relative — in fact, my nephew.

2 Thus under King Esarhaddon I returned to my home, and my wife Anna and my son Tobiah were restored to me. Then on our festival of Pentecost, the feast of Weeks, a fine dinner was prepared for me, and I reclined to eat. 2 The table was set for me, and when many different dishes were placed before me, I said to my son Tobiah: "My son, go out and try to find a poor man from among our kinsmen exiled in Nineveh. If he is a sincere worshiper of God, bring him back with you, so that he can share this meal with me. Indeed, son, I shall wait for you to come back."

3 Tobiah went out to look for some poor kinsman of ours. When he returned he exclaimed, "Father!" I said to him, "What is it, son?" He answered, "Father, one of our people has been murdered! His body lies in the market place where he was just strangled!" 4 I sprang to my feet, leaving the dinner untouched; and I carried the dead man from the street and put him in one of the rooms, so that I might bury him after sunset. 5 Returning to my own quarters, I washed myself and ate my food in sorrow. 6 I was reminded of the oracle pronounced by the prophet Amos against Bethel:

"Your festivals shall be returned into mourning,
And all your songs into lamentation."

7 And I wept. Then at sunset I went out, dug a grave, and buried him.

8 The neighbors mocked me, saying to one another: "Will this man never learn! Once before he was hunted down for execution because of this very thing; yet now that he has escaped, here he is again burying the dead!"

9 That same night I bathed, and went to sleep next to the wall of my courtyard. Because of the heat I left my face uncovered. 10 I did not know there were birds perched on

the hungry and clothes to those who lacked them; and I buried, when I saw them, the bodies of my country-folk thrown over the walls of Nineveh.

18 I also buried those who were killed by Sennacherib. When Sennacherib was beating a disorderly retreat from Judaea after the King of heaven had punished his blasphemies, he killed a great number of Israelites in his rage. So I stole their bodies to bury them; Sennacherib looked for them and could not find them. 19 A Ninevite went and told the king it was I who had buried them secretly. When I knew that the king had been told about me and saw myself being hunted by men who would put me to death, I was afraid and fled. 20 All my goods were seized; they were all confiscated by the treasury; nothing was left me but my wife Anna and my son Tobias.

21 Less than forty days after this, the king was murdered by his two sons, who then fled to the mountains of Ararat. His son Esarhaddon succeeded. Ahikar, son of my brother Anael, was appointed chancellor of the exchequer for the kingdom and given the main ordering of affairs. 22 Ahikar then interceded for me and I was allowed to return to Nineveh, since Ahikar had been chief cupbearer, keeper of the signet, administrator and treasurer under Sennacherib king of Assyria, and Esarhaddon had kept him in office. He was a relation of mine; he was my nephew.

2 In the reign of Esarhaddon, therefore, I returned home, and my wife Anna was restored to me with my son Tobias. At our feast of Pentecost (the feast of Weeks) there was a good dinner. I took my place for the meal; 2 the table was brought to me and various dishes were brought. I then said to my son Tobias, 'Go, my child, and seek out some poor, loyal-hearted man among our brothers exiled in Nineveh, and bring him to share my meal. I will wait until you come back, my child.' 3 So Tobias went out to look for some poor man among our brothers, but he came back again and said, 'Father!' I replied, 'What is it, my child?' He went on, 'Father, one of our nation has just been murdered; he has been strangled and then thrown down in the market place; he is there still.' 4 I sprang up at once, left my meal untouched, took the man from the market place and laid him in one of my rooms, waiting until sunset to bury him. 5 I came in again and washed myself and ate my bread in sorrow, 6 remembering the words of the prophet Amos concerning Bethel:

I shall turn your festivals into mourning
and all your singing into lamentation.[a]

7 And I wept. When the sun was down, I went and dug a grave and buried him. 8 My neighbours laughed and said, 'See! He is not afraid any more.' (You must remember that a price had been set on my head earlier for this very thing.) 'Once before he had to flee, yet here he is, beginning to bury the dead again.'

9 That night I took a bath; then I went into the courtyard and lay down by the courtyard wall. Since it was hot I left my face uncovered. 10 I did not know that there were spar-

a 2 Am 8:10.

did not know that there were sparrows on the wall; their fresh droppings fell into my eyes and produced white films. I went to physicians to be healed, but the more they treated me with ointments the more my vision was obscured by the white films, until I became completely blind. For four years I remained unable to see. All my kindred were sorry for me, and Ahikar took care of me for two years before he went to Elymais.

11 At that time, also, my wife Anna earned money at women's work. 12 She used to send what she made to the owners and they would pay wages to her. One day, the seventh of Dystrus, when she cut off a piece she had woven and sent it to the owners, they paid her full wages and also gave her a young goat for a meal. 13 When she returned to me, the goat began to bleat. So I called her and said, "Where did you get this goat? It is surely not stolen, is it? Return it to the owners; for we have no right to eat anything stolen." 14 But she said to me, "It was given to me as a gift in addition to my wages." But I did not believe her, and told her to return it to the owners. I became flushed with anger against her over this. Then she replied to me, "Where are your acts of charity? Where are your righteous deeds? These things are known about you!"*o*

3 Then with much grief and anguish of heart I wept, and with groaning began to pray:
2 "You are righteous, O Lord,
　　and all your deeds are just;
　all your ways are mercy and truth;
　　you judge the world.*p*
3 And now, O Lord, remember me
　　and look favorably upon me.
　Do not punish me for my sins
　　and for my unwitting offenses
　　and those that my ancestors committed before
　　　you.
　They sinned against you,
4 　　and disobeyed your commandments.
　So you gave us over to plunder, exile, and death,
　　to become the talk, the byword, and an object
　　　of reproach
　　among all the nations among whom you have
　　　dispersed us.
5 And now your many judgments are true
　　in exacting penalty from me for my sins.
　For we have not kept your commandments
　　and have not walked in accordance with truth
　　　before you.
6 So now deal with me as you will;
　　command my spirit to be taken from me,
　　so that I may be released from the face of the
　　　earth and become dust.
　For it is better for me to die than to live,
　　because I have had to listen to undeserved
　　　insults,
　　and great is the sorrow within me.
　Command, O Lord, that I be released from this
　　　distress;
　release me to go to the eternal home,
　　and do not, O Lord, turn your face away from
　　　me.
　For it is better for me to die
　　than to see so much distress in my life
　　and to listen to insults."

7 On the same day, at Ecbatana in Media, it also happened that Sarah, the daughter of Raguel, was reproached by one of her father's maids. 8 For she had been married to

o Or *to you*; Gk *with you*　*p* Other ancient authorities read *you render true and righteous judgment forever*

that there were sparrows in the wall above me, and their droppings fell, still warm, right into my eyes and produced white patches. I went to the doctors to be cured, but the more they treated me with their ointments, the more my eyes became blinded by the white patches, until I lost my sight. I was blind for four years; my kinsmen all grieved for me, and for two years Ahikar looked after me, until he moved to Elymais.

11 At that time Anna my wife used to earn money by women's work, spinning and weaving, 12 and her employers would pay her when she took them what she had done. One day, the seventh of Dystrus, after she had cut off the piece she had woven and delivered it, they not only paid her wages in full, but also gave her a kid from their herd of goats to take home. 13 When my wife came into the house to me, the kid began to bleat, and I called out to her: 'Where does that kid come from? I hope it was not stolen? Return it to its owners; we have no right to eat anything stolen.' 14 But she assured me: 'It was given me as a present, over and above my wages.' I did not believe her and insisted that she return it, and I blushed with shame for what she had done. Her rejoinder was: 'So much for all your acts of charity and all your good works! Everyone can now see what you are really like.'

3 In deep distress I groaned and wept aloud, and as I groaned I prayed: 2 'O Lord, you are just and all your acts are just; in all your ways you are merciful and true; you are the Judge of the world. 3 Now bear me in mind, Lord, and look upon me. Do not punish me for the sins and errors which I and my fathers have committed. 4 We have sinned against you and disobeyed your commandments, and you have given us up to the despoiler, to captivity and death, until we have become a proverb and a byword; we are taunted by all the nations among whom you have scattered us. 5 I acknowledge the justice of your many judgements, the due penalty for our sins, for we have not carried out your commandments or lived in true obedience before you. 6 And now deal with me as you will. Command that my life be taken away from me so that I may be removed from the face of the earth and turned to dust. I would be better dead than alive, for I have had to listen to taunts I have not deserved and my grief is great. Lord, command that I be released from this misery; let me go to the eternal resting-place. Do not turn your face from me, Lord; I had rather die than live in such misery, listening to such taunts.'

7 On the same day it happened that Sarah, the daughter of Raguel who lived at Ecbatana in Media, also had to listen to taunts, from one of her father's servant-girls. 8 Sarah had

the wall above me, till their warm droppings settled in my eyes, causing cataracts. I went to see some doctors for a cure, but the more they anointed my eyes with various salves, the worse the cataracts became, until I could see no more. For four years I was deprived of eyesight, and all my kinsmen were grieved at my condition. Ahiqar, however, took care of me for two years, until he left for Elymais. 11 At that time my wife Anna worked for hire at weaving cloth, the kind of work women do. 12 When she sent back the goods to their owners, they would pay her. Late in winter she finished the cloth and sent it back to the owners. They paid her the full salary, and also gave her a young goat for the table. 13 On entering my house the goat began to bleat. I called to my wife and said: "Where did this goat come from? Perhaps it was stolen! Give it back to its owners; we have no right to eat stolen food!" 14 But she said to me, "It was given to me as a bonus over and above my wages." Yet I would not believe her; and told her to give it back to its owners. I became very angry with her over this. So she retorted: "Where are your charitable deeds now? Where are your virtuous acts? See! Your true character is finally showing itself!"

3 Grief-stricken in spirit, I groaned and wept aloud. Then with sobs I began to pray:

2 "You are righteous, O Lord,
    and all your deeds are just;
All your ways are mercy and truth;
    you are the judge of the world.
3 And now, O Lord, may you be mindful of me,
    and look with favor upon me.
Punish me not for my sins,
    nor for my inadvertent offenses,
    nor for those of my fathers.

"They sinned against you,
4   and disobeyed your commandments.
So you handed us over to plundering, exile,
    and death,
    till we were an object lesson, a byword,
    a reproach
    in all the nations among whom you scattered us.

5 "Yes, your judgments are many and true
    in dealing with me as my sins
    and those of my fathers deserve.
For we have not kept your commandments,
    nor have we trodden the paths of truth
    before you.

6 "So now, deal with me as you please,
    and command my life breath to be taken
        from me,
    that I may go from the face of the earth
        into dust.
It is better for me to die than to live,
    because I have heard insulting calumnies,
    and I am overwhelmed with grief.

"Lord, command me to be delivered from
        such anguish;
    let me go to the everlasting abode;
    Lord, refuse me not.
For it is better for me to die
    than to endure so much misery in life,
    and to hear these insults!"

7 On the same day, at Ecbatana in Media, it so happened that Raguel's daughter Sarah also had to listen to abuse, from one of her father's maids. 8 For she had been married

rows in the wall above my head; their hot droppings fell into my eyes. This caused white spots to form, which I went to have treated by the doctors. But the more ointments they tried me with, the more the spots blinded me, and in the end, I became completely blind. I remained without sight four years; all my brothers were distressed on my behalf; and Ahikar provided for my upkeep for two years, until he left for Elymais. 11 My wife Anna then undertook woman's work; she would spin wool and take cloth to weave; 12 she used to deliver whatever had been ordered from her and then receive payment. Now on the seventh day of the month of Dystros, she finished a piece of work and delivered it to her customers. They paid her all that was due, and into the bargain presented her with a kid for a meal. 13 When the kid came into my house, it began to bleat. I called to my wife and said, 'Where does this creature come from? Suppose it has been stolen! Let the owners have it back; we have no right to eat stolen goods'. 14 She said, 'No, it was a present given me over and above my wages.' I did not believe her, and told her to give it back to the owners (I felt deeply ashamed of her). To which, she replied, 'What about your own alms? What about your own good works? Everyone knows what return you have had for them.'

3 Then, sad at heart, I sighed and wept, and began this prayer of lamentation:

2 You are just, O Lord,
    and just are all your works.
All your ways are grace and truth,
    and you are the Judge of the world.

3 Therefore, Lord,
    remember me, look on me.
Do not punish me for my sins
    or for my needless faults
    or those of my ancestors.

4 For we have sinned against you
    and broken your commandments;
    and you have given us over to be plundered,
to captivity and death,
    to be the talk, the laughing-stock and scorn
    of all the nations among whom you have dispersed
        us.

5 And now all your decrees are true
    when you deal with me as my faults deserve,
    and those of my ancestors.
For we have neither kept your commandments
    nor walked in truth before you.

6 So now, do with me as you will;
    be pleased to take my life from me;
    so that I may be delivered from earth
    and become earth again.
Better death than life for me,
    for I have endured groundless insult
    and am in deepest sorrow.

Lord, be pleased
    to deliver me from this affliction.
Let me go away to my everlasting home;
    do not turn your face from me, O Lord.
Better death for me than life prolonged
    in the face of unrelenting misery:
    I can no longer bear to listen to insults.

7 It chanced on the same day that Sarah the daughter of Raguel, who lived in Media at Ecbatana, also heard insults from one of her father's maids. 8 For she had been given in

seven husbands, and the wicked demon Asmodeus had killed each of them before they had been with her as is customary for wives. So the maid said to her, "You are the one who kills*q* your husbands! See, you have already been married to seven husbands and have not borne the name of*r* a single one of them. 9 Why do you beat us? Because your husbands are dead? Go with them! May we never see a son or daughter of yours!"

10 On that day she was grieved in spirit and wept. When she had gone up to her father's upper room, she intended to hang herself. But she thought it over and said, "Never shall they reproach my father, saying to him, 'You had only one beloved daughter but she hanged herself because of her distress.' And I shall bring my father in his old age down in sorrow to Hades. It is better for me not to hang myself, but to pray the Lord that I may die and not listen to these reproaches anymore." 11 At that same time, with hands outstretched toward the window, she prayed and said,

"Blessed are you, merciful God!
Blessed is your name forever;
    let all your works praise you forever.
12 And now, Lord,*s* I turn my face to you,
    and raise my eyes toward you.
13 Command that I be released from the earth
    and not listen to such reproaches any more.
14 You know, O Master, that I am innocent
    of any defilement with a man,
15 and that I have not disgraced my name
    or the name of my father in the land of my
        exile.
I am my father's only child;
    he has no other child to be his heir;
and he has no close relative or other kindred
    for whom I should keep myself as wife.
Already seven husbands of mine have died.
    Why should I still live?
But if it is not pleasing to you, O Lord, to take
        my life,
    hear me in my disgrace."

16 At that very moment, the prayers of both of them were heard in the glorious presence of God. 17 So Raphael was sent to heal both of them: Tobit, by removing the white films from his eyes, so that he might see God's light with his eyes; and Sarah, daughter of Raguel, by giving her in marriage to Tobias son of Tobit, and by setting her free from the wicked demon Asmodeus. For Tobias was entitled to have her before all others who had desired to marry her. At the same time that Tobit returned from the courtyard into his house, Sarah daughter of Raguel came down from her upper room.

4 That same day Tobit remembered the money that he had left in trust with Gabael at Rages in Media, 2 and he said to himself, "Now I have asked for death. Why do I not call my son Tobias and explain to him about the money before I die?" 3 Then he called his son Tobias, and when he came to him he said, "My son, when I die,*t* give me a proper burial. Honor your mother and do not abandon her all the days of her life. Do whatever pleases her, and do not grieve her in anything. 4 Remember her, my son, because

been given in marriage to seven husbands and, before the marriages could be duly consummated, each one of them had been killed by the evil demon Asmodaeus. The servant said to her: 'It is you who kill your husbands! You have already been given in marriage to seven, and you have not borne the name of any one of them. 9 Why punish us because they are dead? Go and join your husbands. I hope we never see son or daughter of yours!'

10 Deeply distressed at that, she went in tears to the roof-chamber of her father's house, meaning to hang herself. But she had second thoughts and said to herself: 'Perhaps they will taunt my father and say, "You had one dear daughter and she hanged herself because of her troubles," and so I shall bring my aged father in sorrow to his grave. No, I will not hang myself; it would be better to beg the Lord to let me die and not live on to hear such reproaches.' 11 Thereupon she spread out her hands towards the window in prayer saying: 'Praise be to you, merciful God, praise to your name for evermore; let all your creation praise you for ever! 12 And now I lift up my eyes and look to you. 13 Command that I be removed from the earth, never again to hear such taunts.

14 'You know, Lord, that I am a virgin, guiltless of intercourse with any man; 15 I have not dishonoured my name or my father's name in the land of my exile. I am my father's only child; he has no other to be his heir, nor has he any near kinsman or relative who might marry me and for whom I should stay alive. Already seven husbands of mine have died; what have I to live for any longer? But if it is not your will, Lord, to let me die, have regard to me in your mercy and spare me those taunts.'

16 At that very moment the prayers of both were heard in the glorious presence of God, 17 and Raphael was sent to cure the two of them: Tobit by removing the white patches from his eyes so that he might see God's light again, and Sarah daughter of Raguel by giving her in marriage to Tobias son of Tobit and by setting her free from the evil demon Asmodaeus, for it was the destiny of Tobias and of no other suitor to possess her. At the moment when Tobit went back into his house from the courtyard, Sarah came down from her father's roof-chamber.

4 THAT same day Tobit remembered the money he had deposited with Gabael at Rages in Media, 2 and he said to himself, 'I have asked for death; before I die I ought to send for my son Tobias and explain to him about this money.' 3 So he sent for Tobias and, when he came, said to him: 'When I die, give me decent burial. Honour your mother, and do not abandon her as long as she lives; do what will please her, and never grieve her heart in any way. 4 Remem-

---

q Other ancient authorities read *strangles*   *r* Other ancient
authorities read *have had no benefit from*   *s* Other ancient
authorities lack *Lord*   *t* Lat

to seven husbands, but the wicked demon Asmodeus killed them off before they could have intercourse with her, as it is prescribed for wives. So the maid said to her: "You are the one who strangles your husbands! Look at you! You have already been married seven times, but you have had no joy with any one of your husbands. 9 Why do you beat us? Because your husbands are dead? Then why not join them! May we never see a son or daughter of yours!"

10 That day she was deeply grieved in spirit. She went in tears to an upstairs room in her father's house with the intention of hanging herself. But she reconsidered, saying to herself: "No! People would level this insult against my father: 'You had only one beloved daughter, but she hanged herself because of ill fortune!' And thus would I cause my father in his old age to go down to the nether world laden with sorrow. It is far better for me not to hang myself, but to beg the Lord to have me die, so that I need no longer live to hear such insults."

11 At that time, then, she spread out her hands, and facing the window, poured out this prayer:

"Blessed are you, O Lord, merciful God!
Forever blessed and honored is your holy name;
may all your works forever bless you.
12 And now, O Lord, to you I turn my face
and raise my eyes.
13 Bid me to depart from the earth,
never again to hear such insults.

14 "You know, O Master, that I am innocent
of any impure act with a man,
15 And that I have never defiled my own name
or my father's name in the land of my exile.

"I am my father's only daughter,
and he has no other child to make his heir,
Nor does he have a close kinsman or other relative
whom I might bide my time to marry.
I have already lost seven husbands;
why then should I live any longer?
But if it please you, Lord, not to slay me,
look favorably upon me and have pity on me;
never again let me hear these insults!"

16 At that very time, the prayer of these two suppliants was heard in the glorious presence of Almighty God. 17 So Raphael was sent to heal them both: to remove the cataracts from Tobit's eyes, so that he might again see God's sunlight; and to marry Raguel's daughter Sarah to Tobit's son Tobiah, and then drive the wicked demon Asmodeus from her. For Tobiah had the right to claim her before any other who might wish to marry her.

In the very moment that Tobit returned from the courtyard to his house, Raguel's daughter Sarah came downstairs from her room.

4 That same day Tobit remembered the money he had deposited with Gabael at Rages in Media, and he thought, 2 "Now that I have asked for death, why should I not call my son Tobiah and let him know about this money before I die?" 3 So he called his son Tobiah; and when he came, he said to him: "My son, when I die, give me a decent burial. Honor your mother, and do not abandon her as long as she lives. Do whatever pleases her, and do not grieve her spirit in any way. 4 Remember, my son, that she

marriage seven times, and Asmodeus, the worst of demons, had killed her bridegrooms one after another before ever they had slept with her as man with wife. The servant-girl said, 'Yes, you kill your bridegrooms yourself. That makes seven already to whom you have been given, and you have not once been in luck yet. 9 Just because your bridegrooms have died, that is no reason for punishing us. Go and join them, and may we be spared the sight of any child of yours!' 10 That day, she grieved, she sobbed, and she went up to her father's room intending to hang herself. But then she thought, 'Suppose they were to blame my father! They would say, "You had an only daughter whom you loved, and now she has hanged herself for grief." I cannot cause my father a sorrow which would bring down his old age to the dwelling of the dead. I should do better not to hang myself, but to beg the Lord to let me die and not live to hear any more insults.' 11 And at this, by the window, with outstretched arms she said this prayer:

You are blessed, O God of mercy!
May your name be blessed for ever,
and may all things you have made
bless you everlastingly.
12 And now I turn my face
and I raise my eyes to you.
13 Let your word deliver me from earth;
I can hear myself insulted no longer.

14 O Lord, you know
that I have remained pure;
no man has touched me;
15 I have not dishonoured your name
or my father's name
in this land of exile.

I am my father's only daughter,
he has no other child as heir;
he has no brother at his side,
nor has he any kinsman left
for whom I ought to keep myself.

I have lost seven husbands already;
why should I live any longer?
If it does not please you to take my life,
then look on me with pity;
I can no longer bear to hear myself defamed.

16 This time the prayer of each of them found favour before the glory of God, 17 and Raphael was sent to bring remedy to them both. He was to take the white spots from the eyes of Tobit, so that he might see God's light with his own eyes; and he was to give Sarah the daughter of Raguel as bride to Tobias son of Tobit, and to rid her of Asmodeus, that worst of demons. For it was to Tobias before all other suitors that she belonged by right. Tobit was coming back from the courtyard into the house at the same moment as Sarah the daughter of Raguel was coming down from the upper room.

4 The same day Tobit remembered the silver that he had left with Gabael at Rhages in Media 2 and thought, 'I have come to the point of praying for death; I should do well to call my son Tobias and tell him about the money before I die.' 3 He summoned his son Tobias and told him, 'When I die, give me an honourable burial. Honour your mother, and never abandon her all the days of your life. Do all that she wants, and give her no reason for sorrow. 4 Remember,

NEW REVISED STANDARD VERSION

she faced many dangers for you while you were in her womb. And when she dies, bury her beside me in the same grave.

5 "Revere the Lord all your days, my son, and refuse to sin or to transgress his commandments. Live uprightly all the days of your life, and do not walk in the ways of wrongdoing; 6 for those who act in accordance with truth will prosper in all their activities. To all those who practice righteousness[u] 7 give alms from your possessions, and do not let your eye begrudge the gift when you make it. Do not turn your face away from anyone who is poor, and the face of God will not be turned away from you. 8 If you have many possessions, make your gift from them in proportion; if few, do not be afraid to give according to the little you have. 9 So you will be laying up a good treasure for yourself against the day of necessity. 10 For almsgiving delivers from death and keeps you from going into the Darkness. 11 Indeed, almsgiving, for all who practice it, is an excellent offering in the presence of the Most High.

12 "Beware, my son, of every kind of fornication. First of all, marry a woman from among the descendants of your ancestors; do not marry a foreign woman, who is not of your father's tribe; for we are the descendants of the prophets. Remember, my son, that Noah, Abraham, Isaac, and Jacob, our ancestors of old, all took wives from among their kindred. They were blessed in their children, and their posterity will inherit the land. 13 So now, my son, love your kindred, and in your heart do not disdain your kindred, the sons and daughters of your people, by refusing to take a wife for yourself from among them. For in pride there is ruin and great confusion. And in idleness there is loss and dire poverty, because idleness is the mother of famine.

14 "Do not keep over until the next day the wages of those who work for you, but pay them at once. If you serve God you will receive payment. "Watch yourself, my son, in everything you do, and discipline yourself in all your conduct. 15 And what you hate, do not do to anyone. Do not drink wine to excess or let drunkenness go with you on your way. 16 Give some of your food to the hungry, and some of your clothing to the naked. Give all your surplus as alms, and do not let your eye begrudge your giving of alms. 17 Place your bread on the grave of the righteous, but give none to sinners. 18 Seek advice from every wise person and do not despise any useful counsel. 19 At all times bless the Lord God, and ask him that your ways may be made straight and that all your paths and plans may prosper. For none of the nations has understanding, but the Lord himself will give them good counsel; but if he chooses otherwise, he casts down to deepest Hades. So now, my child, remember these commandments, and do not let them be erased from your heart.

20 "And now, my son, let me explain to you that I left ten talents of silver in trust with Gabael son of Gabrias, at Rages in Media. 21 Do not be afraid, my son, because we have become poor. You have great wealth if you fear God and flee from every sin and do what is good in the sight of the Lord your God."

5 Then Tobias answered his father Tobit, "I will do everything that you have commanded me, father; 2 but

REVISED ENGLISH BIBLE

ber, my son, all the hazards she faced for your sake while you were in her womb. When she dies, bury her beside me in the same grave.

5 'Keep the Lord in mind every day of your life, my son, and never deliberately do what is wrong or violate his commandments. As long as you live do what is right, and avoid evil ways; 6 for an honest life leads to success in any undertaking, and to all who do right the Lord will give good counsel.

7 'Distribute alms from what you possess and never with a grudging eye. Do not turn your face away from any poor man, and God will not turn away his face from you. 8 Let your almsgiving match your means. If you have little, do not be ashamed to give the little you can afford; 9 you will be laying up sound insurance against the day of adversity. 10 Almsgiving preserves the giver from death and keeps him from going down into darkness. 11 All who give alms are making an offering acceptable to the Most High.

12 'Be on your guard, my son, against fornication; and above all choose your wife from the race of your ancestors. Do not take a foreign wife, one not of your father's tribe, for we are descendants of the prophets. My son, remember that back to the earliest days our ancestors, Noah, Abraham, Isaac, Jacob, all chose wives from their kindred. They were blessed in their children, and their descendants will possess the land. 13 So you too, my son, must love your kindred; do not be too proud to take a wife from among the women of your own nation. Such pride breeds ruin and disorder, and the waster declines into poverty; waste is the mother of starvation.

14 'Pay any man who works for you his wages that same day; let no one wait for his money. If you serve God, you will be repaid. Be circumspect, my son, in all that you do, and in all your behaviour be true to your upbringing. 15 Do to no one what you yourself would hate. Do not drink to excess or let drunkenness become a habit. 16 Share your food with the hungry, your clothes with those who have none. Whatever you have beyond your own needs, distribute in alms, and do not give with a grudging look. 17 Pour out your wine and offer your bread on the tombs of the righteous; but give nothing to sinners. 18 Seek advice from every sensible person; do not despise any advice that may be of use. 19 Praise the Lord God at all times and ask him to guide your steps; then all you do and all you plan will be crowned with success. The heathen lack such guidance; it is the Lord himself who gives all good things and who humbles whomsoever he chooses to the lowly grave. Now remember those injunctions, my son; let them never be effaced from your mind.

20 'And now, my son, I should tell you that I have ten talents of silver on deposit with Gabael son of Gabri at Rages in Media. 21 Do not be anxious because we have become poor; there is great wealth awaiting you, if only you fear God and avoid all wickedness and do what is good in the sight of the Lord your God.'

5 Tobias said: 'I will do all that you have told me, father. 2 But how shall I be able to recover this money from

---

[u] The text of codex Sinaiticus goes directly from verse 6 to verse 19, reading *To those who practice righteousness* 19*the Lord will give good counsel.* In order to fill the lacuna verses 7 to 18 are derived from other ancient authorities

went through many trials for your sake while you were in her womb. And when she dies, bury her in the same grave with me.

5 "Through all your days, my son, keep the Lord in mind, and suppress every desire to sin or to break his commandments. Perform good works all the days of your life, and do not tread the paths of wrongdoing. 6 For if you are steadfast in your service, your good works will bring success, not only to you, but also to all those who live uprightly.

7 "Give alms from your possessions. Do not turn your face away from any of the poor, and God's face will not be turned away from you. 8 Son, give alms in proportion to what you own. If you have great wealth, give alms out of your abundance; if you have but little, distribute even some of that. But do not hesitate to give alms; 9 you will be storing up a goodly treasure for yourself against the day of adversity. 10 Almsgiving frees one from death, and keeps one from going into the dark abode. 11 Alms are a worthy offering in the sight of the Most High for all who give them.

12 "Be on your guard, son, against every form of immorality, and above all, marry a woman of the lineage of your forefathers. Do not marry a stranger who is not of your father's tribe, because we are sons of the prophets. My boy, keep in mind Noah, Abraham, Isaac, and Jacob, our fathers from of old; all of them took wives from among their own kinsmen and were blessed in their children. Remember that their posterity shall inherit the land. 13 Therefore, my son, love your kinsmen. Do not be so proudhearted toward your kinsmen, the sons and daughters of your people, as to refuse to take a wife for yourself from among them. For in such arrogance there is ruin and great disorder. Likewise, in worthlessness there is decay and dire poverty, for worthlessness is the mother of famine.

14 "Do not keep with you overnight the wages of any man who works for you, but pay him immediately. If you thus behave as God's servant, you will receive your reward. Keep a close watch on yourself, my son, in everything you do, and discipline yourself in all your conduct. 15 Do to no one what you yourself dislike. Do not drink wine till you become drunk, nor let drunkenness accompany you on your way.

16 "Give to the hungry some of your bread, and to the naked some of your clothing. Whatever you have left over, give away as alms; and do not begrudge the alms you give. 17 Be lavish with your bread and wine at the burial of the virtuous, but do not share them with sinners.

18 "Seek counsel from every wise man, and do not think lightly of any advice that can be useful. 19 At all times bless the Lord God, and ask him to make all your paths straight and to grant success to all your endeavors and plans. For no pagan nation possesses good counsel, but the Lord himself gives all good things. If the Lord chooses, he raises a man up; but if he should decide otherwise, he casts him down to the deepest recesses of the nether world. So now, my son, keep in mind my commandments, and never let them be erased from your heart.

20 "And now, son, I wish to inform you that I have deposited a great sum of money with Gabri's son Gabael at Rages in Media. 21 Do not be discouraged, my child, because of our poverty. You will be a rich man if you fear God, avoid all sin, and do what is right before the Lord your God."

5 Then Tobiah replied to his father Tobit: "Everything that you have commanded me, father, I will do. 2 But

my child, all the risks she ran for your sake when you were in her womb. And when she dies, bury her at my side in the same grave.

5 'My child, be faithful to the Lord all your days. Never entertain the will to sin or to transgress his laws. Do good works all the days of your life, never follow ways that are not upright; 6 for if you act in truthfulness, you will be successful in all your actions, as everyone is who practises what is upright.

7 'Set aside part of your goods for almsgiving. Never turn your face from the poor and God will never turn his from you. 8 Measure your alms by what you have; if you have much, give more; if you have little, do not be afraid to give less in alms. 9 So doing, you will lay up for yourself a great treasure for the day of necessity. 10 For almsgiving delivers from death and saves people from passing down to darkness. 11 Almsgiving is a most effective offering for all those who do it in the presence of the Most High.

12 'My child, avoid all loose conduct. Choose a wife of your father's stock. Do not take a foreign wife outside your father's tribe, because we are the children of the prophets. Remember Noah, Abraham, Isaac and Jacob, our ancestors from the beginning. All of them took wives from their own kindred, and they were blessed in their children, and their race will inherit the earth. 13 You, too, my child, must love your own brothers; never presume to despise your brothers, the sons and daughters of your people; choose your wife from among them. For pride brings ruin and much worry; idleness causes need and poverty, for the mother of famine is idleness.

14 'Do not keep back until next day the wages of those who work for you; pay them at once. If you serve God you will be rewarded. Be careful, my child, in all you do, well-disciplined in all your behaviour. 15 Do to no one what you would not want done to you. Do not drink wine to the point of drunkenness; do not let excess be your travelling companion.

16 'Give your bread to those who are hungry, and your clothes to those who lack clothing. Of whatever you own in plenty, devote a proportion to almsgiving; and when you give alms, do it ungrudgingly. 17 Be generous with bread and wine on the graves of upright people, but not for the sinner.

18 'Ask advice of every wise person; never scorn any profitable advice. 19 Bless the Lord God in everything; beg him to guide your ways and bring your paths and purposes to their end. For wisdom is not the property of every nation; their desire for what is good is conferred by the Lord. At his will he lifts up or he casts down to the depths of the dwelling of the dead. So now, my child, remember these precepts and never let them fade from your heart.

20 'Now, my child, I must tell you I have left ten talents of silver with Gabael son of Gabrias, at Rhages in Media. 21 Do not be afraid, my child, if we have grown poor. You have great wealth if you fear God, if you shun every kind of sin and if you do what is pleasing to the Lord your God.'

5 Tobias then replied to his father Tobit, 'Father, I shall do everything you have told me. 2 But how am I to

how can I obtain the money^y from him, since he does not know me and I do not know him? What evidence^w am I to give him so that he will recognize and trust me, and give me the money? Also, I do not know the roads to Media, or how to get there." 3 Then Tobit answered his son Tobias, "He gave me his bond and I gave him my bond. I^x divided his in two; we each took one part, and I put one with the money. And now twenty years have passed since I left this money in trust. So now, my son, find yourself a trustworthy man to go with you, and we will pay him wages until you return. But get back the money from Gabael."^y

4 So Tobias went out to look for a man to go with him to Media, someone who was acquainted with the way. He went out and found the angel Raphael standing in front of him; but he did not perceive that he was an angel of God. 5 Tobias^z said to him, "Where do you come from, young man?" "From your kindred, the Israelites," he replied, "and I have come here to work." Then Tobias^a said to him, "Do you know the way to go to Media?" 6 "Yes," he replied, "I have been there many times; I am acquainted with it and know all the roads. I have often traveled to Media, and would stay with our kinsman Gabael who lives in Rages of Media. It is a journey of two days from Ecbatana to Rages; for it lies in a mountainous area, while Ecbatana is in the middle of the plain." 7 Then Tobias said to him, "Wait for me, young man, until I go in and tell my father; for I do need you to travel with me, and I will pay you your wages." 8 He replied, "All right, I will wait; but do not take too long."

9 So Tobias^a went in to tell his father Tobit and said to him, "I have just found a man who is one of our own Israelite kindred!" He replied, "Call the man in, my son, so that I may learn about his family and to what tribe he belongs, and whether he is trustworthy enough to go with you."

10 Then Tobias went out and called him, and said, "Young man, my father is calling for you." So he went in to him, and Tobit greeted him first. He replied, "Joyous greetings to you!" But Tobit retorted, "What joy is left for me any more? I am a man without eyesight; I cannot see the light of heaven, but I lie in darkness like the dead who no longer see the light. Although still alive, I am among the dead. I hear people but I cannot see them." But the young man^a said, "Take courage; the time is near for God to heal you; take courage." Then Tobit said to him, "My son Tobias wishes to go to Media. Can you accompany him and guide him? I will pay your wages, brother." He answered, "I can go with him and I know all the roads, for I have often gone to Media and have crossed all its plains, and I am familiar with its mountains and all of its roads."

11 Then Tobit^a said to him, "Brother, of what family are you and from what tribe? Tell me, brother." 12 He replied, "Why do you need to know my tribe?" But Tobit^a said, "I want to be sure, brother, whose son you are and what your name is." 13 He replied, "I am Azariah, the son of the great Hananiah, one of your relatives." 14 Then Tobit said to him, "Welcome! God save you, brother. Do not feel bitter toward me, brother, because I wanted to be sure about your ancestry. It turns out that you are a kinsman, and of good and noble lineage. For I knew Hananiah and Nathan,^b the two sons of Shemeliah,^c and they used to go with me to Jerusalem and worshiped with me there, and were not led astray. Your kindred are good people; you come of good stock. Hearty welcome!"

Gabael, since he does not know me and I do not know him? What proof of identity shall I give him to make him trust me and give me the money? Besides, I do not know the roads which would get me to Media.' 3 To this Tobit replied: 'He gave me his note of hand, and I divided it in two and we took one part each. I kept one half of it and put half with the money. It is all of twenty years since I deposited that money! Now, my son, find someone reliable to go with you, and we shall pay him his wages up to the time of your return; then go and recover the money from Gabael.'

4 Tobias went out to look for someone who knew the way and would accompany him to Media, and found himself face to face with the angel Raphael. 5 Not knowing he was an angel of God, he questioned him: 'Where do you come from, young man?' 'I am an Israelite,' he replied, 'one of your fellow-countrymen, and I have come here to find work.' Tobias asked, 'Do you know the road to Media?' 6 'Yes,' he said, 'I have been there many times; I am familiar with all the routes, I know them well. I have frequently travelled into Media and used to stay with Gabael our fellow-countryman who lives there in Rages. It is two full days' journey to Rages from Ecbatana; for Rages is situated in the hills, and Ecbatana lies in the middle of the plain.' 7 Tobias said: 'Wait for me, young man, while I go in and tell my father. I need you to go with me and I shall pay you for it.' 8 'Very well, I shall wait,' he answered, 'only do not be long.'

Tobias went in and told his father. 'I have found a fellow-Israelite to accompany me,' he said. His father replied, 'Call him in; I must find out the man's family and tribe and make sure, my son, that he will be a trustworthy companion for you.'

9 Tobias went out and called him: 'Young man, my father is asking for you.' When he entered, Tobit greeted him first. To Raphael's reply, 'May all be well with you!' Tobit retorted: 'How can anything be well with me any more? I am now blind; I cannot see the light of heaven, but lie in darkness like the dead who can no longer see the light. Though still alive, I am as good as dead. I hear voices, but I cannot see those speaking.' Raphael answered: 'Take heart; in God's design your cure is at hand. Take heart!' Tobit went on: 'My son Tobias wishes to travel to Media. Can you go with him as his guide? I shall pay you, my friend.' 'Yes,' he said, 'I can go with him. I know all the roads, for I have often been to Media. I have travelled over all the plains and mountains there and am familiar with the whole way.' 10 Tobit said to him, 'Tell me, my friend, what family and tribe do you belong to?' 11 He asked, 'Why do you need to know my tribe?' Tobit said, 'I wish to know whose son you are, my friend, and what your name is.' 12 'I am Azarias,' he replied, 'son of the older Ananias, one of your kinsmen.'

13 Tobit said to him: 'Welcome, may all be well with you! Do not be angry with me, my friend, for wanting to know all about you and your parentage. You are, as it turns out, a kinsman and a man of good and honourable family. I knew Ananias and Nathan, the two sons of the older Semelias. They used to go with me to Jerusalem and worship with me there; they were never led into error. Your kinsmen are worthy men; you come of a sound stock. You are indeed

---

^vGk it   ^wGk sign   ^xOther authorities read He   ^yGk from him   ^zGk He   ^aGk he   ^bOther ancient authorities read Jathan or Nathamiah   ^cOther ancient authorities read Shemaiah

5:6 **in Rages:** so one Vs. (cp. 4:1); Gk in Ecbatana.

how shall I be able to obtain the money from him, since he does not know me nor do I know him? What can I show him to make him recognize me and trust me, so that he will give me the money? I do not even know which roads to take for the journey into Media!" ³Tobit answered his son Tobiah: "We exchanged signatures on a document written in duplicate; I divided it into two parts, and each of us kept one; his copy I put with the money. Think of it, twenty years have already passed since I deposited that money! So now, my son, find yourself a trustworthy man who will make the journey with you. We will, of course, give him a salary when you return; but get back that money from Gabael."

⁴Tobiah went to look for someone acquainted with the roads who would travel with him to Media. As soon as he went out, he found the angel Raphael standing before him, though he did not know that this was an angel of God. ⁵Tobiah said to him, "Who are you, young man?" He replied, "I am an Israelite, one of your kinsmen. I have come here to work." Tobiah said, "Do you know the way to Media?" ⁶The other replied: "Yes, I have been there many times. I know the place well and I know all the routes. I have often traveled to Media; I used to stay with our kinsman Gabael, who lives at Rages in Media. It is a good two days' travel from Ecbatana to Rages, for Rages is situated at the mountains, Ecbatana out on the plateau." ⁷Tobiah said to him, "Wait for me, young man, till I go back and tell my father; for I need you to make the journey with me. I will, of course, pay you." ⁸Raphael replied, "Very well, I will wait for you; but do not be long."

⁹Tobiah went back to tell his father Tobit what had happened. He said to him, "I have just found a man who is one of our own Israelite kinsmen!" Tobit said, "Call the man, so that I may find out what family and tribe he comes from, and whether he is trustworthy enough to travel with you, son." Tobiah went out to summon the man saying, "Young man, my father would like to see you."

¹⁰When Raphael entered the house, Tobit greeted him first. Raphael said, "Hearty greetings to you!" Tobit replied: "What joy is left for me any more? Here I am, a blind man who cannot see God's sunlight, but must remain in darkness, like the dead who no longer see the light! Though alive, I am among the dead. I can hear a man's voice, but I cannot see him." Raphael said, "Take courage! God has healing in store for you; so take courage!" Tobit then said: "My son Tobiah wants to go to Media. Can you go with him to show him the way? I will of course pay you, brother." Raphael answered: "Yes, I can go with him, for I know all the routes. I have often traveled to Media and crossed all its plains and mountains; so I know every road well." ¹¹Tobit asked, "Brother, tell me, please, what family and tribe are you from?" ¹²Raphael said: "Why? Do you need a tribe and a family? Or are you looking for a hired man to travel with your son?" Tobit replied, "I wish to know truthfully whose son you are, brother, and what your name is."

¹³Raphael answered, "I am Azariah, son of Hananiah the elder, one of your own kinsmen." ¹⁴Tobit exclaimed: "Welcome! God save you, brother! Do not be provoked with me, brother, for wanting to learn the truth about your family. So it turns out that you are a kinsman, and from a noble and good line! I knew Hananiah and Nathaniah, the two sons of Shemaiah the elder; with me they used to make the pilgrimage to Jerusalem, where we would worship together. No, they did not stray from the right path; your kinsmen are good men. You are certainly of good lineage, and welcome!"

recover the silver from him? He does not know me, nor I him. What token am I to give him for him to believe me and hand the silver over to me? And besides, I do not know what roads to take for this journey into Media.' ³Then Tobit answered his son Tobias, 'Each of us set his signature to a note which I cut in two, so that each could keep half of it. I took one piece, and put the other with the silver. To think it was twenty years ago I left this silver in his keeping! And now, my child, find a trustworthy travelling companion — we shall pay him for his time until you arrive back — and then go and collect the silver from Gabael.'

⁴Tobias went out to look for a man who knew the way to go with him to Media. Outside he found Raphael the angel standing facing him, though he did not guess he was an angel of God. ⁵He said, 'Where do you come from, friend?' The angel replied, 'I am one of your brother Israelites; I have come to these parts to look for work.' Tobias asked, 'Do you know the road to Media?' ⁶The other replied, 'Certainly I do, I have been there many times; I have knowledge and experience of all the ways. I have often been to Media and stayed with Gabael one of our kinsmen who lives at Rhages in Media. It usually takes two full days to get from Ecbatana to Rhages; Rhages lies in the mountains, and Ecbatana is in the middle of the plain.' ⁷Tobias said, 'Wait for me, friend, while I go and tell my father; I need you to come with me; I shall pay you for your time.' ⁸The other replied, 'Good, I shall wait; but do not be long.'

⁹Tobias went in and told his father that he had found one of their brother Israelites. And the father said, 'Fetch him in; I want to find out about his family and tribe. I must see if he is going to be a reliable companion for you, my child.' So Tobias went out and called him, 'Friend,' he said, 'my father wants you.'

¹⁰The angel came into the house; Tobit greeted him, and the other answered, wishing him happiness in plenty. Tobit replied, 'Can I ever be happy again? I am a blind man; I no longer see the light of heaven; I am sunk in darkness like the dead who see the light no more. I am a man buried alive; I hear people speak but cannot see them.' The angel said, 'Take comfort; before long God will heal you. Take comfort.' Tobit said, 'My son Tobias wishes to go to Media. Will you join him as his guide? Brother, I will pay you.' He replied, 'I am willing to go with him; I know all the ways; I have often been to Media, I have crossed all its plains and mountains, and I know all its roads.' ¹¹Tobit said, 'Brother, what family and what tribe do you belong to? Will you tell me, brother?' ¹²'What does my tribe matter to you?' the angel said. Tobit said, 'I want to be quite sure whose son you are and what your name is.' ¹³The angel said, 'I am Azarias, son of the great Ananias, one of your kinsmen.' ¹⁴'Welcome and greetings, brother! Do not be offended at my wanting to know the name of your family; I find you are my kinsman of a good and honourable line. I know Ananias and Nathan, the two sons of the great Shemaiah. They used to go to Jerusalem with me; we have worshipped together there and they have never strayed from the right path. Your brothers are worthy men; you come of good stock; welcome.'

NEW REVISED STANDARD VERSION

15 Then he added, "I will pay you a drachma a day as wages, as well as expenses for yourself and my son. So go with my son, 16 and *d* I will add something to your wages." Raphael *e* answered, "I will go with him; so do not fear. We shall leave in good health and return to you in good health, because the way is safe." 17 So Tobit *f* said to him, "Blessings be upon you, brother."

Then he called his son and said to him, "Son, prepare supplies for the journey and set out with your brother. May God in heaven bring you safely there and return you in good health to me; and may his angel, my son, accompany you both for your safety."

Before he went out to start his journey, he kissed his father and mother. Tobit then said to him, "Have a safe journey."

18 But his mother *g* began to weep, and said to Tobit, "Why is it that you have sent my child away? Is he not the staff of our hand as he goes in and out before us? 19 Do not heap money upon money, but let it be a ransom for our child. 20 For the life that is given to us by the Lord is enough for us." 21 Tobit *e* said to her, "Do not worry; our child will leave in good health and return to us in good health. Your eyes will see him on the day when he returns to you in good health. Say no more! Do not fear for them, my sister. 22 For a good angel will accompany him; his journey will be successful, and he will come back in good health."

6 1 So she stopped weeping.

The young man went out and the angel went with him; 2 and the dog came out with him and went along with them. So they both journeyed along, and when the first night overtook them they camped by the Tigris river. 3 Then the young man went down to wash his feet in the Tigris river. Suddenly a large fish leaped up from the water and tried to swallow the young man's foot, and he cried out. 4 But the angel said to the young man, "Catch hold of the fish and hang on to it!" So the young man grasped the fish and drew it up on the land. 5 Then the angel said to him, "Cut open the fish and take out its gall, heart, and liver. Keep them with you, but throw away the intestines. For its gall, heart, and liver are useful as medicine." 6 So after cutting open the fish the young man gathered together the gall, heart, and liver; then he roasted and ate some of the fish, and kept some to be salted.

The two continued on their way together until they were near Media. *h* 7 Then the young man questioned the angel and said to him, "Brother Azariah, what medicinal value is there in the fish's heart and liver, and in the gall?" 8 He replied, "As for the fish's heart and liver, you must burn them to make a smoke in the presence of a man or woman afflicted by a demon or evil spirit, and every affliction will flee away and never remain with that person any longer. 9 And as for the gall, anoint a person's eyes where white films have appeared on them; blow upon them, upon the white films, and the eyes *i* will be healed."

10 When he entered Media and already was approaching Ecbatana, *j* 11 Raphael said to the young man, "Brother Tobias." "Here I am," he answered. Then Raphael *f* said to him, "We must stay this night in the home of Raguel. He is your relative, and he has a daughter named Sarah. 12 He has no male heir and no daughter except Sarah only, and you, as next of kin to her, have before all other men a hereditary claim on her. Also it is right for you to inherit her father's possessions. Moreover, the girl is sensible, brave, and very beautiful, and her father is a good man." 13 He

REVISED ENGLISH BIBLE

welcome.' 14 And he added: 'I shall pay you a drachma a day and allow you the same expenses as my son. 15 Accompany him, and I shall give you something over and above your wage.' 16 Raphael agreed: 'I shall go with him. Never fear; we shall travel there and back without mishap, for the road is not dangerous.' Tobit said to him, 'God bless you, my friend!' He called his son and said: 'My son, get ready what you need for the journey and go with your kinsman. May God in heaven preserve you both on your journey there, and restore you to me safe and sound. May his angel safely escort you both, my son.' Before setting out Tobias kissed his father and mother, and Tobit wished him a safe journey.

17 Then his mother burst into tears. 'Why must you send my boy away?' she said to Tobit. 'Is he not the staff on which we lean? Do we not depend on him at every turn? 18 Why the haste to lay out money for money? For the sake of our boy write it off! 19 Let us be content to live the life appointed for us by the Lord.' 20 'Do not worry,' replied Tobit, 'our son will go safely and come back safely, and you will see him with your own eyes on the day of his return. Do not worry or be anxious about them, my dear. 21 A good angel will go with him; his journey will prosper and he will come back without mishap.' 22 At that she stopped weeping.

6 THE youth and the angel left the house together; the dog followed Tobias out and accompanied them. They travelled until night overtook them, and then camped by the river Tigris. 2 Tobias went down to bathe his feet in the river, and a huge fish leapt out of the water and tried to swallow his foot. He cried out, 3 and the angel said to him, 'Seize the fish and hold it fast.' So Tobias caught hold of it and dragged it up on the bank. 4 The angel said: 'Split open the fish and take out its gall, heart, and liver; keep them by you, but throw the guts away; the gall, heart, and liver can be used as remedies.' 5 Tobias split the fish open, and put its gall, heart, and liver on one side. He broiled and ate part of the fish; the rest he salted and kept.

They continued the journey together, and when they came near to Media 6 the youth asked the angel: 'Azarias, my friend, what remedy is there in the fish's heart and liver and in its gall?' 7 He replied: 'You can use the heart and liver as a fumigation for any man or woman attacked by a demon or evil spirit; the attack will cease, and it will give no further trouble. 8 The gall is for anointing a person's eyes when white patches have spread over them; after one has blown on the patches, the eyes will recover.'

9 When he had entered Media and was already approaching Ecbatana, 10 Raphael said to the youth, 'Tobias, my friend.' 'Yes?' he replied. Raphael said: 'We must stay tonight with Raguel, who is a relative of yours. He has a daughter named Sarah, but no other children, neither sons nor daughters. 11 You as her next of kin have the right to marry her and inherit her father's property. 12 The girl is sensible, brave, and very beautiful indeed, and her father is

---

d Other ancient authorities add *when you return safely*   *e* Gk He
f Gk *he*   *g* Other ancient authorities add *Anna*   *h* Other ancient authorities read *Ecbatana*   *i* Gk *they*   *j* Other ancient authorities read *Rages*

15 Then he added: "For each day you are away I will give you the normal wages, plus expenses for you and for my son. If you go with my son, 16 I will even add a bonus to your wages!" Raphael replied: "I will go with him; have no fear. In good health we shall leave you, and in good health we shall return to you, for the way is safe." 17 Tobit said, "God bless you, brother." Then he called his son and said to him: "My son, prepare whatever you need for the journey, and set out with your kinsman. May God in heaven protect you on the way and bring you back to me safe and sound; and may his angel accompany you for safety, my son."

Before setting out on his journey, Tobiah kissed his father and mother. Tobit said to him, "Have a safe journey." 18 But his mother began to weep. She said to Tobit: "Why have you decided to send my child away? Is he not the staff to which we cling, ever there with us in all that we do? 19 I hope more money is not your chief concern! Rather let it be a ransom for our son! 20 What the Lord has given us to live on is certainly enough for us." 21 Tobit reassured her: "Have no such thought. Our son will leave in good health and come back to us in good health. Your own eyes will see the day when he returns to you safe and sound. 22 So, no such thought; do not worry about them, my love. For a good angel will go with him, his journey will be successful, and he will return unharmed." 1 Then she 6 stopped weeping.

2 When the boy left home, accompanied by the angel, the dog followed Tobiah out of the house and went with him. The travelers walked till nightfall, and made camp beside the Tigris River. 3 Now when the boy went down to wash his feet in the river, a large fish suddenly leaped out of the water and tried to swallow his foot. He shouted in alarm. 4 But the angel said to him, "Take hold of the fish and don't let it get away!" The boy seized the fish and hauled it up on the shore. 5 The angel then told him: "Cut the fish open and take out its gall, heart, and liver, and keep them with you; but throw away the entrails. Its gall, heart, and liver make useful medicines." 6 After the lad had cut the fish open, he put aside the gall, heart, and liver. Then he broiled and ate part of the fish; the rest he salted and kept for the journey.

7 Afterward they traveled on together till they were near Media. The boy asked the angel this question: "Brother Azariah, what medicinal value is there in the fish's heart, liver, and gall?" 8 He answered: "As regards the fish's heart and liver, if you burn them so that the smoke surrounds a man or a woman who is afflicted by a demon or evil spirit, the affliction will leave him completely, and no demons will ever return to him again. 9 And as for the gall, if you rub it on the eyes of a man who has cataracts, blowing into his eyes right on the cataracts, his sight will be restored."

10 When they had entered Media and were getting close to Ecbatana, 11 Raphael said to the boy, "Brother Tobiah!" He answered, "Yes, what is it?" Raphael continued: "Tonight we must stay with Raguel, who is a relative of yours. He has a daughter named Sarah, 12 but no other child. Since you are Sarah's closest relative, you before all other men have the right to marry her. Also, her father's estate is rightfully yours to inherit. Now the girl is sensible, courageous, and very beautiful; and her father loves her dearly."

15 He went on, 'I engage you at a drachma a day, with the same expenses as my own son's. Complete the journey with my son 16 and I shall go beyond the agreed wage.' The angel replied, 'I shall complete the journey with him. Do not be afraid. On the journey outward all will be well; on the journey back all will be well; the road is safe.' 17 Tobit said, 'Blessings on you, brother!' Then he turned to his son. 'My child', he said, 'prepare what you need for the journey, and set off with your brother. May God in heaven protect you abroad and bring you both back to me safe and sound! May his angel go with you and protect you, my child!'

Tobias left the house to set out and kissed his father and mother. Tobit said, 'A happy journey!' 18 His mother burst into tears and said to Tobit, 'Why must you send my child away? Is he not the staff of our hands, as he goes about before us? 19 Surely money is not the only thing that matters? Surely it is not as precious as our child? 20 The way of life God had already given us was good enough.' 21 He said, 'Do not think such thoughts. Going away and coming back, all will be well with our child. You will see for yourself when he comes back safe and sound! Do not think such thoughts; do not worry on their account, my sister. 22 A good angel will go with him; he will have a good journey and come back to us well and happy.'

6 And she dried her tears.

2 The boy left with the angel, and the dog followed behind. The two walked on, and when the first evening came they camped beside the Tigris. 3 The boy had gone down to the river to wash his feet, when a great fish leapt out of the water and tried to swallow his foot. The boy gave a shout 4 and the angel said, 'Catch the fish; do not let it go.' The boy mastered the fish and pulled it onto the bank. 5 The angel said, 'Cut it open; take out gall, heart and liver; set these aside and throw the entrails away, for gall and heart and liver have curative properties.' 6 The boy cut the fish open and took out gall and heart and liver. He fried part of the fish for his meal and kept some for salting. Then they walked on again together until they were nearly in Media.

7 Then the boy asked the angel this question, 'Brother Azarias, what can the fish's heart, liver and gall cure?' 8 He replied, 'You burn the fish's heart and liver, and their smoke is used in the case of a man or woman plagued by a demon or evil spirit; any such affliction disappears for good, leaving no trace. 9 As regards the gall, this is used as an eye ointment for anyone having white spots on his eyes; after using it, you have only to blow on the spots to cure them.'

10 They entered Media and had nearly reached Ecbatana 11 when Raphael said to the boy, 'Brother Tobias.' 'Yes?' he replied. The angel went on, 'Tonight we are to stay with Raguel, who is a kinsman of yours. He has a daughter called Sarah, 12 but apart from Sarah he has no other son or daughter. Now you are her next of kin; she belongs to you before anyone else and you may claim her father's inheritance. She is a thoughtful, courageous and very lovely girl, and her father loves her dearly. 13 You have the right to

continued, "You have every right to take her in marriage. So listen to me, brother; tonight I will speak to her father about the girl, so that we may take her to be your bride. When we return from Rages we will celebrate her marriage. For I know that Raguel can by no means keep her from you or promise her to another man without incurring the penalty of death according to the decree of the book of Moses. Indeed he knows that you, rather than any other man, are entitled to marry his daughter. So now listen to me, brother, and tonight we shall speak concerning the girl and arrange her engagement to you. And when we return from Rages we will take her and bring her back with us to your house."

14 Then Tobias said in answer to Raphael, "Brother Azariah, I have heard that she already has been married to seven husbands and that they died in the bridal chamber. On the night when they went in to her, they would die. I have heard people saying that it was a demon that killed them. 15 It does not harm her, but it kills anyone who desires to approach her. So now, since I am the only son my father has, I am afraid that I may die and bring my father's and mother's life down to their grave, grieving for me — and they have no other son to bury them."

16 But Raphael[k] said to him, "Do you not remember your father's orders when he commanded you to take a wife from your father's house? Now listen to me, brother, and say no more about this demon. Take her. I know that this very night she will be given to you in marriage. 17 When you enter the bridal chamber, take some of the fish's liver and heart, and put them on the embers of the incense. An odor will be given off; 18 the demon will smell it and flee, and will never be seen near her any more. Now when you are about to go to bed with her, both of you must first stand up and pray, imploring the Lord of heaven that mercy and safety may be granted to you. Do not be afraid, for she was set apart for you before the world was made. You will save her, and she will go with you. I presume that you will have children by her, and they will be as brothers to you. Now say no more!" When Tobias heard the words of Raphael and learned that she was his kinswoman,[l] related through his father's lineage, he loved her very much, and his heart was drawn to her.

7 Now when they[m] entered Ecbatana, Tobias[k] said to him, "Brother Azariah, take me straight to our brother Raguel." So he took him to Raguel's house, where they found him sitting beside the courtyard door. They greeted him first, and he replied, "Joyous greetings, brothers; welcome and good health!" Then he brought them into his house. 2 He said to his wife Edna, "How much the young man resembles my kinsman Tobit!" 3 Then Edna questioned them, saying, "Where are you from, brothers?" They answered, "We belong to the descendants of Naphtali who are exiles in Nineveh." 4 She said to them, "Do you know our kinsman Tobit?" And they replied, "Yes, we know him." Then she asked them, "Is he[n] in good health?" 5 They replied, "He is alive and in good health." And Tobias added, "He is my father!" 6 At that Raguel jumped up and kissed him and wept. 7 He also spoke to him as follows, "Blessings on you, my child, son of a good and noble father!"[o] "O most miserable of calamities that such an upright and beneficent man has become blind!" He then embraced his kinsman Tobias and wept. 8 His wife Edna also wept for him, and their daughter Sarah likewise wept.

an honourable man.' He went on: 'It is your right to marry her. Be guided by me, my friend; I shall speak to her father this very night and ask him to promise us the girl as your bride, and on our return from Rages we shall celebrate her marriage. I know that Raguel cannot withhold her from you or betroth her to another without incurring the death penalty according to the decree in the book of Moses; and he is aware that his daughter belongs by right to you rather than to any other man. Now be guided by me, my friend; we shall talk about the girl tonight and betroth her to you, and when we return from Rages we shall take her back with us to your home.'

13 At this Tobias protested: 'Azarias, my friend, I have heard she has already been given to seven husbands who died in the bridal chamber; the very night they went into the bridal chamber to her they died. 14 A demon kills them, I have been told. And now it is my turn to be afraid; he does her no harm, because he loves her, but he kills any man who tries to come near her. I am my father's only child, and I fear that, were I to die, grief for me would bring my father and mother to their grave; and they have no other son to bury them.'

15 Raphael said: 'But have you forgotten your father's instructions? He told you to take a wife from your father's kindred. Now be guided by me, my friend: marry Sarah, and do not worry about the demon. I am sure that this night she will be given to you as your wife. 16 When you enter the bridal chamber, take some of the fish's liver and its heart, and put them on the burning incense. The smell will spread, 17 and when it reaches the demon he will make off, never to be seen near her any more. When you are about to go to bed with her, both of you must first stand up and pray, beseeching the Lord of heaven to grant you mercy and protection. Have no fear; she was destined for you before the world was made. You will rescue her and she will go with you. I have no doubt that you will have children by her and they will be very dear to you. Now do not worry!' When Tobias heard what Raphael said, and learnt that Sarah was his kinswoman and of his father's house, he was filled with love for her and set his heart on her.

7 As they entered Ecbatana Tobias said, 'Azarias, my friend, take me straight to our kinsman Raguel.' So he took him to Raguel's house, where they found him sitting by the courtyard gate. They greeted him first, and he replied, 'Greetings to you, my friends. You are indeed welcome.' When he brought them into his house, 2 he said to Edna his wife, 'Is not this young man like my kinsman Tobit? 3 Edna questioned them, 'Friends, where do you come from?' 'We belong to the tribe of Naphtali, now in captivity at Nineveh,' they answered. 4 'Do you know our kinsman Tobit?' she asked, and they replied, 'Yes, we do.' 'Is he well?' she said. 5 'He is alive and well,' they answered, and Tobias added, 'He is my father.' 6 Raguel jumped up and, with tears in his eyes, he kissed him. 7 'God bless you, my boy,' he said, 'son of a good and upright father. But what a calamity that so just and charitable a man has lost his sight!' He embraced Tobias his kinsman and wept; 8 Edna his wife and their daughter Sarah also wept for Tobit.

k Gk he   l Gk sister   m Other ancient authorities read he
n Other ancient authorities add alive and   o Other ancient authorities
add When he heard that Tobit had lost his sight, he was stricken with
grief and wept. Then he said,

6:17 be very dear to you: lit. be like brothers to you.

13 He continued: "Since you have the right to marry her, listen to me, brother. Tonight I will ask the girl's father to let us have her as your bride. When we return from Rages, we will hold the wedding feast for her. I know that Raguel cannot keep her from you or let her become engaged to another man; that would be a capital crime according to the decree in the Book of Moses, and he knows that it is your right, before all other men, to marry his daughter. So heed my words, brother; tonight we must speak for the girl, so that we may have her engaged to you. And when we return from Rages, we will take her and bring her back with us to your house."

14 Tobiah objected, however: "Brother Azariah, I have heard that this woman has already been married seven times, and that her husbands died in their bridal chambers. On the very night they approached her, they dropped dead. And I have heard it said that it was a demon who killed them. 15 So now I too am afraid of this demon. Because he loves her, he does not harm her; but he does slay any man who wishes to come close to her. I am my father's only child. If I should die, I would bring my father and mother down to their grave in sorrow over me. And they have no other son to bury them!"

16 Raphael said to him: "Do you not remember your father's orders? He commanded you to marry a woman from your own family. So now listen to me, brother; do not give another thought to this demon, but marry Sarah. I know that tonight you shall have her for your wife! 17 When you go into the bridal chamber, take the fish's liver and heart, and place them on the embers for the incense. 18 As soon as the demon smells the odor they give off, he will flee and never again show himself near her. Then when you are about to have intercourse with her, both of you first rise up to pray. Beg the Lord of heaven to show you mercy and grant you deliverance. But do not be afraid, for she was set apart for you before the world existed. You will save her, and she will go with you. And I suppose that you will have children by her, who will take the place of brothers for you. So do not worry."

When Tobiah heard Raphael say that she was his kinswoman, of his own family's lineage, he fell deeply in love with her, and his heart became set on her.

7 When they entered Ecbatana, Tobiah said, "Brother Azariah, lead me straight to our kinsman Raguel." So he brought him to the house of Raguel, whom they found seated by his courtyard gate. They greeted him first. He said to them, "Greetings to you too, brothers! Good health to you, and welcome!" When he brought them into his home, 2 he said to his wife Edna, "This young man looks just like my kinsman Tobit!" 3 So Edna asked them, "Who are you, brothers?" They answered, "We are of the exiles from Naphtali at Nineveh." 4 She said, "Do you know our kinsman Tobit?" They answered, "Indeed we do!" She asked, "Is he well?" 5 They answered, "Yes, he is alive and well." Then Tobiah exclaimed, "He is my father!" 6 Raguel sprang up and kissed him, shedding tears of joy. 7 But when he heard that Tobit had lost his eyesight, he was grieved and wept aloud. He said to Tobiah: "My child, God bless you! You are the son of a noble and good father. But what a terrible misfortune that such a righteous and charitable man should be afflicted with blindness!" He continued to weep in the arms of his kinsman Tobiah. 8 His wife Edna also wept for Tobit; and even their daughter Sarah began to weep.

marry her. Listen, brother; this very evening I shall speak about the girl to her father and arrange for her to be betrothed to you, and when we come back from Rhages we can celebrate the marriage. I assure you, Raguel has no right whatever to refuse you or to betroth her to anyone else. That would be asking for death, as prescribed in the Book of Moses, once he is aware that kinship gives you the pre-eminent right to marry his daughter. So listen, brother. This very evening we shall speak about the girl and ask for her hand in marriage. When we come back from Rhages we shall fetch her and take her home with us.'

14 Tobias replied to Raphael, 'Brother Azarias, I have been told that she has already been given in marriage seven times and that each time her bridegroom has died in the bridal room. He died the same night as he entered her room; and I have heard people say it was a demon that killed them, 15 and this makes me afraid. To her the demon does no harm because he loves her, but as soon as a man tries to approach her, he kills him. I am my father's only son, and I have no wish to die. I do not want my father and mother to grieve over me for the rest of their lives; they have no other son to bury them.' 16 The angel said, 'Have you forgotten your father's advice? After all, he urged you to choose a wife from your father's family. Listen then, brother. Do not worry about the demon; take her. This very evening, I promise, she will be given you as your wife. 17 Then once you are in the bridal room, take the heart and liver of the fish and lay a little of it on the burning incense. The reek will rise, 18 the demon will smell it and flee, and there is no danger that he will ever be found near the girl again. Then, before you sleep together, first stand up, both of you, and pray. Ask the Lord of heaven to grant you his grace and protection. Do not be afraid; she was destined for you from the beginning, and you are the one to save her. She will follow you, and I pledge my word she will give you children who will be like brothers to you. Do not worry.' And when Tobias heard Raphael say this, when he understood that Sarah was his sister, a kinswoman of his father's family, he fell so deeply in love with her that he could no longer call his heart his own.

7 As they entered Ecbatana, Tobias said, 'Brother Azarias, take me at once to our brother Raguel's.' And he showed him the way to the house of Raguel, whom they found sitting beside his courtyard door. They greeted him first, and he replied, 'Welcome and greetings, brothers.' And he took them into his house. 2 He said to his wife Edna, 'How like my brother Tobit this young man is!' 3 Edna asked them where they came from; they said, 'We are sons of Naphtali exiled in Nineveh.' 4 'Do you know our brother Tobit?' 'Yes.' 'How is he?' 5 'He is alive and well.' And Tobias added, 'He is my father.' 6 Raguel leapt to his feet and kissed him and wept. 7 Then, finding words, he said, 'Blessings on you, child! You are the son of a noble father. How sad it is that someone so bright and full of good deeds should have gone blind!' He fell on the neck of his kinsman Tobias and wept. 8 And his wife Edna wept for him, and so

9 Then Raguel*p* slaughtered a ram from the flock and received them very warmly.

When they had bathed and washed themselves and had reclined to dine, Tobias said to Raphael, "Brother Azariah, ask Raguel to give me my kinswoman*q* Sarah." 10 But Raguel overheard it and said to the lad, "Eat and drink, and be merry tonight. For no one except you, brother, has the right to marry my daughter Sarah. Likewise I am not at liberty to give her to any other man than yourself, because you are my nearest relative. But let me explain to you the true situation more fully, my child. 11 I have given her to seven men of our kinsmen, and all died on the night when they went in to her. But now, my child, eat and drink, and the Lord will act on behalf of you both." But Tobias said, "I will neither eat nor drink anything until you settle the things that pertain to me." So Raguel said, "I will do so. She is given to you in accordance with the decree in the book of Moses, and it has been decreed from heaven that she be given to you. Take your kinswoman;*q* from now on you are her brother and she is your sister. She is given to you from today and forever. May the Lord of heaven, my child, guide and prosper you both this night and grant you mercy and peace." 12 Then Raguel summoned his daughter Sarah. When she came to him he took her by the hand and gave her to Tobias,*r* saying, "Take her to be your wife in accordance with the law and decree written in the book of Moses. Take her and bring her safely to your father. And may the God of heaven prosper your journey with his peace." 13 Then he called her mother and told her to bring writing material; and he wrote out a copy of a marriage contract, to the effect that he gave her to him as wife according to the decree of the law of Moses. 14 Then they began to eat and drink.

15 Raguel called his wife Edna and said to her, "Sister, get the other room ready, and take her there." 16 So she went and made the bed in the room as he had told her, and brought Sarah*s* there. She wept for her daughter.*s* Then, wiping away the tears,*t* she said to her, "Take courage, my daughter; the Lord of heaven grant you joy*u* in place of your sorrow. Take courage, my daughter." Then she went out.

8 When they had finished eating and drinking they wanted to retire; so they took the young man and brought him into the bedroom. 2 Then Tobias remembered the words of Raphael, and he took the fish's liver and heart out of the bag where he had them and put them on the embers of the incense. 3 The odor of the fish so repelled the demon that he fled to the remotest parts*v* of Egypt. But Raphael followed him, and at once bound him there hand and foot.

4 When the parents*w* had gone out and shut the door of the room, Tobias got out of bed and said to Sarah,*s* "Sister, get up, and let us pray and implore our Lord that he grant us mercy and safety." 5 So she got up, and they began to pray and implore that they might be kept safe. Tobias*x* began by saying,

"Blessed are you, O God of our ancestors,
  and blessed is your name in all generations
    forever.
Let the heavens and the whole creation bless you
    forever.

Raguel slaughtered a ram from the flock and entertained them royally. They bathed and then, after washing their hands, took their places for the meal. Tobias said to Raphael, 'Azarias, my friend, ask Raguel to give me Sarah my kinswoman.' 9 Raguel overheard this and said to the young man: 'Eat and drink tonight, and enjoy yourself. 10 There is no one but yourself who should have my daughter Sarah; indeed I ought not to give her to anyone else, since you are my nearest kinsman. However, I must reveal the truth to you, my son: 11 I have given her in marriage to seven of our kinsmen, and they all died on their wedding night. My son, eat and drink now, and may the Lord deal kindly with you both.' Tobias answered, 'I shall not eat again or drink until you have disposed of this business of mine.' 12 Raguel said to him, 'I shall do so: I give her to you in accordance with the decree in the book of Moses, and Heaven itself has decreed that she shall be yours. Take your kinsman; from now on you belong to her and she to you, from today she is yours for ever. May all go well with you both this night, my son; may the Lord of heaven grant you mercy and peace.'

13 Raguel called for Sarah and, when she came, he took her by the hand and gave her to Tobias with these words: 'Receive my daughter as your wedded wife in accordance with the law, the decree written in the book of Moses; keep her and take her safely home to your father. And may the God of heaven grant you prosperity and peace.' 14 Then he sent for her mother and told her to fetch a roll of papyrus, and he wrote out and put his seal on a marriage contract giving Sarah to Tobias as his wife according to this decree. 15 After that they began to eat and drink.

16 Raguel called his wife and said, 'My dear, get the other bedroom ready and take her in there.' 17 Edna went and prepared the room as he had told her, and brought Sarah into it. She wept over her, and then drying her tears said: 18 'Take heart, dear daughter; the Lord of heaven give you gladness instead of sorrow. Take heart, daughter!' Then she went out.

8 When they had finished eating and drinking and were ready for bed, the young man was escorted to the bedroom. 2 Tobias recalled what Raphael told him; he removed the fish's liver and heart from the bag in which he had them, and put them on the burning incense. 3 The smell from the fish kept the demon away, and he made off into Upper Egypt. Raphael followed him there and promptly bound him hand and foot.

4 After they were left alone and the door was shut, Tobias got up from the bed, saying to Sarah, 'Rise, my love; let us pray and beseech our Lord to show us mercy and keep us in safety.' 5 She got up, and they began to pray that they might be kept safe. Tobias said: 'We praise you, God of our fathers, we praise your name for ever and ever. Let the heavens and all your creation praise you for ever. 6 You

---

p Gk *he*   *q* Gk *sister*   *r* Gk *him*   *s* Gk *her*   *t* Other ancient
authorities read *the tears of her daughter*   *u* Other ancient
authorities read *favor*   *v* Or *fled through the air to the parts*
w Gk *they*   *x* Gk *He*

9 Afterward, Raguel slaughtered a ram from the flock and gave them a cordial reception. When they had bathed and reclined to eat, Tobiah said to Raphael, "Brother Azariah, ask Raguel to let me marry my kinswoman Sarah." 10 Raguel overheard the words; so he said to the boy: "Eat and drink and be merry tonight, for no man is more entitled to marry my daughter Sarah than you, brother. Besides, not even I have the right to give her to anyone but you, because you are my closest relative. But I will explain the situation to you very frankly. 11 I have given her in marriage to seven men, all of whom were kinsmen of ours, and all died on the very night they approached her. But now, son, eat and drink. I am sure the Lord will look after you both." Tobiah answered, "I will eat or drink nothing until you set aside what belongs to me."

Raguel said to him: "I will do it. She is yours according to the decree of the Book of Moses. Your marriage to her has been decided in heaven! Take your kinswoman; from now on you are her love, and she is your beloved. She is yours today and ever after. And tonight, son, may the Lord of heaven prosper you both. May he grant you mercy and peace." 12 Then Raguel called his daughter Sarah, and she came to him. He took her by the hand and gave her to Tobiah with the words: "Take her according to the law. According to the decree written in the Book of Moses she is your wife. Take her and bring her back safely to your father. And may the God of heaven grant both of you peace and prosperity." 13 He then called her mother and told her to bring a scroll, so that he might draw up a marriage contract stating that he gave Sarah to Tobiah as his wife according to the decree of the Mosaic law. Her mother brought the scroll, and he drew up the contract, to which they affixed their seals.

14 Afterward they began to eat and drink. 15 Later Raguel called his wife Edna and said, "My love, prepare the other bedroom and bring the girl there." 16 She went and made the bed in the room, as she was told, and brought the girl there. After she had cried over her, she wiped away the tears and said: 17 "Be brave, my daughter. May the Lord of heaven grant you joy in place of your grief. Courage, my daughter." Then she left.

8 When they had finished eating and drinking, the girl's parents wanted to retire. They brought the young man out of the dining room and led him into the bedroom. 2 At this point Tobiah, mindful of Raphael's instructions, took the fish's liver and heart from the bag which he had with him, and placed them on the embers for the incense. 3 The demon, repelled by the odor of the fish, fled into Upper Egypt; Raphael pursued him there and bound him hand and foot. Then Raphael returned immediately.

4 When the girl's parents left the bedroom and closed the door behind them, Tobiah arose from bed and said to his wife, "My love, get up. Let us pray and beg our Lord to have mercy on us and to grant us deliverance." 5 She got up, and they started to pray and beg that deliverance might be theirs. He began with these words:

"Blessed are you, O God of our fathers;
    praised be your name forever and ever.
Let the heavens and all your creation
    praise you forever.

did his daughter Sarah. 9 Raguel killed a ram from the flock, and they gave him a warm welcome.

They washed and bathed and sat down to table. Then Tobias said to Raphael, 'Brother Azarias, will you ask Raguel to give me my sister Sarah?' 10 Raguel overheard the words, and said to the young man, 'Eat and drink, and make the most of your evening; no one else has the right to take my daughter Sarah — no one but you, my brother. In any case even I am not at liberty to give her to anyone else, since you are her next of kin. However, my boy, I must be frank with you: 11 I have tried to find a husband for her seven times among our kinsmen, and all of them have died the first evening, on going to her room. But for the present, my boy, eat and drink; the Lord will grant you his grace and peace.' Tobias spoke out, 'I will not hear of eating and drinking till you have come to a decision about me.' Raguel answered, 'Very well. Since, by the prescription of the Book of Moses she is given to you, Heaven itself decrees she shall be yours. I therefore entrust your sister to you. From now on you are her brother and she is your sister. She is given to you from today for ever. The Lord of heaven favour you tonight, my child, and grant you his grace and peace.' 12 Raguel called for his daughter Sarah, took her by the hand and gave her to Tobias with these words, 'I entrust her to you; the law and the ruling recorded in the Book of Moses assign her to you as your wife. Take her; bring her home safe and sound to your father's house. The God of heaven grant you a good journey in peace.' 13 Then he turned to her mother and asked her to fetch him writing paper. He drew up the marriage contract, and so he gave his daughter as bride to Tobias according to the ordinance of the Law of Moses.

14 After this they began to eat and drink. 15 Raguel called his wife Edna and said, 'My sister, prepare the second room and take her there.' 16 She went and made the bed in this room as he had ordered, and took her daughter to it. She wept over her, then wiped away her tears and said, 'Courage, daughter! May the Lord of heaven turn your grief to joy! Courage, daughter!' And she went out.

8 When they had finished eating and drinking and it seemed time to go to bed, the young man was taken from the dining room to the bedroom. 2 Tobias remembered Raphael's advice; he went to his bag, took the fish's heart and liver out of it and put some on the burning incense. 3 The reek of the fish distressed the demon, who fled through the air to Egypt. Raphael pursued him there, shackled him and strangled him forthwith.

4 The parents meanwhile had gone out and shut the door behind them. Tobias rose from the bed, and said to Sarah, 'Get up, my sister! You and I must pray and petition our Lord to win his grace and his protection.' 5 She stood up, and they began praying for protection, and this was how he began:

You are blessed, O God of our fathers;
    blessed too is your name
    for ever and ever.
Let the heavens bless you
and all things you have made
    for evermore.

6 You made Adam, and for him you made his wife
Eve
as a helper and support.
From the two of them the human race has
sprung.
You said, 'It is not good that the man should be
alone;
let us make a helper for him like himself.'
7 I now am taking this kinswoman of mine,
not because of lust,
but with sincerity.
Grant that she and I may find mercy
and that we may grow old together."
8 And they both said, "Amen, Amen." 9 Then they went to
sleep for the night.

But Raguel arose and called his servants to him, and they
went and dug a grave, 10 for he said, "It is possible that he
will die and we will become an object of ridicule and derision." 11 When they had finished digging the grave, Raguel
went into his house and called his wife, 12 saying, "Send
one of the maids and have her go in to see if he is alive. But
if he is dead, let us bury him without anyone knowing it."
13 So they sent the maid, lit a lamp, and opened the door;
and she went in and found them sound asleep together.
14 Then the maid came out and informed them that he was
alive and that nothing was wrong. 15 So they blessed the
God of heaven, and Raguel *y* said,
"Blessed are you, O God, with every pure
blessing;
let all your chosen ones bless you. *z*
Let them bless you forever.
16 Blessed are you because you have made me glad.
It has not turned out as I expected,
but you have dealt with us according to your
great mercy.
17 Blessed are you because you had compassion
on two only children.
Be merciful to them, O Master, and keep them
safe;
bring their lives to fulfillment
in happiness and mercy."
18 Then he ordered his servants to fill in the grave before
daybreak.
19 After this he asked his wife to bake many loaves of
bread; and he went out to the herd and brought two steers
and four rams and ordered them to be slaughtered. So they
began to make preparations. 20 Then he called for Tobias
and swore on oath to him in these words: *a* "You shall not
leave here for fourteen days, but shall stay here eating and
drinking with me; and you shall cheer up my daughter, who
has been depressed. 21 Take at once half of what I own and
return in safety to your father; the other half will be yours
when my wife and I die. Take courage, my child. I am your
father and Edna is your mother, and we belong to you as
well as to your wife *b* now and forever. Take courage, my
child."

9 Then Tobias called Raphael and said to him, 2 "Brother
Azariah, take four servants and two camels with you
and travel to Rages. Go to the home of Gabael, give him the
bond, get the money, and then bring him with you to the
wedding celebration. 4 For you know that my father must be
counting the days, and if I delay even one day I will upset
him very much. 3 You are witness to the oath Raguel has
sworn, and I cannot violate his oath." *c* 5 So Raphael with

made Adam and also Eve his wife, who was to be his
partner and support; and those two were the parents of the
human race. This was your word: "It is not good for the man
to be alone; let us provide a partner suited to him." 7 So now
I take this my beloved to wife, not out of lust but in true
marriage. Grant that she and I may find mercy and grow old
together.' 8 They both said 'Amen, Amen,' 9 and they slept
through the night.

Raguel rose and summoned his servants, and they went
out and dug a grave, 10 for he thought, 'Tobias may be dead,
and then we shall have to face scorn and taunts.' 11 When
they had finished digging the grave, Raguel went into the
house and called his wife: 12 'Send one of the servant-girls',
he said, 'to go in and see whether he is alive; for if he is
dead, let us bury him so that no one may know.' 13 They lit
a lamp, opened the door, and sent a servant in; and she
found them sound asleep together. 14 She came out and told
them, 'He is alive and has come to no harm.'
15 Then Raguel praised the God of heaven: 'All praise to
you, O God, all perfect praise! Let men praise you throughout the ages. 16 Praise to you for the joy you have given me:
the thing I feared has not happened, but you have shown us
your great mercy. 17 Praise to you for the mercy you have
shown to these two, these only children. Lord, show them
mercy, keep them safe, and grant them a long life of happiness and affection.' 18 And he ordered his servants to fill in
the grave before dawn came.
19 Telling his wife to bake a great batch of bread, he went
to the herd and brought two oxen and four rams and ordered
his servants to get them ready; so they set about the preparations. 20 Then calling Tobias he said: 'You shall not stir
from here for two weeks. Stay; eat and drink with us, and
cheer my daughter's heart after all her suffering. 21 Here and
now take half of all I possess, and may you have a safe
journey back to your father; the other half will come to you
both when I and my wife die. Be reassured, my son, I am
your father and Edna is your mother; now and always we
are as close to you as we are to your wife. You have nothing
to fear, my son.'

9 Tobias sent for Raphael and said: 2 'Azarias, my
friend, take four servants and two camels with you,
and go to Rages. Make your way to Gabael's house, give
him the note of hand and collect the money; then bring him
with you to the wedding feast. 3-4 My father, as you know,
will be counting the days, and if I am even one day late it
will distress him. Yet you see what Raguel has sworn, and
I cannot go against his oath.' 5 So Raphael went with the

---

y Gk *they*   *z* Other ancient authorities lack this line   *a* Other
ancient authorities read *Tobias and said to him*   *b* Gk *sister*
c In other ancient authorities verse 3 precedes verse 4

6 You made Adam and you gave him his wife Eve
    to be his help and support;
    and from these two the human race descended.
You said, 'It is not good for the man to be alone;
    let us make him a partner like himself.'
7 Now, Lord, you know that I take this wife of mine
    not because of lust,
    but for a noble purpose.
Call down your mercy on me and on her,
    and allow us to live together to a happy
    old age."

8 They said together, "Amen, amen," 9 and went to bed for
the night.
    But Raguel got up and summoned his servants. With him
they went out to dig a grave, 10 for he said, "I must do this,
because if Tobiah should die, we would be subjected to
ridicule and insult." 11 When they had finished digging the
grave, Raguel went back into the house and called his wife,
12 saying, "Send one of the maids in to see whether Tobiah
is alive or dead, so that if necessary we may bury him
without anyone's knowing about it." 13 She sent the maid,
who lit a lamp, opened the bedroom door, went in, and
found them sound asleep together. 14 The maid went out and
told the girl's parents that Tobiah was alive, and that there
was nothing wrong. 15 Then Raguel praised the God of
heaven in these words:

    "Blessed are you, O God, with every holy and
        pure blessing!
    Let all your chosen ones praise you;
        let them bless you forever!
16 Blessed are you, who have made me glad;
        what I feared did not happen.
    Rather you have dealt with us
        according to your great mercy.
17 Blessed are you, for you were merciful
        toward two only children.
    Grant them, Master, mercy and deliverance,
        and bring their lives to fulfillment
        with happiness and mercy."

18 Then he told his servants to fill in the grave before dawn.
    19 He asked his wife to bake many loaves of bread; he
himself went out to the herd and picked out two steers and
four rams which he ordered to be slaughtered. So the servants began to prepare the feast. 20 He summoned Tobiah
and made an oath in his presence, saying: "For fourteen
days you shall not stir from here, but shall remain here
eating and drinking with me; and you shall bring joy to my
daughter's sorrowing spirit. 21 Take, to begin with, half of
whatever I own when you go back in good health to your
father; the other half will be yours when I and my wife die.
Be of good cheer, my son! I am your father, and Edna is
your mother; and we belong to you and to your beloved now
and forever. So be happy, son!"

9 Then Tobiah called Raphael and said to him: 2 "Brother
    Azariah, take along with you your servants and two
camels and travel to Rages. Go to Gabael's house and give
him this bond. Get the money and then bring him along with
you to the wedding celebration. 4 For you know that my
father is counting the days. If I should delay my return by
a single day, I would cause him intense grief. 3 You witnessed the oath that Raguel has sworn; I cannot violate his
oath." 5 So Raphael, together with the four servants and two

6 You it was who created Adam,
    you who created Eve his wife
    to be his help and support;
    and from these two the human race was born.
You it was who said,
    'It is not right that the man should be alone;
    let us make him a helper like him.' [b]
7 And so I take my sister
    not for any lustful motive,
    but I do it in singleness of heart.
Be kind enough to have pity on her and on me
    and bring us to old age together.

8 And together they said, 'Amen, Amen,' 9 and lay down for
the night.
    But Raguel rose and called his servants, who came and
helped him dig a grave. 10 He had thought, 'Heaven grant he
does not die! We should be overwhelmed with ridicule and
shame.' 11 When the grave was ready, Raguel went back to
the house, called his wife 12 and said, 'Will you send a maid
to the room to see if Tobias is still alive? For if he is dead,
we may be able to bury him without anyone else knowing.'
13 They sent the maid, lit the lamp, opened the door and the
maid went in. She found the two fast asleep together; 14 she
came out again and whispered, 'He is not dead; all is well.'
15 Then Raguel blessed the God of heaven with these words:

    You are blessed, my God,
        with every blessing that is pure;
        may you be blessed for evermore!
16 You are blessed for having made me glad.
        What I feared has not happened,
        instead you have shown us
        your boundless mercy.
17 You are blessed for taking pity
        on this only son, this only daughter.
    Grant them, Master, your mercy and your
        protection;
        let them live out their lives
        in happiness and in mercy.

18 And he made his servants fill the grave in before dawn
broke.
    19 He told his wife to make an ovenful of bread; he went
to his flock, brought back two oxen and four sheep and gave
orders for them to be cooked; and preparations began. 20 He
called Tobias and said, 'I will not hear of your leaving here
for a fortnight. You are to stay where you are, eating and
drinking, with me. You will make my daughter happy again
after all her troubles. 21 After that, take away a half of all I
have, and take her safe and sound back to your father.
When my wife and I are dead you shall have the other half.
Courage, my boy! I am your father, and Edna is your
mother. We are your parents in future, as we are your
sister's. Courage, my son!'

9 Then Tobias turned to Raphael. 2 'Brother Azarias,' he
    said, 'take four servants and two camels and leave for
Rhages. 3 Go to Gabael's house, give him the receipt and
see about the money; then invite him to come with you to
my wedding feast. 4 You know that my father must be
counting the days and that I cannot lose a single one without
worrying him. 5 You see what Raguel has pledged himself

b 8 Gn 2:18.

the four servants and two camels went to Rages in Media and stayed with Gabael. Raphael[d] gave him the bond and informed him that Tobit's son Tobias had married and was inviting him to the wedding celebration. So Gabael[e] got up and counted out to him the money bags, with their seals intact; then they loaded them on the camels.[f] 6 In the morning they both got up early and went to the wedding celebration. When they came into Raguel's house they found Tobias reclining at table. He sprang up and greeted Gabael,[g] who wept and blessed him with the words, "Good and noble son of a father good and noble, upright and generous! May the Lord grant the blessing of heaven to you and your wife, and to your wife's father and mother. Blessed be God, for I see in Tobias the very image of my cousin Tobit."

10 Now, day by day, Tobit kept counting how many days Tobias[e] would need for going and for returning. And when the days had passed and his son did not appear, 2 he said, "Is it possible that he has been detained? Or that Gabael has died, and there is no one to give him the money?" 3 And he began to worry. 4 His wife Anna said, "My child has perished and is no longer among the living." And she began to weep and mourn for her son, saying, 5 "Woe to me, my child, the light of my eyes, that I let you make the journey." 6 But Tobit kept saying to her, "Be quiet and stop worrying, my dear;[h] he is all right. Probably something unexpected has happened there. The man who went with him is trustworthy and is one of our own kin. Do not grieve for him, my dear;[h] he will soon be here." 7 She answered him, "Be quiet yourself! Stop trying to deceive me! My child has perished." She would rush out every day and watch the road her son had taken, and would heed no one.[i] When the sun had set she would go in and mourn and weep all night long, getting no sleep at all.

Now when the fourteen days of the wedding celebration had ended that Raguel had sworn to observe for his daughter, Tobias came to him and said, "Send me back, for I know that my father and mother do not believe that they will see me again. So I beg of you, father, to let me go so that I may return to my own father. I have already explained to you how I left him." 8 But Raguel said to Tobias, "Stay, my child, stay with me; I will send messengers to your father Tobit and they will inform him about you." 9 But he said, "No! I beg you to send me back to my father." 10 So Raguel promptly gave Tobias his wife Sarah, as well as half of all his property: male and female slaves, oxen and sheep, donkeys and camels, clothing, money, and household goods. 11 Then he saw them safely off; he embraced Tobias[g] and said, "Farewell, my child; have a safe journey. The Lord of heaven prosper you and your wife Sarah, and may I see children of yours before I die." 12 Then he kissed his daughter Sarah and said to her, "My daughter, honor your father-in-law and your mother-in-law,[j] since from now on they are as much your parents as those who gave you birth. Go in peace, daughter, and may I hear a good report about you as long as I live." Then he bade them farewell and let them go. Then Edna said to Tobias, "My child and dear brother, the Lord of heaven bring you back safely, and may I live long enough to see children of you and of my daughter Sarah before I die. In the sight of the Lord I entrust my daughter to you; do nothing to grieve her all the days of your life. Go in peace, my child. From now on I am your mother and Sarah is your beloved wife.[h] May we all prosper together all the days of our lives." Then she kissed them both and saw them safely off. 13 Tobias parted from Raguel

four servants and two camels to Rages in Media and stayed the night with Gabael. He delivered the note of hand and informed him that Tobit's son Tobias had taken a wife and was inviting him to the wedding feast. At once Gabael counted out to him the bags with their seals intact, and they put them together. 6 They all made an early start and came to the wedding. Entering Raguel's house they found Tobias at the feast, and he jumped up and greeted Gabael. With tears in his eyes Gabael blessed him and said: 'Good and worthy son of a worthy father, that just and charitable man, may the Lord give Heaven's blessing to you, your wife, and your parents-in-law. Praise be to God, for I have seen my cousin Tobias, the very likeness of his father.'

10 Day by day Tobit was keeping count of the time Tobias would take for his journey there and for his journey back. When the time was up and his son had not made his appearance, 2 Tobit said: 'Perhaps he has been detained there? Or perhaps Gabael is dead and there is no one to give him the money?' 3 And he grew anxious. 4 Anna his wife said: 'My child has perished. He is no longer in the land of the living.' She began to weep, lamenting for her son: 5 'O my child, the light of my eyes, why did I let you go?' 6 Tobit said to her: 'Hush! Do not worry, my dear; he is all right. Something has happened there to distract them. The man who went with him is one of our kinsmen and can be trusted. My dear, do not grieve for him; he will be back.' 7 'Hush yourself!' she retorted. 'Do not try to deceive me. My child has perished.' Each day she would rush out to keep watch on the road her son had taken, and would listen to no one; and when she came indoors at sunset she was unable to sleep, but lamented and wept the whole night long.

After the two weeks of wedding celebrations which Raguel had sworn to hold for his daughter came to an end, Tobias approached him. 'Let me be on my way,' he said, 'for I am sure that my parents are thinking they will never see me again. I beg you, father, let me go home now to my father Tobit. I have already told you how I left him.' 8 Raguel replied: 'Stay, my son, stay with me, and I shall send messengers to your father to explain matters to him.' 9 But Tobias insisted: 'No, please let me go home to my father.' 10 Then without more ado Raguel handed over to Tobias Sarah his bride along with half of all that he possessed, male and female slaves, cattle and sheep, donkeys and camels, clothes, money, and household goods. 11 He bade them farewell. Embracing Tobias he said: 'Goodbye, my son, goodbye; a safe journey to you! May the Lord of heaven prosper you and Sarah your wife; and may I live to see your children.' 12 To his daughter Sarah he said: 'Honour your husband's father and mother; they are now your parents as much as if you were their own child. Go in peace, my daughter; as long as I live I hope to hear nothing but good news of you.' After bidding them both goodbye, he sent them on their way. Edna said to Tobias: 'My very dear cousin, may the Lord bring you safely home, you and my daughter Sarah, and may I live long enough to see your children. In the sight of the Lord I entrust my daughter to your keeping; do nothing to cause her distress throughout your life. Go in peace, my son. From now on I am your mother and Sarah is your beloved wife. May we all be blessed with prosperity to the end of our days!' She kissed them both goodbye and let them go.

d Gk He   e Gk he   f Other ancient authorities lack *on the camels*   g Gk him   h Gk sister   i Other ancient authorities read *and she would eat nothing*   j Other ancient authorities lack parts of *Then . . . mother-in-law*

camels, traveled to Rages in Media, where they stayed at Gabael's house. Raphael gave Gabael his bond and told him about Tobit's son Tobiah, and that he had married and was inviting him to the wedding celebration. Gabael promptly checked over the sealed moneybags, and they placed them on the camels.

6 The following morning they got an early start and traveled to the wedding celebration. When they entered Raguel's house, they found Tobiah reclining at table. He sprang up and greeted Gabael, who wept and blessed him, exclaiming: "O noble and good child, son of a noble and good, upright and charitable man, may the Lord grant heavenly blessing to you and to your wife, and to your wife's father and mother. Blessed be God, because I have seen the very image of my cousin Tobit!"

10 Meanwhile, day by day, Tobit was keeping track of the time Tobiah would need to go and to return. When the number of days was reached and his son did not appear, 2 he said, "I wonder what has happened. Perhaps he has been detained there; or perhaps Gabael is dead, and there is no one to give him the money." 3 And he began to worry. 4 His wife Anna said, "My son has perished and is no longer among the living!" And she began to weep aloud and to wail over her son: 5 "Alas, my child, light of my eyes, that I let you make this journey!" 6 But Tobit kept telling her: "Hush, do not think about it, my love; he is safe! Probably they have to take care of some unexpected business there. The man who is traveling with him is trustworthy, and is one of our own kinsmen. So do not worry over him, my love. He will be here soon." 7 But she retorted, "Stop it, and do not lie to me! My child has perished!" She would go out and keep watch all day at the road her son had taken, and she ate nothing. At sunset she would go back home to wail and cry the whole night through, getting no sleep at all.

Now at the end of the fourteen-day wedding celebration which Raguel had sworn to hold for his daughter, Tobiah went to him and said: "Please let me go, for I know that my father and mother do not believe they will ever see me again. So I beg you, father, let me go back to my father. I have already told you how I left him." 8 Raguel said to Tobiah: "Stay, my child, stay with me. I am sending messengers to your father Tobit, and they will give him news of you." 9 But Tobiah insisted, "No, I beg you to let me go back to my father."

10 Raguel then promptly handed over to Tobiah Sarah his wife, together with half of all his property: male and female slaves, oxen and sheep, asses and camels, clothing, money, and household goods. 11 Bidding them farewell, he let them go. He embraced Tobiah and said to him: "Good-bye, my son. Have a safe journey. May the Lord of heaven grant prosperity to you and to your wife Sarah. And may I see children of yours before I die!" 12 Then he kissed his daughter Sarah and said to her: "My daughter, honor your father-in-law and your mother-in-law, because from now on they are as much your parents as the ones who brought you into the world. Go in peace, my daughter; let me hear good reports about you as long as I live." Finally he said good-bye to them and sent them away.

13 Then Edna said to Tobiah: "My child and beloved kinsman, may the Lord bring you back safely, and may I live long enough to see children of you and of my daughter Sarah before I die. Before the Lord, I entrust my daughter to your care. Never cause her grief at any time in your life. Go in peace, my child. From now on I am your mother, and Sarah is your beloved. May all of us be prosperous all the days of our lives." She kissed them both and sent them away in peace.

to do; I am bound by his oath.' So Raphael left for Rhages in Media with the four servants and two camels. They stayed with Gabael, and Raphael showed him the receipt. He told him about the marriage of Tobias son of Tobit and gave him his invitation to the wedding feast. Gabael started counting out the sacks to him — the seals were intact — and they loaded them on to the camels. 6 Early in the morning they set off together for the feast, and reached Raguel's house where they found Tobias dining. He rose to greet Gabael, who burst into tears and blessed him with the words, 'Excellent son of a father beyond reproach, just and generous in his dealings! The Lord give heaven's blessing to you, to your wife, to your wife's father and mother! Blessed be God for granting me the sight of this living image of my cousin Tobit!'

10 Every day, meanwhile, Tobit kept reckoning the days required for the journey there and the journey back. The full number went by, and still his son had not come. 2 Then he thought, 'I hope he has not been delayed there! I hope Gabael is not dead, so that no one will give him the silver.' 3 And he began to worry. 4 His wife Anna kept saying, 'My son is dead! He is no longer among the living!' And she began to weep and mourn over her son. She kept saying, 5 'Alas! I should never have let you leave me, my child, you, the light of my eyes.' 6 And Tobit would reply, 'Hush, my sister! Do not worry. All is well with him. Something has happened there to delay them. His companion is someone we can trust, one of our kinsmen at that. Do not lose heart, my sister. 7 He will soon be here.' But all she would say was, 'Leave me alone; do not try to deceive me. My child is dead.' And every day she would go abruptly out to watch the road by which her son had left. She trusted no eyes but her own. Once the sun had set she would come home again, only to weep and moan all night, unable to sleep.

After the fourteen days of feasting that Raguel had sworn to keep for his daughter's marriage, Tobias came to him and said, 'Let me go now; my father and mother must have lost all hope of seeing me again. So I beg you, father, to let me return to my father's house; I have told you the plight he was in when I left him.' 8 Raguel said to Tobias, 'Stay, my son, stay with me. I shall send messengers to your father Tobit to give him news of you.' 9 But Tobias pressed him, 'No, I beg you to let me go back to my father's house.'

10 Without more ado, Raguel committed Sarah his bride into his keeping. He gave Tobias half his wealth, slaves, men and women, oxen and sheep, donkeys and camels, clothes and money and household things. 11 And so he let them leave happily. To Tobias he said these parting words, 'Good health, my son, and a happy journey! May the Lord of heaven be gracious to you and to your wife Sarah! I hope to see your children before I die.' 12 To his daughter Sarah he said, 'Go now to your father-in-law's house, since henceforward they are as much your parents as those who gave you life. Go in peace, my daughter, I hope to hear nothing but good of you, as long as I live.' He said goodbye to them and let them go.

Edna in her turn said to Tobias, 'Dear son and brother, may it please the Lord to bring you back again! I hope to live long enough to see the children of you and my daughter Sarah before I die. In the sight of the Lord I give my daughter into your keeping. Never make her unhappy as long as you live. Go in peace, my son. Henceforward I am your mother and Sarah is your sister. May we all live happily for the rest of our lives!' And she kissed them both and saw them set out happily.

with happiness and joy, praising the Lord of heaven and earth, King over all, because he had made his journey a success. Finally, he blessed Raguel and his wife Edna, and said, "I have been commanded by the Lord to honor you all the days of my life."*k*

11 When they came near to Kaserin, which is opposite Nineveh, Raphael said, 2 "You are aware of how we left your father. 3 Let us run ahead of your wife and prepare the house while they are still on the way." 4 As they went on together Raphael*l* said to him, "Have the gall ready." And the dog*m* went along behind them.

5 Meanwhile Anna sat looking intently down the road by which her son would come. 6 When she caught sight of him coming, she said to his father, "Look, your son is coming, and the man who went with him!"

7 Raphael said to Tobias, before he had approached his father, "I know that his eyes will be opened. 8 Smear the gall of the fish on his eyes; the medicine will make the white films shrink and peel off from his eyes, and your father will regain his sight and see the light."

9 Then Anna ran up to her son and threw her arms around him, saying, "Now that I have seen you, my child, I am ready to die." And she wept. 10 Then Tobit got up and came stumbling out through the courtyard door. Tobias went up to him, 11 with the gall of the fish in his hand, and holding him firmly, he blew into his eyes, saying, "Take courage, father." With this he applied the medicine on his eyes, 12 and it made them smart.*k* 13 Next, with both his hands he peeled off the white films from the corners of his eyes. Then Tobit*l* saw his son and*n* threw his arms around him, 14 and he wept and said to him, "I see you, my son, the light of my eyes!" Then he said,

"Blessed be God,
and blessed be his great name,
and blessed be all his holy angels.
May his holy name be blessed*o*
throughout all the ages.
15 Though he has afflicted me,
he has had mercy upon me.*p*
Now I see my son Tobias!"

So Tobit went in rejoicing and praising God at the top of his voice. Tobias reported to his father that his journey had been successful, that he had brought the money, that he had married Raguel's daughter Sarah, and that she was, indeed, on her way there, very near to the gate of Nineveh.

16 Then Tobit, rejoicing and praising God, went out to meet his daughter-in-law at the gate of Nineveh. When the people of Nineveh saw him coming, walking along in full vigor and with no one leading him, they were amazed. 17 Before them all, Tobit acknowledged that God had been merciful to him and had restored his sight. When Tobit met Sarah the wife of his son Tobias, he blessed her saying, "Come in, my daughter, and welcome. Blessed be your God who has brought you to us, my daughter. Blessed be your father and your mother, blessed be my son Tobias, and blessed be you, my daughter. Come in now to your home, and welcome, with blessing and joy. Come in, my daughter." So on that day there was rejoicing among all the Jews who were in Nineveh. 18 Ahikar and his nephew Nadab were also present to share Tobit's joy. With merriment they celebrated Tobias's wedding feast for seven days, and many gifts were given to him.*q*

11 Tobias parted from Raguel in good health and spirits, praising the Lord of heaven and earth, the King of all, for the success of his journey. He gave his blessing to Raguel and Edna his wife, saying, 'It is the Lord's command that I should honour you all your days.'

2 When they reached Caserin close to Nineveh, Raphael said: 'You know how your father was when we left him. 3 Let us hurry on ahead of your wife and see that the house is ready before the others arrive'; 4 and as the two of them went on together he added, 'Bring the fish-gall in your hand.' The dog went with the angel and Tobias, following at their heels.

5 Anna sat watching the road by which her son would return. 6 She caught sight of him coming and exclaimed to his father, 'Here he comes—your son and the man who went with him!' 7 Before Tobias reached his father's house Raphael said: 'I know for certain that his eyes will be opened. 8 Spread the fish-gall on them; this remedy will make the white patches shrink and peel off. Your father will get his sight back and see the light of day.' 9 Anna ran forward, flung her arms round her son, and said to him: 'Now that I have seen you again, my child, I am ready to die.' And she wept.

10 As Tobit rose to his feet and came stumbling out through the courtyard gate, 11 Tobias went up to him with the fish-gall in his hand. He blew into his father's eyes and then, taking him by the arm and saying, 'Do not be alarmed, father,' 12 he applied the remedy carefully 13 and with both hands peeled off the patches from the corners of Tobit's eyes. Tobit threw his arms round him 14 and burst into tears. 'I can see you, my son, the light of my eyes!' he cried. 'Praise be to God, and praise to his great name and to all his holy angels. May his great name rest on us. Praised be all the angels for ever and ever. 15 He laid his scourge on me, and now, look, I see my son Tobias!'

Tobias went inside, rejoicing and praising God with all his might. He told his father about the success of his journey and the recovery of the money, and how he had married Raguel's daughter Sarah. 'She is on her way,' he said, 'quite close to the city gate.' 16 Tobit went out joyfully to meet his daughter-in-law at the gate, praising God as he went. At the sight of him passing through the city in full vigour and walking without anyone to guide his steps, the people of Nineveh were amazed; 17 and Tobit gave thanks to God before them all for his mercy in opening his eyes.

When he met Sarah, the wife of his son Tobias, he blessed her and said to her: 'Come in, daughter, welcome! Praise be to God who has brought you to us. Blessings on your father and mother, and on my son Tobias, and blessings on you, my daughter. Come into your home, and may health, blessings, and joy be yours; come in, my daughter.' For all the Jews in Nineveh it was a day of joy, 18 and Ahikar and Nadab, Tobit's cousins, came to share his happiness. The joyful celebrations went on for a week, and many were the presents given to them.

---

k Lat: Meaning of Gk uncertain   *l* Gk he   *m* Codex Sinaiticus reads *And the Lord*   *n* Other ancient authorities lack *saw his son and*   *o* Codex Sinaiticus reads *May his great name be upon us and blessed be all the angels*   *p* Lat: Gk lacks this line   *q* Other ancient authorities lack parts of this sentence

NEW AMERICAN BIBLE

14When Tobiah left Raguel, he was full of happiness and joy, and he blessed the Lord of heaven and earth, the King of all, for making his journey so successful. Finally he said good-bye to Raguel and his wife Edna, and added, "May I honor you all the days of my life!"

11 Then they left and began their return journey. When they were near Kaserin, just before Nineveh, 2Raphael said: "You know how we left your father. 3Let us hurry on ahead of your wife to prepare the house while the rest of the party are still on the way." 4So they both went on ahead and Raphael said to Tobiah, "Have the gall in your hand!" And the dog ran along behind them.

5Meanwhile, Anna sat watching the road by which her son was to come. 6When she saw him coming, she exclaimed to his father, "Tobit, your son is coming, and the man who traveled with him!"

7Raphael said to Tobiah before he reached his father: "I am certain that his eyes will be opened. 8Smear the fish gall on them. This medicine will make the cataracts shrink and peel off from his eyes; then your father will again be able to see the light of day."

9Then Anna ran up to her son, threw her arms around him, and said to him, "Now that I have seen you again, son, I am ready to die!" And she sobbed aloud. 10Tobit got up and stumbled out through the courtyard gate. Tobiah went up to him 11with the fish gall in his hand, and holding him firmly, blew into his eyes. "Courage, father," he said. 12Next he smeared the medicine on his eyes, 13and it made them smart. Then, beginning at the corners of Tobit's eyes, Tobiah used both hands to peel off the cataracts. When Tobit saw his son, he threw his arms around him 14and wept. He exclaimed, "I can see you, son, the light of my eyes!" Then he said:

"Blessed be God,
　and praised be his great name,
　and blessed be all his holy angels.
May his holy name be praised
　throughout all the ages,
15Because it was he who scourged me,
　and it is he who has had mercy on me.
Behold, I now see my son Tobiah!"

Then Tobit went back in, rejoicing and praising God with full voice. Tobiah told his father that his journey had been a success; that he had brought back the money; and that he had married Raguel's daughter Sarah, who would arrive shortly, for she was approaching the gate of Nineveh.

16Rejoicing and praising God, Tobit went out to the gate of Nineveh to meet his daughter-in-law. When the people of Nineveh saw him walking along briskly, with no one leading him by the hand, they were amazed. 17Before them all Tobit proclaimed how God had mercifully restored sight to his eyes. When Tobit reached Sarah, the wife of his son Tobiah, he greeted her: "Welcome, my daughter! Blessed be your God for bringing you to us, daughter! Blessed are your father and your mother. Blessed is my son Tobiah, and blessed are you, daughter! Welcome to your home with blessing and joy. Come in, daughter!" That day there was joy for all the Jews who lived in Nineveh. 18Ahiqar and his nephew Nadab also came to rejoice with Tobit. They celebrated Tobiah's wedding feast for seven happy days, and he received many gifts.

NEW JERUSALEM BIBLE

13Tobias left Raguel's house with his mind at ease. In his gladness he blessed the Lord of heaven and earth, the King of all that is, for the happy issue of his travels. He gave this blessing to Raguel and his wife Edna, 'May it be my happiness to honour you for the rest of my life!'

11 They were nearly at Kaserin, opposite Nineveh, 2when Raphael said, 'You know the plight in which we left your father; 3let us go on ahead of your wife and prepare the house ourselves while she travels behind with the others.' 4They went on together (Raphael warned Tobias to take the gall with him) and the dog followed them.

5Anna was sitting, watching the road by which her son would come. 6She was sure at once it must be he and said to the father, 'Here comes your son, with his companion.'

7Raphael said to Tobias before he reached his father, 'I give you my word that your father's eyes will open. 8You must put the fish's gall to his eyes; the medicine will smart and will draw a filmy white skin off his eyes. And your father will no more be blind but will be able to see the light.'

9The mother ran forward and threw her arms round her son's neck. 'Now I can die,' she said, 'I have seen you again.' And she wept. 10Tobit rose to his feet and stumbled across the courtyard through the door. Tobias came on towards him 11(he had the fish's gall in his hand). He blew into his eyes and said, steadying him, 'Take courage, father!' With this he applied the medicine, left it there a while, 12then with both hands peeled away a filmy skin from the corners of his eyes. 13Then his father fell on his neck 14and wept. He exclaimed, 'I can see you, my son, the light of my eyes!' And he said:

Blessed be God!
Blessed be his great name!
Blessed be all his holy angels!
Blessed be his great name
for evermore!

15For, having afflicted me,
he has had pity on me
and now I see my son Tobias!

Tobias went indoors, joyfully blessing God at the top of his voice. Then he told his father everything; how his journey had been successful and he had brought the silver back; how he had married Sarah the daughter of Raguel; how she was following him now, close behind, and could not be far from the gates of Nineveh.

16Tobit set off to the gates of Nineveh to meet his daughter-in-law, giving joyful praise to God as he went. When the people of Nineveh saw him walking without a guide and stepping forward as briskly as of old, they were astonished. 17Tobit described to them how God had taken pity on him and had opened his eyes. Then Tobit met Sarah the bride of his son Tobias, and blessed her in these words. 'Welcome, daughter! Blessed be your God for sending you to us, my daughter. Blessings on your father, blessings on my son Tobias, blessings on yourself, my daughter. Welcome now to your own house in joyfulness and in blessedness. Come in, my daughter.' That day brought joy to the Jews of Nineveh, 18and his cousins Ahikar and Nadab came to share in Tobit's happiness.

12 When the wedding celebration was ended, Tobit called his son Tobias and said to him, "My child, see to paying the wages of the man who went with you, and give him a bonus as well." 2 He replied, "Father, how much shall I pay him? It would do no harm to give him half of the possessions brought back with me. 3 For he has led me back to you safely, he cured my wife, he brought the money back with me, and he healed you. How much extra shall I give him as a bonus?" 4 Tobit said, "He deserves, my child, to receive half of all that he brought back." 5 So Tobias*r* called him and said, "Take for your wages half of all that you brought back, and farewell."

6 Then Raphael*r* called the two of them privately and said to them, "Bless God and acknowledge him in the presence of all the living for the good things he has done for you. Bless and sing praise to his name. With fitting honor declare to all people the deeds*s* of God. Do not be slow to acknowledge him. 7 It is good to conceal the secret of a king, but to acknowledge and reveal the works of God, and with fitting honor to acknowledge him. Do good and evil will not overtake you. 8 Prayer with fasting*t* is good, but better than both is almsgiving with righteousness. A little with righteousness is better than wealth with wrongdoing.*u* It is better to give alms than to lay up gold. 9 For almsgiving saves from death and purges away every sin. Those who give alms will enjoy a full life, 10 but those who commit sin and do wrong are their own worst enemies.

11 "I will now declare the whole truth to you and will conceal nothing from you. Already I have declared it to you when I said, 'It is good to conceal the secret of a king, but to reveal with due honor the works of God.' 12 So now when you and Sarah prayed, it was I who brought and read*v* the record of your prayer before the glory of the Lord, and likewise whenever you would bury the dead. 13 And that time when you did not hesitate to get up and leave your dinner to go and bury the dead, 14 I was sent to test you. And at the same time God sent me to heal you and Sarah your daughter-in-law. 15 I am Raphael, one of the seven angels who stand ready and enter before the glory of the Lord."

16 The two of them were shaken; they fell face down, for they were afraid. 17 But he said to them, "Do not be afraid; peace be with you. Bless God forevermore. 18 As for me, when I was with you, I was not acting on my own will, but by the will of God. Bless him each and every day; sing his praises. 19 Although you were watching me, I really did not eat or drink anything — but what you saw was a vision. 20 So now get up from the ground,*w* and acknowledge God. See, I am ascending to him who sent me. Write down all these things that have happened to you." And he ascended. 21 Then they stood up, and could see him no more. 22 They kept blessing God and singing his praises, and they acknowledged God for these marvelous deeds of his, when an angel of God had appeared to them.

13 Then Tobit*r* said:
"Blessed be God who lives forever,
   because his kingdom*x* lasts throughout all
      ages.

12 After the wedding celebrations were over, Tobit sent for Tobias. 'My son,' he said, 'when you pay the man who went with you, see that you give him something extra, over and above his wages.' 2 Tobias asked: 'How much shall I pay him, father? It would not hurt to give him half the money he and I brought back. 3 He has kept me safe, cured my wife, helped me bring the money, and healed you. How much extra shall I pay him?' 4 Tobit replied, 'It would be right, my son, for him to be given half of all that he has brought with him.' 5 So Tobias called him and said, 'Half of all that you have brought with you is to be yours for your wages; take it, and may you fare well.'

6 Then Raphael called them both aside and said to them: 'Praise God, and in the presence of all living creatures thank him for the good he has done you, so that they may sing hymns of praise to his name. Proclaim to all the world what God has done; pay him honour and give him willing thanks. 7 A king's secret ought to be kept, but the works of God should be publicly acknowledged. Acknowledge them, therefore, and pay him honour. Do good, and no evil will befall you. 8 Better prayer with sincerity, and almsgiving with righteousness, than wealth with wickedness. Better give alms than hoard up gold. 9 Almsgiving preserves from death and wipes out every sin. Givers of alms will enjoy long life; 10 but sinners and wrongdoers are their own enemies.

11 'I will tell you the whole truth, hiding nothing from you. I have already made it clear to you that while a king's secret ought to be kept, the works of God should be glorified in public. 12 Now Tobit, when you and Sarah prayed, it was I who brought your prayers to be remembered in the glorious presence of the Lord. 13 So too when you buried the dead: that day when without hesitation you got up from your meal to go and bury the dead man, I was sent to test you. 14 At the same time God sent me to cure both you and Sarah your daughter-in-law. 15 I am Raphael, one of the seven angels who stand in attendance on the Lord and enter his glorious presence.'

16 Both of them were deeply shaken and prostrated themselves in fear. 17 But he said to them: 'Do not be afraid, peace be with you; praise God for ever. 18 It is no thanks to me that I have been with you; it was the will of God. To him all your life long sing hymns of praise. 19 Take note that I ate no food; what you saw was an apparition. 20 And now praise the Lord, give thanks to God here on earth; I am about to ascend to him who sent me. Write down everything that has happened to you.' 21 He then ascended and, when they rose to their feet, was no longer to be seen. 22 They sang hymns of praise to God, giving him thanks for the great deeds he had done when an angel of God appeared to them.

13 IN the fullness of his joy Tobit wrote this prayer:

Praise to the ever-living God and to his
   kingdom.

---

r Gk *he*   *s* Gk *words*; other ancient authorities read *words of the deeds*   *t* Codex Sinaiticus *with sincerity*   *u* Lat   *v* Lat: Gk lacks *and read*   *w* Other ancient authorities read *now bless the Lord on earth*   *x* Other ancient authorities read *forever, and his kingdom*

12:8 **sincerity:** or, *in some texts*, fasting.

12 When the wedding celebration came to an end, Tobit called his son Tobiah and said to him, "Son, see to it that you give what is due to the man who made the journey with you; give him a bonus too." 2 Tobiah said: "Father, how much shall I pay him? It would not hurt me at all to give him half of all the wealth he brought back with me. 3 He led me back safe and sound; he cured my wife; he brought the money back with me; and he cured you. How much of a bonus should I give him?" 4 Tobit answered, "It is only fair, son, that he should receive half of all that he brought back." 5 So Tobiah called Raphael and said, "Take as your wages half of all that you have brought back, and go in peace."

6 Raphael called the two men aside privately and said to them: "Thank God! Give him the praise and the glory. Before all the living, acknowledge the many good things he has done for you, by blessing and extolling his name in song. Before all men, honor and proclaim God's deeds, and do not be slack in praising him. 7 A king's secret it is prudent to keep, but the works of God are to be declared and made known. Praise them with due honor. Do good, and evil will not find its way to you. 8 Prayer and fasting are good, but better than either is almsgiving accompanied by righteousness. A little with righteousness is better than abundance with wickedness. It is better to give alms than to store up gold; 9 for almsgiving saves one from death and expiates every sin. Those who regularly give alms shall enjoy a full life; 10 but those habitually guilty of sin are their own worst enemies.

11 "I will now tell you the whole truth; I will conceal nothing at all from you. I have already said to you, 'A king's secret it is prudent to keep, but the works of God are to be made known with due honor.' 12 I can now tell you that when you, Tobit, and Sarah prayed, it was I who presented and read the record of your prayer before the Glory of the Lord; and I did the same thing when you used to bury the dead. 13 When you did not hesitate to get up and leave your dinner in order to go and bury the dead, 14 I was sent to put you to the test. At the same time, however, God commissioned me to heal you and your daughter-in-law Sarah. 15 I am Raphael, one of the seven angels who enter and serve before the Glory of the Lord."

16 Stricken with fear, the two men fell to the ground. 17 But Raphael said to them: "No need to fear; you are safe. Thank God now and forever. 18 As for me, when I came to you it was not out of any favor on my part, but because it was God's will. So continue to thank him every day; praise him with song. 19 Even though you watched me eat and drink, I did not really do so; what you were seeing was a vision. 20 So now get up from the ground and praise God. Behold, I am about to ascend to him who sent me; write down all these things that have happened to you." 21 When Raphael ascended, they rose to their feet and could no longer see him. 22 They kept thanking God and singing his praises; and they continued to acknowledge these marvelous deeds which he had done when the angel of God appeared to them.

13 Then Tobit composed this joyful prayer:

Blessed be God who lives forever,
  because his kingdom lasts for all ages.

12 When the wedding feast was over, Tobit called his son Tobias and said, 'My son, you ought to think about paying the amount due to your fellow traveller; give him more than the figure agreed on.' 2 'Father,' he replied, 'how much am I to give him for his help? Even if I give him half the goods he brought back with me, I shall not be the loser. 3 He has brought me back safe and sound, he has cured my wife, he has brought the money back too, and now he has cured you as well. How much am I to give him for all this?' 4 Tobit said, 'He has richly earned half what he brought back'. 5 So Tobias called his companion and said, 'Take half of what you brought back, in payment for all you have done, and go in peace.'

6 Then Raphael took them both aside and said, 'Bless God, utter his praise before all the living for the favour he has shown you. Bless and extol his name. Proclaim before all people the deeds of God as they deserve, and never tire of giving him thanks. 7 It is right to keep the secret of a king, yet right to reveal and publish the works of God as they deserve. Do what is good, and no evil can befall you.

8 'Prayer with fasting and alms with uprightness are better than riches with iniquity. Better to practise almsgiving than to hoard up gold. 9 Almsgiving saves from death and purges every kind of sin. Those who give alms have their fill of days; 10 those who commit sin and do evil bring harm on themselves.

11 'I am going to tell you the whole truth, hiding nothing from you. I have already told you that it is right to keep the secret of a king, yet right too to reveal in a worthy way the words of God. 12 So you must know that when you and Sarah were at prayer, it was I who offered your supplications before the glory of the Lord and who read them; so too when you were burying the dead. 13 When you did not hesitate to get up and leave the table to go and bury a dead man, 14 I was sent to test your faith, 14 and at the same time God sent me to heal you and your daughter-in-law Sarah. 15 I am Raphael, one of the seven angels who stand ever ready to enter the presence of the glory of the Lord.'

16 They were both overwhelmed with awe; they fell on their faces in terror. 17 But the angel said, 'Do not be afraid; peace be with you. Bless God for ever. 18 As far as I was concerned, when I was with you, my presence was not by any decision of mine, but by the will of God; he is the one whom you must bless as long as you live, he is the one that you must praise. 19 You thought you saw me eating, but that was appearance and no more. 20 Now bless the Lord on earth and give thanks to God. I am about to return to him who sent me from above. Write down all that has happened.' And he rose in the air. 21 When they stood up again, he was no longer visible. They praised God with hymns; they thanked him for having performed such wonders; had not an angel of God appeared to them?

13 And he said:

Blessed be God who lives for ever,
  for his reign endures throughout all ages!

2 For he afflicts, and he shows mercy;
   he leads down to Hades in the lowest regions
      of the earth,
   and he brings up from the great abyss,*y*
   and there is nothing that can escape his hand.
3 Acknowledge him before the nations, O children
      of Israel;
   for he has scattered you among them.
4   He has shown you his greatness even there.
   Exalt him in the presence of every living being,
      because he is our Lord and he is our God;
   he is our Father and he is God forever.
5 He will afflict*z* you for your iniquities,
   but he will again show mercy on all of you.
   He will gather you from all the nations
      among whom you have been scattered.
6 If you turn to him with all your heart and with all
         your soul,
   to do what is true before him,
   then he will turn to you
      and will no longer hide his face from you.
   So now see what he has done for you;
      acknowledge him at the top of your voice.
   Bless the Lord of righteousness,
      and exalt the King of the ages.*a*
   In the land of my exile I acknowledge him,
      and show his power and majesty to a nation of
         sinners:
   'Turn back, you sinners, and do what is right
         before him;
      perhaps he may look with favor upon you and
         show you mercy.'
7   As for me, I exalt my God,
      and my soul rejoices in the King of heaven.
8 Let all people speak of his majesty,
      and acknowledge him in Jerusalem.
9 O Jerusalem, the holy city,
   he afflicted*b* you for the deeds of your
         hands,*c*
   but will again have mercy on the children of
      the righteous.
10 Acknowledge the Lord, for he is good,*d*
      and bless the King of the ages,
   so that his tent*e* may be rebuilt in you in joy.
   May he cheer all those within you who are
         captives,
      and love all those within you who are
         distressed,
         to all generations forever.
11 A bright light will shine to all the ends of the
      earth;
   many nations will come to you from far away,
   the inhabitants of the remotest parts of the earth
      to your holy name,
   bearing gifts in their hands for the King of
         heaven.
   Generation after generation will give joyful praise
      in you,
      the name of the chosen city will endure
         forever.

2 He both punishes and shows mercy;
   he brings men down to the grave below,
   and he brings them up from the great destruction;
   nothing can escape his power.
3 Israelites, give him thanks in the sight of the
      nations,
   for, having scattered you among them,
4 he has shown you his greatness there.
   In the sight of every living creature exalt him,
   for he is our Lord and our God,
   our Father and God for ever.
5 Though for your wickedness he will punish you,
   yet he will show mercy to you all,
   wherever you may be dispersed among the nations.
6 When you turn to him with all your heart and soul
   and act in loyal obedience to him,
   then he will turn to you;
   he will hide his face from you no longer.
   Consider now what he has done for you,
   and with full voice give him thanks;
   praise the righteous Lord
   and exalt the eternal King.

   In the land of my exile I give thanks to him
   and declare his might and greatness to a sinful
         nation.
   Sinners, turn and do what is right in his eyes;
   who knows, he may yet welcome you and show
         mercy.
7 I shall exalt my God
   and rejoice in the King of heaven.
8 Let all men tell of his majesty
   and in Jerusalem give him thanks.
9 O Jerusalem, Holy City,
   he will punish you for what your sons have done,
   but he will have mercy once more on the
      righteous.
10 Give thanks to the Lord for his goodness
   and praise to the eternal King.
   Your sanctuary will be rebuilt for you with
         rejoicing.
   May he give happiness to all your exiles
   and cherish for all generations those in distress.

11 Your radiance will shine to the ends of the earth.
   Many nations will come to you from afar,
   to your holy name from every corner of the earth,
   bearing gifts in their hands for the King of heaven.
   In you endless generations will utter their joy;
   the name of the chosen city will endure for ever
      and ever.

---

y Gk *from destruction*   *z* Other ancient authorities read *He afflicted*
a The lacuna in codex Sinaiticus, verses 6b to 10a, is filled in from
other ancient authorities   *b* Other ancient authorities read *will afflict*
c Other ancient authorities read *your children*   *d* Other ancient
authorities read *Lord worthily*   *e* Or *tabernacle*

NEW AMERICAN BIBLE

2 For he scourges and then has mercy;
　he casts down to the depths of the netherworld,
　and he brings up from the great abyss.
No one can escape his hand.

3 Praise him, you Israelites, before the Gentiles,
　for though he has scattered you among them,
4 　he has shown you his greatness even there.
Exalt him before every living being,
　because he is the Lord our God,
　our Father and God forever.
5 He scourged you for your iniquities,
　but will again have mercy on you all.
He will gather you from all the Gentiles
　among whom you have been scattered.

6 When you turn back to him with all your heart,
　to do what is right before him,
Then he will turn back to you,
　and no longer hide his face from you.
So now consider what he has done for you,
　and praise him with full voice.
Bless the Lord of righteousness,
　and exalt the King of the ages.

In the land of my exile I praise him,
　and show his power and majesty to a
　　sinful nation.
"Turn back, you sinners! do the right before him:
　perhaps he may look with favor upon you
　and show you mercy.
7 "As for me, I exalt my God,
　and my spirit rejoices in the King of heaven.
8 Let all men speak of his majesty,
　and sing his praises in Jerusalem."

9 O Jerusalem, holy city,
　he scourged you for the works of your hands,
　but will again pity the children of the righteous.
10 Praise the Lord for his goodness,
　and bless the King of the ages,
　so that his tent may be rebuilt in you with joy.
May he gladden within you all who were captives;
　all who were ravaged may he cherish within you
　for all generations to come.

11 A bright light will shine to all parts of the earth;
　many nations shall come to you from afar,
And the inhabitants of all the limits of the earth,
　drawn to you by the name of the Lord God,
Bearing in their hands their gifts for the King
　　of heaven.
Every generation shall give joyful praise in you,
　and shall call you the chosen one,
　through all ages forever.

NEW JERUSALEM BIBLE

2 For he both punishes and pardons;
　he sends people down to the depths of the
　　underworld
　and draws them up from utter Destruction;
　no one can escape his hand.
3 Declare his praise before the nations,
　you who are the children of Israel!
For if he has scattered you among them,
4 there too he has shown you his greatness.
Extol him before all the living;
　he is our Lord
　and he is our God;
　he is our Father,
　and he is God for ever and ever.

5 Though he punishes you for your iniquities,
　he will take pity on you all;
　he will gather you from every nation
　wherever you have been scattered.
6 If you return to him
　with all your heart and all your soul,
　behaving honestly towards him,
　then he will return to you
　and hide his face from you no longer.
Consider how well he has treated you;
　loudly give him thanks.
Bless the Lord of justice
　and extol the King of the ages.

I for my part sing his praise
　in the country of my exile;
I make his power and greatness known
　to a nation that has sinned.
Sinners, return to him;
　let your conduct be upright before him;
　perhaps he will be gracious to you
　and take pity on you.
7 I for my part extol God
　and my soul rejoices
　in the King of heaven.
Let his greatness 8 be on every tongue,
　his praises be sung in Jerusalem.

9 Jerusalem, Holy City,
　God has scourged you for what you have done
　but will still take pity on the children of the
　　upright.
10 Thank the Lord as he deserves
　and bless the King of the ages,
　that your Temple may be rebuilt with joy within
　　you;
　within you he may comfort every exile,
　and within you he may love all those who are
　　distressed,
　for all generations to come.

11 A bright light will shine
　over all the regions of the earth;
　many nations will come from far away,
　from all the ends of the earth,
　to dwell close to the holy name of the Lord God,
　with gifts in their hands for the King of heaven.
Within you, generation after generation
　will proclaim their joy,
　and the name of her who is Elect will endure
　through the generations to come.

NEW REVISED STANDARD VERSION	REVISED ENGLISH BIBLE

NEW REVISED STANDARD VERSION

12 Cursed are all who speak a harsh word against
you;
cursed are all who conquer you
and pull down your walls,
all who overthrow your towers
and set your homes on fire.
But blessed forever will be all who revere
you.*f*

13 Go, then, and rejoice over the children of the
righteous,
for they will be gathered together
and will praise the Lord of the ages.

14 Happy are those who love you,
and happy are those who rejoice in your
prosperity.
Happy also are all people who grieve with you
because of your afflictions;
for they will rejoice with you
and witness all your glory forever.

15 My soul blesses*g* the Lord, the great King!

16 For Jerusalem will be built*h* as his house for
all ages.
How happy I will be if a remnant of my
descendants should survive
to see your glory and acknowledge the King of
heaven.
The gates of Jerusalem will be built with sapphire
and emerald,
and all your walls with precious stones.
The towers of Jerusalem will be built with gold,
and their battlements with pure gold.
The streets of Jerusalem will be paved
with ruby and with stones of Ophir.

17 The gates of Jerusalem will sing hymns of joy,
and all her houses will cry, 'Hallelujah!
Blessed be the God of Israel!'
and the blessed will bless the holy name
forever and ever."

14 So ended Tobit's words of praise.
2 Tobit*i* died in peace when he was one hundred
twelve years old, and was buried with great honor in Nineveh. He was sixty-two*j* years old when he lost his eyesight, and after regaining it he lived in prosperity, giving
alms and continually blessing God and acknowledging
God's majesty.

3 When he was about to die, he called his son Tobias
and the seven sons of Tobias*k* and gave this command:
"My son, take your children 4 and hurry off to Media, for I
believe the word of God that Nahum spoke about Nineveh,
that all these things will take place and overtake Assyria and
Nineveh. Indeed, everything that was spoken by the prophets of Israel, whom God sent, will occur. None of all their
words will fail, but all will come true at their appointed
times. So it will be safer in Media than in Assyria and
Babylon. For I know and believe that whatever God has
said will be fulfilled and will come true; not a single word
of the prophecies will fail. All of our kindred, inhabitants of
the land of Israel, will be scattered and taken as captives
from the good land; and the whole land of Israel will be
desolate, even Samaria and Jerusalem will be desolate. And
the temple of God in it will be burned to the ground, and it
will be desolate for a while.*l*

REVISED ENGLISH BIBLE

12 Accursed will be all who speak harshly to you,
all who wreak destruction, pulling down your
walls,
overthrowing your towers, and burning your
houses;
but for ever blessed will be those who rebuild you.

13 Come then, be joyful for the righteous,
for they will all be gathered together
and will praise the eternal Lord.

14 How happy will they be who love you
and happy those who rejoice in your prosperity,
happy those who grieve for you in all your
afflictions!
They will rejoice over you
and behold all your joy for ever.

15 My soul, praise the Lord, the great King,

16 for Jerusalem will be built again
to be his dwelling-place for all time.
How happy I shall be when the remnant of my
descendants
see your splendour and give thanks to the King of
heaven!
The gates of Jerusalem will be built of sapphire
and emerald,
and all the walls of costly stones.
The towers of Jerusalem will be built of gold,
their battlements of the finest gold.

17 The streets of Jerusalem will be paved
with garnets and jewels of Ophir.

18 Jerusalem's gates will sing hymns of joy
and all the houses in her will say,
'Alleluia! Praise to the God of Israel!'
In you, O Jerusalem, his holy name
will be praised for ever and ever.

14 So ended Tobit's thanksgiving. He died peacefully
at the age of a hundred and twelve, and was buried
in Nineveh with all honour. 2 He was sixty-two years old
when his eyes were damaged, and after he recovered his
sight he lived in prosperity, doing acts of charity and never
ceasing to praise God and to proclaim his majesty.

3 When he was dying, he sent for his son Tobias and gave
him these instructions: 'My son, you must take your children 4 and be off to Media with all haste, for I believe God's
word spoken against Nineveh by Nahum. It will all come
true; everything will happen to Asshur and Nineveh that
was spoken by the prophets of Israel who were sent by God.
Not a word of it will fall short; all will take place in due
time. It will be safer in Media than in Assyria or Babylon.
I know, I am convinced, that all God's words will be fulfilled. It will be so: not one of them will fail. Our countrymen who live in Israel will all be scattered and carried off
into captivity out of that good land. The whole of Israel's
territory with Samaria and Jerusalem will lie waste; and for
a time the house of God will be in mourning, burnt to the
ground.

*f*Other ancient authorities read *who build you up*   *g*Or *O my soul,*
bless   *h*Other ancient authorities add *for a city*   *i*Gk *He*
*j*Other ancient authorities read *fifty-eight*   *k*Lat: Gk lacks *and the*
seven sons of Tobias   *l*Lat: Other ancient authorities read *of God*
will be in distress and will be burned for a while

12 Accursed are all who speak a harsh word
  against you;
  accursed are all who destroy you
  and pull down your walls,
And all who overthrow your towers
  and set fire to your homes;
  but forever blessed are all those who build you
    up.

13 Go, then, rejoice over the children of
    the righteous,
  who shall all be gathered together
  and shall bless the Lord of the ages.
14 Happy are those who love you,
  and happy those who rejoice in your prosperity.

Happy are all the men who shall grieve over you,
  over all your chastisements,
For they shall rejoice in you
  as they behold all your joy forever.

15 My spirit blesses the Lord, the great King;
16   Jerusalem shall be rebuilt as his home forever.
  Happy for me if a remnant of my offspring survive
  to see your glory and to praise the King
    of heaven!

The gates of Jerusalem shall be built with sapphire
    and emerald,
  and all your walls with precious stones.
The towers of Jerusalem shall be built with gold,
  and their battlements with pure gold.
17 The streets of Jerusalem shall be paved
  with rubies and stones of Ophir;
18 The gates of Jerusalem shall sing hymns
    of gladness,
  and all her houses shall cry out, "Alleluia!"

  "Blessed be God who has raised you up!
    may he be blessed for all ages!"
  For in you they shall praise his holy name forever.

The end of Tobit's hymn of praise.

14 Tobit died peacefully at the age of a hundred and
twelve, and received an honorable burial in Nineveh. 2 He was sixty-two years old when he lost his eyesight,
and after he recovered it he lived in prosperity, giving alms
and continually blessing God and praising the divine Majesty.
3 Just before he died, he called his son Tobiah and Tobiah's seven sons, and gave him this command: "Son, take
your children 4 and flee into Media, for I believe God's
word which was spoken by Nahum against Nineveh. It shall
all happen, and shall overtake Assyria and Nineveh; indeed,
whatever was said by Israel's prophets, whom God commissioned, shall occur. Not one of all the oracles shall
remain unfulfilled, but everything shall take place in the
time appointed for it. So it will be safer in Media than in
Assyria or Babylon. For I know and believe that whatever
God has spoken will be accomplished. It shall happen, and
not a single word of the prophecies shall prove false.
  "As for our kinsmen who dwell in Israel, they shall all be
scattered and led away into exile from the Good Land. The
entire country of Israel shall become desolate; even Samaria
and Jerusalem shall become desolate! God's temple there
shall be burnt to the ground and shall be desolate for a

12 Cursed be any who affront you,
  cursed be any who destroy you,
  who throw down your walls,
  who rase your towers,
  who burn your houses!
  Eternally blessed be he who rebuilds you!
13 Then you will exult, and rejoice
  over the children of the upright,
  for they will all have been gathered in
  and will bless the Lord of the ages.

14 Blessed are those who love you,
  blessed those who rejoice over your peace,
  blessed those who have mourned
  over all your punishment!
  For they will soon rejoice within you,
  witness all your blessedness in days to come.
15 My soul blesses the Lord, the great King
16 because Jerusalem will be built anew
  and his house for ever and ever.

What bliss, if one of my family be left
  to see your glory and praise the King of heaven!
The gates of Jerusalem will be built
  of sapphire and of emerald,
  and all your walls of precious stone,
  the towers of Jerusalem will be built of gold
  and their battlements of pure gold.
17 The streets of Jerusalem will be paved
  with ruby and with stones from Ophir;
  the gates of Jerusalem will resound
  with songs of exultation;
  and all her houses will say,
  'Alleluia! Blessed be the God of Israel.'
  Within you they will bless the holy name
  for ever and ever.

14 The end of the hymns of Tobit.

  Tobit died when he was a hundred and twelve years old
and received an honourable burial in Nineveh. 2 He had
been sixty-two when he went blind; and after his cure, he
lived in comfort, practising almsgiving and continually
praising God and extolling his greatness. 3 When he was at
the point of death he summoned his son Tobias and gave
him these instructions, 4 'My son, take your children and
hurry away to Media, since I believe the word of God
pronounced over Nineveh by Nahum. Everything will come
true, everything happen that the emissaries of God, the
prophets of Israel, have predicted against Assyria and
Nineveh; not one of their words will prove false. It will all
take place in due time. You will be safer in Media than in
Assyria or in Babylonia. Since I for my part know and
believe that everything God has said will come true; so it
will be, and not a word of the prophecies will fail.
  'A census will be taken of our brothers living in the land
of Israel and they will be exiled far from their own fair
country. The entire territory of Israel will become a desert,
and Samaria and Jerusalem will become a desert, and the
house of God, for a time, will be laid waste and burnt.

5 "But God will again have mercy on them, and God will bring them back into the land of Israel; and they will rebuild the temple of God, but not like the first one until the period when the times of fulfillment shall come. After this they all will return from their exile and will rebuild Jerusalem in splendor; and in it the temple of God will be rebuilt, just as the prophets of Israel have said concerning it. 6 Then the nations in the whole world will all be converted and worship God in truth. They will all abandon their idols, which deceitfully have led them into their error; 7 and in righteousness they will praise the eternal God. All the Israelites who are saved in those days and are truly mindful of God will be gathered together; they will go to Jerusalem and live in safety forever in the land of Abraham, and it will be given over to them. Those who sincerely love God will rejoice, but those who commit sin and injustice will vanish from all the earth. 8,9 So now, my children, I command you, serve God faithfully and do what is pleasing in his sight. Your children are also to be commanded to do what is right and to give alms, and to be mindful of God and to bless his name at all times with sincerity and with all their strength. So now, my son, leave Nineveh; do not remain here. 10 On whatever day you bury your mother beside me, do not stay overnight within the confines of the city. For I see that there is much wickedness within it, and that much deceit is practiced within it, while the people are without shame. See, my son, what Nadab did to Ahikar who had reared him. Was he not, while still alive, brought down into the earth? For God repaid him to his face for this shameful treatment. Ahikar came out into the light, but Nadab went into the eternal darkness, because he tried to kill Ahikar. Because he gave alms, Ahikar[m] escaped the fatal trap that Nadab had set for him, but Nadab fell into it himself, and was destroyed. 11 So now, my children, see what almsgiving accomplishes, and what injustice does — it brings death! But now my breath fails me."

Then they laid him on his bed, and he died; and he received an honorable funeral. 12 When Tobias's mother died, he buried her beside his father. Then he and his wife and children[n] returned to Media and settled in Ecbatana with Raguel his father-in-law. 13 He treated his parents-in-law[o] with great respect in their old age, and buried them in Ecbatana of Media. He inherited both the property of Raguel and that of his father Tobit. 14 He died highly respected at the age of one hundred seventeen[p] years. 15 Before he died he heard[q] of the destruction of Nineveh, and he saw its prisoners being led into Media, those whom King Cyaxares[r] of Media had taken captive. Tobias[s] praised God for all he had done to the people of Nineveh and Assyria; before he died he rejoiced over Nineveh, and he blessed the Lord God forever and ever. Amen.[t]

m Gk *he*; other ancient authorities read *Manasses*   n Codex Sinaiticus lacks *and children*   o Gk *them*   p Other authorities read other numbers   q Codex Sinaiticus reads *saw and heard*   r Cn: Codex Sinaiticus *Ahikar*; other ancient authorities read *Nebuchadnezzar and Ahasuerus*   s Gk *He*   t Other ancient authorities lack *Amen*

5 'But God will have mercy on them again and bring them back to the land of Israel. They will rebuild the house of God, yet not as it was at first, not until the time of fulfilment comes. Then they will all return from their captivity and rebuild Jerusalem in splendour; then indeed God's house will be built in her as the prophets of Israel foretold. 6 All the nations in the whole world will be converted to the true worship of God; they will renounce the idols which led them astray into error, 7 and will praise the eternal God in righteousness. All the Israelites who survive at that time and are firm in their loyalty to God will be brought together; they will come to Jerusalem to take possession of the land of Abraham and will live there securely for ever. Those who love God in sincerity will rejoice; sinners and wrongdoers will disappear from the earth.

8 'My children, I give you this command: serve God in truth and do what is pleasing to him. 9 Teach your children to do what is right and give alms, to be mindful of God and praise his name sincerely at all times and with all their strength.

10 'Now, my son, you must leave Nineveh; do not stay here. Once you have laid your mother in the grave beside me, do not spend another night within the city boundaries, for I observe that the place is full of wickedness and shameless dishonesty. My son, think what Nadab did to Ahikar who brought him up: he forced him to hide in a living grave. Ahikar survived to see God requite the disgrace brought on him; he came out into the light of day, but Nadab passed into everlasting darkness for his attempt to kill Ahikar. Because he gave alms, Ahikar escaped from the deadly trap Nadab set for him, and it was Nadab who fell into the trap and was destroyed. 11 See what comes of almsgiving, my children; and see what comes of wickedness — death. But now my strength is failing.' They laid him on his bed and he died, and he was given honourable burial.

12 When his mother died, Tobias buried her beside his father; then he and his wife and children went to Media, where they settled at Ecbatana with his father-in-law Raguel. 13 He honoured and cared for his wife's parents in their old age. He buried them at Ecbatana in Media, and he inherited the estate of Raguel as well as that of his father Tobit. 14 At the age of a hundred and seventeen he died, greatly respected. 15 Tobias lived long enough to hear of the destruction of Nineveh by King Ahasuerus of Media and to see the prisoners of war brought from there into Media. He praised God for all that he had done to the inhabitants of Nineveh and Asshur; before he died he rejoiced over the fate of Nineveh, and he praised the Lord God who lives for ever and ever.

Amen.

14:10 **he gave alms**: *prob. rdg; Gk* I gave alms.

while. 5 But God will again have mercy on them and bring them back to the land of Israel. They shall rebuild the temple, but it will not be like the first one, until the era when the appointed times shall be completed. Afterward all of them shall return from their exile, and they shall rebuild Jerusalem with splendor. In her the temple of God shall also be rebuilt; yes, it will be rebuilt for all generations to come, just as the prophets of Israel said of her. 6 All the nations of the world shall be converted and shall offer God true worship; all shall abandon their idols which have deceitfully led them into error, 7 and shall bless the God of the ages in righteousness. Because all the Israelites who are to be saved in those days will truly be mindful of God, they shall be gathered together and go to Jerusalem; in security shall they dwell forever in the land of Abraham, which will be given over to them. Those who sincerely love God shall rejoice, but those who become guilty of sin shall completely disappear from the land.

9 "Now, children, I give you this command: serve God faithfully and do what is right before him; you must tell your children to do what is upright and to give alms, to be mindful of God and at all times to bless his name sincerely and with all their strength.

8 "Now, as for you, my son, depart from Nineveh; do not remain here. 10 The day you bury your mother next to me, do not even stay overnight within the confines of the city. For I see that people here shamelessly commit all sorts of wickedness and treachery. Think, my son, of all that Nadab did to Ahiqar, the very one who brought him up: Ahiqar went down alive into the earth! Yet God made Nadab's disgraceful crime rebound against him. Ahiqar came out again into the light, but Nadab went into the everlasting darkness, for he had tried to kill Ahiqar. Because Ahiqar had given alms to me, he escaped from the deadly trap Nadab had set for him. But Nadab himself fell into the deadly trap, and it destroyed him. 11 So, my children, note well what almsgiving does, and also what wickedness does — it kills! But now my spirit is about to leave me."

12 They placed him on his bed and he died; and he received an honorable burial. When Tobiah's mother died, he buried her next to his father. He then departed with his wife and children for Media, where he settled in Ecbatana with his father-in-law Raguel. 13 He took respectful care of his aging father-in-law and mother-in-law; and he buried them at Ecbatana in Media. Then he inherited Raguel's estate as well as that of his father Tobit. 14 He died at the venerable age of a hundred and seventeen. 15 But before he died, he heard of the destruction of Nineveh and saw its effects. He witnessed the exile of the city's inhabitants when Cyaxares, king of Media, led them captive into Media. Tobiah praised God for all that he had done against the citizens of Nineveh and Assyria. Before dying he rejoiced over Nineveh's destruction, and he blessed the Lord God forever and ever. Amen.

5 Then once again God will take pity on them and bring them back to the land of Israel. They will rebuild his house, although it will be less beautiful than the first, until the time is fulfilled. But after this, all will return from captivity and rebuild Jerusalem in all her glory, and the house of God will be rebuilt within her as the prophets of Israel have foretold. 6 And all the people of the whole earth will be converted and will reverence God with all sincerity. All will renounce their false gods who have led them astray into error, 7 and will bless the God of ages in uprightness. All the Israelites spared in those days will remember God in sincerity of heart. They will come and gather in Jerusalem and thereafter dwell securely in the land of Abraham, which will be theirs. And those who sincerely love God will rejoice. And those who commit sin and wickedness will vanish from the earth.

8 'And now, my children, I lay this duty on you; serve God sincerely, and do what is pleasing to him. And lay on your children the obligation to behave uprightly, to give alms, to keep God in mind and to bless his name always, sincerely and with all their might.

9 'So then, my son, leave Nineveh, do not stay here. 10 As soon as you have buried your mother next to me, go the same day, whenever it may be, and do not linger in this country where I see wickedness and perfidy unashamedly triumphant. Consider, my child, all the things done by Nadab to his foster-father Ahikar. Was not Ahikar forced to go underground, though still a living man? But God made the criminal pay for his outrage before his victim's eyes, since Ahikar came back to the light of day, while Nadab went down to everlasting darkness in punishment for plotting against Ahikar's life. Because of his good works Ahikar escaped the deadly snare Nadab had laid for him, and Nadab fell into it to his own ruin. 11 So, my children, you see what comes of almsgiving, and what wickedness leads to, I mean to death. But now breath fails me.'

They laid him back on his bed; he died and was buried with honour.

12 When his mother died, Tobias buried her beside his father. Then he left for Media with his wife and children. He lived in Ecbatana with Raguel, his father-in-law. 13 He treated the ageing parents of his wife with every care and respect, and later buried them in Ecbatana in Media. Tobias inherited the patrimony of Raguel besides that of his father Tobit. 14 Much honoured, he lived to the age of a hundred and seventeen years. 15 Before he died he witnessed the ruin of Nineveh. He saw the Ninevites taken prisoner and deported to Media by Cyaxares king of Media. He blessed God for everything he inflicted on the Ninevites and Assyrians. Before his death he had the opportunity of rejoicing over the fate of Nineveh, and he blessed the Lord God for ever and ever. Amen.

Judith

1 It was the twelfth year of the reign of Nebuchadnezzar, who ruled over the Assyrians in the great city of Nineveh. In those days Arphaxad ruled over the Medes in Ecbatana. 2 He built walls around Ecbatana with hewn stones three cubits thick and six cubits long; he made the walls seventy cubits high and fifty cubits wide. 3 At its gates he raised towers one hundred cubits high and sixty cubits wide at the foundations. 4 He made its gates seventy cubits high and forty cubits wide to allow his armies to march out in force and his infantry to form their ranks. 5 Then King Nebuchadnezzar made war against King Arphaxad in the great plain that is on the borders of Ragau. 6 There rallied to him all the people of the hill country and all those who lived along the Euphrates, the Tigris, and the Hydaspes, and, on the plain, Arioch, king of the Elymeans. Thus, many nations joined the forces of the Chaldeans. *a*

7 Then Nebuchadnezzar, king of the Assyrians, sent messengers to all who lived in Persia and to all who lived in the west, those who lived in Cilicia and Damascus, Lebanon and Antilebanon, and all who lived along the seacoast, 8 and those among the nations of Carmel and Gilead, Upper Galilee and the great plain of Esdraelon, 9 and all who were in Samaria and its towns, and beyond the Jordan as far as Jerusalem and Bethany and Chelous and Kadesh and the river of Egypt, and Tahpanhes and Raamses and the whole land of Goshen 10 even beyond Tanis and Memphis, and all who lived in Egypt as far as the borders of Ethiopia. 11 But all who lived in the whole region disregarded the summons of Nebuchadnezzar, king of the Assyrians, and refused to join him in the war; for they were not afraid of him, but regarded him as only one man. *b* So they sent back his messengers empty-handed and in disgrace.

12 Then Nebuchadnezzar became very angry with this whole region, and swore by his throne and kingdom that he would take revenge on the whole territory of Cilicia and Damascus and Syria, that he would kill with his sword also all the inhabitants of the land of Moab, and the people of Ammon, and all Judea, and every one in Egypt, as far as the coasts of the two seas.

13 In the seventeenth year he led his forces against King Arphaxad and defeated him in battle, overthrowing the whole army of Arphaxad and all his cavalry and all his chariots. 14 Thus he took possession of his towns and came to Ecbatana, captured its towers, plundered its markets, and turned its glory into disgrace. 15 He captured Arphaxad in the mountains of Ragau and struck him down with his spears, thus destroying him once and for all. 16 Then he returned to Nineveh, he and all his combined forces, a vast body of troops; and there he and his forces rested and feasted for one hundred twenty days.

2 In the eighteenth year, on the twenty-second day of the first month, there was talk in the palace of Nebuchadnezzar, king of the Assyrians, about carrying out his revenge on the whole region, just as he had said. 2 He summoned all his ministers and all his nobles and set before them his secret plan and recounted fully, with his own lips, all the wickedness of the region. *c* 3 They decided that every one who had not obeyed his command should be destroyed.

4 When he had completed his plan, Nebuchadnezzar, king of the Assyrians, called Holofernes, the chief general of his army, second only to himself, and said to him,

Judith

1 IN the twelfth year of the reign of Nebuchadnezzar, who ruled the Assyrians from his great city of Nineveh, Arphaxad was ruling the Medes from Ecbatana. 2 Arphaxad encircled Ecbatana with a wall built of hewn stones, each four and a half feet thick and nine feet long. He made the wall a hundred and five feet high and seventy-five feet thick, 3 and at the city gates he set up towers a hundred and fifty feet high with foundations ninety feet thick; 4 the gates themselves he made a hundred and five feet high, and he made them sixty feet wide to allow his army to march out in full force with the infantry in formation. 5 It was in those days, then, that King Nebuchadnezzar waged war against King Arphaxad in the great plain on the borders of Ragau. 6 All the inhabitants of the hill-country, all who lived along the Euphrates, the Tigris, and the Hydaspes, and, on the plain, King Arioch of Elam, these rallied to Nebuchadnezzar; and many tribes of the Chelodites joined forces with them.

7 King Nebuchadnezzar of Assyria sent a summons to all the inhabitants of Persia, and to all who lived in the west: the inhabitants of Cilicia and Damascus, Lebanon and Antilebanon, all who lived along the coast, 8 the peoples in Carmel and Gilead, Upper Galilee, and the great plain of Esdraelon, 9 all who were in Samaria and its towns, and those to the west of the Jordan as far as Jerusalem, Betane, Chelus, Kadesh, and the wadi of Egypt, those who lived in Tahpanhes, Rameses, and the whole land of Goshen 10 as far as Tanis and Memphis, and all the inhabitants of Egypt as far as the borders of Ethiopia. 11 But the king's summons was flouted by the entire region, and they did not join him for the campaign. They were not afraid of him; they regarded him as a mere man, and treating his envoys with contempt, they sent them back empty-handed.

12 This roused Nebuchadnezzar to fury against the whole region; he swore by his throne and kingdom to exact vengeance from all the territories of Cilicia, Damascus, and Syria, and to put their inhabitants to the sword, along with the Moabites, the Ammonites, the people throughout Judaea, and everyone in Egypt, the whole region within the limits of the two seas.

13 In the seventeenth year of his reign he marshalled his forces against King Arphaxad and defeated him in battle, with the complete rout of his army, all his cavalry and chariots. 14 He occupied his towns, and advancing on Ecbatana he captured its towers, looted the bazaars, and reduced its splendour to abject ruin. 15 He caught Arphaxad in the mountains of Ragau and ran him through with his spear, and so made an end of him. 16 Then he and his combined forces, an immense host of warriors, went back with the spoil to Nineveh, where for four months he relaxed and feasted with his army.

2 In the eighteenth year, on the twenty-second day of the first month, there was a conference in King Nebuchadnezzar's palace about implementing his threat of vengeance on the whole region. 2 Calling together all his officers and nobles, the king laid before them his secret plan for the region and declared his determination to put an end to the disaffection. 3 It was resolved by them that everyone who had not obeyed the king's summons should die.

4 When his plans were completed, King Nebuchadnezzar of Assyria summoned his commander-in-chief Holophernes, who was second only to himself, and said, 5 'This

---

a Syr: Gk *Cheleoudites*   *b* Or *a man*   *c* Meaning of Gk uncertain   1:15 **made an end of him**: *prob. rdg; Gk adds* up to that day.

THE BOOK OF
Judith

Judith

1 It was the twelfth year of the reign of Nebuchadnezzar, king of the Assyrians in the great city of Nineveh. At that time Arphaxad ruled over the Medes in Ecbatana. ² Around this city he built a wall of blocks of stone, each three cubits in height and six in length. He made the wall seventy cubits high and fifty thick. ³ At the gates he raised towers of a hundred cubits, with a thickness of sixty cubits at the base. ⁴ The gateway he built to a height of seventy cubits, with an opening forty cubits wide for the passage of his chariot forces and the marshaling of his infantry. ⁵ Then King Nebuchadnezzar waged war against King Arphaxad in the vast plain, in the district of Ragae. ⁶ To him there rallied all the inhabitants of the mountain region, all who dwelt along the Euphrates, the Tigris, and the Hydaspes, and King Arioch of the Elamites, in the plain. Thus many nations came together to resist the people of Cheleoud.

⁷ Now Nebuchadnezzar, king of the Assyrians, sent messengers to all the inhabitants of Persia, and to all those who dwelt in the West: to the inhabitants of Cilicia and Damascus, Lebanon and Anti-Lebanon, to all who dwelt along the seacoast, ⁸ to the peoples of Carmel, Gilead, Upper Galilee, and the vast plain of Esdraelon, ⁹ to all those in Samaria and its cities, and west of the Jordan as far as Jerusalem, Bethany, Chelous, Kadesh, and the River of Egypt; to Tahpanhes, Raamses, all the land of Goshen, ¹⁰ Tanis, Memphis and beyond, and to all the inhabitants of Egypt as far as the borders of Ethiopia.

¹¹ But the inhabitants of all that land disregarded the summons of Nebuchadnezzar, king of the Assyrians, and would not go with him to the war. They were not afraid of him but regarded him as a lone individual opposed to them, and turned away his envoys empty-handed, in disgrace. ¹² Then Nebuchadnezzar fell into a violent rage against all that land, and swore by his throne and his kingdom that he would avenge himself on all the territories of Cilicia and Damascus and Syria, and also destroy with his sword all the inhabitants of Moab, Ammon, the whole of Judea, and those living anywhere in Egypt as far as the borders of the two seas.

¹³ In the seventeenth year he proceeded with his army against King Arphaxad, and was victorious in his campaign. He routed the whole force of Arphaxad, his entire cavalry and all his chariots, ¹⁴ and took possession of his cities. He pressed on to Ecbatana and took its towers, sacked its marketplaces, and turned its glory into shame. ¹⁵ Arphaxad himself he overtook in the mountains of Ragae, ran him through with spears, and utterly destroyed him. ¹⁶ Then he returned home with all his numerous, motley horde of warriors; and there he and his army relaxed and feasted for a hundred and twenty days.

2 In the eighteenth year, on the twenty-second day of the first month, there was a discussion in the palace of Nebuchadnezzar, king of the Assyrians, about taking revenge on the whole world, as he had threatened. ² He summoned all his ministers and nobles, laid before them his secret plan, and urged the total destruction of those countries. ³ They decided to do away with all those who had refused to comply with the order he had issued.

⁴ When he had completed his plan, Nebuchadnezzar, king of the Assyrians, summoned Holofernes, general in chief of his forces, second to himself in command, and said to him:

1 It was the twelfth year of Nebuchadnezzar who reigned over the Assyrians in the great city of Nineveh. Arphaxad was then reigning over the Medes in Ecbatana. ² He surrounded this city with walls of dressed stones three cubits thick and six cubits long, making the rampart seventy cubits high and fifty cubits wide. ³ At the gates he placed towers one hundred cubits high and, at the foundations, sixty cubits wide, ⁴ the gates themselves being seventy cubits high and forty cubits wide to allow his forces to march out in a body and his infantry to parade freely. ⁵ About this time King Nebuchadnezzar gave battle to King Arphaxad in the great plain lying in the territory of Ragae. ⁶ Supporting him were all the peoples from the highlands, all from the Euphrates and Tigris and Hydaspes, and those from the plains who were subject to Arioch, king of the Elymaeans. Thus many nations had mustered to take part in the battle of the Cheleoudites.

⁷ Nebuchadnezzar king of the Assyrians sent a message to all the inhabitants of Persia, to all the inhabitants of the western countries, Cilicia, Damascus, Lebanon, Anti-Lebanon, to all those along the coast, ⁸ to the peoples of Carmel, Gilead, Upper Galilee, the great plain of Esdraelon, ⁹ to the people of Samaria and its outlying towns, to those beyond Jordan, as far away as Jerusalem, Bethany, Chelous, Kadesh, the river of Egypt, Tahpanhes, Rameses and the whole territory of Goshen, ¹⁰ beyond Tanis too and Memphis, and to all the inhabitants of Egypt as far as the frontiers of Ethiopia. ¹¹ But the inhabitants of these countries ignored the summons of Nebuchadnezzar king of Assyria and did not rally to him to make war. They were not afraid of him, since in their view he appeared isolated. Hence they sent his ambassadors back with nothing achieved and in disgrace. ¹² Nebuchadnezzar was furious with all these countries. He swore by his throne and kingdom to take revenge on all the territories of Cilicia, Damascus and Syria, of the Moabites and of the Ammonites, of Judaea and Egypt as far as the limits of the two seas, and to ravage them with the sword.

¹³ In the seventeenth year, he gave battle with his whole army to King Arphaxad and in this battle defeated him. He routed Arphaxad's entire army and all his cavalry and chariots; ¹⁴ he occupied his towns and advanced on Ecbatana; he seized its towers and plundered its market places, reducing its former magnificence to a mockery. ¹⁵ He later captured Arphaxad in the mountains of Ragae and, thrusting him through with his spears, destroyed him once and for all. ¹⁶ He then retired with his troops and all who had joined forces with him: a vast horde of armed men. Then he and his army gave themselves up to carefree feasting for a hundred and twenty days.

2 In the eighteenth year, on the twenty-second day of the first month, a rumour ran through the palace that Nebuchadnezzar king of the Assyrians was to have his revenge on all the countries, as he had threatened. ² Summoning his general staff and senior officers, he held a secret conference with them, and with his own lips pronounced utter destruction on the entire area. ³ It was then decreed that everyone should be put to death who had not answered the king's appeal.

⁴ When the council was over, Nebuchadnezzar king of the Assyrians sent for Holofernes, general-in-chief of his armies and subordinate only to himself. He said to him,

NEW REVISED STANDARD VERSION

5 "Thus says the Great King, the lord of the whole earth: Leave my presence and take with you men confident in their strength, one hundred twenty thousand foot soldiers and twelve thousand cavalry. 6 March out against all the land to the west, because they disobeyed my orders. 7 Tell them to prepare earth and water, for I am coming against them in my anger, and will cover the whole face of the earth with the feet of my troops, to whom I will hand them over to be plundered. 8 Their wounded shall fill their ravines and gullies, and the swelling river shall be filled with their dead. 9 I will lead them away captive to the ends of the whole earth. 10 You shall go and seize all their territory for me in advance. They must yield themselves to you, and you shall hold them for me until the day of their punishment. 11 But to those who resist show no mercy, but hand them over to slaughter and plunder throughout your whole region. 12 For as I live, and by the power of my kingdom, what I have spoken I will accomplish by my own hand. 13 And you— take care not to transgress any of your lord's commands, but carry them out exactly as I have ordered you; do it without delay."

14 So Holofernes left the presence of his lord, and summoned all the commanders, generals, and officers of the Assyrian army. 15 He mustered the picked troops by divisions as his lord had ordered him to do, one hundred twenty thousand of them, together with twelve thousand archers on horseback, 16 and he organized them as a great army is marshaled for a campaign. 17 He took along a vast number of camels and donkeys and mules for transport, and innumerable sheep and oxen and goats for food; 18 also ample rations for everyone, and a huge amount of gold and silver from the royal palace.

19 Then he set out with his whole army, to go ahead of King Nebuchadnezzar and to cover the whole face of the earth to the west with their chariots and cavalry and picked foot soldiers. 20 Along with them went a mixed crowd like a swarm of locusts, like the dust*d* of the earth—a multitude that could not be counted.

21 They marched for three days from Nineveh to the plain of Bectileth, and camped opposite Bectileth near the mountain that is to the north of Upper Cilicia. 22 From there Holofernes*e* took his whole army, the infantry, cavalry, and chariots, and went up into the hill country. 23 He ravaged Put and Lud, and plundered all the Rassisites and the Ishmaelites on the border of the desert, south of the country of the Chelleans. 24 Then he followed*f* the Euphrates and passed through Mesopotamia and destroyed all the fortified towns along the brook Abron, as far as the sea. 25 He also seized the territory of Cilicia, and killed everyone who resisted him. Then he came to the southern borders of Japheth, facing Arabia. 26 He surrounded all the Midianites, and burned their tents and plundered their sheepfolds. 27 Then he went down into the plain of Damascus during the wheat harvest, and burned all their fields and destroyed their flocks and herds and sacked their towns and ravaged their lands and put all their young men to the sword.

28 So fear and dread of him fell upon all the people who lived along the seacoast, at Sidon and Tyre, and those who lived in Sur and Ocina and all who lived in Jamnia. Those who lived in Azotus and Ascalon feared him greatly.

3 They therefore sent messengers to him to sue for peace in these words: 2 "We, the servants of Nebuchadnezzar, the Great King, lie prostrate before you. Do with us whatever you will. 3 See, our buildings and all our land and all our wheat fields and our flocks and herds and all our encampments*g* lie before you; do with them as you please.

is the decree of the Great King, lord of all the earth: Directly you leave my presence, you are to take under your command an army of seasoned troops, a hundred and twenty thousand infantry with a force of twelve thousand cavalry, 6 and march against all the peoples of the west who have dared to disobey the order I issued. 7 Bid them have earth and water ready in token of submission, for I am coming to vent my wrath on them. Every corner of their land will be overrun by my army, and I shall give them up to be plundered by my troops; 8 their wounded will fill the ravines and wadis, and every river will be choked with their dead; 9 and I shall send them into captivity to the ends of the earth. 10 Go, and occupy all their territory for me. If they submit, hold them for me until the time comes to punish them. 11 But to those who resist show no mercy; throughout the whole region give them up to be slaughtered and plundered. 12 By my life and royal power I have spoken and shall act accordingly. 13 You are to obey these orders to the letter; see that you discharge them exactly as I your sovereign have commanded you, and do so without delay!'

14 Withdrawing from the royal presence, Holophernes summoned all the marshals, generals, and officers of the Assyrian army. 15 He mustered, as the king had commanded, a hundred and twenty thousand infantry and twelve thousand mounted archers, all picked men, 16 and marshalled them in the regular battle order of a great army. 17 He took an immense number of camels, donkeys, and mules for the baggage, innumerable sheep, oxen, and goats for provisions, 18 ample rations for every man, as well as a great quantity of gold and silver from the royal palace. 19 With his whole army he set off in advance of King Nebuchadnezzar to overrun the entire region to the west with his chariots, cavalry, and picked infantry. 20 Accompanying them went a motley host like a swarm of locusts, countless as the dust of the earth.

21 From Nineveh they marched for three days towards the plain of Bectileth, and encamped near Bectileth near the mountain to the north of Upper Cilicia. 22 From there Holophernes pushed on into the hill-country with his whole army—infantry, cavalry, and chariots. 23 He devastated Put and Lud, and plundered all the people of Rassis, and the Ishmaelites on the edge of the desert south of the land of the Cheleans. 24 Then following the Euphrates he traversed Mesopotamia and destroyed every fortified town along the wadi Abron as far as the sea. 25 He occupied the territory of Cilicia, cutting down any who resisted. He marched south to the borders of Japheth which fronts Arabia. 26 He encircled the Midianites, set their encampments on fire, and plundered their sheepfolds. 27 He went down into the plain of Damascus at the time of the wheat harvest, and set fire to the crops; he slaughtered the flocks and herds, sacked the towns, laid waste the countryside, and put all the young men to the sword.

28 Fear and dread of him assailed the inhabitants of the coast at Sidon and Tyre, and the people of Sur and Okina, and of Jemnaan; terror seized the populations of Azotus and Ascalon.

3 1 They sent envoys to sue for peace. 2 'We, the servants of the Great King, Nebuchadnezzar, lie prostrate before you,' they said; 'do with us as you please. 3 Our homesteads, all our territory and wheatfields, our flocks and herds with every sheepfold in our encampments, all are yours to deal with as you will. 4 Our towns along with their

d Gk sand   *e* Gk he   *f* Or crossed   *g* Gk all the sheepfolds of our tents

2:24 **following:** or crossing.

5 "Thus says the great king, the lord of all the earth: Go forth from my presence, take with you men of proven valor, a hundred and twenty thousand infantry and twelve thousand cavalry, 6 and proceed against all the land of the West, because they did not comply with the order I issued. 7 Tell them to have earth and water ready, for I will come against them in my wrath; I will cover all the land with the feet of my soldiers, to whom I will deliver them as spoils. 8 Their slain shall fill their ravines and wadies, the swelling torrent shall be choked with their dead; 9 and I will deport them as exiles to the very ends of the earth.

10 "You go before me and take possession of all their territories for me. If they surrender to you, guard them for me till the day of their punishment. 11 As for those who resist, show them no quarter, but deliver them up to slaughter and plunder in each country you occupy. 12 For as I live, and by the strength of my kingdom, what I have spoken I will accomplish by my power. 13 Do not disobey a single one of the orders of your lord; fulfill them exactly as I have commanded you, and do it without delay."

14 So Holofernes left the presence of his lord, and summoned all the princes, and the generals and officers of the Assyrian army. 15 He mustered a hundred and twenty thousand picked troops, as his lord had commanded, and twelve thousand mounted archers, 16 and grouped them into a complete combat force. 17 He took along a very large number of camels, asses, and mules for their baggage; innumerable sheep, cattle, and goats for their food supply; 18 abundant provisions for each man, and much gold and silver from the royal palace.

19 Then he and his whole army proceeded on their expedition in advance of King Nebuchadnezzar, to cover all the western region with their chariots and cavalry and regular infantry. 20 A huge, irregular force, too many to count, like locusts or the dust of the earth, went along with them.

21 After a three-day march from Nineveh, they reached the plain of Bectileth, and from Bectileth they next encamped near the mountains to the north of Upper Cilicia. 22 From there Holofernes took his whole force, the infantry, calvary, and chariots, and marched into the mountain region. 23 He devastated Put and Lud, and plundered all the Rassisites and the Ishmaelites on the border of the desert toward the south of Chaldea.

24 Then, following the Euphrates, he went through Mesopotamia, and battered down every fortified city along the Wadi Abron, until he reached the sea. 25 He seized the territory of Cilicia, and cut down everyone who resisted him. Then he proceeded to the southern borders of Japheth, toward Arabia. 26 He surrounded all the Midianites, burned their tents, and plundered their sheepfolds. 27 Descending to the plain of Damascus at the time of the wheat harvest, he set fire to all their fields, destroyed their flocks and herds, despoiled their cities, devastated their plains, and put all their youths to the sword.

28 The fear and dread of him fell upon all the inhabitants of the coastland, upon those in Sidon and Tyre, and those who dwelt in Sur and Ocina, and the inhabitants of Jamnia. Those in Azotus and Ascalon also feared him greatly.

3 They therefore sent messengers to him to sue for peace in these words: 2 "We, the servants of Nebuchadnezzar the great king, lie prostrate before you; do with us as you will. 3 Our dwellings and all our wheat fields, our flocks and herds, and all our encampments are at your disposal; make use of them as you please. 4 Our cities and their inhabitants

5 'Thus speaks the Great King, lord of the whole world, "Go; take men of proven valour, about a hundred and twenty thousand foot soldiers and a strong company of horse with twelve thousand cavalrymen; 6 then advance against all the western lands, since these people have disregarded my call. 7 Bid them have earth and water ready, because in my rage I am about to march on them; the feet of my soldiers will cover the whole face of the earth, and I shall plunder it. 8 Their wounded will fill the valleys and the torrents, and rivers, blocked with their dead, will overflow. 9 I shall lead them captive to the ends of the earth. 10 Now go! Begin by conquering this whole region for me. If they surrender to you, hold them for me until the time comes to punish them. 11 But if they resist, look on no one with clemency, hand them over to slaughter and plunder throughout the territory entrusted to you. 12 For by my life and by the living power of my kingdom I have spoken. All this I shall do by my power. 13 And you, neglect none of your master's commands, act strictly according to my orders without further delay." '

14 Leaving the presence of his sovereign, Holofernes immediately summoned all the marshals, generals and officers of the Assyrian army 15 and detailed the picked troops as his master had ordered, about a hundred and twenty thousand men and a further twelve thousand mounted archers. 16 He organised these in the normal battle formation. 17 He then secured vast numbers of camels, donkeys and mules to carry the baggage, and innumerable sheep, oxen and goats for food supplies. 18 Every man received full rations and a generous sum of gold and silver from the king's purse.

19 He then set out for the campaign with his whole army, in advance of King Nebuchadnezzar, to overwhelm the whole western region with his chariots, his horsemen and his picked body of foot. 20 A motley gathering followed in his rear, as numerous as locusts or the grains of sand on the ground; there was no counting their multitude.

21 Thus they set out from Nineveh and marched for three days towards the Plain of Bectileth. From Bectileth they went on to pitch camp near the mountains that lie to the north of Upper Cilicia. 22 From there Holofernes advanced into the highlands with his whole army, infantry, horsemen, chariots. 23 He cut his way through Put and Lud, carried away captive all the sons of Rassis and sons of Ishmael living on the verge of the desert south of Cheleon, 24 marched along the Euphrates, crossed Mesopotamia, rased all the fortified towns controlling the Wadi Abron and reached the sea. 25 Next he attacked the territories of Cilicia, butchering all who offered him resistance, advanced on the southern frontiers of Japheth, facing Arabia, 26 completely encircled the Midianites, burned their tents and plundered their sheep-folds, 27 made his way down to the Damascus plain at the time of the wheat harvest, set fire to the fields, destroyed the flocks and herds, sacked the towns, laid the countryside waste and put all the young men to the sword. 28 Fear and trembling seized all the coastal peoples; those of Sidon and Tyre, those of Sur, Ocina and Jamnia. The populations of Azotos and Ascalon were panic-stricken.

3 They therefore sent envoys to him to sue for peace, to say, 2 'We are servants of the great King Nebuchadnezzar; we lie prostrate before you. Treat us as you think fit. 3 Our cattle-farms, all our land, all our wheat fields, our flocks and herds, all the sheep-folds in our encampments are at your disposal. Do with them as you please. 4 Our

| NEW REVISED STANDARD VERSION | REVISED ENGLISH BIBLE |

4 Our towns and their inhabitants are also your slaves; come and deal with them as you see fit."

5 The men came to Holofernes and told him all this. 6 Then he went down to the seacoast with his army and stationed garrisons in the fortified towns and took picked men from them as auxiliaries. 7 These people and all in the countryside welcomed him with garlands and dances and tambourines. 8 Yet he demolished all their shrines[h] and cut down their sacred groves; for he had been commissioned to destroy all the gods of the land, so that all nations should worship Nebuchadnezzar alone, and that all their dialects and tribes should call upon him as a god.

9 Then he came toward Esdraelon, near Dothan, facing the great ridge of Judea; 10 he camped between Geba and Scythopolis, and remained for a whole month in order to collect all the supplies for his army.

4 When the Israelites living in Judea heard of everything that Holofernes, the general of Nebuchadnezzar, the king of the Assyrians, had done to the nations, and how he had plundered and destroyed all their temples, 2 they were therefore greatly terrified at his approach; they were alarmed both for Jerusalem and for the temple of the Lord their God. 3 For they had only recently returned from exile, and all the people of Judea had just now gathered together, and the sacred vessels and the altar and the temple had been consecrated after their profanation. 4 So they sent word to every district of Samaria, and to Kona, Beth-horon, Belmain, and Jericho, and to Choba and Aesora, and the valley of Salem. 5 They immediately seized all the high hilltops and fortified the villages on them and stored up food in preparation for war—since their fields had recently been harvested.

6 The high priest, Joakim, who was in Jerusalem at the time, wrote to the people of Bethulia and Betomesthaim, which faces Esdraelon opposite the plain near Dothan, 7 ordering them to seize the mountain passes, since by them Judea could be invaded; and it would be easy to stop any who tried to enter, for the approach was narrow, wide enough for only two at a time to pass.

8 So the Israelites did as they had been ordered by the high priest Joakim and the senate of the whole people of Israel, in session at Jerusalem. 9 And every man of Israel cried out to God with great fervor, and they humbled themselves with much fasting. 10 They and their wives and their children and their cattle and every resident alien and hired laborer and purchased slave—they all put sackcloth around their waists. 11 And all the Israelite men, women, and children living at Jerusalem prostrated themselves before the temple and put ashes on their heads and spread out their sackcloth before the Lord. 12 They even draped the altar with sackcloth and cried out in unison, praying fervently to the God of Israel not to allow their infants to be carried off and their wives to be taken as booty, and the towns they had inherited to be destroyed, and the sanctuary to be profaned and desecrated to the malicious joy of the Gentiles.

13 The Lord heard their prayers and had regard for their distress; for the people fasted many days throughout Judea and in Jerusalem before the sanctuary of the Lord Almighty. 14 The high priest Joakim and all the priests who stood before the Lord and ministered to the Lord, with sackcloth around their loins, offered the daily burnt offerings, the votive offerings, and freewill offerings of the people. 15 With ashes on their turbans, they cried out to the Lord with all their might to look with favor on the whole house of Israel.

inhabitants are yours to enslave; come and dispose of them as you think fit.'

5 When the envoys brought this message to Holofernes, 6 he went down with his army to the coast, where he established garrisons in all the fortified towns, and, at the same time, took from them picked men to serve as auxiliaries. 7 Both there and throughout the surrounding country he was welcomed with garlands and dancing and the sound of tambourines. 8 He demolished all their sanctuaries[3:8] and cut down their sacred groves, for his commission was to destroy all the gods of the land, so that Nebuchadnezzar alone should be worshipped by every nation, and he alone be invoked as a god by men of every tongue and tribe.

9 Holofernes then advanced towards Esdraelon, near Dothan, which faces the Judaean ridge, 10 and encamped between Geba and Scythopolis, where he remained for a whole month to collect whatever supplies were needed for his army.

4 A FULL report of the measures undertaken by Holofernes, King Nebuchadnezzar's commander-in-chief, how he had despoiled all the temples of the nations and razed them to the ground, reached the ears of the Israelites living in Judaea. 2 His approach filled them with terror, and they trembled for the fate of Jerusalem and the sanctuary of the Lord their God. 3 They had just returned from captivity, and only recently had all the people been reunited in Judaea, and the sacred vessels, the altar, and the temple been sanctified after their desecration. 4 Accordingly they sent out a warning to the whole of Samaria, Cona, Beth-horon, Belmain and Jericho, Choba and Aesora, and the valley of Salem; 5 the tops of all the high hills were occupied, the hill villages fortified, and stores of food from the newly harvested fields laid up in preparation for war. 6 Joakim, high priest in Jerusalem at that time, wrote to the people of Bethulia and Bethomesthaim, which is opposite Esdraelon facing the plain near Dothan, 7 directing them to hold the passes into the hill-country, because they gave access to Judaea; as the approaches were wide enough for only two men at most, it was easy to prevent the passage of an invader.

8 The Israelites complied with the orders issued by Joakim the high priest and by the senate of all Israel in Jerusalem. 9 They all cried to God with great fervour, fasting and humbling themselves; 10 they put on sackcloth—they, their wives and children, their livestock, and every resident foreigner, hired labourer, and slave. 11 In Jerusalem the Israelites, men, women, and children, all prostrated themselves in front of the sanctuary, and, with ashes on their heads, spread out their sackcloth before the Lord. They draped the altar in sackcloth, 12 and with one voice they fervently implored the God of Israel not to allow their infants to be captured, their wives carried off, their ancestral cities destroyed, and the temple desecrated and dishonoured, so giving the heathen cause for gloating. 13 The Lord heard their prayer and took pity on their distress.

For many days the entire population of Judaea and Jerusalem fasted before the temple of the Lord Almighty. 14 Joakim the high priest and the priests who stood in the presence of the Lord, and all who served him, wore sackcloth when they offered the regular whole-offering and the votive and freewill-offerings of the people; 15 they put ashes on their turbans, and they cried with all their might to the Lord to look favourably on the whole house of Israel.

---

[h] Syr: Gk borders

3:8 **sanctuaries**: so one Vs.; Gk borders.

are also at your service; come and deal with them as you see fit." 5 After the spokesmen had reached Holofernes and given him this message, 6 he went down with his army to the seacoast, and stationed garrisons in the fortified cities; from them he impressed picked troops as auxiliaries. 7 The people of these cities and all the inhabitants of the countryside received him with garlands and dancing to the sound of timbrels. 8 Nevertheless, he devastated their whole territory and cut down their sacred groves, for he had been commissioned to destroy all the gods of the earth, so that every nation might worship Nebuchadnezzar alone, and every people and tribe invoke him as a god. 9 At length Holofernes reached Esdraelon in the neighborhood of Dothan, the approach to the main ridge of the Judean mountains; 10 he set up his camp between Geba and Scythopolis, and stayed there a whole month to refurbish all the equipment of his army.

4 When the Israelites who dwelt in Judea heard of all that Holofernes, commander in chief of Nebuchadnezzar, king of the Assyrians, had done to the nations, and how he had despoiled all their temples and destroyed them, 2 they were in extreme dread of him, and greatly alarmed for Jerusalem and the temple of the LORD, their God. 3 Now, they had lately returned from exile, and only recently had all the people of Judea been gathered together, and the vessels, the altar, and the temple been purified from profanation. 4 So they sent word to the whole region of Samaria, to Kona, Beth-horon, Belmain, and Jericho, to Choba and Aesora, and to the valley of Salem. 5 The people there posted guards on all the summits of the high mountains, fortified their villages, and since their fields had recently been harvested, stored up provisions in preparation for war. 6 Joakim, who was high priest in Jerusalem in those days, wrote to the inhabitants of Bethulia [and Betomesthaim], which is on the way to Esdraelon, facing the plain near Dothan, 7 and instructed them to keep firm hold of the mountain passes, since these offered access to Judea. It would be easy to ward off the attacking forces, as the defile was only wide enough for two abreast. 8 The Israelites carried out the orders given them by Joakim, the high priest, and the senate of the whole people of Israel, which met in Jerusalem.

9 All the men of Israel cried to God with great fervor and did penance — 10 they, along with their wives, and children, and domestic animals. All their resident aliens, hired laborers, and slaves also girded themselves with sackcloth. 11 And all the Israelite men, women, and children who lived in Jerusalem prostrated themselves in front of the temple building, with ashes strewn on their heads, displaying their sackcloth covering before the LORD. 12 The altar, too, they draped in sackcloth; and with one accord they cried out fervently to the God of Israel not to allow their children to be seized, their wives to be taken captive, the cities of their inheritance to be ruined, or the sanctuary to be profaned and mocked for the nations to gloat over.

13 The LORD heard their cry and had regard for their distress. For the people observed a fast of many days' duration throughout Judea, and before the sanctuary of the LORD Almighty in Jerusalem. 14 The high priest Joakim, and all the priests in attendance on the LORD who served his altar, were also girded with sackcloth as they offered the daily holocaust, the votive offerings, and the free-will offerings of the people. 15 With ashes upon their turbans, they cried to the LORD with all their strength to look with favor on the whole house of Israel.

towns and their inhabitants too are at your service; go and treat them as you think fit.' 5 These men came to Holofernes and delivered the message as above.

6 He then made his way down to the coast with his army and stationed garrisons in all the fortified towns, levying outstanding men there as auxiliaries. 7 The people of these cities and of all the other towns in the neighbourhood welcomed him, wearing garlands and dancing to the sound of tambourines. 8 But he demolished their shrines and cut down their sacred trees, carrying out his commission to destroy all local gods so that the nations should worship Nebuchadnezzar alone and people of every language and nationality should hail him as a god.

9 Thus he reached the edge of Esdraelon, in the neighbourhood of Dothan, a village facing the great ridge of Judaea. 10 He pitched camp between Geba and Scythopolis and stayed there a full month to re-provision his forces.

4 When the Israelites living in Judaea heard how Holofernes, general-in-chief of Nebuchadnezzar king of the Assyrians, had treated the various nations, plundering their temples and destroying them, 2 they were thoroughly alarmed at his approach and trembled for Jerusalem and the Temple of the Lord their God. 3 They had returned from captivity only a short time before, and the resettlement of the people in Judaea and the reconsecration of the sacred furnishings, of the altar, and of the Temple, which had been profaned, were of recent date.

4 They therefore alerted the whole of Samaria, Kona, Beth-Horon, Belmain, Jericho, Choba, Aesora and the Salem valley. 5 They occupied the summits of the highest mountains and fortified the villages on them; they laid in supplies for the coming war, as the fields had just been harvested. 6 Joakim the high priest, resident in Jerusalem at the time, wrote to the inhabitants of Bethulia and of Betomesthaim, two towns facing Esdraelon, towards the plain of Dothan. 7 He ordered them to occupy the mountain passes, the only means of access to Judaea, for there it would be easy for them to halt an attacking force, the narrowness of the approach not allowing men to advance more than two abreast. 8 The Israelites carried out the orders of Joakim the high priest and of the people's Council of Elders in session at Jerusalem.

9 All the men of Israel cried most fervently to God and humbled themselves before him. 10 They, their wives, their children, their cattle, all their resident aliens, hired or slave, wrapped sackcloth round their loins. 11 All the Israelites in Jerusalem, including women and children, lay prostrate in front of the Temple, and with ashes on their heads stretched out their hands before the Lord. 12 They draped the altar itself in sackcloth and fervently joined together in begging the God of Israel not to let their children be carried off, their wives distributed as booty, the towns of their heritage destroyed, the Temple profaned and desecrated for the heathen to gloat over. 13 The Lord heard them and looked kindly on their distress.

The people fasted for many days throughout Judaea as well as in Jerusalem before the sanctuary of the Lord Almighty. 14 Joakim the high priest and all who stood before the Lord, the Lord's priests and ministers, wore sackcloth round their loins as they offered the perpetual burnt offering and the votive and voluntary offerings of the people. 15 With ashes on their turbans they earnestly called on the Lord to look kindly on the House of Israel.

5 It was reported to Holofernes, the general of the Assyrian army, that the people of Israel had prepared for war and had closed the mountain passes and fortified all the high hilltops and set up barricades in the plains. 2 In great anger he called together all the princes of Moab and the commanders of Ammon and all the governors of the coastland, 3 and said to them, "Tell me, you Canaanites, what people is this that lives in the hill country? What towns do they inhabit? How large is their army, and in what does their power and strength consist? Who rules over them as king and leads their army? 4 And why have they alone, of all who live in the west, refused to come out and meet me?"

5 Then Achior, the leader of all the Ammonites, said to him, "May my lord please listen to a report from the mouth of your servant, and I will tell you the truth about this people that lives in the mountain district near you. No falsehood shall come from your servant's mouth. 6 These people are descended from the Chaldeans. 7 At one time they lived in Mesopotamia, because they did not wish to follow the gods of their ancestors who were in Chaldea. 8 Since they had abandoned the ways of their ancestors, and worshiped the God of heaven, the God they had come to know, their ancestors*i* drove them out from the presence of their gods. So they fled to Mesopotamia, and lived there for a long time. 9 Then their God commanded them to leave the place where they were living and go to the land of Canaan. There they settled, and grew very prosperous in gold and silver and very much livestock. 10 When a famine spread over the land of Canaan they went down to Egypt and lived there as long as they had food. There they became so great a multitude that their race could not be counted. 11 So the king of Egypt became hostile to them; he exploited them and forced them to make bricks. 12 They cried out to their God, and he afflicted the whole land of Egypt with incurable plagues. So the Egyptians drove them out of their sight. 13 Then God dried up the Red Sea before them, 14 and he led them by the way of Sinai and Kadesh-barnea. They drove out all the people of the desert, 15 and took up residence in the land of the Amorites, and by their might destroyed all the inhabitants of Heshbon; and crossing over the Jordan they took possession of all the hill country. 16 They drove out before them the Canaanites, the Perizzites, the Jebusites, the Shechemites, and all the Gergesites, and lived there a long time.

17 "As long as they did not sin against their God they prospered, for the God who hates iniquity is with them. 18 But when they departed from the way he had prescribed for them, they were utterly defeated in many battles and were led away captive to a foreign land. The temple of their God was razed to the ground, and their towns were occupied by their enemies. 19 But now they have returned to their God, and have come back from the places where they were scattered, and have occupied Jerusalem, where their sanctuary is, and have settled in the hill country, because it was uninhabited.

20 "So now, my master and lord, if there is any oversight in this people and they sin against their God and we find out their offense, then we can go up and defeat them. 21 But if they are not a guilty nation, then let my lord pass them by; for their Lord and God will defend them, and we shall become the laughingstock of the whole world."

22 When Achior had finished saying these things, all the people standing around the tent began to complain; Holofernes' officers and all the inhabitants of the seacoast and Moab insisted that he should be cut to pieces. 23 They said,

5 When it was reported to Holophernes that the Israelites had prepared for war by closing the passes through the hill-country, fortifying all the heights, and putting obstructions in the plains, 2 his anger knew no bounds. He summoned all the rulers of Moab and the Ammonite generals, and all the governors of the coastal region. 3 'Tell me, you Canaanites,' he demanded, 'what people is this that lives in the hill-country? What are their cities? How large is their army, and wherein lies their power and strength? Who has set up as king at the head of their forces? 4 Of all the people of the west, why do they alone disdain to come to meet me?'

5 Achior, the commander of the Ammonites, replied: 'My lord, if you will allow your servant to speak, I shall give you the true facts about this people that lives close at hand in the hill-country; no lie will pass your servant's lips. 6 They are descended from the Chaldaeans; 7 and at one time they settled in Mesopotamia, because they refused to worship the gods their fathers had worshipped in Chaldaea. 8 They abandoned the ways of their ancestors and worshipped the God of heaven, the God whom they acknowledge today. When they were driven from the presence of their fathers' gods, they fled to Mesopotamia and lived there for a long time. 9 Commanded by their God to leave their new home and move to Canaan, they settled there and acquired great wealth in gold and silver, and livestock in plenty.

10 'Because of a famine which spread throughout Canaan, they went down to Egypt, where they lived as long as they found food. While there, they multiplied so greatly that their numbers were past counting, 11 and the king of Egypt took precautionary action by setting them to labour at brickmaking and by reducing them to slavery. 12 They cried to their God, and he inflicted incurable plagues on the whole of Egypt. When the Egyptians expelled them, 13 their God dried up the Red Sea for them 14 and led them towards Sinai and Kadesh-barnea. They drove out all the inhabitants of the wilderness 15 and settled in the land of the Amorites, and by force of arms exterminated the whole population of Heshbon. Then they crossed the Jordan and took possession of the entire hill-country, 16 driving out the Canaanites, the Perizzites, the Jebusites, the Shechemites, and all the Girgashites; and there they lived for a long time.

17 'As long as they did not sin against their God, they prospered, for they had the support of a God who hates wickedness. 18 When, however, they strayed from the path he had marked out for them, they suffered heavy losses in many wars; they were carried captive to a foreign country, the sanctuary of their God was razed to the ground, and their towns were seized by enemies. 19 But now that they have turned again to their God, they have come back from the lands to which they had been dispersed; they have occupied Jerusalem, the site of their holy place, and have settled in the hill-country, which lay uninhabited. 20 Now, my sovereign lord, if these people have fallen into the error of sinning against their God, and if we find that in so doing they have put themselves at a disadvantage, then we can go up and attack them. 21 But if these people have not violated their law, then let my lord leave them alone, for fear that the God they serve should defend and protect them, and we become the laughing-stock of the whole world.'

22 When Achior finished speaking there were protests from all who stood round the tent. Holophernes' officers, together with the people from the coastal region and from Moab, demanded that Achior be hacked to pieces. 23 'We

5 It was reported to Holofernes, commander in chief of the Assyrian army, that the Israelites were ready for battle, and had blocked the mountain passes, fortified the summits of all the higher peaks, and placed roadblocks in the plains. 2 In great anger he summoned all the rulers of the Moabites, the generals of the Ammonites, and all the satraps of the seacoast 3 and said to them: "Now tell me, you Canaanites, what sort of people is this that dwells in the mountains? Which cities do they inhabit? How large is their army? In what does their power and strength consist? Who has set himself up as their king and the leader of their army? 4 Why have they refused to come out to meet me along with all the other inhabitants of the West?"

5 Then Achior, the leader of all the Ammonites, said to him: "My lord, hear this account from your servant; I will tell you the truth about this people that lives near you [that inhabits this mountain region]; no lie shall escape your servant's lips.

6 "These people are descendants of the Chaldeans. 7 They formerly dwelt in Mesopotamia, for they did not wish to follow the gods of their forefathers who were born in the land of the Chaldeans. 8 Since they abandoned the way of their ancestors, and acknowledged with divine worship the God of heaven, their forefathers expelled them from the presence of their gods. So they fled to Mesopotamia and dwelt there a long time. 9 Their God bade them leave their abode and proceed to the land of Canaan. Here they settled, and grew very rich in gold, silver, and a great abundance of livestock. 10 Later, when famine had gripped the whole land of Canaan, they went down into Egypt. They stayed there as long as they found sustenance, and grew into such a great multitude that the number of their race could not be counted. 11 The king of Egypt, however, rose up against them, shrewdly forced them to labor at brickmaking, oppressed and enslaved them. 12 But they cried to their God, and he struck the land of Egypt with plagues for which there was no remedy. When the Egyptians expelled them, 13 God dried up the Red Sea before them, 14 and led them along the route to Sinai and Kadesh-barnea. First they drove out all the inhabitants of the desert; 15 then they settled in the land of the Amorites, destroyed all the Heshbonites by main force, crossed the Jordan, and took possession of the whole mountain region. 16 They expelled the Canaanites, the Perizzites, the Jebusites, the Shechemites, and all the Gergesites; and they lived in these mountains a long time.

17 "As long as the Israelites did not sin in the sight of their God, they prospered, for their God, who hates wickedness, was with them. 18 But when they deviated from the way he prescribed for them, they were ground down steadily, more and more, by frequent wars, and finally taken as captives into foreign lands. The temple of their God was razed to the ground, and their cities were occupied by their enemies. 19 But now that they have returned to their God, they have come back from the Dispersion wherein they were scattered, and have repossessed Jerusalem, where their sanctuary is, and have settled again in the mountain region which was unoccupied.

20 "So now, my lord and master, if these people are at fault, and are sinning against their God, and if we verify this offense of theirs, then we shall be able to go up and conquer them. 21 But if they are not a guilty nation, then your lordship should keep his distance; otherwise their LORD and God will shield them, and we shall become the laughing-stock of the whole world."

22 Now when Achior had concluded his recommendation, all the people standing round about the tent murmured; and the officers of Holofernes and all the inhabitants of the seacoast and of Moab alike said he should be cut to pieces.

5 Holofernes, general-in-chief of the Assyrian army, received the intelligence that the Israelites were preparing for war, that they had closed the mountain passes, fortified all the high peaks and laid obstructions in the plains. 2 Holofernes was furious. He summoned all the princes of Moab, all the generals of Ammon and all the satraps of the coastal regions. 3 'Men of Canaan,' he said, 'tell me: what people is this that occupies the hill-country? What towns does it inhabit? How large is its army? What are the sources of its power and strength? Who is the king who rules it and commands its army? 4 Why have they disdained to wait on me, as all the western peoples have?'

5 Achior, leader of all the Ammonites, replied, 'May my lord be pleased to listen to what your servant is going to say. I shall give you the facts about these mountain folk whose home lies close to you. You will hear no lie from the mouth of your servant. 6 These people are descended from the Chaldaeans. 7 They once came to live in Mesopotamia, because they did not want to follow the gods of their ancestors who lived in Chaldaea. 8 They abandoned the way of their ancestors to worship the God of heaven, the God they learnt to acknowledge. Banished from the presence of their own gods, they fled to Mesopotamia where they lived for a long time. 9 When God told them to leave their home and set out for Canaan, they settled there and accumulated gold and silver and great herds of cattle. 10 Next, famine having overwhelmed the land of Canaan, they went down to Egypt where they stayed till they were well nourished. There they became a great multitude, a race beyond counting. 11 But the king of Egypt turned against them and exploited them by forcing them to make bricks; he degraded them, reducing them to slavery. 12 They cried to their God, who struck the entire land of Egypt with incurable plagues, and the Egyptians expelled them. 13 God dried up the Red Sea before them 14 and led them forward by way of Sinai and Kadesh-Barnea. Having driven off all the inhabitants of the desert, 15 they settled in the land of the Amorites and in their strength exterminated the entire population of Heshbon. Then, having crossed the Jordan, they took possession of all the hill-country, 16 driving out the Canaanites before them and the Perizzites, Jebusites, Shechemites and all the Girgashites, and lived there for many years. 17 All the while they did not sin before their God, prosperity was theirs, for they have a God who hates wickedness. 18 But when they turned from the path he had marked out for them some were exterminated in a series of battles, others were taken captive to a foreign land. The Temple of their God was rased to the ground and their towns were seized by their enemies. 19 Then having turned once again to their God, they came back from the places to which they had been dispersed and scattered, regained possession of Jerusalem, where they have their Temple, and reoccupied the hill-country which had been left deserted. 20 So, now, master and lord, if this people has committed any fault, if they have sinned against their God, let us be sure that they really have this reason to fail, then advance and attack them. 21 But if their nation is guiltless, my lord would do better to abstain, for fear that their Lord and God should protect them. We should then become the laughing-stock of the whole world.'

22 When Achior had ended this speech, all the people crowding round the tent began protesting. Holofernes' own senior officers, as well as all the coastal peoples and the Moabites, threatened to tear him limb from limb. 23 'Why

"We are not afraid of the Israelites; they are a people with no strength or power for making war. 24 Therefore let us go ahead, Lord Holofernes, and your vast army will swallow them up."

6 When the disturbance made by the people outside the council had died down, Holofernes, the commander of the Assyrian army, said to Achior*j* in the presence of all the foreign contingents:

2 "Who are you, Achior and you mercenaries of Ephraim, to prophesy among us as you have done today and tell us not to make war against the people of Israel because their God will defend them? What god is there except Nebuchadnezzar? He will send his forces and destroy them from the face of the earth. Their God will not save them; 3 we the king's*k* servants will destroy them as one man. They cannot resist the might of our cavalry. 4 We will overwhelm them;*l* their mountains will be drunk with their blood, and their fields will be full of their dead. Not even their footprints will survive our attack; they will utterly perish. So says King Nebuchadnezzar, lord of the whole earth. For he has spoken; none of his words shall be in vain.

5 "As for you, Achior, you Ammonite mercenary, you have said these words in a moment of perversity; you shall not see my face again from this day until I take revenge on this race that came out of Egypt. 6 Then at my return the sword of my army and the spear*m* of my servants shall pierce your sides, and you shall fall among their wounded. 7 Now my slaves are going to take you back into the hill country and put you in one of the towns beside the passes. 8 You will not die until you perish along with them. 9 If you really hope in your heart that they will not be taken, then do not look downcast! I have spoken, and none of my words shall fail to come true."

10 Then Holofernes ordered his slaves, who waited on him in his tent, to seize Achior and take him away to Bethulia and hand him over to the Israelites. 11 So the slaves took him and led him out of the camp into the plain, and from the plain they went up into the hill country and came to the springs below Bethulia. 12 When the men of the town saw them,*n* they seized their weapons and ran out of the town to the top of the hill, and all the slingers kept them from coming up by throwing stones at them. 13 So having taken shelter below the hill, they bound Achior and left him lying at the foot of the hill, and returned to their master.

14 Then the Israelites came down from their town and found him; they untied him and brought him into Bethulia and placed him before the magistrates of their town, 15 who in those days were Uzziah son of Micah, of the tribe of Simeon, and Chabris son of Gothoniel, and Charmis son of Melchiel. 16 They called together all the elders of the town, and all their young men and women ran to the assembly. They set Achior in the midst of all their people, and Uzziah questioned him about what had happened. 17 He answered and told them what had taken place at the council of Holofernes, and all that he had said in the presence of the Assyrian leaders, and all that Holofernes had boasted he would do against the house of Israel. 18 Then the people fell down and worshiped God, and cried out:

19 "O Lord God of heaven, see their arrogance, and have pity on our people in their humiliation, and look kindly today on the faces of those who are consecrated to you."

20 Then they reassured Achior, and praised him highly. 21 Uzziah took him from the assembly to his own house and gave a banquet for the elders; and all that night they called on the God of Israel for help.

are not going to be scared of the Israelites,' they said, 'a people incapable of putting a force of any strength in the field. 24 Let us march into the hill-country, Lord Holophernes; your great army will swallow them whole.'

6 When the uproar among the men surrounding the council had died down, Holophernes, the Assyrian commander-in-chief, addressed Achior in front of all the assembled foreigners: 2 'And who are you, Achior, you and your Ephraimite mercenaries, to play the prophet in our presence as you have done today, telling us not to make war against this people, Israel, because their God will protect them? What god is there besides Nebuchadnezzar? 3 When he exerts his power he will wipe them off the face of the earth; their God will assuredly not come to their rescue. We who serve Nebuchadnezzar shall strike them down as if they were but one man. They will not be able to withstand the weight of our cavalry; 4 we shall overwhelm them. Their mountains will be drenched with their blood, and the plains filled with their dead. They cannot stand against us; they will perish without trace. So says King Nebuchadnezzar, lord of all the earth; he has spoken, and his words are no empty threat.

5 'As for you, Achior, you Ammonite mercenary, this is treasonable talk. You shall not see my face again from this day until I have taken vengeance on that brood of fugitives from Egypt; 6 but when I come back my warriors will run you through with sword and spear and add you to their victims. 7 My men will now take you away to the hill-country and leave you in one of the towns in the passes; 8 you will be allowed to live until you share their fate. 9 If you are so confident that these places will not fall into our hands, you need not look downcast. I have spoken, and not a single word of mine will go unfulfilled.'

10 Holophernes ordered the slaves standing by in the tent to seize Achior, escort him to Bethulia, and hand him over to the Israelites. 11 So laying hold of him they took him outside the camp into the plain, and from there up into the hill-country, until they arrived at the springs below Bethulia. 12 The moment the men of Bethulia sighted them, they picked up their weapons and sallied forth from the town to the top of the hill, and the slingers all pelted the enemy with stones to prevent them from coming up. 13 But they slipped through under cover of the hill, bound Achior and left him lying there at the foot, and then returned to their master.

14 When the Israelites came down from the town and found Achior, they untied him and took him into Bethulia, where they brought him before the town magistrates 15 then in office, Ozias son of Mica, of the tribe of Simeon, and Chabris son of Gothoniel, and Charmis son of Melchiel. 16 The magistrates summoned the elders of the town, and all the young men and women also came running to the assembly. When Achior had been put in the centre of the crowd, Ozias questioned him as to what had happened. 17 He answered by telling them everything that had taken place in Holophernes' council, what he himself had said in the presence of the Assyrian commanders, and how Holophernes had boasted of what he would do to Israel. 18 At this the people prostrated themselves in worship and cried out to God: 19 'O Lord, God of heaven, consider their arrogance; have pity on us and our nation in our humiliation; show favour this day to your own people.' 20 Then they reassured Achior and commended him warmly. 21 Ozias brought him from the assembly to his own house, where he gave a feast for the elders; and all night long they invoked the help of the God of Israel.

---

j Other ancient authorities add *and to all the Moabites*   *k* Gk *his*
l Other ancient authorities add *with it*   *m* Lat Syr: Gk *people*
n Other ancient authorities add *on the top of the hill*

23 "We are not afraid of the Israelites," they said, "for they are a powerless people, incapable of a strong defense. 24 Let us therefore attack them; your great army, Lord Holofernes, will swallow them up."

6 When the noise of the crowd surrounding the council had subsided, Holofernes, commander in chief of the Assyrian army, said to Achior, in the presence of the whole throng of coastland peoples, of the Moabites, and of the Ammonite mercenaries: 2 "Who are you, Achior, to prophesy among us as you have done today, and to tell us not to fight against the Israelites because their God protects them? What god is there beside Nebuchadnezzar? He will send his force and destroy them from the face of the earth. Their God will not save them; 3 but we, the servants of Nebuchadnezzar, will strike them down as one man, for they will be unable to withstand the force of our cavalry. 4 We will overwhelm them with it, and the mountains shall be drunk with their blood, and their plains filled with their corpses. Not a trace of them shall survive our attack: they shall utterly perish, says King Nebuchadnezzar, lord of all the earth; for he has spoken, and his words shall not remain unfulfilled. 5 As for you, Achior, you Ammonite mercenary, for saying these things in a moment of perversity you shall not see my face after today, until I have taken revenge on this race of people from Egypt. 6 Then at my return, the sword of my army or the spear of my servants will pierce your sides, and you shall fall among their slain. 7 My servants will now conduct you to the mountain region, and leave you at one of the towns along the ascent. 8 You shall not die till you are destroyed together with them. 9 If you still cherish the hope that they will not be taken, then there is no need for you to be downcast. I have spoken, and my words shall not prove false in any respect."

10 Then Holofernes ordered the servants who were standing by in his tent to seize Achior, conduct him to Bethulia, and hand him over to the Israelites. 11 So the servants took him in custody and brought him out of the camp into the plain. From there they led him into the mountain region till they reached the springs below Bethulia. 12 When the men of the city saw them, they seized their weapons and ran out of the city to the crest of the ridge; and all the slingers blocked the ascent of Holofernes' servants by hurling stones upon them. 13 So they took cover below the mountain, where they bound Achior and left him lying at the foot of the mountain; then they returned to their lord.

14 The Israelites came down to him from their city, loosed him, and brought him into Bethulia. They haled him before the rulers of the city, 15 who in those days were Uzziah, son of Micah of the tribe of Simeon, Chabris, son of Gothoniel, and Charmis, son of Melchiel. 16 They then convened all the elders of the city; and all their young men, as well as the women, gathered in haste at the place of assembly. They placed Achior in the center of the throng, and Uzziah questioned him about what had happened. 17 He replied by giving them an account of what was said in the council of Holofernes, and of all his own words among the Assyrian officers, and of all the boasting threats of Holofernes against the house of Israel. 18 At this the people fell prostrate and worshiped God; and they cried out: 19 "Lord, God of heaven, behold their arrogance! Have pity on the lowliness of our people, and look with favor this day on those who are consecrated to you." 20 Then they reassured Achior and praised him highly. 21 Uzziah brought him from the assembly to his home, where he gave a banquet for the elders. That whole night they called upon the God of Israel for help.

should we be afraid of the Israelites? They are a weak and powerless people, quite unable to stand a stiff attack. 24 Forward! Advance! Your army, Holofernes our master, will swallow them in one mouthful!'

6 When the uproar of those crowding round the council had subsided, Holofernes, general-in-chief of the Assyrian army, reprimanded Achior in front of the whole crowd of foreigners and Ammonites. 2 'Achior, who do you think you are, you and the Ephraimite mercenaries, playing the prophet like this with us today, and trying to dissuade us from making war on the people of Israel? You claim their God will protect them. And who is God if not Nebuchadnezzar? He himself will display his power and wipe them off the face of the earth, and their God will certainly not save them. 3 But we, his servants, shall destroy them as easily as a single individual. They can never resist the strength of our cavalry. 4 We shall burn them all. Their mountains will be drunk with their blood and their plains filled with their corpses. Far from being able to resist us, every one of them will die; thus says King Nebuchadnezzar, lord of the whole world. For he has spoken, and his words will not prove empty. 5 As for you, Achior, you Ammonite mercenary, who in a rash moment said these words, you will not see my face again until the day when I have taken my revenge on this brood from Egypt. 6 And then the swords of my soldiers and the spears of my officers will pierce your sides. You will fall among their wounded, the moment I turn on Israel. 7 My servants will now take you into the hill-country and leave you near one of the towns in the passes; 8 you will not die, until you share their ruin. 9 No need to look so sad if you cherish the secret hope that they will not be captured! I have spoken; none of my words will prove idle.'

10 Holofernes having commanded his tent-orderlies to seize Achior, to take him to Bethulia and to hand him over to the Israelites, 11 the orderlies took him, escorted him out of the camp and across the plain, and then, making for the hill-country, reached the springs below Bethulia. 12 As soon as the men of the town sighted them, they snatched up their weapons, left the town and made for the mountain tops, while all the slingers pelted them with stones to prevent them from coming up. 13 However, they managed to take cover at the foot of the slope, where they bound Achior and left him lying at the bottom of the mountain and returned to their master.

14 The Israelites then came down from their town, stopped by him, unbound him and took him to Bethulia, where they brought him before the chief men of the town, 15 who at that time were Uzziah son of Micah of the tribe of Simeon, Chabris son of Gothoniel and Charmis son of Melchiel. 16 These summoned all the elders of the town. The young men and the women also hurried to the assembly. Achior was made to stand with all the people surrounding him, and Uzziah questioned him about what had happened. 17 He answered by telling them what had been said at Holofernes' council, and what he himself had said in the presence of the Assyrian leaders, and how Holofernes had bragged of what he would do to the House of Israel. 18 At this the people fell to the ground and worshipped God. 19 'Lord God of heaven,' they cried, 'take notice of their arrogance and have pity on the humiliation of our race. Look kindly today on those who are consecrated to you.' 20 They then spoke reassuringly to Achior and praised him warmly. 21 After the assembly Uzziah took him home and gave a banquet for the elders; all that night they called on the God of Israel for help.

7 The next day Holofernes ordered his whole army, and all the allies who had joined him, to break camp and move against Bethulia, and to seize the passes up into the hill country and make war on the Israelites. 2 So all their warriors marched off that day; their fighting forces numbered one hundred seventy thousand infantry and twelve thousand cavalry, not counting the baggage and the foot soldiers handling it, a very great multitude. 3 They encamped in the valley near Bethulia, beside the spring, and they spread out in breadth over Dothan as far as Balbaim and in length from Bethulia to Cyamon, which faces Esdraelon.

4 When the Israelites saw their vast numbers, they were greatly terrified and said to one another, "They will now strip clean the whole land; neither the high mountains nor the valleys nor the hills will bear their weight." 5 Yet they all seized their weapons, and when they had kindled fires on their towers, they remained on guard all that night.

6 On the second day Holofernes led out all his cavalry in full view of the Israelites in Bethulia. 7 He reconnoitered the approaches to their town, and visited the springs that supplied their water; he seized them and set guards of soldiers over them, and then returned to his army.

8 Then all the chieftains of the Edomites and all the leaders of the Moabites and the commanders of the coastland came to him and said, 9 "Listen to what we have to say, my lord, and your army will suffer no losses. 10 This people, the Israelites, do not rely on their spears but on the height of the mountains where they live, for it is not easy to reach the tops of their mountains. 11 Therefore, my lord, do not fight against them in regular formation, and not a man of your army will fall. 12 Remain in your camp, and keep all the men in your forces with you; let your servants take possession of the spring of water that flows from the foot of the mountain, 13 for this is where all the people of Bethulia get their water. So thirst will destroy them, and they will surrender their town. Meanwhile, we and our people will go up to the tops of the nearby mountains and camp there to keep watch to see that no one gets out of the town. 14 They and their wives and children will waste away with famine, and before the sword reaches them they will be strewn about in the streets where they live. 15 Thus you will pay them back with evil, because they rebelled and did not receive you peaceably."

16 These words pleased Holofernes and all his attendants, and he gave orders to do as they had said. 17 So the army of the Ammonites moved forward, together with five thousand Assyrians, and they encamped in the valley and seized the water supply and the springs of the Israelites. 18 And the Edomites and Ammonites went up and encamped in the hill country opposite Dothan; and they sent some of their men toward the south and the east, toward Egrebeh, which is near Chusi beside the Wadi Mochmur. The rest of the Assyrian army encamped in the plain, and covered the whole face of the land. Their tents and supply trains spread out in great number, and they formed a vast multitude.

19 The Israelites then cried out to the Lord their God, for their courage failed, because all their enemies had surrounded them, and there was no way of escape from them. 20 The whole Assyrian army, their infantry, chariots, and cavalry, surrounded them for thirty-four days, until all the water containers of every inhabitant of Bethulia were empty; 21 their cisterns were going dry, and on no day did they have enough water to drink, for their drinking water was rationed. 22 Their children were listless, and the women and young men fainted from thirst and were collapsing in the streets of the town and in the gateways; they no longer had any strength.

7 THE next day Holophernes gave orders to his whole army together with all his allies to strike camp and march on Bethulia, to seize the passes up into the hill-country, and engage the Israelites in battle. 2 The entire force moved off, an army of a hundred and seventy thousand infantry and twelve thousand cavalry, not counting the baggage train of the infantry, an immense host. 3 They encamped in the valley near Bethulia, beside the spring; and their camp extended in breadth towards Dothan as far as Belbaim, and in length from Bethulia to Cyamon which faces Esdraelon. 4 The Israelites viewed the enemy's numbers with great alarm. 'These men will devour the whole country,' they said to one another; 'neither the high mountains nor the valleys, nor yet the hills, will ever be able to support the burden of them.' 5 Each man stood to arms; they lit beacons on their towers and remained on guard throughout the night.

6 On the following day Holophernes led out all his cavalry in full view of the Israelites in Bethulia. 7 He reconnoitred the approaches to the town and in the course of his tour seized the springs which were its water supply; he stationed detachments of soldiers to picket them, before returning to his main force.

8 The rulers of Esau's descendants and the Moabite leaders, along with the commanders of the coastal region, made a joint approach to him. 9 'Be pleased to listen to our proposal,' they said, 'so that no disaster may befall the army of our lord. 10 These Israelites rely, not on their spears, but on the height of the mountains where they live, for it is no easy task to assault those mountain peaks. 11 Therefore, Lord Holophernes, avoid a pitched battle with them, and not one of your men will be lost. 12 Remain in the camp and keep all your soldiers in their quarters; but permit us, my lord, to take possession of the spring at the foot of the hill, 13 for that is where the whole population of Bethulia draws its water. When they are dying of thirst they will surrender the town. Meanwhile, we and our troops shall scale the neighbouring hills and make our camp there to see that not a man escapes from the place. 14 They and their wives and children will waste away with famine; even before the sword reaches them, the streets will be strewn with their corpses. 15 So you will make them pay dearly for rebelling against you and refusing to receive you peaceably.'

16 Their plan met with the approval of Holophernes and his entire staff, and he gave orders for it to be carried out. 17 A Moabite force, along with five thousand Assyrians, moved camp into the valley, where they seized the springs which were the Israelites' water supply. 18 Esau's descendants and the Ammonites went up into the hill-country and pitched camp opposite Dothan, and they sent a detachment south-east in the direction of Egrebel, which is near Chus by the wadi Mochmur. The rest of the Assyrian army, a vast host, made their camp on the plain; they filled the entire countryside, forming, with their tents and baggage train, an immense encampment.

19 The Israelites cried to the Lord their God. They were encircled by their enemies; there was no way of escape, and their courage failed. 20 For thirty-four days the whole Assyrian army, infantry, chariots, and cavalry, kept them blockaded. The people of Bethulia came to the end of their household supplies of water, 21 and the cisterns too were running dry; drinking water was so strictly rationed that there was never a day when their needs were satisfied. 22 Infants were listless, women and young men, faint with thirst, collapsed in the streets and gateways from sheer exhaustion.

7:17 **Moabite:** *so Old Lat.; Gk* Ammonite.

7 The following day Holofernes ordered his whole army, and all the allied troops that had come to his support, to move against Bethulia, seize the mountain passes, and engage the Israelites in battle. 2 That same day all their fighting men went into action. Their forces numbered a hundred and seventy thousand infantry and twelve thousand horsemen, not counting the baggage train or the men who accompanied it on foot—a very great army. 3 They encamped at the spring in the valley near Bethulia, and spread out in breadth toward Dothan as far as Balbaim, and in length from Bethulia to Cyamon, which faces Esdraelon.

4 When the Israelites saw how many there were, they said to one another in great dismay: "Soon they will devour the whole country. Neither the high mountains nor the valleys and hills can support the mass of them." 5 Yet they all seized their weapons, lighted fires on their bastions, and kept watch throughout the night.

6 On the second day Holofernes led out all his cavalry in the sight of the Israelites who were in Bethulia. 7 He reconnoitered the approaches to their city and located their sources of water; these he seized, stationing armed detachments around them, while he himself returned to his troops.

8 All the commanders of the Edomites and all the leaders of the Ammonites, together with the generals of the sea-coast, came to Holofernes and said: 9 "Sir, listen to what we have to say, that there may be no losses among your troops. 10 These Israelites do not rely on their spears, but on the height of the mountains where they dwell; it is not easy to reach the summit of their mountains. 11 Therefore, sir, do not attack them in regular formation; thus not a single one of your troops will fall. 12 Stay in your camp, and spare all your soldiers. Have some of your servants keep control of the source of water that flows out at the base of the mountain, 13 for that is where the inhabitants of Bethulia get their water. Then thirst will begin to carry them off, and they will surrender their city. Meanwhile, we and our men will go up to the summits of the nearby mountains, and encamp there to guard against anyone's leaving the city. 14 They and their wives and children will languish with hunger, and even before the sword strikes them they will be laid low in the streets of their city. 15 Thus you will render them dire punishment for their rebellion and their refusal to meet you peacefully."

16 Their words pleased Holofernes and all his ministers, and he ordered their proposal to be carried out. 17 Thereupon the Moabites moved camp, together with five thousand Assyrians. They encamped in the valley, and held the water supply and the springs of the Israelites. 18 The Edomites and the Ammonites went up and encamped in the mountain region opposite Dothan; and they sent some of their men to the south and to the east opposite Egrebel, near Chusi, which is on Wadi Mochmur. The rest of the Assyrian army was encamped in the plain, covering the whole countryside. Their enormous store of tents and equipment was spread out in profusion everywhere.

19 The Israelites cried to the LORD, their God, for they were disheartened, since all their enemies had them surrounded, and there was no way of slipping through their lines. 20 The whole Assyrian camp, infantry, chariots, and cavalry, kept them thus surrounded for thirty-four days. All the reservoirs of water failed the inhabitants of Bethulia, 21 and the cisterns ran dry, so that on no day did they have enough to drink, but their drinking water was rationed. 22 Their children fainted away, and the women and youths were consumed with thirst and were collapsing in the streets and gateways of the city, with no strength left in them.

7 The following day Holofernes issued orders to his whole army and to the whole host of auxiliaries who had joined him, to break camp and march on Bethulia, to occupy the mountain passes and so open the campaign against the Israelites. 2 The troops broke camp that same day. The actual fighting force numbered one hundred and twenty thousand infantry and twelve thousand cavalry, not to mention the baggage train with the vast number of men on foot concerned with that. 3 They penetrated the valley in the neighbourhood of Bethulia, near the spring, and deployed on a wide front from Dothan to Balbaim and, in depth, from Bethulia to Cyamon, which faces Esdraelon. 4 When the Israelites saw this horde, they were all appalled and said to each other, 'Now they will lick the whole country clean. Not even the loftiest peaks, the gorges or the hills will be able to stand the weight of them.' 5 Each man snatched up his arms; they lit beacons on their towers and spent the whole night on watch.

6 On the second day Holofernes deployed his entire cavalry in sight of the Israelites in Bethulia. 7 He reconnoitred the slopes leading up to the town, located the water-points, seized them and posted pickets over them and returned to the main body. 8 The chieftains of the sons of Esau, all the leaders of the Moabites and the generals of the coastal district then came to him and said, 9 'If our master will be pleased to listen to us, his forces will not sustain a single wound. 10 These Israelites do not rely so much on their spears as on the height of the mountains where they live. And admittedly it is not at all easy to scale these heights of theirs.

11 'This being the case, master, avoid engaging them in a pitched battle and then you will not lose a single man. 12 Stay in camp, keep all your troops there too, while your servants seize the spring which rises at the foot of the mountain, 13 since that is what provides the population of Bethulia with their water supply. Thirst will then force them to surrender their town. Meanwhile, we and our men will climb the nearest mountain tops and form advance posts there to prevent anyone from leaving the town. 14 Hunger will waste them, with their wives and children, and before the sword can reach them they will already be lying in the streets outside their houses. 15 And you will make them pay dearly for their defiance and their refusal to meet you peaceably.'

16 Their words pleased Holofernes as well as all his officers, and he decided to do as they suggested. 17 Accordingly, a troop of Moabites moved forward with a further five thousand Assyrians. They penetrated the valley and seized the Israelites' waterpoints and springs. 18 Meanwhile the Edomites and Ammonites went and took up positions in the highlands opposite Dothan, sending some of their men to the south-east opposite Egrebel near Chous on the Wadi Mochmur. The rest of the Assyrian army took up positions in the plain, covering every inch of the ground; their tents and equipment made an immense encampment, so vast were their numbers.

19 The Israelites called on the Lord their God, dispirited because the enemy had surrounded them and cut all line of retreat. 20 For thirty-four days the Assyrian army, infantry, chariots, cavalrymen, had them surrounded. Every water-jar the inhabitants of Bethulia had was empty, 21 their storage-wells were drying up; on no day could a man drink his fill, since their water was rationed. 22 Their little children pined away, the women and young men grew weak with thirst; they collapsed in the streets and gateways of the town; they had no strength left.

NEW REVISED STANDARD VERSION

23 Then all the people, the young men, the women, and the children, gathered around Uzziah and the rulers of the town and cried out with a loud voice, and said before all the elders, 24 "Let God judge between you and us! You have done us a great injury in not making peace with the Assyrians. 25 For now we have no one to help us; God has sold us into their hands, to be strewn before them in thirst and exhaustion. 26 Now summon them and surrender the whole town as booty to the army of Holofernes and to all his forces. 27 For it would be better for us to be captured by them.*o* We shall indeed become slaves, but our lives will be spared, and we shall not witness our little ones dying before our eyes, and our wives and children drawing their last breath. 28 We call to witness against you heaven and earth and our God, the Lord of our ancestors, who punishes us for our sins and the sins of our ancestors; do today the things that we have described!"

29 Then great and general lamentation arose throughout the assembly, and they cried out to the Lord God with a loud voice. 30 But Uzziah said to them, "Courage, my brothers and sisters!*p* Let us hold out for five days more; by that time the Lord our God will turn his mercy to us again, for he will not forsake us utterly. 31 But if these days pass by, and no help comes for us, I will do as you say."

32 Then he dismissed the people to their various posts, and they went up on the walls and towers of their town. The women and children he sent home. In the town they were in great misery.

8 Now in those days Judith heard about these things: she was the daughter of Merari son of Ox son of Joseph son of Oziel son of Elkiah son of Ananias son of Gideon son of Raphain son of Ahitub son of Elijah son of Hilkiah son of Eliab son of Nathanael son of Salamiel son of Sarasadai son of Israel. 2 Her husband Manasseh, who belonged to her tribe and family, had died during the barley harvest. 3 For as he stood overseeing those who were binding sheaves in the field, he was overcome by the burning heat, and took to his bed and died in his town Bethulia. So they buried him with his ancestors in the field between Dothan and Balamon. 4 Judith remained as a widow for three years and four months 5 at home where she set up a tent for herself on the roof of her house. She put sackcloth around her waist and dressed in widow's clothing. 6 She fasted all the days of her widowhood, except the day before the sabbath and the sabbath itself, the day before the new moon and the day of the new moon, and the festivals and days of rejoicing of the house of Israel. 7 She was beautiful in appearance, and was very lovely to behold. Her husband Manasseh had left her gold and silver, men and women slaves, livestock, and fields; and she maintained this estate. 8 No one spoke ill of her, for she feared God with great devotion.

9 When Judith heard the harsh words spoken by the people against the ruler, because they were faint for lack of water, and when she heard all that Uzziah said to them, and how he promised them under oath to surrender the town to the Assyrians after five days, 10 she sent her maid, who was in charge of all she possessed, to summon Uzziah and*q* Chabris and Charmis, the elders of her town. 11 They came to her, and she said to them,

"Listen to me, rulers of the people of Bethulia! What you have said to the people today is not right; you have even sworn and pronounced this oath between God and you, promising to surrender the town to our enemies unless the Lord turns and helps us within so many days. 12 Who are you to put God to the test today, and to set yourselves up in the place of*r* God in human affairs? 13 You are putting

REVISED ENGLISH BIBLE

23 The people — young men, women, and children — all gathered round Ozias and the magistrates of the town, protesting loudly and saying in the presence of the elders: 24 'May God judge between us, for you have done us a great wrong in not suing for terms from the Assyrians. 25 Now we have no one to help us; God has sold us into their power, and they will find us struck down, all dead of thirst. 26 Surrender to them even now; let Holophernes' people and his army sack the whole town. 27 It is better for us to be carried off by them, for even as slaves we shall at least be alive, and we shall not have to watch our little ones dying before our eyes, the women and children at their last gasp. 28 We call heaven and earth to witness against you, we call our God, the Lord of our fathers, who is punishing us for our sins and the sins of our fathers. We pray that he may not let our forebodings come true this day.' 29 The whole assembly broke into a chorus of lamentation and cried loudly to the Lord God.

30 Ozias said to them, 'Courage, my friends! Let us hold out for five more days; by that time the Lord our God will again show us his mercy, for he will not abandon us for ever. 31 But if by the end of that time no help has reached us, I shall do what you ask.' 32 He dismissed the men, each to his post, and they went off to the walls and towers of the town; the women and children were sent to their homes. And throughout the town there was deep dejection.

8 News of what was happening reached Judith, daughter of Merari who was the son of Ox, son of Joseph, son of Oziel, son of Helkias, son of Ananias, son of Gideon, son of Raphaim, son of Ahitob, son of Elias, son of Chelkias, son of Eliab, son of Nathanael, son of Salamiel, son of Sarasadae, son of Israel. 2 Her husband Manasses, who belonged to the same tribe and clan as she did, had died during the barley harvest. 3 While he was out in the fields supervising the binding of the sheaves, he suffered sunstroke; he took to his bed and died in Bethulia his native town and was buried beside his ancestors in the field between Dothan and Balamon. 4 For three years and four months Judith had lived in her house as a widow; 5 she had a shelter erected on the roof, and she put on sackcloth and always wore mourning. 6 After she became a widow she used to fast every day except sabbath eve, the sabbath itself, the eve of the new moon, the day of the new moon, and the Israelite feasts and days of public rejoicing. 7 She was beautiful and very attractive. Manasses had left her gold and silver, slaves and slave-girls, livestock and land, and she lived on her property. 8 No one had a word to say against her, for she was a deeply religious woman.

9 When Judith heard how the people, demoralized by the shortage of water, had made shameful demands on Ozias the magistrate, and how he had given them his oath to surrender the town to the Assyrians at the end of five days, 10 she sent her maid who had charge of everything she owned to ask Ozias, Chabris, and Charmis, the elders of the town, to come and see her.

11 On their arrival she said: 'Listen to me, magistrates of Bethulia. It was wrong of you to speak as you did to the people today, binding yourselves and God in a solemn contract to surrender the town to our enemies unless the Lord sends relief within so many days. 12 Who are you to put God to the test at a time like this, and to usurp his role in human affairs? 13 It is the Lord Almighty you are now putting to the

---

o Other ancient authorities add *than to die of thirst*   *p* Gk *Courage, brothers*   *q* Other ancient authorities lack *Uzziah and* (see verses 28 and 35)   *r* Or *above*

23 All the people, therefore, including youths, women, and children, went in a crowd to Uzziah and the rulers of the city. They set up a great clamor and said before the elders: 24 "God judge between you and us! You have done us grave injustice in not making peace with the Assyrians. 25 There is no help for us now! Instead, God has sold us into their power by laying us prostrate before them in thirst and utter exhaustion. 26 Therefore, summon them and deliver the whole city as booty to the troops of Holofernes and to all his forces; 27 we would be better off to become their prey. We should indeed be made slaves, but at least we should live, and not have to behold our little ones dying before our eyes and our wives and children breathing out their souls. 28 We adjure you by heaven and earth, and by our God, the LORD of our forefathers, who is punishing us for our sins and those of our forefathers, to do as we have proposed, this very day."

29 All in the assembly with one accord broke into shrill wailing and loud cries to the LORD their God. 30 But Uzziah said to them, "Courage, my brothers! Let us wait five days more for the LORD our God, to show his mercy toward us; he will not utterly forsake us. 31 But if those days pass without help coming to us, I will do as you say." 32 Then he dispersed the men to their posts, and they returned to the walls and towers of the city; the women and children he sent to their homes. Throughout the city they were in great misery.

8 Now in those days Judith, daughter of Merari, son of Joseph, son of Oziel, son of Elkiah, son of Ananias, son of Gideon, son of Raphain, son of Ahitob, son of Elijah, son of Hilkiah, son of Eliab, son of Nathanael, son of Salamiel, son of Sarasadai, son of Simeon, son of Israel, heard of this. 2 Her husband, Manasseh, of her own tribe and clan, had died at the time of the barley harvest. 3 While he was in the field supervising those who bound the sheaves, he suffered sunstroke; and he died of this illness in Bethulia, his native city. He was buried with his forefathers in the field between Dothan and Balamon. 4 The widowed Judith remained three years and four months at home, 5 where she set up a tent for herself on the roof of her house. She put sackcloth about her loins and wore widow's weeds. 6 She fasted all the days of her widowhood, except sabbath eves and sabbaths, new moon eves and new moons, feast-days and holidays of the house of Israel. 7 She was beautifully formed and lovely to behold. Her husband, Manasseh, had left her gold and silver, servants and maids, livestock and fields, which she was maintaining. 8 No one had a bad word to say about her, for she was a very God-fearing woman.

9 When Judith, therefore, heard of the harsh words which the people, discouraged by their lack of water, had spoken against their ruler, and of all that Uzziah had said to them in reply, swearing that he would hand over the city to the Assyrians at the end of five days, 10 she sent the maid who was in charge of all her things to ask Uzziah, Chabris, and Charmis, the elders of the city, to visit her. 11 When they came, she said to them: "Listen to me, you rulers of the people of Bethulia. What you said to the people today is not proper. When you promised to hand over the city to our enemies at the end of five days unless within that time the LORD comes to our aid, you interposed between God and yourselves this oath which you took. 12 Who are you, then, that you should have put God to the test this day, setting yourselves in the place of God in human affairs? 13 It is the

23 Young men, women, children, the whole people thronged clamouring round Uzziah and the chief men of the town, shouting in the presence of the assembled elders, 24 'May God be judge between you and us! For you have done us great harm, by not suing for peace with the Assyrians. 25 And now there is no one to help us. God has delivered us into their hands to be prostrated before them in thirst and utter helplessness. 26 Call them in at once; hand the whole town over to be sacked by Holofernes' men and all his army. 27 After all, we should be much better off as their booty than we are now; no doubt we shall be enslaved, but at least we shall be alive and not see our little ones dying before our eyes or our wives and children perishing. 28 By heaven and earth and by our God, the Lord of our fathers, who is punishing us for our sins and the sins of our ancestors, we implore you to take this course now, today.' 29 Bitter lamentations rose from the whole assembly, and they all cried loudly to the Lord God.

30 Then Uzziah spoke to them, 'Take heart, brothers! Let us hold out five days more. By then the Lord our God will take pity on us, for he will not desert us altogether. 31 At the end of this time, if no help is forthcoming, I shall do as you have said.' 32 With that he dismissed the people to their various quarters. The men went to man the walls and towers of the town, sending the women and children home. The town was full of despondency.

8 Judith was informed at the time of what had happened. She was the daughter of Merari son of Ox, son of Joseph, son of Oziel, son of Elkiah, son of Ananias, son of Gideon, son of Raphaim, son of Ahitub, son of Elijah, son of Hilkiah, son of Eliab, son of Nathanael, son of Salamiel, son of Sarasadai, son of Israel. 2 Her husband Manasseh, of her own tribe and family, had died at the time of the barley harvest. 3 He was supervising the men as they bound up the sheaves in the field when he caught sunstroke and had to take to his bed. He died in Bethulia, his home town, and was buried with his ancestors in the field that lies between Dothan and Balamon. 4 As a widow, Judith stayed inside her home for three years and four months. 5 She had had an upper room built for herself on the roof. She wore sackcloth next to the skin and dressed in widow's weeds. 6 She fasted every day of her widowhood except for the Sabbath eve, the Sabbath itself, the eve of New Moon, the feast of New Moon and the joyful festivals of the House of Israel. 7 Now she was very beautiful, charming to see. Her husband Manasseh had left her gold and silver, menservants and maidservants, herds and land; and she lived among all her possessions 8 without anyone finding a word to say against her, so devoutly did she fear God.

9 Hearing how the water shortage had demoralised the people and how they had complained bitterly to the headman of the town, and being also told what Uzziah had said to them and how he had given them his oath to surrender the town to the Assyrians in five days' time, 10 Judith immediately sent the serving-woman who ran her household to summon Chabris and Charmis, two elders of the town. 11 When these came in she said:

'Listen to me, leaders of the people of Bethulia. You were wrong to speak to the people as you did today and to bind yourself by oath, in defiance of God, to surrender the town to our enemies if the Lord did not come to your help within a set number of days. 12 Who are you, to put God to the test today, you, of all people, to set yourselves above him? 13 You put the Lord Almighty to the test! You do not

the Lord Almighty to the test, but you will never learn anything! 14 You cannot plumb the depths of the human heart or understand the workings of the human mind; how do you expect to search out God, who made all these things, and find out his mind or comprehend his thought? No, my brothers, do not anger the Lord our God. 15 For if he does not choose to help us within these five days, he has power to protect us within any time he pleases, or even to destroy us in the presence of our enemies. 16 Do not try to bind the purposes of the Lord our God; for God is not like a human being, to be threatened, or like a mere mortal, to be won over by pleading. 17 Therefore, while we wait for his deliverance, let us call upon him to help us, and he will hear our voice, if it pleases him.

18 "For never in our generation, nor in these present days, has there been any tribe or family or people or town of ours that worships gods made with hands, as was done in days gone by. 19 That was why our ancestors were handed over to the sword and to pillage, and so they suffered a great catastrophe before our enemies. 20 But we know no other god but him, and so we hope that he will not disdain us or any of our nation. 21 For if we are captured, all Judea will be captured and our sanctuary will be plundered; and he will make us pay for its desecration with our blood. 22 The slaughter of our kindred and the captivity of the land and the desolation of our inheritance — all this he will bring on our heads among the Gentiles, wherever we serve as slaves; and we shall be an offense and a disgrace in the eyes of those who acquire us. 23 For our slavery will not bring us into favor, but the Lord our God will turn it to dishonor.

24 "Therefore, my brothers, let us set an example for our kindred, for their lives depend upon us, and the sanctuary — both the temple and the altar — rests upon us. 25 In spite of everything let us give thanks to the Lord our God, who is putting us to the test as he did our ancestors. 26 Remember what he did with Abraham, and how he tested Isaac, and what happened to Jacob in Syrian Mesopotamia, while he was tending the sheep of Laban, his mother's brother. 27 For he has not tried us with fire, as he did them, to search their hearts, nor has he taken vengeance on us; but the Lord scourges those who are close to him in order to admonish them."

28 Then Uzziah said to her, "All that you have said was spoken out of a true heart, and there is no one who can deny your words. 29 Today is not the first time your wisdom has been shown, but from the beginning of your life all the people have recognized your understanding, for your heart's disposition is right. 30 But the people were so thirsty that they compelled us to do for them what we have promised, and made us take an oath that we cannot break. 31 Now since you are a God-fearing woman, pray for us, so that the Lord may send us rain to fill our cisterns. Then we will no longer feel faint from thirst."

32 Then Judith said to them, "Listen to me. I am about to do something that will go down through all generations of our descendants. 33 Stand at the town gate tonight so that I may go out with my maid; and within the days after which you have promised to surrender the town to our enemies, the Lord will deliver Israel by my hand. 34 Only, do not try to find out what I am doing; for I will not tell you until I have finished what I am about to do."

35 Uzziah and the rulers said to her, "Go in peace, and may the Lord God go before you, to take vengeance on our enemies." 36 So they returned from the tent and went to their posts.

proof! Will you never understand? 14 You are unable to plumb the depths of the human heart or grasp the way the mind works; how then can you fathom the Maker of mortal beings? How can you know God's mind and understand his thought? No, my friends, do not provoke the anger of the Lord our God. 15 For even if he does not choose to help us within the five days, he has the power to shield us at any time he pleases, or equally he can let us be destroyed by our enemies. 16 It is not for you to impose conditions on the Lord our God, because God will neither yield to threats nor be bargained with like a mere mortal. 17 So while we wait for the deliverance which is his to give, let us appeal to him for help. If he sees fit, he will hear us.

18 'At the present day there is not one of our tribes or clans, districts or towns, that worships man-made gods, or has done so within living memory. This did take place in days gone by, 19 and that was why our forefathers were abandoned to slaughter and pillage, and great was their downfall at the hand of the enemy. 20 We, however, acknowledge no god but the Lord, and so have confidence that he will not spurn us or any of our nation. 21 If we should lose Bethulia, then all Judaea will be lost; the temple will be sacked, and God will hold us responsible for its desecration. 22 The slaughter and deportation of our fellow-countrymen and the devastation of our ancestral land will bring his judgement on our heads, wherever among the Gentiles we become slaves. Our masters will regard us with disgust and contempt. 23 There will be no happy ending to our servitude, no return to favour; the Lord our God will use it to dishonour us.

24 'My friends, let us now set an example to our fellow-countrymen, for their lives depend on us, and with us rests the fate of the temple, its precincts, and the altar. 25 Despite our peril let us give thanks to the Lord our God, for he is putting us to the test as he did our forefathers. 26 Remember how he dealt with Abraham, and how he tested Isaac, and what happened to Jacob in Syrian Mesopotamia while he was working as a shepherd for his uncle Laban. 27 The Lord is subjecting us to the same fiery ordeal by which he tested their loyalty, not taking vengeance on us: it is as a warning that he scourges his worshippers.'

28 Ozias replied, 'You have spoken from the wisdom of your heart, and what you say no one can deny. 29 This is not the first time you have given proof of your wisdom; throughout your life we have all recognized your good sense and sound judgement. 30 But the people were desperate with thirst, and drove us to make this promise and bind ourselves by an oath we may not break. 31 You are a devout woman; pray for us now and ask the Lord to send the rain to fill our cisterns, and then we shall be faint no more.'

32 'Listen to me,' said Judith. 'I am going to do something which will be remembered among our countrymen for all generations. 33 Be at the gate tonight; I shall go out with my maid and, before the day on which you have promised to surrender the town to our enemies, the Lord will deliver Israel by my hand. 34 But do not question me about my plan; I shall tell you nothing until I have accomplished what I mean to do.' 35 Ozias and the magistrates said to her, 'Go with our blessing, and may you have the guidance of the Lord God as you take vengeance on our enemies.' 36 They then left her roof-shelter and returned to their posts.

LORD Almighty for whom you are laying down conditions; will you never understand anything? 14 You cannot plumb the depths of the human heart or grasp the workings of the human mind; how then can you fathom God, who has made all these things, discern his mind, and understand his plan?

"No, my brothers, do not anger the LORD our God. 15 For if he does not wish to come to our aid within the five days, he has it equally within his power to protect us at such time as he pleases, or to destroy us in the face of our enemies. 16 It is not for you to make the LORD our God give surety for his plans.

"God is not man that he should be moved
        by threats,
    nor human, that he may be given an ultimatum.

17 "So while we wait for the salvation that comes from him, let us call upon him to help us, and he will hear our cry if it is his good pleasure. 18 For there has not risen among us in recent generations, nor does there exist today, any tribe, or clan, or town, or city of ours that worships gods made by hands, as happened in former days. 19 It was for such conduct that our forefathers were handed over to the sword and to pillage, and fell with great destruction before our enemies. 20 But since we acknowledge no other god but the LORD, we hope that he will not disdain us or any of our people. 21 If we are taken, all Judea will fall, our sanctuary will be plundered, and God will make us pay for its profanation with our life's blood. 22 For the slaughter of our kinsmen, for the taking of exiles from the land, and for the devastation of our inheritance, he will lay the guilt on our heads. Wherever we shall be enslaved among the nations, we shall be a mockery and a reproach in the eyes of our masters. 23 Our enslavement will not be turned to our benefit, but the LORD our God will maintain it to our disgrace.

24 "Therefore, my brothers, let us set an example for our kinsmen. Their lives depend on us, and the defense of the sanctuary, the temple, and the altar rests with us. 25 Besides all this, we should be grateful to the LORD our God, for putting us to the test, as he did our forefathers. 26 Recall how he dealt with Abraham, and how he tried Isaac, and all that happened to Jacob in Syrian Mesopotamia while he was tending the flocks of Laban, his mother's brother. 27 Not for vengeance did the LORD put them in the crucible to try their hearts, nor has he done so with us. It is by way of admonition that he chastises those who are close to him."

28 Then Uzziah said to her: "All that you have said was spoken with good sense, and no one can gainsay your words. 29 Not today only is your wisdom made evident, but from your earliest years all the people have recognized your prudence, which corresponds to the worthy dispositions of your heart. 30 The people, however, were so tortured with thirst that they forced us to speak to them as we did, and to bind ourselves by an oath that we cannot break. 31 But now, God-fearing woman that you are, pray for us that the LORD may send rain to fill up our cisterns, lest we be weakened still further."

32 Then Judith said to them: "Listen to me! I will do something that will go down from generation to generation among the descendants of our race. 33 Stand at the gate tonight to let me pass through with my maid; and within the days you have specified before you will surrender the city to our enemies, the LORD will rescue Israel by my hand. 34 You must not inquire into what I am doing, for I will not tell you until my plan has been accomplished." 35 Uzziah and the rulers said to her, "Go in peace, and may the LORD God go before you to take vengeance upon our enemies!" 36 Then they withdrew from the tent and returned to their posts.

understand anything, and never will. 14 If you cannot sound the depths of the human heart or unravel the arguments of the human mind, how can you fathom the God who made all things, or sound his mind or unravel his purposes? No, brothers, do not provoke the anger of the Lord our God. 15 Although it may not be his will to help us within the next five days, he has the power to protect us for as many days as he pleases, just as he has the power to destroy us before our enemies. 16 But you have no right to demand guarantees where the designs of the Lord our God are concerned. For God is not to be threatened as a human being is, nor is he, like a mere human, to be cajoled. 17 Rather, as we wait patiently for him to save, let us plead with him to help us. He will hear our voice if such is his good pleasure.

18 'And indeed of recent times and still today there is not one tribe of ours, or family, or village, or town that has worshipped gods made by human hand, as once was done, 19 which was the reason why our ancestors were delivered over to sword and sack, and perished in misery at the hands of our enemies. 20 We for our part acknowledge no other God but him; and so we may hope he will not look on us disdainfully or desert our nation.

21 'If indeed they capture us, as you expect, then all Judaea will be captured too, and our holy places plundered, and we shall answer with our blood for their profanation. 22 The slaughter of our brothers, the captivity of our country, the unpeopling of our heritage, will recoil on our own heads among the nations whose slaves we shall become, and our new masters will look down on us as an outrage and a disgrace; 23 for our surrender will not reinstate us in their favour; no, the Lord our God will make it a thing to be ashamed of. 24 So now, brothers, let us set an example to our brothers, since their lives depend on us, and the sanctuary — Temple and altar — rests on us.

25 'All this being so, let us rather give thanks to the Lord our God who, as he tested our ancestors, is now testing us. 26 Remember how he treated Abraham, all the ordeals of Isaac, all that happened to Jacob in Syrian Mesopotamia while he kept the sheep of Laban, his mother's brother. 27 For as these ordeals were intended by him to search their hearts, so now this is not vengeance that God is exacting on us, but a warning inflicted by the Lord on those who are near his heart.'

28 Uzziah replied, 'Everything you have just said comes from an honest heart and no one will contradict a word of it. 29 Not that today is the first time your wisdom has been displayed; from your earliest years all the people have known how shrewd you are and of how sound a heart. 30 But, parched with thirst, the people forced us to act as we had promised them and to bind ourselves by an inviolable oath. 31 You are a devout woman; pray to the Lord, then, to send us a downpour to fill our storage-wells, so that our faintness may pass.'

32 Judith replied, 'Listen to me, I intend to do something, the memory of which will be handed down to the children of our race from age to age. 33 Tonight you must be at the gate of the town. I shall make my way out with my attendant. Before the time fixed by you for surrendering the town to our enemies, the Lord will make use of me to rescue Israel. 34 You must not ask what I intend to do; I shall not tell you until I have done it.' 35 Uzziah and the chief men said, 'Go in peace. May the Lord show you a way to take revenge on our enemies.' 36 And leaving the upper room they went back to their posts.

NEW REVISED STANDARD VERSION	REVISED ENGLISH BIBLE

NEW REVISED STANDARD VERSION

9 Then Judith prostrated herself, put ashes on her head, and uncovered the sackcloth she was wearing. At the very time when the evening incense was being offered in the house of God in Jerusalem, Judith cried out to the Lord with a loud voice, and said,

2 "O Lord God of my ancestor Simeon, to whom you gave a sword to take revenge on those strangers who had torn off a virgin's clothing[s] to defile her, and exposed her thighs to put her to shame, and polluted her womb to disgrace her; for you said, 'It shall not be done' — yet they did it. 3 So you gave up their rulers to be killed, and their bed, which was ashamed of the deceit they had practiced, was stained with blood, and you struck down slaves along with princes, and princes on their thrones. 4 You gave up their wives for booty and their daughters to captivity, and all their booty to be divided among your beloved children who burned with zeal for you and abhorred the pollution of their blood and called on you for help — O God, my God, hear me also — a widow.

5 "For you have done these things and those that went before and those that followed. You have designed the things that are now, and those that are to come. What you had in mind has happened; 6 the things you decided on presented themselves and said, 'Here we are!' For all your ways are prepared in advance, and your judgment is with foreknowledge.

7 "Here now are the Assyrians, a greatly increased force, priding themselves in their horses and riders, boasting in the strength of their foot soldiers, and trusting in shield and spear, in bow and sling. They do not know that you are the Lord who crushes wars; the Lord is your name. 8 Break their strength by your might, and bring down their power in your anger; for they intend to defile your sanctuary, and to pollute the tabernacle where your glorious name resides, and to break off the horns[t] of your altar with the sword. 9 Look at their pride, and send your wrath upon their heads. Give to me, a widow, the strong hand to do what I plan. 10 By the deceit of my lips strike down the slave with the prince and the prince with his servant; crush their arrogance by the hand of a woman.

11 "For your strength does not depend on numbers, nor your might on the powerful. But you are the God of the lowly, helper of the oppressed, upholder of the weak, protector of the forsaken, savior of those without hope.

REVISED ENGLISH BIBLE

9 Judith prostrated herself; she put ashes on her head and uncovered the sackcloth she was wearing, and at the moment when the evening incense was being offered in the house of God at Jerusalem, she raised her voice and cried to the Lord: 2 'Lord, the God of my forefather Simeon, you put a sword in Simeon's hand for him to take vengeance on those foreigners who had stripped off a virgin's veil to defile her, uncovered her thighs to shame her, and violated her womb to dishonour her. Though you said, "Such a thing shall not be done," yet they did so. 3 That was why you gave up their rulers to be slain, and the bed they had disgraced with their treachery to be stained with blood; beneath your stroke both slaves and princes fell, even princes upon their thrones. 4 You gave their wives as booty, and their daughters as captives, and all the spoils to be apportioned among your beloved sons, who, aflame with zeal for your cause and aghast at the pollution of their blood, called on you for help. God, my God, hear also a widow's prayer. 5 All that happened then, and all that happened before and after, was your work. What is now and what is yet to be, you have planned; and what you have planned has come to pass. 6 The things you have foreordained present themselves and say, "We are here." All your ways are prepared beforehand: your judgement rests on foreknowledge.

7 'Here are the Assyrians massed in force, exultant in their horses and riders, boasting of the might of their infantry, confident in shield and javelin, bow and sling. They do not know that you are the Lord who stamps out wars; the Lord is your name. 8 Overthrow their strength by your power and crush their might in your anger, for their aim is to desecrate your temple, to defile the dwelling-place of your glorious name, and to lay low the horns of your altar with the sword. 9 See how arrogant they are! Bring down your wrath on their heads, and give to me, widow though I am, the strength to achieve my end. 10 Use the guile of my words to strike them down, the slave with the ruler, the ruler with the servant; shatter their pride by a woman's hand. 11 Your might lies not in numbers nor your sovereign power in strong men, but you are the God of the humble, the help of the poor, the support of the weak, the protector of the despairing, the deliverer of those who have lost all hope.

---

[s] Cn: Gk *loosed her womb*   [t] Syr: Gk *horn*

NEW AMERICAN BIBLE

9 Judith threw herself down prostrate, with ashes strewn upon her head, and wearing nothing over her sackcloth. While the incense was being offered in the temple of God in Jerusalem that evening, Judith prayed to the LORD with a loud voice: 2"LORD, God of my forefather Simeon! You put a sword into his hand to take revenge upon the foreigners who had immodestly loosened the maiden's girdle, shamefully exposed her thighs, and disgracefully violated her body. This they did, though you forbade it. 3Therefore you had their rulers slaughtered; and you covered with their blood the bed in which they lay deceived, the same bed that had felt the shame of their own deceiving. You smote the slaves together with their princes, and the princes together with their servants. 4Their wives you handed over to plunder, and their daughters to captivity; and all the spoils you divided among your favored sons, who burned with zeal for you, and in their abhorrence of the defilement of their kinswoman, called on you for help.

5"O God, my God, hear me also, a widow. It is you who were the author of those events and of what preceded and followed them. The present, also, and the future you have planned. Whatever you devise comes into being; 6the things you decide on come forward and say, 'Here we are!' All your ways are in readiness, and your judgment is made with foreknowledge.

7"Here are the Assyrians, a vast force, priding themselves on horse and rider, boasting of the power of their infantry, trusting in shield and spear, bow and sling. They do not know that

8" 'You, the LORD, crush warfare;
Lord is your name.'

"Shatter their strength in your might, and crush their force in your wrath; for they have resolved to profane your sanctuary, to defile the tent where your glorious name resides, and to overthrow with iron the horns of your altar. 9See their pride, and send forth your wrath upon their heads. Give me, a widow, the strong hand to execute my plan. 10With the guile of my lips, smite the slave together with the ruler, the ruler together with his servant; crush their pride by the hand of a woman.

11"Your strength is not in numbers, nor does your power depend upon stalwart men; but you are the God of the lowly, the helper of the oppressed, the supporter of the weak, the protector of the forsaken, the savior of those without hope.

NEW JERUSALEM BIBLE

9 Judith threw herself face to the ground, scattered ashes on her head, undressed as far as the sackcloth she was wearing and cried loudly to the Lord. At the same time in Jerusalem the evening incense was being offered in the Temple of God. Judith said:

2Lord, God of my ancestor Simeon,
you armed him with a sword to take vengeance on the foreigners
who had undone a virgin's belt to her shame,
laid bare her thigh to her confusion,
violated her womb to her dishonour,
since, though you said, 'This must not be,' they did it.

3For this you handed their leaders over to slaughter,
and their bed, defiled by their treachery,
was itself betrayed in blood.
You struck the slaves with the chieftains
and the chieftains with their retainers.

4You left their wives to be carried off,
their daughters to be taken captive,
and their spoils to be shared out
among the sons you loved,
who had been so zealous for you,
had loathed the stain put on their blood
and called on you for help.

O God, my God,
now hear this widow too;
5for you have made the past,
and what is happening now, and what will follow.
What is, what will be, you have planned;
what has been, you designed.

6Your purposes stood forward;
'See, here we are!' they said.
For all your ways are prepared
and your judgements delivered with foreknowledge.

7See the Assyrians, with their army abounding
glorying in their horses and their riders,
exulting in the strength of their infantry.
Trust as they may in shield and spear,
in bow and sling,
in you they have not recognised the Lord,
the breaker of battle-lines;
8yours alone is the title of Lord.

Break their violence with your might,
in your anger bring down their strength.
For they plan to profane your holy places,
to defile the tabernacle, the resting place of your
glorious name,
and to hack down the horn of your altar.
9Observe their arrogance,
send your fury on their heads,
give the strength I have in mind
to this widow's hand.
10By guile of my lips
strike down slave with master,
and master with retainer.
Break their pride
by a woman's hand.

11Your strength does not lie in numbers,
nor your might in strong men;
since you are the God of the humble,
the help of the oppressed,
the support of the weak,
the refuge of the forsaken,
the Saviour of the despairing.

12 Please, please, God of my father, God of the heritage of Israel, Lord of heaven and earth, Creator of the waters, King of all your creation, hear my prayer! 13 Make my deceitful words bring wound and bruise on those who have planned cruel things against your covenant, and against your sacred house, and against Mount Zion, and against the house your children possess. 14 Let your whole nation and every tribe know and understand that you are God, the God of all power and might, and that there is no other who protects the people of Israel but you alone!"

10 When Judith[u] had stopped crying out to the God of Israel, and had ended all these words, 2 she rose from where she lay prostrate. She called her maid and went down into the house where she lived on sabbaths and on her festal days. 3 She removed the sackcloth she had been wearing, took off her widow's garments, bathed her body with water, and anointed herself with precious ointment. She combed her hair, put on a tiara, and dressed herself in the festive attire that she used to wear while her husband Manasseh was living. 4 She put sandals on her feet, and put on her anklets, bracelets, rings, earrings, and all her other jewelry. Thus she made herself very beautiful, to entice the eyes of all the men who might see her. 5 She gave her maid a skin of wine and a flask of oil, and filled a bag with roasted grain, dried fig cakes, and fine bread;[v] then she wrapped up all her dishes and gave them to her to carry.

6 Then they went out to the town gate of Bethulia and found Uzziah standing there with the elders of the town, Chabris and Charmis. 7 When they saw her transformed in appearance and dressed differently, they were very greatly astounded at her beauty and said to her, 8 "May the God of our ancestors grant you favor and fulfill your plans, so that the people of Israel may glory and Jerusalem may be exalted." She bowed down to God.

9 Then she said to them, "Order the gate of the town to be opened for me so that I may go out and accomplish the things you have just said to me." So they ordered the young men to open the gate for her, as she requested. 10 When they had done this, Judith went out, accompanied by her maid. The men of the town watched her until she had gone down the mountain and passed through the valley, where they lost sight of her.

11 As the women[w] were going straight on through the valley, an Assyrian patrol met her 12 and took her into custody. They asked her, "To what people do you belong, and where are you coming from, and where are you going?" She replied, "I am a daughter of the Hebrews, but I am fleeing from them, for they are about to be handed over to you to be devoured. 13 I am on my way to see Holofernes the commander of your army, to give him a true report; I will show him a way by which he can go and capture all the hill country without losing one of his men, captured or slain." 14 When the men heard her words, and observed her face — she was in their eyes marvelously beautiful — they said to her, 15 "You have saved your life by hurrying down to see our lord. Go at once to his tent; some of us will escort you and hand you over to him. 16 When you stand before him, have no fear in your heart, but tell him what you have just said, and he will treat you well." 17 They chose from their number a hundred men to accompany her and her maid, and they brought them to the tent of Holofernes. 18 There was great excitement in the

12 God of my forefather, God of Israel's heritage, Lord of heaven and earth, Creator of the waters, King of all your creation, hear my prayer! 13 Grant that my deceiving words may wound and bruise those who harbour cruel designs against your covenant and against your temple, the summit of Zion, and the home and possession of your children. 14 May your whole nation, every tribe, be made aware that you are God, God of all power and might, and that you and you alone are Israel's shield.'

10 When Judith had ended this prayer to the God of Israel, 2 she rose from where she had been lying prostrate, called her maid, and went down into the house in which she spent her sabbaths and days of festival. 3 She removed the sackcloth she was wearing and laid aside her widow's dress. After bathing, she anointed herself with rich perfume. She arranged her hair elaborately, tied it with a ribbon, and arrayed herself in her gayest clothes, those she used to wear while her husband Manasses was still alive. 4 She put sandals on her feet and adorned herself with anklets, bracelets and rings, her ear-rings, and all her ornaments, and made herself very attractive, to catch the eye of any man who saw her. 5 She gave her maid a skin of wine and a flask of oil; she filled a bag with roasted grain, cakes of dried figs, and loaves of fine bread, packed up her utensils, and gave it all to her maid to carry.

6 From the house they made their way to the town gate of Bethulia, where they found Ozias standing with Chabris and Charmis, the elders of the town. 7 When they beheld Judith transformed in appearance and quite differently dressed, they marvelled at her beauty and said to her, 8 'The God of our fathers grant that you meet with favour and accomplish what you are undertaking, so that Israel may triumph and Jerusalem be exalted!' Judith bowed in worship to God 9 and then said, 'Give the order for the gate to be opened for me, and I shall go and carry out all we have spoken of.' They ordered the young men to do as she asked, 10 and when the gate was opened Judith went out, accompanied by her maid. The men of the town gazed after her until she had gone down the hillside and along the valley, where they lost sight of her.

11 As the two women were making their way straight down the valley, they were confronted by an Assyrian outpost 12 who stopped Judith and questioned her: 'What is your nationality? Where have you come from, and where are you going?' 'I am a Hebrew,' she replied; 'but I am running away from my people, because they are about to fall into your hands and become your prey. 13 I am on my way to Holophernes, your commander-in-chief, with accurate information for him: I shall show him a route by which he can gain control of the entire hill-country without one of you suffering injury or worse.'

14 The men listened to her story, looking at her face and marvelling at her beauty. 15 'By coming down at once to see our master you have saved your life,' they said. 'You must go to his tent straight away; some of us will escort you and hand you over. 16 When you are in his presence, do not be afraid; just tell him what you have told us, and he will treat you well.' 17 They detailed a hundred of their number to accompany her and her maid, and the two women were conducted to Holophernes' tent.

---

[u] Gk *she*   [v] Other ancient authorities add *and cheese*   [w] Gk *they*

NEW AMERICAN BIBLE

NEW JERUSALEM BIBLE

12 "Please, please, God of my forefather, God of the heritage of Israel, LORD of heaven and earth, Creator of the waters, King of all you have created, hear my prayer! 13 Let my guileful speech bring wound and wale on those who have planned dire things against your covenant, your holy temple, Mount Zion, and the homes your children have inherited. 14 Let your whole nation and all the tribes know clearly that you are the God of all power and might, and that there is no other who protects the people of Israel but you alone."

12 Please, please, God of my father,
God of the heritage of Israel,
Master of heaven and earth,
Creator of the waters,
King of your whole creation,
hear my prayer.
13 Give me a beguiling tongue
to wound and kill
those who have formed such cruel designs
against your covenant,
against your holy dwelling-place,
against Mount Zion,
against the house belonging to your sons.
14 And demonstrate to every nation, every tribe,
that you are the Lord, God of all power, all might,
and that the race of Israel has no protector but you.

10 As soon as Judith had thus concluded, and ceased her invocation to the God of Israel, 2 she rose from the ground. She called her maid and they went down into the house, which she used only on sabbaths and feast days. 3 She took off the sackcloth she had on, laid aside the garments of her widowhood, washed her body with water, and anointed it with rich ointment. She arranged her hair and bound it with a fillet, and put on the festive attire she had worn while her husband, Manasseh, was living. 4 She chose sandals for her feet, and put on her anklets, bracelets, rings, earrings, and all her other jewelry. Thus she made herself very beautiful, to captivate the eyes of all the men who should see her.

5 She gave her maid a leather flask of wine and a cruse of oil. She filled a bag with roasted grain, fig cakes, bread and cheese; all these provisions she wrapped up and gave to the maid to carry. 6 Then they went out to the gate of the city of Bethulia and found Uzziah and the elders of the city, Chabris and Charmis, standing there. 7 When these men saw Judith transformed in looks and differently dressed, they were very much astounded at her beauty and said to her, 8 "May the God of our fathers bring you to favor, and make your undertaking a success, for the glory of the Israelites and the exaltation of Jerusalem."

Judith bowed down to God. Then she said to them, 9 "Order the gate of the city opened for me, that I may go to carry out the business we discussed." So they ordered the youths to open the gate for her as she requested. 10 When they did so, Judith and her maid went out. The men of the city kept her in view as she went down the mountain and crossed the valley; then they lost sight of her.

11 As Judith and her maid walked directly across the valley, they encountered the Assyrian outpost. 12 The men took her in custody and asked her, "To what people do you belong? Where do you come from, and where are you going?" She replied: "I am a daughter of the Hebrews, and I am fleeing from them, because they are about to be delivered up to you as prey. 13 I have come to see Holofernes, the general in chief of your forces, to give him a trustworthy report; I will show him the route by which he can ascend and take possession of the whole mountain district without a single one of his men suffering injury or loss of life." 14 When the men heard her words and gazed upon her face, which appeared wondrously beautiful to them, they said to her, 15 "By coming down thus promptly to see our master, you have saved your life. Now go to his tent; some of our men will accompany you to present you to him. 16 When you stand before him, have no fear in your heart; give him the report you speak of, and he will treat you well." 17 So they detailed a hundred of their men as an escort for her and her maid, and these conducted them to the tent of Holofernes.

10 Thus Judith called on the God of Israel. When she had finished praying, 2 she got up from the floor, summoned her maid and went down into the rooms which she used on Sabbath days and festivals. 3 There she removed the sackcloth she was wearing and taking off her widow's dress, she washed all over, anointed herself plentifully with perfumes, dressed her hair, wrapped a turban round it and put on the robe of joy she used to wear when her husband Manasseh was alive. 4 She put sandals on her feet, put on her necklaces, bracelets, rings, earrings and all her jewellery, and made herself beautiful enough to beguile the eye of any man who saw her. 5 Then she handed her maid a skin of wine and a flask of oil, filled a bag with barley girdle-cakes, cakes of dried fruit and pure loaves, and wrapping all these provisions up gave them to her as well. 6 They then went out, making for the town gate of Bethulia. There they found Uzziah waiting with the two elders of the town, Chabris and Charmis. 7 When they saw Judith, her face so changed and her clothes so different, they were lost in admiration of her beauty. They said to her:

8 May the God of our ancestors keep you in his favour!
May he crown your designs with success
to the glory of the children of Israel,
to the greater glory of Jerusalem!

9 Judith worshipped God, and then she said, 'Have the town gate opened for me so that I can go out and fulfil all the wishes you expressed to me.' They did as she asked and gave orders to the young men to open the gate for her. 10 This done, Judith went out accompanied by her maid, while the men of the town watched her all the way down the mountain and across the valley, until they lost sight of her.

11 As the women were making straight through the valley, an advance unit of Assyrians intercepted them, 12 and, seizing Judith, began to question her. 'Which side are you on? Where do you come from? Where are you going?' 'I am a daughter of the Hebrews,' she replied, 'and I am fleeing from them since they will soon be your prey. 13 I am on my way to see Holofernes, the general of your army, to give him trustworthy information. I shall show him the road to take if he wants to capture all the hill-country without losing one man or one life.' 14 As the men listened to what she was saying, they stared in astonishment at the sight of such a beautiful woman. 15 'It will prove the saving of you,' they said to her, 'coming down to see our master of your own accord. You had better go to his tent; some of our men will escort you and hand you over to him. 16 Once you are in his presence do not be afraid. Tell him what you have just told us and you will be well treated.' 17 They then detailed a hundred of their men as escort for herself and her attendant, and these led them to the tent of Holofernes.

NEW REVISED STANDARD VERSION	REVISED ENGLISH BIBLE

whole camp, for her arrival was reported from tent to tent. They came and gathered around her as she stood outside the tent of Holofernes, waiting until they told him about her. 19 They marveled at her beauty and admired the Israelites, judging them by her. They said to one another, "Who can despise these people, who have women like this among them? It is not wise to leave one of their men alive, for if we let them go they will be able to beguile the whole world!" 20 Then the guards of Holofernes and all his servants came out and led her into the tent. 21 Holofernes was resting on his bed under a canopy that was woven with purple and gold, emeralds and other precious stones. 22 When they told him of her, he came to the front of the tent, with silver lamps carried before him. 23 When Judith came into the presence of Holofernes *x* and his servants, they all marveled at the beauty of her face. She prostrated herself and did obeisance to him, but his slaves raised her up.

11 Then Holofernes said to her, "Take courage, woman, and do not be afraid in your heart, for I have never hurt anyone who chose to serve Nebuchadnezzar, king of all the earth. 2 Even now, if your people who live in the hill country had not slighted me, I would never have lifted my spear against them. They have brought this on themselves. 3 But now tell me why you have fled from them and have come over to us. In any event, you have come to safety. Take courage! You will live tonight and ever after. 4 No one will hurt you. Rather, all will treat you well, as they do the servants of my lord King Nebuchadnezzar."

5 Judith answered him, "Accept the words of your slave, and let your servant speak in your presence. I will say nothing false to my lord this night. 6 If you follow out the words of your servant, God will accomplish something through you, and my lord will not fail to achieve his purposes. 7 By the life of Nebuchadnezzar, king of the whole earth, and by the power of him who has sent you to direct every living being! Not only do human beings serve him because of you, but also the animals of the field and the cattle and the birds of the air will live, because of your power, under Nebuchadnezzar and all his house. 8 For we have heard of your wisdom and skill, and it is reported throughout the whole world that you alone are the best in the whole kingdom, the most informed and the most astounding in military strategy.

9 "Now as for Achior's speech in your council, we have heard his words, for the people of Bethulia spared him and he told them all he had said to you. 10 Therefore, lord and master, do not disregard what he said, but keep it in your mind, for it is true. Indeed our nation cannot be punished, nor can the sword prevail against them, unless they sin against their God. 11 "But now, in order that my lord may not be defeated and his purpose frustrated, death will fall upon them, for a sin has overtaken them by which they are about to provoke their God to anger when they do what is wrong. 12 Since their food supply is exhausted and their water has almost given out, they have planned to kill their livestock and have determined to use all that God by his laws has forbidden them to eat. 13 They have decided to consume the first fruits of the grain and the tithes of the wine and oil, which they had consecrated and set aside for the priests who minister in the presence of our God in Jerusalem — things it is not lawful for any of the people even to touch with their hands. 14 Since even the people in Jerusalem have been doing this, they have sent messengers there in order to bring back permission from the council of the elders. 15 When the re-

18 AS THE news of her coming spread from tent to tent, men ran from all parts of the camp and gathered in a circle round her as she stood outside Holophernes' tent waiting for him to be told about her. 19 Admiration for her beauty led them to feel admiration for all Israelites; they said to each other, 'Who could despise a nation whose women are like these? We had better not leave a man of them alive, for if they get away they will be able to outwit the whole world.' 20 Holophernes' bodyguard and all his attendants came out and escorted her into the tent, 21 where he was resting on his bed under a mosquito-net of purple interwoven with gold, emeralds, and precious stones. 22 When Judith was announced he came out to the front part of the tent, with silver lamps carried before him. 23 She entered his presence, and he and his attendants all marvelled at the beauty of her face. She prostrated herself and did obeisance to him, but his slaves raised her up.

11 'Do not be alarmed, madam,' said Holophernes; 'there is no cause for fear. I have never injured anyone who chose to serve Nebuchadnezzar, king of all the earth. 2 I should never have raised my spear against your people in the hill-country had they not insulted me; they have brought it on themselves. 3 Now tell me why you have run away from them and joined us. You have saved your life by coming. Be reassured! You are in no danger, this night or at any time; 4 no one will harm you. On the contrary, you will enjoy the benefits that are accorded to the subjects of my master, King Nebuchadnezzar.'

5 Judith replied, 'My lord, grant your slave a hearing and listen to what I have to say to you. The information I am giving you tonight is the truth. 6 If you follow my advice, through you God will accomplish a great thing, and my lord will not fail to attain his ends: 7 I swear this by the life of Nebuchadnezzar, king of all the earth, and by the living might of him who sent you to bring order to all creatures. Thanks to you and to your power, not only do men serve him, but wild animals, cattle, and birds will live at the disposal of Nebuchadnezzar and his whole house. 8 We have heard how wise and clever you are; you are known throughout the world as a man of ability who has no peer in all the empire, a man of powerful intellect and amazing skill in the arts of war.

9 'Now, we have heard about the speech that Achior made in your council; the men of Bethulia rescued him and he told them everything he had said in your presence. 10 Do not disregard his words, my sovereign lord, but give them full weight. They are true: no punishment ever befalls our race nor does the sword subdue them, except when they sin against their God. 11 And yet, my lord, you are not to be thwarted and cheated of success; they are doomed to die, and sin has them in its power, for whenever they do wrong they arouse their God's anger. 12 Since they have run out of food and their water supply is desperately low, they have decided to lay hands on their cattle, proposing to eat all the things that God by his laws has strictly prohibited; 13 they have resolved to use up the firstfruits of the grain and the tithes of wine and oil, although these are dedicated and reserved for the priests who stand in attendance before our God in Jerusalem, and no layman may so much as touch them. 14 They have sent to Jerusalem for permission from the senate, because even the people there have done this.'

x Gk *him*

18 When the news of her arrival spread among the tents, a crowd gathered in the camp. They came and stood around her as she waited outside the tent of Holofernes, while he was being informed about her. 19 They marveled at her beauty, regarding the Israelites with wonder because of her, and they said to one another, "Who can despise this people that has such women among them? It is not wise to leave one man of them alive, for if any were to be spared they could beguile the whole world." 20 The guard of Holofernes and all his servants came out and ushered her into the tent. 21 Now Holofernes was reclining on his bed under a canopy with a netting of crimson and gold, emeralds and other precious stones. 22 When they announced her to him, he came out to the antechamber, preceded by silver lamps; 23 and when Holofernes and his servants beheld Judith, they all marveled at the beauty of her face. She threw herself down prostrate before him, but his servants raised her up.

11 Then Holofernes said to her: "Take courage, lady; have no fear in your heart! Never have I harmed anyone who chose to serve Nebuchadnezzar, king of all the earth. 2 Nor would I have raised my spear against your people who dwell in the mountain region, had they not despised me and brought this upon themselves. 3 But now tell me why you fled from them and came to us. In any case, you have come to safety. Take courage! Your life is spared tonight and for the future. 4 No one at all will harm you. Rather, you will be well treated, as are all the servants of my lord, King Nebuchadnezzar."

5 Judith answered him: "Listen to the words of your servant, and let your handmaid speak in your presence! I will tell no lie to my lord this night, 6 and if you follow out the words of your handmaid, God will give you complete success, and my lord will not fail in any of his undertakings. 7 By the life of Nebuchadnezzar, king of all the earth, and by the power of him who has sent you to set all creatures aright! not only do men serve him through you; but even the wild beasts and the cattle and the birds of the air, because of your strength, will live for Nebuchadnezzar and his whole house. 8 Indeed, we have heard of your wisdom and sagacity, and all the world is aware that throughout the kingdom you alone are competent, rich in experience, and distinguished in military strategy.

9 "As for Achior's speech in your council, we have heard of it. When the men of Bethulia spared him, he told them all he had said to you. 10 So then, my lord and master, do not disregard his word, but bear it in mind, for it is true. For our people are not punished, nor does the sword prevail against them, except when they sin against their God. 11 But now their guilt has caught up with them by which they bring the wrath of their God upon them whenever they do wrong; so that my lord will not be repulsed and fail, but death will overtake them. 12 Since their food gave out and all their water ran low, they decided to kill their animals, and determined to consume all the things which God in his laws forbade them to eat. 13 They decreed that they would use up the first fruits of grain and the tithes of wine and oil which they had sanctified and reserved for the priests who minister in the presence of our God in Jerusalem: things which no layman should even touch with his hands. 14 They have sent messengers to Jerusalem to bring back to them authorization from the council of the elders; for the inhabitants there have also done these things. 15 On the very day when the re-

18 News of her coming had already spread through the tents, and there was a general stir in the camp. She was still outside the tent of Holofernes waiting to be announced, when a crowd began forming round her. 19 They were immediately impressed by her beauty and impressed with the Israelites because of her. 'Who could despise a people who have women like this?' they kept saying. 'Better not leave one of them alive; let any go and they could twist the whole world round their fingers!' 20 The bodyguard and adjutants of Holofernes then came out and led Judith into the tent. 21 Holofernes was resting on his bed under a canopy of purple and gold studded with emeralds and precious stones. 22 The men announced her and he came out to the entrance to the tent, with silver torches carried before him.

23 When Judith confronted the general and his adjutant, the beauty of her face astonished them all. She fell on her face and did homage to him, but his servants raised her from the ground.

11 'Courage, woman,' Holofernes said, 'do not be afraid. I have never hurt anyone who chose to serve Nebuchadnezzar, king of the whole world. 2 Even now, if your nation of mountain dwellers had not insulted me, I would not have raised a spear against them. This was their fault, not mine. 3 But tell me, why have you fled from them and come to us? . . . Anyhow, this will prove the saving of you. Courage! You will live through this night, and many after. 4 No one will hurt you. On the contrary, you will be treated as well as any who serve my lord King Nebuchadnezzar.'

5 Judith said, 'Please listen favourably to what your slave has to say. Permit your servant to speak in your presence, I shall speak no word of a lie to my lord tonight. 6 You have only to follow your servant's advice and God will bring your work to a successful conclusion; in what my lord undertakes he will not fail. 7 Long life to Nebuchadnezzar, king of the whole world, who has sent you to set every living soul to rights; may his power endure! Since, thanks to you, he is served not only by human beings, but because of your might the wild animals themselves, the cattle, and the birds of the air are to live in the service of Nebuchadnezzar and his whole House.

8 'We have indeed heard of your genius and adroitness of mind. It is known everywhere in the world that throughout the empire you have no rival for ability, wealth of experience and brilliance in waging war. 9 We have also heard what Achior said in his speech to your council. The men of Bethulia having spared him, he has told them everything that he said to you. 10 Now, master and lord, do not disregard what he said; keep it in your mind, since it is true; our nation will not be punished, the sword will indeed have no power over them, unless they sin against their God. 11 But as it is, my lord need expect no repulse or setback, since death is about to fall on their heads, for sin has gained a hold over them, provoking the anger of their God each time that they commit it. 12 As they are short of food and their water is giving out, they have resolved to fall back on their cattle and decided to make use of all the things that God has, by his laws, forbidden them to eat. 13 Not only have they made up their minds to eat the first-fruits of corn and the tithes of wine and oil, though these have been consecrated by them and set apart for the priests who serve in Jerusalem in the presence of our God, and may not lawfully even be handled by ordinary people, 14 but they have sent men to Jerusalem—where the inhabitants are doing much the same—to bring them back authorisation from the Council of Elders. 15 Now this will be the outcome: when the

NEW REVISED STANDARD VERSION

sponse reaches them and they act upon it, on that very day they will be handed over to you to be destroyed.

16 "So when I, your slave, learned all this, I fled from them. God has sent me to accomplish with you things that will astonish the whole world wherever people shall hear about them. 17 Your servant is indeed God-fearing and serves the God of heaven night and day. So, my lord, I will remain with you; but every night your servant will go out into the valley and pray to God. He will tell me when they have committed their sins. 18 Then I will come and tell you, so that you may go out with your whole army, and not one of them will be able to withstand you. 19 Then I will lead you through Judea, until you come to Jerusalem; there I will set your throne.y You will drive them like sheep that have no shepherd, and no dog will so much as growl at you. For this was told me to give me foreknowledge; it was announced to me, and I was sent to tell you."

20 Her words pleased Holofernes and all his servants. They marveled at her wisdom and said, 21 "No other woman from one end of the earth to the other looks so beautiful or speaks so wisely!" 22 Then Holofernes said to her, "God has done well to send you ahead of the people, to strengthen our hands and bring destruction on those who have despised my lord. 23 You are not only beautiful in appearance, but wise in speech. If you do as you have said, your God shall be my God, and you shall live in the palace of King Nebuchadnezzar and be renowned throughout the whole world."

12 Then he commanded them to bring her in where his silver dinnerware was kept, and ordered them to set a table for her with some of his own delicacies, and with some of his own wine to drink. 2 But Judith said, "I cannot partake of them, or it will be an offense; but I will have enough with the things I brought with me." 3 Holofernes said to her, "If your supply runs out, where can we get you more of the same? For none of your people are here with us." 4 Judith replied, "As surely as you live, my lord, your servant will not use up the supplies I have with me before the Lord carries out by my hand what he has determined."

5 Then the servants of Holofernes brought her into the tent, and she slept until midnight. Toward the morning watch she got up 6 and sent this message to Holofernes: "Let my lord now give orders to allow your servant to go out and pray." 7 So Holofernes commanded his guards not to hinder her. She remained in the camp three days. She went out each night to the valley of Bethulia, and bathed at the spring in the camp.z 8 After bathing, she prayed the Lord God of Israel to direct her way for the triumph of hisa people. 9 Then she returned purified and stayed in the tent until she ate her food toward evening.

10 On the fourth day Holofernes held a banquet for his personal attendants only, and did not invite any of his officers. 11 He said to Bagoas, the eunuch who had charge of his personal affairs, "Go and persuade the Hebrew woman who is in your care to join us and to eat and drink with us. 12 For it would be a disgrace if we let such a woman go without having intercourse with her. If we do not seduce her, she will laugh at us."

13 So Bagoas left the presence of Holofernes, and approached her and said, "Let this pretty girl not hesitate to come to my lord to be honored in his presence, and to enjoy drinking wine with us, and to become today like one of the Assyrian women who serve in the palace of Nebuchadnezzar." 14 Judith replied, "Who am I to refuse my lord? Whatever pleases him I will do at once, and it will be a joy to me until the day of my death." 15 So she proceeded to dress

REVISED ENGLISH BIBLE

15 As soon as ever the word comes and they act on it, that same day they will be given up to you to be destroyed.

16 'When I learnt all this, my lord, I left them and made my escape; the things that God has sent me to do with you will be the wonder of the whole world, wherever men hear about them. 17 For I, your servant, am a godfearing woman: day and night I worship the God of heaven. I shall stay with you now, my lord, and each night I shall go out into the valley and pray to God, and when they have committed their sins he will tell me. 18 Immediately I bring you word, you may go out at the head of your army; you will meet with no resistance. 19 I shall guide you across Judaea until you reach Jerusalem, and I shall set up your throne in the heart of the city. You will drive them like sheep that have lost their shepherd, and not a dog will so much as growl at you. I have been given foreknowledge of this; it has been revealed to me, and I have been sent to announce it to you.'

20 Judith's words delighted Holophernes and all those in attendance on him and, amazed at her wisdom, 21 they declared, 'From one end of the earth to the other there is not a woman to compare with her for beauty of face or shrewdness of speech.' 22 Holophernes assured her, 'Your God has done well in sending you out from your people, to bring strength to us and destruction to those who have insulted my lord! 23 Your looks are striking and your words are wise. Do as you have promised, and your God shall be my god, and you shall live in King Nebuchadnezzar's palace and be renowned throughout the whole world.'

12 Holophernes then told them to bring her in where his silver was set out, and gave orders for a meal to be served to her from his own food and wine. 2 But Judith said, 'I must not eat of it for fear I should be breaking our law. What I have brought will be sufficient for my needs.' 3 'But', asked Holophernes, 'where can we get you a fresh supply of the same kind if you use up all you have with you? There is no one from your people here among us.' 4 Judith replied, 'As sure as you live, my lord, I shall not finish what I have with me before God accomplishes by my hand what he has purposed.'

5 Holophernes' attendants conducted her to a tent, and she slept until midnight. Shortly before the dawn watch she rose 6 and sent this request to Holophernes: 'May it please my lord to give orders for me to be allowed to go out and pray.' 7 Holophernes ordered his bodyguard not to prevent her. She stayed in the camp for three days, going out each night into the valley of Bethulia and bathing in the spring at the camp. 8 When she came up out of the water she would pray the Lord, the God of Israel, to prosper her undertaking to restore his people. 9 Then she returned to the camp purified, and remained in the tent until she took her evening meal.

10 On the fourth day Holophernes gave a banquet for his personal servants only; none of the army officers were invited. 11 He said to Bagoas, the eunuch in charge of all his personal affairs: 'Go to the Hebrew woman who is in your care, and persuade her to join us at our feast. 12 We shall lose face if we let such a woman go without enjoying her favours; if we do not win her, she will laugh us to scorn.' 13 Bagoas withdrew from Holophernes' presence and went in to Judith. 'Now, my fair one,' he said, 'do not be bashful; come along to my master and give yourself the honour of his company. Drink with us and enjoy yourself, and behave today like one of the Assyrian women in attendance at Nebuchadnezzar's palace.' 14 'Who am I to refuse my lord?' answered Judith. 'I am eager to do whatever pleases him, and it will be something to boast of till my dying day.'

y Or chariot   z Other ancient authorities lack in the camp
a Other ancient authorities read her

sponse reaches them and they act upon it, they will be handed over to you for destruction.

16"As soon as I, your handmaid, learned all this, I fled from them. God has sent me to perform with you such deeds that people throughout the world will be astonished on hearing of them. 17 Your handmaid is, indeed, a God-fearing woman, serving the God of heaven night and day. Now I will remain with you, my lord; but each night your handmaid will go out to the ravine and pray to God. He will tell me when the Israelites have committed their crimes. 18 Then I will come and let you know, so that you may go out with your whole force, and not one of them will be able to withstand you. 19 I will lead you through Judea, till you come to Jerusalem, and there I will set up your judgment seat. You will drive them like sheep that have no shepherd, and not even a dog will growl at you. This was told me, and announced to me in advance, and I in turn have been sent to tell you."

20 Her words pleased Holofernes and all his servants; they marveled at her wisdom and exclaimed, 21"No other woman from one end of the world to the other looks so beautiful and speaks so wisely!" 22 Then Holofernes said to her: "God has done well in sending you ahead of your people, to bring victory to our arms, and destruction to those who have despised my lord. 23 You are fair to behold, and your words are well spoken. If you do as you have said, your God will be my God; you shall dwell in the palace of King Nebuchadnezzar, and shall be renowned throughout the earth."

12 Then he ordered them to lead her into the room where his silverware was kept, and bade them set a table for her with his own delicacies to eat and his own wine to drink. 2 But Judith said, 'I will not partake of them, lest it be an occasion of sin; but I shall be amply supplied from the things I brought with me." 3 Holofernes asked her: "But if your provisions give out, where shall we get more of the same to provide for you? None of your people are with us." 4 Judith answered him, "As surely as you, my lord, live, your handmaid will not use up her supplies till the LORD accomplishes by my hand what he has determined."

5 Then the servants of Holofernes led her into the tent, where she slept till midnight. In the night watch just before dawn, she rose 6 and sent this message to Holofernes, "Give orders, my lord, to let your handmaid go out for prayer." 7 So Holofernes ordered his bodyguard not to hinder her. Thus she stayed in the camp three days. Each night she went out to the ravine of Bethulia, where she washed herself at the spring of the camp. 8 After bathing, she besought the LORD, the God of Israel, to direct her way for the triumph of his people. 9 Then she returned purified to the tent, and remained there until her food was brought to her toward evening.

10 On the fourth day Holofernes gave a banquet for his servants alone, to which he did not invite any of the officers. 11 And he said to Bagoas, the eunuch in charge of his household: "Go and persuade this Hebrew woman in your care to come and to eat and drink with us. 12 It would be a disgrace for us to have such a woman with us without enjoying her company. If we do not entice her, she will laugh us to scorn."

13 So Bagoas left the presence of Holofernes, and came to Judith and said, "So fair a maiden should not be reluctant to come to my lord to be honored by him, to enjoy drinking wine with us, and to be like one of the Assyrian women who live in the palace of Nebuchadnezzar." 14 She replied, "Who am I to refuse my lord? Whatever is pleasing to him I will promptly do. This will be a joy for me till the day of my death."

permission arrives and they act on it, that very day they will be delivered over to you for destruction.

16 'When I, your servant, came to know all this, I fled from them. God has sent me to do things with you at which the world will be astonished when it hears. 17 Your servant is a devout woman; she honours the God of heaven day and night. I therefore propose, my lord, to stay with you. I, your servant, shall go out every night into the valley and pray to God to let me know when they have committed their sin. 18 I shall then come and tell you, so that you can march out with your whole army; and none of them will be able to resist you. 19 I shall be your guide right across Judaea until you reach Jerusalem; there I shall enthrone you in the very middle of the city. And then you can round them up like shepherd-less sheep, with never a dog daring to bark at you. Foreknowledge tells me this; this has been foretold to me and I have been sent to reveal it to you.'

20 Her words pleased Holofernes, and all his adjutants. Full of admiration at her wisdom they exclaimed, 21 'There is no woman like her from one end of the earth to the other, so lovely of face and so wise of speech!' 22 Holofernes said, 'God has done well to send you ahead of the others. Strength will be ours, and ruin theirs who have insulted my lord. 23 As for you, you are as beautiful as you are eloquent; if you do as you have promised, your God shall be my God, and you yourself shall make your home in the palace of King Nebuchadnezzar and be famous throughout the world.'

12 With that he had her brought in to where his silver dinner service was already laid, and had his own food served to her and his own wine poured out for her. 2 But Judith said, 'I would rather not eat this, in case I incur some fault. What I have brought will be enough for me.' 3 'Suppose your provisions run out,' Holofernes asked, 'how could we get more of the same sort? We have no one belonging to your race here.' 4 'May your soul live, my lord,' Judith answered, 'the Lord will have used me to accomplish his plan, before your servant has finished these provisions.' 5 Holofernes' adjutants then took her to a tent where she slept until midnight. A little before the morning watch, she got up. 6 She had already sent this request to Holofernes, 'Let my lord kindly give orders for your servant to be allowed to go out and pray,' 7 and Holofernes had ordered his guards not to prevent her. She stayed in the camp for three days; she went out each night to the valley of Bethulia and washed at the spring where the picket had been posted. 8 As she went she prayed to the Lord God of Israel to guide her in her plan to relieve the children of her people. 9 Having purified herself, she would return and stay in her tent until her meal was brought her in the evening.

10 On the fourth day Holofernes gave a banquet, inviting only his own staff and none of the other officers. 11 He said to Bagoas, the officer in charge of his personal affairs, 'Go and persuade that Hebrew woman you are looking after to come and join us and eat and drink in our company. 12 We shall be disgraced if we let a woman like this go without seducing her. If we do not seduce her, everyone will laugh at us!' 13 Bagoas then left Holofernes and went to see Judith. 'Would this young and lovely woman condescend to come to my lord?' he asked. 'She will occupy the seat of honour opposite him, drink the joyful wine with us and be treated today like one of the Assyrian ladies who stand in the palace of Nebuchadnezzar.' 14 'Who am I', Judith replied, 'to resist my lord? I shall not hesitate to do whatever he wishes, and doing this will be my joy to my dying day.'

herself in all her woman's finery. Her maid went ahead and spread for her on the ground before Holofernes the lamb-skins she had received from Bagoas for her daily use in reclining.

16 Then Judith came in and lay down. Holofernes' heart was ravished with her and his passion was aroused, for he had been waiting for an opportunity to seduce her from the day he first saw her. 17 So Holofernes said to her, "Have a drink and be merry with us!" 18 Judith said, "I will gladly drink, my lord, because today is the greatest day in my whole life." 19 Then she took what her maid had prepared and ate and drank before him. 20 Holofernes was greatly pleased with her, and drank a great quantity of wine, much more than he had ever drunk in any one day since he was born.

13 When evening came, his slaves quickly withdrew. Bagoas closed the tent from outside and shut out the attendants from his master's presence. They went to bed, for they all were weary because the banquet had lasted so long. 2 But Judith was left alone in the tent, with Holofernes stretched out on his bed, for he was dead drunk.

3 Now Judith had told her maid to stand outside the bedchamber and to wait for her to come out, as she did on the other days; for she said she would be going out for her prayers. She had said the same thing to Bagoas. 4 So every-one went out, and no one, either small or great, was left in the bedchamber. Then Judith, standing beside his bed, said in her heart, "O Lord God of all might, look in this hour on the work of my hands for the exaltation of Jerusalem. 5 Now indeed is the time to help your heritage and to carry out my design to destroy the enemies who have risen up against us."

6 She went up to the bedpost near Holofernes' head, and took down his sword that hung there. 7 She came close to his bed, took hold of the hair of his head, and said, "Give me strength today, O Lord God of Israel!" 8 Then she struck his neck twice with all her might, and cut off his head. 9 Next she rolled his body off the bed and pulled down the canopy from the posts. Soon afterward she went out and gave Holo-fernes' head to her maid, 10 who placed it in her food bag.

Then the two of them went out together, as they were accustomed to do for prayer. They passed through the camp, circled around the valley, and went up the mountain to Bethulia, and came to its gates. 11 From a distance Judith called out to the sentries at the gates, "Open, open the gate! God, our God, is with us, still showing his power in Israel and his strength against our enemies, as he has done today!"

12 When the people of her town heard her voice, they hurried down to the town gate and summoned the elders of the town. 13 They all ran together, both small and great, for it seemed unbelievable that she had returned. They opened the gate and welcomed them. Then they lit a fire to give light, and gathered around them. 14 Then she said to them with a loud voice, "Praise God, O praise him! Praise God, who has not withdrawn his mercy from the house of Israel, but has destroyed our enemies by my hand this very night!"

15 Then she pulled the head out of the bag and showed it to them, and said, "See here, the head of Holofernes, the commander of the Assyrian army, and here is the canopy beneath which he lay in his drunken stupor. The Lord has struck him down by the hand of a woman. 16 As the Lord lives, who has protected me in the way I went, I swear that it was my face that seduced him to his destruction, and that he committed no sin with me, to defile and shame me."

15 She proceeded to dress herself up, putting on all her femi-nine finery. Her maid went ahead of her, and spread on the ground in front of Holophernes the fleeces which Bagoas had provided for her daily use, so that she might recline on them while eating.

16 As Judith came in and took her place, Holophernes was beside himself with desire for her. He trembled with passion and was filled with an ardent longing to possess her; indeed ever since he first set eyes on her he had been seeking an opportunity to seduce her. 17 He said to her, 'Drink, and join in our merriment.' 18 'Certainly I shall, my lord,' re-plied Judith, 'for today is the greatest day of my life.' 19 Then she took what her servant had prepared, and ate and drank in his presence. 20 Holophernes was entranced with her, and he drank a great deal of wine, more than he had ever drunk on any single day in his whole life.

13 When it grew late, Holophernes' servants made haste to withdraw, and Bagoas closed the tent from outside, shutting out the attendants from his master's pres-ence, and they went off to their beds; the banquet had lasted so long that they were all exhausted. 2 Judith was now alone in the tent, with Holophernes lying sprawled on his bed, dead drunk. 3 Judith had told her maid to stand outside the sleeping apartment and wait for her to go out as she did on other days; she had said that she would be going out to pray, and had explained this to Bagoas also.

4 When all had left and not a soul remained, Judith stood beside Holophernes' bed and prayed silently: 'O Lord, God of all power, look favourably now on what I am doing to bring glory to Jerusalem, 5 for this is the moment to come to the aid of your heritage and to prosper my plan for crushing the enemies who have attacked us.' 6 She went to the bed-rail beside Holophernes' head, reached down his sword, 7 and drawing close to the bed she gripped him by the hair. 'Now give me strength, O Lord, God of Israel,' she said, 8 and struck at his neck twice with all her might and cut off his head. 9 She rolled the body off the bed and removed the mosquito-net from its posts; quickly she came out and gave Holophernes' head to her maid, 10 who put it in the food-bag. Then the two of them went out together as they always did when they went to pray. They passed through the camp, and went round the valley and up the hill to Bethulia till they approached its gates.

11 From a distance Judith called to the guards: 'Open up! Open the gate! God, our God, is with us, still showing his strength in Israel and his might against our enemies. Today he has shown it!' 12 When the townspeople heard her voice, they hurried down to the gate and summoned the elders of the town. 13 Everyone, high and low, came running, hardly able to believe that Judith had returned. They opened the gate, and welcomed in the two women. Then, kindling a fire to give light, they gathered round them. 14 Judith raised her voice: 'Praise God! O praise him!' she cried. 'Give praise to God who has not withdrawn his mercy from the house of Israel, but has crushed our enemies by my hand this very night!' 15 She took the head from the bag and showed it to them. 'Look!' she said. 'The head of Holo-phernes, the Assyrian commander-in-chief! And here is the net under which he lay drunk! The Lord has struck him down by a woman's hand! 16 And I swear by the Lord who has brought me safely along the way I have travelled, that, though my face lured him to his destruction, he committed no sin with me, and my honour is unblemished.'

15 Thereupon she proceeded to put on her festive garments and all her feminine adornments. Meanwhile her maid went ahead and spread out on the ground for her in front of Holofernes the fleece Bagoas had furnished for her daily use in reclining at her dinner. 16 Then Judith came in and reclined on it. The heart of Holofernes was in rapture over her, and his spirit was shaken. He was burning with the desire to possess her, for he had been biding his time to seduce her from the day he saw her. 17 Holofernes said to her, "Drink and be merry with us!" 18 Judith replied, "I will gladly drink, my lord, for at no time since I was born have I ever enjoyed life as much as I do today." 19 She then took the things her maid had prepared, and ate and drank in his presence. 20 Holofernes, charmed by her, drank a great quantity of wine, more than he had ever drunk on one single day in his life.

13 When it grew late, his servants quickly withdrew. Bagoas closed the tent from the outside and excluded the attendants from their master's presence. They went off to their beds, for they were all tired from the prolonged banquet. 2 Judith was left alone in the tent with Holofernes, who lay prostrate on his bed, for he was sodden with wine. 3 She had ordered her maid to stand outside the bedroom and wait, as on the other days, for her to come out; she said she would be going out for her prayer. To Bagoas she had said this also.

4 When all had departed, and no one, small or great, was left in the bedroom, Judith stood by Holofernes' bed and said within herself: "O LORD, God of all might, in this hour look graciously on my undertaking for the exaltation of Jerusalem; 5 now is the time for aiding your heritage and for carrying out my design to shatter the enemies who have risen against us." 6 She went to the bedpost near the head of Holofernes, and taking his sword from it, 7 drew close to the bed, grasped the hair of his head, and said, "Strengthen me this day, O God of Israel!" 8 Then with all her might she struck him twice in the neck and cut off his head. 9 She rolled his body off the bed and took the canopy from its supports. Soon afterward, she came out and handed over the head of Holofernes to her maid, 10 who put it into her food pouch; and the two went off together as they were accustomed to do for prayer.

They passed through the camp, and skirting the ravine, reached Bethulia on the mountain. As they approached its gates, 11 Judith shouted to the guards from a distance: "Open! Open the gate! God, our God, is with us. Once more he has made manifest his strength in Israel and his power against our enemies; he has done it this very day." 12 When the citizens heard her voice, they quickly descended to their city gate and summoned the city elders. 13 All the people, from the least to the greatest, hurriedly assembled, for her return seemed unbelievable. They opened the gate and welcomed the two women. They made a fire for light; and when they gathered around the two, 14 Judith urged them with a loud voice: "Praise God, praise him! Praise God, who has not withdrawn his mercy from the house of Israel, but has shattered our enemies by my hand this very night." 15 Then she took the head out of the pouch, showed it to them, and said: "Here is the head of Holofernes, general in charge of the Assyrian army, and here is the canopy under which he lay in his drunkenness. The LORD struck him down by the hand of a woman. 16 As the LORD lives, who has protected me in the path I have followed, I swear that it was my face that seduced Holofernes to his ruin, and that he did not sin with me to my defilement or disgrace."

15 So she got up and put on her dress and all her feminine adornments. Her maid preceded her, and on the floor in front of Holofernes spread the fleece Bagoas had given Judith for her daily use to lie on as she ate. 16 Judith came in and took her place. The heart of Holofernes was ravished at the sight; his very soul was stirred. He was seized with a violent desire to sleep with her; and indeed since the first day he saw her, he had been waiting for an opportunity to seduce her. 17 'Drink then!' Holofernes said. 'Enjoy yourself with us!' 18 'I am delighted to do so, my lord, for since my birth I have never felt my life more worthwhile than today.' 19 She took what her maid had prepared, and ate and drank facing him. 20 Holofernes was so enchanted with her that he drank far more wine than he had drunk on any other day of his life.

13 It grew late and his staff hurried away. Bagoas closed the tent from the outside, having shown out those who still lingered in his lord's presence. They went to their beds wearied with too much drinking, 2 and Judith was left alone in the tent with Holofernes who had collapsed wine-sodden on his bed. 3 Judith then told her maid to stay just outside the bedroom and wait for her to come out, as she did every morning. She had let it be understood she would be going out to her prayers and had also spoken of her intention to Bagoas.

4 By now everyone had left Holofernes, and no one, either important or unimportant, was left in the bedroom. Standing beside the bed, Judith murmured to herself:

Lord God, to whom all strength belongs,
prosper what my hands are now to do
for the greater glory of Jerusalem;
5 now is the time to recover your heritage
and to further my plans
to crush the enemies arrayed against us.

6 With that she went up to the bedpost by Holofernes' head and took down his scimitar; 7 coming closer to the bed she caught him by the hair and said, 'Make me strong today, Lord God of Israel!' 8 Twice she struck at his neck with all her might, and cut off his head. 9 She then rolled his body off the bed and pulled down the canopy from the bedposts. After which, she went out and gave the head of Holofernes to her maid 10 who put it in her food bag. The two then left the camp together, as they always did when they went to pray. Once they were out of the camp, they skirted the ravine, climbed the slope to Bethulia and made for the gates.

11 From a distance, Judith shouted to the guards on the gates, 'Open the gate! Open! For the Lord our God is with us still, displaying his strength in Israel and his might against our enemies, as he has done today!' 12 Hearing her voice, the townsmen hurried down to the town gate and summoned the elders. 13 Everyone, great and small, came running down, since her arrival was unexpected. They threw the gate open, welcomed the women, lit a fire to see by and crowded round them. 14 Then Judith raised her voice and said, 'Praise God! Praise him! Praise the God who has not withdrawn his mercy from the House of Israel, but has shattered our enemies by my hand tonight!' 15 She pulled the head out of the bag and held it for them to see. 'This is the head of Holofernes, general-in-chief of the Assyrian army; here is the canopy under which he lay drunk! The Lord has struck him down by the hand of a woman! 16 Glory to the Lord who has protected me in the course I took! My face seduced him, only to his own undoing; he committed no sin with me to shame or disgrace me.'

17 All the people were greatly astonished. They bowed down and worshiped God, and said with one accord, "Blessed are you our God, who have this day humiliated the enemies of your people."

18 Then Uzziah said to her, "O daughter, you are blessed by the Most High God above all other women on earth; and blessed be the Lord God, who created the heavens and the earth, who has guided you to cut off the head of the leader of our enemies. 19 Your praise[b] will never depart from the hearts of those who remember the power of God. 20 May God grant this to be a perpetual honor to you, and may he reward you with blessings, because you risked your own life when our nation was brought low, and you averted our ruin, walking in the straight path before our God." And all the people said, "Amen. Amen."

14 Then Judith said to them, "Listen to me, my friends. Take this head and hang it upon the parapet of your wall. 2 As soon as day breaks and the sun rises on the earth, each of you take up your weapons, and let every able-bodied man go out of the town; set a captain over them, as if you were going down to the plain against the Assyrian outpost; only do not go down. 3 Then they will seize their arms and go into the camp and rouse the officers of the Assyrian army. They will rush into the tent of Holofernes and will not find him. Then panic will come over them, and they will flee before you. 4 Then you and all who live within the borders of Israel will pursue them and cut them down in their tracks. 5 But before you do all this, bring Achior the Ammonite to me so that he may see and recognize the man who despised the house of Israel and sent him to us as if to his death."

6 So they summoned Achior from the house of Uzziah. When he came and saw the head of Holofernes in the hand of one of the men in the assembly of the people, he fell down on his face in a faint. 7 When they raised him up he threw himself at Judith's feet, and did obeisance to her, and said, "Blessed are you in every tent of Judah! In every nation those who hear your name will be alarmed. 8 Now tell me what you have done during these days."

So Judith told him in the presence of the people all that she had done, from the day she left until the moment she began speaking to them. 9 When she had finished, the people raised a great shout and made a joyful noise in their town. 10 When Achior saw all that the God of Israel had done, he believed firmly in God. So he was circumcised, and joined the house of Israel, remaining so to this day.

11 As soon as it was dawn they hung the head of Holofernes on the wall. Then they all took their weapons, and they went out in companies to the mountain passes. 12 When the Assyrians saw them they sent word to their commanders, who then went to the generals and the captains and to all their other officers. 13 They came to Holofernes' tent and said to the steward in charge of all his personal affairs, "Wake up our lord, for the slaves have been so bold as to come down against us to give battle, to their utter destruction."

14 So Bagoas went in and knocked at the entry of the tent, for he supposed that he was sleeping with Judith.

17 The people were all astounded at what she had done; and bowing in worship to God, they spoke with one voice: 'Praise be to you, our God, who has this day humiliated the enemies of your people!' 18 Ozias addressed Judith: 'Daughter, the blessing of God Most High rests on you more than on any other woman on earth; praise be to the Lord God who created heaven and earth; under his guidance you struck off the head of the leader of our enemies. 19 As long as men commemorate the power of God, the sure hope which inspired you will never fade from their minds. 20 May God make your deed redound to your honour for ever, and may he shower blessings on you! You risked your life for our nation when it was faced with humiliation. Boldly you went to meet the disaster that threatened us, and firmly you held to God's straight road.' All the people responded, 'Amen, Amen.'

14 JUDITH said to them: 'Listen to me, my friends; take this head and hang it out on the battlements. 2 Then at daybreak, as soon as the sun rises, let every able-bodied man among you arm himself; march out of the town with a leader before you, as if you were going down to the plain to attack the Assyrian outpost, but do not go down. 3 The men there will pick up their weapons and make for the camp to rouse their commanders, who will rush to Holophernes' tent. When he is not to be found, panic will seize them and they will flee from you; 4 pursue them, you and all who live within Israel's borders, and cut them down in their tracks. 5 But first of all, summon Achior the Ammonite to me, so that he may see for himself and identify the man who treated Israel with contempt and sent him to us as if to his death.'

6 Achior was summoned from Ozias's house. He came, and when he saw Holophernes' head held by one of the men among the assembled people, he fell down in a faint. 7 After they revived him, he threw himself at Judith's feet and did obeisance to her. 'Your praises will be sung in every home in Judah and among all nations,' he declared; 'they will tremble when they hear your name. 8 And now tell me what you have done during these days.' So while the people listened, Judith told him everything from the day she left until that very moment. 9 As she ended her story, the people raised a shout of acclamation, making the town resound with their cheers. 10 Achior, realizing all that the God of Israel had done, believed wholeheartedly in him; he was circumcised, and admitted as a member of the community of Israel, as his descendants are to this day.

11 At dawn they hung Holophernes' head on the wall; then every man took up his weapons, and they marched out in companies towards the approaches to the town. 12 The moment the Assyrians set eyes on them, they passed word to their leaders, who went to the commanders, captains, and all the other officers. 13 They presented themselves at Holophernes' tent and said to his steward: 'Wake our master! These slaves have had the audacity to come down and offer battle. They are asking to be utterly wiped out.' 14 Bagoas went in and knocked at the screen of the inner tent, supposing that Holophernes was sleeping with Judith. 15 When

b Other ancient authorities read hope

17 All the people were greatly astonished. They bowed down and worshiped God, saying with one accord, "Blessed are you, our God, who today have brought to nought the enemies of your people." 18 Then Uzziah said to her: "Blessed are you, daughter, by the Most High God, above all the women on earth; and blessed be the LORD God, the creator of heaven and earth, who guided your blow at the head of the chief of our enemies. 19 Your deed of hope will never be forgotten by those who tell of the might of God. 20 May God make this redound to your everlasting honor, rewarding you with blessings, because you risked your life when your people were being oppressed, and you averted our disaster, walking uprightly before our God." And all the people answered, "Amen! Amen!"

14 Then Judith said to them: "Listen to me, my brothers. Take this head and hang it on the parapet of your wall. 2 At daybreak, when the sun rises on the earth, let each of you seize his weapons, and let all the able-bodied men rush out of the city under command of a captain, as if about to go down into the plain against the advance guard of the Assyrians, but without going down. 3 They will seize their armor and hurry to their camp to awaken the generals of the Assyrian army. When they run to the tent of Holofernes and do not find him, panic will seize them, and they will flee before you. 4 Then you and all the other inhabitants of the whole territory of Israel will pursue them and strike them down in their tracks. 5 But before doing this, summon for me Achior the Ammonite, that he may see and recognize the one who despised the house of Israel and sent him here to meet his death."

6 So they called Achior from the house of Uzziah. When he came and saw the head of Holofernes in the hand of one of the men in the assembly of the people, he fell forward in a faint. 7 Then, after they lifted him up, he threw himself at the feet of Judith in homage, saying: "Blessed are you in every tent of Judah; and in every foreign nation, all who hear of you will be struck with terror. 8 But now, tell me all that you did during these days." So Judith told him, in the presence of the people, all that she had been doing from the day she left till the time she began speaking to them. 9 When she finished her account, the people cheered loudly, and their city resounded with shouts of joy. 10 Now Achior, seeing all that the God of Israel had done, believed firmly in him. He had the flesh of his foreskin circumcised, and he has been united with the house of Israel to the present day.

11 At daybreak they hung the head of Holofernes on the wall. Then all the Israelite men took up their arms and went to the slopes of the mountain. 12 When the Assyrians saw them, they notified their captains; these, in turn, went to the generals and division leaders and all their other commanders. 13 They came to the tent of Holofernes and said to the one in charge of all his things, "Waken our master, for the slaves have dared come down to give us battle, to their utter destruction." 14 Bagoas went in, and knocked at the entry of the tent, presuming that he was sleeping with Judith. 15 As

17 Overcome with emotion, the people all prostrated themselves and worshipped God, exclaiming with one voice, 'Blessings on you, our God, for confounding your people's enemies today!' 18 Uzziah then said to Judith:

May you be blessed, my daughter, by God Most
  High,
beyond all women on earth;
and blessed be the Lord God,
Creator of heaven and earth,
who guided you to cut off the head
of the leader of our enemies!
19 The trust which you have shown
will not pass from human hearts,
as they commemorate
the power of God for evermore.
20 God grant you may be always held in honour
and rewarded with blessings,
since you did not consider your own life
when our nation was brought to its knees,
but warded off our ruin,
walking in the right path before our God.
And the people all said, 'Amen! Amen!'

14 Judith said, 'Listen to me, brothers. Take this head and hang it on your battlements. 2 When morning comes and the sun is up, let every man take his arms and every able-bodied man leave the town. Appoint a leader for them, as if you meant to march down to the plain against the Assyrian advanced post. But you must not do this. 3 The Assyrians will gather up their equipment, make for their camp and wake up their commanders; they in turn will rush to the tent of Holofernes and not be able to find him. They will then be seized with panic and flee at your advance. 4 All you and the others who live in the territory of Israel will have to do is to give chase and slaughter them as they retreat.

5 'But before you do this, call me Achior the Ammonite, for him to see and identify the man who held the House of Israel in contempt, the man who sent him to us as someone already doomed to die.' 6 So they had Achior brought from Uzziah's house. No sooner had he arrived and seen the head of Holofernes held by a member of the people's assembly than he fell on his face in a faint. 7 They lifted him up. He then threw himself at Judith's feet and, prostrate before her, exclaimed:

May you be blessed in all the tents of Judah
and in every nation;
those who hear your name
will be seized with dread!

8 'Now tell me everything that you have done in these past few days.' And surrounded by the people, Judith told him everything she had done from the day she left Bethulia to the moment when she was speaking. 9 When she came to the end, the people cheered at the top of their voices until the town echoed. 10 Achior, recognising all that the God of Israel had done, believed ardently in him, and, accepting circumcision, was permanently incorporated into the House of Israel.

11 At daybreak they hung the head of Holofernes on the ramparts. Every man took his arms and they all went out in groups to the slopes of the mountain. 12 Seeing this, the Assyrians sent word to their leaders, who in turn reported to the generals, the captains of thousands and all the other officers; 13 and these in their turn reported to the tent of Holofernes. 'Rouse our master,' they said to his major-domo, 'these slaves have dared to march down on us to attack — and to be wiped out to a man!' 14 Bagoas went inside and struck the curtain dividing the tent, thinking that Holofernes was sleeping with Judith. 15 But as no one

NEW REVISED STANDARD VERSION

15 But when no one answered, he opened it and went into the bedchamber and found him sprawled on the floor dead, with his head missing. 16 He cried out with a loud voice and wept and groaned and shouted, and tore his clothes. 17 Then he went to the tent where Judith had stayed, and when he did not find her, he rushed out to the people and shouted, 18 "The slaves have tricked us! One Hebrew woman has brought disgrace on the house of King Nebuchadnezzar. Look, Holofernes is lying on the ground, and his head is missing!"

19 When the leaders of the Assyrian army heard this, they tore their tunics and were greatly dismayed, and their loud cries and shouts rose up throughout the camp.

15 When the men in the tents heard it, they were amazed at what had happened. 2 Overcome with fear and trembling, they did not wait for one another, but with one impulse all rushed out and fled by every path across the plain and through the hill country. 3 Those who had camped in the hills around Bethulia also took to flight. Then the Israelites, everyone that was a soldier, rushed out upon them. 4 Uzziah sent men to Betomasthaim[c] and Choba and Kola, and to all the frontiers of Israel, to tell what had taken place and to urge all to rush out upon the enemy to destroy them. 5 When the Israelites heard it, with one accord they fell upon the enemy,[d] and cut them down as far as Choba. Those in Jerusalem and all the hill country also came, for they were told what had happened in the camp of the enemy. The men in Gilead and in Galilee outflanked them with great slaughter, even beyond Damascus and its borders. 6 The rest of the people of Bethulia fell upon the Assyrian camp and plundered it, acquiring great riches. 7 And the Israelites, when they returned from the slaughter, took possession of what remained. Even the villages and towns in the hill country and in the plain got a great amount of booty, since there was a vast quantity of it.

8 Then the high priest Joakim and the elders of the Israelites who lived in Jerusalem came to witness the good things that the Lord had done for Israel, and to see Judith and to wish her well. 9 When they met her, they all blessed her with one accord and said to her, "You are the glory of Jerusalem, you are the great boast of Israel, you are the great pride of our nation! 10 You have done all this with your own hand; you have done great good to Israel, and God is well pleased with it. May the Almighty Lord bless you forever!" And all the people said, "Amen."

11 All the people plundered the camp for thirty days. They gave Judith the tent of Holofernes and all his silver dinnerware, his beds, his bowls, and all his furniture. She took them and loaded her mules and hitched up her carts and piled the things on them.

12 All the women of Israel gathered to see her, and blessed her, and some of them performed a dance in her honor. She took ivy-wreathed wands and distributed them to the women who were with her; 13 and she and those who were with her crowned themselves with olive wreaths. She went before all the people in the dance, leading all the women, while all the men of Israel followed, bearing their arms and wearing garlands and singing hymns.

REVISED ENGLISH BIBLE

there was no reply, he drew aside the screen, entered the sleeping apartment, and found the dead body sprawled over a footstool, with the head gone. 16 He gave a great cry, wailing and groaning aloud, and tearing his clothes. 17 He went into the tent which Judith had occupied, and not finding her there he burst out, shouting to the troops, 18 'The slaves have fooled us. One Hebrew woman has brought shame on Nebuchadnezzar's house. Look! Holophernes is lying on the ground, headless!' 19 At his words the officers of the Assyrian army were appalled and tore their clothes, and the camp rang with their shouting and wild cries.

15 When news of those events spread to the men in the camp, they were thrown into confusion. 2 Terrified and panic-stricken and making no attempt to keep together, they streamed out as if by a common impulse, seeking to escape by any and every path across the plain and the hill-country, 3 while those who were encamped in the hills around Bethulia also took to flight. Thereupon all the fighting men of Israel poured out in pursuit. 4 Ozias sent messengers to Bethomesthaim, Choba, and Chola, and throughout the whole territory of Israel, to report what had happened and to encourage all to attack and destroy the enemy. 5 At this every man in Israel joined in the onslaught, cutting down the fugitives the whole way to Choba. So also the men from Jerusalem and the entire hill-country rallied in support, for word had reached them of what had happened to the enemy camp. The men of Gilead and Galilee outflanked the Assyrians and inflicted heavy losses on them, pressing on beyond Damascus and its surrounding district. 6 The rest of the inhabitants of Bethulia fell on the Assyrian camp and made themselves rich with the spoils. 7 When the Israelites returned from the slaughter, they helped themselves to what remained; there was a huge quantity, and the villages and hamlets in the hill-country and in the plain secured booty in plenty.

8 Joakim the high priest and the senate of Israel came from Jerusalem to see for themselves the great things the Lord had done for his people, and to greet Judith in person. 9 When they came into her presence, they all with one accord praised her: 'You are the glory of Jerusalem, the great pride of Israel, the great boast of our people! 10 With your own hand you have done all this, bestowing these benefits on Israel, and God has shown his approval. Blessings on you from the Lord Almighty, for all time to come!' And the people responded, 'Amen.'

11 The looting of the camp went on for thirty days. Judith was given Holophernes' tent, with all its silver, and his couches, bowls, and furniture. She loaded her mule, then got her wagons ready and piled the goods on them. 12 The Israelite women all came flocking to see her; they sang her praises, and some performed a dance in her honour. She took garlanded wands and distributed them among the women who accompanied her, 13 and she and those who were with her crowned themselves with olive leaves. Then, at the head of the people, she led the women in the dance; the men of Israel, in full armour, followed, all wearing garlands on their heads and singing hymns.

[c] Other ancient authorities add and Bebai   [d] Gk them

2180

no one answered, he parted the curtains, entered the bedroom, and found him lying on the floor, a headless corpse. 16 He broke into a loud clamor of weeping, groaning, and howling, and rent his garments. 17 Then he entered the tent where Judith had her quarters; and, not finding her, he rushed out to the troops and cried: 18 "The slaves have duped us! A single Hebrew woman has brought disgrace on the house of King Nebuchadnezzar. Here is Holofernes headless on the ground!"

19 When the commanders of the Assyrian army heard these words, they rent their tunics and were seized with consternation. Loud screaming and howling arose in the camp.

15 On hearing what had happened, those still in their tents were amazed, 2 and overcome with fear and trembling. No one kept ranks any longer; they scattered in all directions, and fled along every road, both through the valley and in the mountains. 3 Those also who were stationed in the mountain district around Bethulia took to flight. Then all the Israelite warriors overwhelmed them.

4 Uzziah sent messengers to Betomasthaim, to Choba and Kona, and to the whole country of Israel to report what had happened, that all might fall upon the enemy and destroy them. 5 On hearing this, all the Israelites, with one accord, attacked them and cut them down as far as Choba. Even those from Jerusalem and the rest of the mountain region took part in this, for they too had been notified of the happenings in the camp of their enemies. The Gileadites and the Galileans struck the enemy's flanks with great slaughter, even beyond Damascus and its territory. 6 The remaining inhabitants of Bethulia swept down on the camp of the Assyrians, plundered it, and acquired great riches. 7 The Israelites who returned from the slaughter took possession of what was left, till the towns and villages in the mountains and on the plain were crammed with the enormous quantity of booty they had seized.

8 The high priest Joakim and the elders of the Israelites, who dwelt in Jerusalem, came to see for themselves the good things that the LORD had done for Israel, and to meet and congratulate Judith. 9 When they had visited her, all with one accord blessed her, saying:

> "You are the glory of Jerusalem,
>   the surpassing joy of Israel;
>   you are the splendid boast of our people.
> 10 With your own hand you have done all this;
>   you have done good to Israel,
>   and God is pleased with what you have wrought.
> May you be blessed by the LORD Almighty
>   forever and ever!"

And all the people answered, "Amen!"

11 For thirty days the whole populace plundered the camp, giving Judith the tent of Holofernes, with all his silver, his couches, his dishes, and all his furniture, which she accepted. She harnessed her mules, hitched her wagons to them, and loaded these things on them.

12 All the women of Israel gathered to see her; and they blessed her and performed a dance in her honor. She took branches in her hands and distributed them to the women around her, 13 and she and the other women crowned themselves with garlands of olive leaves. At the head of all the people, she led the women in the dance, while the men of Israel followed in their armor, wearing garlands and singing hymns.

seemed to hear, he drew the curtain and went into the bedroom, to find him thrown down dead on the threshold, with his head cut off. 16 He gave a great shout, wept, sobbed, shrieked and rent his clothes. 17 He then went into the tent which Judith had occupied and could not find her either. Then, rushing out to the men, he shouted, 18 'The slaves have rebelled! A single Hebrew woman has brought shame on the House of Nebuchadnezzar. Holofernes is lying dead on the ground, without his head!'

19 When they heard this, the leaders of the Assyrian army tore their tunics in consternation, and the camp rang with their wild cries and their shouting.

15 When the men who were still in their tents heard the news they were appalled. 2 Panic-stricken and trembling, no two of them could keep together, the rout was complete, with one accord they fled along every track across the plain or through the mountains. 3 The men who had been bivouacking in the mountains round Bethulia were fleeing too. Then all the Israelite warriors charged down on them. 4 Uzziah sent messengers to Betomasthaim, Bebai, Choba, Kola, throughout the whole territory of Israel, to inform them of what had happened and to urge them all to hurl themselves on the enemy and annihilate them. 5 As soon as the Israelites heard the news, they fell on them as one man and massacred them all the way to Choba. The men of Jerusalem and the entire mountain country also rallied to them, once they had been informed of the events in the enemy camp. Then the men of Gilead and Galilee attacked them on the flank and struck at them fiercely till they neared Damascus and its territory. 6 All the other inhabitants of Bethulia fell on the Assyrian camp and looted it to their great profit. 7 The Israelites returning from the slaughter seized what was left. The hamlets and villages of the mountain country and the plain also captured a great deal of booty, since there were vast stores of it.

8 Joakim the high priest and the entire Council of Elders of Israel, who were in Jerusalem, came to gaze on the benefits that the Lord had lavished on Israel and to see Judith and congratulate her. 9 On coming to her house, they blessed her with one accord, saying:

> You are the glory of Jerusalem!
> You are the great pride of Israel!
> You are the highest honour of our race!
>
> 10 By doing all this with your own hand
> you have deserved well of Israel,
> and God has approved what you have done.
> May you be blessed by the Lord Almighty
> in all the days to come!

And the people all said, 'Amen!'

11 The people looted the camp for thirty days. They gave Judith the tent of Holofernes, all his silver plate, his divans, his drinking bowls and all his furniture. She took this, loaded her mule, harnessed her carts and heaped the things into them. 12 All the women of Israel, hurrying to see her, formed choirs of dancers in her honour. Judith took wands of vine-leaves in her hand and distributed them to the women who accompanied her; 13 she and her companions put on wreaths of olive. Then she took her place at the head of the procession and led the women as they danced. All the men of Israel, armed and garlanded, followed them, singing

NEW REVISED STANDARD VERSION	REVISED ENGLISH BIBLE

NEW REVISED STANDARD VERSION

16 14 Judith began this thanksgiving before all Israel, and all the people loudly sang this song of praise. 1 And Judith said,

Begin a song to my God with tambourines,
    sing to my Lord with cymbals.
Raise to him a new psalm;*e*
    exalt him, and call upon his name.
2 For the Lord is a God who crushes wars;
    he sets up his camp among his people;
    he delivered me from the hands of my
        pursuers.
3 The Assyrian came down from the mountains of
    the north;
    he came with myriads of his warriors;
    their numbers blocked up the wadis,
    and their cavalry covered the hills.
4 He boasted that he would burn up my territory,
    and kill my young men with the sword,
    and dash my infants to the ground,
    and seize my children as booty,
    and take my virgins as spoil.
5 But the Lord Almighty has foiled them
    by the hand of a woman.*f*
6 For their mighty one did not fall by the hands of
    the young men,
    nor did the sons of the Titans strike him down,
    nor did tall giants set upon him;
    but Judith daughter of Merari
    with the beauty of her countenance undid him.
7 For she put away her widow's clothing
    to exalt the oppressed in Israel.
    She anointed her face with perfume;
8   she fastened her hair with a tiara
    and put on a linen gown to beguile him.
9 Her sandal ravished his eyes,
    her beauty captivated his mind,
    and the sword severed his neck!
10 The Persians trembled at her boldness,
    the Medes were daunted at her daring.

11 Then my oppressed people shouted;
    my weak people cried out,*g* and the enemy*h*
        trembled;
    they lifted up their voices, and the enemy*h*
        were turned back.
12 Sons of slave-girls pierced them through
    and wounded them like the children of
        fugitives;
    they perished before the army of my Lord.

13 I will sing to my God a new song:
    O Lord, you are great and glorious,
    wonderful in strength, invincible.
14 Let all your creatures serve you,
    for you spoke, and they were made.
    You sent forth your spirit,*i* and it formed
        them;*j*
    there is none that can resist your voice.
15 For the mountains shall be shaken to their
    foundations with the waters;
    before your glance the rocks shall melt like
        wax.
    But to those who fear you
    you show mercy.

REVISED ENGLISH BIBLE

16 IN the presence of all Israel, Judith began this hymn of praise and thanksgiving, which was echoed by the people:

2 'Strike up a song to my God with tambourines;
    sing to the Lord with cymbals;
    raise a psalm of praise to him;
    honour him and invoke his name.
3 The Lord is a God who stamps out wars;
    he has brought me safe from my pursuers;
    he has stationed his camp among his people.
4 'The Assyrian came from the mountains of the
        north;
    his armies came in such myriads
    that his troops choked the valleys,
    the cavalry covered the hills.
5 He threatened to set my whole land on fire,
    to put my young men to the sword
    and dash my infants to the ground,
    to take my children as booty, my maidens as spoil.
6 'The Lord Almighty has thwarted them by a
        woman's hand.
7 It was no young man that brought their champion
        low;
    no Titan struck him down,
    no tall giant set upon him;
    but Judith, Merari's daughter, disarmed him by her
        beauty.
8 To raise up the afflicted in Israel
    she laid aside her widow's dress;
    she anointed her face with perfume,
    bound her hair with a ribbon,
    and chose a linen gown to beguile him.
9 Her sandal entranced his eye,
    her beauty took his heart captive—
    and the sword cut through his neck!

10 'The Persians shuddered at her daring,
    the Medes were daunted by her boldness.
11 Then my lowly ones shouted in triumph
    and the enemy were dismayed;
    my weak ones shouted
    and the enemy cowered in fear;
    they raised their voices and the enemy took to
        flight.
12 The sons of maidservants ran them through,
    wounding them like runaway slaves;
    they were destroyed by the army of my Lord.

13 'I will sing a new hymn to my God:
    O Lord, you are great and glorious,
    you are marvellous in your strength, invincible.
14 Let your whole creation serve you;
    for you spoke, and all things came to be;
    you sent out your spirit, and it gave them form;
    none can oppose your word.
15 Mountains will shake to their depths like water,
    rocks melt like wax at your presence;
    but you still show compassion
    to those who fear you.

---

e Other ancient authorities read *a psalm and praise* *f* Other ancient authorities add *he has confounded them* *g* Other ancient authorities read *feared* *h* Gk *they* *i* Or *breath* *j* Other ancient authorities read *they were created*

14 Judith led all Israel in this song of thanksgiving, and the people swelled this hymn of praise:

16 "Strike up the instruments,
　　　a song to my God with timbrels,
　chant to the LORD with cymbals;
　Sing to him a new song,
　　　exalt and acclaim his name.
2 For the LORD is God; he crushes warfare,
　and sets his encampment among his people;
　　　he snatched me from the hands of my
　　　　　persecutors.

3 "The Assyrian came from the mountains of
　　　the north,
　with the myriads of his forces he came;
　Their numbers blocked the torrents, their horses
　　　covered the hills.
4 He threatened to burn my land,
　　　put my youths to the sword,
　Dash my babes to the ground,
　　　make my children a prey,
　　　and seize my virgins as spoil.

5 "But the LORD Almighty thwarted them,
　　　by a woman's hand he confounded them.
6 Not by youths was their mighty one struck down,
　　　nor did titans bring him low,
　　　nor huge giants attack him;
　But Judith, the daughter of Merari,
　　　by the beauty of her countenance disabled him.
7 She took off her widow's garb
　　　to raise up the afflicted in Israel.
　She anointed her face with fragrant oil;
8 　with a fillet she fastened her tresses
　　　and put on a linen robe to beguile him.
9 Her sandals caught his eyes,
　　　and her beauty captivated his mind.
　The sword cut through his neck.

10 "The Persians were dismayed at her daring,
　　　the Medes appalled at her boldness.
11 When my lowly ones shouted, they were terrified;
　　　when my weaklings cried out, they trembled;
　at the sound of their war cry, they took to flight.
12 The sons of slave girls pierced them through;
　　　the supposed sons of rebel mothers cut
　　　　　them down;
　they perished before the ranks of my LORD.

13 "A new hymn I will sing to my God.
　O LORD, great are you and glorious,
　　　wonderful in power and unsurpassable.
14 Let your every creature serve you;
　　　for you spoke, and they were made,
　You sent forth your spirit, and they were created;
　　　no one can resist your word.
15 The mountains to their bases, and the seas,
　　　are shaken;
　　　the rocks, like wax, melt before your glance.

　"But to those who fear you,
　　　you are very merciful.

hymns. 14 With all Israel round her, Judith broke into this song of thanksgiving and the whole people sang this hymn:

16 Break into song for my God, to the tambourine,
　　　sing in honour of the Lord, to the cymbal,
　let psalm and canticle mingle for him,
　extol his name, invoke it!
2 For the Lord is a God who breaks battle-lines;
　he has pitched his camp in the middle of his
　　　people
　to deliver me from the hands of my oppressors.

3 Assyria came down from the mountains of the
　　　north,
　came with tens of thousands of his army.
　Their multitude blocked the ravines,
　their horses covered the hills.
4 He threatened to burn up my country,
　destroy my young men with the sword,
　dash my sucklings to the ground,
　make prey of my little ones,
　carry off my maidens;
5 but the Lord Almighty has thwarted them
　by a woman's hand.

6 For their hero did not fall at the young men's
　　　hands,
　it was not the sons of Titans struck him down,
　no proud giants made that attack,
　but Judith, the daughter of Merari,
　who disarmed him with the beauty of her face.
7 She laid aside her widow's dress
　to raise up those who were oppressed in Israel;
　she anointed her face with perfume,
8 bound her hair under a turban,
　put on a linen gown to seduce him.
9 Her sandal ravished his eye,
　her beauty took his soul prisoner
　and the scimitar cut through his neck!

10 The Persians trembled at her boldness,
　the Medes were daunted by her daring.
11 These were struck with fear when my lowly ones
　　　raised the war cry,
　these were seized with terror when my weak ones
　　　shouted,
　and when they raised their voices these gave
　　　ground.
12 The children of mere girls ran them through,
　pierced them like the offspring of deserters.
　They perished in the battle of my Lord!

13 I shall sing a new song to my God.
　Lord, you are great, you are glorious,
　wonderfully strong, unconquerable.
14 May your whole creation serve you!
　For you spoke and things came into being,
　you sent your breath and they were put together,
　and no one can resist your voice.

15 Should mountains be tossed from their foundations
　to mingle with the waves,
　should rocks melt
　like wax before your face,
　to those who fear you,
　you would still be merciful.

16 For every sacrifice as a fragrant offering is a
small thing,
and the fat of all whole burnt offerings to you
is a very little thing;
but whoever fears the Lord is great forever.

17 Woe to the nations that rise up against my
people!
The Lord Almighty will take vengeance on
them in the day of judgment;
he will send fire and worms into their flesh;
they shall weep in pain forever.

18 When they arrived at Jerusalem, they worshiped
God. As soon as the people were purified, they offered their
burnt offerings, their freewill offerings, and their gifts.
19 Judith also dedicated to God all the possessions of Holofernes, which the people had given her; and the canopy that
she had taken for herself from his bedchamber she gave as
a votive offering. 20 For three months the people continued
feasting in Jerusalem before the sanctuary, and Judith remained with them.

21 After this they all returned home to their own inheritances. Judith went to Bethulia, and remained on her estate.
For the rest of her life she was honored throughout the
whole country. 22 Many desired to marry her, but she gave
herself to no man all the days of her life after her husband
Manasseh died and was gathered to his people. 23 She became more and more famous, and grew old in her husband's
house, reaching the age of one hundred five. She set her
maid free. She died in Bethulia, and they buried her in the
cave of her husband Manasseh; 24 and the house of Israel
mourned her for seven days. Before she died she distributed
her property to all those who were next of kin to her husband Manasseh, and to her own nearest kindred. 25 No one
ever again spread terror among the Israelites during the
lifetime of Judith, or for a long time after her death.

16 All sacrifices with their fragrance are but a small
thing,
all the fat for whole-offerings is of no significance
to you;
but he who fears the Lord is great always.
17 Woe to the nations which attack my people!
The Lord Almighty will punish them on the day of
judgement;
he will consign their bodies to fire and worms;
in pain they will weep for ever.'

18 They went to worship God at Jerusalem, and as soon as
the people were purified, they presented their whole-offerings, freewill-offerings, and gifts. 19 Judith dedicated to
God all Holophernes' possessions which the people had
given to her; the net, which she herself had taken from the
sleeping apartment, she gave to God as a votive offering.
20 For three months the people continued their celebrations
before the temple at Jerusalem; and Judith remained with
them.

21 At the end of that time they all returned to their own
homes. Judith went back to Bethulia, where she lived on her
estate, and throughout her lifetime was renowned in the
whole country. 22 Though she had many suitors, she remained a widow all her days after her husband Manasses
died and was gathered to his fathers. 23 Her fame continued
to increase, and she lived on in her husband's house until
she was a hundred and five years old. She gave her maid her
liberty. She died in Bethulia and was laid in the burial cave
beside her husband Manasses, 24 and Israel observed
mourning for seven days. Before her death she divided her
property among all those who were most closely related to
her husband, and among her own nearest relations.

25 No one dared to threaten the Israelites again in Judith's
lifetime, or indeed for a long time after her death.

16 Though the sweet odor of every sacrifice is a trifle,
and the fat of all holocausts but little in
your sight,
one who fears the LORD is forever great.

17 "Woe to the nations that rise against my people!
The LORD Almighty will requite them;
in the day of judgment he will punish them:
He will send fire and worms into their flesh,
and they shall burn and suffer forever."

18 The people then went to Jerusalem to worship God; when they were purified, they offered their holocausts, free-will offerings, and gifts. 19 Judith dedicated, as a votive offering to God, all the things of Holofernes that the people had given her, as well as the canopy that she herself had taken from his bedroom. 20 For three months the people continued their celebration in Jerusalem before the sanctuary, and Judith remained with them.

21 When those days were over, each one returned to his inheritance. Judith went back to Bethulia and remained on her estate. For the rest of her life she was renowned throughout the land. 22 Many wished to marry her, but she gave herself to no man all the days of her life from the time of the death and burial of her husband, Manasseh. 23 She lived to be very old in the house of her husband, reaching the advanced age of a hundred and five. She died in Bethulia, where they buried her in the tomb of her husband, Manasseh; 24 and the house of Israel mourned her for seven days. Before she died, she distributed her goods to the relatives of her husband, Manasseh, and to her own relatives; and to the maid she gave her freedom.

25 During the life of Judith and for a long time after her death, no one again disturbed the Israelites.

16 A little thing indeed
is a sweetly smelling sacrifice,
still less the fat
burned for you in burnt offering;
but whoever fears the Lord
is great for ever.

17 Woe to the nations
who rise against my race!
The Lord Almighty
will punish them on judgement day.
He will send fire and worms in their flesh
and they will weep with pain for evermore.

18 When they reached Jerusalem they fell on their faces before God, and once the people had been purified, they presented their burnt offerings, voluntary offerings and gifts. 19 All Holofernes' property given her by the people, and the canopy she herself had stripped from his bed, Judith vowed to God as a dedicated offering. 20 For three months the people gave themselves up to rejoicings in front of the Temple in Jerusalem, where Judith stayed with them.

21 When this was over, everyone returned home. Judith went back to Bethulia and lived on her property; as long as she lived, she enjoyed a great reputation throughout the country. 22 She had many suitors, but all her days, from the time her husband Manasseh died and was gathered to his people, she never gave herself to another man. 23 Her fame spread more and more, the older she grew in her husband's house; she lived to the age of one hundred and five. She emancipated her maid, then died in Bethulia and was buried in the cave where Manasseh her husband lay. 24 The House of Israel mourned her for seven days. Before her death she had distributed her property among her own relations and those of her husband Manasseh.

25 Never again during the lifetime of Judith, nor indeed for a long time after her death, did anyone trouble the Israelites.

The deuterocanonical portions of the Book of Esther are several additional passages found in the Greek translation of the Hebrew Book of Esther, a translation that differs also in other respects from the Hebrew text (the latter is translated in the NRSV Old Testament). The disordered chapter numbers come from the displacement of the additions to the end of the canonical Book of Esther by Jerome in his Latin translation and from the subsequent division of the Bible into chapters by Stephen Langton, who numbered the additions consecutively as though they formed a direct continuation of the Hebrew text. So that the additions may be read in their proper context, the whole of the Greek version is here translated, though certain familiar names are given according to their Hebrew rather than their Greek form; for example, Mordecai and Vashti instead of Mardocheus and Astin. The order followed is that of the Greek text, but the chapter and verse numbers conform to those of the King James or Authorized Version. The additions, conveniently indicated by the letters A–F, are located as follows: A, before 1.1; B, after 3.13; C and D, after 4.17; E, after 8.12; F, after 10.3.

The portions of the Book of Esther commonly included in the Apocrypha are extracts from the Greek version of the book, which differs substantially from the Hebrew text (translated in *The Revised English Bible: Old Testament*). In order that they may be read in their original sequence, the whole of the Greek version is here translated, those portions which are not normally printed in the Apocrypha being enclosed in square brackets, with the chapter and verse numbers in italic figures. The order followed is that of the Greek text, but the chapter and verse numbers are made to conform to those of the Authorized Version. Proper names are given in the form in which they occur in the Greek version.

Esther

(The Greek Version Containing the Additional Chapters)

THE REST OF THE CHAPTERS OF THE BOOK OF

Esther

Which Are Found Neither in the Hebrew Nor in the Syriac

ADDITION A

11 *a* **2** In the second year of the reign of Artaxerxes the Great, on the first day of Nisan, Mordecai son of Jair son of Shimei*b* son of Kish, of the tribe of Benjamin, had a dream. 3 He was a Jew living in the city of Susa, a great man, serving in the court of the king. 4 He was one of the captives whom King Nebuchadnezzar of Babylon had brought from Jerusalem with King Jeconiah of Judea. And this was his dream: 5 Noises*c* and confusion, thunders and earthquake, tumult on the earth! 6 Then two great dragons came forward, both ready to fight, and they roared terribly. 7 At their roaring every nation prepared for war, to fight against the righteous nation. 8 It was a day of darkness and gloom, of tribulation and distress, affliction and great tumult on the earth! 9 And the whole righteous nation was troubled; they feared the evils that threatened them,*d* and were ready to perish. 10 Then they cried out to God; and at their outcry, as though from a tiny spring, there came a great river, with abundant water; 11 light came, and the sun rose, and the lowly were exalted and devoured those held in honor.

12 Mordecai saw in this dream what God had determined to do, and after he awoke he had it on his mind, seeking all day to understand it in every detail.

12 Now Mordecai took his rest in the courtyard with Gabatha and Tharra, the two eunuchs of the king who kept watch in the courtyard. 2 He overheard their conversation and inquired into their purposes, and learned that they were preparing to lay hands on King Artaxerxes; and he informed the king concerning them. 3 Then the king examined the two eunuchs, and after they had confessed it, they were led away to execution. 4 The king made a permanent record of these things, and Mordecai wrote an account of them. 5 And the king ordered Mordecai to serve in the court, and rewarded him for these things. 6 But Haman son of Hammedatha, a Bougean, who was in great honor with the king, determined to injure Mordecai and his people because of the two eunuchs of the king.

END OF ADDITION A

11 *2* In the second year of the reign of Artaxerxes the Great King, on the first day of the month of Nisan, Mardochaeus son of Jairus, son of Semeius, son of Kisaeus, of the tribe of Benjamin, had a dream. 3 Mardochaeus, who was in the royal service at court, was a Jew living in the city of Susa and a man of high standing; 4 he was one of the exiles, a descendant of those whom King Nebuchadnezzar of Babylon had carried away from Jerusalem with King Jechonias of Judah. This was his dream: 5 first came din and tumult, peals of thunder and an earthquake, turmoil on the earth. 6 Then two great dragons appeared, each poised to grapple with the other. They gave a mighty roar, 7 and every nation was roused by it to prepare for war and fight against the righteous nation. 8 It was a day of darkness and gloom, distress and anguish, oppression and great turmoil on the earth. 9 The whole righteous nation, dreading the evils in store, was troubled and prepared for death. 10 They cried aloud to God, and in answer there came as though from a little spring a great river brimming with water. 11 As the sun rose it grew light; the humble were exalted and they devoured those of high degree. 12 After this dream, in which he saw what God had resolved to do, Mardochaeus woke; he pondered over the dream until nightfall, trying in every way to understand it.

12 Once, while Mardochaeus was taking his rest in the royal courtyard with Gabatha and Tharra, the two eunuchs in the king's service who were on guard in the courtyard, 2 he overheard them deep in discussion. He listened carefully to discover what was on their minds, and found they were plotting violence against King Artaxerxes. He denounced them to the king, 3 who had the two eunuchs interrogated; on their confessing, they were led away to execution. 4 The king wrote an account of this affair to have it on record; Mardochaeus also wrote an account of it. 5 The king gave him an appointment at court, and rewarded him for his services. 6 But Haman son of Hamadathus, a Bugaean, who enjoyed the royal favour, looked for a chance to harm Mardochaeus and his people because of the king's two eunuchs.

---

a Chapters 11.2—12.6 correspond to chapter A 1-17 in some translations. *b* Gk *Semeios* *c* Or *Voices* *d* Gk *their own evils*

The text of Esther, written originally in Hebrew, was transmitted in two forms: a short Hebrew form and a longer Greek version. The latter contains 107 additional verses, inserted at appropriate places within the Hebrew form of the text. A few of these seem to have a Hebrew origin while the rest are Greek in original composition. It is possible that the Hebrew form of the text is original throughout. If it systematically omits reference to God and his Providence over Israel, this is perhaps due to fear of irreverent response. The Greek text with the above-mentioned additions is possibly a later literary paraphrase in which the author seeks to have the reader share his sentiments. This standard Greek text is pre-Christian in origin. The church has accepted the additions as equally inspired with the rest of the book.

In present translations, the portions preceded by the letters A through F indicate the underlying Greek additions referred to above. The regular chapter numbers apply to the Hebrew text.

Since the New American Bible version of Esther inserts translations of the additional Greek passages into a translation of the Hebrew text, the designation "deuterocanonical" properly applies only to the Greek insertions.

The Book of Esther has two forms: one short, in Hebrew; one long, in Greek. The Greek version contains the following passages not found in the Hebrew: the dream of Mordecai, 1:1^{a-r} and its explanation, 10:3^{a-k}; two edicts of Ahasuerus, 3:13^{a-g} and 8:12^{a-v}, the prayer of Mordecai, 4:17^{a-i} the prayer of Esther, 4:17^{k-z} a second account of Esther's appeal to Ahasuerus, 5:1^{a-f} and 5:2^{a-b}; an appendix explaining the origin of the Greek version, 10:3^l. Jerome placed his translation of these passages after the translated Hebrew text (Vulg. 10:4–16:24); in our own translation they have been left where the Greek text has them, but in italics.

Since the New Jerusalem Bible version of Esther inserts translations of the additional Greek passages into a translation of the Hebrew text, the designation "deuterocanonical" properly applies only to the Greek insertions.

THE BOOK OF
Esther

Esther

A In the second year of the reign of the great King Ahasuerus, on the first day of Nisan, Mordecai, son of Jair, son of Shimei, son of Kish, of the tribe of Benjamin, had a dream. 2 He was a Jew residing in the city of Susa, a prominent man who served at the king's court, 3 and one of the captives whom Nebuchadnezzar, king of Babylon, had taken from Jerusalem with Jeconiah, king of Judah.

4 This was his dream. There was noise and tumult, thunder and earthquake — confusion upon the earth. 5 Two great dragons came on, both poised for combat. They uttered a mighty cry, 6 and at their cry every nation prepared for war, to fight against the race of the just. 7 It was a dark and gloomy day. Tribulation and distress, evil and great confusion, lay upon the earth. 8 The whole race of the just were dismayed with fear of the evils to come upon them, and were at the point of destruction. 9 Then they cried out to God, and as they cried, there appeared to come forth a great river, a flood of water from a little spring. 10 The light of the sun broke forth; the lowly were exalted and they devoured the nobles.

11 Having seen this dream and what God intended to do, Mordecai awoke. He kept it in mind, and tried in every way, until night, to understand its meaning.

12 Mordecai lodged at the court with Bagathan and Thares, two eunuchs of the king who were court guards. 13 He overheard them plotting, investigated their plans, and discovered that they were preparing to lay hands on King Ahasuerus. So he informed the king about them, 14 and the king had the two eunuchs questioned and, upon their confession, put to death. 15 Then the king had these things recorded; Mordecai, too, put them into writing. 16 The king also appointed Mordecai to serve at the court, and rewarded him for his actions.

17 Haman, however, son of Hammedatha the Agagite, who was in high honor with the king, sought to harm Mordecai and his people because of the two eunuchs of the king.

1 1a *aIn the second year of the reign of the Great King, Ahasuerus, on the first day of Nisan, a dream came to Mordecai son of Jair, son of Shimei, son of Kish, of the tribe of Benjamin, 1b a Jew living at Susa and holding high office at the royal court.* 1c *He was one of the captives whom Nebuchadnezzar king of Babylon had deported from Jerusalem with Jeconiah king of Judah.*

1d *This was his dream. There were cries and noise, thunder and earthquakes, and disorder over the whole earth.* 1e *Then two great dragons came forward, each ready for the fray, and set up a great roar.* 1f *At the sound of them every nation made ready to wage war against the nation of the just.* 1g *A day of darkness and gloom, of affliction and distress, oppression and great disturbance on earth!* 1h *The entire upright nation was thrown into consternation at the fear of the evils awaiting it and prepared for death, crying out to God.* 1i *Then from its cry, as from a little spring, there grew a great river, a flood of water.* 1k *Light came as the sun rose, and the humble were raised up and devoured the mighty.*

1l *On awakening from this dream and vision of God's designs, Mordecai thought deeply about the matter, trying his best all day to discover what its meaning might be.*

1m *Mordecai was lodging at court with Bigthan and Teresh, two of the king's eunuchs who guarded the palace.* 1n *Having got wind of their plotting and gained knowledge of their designs, he discovered that they were preparing to assassinate King Ahasuerus, and he warned the king against them.* 1o *The king gave orders for the two officers to be tortured; they confessed and were executed.* 1p *He then had these events entered in his Record Book, while Mordecai himself also wrote an account of them.* 1q *The king then appointed Mordecai to an office at court and rewarded him with presents.* 1r *But Haman son of Hammedatha, the Agagite, who enjoyed high favour with the king, determined to injure Mordecai in revenge for the affair of the king's two officers.*

a 1 Throughout the book the passages printed in italics are contained in the Gk text but are not in the Hebr.

1 It was after this that the following things happened in the days of Artaxerxes, the same Artaxerxes who ruled over one hundred twenty-seven provinces from India to Ethiopia.*e* 2 In those days, when King Artaxerxes was enthroned in the city of Susa, 3 in the third year of his reign, he gave a banquet for his Friends and other persons of various nations, the Persians and Median nobles, and the governors of the provinces. 4 After this, when he had displayed to them the riches of his kingdom and the splendor of his bountiful celebration during the course of one hundred eighty days, 5 at the end of the festivity*f* the king gave a drinking party for the people of various nations who lived in the city. This was held for six days in the courtyard of the royal palace, 6 which was adorned with curtains of fine linen and cotton, held by cords of purple linen attached to gold and silver blocks on pillars of marble and other stones. Gold and silver couches were placed on a mosaic floor of emerald, mother-of-pearl, and marble. There were coverings of gauze, embroidered in various colors, with roses arranged around them. 7 The cups were of gold and silver, and a miniature cup was displayed, made of ruby, worth thirty thousand talents. There was abundant sweet wine, such as the king himself drank. 8 The drinking was not according to a fixed rule; but the king wished to have it so, and he commanded his stewards to comply with his pleasure and with that of the guests.

9 Meanwhile, Queen Vashti*g* gave a drinking party for the women in the palace where King Artaxerxes was.

10 On the seventh day, when the king was in good humor, he told Haman, Bazan, Tharra, Boraze, Zatholtha, Abataza, and Tharaba, the seven eunuchs who served King Artaxerxes, 11 to escort the queen to him in order to proclaim her as queen and to place the diadem on her head, and to have her display her beauty to all the governors and the people of various nations, for she was indeed a beautiful woman. 12 But Queen Vashti*g* refused to obey him and would not come with the eunuchs. This offended the king and he became furious. 13 He said to his Friends, "This is how Vashti*g* has answered me.*h* Give therefore your ruling and judgment on this matter." 14 Arkesaeus, Sarsathaeus, and Malesear, then the governors of the Persians and Medes who were closest to the king — Arkesaeus, Sarsathaeus, and Malesear, who sat beside him in the chief seats — came to him 15 and told him what must be done to Queen Vashti*g* for not obeying the order that the king had sent her by the eunuchs. 16 Then Muchaeus said to the king and the governors, "Queen Vashti*g* has insulted not only the king but also all the king's governors and officials" 17 (for he had reported to them what the queen had said and how she had defied the king). "And just as she defied King Artaxerxes, 18 so now the other ladies who are wives of the Persian and Median governors, on hearing what she has said to the king, will likewise dare to insult their husbands. 19 If therefore it pleases the king, let him issue a royal decree, inscribed in accordance with the laws of the Medes and Persians so that it may not be altered, that the queen may no longer come into his presence; but let the king give her royal rank to a woman better than she. 20 Let whatever law the king enacts be proclaimed in his kingdom, and thus all women will give honor to their husbands, rich and poor alike." 21 This speech pleased the king and the governors, and the king did as Muchaeus had recommended. 22 The king sent the decree into all his kingdom, to every province in its own language, so that in every house respect would be shown to every husband.

1 [THOSE events happened in the days of Artaxerxes, that Artaxerxes who ruled from India to Ethiopia, a hundred and twenty-seven provinces, 2 at the time when he had taken his seat on the royal throne in the city of Susa. 3 In the third year of his reign he gave a reception for the king's Friends and for others of various races, the Persian and Median nobles, and the leading provincial governors. 4 Afterwards he put on display to them the wealth of his kingdom and the dazzling splendour of his riches for a hundred and eighty days. 5 When these days of feasting were over, the king held a banquet for all the people of various races present in the city of Susa; it lasted six days and took place in the palace court, 6 which was decorated with white curtains of linen and cotton stretched on cords of purple, and these were attached to blocks of gold and silver resting on stone and marble columns. There were gold and silver couches placed on a pavement of malachite, marble, and mother-of-pearl, and there were coverings of transparent weave elaborately embroidered with roses arranged in a circle. 7 The cups were of gold and silver, and on display was a miniature cup made from a ruby worth thirty thousand talents. The wine, which was from the king's own cellar, was abundant and sweet. 8 The drinking was according to no fixed rule, for the king had laid down that all the palace stewards should respect his wishes and those of the guests. 9 Queen Astin gave a banquet for the women inside King Artaxerxes' palace.

10 On the seventh day, when he was feeling merry, the king ordered Haman, Mazan, Tharra, Borazes, Zatholtha, Abataza, and Tharaba, the seven eunuchs who were in attendance on the king's person, 11 to bring the queen into his presence, so that she might place the royal diadem on her head and display her beauty to the officers and people of various races; for she was indeed a beautiful woman. 12 But Queen Astin refused to obey and accompany the eunuchs. This incensed the king and his anger flared up. 13 He said to his courtiers, 'You hear how Astin spoke. Give your ruling and judgement in the matter.' 14 Harkesaeus, Sarathaeus, and Malesear, the nobles of Persia and Media who were closest to the king and occupied the seats of honour by him, approached 15 and made known to him what, according to the law, should be done to Queen Astin for disobeying the royal command conveyed to her by the eunuchs.

16 Muchaeus made this reply to the king and the nobles: 'Queen Astin has done wrong, not to the king alone, but also to all the nobles and officers of the king.' 17 (For he had repeated to them what the queen had said and how she had defied the king.) 18 'Just as she defied King Artaxerxes, so now the nobles of Persia and Media will find that all the great ladies are emboldened to treat their husbands with disrespect, when they hear what she said to the king. 19 If it please your majesty, let a royal decree be issued once and for all, and let it be inscribed among the laws of the Medes and Persians, that Astin shall not come in again to the king; and let your majesty give her place as queen to another who is more worthy of it than she. 20 Let whatever law the king makes be proclaimed throughout the kingdom, and so all women, rich and poor alike, will give honour to their husbands.' 21 The advice pleased the king and the princes, and the king did as Muchaeus had proposed. 22 Dispatches were sent to all the provinces of the kingdom, to every province in its own language, in order that each man should be treated with deference in his own house.

---

e Other ancient authorities lack *to Ethiopia*   *f* Gk *marriage feast*
g Gk *Astin*   *h* Gk *Astin has said thus and so*

NEW AMERICAN BIBLE

1 During the reign of Ahasuerus—this was the Ahasuerus who ruled over a hundred and twenty-seven provinces from India to Ethiopia— [2] while he was occupying the royal throne in the stronghold of Susa, [3] in the third year of his reign, he presided over a feast for all his officers and ministers: the Persian and Median aristocracy, the nobles, and the governors of the provinces. [4] For as many as a hundred and eighty days, he displayed the glorious riches of his kingdom and the resplendent wealth of his royal estate.

[5] At the end of this time the king gave a feast of seven days in the garden court of the royal palace for all the people, great and small, who were in the stronghold of Susa. [6] There were white cotton draperies and violet hangings, held by cords of crimson byssus from silver rings on marble pillars. Gold and silver couches were on the pavement, which was of porphyry, marble, mother-of-pearl, and colored stones. [7] Liquor was served in a variety of golden cups, and the royal wine flowed freely, as befitted the king's munificence. [8] By ordinance of the king the drinking was unstinted, for he had instructed all the stewards of his household to comply with the good pleasure of everyone.

[9] Queen Vashti also gave a feast for the women inside the royal palace of King Ahasuerus.

[10] On the seventh day, when the king was merry with wine, he instructed Mehuman, Biztha, Harbona, Bigtha, Abagtha, Zethar, and Carkas, the seven eunuchs who attended King Ahasuerus, [11] to bring Queen Vashti into his presence wearing the royal crown, that he might display her beauty to the populace and the officials, for she was lovely to behold. [12] But Queen Vashti refused to come at the royal order issued through the eunuchs. At this the king's wrath flared up, and he burned with fury. [13] He conferred with the wise men versed in the law, because the king's business was conducted in general consultation with lawyers and jurists. [14] He summoned Carshena, Shethar, Admatha, Tarshish, Meres, Marsena and Memucan, the seven Persian and Median officials who were in the king's personal service and held first rank in the realm, [15] and asked them, "What is to be done by law with Queen Vashti for disobeying the order of King Ahasuerus issued through the eunuchs?"

[16] In the presence of the king and of the officials, Memucan answered: "Queen Vashti has not wronged the king alone, but all the officials and the populace throughout the provinces of King Ahasuerus. [17] For the queen's conduct will become known to all the women, and they will look with disdain upon their husbands when it is reported, 'King Ahasuerus commanded that Queen Vashti be ushered into his presence, but she would not come.' [18] This very day the Persian and Median ladies who hear of the queen's conduct will rebel against all the royal officials, with corresponding disdain and rancor. [19] If it please the king, let an irrevocable royal decree be issued by him and inscribed among the laws of the Persians and Medes, forbidding Vashti to come into the presence of King Ahasuerus and authorizing the king to give her royal dignity to one more worthy than she. [20] Thus, when the decree which the king will issue is published throughout his realm, vast as it is, all wives will honor their husbands, from the greatest to the least."

[21] This proposal found acceptance with the king and the officials, and the king acted on the advice of Memucan. [22] He sent letters to all the royal provinces, to each province in its own script and to each people in its own language, to the effect that every man should be lord in his own home.

NEW JERUSALEM BIBLE

1 It was in the days of Ahasuerus, the Ahasuerus whose empire stretched from India to Ethiopia and comprised one hundred and twenty-seven provinces. [2] In those days, when King Ahasuerus was sitting on his royal throne in the citadel of Susa, [3] in the third year of his reign, he gave a banquet at his court for all his officers-of-state and ministers, Persian and Median army-commanders, nobles and provincial governors. [4] Thus he displayed the riches and splendour of his empire and the pomp and glory of his majesty; the festivities went on for a long time, a hundred and eighty days.

[5] When this period was over, for seven days the king gave a banquet for all the people living in the citadel of Susa, to high and low alike, on the esplanade in the gardens of the royal palace. [6] There were white and violet hangings fastened with cords of fine linen and purple thread to silver rings on marble columns, couches of gold and silver on a pavement of porphyry, marble, mother-of-pearl and precious stones. [7] For drinking there were golden cups of various design and plenty of wine provided by the king with royal liberality. [8] The royal edict did not, however, make drinking obligatory, the king having instructed the officials of his household to treat each guest according to the guest's own wishes.

[9] Queen Vashti, for her part, gave a banquet for the women in the royal palace of King Ahasuerus. [10] On the seventh day, when the king was merry with wine, he commanded Mehuman, Biztha, Harbona, Bigtha, Abagtha, Zethar and Carkas, the seven officers in attendance on the person of King Ahasuerus, [11] to bring Queen Vashti before the king, crowned with her royal diadem, in order to display her beauty to the people and the officers-of-state, since she was very beautiful. [12] But Queen Vashti refused to come at the king's command delivered by the officers. The king was very angry at this and his rage grew hot. [13] Addressing himself to the wise men who were versed in the law—it being the practice to refer matters affecting the king to expert lawyers and jurists—[14] he summoned Carshena, Shethar, Admatha, Tarshish, Meres, Marsena and Memucan, seven Persian and Median officers-of-state who had privileged access to the royal presence and occupied the leading positions in the kingdom. [15] 'According to law,' he said, 'what is to be done to Queen Vashti for not obeying the command of King Ahasuerus delivered by the officers?' [16] In the presence of the king and the officers-of-state, Memucan replied, 'Queen Vashti has wronged not only the king but also all the officers-of-state and all the peoples inhabiting the provinces of King Ahasuerus. [17] The queen's conduct will soon become known to all the women, who will adopt a contemptuous attitude towards their own husbands. They will say, "King Ahasuerus himself commanded Queen Vashti to appear before him and she did not come." [18] Before the day is out, the wives of the Persian and Median officers-of-state will be telling every one of the king's officers-of-state what they have heard about the queen's behaviour; and that will mean contempt and anger all round. [19] If it is the king's pleasure, let him issue a royal edict, to be irrevocably incorporated into the laws of the Persians and Medes, to the effect that Vashti is never to appear again before King Ahasuerus, and let the king confer her royal dignity on a worthier woman. [20] Let this edict issued by the king be proclaimed throughout his empire—which is great—and all the women will henceforth bow to the authority of their husbands, both high and low alike.'

[21] This speech pleased the king and the officers-of-state, and the king did as Memucan advised. [22] He sent letters to all the provinces of the kingdom, to each province in its own script and to each nation in its own language, ensuring that every husband should be master in his own house.

2 After these things, the king's anger abated, and he no longer was concerned about Vashti[i] or remembered what he had said and how he had condemned her. 2 Then the king's servants said, "Let beautiful and virtuous girls be sought out for the king. 3 The king shall appoint officers in all the provinces of his kingdom, and they shall select beautiful young virgins to be brought to the harem in Susa, the capital. Let them be entrusted to the king's eunuch who is in charge of the women, and let ointments and whatever else they need be given them. 4 And the woman who pleases the king shall be queen instead of Vashti.[i] This pleased the king, and he did so.

5 Now there was a Jew in Susa the capital whose name was Mordecai son of Jair son of Shimei[j] son of Kish, of the tribe of Benjamin; 6 he had been taken captive from Jerusalem among those whom King Nebuchadnezzar of Babylon had captured. 7 And he had a foster child, the daughter of his father's brother, Aminadab, and her name was Esther. When her parents died, he brought her up to womanhood as his own. The girl was beautiful in appearance. 8 So, when the decree of the king was proclaimed, and many girls were gathered in Susa the capital in custody of Gai, Esther also was brought to Gai, who had custody of the women. 9 The girl pleased him and won his favor, and he quickly provided her with ointments and her portion of food,[k] as well as seven maids chosen from the palace; he treated her and her maids with special favor in the harem. 10 Now Esther had not disclosed her people or country, for Mordecai had commanded her not to make it known. 11 And every day Mordecai walked in the courtyard of the harem, to see what would happen to Esther.

12 Now the period after which a girl was to go to the king was twelve months. During this time the days of beautification are completed — six months while they are anointing themselves with oil of myrrh, and six months with spices and ointments for women. 13 Then she goes in to the king; she is handed to the person appointed, and goes with him from the harem to the king's palace. 14 In the evening she enters and in the morning she departs to the second harem, where Gai the king's eunuch is in charge of the women; and she does not go in to the king again unless she is summoned by name.

15 When the time was fulfilled for Esther daughter of Aminadab, the brother of Mordecai's father, to go in to the king, she neglected none of the things that Gai, the eunuch in charge of the women, had commanded. Now Esther found favor in the eyes of all who saw her. 16 So Esther went in to King Artaxerxes in the twelfth month, which is Adar, in the seventh year of his reign. 17 And the king loved Esther and she found favor beyond all the other virgins, so he put on her the queen's diadem. 18 Then the king gave a banquet lasting seven days for all his Friends and the officers to celebrate his marriage to Esther; and he granted a remission of taxes to those who were under his rule.

19 Meanwhile Mordecai was serving in the courtyard. 20 Esther had not disclosed her country — such were the instructions of Mordecai; but she was to fear God and keep his laws, just as she had done when she was with him. So Esther did not change her mode of life.

2 Some time later, when the anger of King Artaxerxes had died down, he called Astin to mind, remembering what she had done and how he had given judgement against her. 2 So the king's attendants said: 'Let there be sought out for your majesty beautiful young virgins; 3 let your majesty appoint commissioners in every province of your kingdom to select these beautiful virgins and bring them to the women's quarters in the city of Susa. Have them placed under the care of the king's eunuch who has charge of the women, and let them be provided with cosmetics and everything else they need. 4 The girl who is most acceptable to the king shall become queen in place of Astin.' The advice pleased the king, and he acted on it.

5 In the city of Susa there lived a Jew named Mardochaeus son of Jairus, son of Semeius, son of Kisaeus, of the tribe of Benjamin; 6 he had been taken into exile from Jerusalem when it was captured by King Nebuchadnezzar of Babylon. 7 He had a foster-child named Esther, the daughter of his father's brother Aminadab; and after the death of her parents he had brought her up, intending to make her his wife. She was a beautiful girl. 8 When the king's edict was proclaimed and many girls were brought to Susa to be committed to the care of Gai, who had charge of the women, Esther too was entrusted to him. 9 He found her pleasing and she received his special favour: he promptly supplied her with cosmetics and with her allowance of food, and also with seven maids assigned to her from the king's palace. She and her maids were accorded favourable treatment in the women's quarters. 10 Esther had not disclosed her race or country, because Mardochaeus had forbidden her to do so. 11 Every day Mardochaeus would walk past the forecourt of the women's quarters to keep an eye on what was happening to Esther.

12 The full period of preparation before a girl went to the king was twelve months: six months' treatment with oil of myrrh, and six months' with perfumes and cosmetics. At the end of this the girl went to the king. 13 She was handed to the person appointed and accompanied him from the women's quarters to the king's palace. 14 She entered the palace in the evening and returned in the morning to another part of the women's quarters, to be under the care of Gai, the king's eunuch in charge of the women. She did not go again to the king unless summoned by name.

15 When the time came for Esther, the daughter of Aminadab, uncle of Mardochaeus, to go to the king, she neglected none of the instructions given her by the king's eunuch in charge of the women. Esther charmed all who saw her, 16 and when she went to King Artaxerxes in the twelfth month, that is, the month of Adar, in the seventh year of his reign, 17 the king fell in love with her. He treated her with greater favour than all the rest of the virgins, and put the queen's diadem on her head. 18 Then, to celebrate his marriage with Esther, the king gave a banquet lasting seven days for all the king's Friends and the officers. He also granted a remission of taxation to all the subjects of his kingdom.

19 MARDOCHAEUS was in attendance in the court. 20 On his instructions Esther had not disclosed her country; she was to fear God and keep the commandments, as she used to do when she was with him. So Esther made no change in her rule of life.

[i] Gk Astin   [j] Gk Semeios   [k] Gk lacks of food

2 After this, when King Ahasuerus' wrath had cooled, he thought over what Vashti had done and what had been decreed against her. 2 Then the king's personal attendants suggested: "Let beautiful young virgins be sought for the king. 3 Let the king appoint commissaries in all the provinces of his realm to bring together all beautiful young virgins to the harem in the stronghold of Susa. Under the care of the royal eunuch Hegai, custodian of the women, let cosmetics be given them. 4 Then the girl who pleases the king shall reign in place of Vashti." This suggestion pleased the king, and he acted accordingly.

5 There was in the stronghold of Susa a certain Jew named Mordecai, son of Jair, son of Shimei, son of Kish, a Benjaminite, 6 who had been exiled from Jerusalem with the captives taken with Jeconiah, king of Judah, whom Nebuchadnezzar, king of Babylon, had deported. 7 He was foster father to Hadassah, that is, Esther, his cousin; for she had lost both father and mother. The girl was beautifully formed and lovely to behold. On the death of her father and mother, Mordecai had taken her as his own daughter.

8 When the king's order and decree had been obeyed and many maidens brought together to the stronghold of Susa under the care of Hegai, Esther also was brought in to the royal palace under the care of Hegai, custodian of the women. 9 The girl pleased him and won his favor. So he promptly furnished her with cosmetics and provisions. Then picking out seven maids for her from the royal palace, he transferred both her and her maids to the best place in the harem. 10 Esther did not reveal her nationality or family, for Mordecai had commanded her not to do so.

11 Day by day Mordecai would walk about in front of the court of the harem, to learn how Esther was faring and what was to become of her.

12 Each girl went in turn to visit King Ahasuerus after the twelve months' preparation decreed for the women. Of this period of beautifying treatment, six months were spent with oil of myrrh, and the other six months with perfumes and cosmetics. 13 Then, when the girl was to visit the king, she was allowed to take with her from the harem to the royal palace whatever she chose. 14 She would go in the evening and return in the morning to a second harem under the care of the royal eunuch Shaashgaz, custodian of the concubines. She could not return to the king unless he was pleased with her and had her summoned by name.

15 As for Esther, daughter of Abihail and adopted daughter of his nephew Mordecai, when her turn came to visit the king, she did not ask for anything but what the royal eunuch Hegai, custodian of the women, suggested. Yet she won the admiration of all who saw her. 16 Esther was led to King Ahasuerus in his palace in the tenth month, Tebeth, in the seventh year of his reign. 17 The king loved Esther more than all other women, and of all the virgins she won his favor and benevolence. So he placed the royal diadem on her head and made her queen in place of Vashti. 18 Then the king gave a great feast in honor of Esther to all his officials and ministers, granting a holiday to the provinces and bestowing gifts with royal bounty.

19 [To resume: From the time the virgins had been brought together, and while Mordecai was passing his time at the king's gate, 20 Esther had not revealed her family or nationality, because Mordecai had told her not to; and Esther continued to follow Mordecai's instructions, just as she had when she was being brought up by him. 21 And during

2 Some time after this, when the king's wrath had subsided, Ahasuerus remembered Vashti, how she had behaved, and the measures taken against her. 2 The king's gentlemen-in-waiting said, 'A search should be made on the king's behalf for beautiful young virgins, 3 and the king appoint commissioners throughout the provinces of his realm to bring all these beautiful young virgins to the citadel of Susa, to the harem under the authority of Hegai the king's eunuch, custodian of the women. Here he will give them whatever they need for enhancing their beauty, 4 and the girl who pleases the king can take Vashti's place as queen.' This advice pleased the king and he acted on it.

5 Now in the citadel of Susa there lived a Jew called Mordecai son of Jair, son of Shimei, son of Kish, of the tribe of Benjamin, 6 who had been deported from Jerusalem among the captives taken away with Jeconiah king of Judah by Nebuchadnezzar king of Babylon, 7 and was now bringing up a certain Hadassah, otherwise called Esther, his uncle's daughter, who had lost both father and mother; the girl had a good figure and a beautiful face, and on the death of her parents Mordecai had adopted her as his daughter.

8 On the promulgation of the royal command and edict a great number of girls were brought to the citadel of Susa where they were entrusted to Hegai. Esther, too, was taken to the king's palace and entrusted to Hegai, the custodian of the women. 9 The girl pleased him and won his favour. Not only did he quickly provide her with all she needed for her dressing room and her meals, but he gave her seven special maids from the king's household and transferred her and her maids to the best part of the harem. 10 Esther had not divulged her race or parentage, since Mordecai had forbidden her to do so. 11 Mordecai walked up and down in front of the courtyard of the harem all day and every day, to learn how Esther was and how she was being treated.

12 Each girl had to appear in turn before King Ahasuerus after a delay of twelve months fixed by the regulations for the women; this preparatory period was occupied as follows: six months with oil of myrrh, and six months with spices and lotions commonly used for feminine beauty treatment. 13 When each girl went to the king, she was given whatever she wanted to take with her, since she then moved from the harem into the royal household. 14 She went there in the evening, and the following morning returned to another harem entrusted to the care of Shaashgaz, the king's officer, custodian of the concubines. She did not go to the king any more, unless he was particularly pleased with her and had her summoned by name.

15 But when it was the turn of Esther the daughter of Abihail, whose nephew Mordecai had adopted her as his own daughter, to go into the king's presence, she did not ask for anything beyond what had been assigned her by Hegai, the king's officer, custodian of the women. Esther won the approval of all who saw her. 16 She was brought to King Ahasuerus in his royal apartments in the tenth month, which is called Tebeth, in the seventh year of his reign; 17 and the king liked Esther better than any of the other women; none of the other girls found so much favour and approval with him. So he set the royal diadem on her head and proclaimed her queen instead of Vashti.

18 The king then gave a great banquet, Esther's banquet, for all his officers-of-state and ministers, decreed a holiday for all the provinces and distributed largesse with royal prodigality.

19 When Esther, like the other girls, had been transferred to the second harem, 20 she did not divulge her parentage or race, in obedience to the orders of Mordecai, whose instructions she continued to follow as when she had been under his care. 21 At this time Mordecai was attached to the Chan-

2, 19-23: This is a resumption, in a slightly different form, of the story already told in Est A, 12-15.

21 Now the king's eunuchs, who were chief body-guards, were angry because of Mordecai's advancement, and they plotted to kill King Artaxerxes. 22 The matter became known to Mordecai, and he warned Esther, who in turn revealed the plot to the king. 23 He investigated the two eunuchs and hanged them. Then the king ordered a memorandum to be deposited in the royal library in praise of the goodwill shown by Mordecai.

3 After these events King Artaxerxes promoted Haman son of Hammedatha, a Bougean, advancing him and granting him precedence over all the king's[l] Friends. 2 So all who were at court used to do obeisance to Haman,[m] for so the king had commanded to be done. Mordecai, however, did not do obeisance. 3 Then the king's courtiers said to Mordecai, "Mordecai, why do you disobey the king's command?" 4 Day after day they spoke to him, but he would not listen to them. Then they informed Haman that Mordecai was resisting the king's command. Mordecai had told them that he was a Jew. 5 So when Haman learned that Mordecai was not doing obeisance to him, he became furiously angry, 6 and plotted to destroy all the Jews under Artaxerxes' rule.

7 In the twelfth year of King Artaxerxes Haman[n] came to a decision by casting lots, taking the days and the months one by one, to fix on one day to destroy the whole race of Mordecai. The lot fell on the fourteenth[o] day of the month of Adar.

8 Then Haman[n] said to King Artaxerxes, "There is a certain nation scattered among the other nations in all your kingdom; their laws are different from those of every other nation, and they do not keep the laws of the king. It is not expedient for the king to tolerate them. 9 If it pleases the king, let it be decreed that they are to be destroyed, and I will pay ten thousand talents of silver into the king's treasury." 10 So the king took off his signet ring and gave it to Haman to seal the decree[p] that was to be written against the Jews. 11 The king told Haman, "Keep the money, and do whatever you want with that nation."

12 So on the thirteenth day of the first month the king's secretaries were summoned, and in accordance with Haman's instructions they wrote in the name of King Artaxerxes to the magistrates and the governors in every province from India to Ethiopia. There were one hundred twenty-seven provinces in all, and the governors were addressed each in his own language. 13 Instructions were sent by couriers throughout all the empire of Artaxerxes to destroy the Jewish people on a given day of the twelfth month, which is Adar, and to plunder their goods.

ADDITION B

13 [q] This is a copy of the letter: "The Great King, Artaxerxes, writes the following to the governors of the hundred twenty-seven provinces from India to Ethiopia and to the officials under them:

21 Two of the king's eunuchs, officers of the bodyguard, were offended at the advancement of Mardochaeus and plotted to murder King Artaxerxes. 22 This became known to Mardochaeus, who told Esther, and she revealed the plot to the king. 23 The king interrogated the two eunuchs and had them hanged, and he ordered that the service Mardochaeus had rendered should be recorded to his honour in the royal archives.

3 It was after those events that King Artaxerxes promoted Haman, son of Hamadathus, a Bugaean, advancing him and giving him precedence above all the king's Friends. 2 Everyone at court did obeisance to Haman, for so the king had commanded it should be done; but Mardochaeus did not do obeisance. 3 The courtiers said, 'Mardochaeus, why do you flout his majesty's command?' 4 They challenged him day after day, and when he refused to listen they informed Haman that Mardochaeus was defying the king's order. Mardochaeus had told them he was a Jew. 5 Haman was furious when he learnt that Mardochaeus was not doing obeisance to him, and 6 he plotted to exterminate all the Jews throughout the kingdom.

7 In the twelfth year of Artaxerxes' reign Haman made an order for lots to be cast, taking the days and months one by one, to decide on a day for the destruction of Mardochaeus's whole race. The lot fell on the thirteenth day of the month of Adar.

8 Then Haman said to King Artaxerxes: 'Dispersed among the nations throughout your whole kingdom, there is one whose laws are different from those of every other nation. They flout your majesty's laws, and it is not in your majesty's interest to tolerate them. 9 If it please you, sire, let an order be issued for their destruction; and I shall make over to the royal treasury the sum of ten thousand talents of silver.' 10 The king drew off his signet ring and, handing it to Haman to seal the decree against the Jews, 11 he said, 'Keep the money, and deal with the people as you think fit.'

12 On the thirteenth day of the first month the king's secretaries were summoned, and in accordance with Haman's instructions they wrote in the name of King Artaxerxes to his army commanders and governors of every province from India to Ethiopia; there were a hundred and twenty-seven provinces in all, and each was addressed in its own language. 13 Dispatches were sent by courier throughout the kingdom of Artaxerxes ordering the extermination of the Jewish race, on a given day of the twelfth month, Adar; and their goods were to be treated as spoil.]

13 THIS is a copy of the letter:

Artaxerxes the Great King to the Governors of the one hundred and twenty-seven provinces from India to Ethiopia and to their regional officials.

---

[l] Gk all his   [m] Gk him   [n] Gk he   [o] Other ancient witnesses read *thirteenth*; see 8.12   [p] Gk lacks *the decree*   [q] Chapter 13.1-7 corresponds to chapter B 1-7 in some translations.

[3:7] **thirteenth:** *so some witnesses (cp.* [8:12]*); other witnesses read* fourteenth.

the time that Mordecai spent at the king's gate, Bagathan and Thares, two of the royal eunuchs who guarded the entrance, had plotted in anger to lay hands on King Ahasuerus. 22 When the plot became known to Mordecai, he told Queen Esther, who in turn informed the king for Mordecai. 23 The matter was investigated and verified, and both of them were hanged on a gibbet. This was written in the annals for the king's use.]

3 After these events King Ahasuerus raised Haman, son of Hammedatha the Agagite, to high rank, seating him above all his fellow officials. 2 All the king's servants who were at the royal gate would kneel and bow down to Haman, for that is what the king had ordered in his regard. Mordecai, however, would not kneel and bow down. 3 The king's servants who were at the royal gate said to Mordecai, "Why do you disobey the king's order?" 4 When they had reminded him day after day and he would not listen to them, they informed Haman, to see whether Mordecai's explanation was acceptable, since he had told them that he was a Jew.

5 When Haman observed that Mordecai would not kneel and bow down to him, he was filled with anger. 6 Moreover, he thought it was not enough to lay hands on Mordecai alone. Since they had told Haman of Mordecai's nationality, he sought to destroy all the Jews, Mordecai's people, throughout the realm of King Ahasuerus. 7 In the first month, Nisan, in the twelfth year of King Ahasuerus, the *pur*, or lot, was cast in Haman's presence, to determine the day and the month for the destruction of Mordecai's people on a single day, and the lot fell on the thirteenth day of the twelfth month, Adar.

8 Then Haman said to King Ahasuerus: "Dispersed among the nations throughout the provinces of your kingdom, there is a certain people living apart, with laws differing from those of every other people. They do not obey the laws of the king, and so it is not proper for the king to tolerate them. 9 If it please the king, let a decree be issued to destroy them; and I will deliver to the procurators ten thousand silver talents for deposit in the royal treasury." 10 The king took the signet ring from his hand and gave it to Haman, son of Hammedatha the Agagite, the enemy of the Jews. 11 "The silver you may keep," the king said to Haman, "but as for this people, do with them whatever you please."

12 So the royal scribes were summoned; and on the thirteenth day of the first month they wrote, at the dictation of Haman, an order to the royal satraps, the governors of every province, and the officials of every people, to each province in its own script and to each people in its own language. It was written in the name of King Ahasuerus and sealed with the royal signet ring. 13 Letters were sent by couriers to all the royal provinces, that all the Jews, young and old, including women and children, should be killed, destroyed, wiped out in one day, the thirteenth day of the twelfth month, Adar, and that their goods should be seized as spoil.

B This is a copy of the letter:

"The great King Ahasuerus writes to the satraps of the hundred and twenty-seven provinces from India to Ethiopia, and the governors subordinate to them, as follows:

cellery and two malcontents, Bigthan and Teresh, officers in the king's service as Guards of the Threshold, plotted to assassinate King Ahasuerus. 22 Mordecai came to hear of this and informed Queen Esther, who in turn, on Mordecai's authority, told the king. 23 The matter was investigated and proved to be true. The two conspirators were sent to the gallows, and the incident was recorded in the Annals, in the royal presence.

3 Shortly afterwards, King Ahasuerus singled out Haman son of Hammedatha, a native of Agag, for promotion. He raised him in rank, granting him precedence over all his colleagues, the other officers-of-state, 2 and all the royal officials employed at the Chancellery used to bow low and prostrate themselves whenever Haman appeared — such was the king's command. Mordecai refused either to bow or to prostrate himself. 3 'Why do you flout the royal command?' the officials of the Chancellery asked Mordecai. 4 Day after day they asked him this, but he took no notice of them. In the end they reported the matter to Haman, to see whether Mordecai would persist in his attitude, since he had told them that he was a Jew. 5 Haman could see for himself that Mordecai did not bow or prostrate himself in his presence; he became furiously angry. 6 And, on being told what race Mordecai belonged to, he thought it beneath him merely to get rid of Mordecai, but made up his mind to wipe out all the members of Mordecai's race, the Jews, living in Ahasuerus' entire empire.

7 In the first month, that is the month of Nisan, of the twelfth year of King Ahasuerus, the *pur*[b] (that is, the lot) was cast in Haman's presence, to determine the day and the month. The lot falling on the twelfth month, which is Adar, 8 Haman said to King Ahasuerus, 'There is a certain unassimilated nation scattered among the other nations throughout the provinces of your realm; their laws are different from those of all the other nations, and the royal laws they ignore; hence it is not in the king's interests to tolerate them. 9 If their destruction be signed, so please the king, I am ready to pay ten thousand talents of silver to the king's receivers, to be credited to the royal treasury.' 10 The king then took his signet ring off his hand and gave it to Haman son of Hammedatha, the persecutor of the Jews. 11 'Keep the money,' he said, 'and you can have the people too; do what you like with them.'

12 The royal scribes were therefore summoned for the thirteenth day of the first month, when they wrote out the orders addressed by Haman to the king's satraps, to the governors ruling each province and to the principal officials of each people, to each province in its own script and to each people in its own language. The edict was signed in the name of King Ahasuerus and sealed with his ring, 13 and letters were sent by runners to every province of the realm, ordering the destruction, slaughter and annihilation of all Jews, young and old, including women and children, on the same day — the thirteenth day of the twelfth month, which is Adar — and the seizing of their possessions.

13a *The text of the letter was as follows:*

'*The Great King, Ahasuerus, to the governors of the hundred and twenty-seven provinces stretching from India to Ethiopia, and to their subordinate district commissioners:*

3, 7: Pur: This word is preserved in the text because its plural, purim, became the name of the feast of Purim commemorating the deliverance of the Jews.

b 3 From this the name of the feast on which the book is read, Purim, is derived. It is a joyful feast, characterised by banquets.

2 "Having become ruler of many nations and master of the whole world (not elated with presumption of authority but always acting reasonably and with kindness), I have determined to settle the lives of my subjects in lasting tranquility and, in order to make my kingdom peaceable and open to travel throughout all its extent, to restore the peace desired by all people.

3 "When I asked my counselors how this might be accomplished, Haman — who excels among us in sound judgment, and is distinguished for his unchanging goodwill and steadfast fidelity, and has attained the second place in the kingdom — 4 pointed out to us that among all the nations in the world there is scattered a certain hostile people, who have laws contrary to those of every nation and continually disregard the ordinances of kings, so that the unifying of the kingdom that we honorably intend cannot be brought about. 5 We understand that this people, and it alone, stands constantly in opposition to every nation, perversely following a strange manner of life and laws, and is ill-disposed to our government, doing all the harm they can so that our kingdom may not attain stability.

6 "Therefore we have decreed that those indicated to you in the letters written by Haman, who is in charge of affairs and is our second father, shall all — wives and children included — be utterly destroyed by the swords of their enemies, without pity or restraint, on the fourteenth day of the twelfth month, Adar, of this present year, 7 so that those who have long been hostile and remain so may in a single day go down in violence to Hades, and leave our government completely secure and untroubled hereafter."

END OF ADDITION B

3 14 Copies of the document were posted in every province, and all the nations were ordered to be prepared for that day. 15 The matter was expedited also in Susa. And while the king and Haman caroused together, the city of Susa^r was thrown into confusion.

4 When Mordecai learned of all that had been done, he tore his clothes, put on sackcloth, and sprinkled himself with ashes; then he rushed through the street of the city, shouting loudly: "An innocent nation is being destroyed!" 2 He got as far as the king's gate, and there he stopped, because no one was allowed to enter the courtyard clothed in sackcloth and ashes. 3 And in every province where the king's proclamation had been posted there was a loud cry of mourning and lamentation among the Jews, and they put on sackcloth and ashes. 4 When the queen's^s maids and eunuchs came and told her, she was deeply troubled by what she heard had happened, and sent some clothes to Mordecai to put on instead of sackcloth; but he would not consent. 5 Then Esther summoned Hachratheus, the eunuch who attended her, and ordered him to get accurate information for her from Mordecai.^{t}

7 So Mordecai told him what had happened and how Haman had promised to pay ten thousand talents into the royal treasury to bring about the destruction of the Jews. 8 He also gave him a copy of what had been posted in Susa for their destruction, to show to Esther; and he told him to charge her to go in to the king and plead for his favor in behalf of the people. "Remember," he said, "the days when you were an ordinary person, being brought up under my care — for Haman, who stands next to the king, has spoken against us and demands our death. Call upon the Lord; then speak to the king in our behalf, and save us from death."

^{r} Gk the city ^{s} Gk When her ^{t} Other ancient witnesses add 6 So Hachratheus went out to Mordecai in the street of the city opposite the city gate.

2 As ruler over many nations and master of the whole world, it is my will — not in the arrogance of power, but because my rule is equitable and mild — to ensure for my subjects a life permanently free from disturbance, to make my kingdom quiet and safe for travel to its farthest limits, and to restore the peace that all men desire. 3 I have enquired of my counsellors how this object might be achieved. Among us Haman is eminent for sound judgement, one whose worth is proved by his constant goodwill and steadfast loyalty, and who has gained the honour of the second place at our court. 4 He has represented to us that dispersed among all the races of the world is a disaffected people, opposed in its laws to every nation, and continually ignoring the royal ordinances, so that our perfected plans for the unified administration of the empire cannot be accomplished. 5 We understand that this nation stands quite alone in its continual hostility to the human race, that it evades the laws by its strange manner of life, and in disloyalty to our government commits the most grave offences, thus undermining the stability of our kingdom. 6 Accordingly we have given orders that all those who are designated to you in the indictments drawn up by Haman our vicegerent and second father shall, with their wives and children, be utterly destroyed by their enemies' swords without mercy or pity, on the thirteenth day of Adar, the twelfth month of the present year. 7 Therefore these persons, who have long been disaffected, shall in a single day meet a violent end, so that our government may henceforth be stable and untroubled.

3 14 [Copies of the dispatch were posted up in every province, and all the peoples were ordered to be ready for that day. 15 The matter was expedited also in Susa. The king and Haman caroused together, but in the city of Susa confusion reigned.

4 WHEN Mardochaeus learnt of all that had been done, he tore his clothes, put on sackcloth, and sprinkled himself with ashes. He rushed out through the city square, crying loudly: 'A nation that has committed no crime is being destroyed.' 2 He went right up to the palace gate, and there he halted, because no one wearing sackcloth and ashes was allowed to enter the courtyard. 3 In every province where the king's decree was posted up, there was a great cry of mourning and lamentation among the Jews, and they put on sackcloth and ashes. 4 When the queen's maids and eunuchs came in and told her, she was distraught at what she heard. She sent clothes for Mardochaeus and urged him to put off his sackcloth, but he refused. 5 Esther then summoned Hachrathaeus, the eunuch who waited upon her, and sent him to Mardochaeus to obtain accurate information for her. 7 Mardochaeus told him all that had happened, and how Haman had promised the king to pay ten thousand talents into the treasury to bring about the destruction of the Jews. 8 He also gave him a copy of the written decree for their destruction which had been posted up in Susa, that he might show it to Esther; and he told him to bid her go to the king to implore his favour and intercede for her people. 'Say to her,' he added, ' "Do not forget your humble origins and your upbringing in my house. Because Haman, who stands next to the king, has spoken against us and demanded our death, call on the Lord, and then speak to the king on our behalf and save our lives." ' 9 When Hachrathaeus came in

13:6 **thirteenth:** *prob. rdg; Gk* fourteenth; *see note on* [3:7].
[4:5] **information for her:** *some witnesses add* 6 So he went out to Mardochaeus in the square opposite the city gate.

NEW AMERICAN BIBLE

NEW JERUSALEM BIBLE

2 When I came to rule many peoples and to hold sway over the whole world, I determined not to be carried away with the sense of power, but always to deal fairly and with clemency; to provide for my subjects a life of complete tranquillity; and by making my government humane and effective as far as the borders, to restore the peace desired by all men. 3 When I consulted my counselors as to how this might be accomplished, Haman, who excels among us in wisdom, who is outstanding for constant devotion and steadfast loyalty, and who has gained the second rank in the kingdom, 4 brought it to our attention that, mixed in with all the races throughout the world, there is one people of bad will, which by its laws is opposed to every other people and continually disregards the decrees of kings, so that the unity of empire blamelessly designed by us cannot be established.

5 "Having noted, therefore, that this most singular people is continually at variance with all men, lives by divergent and alien laws, is inimical to our interests, and commits the worst crimes, so that stability of government cannot be obtained, 6 we hereby decree that all those who are indicated to you in the letters of Haman, who is in charge of the administration and is a second father to us, shall, together with their wives and children, be utterly destroyed by the swords of their enemies, without any pity or mercy, on the fourteenth day of the twelfth month, Adar, of the current year; 7 so that when these people, whose present ill will is of long standing, have gone down into the nether world by a violent death on one same day, they may at last leave our affairs stable and undisturbed for the future."

(3) 14 A copy of the decree to be promulgated as law in every province was published to all the peoples, that they might be prepared for that day. 15 The couriers set out in haste at the king's command; meanwhile, the decree was promulgated in the stronghold of Susa. The king and Haman then sat down to feast, but the city of Susa was thrown into confusion.

4 When Mordecai learned all that was happening, he tore his garments, put on sackcloth and ashes, and walked through the city, crying out loudly and bitterly, 2 till he came before the royal gate, which no one clothed in sackcloth might enter. 3 (Likewise in each of the provinces, wherever the king's legal enactment reached, the Jews went into deep mourning, with fasting, weeping, and lament; they all slept on sackcloth and ashes.)

4 Queen Esther's maids and eunuchs came and told her. Overwhelmed with anguish, she sent garments for Mordecai to put on, so that he might take off his sackcloth; but he refused. 5 Esther then summoned Hathach, one of the king's eunuchs whom he had placed at her service, and commanded him to find out what this action of Mordecai meant and the reason for it. 6 So Hathach went out to Mordecai in the public square in front of the royal gate, 7 and Mordecai told him all that had happened, as well as the exact amount of silver Haman had promised to pay to the royal treasury for the slaughter of the Jews. 8 He also gave him a copy of the written decree for their destruction which had been promulgated in Susa, to show and explain to Esther. He was to instruct her to go to the king; she was to plead and intercede with him in behalf of her people. B, 8 "Remember the days of your lowly estate," Mordecai had him say, "when you were brought up in my charge; for Haman, who is second to the king, has asked for our death. B, 9 Invoke the LORD and speak to the king for us; save us from death."

13b 'Being placed in authority over many nations and ruling the whole world, I have resolved never to be carried away by the insolence of power, but always to rule with moderation and clemency, so as to assure for my subjects a life ever free from storms and, offering my kingdom the benefits of civilisation and free transit from end to end, to restore that peace which all men desire. 13c In consultation with our advisers as to how this aim is to be effected, we have been informed by one of them, eminent among us for prudence and well proved for his unfailing devotion and unshakeable trustworthiness, and in rank second only to our majesty, Haman by name, 13d that there is, mingled among all the tribes of the earth, a certain ill-disposed people, opposed by its laws to every other nation and continually defying the royal ordinances, in such a way as to obstruct that form of government assured by us to the general good.

13e 'Considering therefore that this people, unique of its kind, is in complete opposition to all humanity from which it differs by its outlandish laws, that it is hostile to our interests and that it commits the most heinous crimes, to the point of endangering the stability of the realm: 13f 'We command that those persons designated to you in the letters written by Haman, who was appointed to watch over our interests and is a second father to us, be all destroyed, root and branch, including women and children, by the swords of their enemies, without any pity or mercy, on the fourteenth day of the twelfth month, Adar, of the present year, 13g so that these past and present malcontents being in one day forcibly thrown down to Hades, our government may henceforward enjoy perpetual stability and peace.'

14 Copies of this decree, to be promulgated as law in each province, were published to the various peoples, so that each might be ready for the day aforementioned. 15 At the king's command, the runners set out with all speed; the decree was first promulgated in the citadel of Susa.

While the king and Haman gave themselves up to feasting and drinking, consternation reigned in the city of Susa.

4 When Mordecai learned what had happened, he tore his garments and put on sackcloth and ashes. Then he walked into the centre of the city, wailing loudly and bitterly, 2 until he arrived in front of the Chancellery, which no one clothed in sackcloth was allowed to enter. 3 And in every province, no sooner had the royal command and edict arrived, than among the Jews there was great mourning, fasting, weeping and wailing, and many lay on sackcloth and ashes.

4 When Queen Esther's maids and officers came and told her, she was overcome with grief. She sent clothes for Mordecai to put on instead of his sackcloth, but he refused them. 5 Esther then summoned Hathach, an officer whom the king had appointed to wait on her, and ordered him to go to Mordecai and enquire what the matter was and why he was acting in this way.

6 Hathach went out to Mordecai in the city square in front of the Chancellery, 7 and Mordecai told him what had happened to him personally, and also about the sum of money which Haman had offered to pay into the royal treasury to procure the destruction of the Jews. 8 He also gave him a copy of the edict of extermination published in Susa for him to show Esther for her information, with the message that she was to go to the king and implore his favour and plead with him for the race to which she belonged. 8a 'Remember your humbler circumstances,' he said, 'when you were fed by my hand. Since Haman, the second person in the realm, has petitioned the king for our deaths, 8b invoke the Lord, speak to the king for us and save us from death!'

B,8f: These verses belong to ch B.

9 Hachratheus went in and told Esther all these things. 10 And she said to him, "Go to Mordecai and say, 11 'All nations of the empire know that if any man or woman goes to the king inside the inner court without being called, there is no escape for that person. Only the one to whom the king stretches out the golden scepter is safe — and it is now thirty days since I was called to go to the king.' "

12 When Hachratheus delivered her entire message to Mordecai, 13 Mordecai told him to go back and say to her, "Esther, do not say to yourself that you alone among all the Jews will escape alive. 14 For if you keep quiet at such a time as this, help and protection will come to the Jews from another quarter, but you and your father's family will perish. Yet, who knows whether it is not for such a time as this that you were made queen?" 15 Then Esther gave the messenger this answer to take back to Mordecai: 16 "Go and gather all the Jews who are in Susa and fast on my behalf; for three days and nights do not eat or drink, and my maids and I will also go without food. After that I will go to the king, contrary to the law, even if I must die." 17 So Mordecai went away and did what Esther had told him to do.

and told Esther all Mardochaeus had said, 10 she bade him take back this message: 11 'Every nation in the kingdom knows that there is no hope for any person, man or woman, who enters the king's presence in the inner court without being summoned; only one to whom the king holds out the gold sceptre is spared. Further, I have not been summoned to go to the king these thirty days.'

12 When Hachrathaeus delivered Esther's message, 13 Mardochaeus sent this reply: 'Do not imagine, Esther, that of all the Jews in the kingdom your alone will be safe. 14 If you remain silent at such a time as this, relief and deliverance for the Jews will come from another quarter, but you and your father's family will perish. And who knows whether it is not for a time like this that you have become queen?' 15 Esther gave the messenger this answer to take back to Mardochaeus: 16 'Go and assemble the Jews that are in Susa and hold a fast for me; for three days, night and day, take neither food nor drink, and I and my maids shall also fast. After that, in defiance of the law, I shall go to the king, even if it costs me my life.' 17 Mardochaeus then went away and did everything Esther had bidden him.]

ADDITION C

13 8u Then Mordecai[v] prayed to the Lord, calling to remembrance all the works of the Lord.

9 He said, "O Lord, Lord, you rule as King over all things, for the universe is in your power and there is no one who can oppose you when it is your will to save Israel, 10 for you have made heaven and earth and every wonderful thing under heaven. 11 You are Lord of all, and there is no one who can resist you, the Lord. 12 You know all things; you know, O Lord, that it was not in insolence or pride or for any love of glory that I did this, and refused to bow down to this proud Haman; 13 for I would have been willing to kiss the soles of his feet to save Israel! 14 But I did this so that I might not set human glory above the glory of God, and I will not bow down to anyone but you, who are my Lord; and I will not do these things in pride. 15 And now, O Lord God and King, God of Abraham, spare your people; for the eyes of our foes are upon us[w] to annihilate us, and they desire to destroy the inheritance that has been yours from the beginning. 16 Do not neglect your portion, which you redeemed for yourself out of the land of Egypt. 17 Hear my prayer, and have mercy upon your inheritance; turn our mourning into feasting that we may live and sing praise to your name, O Lord; do not destroy the lips[x] of those who praise you."

18 And all Israel cried out mightily, for their death was before their eyes.

13 8 CALLING to mind all that the Lord had done, Mardochaeus uttered this prayer. 9 'O Lord, Lord and King, Ruler over all, for the whole creation is under your authority, and when it is your will to save Israel there is none who can oppose you: 10 you made heaven and earth and every wonderful thing under heaven; 11 you are Lord of all, and there is none who can resist you, the Lord. 12 You know all things; you know, Lord, that it was not from insolence or arrogance or vainglory that I refused to bow before this proud Haman, 13 for to save Israel I would gladly have kissed the soles of his feet! 14 But I acted in this way so as not to hold a man in greater honour than God; I shall not bow before any but you, my Lord, and it is not from arrogance that I refuse this homage. 15 Now, O Lord, God and King, God of Abraham, spare your people, for our enemies are bent on bringing us to ruin, and they have set their hearts upon the destruction of your chosen people, yours from the beginning. 16 Do not disregard your own possession which you ransomed and brought out of Egypt for yourself. 17 Hear my prayer, and have mercy on your heritage; turn our mourning into feasting, that we may live to sing of your name, O Lord. Do not put to silence the lips that give you praise.' 18 The Israelites cried aloud with all their might, for death stared them in the face.

---

u Chapters 13.8 — 15.16 correspond to chapters C 1-30 and D 1-16 in some translations. v Gk he w Gk for they are eying us x Gk mouth

9 Hathach returned to Esther and told her what Mordecai had said. 10 Then Esther replied to Hathach and gave him this message for Mordecai: 11 "All the servants of the king and the people of his provinces know that any man or woman who goes to the king in the inner court without being summoned, suffers the automatic penalty of death, unless the king extends to him the golden scepter, thus sparing his life. Now as for me, I have not been summoned to the king for thirty days."

12 When Esther's words were reported to Mordecai, 13 he had this reply brought to her: "Do not imagine that because you are in the king's palace, you alone of all the Jews will escape. 14 Even if you now remain silent, relief and deliverance will come to the Jews from another source; but you and your father's house will perish. Who knows but that it was for a time like this that you obtained the royal dignity?"

15 Esther sent back to Mordecai the response: 16 "Go and assemble all the Jews who are in Susa; fast on my behalf, all of you, not eating or drinking, night or day, for three days. I and my maids will also fast in the same way. Thus prepared, I will go to the king, contrary to the law. If I perish, I perish!"

C Mordecai went away and did exactly as Esther had commanded. 1 Recalling all that the Lord had done, he prayed to him 2 and said: "O Lord God, almighty King, all things are in your power, and there is no one to oppose you in your will to save Israel. 3 You made heaven and earth and every wonderful thing under the heavens. 4 You are Lord of all, and there is no one who can resist you, Lord. 5 You know all things. You know, O Lord, that it was not out of insolence or pride or desire for fame that I acted thus in not bowing down to the proud Haman. 6 Gladly would I have kissed the soles of his feet for the salvation of Israel. 7 But I acted as I did so as not to place the honor of man above that of God. I will not bow down to anyone but you, my Lord. It is not out of pride that I am acting thus. 8 And now, Lord God, King, God of Abraham, spare your people, for our enemies plan our ruin and are bent upon destroying the inheritance that was yours from the beginning. 9 Do not spurn your portion, which you redeemed for yourself out of Egypt. 10 Hear my prayer; have pity on your inheritance and turn our sorrow into joy: thus we shall live to sing praise to your name, O Lord. Do not silence those who praise you."

11 All Israel, too, cried out with all their strength, for death was staring them in the face.

9 Hathach came back and told Esther what Mordecai had said; 10 and she replied with the following message for Mordecai, 11 'Royal officials and people living in the provinces alike all know that for anyone, man or woman, who approaches the king in the private apartments without having been summoned there, there is only one law: he must die, unless the king, by pointing his golden sceptre towards him, grants him his life. And I have not been summoned to the king for the last thirty days.'

12 These words of Esther were reported to Mordecai, 13 who sent back the following reply, 'Do not suppose that, because you are in the king's palace, you are going to be the one Jew to escape. 14 No; if you persist in remaining silent at such a time, relief and deliverance will come to the Jews from another quarter, but both you and your father's whole family will perish. Who knows? Perhaps you have come to the throne for just such a time as this.'

15 Whereupon Esther sent this reply to Mordecai, 16 'Go and assemble all the Jews now in Susa and fast for me. Do not eat or drink day or night for three days. For my part, I and my waiting-women shall keep the same fast, after which I shall go to the king in spite of the law; and if I perish, I perish.' 17 Mordecai went away and carried out Esther's instructions.

17a *Then calling to mind all the wonderful works of the Lord, he offered this prayer:*

17b *Lord, Lord, Almighty King,*
everything is subject to your power,
and there is no one who can withstand you
in your determination to save Israel.

17c *You have made heaven and earth,*
and all the marvels that are under heaven.
You are the Master of the universe
and no one can resist you, Lord.

17d *You know all things,*
you, Lord, know
that neither pride, self-esteem nor vainglory
prompted me to do what I have done:
to refuse to prostrate myself
before proud Haman.
Gladly would I have kissed the soles of his feet,
had this assured the safety of Israel.

17e *But what I have done, I have done,*
rather than place the glory of a man
above the glory of God;
and I shall not prostrate myself to anyone
except, Lord, to you,
and, in so doing, I shall not be acting in pride.

17f *And now, Lord God,*
King, God of Abraham
spare your people!
For our ruin is being plotted,
there are plans to destroy your ancient heritage.
17g *Do not overlook your inheritance,*
which you redeemed from Egypt to be yours.
17h *Hear my supplication,*
have mercy on your heritage,
and turn our grief into rejoicing,
so that we may live, Lord, to hymn your name.
Do not suffer the mouths
of those who praise you to perish.

17i *And all Israel cried out with all their might, since death was staring them in the face.*

NEW REVISED STANDARD VERSION

14 Then Queen Esther, seized with deadly anxiety, fled to the Lord. 2 She took off her splendid apparel and put on the garments of distress and mourning, and instead of costly perfumes she covered her head with ashes and dung, and she utterly humbled her body; every part that she loved to adorn she covered with her tangled hair. 3 She prayed to the Lord God of Israel, and said: "O my Lord, you only are our king; help me, who am alone and have no helper but you, 4 for my danger is in my hand. 5 Ever since I was born I have heard in the tribe of my family that you, O Lord, took Israel out of all the nations, and our ancestors from among all their forebears, for an everlasting inheritance, and that you did for them all that you promised. 6 And now we have sinned before you, and you have handed us over to our enemies 7 because we glorified their gods. You are righteous, O Lord! 8 And now they are not satisfied that we are in bitter slavery, but they have covenanted with their idols 9 to abolish what your mouth has ordained, and to destroy your inheritance, to stop the mouths of those who praise you and to quench your altar and the glory of your house, 10 to open the mouths of the nations for the praise of vain idols, and to magnify forever a mortal king.

11 "O Lord, do not surrender your scepter to what has no being; and do not let them laugh at our downfall; but turn their plan against them, and make an example of him who began this against us. 12 Remember, O Lord; make yourself known in this time of our affliction, and give me courage, O King of the gods and Master of all dominion! 13 Put eloquent speech in my mouth before the lion, and turn his heart to hate the man who is fighting against us, so that there may be an end of him and those who agree with him. 14 But save us by your hand, and help me, who am alone and have no helper but you, O Lord. 15 You have knowledge of all things, and you know that I hate the splendor of the wicked and abhor the bed of the uncircumcised and of any alien. 16 You know my necessity—that I abhor the sign of my proud position, which is upon my head on days when I appear in public. I abhor it like a filthy rag, and I do not wear it on the days when I am at leisure. 17 And your servant

REVISED ENGLISH BIBLE

14 QUEEN Esther, in the grip of mortal anxiety, sought refuge in the Lord. 2 She took off her royal robes and put on the garb of distress and mourning. Instead of rich perfumes she strewed ashes and dirt over her head; she abased her body, and every part that she had delighted to adorn she covered with her dishevelled hair. 3 Then she prayed to the Lord God of Israel.

'O my Lord, you alone are our King; come to my help who am alone and have no other helper but you, 4 for I am taking my life in my hands. 5 From my earliest days I have been taught by my father's family and tribe that you, Lord, chose Israel out of all the nations, and from all who went before them you chose our fathers as an everlasting possession, and you have performed for them whatever you promised. 6 But now we have sinned against you, and you have handed us over to our enemies 7 because we paid honour to their gods. O Lord, you are just. 8 Yet even now our enemies are not content that we are in bitter servitude; they have taken a vow 9 to annul the decree you have proclaimed and to destroy Israel, your possession, silencing those who praise you, extinguishing the glory of your house and the flame on your altar. 10 They would give the heathen cause to sing the praises of their worthless gods, and would have a mortal king held in everlasting honour.

11 'Do not yield your sceptre, Lord, to gods that have no real existence; let not our enemies mock at our ruin, but turn their plot against them, and make an example of the man who planned it. 12 Be mindful of us, Lord; reveal yourself in the time of our distress, and give me courage, O King of gods, Sovereign over every power. 13 Put the right words into my mouth when I enter this lion's den, and divert his hatred to him who is our enemy, so that there may be an end of him and his associates.

14 'By your power save us, and help me who am alone and have no one but you, Lord. 15 You know all things; you know that I hate the splendour of the heathen; I abhor the bed of the uncircumcised or of any Gentile. 16 You know in what straits I am: I loathe that symbol of pride, the headdress that I wear when I show myself in public, I loathe it as one loathes a filthy rag and in private never wear it. 17 I,

14:1 in . . . anxiety: *or* caught up in this deadly struggle.

12 Queen Esther, seized with mortal anguish, likewise had recourse to the LORD. 13 Taking off her splendid garments, she put on garments of distress and mourning. In place of her precious ointments she covered her head with dirt and ashes. She afflicted her body severely; all her festive adornments were put aside, and her hair was wholly disheveled.

14 Then she prayed to the LORD, the God of Israel, saying: "My LORD, our King, you alone are God. Help me, who am alone and have no help but you, 15 for I am taking my life in my hand. 16 As a child I was wont to hear from the people of the land of my forefathers that you, O LORD, chose Israel from among all peoples, and our fathers from among all their ancestors, as a lasting heritage, and that you fulfilled all your promises to them. 17 But now we have sinned in your sight, and you have delivered us into the hands of our enemies, 18 because we worshiped their gods. You are just, O LORD. 19 But now they are not satisfied with our bitter servitude, but have undertaken 20 to do away with the decree you have pronounced, and to destroy your heritage; to close the mouths of those who praise you, and to extinguish the glory of your temple and your altar; 21 to open the mouths of the heathen to acclaim their false gods, and to extol an earthly king forever.

22 "O LORD, do not relinquish your scepter to those that are nought. Let them not gloat over our ruin, but turn their own counsel against them and make an example of our chief enemy. 23 Be mindful of us, O LORD. Manifest yourself in the time of our distress and give me courage, King of gods and Ruler of every power. 24 Put in my mouth persuasive words in the presence of the lion and turn his heart to hatred for our enemy, so that he and those who are in league with him may perish. 25 Save us by your power, and help me, who am alone and have no one but you, O LORD.

"You know all things. 26 You know that I hate the glory of the pagans, and abhor the bed of the uncircumcised or of any foreigner. 27 You know that I am under constraint, that I abhor the sign of grandeur which rests on my head when I appear in public; abhor it like a polluted rag, and do not

17k *Queen Esther also took refuge with the Lord in the mortal peril which had overtaken her. She took off her sumptuous robes and put on sorrowful mourning. Instead of expensive perfumes, she covered her head with ashes and dung. She mortified her body severely, and the former scenes of her happiness and elegance were now littered with tresses torn from her hair. She besought the Lord God of Israel in these words:*

17l *My Lord, our King, the Only One,*
   come to my help, for I am alone
   and have no helper but you
   and am about to take my life in my hands.

17m *I have been taught from infancy*
   in the bosom of my family
   that you, Lord, have chosen
   Israel out of all the nations
   and our ancestors out of all before them,
   to be your heritage for ever;
   and that you have treated them as you promised.

17n *But we have sinned against you*
   and you have handed us over to our enemies
   for paying honour to their gods.
   Lord, you are upright.

17o *But they are not satisfied*
   with the bitterness of our slavery:
   they have pledged themselves to their idols
   to abolish the decree that your own lips have
      uttered,
   to blot out your heritage,
   to stop the mouths of those who praise you,
   to quench your altar and the glory of your House,

17p *and instead to open the mouths of the heathen,*
   to sing the praise of worthless idols
   and for ever to idolise a king of flesh.

17q *Do not yield your sceptre, Lord,*
   to what does not exist.
   Never let our ruin be matter for laughter.
   Turn these plots against their authors,
   and make an example
   of the man who leads the attack on us.

17r *Remember, Lord; reveal yourself*
   in the time of our distress.

   As for me, give me courage,
   King of gods and Master of all powers!

17s *Put persuasive words into my mouth*
   when I face the lion;
   change his feeling into hatred for our enemy,
   so that he may meet his end,
   and all those like him!

17t *As for ourselves, save us by your hand,*
   and come to my help, for I am alone
   and have no one but you, Lord.

17u *You have knowledge of all things,*
   and you know that I hate honours from the
      godless,
   that I loathe the bed of the uncircumcised,
   of any foreigner whatever.

17w *You know I am under constraint,*
   that I loathe the symbol of my high position
   bound round my brow when I appear at court;
   I loathe it as if it were a filthy rag
   and do not wear it on my days of leisure.

has not eaten at Haman's table, and I have not honored the king's feast or drunk the wine of libations. 18 Your servant has had no joy since the day that I was brought here until now, except in you, O Lord God of Abraham. 19 O God, whose might is over all, hear the voice of the despairing, and save us from the hands of evildoers. And save me from my fear!"

END OF ADDITION C

ADDITION D

15 On the third day, when she ended her prayer, she took off the garments in which she had worshiped, and arrayed herself in splendid attire. 2 Then, majestically adorned, after invoking the aid of the all-seeing God and Savior, she took two maids with her; 3 on one she leaned gently for support, 4 while the other followed, carrying her train. 5 She was radiant with perfect beauty, and she looked happy, as if beloved, but her heart was frozen with fear. 6 When she had gone through all the doors, she stood before the king. He was seated on his royal throne, clothed in the full array of his majesty, all covered with gold and precious stones. He was most terrifying.

7 Lifting his face, flushed with splendor, he looked at her in fierce anger. The queen faltered, and turned pale and faint, and collapsed on the head of the maid who went in front of her. 8 Then God changed the spirit of the king to gentleness, and in alarm he sprang from his throne and took her in his arms until she came to herself. He comforted her with soothing words, and said to her, 9 "What is it, Esther? I am your husband.y Take courage; 10 You shall not die, for our law applies only to our subjects.z Come near."

11 Then he raised the golden scepter and touched her neck with it; 12 he embraced her, and said, "Speak to me." 13 She said to him, "I saw you, my lord, like an angel of God, and my heart was shaken with fear at your glory. 14 For you are wonderful, my lord, and your countenance is full of grace." 15 And while she was speaking, she fainted and fell. 16 Then the king was agitated, and all his servants tried to comfort her.

END OF ADDITION D

5 a 3 The king said to her, "What do you wish, Esther? What is your request? It shall be given you, even to half of my kingdom." 4 And Esther said, "Today is a special day for me. If it pleases the king, let him and Haman come to the dinner that I shall prepare today." 5 Then the king said, "Bring Haman quickly, so that we may do as Esther desires." So they both came to the dinner that Esther had spoken about. 6 While they were drinking wine, the king

your servant, have not eaten at Haman's table, nor have I graced a banquet of the king nor touched the wine of his drink-offerings. 18 From the day of my preferment until now I have known no joy except in you, Lord God of Abraham. 19 O God, the all-prevailing, give heed to the cry of those driven to despair: deliver us from the power of the wicked, and rescue me from what I dread.'

15 On the third day, after ending her prayers, Esther put off the clothes she had worn while she worshipped, and arrayed herself in her robes of state. 2 When she was attired in all her splendour and had invoked the all-seeing God, her preserver, she took her two maids with her; 3 on one she leaned for support, as befitted a fine lady, 4 while the other followed, bearing her train. 5 She was radiant and in the height of her beauty; her face was as cheerful as it was lovely, but her heart was constricted with fear. 6 She passed through all the doors until she stood in the royal presence. The king was seated on his throne in the full array of his majesty, all gold and precious stones, an awe-inspiring figure. 7 He looked up, his face aglow with regal dignity, and regarded her with towering anger. The queen sank down, changing colour and fainting, and she swooned on the shoulder of the maid who went before her.

8 But the king's mood was changed by God to one of gentleness. In deep concern he started up from his throne and held her in his arms until she came to herself. He soothed her with reassuring words: 9 'Esther, what is it? Have no fear of me, your loving husband; 10 you shall not die, for our order is only for our subjects. You may approach.' 11 The king raised his gold sceptre and touched her neck; 12 then he kissed her and said, 'You may speak to me.' 13 She answered, 'My lord, I saw you like an angel of God; I was awestruck at your glorious appearance. 14 Your countenance is so full of grace, my lord, that I look in wonder.' 15 But while she was speaking she sank down fainting; 16 the king was distressed, and his attendants all tried to reassure her.

5 3 [THE king said, 'What is your wish, Esther? Whatever you request, up to half my kingdom, shall be given you.' 4 'This is a festive day for me,' she answered; 'if it please your majesty, will you come, and Haman with you, to a banquet I am preparing today?' 5 The king gave orders for Haman to be brought with all speed to meet Esther's wishes; and they both went to the banquet to which she had invited them. 6 Over the wine the king said to her,

---

y Gk brother   z Meaning of Gk uncertain   a In Greek, Chapter D replaces verses 1 and 2 in Hebrew.

wear it in private. 28 I, your handmaid, have never eaten at the table of Haman, nor have I graced the banquet of the king or drunk the wine of libations. 29 From the day I was brought here till now, your handmaid has had no joy except in you, O LORD, God of Abraham. 30 O God, more powerful than all, hear the voice of those in despair. Save us from the power of the wicked, and deliver me from my fear."

D On the third day, putting an end to her prayers, she took off her penitential garments and arrayed herself in her royal attire. 2 In making her state appearance, after invoking the all-seeing God and savior, she took with her two maids; 3 on the one she leaned gently for support, 4 while the other followed her, bearing her train. 5 She glowed with the perfection of her beauty and her countenance was as joyous as it was lovely, though her heart was shrunk with fear. 6 She passed through all the portals till she stood face to face with the king, who was seated on his royal throne, clothed in full robes of state, and covered with gold and precious stones, so that he inspired great awe. 7 As he looked up, his features ablaze with the height of majestic anger, the queen staggered, changed color, and leaned weakly against the head of the maid in front of her. 8 But God changed the king's anger to gentleness. In great anxiety he sprang from his throne, held her in his arms until she recovered, and comforted her with reassuring words. 9 "What is it, Esther?" he said to her. "I am your brother. Take courage! 10 You shall not die because of this general decree of ours. 11 Come near!" 12 Raising the golden scepter, he touched her neck with it, embraced her, and said, "Speak to me."

13 She replied: "I saw you, my lord, as an angel of God, and my heart was troubled with fear of your majesty. 14 For you are awesome, my lord, though your glance is full of kindness." 15 As she said this, she fainted. 16 The king became troubled and all his attendants tried to revive her.

5 [Now on the third day, Esther put on her royal garments and stood in the inner courtyard, looking toward the royal palace, while the king was seated on his royal throne in the audience chamber, facing the palace doorway. 2 He saw Queen Esther standing in the courtyard, and made her welcome by extending toward her the golden staff which he held. She came up to him, and touched the top of the staff.]

3 Then the king said to her, "What is it, Queen Esther? What is your request? Even if it is half of my kingdom, it shall be granted you." 4 "If it please your majesty," Esther replied, "come today with Haman to a banquet I have prepared." 5 And the king ordered, "Have Haman make haste to fulfill the wish of Esther."

So the king went with Haman to the banquet Esther had prepared. 6 During the drinking of the wine, the king said to

17x *Your servant has not eaten at Haman's table,*
nor taken pleasure in the royal banquets,
nor drunk the wine of libations.
17y *Nor has your servant found pleasure*
from the day of her promotion until now
except in you, Lord, God of Abraham.
17z *O God, whose strength prevails over all,*
listen to the voice of the desperate,
save us from the hand of the wicked,
and free me from my fear!

5 1a *On the third day, when she had finished praying, she took off her suppliant's mourning attire and dressed herself in her full splendour. Radiant as she then appeared, she invoked God who watches over all people and saves them. With her, she took two ladies-in-waiting. With a delicate air she leaned on one, while the other accompanied her carrying her train.* 1b *Rosy with the full flush of her beauty, her face radiated joy and love: but her heart shrank with fear.* 1c *Having passed through door after door, she found herself in the presence of the king. He was sitting on his royal throne, dressed in all his robes of state, glittering with gold and precious stones — a formidable sight.* 1d *He looked up, afire with majesty and, blazing with anger, saw her. The queen sank to the floor. As she fainted, the colour drained from her face and her head fell against the lady-in-waiting beside her.* 1e *But God changed the king's heart, inducing a milder spirit. He sprang from his throne in alarm and took her in his arms until she recovered, comforting her with soothing words.* 1f *'What is the matter, Esther?' he said. 'I am your brother. Take heart, you are not going to die; our order applies only to ordinary people. Come to me.'* 2 *And raising his golden sceptre he laid it on Esther's neck, embraced her and said, 'Speak to me.'* 2a *'Sire,' she said, 'to me you looked like one of God's angels, and my heart was moved with fear of your majesty. For you are a figure of wonder, my lord, and your face is full of graciousness.'* 2b *But as she spoke she fell down in a faint. The king grew more agitated, and his courtiers all set about reviving her.*

3 'What is the matter, Queen Esther?' the king said. 'Tell me what you want; even if it is half my kingdom, I grant it you.' 4 'Would it please the king,' Esther replied, 'to come with Haman today to the banquet I have prepared for him?' 5 The king said, 'Tell Haman to come at once, so that Esther may have her wish.'

6 So the king and Haman came to the banquet that Esther had prepared and, during the banquet, the king again said to

---

5, 1f: The Hebrew text here translated is a short form of the account already given in Greek.

said to Esther, "What is it, Queen Esther? It shall be granted you." 7 She said, "My petition and request is: 8 if I have found favor in the sight of the king, let the king and Haman come to the dinner that I shall prepare them, and tomorrow I will do as I have done today."

9 So Haman went out from the king joyful and glad of heart. But when he saw Mordecai the Jew in the courtyard, he was filled with anger. 10 Nevertheless, he went home and summoned his friends and his wife Zosara. 11 And he told them about his riches and the honor that the king had bestowed on him, and how he had advanced him to be the first in the kingdom. 12 And Haman said, "The queen did not invite anyone to the dinner with the king except me; and I am invited again tomorrow. 13 But these things give me no pleasure as long as I see Mordecai the Jew in the courtyard." 14 His wife Zosara and his friends said to him, "Let a gallows be made, fifty cubits high, and in the morning tell the king to have Mordecai hanged on it. Then, go merrily with the king to the dinner." This advice pleased Haman, and so the gallows was prepared.

6 That night the Lord took sleep from the king, so he gave orders to his secretary to bring the book of daily records, and to read to him. 2 He found the words written about Mordecai, how he had told the king about the two royal eunuchs who were on guard and sought to lay hands on King Artaxerxes. 3 The king said, "What honor or dignity did we bestow on Mordecai?" The king's servants said, "You have not done anything for him." 4 While the king was inquiring about the goodwill shown by Mordecai, Haman was in the courtyard. The king asked, "Who is in the courtyard?" Now Haman had come to speak to the king about hanging Mordecai on the gallows that he had prepared. 5 The servants of the king answered, "Haman is standing in the courtyard." And the king said, "Summon him." 6 Then the king said to Haman, "What shall I do for the person whom I wish to honor?" And Haman said to himself, "Whom would the king wish to honor more than me?" 7 So he said to the king, "For a person whom the king wishes to honor, 8 let the king's servants bring out the fine linen robe that the king has worn, and the horse on which the king rides, 9 and let both be given to one of the king's honored Friends, and let him robe the person whom the king loves and mount him on the horse, and let it be proclaimed through the open square of the city, saying, 'Thus shall it be done to everyone whom the king honors.' " 10 Then the king said to Haman, "You have made an excellent suggestion! Do just as you have said for Mordecai the Jew, who is on duty in the courtyard. And let nothing be omitted from what you have proposed." 11 So Haman got the robe and the horse; he put the robe on Mordecai and made him ride through the open square of the city, proclaiming, "Thus shall it be done to everyone whom the king wishes to honor." 12 Then Mordecai returned to the courtyard, and Haman hurried back to his house, mourning and with his head covered. 13 Haman told his wife Zosara and his friends what had befallen him. His friends and his wife said to him, "If Mordecai is of the Jewish people, and you have begun to be humiliated before him, you will surely fall. You will not be able to defend yourself, because the living God is with him."

'What is it, Queen Esther? Whatever you request shall be yours.' 7 She said, 'This is my petition and request: 8 if I have found favour with your majesty, will your majesty and Haman come again tomorrow to the banquet that I shall prepare for you both? Tomorrow I shall do as I have done today.'

9 Although Haman left the royal presence overjoyed and in the best of spirits, as soon as he saw Mardochaeus the Jew in the king's court he was furious. 10 When he arrived home, he sent for his friends and for Zosara, his wife, 11 and held forth to them about his wealth and the honours with which the king had invested him, and how he had advanced him to the chief position in the kingdom. 12 'The queen', Haman went on, 'had no one but myself come with the king to her banquet; and I am invited tomorrow. 13 Yet all this gives me no satisfaction so long as I see that Jew Mardochaeus at court.' 14 His wife Zosara and his friends said to him: 'Have a gallows set up, seventy-five feet high, and in the morning propose to the king that Mardochaeus be hanged on it. Then you can go with the king to the banquet and enjoy yourself.' This advice seemed good to Haman, and the gallows was made ready.

6 THAT night the Lord prevented the king from sleeping, so he ordered his secretary to bring the court chronicle and read it to him. 2 In it he found recorded an entry concerning Mardochaeus, how he had furnished information for the king about the two royal eunuchs on guard who had plotted to assassinate Artaxerxes. 3 When the king asked, 'What honour or favour did we confer on Mardochaeus?' his attendants said, 'You have not done anything for him.' 4 While the king was enquiring about Mardochaeus's service to him, Haman appeared in the courtyard. 'Who is in court?' said the king. As Haman had just then entered to propose to the king that Mardochaeus should be hanged on the gallows he had prepared, 5 the king's servants replied, 'Haman is standing there in the court.' 'Let him enter!' commanded the king. 6 Then he asked him, 'What shall I do for the man I wish to honour?' Haman thought, 'Whom other than myself would the king wish to honour?' 7 So he answered, 'For the man whom the king wishes to honour? 8 Let the king's attendants bring a robe of fine linen which the king himself has worn, and a horse on which the king rides. 9 Let both be handed over to one of the king's most noble Friends, and let him invest the man whom the king loves and mount him on the horse, and let him proclaim through the city square: "This shall be done for any man whom the king honours." ' 10 The king said to Haman, 'Well spoken! Do this for Mardochaeus the Jew who serves in the courtyard. Let nothing be omitted of what you have proposed.' 11 Haman took the robe and the horse; he invested Mardochaeus, mounted him on horseback, and went through the city square proclaiming: 'See what is done for any man whom the king wishes to honour.'

12 Mardochaeus then returned to the courtyard, while Haman hurried off home in grief with his head veiled. 13 When he told his wife Zosara and his friends what had happened to him, the response he got was: 'If you have begun to be humiliated before Mardochaeus, and he is a Jew, your downfall is certain; you cannot get the better of him, because the living God is on his side.'

[5:14] **seventy-five feet:** lit. fifty cubits.

NEW AMERICAN BIBLE

Esther, "Whatever you ask for shall be granted, and whatever request you make shall be honored, even if it is for half my kingdom." 7 Esther replied: "This is my petition and request: 8 if I have found favor with the king and if it pleases your majesty to grant my petition and honor my request, come with Haman tomorrow to a banquet which I shall prepare for you; and then I will do as you ask."

9 That day Haman left happy and in good spirits. But when he saw that Mordecai at the royal gate did not rise, and showed no fear of him, he was filled with anger toward him. 10 Haman restrained himself, however, and went home, where he summoned his friends and his wife Zeresh. 11 He recounted the greatness of his riches, the large number of his sons, and just how the king had promoted him and placed him above the officials and royal servants. 12 "Moreover," Haman added, "Queen Esther invited no one but me to the banquet with the king; again tomorrow I am to be her guest, with the king. 13 Yet none of this satisfies me as long as I continue to see the Jew Mordecai sitting at the royal gate." 14 His wife Zeresh and all his friends said to him, "Have a gibbet set up, fifty cubits in height, and in the morning ask the king to have Mordecai hanged on it. Then go to the banquet with the king in good cheer." This suggestion pleased Haman, and he had the gibbet erected.

6 That night the king, unable to sleep, asked that the chronicle of notable events be brought in. While this was being read to him, 2 the passage occurred in which Mordecai reported Bagathan and Teresh, two of the royal eunuchs who guarded the entrance, for seeking to lay hands on King Ahasuerus. 3 The king asked, "What was done to reward and honor Mordecai for this?" The king's attendants replied, "Nothing was done for him."

4 "Who is in the court?" the king asked. Now Haman had entered the outer court of the king's palace to suggest to the king that Mordecai should be hanged on the gibbet he had raised for him. 5 The king's servants answered him, "Haman is waiting in the court." "Let him come in," the king said. 6 When Haman entered, the king said to him, "What should be done for the man whom the king wishes to reward?" Now Haman thought to himself, "Whom would the king more probably wish to reward than me?" 7 So he replied to the king: "For the man whom the king wishes to reward 8 there should be brought the royal robe which the king wore and the horse on which the king rode when the royal crown was placed on his head. 9 The robe and the horse should be consigned to one of the noblest of the king's officials, who must clothe the man the king wishes to reward, have him ride on the horse in the public square of the city, and cry out before him, 'This is what is done for the man whom the king wishes to reward.' " 10 Then the king said to Haman: "Hurry! Take the robe and horse as you have proposed, and do this for the Jew Mordecai, who is sitting at the royal gate. Do not omit anything you proposed." 11 So Haman took the robe and horse, clothed Mordecai, had him ride in the public square of the city, and cried out before him, "This is what is done for the man whom the king wishes to reward."

12 Mordecai then returned to the royal gate, while Haman hurried home, his head covered in grief. 13 When he told his wife Zeresh and all his friends everything that had happened to him, his advisers and his wife Zeresh said to him, "If Mordecai, before whom you are beginning to decline, is of the Jewish race, you will not prevail against him, but will surely be defeated by him."

NEW JERUSALEM BIBLE

Esther, 'Tell me your request; I grant it to you. Tell me what you want; even if it is half my kingdom, it is yours for the asking.' 7 'What do I want, what is my request?' Esther replied. 8 'If I have found favour in the king's eyes, and if it is his pleasure to grant what I ask and to agree to my request, let the king and Haman come to the banquet I intend to give them tomorrow, and then I shall do as the king says.'

9 Haman left full of joy and high spirits that day; but when he saw Mordecai at the Chancellery, neither standing up nor stirring at his approach, he felt a gust of anger. 10 He restrained himself, however. Returning home, he sent for his friends and Zeresh his wife 11 and held forth to them about his dazzling wealth, his many children, how the king had raised him to a position of honour and promoted him over the heads of the king's officers-of-state and ministers. 12 'What is more,' he added, 'Queen Esther has just invited me and the king — no one else except me — to a banquet she was giving, and better still she has invited me and the king again tomorrow. 13 But what do I care about all this when all the while I see Mordecai the Jew sitting there at the Chancellery?' 14 'Have a fifty-cubit gallows run up,' said Zeresh his wife and all his friends, 'and in the morning ask the king to have Mordecai hanged on it. Then you can go with the king to the banquet, without a care in the world!' Delighted with this advice, Haman had the gallows erected.

6 That night the king could not sleep; he called for the Record Book, or Annals, to be brought and read to him. 2 They contained an account of how Mordecai had denounced Bigthan and Teresh, two of the king's eunuchs serving as Guards of the Threshold, who had plotted to assassinate King Ahasuerus. 3 'And what honour and dignity', the king asked, 'was conferred on Mordecai for this?' 'Nothing has been done for him,' the gentlemen-in-waiting replied. 4 The king then said, 'Who is outside in the antechamber?' Haman had, that very moment, entered the outer antechamber of the private apartments, to ask the king to have Mordecai hanged on the gallows which he had just put up for the purpose. 5 So the king's gentlemen-in-waiting replied, 'It is Haman out in the antechamber.' 'Bring him in,' the king said, 6 and, as soon as Haman came in, went on to ask, 'What is the right way to treat a man whom the king wishes to honour?' 'Whom', thought Haman, 'would the king wish to honour, if not me?' 7 So he replied, 'If the king wishes to honour someone, 8 royal robes should be brought from the king's wardrobe, and a horse from the king's stable, sporting a royal diadem on its head. 9 The robes and horse should be entrusted to one of the noblest of the king's officers-of-state, who should then array the man whom the king wishes to honour and lead him on horseback through the city square, proclaiming before him: "This is the way a man shall be treated whom the king wishes to honour." ' 10 'Hurry,' the king said to Haman, 'take the robes and the horse, and do everything you have just said to Mordecai the Jew, who works at the Chancellery. On no account leave out anything that you have mentioned.'

11 So taking the robes and the horse, Haman arrayed Mordecai and led him on horseback through the city square, proclaiming before him: 'This is the way a man shall be treated whom the king wishes to honour.' 12 After this Mordecai returned to the Chancellery, while Haman went hurrying home in dejection and covering his face. 13 He told his wife Zeresh and all his friends what had just happened. His wife Zeresh and his friends said, 'You are beginning to fall, and Mordecai to rise; if he is Jewish, you will never get the better of him. With him against you, your fall is certain.'

14 While they were still talking, the eunuchs arrived and hurriedly brought Haman to the banquet that Esther had prepared. 7 1 So the king and Haman went in to drink with the queen. 2 And the second day, as they were drinking wine, the king said, "What is it, Queen Esther? What is your petition and what is your request? It shall be granted to you, even to half of my kingdom." 3 She answered and said, "If I have found favor with the king, let my life be granted me at my petition, and my people at my request. 4 For we have been sold, I and my people, to be destroyed, plundered, and made slaves—we and our children—male and female slaves. This has come to my knowledge. Our antagonist brings shame on*b* the king's court." 5 Then the king said, "Who is the person that would dare to do this thing?" 6 Esther said, "Our enemy is this evil man Haman!" At this, Haman was terrified in the presence of the king and queen.

7 The king rose from the banquet and went into the garden, and Haman began to beg for his life from the queen, for he saw that he was in serious trouble. 8 When the king returned from the garden, Haman had thrown himself on the couch, pleading with the queen. The king said, "Will he dare even assault my wife in my own house?" Haman, when he heard, turned away his face. 9 Then Bugathan, one of the eunuchs, said to the king, "Look, Haman has even prepared a gallows for Mordecai, who gave information of concern to the king; it is standing at Haman's house, a gallows fifty cubits high." So the king said, "Let Haman be hanged on that." 10 So Haman was hanged on the gallows that he had prepared for Mordecai. With that the anger of the king abated.

8 On that very day King Artaxerxes granted to Esther all the property of the persecutor*c* Haman. Mordecai was summoned by the king, for Esther had told the king*d* that he was related to her. 2 The king took the ring that had been taken from Haman, and gave it to Mordecai; and Esther set Mordecai over everything that had been Haman's.

3 Then she spoke once again to the king and, falling at his feet, she asked him to avert all the evil that Haman had planned against the Jews. 4 The king extended his golden scepter to Esther, and she rose and stood before the king. 5 Esther said, "If it pleases you, and if I have found favor, let an order be sent rescinding the letters that Haman wrote and sent to destroy the Jews in your kingdom. 6 How can I look on the ruin of my people? How can I be safe if my ancestral nation*e* is destroyed?" 7 The king said to Esther, "Now that I*f* have granted all of Haman's property to you and have hanged him on a tree because he acted against the Jews, what else do you request? 8 Write in my name what you think best and seal it with my ring; for whatever is written at the king's command and sealed with my ring cannot be contravened."

14 While they were still talking, the eunuchs arrived and Haman was hurried off to the banquet Esther had prepared. 7 So the king and Haman went to the queen's banquet, 2 and on that second day, over the wine, the king said, 'What is it, Queen Esther? What is your petition? What is your request? You shall have it, up to half my kingdom.' 3 She answered: 'If I have found favour with your majesty, my petition and request is that my own life and the lives of my people be spared. 4 For we have been sold, I and my people, to be destroyed, plundered, and enslaved, we and our children, male and female—or so I have heard. Our adversary brings discredit on the king's court.' 5 The king demanded, 'Who is he that has dared to do such a thing?' 6 She answered, 'An enemy, this wicked Haman!' Haman stood dumbfounded before the king and queen. 7 The king rose from the banquet and went into the garden, while Haman began to plead with the queen, for he saw that things looked very black for him. 8 When the king returned from the garden, Haman in his entreaties had flung himself across the queen's couch. The king exclaimed, 'What! You even assault the queen in my own palace?' At those words Haman turned away in despair. 9 Bugathan, one of the eunuchs, said to the king, 'There is actually a gallows seventy-five feet high, standing in Haman's grounds; he prepared it for Mardochaeus, the man who reported the plot against your majesty.' 'Let Haman be hanged on it!' said the king. 10 Haman was hanged on the gallows that had been prepared for Mardochaeus, and the king's anger subsided.

8 The same day King Artaxerxes gave Esther all that had belonged to Haman, the adversary of the Jews, and Mardochaeus was summoned to the king's presence, for Esther had revealed his relationship to her. 2 The king took off his signet ring, which he had taken back from Haman, and gave it to Mardochaeus. Esther put Mardochaeus in charge of all Haman's property.

3 Once again Esther addressed the king, falling at his feet and imploring him to thwart the wickedness of Haman and all he had devised against the Jews. 4 The king extended his gold sceptre to her, and she rose and stood before the king. 5 'If it pleases you,' she said, 'and if I have found favour, let a writ be issued to recall the dispatches sent by Haman in pursuance of his plan to destroy the Jews in your kingdom. 6 For how can I bear to witness the ill-treatment of my people? How can I bear to survive the destruction of my kindred?' 7 The king replied: 'What more do you want? To please you I have given you the whole of Haman's property, and hanged him on the gallows because he threatened the lives of the Jews. 8 Now you may issue a writ in my name, in whatever terms you think fit, and seal it with my signet; no order written at the king's direction and sealed with his signet can be gainsaid.'

b Gk *is not worthy of*   *c* Gk *slanderer*   *d* Gk *him*   *e* Gk *country*
f Gk *If I*

14 While they were speaking with him, the king's eunuchs arrived and hurried Haman off to the banquet Esther had prepared.

7 So the king and Haman went to the banquet with Queen Esther. 2 Again, on this second day, during the drinking of the wine, the king said to Esther, "Whatever you ask, Queen Esther, shall be granted you. Whatever request you make shall be honored, even for half the kingdom." 3 Queen Esther replied: "If I have found favor with you, O king, and if it pleases your majesty, I ask that my life be spared, and I beg that you spare the lives of my people. 4 For my people and I have been delivered to destruction, slaughter, and extinction. If we were to be sold into slavery I would remain silent, but as it is, the enemy will be unable to compensate for the harm done to the king." 5 "Who and where," said King Ahasuerus to Queen Esther, "is the man who has dared to do this?" 6 Esther replied, "The enemy oppressing us is this wicked Haman." At this, Haman was seized with dread of the king and queen.

7 The king left the banquet in anger and went into the garden of the palace, but Haman stayed to beg Queen Esther for his life, since he saw that the king had decided on his doom. 8 When the king returned from the garden of the palace to the banquet hall, Haman had thrown himself on the couch on which Esther was reclining; and the king exclaimed, "Will he also violate the queen while she is with me in my own house!" Scarcely had the king spoken, when the face of Haman was covered over.

9 Harbona, one of the eunuchs who attended the king, said, "At the house of Haman stands a gibbet fifty cubits high. Haman prepared it for Mordecai, who gave the report that benefited the king." The king answered, "Hang him on it." 10 So they hanged Haman on the gibbet which he had made ready for Mordecai, and the anger of the king abated.

8 That day King Ahasuerus gave the house of Haman, enemy of the Jews, to Queen Esther; and Mordecai was admitted to the king's presence, for Esther had revealed his relationship to her. 2 The king removed his signet ring from Haman, and transferred it into the keeping of Mordecai; and Esther put Mordecai in charge of the house of Haman.

3 In another audience with the king, Esther fell at his feet and tearfully implored him to revoke the harm done by Haman the Agagite, and the plan he had devised against the Jews. 4 The king stretched forth the golden scepter to Esther. So she rose and, standing in his presence, 5 said: "If it pleases your majesty and seems proper to you, and if I have found favor with you and you love me, let a document be issued to revoke the letters which that schemer Haman, son of Hammedatha the Agagite, wrote for the destruction of the Jews in all the royal provinces. 6 For how can I witness the evil that is to befall my people, and how can I behold the destruction of my race?"

7 King Ahasuerus then said to Queen Esther and to the Jew Mordecai: "Now that I have given Esther the house of Haman, and they have hanged him on the gibbet because he attacked the Jews, 8 you in turn may write in the king's name what you see fit concerning the Jews and seal the letter with the royal signet ring." For whatever is written in the name of the king and sealed with the royal signet ring cannot be revoked.

14 While they were still talking, the king's officers arrived in a hurry to escort Haman to the banquet that Esther was giving.

7 The king and Haman went to Queen Esther's banquet, 2 and this second day, during the banquet, the king again said to Esther, 'Tell me your request, Queen Esther. I grant it to you. Whatever you want; even if it is half my kingdom, it is yours for the asking.' 3 'If I have found favour in your eyes, O king,' Queen Esther replied, 'and if it please your majesty, grant me my life — that is my request; and the lives of my people — that is what I want. 4 For we have been handed over, my people and I, to destruction, slaughter and annihilation; had we merely been sold as slaves and servant-girls, I should not have said anything; but in the present case, it will be beyond the persecutor's means to make good the loss that the king is about to sustain.' 5 King Ahasuerus interrupted Queen Esther, 'Who is this man?' he exclaimed. 'Where is the man who has thought of doing such a thing?' 6 Esther replied, 'The persecutor, the enemy? Why, this wretch Haman!' Haman quaked with terror in the presence of the king and queen.

7 In a rage the king got up from the banquet and went into the palace garden; while Haman, realising that the king was determined on his ruin, stayed behind to beg Queen Esther for his life.

8 When the king came back from the palace garden into the banqueting hall, he found Haman sprawled across the couch where Esther was reclining. 'What!' the king exclaimed. 'Is he going to rape the queen in my own palace?' The words were scarcely out of his mouth than a veil was thrown over Haman's face. 9 In the royal presence, Harbona, one of the officers, said, 'There is that fifty-cubit gallows, too, which Haman ran up for Mordecai, who spoke up to the king's great advantage. It is all ready at his house.' 'Hang him on it,' said the king. 10 So Haman was hanged on the gallows which he had erected for Mordecai, and the king's wrath subsided.

8 That same day King Ahasuerus gave Queen Esther the house of Haman, the persecutor of the Jews. Mordecai was presented to the king, Esther having revealed their mutual relationship. 2 The king, who had recovered his signet ring from Haman, took it off and gave it to Mordecai, while Esther gave Mordecai charge of Haman's house.

3 Esther again went to speak to the king. She fell at his feet, weeping and imploring his favour, to frustrate the malice that Haman the Agagite had been plotting against the Jews. 4 The king held out the golden sceptre to her, whereupon Esther stood up and faced him. 5 'If such is the king's good pleasure,' she said, 'and if I have found favour before him, if my petition seems proper to him and if I myself am pleasing to his eyes, may he be pleased to issue a written revocation of the letters which Haman son of Hammedatha, the Agagite, has had written, ordering the destruction of the Jews throughout the royal provinces. 6 For how can I look on, while my people suffer what is proposed for them? How can I bear to witness the extermination of my relatives?'

7 King Ahasuerus said to Queen Esther and to Mordecai the Jew, 'I for my part have given Esther Haman's house, and have had him hanged on the gallows for planning to destroy the Jews. 8 You, for your part, write what you please as regards the Jews, in the king's name, and seal it with the king's signet; for any edict written in the king's name and sealed with his signet is irrevocable.' 9 The royal

9 The secretaries were summoned on the twenty-third day of the first month, that is, Nisan, in the same year; and all that he commanded with respect to the Jews was given in writing to the administrators and governors of the provinces from India to Ethiopia, one hundred twenty-seven provinces, to each province in its own language. 10 The edit was written*g* with the king's authority and sealed with his ring, and sent out by couriers. 11 He ordered the Jews in every city to observe their own laws, to defend themselves, and to act as they wished against their opponents and enemies 12 on a certain day, the thirteenth of the twelfth month, which is Adar, throughout all the kingdom of Artaxerxes.

9 On the twenty-third day of the first month, Nisan, in the same year, the secretaries were summoned; and the Jews were informed in writing of the instructions given to the administrators and chief governors in the hundred and twenty-seven provinces from India to Ethiopia, to each province in its own language. 10 The writ was drawn up in the king's name and sealed with his signet, and dispatches were sent by courier. 11 By these dispatches permission was granted to the Jews in every city to observe their own laws and to defend themselves, and to deal as they wished with their opponents and enemies, 12 throughout the kingdom of Artaxerxes, in one day, the thirteenth of Adar, the twelfth month.]

ADDITION E

16 *h* The following is a copy of this letter:
"The Great King, Artaxerxes, to the governors of the provinces from India to Ethiopia, one hundred twenty-seven provinces, and to those who are loyal to our government, greetings.

2 "Many people, the more they are honored with the most generous kindness of their benefactors, the more proud do they become, 3 and not only seek to injure our subjects, but in their inability to stand prosperity, they even undertake to scheme against their own benefactors. 4 They not only take away thankfulness from others, but, carried away by the boasts of those who know nothing of goodness, they even assume that they will escape the evil-hating justice of God, who always sees everything. 5 And often many of those who are set in places of authority have been made in part responsible for the shedding of innocent blood, and have been involved in irremediable calamities, by the persuasion of friends who have been entrusted with the administration of public affairs, 6 when these persons by the false trickery of their evil natures beguile the sincere goodwill of their sovereigns.

7 "What has been wickedly accomplished through the pestilent behavior of those who exercise authority unworthily can be seen, not so much from the more ancient records that we hand on, as from investigation of matters close at hand.*i* 8 In the future we will take care to render our kingdom quiet and peaceable for all, 9 by changing our methods and always judging what comes before our eyes with more equitable consideration. 10 For Haman son of Hammedatha, a Macedonian (really an alien to the Persian blood, and quite devoid of our kindliness), having become our guest, 11 enjoyed so fully the goodwill that we have for every nation that he was called our father and was continually bowed down to by all as the person second to the royal throne. 12 But, unable to restrain his arrogance, he undertook to deprive us of our kingdom and our life,*j* 13 and with intricate craft and deceit asked for the destruction of Mordecai, our savior and perpetual benefactor, and of Esther, the blameless partner of our kingdom, together with their whole nation. 14 He thought that by these methods he would catch us undefended and would transfer the kingdom of the Persians to the Macedonians.

15 "But we find that the Jews, who were consigned to annihilation by this thrice-accursed man, are not evildoers, but are governed by most righteous laws 16 and are children

16 THE following is a copy of the letter:

From Artaxerxes the Great King to the Governors of the one hundred and twenty-seven provinces from India to Ethiopia, and to our loyal subjects.

Greeting.

2 Many who have been repeatedly honoured by the bountiful goodness of their benefactors have grown arrogant, 3 and not only attempt to injure our subjects but, unable to keep their insolence within bounds, even plot mischief against those same benefactors. 4 Not content with destroying gratitude among men, they are so carried away by the presumption of those who are strangers to good breeding that they even suppose they will escape the avenging justice of the all-seeing God. 5 Often, when the king's business has been entrusted to those he counts his friends, they have, by their plausibility, made those in supreme authority partners in the shedding of innocent blood and involved them in irreparable misfortunes, 6 for their malevolence with its misleading sophistries has imposed upon the sincere goodwill of their rulers. 7 The evil brought about by those who wield power unworthily you can observe, not only in the accounts handed down to us from the past, but also in your familiar experience, 8 and the lesson can be applied to the future. Thus we shall ensure the peace and stability of the realm for the benefit of all; 9 we shall make no changes but shall always decide such matters as come to our notice with firmness and equity.

10 Now Haman son of Hamadathus, a Macedonian, an alien in fact with no Persian blood and not a trace of our kindly nature, was accepted by us 11 and enjoyed so fully the benevolence which we extend to every nation that he was given the title of Father and used to receive obeisance from everyone as second only to our royal throne. 12 But this man in his unbridled arrogance schemed to deprive us of our kingdom and our life; 13 by deceitfulness and tortuous cunning he sought to bring about the destruction of Mardochaeus, our constant benefactor who had saved our life, and of Esther, our blameless consort, together with their whole nation. 14 He thought, by these means, to catch us without support and transfer to the Macedonians the sovereignty now held by the Persians.

15 We find, however, that the Jews whom this double-dyed villain had consigned to extinction are no evildoers; on the contrary, they order their lives by the most just of laws 16 and are children of the living God, the Most High

---

g Gk *It was written*   *h* Chapter 16.1-24 corresponds to chapter E 1-24 in some translations.   *i* Gk *matters beside* (your) *feet*
j Gk *our spirit*

9 At that time, on the twenty-third day of the third month, Sivan, the royal scribes were summoned. Exactly as Mordecai dictated, they wrote to the Jews and to the satraps, governors, and officials of the hundred and twenty-seven provinces from India to Ethiopia: to each province in its own script and to each people in its own language, and to the Jews in their own script and language. 10 These letters, which he wrote in the name of King Ahasuerus and sealed with the royal signet ring, he sent by mounted couriers riding thoroughbred royal steeds. 11 In these letters the king authorized the Jews in each and every city to group together and defend their lives, and to kill, destroy, wipe out, along with their wives and children, every armed group of any nation or province which should attack them, and to seize their goods as spoil 12 throughout the provinces of King Ahasuerus, on a single day, the thirteenth of the twelfth month, Adar.

E The following is a copy of the letter: "King Ahasuerus the Great to the governors of the provinces in the hundred and twenty-seven satrapies from India to Ethiopia, and to those responsible for our interests: Greetings! 2 "Many have become the more ambitious the more they were showered with honors through the bountiful generosity of their patrons. 3 Not only do they seek to do harm to our subjects; incapable of bearing such greatness, they even begin plotting against their own benefactors. 4 Not only do they drive out gratitude from among men; with the arrogant boastfulness of those to whom goodness has no meaning, they suppose they will escape the vindictive judgment of the all-seeing God. 5 "Often, too, the fair speech of friends entrusted with the administration of affairs has induced many placed in authority to become accomplices in the shedding of innocent blood, and has involved them in irreparable calamities 6 by deceiving with malicious slander the sincere good will of rulers. 7 This can be verified in the ancient stories that have been handed down to us, but more fully when one considers the wicked deeds perpetrated in your midst by the pestilential influence of those undeserving of authority. 8 We must provide for the future, so as to render the kingdom undisturbed and peaceful for all men, 9 taking advantage of changing conditions and deciding always with equitable treatment matters coming to our attention. 10 "For instance, Haman, son of Hammedatha, a Macedonian, certainly not of Persian blood, and very different from us in generosity, was hospitably received by us. 11 He so far enjoyed the good will which we have toward all peoples that he was proclaimed 'father of the king,' before whom everyone was to bow down; he attained the rank second to the royal throne. 12 But, unequal to this dignity, he strove to deprive us of kingdom and of life; 13 and by weaving intricate webs of deceit, he demanded the destruction of Mordecai, our savior and constant benefactor, and of Esther, our blameless royal consort, together with their whole race. 14 For by such measures he hoped to catch us defenseless and to transfer the rule of the Persians to the Macedonians. 15 But we find that the Jews, who were doomed to extinction by this arch-criminal, are not evildoers, but rather are governed by very just laws 16 and are the children of the Most

scribes were summoned at once — it was the third month, the month of Sivan, on the twenty-third day — and at Mordecai's dictation an order was written to the Jews, the satraps, governors and principal officials of the provinces stretching from India to Ethiopia, a hundred and twenty-seven provinces, to each province in its own script, and to each people in its own language, and to the Jews in their own script and language. 10 These letters, written in the name of King Ahasuerus and sealed with the king's signet, were carried by couriers mounted on horses from the king's own stud-farms. 11 In them the king granted the Jews, in whatever city they lived, the right to assemble in self-defence, with permission to destroy, slaughter and annihilate any armed force of any people or province that might attack them, together with their women and children, and to plunder their possessions, 12 with effect from the same day throughout the provinces of King Ahasuerus — the thirteenth day of the twelfth month, which is Adar.

12a *The text of the letter was as follows:*

12b *'The Great King, Ahasuerus, to the satraps of the hundred and twenty-seven provinces which stretch from India to Ethiopia, to the provincial governors and to all our loyal subjects, greeting:*
12c *'Many people, repeatedly honoured by the extreme bounty of their benefactors, only grow the more arrogant. It is not enough for them to seek our subjects' injury, but unable as they are to support the weight of their own surfeit they turn to scheming against their benefactors themselves.* 12d *Not content with banishing gratitude from the human heart, but elated by the plaudits of people unacquainted with goodness, notwithstanding that all is for ever under the eye of God, they expect to escape his justice, so hostile to the wicked.* 12e *Thus it has often happened to those placed in authority that, having entrusted friends with the conduct of affairs and allowed themselves to be influenced by them, they find themselves sharing with these the guilt of innocent blood and involved in irremediable misfortunes,* 12f *the upright intentions of rulers having been misled by false arguments of the evilly disposed.* 12g *This may be seen without recourse to the history of earlier times to which we have referred; you have only to look at what is before you, at the crimes perpetrated by a plague of unworthy officials.* 12h *For the future, we shall exert our efforts to assure the tranquillity and peace of the realm for all,* 12i *by adopting new policies and by always judging matters that are brought to our notice in the most equitable spirit.*

12k *'Thus Haman son of Hammedatha, a Macedonian, without a drop of Persian blood and far removed from our goodness, enjoyed our hospitality* 12l *and was treated by us with the benevolence which we show to every nation, even to the extent of being proclaimed our 'father' and being accorded universally the prostration of respect as second in dignity to the royal throne.* 12m *But he, unable to keep within his own high rank, schemed to deprive us of our realm and of our life.* 12n *Furthermore, by tortuous wiles and arguments, he would have had us destroy Mordecai, our saviour and constant benefactor, with Esther the blameless partner of our majesty, and their whole nation besides.* 12o *He thought by these means to leave us without support and so to transfer the Persian empire to the Macedonians.*

12p *'But we find that the Jews, marked out for annihilation by this arch-scoundrel, are not criminals: they are in fact governed by the most just of laws.* 12q *They are*

of the living God, most high, most mighty,*k* who has directed the kingdom both for us and for our ancestors in the most excellent order.

17 "You will therefore do well not to put in execution the letters sent by Haman son of Hammedatha, 18 since he, the one who did these things, has been hanged at the gate of Susa with all his household — for God, who rules over all things, has speedily inflicted on him the punishment that he deserved.

19 "Therefore post a copy of this letter publicly in every place, and permit the Jews to live under their own laws. 20 And give them reinforcements, so that on the thirteenth day of the twelfth month, Adar, on that very day, they may defend themselves against those who attack them at the time of oppression. 21 For God, who rules over all things, has made this day to be a joy for his chosen people instead of a day of destruction for them.

22 "Therefore you shall observe this with all good cheer as a notable day among your commemorative festivals, 23 so that both now and hereafter it may represent deliverance for you*l* and the loyal Persians, but that it may be a reminder of destruction for those who plot against us.

24 "Every city and country, without exception, that does not act accordingly shall be destroyed in wrath with spear and fire. It shall be made not only impassable for human beings, but also most hateful to wild animals and birds for all time.

END OF ADDITION E

8 13 "Let copies of the decree be posted conspicuously in all the kingdom, and let all the Jews be ready on that day to fight against their enemies."

14 So the messengers on horseback set out with all speed to perform what the king had commanded; and the decree was published also in Susa. 15 Mordecai went out dressed in the royal robe and wearing a gold crown and a turban of purple linen. The people in Susa rejoiced on seeing him. 16 And the Jews had light and gladness 17 in every city and province wherever the decree was published; wherever the proclamation was made, the Jews had joy and gladness, a banquet and a holiday. And many of the Gentiles were circumcised and became Jews out of fear of the Jews.

9 Now on the thirteenth day of the twelfth month, which is Adar, the decree written by the king arrived. 2 On that same day the enemies of the Jews perished; no one resisted, because they feared them. 3 The chief provincial governors, the princes, and the royal secretaries were paying honor to the Jews, because fear of Mordecai weighed upon them. 4 The king's decree required that Mordecai's name be held in honor throughout the kingdom.*m* 6 Now in the city of Susa the Jews killed five hundred people, 7 including Pharsannestain, Delphon, Phasga, 8 Pharadatha, Barea, Sarbacha, 9 Marmasima, Aruphaeus, Arsaeus, Zabutheus, 10 the ten sons of Haman son of Hammedatha, the Bougean, the enemy of the Jews — and they indulged*n* themselves in plunder.

11 That very day the number of those killed in Susa was reported to the king. 12 The king said to Esther, "In Susa,

and Most Mighty, who for us as for our ancestors has maintained the kingdom in excellent order. 17 You will, therefore, disregard the letters sent by Haman son of Hamadathus, 18 because he, the contriver of all this, has been hanged at the gate of Susa, he and his whole household, for God who controls all things brought on him speedily the punishment he deserved.

19 Copies of this letter are to be posted up in all public places. The Jews are to live under their own laws, 20 and be given every assistance so that on the very same day, the thirteenth day of Adar, the twelfth month, they may avenge themselves on their assailants in the time of oppression. 21 God, who has all things in his power, has made that a day of joy, not of ruin, for his chosen people.

22 Therefore you also must keep it with all good cheer, as a notable day among your feasts of commemoration, 23 so that henceforth it may be a standing symbol of deliverance to us and our loyal Persians, but a reminder of destruction to those who plot against us. 24 Any city or country whatsoever which does not act upon these orders will incur our wrath and be destroyed with fire and sword. Not only will no man set foot in it, but it will also be shunned by beast and bird for all time.

8 13 [Let copies be posted up prominently throughout the kingdom, so that all the Jews may be prepared for that day, to fight against their enemies.

14 Mounted couriers set out post-haste to do what the king commanded; and the decree was published also in Susa.

15 When Mardochaeus went out in a royal robe, wearing a gold crown and a turban of fine linen dyed purple, the people in Susa rejoiced to see him. 16 For the Jews all was light and gladness 17 in every city and province, wherever the decree was posted up; there was joy and gladness for them, feasting and merrymaking. And many of the Gentiles were circumcised and professed Judaism, because of fear of the Jews.

9 On the thirteenth day of Adar, the twelfth month, the decree drawn up by the king arrived. That same day the enemies of the Jews perished, 2 for in their fear none offered resistance. 3 The leading provincial governors, the princes, and the royal secretaries paid honour to the Jews out of fear of Mardochaeus, 4 for they had received the king's decree that his name should be honoured throughout the kingdom. 6 In the capital itself the Jews slaughtered five hundred men, 7 including Pharsanestan, Delphon, Phasga, 8 Pharadatha, Barsa, Sarbach, 9 Marmasima, Ruphaeus, Arsaeus, and Zabuthaeus, 10 the ten sons of Haman son of Hamadathus, the Bugaean and enemy of the Jews; and they took plunder.

11 When the number of those killed in Susa was reported to the king that day, 12 he said to Esther, 'In the city of Susa

---

k Gk *greatest* *l* Other ancient authorities read *for us* *m* Meaning of Gk uncertain. Some ancient authorities add verse 5, *So the Jews struck down all their enemies with the sword, killing and destroying them, and they did as they pleased to those who hated them.* *n* Other ancient authorities read *did not indulge*

[9:4] **the kingdom:** *some witnesses add from the Heb.* 5 The Jews put their enemies to the sword. There was great slaughter and destruction, and they worked their will on those who hated them.

High, the living God of majesty, who has maintained the kingdom in a flourishing condition for us and for our forebears. 17"You will do well, then, to ignore the letter sent by Haman, son of Hammedatha, 18 for he who composed it has been hanged, together with his entire household, before the gates of Susa. Thus swiftly has God, who governs all, brought just punishment upon him.

19"You shall exhibit a copy of this letter publicly in every place, to certify that the Jews may follow their own laws, 20 and that you may help them on the day set for their ruin, the thirteenth day of the twelfth month, Adar, to defend themselves against those who attack them. 21 For God, the ruler of all, has turned that day for them from one of destruction of the chosen race into one of joy. 22 Therefore, you too must celebrate this memorable day among your designated feasts with all rejoicing, 23 so that both now and in the future it may be, for us and for loyal Persians, a celebration of victory, and for those who plot against us a reminder of destruction.

24"Every city and province, without exception, that does not observe this decree shall be ruthlessly destroyed with fire and sword, so that it will be left not merely untrodden by men, but even shunned by wild beasts and birds forever."

children of the Most High, the great and living God to whom we and our ancestors owe the continuing prosperity of our realm. 12r You will therefore do well not to act on the letters sent by Haman son of Hammedatha, since their author has been hanged at the gates of Susa with his whole household: a fitting punishment, which God, Master of the Universe, has speedily inflicted on him. 12s Put up copies of this letter everywhere, allow the Jews to observe their own customs without fear, and come to their help against anyone who attacks them on the day originally chosen for their maltreatment, that is, the thirteenth day of the twelfth month, which is Adar. 12t For the all-powerful God has made this day a day of joy and not of ruin for the chosen people. 12u You, for your part, among your solemn festivals celebrate this as a special day with every kind of feasting, so that now and in the future, for you and for Persians of good will, it may commemorate your rescue, and for your enemies may stand as a reminder of their ruin.

12v 'Every city and, more generally, every country, which does not follow these instructions, will be mercilessly devastated with fire and sword, and made not only inaccessible to human beings but hateful to wild animals and even birds for ever.'

(8) 13 A copy of the letter to be promulgated as law in each and every province was published among all the peoples, so that the Jews might be prepared on that day to avenge themselves on their enemies. 14 Couriers mounted on royal steeds sped forth in haste at the king's order, and the decree was promulgated in the stronghold of Susa. 15 Mordecai left the king's presence clothed in a royal robe of violet and of white cotton, with a large crown of gold and a cloak of crimson byssus. The city of Susa shouted with joy, 16 and there was splendor and merriment for the Jews, exultation and triumph. 17 In each and every province and in each and every city, wherever the king's order arrived, there was merriment and exultation, banqueting and feasting for the Jews. And many of the peoples of the land embraced Judaism, for they were seized with a fear of the Jews.

9 When the day arrived on which the order decreed by the king was to be carried out, the thirteenth day of the twelfth month, Adar, on which the enemies of the Jews had expected to become masters of them, the situation was reversed: the Jews became masters of their enemies. 2 The Jews mustered in their cities throughout the provinces of King Ahasuerus to attack those who sought to do them harm, and no one could withstand them, but all peoples were seized with a fear of them. 3 Moreover, all the officials of the provinces, the satraps, governors, and royal procurators supported the Jews from fear of Mordecai; 4 for Mordecai was powerful in the royal palace, and the report was spreading through all the provinces that he was continually growing in power.

5 The Jews struck down all their enemies with the sword, killing and destroying them; they did to their enemies as they pleased. 6 In the stronghold of Susa, the Jews killed and destroyed five hundred men. 7 They also killed Parshandatha, Dalphon, Aspatha, 8 Porathai, Adalia, Aridatha, 9 Parmashta, Arisai, Aridai, and Vaizatha, 10 the ten sons of Haman, son of Hammedatha, the foe of the Jews. However, they did not engage in plundering. 11 On the same day, when the number of those killed in the stronghold of Susa was reported to the king, 12 he said

13 Copies of this edict, to be promulgated as law in each province, were published to the various peoples, so that the Jews could be ready on the day stated to avenge themselves on their enemies. 14 The couriers, mounted on the king's horses, set out in great haste and urgency at the king's command. The edict was also published in the citadel of Susa. 15 Mordecai left the royal presence in a princely gown of violet and white, with a great golden crown and a cloak of fine linen and purple. The city of Susa shouted for joy. 16 For the Jews there was light and gladness, joy and honour. 17 In every province and in every city, wherever the king's command and decree arrived, there was joy and gladness among the Jews, with feasting and holiday-making. Of the country's population many became Jews, since now the Jews were feared.

9 The king's command and decree came into force on the thirteenth day of the twelfth month, Adar, and the day on which the enemies of the Jews had hoped to crush them produced the very opposite effect: the Jews it was who crushed their enemies. 2 In their towns throughout the provinces of King Ahasuerus, the Jews assembled to strike at those who had planned to injure them. No one resisted them, since the various peoples were now all afraid of them. 3 Provincial officers-of-state, satraps, governors and royal officials, all supported the Jews for fear of Mordecai. 4 And indeed Mordecai was a power in the palace and his fame was spreading through all the provinces; Mordecai was steadily growing more powerful.

5 So the Jews struck down all their enemies with the sword, with resulting slaughter and destruction, and worked their will on their opponents. 6 In the citadel of Susa alone, the Jews put to death and slaughtered five hundred men, 7 notably Parshandatha, Dalphon, Aspatha, 8 Poratha, Adalia, Aridatha, 9 Parmashta, Arisai, Aridai and Jezatha, 10 the ten sons of Haman son of Hammedatha, the persecutor of the Jews. But they took no plunder.

11 The number of those killed in the citadel of Susa was reported to the king that same day. 12 The king said to

the capital, the Jews have destroyed five hundred people. What do you suppose they have done in the surrounding countryside? Whatever more you ask will be done for you." 13 And Esther said to the king, "Let the Jews be allowed to do the same tomorrow. Also, hang up the bodies of Haman's ten sons." 14 So he permitted this to be done, and handed over to the Jews of the city the bodies of Haman's sons to hang up. 15 The Jews who were in Susa gathered on the fourteenth and killed three hundred people, but took no plunder.

16 Now the other Jews in the kingdom gathered to defend themselves, and got relief from their enemies. They destroyed fifteen thousand of them, but did not engage in plunder. 17 On the fourteenth day they rested and made that same day a day of rest, celebrating it with joy and gladness. 18 The Jews who were in Susa, the capital, came together also on the fourteenth, but did not rest. They celebrated the fifteenth with joy and gladness. 19 On this account then the Jews who are scattered around the country outside Susa keep the fourteenth of Adar as a joyful holiday, and send presents of food to one another, while those who live in the large cities keep the fifteenth day of Adar as their joyful holiday, also sending presents to one another.

20 Mordecai recorded these things in a book, and sent it to the Jews in the kingdom of Artaxerxes both near and far, 21 telling them that they should keep the fourteenth and fifteenth days of Adar, 22 for on these days the Jews got relief from their enemies. The whole month (namely, Adar), in which their condition had been changed from sorrow into gladness and from a time of distress to a holiday, was to be celebrated as a time for feasting*o* and gladness and for sending presents of food to their friends and to the poor.

23 So the Jews accepted what Mordecai had written to them 24 — how Haman son of Hammedatha, the Macedonian,*p* fought against them, how he made a decree and cast lots*q* to destroy them, 25 and how he went in to the king, telling him to hang Mordecai; but the wicked plot he had devised against the Jews came back upon himself, and he and his sons were hanged. 26 Therefore these days were called "Purim," because of the lots (for in their language this is the word that means "lots"). And so, because of what was written in this letter, and because of what they had experienced in this affair and what had befallen them, Mordecai established this festival,*r* 27 and the Jews took upon themselves, upon their descendants, and upon all who would join them, to observe it without fail.*s* These days of Purim should be a memorial and kept from generation to generation, in every city, family, and country. 28 These days of Purim are to be observed for all time, and the commemoration of them was never to cease among their descendants.

29 Then Queen Esther daughter of Aminadab along with Mordecai the Jew wrote down what they had done, and gave full authority to the letter about Purim.*t* 31 And Mordecai and Queen Esther established this decision on their own responsibility, pledging their own well-being to the plan.*s* 32 Esther established it by a decree forever, and it was written for a memorial.

the Jews have killed five hundred men; what do you suppose they have done in the surrounding country? Whatever further request you have, it shall be granted.' 13 Esther replied, 'Let the Jews be permitted to do the same tomorrow, and hang up the bodies of Haman's ten sons.' 14 He allowed this to be done, and he handed over the bodies of Haman's ten sons to the Jews of the city to be hung up. 15 The Jews in Susa assembled on the fourteenth day of Adar also, and killed three hundred men, but they took no plunder.

16 The rest of the Jews throughout the kingdom rallied in self-defence, and so had respite from their enemies, for they slaughtered fifteen thousand on the thirteenth of Adar, but they took no plunder. 17 On the fourteenth of the month they rested, and made it a day of rest, with rejoicing and merrymaking. 18 The Jews in the city of Susa had assembled also on the fourteenth day; they did not rest on that day, but they kept the fifteenth with rejoicing and merrymaking. 19 That is why Jews who are dispersed over the remoter parts observe the fourteenth of Adar as a holiday with merrymaking, sending presents of food to one another; but those who live in the principal cities keep the fifteenth of Adar as a holiday, for merrymaking and sending presents of food to one another.

20 MARDOCHAEUS put these things on record in a book and sent it to the Jews in Artaxerxes' kingdom, both near and far, 21 requiring them to establish these holidays, and to observe the fourteenth and fifteenth of Adar, 22 because these were the days on which the Jews had respite from their enemies; and they were to observe the whole month of Adar, in which came the change from sorrow to joy and from a time of mourning to holiday, as days for weddings and merrymaking, days for sending presents of food to friends and to the poor.

23 The Jews welcomed the account which Mardochaeus wrote: 24 how Haman son of Hamadathus, the Macedonian, fought against them, how he made a decree and cast lots with intent to destroy them, 25 how he came before the king with a proposal to hang Mardochaeus, how all the evils which he had plotted against the Jews recoiled upon him, and how he and his sons were hanged. 26 This is why these days were named Purim, because in the Jews' language it means 'Lots'. Because of all that was written in this letter, because of all that they had experienced, and all that had happened and been done, 27 the Jews gladly undertook, on behalf of themselves, their descendants, and those who should join them, to observe these days without fail; 28 they were to be days of commemoration, duly celebrated generation after generation in every city, family, and province; further, these days of Purim were to be observed for all time, and the commemoration was never to cease throughout all ages.

29 Queen Esther daughter of Aminadab, and Mardochaeus the Jew, recorded in writing all that they had done, and confirmed the letter about Purim; 30–31 they had made themselves responsible for this decision and staked their life upon the plan. 32 Esther established it for all time by her decree, and it was put on record.

---

o Gk *of weddings*   *p* Other ancient witnesses read *the Bougean*
q Gk *a lot*   *r* Gk *he established* (it)   *s* Meaning of Gk uncertain
t Verse 30 in Heb is lacking in Gk: *Letters were sent to all the Jews, to the one hundred twenty-seven provinces of the kingdom of Ahasuerus, in words of peace and truth.*

[9:27] observe . . . days: *prob. rdg; cp. Heb.*

|

to Queen Esther: "In the stronghold of Susa the Jews have killed and destroyed five hundred men, as well as the ten sons of Haman. What must they have done in the other royal provinces! You shall again be granted whatever you ask, and whatever you request shall be honored." 13 So Esther said, "If it pleases your majesty, let the Jews in Susa be permitted again tomorrow to act according to today's decree, and let the ten sons of Haman be hanged on gibbets." 14 The king then gave an order to this effect, and the decree was published in Susa. So the ten sons of Haman were hanged, 15 and the Jews in Susa mustered again on the fourteenth of the month of Adar and killed three hundred men in Susa. However, they did not engage in plundering.

16 The other Jews, who dwelt in the royal provinces, also mustered and defended themselves, and obtained rest from their enemies. They killed seventy-five thousand of their foes, without engaging in plunder, 17 on the thirteenth day of the month of Adar. On the fourteenth of the month they rested, and made it a day of feasting and rejoicing.

18 (The Jews in Susa, however, mustered on the thirteenth and fourteenth of the month. But on the fifteenth they rested, and made it a day of feasting and rejoicing.) 19 That is why the rural Jews, who dwell in villages, celebrate the fourteenth of the month of Adar as a day of rejoicing and feasting, a holiday on which they send gifts of food to one another.

20 Mordecai recorded these events and sent letters to all the Jews, both near and far, in all the provinces of King Ahasuerus. 21 He ordered them to celebrate every year both the fourteenth and the fifteenth of the month of Adar 22 as the day on which the Jews obtained rest from their enemies and as the month which was turned for them from sorrow into joy, from mourning into festivity. They were to observe these days with feasting and gladness, sending food to one another and gifts to the poor. 23 The Jews took upon themselves for the future this observance which they instituted at the written direction of Mordecai.

24 Haman, son of Hammedatha the Agagite, the foe of all the Jews, had planned to destroy them and had cast the *pur,* or lot, for the time of their defeat and destruction. 25 Yet, when Esther entered the royal presence, the king ordered in writing that the wicked plan Haman had devised against the Jews should instead be turned against Haman and that he and his sons should be hanged on gibbets. 26 And so these days have been named Purim after the word *pur.*

Thus, because of all that was contained in this letter, and because of what they had witnessed and experienced in this affair, 27 the Jews established and took upon themselves, their descendants, and all who should join them, the inviolable obligation of celebrating these two days every year in the manner prescribed by this letter, and at the time appointed. 28 These days were to be commemorated and kept in every generation, by every clan, in every province, and in every city. These days of Purim were never to fall into disuse among the Jews, nor into oblivion among their descendants.

29 Queen Esther, daughter of Abihail and of Mordecai the Jew, wrote to confirm with full authority this second letter about Purim, 30 when Mordecai sent documents concerning peace and security to all the Jews in the hundred and twenty-seven provinces of Ahasuerus' kingdom. 31 Thus were established, for their appointed time, these days of Purim which Mordecai the Jew and Queen Esther had designated for the Jews, just as they had previously enjoined upon themselves and upon their race the duty of fasting and supplication. 32 The command of Esther confirmed these prescriptions for Purim and was recorded in the book.

Queen Esther, 'In the citadel of Susa the Jews have killed five hundred men and also the ten sons of Haman. What must they have done in the other provinces of the realm? Tell me your request; I grant it to you. Tell me what else you would like; it is yours for the asking.' 13 'If such is the king's pleasure,' Esther replied, 'let the Jews of Susa be allowed to enforce today's decree tomorrow as well. And as for the ten sons of Haman, let their bodies be hanged on the gallows.' 14 Whereupon, the king having given the order, the edict was promulgated in Susa and the ten sons of Haman were hanged. 15 Thus the Jews of Susa reassembled on the fourteenth day of the month of Adar and killed three hundred men in the city. But they took no plunder.

16 The other Jews who lived in the king's provinces also assembled to defend their lives and rid themselves of their enemies. They slaughtered seventy-five thousand of their opponents. But they took no plunder. 17 This was on the thirteenth day of the month of Adar. On the fourteenth day they rested and made it a day of feasting and gladness. 18 But for the Jews of Susa, who had assembled on the thirteenth and fourteenth days, the fifteenth was the day they rested, making that a day of feasting and gladness. 19 This is why Jewish country people, those who live in undefended villages, keep the fourteenth day of the month of Adar as a day of gladness, feasting and holiday-making, and the exchanging of presents with one another, 19a *whereas for those who live in cities the day of rejoicing and exchanging presents with their neighbours is the fifteenth day of Adar.*

20 Mordecai committed these events to writing. Then he sent letters to all the Jews living in the provinces of King Ahasuerus, both near and far, 21 enjoining them to celebrate the fourteenth and fifteenth days of the month of Adar every year, 22 as the days on which the Jews had rid themselves of their enemies, and the month in which their sorrow had been turned into gladness, and mourning into a holiday. He therefore told them to keep these as days of festivity and gladness when they were to exchange presents and make gifts to the poor.

23 Once having begun, the Jews continued observing these practices, Mordecai having written them an account 24 of how Haman son of Hammedatha, the Agagite, the persecutor of all the Jews, had plotted their destruction and had cast the *pur,* that is, the lot, for their overthrow and ruin; 25 but how, when he went back to the king to ask him to order the hanging of Mordecai, the wicked scheme which he had devised against the Jews recoiled on his own head, and both he and his sons were hanged on the gallows; 26 and that, hence, these days were called Purim, from the word *pur.* And so, because of what was written in this letter, and because of what they had seen for themselves and of what had happened to them, 27 the Jews willingly bound themselves, their descendants and all who should join them, to celebrate these two days without fail, in the manner prescribed and at the time appointed, year after year. 28 Thus commemorated and celebrated from generation to generation, in every family, in every province, in every city, these days of Purim will never be abrogated among the Jews, nor will their memory perish from their race.

29 Queen Esther, the daughter of Abihail, wrote with full authority to ratify this second letter, 30 and sent letters to all the Jews of the hundred and twenty-seven provinces of the realm of Ahasuerus, in terms of peace and loyalty 31 enjoining them to observe these days of Purim at the appointed time, as Mordecai the Jew had recommended, and in the manner prescribed for themselves and their descendants, with additional ordinances for fasts and lamentations. 32 The ordinance of Esther fixed the law of Purim, which was then recorded in a book.

NEW REVISED STANDARD VERSION	REVISED ENGLISH BIBLE

10 The king levied a tax upon his kingdom both by land and sea. 2 And as for his power and bravery, and the wealth and glory of his kingdom, they were recorded in the annals of the kings of the Persians and the Medes. 3 Mordecai acted with authority on behalf of King Artaxerxes and was great in the kingdom, as well as honored by the Jews. His way of life was such as to make him beloved to his whole nation.

ADDITION F

4*u* And Mordecai said, "These things have come from God; 5 for I remember the dream that I had concerning these matters, and none of them has failed to be fulfilled. 6 There was the little spring that became a river, and there was light and sun and abundant water—the river is Esther, whom the king married and made queen. 7 The two dragons are Haman and myself. 8 The nations are those that gathered to destroy the name of the Jews. 9 And my nation, this is Israel, who cried out to God and were saved. The Lord has saved his people; the Lord has rescued us from all these evils; God has done great signs and wonders, wonders that have never happened among the nations. 10 For this purpose he made two lots, one for the people of God and one for all the nations, 11 and these two lots came to the hour and moment and day of decision before God and among all the nations. 12 And God remembered his people and vindicated his inheritance. 13 So they will observe these days in the month of Adar, on the fourteenth and fifteenth*v* of that month, with an assembly and joy and gladness before God, from generation to generation forever among his people

11 Israel." 1 In the fourth year of the reign of Ptolemy and Cleopatra, Dositheus, who said that he was a priest and a Levite,*w* and his son Ptolemy brought to Egypt*x* the preceding Letter about Purim, which they said was authentic and had been translated by Lysimachus son of Ptolemy, one of the residents of Jerusalem.

END OF ADDITION F

u Chapter 10.4-13 and 11.1 correspond to chapter F 1-11 in some translations. *v* Other ancient authorities lack *and fifteenth* *w* Or *priest, and Levitas* *x* Cn: Gk *brought in*

10 The king made decrees for his kingdom over land and sea. 2 His strength and courage, his wealth and the splendour of his kingdom, are recorded in the book of the kings of the Persians and Medes. 3 Mardochaeus was viceroy for King Artaxerxes; he was a great man in the kingdom and honoured by the Jews. His way of life won him the affection of his whole nation.]

10 4 MARDOCHAEUS said, 'This is God's doing, 5 for I have been reminded of the dream I had about these matters; every one of the visions I saw has been fulfilled. 6 There was the little spring which became a river, and there was light and sun and abundant water: the river is Esther, whom the king married and made queen; 7 the two dragons are Haman and myself; 8 the nations are those who combined to blot out all memory of the Jews; 9 my nation is Israel, which cried out to God and was delivered. The Lord has delivered his people, he has rescued us from all these evils. God performed great signs and portents, such as have never occurred among the nations. 10 He prepared two lots, one for the people of God and one for all the nations; 11 then came the hour and the time for these two lots to be cast, the judgement by God upon all the nations; 12 he remembered his people and gave the verdict for his heritage. 13 'So they are to keep these days in the month of Adar, the fourteenth and fifteenth of that month, by assembling with joy and gladness before God from one generation of his people Israel to another for ever.'

11 1 In the fourth year of the reign of Ptolemy and Cleopatra, Dositheus, who declared he was a levitical priest, and Ptolemaeus his son, brought the foregoing letter about Purim; according to their declaration it was authentic and had been translated by Lysimachus son of Ptolemaeus, a resident in Jerusalem.

NEW AMERICAN BIBLE

10 King Ahasuerus laid tribute on the land and on the islands of the sea. ²All the acts of his power and valor, as well as a detailed account of the greatness of Mordecai, whom the king promoted, are recorded in the chronicles of the kings of Media and Persia. ³The Jew Mordecai was next in rank to King Ahasuerus, in high standing among the Jews, and was regarded with favor by his many brethren, as the promoter of his people's welfare and the herald of peace for his whole race.

F Then Mordecai said: "This is the work of God. ²I recall the dream I had about these very things, and not a single detail has been left unfulfilled — ³the tiny spring that grew into a river, the light of the sun, the many waters. The river is Esther, whom the king married and made queen. ⁴The two dragons are myself and Haman. ⁵The nations are those who assembled to destroy the name of the Jews, ⁶but my people is Israel, who cried to God and was saved.

"The LORD saved his people and delivered us from all these evils. God worked signs and great wonders, such as have not occurred among the nations. ⁷For this purpose he arranged two lots: one for the people of God, the second for all the other nations. ⁸These two lots were fulfilled in the hour, the time, and the day of judgment before God and among all the nations. ⁹God remembered his people and rendered justice to his inheritance.

¹⁰"Gathering together with joy and happiness before God, they shall celebrate these days on the fourteenth and fifteenth of the month Adar throughout all future generations of his people Israel."

F, 10: The Greek text of Esther contains a postscript as follows: In the fourth year of the reign of Ptolemy and Cleopatra, Dositheus, who said he was a priest and Levite, and his son Ptolemy brought the present letter of Purim, saying that it was genuine and that Lysimachus, son of Ptolemy, of the community of Jerusalem, had translated it. The date referred to in this postscript is most probably 78-77 B.C., in the reign of Ptolemy XII and Cleopatra V.

NEW JERUSALEM BIBLE

10 King Ahasuerus put not only the mainland under tribute but the Mediterranean islands as well. ²All his feats of power and valour, and the account of the high honour to which he raised Mordecai: all this is recorded in the Book of the Annals of the Kings of Media and Persia.

³And Mordecai the Jew was next in rank to King Ahasuerus. He was a man held in respect among the Jews, esteemed by thousands of his brothers, a man who sought the good of his people and cared for the welfare of his entire race.

³ᵃ*And Mordecai said, 'All this is God's doing. ³ᵇI remember the dream I had about these matters, nothing of which has failed to come true: ³ᶜthe little spring that became a river, the light that shone, the sun, the flood of water. Esther is the river — she whom the king married and made queen. ³ᵈThe two dragons are Haman and myself. ³ᵉThe nations are those that banded together to blot out the name of Jew. ³ᶠThe single nation, mine, is Israel, those who cried out to God and were saved. Yes, the Lord has saved his people, the Lord has delivered us from all these evils, God has worked such signs and great wonders as have never occurred among the nations.*

³ᵍ*'Two destinies he appointed, one for his own people, one for the nations at large. ³ʰAnd these two destinies were worked out at the hour and time and day laid down by God, involving all the nations. ³ⁱIn this way God has remembered his people and vindicated his heritage; ³ᵏand for them these days, the fourteenth and fifteenth of the month of Adar, are to be days of assembly, of joy and of gladness before God, through all generations and for ever among his people Israel.'*

³ˡ*In the fourth year of the reign of Ptolemy and Cleopatra, Dositheus, who affirmed that he was a priest and Levite, and Ptolemy his son brought the foregoing letter concerning Purim. They vouched for its authenticity, the translation having been made by Lysimachus son of Ptolemy, a member of the Jerusalem community.*

The Wisdom of Solomon

1 Love righteousness, you rulers of the earth,
   think of the Lord in goodness
   and seek him with sincerity of heart;
2 because he is found by those who do not put him
      to the test,
   and manifests himself to those who do not
      distrust him.
3 For perverse thoughts separate people from God,
   and when his power is tested, it exposes the
      foolish;
4 because wisdom will not enter a deceitful soul,
   or dwell in a body enslaved to sin.
5 For a holy and disciplined spirit will flee from
      deceit,
   and will leave foolish thoughts behind,
   and will be ashamed at the approach of
      unrighteousness.

6 For wisdom is a kindly spirit,
   but will not free blasphemers from the guilt of
      their words;
   because God is witness of their inmost feelings,
   and a true observer of their hearts, and a hearer
      of their tongues.
7 Because the spirit of the Lord has filled the
      world,
   and that which holds all things together knows
      what is said,
8 therefore those who utter unrighteous things will
      not escape notice,
   and justice, when it punishes, will not pass them
      by.
9 For inquiry will be made into the counsels of the
      ungodly,
   and a report of their words will come to the
      Lord,
   to convict them of their lawless deeds;
10 because a jealous ear hears all things,
   and the sound of grumbling does not go unheard.
11 Beware then of useless grumbling,
   and keep your tongue from slander;
   because no secret word is without result,a
   and a lying mouth destroys the soul.

12 Do not invite death by the error of your life,
   or bring on destruction by the works of your
      hands;
13 because God did not make death,
   and he does not delight in the death of the living.
14 For he created all things so that they might exist;
   the generative forcesb of the world are
      wholesome,
   and there is no destructive poison in them,
   and the dominionc of Hades is not on earth.
15 For righteousness is immortal.

The Wisdom of Solomon

1 LOVE justice, you rulers of the earth; set your mind upon the Lord in the right way, and seek him in single-ness of heart; 2 for he is to be found by those who trust him without question, and he makes himself known to those who never doubt him. 3 Dishonest thinking cuts people off from God, and if fools take liberties with his power he shows them up for what they are. 4 Wisdom will not enter a shifty soul, nor make her home in a body that is mort-gaged to sin. 5 This holy spirit of discipline will shun false-hood; she cannot stay in the presence of unreason, and will withdraw at the approach of injustice.

6 The spirit of wisdom is kindly towards mortals, but she will not hold a blasphemer blameless for his words, because God, who sees clearly into his heart and hears every word he speaks, is a witness of his inmost being. 7 For the spirit of the Lord fills the whole earth, and that which holds all things together knows well everything that is said. 8 Hence no one can utter injustice and not be found out, nor will justice overlook him when she passes sentence. 9 The de-vices of a godless person will be brought to account, and a report of his words will come before the Lord as proof of his iniquity; 10 no muttered syllable escapes that vigilant ear. 11 Beware, then, of futile grumbling, and avoid all bitter talk; for even a secret whisper will not go unheeded, and a lying tongue brings destruction on its owner.

12 Do not court death by a crooked life; do not draw disaster on yourselves by your own actions. 13 For God did not make death, and takes no pleasure in the destruction of any living thing; 14 he created all things that they might have being. The creative forces of the world make for life; there is no deadly poison in them. Death has no sovereignty on earth, 15 for justice is immortal; 16 but the godless by their

THE BOOK OF
Wisdom

1 Love justice, you who judge the earth;
 think of the LORD in goodness,
 and seek him in integrity of heart;
² Because he is found by those who test him not,
 and he manifests himself to those who do not
 disbelieve him.
³ For perverse counsels separate a man from God,
 and his power, put to the proof, rebukes
 the foolhardy;
⁴ Because into a soul that plots evil wisdom
 enters not,
 nor dwells she in a body under debt of sin.
⁵ For the holy spirit of discipline flees deceit
 and withdraws from senseless counsels;
 and when injustice occurs it is rebuked.
⁶ For wisdom is a kindly spirit,
 yet she acquits not the blasphemer of his
 guilty lips;
Because God is the witness of his inmost self
 and the sure observer of his heart
 and the listener to his tongue.
⁷ For the spirit of the LORD fills the world,
 is all-embracing, and knows what man says.
⁸ Therefore no one who utters wicked things can
 go unnoticed,
 nor will chastising condemnation pass him by.
⁹ For the devices of the wicked man shall
 be scrutinized,
 and the sound of his words shall reach the LORD,
 for the chastisement of his transgressions;
¹⁰ Because a jealous ear hearkens to everything,
 and discordant grumblings are no secret.
¹¹ Therefore guard against profitless grumbling,
 and from calumny withhold your tongues;
For a stealthy utterance does not go unpunished,
 and a lying mouth slays the soul.
¹² Court not death by your erring way of life,
 nor draw to yourselves destruction by the works
 of your hands.
¹³ Because God did not make death,
 nor does he rejoice in the destruction of
 the living.
¹⁴ For he fashioned all things that they might
 have being;
 and the creatures of the world are wholesome,
And there is not a destructive drug among them
 nor any domain of the nether world on earth,
¹⁵ For justice is undying.

THE BOOK OF
Wisdom

1 Love uprightness you who are rulers on earth,
 be properly disposed towards the Lord
 and seek him in simplicity of heart;
² for he will be found by those who do not put him
 to the test,
 revealing himself to those who do not mistrust
 him.
³ Perverse thoughts, however, separate people from
 God,
 and power, when put to the test, confounds the
 stupid.
⁴ Wisdom will never enter the soul of a wrong-doer,
 nor dwell in a body enslaved to sin;
⁵ for the holy spirit of instruction flees deceitfulness,
 recoils from unintelligent thoughts,
 is thwarted by the onset of vice.
⁶ Wisdom is a spirit friendly to humanity,
 though she will not let a blasphemer's words go
 unpunished;
 since God observes the very soul
 and accurately surveys the heart,
 listening to every word.
⁷ For the spirit of the Lord fills the world,
 and that which holds everything together knows
 every word said.
⁸ No one who speaks what is wrong will go
 undetected,
 nor will avenging Justice pass by such a one.
⁹ For the schemes of the godless will be examined,
 and a report of his words will reach the Lord
 to convict him of his crimes.
¹⁰ There is a jealous ear that overhears everything,
 not even a murmur of complaint escapes it.
¹¹ So beware of uttering frivolous complaints,
 restrain your tongue from finding fault;
 even what is said in secret has repercussions,
 and a lying mouth deals death to the soul.
¹² Do not court death by the errors of your ways,
 nor invite destruction through the work of your
 hands.
¹³ For God did not make Death,
 he takes no pleasure in destroying the living.
¹⁴ To exist — for this he created all things;
 the creatures of the world have health in them,
 in them is no fatal poison,
 and Hades has no power over the world:
¹⁵ for uprightness is immortal.

| NEW REVISED STANDARD VERSION | REVISED ENGLISH BIBLE |

16 But the ungodly by their words and deeds
    summoned death;[d]
considering him a friend, they pined away
    and made a covenant with him,
because they are fit to belong to his company.

2 For they reasoned unsoundly, saying to
        themselves,
"Short and sorrowful is our life,
    and there is no remedy when a life comes to its
        end,
    and no one has been known to return from
        Hades.
2 For we were born by mere chance,
    and hereafter we shall be as though we had never
        been,
for the breath in our nostrils is smoke,
    and reason is a spark kindled by the beating of
        our hearts;
3 when it is extinguished, the body will turn to
        ashes,
    and the spirit will dissolve like empty air.
4 Our name will be forgotten in time,
    and no one will remember our works;
our life will pass away like the traces of a cloud,
    and be scattered like mist
that is chased by the rays of the sun
    and overcome by its heat.
5 For our allotted time is the passing of a shadow,
    and there is no return from our death,
because it is sealed up and no one turns back.

6 "Come, therefore, let us enjoy the good things
        that exist,
    and make use of the creation to the full as in
        youth.
7 Let us take our fill of costly wine and perfumes,
    and let no flower of spring pass us by.
8 Let us crown ourselves with rosebuds before they
        wither.
9 Let none of us fail to share in our revelry;
    everywhere let us leave signs of enjoyment,
because this is our portion, and this our lot.
10 Let us oppress the righteous poor man;
    let us not spare the widow
    or regard the gray hairs of the aged.
11 But let our might be our law of right,
    for what is weak proves itself to be useless.

12 "Let us lie in wait for the righteous man,
    because he is inconvenient to us and opposes our
        actions;
he reproaches us for sins against the law,
    and accuses us of sins against our training.
13 He professes to have knowledge of God,
    and calls himself a child[e] of the Lord.
14 He became to us a reproof of our thoughts;
15 the very sight of him is a burden to us,
    because his manner of life is unlike that of
        others,
    and his ways are strange.
16 We are considered by him as something base,
    and he avoids our ways as unclean;
he calls the last end of the righteous happy,
    and boasts that God is his father.
17 Let us see if his words are true,
    and let us test what will happen at the end of his
        life;

deeds and words have asked death for his company. Thinking him their friend and pining for him, they have made a
pact with him because they are fit members of his party.

2 They said to themselves in their deluded way: 'Our life
    is short and full of trouble, and when a person comes
to the end there is no remedy; no one has been known to
return from the grave. 2 By mere chance were we born, and
afterwards we shall be as though we had never existed, for
the breath in our nostrils is but a wisp of smoke; our reason
is a mere spark kept alive by the beating of our hearts, 3 and
when that goes out, our body will turn to ashes and the
breath of our life disperse like empty air. 4 With the passing
of time our names will be forgotten, and no one will remember anything we did. Our life will vanish like the last vestige
of a cloud; and as a mist is chased away by the sun's rays
and overborne by its heat, so too will life be dispersed. 5 A
fleeting shadow — such is our life, and there is no postpone-
ment of our end. Man's fate is sealed: no one returns.

6 'Come then, let us enjoy the good things while we can
and, with all the eagerness of youth, make full use of the
creation. 7 Let us have costly wines and perfumes to our
heart's content, and let no flower of spring escape us. 8 Let
us crown ourselves with rosebuds before they wither. 9 Let
none of us fail to share in the good things that are ours; let
us leave behind on every side traces of our revelry. This is
the life for us, this our birthright.

10 'Down with the poor and honest man! Let us show no
mercy to the widow, no reverence to the grey hairs of old
age. 11 For us let might be right! Weakness is proved to be
good for nothing. 12 Let us set a trap for the just man; he
stands in our way, a check to us at every turn; he girds at
us as breakers of the law, and calls us traitors to our upbringing. 13 He knows God, so he says; he styles himself
"child of the Lord". 14 He is a living condemnation of all our
way of thinking. 15 The very sight of him is an affliction to
us, because his life is not like other people's, and the paths
he follows are quite different. 16 He rejects us like base
coin, and avoids us and our ways as if we were filth; he says
that the just die happy, and boasts that God is his father.
17 Let us test the truth of his claim, let us see what will
happen to him in the end; 18 for if the just man is God's son,

NEW AMERICAN BIBLE

16 It was the wicked who with hands and words
    invited death,
  considered it a friend, and pined for it,
  and made a covenant with it,
  Because they deserve to be in its possession,

2 ¹ they who said among themselves, thinking
    not aright:
  "Brief and troublous is our lifetime;
    neither is there any remedy for man's dying,
    nor is anyone known to have come back from
      the nether world.
² For haphazard were we born,
    and hereafter we shall be as though we had
      not been;
  Because the breath in our nostrils is a smoke
    and reason is a spark at the beating of
      our hearts,
³ And when this is quenched, our body will be ashes
    and our spirit will be poured abroad like
      unresisting air.
⁴ Even our name will be forgotten in time,
    and no one will recall our deeds.
  So our life will pass away like the traces of
    a cloud,
    and will be dispersed like a mist
  pursued by the sun's rays
    and overpowered by its heat.
⁵ For our lifetime is the passing of a shadow;
    and our dying cannot be deferred
    because it is fixed with a seal; and no
      one returns.
⁶ Come, therefore, let us enjoy the good things that
    are real,
    and use the freshness of creation avidly.
⁷ Let us have our fill of costly wine and perfumes,
    and let no springtime blossom pass us by;
⁸ let us crown ourselves with rosebuds ere
    they wither.
⁹ Let no meadow be free from our wantonness;
    everywhere let us leave tokens of our rejoicing,
    for this our portion is, and this our lot.
¹⁰ Let us oppress the needy just man;
    let us neither spare the widow
    nor revere the old man for his hair grown white
      with time.
¹¹ But let our strength be our norm of justice;
    for weakness proves itself useless.
¹² Let us beset the just one, because he is obnoxious
      to us;
    he sets himself against our doings,
  Reproaches us for transgressions of the law
    and charges us with violations of our training.
¹³ He professes to have knowledge of God
    and styles himself a child of the LORD.
¹⁴ To us he is the censure of our thoughts;
    merely to see him is a hardship for us,
¹⁵ Because his life is not like other men's,
    and different are his ways.
¹⁶ He judges us debased;
    he holds aloof from our paths as from
      things impure.
  He calls blest the destiny of the just
    and boasts that God is his Father.
¹⁷ Let us see whether his words be true;
    let us find out what will happen to him.

NEW JERUSALEM BIBLE

16 But the godless call for Death with deed and word,
    counting him friend, they wear themselves out for
      him;
  with him they make a pact,
    worthy as they are to belong to him.

2 And this is the false argument they use,
  'Our life is short and dreary,
    there is no remedy when our end comes,
    no one is known to have come back from Hades.
² We came into being by chance
    and afterwards shall be as though we had never
      been.
  The breath in our nostrils is a puff of smoke,
    reason a spark from the beating of our hearts;
³ extinguish this and the body turns to ashes,
    and the spirit melts away like the yielding air.
⁴ In time, our name will be forgotten,
    nobody will remember what we have done;
  our life will pass away like wisps of cloud,
    dissolving like the mist
    that the sun's rays drive away
    and that its heat dispels.
⁵ For our days are the passing of a shadow,
    our end is without return,
    the seal is affixed and nobody comes back.

⁶ 'Come then, let us enjoy the good things of today,
    let us use created things with the zest of youth:
⁷ take our fill of the dearest wines and perfumes,
    on no account forgo the flowers of spring
⁸ but crown ourselves with rosebuds before they
      wither,
⁹ no meadow excluded from our orgy;
    let us leave the signs of our revelry everywhere,
    since this is our portion, this our lot!

¹⁰ 'As for the upright man who is poor, let us oppress
      him;
    let us not spare the widow,
    nor respect old age, white-haired with many years.
¹¹ Let our might be the yardstick of right,
    since weakness argues its own futility.
¹² Let us lay traps for the upright man, since he
      annoys us
    and opposes our way of life,
    reproaches us for our sins against the Law,
    and accuses us of sins against our upbringing.
¹³ He claims to have knowledge of God,
    and calls himself a child of the Lord.
¹⁴ We see him as a reproof to our way of thinking,
    the very sight of him weighs our spirits down;
¹⁵ for his kind of life is not like other people's,
    and his ways are quite different.
¹⁶ In his opinion we are counterfeit;
    he avoids our ways as he would filth;
    he proclaims the final end of the upright as blessed
    and boasts of having God for his father.
¹⁷ Let us see if what he says is true,
    and test him to see what sort of end he will have.

| NEW REVISED STANDARD VERSION | REVISED ENGLISH BIBLE |

18 for if the righteous man is God's child, he will
   help him,
   and will deliver him from the hand of his
   adversaries.
19 Let us test him with insult and torture,
   so that we may find out how gentle he is,
   and make trial of his forbearance.
20 Let us condemn him to a shameful death,
   for, according to what he says, he will be
   protected."

21 Thus they reasoned, but they were led astray,
   for their wickedness blinded them,
22 and they did not know the secret purposes of
   God,
   nor hoped for the wages of holiness,
   nor discerned the prize for blameless souls;
23 for God created us for incorruption,
   and made us in the image of his own eternity,f
24 but through the devil's envy death entered the
   world,
   and those who belong to his company experience
   it.

3 But the souls of the righteous are in the hand of
   God,
   and no torment will ever touch them.
2 In the eyes of the foolish they seemed to have
   died,
   and their departure was thought to be a disaster,
3 and their going from us to be their destruction;
   but they are at peace.
4 For though in the sight of others they were
   punished,
   their hope is full of immortality.
5 Having been disciplined a little, they will receive
   great good,
   because God tested them and found them worthy
   of himself;
6 like gold in the furnace he tried them,
   and like a sacrificial burnt offering he accepted
   them.
7 In the time of their visitation they will shine
   forth,
   and will run like sparks through the stubble.
8 They will govern nations and rule over peoples,
   and the Lord will reign over them forever.
9 Those who trust in him will understand truth,
   and the faithful will abide with him in love,
   because grace and mercy are upon his holy ones,
   and he watches over his elect.g

10 But the ungodly will be punished as their
   reasoning deserves,
   those who disregarded the righteoush
   and rebelled against the Lord;
11 for those who despise wisdom and instruction are
   miserable.
   Their hope is vain, their labors are unprofitable,
   and their works are useless.
12 Their wives are foolish, and their children evil;
13 their offspring are accursed.
   For blessed is the barren woman who is
   undefiled,
   who has not entered into a sinful union;
   she will have fruit when God examines souls.

God will stretch out a hand to him and save him from the
clutches of his enemies. 19 Insult and torture are the means
to put him to the test, to measure his forbearance and learn
how long his patience lasts. 20 Let us condemn him to a
shameful death, for, if what he says is true, he will have a
protector.'

21 So they argued, and how wrong they were! Blinded by
their own malevolence, 22 they failed to understand God's
hidden plan; they never expected that holiness of life would
have its recompense, never thought that innocence would
have its reward. 23 But God created man imperishable, and
made him the image of his own eternal self; 24 it was the
devil's spite that brought death into the world, and the
experience of it is reserved for those who take his side.

3 But the souls of the just are in God's hand; no torment
   will touch them. 2 In the eyes of the foolish they
seemed to be dead; their departure was reckoned as defeat,
3 and their going from us as disaster. But they are at peace,
4 for though in the sight of men they may suffer punishment,
they have a sure hope of immortality; 5 and after a little
chastisement they will receive great blessings, because God
has tested them and found them worthy to be his. 6 He put
them to the proof like gold in a crucible, and found them
acceptable like an offering burnt whole on the altar. 7 In the
hour of their judgement they will shine in glory, and will
sweep over the world like sparks through stubble. 8 They
will be judges and rulers over nations and peoples, and the
Lord will be their King for ever. 9 Those who have put their
trust in him will understand that he is true, and the faithful
will attend upon him in love; they are his chosen, and grace
and mercy will be theirs.

10 But the godless will meet with the punishment their
evil thoughts deserve, because they took no heed of justice
and rebelled against the Lord. 11 Wretched indeed is he who
thinks nothing of wisdom and discipline; the hopes of such
people are void, their labours unprofitable, their actions
futile; 12 their wives are wanton, their children depraved,
13 their parenthood is under a curse. But blessed is the childless woman if she is innocent, if she has never slept with a
man in sin; at the great assize of souls she will find a
fruitfulness of her own. 14 Blessed also is the eunuch, if he

---

f Other ancient authorities read *nature*   g Text of this line uncertain;
omitted by some ancient authorities. Compare 4.15   h Or *what is
right*

18 For if the just one be the son of God, he will
defend him
and deliver him from the hand of his foes.
19 With revilement and torture let us put him to
the test
that we may have proof of his gentleness
and try his patience.
20 Let us condemn him to a shameful death;
for according to his own words, God will take
care of him."
21 These were their thoughts, but they erred;
for their wickedness blinded them,
22 And they knew not the hidden counsels of God;
neither did they count on a recompense
of holiness
nor discern the innocent souls' reward.
23 For God formed man to be imperishable;
the image of his own nature he made him.
24 But by the envy of the devil, death entered
the world,
and they who are in his possession experience it.

3 But the souls of the just are in the hand of God,
and no torment shall touch them.
2 They seemed, in the view of the foolish, to
be dead;
and their passing away was thought an affliction
3 and their going forth from us, utter destruction.
But they are in peace.
4 For if before men, indeed, they be punished,
yet is their hope full of immortality;
5 Chastised a little, they shall be greatly blessed,
because God tried them
and found them worthy of himself.
6 As gold in the furnace, he proved them,
and as sacrificial offerings he took them
to himself.
7 In the time of their visitation they shall shine,
and shall dart about as sparks through stubble;
8 They shall judge nations and rule over peoples,
and the LORD shall be their King forever.
9 Those who trust in him shall understand truth,
and the faithful shall abide with him in love:
Because grace and mercy are with his holy ones,
and his care is with his elect.
10 But the wicked shall receive a punishment to match
their thoughts,
since they neglected justice and forsook
the LORD.
11 For he who despises wisdom and instruction
is doomed.
Vain is their hope, fruitless are their labors,
and worthless are their works.
12 Their wives are foolish and their children wicked;
accursed is their brood.
13 Yes, blessed is she who, childless and undefiled,
knew not transgression of the marriage bed;
she shall bear fruit at the visitation of souls.

18 For if the upright man is God's son, God will help
him
and rescue him from the clutches of his enemies.
19 Let us test him with cruelty and with torture,
and thus explore this gentleness of his
and put his patience to the test.
20 Let us condemn him to a shameful death
since God will rescue him — or so he claims.'
21 This is the way they reason, but they are misled,
since their malice makes them blind.
22 They do not know the hidden things of God,
they do not hope for the reward of holiness,
they do not believe in a reward for blameless
souls.
23 For God created human beings to be immortal,
he made them as an image of his own nature;
24 Death came into the world only through the Devil's
envy,
as those who belong to him find to their cost.

3 But the souls of the upright are in the hands of
God,
and no torment can touch them.
2 To the unenlightened, they appeared to die,
their departure was regarded as disaster,
3 their leaving us like annihilation;
but they are at peace.
4 If, as it seemed to us, they suffered punishment,
their hope was rich with immortality;
5 slight was their correction, great will their
blessings be.
God was putting them to the test
and has proved them worthy to be with him;
6 he has tested them like gold in a furnace,
and accepted them as a perfect burnt offering.
7 At their time of visitation, they will shine out;
as sparks run through the stubble, so will they.
8 They will judge nations, rule over peoples,
and the Lord will be their king for ever.
9 Those who trust in him will understand the truth,
those who are faithful will live with him in love;
for grace and mercy await his holy ones,
and he intervenes on behalf of his chosen.
10 But the godless will be duly punished for their
reasoning,
for having neglected the upright and deserted the
Lord.
11 Yes, wretched are they who scorn wisdom and
discipline:
their hope is void,
their toil unavailing,
their achievements unprofitable;
12 their wives are reckless,
their children depraved,
their descendants accursed.
13 Blessed the sterile woman if she be blameless,
and has not known an unlawful bed,
for she will have fruit at the visitation of souls.

NEW REVISED STANDARD VERSION

14 Blessed also is the eunuch whose hands have
    done no lawless deed,
    and who has not devised wicked things against
        the Lord;
    for special favor will be shown him for his
        faithfulness,
    and a place of great delight in the temple of the
        Lord.
15 For the fruit of good labors is renowned,
    and the root of understanding does not fail.
16 But children of adulterers will not come to
        maturity,
    and the offspring of an unlawful union will
        perish.
17 Even if they live long they will be held of no
        account,
    and finally their old age will be without honor.
18 If they die young, they will have no hope
    and no consolation on the day of judgment;
19 For the end of an unrighteous generation is
        grievous.

4 Better than this is childlessness with virtue,
    for in the memory of virtue[i] is immortality,
    because it is known both by God and by mortals.
2 When it is present, people imitate[j] it,
    and they long for it when it has gone;
    throughout all time it marches, crowned in
        triumph,
    victor in the contest for prizes that are undefiled.
3 But the prolific brood of the ungodly will be of
        no use,
    and none of their illegitimate seedlings will strike
        a deep root
    or take a firm hold.
4 For even if they put forth boughs for a while,
    standing insecurely they will be shaken by the
        wind,
    and by the violence of the winds they will be
        uprooted.
5 The branches will be broken off before they come
        to maturity,
    and their fruit will be useless,
    not ripe enough to eat, and good for nothing.
6 For children born of unlawful unions
    are witnesses of evil against their parents when
        God examines them.[k]
7 But the righteous, though they die early, will be
        at rest.
8 For old age is not honored for length of time,
    or measured by number of years;
9 but understanding is gray hair for anyone,
    and a blameless life is ripe old age.
10 There were some who pleased God and were
        loved by him,
    and while living among sinners were taken up.
11 They were caught up so that evil might not
        change their understanding
    or guile deceive their souls.
12 For the fascination of wickedness obscures what
        is good,
    and roving desire perverts the innocent mind.
13 Being perfected in a short time, they fulfilled
        long years;
14 for their souls were pleasing to the Lord,
    therefore he took them quickly from the midst of
        wickedness.

REVISED ENGLISH BIBLE

has never done anything against the law and never harboured a wicked thought against the Lord; in return for his faith he will receive special favour, and a place in the Lord's temple to delight his heart the more. 15 Honest work bears glorious fruit, and wisdom grows from roots that are imperishable. 16 But the children of adultery are like fruit that never ripens; they have sprung from a union forbidden by the law and will come to nothing. 17 Even if they attain length of life, they will be held of no account, and at the end their old age will be without honour. 18 If they die young, they will have no hope, no consolation in the day of judgement; 19 the unjust generation has a harsh fate in store.

4 It is better to be childless, provided one is virtuous; for virtue held in remembrance is a kind of immortality, because it wins recognition from God, and also from mankind; 2 they follow the good person's example while it is with them, and when it is gone they mourn its loss. Through all time virtue makes its triumphal progress, crowned with victory in the contest for prizes that nothing can tarnish. 3 But the swarming progeny of the godless will come to no good; none of their bastard offshoots will strike deep root or take firm hold. 4 For a time their branches may flourish, but as they have no sure footing they will be shaken by the wind, and uprooted by the violence of the gales. 5 Their boughs will be snapped off half grown, and their fruit will be worthless, unripe, uneatable, and fit for nothing. 6 Children engendered in unlawful union are living evidence of their parents' sin when God brings them to account.

7 But the just person, even one who dies an untimely death, will be at rest. 8 It is not length of life and number of years which bring the honour due to age; 9 if people have understanding, they may have grey hairs enough, and an unblemished life is the true ripeness of age. 10 There was once such a man who pleased God, and God accepted him and took him while still living from among sinners. 11 He was snatched away before his mind could be perverted by wickedness or his soul deceived by falsehood 12 (because evil is like witchcraft: it dims the radiance of good, and the waywardness of desire unsettles an innocent mind); 13 in a short time he came to the perfection of a full span of years. 14 His soul was pleasing to the Lord, who removed him early from

---

[i] Gk it   [j] Other ancient authorities read *honor*   [k] Gk *at their examination*

14 So also the eunuch whose hand wrought
    no misdeed,
  who held no wicked thoughts against
    the LORD —
For he shall be given fidelity's choice reward
  and a more gratifying heritage in the
    LORD's temple.
15 For the fruit of noble struggles is a glorious one;
  and unfailing is the root of understanding.
16 But the children of adulterers will remain
    without issue,
  and the progeny of an unlawful bed
    will disappear.
17 For should they attain long life, they will be held
    in no esteem,
  and dishonored will their old age be at last;
18 While should they die abruptly, they have no hope
  nor comfort in the day of scrutiny;
19   for dire is the end of the wicked generation.

4 Better is childlessness with virtue;
  for immortal is its memory:
    because both by God is it acknowledged, and
    by men.
2 When it is present men imitate it,
  and they long for it when it is gone;
And forever it marches crowned in triumph,
  victorious in unsullied deeds of valor.
3 But the numerous progeny of the wicked shall be
    of no avail;
  their spurious offshoots shall not strike deep root
    nor take firm hold.
4 For even though their branches flourish for a time,
  they are unsteady and shall be rocked by
    the wind
  and, by the violence of the winds, uprooted;
5 Their twigs shall be broken off untimely,
  and their fruit be useless, unripe for eating,
  and fit for nothing.
6 For children born of lawless unions
  give evidence of the wickedness of their parents,
    when they are examined.
7 But the just man, though he die early, shall be
    at rest.
8 For the age that is honorable comes not with the
    passing of time,
  nor can it be measured in terms of years.
9 Rather, understanding is the hoary crown for men,
  and an unsullied life, the attainment of old age.
10 He who pleased God was loved;
  he who lived among sinners was transported —
11 Snatched away, lest wickedness pervert his mind
  or deceit beguile his soul;
12 For the witchery of paltry things obscures what
    is right
  and the whirl of desire transforms the
    innocent mind.
13 Having become perfect in a short while,
  he reached the fullness of a long career;
14   for his soul was pleasing to the LORD,
  therefore he sped him out of the midst
    of wickedness.

14 Blessed, too, the eunuch whose hand commits no
    crime,
  and who harbours no resentment against the Lord:
    a special favour will be granted to him for his
    loyalty,
  a most desirable portion in the temple of the Lord.
15 For the fruit of honest labours is glorious,
  and the root of understanding does not decay.
16 But the children of adulterers will not reach
    maturity,
  the offspring of an unlawful bed will disappear.
17 Even if they live long, they will count for nothing,
  their old age will go unhonoured at the last;
18 while if they die early, they have neither hope
  nor comfort on the day of judgement,
19 for the end of a race of evil-doers is harsh.

4 Better to have no children yet to have virtue,
  since immortality perpetuates its memory;
  for God and human beings both recognise it.
2 Present, we imitate it,
  absent, we long for it;
  crowned, it holds triumph through eternity,
  having striven for untainted prizes and emerged the
    victor.
3 But the offspring of the godless come to nothing,
    however prolific,
  sprung from a bastard stock, they will never strike
    deep roots,
  never put down firm foundations.
4 They may branch out for a time,
  but, on unsteady foundations, they will be rocked
    by the wind
  and uprooted by the force of the storm;
5 their branches, yet unformed, will be snapped off,
  their fruit is useless,
  too unripe to eat,
  fit for nothing.
6 For children begotten of unlawful bed
  witness, when put on trial, to their parents'
    wickedness.
7 The upright, though he die before his time, will
    find rest.
8 Length of days is not what makes age honourable,
  nor number of years the true measure of life;
9 understanding, this is grey hairs,
  untarnished life, this is ripe old age.
10 Having won God's favour, he has been loved
  and, as he was living among sinners, has been
    taken away.
11 He has been carried off so that evil may not warp
    his understanding
  or deceitfulness seduce his soul;
12 for the fascination of evil throws good things into
    the shade,
  and the whirlwind of desire corrupts a simple
    heart.
13 Having come to perfection so soon, he has lived
    long;
14 his soul being pleasing to the Lord,
  he has hurried away from the wickedness around
    him.

15 Yet the peoples saw and did not understand,
or take such a thing to heart,
that God's grace and mercy are with his elect,
and that he watches over his holy ones.

16 The righteous who have died will condemn the
ungodly who are living,
and youth that is quickly perfected[1] will
condemn the prolonged old age of the
unrighteous.

17 For they will see the end of the wise,
and will not understand what the Lord purposed
for them,
and for what he kept them safe.

18 The unrighteous[m] will see, and will have
contempt for them,
but the Lord will laugh them to scorn.
After this they will become dishonored corpses,
and an outrage among the dead forever;

19 because he will dash them speechless to the
ground,
and shake them from the foundations;
they will be left utterly dry and barren,
and they will suffer anguish,
and the memory of them will perish.

20 They will come with dread when their sins are
reckoned up,
and their lawless deeds will convict them to their
face.

5 Then the righteous will stand with great
confidence
in the presence of those who have oppressed them
and those who make light of their labors.

2 When the unrighteous[n] see them, they will be
shaken with dreadful fear,
and they will be amazed at the unexpected
salvation of the righteous.

3 They will speak to one another in repentance,
and in anguish of spirit they will groan, and say,

4 "These are persons whom we once held in
derision
and made a byword of reproach—fools that we
were!
We thought that their lives were madness
and that their end was without honor.

5 Why have they been numbered among the
children of God?
And why is their lot among the saints?

6 So it was we who strayed from the way of truth,
and the light of righteousness did not shine on us,
and the sun did not rise upon us.

7 We took our fill of the paths of lawlessness and
destruction,
and we journeyed through trackless deserts,
but the way of the Lord we have not known.

8 What has our arrogance profited us?
And what good has our boasted wealth brought
us?

9 "All those things have vanished like a shadow,
and like a rumor that passes by;

10 like a ship that sails through the billowy water,
and when it has passed no trace can be found,
no track of its keel in the waves;

a wicked world. 15 People see this but give it no thought;
they do not lay to heart the truth, that those whom God has
chosen enjoy his grace and mercy, and that he comes to the
help of his holy people.

16 Even after his death the just person will shame the
godless who are still alive; youth come quickly to perfection
will shame the person who has grown old in sin. 17 The
godless will see the end of the wise person, without understanding what the Lord had purposed for him and why he
took him into safe keeping; 18 they will see it and make light
of him, but it is they whom the Lord will laugh to scorn. In
death their bodies will be dishonoured, and among the dead
they will be an object of lasting contempt; 19 for he will fling
them speechless to the ground, shake them from their foundations, and leave them barren as a desert; they will be in
anguish, and all memory of them will perish. 20 So, on the
day of reckoning for their sins, they will come cringing,
convicted to their face by their own lawless actions.

5 Then the just man will take his stand, full of assurance,
to confront those who oppressed him and made light of
his sufferings; 2 at the sight of him there will be terror and
confusion, and they will be astounded at his unforeseen
deliverance. 3 Remorseful, groaning and gasping for breath,
they will say among themselves: 'Was not this the man who
was once our butt, a target for our contempt? 4 Fools that we
were, we held his way of life to be madness and his end
dishonourable. 5 To think he is now counted one of the sons
of God and assigned a place of his own among God's people! 6 How far we strayed from the way of truth! The lamp
of justice never gave us light, the sun never rose on us. 7 We
roamed to our heart's content along the paths of wickedness
and ruin, wandering through trackless deserts and ignoring
the Lord's highway. 8 What good has pride been to us?
What can we show for all our vaunted wealth? 9 All those
things have passed like a shadow, like a messenger galloping by; 10 like a ship that cleaves the surging sea and, when
she has passed, not a trace is to be found, no wake from her
keel in the waves; 11 or as when a bird flies through the air,

---

[1]Or ended   [m] Gk They   [n] Gk they

|

But the people saw and did not understand,
nor did they take this into account.

16 Yes, the just man dead condemns the sinful
who live,
and youth swiftly completed
condemns the many years of the wicked man
grown old.
17 For they see the death of the wise man
and do not understand what the LORD intended
for him,
or why he made him secure.
18 They see, and hold him in contempt;
but the LORD laughs them to scorn.
19 And they shall afterward become
dishonored corpses
and an unceasing mockery among the dead.
For he shall strike them down speechless
and prostrate
and rock them to their foundations;
They shall be utterly laid waste
and shall be in grief
and their memory shall perish.

20 Fearful shall they come, at the counting up of
their sins,
and their lawless deeds shall convict them to
their face.

5 Then shall the just one with great
assurance confront
his oppressors who set at nought his labors.
2 Seeing this, they shall be shaken with
dreadful fear,
and amazed at the unlooked-for salvation.
3 They shall say among themselves, rueful
and groaning through anguish of spirit:
"This is he whom once we held as a laughingstock
and as a type for mockery, 4 fools that we were!
His life we accounted madness,
and his death dishonored.
5 See how he is accounted among the sons of God;
how his lot is with the saints!
6 We, then, have strayed from the way of truth,
and the light of justice did not shine for us,
and the sun did not rise for us.
7 We had our fill of the ways of mischief and
of ruin;
we journeyed through impassable deserts,
but the way of the LORD we knew not.
8 What did our pride avail us?
What have wealth and its boastfulness
afforded us?
9 All of them passed like a shadow
and like a fleeting rumor;
10 Like a ship traversing the heaving water,
of which, when it has passed, no trace can
be found,
no path of its keel in the waves.

Yet people look on, uncomprehending;
and it does not enter their heads
15 that grace and mercy await his chosen ones
and that he intervenes on behalf of his holy ones.
16 The upright who dies condemns the godless who
survive,
and youth quickly perfected condemns the lengthy
old age of the wicked.
17 These people see the end of the wise
without understanding what the Lord has in store
or why he has taken such a one to safety;
18 they look on and sneer,
but the Lord will laugh at them.
19 Soon they will be corpses without honour,
objects of horror among the dead for ever.
For he will shatter them and fling them headlong
and dumbfounded.
He will shake them from their foundations;
they will be utterly laid waste,
a prey to grief,
and their memory will perish.

20 When the count of their sins has been drawn up, in
terror they will come,
and their crimes, confronting them, will accuse
them.

5 Then the upright will stand up boldly
to face those who had oppressed him
and had thought so little of his sufferings.
2 And, seeing him, they will be seized with terrible
fear,
amazed that he should have been so unexpectedly
saved.
3 Stricken with remorse, they will say to one another
with groans and labouring breath,
4 'This is the one whom we used to mock,
making him the butt of our insults, fools that we
were!
His life we regarded as madness,
his ending as without honour.
5 How has he come to be counted as one of the
children of God
and to have his lot among the holy ones?
6 Clearly we have strayed from the way of truth;
the light of justice has not shone for us,
the sun has not risen for us.
7 We have left no path of lawlessness or ruin
unexplored,
we have crossed deserts where there was no track,
but the way of the Lord is one we have never
known.
8 What good has arrogance been to us?
What has been the purpose of our riches and
boastfulness?
9 All those things have passed like a shadow,
passed like a fleeting rumour.
10 Like a ship that cuts through heaving waves —
leaving no trace to show where it has passed,
no wake from its keel in the waves.

4, 15: The verse here omitted repeats the last two lines of Wis 3, 9.

| NEW REVISED STANDARD VERSION | REVISED ENGLISH BIBLE |

NEW REVISED STANDARD VERSION

11 or as, when a bird flies through the air,
 no evidence of its passage is found;
 the light air, lashed by the beat of its pinions
 and pierced by the force of its rushing flight,
 is traversed by the movement of its wings,
 and afterward no sign of its coming is found
  there;

12 or as, when an arrow is shot at a target,
 the air, thus divided, comes together at once,
 so that no one knows its pathway.

13 So we also, as soon as we were born, ceased to
  be,
 and we had no sign of virtue to show,
 but were consumed in our wickedness."

14 Because the hope of the ungodly is like
  thistledown[o] carried by the wind,
 and like a light frost[p] driven away by a storm;
 it is dispersed like smoke before the wind,
 and it passes like the remembrance of a guest
  who stays but a day.

15 But the righteous live forever,
 and their reward is with the Lord;
 the Most High takes care of them.

16 Therefore they will receive a glorious crown
 and a beautiful diadem from the hand of the
  Lord,
 because with his right hand he will cover them,
 and with his arm he will shield them.

17 The Lord[q] will take his zeal as his whole armor,
 and will arm all creation to repel[r] his enemies;

18 he will put on righteousness as a breastplate,
 and wear impartial justice as a helmet;

19 he will take holiness as an invincible shield,

20 and sharpen stern wrath for a sword,
 and creation will join with him to fight against
  his frenzied foes.

21 Shafts of lightning will fly with true aim,
 and will leap from the clouds to the target, as
  from a well-drawn bow,

22 and hailstones full of wrath will be hurled as
  from a catapult;
 the water of the sea will rage against them,
 and rivers will relentlessly overwhelm them;

23 a mighty wind will rise against them,
 and like a tempest it will winnow them away.
 Lawlessness will lay waste the whole earth,
 and evildoing will overturn the thrones of rulers.

6 Listen therefore, O kings, and understand;
 learn, O judges of the ends of the earth.

2 Give ear, you that rule over multitudes,
 and boast of many nations.

3 For your dominion was given you from the Lord,
 and your sovereignty from the Most High;
 he will search out your works and inquire into
  your plans.

4 Because as servants of his kingdom you did not
  rule rightly,
 or keep the law,
 or walk according to the purpose of God,

5 he will come upon you terribly and swiftly,
 because severe judgment falls on those in high
  places.

6 For the lowliest may be pardoned in mercy,
 but the mighty will be mightily tested.

REVISED ENGLISH BIBLE

there is no sign of her passage, but with the stroke of her pinions she lashes the insubstantial breeze and parts it with the whirr and the rush of her beating wings, and so she passes through it, and thereafter it bears no mark of her assault; 12 or as when a shaft is shot at a target, the air is parted and instantly closes up again and no one can tell where the arrow passed. 13 So too with us, as soon as we were born we ceased to be; we had no token of virtue to show, and in our wickedness we frittered our lives away.'

14 The hope of the godless is like down flying on the wind, like spindrift swept before a storm, like smoke which the wind whirls away, transient like the memory of a guest who stayed but one day.

15 But the just live for ever; their reward is in the Lord's keeping, and the Most High has them in his care. 16 Therefore royal splendour will be theirs, and a fair diadem from the Lord himself; he will protect them with his right hand and shield them with his arm. 17 He will array himself from head to foot with the armour of his wrath, and make all creation his weapon against his enemies. 18 With the cuirass of justice on his breast, and on his head the helmet of inflexible judgement, 19 he will take holiness for his invincible shield 20 and sharpen his relentless anger for a sword; and his whole world will join him in the fight against his frenzied foes. 21 The bolts of his lightning will fly straight upon the mark, they will leap upon the target as if his bow in the clouds were drawn in its full arc, 22 and the artillery of his resentment will let fly a fury of hail. The waters of the sea will rage over them, and the rivers wash them relentlessly away; 23 a great tempest will arise against them, and scatter them like chaff before a whirlwind. So lawlessness will make the whole world desolate, and evildoing will overturn the thrones of princes.

6 HEAR then, you kings, take this to heart; lords of the wide world, learn this lesson; 2 give ear, you rulers of the multitude, who take pride in the myriads of your people. 3 Your authority was bestowed on you by the Lord, your power comes from the Most High. He will probe your actions and scrutinize your intentions. 4 Though you are servants appointed by the King, you have not been upright judges; you have not maintained the law or guided your steps by the will of God. 5 Swiftly and terribly he will descend on you, for judgement falls relentlessly on those in high places. 6 The lowest may find pity and forgiveness, but those in power will be called powerfully to account; 7 for he

---

o Other ancient authorities read *dust*   p Other ancient authorities
read *spider's web*   q Gk He   r Or *punish*

NEW AMERICAN BIBLE

11 Or like a bird flying through the air;
   no evidence of its course is to be found—
But the fluid air, lashed by the beat of pinions,
   and cleft by the rushing force
Of speeding wings, is traversed:
   and afterward no mark of passage can be found
      in it.
12 Or as, when an arrow has been shot at a mark,
   the parted air straightway flows together again
      so that none discerns the way it went through—
13 Even so we, once born, abruptly came to nought
   and held no sign of virtue to display,
      but were consumed in our wickedness."
14 Yes, the hope of the wicked is like thistledown
      borne on the wind,
   and like fine, tempest-driven foam;
Like smoke scattered by the wind,
   and like the passing memory of the nomad
      camping for a single day.
15 But the just live forever,
   and in the LORD is their recompense,
      and the thought of them is with the Most High.
16 Therefore shall they receive the splendid crown,
   the beauteous diadem, from the hand of
      the LORD—
For he shall shelter them with his right hand,
   and protect them with his arm.
17 He shall take his zeal for armor
   and he shall arm creation to requite the enemy;
18 He shall don justice for a breastplate
   and shall wear sure judgment for a helmet;
19 He shall take invincible rectitude as a shield
20   and whet his sudden anger for a sword,
And the universe shall war with him against
      the foolhardy.
21 Well-aimed shafts of lightnings shall go forth
   and from the clouds as from a well-drawn bow
      shall leap to the mark;
22   and as from his sling, wrathful hailstones shall
      be hurled.
The water of the sea shall be enraged against them
   and the streams shall abruptly overflow;
23 A mighty wind shall confront them
   and a tempest winnow them out;
Thus lawlessness shall lay the whole earth waste
   and evildoing overturn the thrones of potentates.

6 Hear, therefore, kings, and understand;
   learn, you magistrates of the earth's expanse!
2 Hearken, you who are in power over the multitude
   and lord it over throngs of peoples!
3 Because authority was given you by the LORD
   and sovereignty by the Most High,
who shall probe your works and scrutinize
   your counsels!
4 Because, though you were ministers of his
      kingdom, you judged not rightly,
   and did not keep the law,
      nor walk according to the will of God,
5 Terribly and swiftly shall he come against you,
   because judgment is stern for the exalted—
6 For the lowly may be pardoned out of mercy
   but the mighty shall be mightily put to the test.

NEW JERUSALEM BIBLE

11 Or like a bird flying through the air—
   leaving no proof of its passing;
it whips the light air with the stroke of its pinions,
   tears it apart in its whirring rush,
drives its way onward with sweeping wing,
   and afterwards no sign is seen of its passage.
12 Or like an arrow shot at a mark,
   the pierced air closing so quickly on itself,
there is no knowing which way the arrow has
      passed.
13 So with us: scarcely born, we disappear;
   of virtue not a trace have we to show,
we have spent ourselves in our own wickedness!'
14 For the hope of the godless is like chaff carried on
      the wind,
   like fine spray driven by the storm;
it disperses like smoke before the wind,
   goes away like the memory of a one-day guest.
15 But the upright live for ever,
   their recompense is with the Lord,
      and the Most High takes care of them.
16 So they will receive the glorious crown
   and the diadem of beauty from the Lord's hand;
for he will shelter them with his right hand
   and with his arm he will shield them.
17 For armour he will take his jealous love,
   he will arm creation to punish his enemies;
18 he will put on justice as a breastplate,
   and for helmet wear his forthright judgement;
19 he will take up invincible holiness for shield,
20 of his pitiless wrath he will forge a sword,
   and the universe will march with him to fight the
      reckless.
21 Bolts truly aimed, the shafts of lightning will leap,
   and from the clouds, as from a full-drawn bow, fly
      to their mark;
22 and the catapult will hurl hailstones charged with
      fury.
The waters of the sea will rage against them,
   the rivers engulf them without pity,
23 a mighty gale will rise against them
   and winnow them like a hurricane.
Thus wickedness will lay the whole earth waste
   and evil-doing bring down the thrones of the
      mighty.

6 Listen then, kings, and understand;
   rulers of remotest lands, take warning;
2 hear this, you who govern great populations,
   taking pride in your hosts of subject nations!
3 For sovereignty is given to you by the Lord
   and power by the Most High,
who will himself probe your acts and scrutinise
   your intentions.
4 If therefore, as servants of his kingdom, you have
      not ruled justly
   nor observed the law,
      nor followed the will of God,
5 he will fall on you swiftly and terribly.
On the highly placed a ruthless judgement falls;
6 the lowly are pardoned, out of pity,
   but the mighty will be mightily tormented.

7 For the Lord of all will not stand in awe of
    anyone,
or show deference to greatness;
because he himself made both small and great,
    and he takes thought for all alike.
8 But a strict inquiry is in store for the mighty.
9 To you then, O monarchs, my words are
    directed,
so that you may learn wisdom and not transgress.
10 For they will be made holy who observe holy
    things in holiness,
and those who have been taught them will find a
    defense.
11 Therefore set your desire on my words;
long for them, and you will be instructed.

12 Wisdom is radiant and unfading,
and she is easily discerned by those who love
    her,
and is found by those who seek her.
13 She hastens to make herself known to those who
    desire her.
14 One who rises early to seek her will have no
    difficulty,
for she will be found sitting at the gate.
15 To fix one's thought on her is perfect
    understanding,
and one who is vigilant on her account will soon
    be free from care,
16 because she goes about seeking those worthy of
    her,
and she graciously appears to them in their paths,
    and meets them in every thought.

17 The beginning of wisdom[s] is the most sincere
    desire for instruction,
and concern for instruction is love of her,
18 and love of her is the keeping of her laws,
and giving heed to her laws is assurance of
    immortality,
19 and immortality brings one near to God;
20 so the desire for wisdom leads to a kingdom.

21 Therefore if you delight in thrones and scepters,
    O monarchs over the peoples,
honor wisdom, so that you may reign forever.
22 I will tell you what wisdom is and how she came
    to be,
and I will hide no secrets from you,
but I will trace her course from the beginning of
    creation,
and make knowledge of her clear,
and I will not pass by the truth;
23 nor will I travel in the company of sickly envy,
for envy[t] does not associate with wisdom.
24 The multitude of the wise is the salvation of the
    world,
and a sensible king is the stability of any people.
25 Therefore be instructed by my words, and you
    will profit.

7 I also am mortal, like everyone else,
    a descendant of the first-formed child of earth;
and in the womb of a mother I was molded into
    flesh,

who is Master of all is obsequious to none, and shows no deference to greatness. Small and great alike are of his making, and all are under his providence equally; [8] but it is for those who wield authority that he reserves the sternest inquisition. [9] To you, then, who have absolute power I speak, in hope that you may learn wisdom and not go astray; [10] those who in holiness have kept a holy course will be accounted holy, and those who have learnt that lesson will be able to make their defence. [11] Therefore be eager to hear me; long for my teaching, and you will learn.

[12] Wisdom shines brightly and never fades; she is readily discerned by those who love her, and by those who seek her she is found. [13] She is quick to make herself known to all who desire knowledge of her; [14] he who rises early in search of her will not grow weary in the quest, for he will find her seated at his door. [15] To meditate on her is prudence in its perfect shape, and to be vigilant in her cause is the short way to freedom from care; [16] she herself searches far and wide for those who are worthy of her, and on their daily path she appears to them with kindly intent, meeting them half-way in all their purposes.

[17] The true beginning of wisdom is the desire to learn, and a concern for learning means love towards her; [18] the love of her means the keeping of her laws; to keep her laws is a warrant of immortality; [19] and immortality brings a person near to God. [20] Thus desire for wisdom leads to a kingdom. [21] If, therefore, you value your thrones and your sceptres, you rulers of the nations, you must honour wisdom so that you may reign for ever.

[22] What wisdom is, and how she came into being, I shall tell you; I shall not conceal her mysteries from you. I shall trace out her course from her first beginnings, and bring the knowledge of her into the light of day; I shall not leave the truth untold. [23] Pale envy will not travel in my company, for the spiteful will have no share in wisdom. [24] Wise men in plenty are the world's salvation, and a prudent king is the sheet-anchor of his people. [25] Therefore learn what I have to teach you, and it will be for your good.

7 I too am a mortal like everyone else, descended from the first man, who was made of dust, [2] and in my

7 For the Lord of all shows no partiality,
  nor does he fear greatness,
Because he himself made the great as well as
    the small,
  and he provides for all alike;
8   but for those in power a rigorous
    scrutiny impends.
9 To you, therefore, O princes, are my
    words addressed
  that you may learn wisdom and that you may
    not sin.
10 For those who keep the holy precepts hallowed
    shall be found holy,
  and those learned in them will have ready
    a response.
11 Desire therefore my words;
  long for them and you shall be instructed.
12 Resplendent and unfading is Wisdom,
  and she is readily perceived by those who
    love her,
  and found by those who seek her.
13 She hastens to make herself known in anticipation
    of men's desire;
14   he who watches for her at dawn shall not
    be disappointed,
  for he shall find her sitting by his gate.
15 For taking thought of her is the perfection
    of prudence,
  and he who for her sake keeps vigil shall quickly
    be free from care;
16 Because she makes her own rounds, seeking those
    worthy of her,
  and graciously appears to them in the ways,
  and meets them with all solicitude.
17 For the first step toward discipline is a very earnest
    desire for her;
  then, care for discipline is love of her;
18   love means the keeping of her laws;
  To observe her laws is the basis
    for incorruptibility;
19   and incorruptibility makes one close to God;
20   thus the desire for Wisdom leads up to
    a kingdom.
21 If, then, you find pleasure in throne and scepter,
    you princes of the peoples,
  honor Wisdom, that you may reign as
    kings forever.
22 Now what Wisdom is, and how she came to be, I
    shall relate;
  and I shall hide no secrets from you,
  But from the very beginning I shall search out
  and bring to light knowledge of her,
  nor shall I diverge from the truth.
23 Neither shall I admit consuming jealousy to
    my company,
  because that can have no fellowship
    with Wisdom.
24 A great number of wise men is the safety of
    the world,
  and a prudent king, the stability of his people;
25   so take instruction from my words, to
    your profit.

7 I too am a mortal man, the same as all the rest,
  and a descendant of the first man formed
    of earth.
And in my mother's womb I was molded into flesh

7 For the Lord of all does not cower before anyone,
  he does not stand in awe of greatness,
  since he himself has made small and great
  and provides for all alike;
8 but a searching trial awaits those who wield power.
9 So, monarchs, my words are meant for you,
  so that you may learn wisdom and not fall into
    error;
10 for those who in holiness observe holy things will
    be adjudged holy,
  and, accepting instruction from them, will find
    their defence in them.
11 Set your heart, therefore, on what I have to say,
  listen with a will, and you will be instructed.
12 Wisdom is brilliant, she never fades.
  By those who love her, she is readily seen,
  by those who seek her, she is readily found.
13 She anticipates those who desire her by making
    herself known first.
14 Whoever gets up early to seek her will have no
    trouble
  but will find her sitting at the door.
15 Meditating on her is understanding in its perfect
    form,
  and anyone keeping awake for her will soon be
    free from care.
16 For she herself searches everywhere for those who
    are worthy of her,
  benevolently appearing to them on their ways,
  anticipating their every thought.
17 For Wisdom begins with the sincere desire for
    instruction,
  care for instruction means loving her,
18 loving her means keeping her laws,
  attention to her laws guarantees incorruptibility,
19 and incorruptibility brings us near to God;
20 the desire for Wisdom thus leads to sovereignty.
21 If then thrones and sceptres delight you, monarchs
    of the nations,
  honour Wisdom, so that you may reign for ever.
22 What Wisdom is and how she was born, I shall
    now explain;
  I shall hide no mysteries from you,
  but shall follow her steps from the outset of her
    origin,
  setting out what we know of her in full light,
  without departing from the truth.
23 Blighting envy is no companion for me,
  for envy has nothing in common with Wisdom.
24 In the greatest number of the wise lies the world's
    salvation,
  in a sagacious king the stability of a people.
25 Learn, therefore, from my words; the gain will be
    yours.

7 I too am mortal like everyone else,
  a descendant of the first man formed from
    the earth.
  I was modelled in flesh inside a mother's womb,

2 within the period of ten months, compacted with
     blood,
   from the seed of a man and the pleasure of
     marriage.

3 And when I was born, I began to breathe the
     common air,
   and fell upon the kindred earth;
   my first sound was a cry, as is true of all.

4 I was nursed with care in swaddling cloths.

5 For no king has had a different beginning of
     existence;

6 there is for all one entrance into life, and one
     way out.

7 Therefore I prayed, and understanding was given
     me;
   I called on God, and the spirit of wisdom came
     to me.

8 I preferred her to scepters and thrones,
   and I accounted wealth as nothing in comparison
     with her.

9 Neither did I liken to her any priceless gem,
   because all gold is but a little sand in her sight,
   and silver will be accounted as clay before her.

10 I loved her more than health and beauty,
    and I chose to have her rather than light,
    because her radiance never ceases.

11 All good things came to me along with her,
    and in her hands uncounted wealth.

12 I rejoiced in them all, because wisdom leads
      them;
    but I did not know that she was their mother.

13 I learned without guile and I impart without
      grudging;
    I do not hide her wealth,

14 for it is an unfailing treasure for mortals,
    those who get it obtain friendship with God,
    commended for the gifts that come from
      instruction.

15 May God grant me to speak with judgment,
    and to have thoughts worthy of what I have
      received;
    for he is the guide even of wisdom
    and the corrector of the wise.

16 For both we and our words are in his hand,
    as are all understanding and skill in crafts.

17 For it is he who gave me unerring knowledge of
      what exists,
    to know the structure of the world and the
      activity of the elements;

18 the beginning and end and middle of times,
    the alternations of the solstices and the changes of
      the seasons,

19 the cycles of the year and the constellations of
      the stars,

20 the natures of animals and the tempers of wild
      animals,
    the powers of spirits[u] and the thoughts of human
      beings,
    the varieties of plants and the virtues of roots;

21 I learned both what is secret and what is
      manifest,

mother's womb I was wrought into flesh during a ten-month
space, compacted in blood from the seed of her husband and
the pleasure that accompanies sleep. 3 When I was born, I
breathed the common air and was laid on the earth that all
mortals tread; and the first sound I uttered, as all do, was a
cry; 4 they wrapped me up and nursed me and cared for me.
5 No king begins life in any other way; 6 for all come into
life by a single path, and by a single path they go out again.

7 Therefore I prayed, and prudence was given me; I called
for help, and there came to me a spirit of wisdom. 8 I valued
her above sceptre and throne, and reckoned riches as nothing beside her; 9 I counted no precious stone her equal,
because compared with her all the gold in the world is but
a handful of sand, and silver worth no more than clay. 10 I
loved her more than health and beauty; I preferred her to the
light of day, for her radiance is unsleeping. 11 So all good
things together came to me with her, and in her hands was
wealth past counting. 12 Everything was mine to enjoy, for
all follow where wisdom leads; yet I was in ignorance that
she is the source of them all. 13 What I learnt with pure
intention I now share ungrudgingly, nor do I hoard for
myself the wealth that comes from her. 14 She is an inexhaustible treasure for mortals, and those who profit by it
become God's friends, commended to him by the gifts they
derive from her instruction.

15 God grant that I may speak according to his will, and
that my own thoughts may be worthy of his gifts, for even
wisdom is under God's direction and he corrects the wise;
16 we and our words, prudence and knowledge and craftsmanship, all are in his hand. 17 He it was who gave me true
understanding of things as they are: a knowledge of the
structure of the world and the operation of the elements;
18 the beginning and end of epochs and their middle course;
the alternating solstices and changing seasons; 19 the cycles
of the years and the constellations; 20 the nature of living
creatures and behaviour of wild beasts; the violent force of
winds and human thought; the varieties of plants and the
virtues of roots. 21 I learnt it all, hidden or manifest, 22 for

2 in a ten-months' period — body and blood,
from the seed of man, and the pleasure that
accompanies marriage.
3 And I too, when born, inhaled the common air,
and fell upon the kindred earth;
wailing, I uttered that first sound common to all.
4 In swaddling clothes and with constant care I
was nurtured.
5 For no king has any different origin or birth,
6 but one is the entry into life for all; and in one
same way they leave it.
7 Therefore I prayed, and prudence was given me;
I pleaded, and the spirit of Wisdom came to me.
8 I preferred her to scepter and throne,
And deemed riches nothing in comparison
with her,
9 nor did I liken any priceless gem to her;
Because all gold, in view of her, is a little sand,
and before her, silver is to be accounted mire.
10 Beyond health and comeliness I loved her,
And I chose to have her rather than the light,
because the splendor of her never yields
to sleep.
11 Yet all good things together came to me in
her company,
and countless riches at her hands;
12 And I rejoiced in them all, because Wisdom is
their leader,
though I had not known that she is the mother
of these.
13 Simply I learned about her, and ungrudgingly do
I share —
her riches I do not hide away;
14 For to men she is an unfailing treasure;
those who gain this treasure win the friendship
of God,
to whom the gifts they have from discipline
commend them.
15 Now God grant I speak suitably
and value these endowments at their worth:
For he is the guide of Wisdom
and the director of the wise.
16 For both we and our words are in his hand,
as well as all prudence and knowledge of crafts.
17 For he gave me sound knowledge of
existing things,
that I might know the organization of the
universe and the force of its elements,
18 The beginning and the end and the midpoint
of times,
the changes in the sun's course and the
variations of the seasons.
19 Cycles of years, positions of the stars,
20 natures of animals, tempers of beasts,
Powers of the winds and thoughts of men,
uses of plants and virtues of roots —
21 Such things as are hidden I learned, and such as
are plain;

2 where, for ten months, in blood I acquired
substance —
the result of virile seed and pleasure, sleep's
companion.
3 I too, when I was born, drew in the common air,
I fell on the same ground that bears us all,
and crying was the first sound I made, like
everyone else.
4 I was nurtured in swaddling clothes, with every
care.
5 No king has known any other beginning of
existence;
6 for there is only one way into life, and one way
out of it.
7 And so I prayed,*a* and understanding was given
me;
I entreated, and the spirit of Wisdom came to me.
8 I esteemed her more than sceptres and thrones;
compared with her, I held riches as nothing.
9 I reckoned no precious stone to be her equal,
for compared with her, all gold is a pinch of sand,
and beside her, silver ranks as mud.
10 I loved her more than health or beauty,
preferred her to the light,
since her radiance never sleeps.
11 In her company all good things came to me,
and at her hands incalculable wealth.
12 All these delighted me, since Wisdom brings them,
though I did not then realise that she was their
mother.
13 What I learned diligently, I shall pass on liberally,
I shall not conceal how rich she is.
14 For she is to human beings an inexhaustible
treasure,
and those who acquire this win God's friendship,
commended to him by the gifts of instruction.
15 May God grant me to speak as he would wish
and conceive thoughts worthy of the gifts I have
received,
since he is both guide to Wisdom and director of
sages;
16 for we are in his hand, yes, ourselves and our
sayings,
and all intellectual and all practical knowledge.
17 He it was who gave me sure knowledge of what
exists,
to understand the structure of the world and the
action of the elements,
18 the beginning, end and middle of the times,
the alternation of the solstices and the succession
of the seasons,
19 the cycles of the year and the position of the stars,
20 the natures of animals and the instincts of wild
beasts,
the powers of spirits and human mental processes,
the varieties of plants and the medical properties of
roots.
21 And now I understand everything, hidden or
visible,

a 7 Cf. 1 K 3:4–14.

22 for wisdom, the fashioner of all things, taught
    me.

There is in her a spirit that is intelligent, holy,
    unique, manifold, subtle,
mobile, clear, unpolluted,
distinct, invulnerable, loving the good, keen,
    irresistible, 23 beneficent, humane,
steadfast, sure, free from anxiety,
all-powerful, overseeing all,
and penetrating through all spirits
    that are intelligent, pure, and altogether subtle.
24 For wisdom is more mobile than any motion;
    because of her pureness she pervades and
        penetrates all things.
25 For she is a breath of the power of God,
    and a pure emanation of the glory of the
        Almighty;
therefore nothing defiled gains entrance into her.
26 For she is a reflection of eternal light,
    a spotless mirror of the working of God,
    and an image of his goodness.
27 Although she is but one, she can do all things,
    and while remaining in herself, she renews all
        things;
in every generation she passes into holy souls
and makes them friends of God, and prophets;
28 for God loves nothing so much as the person who
    lives with wisdom.
29 She is more beautiful than the sun,
    and excels every constellation of the stars.
Compared with the light she is found to be
        superior,
30 for it is succeeded by the night,
    but against wisdom evil does not prevail.

8   She reaches mightily from one end of the earth to
        the other,
and she orders all things well.
2 I loved her and sought her from my youth;
    I desired to take her for my bride,
and became enamored of her beauty.
3 She glorifies her noble birth by living with God,
    and the Lord of all loves her.
4 For she is an initiate in the knowledge of God,
    and an associate in his works.
5 If riches are a desirable possession in life,
    what is richer than wisdom, the active cause of
        all things?
6 And if understanding is effective,
    who more than she is fashioner of what exists?
7 And if anyone loves righteousness,
    her labors are virtues;
for she teaches self-control and prudence,
    justice and courage;
nothing in life is more profitable for mortals than
        these.
8 And if anyone longs for wide experience,
    she knows the things of old, and infers the things
        to come;
she understands turns of speech and the solutions
        of riddles;
she has foreknowledge of signs and wonders
and of the outcome of seasons and times.
9 Therefore I determined to take her to live with
    me,
knowing that she would give me good counsel
and encouragement in cares and grief.

I was taught by wisdom, by her whose skill made all things.
In wisdom there is a spirit intelligent and holy, unique in
its kind yet made up of many parts, subtle, free-moving,
lucid, spotless, clear, neither harmed nor harming, loving
what is good, eager, unhampered, beneficent, 23 kindly towards mortals, steadfast, unerring, untouched by care, all-
powerful, all-surveying, and permeating every intelligent,
pure, and most subtle spirit. 24 For wisdom moves more
easily than motion itself; she is so pure she pervades and
permeates all things. 25 Like a fine mist she rises from the
power of God, a clear effluence from the glory of the Almighty; so nothing defiled can enter into her by stealth.
26 She is the radiance that streams from everlasting light, the
flawless mirror of the active power of God, and the image
of his goodness. 27 She is but one, yet can do all things;
herself unchanging, she makes all things new; age after age
she enters into holy souls, and makes them friends of God
and prophets, 28 for nothing is acceptable to God but the
person who makes his home with wisdom. 29 She is more
beautiful than the sun, and surpasses every constellation.
Compared with the light of day, she is found to excel, 30 for
day gives place to night, but against wisdom no evil can
prevail.

8 1 She spans the world in power from end to end, and
    gently orders all things.

2 WISDOM I loved; I sought her out when I was young and
longed to win her for my bride; I was in love with her
beauty. 3 She adds lustre to her noble birth, because it is
given her to live with God; the Lord of all things has accepted her. 4 She is initiated into the knowledge that belongs to
God, and she chooses what his works are to be. 5 If riches
are a possession to be desired in life, what is richer than
wisdom, the active cause of all things? 6 If prudence shows
itself in action, who more than wisdom is the artificer of all
that is? 7 If someone loves uprightness, the fruits of wisdom's labours are the virtues; temperance and prudence,
justice and fortitude, these are her teaching, and life can
offer nothing of more value than these. 8 If someone longs,
perhaps, for great experience, she knows the past, she can
infer what is yet to come; she understands the subtleties of
argument and the solving of hard questions; she can read
signs and portents and foretell what the different times and
seasons will bring about.

9 So I determined to take her home to live with me, knowing that she would be my counsellor in prosperity and my
comfort in anxiety and grief. 10 Through her, I thought, I

7:26 **the radiance . . . from:** *or* the reflection of.

22 for Wisdom, the artificer of all, taught me.

For in her is a spirit
  intelligent, holy, unique,
Manifold, subtle, agile,
  clear, unstained, certain,
Not baneful, loving the good, keen,
  unhampered, beneficent, 23 kindly,
Firm, secure, tranquil,
  all-powerful, all-seeing,
And pervading all spirits,
  though they be intelligent, pure and very subtle.
24 For Wisdom is mobile beyond all motion,
  and she penetrates and pervades all things by
    reason of her purity.
25 For she is an aura of the might of God
  and a pure effusion of the glory of the Almighty;
    therefore nought that is sullied enters into her.
26 For she is the refulgence of eternal light,
  the spotless mirror of the power of God,
  the image of his goodness.
27 And she, who is one, can do all things,
  and renews everything while herself perduring;
And passing into holy souls from age to age,
  she produces friends of God and prophets.
28 For there is nought God loves, be it not one who
    dwells with Wisdom.
29 For she is fairer than the sun
  and surpasses every constellation of the stars.
Compared to light, she takes precedence;
30   for that, indeed, night supplants,
  but wickedness prevails not over Wisdom.

8 Indeed, she reaches from end to end mightily
  and governs all things well.
2 Her I loved and sought after from my youth;
  I sought to take her for my bride
  and was enamored of her beauty.
3 She adds to nobility the splendor of companionship
    with God;
  even the LORD of all loved her.
4 For she is instructress in the understanding of God,
  the selector of his works.
5 And if riches be a desirable possession in life,
  what is more rich than Wisdom, who produces
    all things?
6 And if prudence renders service,
  who in the world is a better craftsman than she?
7 Or if one loves justice,
  the fruits of her works are virtues;
For she teaches moderation and prudence,
  justice and fortitude,
  and nothing in life is more useful for men
    than these.
8 Or again, if one yearns for copious learning,
  she knows the things of old, and infers those yet
    to come.
She understands the turns of phrases and the
    solutions of riddles;
signs and wonders she knows in advance
  and the outcome of times and ages.
9 So I determined to take her to live with me,
  knowing that she would be my counselor while
    all was well,
  and my comfort in care and grief.

for Wisdom, the designer of all things, has
  instructed me.
22 For within her is a spirit[b] intelligent, holy,
  unique, manifold, subtle,
  mobile, incisive, unsullied,
  lucid, invulnerable, benevolent, shrewd,
23 irresistible, beneficent, friendly to human beings,
  steadfast, dependable, unperturbed,
  almighty, all-surveying,
  penetrating all intelligent, pure and most subtle
    spirits.
24 For Wisdom is quicker to move than any motion;
  she is so pure, she pervades and permeates all
    things.
25 She is a breath of the power of God,
  pure emanation of the glory of the Almighty;
  so nothing impure can find its way into her.
26 For she is a reflection of the eternal light,
  untarnished mirror of God's active power,
  and image of his goodness.
27 Although she is alone, she can do everything;
  herself unchanging, she renews the world,
  and, generation after generation, passing into holy
    souls,
  she makes them into God's friends and prophets;
28 for God loves only those who dwell with Wisdom.
29 She is indeed more splendid than the sun,
  she outshines all the constellations;
  compared with light, she takes first place,
30 for light must yield to night,
  but against Wisdom evil cannot prevail.

8 Strongly she reaches from one end of the world to
  the other
  and she governs the whole world for its good.
2 Wisdom I loved and searched for from my youth;
  I resolved to have her as my bride,
  I fell in love with her beauty.
3 She enhances her noble birth by sharing God's life,
  for the Master of All has always loved her.
4 Indeed, she shares the secrets of God's knowledge,
  and she chooses what he will do.
5 If in this life wealth is a desirable possession,
  what is more wealthy than Wisdom whose work is
    everywhere?
6 Or if it be the intellect that is at work,
  who, more than she, designs whatever exists?
7 Or if it be uprightness you love,
  why, virtues are the fruit of her labours,
  since it is she who teaches temperance and
    prudence,
  justice and fortitude;
  nothing in life is more useful for human beings.
8 Or if you are eager for wide experience,
  she knows the past, she forecasts the future;
  she knows how to turn maxims, and solve riddles;
  she has foreknowledge of signs and wonders,
  and of the unfolding of the ages and the times.
9 I therefore determined to take her to share my life,
  knowing that she would be my counsellor in
    prosperity
  and comfort me in cares and sorrow.

b 7 The peak of OT writing on Wisdom (cf. Jb 28; Pr 8:22). The
twenty-one qualities show Wisdom originating and participating in
God, inseparable from him but working in the world.

NEW REVISED STANDARD VERSION	REVISED ENGLISH BIBLE

10 Because of her I shall have glory among the
   multitudes
   and honor in the presence of the elders, though I
   am young.
11 I shall be found keen in judgment,
   and in the sight of rulers I shall be admired.
12 When I am silent they will wait for me,
   and when I speak they will give heed;
   if I speak at greater length,
   they will put their hands on their mouths.
13 Because of her I shall have immortality,
   and leave an everlasting remembrance to those
   who come after me.
14 I shall govern peoples,
   and nations will be subject to me;
15 dread monarchs will be afraid of me when they
   hear of me;
   among the people I shall show myself capable,
   and courageous in war.
16 When I enter my house, I shall find rest with her;
   for companionship with her has no bitterness,
   and life with her has no pain, but gladness and
   joy.
17 When I considered these things inwardly,
   and pondered in my heart
   that in kinship with wisdom there is immortality,
18 and in friendship with her, pure delight,
   and in the labors of her hands, unfailing wealth,
   and in the experience of her company,
      understanding,
   and renown in sharing her words,
   I went about seeking how to get her for myself.
19 As a child I was naturally gifted,
   and a good soul fell to my lot;
20 or rather, being good, I entered an undefiled
   body.
21 But I perceived that I would not possess wisdom
      unless God gave her to me—
   and it was a mark of insight to know whose gift
      she was—
   so I appealed to the Lord and implored him,
   and with my whole heart I said:

9 "O God of my ancestors and Lord of mercy,
      who have made all things by your word,
2 and by your wisdom have formed humankind
   to have dominion over the creatures you have
      made,
3 and rule the world in holiness and righteousness,
   and pronounce judgment in uprightness of soul,
4 give me the wisdom that sits by your throne,
   and do not reject me from among your servants.
5 For I am your servant[v] the son of your serving
      girl,
   a man who is weak and short-lived,
   with little understanding of judgment and laws;
6 for even one who is perfect among human beings
   will be regarded as nothing without the wisdom
      that comes from you.
7 You have chosen me to be king of your people
   and to be judge over your sons and daughters.
8 You have given command to build a temple on
      your holy mountain,
   and an altar in the city of your habitation,
   a copy of the holy tent that you prepared from
      the beginning.

shall win fame in the eyes of the people and honour among
older men, young though I am. 11 When I sit in judgement,
I shall prove myself acute, and the great will admire me;
12 when I say nothing, they will wait for me to speak; when
I speak, they will attend and, though I talk at some length,
they will lay a finger to their lips and listen. 13 Through her
I shall have immortality and leave an undying memory to
those who come after me. 14 I shall govern peoples, and
nations will become subject to me. 15 Tyrants, however
dread, will be afraid when they hear of me; among my own
people I shall show myself a good king, and on the battlefield a brave one. 16 When I come home, I shall find rest
with her; for there is no bitterness in her company, no pain
in life with her, only gladness and joy.

17 I turned this over in my mind, and I perceived that
there is immortality in kinship with wisdom, 18 and in her
friendship there is pure delight; that in doing her work is
wealth inexhaustible, to be taught in her school gives understanding, and an honourable name is won by converse with
her. So I went about in search of some way to win her for
my own. 19 As a child I was born to excellence, and a noble
soul fell to my lot; 20 or rather, I myself was noble, and I
entered into an undefiled body; 21 but I saw that there was
no way to gain possession of her except by gift of God—
and it was itself a mark of understanding to know from
whom that gift must come. So I pleaded with the Lord, and
from the depths of my heart I prayed to him in these words:

9 1 God of our forefathers, merciful Lord, who made all
   things by your word, 2 and in your wisdom fashioned
man to have sovereignty over your whole creation, 3 and to
be steward of the world in holiness and righteousness, and
to administer justice with an upright heart: 4 give me wisdom, who sits beside your throne, and do not refuse me a
place among your servants. 5 I am your slave, your slave-
girl's son, weak and with but a short time to live, too feeble
to understand justice and law; 6 for let someone be never so
perfect in the eyes of his fellows, if the wisdom that comes
from you is wanting, he will be of no account. 7 You chose
me to be king of your own people and judge of your sons
and daughters; 8 you told me to build a temple on your
sacred mountain and an altar in the city which is your dwelling-place, a copy of the sacred tabernacle prepared by you
from the beginning. 9 With you is wisdom, who is familiar

---

v Gk slave

10 For her sake I should have glory among
the masses,
and esteem from the elders, though I be but
a youth.
11 I should become keen in judgment,
and should be a marvel before rulers.
12 They would abide my silence and attend
my utterance;
and as I spoke on further,
they would place their hands upon their mouths.
13 For her sake I should have immortality
and leave to those after me an
everlasting memory.
14 I should govern peoples, and nations would be
my subjects —
15 terrible princes, hearing of me, would be afraid;
in the assembly I should appear noble, and in
war courageous.
16 Within my dwelling, I should take my repose
beside her;
For association with her involves no bitterness
and living with her no grief,
but rather joy and gladness.
17 Thinking thus within myself,
and reflecting in my heart
That there is immortality in kinship with Wisdom,
18 and good pleasure in her friendship,
and unfailing riches in the works of her hands,
And that in frequenting her society there
is prudence,
and fair renown in sharing her discourses,
I went about seeking to take her for my own.
19 Now, I was a well-favored child,
and I came by a noble nature;
20 or rather, being noble, I attained an
unsullied body.
21 And knowing that I could not otherwise possess
her except God gave it —
and this, too, was prudence, to know whose is
the gift —
I went to the LORD and besought him,
and said with all my heart:

9

God of my fathers, LORD of mercy,
you who have made all things by your word
2 And in your wisdom have established man
to rule the creatures produced by you,
3 To govern the world in holiness and justice,
and to render judgment in integrity of heart:
4 Give me Wisdom, the attendant at your throne,
and reject me not from among your children:
5 For I am your servant, the son of your handmaid,
a man weak and short-lived
and lacking in comprehension of judgment and
of laws.
6 Indeed, though one be perfect among the sons
of men,
if Wisdom, who comes from you, be not
with him,
he shall be held in no esteem.
7 You have chosen me king over your people
and magistrate for your sons and daughters.
8 You have bid me build a temple on your
holy mountain
and an altar in the city that is your
dwelling place,
a copy of the holy tabernacle which you had
established from of old.

10 'Thanks to her, I shall be admired by the masses
and honoured, though young, by the elders.
11 I shall be reckoned shrewd as a judge,
and the great will be amazed at me.
12 They will wait on my silences,
and pay attention when I speak;
if I speak at some length, they will lay their hand
on their lips.
13 By means of her, immortality will be mine,
I shall leave an everlasting memory to my
successors.
14 I shall govern peoples, and nations will be subject
to me;
15 at the sound of my name fearsome despots will be
afraid;
I shall show myself kind to the people and valiant
in battle.
16 'When I go home I shall take my ease with her,
for nothing is bitter in her company,
when life is shared with her there is no pain,
nothing but pleasure and joy.'
17 Having meditated on all this,
and having come to the conclusion
that immortality resides in kinship with Wisdom,
18 noble contentment in her friendship,
inexhaustible riches in her activities,
understanding in cultivating her society,
and renown in conversing with her,
I went all ways, seeking how to get her.
19 I was a boy of happy disposition,
I had received a good soul as my lot,
20 or rather, being good, I had entered an undefiled
body;
21 but, realising that I could never possess Wisdom
unless God gave her to me,
—a sign of intelligence in itself, to know in whose
gift she lay —
I prayed[c] to the Lord and entreated him,
and with all my heart I said:

9

'God of our ancestors, Lord of mercy,
who by your word have made the universe,
2 and in your wisdom have fitted human beings
to rule the creatures that you have made,
3 to govern the world in holiness and saving justice
and in honesty of soul to dispense fair judgement,
4 grant me Wisdom, consort of your throne,
and do not reject me from the number of your
children.
5 For I am your servant, son of your serving maid,
a feeble man, with little time to live,
with small understanding of justice and the laws.
6 Indeed, were anyone perfect among the sons of
men,
if he lacked the Wisdom that comes from you, he
would still count for nothing.
7 'You have chosen me to be king over your people,
to be judge of your sons and daughters.
8 You have bidden me build a temple on your holy
mountain,
and an altar in the city where you have pitched
your tent,
a copy of the holy Tent which you prepared at the
beginning.

---

[c] **8** Cf. 1 K 3:6–9.

NEW REVISED STANDARD VERSION

REVISED ENGLISH BIBLE

9 With you is wisdom, she who knows your works
and was present when you made the world;
she understands what is pleasing in your sight
and what is right according to your
commandments.
10 Send her forth from the holy heavens,
and from the throne of your glory send her,
that she may labor at my side,
and that I may learn what is pleasing to you.
11 For she knows and understands all things,
and she will guide me wisely in my actions
and guard me with her glory.
12 Then my works will be acceptable,
and I shall judge your people justly,
and shall be worthy of the throne[w] of my father.
13 For who can learn the counsel of God?
Or who can discern what the Lord wills?
14 For the reasoning of mortals is worthless,
and our designs are likely to fail;
15 for a perishable body weighs down the soul,
and this earthy tent burdens the thoughtful[x]
mind.
16 We can hardly guess at what is on earth,
and what is at hand we find with labor;
but who has traced out what is in the heavens?
17 Who has learned your counsel,
unless you have given wisdom
and sent your holy spirit from on high?
18 And thus the paths of those on earth were set
right,
and people were taught what pleases you,
and were saved by wisdom."

with your works and was present when you created the
universe, who is aware of what is acceptable to you and in
keeping with your commandments. 10 Send her forth from
your holy heaven, and from your glorious throne bid her
come down, so that she may labour at my side and I may
learn what is pleasing to you. 11 She knows and understands
all things; she will guide me prudently in whatever I do, and
guard me with her glory. 12 So my life's work will be acceptable, and I shall judge your people justly, and be worthy of my father's throne.

13 How can any human being learn what is God's plan?
Who can apprehend what is the will of the Lord? 14 The
reasoning of mortals is uncertain, and our plans are fallible,
15 because a perishable body weighs down the soul, and its
frame of clay burdens the mind already so full of care.
16 With difficulty we guess even at things on earth, and
laboriously find out what lies within our reach; but who has
ever traced out what is in heaven? 17 Who ever came to
know your purposes, unless you had given him wisdom and
sent your holy spirit from heaven on high? 18 Thus it was
that those on earth were set on the right path, and mortals
were taught what pleases you; thus were they kept safe by
wisdom.

10 Wisdom[y] protected the first-formed father of the
world, when he alone had been created;
she delivered him from his transgression,
2 and gave him strength to rule all things.
3 But when an unrighteous man departed from her
in his anger,
he perished because in rage he killed his brother.
4 When the earth was flooded because of him,
wisdom again saved it,
steering the righteous man by a paltry piece of
wood.
5 Wisdom[y] also, when the nations in wicked
agreement had been put to confusion,
recognized the righteous man and preserved him
blameless before God,
and kept him strong in the face of his compassion
for his child.
6 Wisdom[y] rescued a righteous man when the
ungodly were perishing;
he escaped the fire that descended on the Five
Cities.[z]
7 Evidence of their wickedness still remains:
a continually smoking wasteland,
plants bearing fruit that does not ripen,
and a pillar of salt standing as a monument to an
unbelieving soul.
8 For because they passed wisdom by,
they not only were hindered from recognizing the
good,
but also left for humankind a reminder of their
folly,
so that their failures could never go unnoticed.

10 WISDOM it was who kept guard over the first father
of the human race, created alone as he was; after he
had sinned she saved him 2 and gave him the strength to rule
over all things. 3 It was because a wicked man forsook her
in his anger that he murdered his brother in a fit of rage, and
so destroyed himself. 4 Through his fault the earth was overwhelmed by a flood, and again wisdom came to the rescue,
teaching the one good man to pilot his plain wooden hulk.
5 When heathen nations leagued in wickedness were thrown
into confusion, she it was who recognized one good man
and kept him blameless in God's sight, giving him strength
to resist his pity for his child. 6 She saved a good man when
the godless were being destroyed, and he escaped the fire
that rained down on the Five Cities, 7 cities whose wickedness is still attested by a smoking waste, by plants whose
fruit can never ripen, and by a pillar of salt standing there
as a memorial of a disbelieving soul. 8 They ignored wisdom and suffered for it, losing the power to recognize what
is good and leaving for mankind a monument to their folly,
such that their enormities can never be forgotten. 9 But wis-

---

[w] Gk thrones   [x] Or anxious   [y] Gk She   [z] Or on Pentapolis

NEW AMERICAN BIBLE

9 Now with you is Wisdom, who knows your works
  and was present when you made the world;
Who understands what is pleasing in your eyes
  and what is conformable with your commands.
10 Send her forth from your holy heavens
  and from your glorious throne dispatch her
That she may be with me and work with me,
  that I may know what is your pleasure.
11 For she knows and understands all things,
  and will guide me discreetly in my affairs
  and safeguard me by her glory;
12 Thus my deeds will be acceptable,
  and I shall judge your people justly
  and be worthy of my father's throne.
13 For what man knows God's counsel,
  or who can conceive what the LORD intends?
14 For the deliberations of mortals are timid,
  and unsure are our plans.
15 For the corruptible body burdens the soul
  and the earthen shelter weighs down the mind
  that has many concerns.
16 And scarce do we guess the things on earth,
  and what is within our grasp we find
  with difficulty;
  but when things are in heaven, who can search
  them out?
17 Or who ever knew your counsel, except you had
  given Wisdom
  and sent your holy spirit from on high?
18 And thus were the paths of those on earth
  made straight,
  and men learned what was your pleasure,
  and were saved by Wisdom.

10 She preserved the first-formed father of
  the world
  when he alone had been created;
And she raised him up from his fall,
2 and gave him power to rule all things.
3 But when the unjust man withdrew from her in
  his anger,
  he perished through his fratricidal wrath.
4 When on his account the earth was flooded,
  Wisdom again saved it,
  piloting the just man on frailest wood.
5 She, when the nations were sunk in
  universal wickedness,
  knew the just man, kept him blameless
  before God,
  and preserved him resolute against pity for
  his child.
6 She delivered the just man from among the wicked
  who were being destroyed,
  when he fled as fire descended
  upon Pentapolis —
7 Where as a testimony to its wickedness,
  there yet remain a smoking desert,
Plants bearing fruit that never ripens,
  and the tomb of a disbelieving soul, a standing
  pillar of salt.
8 For those who forsook Wisdom
  first were bereft of knowledge of the right,
And then they left mankind a memorial of
  their folly —
  so that they could not even be hidden in
  their fall.

NEW JERUSALEM BIBLE

9 With you is Wisdom, she who knows your works,
  she who was present when you made the world;
  she understands what is pleasing in your eyes
  and what agrees with your commandments.
10 Despatch her from the holy heavens,
  send her forth from your throne of glory
  to help me and to toil with me
  and teach me what is pleasing to you;
11 since she knows and understands everything
  she will guide me prudently in my actions
  and will protect me with her glory.
12 Then all I do will be acceptable,
  I shall govern your people justly
  and be worthy of my father's throne.
13 'What human being indeed can know the intentions
  of God?
  And who can comprehend the will of the Lord?
14 For the reasoning of mortals is inadequate,
  our attitudes of mind unstable;
15 for a perishable body presses down the soul,
  and this tent of clay weighs down the mind with its
  many cares.
16 It is hard enough for us to work out what is on
  earth,
  laborious to know what lies within our reach;
  who, then, can discover what is in the heavens?
17 And who could ever have known your will, had
  you not given Wisdom
  and sent your holy Spirit from above?
18 Thus have the paths of those on earth been
  straightened
  and people have been taught what pleases you,
  and have been saved, by Wisdom.'

10 d It was Wisdom who protected the first man to
  be fashioned,
  the father of the world, who had been created all
  alone,
  she it was who rescued him from his fall
2 and gave him the strength to subjugate all things.
3 But when in his wrath a wicked man deserted her,
  he perished in his fratricidal fury.
4 When because of him the earth was drowned, it
  was Wisdom again who saved it,
  piloting the upright man on valueless timber.
5 Again, when, concurring in wickedness, the
  nations had been thrown into confusion,
  she singled out the upright man, preserved him
  blameless before God
  and fortified him against pity for his child.
6 She it was who, while the godless perished, saved
  the upright man
  as he fled from the fire raining down on the Five
  Cities,
7 in witness against whose evil ways
  a desolate land still smokes,
  where plants bear fruit that never ripens
  and where, monument to an unbelieving soul, there
  stands a pillar of salt.
8 For, by ignoring the path of Wisdom,
  not only did they suffer the loss of not knowing
  the good,
  but they left the world a memorial to their folly,
  so that their offences could not pass unnoticed.

d 10 v. 1 Adam, v. 3 Cain, v. 4 Noah, v. 5 Abraham, v. 6 Lot, v. 10
Jacob, v. 13 Joseph.

| NEW REVISED STANDARD VERSION | REVISED ENGLISH BIBLE |

9 Wisdom rescued from troubles those who served her.

10 When a righteous man fled from his brother's wrath,
she guided him on straight paths;
she showed him the kingdom of God,
and gave him knowledge of holy things;
she prospered him in his labors,
and increased the fruit of his toil.

11 When his oppressors were covetous,
she stood by him and made him rich.

12 She protected him from his enemies,
and kept him safe from those who lay in wait for him;
in his arduous contest she gave him the victory,
so that he might learn that godliness is more powerful than anything else.

13 When a righteous man was sold, wisdom[a] did not desert him,
but delivered him from sin.
She descended with him into the dungeon,

14 and when he was in prison she did not leave him,
until she brought him the scepter of a kingdom
and authority over his masters.
Those who accused him she showed to be false,
and she gave him everlasting honor.

15 A holy people and blameless race
wisdom delivered from a nation of oppressors.

16 She entered the soul of a servant of the Lord,
and withstood dread kings with wonders and signs.

17 She gave to holy people the reward of their labors;
she guided them along a marvelous way,
and became a shelter to them by day,
and a starry flame through the night.

18 She brought them over the Red Sea,
and led them through deep waters;

19 but she drowned their enemies,
and cast them up from the depth of the sea.

20 Therefore the righteous plundered the ungodly;
they sang hymns, O Lord, to your holy name,
and praised with one accord your defending hand;

21 for wisdom opened the mouths of those who were mute,
and made the tongues of infants speak clearly.

11 Wisdom[b] prospered their works by the hand of a holy prophet.

2 They journeyed through an uninhabited wilderness,
and pitched their tents in untrodden places.

3 They withstood their enemies and fought off their foes.

4 When they were thirsty, they called upon you,
and water was given them out of flinty rock,
and from hard stone a remedy for their thirst.

5 For through the very things by which their enemies were punished,
they themselves received benefit in their need.

6 Instead of the fountain of an ever-flowing river,
stirred up and defiled with blood

7 in rebuke for the decree to kill the infants,
you gave them abundant water unexpectedly,

8 showing by their thirst at that time
how you punished their enemies.

---

dom brought her servants safely out of their troubles. 10 When a good man was a fugitive from his brother's anger, she it was who guided him on straight paths; she gave him a vision of God's kingdom and a knowledge of holy things; she prospered his labours and made his toil fruitful. 11 When others in their rapacity sought to exploit him, she stood by him and made him rich. 12 She kept him safe from his enemies, and preserved him from treacherous attacks; after his hard struggle she gave him victory, and taught him that godliness is the mightiest power of all. 13 It was she who refused to desert a good man when he was sold into slavery; she preserved him from sin and went down into the dungeon with him, 14 nor did she leave him when he was in chains until she had brought him a kingdom's sceptre with authority over his persecutors; she gave the lie to his accusers, and bestowed on him undying fame.

15 It was wisdom who rescued a godfearing people, a blameless race, from a nation of oppressors; 16 she inspired a servant of the Lord, and with his signs and wonders he defied formidable kings. 17 She rewarded the labours of a godfearing people, she guided them on a miraculous journey, and became a covering for them by day and a blaze of stars by night. 18 She brought them over the Red Sea, leading them through its deep waters; 19 but their enemies she engulfed, and cast them up again out of the fathomless deep. 20 So the good despoiled the ungodly; they sang the glories of your holy name, O Lord, and with one accord praised your power, their champion; 21 for wisdom enabled the dumb to speak, and made the tongues of infants eloquent.

11 Wisdom, working through a holy prophet, gave them success in all they did. 2 They made their way across an unpeopled desert and pitched camp in untrodden wastes; 3 they stood firm against their enemies, and fought off hostile assaults. 4 When they were thirsty they cried to you, and water to slake their thirst was given them out of the hard stone of a rocky cliff. 5 The selfsame means by which their oppressors had been punished were used to help them in their hour of need: 6 those others found their river no unfailing stream of water, but putrid and befouled with blood, 7 a punishment for their order that all the infants should be killed; to these, however, when they had lost hope, you gave abundant water. 8 So, from the thirst they then endured, they learnt how you had punished their ene-

---

[a] Gk she   [b] Gk She

9 But Wisdom delivered from tribulations those who
served her.
10 She, when the just man fled from his
brother's anger,
guided him in direct ways,
Showed him the kingdom of God
and gave him knowledge of holy things;
She prospered him in his labors
and made abundant the fruit of his works,
11 Stood by him against the greed of his defrauders,
and enriched him;
12 She preserved him from foes,
and secured him against ambush,
And she gave him the prize for his stern struggle
that he might know that devotion to God
is mightier than all else.
13 She did not abandon the just man when he
was sold,
but delivered him from sin.
14 She went down with him into the dungeon,
and did not desert him in his bonds,
Until she brought him the scepter of royalty
and authority over his oppressors,
Showed those who had defamed him false,
and gave him eternal glory.
15 The holy people and blameless race — it was she
who delivered them from the nation that
oppressed them.
16 She entered the soul of the LORD's servant,
and withstood fearsome kings with signs
and portents;
17 she gave the holy ones the recompense of
their labors,
Conducted them by a wondrous road,
and became a shelter for them by day
and a starry flame by night.
18 She took them across the Red Sea,
and brought them through the deep waters —
19 But their enemies she overwhelmed,
and cast them up from the bottom of the depths.
20 Therefore the just despoiled the wicked;
and they sang, O LORD, your holy name and
praised in unison your conquering hand —
21 Because Wisdom opened the mouths of the dumb,
and gave ready speech to infants.

11 She made their affairs prosper through the
holy prophet.
2 They journeyed through the uninhabited desert,
and in solitudes they pitched their tents;
3 they withstood enemies and took vengeance on
their foes.
4 When they thirsted, they called upon you,
and water was given them from the sheer rock,
assuagement for their thirst from the hard stone.
5 For by the things through which their foes
were punished
they in their need were benefited.
6 Instead of a spring, when the perennial river
was troubled with impure blood
7 as a rebuke to the decree for the slaying
of infants,
You gave them abundant water in an
unhoped-for way,
8 once you had shown by the thirst they then had
how you punished their adversaries.

9 But Wisdom delivered her servants from their
ordeals.
10 The upright man, fleeing from the anger of his
brother,
was led by her along straight paths.
She showed him the kingdom of God
and taught him the knowledge of holy things.
She brought him success in his labours
and gave him full return for all his efforts;
11 she stood by him against grasping and oppressive
men
and she made him rich.
12 She preserved him from his enemies
and saved him from the traps they set for him.
In an arduous struggle she awarded him the prize,
to teach him that piety is stronger than all.
13 She did not forsake the upright man when he was
sold,
but snatched him away from sin;
14 she accompanied him down into the pit,
nor did she abandon him in his chains
until she had brought him the sceptre of a kingdom
and authority over his despotic masters,
thus exposing as liars those who had traduced him,
and giving him honour everlasting.
15 It was Wisdom who delivered a holy people,
a blameless race, from a nation of oppressors.
16 She entered the soul of a servant of the Lord,
and withstood fearsome kings with wonders and
signs.
17 To the holy people she gave the wages of their
labours;
she guided them by a marvellous road,
herself their shelter by day —
and their starlight through the night.
18 She brought them across the Red Sea,
leading them through an immensity of water,
19 whereas she drowned their enemies,
then spat them out from the depths of the abyss.
20 So the upright despoiled the godless;
Lord, they extolled your holy name,
and with one accord praised your protecting hand;
21 for Wisdom opened the mouths of the dumb
and made eloquent the tongues of babes.

11 She made their actions successful, by means of a
holy prophet.
2 They journeyed through an unpeopled desert
and pitched their tents in inaccessible places.
3 They stood firm against their enemies, fought off
their foes.
4 On you they called when they were thirsty,
and from the rocky cliff water was given them,
from hard stone a remedy for their thirst.
5 Thus, what had served to punish their enemies
became a benefit for them in their difficulties.
6 Whereas their enemies had only the ever-flowing
source
of a river fouled with mingled blood and mud,
7 to punish them for their decree of infanticide,
you gave your people, against all hope, water in
abundance,
8 once you had shown by the thirst that they were
experiencing
how severely you were punishing their enemies.

9　For when they were tried, though they were being
　　　disciplined in mercy,
　they learned how the ungodly were tormented
　　　when judged in wrath.
10　For you tested them as a parent*c* does in
　　　warning,
　but you examined the ungodly*d* as a stern king
　　　does in condemnation.
11　Whether absent or present, they were equally
　　　distressed,
12　for a twofold grief possessed them,
　and a groaning at the memory of what had
　　　occurred.
13　For when they heard that through their own
　　　punishments
　the righteous*e* had received benefit, they
　　　perceived it was the Lord's doing.
14　For though they had mockingly rejected him who
　　　long before had been cast out and
　　　exposed,
　at the end of the events they marveled at him,
　when they felt thirst in a different way from the
　　　righteous.
15　In return for their foolish and wicked thoughts,
　which led them astray to worship irrational
　　　serpents and worthless animals,
　you sent upon them a multitude of irrational
　　　creatures to punish them,
16　so that they might learn that one is punished by
　　　the very things by which one sins.
17　For your all-powerful hand,
　which created the world out of formless matter,
　did not lack the means to send upon them a
　　　multitude of bears, or bold lions,
18　or newly-created unknown beasts full of rage,
　or such as breathe out fiery breath,
　or belch forth a thick pall of smoke,
　or flash terrible sparks from their eyes;
19　not only could the harm they did destroy
　　　people,*f*
　but the mere sight of them could kill by fright.
20　Even apart from these, people*e* could fall at a
　　　single breath
　when pursued by justice
　and scattered by the breath of your power.
　But you have arranged all things by measure and
　　　number and weight.
21　For it is always in your power to show great
　　　strength,
　and who can withstand the might of your arm?
22　Because the whole world before you is like a
　　　speck that tips the scales,
　and like a drop of morning dew that falls on the
　　　ground.
23　But you are merciful to all, for you can do all
　　　things,
　and you overlook people's sins, so that they may
　　　repent.
24　For you love all things that exist,
　and detest none of the things that you have made,
　for you would not have made anything if you had
　　　hated it.
25　How would anything have endured if you had not
　　　willed it?
　Or how would anything not called forth by you
　　　have been preserved?

mies; 9when they themselves were put to the test, though
chastisement was tempered with mercy, they understood the
tortures of the godless who were sentenced in anger. 10Your
own people you subjected to an ordeal, disciplining them
like a father, but those others you put to the torture like a
stern king passing sentence. 11Whether at home or abroad,
they were equally in distress, 12for double misery had come
upon them, and they groaned as they recalled the past.
13When they heard that the means of their own punishment
had been used to benefit your people, they saw your hand
in it, Lord. 14The man who long ago had been abandoned
and exposed, whom they had rejected with contumely, became in the event the object of their wonder and admiration;
their thirst was such as the godly never knew.

15In return for the foolish imagination of those wicked
people, which deluded them into worshipping reptiles incapable of reason, and mere vermin, you sent upon them in
your vengeance mindless swarms 16to teach them that the
instruments of someone's sin are the instruments of his
punishment. 17For your almighty hand, which created the
world out of formless matter, was not without other resource: it could have let loose on those wicked people a
horde of bears or ravening lions 18or unknown ferocious
monsters newly created, breathing out blasts of fire, or
roaring and belching smoke, or flashing terrible sparks like
lightning from their eyes, 19beasts with power not only to
exterminate them by the wounds they inflicted, but by their
mere appearance to kill them with fright. 20Even without
these, a single breath would have sufficed to lay them low,
with justice in pursuit and the breath of your power to blow
them away; but you have set all things in order by measure
and number and weight.

21Great strength is yours to exert at any moment, and the
power of your arm no one can resist, 22for in your sight the
whole world is like a grain that just tips the scale or like a
drop of dew alighting on the ground at dawn. 23But you are
merciful to all because you can do all things; you overlook
people's sins in order to bring them to repentance; 24for all
existing things are dear to you and you hate nothing that you
have created—why else would you have made it? 25How
could anything have continued in existence, had it not been
your will? How could it have endured unless called into

---

c Gk *a father*　　*d* Gk *those*　　*e* Gk *they*　　*f* Gk *them*

9 For when they had been tried, though only
mildly chastised,
they recognized how the wicked, condemned in
anger, were being tormented.
11 Both those afar off and those close by
were afflicted:
10 the latter you tested, admonishing them as
a father;
the former as a stern king you probed
and condemned.
12 For a twofold grief took hold of them
and a groaning at the remembrance of the ones
who had departed.
13 For when they heard that the cause of their
own torments
was a benefit to these others, they recognized
the LORD.
14 Him who of old had been cast out in exposure they
indeed mockingly rejected;
but in the end of events, they marveled at him,
since their thirst proved unlike that of the just.
15 And in return for their senseless, wicked thoughts,
which misled them into worshiping dumb
serpents and worthless insects,
You sent upon them swarms of dumb creatures
for vengeance;
16 that they might recognize that a man is punished
by the very things through which he sins.
17 For not without means was your almighty hand,
that had fashioned the universe from
formless matter,
to send upon them a drove of bears or
fierce lions,
18 Or new-created, wrathful, unknown beasts
to breathe forth fiery breath,
Or pour out roaring smoke,
or flash terrible sparks from their eyes.
19 Not only could these attack and completely
destroy them;
even their frightful appearance itself could slay.
20 Even without these, they could have been killed at
a single blast,
pursued by retribution
and winnowed out by your mighty spirit;
But you have disposed all things by measure and
number and weight.
21 For with you great strength abides always;
who can resist the might of your arm?
22 Indeed, before you the whole universe is as a grain
from a balance,
or a drop of morning dew come down upon
the earth.
23 But you have mercy on all, because you can do
all things;
and you overlook the sins of men that they
may repent.
24 For you love all things that are
and loathe nothing that you have made;
for what you hated, you would not
have fashioned.
25 And how could a thing remain, unless you
willed it;
or be preserved, had it not been called forth
by you?

9 From their own ordeals, which were only loving
correction,
they realised how an angry sentence was
tormenting the godless;
10 for you had tested your own as a father
admonishes,
but the others you had punished as a pitiless king
condemns,
11 and, whether far or near, they were equally
afflicted.
12 For a double sorrow seized on them,
and a groaning at the memory of the past;
13 when they learned that the punishments they were
receiving
were beneficial to the others, they realised it was
the Lord,
14 while for the man whom long before they had
exposed and later mockingly rebuffed,
they felt only admiration when all was done,
having suffered a thirst so different from that of the
upright.
15 For their foolish and wicked notions which led
them astray
into worshipping mindless reptiles and contemptible
beetles,
you sent a horde of mindless animals to punish
them
16 and to teach them that the agent of sin is the agent
of punishment.
17 And indeed your all-powerful hand which created
the world from formless matter, did not lack means
to unleash a horde of bears or savage lions on
them
18 or unknown beasts, newly created, full of rage,
breathing out fire,
or puffing out stinking smoke,
or flashing fearful sparks from their eyes,
19 beasts able not only to destroy them, being so
savage,
but even to strike them dead by their terrifying
appearance.
20 However, without these, one breath could have
blown them over,
pursued by Justice,
whirled away by the breath of your power.
You, however, ordered all things by measure,
number and weight.
21 For your great power is always at your service,
and who can withstand the might of your arm?
22 The whole world, for you, can no more than tip a
balance,
like a drop of morning dew falling on the ground.
23 Yet you are merciful to all, because you are
almighty,
you overlook people's sins, so that they can repent.
24 Yes, you love everything that exists,
and nothing that you have made disgusts you,
since, if you had hated something, you would not
have made it.
25 And how could a thing subsist, had you not willed
it?
Or how be preserved, if not called forth by you?

26 You spare all things, for they are yours, O Lord,
    you who love the living.

12 For your immortal spirit is in all
    things.

2 Therefore you correct little by little those
    who trespass,
and you remind and warn them of the things
    through which they sin,
so that they may be freed from wickedness and
    put their trust in you, O Lord.

3 Those who lived long ago in your holy land
4 you hated for their detestable practices,
    their works of sorcery and unholy rites,
5 their merciless slaughter*g* of children,
    and their sacrificial feasting on human flesh and
    blood.
These initiates from the midst of a heathen cult,*h*
6 these parents who murder helpless lives,
you willed to destroy by the hands of our
    ancestors,
7 so that the land most precious of all to you
might receive a worthy colony of the servants*i*
    of God.
8 But even these you spared, since they were but
    mortals,
and sent wasps*j* as forerunners of your army
to destroy them little by little.
9 though you were not unable to give the ungodly
    into the hands of the righteous in battle,
or to destroy them at one blow by dread wild
    animals or your stern word.
10 But judging them little by little you gave them an
    opportunity to repent,
though you were not unaware that their origin*k*
    was evil
and their wickedness inborn,
and that their way of thinking would never
    change.
11 For they were an accursed race from the
    beginning,
and it was not through fear of anyone that you
    left them unpunished for their sins.

12 For who will say, "What have you done?"
Or will resist your judgment?
Who will accuse you for the destruction of
    nations that you made?
Or who will come before you to plead as an
    advocate for the unrighteous?
13 For neither is there any god besides you, whose
    care is for all people,*l*
to whom you should prove that you have not
    judged unjustly;
14 nor can any king or monarch confront you about
    those whom you have punished.
15 You are righteous and you rule all things
    righteously,
deeming it alien to your power
to condemn anyone who does not deserve to be
    punished.
16 For your strength is the source of righteousness,
and your sovereignty over all causes you to spare
    all.
17 For you show your strength when people doubt
    the completeness of your power,
and you rebuke any insolence among those who
    know it.*h*

being by you? 26 You spare all things because they are
12 yours, O Lord, who love all that lives; 1 for your
imperishable breath is in every one of them.

2 For this reason you correct offenders little by little,
disciplining them and reminding them of their sins, in order
that they may abandon their evil ways and put their trust in
you, Lord. 3 There were the ancient inhabitants of your holy
land: 4 you hated them for their loathsome practices, their
sorcery and unholy rites, 5 their pitiless killing of children,
their cannibal feasts of human flesh and blood; 6 they were
initiates of a secret ritual in which parents slaughtered their
defenceless children. Therefore it was your will to destroy
them at the hands of our forefathers, 7 so that the land which
is of all lands most precious in your eyes might receive in
God's children settlers worthy of it. 8 And yet you spared
them because they too were human beings, and you sent
hornets as the advance guard of your army to exterminate
them by stages. 9 It was well within your power to have the
godly overwhelm the godless in a pitched battle, or to wipe
them out in an instant by fearsome beasts or with one relentless word. 10 But instead you carried out the sentence by
stages to give them room for repentance, knowing well
enough that they came of evil stock, that their wickedness
was innate, and that their way of thinking would not change
to the end of time, 11 for there was a curse on their race from
the beginning.
Nor was it out of deference to anyone else that you gave
them an amnesty for their misdeeds, 12 for no one can say
'What have you done?' Who can challenge your verdict?
Who can bring a charge against you for destroying nations
which were of your own making? Who can appear against
you in court to plead the cause of the guilty? 13 For there is
no other god but you; all the world is your concern, and
there is none to whom you must prove the justice of your
sentence. 14 There is no king or other ruler who can outface
you on behalf of those whom you have punished. 15 But you
are just and you order all things justly, counting it alien to
your power to condemn anyone to undeserved punishment.
16 For your strength is the source of justice, and it is because
you are Master of all that you are lenient to all. 17 You show
your strength when people doubt whether your power is
absolute; it is when they know it and yet are insolent that
you punish them. 18 But you, with strength at your com-

g Gk *slaughterers*   *h* Meaning of Gk uncertain   *i* Or *children*
j Or *hornets*   *k* Or *nature*   *l* Or *all things*

26 But you spare all things, because they
    are yours, O LORD and lover of souls,

12

1 for your imperishable spirit is in all things!
2 Therefore you rebuke offenders little
    by little,
warn them, and remind them of the sins they
    are committing,
that they may abandon their wickedness and
    believe in you, O LORD!
3 For, truly, the ancient inhabitants of your
    holy land,
4   whom you hated for deeds most odious —
Works of witchcraft and impious sacrifices;
5   a cannibal feast of human flesh
    and of blood, from the midst of . . . —
These merciless murderers of children,
6   and parents who took with their own hands
    defenseless lives,
You willed to destroy by the hands of our fathers,
7   that the land that is dearest of all to you
    might receive a worthy colony of
    God's children.
8 But even these, as they were men, you spared,
    and sent wasps as forerunners of your army,
that they might exterminate them by degrees.
9 Not that you were without power to have the
    wicked vanquished in battle by the just,
or wiped out at once by terrible beasts or by one
    decisive word;
10 But condemning them bit by bit, you gave them
    space for repentance.
You were not unaware that their race was wicked
    and their malice ingrained,
And that their dispositions would never change;
11   for they were a race accursed from
    the beginning.
Neither out of fear for anyone
    did you grant amnesty for their sins.
12 For who can say to you, "What have you done?"
    or who can oppose your decree?
Or when peoples perish, who can challenge you,
    their maker;
or who can come into your presence as
    vindicator of unjust men?
13 For neither is there any god besides you who have
    the care of all,
that you need show you have not
    unjustly condemned;
14 Nor can any king or prince confront you on behalf
    of those you have punished.
15 But as you are just, you govern all things justly;
you regard it as unworthy of your power
to punish one who has incurred no blame.
16 For your might is the source of justice;
your mastery over all things makes you lenient
    to all.
17 For you show your might when the perfection of
    your power is disbelieved;
and in those who know you, you
    rebuke temerity.

26 No, you spare all, since all is yours, Lord, lover of
    life!

12

1 For your imperishable spirit is in everything!
2 And thus, gradually, you correct those who
    offend;
you admonish and remind them of how they have
    sinned,
so that they may abstain from evil and trust in you,
    Lord.
3 The ancient inhabitants of your holy land
4 you hated for their loathsome practices,
    their acts of sorcery, and unholy rites.
5 Those ruthless murderers of children,
    those eaters of entrails at feasts of human flesh and
    of blood,
    those initiates of secret brotherhoods,
6 those murderous parents of defenceless beings,
    you determined to destroy at our ancestors' hands,
7 so that this land, dearer to you than any other,
    might receive a worthy colony of God's children.
8 Even so, since these were human, you treated them
    leniently,
sending hornets as forerunners of your army,
    to exterminate them little by little.
9 Not that you were unable to hand the godless over
    to the upright in pitched battle
or destroy them at once by savage beasts or one
    harsh word;
10 but, by carrying out your sentences gradually, you
    gave them a chance to repent,
although you knew that they were inherently evil,
    innately wicked,
11 and fixed in their cast of mind;
    for they were a race accursed from the beginning.

Nor was it from awe of anyone that you let their
    sins go unpunished.
12 For who is there to ask, 'What have you done?'
Or who is there to disagree with your sentence?
Who to arraign you for destroying nations which
    you have created?
Who to confront you by championing the wicked?
13 For there is no god, other than you, who cares for
    every one,
to whom you have to prove that your sentences
    have been just.
14 No more could any king or despot challenge you
    over those whom you have punished.
15 For, being upright yourself, you rule the universe
    uprightly,
and hold it as incompatible with your power
to condemn anyone who has not deserved to be
    punished.
16 For your strength is the basis of your saving
    justice,
and your sovereignty over all makes you lenient to
    all.
17 You show your strength when people will not
    believe in your absolute power,
and you confound any insolence in those who do
    know it.

12, 5: And of blood, from the midst of . . . : this line is obscure in
the current Greek text and in all extant translations.

18 Although you are sovereign in strength, you
judge with mildness,
and with great forbearance you govern us;
for you have power to act whenever you choose.

19 Through such works you have taught your people
that the righteous must be kind,
and you have filled your children with good
hope,
because you give repentance for sins.

20 For if you punished with such great care and
indulgence[m]
the enemies of your servants[n] and those
deserving of death,
granting them time and opportunity to give up
their wickedness,

21 with what strictness you have judged your
children,
to whose ancestors you gave oaths and covenants
full of good promises!

22 So while chastening us you scourge our enemies
ten thousand times more,
so that, when we judge, we may meditate upon
your goodness,
and when we are judged, we may expect mercy.

23 Therefore those who lived unrighteously, in a life
of folly,
you tormented through their own abominations.

24 For they went far astray on the paths of error,
accepting as gods those animals that even their
enemies[o] despised;
they were deceived like foolish infants.

25 Therefore, as though to children who cannot
reason,
you sent your judgment to mock them.

26 But those who have not heeded the warning of
mild rebukes
will experience the deserved judgment of God.

27 For when in their suffering they became incensed
at those creatures that they had thought to be
gods, being punished by means of them,
they saw and recognized as the true God the one
whom they had before refused to know.
Therefore the utmost condemnation came upon
them.

13 For all people who were ignorant of God were
foolish by nature;
and they were unable from the good things that
are seen to know the one who exists,
nor did they recognize the artisan while paying
heed to his works;

2 but they supposed that either fire or wind or swift
air,
or the circle of the stars, or turbulent water,
or the luminaries of heaven were the gods that
rule the world.

3 If through delight in the beauty of these things
people assumed them to be gods,
let them know how much better than these is
their Lord,
for the author of beauty created them.

4 And if people[o] were amazed at their power and
working,
let them perceive from them
how much more powerful is the one who formed
them.

mand, judge in mercy and rule us in great forbearance; for
the power is yours to exercise whenever you choose.

19 By acts like these you taught your people that he who
is just must also be kind-hearted, and you have filled your
children with hope by the offer of repentance for their sins.
20 If you used such care and such indulgence even in punishing your children's enemies who deserved to die, granting
them time and opportunity to win free of their wickedness,
21 with what discrimination you passed judgement on your
people, to whose forefathers you gave sworn covenants full
of the promise of good!

22 So we are chastened by you, but you scourge our enemies ten thousand times more, so that we may lay your
goodness to heart when we sit in judgement, and may hope
for mercy when we ourselves are judged. 23 This is why the
wicked who had lived their lives in heedless folly were
tormented by you with their own abominations. 24 They had
strayed far down the paths of error, taking for gods the most
despised and hideous creatures; they were deluded like
thoughtless infants. 25 And so, as though they were children
who had not learnt reason, you imposed on them a sentence
that made them ridiculous; 26 but those who are not disciplined by such derisive correction will experience the full
weight of divine judgement. 27 They were indignant at their
own sufferings, but, finding themselves chastised through
the very creatures they had deemed to be gods, they recognized that the true God was he whom they had formerly
refused to know. For this reason the full rigour of condemnation overtook them.

13 WHAT born fools were all who lived in ignorance of
God! From the good things before their eyes they
could not learn to know him who is, and failed to recognize
the artificer though they observed his handiwork! 2 Fire,
wind, swift air, the circle of the starry signs, rushing water,
or the great lights in heaven that rule the world — these they
accounted gods. 3 If it was through delight in the beauty of
these things that people supposed them gods, they ought to
have understood how much better is the Lord and Master of
them all; for it was by the prime author of all beauty they
were created. 4 If it was through astonishment at their power
and influence, people should have learnt from these how
much more powerful is he who made them. 5 For the great-

---

[m] Other ancient authorities lack *and indulgence*; others read *and
entreaty*   [n] Or *children*   [o] Gk *they*

18 But though you are master of might, you judge
        with clemency,
    and with much lenience you govern us;
    for power, whenever you will, attends you.
19 And you taught your people, by these deeds,
        that those who are just must be kind;
    And you gave your sons good ground for hope
        that you would permit repentance for their sins.
20 For these were enemies of your servants, doomed
        to death;
    yet, while you punished them with such
        solicitude and pleading,
        granting time and opportunity to
        abandon wickedness,
21 With what exactitude you judged your sons,
    to whose fathers you gave the sworn covenants
        of goodly promises!
22 Us, therefore, you chastise, and our enemies with a
        thousand blows you punish,
    that we may think earnestly of your goodness
        when we judge,
    and, when being judged, may look for mercy.
23 Hence those unjust also, who lived a life of folly,
    you tormented through their own abominations.
24 For they went far astray in the paths of error,
    taking for gods the worthless and disgusting
        among beasts,
    deceived like senseless infants.
25 Therefore as though upon unreasoning children,
    you sent your judgment on them as a mockery;
26 But they who took no heed of punishment which
        was but child's play
    were to experience a condemnation worthy
        of God.
27 For in the things through which they
        suffered distress,
    since they were tortured by the very things they
        deemed gods,
    They saw and recognized the true God
    whom before they had refused to know;
    with this, their final condemnation came
        upon them.

13 For all men were by nature foolish who were in
        ignorance of God,
    and who from the good things seen did not
        succeed in knowing him who is,
    and from studying the works did not discern
        the artisan;
2 But either fire, or wind, or the swift air,
    or the circuit of the stars, or the mighty water,
    or the luminaries of heaven, the governors of the
        world, they considered gods.
3 Now if out of joy in their beauty they thought
        them gods,
    let them know how far more excellent is the
        Lord than these;
    for the original source of beauty fashioned them.
4 Or if they were struck by their might and energy,
    let them from these things realize how much
        more powerful is he who made them.

18 But you, controlling your strength, are mild in
        judgement, and govern us with great
        lenience,
    for you have only to will, and your power is there.
19 By acting thus, you have taught your people
    that the upright must be kindly to his fellows,
    and you have given your children the good hope
    that after sins you will grant repentance.
20 For, if with such care and indulgence you have
        punished
    your children's enemies, though doomed to death,
    and have given them time and place to be rid of
        their wickedness,
21 with what exact attention have you not judged your
        children,
    to whose ancestors, by oaths and covenants, you
        made such generous promises?
22 Thus, you instruct us, when you punish our
        enemies in moderation,
    that we should reflect on your kindness when we
        judge,
    and, when we are judged, we should look for
        mercy.
23 And this is why people leading foolish and wicked
        lives
    were tortured by you with their own abominations;
24 for they had strayed too far on the paths of error
    by taking the vilest and most despicable of animals
        for gods,
    being deluded like silly little children.
25 So, as to children with no sense,
    you gave them a sentence making fools of them.
26 Those, however, who would not take warning from
        a mocking reproof
    were soon to endure a sentence worthy of God.
27 The creatures that made them suffer and against
        which they protested,
    those very creatures that they had taken for gods
        and by which they were punished they saw
        in their true light;
    and he whom hitherto they had refused to know,
        they realised was true God.
    And this is why the final condemnation fell on
        them.

13 Yes, naturally stupid are all who are unaware of
        God,
    and who, from good things seen, have not been
        able to discover Him-who-is,
    or, by studying the works, have not recognised the
        Artificer.
2 Fire, however, or wind, or the swift air,
    the sphere of the stars, impetuous water, heaven's
        lamps,
    are what they have held to be the gods who govern
        the world.
3 If, charmed by their beauty, they have taken these
        for gods,
    let them know how much the Master of these
        excels them,
    since he was the very source of beauty that created
        them.
4 And if they have been impressed by their power
        and energy,
    let them deduce from these how much mightier is
    he that has formed them,

5 For from the greatness and beauty of created
things
comes a corresponding perception of their
Creator.
6 Yet these people are little to be blamed,
for perhaps they go astray
while seeking God and desiring to find him.
7 For while they live among his works, they keep
searching,
and they trust in what they see, because the
things that are seen are beautiful.
8 Yet again, not even they are to be excused;
9 for if they had the power to know so much
that they could investigate the world,
how did they fail to find sooner the Lord of these
things?
10 But miserable, with their hopes set on dead
things, are those
who give the name "gods" to the works of human
hands,
gold and silver fashioned with skill,
and likenesses of animals,
or a useless stone, the work of an ancient hand.
11 A skilled woodcutter may saw down a tree easy
to handle
and skillfully strip off all its bark,
and then with pleasing workmanship
make a useful vessel that serves life's needs,
12 and burn the cast-off pieces of his work
to prepare his food, and eat his fill.
13 But a cast-off piece from among them, useful for
nothing,
a stick crooked and full of knots,
he takes and carves with care in his leisure,
and shapes it with skill gained in idleness;*p*
he forms it in the likeness of a human being,
14 or makes it like some worthless animal,
giving it a coat of red paint and coloring its
surface red
and covering every blemish in it with paint;
15 then he makes a suitable niche for it,
and sets it in the wall, and fastens it there with
iron.
16 He takes thought for it, so that it may not fall,
because he knows that it cannot help itself,
for it is only an image and has need of help.
17 When he prays about possessions and his
marriage and children,
he is not ashamed to address a lifeless thing.
18 For health he appeals to a thing that is weak;
for life he prays to a thing that is dead;
for aid he entreats a thing that is utterly
inexperienced;
for a prosperous journey, a thing that cannot take
a step;
19 for money-making and work and success with his
hands
he asks strength of a thing whose hands have no
strength.

14 Again, one preparing to sail and about to voyage
over raging waves
calls upon a piece of wood more fragile than the
ship that carries him.
2 For it was desire for gain that planned that
vessel,
and wisdom was the artisan who built it;

ness and beauty of created things give us a corresponding
idea of their Creator. 6 Yet these people are not greatly to be
blamed, for when they go astray they may be seeking God
and really wishing to find him. 7 Passing their lives among
his works and making a close study of them, they are persuaded by appearances because of the beauty of what they
see. 8 Yet even so they do not deserve to be excused, 9 for
with enough understanding to speculate about the universe,
why did they not sooner discover its Lord and Master?

10 The really degraded ones are those whose hopes are set
on lifeless things, who give the title of gods to the work of
human hands, to gold and silver fashioned by art into images of living creatures, or to a useless stone carved by a
craftsman long ago. 11 Suppose some skilled worker in
wood fells with his saw a convenient tree and deftly strips
off all the bark, then works it up elegantly into some household vessel suitable for everyday use; 12 and the bits left
over from his work he uses to cook his food, and then eats
his fill. 13 But among what is left over there is one useless
piece, crooked and full of knots, and this he takes and
carves to occupy his idle moments. He shapes it with lei-
surely skill into the image of a human being, 14 or else he
gives it the form of some worthless creature, smearing it
over with vermilion and raddling its surface with red paint,
so that every flaw in it is daubed over. 15 Then he makes a
suitable shrine for it and fixes it on the wall, securing it with
nails. 16 It is he who has to take the precautions on its behalf
to save it from falling, for he well knows that it cannot fend
for itself: it needs help, for it is only an image. 17 Yet he
prays to it about his possessions and his wife and children,
and feels no shame in addressing this inanimate object;
18 for health he appeals to a thing that is weak, for life he
prays to a thing that is dead, for aid he asks help from
something utterly incapable, for a prosperous journey from
something that cannot put one foot before the other;
19 where earnings or business or success in handicraft are in
question he asks effectual help from a thing whose hands
are entirely ineffectual.

14 Again, the man who gets ready for a voyage and
plans to set his course through the wild waves invokes a piece of wood more fragile than the ship which is
to carry him. 2 Desire for gain invented the ship, and the
shipwright with his skill built it; 3 but your providence,

14:2 **and the shipwright . . . built it:** *other witnesses read* and
wisdom was the shipwright who built it.

p Other ancient authorities read *with intelligent skill*

5 For from the greatness and the beauty of
    created things
      their original author, by analogy, is seen.
6 But yet, for these the blame is less;
  For they indeed have gone astray perhaps,
    though they seek God and wish to find him.
7 For they search busily among his works,
  but are distracted by what they see, because the
    things seen are fair.
8 But again, not even these are pardonable.
9 For if they so far succeeded in knowledge
  that they could speculate about the world,
    how did they not more quickly find its Lord?

10 But doomed are they, and in dead things are
    their hopes,
  who termed gods things made by human hands:
Gold and silver, the product of art, and likenesses
    of beasts,
  or useless stone, the work of an ancient hand.
11 A carpenter may saw out a suitable tree
  and skillfully scrape off all its bark,
And deftly plying his art,
  produce something fit for daily use,
12 and use up the refuse from his handiwork in
    preparing his food, and have his fill;
13 Then the good-for-nothing refuse from
    these remnants,
  crooked wood grown full of knots,
  he takes and carves to occupy his spare time.
This wood he models with listless skill,
  and patterns it on the image of a man
14 or makes it resemble some worthless beast.
When he has daubed it with red and crimsoned its
    surface with red stain,
  and daubed over every blemish in it,
15 He makes a fitting shrine for it
  and puts it on the wall, fastening it with a nail.
16 Thus lest it fall down he provides for it,
  knowing that it cannot help itself;
  for, truly, it is an image and needs help.
17 But when he prays about his goods or marriage
    or children,
  he is not ashamed to address the thing without
    a soul.
And for vigor he invokes the powerless;
18 and for life he entreats the dead;
And for aid he beseeches the wholly incompetent,
  and about travel, something that cannot
    even walk.
19 And for profit in business and success with
    his hands
  he asks facility of a thing with hands
    completely inert.

5 since through the grandeur and beauty of the
    creatures
  we may, by analogy, contemplate their Author.
6 Small blame, however, attaches to them,
  for perhaps they go astray
  only in their search for God and their eagerness to
    find him;
7 familiar with his works, they investigate them
  and fall victim to appearances, seeing so much
    beauty.
8 But even so, they have no excuse:
9 if they are capable of acquiring enough knowledge
  to be able to investigate the world,
  how have they been so slow to find its Master?

10 But wretched are they, with their hopes set on dead
    things,
  who have given the title of gods to human
    artefacts,
  gold or silver, skilfully worked,
  figures of animals,
  or useless stone, carved by some hand long ago.
11 Take a woodcutter. He fells a suitable tree,
  neatly strips off the bark all over
  and then with admirable skill
  works the wood into an object useful in daily life.
12 The bits left over from his work
  he uses for cooking his food, then eats his fill.
13 There is still a good-for-nothing bit left over,
  a gnarled and knotted billet:
  he takes it and whittles it with the concentration of
    his leisure hours,
  he shapes it with the skill of experience,
  he gives it a human shape
14 or perhaps he makes it into some vile animal,
  smears it with ochre, paints its surface red,
  coats over all its blemishes.
15 He next makes a worthy home for it,
  lets it into the wall, fixes it with an iron clamp.
16 Thus he makes sure that it will not fall down—
  being well aware that it cannot help itself,
  since it is only an image, and needs to be helped.
17 And yet, if he wishes to pray for his goods, for his
    marriage, for his children,
  he does not blush to harangue this lifeless thing—
  for health, he invokes what is weak,
18 for life, he pleads with what is dead,
  for help, he goes begging to total inexperience,
  for a journey, what cannot even use its feet,
19 for profit, an undertaking, and success in pursuing
    his craft,
  he asks skill from something whose hands have no
    skill whatever.

14 Again, one preparing for a voyage and about to
    traverse the wild waves
  cries out to wood more unsound than the boat
    that bears him.
2 For the urge for profits devised this latter,
  and Wisdom the artificer produced it.

14 Or someone else, taking ship to cross the wild
    waves,
  loudly invokes a piece of wood*e* frailer than the
    vessel that bears him.
2 Agreed, the ship is the product of a craving for
    gain,
  its building embodies the wisdom of the
    shipwright;

e **14** A ship's figurehead.

3 but it is your providence, O Father, that steers its
course,
because you have given it a path in the sea,
and a safe way through the waves,
4 showing that you can save from every danger,
so that even a person who lacks skill may put to
sea.
5 It is your will that works of your wisdom should
not be without effect;
therefore people trust their lives even to the
smallest piece of wood,
and passing through the billows on a raft they
come safely to land.
6 For even in the beginning, when arrogant giants
were perishing,
the hope of the world took refuge on a raft,
and guided by your hand left to the world the
seed of a new generation.
7 For blessed is the wood by which righteousness
comes.

8 But the idol made with hands is accursed, and so
is the one who made it—
he for having made it, and the perishable thing
because it was named a god.
9 For equally hateful to God are the ungodly and
their ungodliness;
10 for what was done will be punished together with
the one who did it.
11 Therefore there will be a visitation also upon the
heathen idols,
because, though part of what God created, they
became an abomination,
snares for human souls
and a trap for the feet of the foolish.

12 For the idea of making idols was the beginning of
fornication,
and the invention of them was the corruption of
life;
13 for they did not exist from the beginning,
nor will they last forever.
14 For through human vanity they entered the world,
and therefore their speedy end has been planned.

15 For a father, consumed with grief at an untimely
bereavement,
made an image of his child, who had been
suddenly taken from him;
he now honored as a god what was once a dead
human being,
and handed on to his dependents secret rites and
initiations.
16 Then the ungodly custom, grown strong with
time, was kept as a law,
and at the command of monarchs carved images
were worshiped.
17 When people could not honor monarchs[q] in their
presence, since they lived at a distance,
they imagined their appearance far away,
and made a visible image of the king whom they
honored,
so that by their zeal they might flatter the absent
one as though present.
18 Then the ambition of the artisan impelled
even those who did not know the king to
intensify their worship.

Father, is the pilot, for you have given it a pathway through
the sea and a safe course among the waves, 4 showing that
you can save from every danger, so that even the inexpert
can put to sea. 5 It is your will that the things made by your
wisdom should not lie unused; and therefore people entrust
their lives even to the frailest spar, and passing through the
billows on a mere raft come safe to land. 6 So in the beginning, when the proud race of giants was being brought to an
end, the hope of mankind escaped on a raft and, piloted by
your hand, bequeathed to the world a new breed of people.
7 While a blessing is on the wood through which right prevails, 8 the wooden idol made by human hands is accursed,
and so is its maker—he because he made it, and the perishable thing because it was called a god. 9 Equally hateful to
God are the godless and their ungodliness; 10 the doer and
the deed will both be punished. 11 Therefore retribution will
fall on the idols of the heathen, because although part of
God's creation they have been made into an abomination, to
make people stumble and to catch the feet of the foolish.
12 The devising of idols is the beginning of immorality; they
are an invention which has blighted human life. 13 They did
not exist from the beginning, nor will they be with us for
ever; 14 superstition brought them into the world, and for
good reason a speedy end is in store for them.

15 Some father, overwhelmed with untimely grief for the
child suddenly taken from him, made an image of his child
and honoured thenceforth as a god what was once a dead
human being, handing on to his household the observance
of rites and ceremonies. 16 Then this impious custom, established by the passage of time, was observed as law. Or
again, graven images came to be worshipped at the command of despotic princes. 17 When people could not do
honour to such a prince before his face because he lived too
far away, they made a likeness of that distant face, and
produced a visible image of the king they sought to honour,
in order that by their zeal they might gratify the absent
prince as though he were present. 18 Then the cult grows in
fervour as those to whom the king is unknown are spurred
on by ambitious craftsmen. 19 In his desire, it may be, to

3 But your providence, O Father! guides it,
  for you have furnished even in the sea a road,
  and through the waves a steady path,
4 Showing that you can save from any danger,
  so that even one without skill may embark.
5 But you will that the products of your Wisdom be
    not idle;
  therefore men trust their lives even to
    frailest wood,
  and have been safe crossing the surge on a raft.
6 For of old, when the proud giants were
    being destroyed,
  the hope of the universe, who took refuge on
    a raft,
  left to the world a future for his race, under the
    guidance of your hand.
7 For blest is the wood through which justice
    comes about;
8   but the handmade idol is accursed, and its maker
    as well:
  he for having produced it, and it, because
    though corruptible, it was termed a god.
9 Equally odious to God are the evildoer and his
    evil deed;
10   and the thing made shall be punished with
    its contriver.
11 Therefore upon even the idols of the nations shall a
    visitation come,
  since they have become abominable amid
    God's works,
  Snares for the souls of men
  and a trap for the feet of the senseless.
12 For the source of wantonness is the devising
    of idols;
  and their invention was a corruption of life.
13 For in the beginning they were not,
  nor shall they continue forever;
14   for by the vanity of men they came into
    the world,
  and therefore a sudden end is devised for them.
15 For a father, afflicted with untimely mourning,
  made an image of the child so quickly taken
    from him,
  And now honored as a god what was formerly a
    dead man
  and handed down to his subjects mysteries
    and sacrifices.
16 Then, in time, the impious practice gained strength
    and was observed as law,
  and graven things were worshiped by
    princely decrees.
17 Men who lived so far away that they could not
    honor him in his presence
  copied the appearance of the distant king
  And made a public image of him they wished
    to honor,
  out of zeal to flatter him when absent, as
    though present.
18 And to promote this observance among those to
    whom it was strange,
  the artisan's ambition provided a stimulus.

3 but your providence, Father, is what steers it,
  you having opened a pathway even through the
    sea,
  and a safe way over the waves,
4 showing that you can save, whatever happens,
  so that, even without experience, someone may put
    to sea.
5 It is not your will that the works of your Wisdom
    should be sterile,
  so people entrust their lives to the smallest piece of
    wood,
  cross the waves on a raft, yet are kept safe and
    sound.
6 Why, in the beginning, when the proud giants were
    perishing,
  the hope of the world took refuge on a raft
  and, steered by your hand, preserved the seed of a
    new generation for the ages to come.
7 For blessed is the wood which serves the cause of
    uprightness
8 but accursed the man-made idol, yes, it and its
    maker,
  he for having made it, and it because, though
    perishable, it has been called god.
9 For God holds the godless and his godlessness in
    equal hatred;
10 both work and workman will alike be punished.
11 Hence even the idols of the nations will have a
    visitation
  since, in God's creation, they have become an
    abomination,
  a scandal for human souls,
  a snare for the feet of the foolish.
12 The idea of making idols was the origin of
    fornication,
  their discovery corrupted life.
13 They did not exist at the beginning, they will not
    exist for ever;
14 human vanity brought them into the world,
  and a quick end is therefore reserved for them.
15 A father afflicted by untimely mourning
  has an image made of his child so soon carried
    off, f
  and now pays divine honours to what yesterday
    was only a corpse,
  handing on mysteries and ceremonies to his people;
16 time passes, the custom hardens and is observed as
    law.
17 Rulers were the ones who ordered that statues
    should be worshipped:
  people who could not honour them in person,
    because they lived too far away,
  would have a portrait made of their distant
    countenance,
  to have an image that they could see of the king
    whom they honoured;
  meaning, by such zeal, to flatter the absent as if he
    were present.
18 Even people who did not know him
  were stimulated into spreading his cult by the
    artist's enthusiasm;

f **14** The Gk custom of giving the dead divine rank.

| NEW REVISED STANDARD VERSION | REVISED ENGLISH BIBLE |

19 For he, perhaps wishing to please his ruler,
   skillfully forced the likeness to take more
      beautiful form,
20 and the multitude, attracted by the charm of his
   work,
   now regarded as an object of worship the one
      whom shortly before they had honored as
      a human being.
21 And this became a hidden trap for humankind,
   because people, in bondage to misfortune or to
      royal authority,
   bestowed on objects of stone or wood the name
      that ought not to be shared.
22 Then it was not enough for them to err about the
      knowledge of God,
   but though living in great strife due to ignorance,
   they call such great evils peace.
23 For whether they kill children in their initiations,
      or celebrate secret mysteries,
   or hold frenzied revels with strange customs,
24 they no longer keep either their lives or their
      marriages pure,
   but they either treacherously kill one another, or
      grieve one another by adultery,
25 and all is a raging riot of blood and murder, theft
      and deceit, corruption, faithlessness,
      tumult, perjury,
26 confusion over what is good, forgetfulness of
      favors,
   defiling of souls, sexual perversion,
   disorder in marriages, adultery, and debauchery.
27 For the worship of idols not to be named
   is the beginning and cause and end of every evil.
28 For their worshipers[r] either rave in exultation,
   or prophesy lies, or live unrighteously, or readily
      commit perjury;
29 for because they trust in lifeless idols
   they swear wicked oaths and expect to suffer no
      harm.
30 But just penalties will overtake them on two
      counts:
   because they thought wrongly about God in
      devoting themselves to idols,
   and because in deceit they swore unrighteously
      through contempt for holiness.
31 For it is not the power of the things by which
      people swear,[s]
   but the just penalty for those who sin,
   that always pursues the transgression of the
      unrighteous.

15 But you, our God, are kind and true,
   patient, and ruling all things[t] in mercy.
2 For even if we sin we are yours, knowing your
      power;
   but we will not sin, because we know that you
      acknowledge us as yours.
3 For to know you is complete righteousness,
   and to know your power is the root of
      immortality.
4 For neither has the evil intent of human art
      misled us,
   nor the fruitless toil of painters,
   a figure stained with varied colors,
5 whose appearance arouses yearning in fools,
   so that they desire[u] the lifeless form of a dead
      image.

please the monarch, a craftsman skilfully distorts the likeness into an ideal form, 20 and the common people, beguiled by the beauty of the workmanship, take for an object of worship him whom lately they honoured as a man. 21 So this becomes a snare in the life of a people: enslaved by mischance or misgovernment, they confer on stocks and stones the name that none may share.

22 Then, not content with crass error in their knowledge of God, people live in the constant warfare of ignorance and call this monstrous evil peace. 23 They perform ritual killing of children and secret ceremonies and the frenzied orgies of unnatural cults; 24 the purity of life and marriage is abandoned; and a man treacherously murders a neighbour or by corrupting his wife breaks his heart. 25 All is chaos — bloody murder, theft and fraud, corruption, treachery, riot, perjury, 26 honest folk driven to distraction; ingratitude, depravity, sexual perversion, breakdown of marriage, adultery, debauchery. 27 For the worship of idols, whose names it is wrong even to mention, is the beginning, the cause, and the end of every evil. 28 People either indulge themselves to the point of madness, or pass off lies as prophecies, or live dishonest lives, or break their oath without scruple. 29 They perjure themselves and expect no harm because the idols they trust in are lifeless. 30 But judgement will overtake them on two counts: both because in their devotion to idols they have thought wrongly about God, and also because in their contempt for religion they have deliberately perjured themselves. 31 It is not any power in what they swear by, but the nemesis of sin, that ever pursues the transgressions of the wicked.

15 But you, our God, are kind and true and patient, a merciful ruler of all that is. 2 Even if we sin, we are yours, since we acknowledge your power. But because we know that we are accounted yours we shall not sin. 3 To know you is the whole of righteousness, and to acknowledge your power is the root of immortality. 4 We have not been led astray by the perverted inventions of human skill or the barren labour of painters, by some gaudily coloured shape, 5 the sight of which arouses in fools a passionate desire for an image without life or breath. 6 They are in love

---

[r] Gk they   [s] Or of the oaths people swear   [t] Or ruling the universe   [u] Gk and he desires

19 For he, mayhap in his determination to please the ruler,
labored over the likeness to the best of his skill;
20 And the masses, drawn by the charm of the workmanship,
soon thought he should be worshiped who shortly before was honored as a man.
21 And this became a snare for mankind,
that men enslaved to either grief or tyranny conferred the incommunicable Name on stocks and stones.
22 Then it was not enough for them to err in their knowledge of God;
but even though they live in a great war of ignorance,
they call such evils peace.
23 For while they celebrate either child-slaying sacrifices or clandestine mysteries,
or frenzied carousals in unheard-of rites,
24 They no longer safeguard either lives or pure wedlock;
but each either waylays and kills his neighbor,
or aggrieves him by adultery.
25 And all is confusion — blood and murder, theft and guile,
corruption, faithlessness, turmoil, perjury,
26 Disturbance of good men, neglect of gratitude,
besmirching of souls, unnatural lust,
disorder in marriage, adultery and shamelessness.
27 For the worship of infamous idols
is the reason and source and extremity of all evil.
28 For they either go mad with enjoyment, or prophesy lies,
or live lawlessly or lightly forswear themselves.
29 For as their trust is in soulless idols,
they expect no harm when they have sworn falsely.
30 But on both counts shall justice overtake them:
because they thought ill of God and devoted themselves to idols,
and because they deliberately swore false oaths, despising piety.
31 For not the might of those that are sworn by but the retribution of sinners
ever follows upon the transgression of the wicked.

15 But you, our God, are good and true,
slow to anger, and governing all with mercy.
2 For even if we sin, we are yours, and know your might;
but we will not sin, knowing that we belong to you.
3 For to know you well is complete justice,
and to know your might is the root of immortality.
4 For neither did the evil creation of men's fancy deceive us,
nor the fruitless labor of painters,
A form smeared with varied colors,
5 the sight of which arouses yearning in the senseless man,
till he longs for the inanimate form of a dead image.

19 for the latter, doubtless wishing to please his ruler,
exerted all his skill to surpass the reality,
20 and the crowd, attracted by the beauty of the work,
mistook for a god someone whom recently they had honoured as a man.
21 And this became a snare for life:
that people, whether enslaved by misfortune or by tyranny,
should have conferred the ineffable Name on sticks and stones.
22 It is not enough, however, for them to have such misconceptions about God;
for, living in the fierce warfare of ignorance,
they call these terrible evils peace.
23 With their child-murdering rites, their occult mysteries,
or their frenzied orgies with outlandish customs,
24 they no longer retain any purity in their lives or their marriages,
one treacherously murdering another or wronging him by adultery.
25 Everywhere a welter of blood and murder, theft and fraud,
corruption, treachery, riot, perjury,
26 disturbance of decent people, forgetfulness of favours,
pollution of souls, sins against nature,
disorder in marriage, adultery and debauchery.
27 For the worship of idols with no name
is the beginning, cause, and end of every evil.
28 For these people either carry their merrymaking to the point of frenzy,
or they prophesy what is not true, or they live wicked lives,
or they perjure themselves without hesitation;
29 since they put their trust in lifeless idols
they do not reckon their false oaths can harm them.
30 But they will be justly punished for this double crime:
for degrading the concept of God by adhering to idols;
and for wickedly perjuring themselves in contempt for what is holy.
31 For it is not the power of the things by which they swear
but the punishment reserved for sinners
that always follows the offences of wicked people.

15 But you, our God, are kind and true,
slow to anger, governing the universe with mercy.
2 Even if we sin, we are yours, since we acknowledge your power,
but we will not sin, knowing we count as yours.
3 To know you is indeed the perfect virtue,
and to know your power is the root of immortality.
4 We have not been duped by inventions of misapplied human skill,
or by the sterile work of painters,
by figures daubed with assorted colours,
5 the sight of which sets fools yearning
and hankering for the lifeless form of an unbreathing image.

6 Lovers of evil things and fit for such objects of
hope[v]
are those who either make or desire or worship
them.

7 A potter kneads the soft earth
and laboriously molds each vessel for our service,
fashioning out of the same clay
both the vessels that serve clean uses
and those for contrary uses, making all alike;
but which shall be the use of each of them
the worker in clay decides.

8 With misspent toil, these workers form a futile
god from the same clay —
these mortals who were made of earth a short
time before
and after a little while go to the earth from which
all mortals are taken,
when the time comes to return the souls that were
borrowed.

9 But the workers are not concerned that mortals
are destined to die
or that their life is brief,
but they compete with workers in gold and silver,
and imitate workers in copper;
and they count it a glorious thing to mold
counterfeit gods.

10 Their heart is ashes, their hope is cheaper than
dirt,
and their lives are of less worth than clay,

11 because they failed to know the one who formed
them
and inspired them with active souls
and breathed a living spirit into them.

12 But they considered our existence an idle game,
and life a festival held for profit,
for they say one must get money however one
can, even by base means.

13 For these persons, more than all others, know
that they sin
when they make from earthy matter fragile
vessels and carved images.

14 But most foolish, and more miserable than an
infant,
are all the enemies who oppressed your people.

15 For they thought that all their heathen idols were
gods,
though these have neither the use of their eyes to
see with,
nor nostrils with which to draw breath,
nor ears with which to hear,
nor fingers to feel with,
and their feet are of no use for walking.

16 For a human being made them,
and one whose spirit is borrowed formed them;
for none can form gods that are like themselves.

17 People are mortal, and what they make with
lawless hands is dead;
for they are better than the objects they worship,
since[w] they have life, but the idols[x] never had.

18 Moreover, they worship even the most hateful
animals,
which are worse than all others when judged by
their lack of intelligence;

with evil and do not deserve anything better to trust in,
those who make such evil things, those who hanker after
them, and those who worship them.

7 A potter laboriously kneading the soft clay shapes every
vessel for our use. Out of the selfsame clay he fashions
without distinction the pots that are to serve for clean uses
and the opposite; and what the purpose of each one is to be,
the moulder of the clay decides. 8 Then with ill-directed toil
he makes a false god out of the same clay, this man who not
long before was himself fashioned out of earth and soon
returns to the place whence he was taken, when the living
soul that was lent to him must be returned on demand. 9 His
concern is not that he must one day fall sick or that his span
of life is short; but he must vie with goldsmiths and silversmiths and emulate the workers in bronze, and he thinks it
does him credit to contrive fakes. 10 His heart is ashes, his
hope worth less than common earth, and his life cheaper
than clay, 11 because he did not recognize by whom he
himself was moulded, or who it was that inspired him with
an active soul and breathed into him the breath of life.
12 No, he reckons this life of ours a game, and our existence
a market where money can be made: 'By fair means or
foul', he says, 'one must get a living.' 13 But this maker of
fragile pots and idols from the same earthy stuff knows
better than anyone that he is doing wrong.

14 The greatest fools of all, and worse than infantile, were
the enemies and oppressors of your people, 15 for they supposed all their heathen idols to be gods, although they have
eyes that cannot see, nostrils that cannot draw breath, ears
that cannot hear, fingers that cannot feel, and feet that are
useless for walking; 16 for it was a man who made them, one
drawing borrowed breath who gave them their shape. But
no human being has the power to shape a god in his own
likeness: 17 he is only mortal, but what he makes with his
impious hands is dead. So he is better than the objects of his
worship, for at least he is alive — they never can be.

18 Moreover, these people worship animals, the most revolting animals. Compared with the rest of the brute creation, their divinities are the least intelligent. 19 Even as

<table>
<tr>
<td>

6 Lovers of evil things, and worthy of such hopes
    are they who make them and long for them and
      worship them.

7 For truly the potter, laboriously working the
      soft earth,
    molds for our service each several article:
Both the vessels that serve for clean purposes
    and their opposites, all alike;
As to what shall be the use of each vessel of
      either class
    the worker in clay is the judge.

8 And with misspent toil he molds a meaningless god
    from the selfsame clay;
    though he himself shortly before was made from
      the earth
And after a little, is to go whence he was taken,
    when the life that was lent him is
      demanded back.

9 But his concern is not that he is to die
    nor that his span of life is brief;
Rather, he vies with goldsmiths and silversmiths
    and emulates molders of bronze,
    and takes pride in modeling counterfeits.

10 Ashes his heart is! more worthless than earth is
      his hope,
    and more ignoble than clay his life;

11 Because he knew not the one who fashioned him,
    and breathed into him a quickening soul,
    and infused a vital spirit.

12 Instead, he esteemed our life a plaything,
    and our span of life a holiday for gain;
    "For one must," says he, "make profit every
      way, be it even out of evil."

13 For this man more than any knows that he
      is sinning,
    when out of earthen stuff he creates fragile
      vessels and idols alike.

14 But all quite senseless, and worse than childish
      in mind,
    are the enemies of your people who
      enslaved them.

15 For they esteemed all the idols of the
      nations, gods,
    which have no use of the eyes for vision,
    nor nostrils to snuff the air,
Nor ears to hear,
    nor fingers on their hands for feeling;
    even their feet are useless to walk with.

16 For a man made them;
    one whose spirit has been lent him
      fashioned them.
For no man succeeds in fashioning a god
    like himself;

17   being mortal, he makes a dead thing with his
      lawless hands.
For he is better than the things he worships;
    he at least lives, but never they.

18 And besides, they worship the most
      loathsome beasts —
    for compared as to folly, these are worse than
      the rest,

</td>
<td>

6 Lovers of evil and worthy of such hopes
    are those who make them, those who want them
      and those who worship them.

7 Take a potter, now, laboriously working the soft
      earth,
    shaping each object for us to use.
Out of the self-same clay,
    he models vessels intended for a noble use
    and those for a contrary purpose, all alike:
but which of these two uses each will have
    is for the potter himself to decide.

8 Then — ill-spent effort! — from the same clay he
      models a futile god,
although so recently made out of earth himself
    and shortly to return to what he was taken from,
when asked to give back the soul that has been lent
      to him.

9 Even so, he does not worry about having to die
    or about the shortness of his life,
but strives to outdo the goldsmiths and
      silversmiths,
imitates the bronzeworkers,
    and prides himself on modelling counterfeits.

10 Ashes, his heart;
    more vile than earth, his hope;
    more wretched than clay, his life!

11 For he has misconceived the One who has
      modelled him,
who breathed an active soul into him
    and inspired a living spirit.

12 What is more, he looks on this life of ours as a
      kind of game,
and our time here like a fair, full of bargains.
'However foul the means,' he says, 'a man must
      make a living.'

13 He, more than any other, knows he is sinning,
he who from one earthy stuff makes both brittle
      pots and idols.

14 But most foolish, more pitiable even than the soul
      of a little child,
are the enemies who once played the tyrant with
      your people,

15 and have taken all the idols of the heathen for
      gods;
these can use neither their eyes for seeing
    nor their nostrils for breathing the air
nor their ears for hearing
    nor the fingers on their hands for handling
nor their feet for walking.

16 They have been made, you see, by a human being,
    modelled by a being whose own breath is
      borrowed.
No man can model a god to resemble himself;

17 subject to death, his impious hands can produce
    only something dead.
He himself is worthier than the things he worships;
    he will at least have lived, but never they.

18 And they worship even the most loathsome of
      animals,
worse than the rest in their degree of stupidity,

</td>
</tr>
</table>

| NEW REVISED STANDARD VERSION | REVISED ENGLISH BIBLE |

19 and even as animals they are not so beautiful in
    appearance that one would desire them,
but they have escaped both the praise of God and
    his blessing.

16 Therefore those people*y* were deservedly
    punished through such creatures,
and were tormented by a multitude of animals.
2 Instead of this punishment you showed kindness
    to your people,
and you prepared quails to eat,
    a delicacy to satisfy the desire of appetite;
3 in order that those people, when they desired
    food,
might lose the least remnant of appetite*z*
because of the odious creatures sent to them,
while your people,*y* after suffering want a short
    time,
might partake of delicacies.

4 For it was necessary that upon those oppressors
    inescapable want should come,
while to these others it was merely shown how
    their enemies were being tormented.

5 For when the terrible rage of wild animals came
    upon your people*a*
and they were being destroyed by the bites of
    writhing serpents,
your wrath did not continue to the end;
6 they were troubled for a little while as a warning,
and received a symbol of deliverance to remind
    them of your law's command.

7 For the one who turned toward it was saved, not
    by the thing that was beheld,
but by you, the Savior of all.
8 And by this also you convinced our enemies
    that it is you who deliver from every evil.
9 For they were killed by the bites of locusts and
    flies,
and no healing was found for them,
because they deserved to be punished by such
    things.
10 But your children were not conquered even by the
    fangs of venomous serpents,
for your mercy came to their help and healed
    them.
11 To remind them of your oracles they were bitten,
    and then were quickly delivered,
so that they would not fall into deep forgetfulness
    and become unresponsive*b* to your kindness.
12 For neither herb nor poultice cured them,
but it was your word, O Lord, that heals all
    people.
13 For you have power over life and death;
you lead mortals down to the gates of Hades and
    back again.
14 A person in wickedness kills another,
but cannot bring back the departed spirit,
or set free the imprisoned soul.

15 To escape from your hand is impossible;
16 for the ungodly, refusing to know you,
were flogged by the strength of your arm,
pursued by unusual rains and hail and relentless
    storms,
and utterly consumed by fire.

animals they are without a trace of beauty which might
make them desirable. When God approved and blessed his
work, they were left out.

16 For that reason it was fitting that the oppressors
were chastised by creatures like these: they were
tormented by swarms of vermin. 2 They were punished; but
your own people you treated with kindness, sending quails
for them to eat, a novel food to satisfy their hunger. 3 Your
purpose was that whereas those others, hungry as they
were, should turn in loathing even from essential food because the creatures sent against them were so repulsive,
your people, after a short spell of scarcity, should partake
of novel delicacies. 4 It was right that the scarcity falling on
the oppressors should be inexorable, and that your people
should learn by brief experience how their enemies were
tortured.

5 Even when fierce and venomous snakes attacked your
people and the bites of writhing serpents were spreading
death, your anger did not continue to the bitter end. 6 Their
short-lived trouble was sent them as a lesson, and they were
given a symbol of salvation to remind them of the requirements of your law. 7 Anyone turning towards it was saved,
not by what he looked at but by you, the saviour of all. 8 In
this way also you convinced our enemies that you are the
deliverer from every evil. 9 Those others died from the bites
of locusts and flies, and no remedy to save their lives was
found, because they deserved to be punished by such creatures.

10 But your people did not succumb to the fangs of
snakes, however poisonous, because your mercy came to
their aid and healed them. 11 It was to remind them of your
decrees that they were bitten, and they were quickly healed
for fear they might fall into deep forgetfulness and become
unresponsive to your kindness. 12 It was neither herb nor
poultice that cured them, but your all-healing word, O
Lord. 13 You have the power of life and death, you bring a
person down to the gates of death and you bring him up
again. 14 In his wickedness a human being may kill, but he
cannot bring back the breath of life that has gone or release
a soul that death has arrested.

15 But from your hand there is no escape; 16 for the godless who refused to acknowledge you were scourged by
your mighty arm, they were pursued by unwonted storms of
rain and hail falling in relentless torrents, and were utterly
destroyed by fire. 17 Strangest of all, in water, that quenches

---

y Gk *they*   *z* Gk *loathed the necessary appetite*   *a* Gk *them*
b Meaning of Gk uncertain

19 Nor for their looks are they good or
  desirable beasts,
  but they have escaped both the approval of God
  and his blessing.

16 Therefore they were fittingly punished by
  similar creatures,
  and were tormented by a swarm of insects.
2 Instead of this punishment, you benefited
  your people
  with a novel dish, the delight they craved,
  by providing quail for their food;
3 That those others, when they desired food,
  since the creatures sent to plague them were
  so loathsome,
  should be turned from even the craving
  of necessities,
  While these, after a brief period of privation,
  partook of a novel dish.
4 For upon those oppressors, inexorable want had
  to come;
  but these needed only be shown how their
  enemies were being tormented.
5 For when the dire venom of beasts came
  upon them
  and they were dying from the bite of
  crooked serpents,
  your anger endured not to the end.
6 But as a warning, for a short time they
  were terrorized,
  though they had a sign of salvation, to remind
  them of the precept of your law.
7 For he who turned toward it was saved,
  not by what he saw,
  but by you, the savior of all.
8 And by this also you convinced our foes
  that you are he who delivers from all evil.
9 For the bites of locusts and of flies slew them,
  and no remedy was found to save their lives
  because they deserved to be punished by
  such means;
10 But not even the fangs of poisonous reptiles
  overcame your sons,
  for your mercy brought the antidote to
  heal them.
11 For as a reminder of your injunctions, they
  were stung,
  and swiftly they were saved,
  Lest they should fall into deep forgetfulness
  and become unresponsive to your beneficence.
12 For indeed, neither herb nor application
  cured them,
  but your all-healing word, O Lord!
13 For you have dominion over life and death;
  you lead down to the gates of the nether world,
  and lead back.
14 Man, however, slays in his malice,
  but when the spirit has come away, it does
  not return,
  nor can he bring back the soul once it
  is confined.
15 But your hand none can escape.
16 For the wicked who refused to know you
  were punished by the might of your arm,
  Pursued by unwonted rains and hailstorms and
  unremitting downpours,
  and consumed by fire.

19 without a trace of beauty—if that is what is
  attractive in animals—
  and excluded from God's praises and blessing.

16 Thus they were appropriately punished by similar
  creatures
  and tormented by swarms of vermin.
2 In contrast to this punishment, you did your people
  a kindness
  and, to satisfy their sharp appetite,
  provided quails—a luscious rarity—for them to
  eat.
3 Thus the Egyptians,
  at the repulsive sight of the creatures sent against
  them,
  were to find that, though they longed for food,
  they had lost their natural appetite;
  whereas your own people, after a short privation,
  were to have a rare relish for their portion.
4 Inevitable that relentless want should seize on the
  former oppressors;
  enough for your people to be shown
  how their enemies were being tortured.
5 Even when the fearful rage of wild animals
  overtook them
  and they were perishing from the bites of writhing
  snakes,
  your retribution did not continue to the end.
6 Affliction struck them briefly, by way of warning,
  and they had a saving token$g$ to remind them of
  the commandment of your Law,
7 for whoever turned to it was saved, not by what he
  looked at,
  but by you, the Saviour of all.
8 And by such means you proved to our enemies
  that you are the one who delivers from every evil;
9 for them, the bites of locusts and flies proved fatal
  and no remedy could be found to save their lives,
  since they deserved to be punished by such
  creatures.
10 But your children,
  not even the fangs of poisonous snakes could bring
  them down;
  for your mercy came to their help and cured them.
11 One sting—how quickly healed!—
  to remind them of your pronouncements
  rather than that, by sinking into deep forgetfulness,
  they should be cut off from your kindness.
12 No herb, no poultice cured them,
  but your all-healing word, Lord.
13 Yes, you are the one with power over life and
  death,
  bringing to the gates of Hades and back again.
14 A human being out of malice may put to death,
  but cannot bring the departed spirit back
  or free the soul that Hades has once received.
15 It is not possible to escape your hand.
16 The godless who refused to acknowledge you
  were scourged by the strength of your arm,
  pursued by no ordinary rains, hail and unrelenting
  downpours,
  and consumed by fire.

g **16** The bronze snake, Nb 21:4–9.

17 For — most incredible of all — in water, which
    quenches all things,
  the fire had still greater effect,
    for the universe defends the righteous.
18 At one time the flame was restrained,
  so that it might not consume the creatures sent
    against the ungodly,
  but that seeing this they might know
  that they were being pursued by the judgment of
    God;
19 and at another time even in the midst of water it
    burned more intensely than fire,
  to destroy the crops of the unrighteous land.
20 Instead of these things you gave your people food
    of angels,
  and without their toil you supplied them from
    heaven with bread ready to eat,
  providing every pleasure and suited to every
    taste.
21 For your sustenance manifested your sweetness
    toward your children;
  and the bread, ministering*c* to the desire of the
    one who took it,
  was changed to suit everyone's liking.
22 Snow and ice withstood fire without melting,
  so that they might know that the crops of their
    enemies
  were being destroyed by the fire that blazed in
    the hail
  and flashed in the showers of rain;
23 whereas the fire,*d* in order that the righteous
    might be fed,
  even forgot its native power.
24 For creation, serving you who made it,
  exerts itself to punish the unrighteous,
  and in kindness relaxes on behalf of those who
    trust in you.
25 Therefore at that time also, changed into all
    forms,
  it served your all-nourishing bounty,
  according to the desire of those who had need,*e*
26 so that your children, whom you loved, O Lord,
    might learn
  that it is not the production of crops that feeds
    humankind
  but that your word sustains those who trust in
    you.
27 For what was not destroyed by fire
  was melted when simply warmed by a fleeting
    ray of the sun,
28 to make it known that one must rise before the
    sun to give you thanks,
  and must pray to you at the dawning of the light;
29 for the hope of an ungrateful person will melt
    like wintry frost,
  and flow away like waste water.

17

Great are your judgments and hard to describe;
  therefore uninstructed souls have gone astray.
2 For when lawless people supposed that they held
    the holy nation in their power,
  they themselves lay as captives of darkness and
    prisoners of long night,
  shut in under their roofs, exiles from eternal
    providence.

everything, the fire burned more fiercely; creation itself fights to defend the righteous. 18 At one time the flame was moderated, so that it should not burn up the living creatures inflicted on the godless, who were to learn from this that it was by God's judgement they were pursued; 19 at another time it blazed even in water with more than the natural power of fire, to destroy the produce of a sinful land.

20 In contrast to this your own people were given angels' food. You sent to them from heaven, without labour on their part, bread ready to eat, rich in every kind of delight and suited to every taste. 21 The sustenance you supplied showed the sweetness of your disposition towards your children, and the bread, serving the appetite of every person who ate it, was transformed into what each wished. 22 Though like snow and ice, yet it resisted fire and did not melt, to teach them that whereas their enemies' crops had been destroyed by fire blazing in the hail and flashing through the teeming rain, 23 that same fire had now forgotten its own power, in order that the godly might be fed.

24 For creation, serving you its Maker, strains to punish the unrighteous and relaxes into benevolence towards those who put their trust in you. 25 It was so at that time too: it adapted itself endlessly in the service of your universal bounty, according to the desire of your suppliants. 26 So your people, whom you, Lord, have loved, were to learn that it is not by the growing of crops that mankind is nourished, but it is by your word that those who trust in you are sustained. 27 That substance, which fire did not destroy, simply melted away when warmed by the sun's first rays, 28 to teach us that we must rise before the sun to give you thanks and pray to you as daylight dawns. 29 The hope of the ungrateful will melt like wintry hoar-frost, and drain away like water that runs to waste.

17

Great are your judgements and hard to expound; and this was why uninstructed souls went astray. 2 The heathen imagined that they could lord it over your holy nation, but, prisoners of darkness and captives of unending night, they themselves lay immured each under his own roof, fugitives from eternal providence. 3 Thinking that

---

c Gk *and it, ministering*   *d* Gk *this*   *e* Or *who made supplication*

NEW AMERICAN BIBLE

17 For against all expectation, in water which
quenches anything,
the fire grew more active;
For the universe fights on behalf of the just.
18 For now the flame was tempered
so that the beasts might not be burnt up that
were sent upon the wicked,
but that these might see and know they were
struck by the judgment of God;
19 And again, even in the water, fire blazed beyond
its strength
so as to consume the produce of the
wicked land.
20 Instead of this, you nourished your people with
food of angels
and furnished them bread from heaven, ready to
hand, untoiled-for,
endowed with all delights and conforming to
every taste.
21 For this substance of yours revealed your sweetness
toward your children,
and serving the desire of him who received it,
was blended to whatever flavor each one wished.
22 Yet snow and ice withstood fire and were
not melted,
that they might know that their enemies' fruits
Were consumed by a fire that blazed in the hail
and flashed lightning in the rain.
23 But this fire, again, that the just might
be nourished,
forgot even its proper strength;
24 For your creation, serving you, its maker,
grows tense for punishment against the wicked,
but is relaxed in benefit for those who trust
in you.
25 Therefore at that very time, transformed in all sorts
of ways,
it was serving your all-nourishing bounty
according to what they needed and desired;
26 That your sons whom you loved might learn,
O LORD,
that it is not the various kinds of fruits that
nourish man,
but it is your word that preserves those who
believe you!
27 For what was not destroyed by fire,
when merely warmed by a momentary
sunbeam, melted;
28 So that men might know that one must give you
thanks before the sunrise,
and turn to you at daybreak.
29 For the hope of the ingrate melts like a wintry frost
and runs off like useless water.

17 For great are your judgments, and hardly to
be described;
therefore the unruly souls were wrong.
2 For when the lawless thought to enslave the
holy nation,
shackled with darkness, fettered by the
long night,
they lay confined beneath their own roofs as
exiles from the eternal providence.

NEW JERUSALEM BIBLE

17 Even more wonderful, in the water—which
quenches all—
the fire[h] raged fiercer than ever;
for the elements fight for the upright.
18 At one moment, the fire would die down,
to avoid consuming the animals sent against the
godless
and to make clear to them by that sight, that the
sentence of God was pursuing them;
19 at another, in the very heart of the water, it would
burn more fiercely than fire
to ruin the produce of a wicked land.
20 How differently with your people! You gave them
the food of angels,
from heaven untiringly providing them bread
already prepared,
containing every delight, to satisfy every taste.
21 And the substance you gave
showed your sweetness towards your children,
for, conforming to the taste of whoever ate it,
it transformed itself into what each eater wished.
22 Snow and ice endured the fire, without melting:
this was to show them that, to destroy the harvests
of their enemies,
fire would burn even in hail and flare in falling
rain,
23 whereas, on the other hand, it would even forget
its own strength
in the service of feeding the upright.

24 For the creation, being at the service of you, its
Creator,
tautens to punish the wicked
and slackens for the benefit of those who trust in
you.
25 And this is why, by changing into all things,
it obediently served your all-nourishing bounty,
conforming to the wishes of those who were in
need;
26 so that your beloved children, Lord, might learn
that the various crops are not what provide
nourishment,
but your word which preserves all who believe in
you.
27 For that which fire could not destroy
melted in the heat of a single fleeting sunbeam,
28 to show that, to give you thanks, we must rise
before the sun
and meet you at the dawning of the day;
29 whereas the hope of the ungrateful melts like
winter frost
and flows away like water running to waste.

17 Yes, your judgements are great and impenetrable,
which is why uninstructed souls have gone
astray.
2 While the wicked supposed they had a holy nation
in their power,
they themselves lay prisoners of the dark,[i] in the
fetters of long night,
confined under their own roofs, banished from
eternal providence.

h 16 Cf. the lightning of Ex 9:24.   i 17 Cf. Ex 10:21–23. It is here
supposed that darkness came on some while light continued for
others.

NEW REVISED STANDARD VERSION	REVISED ENGLISH BIBLE

3 For thinking that in their secret sins they were
  unobserved
behind a dark curtain of forgetfulness,
they were scattered, terribly*f* alarmed,
and appalled by specters.

4 For not even the inner chamber that held them
    protected them from fear,
but terrifying sounds rang out around them,
and dismal phantoms with gloomy faces
    appeared.

5 And no power of fire was able to give light,
nor did the brilliant flames of the stars
avail to illumine that hateful night.

6 Nothing was shining through to them
except a dreadful, self-kindled fire,
and in terror they deemed the things that they
    saw
to be worse than that unseen appearance.

7 The delusions of their magic art lay humbled,
and their boasted wisdom was scornfully rebuked.

8 For those who promised to drive off the fears and
    disorders of a sick soul
were sick themselves with ridiculous fear.

9 For even if nothing disturbing frightened them,
yet, scared by the passing of wild animals and
    the hissing of snakes

10 they perished in trembling fear,
refusing to look even at the air, though it
    nowhere could be avoided.

11 For wickedness is a cowardly thing, condemned
    by its own testimony;*g*
distressed by conscience, it has always
    exaggerated*h* the difficulties.

12 For fear is nothing but a giving up of the helps
    that come from reason;

13 and hope, defeated by this inward weakness,
prefers ignorance of what causes the torment.

14 But throughout the night, which was really
    powerless
and which came upon them from the recesses of
    powerless Hades,
they all slept the same sleep,

15 and now were driven by monstrous specters,
and now were paralyzed by their souls' surrender;
for sudden and unexpected fear overwhelmed
    them.

16 And whoever was there fell down,
and thus was kept shut up in a prison not made
    of iron;

17 for whether they were farmers or shepherds
or workers who toiled in the wilderness,
they were seized, and endured the inescapable
    fate;
for with one chain of darkness they all were
    bound.

18 Whether there came a whistling wind,
or a melodious sound of birds in wide-spreading
    branches,
or the rhythm of violently rushing water,

19 or the harsh crash of rocks hurled down,
or the unseen running of leaping animals,
or the sound of the most savage roaring beasts,
or an echo thrown back from a hollow of the
    mountains,
it paralyzed them with terror.

their secret sins might escape detection beneath a dark pall of oblivion, they lay in disorder, dreadfully afraid, terrified by apparitions. 4 Not even the dark corner that hid them offered refuge from fear, but loud, unnerving noises resounded about them, and phantoms with faces grim and downcast passed before their eyes. 5 No fire, however intense, was strong enough to give them light, nor were the brilliant, flaming stars adequate to pierce that hideous darkness. 6 There shone on them only a terrifying blaze of no human making, and in their panic they thought the real world even worse than the sight their imagination conjured up. 7 The tricks of the sorcerer's art failed, and their boasted wisdom was exposed and put to shame; 8 for those who professed to drive out fear and trouble from sick souls were themselves sick with dread that made them ridiculous. 9 Even if there was nothing frightful to terrify them, yet having once been scared by the advance of the vermin and the hissing of the serpents, 10 they collapsed in terror, even refusing to look upon the air from which there could be no escape. 11 For wickedness proves a cowardly thing when condemned by an inner witness, and in the grip of conscience gives way to forebodings of disaster. 12 Fear is nothing but an abandonment of the aid that reason affords; 13 and hope, defeated by this inward weakness, capitulates in ignorance of the cause by which the torment comes.

14 So all that night, which really had no power over them because it came upon them from the powerless depths of hell, they slept the same haunted sleep, 15 now harried by portentous spectres, now paralysed by the treachery of their own souls; sudden and unforeseen, fear came upon them. 16 Thus someone would fall down wherever he was and be held captive, locked in a prison that had no bars. 17 Farmer or shepherd or a labourer toiling out in the wilderness, he was overtaken, and awaited the inescapable doom; the same chain of darkness bound all alike. 18 The whispering breeze, the sweet melody of birds in spreading branches, the steady noise of rushing water, 19 the headlong crash of rocks falling, the racing of creatures as they bound along unseen, the roar of savage wild beasts, or an echo reverberating from hollows in the hills — all these sounds paralysed them with fear. 20 The whole world was bathed in the bright light of

---

f Other ancient authorities read *unobserved, they were darkened behind a dark curtain of forgetfulness, terribly*   *g* Meaning of Gk uncertain   *h* Other ancient authorities read *anticipated*

3 For they who supposed their secret sins were hid
   under the dark veil of oblivion
Were scattered in fearful trembling,
   terrified by apparitions.
4 For not even their inner chambers kept
      them fearless,
   for crashing sounds on all sides terrified them,
   and mute phantoms with somber looks appeared.
5 No force, even of fire, was able to give light,
   nor did the flaming brilliance of the stars
   succeed in lighting up that gloomy night.
6 But only intermittent, fearful fires
   flashed through upon them;
And in their terror they thought beholding these
      was worse
   than the times when that sight was no longer to
      be seen.
7 And mockeries of the magic art were in readiness,
   and a jeering reproof of their
      vaunted shrewdness.
8 For they who undertook to banish fears and terrors
   from the sick soul
   themselves sickened with a ridiculous fear.
9 For even though no monstrous thing
      frightened them,
   they shook at the passing of insects and the
      hissing of reptiles,
10 And perished trembling,
   reluctant to face even the air that they could
      nowhere escape.
11 For wickedness, of its nature cowardly, testifies in
      its own condemnation,
   and because of a distressed conscience, always
      magnifies misfortunes.
12 For fear is nought but the surrender of the helps
      that come from reason;
13   and the more one's expectation is of
      itself uncertain,
   the more one makes of not knowing the cause
      that brings on torment.
14 So they, during that night, powerless though
      it was,
   that had come upon them from the recesses of a
      powerless nether world,
   while all sleeping the same sleep,
15 Were partly smitten by fearsome apparitions
   and partly stricken by their soul's surrender;
   for fear came upon them, sudden
      and unexpected.
16 Thus, then, whoever was there fell
   into that unbarred prison and was kept confined.
17 For whether one was a farmer, or a shepherd,
   or a worker at tasks in the wasteland,
Taken unawares, he served out the
      inescapable sentence;
18   for all were bound by the one bond of darkness.
And were it only the whistling wind,
   or the melodious song of birds in the
      spreading branches,
Or the steady sound of rushing water,
19   or the rude crash of overthrown rocks,
Or the unseen gallop of bounding animals,
   or the roaring cry of the fiercest beasts,
Or an echo resounding from the hollow of
      the hills,
   these sounds, inspiring terror, paralyzed them.

3 While they thought to remain unnoticed with their
      secret sins,
   curtained by dark forgetfulness,
   they were scattered in fearful dismay,
   terrified by apparitions.
4 The hiding place sheltering them could not ward
      off their fear;
   terrifying noises echoed round them;
   and gloomy, grim-faced spectres haunted them.
5 No fire had power enough to give them light,
   nor could the brightly blazing stars
   illuminate that dreadful night.
6 The only light for them was a great, spontaneous
      blaze —
   a fearful sight to see!
And in their terror, once that sight had vanished,
   they thought what they had seen more terrible than
      ever.
7 Their magical illusions were powerless now,
   and their claims to intelligence were ignominiously
      confounded;
8 for those who promised to drive out fears and
      disorders from sick souls
   were now themselves sick with ludicrous fright.
9 Even when there was nothing frightful to scare
      them,
   the vermin creeping past and the hissing of reptiles
      filled them with panic;
10 they died convulsed with fright,
   refusing even to look at empty air, which cannot
      be eluded anyhow!
11 Wickedness is confessedly very cowardly, and it
      condemns itself;
   under pressure from conscience it always assumes
      the worst.
12 Fear, indeed, is nothing other
   than the failure of the help offered by reason;
13 the less you rely within yourself on this,
   the more alarming it is not to know the cause of
      your suffering.
14 And they, all locked in the same sleep,
   while that darkness lasted — which was in fact quite
      powerless
   and had issued from the depths of equally
      powerless Hades —
15 were now chased by monstrous spectres,
   now paralysed by the fainting of their souls;
   for a sudden, unexpected terror had attacked them.
16 And thus, whoever it might be that fell there
   stayed clamped to the spot in this prison without
      bars.
17 Whether he was ploughman or shepherd,
   or somebody at work in the desert,
   he was still overtaken and suffered the inevitable
      fate,
   for all had been bound by the one same chain of
      darkness.
18 The soughing of the wind,
   the tuneful noise of birds in the spreading
      branches,
   the measured beat of water in its powerful course,
   the headlong din of rocks cascading down,
19 the unseen course of bounding animals,
   the roaring of the most savage of wild beasts,
   the echo rebounding from the clefts in the
      mountains,
   all held them paralysed with fear.

| NEW REVISED STANDARD VERSION | REVISED ENGLISH BIBLE |

20 For the whole world was illumined with brilliant light,
and went about its work unhindered,
21 while over those people alone heavy night was spread,
an image of the darkness that was destined to receive them;
but still heavier than darkness were they to themselves.

18 But for your holy ones there was very great light.
Their enemies[i] heard their voices but did not see their forms,
and counted them happy for not having suffered,
2 and were thankful that your holy ones,[j] though previously wronged, were doing them no injury;
and they begged their pardon for having been at variance with them.[j]
3 Therefore you provided a flaming pillar of fire as a guide for your people's[k] unknown journey,
and a harmless sun for their glorious wandering.
4 For their enemies[l] deserved to be deprived of light and imprisoned in darkness,
those who had kept your children imprisoned,
through whom the imperishable light of the law was to be given to the world.

5 When they had resolved to kill the infants of your holy ones,
and one child had been abandoned and rescued,
you in punishment took away a multitude of their children;
and you destroyed them all together by a mighty flood.
6 That night was made known beforehand to our ancestors,
so that they might rejoice in sure knowledge of the oaths in which they trusted.
7 The deliverance of the righteous and the destruction of their enemies
were expected by your people.
8 For by the same means by which you punished our enemies
you called us to yourself and glorified us.
9 For in secret the holy children of good people offered sacrifices,
and with one accord agreed to the divine law,
so that the saints would share alike the same things,
both blessings and dangers;
and already they were singing the praises of the ancestors.[m]
10 But the discordant cry of their enemies echoed back,
and their piteous lament for their children was spread abroad.
11 The slave was punished with the same penalty as the master,
and the commoner suffered the same loss as the king;
12 and they all together, by the one form[n] of death, had corpses too many to count.
For the living were not sufficient even to bury them,
since in one instant their most valued children had been destroyed.

day, and went about its tasks unimpeded; 21 those people alone were overspread with heavy night, fit image of the darkness that awaited them. But heavier than the darkness was the burden each was to himself.

18 For your holy ones, however, there shone a very great light. Their enemies, hearing their voices but not seeing them, counted them happy because they had not suffered as they themselves had; 2 they thanked them for their forbearance under provocation, and begged as a favour that they should part company. 3 In place of the darkness you provided a pillar of fire to be the guide of their uncharted journey, a sun that would not scorch them on that glorious expedition. 4 Their enemies did indeed deserve to lose the light of day and be imprisoned in darkness, for they had kept in durance your people, through whom the imperishable light of the law was to be given to the world.

5 They planned to kill the new-born infants among your holy people but, when one babe had been exposed and rescued, you deprived them of their children in requital, and drowned them all together in the swelling waves. 6 Of that night our forefathers were given warning in advance, so that, having sure knowledge, they might be heartened by the promises which they trusted. 7 Your people were looking for the deliverance of the godly and the destruction of their enemies; 8 for you used the same means to punish our assailants and to make us glorious when we heard your call. 9 The devout children of a virtuous race were offering sacrifices in secret, and covenanted with one accord to keep the law of God and to share alike in the same benefits and the same dangers; already they were singing their ancestral sacred songs of praise.

10 In discordant contrast there came a clamour from their enemies, as piteous lamentation for their children spread abroad. 11 Master and slave were punished together with the same penalty; king and commoner suffered the selfsame fate. 12 All alike had dead past counting, struck down by one common form of death; there were not even enough living to bury the dead; at one stroke the most precious of their offspring had perished. 13 Relying on their magic arts,

---

[i] Gk They   [j] Meaning of Gk uncertain   [k] Gk their   [l] Gk those persons   [m] Other ancient authorities read dangers, the ancestors already leading the songs of praise   [n] Gk name

20 For the whole world shone with brilliant light
    and continued its works without interruption;
21 Over them alone was spread oppressive night,
    an image of the darkness that next should come
        upon them;
    yet they were to themselves more burdensome
        than the darkness.

18 But your holy ones had very great light;
    And those others, who heard their voices
        but did not see their forms,
    since now they themselves had suffered, called
        them blest;
2 And because they who formerly had been wronged
    did not harm them, they thanked them,
    and pleaded with them, for the sake of the
        difference between them.
3 Instead of this, you furnished the flaming pillar
    which was a guide on the unknown way,
    and the mild sun for an honorable migration.
4 For those deserved to be deprived of light and
        imprisoned by darkness,
    who had kept your sons confined
    through whom the imperishable light of the law
        was to be given to the world.

5 When they determined to put to death the infants
    of the holy ones,
    and when a single boy had been cast forth
        but saved,
  As a reproof you carried off their multitude of sons
    and made them perish all at once in the
        mighty water.
6 That night was known beforehand to our fathers,
    that, with sure knowledge of the oaths in which
    they put their faith, they might
    have courage.
7 Your people awaited
    the salvation of the just and the destruction of
    their foes.
8 For when you punished our adversaries,
    in this you glorified us whom you
    had summoned.
9 For in secret the holy children of the good were
    offering sacrifice
    and putting into effect with one accord the
    divine institution,
  That your holy ones should share alike the same
    good things and dangers,
    having previously sung the praises of the fathers.
10 But the discordant cry of their enemies responded,
    and the piteous wail of mourning for children
    was borne to them.
11 And the slave was smitten with the same
    retribution as his master;
    even the plebeian suffered the same as the king.
12 And all alike by a single death
    had countless dead;
  For the living were not even sufficient for
    the burial,
    since at a single instant their nobler offspring
    were destroyed.

20 For the whole world shone with the light of day
    and, unhindered, went about its work;
21 over them alone there spread a heavy darkness,
    image of the dark that would receive them.
  But heavier than the darkness was the burden they
    were to themselves.

18 For your holy ones, however, there was a very
    great light.
  The Egyptians, who could hear them but not see
    them,
  called them fortunate because they had not suffered
    too;
2 they thanked them for doing no injury in return for
    previous wrongs
  and asked forgiveness for their past ill-will.
3 In contrast to the darkness, you gave your people a
    pillar of blazing fire
  to guide them on their unknown journey,
  a mild sun for their ambitious migration.
4 But well those others deserved to be deprived of
    light
  and imprisoned in darkness,
  for they had kept in captivity your children,
  by whom the incorruptible light of the Law was to
    be given to the world.

5 As they had resolved to kill the infants of the holy
    ones,
  and as of those exposed only one child had been
    saved,
  you punished them by carrying off their horde of
    children
  and by destroying them all in the wild water.
6 That night had been known in advance to our
    ancestors,
  so that, well knowing him in whom they had put
    their trust, they would be sure of his
    promises.
7 Your people thus were waiting
  both for the rescue of the upright and for the ruin
    of the enemy;
8 for by the very vengeance that you exacted on our
    adversaries,
  you glorified us by calling us to you.
9 So the holy children of the good offered sacrifice
    in secret
  and with one accord enacted this holy law:
  that the holy ones should share good things and
    dangers alike;
  and forthwith they chanted the hymns of the
    ancestors.

10 In echo came the discordant cries of their enemies,
  and the pitiful wails of people mourning for their
    children
  could be heard from far away.
11 One and the same punishment had struck slave and
    master alike,
  and now commoner and king had the same
    sufferings to endure.
12 Struck by the same death, all had innumerable
    dead.
  There were not enough living left to bury them,
  for, at one stroke, the flower of their offspring had
    perished.

13 For though they had disbelieved everything
because of their magic arts,
yet, when their firstborn were destroyed, they
acknowledged your people to be God's
child.

14 For while gentle silence enveloped all things,
and night in its swift course was now half gone,

15 your all-powerful word leaped from heaven, from
the royal throne,
into the midst of the land that was doomed,
a stern warrior

16 carrying the sharp sword of your authentic
command,
and stood and filled all things with death,
and touched heaven while standing on the earth.

17 Then at once apparitions in dreadful dreams
greatly troubled them,
and unexpected fears assailed them;

18 and one here and another there, hurled down half
dead,
made known why they were dying;

19 for the dreams that disturbed them forewarned
them of this,
so that they might not perish without knowing
why they suffered.

20 The experience of death touched also the
righteous,
and a plague came upon the multitude in the
desert,
but the wrath did not long continue.

21 For a blameless man was quick to act as their
champion;
he brought forward the shield of his ministry,
prayer and propitiation by incense;
he withstood the anger and put an end to the
disaster,
showing that he was your servant.

22 He conquered the wrath*o* not by strength of
body,
not by force of arms,
but by his word he subdued the avenger,
appealing to the oaths and covenants given to our
ancestors.

23 For when the dead had already fallen on one
another in heaps,
he intervened and held back the wrath,
and cut off its way to the living.

24 For on his long robe the whole world was
depicted,
and the glories of the ancestors were engraved on
the four rows of stones,
and your majesty was on the diadem upon his
head.

25 To these the destroyer yielded, these he*p* feared;
for merely to test the wrath was enough.

19 But the ungodly were assailed to the end by
pitiless anger,
for God*q* knew in advance even their future
actions:

2 how, though they themselves had permitted*r*
your people to depart
and hastily sent them out,
they would change their minds and pursue them.

they had scouted all warnings; but when they saw the destruction of their firstborn, they acknowledged that your
people have God as their Father.

14 All things were lying in peace and silence, and night in
her swift course was half spent, 15 when your all-powerful
word leapt from your royal throne in heaven into the midst
of that doomed land like a relentless warrior, 16 bearing the
sharp sword of your inflexible decree; with his head touching the heavens and his feet on earth he stood and spread
death everywhere. 17 Then all at once nightmare phantoms
appalled the godless, and fears unlooked-for beset them;
18 flinging themselves half dead to the ground, one here,
another there, they made clear why they were dying; 19 for
the dreams that tormented them had taught them before they
died, so that they should not perish still ignorant of why
they suffered.

20 The godly also had a taste of death when large numbers
were struck down in the wilderness. But the divine wrath
did not long continue, 21 for a blameless man was quick to
be their champion, bearing the weapons of his priestly ministry, prayer and the incense that propitiates; he withstood
the divine anger and set a limit to the disaster, thus showing
that he was indeed your servant. 22 He overcame the anger
neither by bodily strength nor by force of arms; but by
words he subdued the avenger, appealing to the sworn covenants made with our forefathers. 23 The dead were already
fallen in heaps when he interposed himself and drove back
the divine wrath, barring its line of attack on those still
alive. 24 On his long-skirted robe the whole world was represented; the glories of the fathers were engraved on his four
rows of precious stones; and your majesty was on the diadem upon his head. 25 To these the destroyer yielded, for
they made him afraid. It was only a taste of the wrath, but
it was enough.

19 But the godless were assailed by pitiless anger to
the very end, for God knew their future also: 2 how
after allowing your people to go, and even urging their
departure, they would have a change of heart and set out in
pursuit. 3 While they were still mourning, still lamenting at

---

o Cn: Gk *multitude*   *p* Other ancient authorities read *they*
q Gk *he*   *r* Other ancient authorities read *had changed their minds
to permit*

18:22 **anger:** *prob. rdg; Gk* crowd.

2260

13 For though they disbelieved at every turn on
   account of sorceries,
   at the destruction of the first-born they
   acknowledged that the people was
   God's son.
14 For when peaceful stillness compassed everything
   and the night in its swift course was half spent,
15 Your all-powerful word from heaven's royal throne
   bounded, a fierce warrior, into the doomed land,
16   bearing the sharp sword of your
      inexorable decree.
   And as he alighted, he filled every place
      with death;
   he still reached to heaven, while he stood upon
      the earth.
17 Then, forthwith, visions in horrible dreams
      perturbed them
   and unexpected fears assailed them;
18 And cast half-dead, one here, another there,
   each was revealing the reason for his dying.
19 For the dreams that disturbed them had proclaimed
      this beforehand,
   lest they perish unaware of why they suffered ill.
20 But the trial of death touched at one time even
      the just,
   and in the desert a plague struck the multitude;
   Yet not for long did the anger last.
21 For the blameless man hastened to be
      their champion,
   bearing the weapon of his special office,
   prayer and the propitiation of incense;
   He withstood the wrath and put a stop to
      the calamity,
   showing that he was your servant.
22 And he overcame the bitterness
   not by bodily strength, not by force of arms;
   But by word he overcame the smiter,
   recalling the sworn covenants with their fathers.
23 For when corpses had already fallen one on another
      in heaps,
   he stood in the midst and checked the anger,
   and cut off the way to the living.
24 For on his full-length robe was the whole world,
   and the glories of the fathers were carved in four
      rows upon the stones,
   and your grandeur was on the crown upon
      his head.
25 To these names the destroyer yielded, and these
      he feared;
   for the mere trial of anger was enough.

13 Those whose spells had made them completely
      incredulous,
   when faced with the destruction of their first-born,
   acknowledged this people to be child of God.
14 When peaceful silence lay over all,
   and night had run the half of her swift course,
15 down from the heavens, from the royal throne,
   leapt your all-powerful Word
   like a pitiless warrior into the heart of a land
      doomed to destruction.
   Carrying your unambiguous command like a sharp
      sword,
16 it stood, and filled the universe with death;
   though standing on the earth, it touched the sky.
17 Immediately, dreams and gruesome visions
   overwhelmed them with terror,
   unexpected fears assailed them.
18 Hurled down, some here, some there, half dead,
   they were able to say why they were dying;
19 for the dreams that had troubled them
   had warned them why beforehand,
   so that they should not perish without knowing
      why they were being afflicted.
20 Experience of death, however, touched the upright
      too,
   and a great many were struck down in the desert.
   But the Retribution did not last long,
21 for a blameless man hurried to their defence.
   Wielding the weapons of his sacred office,
   prayer and expiating incense,
   he confronted Retribution and put an end to the
      plague,
   thus showing that he was your servant.
22 He overcame Hostility, not by physical strength,
   nor by force of arms;
   but by word he prevailed over the Punisher,
   by recalling the oaths made to the Fathers, and the
      covenants.
23 Already the corpses lay piled in heaps,
   when he interposed and beat Retribution back
   and cut off its approach to the living.
24 For the whole world was on his flowing robe,
   the glorious names of the Fathers engraved on the
      four rows of stones,
   and your Majesty on the diadem on his head.
25 From these the Destroyer recoiled, he was afraid of
      these.
   This one experience of Retribution was enough.

19 But the wicked, merciless wrath assailed until
   the end.
   For he knew beforehand what they were yet
      to do:
2 That though they themselves had agreed to
      the departure
   and had anxiously sent them on their way,
   they would regret it and pursue them.

19 But the godless were assailed by merciless anger
   to the very end,
   for he knew beforehand what they would do,
2 how, after letting his people leave and hastening
      their departure,
   they would change their minds and give chase.

3 For while they were still engaged in mourning,
 and were lamenting at the graves of their dead,
 they reached another foolish decision,
 and pursued as fugitives those whom they had
   begged and compelled to leave.
4 For the fate they deserved drew them on to this
   end,
 and made them forget what had happened,
 in order that they might fill up the punishment
   that their torments still lacked,
5 and that your people might experience[s] an
   incredible journey,
 but they themselves might meet a strange death.

6 For the whole creation in its nature was fashioned
   anew,
 complying with your commands,
 so that your children[t] might be kept unharmed.
7 The cloud was seen overshadowing the camp,
 and dry land emerging where water had stood
   before,
 an unhindered way out of the Red Sea,
 and a grassy plain out of the raging waves,
8 where those protected by your hand passed
   through as one nation,
 after gazing on marvelous wonders.
9 For they ranged like horses,
 and leaped like lambs,
 praising you, O Lord, who delivered them.
10 For they still recalled the events of their sojourn,
 how instead of producing animals the earth
   brought forth gnats,
 and instead of fish the river spewed out vast
   numbers of frogs.
11 Afterward they saw also a new kind[u] of birds,
 when desire led them to ask for luxurious food;
12 for, to give them relief, quails came up from the
   sea.
13 The punishments did not come upon the sinners
 without prior signs in the violence of thunder,
 for they justly suffered because of their wicked
   acts;
 for they practiced a more bitter hatred of
   strangers.
14 Others had refused to receive strangers when they
   came to them,
 but these made slaves of guests who were their
   benefactors.
15 And not only so — but, while punishment of some
   sort will come upon the former
 for having received strangers with hostility,
16 the latter, having first received them with festal
   celebrations,
 afterward afflicted with terrible sufferings
 those who had already shared the same rights.
17 They were stricken also with loss of sight —
 just as were those at the door of the righteous
   man —
 when, surrounded by yawning darkness,
 all of them tried to find the way through their
   own doors.

the graves of their dead, they rushed into another foolish decision, and pursued as runaways those whom they had entreated to leave. 4 For a well-deserved fate was drawing them on to this conclusion and made them forget what had happened, so that they might suffer the torments still needed to complete their punishment, 5 and so that your people might achieve an incredible journey but their enemies meet a strange death.

6 The whole creation, with all its elements, was refashioned in subservience to your commands, in order that your servants might be preserved unscathed. 7 They gazed at the cloud that overshadowed the camp, at dry land emerging where before was only water, at an open road leading out of the Red Sea, and a grassy plain in place of stormy waves, 8 across which the whole nation passed under the protection of your hand, after witnessing amazing portents. 9 They were like horses at pasture, like skipping lambs, as they praised you, O Lord, by whom they were rescued. 10 They still remembered their life in a foreign land: how instead of cattle the earth bred lice, and instead of fish the river disgorged swarms of frogs; 11 and how, at a later stage, they had seen a new sort of bird when, driven by appetite, they had begged for delicacies to eat, 12 and for their relief quails came up from the sea.

13 On the sinners, however, punishment came, heralded by violent thunderbolts. They suffered justly for their own wickedness, because their hatred of strangers was on a new level of bitterness. 14 While others there had been who refused to welcome strangers when they came to them, these made slaves of guests who were their benefactors. 15 There will indeed be a judgement for those whose reception of foreigners was hostile; 16 but these, after a festal welcome, oppressed with hard labour men who had earlier shared their rights. 17 They were struck with blindness also, like the men at the door of the one good man, when yawning darkness fell upon them and each went groping for his own doorway.

---

[s] Other ancient authorities read *accomplish*   [t] Or *servants*
[u] Or *production*

3 For while they were still engaged in funeral rites
  and were mourning at the burials of the dead,
They adopted another senseless plan;
  and those whom they had sent away
    with entreaty,
  they pursued as fugitives.
4 For a compulsion suited to this ending drew
    them on,
  and made them forgetful of what had
    befallen them,
That they might fill out the torments of
    their punishment,
5 and your people might experience a
    glorious journey
  while those others met an extraordinary death.
6 For all creation, in its several kinds, was being
    made over anew,
  serving its natural laws,
  that your children might be preserved unharmed.
7 The cloud overshadowed their camp;
  and out of what had before been water, dry land
    was seen emerging:
Out of the Red Sea an unimpeded road,
  and a grassy plain out of the mighty flood.
8 Over this crossed the whole nation sheltered by
    your hand,
  after they beheld stupendous wonders.
9 For they ranged about like horses,
  and bounded about like lambs,
  praising you, O Lord! their deliverer.
10 For they were still mindful of what had happened
    in their sojourn:
  how instead of the young of animals the land
    brought forth gnats,
  and instead of fishes the river swarmed with
    countless frogs.
11 And later they saw also a new kind of bird
  when, prompted by desire, they asked for
    pleasant foods;
12 For to appease them quail came to them from
    the sea.
13 And the punishments came upon the sinners
  only after forewarnings from the violence of
    the thunderbolts.
  For they justly suffered for their own misdeeds,
  since indeed they treated their guests with the
    more grievous hatred.
14 For those others did not receive unfamiliar visitors,
  but these were enslaving beneficent guests.
15 And not that only; but what punishment was to
    be theirs
  since they received strangers unwillingly!
16 Yet these, after welcoming them with festivities,
  oppressed with awful toils
  those who now shared with them the
    same rights.
17 And they were struck with blindness,
  as those others had been at the portals of
    the just —
  When, surrounded by yawning darkness,
  each sought the entrance of his own gate.

3 They were actually still conducting their mourning
    rites
  and lamenting at the tombs of their dead,
  when another mad scheme came into their heads
  and they set out to pursue, as though runaways,
  the people whom they had expelled and begged to
    go.
4 A well-deserved fate urged them to this extreme
  and made them forget what had already happened,
  so that they would add to their torments
  the one punishment outstanding
5 and, while your people were experiencing a
    journey
  contrary to all expectations,
  would themselves meet an extraordinary death.
6 For the whole creation, submissive to your
    commands,
  had its very nature re-created,
  so that your children should be preserved from
    harm.
7 Overshadowing the camp there was the cloud;
  where there had been water, dry land was seen to
    rise;
  the Red Sea became an unimpeded way,
  the tempestuous waves, a green plain;
8 sheltered by your hand, the whole nation passed
    across,
  gazing at these amazing prodigies.
9 They were like horses at pasture,
  they skipped like lambs,
  singing your praises, Lord, their deliverer.
10 For they still remembered the events of their exile,
  how the land had bred mosquitoes instead of
    animals
  and the River had disgorged millions of frogs
    instead of fish.
11 Later they were to see a new way for birds to
    come into being,
  when, goaded by greed, they demanded something
    tasty,
12 and quails came up out of the sea to satisfy them.
13 On the sinners, however, punishments rained down
  not without violent thunder as early warning;
  and they suffered what their own crimes had justly
    deserved
  since they had shown such bitter hatred to
    foreigners.
14 Others, indeed, had failed to welcome strangers
    who came to them,
  but the Egyptians had enslaved their own guests
    and benefactors.
15 The sinners, moreover, will certainly be punished
    for it,
  since they gave the foreigners a hostile welcome;
16 but the latter, having given a festive reception
  to people who already shared the same rights as
    themselves,
  later overwhelmed them with terrible labours.
17 Hence they were struck with blindness,
  like the sinners at the gate of the upright,
  when, yawning darkness all around them,
  each had to grope his way through his own door.

18 For the elements changed^v places with one
    another,
    as on a harp the notes vary the nature of the
        rhythm,
    while each note remains the same.^w
    This may be clearly inferred from the sight of
        what took place.
19 For land animals were transformed into water
        creatures,
    and creatures that swim moved over to the land.
20 Fire even in water retained its normal power,
    and water forgot its fire-quenching nature.
21 Flames, on the contrary, failed to consume
    the flesh of perishable creatures that walked
        among them,
    nor did they melt^x the crystalline, quick-melting
        kind of heavenly food.

22 For in everything, O Lord, you have exalted and
        glorified your people,
    and you have not neglected to help them at all
        times and in all places.

^v Gk *changing*   ^w Meaning of Gk uncertain   ^x Cn: Gk *nor could
be melted*

18 As the strings of a harp can make various tunes with
different names though each string retains its own pitch, so
the elements combined among themselves in different
ways, as can be accurately inferred from the observation of
what happened. 19 Land animals took to the water and creatures that swim migrated to dry land; 20 fire retained its
normal power even in water, and water forgot its fire-
quenching properties. 21 Flames on the other hand failed to
consume the flesh of perishable creatures that walked in
them, and the substance of heavenly food, like ice and
prone to melt, no longer melted.

22 In everything, O Lord, you have made your people
great and glorious, and in every time and place you have
been their unfailing helper.

18 For the elements, in variable harmony
    among themselves,
  like strings of the harp, produce new melody,
  while the flow of music steadily persists.
  And this can be perceived exactly from a review of
    what took place.
19 For land creatures were changed into
    water creatures,
  and those that swam went over on to the land.
20 Fire in water maintained its own strength,
  and water forgot its quenching nature;
21 Flames, by contrast, neither consumed the flesh
  of the perishable animals that went about
    in them,
  nor melted the icelike, quick-melting kind of
    ambrosial food.
22 For every way, O LORD! you magnified and
    glorified your people;
  unfailing, you stood by them in every time
    and circumstance.

18 A new attuning of the elements occurred,
  as on a harp the notes may change their rhythm,
  though all the while preserving the same tone;
  and this is just what happened:
19 land animals became aquatic,
  swimming ones took to the land,
20 fire reinforced its strength in water,
  and water forgot the power of extinguishing it;
21 flames, on the other hand, did not char the flesh
  of delicate animals that ventured into them;
  nor did they melt the heavenly food
  resembling ice and as easily melted.

22 Yes, Lord, in every way you have made your
    people great and glorious;
  you have never failed to help them at any time or
    place.

ECCLESIASTICUS, OR THE
WISDOM OF JESUS SON OF
Sirach

Ecclesiasticus

OR THE WISDOM OF JESUS
SON OF SIRACH

THE PROLOGUE

Many great teachings have been given to us through the Law and the Prophets and the others[a] that followed them, and for these we should praise Israel for instruction and wisdom. Now, those who read the scriptures must not only themselves understand them, but must also as lovers of learning be able through the spoken and written word to help the outsiders. So my grandfather Jesus, who had devoted himself especially to the reading of the Law and the Prophets and the other books of our ancestors, and had acquired considerable proficiency in them, was himself also led to write something pertaining to instruction and wisdom, so that by becoming familiar also with his book[b] those who love learning might make even greater progress in living according to the law.

You are invited therefore to read it with goodwill and attention, and to be indulgent in cases where, despite our diligent labor in translating, we may seem to have rendered some phrases imperfectly. For what was originally expressed in Hebrew does not have exactly the same sense when translated into another language. Not only this book, but even the Law itself, the Prophecies, and the rest of the books differ not a little when read in the original.

When I came to Egypt in the thirty-eighth year of the reign of Euergetes and stayed for some time, I found opportunity for no little instruction.[c] It seemed highly necessary that I should myself devote some diligence and labor to the translation of this book. During that time I have applied my skill day and night to complete and publish the book for those living abroad who wished to gain learning and are disposed to live according to the law.

A LEGACY of great value has come down to us through the law, the prophets, and the writers who followed in their steps, and Israel deserves recognition for its traditions of learning and wisdom. It is the duty of those who study the scriptures not only to become expert themselves, but also to use their scholarship for the benefit of the world outside through both the spoken and the written word. For that reason my grandfather Jesus, who had applied himself diligently to the study of the law, the prophets, and the other writings of our ancestors, and had gained a considerable proficiency in them, was moved to compile a book of his own on the themes of learning and wisdom, in order that, with this further help, scholars might make greater progress in their studies by living as the law directs.

You are asked, then, to read with sympathetic attention, and to make allowances wherever you think that, in spite of all the devoted work that has been put into the translation, some of the expressions I have used are inadequate. For what is said in Hebrew does not have the same force when translated into another tongue. Not only the present work, but even the law itself, as well as the prophets and the other writings, are not a little different when spoken in the original.

When I came to Egypt and settled there in the thirty-eighth year of the reign of King Euergetes, I found much scope for giving instruction; and I thought it very necessary to spend some energy and labour on the translation of this book. Ever since then I have applied my skill night and day to complete it, and to publish it for the use of those who have made their home in a foreign land, and wish to study and so train themselves to live according to the law.

1 All wisdom is from the Lord,
and with him it remains forever.
2 The sand of the sea, the drops of rain,
and the days of eternity — who can count them?
3 The height of heaven, the breadth of the earth,
the abyss, and wisdom[d] — who can search them out?
4 Wisdom was created before all other things,
and prudent understanding from eternity.[e]
6 The root of wisdom — to whom has it been revealed?
Her subtleties — who knows them?[f]
8 There is but one who is wise, greatly to be feared,
seated upon his throne — the Lord.
9 It is he who created her;
he saw her and took her measure;
he poured her out upon all his works,

1 ALL wisdom is from the Lord;
she dwells with him for ever.
2 Who can count the sands of the sea,
the raindrops, or the days of unending time?
3 Who can measure the height of the sky,
the breadth of the earth, or the depth of the abyss?
4 Wisdom was first of all created things;
intelligent purpose has existed from the beginning.
6 To whom has the root of wisdom been revealed?
Who has understanding of her subtlety?
8 One alone is wise, the Lord most terrible,
seated upon his throne.
9 It is he who created her, beheld and measured her,
and infused her into all his works.

---

[a] Or *other books*   [b] Gk *with these things*   [c] Other ancient authorities read *I found a copy affording no little instruction*   [d] Other ancient authorities read *the depth of the abyss*   [e] Other ancient authorities add as verse 5, *The source of wisdom is God's word in the highest heaven, and her ways are the eternal commandments.*   [f] Other ancient authorities add as verse 7, *The knowledge of wisdom—to whom was it manifested? And her abundant experience—who has understood it?*

1:3 **of the abyss:** *prob. rdg; Gk adds* or wisdom.   1:4 **from the beginning:** *some witnesses add* 5The fountain of wisdom is God's word on high, and her ways are eternal commandments.   1:6 **of her subtlety:** *some witnesses add* 7Who has discovered all that wisdom knows, or understood her wealth of experience?

THE BOOK OF

Sirach

(Ecclesiasticus)

NOTE: The numbering of the verses is based on a Latin text which included several additions to the original. In some cases whole verses are missed out in this edition.

FOREWORD

Many important truths have been handed down to us through the law, the prophets, and the later authors; and for these the instruction and wisdom of Israel merit praise. Now, those who are familiar with these truths must not only understand them themselves but, as lovers of wisdom, be able, in speech and in writing, to help others less familiar. Such a one was my grandfather, Jesus, who, having devoted himself for a long time to the diligent study of the law, the prophets, and the rest of the books of our ancestors, and having developed a thorough familiarity with them, was moved to write something himself in the nature of instruction and wisdom, in order that those who love wisdom might, by acquainting themselves with what he too had written, make even greater progress in living in conformity with the divine law.

You therefore are now invited to read it in a spirit of attentive good will, with indulgence for any apparent failure on our part, despite earnest efforts, in the interpretation of particular passages. For words spoken originally in Hebrew are not as effective when they are translated into another language. That is true not only of this book but of the law itself, the prophets and the rest of the books, which differ no little when they are read in the original.

I arrived in Egypt in the thirty-eighth year of the reign of King Euergetes, and while there, I found a reproduction of our valuable teaching. I therefore considered myself in duty bound to devote some diligence and industry to the translation of this book. Many sleepless hours of close application have I devoted in the interval to finishing the book for publication, for the benefit of those living abroad who wish to acquire wisdom and are disposed to live their lives according to the standards of the law.

1   All wisdom comes from the LORD
      and with him it remains forever.
2 The sand of the seashore, the drops of rain,
      the days of eternity: who can number these?
3 Heaven's height, earth's breadth,
      the depths of the abyss: who can explore these?
4 Before all things else wisdom was created;
      and prudent understanding, from eternity.
5 To whom has wisdom's root been revealed?
      Who knows her subtleties?
6 There is but one, wise and truly awe-inspiring,
      seated upon his throne:
7 It is the LORD; he created her,
      has seen her and taken note of her.
8 He has poured her forth upon all his works,

Ecclesiasticus

TRANSLATOR'S FOREWORD

1 The Law, the Prophets, 2 and the other writers succeeding them have passed on to us great lessons, 3 in consequence of which Israel must be commended for learning and wisdom. 4 Furthermore, it is a duty, not only to acquire learning by reading, 5 but also, once having acquired it, to make oneself of use to people outside 6 by what one can say or write. 7 My grandfather Jesus, having long devoted himself to the reading 8 of the Law, 9 the Prophets 10 and other books of the Fathers 11 and having become very learned in them, 12 himself decided to write something on the subjects of learning and wisdom, 13 so that people who wanted to learn might, by themselves accepting these disciplines, 14 learn how better to live according to the Law.

15 You are therefore asked 16 to read this book 17 with good will and attention 18 and to show indulgence 19 in those places where, notwithstanding our efforts at interpretation, we may seem 20 to have failed to give an adequate rendering of this or that expression; 21 the fact is that there is no equivalent 22 for things originally written in Hebrew when it is a question of translating them into another language; 23 what is more, 24 the Law itself, the Prophets 25 and the other books 26 differ considerably in translation from what appears in the original text.

27 It was in the thirty-eighth year of the late King Euergetes*a* 28 that, coming to Egypt and spending some time here, 29 and finding life here consistent with a high degree of wisdom, 30 I became convinced of an immediate duty to apply myself in my turn with pains and diligence to the translation of the book that follows; 31 and I spent much time and learning on it 32 in the course of this period, 33 to complete the work and to publish the book 34 for the benefit of those too who, domiciled abroad, wish to study, 35 to reform their behaviour, and to live as the Law requires.

1   All wisdom comes from the Lord,
      she is with him for ever.
2 The sands of the sea, the drops of rain,
      the days of eternity — who can count them?
3 The height of the sky, the breadth of the earth,
      the depth of the abyss — who can explore them?
4 Wisdom was created before everything,
      prudent understanding subsists from remotest
      ages.
6 For whom has the root of wisdom ever been
      uncovered?
      Her resourceful ways, who knows them?
8 One only is wise, terrible indeed,
9   seated on his throne, the Lord.
  It was he who created, inspected and weighed her
      up,
      and then poured her out on all his works —

a **Foreword** Ptolemy VII Euergetes Physcon (170–117 BC). So the date is 132 BC.

NEW REVISED STANDARD VERSION	REVISED ENGLISH BIBLE

10 upon all the living according to his gift;
   he lavished her upon those who love him. g

11 The fear of the Lord is glory and exultation,
   and gladness and a crown of rejoicing.
12 The fear of the Lord delights the heart,
   and gives gladness and joy and long life. h
13 Those who fear the Lord will have a happy end;
   on the day of their death they will be blessed.
14 To fear the Lord is the beginning of wisdom;
   she is created with the faithful in the womb.
15 She made i among human beings an eternal
        foundation,
   and among their descendants she will abide
        faithfully.
16 To fear the Lord is fullness of wisdom;
   she inebriates mortals with her fruits;
17 she fills their j whole house with desirable goods,
   and their j storehouses with her produce.
18 The fear of the Lord is the crown of wisdom,
   making peace and perfect health to flourish. k
19 She rained down knowledge and discerning
        comprehension,
   and she heightened the glory of those who held
        her fast.
20 To fear the Lord is the root of wisdom,
   and her branches are long life. l

22 Unjust anger cannot be justified,
   for anger tips the scale to one's ruin.
23 Those who are patient stay calm until the right
        moment,
   and then cheerfulness comes back to them.
24 They hold back their words until the right
        moment;
   then the lips of many tell of their good sense.
25 In the treasuries of wisdom are wise sayings,
   but godliness is an abomination to a sinner.
26 If you desire wisdom, keep the commandments,
   and the Lord will lavish her upon you.
27 For the fear of the Lord is wisdom and discipline,
   fidelity and humility are his delight.
28 Do not disobey the fear of the Lord;
   do not approach him with a divided mind.
29 Do not be a hypocrite before others,
   and keep watch over your lips.
30 Do not exalt yourself, or you may fall
   and bring dishonor upon yourself.
   The Lord will reveal your secrets
   and overthrow you before the whole
        congregation,
   because you did not come in the fear of the Lord,
   and your heart was full of deceit.

2 My child, when you come to serve the Lord,
     prepare yourself for testing. m
2 Set your heart right and be steadfast,
   and do not be impetuous in time of calamity.
3 Cling to him and do not depart,
   so that your last days may be prosperous.

10 To everyone he has given her in some degree,
   but without stint to those who love him.

11 THE fear of the Lord brings honour and pride,
   cheerfulness and a garland of joy.
12 The fear of the Lord gladdens the heart;
   it brings cheerfulness and joy and long life.
13 Whoever fears the Lord, it will be well with him at
        the last,
   and on the day of his death blessings will be his.
14 The beginning of wisdom is the fear of the Lord;
   she is created with the faithful in their mother's
        womb.
15 she has built an everlasting home among mortals,
   and with their descendants she will keep faith.
16 The full measure of wisdom is the fear of the
        Lord;
   she gives to mortals deep draughts of her wine.
17 She fills her home with all that the heart can
        desire,
   and her storehouses with her produce.
18 Wisdom's garland is the fear of the Lord,
   flowering with peace and perfect health.
19 She showers down knowledge and discernment,
   and bestows high honour on those who hold fast to
        her.
20 Wisdom is rooted in the fear of the Lord,
   and long life grows on her branches.

22 Unjust rage can never be excused;
   when anger tips the scale it is a person's downfall.
23 Until the right moment comes, he who is patient
        restrains himself,
   and afterwards cheerfulness breaks through again;
24 until the right moment he keeps his thoughts to
        himself,
   and later his good sense is on everyone's lips.
25 In wisdom's treasure house are wise proverbs,
   but godliness is detestable to a sinner.
26 If you long for wisdom, keep the commandments,
   and the Lord will give it you without stint.
27 The fear of the Lord is wisdom and instruction;
   fidelity and gentleness are his delight.
28 Do not disregard the fear of the Lord
   or approach him without sincerity.
29 Do not act a part before the eyes of the world;
   keep guard over your lips.
30 Never be arrogant, or you will fall
   and bring disgrace on yourself;
   the Lord will reveal your secrets
   and humble you before the assembly,
   because what prompted you was not the fear of the
        Lord:
   guile filled your heart.

2 MY son, if you aspire to be a servant of the Lord,
     prepare yourself for testing.
2 Set a straight course and keep to it,
   and do not be dismayed in the face of adversity.
3 Hold fast to him and never let go,
   if you would end your days in prosperity.

---

g Other ancient authorities add Love of the Lord is glorious wisdom;
to those to whom he appears he apportions her, that they may see
him.   h Other ancient authorities add The fear of the Lord is a gift
from the Lord; also for love he makes firm paths.   i Gk made as a
nest   j Other ancient authorities read her   k Other ancient
authorities add Both are gifts of God for peace; glory opens up for
those who love him. He saw her and took her measure.   l Other
ancient authorities add as verse 21, The fear of the Lord drives away
sins; and where it abides, it will turn away all anger.   m Or trials

1:20 on her branches: some witnesses add 21 The fear of the Lord
drives away sins, and wherever it dwells it averts his anger.
1:30 because . . . the Lord: or because you had no concern for the
fear of the Lord.

upon every living thing according to his bounty;
he has lavished her upon his friends.

9 Fear of the LORD is glory and splendor,
gladness and a festive crown.
10 Fear of the LORD warms the heart,
giving gladness and joy and length of days.
11 He who fears the LORD will have a happy end;
even on the day of his death he will be blessed.
12 The beginning of wisdom is fear of the LORD,
which is formed with the faithful in the womb.
13 With devoted men was she created from of old,
and with their children her beneficence abides.
14 Fullness of wisdom is fear of the LORD;
she inebriates men with her fruits.
15 Her entire house she fills with choice foods,
her granaries with her harvest.
16 Wisdom's garland is fear of the LORD,
with blossoms of peace and perfect health.
17 Knowledge and full understanding she
showers down;
she heightens the glory of those who
possess her.
18 The root of wisdom is fear of the LORD;
her branches are length of days.

19 One cannot justify unjust anger;
anger plunges a man to his downfall.
20 A patient man need stand firm but for a time,
and then contentment comes back to him.
21 For a while he holds back his words,
then the lips of many herald his wisdom.
22 Among wisdom's treasures is the paragon
of prudence;
but fear of the LORD is an abomination to
the sinner.
23 If you desire wisdom, keep the commandments,
and the LORD will bestow her upon you.
24 For fear of the LORD is wisdom and culture;
loyal humility is his delight.
25 Be not faithless to the fear of the LORD,
nor approach it with duplicity of heart.
26 Play not the hypocrite before men;
over your lips keep watch.
27 Exalt not yourself lest you fall
and bring upon you dishonor;
28 For then the LORD will reveal your secrets
and publicly cast you down,
29 Because you approached the fear of the LORD
with your heart full of guile.

2 My son, when you come to serve the LORD,
prepare yourself for trials.
2 Be sincere of heart and steadfast,
undisturbed in time of adversity.
3 Cling to him, forsake him not;
thus will your future be great.

10 as much to each living creature as he chose —
bestowing her on those who love him.

11 The fear of the Lord is glory and pride,
happiness and a crown of joyfulness.
12 The fear of the Lord gladdens the heart,
giving happiness, joy and long life.
13 For those who fear the Lord, all will end well:
on their dying day they will be blessed.
14 The basis of wisdom is to fear the Lord;
she was created with the faithful in their
mothers' womb;
15 she has made a home in the human race, an
age-old foundation,
and to their descendants will she faithfully cling.
16 The fullness of wisdom is to fear the Lord;
she intoxicates them with her fruits;
17 she fills their entire house with treasures
and their storerooms with her produce.
18 The crown of wisdom is to fear the Lord:
she makes peace and health flourish.
19 The Lord has seen and assessed her,
he has showered down knowledge and
intelligence,
he has exalted the renown of those who possess
her.
20 The root of wisdom is to fear the Lord,
and her branches are long life.

22 The rage of the wicked cannot put him in the right,
for the weight of his rage is his downfall.
23 A patient person puts up with things until the right
time comes:
but his joy will break out in the end.
24 Till the time comes he keeps his thoughts to
himself,
and many a lip will affirm how wise he is.

25 Wisdom's treasures contain the maxims of
knowledge,
the sinner, however, holds piety in abhorrence.
26 If you desire wisdom, keep the commandments,
and the Lord will bestow it on you.
27 For the fear of the Lord is wisdom and instruction,
and what pleases him is faithfulness and
gentleness.
28 Do not stand out against fear of the Lord,
do not practise it with a double heart.
29 Do not act a part in public',
keep watch over your lips.
30 Do not grow too high and mighty, for fear you fall
and cover yourself in disgrace;
for the Lord would then reveal your secrets
and overthrow you before the whole community
for not having practised fear of the Lord
and for having a heart full of deceit.

2 My child, if you aspire to serve the Lord,
prepare yourself for an ordeal.
2 Be sincere of heart, be steadfast,
and do not be alarmed when disaster comes.
3 Cling to him and do not leave him,
so that you may be honoured at the end of your
days.

NEW REVISED STANDARD VERSION	REVISED ENGLISH BIBLE

NEW REVISED STANDARD VERSION

4 Accept whatever befalls you,
and in times of humiliation be patient.
5 For gold is tested in the fire,
and those found acceptable, in the furnace of
humiliation.[n]
6 Trust in him, and he will help you;
make your ways straight, and hope in him.

7 You who fear the Lord, wait for his mercy;
do not stray, or else you may fall.
8 You who fear the Lord, trust in him,
and your reward will not be lost.
9 You who fear the Lord, hope for good things,
for lasting joy and mercy.[o]
10 Consider the generations of old and see:
has anyone trusted in the Lord and been
disappointed?
Or has anyone persevered in the fear of the
Lord[p] and been forsaken?
Or has anyone called upon him and been
neglected?
11 For the Lord is compassionate and merciful;
he forgives sins and saves in time of distress.

12 Woe to timid hearts and to slack hands,
and to the sinner who walks a double path!
13 Woe to the fainthearted who have no trust!
Therefore they will have no shelter.
14 Woe to you who have lost your nerve!
What will you do when the Lord's reckoning
comes?

15 Those who fear the Lord do not disobey his
words,
and those who love him keep his ways.
16 Those who fear the Lord seek to please him,
and those who love him are filled with his law.
17 Those who fear the Lord prepare their hearts,
and humble themselves before him.
18 Let us fall into the hands of the Lord,
but not into the hands of mortals;
for equal to his majesty is his mercy,
and equal to his name are his works.[q]

3 Listen to me your father, O children;
act accordingly, that you may be kept in
safety.
2 For the Lord honors a father above his children,
and he confirms a mother's right over her
children.
3 Those who honor their father atone for sins,
4 and those who respect their mother are like
those who lay up treasure.
5 Those who honor their father will have joy in
their own children,
and when they pray they will be heard.
6 Those who respect their father will have long life,
and those who honor[r] their mother obey the
Lord;
7 they will serve their parents as their masters.[s]
8 Honor your father by word and deed,
that his blessing may come upon you.
9 For a father's blessing strengthens the houses of
the children,
but a mother's curse uproots their foundations.

REVISED ENGLISH BIBLE

4 Bear every hardship that is sent you,
and whenever humiliation comes, be patient;
5 for gold is assayed in the fire,
and the chosen ones in the furnace of humiliation.
6 Trust him and he will help you;
steer a straight course and fix your hope on him.

7 You that fear the Lord, wait for his mercy;
do not stray, for fear you will fall.
8 You that fear the Lord, trust in him,
and you will not be baulked of your reward.
9 You that fear the Lord, hope for prosperity
and lasting joy and favour.
10 Consider the past generations and see:
was anyone who trusted the Lord ever
disappointed?
Was anyone who stood firm in the fear of him ever
abandoned?
Did he ever ignore anyone who called to him?
11 For the Lord is compassionate and merciful;
he forgives sins and saves in time of trouble.

12 Woe to faint hearts and nerveless hands
and to the sinner who leads a double life!
13 Woe to the feeble-hearted! They have no faith,
and therefore will go unprotected.
14 Woe to you who have given up the struggle!
What will you do at the Lord's coming?

15 Those who fear the Lord never disobey his words,
and all who love him keep to his ways.
16 Those who fear the Lord try to do his will,
and all who love him steep themselves in the law.
17 Those who fear the Lord will always be ready;
they humble themselves before him and say,
18 'Let us fall into the Lord's hands, not into the
hands of men,'
for his majesty is equalled by his mercy.

3 CHILDREN, listen to me, for I am your father;
do what I tell you, that you may be safe.
2 The Lord has given the father honour in his
children's eyes
and confirmed a mother's rights in the eyes of her
sons.
3 Respect for a father atones for sins;
4 to honour your mother is like laying up treasure.
5 He who respects his father will be made happy by
children,
and when he prays, he will be heard.
6 He who honours his father will have a long life,
and he who obeys the Lord gives comfort to his
mother;
7 he submits to his parents as though he were their
servant.
8 Honour your father by deed and word,
so that you may receive his blessing;
9 for a father's blessing strengthens his children's
houses,
but a mother's curse uproots their foundations.

---

[n] Other ancient authorities add *in sickness and poverty put your trust
in him* [o] Other ancient authorities add *For his reward is an
everlasting gift with joy.* [p] Gk *of him* [q] Syr: Gk lacks this line
[r] Heb: Other ancient authorities read *comfort* [s] In other ancient
authorities this line is preceded by *Those who fear the Lord honor
their father,*

NEW AMERICAN BIBLE

NEW JERUSALEM BIBLE

⁴Accept whatever befalls you,
in crushing misfortune be patient;
⁵For in fire gold is tested,
and worthy men in the crucible of humiliation.
⁶Trust God and he will help you;
make straight your ways and hope in him.

⁷You who fear the LORD, wait for his mercy,
turn not away lest you fall.
⁸You who fear the LORD, trust him,
and your reward will not be lost.
⁹You who fear the LORD, hope for good things,
for lasting joy and mercy.
¹⁰Study the generations long past and understand;
has anyone hoped in the LORD and
been disappointed?
Has anyone persevered in his fear and
been forsaken?
has anyone called upon him and been rebuffed?
¹¹Compassionate and merciful is the LORD;
he forgives sins, he saves in time of trouble.

¹²Woe to craven hearts and drooping hands,
to the sinner who treads a double path!
¹³Woe to the faint of heart who trust not,
who therefore will have no shelter!
¹⁴Woe to you who have lost hope!
what will you do at the visitation of the LORD?
¹⁵Those who fear the LORD disobey not his words;
those who love him keep his ways.
¹⁶Those who fear the LORD seek to please him,
those who love him are filled with his law.
¹⁷Those who fear the LORD prepare their hearts
and humble themselves before him.
¹⁸Let us fall into the hands of the LORD
and not into the hands of men,
For equal to his majesty
is the mercy that he shows.

⁴Whatever happens to you, accept it,
and in the uncertainties of your humble state, be
patient,
⁵since gold is tested in the fire,
and the chosen in the furnace of humiliation.
⁶Trust him and he will uphold you,
follow a straight path and hope in him.
⁷You who fear the Lord, wait for his mercy;
do not turn aside, for fear you fall.
⁸You who fear the Lord, trust him,
and you will not be robbed of your reward.
⁹You who fear the Lord, hope for those good gifts
of his,
everlasting joy and mercy.
¹⁰Look at the generations of old and see:
whoever trusted in the Lord and was put to
shame?
Or whoever, steadfastly fearing him, was forsaken?
Or whoever called to him and was ignored?
¹¹For the Lord is compassionate and merciful,
he forgives sins and saves in the time of distress.
¹²Woe to faint hearts and listless hands,
and to the sinner who treads two paths!
¹³Woe to the listless heart that has no faith,
for such will have no protection.
¹⁴Woe to you who have lost the strength to endure;
what will you do at the Lord's visitation?
¹⁵Those who fear the Lord do not disdain his words,
and those who love him keep his ways.
¹⁶Those who fear the Lord do their best to please
him,
and those who love him will find satisfaction in
the Law.
¹⁷Those who fear the Lord keep their hearts prepared
and humble themselves in his presence.
¹⁸Let us fall into the hands of the Lord, not into any
human clutches;
for as his majesty is, so too is his mercy.

3 Children, pay heed to a father's right;
do so that you may live.
²For the LORD sets a father in honor over
his children;
a mother's authority he confirms over her sons.
³He who honors his father atones for sins;
⁴ he stores up riches who reveres his mother.
⁵He who honors his father is gladdened by children,
and when he prays he is heard.
⁶He who reveres his father will live a long life;
he obeys the LORD who brings comfort to
his mother.

⁷He who fears the LORD honors his father,
and serves his parents as rulers.
⁸In word and deed honor your father
that his blessing may come upon you;
⁹For a father's blessing gives a family firm roots,
but a mother's curse uproots the growing plant.

3 Children, listen to me for I am your father:
do what I tell you, and so be safe;
²for the Lord honours the father above his children
and upholds the rights of a mother over her
sons.
³Whoever respects a father expiates sins,
⁴ whoever honours a mother is like someone
amassing a fortune.
⁵Whoever respects a father will in turn be happy
with children,
the day he prays for help, he will be heard.
⁶Long life comes to anyone who honours a father,
whoever obeys the Lord makes a mother happy.
⁷ Such a one serves parents as well as the Lord.
⁸Respect your father in deed as well as word,
so that blessing may come on you from him;
⁹since a father's blessing makes his children's house
firm,
while a mother's curse tears up its foundations.

NEW REVISED STANDARD VERSION	REVISED ENGLISH BIBLE

NEW REVISED STANDARD VERSION

10 Do not glorify yourself by dishonoring your
father,
for your father's dishonor is no glory to you.
11 The glory of one's father is one's own glory,
and it is a disgrace for children not to respect
their mother.
12 My child, help your father in his old age,
and do not grieve him as long as he lives;
13 even if his mind fails, be patient with him;
because you have all your faculties do not
despise him.
14 For kindness to a father will not be forgotten,
and will be credited to you against your sins;
15 in the day of your distress it will be remembered
in your favor;
like frost in fair weather, your sins will melt
away.
16 Whoever forsakes a father is like a blasphemer,
and whoever angers a mother is cursed by the
Lord.
17 My child, perform your tasks with humility;[t]
then you will be loved by those whom God
accepts.
18 The greater you are, the more you must humble
yourself;
so you will find favor in the sight of the
Lord.[u]
20 For great is the might of the Lord;
but by the humble he is glorified.
21 Neither seek what is too difficult for you,
nor investigate what is beyond your power.
22 Reflect upon what you have been commanded,
for what is hidden is not your concern.
23 Do not meddle in matters that are beyond you,
for more than you can understand has been
shown you.
24 For their conceit has led many astray,
and wrong opinion has impaired their
judgment.
25 Without eyes there is no light;
without knowledge there is no wisdom.[v]
26 A stubborn mind will fare badly at the end,
and whoever loves danger will perish in it.
27 A stubborn mind will be burdened by troubles,
and the sinner adds sin to sins.
28 When calamity befalls the proud, there is no
healing,
for an evil plant has taken root in him.
29 The mind of the intelligent appreciates proverbs,
and an attentive ear is the desire of the wise.
30 As water extinguishes a blazing fire,
so almsgiving atones for sin.
31 Those who repay favors give thought to the
future;
when they fall they will find support.

4 My child, do not cheat the poor of their living,
and do not keep needy eyes waiting.
2 Do not grieve the hungry,
or anger one in need.
3 Do not add to the troubles of the desperate,
or delay giving to the needy.

REVISED ENGLISH BIBLE

10 Never seek honour at the cost of discredit to your
father;
how can his discredit bring honour to you?
11 A man gets honour from his father's honour;
a mother's dishonour is disgrace to her children.
12 My son, look after your father in his old age,
and as long as he lives do nothing to grieve him.
13 Even if his mind fails, make allowances
and do not despise him because you are in your
prime.
14 If you support your father it will never be forgotten
and will stand to your credit against your sins;
15 when you are in trouble, it will be remembered in
your favour,
and your sins will melt away like frost in sunshine.
16 To leave your father in the lurch is like blasphemy;
to curse your mother is to provoke your Creator's
wrath.
17 My son, in all you do be unassuming,
and those whom the Lord approves will love you.
18 The greater you are, the humbler must you be,
and the Lord will show you favour;
20 for his power is great,
yet he reveals his secrets to the humble.
21 Do not pry into things too hard for you
or investigate what is beyond your reach.
22 Meditate on what the Lord has commanded;
what he has kept hidden need not concern you.
23 Do not busy yourself with matters that are beyond
you;
even what has been shown you is above the grasp
of mortals.
24 Many have been led astray by their theorizing,
and evil imaginings have impaired their
judgements.
26 Stubbornness will come to a bad end,
and he who flirts with danger will lose his life.
27 Stubbornness brings a load of troubles;
the sinner piles sin on sin.
28 When calamity befalls the arrogant, there is no
cure;
wickedness is too deeply rooted in them.
29 A sensible person will take a proverb to heart;
an attentive audience is the desire of the wise.
30 As water quenches a blazing fire,
so almsgiving atones for sin.
31 He who repays a favour is mindful of his future;
when he is falling, he will have support at hand.

4 My son, do not cheat a poor person of his
livelihood
or keep him waiting with hungry eyes.
2 Do not tantalize one who is starving
or drive him to desperation in his need.
3 If someone is desperate, do not add to his troubles
or keep him waiting for the charity he asks.

---

[t] Heb: Gk *meekness*   [u] Other ancient authorities add as verse 19,
*Many are lofty and renowned, but to the humble he reveals his
secrets.*   [v] Heb: Other ancient authorities lack verse 25

3:18 **show you favour:** *some witnesses add* [19]Many are high and
illustrious, but he reveals his secrets to the humble.   3:24 **their
judgements:** *some witnesses add* [25]Without the apple of the eye, light
is lacking; without knowledge, wisdom is lacking.

10 Glory not in your father's shame,
    for his shame is no glory to you!
11 His father's honor is a man's glory;
    disgrace for her children, a mother's shame.
12 My son, take care of your father when he is old;
    grieve him not as long as he lives.
13 Even if his mind fail, be considerate with him;
    revile him not in the fullness of your strength.
14 For kindness to a father will not be forgotten,
    it will serve as a sin offering — it will take
        lasting root.
15 In time of tribulation it will be recalled to
        your advantage,
    like warmth upon frost it will melt away
        your sins.
16 A blasphemer is he who despises his father;
    accursed of his Creator, he who angers
        his mother.
17 My son, conduct your affairs with humility,
    and you will be loved more than a giver of gifts.
18 Humble yourself the more, the greater you are,
    and you will find favor with God.
19 For great is the power of God;
    by the humble he is glorified.
20 What is too sublime for you, seek not,
    into things beyond your strength search not.
21 What is committed to you, attend to;
    for what is hidden is not your concern.
22 With what is too much for you meddle not,
    when shown things beyond
        human understanding.
23 Their own opinion has misled many,
    and false reasoning unbalanced their judgment.
24 Where the pupil of the eye is missing, there is
        no light,
    and where there is no knowledge, there is
        no wisdom.
25 A stubborn man will fare badly in the end,
    and he who loves danger will perish in it.
26 A stubborn man will be burdened with sorrow;
    a sinner will heap sin upon sin.
27 For the affliction of the proud man there is
        no cure;
    he is the offshoot of an evil plant.
28 The mind of a sage appreciates proverbs,
    and an attentive ear is the wise man's joy.
29 Water quenches a flaming fire,
    and alms atone for sins.
30 He who does a kindness is remembered afterward;
    when he falls, he finds a support.

4 My son, rob not the poor man of his livelihood:
    force not the eyes of the needy to turn away.
2 A hungry man grieve not,
    a needy man anger not;
3 Do not exasperate the downtrodden;
    delay not to give to the needy.

10 Do not make a boast of disgrace overtaking your
        father,
    your father's disgrace reflects no honour on you;
11 for a person's own honour derives from the respect
        shown to his father,
    and a mother held in dishonour is a reproach to
        her children.
12 My child, support your father in his old age,
    do not grieve him during his life.
13 Even if his mind should fail, show him sympathy,
    do not despise him in your health and strength;
14 for kindness to a father will not be forgotten
    but will serve as reparation for your sins.
15 On your own day of ordeal God will remember
        you:
    like frost in sunshine, your sins will melt away.
16 Whoever deserts a father is no better than a
        blasphemer,
    and whoever distresses a mother is accursed of
        the Lord.
17 My child, be gentle in carrying out your business,
    and you will be better loved than a lavish giver.
18 The greater you are, the more humbly you should
        behave,
    and then you will find favour with the Lord;
20 for great though the power of the Lord is,
    he accepts the homage of the humble.
21 Do not try to understand things that are too
        difficult for you,
    or try to discover what is beyond your powers.
22 Concentrate on what has been assigned you,
    you have no need to worry over mysteries.
23 Do not meddle with matters that are beyond you;
    what you have been taught already exceeds the
        scope of the human mind.
24 For many have been misled by their own notions,
    wicked presumption having warped their
        judgement.
26 A stubborn heart will come to a bad end,
    and whoever dallies with danger will perish
        in it.
27 A stubborn heart is weighed down with troubles,
    the sinner heaps sin on sin.
28 For the disease of the proud there is no cure,
    since an evil growth has taken root there.
29 The heart of the sensible will reflect on
        parables,
    an attentive ear is the sage's dream.
30 Water puts out a blazing fire,
    almsgiving expiates sins.
31 Whoever gives favours in return is mindful of the
        future;
    at the moment of falling, such a person will find
        support.

4 My child, do not refuse the poor a livelihood,
    do not tantalise the needy.
2 Do not add to the sufferings of the hungry,
    do not bait anyone in distress.
3 Do not aggravate a heart already angry,
    nor keep the destitute waiting for your alms.

NEW REVISED STANDARD VERSION	REVISED ENGLISH BIBLE

NEW REVISED STANDARD VERSION

4 Do not reject a suppliant in distress,
   or turn your face away from the poor.
5 Do not avert your eye from the needy,
   and give no one reason to curse you;
6 for if in bitterness of soul some should curse you,
   their Creator will hear their prayer.

7 Endear yourself to the congregation;
   bow your head low to the great.
8 Give a hearing to the poor,
   and return their greeting politely.
9 Rescue the oppressed from the oppressor;
   and do not be hesitant in giving a verdict.
10 Be a father to orphans,
   and be like a husband to their mother;
   you will then be like a son of the Most High,
   and he will love you more than does your
   mother.

11 Wisdom teaches[w] her children
   and gives help to those who seek her.
12 Whoever loves her loves life,
   and those who seek her from early morning are
   filled with joy.
13 Whoever holds her fast inherits glory,
   and the Lord blesses the place she[x] enters.
14 Those who serve her minister to the Holy One;
   the Lord loves those who love her.
15 Those who obey her will judge the nations,
   and all who listen to her will live secure.
16 If they remain faithful, they will inherit her;
   their descendants will also obtain her.
17 For at first she will walk with them on tortuous
   paths;
   she will bring fear and dread upon them,
   and will torment them by her discipline
   until she trusts them,[y]
   and she will test them with her ordinances.
18 Then she will come straight back to them again
   and gladden them,
   and will reveal her secrets to them.
19 If they go astray she will forsake them,
   and hand them over to their ruin.

20 Watch for the opportune time, and beware of
   evil,
   and do not be ashamed to be yourself.
21 For there is a shame that leads to sin,
   and there is a shame that is glory and favor.
22 Do not show partiality, to your own harm,
   or deference, to your downfall.
23 Do not refrain from speaking at the proper
   moment,[z]
   and do not hide your wisdom.[a]
24 For wisdom becomes known through speech,
   and education through the words of the tongue.
25 Never speak against the truth,
   but be ashamed of your ignorance.
26 Do not be ashamed to confess your sins,
   and do not try to stop the current of a river.
27 Do not subject yourself to a fool,
   or show partiality to a ruler.
28 Fight to the death for truth,
   and the Lord God will fight for you.

29 Do not be reckless in your speech,
   or sluggish and remiss in your deeds.

REVISED ENGLISH BIBLE

4 Do not reject the appeal of someone in distress
   or turn your back on the poor;
5 when one begs for alms, do not look the other
   way,
   so giving him cause to curse you,
6 for if he curses you in his bitterness,
   his Creator will hear his prayer.
7 Make yourself popular in the assembly,
   and show deference to the great.
8 When anyone who is poor speaks to you, give him
   your attention
   and answer his greeting courteously.
9 Rescue the downtrodden from the oppressor
   and be firm when giving a verdict.
10 Be as a father to the fatherless
   and like a husband to their mother;
   then the Most High will call you his son,
   and greater than a mother's love will be his love
   for you.

11 WISDOM raises her sons to greatness
   and gives help to those who seek her.
12 To love her is to love life;
   those who rise early to greet her will be filled with
   joy.
13 He who holds fast to her will gain honour;
   the Lord's blessing rests on the house she enters.
14 To serve her is to serve the Holy One,
   and the Lord loves those who love her.
15 He who is obedient to her will give true
   judgement,
   and, because he listens to her, his home will be
   secure.
16 If he trusts her, he will possess her
   and bequeath her to his descendants.
17 At first she will lead him by tortuous ways,
   filling him with craven fears.
   Her discipline will be a torment to him,
   and her decrees a hard test,
   until he trusts her with all his heart;
18 then she will come straight back to him,
   bringing gladness and revealing to him her secrets.
19 But if he strays, she will abandon him
   and leave him to his fate.

20 BE on your guard at all times and beware of evil;
   do not be over-modest in your own cause,
21 for there is a modesty that leads to sin,
   as well as a modesty that brings honour and
   favour.
22 Do not be untrue to yourself in deference to
   another,
   or diffident to your own undoing.
23 Never remain silent when a word might put things
   right,
   and do not hide your wisdom,
24 for it is by the spoken word that wisdom is known,
   and learning finds expression in speech.
25 Do not argue against the truth,
   but have a proper sense of your own ignorance.
26 Never be ashamed to admit your mistakes,
   and do not try to swim against the current.
27 Do not let yourself be a doormat to a fool
   or curry favour with the powerful.
28 Fight to the death for truth,
   and the Lord God will fight on your side.

29 Do not be forward in your speech
   while slack and feeble in deeds.

---

w Heb Syr: Gk *exalts*   x Or *he*   y Or *until they remain faithful in
their heart*   z Heb: Gk *at a time of salvation*   a So some Gk Mss
and Heb Syr Lat: Other Gk Mss lack *and do not hide your wisdom*   4:13 **she:** or *he.*

NEW AMERICAN BIBLE

NEW JERUSALEM BIBLE

4 A beggar in distress do not reject;
  avert not your face from the poor.
5 From the needy turn not your eyes,
  give no man reason to curse you;
6 For if in the bitterness of his soul he curse you,
  his Creator will hear his prayer.
7 Endear yourself to the assembly;
  before a ruler bow your head.
8 Give a hearing to the poor man,
  and return his greeting with courtesy;
9 Deliver the oppressed from the hand of
  the oppressor;
  let not justice be repugnant to you.
10 To the fatherless be as a father,
  and help their mother as a husband would;
  Thus will you be like a son to the Most High,
  and he will be more tender to you than
  a mother.
11 Wisdom instructs her children
  and admonishes those who seek her.
12 He who loves her loves life;
  those who seek her out win her favor.
13 He who holds her fast inherits glory;
  wherever he dwells, the LORD bestows blessings.
14 Those who serve her serve the Holy One;
  those who love her the LORD loves.
15 He who obeys her judges nations;
  he who hearkens to her dwells in her
  inmost chambers.
16 If one trusts her, he will possess her;
  his descendants too will inherit her.
17 She walks with him as a stranger,
  and at first she puts him to the test;
  Fear and dread she brings upon him
  and tries him with her discipline;
  With her precepts she puts him to the proof,
  until his heart is fully with her.
18 Then she comes back to bring him happiness
  and reveal her secrets to him.
19 But if he fails her, she will abandon him
  and deliver him into the hands of despoilers.
20 Use your time well; guard yourself from evil,
  and bring upon yourself no shame.
21 There is a sense of shame laden with guilt,
  and a shame that merits honor and respect.
22 Show no favoritism to your own discredit;
  let no one intimidate you to your own downfall.
23 Refrain not from speaking at the proper time,
  and hide not away your wisdom;
24 For it is through speech that wisdom
  becomes known,
  and knowledge through the tongue's rejoinder.
25 Never gainsay the truth,
  and struggle not against the rushing stream.
26 Be not ashamed to acknowledge your guilt,
  but of your ignorance rather be ashamed.
27 Do not abase yourself before an impious man,
  nor refuse to do so before rulers.
28 Even to the death fight for truth,
  and the LORD your God will battle for you.
29 Be not surly in your speech,
  nor lazy and slack in your deeds.

4 Do not repulse a hard-pressed beggar,
  nor turn your face from the poor.
5 Do not avert your eyes from the needy,
  give no one occasion to curse you;
6 for if someone curses you in distress,
  his Maker will give ear to the imprecation.
7 Gain the love of the community,
  in the presence of the great bow your head.
8 To the poor lend an ear,
  and courteously return the greeting.
9 Save the oppressed from the hand of the oppressor,
  and do not be mean-spirited in your judgements.
10 Be like a father to the fatherless
  and as good as a husband to their mothers.
  And you will be like a child to the Most High,
  who will love you more than your own mother
  does.
11 Wisdom brings up her own children
  and cares for those who seek her.
12 Whoever loves her loves life,
  those who seek her early will be filled with joy.
13 Whoever possesses her will inherit honour,
  and wherever he walks the Lord will bless him.
14 Those who serve her minister to the Holy One,
  and the Lord loves those who love her.
15 Whoever obeys her rules the nations,
  whoever pays attention to her dwells secure.
16 If he trusts himself to her he will inherit her,
  and his descendants will remain in possession of
  her;
17 for though she takes him at first through winding
  ways,
  bringing fear and faintness on him,
  trying him out with her discipline till she can trust
  him,
  and testing him with her ordeals,
18 she then comes back to him on the straight road,
  makes him happy
  and reveals her secrets to him.
19 If he goes astray, however, she abandons him
  and leaves him to his own destruction.
20 Take circumstances into account and beware of
  evil,
  and have no cause to be ashamed of yourself;
21 for there is a shame that leads to sin
  and a shame that is honourable and gracious.
22 Do not be too severe on yourself,
  do not let shame lead you to ruin.
23 Do not refrain from speaking when it will do good,
  and do not hide your wisdom;
24 for your wisdom is made known by what you say,
  your erudition by the words you utter.
25 Do not contradict the truth,
  rather blush for your own ignorance.
26 Do not be ashamed to confess your sins,
  do not struggle against the current of the river.
27 Do not grovel to the foolish,
  do not show partiality to the influential.
28 Fight to the death for truth,
  and the Lord God will war on your side.
29 Do not be bold of tongue,
  yet idle and slack in deed;

30 Do not be like a lion in your home,
  or suspicious of your servants.
31 Do not let your hand be stretched out to receive
  and closed when it is time to give.

5 Do not rely on your wealth,
  or say, "I have enough."
2 Do not follow your inclination and strength
  in pursuing the desires of your heart.
3 Do not say, "Who can have power over me?"
  for the Lord will surely punish you.
4 Do not say, "I sinned, yet what has happened to me?"
  for the Lord is slow to anger.
5 Do not be so confident of forgiveness[b]
  that you add sin to sin.
6 Do not say, "His mercy is great,
  he will forgive[c] the multitude of my sins,"
  for both mercy and wrath are with him,
  and his anger will rest on sinners.
7 Do not delay to turn back to the Lord,
  and do not postpone it from day to day;
  for suddenly the wrath of the Lord will come upon you,
  and at the time of punishment you will perish.
8 Do not depend on dishonest wealth,
  for it will not benefit you on the day of calamity.
9 Do not winnow in every wind,
  or follow every path.[d]
10 Stand firm for what you know,
  and let your speech be consistent.
11 Be quick to hear,
  but deliberate in answering.
12 If you know what to say, answer your neighbor;
  but if not, put your hand over your mouth.
13 Honor and dishonor come from speaking,
  and the tongue of mortals may be their downfall.
14 Do not be called double-tongued[e]
  and do not lay traps with your tongue;
  for shame comes to the thief,
  and severe condemnation to the double-tongued.
15 In great and small matters cause no harm,[f]

6 1 and do not become an enemy instead of a friend;
  for a bad name incurs shame and reproach;
  so it is with the double-tongued sinner.
2 Do not fall into the grip of passion,[g]
  or you may be torn apart as by a bull.[h]
3 Your leaves will be devoured and your fruit destroyed,
  and you will be left like a withered tree.
4 Evil passion destroys those who have it,
  and makes them the laughingstock of their enemies.
5 Pleasant speech multiplies friends,
  and a gracious tongue multiplies courtesies.
6 Let those who are friendly with you be many,
  but let your advisers be one in a thousand.

30 Do not play the lion in your home
  or swagger among your servants.
31 Do not keep your hand wide open to receive,
  but closed when it is time to repay.

5 Do not rely on your money
  and say, 'This makes me self-sufficient.'
2 Do not yield to every impulse you can gratify
  or follow the desires of your heart.
3 Do not say, 'I have no master';
  the Lord, you may be sure, will call you to account.
4 Do not say, 'I sinned, yet nothing happened to me';
  it is only that the Lord is very patient.
5 Do not be so confident of pardon
  that you pile up sin on sin;
6 do not say, 'His compassion is so great
  he will pardon my sins, however many.'
  To him belong both mercy and anger,
  and sinners feel the weight of his retribution.
7 Turn back to the Lord without delay,
  and do not defer action from one day to the next;
  for the Lord's anger can suddenly pour out,
  and at the time of reckoning you will perish.
8 Do not rely on ill-gotten gains,
  for they will not avail on the day of calamity.
9 Do NOT winnow in every wind
  or walk along every path:
  this is the mark of duplicity.
10 Stand firmly by what you know,
  and be consistent in what you say.
11 Be quick to listen,
  but over your answer take time.
12 Give an answer if you know what to say,
  but if not, hold your tongue.
13 Through speaking come both honour and dishonour,
  and the tongue can be its owner's downfall.
14 Do not get a name for tale-bearing
  or lay traps with your tongue,
  for, as there is shame in store for the thief,
  so there is harsh censure for duplicity.
15 Avoid all faults, both great and small.

6 Do not change from a friend into an enemy,
  for a bad name earns shame and disgrace:
  this is the mark of duplicity.
2 Never let violent passions rouse you;
  they will tear you apart like a bull;
3 they will devour your foliage, destroy your fruit,
  and leave you a withered tree.
4 Evil passion ruins anyone who harbours it,
  and gives his enemies cause to gloat over him.
5 Pleasant words win many friends,
  and affable talk makes acquaintance easy.
6 Live at peace with everyone;
  accept advice, however, from but one in a thousand.

---

b Heb: Gk *atonement*   c Heb: Gk *he* (or *it*) *will atone for*
d Gk adds *so it is with the double-tongued sinner* (see 6.1)   e Heb:
Gk *a slanderer*   f Heb Syr: Gk *be ignorant*   g Heb: Meaning of
Gk uncertain   h Meaning of Gk uncertain

6:2 **they . . . bull:** *prob. mng; Gk obscure.*

30 Be not a lion at home,
   nor sly and suspicious at work.
31 Let not your hand be open to receive
   and clenched when it is time to give.

5 Rely not on your wealth;
   say not: "I have the power."
2 Rely not on your strength
   in following the desires of your heart.
3 Say not: "Who can prevail against me?"
   for the LORD will exact the punishment.
4 Say not: "I have sinned, yet what has
      befallen me?"
   for the LORD bides his time.
5 Of forgiveness be not overconfident,
   adding sin upon sin.
6 Say not: "Great is his mercy;
   my many sins he will forgive."
7 For mercy and anger alike are with him;
   upon the wicked alights his wrath.
8 Delay not your conversion to the LORD,
   put it not off from day to day;
9 For suddenly his wrath flames forth;
   at the time of vengeance, you will be destroyed.
10 Rely not upon deceitful wealth,
   for it will be no help on the day of wrath.

11 Winnow not in every wind,
   and start not off in every direction.
12 Be consistent in your thoughts;
   steadfast be your words.
13 Be swift to hear,
   but slow to answer.
14 If you have the knowledge, answer your neighbor;
   if not, put your hand over your mouth.
15 Honor and dishonor through talking!
   A man's tongue can be his downfall.
16 Be not called a detractor;
   use not your tongue for calumny;
17 For shame has been created for the thief,
   and the reproach of his neighbor for
      the double-tongued.

6 Say nothing harmful, small or great;
   be not a foe instead of a friend;
   A bad name and disgrace will you acquire:
   "That for the evil man with double tongue!"
2 Fall not into the grip of desire,
   lest, like fire, it consume your strength;
3 Your leaves it will eat, your fruits destroy,
   and you will be left a dry tree,
4 For contumacious desire destroys its owner
   and makes him the sport of his enemies.

5 A kind mouth multiplies friends,
   and gracious lips prompt friendly greetings.
6 Let your acquaintants be many,
   but one in a thousand your confidant.

30 do not be like a lion at home,
   or cowardly towards your servants.
31 Do not let your hands be outstretched to receive,
   yet tight-fisted when the time comes to give
      back.

5 Do not put your confidence in your money
   or say, 'With this I am self-sufficient.'
2 Do not be led by your appetites and energy
   to follow the passions of your heart.
3 And do not say, 'Who has authority over me?'
   for the Lord will certainly give you your
      deserts.
4 Do not say, 'I have sinned, but what harm has
      befallen me?'
   for the Lord's forbearance is long.
5 Do not be so sure of forgiveness
   that you add sin to sin.
6 And do not say, 'His compassion is great,
   he will forgive me my many sins';
   for with him are both mercy and retribution,
   and his anger does not pass from sinners.
7 Do not delay your return to the Lord,
   do not put it off day after day;
   for suddenly the Lord's wrath will blaze out,
   and on the day of punishment you will be utterly
      destroyed.
8 Do not set your heart on ill-gotten gains,
   they will be of no use to you on the day of
      disaster.
9 Do not winnow in every wind,
   or walk along every by-way
   (as the double-talking sinner does).
10 Be steady in your convictions,
   and be a person of your word.
11 Be quick to listen,
   and deliberate in giving an answer.
12 If you understand the matter, give your neighbour
      an answer,
   if not, keep your hand over your mouth.
13 Both honour and disgrace come from talking,
   the tongue is its owner's downfall.
14 Do not get a name for scandal-mongering,
   do not set traps with your tongue;
   for as shame lies in store for the thief,
   so harsh condemnation awaits the
      deceitful.
15 Avoid offences in great as in small matters,
   and do not exchange friendship for enmity,

6 1 for a bad name will earn you shame and reproach,
   as happens to the double-talking sinner.
2 Do not get carried aloft on the wings of passion,
   for fear your strength tear itself apart like a bull,
3 and you devour your own foliage and destroy your
      own fruit
   and end by making yourself like a piece of
      dried-up wood.
4 An evil temper destroys the person who has it
   and makes him the laughing-stock of his
      enemies.

5 A kindly turn of speech attracts new friends,
   a courteous tongue invites many a friendly
      response.
6 Let your acquaintances be many,
   but for advisers choose one out of a thousand.

7 When you gain friends, gain them through
testing,
and do not trust them hastily.
8 For there are friends who are such when it suits
them,
but they will not stand by you in time of
trouble.
9 And there are friends who change into enemies,
and tell of the quarrel to your disgrace.
10 And there are friends who sit at your table,
but they will not stand by you in time of
trouble.
11 When you are prosperous, they become your
second self,
and lord it over your servants;
12 but if you are brought low, they turn against you,
and hide themselves from you.
13 Keep away from your enemies,
and be on guard with your friends.
14 Faithful friends are a sturdy shelter:
whoever finds one has found a treasure.
15 Faithful friends are beyond price;
no amount can balance their worth.
16 Faithful friends are life-saving medicine;
and those who fear the Lord will find them.
17 Those who fear the Lord direct their friendship
aright,
for as they are, so are their neighbors also.
18 My child, from your youth choose discipline,
and when you have gray hair you will still find
wisdom.
19 Come to her like one who plows and sows,
and wait for her good harvest.
For when you cultivate her you will toil but little,
and soon you will eat of her produce.
20 She seems very harsh to the undisciplined;
fools cannot remain with her.
21 She will be like a heavy stone to test them,
and they will not delay in casting her aside.
22 For wisdom is like her name;
she is not readily perceived by many.
23 Listen, my child, and accept my judgment;
do not reject my counsel.
24 Put your feet into her fetters,
and your neck into her collar.
25 Bend your shoulders and carry her,
and do not fret under her bonds.
26 Come to her with all your soul,
and keep her ways with all your might.
27 Search out and seek, and she will become known
to you;
and when you get hold of her, do not let her
go.
28 For at last you will find the rest she gives,
and she will be changed into joy for you.
29 Then her fetters will become for you a strong
defense,
and her collar a glorious robe.
30 Her yoke*i* is a golden ornament,
and her bonds a purple cord.
31 You will wear her like a glorious robe,
and put her on like a splendid crown.*j*
32 If you are willing, my child, you can be
disciplined,
and if you apply yourself you will become
clever.

7 When you make a friend, begin by testing him,
and be in no hurry to give him your trust.
8 Some friends are loyal when it suits them
but desert you in time of trouble.
9 Some friends turn into enemies
and shame you by making the quarrel public.
10 Another may sit at your table
but in time of trouble is nowhere to be found;
11 when you are prosperous, he is your second self
and talks familiarly with your servants,
12 but if you come down in the world, he turns
against you
and you will not see his face again.
13 Hold your enemies at a distance,
and keep a wary eye on your friends.
14 A faithful friend is a secure shelter;
whoever finds one, finds a treasure.
15 A faithful friend is beyond price;
there is no measure of his worth.
16 A faithful friend is an elixir of life,
found only by those who fear the Lord.
17 Whoever fears the Lord directs his friendship
aright,
for he treats a neighbour as himself.
18 My son, seek wisdom's instruction while you are
young,
and you will still find her when your hair turns
white.
19 Come to her like a farmer who ploughs and sows;
then wait for the good fruits she supplies.
If you cultivate her, you will labour for a little
while,
but soon you will be enjoying the harvest.
20 How harsh she seems to the uninstructed!
The fool cannot abide her;
21 like a boulder she tests and strains his strength,
and he is not slow to let her drop.
22 Wisdom well deserves her name;
she is not accessible to many.
23 Listen, my son: accept my opinion
and do not reject my advice.
24 Put your feet in wisdom's fetters
and your neck into her collar.
25 Stoop to carry her on your shoulders
and do not chafe at her bonds.
26 Come to her wholeheartedly,
and with all your might keep to her ways.
27 Follow her track, and she will make herself known;
once you have grasped her, do not let her go.
28 In the end you will find the refreshment she offers;
she will transform herself for you into joy:
29 her fetters will become your strong defence
and her collar a splendid robe.
30 Her yoke is a golden ornament
and her bonds a violet cord;
31 you will put her on like a splendid robe
and wear her like a garland of joy.
32 If it is your wish, my son, you will be instructed;
if you give your mind to it, you will become
clever;

*i*Heb: Gk *Upon her*   *j*Heb: Gk *crown of gladness*   6:30 **Her yoke:** so Heb.; Gk *Upon her.*

NEW AMERICAN BIBLE

NEW JERUSALEM BIBLE

7 When you gain a friend, first test him,
and be not too ready to trust him.
8 For one sort of friend is a friend when it suits him,
but he will not be with you in time of distress.
9 Another is a friend who becomes an enemy,
and tells of the quarrel to your shame.
10 Another is a friend, a boon companion,
who will not be with you when sorrow comes.
11 When things go well, he is your other self,
and lords it over your servants;
12 But if you are brought low, he turns against you
and avoids meeting you.
13 Keep away from your enemies;
be on your guard with your friends.
14 A faithful friend is a sturdy shelter;
he who finds one finds a treasure.
15 A faithful friend is beyond price,
no sum can balance his worth.
16 A faithful friend is a life-saving remedy,
such as he who fears God finds;
17 For he who fears God behaves accordingly,
and his friend will be like himself.

18 My son, from your youth embrace discipline;
thus will you find wisdom with graying hair.
19 As though plowing and sowing, draw close to her;
then await her bountiful crops.
20 For in cultivating her you will labor but little,
and soon you will eat of her fruits.
21 How irksome she is to the unruly!
The fool cannot abide her.
22 She will be like a burdensome stone to test him,
and he will not delay in casting her aside.
23 For discipline is like her name,
she is not accessible to many.

24 Listen, my son, and heed my advice;
refuse not my counsel.
25 Put your feet into her fetters,
and your neck under her yoke.
26 Stoop your shoulders and carry her
and be not irked at her bonds.
27 With all your soul draw close to her;
with all your strength keep her ways.
28 Search her out, discover her; seek her and you will
find her.
Then when you have her, do not let her go;
29 Thus will you afterward find rest in her,
and she will become your joy.
30 Her fetters will be your throne of majesty;
her bonds, your purple cord.
31 You will wear her as your robe of glory,
bear her as your splendid crown.

32 My son, if you wish, you can be taught;
if you apply yourself, you will be shrewd.

7 If you want to make a friend, take him on trial,
and do not be in a hurry to trust him;
8 for one kind of friend is so only when it suits him
but will not stand by you in your day of trouble.
9 Another kind of friend will fall out with you
and to your dismay make your quarrel public,
10 and a third kind of friend will share your table,
but not stand by you in your day of trouble:
11 when you are doing well he will be your second
self,
ordering your servants about;
12 but, if disaster befalls you, he will recoil from you
and keep out of your way.
13 Keep well clear of your enemies,
and be wary of your friends.
14 A loyal friend is a powerful defence:
whoever finds one has indeed found a treasure.
15 A loyal friend is something beyond price,
there is no measuring his worth.
16 A loyal friend is the elixir of life,
and those who fear the Lord will find one.
17 Whoever fears the Lord makes true friends,
for as a person is, so is his friend too.

18 My child, from your earliest youth choose
instruction,
and till your hair is white you will keep finding
wisdom.
19 Like ploughman and sower, cultivate her
and wait for her fine harvest,
for in tilling her you will toil a little while,
but very soon you will be eating her crops.
20 How very harsh she is to the undisciplined!
The senseless does not stay with her for long:
21 she will weigh as heavily on the senseless as a
touchstone
and such a person will lose no time in throwing
her off;
22 for Wisdom is true to her name,
she is not accessible to many.
23 Listen, my child, and take my advice,
do not reject my counsel:
24 put your feet into her fetters,
and your neck into her collar;
25 offer your shoulder to her burden,
do not be impatient of her bonds;
26 court her with all your soul,
and with all your might keep in her ways;
27 search for her, track her down: she will reveal
herself;
once you hold her, do not let her go.
28 For in the end you will find rest in her
and she will take the form of joy for you:
29 her fetters will find a mighty defence,
her collars, a precious necklace.
30 Her yoke will be a golden ornament,
and her bonds be purple ribbons;
31 you will wear her like a robe of honour,
you will put her on like a crown of joy.
32 If you wish it, my child, you can be taught;
apply yourself, and you will become intelligent.

| NEW REVISED STANDARD VERSION | REVISED ENGLISH BIBLE |

NEW REVISED STANDARD VERSION

33 If you love to listen you will gain knowledge,
and if you pay attention you will become wise.
34 Stand in the company of the elders.
Who is wise? Attach yourself to such a one.
35 Be ready to listen to every godly discourse,
and let no wise proverbs escape you.
36 If you see an intelligent person, rise early to visit
him;
let your foot wear out his doorstep.
37 Reflect on the statutes of the Lord,
and meditate at all times on his
commandments.
It is he who will give insight to[k] your mind,
and your desire for wisdom will be granted.

7 Do no evil, and evil will never overtake you.
2 Stay away from wrong, and it will turn
away from you.
3 Do[l] not sow in the furrows of injustice,
and you will not reap a sevenfold crop.
4 Do not seek from the Lord high office,
or the seat of honor from the king.
5 Do not assert your righteousness before the Lord,
or display your wisdom before the king.
6 Do not seek to become a judge,
or you may be unable to root out injustice;
you may be partial to the powerful,
and so mar your integrity.
7 Commit no offense against the public,
and do not disgrace yourself among the people.
8 Do not commit a sin twice;
not even for one will you go unpunished.
9 Do not say, "He will consider the great number
of my gifts,
and when I make an offering to the Most High
God, he will accept it."
10 Do not grow weary when you pray;
do not neglect to give alms.
11 Do not ridicule a person who is embittered in
spirit,
for there is One who humbles and exalts.
12 Do not devise[m] a lie against your brother,
or do the same to a friend.
13 Refuse to utter any lie,
for it is a habit that results in no good.
14 Do not babble in the assembly of the elders,
and do not repeat yourself when you pray.
15 Do not hate hard labor
or farm work, which was created by the Most
High.
16 Do not enroll in the ranks of sinners;
remember that retribution does not delay.
17 Humble yourself to the utmost,
for the punishment of the ungodly is fire and
worms.[n]
18 Do not exchange a friend for money,
or a real brother for the gold of Ophir.
19 Do not dismiss[o] a wise and good wife,
for her charm is worth more than gold.
20 Do not abuse slaves who work faithfully,
or hired laborers who devote themselves to
their task.
21 Let your soul love intelligent slaves;[p]
do not withhold from them their freedom.

REVISED ENGLISH BIBLE

33 if you are content to listen, you will learn;
if you are attentive, you will grow wise.
34 When you stand among the assembled elders,
see who is wise and stick close by him.
35 Listen gladly to every godly conversation;
let no wise maxim escape you.
36 If you discover anyone who is wise, rise early to
visit him;
let your feet wear out his doorstep.
37 Ponder the decrees of the Lord
and study his commandments at all times.
He will instruct your mind,
and your desire for wisdom shall be met.

7 Do NO evil, and no evil will befall you;
2 keep clear of wrong, and it will avoid you.
3 Do not sow in the furrows of injustice,
for fear of reaping a sevenfold crop.
4 Do not ask the Lord for high office
or the king for preferment.
5 Do not pose as righteous before the Lord
or act the sage in the king's presence.
6 Do not aspire to be a judge;
you may lack the strength to root out injustice,
or you may be intimidated by rank
and so compromise your integrity.
7 Do not commit an offence against the community
and so incur a public disgrace.
8 Do not pile up sin on sin,
for just one is enough to make you guilty.
9 Do not say, 'All my gifts to God will be taken into
account;
when I make an offering to the Most High he will
accept it.'
10 Do not grow weary of praying
or neglect almsgiving.
11 Never laugh at anyone in his bitter humiliation,
for there is One who both humbles and exalts.
12 Do not plot to deceive your brother
or do the like to your friend.
13 Refuse ever to tell a lie;
it is a habit from which no good comes.
14 Do not be loquacious among the assembled elders,
and when you pray do not repeat yourself.
15 Do not resent manual labour;
work on the land was ordained by the Most High.
16 Do not enlist in the ranks of sinners;
remember that retribution will not tarry.
17 Humble yourself to the uttermost,
for the doom of the ungodly is fire and worms.
18 Do not part with a friend for gain,
or a true brother for all the gold of Ophir.
19 Do not miss the chance of a wise and good wife;
her attractions are worth more than gold.
20 Do not ill-treat a servant who works honestly
or a hireling whose heart is in his work.
21 Regard a good servant with deep affection
and do not withhold his freedom from him.

---

k Heb: Gk *will confirm*   l Gk *My child, do*   m Heb: Gk *plow*
n Heb *for the expectation of mortals is worms*   o Heb: Gk *deprive*
yourself of   p Heb *Love a wise slave as yourself*   7:18 **gain:** *prob. rdg; Gk* a trifle.

NEW AMERICAN BIBLE

33 If you are willing to listen, you will learn;
   if you give heed, you will be wise.
34 Frequent the company of the elders;
   whoever is wise, stay close to him.
35 Be eager to hear every godly discourse;
   let no wise saying escape you.
36 If you see a man of prudence, seek him out;
   let your feet wear away his doorstep!
37 Reflect on the precepts of the LORD,
   let his commandments be your
      constant meditation;
   Then he will enlighten your mind,
   and the wisdom you desire he will grant.

7 Do no evil, and evil will not overtake you;
 2   avoid wickedness, and it will turn aside
        from you.
 3 Sow not in the furrows of injustice,
   lest you harvest it sevenfold.
 4 Seek not from the LORD authority,
   nor from the king a place of honor.
 5 Parade not your justice before the LORD,
   and before the king flaunt not your wisdom.
 6 Seek not to become a judge
   if you have not strength to root out crime,
   Or you will show favor to the ruler
   and mar your integrity.
 7 Be guilty of no evil before the city's populace,
   nor disgrace yourself before the assembly.
 8 Do not plot to repeat a sin;
   not even for one will you go unpunished.
 9 Say not: "He will appreciate my many gifts;
   the Most High will accept my offerings."
10 Be not impatient in prayers,
   and neglect not the giving of alms.
11 Laugh not at an embittered man;
   be mindful of him who exalts and humbles.
12 Plot no mischief against your brother,
   nor against your friend and companion.
13 Delight not in telling lie after lie,
   for it never results in good.
14 Thrust not yourself into the deliberations
      of princes,
   and repeat not the words of your prayer.
15 Hate not laborious tasks,
   nor farming, which was ordained by the
      Most High.
16 Do not esteem yourself better than your fellows;
   remember, his wrath will not delay.
17 More and more, humble your pride;
   what awaits man is worms.
18 Barter not a friend for money,
   nor a dear brother for the gold of Ophir.
19 Dismiss not a sensible wife;
   a gracious wife is more precious than corals.
20 Mistreat not a servant who faithfully serves,
   nor a laborer who devotes himself to his task.
21 Let a wise servant be dear to you as your own self;
   refuse him not his freedom.

NEW JERUSALEM BIBLE

33 If you love listening, you will learn,
   if you pay attention, you will become wise.
34 Attend the gathering of elders;
   if there is a wise man there, attach yourself to
      him.
35 Listen willingly to any discourse coming from
      God,
   do not let wise proverbs escape you.
36 If you see a man of understanding, visit him early,
   let your feet wear out his doorstep.
37 Reflect on the injunctions of the Lord,
   busy yourself at all times with his
      commandments.
   He will strengthen your mind,
   and the wisdom you desire will be granted you.

7 Do no evil, and evil will not befall you;
 2   shun wrong, and it will avoid you.
 3 My child, do not sow in the furrows of
      wickedness,
   for fear you have to reap them seven times over.
 4 Do not ask the Lord for the highest place,
   or the king for a seat of honour.
 5 Do not parade your uprightness before the Lord,
   or your wisdom before the king.
 6 Do not scheme to be appointed judge,
   for fear you should not be strong enough to
      stamp out injustice,
   for fear of being swayed by someone influential
   and so of risking the loss of your integrity.
 7 Do not wrong the general body of citizens
   and so lower yourself in popular esteem.
 8 Do not be drawn to sin twice over,
   for you will not go unpunished even once.
 9 Do not say, 'God will be impressed by my
      numerous offerings;
   when I sacrifice to God Most High, he is bound
      to accept.'
10 Do not be hesitant in prayer;
   do not neglect to give alms.
11 Do not laugh at someone who is sad of heart,
   for he who brings low can lift up high.
12 Do not make up lies against your brother,
   nor against a friend either.
13 Mind you tell no lies,
   for no good can come of it.
14 Do not talk too much at the gathering of elders,
   and do not repeat yourself at your prayers.
15 Do not shirk tiring jobs
   or farm work, ordained by the Most High.
16 Do not swell the ranks of sinners,
   remember that the retribution will not delay.
17 Be very humble,
   since the recompense for the godless is fire and
      worms.
18 Do not barter a friend away for the sake of profit,
   nor a true brother for the gold of Ophir.
19 Do not turn against a wise and good wife;
   her gracious presence is worth more than gold.
20 Do not ill-treat a slave who is an honest worker,
   or a wage-earner who is devoted to you.
21 Love an intelligent slave with all your heart,
   and do not deny such a slave his freedom.

NEW REVISED STANDARD VERSION	REVISED ENGLISH BIBLE

NEW REVISED STANDARD VERSION

22 Do you have cattle? Look after them;
   if they are profitable to you, keep them.
23 Do you have children? Discipline them,
   and make them obedient*q* from their youth.
24 Do you have daughters? Be concerned for their
      chastity,*r*
   and do not show yourself too indulgent with
      them.
25 Give a daughter in marriage, and you complete a
      great task;
   but give her to a sensible man.
26 Do you have a wife who pleases you?*s* Do not
      divorce her;
   but do not trust yourself to one whom you
      detest.
27 With all your heart honor your father,
   and do not forget the birth pangs of your
      mother.
28 Remember that it was of your parents*t* you were
      born;
   how can you repay what they have given to
      you?
29 With all your soul fear the Lord,
   and revere his priests.
30 With all your might love your Maker,
   and do not neglect his ministers.
31 Fear the Lord and honor the priest,
   and give him his portion, as you have been
      commanded:
   the first fruits, the guilt offering, the gift of the
      shoulders,
   the sacrifice of sanctification, and the first
      fruits of the holy things.
32 Stretch out your hand to the poor,
   so that your blessing may be complete.
33 Give graciously to all the living;
   do not withhold kindness even from the dead.
34 Do not avoid those who weep,
   but mourn with those who mourn.
35 Do not hesitate to visit the sick,
   because for such deeds you will be loved.
36 In all you do, remember the end of your life,
   and then you will never sin.

8 Do not contend with the powerful,
   or you may fall into their hands.
2 Do not quarrel with the rich,
   in case their resources outweigh yours;
   for gold has ruined many,
   and has perverted the minds of kings.
3 Do not argue with the loud of mouth,
   and do not heap wood on their fire.
4 Do not make fun of one who is ill-bred,
   or your ancestors may be insulted.
5 Do not reproach one who is turning away from
      sin;
   remember that we all deserve punishment.
6 Do not disdain one who is old,
   for some of us are also growing old.
7 Do not rejoice over any one's death;
   remember that we must all die.
8 Do not slight the discourse of the sages,
   but busy yourself with their maxims;
   because from them you will learn discipline
   and how to serve princes.

REVISED ENGLISH BIBLE

22 Have you cattle? Take care of them,
   and if they bring you profit, do not part with them.
23 Have you sons? Discipline them
   and break them in from their earliest years.
24 Have you daughters? Keep a close watch over
      them,
   and do not look on them with indulgence.
25 Marry off your daughter, and you will have done
      well;
   but give her to a sensible husband.
26 If you have a wife after your own heart, do not
      divorce her;
   but do not trust yourself to one you cannot love.
27 Honour your father with all your heart
   and do not forget your mother's birth-pangs.
28 Remember that your parents brought you into the
      world;
   how can you repay them for all that they have
      done?
29 Reverence the Lord wholeheartedly
   and show respect to his priests.
30 Love your Maker with all your might
   and do not leave his ministers without support.
31 Fear the Lord and honour the priest,
   and give them their due as you have been
      commanded:
   the firstfruits, the guilt-offering, and the shoulder
      of the victim,
   the sacred grain-offering, and the firstfruits of holy
      things.
32 Be open-handed also with the poor,
   that your blessedness may be complete.
33 Every living being appreciates generosity;
   do not withhold kindness even from the dead.
34 Do not turn your back on those who weep,
   but mourn with those who mourn.
35 Do not hesitate to visit the sick,
   for by such acts you will win affection.
36 In whatever you are doing, remember the end that
      awaits you;
   then all your life you will never go wrong.

8 Do not pit yourself against the great,
   for fear of falling into their power.
2 Do not quarrel with the rich,
   for fear they will outbid you;
   for gold has brought ruin on many
   and has perverted the minds of kings.
3 Do not argue with a garrulous person
   and so add fuel to his fire.
4 Never make fun of the ill-mannered,
   or you may hear your ancestors insulted.
5 Do not taunt a repentant sinner;
   remember that we are all guilty.
6 Despise nobody in his old age;
   some of us are growing old as well.
7 Do not gloat over the death of anyone;
   remember we all must die.
8 Do not neglect the discourse of the wise,
   but apply yourself to their maxims;
   from these you will gain instruction
   and learn how to serve the great.

---

q Gk bend their necks   *r* Gk body   *s* Heb Syr lack *who pleases
you*   *t* Gk them

7:31 **guilt-offering:** *or* reparation-offering. **sacred grain-offering:** *lit.*
sacrifice of consecration.

22 If you have livestock, look after them;
    if they are dependable, keep them.
23 If you have sons, chastise them;
    bend their necks from childhood.
24 If you have daughters, keep them chaste,
    and be not indulgent to them.
25 Giving your daughter in marriage ends a great task;
    but give her to a worthy man.
26 If you have a wife, let her not seem odious to you;
    but where there is ill-feeling, trust her not.
27 With your whole heart honor your father;
    your mother's birthpangs forget not.
28 Remember, of these parents you were born;
    what can you give them for all they gave you?
29 With all your soul, fear God,
    revere his priests.
30 With all your strength, love your Creator,
    forsake not his ministers.
31 Honor God and respect the priest;
    give him his portion as you have
        been commanded:
  First fruits and contributions,
    due sacrifices and holy offerings.
32 To the poor man also extend your hand,
    that your blessing may be complete;
33 Be generous to all the living,
    and withhold not your kindness from the dead.
34 Avoid not those who weep,
    but mourn with those who mourn;
35 Neglect not to visit the sick —
    for these things you will be loved.
36 In whatever you do, remember your last days,
    and you will never sin.

22 Have you cattle? Look after them;
    if they are making you a profit, keep them.
23 Have you children? Educate them,
    from childhood make them bow the neck.
24 Have you daughters? Take care of their bodies,
    but do not be over-indulgent.
25 Marry a daughter off, and you have finished a
        great work;
    but give her to a man of sense.
26 Have you a wife to your liking? Do not turn her
        out;
    but if you do not love her, never trust her.
27 With all your heart honour your father,
    never forget the birthpangs of your mother.
28 Remember that you owe your birth to them;
    how can you repay them for what they have
        done for you?
29 With all your soul, fear the Lord
    and revere his priests.
30 With all your might love him who made you,
    and do not abandon his ministers.
31 Fear the Lord and honour the priest
    and give him the portion enjoined on you:
  first-fruits, sacrifice of reparation, shoulder-gift,
    sanctification sacrifice, first-fruits of the holy
        things.
32 And also give generously to the poor,
    so that your blessing may lack nothing.
33 Let your generosity extend to all the living,
    do not withhold it even from the dead.
34 Do not turn your back on those who weep,
    but share the grief of the grief-stricken.
35 Do not shrink from visiting the sick;
    in this way you will make yourself loved.
36 In everything you do, remember your end,
    and you will never sin.

8   Contend not with an influential man,
    lest you fall into his power.
2 Quarrel not with a rich man,
    lest he pay out the price of your downfall;
For gold has dazzled many,
    and perverts the character of princes.
3 Dispute not with a man of railing speech,
    heap no wood upon his fire.
4 Be not too familiar with an unruly man,
    lest he speak ill of your forebears.
5 Shame not a repentant sinner;
    remember, we all are guilty.
6 Insult no man when he is old,
    for some of us, too, will grow old.
7 Rejoice not when a man dies;
    remember, we are all to die.
8 Spurn not the discourse of the wise,
    but acquaint yourself with their proverbs;
From them you will acquire the training
    to serve in the presence of princes.

8   Do not try conclusions with anyone influential,
    in case you later fall into his clutches.
2 Do not quarrel with anyone rich,
    in case he puts his weight against you;
for gold has destroyed many,
    and has swayed the hearts of kings.
3 Do not argue with anyone argumentative,
    do not pile wood on that fire.
4 Do not joke with anyone uncouth,
    for fear of hearing your ancestors insulted.
5 Do not revile a repentant sinner;
    remember that we all are guilty.
6 Do not despise anyone in old age;
    after all, some of us too are growing old.
7 Do not gloat over anyone's death;
    remember that we all have to die.
8 Do not scorn the discourse of the wise,
    but make yourself familiar with their maxims,
since from these you will learn the theory
    and the art of serving the great.

9 Do not ignore the discourse of the aged,
 for they themselves learned from their
  parents;*u*
from them you learn how to understand
 and to give an answer when the need arises.

10 Do not kindle the coals of sinners,
 or you may be burned in their flaming fire.

11 Do not let the insolent bring you to your feet,
 or they may lie in ambush against your words.

12 Do not lend to one who is stronger than you;
 but if you do lend anything, count it as a loss.

13 Do not give surety beyond your means;
 but if you give surety, be prepared to pay.

14 Do not go to law against a judge,
 for the decision will favor him because of his
  standing.

15 Do not go traveling with the reckless,
 or they will be burdensome to you;
for they will act as they please,
 and through their folly you will perish with
  them.

16 Do not pick a fight with the quick-tempered,
 and do not journey with them through lonely
  country,
because bloodshed means nothing to them,
 and where no help is at hand, they will strike
  you down.

17 Do not consult with fools,
 for they cannot keep a secret.

18 In the presence of strangers do nothing that is to
 be kept secret,
for you do not know what they will divulge.*v*

19 Do not reveal your thoughts to anyone,
 or you may drive away your happiness.*w*

9 Do not be jealous of the wife of your bosom,
 or you will teach her an evil lesson to your
  own hurt.

2 Do not give yourself to a woman
 and let her trample down your strength.

3 Do not go near a loose woman,
 or you will fall into her snares.

4 Do not dally with a singing girl,
 or you will be caught by her tricks.

5 Do not look intently at a virgin,
 or you may stumble and incur penalties for her.

6 Do not give yourself to prostitutes,
 or you may lose your inheritance.

7 Do not look around in the streets of a city,
 or wander about in its deserted sections.

8 Turn away your eyes from a shapely woman,
 and do not gaze at beauty belonging to another;
many have been seduced by a woman's beauty,
 and by it passion is kindled like a fire.

9 Never dine with another man's wife,
 or revel with her at wine;
or your heart may turn aside to her,
 and in blood*x* you may be plunged into
  destruction.

10 Do not abandon old friends,
 for new ones cannot equal them.
A new friend is like new wine;
 when it has aged, you can drink it with
  pleasure.

9 Attend to the discourse of your elders,
 for they themselves learned from their fathers;
they can teach you to understand
 and to have an answer ready when you need one.

10 Do not fan a sinner's embers into a blaze,
 for fear of being burnt in the flames.

11 Do not let anyone's insolence bring you to your
 feet;
he is but waiting to trap you with your own words.

12 Do not lend to someone more powerful than
 yourself,
or, if you do, write off the loan as a loss.

13 Do not stand surety beyond your means,
 and, when you do stand surety, be prepared to pay.

14 Do not go to law with a judge;
 in deference to his position he will be given the
  verdict.

15 Do not go on a journey with a reckless man,
 for you may find him a burden;
he will take the way he fancies,
 and through his folly you also will come to ruin.

16 Do not fall out with a hot-tempered man
 or travel with him across the desert;
he thinks nothing of bloodshed,
 and where no help is at hand he will set upon you.

17 Never discuss your plans with a fool,
 for he cannot keep anything to himself.

18 Do nothing private in the presence of a stranger;
 you do not know what use he will make of it.

19 Do not tell what is in your mind to all comers
 or accept favours from them.

9 Do not be jealous over your dear wife;
 what you teach her may cause you harm.

2 Do not surrender yourself to a woman
 for her to trample your strength underfoot.

3 Do not go near a loose woman
 or you may fall into her snares.

4 Do not keep company with a dancing-girl
 or you may be caught by her advances.

5 Do not stare at a virgin
 or you may be trapped into paying damages for
  her.

6 Never surrender yourself to prostitutes,
 for fear of losing all you possess.

7 Do not gaze about you in the city streets
 or wander in its unfrequented areas.

8 Do not let your eye linger on a comely figure
 or stare at beauty not yours to possess.
Many have been seduced by the beauty of a
  woman;
it kindles passion like fire.

9 Never sit down with another man's wife
 or join her in a drinking party,
for fear of succumbing to her charms
 and slipping into fatal disaster.

10 Do not desert an old friend;
 a new one is not on a par with him.
A new friend is like new wine:
 until it has matured, you do not enjoy it.

---

u Or *ancestors* *v* Or *it will bring forth* *w* Heb: Gk *and let him
not return a favor to you* *x* Heb: Gk *by your spirit*

9 Reject not the tradition of old men
   which they have learned from their fathers;
From it you will obtain the knowledge
   how to answer in time of need.
10 Kindle not the coals of a sinner,
   lest you be consumed in his flaming fire.
11 Let not the impious man intimidate you;
   it will set him in ambush against you.
12 Lend not to one more powerful than yourself;
   and whatever you lend, count it as lost.
13 Go not surety beyond your means;
   think any pledge a debt you must pay.
14 Contend not at law with a judge,
   for he will settle it according to his whim.
15 Travel not with a ruthless man,
   lest he weigh you down with calamity;
For he will go his own way straight,
   and through his folly you will perish with him.
16 Provoke no quarrel with a quick-tempered man
   nor ride with him through the desert;
For bloodshed is nothing to him;
   when there is no one to help you, he will
      destroy you.
17 Take no counsel with a fool,
   for he can keep nothing to himself.
18 Before a stranger do nothing that should be
      kept secret,
   for you know not what it will engender.
19 Open your heart to no man,
   and banish not your happiness.

9 Be not jealous of the wife of your bosom,
   lest you teach her to do evil against you.
2 Give no woman power over you
   to trample upon your dignity.
3 Be not intimate with a strange woman,
   lest you fall into her snares.
4 With a singing girl be not familiar,
   lest you be caught in her wiles.
5 Entertain no thoughts against a virgin,
   lest you be enmeshed in damages for her.
6 Give not yourself to harlots,
   lest you surrender your inheritance.
7 Gaze not about the lanes of the city
   and wander not through its squares;
8 Avert your eyes from a comely woman;
   gaze not upon the beauty of another's wife—
Through woman's beauty many perish,
   for lust for it burns like fire.
9 With a married woman dine not,
   recline not at table to drink by her side,
Lest your heart be drawn to her
   and you go down in blood to the grave.

10 Discard not an old friend,
   for the new one cannot equal him.
A new friend is like new wine
   which you drink with pleasure only when it
      has aged.

9 Do not dismiss what the old people have to say,
   for they too were taught by their parents;
from them you will learn how to think,
   and the art of the timely answer.
10 Do not kindle the coals of the sinner,
   in case you scorch yourself in his blaze.
11 Refuse to be provoked by the insolent,
   for fear that such a one try to trap you in your
      words.
12 Do not lend to anyone who is stronger than you
      are —
   if you do lend, resign yourself to loss.
13 Do not stand surety beyond your means;
   if you do stand surety, be prepared to pay up.
14 Do not go to law with a judge,
   since judgement will be given in his favour.
15 Do not go travelling with a rash man,
   for fear he becomes burdensome to you;
he will act as the whim takes him,
   and you will both be ruined by his folly.
16 Do not argue with a quick-tempered man,
   do not go with him where there are no other
      people,
since blood counts for nothing in his eyes,
   and where no help is to be had, he will strike
      you down.
17 Do not ask a fool for advice,
   since a fool will not be able to keep a
      confidence.
18 In a stranger's presence do nothing that should be
      kept secret,
   since you cannot tell what use the stranger will
      make of it.
19 Do not open your heart to all comers,
   nor lay claim to their good offices.

9 Do not be jealous of the wife you love,
   do not teach her lessons in how to harm you.
2 Do not put yourself in a woman's hands
   or she may come to dominate you completely.
3 Do not keep company with a prostitute,
   in case you get entangled in her snares.
4 Do not dally with a singing girl,
   in case you get caught by her wiles.
5 Do not stare at a pretty girl,
   in case you and she incur the same punishment.
6 Do not give your heart to whores,
   or you will ruin your inheritance.
7 Keep your eyes to yourself in the streets of a town,
   do not prowl about its unfrequented quarters.
8 Turn your eyes away from a handsome woman,
   do not stare at a beauty belonging to someone
      else.
Because of a woman's beauty, many have been
      undone;
   this makes passion flare up like a fire.
9 Never sit down with a married woman,
   or sit at table with her drinking wine,
in case you let your heart succumb to her
   and you lose all self-control and slide to disaster.

10 Do not desert an old friend;
   the new one will not be his match.
New friend, new wine;
   when it grows old, you drink it with pleasure.

11 Do not envy the success of sinners,
  for you do not know what their end will be
    like.
12 Do not delight in what pleases the ungodly;
  remember that they will not be held guiltless
    all their lives.
13 Keep far from those who have power to kill,
  and you will not be haunted by the fear of
    death.
  But if you approach them, make no misstep,
    or they may rob you of your life.
  Know that you are stepping among snares,
    and that you are walking on the city
      battlements.

14 As much as you can, aim to know your
    neighbors,
  and consult with the wise.
15 Let your conversation be with intelligent people,
  and let all your discussion be about the law of
    the Most High.
16 Let the righteous be your dinner companions,
  and let your glory be in the fear of the Lord.

17 A work is praised for the skill of the artisan;
  so a people's leader is proved wise by his
    words.
18 The loud of mouth are feared in their city,
  and the one who is reckless in speech is hated.

10 A wise magistrate educates his people,
  and the rule of an intelligent person is well
    ordered.
2 As the people's judge is, so are his officials;
  as the ruler of the city is, so are all its
    inhabitants.
3 An undisciplined king ruins his people,
  but a city becomes fit to live in through the
    understanding of its rulers.
4 The government of the earth is in the hand of the
    Lord,
  and over it he will raise up the right leader for
    the time.
5 Human success is in the hand of the Lord,
  and it is he who confers honor upon the
    lawgiver.y
6 Do not get angry with your neighbor for every
    injury,
  and do not resort to acts of insolence.
7 Arrogance is hateful to the Lord and to mortals,
  and injustice is outrageous to both.
8 Sovereignty passes from nation to nation
  on account of injustice and insolence and
    wealth.z
9 How can dust and ashes be proud?
  Even in life the human body decays.a
10 A long illness baffles the physician;b
  the king of today will die tomorrow.
11 For when one is dead
  he inherits maggots and verminc and worms.
12 The beginning of human pride is to forsake the
    Lord;
  the heart has withdrawn from its Maker.

11 Do not envy a bad man his success;
  you do not know what is in store for him.
12 Take no pleasure in the pleasures of the ungodly;
  remember that before they die punishment will
    overtake them.
13 Keep clear of a man who has power to kill,
  and you will not be haunted by the fear of death;
  but if you should approach him, make no false step
    or you will risk losing your life.
  Be aware that you are moving among pitfalls,
    or walking on the battlements of the city.
14 Take the measure of your neighbours as best you
    can,
  and accept advice from those who are wise.
15 Let your discussion be with intelligent men
  and all your talk about the law of the Most High.
16 At table choose the company of good men
  whose pride is in the fear of the Lord.

17 A craftsman is recognized by the skill of his hands
  and a councillor by his words of wisdom.
18 A garrulous person is the terror of his town,
  and one who is unguarded in his speech is
    detested.

10 A wise ruler instructs his people
  and gives them sound and orderly government.
2 Like ruler, like ministers;
  like sovereign, like subjects;
3 a king lacking instruction is his people's ruin,
  but sound judgement in a prince upholds a city.

4 THE government of the world is in the hand of the
    Lord;
  at the right time he will find the right man to rule
    it.
5 In the Lord's hand is all human success;
  it is he who confers honour on the legislator.

6 Do not be angry with your neighbour for every
    offence,
  and do not resort to acts of insolence.
7 Arrogance is hateful in the sight of God and man,
  and injustice is offensive to both.
8 Because of injustice, insolence, and greed,
  empire passes from nation to nation.
9 What has a mortal to be so proud of? He is only
    dust and ashes,
  subject even in life to bodily decay.
10 A long illness mocks the doctor's skill;
  today's king is tomorrow's corpse.
11 When anyone dies, he comes into an inheritance
  of maggots and vermin and worms.
12 The beginning of pride is to forsake the Lord,
  when the human heart revolts against its Maker;

---

y Heb: Gk *scribe* z Other ancient authorities add here or after
verse 9a, *Nothing is more wicked than one who loves money, for such
a person puts his own soul up for sale.* a Heb: Meaning of Gk
uncertain b Heb Lat: Meaning of Gk uncertain c Heb: Gk *wild
animals*

10:9 **even . . . decay:** *prob. mng, based on Heb.; Gk obscure.*

11 Envy not a sinner's fame,
   for you know not what disaster awaits him.
12 Rejoice not at a proud man's success;
   remember he will not reach death unpunished.
13 Keep far from the man who has power to kill,
   and you will not be filled with the dread
      of death.
   But if you approach him, offend him not,
   lest he take away your life;
   Know that you are stepping among snares
   and walking over a net.
14 As best you can, take your neighbors' measure,
   and associate with the wise.
15 With the learned be intimate;
   let all your conversation be about the law of
      the LORD.
16 Have just men for your table companions;
   in the fear of God be your glory.

17 Skilled artisans are esteemed for their deftness;
   but the ruler of his people is the skilled sage.
18 Feared in the city is the man of railing speech,
   and he who talks rashly is hated.

11 Do not envy the sinner his success;
   you do not know how that will end.
12 Do not take pleasure in what pleases the godless;
   remember they will not go unpunished here
      below.
13 Keep your distance from the man who has the
      power to put to death,
   and you will not be haunted by the fear of
      dying.
   If you do approach him, make no false move,
   or he may take your life.
   Realise that you are treading among trip-lines,
   that you are strolling on the battlements.
14 Cultivate your neighbours to the best of your
      ability,
   and consult with the wise.
15 For conversation seek the intelligent,
   let all your discussions bear on the law of the
      Most High.
16 Have the upright for your table companions,
   and let your pride be in fearing the Lord.
17 Work from skilled hands will earn its praise,
   but a leader of the people must be skilful in
      words.
18 A chatterbox is a terror to his town,
   a loose talker is detested.

10 A wise magistrate lends stability to his people,
   and the government of a prudent man is
      well ordered.
2 As the people's judge, so are his ministers;
   as the head of a city, its inhabitants.
3 A wanton king destroys his people,
   but a city grows through the wisdom of
      its princes.
4 Sovereignty over the earth is in the hand of God,
   who raises up on it the man of the hour;
5 Sovereignty over every man is in the hand of God,
   who imparts his majesty to the ruler.

6 No matter the wrong, do no violence to
      your neighbor,
   and do not walk the path of arrogance.
7 Odious to the LORD and to men is arrogance,
   and the sin of oppression they both hate.
8 Dominion is transferred from one people to another
   because of the violence of the arrogant.
9 Why are dust and ashes proud?
   even during life man's body decays;
10 A slight illness — the doctor jests,
   a king today — tomorrow he is dead.
11 When a man dies, he inherits corruption;
   worms and gnats and maggots.
12 The beginning of pride is man's stubbornness
   in withdrawing his heart from his Maker;

10 A sagacious ruler educates his people,
   and he makes his subjects understand order.
2 As the magistrate is, so will his officials be,
   as the governor is, so will be the inhabitants of
      his city.
3 An undisciplined king will be the ruin of his
      people,
   a city owes its prosperity to the intelligence of
      its leading men.
4 The government of the earth is in the hands of the
      Lord,
   he sets the right leader over it at the right time.
5 Human success is in the hands of the Lord.
   He invests the scribe with honour.

6 Do not resent your neighbour's every offence,
   and never act in a fit of passion.
7 Pride is hateful to God and humanity,
   and injustice is abhorrent to both.
8 Sovereignty passes from nation to nation
   because of injustice, arrogance and money.
9 What has dust and ashes to pride itself on?
   Even in life its entrails are repellent.
10 A long illness makes a fool of the doctor;
   a king today is a corpse tomorrow.
11 For in death the portion of all alike will be
   insects, wild animals and worms.
12 The first stage of pride is to desert the Lord
   and to turn one's heart away from one's Maker.

13 For the beginning of pride is sin,
　　and the one who clings to it pours out
　　　abominations.
　　Therefore the Lord brings upon them unheard-of
　　　calamities,
　　and destroys them completely.
14 The Lord overthrows the thrones of rulers,
　　and enthrones the lowly in their place.
15 The Lord plucks up the roots of the nations,*d*
　　and plants the humble in their place.
16 The Lord lays waste the lands of the nations,
　　and destroys them to the foundations of the
　　　earth.
17 He removes some of them and destroys them,
　　and erases the memory of them from the earth.
18 Pride was not created for human beings,
　　or violent anger for those born of women.
19 Whose offspring are worthy of honor?
　　Human offspring.
　　Whose offspring are worthy of honor?
　　Those who fear the Lord.
　　Whose offspring are unworthy of honor?
　　Human offspring.
　　Whose offspring are unworthy of honor?
　　Those who break the commandments.
20 Among family members their leader is worthy of
　　　honor,
　　but those who fear the Lord are worthy of
　　　honor in his eyes.*e*
22 The rich, and the eminent, and the poor—
　　their glory is the fear of the Lord.
23 It is not right to despise one who is intelligent but
　　　poor,
　　and it is not proper to honor one who is sinful.
24 The prince and the judge and the ruler are
　　　honored,
　　but none of them is greater than the one who
　　　fears the Lord.
25 Free citizens will serve a wise servant,
　　and an intelligent person will not complain.

26 Do not make a display of your wisdom when you
　　　do your work,
　　and do not boast when you are in need.
27 Better is the worker who has goods in plenty
　　than the boaster who lacks bread.

28 My child, honor yourself with humility,
　　and give yourself the esteem you deserve.
29 Who will acquit those who condemn*f*
　　　themselves?
　　And who will honor those who dishonor
　　　themselves?*g*
30 The poor are honored for their knowledge,
　　while the rich are honored for their wealth.
31 One who is honored in poverty, how much more
　　　in wealth!
　　And one dishonored in wealth, how much more
　　　in poverty!

11 The wisdom of the humble lifts their heads high,
　　and seats them among the great.
2 Do not praise individuals for their good looks,
　　or loathe anyone because of appearance alone.
3 The bee is small among flying creatures,
　　but what it produces is the best of sweet things.

d Other ancient authorities read *proud nations*　　*e* Other ancient
authorities add as verse 21, *The fear of the Lord is the beginning of
acceptance; obduracy and pride are the beginning of rejection.*
f Heb: Gk *sin against*　　*g* Heb Lat: Gk *their own life*

13 as its beginning is sin,
　　so persistence in it brings on a deluge of depravity.
　　Therefore the Lord inflicts signal punishments on
　　　the proud
　　and brings them to utter disaster.
14 The Lord overturns the thrones of princes
　　and installs the meek in their place.
15 The Lord uproots nations
　　and plants the humble in their place.
16 The Lord lays waste the territory of nations,
　　destroying them to the very foundations of the
　　　earth;
17 some he shrivels away to nothing,
　　so that all memory of them vanishes from the
　　　earth.
18 Pride was not the Creator's design for man
　　nor violent anger for those born of woman.
19 What creature is worthy of honour? Man.
　　What men? Those who fear the Lord.
　　What creature is worthy of contempt? Man.
　　What men? Those who break the commandments.
20 The members of the family honour their head;
　　the Lord honours those who fear him.
22 The convert, the stranger, and the poor—
　　their pride is in the fear of the Lord.
23 It is not right to despise a poor man whose
　　　judgement is sound,
　　and it is wrong to honour a rich man who is a
　　　sinner.
24 The mighty, the judge, and the prince win high
　　　renown,
　　but none is as great as he who fears the Lord.
25 When a wise servant is waited on by free men,
　　the sensible person will not protest.

26 Do NOT be too clever to do a day's work
　　or give yourself airs when you have nothing to live
　　　on.
27 It is better to work and have more than enough
　　than to be full of conceit on an empty stomach.
28 My son, be modest, but keep your self-respect
　　and value yourself at your true worth.
29 Who will speak up for anyone who is his own
　　　enemy,
　　or respect someone who disparages himself?
30 The poor may be honoured for good sense,
　　the rich for wealth.
31 If someone is honoured in poverty, how much
　　　more in wealth!
　　If he is dishonoured in wealth, how much more in
　　　poverty!

11 Someone poor but wise can hold his head high
　　and take his seat among the great.
2 Do not overrate one person for his good looks
　　or be repelled by another's appearance.
3 The bee is small among winged creatures,
　　yet her produce takes first place for sweetness.

10:20 **fear him:** *some witnesses add* 21Fear the Lord, and you will be
accepted; be obstinate and proud, and you will be rejected.
10:22 **convert:** *so Heb.;* Gk *rich.*　　10:23 **rich:** *so Syriac;* Gk
omits.

13 For pride is the reservoir of sin,
  a source which runs over with vice;
  Because of it God sends unheard-of afflictions
  and brings men to utter ruin.
14 The thrones of the arrogant God overturns
  and establishes the lowly in their stead.
15 The roots of the proud God plucks up,
  to plant the humble in their place:
16 He breaks down their stem to the level of
  the ground,
  then digs their roots from the earth.
17 The traces of the proud God sweeps away
  and effaces the memory of them from the earth.
18 Insolence is not allotted to a man,
  nor stubborn anger to one born of woman.

19 Whose offspring can be in honor? Those of men.
  Which offspring are in honor? Those who
  fear God.
  Whose offspring can be in disgrace? Those of men.
  Which offspring are in disgrace? Those who
  transgress the commandments.
20 Among brethren their leader is in honor;
  he who fears God is in honor among his people.
21 Be it tenant or wayfarer, alien or pauper,
  his glory is the fear of the LORD.
22 It is not just to despise a man who is wise
  but poor,
  nor proper to honor any sinner.
23 The prince, the ruler, the judge are in honor;
  but none is greater than he who fears God.
24 When free men serve a prudent slave,
  the wise man does not complain.
25 Flaunt not your wisdom in managing your affairs,
  and boast not in your time of need.
26 Better the worker who has plenty of everything
  than the boaster who is without bread.
27 My son, with humility have self-esteem;
  prize yourself as you deserve.
28 Who will acquit him who condemns himself?
  who will honor him who discredits himself?
29 The poor man is honored for his wisdom
  as the rich man is honored for his wealth;
30 Honored in poverty, how much more so in wealth!
  Dishonored in wealth, in poverty how much
  the more!

13 Since the first stage of pride is sin,
  whoever clings to it will pour forth filth.
  This is why the Lord inflicts unexpected
  punishments
  on such people, utterly destroying them.
14 The Lord has turned mighty princes off their
  thrones
  and seated the humble there instead.
15 The Lord has plucked up the proud by the roots,
  and planted the lowly in their place.
16 The Lord has overthrown the lands of the nations
  and destroyed them to the very foundations of
  the earth.
17 Sometimes he has taken them away and destroyed
  them,
  and blotted out their memory from the earth.
18 Pride was not created for human beings,
  nor furious rage for those born of woman.

19 What race deserves honour? The human race.
  What race deserves honour? Those who fear the
  Lord.
  What race deserves contempt? The human race.
  What race deserves contempt? Those who break
  the Law.
20 A leader is honoured by his brothers,
  and those who fear the Lord are honoured by
  him.
22 The rich, the noble, the poor,
  let them pride themselves on fearing the Lord.
23 It is not right to despise one who is poor but
  intelligent,
  and it is not good to honour one who is a sinner.
24 Magnate, magistrate, potentate, all are to be
  honoured,
  but none is greater than the one who fears the
  Lord.
25 A wise slave will have free men waiting on him,
  and the enlightened will not complain.

26 Do not try to be smart when you do your work,
  do not put on airs when you are in difficulties.
27 Better the hardworking who has plenty of
  everything,
  than the pretentious at a loss for a meal.
28 My child, be modest in your self-esteem,
  and value yourself at your proper worth.
29 Who can justify one who inflicts injuries on
  himself,
  or respect one who is full of self-contempt?
30 The poor is honoured for wit,
  and the rich for wealth.
31 Honoured in poverty, how much the more in
  wealth!
  Dishonoured in wealth, how much the more in
  poverty!

11 The poor man's wisdom lifts his head high
  and sets him among princes.
2 Praise not a man for his looks;
  despise not a man for his appearance.
3 Least is the bee among winged things,
  but she reaps the choicest of all harvests.

11 Wisdom enables the poor to stand erect,
  and gives to the poor a place with the great.
2 Do not praise anyone for good looks,
  nor dislike anyone for mere appearance.
3 Small among winged creatures is the bee
  but her produce is the sweetest of the sweet.

NEW REVISED STANDARD VERSION	REVISED ENGLISH BIBLE

NEW REVISED STANDARD VERSION

4 Do not boast about wearing fine clothes,
  and do not exalt yourself when you are
    honored;
for the works of the Lord are wonderful,
  and his works are concealed from humankind.
5 Many kings have had to sit on the ground,
  but one who was never thought of has worn a
    crown.
6 Many rulers have been utterly disgraced,
  and the honored have been handed over to
    others.

7 Do not find fault before you investigate;
  examine first, and then criticize.
8 Do not answer before you listen,
  and do not interrupt when another is speaking.
9 Do not argue about a matter that does not
    concern you,
  and do not sit with sinners when they judge a
    case.

10 My child, do not busy yourself with many
    matters;
  if you multiply activities, you will not be held
    blameless.
  If you pursue, you will not overtake,
    and by fleeing you will not escape.
11 There are those who work and struggle and hurry,
  but are so much the more in want.
12 There are others who are slow and need help,
  who lack strength and abound in poverty;
  but the eyes of the Lord look kindly upon them;
  he lifts them out of their lowly condition
13 and raises up their heads
  to the amazement of the many.

14 Good things and bad, life and death,
  poverty and wealth, come from the Lord. *h*
17 The Lord's gift remains with the devout,
  and his favor brings lasting success.
18 One becomes rich through diligence and
    self-denial,
  and the reward allotted to him is this:
19 when he says, "I have found rest,
    and now I shall feast on my goods!"
  he does not know how long it will be
    until he leaves them to others and dies.
20 Stand by your agreement and attend to it,
  and grow old in your work.
21 Do not wonder at the works of a sinner,
  but trust in the Lord and keep at your job;
  for it is easy in the sight of the Lord
    to make the poor rich suddenly, in an instant.
22 The blessing of the Lord is*i* the reward of the
    pious,
  and quickly God causes his blessing to
    flourish.
23 Do not say, "What do I need,
    and what further benefit can be mine?"
24 Do not say, "I have enough,
    and what harm can come to me now?"
25 In the day of prosperity, adversity is forgotten,
  and in the day of adversity, prosperity is not
    remembered.

REVISED ENGLISH BIBLE

4 Do not brag about your fine clothes
  or be elated when honours come your way.
  Remember, the Lord can perform marvels
  which are hidden from mortal eyes:
5 many a king has been reduced to sitting on the
    ground,
  while crowns have gone where least expected;
6 many a ruler has been stripped of every honour,
  and the eminent have found themselves at the
    mercy of others.

7 Do not find fault before examining the evidence;
  think first, and criticize afterwards.
8 Do not answer without first listening,
  and do not interrupt while another is speaking.
9 Never take sides in a quarrel not your own
  or become involved in the disputes of the wicked.

10 My son, do not engage in too many transactions;
  attempting too much, you will come to grief;
  in pursuit you will not overtake;
  in flight you will not escape.
11 One person slaves and toils and presses on,
  and yet falls farther behind.
12 Another is slow and in need of help,
  poor in strength, rich only in poverty;
  yet the Lord turns on him a kindly eye,
  lifts him up out of his miserable plight,
13 and, to the amazement of many, raises him to
    dignity.

14 Good fortune and bad, life and death,
  poverty and wealth, all are from the Lord.
17 His gifts to the devout endure;
  his approval brings unending prosperity.
18 Someone may grow rich by stinting and sparing,
  but what does he get for his pains?
19 When he says, 'I have earned my rest
    and now I can live on my savings,'
  he does not know how long it will be
  before he must die and leave them to others.

20 Stand by your contract and give your mind to it;
  grow old at your work.
21 Do not envy the wicked their achievements;
  trust the Lord and stick to your job,
  for it is very easy for the Lord
  to make the poor rich all in a moment.
22 Piety is rewarded by the Lord's blessing,
  which blossoms in a single hour.
23 Do not say, 'What use am I?
  What good can the future hold for me?'
24 And do not say, 'I am self-sufficient;
  nothing can ever go wrong for me.'
25 Hardship is forgotten in time of prosperity,
  and prosperity in time of hardship.

---

h Other ancient authorities add as verses 15 and 16, *15Wisdom,
understanding, and knowledge of the law come from the Lord;
affection and the ways of good works come from him. 16Error and
darkness were created with sinners; evil grows old with those who
take pride in malice.* *i* Heb: Gk *is in*

11:14 **from the Lord:** *some witnesses add* 15From the Lord come
wisdom, understanding, and knowledge of the law, love, and the
doing of good works. 16 Error and darkness have been with sinners
from their birth, and evil grows old with them who delight in it.

NEW AMERICAN BIBLE

4 Mock not the worn cloak
   and jibe at no man's bitter day:
 For strange are the works of the LORD,
   hidden from men his deeds.
5 The oppressed often rise to a throne,
   and some that none would consider wear
     a crown.
6 The exalted often fall into utter disgrace;
   the honored are given into enemy hands.

7 Before investigating, find no fault;
   examine first, then criticize.
8 Before hearing, answer not,
   and interrupt no one in the middle of his speech.
9 Dispute not about what is not your concern;
   in the strife of the arrogant take no part.
10 My son, why increase your cares,
    since he who is avid for wealth will not
      be blameless?
 Even if you run after it, you will never overtake it;
   however you seek it, you will not find it.
11 One may toil and struggle and drive,
    and fall short all the more.
12 Another goes his way a weakling and a failure,
    with little strength and great misery—
 Yet the eyes of the LORD look favorably upon him;
   he raises him free of the vile dust,
13 Lifts up his head and exalts him
    to the amazement of the many.
14 Good and evil, life and death,
    poverty and riches, are from the LORD.
15 Wisdom and understanding and knowledge
      of affairs,
    love and virtuous paths are from the LORD.
16 Error and darkness were formed with sinners from
      their birth,
    and evil grows old with evildoers.
17 The LORD's gift remains with the just;
    his favor brings continued success.
18 A man may become rich through a miser's life,
    and this is his allotted reward:
19 When he says: "I have found rest,
    now I will feast on my possessions,"
 He does not know how long it will be
   till he dies and leaves them to others.

20 My son, hold fast to your duty, busy yourself
      with it,
    grow old while doing your task.
21 Admire not how sinners live,
    but trust in the LORD and wait for his light;
 For it is easy with the LORD
   suddenly, in an instant, to make a poor
     man rich.
22 God's blessing is the lot of the just man,
    and in due time his hopes bear fruit.
23 Say not: "What do I need?
    What further pleasure can be mine?"
24 Say not: "I am independent.
    What harm can come to me now?"
25 The day of prosperity makes one forget adversity;
    the day of adversity makes one forget prosperity.

NEW JERUSALEM BIBLE

4 Do not grow proud when people honour you;
   for the works of the Lord are wonderful
     but hidden from human beings.
5 Many monarchs have been made to sit on the
      ground,
    and the person nobody thought of has worn the
      crown.
6 Many influential people have been utterly
      disgraced,
    and prominent people have fallen into the power
      of others.
7 Do not find fault before making thorough enquiry;
   first reflect, then give a reprimand.
8 Listen before you answer,
   and do not interrupt a speech before it is
     finished.
9 Do not wrangle about something that does not
      concern you,
    do not interfere in the quarrels of sinners.
10 My child, do not take on a great amount of
      business;
    if you multiply your interests, you are bound to
      suffer for it;
 hurry as fast as you can, yet you will never arrive,
   nor will you escape by running away.
11 Some people work very hard at top speed,
    only to find themselves falling further behind.
12 Or there is the slow kind of person, needing help,
    poor in possessions and rich in poverty;
 and the Lord turns a favourable eye on him,
   lifts him out of his wretched condition,
13 and enables him to hold his head high,
    thus causing general astonishment.
14 Good and bad, life and death,
    poverty and wealth, all come from the Lord.
17 To the devout the Lord's gift remains constant,
    and his favour will be there to lead them for
      ever.
18 Others grow rich by pinching and scraping,
    and here is the reward they receive for it:
19 although they say, 'Now I can sit back
    and enjoy the benefit of what I have got,'
 they do not know how long this will last;
   they will have to leave their goods to others and
     die.
20 Stick to your job, work hard at it
    and grow old at your work.
21 Do not admire the achievements of sinners,
    trust the Lord and mind your own business;
 since it is a trifle in the eyes of the Lord,
   in a moment, suddenly to make the poor rich.
22 The blessing of the Lord is the reward of the
      devout,
    in a moment God brings his blessing to flower.
23 Do not say, 'What are my needs,
    how much shall I have in the future?'
24 And do not say, 'I am self-sufficient,
    what disaster can affect me now?'
25 In prosperous times, disasters are forgotten
    and in times of disaster, no one remembers
      prosperity.

NEW REVISED STANDARD VERSION

REVISED ENGLISH BIBLE

26 For it is easy for the Lord on the day of death
    to reward individuals according to their
    conduct.
27 An hour's misery makes one forget past delights,
    and at the close of one's life one's deeds are
    revealed.
28 Call no one happy before his death;
    by how he ends, a person becomes known.*j*

29 Do not invite everyone into your home,
    for many are the tricks of the crafty.
30 Like a decoy partridge in a cage, so is the mind
    of the proud,
    and like spies they observe your weakness;*k*
31 for they lie in wait, turning good into evil,
    and to worthy actions they attach blame.
32 From a spark many coals are kindled,
    and a sinner lies in wait to shed blood.
33 Beware of scoundrels, for they devise evil,
    and they may ruin your reputation forever.
34 Receive strangers into your home and they will
    stir up trouble for you,
    and will make you a stranger to your own
    family.

12 If you do good, know to whom you do it,
    and you will be thanked for your good deeds.
2 Do good to the devout, and you will be repaid—
    if not by them, certainly by the Most High.
3 No good comes to one who persists in evil
    or to one who does not give alms.
4 Give to the devout, but do not help the sinner.
5 Do good to the humble, but do not give to the
    ungodly;
    hold back their bread, and do not give it to them,
    for by means of it they might subdue you;
    then you will receive twice as much evil
    for all the good you have done to them.
6 For the Most High also hates sinners
    and will inflict punishment on the ungodly.*l*
7 Give to the one who is good, but do not help the
    sinner.
8 A friend is not known*m* in prosperity,
    nor is an enemy hidden in adversity.
9 One's enemies are friendly*n* when one prospers,
    but in adversity even one's friend disappears.
10 Never trust your enemy,
    for like corrosion in copper, so is his
    wickedness.
11 Even if he humbles himself and walks bowed
    down,
    take care to be on your guard against him.
    Be to him like one who polishes a mirror,
    to be sure it does not become completely
    tarnished.
12 Do not put him next to you,
    or he may overthrow you and take your place.
    Do not let him sit at your right hand,
    or else he may try to take your own seat,
    and at last you will realize the truth of my words,
    and be stung by what I have said.

26 Even on the day a person dies it is easy for the
    Lord
    to give him what he deserves.
27 An hour's misery wipes out all memory of delight,
    and someone's end reveals how he has lived.
28 Call no one happy before he dies,
    for not until death is a person known for what he
    is.

29 Do NOT invite all comers into your home;
    dishonesty wears many a guise.
30 A proud person's mind is like a decoy partridge in
    its cage,
    or like a spy watching for a false step;
31 he waits for a chance to twist good into evil
    or to cast blame on praiseworthy actions.
32 One spark kindles many coals,
    and a plot laid by a bad man ends in bloodshed.
33 Beware of a scoundrel and his evil schemes,
    or he may ruin your reputation forever.
34 Admit a stranger to your home and he will stir up
    trouble
    and estrange you from your own flesh and blood.

12 If you do a good turn, make sure to whom you
    are doing it;
    then you will have credit for your kindness.
2 A good turn done to a godfearing person will be
    repaid,
    if not by him, then by the Most High.
3 There is no prosperity for the persistent wrongdoer
    or for him who never gives alms.
4 Give to the godfearing, but never help the sinner.
5 Keep your good works for the humble, not the
    godless;
    put away your bread, do not give him any;
    he will use your gift to get the better of you,
    and for every favour you have done him
    you will suffer a twofold injury;
6 for the Most High himself hates sinners
    and sends the ungodly what they deserve.
7 Give to anyone who is good, but never help a
    sinner.
8 Prosperity does not reveal your friends,
    nor does adversity conceal your enemies.
9 When all goes well with someone his enemies are
    friendly;
    when things go badly even a friend will shun him.
10 Never trust an enemy;
    he will turn vicious as surely as bronze corrodes.
11 Even if he appears humble and cringing,
    keep your distance and be on your guard.
    Behave towards him like someone who polishes a
    mirror
    to ensure it does not tarnish.
12 Do not place him by your side,
    or he will trip you up and supplant you;
    do not seat him at your right hand,
    or he will thrust you out and take your place;
    and in the end you will admit the force of my
    words
    and recall my warning with regret.

---

j Heb: Gk *and through his children a person becomes known*
k Heb: Gk *downfall*   *l* Other ancient authorities add *and he is
keeping them for the day of their punishment*   *m* Other ancient
authorities read *punished*   *n* Heb: Gk *grieved*

NEW AMERICAN BIBLE

NEW JERUSALEM BIBLE

26 For it is easy with the LORD on the day of death
　to repay man according to his deeds.
27 A moment's affliction brings forgetfulness of
　　past delights;
　when a man dies, his life is revealed.
28 Call no man happy before his death,
　for by how he ends, a man is known.

29 Bring not every man into your house,
　for many are the snares of the crafty one;
30 Though he seem like a bird confined in a cage,
　yet like a spy he will pick out the weak spots.
31 The talebearer turns good into evil;
　with a spark he sets many coals afire.
32 The evil man lies in wait for blood,
　and plots against your choicest possessions.
33 Avoid a wicked man, for he breeds only evil,
　lest you incur a lasting stain.
34 Lodge a stranger with you, and he will subvert
　　your course,
　and make a stranger of you to your
　　own household.

12 If you do good, know for whom you are
　　doing it,
　and your kindness will have its effect.
2 Do good to the just man and reward will be yours,
　if not from him, from the LORD.
3 No good comes to him who gives comfort to
　　the wicked,
　nor is it an act of mercy that he does.
4 Give to the good man, refuse the sinner;
　refresh the downtrodden, give nothing to the
　　proud man.
5 No arms for combat should you give him,
　lest he use them against yourself;
6 With twofold evil you will meet
　for every good deed you do for him.
7 The Most High himself hates sinners,
　and upon the wicked he takes vengeance.

8 In our prosperity we cannot know our friends;
　in adversity an enemy will not remain concealed.
9 When a man is successful even his enemy
　　is friendly;
　in adversity even his friend disappears.
10 Never trust your enemy,
　for his wickedness is like corrosion in bronze.
11 Even though he acts humbly and peaceably
　　toward you,
　take care to be on your guard against him.
　Rub him as one polishes a brazen mirror,
　and you will find that there is still corrosion.
12 Let him not stand near you,
　lest he oust you and take your place.
　Let him not sit at your right hand,
　lest he then demand your seat,
　And in the end you appreciate my advice,
　when you groan with regret, as I warned you.

26 Yet it is a trifle for the Lord on the day someone
　　dies
　to repay him as his conduct deserves.
27 A moment's adversity, and pleasures are forgotten;
　in a person's last hour his deeds will stand
　　revealed.
28 Call no one fortunate before his death;
　it is by his end that someone will be known.

29 Do not bring everyone home with you,
　for many are the traps of the crafty.
30 Like a captive partridge in a cage, so is the heart
　　of the proud:
　like a spy he watches for your downfall,
31 ever on the look-out, turning good into bad
　and finding fault with what is praiseworthy.
32 A heartful of glowing coals starts from a single
　　spark,
　and the sinner lurks for the chance to spill
　　blood.
33 Beware of a scoundrel and his evil contrivances,
　in case he puts a smear on you for ever.
34 Give a home to a stranger and he will start trouble
　and estrange you from your own family.

12 If you mean to do a kindness, choose the right
　　person,
　then your good deeds will not be wasted.
2 Do good to someone devout, and you will be
　　rewarded,
　if not by that person, then certainly by the Most
　　High.
3 No good will come to one who persists in evil,
　or who refuses to give alms.
4 Give to the devout,
　do not go to the help of a sinner.
5 Do good to the humble,
　give nothing to the godless.
　Refuse him bread, do not give him any,
　it might make him stronger than you are;
　then you would be repaid evil twice over
　for all the good you had done him.
6 For the Most High himself detests sinners,
　and will repay the wicked with what they
　　deserve.
7 Give to the good,
　and do not go to the help of a sinner.
8 In prosperity you cannot always tell a true friend,
　but in adversity you cannot mistake an enemy.
9 When someone is doing well that person's enemies
　　are sad,
　when someone is doing badly, even a friend will
　　keep at a distance.
10 Do not ever trust an enemy;
　as bronze tarnishes, so does an enemy's malice.
11 Even if he behaves humbly and comes bowing and
　　scraping,
　maintain your reserve and be on your guard
　　against him.
　Behave towards him as if you were polishing a
　　mirror,
　you will find that his tarnish cannot last.
12 Do not stand him beside you
　in case he thrusts you out and takes your place.
　Do not seat him on your right,
　or he will be after your position,
　and then you will remember what I have said
　and sadly admit that I was right.

NEW REVISED STANDARD VERSION

13 Who pities a snake charmer when he is bitten,
or all those who go near wild animals?
14 So no one pities a person who associates with a sinner
and becomes involved in the other's sins.
15 He stands by you for a while,
but if you falter, he will not be there.
16 An enemy speaks sweetly with his lips,
but in his heart he plans to throw you into a pit;
an enemy may have tears in his eyes,
but if he finds an opportunity he will never have enough of your blood.
17 If evil comes upon you, you will find him there ahead of you;
pretending to help, he will trip you up.
18 Then he will shake his head, and clap his hands,
and whisper much, and show his true face.

13 Whoever touches pitch gets dirty,
and whoever associates with a proud person becomes like him.
2 Do not lift a weight too heavy for you,
or associate with one mightier and richer than you.
How can the clay pot associate with the iron kettle?
The pot will strike against it and be smashed.
3 A rich person does wrong, and even adds insults;
a poor person suffers wrong, and must add apologies.
4 A rich person[o] will exploit you if you can be of use to him,
but if you are in need he will abandon you.
5 If you own something, he will live with you;
he will drain your resources without a qualm.
6 When he needs you he will deceive you,
and will smile at you and encourage you;
he will speak to you kindly and say, "What do you need?"
7 He will embarrass you with his delicacies,
until he has drained you two or three times,
and finally he will laugh at you.
Should he see you afterwards, he will pass you by
and shake his head at you.

8 Take care not to be led astray
and humiliated when you are enjoying yourself.[p]
9 When an influential person invites you, be reserved,
and he will invite you more insistently.
10 Do not be forward, or you may be rebuffed;
do not stand aloof, or you will be forgotten.
11 Do not try to treat him as an equal,
or trust his lengthy conversations;
for he will test you by prolonged talk,
and while he smiles he will be examining you.
12 Cruel are those who do not keep your secrets;
they will not spare you harm or imprisonment.
13 Be on your guard and very careful,
for you are walking about with your own downfall.[q]

[o] Gk *He* [p] Other ancient authorities read *in your folly* [q] Other ancient authorities add as verse 14, *When you hear these things in your sleep, wake up! During all your life love the Lord, and call on him for your salvation.*

REVISED ENGLISH BIBLE

13 Who sympathizes with a snake-charmer when he is bitten,
or with those who deal with wild animals?
14 So is it with the person who keeps bad company
and is involved in another's wickedness.
15 He may stand by you for a while,
but if your fortunes decline, his friendship will not last.
16 An enemy speaks honeyed words,
but in his heart he plans to topple you into the ditch.
He may have tears in his eyes,
but given the chance he will not stop at bloodshed.
17 If disaster overtakes you, you will find him there ahead of you,
and while pretending to help, he will catch you by the heel.
18 Then he will wag his head and rub his hands
and with many a whispered slander reveal his true colours.

13 Handle pitch and it will make you dirty;
associate with the arrogant and you will grow like them.
2 Do not lift a weight too heavy for you,
nor associate with someone greater and richer than yourself.
How can a jug be friends with a kettle?
If they knock together, it will be smashed.
3 A rich person does wrong, and then adds insult to injury;
a poor person is wronged, and must apologize into the bargain.
4 If you can serve his turn, a rich person will exploit you,
but if you are in need, he will drop you.
5 If you are in funds, he will be your constant companion
and without a twinge of remorse drain you dry.
6 He may need you, and then he will deceive you
and be all smiles and encouragement,
paying you compliments and asking, 'What can I do for you?'
7 embarrassing you with his hospitality,
until he has drained you two or three times over;
but he will end up by laughing at you.
Afterwards, when he sees you, he will pass you by
and wag his head over you.
8 Take care not to be led astray
and humiliated when you are enjoying yourself.
9 If a great man invites you, be slow to accept,
and he will be the more pressing in his invitation.
10 Do not push yourself forward, for fear of a rebuff,
but do not keep aloof, or you may be forgotten.
11 Do not presume to converse with him as an equal,
and put no trust in his effusive speeches;
the more he speaks, the more he is testing you,
weighing you up even while he smiles.
12 The person who betrays a confidence is without compunction
and will not spare you injury or imprisonment.
13 Confide in no one and be on your guard,
for you are walking with disaster.

13:13 **with disaster:** *some witnesses add* When you hear this in your sleep, wake up! 14 Love the Lord all your life, and appeal to him to keep you safe.

<table>
<tr><td>

13 Who pities a snake charmer when he is bitten,
  or anyone who goes near a wild beast?
14 So is it with the companion of the proud man,
  who is involved in his sins:
15 While you stand firm, he makes no bold move;
  but if you slip, he cannot hold back.
16 With his lips an enemy speaks sweetly,
  but in his heart he schemes to plunge you into
   the abyss.
Though your enemy has tears in his eyes,
  if given the chance, he will never have enough
   of your blood.
17 If evil comes upon you, you will find him at hand;
  feigning to help, he will trip you up,
18 Then he will nod his head and clap his hands
  and hiss repeatedly, and show his true face.

</td><td>

13 Who feels sorry for a snake-charmer bitten by a
  snake,
  or for those who take risks with savage
   animals? —
14 just so for one who consorts with a sinner,
  and becomes an accomplice in his sins.
15 He will stay with you for a while,
  but if you once give way he will press his
   advantage.
16 An enemy may have sweetness on his lips,
  and in his heart a scheme to throw you into the
   ditch.
An enemy may have tears in his eyes,
  but if he gets a chance there can never be too
   much blood for him.
17 If you meet with misfortune, you will find him
   there before you,
  and, pretending to help you, he will trip you up.
18 He will wag his head and clap his hands,
  he will whisper a lot and his expression will
   change.

</td></tr>
</table>

13 He who touches pitch blackens his hand;
  he who associates with an impious man learns
   his ways.
2 Bear no burden too heavy for you;
  go with no one greater or wealthier
   than yourself.
How can the earthen pot go with the
   metal cauldron?
When they knock together, the pot will
   be smashed:
3 The rich man does wrong and boasts of it,
  the poor man is wronged and begs forgiveness.
4 As long as the rich man can use you he will
   enslave you,
  but when you are exhausted, he will
   abandon you.
5 As long as you have anything he will speak fair
   words to you,
  and with smiles he will win your confidence;
6 When he needs something from you he will
   cajole you,
  then without regret he will impoverish you.
7 While it serves his purpose he will beguile you,
  then twice or three times he will terrify you;
When later he sees you he will pass you by,
  and shake his head over you.
8 Guard against being presumptuous;
  be not as those who lack sense.
9 When invited by a man of influence, keep
   your distance;
  then he will urge you all the more.
10 Be not bold with him lest you be rebuffed,
  but keep not too far away lest you be forgotten.
11 Engage not freely in discussion with him,
  trust not his many words;
For by prolonged talk he will test you,
  and though smiling he will probe you.
12 Mercilessly he will make of you a laughingstock,
  and will not refrain from injury or chains.
13 Be on your guard and take care
  never to accompany men of violence.

13 Whoever touches pitch will be defiled,
  and anyone who associates with the proud will
   come
  to be like them.
2 Do not try to carry a burden too heavy for you,
  do not associate with someone more powerful
   and wealthy than yourself.
Why put the clay pot next to the iron cauldron?
  It will only break when they bang against each
   other.
3 The rich does wrong and takes a high line;
  the poor is wronged and has to beg for pardon.
4 If you are useful the rich will exploit you,
  if you go bankrupt he will desert you.
5 Are you well off? — he will live with you,
  he will clean you out without a single qualm.
6 Does he need you? — he will hoodwink you,
  smile at you and raise your hopes;
he will speak politely to you
  and say, 'Is there anything you need?'
7 He will make you feel small at his dinner parties
  and, having cleaned you out two or three times
   over,
  will end by laughing at you.
Afterwards, when he sees you, he will avoid you
  and shake his head about you.
8 Take care you are not hoodwinked
  and thus humiliated through your own stupidity.
9 When an influential person invites you, show
   reluctance,
  and he will press his invitation all the more.
10 Do not thrust yourself forward, in case you are
   pushed aside,
  but do not stand aloof, or you will be
   overlooked.
11 Do not affect to treat him as an equal,
  do not trust his flow of words;
since all this talking is expressly meant to test you,
  under cover of geniality he will be weighing you
   up.
12 Pitiless is anyone who retails gossip;
  he will not spare you either blows or chains.
13 Be wary, take very great care,
  because you are walking with your own
   downfall.

15 Every creature loves its like,
  and every person the neighbor.
16 All living beings associate with their own kind,
  and people stick close to those like themselves.
17 What does a wolf have in common with a lamb?
  No more has a sinner with the devout.
18 What peace is there between a hyena and a dog?
  And what peace between the rich and the poor?
19 Wild asses in the wilderness are the prey of lions;
  likewise the poor are feeding grounds for the
  rich.
20 Humility is an abomination to the proud;
  likewise the poor are an abomination to the
  rich.

21 When the rich person totters, he is supported by
  friends,
  but when the humble*r* falls, he is pushed away
  even by friends.
22 If the rich person slips, many come to the rescue;
  he speaks unseemly words, but they justify
  him.
  If the humble person slips, they even criticize
  him;
  he talks sense, but is not given a hearing.
23 The rich person speaks and all are silent;
  they extol to the clouds what he says.
  The poor person speaks and they say, "Who is
  this fellow?"
  And should he stumble, they even push him
  down.
24 Riches are good if they are free from sin;
  poverty is evil only in the opinion of the
  ungodly.

25 The heart changes the countenance,
  either for good or for evil.*s*
26 The sign of a happy heart is a cheerful face,
  but to devise proverbs requires painful
  thinking.

14 Happy are those who do not blunder with their
  lips,
  and need not suffer remorse for sin.
2 Happy are those whose hearts do not condemn
  them,
  and who have not given up their hope.

3 Riches are inappropriate for a small-minded
  person;
  and of what use is wealth to a miser?
4 What he denies himself he collects for others;
  and others will live in luxury on his goods.
5 If one is mean to himself, to whom will he be
  generous?
  He will not enjoy his own riches.
6 No one is worse than one who is grudging to
  himself;
  this is the punishment for his meanness.
7 If ever he does good, it is by mistake;
  and in the end he reveals his meanness.
8 The miser is an evil person;
  he turns away and disregards people.
9 The eye of the greedy person is not satisfied with
  his share;
  greedy injustice withers the soul.
10 A miser begrudges bread,
  and it is lacking at his table.

15 Every living thing loves its like,
  and every person his own sort.
16 All creatures flock together with their kind,
  and human beings stick close to their fellows.
17 What has a wolf in common with a lamb,
  or a sinner with someone who fears God?
18 What peace can there be between hyena and dog,
  what peace between rich and poor?
19 As lions prey on the wild asses of the desert,
  so the rich live off the poor.
20 As humility disgusts the proud,
  so the rich are disgusted by the poor.

21 If a rich person staggers, he is steadied by his
  friends;
  a poor one falls, and his friends promptly disown
  him.
22 When a rich person slips, many come to his
  rescue;
  if he says something outrageous, they make
  excuses for him.
  A poor one makes a slip, and at once he is
  criticized;
  even if he talks sense, he is not given a hearing.
23 A rich person speaks, and all keep silent;
  then they praise his speech to the skies.
  A poor one speaks, and they say, 'Who is this?'
  and if he stumbles, they push him farther.

24 WEALTH untainted by sin is good;
  poverty brought on by godless conduct is evil.
25 It is the heart that changes the look on the face
  either for better or for worse.
26 A cheerful face betokens someone in good heart,
  but the invention of proverbs involves wearisome
  thought.

14 Happy is the one who has never let slip a
  careless word,
  who has never felt the sting of remorse!
2 Happy is the one whose conscience does not
  accuse him,
  whose hopes have never been dashed!

3 Meanness and wealth do not go well together:
  what use is money to a miser?
4 He deprives himself only to hoard for others;
  on his possessions someone else will lead a life of
  luxury.
5 How can anyone who is hard on himself be kind to
  others?
  His money brings him no enjoyment.
6 No one is worse than he who is grudging to
  himself:
  his niggardliness is its own retribution.
7 If ever he does good, he does it by mistake,
  and his villainy comes out at the finish.
8 He is hard who has a grudging eye,
  who turns his back on need and looks the other
  way.
9 The covetous eye is not satisfied with its share;
  greedy injustice shrivels the soul.
10 Someone with a miserly outlook begrudges bread
  and keeps a bare table.

r Other ancient authorities read *poor*   *s* Other ancient authorities add
and a glad heart makes a cheerful countenance

14 Every living thing loves its own kind,
    every man a man like himself.
15 Every being is drawn to its own kind;
    with his own kind every man associates.
16 Is a wolf ever allied with a lamb?
    So it is with the sinner and the just.
17 Can there be peace between the hyena and
    the dog?
    Or between the rich and the poor can there
    be peace?
18 Lion's prey are the wild asses of the desert;
    so too the poor are feeding grounds for the rich.
19 A proud man abhors lowliness;
    so does the rich man abhor the poor.
20 When a rich man stumbles he is supported by
    a friend;
    when a poor man trips he is pushed down by
    a friend.
21 Many are the supporters for a rich man when
    he speaks;
    though what he says is odious, it wins approval.
    When a poor man speaks they make sport of him;
    he speaks wisely and no attention is paid him.
22 A rich man speaks and all are silent,
    his wisdom they extol to the clouds.
    A poor man speaks and they say: "Who is that?"
    If he slips they cast him down.
23 Wealth is good when there is no sin;
    but poverty is evil by the standards of the proud.
24 The heart of a man changes his countenance,
    either for good or for evil.
25 The sign of a good heart is a cheerful countenance;
    withdrawn and perplexed is the
    laborious schemer.

14 Happy the man whose mouth brings him
    no grief,
    who is not stung by remorse for sin.
2 Happy the man whose conscience does not
    reproach him,
    who has not lost hope.
3 Wealth ill becomes the mean man;
    and to the miser, of what use is gold?
4 What he denies himself he collects for others,
    and in his possessions a stranger will revel.
5 To whom will he be generous who is stingy
    with himself
    and does not enjoy what is his own?
6 None is more stingy than he who is stingy
    with himself;
    he punishes his own miserliness.
7 If ever he is generous, it is by mistake;
    and in the end he displays his greed.
8 In the miser's opinion his share is too small;
9   he refuses his neighbor and brings ruin
    on himself.
10 The miser's eye is rapacious for bread,
    but on his own table he sets it stale.

15 Every living thing loves its own sort,
    and every man his fellow.
16 Every creature mixes with its kind,
    and human beings stick to their own sort.
17 How can wolf and lamb agree? —
    Just so with sinner and devout.
18 What peace can there be between hyena and dog?
    And what peace between rich and poor?
19 Wild desert donkeys are the prey of lions;
    so too, the poor is the quarry of the rich.
20 The proud thinks humility abhorrent;
    so too, the rich abominates the poor.
21 When the rich stumbles he is supported by friends;
    when the poor falls, his friends push him away.
22 When the rich slips, there are many hands to catch
    him,
    if he talks nonsense he is congratulated.
    The poor slips, and is blamed for it,
    he may talk good sense, but no room is made
    for him.
23 The rich speaks and everyone stops talking,
    and then they praise his discourse to the skies.
    The poor speaks and people say, 'Who is this?'
    and if he stumbles, they trip him up yet more.

24 Wealth is good where there is no sin,
    poverty is evil, the godless say.
25 The heart moulds a person's expression
    whether for better or worse.
26 Happy heart, cheerful expression;
    but wearisome work, inventing proverbs.

14 Blessed is anyone who has not sinned in speech
    and who needs feel no remorse for sins.
2 Blessed is anyone whose conscience brings no
    reproach
    and who has never given up hope.
3 Wealth is not the right thing for the niggardly,
    and what use are possessions to the covetous?
4 Whoever hoards by stinting himself is hoarding for
    others,
    and others will live sumptuously on his riches.
5 If someone is mean to himself, whom does he
    benefit?
    he does not even enjoy what is his own.
6 No one is meaner than the person who is mean to
    himself,
    this is how his wickedness repays him.
7 If he does any good, he does it unintentionally,
    and in the end he himself reveals his
    wickedness.
8 Wicked the person who has an envious eye,
    averting his face, and careless of others' lives.
9 The eye of the grasping is not content with what
    he has,
    greed shrivels up the soul.
10 The miser is grudging of bread,
    there is famine at his table.

NEW REVISED STANDARD VERSION	REVISED ENGLISH BIBLE

11 My child, treat yourself well, according to your means,
    and present worthy offerings to the Lord.

12 Remember that death does not tarry,
    and the decree[t] of Hades has not been shown to you.

13 Do good to friends before you die,
    and reach out and give to them as much as you can.

14 Do not deprive yourself of a day's enjoyment;
    do not let your share of desired good pass by you.

15 Will you not leave the fruit of your labors to another,
    and what you acquired by toil to be divided by lot?

16 Give, and take, and indulge yourself,
    because in Hades one cannot look for luxury.

17 All living beings become old like a garment,
    for the decree[u] from of old is, "You must die!"

18 Like abundant leaves on a spreading tree
    that sheds some and puts forth others,
so are the generations of flesh and blood:
    one dies and another is born.

19 Every work decays and ceases to exist,
    and the one who made it will pass away with it.

20 Happy is the person who meditates on[v] wisdom
    and reasons intelligently,

21 who[w] reflects in his heart on her ways
    and ponders her secrets,

22 pursuing her like a hunter,
    and lying in wait on her paths;

23 who peers through her windows
    and listens at her doors;

24 who camps near her house
    and fastens his tent peg to her walls;

25 who pitches his tent near her,
    and so occupies an excellent lodging place;

26 who places his children under her shelter,
    and lodges under her boughs;

27 who is sheltered by her from the heat,
    and dwells in the midst of her glory.

15

Whoever fears the Lord will do this,
    and whoever holds to the law will obtain wisdom.[x]

2 She will come to meet him like a mother,
    and like a young bride she will welcome him.

3 She will feed him with the bread of learning,
    and give him the water of wisdom to drink.

4 He will lean on her and not fall,
    and he will rely on her and not be put to shame.

5 She will exalt him above his neighbors,
    and will open his mouth in the midst of the assembly.

6 He will find gladness and a crown of rejoicing,
    and will inherit an everlasting name.

7 The foolish will not obtain her,
    and sinners will not see her.

8 She is far from arrogance,
    and liars will never think of her.

9 Praise is unseemly on the lips of a sinner,
    for it has not been sent from the Lord.

---

11 My son, treat yourself well if you can afford it,
    and present worthy sacrifices to the Lord.

12 Remember that death will not tarry;
    the hour of your appointment with the grave is undisclosed.

13 Before you die, treat your friend well;
    reach out as far as you can to help him.

14 Do not miss a day's enjoyment
    or forgo your share of innocent pleasure.

15 Are you to leave to others all you have laboured for
    and let them draw lots for your hard-earned wealth?

16 Give and take; pamper yourself,
    expect no luxury in the grave.

17 The body wears out like a garment;
    for the age-old sentence stands: you shall die.

18 In the thick foliage of a spreading tree
    some leaves fall and others grow in their stead;
so too with the generations of flesh and blood;
    one dies and another comes to birth.

19 All human works decay and vanish,
    and the worker follows them into oblivion.

20 HAPPY is he who gives his mind to wisdom
    and meditates on understanding;

21 happy is he who reflects on her ways
    and ponders her secrets!

22 Stalk her like a hunter
    and lie in wait by her paths.

23 He who peeps in at her window
    and listens at her door,

24 who camps beside her house,
    driving his tent-peg into her wall,

25 who pitches his tent close by her,
    having found a good place to live—

26 that man will put his children under her shade
    and camp beneath her branches;

27 sheltered by her from the heat,
    he will dwell in her glory.

15

He who fears the Lord will act thus,
    and if he masters the law, wisdom will be his.

2 She will come out to meet him like a mother;
    she will receive him like a young bride.

3 For food she will give him the bread of understanding
    and for drink the water of wisdom.

4 He will lean on her and will not fall,
    he will rely on her and not be put to shame.

5 She will advance him above his neighbours
    and find words for him when he speaks in the assembly.

6 He will be crowned with joy and exultation;
    lasting renown will be his heritage from her.

7 Fools will never possess wisdom,
    nor will sinners catch a glimpse of her.

8 She holds aloof from arrogance;
    liars never call her to mind.

9 Praise is out of place on the lips of a sinner,
    because it has not come from the Lord;

---

t Heb Syr: Gk *covenant*   u Heb: Gk *covenant*   v Other ancient authorities read *dies in*   w The structure adopted in verses 21-27 follows the Heb   x Gk *her*

NEW AMERICAN BIBLE

NEW JERUSALEM BIBLE

11 My son, use freely whatever you have
and enjoy it as best you can;
12 Remember that death does not tarry,
nor have you been told the grave's
appointed time.
13 Before you die, be good to your friend,
and give him a share in what you possess.
14 Deprive not yourself of present good things,
let no choice portion escape you.
15 Will you not leave your riches to others,
and your earnings to be divided by lot?
16 Give, take, and treat yourself well,
for in the nether world there are no joys to seek.
17 All flesh grows old, like a garment;
the age-old law is: All must die.
18 As with the leaves that grow on a vigorous tree:
one falls off and another sprouts —
So with the generations of flesh and blood:
one dies and another is born.
19 All man's works will perish in decay,
and his handiwork will follow after him.

20 Happy the man who meditates on wisdom,
and reflects on knowledge;
21 Who ponders her ways in his heart,
and understands her paths;
22 Who pursues her like a scout,
and lies in wait at her entry way;
23 Who peeps through her windows,
and listens at her doors;
24 Who encamps near her house,
and fastens his tent pegs next to her walls;
25 Who pitches his tent beside her,
and lives as her welcome neighbor;
26 Who builds his nest in her leafage,
and lodges in her branches;
27 Who takes shelter with her from the heat,
and dwells in her home.

11 My child, treat yourself as well as you can afford,
and bring worthy offerings to the Lord.
12 Remember that death will not delay,
and that you have never seen Sheol's contract.
13 Be kind to your friend before you die,
treat him as generously as you can afford.
14 Do not refuse yourself the good things of today,
do not let your share of what is lawfully desired
pass you by.
15 Will you not have to leave your fortune to another,
and the fruit of your labour to be divided by lot?
16 Give and receive, enjoy yourself —
there are no pleasures to be found in Sheol.
17 Like clothes, every body will wear out,
the age-old law is, 'Everyone must die.'
18 Like foliage growing on a bushy tree,
some leaves falling, others growing,
so are the generations of flesh and blood:
one dies, another is born.
19 Every achievement rots away and perishes,
and with it goes its author.

20 Blessed is anyone who meditates on wisdom,
and reasons with intelligence,
21 who studies her ways in his heart,
and ponders her secrets.
22 He pursues her like a hunter,
and lies in wait by her path;
23 he peeps in at her windows,
and listens at her doors;
24 he lodges close to her house,
and fixes his peg in her walls;
25 he pitches his tent at her side,
and lodges in an excellent lodging;
26 he sets his children in her shade,
and camps beneath her branches;
27 he is sheltered by her from the heat,
and in her glory he makes his home.

15 He who fears the LORD will do this;
he who is practiced in the law will come
to wisdom.
2 Motherlike she will meet him,
like a young bride she will embrace him,
3 Nourish him with the bread of understanding,
and give him the water of learning to drink.
4 He will lean upon her and not fall,
he will trust in her and not be put to shame.
5 She will exalt him above his fellows;
in the assembly she will make him eloquent.
6 Joy and gladness he will find,
an everlasting name inherit.
7 Worthless men will not attain to her,
haughty men will not behold her.
8 Far from the impious is she,
not to be spoken of by liars.
9 Unseemly is praise on a sinner's lips,
for it is not accorded to him by God.

15 Whoever fears the Lord will act like this,
and whoever grasps the Law will obtain
wisdom.
2 She will come to meet him like a mother,
and receive him like a virgin bride.
3 She will give him the bread of understanding to
eat,
and the water of wisdom to drink.
4 He will lean on her and will not fall,
he will rely on her and not be put to shame.
5 She will raise him high above his neighbours,
and in full assembly she will open his mouth.
6 He will find happiness and a crown of joy,
he will inherit an everlasting name.
7 Fools will not gain possession of her,
nor will sinners set eyes on her.
8 She stands remote from pride,
and liars cannot call her to mind.
9 Praise is unseemly in a sinner's mouth,
since it has not been put there by the Lord.

10 For in wisdom must praise be uttered,
  and the Lord will make it prosper.
11 Do not say, "It was the Lord's doing that I fell
    away";
  for he does not do *y* what he hates.
12 Do not say, "It was he who led me astray";
  for he has no need of the sinful.
13 The Lord hates all abominations;
  such things are not loved by those who fear
    him.
14 It was he who created humankind in the
    beginning,
  and he left them in the power of their own free
    choice.
15 If you choose, you can keep the commandments,
  and to act faithfully is a matter of your own
    choice.
16 He has placed before you fire and water;
  stretch out your hand for whichever you
    choose.
17 Before each person are life and death,
  and whichever one chooses will be given.
18 For great is the wisdom of the Lord;
  he is mighty in power and sees everything;
19 his eyes are on those who fear him,
  and he knows every human action.
20 He has not commanded anyone to be wicked,
  and he has not given anyone permission to sin.

16 Do not desire a multitude of worthless *z* children,
  and do not rejoice in ungodly offspring.
2 If they multiply, do not rejoice in them,
  unless the fear of the Lord is in them.
3 Do not trust in their survival,
  or rely on their numbers; *a*
  for one can be better than a thousand,
  and to die childless better than to have ungodly
    children.
4 For through one intelligent person a city can be
    filled with people,
  but through a clan of outlaws it becomes
    desolate.
5 Many such things my eye has seen,
  and my ear has heard things more striking than
    these.
6 In an assembly of sinners a fire is kindled,
  and in a disobedient nation wrath blazes up.
7 He did not forgive the ancient giants
  who revolted in their might.
8 He did not spare the neighbors of Lot,
  whom he loathed on account of their
    arrogance.
9 He showed no pity on the doomed nation,
  on those dispossessed because of their sins; *b*
10 or on the six hundred thousand foot soldiers
  who assembled in their stubbornness. *c*
11 Even if there were only one stiff-necked person,
  it would be a wonder if he remained
    unpunished.
  For mercy and wrath are with the Lord; *d*
  he is mighty to forgive—but he also pours out
    wrath.

10 for praise is the outward expression of wisdom,
  and the Lord himself prompts it.
11 Do not say, 'The Lord is to blame for my going
    astray';
  it is for you to avoid what he hates.
12 Do not say, 'It was he who led me into error';
  he has no use for a sinner.
13 The Lord hates every kind of vice;
  you cannot love vice and still fear him.
14 When in the beginning God created the human
    race,
  he left them free to take their own decisions:
15 if you choose, you can observe the
    commandments;
  you can keep faith if you are so minded.
16 He has set before you fire and water:
  reach out and make your choice.
17 Mortals are offered life or death:
  whichever they prefer will be given them.
18 For great is the wisdom of the Lord;
  he is mighty in power, all-seeing;
19 his eyes are on those who fear him;
  no human action escapes his notice.
20 He has commanded no one to be impious;
  to none has he given licence to sin.

16 DO NOT set your heart on a large family of
  ne'er-do-wells
  or think yourself happy in sons who are godless.
2 However many your children, do not think yourself
    happy
  unless the fear of the Lord is in them.
3 Do not count on their living to be old
  or rely on their number,
  for one son can be better than a thousand.
  Better indeed to die childless than to have ungodly
    children!
4 One person of good sense can establish a city,
  but a tribe of lawless people can turn it into a
    desert.
5 Many such things have I seen with my own eyes,
  and still weightier examples have come to my ears.
6 Where sinners assemble, fire breaks out;
  retribution blazes up when a nation is disobedient.
7 There was no pardon for the giants of old,
  who rebelled in all their strength.
8 There was no reprieve for Lot's adopted home,
  abhorrent in its arrogance.
9 There was no mercy for the doomed nation,
  exterminated in its sin,
10 and no mercy for those six hundred thousand
    warriors
  assembled in stubborn defiance.
11 Even if there were but one stubborn person,
  it would be a miracle for him to escape
    punishment,
  for mercy and anger belong to the Lord:
  he shows his power now in forgiveness, now in
    overflowing anger.

---

y Heb: Gk *you ought not do*　*z* Heb: Gk *unprofitable*　*a* Other
ancient authorities add *For you will groan in untimely mourning, and
will know of their sudden end.*　*b* Other ancient authorities add *All
these things he did to the hard-hearted nations, and by the multitude
of his holy ones he was not appeased.*　*c* Other ancient authorities
add *Chastising, showing mercy, striking, healing, the Lord persisted
in mercy and discipline.*　*d* Gk *him*

|

10 But praise is offered by the wise man's tongue;
    its rightful steward will proclaim it.

11 Say not: "It was God's doing that I fell away";
    for what he hates he does not do.

12 Say not: "It was he who set me astray";
    for he has no need of wicked man.

13 Abominable wickedness the LORD hates,
    he does not let it befall those who fear him.

14 When God, in the beginning, created man,
    he made him subject to his own free choice.

15 If you choose you can keep the commandments;
    it is loyalty to do his will.

16 There are set before you fire and water;
    to whichever you choose, stretch forth
        your hand.

17 Before man are life and death,
    whichever he chooses shall be given him.

18 Immense is the wisdom of the LORD;
    he is mighty in power, and all-seeing.

19 The eyes of God see all he has made;
    he understands man's every deed.

20 No man does he command to sin,
    to none does he give strength for lies.

10 For praise should be uttered only in wisdom,
    and the Lord himself then prompts it.

11 Do not say, 'The Lord was responsible for my
        sinning,'
    for he does not do what he hates.

12 Do not say, 'It was he who led me astray,'
    for he has no use for a sinner.

13 The Lord hates all that is foul,
    and no one who fears him will love it either.

14 He himself made human beings in the beginning,
    and then left them free to make their own
        decisions.

15 If you choose, you will keep the commandments
    and so be faithful to his will.

16 He has set fire and water before you;
    put out your hand to whichever you prefer.

17 A human being has life and death before him;
    whichever he prefers will be given him.

18 For vast is the wisdom of the Lord;
    he is almighty and all-seeing.

19 His eyes are on those who fear him,
    he notes every human action.

20 He never commanded anyone to be godless,
    he has given no one permission to sin.

16 Desire not a brood of worthless children,
    nor rejoice in wicked offspring.

2 Many though they be, exult not in them
    if they have not the fear of the LORD.

3 Count not on their length of life,
    have no hope in their future.
  For one can be better than a thousand;
    rather die childless than have godless children!

4 Through one wise man can a city be peopled;
    through a clan of rebels it becomes desolate.

5 Many such things has my eye seen,
    even more than these has my ear heard.

6 Against a sinful band fire is enkindled,
    upon a godless people wrath flames out.

7 He forgave not the leaders of old
    who rebelled long ago in their might;

8 He spared not the neighbors of Lot
    whom he detested for their pride;

9 Nor did he spare the doomed people
    who were uprooted because of their sin;

10 Nor the six hundred thousand foot soldiers
    who perished for the impiety of their hearts.

11 And had there been but one stiffnecked man,
    it were a wonder had he gone unpunished.
  For mercy and anger alike are with him
    who remits and forgives, though on the wicked
        alights his wrath.

16 Do not long for a brood of worthless children,
    and do not take pleasure in godless sons.

2 However many you have, take no pleasure in
        them,
    unless the fear of the Lord lives among them.

3 Do not count on their having long life,
    do not put too much faith in their number;
  for better have one than a thousand,
    better die childless than have children who are
        godless.

4 One person of sense can populate a city,
    but a race of lawless people will be destroyed.

5 My eyes have seen many such things,
    my ears have heard things even more
        impressive.

6 Fire is kindled in a sinful society,
    Retribution blazes in a rebellious nation.

7 God did not pardon the giants of old
    who, confident in their strength, had rebelled.

8 He did not spare the people with whom Lot lived;
    he abhorred them, rather, for their pride.

9 He was pitiless to the nation of perdition —
    those people who gloried in their sins —

10 as also to the six hundred thousand men on the
        march,
    who had banded together in their obstinacy.

11 And had there been only one man stubborn,
    it would have been amazing had he escaped
        unpunished,
  since mercy and wrath alike belong to the Lord
    who is mighty to forgive and to pour out wrath.

NEW REVISED STANDARD VERSION	REVISED ENGLISH BIBLE

12 Great as his mercy, so also is his chastisement;
   he judges a person according to one's deeds.
13 The sinner will not escape with plunder,
   and the patience of the godly will not be
      frustrated.
14 He makes room for every act of mercy;
   everyone receives in accordance with one's
      deeds.*e*

17 Do not say, "I am hidden from the Lord,
   and who from on high has me in mind?
   Among so many people I am unknown,
   for what am I in a boundless creation?
18 Lo, heaven and the highest heaven,
   the abyss and the earth, tremble at his
      visitation!*f*
19 The very mountains and the foundations of the
      earth
   quiver and quake when he looks upon them.
20 But no human mind can grasp this,
   and who can comprehend his ways?
21 Like a tempest that no one can see,
   so most of his works are concealed.*g*
22 Who is to announce his acts of justice?
   Or who can await them? For his decree*h* is far
      off."*i*
23 Such are the thoughts of one devoid of
      understanding;
   a senseless and misguided person thinks
      foolishly.

24 Listen to me, my child, and acquire knowledge,
   and pay close attention to my words.
25 I will impart discipline precisely*j*
   and declare knowledge accurately.

26 When the Lord created*k* his works from the
      beginning,
   and, in making them, determined their
      boundaries,
27 he arranged his works in an eternal order,
   and their dominion*l* for all generations.
   They neither hunger nor grow weary,
   and they do not abandon their tasks.
28 They do not crowd one another,
   and they never disobey his word.
29 Then the Lord looked upon the earth,
   and filled it with his good things.
30 With all kinds of living beings he covered its
      surface,
   and into it they must return.

17 The Lord created human beings out of earth,
   and makes them return to it again.
2 He gave them a fixed number of days,
   but granted them authority over everything on
      the earth.*m*
3 He endowed them with strength like his own,*n*
   and made them in his own image.
4 He put the fear of them*o* in all living beings,

12 His mercy is great, but great also his
      condemnation;
   he judges each by what he has done.
13 He does not let the wrongdoer escape with his
      plunder
   or try the patience of the godly too long.
14 He gives scope freely to his mercy,
   and everyone is treated according to his deeds.

17 Do not say, 'I am hidden from the Lord;
   who is there up above to give a thought to me?
   Among so many I shall not be noticed;
   what am I in the immensity of creation?'
18 Heaven itself, the highest heaven,
   the abyss, and the earth are shaken at his coming;
19 the mountains also and the foundations of the
      world
   quiver and tremble when he looks upon them.
20 What mortal mind can grasp this
   or comprehend his ways?
21 As a squall takes people unawares,
   so his works for the most part are done in secret.
22 'Who is to declare his acts of justice
   or who will wait for them,
   their fulfilment being so remote?'
23 These are the thoughts of a small mind,
   the absurdities of a senseless and misguided
      person.

24 My son, listen to me and acquire knowledge;
   pay heed to what I say.
25 I will offer you correct instruction
   and teach you accurate knowledge.
26 When in the beginning the Lord created his works
   and, after making them, defined their boundaries,
27 he disposed them in an eternal order
   and fixed their domains for all time.
   They do not grow hungry or weary,
   or abandon their tasks;
28 one does not jostle another,
   nor will they ever disobey his word.
29 Then the Lord looked at the earth
   and filled it with his good things.
30 With every kind of living creature he covered its
      surface,
   and to the earth they must all return.

17 The Lord created human beings from the earth
   and to it he turns them back again.
2 He set a fixed span of life for mortals
   and gave them authority over everything on earth.
3 He clothed them with power like his own
   and made them in his own image.
4 He put the fear of them into all creatures

---

e Other ancient authorities add *15The Lord hardened Pharaoh so that
he did not recognize him, in order that his works might be known
under heaven. 16His mercy is manifest to the whole of creation, and
he divided his light and darkness with a plumb line.*   *f* Other
ancient authorities add *The whole world past and present is in his
will.*   *g* Meaning of Gk uncertain: Heb Syr *If I sin, no eye can see
me, and if I am disloyal in all secret, who is to know?*   *h* Heb *the
decree:* Gk *the covenant*   *i* Other ancient authorities add *and a
scrutiny for all comes at the end*   *j* Gk *by weight*   *k* Heb: Gk
judged   *l* Or *elements*   *m* Lat: Gk *it*   *n* Lat: Gk *proper to them*
o Syr: Gk *him*

16:14 **his deeds:** *some witnesses add* 15The Lord made Pharaoh too
stubborn to acknowledge him, so that his deeds might be published to
the world. 16He displays his mercy to the whole creation, and has
assigned his light and his darkness for human beings.

NEW AMERICAN BIBLE

12 Great as his mercy is his punishment;
   he judges men, each according to his deeds.
13 A criminal does not escape with his plunder;
   a just man's hope God does not
       leave unfulfilled.
14 Whoever does good has his reward,
   which each receives according to his deeds.
15 Say not: "I am hidden from God;
   in heaven who remembers me?
   Among so many people I cannot be known;
   what am I in the world of spirits?
16 Behold, the heavens, the heaven of heavens,
   the earth and the abyss tremble at his visitation;
17 The roots of the mountains, the
       earth's foundations,
   at his mere glance, quiver and quake.
18 Of me, therefore, he will take no thought;
   with my ways who will concern himself?
19 If I sin, no eye will see me;
   if all in secret I am disloyal, who is to know?
20 Who tells him of just deeds
   and what could I expect for doing my duty?"
21 Such are the thoughts of senseless men,
   which only the foolish knave will think.

22 Hearken to me, my son, take my advice,
   apply your mind to my words,
23 While I propose measured wisdom,
   and impart accurate knowledge.
24 When at the first God created his works
   and, as he made them, assigned their tasks,
25 He ordered for all time what they were to do
   and their domains from generation to generation.
   They were not to hunger, nor grow weary,
   nor ever cease from their tasks.
26 Not one should ever crowd its neighbor,
   nor should they ever disobey his word.
27 Then the LORD looked upon the earth,
   and filled it with his blessings.
28 Its surface he covered with all manner of life
   which must return into it again.

17 The LORD from the earth created man,
   and in his own image he made him.
2 Limited days of life he gives him
   and makes him return to earth again.
3 He endows man with a strength of his own,
   and with power over all things else on earth.
4 He puts the fear of him in all flesh,

NEW JERUSALEM BIBLE

12 As great as his mercy, so is his severity;
   he judges each person as his deeds deserve:
13 the sinner will not escape with his ill-gotten gains
   nor the patience of the devout go for nothing.
14 He takes note of every charitable action,
   and everyone is treated as he deserves.

17 Do not say, 'I shall hide from the Lord;
   who is going to remember me up there?
   I shall not be noticed among so many people;
   what am I in the immensity of creation?'
18 For see, the sky and the heavens above the sky,
   the abyss and the earth shake at his visitation.
19 The mountains and earth's foundations alike
   quail and tremble when he looks at them.
20 But to all this no one gives thought.
   Who keeps his movements in mind?
21 The storm wind itself is invisible,
   and most of what he does goes undetected.
22 'Who will report whether justice has been done?
   Who will be watching? The covenant is remote!'
23 Such are the thoughts of the person of little sense,
   stupid, misguided, cherishing his folly.

24 Listen to me, my child, and learn knowledge,
   and give your whole mind to my words.
25 I shall expound discipline methodically
   and proclaim knowledge with precision.
26 When God created his works in the beginning,
   he assigned them their places as soon as they
       were made.
27 He determined his works for all time,
   from their origins to their distant generations.
   They know neither hunger nor weariness,
   and they never desert their duties.
28 Not one has ever got in the way of another,
   and they will never disobey his word.
29 And afterwards the Lord looked at the earth,
   and filled it with his good things.
30 He covered its surface with every kind of animal,
   and to it they will return.

17 The Lord fashioned human beings from the
       earth,
   to consign them back to it.
2 He gave them so many days and so much time,
   he gave them authority over everything on earth.
3 He clothed them in strength, like himself,
   and made them in his own image.
4 He filled all living things with dread of human
       beings,

NEW REVISED STANDARD VERSION	REVISED ENGLISH BIBLE

and gave them dominion over beasts and
 birds. *p*

6 Discretion and tongue and eyes,
 ears and a mind for thinking he gave them.

7 He filled them with knowledge and
  understanding,
 and showed them good and evil.

8 He put the fear of him into *q* their hearts
 to show them the majesty of his works. *r*

10 And they will praise his holy name,

9 to proclaim the grandeur of his works.

11 He bestowed knowledge upon them,
 and allotted to them the law of life. *s*

12 He established with them an eternal covenant,
 and revealed to them his decrees.

13 Their eyes saw his glorious majesty,
 and their ears heard the glory of his voice.

14 He said to them, "Beware of all evil."
 And he gave commandment to each of them
  concerning the neighbor.

15 Their ways are always known to him;
 they will not be hid from his eyes. *t*

17 He appointed a ruler for every nation,
 but Israel is the Lord's own portion. *u*

19 All their works are as clear as the sun before
  him,
 and his eyes are ever upon their ways.

20 Their iniquities are not hidden from him,
 and all their sins are before the Lord. *v*

22 One's almsgiving is like a signet ring with the
  Lord, *w*
 and he will keep a person's kindness like the
  apple of his eye. *x*

23 Afterward he will rise up and repay them,
 and he will bring their recompense on their
  heads.

24 Yet to those who repent he grants a return,
 and he encourages those who are losing hope.

25 Turn back to the Lord and forsake your sins;
 pray in his presence and lessen your offense.

26 Return to the Most High and turn away from
  iniquity, *y*
 and hate intensely what he abhors.

27 Who will sing praises to the Most High in Hades
 in place of the living who give thanks?

28 From the dead, as from one who does not exist,
 thanksgiving has ceased;
 those who are alive and well sing the Lord's
  praises.

29 How great is the mercy of the Lord,
 and his forgiveness for those who return to
  him!

and granted them lordship over beasts and birds.

6 He fashioned tongues, eyes, and ears for them,
 and gave them minds with which to think.

7 He filled them with understanding and knowledge
 and showed them good and evil.

8 He kept watch over their hearts,
 to display to them the majesty of his works.

10 They will praise his holy name,
 proclaiming the grandeur of his works.

11 He gave them knowledge
 and endowed them with the life-bringing law.

12 He established with them an everlasting covenant
 and revealed to them his decrees.

13 Their eyes saw his glorious majesty,
 and their ears heard the glory of his voice.

14 He said to them, 'Refrain from all wrongdoing,'
 and he taught each his duty towards his neighbour.

15 Their conduct lies open before him at all times,
 never hidden from his sight.

17 For every nation he appointed a ruler,
 but Israel is the Lord's portion.

19 Whatever they do is as clear as the sun to him;
 his eyes are always on their ways.

20 Their misdeeds are not hidden from the Lord;
 he observes all their sins.

22 Charitable giving he treasures like a signet ring,
 and kindness like the apple of his eye.

23 In the end he will arise and give the wicked their
  deserts,
 bringing down retribution on their heads.

24 Yet he leaves a way open for the penitent to return
  to him
 and endows the waverer with strength to endure.

25 Return to the Lord and have done with sin;
 make your prayer in his presence and lessen your
  offence.

26 Come back to the Most High, renounce
  wrongdoing,
 and hate intensely what he abhors.

27 The living give him thanks,
 but who will praise the Most High from the grave?

28 When the dead cease to be, their gratitude dies
  with them;
 only when alive and well do they praise the Lord.

29 How great is the Lord's mercy
 and his forgiveness to those who turn to him!

---

p Other ancient authorities add as verse 5, *They obtained the use of
the five faculties of the Lord; as sixth he distributed to them the gift
of mind, and as seventh, reason, the interpreter of one's faculties.*
q Other ancient authorities read *He set his eye upon*   *r* Other ancient
authorities add *and he gave them to boast of his marvels forever*
s Other ancient authorities add *so that they may know that they who
are alive now are mortal*   *t* Other ancient authorities add *16 Their
ways from youth tend toward evil, and they are unable to make for
themselves hearts of flesh in place of their stony hearts. 17 For in the
division of the nations of the whole earth, he appointed*   *u* Other
ancient authorities add as verse 18, *whom, being his firstborn, he
brings up with discipline, and allotting to him the light of his love, he
does not neglect him.*   *v* Other ancient authorities add as verse 21,
But the Lord, who is gracious and knows how they are formed, has
neither left them nor abandoned them, but has spared them.*
w Gk *him*   *x* Other ancient authorities add *apportioning repentance
to his sons and daughters*   *y* Other ancient authorities add *for he
will lead you out of darkness to the light of health.*

17:4 **beasts and birds:** *some witnesses add* 5 The Lord gave them the
use of the five faculties; as a sixth gift he assigned to them mind, and
as a seventh, reason, the interpreter of those faculties.   17:8 **his
works:** *some witnesses add* 9 To them it is given to boast for ever of
his marvels.   17:15–17 **his sight . . . nation:** *some witnesses read*
his sight. 16 Everyone from his youth tended towards evil; they could
not make themselves hearts of flesh in place of their hearts of stone.
17 When he dispersed the nations over all the earth, for every nation.
17:17 **portion:** *some witnesses add* 18 He rears them with discipline as
his firstborn, imparting to them the light of love and never neglecting
them.   17:20 **their sins:** *some witnesses add* 21 The Lord who is
gracious and knows of what they are made has neither rejected nor
deserted them, but spared them.

and gives him rule over beasts and birds.
5 He forms men's tongues and eyes and ears,
  and imparts to them an understanding heart.
6 With wisdom and knowledge he fills them;
  good and evil he shows them.
7 He looks with favor upon their hearts,
  and shows them his glorious works,
8 That they may describe the wonders of his deeds
  and praise his holy name.
9 He has set before them knowledge,
  a law of life as their inheritance;
10 An everlasting covenant he has made with them,
  his commandments he has revealed to them.
11 His majestic glory their eyes beheld,
  his glorious voice their ears heard.
12 He says to them, "Avoid all evil";
  each of them he gives precepts about his
    fellow men.
13 Their ways are ever known to him,
  they cannot be hidden from his eyes.
14 Over every nation he places a ruler,
  but the LORD's own portion is Israel.
15 All their actions are clear as the sun to him,
  his eyes are ever upon their ways.
16 Their wickedness cannot be hidden from him;
  all of their sins are before the LORD.
17 A man's goodness God cherishes like a signet ring,
  a man's virtue, like the apple of his eye.
18 Later he will rise up and repay them,
  and requite each one of them as they deserve.
19 But to the penitent he provides a way back,
  he encourages those who are losing hope!
20 Return to the LORD and give up sin,
  pray to him and make your offenses few.
21 Turn again to the Most High and away from sin,
  hate intensely what he loathes;
22 Who in the nether world can glorify the Most High
  in place of the living who offer their praise?
23 No more can the dead give praise than those who
    have never lived;
  they glorify the LORD who are alive and well.
24 How great the mercy of the LORD,
  his forgiveness of those who return to him!

making them masters over beasts and birds.
6 He made them a tongue, eyes and ears,
  and gave them a heart to think with.
7 He filled them with knowledge and intelligence,
  and showed them what was good and what evil.
8 He put his own light in their hearts
  to show them the magnificence of his works,
10 so that they would praise his holy name
  as they told of his magnificent works.
11 He set knowledge before them,
  he endowed them with the law of life.
12 He established an eternal covenant with them,
  and revealed his judgements to them.
13 Their eyes saw the majesty of his glory,
  and their ears heard the glory of his voice.
14 He said to them, 'Beware of all wrong-doing';
  he gave each a commandment concerning his
    neighbour.
15 Their ways are always under his eye,
  they cannot be hidden from his sight.
17 Over each nation he has set a governor,
  but Israel is the Lord's own portion.
19 Their actions are all as plain as the sun to him,
  and his eyes rest constantly on their conduct.
20 Their iniquities are not hidden from him,
  all their sins are before the Lord.
22 Almsgiving is like a signet ring to him,
  he cherishes generosity like the pupil of an eye.
23 One day he will rise and reward them,
  he will repay their deserts on their own heads.
24 But to those who repent he permits return,
  and he encourages those who have lost hope.
25 Return to the Lord and renounce your sins,
  plead before his face, stop offending him.
26 Come back to the Most High, turn away from
    iniquity
  and hold all that is foul in abhorrence.
27 Who is going to praise the Most High in Sheol
  if we do not glorify him while we are alive?
28 The dead can praise no more than those who do
    not exist,
  only those with life and health can praise the
    Lord.
29 How great is the mercy of the Lord,
  his pardon for those who turn to him!

NEW REVISED STANDARD VERSION	REVISED ENGLISH BIBLE

NEW REVISED STANDARD VERSION

30 For not everything is within human capability,
  since human beings are not immortal.
31 What is brighter than the sun? Yet it can be
  eclipsed.
  So flesh and blood devise evil.
32 He marshals the host of the height of heaven;
  but all human beings are dust and ashes.

18 He who lives forever created the whole universe;
2   the Lord alone is just. *z*
4 To none has he given power to proclaim his
  works;
  and who can search out his mighty deeds?
5 Who can measure his majestic power?
  And who can fully recount his mercies?
6 It is not possible to diminish or increase them,
  nor is it possible to fathom the wonders of the
  Lord.
7 When human beings have finished, they are just
  beginning,
  and when they stop, they are still perplexed.
8 What are human beings, and of what use are
  they?
  What is good in them, and what is evil?
9 The number of days in their life is great if they
  reach one hundred years. *a*
10 Like a drop of water from the sea and a grain of
  sand,
  so are a few years among the days of eternity.
11 That is why the Lord is patient with them
  and pours out his mercy upon them.
12 He sees and recognizes that their end is
  miserable;
  therefore he grants them forgiveness all the
  more.
13 The compassion of human beings is for their
  neighbors,
  but the compassion of the Lord is for every
  living thing.
  He rebukes and trains and teaches them,
  and turns them back, as a shepherd his flock.
14 He has compassion on those who accept his
  discipline
  and who are eager for his precepts.
15 My child, do not mix reproach with your good
  deeds,
  or spoil your gift by harsh words.
16 Does not the dew give relief from the scorching
  heat?
  So a word is better than a gift.
17 Indeed, does not a word surpass a good gift?
  Both are to be found in a gracious person.
18 A fool is ungracious and abusive,
  and the gift of a grudging giver makes the eyes
  dim.
19 Before you speak, learn;
  and before you fall ill, take care of your
  health.
20 Before judgment comes, examine yourself;
  and at the time of scrutiny you will find
  forgiveness.
21 Before falling ill, humble yourself;
  and when you have sinned, repent.

REVISED ENGLISH BIBLE

30 Not everything is within human reach,
  for we are not immortal.
31 Is anything brighter than the sun? Yet it suffers
  eclipse;
  so flesh and blood have evil thoughts.
32 The Lord judges the armies of high heaven,
  and humankind, who are but dust and ashes.

18 He who lives for ever is the Creator of the whole
  universe;
2 the Lord alone will be proved supreme.
4 To whom is it given to unfold the story of his
  works?
  Who can fathom his mighty acts?
5 No one can measure his majestic power,
  still less tell the full tale of his mercies.
6 They can neither be diminished nor increased,
  and the wonders of the Lord cannot be fathomed.
7 When anyone finishes he is still only beginning,
  and when he stops he will still be at a loss.
8 What is a human being, and what use is he?
  His good or evil deeds, what do they signify?
9 His span of life is at the most a hundred years;
10 compared with unending time, his few years
  are like one drop from the ocean or a single grain
  of sand.
11 That is why the Lord is patient with people;
  that is why he lavishes his mercy upon them.
12 He sees and knows the harsh fate in store for
  them,
  and therefore gives full play to his forgiveness.
13 Their compassion is only for their own kin,
  but the Lord's compassion is for all mankind.
  He corrects, disciplines and teaches,
  and brings them back as a shepherd brings his
  flock.
14 He has compassion on those who accept discipline
  and are eager to obey his decrees.
15 Do GOOD, my son, but without scolding;
  do not spoil your generosity with hurtful words.
16 Does not the dew give respite from the scorching
  heat?
  So a word can do more than a gift.
17 Does not a kind word count for more than a rich
  present?
  With someone gracious you will find both.
18 A graceless fool must always be taunting,
  and a grudging giver makes no eyes sparkle.
19 Before you speak, learn;
  before sickness comes, attend to your health.
20 Before judgement, examine yourself,
  and you will find pardon in your hour of trial.
21 Before you fall ill, humble yourself;
  whenever you sin, show your penitence.

---

z Other ancient authorities add *and there is no other beside him;* *3he steers the world with the span of his hand, and all things obey his will; for he is king of all things by his power, separating among them the holy things from the profane.* *a* Other ancient authorities add *but the death of each one is beyond the calculation of all*

17:32 The Lord . . . ashes: *so Syriac.* **18:2 proved supreme:** *some witnesses add* and there is none beside him *3*who can steer the world with a touch of his hand, so that all things obey his will; as King of the universe, he has power to fix the bounds between what is holy and what is profane.

25 The like cannot be found in men,
   for not immortal is any son of man.
26 Is anything brighter than the sun? Yet it can
      be eclipsed.
   How obscure then the thoughts of flesh and blood!
27 God watches over the hosts of highest heaven,
   while all men are dust and ashes.

18 The Eternal is the judge of all things
         without exception;
   the LORD alone is just.
2 Whom has he made equal to describing his works,
   and who can probe his mighty deeds?
3 Who can measure his majestic power,
   or exhaust the tale of his mercies?
4 One cannot lessen, nor increase,
   nor penetrate the wonders of the LORD.
5 When a man ends he is only beginning,
   and when he stops he is still bewildered.
6 What is man, of what worth is he?
   the good, the evil in him, what are these?
7 The sum of a man's days is great
   if it reaches a hundred years:
8 Like a drop of sea water, like a grain of sand,
   so are these few years among the days
      of eternity.
9 That is why the LORD is patient with men
   and showers upon them his mercy.
10 He sees and understands that their death
      is grievous,
   and so he forgives them all the more.
11 Man may be merciful to his fellow man,
   but the LORD's mercy reaches all flesh,
12 Reproving, admonishing, teaching,
   as a shepherd guides his flock;
13 Merciful to those who accept his guidance,
   who are diligent in his precepts.

14 My son, to your charity add no reproach,
   nor spoil any gift by harsh words.
15 Like dew that abates a burning wind,
   so does a word improve a gift.
16 Sometimes the word means more than the gift;
   both are offered by a kindly man.
17 Only a fool upbraids before giving;
   a grudging gift wears out the expectant eyes.
18 Be informed before speaking;
   before sickness prepare the cure.
19 Before you are judged, seek merit for yourself,
   and at the time of visitation you will have
      a ransom.
20 Before you have fallen, humble yourself;
   when you have sinned, show repentance.
21 Delay not to forsake sins,
   neglect it not till you are in distress.

30 For we cannot have everything,
   human beings are not immortal.
31 What is brighter than the sun? And yet it fades.
   Flesh and blood think of nothing but evil.
32 He surveys the armies of the lofty sky,
   and all of us are only dust and ashes.

18 He who lives for ever has created the sum of
         things.
2   The Lord alone will be found just.
4 He has given no one the power to proclaim his
      works to the end,
   and who can fathom his magnificent deeds?
5 Who can assess his magnificent strength,
   and who can go further and tell all of his
      mercies?
6 Nothing can be added to them, nothing subtracted,
   it is impossible to fathom the marvels of the
      Lord.
7 When someone finishes he is only beginning,
   and when he stops he is as puzzled as ever.
8 What is a human being, what purpose does he
      serve?
   What is good and what is bad for him?
9 The length of his life: a hundred years at most.
10 Like a drop of water from the sea, or a grain of
      sand,
   such are these few years compared with eternity.
11 This is why the Lord is patient with them
   and pours out his mercy on them.
12 He sees and recognises how wretched their end is,
   and so he makes his forgiveness the greater.
13 Human compassion extends to neighbours,
   but the Lord's compassion extends to everyone;
   rebuking, correcting and teaching,
   bringing them back as a shepherd brings his
      flock.
14 He has compassion on those who accept correction,
   and who fervently search for his judgements.

15 My child, do not temper your favours with blame
   nor any of your gifts with words that hurt.
16 Does not dew relieve the heat?
   In the same way a word is worth more than a
      gift.
17 Why surely, a word is better than a good present,
   but a generous person is ready with both.
18 A fool will offer nothing but insult,
   and a grudging gift makes the eyes smart.

19 Learn before you speak,
   take care of yourself before you fall ill.
20 Examine yourself before judgement comes,
   and on the day of visitation you will be
      acquitted.
21 Humble yourself before you fall ill,
   repent as soon as the sin is committed.

NEW REVISED STANDARD VERSION	REVISED ENGLISH BIBLE

22 Let nothing hinder you from paying a vow
  promptly,
  and do not wait until death to be released from
  it.
23 Before making a vow, prepare yourself;
  do not be like one who puts the Lord to the
  test.
24 Think of his wrath on the day of death,
  and of the moment of vengeance when he turns
  away his face.
25 In the time of plenty think of the time of hunger;
  in days of wealth think of poverty and need.
26 From morning to evening conditions change;
  all things move swiftly before the Lord.

27 One who is wise is cautious in everything;
  when sin is all around, one guards against
  wrongdoing.
28 Every intelligent person knows wisdom,
  and praises the one who finds her.
29 Those who are skilled in words become wise
  themselves,
  and pour forth apt proverbs. *b*

SELF-CONTROL *c*
30 Do not follow your base desires,
  but restrain your appetites.
31 If you allow your soul to take pleasure in base
  desire,
  it will make you the laughingstock of your
  enemies.
32 Do not revel in great luxury,
  or you may become impoverished by its
  expense.
33 Do not become a beggar by feasting with
  borrowed money,
  when you have nothing in your purse. *d*

19 The one who does this *e* will not become rich;
  one who despises small things will fail little by
  little.
2 Wine and women lead intelligent men astray,
  and the man who consorts with prostitutes is
  reckless.
3 Decay and worms will take possession of him,
  and the reckless person will be snatched away.

4 One who trusts others too quickly has a shallow
  mind,
  and one who sins does wrong to oneself.
5 One who rejoices in wickedness *f* will be
  condemned, *g*
6 but one who hates gossip has less evil.
7 Never repeat a conversation,
  and you will lose nothing at all.
8 With friend or foe do not report it,
  and unless it would be a sin for you, do not
  reveal it;
9 for someone may have heard you and watched
  you,
  and in time will hate you.
10 Have you heard something? Let it die with you.
  Be brave, it will not make you burst!

22 Let nothing hinder the prompt discharge of your
  vows;
  do not wait until death to be absolved.
23 Before you make a vow, give it due thought;
  do not be like those who try the Lord's patience.
24 Think of the wrath you must face in the hour of
  death,
  when the time of reckoning comes and he turns
  away his face.
25 Remember in time of plenty the time of famine,
  poverty and need in your days of wealth.
26 Between dawn and dusk times may alter;
  before the Lord all change comes quickly.
27 The wise are always on their guard;
  when sin is rife they will beware of negligence.
28 Everybody with sense makes acquaintance with
  wisdom,
  and to him who finds her she gives cause for
  thankfulness.
29 They who are trained in learning prove wise
  themselves
  and pour forth apt proverbs.

30 Do not let your passions be your guide;
  keep your lusts under control.
31 If you indulge yourself with all that passion
  fancies,
  it will give your enemies cause to gloat over you.
32 Do not revel in great luxury,
  or the expense of it may ruin you.
33 Squandering and drunkenness
  will leave you with nothing in your purse.

19 A drunken workman will never grow rich;
  carelessness in small things leads by degrees to
  ruin.
2 Wine and women rob the wise of their wits,
  and a frequenter of prostitutes becomes more and
  more reckless;
3 decay and worms take possession of him;
  through his recklessness he is destroyed.

4 To trust anyone hastily shows a shallow mind,
  and to sin is to do oneself an injury.
5 To delight in wickedness is to court condemnation,
6 but evil loses its hold on him who hates gossip.
7 Never repeat what you hear,
  and you will never be the loser.
8 Tell no tales before friend or foe;
  unless silence makes you an accomplice, never
  betray a secret.
9 Suppose someone has heard you and learnt to
  distrust you,
  he will seize a chance to show his hatred.
10 Have you heard a rumour? Let it die with you.
  Never fear, it will not make you burst!

---

b Other ancient authorities add *Better is confidence in the one Lord
than clinging with a dead heart to a dead one.* *c* This heading is
included in the Gk text. *d* Other ancient authorities add *for you
will be plotting against your own life* *e* Heb: Gk *A worker who is
a drunkard* *f* Other ancient authorities read *heart* *g* Other
ancient authorities add *but one who withstands pleasures crowns his
life.* *6 One who controls the tongue will live without strife,*

22 Let nothing prevent the prompt payment of
  your vows;
    wait not to fulfill them when you are dying.
23 Before making a vow have the means to fulfill it;
    be not one who tries the LORD.
24 Think of wrath and the day of death,
    the time of vengeance when he will hide
      his face.
25 Remember the time of hunger in the time
    of plenty,
      poverty and want in the day of wealth.
26 Between morning and evening the weather changes;
    before the LORD all things are fleeting.
27 A wise man is circumspect in all things;
    when sin is rife he keeps himself
      from wrongdoing.
28 Any learned man should make wisdom known,
    and he who attains to her should declare
      her praise;
29 Those trained in her words must show
    their wisdom,
      dispensing sound proverbs like
        life-giving waters.

30 Go not after your lusts,
    but keep your desires in check.
31 If you satisfy your lustful appetites
    they will make you the sport of your enemies.
32 Have no joy in the pleasures of a moment
    which bring on poverty redoubled;
33 Become not a glutton and a winebibber
    with nothing in your purse.

22 Let nothing prevent your discharging a vow in
  good time,
    and do not wait till death to set matters right.
23 Prepare yourself before making a vow,
    and do not be like someone who tempts the
      Lord.
24 Bear in mind the retribution of the last days,
    the time of vengeance when God averts his face.
25 In a time of plenty remember times of famine,
    think of poverty and want when you are rich.
26 The time slips by between dawn and dusk,
    everything passes quickly for the Lord.
27 The wise will be cautious in everything,
    in sinful times will take care not to offend.
28 Every person of sense recognises wisdom,
    and will respect anyone who has found her.
29 Those who understand sayings have toiled for their
  wisdom
    and have poured out accurate maxims.

30 Do not be governed by your passions,
    restrain your desires.
31 If you allow yourself to satisfy your desires,
    this will make you the laughing-stock of your
      enemies.
32 Do not indulge in luxurious living,
    do not get involved in such society.
33 Do not beggar yourself by banqueting on credit
    when there is nothing in your pocket.

19 He who does so grows no richer;
  he who wastes the little he has will be
    stripped bare.
2 Wine and women make the mind giddy,
    and the companion of harlots becomes reckless.
4 He who lightly trusts in them has no sense,
    and he who strays after them sins against his
      own life.
3 Rottenness and worms will possess him,
    for contumacious desire destroys its owner.

5 He who gloats over evil will meet with evil,
    and he who repeats an evil report has no sense.
6 Never repeat gossip,
    and you will not be reviled.
7 Tell nothing to friend or foe;
    if you have a fault, reveal it not,
8 For he who hears it will hold it against you,
    and in time become your enemy.
9 Let anything you hear die within you;
    be assured it will not make you burst.

19 1 A drunken workman will never grow rich,
    and one who makes light of small matters will
      gradually sink.
2 Wine and women corrupt intelligent men,
    the customer of whores loses all sense of shame.
3 Grubs and worms will have him as their legacy,
    and the man who knows no shame will lose his
      life.
4 Being too ready to trust shows shallowness of
  mind,
    and sinning harms the sinner.
5 Taking pleasure in evil earns condemnation;
6   by hating gossip one avoids evil.
7 Never repeat what you are told
    and you will come to no harm;
8 whether to friend or foe, do not talk about it,
    unless it would be sinful not to, do not reveal it;
9 you would be heard out, then mistrusted,
    and in due course you would be hated.
10 Have you heard something? Let it die with you.
    Courage! It will not burst you!

NEW REVISED STANDARD VERSION

REVISED ENGLISH BIBLE

11 Having heard something, the fool suffers birth
 pangs
 like a woman in labor with a child.
12 Like an arrow stuck in a person's thigh,
 so is gossip inside a fool.
13 Question a friend; perhaps he did not do it;
 or if he did, so that he may not do it again.
14 Question a neighbor; perhaps he did not say it;
 or if he said it, so that he may not repeat it.
15 Question a friend, for often it is slander;
 so do not believe everything you hear.
16 A person may make a slip without intending it.
 Who has not sinned with his tongue?
17 Question your neighbor before you threaten him;
 and let the law of the Most High take its
 course.[h]

20 The whole of wisdom is fear of the Lord,
 and in all wisdom there is the fulfillment of the
 law.[i]
22 The knowledge of wickedness is not wisdom,
 nor is there prudence in the counsel of sinners.
23 There is a cleverness that is detestable,
 and there is a fool who merely lacks wisdom.
24 Better are the God-fearing who lack
 understanding
 than the highly intelligent who transgress the
 law.
25 There is a cleverness that is exact but unjust,
 and there are people who abuse favors to gain
 a verdict.
26 There is the villain bowed down in mourning,
 but inwardly he is full of deceit.
27 He hides his face and pretends not to hear,
 but when no one notices, he will take
 advantage of you.
28 Even if lack of strength keeps him from sinning,
 he will nevertheless do evil when he finds the
 opportunity.
29 A person is known by his appearance,
 and a sensible person is known when first met,
 face to face.
30 A person's attire and hearty laughter,
 and the way he walks, show what he is.

20 There is a rebuke that is untimely,
 and there is the person who is wise enough to
 keep silent.
2 How much better it is to rebuke than to fume!
3 And the one who admits his fault will be kept
 from failure.
4 Like a eunuch lusting to violate a girl
 is the person who does right under compulsion.
5 Some people keep silent and are thought to be
 wise,
 while others are detested for being talkative.
6 Some people keep silent because they have
 nothing to say,
 while others keep silent because they know
 when to speak.

11 A fool with a rumour goes through agony
 like a woman in labour.
12 As painful as an arrow through the thigh
 is a rumour in the heart of a fool.
13 Put it to your friend; he may not have done it,
 or if he did, he will know not to do it again.
14 Put it to your neighbour; he may not have said it,
 or if he did, he will know not to say it again.
15 Put it to your friend; it will often turn out to be
 slander;
 so do not believe everything you hear.
16 Someone may let slip what he does not intend;
 is anyone's tongue free from guilt?
17 Put your case to your neighbour before you
 threaten him,
 and let the law of the Most High take its course.

20 All wisdom is the fear of the Lord
 and includes the fulfilling of the law.
22 To know about wickedness is not wisdom,
 nor is there good sense in the advice of sinners.
23 There is a cleverness that repels,
 and some fools are merely ignorant.
24 Better to lack brains and be godfearing
 than to have great intelligence and transgress the
 law.
25 A meticulous cleverness may lead to injustice,
 and crooked means may be used to uncover the
 right.
26 A scoundrel may bow his head and wear
 mourning,
 but at heart be an out-and-out fraud.
27 He hides his face and pretends to be deaf,
 but when no one is looking, he steals a march on
 you;
28 and if lack of strength prevents him from doing
 wrong,
 he will still harm you at the first opportunity.
29 You can tell a person by his appearance
 and recognize good sense at first sight.
30 His clothes, the way he laughs,
 his gait — these reveal his character.

20 A reproof may be untimely,
 and silence may show a man's good sense.
2 How much better to rebuke than to nurse one's
 anger!
 Confession may save someone from losing face.
4 Like a eunuch longing to ravish a young girl
 is he who resorts to force to secure right.
5 One person is silent, and is reckoned to be wise;
 another chatters, and is detested for it.
6 There is the person who is silent, at a loss for an
 answer;
 another is silent, biding his time.

h Other ancient authorities add *and do not be angry.* *18The fear of the
Lord is the beginning of acceptance, and wisdom obtains his love.*
*19The knowledge of the Lord's commandments is life-giving
discipline; and those who do what is pleasing to him enjoy the fruit
of the tree of immortality.* *i* Other ancient authorities add *and the
knowledge of his omnipotence.* *21When a slave says to his master, "I
will not act as you wish,"* even if later he does it, he angers the one
who supports him.*

19:17 **its course:** *some witnesses add* without giving way to anger.
18The fear of the Lord is the beginning of acceptance by him, and
wisdom wins love from him. 19The knowledge of the Lord's
commandments is discipline for life, and those who do what pleases
him pluck the fruit of the tree of immortality.   19:20 **the law:**
some witnesses add and a knowledge of his omnipotence. 21A servant
who says to his master, 'I will not do as you wish,' even if he does
it later, angers him who feeds him.   20:2 **losing face:** *some
witnesses add* 3How good it is to meet reproof with repentance, and
so escape deliberate sin!

10 When a fool hears something, he is in labor,
   like a woman giving birth to a child.
11 Like an arrow lodged in a man's thigh
   is gossip in the breast of a fool.
12 Admonish your friend — he may not have done it;
   and if he did, that he may not do it again.
13 Admonish your neighbor — he may not have said it;
   and if he did, that he may not say it again.
14 Admonish your friend — often it may be slander;
   every story you must not believe.
15 Then, too, a man can slip and not mean it;
   who has not sinned with his tongue?
16 Admonish your neighbor before you break
      with him;
   thus will you fulfill the law of the Most High.

17 All wisdom is fear of the LORD;
   perfect wisdom is the fulfillment of the law.
18 The knowledge of wickedness is not wisdom,
   nor is there prudence in the counsel of sinners.
19 There is a shrewdness that is detestable,
   while the simple man may be free from sin.
20 There are those with little understanding who
      fear God,
   and those of great intelligence who violate
      the law.
21 There is a shrewdness keen but dishonest,
   which by duplicity wins a judgment.
22 There is the wicked man who is bowed in grief,
   but is full of guile within;
23 He bows his head and feigns not to hear,
   but when not observed, he will take advantage
      of you:
24 Even though his lack of strength keeps him
      from sinning,
   when he finds the opportunity, he will do harm.
25 One can tell a man by his appearance;
   a wise man is known as such when first met.
26 A man's attire, his hearty laughter and his gait,
   proclaim him for what he is.

20 An admonition can be inopportune,
   and a man may be wise to hold his peace.
2 It is much better to admonish than to lose
      one's temper,
   for one who admits his fault will be kept
      from disgrace.
3 Like a eunuch lusting for intimacy with a maiden
   is he who does right under compulsion.
4 One man is silent and is thought wise,
   another is talkative and is disliked.
5 One man is silent because he has nothing to say;
   another is silent, biding his time.

11 A fool will suffer birthpangs over a piece of news,
   like a woman labouring with child.
12 Like an arrow stuck in the flesh of the thigh,
   so is a piece of news inside a fool.

13 Question your friend, he may have done nothing at
      all;
   and if he has done anything, he will not do it
      again.
14 Question your neighbour, he may have said
      nothing at all;
   and if he has said anything, he will not say it
      again.
15 Question your friend, for slander is very common,
   do not believe all you hear.
16 People sometimes make a slip, without meaning
      what they say;
   and which of us has never sinned by speech?
17 Question your neighbour before you threaten him,
   and defer to the Law of the Most High.

20 Wisdom consists entirely in fearing the Lord,
   and wisdom is entirely constituted by the
      fulfilling of the Law.
22 Being learned in evil, however, is not wisdom,
   there is no prudence in the advice of sinners.
23 There is a cleverness that is detestable;
   whoever has no wisdom is a fool.
24 Better be short of sense and full of fear,
   than abound in shrewdness and violate the Law.
25 There is a wickedness which is scrupulous but
      nonetheless dishonest,
   and there are those who misuse kindness to win
      their case.
26 There is the person who will walk bowed down
      with grief,
   when inwardly this is nothing but deceit:
27 he hides his face and pretends to be deaf,
   if he is not unmasked, he will take advantage of
      you.
28 There is the person who is prevented from sinning
      by lack of strength,
   yet he will do wrong when he gets the chance.
29 You can tell a person by his appearance,
   you can tell a thinker by the look on his face.
30 The way a person dresses, the way he laughs,
   the way he walks, tell you what he is.

20 There is the rebuke that is untimely,
   and there is the person who keeps quiet, and he
      is the shrewd one.
2 But how much better to rebuke than to fume!
3   The person who acknowledges a fault wards off
      punishment.

4 Like a eunuch trying to take a girl's virginity
   is someone who tries to impose justice by force.

5 There is the person who keeps quiet and is
      considered wise,
   another incurs hatred for talking too much.

6 There is the person who keeps quiet, not knowing
      how to answer,
   another keeps quiet, knowing when to speak.

NEW REVISED STANDARD VERSION

7 The wise remain silent until the right moment,
  but a boasting fool misses the right moment.
8 Whoever talks too much is detested,
  and whoever pretends to authority is hated. *j*
9 There may be good fortune for a person in
    adversity,
  and a windfall may result in a loss.
10 There is the gift that profits you nothing,
  and the gift to be paid back double.
11 There are losses for the sake of glory,
  and there are some who have raised their heads
    from humble circumstances.
12 Some buy much for little,
  but pay for it seven times over.
13 The wise make themselves beloved by only few
    words, *k*
  but the courtesies of fools are wasted.
14 A fool's gift will profit you nothing, *l*
  for he looks for recompense sevenfold. *m*
15 He gives little and upbraids much;
  he opens his mouth like a town crier.
  Today he lends and tomorrow he asks it back;
  such a one is hateful to God and humans. *n*
16 The fool says, "I have no friends,
  and I get no thanks for my good deeds.
  Those who eat my bread are evil-tongued."
17 How many will ridicule him, and how often! *o*
18 A slip on the pavement is better than a slip of the
    tongue;
  the downfall of the wicked will occur just as
    speedily.
19 A coarse person is like an inappropriate story,
  continually on the lips of the ignorant.
20 A proverb from a fool's lips will be rejected,
  for he does not tell it at the proper time.
21 One may be prevented from sinning by poverty;
  so when he rests he feels no remorse.
22 One may lose his life through shame,
  or lose it because of human respect. *p*
23 Another out of shame makes promises to a friend,
  and so makes an enemy for nothing.
24 A lie is an ugly blot on a person;
  it is continually on the lips of the ignorant.
25 A thief is preferable to a habitual liar,
  but the lot of both is ruin.
26 A liar's way leads to disgrace,
  and his shame is ever with him.

PROVERBIAL SAYINGS *q*

27 The wise person advances himself by his words,
  and one who is sensible pleases the great.
28 Those who cultivate the soil heap up their
    harvest,
  and those who please the great atone for
    injustice.
29 Favors and gifts blind the eyes of the wise;
  like a muzzle on the mouth they stop reproofs.

REVISED ENGLISH BIBLE

7 The wise are silent until the right moment,
  but a swaggering fool is always speaking out of
    turn.
8 The garrulous get themselves detested,
  and one who abuses his position arouses hatred.
9 SOME find profit in adversity,
  while good fortune may turn into loss.
10 Sometimes liberality does not benefit the giver;
  sometimes it brings a double return.
11 The quest for honour may lead some to loss of
    position,
  while others may rise from obscurity to eminence.
12 Someone may make a good bargain,
  yet pay for it seven times over.
13 A wise person endears himself when he speaks,
  but a fool makes himself agreeable to no purpose.
14 A gift from a fool will bring you no profit;
  it looks bigger to him than to you.
15 He gives small gifts accompanied by long lectures
  and opens his mouth as wide as the town crier.
  Today he gives a loan, and tomorrow demands it
    back.
  Such conduct is detestable!
16 The fool says, 'I have not one friend
  and I get no thanks for my kindnesses;
  those who eat my bread speak ill of me.'
17 How everyone will laugh at him—and how often!
18 Better a slip on the floor than a slip of the tongue;
  the downfall of the wicked comes just as suddenly.
19 An ill-mannered man is like an ill-timed story,
  continually on the lips of the ill-bred.
20 A proverb will fall flat when uttered by a fool;
  he is sure to bring it out at the wrong moment.
21 Poverty may keep someone from doing wrong;
  when he goes to rest, conscience will not trouble
    him.
22 Diffidence may be someone's undoing,
  or a foolish appearance may bring him disaster.
23 Someone may be shamed into making promises to
    a friend
  and needlessly turn him into an enemy.
24 A lie is an ugly blot on anyone's name
  and is continually on the lips of the ill-bred.
25 Better be a thief than a habitual liar,
  but both will come to a bad end.
26 A lying disposition brings disgrace,
  shame that can never be shaken off.
27 He that is wise in discourse advances himself,
  and he that has sense is pleasing to the great.
28 He who cultivates his land heaps up a harvest;
  he who pleases the great secures pardon for his
    offence.
29 Hospitality and gifts make the wise blind;
  like a gag in the mouth they silence criticism.

---

j Other ancient authorities add *How good it is to show repentance
when you are reproved, for so you will escape deliberate sin!*
k Heb: Gk *by words*   *l* Other ancient authorities add *so it is with the
envious who give under compulsion*   *m* Syr: Gk *he has many eyes
instead of one*   *n* Other ancient authorities lack *to God and humans*
o Other ancient authorities add *for he has not honestly received what
he has, and what he does not have is unimportant to him*   *p* Other
ancient authorities read *his foolish look*   *q* This heading is included
in the Gk text.

6 A wise man is silent till the right time comes,
  but a boasting fool ignores the proper time.
7 He who talks too much is detested;
  he who pretends to authority is hated.

8 Some misfortunes bring success;
  some things gained are a man's loss.
9 Some gifts do one no good,
  and some must be paid back double.
10 Humiliation can follow fame,
  while from obscurity a man can lift up his head.
11 A man may buy much for little,
  but pay for it seven times over.
12 A wise man makes himself popular by a
    few words,
  but fools pour forth their blandishments in vain.
13 A gift from a rogue will do you no good,
  for in his eyes his one gift is equal to seven.
14 He gives little and criticizes often,
  and like a crier he shouts aloud.
  He lends today, he asks it back tomorrow;
  hateful indeed is such a man.
15 A fool has no friends,
  nor thanks for his generosity;
16 Those who eat his bread have an evil tongue.
  How many times they laugh him to scorn!

17 A fall to the ground is less sudden than a slip of
    the tongue;
  that is why the downfall of the wicked comes
    so quickly.
18 Insipid food is the untimely tale;
  the unruly are always ready to offer it.
19 A proverb when spoken by a fool is unwelcome,
  for he does not utter it at the proper time.
20 A man through want may be unable to sin,
  yet in this tranquility he cannot rest.
21 One may lose his life through shame,
  and perish through a fool's intimidation.
22 A man makes a promise to a friend out of shame,
  and has him for his enemy needlessly.
23 A lie is a foul blot in a man,
  yet it is constantly on the lips of the unruly.
24 Better a thief than an inveterate liar,
  yet both will suffer disgrace.
25 A liar's way leads to dishonor,
  his shame remains ever with him.
26 A wise man advances himself by his words,
  a prudent man pleases the great.
27 He who works his land has abundant crops,
  he who pleases the great is pardoned his faults.
28 Favors and gifts blind the eyes;
  like a muzzle over the mouth they
    silence reproof.

7 The wise will keep quiet till the right moment,
  but a garrulous fool will always misjudge it.
8 Someone who talks too much will earn dislike,
  and someone who usurps authority will earn
    hatred.
9 There is the person who finds misfortune a boon,
  and the piece of luck that turns to loss.
10 There is the gift that affords you no profit,
  and the gift that repays you double.
11 There is the honour that leads to humiliation,
  and there are people in a low state who raise
    their heads.
12 There is the person who buys much for little,
  yet pays for it seven times over.
13 The wise wins love with words,
  while fools may shower favours in vain.
14 The gift of the stupid will bring you no advantage,
  his eyes look for seven times as much in return.
15 He gives little and reviles much,
  he opens his mouth like the town crier,
  he lends today and demands payment tomorrow;
  he is a detestable fellow.
16 The fool will say, 'I have no friends,
  I get no gratitude for my good deeds;
17 those who eat my bread have malicious tongues.'
  How often he will be laughed at, and by how
    many!

18 Better a slip on the pavement than a slip of the
    tongue;
  this is how ruin takes the wicked by surprise.

19 A coarse-grained person is like an indiscreet story
  endlessly retold by the ignorant.

20 A maxim is rejected when coming from a fool,
  since the fool does not utter it on the apt
    occasion.

21 There is a person who is prevented from sinning by
    poverty;
  no qualms of conscience disturb that person's
    rest.

22 There is a person who courts destruction out of
    false shame,
  courts destruction for the sake of a fool's
    opinion.

23 There is a person who out of false shame makes
    promises to a friend,
  and so makes an enemy for nothing.

24 Lying is an ugly blot on anyone,
  and ever on the lips of the undisciplined.

25 A thief is preferable to an inveterate liar,
  but both are heading for ruin.

26 Lying is an abominable habit,
  the liar's disgrace lasts for ever.

27 The wise gains advancement by words,
  the shrewd wins favour from the great.

28 Whoever tills the soil will have a full harvest,
  whoever wins favour from the great will secure
    pardon for offences.

29 Presents and gifts blind the eyes of the wise
  and stifle rebukes like a muzzle on the mouth.

NEW REVISED STANDARD VERSION	REVISED ENGLISH BIBLE

NEW REVISED STANDARD VERSION

30 Hidden wisdom and unseen treasure,
   of what value is either?
31 Better are those who hide their folly
   than those who hide their wisdom.*r*

21 Have you sinned, my child? Do so no more,
   but ask forgiveness for your past sins.
2 Flee from sin as from a snake;
   for if you approach sin, it will bite you.
   Its teeth are lion's teeth,
   and can destroy human lives.
3 All lawlessness is like a two-edged sword;
   there is no healing for the wound it inflicts.
4 Panic and insolence will waste away riches;
   thus the house of the proud will be laid
   waste.*s*
5 The prayer of the poor goes from their lips to the
   ears of God,*t*
   and his judgment comes speedily.
6 Those who hate reproof walk in the sinner's
   steps,
   but those who fear the Lord repent in their
   heart.
7 The mighty in speech are widely known;
   when they slip, the sensible person knows it.
8 Whoever builds his house with other people's
   money
   is like one who gathers stones for his burial
   mound.*u*
9 An assembly of the wicked is like a bundle of
   tow,
   and their end is a blazing fire.
10 The way of sinners is paved with smooth stones,
   but at its end is the pit of Hades.
11 Whoever keeps the law controls his thoughts,
   and the fulfillment of the fear of the Lord is
   wisdom.
12 The one who is not clever cannot be taught,
   but there is a cleverness that increases
   bitterness.
13 The knowledge of the wise will increase like a
   flood,
   and their counsel like a life-giving spring.
14 The mind*v* of a fool is like a broken jar;
   it can hold no knowledge.
15 When an intelligent person hears a wise saying,
   he praises it and adds to it;
   when a fool*w* hears it, he laughs at*x* it
   and throws it behind his back.
16 A fool's chatter is like a burden on a journey,
   but delight is found in the speech of the
   intelligent.
17 The utterance of a sensible person is sought in
   the assembly,
   and they ponder his words in their minds.
18 Like a house in ruins is wisdom to a fool,
   and to the ignorant, knowledge is talk that has
   no meaning.
19 To a senseless person education is fetters on his
   feet,
   and like manacles on his right hand.

REVISED ENGLISH BIBLE

30 Hidden wisdom and buried treasure—
   what is the use of either?
31 Better one who hides his folly
   than one who hides his wisdom!

21 My son, have you done wrong? Do no more,
   and for your past wrongdoing ask pardon.
2 Avoid wrong as you would a viper,
   for it will bite you if you go near;
   its teeth are like a lion's teeth
   and can deprive men of their lives.
3 Every breach of the law is a two-edged sword;
   the wound it inflicts is incurable.
4 Bullying and insolence are destroyers of wealth;
   thus a proud man will be bereft of his home.
5 The Lord listens to the appeal of the poor,
   and his verdict follows promptly.
6 To hate reproof is to go the way of sinners,
   but whoever fears the Lord will repent
   wholeheartedly.
7 A great talker is known far and wide;
   a sensible person is aware of his own failings.
8 To build a house with borrowed money
   is like gathering the stones for one's own tomb.
9 An assembly of the wicked is like a bundle of tow;
   they end in flames.
10 The sinners' road is smoothly paved,
   but it leads straight down to the grave.
11 WHOEVER keeps the law keeps control of his
   thoughts;
   the fear of the Lord has its outcome in wisdom.
12 He who is not clever cannot be taught,
   but there is a cleverness which breeds bitterness.
13 The knowledge of the wise is like a river in full
   flood;
   advice from such is like a fountain of life.
14 A fool's mind is like a broken jug:
   it cannot retain anything it learns.
15 If an instructed man hears a wise saying,
   he applauds it and improves on it;
   if a dissolute man hears it, he is annoyed
   and flings it away out of his sight.
16 Listening to a fool is like travelling with a heavy
   pack,
   but delight is to be found in learned conversation.
17 The assembly welcomes a word from a wise man
   and ponders what he says.

18 To a fool, wisdom is like a derelict house;
   the knowledge of the stupid is a string of
   ill-digested sayings.
19 To the ignorant, instruction is like fetters,
   like a manacle on the right wrist.

---

r Other ancient authorities add *32Unwearied endurance in seeking the
Lord is better than a masterless charioteer of one's own life.*
s Other ancient authorities read *uprooted*   *t* Gk *his ears*   *u* Other
ancient authorities read *for the winter*   *v* Syr Lat: Gk *entrails*
w Syr: Gk *reveler*   *x* Syr: Gk *dislikes*

20:31 **his wisdom:** *some witnesses add* *32Better to seek the Lord with
unremitting patience than to drive one's way through life on one's
own.*

29 Hidden wisdom and unseen treasure —
  of what value is either?
30 Better the man who hides his folly
  than the one who hides his wisdom.

21 My son, if you have sinned, do so no more,
  and for your past sins pray to be forgiven.
2 Flee from sin as from a serpent
  that will bite you if you go near it;
  Its teeth are lion's teeth,
  destroying the souls of men.
3 Every offense is a two-edged sword;
  when it cuts, there can be no healing.
4 Violence and arrogance wipe out wealth;
  so too a proud man's home is destroyed.
5 Prayer from a poor man's lips is heard at once,
  and justice is quickly granted him.
6 He who hates correction walks the sinner's path,
  but he who fears the LORD repents in his heart.
7 Widely known is the boastful speaker,
  but the wise man knows his own faults.
8 He who builds his house with another's money
  is collecting stones for his funeral mound.
9 A band of criminals is like a bundle of tow;
  they will end in a flaming fire.
10 The path of sinners is smooth stones
  that end in the depths of the nether world.
11 He who keeps the law controls his impulses;
  he who is perfect in fear of the LORD
    has wisdom.
12 He can never be taught who is not shrewd,
  but one form of shrewdness is thoroughly bitter.
13 A wise man's knowledge wells up in a flood,
  and his counsel, like a living spring;
14 A fool's mind is like a broken jar —
  no knowledge at all can it hold.
15 When an intelligent man hears words of wisdom,
  he approves them and adds to them;
  The wanton hears them with scorn
  and casts them behind his back.
16 A fool's chatter is like a load on a journey,
  but there is charm to be found upon the lips of
    the wise.
17 The views of a prudent man are sought in
    an assembly,
  and his words are considered with care.
18 Like a house in ruins is wisdom to a fool;
  the stupid man knows it only as
    inscrutable words.
19 Like fetters on the legs is learning to a fool,
  like a manacle on his right hand.

30 Wisdom concealed, and treasure undiscovered,
  what use is either of these?
31 Better one who conceals his folly
  than one who conceals his wisdom. *b*

21 My child, have you sinned? Do so no more,
  and ask forgiveness for your previous faults.
2 Flee from sin as from a snake,
  if you approach it, it will bite you;
  its teeth are lion's teeth,
  they take human life away.
3 All law-breaking is like a two-edged sword,
  the wounds it inflicts are beyond cure.
4 Terror and violence make havoc of riches,
  similarly, desolation overtakes the houses of the
    proud.
5 A plea from the mouth of the poor goes straight to
    the ear of God,
  whose judgement comes without delay.
6 Whoever resents reproof walks in the sinner's
    footsteps;
  whoever fears the Lord is repentant of heart.
7 The glib speaker is known far and wide,
  but the wary detects every slip.
8 To build your house with other people's money
  is like collecting stones for your own tomb.
9 A meeting of the lawless is like a heap of tow:
  they will end in a blazing fire.
10 The sinner's road is smoothly paved,
  but it ends at the pit of Sheol.
11 Whoever keeps the Law will master his instincts;
  the fear of the Lord is made perfect in wisdom.
12 No one who lacks aptitude can be taught,
  but certain aptitudes give rise to bitterness.
13 The sage's knowledge is as rich as the abyss
  and his advice is like a living spring.
14 The heart of a fool is like a broken jar,
  it will not hold any knowledge.
15 If the educated hears a wise saying,
  he praises it and caps it with another;
  if a debauchee hears it, he does not like it
  and tosses it behind his back.
16 The talk of a fool is like a load on a journey,
  but it is a pleasure to listen to the intelligent.
17 The utterance of the shrewd will be eagerly
    awaited in the assembly,
  what he says will be given serious consideration.
18 The wisdom of a fool is like the wreckage of a
    house,
  the knowledge of a dolt is incoherent talk.
19 To the senseless fellow instruction is like fetters on
    the feet,
  like manacles on the right hand.

b 20 = 41:14–15.

20 A fool raises his voice when he laughs,
  but the wise^y smile quietly.
21 To the sensible person education is like a golden
    ornament,
  and like a bracelet on the right arm.
22 The foot of a fool rushes into a house,
  but an experienced person waits respectfully
    outside.
23 A boor peers into the house from the door,
  but a cultivated person remains outside.
24 It is ill-mannered for a person to listen at a door;
  the discreet would be grieved by the disgrace.
25 The lips of babblers speak of what is not their
    concern,^z
  but the words of the prudent are weighed in the
    balance.
26 The mind of fools is in their mouth,
  but the mouth of the wise is in^a their mind.
27 When an ungodly person curses an adversary,^b
  he curses himself.
28 A whisperer degrades himself
  and is hated in his neighborhood.

22 The idler is like a filthy stone,
  and every one hisses at his disgrace.
2 The idler is like the filth of dunghills;
  anyone that picks it up will shake it off his
    hand.
3 It is a disgrace to be the father of an
    undisciplined son,
  and the birth of a daughter is a loss.
4 A sensible daughter obtains a husband of her
    own,
  but one who acts shamefully is a grief to her
    father.
5 An impudent daughter disgraces father and
    husband,
  and is despised by both.
6 Like music in time of mourning is ill-timed
    conversation,
  but a thrashing and discipline are at all times
    wisdom.^c
9 Whoever teaches a fool is like one who glues
    potsherds together,
  or who rouses a sleeper from deep slumber.
10 Whoever tells a story to a fool tells it to a drowsy
    man;
  and at the end he will say, "What is it?"
11 Weep for the dead, for he has left the light
    behind;
  and weep for the fool, for he has left
    intelligence behind.
  Weep less bitterly for the dead, for he is at rest;
  but the life of the fool is worse than death.
12 Mourning for the dead lasts seven days,
  but for the foolish or the ungodly it lasts all the
    days of their lives.

21 To the wise, instruction is a gold ornament
  like a bracelet on the right arm.
20 A fool guffaws,
  but a clever man smiles quietly, if at all.
22 A fool rushes into a house,
  while someone of experience hangs back politely.
23 A boor peers into a house from the doorstep,
  while a well-bred person stands outside.
24 It is bad manners to eavesdrop at doors;
  anyone with sense would think it an intolerable
    disgrace.
25 The glib only repeat what others have said,
  but the wise weigh every word.
26 Fools speak before they think,
  but the wise think before they speak.
27 When the ungodly curses his adversary,
  he is really cursing himself.
28 A tale-bearer blackens his own character
  and gets himself detested throughout the
    neighbourhood.

22 A sluggard is like a filthy stone:
  everyone jeers at his disgrace.
2 A sluggard is like a lump of dung:
  whoever picks it up shakes it off his hand.
3 There is shame in being father to an ill-mannered
    son,
  and the birth of a daughter means loss.
4 A sensible daughter wins a husband,
  but an immodest one is a grief to her father.
5 A brazen daughter brings shame on father and
    husband,
  and is despised by both.
6 Unseasonable talk is like music in time of
    mourning,
  but the lash of wisdom's discipline is always in
    season.
7 Teaching a fool is like mending pottery with paste,
  or like rousing a sleeper from heavy slumber.
8 As well talk with someone dozing as with a fool;
  when you have finished, he will say, 'What was
    that?'
11 Weep for the dead: he has taken leave of the light;
  weep for the fool: he has taken leave of his wits.
  Weep less bitterly for the dead, for he is at rest;
  but the fool's life is worse than death.
12 Mourning for the dead lasts seven days;
  for an impious fool it lasts all the days of his life.

---

^ySyr Lat: Gk *clever*   ^zOther ancient authorities read *of strangers speak
of these things*   ^aOther ancient authorities omit *in*   ^bOr *curses
Satan*   ^cOther ancient authorities add ⁷*Children who are brought up
in a good life, conceal the lowly birth of their parents.* ⁸*Children who are
disdainfully and boorishly haughty stain the nobility of their kindred.*

22:8 '**What was that?**': *some witnesses add* ⁹Children nurtured in a
good life do not show the low birth of their parents; ¹⁰but those who
run riot, haughty and undisciplined, sully the good name of their
family.

20 A fool raises his voice in laughter,
    but a prudent man at the most smiles gently.
21 Like a chain of gold is learning to a wise man,
    like a bracelet on his right arm.

22 The fool steps boldly into a house,
    while the well-bred man remains outside;
23 A boor peeps through the doorway of a house,
    but a cultured man keeps his glance cast down.
24 It is rude for one to listen at a door;
    a cultured man would be overwhelmed by the
       disgrace of it.
25 The lips of the impious talk of what is not
       their concern,
    but the words of the prudent are
       carefully weighed.
26 Fools' thoughts are in their mouths,
    wise men's words are in their hearts.
27 When a godless man curses his adversary,
    he really curses himself.
28 A slanderer besmirches himself,
    and is hated by his neighbors.

22 The sluggard is like a stone in the mud;
    everyone hisses at his disgrace.
2 The sluggard is like a lump of dung;
    whoever touches him wipes his hands.
3 An unruly child is a disgrace to its father;
    if it be a daughter, she brings him to poverty.
4 A thoughtful daughter becomes a treasure to
       her husband,
    a shameless one is her father's grief.
5 A hussy shames her father and her husband;
    by both she is despised.
6 Like a song in time of mourning is
       inopportune talk,
    but lashes and discipline are at all times wisdom.
7 Teaching a fool is like gluing a broken pot,
    or like disturbing a man in the depths of sleep;
8 He talks with a slumberer who talks with a fool,
    for when it is over, he will say, "What
       was that?"
9 Weep over the dead man, for his light has
       gone out;
    weep over the fool, for sense has left him.
10 Weep but a little over the dead man, for he is
       at rest;
    but worse than death is the life of a fool.
11 Seven days of mourning for the dead,
    but for the wicked fool a whole lifetime.

20 A fool laughs at the top of his voice,
    but the intelligent quietly smiles.
21 To the shrewd instruction is like a golden
       ornament,
    like a bracelet on the right arm.

22 The step of a fool goes straight into a house,
    but a person of much experience makes a
       respectful approach;
23 the stupid peeps inside through the door,
    a well-bred person waits outside.
24 Listening at doors is a sign of bad upbringing,
    the perceptive would be ashamed to do so.

25 The lips of gossips repeat the words of others,
    the words of the wise are carefully weighed.
26 The heart of fools is in their mouth,
    but the mouth of the wise is in their heart.
27 When the godless curses Satan,
    he is cursing himself.
28 The scandal-monger sullies himself
    and earns the hatred of the neighbourhood.

22 An idler is like a stone covered in filth,
    everyone whistles at his disgrace.
2 An idler is like a lump of dung,
    anyone picking it up shakes it off his hand.

3 It is a disgrace to have fathered a badly brought-up
       son,
    but the birth of any daughter is a loss;
4 a sensible daughter will find a husband,
    but a shameless one is a grief to her father.
5 A brazen daughter puts father and mother to
       shame,
    and will be disowned by both.

6 An untimely remonstrance is like music at a
       funeral,
    but a thrashing and correction are wisdom at all
       times.

9 Teaching a fool is like gluing bits of pottery
       together —
    you are rousing someone who is besotted with
       sleep.
10 You might as well talk to someone sound asleep;
    when you have finished the fool will say,
       'What's up?'

11 Shed tears for the dead, who has left the light
       behind;
    shed tears for the fool, who has left his wits
       behind.
    Shed quieter tears for the dead who is at rest,
    for the fool life is worse than death.
12 Mourning for the dead lasts seven days,
    for the foolish and ungodly all the days of their
       lives.

NEW REVISED STANDARD VERSION	REVISED ENGLISH BIBLE

NEW REVISED STANDARD VERSION

13 Do not talk much with a senseless person
  or visit an unintelligent person.*d*
Stay clear of him, or you may have trouble,
  and be spattered when he shakes himself off.
Avoid him and you will find rest,
  and you will never be wearied by his lack of
    sense.
14 What is heavier than lead?
  And what is its name except "Fool"?
15 Sand, salt, and a piece of iron
  are easier to bear than a stupid person.
16 A wooden beam firmly bonded into a building
  is not loosened by an earthquake;
so the mind firmly resolved after due reflection
  will not be afraid in a crisis.
17 A mind settled on an intelligent thought
  is like stucco decoration that makes a wall
    smooth.
18 Fences*e* set on a high place
  will not stand firm against the wind;
so a timid mind with a fool's resolve
  will not stand firm against any fear.

19 One who pricks the eye brings tears,
  and one who pricks the heart makes clear its
    feelings.
20 One who throws a stone at birds scares them
    away,
  and one who reviles a friend destroys a
    friendship.
21 Even if you draw your sword against a friend,
  do not despair, for there is a way back.
22 If you open your mouth against your friend,
  do not worry, for reconciliation is possible.
But as for reviling, arrogance, disclosure of
    secrets, or a treacherous blow —
  in these cases any friend will take to flight.

23 Gain the trust of your neighbor in his poverty,
  so that you may rejoice with him in his
    prosperity.
Stand by him in time of distress,
  so that you may share with him in his
    inheritance.*f*
24 The vapor and smoke of the furnace precede the
    fire;
  so insults precede bloodshed.
25 I am not ashamed to shelter a friend,
  and I will not hide from him.
26 But if harm should come to me because of him,
  whoever hears of it will beware of him.

27 Who will set a guard over my mouth,
  and an effective seal upon my lips,
so that I may not fall because of them,
  and my tongue may not destroy me?

23 O Lord, Father and Master of my life,
    do not abandon me to their designs,
  and do not let me fall because of them!
2 Who will set whips over my thoughts,
  and the discipline of wisdom over my mind,
so as not to spare me in my errors,
  and not overlook my*g* sins?

REVISED ENGLISH BIBLE

13 Do not prolong talk with a fool
  or visit one who is stupid.
Beware of him, or you may be in trouble
  and find yourself bespattered when he shakes
    himself.
Avoid him, if you are looking for peace,
  and you will not be worn out by his folly.
14 What is heavier than lead?
  What is its name but 'Fool'?
15 Sand, salt, and a lump of iron
  are less of a burden than a stupid person.
16 A tie-beam fixed firmly into a building
  is not shaken loose by an earthquake;
so a mind kept steadfast by sensible advice
  will not be daunted in a crisis.
17 A mind solidly backed by intelligent thought
  is like stucco decorating a well-prepared wall.
18 As a fence set on a hilltop
  will not stand against the wind,
so a mind made timid by foolish fancies
  is not proof against any terror.

19 Prick the eye and tears will flow;
  prick the heart and you will find it sensitive.
20 Throw a stone at birds and you scare them away;
  taunt a friend and you destroy a friendship.
21 If you have drawn your sword on a friend,
  do not despair; a way back is still open.
22 If you have quarrelled with a friend,
  do not hold aloof, for there can still be
    reconciliation.
But taunts, scorn, a secret betrayed, a stab in the
    back —
  these will make any friend keep his distance.
23 Win your neighbour's confidence while he is poor,
  that you may share fully in his prosperity;
stand by him in time of trouble,
  that you may be his partner when he comes into a
    fortune.
24 As furnace fumes and smoke precede the flame,
  so insults come before bloodshed.
25 I shall not be ashamed to protect a friend,
  nor shall I turn my back on him;
26 and if on his account harm should befall me,
  everyone who hears of it will beware of him.

27 O FOR a sentry to guard my mouth
  and a seal of discretion to close my lips,
to prevent them from being my downfall,
  to keep my tongue from causing my ruin!

23 Lord, Father, and Ruler of my life,
    do not abandon me to the tongue's control
  or allow it to bring about my downfall.
2 O for wisdom's rod to curb my thoughts
  and to discipline my mind,
that my shortcomings may not be overlooked
  or any sin of mine be condoned!

---

*d*Other ancient authorities add *For being without sense he will despise
everything about you*   *e*Other ancient authorities read *Pebbles*
*f*Other ancient authorities add *For one should not always despise
restricted circumstances, or admire a rich person who is stupid.*
*g*Gk *their*

22:18 **a fence:** or pebbles.

12 Speak but seldom with the stupid man,
    be not the companion of a brute;
13 Beware of him lest you have trouble
    and be spattered when he shakes himself;
  Turn away from him and you will find rest
    and not be wearied by his lack of sense.
14 What is heavier than lead,
    and what is its name but "Fool"?
15 Sand and salt and an iron mass
    are easier to bear than a stupid man.

16 Masonry bonded with wooden beams
    is not loosened by an earthquake;
  Neither is a resolve constructed with
      careful deliberation
    shaken in a moment of fear.
17 A resolve that is backed by prudent understanding
    is like the polished surface of a smooth wall.
18 Small stones lying on an open height
    will not remain when the wind blows;
  Neither can a timid resolve based on foolish plans
    withstand fear of any kind.

19 One who jabs the eye brings tears:
    he who pierces the heart bares its feelings.
20 He who throws stones at birds drives them away,
    and he who insults a friend breaks up
      the friendship.
21 Should you draw a sword against a friend,
    despair not, it can be undone.
22 Should you speak sharply to a friend,
    fear not, you can be reconciled.
  But a contemptuous insult, a confidence broken,
    or a treacherous attack will drive away
      any friend.

23 Make fast friends with a man while he is poor;
    thus will you enjoy his prosperity with him.
  In time of trouble remain true to him,
    so as to share in his inheritance when it comes.
24 Before flames burst forth an oven smokes;
    so does abuse come before bloodshed.
25 From a friend in need of support
    no one need hide in shame;
26 But from him who brings harm to his friend
    all will stand aloof who hear of it.

27 Who will set a guard over my mouth,
    and upon my lips an effective seal,
  That I may not fail through them,
    that my tongue may not destroy me?

23 Lord, Father and Master of my life,
    permit me not to fall by them!
2 Who will apply the lash to my thoughts,
    to my mind the rod of discipline,
  That my failings may not be spared,
    nor the sins of my heart overlooked;

---

13 Do not waste many words on the stupid,
    do not go near a dolt.

  Beware of him, or you will have trouble
    and be soiled by contact with him;
  keep away from him, and you will have peace of
      mind
    and not be exasperated by his folly.

14 What is heavier than lead,
    and what is its name if not 'fool'?
15 Sand and salt and a lump of iron
    are a lighter burden than a dolt.

16 A tie-beam bonded into a building
    will not be dislodged by an earthquake;
  so too, a heart resolved after due reflection
    will not flinch at the critical moment.

17 A heart founded on intelligent reflection
    is like a stucco decoration on a smooth wall.

18 Pebbles placed on top of a wall
    will not stand up to the wind;
  no more can the heart of a fool frightened at his
      own thoughts
    stand up to fear.

19 Prick an eye and you will draw a tear,
    prick a heart and you reveal its feelings.

20 Throw stones at birds and you scare them away,
    reproach a friend and you destroy a friendship.

21 If you have drawn your sword on a friend,
    do not despair; there is a way back.
22 If you have opened your mouth against your
      friend,
    do not worry; there is hope for reconciliation;
  but insult, arrogance, betrayal of secrets, and the
      stab in the back—
    in these cases any friend is lost.

23 Win your neighbour's confidence when he is poor,
    so that you may enjoy his later good fortune
      with him;
  stand by him in times of trouble,
    in order to have your share when he comes into
      a legacy.

24 Fire is heralded by the reek of the furnace and
      smoke,
    so too, bloodshed by insults.

25 I shall not be ashamed to shelter a friend
    nor shall I hide away from him,
26 and if evil comes to me through him,
    everyone who hears about it will beware of him.

27 Who will set a guard on my mouth,
    and an efficient seal on my lips,
  to keep me from falling,
    and my tongue from causing my ruin?

23 Lord, father and master of my life,
    do not abandon me to their whims,
    do not let me fall because of them.
2 Who will lay whips to my thoughts,
    and the discipline of wisdom to my heart,
  to be merciless to my errors
    and not let my sins go unchecked,

3 Otherwise my mistakes may be multiplied,
    and my sins may abound,
    and I may fall before my adversaries,
    and my enemy may rejoice over me. *h*

4 O Lord, Father and God of my life,
    do not give me haughty eyes,

5   and remove evil desire from me.

6 Let neither gluttony nor lust overcome me,
    and do not give me over to shameless passion.

DISCIPLINE OF THE TONGUE *i*

7 Listen, my children, to instruction concerning the
    mouth;
    the one who observes it will never be caught.

8 Sinners are overtaken through their lips;
    by them the reviler and the arrogant are tripped
    up.

9 Do not accustom your mouth to oaths,
    nor habitually utter the name of the Holy One;

10 for as a servant who is constantly under scrutiny
    will not lack bruises,
    so also the person who always swears and utters
    the Name
    will never be cleansed *j* from sin.

11 The one who swears many oaths is full of
    iniquity,
    and the scourge will not leave his house.
    If he swears in error, his sin remains on him,
    and if he disregards it, he sins doubly;
    if he swears a false oath, he will not be justified,
    for his house will be filled with calamities.

12 There is a manner of speaking comparable to
    death; *k*
    may it never be found in the inheritance of
    Jacob!
    Such conduct will be far from the godly,
    and they will not wallow in sins.

13 Do not accustom your mouth to coarse, foul
    language,
    for it involves sinful speech.

14 Remember your father and mother
    when you sit among the great,
    or you may forget yourself in their presence,
    and behave like a fool through bad habit;
    then you will wish that you had never been born,
    and you will curse the day of your birth.

15 Those who are accustomed to using abusive
    language
    will never become disciplined as long as they
    live.

16 Two kinds of individuals multiply sins,
    and a third incurs wrath.
    Hot passion that blazes like a fire
    will not be quenched until it burns itself out;
    one who commits fornication with his near of kin
    will never cease until the fire burns him up.

17 To a fornicator all bread is sweet;
    he will never weary until he dies.

18 The one who sins against his marriage bed
    says to himself, "Who can see me?
    Darkness surrounds me, the walls hide me,
    and no one sees me. Why should I worry?
    The Most High will not remember sins."

3 Then my errors would not multiply
    or my sins increase in number,
    humiliating me before my opponents
    and giving my enemy cause to gloat.

4 Lord, Father, and God of my life,
    do not let me wear a supercilious look.

5 Protect me from the onslaught of desire;

6 let neither gluttony nor lust take hold of me,
    and do not give me over to shamelessness.

7 Hear how to discipline the mouth, my sons;
    he that does so will never be caught out.

8 It is by his own words that the sinner is ensnared;
    by his own scurrility and pride he is tripped.

9 Do not accustom your mouth to oaths
    or make a habit of using the Holy One's name.

10 As a servant constantly questioned under the lash
    is never free from weals,
    so also anyone who has oaths and the sacred name
    forever on his lips
    will never be clear of guilt.

11 One given to oaths is wicked to the core;
    the rod will never be far from his house.
    If he goes back on his word, he must bear the
    blame;
    if he wilfully neglects it, he sins twice over;
    if his oath was insincere, punishment will overtake
    him
    and his house will be filled with trouble.

12 There is a kind of speech that is the counterpart of
    death;
    may it never be found among Jacob's descendants!
    The godly will keep clear of such conduct
    and will not wallow in sin.

13 Do not make a habit of coarse and filthy talk,
    or you will be bound to say something sinful.

14 Remember your father and mother
    when you take your seat among the great;
    otherwise you may forget yourself in their presence
    and through such habits make a fool of yourself;
    then you will wish you had never been born,
    and curse the day of your birth.

15 Someone addicted to scurrilous talk
    will never learn better as long as he lives.

16 Two KINDS of people add sin to sin,
    and a third brings God's wrath on himself.
    Hot lust that blazes like a fire
    can never be suppressed till life itself is quenched.
    A man whose whole body is given to sensuality
    never stops till the fire consumes him.

17 To the profligate every cake is as sweet as the last,
    and he will not leave off until he dies.

18 The man who strays from his own bed
    says to himself, 'Who can see me?
    All around is dark and the walls hide me;
    nobody can see me; why need I worry?
    The Most High will take no note of my sins.'

---

h Other ancient authorities add *From them the hope of your mercy is
remote*   *i* This heading is included in the Gk text.   *j* Syr *be free*
k Other ancient authorities read *clothed about with death*

3 Lest my failings increase,
and my sins be multiplied;
Lest I succumb to my foes,
and my enemy rejoice over me?

4 LORD, Father and God of my life,
abandon me not into their control!

5 A brazen look allow me not;
ward off passion from my heart,

6 Let not the lustful cravings of the flesh master me,
surrender me not to shameless desires.

7 Give heed, my children, to the instruction that
I pronounce,
for he who keeps it will not be enslaved.

8 Through his lips is the sinner ensnared;
the railer and the arrogant man fall thereby.

9 Let not your mouth form the habit of swearing,
or becoming too familiar with the Holy Name.

10 Just as a slave that is constantly under scrutiny
will not be without welts,
So one who swears continually by the Holy Name
will not remain free from sin.

11 A man who often swears heaps up obligations;
the scourge will never be far from his house.
If he swears in error, he incurs guilt;
if he neglects his obligation, his sin is
doubly great.
If he swears without reason he cannot be
found just,
and all his house will suffer affliction.

12 There are words which merit death;
may they never be heard among Jacob's heirs.
For all such words are foreign to the devout,
who do not wallow in sin.

13 Let not your mouth become used to coarse talk,
for in it lies sinful matter.

14 Keep your father and mother in mind
when you sit among the mighty,
Lest in their presence you commit a blunder
and disgrace your upbringing,
By wishing you had never been born
or cursing the day of your birth.

15 A man who has the habit of abusive language
will never mature in character as long as
he lives.

16 Two types of men multiply sins,
a third draws down wrath;
For burning passion is a blazing fire,
not to be quenched till it burns itself out:
A man given to sins of the flesh,
who never stops until the fire breaks forth;

17 The rake to whom all bread is sweet
and who is never through till he dies;

18 And the man who dishonors his marriage bed
and says to himself, "Who can see me?
Darkness surrounds me, walls hide me;
no one sees me; why should I fear to sin?"
Of the Most High he is not mindful,

3 for fear my errors should multiply
and my sins then abound
and I fall before my adversaries,
and my enemy gloat over me?

4 Lord, father and God of my life,
do not let my eyes be proud,

5 turn envy away from me,

6 do not let lechery and lust grip me,
do not leave me a prey to shameless desire.

7 Children, listen to what I teach,
no one who keeps it will be caught out.

8 The sinner is ensnared by his own lips,
both the abusive and the proud are tripped by
them.

9 Do not get into the habit of swearing,
do not make a habit of naming the Holy One;

10 for just as a slave who is constantly overseen
will never be without bruises,
so someone who is always swearing and uttering
the Name
will not be exempt from sin.

11 A man for ever swearing is full of iniquity,
and the scourge will not depart from his house.
If he offends, his sin will be on him,
if he did it unheedingly, he has doubly sinned;
if he swears a false oath, he will not be treated as
innocent,
for his house will be filled with calamities.

12 One way of talking is like death,
let it not be found in the heritage of Jacob
since devout people have nothing to do with that:
they will not wallow in sin.

13 Do not get into the habit of using coarse and foul
language
since this involves sinful words.

14 Remember your father and mother
when you are sitting with the great,
for fear you forget yourself in their presence
and behave like a fool,
and then wish you had not been born
and curse the day of your birth.

15 No one in the habit of using shameful language
will break himself of it as long as he lives.

16 There are two types of people who commit sin
after sin
and a third who attracts retribution—

17 desire, blazing like a furnace,
will not die down until it has been sated—
the man who lusts after members of his own family
is not going to stop until he is quite burnt out;
every food is sweet to the promiscuous,
and he will not desist until he dies;

18 and the man who sins against the marriage bed
and says to himself, 'Who can see me?
There is darkness all round me, the walls hide me,
no one can see me, why should I worry?
The Most High will not remember my sins.'

19 His fear is confined to human eyes
  and he does not realize that the eyes of the
      Lord
  are ten thousand times brighter than the sun;
  they look upon every aspect of human behavior
      and see into hidden corners.
20 Before the universe was created, it was known to
      him,
  and so it is since its completion.
21 This man will be punished in the streets of the
      city,
  and where he least suspects it, he will be
      seized.
22 So it is with a woman who leaves her husband
  and presents him with an heir by another man.
23 For first of all, she has disobeyed the law of the
      Most High;
  second, she has committed an offense against
      her husband;
  and third, through her fornication she has
      committed adultery
  and brought forth children by another man.
24 She herself will be brought before the assembly,
  and her punishment will extend to her children.
25 Her children will not take root,
  and her branches will not bear fruit.
26 She will leave behind an accursed memory
  and her disgrace will never be blotted out.
27 Those who survive her will recognize
  that nothing is better than the fear of the Lord,
  and nothing sweeter than to heed the
      commandments of the Lord. [l]

THE PRAISE OF WISDOM [m]

24 Wisdom praises herself,
  and tells of her glory in the midst of her
      people.
2 In the assembly of the Most High she opens her
      mouth,
  and in the presence of his hosts she tells of her
      glory:
3 "I came forth from the mouth of the Most High,
  and covered the earth like a mist.
4 I dwelt in the highest heavens,
  and my throne was in a pillar of cloud.
5 Alone I compassed the vault of heaven
  and traversed the depths of the abyss.
6 Over waves of the sea, over all the earth,
  and over every people and nation I have held
      sway. [n]
7 Among all these I sought a resting place;
  in whose territory should I abide?
8 "Then the Creator of all things gave me a
      command,
  and my Creator chose the place for my tent.
  He said, 'Make your dwelling in Jacob,
  and in Israel receive your inheritance.'
9 Before the ages, in the beginning, he created me,
  and for all the ages I shall not cease to be.
10 In the holy tent I ministered before him,
  and so I was established in Zion.
11 Thus in the beloved city he gave me a resting
      place,
  and in Jerusalem was my domain.

19 The eyes of human beings are all he fears;
  he forgets that the eyes of the Lord
  are ten thousand times brighter than the sun,
  observing every step that mortals take
  and penetrating to every secret place;
20 before all things were created, they were known to
      him,
  and so it is since their completion.
21 Such a man will pay the penalty in the public
      street,
  caught where he least expected it.
22 So too with the woman who is unfaithful to her
      husband,
  presenting him with an heir by another man:
23 first, she disobeys the law of the Most High;
  secondly, she commits an offence against her
      husband;
  thirdly, she has prostituted herself
  by bearing bastard children.
24 She shall be brought before the assembly for
      judgement,
  and the consequences will fall on her children.
25 Her children will not take root,
  nor will fruit grow on her branches.
26 A curse will rest on her memory,
  and her shame will never be wiped out.
27 All who survive her will learn
  that nothing is better than the fear of the Lord,
  nothing sweeter than obeying his commandments.

24 HEAR the praise of wisdom from her own mouth,
  as she speaks with pride among her people,
2 before the assembly of the Most High
  and in the presence of the heavenly host:
3 'I am the word spoken by the Most High;
  it was I who covered the earth like a mist.
4 My dwelling-place was in high heaven;
  my throne was in a pillar of cloud.
5 Alone I made a circuit of the sky
  and traversed the depths of the abyss.
6 The waves of the sea, the whole earth,
  every people and nation were under my sway.
7 Among them all I sought where I might come to
      rest:
  in whose territory was I to settle?
8 Then the Creator of all things laid a command on
      me;
  he who created me decreed where I should dwell.
  He said, "Make your home in Jacob;
  enter on your heritage in Israel."
9 Before time began he created me,
  and until the end of time I shall endure.
10 In the sacred tent I ministered in his presence,
  and thus I came to be established in Zion.
11 He settled me in the city he loved
  and gave me authority in Jerusalem.

---

[l] Other ancient authorities add as verse 28, *It is a great honor to
follow God, and to be received by him is long life.* [m] This heading
is included in the Gk text. [n] Other ancient authorities read *I have
acquired a possession*

23:27 **his commandments:** *some witnesses add* 28 To follow God
brings great honour; to win his approval means length of days.

NEW AMERICAN BIBLE

NEW JERUSALEM BIBLE

19 fearing only the eyes of men;
He does not understand that the eyes of the LORD,
  ten thousand times brighter than the sun,
Observe every step a man takes
  and peer into hidden corners.
20 He who knows all things before they exist
  still knows them all after they are made.
21 Such a man will be punished in the streets of
    the city;
  when he least expects it, he will
    be apprehended.

22 So also with the woman who is unfaithful to
    her husband
  and offers as heir her son by a stranger.
23 First, she has disobeyed the law of the Most High;
  secondly, she has wronged her husband;
Thirdly, in her wanton adultery
  she has borne children by another man.
24 Such a woman will be dragged before
    the assembly,
  and her punishment will extend to her children;
25 Her children will not take root,
  her branches will not bring forth fruit.
26 She will leave an accursed memory;
  her disgrace will never be blotted out.
27 Thus all who dwell on the earth shall know,
  and all who inhabit the world shall understand,
That nothing is better than the fear of the LORD,
  nothing more salutary than to obey
    his commandments.

19 What he fears are human eyes,
he does not realise that the eyes of the Lord
  are ten thousand times brighter than the sun,
observing every aspect of human behaviour,
  seeing into the most secret corners.
20 All things were known to him before they were
    created,
  and are still, now that they are finished.
21 This man will be punished in view of the whole
    town,
  and will be seized when he least expects it.

22 Similarly the woman unfaithful to her husband,
  who provides him with an heir by another man:
23 first, she has disobeyed the Law of the Most High;
  secondly, she has been false to her husband;
  and thirdly, she has gone whoring in adultery
24   and conceived children by another man.
She will be led before the assembly,
  an enquiry will be held about her children.
25 Her children will strike no root,
  her branches will bear no fruit.
26 She will leave an accursed memory behind her,
  her shame will never be wiped out.
27 And those who survive her will recognise
  that nothing is better than fearing the Lord,
  and nothing sweeter than adherence to the Lord's
    commandments.

24 Wisdom sings her own praises,
  before her own people she proclaims her glory;
2 In the assembly of the Most High she opens
    her mouth,
  in the presence of his hosts she declares
    her worth:
3 "From the mouth of the Most High I came forth,
  and mistlike covered the earth.
4 In the highest heavens did I dwell,
  my throne on a pillar of cloud.
5 The vault of heaven I compassed alone,
  through the deep abyss I wandered.
6 Over waves of the sea, over all the land,
  over every people and nation I held sway.
7 Among all these I sought a resting place;
  in whose inheritance should I abide?
8 "Then the Creator of all gave me his command,
  and he who formed me chose the spot for
    my tent,
Saying, 'In Jacob make your dwelling,
  in Israel your inheritance.'
9 Before all ages, in the beginning, he created me,
  and through all ages I shall not cease to be.
10 In the holy tent I ministered before him,
  and in Zion I fixed my abode.
11 Thus in the chosen city he has given me rest,
  in Jerusalem is my domain.

24 Wisdom[c] speaks her own praises,
  in the midst of her people she glories in herself.
2 She opens her mouth in the assembly of the Most
    High,
  she glories in herself in the presence of the
    Mighty One:
3 'I came forth from the mouth of the Most High,
  and I covered the earth like mist.
4 I had my tent in the heights,
  and my throne was a pillar of cloud.
5 Alone, I have made the circuit of the heavens
  and walked through the depths of the abyss.
6 Over the waves of the sea and over the whole
    earth,
  and over every people and nation I have held
    sway.
7 Among all these I searched for rest,
  and looked to see in whose territory I might
    pitch camp.
8 Then the Creator of all things instructed me
  and he who created me fixed a place for my
    tent.
He said, "Pitch your tent in Jacob,
  make Israel your inheritance."
9 From eternity, in the beginning, he created me,
  and for eternity I shall remain.
10 In the holy tent I ministered before him
  and thus became established in Zion.
11 In the beloved city he has given me rest,
  and in Jerusalem I wield my authority.

[c] 24 A high point: personified Wisdom shares God's throne (the cloud)
but also chooses Israel for an inheritance and more specifically serves
in the Temple. Sira then identifies Wisdom with the Law.

NEW REVISED STANDARD VERSION	REVISED ENGLISH BIBLE

12 I took root in an honored people,
    in the portion of the Lord, his heritage.
13 "I grew tall like a cedar in Lebanon,
    and like a cypress on the heights of Hermon.
14 I grew tall like a palm tree in En-gedi,*o*
    and like rosebushes in Jericho;
    like a fair olive tree in the field,
    and like a plane tree beside water*p* I grew tall.
15 Like cassia and camel's thorn I gave forth
      perfume,
    and like choice myrrh I spread my fragrance,
    like galbanum, onycha, and stacte,
    and like the odor of incense in the tent.
16 Like a terebinth I spread out my branches,
    and my branches are glorious and graceful.
17 Like the vine I bud forth delights,
    and my blossoms become glorious and
      abundant fruit.*q*

19 "Come to me, you who desire me,
    and eat your fill of my fruits.
20 For the memory of me is sweeter than honey,
    and the possession of me sweeter than the
      honeycomb.
21 Those who eat of me will hunger for more,
    and those who drink of me will thirst for more.
22 Whoever obeys me will not be put to shame,
    and those who work with me will not sin."
23 All this is the book of the covenant of the Most
      High God,
    the law that Moses commanded us
    as an inheritance for the congregations of
      Jacob.*r*
25 It overflows, like the Pishon, with wisdom,
    and like the Tigris at the time of the first
      fruits.
26 It runs over, like the Euphrates, with
      understanding,
    and like the Jordan at harvest time.
27 It pours forth instruction like the Nile,*s*
    like the Gihon at the time of vintage.
28 The first man did not know wisdom*t* fully,
    nor will the last one fathom her.
29 For her thoughts are more abundant than the sea,
    and her counsel deeper than the great abyss.
30 As for me, I was like a canal from a river,
    like a water channel into a garden.
31 I said, "I will water my garden
    and drench my flower-beds."
    And lo, my canal became a river,
    and my river a sea.
32 I will again make instruction shine forth like the
      dawn,
    and I will make it clear from far away.
33 I will again pour out teaching like prophecy,
    and leave it to all future generations.
34 Observe that I have not labored for myself alone,
    but for all who seek wisdom.*t*

12 I took root among the people whom the Lord had
      honoured
    by choosing them to be his own portion.
13 'There I grew like a cedar of Lebanon,
    like a cypress on the slopes of Hermon,
14 like a date-palm at En-gedi,
    like roses at Jericho.
    I grew like a fair olive tree in the vale,
    or like a plane tree planted beside the water.
15 Like cinnamon or camel-thorn I was redolent of
      spices;
    like choice myrrh I spread my fragrance,
    like galbanum, aromatic shell, and gum resin,
    like the smoke of frankincense in the sacred tent.
16 Like a terebinth I spread out my branches,
    laden with honour and grace.
17 I put forth graceful shoots like the vine,
    and my blossoms were a harvest of honour and
      wealth.

19 'Come to me, all you who desire me,
    and eat your fill of my fruit.
20 To think of me is sweeter than honey,
    to possess me sweeter than the honeycomb.
21 Whoever feeds on me will hunger for more;
    whoever drinks from me will thirst for more.
22 To obey me is to be safe from disgrace;
    those who make me their business will not go
      astray.'
23 All this is the book of the covenant of God Most
      High,
    the law laid on us by Moses,
    a possession for the assemblies of Jacob.
25 It sends out wisdom in full flood like the river
      Pishon
    or like the Tigris at the time of firstfruits;
26 it overflows like the Euphrates with understanding
    or like the Jordan at the harvest season.
27 It pours forth instruction like the Nile,
    like the Gihon at the time of vintage.
28 No one has ever known wisdom fully
    and from first to last no one has fathomed her,
29 for her thoughts are vaster than the ocean,
    her purpose more profound than the great abyss.
30 As for me, I was like a watercourse leading from a
      river,
    like a conduit into a pleasure garden.
31 I said, 'I will water my garden,
    soaking its flower beds';
    all at once my watercourse became a river
    and my river a sea.
32 I will again make learning shine like the dawn,
    that its light may be seen from afar.
33 I will again pour out my teaching like prophecy
    and bequeath it to future generations.
34 Truly, I have not toiled for myself alone
    but for all who seek wisdom.

---

o Other ancient authorities read *on the beaches*   *p* Other ancient
authorities omit *beside water*   *q* Other ancient authorities add as
verse 18, *I am the mother of beautiful love, of fear, of knowledge,
and of holy hope; being eternal, I am given to all my children, to
those who are named by him.*   *r* Other ancient authorities add as
verse 24, *"Do not cease to be strong in the Lord, cling to him so that
he may strengthen you; the Lord Almighty alone is God, and besides
him there is no savior."*   *s* Syr: Gk *It makes instruction shine forth
like light*   *t* Gk *her*

24:17 **honour and wealth:** *some witnesses add* 18I give birth to
honourable love, to reverence, knowledge, and holy hope; all these
my eternal progeny I give to God's elect *(prob. mng; Gk obscure).*
24:23 **assemblies of Jacob:** *some witnesses add* 24Never fail to be
strong in the Lord; hold fast to him, so that he may strengthen you.
The Lord Almighty is God alone, and beside him there is no saviour.
24:25, 26, 27 **It:** *or* He.   24:27 **pours . . . Nile:** *so one Vs.; Gk*
makes instruction shine like light.

12 I have struck root among the glorious people,
in the portion of the LORD, his heritage.
13 "Like a cedar on Lebanon I am raised aloft,
like a cypress on Mount Hermon,
14 Like a palm tree in Engedi,
like a rosebush in Jericho,
Like a fair olive tree in the field,
like a plane tree growing beside the water.
15 Like cinnamon, or fragrant balm, or
precious myrrh,
I give forth perfume;
Like galbanum and onycha and sweet spices,
like the odor of incense in the holy place.
16 I spread out my branches like a terebinth,
my branches so bright and so graceful.
17 I bud forth delights like the vine,
my blossoms become fruit fair and rich.
18 Come to me, all you that yearn for me,
and be filled with my fruits;
19 You will remember me as sweeter than honey,
better to have than the honeycomb.
20 He who eats of me will hunger still,
he who drinks of me will thirst for more;
21 He who obeys me will not be put to shame,
he who serves me will never fail."

22 All this is true of the book of the Most
High's covenant,
the law which Moses commanded us
as an inheritance for the community of Jacob.
23 It overflows, like the Pishon, with wisdom —
like the Tigris in the days of the new fruits.
24 It runs over, like the Euphrates,
with understanding,
like the Jordan at harvest time.
25 It sparkles like the Nile with knowledge,
like the Gihon at vintage time.
26 The first man never finished
comprehending wisdom,
nor will the last succeed in fathoming her.
27 For deeper than the sea are her thoughts;
her counsels, than the great abyss.

28 Now I, like a rivulet from her stream,
channeling the waters into a garden,
29 Said to myself, "I will water my plants,
my flower bed I will drench";
And suddenly this rivulet of mine became a river,
then this stream of mine, a sea.
30 Thus do I send my teachings forth shining like
the dawn,
to become known afar off.
31 Thus do I pour out instruction like prophecy
and bestow it on generations to come.

12 I have taken root in a privileged people,
in the Lord's property, in his inheritance.
13 I have grown tall as a cedar on Lebanon,
as a cypress on Mount Hermon;
14 I have grown tall as a palm in En-Gedi,
as the rose bushes of Jericho;
as a fine olive in the plain,
as a plane tree, I have grown tall.
15 Like cinnamon and acanthus, I have yielded a
perfume,
like choice myrrh, have breathed out a scent,
like galbanum, onycha, labdanum,
like the smoke of incense in the tent.
16 I have spread my branches like a terebinth,
and my branches are glorious and graceful.
17 I am like a vine putting out graceful shoots,
my blossoms bear the fruit of glory and wealth.
19 Approach me, you who desire me,
and take your fill of my fruits,
20 for memories of me are sweeter than honey,
inheriting me is sweeter than the honeycomb.
21 They who eat me will hunger for more,
they who drink me will thirst for more.
22 No one who obeys me will ever have to blush,
no one who acts as I dictate will ever sin.'

23 All this is no other than the Book of the Covenant
of the Most High God,
the Law that Moses enjoined on us,
an inheritance for the communities of Jacob.
25 This is what makes wisdom brim over like the
Pishon,
like the Tigris in the season of fruit,
26 what makes intelligence overflow like the
Euphrates,
like the Jordan at harvest time;
27 and makes discipline flow like the Nile,
like the Gihon when the grapes are harvested.
28 The first man did not finish discovering about her,
nor has the most recent tracked her down;
29 for her thoughts are wider than the sea,
and her designs more profound than the abyss.
30 And I, like a conduit from a river,
like a watercourse running into a garden,
31 I said, 'I am going to water my orchard,
I intend to irrigate my flower beds.'
And see, my conduit has grown into a river,
and my river has grown into a sea.
32 Making discipline shine forth from daybreak,
I shall send its light far and wide.
33 I shall pour out teaching like prophecy,
as a legacy to all future generations.
34 And note, I have been working not merely for
myself,
but for all who are seeking wisdom.

25 I take pleasure in three things,
and they are beautiful in the sight of God and
of mortals:*u*
agreement among brothers and sisters, friendship
among neighbors,
and a wife and a husband who live in
harmony.
2 I hate three kinds of people,
and I loathe their manner of life:
a pauper who boasts, a rich person who lies,
and an old fool who commits adultery.

3 If you gathered nothing in your youth,
how can you find anything in your old age?
4 How attractive is sound judgment in the
gray-haired,
and for the aged to possess good counsel!
5 How attractive is wisdom in the aged,
and understanding and counsel in the
venerable!
6 Rich experience is the crown of the aged,
and their boast is the fear of the Lord.

7 I can think of nine whom I would call blessed,
and a tenth my tongue proclaims:
a man who can rejoice in his children;
a man who lives to see the downfall of his
foes.
8 Happy the man who lives with a sensible wife,
and the one who does not plow with ox and
ass together.*v*
Happy is the one who does not sin with the
tongue,
and the one who has not served an inferior.
9 Happy is the one who finds a friend,*w*
and the one who speaks to attentive listeners.
10 How great is the one who finds wisdom!
But none is superior to the one who fears the
Lord.
11 Fear of the Lord surpasses everything;
to whom can we compare the one who has
it?*x*

13 Any wound, but not a wound of the heart!
Any wickedness, but not the wickedness of a
woman!
14 Any suffering, but not suffering from those who
hate!
And any vengeance, but not the vengeance of
enemies!
15 There is no venom*y* worse than a snake's
venom,*y*
and no anger worse than a woman's*z* wrath.*z*
16 I would rather live with a lion and a dragon
than live with an evil woman.
17 A woman's wickedness changes her appearance,
and darkens her face like that of a bear.
18 Her husband sits*a* among the neighbors,
and he cannot help sighing*b* bitterly.
19 Any iniquity is small compared to a woman's
iniquity;
may a sinner's lot befall her!

25 THERE are three sights which warm my heart
and are beautiful in the eyes of the Lord and of
men:
concord among brothers, amity among neighbours,
and a man and wife who are inseparable.
2 There are three kinds of men who arouse my
hatred
and disgust me by their manner of life:
a poor man who boasts, a rich man who lies,
and an old fool who commits adultery.

3 If you have not gathered wisdom in your youth,
will you find it when you are old?
4 How well sound judgement befits grey hairs,
as wise advice does those advanced in years!
5 How well wisdom befits the aged,
and ripe counsel persons of eminence!
6 Long experience is the crown of the aged,
and their pride is the fear of the Lord.

7 I can think of nine men I count happy,
and I can tell you of a tenth:
a man who delights in his children,
and one who lives to see the downfall of his
enemy.
8 Happy the husband of a sensible wife,
the farmer who does not plough with ox and ass
together,
he whose tongue never trips him,
and he who has never had to work for his inferior!
9 Happy the man who has found a friend,
and the speaker who has an attentive audience!
10 How great is he who finds wisdom!
But no greater than he who fears the Lord.
11 The fear of the Lord excels all other gifts;
to whom can its possessor be compared?

13 ANY wound but a wound in the heart,
any malice but a woman's!
14 Any disaster but one caused by hate,
any vengeance but the vengeance of an enemy!
15 There is no venom deadlier than a snake's
and no anger deadlier than a woman's.

16 I would sooner live with a lion or a serpent
than share a house with a malicious wife.
17 Her spite changes her expression,
making her look as surly as a bear.
18 Her husband goes to a neighbour for his meals
and cannot repress a bitter sigh.

19 There is nothing so bad as a bad wife;
may the fate of the wicked overtake her!

---

u Syr Lat: Gk *In three things I was beautiful and I stood in beauty
before the Lord and mortals.*   *v* Heb Syr: Gk lacks *and the one
who does not plow with ox and ass together*   *w* Lat Syr: Gk *good
sense*   *x* Other ancient authorities add as verse 12, *The fear of the
Lord is the beginning of love for him, and faith is the beginning of
clinging to him.*   *y* Syr: Gk *head*   *z* Other ancient authorities read
an enemy's   *a* Heb Syr: Gk *loses heart*   *b* Other ancient
authorities read *and listening he sighs*

25:8 **the farmer ... together:** so Heb.; Gk omits.   25:9 **found a
friend:** so Vss.; Gk found good sense.   25:11 **be compared:** *some
witnesses add* 12 The fear of the Lord is the source of love for him,
and faith is the source of adherence to him.   25:15 **venom:** *prob.
mng;* Gk head. **a woman's:** *so some* Vss.; Gk an enemy's.

NEW AMERICAN BIBLE

NEW JERUSALEM BIBLE

25 With three things I am delighted,
for they are pleasing to the LORD and to men:
Harmony among brethren, friendship
among neighbors,
and the mutual love of husband and wife.
2 Three kinds of men I hate;
their manner of life I loathe indeed:
A proud pauper, a rich dissembler,
and an old man lecherous in his dotage.

3 What you have not saved in your youth,
how will you acquire in your old age?
4 How becoming to the gray-haired is judgment,
and a knowledge of counsel to those on in years!
5 How becoming to the aged is wisdom,
understanding and prudence to the venerable!
6 The crown of old men is wide experience;
their glory, the fear of the LORD.

7 There are nine who come to my mind as blessed,
a tenth whom my tongue proclaims:
The man who finds joy in his children,
and he who lives to see his enemies' downfall.
8 Happy is he who dwells with a sensible wife,
and he who plows not like a donkey yoked with
an ox.
Happy is he who sins not with his tongue,
and he who serves not his inferior.
9 Happy is he who finds a friend
and he who speaks to attentive ears.
10 He who finds wisdom is great indeed,
but not greater than he who fears the LORD.
11 Fear of the LORD surpasses all else,
its possessor is beyond compare.

12 Worst of all wounds is that of the heart,
worst of all evils is that of a woman.
13 Worst of all sufferings is that from one's foes,
worst of all vengeance is that of one's enemies:
14 No poison worse than that of a serpent,
no venom greater than that of a woman.
15 With a dragon or a lion I would rather dwell
than live with an evil woman.
16 Wickedness changes a woman's looks,
and makes her sullen as a female bear.
17 When her husband sits among his neighbors,
a bitter sigh escapes him unawares.
18 There is scarce any evil like that in a woman;
may she fall to the lot of the sinner!

25 There are three things my soul delights in,
and which are delightful to God and to all
people:
concord between brothers, friendship between
neighbours,
and a wife and husband who live happily
together.
2 There are three sorts of people my soul hates,
and whose existence I consider an outrage:
the poor swollen with pride, the rich who is a liar
and an adulterous old man who has no sense.

3 If you have gathered nothing in your youth,
how can you discover anything in your old age?
4 How fine a thing: sound judgement with grey
hairs,
and for greybeards to know how to advise!
5 How fine a thing: wisdom in the aged,
and considered advice coming from people of
distinction!
6 The crown of the aged is ripe experience,
their glory, the fear of the Lord.

7 There are nine things I can think of which strike
me as happy,
and a tenth which is now on my tongue:
the man who can be proud of his children,
he who lives to see the downfall of his enemies;
8 happy is he who keeps house with a sensible wife;
he who does not toil with ox and donkey;[d]
he who has never sinned with his tongue;
he who does not serve a man less worthy than
himself;
9 happy is he who has acquired good sense
and can find attentive ears for what he has to
say;
10 how great is he who has acquired wisdom;
but unsurpassed is one who fears the Lord.
11 The fear of the Lord surpasses everything;
what can compare with someone who has
mastered that?

13 Any wound rather than a wound of the heart!
Any spite rather than the spite of woman!
14 Any evil rather than an evil caused by an enemy!
Any vengeance rather than the vengeance of a
foe!
15 There is no poison worse than the poison of a
snake,
there is no fury worse than the fury of an
enemy.
16 I would sooner keep house with a lion or a dragon
than keep house with a spiteful wife.
17 A woman's spite changes her appearance
and makes her face as grim as a bear's.
18 When her husband goes out to dinner with his
neighbours,
he cannot help heaving bitter sighs.
19 No spite can approach the spite of a woman,
may a sinner's lot be hers!

---

[d] **25** Such an uneven team is prohibited by Dt 22:10.

NEW REVISED STANDARD VERSION	REVISED ENGLISH BIBLE

NEW REVISED STANDARD VERSION

20 A sandy ascent for the feet of the aged—
   such is a garrulous wife to a quiet husband.
21 Do not be ensnared by a woman's beauty,
   and do not desire a woman for her
   possessions.*c*
22 There is wrath and impudence and great disgrace
   when a wife supports her husband.
23 Dejected mind, gloomy face,
   and wounded heart come from an evil wife.
   Drooping hands and weak knees
   come from the wife who does not make her
   husband happy.
24 From a woman sin had its beginning,
   and because of her we all die.
25 Allow no outlet to water,
   and no boldness of speech to an evil wife.
26 If she does not go as you direct,
   separate her from yourself.

26 Happy is the husband of a good wife;
   the number of his days will be doubled.
2 A loyal wife brings joy to her husband,
   and he will complete his years in peace.
3 A good wife is a great blessing;
   she will be granted among the blessings of the
   man who fears the Lord.
4 Whether rich or poor, his heart is content,
   and at all times his face is cheerful.
5 Of three things my heart is frightened,
   and of a fourth I am in great fear:*d*
   Slander in the city, the gathering of a mob,
   and false accusation—all these are worse than
   death.
6 But it is heartache and sorrow when a wife is
   jealous of a rival,
   and a tongue-lashing makes it known to all.
7 A bad wife is a chafing yoke;
   taking hold of her is like grasping a scorpion.
8 A drunken wife arouses great anger;
   she cannot hide her shame.
9 The haughty stare betrays an unchaste wife;
   her eyelids give her away.
10 Keep strict watch over a headstrong daughter,
   or else, when she finds liberty, she will make
   use of it.
11 Be on guard against her impudent eye,
   and do not be surprised if she sins against you.
12 As a thirsty traveler opens his mouth
   and drinks from any water near him,
   so she will sit in front of every tent peg
   and open her quiver to the arrow.
13 A wife's charm delights her husband,
   and her skill puts flesh on his bones.
14 A silent wife is a gift from the Lord,
   and nothing is so precious as her
   self-discipline.
15 A modest wife adds charm to charm,
   and no scales can weigh the value of her
   chastity.
16 Like the sun rising in the heights of the Lord,
   so is the beauty of a good wife in her
   well-ordered home.
17 Like the shining lamp on the holy lampstand,
   so is a beautiful face on a stately figure.

REVISED ENGLISH BIBLE

20 It is as easy for an old man to climb a sand-dune
   as for a quiet husband to live with a garrulous wife.
21 Do not be enticed by a woman's beauty
   or set your heart on possessing one who has
   wealth.
22 If a man is supported by his wife
   he must expect tantrums, effrontery, and much
   humiliation.
23 Depression, downcast looks, and a broken heart:
   these are caused by a worthless wife.
   Feeble of hand and weak at the knees
   is the man whose wife fails to bring him happiness.
24 Sin began with a woman,
   and because of her we all die.
25 Do not leave a leaky cistern to drip
   or allow a worthless wife to say whatever she
   likes.
26 If she does not accept your control,
   bring the marriage to an end.

26 A good wife makes a happy husband;
   she doubles the length of his life.
2 A staunch wife is her husband's joy;
   he will live out his days in peace.
3 A good wife is a blessing;
   she is one of the Lord's gifts to those who fear
   him.
4 Rich or poor, they are in good heart,
   with always a smile on their faces.
5 Three things there are that alarm me,
   and a fourth I am afraid to face:
   scandalmongering in the city, a mob controlling the
   assembly,
   and false accusation—all harder to bear than death;
6 but a wife's jealousy of a rival brings heartache
   and grief,
   and everyone alike feels the lash of her tongue.
7 A bad wife is a yoke that chafes;
   controlling her is like handling a scorpion.
8 A drunken wife provokes much anger;
   she will not conceal her excesses.
9 A loose woman betrays herself by her bold looks;
   you can tell her by her glance.
10 Keep close watch over a headstrong daughter;
   if she finds you off your guard, she will take her
   chance.
11 Beware of her impudent looks
   and do not be surprised if she disobeys you.
12 As a parched traveller with gaping mouth
   drinks from any spring that offers,
   she will open her arms to every embrace
   and her quiver to every arrow.
13 A wife's charm is the delight of her husband,
   and her womanly skill puts flesh on his bones.
14 A silent wife is a gift from the Lord;
   her good breeding is more than money can buy.
15 A modest wife has infinite charm;
   no scales can weigh the worth of her self-control.
16 As beautiful as the sunrise in the Lord's heavens
   is a good wife in a well-ordered home.
17 As bright as the light on the sacred lampstand
   is a beautiful face with a stately figure.

---

c Heb Syr: Other Gk authorities read *for her beauty*   *d* Syr: Meaning
of Gk uncertain

26:3 **blessing:** *lit.* good portion.

19 Like a sandy hill to aged feet
   is a railing wife to a quiet man.
	20 Like the climbing of a sandhill for elderly feet,
	   such is a garrulous wife for a quiet husband.

20 Stumble not through woman's beauty,
   nor be greedy for her wealth;
	21 Do not be taken in by a woman's beauty,
	   never lose your head over a woman.

21 The man is a slave, in disgrace and shame,
   when a wife supports her husband.
	22 Bad temper, insolence and shame hold sway
	   where the wife supports the husband.

22 Depressed mind, saddened face,
   broken heart — this from an evil wife.
   Feeble hands and quaking knees —
   from a wife who brings no happiness to
   her husband.
	23 Low spirits, gloomy face, stricken heart:
	   such is a spiteful wife.
	   Slack hands and sagging knees:
	   such is the wife who does not make her husband
	   happy.

23 In woman was sin's beginning,
   and because of her we all die.
	24 Sin began with a woman,
	   and thanks to her we must all die.

24 Allow water no outlet,
   and be not indulgent to an erring wife.
	25 Do not let water find a leak,
	   nor a spiteful woman give free rein to her
	   tongue.

25 If she walks not by your side,
   cut her away from you.
	26 If she will not do as you tell her,
	   get rid of her.

26 Happy the husband of a good wife,
   twice-lengthened are his days;

26 How blessed is the husband of a really good
   wife;
   the number of his days will be doubled.

2 A worthy wife brings joy to her husband,
   peaceful and full is his life.
	2 A perfect wife is the joy of her husband,
	   he will live out the years of his life in peace.

3 A good wife is a generous gift
   bestowed upon him who fears the Lord;
	3 A good wife is the best of portions,
	   reserved for those who fear the Lord;

4 Be he rich or poor, his heart is content,
   and a smile is ever on his face.
	4 rich or poor, their hearts will be glad,
	   their faces cheerful, whatever the season.

5 There are three things at which my heart quakes,
   a fourth before which I quail:
   Though false charges in public, trial before all
   the people,
   and lying testimony are harder to bear
   than death,
	5 There are three things that I dread,
	   and a fourth which terrifies me:
	   slander by a whole town, the gathering of a mob,
	   and a false accusation — these are all worse than
	   death;

6 A jealous wife is heartache and mourning
   and a scourging tongue like the other three.
	6 but a woman jealous of a woman means heartbreak
	   and sorrow,
	   and all this is the scourge of the tongue.

7 A bad wife is a chafing yoke;
   he who marries her seizes a scorpion.
	7 A bad wife is a badly fitting ox-yoke,
	   trying to master her is like grasping a scorpion.

8 A drunken wife arouses great anger,
   for she does not hide her shame.
	8 A drunken wife will goad anyone to fury,
	   she cannot conceal her own degradation.

9 By her eyelids and her haughty stare
   an unchaste wife can be recognized.
	9 A woman's wantonness shows in her wide-eyed
	   look,
	   her eyelashes leave no doubt.

10 Keep a strict watch over an unruly wife,
   lest, finding an opportunity, she make use of it;
	10 Keep a headstrong daughter under firm control,
	   or, feeling free, she will take advantage of it.

11 Follow close if her eyes are bold,
   and be not surprised if she betrays you:
	11 Keep a strict watch on her shameless eye,
	   do not be surprised if she disgraces you.

12 As a thirsty traveler with eager mouth
   drinks from any water that he finds,
   So she settles down before every tent peg
   and opens her quiver for every arrow.
	12 Like a thirsty traveller she will open her mouth
	   and drink any water she comes across;
	   she will sit down in front of every tent-peg
	   and open her quiver to any arrow.

13 A gracious wife delights her husband,
   her thoughtfulness puts flesh on his bones;
	13 The grace of a wife will charm her husband,
	   her understanding will make him the stronger.

14 A gift from the Lord is her governed speech,
   and her firm virtue is of surpassing worth.
	14 A silent wife is a gift from the Lord,
	   no price can be put on a well-trained character.

15 Choicest of blessings is a modest wife,
   priceless her chaste person.
	15 A modest wife is a boon twice over,
	   a chaste character cannot be over-valued.

16 Like the sun rising in the Lord's heavens,
   the beauty of a virtuous wife is the radiance of
   her home.
	16 Like the sun rising over the mountains of the Lord,
	   such is the beauty of a good wife in a well-run
	   house.

17 Like the light which shines above the
   holy lampstand,
   are her beauty of face and graceful figure.
	17 Like a lamp shining on the sacred lamp-stand,
	   such is a beautiful face on a well-proportioned
	   body.

NEW REVISED STANDARD VERSION	REVISED ENGLISH BIBLE

18 Like golden pillars on silver bases,
    so are shapely legs and steadfast feet.

Other ancient authorities add verses 19–27:

19 *My child, keep sound the bloom of your youth,*
    and do not give your strength to strangers.
20 *Seek a fertile field within the whole plain,*
    and sow it with your own seed, trusting in your
    fine stock.
21 *So your offspring will prosper,*
    and, having confidence in their good descent,
    will grow great.
22 *A prostitute is regarded as spittle,*
    and a married woman as a tower of death to
    her lovers.
23 *A godless wife is given as a portion to a lawless*
    man,
    but a pious wife is given to the man who fears
    the Lord.
24 *A shameless woman constantly acts disgracefully,*
    but a modest daughter will even be
    embarrassed before her husband.
25 *A headstrong wife is regarded as a dog,*
    but one who has a sense of shame will fear the
    Lord.
26 *A wife honoring her husband will seem wise to*
    all,
    but if she dishonors him in her pride she will
    be known to all as ungodly.
    Happy is the husband of a good wife;
    for the number of his years will be doubled.
27 *A loud-voiced and garrulous wife is like a*
    trumpet sounding the charge,
    and every person like this lives in the anarchy
    of war.

28 At two things my heart is grieved,
    and because of a third anger comes over me:
    a warrior in want through poverty,
      intelligent men who are treated
      contemptuously,
    and a man who turns back from righteousness to
      sin —
    the Lord will prepare him for the sword!
29 A merchant can hardly keep from wrongdoing,
    nor is a tradesman innocent of sin.

27 Many have committed sin for gain,[e]
    and those who seek to get rich will avert their
      eyes.
2 As a stake is driven firmly into a fissure between
      stones,
    so sin is wedged in between selling and
      buying.
3 If a person is not steadfast in the fear of the
      Lord,
    his house will be quickly overthrown.
4 When a sieve is shaken, the refuse appears;
    so do a person's faults when he speaks.
5 The kiln tests the potter's vessels;
    so the test of a person is in his conversation.
6 Its fruit discloses the cultivation of a tree;
    so a person's speech discloses the cultivation of
      his mind.
7 Do not praise anyone before he speaks,
    for this is the way people are tested.

---

18 Like a golden pillar on a silver base
    is a shapely leg with a firm foot.

Some witnesses add verses 19–27:

19 *My son, guard your health in the bloom of your*
    youth,
    and do not waste your vigour on strange women.
20 *Search the whole plain for a fertile plot;*
    sow your own seed, trusting in your sound stock.
21 *Then the children you leave behind*
    will prosper, confident in their parentage.
22 *A woman of the streets is no better than spittle;*
    a married woman is a mortuary for her lovers.
23 *A godless woman is a good match for a lawless*
    husband,
    a godly one for a man who fears the Lord.
24 *A brazen woman courts disgrace,*
    but a virtuous daughter is modest even before her
    husband.
25 *A headstrong woman is a shameless bitch,*
    but a modest one fears the Lord.
26 *A woman who honours her husband is accounted*
    wise by all,
    but if she despises him, all know her as proud and
    godless.
    A good wife makes a happy husband;
    she doubles the length of his life.
27 *A strident, garrulous wife is like a trumpet*
    sounding the charge;
    in a home like hers a man lives in the confusions
    of war.

---

28 Two THINGS grieve my heart,
    and a third excites my anger:
    a soldier in distress through poverty,
    the wise treated with contempt,
    and someone deserting right conduct for wrong —
    for such a one the Lord will get ready the sword.
29 How rare it is for a merchant to keep clear of
      wrong
    or a shopkeeper to be acquitted of dishonesty!

27 Many have cheated for gain;
    a money-grubber will always turn a blind eye.
2 As a peg is fixed in the joint between stones,
    so dishonesty squeezes in between selling and
      buying.
3 Unless a person holds resolutely to the fear of the
      Lord,
    his house will soon collapse in ruins.
4 Shake a sieve, and the rubbish remains;
    start an argument, and a man's faults show up.
5 As the work of a potter is tested in the kiln,
    so a man is tried in debate.
6 As a tree's fruit reveals the skill of the grower,
    so the expression of a man's thoughts reveals his
      character.
7 Do not praise a man till you hear him in argument,
    for that is the test.

---

[e] Other ancient authorities read *a trifle*

26:18 **a firm foot:** *In standard editions of the* Revised English Bible
the italicized verses that follow appear in a footnote.

NEW AMERICAN BIBLE	NEW JERUSALEM BIBLE

18 Golden columns on silver bases
 are her shapely limbs and steady feet.

18 Like golden pillars on a silver base,
 such are shapely legs on firm-set heels.

Among the additions found here in some manuscripts
are the following lines:

"My son, take care in the prime of life
* not to surrender your strength to strangers;*
Single out from the land a goodly field
* and there with confidence sow the seed of your*
*   increase;*
So shall you have your offspring around you,
* and in confidence shall they grow up.*
"Though a woman for hire be thought of as a
*   trifle,*
* a married woman is a deadly snare for those*
*   who embrace her.*
"A wife's complaint should be made in meekness,
* and show itself in a slight flush;*
But a loud-mouthed, scolding wife
* is a trumpet signaling for battle:*
Any human being who answers that challenge
* will spend his life amid the turbulence of war."*

19 These two bring grief to my heart,
 and the third arouses my horror:
 A wealthy man reduced to want;
 illustrious men held in contempt;
 And the man who passes from justice to sin,
 for whom the LORD makes ready the sword.

20 A merchant can hardly remain upright,
 nor a shopkeeper free from sin;

28 There are two things which grieve my heart
 and a third arouses my anger:
 a warrior wasting away through poverty,
 the intelligent treated with contempt,
 someone turning back from virtue to sin—
 the Lord marks out such a person for a violent
 death.

29 It is difficult for a merchant to avoid doing wrong
 and for a trader not to incur sin.

27 For the sake of profit many sin,
 and the struggle for wealth blinds the eyes.
2 Like a peg driven between fitted stones,
 between buying and selling sin is wedged in.
3 Unless you earnestly hold fast to the fear of
 the LORD,
 suddenly your house will be thrown down.
4 When a sieve is shaken, the husks appear;
 so do a man's faults when he speaks.
5 As the test of what the potter molds is in
 the furnace,
 so in his conversation is the test of a man.
6 The fruit of a tree shows the care it has had;
 so too does a man's speech disclose the bent of
 his mind.
7 Praise no man before he speaks,
 for it is then that men are tested.

27 Many have sinned for the sake of profit,
 one who hopes to be rich must turn a blind eye.
2 A peg will stick in the joint between two stones,
 and sin will wedge itself between selling and
 buying.
3 Whoever does not firmly hold to the fear of the
 Lord,
 his house will soon be overthrown.
4 In a shaken sieve the rubbish is left behind,
 so too the defects of a person appear in speech.
5 The kiln tests the work of the potter,
 the test of a person is in conversation.
6 The orchard where the tree grows is judged by its
 fruit,
 similarly words betray what a person feels.
7 Do not praise anyone who has not yet spoken,
 since this is where people are tested.

26, 18 In standard editions of the *New American Bible* the italicized
verses that follow appear in a footnote.

8 If you pursue justice, you will attain it
  and wear it like a glorious robe.
9 Birds roost with their own kind,
  so honesty comes home to those who practice
  it.
10 A lion lies in wait for prey;
  so does sin for evildoers.
11 The conversation of the godly is always wise,
  but the fool changes like the moon.
12 Among stupid people limit your time,
  but among thoughtful people linger on.
13 The talk of fools is offensive,
  and their laughter is wantonly sinful.
14 Their cursing and swearing make one's hair stand
  on end,
  and their quarrels make others stop their ears.
15 The strife of the proud leads to bloodshed,
  and their abuse is grievous to hear.

16 Whoever betrays secrets destroys confidence,
  and will never find a congenial friend.
17 Love your friend and keep faith with him;
  but if you betray his secrets, do not follow
  after him.
18 For as a person destroys his enemy,
  so you have destroyed the friendship of your
  neighbor.
19 And as you allow a bird to escape from your
  hand,
  so you have let your neighbor go, and will not
  catch him again.
20 Do not go after him, for he is too far off,
  and has escaped like a gazelle from a snare.
21 For a wound may be bandaged,
  and there is reconciliation after abuse,
  but whoever has betrayed secrets is without
  hope.

22 Whoever winks the eye plots mischief,
  and those who know him will keep their
  distance.
23 In your presence his mouth is all sweetness,
  and he admires your words;
  but later he will twist his speech
  and with your own words he will trip you up.
24 I have hated many things, but him above all;
  even the Lord hates him.
25 Whoever throws a stone straight up throws it on
  his own head,
  and a treacherous blow opens up many
  wounds.
26 Whoever digs a pit will fall into it,
  and whoever sets a snare will be caught in it.
27 If a person does evil, it will roll back upon him,
  and he will not know where it came from.
28 Mockery and abuse issue from the proud,
  but vengeance lies in wait for them like a lion.
29 Those who rejoice in the fall of the godly will be
  caught in a snare,
  and pain will consume them before their death.

30 Anger and wrath, these also are abominations,
  yet a sinner holds on to them.

28 The vengeful will face the Lord's vengeance,
  for he keeps a strict account of *f* their sins.
2 Forgive your neighbor the wrong he has done,
  and then your sins will be pardoned when you
  pray.
3 Does anyone harbor anger against another,

f Other ancient authorities read *for he firmly establishes*

8 If justice is what you seek, you will succeed
  and wear it like a splendid robe.
9 Birds of a feather roost together,
  and honesty comes home to those who practise it.
10 A lion lies in wait for its prey;
  so does sin for those whose conduct is evil.
11 The conversation of the godly is constantly wise,
  but a fool is as changeable as the moon.
12 Grudge every minute spent among fools,
  but linger among the thoughtful.
13 The conversation of fools provokes disgust;
  to them a life of licence is just a joke.
14 The chatter of the profane makes the hair stand on
  end;
  when such folk quarrel, others stop their ears.
15 The quarrels of the proud lead to bloodshed;
  their abuse makes sorry hearing.

16 The betrayer of secrets forfeits all trust;
  he will never find an intimate friend.
17 Love your friend and keep faith with him;
  but if you betray his secrets, steer clear of him,
18 for as one kills an enemy,
  so you have killed your neighbour's friendship.
19 As a bird that is allowed to fly out of your hand,
  your neighbour, once lost, will not be caught
  again.
20 He has gone too far for you to pursue him;
  he has escaped like a gazelle from a trap.
21 A wound may be bandaged, an insult pardoned,
  but the betrayer of secrets has renounced all hope.

22 Someone who winks is plotting mischief;
  those who know him will keep their distance.
23 He speaks sweetly enough to your face
  and admires whatever you say,
  but later he will change his tune
  and use your own words to trip you.
24 There are many things I hate, but him above all;
  and the Lord will hate him too.
25 Throw a stone in the air and you throw it on your
  own head;
  and a treacherous blow means wounds all round.
26 Dig a pit and you will fall into it;
  set a trap and you will be caught by it.
27 The wrong anyone does recoils on him,
  and he has no idea where it comes from.
28 The arrogant deal in mockery and taunts,
  but like a lion retribution lies in wait for them.
29 Those who rejoice at the downfall of the good will
  be trapped,
  and before they die they will be consumed with
  pain.

30 Rage and anger, these also I abhor,
  but a sinner has them ready at hand.

28 Whoever acts vengefully will face the vengeance
  of the Lord,
  who keeps strict account of sins.
2 Forgive your neighbour any wrong he has done
  you;
  then, when you pray, your sins will be forgiven.
3 If anyone harbours anger against another,

8 If you strive after justice you will attain it,
   and put it on like a splendid robe.
9 Birds nest with their own kind,
   and fidelity comes to those who live by it.
10 As a lion crouches in wait for prey,
   so do sins for evildoers.
11 Ever wise are the discourses of the devout,
   but the godless man, like the moon,
     is inconstant.
12 Limit the time you spend among fools,
   but frequent the company of thoughtful men.
13 The conversation of the wicked is offensive,
   their laughter is wanton guilt.
14 Their oath-filled talk makes the hair stand on end,
   their brawls make one stop one's ears.
15 Wrangling among the haughty ends in bloodshed,
   their cursing is painful to hear.

16 He who betrays a secret cannot be trusted,
   he will never find an intimate friend.
17 Cherish your friend, keep faith with him;
   but if you betray his confidence, follow him not;
18 For as an enemy might kill a man,
   you have killed your neighbor's friendship.
19 Like a bird released from the hand,
   you have let your friend go and cannot
     recapture him;
20 Follow him not, for he is far away,
   he has fled like a gazelle from the trap.
21 A wound can be bound up, and an insult forgiven,
   but he who betrays secrets does
     hopeless damage.

22 He who has shifty eyes plots mischief
   and no one can ward him off;
23 In your presence he uses honeyed talk,
   and admires your every word,
   But later he changes his tone
   and twists your words to your ruin.
24 There is nothing that I hate so much,
   and the LORD hates him as well.
25 As a stone falls back on him who throws it up,
   so a blow struck in treachery injures more
     than one.
26 As he who digs a pit falls into it,
   and he who lays a snare is caught in it,
27 Whoever does harm will be involved in it
   without knowing how it came upon him.

28 Mockery and abuse will be the lot of the proud,
   and vengeance lies in wait for them like a lion.
29 The trap seizes those who rejoice in pitfalls,
   and pain will consume them before they die;
30 Wrath and anger are hateful things,
   yet the sinner hugs them tight.

28 The vengeful will suffer the LORD's vengeance,
   for he remembers their sins in detail.
2 Forgive your neighbor's injustice;
   then when you pray, your own sins will
     be forgiven.
3 Should a man nourish anger against his fellows

8 If you pursue virtue, you will attain it
   and put it on like a festal gown.
9 Birds consort with their kind,
   truth comes home to those who practise it.
10 The lion lies in wait for its prey,
   so does sin for those who do wrong.
11 The conversation of the devout is wisdom at all
     times,
   but the fool is as changeable as the moon.
12 When visiting stupid people, choose the right
     moment,
   but among the thoughtful take your time.
13 The conversation of fools is disgusting,
   raucous their laughter in their sinful pleasures.
14 The talk of hard-swearing people makes your hair
     stand on end,
   their brawling makes you stop your ears.
15 A quarrel between the proud leads to bloodshed,
   and their insults are embarrassing to hear.

16 A betrayer of secrets forfeits all trust
   and will never find the kind of friend he wants.
17 Be fond of a friend and keep faith with him,
   but if you have betrayed his secrets, do not go
     after him any more;
18 for, as one destroys a person by killing him,
   so you have killed your neighbour's friendship,
19 and as you let a bird slip through your fingers,
   so you have let your friend go, and will not
     catch him.
20 Do not go after him — he is far away,
   he has fled like a gazelle from the snare.
21 For a wound can be bandaged and abuse forgiven,
   but for the betrayer of a secret there is no hope.

22 Someone with a sly wink is plotting mischief,
   no one can dissuade him from it.
23 Honey-tongued to your face,
   he is lost in admiration at your words;
   but behind your back he has other things to say,
   and turns your words into a stumbling-block.
24 I have found many things to hate, but nothing as
     much as him,
   and the Lord hates him too.
25 Whoever throws a stone in the air, throws it on to
     his own head;
   a treacherous blow cuts both ways.
26 The man who digs a pit falls into it,
   whoever sets a snare will be caught by it.
27 On anyone who does evil, evil will recoil,
   without his knowing where it comes from.

28 Sarcasm and abuse are the mark of the arrogant,
   but vengeance lies in wait like a lion for such a
     one.
29 The trap will close on all who rejoice in the
     downfall of the devout,
   and pain will eat them up before they die.

30 Resentment and anger, these are foul things too,
   and a sinner is a master at both.

28 Whoever exacts vengeance will experience the
     vengeance of the Lord,
   who keeps strict account of sin.
2 Pardon your neighbour any wrongs done to you,
   and when you pray, your sins will be forgiven.
3 If anyone nurses anger against another,

NEW REVISED STANDARD VERSION	REVISED ENGLISH BIBLE
and expect healing from the Lord?	can he expect help from the Lord?
4 If one has no mercy toward another like himself, can he then seek pardon for his own sins?	4 If he refuses mercy to his fellow, can he ask forgiveness for his own sins?
5 If a mere mortal harbors wrath, who will make an atoning sacrifice for his sins?	5 If a mere mortal cherishes rage, where is he to look for pardon?
6 Remember the end of your life, and set enmity aside; remember corruption and death, and be true to the commandments.	6 Think of the end that awaits you, and have done with hate; think of mortality and death, and be true to the commandments;
7 Remember the commandments, and do not be angry with your neighbor; remember the covenant of the Most High, and overlook faults.	7 think of the commandments, and do not be enraged at your neighbour; think of the covenant of the Most High, and overlook errors.
8 Refrain from strife, and your sins will be fewer; for the hot-tempered kindle strife,	8 To avoid a quarrel is a setback for sin, for quarrels are kindled by a hot temper.
9 and the sinner disrupts friendships and sows discord among those who are at peace.	9 A sinner sets friends at odds and spreads enmity where before there was peace.
10 In proportion to the fuel, so will the fire burn, and in proportion to the obstinacy, so will strife increase;g in proportion to a person's strength will be his anger, and in proportion to his wealth he will increase his wrath.	10 The more fuel, the fiercer the blaze; the more stubborn the defence, the fiercer the fight. The greater a person, the greater his anger; the more his wealth, the higher his temper will flare.
11 A hasty quarrel kindles a fire, and a hasty dispute sheds blood.	11 A hasty dispute kindles a fire; a hasty quarrel leads to bloodshed.
12 If you blow on a spark, it will glow; if you spit on it, it will be put out; yet both come out of your mouth.	12 Blow on a spark to make it glow, or spit on it to put it out; both results come from your mouth.
13 Curse the gossips and the double-tongued, for they destroy the peace of many.	13 Curses on tale-bearing and duplicity! For they have been the ruin of many who were living peaceably.
14 Slanderh has shaken many, and scattered them from nation to nation; it has destroyed strong cities, and overturned the houses of the great.	14 A third party's talk has wrecked the lives of many and driven them from country to country; it has destroyed strong cities and overthrown the houses of the great.
15 Slanderi has driven virtuous women from their homes, and deprived them of the fruit of their toil.	15 A third party's talk has brought divorce on staunch wives and deprived them of the fruits of their industry;
16 Those who pay heed to slanderj will not find rest, nor will they settle down in peace.	16 whoever heeds it will never again find rest or live in peace of mind.
17 The blow of a whip raises a welt, but a blow of the tongue crushes the bones.	17 The lash of a whip raises weals, but the lash of a tongue will break bones.
18 Many have fallen by the edge of the sword, but not as many as have fallen because of the tongue.	18 Many have been killed by the edge of the sword, but not so many as by the tongue.
19 Happy is the one who is protected from it, who has not been exposed to its anger, who has not borne its yoke, and has not been bound with its fetters.	19 Happy are they who are sheltered from its onslaught, who have not been exposed to its fury, who have not borne its yoke or been chained with its fetters;
20 For its yoke is a yoke of iron, and its fetters are fetters of bronze;	20 for its yoke is of iron, its fetters are of bronze!
21 its death is an evil death, and Hades is preferable to it.	21 The death it inflicts is a horrible death; better the grave than the tongue!
22 It has no power over the godly; they will not be burned in its flame.	22 But it has no power over the godfearing; they cannot be burnt in its flames.
23 Those who forsake the Lord will fall into its power; it will burn among them and will not be put out. It will be sent out against them like a lion; like a leopard it will mangle them.	23 Rather, those who desert the Lord fall victim to it; among them it will blaze up and never be quenched. It will launch itself against them like a lion and tear them like a leopard.
24a As you fence in your property with thorns, 25b so make a door and a bolt for your mouth.	24 As you enclose your garden with a thorn hedge, and as you tie up securely your silver and gold,

g Other ancient authorities read *burn*   h Gk *A third tongue*
i Gk *A third tongue*   j Gk *it*

and expect healing from the LORD?

4 Should a man refuse mercy to his fellows,
  yet seek pardon for his own sins?
5 If he who is but flesh cherishes wrath,
  who will forgive his sins?
6 Remember your last days, set enmity aside;
  remember death and decay, and cease from sin!
7 Think of the commandments, hate not
    your neighbor;
  of the Most High's covenant, and
    overlook faults.

8 Avoid strife and your sins will be fewer,
  for a quarrelsome man kindles disputes,
9 Commits the sin of disrupting friendship
  and sows discord among those at peace.
10 The more wood, the greater the fire,
  the more underlying it, the fiercer the fight;
  The greater a man's strength, the sterner his anger,
  the greater his power, the greater his wrath.
11 Pitch and resin make fires flare up,
  and insistent quarrels provoke bloodshed.

12 If you blow upon a spark, it quickens into flame,
  if you spit on it, it dies out;
  yet both you do with your mouth!
13 Cursed be gossips and the double-tongued,
  for they destroy the peace of many.
14 A meddlesome tongue subverts many,
  and makes them refugees among the peoples;
  It destroys walled cities,
  and overthrows powerful dynasties.
15 A meddlesome tongue can drive virtuous women
    from their homes
  and rob them of the fruit of their toil;
16 Whoever heeds it has no rest,
  nor can he dwell in peace.

17 A blow from a whip raises a welt,
  but a blow from the tongue smashes bones;
18 Many have fallen by the edge of the sword,
  but not as many as by the tongue.
19 Happy he who is sheltered from it,
  and has not endured its wrath;
  Who has not borne its yoke
  nor been fettered with its chains;
20 For its yoke is a yoke of iron
  and its chains are chains of bronze!
21 Dire is the death it inflicts,
  besides which even the nether world is a gain;
22 It will not take hold among the just
  nor scorch them in its flame,
23 But those who forsake the LORD will fall victims
    to it,
  as it burns among them unquenchably!
  It will hurl itself against them like a lion;
  like a panther, it will tear them to pieces.
24 As you hedge round your vineyard with thorns,
  set barred doors over your mouth;

can one then demand compassion from the Lord?
4 Showing no pity for someone like oneself,
  can one then plead for one's own sins?
5 Mere creature of flesh, yet cherishing
    resentment! —
  who will forgive one for sinning?
6 Remember the last things, and stop hating,
  corruption and death, and be faithful to the
    commandments.
7 Remember the commandments, and do not bear
    your fellow ill-will,
  remember the covenant of the Most High, and
    ignore the offence.

8 Avoid quarrelling and you will sin less;
  for the hot-tempered provokes quarrels,
9 a sinner sows trouble between friends,
  introducing discord among the peaceful.
10 The way a fire burns depends on its fuel,
  a quarrel spreads in proportion to its violence;
  a man's rage depends on his strength,
  his fury grows fiercer in proportion to his
    wealth.
11 A sudden quarrel kindles fire,
  a hasty dispute leads to bloodshed.
12 Blow on a spark and up it flares,
  spit on it and out it goes;
  both are the effects of your mouth.

13 A curse on the scandal-monger and double-talker,
  such a person has ruined many who lived in
    concord.
14 That third tongue has shattered the peace of many
  and driven them from nation to nation;
  it has pulled down fortified cities,
  and overthrown the houses of the great.
15 The third tongue has had upright wives divorced,
  depriving them of reward for their hard work.
16 No one who listens to it will ever know peace of
    mind,
  will ever live in peace again.
17 A stroke of the whip raises a weal,
  but a stroke of the tongue breaks bones.
18 Many have fallen by the edge of the sword,
  but many more have fallen by the tongue.
19 Blessed is anyone who has been sheltered from it,
  and has not experienced its fury,
  who has not dragged its yoke about,
  or been bound in its chains;
20 for its yoke is an iron yoke,
  its chains are bronze chains;
21 the death it inflicts is a miserable death,
  Sheol is preferable to it.
22 It cannot gain a hold over the devout,
  they are not burnt by its flames.
23 Those who desert the Lord will fall into it,
  it will flare up inextinguishably among them,
  it will be let loose against them like a lion,
  it will tear them like a leopard.
24 Be sure you put a thorn-hedge round your
    property,
  lock away your silver and gold;

NEW REVISED STANDARD VERSION	REVISED ENGLISH BIBLE

24b As you lock up your silver and gold,
25a   so make balances and scales for your words.
26 Take care not to err with your tongue,*k*
  and fall victim to one lying in wait.

25 so weigh your words and measure them,
  and make for your mouth a door that locks.
26 Take care you are not tripped by your tongue
  to fall before a waiting enemy.

29 The merciful lend to their neighbors;
  by holding out a helping hand they keep the
    commandments.
2 Lend to your neighbor in his time of need;
  repay your neighbor when a loan falls due.
3 Keep your promise and be honest with him,
  and on every occasion you will find what you
    need.
4 Many regard a loan as a windfall,
  and cause trouble to those who help them.
5 One kisses another's hands until he gets a loan,
  and is deferential in speaking of his neighbor's
    money;
  but at the time for repayment he delays,
  and pays back with empty promises,
  and finds fault with the time.
6 If he can pay, his creditor*l* will hardly get back
    half,
  and will regard that as a windfall.
  If he cannot pay, the borrower*l* has robbed the
    other of his money,
  and he has needlessly made him an enemy;
  he will repay him with curses and reproaches,
  and instead of glory will repay him with
    dishonor.
7 Many refuse to lend, not because of meanness,
  but from fear*m* of being defrauded needlessly.
8 Nevertheless, be patient with someone in humble
    circumstances,
  and do not keep him waiting for your alms.
9 Help the poor for the commandment's sake,
  and in their need do not send them away
    empty-handed.
10 Lose your silver for the sake of a brother or a
    friend,
  and do not let it rust under a stone and be lost.
11 Lay up your treasure according to the
    commandments of the Most High,
  and it will profit you more than gold.
12 Store up almsgiving in your treasury,
  and it will rescue you from every disaster;
13 better than a stout shield and a sturdy spear,
  it will fight for you against the enemy.
14 A good person will be surety for his neighbor,
  but the one who has lost all sense of shame
    will fail him.
15 Do not forget the kindness of your guarantor,
  for he has given his life for you.
16 A sinner wastes the property of his guarantor,
17   and the ungrateful person abandons his rescuer.
18 Being surety has ruined many who were
    prosperous,
  and has tossed them about like waves of the
    sea;
  it has driven the influential into exile,
  and they have wandered among foreign
    nations.
19 The sinner comes to grief through surety;
  his pursuit of gain involves him in lawsuits.
20 Assist your neighbor to the best of your ability,
  but be careful not to fall yourself.

29 HE who is compassionate lends to his neighbour;
  by giving a helping hand he fulfils the
    commandments.
2 Lend to your neighbour in his hour of need;
  repay your neighbour punctually.
3 Be as good as your word and keep faith with him,
  and your needs will always be met.
4 Many treat a loan as a windfall
  and create trouble for those who helped them.
5 Until he gets a loan, a man kisses his neighbour's
    hand
  and at the sight of his wealth drops his voice;
  when repayment is due, he delays,
  pays back only perfunctory promises,
  and claims that times are hard.
6 If the creditor presses, he will get back scarcely
    half,
  and will count himself lucky at that;
  if he does not press, he has deprived himself of the
    money,
  and made an enemy into the bargain.
  The debtor will pay him back in curses and insults,
  with dishonour in place of honour.
7 Because of such knavery many refuse to lend,
  for fear of being parted from their money to no
    purpose.
8 Nevertheless be patient with the penniless,
  and do not keep them waiting for your charity;
9 for the commandment's sake help the poor,
  and in their need do not send them away
    empty-handed.
10 Be ready to lose money for a brother or a friend
  rather than leave it to rust away under a stone.
11 Dispose of your treasure as commanded by the
    Most High;
  that will benefit you more than gold.
12 Let almsgiving be the treasure in your strong-room,
  and it will deliver you from every misfortune;
13 better than stout shield or strong spear,
  it will arm you against the enemy.
14 A good person will stand surety for his neighbour;
  only he who is lost to shame will let him down.
15 If someone stands surety for you, do not forget the
    favour;
  he has staked his very self on your behalf.
16 A sinner ruins the property of his surety,
17 and one who is ungrateful leaves his rescuer in the
    lurch.
18 Standing surety has overturned the prosperity of
    many
  and wrecked them like a storm at sea;
  it has driven people of influence into exile
  and set them wandering in foreign countries.
19 When a sinner involves himself in accepting
    surety,
  his pursuit of gain will land him in lawsuits.
20 So help your neighbour to the best of your ability,
  but beware of becoming too deeply involved.

---

*k Gk with it   l Gk he   m Other ancient authorities read many
refuse to lend, therefore, because of such meanness; they are afraid*

25 As you seal up your silver and gold,
    so balance and weigh your words.
26 Take care not to slip by your tongue
    and fall victim to your foe waiting in ambush.

29
He does a kindness who lends to his neighbor,
    and he fulfills the precepts who holds out a
    helping hand.
2 Lend to your neighbor in his hour of need,
    and pay back your neighbor when a loan
    falls due;
3 Keep your promise, be honest with him,
    and you will always come by what you need.
4 Many a man who asks for a loan
    adds to the burdens of those who help him;
5 When he borrows, he kisses the lender's hand
    and speaks with respect of his creditor's wealth;
But when payment is due he disappoints him
    and says he is helpless to meet the claim.
6 If the lender is able to recover barely half,
    he considers this an achievement;
If not, he is cheated of his wealth
    and acquires an enemy at no extra charge;
With curses and insults the borrower pays
    him back,
    with abuse instead of honor.
7 Many refuse to lend, not out of meanness,
    but from fear of being cheated.

8 To a poor man, however, be generous;
    keep him not waiting for your alms;
9 Because of the precept, help the needy,
    and in their want, do not send them away
    empty-handed.

10 Spend your money for your brother and friend,
    and hide it not under a stone to perish;
11 Dispose of your treasure as the Most
    High commands,
    for that will profit you more than the gold.
12 Store up almsgiving in your treasure house,
    and it will save you from every evil;
13 Better than a stout shield and a sturdy spear
    it will fight for you against the foe.

14 A good man goes surety for his neighbor,
    and only the shameless would play him false;
15 Forget not the kindness of your backer,
    for he offers his very life for you.
16 The wicked turn a pledge on their behalf
    into misfortune,
    and the ingrate abandons his protector;
17 Going surety has ruined many prosperous men
    and tossed them about like waves of the sea,
18 Has exiled men of prominence
    and sent them wandering through foreign lands.
19 The sinner through surety comes to grief,
    and he who undertakes too much falls
    into lawsuits.
20 Go surety for your neighbor according to
    your means,
    but take care lest you fall thereby.

25 then make scales and weights for your words,
    and put a door with bolts across your mouth.
26 Take care you take no false step through it,
    in case you fall a prey to him who lies in wait.

29
Making your neighbour a loan is an act of
    mercy,
    to lend him a helping hand is to keep the
    commandments.
2 Lend to your neighbour in his time of need,
    and in your turn repay your neighbour on time.
3 Be as good as your word and keep faith with him,
    and you will find your needs met every time.
4 Many treat a loan as a windfall,
    and embarrass those who have come to their
    rescue.
5 Until he gets something, a man will kiss his
    neighbour's hand,
    and refer diffidently to his wealth;
but when the loan falls due, he puts this off,
    he repays with offhand words,
    and pleads the inconvenience of the time.
6 Even if he can be made to pay, his creditor will
    recover barely half,
    and consider even that a windfall.
But otherwise he will be cheated of his money,
    and undeservedly gain himself an enemy;
the man will pay him back in curses and abuse,
    and with insults instead of honour.
7 Many, not out of malice, refuse to lend;
    they are merely anxious not to be cheated for
    nothing.

8 Nevertheless, be patient with those who are badly
    off,
    do not keep them waiting on your generosity.
9 In obedience to the commandment, help the poor;
    do not turn the poor away empty-handed in their
    need.
10 Spend your money on your brother or your friend,
    do not leave it under a stone to rust away.
11 Use your wealth as the Most High has decreed;
    you will find that more profitable than gold.
12 Stock your store-rooms with almsgiving;
    this will save you from all misfortune.
13 Better than sturdy shield or weighty spear,
    this will fight for you against the enemy.

14 A good man will go surety for his neighbour;
    only a shameless wretch would desert him.
15 Do not forget the favour your guarantor has done
    you;
    he has given his life for you.
16 A sinner is careless of his guarantor's prosperity,
    the ungrateful forgets his deliverer.
17 Going surety has ruined many who were
    prosperous,
    tossing them about in a heavy sea.
18 It has driven the powerful from home
    to wander among foreign nations.
19 A wicked man in a hurry to stand guarantor
    in the hope of profit, is hurrying to be
    sentenced.
20 Come to your neighbour's help as far as you can,
    but take care not to fall into the same plight.

NEW REVISED STANDARD VERSION	REVISED ENGLISH BIBLE

21 The necessities of life are water, bread, and
    clothing,
    and also a house to assure privacy.
22 Better is the life of the poor under their own
    crude roof
    than sumptuous food in the house of others.
23 Be content with little or much,
    and you will hear no reproach for being a
    guest.[n]
24 It is a miserable life to go from house to house;
    as a guest you should not open your mouth;
25 you will play the host and provide drink without
    being thanked,
    and besides this you will hear rude words like
    these:
26 "Come here, stranger, prepare the table;
    let me eat what you have there."
27 "Be off, stranger, for an honored guest is here;
    my brother has come for a visit, and I need the
    guest-room."
28 It is hard for a sensible person to bear
    scolding about lodging[o] and the insults of the
    moneylender.

CONCERNING CHILDREN[p]

30 He who loves his son will whip him often,
    so that he may rejoice at the way he turns out.
2 He who disciplines his son will profit by him,
    and will boast of him among acquaintances.
3 He who teaches his son will make his enemies
    envious,
    and will glory in him among his friends.
4 When the father dies he will not seem to be dead,
    for he has left behind him one like himself,
5 whom in his life he looked upon with joy
    and at death, without grief.
6 He has left behind him an avenger against his
    enemies,
    and one to repay the kindness of his friends.
7 Whoever spoils his son will bind up his wounds,
    and will suffer heartache at every cry.
8 An unbroken horse turns out stubborn,
    and an unchecked son turns out headstrong.
9 Pamper a child, and he will terrorize you;
    play with him, and he will grieve you.
10 Do not laugh with him, or you will have sorrow
    with him,
    and in the end you will gnash your teeth.
11 Give him no freedom in his youth,
    and do not ignore his errors.
12 Bow down his neck in his youth,[q]
    and beat his sides while he is young,
    or else he will become stubborn and disobey you,
    and you will have sorrow of soul from him.[r]
13 Discipline your son and make his yoke heavy,[s]
    so that you may not be offended by his
    shamelessness.
14 Better off poor, healthy, and fit
    than rich and afflicted in body.
15 Health and fitness are better than any gold,
    and a robust body than countless riches.

21 The basis of life is water, bread, and clothing,
    and a home with decent privacy.
22 Better the life of the poor in his own hut
    than a sumptuous banquet in someone else's house!
23 Rest content with whatever you have, be it much
    or little,
    and do not become known for living on hospitality.
24 It is a miserable life going from house to house,
    keeping your mouth shut because you are a visitor.
25 Without thanks you play the host and hand round
    the drinks,
    and into the bargain must listen to things that
    rankle:
26 'Come here, you stranger, and lay the table;
    whatever you have there, hand it to me.'
27 'Be off, stranger! Make way for a more important
    guest;
    my brother has come to stay, and I need the guest
    room.'
28 Two things a sensitive person finds hard to bear:
    criticism at home and abuse from a creditor!

30 A MAN who loves his son will not spare the rod,
    and then in his old age he may have joy of him.
2 He who disciplines his son will find profit in him
    and take pride in him among his acquaintances.
3 He who educates his son makes his enemy envious
    and will boast of him among friends.
4 When the father dies, it is as if he were still alive,
    for he has left behind a copy of himself.
5 During his lifetime he saw and rejoiced,
    and on his deathbed he had no regrets.
6 He has left an heir to take vengeance on his
    enemies
    and to repay friends for their kindness.
7 A man who coddles his son will bandage every
    scratch
    and be on tenterhooks at every cry.
8 An unbroken horse turns out stubborn,
    and an unchecked son turns out headstrong.
9 Pamper a boy and he will shock you;
    join in his games and he will grieve you.
10 Do not share his laughter, or you will share his
    pain
    and end by grinding your teeth.
11 While he is young do not give him freedom
    or overlook his errors.
12 While he is young break him in,
    and beat him soundly while he is still a child;
    otherwise he may grow stubborn and disobedient
    and cause you distress.
13 Discipline your son and take pains with him
    or he may affront you by some disgraceful act.
14 BETTER to be poor and healthy and fit
    than to be rich and racked by disease.
15 Health and fitness are better than any amount of
    gold,
    and vigour of body than boundless prosperity.

---

[n] Lat: Gk *reproach from your family*; other ancient authorities lack
this line   [o] Or *scolding from the household*   [p] This heading is
included in the Gk text.   [q] Other ancient authorities lack this line
and the preceding line   [r] Other ancient authorities lack this line
[s] Heb: Gk *take pains with him*

NEW AMERICAN BIBLE

NEW JERUSALEM BIBLE

21 Life's prime needs are water, bread, and clothing,
    a house, too, for decent privacy.
22 Better a poor man's fare under the shadow of one's
    own roof
    than sumptuous banquets among strangers.
23 Be it little or much, be content with what
    you have,
    and pay no heed to him who would disparage
    your home;
24 A miserable life it is to go from house to house,
    for as a guest you dare not open your mouth.
25 The visitor has no thanks for filling the cups;
    besides, you will hear these bitter words:
26 "Come here, stranger, set the table,
    give me to eat the food you have!
27 Away, stranger, for one more worthy;
    for my brother's visit I need the room!"
28 Painful things to a sensitive man
    are abuse at home and insults from his creditors.

21 The first thing in life is water, and bread, and
    clothing,
    and a house for the sake of privacy.
22 Better the life of the poor under a roof of planks,
    than lavish fare in somebody else's house.
23 Whether you have little or much, be content with
    it,
    and you will not hear your household
    complaining.
24 It is a miserable life, going from house to house;
    wherever you stay, you dare not open your
    mouth,
25 you do not belong, you receive no thanks for the
    drink you pour out
    and hear embittering words into the bargain:
26 'Come along, stranger, lay the table,
    what have you got ready? give me something to
    eat!'
27 'Go away, stranger, make room for someone
    important;
    my brother is coming to stay, I need the house.'
28 It is hard for the reasonable
    to be begrudged hospitality
    to be shamed like a debtor.

30 He who loves his son chastises him often,
    that he may be his joy when he grows up.
2 He who disciplines his son will benefit from him,
    and boast of him among his intimates.
3 He who educates his son makes his enemy jealous,
    and shows his delight in him among his friends.
4 At the father's death, he will seem not dead,
    since he leaves after him one like himself,
5 Whom he looks upon through life with joy,
    and even in death, without regret:
6 The avenger he leaves against his foes,
    and the one to repay his friends with kindness.

7 He who spoils his son will have wounds
    to bandage,
    and will quake inwardly at every outcry.
8 A colt untamed turns out stubborn;
    a son left to himself grows up unruly.
9 Pamper your child and he will be a terror for you,
    indulge him and he will bring you grief.
10 Share not in his frivolity lest you share in
    his sorrow,
    when finally your teeth are clenched in remorse.
11 Give him not his own way in his youth,
    and close not your eyes to his follies.
12 Bend him to the yoke when he is young,
    thrash his sides while he is still small,
    Lest he become stubborn, disobey you,
    and leave you disconsolate.
13 Discipline your son, make heavy his yoke,
    lest his folly humiliate you.

14 Better a poor man strong and robust,
    than a rich man with wasted frame.
15 More precious than gold is health and well-being,
    contentment of spirit than coral.

30 Whoever loves his son will beat him frequently
    so that in after years the son may be his
    comfort.
2 Whoever is strict with his son will reap the benefit,
    and be able to boast of him to his acquaintances.
3 Whoever educates his son will be the envy of his
    enemy,
    and will be proud of him among his friends.
4 Even when the father dies, he might well not be
    dead,
    since he leaves his likeness behind him.
5 In life he has had the joy of his company,
    dying, he has no anxieties.
6 He leaves an avenger against his enemies
    and a rewarder of favours for his friends.

7 Whoever coddles his son will bandage his wounds,
    his heart will turn over at every cry.
8 A badly broken-in horse turns out stubborn,
    a son left to himself turns out headstrong.
9 Pamper your child and he will terrorise you,
    play along with him and he will bring you
    sorrow.

10 Do not laugh with him, or one day you will weep
    with him
    and end up gnashing your teeth.
11 While he is young, do not allow him his freedom
    and do not wink at his mistakes.
12 Bend his neck in youth,
    bruise his ribs while he is a child,
    or else he will grow stubborn and disobedient,
    and hurt you very deeply.
13 Be strict with your son, and persevere with him,
    or you will rue his insolence.

14 Better be poor if healthy and fit
    than rich if tormented in body.
15 Health and strength are better than any gold,
    a robust body than untold wealth.

16 There is no wealth better than health of body,
  and no gladness above joy of heart.
17 Death is better than a life of misery,
  and eternal sleep *t* than chronic sickness.

CONCERNING FOODS *u*

18 Good things poured out upon a mouth that is
    closed
  are like offerings of food placed upon a grave.
19 Of what use to an idol is a sacrifice?
  For it can neither eat nor smell.
  So is the one punished by the Lord;
20 he sees with his eyes and groans
  as a eunuch groans when embracing a girl. *v*

21 Do not give yourself over to sorrow,
  and do not distress yourself deliberately.
22 A joyful heart is life itself,
  and rejoicing lengthens one's life span.
23 Indulge yourself *w* and take comfort,
  and remove sorrow far from you,
  for sorrow has destroyed many,
  and no advantage ever comes from it.
24 Jealousy and anger shorten life,
  and anxiety brings on premature old age.
25 Those who are cheerful and merry at table
  will benefit from their food.

31 Wakefulness over wealth wastes away one's
    flesh,
  and anxiety about it drives away sleep.
2 Wakeful anxiety prevents slumber,
  and a severe illness carries off sleep. *x*
3 The rich person toils to amass a fortune,
  and when he rests he fills himself with his
    dainties.
4 The poor person toils to make a meager living,
  and if ever he rests he becomes needy.

5 One who loves gold will not be justified;
  one who pursues money will be led astray *y* by
    it.
6 Many have come to ruin because of gold,
  and their destruction has met them face to face.
7 It is a stumbling block to those who are avid for
    it,
  and every fool will be taken captive by it.
8 Blessed is the rich person who is found
    blameless,
  and who does not go after gold.
9 Who is he, that we may praise him?
  For he has done wonders among his people.
10 Who has been tested by it and been found
    perfect?
  Let it be for him a ground for boasting.
  Who has had the power to transgress and did not
    transgress,
  and to do evil and did not do it?
11 His prosperity will be established, *z*
  and the assembly will proclaim his acts of
    charity.

16 There is no wealth to compare with bodily health,
  no joy to surpass gladness of heart.
17 Better death than a life of misery,
  eternal rest than a long illness.
18 Delicacies heaped before someone with no appetite
  are like offerings of food placed on a tomb.
19 What use is a sacrifice to an idol
  which can neither taste nor smell?
  So it is with one afflicted by the Lord:
20 he gazes at the food before him and groans
  as a eunuch groans when he embraces a virgin.

21 Do not abandon yourself to grief
  or go out of your way to distress yourself.
22 A merry heart keeps a person alive,
  and joy lengthens his span of days.
23 Indulge yourself, take comfort,
  and banish grief far from you;
  for grief has been the death of many
  and no advantage ever came of it.
24 Envy and anger shorten life,
  and anxiety brings premature old age.
25 He who has a light heart has a good appetite
  and relishes the food he eats.

31 Wakeful nights make the rich person lose weight,
    when the cares of wealth drive sleep away;
2 sleepless worry keeps him wide awake,
  just as serious illness banishes sleep.
3 The rich man toils to amass a fortune,
  and when he relaxes he enjoys every luxury.
4 The poor man toils to make a slender living,
  and when he relaxes he finds himself in want.

5 Passion for gold can never be right;
  the pursuit of profit leads astray.
6 Because of gold many a one has met his downfall
  and found himself face to face with ruin.
7 Gold is a pitfall to those who make it their god,
  and every fool is ensnared by it.
8 Happy are the rich who have remained blameless
  and have not let gold become their guide!
9 Show us such a person, and we will congratulate
    him;
  he has performed a miracle among his people.
10 Has anyone come through this test unscathed?
  Then he has good cause to be proud.
  Has anyone had it in his power to sin and
    refrained,
  to do wrong and not done it?
11 Then he will be confirmed in his prosperity,
  and the assembly will hail him as a benefactor.

---

t Other ancient authorities lack *eternal sleep*   *u* This heading is
included in the Gk text; other ancient authorities place the heading
before verse 16   *v* Other ancient authorities add *So is the person
who does right under compulsion*   *w* Other ancient authorities read
Beguile yourself   *x* Other ancient authorities read *sleep carries off a
severe illness*   *y* Heb Syr: Gk *pursues destruction will be filled*
z Other ancient authorities add *because of this*

NEW AMERICAN BIBLE

16No treasure greater than a healthy body;
   no happiness, than a joyful heart!
17Preferable is death to a bitter life,
   unending sleep to constant illness.
18Dainties set before one who cannot eat
   are like the offerings placed before a tomb.
19What good is an offering to an idol
   that can neither taste nor smell?
20So it is with the afflicted man
   who groans at the good things his eyes behold!

21Do not give in to sadness,
   torment not yourself with brooding;
22Gladness of heart is the very life of man,
   cheerfulness prolongs his days.
23Distract yourself, renew your courage,
   drive resentment far away from you;
For worry has brought death to many,
   nor is there aught to be gained from resentment.
24Envy and anger shorten one's life,
   worry brings on premature old age.
25One who is cheerful and gay while at table
   benefits from his food.

31 Keeping watch over riches wastes the flesh,
   and the care of wealth drives away rest.
2Concern for one's livelihood banishes slumber;
   more than a serious illness it disturbs repose.
3The rich man labors to pile up wealth,
   and his only rest is wanton pleasure;
4The poor man toils for a meager subsistence,
   and if ever he rests, he finds himself in want.
5The lover of gold will not be free from sin,
   for he who pursues wealth is led astray by it.
6Many have been ensnared by gold,
   though destruction lay before their eyes;
7It is a stumbling block to those who are avid for it,
   a snare for every fool.
8Happy the rich man found without fault,
   who turns not aside after gain!
9Who is he, that we may praise him?
   he, of all his kindred, has done wonders,
10For he has been tested by gold and come off safe,
   and this remains his glory;
He could have sinned but did not,
   could have done evil but would not,
11So that his possessions are secure,
   and the assembly recounts his praises.

16No riches can outweigh bodily health,
   no enjoyment surpass a cheerful heart.
17Better death than a wretched life,
   and everlasting rest than chronic illness.
18Good things lavished on a closed mouth
   are like food offerings put on a grave.
19What use is an offering to an idol
   which can neither eat nor smell?
How describe someone pursued by the Lord's
   displeasure?
20   He looks and sighs
   like a eunuch embracing a pretty girl—how he
   sighs!
21Do not abandon yourself to sorrow,
   do not torment yourself with brooding.
22Gladness of heart is life to anyone,
   joy is what gives length of days.
23Give your cares the slip, console your heart,
   chase sorrow far away;
for sorrow has been the ruin of many,
   and is no use to anybody.
24Jealousy and anger shorten your days,
   and worry brings premature old age.
25A genial heart makes a good trencherman,
   someone who enjoys a good meal.

31 The sleeplessness brought by wealth makes a
   person lose weight,
   the worry it causes drives away sleep.
2The worries of the daytime prevent you from
   sleeping,
   like a serious illness, they keep sleep at bay.
3The rich for ever toils, piling up money,
   and then, leaving off, he is gorged with luxuries;
4the poor for ever toils, barely making a living,
   and then, leaving off, is poorer than ever.
5No one who loves money can easily avoid sinning,
   whoever pursues profit will be corrupted by it.
6Gold has been the ruin of many;
   their coming destruction was self-evident,
7since it is a snare for those who sacrifice to it
   and stupid people all get caught in it.
8Happy the rich who is found to be blameless
   and does not go chasing after gold.
9Who is he, so that we can congratulate him,
   for he has achieved marvels among his fellows?
10Who has been through this test and emerged
   perfect?
He may well be proud of that!
Who has had the chance to sin and has not sinned,
   had the chance to do wrong and has not done it?
11His fortune will be firmly based
   and the assembly will acclaim his generosity.

NEW REVISED STANDARD VERSION	REVISED ENGLISH BIBLE

12 Are you seated at the table of the great?*a*
  Do not be greedy at it,
    and do not say, "How much food there is
      here!"
13 Remember that a greedy eye is a bad thing.
    What has been created more greedy than the
      eye?
    Therefore it sheds tears for any reason.
14 Do not reach out your hand for everything you
      see,
    and do not crowd your neighbor*b* at the dish.
15 Judge your neighbor's feelings by your own,
    and in every matter be thoughtful.
16 Eat what is set before you like a well brought-up
      person,*c*
    and do not chew greedily, or you will give
      offense.
17 Be the first to stop, as befits good manners,
    and do not be insatiable, or you will give
      offense.
18 If you are seated among many persons,
    do not help yourself*d* before they do.
19 How ample a little is for a well-disciplined
      person!
    He does not breathe heavily when in bed.
20 Healthy sleep depends on moderate eating;
    he rises early, and feels fit.
    The distress of sleeplessness and of nausea
    and colic are with the glutton.
21 If you are overstuffed with food,
    get up to vomit, and you will have relief.
22 Listen to me, my child, and do not disregard me,
    and in the end you will appreciate my words.
    In everything you do be moderate,*e*
    and no sickness will overtake you.
23 People bless the one who is liberal with food,
    and their testimony to his generosity is
      trustworthy.
24 The city complains of the one who is stingy with
      food,
    and their testimony to his stinginess is
      accurate.
25 Do not try to prove your strength by
      wine-drinking,
    for wine has destroyed many.
26 As the furnace tests the work of the smith,*f*
    so wine tests hearts when the insolent quarrel.
27 Wine is very life to human beings
    if taken in moderation.
    What is life to one who is without wine?
    It has been created to make people happy.
28 Wine drunk at the proper time and in moderation
    is rejoicing of heart and gladness of soul.
29 Wine drunk to excess leads to bitterness of spirit,
    to quarrels and stumbling.
30 Drunkenness increases the anger of a fool to his
      own hurt,
    reducing his strength and adding wounds.
31 Do not reprove your neighbor at a banquet of
      wine,
    and do not despise him in his merrymaking;
  speak no word of reproach to him,
    and do not distress him by making demands of
      him.

12 WHEN seated at a grand table
    do not smack your lips and exclaim, 'What a
      feast!'
13 Remember, it is a bad thing to have a greedy eye.
    There is no greater evil in creation than the eye;
    for that reason it must shed tears at every turn.
14 Do not reach for everything within sight,
    or jostle your fellow-guest at the dish;
15 judge his feelings by your own,
    and always behave with consideration.
16 Eat what is set before you, but not like a beast;
    do not munch your food and make yourself
      objectionable.
17 Be the first to stop for good manners' sake
    and do not be a glutton, or you will give offence.
18 If you are dining in a large company,
    do not reach out your hand before others.
19 A person of good upbringing is content with little,
    so when he goes to bed he is not short of breath.
20 The moderate eater enjoys healthy sleep:
    he rises early, feeling refreshed;
    but sleeplessness, nausea, and colic
    are the lot of the glutton.
21 If you cannot avoid overeating at a banquet,
    leave the table and find relief by vomiting.
22 Listen to me, my son; do not disregard me,
    and in the end my words will come home to you.
    In all you do avoid extremes,
    and no illness will come your way.
23 Everyone has a good word for a liberal host;
    the evidence of his generosity is convincing.
24 The whole town grumbles at a mean host,
    and there is sure evidence of his meanness.
25 Do not use wine to prove your manhood,
    for wine has been the ruin of many.
26 As the furnace tests iron when it is being
      tempered,
    so wine tests character when boasters are
      wrangling.
27 Wine puts life into anyone
    who drinks it in moderation.
    What is life to somebody deprived of wine?
    Was it not created to gladden the heart?
28 Wine brings gaiety and high spirits
    if people know when to drink and when to stop;
29 but wine in excess makes for bitter feelings
    and leads to offence and retaliation.
30 Drunkenness inflames a fool's anger to his own
      hurt;
    it saps his strength and exposes him to injury.
31 At a banquet do not rebuke your fellow-guest
    or make him feel small while he is enjoying
      himself.
    That is no time to upbraid him
    or pester him to pay his debts.

---

a Heb Syr: Gk *at a great table*   *b* Gk *him*   *c* Heb: Gk *like a human being*   *d* Gk *reach out your hand*   *e* Heb Syr: Gk *industrious*   *f* Heb: Gk *tests the hardening of steel by dipping*

NEW AMERICAN BIBLE

NEW JERUSALEM BIBLE

12 If you are dining with a great man,
bring not a greedy gullet to his table,
Nor cry out, "How much food there is here?"
13 Remember that gluttony is evil.
No creature is greedier than the eye:
therefore it weeps for any cause.
15 Recognize that your neighbor feels as you do,
and keep in mind your own dislikes:
14 Toward what he eyes, do not put out a hand;
nor reach when he does for the same dish.
16 Behave at table like a favored guest,
and be not greedy, lest you be despised.
17 Be the first to stop, as befits good manners;
gorge not yourself, lest you give offense.
18 If there are many with you at table,
be not the first to reach out your hand.
19 Does not a little suffice for a well-bred man?
When he lies down, it is without discomfort.
20 Distress and anguish and loss of sleep,
and restless tossing for the glutton!
Moderate eating ensures sound slumber
and a clear mind next day on rising.
21 If perforce you have eaten too much,
once you have emptied your stomach, you will
have relief.
22 Listen to me, my son, and scorn me not;
later you will find my advice good.
In whatever you do, be moderate,
and no sickness will befall you.
23 On a man generous with food, blessings
are invoked,
and this testimony to his goodness is lasting;
24 He who is miserly with food is denounced
in public,
and this testimony to his stinginess is lasting.
25 Let not wine-drinking be the proof of
your strength,
for wine has been the ruin of many.
26 As the furnace probes the work of the smith,
so does wine the hearts of the insolent.
27 Wine is very life to man
if taken in moderation.
Does he really live who lacks the wine
which was created for his joy?
28 Joy of heart, good cheer and merriment
are wine drunk freely at the proper time.
29 Headache, bitterness and disgrace
is wine drunk amid anger and strife.
30 More and more wine is a snare for the fool;
it lessens his strength and multiplies his wounds.
31 Rebuke not your neighbor when wine is served,
nor put him to shame while he is merry;
Use no harsh words with him
and distress him not in the presence of others.

12 If you are sitting down to a lavish table,
do not display your greed,
do not say, 'What a lot to eat!'
13 Remember, it is bad to have a greedy eye.
Is any creature more wicked than the eye?
—That is why it is always weeping!
14 Do not reach out for anything your host has his
eye on,
do not jostle him at the dish.
15 Judge your fellow-guest's needs by your own,
be thoughtful in every way.
16 Eat what is offered you like a well brought-up
person,
do not wolf your food or you will earn dislike.
17 For politeness' sake be the first to stop;
do not act the glutton, or you will give offence,
18 and if you are sitting with a large party,
do not help yourself before the others do.
19 A little is quite enough for a well-bred person;
his breathing is easy when he lies in bed.
20 A moderate diet ensures sound sleep,
one gets up early, in the best of spirits.
Sleeplessness, biliousness and gripe
are what the glutton has to endure.
21 If you are forced to eat too much,
get up, go and vomit, and you will feel better.
22 Listen to me, my child, do not disregard me,
eventually you will see the force of my words.
Be moderate in all your activities
and illness will never overtake you.
23 People praise the person who keeps a splendid
table,
and their opinion of his munificence is sound.
24 But a niggardly host provokes universal resentment
and people will retail instances of his meanness.
25 Do not play the valiant at your wine,
for wine has been the undoing of many.
26 The furnace proves the temper of steel,
and wine proves hearts in the drinking bouts of
braggarts.
27 Wine gives life
if drunk in moderation.
What is life worth without wine?
It came into being to make people happy.
28 Drunk at the right time and in the right amount,
wine makes for a glad heart and a cheerful
mind.
29 Bitterness of soul comes of wine drunk to excess
out of temper or bravado.
30 Drunkenness excites the stupid to a fury to his own
harm,
it reduces his strength while leading to blows.
31 Do not provoke your fellow-guest at a wine feast,
do not make fun of him when he is enjoying
himself,
do not take him to task
or annoy him by reclaiming money owed.

NEW REVISED STANDARD VERSION	REVISED ENGLISH BIBLE

32 If they make you master of the feast, do not exalt
yourself;
be among them as one of their number.
Take care of them first and then sit down;
2 when you have fulfilled all your duties, take
your place,
so that you may be merry along with them
and receive a wreath for your excellent
leadership.

3 Speak, you who are older, for it is your right,
but with accurate knowledge, and do not
interrupt the music.
4 Where there is entertainment, do not pour out
talk;
do not display your cleverness at the wrong
time.
5 A ruby seal in a setting of gold
is a concert of music at a banquet of wine.
6 A seal of emerald in a rich setting of gold
is the melody of music with good wine.

7 Speak, you who are young, if you are obliged to,
but no more than twice, and only if asked.
8 Be brief; say much in few words;
be as one who knows and can still hold his
tongue.
9 Among the great do not act as their equal;
and when another is speaking, do not babble.

10 Lightning travels ahead of the thunder,
and approval goes before one who is modest.
11 Leave in good time and do not be the last;
go home quickly and do not linger.
12 Amuse yourself there to your heart's content,
but do not sin through proud speech.
13 But above all bless your Maker,
who fills you with his good gifts.

14 The one who seeks God*g* will accept his
discipline,
and those who rise early to seek him*h* will
find favor.
15 The one who seeks the law will be filled with it,
but the hypocrite will stumble at it.
16 Those who fear the Lord will form true
judgments,
and they will kindle righteous deeds like a
light.
17 The sinner will shun reproof,
and will find a decision according to his liking.

18 A sensible person will not overlook a thoughtful
suggestion;
an insolent*i* and proud person will not be
deterred by fear.*j*
19 Do nothing without deliberation,
but when you have acted, do not regret it.
20 Do not go on a path full of hazards,
and do not stumble at an obstacle twice.*k*
21 Do not be overconfident on a smooth*l* road,
22 and give good heed to your paths. *m*
23 Guard*n* yourself in every act,
for this is the keeping of the commandments.

32 ARE you chosen to preside at a feast? Do not put
on airs;
mix with the others as one of them.
Look after them and only then sit down yourself;
discharge your duties before you take your place.
2 Let the enjoyment of others be your pleasure,
and you will win a garland for good manners.

3 When you are old, you are entitled to speak,
but come to the point and do not interrupt the
music.
4 Where entertainment is provided, do not keep up a
stream of talk;
it is the wrong moment to show off your wisdom.
5 Like a garnet set in a gold ring
is a concert of music at a banquet.
6 Like an emerald in a setting of gold
is tuneful music with good wine.

7 When you are young, speak if the need arises,
but twice at the most, and only when asked.
8 Be brief, say much in few words,
like someone who knows and can still hold his
tongue.
9 In the company of the great do not make yourself
their equal
or go on chattering when another is speaking.
10 As lightning streaks ahead of thunder,
so esteem goes before a modest person.
11 Leave in good time and do not be the last to go;
go straight off home without lingering.
12 There you may amuse yourself to your heart's
content
without giving offence by arrogant talk.
13 And one thing more: give praise to your Maker,
who has filled your cup with his benefits.

14 WHOEVER fears the Lord will accept his discipline;
those diligent in their search for him win his
approval.
15 Those who study the law will find satisfaction
therein,
but the law will prove a stumbling block to the
insincere.
16 Those who fear the Lord discover his will
and make his decrees shine out like a beacon.
17 A sinner does not accept criticism;
he will find precedents to justify his choice.

18 A thoughtful person can always take a hint,
but an arrogant upstart lacks all diffidence.
19 Never do anything without due thought,
and once started do not change your mind.
20 Do not travel by a road full of obstacles
and stumble along among its boulders.
21 Do not be careless on a clear road;
22 watch where you go.
23 Whatever you are doing, keep yourself safe,
for this too is fulfilling the commandments.

---

g Heb: Gk *who fears the Lord*   *h* Other ancient authorities lack *to
seek him*   *i* Heb: Gk *alien*   *j* Meaning of Gk uncertain. Other
ancient authorities add *and after acting, with him, without
deliberation*   *k* Heb: Gk *stumble on stony ground*   *l* Or *an
unexplored*   *m* Heb Syr: Gk *and beware of your children*
n Heb Syr: Gk *Trust*

32 If you are chosen to preside at dinner, be not puffed up,
   but with the guests be as one of themselves;
Take care of them first before you sit down;
2   when you have fulfilled your duty, then take your place,
To share in their joy
   and win praise for your hospitality.
3 Being older, you may talk; that is only your right,
   but temper your wisdom, not to disturb the singing.
4 When wine is present, do not pour out discourse,
   and flaunt not your wisdom at the wrong time.
5 Like a seal of carnelian in a setting of gold
   is a concert when wine is served.
6 Like a gold mounting with an emerald seal
   is string music with delicious wine.
7 Young man, speak only when necessary,
   when they have asked you more than once;
8 Be brief, but say much in those few words,
   be like the wise man, taciturn.
9 When among your elders be not forward,
   and with officials be not too insistent.
10 Like the lightning that flashes before a storm
   is the esteem that shines on modesty.
11 When it is time to leave, tarry not;
   be off for home! There take your ease,
12 And there enjoy doing as you wish,
   but without sin or words of pride.
13 Above all, give praise to your Creator,
   who showers his favors upon you.

14 He who would find God must accept discipline;
   he who seeks him obtains his request.
15 He who studies the law masters it,
   but the hypocrite finds it a trap.
16 His judgment is sound who fears the LORD;
   out of obscurity he draws forth a clear plan.
17 The sinner turns aside reproof
   and distorts the law to suit his purpose.
18 The thoughtful man will not neglect direction;
   the proud and insolent man is deterred by nothing.
19 Do nothing without counsel,
   and then you need have no regrets.
20 Go not on a way that is set with snares,
   and let not the same thing trip you twice.
21 Be not too sure even of smooth roads,
22   be careful on all your paths.
23 Whatever you do, be on your guard,
   for in this way you will keep the commandments.

32 Have they made you the presider? Do not let it go to your head,
   behave like everyone else in the party,
   see that they are happy and then sit down yourself.
2 Having discharged your duties, take your place
   so that your joy may be through theirs,
   and you may receive the crown for your competence.
3 Speak, old man — it is proper that you should —
   but with discretion: do not spoil the music.
4 If someone is singing, do not ramble on
   and do not play the sage at the wrong moment.
5 An amber seal on a precious stone,
   such is a concert of music at a wine feast.
6 An emerald seal in a golden setting,
   such are strains of music with a vintage wine.
7 Speak, young man, when you must,
   but twice at most, and then only if questioned.
8 Keep to the point, say much in few words;
   give the impression of knowing but not wanting to speak.
9 Among eminent people do not behave as though you were their equal;
   do not make frivolous remarks when someone else is speaking.
10 Lightning comes before the thunder,
   favour goes ahead of a modest person.
11 Leave in good time, do not bring up the rear,
   and hurry home without loitering.
12 There amuse yourself, and do what you have a mind to,
   but do not sin by arrogant talk.
13 And for all this bless your Creator,
   who intoxicates you with his favours.

14 Whoever fears the Lord will accept his correction;
   those who look for him will win his favour.
15 Whoever seeks the Law will be nourished by it,
   the hypocrite will find it a stumbling-block.
16 Those who fear the Lord win his approval,
   their good deeds shining like a light.
17 The sinner waves reproof aside,
   he finds an excuse for headstrong behaviour.
18 A sensible person never scorns a warning;
   foreigners and the proud do not know about fear.
19 Never act without reflection,
   and you will not regret your actions.
20 Do not venture on a rough road,
   for fear of stumbling over the stones.
21 Do not be over-confident on an even road
22   and beware of your own children.
23 Watch yourself in everything you do;
   this is also the way to keep the commandments.

NEW REVISED STANDARD VERSION	REVISED ENGLISH BIBLE

NEW REVISED STANDARD VERSION

24 The one who keeps the law preserves himself,[o]
and the one who trusts the Lord will not suffer
loss.

33 No evil will befall the one who fears the Lord,
but in trials such a one will be rescued again
and again.

2 The wise will not hate the law,
but the one who is hypocritical about it is like
a boat in a storm.

3 The sensible person will trust in the law;
for such a one the law is as dependable as a
divine oracle.

4 Prepare what to say, and then you will be
listened to;
draw upon your training, and give your
answer.

5 The heart of a fool is like a cart wheel,
and his thoughts like a turning axle.

6 A mocking friend is like a stallion
that neighs no matter who the rider is.

7 Why is one day more important than another,
when all the daylight in the year is from the
sun?

8 By the Lord's wisdom they were distinguished,
and he appointed the different seasons and
festivals.

9 Some days he exalted and hallowed,
and some he made ordinary days.

10 All human beings come from the ground,
and humankind[p] was created out of the dust.

11 In the fullness of his knowledge the Lord
distinguished them
and appointed their different ways.

12 Some he blessed and exalted,
and some he made holy and brought near to
himself;
but some he cursed and brought low,
and turned them out of their place.

13 Like clay in the hand of the potter,
to be molded as he pleases,
so all are in the hand of their Maker,
to be given whatever he decides.

14 Good is the opposite of evil,
and life the opposite of death;
so the sinner is the opposite of the godly.

15 Look at all the works of the Most High;
they come in pairs, one the opposite of the
other.

16 Now I was the last to keep vigil;
I was like a gleaner following the
grape-pickers;

17 by the blessing of the Lord I arrived first,
and like a grape-picker I filled my wine press.

18 Consider that I have not labored for myself alone,
but for all who seek instruction.

19 Hear me, you who are great among the people,
and you leaders of the congregation, pay heed!

20 To son or wife, to brother or friend,
do not give power over yourself, as long as
you live;
and do not give your property to another,
in case you change your mind and must ask for
it.

21 While you are still alive and have breath in you,
do not let anyone take your place.

REVISED ENGLISH BIBLE

24 To rely on the law is to heed its commandments;
trust the Lord and suffer no loss.

33 No misfortune ever befalls him who fears the
Lord:
in trials he will be rescued time and again.

2 A wise person does not hate the law,
but he who is insincere about it is like a skiff in a
squall.

3 A sensible person puts his trust in the law,
finding it reliable like the oracle of God.

4 If you want a hearing, prepare what you have to
say;
marshal your learning, then give your answer.

5 The feelings of a fool turn like a cartwheel,
and his thoughts spin like an axle.

6 A sarcastic friend is like a stallion
which neighs no matter who is on its back.

7 Why is one day more important than another,
when every day in the year has its light from the
sun?

8 It was by the Lord's decision that they were
distinguished;
he appointed the various seasons and festivals:

9 some days he made high and holy,
and others he assigned to the common run of days.

10 All mankind comes from the ground—
Adam himself was created out of earth—

11 yet in his great wisdom the Lord distinguished
them
and made them go their various ways:

12 some he blessed and lifted high,
some he hallowed and brought near to himself,
others he cursed and humbled
and removed from their place.

13 As clay is in the potter's hands
to be moulded just as he chooses,
so are human beings in the hands of their Maker
to be dealt with as he decides.

14 Good is the opposite of evil, and life of death;
so the sinner is the opposite of the godly.

15 Look at all the works of the Most High—
they are in pairs, one the counterpart of the other.

16 I, last of all, kept watch.
I was like a gleaner following the grape-pickers,
and by the Lord's blessing I arrived in time
to fill my winepress as full as any of them.

17 Note that I did not toil for myself alone,
but for all who seek learning.

18 Listen to me, you dignitaries among the people;
you leaders of the assembly, give me your
attention.

19 As long as you live, give no one power over
yourself—
son or wife, brother or friend.
Do not give your possessions to another,
in case you change your mind and want them back.

20 As long as you have life and breath,
do not let anyone take your place.

o Heb: Gk *who believes the law heeds the commandments*
p Heb: Gk *Adam*

²⁴He who keeps the law preserves himself;
and he who trusts in the LORD shall not be put
to shame.

33 No evil can harm the man who fears the LORD;
through trials, again and again he is safe.
²He who hates the law is without wisdom,
and is tossed about like a boat in a storm.
³The prudent man trusts in the word of the LORD,
and the law is dependable for him as a
divine oracle.
⁴Prepare your words and you will be listened to;
draw upon your training, and then give
your answer.

⁵Like the wheel of a cart is the mind of a fool;
his thoughts revolve in circles.
⁶A fickle friend is like the stallion
that neighs, no matter who the rider.
⁷Why is one day more important than another,
when it is the sun that lights up every day?
⁸It is due to the LORD'S wisdom that they differ;
it is through him the seasons and feasts come
and go.
⁹Some he dignifies and sanctifies,
and others he lists as ordinary days.
¹⁰So too, all men are of clay,
for from earth man was formed;
¹¹Yet with his great knowledge the LORD makes
men unlike;
in different paths he has them walk.
¹²Some he blesses and makes great,
some he sanctifies and draws to himself.
Others he curses and brings low,
and expels them from their place.
¹³Like clay in the hands of a potter,
to be molded according to his pleasure,
So are men in the hands of their Creator,
to be assigned by him their function.
¹⁴As evil contrasts with good, and death with life,
so are sinners in contrast with the just;
¹⁵See now all the works of the Most High:
they come in pairs, the one the opposite of
the other.

¹⁶Now I am the last to keep vigil,
like a gleaner after the vintage;
¹⁷Since by the LORD'S blessing I have made progress
till like a vintager I have filled my winepress,
¹⁸I would inform you that not for myself only have
I toiled,
but for every seeker after wisdom.

¹⁹Listen to me, O leaders of the multitude;
O rulers of the assembly, give ear!
²⁰Let neither son nor wife, neither brother nor friend,
have power over you as long as you live.
²¹While breath of life is still in you,
let no man have dominion over you.
Give not to another your wealth,
lest then you have to plead with him;

²⁴Anyone who trusts in the Law obeys its precepts,
no one who has confidence in the Lord will
come to harm.

33 No evil will befall one who fears the Lord,
such a one will be rescued even in the ordeal.
²No one who hates the Law is wise,
one who is hypocritical about it is like a
storm-tossed ship.
³An intelligent person will put faith in the Law,
for such a one the Law is as dependable as a
prophecy.
⁴Prepare what you have to say and you will get a
hearing,
marshal your information before you answer.

⁵The feelings of a fool are like a cart-wheel,
a fool's thought revolves like a turning axle.
⁶A rutting stallion is like a sarcastic friend;
he neighs, whoever rides him.
⁷Why is one day better than another,
though the sun gives the same daylight
throughout the year?
⁸They have been differentiated in the mind of the
Lord,
who has diversified the seasons and feasts;
⁹some he has made more important and has
hallowed,
others he has made ordinary days.
¹⁰Human beings come from the ground,
Adam himself was formed out of earth;
¹¹in the fullness of his wisdom
the Lord has made distinctions between them,
and diversified their conditions.
¹²Some of them he has blessed,
hallowing and setting them near him;
others he has cursed and humiliated
by degrading them from their positions.
¹³Like clay in the hands of the potter
to mould as it pleases him,
so are human beings in the hands of their Maker
to reward as he judges right.
¹⁴Opposite evil stands good,
opposite death, life;
so too opposite the devout stands the sinner.
¹⁵Contemplate all the works of the Most High,
you will find they go in pairs, by opposites.

¹⁶Although the last to come, I have kept my eyes
open
like a man picking up what the grape-pickers
have left.
¹⁷By the blessing of the Lord I have come in first,
and like a true grape-picker have filled my
winepress.
¹⁸And note, I have not been working merely for
myself,
but for all who seek instruction.

¹⁹Listen to me, important public figures,
presidents of the assembly, give ear!

²⁰Neither to son nor wife, brother nor friend,
give power over yourself during your own
lifetime.
And do not give your property to anyone else,
in case you regret it and have to ask for it back.
²¹As long as you live and there is breath in your
body,
do not yield power over yourself to anyone;

22 For it is better that your children should ask from
you
than that you should look to the hand of your
children.
23 Excel in all that you do;
bring no stain upon your honor.
24 At the time when you end the days of your life,
in the hour of death, distribute your
inheritance.
25 Fodder and a stick and burdens for a donkey;
bread and discipline and work for a slave.
26 Set your slave to work, and you will find rest;
leave his hands idle, and he will seek liberty.
27 Yoke and thong will bow the neck,
and for a wicked slave there are racks and
tortures.
28 Put him to work, in order that he may not be
idle,
29 for idleness teaches much evil.
30 Set him to work, as is fitting for him,
and if he does not obey, make his fetters
heavy.
Do not be overbearing toward anyone,
and do nothing unjust.
31 If you have but one slave, treat him like yourself,
because you have bought him with blood.
If you have but one slave, treat him like a
brother,
for you will need him as you need your life.
32 If you ill-treat him, and he leaves you and runs
away,
33 which way will you go to seek him?

34 The senseless have vain and false hopes,
and dreams give wings to fools.
2 As one who catches at a shadow and pursues the
wind,
so is anyone who believes in*q* dreams.
3 What is seen in dreams is but a reflection,
the likeness of a face looking at itself.
4 From an unclean thing what can be clean?
And from something false what can be true?
5 Divinations and omens and dreams are unreal,
and like a woman in labor, the mind has
fantasies.
6 Unless they are sent by intervention from the
Most High,
pay no attention to them.
7 For dreams have deceived many,
and those who put their hope in them have
perished.
8 Without such deceptions the law will be fulfilled,
and wisdom is complete in the mouth of the
faithful.
9 An educated*r* person knows many things,
and one with much experience knows what he
is talking about.
10 An inexperienced person knows few things,
11 but he that has traveled acquires much
cleverness.
12 I have seen many things in my travels,
and I understand more than I can express.
13 I have often been in danger of death,
but have escaped because of these experiences.
14 The spirit of those who fear the Lord will live,
15 for their hope is in him who saves them.

21 It is better for your children to ask help from you
than for you to be dependent on them.
22 In all that you do, keep the upper hand
and allow no stain on your reputation.
23 Let your life run its full course
and then, at the hour of death, distribute your
property.
24 Fodder, the stick, and burdens for a donkey;
for a servant—bread, discipline, and work!
25 Keep your slave at work, if you want rest for
yourself;
if you let him slack, he will be looking for his
liberty.
26 The ox is tamed by yoke and harness,
the bad servant by rack and torture.
27 Set him to work to keep him from being idle,
for idleness is a great teacher of mischief.
28 Give him work to do, for that is what he is for,
and if he disobeys you, load him with fetters.
29 Do not be too exacting towards anyone
or do anything contrary to justice.
30 If you have only one servant, treat him as you do
yourself,
because you bought him at a high price.
31 If you have only one servant, treat him like a
brother;
you will need him as much as you need yourself.
If you ill-treat him and he takes to his heels,
where will you go to look for him?

34 VAIN hopes delude the senseless,
and dreams give wings to a fool's fancy.
2 Paying heed to dreams
is like clutching a shadow or chasing the wind.
3 What you see in a dream is nothing but a
reflection,
the image of a face in a mirror.
4 Truth can no more come from illusion
than purity can come from impurity.
5 Divination, omens, and dreams are all futile,
mere fantasies, like those of a woman in labour.
6 Unless they are sent by intervention from the Most
High,
pay no attention to them.
7 Dreams have led many astray
and disappointed those who built their hopes on
them.
8 The law is perfect without such illusions;
wisdom spoken by those faithful to the law is
complete.
9 He who is well travelled knows much,
and a person of experience understands what he is
talking about.
10 He who has little experience knows little,
but travel increases a person's resources.
11 In the course of my own journeyings I have seen
much
and understand more than I can put into words.
12 I have often been in deadly danger
but escaped, thanks to the experience I had gained.
13 THOSE who fear the Lord will live,
for their trust is in him who can keep them safe.

---

q Syr: Gk *pays heed to*   *r* Other ancient authorities read A *traveled*   33:30 **at a high price:** Gk *with blood.*

22 Far better that your children plead with you
    than that you should look to their generosity.
	22 better for your children to come begging to you,
	    than for you to have to go begging to them.

23 Keep control over all your affairs;
    let no one tarnish your glory.
	23 In all you do be the master,
	    and leave a reputation unstained.

24 When your few days reach their limit,
    at the time of death distribute your inheritance.
	24 The day your life draws to a close,
	    at the hour of death, then distribute your
	        heritage.

25 Fodder and whip and loads for an ass;
    the yoke and harness and the rod of his master.
	25 Fodder, the stick and burdens for a donkey,
	    bread, discipline and work for a slave.

27 Food, correction and work for a slave;
    and for a wicked slave, punishment in
        the stocks.
	26 Work your slave hard, and you will have peace of
	        mind,
	    leave his hands idle, and he will be asking for
	        his freedom.

26 Make a slave work and he will look for his rest;
    let his hands be idle and he will seek to be free.
	27 Yoke and harness will bow the neck,
	    for a bad servant, torments and the rack.

28 Force him to work that he be not idle,
    for idleness is an apt teacher of mischief.
	28 Set him to work, so that he will not be idle;
	    idleness teaches every kind of mischief.

29 Put him to work, for that is what befits him;
    if he becomes unruly, load him with chains.
	29 Keep him at his duties, where he should be,
	    if he is disobedient, clap him in irons.

30 But never lord it over any human being,
    and do nothing unjust.
	30 But do not be over-exacting with anyone,
	    and do nothing contrary to justice.

31 If you have but one slave, treat him like yourself,
    for you have acquired him with your
        life's blood;
	31 You have only one slave? Treat him like yourself,
	    since you have acquired him with blood.

32 If you have but one slave, deal with him as
        a brother,
    for you need him as you need your life:
	32 You have only one slave? Treat him as a brother,
	    since you need him as you need yourself.

33 If you mistreat him and he runs away,
    in what direction will you look for him?
	33 If you ill-treat him and he runs away,
	    which way will you go to look for him?

34 Empty and false are the hopes of the senseless,
    and fools are borne aloft by dreams.
	34 Vain and deceptive hopes are for the foolish,
	    and dreams lend wings to fools.

2 Like a man who catches at shadows or chases
        the wind,
    is the one who believes in dreams.
	2 As well clutch at shadows and chase the wind
	    as put any faith in dreams.

3 What is seen in dreams is to reality
    what the reflection of a face is to the face itself.
	3 Dreams are no different from mirrors;
	    confronting a face, the reflection of that face.

4 Can the unclean produce the clean?
    can the liar ever speak the truth?
	4 What can be cleansed by uncleanness,
	    what can be verified by falsehood?

5 Divination, omens and dreams all are unreal;
    what you already expect, the mind depicts.
	5 Divinations, auguries and dreams are nonsense,
	    like the fantasies of a pregnant woman.

6 Unless it be a vision specially sent by the
        Most High,
    fix not your heart on it;
	6 Unless sent as emissaries from the Most High,
	    do not give them a thought;

7 For dreams have led many astray,
    and those who believed in them have perished.
	7 for dreams have led many astray,
	    and those who relied on them have come to
	        grief.

8 The law is fulfilled without fail,
    and perfect wisdom is found in the mouth of the
        faithful man.
	8 Fulfilling the Law requires no such falsehood,
	    and wisdom is perfected in veracity.

9 A man with training gains wide knowledge;
    a man of experience speaks sense.
	9 A much travelled man knows many things,
	    and a man of great experience will talk sound
	        sense.

10 One never put to the proof knows little,
    whereas with travel a man adds to
        his resourcefulness.
	10 Someone who has never had his trials knows little;
	    but the travelled man is master of every
	        situation.

11 I have seen much in my travels,
    learned more than ever I could say.
	11 I have seen many things on my travels,
	    I have understood more than I can put into
	        words.

12 Often I was in danger of death,
    but by these attainments I was saved.
	12 I have often been in danger of death,
	    but I have been spared, and this is why:

13 Lively is the courage of those who fear the LORD,
    for they put their hope in their savior;
	13 the spirit of those who fear the Lord can survive,
	    for their hope is in someone with power to save
	        them.

NEW REVISED STANDARD VERSION	REVISED ENGLISH BIBLE

NEW REVISED STANDARD VERSION

16 Those who fear the Lord will not be timid,
    or play the coward, for he is their hope.
17 Happy is the soul that fears the Lord!
18 To whom does he look? And who is his
    support?
19 The eyes of the Lord are on those who love him,
    a mighty shield and strong support,
    a shelter from scorching wind and a shade from
        noonday sun,
    a guard against stumbling and a help against
        falling.
20 He lifts up the soul and makes the eyes sparkle;
    he gives health and life and blessing.
21 If one sacrifices ill-gotten goods, the offering is
    blemished;[s]
22 the gifts[t] of the lawless are not acceptable.
23 The Most High is not pleased with the offerings
    of the ungodly,
    nor for a multitude of sacrifices does he forgive
        sins.
24 Like one who kills a son before his father's eyes
    is the person who offers a sacrifice from the
        property of the poor.
25 The bread of the needy is the life of the poor;
    whoever deprives them of it is a murderer.
26 To take away a neighbor's living is to commit
    murder;
27 to deprive an employee of wages is to shed
    blood.
28 When one builds and another tears down,
    what do they gain but hard work?
29 When one prays and another curses,
    to whose voice will the Lord listen?
30 If one washes after touching a corpse, and
    touches it again,
    what has been gained by washing?
31 So if one fasts for his sins,
    and goes again and does the same things,
    who will listen to his prayer?
    And what has he gained by humbling himself?

35 The one who keeps the law makes many
    offerings;
2 one who heeds the commandments makes an
    offering of well-being.
3 The one who returns a kindness offers choice
    flour,
4 and one who gives alms sacrifices a thank
    offering.
5 To keep from wickedness is pleasing to the Lord,
    and to forsake unrighteousness is an atonement.
6 Do not appear before the Lord empty-handed,
7 for all that you offer is in fulfillment of the
    commandment.
8 The offering of the righteous enriches the altar,
    and its pleasing odor rises before the Most
        High.
9 The sacrifice of the righteous is acceptable,
    and it will never be forgotten.
10 Be generous when you worship the Lord,
    and do not stint the first fruits of your hands.
11 With every gift show a cheerful face,
    and dedicate your tithe with gladness.

REVISED ENGLISH BIBLE

14 Fear the Lord and have nothing else to fear;
    he whose trust is in him will never be daunted.
15 How happy is he who fears the Lord!
    He knows where to look for support.
16 The Lord keeps watch over those who love him;
    he is their strong shield and firm support,
    a shelter from scorching wind and noonday heat,
    a safeguard against stumbling, a help against
        falling.
17 He raises the spirits and makes the eyes sparkle;
    he gives healing and life and blessing.
18 A sacrifice from ill-gotten gains is tainted,
    and the gifts of the wicked win no approval.
19 The Most High has no pleasure in the offerings of
    the godless,
    nor do countless sacrifices win his forgiveness.
20 To offer a sacrifice from the possessions of the
    poor
    is like killing a son before his father's eyes.
21 Bread is life to the destitute,
    and to deprive them of it is murder.
22 To rob your neighbour of his livelihood is to kill
    him,
    and he who defrauds a worker of his wages sheds
        blood.
23 WHEN one builds and another pulls down,
    what have they gained except hard work?
24 When one prays and another curses,
    which is the Lord to listen to?
25 Bathe after touching a corpse and then touch it
    again,
    and what have you gained by your washing?
26 So it is with the one who fasts for his sins
    and goes and repeats his offence;
    who will listen to his prayer?
    What has he gained by his penance?

35 To keep the law is worth many offerings;
    to heed the commandments is a shared-offering.
2 A kindness repaid is a grain-offering,
    and to give alms is a thank-offering.
3 The way to please the Lord is to keep clear of evil,
    and to keep clear of wrongdoing is to make
        atonement.
4 Yet do not appear before the Lord empty-handed;
5 perform all the sacrifices, for they are commanded.
6 When the just person brings his offering of fat to
    the altar,
    its fragrance rises to the presence of the Most
        High.
7 The sacrifice of the just is acceptable,
    and such a memorial will never be forgotten.
8 Be generous in your worship of the Lord
    and do not stint the firstfruits of your labour.
9 Give all your gifts cheerfully,
    and with gladness dedicate your tithe.

[s] Other ancient authorities read *is made in mockery*   [t] Other ancient
authorities read *mockeries*

14 He who fears the LORD is never alarmed,
  never afraid; for the LORD is his hope.
15 Happy the soul that fears the LORD!
  In whom does he trust, and who is his support?
16 The eyes of the LORD are upon those who
    love him;
  he is their mighty shield and strong support,
  A shelter from the heat, a shade from the
    noonday sun,
  a guard against stumbling, a help against falling.
17 He buoys up the spirits, brings a sparkle to
    the eyes,
  gives health and life and blessing.

18 Tainted his gifts who offers in sacrifice
    ill-gotten goods!
  Mock presents from the lawless win not
    God's favor.
19 The Most High approves not the gifts of
    the godless,
  nor for their many sacrifices does he forgive
    their sins.
20 Like the man who slays a son in his
    father's presence
  is he who offers sacrifice from the possessions
    of the poor.
21 The bread of charity is life itself for the needy;
  he who withholds it is a man of blood.
22 He slays his neighbor who deprives him of
    his living;
  he sheds blood who denies the laborer
    his wages.
23 If one man builds up and another tears down,
  what do they gain but trouble?
24 If one man prays and another curses,
  whose voice will the LORD hear?
25 If a man again touches a corpse after he
    has bathed,
  what did he gain by the purification?
26 So with a man who fasts for his sins,
  but then goes and commits them again:
  Who will hear his prayer,
  and what has he gained by his mortification?

35 To keep the law is a great oblation,
    and he who observes the commandments
    sacrifices a peace offering.
2 In works of charity one offers fine flour,
  and when he gives alms he presents his sacrifice
    of praise.
3 To refrain from evil pleases the LORD,
  and to avoid injustice is an atonement.
4 Appear not before the LORD empty-handed,
  for all that you offer is in fulfillment of
    the precepts.
5 The just man's offering enriches the altar
  and rises as a sweet odor before the Most High.
6 The just man's sacrifice is most pleasing,
  nor will it ever be forgotten.
7 In generous spirit pay homage to the LORD,
  be not sparing of freewill gifts.
8 With each contribution show a
    cheerful countenance,
  and pay your tithes in a spirit of joy.

14 No one who fears the Lord need ever hesitate,
  or ever be daunted, since the Lord is his hope.
15 Happy the soul of one who fears the Lord.
  On whom does he rely? Who supports him?
16 The eyes of the Lord watch over those who love
    him,
  he is their powerful protection and their strong
    support,
  their screen from the desert wind, their shelter
    from the midday sun,
  a guard against stumbling, an assurance against a
    fall.
17 He revives the spirit and brightens the eyes,
  he gives health, life and blessing.

18 The sacrifice of an offering unjustly acquired is a
    mockery;
  the gifts of the impious are unacceptable.
19 The Most High takes no pleasure in offerings from
    the godless,
  multiplying sacrifices will not gain pardon for
    sin.
20 Offering sacrifice from the property of the poor
  is as bad as slaughtering a son before his father's
    eyes.
21 A meagre diet is the very life of the poor,
  to deprive them of it is to commit murder.
22 To take away a fellow-man's livelihood is to kill
    him,
  to deprive an employee of his wages is to shed
    blood.
23 If one person builds while another pulls down,
  what will they get out of it but trouble?
24 If one person prays and another calls down a curse,
  to which one's voice is the Master going to
    listen?
25 If someone washes after touching a corpse, and
    then touches it again,
  what is the good of his washing?
26 Just so with someone who fasts for sin,
  and then goes and commits it again.
  Who is going to hear that person's prayer?
  What is the good of the self-abasement?

35 One who keeps the Law multiplies offerings;
    one who follows the commandments offers
    communion sacrifices.
2 Proof of gratitude is an offering of fine flour,
  almsgiving a sacrifice of praise.
3 To abandon wickedness is what pleases the Lord,
  to give up wrong-doing is an expiatory sacrifice.
4 Do not appear empty-handed in the Lord's
    presence;
  for all these things are due under the
    commandment.
5 The offering of the upright graces the altar,
  and its savour rises before the Most High.
6 The sacrifice of the upright is acceptable,
  its memorial will not be forgotten.
7 Honour the Lord with generosity,
  do not stint the first-fruits you bring.
8 Add a smiling face to all your gifts,
  and be cheerful as you dedicate your tithes.

NEW REVISED STANDARD VERSION	REVISED ENGLISH BIBLE

NEW REVISED STANDARD VERSION

12 Give to the Most High as he has given to you,
  and as generously as you can afford.
13 For the Lord is the one who repays,
  and he will repay you sevenfold.
14 Do not offer him a bribe, for he will not accept
  it;
15 and do not rely on a dishonest sacrifice;
  for the Lord is the judge,
  and with him there is no partiality.
16 He will not show partiality to the poor;
  but he will listen to the prayer of one who is
  wronged.
17 He will not ignore the supplication of the orphan,
  or the widow when she pours out her
  complaint.
18 Do not the tears of the widow run down her
  cheek
19 as she cries out against the one who causes
  them to fall?
20 The one whose service is pleasing to the Lord
  will be accepted,
  and his prayer will reach to the clouds.
21 The prayer of the humble pierces the clouds,
  and it will not rest until it reaches its goal;
  it will not desist until the Most High responds
22 and does justice for the righteous, and executes
  judgment.
  Indeed, the Lord will not delay,
  and like a warrior*u* will not be patient
  until he crushes the loins of the unmerciful
23 and repays vengeance on the nations;
  until he destroys the multitude of the insolent,
  and breaks the scepters of the unrighteous;
24 until he repays mortals according to their deeds,
  and the works of all according to their
  thoughts;
25 until he judges the case of his people
  and makes them rejoice in his mercy.
26 His mercy is as welcome in time of distress
  as clouds of rain in time of drought.

36 Have mercy upon us, O God*v* of all,
2 and put all the nations in fear of you.
3 Lift up your hand against foreign nations
  and let them see your might.
4 As you have used us to show your holiness to
  them,
  so use them to show your glory to us.
5 Then they will know,*w* as we have known
  that there is no God but you, O Lord.
6 Give new signs, and work other wonders;
7 make your hand and right arm glorious.
8 Rouse your anger and pour out your wrath;
9 destroy the adversary and wipe out the enemy.
10 Hasten the day, and remember the appointed
  time,*x*
  and let people recount your mighty deeds.
11 Let survivors be consumed in the fiery wrath,
  and may those who harm your people meet
  destruction.
12 Crush the heads of hostile rulers
  who say, "There is no one but ourselves."
13 Gather all the tribes of Jacob,*y*
16 and give them their inheritance, as at the
  beginning.

REVISED ENGLISH BIBLE

10 Give to the Most High as he has given to you,
  as generously as your means allow,
11 for the Lord always repays
  and you will be repaid seven times over.
12 Do not offer him a bribe, for he will not accept it,
  and do not rely on an ill-gotten sacrifice.
  The Lord is a judge
  who is no respecter of persons.
13 He has no favourites at the expense of the poor,
  and he listens to the prayer of the wronged.
14 He never ignores the appeal of the orphan
  or of the widow as she pours out her complaint.
15 How the tears run down the widow's cheeks,
  and her cries accuse him who caused them!
16 To be accepted a man must serve the Lord as he
  requires,
  and then his prayer will reach the clouds.
17 The prayer of the humble pierces the clouds;
  before it reaches its goal there is no comfort for
  him.
  He does not desist until the Most High intervenes,
  giving the just their rights and seeing justice done.
18 The Lord will not be slow,
  neither will he be patient with the wicked,
  until he breaks the bones of the merciless
  and sends retribution on the heathen;
  until he blots out the insolent, one and all,
  and shatters the power of the unjust;
19 until he gives all people their deserts,
  measuring their actions by their intentions;
  until he gives his people their rights
  and gladdens them with his mercy.
20 When affliction comes, mercy is as timely
  as rain-clouds in a time of drought.

36 Look on us with pity, Lord God of all,
2 and strike fear into every nation.
3 Lift your hand against the heathen,
  and let them behold your power.
4 As they have seen your holiness displayed among
  us,
  so let us see your greatness displayed among them.
5 Let them learn, as we ourselves have learned,
  that there is no god but you, O Lord.
6 Renew your signs, repeat your miracles,
  win glory for your mighty hand and right arm.
7 Rouse your anger, pour out your wrath,
  to destroy the adversary and wipe out the enemy.
8 Remember the day you have appointed and hasten
  it,
  and give men cause to recount your wonders.
9 Let burning wrath devour the survivors,
  and let the oppressors of your people meet their
  doom.
10 Crush the heads of hostile princes
  who say, 'No one counts but us.'
11 Gather all the tribes of Jacob,
  and grant them their inheritance, as you did long
  ago.

---

*u*Heb: Gk *and with them*   *v*Heb: Gk *O Master, the God*
*w*Heb: Gk *And let them know you*   *x*Other ancient authorities read
remember your oath   *y*Owing to a dislocation in the Greek Mss of
Sirach, the verse numbers 14 and 15 are not used in chapter 36,
though no text is missing.

NEW AMERICAN BIBLE

9 Give to the Most High as he has given to you,
   generously, according to your means.
10 For the LORD is one who always repays,
   and he will give back to you sevenfold.
11 But offer no bribes, these he does not accept!
   Trust not in sacrifice of the fruits of extortion,
12 For he is a God of justice,
   who knows no favorites.
13 Though not unduly partial toward the weak,
   yet he hears the cry of the oppressed.
14 He is not deaf to the wail of the orphan,
   nor to the widow when she pours out
     her complaint;
15 Do not the tears that stream down her cheek
   cry out against him that causes them to fall?
16 He who serves God willingly is heard;
   his petition reaches the heavens.
17 The prayer of the lowly pierces the clouds;
   it does not rest till it reaches its goal,
18 Nor will it withdraw till the Most High responds,
   judges justly and affirms the right.
19 God indeed will not delay,
   and like a warrior, will not be still
20 Till he breaks the backs of the merciless
   and wreaks vengeance upon the proud;
21 Till he destroys the haughty root and branch,
   and smashes the scepter of the wicked;
22 Till he requites mankind according to its deeds,
   and repays men according to their thoughts;
23 Till he defends the cause of his people,
   and gladdens them by his mercy.
24 Welcome is his mercy in time of distress
   as rain clouds in time of drought.

36 Come to our aid, O God of the universe,
   and put all the nations in dread of you!
2 Raise your hand against the heathen,
   that they may realize your power.
3 As you have used us to show them your holiness,
   so now use them to show us your glory.
4 Thus they will know, as we know,
   that there is no God but you.
5 Give new signs and work new wonders;
   show forth the splendor of your right hand
     and arm;
6 Rouse your anger, pour out wrath,
   humble the enemy, scatter the foe.
7 Hasten the day, bring on the time;
9   crush the heads of the hostile rulers.
8 Let raging fire consume the fugitive,
   and your people's oppressors meet destruction.
10 Gather all the tribes of Jacob,
   that they may inherit the land as of old.
11 Show mercy to the people called by your name;
   Israel, whom you named your first-born.

NEW JERUSALEM BIBLE

9 Give to the Most High as he has given to you,
   as generously as your means can afford;
10 for the Lord is a good rewarder,
   he will reward you seven times over.
11 Do not try to bribe him with presents, he will not
     accept them,
   do not put your faith in wrongly motivated
     sacrifices;
12 for the Lord is a judge
   who is utterly impartial.
13 He never shows partiality to the detriment of the
     poor,
   he listens to the plea of the injured party.
14 He does not ignore the orphan's supplication,
   nor the widow's as she pours out her complaint.
15 Do the widow's tears not run down her cheeks,
   as she accuses the man who is the cause of
     them?
16 Whoever wholeheartedly serves God will be
     accepted,
   his petitions will carry to the clouds.
17 The prayer of the humble pierces the clouds:
   and until it does, he is not to be consoled,
18 nor will he desist until the Most High takes notice
     of him,
   acquits the upright and delivers judgement.
19 And the Lord will not be slow,
   nor will he be dilatory on their behalf,
20 until he has crushed the loins of the merciless
   and exacted vengeance on the nations,
21 until he has eliminated the hordes of the arrogant
   and broken the sceptres of the wicked,
22 until he has repaid all people as their deeds deserve
   and human actions as their intentions merit,
23 until he has judged the case of his people
   and made them rejoice in his mercy.
24 Mercy is welcome in time of trouble,
   like rain clouds in time of drought.

36 Take pity on us, Master, Lord of the universe,
   look at us,
   spread fear of yourself throughout all other
     nations.
2 Raise your hand against the foreign nations
   and let them see your might.
3 As, in their sight, you have proved yourself holy to
     us,
   so now, in our sight, prove yourself great to
     them.
4 Let them acknowledge you, just as we have
     acknowledged
   that there is no God but you, Lord.
5 Send new portents, do fresh wonders,
   win glory for your hand and your right arm.
6 Rouse your fury, pour out your rage,
   destroy the opponent, annihilate the enemy.
7 Hasten the day, remember the oath,
   and let people tell of your mighty deeds.
8 Let fiery wrath swallow up the survivor,
   and destruction overtake those who oppress your
     people.
9 Crush the heads of hostile rulers
   who say, 'There is no one else but us!'
10 Gather together all the tribes of Jacob,
   restore them their heritage as at the beginning.
11 Take pity, Lord, on the people called by your
     name,
   on Israel whom you have made your first-born.

NEW REVISED STANDARD VERSION	REVISED ENGLISH BIBLE

NEW REVISED STANDARD VERSION

17 Have mercy, O Lord, on the people called by
     your name,
     on Israel, whom you have named*z* your
          firstborn.
18 Have pity on the city of your sanctuary,*a*
     Jerusalem, the place of your dwelling.*b*
19 Fill Zion with your majesty,*c*
     and your temple*d* with your glory.
20 Bear witness to those whom you created in the
          beginning,
     and fulfill the prophecies spoken in your name.
21 Reward those who wait for you
     and let your prophets be found trustworthy.
22 Hear, O Lord, the prayer of your servants,
     according to your goodwill toward*e* your
          people,
     and all who are on the earth will know
     that you are the Lord, the God of the ages.

23 The stomach will take any food,
     yet one food is better than another.
24 As the palate tastes the kinds of game,
     so an intelligent mind detects false words.
25 A perverse mind will cause grief,
     but a person with experience will pay him
          back.
26 A woman will accept any man as a husband,
     but one girl is preferable to another.
27 A woman's beauty lights up a man's face,
     and there is nothing he desires more.
28 If kindness and humility mark her speech,
     her husband is more fortunate than other men.
29 He who acquires a wife gets his best
          possession,*f*
     a helper fit for him and a pillar of support.*g*
30 Where there is no fence, the property will be
          plundered;
     and where there is no wife, a man will become
          a fugitive and a wanderer.*h*
31 For who will trust a nimble robber
     that skips from city to city?
     So who will trust a man that has no nest,
     but lodges wherever night overtakes him?

37 Every friend says, "I too am a friend";
     but some friends are friends only in name.
2 Is it not a sorrow like that for death itself
     when a dear friend turns into an enemy?
3 O inclination to evil, why were you formed
     to cover the land with deceit?
4 Some companions rejoice in the happiness of a
          friend,
     but in time of trouble they are against him.
5 Some companions help a friend for their
          stomachs' sake,
     yet in battle they will carry his shield.
6 Do not forget a friend during the battle,*i*
     and do not be unmindful of him when you
          distribute your spoils.*j*

7 All counselors praise the counsel they give,
     but some give counsel in their own interest.

REVISED ENGLISH BIBLE

12 Have pity, Lord, on the people called by your
          name,
     on Israel, whom you have named your firstborn.
13 Show mercy to the city of your sanctuary,
     to the city of Jerusalem, your dwelling-place.
14 Fill Zion with the praise of your triumph
     and the temple with your glory.
15 Acknowledge those you created at the beginning
     and fulfil the prophecies spoken in your name.
16 Reward those who look to you in trust;
     prove your prophets worthy of credence.
17 Listen, O Lord, to the prayer of your servants,
     who claim Aaron's blessing on your people.
     Let all who live on earth acknowledge
     that you are the Lord, the eternal God.

18 THE stomach will accept any food,
     but one food is better than another.
19 As the palate identifies game by its taste,
     so the discerning mind detects lies.
20 A warped mind makes trouble,
     but he who has wide experience can get his own
          back.
21 A woman will take any man for husband,
     but a man may prefer one girl to another.
22 A woman's beauty makes a man happy,
     and there is nothing he desires more.
23 If she has a kind and gentle tongue,
     then her husband has no peer among men.
24 He who acquires a wife has the beginnings of a
          fortune,
     a helper to match his needs and a pillar to give
          him support.
25 Where there is no hedge, a vineyard is plundered;
     where there is no wife, a man wanders about in
          misery.
26 Does anyone trust the swift-moving bandit
     who swoops on town after town?
     No more will they trust a homeless man
     who lodges wherever night overtakes him.

37 Every friend says, 'I too am your friend';
     but some are friends in name only.
2 What a mortal grief it is
     when a dear friend turns into an enemy!
3 O propensity to evil, how did you creep in
     to cover the earth with treachery?
4 A friend may be all smiles when you are joyful,
     but turn against you when trouble comes.
5 Another shares your toil for the sake of a meal,
     and yet may shield you against an enemy.
6 Do not forget a friend in the fight,
     and do not neglect him when prosperity comes
          your way.

7 Every counsellor says his advice is best,
     but he may have in view his own advantage.

---

z Other ancient authorities read *you have likened to*   *a* Or *on your
holy city*   *b* Heb: Gk *your rest*   *c* Heb Syr: Gk *the celebration of
your wondrous deeds*   *d* Heb Syr: Gk Lat *people*   *e* Heb and two
Gk witnesses: Lat and most Gk witnesses read *according to the
blessing of Aaron for*   *f* Heb: Gk *enters upon a possession*
g Heb: Gk *rest*   *h* Heb: Gk *wander about and sigh*   *i* Heb: Gk *in
your heart*   *j* Heb: Gk *him in your wealth*

NEW AMERICAN BIBLE

12 Take pity on your holy city,
   Jerusalem, your dwelling place.
13 Fill Zion with your majesty,
   your temple with your glory.

14 Give evidence of your deeds of old;
   fulfill the prophecies spoken in your name,
15 Reward those who have hoped in you,
   and let your prophets be proved true.
16 Hear the prayer of your servants,
   for you are ever gracious to your people;
17 Thus it will be known to the very ends of the earth
   that you are the eternal God.

18 The throat can swallow any food,
   yet some foods are more agreeable than others;
19 As the palate tests meat by its savor,
   so does a keen mind insincere words.
20 A deceitful character causes grief,
   but an experienced man can turn the tables
   on him.
21 Though any man may be accepted as a husband,
   yet one girl will be more suitable than another:
22 A woman's beauty makes her husband's face
   light up,
   for it surpasses all else that charms the eye;
23 And if, besides, her speech is kindly,
   his lot is beyond that of mortal men.
24 A wife is her husband's richest treasure,
   a helpmate, a steadying column.
25 A vineyard with no hedge will be overrun;
   a man with no wife becomes a
   homeless wanderer.
26 Who will trust an armed band
   that shifts from city to city?
27 Or a man who has no nest,
   but lodges where night overtakes him?

37 Every friend declares his friendship,
   but there are friends who are friends in
   name only.
2 Is it not a sorrow unto death
   when your bosom companion becomes
   your enemy?
3 "Alas, my companion! Why were you created
   to blanket the earth with deceit?"
4 A false friend will share your joys,
   but in time of trouble he stands afar off.
5 A true friend will fight with you against the foe,
   against your enemies he will be
   your shield-bearer.
6 Forget not your comrade during the battle,
   and neglect him not when you distribute
   your spoils.

7 Every counselor points out a way,
   but some counsel ways of their own;

NEW JERUSALEM BIBLE

12 Have compassion on your holy city,
   on Jerusalem, the place where you rest.
13 Fill Zion with your praises
   and your sanctuary with your glory.

14 Vindicate those whom you created first,
   fulfil what has been prophesied in your name.
15 Give those who wait for you their reward,
   let your prophets be proved true.
16 Grant, Lord, the prayer of your servants,
   in the terms of Aaron's blessing on your people,
17 so that all the earth's inhabitants may acknowledge
   that you are the Lord, the everlasting God.

18 The stomach takes in all kinds of food,
   but some foods are better than others.
19 As the palate discerns the flavour of game,
   so a shrewd listener detects lying words.
20 A perverse character causes depression in others;
   it needs experience to know how to repay such a
   one.
21 A woman will accept any husband,
   but some daughters are better than others.
22 A woman's beauty delights the beholder,
   a man likes nothing better.
23 If her tongue is kind and gentle,
   her husband is the happiest of men.
24 The man who takes a wife has the makings of a
   fortune,
   a helper to match himself, a pillar of support.
25 When property has no fence, it is open to plunder,
   when a man has no wife, he is aimless and
   querulous.
26 Will anyone trust an armed thief
   who flits from town to town?
27 So it is with the man who has no nest,
   and lodges wherever night overtakes him.

37 Any friend will say, 'I am your friend too,'
   but some friends are friends only in name.
2 Is it not a deadly sorrow
   when a comrade or a friend turns enemy?
3 O evil inclination, why were you created,
   to cover the earth with deceit?
4 One kind of comrade congratulates a friend in
   prosperity
   but in time of trouble appears on the other side.
5 One kind of comrade genuinely feels for a friend
   and when it comes to a fight, springs to arms.
6 Do not forget the genuine friend,
   do not push him out of mind once you are rich.

7 Any adviser will offer advice,
   but some are governed by self-interest.

8 Be wary of a counselor,
and learn first what is his interest,
for he will take thought for himself.
He may cast the lot against you
9 and tell you, "Your way is good,"
and then stand aside to see what happens to
you.
10 Do not consult the one who regards you with
suspicion;
hide your intentions from those who are jealous
of you.
11 Do not consult with a woman about her rival
or with a coward about war,
with a merchant about business
or with a buyer about selling,
with a miser about generosity^k
or with the merciless about kindness,
with an idler about any work
or with a seasonal laborer about completing his
work,
with a lazy servant about a big task —
pay no attention to any advice they give.
12 But associate with a godly person
whom you know to be a keeper of the
commandments,
who is like-minded with yourself,
and who will grieve with you if you fail.
13 And heed^l the counsel of your own heart,
for no one is more faithful to you than it is.
14 For our own mind sometimes keeps us better
informed
than seven sentinels sitting high on a
watchtower.
15 But above all pray to the Most High
that he may direct your way in truth.

16 Discussion is the beginning of every work,
and counsel precedes every undertaking.
17 The mind is the root of all conduct;
18 it sprouts four branches,^{m}
good and evil, life and death;
and it is the tongue that continually rules them.
19 Some people may be clever enough to teach
many,
and yet be useless to themselves.
20 A skillful speaker may be hated;
he will be destitute of all food,
21 for the Lord has withheld the gift of charm,
since he is lacking in all wisdom.
22 If a person is wise to his own advantage,
the fruits of his good sense will be
praiseworthy.^{n}
23 A wise person instructs his own people,
and the fruits of his good sense will endure.
24 A wise person will have praise heaped upon him,
and all who see him will call him happy.
25 The days of a person's life are numbered,
but the days of Israel are without number.
26 One who is wise among his people will inherit
honor,^{o}
and his name will live forever.

27 My child, test yourself while you live;
see what is bad for you and do not give in to
it.

8 Be on your guard against him who proffers advice;
find out first where his interest lies,
for his advice will be weighted in his own favour.
He may tip the scales against you;
9 he may say, 'Your road is clear,'
and then stand aside to see what befalls you.
10 Do not consult anyone who regards you with
suspicion,
or reveal your intentions to those who envy you.
11 Never consult a woman about her rival
or a coward about war,
a merchant about a bargain
or a buyer about a sale,
a grudging person about gratitude
or a hard-hearted person about a kind action,
an idler about work of any sort,
a seasonal worker about the end of the job,
or a lazy servant about an exacting task —
do not turn to them for any advice.
12 Rely rather on a godfearing person
whom you know to be a keeper of the
commandments,
one who is with you heart and soul
and will show you sympathy if you have a setback.
13 But trust your own judgement also,
for you have no more reliable counsellor.
14 One's own mind has sometimes a way of bringing
word
better than seven watchmen posted on a tower.
15 But above all pray to the Most High
to guide you on the path of truth.

16 Every undertaking begins in discussion,
and deliberation precedes every action.
17 The roots of choice are in the heart:
18 destiny takes four forms,
good and evil, life and death;
and always it is the tongue that decides the issue.
19 Someone may be clever enough to teach many
and yet be of no use to himself.
20 A brilliant speaker may make enemies
and end by dying of hunger,
21 if the Lord has withheld grace and charm
by depriving him of wisdom.
22 If someone is wise in the conduct of his own life,
his good sense can be trusted when he gives
advice.
23 If someone is wise and instructs his people,
then his good sense can be trusted.
24 A wise person will have praise heaped on him,
and all who see him will count him happy.
25 Human life can be numbered in days,
but the days of Israel are countless.
26 A person who is wise will possess the confidence
of his people,
and his name will live for ever.

27 My son, test yourself all your life long;
note what is bad for you, and do not indulge in it;

---

^{k} Heb: Gk gratitude ^{l} Heb: Gk establish ^{m} Heb: Gk As a clue to
changes of heart four kinds of destiny appear ^{n} Other ancient
witnesses read trustworthy ^{o} Other ancient authorities read
confidence

8 Be on the alert when one proffers advice,
    find out first of all what he wants.
For he may be thinking of himself alone;
    why should the profit fall to him?
9 He may tell you how good your way will be,
    and then stand by to watch your misfortune.
10 Seek no advice from one who regards you
        with hostility;
    from those who envy you, keep your
        intentions hidden.
11 Speak not to a woman about her rival,
    nor to a coward about war,
    to a merchant about business,
    to a buyer about value,
    to a miser about generosity,
    to a cruel man about mercy,
    to a lazy man about work,
    to a seasonal laborer about the harvest,
    to an idle slave about a great task:
    pay no attention to any advice they give.
12 Instead, associate with a religious man,
    who you are sure keeps the commandments;
Who is like-minded with yourself
    and will feel for you if you fall.
13 Then, too, heed your own heart's counsel;
    for what have you that you can depend on more?
14 A man's conscience can tell him his situation
    better than seven watchmen in a lofty tower.
15 Most important of all, pray to God
    to set your feet in the path of truth.

16 A word is the source of every deed;
    a thought, of every act.
17 The root of all conduct is the mind;
    four branches it shoots forth:
18 Good and evil, death and life,
    their absolute mistress is the tongue.
19 A man may be wise and benefit many,
    yet be of no use to himself.
20 Though a man may be wise, if his words
        are rejected
    he will be deprived of all enjoyment.
21 When a man is wise to his own advantage,
    the fruits of his knowledge are seen in his
        own person;
22 When a man is wise to his people's advantage,
    the fruits of his knowledge are enduring:
23 Limited are the days of one man's life,
    but the life of Israel is days without number.
24 One wise for himself has full enjoyment,
    and all who see him praise him;
25 One wise for his people wins a heritage of glory,
    and his name endures forever.

26 My son, while you are well, govern your appetite
    so that you allow it not what is bad for you;

8 Beware of someone who offers advice;
    first find out what he wants himself —
since his advice coincides with his own interest —
    in case he has designs on you
9 and tells you, 'You are on the right road,'
    but stands well clear to see what will happen to
        you.
10 Do not consult anyone who looks at you askance,
    conceal your plans from people jealous of you.
11 Do not consult a woman about her rival,
    or a coward about war,
    a merchant about prices,
    or a buyer about selling,
    anyone mean about gratitude,
    or anyone selfish about kindness,
    a lazy fellow about any sort of work,
    or a casual worker about finishing a job,
    an idle servant about a major undertaking —
    do not rely on these for any advice.
12 But have constant recourse to some devout person,
    whom you know to be a keeper of the
        commandments,
    whose soul matches your own,
    and who, if you go wrong, will be sympathetic.
13 Finally, stick to the advice your own heart gives
        you,
    no one can be truer to you than that;
14 since a person's soul often gives a clearer warning
    than seven watchmen perched on a watchtower.
15 And besides all this beg the Most High
    to guide your steps into the truth.

16 Reason should be the basis for every activity,
    reflection must come before any undertaking.
17 Thoughts are rooted in the heart,
    and this sends out four branches:
18 good and evil, life and death,
    and mistress of them always is the tongue.
19 One kind of person is clever at teaching others,
    yet is no good whatever to himself;
20 another, very eloquent, is detested
    and ends by starving to death,
21 not having won the favour of the Lord,
    and being destitute of all wisdom.
22 Another considers himself wise
    and proclaims his intellectual conclusions as
        certainties.
23 But the truly wise instructs his people
    and his intellectual conclusions are certainties.
24 The wise is showered with blessings,
    and all who see him will call him happy.
25 Human life lasts a number of days,
    but the days of Israel are beyond counting.
26 The wise will earn confidence among the people,
    his name will live for ever.

27 During your life, my child, see what suits your
        constitution,
    do not give it what you find disagrees with it;

| NEW REVISED STANDARD VERSION | REVISED ENGLISH BIBLE |

NEW REVISED STANDARD VERSION

28 For not everything is good for everyone,
  and no one enjoys everything.
29 Do not be greedy for every delicacy,
  and do not eat without restraint;
30 for overeating brings sickness,
  and gluttony leads to nausea.
31 Many have died of gluttony,
  but the one who guards against it prolongs his
    life.

38 Honor physicians for their services,
    for the Lord created them;
2 for their gift of healing comes from the Most
    High,
  and they are rewarded by the king.
3 The skill of physicians makes them distinguished,
  and in the presence of the great they are
    admired.
4 The Lord created medicines out of the earth,
  and the sensible will not despise them.
5 Was not water made sweet with a tree
  in order that its *p* power might be known?
6 And he gave skill to human beings
  that he *q* might be glorified in his marvelous
    works.
7 By them the physician *r* heals and takes away
    pain;
8 the pharmacist makes a mixture from them.
  God's *s* works will never be finished;
  and from him health *t* spreads over all the
    earth.
9 My child, when you are ill, do not delay,
  but pray to the Lord, and he will heal you.
10 Give up your faults and direct your hands rightly,
  and cleanse your heart from all sin.
11 Offer a sweet-smelling sacrifice, and a memorial
    portion of choice flour,
  and pour oil on your offering, as much as you
    can afford. *u*
12 Then give the physician his place, for the Lord
    created him;
  do not let him leave you, for you need him.
13 There may come a time when recovery lies in the
    hands of physicians, *v*
14 for they too pray to the Lord
  that he grant them success in diagnosis *w*
  and in healing, for the sake of preserving life.
15 He who sins against his Maker,
  will be defiant toward the physician. *x*

16 My child, let your tears fall for the dead,
  and as one in great pain begin the lament.
  Lay out the body with due ceremony,
  and do not neglect the burial.
17 Let your weeping be bitter and your wailing
    fervent;
  make your mourning worthy of the departed,
  for one day, or two, to avoid criticism;
  then be comforted for your grief.
18 For grief may result in death,
  and a sorrowful heart saps one's strength.
19 When a person is taken away, sorrow is over;
  but the life of the poor weighs down the heart.
20 Do not give your heart to grief;
  drive it away, and remember your own end.

REVISED ENGLISH BIBLE

28 for not everything is good for everyone,
  nor do we all enjoy the same things.
29 Do not be greedy for every delicacy
  or eat without restraint,
30 for illness is a sure result of overeating,
  and gluttony is next door to nausea.
31 Gluttony has been the death of many,
  but he who is careful prolongs his life.

38 Value the services of a doctor
    for he has his place assigned him by the Lord.
2 His skill comes from the Most High,
  and he is rewarded by kings.
3 The doctor's knowledge gives him high standing
  and wins him the admiration of the great.
4 The Lord has created remedies from the earth,
  and a sensible man will not disparage them.
5 Was not water sweetened by a log,
  and so the power of the Lord was revealed?
6 The Lord has imparted knowledge to mortals,
  that by their use of his marvels he may win praise;
7 by means of them the doctor relieves pain
8 and from them the pharmacist compounds his
    mixture.
  There is no limit to the works of the Lord,
  who spreads health over the whole world.

9 My son, in time of illness do not be remiss,
  but pray to the Lord and he will heal you.
10 Keep clear of wrongdoing, amend your ways,
  and cleanse your heart from all sin.
11 Bring a fragrant offering and a memorial sacrifice
    of flour;
  pour oil on the sacrifice; be as lavish as you can.
12 And the doctor should be called;
  keep him by you, for you need him also.
13 A time may come when your recovery is in his
    hands;
14 then he too will pray to the Lord
  to grant success in relieving pain
  and finding a cure to save the patient's life.
15 He who sins before his Maker
  shows himself arrogant before the doctor.

16 My son, shed tears for one who has died;
  raise a lament for your grievous loss.
  Shroud the body with proper ceremony
  and do not neglect his burial.
17 With bitter weeping and passionate wailing
  make your mourning worthy of him.
  Mourn for a few days and avoid criticism;
  then take comfort in your grief,
18 for grief may lead to death,
  and a grieving heart saps the strength.
19 With the burial, grief should pass;
  a life of misery is an affliction to the heart.
20 Do not abandon yourself to grief;
  put it from you and think of your own end.

---

p Or *his*   *q* Or *they*   *r* Heb: Gk *he*   *s* Gk *His*   *t* Or *peace*
u Heb: Lat lacks *as much as you can afford*; Meaning of Gk uncertain
v Gk *in their hands*   *w* Heb: Gk *rest*   *x* Heb: Gk *may he fall into
the hands of the physician*

27 For not every food is good for everyone,
    nor is everything suited to every taste.
28 Be not drawn after every enjoyment,
    neither become a glutton for choice foods,
29 For sickness comes with overeating,
    and gluttony brings on biliousness.
30 Through lack of self-control many have died,
    but the abstemious man prolongs his life.

38 Hold the physician in honor, for he is essential
        to you,
    and God it was who established his profession.
2 From God the doctor has his wisdom,
    and the king provides for his sustenance.
3 His knowledge makes the doctor distinguished,
    and gives him access to those in authority.
4 God makes the earth yield healing herbs
    which the prudent man should not neglect;
5 Was not the water sweetened by a twig
    that men might learn his power?
6 He endows men with the knowledge
    to glory in his mighty works,
7 Through which the doctor eases pain
    and the druggist prepares his medicines;
8 Thus God's creative work continues without cease
    in its efficacy on the surface of the earth.

9 My son, when you are ill, delay not,
    but pray to God, who will heal you:
10 Flee wickedness; let your hands be just,
    cleanse your heart of every sin;
11 Offer your sweet-smelling oblation and petition,
    a rich offering according to your means.
12 Then give the doctor his place
    lest he leave; for you need him too.
13 There are times that give him an advantage,
14   and he too beseeches God
    That his diagnosis may be correct
    and his treatment bring about a cure.
15 He who is a sinner toward his Maker
    will be defiant toward the doctor.

16 My son, shed tears for one who is dead
    with wailing and bitter lament;
    As is only proper, prepare the body,
    absent not yourself from his burial:
17 Weeping bitterly, mourning fully,
    pay your tribute of sorrow, as he deserves,
18 One or two days, to prevent gossip;
    then compose yourself after your grief,
19 For grief can bring on an extremity
    and heartache destroy one's health.
20 Turn not your thoughts to him again;
    cease to recall him; think rather of the end.

28 for not everything is good for everybody,
    nor does everybody like everything.
29 Do not be insatiable for any delicacy,
    do not be greedy for food,
30 for over-eating leads to illness
    and excess leads to liver-attacks.
31 Many people have died from over-eating;
    control yourself, and so prolong your life.

38 Treat the doctor with the honour that is his due,
        in consideration of his services;
    for he too has been created by the Lord.
2 Healing itself comes from the Most High,
    like a gift received from a king.
3 The doctor's learning keeps his head high,
    and the great regard him with awe.
4 The Lord has brought forth medicinal herbs from
    the ground,
    and no one sensible will despise them.
5 Did not a piece of wood once sweeten the water,
    thus giving proof of its power?*e*
6 He has also given some people knowledge,
    so that they may draw credit from his mighty
       works.
7 He uses these for healing and relieving pain;
    the druggist makes up a mixture from them.
8 Thus, there is no end to his activities;
    thanks to him, well-being exists throughout the
       world.

9 My child, when you are ill, do not rebel,
    but pray to the Lord and he will heal you.
10 Renounce your faults, keep your hands unsoiled,
    and cleanse your heart from all sin.
11 Offer incense and a memorial of fine flour,
    make as rich an offering as you can afford.
12 Then let the doctor take over — the Lord created
      him too —
    do not let him leave you, for you need him.
13 There are times when good health depends on
      doctors.
14   For they, in their turn, will pray the Lord
    to grant them the grace to relieve
    and to heal, and so prolong your life.
15 Whoever sins in the eyes of his Maker,
    let such a one come under the care of the
      doctor!

16 My child, shed tears over the dead,
    lament for the dead to show your sorrow,
    then bury the body with due ceremony
    and do not fail to honour the grave.
17 Weep bitterly, beat your breast,
    observe the mourning the dead deserves
    for a day or two, to avoid censorious comment,
    and then be comforted in your sorrow;
18 for grief can lead to death,
    a grief-stricken heart loses all energy.
19 In affliction sorrow persists,
    a life of grief is hard to bear.
20 Do not abandon your heart to grief,
    drive it away, bear your own end in mind.

e **38** Ex 15:23–25.

NEW REVISED STANDARD VERSION	REVISED ENGLISH BIBLE

21 Do not forget, there is no coming back;
  you do the dead[y] no good, and you injure
    yourself.
22 Remember his[z] fate, for yours is like it;
  yesterday it was his,[a] and today it is yours.
23 When the dead is at rest, let his remembrance
    rest too,
  and be comforted for him when his spirit has
    departed.

24 The wisdom of the scribe depends on the
    opportunity of leisure;
  only the one who has little business can
    become wise.
25 How can one become wise who handles the plow,
  and who glories in the shaft of a goad,
  who drives oxen and is occupied with their work,
  and whose talk is about bulls?
26 He sets his heart on plowing furrows,
  and he is careful about fodder for the heifers.
27 So too is every artisan and master artisan
  who labors by night as well as by day;
  those who cut the signets of seals,
  each is diligent in making a great variety;
  they set their heart on painting a lifelike image,
  and they are careful to finish their work.
28 So too is the smith, sitting by the anvil;
    intent on his iron-work;
  the breath of the fire melts his flesh,
  and he struggles with the heat of the furnace;
  the sound of the hammer deafens his ears,[b]
  and his eyes are on the pattern of the object.
  He sets his heart on finishing his handiwork,
  and he is careful to complete its decoration.
29 So too is the potter sitting at his work
  and turning the wheel with his feet;
  he is always deeply concerned over his products,
  and he produces them in quantity.
30 He molds the clay with his arm
  and makes it pliable with his feet;
  he sets his heart to finish the glazing,
  and he takes care in firing[c] the kiln.

31 All these rely on their hands,
  and all are skillful in their own work.
32 Without them no city can be inhabited,
  and wherever they live, they will not go
    hungry.[d]
  Yet they are not sought out for the council of the
    people,[e]
33 nor do they attain eminence in the public
    assembly.
  They do not sit in the judge's seat,
  nor do they understand the decisions of the
    courts;
  they cannot expound discipline or judgment,
  and they are not found among the rulers.[f]
34 But they maintain the fabric of the world,
  and their concern is for[g] the exercise of their
    trade.

  How different the one who devotes himself
    to the study of the law of the Most High!

39 He seeks out the wisdom of all the ancients,
    and is concerned with prophecies;
2 he preserves the sayings of the famous
  and penetrates the subtleties of parables;

---

21 Never forget: there is no returning;
  you cannot help the dead and can only harm
    yourself.
22 Remember that his fate will also be yours:
  'Mine today, yours tomorrow.'
23 When the dead is at rest, let his memory rest too;
  be comforted for him as soon as his spirit departs.

24 A SCHOLAR's wisdom comes of ample leisure;
  to be wise he must be relieved of other tasks.
25 How can one become wise who follows the
    plough,
  whose pride is in wielding the goad,
  who is absorbed in the task of driving oxen,
  whose talk is all about cattle?
26 He concentrates on ploughing his furrows,
  and toils late to give the heifers their fodder.
27 So it is with every craftsman and designer
  working both day and night.
  Such are those who make engravings on signets
  and patiently vary the design;
  they concentrate on making an exact likeness
  and stay up to all hours to finish their task.
28 So it is with the smith, sitting by his anvil,
  intent on his ironwork.
  The fiery vapours shrivel his flesh
  as he wrestles in the heat of the furnace;
  the hammer rings in his ears again and again,
  and his eyes are on the pattern he is copying.
  He concentrates on completing the task
  and stays up late to give it a perfect finish.
29 So it is with the potter, sitting at his work,
  turning the wheel with his feet,
  always engrossed in the task
  of making up his tally of vessels;
30 he moulds the clay with his arm,
  crouching forward to exert his strength.
  He concentrates on finishing the glazing,
  and stays up to clean out the furnace.

31 All those rely on their hands,
  and each is skilful at his own craft.
32 Without them a city would have no inhabitants;
  no settlers or travellers would come to it.
33 Yet they are not in demand at public discussions,
  nor do they attain to high office in the assembly.
  They do not sit on the judge's bench
  or understand the decisions of the courts.
  They cannot expound moral or legal principles
  and are not ready with maxims.
34 But they maintain the fabric of this world,
  and the practice of their craft is their prayer.

39 How different it is with one who devotes himself
    to reflecting on the law of the Most High,
  who explores all the wisdom of the past
  and occupies himself with the study of prophecies!
2 He preserves the sayings of the famous
  and penetrates the subtleties of parables.

---

[y] Gk him [z] Heb: Gk *my* [a] Heb: Gk *mine* [b] Cn: Gk *renews his
ear* [c] Cn: Gk *cleaning* [d] Syr: Gk *and people can neither live
nor walk there* [e] Most ancient authorities lack this line
[f] Cn: Gk *among parables* [g] Syr: Gk *prayer is in*

21 Recall him not, for there is no hope of his return;
  it will not help him, but will do you harm.
	21 Do not forget, there is no coming back;
	  you cannot help the dead, and you will harm
	    yourself.

22 Remember that his fate will also be yours;
  for him it was yesterday, for you today.
	22 'Remember my doom, since it will be yours too;
	  I yesterday, you today!'

23 With the departed dead, let memory fade;
  rally your courage, once the soul has left.
	23 Once the dead are laid to rest, let their memory
	    rest,
	  do not fret for them, once their spirit departs.

24 The scribe's profession increases his wisdom;
  whoever is free from toil can become a
    wise man.
	24 Leisure gives the scribe the chance to acquire
	    wisdom;
	  a man with few commitments can grow wise.

25 How can he become learned who guides the plow,
  who thrills in wielding the goad like a lance,
Who guides the ox and urges on the bullock,
  and whose every concern is for cattle?
	25 How can the ploughman become wise,
	  whose sole ambition is to wield the goad,
	  driving his oxen, engrossed in their work,
	  his conversation limited to bullocks,

26 His care is for plowing furrows,
  and he keeps a watch on the beasts in the stalls.
	26 his thoughts absorbed in the furrows he traces
	  and his long evenings spent in fattening heifers?

27 So with every engraver and designer
  who, laboring night and day,
Fashions carved seals,
  and whose concern is to vary the pattern.
His care is to produce a vivid impression,
  and he keeps watch till he finishes his design.
	27 Similarly with all workmen and craftsmen,
	  toiling day and night;
	those who engrave seals,
	  for ever trying to think of a new design,
	concentrating on catching a good likeness
	  and staying up late to get the work done.

28 So with the smith standing near his anvil,
  forging crude iron.
The heat from the fire sears his flesh,
  yet he toils away in the furnace heat.
The clang of the hammer deafens his ears,
  his eyes are fixed on the tool he is shaping.
His care is to finish his work,
  and he keeps watch till he perfects it in detail.
	28 Similarly with the blacksmith sitting by his anvil;
	  he considers what to do with the pig-iron,
	the breath of the fire scorches his skin,
	  as he contends with the heat of the furnace;
	the noise of the hammer deafens him,
	  his eyes are fixed on the pattern;
	he concentrates on getting the job done well
	  and stays up late to apply the finishing touches.

29 So with the potter sitting at his labor
  revolving the wheel with his feet.
He is always concerned for his products,
  and turns them out in quantity.
	29 Similarly with the potter, sitting at his work,
	  turning the wheel with his feet;
	constantly on the alert over his work,
	  each flick of the finger premeditated;

30 With his hands he molds the clay,
  and with his feet softens it.
His care is for proper coloring,
  and he keeps watch on the fire of his kiln.
	30 he pummels the clay with his arm,
	  and with his feet he kneads it;
	he concentrates on applying the glaze right
	  and stays up late to clean the kiln.

31 All these men are skilled with their hands,
  each one an expert at his own task;
	31 All these people rely on their hands
	  and each is skilled at his own craft.

32 Without them no city could be lived in,
  and wherever they stay, they need not hunger.
	32 A town could not be inhabited without them,
	  there would be no settling, no travelling.

33 They do not occupy the judge's bench,
  nor are they prominent in the assembly;
They set forth no decisions or judgments,
  nor are they found among the rulers;
	33 But you will not find them in the parliament,
	  they do not hold high rank in the assembly.
	They do not sit on the judicial bench,
	  and they do not meditate on the Law.

34 Yet they maintain God's ancient handiwork,
  and their concern is for exercise of their skill.
	34 They are not remarkable for their culture or
	    judgement,
	  nor are they found frequenting the philosophers.
	They sustain the structure of the world,
	  and their prayer is concerned with their trade.

39 How different the man who devotes himself
  to the study of the law of the Most High!
He explores the wisdom of the men of old
  and occupies himself with the prophecies;
2 He treasures the discourses of famous men,
  and goes to the heart of involved sayings;

39 Not so with one who concentrates his mind
  and his meditation on the Law of the Most High.
He researches into the wisdom of all the Ancients,
  he occupies his time with the prophecies.
2 He preserves the discourses of famous men,
  he is at home with the niceties of parables.

3 he seeks out the hidden meanings of proverbs
   and is at home with the obscurities of parables.
4 He serves among the great
   and appears before rulers;
   he travels in foreign lands
   and learns what is good and evil in the human
      lot.
5 He sets his heart to rise early
   to seek the Lord who made him,
   and to petition the Most High;
   he opens his mouth in prayer
   and asks pardon for his sins.

6 If the great Lord is willing,
   he will be filled with the spirit of
      understanding;
   he will pour forth words of wisdom of his own
   and give thanks to the Lord in prayer.
7 The Lord[h] will direct his counsel and
      knowledge,
   as he meditates on his mysteries.
8 He will show the wisdom of what he has learned,
   and will glory in the law of the Lord's
      covenant.
9 Many will praise his understanding;
   it will never be blotted out.
   His memory will not disappear,
   and his name will live through all generations.
10 Nations will speak of his wisdom,
   and the congregation will proclaim his praise.
11 If he lives long, he will leave a name greater than
      a thousand,
   and if he goes to rest, it is enough[i] for him.

12 I have more on my mind to express;
   I am full like the full moon.
13 Listen to me, my faithful children, and blossom
   like a rose growing by a stream of water.
14 Send out fragrance like incense,
   and put forth blossoms like a lily.
   Scatter the fragrance, and sing a hymn of praise;
   bless the Lord for all his works.
15 Ascribe majesty to his name
   and give thanks to him with praise,
   with songs on your lips, and with harps;
   this is what you shall say in thanksgiving:

16 "All the works of the Lord are very good,
   and whatever he commands will be done at the
      appointed time.
17 No one can say, 'What is this?' or 'Why is
      that?' —
   for at the appointed time all such questions will
      be answered.
   At his word the waters stood in a heap,
   and the reservoirs of water at the word of his
      mouth.
18 When he commands, his every purpose is
      fulfilled,
   and none can limit his saving power.
19 The works of all are before him,
   and nothing can be hidden from his eyes.
20 From the beginning to the end of time he can see
      everything,
   and nothing is too marvelous for him.
21 No one can say, 'What is this?' or 'Why is
      that?' —
   for everything has been created for its own
      purpose.

3 He explores the hidden meaning of proverbs
   and knows his way among enigmatic parables.
4 The great avail themselves of his services,
   and he appears in the presence of rulers.
   He travels in foreign countries,
   learning at first hand human good and human evil.
5 He makes a point of rising early
   to seek the Lord, his Maker;
   he prays to the Most High,
   asking pardon for his sins.
6 If it is the will of the mighty Lord,
   he will be filled with a spirit of intelligence;
   then he will pour forth wise sayings of his own
   and give thanks to the Lord in prayer.
7 He is directed in his counsel and knowledge by the
      Lord,
   whose secrets are his constant study.
8 In his teaching he will reveal his learning,
   and his pride will be in the law of the Lord's
      covenant.
9 Many will praise his intelligence,
   and it will never be forgotten.
   The memory of him will not die,
   and his name will live for ever and ever.
10 The nations will tell of his wisdom,
   and the assembled people will sing his praise.
11 If he lives long, he will leave a name in a
      thousand;
   when he goes to his long rest, his reputation is
      secure.

12 I HAVE still more thoughts to express;
   I am as full as the moon at mid-month.
13 Listen to me, my devout sons, and blossom
   like a rose planted by a stream.
14 Spread your fragrance like frankincense,
   and bloom like a lily.
   Scatter your fragrance; lift your voices in song,
   praising the Lord for all he has done.
15 Ascribe majesty to his name
   and give thanks to him with praise,
   with harps and the singing of songs.
   Let these be your words of thanksgiving:
16 'All that the Lord has done is excellent;
   all that he commands will in due time take place.'
17 Let no one ask, 'What is this?' or 'Why is that?'
   In due time all such questions will be answered.

   At his bidding the waters stood up like a heap,
   and his word created reservoirs for them.
18 When he commands, his will is done,
   and no one can thwart his saving power.
19 The deeds of all mankind lie plain before him,
   and there is no hiding from his eyes.
20 From the beginning to the end of time he keeps
      watch;
   nothing is too marvellous or too difficult for him.
21 Let no one ask, 'What is this?' or 'Why is that?'
   for everything has been created for its own
      purpose.

---

[h] Gk *He himself*   [i] Cn: Meaning of Gk uncertain

3 He studies obscure parables,
  and is busied with the hidden meanings of
    the sages.
4 He is in attendance on the great,
  and has entrance to the ruler.
5 He travels among the peoples of foreign lands
  to learn what is good and evil among men.
6 His care is to seek the LORD, his Maker,
  to petition the Most High,
To open his lips in prayer,
  to ask pardon for his sins.
Then, if it pleases the LORD Almighty,
  he will be filled with the spirit of understanding;
He will pour forth his words of wisdom
  and in prayer give thanks to the LORD,
7 Who will direct his knowledge and his counsel,
  as he meditates upon his mysteries.
8 He will show the wisdom of what he has learned
  and glory in the law of the LORD's covenant.
9 Many will praise his understanding;
  his fame can never be effaced;
Unfading will be his memory,
  through all generations his name will live;
10 Peoples will speak of his wisdom,
  and in assembly sing his praises.
11 While he lives he is one out of a thousand,
  and when he dies his renown will not cease.

12 Once more I will set forth my theme
  to shine like the moon in its fullness!
13 Listen, my faithful children: open up your petals,
  like roses planted near running waters;
14 Send up the sweet odor of incense,
  break forth in blossoms like the lily.
Send up the sweet odor of your hymn of praise;
  bless the LORD for all he has done!
15 Proclaim the greatness of his name,
  loudly sing his praises,
With music on the harp and all
    stringed instruments;
  sing out with joy as you proclaim:

16 The works of God are all of them good;
  in its own time every need is supplied.
17 At his word the waters become still as in a flask;
  he had but to speak and the reservoirs
    were made.
18 He has but to command and his will is done;
  nothing can limit his achievement.
19 The works of all mankind are present to him;
  not a thing escapes his eye.
20 His gaze spans all the ages;
  to him there is nothing unexpected.
21 No cause then to say: "What is the purpose
    of this?"
  Everything is chosen to satisfy a need.

3 He researches into the hidden sense of proverbs,
  he ponders the obscurities of parables.
4 He enters the service of princes,
  he is seen in the presence of rulers.
He travels in foreign countries,
  he has experienced human good and human evil.
5 At dawn and with all his heart
  he turns to the Lord his Creator;
he pleads in the presence of the Most High,
  he opens his mouth in prayer
  and makes entreaty for his sins.
6 If such be the will of the great Lord,
  he will be filled with the spirit of intelligence,
he will shower forth words of wisdom,
  and in prayer give thanks to the Lord.
7 He will grow upright in purpose and learning,
  he will ponder the Lord's hidden mysteries.
8 He will display the instruction he has received,
  taking his pride in the Law of the Lord's
    covenant.
9 Many will praise his intelligence
  and it will never be forgotten.
His memory will not disappear,
  generation after generation his name will live.
10 Nations will proclaim his wisdom,
  the assembly will celebrate his praises.ƒ
11 If he lives long, his name will be more glorious
    than a thousand others,
  and if he dies, that will satisfy him just as well.

12 And here are some more of my reflections:
  yes, I am as full as the moon at the full!
13 Listen to me, devout children, and blossom
  like the rose that grows on the bank of a
    watercourse.
14 Give off a sweet smell like incense,
  flower like the lily, spread your fragrance
    abroad,
sing a song of praise
  blessing the Lord for all his works.
15 Declare the greatness of his name,
  proclaim his praise
with song and with lyre,
  and this is how you must sing his praises:
16 'How wonderful, the actions of the Lord!
  Whatever he orders is done at the proper time!'
You must not say, 'What is this? Why is that?'
  There is a proper time for every question.
17 At his word, the water stops and piles up high,
  at his voice, the watery reservoirs take shape,
18 at his command, whatever he wants is done,
  no one can stop him, if he intends to save.
19 He can see whatever human beings are doing,
  nothing can be hidden from his eye;
20 his gaze stretches from eternity to eternity,
  and nothing can astonish him.
21 You must not say, 'What is this? Why is that?'
  for everything has been made for a purpose.

ƒ39 = 44:15.

NEW REVISED STANDARD VERSION	REVISED ENGLISH BIBLE

NEW REVISED STANDARD VERSION

22 "His blessing covers the dry land like a river,
and drenches it like a flood.
23 But his wrath drives out the nations,
as when he turned a watered land into salt.
24 To the faithful his ways are straight,
but full of pitfalls for the wicked.
25 From the beginning good things were created for
the good,
but for sinners good things and bad.*j*
26 The basic necessities of human life
are water and fire and iron and salt
and wheat flour and milk and honey,
the blood of the grape and oil and clothing.
27 All these are good for the godly,
but for sinners they turn into evils.

28 "There are winds created for vengeance,
and in their anger they can dislodge
mountains;*k*
on the day of reckoning they will pour out their
strength
and calm the anger of their Maker.
29 Fire and hail and famine and pestilence,
all these have been created for vengeance;
30 the fangs of wild animals and scorpions and
vipers,
and the sword that punishes the ungodly with
destruction.
31 They take delight in doing his bidding,
always ready for his service on earth;
and when their time comes they never disobey
his command."

32 So from the beginning I have been convinced of
all this
and have thought it out and left it in writing:
33 All the works of the Lord are good,
and he will supply every need in its time.
34 No one can say, "This is not as good as that,"
for everything proves good in its appointed
time.
35 So now sing praise with all your heart and voice,
and bless the name of the Lord.

40 Hard work was created for everyone,
and a heavy yoke is laid on the children of
Adam,
from the day they come forth from their mother's
womb
until the day they return to*l* the mother of all
the living.*m*
2 Perplexities and fear of heart are theirs,
and anxious thought of the day of their death.
3 From the one who sits on a splendid throne
to the one who grovels in dust and ashes,
4 from the one who wears purple and a crown
to the one who is clothed in burlap,
5 there is anger and envy and trouble and unrest,
and fear of death, and fury and strife.
And when one rests upon his bed,
his sleep at night confuses his mind.
6 He gets little or no rest;
he struggles in his sleep as he did by day.*n*
He is troubled by the visions of his mind
like one who has escaped from the battlefield.
7 At the moment he reaches safety he wakes up,
astonished that his fears were groundless.

REVISED ENGLISH BIBLE

22 His blessing is like a river in full flood
which soaks the parched ground.
23 As surely as he turned fresh water into brine,
so shall the heathen incur his anger.
24 For the devout his ways are straight;
for the wicked they are full of pitfalls.
25 From the beginning good was created for the good,
and evil for sinners.
26 The basic necessities of human life
are water, fire, iron, and salt,
flour, honey, and milk,
the juice of the grape, oil, and clothing—
27 all these are good for the godfearing,
but turn to evil for sinners.

28 There are winds created to be agents of retribution,
with great whips to give play to their fury;
on the day of reckoning they exert their force
and so allay the anger of their Maker.
29 Fire and hail, famine and pestilence,
all these were created for retribution;
30 beasts of prey, scorpions, and vipers,
and the avenging sword to destroy the ungodly.
31 They delight in carrying out his commandments,
always standing ready for his service on the earth;
and when the time comes, they never disobey his
word.

32 I have been convinced of all this from the
beginning;
I have thought it over and left it in writing:
33 all that the Lord has made is good,
and he supplies every need as it arises.
34 Let no one say, 'This is less good than that,'
for all things prove good at their proper time.
35 Come now, sing with full heart and voice,
and to the name of the Lord give praise!

40 HARD work is the lot of every mortal,
and a heavy yoke is laid on the children of Adam
from the day when they come from their mothers'
womb
until the day of their return to the earth, the mother
of all;
2 troubled thoughts and fears are theirs,
and anxious expectation of the day of their death.
3 Whether someone sits in royal splendour on a
throne
or lies humbled in dust and ashes,
4 whether he wears the purple and a crown
or is clothed in sackcloth,
5 his life is nothing but anger and envy,
a troubled and anxious mind,
fear of death, and guilt, and contention.
Even at night when he goes to bed,
sleep brings fresh confusion to his mind.
6 There is little or no rest for him;
he is as confused in his sleep as in the daytime.
Disturbed by nightmares,
he fancies himself a fugitive from the line of battle;
7 and at the moment when he reaches safety, he
wakes up,
amazed to find his fears groundless.

---

j Heb Lat: Gk *sinners bad things*   *k* Heb Syr: Gk *can scourge*
mightily   *l* Other Gk and Lat authorities read *are buried in*
m Heb: Gk *of all*   *n* Arm: Meaning of Gk uncertain

<table>
<tr><td>

22 His blessing overflows like the Nile;
   like the Euphrates it enriches the surface of
      the earth.
23 Again, his wrath expels the nations
   and turns fertile land into a salt marsh.
24 For the virtuous his paths are level,
   to the haughty they are steep;
25 Good things for the good he provided from
      the beginning,
   but for the wicked good things and bad.
26 Chief of all needs for human life
   are water and fire, iron and salt,
   The heart of the wheat, milk and honey,
      the blood of the grape, and oil, and cloth;
27 For the good all these are good,
   but for the wicked they turn out evil.
28 There are storm winds created to punish,
   which in their fury can dislodge mountains;
   When destruction must be, they hurl all their force
      and appease the anger of their Maker.
29 In his treasury also, kept for the proper time,
   are fire and hail, famine, disease,
30 Ravenous beasts, scorpions, vipers,
   and the avenging sword to exterminate
      the wicked;
31 In doing his bidding they rejoice,
   in their assignments they disobey not
      his command.
32 So from the first I took my stand,
   and wrote down as my theme:
33 The works of God are all of them good;
   every need when it comes he fills.
34 No cause then to say: "This is not as good as that";
   for each shows its worth at the proper time.
35 So now with full joy of heart proclaim
   and bless the name of the Holy One.

</td><td>

22 As his blessing covers the dry land like a river
   and soaks it like a flood,
23 so retribution is his legacy to the nations,
   just as he has turned fresh waters to salt.
24 His ways are as smooth for the devout,
   as they are full of obstacles for the wicked.
25 Good things were created from the beginning for
      good people,
   as bad ones were for sinners.
26 The prime needs of human beings for living
   are water and fire, iron and salt,
   wheat-flour, milk and honey,
      the juice of the grape, oil and clothing.
27 All these are good for those who are good,
   but turn out bad for sinners.
28 Some winds have been created for punishing,
   in his fury, he uses them as scourges;
   on the day of doom, they unleash their violence
      and appease the wrath of their Creator.
29 Fire and hail, famine and death,
   have all been created for punishing.
30 Wild animals' fangs, scorpions, vipers,
   the avenging sword for the ruin of the godless:
31 all of them exult in discharging his orders,
   ready on earth whenever the need arises
   and, when their time comes, not falling short of
      his word.
32 That is why I was determined from the outset,
   why I have pondered and why I have written,
33 'The works of the Lord are all good,
   when the time is right, he gives whatever is
      needed.
34 You must not say, "This is worse than that,"
   for, sooner or later, everything proves its worth.
35 So now, sing with all your heart and voice,
   and bless the name of the Lord!'

</td></tr>
</table>

<table>
<tr><td>

40 A great anxiety has God allotted,
   and a heavy yoke, to the sons of men;
   From the day one leaves his mother's womb
   to the day he returns to the mother of all
      the living,
2 His thoughts, the fear in his heart,
   and his troubled forebodings till the day
      he dies —
3 Whether he sits on a lofty throne
   or grovels in dust and ashes,
4 Whether he bears a splendid crown
   or is wrapped in the coarsest of cloaks —
5 Are of wrath and envy, trouble and dread,
   terror of death, fury and strife.
   Even when he lies on his bed to rest,
      his cares at night disturb his sleep.
6 So short is his rest it seems like none,
   till in his dreams he struggles as he did by day,
   Terrified by what his mind's eye sees,
      like a fugitive being pursued;
7 As he reaches safety, he wakes up
   astonished that there was nothing to fear.

</td><td>

40 A hard lot has been created for human beings,
   a heavy yoke lies on the children of Adam
   from the day they come out of their mother's
      womb,
   till the day they return to the mother of them all.
2 What fills them with foreboding and their hearts
      with fear
   is dread of the day of death.
3 From the one who sits on a glorious throne
   to the wretch in dust and ashes,
4 from the one who wears purple and a crown
   to the one dressed in sacking,
   all is fury and jealousy, turmoil and unrest,
      fear of death, rivalry, strife.
5 And even at night while he rests on his bed
   his sleep only gives a new twist to his worries:
6 scarcely has he lain down to rest,
   when in his sleep, as if in broad daylight,
   he is troubled with nightmares,
      like one who has escaped from a battle,
7 and at the moment of rescue he wakes up,
   amazed that there was nothing to be afraid of!

</td></tr>
</table>

NEW REVISED STANDARD VERSION	REVISED ENGLISH BIBLE

8 To all creatures, human and animal,
  but to sinners seven times more,
9 come death and bloodshed and strife and sword,
  calamities and famine and ruin and plague.
10 All these were created for the wicked,
  and on their account the flood came.
11 All that is of earth returns to earth,
  and what is from above returns above.*o*
12 All bribery and injustice will be blotted out,
  but good faith will last forever.
13 The wealth of the unjust will dry up like a river,
  and crash like a loud clap of thunder in a
    storm.
14 As a generous person has cause to rejoice,
  so lawbreakers will utterly fail.
15 The children of the ungodly put out few branches;
  they are unhealthy roots on sheer rock.
16 The reeds by any water or river bank
  are plucked up before any grass;
17 but kindness is like a garden of blessings,
  and almsgiving endures forever.
18 Wealth and wages make life sweet,*p*
  but better than either is finding a treasure.
19 Children and the building of a city establish one's
    name,
  but better than either is the one who finds
    wisdom.
  Cattle and orchards make one prosperous;*q*
  but a blameless wife is accounted better than
    either.
20 Wine and music gladden the heart,
  but the love of friends*r* is better than either.
21 The flute and the harp make sweet melody,
  but a pleasant voice is better than either.
22 The eye desires grace and beauty,
  but the green shoots of grain more than either.
23 A friend or companion is always welcome,
  but a sensible wife*s* is better than either.
24 Kindred and helpers are for a time of trouble,
  but almsgiving rescues better than either.
25 Gold and silver make one stand firm,
  but good counsel is esteemed more than either.
26 Riches and strength build up confidence,
  but the fear of the Lord is better than either.
  There is no want in the fear of the Lord,
  and with it there is no need to seek for help.
27 The fear of the Lord is like a garden of blessing,
  and covers a person better than any glory.
28 My child, do not lead the life of a beggar;
  it is better to die than to beg.
29 When one looks to the table of another,
  one's way of life cannot be considered a life.
  One loses self-respect with another person's food,
  but one who is intelligent and well instructed
    guards against that.
30 In the mouth of the shameless begging is sweet,
  but it kindles a fire inside him.

41 O death, how bitter is the thought of you
  to the one at peace among possessions,
  who has nothing to worry about and is prosperous
    in everything,
  and still is vigorous enough to enjoy food!

8 To all living creatures, human and animal—
  and seven times over to sinners—
9 come death and bloodshed, quarrelling and the
    sword,
  disaster, famine, havoc, and plague.
10 All these were created for the wicked,
  on whose account the flood came.
11 All that is of earth returns to earth again,
  and all that is of water finds its way back to the
    sea.
12 Bribery and injustice will vanish completely,
  but good faith will stand for ever.
13 Wealth from wickedness will dry up like a wadi
  and die away like a clap of thunder in a storm;
14 when the torrent rises, rocks are rolled away;
  yet suddenly it ceases for ever.
15 The branches of an impious stock put out few
    shoots;
  their tainted roots are planted on sheer rock.
16 The rush that grows on every river bank
  dries up before any other grass.
17 But kindness is a paradise in its blessings,
  and almsgiving lasts for ever.
18 To be employed and to be one's own master, both
    are sweet,
  but to find a treasure is better still.
19 Offspring and the founding of a city perpetuate a
    name,
  but better still is a perfect wife.
20 Wine and music gladden the heart,
  but better still is the love of wisdom.
21 Flute and harp make pleasant melody,
  but better still is a pleasant voice.
22 The eye likes to look on grace and beauty,
  but better still on the green shoots in a cornfield.
23 A friend or companion is a welcome partner,
  but better still to be man and wife.
24 Brothers and helpers are a stand-by in time of
    trouble,
  but better still is almsgiving.
25 Gold and silver make a person stand firm,
  but better still is good advice.
26 Wealth and strength uplift the heart,
  but better still is the fear of the Lord.
  To fear the Lord is to lack nothing,
  never to be in need of support.
27 The fear of the Lord is a paradise in its blessings;
  it affords better protection than high position.
28 My son, do not live the life of a beggar;
  better die than beg!
29 When someone starts looking to another's table,
  his existence is not worth calling life.
  It is demoralizing to live on the food of another,
  and he who is wise and well disciplined will guard
    against it.
30 He who has lost all shame speaks as if begging
    were sweet,
  but in his breast resentment burns.

41 How bitter the thought of you, O Death,
  to anyone at ease among his possessions,
  free from cares, prosperous in all things,
  and still vigorous enough to enjoy a good meal!

o Heb Syr: Gk Lat *from the waters returns to the sea*   *p* Heb: Gk
Life is sweet for the self-reliant worker   *q* Heb Syr: Gk lacks *but
better . . . prosperous*   *r* Heb: Gk *wisdom*   *s* Heb Compare Syr:
Gk *wife with her husband*

NEW AMERICAN BIBLE

8 So it is with all flesh, with man and with beast,
  but for sinners seven times more.
9 Plague and bloodshed, wrath and the sword,
  plunder and ruin, famine and death:
10 For the wicked, these were created evil,
  and it is they who bring on destruction.

11 All that is of earth returns to earth,
  and what is from above returns above.
12 All that comes from bribes or injustice will be
  wiped out,
  but loyalty remains for ages.
13 Wealth out of wickedness is like a wadi in spate:
  like a mighty stream with lightning and thunder,
14 Which, in its rising, rolls along the stones,
  but suddenly, once and for all, comes to an end.
15 The offshoot of violence will not flourish,
  for the root of the godless is on sheer rock;
16 Or they are like reeds on the riverbank,
  withered before all other plants.
17 But goodness will never be cut off,
  and justice endures forever.

  Wealth or wages can make life sweet,
  but better than either is finding a treasure.
18 A child or a city will preserve one's name,
  but better than either, attaining wisdom.
19 Sheepfolds and orchards bring flourishing health;
  but better than either, a devoted wife;
20 Wine and music delight the soul,
  but better than either, conjugal love.
21 The flute and the harp offer sweet melody,
  but better than either, a voice that is true.
22 Charm and beauty delight the eye,
  but better than either, the flowers of the field.
23 A friend, a neighbor, are timely guides,
  but better than either, a prudent wife.
24 A brother, a helper, for times of stress;
  but better than either, charity that rescues.
25 Gold and silver make one's way secure,
  but better than either, sound judgment.
26 Wealth and vigor build up confidence,
  but better than either, fear of God.
  Fear of the LORD leaves nothing wanting;
  he who has it need seek no other support:
27 The fear of God is a paradise of blessings;
  its canopy, all that is glorious.

28 My son, live not the life of a beggar,
  better to die than to beg;
29 When one has to look to another's table,
  his life is not really a life.
  His neighbor's delicacies bring revulsion of spirit
  to one who understands inward feelings:
30 In the mouth of the shameless man begging
  is sweet,
  but within him it burns like fire.

41 O death! how bitter the thought of you
  for the man at peace amid his possessions,
For the man unruffled and always successful,
  who still can enjoy life's pleasures.

NEW JERUSALEM BIBLE

8 For all creatures, human and animal —
  and seven times more for sinners —
9 there is death and blood and strife and the sword,
  disasters, famine, affliction, plague.
10 These things were all created for the wicked,
  and the Flood came because of them.
11 All that comes from the earth returns to the
  earth, g
  and what comes from the water returns to the
  sea.

12 All bribery and injustice will be blotted out,
  but good faith will stand for ever.
13 Ill-gotten wealth will vanish like a torrent,
  like the single thunder-clap that heralds rain.
14 When he opens his hand, he rejoices,
  by the same token, sinners come to ruin.
15 The sprigs of the godless will not make many
  branches,
  tainted roots find only hard rock.
16 The reed that grows by every lake and river's edge
  is the first plant to be uprooted.
17 Charity is a very paradise of blessing
  and almsgiving endures for ever.
18 For a person of private means and one who works
  hard, life is pleasant,
  better off than either, one who finds a treasure.
19 Children and the founding of a city perpetuate a
  name:
  more esteemed than either, a perfect wife.
20 Wine and music cheer the heart;
  better than either, the love of wisdom.
21 Flute and harp add sweetness to a song;
  better than either, a melodious voice.
22 The eye longs for grace and beauty;
  better than either, the green of spring corn.
23 Friend or comrade — it is always well met;
  better than either, a wife and husband.
24 Brothers and allies are good in times of trouble;
  better than either, almsgiving to the rescue.
25 Gold and silver will steady your feet;
  more esteemed than either, good advice.
26 Money and strength make a confident heart;
  better than either, the fear of the Lord.
  With fear of the Lord, nothing is lacking:
  no need to seek for other help.
27 Fear of the Lord is a paradise of blessing,
  a better protection than the highest reputation.

28 My child, do not live by sponging off others,
  better be dead than be a sponger.
29 A life spent in eyeing someone else's table
  cannot be accounted a life at all.
  Other people's food defiles the gullet;
  a wise, well-brought-up person will beware of
  doing this.
30 What a sponger says may sound very sweet
  but in his belly there burns a fire.

41 O death, how bitter it is to remember you
  for someone peacefully living with his
  possessions,
  for someone with no worries and everything going
  well
  and who can still enjoy his food!

g **40** = 41:10.

NEW REVISED STANDARD VERSION	REVISED ENGLISH BIBLE

NEW REVISED STANDARD VERSION

2 O death, how welcome is your sentence
  to one who is needy and failing in strength,
worn down by age and anxious about everything;
  to one who is contrary, and has lost all
      patience!
3 Do not fear death's decree for you;
  remember those who went before you and
      those who will come after.
4 This is the Lord's decree for all flesh;
  why then should you reject the will of the
      Most High?
  Whether life lasts for ten years or a hundred or a
      thousand,
  there are no questions asked in Hades.

5 The children of sinners are abominable children,
  and they frequent the haunts of the ungodly.
6 The inheritance of the children of sinners will
      perish,
  and on their offspring will be a perpetual
      disgrace.
7 Children will blame an ungodly father,
  for they suffer disgrace because of him.
8 Woe to you, the ungodly,
  who have forsaken the law of the Most High
      God!
9 If you have children, calamity will be theirs;
  you will beget them only for groaning.
  When you stumble, there is lasting joy;[t]
  and when you die, a curse is your lot.
10 Whatever comes from earth returns to earth;
  so the ungodly go from curse to destruction.

11 The human body is a fleeting thing,
  but a virtuous name will never be blotted out.[u]
12 Have regard for your name, since it will outlive
      you
  longer than a thousand hoards of gold.
13 The days of a good life are numbered,
  but a good name lasts forever.

14 My children, be true to your training and be at
      peace;
  hidden wisdom and unseen treasure—
  of what value is either?
15 Better are those who hide their folly
  than those who hide their wisdom.

16 Therefore show respect for my words;
  for it is not good to feel shame in every
      circumstance,
  nor is every kind of abashment to be
      approved.[v]

17 Be ashamed of sexual immorality, before your
      father or mother;
  and of a lie, before a prince or a ruler;
18 of a crime, before a judge or magistrate;
  and of a breach of the law, before the
      congregation and the people;
  of unjust dealing, before your partner or your
      friend;
19 and of theft, in the place where you live.
  Be ashamed of breaking an oath or agreement,[w]
  and of leaning on your elbow at meals;
  of surliness in receiving or giving,
20 and of silence, before those who greet you;

REVISED ENGLISH BIBLE

2 How welcome your sentence, O Death,
  to a destitute person whose strength is failing,
  who is worn down by age and endless anxiety,
  resentful and at the end of his patience!
3 Do not fear death's sentence;
  remember those before you and those coming after.
4 This is the Lord's decree for all mortals;
  why try to argue with the will of the Most High?
  Whether life lasts ten years, or a hundred, or a
      thousand,
  no questions will be asked about it in the grave.

5 What a loathsome brood are the children of
      sinners,
  brought up in the haunts of the godless!
6 Their inheritance disappears,
  and their descendants live in lasting disgrace.
7 A godless father is taunted by his children
  for the disgrace they endure on his account.
8 Woe to you who are impious,
  who have abandoned the law of God Most High!
9 When you are born, you are born to a curse,
  and when you die, a curse is your lot.
10 All that is of earth returns to earth;
  so too the godless go from curse to destruction.
11 There is grief over the death of the body,
  but sinners have no good name to survive them.
12 Take thought for your name: it will outlive you
  longer than thousands of great hoards of gold.
13 The days of a good life are numbered,
  but a good name lasts for all time.

14 BE true to your upbringing, my children, and live
      in peace.
  Hidden wisdom and buried treasure—
  what is the use of either?
15 Better someone who hides his folly
  than one who hides his wisdom.

16 Show deference, then, to my teaching:
  shame is not appropriate on all occasions,
  nor are all things held in high repute by everyone.
17 Be ashamed to be detected in fornication by your
      parents,
  or in lies by a ruler or prince;
18 in crime by a judge or magistrate,
  or in a breach of God's law by the assembly and
      people;
  in dishonesty by a partner or friend,
19 or in theft by the neighbourhood.
  Be ashamed of breach of oath or contract.

  Be ashamed of leaning your elbow on the table,
  of giving or receiving with ill grace,
20 of refusing to return a greeting,

---

t Heb: Meaning of Gk uncertain   *u* Heb: Gk *People grieve over the
death of the body, but the bad name of sinners will be blotted out*
v Heb: Gk *and not everything is confidently esteemed by everyone*
w Heb: Gk *before the truth of God and the covenant*

2 O death! how welcome your sentence
   to the weak man of failing strength,
Tottering and always rebuffed,
   with no more sight, with vanished hope.
3 Fear not death's decree for you;
   remember, it embraces those before you, and
      those after.
4 Thus God has ordained for all flesh;
   why then should you reject the will of the
      Most High?
Whether one has lived a thousand years, a
   hundred, or ten,
   in the nether world he has no claim on life.

5 A reprobate line are the children of sinners,
   and witless offspring are in the homes of
      the wicked.
6 Their dominion is lost to sinners' children,
   and reproach abides with their descendants.
7 Children curse their wicked father,
   for they suffer disgrace through him.
8 Woe to you, O sinful men,
   who forsake the law of the Most High.
9 If you have children, calamity will seize them;
   you will beget them only for groaning.
When you stumble, there is lasting joy;
   at death, you become a curse.
10 Whatever is of nought returns to nought,
   so too the godless from void to void.
11 Man's body is a fleeting thing,
   but a virtuous name will never be annihilated.
12 Have a care for your name, for it will stand by you
   better than precious treasures in the thousands;
13 The boon of life is for limited days,
   but a good name, for days without number.

14 My children, heed my instruction about shame;
   judge of disgrace only according to my rules,
For it is not always well to be ashamed,
   nor is it always the proper thing to blush:
15 Before father and mother be ashamed
   of immorality,
   before master and mistress, of falsehood;
16 Before prince and ruler, of flattery;
   before the public assembly, of crime;
17 Before friend and companion, of disloyalty,
   and of breaking an oath or agreement.
18 Be ashamed of theft from the people where
      you settle,
   and of stretching out your elbow when you dine;
19 Of refusing to give when asked,
   of defrauding another of his appointed share,
20 Of failing to return a greeting,
   and of rebuffing a friend;

2 O death, your sentence is welcome
   to one in want, whose strength is failing,
to one worn out with age and a thousand worries,
   resentful and impatient!
3 Do not dread death's sentence;
   remember those who came before you and those
      who will come after.
4 This is the sentence passed on all living creatures
   by the Lord,
   so why object to what seems good to the Most
      High?
Whether your life lasts ten or a hundred or a
   thousand years,
   its length will not be held against you in Sheol.

5 Hateful brats, such are the children of sinners,
   who foregather in the haunts of the godless.
6 The inheritance of sinners' children is doomed to
      perish,
   their posterity will endure lasting reproach.
7 A godless father will be blamed by his children
   for the reproach he has brought on them.
8 A bad outlook for you, godless people,
   who have forsaken the Law of God Most High.
9 When you were born, you were born to be
      accursed,
   and when you die, that curse will be your
      portion.
10 All that comes from the earth returns to the
      earth,[h]
   so too the wicked proceed from curse to
      destruction.
11 Mourning concerns only the bodies of the dead,
   but the worthless name of sinners will be blotted
      out.
12 Be careful of your reputation, for it will last you
      longer
   than a thousand great hoards of gold.
13 A good life lasts a certain number of days,
   but a good reputation lasts for ever.

14 Keep my instructions and be at peace, my children.

   Wisdom[i] hidden away and treasure undisplayed,
      what use is either of these?
15 Better someone who hides his folly
   than one who hides his wisdom.
16 Preserve a sense of shame in the following matters,
   for not every kind of shame is right to harbour,
   nor is every situation correctly appraised by all.
17 Be ashamed, before father and mother, of depraved
      behaviour,
   and before prince or potentate of telling lies;
18 of wrong-doing before judge or magistrate,
   and of impiety before the assembly of the
      people;
19 of sharp practice before your companion and your
      friend,
   and of theft before the neighbourhood you live
      in.
20 Before the truth and covenant of God,
   be ashamed of leaning elbows on the table,
21 of being ungracious when giving or receiving,
   of ignoring those who greet you,

NEW REVISED STANDARD VERSION	REVISED ENGLISH BIBLE

NEW REVISED STANDARD VERSION

of looking at a prostitute,
21 and of rejecting the appeal of a relative;
of taking away someone's portion or gift,
and of gazing at another man's wife;
22 of meddling with his servant-girl—
and do not approach her bed;
of abusive words, before friends—
and do not be insulting after making a
gift.

42 Be ashamed of repeating what you hear,
and of betraying secrets.
Then you will show proper shame,
and will find favor with everyone.

Of the following things do not be ashamed,
and do not sin to save face:
2 Do not be ashamed of the law of the Most High
and his covenant,
and of rendering judgment to acquit the
ungodly;
3 of keeping accounts with a partner or with
traveling companions,
and of dividing the inheritance of friends;
4 of accuracy with scales and weights,
and of acquiring much or little;
5 of profit from dealing with merchants,
and of frequent disciplining of children,
and of drawing blood from the back of a
wicked slave.
6 Where there is an untrustworthy wife, a seal is a
good thing;
and where there are many hands, lock things
up.
7 When you make a deposit, be sure it is counted
and weighed,
and when you give or receive, put it all in
writing.
8 Do not be ashamed to correct the stupid or
foolish
or the aged who are guilty of sexual
immorality.
Then you will show your sound training,
and will be approved by all.

9 A daughter is a secret anxiety to her father,
and worry over her robs him of sleep;
when she is young, for fear she may not marry,
or if married, for fear she may be disliked;
10 while a virgin, for fear she may be seduced
and become pregnant in her father's house;
or having a husband, for fear she may go astray,
or, though married, for fear she may be barren.
11 Keep strict watch over a headstrong daughter,
or she may make you a laughingstock to your
enemies,
a byword in the city and the assembly of[x] the
people,
and put you to shame in public gatherings.[y]
See that there is no lattice in her room,
no spot that overlooks the approaches to the
house.[z]
12 Do not let her parade her beauty before any man,
or spend her time among married women;[x]
13 for from garments comes the moth,
and from a woman comes woman's wickedness.
14 Better is the wickedness of a man than a woman
who does good;
it is woman who brings shame and disgrace.

REVISED ENGLISH BIBLE

or of ogling a prostitute.
21 Be ashamed of turning away a relative,
of robbing someone of his rightful share,
or of eyeing another man's wife.
22 Be ashamed of meddling with his slave-girl
or of visiting her bed.
Be ashamed of taunting your friends
or following up your charity with a lecture.
23 Be ashamed of repeating what you have
heard
and of betraying a confidence.
24 Then you will show a proper sense of shame
and be popular with everyone.

42 But at other times you must not be ashamed,
or you will do wrong out of deference to others.
2 Do not be ashamed of the law and covenant of the
Most High,
or of acting justly even if you acquit the ungodly;
3 of settling an account with a partner or travelling
companion,
or of sharing an inheritance with the other heirs;
4 of using accurate weights and measures,
or of acquiring possessions, many or few,
5 or of making a profit out of trade;
of frequent disciplining of children,
or of drawing blood from the back of a worthless
servant.
6 If your wife is untrustworthy, bolt your door;
where there are many hands, keep things under
lock and key.
7 When you make a deposit, see it counted and
weighed,
and when you give or receive, have it all in
writing.
8 Do not be ashamed to discipline the ignorant and
foolish,
or a greybeard on trial for fornication.
You will be showing your sound upbringing
and win universal approval.

9 A daughter is a secret anxiety to her father,
and worry about her keeps him awake at night:
when she is young, for fear she may grow too old
to marry,
and when she is married, for fear her husband may
divorce her;
10 when she is a virgin, for fear she may be seduced
and become pregnant in her father's house;
when she has a husband, for fear she may prove
unfaithful,
and after marriage, for fear she may be barren.
11 Keep close watch over a headstrong daughter,
or she may give your enemies cause to gloat,
making you the talk of the town, a byword among
the people,
shaming you in the eyes of the world.
12 Give her a bedroom without windows,
a room that does not overlook the entrance.
Do not let her display her beauty to any man,
or sit gossiping in the women's quarters;
13 for out of clothes comes the moth,
and out of woman comes woman's wickedness.
14 Better a man's wickedness than a woman's
goodness;
it is woman who brings shame and disgrace.

---

x Heb: Meaning of Gk uncertain   y Heb: Gk to shame before the
great multitude   z Heb: Gk lacks See . . . house

21 Of gazing at a married woman,
and of entertaining thoughts about
another's wife;
Of trifling with a servant girl you have,
and of violating her couch;
22 Of using harsh words with friends,
and of following up your gifts with insults;
23 Of repeating what you hear,
and of betraying secrets —
24 These are the things you should rightly avoid
as shameful
if you would be looked upon by everyone
with favor.

42 But of these things be not ashamed,
lest you sin through human respect:
2 Of the law of the Most High and his precepts,
or of the sentence to be passed upon the sinful;
3 Of sharing the expenses of a business or a journey,
or of dividing an inheritance or property;
4 Of accuracy of scales and balances,
or of tested measures and weights;
5 Of acquiring much or little,
or of bargaining in dealing with a merchant;
Of constant training of children,
or of beating the sides of a disloyal servant;
6 Of a seal to keep an erring wife at home,
or of a lock placed where there are many hands;
7 Of numbering every deposit,
or of recording all that is given or received;
8 Of chastisement of the silly and the foolish,
or of the aged and infirm answering for
wanton conduct.
Thus you will be truly cautious
and recognized by all men as discreet.

9 A daughter is a treasure that keeps her
father wakeful,
and worry over her drives away rest:
Lest she pass her prime unmarried,
or when she is married, lest she be disliked;
10 While unmarried, lest she be seduced,
or, as a wife, lest she prove unfaithful;
Lest she conceive in her father's home,
or be sterile in that of her husband.
11 Keep a close watch on your daughter,
lest she make you the sport of your enemies,
A byword in the city, a reproach among
the people,
an object of derision in public gatherings.
See that there is no lattice in her room,
no place that overlooks the approaches to
the house.
12 Let her not parade her charms before men,
or spend her time with married women;
13 For just as moths come from garments,
so harm to women comes from women:
14 Better a man's harshness than a
woman's indulgence,
and a frightened daughter than any disgrace.

22 of gazing at a loose woman,
of repulsing your fellow-countryman,
23 of misappropriating another's portion or
gift,
of paying court to another man's wife,
24 of making advances to his servant-girl
—do not go near her bed—
25 of saying disagreeable things to friends
—do not follow up a gift with a taunt—
26 of repeating everything you hear
and of betraying confidences.
27 Then you will know what true shame is,
and you will find yourself in everyone's graces.

42 The following things you should not be ashamed
of,
and do not sin from fear of what others think:
2 of the Law of the Most High or of the covenant,
of a verdict that acquits the godless,
3 of keeping accounts with a travelling companion,
of settling property on your friends,
4 of being accurate over scales and weights,
of making small and large profits,
5 of gaining from commercial transactions,
of disciplining your children strictly,
of lashing a wicked slave till you draw blood.
6 With an interfering wife, it is as well to use your
seal,
and where there are many hands, lock things up.
7 Whatever stores you issue, do it by number and
weight,
spendings and takings, put everything in writing.
8 Do not be ashamed to correct a stupid person or a
fool,
or an old dotard who bickers with young people.
Then you will show yourself really educated
and win the approval of everyone.

9 Unknown to her, a daughter keeps her father
awake,
the worry she gives him drives away his sleep:
in her youth, in case she never marries,
married, in case she should be disliked,
10 as a virgin, in case she should be defiled
and found with child in her father's house,
having a husband, in case she goes astray,
married, in case she should be sterile!
11 Your daughter is headstrong? Keep a sharp
look-out
that she does not make you the laughing-stock of
your enemies,
the talk of the town, the object of common gossip,
and put you to public shame.
12 Do not stare at any man for his good looks,
do not sit down with women;
13 for moth comes out of clothes,
and woman's spite out of woman.
14 Better a man's spite than a woman's kindness:
women give rise to shame and reproach.

NEW REVISED STANDARD VERSION	REVISED ENGLISH BIBLE

NEW REVISED STANDARD VERSION

15 I will now call to mind the works of the Lord,
    and will declare what I have seen.
By the word of the Lord his works are made;
    and all his creatures do his will. *a*
16 The sun looks down on everything with its light,
    and the work of the Lord is full of his glory.
17 The Lord has not empowered even his holy ones
    to recount all his marvelous works,
which the Lord the Almighty has established
    so that the universe may stand firm in his
      glory.
18 He searches out the abyss and the human heart;
    he understands their innermost secrets.
For the Most High knows all that may be known;
    he sees from of old the things that are to
      come. *b*
19 He discloses what has been and what is to be,
    and he reveals the traces of hidden things.
20 No thought escapes him,
    and nothing is hidden from him.
21 He has set in order the splendors of his wisdom;
    he is from all eternity one and the same.
Nothing can be added or taken away,
    and he needs no one to be his counselor.
22 How desirable are all his works,
    and how sparkling they are to see! *c*
23 All these things live and remain forever;
    each creature is preserved to meet a particular
      need. *d*
24 All things come in pairs, one opposite the other,
    and he has made nothing incomplete.
25 Each supplements the virtues of the other.
    Who could ever tire of seeing his glory?

43 The pride of the higher realms is the clear vault
      of the sky,
    as glorious to behold as the sight of the
      heavens.
2 The sun, when it appears, proclaims as it rises
    what a marvelous instrument it is, the work of
      the Most High.
3 At noon it parches the land,
    and who can withstand its burning heat?
4 A man tending *e* a furnace works in burning heat,
    but three times as hot is the sun scorching the
      mountains;
it breathes out fiery vapors,
    and its bright rays blind the eyes.
5 Great is the Lord who made it;
    at his orders it hurries on its course.
6 It is the moon that marks the changing seasons, *f*
    governing the times, their everlasting sign.
7 From the moon comes the sign for festal days,
    a light that wanes when it completes its course.
8 The new moon, as its name suggests, renews
      itself; *g*
how marvelous it is in this change,
a beacon to the hosts on high,
    shining in the vault of the heavens!
9 The glory of the stars is the beauty of heaven,
    a glittering array in the heights of the Lord.

REVISED ENGLISH BIBLE

15 Now I SHALL call to mind the works of the Lord
    and describe what I have seen,
his works which by his word were made.
16 As everything is illumined by the rays of the sun,
    so the works of the Lord are full of his glory.
17 Even to the angels the Lord has not given the
      power
to tell the full tale of the marvels
accomplished by the Lord Almighty,
    so that the universe may stand firm in his glory.
18 He fathoms both the abyss and the human heart,
    he is versed in their intricacies;
for the Most High possesses all knowledge,
    and the signs of the times are under his eye.
19 He discloses both past and future,
    and lays bare the traces of secret things.
20 No thought escapes his notice,
    and not a single word is hidden from him.
21 He has set in order the masterpieces of his
      wisdom,
he who is One from eternity to eternity;
nothing is added, nothing taken away,
    and he needs none to give him counsel.
22 How pleasing is all that he has made,
    even the smallest spark the eye can see!
23 His works endure, all of them active for ever
    and all responsive to their several functions.
24 All things go in pairs, one the counterpart of the
      other;
he has made nothing incomplete.
25 One thing supplements the virtues of another.
    Of his glory who can ever see too much?

43 How splendid is the clear vault of the sky,
    how glorious the spectacle of the heavens!
2 The sun comes into view proclaiming as it rises
    how marvellous it is, the handiwork of the Most
      High.
3 At noon it parches the earth,
    and no one can endure its blazing heat.
4 The stoker of a furnace works in the heat,
    but three times as hot is the hill-scorching sun.
It breathes out fiery vapours;
    the glare of its rays blinds the eyes.
5 Great is the Lord, its Creator,
    whose word speeds it on its course.
6 He made the moon also to serve in its turn,
    a perpetual sign to mark the divisions of time.
7 From the moon, feast days are reckoned;
    it is a light that wanes as it completes its course.
8 The moon gives its name to the month;
    it waxes marvellously as its phases change,
a beacon to the armies of heaven,
    shining in the vault of the sky.
9 The stars in their brilliance adorn the heavens,
    a glittering array in the heights of the Lord.

---

a Syr Compare Heb: most Gk witnesses lack *and all . . . will*
b Heb: Gk *he sees the sign(s) of the age*   *c* Meaning of Gk
uncertain   *d* Heb: Gk *forever for every need, and all are obedient*
e Other ancient authorities read *blowing upon*   *f* Heb: Meaning of
Gk uncertain   *g* Heb: Gk *The month is named after the moon*

15 Now will I recall God's works;
   what I have seen, I will describe.
At God's word were his works brought into being;
   they do his will as he has ordained for them.
16 As the rising sun is clear to all,
   so the glory of the LORD fills all his works;
17 Yet even God's holy ones must fail
   in recounting the wonders of the LORD,
Though God has given these, his hosts,
   the strength
   to stand firm before his glory.
18 He plumbs the depths and penetrates the heart;
   their innermost being he understands.
The Most High possesses all knowledge,
   and sees from of old the things that are to come:
19 He makes known the past and the future,
   and reveals the deepest secrets.
20 No understanding does he lack;
   no single thing escapes him.
21 Perennial is his almighty wisdom;
   he is from all eternity one and the same,
22 With nothing added, nothing taken away;
   no need of a counselor for him!
23 How beautiful are all his works!
   even to the spark and fleeting vision!
24 The universe lives and abides forever;
   to meet each need, each creature is preserved.
25 All of them differ, one from another,
   yet none of them has he made in vain,
For each in turn, as it comes, is good;
   can one ever see enough of their splendor?

43 The clear vault of the sky shines forth
   like heaven itself, a vision of glory.
2 The orb of the sun, resplendent at its rising:
   what a wonderful work of the Most High!
3 At noon it seethes the surface of the earth,
   and who can bear its fiery heat?
4 Like a blazing furnace of solid metal,
   it sets the mountains aflame with its rays;
By its fiery darts the land is consumed;
   the eyes are dazzled by its light.
5 Great indeed is the LORD who made it,
   at whose orders it urges on its steeds.
6 The moon, too, that marks the changing times,
   governing the seasons, their lasting sign,
7 By which we know the feast days and fixed dates,
   this light-giver which wanes in its course:
8 As its name says, each month it renews itself;
   how wondrous in this change!
9 The beauty, the glory, of the heavens are the stars
   that adorn with their sparkling the heights
   of God,

15 Next, I shall remind you of the works of the Lord,
   and tell of what I have seen.
By the words of the Lord his works come into
   being
   and all creation obeys his will.
16 The shining sun looks down on all things,
   and the work of the Lord is full of his glory.
17 The Lord has not granted the Holy Ones the power
   to tell of all his marvels
which the Almighty Lord has solidly constructed
   for the universe to stand firm in his glory.
18 He has fathomed both the abyss and the human
   heart
   and seen into their devious ways;
for the Most High knows all there is to know
   and sees the signs of the times.
19 He declares what is past and what will be,
   and reveals the trend of hidden things.
20 Not a thought escapes him,
   not a single word is hidden from him.
21 He has embellished the magnificent works of his
   wisdom,
   he is from everlasting to everlasting,
nothing can be added to him, nothing taken away,
   he needs no one's advice.
22 How lovely, all his works,
   how dazzling to the eye!
23 They all live and last for ever,
   and, whatever the circumstances, all obey.
24 All things go in pairs, by opposites,
   he has not made anything imperfect:
25 one thing complements the excellence of another.
   Who could ever grow tired of gazing at his
   glory?

43 Pride of the heights, a clear vault of the sky —
   such is the beauty of the heavens, a glorious
   sight.
2 The sun, as he emerges, proclaims at his rising,
   'How wonderful a thing, the work of the Most
   High!'
3 At his zenith, he parches the ground,
   who can withstand his blaze?
4 We have to blow the furnace to produce any heat,
   the sun burns the mountains three times as
   much;
breathing out blasts of fire,
   flashing his rays, he dazzles the eyes.
5 Great is the Lord who created him
   and whose word speeds him on his course.

6 And then the moon, ever punctual
   to mark the times, an everlasting sign:
7 It is the moon that signals the feasts,
   a luminary that wanes after being full.
8 The month derives its name from hers,
   she waxes wonderfully in her phases,
banner of the hosts on high,
   shining in the vault of heaven.

9 The glory of the stars makes the beauty of the sky,
   a brilliant adornment of the Lord on High.

NEW REVISED STANDARD VERSION	REVISED ENGLISH BIBLE

10 On the orders of the Holy One they stand in their
   appointed places;
   they never relax in their watches.

11 Look at the rainbow, and praise him who made
   it;
   it is exceedingly beautiful in its brightness.

12 It encircles the sky with its glorious arc;
   the hands of the Most High have stretched it
   out.

13 By his command he sends the driving snow
   and speeds the lightnings of his judgment.

14 Therefore the storehouses are opened,
   and the clouds fly out like birds.

15 In his majesty he gives the clouds their strength,
   and the hailstones are broken in pieces.

17a The voice of his thunder rebukes the earth;

16 when he appears, the mountains shake.
   At his will the south wind blows;

17b so do the storm from the north and the
   whirlwind.
   He scatters the snow like birds flying down,
   and its descent is like locusts alighting.

18 The eye is dazzled by the beauty of its whiteness,
   and the mind is amazed as it falls.

19 He pours frost over the earth like salt,
   and icicles form like pointed thorns.

20 The cold north wind blows,
   and ice freezes on the water;
   it settles on every pool of water,
   and the water puts it on like a breastplate.

21 He consumes the mountains and burns up the
   wilderness,
   and withers the tender grass like fire.

22 A mist quickly heals all things;
   the falling dew gives refreshment from the
   heat.

23 By his plan he stilled the deep
   and planted islands in it.

24 Those who sail the sea tell of its dangers,
   and we marvel at what we hear.

25 In it are strange and marvelous creatures,
   all kinds of living things, and huge
   sea-monsters.

26 Because of him each of his messengers succeeds,
   and by his word all things hold together.

27 We could say more but could never say enough;
   let the final word be: "He is the all."

28 Where can we find the strength to praise him?
   For he is greater than all his works.

29 Awesome is the Lord and very great,
   and marvelous is his power.

30 Glorify the Lord and exalt him as much as you
   can,
   for he surpasses even that.
   When you exalt him, summon all your strength,
   and do not grow weary, for you cannot praise
   him enough.

31 Who has seen him and can describe him?
   Or who can extol him as he is?

32 Many things greater than these lie hidden,
   for I[h] have seen but few of his works.

33 For the Lord has made all things,
   and to the godly he has given wisdom.

HYMN IN HONOR OF OUR ANCESTORS[i]

44 Let us now sing the praises of famous men,
   our ancestors in their generations.

---

10 At the Holy One's command each stands in its
   place,
   never defaulting at its post.

11 Look at the rainbow and praise its Maker;
   it shines with a surpassing beauty,

12 spanning the heavens with its gleaming arc,
   a bow bent by the hands of the Most High.

13 His command speeds the snowstorm
   and sends the swift lightning to execute his
   sentence.

14 To that end the storehouses are opened,
   and the clouds fly out like birds.

15 By his mighty power the clouds are massed
   and the hailstones broken small.

16-17 The thunder of his voice makes the earth writhe,
   and on his appearing the hills are shaken.
   At his will the south wind blows,
   the squall from the north and the hurricane.
   He scatters the snowflakes like birds alighting;
   they settle like a swarm of locusts.

18 The eye is dazzled by their beautiful whiteness,
   and the mind is entranced as they fall.

19 He sprinkles hoar-frost on the earth like salt,
   and icicles congeal like pointed stakes.

20 A cold blast from the north
   and ice freezes hard on the water,
   settling on every pool
   as though the water were putting on a breastplate.

21 He consumes the hills, burns up the wilderness,
   and like fire shrivels the grass.

22 Cloudy weather quickly puts all to rights,
   and dew brings welcome relief after the scorching
   heat.

23 In his design he curbed the deep
   and planted islands there.

24 Those who sail the sea have tales of its dangers
   which astonish all of us who hear them;

25 in it are strange and wonderful creatures,
   all kinds of living things and great sea monsters.

26 By his own action his purpose succeeds,
   and by his word all things are held together.

27 However much we say, our words will always fall
   short;
   the end of the matter is: God is all.

28 Where can we find the skill to sing his praises?
   For he is greater than all his works.

29 The Lord is terrible and very great;
   marvellous is his power.

30 Honour the Lord to the best of your ability,
   yet still is he high above all praise.
   Summon all your strength to extol him,
   and be untiring, for you will always fall short.

31 Who has seen him, that he can describe him?
   Can anyone praise him as he truly is?

32 We have seen but a small part of his works,
   and there remain many mysteries greater still.

33 The Lord has created all things,
   and to the godly he has granted wisdom.

44 LET us now praise famous men,
   the fathers of our people in their generations;

---

h Heb: Gk *we*   i This title is included in the Gk text.

NEW AMERICAN BIBLE

NEW JERUSALEM BIBLE

10 At whose command they keep their place
and never relax in their vigils.
A weapon against the flood waters stored on high,
lighting up the firmament by its brilliance,
11 Behold the rainbow! Then bless its Maker,
for majestic indeed is its splendor;
12 It spans the heavens with its glory,
this bow bent by the mighty hand of God.

13 His rebuke marks out the path for the lightning,
and speeds the arrows of his judgment to
their goal.
14 At it the storehouse is opened,
and like vultures the clouds hurry forth.
15 In his majesty he gives the storm its power
and breaks off the hailstones.
16 The thunder of his voice makes the earth writhe;
before his might the mountains quake.
17 A word from him drives on the south wind,
the angry north wind, the hurricane and
the storm.
18 He sprinkles the snow like fluttering birds;
it comes to settle like swarms of locusts.
19 Its shining whiteness blinds the eyes,
the mind is baffled by its steady fall.
20 He scatters frost like so much salt;
it shines like blossoms on the thornbush.
21 Cold northern blasts he sends
that turn the ponds to lumps of ice.
He freezes over every body of water,
and clothes each pool with a coat of mail.
22 When the mountain growth is scorched with heat,
and the flowering plains as though by flames,
23 The dripping clouds restore them all,
and the scattered dew enriches the parched land.
24 His is the plan that calms the deep,
and plants the islands in the sea.
25 Those who go down to the sea tell part of its story,
and when we hear them we are thunderstruck;
26 In it are his creatures, stupendous, amazing,
all kinds of life, and the monsters of the deep.
27 For him each messenger succeeds,
and at his bidding accomplishes his will.
28 More than this we need not add;
let the last word be, he is all in all!
29 Let us praise him the more, since we cannot
fathom him,
for greater is he than all his works;
30 Awful indeed is the LORD's majesty,
and wonderful is his power.
31 Lift up your voices to glorify the LORD,
though he is still beyond your power to praise;
32 Extol him with renewed strength,
and weary not, though you cannot reach the end:
33 For who can see him and describe him?
or who can praise him as he is?
34 Beyond these, many things lie hid;
only a few of his works have we seen.
35 It is the LORD who has made all things,
and to those who fear him he gives wisdom.

10 At the words of the Holy One they stand as he
decrees,
and never grow slack at their watch.
11 See the rainbow and praise its Maker,
so superbly beautiful in its splendour.
12 Across the sky it forms a glorious arc
drawn by the hands of the Most High.

13 By his command he sends the snow,
he speeds the lightning by his command.
14 In the same way, his treasuries open
and the clouds fly out like birds.
15 His great power solidifies the clouds,
then pulverises them into hail.
17a At the roar of his thunder, the earth writhes in
labour,
16 at the sight of him, the mountains quake.
At his will the south wind blows,
17b or the storm from the north and the whirlwind.
18 He sprinkles snow like birds alighting,
it comes down like locusts settling.
The eye marvels at the beauty of its whiteness,
and the mind is amazed at its falling.
19 Over the earth, like salt, he also pours hoarfrost,
which, when it freezes, bristles like thorns.
20 The cold wind blows from the north,
and ice forms on the water;
it forms on every piece of standing water, ·
covering it like a breastplate.
21 The wind swallows up the mountains and scorches
the desert,
like a fire it consumes the vegetation.
22 But cloud brings swift healing,
and dew brings joy after the heat.

23 By his own resourcefulness he has tamed the
abyss,
and planted it with islands.
24 Those who sail the sea tell of its dangers,
their accounts fill our ears with amazement:
25 for there too exist strange and wonderful works,
animals of every kind and huge sea creatures.
26 Thanks to God, his messenger reaches port,
everything works out according to his word.

27 We could say much more and still fall short;
to put it concisely, 'He is all.'
28 Where shall we find sufficient power to glorify
him,
since he is the Great One, above all his works,
29 the awe-inspiring Lord, stupendously great,
and wonderful in his power?
30 Exalt the Lord in your praises
as high as you may—still he surpasses you.
Exert all your strength when you exalt him,
do not grow tired—you will never come to the
end.
31 Who has ever seen him to describe him?
Who can glorify him as he deserves?
32 Many mysteries remain even greater than these,
for we have seen only a few of his works,
33 the Lord himself having created all things
and given wisdom to those who are devout.

44 Now will I praise those godly men,
our ancestors, each in his own time:

44 Next let us praise illustrious men,
our ancestors in their successive generations.

NEW REVISED STANDARD VERSION	REVISED ENGLISH BIBLE

NEW REVISED STANDARD VERSION

2 The Lord apportioned to them*j* great glory,
  his majesty from the beginning.
3 There were those who ruled in their kingdoms,
  and made a name for themselves by their valor;
  those who gave counsel because they were
      intelligent;
  those who spoke in prophetic oracles;
4 those who led the people by their counsels
  and by their knowledge of the people's lore;
  they were wise in their words of instruction;
5 those who composed musical tunes,
  or put verses in writing;
6 rich men endowed with resources,
  living peacefully in their homes —
7 all these were honored in their generations,
  and were the pride of their times.
8 Some of them have left behind a name,
  so that others declare their praise.
9 But of others there is no memory;
  they have perished as though they had never
      existed;
  they have become as though they had never been
      born,
  they and their children after them.
10 But these also were godly men,
  whose righteous deeds have not been forgotten;
11 their wealth will remain with their descendants,
  and their inheritance with their children's
      children.*k*
12 Their descendants stand by the covenants;
  their children also, for their sake.
13 Their offspring will continue forever,
  and their glory will never be blotted out.
14 Their bodies are buried in peace,
  but their name lives on generation after
      generation.
15 The assembly declares*l* their wisdom,
  and the congregation proclaims their praise.

16 Enoch pleased the Lord and was taken up,
  an example of repentance to all generations.

17 Noah was found perfect and righteous;
  in the time of wrath he kept the race alive;*m*
  therefore a remnant was left on the earth
  when the flood came.
18 Everlasting covenants were made with him
  that all flesh should never again be blotted out
      by a flood.

19 Abraham was the great father of a multitude of
      nations,
  and no one has been found like him in glory.
20 He kept the law of the Most High,
  and entered into a covenant with him;
  he certified the covenant in his flesh,
  and when he was tested he proved faithful.
21 Therefore the Lord*n* assured him with an oath
  that the nations would be blessed through his
      offspring;
  that he would make him as numerous as the dust
      of the earth,
  and exalt his offspring like the stars,
  and give them an inheritance from sea to sea
  and from the Euphrates*o* to the ends of the
      earth.

REVISED ENGLISH BIBLE

2 to them the Lord assigned great glory,
  his majestic greatness from of old.
3 Some held sway over kingdoms
  and gained renown by their might.
  Others were far-seeing counsellors
  who spoke out with prophetic power.
4 Some guided the people by their deliberations
  and by their knowledge of the nation's law,
  giving instruction from their fund of wisdom.
5 Some were composers of music;
  some were writers of poetry.
6 Others were endowed with wealth and strength,
  living at ease in their homes.
7 All those won glory in their own generation
  and were the pride of their times.
8 Some there are who have left behind them a name
  to be commemorated in story.
9 Others are unremembered;
  they have perished as though they had never
      existed,
  as though they had never been born;
  so too it was with their children after them.
10 But not so our forefathers, men true to their faith,
  whose virtuous deeds have not been forgotten.
11 Their prosperity is handed on to their descendants,
  their inheritance to future generations.
12 Through them their children are within the
      covenants —
  the whole race of their descendants.
13 Their line will endure for all time;
  their glory will never die.
14 Their bodies are buried in peace
  and their name lives for ever.
15 Nations will tell of their wisdom,
  and the assembled people will sing their praise.

16 Enoch pleased the Lord and was taken up to
      heaven,
  an example of repentance to future ages.

17 Noah was found perfect and righteous,
  and thus he made amends in the time of God's
      wrath;
  that was why when the flood came
  a remnant survived on the earth.
18 An everlasting covenant was established with him,
  that never again should all life be swept away by a
      flood.

19 Abraham was the great father of a host of nations;
  no one has ever been found to equal him in fame.
20 He kept the law of the Most High;
  he entered into a covenant with him,
  setting the mark of it on his body.
  When put to the test he proved steadfast.
21 Therefore the Lord assured him on oath
  that through his descendants nations should find
      blessing,
  and that his family should be countless as the dust
      of the earth
  and be exalted as high as the stars;
  that their territories should extend from sea to sea,
  from the river to the ends of the earth.

j Heb: Gk *created*   *k* Heb Compare Lat Syr: Meaning of Gk
uncertain   *l* Heb: Gk *Peoples declare*   *m* Heb: Gk *was taken in
exchange*   *n* Gk *he*   *o* Syr: Heb Gk *River*

| NEW AMERICAN BIBLE | NEW JERUSALEM BIBLE |

NEW AMERICAN BIBLE

2 The abounding glory of the Most High's portion,
   his own part, since the days of old.
Subduers of the land in kingly fashion,
   men of renown for their might,
3 Or counselors in their prudence,
   or seers of all things in prophecy;
4 Resolute princes of the folk,
   and governors with their staves;
Authors skilled in composition,
   and forgers of epigrams with their spikes;
5 Composers of melodious psalms,
   or discoursers on lyric themes;
6 Stalwart men, solidly established
   and at peace in their own estates —
7 All these were glorious in their time,
   each illustrious in his day.
8 Some of them have left behind a name
   and men recount their praiseworthy deeds;
9 But of others there is no memory,
   for when they ceased, they ceased.
And they are as though they had not lived,
   they and their children after them.
10 Yet these also were godly men
   whose virtues have not been forgotten;
11 Their wealth remains in their families,
   their heritage with their descendants;
12 Through God's covenant with them their
      family endures,
   their posterity for their sake.
13 And for all time their progeny will endure,
   their glory will never be blotted out;
14 Their bodies are peacefully laid away,
   but their name lives on and on.
15 At gatherings their wisdom is retold,
   and the assembly proclaims their praise.
16 [ENOCH walked with the LORD and was taken up,
   that succeeding generations might learn by
      his example.]
17 NOAH, found just and perfect,
   renewed the race in the time of devastation.
Because of his worth there were survivors,
   and with a sign to him the deluge ended;
18 A lasting agreement was made with him,
   that never should all flesh be destroyed.
19 ABRAHAM, father of many peoples,
   kept his glory without stain:
20 He observed the precepts of the Most High,
   and entered into an agreement with him;
In his own flesh he incised the ordinance,
   and when tested he was found loyal.
21 For this reason, God promised him with an oath
   that in his descendants the nations would
      be blessed,
That he would make him numerous as the grains
      of dust,
   and exalt his posterity like the stars;
That he would give them an inheritance from sea
      to sea,
   and from the River to the ends of the earth.

NEW JERUSALEM BIBLE

2 The Lord has created an abundance of glory,
   and displayed his greatness from earliest times.
3 Some wielded authority as kings
   and were renowned for their strength;
others were intelligent advisers
   and uttered prophetic sayings.
4 Others directed the people by their advice,
   by their understanding of the popular mind,
   and by the wise words of their teaching;
5 others composed musical melodies
   and set down ballads;
6 others were rich and powerful,
   living peacefully in their homes.
7 All these were honoured by their contemporaries
   and were the glory of their day.
8 Some of them left a name behind them,
   so that their praises are still sung.
9 While others have left no memory,
   and disappeared as though they had not existed.
They are now as though they had never been,
   and so too, their children after them.
10 But here is a list of illustrious men
   whose good works have not been forgotten.
11 In their descendants they find
   a rich inheritance, their posterity.
12 Their descendants stand by the commandments
   and, thanks to them, so do their children's
      children.
13 Their offspring will last for ever,
   their glory will not fade.
14 Their bodies have been buried in peace,
   and their name lives on for all generations.
15 The peoples will proclaim their wisdom,
   the assembly will celebrate their praises.*j*
16 Enoch pleased the Lord and was transferred to
      heaven,
an example for the conversion of all generations.
17 Noah was found perfectly upright,
   in the time of retribution he became the heir:
because of him a remnant was preserved for the
      earth
   at the coming of the Flood.
18 Everlasting covenants were made with him
   that never again should every living creature
      perish by flood.
19 Abraham, the great ancestor of a host of nations,
   no one was ever his equal in glory.
20 He observed the Law of the Most High,
   and entered into a covenant with him.
He confirmed the covenant in his own flesh,
   and proved himself faithful under ordeal.
21 The Lord therefore promised him on oath
   to bless the nations through his descendants,
to multiply him like the dust on the ground,
to exalt his descendants like the stars,
and to give them the land as their heritage,
   from one sea to the other,
from the River to the ends of the earth.

44, 16: The present verse is an expansion of the original text.   *j* 44 = 39:10.

NEW REVISED STANDARD VERSION	REVISED ENGLISH BIBLE

NEW REVISED STANDARD VERSION

22 To Isaac also he gave the same assurance
   for the sake of his father Abraham.
The blessing of all people and the covenant
23   he made to rest on the head of Jacob;
he acknowledged him with his blessings,
   and gave him his inheritance;
he divided his portions,
   and distributed them among twelve tribes.

From his descendants the Lord*p* brought forth a
   godly man,
   who found favor in the sight of all

45 ¹ and was beloved by God and people,
   Moses, whose memory is blessed.
2 He made him equal in glory to the holy ones,
   and made him great, to the terror of his
      enemies.
3 By his words he performed swift miracles;*q*
   the Lord*p* glorified him in the presence of
      kings.
He gave him commandments for his people,
   and revealed to him his glory.
4 For his faithfulness and meekness he consecrated
      him,
   choosing him out of all humankind.
5 He allowed him to hear his voice,
   and led him into the dark cloud,
and gave him the commandments face to face,
   the law of life and knowledge,
so that he might teach Jacob the covenant,
   and Israel his decrees.

6 He exalted Aaron, a holy man like Moses*r*
   who was his brother, of the tribe of Levi.
7 He made an everlasting covenant with him,
   and gave him the priesthood of the people.
He blessed him with stateliness,
   and put a glorious robe on him.
8 He clothed him in perfect splendor,
   and strengthened him with the symbols of
      authority,
   the linen undergarments, the long robe, and the
      ephod.
9 And he encircled him with pomegranates,
   with many golden bells all around,
to send forth a sound as he walked,
   to make their ringing heard in the temple
   as a reminder to his people;
10 with the sacred vestment, of gold and violet
   and purple, the work of an embroiderer;
with the oracle of judgment, Urim and
      Thummim;
11 with twisted crimson, the work of an artisan;
with precious stones engraved like seals,
   in a setting of gold, the work of a jeweler,
to commemorate in engraved letters
   each of the tribes of Israel;
12 with a gold crown upon his turban,
   inscribed like a seal with "Holiness,"
a distinction to be prized, the work of an expert,
   a delight to the eyes, richly adorned.
13 Before him such beautiful things did not exist.
   No outsider ever put them on,
but only his sons
   and his descendants in perpetuity.
14 His sacrifices shall be wholly burned
   twice every day continually.

REVISED ENGLISH BIBLE

22 To Isaac, for the sake of Abraham his father,
   he gave the same assurance
   of a blessing for all mankind and a covenant.
23 He made the blessing rest on the head of Jacob,
   who was confirmed in the blessings he had
      received
   and was given the land for his inheritance,
   divided into portions
   which were allotted to the twelve tribes.

45 From Jacob's stock the Lord raised up a man of
   faith
who won favour in the eyes of all:
   Moses of blessed memory, beloved by God and his
      people.
2 The Lord made him equal in glory to the angels,
   giving him power to the terror of his enemies.
3 He sent sign after sign at his request,
   so enhancing his reputation with the king.
He gave him a commission to his people
   and revealed to him some part of his glory.
4 For his loyalty and humility he consecrated him,
   choosing him above everyone else.
5 He let him hear his voice
   and brought him into the dark cloud,
   where face to face he gave him the
      commandments,
   law which is the source of life and knowledge,
   so that he might teach his covenant to Jacob,
   his decrees to Israel.

6 He raised up Aaron of the tribe of Levi,
   a holy man like his brother.
7 He made an everlasting covenant with him,
   conferring on him the priesthood of the nation.
He honoured and adorned him,
   clothing him in splendid vestments,
8 robing him in full and proud array.
He gave him the emblems of his station,
   the linen trousers, the mantle, and the tunic.
9 Round his robe he put pomegranates
   and a circle of many golden bells
to make music as he walked,
   ringing aloud throughout the temple
   as a reminder to his people.
10 He gave him the sacred vestment adorned with
      embroidery,
   gold and violet and purple;
   the oracle of judgement with the tokens of truth;
11 the scarlet thread spun with a craftsman's art;
   the precious stones, engraved like signets,
   and mounted by the jeweller in a setting of gold,
   with inscriptions to serve as reminders,
   one for each of the tribes of Israel;
12 the gold diadem upon his turban,
   engraved like a signet with 'Holy to the Lord'.
A proud adornment! A miracle of art!
   What rich decoration to delight the eyes!
13 Before him there had not been such things of
      beauty.
Only his family has ever worn them,
   throughout the ages only his sons and his
      descendants.
14 Twice each day without fail
   they present his sacrifice, a complete offering.

45:10 **the oracle . . . truth:** *or* the breastpiece of judgement with the
Urim and Thummim (Exod. 28:30).   45:12 **signet . . . Lord:** *cp.*
Exod. 28:36; *lit.* signet of holiness.

p Gk *he*   *q* Heb: Gk *caused signs to cease*   *r* Gk *him*

22 And for Isaac he renewed the same promise
    because of Abraham, his father.
The covenant with all his forebears was confirmed,
    and the blessing rested upon the head of Jacob.
23 God acknowledged him as the first-born,
    and gave him his inheritance.
He fixed the boundaries for his tribes,
    and their division into twelve.

45 From him was to spring the man
    who won the favor of all:
Dear to God and men,
    Moses, whose memory is held in benediction.
2 God's honor devolved upon him,
    and the Lord strengthened him with
        fearful powers;
3 God wrought swift miracles at his words
    and sustained him in the king's presence.
He gave him the commandments for his people,
    and revealed to him his glory.
4 For his trustworthiness and meekness
    God selected him from all mankind;
5 He permitted him to hear his voice,
    and led him into the cloud,
Where, face to face, he gave him
    the commandments,
    the law of life and understanding,
That he might teach his precepts to Jacob,
    his judgments and decrees to Israel.

6 He raised up also, like Moses in holiness,
    his brother Aaron, of the tribe of Levi.
7 He made him perpetual in his office
    when he bestowed on him the priesthood of
        his people;
He established him in honor
    and crowned him with lofty majesty;
8 He clothed him with splendid apparel,
    and adorned him with the glorious vestments:
Breeches and tunic and robe
    with pomegranates around the hem,
9 And a rustle of bells round about,
    through whose pleasing sound at each step
He would be heard within the sanctuary,
    and the children of his race would
        be remembered;
10 The sacred vestments of gold, of violet,
    and of crimson, wrought with embroidery;
The breastpiece for decision, the ephod
    and cincture
11   with scarlet yarn, the work of the weaver;
Precious stones with seal engravings
    in golden settings, the work of the jeweler,
To commemorate in incised letters
    each of the tribes of Israel;
12 On his turban the diadem of gold,
    its plate wrought with the insignia of holiness,
Majestic, glorious, renowned for splendor,
    a delight to the eyes, beauty supreme.
13 Before him, no one was adorned with these,
    nor may they ever be worn by any
Except his sons and them alone,
    generation after generation, for all time.
14 His cereal offering is wholly burnt
    with the established sacrifice twice each day;

22 To Isaac too, for the sake of Abraham his father,
    he assured 23 the blessing of all humanity;
    he caused the covenant to rest on the head of
        Jacob.
He confirmed him in his blessings
    and gave him the land as his inheritance;
he divided it into portions,
    and shared it out among the twelve tribes.

45 From Jacob's stock he produced a generous man
    who found favour in the eyes of all humanity,
beloved by God and people,
    Moses, of blessed memory.
2 He made him the equal of the holy ones in glory
    and made him strong, to the terror of his
        enemies.
3 By the word of Moses, he made prodigies cease
    and raised him high in the respect of kings;
he gave him commandments for his people,
    and showed him something of his glory.
4 For his loyalty and gentleness he sanctified him,
    choosing him alone out of all human beings;
5 he allowed him to hear his voice,
    and led him into the darkness;
6 he gave him the commandments face to face,
    the law of life and knowledge,
to teach Jacob his ordinances
    and Israel his decrees.

He raised up Aaron, a holy man like Moses,
    his brother, of the tribe of Levi.
7 He made an everlasting covenant with him,
    and gave him the priesthood of the people.
He adorned him with impressive vestments,
    he dressed him in a robe of glory.
8 He clothed him in glorious perfection
    and invested him with rich ornaments,
    the breeches, the long robe, the *ephod*.
9 To surround the robe he gave him pomegranates,
    and many gold bells all round
to chime at every step,
    for their sound to be heard in the Temple
    as a reminder to the children of his people;
10 and a sacred vestment of gold and aquamarine
    and scarlet, the work of an embroiderer;
the pectoral of judgement, the *urim* and *thummim*,
    of plaited crimson, the work of a craftsman;
11 precious stones cut like seals
    mounted in gold, the work of a jeweller,
as a reminder with their engraved inscriptions
    of the number of the tribes of Israel;
12 and a golden diadem on his turban,
    engraved with the seal of consecration;
superb ornamentation, magnificent work,
    adornment to delight the eye.
13 There had never been such lovely things before
    him,
    and no one else has ever put them on,
but only his own sons,
    and his descendants for all time.
14 His sacrifices were to be burnt entirely,
    twice each day and for ever.

15 Moses ordained him,
   and anointed him with holy oil;
it was an everlasting covenant for him
   and for his descendants as long as the heavens
      endure,
to minister to the Lord[s] and serve as priest
   and bless his people in his name.
16 He chose him out of all the living
   to offer sacrifice to the Lord,
incense and a pleasing odor as a memorial
      portion,
   to make atonement for the[t] people.
17 In his commandments he gave him
   authority and statutes and[u] judgments,
to teach Jacob the testimonies,
   and to enlighten Israel with his law.
18 Outsiders conspired against him,
   and envied him in the wilderness,
Dathan and Abiram and their followers
   and the company of Korah, in wrath and anger.
19 The Lord saw it and was not pleased,
   and in the heat of his anger they were
      destroyed;
he performed wonders against them
   to consume them in flaming fire.
20 He added glory to Aaron
   and gave him a heritage;
he allotted to him the best of the first fruits,
   and prepared bread of first fruits in abundance;
21 for they eat the sacrifices of the Lord,
   which he gave to him and his descendants.
22 But in the land of the people he has no
      inheritance,
   and he has no portion among the people;
for the Lord[v] himself is his[w] portion and
      inheritance.

23 Phinehas son of Eleazar ranks third in glory
   for being zealous in the fear of the Lord,
and standing firm, when the people turned away,
   in the noble courage of his soul;
   and he made atonement for Israel.
24 Therefore a covenant of friendship was
      established with him,
   that he should be leader of the sanctuary and of
      his people,
that he and his descendants should have
   the dignity of the priesthood forever.
25 Just as a covenant was established with David
   son of Jesse of the tribe of Judah,
that the king's heritage passes only from son to
      son,
so the heritage of Aaron is for his descendants
      alone.

26 And now bless the Lord
   who has crowned you with glory.[x]
May the Lord[v] grant you wisdom of mind
   to judge his people with justice,
so that their prosperity may not vanish,
   and that their glory may endure through all
      their generations.

15 It was Moses who installed him
   and anointed him with sacred oil,
to mark the everlasting covenant made with him
   and with his descendants as long as the heavens
      endure,
that he should be the Lord's minister in the priestly
      office
   and bless his people in his name.
16 The Lord chose him out of all mankind
   to bring offerings to him,
incense and the fragrance of memorial sacrifice,
   to make expiation for the people.
17 He entrusted to him his commandments,
   with authority to pronounce legal decisions,
to teach Jacob his decrees
   and enlighten Israel about his law.
18 Upstarts became envious of him
   and conspired against him in the wilderness:
Dathan and Abiram with their supporters
   and Korah's men inflamed with anger.
19 The Lord saw and was displeased;
   in the heat of his wrath he destroyed them;
amid portents he consumed them with blazing fire.
20 But he added to Aaron's glory
   and gave him a heritage
by allotting to the priests the choicest firstfruits,
   thus ensuring that they above all should have bread
      in plenty;
21 for they eat the sacrifices of the Lord,
   which he gave to Aaron and his descendants.
22 But Aaron was to have no holding in the land of
      his people,
no portion among them was allotted to him;
   the Lord himself is his portion and holding.
23 Phinehas son of Eleazar ranks third in renown
   for being zealous in reverence towards the Lord,
and for standing firm with noble courage
   when the people defected;
by so doing he made expiation for Israel.
24 Therefore a covenant was established with him,
   assuring him charge of the sanctuary and the
      people,
conferring on him and on his descendants
   the high-priesthood for ever.

25 As by a covenant with David son of Jesse of the
      tribe of Judah
the royal succession should always pass from father
      to son,
so the priestly succession was to pass from Aaron
      to his descendants.
26 Now praise the Lord who is good
   and gives you a crown of glory!
May he grant you a wise mind
   to judge his people with justice,
so that their prosperity may never vanish
   and their glory may be passed on to future
      generations!

[s] Gk him   [t] Other ancient authorities read *his* or *your*   [u] Heb: Gk
authority in covenants of   [v] Gk he   [w] Other ancient authorities
read *your*   [x] Heb: Gk lacks *who . . . glory*

15 For Moses ordained him
  and anointed him with the holy oil,
In a lasting covenant with him
  and with his family, as permanent as
    the heavens,
That he should serve God in his priesthood
  and bless his people in his name.
16 He chose him from all mankind
  to offer holocausts and choice offerings,
To burn sacrifices of sweet odor for a memorial,
  and to atone for the people of Israel.
17 He gave to him his laws,
  and authority to prescribe and to judge:
To teach the precepts to his people,
  and the ritual to the descendants of Israel.
18 Men of other families were inflamed against him,
  were jealous of him in the desert,
The followers of Dathan and Abiram,
  and the band of Korah in their defiance.
19 But the LORD saw this and became angry,
  he destroyed them in his burning wrath.
He brought down upon them a miracle,
  and consumed them with his flaming fire.
20 Then he increased the glory of Aaron
  and bestowed upon him his inheritance:
The sacred offerings he allotted to him,
  with the showbread as his portion;
21 The oblations of the LORD are his food,
  a gift to him and his descendants.
22 But he holds no land among the people
  nor shares with them their heritage;
For the LORD himself is his portion,
  his inheritance in the midst of Israel.

23 PHINEHAS too, the son of Eleazar,
  was the courageous third of his line
When, zealous for the God of all,
  he met the crisis of his people
And, at the prompting of his noble heart,
  atoned for the children of Israel.
24 Therefore on him again God conferred the right,
  in a covenant of friendship, to provide for
    the sanctuary,
So that he and his descendants
  should possess the high priesthood forever.
25 For even his covenant with David,
  the son of Jesse of the tribe of Judah,
Was an individual heritage through one son alone;
  but the heritage of Aaron is for all his
    descendants.

26 And now bless the LORD
  who has crowned you with glory!
May he grant you wisdom of heart
  to govern his people in justice,
Lest their welfare should ever be forgotten,
  or your authority, throughout all time.

15 Moses consecrated him
  and anointed him with holy oil;
and this was an everlasting covenant for him,
  and for his descendants as long as the heavens
    endure,
that he should preside over worship, act as priest,
  and bless the people in the name of the Lord.
16 He chose him out of all the living
  to offer sacrifices to the Lord,
incense and perfume as a memorial
  to make expiation for the people.
17 He entrusted him with his commandments,
  committed to him the statutes of the Law
for him to teach Jacob his decrees
  and enlighten Israel on his Law.
18 Others plotted against him,
  they were jealous of him in the desert,
Dathan and Abiram and their men,
  Korah and his crew in fury and rage.
19 The Lord saw it and was displeased,
  his raging fury made an end of them;
he worked miracles on them,
  consuming them by his flaming fire.
20 And he added to Aaron's glory,
  he gave him an inheritance;
he allotted him the offerings of the first-fruits,
  before all else, as much bread as he could want.
21 Thus they eat the sacrifices of the Lord
  which he gave to him and his posterity.
22 But of the people's territory he inherits nothing,
  he alone of all the people has no share,
  'For I myself am your share and heritage.'

23 Phinehas son of Eleazar is third in glory
  because of his zeal in the fear of the Lord,
because he stood firm when the people revolted,
  with a staunch and courageous heart;
  and in this way made expiation for Israel.
24 Hence a covenant of peace was sealed with him,
  making him governor of both sanctuary and
    people,
and securing to him and his descendants
  the high priestly dignity for ever.
25 There was also a covenant with David
  son of Jesse, of the tribe of Judah,
a royal succession by exclusively linear descent,
  but the succession of Aaron passes to all his
    descendants.
26 May God endow your hearts with wisdom
  to judge his people uprightly,
so that the virtues of your ancestors may never
    fade,
  and their glory may pass to all their descendants!

46

Joshua son of Nun was mighty in war,
and was the successor of Moses in the
prophetic office.
He became, as his name implies,
a great savior of God's*y* elect,
to take vengeance on the enemies that rose
against them,
so that he might give Israel its inheritance.

2 How glorious he was when he lifted his hands
and brandished his sword against the cities!

3 Who before him ever stood so firm?
For he waged the wars of the Lord.

4 Was it not through him that the sun stood still
and one day became as long as two?

5 He called upon the Most High, the Mighty One,
when enemies pressed him on every side,
and the great Lord answered him
with hailstones of mighty power.

6 He overwhelmed that nation in battle,
and on the slope he destroyed his opponents,
so that the nations might know his armament,
that he was fighting in the sight of the Lord;
for he was a devoted follower of the Mighty
One.

7 And in the days of Moses he proved his loyalty,
he and Caleb son of Jephunneh:
they opposed the congregation,*z*
restrained the people from sin,
and stilled their wicked grumbling.

8 And these two alone were spared
out of six hundred thousand infantry,
to lead the people*a* into their inheritance,
the land flowing with milk and honey.

9 The Lord gave Caleb strength,
which remained with him in his old age,
so that he went up to the hill country,
and his children obtained it for an inheritance,

10 so that all the Israelites might see
how good it is to follow the Lord.

11 The judges also, with their respective names,
whose hearts did not fall into idolatry
and who did not turn away from the Lord—
may their memory be blessed!

12 May their bones send forth new life from where
they lie,
and may the names of those who have been
honored
live again in their children!

13 Samuel was beloved by his Lord;
a prophet of the Lord, he established the
kingdom
and anointed rulers over his people.

14 By the law of the Lord he judged the
congregation,
and the Lord watched over Jacob.

15 By his faithfulness he was proved to be a
prophet,
and by his words he became known as a
trustworthy seer.

16 He called upon the Lord, the Mighty One,
when his enemies pressed him on every side,
and he offered in sacrifice a suckling lamb.

17 Then the Lord thundered from heaven,

46

Joshua son of Nun was a mighty warrior
and the successor of Moses in the prophetic
office.
He well deserved his name
as a great saviour of the Lord's chosen people.
He wrought vengeance on the enemies who
attacked them,
and so put Israel in possession of its heritage.

2 How glorious he was when with upraised hand
he brandished his sword against the city!

3 He was fighting the Lord's battles
and none could oppose him.

4 Was it not through him that the sun stood still
and made one day as long as two?

5 When the enemy was pressing him hard on every
side,
he called to the Most High, the Mighty One;
his prayer was answered by the great Lord,

6 who displayed his power in a storm of hail.
Joshua overwhelmed the hostile nation
and crushed his assailants as they fled down the
pass,
that the nations should know the source of his
strength
and learn that he fought under the eyes of the Lord,
for he followed where the Mighty One led.

7 In the time of Moses he had proved his
faithfulness,
he and Caleb son of Jephunneh:
they stood their ground against the assembled
Israelites,
restrained the people from sin,
and silenced their wicked grumbling.

8 Out of six hundred thousand warriors
these two alone survived
to bring the people into their heritage,
into a land flowing with milk and honey.

9 The Lord gave Caleb strength,
which even in old age did not fail him,
and he was able to invade the hill-country
and win possession of it for his descendants.

10 Thus all Israel might see
how good it is to follow the Lord.

11 Then there are the judges, name after famous
name;
all of them rejected idolatry
and never turned away from the Lord—
blessings be on their memory!

12 May their bones send forth new life from the
grave!
May the fame of the honoured dead be matched by
their sons!

13 Samuel was beloved by his Lord.
As prophet of the Lord he established the
monarchy
and anointed rulers over his people.

14 He dispensed justice according to the law of the
Lord,
and the Lord kept watch over the people of Jacob.

15 By his fidelity he was proved a trustworthy
prophet,
his faithfulness to his vision was shown by his
words.

16 When enemies were pressing him hard on every
side,
he called to the mighty Lord,
offering a sucking-lamb in sacrifice.

17 Then the Lord thundered from heaven,

46

Valiant leader was JOSHUA, son of Nun
  assistant to Moses in the prophetic office,
Formed to be, as his name implies,
  the great savior of God's chosen ones,
To punish the enemy
  and to win the inheritance for Israel.
² What glory was his when he raised his arm,
  to brandish his javelin against the city!
³ And who could withstand him
  when he fought the battles of the LORD?
⁴ Did he not by his power stop the sun,
  so that one day became two?
⁵ He called upon the Most High God
  when his enemies beset him on all sides,
And God Most High gave answer to him
  in hailstones of tremendous power,
⁶ Which he rained down upon the hostile army
  till on the slope he destroyed the foe;
That all the doomed nations might know
  that the LORD was watching over his
    people's battles.
And because he was a devoted follower of God
⁷ and in Moses' lifetime showed himself loyal,
He and CALEB, son of Jephunneh,
  when they opposed the rebel assembly,
Averted God's anger from the people
  and suppressed the wicked complaint —
⁸ Because of this, they were the only two spared
  from the six hundred thousand infantry,
To lead the people into their inheritance,
  the land flowing with milk and honey.
⁹ And the strength he gave to Caleb
  remained with him even in his old age
Till he won his way onto the summits of the land;
  his family too received an inheritance,
¹⁰ That all the people of Jacob might know
  how good it is to be a devoted follower of
    the LORD.
¹¹ The JUDGES, too, each one of them,
  whose hearts were not deceived,
Who did not abandon God:
  may their memory be ever blessed,
¹² Their bones return to life from their resting place,
  and their names receive fresh luster in
    their children!
¹³ Beloved of his people, dear to his Maker,
  dedicated from his mother's womb,
Consecrated to the LORD as a prophet,
  was SAMUEL, the judge and priest.
At God's word he established the kingdom
  and anointed princes to rule the people.
¹⁴ By the law of the LORD he judged the nation,
  when he visited the encampments of Jacob.
¹⁵ As a trustworthy prophet he was sought out
  and his words proved him true as a seer.
¹⁶ He, too, called upon God,
  and offered him a suckling lamb;
¹⁷ Then the LORD thundered forth from heaven,

46

Mighty in war was Joshua son of Nun,
  successor to Moses in the prophetic office,
who well deserved his name, *k*
  and was a great saviour of the chosen people,
wreaking vengeance on the enemies who opposed
    him,
  and so bringing Israel into its inheritance.
² How splendid he was when, arms uplifted,
  he brandished his sword against cities!
³ Who had ever shown such determination as his?
  He himself led the battles of the Lord.
⁴ Was not the sun held back by his hand,
  and one day drawn out into two?
⁵ He called on the Most High, the Mighty One,
  while pressing the enemies from all directions,
and the great Lord answered him
  with hard and violent hailstones.
⁶ He fell on that enemy nation,
  and at the Descent destroyed all resistance
to make the nations acknowledge his warlike
    prowess
  and that he was waging war on behalf of the
    Lord.
⁷ For he was a follower of the Mighty One,
  in the time of Moses showing his devotion,
he and Caleb son of Jephunneh,
  by opposing the whole community,
by preventing the people from sinning,
  and by silencing the mutters of rebellion.
⁸ Hence these two alone were preserved
  out of six hundred thousand men on the march,
and brought into their inheritance,
  into a land where milk and honey flow.
⁹ And the Lord conferred strength on Caleb too,
  which stayed by him into old age,
so that he could invest the highlands of the country
  which his descendants kept as their inheritance,
¹⁰ so that every Israelite might see
  that it is good to follow the Lord.

¹¹ The Judges too, each when he was called,
  all men whose hearts were never disloyal,
who never turned their backs on the Lord —
  may their memory be blessed!
¹² May their bones flourish again from the tomb,
  and may the names of those illustrious men
    be worthily borne by their sons!

¹³ Samuel was the beloved of his Lord;
  prophet of the Lord, he instituted the kingdom,
    and anointed rulers over his people.
¹⁴ By the Law of the Lord he judged the assembly,
  and the Lord watched over Jacob.
¹⁵ By his loyalty he was recognised as a prophet,
  by his words he was known to be a trustworthy
    seer.
¹⁶ He called on the Lord, the Mighty One,
  when his enemies pressed in from all directions,
  by offering a sucking lamb.
¹⁷ And the Lord thundered from heaven,

---

k 46 *Yehoshua'* (= Joshua) means 'Yahweh saves'.

and made his voice heard with a mighty sound;
18 he subdued the leaders of the enemy[b]
  and all the rulers of the Philistines.
19 Before the time of his eternal sleep,
  Samuel[c] bore witness before the Lord and his
    anointed:
  "No property, not so much as a pair of shoes,
    have I taken from anyone!"
  And no one accused him.
20 Even after he had fallen asleep, he prophesied
  and made known to the king his death,
  and lifted up his voice from the ground
    in prophecy, to blot out the wickedness of the
    people.

47 After him Nathan rose up
  to prophesy in the days of David.
2 As the fat is set apart from the offering of
    well-being,
  so David was set apart from the Israelites.
3 He played with lions as though they were young
    goats,
  and with bears as though they were lambs of
    the flock.
4 In his youth did he not kill a giant,
  and take away the people's disgrace,
  when he whirled the stone in the sling
  and struck down the boasting Goliath?
5 For he called on the Lord, the Most High,
  and he gave strength to his right arm
  to strike down a mighty warrior,
  and to exalt the power[d] of his people.
6 So they glorified him for the tens of thousands he
    conquered,
  and praised him for the blessings bestowed by
    the Lord,
  when the glorious diadem was given to him.
7 For he wiped out his enemies on every side,
  and annihilated his adversaries the Philistines;
  he crushed their power[d] to our own day.
8 In all that he did he gave thanks
    to the Holy One, the Most High, proclaiming
    his glory;
  he sang praise with all his heart,
  and he loved his Maker.
9 He placed singers before the altar,
  to make sweet melody with their voices.[e]
10 He gave beauty to the festivals,
  and arranged their times throughout the year,[f]
  while they praised God's[g] holy name,
  and the sanctuary resounded from early
    morning.
11 The Lord took away his sins,
  and exalted his power[d] forever;
  he gave him a covenant of kingship
  and a glorious throne in Israel.

12 After him a wise son rose up
  who because of him lived in security:[h]
13 Solomon reigned in an age of peace,
  because God made all his borders tranquil,
  so that he might build a house in his name
  and provide a sanctuary to stand forever.
14 How wise you were when you were young!
  You overflowed like the Nile[i] with
    understanding.

making his voice heard in a mighty sound,
18 and routed the leaders of the enemy,
  all the lords of the Philistines.
19 Before the time came for his eternal sleep,
  Samuel called the Lord and his anointed to witness:
  'I have never taken anyone's property,
  not so much as a pair of shoes';
  and no man brought any charge against him.
20 Even after he had gone to his rest he prophesied
  and made the king's fate known to him,
  lifting up his voice in prophecy from the ground
  to wipe out the wickedness of the people.

47 After him there arose Nathan
  to prophesy in the reign of David.
2 As the choice fat is set aside from the sacrifice,
  so David was chosen out of all Israel.
3 He disported himself with lions as though they
    were young goats,
  with bears as though they were lambs.
4 While still a youth he killed a giant
  and removed the shame of his people,
  when he whirled his sling with its stone
  and brought down the arrogant Goliath;
5 for he called to the Lord Most High,
  who gave strength to his right arm
  to strike that mighty warrior down
6 and win victory for his people.
  So they hailed him as conqueror of tens of
    thousands,
  and sang his praises for the blessings bestowed by
    the Lord.
  When he assumed the glorious crown,
7 he fought and subdued enemies on every side;
  he crushed the resistance of the Philistines,
  whose power remains broken to this day.
8 In all he did he gave thanks,
  ascribing glory to the Holy One, the Most High;
  with all his heart he sang hymns of praise
  to show his love for his Maker.
9 He appointed musicians to stand before the altar
  and sing sweet music to the harp.
10 He ordered the festivals with dignity
  and fixed for all time the round of sacred seasons,
  when the Lord's holy name is praised
  and the sanctuary resounds from dawn to dusk.
11 The Lord pardoned his sins
  and endowed him with great power for ever:
  by a covenant he gave him the kingship
  and a glorious throne in Israel.

12 He was succeeded by a wise son, Solomon;
  thanks to David his father, he lived in spacious
    days.
13 He reigned in an age of peace,
  because on every side God gave him tranquillity,
  that he might build a house in God's honour,
  a sanctuary founded to last for ever.
14 How wise you were, Solomon, in your youth,
  full of understanding like a brimming river!

---

[b] Heb: Gk leaders of the people of Tyre   [c] Gk he   [d] Gk horn
[e] Other ancient authorities add and daily they sing his praises
[f] Gk to completion   [g] Gk his   [h] Heb: Gk in a broad place
[i] Heb: Gk a river

46:18 the enemy: so Heb.; Gk Tyre.

and the tremendous roar of his voice was heard.
18 He brought low the rulers of the enemy
and destroyed all the lords of the Philistines.
19 When Samuel approached the end of his life,
he testified before the LORD and his
anointed prince,
"No bribe or secret gift have I taken from
any man!"
and no one dared gainsay him.
20 Even when he lay buried, his guidance was sought;
he made known to the king his fate,
And from the grave he raised his voice
as a prophet, to put an end to wickedness.

47 After him came NATHAN
who served in the presence of David.
2 Like the choice fat of the sacred offerings,
so was DAVID in Israel.
3 He made sport of lions as though they were kids,
and of bears, like lambs of the flock.
4 As a youth he slew the giant
and wiped out the people's disgrace,
When his hand let fly the slingstone
that crushed the pride of Goliath.
5 Since he called upon the Most High God,
who gave strength to his right arm
To defeat the skilled warrior
and raise up the might of his people,
6 Therefore the women sang his praises
and ascribed to him tens of thousands.
When he assumed the royal crown, he battled
7 and subdued the enemy on every side.
He destroyed the hostile Philistines
and shattered their power till our own day.
8 With his every deed he offered thanks
to God Most High, in words of praise.
With his whole being he loved his Maker
and daily had his praises sung;
9 He added beauty to the feasts
and solemnized the seasons of each year
With string music before the altar,
providing sweet melody for the psalms
10 So that when the Holy Name was praised,
before daybreak the sanctuary would resound.
11 The LORD forgave him his sins
and exalted his strength forever;
He conferred on him the rights of royalty
and established his throne in Israel.
12 Because of his merits he had as his successor
a wise son, who lived in security:
13 SOLOMON reigned during an era of peace,
for God made tranquil all his borders.
He built a house to the name of God,
and established a lasting sanctuary.
14 How wise you were when you were young,
overflowing with instruction, like the Nile
in flood!

and made his voice heard in a rolling peal;
18 he massacred the leaders of the enemy,
and all the rulers of the Philistines.
19 Before the time of his everlasting rest
he bore witness to the Lord and his anointed,
'Of no property, not even a pair of sandals,
have I ever deprived a soul.'
Nor did anyone accuse him.
20 And, having fallen asleep, he prophesied again,
warning the king of his end;
he spoke from the depths of the earth in prophecy,
to blot out the wickedness of the people.

47 After him arose Nathan,
to prophesy in the time of David.
2 As the fat is set apart from the communion
sacrifice,
so was David chosen out of the Israelites.
3 He played with lions as though with kids,
and with bears as though with lambs.
4 While still a boy, did he not slay the giant
and take away the people's shame,
by hurling a stone from his sling
and cutting short the boasting of Goliath?
5 For he called on the Lord Most High,
who gave strength to his right arm
to put a mighty warrior to death
and assert the strength of his own people.
6 Hence they gave him credit for ten thousand,
and praised him while they blessed the Lord,
by offering him a crown of glory.
7 For he destroyed the enemies on every front,
he annihilated his foes, the Philistines,
and crushed their strength for ever.
8 In all his activities he gave thanks
to the Holy One Most High in words of glory;
he put all his heart into his songs
out of love for his Creator.
9 He placed singers before the altar,
melodiously to sing;
10 he gave the feasts their splendour,
the festivals their solemn pomp,
causing the Lord's holy name to be praised
and the sanctuary to resound from dawn.
11 The Lord took away his sins,
making his strength ever greater;
he gave him a royal covenant,
and a glorious throne in Israel.
12 A wise son succeeded him,
who lived content, thanks to him.
13 Solomon reigned in a time of peace,
and God gave him peace all round
so that he could raise a house to his name
and prepare an everlasting sanctuary.
14 How wise you were despite your youth,
like a river, brimming over with intelligence!

15 Your influence spread throughout the earth,
　　and you filled it with proverbs having deep
　　　meaning.
16 Your fame reached to far-off islands,
　　and you were loved for your peaceful reign.
17 Your songs, proverbs, and parables,
　　and the answers you gave astounded the
　　　nations.
18 In the name of the Lord God,
　　who is called the God of Israel,
　　you gathered gold like tin
　　and amassed silver like lead.
19 But you brought in women to lie at your side,
　　and through your body you were brought into
　　　subjection.
20 You stained your honor,
　　and defiled your family line,
　　so that you brought wrath upon your children,
　　and they were grieved*j* at your folly,
21 because the sovereignty was divided
　　and a rebel kingdom arose out of Ephraim.
22 But the Lord will never give up his mercy,
　　or cause any of his works to perish;
　　he will never blot out the descendants of his
　　　chosen one,
　　or destroy the family line of him who loved
　　　him.
　　So he gave a remnant to Jacob,
　　and to David a root from his own family.
23 Solomon rested with his ancestors,
　　and left behind him one of his sons,
　　broad in*k* folly and lacking in sense,
　　Rehoboam, whose policy drove the people to
　　　revolt.
　　Then Jeroboam son of Nebat led Israel into sin
　　and started Ephraim on its sinful ways.
24 Their sins increased more and more,
　　until they were exiled from their land.
25 For they sought out every kind of wickedness,
　　until vengeance came upon them.

48 Then Elijah arose, a prophet like fire,
　　　and his word burned like a torch.
2 He brought a famine upon them,
　　and by his zeal he made them few in number.
3 By the word of the Lord he shut up the heavens,
　　and also three times brought down fire.
4 How glorious you were, Elijah, in your wondrous
　　　deeds!
　　Whose glory is equal to yours?
5 You raised a corpse from death
　　and from Hades, by the word of the Most High.
6 You sent kings down to destruction,
　　and famous men, from their sickbeds.
7 You heard rebuke at Sinai
　　and judgments of vengeance at Horeb.
8 You anointed kings to inflict retribution,
　　and prophets to succeed you.*l*
9 You were taken up by a whirlwind of fire,
　　in a chariot with horses of fire.
10 At the appointed time, it is written, you are
　　　destined*m*
　　to calm the wrath of God before it breaks out
　　　in fury,
　　to turn the hearts of parents to their children,
　　and to restore the tribes of Jacob.

15 Your mind embraced the whole world,
　　and you stored it with proverbs and riddles.
16 Your fame reached distant islands,
　　and you were beloved for your peaceful reign.
17 Your songs, your sayings, your proverbs,
　　and the answers you gave were the wonders of the
　　　world.
18 In the name of the Lord God,
　　who is known as the God of Israel,
　　you amassed gold and silver
　　like so much tin and lead.
19 But you took women to lie at your side
　　and let them usurp your authority.
20 You stained your reputation
　　and tainted your line.
　　You brought God's wrath on your children
　　and there was outrage at your folly,
21 because it divided the sovereignty
　　and in Ephraim a rebel dynasty came to power.
22 But the Lord never ceases to be merciful;
　　he does not destroy what he himself has made;
　　he will never wipe out the offspring of his chosen
　　　servant
　　or cut short the line of one who has loved him.
　　So he granted a remnant to Jacob
　　and let a scion of David survive.

23 When Solomon rested with his forefathers,
　　he left one of his sons to succeed him,
　　a man of weak mind, the fool of the nation,
　　Rehoboam, whose policy drove the people to
　　　revolt.
　　Jeroboam son of Nebat led Israel into sin
　　and started Ephraim on its wicked course.
24 Their sins increased beyond measure
　　until they were driven into exile from their native
　　　land;
25 they explored every kind of wickedness
　　until punishment overtook them.

48 Then there arose Elijah, a prophet like fire,
　　　whose word blazed like a torch.
2 He brought famine on the people,
　　and in his zeal reduced them in number.
3 By the word of the Lord he shut up the sky,
　　and three times he called down fire from heaven.
4 How glorious you were, Elijah, in your miracles!
　　Who else can boast such deeds?
5 By the word of the Most High
　　you raised a corpse from death and the grave.
6 You sent kings and famous men
　　from their sick-beds down to destruction.
7 You heard a rebuke at Sinai,
　　a sentence of doom at Horeb.
8 You anointed kings for retribution,
　　and a prophet to succeed you.
9 You were taken up to heaven in a fiery whirlwind,
　　in a chariot drawn by horses of fire.
10 Scripture records that you are to come at the
　　　appointed time
　　to allay the divine wrath before it erupts in fury,
　　to reconcile father and son,
　　and to restore the tribes of Jacob.

---

j Other ancient authorities read *I was grieved*　　*k* Heb (with a play on
the name Rehoboam) Syr: Gk *the people's*　　*l* Heb: Gk *him*
m Heb: Gk *are for reproofs*

15 Your understanding covered the whole earth,
  and, like a sea, filled it with knowledge.
16 Your fame reached distant coasts,
  and their peoples came to hear you;
17 With song and story and riddle,
  and with your answers, you astounded
    the nations.
18 You were called by that glorious name
  which was conferred upon Israel.
Gold you gathered like so much iron,
  you heaped up silver as though it were lead;
19 But you abandoned yourself to women
  and gave them dominion over your body.
20 You brought dishonor upon your reputation,
  shame upon your marriage,
Wrath upon your descendants,
  and groaning upon your domain;
21 Thus two governments came into being,
  when in Ephraim kingship was usurped.
22 But God does not withdraw his mercy,
  nor permit even one of his promises to fail.
He does not uproot the posterity of his chosen one,
  nor destroy the offspring of his friend.
So he gave to Jacob a remnant,
  to David a root from his own family.
23 Solomon finally slept with his fathers,
  and left behind him one of his sons,
Expansive in folly, limited in sense,
  REHOBOAM, who by his policy made the
    people rebel;
Until one arose who should not be remembered,
  the sinner who led Israel into sin,
Who brought ruin to Ephraim
24 and caused them to be exiled from their land.
Their sinfulness grew more and more,
25 and they lent themselves to every evil,

48 Till like a fire there appeared the prophet
  whose words were as a flaming furnace.
2 Their staff of bread he shattered,
  in his zeal he reduced them to straits;
3 By God's word he shut up the heavens
  and three times brought down fire.
4 How awesome are you, ELIJAH!
  Whose glory is equal to yours?
5 You brought a dead man back to life
  from the nether world, by the will of the LORD.
6 You sent kings down to destruction,
  and nobles, from their beds of sickness.
7 You heard threats at Sinai,
  at Horeb avenging judgments.
8 You anointed kings who should inflict vengeance,
  and a prophet as your successor.
9 You were taken aloft in a whirlwind,
  in a chariot with fiery horses.
10 You are destined, it is written, in time to come
  to put an end to wrath before the day of
    the LORD,
To turn back the hearts of fathers toward
    their sons,
  and to re-establish the tribes of Jacob.

15 Your mind ranged the earth,
  you filled it with mysterious sayings.
16 Your name reached the distant islands,
  and you were loved for your peace.[l]
17 Your songs, your proverbs, your sayings
  and your answers were the wonder of the world.
18 In the name of the Lord God,
  of him who is called the God of Israel,
you amassed gold like so much tin,
  and made silver as common as lead.
19 You abandoned your body to women,
  you became the slave of your appetites.
20 You stained your honour,
  you profaned your stock,
so bringing retribution on your children
  and affliction for your folly:
21 the empire split in two,
  from Ephraim arose a rebel kingdom.
22 But the Lord never goes back on his mercy,
  never cancels any of his words,
will neither deny offspring to his elect
  nor stamp out the line of the man who loved
    him.
And hence, he has granted a remnant to Jacob
  and to David a root sprung from him.
23 Solomon rested with his ancestors,
  leaving one of his stock as his successor,
the stupidest member of the nation,
  brainless Rehoboam, who drove the people to
    rebel.
24 Next, Jeroboam son of Nebat, who made Israel
    sin,
  and set Ephraim on the way of evil;
from then on their sins multiplied so excessively
  as to drive them out of their country;
25 for they tried out every kind of wickedness,
  until vengeance overtook them.

48 Then the prophet Elijah arose like a fire,
  his word flaring like a torch.
2 It was he who brought famine on them
  and decimated them in his zeal.
3 By the word of the Lord he shut up the heavens,
  three times also he brought down fire.
4 How glorious you were in your miracles, Elijah!
  Has anyone reason to boast as you have? —
5 rousing a corpse from death,
  from Sheol, by the word of the Most High;
6 dragging kings down to destruction,
  and high dignitaries from their beds;
7 hearing a rebuke on Sinai
  and decrees of punishment on Horeb;
8 anointing kings as avengers,
  and prophets to succeed you;
9 taken up in the whirlwind of fire,
  in a chariot with fiery horses;
10 designated in the prophecies of doom
  to allay God's wrath before the fury breaks,
  to turn the hearts of fathers towards their
    children,[m]
  and to restore the tribes of Jacob.

l **47** Solomon means 'man of peace'. *m* **48** Ml 3:24.

NEW REVISED STANDARD VERSION	REVISED ENGLISH BIBLE

NEW REVISED STANDARD VERSION

11 Happy are those who saw you
    and were adorned[n] with your love!
    For we also shall surely live.[o]
12 When Elijah was enveloped in the whirlwind,
    Elisha was filled with his spirit.
    He performed twice as many signs,
    and marvels with every utterance of his
        mouth.[p]
    Never in his lifetime did he tremble before any
        ruler,
    nor could anyone intimidate him at all.
13 Nothing was too hard for him,
    and when he was dead, his body prophesied.
14 In his life he did wonders,
    and in death his deeds were marvelous.
15 Despite all this the people did not repent,
    nor did they forsake their sins,
    until they were carried off as plunder from their
        land,
    and were scattered over all the earth.
    The people were left very few in number,
    but with a ruler from the house of David.
16 Some of them did what was right,
    but others sinned more and more.
17 Hezekiah fortified his city,
    and brought water into its midst;
    he tunneled the rock with iron tools,
    and built cisterns for the water.
18 In his days Sennacherib invaded the country;
    he sent his commander[q] and departed;
    he shook his fist against Zion,
    and made great boasts in his arrogance.
19 Then their hearts were shaken and their hands
        trembled,
    and they were in anguish, like women in labor.
20 But they called upon the Lord who is merciful,
    spreading out their hands toward him.
    The Holy One quickly heard them from heaven,
    and delivered them through Isaiah.
21 The Lord[r] struck down the camp of the
        Assyrians,
    and his angel wiped them out.
22 For Hezekiah did what was pleasing to the Lord,
    and he kept firmly to the ways of his ancestor
        David,
    as he was commanded by the prophet Isaiah,
    who was great and trustworthy in his visions.
23 In Isaiah's[s] days the sun went backward,
    and he prolonged the life of the king.
24 By his dauntless spirit he saw the future,
    and comforted the mourners in Zion.
25 He revealed what was to occur to the end of
        time,
    and the hidden things before they happened.

49 The name[t] of Josiah is like blended incense
    prepared by the skill of the perfumer;
    his memory[u] is as sweet as honey to every
        mouth,
    and like music at a banquet of wine.
2 He did what was right by reforming the people,
    and removing the wicked abominations.
3 He kept his heart fixed on the Lord;
    in lawless times he made godliness prevail.

REVISED ENGLISH BIBLE

11 Happy are those who see you,
    happy those who have fallen asleep in love!
    (For we also shall certainly live.)
12 After Elijah had vanished in a whirlwind,
    Elisha was filled with his spirit.
    Throughout his life no ruler made him tremble,
    no one lorded it over him.
13 Nothing was too difficult for him,
    and even in the grave his body kept its prophetic
        power.
14 In life he worked miracles;
    in death also his deeds were marvellous.
15 Despite all this the people did not repent
    or renounce their sins,
    until they were carried off captive from their land
    and scattered over the whole world.
    Only a very small nation was left
    under a ruler from the house of David;
16 some of them did what was pleasing to the Lord,
    but others committed sin upon sin.
17 Hezekiah fortified his city
    and brought water within its walls;
    with tools of iron he cut through sheer rock
    and made cisterns for the water.
18 In his reign Sennacherib invaded the country,
    and from Lachish sent Rab-shakeh,
    who came with threats against Zion,
    boasting loudly in his arrogance.
19 At this the people were unnerved in heart and
        hand,
    and suffered the anguish of a woman in labour;
20 they called to the merciful Lord,
    holding out their hands to him in supplication.
    From heaven the Holy One quickly answered their
        prayer:
    he sent Isaiah to the rescue;
21 he struck at the camp of the Assyrians
    and his angel destroyed them.
22 For Hezekiah did what was pleasing to the Lord
    and held firmly to the ways of David his ancestor
    as he was instructed to do by Isaiah,
    the great prophet whose vision could be trusted.
23 In his time the sun went back,
    and he added many years to the king's life.
24 With inspired power he saw the future
    and comforted the mourners in Zion.
25 He revealed what was to be until the end of time,
    the secrets of things still to come.

49 The memory of Josiah is fragrant as incense
    blended by the perfumer's craft,
    sweet as honey to every palate
    or like music at a banquet.
2 He followed a right course, reforming the nation
    and rooting out loathsome and lawless practices.
3 He was wholeheartedly loyal to the Lord
    and in a lawless age made godliness prevail.

---

n Other ancient authorities read *and have died*   o Text and meaning
of Gk uncertain   p Heb: Gk lacks *He performed . . . mouth*
q Other ancient authorities add *from Lachish*   r Gk *He*   s Gk *his*
t Heb: Gk *memory*   u Heb: Gk *it*

NEW AMERICAN BIBLE

11 Blessed is he who shall have seen you before
he dies,
12   O Elijah, enveloped in the whirlwind!

Then ELISHA, filled with a twofold portion of
his spirit,
wrought many marvels by his mere word.
During his lifetime he feared no one,
nor was any man able to intimidate his will.
13 Nothing was beyond his power;
beneath him flesh was brought back into life.
14 In life he performed wonders,
and after death, marvelous deeds.
15 Despite all this the people did not repent,
nor did they give up their sins,
Until they were rooted out of their land
and scattered all over the earth.
But Judah remained, a tiny people,
with its rulers from the house of David.
16 Some of these did what was right,
but others were extremely sinful.

17 HEZEKIAH fortified his city
and had water brought into it;
With iron tools he cut through the rock
and he built reservoirs for water.
18 During his reign Sennacherib led an invasion,
and sent his adjutant;
He shook his fist at Zion
and blasphemed God in his pride.
19 The people's hearts melted within them,
and they were in anguish like that of childbirth.
20 But they called upon the Most High God
and lifted up their hands to him;
He heard the prayer they uttered,
and saved them through ISAIAH.
21 God struck the camp of the Assyrians
and routed them with a plague.
22 For Hezekiah did what was right
and held fast to the paths of David,
As ordered by the illustrious prophet
Isaiah, who saw the truth in visions.
23 In his lifetime he turned back the sun
and prolonged the life of the king.
24 By his powerful spirit he looked into the future
and consoled the mourners of Zion;
25 He foretold what should be till the end of time,
hidden things yet to be fulfilled.

NEW JERUSALEM BIBLE

11 Blessed, those who will see you,
and those who have fallen asleep in love;
for we too shall certainly have life.
12 Such was Elijah, who was enveloped in a
whirlwind;
and Elisha was filled with his spirit;
throughout his life no ruler could shake him,
and no one could subdue him.
13 No task was too hard for him,
and even in death his body prophesied.
14 In his lifetime he performed wonders,
and in death his works were marvellous.

15 Despite all this the people did not repent,
nor did they give up their sins,
until they were herded out of their country
and scattered all over the earth;
16 only a few of the people were left,
with a ruler of the House of David.
Some of them did what pleased the Lord,
others piled sin on sin.

17 Hezekiah fortified his city,
and laid on a water-supply inside it;
with iron he tunnelled through the rock
and constructed storage-tanks.
18 In his days Sennacherib invaded
and sent Rabshakeh;
he lifted his hand against Zion,
and boasted loudly in his arrogance.
19 Then their hearts and hands trembled,
they felt the pangs of a woman in labour,
20 but they called on the merciful Lord,
stretching out their hands towards him.
Swiftly the Holy One heard them from heaven
and delivered them by the agency of Isaiah;
21 he struck the camp of the Assyrians
and his Angel annihilated them.
22 For Hezekiah did what is pleasing to the Lord,
and was steadfast[n] in the ways of David his
father,
enjoined on him by the prophet Isaiah,
a great man trustworthy in his vision.
23 In his days the sun moved back;
he prolonged the life of the king.
24 In the power of the spirit he saw the last things,
he comforted the mourners of Zion,
25 he revealed the future to the end of time,
and hidden things long before they happened.

49 The name JOSIAH is like blended incense,
made lasting by a skilled perfumer.
Precious is his memory, like honey to the taste,
like music at a banquet.
2 For he grieved over our betrayals
and destroyed the abominable idols.
3 He turned to God with his whole heart,
and, though times were evil, he practiced virtue.

49 The memory of Josiah is like blended incense
prepared by the perfumer's art;
it is as sweet as honey to all mouths,
and like music at a wine feast.
2 He took the right course, of converting the people,
he rooted out the iniquitous abominations,
3 he set his heart on the Lord,
in godless times he upheld the cause of religion.

---

[n] 48 Word-play on 'Hezekiah' (= Yahweh makes strong).

4 Except for David and Hezekiah and Josiah,
　　all of them were great sinners,
　for they abandoned the law of the Most High;
　　the kings of Judah came to an end.
5 They[v] gave their power to others,
　　and their glory to a foreign nation,
6 who set fire to the chosen city of the sanctuary,
　　and made its streets desolate,
　　as Jeremiah had foretold.[w]
7 For they had mistreated him,
　　who even in the womb had been consecrated a
　　　prophet,
　to pluck up and ruin and destroy,
　　and likewise to build and to plant.

8 It was Ezekiel who saw the vision of glory,
　　which God[x] showed him above the chariot of
　　　the cherubim.
9 For God[y] also mentioned Job
　　who held fast to all the ways of justice.[z]
10 May the bones of the Twelve Prophets
　　send forth new life from where they lie,
　for they comforted the people of Jacob
　　and delivered them with confident hope.

11 How shall we magnify Zerubbabel?
　　He was like a signet ring on the right hand,
12 and so was Jeshua son of Jozadak;
　in their days they built the house
　　and raised a temple[a] holy to the Lord,
　　destined for everlasting glory.
13 The memory of Nehemiah also is lasting;
　　he raised our fallen walls,
　and set up gates and bars,
　　and rebuilt our ruined houses.

14 Few have[b] ever been created on earth like
　　Enoch,
　　for he was taken up from the earth.
15 Nor was anyone ever born like Joseph;[c]
　　even his bones were cared for.
16 Shem and Seth and Enosh were honored,[d]
　　but above every other created living being was
　　Adam.

50 The leader of his brothers and the pride of his
　　people[e]
　was the high priest, Simon son of Onias,
　who in his life repaired the house,
　　and in his time fortified the temple.
2 He laid the foundations for the high double walls,
　　the high retaining walls for the temple
　　　enclosure.
3 In his days a water cistern was dug,[f]
　　a reservoir like the sea in circumference.
4 He considered how to save his people from ruin,
　　and fortified the city against siege.
5 How glorious he was, surrounded by the people,
　　as he came out of the house of the curtain.
6 Like the morning star among the clouds,
　　like the full moon at the festal season;[f]

4 Except David, Hezekiah, and Josiah,
　　all were guilty of wrongdoing,
　for all abandoned the law of the Most High.
　So the royal line of Judah came to an end;
5 they surrendered their power to others
　　and their glory to a foreign nation.
6 The chosen city, the city of the sanctuary, was set
　　on fire,
　and its streets were left deserted, as Jeremiah had
　　foretold.
7 He was maltreated,
　　even though he was a prophet consecrated from the
　　　womb
　to uproot, to damage, and to demolish,
　　but also to build and to plant.

8 There was revealed to Ezekiel a vision of the Glory
　　which was enthroned on the chariot of the
　　　cherubim.
9 The Lord remembered his enemies and sent a
　　storm,
　but to those who kept to the right path he brought
　　benefits.
10 May the bones of the twelve prophets also
　　send forth new life from the grave!
　For they put new heart into Jacob,
　　and by their confident hope delivered the people.

11 How can we tell the greatness of Zerubbabel,
　　who was like a signet ring on the Lord's right
　　　hand?
12 Jeshua son of Jozadak was with him,
　　and in their day they rebuilt the house,
　　erecting a temple holy to the Lord,
　　destined for eternal glory.
13 Great also is the memory of Nehemiah,
　　who restored for us the fallen walls,
　　who reconstructed their barred gates,
　　and built again our ruined homes.

14 No one to equal Enoch has been created on earth,
　　for from the earth he was taken up into heaven.
15 No man has been born to be Joseph's peer,
　　the ruler of his brothers and the support of the
　　　people;
　over his bones watch was kept.
16 Shem and Seth were honoured among men,
　　but Adam holds pre-eminence over all creation.

50 Greatest among his brothers and the glory of his
　　people
　was the high priest Simon son of Onias
　in whose lifetime the house was repaired,
　in whose days the temple was fortified.
2 He laid the foundation for the high double wall,
　　the high retaining wall of the temple precinct.
3 In his day a reservoir was dug,
　　a cistern broad as the sea.
4 He was concerned to ward off disaster from his
　　people
　and made the city strong against siege.
5 How glorious he was as he processed through the
　　temple,
　emerging from behind the veil of the sanctuary!
6 He was like the morning star appearing through a
　　cloud
　or the full moon on festal days;

v Heb He　　w Gk by the hand of Jeremiah　　x Gk He　　y Gk he
z Heb Compare Syr: Meaning of Gk uncertain　　a Other ancient
authorities read people　　b Heb Syr: Gk No one has　　c Heb Syr:
Gk adds the leader of his brothers, the support of the people
d Heb: Gk Shem and Seth were honored by people　　e Heb Syr: Gk
lacks this line. Compare 49.15　　f Heb: Meaning of Gk uncertain

4 Except for David, Hezekiah and Josiah,
   they all were wicked;
They abandoned the law of the Most High,
   these kings of Judah, right to the very end.
5 So he gave over their power to others,
   their glory to a foolish foreign nation
6 Who burned the holy city
   and left its streets desolate,
As JEREMIAH had foretold; 7 for they had treated
   him badly
who even in the womb had been made
   a prophet,
To root out, pull down, and destroy,
   and then to build and to plant.
8 EZEKIEL beheld the vision
   and described the different creatures of
     the chariot;
9 He also referred to JOB,
   who always persevered in the right path.
10 Then, too, the TWELVE PROPHETS —
   may their bones return to life from their
     resting place! —
Gave new strength to Jacob
   and saved him by their faith and hope.

11 How can we fittingly praise ZERUBBABEL,
   who was like a signet ring on God's right hand,
12 And Jeshua, Jozadak's son?
   In their time they built the house of God;
They erected the holy temple,
   destined for everlasting glory.
13 Extolled be the memory of NEHEMIAH!
   He rebuilt our ruined walls,
Restored our shattered defenses,
   and set up gates and bars.

14 Few on earth have been made the equal of ENOCH,
   for he was taken up bodily.
15 Was ever a man born like JOSEPH?
   Even his dead body was provided for.
16 Glorious, too, were SHEM and SETH and ENOS;
   but beyond that of any living being
   was the splendor of ADAM.

50 The greatest among his brethren, the glory of
     his people,
   was SIMON the priest, son of Jochanan,
In whose time the house of God was renovated,
   in whose days the temple was reinforced.
2 In his time also the wall was built
   with powerful turrets for the temple precincts;
3 In his time the reservoir was dug,
   the pool with a vastness like the sea's.
4 He protected his people against brigands
   and strengthened his city against the enemy.
5 How splendid he was as he appeared from the tent,
   as he came from within the veil!
6 Like a star shining among the clouds,
   like the full moon at the holyday season;

4 Apart from David, Hezekiah and Josiah,
   they all heaped wrong on wrong,
they abandoned the Law of the Most High:
   the kings of Judah disappeared;
5 for they handed their power over to others
   and their honour to a foreign nation.
6 The holy, chosen city was burnt down,
   her streets were left deserted;
7 as Jeremiah had predicted; for they had ill-treated
   him,
though consecrated a prophet in his mother's
     womb,
to tear up and afflict *and destroy,*
   but also *to build up and to plant.o*
8 Ezekiel saw a vision of glory
   which God showed to him
     above the chariot of the great winged
     creatures,
9 for he mentioned the enemies in the downpour
   to the advantage of those who follow the right
     way.
10 As for the twelve prophets,
   may their bones flower again from the tomb,
since they have comforted Jacob
   and redeemed him in faith and hope.

11 How shall we extol Zerubbabel?
   He was like a signet ring on the right hand,
12 so too was Joshua son of Jozadak;
   they who in their days built the Temple
and raised a sanctuary sacred to the Lord,
   destined to everlasting glory.
13 Great too is the memory of Nehemiah,
   who rebuilt our walls which lay in ruins,
erected the bolted gates
   and rebuilt our houses.

14 No one else has ever been created on earth to
     equal Enoch,
   for he was taken up from earth.
15 And no one else ever born has been like Joseph,
   the leader of his brothers, the prop of his people;
   his bones received a visitation.
16 Shem and Seth were the most honoured of men,
   but above every living creature is Adam.

50 It was the High Priest Simon son of Onias p
     who repaired the Temple during his lifetime
   and in his day fortified the sanctuary.
2 He laid the foundations of double depth,
   the high buttresses of the Temple precincts.
3 In his day the pool was excavated,
   a reservoir as huge as the sea.
4 Anxious to save the people from ruin,
   he fortified the city against siege.
5 How splendid he was with the people thronging
     round him,
   when he emerged from the curtained shrine,
6 like the morning star among the clouds,
   like the moon at the full,

o **49** Jr 1:10.   p **50** Simon II, son of Onias III, high priest c.
220–195 BC.

NEW REVISED STANDARD VERSION	REVISED ENGLISH BIBLE

7 like the sun shining on the temple of the Most
 High,
 like the rainbow gleaming in splendid clouds;
8 like roses in the days of first fruits,
 like lilies by a spring of water,
 like a green shoot on Lebanon on a summer
 day;
9 like fire and incense in the censer,
 like a vessel of hammered gold
 studded with all kinds of precious stones;
10 like an olive tree laden with fruit,
 and like a cypress towering in the clouds.
11 When he put on his glorious robe
 and clothed himself in perfect splendor,
 when he went up to the holy altar,
 he made the court of the sanctuary glorious.

12 When he received the portions from the hands of
 the priests,
 as he stood by the hearth of the altar
with a garland of brothers around him,
 he was like a young cedar on Lebanon
 surrounded by the trunks of palm trees.
13 All the sons of Aaron in their splendor
 held the Lord's offering in their hands
 before the whole congregation of Israel.
14 Finishing the service at the altars,*g*
 and arranging the offering to the Most High,
 the Almighty,
15 he held out his hand for the cup
 and poured a drink offering of the blood of the
 grape;
he poured it out at the foot of the altar,
 a pleasing odor to the Most High, the king of
 all.
16 Then the sons of Aaron shouted;
 they blew their trumpets of hammered metal;
 they sounded a mighty fanfare
 as a reminder before the Most High.
17 Then all the people together quickly
 fell to the ground on their faces
 to worship their Lord,
 the Almighty, God Most High.
18 Then the singers praised him with their voices
 in sweet and full-toned melody.*h*
19 And the people of the Lord Most High offered
 their prayers before the Merciful One,
 until the order of worship of the Lord was ended,
 and they completed his ritual.
20 Then Simon*i* came down and raised his hands
 over the whole congregation of Israelites,
 to pronounce the blessing of the Lord with his
 lips,
 and to glory in his name;
21 and they bowed down in worship a second time,
 to receive the blessing from the Most High.

22 And now bless the God of all,
 who everywhere works great wonders,
 who fosters our growth from birth,
 and deals with us according to his mercy.
23 May he give us*j* gladness of heart,
 and may there be peace in our*k* days
 in Israel, as in the days of old.
24 May he entrust to us his mercy,
 and may he deliver us in our*l* days!

7 like the sun shining on the temple of the Most
 High
 or the light of the rainbow on the gleaming clouds;
8 like a rose in springtime
 or lilies by a fountain of water;
 like a green shoot upon Lebanon on a summer's
 day
9 or frankincense burning in the censer;
 like a cup all of beaten gold,
 decorated with every kind of precious stone;
10 like an olive tree laden with fruit
 or a cypress with its summit in the clouds.
11 When he assumed his resplendent vestments,
 robing himself in full and proud array,
 he went up to the holy altar,
 adding lustre to the court of the sanctuary.

12 While he received the sacrificial portions from the
 priests,
 as he stood by the altar hearth
 with his brother priests around him like a garland,
 he was like a young cedar of Lebanon
 in the midst of encircling palms.
13 All the priests of Aaron's line in their splendour
 stood before the whole assembly of Israel,
 holding the Lord's offering in their hands.
14 To complete the ceremonies at the altar
 and adorn the offering of the Most High, the
 Almighty,
15 he reached out his hand for the cup
 and made the libation from the blood of the grape,
 pouring its fragrance at the base of the altar
 to the Most High, the King of all.
16 Then the priests of Aaron's line shouted
 and blew their trumpets of beaten silver;
 they sounded a mighty fanfare
 as a reminder before the Most High.
17 At once all the people prostrated themselves
 to worship their Lord, the Almighty, God Most
 High.
18 The choir broke into praise,
 in the full, sweet strains of resounding song,
19 while the people were making their petitions
 to the Lord Most High, the Merciful One,
 until the liturgy of the Lord was finished
 and the ritual complete.
20 Then Simon came down and raised his hands
 over the whole congregation of Israel
 to pronounce the Lord's blessing
 and to glory in his name;
21 and again they bowed in worship
 to receive the blessing from the Most High.

22 Now COME, let us praise the God of the universe,
 who everywhere works great wonders,
 who from our birth raises us up
 and deals with us in mercy.
23 May he grant us a joyful heart,
 and in our days send Israel lasting peace.
24 May he confirm his mercy towards us,
 and in his own good time grant us deliverance.

g Other ancient authorities read *altar*   h Other ancient authorities
read *in sweet melody throughout the house*   i Gk *he*   j Other
ancient authorities read *you*   k Other ancient authorities read *your*
l Other ancient authorities read *his*

7 Like the sun shining upon the temple,
   like the rainbow appearing in the cloudy sky;
8 Like the blossoms on the branches in springtime,
   like a lily on the banks of a stream;
   Like the trees of Lebanon in summer,
9   like the fire of incense at the sacrifice;
   Like a vessel of beaten gold,
      studded with precious stones;
10 Like a luxuriant olive tree thick with fruit,
   like a cypress standing against the clouds;
11 Vested in his magnificent robes,
   and wearing his garments of splendor,
   As he ascended the glorious altar
      and lent majesty to the court of the sanctuary.

12 When he received the sundered victims from
      the priests
   while he stood before the sacrificial wood,
   His brethren ringed him about like a garland,
      like a stand of cedars on Lebanon;
13 All the sons of Aaron in their dignity
   clustered around him like poplars,
   With the offerings to the LORD in their hands,
      in the presence of the whole assembly of Israel.
14 Once he had completed the services at the altar
   with the arranging of the sacrifices for the
      Most High,
15 And had stretched forth his hand for the cup,
   to offer blood of the grape,
   And poured it out at the foot of the altar,
      a sweet-smelling odor to the Most High God,
16 The sons of Aaron would sound a blast,
   the priests, on their trumpets of beaten metal;
   A blast to resound mightily
      as a reminder before the Most High.
17 Then all the people with one accord
   would quickly fall prostrate to the ground
   In adoration before the Most High,
      before the Holy One of Israel.

18 Then hymns would re-echo,
   and over the throng sweet strains of
      praise resound.
19 All the people of the land would shout for joy,
   praying to the Merciful One,
   As the high priest completed the services at
      the altar
   by presenting to God the sacrifice due;
20 Then coming down he would raise his hands
   over all the congregation of Israel.
   The blessing of the LORD would be upon his lips,
      the name of the LORD would be his glory.
21 Then again the people would lie prostrate
   to receive from him the blessing of the
      Most High.

22 And now, bless the God of all,
   who has done wondrous things on earth;
   Who fosters men's growth from their
      mother's womb,
   and fashions them according to his will!
23 May he grant you joy of heart
   and may peace abide among you;
24 May his goodness toward us endure in Israel
   as long as the heavens are above.

7 like the sun shining on the Temple of the Most
      High,
   like the rainbow gleaming against brilliant
      clouds,
8 like a rose in springtime,
   like a lily by a spring,
   like a branch of the incense tree in summer,
9   like fire and incense in the censer,
   like a massive golden vessel
      encrusted with every kind of precious stone,
10 like an olive tree loaded with fruit,
   like a cypress soaring to the clouds;
11 when he took his ceremonial robe
   and put on his magnificent ornaments,
   when he went up to the holy altar
      and filled the sanctuary precincts with his
         grandeur;
12 when he received the portions from the hands of
      the priests,
   himself standing by the altar hearth,
   crowned by the circle of his brothers,
      as a cedar of Lebanon is by its foliage,
   as though surrounded by the trunks of palm trees.
13   When all the sons of Aaron in their glory,
   with the offerings of the Lord in their hands,
      stood before the whole assembly of Israel,
14 while he completed the rites at the altars,
   nobly presenting the offerings to the Almighty,
      Most High!
15 He would reach out his hand to the cup
   and pour a libation of wine,
   pouring it at the foot of the altar,
      a fragrance pleasing to the Most High, King of
         All;
16 then the sons of Aaron would shout
   and blow their metal trumpets,
   making a mighty sound ring out
      as a reminder before the Most High;
17 and immediately the people all together
   would fall on their faces to the ground,
   in adoration of their Lord,
      the Almighty, God Most High,
18 and with the cantors chanting their hymns of
      praise.
   Sweet was the melody of all these voices,
19 as the people pleaded with the Lord Most High
   and prayed in the presence of the Merciful,
   until the service of the Lord was completed
      and the ceremony at an end.
20 Then he would come down and raise his hands
   over the whole assembly of the Israelites,
   to give them the Lord's blessing from his lips,
      being privileged to pronounce his name;
21 and once again the people would bow low
   to receive the blessing of the Most High.

22 And now bless the God of all things,
   the doer of great deeds everywhere,
   who has exalted our days from the womb
      and has acted mercifully towards us.
23 May he grant us cheerful hearts
   and bring peace in our time,
   in Israel for ages on ages.
24 May his mercy be faithfully with us,
   may he redeem us in our own times!

NEW REVISED STANDARD VERSION	REVISED ENGLISH BIBLE

NEW REVISED STANDARD VERSION

25 Two nations my soul detests,
   and the third is not even a people:
26 Those who live in Seir,[m] and the Philistines,
   and the foolish people that live in Shechem.

27 Instruction in understanding and knowledge
   I have written in this book,
   Jesus son of Eleazar son of Sirach[n] of Jerusalem,
   whose mind poured forth wisdom.
28 Happy are those who concern themselves with
      these things,
   and those who lay them to heart will become
      wise.
29 For if they put them into practice, they will be
      equal to anything,
   for the fear[o] of the Lord is their path.

PRAYER OF JESUS SON OF SIRACH[p]

51 I give you thanks, O Lord and King,
   and praise you, O God my Savior.
   I give thanks to your name,
2   for you have been my protector and helper
   and have delivered me from destruction
      and from the trap laid by a slanderous tongue,
      from lips that fabricate lies.
   In the face of my adversaries
      you have been my helper 3 and delivered me,
      in the greatness of your mercy and of your
         name,
   from grinding teeth about to devour me,
      from the hand of those seeking my life,
      from the many troubles I endured,
4 from choking fire on every side,
   and from the midst of fire that I had not
      kindled,
5 from the deep belly of Hades,
   from an unclean tongue and lying words —
6   the slander of an unrighteous tongue to the
         king.
   My soul drew near to death,
      and my life was on the brink of Hades below.
7 They surrounded me on every side,
      and there was no one to help me;
   I looked for human assistance,
      and there was none.
8 Then I remembered your mercy, O Lord,
      and your kindness[q] from of old,
   for you rescue those who wait for you
      and save them from the hand of their enemies.
9 And I sent up my prayer from the earth,
      and begged for rescue from death.
10 I cried out, "Lord, you are my Father;[r]
      do not forsake me in the days of trouble,
      when there is no help against the proud.
11 I will praise your name continually,
      and will sing hymns of thanksgiving."
   My prayer was heard,
12   for you saved me from destruction
      and rescued me in time of trouble.
   For this reason I thank you and praise you,
      and I bless the name of the Lord.

REVISED ENGLISH BIBLE

25 Two nations I detest,
   and a third is no nation at all:
26 the inhabitants of Mount Seir, the Philistines,
   and the senseless folk that live at Shechem.

27 I, Jesus son of Sirach Eleazar, of Jerusalem,
   whose mind became a fountain of wisdom,
   have provided in this book
   instruction in good sense and understanding.
28 Happy the man who occupies himself with these
      things,
   who lays them to heart and becomes wise!
29 If he follows them he will be equal to anything,
   for the light of the Lord will shine on his path.

51 I SHALL give thanks to you, Lord and King;
   I shall praise you, God my Saviour.
   I give thanks to you
2 because you have been my protector and my
      helper,
   rescuing me from destruction,
   from the trap laid by a slanderous tongue
   and from lips that invent lies.
   In the face of my assailants you came to my help;
3 in the fullness of your mercy and honour you
      rescued me
   from gnashing teeth waiting to devour me,
   from hands that threatened my life,
   from the many troubles I endured,
4 from the choking fire enveloping me,
   from flames I had not kindled,
5 from the deep recesses of the grave,
   from the foul tongue and the lying word —
6 a wicked slander spoken in the king's presence.
   I came very near to death,
   close to the brink of the grave.
7 On every side I was surrounded
   and there was no one to help;
   I looked for human aid and there was none.
8 Then I remembered your mercy, Lord,
   what you did in days long past;
   you deliver those who put their trust in you
   and free them from the power of their enemies.
9 From the earth I sent up my prayer,
   begging to be rescued from death.
10 I cried, 'Lord, you are my Father;
   do not abandon me in time of trouble,
   when I am helpless in the face of arrogance.
11 I shall praise you continually;
   I shall sing hymns of thanksgiving.'
   My petition was granted,
12 for you saved me from destruction,
   bringing me out from my desperate plight.
   Therefore I shall give you thanks and praise;
   I shall bless the name of the Lord.

---

m Heb Compare Lat: Gk *on the mountain of Samaria*
n Heb: Meaning of Gk uncertain   o Heb: Other ancient authorities
read *light*   p This title is included in the Gk text.   q Other
ancient authorities read *work*   r Heb: Gk *the Father of my lord*

50:26 **Mount Seir:** *cp. Heb.*; *Gk* the mountain of Samaria.

25 My whole being loathes two nations,
   the third is not even a people:
26 Those who live in Seir and Philistia,
   and the degenerate folk who dwell in Shechem.

27 Wise instruction, appropriate proverbs,
   I have written in this book,
   I, Jesus, son of Eleazar, son of Sirach,
     as they gushed forth from my
     heart's understanding.
28 Happy the man who meditates upon these things,
   wise the man who takes them to heart!
29 If he puts them into practice, he can cope
     with anything,
   for the fear of the LORD is his lamp.

51   I give you thanks, O God of my father;
     I praise you, O God my savior!
  I will make known your name, refuge of my life;
 2   you have been my helper against my adversaries.
  You have saved me from death,
    and kept back my body from the pit,
  From the clutches of the nether world you have
    snatched my feet;
 3   you have delivered me, in your great mercy,
  From the scourge of a slanderous tongue,
    and from lips that went over to falsehood;
  From the snare of those who watched for
    my downfall,
    and from the power of those who sought my life;
  From many a danger you have saved me,
 4   from flames that hemmed me in on every side;
  From the midst of unremitting fire,
 5   from the deep belly of the nether world;
  From deceiving lips and painters of lies,
 6   from the arrows of dishonest tongues.
  I was at the point of death,
    my soul was nearing the depths of the
    nether world;
 7 I turned every way, but there was no one to
    help me,
  I looked for one to sustain me, but could find
    no one.
 8 But then I remembered the mercies of the LORD,
    his kindness through ages past;
  For he saves those who take refuge in him,
    and rescues them from every evil.
 9 So I raised my voice from the very earth,
    from the gates of the nether world, my cry.
10 I called out: O Lord, you are my father,
    you are my champion and my savior;
  Do not abandon me in time of trouble,
    in the midst of storms and dangers.
11 I will ever praise your name
    and be constant in my prayers to you.
  Thereupon the LORD heard my voice,
    he listened to my appeal;
12 He saved me from evil of every kind
    and preserved me in time of trouble.
  For this reason I thank him and I praise him;
    I bless the name of the LORD.

25 There are two nations that my soul detests,
   the third is not a nation at all:
26 the inhabitants of Mount Seir, the Philistines,
   and the stupid people living at Shechem.

27 Instruction in wisdom and knowledge
   is what has been written in this book,
   by Jesus son of Sira Eleazar of Jerusalem,
   who has poured a rain of wisdom from his heart.
28 Blessed is he who devotes his time to these
   and grows wise by taking them to heart!
29 If he practises them he will be strong enough for
    anything,
   since the light of the Lord is his path.

51   I shall give thanks to you, Lord and King,
    and praise you, God my Saviour,
   I give thanks to your name;
 2 for you have been my guard and support
    and redeemed my body from destruction,
  from the snare of the lying tongue,
    from lips that fabricate falsehood;
  in the presence of my assailants, you were on my
    side;
  you have been my support, you have redeemed
    me,
 3 true to your abounding kindness
    — and the greatness of your name — you
    liberated me
  from the fangs of those seeking to devour me,
    from the clutches of those seeking my life,
    from the many ordeals which I have endured,
 4 from the stifling heat which hemmed me in,
    from the heart of a fire which I had not kindled,
 5 from deep in the belly of Sheol,
 6   treacherous denunciations to the king.
  My soul has been close to death,
    my life had gone down to the brink of Sheol.
 7 I was completely surrounded, there was no one to
    help me;
  I looked for someone to help me, there was no
    one.
 8 Then I remembered your mercy, Lord,
    and your deeds from earliest times,
  how you deliver those who wait for you patiently,
    and save them from the clutches of their
    enemies.
 9 And I sent up my plea from the earth,
    I begged to be delivered from death.
10 I called on the Lord, the father of my Lord,
    'Do not desert me in the days of ordeal,
    in the days of the proud, when we are helpless.
  I shall praise your name unceasingly
    and gratefully sing its praises.'
11 And my plea was heard,
    for you saved me from destruction,
    you delivered me from that time of evil.
12 And therefore I shall thank you and praise you,
    and bless the name of the Lord.

51, 12 In standard editions of the *New American Bible* the italicized
verses that follow appear in a footnote. (Cf. Ps 148,14.)

Heb adds:

Give thanks to the Lord, for he is good,
  for his mercy endures forever;

Give thanks to the God of praises,
  for his mercy endures forever;

Give thanks to the guardian of Israel,
  for his mercy endures forever;

Give thanks to him who formed all things,
  for his mercy endures forever;

Give thanks to the redeemer of Israel,
  for his mercy endures forever;

Give thanks to him who gathers the dispersed of
    Israel,
  for his mercy endures forever;

Give thanks to him who rebuilt his city and his
    sanctuary,
  for his mercy endures forever;

Give thanks to him who makes a horn to sprout
    for the house of David,
  for his mercy endures forever;

Give thanks to him who has chosen the sons of
    Zadok to be priests,
  for his mercy endures forever;

Give thanks to the shield of Abraham,
  for his mercy endures forever;

Give thanks to the rock of Isaac,
  for his mercy endures forever;

Give thanks to the mighty one of Jacob,
  for his mercy endures forever;

Give thanks to him who has chosen Zion,
  for his mercy endures forever;

Give thanks to the King of the kings of kings,
  for his mercy endures forever;

He has raised up a horn for his people,
  praise for all his loyal ones.

For the children of Israel, the people close to
    him.
  Praise the Lord!

13 While I was still young, before I went on my
      travels,
    I sought wisdom openly in my prayer.

14 Before the temple I asked for her,
    and I will search for her until the end.

15 From the first blossom to the ripening grape
    my heart delighted in her;
    my foot walked on the straight path;
    from my youth I followed her steps.

16 I inclined my ear a little and received her,
    and I found for myself much instruction.

17 I made progress in her;
    to him who gives wisdom I will give glory.

18 For I resolved to live according to wisdom,[s]
    and I was zealous for the good,
    and I shall never be disappointed.

13 WHEN I was still young, before I set off on my
      travels,
    in my prayers I asked openly for wisdom.

14 In the forecourt of the sanctuary I laid claim to
      her,
    and I shall seek her to the end.

15 From the first blossom to the ripening of the grape
    she has been the delight of my heart.
    From my youth my steps have followed her
      without swerving.

16 I had hardly begun to listen when I was rewarded,
    and I gained for myself much instruction.

17 I made progress in my studies;
    all glory to God who gives me wisdom!

18 I determined to practise what I learnt;
    I pursued goodness, and shall never regret it.

[s] Gk *her*

After verse 12 the Hebrew text gives the litany of
praise contained below. It is not found in any versions
and is therefore of doubtful authenticity.

Give thanks to the Lord, for he is good, for his
mercy endures forever;
Give thanks to the God of glory, for his mercy
endures forever;
Give thanks to the guardian of Israel, for his
mercy endures forever;
Give thanks to the creator of the universe, for his
mercy endures forever;
Give thanks to the redeemer of Israel, for his
mercy endures forever;
Give thanks to him who gathers the dispersed of
Israel, for his mercy endures forever;
Give thanks to him who builds his city and his
sanctuary, for his mercy endures forever;
Give thanks to him who makes a horn to sprout
forth, for the house of David, for his mercy
endures forever;
Give thanks to him who has chosen for this priests
the sons of Zadok, for his mercy endures
forever;
Give thanks to the shield of Abraham, for his
mercy endures forever;
Give thanks to the rock of Isaac, for his mercy
endures forever;
Give thanks to the mighty one of Jacob, for his
mercy endures forever;
Give thanks to him who has chosen Zion, for his
mercy endures forever;
Give thanks to the king over kings, for his mercy
endures forever;
He has lifted up the horn of his people, be this his
praise from all his faithful ones,
From the children of Israel, the people close to
him.
Alleluia!

13 When I was young and innocent,
   I sought wisdom.
14 She came to me in her beauty,
   and until the end I will cultivate her.
15 As the blossoms yielded to ripening grapes,
   the heart's joy,
   My feet kept to the level path
     because from earliest youth I was familiar
     with her.
16 In the short time I paid heed,
   I met with great instruction.
17 Since in this way I have profited,
   I will give my teacher grateful praise.
18 I became resolutely devoted to her—
   the good I persistently strove for.

13 When I was still a youth, before I went travelling,
   in my prayers I asked outright for wisdom.
14 Outside the sanctuary I would pray for her,
   and to the last I shall continue to seek her.
15 From her blossoming to the ripening of her grape
   my heart has taken its delight in her.
   My foot has pursued a straight path,
   I have sought her ever since my youth.
16 By bowing my ear a little, I have received her,
   and have found much instruction.
17 Thanks to her I have advanced;
   glory be to him who has given me wisdom!
18 For I was determined to put her into practice,
   have earnestly pursued the good, and shall not
     be put to shame.

NEW REVISED STANDARD VERSION	REVISED ENGLISH BIBLE

NEW REVISED STANDARD VERSION

19 My soul grappled with wisdom,*t*
 and in my conduct I was strict;*u*
 I spread out my hands to the heavens,
 and lamented my ignorance of her.
20 I directed my soul to her,
 and in purity I found her.

 With her I gained understanding from the first;
 therefore I will never be forsaken.
21 My heart was stirred to seek her;
 therefore I have gained a prize possession.
22 The Lord gave me my tongue as a reward,
 and I will praise him with it.

23 Draw near to me, you who are uneducated,
 and lodge in the house of instruction.
24 Why do you say you are lacking in these
 things,*v*
 and why do you endure such great thirst?
25 I opened my mouth and said,
 Acquire wisdom*w* for yourselves without
 money.
26 Put your neck under her*x* yoke,
 and let your souls receive instruction;
 it is to be found close by.
27 See with your own eyes that I have labored but
 little
 and found for myself much serenity.
28 Hear but a little of my instruction,
 and through me you will acquire silver and
 gold.*y*
29 May your soul rejoice in God's*z* mercy,
 and may you never be ashamed to praise him.
30 Do your work in good time,
 and in his own time God*a* will give you your
 reward.

t Gk *her* *u* Meaning of Gk uncertain *v* Cn Compare Heb Syr:
Meaning of Gk uncertain *w* Heb: Gk lacks *wisdom* *x* Heb: other
ancient authorities read *the* *y* Syr Compare Heb: Gk *Get*
instruction with a large sum of silver, and you will gain by it much
gold. *z* Gk *his* *a* Gk *he*

REVISED ENGLISH BIBLE

19 With all my might I strove for wisdom
 and was scrupulous in whatever I did.
 I spread out my hands to Heaven above,
 deploring my shortcomings;
20 I set my heart on possessing wisdom,
 and by keeping myself pure I found her.
 With her I gained understanding from the first;
 therefore I shall never be at a loss.
21 Because I passionately yearned to discover her,
 a noble possession was mine:
22 as my reward the Lord gave me eloquence,
 and with it I shall praise him.

23 YOU THAT are uninstructed,
 come to me and lodge in the house of instruction.
24 Why do you still lack these things
 and leave your great thirst unslaked?
25 I have made this proclamation:
 'Buy wisdom for yourselves without money.
26 Bend your neck to the yoke
 and be ready to accept instruction;
 you need not go far to find it.'
27 See for yourselves how little were my labours
 compared with the great refreshment I have found.
28 Your instruction may cost you a large amount of
 silver,
 but it will bring you a large return in gold.
29 May you take delight in the Lord's mercy
 and never be ashamed of praising him.
30 Do your duty in good time,
 and he in his own time will give you your reward.

51:24 *Why . . . things: prob. rdg; Gk obscure.*

19 I burned with desire for her,
  never turning back.
I became preoccupied with her,
  never weary of extolling her.
My hand opened her gate
  and I came to know her secrets.
20 For her I purified my hands;
  in cleanness I attained to her.
At first acquaintance with her, I
    gained understanding
  such that I will never forsake her.
21 My whole being was stirred as I learned about her;
  therefore I have made her my prize possession.
22 The LORD has granted me my lips as a reward,
  and my tongue will declare his praises.

23 Come aside to me, you untutored,
  and take up lodging in the house of instruction;
24 How long will you be deprived of wisdom's food,
  how long will you endure such bitter thirst?
25 I open my mouth and speak of her:
  gain, at no cost, wisdom for yourselves.
26 Submit your neck to her yoke,
  that your mind may accept her teaching.
For she is close to those who seek her,
  and the one who is in earnest finds her.
27 See for yourselves! I have labored only a little,
  but have found much.
28 Acquire but a little instruction;
  you will win silver and gold through her.
29 Let your spirits rejoice in the mercy of God,
  and be not ashamed to give him praise.
30 Work at your tasks in due season,
  and in his own time God will give you
      your reward.

19 My soul has fought to possess her,
  I have been scrupulous in keeping the Law;
I have stretched out my hands to heaven
  and bewailed how little I knew of her;
20 I have directed my soul towards her,
  and in purity I have found her;
having my heart fixed on her from the outset,
  I shall never be deserted;
21 my very core having yearned to discover her,
  I have now acquired a good possession.
22 In reward the Lord has given me a tongue
  with which I shall sing his praises.
23 Come close to me, you ignorant,
  take your place in my school.
24 Why complain about lacking these things
  when your souls are so thirsty for them?
25 I have opened my mouth, I have said:
  'Buy her without money,
26 put your necks under her yoke,
  let your souls receive instruction,
  she is near, within your reach.'
27 See for yourselves: how slight my efforts have
      been
  to win so much peace.
28 Buy instruction with a large sum of silver,
  thanks to her you will gain much gold.
29 May your souls rejoice in the mercy of the Lord,
  may you never be ashamed of praising him.
30 Do your work before the appointed time
  and at the appointed time he will give you your
      reward.

(*Subscript:*) Wisdom of Jesus, son of Sira.

Baruch

1 These are the words of the book that Baruch son of Neriah son of Mahseiah son of Zedekiah son of Hasadiah son of Hilkiah wrote in Babylon, 2 in the fifth year, on the seventh day of the month, at the time when the Chaldeans took Jerusalem and burned it with fire.

3 Baruch read the words of this book to Jeconiah son of Jehoiakim, king of Judah, and to all the people who came to hear the book, 4 and to the nobles and the princes, and to the elders, and to all the people, small and great, all who lived in Babylon by the river Sud.

5 Then they wept, and fasted, and prayed before the Lord; 6 they collected as much money as each could give, 7 and sent it to Jerusalem to the high priest[a] Jehoiakim son of Hilkiah son of Shallum, and to the priests, and to all the people who were present with him in Jerusalem. 8 At the same time, on the tenth day of Sivan, Baruch[b] took the vessels of the house of the Lord, which had been carried away from the temple, to return them to the land of Judah — the silver vessels that Zedekiah son of Josiah, king of Judah, had made, 9 after King Nebuchadnezzar of Babylon had carried away from Jerusalem Jeconiah and the princes and the prisoners and the nobles and the people of the land, and brought them to Babylon.

10 They said: Here we send you money; so buy with the money burnt offerings and sin offerings and incense, and prepare a grain offering, and offer them on the altar of the Lord our God; 11 and pray for the life of King Nebuchadnezzar of Babylon, and for the life of his son Belshazzar, so that their days on earth may be like the days of heaven. 12 The Lord will give us strength, and light to our eyes; we shall live under the protection[c] of King Nebuchadnezzar of Babylon, and under the protection of his son Belshazzar, and we shall serve them many days and find favor in their sight. 13 Pray also for us to the Lord our God, for we have sinned against the Lord our God, and to this day the anger of the Lord and his wrath have not turned away from us. 14 And you shall read aloud this scroll that we are sending you, to make your confession in the house of the Lord on the days of the festivals and at appointed seasons.

15 And you shall say: The Lord our God is in the right, but there is open shame on us today, on the people of Judah, on the inhabitants of Jerusalem, 16 and on our kings, our rulers, our priests, our prophets, and our ancestors, 17 because we have sinned before the Lord. 18 We have disobeyed him, and have not heeded the voice of the Lord our God, to walk in the statutes of the Lord that he set before us. 19 From the time when the Lord brought our ancestors out of the land of Egypt until today, we have been disobedient to the Lord our God, and we have been negligent, in not heeding his voice. 20 So to this day there have clung to us the calamities and the curse that the Lord declared through his servant Moses at the time when he brought our ancestors out of the land of Egypt to give us a land flowing with milk and honey. 21 We did not listen to the voice of the Lord our God in all the words of the prophets whom he sent to us, 22 but all of us followed the intent of our own wicked hearts by serving other gods and doing what is evil in the sight of the Lord our God.

Baruch

1 THIS is the book of Baruch son of Neriah, son of Mahseiah, son of Zedekiah, son of Hasadiah, son of Hilkiah, written by him in Babylon, 2 on the seventh day of the month, in the fifth year after the capture and burning of Jerusalem by the Chaldaeans.

3 Baruch read the book aloud to Jeconiah son of Joakim, king of Judah, and to the whole community assembled to hear it: 4 the nobles, the princes of the royal blood, the elders, and all the people, high and low — in short, all who were living in Babylon by the river Soud. 5 Then with tears and fasting they offered their prayers before the Lord. 6 Each of them got together as much money as he could, 7 and this was sent to Jerusalem, to the high priest Joakim son of Hilkiah, son of Shallum, and to the other priests and all the people who were with him there. 8 At the same time, on the tenth day of the month of Sivan, Baruch took the vessels belonging to the house of the Lord which had been looted from the temple, and returned them to the land of Judah. These were the silver vessels which Zedekiah son of Josiah, king of Judah, had made, 9 after King Nebuchadnezzar of Babylon deported Jeconiah from Jerusalem and carried him off to Babylon, along with the rulers, craftsmen, nobles, and the common people.

10 They sent this message: The money we are sending you is to be used to buy whole-offerings, sin-offerings, and frankincense, and to provide grain-offerings; you are to offer them on the altar of the Lord our God, 11 with prayers for King Nebuchadnezzar of Babylon and for his son Belshazzar, that their life may last as long as the heavens are above the earth. 12 So the Lord will strengthen us and bring light to our eyes, and we shall live under the protection of King Nebuchadnezzar of Babylon and of Belshazzar his son; we shall give them service for many a day and find favour with them. 13 Pray also for us to the Lord our God, because we have sinned against him, and to this day the Lord's anger and wrath have not been averted from us.

14 You shall read this book we are sending you, and on the feast day and throughout the festal season make confession in the house of the Lord 15 in these words: The right is on the side of the Lord our God; the shame, now as ever, belongs to us, the men of Judah and the citizens of Jerusalem, 16 to our kings and rulers, our priests and prophets, and to our forefathers. 17 We have sinned against the Lord 18 and disobeyed him; we paid no heed to the voice of the Lord our God and did not conform to the laws he laid down for us. 19 We have been disobedient to the Lord our God from the day he brought our forefathers out of Egypt until now; we have thoughtlessly disregarded his voice. 20 So we find ourselves in the grip of adversity, suffering under the curse which the Lord commanded his servant Moses to pronounce, when he led our forefathers out of Egypt to give us a land flowing with milk and honey, as it still is today. 21 Moreover, we refused to hear the Lord our God speaking in all the words of the prophets he sent us; 22 we went our own way, each to follow the promptings of his wicked heart, to serve other gods, and to do what was evil in the sight of the Lord our God.

---

a Gk *the priest*   *b* Gk *he*   *c* Gk *in the shadow*

1:9 **craftsmen:** *prob. rdg; Gk* prisoners.   1:10 **sin-offerings:** *or* purification-offerings.

2400

THE BOOK OF
Baruch

1 Now these are the words of the scroll which Baruch, son of Neriah, son of Mahseiah, son of Zedekiah, son of Hasadiah, son of Hilkiah, wrote in Babylon, 2 in the fifth year [on the seventh day of the month, at the time when the Chaldeans took Jerusalem and burnt it with fire]. 3 And Baruch read the words of this scroll for Jeconiah, son of Jehoiakim, king of Judah, to hear it, as well as all the people who came to the reading: 4 the nobles, the kings' sons, the elders, and the whole people, small and great alike — all who lived in Babylon by the river Sud.

5 They wept and fasted and prayed before the LORD, 6 and collected such funds as each could furnish. 7 These they sent to Jerusalem, to Jehoiakim, son of Hilkiah, son of Shallum, the priest, and to the priests and the whole people who were with him in Jerusalem. 8 [This was when he received the vessels of the house of the LORD that had been removed from the temple, to restore them to the land of Judah, on the tenth of Sivan. These silver vessels Zedekiah, son of Josiah, king of Judah, had had made 9 after Nebuchadnezzar, king of Babylon, carried off Jeconiah, and the princes, and the skilled workers, and the nobles, and the people of the land from Jerusalem, as captives, and brought them to Babylon.]

10 Their message was: "We send you funds, with which you are to procure holocausts, sin offerings, and frankincense, and to prepare cereal offerings; offer these on the altar of the LORD our God, 11 and pray for the life of Nebuchadnezzar, king of Babylon, and that of Belshazzar, his son, that their lifetimes may equal the duration of the heavens above the earth; 12 and that the LORD may give us strength, and light to our eyes, that we may live under the protective shadow of Nebuchadnezzar, king of Babylon, and that of Belshazzar, his son, and serve them long, finding favor in their sight.

13 "Pray for us also to the LORD, our God; for we have sinned against the LORD, our God, and the wrath and anger of the LORD have not yet been withdrawn from us at the present day. 14 And read out publicly this scroll which we send you, in the house of the LORD, on the feast day and during the days of assembly:

15 "Justice is with the LORD, our God; and we today are flushed with shame, we men of Judah and citizens of Jerusalem, 16 that we, with our kings and rulers and priests and prophets, and with our fathers, 17 have sinned in the LORD'S sight 18 and disobeyed him. We have neither heeded the voice of the LORD, our God, nor followed the precepts which the LORD set before us. 19 From the time the LORD led our fathers out of the land of Egypt until the present day, we have been disobedient to the LORD, our God, and only too ready to disregard his voice. 20 And the evils and the curse which the LORD enjoined upon Moses, his servant, at the time he led our fathers forth from the land of Egypt to give us the land flowing with milk and honey, cling to us even today. 21 For we did not heed the voice of the LORD, our God, in all the words of the prophets whom he sent us, 22 but each one of us went off after the devices of our own wicked hearts, served other gods, and did evil in the sight of the LORD, our God.

THE BOOK OF
Baruch

1 This is the text of the book written in Babylon by Baruch son of Neraiah, son of Mahseiah, son of Zedekiah, son of Hasadiah, son of Hilkiah, 2 in the fifth year, on the seventh day of the month, at the time when the Chaldaeans had captured Jerusalem and burned it down.

3 Baruch read the text of this book aloud to Jeconiah son of Jehoiakim, king of Judah, and to all the people who had come to hear the reading, 4 to the nobles and the sons of the king, and to the elders; to the whole people, that is, to the least no less than to the greatest, to all who lived in Babylon beside the river Sud. 5 On hearing it they wept, fasted and prayed before the Lord; 6 and they collected as much money as each could afford 7 and sent it to Jerusalem to the priest Jehoiakim son of Hilkiah, son of Shallum, and the other priests, and all the people who were with him in Jerusalem. 8 Also on the tenth day of Sivan he was given the utensils of the house of the Lord, which had been removed from the Temple, to take them back to the land of Judah; these were silver utensils which Zedekiah son of Josiah, king of Judah, had had made 9 after Nebuchadnezzar king of Babylon had deported Jeconiah from Jerusalem to Babylon, together with the princes, the metalworkers, the nobles and the common people.

10 Now, they wrote, we are sending you money to pay for burnt offerings, offerings for sin, and incense. Prepare oblations and offer them on the altar of the Lord our God; 11 and pray for the long life of Nebuchadnezzar king of Babylon, and of his son Belshazzar, that they may endure on earth as long as the heavens endure; 12 and that the Lord may give us strength and enlighten our eyes, so that we may lead our lives under the protection of Nebuchadnezzar king of Babylon and of his son Belshazzar, and that we may serve them for a long time and win their favour. 13 Also pray to the Lord our God for us, because we have sinned against him, and the anger, the fury of the Lord, has still not turned away from us. 14 Lastly, you must read the booklet which we are sending you, publicly in the house of the Lord on the feast-day and appropriate days. 15 You must say:

Saving justice is the Lord's, we have only the look of shame we bear, as is the case today for the people of Judah and the inhabitants of Jerusalem, 16 for our kings and princes, our priests, our prophets, and for our ancestors, 17 because we have sinned before the Lord, 18 have disobeyed him, and have not listened to the voice of the Lord our God telling us to follow the commandments which the Lord had ordained for us. 19 From the day when the Lord brought our ancestors out of Egypt until today we have been disobedient to the Lord our God, and been disloyal, refusing to listen to his voice. 20 And we are not free even today of the disasters and the curse which the Lord pronounced through his servant Moses the day he brought our ancestors out of Egypt to give us a land flowing with milk and honey. 21 We have not listened to the voice of the Lord our God in all the words of those prophets he sent us; 22 but, each following the dictates of our evil heart, we have taken to serving alien gods, and doing what is displeasing to the Lord our God.

2 So the Lord carried out the threat he spoke against us: against our judges who ruled Israel, and against our kings and our rulers and the people of Israel and Judah. 2 Under the whole heaven there has not been done the like of what he has done in Jerusalem, in accordance with the threats that were^d written in the law of Moses. 3 Some of us ate the flesh of their sons and others the flesh of their daughters. 4 He made them subject to all the kingdoms around us, to be an object of scorn and a desolation among all the surrounding peoples, where the Lord has scattered them. 5 They were brought down and not raised up, because our nation^e sinned against the Lord our God, in not heeding his voice.

6 The Lord our God is in the right, but there is open shame on us and our ancestors this very day. 7 All those calamities with which the Lord threatened us have come upon us. 8 Yet we have not entreated the favor of the Lord by turning away, each of us, from the thoughts of our wicked hearts. 9 And the Lord has kept the calamities ready, and the Lord has brought them upon us, for the Lord is just in all the works that he has commanded us to do. 10 Yet we have not obeyed his voice, to walk in the statutes of the Lord that he set before us.

11 And now, O Lord God of Israel, who brought your people out of the land of Egypt with a mighty hand and with signs and wonders and with great power and outstretched arm, and made yourself a name that continues to this day, 12 we have sinned, we have been ungodly, we have done wrong, O Lord our God, against all your ordinances. 13 Let your anger turn away from us, for we are left, few in number, among the nations where you have scattered us. 14 Hear, O Lord, our prayer and our supplication, and for your own sake deliver us, and grant us favor in the sight of those who have carried us into exile; 15 so that all the earth may know that you are the Lord our God, for Israel and his descendants are called by your name.

16 O Lord, look down from your holy dwelling, and consider us. Incline your ear, O Lord, and hear; 17 open your eyes, O Lord, and see, for the dead who are in Hades, whose spirit has been taken from their bodies, will not ascribe glory or justice to the Lord; 18 but the person who is deeply grieved, who walks bowed and feeble, with failing eyes and famished soul, will declare your glory and righteousness, O Lord.

19 For it is not because of any righteous deeds of our ancestors or our kings that we bring before you our prayer for mercy, O Lord our God. 20 For you have sent your anger and your wrath upon us, as you declared by your servants the prophets, saying: 21 Thus says the Lord: Bend your shoulders and serve the king of Babylon, and you will remain in the land that I gave to your ancestors. 22 But if you will not obey the voice of the Lord and will not serve the king of Babylon, 23 I will make to cease from the towns of Judah and from the region around Jerusalem the voice of mirth and the voice of gladness, the voice of the bridegroom and the voice of the bride, and the whole land will be a desolation without inhabitants.

24 But we did not obey your voice, to serve the king of Babylon; and you have carried out your threats, which you spoke by your servants the prophets, that the bones of our kings and the bones of our ancestors would be brought out of their resting place; 25 and indeed they have been thrown out to the heat of day and the frost of night. They perished in great misery, by famine and sword and pestilence. 26 And the house that is called by your name you have made as it is today, because of the wickedness of the house of Israel and the house of Judah.

2 The Lord has made good the warning he gave about us and about our judges in Israel, about our kings and rulers and the people of Israel and Judah. 2 Under the whole of heaven no such things have been done as were done in Jerusalem; they fulfilled what was foretold in the law of Moses: 3 that we should eat the flesh of our children, one his own son and another his own daughter. 4 The Lord made our nation subject to all the kingdoms round about; to all the peoples among whom he had scattered us our name was a byword, our land a wilderness. 5 Instead of rising high, our nation sank low, because in disregarding his voice we sinned against the Lord our God. 6 The right is on the side of the Lord our God; the shame, now as ever, belongs to us and to our forefathers. 7 All those disasters of which the Lord gave us warning have come upon us; 8 yet we did not entreat the Lord to turn each one of us from the thoughts of his wicked heart. 9 The Lord has kept strict watch and brought the disasters on us. In all that he has done to us he is just; 10 yet we did not heed his warning, nor did we conform to the laws he laid down for our guidance.

11 Lord God of Israel, who brought your people out of Egypt by a strong hand, with signs and portents, with great power and arm uplifted, winning for yourself a name that lives on to this day, 12 now, Lord our God, we have broken all your commandments by our sin, our godlessness, and our injustice. 13 Turn your anger away from us, for we are left few in number among the heathen where you have scattered us. 14 Listen, Lord, to our prayer and supplication, deliver us for your own sake, and grant us favour with those who have taken us into exile, 15 so that the whole world may know you are the Lord our God, and yours is the name by which Israel and his posterity are called.

16 Lord, look down from your holy dwelling-place and take thought for us; incline your ear to us, Lord, and hear; 17 open your eyes, Lord, and see. The dead are in their graves, all breath gone from their bodies, and they cannot sing the Lord's praises or applaud his justice; 18 it is the living, mourning their fall from greatness, walking the earth bent and enfeebled, with eyes dimmed and with failing appetite—it is they, Lord, who will sing your praises and applaud your justice.

19 Not for any righteous deeds of our forefathers and our kings do we lay before you our plea for pity, Lord our God. 20 You have vented on us that anger and wrath of which you warned us through your servants the prophets when you said: 21 'These are the words of the Lord: Bow your shoulders and serve the king of Babylon, and you will remain in the land that I gave to your fathers; 22 but if you ignore the Lord's command to serve the king of Babylon, 23 then I shall banish from the cities of Judah and from the streets of Jerusalem the sound of joy and gladness, the voices of bridegroom and bride; the whole land will lie waste and abandoned.' 24 When we went against your command to serve the king of Babylon, you made good the warning given through your servants the prophets: the bones of our kings and of our fathers have been brought out from their resting-place, 25 thrown down, and exposed to the scorching heat by day and the frost by night. They died a painful death by famine, sword, and pestilence. 26 And because of the wickedness of Israel and Judah the house that bears your name has become what it is today.

NEW AMERICAN BIBLE

2 "And the LORD fulfilled the warning he had uttered against us: against our judges, who governed Israel, against our kings and princes, and against the men of Israel and Judah. 2 He brought down upon us evils so great that there has not been done anywhere under heaven what has been done in Jerusalem, as was written in the law of Moses: 3 that one after another of us should eat the flesh of his son or of his daughter. 4 He has made us subject to all the kingdoms round about us, a reproach and a horror among all the nations round about to which the LORD has scattered us. 5 We are brought low, not raised up, because we sinned against the LORD, our God, not heeding his voice.

6 "Justice is with the LORD, our God; and we, like our fathers, are flushed with shame even today. 7 All the evils of which the LORD had warned us have come upon us; 8 and we did not plead before the LORD, or turn, each from the figments of his evil heart. 9 And the LORD kept watch over the evils, and brought them home to us; for the LORD is just in all the works he commanded us to do, 10 but we did not heed his voice, or follow the precepts of the LORD which he set before us.

11 "And now, LORD, God of Israel, you who led your people out of the land of Egypt with your mighty hand, with signs and wonders and great might, and with your upraised arm, so that you have made for yourself a name till the present day: 12 we have sinned, been impious, and violated, O LORD, our God, all your statutes. 13 Let your anger be withdrawn from us, for we are left few in number among the nations to which you scattered us. 14 Hear, O LORD, our prayer of supplication, and deliver us for your own sake: grant us favor in the presence of our captors, 15 that the whole earth may know that you are the LORD, our God, and that Israel and his descendants bear your name. 16 O LORD, look down from your holy dwelling and take thought of us; turn, O LORD, your ear to hear us. 17 Look directly at us, and behold: it is not the dead in the nether world, whose spirits have been taken from within them, who will give glory and vindication to the LORD. 18 He whose soul is deeply grieved, who walks bowed and feeble, with failing eyes and famished soul, will declare your glory and justice, LORD!

19 "Not on the just deeds of our fathers and our kings do we base our plea for mercy in your sight, O LORD, our God. 20 You have brought your wrath and anger down upon us, as you had warned us through your servants the prophets: 21 'Thus says the LORD: Bend your shoulders to the service of the king of Babylon, that you may continue in the land I gave your fathers: 22 for if you do not hear the LORD's voice so as to serve the king of Babylon,

23 I will make to cease from the cities of Judah
   and from the streets of Jerusalem
The sounds of joy and the sounds of gladness,
   the voice of the bridegroom
   and the voice of the bride;
And all the land shall be deserted,
   without inhabitants.'

24 But we did not heed your voice, or serve the king of Babylon, and you fulfilled the threats you had made through your servants the prophets, to have the bones of our kings and the bones of our fathers brought out from their burial places. 25 And indeed, they lie exposed to the heat of day and the frost of night. They died in dire anguish, by hunger and the sword and plague. 26 And you reduced the house which bears your name to what it is today, for the wickedness of the kingdom of Israel and the kingdom of Judah.

NEW JERUSALEM BIBLE

2 And so the Lord has carried out the sentence which he passed on us, on our judges who governed Israel, on our kings and leaders and on the people of Israel and of Judah; 2 what he did to Jerusalem has never been paralleled under the wide heavens — in conformity with what was written in the Law of Moses; 3 we were each reduced to eating the flesh of our own sons and daughters. 4 Furthermore, he has handed them over into the power of all the kingdoms that surround us, to be the contempt and execration of all the neighbouring peoples among whom the Lord scattered them. 5 Instead of being masters, they found themselves enslaved, because we had sinned against the Lord our God by not listening to his voice.

6 Saving justice is the Lord's; we and our ancestors have only the look of shame we bear today. 7 All those disasters which the Lord pronounced against us have now befallen us. 8 And yet we have not tried to win the favour of the Lord by each of us renouncing the dictates of our own wicked heart; 9 so the Lord has been alert to our misdeeds and has brought disaster down on us, since the Lord is upright in everything he had commanded us to do, 10 and we have not listened to his voice so as to follow the commandments which the Lord had ordained for us.

11 And now, Lord, God of Israel, who brought your people out of Egypt with a mighty hand, with signs and wonders, with great power and with outstretched arm, to win yourself a name such as you have today, 12 we have sinned, we have committed sacrilege; Lord our God, we have broken all your precepts. 13 Let your anger turn from us since we are no more than a little remnant among the nations where you have dispersed us. 14 Listen, Lord, to our prayers and our entreaties; deliver us for your own sake and let us win the favour of the people who have deported us, 15 so that the whole world may know that you are the Lord our God, since Israel and his descendants bear your name. 16 Look down, Lord, from your holy dwelling-place and think of us; open your ear, Lord, and listen, 17 open your eyes, Lord, and look; the dead down in Sheol, whose breath has been taken from their bodies, are not the ones to give glory and due recognition to the Lord; 18 whoever is overcome with affliction, who goes along bowed down and frail, with failing eyes and hungering soul, that is the one to give you glory and due recognition, Lord.

19 We do not rely on the merits of our ancestors and of our kings to offer you our humble plea, Lord our God. 20 No, you have sent down your anger and your fury on us, as you threatened through your servants the prophets when they said, 21 'The Lord says this: *Bend your necks and serve the king of Babylon,*[a] and you will remain in the country which I gave to your ancestors. 22 But if you do not listen to the voice of the Lord and serve the king of Babylon 23 then *I shall silence the shouts of rejoicing and mirth and the voices of bridegroom and bride in the towns of Judah and the streets of Jerusalem, and the whole country will be reduced to desert,*[b] with no inhabitants.' 24 But we would not listen to your voice and serve the king of Babylon, and so you carried out what you had threatened through your servants the prophets: that the bones of our kings and of our ancestors would be dragged from their resting places. 25 They were indeed *tossed out to the heat of the day and the frost of the night.*[c] And people died in dreadful agony, from famine, sword and plague. 26 And so, because of the wickedness of the House of Israel and the House of Judah, you have made this House, that bears your name, what it is today.

---

a 2 Jr 27:12.   *b* 2 Jr 7:34.   *c* 2 Jr 36:30.

NEW REVISED STANDARD VERSION

27 Yet you have dealt with us, O Lord our God, in all your kindness and in all your great compassion, 28 as you spoke by your servant Moses on the day when you commanded him to write your law in the presence of the people of Israel, saying, 29 "If you will not obey my voice, this very great multitude will surely turn into a small number among the nations, where I will scatter them. 30 For I know that they will not obey me, for they are a stiff-necked people. But in the land of their exile they will come to themselves 31 and know that I am the Lord their God. I will give them a heart that obeys and ears that hear; 32 they will praise me in the land of their exile, and will remember my name 33 and turn from their stubbornness and their wicked deeds; for they will remember the ways of their ancestors, who sinned before the Lord. 34 I will bring them again into the land that I swore to give to their ancestors, to Abraham, Isaac, and Jacob, and they will rule over it; and I will increase them, and they will not be diminished. 35 I will make an everlasting covenant with them to be their God and they shall be my people; and I will never again remove my people Israel from the land that I have given them."

3 O Lord Almighty, God of Israel, the soul in anguish and the wearied spirit cry out to you. 2 Hear, O Lord, and have mercy, for we have sinned before you. 3 For you are enthroned forever, and we are perishing forever. 4 O Lord Almighty, God of Israel, hear now the prayer of the people*f* of Israel, the children of those who sinned before you, who did not heed the voice of the Lord their God, so that calamities have clung to us. 5 Do not remember the iniquities of our ancestors, but in this crisis remember your power and your name. 6 For you are the Lord our God, and it is you, O Lord, whom we will praise. 7 For you have put the fear of you in our hearts so that we would call upon your name; and we will praise you in our exile, for we have put away from our hearts all the iniquity of our ancestors who sinned against you. 8 See, we are today in our exile where you have scattered us, to be reproached and cursed and punished for all the iniquities of our ancestors, who forsook the Lord our God.

9 Hear the commandments of life, O Israel;
    give ear, and learn wisdom!
10 Why is it, O Israel, why is it that you are in the
        land of your enemies,
    that you are growing old in a foreign country,
    that you are defiled with the dead,
11   that you are counted among those in Hades?
12 You have forsaken the fountain of wisdom.
13 If you had walked in the way of God,
    you would be living in peace forever.
14 Learn where there is wisdom,
    where there is strength,
    where there is understanding,
    so that you may at the same time discern
    where there is length of days, and life,
    where there is light for the eyes, and peace.
15 Who has found her place?
    And who has entered her storehouses?
16 Where are the rulers of the nations,
    and those who lorded it over the animals on
        earth;
17 those who made sport of the birds of the air,
    and who hoarded up silver and gold
    in which people trust,
    and there is no end to their getting;

REVISED ENGLISH BIBLE

27 Yet, Lord our God, you have shown us all your wonted forbearance and all your great mercy. 28 This is as you promised through your servant Moses on the day you commanded him to write down your law in the presence of the Israelites, when you said: 29 'If you will not heed what I say, this great swarming multitude will be reduced to a mere handful among the heathen where I shall scatter them. 30 I know this stubborn people will not listen to me, but in the land of their exile they will come to their right mind 31 and know that I am the Lord their God. I shall give them a mind to understand and ears to hear. 32 They will praise me in the land of their exile and turn their thoughts to me; 33 recalling how their forefathers sinned against the Lord, they will repent of their stubbornness and their wicked practices. 34 Then I shall bring them again to the land that I swore to give to their forefathers, Abraham, Isaac, and Jacob, and they will rule over it. I shall increase their number: they will never dwindle away. 35 I shall enter into an everlasting covenant with them, that I become their God and they become my people. Never again shall I remove my people Israel from the land I have given them.'

3 Lord Almighty, God of Israel, to you the soul in anguish and the fainting spirit cry out. 2 Hear and have mercy, Lord, for we have sinned against you. 3 You are enthroned for ever; we are for ever passing away. 4 Now Lord Almighty, God of Israel, hear the prayer of the men of Israel and of the sons of those who sinned against you. They did not heed the voice of the Lord their God, and so we are in the grip of adversity. 5 Do not call to mind the misdeeds of our forefathers, but remember at this time your power and your name, 6 for you are the Lord our God, and we shall praise you, Lord. 7 It is for this that you have put into our hearts the fear of you: to make us call on your name. And we shall praise you in our exile, for we have renounced all the wrongdoing of our forefathers who sinned against you. 8 Today we are exiled in the lands where you have scattered us; you have made us a byword and a curse, to be punished for all the sins of our forefathers, who rebelled against the Lord our God.

9 Israel, listen to the life-giving commandments;
    hear, and learn understanding.
10 Why is it, Israel, that you are in your enemies'
        country,
    grown old in a foreign land?
    Why have you shared defilement with the dead
11 and been numbered among those that lie in the
        grave?
12 Because you have forsaken the fountain of
        wisdom!
13 If only you had walked in God's ways,
    you would have lived in peace for ever.
14 Where is wisdom, where is strength,
    where is intelligence? Learn that,
    and you will know where are length of days and
        life,
    where happiness and peace.
15 Who has discovered wisdom's dwelling-place,
    who has entered her treasure house?
16 Where are the rulers of the nations now?
    Where are those who had lordship over earth's
        wild beasts,
17 those who made their sport with the birds of the
        air?
    Where are the hoarders of silver and gold
    in which men put their trust,
    those whose greed knew no limit?

---

f Gk dead

3:4 **men:** *prob. rdg; Gk dead.*

NEW AMERICAN BIBLE

27 "But with us, O Lord, our God, you have dealt in all your clemency and in all your great mercy. 28 This was your warning through your servant Moses, the day you ordered him to write down your law in the presence of the Israelites: 29 If you do not heed my voice, surely this great and numerous throng will dwindle away among the nations to which I will scatter them. 30 For I know they will not heed me, because they are a stiff-necked people. But in the land of their captivity they shall have a change of heart; 31 they shall know that I, the LORD, am their God. I will give them hearts, and heedful ears; 32 and they shall praise me in the land of their captivity, and shall invoke my name. 33 Then they shall turn back from their stiff-necked stubbornness, and from their evil deeds, because they shall remember the fate of their fathers who sinned against the LORD. 34 And I will bring them back to the land which with my oath I promised to their fathers, to Abraham, Isaac and Jacob; and they shall rule it. I will make them increase; they shall not then diminish. 35 And I will establish for them, as an eternal covenant, that I will be their God, and they shall be my people; and I will not again remove my people Israel from the land I gave them.

3 "LORD Almighty, God of Israel, afflicted souls and dismayed spirits call to you. 2 Hear, O LORD, for you are a God of mercy; and have mercy on us, who have sinned against you: 3 for you are enthroned forever, while we are perishing forever. 4 LORD Almighty, God of Israel, hear the prayer of Israel's few, the sons of those who sinned against you; they did not heed the voice of the LORD their God, and the evils cling to us. 5 Remember at this time not the misdeeds of our fathers, but your own hand and name: 6 for you are the LORD our God; and you, O LORD, we will praise! 7 For this, you put into our hearts the fear of you: that we may call upon your name, and praise you in our captivity, when we have removed from our hearts all the wickedness of our fathers who sinned against you. 8 Behold us today in our captivity, where you scattered us, a reproach, a curse, and a requital for all the misdeeds of our fathers, who withdrew from the LORD, our God."

9 Hear, O Israel, the commandments of life:
  listen, and know prudence!
10 How is it, Israel,
    that you are in the land of your foes,
    grown old in a foreign land,
  Defiled with the dead,
11   accounted with those destined for the
      nether world?
12 You have forsaken the fountain of wisdom!
13   Had you walked in the way of God,
    you would have dwelt in enduring peace.
14 Learn where prudence is,
    where strength, where understanding;
  That you may know also
    where are length of days, and life,
    where light of the eyes, and peace.

15 Who has found the place of wisdom,
    who has entered into her treasuries?
16 Where are the rulers of the nations,
    they who lorded it over the wild beasts of
      the earth,
17   and made sport of the birds of the heavens:
  They who heaped up the silver
    and the gold in which men trust;
    of whose possessions there was no end?

NEW JERUSALEM BIBLE

27 And yet, Lord our God, you have treated us in a way worthy of all your goodness and boundless tenderness, 28 just as you had promised through your servant Moses, the day you told him to write your Law in the presence of the Israelites, and said, 29 'If you do not listen to my voice, this great and innumerable multitude will certainly be reduced to a tiny few among the nations where I shall scatter them — 30 for I knew that, being an obstinate people, they would not listen to me. But in the country of their exile, they will come to themselves 31 and acknowledge that I am the Lord their God. I shall give them a heart and an attentive ear, 32 and they will sing my praises in the country of their exile, they will remember my name; 33 they will stop being obstinate and, remembering what became of their ancestors who sinned before the Lord, will turn from their evil deeds. 34 Then I shall bring them back to the country which I promised on oath to their ancestors Abraham, Isaac and Jacob, and make them masters in it. I shall make their numbers grow; they will not dwindle again. 35 And I shall make an everlasting covenant with them; so that I am their God and they are my people. And never again shall I drive my people Israel out of the country which I have given them.'

3 Almighty Lord, God of Israel, a soul in anguish, a troubled heart now cries to you: 2 Listen and have pity, Lord, for we have sinned before you. 3 You sit enthroned for ever, while we are perishing for ever. 4 Almighty Lord, God of Israel, hear the prayer of the dead of Israel, of the children of those who have sinned against you and have not listened to the voice of the Lord their God; hence the disasters which dog us. 5 Do not call to mind the misdeeds of our ancestors, but remember instead your power and your name. 6 You are indeed the Lord our God and we will praise you, Lord, 7 since you have put respect for you in our hearts to encourage us to call on your name. We long to praise you in our exile, for we have rid our hearts of the wickedness of our ancestors who sinned against you. 8 Look, today we are still in exile where you have scattered us as something contemptible, accursed, condemned, for all the misdeeds of our ancestors who had abandoned the Lord our God.

9 Listen, Israel, to commands that bring life;
  hear, and learn what knowledge means.
10 Why, Israel, why are you in the country of your
      enemies,
    growing older and older in an alien land,
11 defiling yourselves with the dead,
    reckoned with those who go to Sheol?
12 It is because you have forsaken the fountain of
      wisdom!
13 Had you walked in the way of God,
    you would be living in peace for ever.
14 Learn where knowledge is, where strength,
    where understanding, and so learn
    where length of days is, where life,
    where the light of the eyes and where peace.

15 But who has found out where she lives,
    who has entered her treasure house?
16 Where now are the leaders of the nations
    and those who ruled even the beasts of earth,
17 those who sported with the birds of heaven,
    those who accumulated silver and gold
    on which all people rely,
    and whose possessions had no end,

18 those who schemed to get silver, and were
anxious,
    but there is no trace of their works?
19 They have vanished and gone down to Hades,
    and others have arisen in their place.

20 Later generations have seen the light of day,
    and have lived upon the earth;
    but they have not learned the way to knowledge,
    nor understood her paths,
    nor laid hold of her.
21 Their descendants have strayed far from her*g*
    way.
22 She has not been heard of in Canaan,
    or seen in Teman;
23 the descendants of Hagar, who seek for
    understanding on the earth,
    the merchants of Merran and Teman,
    the story-tellers and the seekers for
    understanding,
    have not learned the way to wisdom,
    or given thought to her paths.

24 O Israel, how great is the house of God,
    how vast the territory that he possesses!
25 It is great and has no bounds;
    it is high and immeasurable.
26 The giants were born there, who were famous of
    old,
    great in stature, expert in war.
27 God did not choose them,
    or give them the way to knowledge;
28 so they perished because they had no wisdom,
    they perished through their folly.

29 Who has gone up into heaven, and taken her,
    and brought her down from the clouds?
30 Who has gone over the sea, and found her,
    and will buy her for pure gold?
31 No one knows the way to her,
    or is concerned about the path to her.
32 But the one who knows all things knows her,
    he found her by his understanding.
    The one who prepared the earth for all time
    filled it with four-footed creatures;
33 the one who sends forth the light, and it goes;
    he called it, and it obeyed him, trembling;
34 the stars shone in their watches, and were glad;
    he called them, and they said, "Here we are!"
    They shone with gladness for him who made
    them.
35 This is our God;
    no other can be compared to him.
36 He found the whole way to knowledge,
    and gave her to his servant Jacob
    and to Israel, whom he loved.
37 Afterward she appeared on earth
    and lived with humankind.

4 She is the book of the commandments of God,
    the law that endures forever.
    All who hold her fast will live,
    and those who forsake her will die.
2 Turn, O Jacob, and take her;
    walk toward the shining of her light.
3 Do not give your glory to another,
    or your advantages to an alien people.
4 Happy are we, O Israel,
    for we know what is pleasing to God.

18 Where are the silversmiths with their patient skill
    and the secrets of their craft?
19 They have vanished, gone down to the grave,
    and others have arisen to take their place.
20 The light of day dawned on a later generation;
    they dwelt in the land,
    but they did not learn the way of knowledge
21 or discover its paths; they did not lay hold of it;
    their children went far astray.
22 Wisdom was not heard of in Canaan
    or seen in Teman.
23 Hagar's descendants who sought for knowledge on
    earth,
    the merchants of Merran and Teman,
    the story-tellers, the seekers after understanding,
    not one of them discovered the way of wisdom
    or had any recollection of her paths.

24 Israel, how great is God's dwelling-place,
    how vast the extent of his domain!
25 Great and boundless it is, lofty and immeasurable.
26 There of old the giants were born,
    a famous race, mighty in stature, skilled in war.
27 But those were not chosen by God
    or shown the way of knowledge.
28 Their race perished for lack of insight;
    they perished in their folly.

29 Has anyone gone up to heaven and gained wisdom
    and brought her down from the clouds?
30 Has anyone crossed the sea and found her,
    or obtained her for fine gold?
31 No one can know the path
    or conceive the way that will lead to her.
32 Only the omniscient God knows her;
    the mind of God discovered her.
    He who established the earth for all time
    filled it with four-footed animals.
33 He sent forth the light and it went on its way;
    he summoned it, and trembling it obeyed.
34 The stars shone in their appointed places and
    rejoiced;
    he summoned them, and they answered, 'We are
    ready,'
    and joyfully they shone for their Maker.
35 This is he who is our God;
    there is none to compare with him.
36 Every way of knowledge he found out
    and gave to Jacob his servant,
    to Israel whom he loved.
37 After that, wisdom appeared on earth
    and lived among men.

4 She is the book of God's commandments,
    the law that endures for ever.
    All who hold fast to her will live,
    but those who forsake her will die.
2 Return, you people of Jacob, and lay hold of her;
    set your course towards the radiance of her light.
3 Do not yield up your glory to another
    or your privileges to a foreign nation.
4 Happy are we, Israel,
    for we know what is pleasing to God!

g Other ancient authorities read their

18 They schemed anxiously for money,
   but there is no trace of their work:
19 They have vanished down into the nether world,
   and others have risen up in their stead.

20 Later generations have seen the light,
   have dwelt in the land,
   But the way to understanding they have
      not known,
21   they have not perceived her paths, or
         reached her;
   their offspring were far from the way to her.
22 She has not been heard of in Canaan,
   nor seen in Teman.
23 The sons of Hagar who seek knowledge on earth,
   the merchants of Midian and Teman,
   the phrasemakers seeking knowledge,
   These have not known the way to wisdom,
   nor have they her paths in mind.

24 O Israel, how vast is the house of God,
   how broad the scope of his dominion:
25 Vast and endless,
   high and immeasurable!
26 In it were born the giants,
   renowned at the first,
   stalwarts, skilled in war.
27 Not these did God choose,
   nor did he give them the way of understanding;
28 They perished for lack of prudence,
   perished through their folly.
29 Who has gone up to the heavens and taken her,
   or brought her down from the clouds?
30 Who has crossed the sea and found her,
   bearing her away rather than choice gold?
31 None knows the way to her,
   nor has any understood her paths.

32 Yet he who knows all things knows her;
   he has probed her by his knowledge—
   He who established the earth for all time,
   and filled it with four-footed beasts;
33 He who dismisses the light, and it departs,
   calls it, and it obeys him trembling;
34 Before whom the stars at their posts
   shine and rejoice;
35 When he calls them, they answer, "Here we are!"
   shining with joy for their Maker.
36 Such is our God;
   no other is to be compared to him:
37 He has traced out all the way of understanding,
   and has given her to Jacob, his servant,
   to Israel, his beloved son.

38 Since then she has appeared on earth,
   and moved among men.

4 She is the book of the precepts of God,
   the law that endures forever;
   All who cling to her will live,
   but those will die who forsake her.
2 Turn, O Jacob, and receive her:
   walk by her light toward splendor.
3 Give not your glory to another,
   your privileges to an alien race.
4 Blessed are we, O Israel;
   for what pleases God is known to us!

18 those who worked so carefully in silver
   —but of whose works no trace is to be found?
19 They have vanished, gone down to Sheol.
   Others have risen to their places,
20 more recent generations have seen the day
   and peopled the earth in their turn,
   but the way of knowledge they have not found;
21 they have not recognised the paths she treads.
   Nor have their children had any grasp of her,
   remaining far from her way.
22 Nothing has been heard of her in Canaan,
   nothing has been seen of her in Teman;
23 the children of Hagar in search of worldly wisdom,
   the merchants of Midian and Teman,
   the tale-spinners and the philosophers have none of
      them found the way to wisdom
   or remembered the paths she treads.

24 How great, Israel, is the house of God,
   how wide his domain,
25 immeasurably wide,
   infinitely lofty!
26 In it were born the giants, famous from the
      beginning,
   immensely tall, expert in war;
27 God's choice did not fall on these,
   he did not show them the way of knowledge;
28 they perished for lack of wisdom,
   perished by their own folly.
29 Who has ever climbed the sky and seized her
   to bring her down from the clouds?
30 Who has ever crossed the ocean and found her
   to bring her back in exchange for the finest gold?
31 No one can learn the way to her,
   no one can understand the path she treads.

32 But the One who knows all discovers her,
   he has grasped her with his own intellect,
   he has set the earth firm for evermore
   and filled it with four-footed beasts,
33 he sends the light—and it goes,
   he recalls it—and trembling it obeys;
34 the stars shine joyfully at their posts;
35 when he calls them, they answer, 'Here we are';
   they shine to delight their Creator.
36 It is he who is our God,
   no other can compare with him.
37 He has uncovered the whole way of knowledge
   and shown it to his servant Jacob,
   to Israel his well-beloved;
38 only then did she appear on earth
   and live among human beings.

4 She is the book of God's commandments,
   the Law that stands for ever;
   those who keep her shall live,
   those who desert her shall die.
2 Turn back, Jacob, seize her,
   in her radiance make your way to light:
3 do not yield your glory to another,
   your privilege to a people not your own.
4 Israel, blessed are we:
   what pleases God has been revealed to us!

5 Take courage, my people,
    who perpetuate Israel's name!
6 It was not for destruction
    that you were sold to the nations,
but you were handed over to your enemies
    because you angered God.
7 For you provoked the one who made you
    by sacrificing to demons and not to God.
8 You forgot the everlasting God, who brought you
    up,
    and you grieved Jerusalem, who reared you.
9 For she saw the wrath that came upon you from
    God,
    and she said:
Listen, you neighbors of Zion,
    God has brought great sorrow upon me;
10 for I have seen the exile of my sons and
    daughters,
    which the Everlasting brought upon them.
11 With joy I nurtured them,
    but I sent them away with weeping and sorrow.
12 Let no one rejoice over me, a widow
    and bereaved of many;
I was left desolate because of the sins of my
    children,
    because they turned away from the law of God.
13 They had no regard for his statutes;
    they did not walk in the ways of God's
        commandments,
    or tread the paths his righteousness showed
        them.
14 Let the neighbors of Zion come;
    remember the capture of my sons and
        daughters,
    which the Everlasting brought upon them.
15 For he brought a distant nation against them,
    a nation ruthless and of a strange language,
    which had no respect for the aged
    and no pity for a child.
16 They led away the widow's beloved sons,
    and bereaved the lonely woman of her
        daughters.
17 But I, how can I help you?
18 For he who brought these calamities upon you
    will deliver you from the hand of your
        enemies.
19 Go, my children, go;
    for I have been left desolate.
20 I have taken off the robe of peace
    and put on sackcloth for my supplication;
    I will cry to the Everlasting all my days.
21 Take courage, my children, cry to God,
    and he will deliver you from the power and
        hand of the enemy.
22 For I have put my hope in the Everlasting to save
        you,
    and joy has come to me from the Holy One,
because of the mercy that will soon come to you
    from your everlasting savior.ʰ
23 For I sent you out with sorrow and weeping,
    but God will give you back to me with joy and
        gladness forever.
24 For as the neighbors of Zion have now seen your
        capture,
    so they soon will see your salvation by God,
which will come to you with great glory
    and with the splendor of the Everlasting.

5 Take heart, my people, who keep Israel's name
    alive.
6 You were sold to the heathen, but not to be
    destroyed.
Because you excited God's wrath
    you were handed over to the foe,
7 for you provoked your Maker
    by sacrificing not to God but to demons.
8 You forgot the eternal God who nurtured you;
    you caused sorrow to Jerusalem who fostered you.
9 She saw how God's wrath had befallen you
    and said: Listen, you neighbours of Zion;
    God has brought on me great grief,
10 for I have witnessed the captivity of my sons and
        daughters
    inflicted on them by the Eternal.
11 With joy I brought them up,
    but with tears and mourning I watched them go.
12 Let no one exult over me, a widow, forsaken by so
        many,
    left desolate through the sins of my children.
    They turned away from the law of God;
13 they would not learn his statutes,
    nor would they follow his commandments,
    nor let God guide and train them in his
        righteousness.
14 Come, you neighbours of Zion,
    bear in mind the captivity of my sons and
        daughters
    inflicted on them by the Eternal;
15 for he let loose on them a nation from afar,
    a ruthless nation speaking a strange tongue
    and with no reverence for the old,
    no pity for the young.
16 They carried off the widow's beloved sons,
    and left her in loneliness, bereft of her daughters.
17 But I, how can I help you?
18 Only the One who brought the disasters on you
    can deliver you from the power of your enemies.
19 Go your way, my children, go,
    for I am left desolate.
20 I have stripped off the robes of peaceful days
    and put on the sackcloth of a suppliant;
    I shall call to the Eternal as long as I live.
21 Take heart, my children! Cry out to God,
    and he will rescue you from tyranny
    and from the power of your enemies.
22 I set my hope of your deliverance on the Eternal;
    the Holy One, your everlasting Saviour, has filled
        me with joy
    for the mercy soon to be granted you.
23 With mourning and tears I watched you go,
    but God will give you back to me
    with gladness and joy for ever.
24 As the neighbours of Zion have now seen your
        captivity,
    so they will soon witness God's deliverance of
        you,
    which will come to you with the great glory
    and the radiance of the Eternal.

ʰ Or from the Everlasting, your savior

5 Fear not, my people!
   Remember, Israel,
6 You were sold to the nations
   not for your destruction;
 It was because you angered God
   that you were handed over to your foes.
7 For you provoked your Maker
   with sacrifices to demons, to no-gods;
8 You forsook the Eternal God who nourished you,
   and you grieved Jerusalem who fostered you.
9 She indeed saw coming upon you
   the anger of God; and she said:

   "Hear, you neighbors of Zion!
   God has brought great mourning upon me,
10 For I have seen the captivity
   that the Eternal God has brought
   upon my sons and daughters.
11 With joy I fostered them;
   but with mourning and lament I let them go.
12 Let no one gloat over me, a widow,
   bereft of many:
 For the sins of my children I am left desolate,
   because they turned from the law of God,
13   and did not acknowledge his statutes;
 In the ways of God's commandments they did
   not walk,
   nor did they tread the disciplined paths of
   his justice.

14 "Let Zion's neighbors come,
   to take note of the captivity of my sons
   and daughters,
   brought upon them by the Eternal God.
15 He has brought against them a nation from afar,
   a nation ruthless and of alien speech,
 That has neither reverence for age
   nor tenderness for childhood:
16 They have led away this widow's cherished sons,
   have left me solitary, without daughters.
17 What can I do to help you?
18   He who has brought this evil upon you
   must himself deliver you from your
   enemies' hands.
19 Farewell, my children, farewell:
   I am left desolate.
20 I have taken off the garment of peace,
   have put on sackcloth for my prayer
   of supplication,
   and while I live I will cry out to the Eternal
   God.

21 "Fear not, my children; call upon God,
   who will deliver you from oppression at
   enemy hands.
22 I have trusted in the Eternal God for your welfare,
   and joy has come to me from the Holy One
 Because of the mercy that will swiftly reach you
   from your eternal savior.
23 With mourning and lament I sent you forth,
   but God will give you back to me
   with enduring gladness and joy.
24 As Zion's neighbors lately saw you taken captive,
   so shall they soon see God's salvation come
   to you,
   with great glory and the splendor of the Eternal
   God.

5 Take courage, my people,
   memorial of Israel!
6 You were sold to the nations,
   but not for extermination.
   You provoked God;
   and so were delivered to your enemies,
7 since you had angered your Creator
   by offering sacrifices to demons, and not to God.
8 You had forgotten the eternal God who reared you.
   You had also grieved Jerusalem who nursed you,
9 for when she saw God's anger
   falling on you, she said:

   Listen, you neighbours of Zion:
   God has sent me great sorrow.
10 I have seen my sons and daughters taken into
   captivity,
   which the Eternal brought down on them.
11 I had reared them joyfully;
   in tears, in sorrow, I watched them go away.
12 Do not, any of you, exult over me,
   a widow, deserted by so many;
   I am bereaved because of the sins of my children,
   who turned away from the Law of God,
13 who did not want to know his precepts
   and would not follow the ways of his
   commandments
   or tread the paths of discipline as his justice
   directed.
14 Come here, neighbours of Zion!
   Remember my sons' and daughters' captivity,
   which the Eternal brought down on them.
15 How he brought a distant nation down on them,
   a ruthless nation speaking a foreign language,
   they showed neither respect for the aged,
   nor pity for the child;
16 they carried off the widow's cherished sons,
   they left her quite alone, bereft of her daughters.
17 For my part, how could I help you?
18 He who brought those disasters down on you,
   is the one to deliver you from your enemies'
   clutches.
19 Go, my children, go your way!
   I must stay bereft and lonely;
20 I have taken off the clothes of peace
   and put on the sackcloth of entreaty;
   all my life I shall cry to the Eternal.
21 Take courage, my children, call on God:
   he will deliver you from tyranny, from the clutches
   of your enemies;
22 for I look to the Eternal for your rescue,
   and joy has come to me from the Holy One
   at the mercy soon to reach you
   from your Saviour, the Eternal.
23 In sorrow and tears I watched you go away,
   but God will give you back to me in joy and
   gladness for ever.
24 As the neighbours of Zion have now witnessed
   your captivity,
   so will they soon see your rescue by God,
   which will come upon you with great glory and
   splendour of the Eternal.

NEW REVISED STANDARD VERSION	REVISED ENGLISH BIBLE

NEW REVISED STANDARD VERSION

25 My children, endure with patience the wrath that
    has come upon you from God.
  Your enemy has overtaken you,
    but you will soon see their destruction
    and will tread upon their necks.
26 My pampered children have traveled rough roads;
    they were taken away like a flock carried off
    by the enemy.
27 Take courage, my children, and cry to God,
    for you will be remembered by the one who
    brought this upon you.
28 For just as you were disposed to go astray from
    God,
    return with tenfold zeal to seek him.
29 For the one who brought these calamities upon
    you
    will bring you everlasting joy with your
    salvation.
30 Take courage, O Jerusalem,
    for the one who named you will comfort you.
31 Wretched will be those who mistreated you
    and who rejoiced at your fall.
32 Wretched will be the cities that your children
    served as slaves;
    wretched will be the city that received your
    offspring.
33 For just as she rejoiced at your fall
    and was glad for your ruin,
    so she will be grieved at her own desolation.
34 I will take away her pride in her great population,
    and her insolence will be turned to grief.
35 For fire will come upon her from the Everlasting
    for many days,
    and for a long time she will be inhabited by
    demons.
36 Look toward the east, O Jerusalem,
    and see the joy that is coming to you from
    God.
37 Look, your children are coming, whom you sent
    away;
    they are coming, gathered from east and west,
  at the word of the Holy One,
    rejoicing in the glory of God.

5 Take off the garment of your sorrow and
    affliction, O Jerusalem,
  and put on forever the beauty of the glory from
    God.
2 Put on the robe of the righteousness that comes
    from God;
  put on your head the diadem of the glory of
    the Everlasting;
3 for God will show your splendor everywhere
    under heaven.
4 For God will give you evermore the name,
    "Righteous Peace, Godly Glory."
5 Arise, O Jerusalem, stand upon the height;
    look toward the east,
  and see your children gathered from west and east
    at the word of the Holy One,
    rejoicing that God has remembered them.
6 For they went out from you on foot,
    led away by their enemies;
  but God will bring them back to you,
    carried in glory, as on a royal throne.

REVISED ENGLISH BIBLE

25 My children, endure in patience
  the wrath God has brought on you;
  your enemy has hunted you down,
  but soon you will see him destroyed,
  soon put your foot on his neck.
26 My pampered children have trodden rough paths,
  driven off like a flock seized by raiders.
27 Take heart, my children! Cry out to God,
  for he who afflicted you will not forget you.
28 Once you were resolved to go astray from God;
  now with tenfold zeal you must turn back and seek
    him.
29 He who brought the disasters on you
  will bring you everlasting joy when he delivers
    you.
30 Take heart, Jerusalem! He who called you by name
  will comfort you.
31 Wretched will they be who maltreated you
  and gloated over your fall;
32 wretched the cities where your children were
    slaves;
  wretched the city that received your sons!
33 She that rejoiced over your downfall
  and was jubilant at your ruin,
  that same city will grieve at her own desolation.
34 I shall strip her of the multitudes that were her
    boast,
  and turn her pride into grief.
35 Fire from the Eternal will be her doom for many a
    day,
  and for a long time to come she will be the haunt
    of demons.
36 Jerusalem, look eastwards and see the joy
  that is coming to you from God.
37 They come, the sons from whom you parted;
  from east to west they come,
  assembling at the word of the Holy One
  and rejoicing in the glory of God.

5 JERUSALEM, strip off your garment of mourning
    and affliction,
  and put on for ever the glorious majesty, the gift
    of God.
2 Wrap about you his robe of righteousness;
  place on your head as a diadem the splendour of
    the Eternal.
3 God will show your radiance to every land under
    heaven;
4 from him you will receive for ever the name
  Righteous Peace, the Splendour of Godliness.
5 Arise, Jerusalem, stand on the height;
  look eastwards and see your children assembled
  from west to east at the word of the Holy One,
  rejoicing that God has remembered them.
6 They went away from you on foot,
  led off by their enemies;
  but God is bringing them home to you,
  borne aloft in glory, as on a royal throne.

NEW AMERICAN BIBLE

25 "My children, bear patiently the anger
    that has come from God upon you;
  Your enemies have persecuted you,
    and you will soon see their destruction
    and trample upon their necks.
26 My pampered children have trodden rough roads,
    carried off by their enemies like sheep in a raid.
27 Fear not, my children; call out to God!
  He who brought this upon you will
    remember you.
28 As your hearts have been disposed to stray
    from God,
  turn now ten times the more to seek him;
29 For he who has brought disaster upon you
    will, in saving you, bring you back
    enduring joy."

30 Fear not, Jerusalem!
  He who gave you your name is
    your encouragement.
31 Fearful are those who harmed you,
  who rejoiced at your downfall;
32 Fearful are the cities where your children
    were enslaved,
  fearful the city that took your sons.
33 As that city rejoiced at your collapse,
  and made merry at your downfall,
  so shall she grieve over her own desolation.
34 I will take from her the joyous throngs,
  and her exultation shall be turned to mourning:
35 For fire shall come upon her
  from the Eternal God, for a long time,
  and demons shall dwell in her from that time on.

36 Look to the east, Jerusalem!
  behold the joy that comes to you from God.
37 Here come your sons whom you once let go,
  gathered in from the east and from the west
  By the word of the Holy One,
  rejoicing in the glory of God.

5 Jerusalem, take off your robe of mourning
    and misery;
  put on the splendor of glory from God forever:
2 Wrapped in the cloak of justice from God,
  bear on your head the mitre
  that displays the glory of the eternal name.
3 For God will show all the earth your splendor:
4   you will be named by God forever
  the peace of justice, the glory of God's worship.
5 Up, Jerusalem! stand upon the heights;
  look to the east and see your children
  Gathered from the east and the west
  at the word of the Holy One,
  rejoicing that they are remembered by God.
6 Led away on foot by their enemies they left you:
  but God will bring them back to you
  borne aloft in glory as on royal thrones.

NEW JERUSALEM BIBLE

25 My children, patiently bear the anger brought on
    you by God.
  Your enemy has persecuted you,
    but soon you will witness his destruction
    and set your foot on his neck.
26 My favourite children have travelled by rough
    roads,
  carried off like a flock by a marauding enemy.
27 Take courage, my children, call on God:
  he who brought this on you will remember you.
28 As by your will you first strayed from God,
  so now turn back and search for him ten times
    harder;
29 for as he has been bringing down those disasters on
    you,
  so will he rescue you and give you eternal joy.

30 Take courage, Jerusalem:
  he who gave you your name will console you.
31 Disaster will come to all who have ill-treated you
  and gloated over your fall.
32 Disaster will come to the cities where your children
    were slaves;
  disaster to whichever one received your children,
33 for just as she rejoiced at your fall
  and was happy to see you ruined,
  so will she grieve over her own desolation.
34 I shall deprive her of the joy of a populous city,
  and her insolence will turn to mourning;
35 fire from the Eternal will befall her for many a
    day,
  and demons will dwell in her for ages.
36 Jerusalem, turn your eyes to the east,
  see the joy that is coming to you from God.
37 Look, the children you watched go away are on
    their way home;
  reassembled from east and west, they are on their
    way home
  at the Holy One's command, rejoicing in God's
    glory.

5 Jerusalem, take off your dress of sorrow and
    distress,
  put on the beauty of God's glory for evermore,
2 wrap the cloak of God's saving justice around you,
  put the diadem of the Eternal One's glory on your
    head,
3 for God means to show your splendour to every
    nation under heaven,
4 and the name God gives you for evermore will be,
  'Peace-through-Justice, and
    Glory-through-Devotion'.
5 Arise, Jerusalem, stand on the heights
  and turn your eyes to the east:
  see your children reassembled from west and east
  at the Holy One's command, rejoicing because
    God has remembered.
6 Though they left you on foot
  driven by enemies,
  now God brings them back to you,
  carried gloriously, like a royal throne.

NEW REVISED STANDARD VERSION

7 For God has ordered that every high mountain
and the everlasting hills be made low
and the valleys filled up, to make level ground,
so that Israel may walk safely in the glory of
God.
8 The woods and every fragrant tree
have shaded Israel at God's command.
9 For God will lead Israel with joy,
in the light of his glory,
with the mercy and righteousness that come
from him.

REVISED ENGLISH BIBLE

7 All the high mountains and everlasting hills
are to be made low as God commanded,
and every ravine is to be filled and levelled,
that Israel may walk securely in the glory of God;
8 and the woods and every fragrant tree
will give Israel shade at God's command.
9 He will lead Israel with joy
by the light of his glory,
in his mercy and his righteousness.

7 For God has commanded
  that every lofty mountain be made low,
And that the age-old depths and gorges
  be filled to level ground,
  that Israel may advance secure in the glory
    of God.
8 The forests and every fragrant kind of tree
  have overshadowed Israel at God's command;
9 For God is leading Israel in joy
  by the light of his glory,
  with his mercy and justice for company.

7 For God has decreed the flattening
  of each high mountain, of the everlasting hills,
  the filling of the valleys to make the ground level
  so that Israel can walk safely in God's glory.
8 And the forests and every fragrant tree will provide
    shade
  for Israel, at God's command;
9 for God will guide Israel in joy by the light of his
    glory,
  with the mercy and saving justice which come
    from him.

The Letter of Jeremiah

A Letter of Jeremiah

6 [a] A copy of a letter that Jeremiah sent to those who were to be taken to Babylon as exiles by the king of the Babylonians, to give them the message that God had commanded him.

2 Because of the sins that you have committed before God, you will be taken to Babylon as exiles by Nebuchadnezzar, king of the Babylonians. 3 Therefore when you have come to Babylon you will remain there for many years, for a long time, up to seven generations; after that I will bring you away from there in peace. 4 Now in Babylon you will see gods made of silver and gold and wood, which people carry on their shoulders, and which cause the heathen to fear. 5 So beware of becoming at all like the foreigners or of letting fear for these gods[b] possess you 6 when you see the multitude before and behind them worshiping them. But say in your heart, "It is you, O Lord, whom we must worship." 7 For my angel is with you, and he is watching over your lives.

8 Their tongues are smoothed by the carpenter, and they themselves are overlaid with gold and silver; but they are false and cannot speak. 9 People[c] take gold and make crowns for the heads of their gods, as they might for a girl who loves ornaments. 10 Sometimes the priests secretly take gold and silver from their gods and spend it on themselves, 11 or even give some of it to the prostitutes on the terrace. They deck their gods[d] out with garments like human beings —these gods of silver and gold and wood 12 that cannot save themselves from rust and corrosion. When they have been dressed in purple robes, 13 their faces are wiped because of the dust from the temple, which is thick upon them. 14 One of them holds a scepter, like a district judge, but is unable to destroy anyone who offends it. 15 Another has a dagger in its right hand, and an ax, but cannot defend itself from war and robbers. 16 From this it is evident that they are not gods; so do not fear them.

17 For just as someone's dish is useless when it is broken, 18 so are their gods when they have been set up in the temples. Their eyes are full of the dust raised by the feet of those who enter. And just as the gates are shut on every side against anyone who has offended a king, as though under sentence of death, so the priests make their temples secure with doors and locks and bars, in order that they may not be plundered by robbers. 19 They light more lamps for them than they light for themselves, though their gods[e] can see none of them. 20 They are[f] just like a beam of the temple, but their hearts, it is said, are eaten away when crawling creatures from the earth devour them and their robes. They do not notice 21 when their faces have been blackened by the smoke of the temple. 22 Bats, swallows, and birds alight on their bodies and heads; and so do cats. 23 From this you will know that they are not gods; so do not fear them.

24 As for the gold that they wear for beauty—it[g] will not shine unless someone wipes off the tarnish; for even when they were being cast, they did not feel it. 25 They are

6 A COPY of a letter sent by Jeremiah to the captives who were to be taken to Babylon by the king of the Babylonians; it conveys a message entrusted to him by God.

2 It is because of the sins you have committed in the sight of God that you are being led away captive to Babylon by Nebuchadnezzar, king of the Babylonians. 3 Once you are in Babylon, your stay there will be long; it will last for many years, up to seven generations; afterwards I will lead you out from there in peace.

4 In Babylon you can now see gods carried on men's shoulders, gods made of silver, gold, and wood, which fill the nations with awe. 5 You must be careful, then, never to become like those foreigners. Do not be overawed by the gods when you see them in the midst of a procession of worshippers, 6 but say in your hearts, 'To you alone, O Lord, is worship due.' 7 For my angel will be with you; your lives will be in his care.

8 The idols are plated with gold and silver. They have tongues fashioned by a craftsman: they are a sham and cannot speak. 9 The people take gold and make crowns for the heads of their gods, as one might for a girl fond of finery. 10 Sometimes the priests filch gold and silver from their gods and spend it on themselves; 11 they will even give some to the temple prostitutes. They dress up the idols in clothes like human beings, their gods of silver, gold, and wood; 12 but the gods, decked in purple though they are, cannot protect themselves against corrosion and moth. 13 The dust in the temple lies thick upon them, so that their faces have to be wiped clean. 14 Like the ruler of a land, the god holds a sceptre, yet he has no power to put to death anyone who offends him. 15 In his right hand he has a dagger and an axe, yet he is powerless to save himself from war and pillage. 16 Clearly they are not gods; therefore have no fear of them.

17 These gods, sitting in their temples, are of no more use than a broken pot. Their eyes get filled with dust from the feet of those who come in. 18 And just as the court of the guardhouse is barricaded when a traitor awaits execution, so the priests secure their temples with doors and bolts and bars to guard against pillage by robbers. 19 The priests light lamps, more than they need for themselves—yet the idols can see none of them. 20 They are like one of the beams of the temple, but, as men admit, their hearts are eaten out, for creatures crawl from the ground and devour both them and their vestments without their being aware of it. 21 Their faces are blackened by the smoke in the temple. 22 Bats and swallows and birds of all kinds perch on their bodies and heads, and cats do likewise. 23 From all this you may be sure that they are not gods; therefore have no fear of them.

24 Though embellished with gold plating, the idols will not shine unless someone rubs off the tarnish. Even when being cast they felt nothing. 25 They were bought regardless

---

[a] The King James Version (like the Latin Vulgate) prints The Letter of Jeremiah as Chapter 6 of the Book of Baruch, and the chapter and verse numbers are here retained. In the Greek Septuagint, the Letter is separated from Baruch by the Book of Lamentations. [b] Gk for them [c] Gk They [d] Gk them [e] Gk they [f] Gk It is [g] Lat Syr: Gk they

6:1 etc. The chapter and verse numbering is that of the Authorized (King James) Version, in which this forms chapter 6 of Baruch.

The Letter of Jeremiah is included as Baruch ch 6 in the New American Bible translation.

The Letter of Jeremiah is included as Baruch ch 6 in the New Jerusalem Bible translation.

BARUCH 6

BARUCH 6

6 A copy of the letter which Jeremiah sent to those who were being led captive to Babylon by the king of the Babylonians, to convey to them what God had commanded him:

For the sins you committed before God, you are being led captive to Babylon by Nebuchadnezzar, king of the Babylonians. ² When you reach Babylon you will be there many years, a period seven generations long; after which I will bring you back from there in peace. ³ And now in Babylon you will see borne upon men's shoulders gods of silver and gold and wood, which cast fear upon the pagans. ⁴ Take care that you yourselves do not imitate their alien example and stand in fear of them, ⁵ when you see the crowd before them and behind worshiping them. Rather, say in your hearts, "You, O Lord, are to be worshiped!"; ⁶ for my angel is with you, and he is the custodian of your lives.

⁷ Their tongues are smoothed by woodworkers; they are covered with gold and silver — but they are a fraud, and cannot speak. ⁸ People bring gold, as to a maiden in love with ornament, ⁹ and furnish crowns for the heads of their gods. Then sometimes the priests take the silver and gold from their gods and spend it on themselves, ¹⁰ or give part of it to the harlots on the terrace. They trick them out in garments like men, these gods of silver and gold and wood; ¹¹ but though they are wrapped in purple clothing, they are not safe from corrosion or insects. ¹² They wipe their faces clean of the house dust which is thick upon them. ¹³ Each has a scepter, like the human ruler of a district; but none does away with those that offend against it. ¹⁴ Each has in its right hand an axe or dagger, but it cannot save itself from war or pillage. Thus it is known they are not gods; do not fear them.

¹⁵ As useless as one's broken tools ¹⁶ are their gods, set up in their houses; their eyes are full of dust from the feet of those who enter. ¹⁷ Their courtyards are walled in like those of a man brought to execution for a crime against the king; the priests reinforce their houses with gates and bars and bolts, lest they be carried off by robbers. ¹⁸ They light more lamps for them than for themselves, yet not one of these can they see. ¹⁹ They are like any beam in the house; it is said their hearts are eaten away. Though the insects out of the ground consume them and their garments, they do not feel it. ²⁰ Their faces are blackened by the smoke of the house. ²¹ Bats and swallows alight on their bodies and on their heads; and cats as well as birds. ²² Know, therefore, that they are not gods, and do not fear them.

²³ Despite the gold that covers them for adornment, unless someone wipes away the corrosion, they do not shine; nor did they feel anything when they were molded. ²⁴ They

A copy of the letter which Jeremiah sent to those about to be led captive to Babylon by the king of the Babylonians, to tell them what he had been commanded by God:

6 'Because of the sins which you have committed before God you are to be deported to Babylon by Nebuchadnezzar king of the Babylonians. ² Once you have reached Babylon you will stay there for many years, as long as seven generations; after which I shall bring you home in peace. ³ Now in Babylon you will see gods made of silver, of gold, of wood, being carried shoulder-high, and filling the gentiles with fear. ⁴ Be on your guard! Do not imitate the foreigners, do not have any fear of their gods ⁵ as you see their worshippers prostrating themselves before and behind them. Instead, say in your hearts, "Master, it is you that we must worship." ⁶ For my angel is with you; your lives will be in his care.

⁷ 'Overlaid with gold and silver, their tongues polished smooth by a craftsman, they are counterfeit and have no power to speak. ⁸ As though for a girl fond of finery, these people take gold and make crowns for the heads of their gods. ⁹ And sometimes, the priests filch gold and silver from their gods to spend on themselves, even giving some of it to the prostitutes on the terrace. ¹⁰ They dress up these gods of silver, gold and wood, in clothes, like human beings; on their own they cannot protect themselves from either tarnish or woodworm; ¹¹ when they have been dressed in purple cloaks, their faces have to be dusted, because of the temple dust which settles thick on them. ¹² One holds a sceptre like the governor of a province, yet is powerless to put to death anyone who offends him; ¹³ another holds sword and mace in his right hand, yet is powerless to defend himself against war or thieves. ¹⁴ From this it is evident that they are not gods; do not be afraid of them.

¹⁵ 'Just as a pot in common use becomes useless once it is broken, so are these gods enshrined inside their temples. ¹⁶ Their eyes are full of dust raised by the feet of those who enter. ¹⁷ Just as the doors are locked on all sides on someone who has offended a king and is under sentence of death, so the priests secure the temples of these gods with gates and bolts and bars for fear of burglary. ¹⁸ They light more lamps for them than they do for themselves, and the gods see none of them. ¹⁹ They are like one of the temple beams, which are said to be gnawed away from within; the termites creep out of the ground and eat them and their clothes too, and they feel nothing. ²⁰ Their faces are blackened by the smoke that rises from the temple. ²¹ Bats, swallows, birds of every kind perch on their bodies and heads, and so do cats. ²² From this, you can see for yourselves that they are not gods; do not be afraid of them.

²³ 'The gold with which they are parading their futility before the world is supposed to make them look beautiful, but if someone does not rub off the tarnish, these gods will not be shining much on their own, and even while they were being cast, they felt nothing. ²⁴ However much was paid for

bought without regard to cost, but there is no breath in them. 26 Having no feet, they are carried on the shoulders of others, revealing to humankind their worthlessness. And those who serve them are put to shame 27 because, if any of these gods falls[h] to the ground, they themselves must pick it up. If anyone sets it upright, it cannot move itself; and if it is tipped over, it cannot straighten itself. Gifts are placed before them just as before the dead. 28 The priests sell the sacrifices that are offered to these gods[i] and use the money themselves. Likewise their wives preserve some of the meat[j] with salt, but give none to the poor or helpless. 29 Sacrifices to them may even be touched by women in their periods or at childbirth. Since you know by these things that they are not gods, do not fear them.

30 For how can they be called gods? Women serve meals for gods of silver and gold and wood; 31 and in their temples the priests sit with their clothes torn, their heads and beards shaved, and their heads uncovered. 32 They howl and shout before their gods as some do at a funeral banquet. 33 The priests take some of the clothing of their gods[k] to clothe their wives and children. 34 Whether one does evil to them or good, they will not be able to repay it. They cannot set up a king or depose one. 35 Likewise they are not able to give either wealth or money; if one makes a vow to them and does not keep it, they will not require it. 36 They cannot save anyone from death or rescue the weak from the strong. 37 They cannot restore sight to the blind; they cannot rescue one who is in distress. 38 They cannot take pity on a widow or do good to an orphan. 39 These things that are made of wood and overlaid with gold and silver are like stones from the mountain, and those who serve them will be put to shame. 40 Why then must anyone think that they are gods, or call them gods?

Besides, even the Chaldeans themselves dishonor them; for when they see someone who cannot speak, they bring Bel and pray that the mute may speak, as though Bel[l] were able to understand! 41 Yet they themselves cannot perceive this and abandon them, for they have no sense. 42 And the women, with cords around them, sit along the passageways, burning bran for incense. 43 When one of them is led off by one of the passers-by and is taken to bed by him, she derides the woman next to her, because she was not as attractive as herself and her cord was not broken. 44 Whatever is done for these idols[m] is false. Why then must anyone think that they are gods, or call them gods?

45 They are made by carpenters and goldsmiths; they can be nothing but what the artisans wish them to be. 46 Those who make them will certainly not live very long themselves; 47 how then can the things that are made by them be gods? They have left only lies and reproach for those who come after. 48 For when war or calamity comes upon them, the priests consult together as to where they can hide themselves and their gods.[m] 49 How then can one fail to see that these are not gods, for they cannot save themselves from war or calamity? 50 Since they are made of wood and overlaid with gold and silver, it will afterward be known that they are false. 51 It will be manifest to all the nations and kings that they are not gods but the work of human hands, and that there is no work of God in them. 52 Who then can fail to know that they are not gods?[n]

53 For they cannot set up a king over a country or give rain to people. 54 They cannot judge their own cause or deliver one who is wronged, for they have no power; 55 they are like crows between heaven and earth. When fire breaks

of price, but there is no breath in them. 26 As they lack feet they are carried on men's shoulders, which proclaims to all how worthless they are. 27 Even those who serve them are put to shame because, if ever an idol topples to the ground, it does not get up by itself; nor, if anyone sets it up again, can it move by its own effort; and if it is tilted it cannot straighten itself. To set an offering before them is like setting it before the dead! 28 The sacrifices made to gods are sold by the priests, who spend the proceeds on themselves. Their wives are no better; they take portions of the sacrifices and cure the meat, and give no share to the needy or helpless. 29 These offerings are handled by women who are menstruating or by mothers fresh from childbirth. Be assured by this that they are not gods; have no fear of them.

30 For how can they be called gods, these gods of silver, gold, and wood, when it is women who serve them food? 31 In the temples are seated the priests, shaven and shorn, with their clothes rent and their heads uncovered. 32 They shout and howl before these gods of theirs, like mourners at a funeral feast. 33 The priests clothe their wives and children with vestments they stripped from the gods. 34 Should anyone do the gods either injury or service they are incapable of repaying it. They cannot set up or depose a king; 35 so too they are quite unable to bestow wealth or money. Anyone making a vow to them and failing to honour it will never be called to account. 36 They will never save anyone from death, never rescue the weak from the strong, 37 never restore the sight of the blind, or rescue a person in distress. 38 They neither pity the widow nor befriend the fatherless. 39 They are like blocks from the quarry, these wooden things plated with gold and silver, and all who serve them will be discredited. 40 How can anyone suppose them to be gods or call them so?

Besides, even the Chaldaeans themselves bring these idols of theirs into disrepute; 41 for when they see a dumb man without the power of articulate speech, they bring him into the temple and ask Bel to give him speech, as if Bel could understand. 42 Because they themselves are void of understanding, they do not see the folly of it and abandon their idols. 43 The women sit in the street with cords round them, burning bran for incense; and when one of them has been drawn aside by a passer-by and she has lain with him, she taunts her neighbour, who has not been thought as attractive as herself and whose cord has not been broken. 44 Everything to do with these idols is a sham. How then can anyone suppose them to be gods or call them so?

45 They are the products of the carpenter and the goldsmith; they can be nothing but what the craftsmen intend them to be. 46 Even their makers' lives cannot be prolonged; how then can the things they make be gods? 47 It is a disgraceful sham they have bequeathed to posterity. 48 If war or disaster overtakes the idols, the priests discuss among themselves where they can hide with their gods. 49 How then can anyone fail to see that these are not gods, when they are powerless to save themselves from war or disaster? 50 Since they are nothing but wood plated all over with gold and silver, they will in such times be recognized for the shams they are. 51 To every nation and king it will be evident that these are not gods but the work of human hands, with no divine power in them whatsoever. 52 Will anyone still not admit that they are not gods?

53 They cannot set up a king over a country; they cannot provide rain; 54 they cannot decide a case or redress an injustice. They are as helpless as crows tossed about in mid-air. 55 When fire breaks out in a temple belonging to

---

[h] Gk *if they fall*   [i] Gk *to them*   [j] Gk *of them*   [k] Gk *some of their clothing*   [l] Gk *he*   [m] Gk *them*   [n] Meaning of Gk uncertain

6:54 **cannot . . . injustice:** *some witnesses read* cannot judge in their own cause, or redress an injustice done them.

are bought at any price, and there is no spirit in them. 25 Having no feet, they are carried on men's shoulders, displaying their shame to all; and those who worship them are put to confusion 26 because, if they fall to the ground, the worshipers must raise them up. They neither move of themselves if one sets them upright, nor come upright if they fall; but one puts gifts beside them as beside the dead. 27 Their priests resell their sacrifices for their own advantage. Even their wives cure parts of the meat, but do not share it with the poor and the weak; 28 the menstruous and women in childbed handle their sacrifices. Knowing from this that they are not gods, do not fear them.

29 How can they be called gods? For women bring the offerings to these gods of silver and gold and wood; 30 and in their temples the priests squat with torn tunic and with shaven hair and beard, and with their heads uncovered. 31 They shout and wail before their gods as others do at a funeral banquet. 32 The priests take some of their clothing and put it on their wives and children. 33 Whether they are treated well or ill by anyone, they cannot requite it; they can neither set up a king nor remove him. 34 Similarly, they cannot give anyone riches or coppers; if one fails to fulfill a vow to them, they cannot exact it of him. 35 They neither save a man from death, nor deliver the weak from the strong. 36 To no blind man do they restore his sight, nor do they save any man in an emergency. 37 They neither pity the widow nor benefit the orphan. 38 These gilded and silvered wooden statues are like stones from the mountains; and their worshipers will be put to shame. 39 How then can it be thought or claimed that they are gods?

40 Even the Chaldeans themselves have no respect for them; for when they see a deaf mute, incapable of speech, they bring forward Bel and ask the god to make noise, as though the man could understand; 41 and they are themselves unable to reflect and abandon these gods, for they have no sense. 42 And their women, girt with cords, sit by the roads, burning chaff for incense; 43 and whenever one of them is drawn aside by some passerby who lies with her, she mocks her neighbor who has not been dignified as she has, and has not had her cord broken. 44 All that takes place around these gods is a fraud: how then can it be thought or claimed that they are gods?

45 They are produced by woodworkers and goldsmiths, and they are nothing else than what these craftsmen wish them to be. 46 Even those who produce them are not long-lived; 47 how then can what they have produced be gods? They have left frauds and opprobrium to their successors. 48 For when war or disaster comes upon them, the priests deliberate among themselves where they can hide with them. 49 How then can one not know that these are no-gods, which do not save themselves either from war or from disaster? 50 They are wooden, gilded and silvered; they will later be known for frauds. To all peoples and kings it will be clear that they are not gods, but human handiwork; and that God's work is not in them.

51 Who does not know that they are not gods? 52 They set no king over the land, nor do they give men rain. 53 They neither vindicate their own rights, nor do they recover what is unjustly taken, for they are unable; 54 they are like crows between heaven and earth. For when fire breaks out in the

them, there is still no breath of life in them. 25 Being unable to walk, they have to be carried on men's shoulders, which shows how futile they are. It is humiliating for their worshippers, too, who have to stand them up again if they fall over. 26 Once they have been stood up, they cannot move on their own; if they tilt askew, they cannot right themselves; offerings made to them might as well be made to the dead. 27 Whatever is sacrificed to them, the priests re-sell and pocket the profit; while their wives salt down part of it, but give nothing to the poor or to the helpless. As to the sacrifices themselves, why, women during their periods and women in childbed are not afraid to touch them! 28 From all this you can tell that they are not gods; do not be afraid of them.

29 'Indeed, how can they even be called gods, when women do the offering to these gods of silver, gold and wood? 30 In their temples, the priests stay sitting down, their garments torn, heads and beard shaved and heads uncovered; 31 they roar and shriek before their gods as people do at funeral feasts. 32 The priests take robes from the gods to clothe their own wives and children. 33 Whether these gods are treated badly or well, they are incapable of paying back either treatment; as incapable too of making or unmaking kings, 34 equally incapable of distributing wealth or money. If anyone fails to honour a vow he has made to them, they cannot call him to account. 35 They can neither save anyone from death nor rescue the weak from the strong, 36 nor restore sight to the blind, nor save anyone in trouble, 37 nor take pity on a widow, nor be generous to an orphan. 38 These wooden gods overlaid with gold and silver are about as much use as rocks cut out of the mountain side. Their worshippers will be confounded! 39 So how can anyone think or say that they are gods?

40 'The Chaldaeans themselves do them no honour; if they find someone who is dumb and cannot speak, they present him to Bel, entreating him for the gift of speech, as though he could perceive it! 41 And they are incapable of drawing the conclusion and abandoning those gods — such is their lack of perception. 42 Women with strings round their waists sit in the streets, burning bran for incense; 43 when one of these has been picked up by a passer-by and been to bed with him, she then gloats over her neighbour for not having been thought as worthy as herself and for not having had her string broken. 44 Whatever is done for them is spurious. So how can anyone think or say that they are gods?

45 'Made by woodworkers and goldsmiths, they are only what those workmen decide to make them. 46 Their makers have not long to live themselves, so how can the things they make be gods? 47 Their legacy to their descendants is nothing but delusion and dishonour. 48 If war or disasters befall them, the priests discuss where best to hide themselves and these gods; 49 how can anyone fail to realise that they are not gods, if they cannot save themselves from war or from disasters? 50 And since they are only made of wood overlaid with gold or silver, it will later become apparent that they are spurious; it will be obvious to everyone, to nations as to kings, that they are not gods but the work of human hands, and that there is no divine activity in them. 51 Does anyone still need convincing that they are not gods?

52 'They can neither appoint a king over a country, nor give rain to humankind, 53 nor regulate their own affairs, nor rescue anyone who suffers a wrong; they are as helpless as crows between sky and ground. 54 If fire falls on the

NEW REVISED STANDARD VERSION

out in a temple of wooden gods overlaid with gold or silver, their priests will flee and escape, but the gods*o* will be burned up like timbers. 56 Besides, they can offer no resistance to king or enemy. Why then must anyone admit or think that they are gods?

57 Gods made of wood and overlaid with silver and gold are unable to save themselves from thieves or robbers. 58 Anyone who can will strip them of their gold and silver and of the robes they wear, and go off with this booty, and they will not be able to help themselves. 59 So it is better to be a king who shows his courage, or a household utensil that serves its owner's need, than to be these false gods; better even the door of a house that protects its contents, than these false gods; better also a wooden pillar in a palace, than these false gods.

60 For sun and moon and stars are bright, and when sent to do a service, they are obedient. 61 So also the lightning, when it flashes, is widely seen; and the wind likewise blows in every land. 62 When God commands the clouds to go over the whole world, they carry out his command. 63 And the fire sent from above to consume mountains and woods does what it is ordered. But these idols *p* are not to be compared with them in appearance or power. 64 Therefore one must not think that they are gods, nor call them gods, for they are not able either to decide a case or to do good to anyone. 65 Since you know then that they are not gods, do not fear them.

66 They can neither curse nor bless kings; 67 they cannot show signs in the heavens for the nations, or shine like the sun or give light like the moon. 68 The wild animals are better than they are, for they can flee to shelter and help themselves. 69 So we have no evidence whatever that they are gods; therefore do not fear them.

70 Like a scarecrow in a cucumber bed, which guards nothing, so are their gods of wood, overlaid with gold and silver. 71 In the same way, their gods of wood, overlaid with gold and silver, are like a thornbush in a garden on which every bird perches; or like a corpse thrown out in the darkness. 72 From the purple and linen*q* that rot upon them you will know that they are not gods; and they will finally be consumed themselves, and be a reproach in the land. 73 Better, therefore, is someone upright who has no idols; such a person will be far above reproach.

o Gk *they*   *p* Gk *these things*   *q* Cn: Gk *marble*, Syr *silk*

REVISED ENGLISH BIBLE

those wooden gods all gilded and silvered, their priests will run for safety, but the gods will go up in flames like timbers. 56 They cannot offer resistance to king or enemy. How then can anyone accept or believe that they are gods?

57 They cannot save themselves from thieves and robbers, these wooden gods, plated with gold and silver. 58 Any able-bodied person can strip them of their gold and silver and make off with the vestments in which they are arrayed; they can in no way help themselves. 59 Better a king who displays his courage than such a sham god, better a household pot that serves its owner's purpose, better even the door of a house that keeps the contents safe, or a wooden pillar in a palace!

60 Sun and moon and the stars that shine so brightly are sent to serve a purpose, and they obey. 61 So too, when the lightning flashes, it is seen far and wide. Likewise the wind blows in every land. 62 When God commands the clouds to travel over all the world, they accomplish their task; 63 and fire, when it is sent down from above to consume mountains and forests, carries out his bidding. But idols are not to be compared with any of these, either in appearance or in power. 64 It follows they are not to be considered gods or given that name, since they are incapable of pronouncing judgement or of conferring benefits on mankind. 65 Being assured, therefore, that they are not gods, have no fear of them.

66 They wield no power over kings, either to curse or to bless; 67 and they cannot provide the nations with signs in the heavens, either by shining like the sun or by giving light like the moon. 68 Wild beasts are better off; they at least can save themselves by taking cover. 69 From first to last there is no evidence that they are gods; so banish all fear of them.

70 These wooden gods of theirs, all plated with gold and silver, give no better protection than a scarecrow in a bed of cucumbers. 71 They are like a thorn bush in a garden, a perch for every bird, or like a corpse cast out in the dark. Such are their wooden gods, with their plating of gold and silver! 72 The purple and fine linen rotting on them proves that they are not gods; in the end they will themselves be eaten away, to the disgrace of the land.

73 Better, then, to be upright and have no idols, for such a one will be in no danger of disgrace.

6:72 **fine linen:** *prob. mng; Gk marble.*

BARUCH 6

NEW AMERICAN BIBLE

temple of these wooden or gilded or silvered gods, though the priests flee and are safe, they themselves are burnt up in the fire like beams. ⁵⁵ They cannot resist a king, or enemy forces. ⁵⁶ How then can it be admitted or thought that they are gods?

They are safe from neither thieves nor bandits, these wooden and silvered and gilded gods; ⁵⁷ those who seize them strip off the gold and the silver, and go away with the clothing that was on them, and they cannot help themselves. ⁵⁸ How much better to be a king displaying his valor, or a handy tool in a house, the joy of its owner, than these false gods; or the door of a house, that keeps safe those who are within, rather than these false gods; or a wooden post in a palace, rather than these false gods! ⁵⁹ The sun and moon and stars are bright, and obedient in the service for which they are sent. ⁶⁰ Likewise the lightning, when it flashes, is a goodly sight; and the same wind blows over all the land. ⁶¹ The clouds, too, when commanded by God to proceed across the whole world, fulfill the order; ⁶² and fire, sent from on high to burn up the mountains and the forests, does what has been commanded. But these false gods are not their equal, whether in beauty or in power; ⁶³ so that it is unthinkable, and cannot be claimed, that they are gods. They can neither execute judgment, nor benefit man. ⁶⁴ Know, therefore, that they are not gods, and do not fear them.

⁶⁵ Kings they neither curse nor bless. ⁶⁶ They show the nations no signs in the heavens, nor are they brilliant like the sun, nor shining like the moon. ⁶⁷ The beasts which can help themselves by fleeing to shelter are better than they are. ⁶⁸ Thus in no way is it clear to us that they are gods; so do not fear them. ⁶⁹ For like a scarecrow in a cucumber patch, that is no protection, are their wooden, gilded, silvered gods. ⁷⁰ Just like a thornbush in a garden on which perches every kind of bird, or like a corpse hurled into darkness, are their silvered and gilded wooden gods. ⁷¹ From the rotting of the purple and the linen upon them, it can be known that they are not gods; they themselves will in the end be consumed, and be a disgrace in the land. ⁷² The better for the just man who has no idols: he shall be far from disgrace!

NEW JERUSALEM BIBLE

temple of these wooden gods overlaid with gold or silver, their priests fly to safety while they for their part stay there like beams, to be burnt. ⁵⁵ They cannot put up any resistance to a king or to enemies. ⁵⁶ So how can anyone think or say that they are gods?

⁵⁷ 'These wooden gods overlaid with gold or silver cannot evade thieves or marauders; strong men may rob them of their gold and silver and make off with the robes they are dressed in; yet they are powerless to help even themselves. ⁵⁸ Better to be a king displaying his prowess, a household pot of use to its owner, than to be these counterfeit gods; or merely the door of a house, protecting what is inside, than these counterfeit gods; or a wooden pillar in a palace than these counterfeit gods. ⁵⁹ The sun, the moon and the stars, which shine and have been given work to do, are obedient; ⁶⁰ similarly, the lightning, as it flashes, is a fine sight; in the same way, the wind blows across every country, ⁶¹ the clouds execute the order God gives them to pass over the whole earth, and the fire, sent from above to consume mountain and forest, carries out its orders. ⁶² Now these gods are not their equals, either in beauty or in power. ⁶³ So, no one can think or say that they are gods, powerless as they are to administer justice or to do anyone any good. ⁶⁴ Therefore, knowing that they are not gods, do not be afraid of them.

⁶⁵ 'For they can neither curse nor bless kings, ⁶⁶ nor produce signs in heaven for the nations, nor shine like the sun, nor shed light like the moon. ⁶⁷ The animals are better off than they are, being able to look after themselves by making for cover. ⁶⁸ There is not the slightest shred of evidence that they are gods; so do not be afraid of them! ⁶⁹ 'Their wooden gods overlaid with gold and silver are like a scarecrow in a field of cucumbers — protecting nothing. ⁷⁰ Or again, their wooden gods overlaid with gold and silver are like a thorn-bush in a garden — any kind of bird may perch on it — or like a corpse thrown out into the dark. ⁷¹ From the purple and linen rotting on their backs you can tell that they are not gods; and in the end, eaten away, they will be the dishonour of the country. ⁷² Better, then, someone upright who has no idols; dishonour will never come near him.'

2419

THE PRAYER OF
Azariah

AND THE SONG OF THE THREE JEWS

THE PRAYER OF
Azariah

AND THE SONG OF THE THREE

An Addition in the Greek Version
of Daniel Between 3:23 and 3:24

(Additions to Daniel, inserted between 3.23 and 3.24)

1 They[a] walked around in the midst of the flames, singing hymns to God and blessing the Lord. 2 Then Azariah stood still in the fire and prayed aloud:

3 "Blessed are you, O Lord, God of our ancestors,
    and worthy of praise;
    and glorious is your name forever!
4 For you are just in all you have done;
    all your works are true and your ways right,
    and all your judgments are true.
5 You have executed true judgments in all you have
        brought upon us
    and upon Jerusalem, the holy city of our
        ancestors;
    by a true judgment you have brought all this
        upon us because of our sins.
6 For we have sinned and broken your law in
        turning away from you;
    in all matters we have sinned grievously.
7 We have not obeyed your commandments,
    we have not kept them or done what you have
        commanded us for our own good.
8 So all that you have brought upon us,
    and all that you have done to us,
    you have done by a true judgment.
9 You have handed us over to our enemies, lawless
        and hateful rebels,
    and to an unjust king, the most wicked in all
        the world.
10 And now we cannot open our mouths;
    we, your servants who worship you, have
        become a shame and a reproach.
11 For your name's sake do not give us up forever,
    and do not annul your covenant.
12 Do not withdraw your mercy from us,
    for the sake of Abraham your beloved
    and for the sake of your servant Isaac
    and Israel your holy one,
13 to whom you promised
    to multiply their descendants like the stars of
        heaven
    and like the sand on the shore of the sea.
14 For we, O Lord, have become fewer than any
        other nation,
    and are brought low this day in all the world
        because of our sins.
15 In our day we have no ruler, or prophet, or
        leader,
    no burnt offering, or sacrifice, or oblation, or
        incense,
    no place to make an offering before you and to
        find mercy.
16 Yet with a contrite heart and a humble spirit may
        we be accepted,

THEY walked in the heart of the fire, praising God and blessing the Lord.

2 AZARIAH stood among the flames and began to pray aloud: 3 'Blessed are you and worthy of praise, Lord, the God of our fathers; your name is glorious for ever: 4 you are just in all you have done to us; all your works are true; your paths are straight, your judgements all true. 5 Just is the sentence in all that you have brought on us and on Jerusalem, the holy city of our ancestors; true and just the sentence you have passed upon our sins. 6 For we sinned and broke your law in rebellion against you; 7 in all we did we sinned. We did not heed your commandments, we did not keep them, we failed to do what you commanded for our good. 8 So in all the punishments you have sent on us, in all you have done to us, your judgements have been just, 9 in that you have handed us over to our enemies, detested rebels against your law, and to a wicked king, the vilest in all the world. 10 Now we are reduced to silence: shame and disgrace have befallen your servants and worshippers.

11 'For the sake of your honour do not abandon us for ever; do not annul your covenant. 12 Do not withdraw your mercy from us, for the sake of Abraham your friend, for the sake of Isaac your servant and Israel your holy one. 13 You promised them that their descendants should be as numerous as the stars in the sky, as the grains of sand on the seashore. 14 Yet, Lord, we have been made the smallest of all nations; for our sins we are today the most abject in the world. 15 Now we have no ruler, no prophet, no leader; there is no whole-offering, no sacrifice, no oblation, no incense, no place to make an offering before you and find mercy. 16 But because we come with contrite heart and

---

a That is, Hananiah, Mishael, and Azariah (Dan 2.17), the original names of Shadrach, Meshach, and Abednego (Dan 1.6-7)

In standard editions of the New American Bible these verses are printed after Daniel 3,23 (p. 1941).

In standard editions of the New Jerusalem Bible these verses are printed after Daniel 3:23 (p. 1941).

DANIEL 3, 24–90

THE SONG OF AZARIAH
IN THE FURNACE AND THE SONG OF
THE THREE YOUNG MEN

(Daniel 3:24–90)

24 They walked about in the flames, singing to God and blessing the Lord. 25 In the fire Azariah stood up and prayed aloud:

26 "Blessed are you, and praiseworthy,
O Lord, the God of our fathers,
and glorious forever is your name.
27 For you are just in all you have done;
all your deeds are faultless, all your ways right,
and all your judgments proper.
28 You have executed proper judgments
in all that you have brought upon us
and upon Jerusalem, the holy city of our fathers.
By a proper judgment you have done all this
because of our sins;
29 For we have sinned and transgressed
by departing from you,
and we have done every kind of evil.
30 Your commandments we have not heeded
or observed,
nor have we done as you ordered us for
our good.
31 Therefore all you have brought upon us,
all you have done to us,
you have done by a proper judgment.
32 You have handed us over to our enemies,
lawless and hateful rebels;
to an unjust king, the worst in all the world.
33 Now we cannot open our mouths;
we, your servants, who revere you,
have become a shame and a reproach.
34 For your name's sake, do not deliver us
up forever,
or make void your covenant.
35 Do not take away your mercy from us,
for the sake of Abraham, your beloved,
Isaac your servant, and Israel your holy one,
36 To whom you promised to multiply their offspring
like the stars of heaven,
or the sand on the shore of the sea.
37 For we are reduced, O Lord, beyond any
other nation,
brought low everywhere in the world this day
because of our sins.
38 We have in our day no prince, prophet, or leader,
no holocaust, sacrifice, oblation, or incense,
no place to offer first fruits, to find favor
with you.
39 But with contrite heart and humble spirit
let us be received;

24 *a* And they walked in the heart of the flames, praising God and blessing the Lord. 25 Azariah stood in the heart of the fire, praying aloud thus:

26 May you be blessed and revered, Lord, God of our
ancestors,
may your name be held glorious for ever.
27 For you are upright in all that you have done for
us,
all your deeds are true,
all your ways right,
all your judgements true.
28 True is the sentence you have given
in all that you have brought down on us
and on Jerusalem, the holy city of our ancestors,
for you have treated us rightly and truly,
as our sins deserve.
29 Yes, we have sinned and committed a crime by
deserting you,
yes, we have greatly sinned;
we have not listened to your commandments,
30 we have not observed them,
we have not done what you commanded us to do
for our own good.
31 Yes, all that you have brought down on us,
all that you have done to us,
you have been fully justified in doing.
32 You have handed us over to our enemies,
to a lawless people, the worst of the godless,
to an unjust king, the worst in the whole world;
33 today we have no right to open our mouths,
shame and dishonour are the lot
of those who serve and worship you.
34 Do not abandon us for ever,
for the sake of your name;
do not repudiate your covenant,
35 do not withdraw your favour from us,
for the sake of Abraham, your friend,
of Isaac, your servant,
and of Israel, your holy one,
36 to whom you promised to make their descendants
as many as the stars of heaven
and as the grains of sand on the seashore.
37 Lord, we have become the least of all nations,
we are put to shame today throughout the world,
because of our sins.
38 We now have no leader, no prophet, no prince,
no burnt offering, no sacrifice, no oblation, no
incense,
no place where we can make offerings to you
39 and win your favour.
But may the contrite soul, the humbled spirit, be as
acceptable to you

3, 24–90: These verses are inspired additions to the Aramaic text of Daniel, translated from the Greek form of the book. They were originally composed in Hebrew or Aramaic, which has not been preserved. The church has always regarded them as part of the canonical Scriptures.

a 3 The following passages are preserved only in Gk.

17 as though it were with burnt offerings of rams
and bulls,
or with tens of thousands of fat lambs;
such may our sacrifice be in your sight today,
and may we unreservedly follow you,*b*
for no shame will come to those who trust in
you.

18 And now with all our heart we follow you;
we fear you and seek your presence.

19 Do not put us to shame,
but deal with us in your patience
and in your abundant mercy.

20 Deliver us in accordance with your marvelous
works,
and bring glory to your name, O Lord.

21 Let all who do harm to your servants be put to
shame;
let them be disgraced and deprived of all
power,
and let their strength be broken.

22 Let them know that you alone are the Lord God,
glorious over the whole world."

23 Now the king's servants who threw them in kept stoking the furnace with naphtha, pitch, tow, and brushwood.
24 And the flames poured out above the furnace forty-nine
cubits, 25 and spread out and burned those Chaldeans who
were caught near the furnace. 26 But the angel of the Lord
came down into the furnace to be with Azariah and his
companions, and drove the fiery flame out of the furnace,
27 and made the inside of the furnace as though a moist wind
were whistling through it. The fire did not touch them at all
and caused them no pain or distress.

28 Then the three with one voice praised and glorified
and blessed God in the furnace:

29 "Blessed are you, O Lord, God of our ancestors,
and to be praised and highly exalted forever;

30 And blessed is your glorious, holy name,
and to be highly praised and highly exalted
forever.

31 Blessed are you in the temple of your holy glory,
and to be extolled and highly glorified forever.

32 Blessed are you who look into the depths from
your throne on the cherubim,
and to be praised and highly exalted forever.

33 Blessed are you on the throne of your kingdom,
and to be extolled and highly exalted forever.

34 Blessed are you in the firmament of heaven,
and to be sung and glorified forever.

35 "Bless the Lord, all you works of the Lord;
sing praise to him and highly exalt him
forever.

36 Bless the Lord, you heavens;
sing praise to him and highly exalt him
forever.

37 Bless the Lord, you angels of the Lord;
sing praise to him and highly exalt him
forever.

38 Bless the Lord, all you waters above the heavens;
sing praise to him and highly exalt him
forever.

39 Bless the Lord, all you powers of the Lord;
sing praise to him and highly exalt him
forever.

40 Bless the Lord, sun and moon;
sing praise to him and highly exalt him
forever.

humbled spirit, may we be accepted. 17 As though we came
with whole-offerings of rams and bullocks and with thousands of fat lambs, let our sacrifice be made before you this
day, that we may obey you in everything, for no shame
shall come to those who put their trust in you. 18 Now we
shall follow you with our whole heart, and in fear seek your
presence. 19 Do not put us to shame, but deal with us in your
forbearance and in the greatness of your mercy. 20 Lord,
Worker of wonders, deliver us, and let your name be glorified. May all who harm your servants be brought low; 21 let
them be put to shame, stripped of all power and sovereignty, and may their strength be crushed; 22 let them know that
you alone are the Lord God, glorious over all the earth.'

23 THE king's servants who had thrown them into the
furnace kept feeding it with naphtha, pitch, tow, and brushwood, 24 so that the flames, blazing above it to a height of
seventy-five feet, 25 leapt out and burnt up those Chaldaeans
who were caught near it. 26 But the angel of the Lord came
down to join Azariah and his companions in the furnace; he
scattered the flames 27 and made the heart of the furnace as
if a moist wind were whistling through. The fire touched
them not at all; it neither harmed nor distressed them.

28 THEN with one voice the three who were in the furnace
praised and glorified and blessed God:

29 Blessed are you, Lord, the God of our fathers;
worthy of praise, highly exalted for ever.

30 Blessed is your holy and glorious name;
highly to be praised, highly exalted for ever.

31 Blessed are you, glorious in your holy temple;
most worthy to be glorified in hymns for ever.

32 Blessed are you, for, enthroned on the cherubim,
you behold the depths;
worthy of praise, highly exalted for ever.

33 Blessed are you on your royal throne;
most worthy to be hymned, highly exalted for
ever.

34 Blessed are you in the vault of heaven;
worthy to be glorified in hymns for ever.

35 Let his whole creation bless the Lord,
sing his praise and exalt him for ever.

36 Bless the Lord, you heavens;
sing his praise and exalt him for ever.

37 Bless the Lord, you that are his angels;
sing his praise and exalt him for ever.

38 Bless the Lord, all you waters above the heavens;
sing his praise and exalt him for ever.

39 Bless the Lord, all you his hosts;
sing his praise and exalt him for ever.

40 Bless the Lord, sun and moon;
sing his praise and exalt him for ever.

---

b Meaning of Gk uncertain

17 **that . . . everything:** *poss. mng; Gk obscure.* 24 **seventy-five
feet:** *Gk forty-nine cubits.*

40 As though it were holocausts of rams and bullocks,
or thousands of fat lambs,
So let our sacrifice be in your presence today
as we follow you unreservedly;
for those who trust in you cannot be put
to shame.
41 And now we follow you with our whole heart,
we fear you and we pray to you.
42 Do not let us be put to shame,
but deal with us in your kindness and
great mercy.
43 Deliver us by your wonders,
and bring glory to your name, O Lord:
44 Let all those be routed
who inflict evils on your servants;
Let them be shamed and powerless,
and their strength broken;
45 Let them know that you alone are the Lord God,
glorious over the whole world."

46 Now the king's men who had thrown them in continued to stoke the furnace with brimstone, pitch, tow, and faggots. 47 The flames rose forty-nine cubits above the furnace, 48 and spread out, burning the Chaldeans nearby. 49 But the angel of the Lord went down into the furnace with Azariah and his companions, drove the fiery flames out of the furnace, 50 and made the inside of the furnace as though a dew-laden breeze were blowing through it. The fire in no way touched them or caused them pain or harm. 51 Then these three in the furnace with one voice sang, glorifying and blessing God:

52 "Blessed are you, O Lord, the God of our fathers,
praiseworthy and exalted above all forever;
And blessed is your holy and glorious name,
praiseworthy and exalted above all for all ages.
53 Blessed are you in the temple of your holy glory,
praiseworthy and glorious above all forever.
54 Blessed are you on the throne of your kingdom,
praiseworthy and exalted above all forever.
55 Blessed are you who look into the depths
from your throne upon the cherubim,
praiseworthy and exalted above all forever.
56 Blessed are you in the firmament of heaven,
praiseworthy and glorious forever.
57 Bless the Lord, all you works of the Lord,
praise and exalt him above all forever.
58 Angels of the Lord, bless the Lord,
praise and exalt him above all forever.
59 You heavens, bless the Lord,
praise and exalt him above all forever.
60 All you waters above the heavens, bless the Lord,
praise and exalt him above all forever.
61 All you hosts of the Lord, bless the Lord;
praise and exalt him above all forever.
62 Sun and moon, bless the Lord;
praise and exalt him above all forever.

40 as burnt offerings of rams and bullocks,
as thousands of fat lambs:
such let our sacrifice be to you today,
and may it please you that we follow you
whole-heartedly,
since those who trust in you will not be shamed.
41 And now we put our whole heart into following
you,
into fearing you and seeking your face once more.
42 Do not abandon us to shame
but treat us in accordance with your gentleness,
in accordance with the greatness of your mercy.
43 Rescue us in accordance with your wonderful
deeds
and win fresh glory for your name, O Lord.
44 Confusion seize all who ill-treat your servants:
may they be covered with shame,
deprived of all their power,
and may their strength be broken.
45 Let them learn that you alone are God and Lord,
glorious over the whole world.

46 All this time, the king's servants, who had thrown them into the furnace, had been stoking it with crude oil, pitch, tow and brushwood 47 until the flames rose forty-nine cubits above the furnace 48 and, leaping out, burnt those Chaldaeans to death who were standing round it. 49 But the angel of the Lord came down into the furnace beside Azariah and his companions; he drove the flames of the fire outwards from the furnace 50 and, in the heart of the furnace, wafted a coolness to them as of the breeze and dew, so that the fire did not touch them at all and caused them no pain or distress.

51 Then all three in unison began to sing, glorifying and blessing God in the furnace, with the words:

52 May you be blessed, Lord, God of our ancestors,
be praised and extolled for ever.
Blessed be your glorious and holy name,
praised and extolled for ever.
53 May you be blessed in the Temple of your sacred
glory,
exalted and glorified above all for ever:
54 blessed on the throne of your kingdom,
exalted above all, glorified for ever:
55 blessed are you who fathom the abyss, enthroned
on the winged creatures,
praised and exalted above all for ever:
56 blessed in the expanse of the heavens,
exalted and glorified for ever.

57 Bless the Lord, all the Lord's creation:
praise and glorify him for ever!
58 Bless the Lord, angels of the Lord,
praise and glorify him for ever!
59 Bless the Lord, heavens,
praise and glorify him for ever!
60 Bless the Lord, all the waters above the heavens,
praise and glorify him for ever!
61 Bless the Lord, powers of the Lord,
praise and glorify him for ever!
62 Bless the Lord, sun and moon,
praise and glorify him for ever!

NEW REVISED STANDARD VERSION	REVISED ENGLISH BIBLE

41 Bless the Lord, stars of heaven;
    sing praise to him and highly exalt him
    forever.

42 "Bless the Lord, all rain and dew;
    sing praise to him and highly exalt him
    forever.

43 Bless the Lord, all you winds;
    sing praise to him and highly exalt him
    forever.

44 Bless the Lord, fire and heat;
    sing praise to him and highly exalt him
    forever.

45 Bless the Lord, winter cold and summer heat;
    sing praise to him and highly exalt him
    forever.

46 Bless the Lord, dews and falling snow;
    sing praise to him and highly exalt him
    forever.

47 Bless the Lord, nights and days;
    sing praise to him and highly exalt him
    forever.

48 Bless the Lord, light and darkness;
    sing praise to him and highly exalt him
    forever.

49 Bless the Lord, ice and cold;
    sing praise to him and highly exalt him
    forever.

50 Bless the Lord, frosts and snows;
    sing praise to him and highly exalt him
    forever.

51 Bless the Lord, lightnings and clouds;
    sing praise to him and highly exalt him
    forever.

52 "Let the earth bless the Lord;
    let it sing praise to him and highly exalt him
    forever.

53 Bless the Lord, mountains and hills;
    sing praise to him and highly exalt him
    forever.

54 Bless the Lord, all that grows in the ground;
    sing praise to him and highly exalt him
    forever.

55 Bless the Lord, seas and rivers;
    sing praise to him and highly exalt him
    forever.

56 Bless the Lord, you springs;
    sing praise to him and highly exalt him
    forever.

57 Bless the Lord, you whales and all that swim in
    the waters;
    sing praise to him and highly exalt him
    forever.

58 Bless the Lord, all birds of the air;
    sing praise to him and highly exalt him
    forever.

59 Bless the Lord, all wild animals and cattle;
    sing praise to him and highly exalt him
    forever.

60 "Bless the Lord, all people on earth;
    sing praise to him and highly exalt him
    forever.

61 Bless the Lord, O Israel;
    sing praise to him and highly exalt him
    forever.

62 Bless the Lord, you priests of the Lord;
    sing praise to him and highly exalt him
    forever.

41 Bless the Lord, you stars of heaven;
    sing his praise and exalt him for ever.

42 Bless the Lord, all rain and dew;
    sing his praise and exalt him for ever.

43 Bless the Lord, all winds that blow;
    sing his praise and exalt him for ever.

44 Bless the Lord, fire and heat;
    sing his praise and exalt him for ever.

45 Bless the Lord, searing blast and bitter cold;
    sing his praise and exalt him for ever.

46 Bless the Lord, sleet and falling snow;
    sing his praise and exalt him for ever.

47 Bless the Lord, you nights and days;
    sing his praise and exalt him for ever.

48 Bless the Lord, light and darkness;
    sing his praise and exalt him for ever.

49 Bless the Lord, frost and cold;
    sing his praise and exalt him for ever.

50 Bless the Lord, rime and snow;
    sing his praise and exalt him for ever.

51 Bless the Lord, lightning and clouds;
    sing his praise and exalt him for ever.

52 Let the earth bless the Lord,
    sing his praise and exalt him for ever.

53 Bless the Lord, you mountains and hills;
    sing his praise and exalt him for ever.

54 Bless the Lord, all that grows in the earth;
    sing his praise and exalt him for ever.

55 Bless the Lord, you flowing springs;
    sing his praise and exalt him for ever.

56 Bless the Lord, you seas and rivers;
    sing his praise and exalt him for ever.

57 Bless the Lord, you whales and everything that
    moves in the waters;
    sing his praise and exalt him for ever.

58 Bless the Lord, all birds of the air;
    sing his praise and exalt him for ever.

59 Bless the Lord, you cattle and wild beasts;
    sing his praise and exalt him for ever.

60 Let all mankind bless the Lord,
    sing his praise and exalt him for ever.

61 Israel, bless the Lord;
    sing his praise and exalt him for ever.

62 Bless the Lord, you that are his priests;
    sing his praise and exalt him for ever.

---

46 **sleet:** *prob. mng; Gk* dew.

63 Stars of heaven, bless the Lord;
  praise and exalt him above all forever.
64 Every shower and dew, bless the Lord;
  praise and exalt him above all forever.
65 All you winds, bless the Lord;
  praise and exalt him above all forever.
66 Fire and heat, bless the Lord;
  praise and exalt him above all forever.
67 [Cold and chill, bless the Lord;
  praise and exalt him above all forever.
68 Dew and rain, bless the Lord;
  praise and exalt him above all forever.]
69 Frost and chill, bless the Lord;
  praise and exalt him above all forever.
70 Ice and snow, bless the Lord;
  praise and exalt him above all forever.
71 Nights and days, bless the Lord;
  praise and exalt him above all forever.
72 Light and darkness, bless the Lord;
  praise and exalt him above all forever.
73 Lightnings and clouds, bless the Lord;
  praise and exalt him above all forever.
74 Let the earth bless the Lord,
  praise and exalt him above all forever.
75 Mountains and hills, bless the Lord;
  praise and exalt him above all forever.
76 Everything growing from the earth, bless the Lord;
  praise and exalt him above all forever.
77 You springs, bless the Lord;
  praise and exalt him above all forever.
78 Seas and rivers, bless the Lord;
  praise and exalt him above all forever.
79 You dolphins and all water creatures, bless
    the Lord;
  praise and exalt him above all forever.
80 All you birds of the air, bless the Lord;
  praise and exalt him above all forever.
81 All you beasts, wild and tame, bless the Lord;
  praise and exalt him above all forever.
82 You sons of men, bless the Lord;
  praise and exalt him above all forever.
83 O Israel, bless the Lord;
  praise and exalt him above all forever.
84 Priests of the Lord, bless the Lord;
  praise and exalt him above all forever.

63 Bless the Lord, stars of heaven,
  praise and glorify him for ever!
64 Bless the Lord, all rain and dew,
  praise and glorify him for ever!
65 Bless the Lord, every wind,
  praise and glorify him for ever!
66 Bless the Lord, fire and heat,
  praise and glorify him for ever!
67 Bless the Lord, cold and warmth,
  praise and glorify him for ever!
68 Bless the Lord, dew and snow-storm,
  praise and glorify him for ever!
69 Bless the Lord, frost and cold,
  praise and glorify him for ever!
70 Bless the Lord, ice and snow,
  praise and glorify him for ever!
71 Bless the Lord, nights and days,
  praise and glorify him for ever!
72 Bless the Lord, light and darkness,
  praise and glorify him for ever!
73 Bless the Lord, lightning and cloud,
  praise and glorify him for ever!
74 Let the earth bless the Lord:
  praise and glorify him for ever!
75 Bless the Lord, mountains and hills,
  praise and glorify him for ever!
76 Bless the Lord, every plant that grows,
  praise and glorify him for ever!
77 Bless the Lord, springs of water,
  praise and glorify him for ever!
78 Bless the Lord, seas and rivers,
  praise and glorify him for ever!
79 Bless the Lord, whales, and everything that moves
    in the waters,
  praise and glorify him for ever!
80 Bless the Lord, every kind of bird,
  praise and glorify him for ever!
81 Bless the Lord, all animals wild and tame,
  praise and glorify him for ever!
82 Bless the Lord, all the human race:
  praise and glorify him for ever!
83 Bless the Lord, O Israel,
  praise and glorify him for ever!
84 Bless the Lord, priests,
  praise and glorify him for ever!

NEW REVISED STANDARD VERSION

63 Bless the Lord, you servants of the Lord;
   sing praise to him and highly exalt him
      forever.
64 Bless the Lord, spirits and souls of the righteous;
   sing praise to him and highly exalt him
      forever.
65 Bless the Lord, you who are holy and humble in
      heart;
   sing praise to him and highly exalt him
      forever.
66 "Bless the Lord, Hananiah, Azariah, and Mishael;
   sing praise to him and highly exalt him
      forever.
   For he has rescued us from Hades and saved us
      from the power[c] of death,
   and delivered us from the midst of the burning
      fiery furnace;
   from the midst of the fire he has delivered us.
67 Give thanks to the Lord, for he is good,
   for his mercy endures forever.
68 All who worship the Lord, bless the God of
      gods,
   sing praise to him and give thanks to him,
   for his mercy endures forever."

c Gk *hand*

REVISED ENGLISH BIBLE

63 Bless the Lord, you that are his servants;
   sing his praise and exalt him for ever.
64 Bless the Lord, spirits and souls of the righteous;
   sing his praise and exalt him for ever.
65 Bless the Lord, you that are devout and humble in
      heart;
   sing his praise and exalt him for ever.

66 Hananiah, Azariah, and Mishael, bless the Lord;
   sing his praise and exalt him for ever.
   He has rescued us from the grave,
   he has saved us from the power of death;
   he has delivered us from the furnace of burning
      flame,
   from the very heart of the fire.
67 Give thanks to the Lord, for he is gracious,
   for his mercy endures for ever.
68 All who worship the Lord, bless the God of gods,
   sing his praise and give him thanks,
   for his mercy endures for ever.

85 Servants of the Lord, bless the Lord;
   praise and exalt him above all forever.
86 Spirits and souls of the just, bless the Lord;
   praise and exalt him above all forever.
87 Holy men of humble heart, bless the Lord;
   praise and exalt him above all forever.
88 Hananiah, Azariah, Mishael, bless the Lord;
   praise and exalt him above all forever.
   For he has delivered us from the nether world,
   and saved us from the power of death,
   He has freed us from the raging flame
   and delivered us from the fire.
89 Give thanks to the Lord, for he is good,
   for his mercy endures forever.
90 Bless the God of gods, all you who fear the Lord;
   praise him and give him thanks,
   because his mercy endures forever."

85 Bless the Lord, his servants,
   praise and glorify him for ever!
86 Bless the Lord, spirits and souls of the upright,
   praise and glorify him for ever!
87 Bless the Lord, faithful, humble-hearted people,
   praise and glorify him for ever!
88 Hananiah, Azariah and Mishael, bless the Lord,
   praise and glorify him for ever! —
   For he has rescued us from the Underworld,
   he has saved us from the hand of Death,
   he has snatched us from the burning fiery furnace,
   he has drawn us from the heart of the flame!
89 Give thanks to the Lord, for he is good,
   for his love is everlasting.
90 Bless the Lord, the God of gods, all who fear him,
   give praise and thanks to him,
   for his love is everlasting!

Susanna

(Chapter 13 of The Greek Version of Daniel)

1 There was a man living in Babylon whose name was Joakim. 2 He married the daughter of Hilkiah, named Susanna, a very beautiful woman and one who feared the Lord. 3 Her parents were righteous, and had trained their daughter according to the law of Moses. 4 Joakim was very rich, and had a fine garden adjoining his house; the Jews used to come to him because he was the most honored of them all.

5 That year two elders from the people were appointed as judges. Concerning them the Lord had said: "Wickedness came forth from Babylon, from elders who were judges, who were supposed to govern the people." 6 These men were frequently at Joakim's house, and all who had a case to be tried came to them there.

7 When the people left at noon, Susanna would go into her husband's garden to walk. 8 Every day the two elders used to see her, going in and walking about, and they began to lust for her. 9 They suppressed their consciences and turned away their eyes from looking to Heaven or remembering their duty to administer justice. 10 Both were overwhelmed with passion for her, but they did not tell each other of their distress, 11 for they were ashamed to disclose their lustful desire to seduce her. 12 Day after day they watched eagerly to see her.

13 One day they said to each other, "Let us go home, for it is time for lunch." So they both left and parted from each other. 14 But turning back, they met again; and when each pressed the other for the reason, they confessed their lust. Then together they arranged for a time when they could find her alone.

15 Once, while they were watching for an opportune day, she went in as before with only two maids, and wished to bathe in the garden, for it was a hot day. 16 No one was there except the two elders, who had hidden themselves and were watching her. 17 She said to her maids, "Bring me olive oil and ointments, and shut the garden doors so that I can bathe." 18 They did as she told them: they shut the doors of the garden and went out by the side doors to bring what they had been commanded; they did not see the elders, because they were hiding.

19 When the maids had gone out, the two elders got up and ran to her. 20 They said, "Look, the garden doors are shut, and no one can see us. We are burning with desire for you; so give your consent, and lie with us. 21 If you refuse, we will testify against you that a young man was with you, and this was why you sent your maids away."

22 Susanna groaned and said, "I am completely trapped. For if I do this, it will mean death for me; if I do not, I cannot escape your hands. 23 I choose not to do it; I will fall into your hands, rather than sin in the sight of the Lord."

24 Then Susanna cried out with a loud voice, and the two elders shouted against her. 25 And one of them ran and opened the garden doors. 26 When the people in the house heard the shouting in the garden, they rushed in at the side door to see what had happened to her. 27 And when the elders told their story, the servants felt very much ashamed, for nothing like this had ever been said about Susanna.

Daniel and Susanna

In Babylon there lived a man named Joakim, 2 who had married Susanna daughter of Hilkiah, a very beautiful and devout woman. 3 Her parents were godfearing people who had brought up their daughter according to the law of Moses. 4 Joakim was very rich, and his house had adjoining it a fine garden; this was a regular meeting-place for the Jews, because he was the man of greatest distinction among them.

5 Now that year the judges appointed were two of the community's elders; of such the Lord had said, 'Wickedness came forth from Babylon, from elders who were judges and were supposed to guide my people.' 6 These men were constantly at Joakim's house, and everyone who had a case to be tried came to them there.

7 At noon, when the people went away, Susanna would go and walk in her husband's garden. 8 Every day the two elders used to see her entering the garden for her walk, and they were inflamed with lust. 9 Their minds were perverted; their thoughts went astray and were no longer turned to God, and they did not keep in mind the demands of justice. 10 Both were infatuated with her; but they did not disclose to each other what torments they suffered, 11 because they were ashamed to confess they wanted to seduce her. 12 Day after day they watched eagerly for a sight of her.

13 One day, having said, 'Let us go home; it is time to eat,' 14 they left and went off in different directions; but turning back they found themselves face to face, and on questioning each other about this, they admitted their passion. Then they agreed on a time when they might find her alone.

15 While they were watching for an opportune moment, Susanna went into the garden as usual, accompanied only by her two maids; it was very hot, and she felt a desire to bathe in the garden. 16 No one else was there apart from the two elders, who had hidden and were spying on her. 17 She said to the maids, 'Bring me olive oil and unguents, and shut the garden doors so that I may bathe.' 18 They did as she said: they made fast the garden doors and went out by the side entrance for the things they had been told to bring; they did not see the elders, because they were in hiding.

19 As soon as the maids had gone, the two elders got up and ran to Susanna. 20 'Look, the garden doors are shut,' they said, 'and no one can see us! We are overcome with desire for you; consent, and yield to us. 21 If you refuse, we shall swear in evidence there was a young man with you and that was why you sent your maids away.' 22 Susanna groaned and said: 'It is a desperate plight I am in! If I do this, the penalty is death; if I do not, you will have me at your mercy. 23 My choice is made: I will not do it! Better to be at your mercy than to sin against the Lord!' 24 With that she called out at the top of her voice, but the two elders shouted her down, 25 and one of them ran and opened the garden door. 26 The household, hearing the uproar in the garden, rushed in through the side entrance to see what had happened to her. 27 When the elders had told their story, the servants were deeply shocked, for no such allegation had ever been made against Susanna.

In standard editions of the New American Bible this chapter is printed after Daniel 12 (p. 1969).

In standard editions of the New Jerusalem Bible this chapter is printed after Daniel 12 (p. 1969).

DANIEL 13

1 In Babylon there lived a man named Joakim, 2 who married a very beautiful and God-fearing woman, Susanna, the daughter of Hilkiah; 3 her pious parents had trained their daughter according to the law of Moses. 4 Joakim was very rich; he had a garden near his house, and the Jews had recourse to him often because he was the most respected of them all.

5 That year, two elders of the people were appointed judges, of whom the Lord said, "Wickedness has come out of Babylon: from the elders who were to govern the people as judges." 6 These men, to whom all brought their cases, frequented the house of Joakim. 7 When the people left at noon, Susanna used to enter her husband's garden for a walk. 8 When the old men saw her enter every day for her walk, they began to lust for her. 9 They suppressed their consciences; they would not allow their eyes to look to heaven, and did not keep in mind just judgments. 10 Though both were enamored of her, they did not tell each other their trouble, 11 for they were ashamed to reveal their lustful desire to have her. 12 Day by day they watched eagerly for her. 13 One day they said to each other, "Let us be off for home, it is time for lunch." So they went out and parted; 14 but both turned back, and when they met again, they asked each other the reason. They admitted their lust, and then they agreed to look for an occasion when they could meet her alone.

15 One day, while they were waiting for the right moment, she entered the garden as usual, with two maids only. She decided to bathe, for the weather was warm. 16 Nobody else was there except the two elders, who had hidden themselves and were watching her. 17 "Bring me oil and soap," she said to the maids, "and shut the garden doors while I bathe." 18 They did as she said; they shut the garden doors and left by the side gate to fetch what she had ordered, unaware that the elders were hidden inside.

19 As soon as the maids had left, the two old men got up and hurried to her. 20 "Look," they said, "the garden doors are shut, and no one can see us; give in to our desire, and lie with us. 21 If you refuse, we will testify against you that you dismissed your maids because a young man was here with you."

22 "I am completely trapped," Susanna groaned. "If I yield, it will be my death; if I refuse, I cannot escape your power. 23 Yet it is better for me to fall into your power without guilt than to sin before the Lord." 24 Then Susanna shrieked, and the old men also shouted at her, 25 as one of them ran to open the garden doors. 26 When the people in the house heard the cries from the garden, they rushed in by the side gate to see what had happened to her. 27 At the accusations by the old men, the servants felt very much ashamed, for never had any such thing been said about Susanna.

SUSANNA AND THE JUDGEMENT OF DANIEL

(Chapter 13 of the Greek Version of Daniel)

1 a In Babylon there lived a man named Joakim. 2 He was married to a woman called Susanna daughter of Hilkiah, a woman of great beauty; and she was God-fearing, 3 for her parents were worthy people and had instructed their daughter in the Law of Moses. 4 Joakim was a very rich man and had a garden by his house; he used to be visited by a considerable number of the Jews, since he was held in greater respect than any other man. 5 Two elderly men had been selected from the people, that year, to act as judges. Of such the Lord had said, 'Wickedness has come to Babylon through the elders and judges posing as guides to the people.' 6 These men were often at Joakim's house, and all who were engaged in litigation used to come to them. 7 At midday, when the people had gone away, Susanna would take a walk in her husband's garden. 8 The two elders, who used to watch her every day as she came in to take her walk, gradually began to desire her. 9 They threw reason aside, making no effort to turn their eyes to Heaven, and forgetting the demands of virtue. 10 Both were inflamed by passion for her, but they hid their desire from each other, 11 for they were ashamed to admit the longing to sleep with her, 12 but they made sure of watching her every day. 13 One day, having parted with the words, 'Let us go home, then, it is time for the midday meal,' they went off in different directions, 14 only to retrace their steps and find themselves face to face again. Obliged then to explain, they admitted their desire and agreed to look for an opportunity of surprising her alone. 15 So they waited for a favourable moment; and one day Susanna came as usual, accompanied only by two young maidservants. The day was hot and she wanted to bathe in the garden. 16 There was no one about except the two elders, spying on her from their hiding place. 17 She said to the servants, 'Bring me some oil and balsam and shut the garden door while I bathe.' 18 They did as they were told, shutting the garden door and going back to the house by a side entrance to fetch what she had asked for; they knew nothing about the elders, for they had concealed themselves.

19 Hardly were the maids gone than the two elders sprang up and rushed upon her. 20 'Look,' they said, 'the garden door is shut, no one can see us. We want to have you, so give in and let us! 21 Refuse, and we shall both give evidence that a young man was with you and that this was why you sent your maids away.' 22 Susanna sighed. 'I am trapped,' she said, 'whatever I do. If I agree, it means death for me; if I resist, I cannot get away from you. 23 But I prefer to fall innocent into your power than to sin in the eyes of the Lord.' 24 She then cried out as loud as she could. The two elders began shouting too, putting the blame on her, 25 and one of them ran to open the garden door. 26 The household, hearing the shouting in the garden, rushed out by the side entrance to see what had happened to her. 27 Once the elders had told their story, the servants were thoroughly taken aback, since nothing of this sort had ever been said of Susanna.

a 13 Ch. 13 occurs in Gk but not in the Hebr. text.

NEW REVISED STANDARD VERSION

28 The next day, when the people gathered at the house of her husband Joakim, the two elders came, full of their wicked plot to have Susanna put to death. In the presence of the people they said, 29 "Send for Susanna daughter of Hilkiah, the wife of Joakim." 30 So they sent for her. And she came with her parents, her children, and all her relatives.

31 Now Susanna was a woman of great refinement and beautiful in appearance. 32 As she was veiled, the scoundrels ordered her to be unveiled, so that they might feast their eyes on her beauty. 33 Those who were with her and all who saw her were weeping.

34 Then the two elders stood up before the people and laid their hands on her head. 35 Through her tears she looked up toward Heaven, for her heart trusted in the Lord. 36 The elders said, "While we were walking in the garden alone, this woman came in with two maids, shut the garden doors, and dismissed the maids. 37 Then a young man, who was hiding there, came to her and lay with her. 38 We were in a corner of the garden, and when we saw this wickedness we ran to them. 39 Although we saw them embracing, we could not hold the man, because he was stronger than we, and he opened the doors and got away. 40 We did, however, seize this woman and asked who the young man was, 41 but she would not tell us. These things we testify."

Because they were elders of the people and judges, the assembly believed them and condemned her to death.

42 Then Susanna cried out with a loud voice, and said, "O eternal God, you know what is secret and are aware of all things before they come to be; 43 you know that these men have given false evidence against me. And now I am to die, though I have done none of the wicked things that they have charged against me!"

44 The Lord heard her cry. 45 Just as she was being led off to execution, God stirred up the holy spirit of a young lad named Daniel, 46 and he shouted with a loud voice, "I want no part in shedding this woman's blood!"

47 All the people turned to him and asked, "What is this you are saying?" 48 Taking his stand among them he said, "Are you such fools, O Israelites, as to condemn a daughter of Israel without examination and without learning the facts? 49 Return to court, for these men have given false evidence against her."

50 So all the people hurried back. And the rest of thea elders said to him, "Come, sit among us and inform us, for God has given you the standing of an elder." 51 Daniel said to them, "Separate them far from each other, and I will examine them."

52 When they were separated from each other, he summoned one of them and said to him, "You old relic of wicked days, your sins have now come home, which you have committed in the past, 53 pronouncing unjust judgments, condemning the innocent and acquitting the guilty, though the Lord said, 'You shall not put an innocent and righteous person to death.' 54 Now then, if you really saw this woman, tell me this: Under what tree did you see them being intimate with each other?" He answered, "Under a mastic tree."b 55 And Daniel said, "Very well! This lie has cost you your head, for the angel of God has received the sentence from God and will immediately cutb you in two."

56 Then, putting him to one side, he ordered them to bring the other. And he said to him, "You offspring of Canaan and not of Judah, beauty has beguiled you and lust has perverted your heart. 57 This is how you have been treating the daughters of Israel, and they were intimate with you through fear; but a daughter of Judah would not tolerate your wickedness. 58 Now then, tell me: Under what tree did

REVISED ENGLISH BIBLE

28 Next day, when the people gathered at her husband Joakim's house, the two elders arrived, intent on their criminal design to have Susanna put to death. 29 In the presence of the people they said, 'Send for Susanna daughter of Hilkiah, Joakim's wife.' She was summoned, 30 and came with her parents and children and all her relatives. 31 Now Susanna was a woman of great beauty and delicate feeling. 32 She was closely veiled, but those scoundrels ordered her to be unveiled so that they might feast their eyes on her beauty. 33 Her family and all who saw her were in tears.

34 Then the two elders stood up before the people and put their hands on her head, 35 she meanwhile looking towards heaven through her tears, for her trust was in the Lord. 36 The elders said: 'As we were walking by ourselves in the garden, this woman came in with her two maids. She shut the garden doors and dismissed her maids, 37 and then a young man, who had been in hiding, came and lay with her. 38 We were in a corner of the garden, and when we saw this wickedness we ran towards them. 39 We saw them in the act, but we could not hold the man; he was too strong for us, he opened the door and got clean away. 40 We seized the woman and asked who the young man was, but she would not tell us. That is our evidence.'

41 Because they were elders of the people and judges, the assembly believed them and condemned her to death. 42 Then raising her voice Susanna cried: 'Eternal God, you know all secrets and foresee all things, 43 you know that their evidence against me is false. And now I am to die, innocent though I am of the charges these wicked men have brought against me.'

44 The Lord heard her cry, 45 and as she was being led off to execution, God inspired a devout young man named Daniel to protest. 46 He shouted out, 'I will not have this woman's blood on my hands.' 47 At this the people all turned towards him and demanded, 'What do you mean?' 48 He stepped forward and said: 'Are you such fools, you Israelites, as to condemn a woman of Israel, without making careful enquiry and finding out the truth? 49 Reopen the trial; the evidence these men have given against her is false.'

50 Everyone hurried back, and the rest of the elders said to Daniel, 'Come, take your place among us and state your case, for God has given you the standing of an elder.' 51 He said, 'Separate these men and keep them at a distance from each other, and I shall examine them.' 52 When they had been separated, Daniel summoned one of them. 'You hardened reprobate,' he began, 'the sins of your past have now come home to you. 53 You have given unjust decisions, condemning the innocent and acquitting the guilty, although the Lord has said, "You must not cause the death of the innocent and guiltless." 54 Now, if you really saw this woman, then tell us, under what tree did you see them together?' He answered, 'Under a clove tree.' 55 Daniel retorted, 'Very good! This lie has cost you your life, for already God's angel has received your sentence from God, and he will cleave you in two.' 56 He ordered him to stand aside, and told them to bring forward the other.

He said to him: 'Spawn of Canaan, no son of Judah, beauty has been your undoing and lust has perverted your heart! 57 So this is how the two of you have been treating the women of Israel, terrifying them into yielding to you! But here is a woman of Judah who would not submit to your villainy. 58 Now tell me, under what tree did you surprise

---

aGk lacks rest of the   bThe Greek words for mastic tree and cut are similar, thus forming an ironic wordplay

54 clove: lit. mastic.   54–55 clove . . . cleave: there is a play on words in the Greek.

NEW AMERICAN BIBLE

NEW JERUSALEM BIBLE

28 When the people came to her husband Joakim the next day, the two wicked elders also came, fully determined to put Susanna to death. Before all the people they ordered: 29 "Send for Susanna, the daughter of Hilkiah, the wife of Joakim." When she was sent for, 30 she came with her parents, children and all her relatives. 31 Susanna, very delicate and beautiful, 32 was veiled; but those wicked men ordered her to uncover her face so as to sate themselves with her beauty. 33 All her relatives and the onlookers were weeping.

34 In the midst of the people the two elders rose up and laid their hands on her head. 35 Through her tears she looked up to heaven, for she trusted in the Lord wholeheartedly. 36 The elders made this accusation: "As we were walking in the garden alone, this woman entered with two girls and shut the doors of the garden, dismissing the girls. 37 A young man, who was hidden there, came and lay with her. 38 When we, in a corner of the garden, saw this crime, we ran toward them. 39 We saw them lying together, but the man we could not hold, because he was stronger than we; he opened the doors and ran off. 40 Then we seized this one and asked who the young man was, 41 but she refused to tell us. We testify to this." The assembly believed them, since they were elders and judges of the people, and they condemned her to death.

42 But Susanna cried aloud: "O eternal God, you know what is hidden and are aware of all things before they come to be: 43 you know that they have testified falsely against me. Here I am about to die, though I have done none of the things with which these wicked men have charged me."

44 The Lord heard her prayer. 45 As she was being led to execution, God stirred up the holy spirit of a young boy named Daniel, 46 and he cried aloud: "I will have no part in the death of this woman." 47 All the people turned and asked him, "What is this you are saying?" 48 He stood in their midst and continued, "Are you such fools, O Israelites! To condemn a woman of Israel without examination and without clear evidence? 49 Return to court, for they have testified falsely against her."

50 Then all the people returned in haste. To Daniel the elders said, "Come, sit with us and inform us, since God has given you the prestige of old age." 51 But he replied, "Separate these two far from one another that I may examine them."

52 After they were separated one from the other, he called one of them and said: "How you have grown evil with age! Now have your past sins come to term: 53 passing unjust sentences, condemning the innocent, and freeing the guilty, although the Lord says, 'The innocent and the just you shall not put to death.' 54 Now, then, if you were a witness, tell me under what tree you saw them together." 55 "Under a mastic tree," he answered. "Your fine lie has cost you your head," said Daniel; "for the angel of God shall receive the sentence from him and split you in two." 56 Putting him to one side, he ordered the other one to be brought. "Offspring of Canaan, not of Judah," Daniel said to him, "beauty has seduced you, lust has subverted your conscience. 57 This is how you acted with the daughters of Israel, and in their fear they yielded to you; but a daughter of Judah did not tolerate your wickedness. 58 Now then, tell me under what tree you

28 Next day a meeting was held at the house of her husband Joakim. The two elders arrived, full of their wicked plea against Susanna, to have her put to death. 29 They addressed the company, 'Summon Susanna daughter of Hilkiah and wife of Joakim.' She was sent for, 30 and came accompanied by her parents, her children and all her relations. 31 Susanna was very graceful and beautiful to look at; 32 she was veiled, so the wretches made her unveil in order to feast their eyes on her beauty. 33 All her own people were weeping, and so were all the others who saw her. 34 The two elders stood up, with all the people round them, and laid their hands on her head. 35 Tearfully she turned her eyes to Heaven, her heart confident in God. 36 The elders then spoke, 'While we were walking by ourselves in the garden, this woman arrived with two maids. She shut the garden door and then dismissed the servants. 37 A young man, who had been hiding, went over to her and they lay together. 38 From the end of the garden where we were, we saw this crime taking place and hurried towards them. 39 Though we saw them together, we were unable to catch the man: he was too strong for us; he opened the door and took to his heels. 40 We did, however, catch this woman and ask her who the young man was. 41 She refused to tell us. That is our evidence.'

Since they were elders of the people and judges, the assembly accepted their word: Susanna was condemned to death. 42 She cried out as loud as she could, 'Eternal God, you know all secrets and everything before it happens; 43 you know that they have given false evidence against me. And now I must die, innocent as I am of everything their malice has invented against me!'

44 The Lord heard her cry 45 and, as she was being led away to die, he roused the holy spirit residing in a young boy called Daniel 46 who began to shout, 'I am innocent of this woman's death!' 47 At this all the people turned to him and asked, 'What do you mean by that?' 48 Standing in the middle of the crowd, he replied, 'Are you so stupid, children of Israel, as to condemn a daughter of Israel unheard, and without troubling to find out the truth? 49 Go back to the scene of the trial: these men have given false evidence against her.'

50 All the people hurried back, and the elders said to Daniel, 'Come and sit with us and tell us what you mean, since God has given you the gifts that elders have.' 51 Daniel said, 'Keep the men well apart from each other, for I want to question them.' 52 When the men had been separated, Daniel had one of them brought to him. 'You have grown old in wickedness,' he said, 'and now the sins of your earlier days have overtaken you, 53 you with your unjust judgements, your condemnation of the innocent, your acquittal of the guilty, although the Lord has said, "You must not put the innocent and upright to death." 54 Now then, since you saw her so clearly, tell me what sort of tree you saw them lying under.' He replied, 'Under an acacia tree.' 55 Daniel said, 'Indeed! Your lie recoils on your own head:[b] the angel of God has already received from him your sentence and will cut you in half.' 56 He dismissed the man, ordered the other to be brought and said to him, 'Son of Canaan, not of Judah, beauty has seduced you, lust has led your heart astray! 57 This is how you have been behaving with the daughters of Israel, and they have been too frightened to resist; but here is a daughter of Judah who could not stomach your wickedness! 58 Now then, tell me what sort of

b 13 In Gk, the punishment and the tree in both cases have similar sounds: schinos/schisei, prinos/kataprisei.

NEW REVISED STANDARD VERSION

you catch them being intimate with each other?" He answered, "Under an evergreen oak."[c] 59 Daniel said to him, "Very well! This lie has cost you also your head, for the angel of God is waiting with his sword to split[c] you in two, so as to destroy you both."

60 Then the whole assembly raised a great shout and blessed God, who saves those who hope in him. 61 And they took action against the two elders, because out of their own mouths Daniel had convicted them of bearing false witness; they did to them as they had wickedly planned to do to their neighbor. 62 Acting in accordance with the law of Moses, they put them to death. Thus innocent blood was spared that day.

63 Hilkiah and his wife praised God for their daughter Susanna, and so did her husband Joakim and all her relatives, because she was found innocent of a shameful deed. 64 And from that day onward Daniel had a great reputation among the people.

[c] The Greek words for *evergreen oak* and *split* are similar, thus forming an ironic wordplay

REVISED ENGLISH BIBLE

them together?' 'Under a yew tree,' he replied. 59 Daniel said to him, 'Very good! This lie has cost you also your life, for the angel of God is waiting sword in hand to hew you down and destroy the pair of you.'

60 At that the whole assembly shouted aloud, praising God, the Saviour of those who trust in him. 61 They turned on the two elders, for out of their own mouths Daniel had convicted them of giving false evidence; 62 they dealt with them according to the law of Moses, putting them to death as they in their wickedness had intended to do to their neighbour. So an innocent life was saved that day. 63 Then Hilkiah and his wife gave praise for their daughter Susanna, as did also her husband Joakim and all her relatives, because she was found innocent of a shameful deed.

64 From that day forward Daniel was held in great esteem among the people.

58 yew: *lit.* oak. 58–59 yew . . . hew: *there is a play on words in the Greek.*

surprised them together." 59 "Under an oak," he said. "Your fine lie has cost you also your head," said Daniel; "for the angel of God waits with a sword to cut you in two so as to make an end of you both."

60 The whole assembly cried aloud, blessing God who saves those that hope in him. 61 They rose up against the two elders, for by their own words Daniel had convicted them of perjury. According to the law of Moses, they inflicted on them the penalty they had plotted to impose on their neighbor: 62 they put them to death. Thus was innocent blood spared that day.

63 Hilkiah and his wife praised God for their daughter Susanna, as did Joakim her husband and all her relatives, because she was found innocent of any shameful deed. 64 And from that day onward Daniel was greatly esteemed by the people.

tree you surprised them under.' He replied, 'Under an aspen tree.' 59 Daniel said, 'Indeed! Your lie recoils on your own head: the angel of God is waiting with a sword to rend you in half, and destroy the pair of you.'

60 Then the whole assembly shouted, blessing God, the Saviour of those who trust in him. 61 And they turned on the two elders whom Daniel had convicted of false evidence out of their own mouths. 62 As the Law of Moses prescribes, they were given the same punishment as they had schemed to inflict on their neighbour. They were put to death. And thus, that day, an innocent life was saved. 63 Hilkiah and his wife gave thanks to God for their daughter Susanna, and so did her husband Joakim and all his relations, because she had been acquitted of anything dishonourable.

64 From that day onwards, Daniel's reputation stood high with the people.

Bel and the Dragon

(Chapter 14 of the Greek Version
of Daniel)

1 When King Astyages was laid to rest with his ancestors, Cyrus the Persian succeeded to his kingdom. 2 Daniel was a companion of the king, and was the most honored of all his friends.

3 Now the Babylonians had an idol called Bel, and every day they provided for it twelve bushels of choice flour and forty sheep and six measures*a* of wine. 4 The king revered it and went every day to worship it. But Daniel worshiped his own God.

So the king said to him, "Why do you not worship Bel?" 5 He answered, "Because I do not revere idols made with hands, but the living God, who created heaven and earth and has dominion over all living creatures."

6 The king said to him, "Do you not think that Bel is a living god? Do you not see how much he eats and drinks every day?" 7 And Daniel laughed, and said, "Do not be deceived, O king, for this thing is only clay inside and bronze outside, and it never ate or drank anything."

8 Then the king was angry and called the priests of Bel*b* and said to them, "If you do not tell me who is eating these provisions, you shall die. 9 But if you prove that Bel is eating them, Daniel shall die, because he has spoken blasphemy against Bel." Daniel said to the king, "Let it be done as you have said."

10 Now there were seventy priests of Bel, besides their wives and children. So the king went with Daniel into the temple of Bel. 11 The priests of Bel said, "See, we are now going outside; you yourself, O king, set out the food and prepare the wine, and shut the door and seal it with your signet. 12 When you return in the morning, if you do not find that Bel has eaten it all, we will die; otherwise Daniel will, who is telling lies about us." 13 They were unconcerned, for beneath the table they had made a hidden entrance, through which they used to go in regularly and consume the provisions. 14 After they had gone out, the king set out the food for Bel. Then Daniel ordered his servants to bring ashes, and they scattered them throughout the whole temple in the presence of the king alone. Then they went out, shut the door and sealed it with the king's signet, and departed. 15 During the night the priests came as usual, with their wives and children, and they ate and drank everything.

16 Early in the morning the king rose and came, and Daniel with him. 17 The king said, "Are the seals unbroken, Daniel?" He answered, "They are unbroken, O king." 18 As soon as the doors were opened, the king looked at the table, and shouted in a loud voice, "You are great, O Bel, and in you there is no deceit at all!"

19 But Daniel laughed and restrained the king from going in. "Look at the floor," he said, "and notice whose footprints these are." 20 The king said, "I see the footprints of men and women and children."

21 Then the king was enraged, and he arrested the priests and their wives and children. They showed him the secret doors through which they used to enter to consume what was on the table. 22 Therefore the king put them to death, and gave Bel over to Daniel, who destroyed it and its temple.

a A little more than fifty gallons   *b* Gk *his priests*

Daniel, Bel, and the Snake

WHEN King Astyages was gathered to his forefathers, he was succeeded on the throne by Cyrus the Persian. 2 Daniel was a companion of the king and the most honoured of all the king's Friends.

3 The Babylonians had an idol called Bel, for which every day they provided twelve bushels of fine flour, forty sheep, and fifty gallons of wine. 4 The king went daily to bow down to it in worship; but Daniel bowed before his own God. When the king asked him, 'Why do you not bow down to Bel?' 5 he replied, 'Because I do not worship man-made idols; I worship the living God who created heaven and earth and is sovereign over all mankind.' 6 The king protested, 'How can you think Bel is not a living god? Do you not see how much he eats and drinks each day?' 7 Daniel laughed. 'Do not be deceived, your majesty,' he said; 'this Bel of yours is just clay inside and bronze outside, and has never eaten or drunk anything.'

8 Angered by this, the king summoned the priests of Bel and said to them, 'If you cannot tell me who it is that consumes these provisions, you shall die; 9 but if you can show it is Bel that eats them, then, for blasphemy against Bel, Daniel shall die.' Daniel said to the king, 'Let it be as you propose.' 10 (There were seventy priests of Bel, and in addition their wives and children.) When the king, along with Daniel, went into the temple of Bel, 11 the priests said, 'We are now leaving; let your majesty set out the food yourself, with the wine you have mixed; then make fast the door and seal it with your signet. 12 In the morning when you return, if you do not find that Bel has eaten it all, let us be put to death; but if Daniel's charges against us turn out to be false, then let him die.' 13 They treated the affair lightly, for beneath the table they had constructed a hidden entrance, by which they used to go in and eat up everything.

14 After the priests had gone, the king set out the food for Bel; and Daniel ordered his servants to bring ashes and sift them over the whole temple with only the king present. They then left the building, closed the door, sealed it with the royal signet, and went away. 15 During the night the priests, with their wives and children, came as usual and ate and drank everything.

16 Next morning the king was up early, and Daniel with him. 17 The king said, 'Are the seals intact, Daniel?' 'They are intact, your majesty,' he answered. 18 As soon as the door was opened, the king took one look at the table and cried aloud, 'Great are you, O Bel! In you there is no deception whatsoever.' 19 But Daniel laughed and held back the king from going in. 'Just look at the floor,' he said, 'and judge whose footprints these are.' 20 The king said, 'I see the footprints of men, women, and children.' In a rage 21 he had the priests arrested together with their wives and children, and they showed him the secret door through which it was their custom to go and eat what was on the table. 22 The king then put them to death, and he handed Bel over to Daniel, who destroyed both idol and temple.

In standard editions of the New American Bible this chapter is printed after Daniel 13.

DANIEL 14

1 After King Astyages was laid with his fathers, Cyrus the Persian succeeded to his kingdom. 2 Daniel was the king's favorite and was held in higher esteem than any of the friends of the king. 3 The Babylonians had an idol called Bel, and every day they provided for it six barrels of fine flour, forty sheep, and six measures of wine. 4 The king worshiped it and went every day to adore it; but Daniel adored only his God. 5 When the king asked him, "Why do you not adore Bel?" Daniel replied, "Because I worship not idols made with hands, but only the living God who made heaven and earth and has dominion over all mankind." 6 Then the king continued, "You do not think Bel is a living god? Do you not see how much he eats and drinks every day?" 7 Daniel began to laugh. "Do not be deceived, O king," he said; "it is only clay inside and bronze outside; it has never taken any food or drink." 8 Enraged, the king called his priests and said to them, "Unless you tell me who it is that consumes these provisions, you shall die. 9 But if you can show that Bel consumes them, Daniel shall die for blaspheming Bel." Daniel said to the king, "Let it be as you say!" 10 There were seventy priests of Bel, besides their wives and children.

When the king went with Daniel into the temple of Bel, 11 the priests of Bel said, "See, we are going to leave. Do you, O king, set out the food and prepare the wine; then shut the door and seal it with your ring. 12 If you do not find that Bel has eaten it all when you return in the morning, we are to die; otherwise Daniel shall die for his lies against us." 13 They were not perturbed, because under the table they had made a secret entrance through which they always came in to consume the food. 14 After they departed the king set the food before Bel, while Daniel ordered his servants to bring some ashes, which they scattered through the whole temple; the king alone was present. Then they went outside, sealed the closed door with the king's ring, and departed. 15 The priests entered that night as usual, with their wives and children, and they ate and drank everything.

16 Early the next morning, the king came with Daniel. 17 "Are the seals unbroken, Daniel?" he asked. And Daniel answered, "They are unbroken, O king." 18 As soon as he had opened the door, the king looked at the table and cried aloud, "Great you are, O Bel; there is no trickery in you." 19 But Daniel laughed and kept the king from entering. "Look at the floor," he said; "whose footprints are these?" 20 "I see the footprints of men, women, and children!" said the king. 21 The angry king arrested the priests, their wives, and their children. They showed him the secret door by which they used to enter to consume what was on the table. 22 He put them to death, and handed Bel over to Daniel, who destroyed it and its temple.

In standard editions of the New Jerusalem Bible this chapter is printed after Daniel 13.

BEL AND THE DRAGON

(Chapter 14 of the Greek Version of Daniel)

1 a When King Astyages joined his ancestors, Cyrus of Persia succeeded him. 2 Daniel was very close to the king, who respected him more than any of his other friends. 3 Now, in Babylon there was an idol called Bel, b to which twelve bushels of the finest flour, forty sheep and six measures of wine were offered every day. 4 The king venerated this idol and used to go and worship it every day. Daniel, however, worshipped his own God. 5 'Why do you not worship Bel?' the king asked Daniel. 'I do not worship idols made by human hand,' Daniel replied, 'I worship the living God who made heaven and earth and who is lord over all living creatures.' 6 'Do you not believe, then,' said the king, 'that Bel is a living god? Can you not see how much he eats and drinks each day?' 7 Daniel laughed. 'Your Majesty,' he said, 'do not be taken in; he is clay inside, and bronze outside, and has never eaten or drunk anything.' 8 This made the king angry; he summoned his priests, 'Tell me who eats all this food,' he said, 'or die. Prove to me that Bel really eats it, and I will have Daniel put to death for blaspheming him.' 9 Daniel said to the king, 'Let it be as you say.'

10 There were seventy of these priests, to say nothing of their wives and children. The king went to the temple of Bel, taking Daniel with him. 11 The priests of Bel said to him, 'We shall now go out, and you, Your Majesty, will lay out the meal and mix the wine and set it out. Then, lock the door and seal it with your personal seal. If, when you return in the morning, you do not find that everything has been eaten by Bel, let us be put to death; otherwise let Daniel, that slanderer!' 12 They were thinking—hence their confidence—of a secret entrance which they had made under the table, and by which they came in regularly and took the offerings away. 13 When the priests had gone and the king had set out the food for Bel, 14 Daniel made his servants bring ashes and spread them all over the temple floor, with no other witness than the king. They then left the building, shut the door and, sealing it with the king's seal, went away. 15 That night, as usual, the priests came with their wives and children; they ate and drank everything.

16 The king was up very early next morning, and Daniel with him. 17 'Daniel,' said the king, 'are the seals intact?' 'They are intact, Your Majesty,' he replied. 18 The king then opened the door, and, taking one look at the table, exclaimed, 'You are great, O Bel! There is no deception in you!' 19 But Daniel laughed; and, restraining the king from going in any further, he said, 'Look at the floor and take note whose footmarks these are!' 20 'I can see the footmarks of men, of women and of children,' said the king, 21 and angrily ordered the priests to be arrested, with their wives and children. They then showed him the secret door through which they used to come and take what was on the table. 22 The king had them put to death and handed Bel over to Daniel who destroyed both the idol and its temple.

a 14 Ch. 14 occurs in Gk but not in the Hebr. text.
b 14 Another name for Marduk, chief god of Babylon.

NEW REVISED STANDARD VERSION

23 Now in that place[c] there was a great dragon, which the Babylonians revered. 24 The king said to Daniel, "You cannot deny that this is a living god; so worship him." 25 Daniel said, "I worship the Lord my God, for he is the living God. 26 But give me permission, O king, and I will kill the dragon without sword or club." The king said, "I give you permission."

27 Then Daniel took pitch, fat, and hair, and boiled them together and made cakes, which he fed to the dragon. The dragon ate them, and burst open. Then Daniel said, "See what you have been worshiping!"

28 When the Babylonians heard about it, they were very indignant and conspired against the king, saying, "The king has become a Jew; he has destroyed Bel, and killed the dragon, and slaughtered the priests." 29 Going to the king, they said, "Hand Daniel over to us, or else we will kill you and your household." 30 The king saw that they were pressing him hard, and under compulsion he handed Daniel over to them.

31 They threw Daniel into the lions' den, and he was there for six days. 32 There were seven lions in the den, and every day they had been given two human bodies and two sheep; but now they were given nothing, so that they would devour Daniel.

33 Now the prophet Habakkuk was in Judea; he had made a stew and had broken bread into a bowl, and was going into the field to take it to the reapers. 34 But the angel of the Lord said to Habakkuk, "Take the food that you have to Babylon, to Daniel, in the lions' den." 35 Habakkuk said, "Sir, I have never seen Babylon, and I know nothing about the den." 36 Then the angel of the Lord took him by the crown of his head and carried him by his hair; with the speed of the wind[d] he set him down in Babylon, right over the den.

37 Then Habakkuk shouted, "Daniel, Daniel! Take the food that God has sent you." 38 Daniel said, "You have remembered me, O God, and have not forsaken those who love you." 39 So Daniel got up and ate. And the angel of God immediately returned Habakkuk to his own place.

40 On the seventh day the king came to mourn for Daniel. When he came to the den he looked in, and there sat Daniel! 41 The king shouted with a loud voice, "You are great, O Lord, the God of Daniel, and there is no other besides you!" 42 Then he pulled Daniel[e] out, and threw into the den those who had attempted his destruction, and they were instantly eaten before his eyes.

[c] Other ancient authorities lack *in that place*   [d] Or *by the power of his spirit*   [e] Gk *him*

REVISED ENGLISH BIBLE

23 THERE was a huge snake which the Babylonians worshipped. 24 The king said to Daniel, 'Bow down to him; you cannot say that this is not a living god.' 25 Daniel answered, 'I shall bow before the Lord my God, for he is a living God. 26 But give me authority, your majesty, and without using sword or staff I shall kill the snake.' 'I grant it,' replied the king. 27 Then Daniel took pitch and fat and hair, boiled them together, and made them into cakes, which he put into the mouth of the snake. The snake swallowed them and burst. Daniel said, 'See what things you people worship!'

28 When they heard of this, the Babylonians in their indignation made common cause against the king. 'The king has turned Jew!' they cried. 'He has pulled down Bel, killed the snake, and put the priests to the sword.' 29 They went to the king. 'Hand Daniel over to us,' they demanded, 'or else we shall kill you and your family.' 30 The king, finding himself thus hard pressed, was compelled to hand him over.

31 They threw Daniel into the lion-pit, and he was there for six days. 32 In the pit were seven lions, and every day two slaves and two sheep were fed to them; now, to make sure they would devour Daniel, they were given nothing.

33 The prophet Habakkuk, who was in Judaea, had made a stew; he broke bread into the bowl, and he was on the way to his field, carrying it to the reapers, 34 when an angel of the Lord said to him, 'Habakkuk, carry that meal you have to Babylon for Daniel, who is in the lion-pit.' 35 'My lord,' replied Habakkuk, 'I have never been to Babylon, and I do not know where the lion-pit is.' 36 The angel took the prophet by the head, and carrying him by his hair swept him to Babylon with the blast of his breath and set him down above the pit. 37 Habakkuk called out, 'Daniel, Daniel! Take the meal that God has sent you.' 38 Daniel said, 'You do indeed remember me, God; you never abandon those who love you.' 39 He got up and ate; and at once God's angel brought Habakkuk home again.

40 On the seventh day the king went to mourn for Daniel, but when he arrived at the pit and looked in, there sat Daniel! 41 The king cried aloud, 'You are indeed great, Lord, the God of Daniel, and there is no god but you alone.' 42 He drew Daniel up, while those men who had plotted to destroy Daniel were flung into the pit, and then and there they were devoured before his eyes.

23 There was a great dragon which the Babylonians worshiped. 24 "Look!" said the king to Daniel, "you cannot deny that this is a living god, so adore it." 25 But Daniel answered, "I adore the Lord, my God, for he is the living God. 26 Give me permission, O king, and I will kill this dragon without sword or club." "I give you permission," the king said. 27 Then Daniel took some pitch, fat, and hair; these he boiled together and made into cakes. He put them into the mouth of the dragon, and when the dragon ate them, he burst asunder. "This," he said, "is what you worshiped."

28 When the Babylonians heard this, they were angry and turned against the king. "The king has become a Jew," they said; "he has destroyed Bel, killed the dragon, and put the priests to death." 29 They went to the king and demanded: "Hand Daniel over to us, or we will kill you and your family." 30 When he saw himself threatened with violence, the king was forced to hand Daniel over to them. 31 They threw Daniel into a lions' den, where he remained six days. 32 In the den were seven lions, and two carcasses and two sheep had been given to them daily. But now they were given nothing, so that they would devour Daniel.

33 In Judea there was a prophet, Habakkuk; he mixed some bread in a bowl with the stew he had boiled, and was going to bring it to the reapers in the field, 34 when an angel of the Lord told him, "Take the lunch you have to Daniel in the lions' den at Babylon." 35 But Habakkuk answered, "Babylon, sir, I have never seen, and I do not know the den!" 36 The angel of the Lord seized him by the crown of his head and carried him by the hair; with the speed of the wind, he set him down in Babylon above the den. 37 "Daniel, Daniel," cried Habakkuk, "take the lunch God has sent you." 38 "You have remembered me, O God," said Daniel; "you have not forsaken those who love you." 39 While Daniel began to eat, the angel of the Lord at once brought Habakkuk back to his own place.

40 On the seventh day the king came to mourn for Daniel. As he came to the den and looked in, there was Daniel, sitting there! 41 The king cried aloud, "You are great, O Lord, the God of Daniel, and there is no other besides you!" 42 Daniel he took out, but those who had tried to destroy him he threw into the den, and they were devoured in a moment before his eyes.

23 There was a great dragon which the Babylonians worshipped too. 24 The king said to Daniel, 'Are you going to tell me that this is made of bronze? Look, it is alive; it eats and drinks; you cannot deny that this is a living god; worship it, then.' 25 Daniel replied, 'I will worship the Lord my God; he is the living God. With your permission, Your Majesty, without using either sword or club, I shall kill this dragon.' 26 'You have my permission,' said the king. 27 Whereupon, Daniel took some pitch, some fat and some hair and boiled them up together, rolled the mixture into balls and fed them to the dragon; the dragon swallowed them and burst. Daniel said, 'Now look at the sort of thing you worship!' 28 The Babylonians were furious when they heard about this and rose against the king. 'The king has turned Jew,' they said, 'he has allowed Bel to be overthrown, and the dragon to be killed, and he has put the priests to death.' 29 So they went to the king and said, 'Hand Daniel over to us or else we shall kill you and your family.' 30 They pressed him so hard that the king found himself forced to hand Daniel over to them.

31 They threw Daniel into the lion pit, and there he stayed for six days. 32 In the pit were seven lions, which were given two human bodies and two sheep every day; but for this period they were not given anything, to make sure they would eat Daniel.

33 Now, the prophet Habakkuk was in Judaea: he had been making a stew and breaking up bread into a basket. He was on his way to the fields, taking this to the harvesters, 34 when the angel of the Lord spoke to him, 'Take the meal you are carrying to Babylon, and give it to Daniel in the lion pit.' 35 'Lord,' replied Habakkuk, 'I have not even seen Babylon and know nothing about this pit.' 36 The angel of the Lord took hold of his head and carried him off by the hair to Babylon where, with a great blast of his breath, he set Habakkuk down on the edge of the pit. 37 'Daniel, Daniel,' Habakkuk shouted, 'take the meal that God has sent you.' 38 And Daniel said, 'You have kept me in mind, O God; you have not deserted those who love you.' 39 Rising to his feet, he ate the meal, while the angel of God carried Habakkuk back in a moment to his own country.

40 On the seventh day, the king came to lament over Daniel; on reaching the pit he looked inside, and there sat Daniel. 41 'You are great, O Lord, God of Daniel,' he exclaimed, 'there is no god but you!' 42 He then had Daniel released from the pit and the plotters of Daniel's ruin thrown in instead, where they were instantly eaten before his eyes.

1 Maccabees

THE FIRST BOOK OF THE
Maccabees

1 After Alexander son of Philip, the Macedonian, who came from the land of Kittim, had defeated[a] King Darius of the Persians and the Medes, he succeeded him as king. (He had previously become king of Greece.) 2 He fought many battles, conquered strongholds, and put to death the kings of the earth. 3 He advanced to the ends of the earth, and plundered many nations. When the earth became quiet before him, he was exalted, and his heart was lifted up. 4 He gathered a very strong army and ruled over countries, nations, and princes, and they became tributary to him.

5 After this he fell sick and perceived that he was dying. 6 So he summoned his most honored officers, who had been brought up with him from youth, and divided his kingdom among them while he was still alive. 7 And after Alexander had reigned twelve years, he died.

8 Then his officers began to rule, each in his own place. 9 They all put on crowns after his death, and so did their descendants after them for many years; and they caused many evils on the earth.

10 From them came forth a sinful root, Antiochus Epiphanes, son of King Antiochus; he had been a hostage in Rome. He began to reign in the one hundred thirty-seventh year of the kingdom of the Greeks.[b]

11 In those days certain renegades came out from Israel and misled many, saying, "Let us go and make a covenant with the Gentiles around us, for since we separated from them many disasters have come upon us." 12 This proposal pleased them, 13 and some of the people eagerly went to the king, who authorized them to observe the ordinances of the Gentiles. 14 So they built a gymnasium in Jerusalem, according to Gentile custom, 15 and removed the marks of circumcision, and abandoned the holy covenant. They joined with the Gentiles and sold themselves to do evil.

16 When Antiochus saw that his kingdom was established, he determined to become king of the land of Egypt, in order that he might reign over both kingdoms. 17 So he invaded Egypt with a strong force, with chariots and elephants and cavalry and with a large fleet. 18 He engaged King Ptolemy of Egypt in battle, and Ptolemy turned and fled before him, and many were wounded and fell. 19 They captured the fortified cities in the land of Egypt, and he plundered the land of Egypt.

20 After subduing Egypt, Antiochus returned in the one hundred forty-third year.[c] He went up against Israel and came to Jerusalem with a strong force. 21 He arrogantly entered the sanctuary and took the golden altar, the lampstand for the light, and all its utensils. 22 He took also the table for the bread of the Presence, the cups for drink offerings, the bowls, the golden censers, the curtain, the crowns, and the gold decoration on the front of the temple; he stripped it all off. 23 He took the silver and the gold, and the costly vessels; he took also the hidden treasures that he found. 24 Taking them all, he went into his own land.

He shed much blood,
> and spoke with great arrogance.
25 Israel mourned deeply in every community,
26   rulers and elders groaned,
> young women and young men became faint,
> the beauty of the women faded.

1 ALEXANDER of Macedon, the son of Philip, marched from the land of Kittim, defeated Darius, king of Persia and Media, and seized his throne, being already king of Greece. 2 During the course of many campaigns, in which he captured strongholds and put kings to death, 3 he traversed the earth to its remotest bounds and plundered countless nations. When at last the world lay quiet under his sway, his pride knew no limits; 4 he built up an extremely powerful army and ruled over countries, nations, and princedoms, all of which rendered him tribute.

5 The time came when Alexander fell ill, and, realizing that he was dying, 6 he summoned his generals, nobles who had been brought up with him from childhood, and divided his empire among them while he was yet alive. 7 At his death he had reigned for twelve years. 8 His generals took over the government, each in his own province, 9 and, when Alexander died, they all assumed royal crowns, and for many years the succession passed to their descendants. They brought untold miseries on the world.

10 An offshoot of this stock was that impious man, Antiochus Epiphanes, son of King Antiochus. He had been a hostage in Rome before he succeeded to the throne in the year 137 of the Greek era.

11 At that time there emerged in Israel a group of renegade Jews, who inveigled many by saying, 'We should go and make an agreement with the Gentiles round about; nothing but disaster has been our lot since we cut ourselves off from them.' 12 This proposal was widely approved, 13 and some of the people in their enthusiasm went to the king and received authority to introduce pagan laws and customs. 14 They built a gymnasium in the gentile style at Jerusalem; 15 they removed their marks of circumcision and repudiated the holy covenant; they intermarried with Gentiles and sold themselves to evil.

16 Once he was firmly established on his throne, Antiochus determined to become king of Egypt and so rule both kingdoms. 17 He invaded Egypt with a powerful force of chariots, elephants, and cavalry, together with a great fleet. 18 When battle was joined, King Ptolemy was routed with heavy loss and took flight. 19 The fortified towns in Egypt were captured and the land pillaged.

20 On his return from the conquest of Egypt in the year 143 Antiochus marched up with a strong force against Israel and Jerusalem. 21 In his arrogance he entered the temple and carried off the gold altar, the lampstand with all its fittings, 22 the table of the Bread of the Presence, the libation cups and bowls, the gold censers, the curtain, and the garlands. He stripped the gold plating from the front of the temple, 23 seized the silver and gold, the precious vessels, and whatever secret treasures he found, 24 and carried them all away when he left for his own country. He had caused much bloodshed, and he boasted arrogantly of what he had done.

25 Great was the mourning throughout Israel,
26 deep the groans of rulers and elders.
> Girls and young men languished;
> the beauty of our women was disfigured.

---

[a] Gk adds and he defeated   [b] 175 B.C.   [c] 169 B.C.

1:1 being . . . Greece: prob. mng; Gk obscure.   1:10 the year . . . era: that is 175 B.C.E.   1:20 143: that is 169 B.C.E.

THE FIRST BOOK OF
Maccabees

1 After Alexander the Macedonian, Philip's son, who came from the land of Kittim, had defeated Darius, king of the Persians and Medes, he became king in his place, having first ruled in Greece. 2 He fought many campaigns, captured fortresses, and put kings to death. 3 He advanced to the ends of the earth, gathering plunder from many nations; the earth fell silent before him, and his heart became proud and arrogant. 4 He collected a very strong army and conquered provinces, nations, and rulers, and they became his tributaries. 5 But after all this he took to his bed, realizing that he was going to die. 6 He therefore summoned his officers, the nobles, who had been brought up with him from his youth, to divide his kingdom among them while he was still alive. 7 Alexander had reigned twelve years when he died.

8 So his officers took over his kingdom, each in his own territory, 9 and after his death they all put on royal crowns, and so did their sons after them for many years, causing much distress over the earth.

10 There sprang from these a sinful offshoot, Antiochus Epiphanes, son of King Antiochus, once a hostage at Rome. He became king in the year one hundred and thirty-seven of the kingdom of the Greeks.

11 In those days there appeared in Israel men who were breakers of the law, and they seduced many people, saying: "Let us go and make an alliance with the Gentiles all around us; since we separated from them, many evils have come upon us." 12 The proposal was agreeable; 13 some from among the people promptly went to the king, and he authorized them to introduce the way of living of the Gentiles. 14 Thereupon they built a gymnasium in Jerusalem according to the Gentile custom. 15 They covered over the mark of their circumcision and abandoned the holy covenant; they allied themselves with the Gentiles and sold themselves to wrongdoing.

16 When his kingdom seemed secure, Antiochus proposed to become king of Egypt, so as to rule over both kingdoms. 17 He invaded Egypt with a strong force, with chariots and elephants, and with a large fleet, 18 to make war on Ptolemy, king of Egypt. Ptolemy was frightened at his presence and fled, leaving many casualties. 19 The fortified cities in the land of Egypt were captured, and Antiochus plundered the land of Egypt.

20 After Antiochus had defeated Egypt in the year one hundred and forty-three, he returned and went up to Israel and to Jerusalem with a strong force. 21 He insolently invaded the sanctuary and took away the golden altar, the lampstand for the light with all its fixtures, 22 the offering table, the cups and the bowls, the golden censers, the curtain, the crowns, and the golden ornament on the façade of the temple. He stripped off everything, 23 and took away the gold and silver and the precious vessels; he also took all the hidden treasures he could find. 24 Taking all this, he went back to his own country, after he had spoken with great arrogance and shed much blood.

25 And there was great mourning for Israel, in every place where they dwelt,
26 and the rulers and the elders groaned.
Virgins and young men languished,
and the beauty of the women was disfigured.

THE FIRST BOOK OF
Maccabees

1 Alexander of Macedon son of Philip had come from the land of Kittim[a] and defeated Darius king of the Persians and Medes, whom he succeeded as ruler, at first of Hellas. 2 He undertook many campaigns, gained possession of many fortresses, and put the local kings to death. 3 So he advanced to the ends of the earth, plundering nation after nation; the earth grew silent before him, and his ambitious heart swelled with pride. 4 He assembled very powerful forces and subdued provinces, nations and princes, and they became his tributaries. 5 But the time came when Alexander took to his bed, in the knowledge that he was dying. 6 He summoned his officers, noblemen who had been brought up with him from his youth, and divided his kingdom among them while he was still alive. 7 Alexander had reigned twelve years when he died. 8 Each of his officers established himself in his own region. 9 All assumed crowns after his death, they and their heirs after them for many years, bringing increasing evils on the world.

10 From these there grew a wicked offshoot, Antiochus Epiphanes son of King Antiochus; once a hostage in Rome, he became king in the 107th year[b] of the kingdom of the Greeks. 11 It was then that there emerged from Israel a set of renegades who led many people astray. 'Come,' they said, 'let us ally ourselves with the gentiles surrounding us, for since we separated ourselves from them many misfortunes have overtaken us.' 12 This proposal proved acceptable, 13 and a number of the people eagerly approached the king, who authorised them to practise the gentiles' observances. 14 So they built a gymnasium in Jerusalem, such as the gentiles have, 15 disguised their circumcision, and abandoned the holy covenant, submitting to gentile rule as willing slaves of impiety.

16 Once Antiochus had seen his authority established, he determined to make himself king of Egypt and the ruler of both kingdoms. 17 He invaded Egypt in massive strength, with chariots and elephants (and cavalry) and a large fleet. 18 He engaged Ptolemy king of Egypt in battle, and Ptolemy turned back and fled before his advance, leaving many casualties. 19 The fortified cities of Egypt were captured, and Antiochus plundered the country. 20 After his conquest of Egypt, in the year 143, Antiochus turned about and advanced on Israel and Jerusalem in massive strength.[c] 21 Insolently breaking into the sanctuary, he removed the golden altar and the lamp-stand for the light with all its fittings, 22 together with the table for the loaves of permanent offering, the libation vessels, the cups, the golden censers, the veil, the crowns, and the golden decoration on the front of the Temple, which he stripped of everything. 23 He made off with the silver and gold and precious vessels; he discovered the secret treasures and seized them 24 and, removing all these, he went back to his own country, having shed much blood and uttered words of extreme arrogance.

25 There was deep mourning for Israel throughout the country:

26 Rulers and elders groaned;
girls and young men wasted away;
the women's beauty suffered a change;

a 1 Term extended from inhabitants of Kition to all Cypriots and then to all Greeks.   b 1 Dates in the text of 1—2 M are of the era starting with the foundation of Antioch in 312 BC.   c 1 // 2 M 5:11–16.

27 Every bridegroom took up the lament;
  she who sat in the bridal chamber was
    mourning.
28 Even the land trembled for its inhabitants,
  and all the house of Jacob was clothed with
    shame.

29 Two years later the king sent to the cities of Judah a chief collector of tribute, and he came to Jerusalem with a large force. 30 Deceitfully he spoke peaceable words to them, and they believed him; but he suddenly fell upon the city, dealt it a severe blow, and destroyed many people of Israel. 31 He plundered the city, burned it with fire, and tore down its houses and its surrounding walls. 32 They took captive the women and children, and seized the livestock. 33 Then they fortified the city of David with a great strong wall and strong towers, and it became their citadel. 34 They stationed there a sinful people, men who were renegades. These strengthened their position; 35 they stored up arms and food, and collecting the spoils of Jerusalem they stored them there, and became a great menace,

36 for the citadel^d became an ambush against the
    sanctuary,
  an evil adversary of Israel at all times.
37 On every side of the sanctuary they shed innocent
    blood;
  they even defiled the sanctuary.
38 Because of them the residents of Jerusalem fled;
  she became a dwelling of strangers;
  she became strange to her offspring,
  and her children forsook her.
39 Her sanctuary became desolate like a desert;
  her feasts were turned into mourning,
  her sabbaths into a reproach,
  her honor into contempt.
40 Her dishonor now grew as great as her glory;
  her exaltation was turned into mourning.

41 Then the king wrote to his whole kingdom that all should be one people, 42 and that all should give up their particular customs. 43 All the Gentiles accepted the command of the king. Many even from Israel gladly adopted his religion; they sacrificed to idols and profaned the sabbath. 44 And the king sent letters by messengers to Jerusalem and the towns of Judah; he directed them to follow customs strange to the land, 45 to forbid burnt offerings and sacrifices and drink offerings in the sanctuary, to profane sabbaths and festivals, 46 to defile the sanctuary and the priests, 47 to build altars and sacred precincts and shrines for idols, to sacrifice swine and other unclean animals, 48 and to leave their sons uncircumcised. They were to make themselves abominable by everything unclean and profane, 49 so that they would forget the law and change all the ordinances. 50 He added,^e "And whoever does not obey the command of the king shall die."

51 In such words he wrote to his whole kingdom. He appointed inspectors over all the people and commanded the towns of Judah to offer sacrifice, town by town. 52 Many of the people, everyone who forsook the law, joined them, and they did evil in the land; 53 they drove Israel into hiding in every place of refuge they had.

54 Now on the fifteenth day of Chislev, in the one hundred forty-fifth year,^f they erected a desolating sacrilege on the altar of burnt offering. They also built altars in the surrounding towns of Judah, 55 and offered incense at the doors of the houses and in the streets. 56 The books of the law that they found they tore to pieces and burned with fire.

27 Every bridegroom took up the lament;
  every bride sat mourning in her bridal chamber.
28 The land trembled for its inhabitants,
  and all the house of Jacob was wrapped in shame.

29 Two years later, the king sent a governor to put the towns of Judaea under tribute. When he arrived at Jerusalem with a powerful force 30 his language, though friendly, was full of guile, for once he had gained the city's confidence he launched a sudden and savage attack. Many of the Israelites were killed, 31 and their city was sacked and set ablaze. On every side the houses and city walls were demolished; 32 the women and children were captured, and the livestock seized.

33 The City of David was turned into a citadel, enclosed by a high, stout wall with strong towers, 34 and garrisoned by impious foreigners and renegades. Having made themselves secure, 35–36 they laid up a store of arms and provisions, and brought in the plunder they had collected from Jerusalem. They lurked there, a snare and threat to the temple and a perpetual menace to Israel.

37 They shed innocent blood all round the temple;
  they defiled the holy place.
38 For fear of them the inhabitants of Jerusalem fled;
  the city became the abode of aliens,
  and alien herself to her offspring:
  her children forsook her.
39 Her temple lay desolate as a wilderness;
  her festivals were turned to mourning,
  her sabbaths to a reproach,
  her honour to contempt.
40 Her present dishonour was equalled only by her
    past renown,
  and her pride was turned to mourning.

41 The king issued an edict throughout his empire: his subjects were all to become one people 42 and abandon their own customs. Everywhere the nations complied with the royal command, 43 and many in Israel willingly adopted the foreign cult, sacrificing to idols and profaning the sabbath. 44 The king sent agents to Jerusalem and the towns of Judaea with written orders that ways and customs foreign to the country should be introduced. 45 Whole-offerings, sacrifices, and drink-offerings were forbidden in the temple; sabbaths and feast days were to be profaned, 46 the temple and its ministers defiled. 47 Pagan altars, idols, and sacred precincts were to be established, swine and other unclean beasts to be offered in sacrifice. 48 The Jews were to leave their sons uncircumcised; they had to make themselves in every way abominable, unclean, and profane, 49 and so forget the law and change all their statutes. 50 The penalty for disobeying the royal command was death.

51 Such were the terms of the edict issued by the king throughout his realm. He appointed superintendents over all the people, and instructed the towns of Judaea to offer sacrifice, town by town. 52 Those of the people who were ready to betray the law all thronged to their side in large numbers. Their wicked conduct throughout the land 53 drove Israel into hiding in every possible place of refuge.

54 On the fifteenth day of the month of Kislev in the year 145, 'the abomination of desolation' was set up on the altar of the Lord. In the towns throughout Judaea pagan altars were built; 55 incense was offered at the doors of houses and in the streets. 56 Every scroll of the law that was found was torn up and consigned to the flames, 57 and anyone discov-

^d Gk it ^e Gk lacks *He added* ^f 167 B.C.   1:54 **145:** *that is* 167 B.C.E.

2440

27 Every bridegroom took up lamentation,
   she who sat in the bridal chamber mourned,
28 And the land was shaken on account of
         its inhabitants,
   and all the house of Jacob was covered
         with shame.

29 Two years later, the king sent the Mysian commander to the cities of Judah, and he came to Jerusalem with a strong force. 30 He spoke to them deceitfully in peaceful terms, and won their trust. Then he attacked the city suddenly, in a great onslaught, and destroyed many of the people in Israel. 31 He plundered the city and set fire to it, demolished its houses and its surrounding walls, 32 took captive the women and children, and seized the cattle. 33 Then they built up the City of David with a high, massive wall and strong towers, and it became their citadel. 34 There they installed a sinful race, perverse men, who fortified themselves inside it, 35 storing up weapons and provisions, and depositing there the plunder they had collected from Jerusalem. And they became a great threat.

36 The citadel became an ambush against
         the sanctuary,
   and a wicked adversary to Israel at all times.
37 And they shed innocent blood around
         the sanctuary;
   they defiled the sanctuary.
38 Because of them the inhabitants of Jerusalem
         fled away,
   and she became the abode of strangers.
   She became a stranger to her own offspring,
   and her children forsook her.
39 Her sanctuary was as desolate as a wilderness;
   her feasts were turned into mourning,
   Her sabbaths to shame,
   her honor to contempt.
40 Her dishonor was as great as her glory had been,
   and her exaltation was turned into mourning.

41 Then the king wrote to his whole kingdom that all should be one people, 42 each abandoning his particular customs. All the Gentiles conformed to the command of the king, 43 and many Israelites were in favor of his religion; they sacrificed to idols and profaned the sabbath. 44 The king sent messengers with letters to Jerusalem and to the cities of Judah, ordering them to follow customs foreign to their land: 45 to prohibit holocausts, sacrifices, and libations in the sanctuary, to profane the sabbaths and feast days, 46 to desecrate the sanctuary and the sacred ministers, to build pagan altars and temples and shrines, 47 to sacrifice swine and unclean animals, 48 to leave their sons uncircumcised, and to let themselves be defiled with every kind of impurity and abomination, 49 so that they might forget the law and change all their observances. 50 Whoever refused to act according to the command of the king should be put to death.

51 Such were the orders he published throughout his kingdom. He appointed inspectors over all the people, and he ordered the cities of Judah to offer sacrifices, each city in turn. 52 Many of the people, those who abandoned the law, joined them and committed evil in the land. 53 Israel was driven into hiding, wherever places of refuge could be found.

54 On the fifteenth day of the month Chislev, in the year one hundred and forty-five, the king erected the horrible abomination upon the altar of holocausts, and in the surrounding cities of Judah they built pagan altars. 55 They also burnt incense at the doors of houses and in the streets. 56 Any scrolls of the law which they found they tore up and burnt. 57 Whoever was found with a scroll of the covenant,

27 every bridegroom took up a dirge,
   the bride sat grief-stricken on her marriage-bed.
28 The earth quaked because of its inhabitants
   and the whole House of Jacob was clothed with
         shame.

29 Two years later the king sent the Mysarch through the cities of Judah. He came to Jerusalem with an impressive force, 30 and addressing them with what appeared to be peaceful words, he gained their confidence; then suddenly he fell on the city, dealing it a terrible blow, and destroying many of the people of Israel. 31 He pillaged the city and set it on fire, tore down its houses and encircling wall, 32 took the women and children captive and commandeered the cattle. 33 They then rebuilt the City of David with a great strong wall and strong towers and made this their Citadel. 34 There they installed a brood of sinners, of renegades, who fortified themselves inside it, 35 storing arms and provisions, and depositing there the loot they had collected from Jerusalem; they were to prove a great trouble.

36 It became an ambush for the sanctuary,
   an evil adversary for Israel at all times.
37 They shed innocent blood all round the sanctuary
   and defiled the sanctuary itself.
38 The citizens of Jerusalem fled because of them,
   she became a dwelling-place of strangers;
   estranged from her own offspring,
   her children forsook her.
39 Her sanctuary became as forsaken as a desert,
   her feasts were turned into mourning,
   her Sabbaths into a mockery,
   her honour into reproach.
40 Her dishonour now fully matched her former glory,
   her greatness was turned into grief.

41 The king then issued a proclamation to his whole kingdom that all were to become a single people, each nation renouncing its particular customs. 42 All the gentiles conformed to the king's decree, 43 and many Israelites chose to accept his religion, sacrificing to idols and profaning the Sabbath. 44 The king also sent edicts by messenger to Jerusalem and the towns of Judah, directing them to adopt customs foreign to the country, 45 banning burnt offerings, sacrifices and libations from the sanctuary, profaning Sabbaths and feasts, 46 defiling the sanctuary and everything holy, 47 building altars, shrines and temples for idols, sacrificing pigs and unclean beasts, 48 leaving their sons uncircumcised, and prostituting themselves to all kinds of impurity and abomination, 49 so that they should forget the Law and revoke all observance of it. 50 Anyone not obeying the king's command was to be put to death. 51 Writing in such terms to every part of his kingdom, the king appointed inspectors for the whole people and directed all the towns of Judah to offer sacrifice city by city. 52 Many of the people — that is, every apostate from the Law — rallied to them and so committed evil in the country, 53 forcing Israel into hiding in any possible place of refuge.

54 On the fifteenth day of Chislev in the year 145 the king built the appalling abomination[d] on top of the altar of burnt offering; and altars were built in the surrounding towns of Judah 55 and incense offered at the doors of houses and in the streets. 56 Any books of the Law that came to light were torn up and burned. 57 Whenever anyone was discovered

---

d 1 An idolatrous altar erected on the Jewish altar of burnt offering.

57 Anyone found possessing the book of the covenant, or anyone who adhered to the law, was condemned to death by decree of the king. 58 They kept using violence against Israel, against those who were found month after month in the towns. 59 On the twenty-fifth day of the month they offered sacrifice on the altar that was on top of the altar of burnt offering. 60 According to the decree, they put to death the women who had their children circumcised, 61 and their families and those who circumcised them; and they hung the infants from their mothers' necks.

62 But many in Israel stood firm and were resolved in their hearts not to eat unclean food. 63 They chose to die rather than to be defiled by food or to profane the holy covenant; and they did die. 64 Very great wrath came upon Israel.

2 In those days Mattathias son of John son of Simeon, a priest of the family of Joarib, moved from Jerusalem and settled in Modein. 2 He had five sons, John surnamed Gaddi, 3 Simon called Thassi, 4 Judas called Maccabeus, 5 Eleazar called Avaran, and Jonathan called Apphus. 6 He saw the blasphemies being committed in Judah and Jerusalem, 7 and said,

"Alas! Why was I born to see this,
    the ruin of my people, the ruin of the holy city,
and to live there when it was given over to the
        enemy,
    the sanctuary given over to aliens?
8 Her temple has become like a person without
        honor;g
9 her glorious vessels have been carried into
        exile.
Her infants have been killed in her streets,
    her youths by the sword of the foe.
10 What nation has not inherited her palacesh
    and has not seized her spoils?
11 All her adornment has been taken away;
    no longer free, she has become a slave.
12 And see, our holy place, our beauty,
    and our glory have been laid waste;
    the Gentiles have profaned them.
13 Why should we live any longer?"

14 Then Mattathias and his sons tore their clothes, put on sackcloth, and mourned greatly.

15 The king's officers who were enforcing the apostasy came to the town of Modein to make them offer sacrifice. 16 Many from Israel came to them; and Mattathias and his sons were assembled. 17 Then the king's officers spoke to Mattathias as follows: "You are a leader, honored and great in this town, and supported by sons and brothers. 18 Now be the first to come and do what the king commands, as all the Gentiles and the people of Judah and those that are left in Jerusalem have done. Then you and your sons will be numbered among the Friends of the king, and you and your sons will be honored with silver and gold and many gifts." 19 But Mattathias answered and said in a loud voice: "Even if all the nations that live under the rule of the king obey him, and have chosen to obey his commandments, everyone of them abandoning the religion of their ancestors, 20 I and my sons and my brothers will continue to live by the covenant of our ancestors. 21 Far be it from us to desert the law and the ordinances. 22 We will not obey the king's words by turning aside from our religion to the right hand or to the left."

23 When he had finished speaking these words, a Jew came forward in the sight of all to offer sacrifice on the altar in Modein, according to the king's command. 24 When Mat-

ered in possession of a Book of the Covenant or conforming to the law was by sentence of the king condemned to die. 58 Thus month after month these wicked men used their power against the Israelites whom they found in their towns. 59 On the twenty-fifth day of each month they offered sacrifice on the pagan altar which was on top of the altar of whole-offering. 60 In accordance with the royal decree, they put to death women who had had their children circumcised; 61 their babies, their families, and those who had performed the circumcisions were hanged by the neck.

62 Yet many in Israel found strength to resist, taking a determined stand against the eating of any unclean food. 63 They welcomed death and died rather than defile themselves and profane the holy covenant. 64 Israel lay under a reign of terror.

2 It was in those days that a certain Mattathias son of John, son of Symeon, came on the scene. He was a priest of the Joarib family from Jerusalem, now settled at Modin, 2 and he had five sons: John called Gaddis, 3 Simon called Thassis, 4 Judas called Maccabaeus, 5 Eleazar called Avaran, and Jonathan called Apphus. 6 When Mattathias saw the sacrilegious acts committed in Judaea and, above all, in Jerusalem, 7 he said:

'Oh! Why was I born to see this,
    the ruin of my people, the ruin of the Holy City,
to sit by while she was surrendered,
    the holy place given up to foreigners?
8 Her temple is like a man robbed of honour;
9 its glorious vessels are carried off as spoil.
Her infants are slain in her streets,
    her young men by the sword of the foe.
10 Is there any nation that has not usurped her
        sovereignty,
    any people that has not taken plunder from her?
11 She has been stripped of all her adornment;
    she is no longer free, she is a slave.

12 'We see the temple, which is our splendour and glory, laid waste and desecrated by the Gentiles. 13 Why should we go on living?' 14 Mattathias and his sons tore their garments, put on sackcloth, and mourned loud and long.

15 The king's officers who were enforcing apostasy came to the town of Modin to see that sacrifice was offered. 16 Many Israelites went over to them, but Mattathias and all his sons stood apart. 17 The officers addressed Mattathias: 'You are a leader here, a man of mark and influence in this town, with your sons and brothers at your back. 18 Now you be the first to come forward; carry out the king's decree as all the nations have done, as well as the leading men in Judaea and the people left in Jerusalem. Then you and your sons will be enrolled among the king's Friends; you will all receive high honours, rich rewards of silver and gold, and many further benefits.' 19 In a ringing voice Mattathias replied: 'Though every nation within the king's dominions obeys and forsakes its ancestral worship, though all have chosen to submit to his commands, 20 yet I and my sons and my brothers will follow the covenant made with our forefathers. 21 Heaven forbid we should ever abandon the law and its statutes! 22 We will not obey the king's command, nor will we deviate one step from our way of worship.'

23 As he finished speaking, a Jew came forward in full view of all to offer sacrifice on the pagan altar at Modin, in obedience to the royal decree. 24 The sight aroused the zeal

---

g Meaning of Gk uncertain   h Other ancient authorities read has not had a part in her kingdom

2:10 **usurped her sovereignty:** or occupied her palaces.

NEW AMERICAN BIBLE

and whoever observed the law, was condemned to death by royal decree. 58 So they used their power against Israel, against those who were caught, each month, in the cities. 59 On the twenty-fifth day of each month they sacrificed on the altar erected over the altar of holocausts. 60 Women who had had their children circumcised were put to death, in keeping with the decree, 61 with the babies hung from their necks; their families also and those who had circumcised them were killed. 62 But many in Israel were determined and resolved in their hearts not to eat anything unclean; 63 they preferred to die rather than to be defiled with unclean food or to profane the holy covenant; and they did die. Terrible affliction was upon Israel.

2 In those days Mattathias, son of John, son of Simeon, a priest of the family of Joarib, left Jerusalem and settled in Modein. 2 He had five sons: John, who was called Gaddi, 3 Simon, who was called Thassi, 4 Judas, who was called Maccabeus, 5 Eleazar, who was called Avaran; and Jonathan, who was called Apphus. 6 When he saw the sacrileges that were being committed in Judah and in Jerusalem, 7 he said: "Woe is me! Why was I born to see the ruin of my people and the ruin of the holy city, and to sit idle while it is given into the hands of enemies, and the sanctuary into the hands of strangers?

8 "Her temple has become like a man disgraced,
9   her glorious ornaments have been carried off
        as spoils,
   Her infants have been murdered in her streets,
        her young men by the sword of the enemy.
10 What nation has not taken its share of her realm,
        and laid its hand on her possessions?
11 All her adornment has been taken away.
        From being free, she has become a slave.
12 We see our sanctuary and our beauty
        and our glory laid waste,
   And the Gentiles have defiled them!
13   Why are we still alive?"

14 Then Mattathias and his sons tore their garments, put on sackcloth, and mourned bitterly.

15 The officers of the king in charge of enforcing the apostasy came to the city of Modein to organize the sacrifices. 16 Many of Israel joined them, but Mattathias and his sons gathered in a group apart. 17 Then the officers of the king addressed Mattathias: "You are a leader, an honorable and great man in this city, supported by sons and kinsmen. 18 Come now, be the first to obey the king's command, as all the Gentiles and the men of Judah and those who are left in Jerusalem have done. Then you and your sons shall be numbered among the King's Friends, and shall be enriched with silver and gold and many gifts." 19 But Mattathias answered in a loud voice: "Although all the Gentiles in the king's realm obey him, so that each forsakes the religion of his fathers and consents to the king's orders, 20 yet I and my sons and my kinsmen will keep to the covenant of our fathers. 21 God forbid that we should forsake the law and the commandments. 22 We will not obey the words of the king nor depart from our religion in the slightest degree."

23 As he finished saying these words, a certain Jew came forward in the sight of all to offer sacrifice on the altar in Modein according to the king's order. 24 When Mattathias

NEW JERUSALEM BIBLE

possessing a copy of the covenant or practising the Law, the king's decree sentenced him to death. 58 Month after month they took harsh action against any offenders they discovered in the towns of Israel. 59 On the twenty-fifth day of each month, sacrifice was offered on the altar erected on top of the altar of burnt offering. 60 Women who had had their children circumcised were put to death according to the edict 61 with their babies hung round their necks, and the members of their household and those who had performed the circumcision were executed with them.

62 Yet there were many in Israel who stood firm and found the courage to refuse unclean food. 63 They chose death rather than contamination by such fare or profanation of the holy covenant, and they were executed. 64 It was a truly dreadful retribution that visited Israel.

2 About then, Mattathias son of John, son of Simeon, a priest of the line of Joarib, left Jerusalem and settled in Modein. 2 He had five sons, John known as Gaddi, 3 Simon called Thassi, 4 Judas called Maccabaeus, 5 Eleazar, called Avaran, and Jonathan called Apphus. 6 When he saw the blasphemies being committed in Judah and Jerusalem, 7 he said, 'Alas that I should have been born to witness the ruin of my people and the ruin of the Holy City, and to sit by while she is delivered over to her enemies, and the sanctuary into the hand of foreigners.

8 'Her Temple has become like someone of no
        repute,
9 the vessels that were her glory have been carried
        off as booty,
   her babies have been slaughtered in her streets,
        her young men by the enemy's sword.
10 Is there a nation that has not claimed
   a share of her royal prerogatives,
   that has not taken some of her spoils?
11 All her ornaments have been snatched from her,
   her former freedom has become slavery.
12 See how the Holy Place, our beauty, our glory,
        is now laid waste,
   see how the gentiles have profaned it!
13 What have we left to live for?'

14 Mattathias and his sons tore their garments, put on sackcloth, and observed deep mourning.

15 The king's commissioners who were enforcing the apostasy came to the town of Modein for the sacrifices. 16 Many Israelites gathered round them, but Mattathias and his sons drew apart. 17 The king's commissioners then addressed Mattathias as follows, 'You are a respected leader, a great man in this town; you have sons and brothers to support you. 18 Be the first to step forward and conform to the king's decree, as all the nations have done, and the leaders of Judah and the survivors in Jerusalem; you and your sons shall be reckoned among the Friends of the King, you and your sons will be honoured with gold and silver and many presents.' 19 Raising his voice, Mattathias retorted, 'Even if every nation living in the king's dominions obeys him, each forsaking its ancestral religion to conform to his decrees, 20 I, my sons and my brothers will still follow covenant of our ancestors. 21 May Heaven preserve us from forsaking the Law and its observances. 22 As for the king's orders, we will not follow them: we shall not swerve from our own religion either to right or to left.' 23 As he finished speaking, a Jew came forward in the sight of all to offer sacrifice on the altar in Modein as the royal edict required.

tathias saw it, he burned with zeal and his heart was stirred. He gave vent to righteous anger; he ran and killed him on the altar. 25 At the same time he killed the king's officer who was forcing them to sacrifice, and he tore down the altar. 26 Thus he burned with zeal for the law, just as Phinehas did against Zimri son of Salu.

27 Then Mattathias cried out in the town with a loud voice, saying: "Let every one who is zealous for the law and supports the covenant come out with me!" 28 Then he and his sons fled to the hills and left all that they had in the town.

29 At that time many who were seeking righteousness and justice went down to the wilderness to live there, 30 they, their sons, their wives, and their livestock, because troubles pressed heavily upon them. 31 And it was reported to the king's officers, and to the troops in Jerusalem the city of David, that those who had rejected the king's command had gone down to the hiding places in the wilderness. 32 Many pursued them, and overtook them; they encamped opposite them and prepared for battle against them on the sabbath day. 33 They said to them, "Enough of this! Come out and do what the king commands, and you will live." 34 But they said, "We will not come out, nor will we do what the king commands and so profane the sabbath day." 35 Then the enemy[i] quickly attacked them. 36 But they did not answer them or hurl a stone at them or block up their hiding places, 37 for they said, "Let us all die in our innocence; heaven and earth testify for us that you are killing us unjustly." 38 So they attacked them on the sabbath, and they died, with their wives and children and livestock, to the number of a thousand persons.

39 When Mattathias and his friends learned of it, they mourned for them deeply. 40 And all said to their neighbors: "If we all do as our kindred have done and refuse to fight with the Gentiles for our lives and for our ordinances, they will quickly destroy us from the earth." 41 So they made this decision that day: "Let us fight against anyone who comes to attack us on the sabbath day; let us not all die as our kindred died in their hiding places."

42 Then there united with them a company of Hasideans, mighty warriors of Israel, all who offered themselves willingly for the law. 43 And all who became fugitives to escape their troubles joined them and reinforced them. 44 They organized an army, and struck down sinners in their anger and renegades in their wrath; the survivors fled to the Gentiles for safety. 45 And Mattathias and his friends went around and tore down the altars; 46 they forcibly circumcised all the uncircumcised boys that they found within the borders of Israel. 47 They hunted down the arrogant, and the work prospered in their hands. 48 They rescued the law out of the hands of the Gentiles and kings, and they never let the sinner gain the upper hand.

49 Now the days drew near for Mattathias to die, and he said to his sons: "Arrogance and scorn have now become strong; it is a time of ruin and furious anger. 50 Now, my children, show zeal for the law, and give your lives for the covenant of our ancestors.

51 "Remember the deeds of the ancestors, which they did in their generations; and you will receive great honor and an everlasting name. 52 Was not Abraham found faithful when tested, and it was reckoned to him as righteousness?

of Mattathias, and, shaking with passion and in a fury of righteous anger, he rushed forward and cut him down on the very altar. 25 At the same time he killed the officer sent by the king to enforce sacrifice, and demolished the pagan altar. 26 So Mattathias showed his fervent zeal for the law, as Phinehas had done when he killed Zimri son of Salu. 27 He shouted for the whole town to hear, 'Follow me, all who are zealous for the law and stand by the covenant!' 28 Then he and his sons took to the hills, leaving behind in the town all they possessed.

29 At that time many who sought to maintain their religion and law went down to live in the desert, 30 taking their children and their wives and their livestock with them, for their miseries were more than they could bear. 31 Word soon reached the king's officers and the forces stationed in Jerusalem, the city of David, that Israelites who had defied the king's order had gone down into hiding-places in the desert. 32 A large body of soldiers, setting off in pursuit, came upon them, and drew up in battle order ready to attack on the sabbath. 33 'There is still time,' they shouted; 'come out, do as the king commands, and your lives will be spared.' 34 'We will not come out,' was the reply; 'we will not obey the king's command to profane the sabbath.' 35 Without more ado the attack was launched, 36 but the Israelites did nothing in reply; they neither hurled stones, nor barricaded their caves. 37 'Let us all meet death with a clear conscience,' they said; 'we call heaven and earth to witness it is contrary to all justice that you are making away with us.' 38 So on the sabbath they were attacked and massacred, men, women, and children, up to a thousand in all, along with their livestock.

39 When Mattathias and his friends learnt of it, their grief was very great, 40 and they said to one another, 'If we all do as our brothers have done and refuse to fight the Gentiles in defence of our lives as well as our laws and customs, then they will soon wipe us off the face of the earth.' 41 That day the decision was taken that if anyone came to fight against them on the sabbath, they would fight back, rather than all perish as their brothers in the caves had done.

42 They were joined at that time by a group of Hasidaeans, stalwarts of Israel, every one of them a volunteer in the cause of the law; 43 and all who were refugees from the troubles came to swell their numbers and add to their strength. 44 Now that they had an organized force, they turned the fierceness of their wrath on the guilty men and renegades; those who escaped their onslaught took refuge with the Gentiles.

45 Mattathias and his friends swept through the country, demolishing the pagan altars 46 and forcibly circumcising all the uncircumcised boys found within the frontiers of Israel. 47 They hunted down their arrogant enemies, and the cause prospered in their hands. 48 Thus they came to the defence of the law against the Gentiles and their kings and withheld power from the wicked.

49 As the time drew near for Mattathias to die, he said to his sons: 'Arrogance now stands secure and gives judgement against us; these are days of calamity and raging fury. 50 Now, my sons, be zealous for the law, and give your lives for the covenant made with your forefathers. 51 If you keep in mind the deeds they did in their generations, great glory and everlasting fame will be yours. 52 Did not Abraham prove faithful under trial, and so win credit as a righteous

NEW AMERICAN BIBLE

saw him, he was filled with zeal; his heart was moved and his just fury was aroused; he sprang forward and killed him upon the altar. 25 At the same time, he also killed the messenger of the king who was forcing them to sacrifice, and he tore down the altar. 26 Thus he showed his zeal for the law, just as Phinehas did with Zimri, son of Salu. 27 Then Mattathias went through the city shouting, "Let everyone who is zealous for the law and who stands by the covenant follow after me!" 28 Thereupon he fled to the mountains with his sons, leaving behind in the city all their possessions. 29 Many who sought to live according to righteousness and religious custom went out into the desert to settle there, 30 they and their sons, their wives and their cattle, because misfortunes pressed so hard on them.

31 It was reported to the officers and soldiers of the king who were in the City of David, in Jerusalem, that certain men who had flouted the king's order had gone out to the hiding places in the desert. 32 Many hurried out after them, and having caught up with them, camped opposite and prepared to attack them on the sabbath. 33 "Enough of this!" the pursuers said to them. "Come out and obey the king's command, and your lives will be spared." 34 But they replied, "We will not come out, nor will we obey the king's command to profane the sabbath." 35 Then the enemy attacked them at once; 36 but they did not retaliate; they neither threw stones, nor blocked up their own hiding places. 37 They said, "Let us all die without reproach; heaven and earth are our witnesses that you destroy us unjustly." 38 So the officers and soldiers attacked them on the sabbath, and they died with their wives, their children and their cattle, to the number of a thousand persons.

39 When Mattathias and his friends heard of it, they mourned deeply for them. 40 "If we all do as our kinsmen have done," they said to one another, "and do not fight against the Gentiles for our lives and our traditions, they will soon destroy us from the earth." 41 On that day they came to this decision: "Let us fight against anyone who attacks us on the sabbath, so that we may not all die as our kinsmen died in the hiding places."

42 Then they were joined by a group of Hasideans, valiant Israelites, all of them devout followers of the law. 43 And all those who were fleeing from the disaster joined them and supported them. 44 They gathered an army and struck down sinners in their anger and lawbreakers in their wrath, and the survivors fled to the Gentiles for safety. 45 Mattathias and his friends went about and tore down the pagan altars; 46 they also forcibly circumcised any uncircumcised boys whom they found in the territory of Israel. 47 They put to flight the arrogant, and the work prospered in their hands. 48 They saved the law from the hands of the Gentiles and of the kings and did not let the sinner triumph.

49 When the time came for Mattathias to die, he said to his sons: "Arrogance and scorn have now grown strong; it is a time of disaster and violent anger. 50 Therefore, my sons, be zealous for the law and give your lives for the covenant of our fathers.

51 "Remember the deeds that our fathers did in
their times,
and you shall win great glory and an
everlasting name.
52 Was not Abraham found faithful in trial,
and it was reputed to him as uprightness?

NEW JERUSALEM BIBLE

24 When Mattathias saw this, he was fired with zeal; stirred to the depth of his being, he gave vent to his legitimate anger, threw himself on the man and slaughtered him on the altar. 25 At the same time he killed the king's commissioner who was there to enforce the sacrifice, and tore down the altar. 26 In his zeal for the Law he acted as Phinehas had against Zimri son of Salu.e 27 Then Mattathias went through the town, shouting at the top of his voice, 'Let everyone who has any zeal for the Law and takes his stand on the covenant come out and follow me.' 28 Then he fled with his sons into the hills, leaving all their possessions behind in the town.

29 Many people who were concerned for virtue and justice went down to the desert and stayed there, 30 taking with them their sons, their wives and their cattle, so oppressive had their sufferings become. 31 Word was brought to the royal officials and forces stationed in Jerusalem, in the City of David, that those who had repudiated the king's edict had gone down to the hiding places in the desert. 32 A strong detachment went after them, and when it came up with them ranged itself against them in battle formation, preparing to attack them on the Sabbath day, 33 and said, 'Enough of this! Come out and do as the king orders and you will be spared.' 34 The others, however, replied, 'We refuse to come out, and we will not obey the king's orders and profane the Sabbath day.' 35 The royal forces at once went into action, 36 but the others offered no opposition; not a stone was thrown, there was no barricading of the hiding places. 37 They only said, 'Let us all die innocent; let heaven and earth bear witness that you are massacring us with no pretence of justice.' 38 The attack was pressed home on the Sabbath itself, and they were slaughtered, with their wives and children and cattle, to the number of one thousand persons.

39 When the news reached Mattathias and his friends, they mourned them bitterly 40 and said to one another, 'If we all do as our brothers have done, and refuse to fight the gentiles for our lives and institutions, they will only destroy us the sooner from the earth.' 41 So then and there they came to this decision, 'If anyone attacks us on the Sabbath day, whoever he may be, we shall resist him; we must not all be killed, as our brothers were in the hiding places.'

42 Soon they were joined by the Hasidaean party,f stout fighting men of Israel, each one a volunteer on the side of the Law. 43 All the refugees from the persecution rallied to them, giving them added support. 44 They organised themselves into an armed force, striking down the sinners in their anger, and the renegades in their fury, and those who escaped them fled to the gentiles for safety. 45 Mattathias and his friends made a tour, overthrowing the altars 46 and forcibly circumcising all the boys they found uncircumcised in the territories of Israel. 47 They hunted down the upstarts and managed their campaign to good effect. 48 They wrested the Law out of the control of the gentiles and the kings and reduced the sinners to impotence.

49 As the days of Mattathias were drawing to a close, he said to his sons, 'Arrogance and outrage are now in the ascendant; it is a period of turmoil and bitter hatred. 50 This is the time, my children, for you to have a burning zeal for the Law and to give your lives for the covenant of our ancestors.

51 Remember the deeds performed by our ancestors,
each in his generation,
and you will win great honour and everlasting
renown.
52 Was not Abraham tested and found faithful,
was that not considered as justifying him?

e 2 Nb 25:6–15.   f 2 lit. 'the devout'. They soon split into two groups, the Pharisees and the Essenes.

NEW REVISED STANDARD VERSION	REVISED ENGLISH BIBLE

53 Joseph in the time of his distress kept the commandment, and became lord of Egypt. 54 Phinehas our ancestor, because he was deeply zealous, received the covenant of everlasting priesthood. 55 Joshua, because he fulfilled the command, became a judge in Israel. 56 Caleb, because he testified in the assembly, received an inheritance in the land. 57 David, because he was merciful, inherited the throne of the kingdom forever. 58 Elijah, because of great zeal for the law, was taken up into heaven. 59 Hananiah, Azariah, and Mishael believed and were saved from the flame. 60 Daniel, because of his innocence, was delivered from the mouth of the lions.

61 "And so observe, from generation to generation, that none of those who put their trust in him will lack strength. 62 Do not fear the words of sinners, for their splendor will turn into dung and worms. 63 Today they will be exalted, but tomorrow they will not be found, because they will have returned to the dust, and their plans will have perished. 64 My children, be courageous and grow strong in the law, for by it you will gain honor.

65 "Here is your brother Simeon who, I know, is wise in counsel; always listen to him; he shall be your father. 66 Judas Maccabeus has been a mighty warrior from his youth; he shall command the army for you and fight the battle against the peoples.j 67 You shall rally around you all who observe the law, and avenge the wrong done to your people. 68 Pay back the Gentiles in full, and obey the commands of the law."

69 Then he blessed them, and was gathered to his ancestors. 70 He died in the one hundred forty-sixth yeark and was buried in the tomb of his ancestors at Modein. And all Israel mourned for him with great lamentation.

man? 53 Joseph, hard pressed though he was, kept God's commandment, and he became overlord of Egypt. 54 Phinehas, our forefather, never flagged in his zeal, and his was the covenant of an everlasting priesthood. 55 Joshua kept the law, and he became a judge in Israel. 56 Caleb bore witness before the congregation, and his reward was a share in the land. 57 David was a man of loyalty, and he was granted the throne of an everlasting kingdom. 58 Elijah never flagged in his zeal for the law, and he was taken up to heaven. 59 Hananiah, Azariah, and Mishael had faith, and they were saved from the flames. 60 Daniel was a man of integrity, and he was rescued from the lions' jaws. 61 So bear in mind how in the history of the generations no one who trusts in Heaven ever lacks strength. 62 Do not fear a wicked man's threats; his success will turn to filth and worms. 63 Today he may be high in honour, but tomorrow not a trace of him will be found; he will have returned to the dust, and his schemes will have come to naught. 64 But you, my sons, draw your courage and strength from the law, for through it glory will be yours.

65 'Now here is Symeon your brother, whom I know to be wise in counsel; listen always to him, for he will be a father to you. 66 Judas Maccabaeus has been strong and brave from boyhood; he is to be your commander in the field, and wage war against the peoples. 67 Assemble to your side all who observe the law, and avenge your people's wrongs. 68 Repay the Gentiles in their own coin, and give heed to what the law decrees.'

69 Mattathias blessed them, and was gathered to his fathers. 70 He died in the year 146, and was buried by his sons in the family tomb at Modin; and there was great lamentation for him throughout Israel.

3 Then his son Judas, who was called Maccabeus, took command in his place. 2 All his brothers and all who had joined his father helped him; they gladly fought for Israel.

3 He extended the glory of his people.
  Like a giant he put on his breastplate;
he bound on his armor of war and waged battles,
  protecting the camp by his sword.
4 He was like a lion in his deeds,
  like a lion's cub roaring for prey.
5 He searched out and pursued those who broke the law;
  he burned those who troubled his people.
6 Lawbreakers shrank back for fear of him;
  all the evildoers were confounded;
  and deliverance prospered by his hand.
7 He embittered many kings,
  but he made Jacob glad by his deeds,
  and his memory is blessed forever.
8 He went through the cities of Judah;
  he destroyed the ungodly out of the land;l
  thus he turned away wrath from Israel.
9 He was renowned to the ends of the earth;
  he gathered in those who were perishing.

3 JUDAS Maccabaeus came forward to take his father's place. 2 He had the support of all his brothers and his father's followers, and they carried on Israel's campaign with zest.

3 He enhanced his people's glory.
  Like a giant he put on his breastplate
  and girt himself with weapons of war.
  He waged many a campaign
  from a camp well guarded with the sword.
4 He was like a lion in his exploits,
  like a young lion roaring for prey.
5 He tracked down and pursued the renegades;
  he consumed with fire the troublers of his people.
6 The renegades cowered in fear of him,
  and all such wrongdoers were utterly confounded,
  while the cause of freedom prospered in his hands.
7 He roused many kings to anger,
  but to Jacob his deeds brought joy.
  He is remembered for ever in blessing.
8 He passed through the towns of Judaea,
  wiping out the apostates there;
  he turned wrath away from Israel.
9 His renown spread to the ends of the earth,
  and he rallied a people near to destruction.

j Or of the people   k 166 B.C.   l Gk it   2:70 146: that is 166 B.C.E.

53 Joseph, when in distress, kept the commandment,
    and he became master of Egypt.
54 Phinehas our father, for his burning zeal,
    received the covenant of an
      everlasting priesthood.
55 Joshua, for executing his commission,
    became a judge in Israel.
56 Caleb, for bearing witness before the assembly,
    received an inheritance in the land.
57 David, for his piety,
    received as a heritage a throne of
      everlasting royalty.
58 Elijah, for his burning zeal for the law,
    was taken up to heaven.
59 Hananiah, Azariah and Mishael, for their faith,
    were saved from the fire.
60 Daniel, for his innocence,
    was delivered from the jaws of lions.
61 And so, consider this from generation
    to generation,
    that none who hope in him shall fail in strength.
62 Do not fear the words of a sinful man,
    for his glory ends in corruption and worms.
63 Today he is exalted, and tomorrow he is not to
    be found,
    because he has returned to his dust,
    and his schemes have perished.
64 Children! be courageous and strong in keeping
    the law,
    for by it you shall be glorified.

65 "Here is your brother Simeon who I know is a wise man;
listen to him always, and he will be a father to you. 66 And
Judas Maccabeus, a warrior from his youth, shall be the
leader of your army and direct the war against the nations.
67 You shall also gather about you all who observe the law,
and you shall avenge the wrongs of your people. 68 Pay back
the Gentiles what they deserve, and observe the precepts of
the law."
69 Then he blessed them, and he was united with his
fathers. 70 He died in the year one hundred and forty-six,
and was buried in the tombs of his fathers in Modein, and
all Israel mourned him greatly.

3 Then his son Judas, who was called Maccabeus, took
his place. 2 All his brothers and all who had joined his
father supported him, and they carried on Israel's war joyfully.

3 He spread abroad the glory of his people,
    and put on his breastplate like a giant.
He armed himself with weapons of war;
    he planned battles and protected the camp with
      his sword.
4 In his actions he was like a lion,
    like a young lion roaring for prey.
5 He pursued the wicked, hunting them out,
    and those who troubled his people he destroyed
      by fire.
6 The lawbreakers were cowed by fear of him,
    and all evildoers were dismayed.
By his hand redemption was happily achieved,
7   and he afflicted many kings;
He made Jacob glad by his deeds,
    and his memory is blessed forever.
8 He went about the cities of Judah
    destroying the impious there.
He turned away wrath from Israel
9   and was renowned to the ends of the earth;
he gathered together those who were perishing.

53 Joseph in the time of his distress maintained the
    Law,
    and so became lord of Egypt.
54 Phinehas, our father, in return for his burning zeal,
    received the covenant of everlasting priesthood.
55 Joshua, for carrying out his task,
    became judge of Israel.
56 Caleb, for his testimony before the assembled
    people,
    received an inheritance in the land.
57 David for his generous heart
    inherited the throne of an everlasting kingdom.
58 Elijah for his consuming fervour for the Law
    was caught up to heaven itself.
59 Hananiah, Azariah and Mishael, for their fidelity,
    were saved from the flame.
60 Daniel for his singleness of heart
    was rescued from the lion's jaws.
61 Know then that, generation after generation,
    no one who hopes in him will be overcome.
62 Do not fear the threats of the sinner,
    all his brave show must come to the dunghill and
      the worms.
63 Exalted today, tomorrow he is nowhere to be
    found,
    for he has returned to the dust he came from
    and his scheming is brought to nothing.
64 My children, be resolute and courageous for the
    Law,
    for it will bring you glory.

65 'Here is your brother Simeon, I know he is a man of
sound judgement. Listen to him all your lives; let him take
your father's place. 66 Judas Maccabaeus, strong and brave
from his youth, let him be your general and conduct the war
against the gentiles. 67 The rest of you are to enrol in your
ranks all those who keep the Law, and to assure the vengeance of your people. 68 Pay back the gentiles to the full,
and hold fast to the ordinance of the Law.' 69 Then he
blessed them and was joined to his ancestors. 70 He died in
the year 146 and was buried in his ancestral tomb at Modein, and all Israel mourned him deeply.

3 His son, Judas, known as Maccabaeus, then took his
place. 2 All his brothers, and all who had attached
themselves to his father, supported him, and they fought for
Israel with a will.

3 He extended the fame of his people.
Like a giant, he put on the breastplate
    and buckled on his war harness;
he engaged in battle after battle,
    protecting the ranks with his sword.
4 He was like a lion in his exploits,
    like a young lion roaring over its prey.
5 He pursued and tracked down the renegades,
    he consigned those who troubled his people to the
      flames.
6 The renegades quailed with the terror he inspired,
    all evil-doers were utterly confounded,
    and deliverance went forward under his leadership.
7 He brought bitterness to many a king
    and rejoicing to Jacob by his deeds,
    his memory is blessed for ever and ever.
8 He went through the towns of Judah
    eliminating the irreligious from them,
    and diverted the Retribution from Israel.
9 His name resounded to the ends of the earth,
    he rallied those who were on the point of
      perishing.

10 Apollonius now gathered together Gentiles and a large force from Samaria to fight against Israel. 11 When Judas learned of it, he went out to meet him, and he defeated and killed him. Many were wounded and fell, and the rest fled. 12 Then they seized their spoils; and Judas took the sword of Apollonius, and used it in battle the rest of his life.

13 When Seron, the commander of the Syrian army, heard that Judas had gathered a large company, including a body of faithful soldiers who stayed with him and went out to battle, 14 he said, "I will make a name for myself and win honor in the kingdom. I will make war on Judas and his companions, who scorn the king's command." 15 Once again a strong army of godless men went up with him to help him, to take vengeance on the Israelites.

16 When he approached the ascent of Beth-horon, Judas went out to meet him with a small company. 17 But when they saw the army coming to meet them, they said to Judas, "How can we, few as we are, fight against so great and so strong a multitude? And we are faint, for we have eaten nothing today." 18 Judas replied, "It is easy for many to be hemmed in by few, for in the sight of Heaven there is no difference between saving by many or by few. 19 It is not on the size of the army that victory in battle depends, but strength comes from Heaven. 20 They come against us in great insolence and lawlessness to destroy us and our wives and our children, and to despoil us; 21 but we fight for our lives and our laws. 22 He himself will crush them before us; as for you, do not be afraid of them."

23 When he finished speaking, he rushed suddenly against Seron and his army, and they were crushed before him. 24 They pursued them[m] down the descent of Beth-horon to the plain; eight hundred of them fell, and the rest fled into the land of the Philistines. 25 Then Judas and his brothers began to be feared, and terror fell on the Gentiles all around them. 26 His fame reached the king, and the Gentiles talked of the battles of Judas.

27 When King Antiochus heard these reports, he was greatly angered; and he sent and gathered all the forces of his kingdom, a very strong army. 28 He opened his coffers and gave a year's pay to his forces, and ordered them to be ready for any need. 29 Then he saw that the money in the treasury was exhausted, and that the revenues from the country were small because of the dissension and disaster that he had caused in the land by abolishing the laws that had existed from the earliest days. 30 He feared that he might not have such funds as he had before for his expenses and for the gifts that he used to give more lavishly than preceding kings. 31 He was greatly perplexed in mind; then he determined to go to Persia and collect the revenues from those regions and raise a large fund.

32 He left Lysias, a distinguished man of royal lineage, in charge of the king's affairs from the river Euphrates to the borders of Egypt. 33 Lysias was also to take care of his son Antiochus until he returned. 34 And he turned over to Lysias[n] half of his forces and the elephants, and gave him orders about all that he wanted done. As for the residents of Judea and Jerusalem, 35 Lysias was to send a force against them to wipe out and destroy the strength of Israel and the remnant of Jerusalem; he was to banish the memory of them from the place, 36 settle aliens in all their territory, and distribute their land by lot. 37 Then the king took the remaining half of his forces and left Antioch his capital in the one hundred and forty-seventh year.[o] He crossed the Euphrates river and went through the upper provinces.

10 Apollonius raised an army, consisting of Gentiles and a large contingent from Samaria, to wage war against Israel. 11 Informed of this, Judas marched out and in the encounter defeated and killed him. Many of the enemy fell; the survivors took flight. 12 From the arms which were captured, Judas obtained the sword of Apollonius, and for the rest of his life he used it in his campaigns.

13 When Seron, the commander of the army in Syria, heard that Judas had mustered a considerable force, all his loyal followers of military age, 14 he said, 'I shall make a name for myself and win renown throughout the empire by taking up arms against Judas and his followers, who set at naught the king's command.' 15 Seron was reinforced by a strong contingent of apostate Jews, who marched up with him to wreak vengeance on Israel. 16 As he reached the pass of Beth-horon, Judas advanced to meet him with a handful of men, 17 who at the sight of the host coming against them said to Judas, 'How can so few of us fight against so many? Besides, we have had nothing to eat all day and are faint with hunger.'

18 Judas replied: 'Many can easily be overpowered by a few; Heaven can save just as well by few as by many. 19 Victory does not depend on numbers; strength is from Heaven alone. 20 Our enemies, inflated with insolence and lawlessness, are coming against us; they mean to kill us and our wives and children for the sake of the plunder they will get. 21 But we are fighting for our lives and for our laws and customs, 22 and Heaven will crush them before our eyes; you have no need to be afraid of them.'

23 As soon as he finished speaking, he launched a surprise attack, which overwhelmed Seron and his army. 24 They were pursued down the pass of Beth-horon as far as the plain; some eight hundred of them fell; the rest fled to Philistia.

25 Judas and his brothers came to be regarded with fear, and alarm spread among the Gentiles round about. 26 His fame reached the ears of the king, and the story of his battles was told in every nation. 27 Incensed by those reports, King Antiochus issued orders for the mobilization of all the forces of his empire, an immensely powerful army. 28 He opened his treasury and gave a year's pay to his troops, with a command to be prepared to serve as required. 29 But he found that his resources were running low; his income from tribute had dwindled as a result of the disaffection and violence he had brought on his empire by abolishing traditional laws and customs. 30 He was worried that, as had happened once or twice before, he might be short of money, both for his normal expenses and for the gifts he had been accustomed to distribute with an even more lavish hand than any of his predecessors on the throne.

31 Greatly disconcerted, he resolved to go to Persia and collect the tribute due from the provinces, and so raise a large sum of ready money. 32 He left Lysias, a distinguished member of the royal family, as viceroy of the territories between the Euphrates and the Egyptian frontier, 33 and he also appointed him guardian of his son Antiochus until his return. 34 He transferred to him half the armed forces, together with the elephants, and gave him detailed instructions about what he wanted done, especially in regard to the inhabitants of Judaea and Jerusalem. 35 Lysias was to dispatch a force against them so as to crush and destroy the power of Israel and those left in Jerusalem, and to blot out all memory of them from the place. 36 Foreigners were to be settled throughout the territory and the land was to be parcelled out among them. 37 The remaining half of his forces the king retained and, setting out with them from Antioch, his capital, in the year 147, he crossed the Euphrates and marched through the upper provinces.

---

m Other ancient authorities read *him*   n Gk *him*   o 165 B.C.   3:37 147: *that is* 165 B.C.E.

³⁸Lysias chose Ptolemy, son of Dorymenes, and Nicanor and Gorgias, capable men among the King's Friends, ³⁹and with them he sent forty thousand men and seven thousand cavalry to invade the land of Judah and ravage it according to the king's orders. ⁴⁰Setting out with all their forces, they came and pitched their camp near Emmaus in the plain. ⁴¹When the merchants of the country heard of their fame, they came to the camp, bringing fetters and a large sum of silver and gold, to buy the Israelites as slaves. A force from Idumea and from Philistia joined with them.

⁴²Judas and his brothers saw that the situation had become critical now that armies were encamped within their territory; they knew of the orders which the king had given to destroy and utterly wipe out the people. ⁴³So they said to one another, "Let us restore our people from their ruined estate, and fight for our people and our sanctuary!"

⁴⁴The assembly gathered together to prepare for battle and to pray and implore mercy and compassion.

⁴⁵Jerusalem was uninhabited, like a desert;
    not one of her children entered or came out.
The sanctuary was trampled on,
    and foreigners were in the citadel;
    it was a habitation of Gentiles.
Joy had disappeared from Jacob,
    and the flute and the harp were silent.

⁴⁶Thus they assembled and went to Mizpah near Jerusalem, because there was formerly at Mizpah a place of prayer for Israel. ⁴⁷That day they fasted and wore sackcloth; they sprinkled ashes on their heads and tore their clothes. ⁴⁸They unrolled the scroll of the law, to learn about the things for which the Gentiles consulted the images of their idols. ⁴⁹They brought with them the priestly vestments, the first fruits, and the tithes; and they brought forward the nazirites who had completed the time of their vows. ⁵⁰And they cried aloud to Heaven: "What shall we do with these men, and where shall we take them? ⁵¹For your sanctuary has been trampled on and profaned, and your priests are in mourning and humiliation. ⁵²Now the Gentiles are gathered together against us to destroy us. You know what they plot against us. ⁵³How shall we be able to resist them unless you help us?" ⁵⁴Then they blew the trumpets and cried out loudly.

⁵⁵After this Judas appointed officers among the people, over thousands, over hundreds, over fifties, and over tens. ⁵⁶He proclaimed that those who were building houses, or were just married, or were planting vineyards, and those who were afraid, could each return to his home, according to the law. ⁵⁷Then the army moved off, and they camped to the south of Emmaus. ⁵⁸Judas said: "Arm yourselves and be brave; in the morning be ready to fight these Gentiles who have assembled against us to destroy us and our sanctuary. ⁵⁹It is better for us to die in battle than to witness the ruin of our nation and our sanctuary. Whatever Heaven wills, he will do."

4 Now Gorgias took five thousand infantry and a thousand picked cavalry, and this detachment set out at night ²in order to attack the camp of the Jews and take them by surprise. Some men from the citadel were their guides. ³Judas heard of it, and himself set out with his soldiers to attack the king's army at Emmaus, ⁴while the latter's forces were still scattered away from the camp. ⁵During the night

³⁸Lysias chose Ptolemy son of Dorymenes, with Nicanor and Gorgias, influential men from among the Friends of the King, ³⁹and, under their command, despatched forty thousand foot and seven thousand horse to invade the land of Judah and devastate it, as the king had ordered. ⁴⁰The entire force set out and reached the neighbourhood of Emmaus in the lowlands, where they pitched camp. ⁴¹The local merchants, hearing the news of this, arrived at the camp, bringing with them a large amount of gold and silver, and fetters as well, proposing to buy the Israelites as slaves; they were accompanied by a company from Idumaea and the Philistine country. ⁴²Judas and his brothers saw that the situation was going from bad to worse and that armies were camping in their territory; they were also well aware that the king had ordered the people's total destruction. ⁴³So they said to each other, 'Let us restore the ruins of our people and fight for our people and our sanctuary.' ⁴⁴The Assembly was summoned, to prepare for war, to offer prayer and to implore compassion and mercy.

⁴⁵Jerusalem was as empty as a desert,
    none of her children to go in and out.
The sanctuary was trodden underfoot,
    men of an alien race held the Citadel,
    which had become a lodging for gentiles.
There was no more rejoicing for Jacob,
    the flute and lyre were mute.

⁴⁶After mustering, they made their way to Mizpah, opposite Jerusalem, since Mizpah was traditionally a place of prayer for Israel. ⁴⁷That day they fasted and put on sackcloth, covering their heads with ashes and tearing their garments. ⁴⁸For the guidance that the gentiles would have sought from the images of their false gods, they opened the Book of the Law. ⁴⁹They also brought out the priestly vestments, with first-fruits and tithes, and marshalled the Nazirites who had completed the period of their vow. ⁵⁰Then, raising their voices to Heaven, they cried, 'What shall we do with these people, and where are we to take them? ⁵¹Your holy place has been trampled underfoot and defiled, your priests mourn in their humiliation, ⁵²and now the gentiles are in alliance to destroy us: you know what they have in mind for us. ⁵³How can we stand up and face them if you do not come to our aid?' ⁵⁴Then they sounded the trumpets and raised a great shout.

⁵⁵Next, Judas appointed leaders for the people, to command a thousand, a hundred, fifty or ten men. ⁵⁶Those who were in the middle of building a house, or were about to be married, or were planting a vineyard, or were afraid, he told to go home again, as the Law allowed. ⁵⁷The column then marched off and took up a position south of Emmaus. ⁵⁸'Stand to your arms,' Judas told them, 'acquit yourselves bravely, in the morning be ready to fight these gentiles massed against us to destroy us and our sanctuary. ⁵⁹Better for us to die in battle than to watch the ruin of our nation and our Holy Place. ⁶⁰Whatever be the will of Heaven, he will perform it.'

4 Gorgias took with him five thousand foot and a thousand picked cavalry, and the force moved off by night ²with the object of attacking the Jewish position and dealing them an unexpected blow; the men from the Citadel were there to guide him. ³Judas got wind of it and himself moved off with his fighters to strike at the royal army at Emmaus, ⁴while its fighting troops were still dispersed outside the camp. ⁵Hence, when Gorgias reached Judas' camp, he

NEW REVISED STANDARD VERSION	REVISED ENGLISH BIBLE

by night, he found no one there, so he looked for them in the hills, because he said, "These men are running away from us."

6 At daybreak Judas appeared in the plain with three thousand men, but they did not have armor and swords such as they desired. 7 And they saw the camp of the Gentiles, strong and fortified, with cavalry all around it; and these men were trained in war. 8 But Judas said to those who were with him, "Do not fear their numbers or be afraid when they charge. 9 Remember how our ancestors were saved at the Red Sea, when Pharaoh with his forces pursued them. 10 And now, let us cry to Heaven, to see whether he will favor us and remember his covenant with our ancestors and crush this army before us today. 11 Then all the Gentiles will know that there is one who redeems and saves Israel."

12 When the foreigners looked up and saw them coming against them, 13 they went out from their camp to battle. Then the men with Judas blew their trumpets 14 and engaged in battle. The Gentiles were crushed, and fled into the plain, 15 and all those in the rear fell by the sword. They pursued them to Gazara, and to the plains of Idumea, and to Azotus and Jamnia; and three thousand of them fell. 16 Then Judas and his force turned back from pursuing them, 17 and he said to the people, "Do not be greedy for plunder, for there is a battle before us; 18 Gorgias and his force are near us in the hills. But stand now against our enemies and fight them, and afterward seize the plunder boldly."

19 Just as Judas was finishing this speech, a detachment appeared, coming out of the hills. 20 They saw that their army[r] had been put to flight, and that the Jews[r] were burning the camp, for the smoke that was seen showed what had happened. 21 When they perceived this, they were greatly frightened, and when they also saw the army of Judas drawn up in the plain for battle, 22 they all fled into the land of the Philistines. 23 Then Judas returned to plunder the camp, and they seized a great amount of gold and silver, and cloth dyed blue and sea purple, and great riches. 24 On their return they sang hymns and praises to Heaven — "For he is good, for his mercy endures forever." 25 Thus Israel had a great deliverance that day.

26 Those of the foreigners who escaped went and reported to Lysias all that had happened. 27 When he heard it, he was perplexed and discouraged, for things had not happened to Israel as he had intended, nor had they turned out as the king had ordered. 28 But the next year he mustered sixty thousand picked infantry and five thousand cavalry to subdue them. 29 They came into Idumea and encamped at Beth-zur, and Judas met them with ten thousand men. 30 When he saw that their army was strong, he prayed, saying, "Blessed are you, O Savior of Israel, who crushed the attack of the mighty warrior by the hand of your servant David, and gave the camp of the Philistines into the hands of Jonathan son of Saul, and of the man who carried his armor. 31 Hem[ ] in this army by the hand of your people Israel, and let them be ashamed of their troops and their cavalry. 32 Fill them with cowardice; melt the boldness of their strength; let them tremble in their destruction. 33 Strike them down with the sword of those who love you, and let all who know your name praise you with hymns."

34 Then both sides attacked, and there fell of the army of Lysias five thousand men; they fell in action.[s] 35 When Lysias saw the rout of his troops and observed the boldness that inspired those of Judas, and how ready they were either to live or to die nobly, he withdrew to Antioch and enlisted mercenaries in order to invade Judea again with an even larger army.

ing the night, but, finding no one there, began to search the hills for them. 'These Jews', he said, 'are running away from us.'

6 Daybreak saw Judas in the plain with three thousand men, though they had not all the armour or swords they needed. 7 They found the gentile camp to be strongly fortified with breastworks, while mounted guards, seasoned troops, patrolled round it.

8 Judas said to his men: 'Do not be afraid of their numbers or panic at their onslaught. 9 Remember how our forefathers were saved at the Red Sea, when pursued by Pharaoh and his army. 10 Now let us call on Heaven to favour our cause and, remembering the covenant made with our forefathers, to crush this army which today opposes us. 11 Then all the Gentiles will know there is One who liberates and saves Israel.'

12 When the foreigners saw them advancing to the attack, 13 they moved out from their camp to give battle. Sounding their trumpets, Judas and his men 14 closed with them, and the Gentiles broke and fled into the plain; 15 all who fell behind were put to the sword. The pursuit was pressed as far as Gazara and the lowlands of Idumaea, to Azotus and Jamnia; some three thousand of the enemy were killed.

16 Judas and his force then broke off the pursuit and withdrew. 17 He said to the people: 'Curb your desire for spoil; there is more fighting ahead of us; 18 Gorgias and his force are in the hills near by. Stand firm now against our enemies and fight; after that, plunder as much as you please.'

19 Before Judas had finished speaking, an enemy patrol appeared, reconnoitring from the hills. 20 They saw that their army had been routed and their camp was being set on fire, for the smoke that met their gaze showed what had happened. 21 They were panic-stricken as they took in the scene, and when, further, they saw the army of Judas in the plain, ready for action, 22 they fled one and all to Philistia.

23 Judas turned back to plunder the camp, and large quantities of gold and silver, violet and purple stuffs, and great riches were seized. 24 At their homecoming there were songs of thanksgiving and praise to Heaven, 'for it is right, because his mercy endures for ever'. 25 That day saw a great deliverance for Israel.

26 Those of the Gentiles who escaped with their lives went to Lysias and reported all that had happened. 27 He was stunned at the news, bitterly disappointed that matters with Israel had not gone as he intended; they had turned out very differently from the king's instructions to him.

28 The following year Lysias mustered sixty thousand picked infantry and five thousand cavalry to bring the war with the Jews to an end. 29 Marching into Idumaea, they encamped at Bethsura, where Judas opposed them with ten thousand men. 30 When he saw the strength of the enemy's army, he prayed: 'All praise to you, Saviour of Israel, who by the hand of your servant David broke the giant's onslaught and who delivered the Philistine army into the hands of Jonathan, Saul's son, and of his armour-bearer. 31 Now let this army be hemmed in by the power of your people Israel, and let the enemy's pride in their troops and mounted men be humbled; 32 fill them with cowardice, make their insolent strength melt away, let them reel under a crushing defeat; 33 may they fall by the sword of those who love you. And let all who know your name praise you with songs of thanksgiving.'

34 Battle was joined, and in the hand-to-hand fighting Lysias lost about five thousand men. 35 When he saw his own army routed and Judas's army in fighting spirit, ready to live or to die nobly, he withdrew to Antioch, where he recruited a force of mercenaries, intending to return to Judaea with a much larger army.

[r] Gk they   [s] Or and some fell on the opposite side

4:35 intending . . . army: prob. mng; Gk obscure.

NEW AMERICAN BIBLE

NEW JERUSALEM BIBLE

Gorgias came into the camp of Judas, and found no one there; so he began to hunt for them in the mountains, saying, "They are fleeing from us."

6 But at daybreak Judas appeared in the plain with three thousand men, who lacked such armor and swords as they would have wished. 7 They saw the army of the Gentiles, strong and breastplated, flanked with cavalry, and made up of expert soldiers. 8 Judas said to the men with him: "Do not be afraid of their numbers or dread their attack. 9 Remember how our fathers were saved in the Red Sea, when Pharaoh pursued them with an army. 10 So now let us cry to Heaven in the hope that he will favor us, remember his covenant with our fathers, and destroy this army before us today. 11 All the Gentiles shall know that there is One who redeems and delivers Israel."

12 When the foreigners looked up and saw them marching toward them, 13 they came out of their camp for battle, and the men with Judas blew the trumpet. 14 The battle was joined and the Gentiles were defeated and fled toward the plain. 15 Their whole rearguard fell by the sword, and they were pursued as far as Gazara and the plains of Judea, to Azotus and Jamnia. About three thousand of their men fell.

16 When Judas and the army returned from the pursuit, 17 he said to the people: "Do not be greedy for the plunder, for there is a fight ahead of us, 18 and Gorgias and his army are near us on the mountain. But now stand firm against our enemies and overthrow them. Afterward you can freely take the plunder."

19 As Judas was finishing this speech, a detachment appeared, looking down from the mountain. 20 They saw that their army had been put to flight and their camp was being burned. The smoke that could be seen indicated what had happened. 21 When they realized this, they were terrified; and when they also saw the army of Judas in the plain ready to attack, 22 they all fled to Philistine territory.

23 Then Judas went back to plunder the camp, and his men collected much gold and silver, violet and crimson cloth, and great treasure. 24 As they returned, they were singing hymns and glorifying Heaven, "for he is good, for his mercy endures forever." 25 Thus Israel had a great deliverance that day.

26 But those of the foreigners who had escaped went and told Lysias all that had occurred. 27 When he heard it he was disturbed and discouraged, because things in Israel had not turned out as he intended and as the king had ordered.

28 So the following year he gathered together sixty thousand picked men and five thousand cavalry, to subdue them. 29 They came into Idumea and camped at Beth-zur, and Judas met them with ten thousand men. 30 Seeing that the army was strong, he prayed thus:

"Blessed are you, O Savior of Israel, who broke the rush of the mighty one by the hand of your servant David, and delivered the camp of the Philistines into the hand of Jonathan, the son of Saul, and his armor-bearer. 31 Give this army into the hands of your people Israel; make them ashamed of their troops and their cavalry. 32 Strike them with fear, weaken the boldness of their strength, and let them tremble at their own destruction. 33 Strike them down by the sword of those who love you, that all who know your name may hymn your praise."

34 Then they engaged in battle, and about five thousand of Lysias' men fell in hand-to-hand fighting. 35 When Lysias saw his ranks beginning to give way, and the increased boldness of Judas, whose men were ready either to live or to die bravely, he withdrew to Antioch and began to recruit mercenaries so as to return to Judea with greater numbers.

found no one and began looking for the Jews in the mountains. 'For', he said, 'we have got them on the run.' 6 First light found Judas in the plain with three thousand men, although these lacked the armour and swords they would have wished. 7 They could now see the gentile encampment with its strong fortifications and cavalry surrounding it, clearly people who understood warfare. 8 Judas said to his men, 'Do not be afraid of their numbers, and do not flinch at their attack. 9 Remember how our ancestors were delivered at the Red Sea when Pharaoh was pursuing them in force. 10 And now let us call on Heaven: if he cares for us, he will remember his covenant with our ancestors and will destroy this army confronting us today; 11 then all the nations will know for certain that there is One who ransoms and saves Israel.'

12 The foreigners looked up and, seeing the Jews advancing against them, 13 came out of the camp to join battle. Judas' men sounded the trumpet 14 and engaged them. The gentiles were defeated and fled towards the plain 15 and all the stragglers fell by the sword. The pursuit continued as far as Gezer and the plains of Idumaea, Azotus and Jamnia, and the enemy lost about three thousand men.

16 Breaking off the pursuit, Judas returned with his men 17 and said to the people, 'Never mind the booty, for we have another battle ahead of us. 18 Gorgias and his troops are still near us in the mountains. First stand up to our enemies and fight them, and then you can safely collect the booty.' 19 The words were hardly out of Judas' mouth, when a detachment came into view, peering down from the mountain. 20 Observing that their own troops had been routed and that the camp had been fired — since the smoke, which they could see, attested the fact — 21 they were panic-stricken at the sight; and when, furthermore, they saw Judas' troops drawn up for battle on the plain, 22 they all fled into Philistine territory. 23 Judas then turned back to plunder the camp, and a large sum in gold and silver, with violet and sea-purple stuffs, and many other valuables were carried off. 24 On their return, the Jews chanted praises to Heaven, singing, 'He is kind and his love is everlasting!' 25 That day had seen a remarkable deliverance in Israel. 26 Those of the foreigners who had escaped came and gave Lysias an account of all that had happened. 27 The news shocked and dismayed him, for affairs in Israel had not gone as he intended, and the result was quite the opposite to what the king had ordered.

28 h The next year he mobilised sixty thousand picked troops and five thousand cavalry with the intention of finishing off the Jews. 29 They advanced into Idumaea and made their base at Beth-Zur, where Judas met them with ten thousand men. 30 When he saw their military strength he offered this prayer, 'Blessed are you, Saviour of Israel, who shattered the mighty warrior's attack at the hand of your servant David, and delivered the Philistine camp into the hands of Jonathan son of Saul, and his armour-bearer. 31 Crush this expedition in the same way at the hands of your people Israel; let their troops and cavalry bring them nothing but shame. 32 Sow panic in their ranks, confound the confidence they put in their numbers and send them reeling in defeat. 33 Overthrow them by the sword of those who love you, and all who acknowledge your name will sing your praises.' 34 The two forces engaged, and five thousand men of Lysias' troops fell in hand-to-hand fighting. 35 Seeing the rout of his army and the courage of Judas' troops and their readiness to live or die nobly, Lysias withdrew to Antioch, where he recruited mercenaries for a further invasion of Judaea in even greater strength.

h 4 4:28seq. // 2 M 11:1–12.

36 Then Judas and his brothers said, "See, our enemies are crushed; let us go up to cleanse the sanctuary and dedicate it." 37 So all the army assembled and went up to Mount Zion. 38 There they saw the sanctuary desolate, the altar profaned, and the gates burned. In the courts they saw bushes sprung up as in a thicket, or as on one of the mountains. They saw also the chambers of the priests in ruins. 39 Then they tore their clothes and mourned with great lamentation; they sprinkled themselves with ashes 40 and fell face down on the ground. And when the signal was given with the trumpets, they cried out to Heaven.

41 Then Judas detailed men to fight against those in the citadel until he had cleansed the sanctuary. 42 He chose blameless priests devoted to the law, 43 and they cleansed the sanctuary and removed the defiled stones to an unclean place. 44 They deliberated what to do about the altar of burnt offering, which had been profaned. 45 And they thought it best to tear it down, so that it would not be a lasting shame to them that the Gentiles had defiled it. So they tore down the altar, 46 and stored the stones in a convenient place on the temple hill until a prophet should come to tell what to do with them. 47 Then they took unhewn*f* stones, as the law directs, and built a new altar like the former one. 48 They also rebuilt the sanctuary and the interior of the temple, and consecrated the courts. 49 They made new holy vessels, and brought the lampstand, the altar of incense, and the table into the temple. 50 Then they offered incense on the altar and lit the lamps on the lampstand, and these gave light in the temple. 51 They placed the bread on the table and hung up the curtains. Thus they finished all the work they had undertaken.

52 Early in the morning on the twenty-fifth day of the ninth month, which is the month of Chislev, in the one hundred forty-eighth year,*u* 53 they rose and offered sacrifice, as the law directs, on the new altar of burnt offering that they had built. 54 At the very season and on the very day that the Gentiles had profaned it, it was dedicated with songs and harps and lutes and cymbals. 55 All the people fell on their faces and worshiped and blessed Heaven, who had prospered them. 56 So they celebrated the dedication of the altar for eight days, and joyfully offered burnt offerings; they offered a sacrifice of well-being and a thanksgiving offering. 57 They decorated the front of the temple with golden crowns and small shields; they restored the gates and the chambers for the priests, and fitted them with doors. 58 There was very great joy among the people, and the disgrace brought by the Gentiles was removed.

59 Then Judas and his brothers and all the assembly of Israel determined that every year at that season the days of dedication of the altar should be observed with joy and gladness for eight days, beginning with the twenty-fifth day of the month of Chislev.

60 At that time they fortified Mount Zion with high walls and strong towers all around, to keep the Gentiles from coming and trampling them down as they had done before. 61 Judas*v* stationed a garrison there to guard it; he also fortified Beth-zur to guard it, so that the people might have a stronghold that faced Idumea.

5 When the Gentiles all around heard that the altar had been rebuilt and the sanctuary dedicated as it was before, they became very angry, 2 and they determined to destroy the descendants of Jacob who lived among them. So they began to kill and destroy among the people. 3 But Judas made war on the descendants of Esau in Idumea, at Akrabattene, because they kept lying in wait for Israel. He dealt them a heavy blow and humbled them and despoiled them.

36 Judas and his brothers said: 'Now that our enemies have been crushed, let us go up to cleanse and rededicate the temple.' 37 When the whole army had assembled, they went up to Mount Zion, 38 where they found the temple laid waste, the altar desecrated, the gates burnt down, the courts overgrown like a thicket or wooded hillside, and the priests' rooms in ruin. 39 They tore their garments, lamented loudly, put ashes on their heads, 40 and threw themselves face downwards on the ground. They cried aloud to Heaven, and the ceremonial trumpets were sounded.

41 Then Judas detailed men to engage the citadel garrison while the temple was being cleansed. 42 He selected priests without blemish and faithful to the law, 43 and they purified the temple, removing to an unclean place the stones which defiled it. 44 They discussed what to do about the desecrated altar of whole-offerings, 45 and rightly decided to demolish it, for fear it might become a lasting reproach to them because it had been defiled by the Gentiles. They therefore pulled down the altar, 46 and stored away the stones in a suitable place on the temple hill, until there should arise a prophet to give a decision about them. 47 They took unhewn stones, as the law directs, and built a new altar on the model of the previous one. 48 They also repaired the temple and restored its interior, and they consecrated the temple courts. 49 New sacred vessels were made; the lampstand, the altar of incense, and the table were brought into the temple. 50 They burnt incense on the altar, and they lit the lamps on the lampstand to shine within the temple. 51 When they had set the Bread of the Presence on the table and spread out the curtains, their work was completed.

52 Early on the twenty-fifth day of the ninth month, the month of Kislev, in the year 148, 53 sacrifice was offered, as laid down by the law, on the newly constructed altar of whole-offerings. 54 On the anniversary of the day of its desecration by the Gentiles, on that very day it was dedicated with hymns of thanksgiving, to the music of harps and lutes and cymbals. 55 All the people prostrated themselves in worship and gave praise to Heaven for prospering their cause.

56 They celebrated the dedication of the altar for eight days; there was rejoicing as they brought whole-offerings and sacrificed shared-offerings and thank-offerings. 57 They decorated the front of the temple with gold garlands and ornamental shields. They renovated the gates and restored the priests' rooms, fitting them with doors. 58 At the lifting of the disgrace brought on them by the Gentiles there was very great rejoicing among the people.

59 Judas, his brothers, and the whole congregation of Israel decreed that, at the same season each year, the dedication of the altar should be observed with joy and gladness for eight days, beginning on the twenty-fifth of Kislev.

60 At that time they encircled Mount Zion with high walls and strong towers to prevent the Gentiles from coming in and overrunning it as they had done before. 61 Judas set a garrison there, and he also fortified Bethsura, so that the people should have a fortress facing Idumaea.

5 The Gentiles round about were greatly incensed when they heard of the building of the altar and rededication of the temple. 2 Determined to wipe out all of Jacob's race living among them, they set about the work of massacre and extermination.

3 Judas made war on the descendants of Esau in Idumaea and attacked Acrabattene, because they had encircled Israel. He inflicted a heavy and humiliating defeat on them and stripped their corpses of armour and weapons. 4 He remem-

---

f Gk whole   *u* 164 B.C.   *v* Gk He   4:52 148: *that is* 164 B.C.E.

2454

36 Then Judas and his brothers said, "Now that our enemies have been crushed, let us go up to purify the sanctuary and rededicate it." 37 So the whole army assembled, and went up to Mount Zion. 38 They found the sanctuary desolate, the altar desecrated, the gates burnt, weeds growing in the courts as in a forest or on some mountain, and the priests' chambers demolished. 39 Then they tore their clothes and made great lamentation; they sprinkled their heads with ashes 40 and fell with their faces to the ground. And when the signal was given with trumpets, they cried out to Heaven.

41 Judas appointed men to attack those in the citadel, while he purified the sanctuary. 42 He chose blameless priests, devoted to the law; 43 these purified the sanctuary and carried away the stones of the Abomination to an unclean place. 44 They deliberated what ought to be done with the altar of holocausts that had been desecrated. 45 The happy thought came to them to tear it down, lest it be a lasting shame to them that the Gentiles had defiled it; so they tore down the altar. 46 They stored the stones in a suitable place on the temple hill, until a prophet should come and decide what to do with them. 47 Then they took uncut stones, according to the law, and built a new altar like the former one. 48 They also repaired the sanctuary and the interior of the temple and purified the courts. 49 They made new sacred vessels and brought the lampstand, the altar of incense, and the table into the temple. 50 Then they burned incense on the altar and lighted the lamps on the lampstand, and these illuminated the temple. 51 They also put loaves on the table and hung up the curtains. Thus they finished all the work they had undertaken.

52 Early in the morning on the twenty-fifth day of the ninth month, that is, the month of Chislev, in the year one hundred and forty-eight, 53 they arose and offered sacrifice according to the law on the new altar of holocausts that they had made. 54 On the anniversary of the day on which the Gentiles had defiled it, on that very day it was reconsecrated with songs, harps, flutes, and cymbals. 55 All the people prostrated themselves and adored and praised Heaven, who had given them success.

56 For eight days they celebrated the dedication of the altar and joyfully offered holocausts and sacrifices of deliverance and praise. 57 They ornamented the façade of the temple with gold crowns and shields; they repaired the gates and the priests' chambers and furnished them with doors. 58 There was great joy among the people now that the disgrace of the Gentiles was removed. 59 Then Judas and his brothers and the entire congregation of Israel decreed that the days of the dedication of the altar should be observed with joy and gladness on the anniversary every year for eight days, from the twenty-fifth day of the month Chislev.

60 At that time they built high walls and strong towers around Mount Zion, to prevent the Gentiles from coming and trampling over it as they had done before. 61 Judas also placed a garrison there to protect it, and likewise fortified Beth-zur, that the people might have a stronghold facing Idumea.

5 When the Gentiles round about heard that the altar had been rebuilt and the sanctuary consecrated as before, they were very angry. 2 So they decided to destroy the descendants of Jacob who were among them, and they began to massacre and persecute the people. 3 Then Judas attacked the sons of Esau at Akrabattene in Idumea, because they were blockading Israel; he defeated them heavily, overcame and despoiled them. 4 He also remembered the malice of the

36 i Judas and his brothers then said, 'Now that our enemies have been defeated, let us go up to purify the sanctuary and dedicate it.' 37 So they marshalled the whole army, and went up to Mount Zion. 38 There they found the sanctuary deserted, the altar desecrated, the gates burned down, and vegetation growing in the courts as it might in a wood or on some mountain, while the storerooms were in ruins. 39 They tore their garments and mourned bitterly, putting dust on their heads. 40 They prostrated themselves on the ground, and when the trumpets gave the signal they cried aloud to Heaven.

41 Judas then ordered his men to keep the Citadel garrison engaged until he had purified the sanctuary. 42 Next, he selected priests who were blameless and zealous for the Law 43 to purify the sanctuary and remove the stones of the 'Pollution' to some unclean place. 44 They discussed what should be done about the altar of burnt offering which had been profaned, 45 and very properly decided to pull it down, rather than later be embarrassed about it since it had been defiled by the gentiles. They therefore demolished it 46 and deposited the stones in a suitable place on the hill of the Dwelling to await the appearance of a prophet who should give a ruling about them. 47 They took unhewn stones, as the Law prescribed, and built a new altar on the lines of the old one. 48 They restored the Holy Place and the interior of the Dwelling, and purified the courts. 49 They made new sacred vessels, and brought the lamp-stand, the altar of incense, and the table into the Temple. 50 They burned incense on the altar and lit the lamps on the lamp-stand, and these shone inside the Temple. 51 They placed the loaves on the table and hung the curtains and completed all the tasks they had undertaken.

52 On the twenty-fifth of the ninth month, Chislev, in the year 148 they rose at dawn 53 and offered a lawful sacrifice on the new altar of burnt offering which they had made. 54 The altar was dedicated, to the sound of hymns, zithers, lyres and cymbals, at the same time of year and on the same day on which the gentiles had originally profaned it. 55 The whole people fell prostrate in adoration and then praised Heaven who had granted them success. 56 For eight days they celebrated the dedication of the altar, joyfully offering burnt offerings, communion and thanksgiving sacrifices. 57 They ornamented the front of the Temple with crowns and bosses of gold, renovated the gates and storerooms, providing the latter with doors. 58 There was no end to the rejoicing among the people, since the disgrace inflicted by the gentiles had been effaced. 59 Judas, with his brothers and the whole assembly of Israel, made it a law that the days of the dedication of the altar should be celebrated yearly at the proper season, for eight days beginning on the twenty-fifth of the month of Chislev, with rejoicing and gladness. j

60 They then proceeded to build high walls with strong towers round Mount Zion, to prevent the gentiles from coming and riding roughshod over it as in the past. 61 Judas stationed a garrison there to guard it; he also fortified Beth-Zur, so that the people would have a fortress confronting Idumaea.

5 When the surrounding nations heard that the altar had been rebuilt and the sanctuary restored to what it had been before, they became very angry 2 and decided to destroy the descendants of Jacob living among them; they began to murder and evict our people. 3 Judas made war on the sons of Esau in Idumaea, k in the region of Acrabattene where they were besieging the Israelites. He dealt them a serious blow, drove them off and despoiled them. 4 He also remembered the wickedness of

i 4 4:36seq. // 2 M 10:1–8.   j 4 The Feast of Hanukkah, a feast of lights.   k 5 // 2 M 10:15–23.

2455

4 He also remembered the wickedness of the sons of Baean, who were a trap and a snare to the people and ambushed them on the highways. 5 They were shut up by him in their[w] towers; and he encamped against them, vowed their complete destruction, and burned with fire their towers and all who were in them. 6 Then he crossed over to attack the Ammonites, where he found a strong band and many people, with Timothy as their leader. 7 He engaged in many battles with them, and they were crushed before him; he struck them down. 8 He also took Jazer and its villages; then he returned to Judea.

9 Now the Gentiles in Gilead gathered together against the Israelites who lived in their territory, and planned to destroy them. But they fled to the stronghold of Dathema, 10 and sent to Judas and his brothers a letter that said, "The Gentiles around us have gathered together to destroy us. 11 They are preparing to come and capture the stronghold to which we have fled, and Timothy is leading their forces. 12 Now then, come and rescue us from their hands, for many of us have fallen, 13 and all our kindred who were in the land of Tob have been killed; the enemy[x] have captured their wives and children and goods, and have destroyed about a thousand persons there."

14 While the letter was still being read, other messengers, with their garments torn, came from Galilee and made a similar report; 15 they said that the people of Ptolemais and Tyre and Sidon, and all Galilee of the Gentiles,[y] had gathered together against them "to annihilate us." 16 When Judas and the people heard these messages, a great assembly was called to determine what they should do for their kindred who were in distress and were being attacked by enemies.[z] 17 Then Judas said to his brother Simon, "Choose your men and go and rescue your kindred in Galilee; Jonathan my brother and I will go to Gilead." 18 But he left Joseph, son of Zechariah, and Azariah, a leader of the people, with the rest of the forces, in Judea to guard it; 19 and he gave them this command, "Take charge of this people, but do not engage in battle with the Gentiles until we return." 20 Then three thousand men were assigned to Simon to go to Galilee, and eight thousand to Judas for Gilead.

21 So Simon went to Galilee and fought many battles against the Gentiles, and the Gentiles were crushed before him. 22 He pursued them to the gate of Ptolemais; as many as three thousand of the Gentiles fell, and he despoiled them. 23 Then he took the Jews[a] of Galilee and Arbatta, with their wives and children, and all they possessed, and led them to Judea with great rejoicing.

24 Judas Maccabeus and his brother Jonathan crossed the Jordan and made three days' journey into the wilderness. 25 They encountered the Nabateans, who met them peaceably and told them all that had happened to their kindred in Gilead: 26 "Many of them have been shut up in Bozrah and Bosor, in Alema and Chaspho, Maked and Carnaim" — all these towns were strong and large — 27 "and some have been shut up in the other towns of Gilead; the enemy[x] are getting ready to attack the strongholds tomorrow and capture and destroy all these people in a single day."

28 Then Judas and his army quickly turned back by the wilderness road to Bozrah; and he took the town, and killed every male by the edge of the sword; then he seized all its spoils and burned it with fire. 29 He left the place at night, and they went all the way to the stronghold of Dathema.[b] 30 At dawn they looked out and saw a large company, which could not be counted, carrying ladders and engines of war to capture the stronghold, and attacking the Jews within.[c]

bered also the wrong done by the Baeanites, who with traps and road-blocks were continually ambushing the Israelites. 5 He shut them up in their forts and positioned his troops against them; then, calling down a solemn curse on them, he set ablaze the forts with all their occupants. 6 He crossed over to attack the Ammonites and was confronted by a strong force and a large crowd of people, all under the leadership of Timotheus. 7 In the course of many engagements, they broke before Judas's attack and were crushed. 8 After Judas had taken Jazer and its dependent villages, he returned to Judaea.

9 The Gentiles in Gilead gathered against the Israelites within their territory, intent on destroying them; but the Israelites took refuge in the fortress of Dathema, 10 from where they sent this letter to Judas and his brothers:

The Gentiles in this region have gathered to wipe us out. 11 With Timotheus in command of their army, they are preparing to come and seize the fortress where we have taken refuge. 12 Therefore come now at once and rescue us from their clutches, for many of our number have already fallen. 13 All our fellow-Jews in the region of Tubias have been massacred, their wives and children seized, and their property carried off, and about a thousand men have lost their lives.

14 While the letter was being read, other messengers with their garments torn arrived from Galilee. 15 'Ptolemais, Tyre and Sidon,' they reported, 'and all heathen Galilee have mobilized armies for our destruction.'

16 When Judas and the people heard this, a full assembly was called to decide what should be done for their fellow-countrymen under persecution and enemy attack. 17 Judas said to his brother Simon, 'You go to the rescue of your countrymen in Galilee with such troops as you need, while I and our brother Jonathan go to Gilead.' 18 The remainder of the forces he left with Josephus son of Zacharias, and Azarias, a leading citizen, for the defence of Judaea. 19 Their orders were: 'Take charge of the people, but on no account engage the Gentiles in battle while we are away.' 20 Simon was allotted three thousand men for the march on Galilee, and Judas eight thousand for the march on Gilead.

21 Simon invaded Galilee and, after many battles, broke the resistance of the Gentiles. 22 Pursuing them as far as the gate of Ptolemais, he killed nearly three thousand of them, and stripped their corpses. 23 He brought back with him the Jews from Galilee and Arbatta, together with their wives and children and all they possessed, and amid great jubilation conducted them to Judaea.

24 Meanwhile Judas Maccabaeus and his brother Jonathan crossed the Jordan and made a three days' march through the desert. 25 They came upon some Nabataeans, who met them peaceably, and gave them a full account of what had happened to the Jews in Gilead: 26 many of them were held prisoner in the large fortified towns of Bozrah and Bezer, in Alema, Casphor, Maked, and Carnaim; 27 some were enclosed in the other towns of Gilead. 'Your enemies,' they reported, 'are marshalling their forces to storm your strongholds tomorrow so as to capture them and destroy all the Jews in them in a single day.'

28 Judas and his army abruptly turned aside to Bozrah by way of the desert, and captured the town. He put the entire male population to the sword, plundered all their property, and set the place on fire. 29 Making a night march from Bozrah he came within reach of the fortress of Dathema. 30 When dawn broke, there in front of them were troops past counting; they were bringing up scaling-ladders and siege-engines to breach the fortress and begin the attack. 31 When

---

[w] Gk her   [x] Gk they   [y] Gk aliens   [z] Gk them   [a] Gk those
[b] Gk lacks of Dathema. See verse 9   [c] Gk and they were attacking them

sons of Baean, who had become a snare and a stumbling-block to the people by ambushing them along the roads. 5He forced them to take refuge in towers, which he besieged; he vowed their annihilation and burned down the towers along with all the persons in them. 6Then he crossed over to the Ammonites, where he found a strong army and a large body of people with Timothy as their leader. 7He fought many battles with them, routed them, and struck them down. 8After seizing Jazer and its villages, he returned to Judea.

9The Gentiles in Gilead assembled to attack and destroy the Israelites who were in their territory; these then fled to the stronghold of Dathema. 10They sent a letter to Judas and his brothers saying: "The Gentiles around us have combined against us to destroy us, 11and they are preparing to come and seize this stronghold to which we have fled. Timothy is the leader of their army. 12Come at once and rescue us from them, for many of us have fallen. 13All our kinsmen who were among the Tobiads have been killed; the Gentiles have carried away their wives and children and their goods, and they have slain there about a thousand men."

14While they were reading this letter, suddenly other messengers, in torn clothes, arrived from Galilee to deliver a similar message: 15that the inhabitants of Ptolemais, Tyre, and Sidon, and the whole of Gentile Galilee had joined forces to destroy them. 16When Judas and the people heard this, a great assembly convened to consider what they should do for their unfortunate kinsmen who were being attacked by enemies.

17Judas said to his brother Simon: "Choose men for yourself, and go, rescue your kinsmen in Galilee; I and my brother Jonathan will go to Gilead." 18In Judea he left Joseph, son of Zechariah, and Azariah, leader of the people, with the rest of the army to guard it. 19"Take charge of these people," he commanded them, "but do not fight against the Gentiles until we return." 20Three thousand men were allotted to Simon, to go into Galilee, and eight thousand men to Judas, for Gilead.

21Simon went into Galilee and fought many battles with the Gentiles. They were crushed before him, 22and he pursued them to the very gate of Ptolemais. About three thousand men of the Gentiles fell, and he gathered their spoils. 23He took with him the Jews who were in Galilee and in Arbatta, with their wives and children and all that they had, and brought them to Judea with great rejoicing.

24Judas Maccabeus and his brother Jonathan crossed the Jordan and marched for three days through the desert. 25There they met some Nabateans, who received them peacefully and told them all that had happened to the Jews in Gilead: 26"Many of them have been imprisoned in Bozrah, in Bosor near Alema, in Chaspho, Maked, and Carnaim"—all of these are large, fortified cities— 27"and some have been imprisoned in the other cities of Gilead. Tomorrow their enemies plan to attack the strongholds and to seize and destroy all these people in one day."

28Thereupon Judas suddenly changed direction with his army, marched across the desert to Bozrah, and captured the city. He slaughtered all the male population, took all their possessions, and set fire to the city. 29He led his army from that place by night, and they marched toward the stronghold of Dathema. 30When morning came, they looked ahead and saw a countless multitude of people, with ladders and devices for capturing the stronghold, and beginning to attack the people within. 31When Judas perceived

the sons of Baean, who were a menace and a trap for the people with their ambushes on the roads. 5Having blockaded them in their town and besieged them, he put them under the curse of destruction; he then set fire to their towers and burned them down with everyone inside. 6Next, he crossed over the Ammonites where he found a strong fighting force and a numerous people, commanded by Timotheus. 7He fought many battles with them, defeated them and cut them to pieces. 8Having captured Jazer and its dependent villages, he retired to Judaea.

9Next, together with those of Gilead banded together to destroy the Israelites living in their territory. The latter, however, took refuge in the fortress of Dathema, 10and sent the following letter to Judas and his brothers:

'The gentiles round us have banded themselves together against us to destroy us, 11and they are preparing to storm the fortress in which we have taken refuge; Timotheus is in command of their forces. 12Come at once and rescue us from their clutches, for we have already suffered great losses. 13All our countrymen living in Tobias' country have been killed, their women and children have been taken into captivity, their property has been seized, and about a thousand men have been destroyed there.'

14While the letter was being read, other messengers arrived from Galilee with their garments torn, bearing similar news, 15'The people of Ptolemais, Tyre and Sidon have joined forces with the whole of gentile Galilee to destroy us!' 16When Judas and the people heard this, they held a great assembly to decide what should be done for their oppressed countrymen who were under attack from their enemies. 17Judas said to his brother Simon, 'Pick your men and go and relieve your countrymen in Galilee, while my brother Jonathan and I make our way into Gilead.' 18He left Joseph son of Zechariah and the people's leader Azariah with the remainder of the army in Judaea to keep guard, and gave them these orders, 19'You are to be responsible for our people. Do not engage the gentiles until we return.' 20Simon was allotted three thousand men for the expedition into Galilee, Judas eight thousand for Gilead.

21Simon advanced into Galilee, engaged the gentiles in several battles and swept all before him; 22he pursued them to the gate of Ptolemais, and they lost about three thousand men, whose spoils he collected. 23With him, he took away the Jews of Galilee and Arbatta, with their wives and children and all their possessions, and brought them into Judaea with great rejoicing.

24Meanwhile Judas Maccabaeus and his brother Jonathan crossed the Jordan[l] and made a three-days' march through the desert, 25where they encountered the Nabataeans,[m] who gave them a friendly reception and told them everything that had been happening to their brothers in Gilead, 26many of whom, they said, were shut up in Bozrah and Bosor, Alema, Chaspho, Maked and Carnaim, all large fortified towns. 27Others were blockaded in the other towns of Gilead, and the enemy planned to attack and capture these strongholds the very next day, and destroy all the people inside them on one day.

28Judas and his army at once turned off by the desert road to Bozrah. He took the town and, having put all the males to the sword and collected the booty, burned it down. 29When night came, he left the place, and they continued their march until they reached the fortress. 30In the light of dawn they looked, and there was an innumerable horde, setting up ladders and engines to capture the fortress; the assault was just beginning. 31When Judas saw that the at-

l 5 // 2 M 12:10–31.   m 5 An Arab people, centred on Petra and
controlling the trade routes for 200 years.

31 So Judas saw that the battle had begun and that the cry of the town went up to Heaven, with trumpets and loud shouts, 32 and he said to the men of his forces, "Fight today for your kindred!" 33 Then he came up behind them in three companies, who sounded their trumpets and cried aloud in prayer. 34 And when the army of Timothy realized that it was Maccabeus, they fled before him, and he dealt them a heavy blow. As many as eight thousand of them fell that day.

35 Next he turned aside to Maapha, *d* and fought against it and took it; and he killed every male in it, plundered it, and burned it with fire. 36 From there he marched on and took Chaspho, Maked, and Bosor, and the other towns of Gilead.

37 After these things Timothy gathered another army and encamped opposite Raphon, on the other side of the stream. 38 Judas sent men to spy out the camp, and they reported to him, "All the Gentiles around us have gathered to him; it is a very large force. 39 They also have hired Arabs to help them, and they are encamped across the stream, ready to come and fight against you." And Judas went to meet them.

40 Now as Judas and his army drew near to the stream of water, Timothy said to the officers of his forces, "If he crosses over to us first, we will not be able to resist him, for he will surely defeat us. 41 But if he shows fear and camps on the other side of the river, we will cross over to him and defeat him." 42 When Judas approached the stream of water, he stationed the officers*e* of the army at the stream and gave them this command, "Permit no one to encamp, but make them all enter the battle." 43 Then he crossed over against them first, and the whole army followed him. All the Gentiles were defeated before him, and they threw away their arms and fled into the sacred precincts at Carnaim. 44 But he took the town and burned the sacred precincts with fire, together with all who were in them. Thus Carnaim was conquered; they could stand before Judas no longer.

45 Then Judas gathered together all the Israelites in Gilead, the small and the great, with their wives and children and goods, a very large company, to go to the land of Judah. 46 So they came to Ephron. This was a large and very strong town on the road, and they could not go around it to the right or to the left; they had to go through it. 47 But the people of the town shut them out and blocked up the gates with stones.

48 Judas sent them this friendly message, "Let us pass through your land to get to our land. No one will do you harm; we will simply pass by on foot." But they refused to open to him. 49 Then Judas ordered proclamation to be made to the army that all should encamp where they were. 50 So the men of the forces encamped, and he fought against the town all that day and all the night, and the town was delivered into his hands. 51 He destroyed every male by the edge of the sword, and razed and plundered the town. Then he passed through the town over the bodies of the dead.

52 Then they crossed the Jordan into the large plain before Beth-shan. 53 Judas kept rallying the laggards and encouraging the people all the way until he came to the land of Judah. 54 So they went up to Mount Zion with joy and gladness, and offered burnt offerings, because they had returned in safety; not one of them had fallen.

55 Now while Judas and Jonathan were in Gilead and their*f* brother Simon was in Galilee before Ptolemais, 56 Joseph son of Zechariah, and Azariah, the commanders of the forces, heard of their brave deeds and of the heroic war they had fought. 57 So they said, "Let us also make a name for ourselves; let us go and make war on the Gentiles

Judas saw that battle was joined, and heard a cry go up to heaven from the town, with the sound of trumpets and loud shouting, 32 he said to his men: 'Fight this day for our brothers!'

33 They advanced in three columns to take the enemy in the rear; they sounded the trumpets and cried aloud in prayer. 34 When the army of Timotheus realized it was Maccabaeus, they fled. In the heavy defeat inflicted on them, there fell that day nearly eight thousand of the enemy.

35 Judas then turned aside to Alema, which he attacked and captured; he killed all the males, plundered the town, and set it on fire. 36 Moving from there, he occupied Casphor, Maked, Bezer, and the other towns of Gilead.

37 After these events Timotheus gathered another army and took up position opposite Raphon, on the far side of the wadi. 38 Judas sent spies to their camp, and they reported that all the Gentiles in the neighbourhood had rallied in very great strength to Timotheus, 39 who had also hired the help of Arab mercenaries. The enemy were encamped on the far side of the wadi, ready to give battle. So Judas marched to meet them.

40 As Judas and his army were approaching the wadi, Timotheus said to his officers: 'If he crosses over to our side first, we shall not be able to stand up to him; he will certainly get the better of us. 41 If, however, his courage fails him and he takes up a position on the other side of the river, then we will cross over and get the better of him.' 42 When Judas reached the wadi, he stationed the officers of the muster on its bank with instructions that the whole army should advance to the battle; no one was to be allowed to take up a fixed position. 43 Thus Judas forestalled the enemy by crossing to attack them at the head of all his people. The gentile army broke before him; one and all they threw away their weapons and sought refuge in the temple at Carnaim. 44 Judas captured the town and burnt the temple and everyone in it. With the overthrow of Carnaim, all resistance came to an end.

45 Judas assembled the Israelites who were in Gilead to escort them all back to Judaea. There was a great host of them, men high and low, women and children, together with their possessions. 46 They arrived at Ephron, a large and strongly fortified town on the road. It was impossible to bypass it on either side; the only route lay through the town. 47 The inhabitants, however, barricaded their gates with boulders and denied them passage. 48 Judas made peaceful overtures to them: 'We have to go through your territory to reach our own. No one will do you any harm: we will simply pass through on foot.' But they refused to open their gates to him.

49 Judas issued orders to those under his command: everyone was to halt where he was. 50 The fighting men took up battle positions and attacked the town all that day and all the night, until it fell into their hands. 51 They put every male to the sword, razed the town to the ground and plundered it, and then marched through it over the bodies of the slain. 52 They crossed the Jordan to the broad plain opposite Beth-shan, 53 while Judas kept the stragglers together and encouraged the people all along the way till he arrived in Judaea. 54 With gladness and jubilation they went up to Mount Zion and offered whole-offerings, because they had returned in safety and without loss.

55 While Judas and Jonathan were in Gilead, and Simon their brother was besieging Ptolemais in Galilee, 56 their heroic military achievements were reported to the two commanders, Azarias and Josephus son of Zacharias, 57 and they said: 'We too must make a name for ourselves; let us undertake a campaign against the Gentiles in our neighbour-

---

d Other ancient authorities read *Alema*   *e* Or *scribes*   *f* Gk *his*

5:35 **Alema:** *some witnesses read* Maapha.

that the struggle had begun and that the noise of the battle was resounding to heaven with trumpet blasts and loud shouting, 32 he said to the men of his army, "Fight for our kinsmen today."

33 He came up behind them with three columns blowing their trumpets and shouting in prayer. 34 When the army of Timothy realized that it was Maccabeus, they fell back before him, and he inflicted on them a crushing defeat. About eight thousand of their men fell that day. 35 Then he turned toward Alema and attacked and captured it; he killed all the male population, plundered the place, and burned it down. 36 From there he moved on and took Chaspho, Maked, Bosor, and the other cities of Gilead.

37 After these events Timothy assembled another army and camped opposite Raphon, on the other side of the stream. 38 Judas sent men to spy on the camp, and they reported to him: "All the Gentiles around us have rallied to him, making a very large force; 39 they have also hired Arabs to help them, and have camped beyond the stream, ready to attack you." So Judas went forward to attack them.

40 As Judas and his army were approaching the running stream, Timothy said to the officers of his army: "If he crosses over to us first, we shall not be able to resist him; he will certainly defeat us. 41 But if he is afraid and camps on the other side of the river, we will cross over to him and defeat him."

42 But when Judas reached the running stream, he stationed the officers of the people beside the stream and gave them this order: "Do not allow any man to pitch a tent; all must go into battle." 43 He was the first to cross to the attack, with all the people behind him, and the Gentiles were crushed before them; they threw away their arms and fled to the temple enclosure at Carnaim. 44 The Jews captured that city and burnt the enclosure with all who were in it. So Carnaim was subdued, and Judas met with no more resistance.

45 Then he assembled all the Israelites, great and small, who were in Gilead, with their wives and children and their goods, a great crowd of people, to go into the land of Judah. 46 When they reached Ephron, a large and strongly fortified city along the way, they found it impossible to encircle it on either the right or the left; they would have to march right through it. 47 But the men in the city shut them out and blocked up the gates with stones. 48 Then Judas sent them his peaceful message: "We wish to cross your territory in order to reach our own; no one will harm you; we will only march through." But they would not open to him.

49 So Judas ordered a proclamation to be made in the camp that everyone make an attack from the place where he was. 50 When the men of the army took up their positions, he assaulted the city all that day and night, and it was delivered to him. 51 He slaughtered every male, razed and plundered the city, and passed through it over the slain.

52 Then they crossed the Jordan to the great plain in front of Beth-shan; 53 and Judas kept rounding up the stragglers and encouraging the people the whole way, until he reached the land of Judah. 54 They ascended Mount Zion in joy and gladness and offered holocausts, because not one of them had fallen; they returned in safety.

55 During the time that Judas and Jonathan were in the land of Gilead, and Simon his brother was in Galilee opposite Ptolemais, 56 Joseph, son of Zechariah, and Azariah, the leaders of the army, heard about the brave deeds and the fighting that they were doing. 57 They said, "Let us also make a name for ourselves by going out and fighting against the Gentiles around us."

tack had begun and that the war cry was rising to heaven from the city, mingled with trumpet calls and a great clamour, 32 he said to the men of his army, 'Into battle today for your brothers!' 33 Dividing them into three commands, he advanced on the enemy's rear, with trumpets sounding and prayers shouted aloud. 34 The troops of Timotheus, recognising that this was Maccabaeus, fled before his advance; Maccabaeus dealt them a crushing defeat; about eight thousand of their men fell that day. 35 Then, wheeling on Alema, he attacked and captured it and, having killed all the males and collected the booty, burned the place down. 36 From there he moved on and took Chaspho, Maked, Bosor and the remaining towns of Gilead. 37 After these events, Timotheus mustered another force and pitched camp opposite Raphon, on the far side of the stream-bed. 38 Judas sent men to reconnoitre the camp, and these reported back as follows, 'With him are massed all the gentiles surrounding us, making a very numerous army, 39 with Arab mercenaries as auxiliaries; they are encamped on the far side of the stream-bed, and ready to launch an attack on you.' Judas then advanced to engage them, 40 and was approaching the watercourse with his troops when Timotheus told the commanders of his army, 'If he crosses first we shall not be able to resist him, because he will have a great advantage over us; 41 but if he is afraid and camps on the other side of the stream, we shall cross over to him and the advantage will then be ours.'

42 As soon as Judas reached the watercourse, he posted people's scribes along it, giving them this order: 'Do not let anyone pitch his tent; all are to go into battle!' 43 He was himself the first across to the enemy side, with all the people following. He defeated all the opposing gentiles, who threw down their arms and ran for refuge in the sanctuary of Carnaim. 44 The Jews first captured the town and then burned down the temple with everyone inside. And so Carnaim was overthrown, and the enemy could offer no further resistance to Judas.

45 Next, Judas assembled all the Israelites living in Gilead, from the least to the greatest, with their wives, children and belongings, an enormous muster, to take them to Judaea. 46 They reached Ephron, a large town straddling the road and strongly fortified. As it was impossible to by-pass it either to right or to left, there was nothing for it but to march straight through. 47 But the people of the town denied them passage and barricaded the gates with stones. 48 Judas sent them a conciliatory message in these terms, 'We want to pass through your territory to reach our own; no one will do you any harm, we only want to go through on foot.' But they would not open up for him. 49 So Judas sent an order down the column for everyone to halt where he stood. 50 The fighting men took up their positions; Judas attacked the town all day and night, and the town fell to him. 51 He put all the males to the sword, rased the town to the ground, plundered it and marched through the town square over the bodies of the dead. 52 They then crossed the Jordan into the Great Plain, opposite Beth-Shean, 53 Judas all the time rallying the stragglers and encouraging the people the whole way until they reached Judaea. 54 They climbed Mount Zion in joy and gladness and presented burnt offerings because they had returned safe and sound without having lost a single man.

55 While Judas and Jonathan were in Gilead and Simon his brother in Galilee outside Ptolemais, 56 Joseph son of Zechariah, and Azariah, who were in command of the army, heard of their valiant deeds and of the battles they had been fighting, 57 and said, 'Let us make a name for ourselves too and go and fight the nations around us.' 58 So

NEW REVISED STANDARD VERSION	REVISED ENGLISH BIBLE

around us." 58 So they issued orders to the men of the forces that were with them and marched against Jamnia. 59 Gorgias and his men came out of the town to meet them in battle. 60 Then Joseph and Azariah were routed, and were pursued to the borders of Judea; as many as two thousand of the people of Israel fell that day. 61 Thus the people suffered a great rout because, thinking to do a brave deed, they did not listen to Judas and his brothers. 62 But they did not belong to the family of those men through whom deliverance was given to Israel.

63 The man Judas and his brothers were greatly honored in all Israel and among all the Gentiles, wherever their name was heard. 64 People gathered to them and praised them.

65 Then Judas and his brothers went out and fought the descendants of Esau in the land to the south. He struck Hebron and its villages and tore down its strongholds and burned its towers on all sides. 66 Then he marched off to go into the land of the Philistines, and passed through Marisa.g 67 On that day some priests, who wished to do a brave deed, fell in battle, for they went out to battle unwisely. 68 But Judas turned aside to Azotus in the land of the Philistines; he tore down their altars, and the carved images of their gods he burned with fire; he plundered the towns and returned to the land of Judah.

6 King Antiochus was going through the upper provinces when he heard that Elymais in Persia was a city famed for its wealth in silver and gold. 2 Its temple was very rich, containing golden shields, breastplates, and weapons left there by Alexander son of Philip, the Macedonian king who first reigned over the Greeks. 3 So he came and tried to take the city and plunder it, but he could not because his plan had become known to the citizens 4 and they withstood him in battle. So he fled and in great disappointment left there to return to Babylon.

5 Then someone came to him in Persia and reported that the armies that had gone into the land of Judah had been routed; 6 that Lysias had gone first with a strong force, but had turned and fled before the Jews;h that the Jewsi had grown strong from the arms, supplies, and abundant spoils that they had taken from the armies they had cut down; 7 that they had torn down the abomination that he had erected on the altar in Jerusalem; and that they had surrounded the sanctuary with high walls as before, and also Beth-zur, his town.

8 When the king heard this news, he was astounded and badly shaken. He took to his bed and became sick from disappointment, because things had not turned out for him as he had planned. 9 He lay there for many days, because deep disappointment continually gripped him, and he realized that he was dying. 10 So he called all his Friends and said to them, "Sleep has departed from my eyes and I am downhearted with worry. 11 I said to myself, 'To what distress I have come! And into what a great flood I now am plunged! For I was kind and beloved in my power.' 12 But now I remember the wrong I did in Jerusalem. I seized all its vessels of silver and gold, and I sent to destroy the inhabitants of Judah without good reason. 13 I know that it is because of this that these misfortunes have come upon me; here I am, perishing of bitter disappointment in a strange land."

14 Then he called for Philip, one of his Friends, and made him ruler over all his kingdom. 15 He gave him the crown and his robe and the signet, so that he might guide his son Antiochus and bring him up to be king. 16 Thus King Antiochus died there in the one hundred forty-ninth year.j

hood.' 58 They gave orders to the forces in their command to advance on Jamnia. 59 When Gorgias and his men marched from the town to give battle, 60 Josephus and Azarias were put to rout and pursued to the frontier of Judaea, with the loss that day of some two thousand Israelites. 61 The people suffered this heavy defeat because those in command of them, thinking to play the hero themselves, had not obeyed Judas and his brothers. 62 Those men were not, however, of that family whose prerogative it was to bring deliverance to Israel.

63 The valiant Judas and his brothers won a great reputation throughout Israel and among all the Gentiles, wherever their fame spread, 64 and crowds flocked to acclaim them.

65 After this, Judas marched out with his brothers and made war on the descendants of Esau in the country to the south. He struck at Hebron and its villages, demolished its fortifications, and everywhere burnt down its forts. 66 He then set out to invade Philistia and marched through Marisa. 67 Several priests who, from a desire to distinguish themselves, had ill-advisedly gone into action, fell in the battle that day. 68 Judas turned aside to Azotus in the territory of the Philistines; he pulled down their altars and burnt the images of their gods; he carried off spoil from the towns, and then went back to Judaea.

6 As King Antiochus made his way through the upper provinces he heard that in Persia there was a city, Elymais, famous for its wealth in silver and gold. 2 Its temple was very rich, full of gold shields, coats of mail, and weapons left there by Philip's son Alexander, king of Macedon and the first to be king over the Greeks. 3 Antiochus came to the city, but in his attempt to take and plunder it he was unsuccessful because his plan had become known to the citizens. 4 They gave battle and drove him off; in bitter disappointment he withdrew towards Babylon.

5 In Persia a messenger brought him the news that the armies which had invaded Judaea had suffered defeat, 6 and that Lysias, who had marched up with an exceptionally strong force, had been flung back in open battle. Further, the strength of the Jews had increased through the capture of weapons, equipment, and spoil in plenty from the armies they destroyed; 7 they had pulled down the abomination built by him on the altar in Jerusalem and surrounded their temple with high walls as before; they had even fortified Bethsura, his city.

8 The king was dismayed and so sorely shaken by this report that he took to his bed, ill with grief at the miscarriage of his plans. 9 There he lay for many days, overcome again and again by bitter grief, and he realized that he was dying. 10 He summoned all his Friends and said: 'Sleep has deserted me; the weight of care has broken my heart. 11 At first I asked myself: Why am I engulfed in this sea of troubles, I who was kind and well loved in the day of my power? 12 But now I recall the wrong I did in Jerusalem: I carried off all the vessels of silver and gold that were there, and with no justification sent armies to wipe out the inhabitants of Judaea. 13 I know that is why these misfortunes have come upon me; and here I am, dying of bitter grief in a foreign land.'

14 He summoned Philip, one of his Friends, and appointed him regent over his whole empire, 15 giving him the crown, his royal robe, and the signet ring, with authority to bring up his son Antiochus and train him for the throne. 16 King Antiochus died in Persia in the year 149.

g Other ancient authorities read Samaria   h Gk them   i Gk they
j 163 B.C.

6:16 149: that is 163 B.C.E.

58 They gave orders to the men of their army who were with them, and marched toward Jamnia. 59 But Gorgias and his men came out of the city to meet them in battle. 60 Joseph and Azariah were beaten, and were pursued to the frontiers of Judea, and about two thousand Israelites fell that day. 61 It was a bad defeat for the people, because they had not obeyed Judas and his brothers, thinking that they would do brave deeds. 62 But they did not belong to the family of those men to whom it was granted to achieve Israel's salvation. 63 The valiant Judas and his brothers were greatly renowned in all Israel and among all the Gentiles, wherever their name was heard; 64 and men gathered about them and praised them.

65 Then Judas and his brothers went out and attacked the sons of Esau in the country toward the south; he took Hebron and its villages, and he destroyed its strongholds and burned the towers around it. 66 He then set out for the land of the Philistines and passed through Marisa. 67 At that time some priests fell in battle who had gone out rashly to fight in their desire to distinguish themselves. 68 Judas then turned toward Azotus in the land of the Philistines. He destroyed their altars and burned the statues of their gods; and after plundering their cities he returned to the land of Judah.

6 As King Antiochus was traversing the inland provinces, he heard that in Persia there was a city called Elymais, famous for its wealth in silver and gold, 2 and that its temple was very rich, containing gold helmets, breastplates, and weapons left there by Alexander, son of Philip, king of Macedon, the first king of the Greeks. 3 He went therefore and tried to capture and pillage the city. But he could not do so, because his plan became known to the people of the city 4 who rose up in battle against him. So he retreated and in great dismay withdrew from there to return to Babylon.

5 While he was in Persia, a messenger brought him news that the armies sent into the land of Judah had been put to flight; 6 that Lysias had gone at first with a strong army and been driven back by the Israelites; that they had grown strong by reason of the arms, men, and abundant possessions taken from the armies they had destroyed; 7 that they had pulled down the Abomination which he had built upon the altar in Jerusalem; and that they had surrounded with high walls both the sanctuary, as it had been before, and his city of Beth-zur.

8 When the king heard this news, he was struck with fear and very much shaken. Sick with grief because his designs had failed, he took to his bed. 9 There he remained many days, overwhelmed with sorrow, for he knew he was going to die.

10 So he called in all his Friends and said to them: "Sleep has departed from my eyes, for my heart is sinking with anxiety. 11 I said to myself: 'Into what tribulation have I come, and in what floods of sorrow am I now! 12 Yet I was kindly and beloved in my rule.' But I now recall the evils I did in Jerusalem, when I carried away all the vessels of gold and silver that were in it, and for no cause gave orders that the inhabitants of Judah be destroyed. 13 I know that this is why these evils have overtaken me; and now I am dying, in bitter grief, in a foreign land.

14 Then he summoned Philip, one of his Friends, and put him in charge of his whole kingdom. 15 He gave him his crown, his robe, and his signet ring, so that he might guide the king's son Antiochus and bring him up to be king. 16 King Antiochus died in Persia in the year one hundred and forty-nine.

they issued orders to the men under their command and marched on Jamnia. 59 Gorgias and his men came out of the town and gave battle. 60 Joseph and Azariah were routed and pursued as far as the frontiers of Judaea. That day about two thousand Israelites lost their lives. 61 Our people thus met with a great reverse, because they had not listened to Judas and his brothers, thinking that they would do something equally valiant. 62 They were not, however, of the same breed of men as those to whom the deliverance of Israel was entrusted.

63 The noble Judas and his brothers, however, were held in high honour throughout Israel and among all the nations wherever their name was heard, 64 and people thronged round to acclaim them. 65 Judas marched out with his brothers to fight the Edomites in the country towards the south; he stormed Hebron and its dependent villages, threw down its fortifications and burned down its encircling towers. 66 Leaving there, he made for the country of the Philistines and passed through Marisa. 67 Among the fallen in that day's fighting were some priests who sought to prove their courage there by joining in the battle, a foolhardy venture. 68 Judas next turned on Azotus, which belonged to the Philistines; he overthrew their altars, burned the statues of their gods and, having pillaged their towns, withdrew to Judaea.

6 [n]King Antiochus, meanwhile, was making his way through the Upper Provinces; he had heard that in Persia there was a city called Elymais, renowned for its riches, its silver and gold, 2 and its very wealthy temple containing golden armour, breastplates and weapons, left there by Alexander son of Philip, the king of Macedon, the first to reign over the Greeks. 3 He therefore went and attempted to take the city and pillage it, but without success, the citizens having been forewarned. 4 They resisted him by force of arms. He was routed, and began retreating, very gloomily, towards Babylon. 5 But, while he was still in Persia, news reached him that the armies which had invaded Judaea had been routed, 6 and that Lysias in particular had advanced in massive strength, only to be forced to turn and flee before the Jews; that the latter were now stronger than ever, thanks to the arms, supplies and abundant spoils acquired from the armies they had cut to pieces, 7 and that they had pulled down the abomination which he had erected on the altar in Jerusalem, had encircled the sanctuary with high walls as in the past, and had fortified Beth-Zur, one of his cities.

8 When the king heard this news he was amazed and profoundly shaken; he threw himself on his bed and fell sick with grief, since things had not turned out for him as he had planned. 9 And there he remained for many days, subject to deep and recurrent fits of melancholy, until he realised that he was dying. 10 Then, summoning all his Friends, he said to them, 'Sleep evades my eyes, and my heart is cowed by anxiety. 11 I have been wondering how I could have come to such a pitch of distress, so great a flood as that which now engulfs me — I who was so generous and well-loved in my heyday. 12 But now I recall how wrongly I acted in Jerusalem when I seized all the vessels of silver and gold there and ordered the extermination of the inhabitants of Judah for no reason at all. 13 This, I am convinced, is why these misfortunes have overtaken me, and why I am dying of melancholy in a foreign land.'

14 He summoned Philip, one of his Friends, and made him regent of the whole kingdom. 15 He entrusted him with his diadem, his robe and his signet, on the understanding that he was to educate his son Antiochus and train him for the throne. 16 King Antiochus then died, in the year 149.

NEW REVISED STANDARD VERSION

17 When Lysias learned that the king was dead, he set up Antiochus the king's[k] son to reign. Lysias[l] had brought him up from boyhood; he named him Eupator.

18 Meanwhile the garrison in the citadel kept hemming Israel in around the sanctuary. They were trying in every way to harm them and strengthen the Gentiles. 19 Judas therefore resolved to destroy them, and assembled all the people to besiege them. 20 They gathered together and besieged the citadel[m] in the one hundred fiftieth year;[n] and he built siege towers and other engines of war. 21 But some of the garrison escaped from the siege and some of the ungodly Israelites joined them. 22 They went to the king and said, "How long will you fail to do justice and to avenge our kindred? 23 We were happy to serve your father, to live by what he said, and to follow his commands. 24 For this reason the sons of our people besieged the citadel[o] and became hostile to us; moreover, they have put to death as many of us as they have caught, and they have seized our inheritances. 25 It is not against us alone that they have stretched out their hands; they have also attacked all the lands on their borders. 26 And see, today they have encamped against the citadel in Jerusalem to take it; they have fortified both the sanctuary and Beth-zur; 27 unless you quickly prevent them, they will do still greater things, and you will not be able to stop them."

28 The king was enraged when he heard this. He assembled all his Friends, the commanders of his forces and those in authority.[p] 29 Mercenary forces also came to him from other kingdoms and from islands of the seas. 30 The number of his forces was one hundred thousand foot soldiers, twenty thousand horsemen, and thirty-two elephants accustomed to war. 31 They came through Idumea and encamped against Beth-zur, and for many days they fought and built engines of war; but the Jews[q] sallied out and burned these with fire, and fought courageously.

32 Then Judas marched away from the citadel and encamped at Beth-zechariah, opposite the camp of the king. 33 Early in the morning the king set out and took his army by a forced march along the road to Beth-zechariah, and his troops made ready for battle and sounded their trumpets. 34 They offered the elephants the juice of grapes and mulberries, to arouse them for battle. 35 They distributed the animals among the phalanxes; with each elephant they stationed a thousand men armed with coats of mail, and with brass helmets on their heads; and five hundred picked horsemen were assigned to each beast. 36 These took their position beforehand wherever the animal was; wherever it went, they went with it, and they never left it. 37 On the elephants[r] were wooden towers, strong and covered; they were fastened on each animal by special harness, and on each were four[s] armed men who fought from there, and also its Indian driver. 38 The rest of the cavalry were stationed on either side, on the two flanks of the army, to harass the enemy while being themselves protected by the phalanxes. 39 When the sun shone on the shields of gold and brass, the hills were ablaze with them and gleamed like flaming torches.

40 Now a part of the king's army was spread out on the high hills, and some troops were on the plain, and they advanced steadily and in good order. 41 All who heard the noise made by their multitude, by the marching of the multitude and the clanking of their arms, trembled, for the army was very large and strong. 42 But Judas and his army advanced to the battle, and six hundred of the king's army fell.

REVISED ENGLISH BIBLE

17 When Lysias learnt that the king was dead, he placed on the throne in succession to his father the young Antiochus, whom he had trained from boyhood, and he gave him the name Eupator.

18 MEANWHILE the garrison of the citadel was confining the Israelites to the neighbourhood of the temple, and, by harassing tactics, giving continual support to the Gentiles. 19 Judas determined to make an end of them; he gathered all the people together to lay siege to the citadel 20 in the year 150, erecting emplacements and siege-engines against the enemy.

21 But some of the beleaguered garrison escaped and were joined by a number of apostate Israelites. 22 They went to the king and complained: 'How long must we wait for you to support our cause and avenge our comrades? 23 We were happy to serve your father, to follow his instructions and obey his decrees. 24 And what was the result? Our own countrymen turned against us; indeed they put to death as many of us as they could lay hold of, and they robbed us of our property. 25 Nor are we the only ones to suffer at their hands; they have attacked all the neighbouring lands as well. 26 At this very moment the citadel in Jerusalem is closely invested, and they are intent on its capture. They have also fortified both the temple and Bethsura. 27 Unless your majesty quickly takes the initiative against them they will go to yet greater lengths. There will be no stopping them!'

28 The king became furious as he listened. He assembled all his Friends, his generals, and cavalry commanders, 29 and he was joined by mercenary troops from other kingdoms and from overseas. 30 His forces numbered one hundred thousand infantry, twenty thousand cavalry, and thirty-two war elephants. 31 They advanced through Idumaea and laid siege to Bethsura, keeping up the attack for many days. They erected siege-engines, but the defenders, fighting back manfully, made a sortie and set them on fire.

32 Judas now withdrew from the citadel and took up his position at Bethzacharia facing towards the royal encampment. 33 Early next morning the king broke camp and after a forced march along the Bethzacharia road he drew up his army in battle order and the trumpets were sounded. 34 The elephants were roused for combat with the blood of grapes and of mulberries. 35 The great beasts were distributed among the phalanxes; by each were stationed a thousand men, equipped with coats of chain-mail and bronze helmets. Five hundred picked horsemen were also assigned to each animal; 36 they were stationed beforehand where the beast was, and wherever it went, they went also, never leaving its side. 37 Each animal had, by way of protection, a strong wooden turret fastened on its back with a special harness, and carried four fighting men as well as an Indian driver. 38 The rest of his cavalry Lysias stationed on either flank of the army, to harass the enemy while themselves protected by the phalanxes. 39 When the sun shone on the gold and bronze shields, the hills gleamed and flashed like blazing torches.

40 Part of the king's army was deployed over the heights, and part over the low ground. They advanced steadily and in good order, 41 and trembling seized all who heard the din and clash of arms of this multitude on the march, for it was indeed a very great and powerful force.

42 Judas drew near with his army and gave battle, and six hundred of the king's men were killed. 43 Eleazar Avaran

---

[k] Gk his   [l] Gk He   [m] Gk it   [n] 162 B.C.   [o] Meaning of Gk uncertain   [p] Gk those over the reins   [q] Gk they   [r] Gk them   [s] Cn: Some authorities read thirty; others thirty-two

6:20 150: that is 162 B.C.E.   6:37 four: prob. rdg; Gk thirty-two.

17 When Lysias learned that the king was dead, he set up the king's son Antiochus, whom he had reared as a child, to be king in his place; and he gave him the title Eupator. 18 The men in the citadel were hemming in Israel around the sanctuary, continually trying to harm them and to strengthen the Gentiles. 19 But Judas planned to destroy them, and called all the people together to besiege them. 20 So in the year one hundred and fifty they assembled and stormed the citadel, for which purpose he constructed catapults and other devices. 21 Some of the besieged escaped, joined by impious Israelites; 22 they went to the king and said:

"How long will you fail to do justice and avenge our kinsmen? 23 We agreed to serve your father and to follow his orders and obey his edicts. 24 And for this the sons of our people have become our enemies; they have put to death as many of us as they could find and have plundered our estates. 25 They have acted aggressively not only against us, but throughout their whole territory. 26 Look! They have now besieged the citadel in Jerusalem in order to capture it, and they have fortified the sanctuary and Beth-zur. 27 Unless you quickly forestall them, they will do even worse things than these, and you will not be able to stop them."

28 When the king heard this he was angry, and he called together all his Friends, the officers of his army, and the commanders of the cavalry. 29 Mercenary forces also came to him from other kingdoms and from the islands of the seas. 30 His army numbered a hundred thousand foot-soldiers, twenty thousand cavalry, and thirty-two elephants trained for war. 31 They passed through Idumea and camped before Beth-zur. For many days they attacked it; they constructed siege-devices, but the besieged made a sortie and burned these, and they fought bravely. 32 Then Judas marched away from the citadel and moved his camp to Beth-zechariah, on the way to the king's camp. 33 The king, rising before dawn, moved his force hastily along the road to Beth-zechariah; and the armies prepared for battle, while the trumpets sounded. 34 They made the elephants drunk on grape and mulberry wine to provoke them to fight. 35 The beasts were distributed along the phalanxes, each elephant having assigned to it a thousand men in coats of mail, with bronze helmets, and five hundred picked cavalry. 36 These anticipated the beast wherever it was; and wherever it moved, they moved too and never left it. 37 A strong wooden tower covering each elephant, and fastened to it by a harness, held, besides the Indian mahout, three soldiers who fought from it. 38 The remaining cavalry were stationed on one or the other of the two flanks of the army, to harass the enemy and to be protected from the phalanxes. 39 When the sun shone on the gold and bronze shields, the mountains gleamed with their brightness and blazed like flaming torches. 40 Part of the king's army extended over the heights, while some were on low ground, but they marched forward steadily and in good order. 41 All who heard the noise of their numbers, the tramp of their marching, and the clashing of the arms, trembled; for the army was very great and strong.

42 Judas with his army advanced to fight, and six hundred men of the king's army fell. 43 Eleazar, called Avaran, saw

17 Lysias, learning that the king was dead, established on the throne in succession to him his son Antiochus, whom he had brought up from childhood — and styled him Eupator. 18 The people in the Citadel at the time were blockading Israel round the sanctuary and were taking every opportunity to harm them and to support the gentiles. 19 Judas decided that they must be destroyed, and he mobilised the whole people to besiege them. 20 They assembled and laid siege to the Citadel in the year 150, building batteries and siege-engines. 21 But some of the besieged broke through the blockade, and to these a number of renegades from Israel attached themselves. 22 They made their way to the king and said, 'How much longer are you going to wait before you see justice done and avenge our fellows? 23 We were content to serve your father, to comply with his orders, and to obey his edicts. 24 As a result our own people will have nothing to do with us; what is more, they have killed all those of us they could catch, and looted our family property. 25 Nor is it on us alone that their blows have fallen, but on all your territories. 26 At this moment, they are laying siege to the Citadel of Jerusalem, to capture it, and they have fortified the sanctuary and Beth-zur. 27 Unless you forestall them at once, they will go on to even bigger things, and then you will never be able to control them.'

28 The king was furious when he heard this and summoned all his Friends, the generals of his forces and the marshals of horse. 29 He recruited mercenaries from other kingdoms and the Mediterranean islands. 30 His forces numbered a hundred thousand foot soldiers, twenty thousand cavalry and thirty-two elephants with experience of battle conditions. 31 They advanced through Idumaea and besieged Beth-Zur, pressing the attack for days on end; they also constructed siege-engines, but the defenders made a sortie and set these on fire, putting up a brave resistance. 32 At this, Judas left the Citadel and pitched camp at Beth-Zechariah opposite the royal encampment. 33 The king rose at daybreak and marched his army at top speed down the road to Beth-Zechariah, where his forces took up their battle formations and sounded the trumpets. 34 The elephants were given a syrup of grapes and mulberries to prepare them for the battle. 35 These animals were distributed among the phalanxes, to each elephant being allocated a thousand men dressed in coats of mail with bronze helmets on their heads; five hundred picked horsemen were also assigned to each beast. 36 The horsemen anticipated every move their elephant made; wherever it went they went with it, never quitting it. 37 On each elephant, to protect it, was a stout wooden tower, kept in position by girths, each with its three combatants, as well as its mahout. 38 The remainder of the cavalry was stationed on one or other of the two flanks of the army, to harass the enemy and cover the phalanxes. 39 When the sun glinted on the bronze and golden shields, the mountains caught the glint and gleamed like fiery torches. 40 One part of the royal army was deployed on the upper slopes of the mountain and the other in the valley below; they advanced in solid, well-disciplined formation. 41 Everyone trembled at the noise made by this vast multitude, the thunder of the troops on the march and the clanking of their armour, for it was an immense and mighty army. 42 Judas and his army advanced to give battle, and six hundred of the king's army were killed. 43 Eleazar, called

43 Now Eleazar, called Avaran, saw that one of the animals was equipped with royal armor. It was taller than all the others, and he supposed that the king was on it. 44 So he gave his life to save his people and to win for himself an everlasting name. 45 He courageously ran into the midst of the phalanx to reach it; he killed men right and left, and they parted before him on both sides. 46 He got under the elephant, stabbed it from beneath, and killed it; but it fell to the ground upon him and he died. 47 When the Jews⟨ saw the royal might and the fierce attack of the forces, they turned away in flight.

48 The soldiers of the king's army went up to Jerusalem against them, and the king encamped in Judea and at Mount Zion. 49 He made peace with the people of Beth-zur, and they evacuated the town because they had no provisions there to withstand a siege, since it was a sabbatical year for the land. 50 So the king took Beth-zur and stationed a guard there to hold it. 51 Then he encamped before the sanctuary for many days. He set up siege towers, engines of war to throw fire and stones, machines to shoot arrows, and catapults. 52 The Jews⟨ also made engines of war to match theirs, and fought for many days. 53 But they had no food in storage,⟨u⟩ because it was the seventh year; those who had found safety in Judea from the Gentiles had consumed the last of the stores. 54 Only a few men were left in the sanctuary; the rest scattered to their own homes, for the famine proved too much for them.

55 Then Lysias heard that Philip, whom King Antiochus while still living had appointed to bring up his son Antiochus to be king, 56 had returned from Persia and Media with the forces that had gone with the king, and that he was trying to seize control of the government. 57 So he quickly gave orders to withdraw, and said to the king, to the commanders of the forces, and to the troops, men, "Daily we grow weaker, our food supply is scant, the place against which we are fighting is strong, and the affairs of the kingdom press urgently on us. 58 Now then let us come to terms with these people, and make peace with them and with all their nation. 59 Let us agree to let them live by their laws as they did before; for it was on account of their laws that we abolished that they became angry and did all these things."

60 The speech pleased the king and the commanders, and he sent to the Jews⟨v⟩ an offer of peace, and they accepted it. 61 So the king and the commanders gave them their oath. On these conditions the Jews⟨ evacuated the stronghold. 62 But when the king entered Mount Zion and saw what a strong fortress the place was, he broke the oath he had sworn and gave orders to tear down the wall all around. 63 Then he set off in haste and returned to Antioch. He found Philip in control of the city, but he fought against him, and took the city by force.

7 In the one hundred fifty-first year⟨w⟩ Demetrius son of Seleucus set out from Rome, sailed with a few men to a town by the sea, and there began to reign. 2 As he was entering the royal palace of his ancestors, the army seized Antiochus and Lysias to bring them to him. 3 But when this act became known to him, he said, "Do not let me see their faces!" 4 So the army killed them, and Demetrius took his seat on the throne of his kingdom.

5 Then there came to him all the renegade and godless men of Israel; they were led by Alcimus, who wanted to be high priest. 6 They brought to the king this accusation against the people: "Judas and his brothers have destroyed all your Friends, and have driven us out of our land. 7 Now

saw that one of the elephants wore royal armour and stood out above all the rest, and, thinking that the king must be on it, 44 he gave his life to save his people and win for himself everlasting renown. 45 He ran boldly towards it, into the middle of the phalanx, dealing death right and left, so that the enemy fell back on either side before him. 46 He got in underneath the elephant, thrust at it from below, and killed it. It sank to the ground on top of him, crushing him to death. 47 When the Jews saw the strength and impetus of the royal forces, they gave ground before them.

48 A part of the royal army marched up to Jerusalem to renew the engagement, and the king encamped against Judaea and Mount Zion. 49 He came to terms with the people of Bethsura, who abandoned the town, not having the food to withstand a siege, as it was a sabbatical year when the land was left fallow. 50 So Bethsura was occupied by the king, who detailed a garrison to hold it.

51 He then subjected the temple to a lengthy siege; he set up emplacements and siege-engines, with flamethrowers, catapults for discharging stones and barbed missiles, and slings. 52 The defenders for their part constructed engines to counter his engines, and put up a prolonged resistance. 53 But there was no food in the storerooms because it was the sabbatical year; those who from time to time had arrived in Judaea as refugees from the Gentiles had consumed all that remained of the provisions. 54 The shortage had been so severe that men had dispersed to their homes, leaving only a few in the temple.

55 Lysias heard that Philip, whom King Antiochus, before he died, had appointed to bring up his son Antiochus and train him for the throne, 56 had now returned from Persia and Media with the late king's expeditionary force and was seeking to take over the government. 57 Hastily he gave orders for departure, saying to the king and to the army officers and men: 'Every day we grow weaker, our provisions are running low, the place we are besieging is strong, and the affairs of the empire are pressing. 58 Let us now offer these men terms, and make peace with them and with their whole nation. 59 Let us guarantee them the right to follow their laws and customs as they used to do, for it was our abolition of these laws and customs that roused their resentment and led to all the troubles.'

60 The proposal having met with approval from both king and commanders, an offer of peace was sent and accepted. 61 The king and his commanders bound themselves by oath, and on the terms agreed the defenders emerged from their stronghold. 62 But when the king entered Mount Zion and saw how strongly the place was fortified, he went back on his oath, and ordered the demolition of the surrounding wall. 63 Then with all speed he departed for Antioch, where he found Philip in possession. In the ensuing battle Antiochus took the city by storm.

7 IN the year 151, Demetrius son of Seleucus left Rome and, landing with a handful of men at a town on the coast, there made himself king. 2 While he was on his way to the palace of his ancestors, the army placed Antiochus and Lysias under arrest, with a view to handing them over to him. 3 But when he was informed of their action, he said, 'Do not let me set eyes on them.' 4 The soldiers accordingly put them to death, and Demetrius ascended the throne of his kingdom.

5 All the apostates and renegades from Israel, led by Alcimus, who aspired to the high-priesthood, came to the king 6 with charges against their people. 'Judas and his brothers have wiped out everybody who supported you and have driven us from our country,' they said. 7 'Be pleased now to

---

⟨t⟩ Gk they   ⟨u⟩ Other ancient authorities read in the sanctuary
⟨v⟩ Gk them   ⟨w⟩ 161 B.C.

6:53 in the storerooms: some witnesses read in the temple.
7:1 151: that is 161 B.C.E.

one of the beasts bigger than any of the others and covered with royal armor, and he thought the king must be on it. 44 So he gave up his life to save his people and win an everlasting name for himself. 45 He dashed up to it in the middle of the phalanx, killing men right and left, so that they fell back from him on both sides. 46 He ran right under the elephant and stabbed it in the belly, killing it. The beast fell to the ground on top of him, and he died there.

47 When the Jews saw the strength of the royal army and the ardor of its forces, they retreated from them. 48 A part of the king's army went up to Jerusalem to attack them, and the king established camps in Judea and at Mount Zion. 49 He made peace with the men of Beth-zur, and they evacuated the city, because they had no food there to enable them to stand a siege, for that was a sabbath year in the land. 50 The king took Beth-zur and stationed a garrison there to hold it. 51 For many days he besieged the sanctuary, setting up artillery and machines, fire-throwers, catapults and mechanical bows for shooting arrows and slingstones. 52 The Jews countered by setting up machines of their own, and kept up the fight a long time. 53 But there were no provisions in the storerooms, because it was the seventh year, and the tide-over provisions had been eaten up by those who had been rescued from the Gentiles and brought to Judea. 54 Few men remained in the sanctuary; the rest scattered, each to his own home, for the famine was too much for them.

55 Lysias heard that Philip, whom King Antiochus, before his death, had appointed to train his son Antiochus to be king, 56 had returned from Persia and Media with the army that accompanied the king, and that he was seeking to take over the government. 57 So he hastily resolved to withdraw. He said to the king, the leaders of the army, and the soldiers: "We are growing weaker every day, our provisions are scanty, the place we are besieging is strong, and it is our duty to take care of the affairs of the kingdom. 58 Therefore let us now come to terms with these men, and make peace with them and all their nation. 59 Let us grant them freedom to live according to their own laws as formerly; it was on account of their laws, which we abolished, that they became angry and did all these things."

60 The proposal found favor with the king and the leaders; he sent peace terms to the Jews, and they accepted. 61 So the king and the leaders swore an oath to them, and on these terms they evacuated the fortification. 62 But when the king entered Mount Zion and saw how the place was fortified, he broke the oath he had sworn and gave orders for the encircling wall to be destroyed. 63 Then he departed in haste and returned to Antioch, where he found Philip in possession of the city. He fought against him and took the city by force.

7 In the year one hundred and fifty-one, Demetrius, son of Seleucus, set out from Rome, arrived with a few men in a city on the seacoast, and began to rule there. 2 As he was preparing to enter the royal palace of his ancestors, the soldiers seized Antiochus and Lysias to bring them to him. 3 When he was informed of this, he said, "Do not show me their faces." 4 So the soldiers killed them, and Demetrius sat on the royal throne.

5 Then all the lawless and impious men of Israel came to him. They were led by Alcimus, who desired to be high priest. 6 They made this accusation to the king against the people: "Judas and his brothers have destroyed all your friends and have driven us out of our country. 7 So now,

Avaran, noticing that one of the elephants was royally caparisoned and was also taller than all the others, and supposing that the king was mounted on it, 44 sacrificed himself to save his people and win an imperishable name. 45 Boldly charging towards the creature through the thick of the phalanx, dealing death to right and left, so that the enemy scattered on either side at his onslaught, 46 he darted in under the elephant, thrust at it from underneath, and killed it. The beast collapsed on top of him, and he died on the spot. 47 The Jews however realising how strong the king was and how ferocious his army, retreated ahead of them.

48 The royal army moved up to encounter them outside Jerusalem, and the king began to blockade Judaea and Mount Zion. 49 He granted peace terms to the people of Beth-Zur, who evacuated the town; it lacked store of provisions to withstand a siege, since the land was enjoying a sabbatical year. 50 Having occupied Beth-Zur, the king stationed a garrison there to hold it. 51 He besieged the sanctuary for a long time, erecting batteries and siege-engines, flame-throwers and ballistas, scorpions to discharge arrows, and catapults. 52 The defenders countered these by constructing their own engines and were thus able to prolong their resistance. 53 But they had no food in their stores since it was the seventh year, and because those who had taken refuge in Judaea from the gentiles had eaten up the last of their reserves. 54 Only a few men were left in the Holy Place, owing to the severity of the famine; the rest had dispersed and gone home.

55 Meanwhile Philip, whom King Antiochus before his death had appointed to train his son Antiochus for the throne, 56 had returned from Persia and Media with the forces that had accompanied the king, and was planning to seize control of affairs. 57 On hearing this, Lysias at once decided to leave,o and said to the king, the generals of the army and the men, 'We are growing weaker every day, we are short of food, and the place we are besieging is well fortified; moreover the affairs of the kingdom demand our attention. 58 Let us offer the hand of friendship to these men and make peace with them and with their whole nation. 59 Let us grant them permission to follow their own customs as before, since it is our abolition of these customs that has provoked them into acting like this.' 60 The king and his commanders approved this argument, and he offered the Jews peace terms, which they accepted. 61 The king and the generals ratified the treaty by oath, and the besieged accordingly left the fortress. 62 The king then entered Mount Zion, but on seeing how impregnable the place was, he broke the oath he had sworn and gave orders for the encircling wall to be demolished. 63 He then hurriedly withdrew, making off for Antioch, where he found Philip already master of the city. Antiochus gave battle and captured the city by force of arms.

7 pIn the year 151, Demetrius son of Seleucus left Rome and arrived with a few men at a town on the coast, where he inaugurated his reign. 2 It so happened that, as he was entering the royal residence of his ancestors, the army captured Antiochus and Lysias, and intended to bring them to him. 3 On hearing this, he said, 'Keep them out of my sight.' 4 The army put them to death, and Demetrius ascended his throne. 5 Next, all those Israelites without law or piety, led by Alcimus, whose ambition was to become high priest, 6 approached the king and denounced our people to him. 'Judas and his brothers', they said, 'have killed all your friends, and he has driven us out of our country. 7 Send

then send a man whom you trust; let him go and see all the ruin that Judas^x has brought on us and on the land of the king, and let him punish them and all who help them." 8 So the king chose Bacchides, one of the king's Friends, governor of the province Beyond the River; he was a great man in the kingdom and was faithful to the king. 9 He sent him, and with him he sent the ungodly Alcimus, whom he made high priest; and he commanded him to take vengeance on the Israelites. 10 So they marched away and came with a large force into the land of Judah; and he sent messengers to Judas and his brothers with peaceable but treacherous words. 11 But they paid no attention to their words, for they saw that they had come with a large force.

12 Then a group of scribes appeared in a body before Alcimus and Bacchides to ask for just terms. 13 The Hasideans were first among the Israelites to seek peace from them, 14 for they said, "A priest of the line of Aaron has come with the army, and he will not harm us." 15 Alcimus^y spoke peaceable words to them and swore this oath to them, "We will not seek to injure you or your Friends." 16 So they trusted him; but he seized sixty of them and killed them in one day, in accordance with the word that was written,

17   "The flesh of your faithful ones and their blood
      they poured out all around Jerusalem,
    and there was no one to bury them."

18 Then the fear and dread of them fell on all the people, for they said, "There is no truth or justice in them, for they have violated the agreement and the oath that they swore."

19 Then Bacchides withdrew from Jerusalem and encamped in Beth-zaith. And he sent and seized many of the men who had deserted to him,^{z} and some of the people, and killed them and threw them into a great pit. 20 He placed Alcimus in charge of the country and left with him a force to help him; then Bacchides went back to the king.

21 Alcimus struggled to maintain his high priesthood, 22 and all who were troubling their people joined him. They gained control of the land of Judah and did great damage in Israel. 23 And Judas saw all the wrongs that Alcimus and those with him had done among the Israelites; it was more than the Gentiles had done. 24 So Judas^x went out into all the surrounding parts of Judea, taking vengeance on those who had deserted and preventing those in the city^a from going out into the country. 25 When Alcimus saw that Judas and those with him had grown strong, and realized that he could not withstand them, he returned to the king and brought malicious charges against them.

26 Then the king sent Nicanor, one of his honored princes, who hated and detested Israel, and commanded him to destroy the people. 27 So Nicanor came to Jerusalem with a large force, and treacherously sent to Judas and his brothers this peaceable message, 28 "Let there be no fighting between you and me; I shall come with a few men to see you face to face in peace."

29 So he came to Judas, and they greeted one another peaceably; but the enemy were preparing to kidnap Judas. 30 It became known to Judas that Nicanor^x had come to him with treacherous intent, and he was afraid of him and would not meet him again. 31 When Nicanor learned that his plan had been disclosed, he went out to meet Judas in battle near Caphar-salama. 32 About five hundred of the army of Nicanor fell, and the rest^b fled into the city of David.

33 After these events Nicanor went up to Mount Zion. Some of the priests from the sanctuary and some of the elders of the people came out to greet him peaceably and to show him the burnt offering that was being offered for the king. 34 But he mocked them and derided them and defiled them and spoke arrogantly, 35 and in anger he swore this

send a man you trust, to go and see what devastation they have brought on us and on the king's territory, and to punish them along with all who aid and abet them.' 8 The king chose one of the royal Friends, Bacchides, who was governor of the province of Beyond-Euphrates, a man of high standing in the empire and loyal to the king; 9 he and Alcimus the apostate, on whom the king had conferred the high-priesthood, were sent with orders to wreak vengeance on Israel. 10 They set out and marched on Judaea with a large force. There Bacchides sent envoys with false offers of friendship, 11 but when Judas and his brothers saw how large an army had come they disregarded those offers.

12 A deputation of doctors of the law appeared before Alcimus and Bacchides, to ask for a just settlement. 13 The Hasidaeans were the first group in Israel to make overtures, 14 for they said, 'A priest of the family of Aaron is come with their forces, and he will not treat us unjustly.' 15 The language of Alcimus was conciliatory; he assured them on oath that no harm was intended to them or to their friends. 16 But once he had gained their confidence, he arrested sixty of them and put them to death all on one day. As scripture says:

17   The bodies of your saints were scattered;
    all round Jerusalem their blood was shed,
    and there was none to give them burial.

18 Fear and dread fell on the whole people. 'There is neither truth nor justice among them,' they said to one another; 'they have broken their agreement and the oath they swore.'

19 Bacchides then left Jerusalem and encamped in Beth-zaith, where he issued orders for the arrest of many of those who had deserted to him, together with some of the people, and had them slaughtered and thrown into a great cistern. 20 He assigned the whole district to Alcimus and detailed troops to assist him, while he himself went back to the king. 21 Alcimus put up a strong fight for his high-priesthood, 22 and all the trouble-makers rallied to him. They gained control over Judaea and inflicted great damage on Israel. 23 When Judas saw the extent of the havoc which Alcimus and his followers had wrought among the Israelites, far worse than anything done by the Gentiles, 24 he went throughout the territory of Judaea and its environs, punishing deserters and debarring them from access to the country districts. 25 Judging that Judas and his supporters had grown too powerful for him to withstand, Alcimus returned to the king and accused them of atrocities.

26 Then the king dispatched Nicanor, one of his most distinguished commanders and a bitter enemy of Israel, with orders to wipe out that people. 27 Nicanor arrived at Jerusalem with a large force and sent envoys to Judas and his brothers with false offers of friendship: 28 'Let there be no quarrel between us,' he said; 'I propose to come with only a small escort to meet you as a friend.'

29 When he came, they greeted one another in friendly fashion, yet the enemy were preparing to kidnap Judas. 30 That Nicanor's visit involved duplicity became known to Judas, and taking alarm he refused to meet him again. 31 Realizing that his plot had been detected, Nicanor marched out to engage Judas near Capharsalama. 32 About five hundred of Nicanor's men were killed; the rest made good their escape to the City of David.

33 After those events, Nicanor went up to Mount Zion, where some of the priests and members of the senate came out from the holy place to extend a friendly welcome to him, and to show him the whole-offering which was being sacrificed for the king. 34 But he mocked and jeered at them and polluted them with his spittle, talking arrogantly 35 and

---

^{x} Gk he ^{y} Gk He ^{z} Or many of his men who had deserted
^{a} Gk and they were prevented ^{b} Gk they

send a man whom you trust to go and see all the havoc Judas has done to us and to the king's land, and let him punish them and all their supporters."

8 Then the king chose Bacchides, one of the King's Friends, governor of West-of-Euphrates, a great man in the kingdom, and faithful to the king. 9 He sent him and the impious Alcimus, to whom he granted the high priesthood, with orders to take revenge on the Israelites. 10 They set out and, on arriving in the land of Judah with a great army, sent messengers who spoke deceitfully to Judas and his brothers in peaceful terms. 11 But these paid no attention to their words, seeing that they had come with a great army. 12 A group of scribes, however, gathered about Alcimus and Bacchides to ask for a just agreement. 13 The Hasideans were the first among the Israelites to seek peace with them, 14 for they said, "A priest of the line of Aaron has come with the army, and he will not do us any wrong." 15 He spoke with them peacefully and swore to them, "We will not try to injure you or your friends." 16 So they trusted him. But he arrested sixty of them and killed them in one day, according to the text of Scripture:

17 "The flesh of your saints they have strewn,
and their blood they have shed round
about Jerusalem,
and there was no one to bury them.

18 Then fear and dread of them came upon all the people, who said: "There is no truth or justice among them; they violated the agreement and the oath that they swore."

19 Bacchides withdrew from Jerusalem and pitched his camp in Beth-zaith. He had many of the men arrested who deserted to him, throwing them into the great pit. 20 He handed the province over to Alcimus, leaving troops to help him, while he himself returned to the king.

21 Alcimus spared no pains to maintain his high priesthood, 22 and all those who were disturbing their people gathered about him. They took possession of the land of Judah and caused great distress in Israel. 23 When Judas saw all the evils that Alcimus and his men were bringing upon the Israelites, more than even the Gentiles had done, 24 he went about all the borders of Judea and took revenge on the men who had deserted, preventing them from going out into the country. 25 But when Alcimus saw that Judas and his followers were gaining strength and realized that he could not oppose them, he returned to the king and accused them of grave crimes.

26 Then the king sent Nicanor, one of his famous officers, who was a bitter enemy of Israel, with orders to destroy the people. 27 Nicanor came to Jerusalem with a large force and deceitfully sent to Judas and his brothers this peaceable message: 28 "Let there be no fight between me and you. I will come with a few men to meet you peaceably."

29 So he came to Judas, and they greeted one another peaceably. But Judas' enemies were prepared to seize him. 30 When he became aware that Nicanor had come to him with treachery in mind, Judas was afraid and would not meet him again. 31 When Nicanor saw that his plan had been discovered, he went out to fight Judas near Caphar-salama. 32 About five hundred men of Nicanor's army fell; the rest fled to the City of David.

33 After this, Nicanor went up to Mount Zion. Some of the priests from the sanctuary and some of the elders of the people came out to greet him peaceably and to show him the holocaust that was being offered for the king. 34 But he mocked and ridiculed them, defiled them, and spoke dis-

someone now whom you can trust; let him go and see the wholesale ruin Judas has brought on us and on the king's dominions, and let him punish the wretches and all who assist them.'

8 The king chose Bacchides, one of the Friends of the King, governor of Transeuphrates, an important personage in the kingdom and loyal to the king. 9 He sent him with the godless Alcimus, whom he confirmed in the high priesthood, with orders to exact retribution from the Israelites. 10 So they set out with a large force and, on reaching Judaea, sent emissaries to Judas and his brothers with proposals peaceable yet treacherous. 11 The latter, however, did not put any faith in their words, aware that they had come with a large force. 12 Nevertheless, a commission of scribes presented themselves before Alcimus and Bacchides, to sue for just terms. 13 The first among the Israelites to ask them for peace terms were the Hasidaeans, 14 who reasoned thus, 'This is a priest of Aaron's line who has come with the armed forces; he will not wrong us.' 15 He did in fact discuss peace terms with them and gave them his oath, 'We shall not attempt to injure you or your friends.' 16 They believed him, but he arrested sixty of them and put them to death on one day, fulfilling the words of scripture: 17 They have scattered the bodies of your faithful, and shed their blood all round Jerusalem, leaving no one to bury them!q

18 At this, fear and dread gripped the whole people. 'There is no truth or virtue in them,' they said, 'they have broken their agreement and their sworn oath.'

19 Bacchides then left Jerusalem and encamped at Beth-Zeth, and from there sent and arrested many of the men who had deserted him and a few of our people too; he had them killed and thrown down the great well. 20 He then put Alcimus in charge of the province, leaving an army with him to support him; Bacchides himself returned to the king. 21 Alcimus continued his struggle to become high priest, 22 and all who were disturbing the peace of their own people rallied to him, and, having won control of Judaea, did much harm in Israel. 23 Seeing that all the wrongs done to the Israelites by Alcimus and his supporters exceeded what the gentiles had done, 24 Judas went right round the whole territory of Judaea to take vengeance on those who had deserted him and to prevent their free movement about the country.

25 When Alcimus saw how strong Judas and his supporters had grown and realised that he was powerless to resist them, he went back to the king, to whom he made malicious accusations against them. 26 The king sent Nicanor, one of his generals ranking as Illustrious and a bitter enemy of Israel, with orders to exterminate the people. 27 Reaching Jerusalem with a large force, Nicanor sent a friendly, yet treacherous, message to Judas and his brothers, as follows: 28 'Let us have no fighting between you and me; I shall come with a small escort for a peaceful meeting with you.' 29 He met Judas and they exchanged friendly greetings; the enemy, however, had made preparations to abduct Judas. 30 When Judas became aware of Nicanor's treacherous purpose in coming to see him, he took fright and refused any further meeting. 31 Nicanor then realised that his plan had been discovered, and took the field against Judas, to give battle near Caphar-Salama. 32 About five hundred of Nicanor's men fell; the rest took refuge in the City of David.

33 After these events Nicanor went up to Mount Zion. Some of the priests came out of the Holy Place with some elders, to give him a friendly welcome and show him the burnt offering being presented for the king. 34 But he ridiculed them, laughed at them, defiled them and used insolent

oath, "Unless Judas and his army are delivered into my hands this time, then if I return safely I will burn up this house." And he went out in great anger. ³⁶ At this the priests went in and stood before the altar and the temple; they wept and said,

³⁷ "You chose this house to be called by your name,
   and to be for your people a house of prayer
      and supplication.
³⁸ Take vengeance on this man and on his army,
      and let them fall by the sword;
   remember their blasphemies,
      and let them live no longer."

39 Now Nicanor went out from Jerusalem and encamped in Beth-horon, and the Syrian army joined him. ⁴⁰ Judas encamped in Adasa with three thousand men. Then Judas prayed and said, ⁴¹ "When the messengers from the king spoke blasphemy, your angel went out and struck down one hundred eighty-five thousand of the Assyrians.ᶜ ⁴² So also crush this army before us today; let the rest learn that Nicanorᵈ has spoken wickedly against the sanctuary, and judge him according to this wickedness."

43 So the armies met in battle on the thirteenth day of the month of Adar. The army of Nicanor was crushed, and he himself was the first to fall in the battle. ⁴⁴ When his army saw that Nicanor had fallen, they threw down their arms and fled. ⁴⁵ The Jewsᵉ pursued them a day's journey, from Adasa as far as Gazara, and as they followed they kept sounding the battle call on the trumpets. ⁴⁶ People came out of all the surrounding villages of Judea, and they outflanked the enemyᶠ and drove them back to their pursuers,ᵍ so that they all fell by the sword; not even one of them was left. ⁴⁷ Then the Jewsᵉ seized the spoils and the plunder; they cut off Nicanor's head and the right hand that he had so arrogantly stretched out, and brought them and displayed them just outside Jerusalem. ⁴⁸ The people rejoiced greatly and celebrated that day as a day of great gladness. ⁴⁹ They decreed that this day should be celebrated each year on the thirteenth day of Adar. ⁵⁰ So the land of Judah had rest for a few days.

8 Now Judas heard of the fame of the Romans, that they were very strong and were well-disposed toward all who made an alliance with them, that they pledged friendship to those who came to them, ² and that they were very strong. He had been told of their wars and of the brave deeds that they were doing among the Gauls, how they had defeated them and forced them to pay tribute, ³ and what they had done in the land of Spain to get control of the silver and gold mines there, ⁴ and how they had gained control of the whole region by their planning and patience, even though the place was far distant from them. They also subdued the kings who came against them from the ends of the earth, until they crushed them and inflicted great disaster on them; the rest paid them tribute every year. ⁵ They had crushed in battle and conquered Philip, and King Perseus of the Macedonians,ʰ and the others who rose up against them. ⁶ They also had defeated Antiochus the Great, king of Asia, who went to fight against them with one hundred twenty elephants and with cavalry and chariots and a very large army. He was crushed by them; ⁷ they took him alive and decreed that he and those who would reign after him should pay a heavy tribute and give hostages and surrender some of their best provinces, ⁸ the countries of India, Media, and Lydia. These they took from him and gave to King Eumenes. ⁹ The Greeks planned to come and destroy them,

vowing in anger: 'Unless Judas and his army are turned over to me at once, I shall burn down this house when I return victorious.' And he departed in a rage. ³⁶ The priests went in again and stood in tears, facing the altar and the temple, and said, ³⁷ 'Lord, you chose this house to bear your name, to be a house of prayer and supplication for your people; ³⁸ take vengeance on this man and his army, and let them perish by the sword. Let their blasphemy not be forgotten; grant them no reprieve.'

³⁹ Nicanor moved from Jerusalem and set up his camp at Beth-horon, where he was joined by an army from Syria. ⁴⁰ Meanwhile Judas, encamping at Adasa with three thousand men, uttered this prayer: ⁴¹ 'When the followers of a certain king were guilty of blasphemy, your angel came forth and struck down one hundred and eighty-five thousand of them. ⁴² In the same way crush this army before us today. Let generations to come know that Nicanor has reviled your holy place; judge him as his wickedness deserves.'

⁴³ Battle was joined on the thirteenth of the month of Adar, and Nicanor's forces suffered a crushing defeat, he himself being the first to fall in the fighting. ⁴⁴ Seeing Nicanor fall, his men threw away their arms and fled. ⁴⁵ The Jews, with their trumpets sounding a signal behind the fleeing enemy, pursued them as far as Gazara, a day's journey from Adasa. ⁴⁶ From every Judaean village round about, the inhabitants came out and, attacking the fugitives on the flanks, forced them back upon their pursuers, so that they all fell by the sword; not one of them survived. ⁴⁷ The Jews gathered up the weapons of the slain and other spoils of war; they cut off Nicanor's head and that right hand he had stretched out so arrogantly, and brought them to be displayed at Jerusalem. ⁴⁸ There was great public rejoicing, and that day was kept as a special day of jubilation. ⁴⁹ It was ordained that the day, the thirteenth of Adar, should be celebrated annually. ⁵⁰ Judaea then entered on a short period of peace.

8 JUDAS had had reports about the Romans: that they were renowned for their military power and for the favour they showed to those who became their allies, and that any who joined them could be sure of their friendship ² and strong military support. He was told of the campaigns they had fought, and the valour they had shown in their conquest of the Gauls, whom they had laid under tribute. ³ He heard of their successes in Spain, where they had seized the silver and gold mines, ⁴ maintaining by perseverance and good judgement their hold on the entire country, distant though it was from their own land. There were kings from the ends of the earth who had marched against them, only to be beaten off, heavily defeated; others there were who paid them annual tribute.

⁵ Philip, and Perseus king of Kittim, and all who had set themselves in opposition to the Romans had been crushed in battle and conquered. ⁶ Antiochus the Great, king of Asia, had advanced against them with one hundred and twenty elephants, with cavalry and chariots and an immense force, only to be totally defeated. ⁷ They had captured the king alive, and had required that he and his successors should pay a large annual tribute, give hostages, ⁸ and cede the territories of India, Media, and Lydia, together with some of their finest provinces; these they had taken from him and handed over to King Eumenes. ⁹ The Greeks planned to attack and destroy them, ¹⁰ but the Romans got to know of

ᶜ Gk of them   ᵈ Gk he   ᵉ Gk they   ᶠ Gk them   ᵍ Gk these
ʰ Or Kittim

dainfully. 35 In a rage he swore: "If Judas and his army are not delivered to me at once, when I return victorious I will burn this temple down." He went away in great anger. 36 The priests, however, went in and stood before the altar and the sanctuary. They wept and said: 37 "You have chosen this house to bear your name, to be a house of prayer and petition for your people. 38 Take revenge on this man and his army, and let them fall by the sword. Remember their blasphemies, and do not let them continue."

39 Nicanor left Jerusalem and pitched his camp at Bethhoron, where the Syrian army joined him. 40 But Judas camped in Adasa with three thousand men. Here Judas uttered this prayer: 41 "When they who were sent by the king blasphemed, your angel went out and killed a hundred and eighty-five thousand of them. 42 In the same way, crush this army before us today, and let the rest know that Nicanor spoke wickedly against your sanctuary; judge him according to his wickedness."

43 The armies met in battle on the thirteenth day of the month Adar. Nicanor's army was crushed, and he himself was the first to fall in the battle. 44 When his army saw that Nicanor was dead, they threw down their arms and fled. 45 The Jews pursued them a day's journey, from Adasa to near Gazara, blowing the trumpets behind them as signals. 46 From all the surrounding villages of Judea people came out and closed in on them. They hemmed them in, and all the enemies fell by the sword; not a single one escaped. 47 Then the Jews collected the spoils and the booty; they cut off Nicanor's head and his right arm, which he had lifted up so arrogantly. These they brought to Jerusalem and displayed there. 48 The people rejoiced greatly, and observed that day as a great festival. 49 They decreed that it should be observed every year on the thirteenth of Adar. 50 And for a short time the land of Judah was quiet.

8 Judas had heard of the reputation of the Romans. They were valiant fighters and acted amiably to all who took their side. They established a friendly alliance with all who applied to them. 2 He was also told of their battles and the brave deeds that they had performed against the Gauls, conquering them and forcing them to pay tribute. 3 They had gotten possession of the silver and gold mines in Spain, 4 and by planning and persistence had conquered the whole country, although it was very remote from their own. They had crushed the kings who had come against them from the far corners of the earth and had inflicted on them severe defeat, and the rest paid tribute to them every year. 5 Philip and Perseus, king of the Macedonians, and the others who opposed them in battle had been overwhelmed and subjugated. 6 Antiochus the Great, king of Asia, who had fought against them with a hundred and twenty elephants and with cavalry and chariots and a very great army, had been defeated by them. 7 They had taken him alive and obliged him and the kings who succeeded him to pay a heavy tribute, to give hostages and a section of 8 Lycia, Mysia, and Lydia from among their best provinces. The Romans took these from him and gave them to King Eumenes. 9 When the men of Greece had planned to come and destroy them, 10 the

language, swearing in his rage, 35 'Unless Judas is handed over to me this time with his army, as soon as I am safely back, I promise you, I shall burn this building down!' 36 Then he went off in a fury. At this, the priests went in again, and stood weeping in front of the altar and the Temple, saying, 37 'You have chosen this house to be called by your name, to be a house of prayer and petition for your people. 38 Take vengeance on this man and on his army, and let them fall by the sword; remember their blasphemies and give them no respite.'

39 Nicanor left Jerusalem and encamped at Beth-Horon, where he was joined by an army from Syria. 40 Judas, meanwhile, camped at Adasa with three thousand men, and offered this prayer, 41 'When the king's envoys blasphemed, your angel went out and struck down one hundred and eighty-five thousand of his men. 42 In the same way let us see you crush this army today, so that everyone else may know that this man has spoken blasphemously against your sanctuary: pass judgement on him as his wickedness deserves!'

43 The armies met in battle on the thirteenth of the month Adar,r and Nicanor's army was crushed, he himself being the first to fall in the battle. 44 When Nicanor's soldiers saw him fall, they threw down their arms and fled. 45 The Jews pursued them a day's journey, from Adasa to the approaches of Gezer; they sounded their trumpets in warning as they followed them, 46 and people came out of all the surrounding Judaean villages to encircle the fugitives, who then turned back on their own men. All fell by the sword, not one being left alive. 47 Having collected the spoils and booty, they cut off Nicanor's head and the right hand he had stretched out in a display of insolence; these were taken and displayed within sight of Jerusalem. 48 The people were overjoyed and kept that day as a great holiday: 49 indeed they decided to celebrate it annually on the thirteenth of Adar. 50 For a short while Judaea enjoyed peace.

8 Now Judas had heard of the reputation of the Romans: how strong they were, and how well disposed towards any who made common cause with them, making a treaty of friendship with anyone who approached them. 2 (And, indeed, they were extremely powerful.) He had been told of their wars and of their prowess among the Gauls, whom they had conquered and put under tribute; 3 and of all they had done in the province of Spain to gain possession of the silver and gold mines there, 4 making themselves masters of the whole country by their determination and perseverance, despite its great distance from their own; of the kings who came from the ends of the earth to attack them, only to be crushed by them and overwhelmed with disaster, and of others who paid them annual tribute; 5 Philip, Perseus king of the Kittim, and others who had dared to make war on them, had been defeated and reduced to subjection, 6 while Antiochus the Great, king of Asia, who had advanced to attack them with a hundred and twenty elephants, cavalry, chariots and a very large army, had also suffered defeat at their hands; 7 they had taken him alive and imposed on him and his successors, on agreed terms, the payment of an enormous tribute, the surrender of hostages, and the cession 8 of the Indian territory, with Media, Lydia, and some of their best provinces, which they took from him and gave to King Eumenes. 9 Judas had also heard how, when the Greeks planned an expedition to destroy the Romans, 10 the

10 but this became known to them, and they sent a general against the Greeks*i* and attacked them. Many of them were wounded and fell, and the Romans*j* took captive their wives and children; they plundered them, conquered the land, tore down their strongholds, and enslaved them to this day. 11 The remaining kingdoms and islands, as many as ever opposed them, they destroyed and enslaved; 12 but with their friends and those who rely on them they have kept friendship. They have subdued kings far and near, and as many as have heard of their fame have feared them. 13 Those whom they wish to help and to make kings, they make kings, and those whom they wish they depose; and they have been greatly exalted. 14 Yet for all this not one of them has put on a crown or worn purple as a mark of pride, 15 but they have built for themselves a senate chamber, and every day three hundred twenty senators constantly deliberate concerning the people, to govern them well. 16 They trust one man each year to rule over them and to control all their land; they all heed the one man, and there is no envy or jealousy among them.

17 So Judas chose Eupolemus son of John son of Accos, and Jason son of Eleazar, and sent them to Rome to establish friendship and alliance, 18 and to free themselves from the yoke; for they saw that the kingdom of the Greeks was enslaving Israel completely. 19 They went to Rome, a very long journey, and they entered the senate chamber and spoke as follows: 20 "Judas, who is also called Maccabeus, and his brothers and the people of the Jews have sent us to you to establish alliance and peace with you, so that we may be enrolled as your allies and friends." 21 The proposal pleased them, 22 and this is a copy of the letter that they wrote in reply, on bronze tablets, and sent to Jerusalem to remain with them there as a memorial of peace and alliance:

23 "May all go well with the Romans and with the nation of the Jews at sea and on land forever, and may sword and enemy be far from them. 24 If war comes first to Rome or to any of their allies in all their dominion, 25 the nation of the Jews shall act as their allies wholeheartedly, as the occasion may indicate to them. 26 To the enemy that makes war they shall not give or supply grain, arms, money, or ships, just as Rome has decided; and they shall keep their obligations without receiving any return. 27 In the same way, if war comes first to the nation of the Jews, the Romans shall willingly act as their allies, as the occasion may indicate to them. 28 And to their enemies there shall not be given grain, arms, money, or ships, just as Rome has decided; and they shall keep these obligations and do so without deceit. 29 Thus on these terms the Romans make a treaty with the Jewish people. 30 If after these terms are in effect both parties shall determine to add or delete anything, they shall do so at their discretion, and any addition or deletion that they may make shall be valid.

31 "Concerning the wrongs that King Demetrius is doing to them, we have written to him as follows, 'Why have you made your yoke heavy on our friends and allies the Jews? 32 If now they appeal again for help against you, we will defend their rights and fight you on sea and on land.' "

9 When Demetrius heard that Nicanor and his army had fallen in battle, he sent Bacchides and Alcimus into the land of Judah a second time, and with them the right wing of the army. 2 They went by the road that leads to Gilgal and

it and sent just one general against them. When battle was joined many of the Greeks fell, and their women and children were made captive. The Romans plundered and annexed their territory, demolishing their strongholds and making the inhabitants slaves, as they remain to this day. 11 The other kingdoms and the islands, any who ever opposed them, they destroyed or reduced to slavery. 12 With their friends, however, and with all who relied on them for protection, they maintained firm friendship.

Thus they overcame rulers near and far, and all who heard of their reputation went in dread of them. 13 Those whom they wished to help and appoint as kings, became kings; those whom they wished to depose, they deposed. By such means they attained to great heights of power. 14 Yet for all this, not one of them ever gave himself the airs of a prince, assuming a crown or putting on the purple. 15 They had established a senate where each day three hundred and twenty senators met for deliberation, giving constant thought to the proper ordering of public affairs. 16 Every year they entrusted their government and the rule of all their dominions to one of their number, all obeying this one man without jealousy or envy.

17 So Judas chose Eupolemus son of John, son of Accos, and Jason son of Eleazar, and sent them to Rome to make a treaty of friendship and alliance, 18 in order that the Romans might rid them of foreign oppression, for it was clear that the Greek empire was reducing Israel to abject slavery. 19 The envoys made the journey to Rome, a very long journey, and when they came into the senate house they spoke as follows: 20 'Judas Maccabeus, his brothers, and the Jewish people have sent us to conclude with you a treaty of alliance, so that we may be enrolled as your allies and friends.' 21 The Romans gave their approval to the proposal, 22 and the following is a copy of the reply which they inscribed on bronze tablets and sent to Jerusalem, so that the Jews might have a record there of the treaty:

23 Success attend the Romans and the Jewish nation by sea and land for ever! May sword and foe be far from them! 24 But if an unprovoked attack is made on Rome or on any of her allies throughout her dominion, 25 then the Jewish nation shall afford them wholehearted support as occasion may require. 26 In accordance with Rome's decision Jews shall neither give nor supply provisions, arms, money, or ships to the enemies of Rome. They are to observe their commitments without compensation.

27 In like manner, if an unprovoked attack is made on the Jewish nation, then the Romans shall afford them wholehearted support as occasion may require. 28 In accordance with Rome's decision there shall be given neither provisions, arms, money, nor ships to the enemies of the Jewish nation. These commitments are to be kept without breach of faith.

29 Those are the terms of the treaty which the Romans have made with the Jewish people. 30 But if, hereafter, both parties agree to add or to rescind anything, what they decide shall be done; any such addition or rescindment shall be valid.

31 To this the Romans added: 'As for the wrongs which King Demetrius is perpetrating against the Jews, we have written to him as follows: "Why have you so harshly oppressed our friends and allies the Jews? 32 If they bring any further complaint against you, we shall open hostilities against you by sea and by land in support of their cause." '

9 When Demetrius heard that Nicanor and his men had fallen in battle, he sent Bacchides and Alcimus a second time into Judaea, and with them the right wing of his army. 2 They marched along the Gilgal road, laid siege to

Romans discovered it, and sent against the Greeks a single general who made war on them. Many were wounded and fell, and the Romans took their wives and children captive. They plundered them, took possession of their land, tore down their strongholds and reduced them to slavery even to this day. 11 All the other kingdoms and islands that had ever opposed them they destroyed and enslaved; 12 with their friends, however, and those who relied on them, they maintained friendship. They had conquered kings both far and near, and all who heard of their fame were afraid of them. 13 In truth, those whom they desired to help to a kingdom became kings, and those whom they wished to depose they deposed; and they were greatly exalted. 14 Yet with all this, none of them put on a crown or wore purple as a display of grandeur. 15 They had made for themselves a senate house, and every day three hundred and twenty men took counsel, deliberating on all that concerned the people and their well-being. 16 They entrusted their government to one man every year, to rule over their entire country, and they all obeyed that one, and there was no envy or jealousy among them.

17 So Judas chose Eupolemus, son of John, son of Accos, and Jason, son of Eleazar, and sent them to Rome to establish an alliance of friendship with them. 18 He did this to get rid of the yoke, for it was obvious that the kingdom of the Greeks was subjecting Israel to slavery. 19 After making a very long journey to Rome, the envoys entered the senate and spoke as follows: 20 "Judas, called Maccabeus, and his brothers, with the Jewish people, have sent us to you to make a peaceful alliance with you, and to enroll ourselves among your allies and friends." 21 The proposal pleased the Romans, 22 and this is a copy of the reply they inscribed on bronze tablets and sent to Jerusalem, to remain there with the Jews as a record of peace and alliance:

23 "May it be well with the Romans and the Jewish nation at sea and on land forever; may sword and enemy be far from them. 24 But if war is first made on Rome, or any of its allies in any of their dominions, 25 the Jewish nation will help them wholeheartedly, as the occasion shall demand; 26 and to those who wage war they shall not give nor provide grain, arms, money, or ships; this is Rome's decision. They shall fulfill their obligations without receiving any recompense. 27 In the same way, if war is made first on the Jewish nation, the Romans will help them willingly, as the occasion shall demand, 28 and to those who are attacking them there shall not be given grain, arms, money, or ships; this is Rome's decision. They shall fulfill their obligations without deception. 29 On these terms the Romans have made an agreement with the Jewish people. 30 But if both parties hereafter decide to add or take away anything, they shall do as they choose, and whatever they shall add or take away shall be valid.

31 "Moreover, concerning the wrongs that King Demetrius has done to them, we have written to him thus: 'Why have you made your yoke heavy upon our friends and allies the Jews? 32 If they complain about you again, we will do them justice and make war on you by land and sea.'"

9 When Demetrius heard that Nicanor and his army had fallen in battle, he again sent Bacchides and Alcimus into the land of Judah, along with the right wing of his army. 2 They took the road to Galilee, and camping opposite

latter had got wind of it and, sending a single general against them, had fought a campaign in which they inflicted heavy casualties, carried their women and children away into captivity, pillaged their goods, subdued their country, tore down their fortresses and reduced them to a slavery lasting to the present day; 11 and how they had destroyed and subjugated all the other kingdoms and islands that resisted them.

12 But where their friends and those who relied on them were concerned, they had always stood by their friendship. They had subdued kings far and near, and all who heard their name went in terror of them. 13 One man, if they determined to help him and advance him to a throne, would certainly occupy it, while another, if they so determined, would find himself deposed; their influence was paramount. 14 In spite of all this, no single one of them had assumed a crown or put on the purple for his own aggrandisement. 15 They had set up a senate, where three hundred and twenty councillors deliberated daily, constantly debating how best to regulate public affairs. 16 They entrusted their government to one man for a year at a time, with absolute power over their whole empire, and this man was obeyed by all without envy or jealousy.

17 Having chosen Eupolemus son of John, of the family of Accos, and Jason son of Eleazar, Judas sent them to Rome to make a treaty of friendship and alliance with these people, 18 in the hope of being rid of the yoke, for they could see that Greek rule was reducing Israel to slavery. 19 The envoys made the lengthy journey to Rome and presented themselves before the Senate with their formal proposal: 20 'Judas Maccabaeus and his brothers, with the Jewish people, have sent us to you to conclude a treaty of alliance and peace with you, and to enrol ourselves as your allies and friends.'

21 The proposal met with the approval of the senators. 22 Here is a copy of the rescript which they engraved on bronze tablets and sent to Jerusalem to be kept there by the Jews as a record of peace and alliance:

23 'Good fortune attend the Romans and the Jewish nation by sea and land for ever; may sword or enemy be far from them!

24 'If war comes first to Rome or any of her allies throughout her dominions, 25 the Jewish nation will take action as her ally, as occasion may require, and do it wholeheartedly. 26 They will not give or supply to the enemy any grain, arms, money or ships: thus has Rome decided, and they are to honour their obligations without guarantees. 27 In the same way, if war comes first to the Jewish nation, the Romans will support them energetically as occasion may offer, 28 and the aggressor will not be furnished with grain, arms, money or ships: such is the Roman decision, and they will honour these obligations without treachery. 29 Such are the articles under which the Romans have concluded their treaty with the Jewish people. 30 If, later, either party should decide to make any addition or deletion, they will be free to do so, and any such addition or deletion will be binding.

31 'As regards the wrongs done to them by King Demetrius, we have written to him in these terms: Why have you made your yoke lie heavy on our friends and allies the Jews? 32 If they appeal against you again, we shall uphold their rights and make war on you by sea and land.'

9 Demetrius, hearing that Nicanor and his army had fallen in battle, sent Bacchides and Alcimus a second time into Judaea, and with them the right wing of his army.

NEW REVISED STANDARD VERSION

REVISED ENGLISH BIBLE

encamped against Mesaloth in Arbela, and they took it and killed many people. 3 In the first month of the one hundred fifty-second year*k* they encamped against Jerusalem; 4 then they marched off and went to Berea with twenty thousand foot soldiers and two thousand cavalry.

5 Now Judas was encamped in Elasa, and with him were three thousand picked men. 6 When they saw the huge number of the enemy forces, they were greatly frightened, and many slipped away from the camp, until no more than eight hundred of them were left.

7 When Judas saw that his army had slipped away and the battle was imminent, he was crushed in spirit, for he had no time to assemble them. 8 He became faint, but he said to those who were left, "Let us get up and go against our enemies. We may have the strength to fight them." 9 But they tried to dissuade him, saying, "We do not have the strength. Let us rather save our own lives now, and let us come back with our kindred and fight them; we are too few." 10 But Judas said, "Far be it from us to do such a thing as to flee from them. If our time has come, let us die bravely for our kindred, and leave no cause to question our honor."

11 Then the army of Bacchides*l* marched out from the camp and took its stand for the encounter. The cavalry was divided into two companies, and the slingers and the archers went ahead of the army, as did all the chief warriors. 12 Bacchides was on the right wing. Flanked by the two companies, the phalanx advanced to the sound of the trumpets; and the men with Judas also blew their trumpets. 13 The earth was shaken by the noise of the armies, and the battle raged from morning until evening.

14 Judas saw that Bacchides and the strength of his army were on the right; then all the stouthearted men went with him, 15 and they crushed the right wing, and he pursued them as far as Mount Azotus. 16 When those on the left wing saw that the right wing was crushed, they turned and followed close behind Judas and his men. 17 The battle became desperate, and many on both sides were wounded and fell. 18 Judas also fell, and the rest fled.

19 Then Jonathan and Simon took their brother Judas and buried him in the tomb of their ancestors at Modein, 20 and wept for him. All Israel made great lamentation for him; they mourned many days and said,

21 "How is the mighty fallen,
the savior of Israel!"

22 Now the rest of the acts of Judas, and his wars and the brave deeds that he did, and his greatness, have not been recorded, but they were very many.

23 After the death of Judas, the renegades emerged in all parts of Israel; all the wrongdoers reappeared. 24 In those days a very great famine occurred, and the country went over to their side. 25 Bacchides chose the godless and put them in charge of the country. 26 They made inquiry and searched for the friends of Judas, and brought them to Bacchides, who took vengeance on them and made sport of them. 27 So there was great distress in Israel, such as had not been since the time that prophets ceased to appear among them.

28 Then all the friends of Judas assembled and said to Jonathan, 29 "Since the death of your brother Judas there has been no one like him to go against our enemies and Bacchides, and to deal with those of our nation who hate us. 30 Now therefore we have chosen you today to take his place as our ruler and leader, to fight our battle." 31 So Jonathan accepted the leadership at that time in place of his brother Judas.

32 When Bacchides learned of this, he tried to kill him.

Messaloth in Arbela, and captured it, inflicting heavy loss of life.

3 In the first month of the year 152, they moved camp to Jerusalem, 4 and from there they marched to Berea with twenty thousand infantry and two thousand cavalry. 5 Judas had established his camp at Alasa. He had with him three thousand picked troops, 6 but, when his men saw the size of the enemy forces, their courage failed and many deserted, until a mere eight hundred remained.

7 Aware that his army had melted away and the campaign was going against him, Judas was greatly disheartened, for there was not time to reassemble his forces. Though himself despondent, 8 he said to those who were left, 'Let us take the offensive and see if we can defeat the enemy.' 9 His men tried to dissuade him: 'Impossible!' they said. 'No, we are too few. Let us save our lives now, and come back later to fight them when we have our comrades with us.' 10 But Judas replied: 'Heaven forbid that I should do such a thing as run away! If our time has come, let us die bravely for our fellow-countrymen, and leave no stain on our honour.'

11 The Syrian army moved from its camp and took up its battle position against Judas's men. The cavalry was divided into two squadrons; the slingers and the archers went ahead of the main force, and the crack troops were in the front line. 12 Bacchides was on the right wing. The phalanx advanced with trumpets sounding and flanked by the two cavalry squadrons; 13 Judas's men also sounded their trumpets. The earth shook as the armies met, and the fighting went on from morning till night.

14 When he saw that Bacchides and the main strength of his army were on the right flank, Judas with all his most valiant troops rallying to him 15 broke the Syrian right and pursued them as far as Mount Azotus. 16 The Syrians on the left, seeing their right wing broken, wheeled about and, following closely after Judas and his men, attacked them from the rear. 17 The fighting became very heavy, and many fell on both sides. 18 Judas was among the fallen; the rest of the Jews fled. 19 Jonathan and Simon carried Judas their brother away and laid him in the family tomb at Modin, 20 and there they wept over him. There was great grief throughout Israel, and the people mourned him for many days, saying,

21 How is our champion fallen,
the saviour of Israel!

22 The rest of the history of Judas, his wars, exploits, and achievements — these were so numerous that they have not been recorded.

23 After the death of Judas, the renegades in every part of Israel emerged from hiding, and all the evildoers reappeared, 24 and the country, afflicted at that time by a terrible famine, went over to their side. 25 Bacchides chose apostates to be in control of the land. 26 They searched out and hunted down the friends of Judas to bring them before Bacchides, who wreaked his vengeance on them and loaded them with indignities. 27 It was a time of harsh oppression for Israel, worse than any since the days when prophets ceased to appear among them. 28 So the friends of Judas all assembled and said to Jonathan, 29 'Since the death of your brother Judas there has not been a man like him to take the lead against our enemies, Bacchides and those of our own nation who are hostile to us. 30 Today, therefore, we have chosen you to succeed him as our ruler and our leader to fight our battles.' 31 From then Jonathan took over the leadership in the place of his brother Judas.

32 When this became known to Bacchides, he sought to

---

the ascent at Arbela, they captured it and killed many people. ³In the first month of the year one hundred and fifty-two, they encamped against Jerusalem. ⁴Then they set out for Berea with twenty thousand men and two thousand cavalry. ⁵Judas, with three thousand picked men, had camped at Elasa. ⁶When his men saw the great number of the troops, they were very much afraid, and many slipped away from the camp, until only eight hundred men remained.

⁷As Judas saw that his army was melting away just when the battle was imminent, he was panic-stricken, because he had no time to gather them together. ⁸But in spite of his discouragement, he said to those who remained: "Let us go forward to meet our enemies; perhaps we can put up a good fight against them." ⁹They tried to dissuade him, saying: "We certainly cannot. Let us save our lives now, and come back with our kinsmen, and then fight against them. Now we are too few." ¹⁰But Judas said: "Far be it from me to do such a thing as to flee from them! If our time has come, let us die bravely for our kinsmen and not leave a stain upon our glory!"

¹¹Then the army of Bacchides moved out of camp and took its position for combat. The cavalry were divided into two squadrons, and the slingers and the archers came on ahead of the army, and all the valiant men were in the front line. ¹²Bacchides was on the right wing. Flanked by the two squadrons, the phalanx attacked as they blew their trumpets. Those who were on Judas' side also blew their trumpets. ¹³The earth shook with the noise of the armies, and the battle raged from morning until evening. ¹⁴Seeing that Bacchides was on the right, with the main force of his army, Judas, with all the most stouthearted rallying to him, ¹⁵drove back the right wing and pursued them as far as the mountain slopes. ¹⁶But when the men on the left wing saw that the right wing was driven back, they turned and followed Judas and his men, taking them in the rear. ¹⁷The battle was fought desperately, and many on both sides fell wounded. ¹⁸Then Judas fell, and the rest fled.

¹⁹Jonathan and Simon took their brother Judas and buried him in the tomb of their fathers at Modein. ²⁰All Israel bewailed him in great grief. They mourned for him many days, and they said, ²¹"How the mighty one has fallen, the savior of Israel!" ²²The other acts of Judas, his battles, the brave deeds he performed, and his greatness have not been recorded; but they were very many.

²³After the death of Judas, the transgressors of the law raised their heads in every part of Israel, and all kinds of evildoers appeared. ²⁴In those days there was a very great famine, and the country deserted to them. ²⁵Bacchides chose impious men and made them masters of the country. ²⁶These sought out and hunted down the friends of Judas and brought them to Bacchides, who punished and derided them. ²⁷There had not been such great distress in Israel since the time prophets ceased to appear among the people.

²⁸Then all the friends of Judas came together and said to Jonathan: ²⁹"Since your brother Judas died, there has been no one like him to oppose our enemies, Bacchides and those who are hostile to our nation. ³⁰Now therefore we have chosen you today to be our ruler and leader in his place, and to fight our battle." ³¹From that moment Jonathan accepted the leadership, and took the place of Judas his brother. ³²When Bacchides learned of it, he sought to kill him.

²They took the road to Galilee and besieged Mesaloth in Arbela, and captured it, putting many people to death. ³In the first month of the year 152, they encamped outside Jerusalem; ⁴they then moved on, making their way to Beer-Zaith with twenty thousand foot and two thousand horse. ⁵Judas lay in camp at Elasa, with three thousand picked men. ⁶When they saw the huge size of the enemy forces they were terrified, and many slipped out of the camp, until no more than eight hundred of the force were left. ⁷With battle now inevitable, Judas realised that his army had melted away; he was aghast, for he had no time to rally them. ⁸Yet, dismayed as he was, he said to those who were left, 'Up! Let us face the enemy; we may yet have the strength to fight them.' ⁹His men tried to dissuade him, declaring, 'We have no strength for anything but to escape with our lives this time; then we can come back with our brothers to fight them; by ourselves we are too few.' ¹⁰Judas retorted, 'That I should do such a thing as run away from them! If our time has come, at least let us die like men for our countrymen, and leave nothing to tarnish our reputation.'

¹¹The army marched out of camp and drew up, facing the enemy. The cavalry was drawn up in two squadrons; the slingers and archers marched in the van of the army, and all the best fighters were put in the front rank; ¹²Bacchides was on the right wing. The phalanx advanced from between the two squadrons, sounding the trumpets; the men on Judas' side also blew their trumpets, ¹³and the earth shook with the noise of the armies. The engagement lasted from morning until evening. ¹⁴Judas saw that Bacchides and the main strength of his army lay on the right; all the stout-hearted rallied to him, ¹⁵and they crushed the right wing, pursuing them as far as the Azara Hills. ¹⁶But when the Syrians on the left wing saw that the right had been broken, they turned and followed hot on the heels of Judas and his men to take them in the rear. ¹⁷The fight became desperate, and there were many casualties on both sides. ¹⁸Judas himself fell, and the remnant fled.

¹⁹Jonathan and Simon took up their brother Judas and buried him in his ancestral tomb at Modein. ²⁰All Israel wept and mourned him deeply and for many days they repeated this dirge. ²¹'What a downfall for the strong man, the man who kept Israel safe!' ²²The other deeds of Judas, the battles he fought, the exploits he performed, and all his titles to greatness have not been recorded; but they were very many.

²³After the death of Judas, the renegades came out of hiding throughout Israel and all the evil-doers reappeared. ²⁴At that time there was a severe famine, and the country went over to their side. ²⁵Bacchides deliberately chose the enemies of religion to administer the country. ²⁶These traced and searched out the friends of Judas and brought them before Bacchides, who ill-treated and mocked them. ²⁷A terrible oppression began in Israel; there had been nothing like it since the disappearance of prophecy among them.

²⁸The friends of Judas then all united in saying to Jonathan, ²⁹'Since your brother Judas died, there has been no one like him to head the resistance against our enemies, people like Bacchides and others who hate our nation. ³⁰Accordingly, we have today chosen you to take his place as our ruler and leader and to fight our campaigns.' ³¹Whereupon, Jonathan took command, in succession to his brother Judas.

³²Bacchides, when he heard the news, made plans to kill

33 But Jonathan and his brother Simon and all who were with him heard of it, and they fled into the wilderness of Tekoa and camped by the water of the pool of Asphar. 34 Bacchides found this out on the sabbath day, and he with all his army crossed the Jordan.

35 So Jonathan[m] sent his brother as leader of the multitude and begged the Nabateans, who were his friends, for permission to store with them the great amount of baggage that they had. 36 But the family of Jambri from Medeba came out and seized John and all that he had, and left with it.

37 After these things it was reported to Jonathan and his brother Simon, "The family of Jambri are celebrating a great wedding, and are conducting the bride, a daughter of one of the great nobles of Canaan, from Nadabath with a large escort." 38 Remembering how their brother John had been killed, they went up and hid under cover of the mountain. 39 They looked out and saw a tumultuous procession with a great amount of baggage; and the bridegroom came out with his friends and his brothers to meet them with tambourines and musicians and many weapons. 40 Then they rushed on them from the ambush and began killing them. Many were wounded and fell, and the rest fled to the mountain; and the Jews[n] took all their goods. 41 So the wedding was turned into mourning and the voice of their musicians into a funeral dirge. 42 After they had fully avenged the blood of their brother, they returned to the marshes of the Jordan.

43 When Bacchides heard of this, he came with a large force on the sabbath day to the banks of the Jordan. 44 And Jonathan said to those with him, "Let us get up now and fight for our lives, for today things are not as they were before. 45 For look! the battle is in front of us and behind us; the water of the Jordan is on this side and on that, with marsh and thicket; there is no place to turn. 46 Cry out now to Heaven that you may be delivered from the hands of our enemies." 47 So the battle began, and Jonathan stretched out his hand to strike Bacchides, but he eluded him and went to the rear. 48 Then Jonathan and the men with him leaped into the Jordan and swam across to the other side, and the enemy[n] did not cross the Jordan to attack them. 49 And about one thousand of Bacchides' men fell that day.

50 Then Bacchides[m] returned to Jerusalem and built strong cities in Judea: the fortress in Jericho, and Emmaus, and Beth-horon, and Bethel, and Timnath, and[o] Pharathon, and Tephon, with high walls and gates and bars. 51 And he placed garrisons in them to harass Israel. 52 He also fortified the town of Beth-zur, and Gazara, and the citadel, and in them he put troops and stores of food. 53 And he took the sons of the leading men of the land as hostages and put them under guard in the citadel at Jerusalem.

54 In the one hundred and fifty-third year,[p] in the second month, Alcimus gave orders to tear down the wall of the inner court of the sanctuary. He tore down the work of the prophets! 55 But he only began to tear it down, for at that time Alcimus was stricken and his work was hindered; his mouth was stopped and he was paralyzed, so that he could no longer say a word or give commands concerning his house. 56 And Alcimus died at that time in great agony. 57 When Bacchides saw that Alcimus was dead, he returned to the king, and the land of Judah had rest for two years.

58 Then all the lawless plotted and said, "See! Jonathan and his men are living in quiet and confidence. So now let us bring Bacchides back, and he will capture them all in one night." 59 And they went and consulted with him. 60 He

kill Jonathan; 33 but Jonathan, his brother Simon, and all who were with them got to know of it and took refuge in the wilderness of Tekoa, where they encamped by the pool of Asphar. 34 Bacchides discovered this on the sabbath, and he crossed the Jordan with his whole army. 35 Jonathan sent his brother John away in charge of the camp followers and appealed to his friends the Nabataeans to look after the baggage train, which was of some size. 36 But the Jambrites, in a sortie from Medaba, kidnapped John and made off with the baggage. 37 Some time afterwards, news was brought to Jonathan and his brother Simon that the Jambrites were celebrating an important wedding and bringing the bride, the daughter of one of the great nobles of Canaan, from Nadabath with a large retinue. 38 The fate of their brother John still fresh in their minds, Jonathan and his men went up and hid themselves under cover of a hill. 39 As they watched, there, coming to meet the bridal party in the middle of a bustling crowd and a train of baggage, was the bridegroom, escorted, to the sound of drums and musical instruments, by his friends and kinsmen all fully armed. 40 Jonathan's men leapt from their ambush and cut them down; many fell, while the survivors made off into the hills, and the Jews took all their goods as spoil. 41 So the wedding was turned into mourning, and the sound of music to lamentation. 42 The blood of their brother fully avenged, Jonathan and Simon returned to the marshes by Jordan.

43 Hearing of this, Bacchides came on the sabbath right to the banks of Jordan with a large force. 44 Jonathan said to his men, 'Up, fight for our lives! Today we are in worse plight than ever: 45 a battle in front, the waters of Jordan behind, to right and left marsh and thicket—there is no escape! 46 Cry to Heaven to save you from the enemy.' 47 Battle was joined, and Jonathan had raised his hand to strike down Bacchides, when the Syrian leader eluded him and got away. 48 Then Jonathan and his men leapt into the Jordan and swam over to the other side; but the enemy did not pursue them across the river. 49 That day the army of Bacchides lost about a thousand men.

50 Bacchides returned to Jerusalem, and he fortified with high walls and barred gates a number of places in Judaea: Jericho's fortress, Emmaus and Beth-horon, Bethel, Timnath-pharathon, and Tephon, 51 in all of which he stationed garrisons to harass Israel. 52 He strengthened the towns of Bethsura and Gazara and the citadel, placing troops and stores of provisions in them. 53 He took as hostages the sons of the leading men of the country and put them under guard in the citadel at Jerusalem.

54 In the second month of the year 153, Alcimus gave orders for the wall of the inner court of the temple to be demolished, thereby destroying the work of the prophets. 55 But he had only begun the work of demolition, when he suffered a stroke which put a stop to his activities. Paralysed and with his speech impaired, he could not utter a word or give final instructions about his property, 56 and subsequently he died in great agony. 57 On learning that Alcimus was dead, Bacchides returned to the king, and for two years Judaea had peace.

58 The renegades all took counsel together: 'Here are Jonathan and his people living in peace and security,' they said; 'if we bring back Bacchides now, he will lay hold of every one of them in a single night.' 59 They went and conferred

[m] Gk he   [n] Gk they   [o] Some authorities omit and   [p] 159 B.C.   9:54 153: that is 159 B.C.E.

2474

33 But Jonathan and his brother Simon and all the men with him discovered this, and they fled to the desert of Tekoa and camped by the waters of the pool of Asphar.

35 Jonathan sent his brother as leader of the convoy to ask permission of his friends, the Nabateans, to deposit with them their great quantity of baggage. 36 But the sons of Jambri from Medaba made a raid and seized and carried off John and everything he had. 37 After this, word was brought to Jonathan and his brother Simon: "The sons of Jambri are celebrating a great wedding, and with a large escort they are bringing the bride, the daughter of one of the great princes of Canaan, from Nadabath." 38 Remembering the blood of John their brother, they went up and hid themselves under cover of the mountain. 39 They watched, and suddenly saw a noisy crowd with baggage; the bridegroom and his friends and kinsmen had come out to meet the bride's party with tambourines and musicians and much equipment. 40 The Jews rose up against them from their ambush and killed them. Many fell wounded, and after the survivors fled toward the mountain, all their spoils were taken. 41 Thus the wedding was turned into mourning, and the sound of music into lamentation. 42 Having taken their revenge for the blood of their brother, the Jews returned to the marshes of the Jordan.

43 When Bacchides heard of it, he came on the sabbath to the banks of the Jordan with a large force. 44 Then Jonathan said to his companions, "Let us get up now and fight for our lives, for today is not like yesterday and the day before. 45 The battle is before us, and behind us are the waters of the Jordan on one side, marsh and thickets on the other, and there is no way of escape. 46 Cry out now to Heaven for deliverance from our enemies." 47 When they joined battle, Jonathan raised his arm to strike Bacchides, but Bacchides backed away from him. 48 Jonathan and his men jumped into the Jordan and swam across to the other side, but the enemy did not pursue them across the Jordan. 49 A thousand men on Bacchides' side fell that day.

50 On returning to Jerusalem, Bacchides built strongholds in Judea: the Jericho fortress, as well as Emmaus, Beth-horon, Bethel, Timnath, Pharathon, and Tephon, with high walls and gates and bars. 51 In each he put a garrison to oppose Israel. 52 He fortified the city of Beth-zur, Gazara and the citadel, and put soldiers in them and stores of provisions. 53 He took as hostages the sons of the leaders of the country and put them in custody in the citadel at Jerusalem.

54 In the year one hundred and fifty-three, in the second month, Alcimus ordered the wall of the inner court of the sanctuary to be torn down, thus destroying the work of the prophets. But he only began to tear it down. 55 Just at that time he had a stroke, and his work was interrupted; his mouth was closed and he was paralyzed, so that he could no longer utter a word to give orders concerning his house. 56 Finally he died in great agony. 57 Seeing that Alcimus was dead, Bacchides returned to the king, and the land of Judah was quiet for two years.

58 Then all the transgressors of the law held a council and said: "Jonathan and his companions are living in peace and security. Now then, let us have Bacchides return, and he will capture all of them in a single night." 59 So they went and took counsel with him. 60 When Bacchides was setting

Jonathan. 33 But this became known to Jonathan, his brother Simon and all his supporters, and they took refuge in the desert of Tekoa, camping by the water-supply at Asphar storage-well. 34 (Bacchides came to know of this on the Sabbath day, and he too crossed the Jordan with his entire army.)

35 Jonathan sent his brother, who was one of his commanders, to ask his friends the Nabataeans to store their considerable baggage for them. 36 The sons of Amrai, however, those of Medeba, intercepted them, captured John and everything he had and made off with their prize. 37 Later, Jonathan and his brother Simon were told that the sons of Amrai were celebrating an important wedding, and were escorting the bride, a daughter of one of the great notables of Canaan, from Nabata with a large retinue. 38 Remembering the bloody end of their brother John, they went up and hid under cover of the mountain. 39 As they were keeping watch, a noisy procession came into sight with a great deal of baggage, and the bridegroom, with his groomsmen and his family, came out to meet it with tambourines and a band, and rich, warlike display. 40 The Jews rushed down on them from their ambush and killed them, inflicting heavy casualties; the survivors escaped to the mountain, leaving their entire baggage train to be captured. 41 Thus, *the wedding was turned into mourning and the music of their band into lamentation.* [s] 42 Having in this way avenged in full the blood of their brother, they returned to the marshes of the Jordan.

43 As soon as Bacchides heard this, he came on the Sabbath day with a considerable force to the steep banks of the Jordan. 44 Jonathan said to his men, 'Up! Let us fight for our lives, for today is not as in the old days. 45 You can see, we shall have to fight on our front and to our rear; we have the waters of the Jordan on one side, the marsh and scrub on the other, and we have no line of withdrawal. 46 This is the moment to call on Heaven, to deliver you from the clutches of your enemies.' 47 The engagement was begun by Jonathan, who aimed a blow at Bacchides, but the Syrian disengaged himself and withdrew, 48 whereupon Jonathan and his men leapt into the Jordan and swam to the other bank; the enemy did not, however, cross the Jordan in pursuit. 49 That day, Bacchides lost about a thousand men.

50 Bacchides went back to Jerusalem and began fortifying some of the Judaean towns: the fortresses of Jericho, Emmaus, Beth-Horon, Bethel, Timnath, Pharathon and Tephon, with high walls and barred gates, 51 and stationed a garrison in each of them to harass Israel. 52 He also fortified the town of Beth-Zur, Gezer and the Citadel, and placed troops in them with supplies of provisions. 53 He took the sons of the leading men of the country as hostages, and had them placed under guard in the Citadel of Jerusalem.

54 In the year 153, in the second month, Alcimus ordered the demolition of the wall of the inner court of the sanctuary, destroying the work of the prophets. Alcimus had just begun the demolition 55 when he suffered a stroke, and his work was interrupted. His mouth became obstructed, and his paralysis made him incapable of speaking at all or giving directions to his household; 56 it was not long before he died in great agony. 57 On the death of Alcimus, Bacchides went back to the king, and Judaea was left in peace for two years.

58 The renegades then all agreed on a plan. 'Now is the time,' they said, 'while Jonathan and his supporters are living in peace and are full of confidence, for us to bring back Bacchides, and he will arrest the lot of them in one night.' 59 So they went to him and reached an understand-

---

9, 34: Omitted, it is a dittography of verse 43.

[s] 9 Am 8:10.

started to come with a large force, and secretly sent letters to all his allies in Judea, telling them to seize Jonathan and his men; but they were unable to do it, because their plan became known. 61 And Jonathan's men*q* seized about fifty of the men of the country who were leaders in this treachery, and killed them.

62 Then Jonathan with his men, and Simon, withdrew to Bethbasi in the wilderness; he rebuilt the parts of it that had been demolished, and they fortified it. 63 When Bacchides learned of this, he assembled all his forces, and sent orders to the men of Judea. 64 Then he came and encamped against Bethbasi; he fought against it for many days and made machines of war.

65 But Jonathan left his brother Simon in the town, while he went out into the country; and he went with only a few men. 66 He struck down Odomera and his kindred and the people of Phasiron in their tents. 67 Then he*r* began to attack and went into battle with his forces; and Simon and his men sallied out from the town and set fire to the machines of war. 68 They fought with Bacchides, and he was crushed by them. They pressed him very hard, for his plan and his expedition had been in vain. 69 So he was very angry at the renegades who had counseled him to come into the country, and he killed many of them. Then he decided to go back to his own land.

70 When Jonathan learned of this, he sent ambassadors to him to make peace with him and obtain release of the captives. 71 He agreed, and did as he said; and he swore to Jonathan*s* that he would not try to harm him as long as he lived. 72 He restored to him the captives whom he had taken previously from the land of Judah; then he turned and went back to his own land, and did not come again into their territory. 73 Thus the sword ceased from Israel. Jonathan settled in Michmash and began to judge the people; and he destroyed the godless out of Israel.

10 In the one hundred sixtieth year*t* Alexander Epiphanes, son of Antiochus, landed and occupied Ptolemais. They welcomed him, and there he began to reign. 2 When King Demetrius heard of it, he assembled a very large army and marched out to meet him in battle. 3 Demetrius sent Jonathan a letter in peaceable words to honor him; 4 for he said to himself, "Let us act first to make peace with him*u* before he makes peace with Alexander against us, 5 for he will remember all the wrongs that we did to him and to his brothers and his nation." 6 So Demetrius*v* gave him authority to recruit troops, to equip them with arms, and to become his ally; and he commanded that the hostages in the citadel should be released to him.

7 Then Jonathan came to Jerusalem and read the letter in the hearing of all the people and of those in the citadel. 8 They were greatly alarmed when they heard that the king had given him authority to recruit troops. 9 But those in the citadel released the hostages to Jonathan, and he returned them to their parents.

10 And Jonathan took up residence in Jerusalem and began to rebuild and restore the city. 11 He directed those who were doing the work to build the walls and encircle Mount Zion with squared stones, for better fortification; and they did so. 12 Then the foreigners who were in the strongholds that Bacchides had built fled; 13 all of them left their places and went back to their own lands. 14 Only in Beth-zur did some remain who had forsaken the law and the commandments, for it served as a place of refuge.

with Bacchides, 60 who set off with a large force. At the same time he sent letters secretly to all his supporters in Judaea, with instructions to seize Jonathan and his men. But because the plan leaked out they were unable to do so, 61 and some fifty of the ringleaders of this villainy in Judaea were taken and put to death. 62 Jonathan and Simon withdrew with their men to Bethbasi in the desert, rebuilt its ruined fortifications, and strengthened it. 63 Informed of this, Bacchides mustered his whole army, summoned his allies in Judaea, 64 and marched against Bethbasi. He took up his position against it, erected siege-engines, and pressed the attack for many days. 65 Jonathan left his brother Simon in the town and, slipping out into the country with a few men, 66 attacked Odomera and his people and the Phasirites in their encampment. 67 Gradually he gained the upper hand and began to advance towards Bethbasi with his forces.

Simon and his men made a sortie from the town, set fire to the siege-engines, 68 and inflicted a shattering attack on Bacchides. They kept up such heavy pressure on him that his plans for an assault were frustrated. 69 Incensed with the renegades at whose instance he had invaded the land, he had many of them put to death. He then decided to return to his own country.

70 When Jonathan learnt of this, he sent envoys to Bacchides to secure peace terms and the return of prisoners. 71 Bacchides agreed and accepted Jonathan's proposals, swearing to him that as long as he lived he would harm him no more. 72 He handed over the prisoners he had taken earlier from Judaea, and then returned to his own country, never again to set foot on Jewish soil. 73 So the war in Israel came to an end. Taking up residence in Michmash, Jonathan began to govern the people and root the apostates out of Israel.

10 IN the year 160, Alexander Epiphanes son of Antiochus arrived by ship and took possession of Ptolemais, where he was welcomed and proclaimed king. 2 On hearing of this King Demetrius raised a very large army and marched out to give battle. 3 At the same time he sent Jonathan a letter in friendly and flattering terms. 4 He said to himself, 'Let us forestall Alexander by making peace with the Jews before Jonathan comes to terms with him against us, 5 for Jonathan will not have forgotten all the harm we did him by our treatment of his brothers and of his nation.' 6 So he granted him authority to raise and equip an army, conferred on him the title of ally, and gave orders for the hostages in the citadel to be handed over to him. 7 Jonathan came to Jerusalem and read out the letter to all the people and also to the men of the garrison in the citadel, 8 who were filled with apprehension on hearing that the king had given Jonathan authority to raise an army. 9 They surrendered the hostages, who were then restored to their parents.

10 Jonathan took up his quarters in Jerusalem and began to rebuild and renovate the city. 11 He instructed those engaged on the work to build the walls and surround Mount Zion with a fortification of squared stones, and this was done. 12 The foreigners who occupied the strongholds built by Bacchides made good their escape, 13 every man of them deserting his post and making off to his own country; 14 only in Bethsura were there still left some of those who had abandoned the law and ordinances and found refuge there.

---

q Gk *they*   *r* Other ancient authorities read *they*   *s* Gk *him*
t 152 B.C.   *u* Gk *them*   *v* Gk *he*   10:1 **160:** *that is* 152 B.C.E.

out with a large force, he sent letters secretly to all his allies in Judea, telling them to seize Jonathan and his companions. They were not able to do this, however, because their plot became known. 61 In fact, Jonathan's men seized about fifty of the men of the country who were ringleaders in the mischief and put them to death. 62 Then Jonathan and Simon and their companions withdrew to Bethbasi in the desert; they rebuilt and strengthened its fortifications that had been demolished. 63 When Bacchides learned of this, he gathered together his whole force and sent word to those who were in Judea. 64 He came and pitched his camp before Bethbasi, and constructing siege-machines, he fought against it for many days.

65 Leaving his brother Simon in the city, Jonathan, accompanied by a small group of men, went out into the field. 66 He struck down Odomera and his kinsmen and the sons of Phasiron in their encampment; these men had set out to go up to the siege with their forces. 67 Simon and his men then sallied forth from the city and set fire to the machines. 68 They fought against Bacchides, and he was beaten. This caused him great distress. Because the enterprise he had planned came to naught, 69 he was angry with the lawless men who had advised him to invade the province. He killed many of them and resolved to return to his own country.

70 Jonathan learned of this and sent ambassadors to make peace with him and to obtain the release of the prisoners. 71 He agreed to do as Jonathan had asked. He swore an oath to him that he would never try to injure him for the rest of his life; 72 and he released the prisoners he had previously taken from the land of Judah. He returned to his own country and never came into their territory again.

73 Then the sword ceased in Israel. Jonathan settled in Michmash; he began to judge the people, and he destroyed the impious in Israel.

10 In the year one hundred and sixty, Alexander, who was called Epiphanes, son of Antiochus, came up and took Ptolemais. He was accepted and began to reign there. 2 When King Demetrius heard of it, he mustered a very large army and marched out to engage him in combat. 3 Demetrius sent a letter to Jonathan written in peaceful terms, to pay him honor; 4 for he said: "Let us be the first to make peace with him, before he makes peace with Alexander against us, 5 since he will remember all the wrongs we have done to him, his brothers, and his nation."

6 So Demetrius authorized Jonathan, as his ally, to gather an army and procure arms; and he ordered that the hostages in the citadel be released to him. 7 Accordingly Jonathan went up to Jerusalem and read the letter to all the people. The men in the citadel 8 were struck with fear when they heard that the king had given him authority to gather an army. 9 They released the hostages to Jonathan, and he gave them back to their parents. 10 Thereafter Jonathan dwelt in Jerusalem, and began to build and restore the city. 11 He ordered the workmen to build the walls and encircle Mount Zion with square stones for its fortification, which they did. 12 The foreigners in the strongholds that Bacchides had built, took flight; 13 each one of them left his place and returned to his own country. 14 Only in Beth-zur did some remain of those who had abandoned the law and the commandments, for they used it as a place of refuge.

ing. 60 Bacchides at once set out with a large force, and sent secret instructions to all his allies in Judaea to seize Jonathan and his supporters. But they were unable to do this because their plan became known, 61 and Jonathan and his men arrested some fifty of the men of the country who were ringleaders in the plot, and put them to death.

62 Jonathan and Simon then retired with their partisans to Beth-Bassi in the desert; they rebuilt the ruinous parts of the place and fortified it. 63 When Bacchides heard this, he mustered his whole force and notified his adherents in Judaea. 64 He then proceeded to lay siege to Beth-Bassi, the fighting was protracted, and he constructed siege-engines. 65 Jonathan, however, leaving his brother Simon in the town, broke out into the countryside with a handful of men. 66 He launched a blow at Odomera and his brothers, and at the sons of Phasiron in their encampment; whereupon, these too came into the struggle, joining forces with him. 67 Simon and his people, meanwhile, made a sortie from the town and set fire to the siege-engines. 68 Taking the offensive against Bacchides, they defeated him. He was greatly disconcerted to find that his plan and his assault had come to nothing, 69 and vented his anger on those renegades who had induced him to enter the country, putting many of them to death; he then decided to take his own troops home.

70 Discovering this, Jonathan sent envoys to negotiate peace terms and the release of prisoners with him. 71 Bacchides agreed to this, accepting his proposals and swearing never to seek occasion to harm him for the rest of his life. 72 Having surrendered to Jonathan those prisoners he had earlier taken in Judaea, he turned about and withdrew to his own country, and never again came near their frontiers. 73 The sword no longer hung over Israel, and Jonathan settled in Michmash, where he began to judge the people and to rid Israel of the godless.

10 In the year 160, Alexander, son of Antiochus Epiphanes, raised an army and occupied Ptolemais. He was well received, and there inaugurated his reign. 2 On hearing this, King Demetrius assembled a very large army and marched off to do battle with him. 3 Demetrius furthermore sent Jonathan a most conciliatory letter, promising to promote him in rank, 4 for, as he said, 'We had better move first to come to terms with these people before he makes common cause with Alexander against us; 5 he will not have forgotten all the wrongs we inflicted on him and his brothers, and on his nation.' 6 He even authorised him to raise an army, to manufacture arms, and to describe himself as his ally, and ordered the hostages in the Citadel to be surrendered to him.

7 Jonathan went straight to Jerusalem and read the letter in the hearing of the whole people and of the men in the Citadel. 8 They were terrified when they heard that the king had given him authority to raise an army. 9 The men in the Citadel surrendered the hostages to Jonathan, who handed them back to their parents. 10 Jonathan then took up residence in Jerusalem and began the rebuilding and restoration of the city. 11 He ordered those responsible for the work to build the walls and the defences round Mount Zion of squared stone blocks to make them stronger, and this was done. 12 The foreigners in the fortresses built by Bacchides abandoned them, 13 one after another leaving his post to go back to his own country. 14 Only at Beth-Zur were a few left of those who had forsaken the Law and the precepts, since this was their refuge.

15 Now King Alexander heard of all the promises that Demetrius had sent to Jonathan, and he heard of the battles that Jonathan[w] and his brothers had fought, of the brave deeds that they had done, and of the troubles that they had endured. 16 So he said, "Shall we find another such man? Come now, we will make him our friend and ally." 17 And he wrote a letter and sent it to him, in the following words:

18 "King Alexander to his brother Jonathan, greetings. 19 We have heard about you, that you are a mighty warrior and worthy to be our friend. 20 And so we have appointed you today to be the high priest of your nation; you are to be called the king's Friend and you are to take our side and keep friendship with us." He also sent him a purple robe and a golden crown.

21 So Jonathan put on the sacred vestments in the seventh month of the one hundred sixtieth year,[x] at the festival of booths,[y] and he recruited troops and equipped them with arms in abundance. 22 When Demetrius heard of these things he was distressed and said, 23 "What is this that we have done? Alexander has gotten ahead of us in forming a friendship with the Jews to strengthen himself. 24 I also will write them words of encouragement and promise them honor and gifts, so that I may have their help." 25 So he sent a message to them in the following words:

"King Demetrius to the nation of the Jews, greetings. 26 Since you have kept your agreement with us and have continued your friendship with us, and have not sided with our enemies, we have heard of it and rejoiced. 27 Now continue still to keep faith with us, and we will repay you with good for what you do for us. 28 We will grant you many immunities and give you gifts.

29 "I now free you and exempt all the Jews from payment of tribute and salt tax and crown levies, 30 and instead of collecting the third of the grain and the half of the fruit of the trees that I should receive, I release them from this day and henceforth. I will not collect them from the land of Judah or from the three districts added to it from Samaria and Galilee, from this day and for all time. 31 Jerusalem and its environs, its tithes and its revenues, shall be holy and free from tax. 32 I release also my control of the citadel in Jerusalem and give it to the high priest, so that he may station in it men of his own choice to guard it. 33 And everyone of the Jews taken as a captive from the land of Judah into any part of my kingdom, I set free without payment; and let all officials cancel also the taxes on their livestock.

34 "All the festivals and sabbaths and new moons and appointed days, and the three days before a festival and the three after a festival — let them all be days of immunity and release for all the Jews who are in my kingdom. 35 No one shall have authority to exact anything from them or annoy any of them about any matter.

36 "Let Jews be enrolled in the king's forces to the number of thirty thousand men, and let the maintenance be given them that is due to all the forces of the king. 37 Let some of them be stationed in the great strongholds of the king, and let some of them be put in positions of trust in the kingdom. Let their officers and leaders be of their own number, and let them live by their own laws, just as the king has commanded in the land of Judah.

38 "As for the three districts that have been added to Judea from the country of Samaria, let them be annexed to Judea so that they may be considered to be under one ruler and obey no other authority than the high priest. 39 Ptole-

15 When King Alexander heard of the promises made to Jonathan by Demetrius, and was given an account of the battles and heroic deeds of Jonathan and his brothers, and of the hardships they had endured, he exclaimed, 16 'Where shall we ever find another man like this? Let us make him our Friend and ally at once.' 17 He therefore wrote Jonathan the following letter:

18 From King Alexander to his brother Jonathan.
Greeting.

19 Reports have reached us of your valour and of how worthy you are to be our Friend. 20 Now this day we appoint you to be high priest of your nation with the title of king's Friend, to support our cause and to maintain friendship with us.

He also sent him a purple robe and a gold crown.

21 Jonathan assumed the sacred vestments in the seventh month of the year 160 at the feast of Tabernacles; he gathered an army and got ready a large supply of weapons. 22 Demetrius was mortified at the news. 23 'How did we come to let Alexander forestall us in gaining the friendship and support of the Jews?' he demanded. 24 'I too shall write to them in cordial terms and offer honours and gifts to keep them on my side.' 25 So he sent the Jews the following message:

From King Demetrius to the Jewish nation.
Greeting.

26 We have heard with much pleasure that you have honoured your agreements and remained in friendship with us and have not gone over to our enemies. 27 Continue now to keep faith with us, and we shall reward you well for what you do in our cause, 28 both by granting you numerous exemptions and by making you gifts.

29 I hereby release and exempt you and all Jews whatsoever from tribute, from the tax on salt, and from the crown-levy. 30 From today and hereafter I exempt you from the one-third of the grain harvest and the half of the fruit harvest due to me; from today and for all time, I shall no longer exact them from Judaea or from the three administrative districts, formerly part of Samaria and Galilee, which I now attach to Judaea. 31 Jerusalem and its environs, with its tithes and tolls, shall be sacred and free of taxes. 32 I surrender also authority over the citadel in Jerusalem and grant the high priest the right to garrison it with men of his own choice. 33 All Jewish prisoners of war taken from Judaea into any part of my realm I now set at liberty without ransom. No one shall exact any levy whatsoever on the livestock of the Jews. 34 All their festivals, sabbaths, new moons, and appointed days, with three days preceding and following each festival, shall be days of exemption and release for all Jews in my kingdom; 35 no one shall have authority to impose on a Jew any exaction or burden whatsoever.

36 Jews shall be enlisted in the forces of the crown to the number of thirty thousand men; they shall receive the standard rate of army pay. 37 Some of them shall be stationed in the important royal strongholds, others placed in positions of trust in the kingdom. Their commanders and officers shall be of their own race, and they may follow their own customs, just as the king has ordered for Judaea.

38 The three districts annexed to Judaea from the territory of Samaria shall be so annexed as to be deemed under a single control and subject to no authority other than that of the high priest.

w Gk he   x 152 B.C.   y Or tabernacles   10:21 **160:** that is 152 B.C.E.

2478

15 King Alexander heard of the promises that Demetrius had made to Jonathan; he was also told of the battles and valiant deeds of Jonathan and his brothers and the troubles that they had endured. 16 He said, "Shall we ever find another man like him? Let us now make him our friend and ally." 17 So he sent Jonathan a letter written in these terms: 18 "King Alexander sends greetings to his brother Jonathan. 19 We have heard of you, that you are a mighty warrior and worthy to be our friend. 20 We have therefore appointed you today to be high priest of your nation; you are to be called the King's Friend, and you are to look after our interests and preserve amity with us." He also sent him a purple robe and a crown of gold.

21 Jonathan put on the sacred vestments in the seventh month of the year one hundred and sixty at the feast of Booths, and he gathered an army and procured many arms. 22 When Demetrius heard of these things, he was distressed and said: 23 "Why have we allowed Alexander to get ahead of us by gaining the friendship of the Jews and thus strengthening himself? 24 I too will write them conciliatory words and offer dignities and gifts, so that they may be an aid to me."

25 So he sent them this message: "King Demetrius sends greetings to the Jewish nation. 26 We have heard how you have kept the treaty with us and continued in our friendship and not gone over to our enemies, and we are glad. 27 Continue, therefore, to keep faith with us, and we will reward you with favors in return for what you do in our behalf. 28 We will grant you many exemptions and will bestow gifts on you.

29 "I now free you, as I also exempt all the Jews, from the tribute, the salt tax, and the crown levies. 30 Instead of collecting the third of the grain and the half of the fruit of the trees that should be my share, I renounce the right from this day forward. Neither now nor in the future will I collect them from the land of Judah or from the three districts annexed from Samaria. 31 Let Jerusalem and her territory, her tithes and her tolls, be sacred and free from tax. 32 I also yield my authority over the citadel in Jerusalem, and I transfer it to the high priest, that he may put in it such men as he shall choose to guard it. 33 Every one of the Jews who has been carried into captivity from the land of Judah into any part of my kingdom I set at liberty without ransom; and let all their taxes, even those on their cattle, be canceled. 34 Let all feast days, sabbaths, new moon festivals, appointed days, and the three days that precede each feast day, and the three days that follow, be days of immunity and exemption for every Jew in my kingdom. 35 Let no man have authority to exact payment from them or to molest any of them in any matter.

36 "Let thirty thousand Jews be enrolled in the king's army and allowances be given them, as is due to all the king's soldiers. 37 Let some of them be stationed in the king's principal strongholds, and of these let some be given positions of trust in the affairs of the kingdom. Let their superiors and their rulers be taken from among them, and let them follow their own laws, as the king has commanded in the land of Judah.

38 "Let the three districts that have been added to Judea from the province of Samaria be incorporated with Judea so that they may be under one man and obey no other authority

15 King Alexander heard of all the promises Demetrius had sent to Jonathan, and he was also given an account of the battles and exploits of this man and his brothers and of the hardships they had endured. 16 'Shall we ever find another man like him?' he exclaimed. 'We must make him our friend and ally!' 17 He therefore wrote him a letter, addressing him in these terms:

18 'King Alexander to his brother Jonathan, greetings.

19 'You have been brought to our notice as a strong man of action and as someone who deserves to be our friend. 20 Accordingly, we have today appointed you high priest of your nation, with the title of "Friend of the King" ' — he also sent him a purple robe and a golden crown — 'and you are to study our interests and maintain friendly relations with us.'

21 Jonathan put on the sacred vestments in the seventh month of the year 160, on the feast of Shelters; he then set about raising troops and manufacturing arms in quantity. 22 Demetrius was displeased when he heard what had happened. 23 'What have we been doing,' he said, 'for Alexander to forestall us in winning the friendship of the Jews and so improving his own position? 24 I too shall address an appeal to them, offering them advancement and riches as an inducement to support me.' 25 And he wrote to them as follows:

'King Demetrius to the Jewish nation, greetings.

26 'We have heard how you have kept your agreement with us and have maintained friendly relations with us and have not gone over to our enemies, and it has given us great satisfaction. 27 If you now continue to keep faith with us, we shall make you a handsome return for what you do on our behalf. 28 We shall accord you many exemptions and grant you privileges.

29 'Henceforth I release you and exempt all the Jews from the tribute, the salt dues and the crown levies, 30 and whereas I am entitled to one-third of the grain and one-half of the fruit of the trees, I release from this levy, from today and for the future, Judaea and the three districts annexed to it from Samaria-Galilee, from this day henceforth in perpetuity. 31 Jerusalem will be sacred and exempt, with its territory, from tithes and dues. 32 I relinquish control of the Citadel in Jerusalem and make it over to the high priest, so that he may man it with a garrison of his own choosing. 33 Every Jewish person taken from Judaea into captivity in any part of my kingdom I set free without ransom, and decree that all will be exempt from taxes, even on their livestock. 34 All festivals, Sabbaths, New Moons and days of special observance, and the three days before and three days after a festival, will be days of exemption and quittance for all the Jews in my kingdom, 35 and no one will have the right to exact payment from, or to molest, any of them for any matter whatsoever.

36 'Jews will be enrolled in the king's forces to the number of thirty thousand men and receive maintenance on the same scale as the rest of the king's forces. 37 Some of them will be stationed in the king's major fortresses, and from among others appointments will be made to positions of trust in the kingdom. Their officers and commanders will be appointed from their own number and will live under their own laws, as the king has prescribed for Judaea.

38 'As regards the three districts annexed to Judaea from the province of Samaria, these will be integrated into Judaea and considered as coming under one governor, obeying the high priest's authority and no other.

mais and the land adjoining it I have given as a gift to the sanctuary in Jerusalem, to meet the necessary expenses of the sanctuary. 40 I also grant fifteen thousand shekels of silver yearly out of the king's revenues from appropriate places. 41 And all the additional funds that the government officials have not paid as they did in the first years,*z* they shall give from now on for the service of the temple.*a* 42 Moreover, the five thousand shekels of silver that my officials*b* have received every year from the income of the services of the temple, this too is canceled, because it belongs to the priests who minister there. 43 And all who take refuge at the temple in Jerusalem, or in any of its precincts, because they owe money to the king or are in debt, let them be released and receive back all their property in my kingdom.

44 "Let the cost of rebuilding and restoring the structures of the sanctuary be paid from the revenues of the king. 45 And let the cost of rebuilding the walls of Jerusalem and fortifying it all around, and the cost of rebuilding the walls in Judea, also be paid from the revenues of the king."

46 When Jonathan and the people heard these words, they did not believe or accept them, because they remembered the great wrongs that Demetrius*c* had done in Israel and how much he had oppressed them. 47 They favored Alexander, because he had been the first to speak peaceable words to them, and they remained his allies all his days.

48 Now King Alexander assembled large forces and encamped opposite Demetrius. 49 The two kings met in battle, and the army of Demetrius fled, and Alexander*d* pursued him and defeated them. 50 He pressed the battle strongly until the sun set, and on that day Demetrius fell.

51 Then Alexander sent ambassadors to Ptolemy king of Egypt with the following message: 52 "Since I have returned to my kingdom and have taken my seat on the throne of my ancestors, and established my rule—for I crushed Demetrius and gained control of our country; 53 I met him in battle, and he and his army were crushed by us, and we have taken our seat on the throne of his kingdom— 54 now therefore let us establish friendship with one another; give me now your daughter as my wife, and I will become your son-in-law, and will make gifts to you and to her in keeping with your position."

55 Ptolemy the king replied and said, "Happy was the day on which you returned to the land of your ancestors and took your seat on the throne of their kingdom. 56 And now I will do for you as you wrote, but meet me at Ptolemais, so that we may see one another, and I will become your father-in-law, as you have said."

57 So Ptolemy set out from Egypt, he and his daughter Cleopatra, and came to Ptolemais in the one hundred sixty-second year.*e* 58 King Alexander met him, and Ptolemy*c* gave him his daughter Cleopatra in marriage, and celebrated her wedding at Ptolemais with great pomp, as kings do.

59 Then King Alexander wrote to Jonathan to come and meet him. 60 So he went with pomp to Ptolemais and met the two kings; he gave them and their Friends silver and gold and many gifts, and found favor with them. 61 A group of malcontents from Israel, renegades, gathered together against him to accuse him; but the king paid no attention to them. 62 The king gave orders to take off Jonathan's garments and to clothe him in purple; and they did so. 63 The king also seated him at his side; and he said to his officers, "Go out with him into the middle of the city and proclaim that no one is to bring charges against him about any matter, and let no one annoy him for any reason." 64 When his

39 Ptolemais and the adjoining land I make over to the temple in Jerusalem, to meet the expenses proper to it. 40 I myself shall make an annual grant of fifteen thousand silver shekels, charged on my own royal accounts, to be drawn from such places as may prove convenient. 41 And the arrears of the subsidy, in so far as it has not been paid by the revenue officials, as it formerly was, shall henceforth be paid in for the needs of the temple. 42 Further, the five thousand silver shekels which used to be taken from the annual income of the temple are also remitted, because they belong to the ministering priests. 43 Whoever takes sanctuary in the temple at Jerusalem or in any part of its precincts, because of a debt to the crown or any other debt, shall be free from distraint on his person or on his property within my kingdom. 44 The cost of the rebuilding and renovation of the temple shall be borne by the royal revenue; 45 in addition, the repair of the walls of Jerusalem and its surrounding fortification, as well as of the fortresses in Judaea, shall become a charge on the royal revenue.

46 Jonathan and the people put no faith in those proposals when they heard them, and declined to accept them, for they recalled the great harm the king had done Israel and his harsh oppression of them. 47 They favoured Alexander, because he had been the first to make overtures of peace, and they remained his allies to the end.

48 King Alexander mustered large forces and took up position over against Demetrius. 49 When the two kings joined battle, Alexander's army was put to flight. Demetrius pursued with vigour, 50 pressing home the attack till sunset; but Demetrius fell that day.

51 Alexander sent envoys to Ptolemy, the king of Egypt, with this message: 52 'I have returned to my kingdom and now sit on the throne of my ancestors. I have assumed the government, defeated Demetrius, and made myself master of our country; 53 when I gave battle, he and his army were routed, and I occupy the throne of his kingdom. 54 Now let us form an alliance; make me your son-in-law by giving me your daughter in marriage, and both to you and to her I shall make gifts worthy of your royal state.'

55 King Ptolemy replied: 'It was a happy day when you returned to the land of your ancestors and ascended the throne of their realm. 56 I now accede to your request; but come to Ptolemais so that we may meet, and I shall become your father-in-law as you propose.'

57 In the year 162, Ptolemy set out from Egypt with his daughter Cleopatra, and arrived at Ptolemais, 58 where King Alexander met him. Ptolemy gave him his daughter in marriage, and the wedding was celebrated there in royal style with great pomp.

59 King Alexander wrote to Jonathan to come and meet him. 60 Jonathan went in state to Ptolemais, where he met the two kings; he presented them with silver and gold, and also made many gifts to their Friends; and so he won their favour.

61 There were some pestilent Jewish renegades who conspired to lodge complaints against Jonathan. The king, however, paid no heed to them, 62 but gave orders for Jonathan to be divested of the garment he wore and to be robed in purple, and this was done. 63 The king then seated him at his side, and bade his officers escort Jonathan into the centre of the city and proclaim that no one should bring any complaint against him or make trouble for him for any reason whatsoever. 64 When this proclamation was made

z Meaning of Gk uncertain   *a* Gk *house*   *b* Gk *they*   *c* Gk *he*
d Other ancient authorities read *Alexander fled, and Demetrius*
e 150 B.C.

10:57 **162:** *that is* 150 B.C.E.

than the high priest. 39 Ptolemais and its confines I give as a present to the sanctuary in Jerusalem for the necessary expenses of the sanctuary. 40 I make a yearly personal grant of fifteen thousand silver shekels out of the royal revenues, from appropriate places. 41 All the additional funds that the officials did not hand over as they had done in the first years, shall henceforth be handed over for the services of the temple. 42 Moreover, the dues of five thousand silver shekels that used to be taken from the revenue of the sanctuary every year shall be canceled, since these funds belong to the priests who perform the services. 43 Whoever takes refuge in the temple of Jerusalem or in any of its precincts, because of money he owes the king, or because of any other debt, shall be released, together with all the goods he possesses in my kingdom. 44 The cost of rebuilding and restoring the structures of the sanctuary shall be covered out of the royal revenue. 45 Likewise the cost of building the walls of Jerusalem and fortifying it all around, and of building walls in Judea, shall be donated from the royal revenue."

46 When Jonathan and the people heard these words, they neither believed nor accepted them, for they remembered the great evil that Demetrius had done in Israel, and how sorely he had afflicted them. 47 They therefore decided in favor of Alexander, for he had been the first to address them peaceably, and they remained his allies for the rest of his life.

48 King Alexander gathered together a large army and encamped opposite Demetrius. 49 The two kings joined battle, and when the army of Demetrius fled, Alexander pursued him, and overpowered his soldiers. 50 He pressed the battle hard until sunset, and Demetrius fell that day.

51 Alexander sent ambassadors to Ptolemy, king of Egypt, with this message: 52 "Now that I have returned to my realm, taken my seat on the throne of my fathers, and established my rule by crushing Demetrius and gaining control of my country — 53 for I engaged him in battle, defeated him and his army, and recovered the royal throne — 54 let us now establish friendship with each other. Give me your daughter for my wife; and as your son-in-law, I will give to you and to her gifts worthy of you."

55 King Ptolemy answered in these words: "Happy the day on which you returned to the land of your fathers and took your seat on their royal throne! 56 I will do for you what you have written; but meet me in Ptolemais, so that we may see each other, and I will become your father-in-law as you have proposed."

57 So Ptolemy with his daughter Cleopatra set out from Egypt and came to Ptolemais in the year one hundred and sixty-two. 58 There King Alexander met him, and Ptolemy gave him his daughter Cleopatra in marriage. Their wedding was celebrated at Ptolemais with great splendor according to the custom of kings.

59 King Alexander also wrote to Jonathan to come and meet him. 60 So he went with pomp to Ptolemais, where he met the two kings and gave them and their friends silver and gold and many gifts and thus won their favor. 61 Some pestilent Israelites, transgressors of the law, united against him to accuse him, but the king paid no heed to them. 62 He ordered Jonathan to be divested of his ordinary garments and to be clothed in royal purple; and so it was done. 63 The king also had him seated at his side. He said to his magistrates: "Go with him to the center of the city and make a proclamation that no one is to bring charges against him on any grounds or be troublesome to him in any way."

39 Ptolemais and the land thereto pertaining I present to the sanctuary in Jerusalem, to meet the necessary expenses of public worship. 40 And I make a personal grant of fifteen thousand silver shekels annually chargeable to the royal revenue from appropriate places. 41 And the entire surplus, which has not been paid in by the officials as in previous years, will henceforth be paid over by them for work on the Temple. 42 In addition, the sum of five thousand silver shekels, levied annually on the profits of the sanctuary, as shown in the annual accounts, is also relinquished as the perquisite of the priests who perform the liturgy. 43 Anyone who takes refuge in the Temple in Jerusalem or any of its precincts, when in debt to the royal exchequer or otherwise, will be discharged in full possession of all the goods he owns in my kingdom. 44 As regards the building and restoration of the sanctuary, the expense of the work will be met from the royal exchequer. 45 The reconstruction of the walls of Jerusalem and the fortification of the perimeter will also be a charge on the royal exchequer, as also the reconstruction of other city walls in Judaea.'

46 When Jonathan and the people heard these proposals, they put no faith in them and refused to accept them, remembering what great wrongs Demetrius had done to Israel and how cruelly he had oppressed them. 47 They decided in favour of Alexander, since he seemed to offer the better inducements of the two, and they became his constant allies. 48 King Alexander now mustered large forces and advanced against Demetrius. 49 The two kings met in battle. Alexander's army was routed, and Demetrius pursued him and defeated his troops. 50 He continued the battle with vigour until sunset. Demetrius himself, however, was killed the same day.

51 Alexander sent ambassadors to Ptolemy king of Egypt, with this message:

52 'Since I have returned to my kingdom, have ascended the throne of my ancestors, have gained control by crushing Demetrius and so recovered our country — 53 for I fought him and we crushed both him and his army, and I now occupy his royal throne — 54 let us now make a treaty of friendship. Give me your daughter in marriage: as your son-in-law, I shall give you, and her, presents which are worthy of you.'

55 King Ptolemy replied as follows:

'Happy the day when you returned to the land of your ancestors and ascended their royal throne! 56 I shall at once do for you what your letter proposes; but meet me at Ptolemais, so that we can see one another, and I shall become your father-in-law, as you have asked.'

57 Ptolemy left Egypt with his daughter Cleopatra and reached Ptolemais in the year 162. 58 King Alexander went to meet him, and Ptolemy gave him the hand of his daughter Cleopatra and celebrated her wedding in Ptolemais with great magnificence, as kings do. 59 King Alexander then wrote to Jonathan to come and meet him. 60 Jonathan made his way in state to Ptolemais and met the two kings; he gave them and their friends silver and gold, and many gifts, and made a favourable impression on them. 61 A number of scoundrels, the pest of Israel, combined to denounce him, but the king paid no attention to them. 62 In fact, the king commanded that Jonathan should be divested of his own garments and clothed in the purple, which was done. 63 The king then seated him by his side and said to his officers, 'Escort him into the centre of the city and proclaim that no one is to bring charges against him on any count; no one is to molest him for any reason.' 64 And so, when his accusers

accusers saw the honor that was paid him, in accord with the proclamation, and saw him clothed in purple, they all fled. 65 Thus the king honored him and enrolled him among his chief*f* Friends, and made him general and governor of the province. 66 And Jonathan returned to Jerusalem in peace and gladness.

67 In the one hundred sixty-fifth year*g* Demetrius son of Demetrius came from Crete to the land of his ancestors. 68 When King Alexander heard of it, he was greatly distressed and returned to Antioch. 69 And Demetrius appointed Apollonius the governor of Coelesyria, and he assembled a large force and encamped against Jamnia. Then he sent the following message to the high priest Jonathan: 70 "You are the only one to rise up against us, and I have fallen into ridicule and disgrace because of you. Why do you assume authority against us in the hill country? 71 If you now have confidence in your forces, come down to the plain to meet us, and let us match strength with each other there, for I have with me the power of the cities. 72 Ask and learn who I am and who the others are that are helping us. People will tell you that you cannot stand before us, for your ancestors were twice put to flight in their own land. 73 And now you will not be able to withstand my cavalry and such an army in the plain, where there is no stone or pebble, or place to flee."

74 When Jonathan heard the words of Apollonius, his spirit was aroused. He chose ten thousand men and set out from Jerusalem, and his brother Simon met him to help him. 75 He encamped before Joppa, but the people of the city closed its gates, for Apollonius had a garrison in Joppa. 76 So they fought against it, and the people of the city became afraid and opened the gates, and Jonathan gained possession of Joppa.

77 When Apollonius heard of it, he mustered three thousand cavalry and a large army, and went to Azotus as though he were going farther. At the same time he advanced into the plain, for he had a large troop of cavalry and put confidence in it. 78 Jonathan*h* pursued him to Azotus, and the armies engaged in battle. 79 Now Apollonius had secretly left a thousand cavalry behind them. 80 Jonathan learned that there was an ambush behind him, for they surrounded his army and shot arrows at his men from early morning until late afternoon. 81 But his men stood fast, as Jonathan had commanded, and the enemy's*i* horses grew tired.

82 Then Simon brought forward his force and engaged the phalanx in battle (for the cavalry was exhausted); they were overwhelmed by him and fled, 83 and the cavalry was dispersed in the plain. They fled to Azotus and entered Beth-dagon, the temple of their idol, for safety. 84 But Jonathan burned Azotus and the surrounding towns and plundered them; and the temple of Dagon, and those who had taken refuge in it, he burned with fire. 85 The number of those who fell by the sword, with those burned alive, came to eight thousand.

86 Then Jonathan left there and encamped against Askalon, and the people of the city came out to meet him with great pomp.

87 He and those with him then returned to Jerusalem with a large amount of booty. 88 When King Alexander heard of these things, he honored Jonathan still more; 89 and he sent to him a golden buckle, such as it is the custom to give to the King's Kinsmen. He also gave him Ekron and all its environs as his possession.

11 Then the king of Egypt gathered great forces, like the sand by the seashore, and many ships; and he tried to get possession of Alexander's kingdom by trickery and add it to his own kingdom. 2 He set out for Syria with

and the men who had planned to lodge complaints saw Jonathan's splendour and the purple robe he wore, one and all decamped. 65 So, honoured by the king, enrolled in the first class of the order of king's Friends, and appointed a general and a provincial governor, 66 Jonathan returned to Jerusalem well pleased with his success.

67 IN the year 165, Demetrius, the son of King Demetrius, arrived in the land of his fathers from Crete, 68 which greatly perturbed King Alexander when he heard of it, and made him return to Antioch. 69 Demetrius appointed as his commander Apollonius the governor of Coele-Syria, who raised a powerful force and encamped at Jamnia. From there he sent this message to Jonathan the high priest: 70 'You are alone in offering resistance to us, and your opposition is bringing me ridicule and disgrace. Why do you defy us up there in the hills? 71 Now if you have confidence in your forces, come down and meet us on the plain, and let us try conclusions with each other there, for I have the power of the cities behind me. 72 Make enquiries; find out who I am, and who are our allies. You will be told that you cannot stand your ground against us: your predecessors were routed twice in their own territory, 73 and now you will not be able to resist my cavalry and such a force as mine on the plain, where there is not so much as a stone or a pebble, or any place to which you can escape.'

74 Provoked by this message from Apollonius, Jonathan marched out from Jerusalem with ten thousand picked men and was joined by his brother Simon with reinforcements. 75 He laid siege to Joppa, where the citizens had closed the gates against him because Apollonius had a garrison there. 76 But when the fighting started, the citizens were frightened and opened the gates; so Jonathan became master of Joppa. 77 Hearing of this, Apollonius with three thousand cavalry and a large body of infantry marched to Azotus as if to pass through it, but at the same time, relying on his numerous cavalry, he advanced into the plain. 78 Jonathan pursued him as far as Azotus, where battle was joined. 79 Apollonius had left behind a thousand cavalry in concealment, 80 and Jonathan now discovered this ambush at his rear. Though surrounded by the enemy raining arrows on them from dawn till dusk, 81 his army stood firm as Jonathan had ordered, and the enemy's horses grew weary. 82 At that point, with the cavalry now exhausted, Simon led out his troops and engaged the enemy phalanx, which, routed by him, took to flight.

83 The horsemen scattered across the plain and the infantry fled to Azotus, where they sought refuge in the temple of Dagon their idol. 84 But Jonathan set fire to Azotus and its surrounding villages, and plundered them; the temple of Dagon, with those who had fled there, he burnt to the ground. 85 The numbers of those who fell by the sword, together with those who lost their lives in the fire, reached eight thousand. 86 Jonathan marched from Azotus, and encamped at Ascalon, where with great pomp the citizens came out to meet him. 87 He and his men returned to Jerusalem loaded with spoil.

88 When these events were reported to King Alexander, he conferred still greater honour on Jonathan, 89 sending him the gold clasp which it is the custom to present to the king's Kinsmen; he also granted him Accaron and all its environs as a personal gift.

11 The king of Egypt gathered a huge army, countless as the sand on the seashore, and with it a great fleet of ships; his intention was to make himself master of Alexander's kingdom by a subterfuge and to add it to his own.

f Gk first   *g* 147 B.C.   *h* Gk he   *i* Gk their   10:67 **165:** *that is* 147 B.C.E.

64 When his accusers saw the honor paid to him in the proclamation, and the purple with which he was clothed, they all fled. 65 The king also honored him by numbering him among his Chief Friends and made him military commander and governor of the province. 66 So Jonathan returned in peace and happiness to Jerusalem.

67 In the year one hundred and sixty-five, Demetrius, son of Demetrius, came from Crete to the land of his fathers. 68 When King Alexander heard of it he was greatly troubled, and returned to Antioch. 69 Demetrius appointed Apollonius governor of Coelesyria. Having gathered a large army, Apollonius pitched his camp at Jamnia. From there he sent this message to Jonathan the high priest:

70 "You are the only one who resists us. I am laughed at and put to shame on your account. Why are you displaying power against us in the mountains? 71 If you have confidence in your forces, come down now to us in the plain, and let us test each other's strength there; the city forces are on my side. 72 Inquire and learn who I am and who the others are who are helping me. Men say that you cannot make a stand against us because your fathers were twice put to flight in their own land. 73 Now you too will be unable to withstand our cavalry and such a force as this in the plain, where there is not a stone or a pebble or a place to flee."

74 When Jonathan heard the message of Apollonius, he was roused. Choosing ten thousand men, he set out from Jerusalem, and Simon his brother joined him to help him. 75 He pitched camp near Joppa, but the men in the city shut him out because Apollonius had a garrison there. When the Jews besieged it, 76 the men of the city became afraid and opened the gates, and so Jonathan took possession of Joppa.

77 When Apollonius heard of it, he drew up three thousand horsemen and an innumerable infantry. He marched on Azotus as though he were going on through the country, but at the same time he advanced into the plain, because he had such a large number of horsemen to rely on. 78 Jonathan followed him to Azotus, and they engaged in battle. 79 Apollonius, however, had left a thousand cavalry in hiding behind them. 80 When Jonathan discovered that there was an ambush behind him, his army was surrounded. From morning until evening they showered his men with arrows. 81 But his men held their ground, as Jonathan had commanded, whereas the enemy's horses became tired out. 82 When the horsemen were exhausted, Simon attacked the phalanx, overwhelmed it and put it to flight. 83 The horsemen too were scattered over the plain. The enemy fled to Azotus and entered Beth-dagon, the temple of their idol, to save themselves. 84 But Jonathan burned and plundered Azotus with its neighboring towns, and destroyed by fire both the temple of Dagon and the men who had taken refuge in it. 85 Those who fell by the sword, together with those who were burned alive, came to about eight thousand men. 86 Then Jonathan left there and pitched his camp at Ashkalon, and the people of that city came out to meet him with great pomp. 87 He and his men then returned to Jerusalem, laden with much booty. 88 When King Alexander heard of these events, he accorded new honors to Jonathan. 89 He sent him a gold buckle, such as is usually given to King's Kinsmen; he also gave him Ekron and all its territory as a possession.

saw the honour done him by this proclamation, and Jonathan himself invested in the purple, they all fled. 65 The king did him the honour of enrolling him among the First Friends, and appointed him commander-in-chief and governor-general. 66 Jonathan then returned to Jerusalem in peace and gladness.

67 In the year 165, Demetrius son of Demetrius came from Crete to the land of his ancestors. 68 When King Alexander heard of it he was plunged into gloom, and retired to Antioch. 69 Demetrius confirmed Apollonius as governor of Coele-Syria; the latter assembled a large force, encamped at Jamnia and sent the following message to Jonathan the high priest:

70 'You are entirely alone in rising against us, and now I find myself ridiculed and reproached on your account. Why do you use your authority to our disadvantage in the mountains? 71 If you are so confident in your forces, come down now to meet us on the plain and let us take each other's measure there; on my side I have the strength of the towns. 72 Ask and learn who I am and who the others supporting us are. You will hear that you cannot stand up to us, since your ancestors were twice routed on their own ground, 73 nor will you now be able to withstand the cavalry or so great an army on the plain, where there is neither rock, nor stone, nor refuge of any kind.'

74 On hearing Apollonius' words, Jonathan's spirit was roused; he picked ten thousand men and left Jerusalem, and his brother Simon joined him with reinforcements. 75 He drew up his forces outside Joppa, the citizens having shut him out, since Apollonius had a garrison in Joppa. When they began the attack, 76 the citizens took fright and opened the gates, and Jonathan occupied Joppa. 77 Hearing this, Apollonius marshalled three thousand cavalry and a large army and made his way to Azotus as though intending to march through, while in fact pressing on into the plain, since he had a great number of cavalry on which he was relying. 78 Jonathan pursued him as far as Azotus, where the armies joined battle. 79 Now, Apollonius had left a thousand horsemen in concealment behind them. 80 Jonathan knew of this enemy position behind him; the horsemen surrounded his army, firing their arrows into his men from morning till evening. 81 But the troops stood firm, as Jonathan had ordered. Once the cavalry was exhausted, 82 Simon sent his own troops into attack against the phalanx, which he cut to pieces and routed. 83 The cavalry scattered over the plain and fled to Azotus, where they took sanctuary in Beth-Dagon, the temple of their idol. 84 Jonathan, however, set fire to Azotus and the surrounding towns, plundered them, and burned down the temple of Dagon, with all the fugitives who had crowded into it. 85 The enemy losses, counting those who fell by the sword and those burnt to death, totalled about eight thousand men. 86 Jonathan then left and pitched camp outside Ascalon, where the citizens came out to meet him with every ceremony. 87 Jonathan then returned to Jerusalem with his followers, laden with booty. 88 In the event, when King Alexander heard what had happened, he awarded Jonathan further honours: 89 he sent him the golden brooch, of the kind customarily presented to the King's Cousins, and gave him proprietary rights over Ekron and the land adjoining it.

11 The king of Egypt gathered his forces, as numerous as the sands of the seashore, and many ships; and he sought by deceit to take Alexander's kingdom and add it to his own. 2 He entered Syria with peaceful words, and the

11 The king of Egypt then assembled an army as numerous as the sands of the seashore, with many ships, and set out to take possession of Alexander's kingdom by a ruse and add it to his own kingdom. 2 He set off

NEW REVISED STANDARD VERSION	REVISED ENGLISH BIBLE

peaceable words, and the people of the towns opened their gates to him and went to meet him, for King Alexander had commanded them to meet him, since he was Alexander's *j* father-in-law. 3 But when Ptolemy entered the towns he stationed forces as a garrison in each town.

4 When he*k* approached Azotus, they showed him the burnt-out temple of Dagon, and Azotus and its suburbs destroyed, and the corpses lying about, and the charred bodies of those whom Jonathan*l* had burned in the war, for they had piled them in heaps along his route. 5 They also told the king what Jonathan had done, to throw blame on him; but the king kept silent. 6 Jonathan met the king at Joppa with pomp, and they greeted one another and spent the night there. 7 And Jonathan went with the king as far as the river called Eleutherus; then he returned to Jerusalem.

8 So King Ptolemy gained control of the coastal cities as far as Seleucia by the sea, and he kept devising wicked designs against Alexander. 9 He sent envoys to King Demetrius, saying, "Come, let us make a covenant with each other, and I will give you in marriage my daughter who was Alexander's wife, and you shall reign over your father's kingdom. 10 I now regret that I gave him my daughter, for he has tried to kill me." 11 He threw blame on Alexander*m* because he coveted his kingdom. 12 So he took his daughter away from him and gave her to Demetrius. He was estranged from Alexander, and their enmity became manifest.

13 Then Ptolemy entered Antioch and put on the crown of Asia. Thus he put two crowns on his head, the crown of Egypt and that of Asia. 14 Now King Alexander was in Cilicia at that time, because the people of that region were in revolt. 15 When Alexander heard of it, he came against him in battle. Ptolemy marched out and met him with a strong force, and put him to flight. 16 So Alexander fled into Arabia to find protection there, and King Ptolemy was triumphant. 17 Zabdiel the Arab cut off the head of Alexander and sent it to Ptolemy. 18 But King Ptolemy died three days later, and his troops in the strongholds were killed by the inhabitants of the strongholds. 19 So Demetrius became king in the one hundred sixty-seventh year.*n*

20 In those days Jonathan assembled the Judeans to attack the citadel in Jerusalem, and he built many engines of war to use against it. 21 But certain renegades who hated their nation went to the king and reported to him that Jonathan was besieging the citadel. 22 When he heard this he was angry, and as soon as he heard it he set out and came to Ptolemais; and he wrote Jonathan not to continue the siege, but to meet him for a conference at Ptolemais as quickly as possible.

23 When Jonathan heard this, he gave orders to continue the siege. He chose some of the elders of Israel and some of the priests, and put himself in danger, 24 for he went to the king at Ptolemais, taking silver and gold and clothing and numerous other gifts. And he won his favor. 25 Although certain renegades of his nation kept making complaints against him, 26 the king treated him as his predecessors had treated him; he exalted him in the presence of all his Friends. 27 He confirmed him in the high priesthood and in as many other honors as he had formerly had, and caused him to be reckoned among his chief*o* Friends. 28 Then Jonathan asked the king to free Judea and the three districts of Samaria*p* from tribute, and promised him three hundred talents. 29 The king consented, and wrote a letter to Jonathan about all these things; its contents were as follows:

2 He set out for Syria with protestations of peace, and the people of the towns proceeded to open their gates to him and went to meet him; this they had been ordered to do by King Alexander, because Ptolemy was his father-in-law. 3 As he continued his progress from town to town, Ptolemy left in each of them a detachment of troops as a garrison. 4 When he reached Azotus, he was shown the burnt-out temple of Dagon, the city itself and its ruined suburbs strewn with corpses and, piled up along his way, the bodies of those burnt in the course of the fighting. 5 The people told the king that it was all Jonathan's doing, for they hoped he would find fault with him; but the king said nothing. 6 When Jonathan met him in state at Joppa, they exchanged greetings and passed the night there, and 7 Jonathan accompanied the king to the river Eleutherus before returning to Jerusalem. 8 King Ptolemy made himself master of the coastal towns as far as Seleucia-by-the-sea, all the time hatching designs hostile to Alexander.

9 He sent envoys to King Demetrius with this message: 'I propose that you and I should make a compact: I will give you my daughter, now Alexander's wife, and you shall reign over the kingdom of your father. 10 I regret having given my daughter to Alexander, for he has tried to kill me.' 11 He maligned him in this way because he coveted his kingdom, 12 and he took back his daughter and gave her to Demetrius. The estrangement between Ptolemy and Alexander turned to open enmity.

13 Ptolemy now entered Antioch, where he assumed the crown of Asia, in addition to the crown of Egypt which he already wore.

14 All this time King Alexander was in Cilicia, because the inhabitants of that region were in revolt, 15 but when he heard what had been taking place he marched against Ptolemy, who met him with a strong force. Alexander was defeated 16 and fled to Arabia for protection; King Ptolemy was triumphant. 17 Zabdiel, an Arab chieftain, cut off Alexander's head and sent it to Ptolemy. 18 On the third day after that, however, King Ptolemy died, and his garrisons in the fortresses were wiped out by the local inhabitants. 19 So in the year 167 Demetrius became king.

20 At this time Jonathan mustered the Judaeans for an attack on the citadel in Jerusalem, and they constructed a large number of siege-engines for the purpose. 21 Some renegades, enemies of their own people, went to the king and reported that Jonathan was laying siege to the citadel, 22 news which excited the king's anger. At once he moved his quarters to Ptolemais, and, in a letter to Jonathan, ordered him to raise the siege and with all speed meet him for conference at Ptolemais.

23 When Jonathan received this summons, he gave orders for the siege to be continued, and then, selecting elders of Israel and priests to accompany him, he set out on his dangerous mission. 24 He took with him silver and gold, and robes, and many other gifts, with which he won the favour of Demetrius when they met at Ptolemais. 25 Although certain renegade Jews tried to lodge complaints against Jonathan, 26 the king treated him just as his predecessors had done, and honoured him in the presence of all his Friends. 27 He confirmed him in the high-priesthood and in all his former dignities, and bestowed on him the rank of head of the first class of king's Friends. 28 Jonathan requested the king to exempt Judaea and the three Samaritan districts from tribute, promising in return three hundred talents. 29 The king gave his consent, and on all these matters wrote as follows:

---

j Gk *his*   *k* Other ancient authorities read *they*   *l* Gk *he*
m Gk *him*   *n* 145 B.C.   *o* Gk *first*   *p* Cn: Gk *the three districts and Samaria*

11:19 **167**: *that is* 145 B.C.E.   11:28 **three . . . districts:** *prob. rdg; Gk* three districts and Samaria.

NEW AMERICAN BIBLE

NEW JERUSALEM BIBLE

people in the cities opened their gates to welcome him, as King Alexander had ordered them to do, since Ptolemy was his father-in-law. 3 But when Ptolemy entered the cities, he stationed garrison troops in each one. 4 When he reached Azotus, he was shown the temple of Dagon destroyed by fire, Azotus and its suburbs demolished, corpses lying about, and the charred bodies of those burned by Jonathan in the war and stacked up along his route. 5 To prejudice the king against Jonathan, he was told what the latter had done; but the king said nothing. 6 Jonathan met the king with pomp at Joppa, and they greeted each other and spent the night there. 7 Jonathan accompanied the king as far as the river called Eleutherus and then returned to Jerusalem.

8 Plotting evil against Alexander, King Ptolemy took possession of the cities along the seacoast as far as Seleucia-by-the-Sea. 9 He sent ambassadors to King Demetrius, saying: "Come, let us make a pact with each other; I will give you my daughter whom Alexander has married, and you shall reign over your father's kingdom. 10 I regret that I gave him my daughter, for he has sought to kill me." 11 His real reason for accusing Alexander, however, was that he coveted Alexander's kingdom. 12 After taking his daughter away and giving her to Demetrius, Ptolemy broke with Alexander; their enmity became open. 13 Then Ptolemy entered Antioch and assumed the crown of Asia; he thus wore two crowns on his head, that of Egypt and that of Asia.

14 King Alexander was in Cilicia at that time, because the people of that region had revolted. 15 When Alexander heard the news, he came to challenge Ptolemy in battle. Ptolemy marched out and met him with a strong force and put him to flight. 16 Alexander fled to Arabia to seek protection. King Ptolemy's triumph was complete 17 when the Arab Zabdiel cut off Alexander's head and sent it to Ptolemy. 18 But three days later King Ptolemy himself died, and his men in the fortified cities were killed by the inhabitants of the strongholds. 19 Thus Demetrius became king in the year one hundred and sixty-seven.

20 At that time Jonathan gathered together the men of Judea to attack the citadel in Jerusalem, and they set up many machines against it. 21 Some transgressors of the law, enemies of their own nation, went to the king and informed him that Jonathan was besieging the citadel. 22 When Demetrius heard this, he was furious, and set out immediately for Ptolemais. He wrote to Jonathan to discontinue the siege and to meet him for a conference at Ptolemais as soon as possible.

23 On hearing this, Jonathan ordered the siege to continue. He selected some elders and priests of Israel and exposed himself to danger 24 by going to the king at Ptolemais. He brought with him silver, gold apparel, and many other presents, and found favor with the king. 25 Although some impious men of his own nation brought charges against him, 26 the king treated him just as his predecessors had done and showed him great honor in the presence of all his Friends. 27 He confirmed him in the high priesthood and in all the honors he had previously held, and had him enrolled among his Chief Friends. 28 Jonathan asked the king to exempt Judea and the three districts of Samaria from tribute, promising him in return three hundred talents. 29 The king agreed and wrote the following letter to Jonathan about all these matters:

for Syria with protestations of peace, and the people of the towns opened their gates to him and came out to meet him, since King Alexander's orders were to welcome him, Ptolemy being his father-in-law. 3 On entering the towns, however, Ptolemy quartered troops as a garrison in each one. 4 When he reached Azotus he was shown the burnt-out temple of Dagon, with Azotus and its suburbs in ruins, corpses scattered here and there, and the charred remains of those whom Jonathan had burnt to death in the battle, piled into heaps along his route. 5 They explained to the king what Jonathan had done, hoping for his disapproval; but the king said nothing. 6 Jonathan went in state to meet the king at Joppa, where they greeted each other and spent the night. 7 Jonathan accompanied the king as far as the river called Eleutherus, and then returned to Jerusalem. 8 King Ptolemy for his part occupied the coastal towns as far as Seleucia on the coast, all the while maturing his wicked designs against Alexander. 9 He sent envoys to King Demetrius to say, 'Come and let us make a treaty; I shall give you my daughter, whom Alexander now has, and you shall rule your father's kingdom. 10 I regret having given my daughter to that man, since he has tried to kill me.' 11 He made this accusation because he coveted his kingdom. 12 Having carried off his daughter and bestowed her on Demetrius, he broke with Alexander, and their enmity became open. 13 Ptolemy next entered Antioch and assumed the crown of Asia; he now wore on his head the two crowns of Egypt and Asia. 14 King Alexander was in Cilicia at the time, since the people of those parts had risen in revolt, 15 but when he heard the news, he advanced on his rival to give battle, while Ptolemy for his part also took the field, met him with a strong force and routed him. 16 Alexander fled to Arabia for refuge, and King Ptolemy reigned supreme. 17 Zabdiel the Arab cut off Alexander's head and sent it to Ptolemy. 18 Three days later King Ptolemy died, and the Egyptian garrisons in the strongholds were killed by the local inhabitants. 19 So Demetrius became king in the year 167.

20 At the same time, Jonathan mustered the men of Judaea for an assault on the Citadel of Jerusalem, and they set up numerous siege-engines against it. 21 But some renegades who hated their nation made their way to the king and told him that Jonathan was besieging the Citadel. 22 The king was angered by the news. No sooner had he been informed than he set out and came to Ptolemais. He wrote to Jonathan, telling him to raise the siege and to meet him for a conference in Ptolemais as soon as possible. 23 When Jonathan heard this, he gave orders for the siege to continue; he then selected a deputation from the elders of Israel and the priests, and took the deliberate risk 24 of himself taking silver and gold, clothing and numerous other presents, and going to Ptolemais to face the king, whose favour he succeeded in winning; 25 and although one or two renegades of his nation brought charges against him, 26 the king treated him as his predecessors had treated him, and promoted him in the presence of all his friends. 27 He confirmed him in the high priesthood and whatever other distinctions he already held, and had him ranked among the First Friends. 28 Jonathan asked the king to exempt Judaea and the three Samaritan districts from taxation, promising him three hundred talents in return. 29 The king consented, and wrote Jonathan a rescript covering the whole matter, in these terms:

30 "King Demetrius to his brother Jonathan and to the nation of the Jews, greetings. 31 This copy of the letter that we wrote concerning you to our kinsman Lasthenes we have written to you also, so that you may know what it says. 32 'King Demetrius to his father Lasthenes, greetings. 33 We have determined to do good to the nation of the Jews, who are our friends and fulfill their obligations to us, because of the goodwill they show toward us. 34 We have confirmed as their possession both the territory of Judea and the three districts of Aphairema and Lydda and Rathamin; the latter, with all the region bordering them, were added to Judea from Samaria. To all those who offer sacrifice in Jerusalem we have granted release from *q* the royal taxes that the king formerly received from them each year, from the crops of the land and the fruit of the trees. 35 And the other payments henceforth due to us of the tithes, and the taxes due to us, and the salt pits and the crown taxes due to us — from all these we shall grant them release. 36 And not one of these grants shall be canceled from this time on forever. 37 Now therefore take care to make a copy of this, and let it be given to Jonathan and put up in a conspicuous place on the holy mountain.' "

38 When King Demetrius saw that the land was quiet before him and that there was no opposition to him, he dismissed all his troops, all of them to their own homes, except the foreign troops that he had recruited from the islands of the nations. So all the troops who had served under his predecessors hated him. 39 A certain Trypho had formerly been one of Alexander's supporters; he saw that all the troops were grumbling against Demetrius. So he went to Imalkue the Arab, who was bringing up Antiochus, the young son of Alexander, 40 and insistently urged him to hand Antiochus *r* over to him, to become king in place of his father. He also reported to Imalkue *r* what Demetrius had done and told of the hatred that the troops of Demetrius *s* had for him; and he stayed there many days.

41 Now Jonathan sent to King Demetrius the request that he remove the troops of the citadel from Jerusalem, and the troops in the strongholds; for they kept fighting against Israel. 42 And Demetrius sent this message back to Jonathan: "Not only will I do these things for you and your nation, but I will confer great honor on you and your nation, if I find an opportunity. 43 Now then you will do well to send me men who will help me, for all my troops have revolted." 44 So Jonathan sent three thousand stalwart men to him at Antioch, and when they came to the king, the king rejoiced at their arrival.

45 Then the people of the city assembled within the city, to the number of a hundred and twenty thousand, and they wanted to kill the king. 46 But the king fled into the palace. Then the people of the city seized the main streets of the city and began to fight. 47 So the king called the Jews to his aid, and they all rallied around him and then spread out through the city; and they killed on that day about one hundred thousand. 48 They set fire to the city and seized a large amount of spoil on that day, and saved the king. 49 When the people of the city saw that the Jews had gained control of the city as they pleased, their courage failed and they cried out to the king with this entreaty: 50 "Grant us peace, and make the Jews stop fighting against us and our city." 51 And they threw down their arms and made peace. So the Jews gained glory in the sight of the king and of all the people in his kingdom, and they returned to Jerusalem with a large amount of spoil.

52 So King Demetrius sat on the throne of his kingdom, and the land was quiet before him. 53 But he broke his word

30 From King Demetrius to his brother Jonathan, and to the Jewish nation.

Greeting.

31 This is what we have written in a letter to our Kinsman Lasthenes about you; we have had a copy made for your information:

32 'From King Demetrius to his respected cousin Lasthenes.

'Greeting.

33 'Since the Jewish people are well disposed towards us and observe their obligations to us, we are resolved to recognize their loyalty by becoming their benefactor. 34 We have, therefore, confirmed them in the possession of the lands of Judaea and the three districts Apherema, Lydda, and Ramathaim, which are now transferred from Samaria to Judaea, together with all the lands adjacent thereto, for the benefit of all who sacrifice at Jerusalem; this is a transfer of the annual payments which the king formerly received from these territories, from the produce of the soil and of the orchards. 35 Other of our revenues, the tithes and tolls now pertaining to us, the salt-pans, and the crown-levy, all these we shall cede to them. 36 'These concessions are from now irrevocable for all future time. 37 See to it then that you make a copy of them to be given to Jonathan for display in a prominent position on the holy mountain.'

38 When King Demetrius saw that the country was quiet under his rule and resistance at an end, he disbanded his forces, dismissing them all to their homes, with the exception of the foreign mercenaries he had recruited from the islands of the Gentiles. As a result the troops who had served under his predecessors all turned against him. 39 A certain Trypho, formerly of the party of Alexander, aware of the widespread disaffection towards Demetrius among the soldiers, went to Imalcue, the Arab chieftain, who had charge of the child Antiochus, Alexander's son, 40 and kept pressing him to hand the boy over to him to be made king in place of his father. He informed Imalcue of all the measures Demetrius was taking and of his unpopularity with his troops; and he remained there for some time.

41 Meanwhile Jonathan sent a request to King Demetrius that the garrisons which were constantly harassing Israel should be withdrawn from the citadel in Jerusalem and from the fortresses. 42 To this Demetrius replied: 'I will not only meet your request, but when opportunity arises I will do you and your people the highest honour. 43 Therefore be so good now as to send men to support me, for my own troops have all defected.'

44 Jonathan dispatched three thousand seasoned fighting men to Antioch, and the king was delighted at their coming. 45 The citizens, a hundred and twenty thousand strong, poured into the centre of the city bent on killing Demetrius, 46 and while they seized control of the streets and fighting broke out, the king took refuge in the palace. 47 He summoned the Jews to his aid, and at once they all rallied to him; they deployed throughout the city and slaughtered as many as a hundred thousand that day, 48 setting the city on fire and taking much booty. And thus the king's life was saved.

49 When the citizens saw that the Jews had the city completely at their mercy, their courage failed and they clamoured to the king 50 to accept their surrender and to stop the Jews making war on them and the city. 51 They threw down their weapons and made peace; and the Jews, now in high repute with the king and his subjects throughout the kingdom, returned to Jerusalem laden with booty. 52 But when King Demetrius was secure on his throne, with the country quiet under him, 53 he went back on all his promises

---

q Or *Samaria, for all those who offer sacrifice in Jerusalem, in place of*   *r* Gk *him*   *s* Gk *his troops*

30 "King Demetrius sends greetings to his brother Jonathan and to the Jewish nation. 31 We are sending you, for your information, a copy of the letter that we wrote to Lasthenes our kinsman concerning you. 32 'King Demetrius sends greetings to his father Lasthenes. 33 Because of the good will they show us, we have decided to bestow benefits on the Jewish nation, who are our friends and who observe their obligations to us. 34 Therefore we confirm their possession, not only of the territory of Judea, but also of the three districts of Aphairema, Lydda, and Ramathaim. These districts, together with all their dependencies, were transferred from Samaria to Judea in favor of all those who offer sacrifices for us in Jerusalem instead of paying the royal taxes that formerly the king received from them each year from the produce of the soil and the fruit of the trees. 35 From this day on we grant them release from payment of all other things that would henceforth be due to us, that is, of tithes and tribute and of the tax on the salt pans and the crown tax. 36 Henceforth none of these provisions shall ever be revoked. 37 Be sure, therefore, to have a copy of these instructions made and given to Jonathan, that it may be displayed in a conspicuous place on the holy hill.' "

38 When King Demetrius saw that the land was peaceful under his rule and that he had no opposition, he dismissed his entire army, every man to his home, except the foreign troops which he had hired from the islands of the nations. So all the soldiers who had served under his predecessors hated him. 39 When a certain Trypho, who had previously belonged to Alexander's party, saw that all the troops were grumbling at Demetrius, he went to Imalkue the Arab, who was bringing up Alexander's young son Antiochus. 40 Trypho kept urging Imalkue to hand over the boy to him, that he might make him king in his father's place. During his stay there of many days, he told him of all that Demetrius had done and of the hatred that his soldiers had for him.

41 Meanwhile Jonathan sent the request to King Demetrius to withdraw his troops from the citadel of Jerusalem and from the other strongholds, for they were constantly hostile to Israel. 42 Demetrius, in turn, sent this word to Jonathan: "I will not only do this for you and your nation, but I will greatly honor you and your nation when I find the opportunity. 43 Do me the favor, therefore, of sending men to fight for me, because all my troops have revolted."

44 So Jonathan sent three thousand good fighting men to him at Antioch. When they came to the king, he was delighted over their arrival, 45 for the populace, one hundred and twenty thousand strong, had massed in the center of the city in an attempt to kill him. 46 But he took refuge in the palace, while the populace gained control of the main streets and began to fight. 47 So the king called the Jews to his aid. They all rallied around him and spread out through the city. On that day they killed about a hundred thousand men in the city, 48 which, at the same time, they set on fire and plundered on a large scale. Thus they saved the king's life. 49 When the populace saw that the Jews held the city at their mercy, they lost courage and cried out to the king in supplication, 50 "Give us your terms and let the Jews stop attacking us and our city." So they threw down their arms and made peace. 51 The Jews thus gained glory in the eyes of the king and all his subjects, and they became renowned throughout his kingdom. Finally they returned to Jerusalem with much spoil.

52 But when King Demetrius was sure of his royal throne, and the land was peaceful under his rule, 53 he broke all his

30 'King Demetrius to Jonathan his brother, and to the Jewish nation, greetings.

31 'We have written to Lasthenes our cousin concerning you, and now send you this copy of our rescript for your own information:

32 "King Demetrius to his father Lasthenes, greetings.

33 "The nation of the Jews is our ally; they fulfil their obligations to us, and in view of their goodwill towards us we have decided to show them our bounty. 34 We confirm them in their possession of the territory of Judaea and the three districts of Aphairema, Lydda and Ramathaim; these were annexed to Judaea from Samaritan territory, with all their dependencies, in favour of all who offer sacrifice in Jerusalem, instead of the royal dues which the king formerly received from them every year, from the yield of the soil and the fruit crops. 35 As regards our other rights over the tithes and taxes due to us, over the salt marshes, and the crown taxes due to us, as from today we release them from them all. 36 None of these grants will be revoked henceforth or anywhere. 37 You will make yourself responsible for having a copy of this made, to be given to Jonathan and displayed on the holy mountain in a conspicuous place." '

38 When King Demetrius saw that the country was at peace under his rule and that no resistance was offered him, he dismissed his forces, and sent all the men home, except for the foreign troops that he had recruited in the foreign island, thus incurring the enmity of the veterans who had served his ancestors. 39 Now Trypho, one of Alexander's former supporters, noting that all the troops were muttering against Demetrius, went to see Iamleku, the Arab who was bringing up Antiochus, Alexander's young son, 40 and repeatedly urged him to let him have the boy, so that he might succeed his father as king; he told him of Demetrius' decision and of the resentment it had aroused among his troops. He spent a long time there. 41 Jonathan, meanwhile, sent to ask King Demetrius to withdraw the garrisons from the Citadel in Jerusalem and from the other fortresses, since they were constantly fighting Israel. 42 Demetrius sent word back to Jonathan, 'Not only will I do this for you and for your nation, but I shall heap honours on you and your nation if I find a favourable opportunity. 43 For the present, you would do well to send me reinforcements, since all my troops have deserted.' 44 Jonathan sent three thousand experienced soldiers to him in Antioch; when they reached the king, he was delighted at their arrival. 45 The citizens crowded together in the centre of the city, to the number of some hundred and twenty thousand, intending to kill the king. 46 The king took refuge in the palace, while the citizens occupied the thoroughfares of the city and began to attack. 47 The king then called on the Jews for help; and these all rallied round him, then fanned out through the city, and that day killed about a hundred thousand of its inhabitants. 48 They fired the city, seizing a great deal of plunder at the same time, and secured the king's safety. 49 When the citizens saw that the Jews had the city at their mercy, their courage failed them, and they made an abject appeal to the king, 50 'Give us the right hand of peace, and let the Jews stop their fight against us and the city.' 51 They threw down their arms and made peace. The Jews were covered in glory, in the eyes of the king and of everyone else in his kingdom. Having won renown in his kingdom, they returned to Jerusalem laden with booty. 52 Thus, King Demetrius sat all the more securely on his royal throne, and the country was quiet under his government. 53 But he gave the

about all that he had promised; he became estranged from Jonathan and did not repay the favors that Jonathan[t] had done him, but treated him very harshly.

54 After this Trypho returned, and with him the young boy Antiochus who began to reign and put on the crown. 55 All the troops that Demetrius had discharged gathered around him; they fought against Demetrius,[u] and he fled and was routed. 56 Trypho captured the elephants[v] and gained control of Antioch. 57 Then the young Antiochus wrote to Jonathan, saying, "I confirm you in the high priesthood and set you over the four districts and make you one of the king's Friends." 58 He also sent him gold plate and a table service, and granted him the right to drink from gold cups and dress in purple and wear a gold buckle. 59 He appointed Jonathan's[w] brother Simon governor from the Ladder of Tyre to the borders of Egypt.

60 Then Jonathan set out and traveled beyond the river and among the towns, and all the army of Syria gathered to him as allies. When he came to Askalon, the people of the city met him and paid him honor. 61 From there he went to Gaza, but the people of Gaza shut him out. So he besieged it and burned its suburbs with fire and plundered them. 62 Then the people of Gaza pleaded with Jonathan, and he made peace with them, and took the sons of their rulers as hostages and sent them to Jerusalem. And he passed through the country as far as Damascus.

63 Then Jonathan heard that the officers of Demetrius had come to Kadesh in Galilee with a large army, intending to remove him from office. 64 He went to meet them, but left his brother Simon in the country. 65 Simon encamped before Beth-zur and fought against it for many days and hemmed it in. 66 Then they asked him to grant them terms of peace, and he did so. He removed them from there, took possession of the town, and set a garrison over it.

67 Jonathan and his army encamped by the waters of Gennesaret. Early in the morning they marched to the plain of Hazor, 68 and there in the plain the army of the foreigners met him; they had set an ambush against him in the mountains, but they themselves met him face to face. 69 Then the men in ambush emerged from their places and joined battle. 70 All the men with Jonathan fled; not one of them was left except Mattathias son of Absalom and Judas son of Chalphi, commanders of the forces of the army. 71 Jonathan tore his clothes, put dust on his head, and prayed. 72 Then he turned back to the battle against the enemy[x] and routed them, and they fled. 73 When his men who were fleeing saw this, they returned to him and joined him in the pursuit as far as Kadesh, to their camp, and there they encamped. 74 As many as three thousand of the foreigners fell that day. And Jonathan returned to Jerusalem.

12 Now when Jonathan saw that the time was favorable for him, he chose men and sent them to Rome to confirm and renew the friendship with them. 2 He also sent letters to the same effect to the Spartans and to other places. 3 So they went to Rome and entered the senate chamber and said, "The high priest Jonathan and the Jewish nation have sent us to renew the former friendship and alliance with them." 4 And the Romans[y] gave them letters to the people in every place, asking them to provide for the envoys[x] safe conduct to the land of Judah.

5 This is a copy of the letter that Jonathan wrote to the Spartans: 6 "The high priest Jonathan, the senate of the nation, the priests, and the rest of the Jewish people to their brothers the Spartans, greetings. 7 Already in time past a

and became estranged from Jonathan; instead of repaying the benefits he had received, he treated him with great harshness.

54 After this Trypho returned, and with him Antiochus, a mere lad, who was now crowned king. 55 The soldiers, so contemptuously discharged by Demetrius, all rallied to Antiochus and fought against Demetrius until he was defeated and fled. 56 Trypho, who had captured the elephants, made himself master of Antioch.

57 The young Antiochus in a letter to Jonathan confirmed him in the high-priesthood, with authority over the four districts, and appointed him one of the king's Friends. 58 He also sent him a service of gold plate, and conferred on him the right to drink from a gold cup, to be robed in purple, and to wear the gold clasp. 59 To Jonathan's brother Simon he assigned command of the area from the Ladder of Tyre to the Egyptian frontier.

60 Jonathan made a tour through the country on the far side of the river, including the towns there, and the whole Syrian army gathered to his support. He went to Ascalon, where he was received with great honour by the citizens. 61 From there he went on to Gaza, but the inhabitants closed the gates against him; so he blockaded it, set fire to its suburbs, and plundered them. 62 The inhabitants of Gaza then sued for peace, and he granted them terms, taking the sons of their magistrates as hostages and sending them off to Jerusalem; he himself continued his progress through the country as far as Damascus.

63 Jonathan heard that Demetrius's officers had arrived at Kedesh-in-Galilee with a large force to divert him from his objective. 64 He went to meet them, leaving his brother Simon in Judaea. 65 Simon took up position against Beth-sura, which he succeeded in blockading after a prolonged attack. 66 Finally the inhabitants sued for terms, which Simon granted; he expelled them from the town, occupied it, and installed a garrison.

67 Jonathan, who had encamped with his army by the lake of Gennesaret, marched out early in the morning into the plain of Hazor. 68 There in the plain were the gentile forces advancing to meet him; they had set an ambush for him in the hills, while they themselves made a frontal attack. 69 When the troops started up from the ambush and joined in the fighting, Jonathan's men took to their heels; 70 except for the two commanders, Mattathias son of Absalom and Judas son of Chalphi, not a man of them stood his ground. 71 Jonathan tore his clothes, threw dust on his head, and prayed. 72 Then he returned to the attack and utterly routed the enemy. 73 Seeing this, the fugitives of Jonathan's army rallied to him and joined in the pursuit as far as the enemy base at Kedesh; there they set up camp. 74 That day about three thousand of the Gentiles fell. Jonathan then returned to Jerusalem.

12 JONATHAN considered that the time was now opportune to select representatives and dispatch them on a mission to Rome to confirm and renew the treaty of friendship with that city. 2 He also sent letters to the same effect to Sparta and elsewhere. 3 The envoys, having reached Rome, entered the senate house, where they said: 'Jonathan the high priest and the Jewish people have sent us to renew their former pact of friendship and alliance.' 4 The Romans provided them with letters requiring the authorities in each place to accord them safe conduct to Judaea.

5 This is a transcript of Jonathan's letter to the Spartans:

6 From Jonathan the High Priest, the Senate of the Jews, the priests, and the rest of the Jewish people, to our brothers of Sparta.
Greeting.

[t] Gk he   [u] Gk him   [v] Gk animals   [w] Gk his   [x] Gk them
[y] Gk they

promises and became estranged from Jonathan. Instead of rewarding Jonathan for all the favors he had received from him, he caused him much trouble. 54 After this, Trypho returned and brought with him the young boy Antiochus, who became king and wore the royal crown. 55 All the soldiers whom Demetrius had discharged rallied around Antiochus and fought against Demetrius, who was routed and fled. 56 Trypho captured the elephants and occupied Antioch. 57 Then young Antiochus wrote to Jonathan: "I confirm you in the high priesthood and appoint you ruler over the four districts and wish you to be one of the King's Friends." 58 He also sent him gold dishes and a dinner service, gave him the right to drink from gold cups, to dress in royal purple, and to wear a gold buckle. 59 Likewise, he made Jonathan's brother Simon governor of the region from the Ladder of Tyre to the frontier of Egypt.

60 Jonathan set out and traveled through West-of-Euphrates and its cities, and all the forces of Syria espoused his cause as allies. When he arrived at Ashkalon, the citizens welcomed him with pomp. 61 But when he set out for Gaza, the people of Gaza locked their gates against him. So he besieged it and burned and plundered its suburbs. 62 Then the people of Gaza appealed to him for mercy, and he granted them peace. He took the sons of their chief men as hostages and sent them to Jerusalem. He then traveled on through the province as far as Damascus.

63 Jonathan heard that the generals of Demetrius had come with a strong force to Kadesh in Galilee, intending to remove him from office. 64 So he went to meet them, leaving his brother Simon in the province. 65 Simon besieged Beth-zur, attacked it for many days, and blockaded the inhabitants. 66 When they sued for peace, he granted it to them. He expelled them from the city, took possession of it, and put a garrison there.

67 Meanwhile, Jonathan and his army pitched their camp near the waters of Gennesaret, and at daybreak they went to the plain of Hazor. 68 There, in front of him on the plain, was the army of the foreigners. This army attacked him in the open, having first detached an ambush against him in the mountains. 69 Then the men in ambush rose out of their places and joined in the battle. 70 All of Jonathan's men fled; no one stayed except the army commanders Mattathias, son of Absalom, and Judas, son of Chalphi. 71 Jonathan tore his clothes, threw earth on his head, and prayed. 72 Then he went back to the combat and so overwhelmed the enemy that they took to flight. 73 Those of his men who were running away saw it and returned to him; and with him they pursued the enemy as far as their camp in Kadesh, where they pitched their own camp. 74 Three thousand of the foreign troops fell on that day. Then Jonathan returned to Jerusalem.

12 When Jonathan saw that the times favored him, he sent selected men to Rome to confirm and renew his friendship with the Romans. 2 He also sent letters to Sparta and other places for the same purpose.

3 After reaching Rome, the men entered the senate chamber and said, "The high priest Jonathan and the Jewish people have sent us to renew the earlier friendship and alliance between you and them." 4 The Romans gave them letters addressed to the authorities in the various places, requesting them to provide the envoys with safe conduct to the land of Judah.

5 This is a copy of the letter that Jonathan wrote to the Spartans: 6 "Jonathan the high priest, the senate of the nation, the priests, and the rest of the Jewish people send greetings to their brothers the Spartans. 7 Long ago a letter

lie to all the promises he had made, and changed his attitude to Jonathan, giving nothing in return for the services Jonathan had rendered him, but thwarting him at every turn. 54 After this, Trypho came back with the little boy Antiochus, who became king and was crowned. 55 All the troops that Demetrius had summarily dismissed rallied to Antiochus, and made war on Demetrius, who turned tail and fled. 56 Trypho captured the elephants and seized Antioch. 57 Young Antiochus then wrote as follows to Jonathan: 'I confirm you in the high priesthood and set you over the four districts and appoint you one of the Friends of the King.' 58 He sent him a service of gold plate, and granted him the right to drink from gold vessels, and to wear the purple and the golden brooch. 59 He appointed his brother Simon commander-in-chief of the region from the Ladder of Tyre to the frontiers of Egypt. 60 Jonathan then set out and made a progress through Transeuphrates and its towns, and the entire Syrian army rallied to his support. He came to Ascalon and was received in state by the inhabitants. 61 From there he proceeded to Gaza, but the people of Gaza shut him out, so he laid siege to it, burning down its suburbs and plundering them. 62 The people of Gaza then pleaded with Jonathan, and he made peace with them; but he took the sons of their chief men as hostages and sent them away to Jerusalem. He then travelled through the country as far as Damascus.

63 Jonathan now learned that Demetrius' generals had arrived at Kadesh in Galilee with a large army, intending to remove him from office, 64 and went to engage them, leaving his brother Simon inside the country. 65 Simon laid siege to Beth-Zur, attacking it day after day, and blockading the inhabitants 66 till they sued for peace, which he granted them, though he expelled them from the town and occupied it, stationing a garrison there. 67 Jonathan and his army, meanwhile, having pitched camp by the Lake of Gennesar, rose early, and by morning were already in the plain of Hazor. 68 The foreigners' army advanced to fight them on the plain, having first positioned an ambush for him in the mountains. While the main body was advancing directly towards the Jews, 69 the troops in ambush broke cover and attacked first. 70 All the men with Jonathan fled; no one was left, except Mattathias son of Absalom and Judas son of Chalphi, the generals of his army. 71 At this, Jonathan tore his garments, put dust on his head, and prayed. 72 Then he returned to the fight and routed the enemy, who fled. 73 When the fugitives from his own forces saw this, they came back to him and joined in the pursuit as far as Kadesh where the enemy encampment was, and there they themselves pitched camp. 74 About three thousand of the foreign troops fell that day. Jonathan then returned to Jerusalem.

12 When Jonathan saw that circumstances were working in his favour, he sent a select mission to Rome to confirm and renew his treaty of friendship with the Romans. 2 He also sent letters to the same effect to the Spartans and to other places. 3 The envoys made their way to Rome, entered the Senate and said, 'Jonathan the high priest and the Jewish nation have sent us to renew your treaty of friendship and alliance with them as before.' 4 The Senate gave them letters to the authorities of each place, to procure their safe conduct to Judaea.

5 The following is the copy of the letter Jonathan wrote to the Spartans:

6 'Jonathan the high priest, the senate of the nation, the priests and the rest of the Jewish people to the Spartans their brothers, greetings.

letter was sent to the high priest Onias from Arius,[z] who was king among you, stating that you are our brothers, as the appended copy shows. 8 Onias welcomed the envoy with honor, and received the letter, which contained a clear declaration of alliance and friendship. 9 Therefore, though we have no need of these things, since we have as encouragement the holy books that are in our hands, 10 we have undertaken to send to renew our family ties and friendship with you, so that we may not become estranged from you, for considerable time has passed since you sent your letter to us. 11 We therefore remember you constantly on every occasion, both at our festivals and on other appropriate days, at the sacrifices that we offer and in our prayers, as it is right and proper to remember brothers. 12 And we rejoice in your glory. 13 But as for ourselves, many trials and many wars have encircled us; the kings around us have waged war against us. 14 We were unwilling to annoy you and our other allies and friends with these wars, 15 for we have the help that comes from Heaven for our aid, and so we were delivered from our enemies, and our enemies were humbled. 16 We therefore have chosen Numenius son of Antiochus and Antipater son of Jason, and have sent them to Rome to renew our former friendship and alliance with them. 17 We have commanded them to go also to you and greet you and deliver to you this letter from us concerning the renewal of our family ties. 18 And now please send us a reply to this."

19 This is a copy of the letter that they sent to Onias:
20 "King Arius of the Spartans, to the high priest Onias, greetings. 21 It has been found in writing concerning the Spartans and the Jews that they are brothers and are of the family of Abraham. 22 And now that we have learned this, please write us concerning your welfare; 23 we on our part write to you that your livestock and your property belong to us, and ours belong to you. We therefore command that our envoys[a] report to you accordingly."

24 Now Jonathan heard that the commanders of Demetrius had returned, with a larger force than before, to wage war against him. 25 So he marched away from Jerusalem and met them in the region of Hamath, for he gave them no opportunity to invade his own country. 26 He sent spies to their camp, and they returned and reported to him that the enemy[a] were being drawn up in formation to attack the Jews[b] by night. 27 So when the sun had set, Jonathan commanded his troops to be alert and to keep their arms at hand so as to be ready all night for battle, and he stationed outposts around the camp. 28 When the enemy heard that Jonathan and his troops were prepared for battle, they were afraid and were terrified at heart; so they kindled fires in their camp and withdrew.[c] 29 But Jonathan and his troops did not know it until morning, for they saw the fires burning. 30 Then Jonathan pursued them, but he did not overtake them, for they had crossed the Eleutherus river. 31 So Jonathan turned aside against the Arabs who are called Zabadeans, and he crushed them and plundered them. 32 Then he broke camp and went to Damascus, and marched through all that region.

33 Simon also went out and marched through the country as far as Askalon and the neighboring strongholds. He turned aside to Joppa and took it by surprise, 34 for he had heard that they were ready to hand over the stronghold to those whom Demetrius had sent. And he stationed a garrison there to guard it.

35 When Jonathan returned he convened the elders of the people and planned with them to build strongholds in Judea, 36 to build the walls of Jerusalem still higher, and to

7 On a former occasion a letter from Arius your king to Onias the high priest acknowledged our kinship; a copy is given below. 8 Onias welcomed your envoy with full honours and accepted the letter in which the terms of alliance and friendship were set forth. 9 We do not regard ourselves as being in need of such alliances, since the sacred books we possess afford us encouragement. 10 Nevertheless, we now venture to make contact with you to renew our pact of brotherhood and friendship so that we may not become estranged, for many years have passed since your previous approach to us. 11 We never neglect any opportunity, on festal and other appropriate days, of making mention of you at our sacrifices and in our prayers, as it is right and proper to remember kinsmen; 12 and we rejoice at your fame.

13 We ourselves have been under the constant pressure of hostile attacks on every side, as the surrounding kings have made war upon us. 14 During the course of these wars we had no wish to trouble you or our other allies and friends. 15 Having had the support of aid from Heaven, we have been saved from our enemies, and they have been humbled. 16 Accordingly, we have chosen Numenius son of Antiochus and Antipater son of Jason and have sent them to the Romans to renew our former friendship and alliance with them. 17 We have instructed them to bear our greetings to you also, and to deliver this letter regarding the renewal of our pact of brotherhood. 18 Now we ask you to favour us with a reply.

19 This is the copy of the letter sent by the Spartans to Onias:

20 From Arius, King of Sparta, to Onias the High Priest. Greeting.

21 A document has come to light which shows that Spartans and Jews are kinsmen, both being descended from Abraham. 22 Now that we have learnt of this, we beg you to write and tell us how your affairs prosper. 23 Our own response is this: 'What is yours, your livestock and every kind of property, is ours, and what is ours is yours.' We are instructing our envoys, therefore, to report to you in these terms.

24 When Jonathan heard that Demetrius's generals had come with an even larger force to renew the attack, 25 he marched out from Jerusalem and met them in the region of Hamath, to give them no chance of setting foot on his territory. 26 Spies sent to the enemy camp reported on their return that dispositions were being made for a night assault. 27 At sunset Jonathan issued orders to his men that throughout the night they were to stay awake and stand to arms ready for battle; he also stationed outposts all round the camp. 28 The enemy were alarmed when they learnt that Jonathan and his men were prepared for their attack; their courage failed them and they withdrew, first lighting watch-fires in their camp. 29 Jonathan and his men saw the fires burning and did not realize what had happened until morning. 30 Though he took up the pursuit, he did not overtake them, for they had crossed the river Eleutherus. 31 Turning aside he attacked and plundered the Arabs called Zabadaeans. 32 He moved on to Damascus, marching through the whole country.

33-34 Meanwhile Simon set out and, after advancing as far as Ascalon and the neighbouring fortresses, he turned towards Joppa. He had heard that the inhabitants intended to hand over the fort to the supporters of Demetrius, but, before they could do so, he occupied it and placed a garrison there for its defence.

35 On his return Jonathan convened the senate and with its agreement decided to build fortresses in Judaea, 36 to in-

was sent to the high priest Onias from Arius, who then reigned over you, stating that you are our brothers, as the attached copy shows. 8 Onias welcomed the envoy with honor and received the letter, which clearly referred to alliance and friendship. 9 Though we have no need of these things, since we have for our encouragement the sacred books that are in our possession, 10 we have ventured to send word to you for the renewal of brotherhood and friendship, so as not to become strangers to you altogether; a long time has passed since your mission to us. 11 We, on our part, have never ceased to remember you in the sacrifices and prayers that we offer on our feasts and other appropriate days, as it is right and proper to remember brothers. 12 We likewise rejoice in your renown. 13 But many hardships and wars have beset us, and the kings around us have attacked us. 14 We did not wish to be troublesome to you and to the rest of our allies and friends in these wars; 15 with the help of Heaven for our support, we have been saved from our enemies, and they have been humbled. 16 So we have chosen Numenius, son of Antiochus, and Antipater, son of Jason, and we have sent them to the Romans to renew our former friendship and alliance with them. 17 We have also ordered them to come to you and greet you, and to deliver to you our letter about the renewal of our brotherhood. 18 Therefore kindly send us an answer on this matter."

19 This is a copy of the letter that was sent to Onias: 20 "Arius, king of the Spartans, sends greetings to Onias the high priest. 21 A document has been found stating that the Spartans and the Jews are brothers; both nations descended from Abraham. 22 Now that we have learned this, kindly write to us about your welfare. 23 We, on our part, are informing you that your cattle and your possessions are ours, and ours are yours. We have, therefore, given orders that you should be told of this."

24 Jonathan heard that the generals of Demetrius had returned to attack him with a stronger army than before. 25 He set out from Jerusalem and went into the country of Hamath to meet them, giving them no time to enter his province. 26 The spies he had sent into their camp came back and reported that the enemy had made ready to attack the Jews that very night. 27 Therefore, when the sun set, Jonathan ordered his men to be on guard and to remain armed, ready for combat, throughout the night. He also set outposts all around the camp. 28 When the enemy heard that Jonathan and his men were ready for battle, their hearts sank with fear and dread. They lighted fires and then withdrew. 29 But because Jonathan and his men were watching the lights burning, they did not know what had happened until morning. 30 Then Jonathan pursued them, but he could not overtake them, for they had crossed the river Eleutherus. 31 So Jonathan turned aside against the Arabs who are called Zabadeans, overwhelming and plundering them. 32 Then he marched on to Damascus and traversed that whole region.

33 Simon also set out and went as far as Ashkalon and its neighboring strongholds. He then turned to Joppa and occupied it, 34 for he heard that its men had intended to hand over this stronghold to the supporters of Demetrius. He left a garrison there to guard it.

35 When Jonathan returned, he assembled the elders of the people, and with them he made plans for building strongholds in Judea, 36 for making the walls of Jerusalem

7 'In the past, a letter was sent to Onias, the high priest, from Areios, one of your kings, stating that you are indeed our brothers, as the copy subjoined attests. 8 Onias received the envoy with honour, and accepted the letter, in which a clear declaration was made of friendship and alliance. 9 For our part, though we have no need of these, having the consolation of the holy books in our possession, 10 we venture to send to renew our fraternal friendship with you, so that we may not become strangers to you, a long time having elapsed since you last wrote to us. 11 We, for our part, on every occasion, at our festivals and on other appointed days, unfailingly remember you in the sacrifices we offer and in our prayers, as it is right and fitting to remember brothers. 12 We rejoice in your renown.

13 'We ourselves, however, have had many trials and many wars, the neighbouring kings making war on us. 14 We were unwilling to trouble you or our other allies and friends during these wars, 15 since we have the support of Heaven to help us, thanks to which we have been delivered from our enemies, and they are the ones who have been brought low. 16 We have therefore chosen Numenius son of Antiochus, and Antipater son of Jason, and sent them to the Romans to renew our former treaty of friendship and alliance, 17 and we have ordered them also to visit you, to greet you and deliver you this letter of ours concerning the renewal of our brotherhood; 18 we shall be grateful for an answer to it.'

19 The following is the copy of the letter sent to Onias:

20 'Areios king of the Spartans, to Onias the high priest, greetings.

21 'It has been discovered in records regarding the Spartans and Jews that they are brothers, and of the race of Abraham. 22 Now that this has come to our knowledge, we shall be obliged if you will send us news of your welfare. 23 Our own message to you is this: your flocks and your possessions are ours, and ours are yours, and we are instructing our envoys to give you a message to this effect.'

24 Jonathan learned that Demetrius' generals had returned with a larger army than before to make war on him. 25 He therefore left Jerusalem and went to engage them in the area of Hamath, not giving them the time to invade his own territory. 26 He sent spies into their camp, who told him on their return that the enemy were taking up positions for a night attack on the Jews. 27 At sunset, Jonathan ordered his men to keep watch with their weapons at hand, in readiness to fight at any time during the night, and posted advance guards all round the camp. 28 On learning that Jonathan and his men were ready to fight, the enemy took fright and, with quaking hearts, lit fires in their bivouac and decamped. 29 Jonathan and his men, watching the glow of the fires, were unaware of their withdrawal until morning, 30 and although Jonathan pursued them, he failed to overtake them, for they had already crossed the river Eleutherus. 31 So Jonathan wheeled round on the Arabs called Zabadaeans, beat them and plundered them; 32 then, breaking camp, he went to Damascus, thus crossing the whole province. 33 Simon, meanwhile, had also set out and had penetrated as far as Ascalon and the neighbouring towns. He then turned on Joppa and moved quickly to occupy it, 34 for he had heard of their intention to hand over this strong point to the supporters of Demetrius; he stationed a garrison there to hold it.

35 Jonathan, on his return, called a meeting of the elders of the people and decided with them to build fortresses in Judaea 36 and to heighten the walls of Jerusalem and erect a

erect a high barrier between the citadel and the city to separate it from the city, in order to isolate it so that its garrison[d] could neither buy nor sell. 37 So they gathered together to rebuild the city; part of the wall on the valley to the east had fallen, and he repaired the section called Chaphenatha. 38 Simon also built Adida in the Shephelah; he fortified it and installed gates with bolts.

39 Then Trypho attempted to become king in Asia and put on the crown, and to raise his hand against King Antiochus. 40 He feared that Jonathan might not permit him to do so, but might make war on him, so he kept seeking to seize and kill him, and he marched out and came to Beth-shan. 41 Jonathan went out to meet him with forty thousand picked warriors, and he came to Beth-shan. 42 When Trypho saw that he had come with a large army, he was afraid to raise his hand against him. 43 So he received him with honor and commended him to all his Friends, and he gave him gifts and commanded his Friends and his troops to obey him as they would himself. 44 Then he said to Jonathan, "Why have you put all these people to so much trouble when we are not at war? 45 Dismiss them now to their homes and choose for yourself a few men to stay with you, and come with me to Ptolemais. I will hand it over to you as well as the other strongholds and the remaining troops and all the officials, and will turn around and go home. For that is why I am here."

46 Jonathan[e] trusted him and did as he said; he sent away the troops, and they returned to the land of Judah. 47 He kept with himself three thousand men, two thousand of whom he left in Galilee, while one thousand accompanied him. 48 But when Jonathan entered Ptolemais, the people of Ptolemais closed the gates and seized him, and they killed with the sword all who had entered with him.

49 Then Trypho sent troops and cavalry into Galilee and the Great Plain to destroy all Jonathan's soldiers. 50 But they realized that Jonathan had been seized and had perished along with his men, and they encouraged one another and kept marching in close formation, ready for battle. 51 When their pursuers saw that they would fight for their lives, they turned back. 52 So they all reached the land of Judah safely, and they mourned for Jonathan and his companions and were in great fear; and all Israel mourned deeply. 53 All the nations around them tried to destroy them, for they said, "They have no leader or helper. Now therefore let us make war on them and blot out the memory of them from humankind."

13 Simon heard that Trypho had assembled a large army to invade the land of Judah and destroy it, 2 and he saw that the people were trembling with fear. So he went up to Jerusalem, and gathering the people together 3 he encouraged them, saying to them, "You yourselves know what great things my brothers and I and the house of my father have done for the laws and the sanctuary; you know also the wars and the difficulties that my brothers and I have seen. 4 By reason of this all my brothers have perished for the sake of Israel, and I alone am left. 5 And now, far be it from me to spare my life in any time of distress, for I am not better than my brothers. 6 But I will avenge my nation and the sanctuary and your wives and children, for all the nations have gathered together out of hatred to destroy us."

7 The spirit of the people was rekindled when they heard these words, 8 and they answered in a loud voice, "You are our leader in place of Judas and your brother Jonathan. 9 Fight our battles, and all that you say to us we will do." 10 So he assembled all the warriors and hurried to complete the walls of Jerusalem, and he fortified it on every side. 11 He sent Jonathan son of Absalom to Joppa, and with

crease the height of the walls of Jerusalem, and to erect a high barrier which would cut off the citadel from the city and so isolate it that the garrison could neither buy nor sell. 37 The people assembled to rebuild the city, for the wall along the ravine to the east had partly collapsed; he also repaired the section called Chaphenatha. 38 Simon rebuilt Adida in the Shephelah, and strengthened it with barred gates.

39 Trypho now aspired to the sovereignty of Asia; he planned to assume the crown and launch an offensive against King Antiochus. 40 But fearing that Jonathan would resort to war to prevent this, he cast about for some means of capturing and killing him. He set off and reached Bethshan. 41 Jonathan went out to confront him with forty thousand picked warriors, and he too reached Bethshan. 42 When Trypho saw the size of the force with Jonathan, he hesitated to take the offensive. 43 Instead he received Jonathan with full honours: he commended him to all his Friends, loaded him with gifts, and ordered his Friends and his troops to obey him as they would himself. 44 He said to him: 'Why have you put all these men to so much trouble? We are not at war! 45 Send them home now and choose a few to accompany you, and come with me to Ptolemais. I shall hand it over to you together with the other fortresses, a large number of troops, and all the officials, and then I shall take my leave. This is the sole purpose of my coming.' 46 Jonathan believed him and did as he said: he dismissed his forces, and they returned to Judaea. 47 He kept back three thousand men, of whom he left two thousand in Galilee, while a thousand accompanied him. 48 But as soon as Jonathan entered Ptolemais, the people closed the gates and seized him, and put to the sword everyone who had come with him.

49 Trypho sent a force of infantry and cavalry into Galilee to the great plain, to wipe out Jonathan's men, 50 who only now learnt that Jonathan had been seized and was lost, along with his escort; however, they put heart into one another and marched off in close formation, ready for battle. 51 When their pursuers saw that they would fight for their lives they turned back. 52 Though all came safely home to Judaea, they were greatly afraid and mourned for Jonathan and those who were with him; the whole of Israel was plunged into grief. 53 The Gentiles round about were all bent on destroying them root and branch. 'The Jews have no leader or champion,' they said; 'so now is the time for us to attack, and we shall blot out all memory of them from among men.'

13 WHEN a report reached Simon that Trypho had got together a large force for the invasion and destruction of Judaea, 2 the people were reduced to a state of panic. Seeing this, Simon went up to Jerusalem, where he called an assembly 3 and to afford them encouragement said: 'I do not need to remind you how much my brothers and I and my father's house have done for the laws and the holy place, what battles we have fought, what hardships we have endured. 4 All my brothers have fallen in this cause, fighting for Israel; only I am left. 5 Now Heaven forbid that I should grudge my life when danger threatens, for I am in no way a better man than my brothers. 6 Rather, since the Gentiles in their hatred have all gathered to destroy us, I shall take up the cause of my nation and of the holy place, of your wives and children.' 7 With these words he rekindled the spirit of the people, 8 and they responded by calling out: 'You shall be our leader in place of Judas and your brother Jonathan. 9 Fight our wars, and we shall do whatever you say.' 10 Simon assembled all the fighting men and hurried on the completion of the walls until Jerusalem was fortified on every side. 11 Jonathan son of Absalom was sent with a

still higher, and for erecting a high barrier between the citadel and the city, that would isolate the citadel and so prevent its garrison from commerce with the city. 37 The people therefore worked together on building up the city, for part of the east wall above the ravine had collapsed. The quarter called Chaphenatha was also repaired. 38 Simon likewise built up Adida in the Shephelah, and strengthened its fortifications by providing them with gates and bars. 39 Trypho was determined to become king of Asia, assume the crown, and do away with King Antiochus. 40 But he was afraid that Jonathan would not permit him, but would fight against him. Looking for a way to seize and kill him, he set out and reached Beth-shan. 41 Jonathan marched out against him with forty thousand picked fighting men and came to Beth-shan. 42 But when Trypho saw that Jonathan had arrived with a large army, he was afraid to offer him violence. 43 Instead, he received him with honor, introduced him to all his friends, and gave him presents. He also ordered his friends and soldiers to obey him as they would himself. 44 Then he said to Jonathan: "Why have you put all your soldiers to so much trouble when we are not at war? 45 Pick out a few men to stay with you, send the rest back home, and then come with me to Ptolemais. I will hand it over to you together with other strongholds and their garrisons, as well as the officials, then I will leave and go home. That is why I came here."

46 Jonathan believed him and did as he said. He dismissed his troops, and they returned to the land of Judah. 47 But he kept with him three thousand men, of whom he sent two thousand to Galilee while one thousand accompanied him. 48 Then as soon as Jonathan had entered Ptolemais, the men of the city closed the gates and seized him; all who had entered with him, they killed with the sword. 49 Trypho sent soldiers and cavalry to Galilee and the Great Plain to destroy all Jonathan's men. 50 These, upon learning that Jonathan had been captured and his companions killed, encouraged one another and went out in compact body ready to fight. 51 As their pursuers saw that they were ready to fight for their lives, they turned back. 52 Thus all these men of Jonathan came safely into the land of Judah. They mourned over Jonathan and his men, and were in great fear, and all Israel fell into deep mourning. 53 All the nations round about sought to destroy them. They said, "Now that they have no leader to help them, let us make war on them and wipe out their memory from among men."

13 When Simon heard that Trypho was gathering a large army to invade and ravage the land of Judah, 2 and saw that the people were in dread and terror, he went up to Jerusalem. There he assembled the people 3 and exhorted them in these words: "You know what I, my brothers, and my father's house have done for the laws and the sanctuary; what battles and disasters we have been through. 4 It was for the sake of these, for the sake of Israel, that all my brothers have perished, and I alone am left. 5 Far be it from me, then, to save my own life in any time of distress, for I am not better than my brothers. 6 Rather will I avenge my nation and the sanctuary, as well as your wives and children, for all the nations out of hatred have united to destroy us."

7 As the people heard these words, their spirit was rekindled. 8 They shouted in reply: "You are our leader in place of your brothers Judas and Jonathan. 9 Fight our battles, and we will do everything that you tell us." 10 So Simon mustered all the men able to fight, and quickly completing the walls of Jerusalem, fortified it on every side. 11 He sent

high barrier between the Citadel and the city, to cut the former off from the city and isolate it, to prevent the occupants from buying or selling. 37 Rebuilding the city was a co-operative effort: part of the wall over the eastern ravine had fallen down; he restored the quarter called Chaphenatha. 38 Simon, meanwhile, rebuilt Adida in the lowlands, fortifying it, and erecting gates with bolts.

39 Trypho's ambition was to become king of Asia, assume the crown, and overpower King Antiochus. 40 He was apprehensive that Jonathan might not allow him to do this, and might even make war on him, so he set out and came to Beth-Shean, in the hopes of finding some pretext for having him arrested and put to death. 41 Jonathan went out to intercept him, with forty thousand picked men in battle order, and arrived at Beth-Shean. 42 When Trypho saw him there with a large force, he hesitated to make any move against him. 43 He even received him with honour, commended him to all his friends, gave him presents and ordered his friends and his troops to obey him as they would himself. 44 He said to Jonathan, 'Why have you given all these people so much trouble, when there is no threat of war between us? 45 Send them back home; pick yourself a few men as your bodyguard, and come with me to Ptolemais, which I am going to hand over to you, with the other fortresses and the remaining troops and all the officials; after which, I shall take the road for home. This was my purpose in coming here.' 46 Jonathan trusted him and did as he said; he dismissed his forces, who went back to Judaea. 47 With him he retained three thousand men, of whom he left two thousand in Galilee, while a thousand accompanied him. 48 But as soon as Jonathan had entered Ptolemais, the people of Ptolemais closed the gates, seized him, and put all those who had entered with him to the sword. 49 Trypho sent troops and cavalry into Galilee and the Great Plain to destroy all Jonathan's supporters. 50 These, concluding that he had been taken and had perished with his companions, encouraged one another, marching with closed ranks and ready to give battle, 51 and when their pursuers saw that they would fight for their lives, they turned back. 52 All reached Judaea safe and sound, and there they lamented Jonathan and his companions, being very frightened indeed; all Israel was plunged into mourning. 53 The surrounding nations were all now looking for ways of destroying them: 'They have no leader,' they said, 'no ally; we have only to attack them now, and we shall blot out their very memory from all peoples.'

13 Simon heard that Trypho had collected a large army to invade and devastate Judaea, 2 and when he saw how the people were quaking with fear, he went up to Jerusalem, called the people together, 3 and exhorted them thus, 'You know yourselves how much I and my brothers and my father's family have done for the laws and the sanctuary; you know what wars and hardships we have experienced. 4 That is why my brothers are all dead, for Israel's sake, and I am the only one left. 5 Far be it from me, then, to be sparing of my own life in any time of oppression, for I am not worth more than my brothers. 6 Rather will I avenge my nation and the sanctuary and your wives and children, now that the foreigners are all united in malice to destroy us.' 7 The people's spirit rekindled as they listened to his words, 8 and they shouted back at him, 'You are our leader in place of Judas and your brother Jonathan. 9 Fight our battles for us, and we will do whatever you tell us.' 10 So he assembled all the fighting men and hurried on with completing the walls of Jerusalem, fortifying the whole perimeter. 11 He sent a considerable force to Joppa

him a considerable army; he drove out its occupants and remained there.

12 Then Trypho left Ptolemais with a large army to invade the land of Judah, and Jonathan was with him under guard. 13 Simon encamped in Adida, facing the plain. 14 Trypho learned that Simon had risen up in place of his brother Jonathan, and that he was about to join battle with him, so he sent envoys to him and said, 15 "It is for the money that your brother Jonathan owed the royal treasury, in connection with the offices he held, that we are detaining him. 16 Send now one hundred talents of silver and two of his sons as hostages, so that when released he will not revolt against us, and we will release him."

17 Simon knew that they were speaking deceitfully to him, but he sent to get the money and the sons, so that he would not arouse great hostility among the people, who might say, 18 "It was because Simon*f* did not send him the money and the sons, that Jonathan*g* perished." 19 So he sent the sons and the hundred talents, but Trypho*g* broke his word and did not release Jonathan.

20 After this Trypho came to invade the country and destroy it, and he circled around by the way to Adora. But Simon and his army kept marching along opposite him to every place he went. 21 Now the men in the citadel kept sending envoys to Trypho urging him to come to them by way of the wilderness and to send them food. 22 So Trypho got all his cavalry ready to go, but that night a very heavy snow fell, and he did not go because of the snow. He marched off and went into the land of Gilead. 23 When he approached Baskama, he killed Jonathan, and he was buried there. 24 Then Trypho turned and went back to his own land.

25 Simon sent and took the bones of his brother Jonathan, and buried him in Modein, the city of his ancestors. 26 All Israel bewailed him with great lamentation, and mourned for him many days. 27 And Simon built a monument over the tomb of his father and his brothers; he made it high so that it might be seen, with polished stone at the front and back. 28 He also erected seven pyramids, opposite one another, for his father and mother and four brothers. 29 For the pyramids*h* he devised an elaborate setting, erecting about them great columns, and on the columns he put suits of armor for a permanent memorial, and beside the suits of armor he carved ships, so that they could be seen by all who sail the sea. 30 This is the tomb that he built in Modein; it remains to this day.

31 Trypho dealt treacherously with the young King Antiochus; he killed him 32 and became king in his place, putting on the crown of Asia; and he brought great calamity on the land. 33 But Simon built up the strongholds of Judea and walled them all around, with high towers and great walls and gates and bolts, and he stored food in the strongholds. 34 Simon also chose emissaries and sent them to King Demetrius with a request to grant relief to the country, for all that Trypho did was to plunder. 35 King Demetrius sent him a favorable reply to this request, and wrote him a letter as follows, 36 "King Demetrius to Simon, the high priest and friend of kings, and to the elders and nation of the Jews, greetings. 37 We have received the gold crown and the palm branch that you*i* sent, and we are ready to make a general peace with you and to write to our officials to grant you release from tribute. 38 All the grants that we have made to you remain valid, and let the strongholds that you have built be your possession. 39 We pardon any errors and offenses committed to this day, and cancel the crown tax that you owe; and whatever other tax has been collected in Jerusalem shall be collected no longer. 40 And if any of you are quali-

f Gk *I*   *g* Gk *he*   *h* Gk *For these*   *i* The word *you* in verses 37-40 is plural

considerable force to Joppa, where he drove out the inhabitants and remained in occupation of the town.

12 Trypho marched from Ptolemais at the head of a large force to invade Judaea, taking Jonathan with him under guard; 13 Simon meanwhile established his camp at Adida on the edge of the plain. 14 When Trypho learnt that Simon had come forward to take the place of his brother Jonathan and was about to offer battle, he sent envoys to him with this message: 15 'We are detaining your brother Jonathan because of certain moneys owed by him to the royal treasury in connection with the offices he held. 16 To ensure that once released he will not again revolt, send now one hundred talents of silver and two of his sons as hostages, and we shall let him go.' 17 Although he was sure the proposal was a trick, Simon had the money and the children brought to him, fearing that otherwise he might arouse widespread animosity among the people, 18 who would say, 'It was because you did not send the money and the children that Jonathan lost his life.' 19 So he sent the children and the hundred talents; but Trypho broke his word and did not release Jonathan.

20 After this, Trypho set out to invade and ravage the country. He made a detour by way of Adora, and Simon with his army marched parallel with him everywhere he went. 21 Meanwhile the garrison of the citadel kept sending emissaries to Trypho, urging him to come by the desert route and to send supplies. 22 Trypho prepared to dispatch the whole of his cavalry, but that night there was a severe storm, and they failed to get through because of the snow; so he withdrew into Gilead. 23 When he was near Bascama, he had Jonathan put to death and buried there. 24 Trypho then turned and went off to his own country.

25 Simon had the body of his brother brought for burial to Modin, the town of his forefathers. 26 There was great grief for Jonathan throughout Israel and the mourning lasted for many days. 27 Over the tomb of his father and brothers Simon raised a lofty monument, visible at a great distance and faced, back and front, with polished stone. 28 He erected seven pyramids, arranged in pairs, for his father and mother and four brothers. 29 He contrived an elaborate setting for the pyramids: he surrounded them with tall columns surmounted with trophies of armour as a perpetual memorial, and with carved ships alongside the trophies, plainly visible to those at sea. 30 This mausoleum which he made at Modin stands to the present day.

31 Trypho now conspired against Antiochus the young king and put him to death. 32 He usurped the throne and assumed the crown of Asia, and he inflicted great damage on the country.

33 Simon rebuilt the fortresses of Judaea, furnishing them with high towers and with massive walls and barred gates; he also stocked the fortresses with provisions. 34 He selected delegates and sent them to King Demetrius to negotiate a remission of taxes for the country, on the ground that all Trypho's exactions had been exorbitant. 35 In reply to this request Demetrius sent a letter in the following terms:

36 From King Demetrius to Simon the High Priest and Friend of kings, and to the elders and nation of the Jews. Greeting.

37 We have received the gold crown and the palm branch which you sent, and we are prepared to make a lasting peace with you and to instruct the revenue officers to grant you remissions of tax. 38 All our agreements with you stand confirmed, and the strongholds which you built shall remain yours. 39 For any errors of omission or commission we grant a free pardon, to take effect from the date of this letter. We remit the crown-levy which you owed us, and every other tax formerly exacted in Jerusalem is henceforth cancelled. 40 Any of you who are suit-

Jonathan, son of Absalom, to Joppa with a large force; Jonathan drove out the occupants and remained there.

12 Then Trypho moved from Ptolemais with a large army to invade the land of Judah, bringing Jonathan with him as prisoner. 13 But Simon pitched his camp at Adida, facing the plain. 14 When Trypho learned that Simon had succeeded his brother Jonathan, and that he intended to fight him, he sent envoys to him with this message: 15 "We have detained your brother Jonathan on account of the money that he owed the royal treasury in connection with the offices that he held. 16 Therefore, if you send us a hundred talents of silver, and two of his sons as hostages to guarantee that when he is set free he will not revolt against us, we will release him."

17 Although Simon knew that they were speaking deceitfully to him, he gave orders to get the money and the boys, for fear of provoking much hostility among the people, who might say 18 that Jonathan perished because Simon would not send Trypho the money and the boys. 19 So he sent the boys and the hundred talents; but Trypho broke his promise and would not let Jonathan go. 20 Next he began to invade and ravage the country. His troops went around by the road that leads to Adora, but Simon and his army moved along opposite him everywhere he went. 21 The men in the citadel sent messengers to Trypho, urging him to come to them by way of the desert, and to send them provisions. 22 Although Trypho got all his cavalry ready to go, there was a heavy fall of snow that night, and he could not go. So he left for Gilead. 23 When he was approaching Baskama, he had Jonathan killed and buried there. 24 Then Trypho returned to his own country.

25 Simon sent for the remains of his brother Jonathan, and buried him in Modein, the city of his fathers. 26 All Israel bewailed him with solemn lamentation, mourning over him for many days. 27 Then Simon erected over the tomb of his father and his brothers a monument of stones, polished front and back, and raised high enough to be seen at a distance. 28 He set up seven pyramids facing one another for his father and his mother and his four brothers. 29 For the pyramids he devised a setting of big columns, on which he carved suits of armor as a perpetual memorial, and next to the armor he placed carved ships, which could be seen by all who sailed the sea. 30 This tomb which he built at Modein is there to the present day.

31 Trypho dealt treacherously with the young King Antiochus. He killed him 32 and assumed the kingship in his place, putting on the crown of Asia. Thus he brought much evil on the land. 33 Simon, on his part, built up the strongholds of Judea, strengthening their fortifications with high towers, thick walls, and gates with bars, and he stored up provisions in the fortresses. 34 Simon also sent chosen men to King Demetrius with the request that he grant the land a release from taxation, for all that Trypho did was to plunder the land. 35 In reply, King Demetrius sent him the following letter:

36 "King Demetrius sends greetings to Simon the high priest, the friend of kings, and to the elders and the Jewish people. 37 We have received the gold crown and the palm branch that you sent. We are willing to be on most peaceful terms with you and to write to our official to grant you release from tribute. 38 Whatever we have guaranteed to you remains in force, and the strongholds that you have built shall remain yours. 39 We remit any oversights and defaults incurred up to now, as well as the crown tax that you owe. Any other tax that may have been collected in Jerusalem shall no longer be collected there. 40 If any of you are quali-

under Jonathan son of Absalom who drove out the inhabitants and remained there in occupation.

12 Trypho now left Ptolemais with a large army to invade Judaea, taking Jonathan with him under guard. 13 Simon pitched camp in Adida, facing the plain. 14 When Trypho learned that Simon had taken the place of his brother Jonathan and that he intended to join battle with him, he sent envoys to him with this message, 15 'Your brother Jonathan was in debt to the royal exchequer for the offices he held; that is why we are detaining him. 16 If you send a hundred talents of silver and two of his sons as hostages, to make sure that on his release he does not revolt against us, we shall release him.' 17 Although Simon was aware that the message was a ruse, he sent for the money and the boys for fear of incurring great hostility from the people, 18 who would have said that Jonathan had died because Simon would not send Trypho the money and the children. 19 He therefore sent both the boys and the hundred talents, but Trypho broke his word and did not release Jonathan. 20 Next, Trypho set about the invasion and devastation of the country; he made a detour along the Adora road, but Simon and his army confronted him wherever he attempted to go. 21 The men in the Citadel kept sending messengers to Trypho, urging him to get through to them by way of the desert and send them supplies. 22 Trypho organised his entire cavalry to go, but that night it snowed so heavily that he could not get through for the snow, so he left there and moved off into Gilead. 23 As he approached Baskama he killed Jonathan, who was buried there. 24 Trypho turned back and regained his own country.

25 Simon sent and recovered the bones of his brother Jonathan, and buried him in Modein, the town of his ancestors. 26 All Israel kept solemn mourning for him and long bewailed him. 27 Over the tomb of his father and brothers, Simon raised a monument high enough to catch the eye, using dressed stone back and front. 28 He erected seven pyramids facing each other, for his father and mother and his four brothers, 29 surrounding them with a structure consisting of tall columns surmounted by trophies of arms to their everlasting memory and, beside the trophies of arms, ships sculpted on a scale to be seen by all who sail the sea. 30 Such was the monument he constructed at Modein, and it is still there today.

31 Now Trypho, betraying the trust of young King Antiochus, put him to death. 32 He usurped his throne, assuming the crown of Asia, and brought great havoc on the country. 33 Simon built up the fortresses of Judaea, surrounding them with high towers, great walls and gates with bolts, and stocked these fortresses with food. 34 He also sent a delegation to King Demetrius, to get him to grant the province a remission, since all Trypho did was to despoil. 35 King Demetrius replied to his request in a letter framed as follows:

36 'King Demetrius to Simon, high priest and Friend of Kings, and to the elders and nation of the Jews, greetings.

37 'It has pleased us to accept the golden crown and the palm you have sent us, and we are disposed to make a general peace with you, and to write to the officials to grant you remissions. 38 Everything that we have decreed concerning you remains in force, and the fortresses you have built may remain in your hands. 39 We pardon all offences, unwitting or intentional, hitherto committed, and remit the crown tax you now owe us; and whatever other taxes were levied in Jerusalem are no longer to be levied. 40 If any of you are suitable for enrolment in our

fied to be enrolled in our bodyguard,*j* let them be enrolled, and let there be peace between us."

41 In the one hundred seventieth year*k* the yoke of the Gentiles was removed from Israel, 42 and the people began to write in their documents and contracts, "In the first year of Simon the great high priest and commander and leader of the Jews."

43 In those days Simon*l* encamped against Gazara*m* and surrounded it with troops. He made a siege engine, brought it up to the city, and battered and captured one tower. 44 The men in the siege engine leaped out into the city, and a great tumult arose in the city. 45 The men in the city, with their wives and children, went up on the wall with their clothes torn, and they cried out with a loud voice, asking Simon to make peace with them; 46 they said, "Do not treat us according to our wicked acts but according to your mercy." 47 So Simon reached an agreement with them and stopped fighting against them. But he expelled them from the city and cleansed the houses in which the idols were located, and then entered it with hymns and praise. 48 He removed all uncleanness from it, and settled in it those who observed the law. He also strengthened its fortifications and built in it a house for himself.

49 Those who were in the citadel at Jerusalem were prevented from going in and out to buy and sell in the country. So they were very hungry, and many of them perished from famine. 50 Then they cried to Simon to make peace with them, and he did so. But he expelled them from there and cleansed the citadel from its pollutions. 51 On the twenty-third day of the second month, in the one hundred seventy-first year,*n* the Jews*o* entered it with praise and palm branches, and with harps and cymbals and stringed instruments, and with hymns and songs, because a great enemy had been crushed and removed from Israel. 52 Simon*p* decreed that every year they should celebrate this day with rejoicing. He strengthened the fortifications of the temple hill alongside the citadel, and he and his men lived there. 53 Simon saw that his son John had reached manhood, and so he made him commander of all the forces; and he lived at Gazara.

14 In the one hundred seventy-second year*q* King Demetrius assembled his forces and marched into Media to obtain help, so that he could make war against Trypho. 2 When King Arsaces of Persia and Media heard that Demetrius had invaded his territory, he sent one of his generals to take him alive. 3 The general*p* went and defeated the army of Demetrius, and seized him and took him to Arsaces, who put him under guard.

4   The land*r* had rest all the days of Simon.
     He sought the good of his nation;
     his rule was pleasing to them,
          as was the honor shown him, all his days.
5   To crown all his honors he took Joppa for a
          harbor,
     and opened a way to the isles of the sea.
6   He extended the borders of his nation,
     and gained full control of the country.
7   He gathered a host of captives;
     he ruled over Gazara and Beth-zur and the
          citadel,
     and he removed its uncleanness from it;
          and there was none to oppose him.
8   They tilled their land in peace;
     the ground gave its increase,
     and the trees of the plains their fruit.

able for enrolment in our retinue shall be so enrolled. Let there be peace between us.'

41 In the year 170, Israel was released from the gentile yoke; 42 the people began to write on their contracts and agreements: 'In the first year of Simon, the great high priest, general, and leader of the Jews'.

43 At that time Simon surrounded and closely invested Gazara with his troops. He constructed a siege-engine, and bringing it up to the town he made a breach in one of the towers and captured it. 44 The men on the siege-engine leapt from it into the town, and there was great commotion. 45 The defenders along with their wives and children climbed on to the city wall with their garments torn, clamouring loudly to Simon to grant them terms. 46 'Do not treat us as our wickedness deserves,' they cried, 'but as your mercy prompts you.' 47 Simon agreed terms and called off the attack. But he expelled them from the town, and after purifying the houses in which there were idols, he made his entry with songs of thanksgiving and praise. 48 Everything which was polluted he threw out, and he settled there men who would keep the law. He strengthened the fortifications, and he built himself a residence in the town.

49 The occupants of the citadel at Jerusalem were prevented from going in and out to buy and sell in the countryside; famine ensued, and many died of starvation. 50 The survivors cried out to Simon to accept their surrender; this he granted; then expelling them from the citadel he cleansed it from its defilement. 51 It was on the twenty-third day of the second month in the year 171 that the Jews entered the city amid a chorus of praise and the waving of palm branches, with lutes, cymbals, and zithers, with hymns and songs, to celebrate Israel's final riddance of a formidable enemy. 52 Simon decreed that this day should be observed as an annual festival. He strengthened the fortifications of the temple hill opposite the citadel, and he and his men made it their base. 53 In recognition of the fact that his son John had now reached manhood, he appointed him commander of all the forces, with Gazara as his headquarters.

14 In the year 172, King Demetrius mustered his army and moved into Media to obtain support for his war against Trypho. 2 When Arsakes king of Persia and Media heard that Demetrius had entered his territory, he dispatched one of his generals to take him alive. 3 The general marched out, defeated and captured Demetrius, and brought him to Arsakes, who kept him under guard.

4 As long as Simon ruled, Judaea was undisturbed. He sought his nation's good, and they lived happily all through the glorious days of his reign. 5 Notable among his achievements was his capture of the port of Joppa to secure his communications overseas. 6 He extended his nation's borders and made himself master of the land. 7 Many prisoners of war were repatriated. He gained control over Gazara and Bethsura and over the citadel, from which he removed all pollution. None could withstand him.

8 The people farmed the land in peace; it produced its crops, and the trees in the plains their fruit. 9 Old men sat

j Or court   *k* 142 B.C.   *l* Gk he   *m* Cn: Gk *Gaza*   *n* 141 B.C.
o Gk *they*   *p* Gk *He*   *q* 140 B.C.   *r* Other ancient authorities add *of Judah*

13:41 **170:** *that is* 142 B.C.E.   13:43 **Gazara:** *prob. rdg: Gk Gaza.*   13:51 **171:** *that is* 141 B.C.E.   14:1 **172:** *that is* 140 B.C.E.

fied for enrollment in our service, let them be enrolled. Let there be peace between us."

41 Thus in the year one hundred and seventy, the yoke of the Gentiles was removed from Israel, 42 and the people began to write in their records and contracts, "In the first year of Simon, high priest, governor, and leader of the Jews."

43 In those days Simon besieged Gazara and surrounded it with troops. He made a siege machine, pushed it up against the city, and attacked and captured one of the towers. 44 The men who had been on the siege machine jumped down into the city and caused a great tumult there. 45 The men of the city, joined by their wives and children, went up on the wall, with their garments rent, and cried out in loud voices, begging Simon to grant them peace. 46 "Do not treat us according to our evil deeds," they said, "but according to your mercy."

47 So Simon came to terms with them and did not destroy them. He made them leave the city, however, and he purified the houses in which there were idols. Then he entered the city with hymns and songs of praise. 48 After removing from it everything that was impure, he settled there men who observed the law. He improved its fortifications and built himself a residence.

49 The men in the citadel in Jerusalem were prevented from going out into the country and back for the purchase of food; they suffered greatly from hunger, and many of them died of starvation. 50 They finally cried out to Simon for peace, and he gave them peace. He expelled them from the citadel and cleansed it of impurities. 51 On the twenty-third day of the second month, in the year one hundred and seventy-one, the Jews entered the citadel with shouts of jubilation, waving of palm branches, the music of harps and cymbals and lyres, and the singing of hymns and canticles, because a great enemy of Israel had been destroyed. 52 Simon decreed that this day should be celebrated every year with rejoicing. He also strengthened the fortifications of the temple hill alongside the citadel, and he and his companions dwelt there. 53 Seeing that his son John was now a grown man, Simon made him commander of all his soldiers, with his residence in Gazara.

14 In the year one hundred and seventy-two, King Demetrius assembled his army and marched into Media to obtain help so that he could fight Trypho. 2 When Arsaces, king of Persia and Media, heard that Demetrius had invaded his territory, he sent one of his generals to take him alive. 3 The general went forth and defeated the army of Demetrius; he captured him and brought him to Arsaces, who put him in prison.

4 The land was at rest all the days of Simon,
 who sought the good of his nation.
His people were delighted with his power
 and his magnificence throughout his reign.
5 As his crowning glory he captured the port
 of Joppa
 and made it a gateway to the isles of the sea.
6 He enlarged the borders of his nation
 and gained control of the country.
7 He took many enemies prisoners of war
 and made himself master of Gazara, Beth-zur,
 and the citadel.

He cleansed the citadel of its impurities;
 there was no one to withstand him.
8 The people cultivated their land in peace;
 the land yielded its produce
 and the trees of the field their fruit.

bodyguard, let them be enrolled, and let there be peace between us.'

41 The gentile yoke was thus lifted from Israel in the year 170, 42 when our people began engrossing their documents and contracts: 'In the first year of Simon, eminent high priest, commander-in-chief and ethnarch of the Jews'.

43 About that time Simon laid siege to Gezer, surrounding it with his troops. He constructed a mobile tower, brought it up to the city, opened a breach in one of the bastions and took it. 44 The men in the mobile tower sprang out into the city, where great confusion ensued. 45 The citizens, accompanied by their wives and children, mounted the ramparts with their garments torn and loudly implored Simon to make peace with them: 46 'Treat us', they said, 'not as our wickedness deserves, but as your mercy prompts you.' 47 Simon came to terms with them and stopped the fighting; but he expelled them from the city, purified the houses which contained idols, and then made his entry with songs of praise. 48 He banished all impurity from it, settled in it people who observed the Law, and having fortified it, built a residence there for himself.

49 The occupants of the Citadel in Jerusalem, prevented as they were from coming out and going into the countryside to buy and sell, were in desperate need of food, and numbers of them were being carried off by starvation. 50 They begged Simon to make peace with them, and he granted this, though he expelled them and purified the Citadel from its pollutions. 51 The Jews made their entry on the twenty-third day of the second month in the year 171, with acclamations and carrying palms, to the sound of lyres, cymbals and harps, chanting hymns and canticles, since a great enemy had been crushed and thrown out of Israel. Simon made it a day of annual rejoicing. 52 He fortified the Temple hill on the Citadel side, and took up residence there with his men. 53 Since his son John had come to manhood, Simon appointed him general-in-chief, with his residence in Gezer.

14 In the year 172, King Demetrius assembled his forces and marched into Media to raise help for the fight against Trypho. 2 When Arsaces king of Persia and Media heard that Demetrius had entered his territory, he sent one of his generals to capture him alive. 3 The general defeated the army of Demetrius, seized him and brought him to Arsaces, who imprisoned him. 4 The country was at peace throughout the days of Simon.

He sought the good of his nation
 and they were well pleased with his authority,
 as with his magnificence, throughout his life.
5 To crown his titles to glory,
 he took Joppa and made it a harbour,
 gaining access to the Mediterranean Isles.
6 He enlarged the frontiers of his nation,
 keeping his mastery over the homeland,
7 resettling a host of captives.
He conquered Gezer, Beth-Zur and the Citadel,
 ridding them of every impurity,
 and no one could resist him.
8 The people farmed their land in peace;
 the land gave its produce,
 the trees of the plain their fruit.

9 Old men sat in the streets;
> they all talked together of good things,
> and the youths put on splendid military attire.
10 He supplied the towns with food,
> and furnished them with the means of defense,
> until his renown spread to the ends of the
> earth.
11 He established peace in the land,
> and Israel rejoiced with great joy.
12 All the people sat under their own vines and fig
> trees,
> and there was none to make them afraid.
13 No one was left in the land to fight them,
> and the kings were crushed in those days.
14 He gave help to all the humble among his people;
> he sought out the law,
> and did away with all the renegades and
> outlaws.
15 He made the sanctuary glorious,
> and added to the vessels of the sanctuary.

16 It was heard in Rome, and as far away as Sparta, that Jonathan had died, and they were deeply grieved. 17 When they heard that his brother Simon had become high priest in his stead, and that he was ruling over the country and the towns in it, 18 they wrote to him on bronze tablets to renew with him the friendship and alliance that they had established with his brothers Judas and Jonathan. 19 And these were read before the assembly in Jerusalem.

20 This is a copy of the letter that the Spartans sent: "The rulers and the city of the Spartans to the high priest Simon and to the elders and the priests and the rest of the Jewish people, our brothers, greetings. 21 The envoys who were sent to our people have told us about your glory and honor, and we rejoiced at their coming. 22 We have recorded what they said in our public decrees, as follows, 'Numenius son of Antiochus and Antipater son of Jason, envoys of the Jews, have come to us to renew their friendship with us. 23 It has pleased our people to receive these men with honor and to put a copy of their words in the public archives, so that the people of the Spartans may have a record of them. And they have sent a copy of this to the high priest Simon.'"

24 After this Simon sent Numenius to Rome with a large gold shield weighing one thousand minas, to confirm the alliance with the Romans.[s]

25 When the people heard these things they said, "How shall we thank Simon and his sons? 26 For he and his brothers and the house of his father have stood firm; they have fought and repulsed Israel's enemies and established its freedom." 27 So they made a record on bronze tablets and put it on pillars on Mount Zion.

This is a copy of what they wrote: "On the eighteenth day of Elul, in the one hundred seventy-second year,[t] which is the third year of the great high priest Simon, 28 in Asaramel,[u] in the great assembly of the priests and the people and the rulers of the nation and the elders of the country, the following was proclaimed to us:

29 "Since wars often occurred in the country, Simon son of Mattathias, a priest of the sons[v] of Joarib, and his brothers, exposed themselves to danger and resisted the enemies of their nation, in order that their sanctuary and the law might be preserved; and they brought great glory to their nation. 30 Jonathan rallied the[w] nation, became their high priest, and was gathered to his people. 31 When their enemies decided to invade their country and lay hands on their sanctuary, 32 then Simon rose up and fought for his

in the streets, talking together of their blessings; and the young men arrayed themselves in splendid military style. 10 Simon supplied the towns with food in plenty and equipped them with weapons for defence, so that his renown spread to the ends of the earth. 11 Peace was restored to the land, and throughout Israel there was great rejoicing. 12 Everyone sat under his own vine and fig tree, and there was none to cause alarm. 13 Those were days when no enemy was seen in the land and every hostile king was crushed. 14 Simon gave his protection to the poor among the people; he fulfilled the demands of the law, and rid the country of renegades and evil men. 15 He enhanced the splendour of the temple and furnished it with a wealth of sacred vessels.

16 The report of Jonathan's death reached Rome and even Sparta, and caused widespread grief. 17 When they heard, however, that his brother Simon had succeeded him as high priest and was firmly in control of both country and towns, 18 they sent him a renewal of the treaty of friendship and alliance they had established with his brothers Judas and Jonathan; this was inscribed on bronze tablets 19 which were read before the assembly in Jerusalem. 20 The following is a copy of the letter which the Spartans sent:

From the magistrates and city of Sparta to the High Priest Simon, to the Senate, the priests, and the rest of the Jewish people, our brothers.
Greeting.
21 The envoys sent to our people have informed us of your honour and fame, and their visit has given us much pleasure. 22 We have entered a record of the message they brought in the minutes of the public assembly; it reads: 'Numenius son of Antiochus and Antipater son of Jason came as envoys of the Jews to renew the treaty of friendship. 23 It was resolved by the public assembly to receive these men with honour and to place a copy of their address in the public archives, so that the people of Sparta might have it on permanent record. A copy of this document has been made for Simon the high priest.'

24 After this, Simon sent Numenius to Rome bearing a large gold shield, worth a thousand minas, to confirm the alliance with the Romans.

25 When the people heard an account of these events they asked themselves how they could show their gratitude to Simon and his sons, 26 for he, with his brothers and his father's family, had proved resolute in repulsing the enemies of Israel and ensuring the nation's freedom. 27 So the people had an inscription engraved on bronze tablets and placed on a monument on Mount Zion; this is a copy of the inscription:

On the eighteenth day of the month of Elul, in the year 172, the third year of Simon's high-priesthood, 28 at Asaramel, before a large assembly of priests, people, rulers of the nation, and elders of the land, the following resolution was passed: 29 'Whereas our land had been subject to frequent wars, Simon son of Mattathias, a priest of the Joarib family, and his brothers put their lives in jeopardy by their resistance to the enemies of the people, in order to safeguard the temple and the law, and they brought great glory to their nation. 30 Jonathan rallied the nation and became high priest, and then was gathered to his forefathers. 31 When enemies resolved to invade and destroy the land and to make an assault on the temple, 32 Simon came forward and fought for his nation.

---

s Gk them   t 140 B.C.   u This word resembles the Hebrew words for *the court of the people of God* or *the prince of the people of God*   v Meaning of Gk uncertain   w Gk *their*

14:27 **172:** *that is* 140 B.C.E.

9 Old men sat in the squares,
  all talking about the good times,
  while the young men wore the glorious apparel
    of war.
10 He supplied the cities with food
  and equipped them with means of defense,
  till his glorious name reached the ends of
    the earth.
11 He brought peace to the land,
  and Israel was filled with happiness.
12 Every man sat under his vine and his fig tree,
  with no one to disturb him.
13 No one was left to attack them in their land;
  the kings in those days were crushed.
14 He strengthened all the lowly among his people
  and was zealous for the law;
  he suppressed all the lawless and the wicked.
15 He made the temple splendid
  and enriched its equipment.

16 When people heard in Rome and even in Sparta that Jonathan had died, they were deeply grieved. 17 But when the Romans heard that his brother Simon had been made high priest in his place and was master of the country and the cities, 18 they sent him inscribed tablets of bronze to renew with him the friendship and alliance that they had established with his brothers Judas and Jonathan. 19 These were read before the assembly in Jerusalem. 20 This is a copy of the letter that the Spartans sent: "The rulers and the citizens of Sparta send greetings to Simon the high priest, the elders, the priests, and the rest of the Jewish people, our brothers. 21 The envoys you sent to our people have informed us of your glory and fame, and we were happy that they came. 22 In accordance with what they said we have recorded the following in the public decrees: Since Numenius, son of Antiochus, and Antipater, son of Jason, envoys of the Jews, have come to us to renew their friendship with us, 23 the people have voted to receive the men with honor, and to deposit a copy of their words in the public archives, so that the people of Sparta may have a record of them. A copy of this decree has been made for Simon the high priest."

24 After this, Simon sent Numenius to Rome with a great gold shield weighing a thousand minas, to confirm the alliance with the Romans.

25 When the people heard of these things, they said, "How can we thank Simon and his sons? 26 He and his brothers and his father's house have stood firm and repulsed Israel's enemies. They have thus preserved its liberty." So they made an inscription on bronze tablets, which they affixed to pillars on Mount Zion. 27 The following is a copy of the inscription:

"On the eighteenth day of Elul, in the year one hundred and seventy-two, that is, the third year under Simon the high priest in Asaramel, 28 in a great assembly of priests, people, rulers of the nation, and elders of the country, the following proclamation was made:

29 " 'Since there have often been wars in our country, Simon, son of the priest Mattathias, descendant of Joarib, and his brothers have put themselves in danger and resisted the enemies of their nation, so that their sanctuary and law might be maintained, and they have thus brought great glory to their nation. 30 After Jonathan had rallied his nation and become their high priest, he was gathered to his kinsmen. 31 When the enemies of the Jews sought to invade and devastate their country and to lay hands on their temple, 32 Si-

9 The elders sat at ease in the squares,
  all their talk was of their prosperity;
  the young men wore splendid armour.
10 He kept the towns supplied with provisions
  and furnished with fortifications,
  until his fame resounded to the ends of the earth.
11 He established peace in the land,
  and Israel knew great joy.
12 Each man sat under his own vine and his own fig
    tree,
  and there was no one to make them afraid.
13 No enemy was left in the land to fight them,
  the very kings of those times had been crushed.
14 He encouraged the afflicted members of his people,
  suppressing every wicked man and renegade.
  He strove to observe the Law,
15 and gave new splendour to the Temple,
  enriching it with many sacred vessels.

16 When it became known in Rome and as far as Sparta that Jonathan was dead, people were deeply grieved. 17 But as soon as they heard that his brother Simon had succeeded him as high priest and was master of the country and the cities in it, 18 they wrote to him on bronze tablets to renew the treaty of friendship and alliance which they had made with his brothers, Judas and Jonathan, 19 and the document was read out before the assembly in Jerusalem. 20 This is the copy of the letter sent by the Spartans:

'The rulers and the city of Sparta, to Simon the high priest and to the elders and priests and the rest of the people of the Jews, greetings.
21 'The ambassadors whom you sent to our people have informed us of your glory and prosperity, and we are delighted with their visit. 22 We have recorded their declarations in the minutes of our public assemblies, as follows, "Numenius son of Antiochus, and Antipater son of Jason, ambassadors of the Jews, came to us to renew their friendship with us. 23 And it was the people's pleasure to receive these personages with honour and to deposit a copy of their statements in the public archives, so that the people of Sparta might preserve a record of them. A copy was also made for Simon the high priest." '

24 After this, Simon sent Numenius to Rome as the bearer of a large golden shield weighing a thousand mina, to confirm the alliance with them.

25 When these events were reported to our people, they said, 'What mark of appreciation shall we give to Simon and his sons? 26 He stood firm, he and his brothers and his father's house: he fought off the enemies of Israel and secured its freedom.' So they recorded an inscription on bronze tablets and set it up on pillars on Mount Zion. 27 This is a copy of the text:

'The eighteenth of Elul, in the year 172, being the third year of Simon, eminent high priest:
28 'In Asaramel, in the Grand Assembly of priests and people, of princes of the nation and of elders of the country:
'We are acquainted with the matters following:
29 'When there was almost incessant fighting in the country Simon, son of Mattathias, a priest of the line of Joarib, and his brothers courted danger and withstood their nation's enemies to safeguard the integrity of their sanctuary and of the Law, and so brought their nation great glory;
30 'For when, Jonathan having rallied his nation and become its high priest and having then been gathered to his ancestors, 31 the enemy planned to invade the country, intending to devastate their territory and to lay hands on their sanctuary, 32 Simon next came forward to fight for

nation. He spent great sums of his own money; he armed the soldiers of his nation and paid them wages. 33 He fortified the towns of Judea, and Beth-zur on the borders of Judea, where formerly the arms of the enemy had been stored, and he placed there a garrison of Jews. 34 He also fortified Joppa, which is by the sea, and Gazara, which is on the borders of Azotus, where the enemy formerly lived. He settled Jews there, and provided in those towns*x* whatever was necessary for their restoration.

35 "The people saw Simon's faithfulness*y* and the glory that he had resolved to win for his nation, and they made him their leader and high priest, because he had done all these things and because of the justice and loyalty that he had maintained toward his nation. He sought in every way to exalt his people. 36 In his days things prospered in his hands, so that the Gentiles were put out of the*z* country, as were also those in the city of David in Jerusalem, who had built themselves a citadel from which they used to sally forth and defile the environs of the sanctuary, doing great damage to its purity. 37 He settled Jews in it and fortified it for the safety of the country and of the city, and built the walls of Jerusalem higher.

38 "In view of these things King Demetrius confirmed him in the high priesthood, 39 made him one of his Friends, and paid him high honors. 40 For he had heard that the Jews were addressed by the Romans as friends and allies and brothers, and that the Romans*a* had received the envoys of Simon with honor.

41 "The Jews and their priests have resolved that Simon should be their leader and high priest forever, until a trustworthy prophet should arise, 42 and that he should be governor over them and that he should take charge of the sanctuary and appoint officials over its tasks and over the country and the weapons and the strongholds, and that he should take charge of the sanctuary, 43 and that he should be obeyed by all, and that all contracts in the country should be written in his name, and that he should be clothed in purple and wear gold.

44 "None of the people or priests shall be permitted to nullify any of these decisions or to oppose what he says, or to convene an assembly in the country without his permission, or to be clothed in purple or put on a gold buckle. 45 Whoever acts contrary to these decisions or rejects any of them shall be liable to punishment."

46 All the people agreed to grant Simon the right to act in accordance with these decisions. 47 So Simon accepted and agreed to be high priest, to be commander and ethnarch of the Jews and priests, and to be protector of them all.*b* 48 And they gave orders to inscribe this decree on bronze tablets, to put them up in a conspicuous place in the precincts of the sanctuary, 49 and to deposit copies of them in the treasury, so that Simon and his sons might have them.

He expended large sums of his own money to arm the soldiers of his nation and to provide their pay. 33 He fortified the towns of Judaea, including Bethsura, a frontier town formerly used by the enemy as an arsenal, and he stationed in it a garrison of Jewish soldiers. 34 The coastal town of Joppa was also fortified, as was Gazara near Azotus, formerly occupied by the enemy. He settled Jews there, and provided these towns with everything requisite for their restoration.

35 'Simon's patriotism and his resolution to win renown for his nation were such that the people made him their leader and high priest, in recognition of his achievements, his just conduct, his loyalty towards the nation, and constant efforts to enhance its power. 36 In his time and under his leadership the Gentiles were successfully evicted from the land; so too were those who had occupied the City of David in Jerusalem and made for themselves a citadel from which they used to sally forth and bring defilement on the whole precinct of the temple and do violence to its purity. 37 He installed Jewish soldiers in it and fortified it for the greater security of the land and city; he also heightened the walls of Jerusalem. 38 In consideration of all this King Demetrius confirmed him in the office of high priest, 39 appointed him one of his Friends, and granted him the highest honours; 40 for he had heard that the Romans were addressing the Jews as friends, allies, and brothers and had received Simon's envoys with much honour.

41 'The Jews and their priests confirmed Simon as their leader and high priest in perpetuity until a true prophet should appear. 42 He was to be their general, and to have full charge of the temple and of the work of reconstruction; in addition the supervision of the country and of the arms and fortifications was to be entrusted to him. 43 He was to be obeyed by the whole people; all official documents throughout the land were to be drawn up in his name. He was to be entitled to wear the purple robe and gold clasp.

44 'None of the people or the priests is to have authority to abrogate any of these decrees, to oppose commands issued by Simon, or to convene any assembly in the land without his permission; none of them is to be robed in purple or to wear the gold clasp. 45 Whoever contravenes these provisions or neglects any of them is to be liable to punishment.

46 'It was the unanimous decision of the people that Simon should officiate in the ways here laid down. 47 Simon accepted, and consented to be high priest, general, and ethnarch of the Jews and the priests, and to be the protector of them all.'

48 This inscription, it was declared, should be engraved on bronze tablets and set up in a prominent position within the precincts of the temple, 49 and copies were to be placed in the treasury in the keeping of Simon and his sons.

15 Antiochus, son of King Demetrius, sent a letter from the islands of the sea to Simon, the priest and ethnarch of the Jews, and to all the nation; 2 its contents were as follows: "King Antiochus to Simon the high priest and ethnarch and to the nation of the Jews, greetings.

15 Antiochus son of King Demetrius sent a letter from overseas to Simon, priest and ethnarch of the Jews, and to the whole nation. 2 It read:

From King Antiochus to Simon, High Priest and Ethnarch, and to the Jewish nation.
Greeting.

---

x Gk *them*   *y* Other ancient authorities read *conduct*   *z* Gk *their*
a Gk *they*   *b* Or *to preside over them all*

mon rose up and fought for his nation, spending large sums of his own money to equip the men of his nation's armed forces and giving them their pay. 33 He fortified the cities of Judea, especially the frontier city of Beth-zur, where he stationed a garrison of Jewish soldiers, and where previously the enemy's arms had been stored. 34 He also fortified Joppa by the sea and Gazara on the border of Azotus, a place previously occupied by the enemy; these cities he resettled with Jews, and furnished them with all that was necessary for their restoration. 35 When the Jewish people saw Simon's loyalty and the glory he planned to bring to his nation, they made him their leader and high priest because of all he had accomplished and the loyalty and justice he had shown his nation. In every way he sought to exalt his people.

36 " 'In his time and under his guidance they succeeded in driving the Gentiles out of their country, especially those in the City of David in Jerusalem, who had built for themselves a citadel from which they used to sally forth to defile the environs of the temple and inflict grave injury on its purity. 37 In this citadel he stationed Jewish soldiers, and he strengthened its fortifications for the defense of the land and the city, while he also raised the wall of Jerusalem to a greater height. 38 Consequently, King Demetrius confirmed him in the high priesthood, 39 made him one of his Friends, and conferred the highest honors on him. 40 He had indeed heard that the Romans had addressed the Jews as friends, allies, and brothers, and that they had received Simon's envoys with honor.

41 " 'The Jewish people and their priest have, therefore, made the following decisions. Simon shall be their permanent leader and high priest until a true prophet arises. 42 He shall act as governor general over them, and shall have charge of the temple, to make regulations concerning its functions and concerning the country, its weapons and strongholds; 43 he shall be obeyed by all. All contracts made in the country shall be dated by his name. He shall have the right to wear royal purple and gold ornaments. 44 It shall not be lawful for any of the people or priests to nullify any of these decisions, or to contradict the orders given by him, or to convene an assembly in the country without his consent, to be clothed in royal purple or wear an official gold brooch. 45 Whoever acts otherwise or violates any of these prescriptions shall be liable to punishment.

46 " 'All the people approved of granting Simon the right to act in accord with these decisions, 47 and Simon accepted and agreed to act as high priest, governor general, and ethnarch of the Jewish people and priests and to exercise supreme authority over all.' "

48 It was decreed that this inscription should be engraved on bronze tablets, to be set up in a conspicuous place in the precincts of the temple, 49 and that copies of it should be deposited in the treasury, where they would be available to Simon and his sons.

15 Antiochus, son of King Demetrius, sent a letter from the islands of the sea to Simon, the priest and ethnarch of the Jews, and to all the nation, 2 which read as follows:

"King Antiochus sends greetings to Simon, the priest and ethnarch, and to the Jewish nation. 3 Whereas certain vil-

his nation: spending much of his personal wealth on arming his nation's fighting men and on providing their pay; 33 fortifying the towns of Judaea, as well as Beth-Zur on the Judaean frontier where the enemy arsenal had formerly been, and stationing in it a garrison of Jewish soldiers; 34 fortifying Joppa on the coast, and Gezer on the borders of Azotus, a place formerly inhabited by the enemy, founding a Jewish colony there, and providing the settlers with everything they needed to set them on their feet;

35 'In consequence of which, the people, aware of Simon's loyalty and of the glory which he was determined to win for his nation, have made him their ethnarch and high priest, for all his services and for the integrity and loyalty which he has shown towards his nation, and for having by every means sought to enhance his people's power;

36 'It has fallen to him in his time to expel the foreigners from his country, including those in the City of David in Jerusalem, who had converted it into a citadel for their own use, from which they would sally out to defile the surroundings of the sanctuary and to violate its sacred character; 37 to station Jewish soldiers there instead for the security of the country and the city; and to heighten the walls of Jerusalem;

38 'And since King Demetrius has heard that the Romans call the Jews their friends, allies and brothers, 39 and that they have given an honourable reception to Simon's ambassadors, and, furthermore, 40 that the Jews and priests are happy that Simon should, pending the advent of a genuine prophet, be their ethnarch and high priest for life 41 therefore he has confirmed him in the high-priestly office, has raised him to the rank of Friend and has showered great honours on him, also confirming him as their commander-in-chief, 42 with the right to appoint officials to oversee the fabric of the sanctuary and to administer the country, munitions and fortresses; 43 he is to have personal charge of the sanctuary, and to be obeyed by all; all official documents in the country must be drawn up in his name; and he may assume the purple and may wear golden ornaments;

44 'Furthermore, it is against the law for any member of the public or of the priesthood to contravene any of these enactments or to contest his decisions, or to convene a meeting anywhere in the country without his permission, or to assume the purple or wear the golden brooch; 45 and anyone acting contrary to, or rejecting any article of, these enactments is liable to punishment;

46 'And since the people have unanimously agreed to grant Simon the right to act as aforesaid, and 47 since Simon, for his part, has given his assent, and has consented to assume the high-priestly office and to be commander-in-chief and ethnarch of the Jews and their priests, and to preside over all:

48 'So, be it now enacted: that this record be inscribed on bronze tablets and be erected at some conspicuous place within the precincts of the Temple, 49 and that copies be deposited in the Treasury for Simon and his descendants.'

15 Antiochus son of King Demetrius addressed a letter from the Mediterranean Isles to Simon, priest and ethnarch of the Jews, and to the whole nation; 2 this was how it read:

'King Antiochus to Simon, high priest and ethnarch, and to the Jewish nation, greetings.

3 Whereas certain scoundrels have gained control of the kingdom of our ancestors, and I intend to lay claim to the kingdom so that I may restore it as it formerly was, and have recruited a host of mercenary troops and have equipped warships, 4 and intend to make a landing in the country so that I may proceed against those who have destroyed our country and those who have devastated many cities in my kingdom, 5 now therefore I confirm to you all the tax remissions that the kings before me have granted you, and a release from all the other payments from which they have released you. 6 I permit you to mint your own coinage as money for your country, 7 and I grant freedom to Jerusalem and the sanctuary. All the weapons that you have prepared and the strongholds that you have built and now hold shall remain yours. 8 Every debt you owe to the royal treasury and any such future debts shall be canceled for you from henceforth and for all time. 9 When we gain control of our kingdom, we will bestow great honor on you and your nation and the temple, so that your glory will become manifest in all the earth."

10 In the one hundred seventy-fourth year[c] Antiochus set out and invaded the land of his ancestors. All the troops rallied to him, so that there were only a few with Trypho. 11 Antiochus pursued him, and Trypho[d] came in his flight to Dor, which is by the sea; 12 for he knew that troubles had converged on him, and his troops had deserted him. 13 So Antiochus encamped against Dor, and with him were one hundred twenty thousand warriors and eight thousand cavalry. 14 He surrounded the town, and the ships joined battle from the sea; he pressed the town hard from land and sea, and permitted no one to leave or enter it.

15 Then Numenius and his companions arrived from Rome, with letters to the kings and countries, in which the following was written: 16 "Lucius, consul of the Romans, to King Ptolemy, greetings. 17 The envoys of the Jews have come to us as our friends and allies to renew our ancient friendship and alliance. They had been sent by the high priest Simon and by the Jewish people 18 and have brought a gold shield weighing one thousand minas. 19 We therefore have decided to write to the kings and countries that they should not seek their harm or make war against them and their cities and their country, or make alliance with those who war against them. 20 And it has seemed good to us to accept the shield from them. 21 Therefore if any scoundrels have fled to you from their country, hand them over to the high priest Simon, so that he may punish them according to their law."

22 The consul[e] wrote the same thing to King Demetrius and to Attalus and Ariarathes and Arsaces, 23 and to all the countries, and to Sampsames,[f] and to the Spartans, and to Delos, and to Myndos, and to Sicyon, and to Caria, and to Samos, and to Pamphylia, and to Lycia, and to Halicarnassus, and to Rhodes, and to Phaselis, and to Cos, and to Side, and to Aradus and Gortyna and Cnidus and Cyprus and Cyrene. 24 They also sent a copy of these things to the high priest Simon.

25 King Antiochus besieged Dor for the second time, continually throwing his forces against it and making engines of war; and he shut Trypho up and kept him from going out or in. 26 And Simon sent to Antiochus[g] two thousand picked troops, to fight for him, and silver and gold and a large amount of military equipment. 27 But he refused to receive them, and broke all the agreements he formerly had made with Simon, and became estranged from him. 28 He sent to him Athenobius, one of his Friends, to confer with

3 Whereas certain rebels have seized control of my ancestral kingdom, now I have decided to assert my claim to it, so that I may restore it to its former state. For this I have recruited a large body of mercenaries and fitted out ships of war. 4 It is my intention to land in my country and to seek out and punish those who have ravaged my kingdom and laid waste many of its cities. 5 Therefore I now confirm all the remissions which my royal predecessors granted you, whether of tribute or of other contributions. 6 I authorize you to mint your own coinage as currency for your country. 7 Jerusalem and the temple is to be free. All the arms you have prepared and the fortresses you have built and now occupy may remain in your hands. 8 All debts now owing to the royal treasury and all future liabilities thereto are cancelled from this time forward for ever. 9 When we have re-established our kingdom, we shall confer the highest honours on you and on your nation and temple, to make your country's fame apparent to the whole world.

10 In the year 174, Antiochus entered the land of his forefathers, and all the armed forces came over to him, leaving Trypho only a few supporters. 11 With Antiochus in pursuit of him, Trypho fled along the coastal road to Dor, 12 for he well knew how desperate was his position now that his troops had deserted. 13 Antiochus, with a hundred and twenty thousand trained soldiers and eight thousand horsemen under his command, laid siege to Dor. 14 He drew a cordon round the town, his ships joining in the blockade from the sea, and thus, both by land and sea, he exerted heavy pressure on it and prevented anyone from leaving or entering.

15 Numenius and his party arrived from Rome with letters to the various kings and nations. That to Ptolemy read as follows:

16 From Lucius, Consul of the Romans, to King Ptolemy. Greeting.

17 Envoys have come to us from our friends and allies the Jews. They were sent by Simon the high priest and the Jewish people, to renew their original treaty of friendship and alliance, 18 and they brought with them a gold shield valued at a thousand minas. 19 We have resolved, therefore, to write to kings and nations, that they do nothing to the detriment of the Jews; they must not make war on them or on their cities or their country, nor are they to ally themselves with those who so make war. 20 We have decided to accept the shield from them. 21 If, therefore, any rebels have escaped from their country to you, they are to be handed over to Simon the high priest to be punished by him according to Jewish law.

22 The same message was sent to King Demetrius, to Attalus, Ariarathes, Arsakes, 23 Sampsakes, and the Spartans, and also to the following places: Delos, Myndos, Sicyon, Caria, Samos, Pamphylia, Lycia, Halicarnassus, Rhodes, Phaselis, Cos, Sideh, Aradus, Gortyna, Cnidus, Cyprus, and Cyrene. 24 A copy was written out for Simon the high priest.

25 King Antiochus laid siege to Dor for the second time, and launched repeated attacks against it; he had siege-engines constructed and blockaded Trypho, preventing all movement in or out of the town.

26 Simon sent two thousand picked men to assist him, as well as silver and gold and much equipment. 27 But Antiochus refused the offer; instead, he repudiated all his previous agreements with Simon and broke off relations. 28 He sent Athenobius, one of the Friends, to convey this mes-

---

c 138 B.C.   d Gk he   e Gk He   f The name is uncertain   g Gk him

15:10 **174:** that is 138 B.C.E.   15:25 **for the second time:** some witnesses read on the second day.

lains have gained control of the kingdom of my ancestors, I intend to reclaim it, that I may restore it to its former state. I have recruited a large number of mercenary troops and equipped warships 4 to make a landing in my country and take revenge on those who have ruined it and laid waste many cities in my realm.

5 "Now, therefore, I confirm to you all the tax exemptions that the kings before me granted you and whatever other privileges they conferred on you. 6 I authorize you to coin your own money, as legal tender in your country. 7 Jerusalem and its temple shall be free. All the weapons you have prepared and all the strongholds you have built and now occupy shall remain in your possession. 8 All debts, present or future, due to the royal treasury shall be canceled for you, now and for all time. 9 When we recover our kingdom, we will greatly honor you and your nation and the temple, so that your glory will be manifest in all the earth."

10 In the year one hundred and seventy-four, Antiochus invaded the land of his ancestors, and all the troops rallied to him, so that few were left with Trypho. 11 Pursued by Antiochus, Trypho fled to Dor, by the sea, 12 realizing what a mass of troubles had come upon him now that his soldiers had deserted him. 13 Antiochus encamped before Dor with a hundred and twenty thousand infantry and eight thousand horsemen. 14 While he invested the city, his ships closed in along the coast, so that he blockaded it by land and sea and let no one go in or out.

15 Meanwhile, Numenius and his companions left Rome with letters such as this addressed to various kings and countries:

16 "Lucius, Consul of the Romans, sends greetings to King Ptolemy. 17 Certain envoys of the Jews, our friends and allies, have come to us to renew their earlier alliance of friendship. They had been sent by Simon the high priest and the Jewish people, 18 and they brought with them a gold shield worth a thousand minas. 19 Therefore we have decided to write to various kings and countries, that they are not to harm them, or wage war against them or their cities or their country, and are not to assist those who fight against them. 20 We have also decided to accept the shield from them. 21 If, then, any troublemakers from their country take refuge among you, hand them over to Simon the high priest, so that he may punish them according to their law."

22 The consul sent similar letters to Kings Demetrius, Attalus, Ariarthes and Arsaces; 23 to all the countries—Sampsames, Sparta, Delos, Myndos, Sicyon, Caria, Samos, Pamphylia, Lycia, Halicarnassus, Rhodes, Phaselis, Cos, Side, Aradus, Gortyna, Cnidus, Cyprus, and Cyrene. 24 A copy of the letter was also sent to Simon the high priest.

25 When King Antiochus was encamped before Dor, he assaulted it continuously both with troops and with the siege machines he had made. He blockaded Trypho by preventing anyone from going in or out. 26 Simon sent to Antiochus' support two thousand elite troops, together with gold and silver and much equipment. 27 But he refused to accept the aid; in fact, he broke all the agreements he had previously made with Simon and became hostile toward him. 28 He sent Athenobius, one of his Friends, to confer with

3 'Whereas certain scoundrels have seized control of the kingdom of our fathers, and I propose to claim back the kingdom so that I may re-establish it as it was before, and whereas I have accordingly recruited very large forces and fitted out warships, 4 intending to make a landing in the country and to hunt down the men who have ruined it and laid waste many towns in my kingdom;

5 'I now, therefore, confirm in your favour all remissions of taxes granted to you by the kings my predecessors, as well as the waiving of whatever presents they may have conceded. 6 I hereby authorise you to mint your own coinage as legal tender for your own country. 7 I declare Jerusalem and the sanctuary to be free; all the arms you have manufactured and the fortresses you have built and now occupy may remain yours. 8 All debts to the royal treasury, present or future, are cancelled henceforth in perpetuity. 9 Furthermore, when we have won back our kingdom, we shall bestow such great honour on yourself, your nation and the sanctuary as will make your glory known throughout the world.'

10 Antiochus invaded the land of his ancestors in the year 174 and, since the troops all rallied to him, Trypho was left with few supporters. 11 Antiochus pursued the usurper, who took refuge in Dora on the coast, 12 knowing that misfortunes were piling up on him and that his troops had deserted him. 13 Antiochus pitched camp outside Dora with a hundred and twenty thousand fighting men and eight thousand cavalry. 14 He laid siege to the city while the ships closed in from the sea, so that he had the city under attack from land and sea, and allowed no one to go in or come out.

15 Numenius and his companions, meanwhile, arrived from Rome, bringing letters addressed to various kings and states, in the following terms:

16 'Lucius, consul of the Romans, to King Ptolemy, greetings.

17 'The Jewish ambassadors have come to us as our friends and allies to renew our original friendship and alliance in the name of the high priest Simon and the Jewish people. 18 They have brought a golden shield worth a thousand *mina*. 19 Accordingly, we have seen fit to write to various kings and states, warning them neither to molest the Jewish people nor to attack either them or their towns or their country, nor to ally themselves with any such aggressors. 20 We have seen fit to accept the shield from them. 21 If, therefore, any scoundrels have fled their country to take refuge with you, hand them over to Simon the high priest, to be punished by him according to their law.'

22 The consul sent the same letter to King Demetrius, to Attalus, Ariarathes and Arsaces, 23 and to all states, including Sampsames, the Spartans, Delos, Myndos, Sicyon, Caria, Samos, Pamphylia, Lycia, Halicarnassus, Rhodes, Phaselis, Cos, Side, Arados, Gortyn, Cyprus and Cyrene. 24 They also drew up a copy for Simon the high priest.

25 Antiochus, meanwhile, from his positions on the outskirts of Dora, was continually throwing detachments against the town. He constructed siege-engines, and blockaded Trypho, preventing movement in or out. 26 Simon sent him two thousand picked men to support him in the fight, with silver and gold and plenty of equipment. 27 But Antiochus would not accept them; instead, he repudiated all his previous agreements with Simon and completely changed his attitude to him. 28 He sent him Athenobius, one of his Friends, to confer with him and say, 'You are now occupy-

him, saying, "You hold control of Joppa and Gazara and the citadel in Jerusalem; they are cities of my kingdom. 29 You have devastated their territory, you have done great damage in the land, and you have taken possession of many places in my kingdom. 30 Now then, hand over the cities that you have seized and the tribute money of the places that you have conquered outside the borders of Judea; 31 or else pay me five hundred talents of silver for the destruction that you have caused and five hundred talents more for the tribute money of the cities. Otherwise we will come and make war on you."

32 So Athenobius, the king's Friend, came to Jerusalem, and when he saw the splendor of Simon, and the sideboard with its gold and silver plate, and his great magnificence, he was amazed. When he reported to him the king's message, 33 Simon said to him in reply: "We have neither taken foreign land nor seized foreign property, but only the inheritance of our ancestors, which at one time had been unjustly taken by our enemies. 34 Now that we have the opportunity, we are firmly holding the inheritance of our ancestors. 35 As for Joppa and Gazara, which you demand, they were causing great damage among the people and to our land; for them we will give you one hundred talents."

Athenobius[h] did not answer him a word, 36 but returned in wrath to the king and reported to him these words, and also the splendor of Simon and all that he had seen. And the king was very angry.

37 Meanwhile Trypho embarked on a ship and escaped to Orthosia. 38 Then the king made Cendebeus commander-in-chief of the coastal country, and gave him troops of infantry and cavalry. 39 He commanded him to encamp against Judea, to build up Kedron and fortify its gates, and to make war on the people; but the king pursued Trypho. 40 So Cendebeus came to Jamnia and began to provoke the people and invade Judea and take the people captive and kill them. 41 He built up Kedron and stationed horsemen and troops there, so that they might go out and make raids along the highways of Judea, as the king had ordered him.

16 John went up from Gazara and reported to his father Simon what Cendebeus had done. 2 And Simon called in his two eldest sons Judas and John, and said to them: "My brothers and I and my father's house have fought the wars of Israel from our youth until this day, and things have prospered in our hands so that we have delivered Israel many times. 3 But now I have grown old, and you by Heaven's[i] mercy are mature in years. Take my place and my brother's, and go out and fight for our nation, and may the help that comes from Heaven be with you."

4 So John[j] chose out of the country twenty thousand warriors and cavalry, and they marched against Cendebeus and camped for the night in Modein. 5 Early in the morning they started out and marched into the plain, where a large force of infantry and cavalry was coming to meet them; and a stream lay between them. 6 Then he and his army lined up against them. He saw that the soldiers were afraid to cross the stream, so he crossed over first; and when his troops saw him, they crossed over after him. 7 Then he divided the army and placed the cavalry in the center of the infantry, for the cavalry of the enemy were very numerous. 8 They sounded the trumpets, and Cendebeus and his army were put to flight; many of them fell wounded and the rest fled into the stronghold. 9 At that time Judas the brother of John was wounded, but John pursued them until Cendebeus[k] reached Kedron, which he had built. 10 They also fled into the towers that were in the fields of Azotus, and John[k] burned it with fire, and about two thousand of them fell. He then returned to Judea safely.

sage: 'You are occupying Joppa and Gazara and the citadel in Jerusalem, cities that belong to my kingdom. 29 You have laid waste their territories and done great damage to the country, and you have made yourselves masters of many places in my kingdom. 30 Therefore I now demand the return of the cities you have seized and the surrender of the tribute exacted from places beyond the frontiers of Judaea over which you have assumed control. 31 Otherwise, you must pay five hundred talents of silver on their account, and another five hundred as compensation for the destruction you have caused and for the loss of tribute from the cities. Failing this, we shall resort to war.'

32 Athenobius, the king's Friend, came to Jerusalem, and when he saw the magnificence of Simon's establishment, and the gold and silver vessels on his sideboard, and his display of wealth, he was amazed. He delivered the king's message, 33 to which Simon replied: 'We have neither occupied other people's land nor taken possession of other people's property; we have taken only our ancestral heritage, unjustly seized for a time by our enemies. 34 We have grasped the opportunity to reclaim our patrimony. 35 But with regard to Joppa and Gazara, which you demand, these towns were doing great damage among our people and in our land; for these we offer one hundred talents.'

Without a word, 36 Athenobius went off in anger to the king, who was furious when Athenobius told him what Simon had said, and described Simon's splendour and all else he had seen.

37 Meanwhile Trypho boarded a ship and made his escape to Orthosia. 38 The king appointed Kendebaeus as commander-in-chief of the coastal zone, and gave him infantry and cavalry, 39 with instructions to blockade Judaea, to rebuild Kedron and strengthen its gates, and to make war on our people; he himself would continue the pursuit of Trypho. 40 Kendebaeus arrived in Jamnia, and by invading Judaea began to harass our people, capturing and killing them. 41 He rebuilt Kedron and stationed cavalry and foot-soldiers there to sally forth and patrol the roads of Judaea, as instructed by the king.

16 John went up from Gazara and reported to Simon, his father, the results of Kendebaeus's campaign. 2 Simon summoned his two eldest sons Judas and John, and said to them: 'My brothers and I and my father's family have fought Israel's battles from our youth until this day, and many a time have we been successful in rescuing Israel. 3 Now I am old, but mercifully you are in the prime of life. Take my brother's place and mine, and go out and fight for our nation. And may help from Heaven be with you!'

4 John levied twenty thousand warriors, foot-soldiers and cavalry, from the country and marched against Kendebaeus. After a night at Modin 5 they advanced early next morning into the plain, where a large force of infantry and cavalry stood ready to meet them on the far side of a wadi. 6 John and his troops were in position facing the enemy, when he realized that his men were afraid to cross the gully. So he himself led the way, and seeing this his men followed him across. 7 John drew up his army with the cavalry in the centre of the infantry, for the opposing cavalry were very numerous. 8 The trumpets sounded for the attack, and Kendebaeus and his army were routed; many fell, and the remainder took refuge in the fortress. 9 John's brother Judas was wounded in the fighting, but John kept up the pursuit until Kendebaeus reached Kedron, which he had rebuilt. 10 The fugitives fled to the forts in the open country round Azotus, whereupon John set fire to Azotus, and some two thousand of the enemy perished. He then returned to Judaea in safety.

---

[h] Gk He   [i] Gk his   [j] Other ancient authorities read he   [k] Gk he

Simon and say: "You are occupying Joppa and Gazara and the citadel of Jerusalem; these are cities of my kingdom. 29 You have laid waste their territories, done great harm to the land, and taken possession of many districts in my realm. 30 Therefore, give up the cities you have seized and the tribute money of the districts outside the territory of Judea of which you have taken possession; 31 or instead, pay me five hundred talents of silver for the devastation you have caused and five hundred talents more for the tribute money of the cities. If you do not do this, we will come and make war on you."

32 So Athenobius, the king's Friend, came to Jerusalem, and on seeing the splendor of Simon's court, the gold and silver plate on the sideboard, and the rest of his rich display, he was amazed. When he gave him the king's message, 33 Simon said to him in reply:

"We have not seized any foreign land; what we took is not the property of others, but our ancestral heritage which for a time had been unjustly held by our enemies. 34 Now that we have the opportunity, we are holding on to the heritage of our ancestors. 35 As for Joppa and Gazara, which you demand, the men of these cities were doing great harm to our people and laying waste our country; however, we are willing to pay you a hundred talents for these cities."

36 Athenobius made no reply, but returned to the king in anger. When he told him of Simon's words, of his splendor, and of all he had seen, the king fell into a violent rage.

37 Trypho had gotten aboard a ship and escaped to Orthosia. 38 Then the king appointed Cendebeus commander in chief of the seacoast, and gave him infantry and cavalry forces. 39 He ordered him to move his troops against Judea and to fortify Kedron and strengthen its gates, so that he could launch attacks against the Jewish people. Meanwhile the king went in pursuit of Trypho. 40 When Cendebeus came to Jamnia, he began to harass the people and to make incursions into Judea, where he took people captive or massacred them. 41 As the king ordered, he fortified Kedron and stationed horsemen and infantry there, so that they could go out and patrol the roads of Judea.

16 John then went up from Gazara and told his father Simon what Cendebeus was doing. 2 Simon called his two oldest sons, Judas and John, and said to them: "I and my brothers and my father's house have fought the battles of Israel from our youth until today, and many times we succeeded in saving Israel. 3 I have now grown old, but you, by the mercy of Heaven, have come to man's estate. Take my place and my brother's, and go out and fight for our nation; and may the help of Heaven be with you!"

4 John then mustered in the land twenty thousand warriors and horsemen. Setting out against Cendebeus, they spent the night at Modein, 5 rose early, and marched into the plain. There, facing them, was an immense army of foot soldiers and horsemen, and between the two armies was a stream. 6 John and his men took their position against the enemy. Seeing that his men were afraid to cross the stream, John crossed first. When his men saw this, they crossed over after him. 7 Then he divided his infantry into two corps and put his cavalry between them, for the enemy's horsemen were very numerous. 8 They blew the trumpets, and Cendebeus and his army were put to flight; many of them fell wounded, and the rest fled toward the stronghold. 9 It was then that John's brother Judas fell wounded; but John pursued them until Cendebeus reached Kidron, which he had fortified. 10 Some took refuge in the towers on the plain of Azotus, but John set fire to these, and about two thousand of the enemy perished. He then returned to Judea in peace.

ing Joppa and Gezer and the Citadel in Jerusalem, which are towns in my kingdom. 29 You have laid waste their territory and done immense harm to the country; and you have seized control of many places properly in my kingdom. 30 Either now surrender the towns you have taken and the taxes from the places you have seized outside the frontiers of Judaea, 31 or else pay me five hundred talents of silver in compensation for them and for the destruction you have done, and another five hundred talents for the taxes from the towns; otherwise we shall come and make war on you.' 32 When the King's Friend, Athenobius, reached Jerusalem and saw Simon's magnificence, his cabinet of gold and silver plate and the state he kept, he was dumbfounded. He delivered the king's message, 33 but Simon gave him this answer, 'We have not taken foreign territory or any alien property but have occupied our ancestral heritage, for some time unjustly wrested from us by our enemies; 34 now that we have a favourable opportunity, we are merely recovering our ancestral heritage. 35 As regards Joppa and Gezer, which you claim, these were towns that did great harm to our people and laid waste our country; we are prepared to give a hundred talents for them.' Without so much as a word in answer, 36 the envoy went back to the king in a rage and reported on Simon's answer and his magnificence, and on everything he had seen, at which the king fell into a fury.

37 Trypho now boarded a ship and escaped to Orthosia. 38 The king appointed Cendebaeus military governor of the coastal region and allotted him a force of infantry and cavalry. 39 He ordered him to deploy his men facing Judaea, and instructed him to rebuild Kedron and fortify its gates, and to make war on our people, while the king himself went in pursuit of Trypho. 40 Cendebaeus arrived at Jamnia and began to provoke our people forthwith, invading Judaea, taking prisoners, and massacring. 41 Having rebuilt Kedron, he stationed cavalry and troops there to make sorties and patrol the roads of Judaea, as the king had ordered.

16 John then went up from Gezer and reported to his father Simon what Cendebaeus was busy doing. 2 At this, Simon summoned his two elder sons, Judas and John, and said to them, 'My brothers and I, and my father's House, have fought the enemies of Israel from our youth until today, and many a time we have been successful in rescuing Israel. 3 But now I am an old man, while you, by the mercy of Heaven, are the right age; take the place of my brother and myself, go out and fight for our nation, and may Heaven's aid be with you.' 4 He then selected twenty thousand of the country's fighting men and cavalry, and these marched against Cendebaeus, spending the night at Modein. 5 Making an early start, they marched into the plain, to find a large army opposing them, both infantry and cavalry; there was, however, a stream-bed in between. 6 John drew up facing them, he and his army and, seeing that the men were afraid to cross the stream-bed, crossed over first himself. When his men saw this, they too crossed after him. 7 He divided his army into two, with the cavalry in the centre and the infantry on either flank, as the opposing cavalry was very numerous. 8 The trumpets rang out; Cendebaeus and his army were put to flight, many of them falling mortally wounded and the rest of them fleeing to the fortress. 9 Then it was that Judas, John's brother, was wounded, but John pursued them until Cendebaeus reached Kedron, which he had rebuilt. 10 Their flight took them as far as the towers in the countryside of Azotus, and John burnt these down. The enemy losses amounted to ten thousand men; John returned safely to Judaea.

11 Now Ptolemy son of Abubus had been appointed governor over the plain of Jericho; he had a large store of silver and gold, 12 for he was son-in-law of the high priest. 13 His heart was lifted up; he determined to get control of the country, and made treacherous plans against Simon and his sons, to do away with them. 14 Now Simon was visiting the towns of the country and attending to their needs, and he went down to Jericho with his sons Mattathias and Judas, in the one hundred seventy-seventh year,*l* in the eleventh month, which is the month of Shebat. 15 The son of Abubus received them treacherously in the little stronghold called Dok, which he had built; he gave them a great banquet, and hid men there. 16 When Simon and his sons were drunk, Ptolemy and his men rose up, took their weapons, rushed in against Simon in the banquet hall and killed him and his two sons, as well as some of his servants. 17 So he committed an act of great treachery and returned evil for good.

18 Then Ptolemy wrote a report about these things and sent it to the king, asking him to send troops to aid him and to turn over to him the towns and the country. 19 He sent other troops to Gazara to do away with John; he sent letters to the captains asking them to come to him so that he might give them silver and gold and gifts; 20 and he sent other troops to take possession of Jerusalem and the temple hill. 21 But someone ran ahead and reported to John at Gazara that his father and brothers had perished, and that "he has sent men to kill you also." 22 When he heard this, he was greatly shocked; he seized the men who came to destroy him and killed them, for he had found out that they were seeking to destroy him.

23 The rest of the acts of John and his wars and the brave deeds that he did, and the building of the walls that he completed, and his achievements, 24 are written in the annals of his high priesthood, from the time that he became high priest after his father.

l 134 B.C.

11 Ptolemaeus son of Abubus had been appointed commander for the plain of Jericho. He had great wealth in silver and gold, 12 for he was the high priest's son-in-law, 13 but he became over-ambitious and, proposing to make himself master of the country, plotted to put Simon and his sons out of the way. 14 When, in the course of a tour to inspect the towns in that region and to attend to their needs, Simon went down to Jericho with his sons Mattathias and Judas in the year 177, in the eleventh month, the month of Shebat, 15 the son of Abubus, with treachery in his heart, received them at the small fort called Dok which he had built, and entertained them lavishly. But he had men in concealment there, 16 and when Simon and his sons were drunk, Ptolemaeus and his accomplices started up and seized their weapons; bursting into the banqueting hall, they attacked Simon and killed him, along with his two sons and some of his servants. 17 It was an act of base treachery in which evil was returned for good.

18 Ptolemaeus forwarded an account of his action to the king, with a request for troops to be sent to his assistance and for him to be given authority over the country and its towns. 19 He ordered some of his men to Gazara to make away with John, and he wrote to the senior officers of the army urging them to come over to him and be given silver and gold and gifts. 20 Other troops he detailed to seize control of Jerusalem and the temple hill. 21 But someone ran ahead and reported to John at Gazara that his father and brothers had been murdered, and that Ptolemaeus had sent men to kill him as well. 22 The news came as a great shock to John, and, learning of the plot against his life, he arrested and put to death the men who came to kill him.

23 The rest of the story of John, his wars and the deeds of valour he performed, the walls he built, and his achievements, 24 are recorded in the annals of his high-priesthood from the time when he succeeded his father.

16:14 *177: that is* 134 B.C.E.

NEW AMERICAN BIBLE

11 Ptolemy, son of Abubus, had been appointed governor of the plain of Jericho, and he had much silver and gold, 12 being the son-in-law of the high priest. 13 But he became ambitious and sought to get control of the country. So he made treacherous plans to do away with Simon and his sons. 14 As Simon was inspecting the cities of the country and providing for their needs, he and his sons Mattathias and Judas went down to Jericho in the year one hundred and seventy-seven, in the eleventh month (that is, the month Shebat). 15 The son of Abubus gave them a deceitful welcome in the little stronghold called Dok which he had built. While serving them a sumptuous banquet, he had his men hidden there. 16 Then, when Simon and his sons had drunk freely, Ptolemy and his men sprang up, weapons in hand, rushed upon Simon in the banquet hall, and killed him, his two sons, and some of his servants. 17 By this vicious act of treason he repaid good with evil.

18 Then Ptolemy wrote an account of this and sent it to the king, asking that troops be sent to help him and that the country be turned over to him. 19 He sent other men to Gazara to do away with John. To the army officers he sent letters inviting them to come to him so that he might present them with silver, gold, and gifts. 20 He also sent others to seize Jerusalem and the mount of the temple. 21 But someone ran ahead and brought word to John at Gazara that his father and his brothers had perished, and that Ptolemy had sent men to kill him also. 22 On hearing this, John was utterly astounded. When the men came to kill him, he had them arrested and put to death, for he knew what they meant to do. 23 Now the rest of the history of John, his wars and the brave deeds he performed, his rebuilding of the walls, and his other achievements — 24 these things are recorded in the chronicle of his pontificate, from the time that he succeeded his father as high priest.

NEW JERUSALEM BIBLE

11 Ptolemy son of Abubos had been appointed general in command of the Plain of Jericho; he owned a great deal of silver and gold, 12 and was the high priest's son-in-law. 13 His ambition was fired; he hoped to make himself master of the whole country and therefore treacherously began to plot the destruction of Simon and his sons. 14 Simon, who was inspecting the towns up and down the country and attending to their administration, had come down to Jericho with his sons Mattathias and Judas, in the year 172, in the eleventh month, the month of Shebat. 15 The son of Abubos lured them into a small fortress called Dok, which he had built, where he offered them a great banquet, having previously hidden men in the place. 16 When Simon and his sons were drunk, Ptolemy and his men reached for their weapons, rushed on Simon in the banqueting hall and killed him with his two sons and some of his servants. 17 He thus committed a great act of treachery and rendered evil for good.

18 Ptolemy wrote a report of the affair and sent it to the king, in the expectation of being sent reinforcements and of having the cities and the province made over to him. 19 He also sent people to Gezer to murder John, and sent written orders to the military commanders to come to him so that he could give them silver, gold and presents; 20 and he also sent others to seize control of Jerusalem and the Temple mount. 21 But someone had been too quick for him and had already informed John in Gezer that his father and brothers had perished, adding, 'He is sending someone to kill you too!' 22 Overcome as John was by the news, he arrested the men who had come to kill him and put them to death, being forewarned of their murderous design. 23 The rest of John's acts, the battles he fought and the exploits he performed, the city walls he built, and all his other achievements, 24 from the day he succeeded his father as high priest, are recorded in the annals of his pontificate.

2 Maccabees

THE SECOND BOOK OF THE

Maccabees

1 The Jews in Jerusalem and those in the land of Judea,
To their Jewish kindred in Egypt,
Greetings and true peace.

2 May God do good to you, and may he remember his covenant with Abraham and Isaac and Jacob, his faithful servants. 3 May he give you all a heart to worship him and to do his will with a strong heart and a willing spirit. 4 May he open your heart to his law and his commandments, and may he bring peace. 5 May he hear your prayers and be reconciled to you, and may he not forsake you in time of evil. 6 We are now praying for you here.

7 In the reign of Demetrius, in the one hundred sixty-ninth year,[a] we Jews wrote to you, in the critical distress that came upon us in those years after Jason and his company revolted from the holy land and the kingdom 8 and burned the gate and shed innocent blood. We prayed to the Lord and were heard, and we offered sacrifice and grain offering, and we lit the lamps and set out the loaves. 9 And now see that you keep the festival of booths in the month of Chislev, in the one hundred eighty-eighth year.[b]

10 The people of Jerusalem and of Judea and the senate and Judas,
To Aristobulus, who is of the family of the anointed priests, teacher of King Ptolemy, and to the Jews in Egypt,
Greetings and good health.

11 Having been saved by God out of grave dangers we thank him greatly for taking our side against the king,[c] 12 for he drove out those who fought against the holy city. 13 When the leader reached Persia with a force that seemed irresistible, they were cut to pieces in the temple of Nanea by a deception employed by the priests of the goddess[d] Nanea. 14 On the pretext of intending to marry her, Antiochus came to the place together with his Friends, to secure most of its treasures as a dowry. 15 When the priests of the temple of Nanea had set out the treasures and Antiochus had come with a few men inside the wall of the sacred precinct, they closed the temple as soon as he entered it. 16 Opening a secret door in the ceiling, they threw stones and struck down the leader and his men; they dismembered them and cut off their heads and threw them to the people outside. 17 Blessed in every way be our God, who has brought judgment on those who have behaved impiously.

18 Since on the twenty-fifth day of Chislev we shall celebrate the purification of the temple, we thought it necessary to notify you, in order that you also may celebrate the festival of booths and the festival of the fire given when Nehemiah, who built the temple and the altar, offered sacrifices.

19 For when our ancestors were being led captive to Persia, the pious priests of that time took some of the fire of the altar and secretly hid it in the hollow of a dry cistern, where they took such precautions that the place was unknown to anyone. 20 But after many years had passed, when

THE SECOND BOOK OF THE

Maccabees

1 FROM the Jews in Jerusalem and in the country of Judaea to their Jewish kinsmen in Egypt.
Greeting and peace.

2 May God prosper you, and may he keep in mind the covenant he made with Abraham, Isaac, and Jacob, his faithful servants. 3 May he give to you all hearts to worship him and to fulfil his purposes with high courage and willing spirit. 4 May he make your minds open to his law and ordinances. May he bring you peace, 5 and grant you an answer to your prayers; may he be reconciled to you and never forsake you in an evil hour. 6 Here and now we are praying for you.

7 In the reign of Demetrius, in the year 169, we wrote to you during the persecution and crisis that we Jews experienced after Jason and his followers defected from the holy land and the kingdom, 8 setting the temple porch on fire and spilling innocent blood. We prayed to the Lord and were answered; we brought a sacrifice and an offering of fine flour, we lit the lamps, and laid out the Bread of the Presence. 9 Now we instruct you to observe the celebration of a feast of Tabernacles in the month of Kislev.

10 Written in the year 188.

FROM the people of Jerusalem and Judaea, from the Senate, and from Judas: to Aristobulus, tutor of King Ptolemy and a member of the family of anointed priests, and to the Jews in Egypt.
Greeting and health.

11 We have been rescued by God from great dangers, for which we give him profound thanks as our champion against the king; 12 God it was who drove out the enemy stationed in the Holy City. 13 When King Antiochus went into Persia with a force that seemed invincible, they were cut to pieces in the temple of the goddess Nanaea through a stratagem employed by her priests. 14 On the pretext of a ritual marriage with the goddess, Antiochus, escorted by his Friends, had come to the temple to secure the considerable treasure by way of dowry. 15 After this was laid out by the priests, he entered the temple precinct with a small bodyguard. As soon as he was inside, the priests shut the sanctuary; 16 then, opening a secret trapdoor in the panelled ceiling, they hurled stones at them, and the king fell as if struck by a thunderbolt. They hacked off limbs and heads and threw them to those outside. 17 Blessed in all things be our God, who handed over the godless to death!

18 We think it right and proper to inform you that we are about to celebrate the purification of the temple on the twenty-fifth of Kislev, so that you also may celebrate a feast of Tabernacles; this is in honour of the fire which appeared when Nehemiah offered sacrifices, after he had rebuilt the temple and the altar. 19 When our forefathers were being carried off to Persia, the devout priests of those days secretly took fire from the altar and concealed it inside a dry well. This proved a safe hiding-place and remained undiscovered. 20 After many years had passed,

---

a 143 B.C.   *b* 124 B.C.   *c* Cn: Gk *as those who array themselves against a king*   *d* Gk lacks *the goddess*

1:7 **169:** *that is* 143 B.C.E.   1:10 **188:** *that is* 124 B.C.E.

THE SECOND BOOK OF
Maccabees

1 The Jews in Jerusalem and in the land of Judea send greetings to their brethren, the Jews in Egypt, and wish them true peace! [2] May God bless you and remember his covenant with his faithful servants, Abraham, Isaac and Jacob. [3] May he give to all of you a heart to worship him and to do his will readily and generously. [4] May he open your heart to his law and his commandments and grant you peace. [5] May he hear your prayers, and be reconciled to you, and never forsake you in time of adversity. [6] Even now we are praying for you here.

[7] In the reign of Demetrius, the year one hundred and sixty-nine, we Jews wrote to you during the trouble and violence that overtook us in those years after Jason and his followers had revolted against the holy land and the kingdom, [8] setting fire to the gatehouse and shedding innocent blood. But we prayed to the LORD, and our prayer was heard; we offered sacrifices and fine flour; we lighted the lamps and set out the loaves of bread. [9] We are now reminding you to celebrate the feast of Booths in the month of Chislev. [10] Dated in the year one hundred and eighty-eight.

The people of Jerusalem and Judea, the senate, and Judas send greetings and good wishes to Aristobulus, counselor of King Ptolemy and member of the family of the anointed priests, and to the Jews in Egypt. [11] Since we have been saved by God from grave dangers, we give him great thanks for having fought on our side against the king; [12] it was he who drove out those who fought against the holy city. [13] When their leader arrived in Persia with his seemingly irresistible army, they were cut to pieces in the temple of the goddess Nanea through a deceitful stratagem employed by Nanea's priests. [14] On the pretext of marrying the goddess, Antiochus with his Friends had come to the place to get its great treasures by way of dowry. [15] When the priests of the Nanaeon had displayed the treasures, Antiochus with a few attendants came to the temple precincts. As soon as he entered the temple, the priests locked the doors. [16] Then they opened a hidden trapdoor in the ceiling, hurled stones at the leader and his companions and struck them down. They dismembered the bodies, cut off their heads and tossed them to the people outside. [17] Forever blessed be our God, who has thus punished the wicked!

[18] We shall be celebrating the purification of the temple on the twenty-fifth day of the month Chislev, so we thought it right to inform you that you too may celebrate the feast of Booths and of the fire that appeared when Nehemiah, the rebuilder of the temple and the altar, offered sacrifices. [19] When our fathers were being exiled to Persia, devout priests of the time took some of the fire from the altar and hid it secretly in the hollow of a dry cistern, making sure that the place would be unknown to anyone. [20] Many years

---

THE SECOND BOOK OF
Maccabees

1 'To their brothers, the Jews living in Egypt, from their brothers, the Jews in Jerusalem and Judaea, greetings and untroubled peace.

[2] 'May God prosper you, remembering his covenant with Abraham, Isaac and Jacob, his faithful servants. [3] May he give you all a heart to worship him and to do his will with a generous mind and a willing spirit. [4] May he open your hearts to his Law and his precepts, and give you peace. [5] May he hear your prayers and be reconciled with you, and not abandon you in time of evil. [6] Such is our prayer for you.

[7] 'During the reign of Demetrius, in the year 169, we Jews wrote to you as follows, "In the extremity of trouble that befell us in the years after Jason and his associates had betrayed the Holy Land and the kingdom, [8] burning down the Temple gateway and shedding innocent blood, we prayed to the Lord and were then heard. And we then offered a sacrifice, with wheat-flour, we lit the lamps and we set out the loaves."

[9] 'And we now recommend you too to keep the feast of Shelters in the month of Chislev, in the year one hundred and eighty-eight.'

[10] 'The people of Jerusalem and of Judaea, the senate and Judas, to Aristobulus, tutor to King Ptolemy and one of the family of the anointed priests, and to the Jews in Egypt, greetings and good health.

[11] 'Since we have been rescued by God from great danger, we give him great thanks for championing our cause against the king, [12] for he it was who carried off those who had taken up arms against the Holy City. [13] For when their leader reached Persia with his seemingly irresistible army, he was cut to pieces in the temple of Nanaea, as the result of a ruse employed by the priests who served that goddess. [14] On the pretext of marrying Nanaea, Antiochus came to the place with his friends, intending to take its treasures as a dowry. [15] The priests of Nanaea had put these on display, and he for his part had entered the temple precincts with only a small retinue. As soon as Antiochus had gone inside the temple, the priests shut him in, [16] opened a trapdoor hidden in the ceiling and struck the leader down by hurling stones like thunderbolts. They then cut him into pieces and threw his head to those who were waiting outside. [17] Blessed in all things be our God, who has delivered the sacrilegious over to death!

[18] 'As we shall be celebrating the purification of the Temple on the twenty-fifth of Chislev, we consider it proper to notify you, so that you too may celebrate it, as you do the feast of Shelters and the fire that appeared when Nehemiah, the builder of the Temple and the altar, offered sacrifice. [19] For when our ancestors were being deported to Persia, the devout priests of the time took some of the fire from the altar and hid it secretly in a hole like a dry well, where they concealed it in such a way that the place was unknown to anyone. [20] When some years had elapsed, in God's good

it pleased God, Nehemiah, having been commissioned by the king of Persia, sent the descendants of the priests who had hidden the fire to get it. And when they reported to us that they had not found fire but only a thick liquid, he ordered them to dip it out and bring it. 21 When the materials for the sacrifices were presented, Nehemiah ordered the priests to sprinkle the liquid on the wood and on the things laid upon it. 22 When this had been done and some time had passed, and when the sun, which had been clouded over, shone out, a great fire blazed up, so that all marveled. 23 And while the sacrifice was being consumed, the priests offered prayer — the priests and everyone. Jonathan led, and the rest responded, as did Nehemiah. 24 The prayer was to this effect:

"O Lord, Lord God, Creator of all things, you are awe-inspiring and strong and just and merciful, you alone are king and are kind, 25 you alone are bountiful, you alone are just and almighty and eternal. You rescue Israel from every evil; you chose the ancestors and consecrated them. 26 Accept this sacrifice on behalf of all your people Israel and preserve your portion and make it holy. 27 Gather together our scattered people, set free those who are slaves among the Gentiles, look on those who are rejected and despised, and let the Gentiles know that you are our God. 28 Punish those who oppress and are insolent with pride. 29 Plant your people in your holy place, as Moses promised."

30 Then the priests sang the hymns. 31 After the materials of the sacrifice had been consumed, Nehemiah ordered that the liquid that was left should be poured on large stones. 32 When this was done, a flame blazed up; but when the light from the altar shone back, it went out. 33 When this matter became known, and it was reported to the king of the Persians that, in the place where the exiled priests had hidden the fire, the liquid had appeared with which Nehemiah and his associates had burned the materials of the sacrifice, 34 the king investigated the matter, and enclosed the place and made it sacred. 35 And with those persons whom the king favored he exchanged many excellent gifts. 36 Nehemiah and his associates called this "nephthar," which means purification, but by most people it is called naphtha. *e*

2 One finds in the records that the prophet Jeremiah ordered those who were being deported to take some of the fire, as has been mentioned, 2 and that the prophet, after giving them the law, instructed those who were being deported not to forget the commandments of the Lord, or to be led astray in their thoughts on seeing the gold and silver statues and their adornment. 3 And with other similar words he exhorted them that the law should not depart from their hearts.

4 It was also in the same document that the prophet, having received an oracle, ordered that the tent and the ark should follow with him, and that he went out to the mountain where Moses had gone up and had seen the inheritance of God. 5 Jeremiah came and found a cave-dwelling, and he brought there the tent and the ark and the altar of incense; then he sealed up the entrance. 6 Some of those who followed him came up intending to mark the way, but could not find it. 7 When Jeremiah learned of it, he rebuked them and declared: "The place shall remain unknown until God gathers his people together again and shows his mercy.

in God's good time Nehemiah was sent back by the king of Persia. He dispatched in search of the fire the descendants of the priests who had hidden it, and they reported to our people that they found, not fire, but a thick liquid. 21 Nehemiah told them to draw some out and bring it to him. When the materials of the sacrifice had been presented, he ordered the priests to sprinkle this liquid over the wood and the sacrifice. 22 This was done, and after some time the sun, till then hidden by clouds, began to shine and to everyone's astonishment there was a great blaze of fire on the altar. 23 While the sacrifice was burning, the priests offered prayer, they and all those present: Jonathan began and the rest responded, led by Nehemiah.

24 The prayer was in this style: 'Lord God, the Creator of all things, the terrible and mighty, the just and merciful, the only King, you alone are gracious; 25 you are the only Giver, the only just and omnipotent and eternal One, the Deliverer of Israel from every evil, who chose the patriarchs and set them apart. 26 Accept, we pray, this sacrifice on behalf of your whole people Israel; watch over them and sanctify them, for they are your own possession. 27 Bring together those of our people who are dispersed, set free those who are enslaved among the heathen, look favourably on those who are despised and detested; so let the heathen know that you are our God. 28 Punish with torments our arrogant and insolent oppressors, 29 and, as promised by Moses, plant your people in your holy land.' 30 The priests then chanted the hymns.

31 After the sacrifice had been consumed, Nehemiah ordered that what remained of the liquid be poured over some great stones. 32 At this a flame shot up, but it burnt itself out as soon as the fire on the altar outshone it.

33 These events became widely known. The king of Persia was told that, in the place where the exiled priests had hidden the fire, a liquid had appeared, which Nehemiah and his companions had used to burn up the materials of the sacrifice. 34 After he had verified this, the king had the site enclosed and declared it sacred. 35 The custodians he appointed received a share of the very substantial revenue the king derived from it. 36 Nehemiah and his companions called the liquid nephthar, which means 'purification'; but most people call it naphtha.

2 The records show that it was Jeremiah the prophet who ordered the exiles to hide the fire, in the way just described. 2 After giving them the law, the prophet charged them not to neglect the ordinances of the Lord, or let their minds be led astray by the sight of gold and silver images in all their finery. 3 In similar terms he appealed to them never to let the law be far from their hearts.

4 It is recorded also that, in obedience to a divine command, the prophet gave orders for the Tent of Meeting and the Ark to accompany him, and he went off to the mountain from the top of which Moses had seen God's promised land. 5 Arriving at the mountain, Jeremiah found a cave-dwelling into which he carried the Tent, the Ark, and the altar of incense; he then blocked up the entrance. 6 Some of his companions went to mark out the way, but were unable to find it. 7 Jeremiah learnt of this and took them to task. 'The place is to remain unknown', he said, 'until God finally gathers his people together and shows them his favour. 8 The Lord will then bring these

1:31 **that what remained . . . stones:** *so some witnesses; others read* that great stones should enclose what remained of the liquid.
1:32 **but . . . outshone it:** *or* but hardly had the light been reflected from the altar, when it burnt itself out.

e Gk *nephthai*

NEW AMERICAN BIBLE

NEW JERUSALEM BIBLE

later, when it so pleased God, Nehemiah, commissioned by the king of Persia, sent the descendants of the priests who had hidden the fire to look for it. 21 When they informed us that they could not find any fire, but only muddy water, he ordered them to scoop some out and bring it. After the material for the sacrifices had been prepared, Nehemiah ordered the priests to sprinkle with the water the wood and what lay on it. 22 When this was done and in time the sun, which had been clouded over, began to shine, a great fire blazed up, so that everyone marveled. 23 While the sacrifice was being burned, the priests recited a prayer, and all present joined in with them, Jonathan leading and the rest responding with Nehemiah.

24 The prayer was as follows: "LORD, LORD God, creator of all things, awesome and strong, just and merciful, the only king and benefactor, 25 who alone are gracious, just, almighty, and eternal, Israel's savior from all evil, who chose our forefathers and sanctified them: 26 accept this sacrifice on behalf of all your people Israel and guard and sanctify your heritage. 27 Gather together our scattered people, free those who are the slaves of the Gentiles, look kindly on those who are despised and detested, and let the Gentiles know that you are our God. 28 Punish those who tyrannize over us and arrogantly mistreat us. 29 Plant your people in your holy place, as Moses promised."

30 Then the priests began to sing hymns. 31 After the sacrifice was burned, Nehemiah ordered the rest of the liquid to be poured upon large stones. 32 As soon as this was done, a flame blazed up, but its light was lost in the brilliance cast from a light on the altar. 33 When the event became known and the king of the Persians was told that, in the very place where the exiled priests had hidden the fire, a liquid was found with which Nehemiah and his people had burned the sacrifices, 34 the king, after verifying the fact, fenced the place off and declared it sacred. 35 To those on whom the king wished to bestow favors he distributed the large revenues he received there. 36 Nehemiah and his companions called the liquid nephthar, meaning purification, but most people name it naphtha.

2 You will find in the records, not only that Jeremiah the prophet ordered the deportees to take some of the aforementioned fire with them, 2 but also that the prophet, in giving them the law, admonished them not to forget the commandments of the LORD or be led astray in their thoughts, when seeing the gold and silver idols and their ornaments. 3 With other similar words he urged them not to let the law depart from their hearts. 4 The same document also tells how the prophet, following a divine revelation, ordered that the tent and the ark should accompany him and how he went off to the mountain which Moses climbed to see God's inheritance. 5 When Jeremiah arrived there, he found a room in a cave in which he put the tent, the ark, and the altar of incense; then he blocked up the entrance. 6 Some of those who followed him came up intending to mark the path, but they could not find it. 7 When Jeremiah heard of this, he reproved them: "The place is to remain unknown until God gathers his people together again and shows them mercy. 8 Then the LORD will disclose these things, and the

time, Nehemiah, commissioned by the king of Persia, sent the descendants of the priests who had hidden the fire to look for it. When they reported that in fact they had found not fire but a thick liquid, Nehemiah ordered them to draw some out and bring it back. 21 When they had done this, Nehemiah ordered the priests to pour this liquid over the sacrificial materials, that is, the wood and what lay on it. 22 When this had been done, and when in due course the sun, which had previously been clouded over, shone out, a great fire flared up, to the astonishment of all. 23 While the sacrifice was being burned, the priests offered prayer, Jonathan intoning with all the priests, and the rest responding with Nehemiah. 24 The prayer took this form, "Lord, Lord God, Creator of all things, awesome, strong, just, merciful, the only king and benefactor, 25 the only provider, who alone are just, almighty and everlasting, the deliverer of Israel from every evil, who made our fathers your chosen ones and sanctified them, 26 accept this sacrifice on behalf of all your people Israel, and protect your heritage and consecrate it. 27 Bring together those of us who are dispersed, set free those in slavery among the heathen, look favourably on those held in contempt or abhorrence, and let the heathen know that you are our God. 28 Punish those who oppress us and affront us by their insolence, 29 and plant your people firmly in your Holy Place, as Moses promised."

30 'The priests then chanted hymns accompanied by the harp. 31 When the sacrifice had been burnt, Nehemiah ordered the remaining liquid to be poured over large stones, 32 and when this was done a flame flared up, to be absorbed in a corresponding blaze of light from the altar. 33 When the matter became known and the king of the Persians heard that, in the place where the exiled priests had hidden the fire, a liquid had appeared, with which Nehemiah and his people had purified the sacrificial offerings, 34 the king, after verifying the facts, had the place enclosed and pronounced sacred. 35 To the people on whom the king bestowed it, he granted a part of the considerable revenue he derived from it. 36 Nehemiah and his people termed this stuff "nephtar", which means "purification", but it is commonly called "naphta".

2 'It is on record that the prophet Jeremiah ordered the deportees to take the fire, as we have described, 2 and how, having given them the Law, the prophet warned the deportees never to forget the Lord's precepts, nor to let their thoughts be tempted by the sight of gold and silver statues or the finery adorning them. 3 Among other similar admonitions, he urged them not to let the Law depart from their hearts.

4 'The same document also describes how the prophet, warned by an oracle, gave orders for the tent and the ark to go with him, when he set out for the mountain which Moses had climbed to survey God's heritage. 5 On his arrival, Jeremiah found a cave-dwelling, into which he put the tent, the ark and the altar of incense, afterwards blocking up the entrance. 6 Some of his companions went back later to mark out the path but were unable to find it. 7 When Jeremiah learned this, he reproached them, "The place is to remain unknown", he said, "until God gathers his people together again and shows them his mercy. 8 Then the Lord will bring

8 Then the Lord will disclose these things, and the glory of the Lord and the cloud will appear, as they were shown in the case of Moses, and as Solomon asked that the place should be specially consecrated."

9 It was also made clear that being possessed of wisdom Solomon*f* offered sacrifice for the dedication and completion of the temple. 10 Just as Moses prayed to the Lord, and fire came down from heaven and consumed the sacrifices, so also Solomon prayed, and the fire came down and consumed the whole burnt offerings. 11 And Moses said, "They were consumed because the sin offering had not been eaten." 12 Likewise Solomon also kept the eight days.

13 The same things are reported in the records and in the memoirs of Nehemiah, and also that he founded a library and collected the books about the kings and prophets, and the writings of David, and letters of kings about votive offerings. 14 In the same way Judas also collected all the books that had been lost on account of the war that had come upon us, and they are in our possession. 15 So if you have need of them, send people to get them for you.

16 Since, therefore, we are about to celebrate the purification, we write to you. Will you therefore please keep the days? 17 It is God who has saved all his people, and has returned the inheritance to all, and the kingship and the priesthood and the consecration, 18 as he promised through the law. We have hope in God that he will soon have mercy on us and will gather us from everywhere under heaven into his holy place, for he has rescued us from great evils and has purified the place.

19 The story of Judas Maccabeus and his brothers, and the purification of the great temple, and the dedication of the altar, 20 and further the wars against Antiochus Epiphanes and his son Eupator, 21 and the appearances that came from heaven to those who fought bravely for Judaism, so that though few in number they seized the whole land and pursued the barbarian hordes, 22 and regained possession of the temple famous throughout the world, and liberated the city, and re-established the laws that were about to be abolished, while the Lord with great kindness became gracious to them— 23 all this, which has been set forth by Jason of Cyrene in five volumes, we shall attempt to condense into a single book. 24 For considering the flood of statistics involved and the difficulty there is for those who wish to enter upon the narratives of history because of the mass of material, 25 we have aimed to please those who wish to read, to make it easy for those who are inclined to memorize, and to profit all readers. 26 For us who have undertaken the toil of abbreviating, it is no light matter but calls for sweat and loss of sleep, 27 just as it is not easy for one who prepares a banquet and seeks the benefit of others. Nevertheless, to secure the gratitude of many we will gladly endure the uncomfortable toil, 28 leaving the responsibility for exact details to the compiler, while devoting our effort to arriving at the outlines of the condensation. 29 For as the master builder of a new house must be concerned with the whole construction, while the one who undertakes its painting and decoration has to consider only what is suitable for its adornment, such in my judgment is the case with us. 30 It is the duty of the original historian to occupy the ground, to discuss matters from every side, and to take trouble with details, 31 but the one who recasts the narrative should be allowed to strive for brevity of expression and to forego exhaustive treatment. 32 At this point therefore let us begin

things to light once more, and his glory will appear together with the cloud, as it was revealed in the time of Moses and also when Solomon prayed that the shrine might be worthily consecrated.'

9 Further, it is related that Solomon, who had the gift of wisdom, offered a dedication sacrifice at the completion of the temple; 10 and that, just as Moses had prayed to the Lord and fire had come down from heaven and burnt up the sacrificial offerings, so in answer to Solomon's prayer the fire came down and consumed the whole-offerings. 11 (Moses said, 'The sin-offering was burnt in the same way because it was not eaten.') 12 The feast celebrated by Solomon went on for eight days.

13 These same facts are set out in the official records and in the memoirs of Nehemiah. Just as Nehemiah collected the chronicles of the kings, the writings of prophets, the works of David, and royal letters about sacred offerings, to found his library, 14 in the same way Judas has collected for us all the documents that had been dispersed as a result of the recent conflict. These are in our possession, 15 and if ever you need any of them, send messengers for them.

16 Since we are about to celebrate the purification of the temple, we are writing to impress upon you the duty of holding this festival. 17 God has rescued his whole people and granted to all of us the holy land, the kingship, the priesthood, and the consecration, 18 as he promised by the law. We have confidence that God will soon show us compassion and gather us from everywhere under heaven to the holy place, for he has delivered us from great evils and purified that place.

19 JASON of Cyrene has set out in five books the story of Judas Maccabaeus and his brothers, of the purification of the great temple, and of the dedication of the altar. 20 He has also given an account of the wars with Antiochus Epiphanes and with his son Eupator, 21 and he has described the apparitions from heaven which appeared to those who, in the cause of the Jewish religion, vied with one another in heroism. Few though they were, they ranged through the whole country, taking booty and routing the foreign hordes; 22 they recovered the world-renowned temple, liberated the city of Jerusalem, and reaffirmed the laws, which were in danger of being abolished. All this they achieved because the Lord showed them clemency and favour.

23 These five books of Jason I shall attempt to summarize in a single work; 24 for I was struck by the mass of statistics and the difficulty which the sheer bulk of the material occasions to those wishing to master the narratives of this history. 25 I have tried to provide entertainment for those who peruse for pleasure, an aid for students who must commit the facts to memory, and in general a service to readers. 26 The task which I have taken on myself in making this summary is no easy one; it means hard work and late nights, 27 just as the man who prepares a banquet and aims to satisfy his guests has no light task. Yet I shall gladly undergo this labour to earn general gratitude 28 and, while concentrating on the main points of my outline, I shall leave to the original author the minute discussion of every particular. 29 While the architect of a new house must concern himself with the whole of the structure, the man who paints in encaustic on the walls needs to discover only what is necessary for the ornamentation; I reckon it is much the same with me. 30 It is the province of the original author of a history to take possession of the field, to spread himself in discussion, and to busy himself with matters of detail; 31 on the other hand, whoever makes an abridgement must be allowed to aim at conciseness of expression and to renounce an exhaustive treatment of the subject matter.

f Gk *he*

2:11 **sin-offering:** *or* purification-offering.

glory of the LORD will be seen in the cloud, just as it appeared in the time of Moses and when Solomon prayed that the Place might be gloriously sanctified."

9 It is also related how Solomon in his wisdom offered a sacrifice at the dedication and the completion of the temple. 10 Just as Moses prayed to the LORD and fire descended from the sky and consumed the sacrifices, so Solomon also prayed and fire came down and burned up the holocausts. 11 Moses had said, "Because it had not been eaten, the sin offering was burned up." 12 Solomon also celebrated the feast in the same way for eight days.

13 Besides these things, it is also told in the records and in Nehemiah's Memoirs how he collected the books about the kings, the writings of the prophets and of David, and the royal letters about sacred offerings. 14 In like manner Judas also collected for us the books that had been scattered because of the war, and we now have them in our possession. 15 If you need them, send messengers to get them for you.

16 As we are about to celebrate the feast of the purification of the temple, we are writing to you requesting you also to please celebrate the feast. 17 It is God who has saved all his people and has restored to all of them their heritage, the kingdom, the priesthood, and the sacred rites, 18 as he promised through the law. We trust in God, that he will soon have mercy on us and gather us together from everywhere under the heavens to his holy Place, for he has rescued us from great perils and has purified his Place.

19 This is the story of Judas Maccabeus and his brothers, of the purification of the great temple, the dedication of the altar, 20 the campaigns against Antiochus Epiphanes and his son Eupator, 21 and of the heavenly manifestations accorded to the heroes who fought bravely for Judaism, so that, few as they were, they seized the whole land, put to flight the barbarian hordes, 22 regained possession of the world-famous temple, liberated the city, and reestablished the laws that were in danger of being abolished, while the LORD favored them with all his generous assistance. 23 All this, which Jason of Cyrene set forth in detail in five volumes, we will try to condense into a single book.

24 In view of the flood of statistics, and the difficulties encountered by those who wish to plunge into historical narratives where the material is abundant, 25 we have aimed to please those who prefer simple reading, as well as to make it easy for the studious who wish to commit things to memory, and to be helpful to all. 26 For us who have taken upon ourselves the labor of making this digest, the task, far from being easy, is one of sweat and of sleepless nights, 27 just as the preparation of a festive banquet is no light matter for one who thus seeks to give enjoyment to others. Similarly, to win the gratitude of many we will gladly endure these inconveniences, 28 while we leave the responsibility for exact details to the original author, and confine our efforts to giving only a summary outline. 29 As the architect of a new house must give his attention to the whole structure, while the man who undertakes the decoration and the frescoes has only to concern himself with what is needed for ornamentation, so I think it is with us. 30 To enter into questions and examine them thoroughly from all sides is the task of the professional historian; 31 but the man who is making an adaptation should be allowed to aim at brevity of expression and to omit detailed treatment of the matter.

these things once more to light, and the glory of the Lord will be seen, and so will the cloud, as it was revealed in the time of Moses[a] and when Solomon[b] prayed that the holy place might be gloriously hallowed."

9 'It was also recorded how Solomon in his wisdom offered the sacrifice of the dedication and completion of the sanctuary. 10 As Moses had prayed to the Lord and fire had come down from heaven and burned up the sacrifice, so Solomon also prayed, and the fire from above consumed the burnt offerings. 11 Moses[c] had said, "Because the sacrifice for sin had not been eaten, it was burnt instead." 12 Solomon[d] similarly observed the eight-day festival.

13 'In addition to the above, it was also recorded, both in these writings and in the Memoirs of Nehemiah, how Nehemiah founded a library and made a collection of the books dealing with the kings and the prophets, the writings of David and the letters of the kings on the subject of offerings. 14 Similarly, Judas made a complete collection of the books dispersed in the late war, and these we still have. 15 If you need any of them, send someone to fetch them.

16 'Since we are about to celebrate the purification, we now write, requesting you to observe the same days. 17 God, who has saved his whole people, conferring heritage, kingdom, priesthood and sanctification on all of us, 18 as he has promised in the Law, will surely, as our hope is in him, be swift to show us mercy and gather us together from everywhere under heaven to the holy place, since he has rescued us from great evils and has purified it.'

19 The story of Judas Maccabaeus and his brothers, the purification of the great Temple, the dedication of the altar, 20 together with the wars against Antiochus Epiphanes and his son Eupator, 21 and the celestial manifestations that came to hearten the brave champions of Judaism, so that, few though they were, they pillaged the whole country, routed the barbarian hordes, 22 recovered the sanctuary renowned the whole world over, liberated the city and reestablished the laws by then all but abolished, the Lord showing his favour by all his gracious help to them — 23 all this, already related in five books by Jason of Cyrene, we shall attempt to condense into a single work. 24 Considering the spate of figures and the difficulty encountered, because of the mass of material, by those who wish to immerse themselves in historical records, 25 we have aimed at providing diversion for those who merely want something to read, a saving of labour for those who enjoy committing things to memory, and profit for each and all. 26 For us who have undertaken the drudgery of this abridgement, it has been no easy task but a matter of sweat and midnight oil, 27 comparable to the exacting task of someone organising a banquet, whose aim is to satisfy a variety of tastes. Nevertheless, for the sake of rendering a general service, we remain glad to endure this drudgery, 28 leaving accuracy of detail to the historian, and concentrating our effort on tracing the outlines in this condensed version. 29 Just as the architect of a new house is responsible for the construction as a whole, while the man undertaking the ceramic painting has to take into consideration only the decorative requirements, so, I think, it is with us. 30 To make the subject his own, to explore its by-ways, to be meticulous about details, is the business of the original historian, 31 but the person making the adaptation must be allowed to aim at conciseness of expression and to forgo any exhaustive treatment of his subject.

a 2 Ex 24:16.   b 2 1 K 8:10–11.   c 2 Lv 10:16–17.
d 2 1 K 8:65–66.

our narrative, without adding any more to what has already been said; for it would be foolish to lengthen the preface while cutting short the history itself.

3 While the holy city was inhabited in unbroken peace and the laws were strictly observed because of the piety of the high priest Onias and his hatred of wickedness, 2 it came about that the kings themselves honored the place and glorified the temple with the finest presents, 3 even to the extent that King Seleucus of Asia defrayed from his own revenues all the expenses connected with the service of the sacrifices.

4 But a man named Simon, of the tribe of Benjamin, who had been made captain of the temple, had a disagreement with the high priest about the administration of the city market. 5 Since he could not prevail over Onias, he went to Apollonius of Tarsus,*g* who at that time was governor of Coelesyria and Phoenicia, 6 and reported to him that the treasury in Jerusalem was full of untold sums of money, so that the amount of the funds could not be reckoned, and that they did not belong to the account of the sacrifices, but that it was possible for them to fall under the control of the king. 7 When Apollonius met the king, he told him of the money about which he had been informed. The king*h* chose Heliodorus, who was in charge of his affairs, and sent him with commands to effect the removal of the reported wealth. 8 Heliodorus at once set out on his journey, ostensibly to make a tour of inspection of the cities of Coelesyria and Phoenicia, but in fact to carry out the king's purpose.

9 When he had arrived at Jerusalem and had been kindly welcomed by the high priest of*i* the city, he told about the disclosure that had been made and stated why he had come, and he inquired whether this really was the situation. 10 The high priest explained that there were some deposits belonging to widows and orphans, 11 and also some money of Hyrcanus son of Tobias, a man of very prominent position, and that it totaled in all four hundred talents of silver and two hundred of gold. To such an extent the impious Simon had misrepresented the facts. 12 And he said that it was utterly impossible that wrong should be done to those people who had trusted in the holiness of the place and in the sanctity and inviolability of the temple that is honored throughout the whole world.

13 But Heliodorus, because of the orders he had from the king, said that this money must in any case be confiscated for the king's treasury. 14 So he set a day and went in to direct the inspection of these funds.

There was no little distress throughout the whole city. 15 The priests prostrated themselves before the altar in their priestly vestments and called toward heaven upon him who had given the law about deposits, that he should keep them safe for those who had deposited them. 16 To see the appearance of the high priest was to be wounded at heart, for his face and the change in his color disclosed the anguish of his soul. 17 For terror and bodily trembling had come over the man, which plainly showed to those who looked at him the pain lodged in his heart. 18 People also hurried out of their houses in crowds to make a general supplication because the holy place was about to be brought into dishonor. 19 Women, girded with sackcloth under their breasts, thronged the streets. Some of the young women who were kept indoors ran together to the gates, and some to the walls, while others peered out of the windows. 20 And holding up their hands to heaven, they all made supplication. 21 There was something pitiable in the prostration of the whole populace and the anxiety of the high priest in his great anguish.

32 Here then, without further comment, I begin my narrative, for it would be absurd to give a lengthy introduction to the history and cut short the history itself.

3 DURING the rule of the high priest Onias, the Holy City enjoyed unbroken peace and prosperity, and there was exemplary observance of the laws, because he was pious and hated wickedness. 2 The kings themselves held the sanctuary in honour and embellished the temple with the most magnificent gifts; 3 King Seleucus of Asia even met the whole cost of the sacrificial worship from his own revenues.

4 But a certain Simon, of the clan Bilgah, who had been appointed administrator of the temple, quarrelled with the high priest about the regulation of the city market. 5 Unable to get the better of Onias, he went to Apollonius son of Thraseus, then governor of Coele-Syria and Phoenicia, 6 and alleged that the treasury at Jerusalem was so packed with untold riches that the total of the accumulated balances was beyond all reckoning; it bore no relation to the account for the sacrifices, and he suggested that these balances might be brought under the control of the king. 7 In the course of a meeting with the king, Apollonius reported what he had been told about the riches, whereupon the king chose Heliodorus, his chief minister, to be sent with orders to effect the removal of these treasures.

8 Heliodorus set off at once, ostensibly to make a tour of inspection of the cities of Coele-Syria and Phoenicia, but in fact to carry out the king's design. 9 When he arrived at Jerusalem and had been cordially received by the high priest and the citizens, he disclosed the purpose of his visit: he told them about the allegations and asked if they were true. 10 The high priest explained that the deposits were held in trust for widows and orphans, 11 apart from what belonged to Hyrcanus son of Tobias, a man of very high standing. The matter was being misrepresented by the godless Simon; the total sum was four hundred talents of silver and two hundred of gold. 12 It was unthinkable, he said, that injury should be done to those who had relied on the sanctity of the place, on the dignity and inviolability of a temple held in reverence the whole world over. 13 But, in virtue of the king's orders, Heliodorus insisted that these deposits must without question be confiscated for the royal treasury.

14 On the day appointed, when he entered the temple to draw up an inventory, there was great distress throughout the city. 15 The priests, prostrating themselves in their vestments before the altar, prayed to Heaven, whose law had made deposits sacred, to keep them intact for their rightful owners. 16 The high priest's looks pierced every beholder to the heart, for his face and changing colour betrayed the anguish of his spirit. 17 Alarm and shuddering gripped him, and the pain he felt was clearly apparent to the onlookers. 18 The people flocked from their houses and rushed to join in universal supplication because of the dishonour which threatened the holy place. 19 Women in sackcloth, their breasts bare, thronged the streets; unmarried girls who were kept in seclusion ran to the gates or the walls, while others leaned out from windows; 20 with outstretched hands all made solemn entreaty to Heaven. 21 It was pitiful to see the crowd lying prostrate in utter disarray and the high priest in an agony of apprehension.

---

g Gk Apollonius son of Tharseas   *h Gk He*   *i Other ancient authorities read and*

3:4 **Bilgah:** *so some witnesses; others read Benjamin.*

32 Here, then, we shall begin our account without further ado; it would be nonsense to write a long preface to a story and then abbreviate the story itself.

3 While the holy city lived in perfect peace and the laws were strictly observed because of the piety of the high priest Onias and his hatred of evil, 2 the kings themselves honored the Place and glorified the temple with the most magnificent gifts. 3 Thus Seleucus, king of Asia, defrayed from his own revenues all the expenses necessary for the sacrificial services. 4 But a certain Simon, of the priestly course of Bilgah, who had been appointed superintendent of the temple, had a quarrel with the high priest about the supervision of the city market. 5 Since he could not prevail against Onias, he went to Apollonius of Tarsus, who at that time was governor of Coelesyria and Phoenicia, and reported to him that the treasury in Jerusalem was so full of untold riches that the total sum of money was incalculable and out of all proportion to the cost of the sacrifices, and that it would be possible to bring it all under the control of the king. 7 When Apollonius had an audience with the king, he informed him about the riches that had been reported to him. The king chose his minister Heliodorus and sent him with instructions to expropriate the aforesaid wealth. 8 So Heliodorus immediately set out on his journey, ostensibly to visit the cities of Coelesyria and Phoenicia, but in reality to carry out the king's purpose. 9 When he arrived in Jerusalem and had been graciously received by the high priest of the city, he told him about the information that had been given, and explained the reason for his presence, and he asked if these things were really true. 10 The high priest explained that part of the money was a care fund for widows and orphans, 11 and a part was the property of Hyrcanus, son of Tobias, a man who occupied a very high position. Contrary to the calumnies of the impious Simon, the total amounted to four hundred talents of silver and two hundred of gold. 12 He added that it was utterly unthinkable to defraud those who had placed their trust in the sanctity of the Place and in the sacred inviolability of a temple venerated all over the world. 13 But because of the orders he had from the king, Heliodorus said that in any case the money must be confiscated for the royal treasury. 14 So on the day he had set he went in to take an inventory of the funds.

There was great distress throughout the city. 15 Priests prostrated themselves in their priestly robes before the altar, and loudly begged him in heaven who had given the law about deposits to keep the deposits safe for those who had made them. 16 Whoever saw the appearance of the high priest was pierced to the heart, for the changed color of his face manifested the anguish of his soul. 17 The terror and bodily trembling that had come over the man clearly showed those who saw him the pain that lodged in his heart. 18 People rushed out of their houses in crowds to make public supplication, because the Place was in danger of being profaned. 19 Women, girded with sackcloth below their breasts, filled the streets; maidens secluded indoors ran together, some to the gates, some to the walls, others peered through the windows, 20 all of them with hands raised toward heaven, making supplication. 21 It was pitiful to see the populace variously prostrated in prayer and the high priest full of dread and anguish.

32 So now let us begin our narrative, without adding any more to what has been said above; there would be no sense in expanding the preface to the history and curtailing the history itself.

3 While the holy city was inhabited in all peace and the laws were observed as perfectly as possible, owing to the piety of Onias the high priest and his hatred of wickedness, 2 it came about that the kings themselves honoured the holy place and enhanced the glory of the Temple with the most splendid offerings, 3 even to the extent that Seleucus king of Asia defrayed from his own revenues all the expenses arising out of the sacrificial liturgy. 4 But a certain Simon, of the tribe of Bilgah, on being appointed administrator of the Temple, came into conflict with the high priest over the regulation of the city markets. 5 Unable to get the better of Onias, he went off to Apollonius, son of Thraseos, who was at that time commander-in-chief of Coele-Syria and Phoenicia, 6 and made out to him that the Treasury in Jerusalem was groaning with untold wealth, that the amount contributed was incalculable and out of all proportion to expenditure on the sacrifice, but that it could all be brought under the control of the king. 7 Apollonius met the king and told him about the wealth that had been disclosed to him; whereupon the king selected Heliodorus, his chancellor, and sent him with instructions to effect the removal of the reported wealth. 8 Heliodorus lost no time in setting out, ostensibly to inspect the towns of Coele-Syria and Phoenicia, but in fact to accomplish the king's purpose. 9 On his arrival in Jerusalem, and after a hospitable reception from the high priest and the city, he announced what had been disclosed, thus revealing the reason for his presence, and asked if this was indeed the true situation. 10 The high priest explained that there were funds set aside for widows and orphans, 11 with some belonging to Hyrcanus son of Tobias, a man occupying a very exalted position, and that the whole sum, in contrast to what the evil Simon had alleged, amounted to four hundred talents of silver and two hundred of gold. 12 He also added that it was entirely out of the question that an injustice should be done to those who had put their trust in the sanctity of the place and in the inviolable majesty of a Temple venerated throughout the entire world.

13 But Heliodorus, because of his instructions from the king, peremptorily insisted that the funds must be confiscated for the royal exchequer. 14 Fixing a day for the purpose, he went in to draw up an inventory of the funds. There was no little consternation throughout the city; 15 the priests in their sacred vestments prostrated themselves before the altar and prayed to Heaven, to the Author of the law governing deposits, to preserve these funds intact for the depositors. 16 The appearance of the high priest was enough to pierce the heart of the beholder, his expression and his altered colour betraying the anguish of his soul; 17 the man was so overwhelmed by fear and bodily trembling that those who saw him could not possibly mistake the distress he was suffering. 18 People rushed headlong from the houses, intent on making public supplication because of the indignity threatening the holy place. 19 Women thronged the streets swathed in sackcloth below their breasts; girls secluded indoors came running, some to the doorways, some to the city walls, while others leaned out of the windows, 20 all stretching out their hands to Heaven in entreaty. 21 It was pitiful to see the people crowding together to prostrate themselves, and the foreboding of the high priest in his deep anguish.

22 While they were calling upon the Almighty Lord that he would keep what had been entrusted safe and secure for those who had entrusted it, 23 Heliodorus went on with what had been decided. 24 But when he arrived at the treasury with his bodyguard, then and there the Sovereign of spirits and of all authority caused so great a manifestation that all who had been so bold as to accompany him were astounded by the power of God, and became faint with terror. 25 For there appeared to them a magnificently caparisoned horse, with a rider of frightening mien; it rushed furiously at Heliodorus and struck at him with its front hoofs. Its rider was seen to have armor and weapons of gold. 26 Two young men also appeared to him, remarkably strong, gloriously beautiful and splendidly dressed, who stood on either side of him and flogged him continuously, inflicting many blows on him. 27 When he suddenly fell to the ground and deep darkness came over him, his men took him up, put him on a stretcher, 28 and carried him away — this man who had just entered the aforesaid treasury with a great retinue and all his bodyguard but was now unable to help himself. They recognized clearly the sovereign power of God.

29 While he lay prostrate, speechless because of the divine intervention and deprived of any hope of recovery, 30 they praised the Lord who had acted marvelously for his own place. And the temple, which a little while before was full of fear and disturbance, was filled with joy and gladness, now that the Almighty Lord had appeared.

31 Some of Heliodorus's friends quickly begged Onias to call upon the Most High to grant life to one who was lying quite at his last breath. 32 So the high priest, fearing that the king might get the notion that some foul play had been perpetrated by the Jews with regard to Heliodorus, offered sacrifice for the man's recovery. 33 While the high priest was making an atonement, the same young men appeared again to Heliodorus dressed in the same clothing, and they stood and said, "Be very grateful to the high priest Onias, since for his sake the Lord has granted you your life. 34 And see that you, who have been flogged by heaven, report to all people the majestic power of God." Having said this they vanished.

35 Then Heliodorus offered sacrifice to the Lord and made very great vows to the Savior of his life, and having bidden Onias farewell, he marched off with his forces to the king. 36 He bore testimony to all concerning the deeds of the supreme God, which he had seen with his own eyes. 37 When the king asked Heliodorus what sort of person would be suitable to send on another mission to Jerusalem, he replied, 38 "If you have any enemy or plotter against your government, send him there, for you will get him back thoroughly flogged, if he survives at all; for there is certainly some power of God about the place. 39 For he who has his dwelling in heaven watches over that place himself and brings it aid, and he strikes and destroys those who come to do it injury." 40 This was the outcome of the episode of Heliodorus and the protection of the treasury.

4 The previously mentioned Simon, who had informed about the money against *j* his own country, slandered Onias, saying that it was he who had incited Heliodorus and had been the real cause of the misfortune. 2 He dared to designate as a plotter against the government the man who was the benefactor of the city, the protector of his compatriots, and a zealot for the laws. 3 When his hatred progressed to such a degree that even murders were committed by one of Simon's approved agents, 4 Onias recognized that the rivalry was serious and that Apollonius son of Menestheus, *k* and governor of Coelesyria and Phoenicia, was intensifying the malice of Simon. 5 So he appealed to the

22 While the people were imploring the Lord Almighty to keep the deposits intact and safe for those who had lodged them, 23 Heliodorus proceeded to put into effect what had been decided. 24 But just as he was arriving with his escort at the treasury, the Ruler of spirits and of all power sent a mighty apparition, so that everyone who had dared to accompany Heliodorus collapsed in terror, stricken with panic before the might of God. 25 There appeared to them a horse, splendidly caparisoned, with a rider of terrifying aspect who was clad all in golden armour; it rushed fiercely at Heliodorus and, rearing up, attacked him with its hooves. 26 There also appeared to Heliodorus two young men of surpassing strength and glorious beauty, magnificently attired. Taking their stand on either side of him, they flogged him, raining on him blow after blow. 27 Suddenly, overwhelmed by a great darkness, he fell to the ground, and his men quickly took him up and placed him on a stretcher. 28 This man, who so recently had entered the treasury accompanied by his whole bodyguard and an attendant crowd, was now borne off utterly helpless, publicly compelled to acknowledge the sovereignty of God.

29 While Heliodorus lay speechless, deprived by this divine act of all hope of recovery, 30 the Jews were praising the Lord for the miracle he had performed in his holy place; the temple, which only a short time before was the scene of alarm and confusion, now overflowed with joy and gladness at the manifestation of the Lord Almighty.

31 Some of Heliodorus's companions lost no time in begging Onias to pray to the Most High that the life of their master, now lying at his very last gasp, might be spared. 32 Fearing that the king might suspect that Heliodorus had met with foul play at the hands of the Jews, the high priest offered a sacrifice for the man's recovery. 33 As the expiation was being made, the same young men, dressed as before, again appeared to Heliodorus, and standing over him said: 'You should be very grateful to Onias the high priest; it is for his sake the Lord has spared your life. 34 You have been scourged by God; now proclaim his mighty power to all men.' With these words they vanished.

35 Heliodorus offered a sacrifice and made lavish freewill-offerings to the Lord who had spared his life; then, taking leave of Onias, he returned with his troops to the king. 36 To everyone he bore witness of the miracles of the supreme God which he had seen with his own eyes. 37 When the king asked him what sort of man would be suitable to send to Jerusalem another time, Heliodorus replied: 38 'If you have an enemy or someone plotting against your government, that is the place to send him; you will receive him back soundly flogged, if he survives at all, for beyond doubt there is a divine power surrounding the place. 39 He whose habitation is in heaven watches over it himself and gives it his aid; those who approach the place with evil intent he strikes down and destroys.'

40 So runs the story of Heliodorus and the preservation of the treasury.

4 But Simon, the man mentioned above, who in the matter of the money had laid information against his country, went on to slander Onias by alleging that it was he who had incited Heliodorus and so been the author of these troubles. 2 He had the effrontery to accuse of conspiracy against the government one who was a benefactor of the city, a protector of his fellow-Jews, and a staunch upholder of the law. 3 The feud reached such a pitch that one of Simon's trusted adherents even resorted to murder. 4 Realizing how dangerous this rivalry had become and that Apollonius son of Menestheus, governor of Coele-Syria and Phoenicia, was encouraging Simon in his evil ways, 5 Onias had

---

j Gk *and*   *k* Vg Compare verse 21: Meaning of Gk uncertain

22 While they were imploring the almighty LORD to keep the deposits safe and secure for those who had placed them in trust, 23 Heliodorus went on with his plan. 24 But just as he was approaching the treasury with his bodyguards, the LORD of spirits who holds all power manifested himself in so striking a way that those who had been bold enough to follow Heliodorus were panic-stricken at God's power and fainted away in terror. 25 There appeared to them a richly caparisoned horse, mounted by a dreadful rider. Charging furiously, the horse attacked Heliodorus with its front hoofs. The rider was seen to be wearing golden armor. 26 Then two other young men, remarkably strong, strikingly beautiful, and splendidly attired, appeared before him. Standing on each side of him, they flogged him unceasingly until they had given him innumerable blows. 27 Suddenly he fell to the ground, enveloped in great darkness. Men picked him up and laid him on a stretcher. 28 The man who a moment before had entered that treasury with a great retinue and his whole bodyguard was carried away helpless, having dearly experienced the sovereign power of God. 29 While he lay speechless and deprived of all hope of aid, due to an act of God's power, 30 the Jews praised the LORD who had marvelously glorified his holy Place; and the temple, charged so shortly before with fear and commotion, was filled with joy and gladness, now that the almighty LORD had manifested himself.

31 Soon some of the companions of Heliodorus begged Onias to invoke the Most High, praying that the life of the man who was about to expire might be spared. 32 Fearing that the king might think that Heliodorus had suffered some foul play at the hands of the Jews, the high priest offered a sacrifice for the man's recovery. 33 While the high priest was offering the sacrifice of atonement, the same young men in the same clothing again appeared and stood before Heliodorus. "Be very grateful to the high priest Onias," they told him. "It is for his sake that the LORD has spared your life. 34 Since you have been scourged by Heaven, proclaim to all men the majesty of God's power." When they had said this, they disappeared.

35 After Heliodorus had offered a sacrifice to the LORD and made most solemn vows to him who had spared his life, he bade Onias farewell, and returned with his soldiers to the king. 36 Before all men he gave witness to the deeds of the most high God that he had seen with his own eyes. 37 When the king asked Heliodorus who would be a suitable man to be sent to Jerusalem next, he answered: 38 "If you have an enemy or a plotter against the government, send him there, and you will receive him back well-flogged, if indeed he survives at all; for there is certainly some special divine power about the Place. 39 He who has his dwelling in heaven watches over that Place and protects it, and he strikes down and destroys those who come to harm it." 40 This was how the matter concerning Heliodorus and the preservation of the treasury turned out.

4 The Simon mentioned above as the informer about the funds against his own country, made false accusations that it was Onias who threatened Heliodorus and instigated the whole miserable affair. 2 He dared to brand as a plotter against the government the man who was a benefactor of the city, a protector of his compatriots, and a zealous defender of the laws. 3 When Simon's hostility reached such a point that murders were being committed by one of his henchmen, 4 Onias saw that the opposition was serious and that Apollonius, son of Menestheus, the governor of Coelesyria and Phoenicia, was abetting Simon's wickedness. 5 So he

22 While they were calling on the all-powerful Lord to preserve the deposits intact for the depositors, in full security, 23 Heliodorus set about his appointed task.

24 He had already arrived with his bodyguard near the Treasury, when the Sovereign of spirits and of every power caused so great an apparition that all who had dared to accompany Heliodorus were dumbfounded at the power of God and reduced to abject terror. 25 Before their eyes appeared a horse richly caparisoned and carrying a fearsome rider. Rearing violently, it struck at Heliodorus with its forefeet. The rider was seen to be accoutred entirely in gold. 26 Two other young men of outstanding strength and radiant beauty, magnificently apparelled, appeared to him at the same time and, taking their stand on each side of him, flogged him unremittingly, inflicting stroke after stroke. 27 Suddenly Heliodorus fell to the ground, enveloped in thick darkness. His men came to his rescue and placed him in a litter, 28 this man who but a moment before had made his way into the Treasury, as we said above, with a great retinue and his whole bodyguard; and as they carried him away, powerless to help himself, they openly acknowledged the sovereign power of God.

29 While Heliodorus lay prostrate under the divine visitation, speechless and bereft of all hope of deliverance, 30 the Jews blessed the Lord who had miraculously glorified his own holy place. And the Temple, which a little while before had been filled with terror and commotion, now overflowed with joy and gladness at the manifestation of the almighty Lord. 31 Some of Heliodorus' companions quickly begged Onias to entreat the Most High to grant the man his life, lying as he did at the very point of death.

32 The high priest, afraid that the king might suspect the Jews of some foul play concerning Heliodorus, did indeed offer a sacrifice for the man's recovery. 33 And while the high priest was performing the rite of expiation, the same young men again appeared to Heliodorus, wearing the same apparel and, standing beside him, said, 'Be very grateful to Onias the high priest, since it is for his sake that the Lord has granted you your life. 34 As for you, who have been scourged by Heaven, you must proclaim to everyone the grandeur of God's power.' So saying, they vanished.

35 Heliodorus offered sacrifice to the Lord and made most solemn vows to the preserver of his life, and then took courteous leave of Onias and marched his forces back to the king. 36 He openly testified to everyone about the works of the supreme God which he had seen with his own eyes. 37 When the king asked Heliodorus what sort of man would be the right person to send to Jerusalem on a second occasion, he replied, 'If you have some enemy or anyone disloyal to the state, send him there, and you will get him back well flogged, if he survives at all, since some peculiarly divine power attaches to the holy place. 39 He who has his dwelling in heaven watches over the place and defends it, and he strikes down and destroys those who come to harm it.' 40 This was the outcome of the affair of Heliodorus and the preservation of the Treasury.

4 The Simon mentioned above as the informer against the funds and against his country began slandering Onias, insinuating that the latter had been responsible for the assault on Heliodorus and himself had contrived this misfortune. 2 Simon now had the effrontery to name this benefactor of the city, this protector of his compatriots, this zealot for the laws, as an enemy of the public good. 3 This hostility reached such proportions that murders were actually committed by some of Simon's agents, 4 and at this point Onias, recognising how mischievous this rivalry was, and aware that Apollonius son of Menestheus, the general commanding Coele-Syria and Phoenicia, was encouraging Simon in his malice, 5 went to see the king, not to play the

king, not accusing his compatriots but having in view the welfare, both public and private, of all the people. 6 For he saw that without the king's attention public affairs could not again reach a peaceful settlement, and that Simon would not stop his folly.

7 When Seleucus died and Antiochus, who was called Epiphanes, succeeded to the kingdom, Jason the brother of Onias obtained the high priesthood by corruption, 8 promising the king at an interview *l* three hundred sixty talents of silver, and from another source of revenue eighty talents. 9 In addition to this he promised to pay one hundred fifty more if permission were given to establish by his authority a gymnasium and a body of youth for it, and to enroll the people of Jerusalem as citizens of Antioch. 10 When the king assented and Jason *m* came to office, he at once shifted his compatriots over to the Greek way of life.

11 He set aside the existing royal concessions to the Jews, secured through John the father of Eupolemus, who went on the mission to establish friendship and alliance with the Romans; and he destroyed the lawful ways of living and introduced new customs contrary to the law. 12 He took delight in establishing a gymnasium right under the citadel, and he induced the noblest of the young men to wear the Greek hat. 13 There was such an extreme of Hellenization and increase in the adoption of foreign ways because of the surpassing wickedness of Jason, who was ungodly and no true *n* high priest, 14 that the priests were no longer intent upon their service at the altar. Despising the sanctuary and neglecting the sacrifices, they hurried to take part in the unlawful proceedings in the wrestling arena after the signal for the discus-throwing, 15 disdaining the honors prized by their ancestors and putting the highest value upon Greek forms of prestige. 16 For this reason heavy disaster overtook them, and those whose ways of living they admired and wished to imitate completely became their enemies and punished them. 17 It is no light thing to show irreverence to the divine laws—a fact that later events will make clear.

18 When the quadrennial games were being held at Tyre and the king was present, 19 the vile Jason sent envoys, chosen as being Antiochian citizens from Jerusalem, to carry three hundred silver drachmas for the sacrifice to Hercules. Those who carried the money, however, thought best not to use it for sacrifice, because that was inappropriate, but to expend it for another purpose. 20 So this money was intended by the sender for the sacrifice to Hercules, but by the decision of its carriers it was applied to the construction of triremes.

21 When Apollonius son of Menestheus was sent to Egypt for the coronation *o* of Philometor as king, Antiochus learned that Philometor *m* had become hostile to his government, and he took measures for his own security. Therefore upon arriving at Joppa he proceeded to Jerusalem. 22 He was welcomed magnificently by Jason and the city, and ushered in with a blaze of torches and with shouts. Then he marched his army into Phoenicia.

23 After a period of three years Jason sent Menelaus, the brother of the previously mentioned Simon, to carry the money to the king and to complete the records of essential business. 24 But he, when presented to the king, extolled him with an air of authority, and secured the high priesthood for himself, outbidding Jason by three hundred talents of silver. 25 After receiving the king's orders he returned, possessing no qualification for the high priesthood, but having the hot temper of a cruel tyrant and the rage of a savage wild beast. 26 So Jason, who after supplanting his own

recourse to the king. He did not appear as an accuser of his fellow-citizens but rather as one concerned for the interests of all the Jews, both as a nation and as individuals. 6 He saw that unless the king intervened there could be no peace in public affairs, nor would Simon be stopped in his mad course.

7 When, on the death of Seleucus, Antiochus known as Epiphanes succeeded to the throne, Jason, Onias's brother, procured for himself the office of high priest by underhand means. 8 In a petition to the king he promised him three hundred and sixty talents in silver coin immediately, and eighty talents from future revenue; 9 further, he undertook to pay an additional hundred and fifty talents if authority were given to set up a gymnasium for the physical education of young men, and to enrol in Jerusalem a group to be known as 'Antiochenes'. 10 The king gave his assent; and Jason, as soon as he had secured the high-priesthood, made his fellow-Jews conform to the Greek way of life.

11 He set aside the royal privileges accorded the Jews through the agency of John, the father of that Eupolemus who at a later date negotiated a treaty of friendship and alliance with the Romans. He abolished the institutions founded on the law and introduced practices which ran counter to it. 12 He lost no time in establishing a gymnasium at the foot of the citadel itself, and he made the most outstanding of the young men adopt the hat worn by Greek athletes. 13 So with the introduction of foreign customs Hellenism reached a high point through the inordinate wickedness of Jason, an apostate and no true high priest. 14 As a result, the priests no longer showed any enthusiasm for their duties at the altar; they treated the temple with disdain, they neglected the sacrifices, and whenever the opening gong called them they hurried to join in the sports at the wrestling school in defiance of the law. 15 They placed no value on dignities prized by their forefathers, but cared above everything for Hellenic honours. 16 This brought misfortune upon them from every side, and the very people whose way of life they admired and tried so hard to emulate turned out to be vindictive enemies. 17 To act profanely against God's laws is no light matter, as will in due course become clear.

18 When the quinquennial games were being held at Tyre in the presence of the king, 19 the villainous Jason sent, as envoys to represent Jerusalem, Antiochenes bearing three hundred drachmas in silver for the sacrifice to Hercules. Even the bearers considered it improper that this money should be used for a sacrifice, and thought it should be spent differently. 20 Thanks to them, the money intended by its sender for the sacrifice to Hercules went in fact to fit out triremes.

21 From Apollonius son of Menestheus, who was sent to Egypt for the coronation of King Philometor, Antiochus learnt that Philometor was now hostile to his interests. Anxious for his own security, he removed to Joppa, and then to Jerusalem, 22 where he was lavishly welcomed by Jason and the city, and received with torchlight processions and ovations. Afterwards he quartered his army in Phoenicia.

23 Three years later, Jason sent Menelaus, brother of the Simon mentioned above, to convey money to the king and to carry out agreed decisions on some urgent business. 24 But Menelaus, once in the king's presence, flattered him with an air of authority, and diverted the high-priesthood to himself, outbidding Jason by three hundred talents in silver. 25 He arrived back with the royal mandate, but with nothing else to make him worthy of the high-priesthood; he had the passions of a cruel tyrant and the temper of a savage beast.

---

l Or *by a petition* *m* Gk *he* *n* Gk lacks *true* *o* Meaning of Gk uncertain

4:9 **enrol . . . 'Antiochenes':** *or* enrol the inhabitants of Jerusalem as citizens of Antioch.

had recourse to the king, not as an accuser of his country-men, but as a man looking to the general and particular good of all the people. 6 He saw that, unless the king inter-vened, it would be impossible to have a peaceful govern-ment, and that Simon would not desist from his folly.

7 But Seleucus died, and when Antiochus surnamed Epiphanes succeeded him on the throne, Onias' brother Jason obtained the high priesthood by corrupt means: 8 in an interview, he promised the king three hundred and sixty talents of silver, as well as eighty talents from another source of income. 9 Besides this he agreed to pay a hundred and fifty more, if he were given authority to establish a gymnasium and a youth club for it and to enroll men in Jerusalem as Antiochians.

10 When Jason received the king's approval and came into office, he immediately initiated his countrymen into the Greek way of life. 11 He set aside the royal concessions granted to the Jews through the mediation of John, father of Eupolemus (that Eupolemus who would later go on an embassy to the Romans to establish a treaty of friendship with them); he abrogated the lawful institutions and intro-duced customs contrary to the law. 12 He quickly estab-lished a gymnasium at the very foot of the acropolis, where he induced the noblest young men to wear the Greek hat. 13 The craze for Hellenism and foreign customs reached such a pitch, through the outrageous wickedness of the ungodly pseudo-high-priest Jason, 14 that the priests no lon-ger cared about the service of the altar. Disdaining the temple and neglecting the sacrifices, they hastened, at the signal for the discus-throwing, to take part in the unlawful exercises on the athletic field. 15 They despised what their ancestors had regarded as honors, while they highly prized what the Greeks esteemed as glory. 16 Precisely because of this, they found themselves in serious trouble: the very people whose manner of life they emulated, and whom they desired to imitate in everything, became their enemies and oppressors. 17 It is no light matter to flout the laws of God, as the following period will show.

18 When the quinquennial games were held at Tyre in the presence of the king, 19 the vile Jason sent envoys as re-presentatives of the Antiochians of Jerusalem, to bring there three hundred silver drachmas for the sacrifice to Hercules. But the bearers themselves decided that the money should not be spent on a sacrifice, as that was not right, but should be used for some other purpose. 20 So the contribution des-tined by the sender for the sacrifice to Hercules was in fact applied, by those who brought it, to the construction of triremes.

21 When Apollonius, son of Menestheus, was sent to Egypt for the coronation of King Philometor, Antiochus learned that the king was opposed to his policies; so he took measures for his own security. 22 After going to Joppa, he proceeded to Jerusalem. There he was received with great pomp by Jason and the people of the city, who escorted him with torchlights and acclamations; following this, he led his army into Phoenicia.

23 Three years later Jason sent Menelaus, brother of the aforementioned Simon, to deliver the money to the king, and to obtain decisions on some important matters. 24 When he had been introduced to the king, he flattered him with such an air of authority that he secured the high priesthood for himself, outbidding Jason by three hundred talents of silver. 25 He returned with the royal commission, but with nothing that made him worthy of the high priesthood; he had the temper of a cruel tyrant and the rage of a wild beast.

accuser of his fellow-citizens, but having the public and private welfare of the entire people at heart. 6 He saw that, without some intervention by the king, an orderly adminis-tration would no longer be possible, nor would Simon put a stop to his folly.

7 When Seleucus had departed this life and Antiochus styled Epiphanes had succeeded to the kingdom, Jason, brother of Onias, usurped the high priesthood: 8 he ap-proached the king with a promise of three hundred and sixty talents of silver, with eighty talents to come from some other source of revenue. 9 He further committed himself to paying another hundred and fifty, if the king would em-power him to set up a gymnasium and youth centre, and to register the Antiochists of Jerusalem. 10 When the king gave his assent, Jason, as soon as he had seized power, imposed the Greek way of life on his fellow-countrymen. 11 He sup-pressed the liberties which the kings had graciously granted to the Jews at the instance of John, father of that Eupolemus who was later to be sent on an embassy to negotiate a treaty of friendship and alliance with the Romans and, overthrow-ing the lawful institutions, introduced new usages contrary to the Law. 12 He went so far as to found a gymnasium at the very foot of the Citadel, and to fit out the noblest of his young men in the petasos. 13 Godless wretch that he was and no true high priest, Jason set no bounds to his impiety; indeed the hellenising process reached such a pitch 14 that the priests ceased to show any interest in serving the altar; but, scorning the Temple and neglecting the sacrifices, they would hurry, on the stroke of the gong, to take part in the distribution, forbidden by the Law, of the oil on the exercise ground; 15 setting no store by the honours of their father-land, they esteemed hellenic glories best of all. 16 But all this brought its own retribution; the very people whose way of life they envied, whom they sought to resemble in every-thing, proved to be their enemies and executioners. 17 It is no small thing to violate the divine laws, as the period that followed will demonstrate.

18 On the occasion of the quadrennial games at Tyre in the presence of the king, 19 the vile Jason sent an embassy of Antiochists from Jerusalem, taking with them three hundred silver drachmas for the sacrifice to Hercules. But even those who brought the money did not think it would be right to spend it on the sacrifice and decided to reserve it for some other item of expenditure; 20 and so what the sender had intended for the sacrifice to Hercules was in fact applied, at the suggestion of those who brought it, to the construction of triremes.

21 Apollonius son of Menestheus had been sent to Egypt to attend the wedding of King Philometor. Antiochus, hav-ing learnt that the latter had become hostile to his affairs, began thinking about his own safety: that was why he had come to Joppa. He then moved to Jerusalem, 22 where he was given a magnificent welcome by Jason and the city, and escorted in by torchlight with acclamation. After which, he marched his army into Phoenicia.

23 When three years had passed, Jason sent Menelaus, brother of the Simon mentioned above, to convey the money to the king and to complete negotiations on various essential matters. 24 But Menelaus, on being presented to the king, flattered him by his own appearance of authority, and so secured the high priesthood for himself, outbidding Jason by three hundred talents of silver. 25 He returned with the royal mandate, bringing nothing worthy of the high priesthood and supported only by the fury of a cruel tyrant and the rage of a savage beast. 26 Thus Jason, who had

brother was supplanted by another man, was driven as a fugitive into the land of Ammon. 27 Although Menelaus continued to hold the office, he did not pay regularly any of the money promised to the king. 28 When Sostratus the captain of the citadel kept requesting payment — for the collection of the revenue was his responsibility — the two of them were summoned by the king on account of this issue. 29 Menelaus left his own brother Lysimachus as deputy in the high priesthood, while Sostratus left Crates, the commander of the Cyprian troops.

30 While such was the state of affairs, it happened that the people of Tarsus and of Mallus revolted because their cities had been given as a present to Antiochis, the king's concubine. 31 So the king went hurriedly to settle the trouble, leaving Andronicus, a man of high rank, to act as his deputy. 32 But Menelaus, thinking he had obtained a suitable opportunity, stole some of the gold vessels of the temple and gave them to Andronicus; other vessels, as it happened, he had sold to Tyre and the neighboring cities. 33 When Onias became fully aware of these acts, he publicly exposed them, having first withdrawn to a place of sanctuary at Daphne near Antioch. 34 Therefore Menelaus, taking Andronicus aside, urged him to kill Onias. Andronicus *p* came to Onias, and resorting to treachery, offered him sworn pledges and gave him his right hand; he persuaded him, though still suspicious, to come out from the place of sanctuary; then, with no regard for justice, he immediately put him out of the way.

35 For this reason not only Jews, but many also of other nations, were grieved and displeased at the unjust murder of the man. 36 When the king returned from the region of Cilicia, the Jews in the city *q* appealed to him with regard to the unreasonable murder of Onias, and the Greeks shared their hatred of the crime. 37 Therefore Antiochus was grieved at heart and filled with pity, and wept because of the moderation and good conduct of the deceased. 38 Inflamed with anger, he immediately stripped off the purple robe from Andronicus, tore off his clothes, and led him around the whole city to that very place where he had committed the outrage against Onias, and there he dispatched the bloodthirsty fellow. The Lord thus repaid him with the punishment he deserved.

39 When many acts of sacrilege had been committed in the city by Lysimachus with the connivance of Menelaus, and when report of them had spread abroad, the populace gathered against Lysimachus, because many of the gold vessels had already been stolen. 40 Since the crowds were becoming aroused and filled with anger, Lysimachus armed about three thousand men and launched an unjust attack, under the leadership of a certain Auranus, a man advanced in years and no less advanced in folly. 41 But when the Jews *r* became aware that Lysimachus was attacking them, some picked up stones, some blocks of wood, and others took handfuls of the ashes that were lying around, and threw them in wild confusion at Lysimachus and his men. 42 As a result, they wounded many of them, and killed some, and put all the rest to flight; the temple robber himself they killed close by the treasury.

43 Charges were brought against Menelaus about this incident. 44 When the king came to Tyre, three men sent by the senate presented the case before him. 45 But Menelaus, already as good as beaten, promised a substantial bribe to Ptolemy son of Dorymenes to win over the king. 46 Therefore Ptolemy, taking the king aside into a colonnade as if for refreshment, induced the king to change his mind. 47 Mene-

26 Jason, who had supplanted his own brother, was now supplanted in his turn and forced to seek refuge in Ammonite territory. 27 Menelaus continued to hold the high-priesthood but without ever paying any of the money he had promised the king, however often it was demanded by Sostratus, the commander of the citadel, 28 who was responsible for collecting the revenues. In consequence both were summoned to appear before the king. 29 Menelaus left as his deputy in the high-priesthood his brother Lysimachus, while Sostratus left Crates, the commander of the Cypriot mercenaries, to act for him.

30 While those events were taking place the inhabitants of Tarsus and Mallus rose in revolt, because their cities had been handed over as a gift to Antiochis, the king's concubine. 31 The king went off hurriedly to restore order, leaving Andronicus, one of his ministers, as regent. 32 Thinking to seize a favourable opportunity, Menelaus made a present to Andronicus of some of the gold plate which he had appropriated from the temple. Some he had already sold to Tyre and neighbouring cities. 33 When Onias learnt of it on good authority, he withdrew to sanctuary at Daphne near Antioch and denounced him. 34 For this, Menelaus approached Andronicus privately and urged him to have Onias put to death. The regent came to Onias and, though bent on treachery, greeted him and with assurances on oath persuaded him to leave the sanctuary in spite of his suspicions. Then at once, with no respect for justice, he made away with him.

35 This wicked murder caused indignation and resentment not only among Jews but among many from other nations as well. 36 When the king returned from Cilicia, the Jews of Antioch sent him a petition about the indefensible killing of Onias, a crime detested equally by the Gentiles. 37 Antiochus, deeply grieved, was moved to pity and tears as he thought of the high character and disciplined conduct of the dead man. 38 His anger flared up and without more ado he stripped Andronicus of the purple and tore off his clothes; then leading him right round the city to that very place where he had committed the sacrilegious crime against Onias, he dispatched the murderer, who was thus repaid by the Lord with richly deserved punishment.

39 Lysimachus, with the connivance of Menelaus, entered on a career of sacrilege and plunder in Jerusalem. When this became widely known and the people heard that much of the gold plate had been disposed of, they combined against Lysimachus. 40 As the crowds, now aroused and furious, were getting out of hand, Lysimachus armed some three thousand men and launched a vicious attack, led by a certain Auranus, a man advanced in years and no less in folly. 41 Recognizing that Lysimachus was behind the attack, some of the crowd seized stones, others blocks of wood, others again handfuls of burning embers that were lying about, and they hurled them indiscriminately at Lysimachus and his men. 42 The result was that many were wounded, some were killed, and the rout was complete; the temple robber himself they put to death near the treasury.

43 A charge was laid against Menelaus in connection with this incident 44 and, on the king's arrival at Tyre, three men sent by the Jewish senate stated their case before him. 45 Menelaus's cause being as good as lost, he promised Ptolemaeus son of Dorymenes a substantial sum of money if he would win over the king. 46 Ptolemaeus led the king aside into a colonnade, as though to take the air, and persuaded him to change his mind. 47 Menelaus, the author of

p Gk He   *q* Or in each city   *r* Gk they

26 Then Jason, who had cheated his own brother and now saw himself cheated by another man, was driven out as a fugitive to the country of the Ammonites.

27 Although Menelaus had obtained the office, he did not make any payments of the money he had promised to the king, 28 in spite of the demand of Sostratus, the commandant of the citadel, whose duty it was to collect the taxes. For this reason, both were summoned before the king. 29 Menelaus left his brother Lysimachus as his substitute in the high priesthood, while Sostratus left Crates, commander of the Cypriots, as his substitute.

30 While these things were taking place, the people of Tarsus and Mallus rose in revolt, because their cities had been given as a gift to Antiochis, the king's mistress. 31 The king, therefore, went off in haste to settle the affair, leaving Andronicus, one of his nobles, as his deputy. 32 Then Menelaus, thinking this a good opportunity, stole some gold vessels from the temple and presented them to Andronicus; he had already sold some other vessels in Tyre and in the neighboring cities. 33 When Onias had clear evidence of the facts, he made a public protest, after withdrawing to the inviolable sanctuary at Daphne, near Antioch. 34 Thereupon Menelaus approached Andronicus privately and asked him to lay hands on Onias. So Andronicus went to Onias, and by treacherously reassuring him through sworn pledges with right hands joined, persuaded him, in spite of his suspicions, to leave the sanctuary. Then, without any regard for justice, he immediately put him to death.

35 As a result, not only the Jews, but many people of other nations as well, were indignant and angry over the unjust murder of the man. 36 When the king returned from the region of Cilicia, the Jews of the city, together with the Greeks who detested the crime, went to see him about the murder of Onias. 37 Antiochus was deeply grieved and full of pity; he wept as he recalled the prudence and noble conduct of the deceased. 38 Inflamed with anger, he immediately stripped Andronicus of his purple robe, tore off his other garments, and had him led through the whole city to the very place where he had committed the outrage against Onias; and there he put the murderer to death. Thus the LORD rendered him the punishment he deserved.

39 Many sacrilegious thefts had been committed by Lysimachus in the city with the connivance of Menelaus. When word was spread that a large number of gold vessels had been stolen, the people assembled in protest against Lysimachus. 40 As the crowds, now thoroughly enraged, began to riot, Lysimachus launched an unjustified attack against them with about three thousand armed men under the leadership of Auranus, a man as advanced in folly as he was in years. 41 Reacting against Lysimachus' attack, the people picked up stones or pieces of wood or handfuls of the ashes lying there and threw them in wild confusion at Lysimachus and his men. 42 As a result, they wounded many of them and even killed a few, while they put all the rest to flight. The sacrilegious thief himself they slew near the treasury.

43 Charges about this affair were brought against Menelaus. 44 When the king came to Tyre, three men sent by the senate presented to him the justice of their cause. 45 But Menelaus, seeing himself on the losing side, promised Ptolemy, son of Dorymenes, a substantial sum of money if he would win the king over. 46 So Ptolemy retired with the king under a colonnade, as if to get some fresh air, and persuaded him to change his mind. 47 Menelaus, who was the

supplanted his own brother, was in turn supplanted by a third, and obliged to take refuge in Ammanitis. 27 As for Menelaus, he secured the office, but defaulted altogether on the sums promised to the king, 28 although Sostratus, the commandant of the Citadel, whose business it was to collect the revenue, kept demanding payment. The pair of them in consequence were summoned before the king, 29 Menelaus leaving his brother Lysimachus as deputy high priest, while Sostratus left Crates, the commander of the Cypriots, to act for him.

30 While all this was going on, it happened that the people of Tarsus and Mallus revolted, because their towns had been given as a present to Antiochis, the king's concubine. 31 The king therefore hurried off to settle the affair, leaving Andronicus, one of his dignitaries, to act as his deputy. 32 Thinking he had found a favourable opportunity, Menelaus abstracted a number of golden vessels from the Temple and presented them to Andronicus, and managed to sell others to Tyre and the surrounding cities. 33 On receiving clear evidence to this effect, Onias retired to a place of sanctuary at Daphne near Antioch and then taxed him with it. 34 Menelaus then had a quiet word with Andronicus, urging him to get rid of Onias. Andronicus sought out Onias and, resorting to the trick of offering him his right hand on oath, succeeded in persuading him, despite the latter's lingering suspicions, to leave sanctuary; whereupon, in defiance of all justice, he immediately put him to death. 35 The result was that not only Jews but many people of other nationalities were appalled and outraged by the unjust murder of this man.

36 On the king's return from the region of Cilicia, the Jews of the capital, and those Greeks who shared their hatred of the crime, appealed to him about the unjustified murder of Onias. 37 Antiochus was profoundly grieved and filled with pity, and he wept for the prudence and moderation of the dead man. 38 Burning with indignation, he immediately stripped Andronicus of the purple, tore his garments off him and, parading him through the length of the city, rid the world of the assassin on the very spot where he had laid impious hands on Onias, the Lord dealing out to him the punishment he deserved.

39 Now Lysimachus with the connivance of Menelaus had committed many sacrilegious thefts in the city, and when the facts became widely known, the populace rose against Lysimachus, who had already disposed of many pieces of gold plate. 40 The infuriated mob was becoming menacing, and Lysimachus armed nearly three thousand men and took aggressive action; the troops were led by a certain Auranus, a man advanced in years and no less in folly. 41 Recognising this act of aggression as the work of Lysimachus, some snatched up stones, others cudgels, while others scooped up handfuls of ashes lying at hand, and all hurled everything indiscriminately at Lysimachus' men, 42 to such effect that they wounded many of them, even killing a few, and routed them all; the sacrilegious thief himself they killed near the Treasury.

43 As a result of this, legal proceedings were taken against Menelaus. 44 When the king came down to Tyre, three men deputed by the Senate pleaded their case before him. 45 Menelaus, seeing the case had gone against him, promised a substantial sum to Ptolemy son of Dorymenes if he would influence the king in his favour. 46 Ptolemy then took the king aside into a colonnade, as though for a breath of fresh air, and persuaded him to change his mind; 47 the king

NEW REVISED STANDARD VERSION	REVISED ENGLISH BIBLE

laus, the cause of all the trouble, he acquitted of the charges against him, while he sentenced to death those unfortunate men, who would have been freed uncondemned if they had pleaded even before Scythians. 48 And so those who had spoken for the city and the villages[s] and the holy vessels quickly suffered the unjust penalty. 49 Therefore even the Tyrians, showing their hatred of the crime, provided magnificently for their funeral. 50 But Menelaus, because of the greed of those in power, remained in office, growing in wickedness, having become the chief plotter against his compatriots.

5 About this time Antiochus made his second invasion of Egypt. 2 And it happened that, for almost forty days, there appeared over all the city golden-clad cavalry charging through the air, in companies fully armed with lances and drawn swords— 3 troops of cavalry drawn up, attacks and counterattacks made on this side and on that, brandishing of shields, massing of spears, hurling of missiles, the flash of golden trappings, and armor of all kinds. 4 Therefore everyone prayed that the apparition might prove to have been a good omen.

5 When a false rumor arose that Antiochus was dead, Jason took no fewer than a thousand men and suddenly made an assault on the city. When the troops on the wall had been forced back and at last the city was being taken, Menelaus took refuge in the citadel. 6 But Jason kept relentlessly slaughtering his compatriots, not realizing that success at the cost of one's kindred is the greatest misfortune, but imagining that he was setting up trophies of victory over enemies and not over compatriots. 7 He did not, however, gain control of the government; in the end he got only disgrace from his conspiracy, and fled again into the country of the Ammonites. 8 Finally he met a miserable end. Accused[t] before Aretas the ruler of the Arabs, fleeing from city to city, pursued by everyone, hated as a rebel against the laws, and abhorred as the executioner of his country and his compatriots, he was cast ashore in Egypt. 9 There he who had driven many from their own country into exile died in exile, having embarked to go to the Lacedaemonians in hope of finding protection because of their kinship. 10 He who had cast out many to lie unburied had no one to mourn for him; he had no funeral of any sort and no place in the tomb of his ancestors.

11 When news of what had happened reached the king, he took it to mean that Judea was in revolt. So, raging inwardly, he left Egypt and took the city by storm. 12 He commanded his soldiers to cut down relentlessly everyone they met and to kill those who went into their houses. 13 Then there was massacre of young and old, destruction of boys, women, and children, and slaughter of young girls and infants. 14 Within the total of three days eighty thousand were destroyed, forty thousand in hand-to-hand fighting, and as many were sold into slavery as were killed.

15 Not content with this, Antiochus[u] dared to enter the most holy temple in all the world, guided by Menelaus, who had become a traitor both to the laws and to his country. 16 He took the holy vessels with his polluted hands, and swept away with profane hands the votive offerings that other kings had made to enhance the glory and honor of the place. 17 Antiochus was elated in spirit, and did not perceive that the Lord was angered for a little while because of the sins of those who lived in the city, and that this was the reason he was disregarding the holy place. 18 But if it had

---

all the mischief, was acquitted and the charges brought against him were dismissed, but the king condemned to death the unfortunate accusers, men who would have been let go as entirely innocent had they appeared even before Scythians. 48 At once those who had pleaded for their city, their people, and their sacred vessels, suffered this undeserved penalty. 49 It caused even some of the Tyrians to show their detestation of the crime by providing a splendid funeral for the victims. 50 Yet thanks to the cupidity of those in power, Menelaus, this arch-plotter against his fellow-citizens, continued in office and went from bad to worse.

5 About that time Antiochus undertook his second expedition against Egypt. 2 For nearly forty days apparitions were seen in the sky all over Jerusalem: galloping horsemen in golden armour, companies of spearmen standing to arms, 3 swordsmen at the ready, and squadrons of cavalry in battle order. Charges and countercharges were made in this direction and that; shields were brandished, spears massed, javelins hurled; breastplates and golden ornaments of every kind blazed with light. 4 That the phenomenon might portend good was the prayer of everyone.

5 On a false report of Antiochus's death, Jason at the head of no less than a thousand men launched a surprise attack on Jerusalem. The defenders on the wall were driven back and, with the city on the point of being taken, Menelaus sought refuge in the citadel. 6 Jason embarked upon an unsparing massacre of his fellow-citizens, for he did not grasp that success against one's own kin is the greatest of failures; he imagined that the trophies he raised marked the defeat of enemies, not of fellow-countrymen. 7 However, he failed to secure control of the government; all he achieved as the result of his scheming was dishonour, and once again he sought asylum in Ammonite territory. 8 His career came to a miserable end, for after being imprisoned by Aretas the ruler of the Arabs he fled from city to city, hunted by all, hated as a renegade against the laws, detested as the butcher of his country and his fellow-citizens, until he landed up in Egypt. 9 Then, having crossed by sea to Sparta, where he hoped to obtain shelter because of the Spartans' kinship with the Jews, he, who had driven so many into exile, himself died an exile. 10 He who had cast out so many to lie unburied was himself unmourned; he had no obsequies of any kind, no resting-place in the ancestral grave.

11 It was clear to the king, when news of those happenings reached him, that Judaea was in a state of insurrection, and he set out from Egypt in savage mood. He took Jerusalem by storm, 12 ordering his troops to cut down unsparingly everyone they met, and to slaughter those who took refuge in the houses. 13 Young and old were murdered, women and children massacred, girls and infants butchered. 14 At the end of three days the victims numbered eighty thousand: forty thousand killed in the fighting, and as many again sold into slavery.

15 Not satisfied with this, and guided by Menelaus, who had turned traitor to both religion and country, the king had the audacity to enter the most holy temple on earth. 16 The villain laid his polluted hands on the sacred vessels, and profanely swept up the votive offerings which other kings had made to enhance the splendour and fame of the shrine. 17 The pride of Antiochus passed all bounds. He did not understand that the sins of the people of Jerusalem had for a short time angered the Lord, and that this was the reason why the temple was left to its fate. 18 Had they not been

---

s Other ancient authorities read the people   t Cn: Gk Imprisoned
u Gk he

cause of all the trouble, the king acquitted of the charges, while he condemned to death those poor men who would have been declared innocent even if they had pleaded their case before Scythians. 48 Thus, those who had prosecuted the case for the city, for the people, and for the sacred vessels, quickly suffered unjust punishment. 49 For this reason, even some Tyrians were indignant over the crime and provided sumptuously for their burial. 50 But Menelaus, thanks to the covetousness of the men in power, remained in office, where he grew in wickedness and became the chief plotter against his fellow citizens.

5 About this time Antiochus sent his second expedition into Egypt. 2 It then happened that all over the city, for nearly forty days, there appeared horsemen charging in midair, clad in garments interwoven with gold — companies fully armed with lances 3 and drawn swords; squadrons of cavalry in battle array, charges and countercharges on this side and that, with brandished shields and bristling spears, flights of arrows and flashes of gold ornaments, together with armor of every sort. 4 Therefore all prayed that this vision might be a good omen.

5 But when a false rumor circulated that Antiochus was dead, Jason gathered fully a thousand men and suddenly attacked the city. As the defenders on the walls were forced back and the city was finally being taken, Menelaus took refuge in the citadel. 6 Jason then slaughtered his fellow citizens without mercy, not realizing that triumph over one's own kindred was the greatest failure, but imagining that he was winning a victory over his enemies, not his fellow countrymen. 7 Even so, he did not gain control of the government, but in the end received only disgrace for his treachery, and once again took refuge in the country of the Ammonites. 8 At length he met a miserable end. Called to account before Aretas, king of the Arabs, he fled from city to city, hunted by all men, hated as a transgressor of the laws, abhorred as the butcher of his country and his countrymen. After being driven into Egypt, 9 he crossed the sea to the Spartans, among whom he hoped to find protection because of his relations with them. There he who had exiled so many from their country perished in exile; 10 and he who had cast out so many to lie unburied went unmourned himself with no funeral of any kind or any place in the tomb of his ancestors.

11 When these happenings were reported to the king, he thought that Judea was in revolt. Raging like a wild animal, he set out from Egypt and took Jerusalem by storm. 12 He ordered his soldiers to cut down without mercy those whom they met and to slay those who took refuge in their houses. 13 There was a massacre of young and old, a killing of women and children, a slaughter of virgins and infants. 14 In the space of three days, eighty thousand were lost, forty thousand meeting a violent death, and the same number being sold into slavery. 15 Not satisfied with this, the king dared to enter the holiest temple in the world; Menelaus, that traitor both to the laws and to his country, served as guide. 16 He laid his impure hands on the sacred vessels and gathered up with profane hands the votive offerings made by other kings for the advancement, the glory, and the honor of the Place. 17 Puffed up in spirit, Antiochus did not realize that it was because of the sins of the city's inhabitants that the LORD was angry for a little while and hence disregarded the holy Place. 18 If they had not become entan-

then dismissed the charges against Menelaus, the cause of all this evil, while he condemned to death the other poor wretches who, had they pleaded even before Scythians, would have been let off scot-free. 48 No time was lost in carrying out this unjust punishment on those who had championed the cause of the city, the townships and the sacred vessels. 49 Some Tyrians even were so outraged by the crime that they provided sumptuously for their funeral, 50 while, as a result of the greed of the powerful, Menelaus remained in power, growing more wicked than ever and establishing himself as the chief enemy of his fellow-citizens.

5 At about this time, Antiochus was preparing for his second attack on Egypt. 2 It then happened that all over the city for nearly forty days there were apparitions of horsemen galloping through the air in cloth of gold, troops of lancers fully armed, 3 squadrons of cavalry in order of battle, attacks and charges this way and that, a flourish of shields, a forest of pikes, a brandishing of swords, a hurling of missiles, a glittering of golden accoutrements and armour of all kinds. 4 So everyone prayed that this manifestation might prove a good omen.

5 Then, on the strength of a false report that Antiochus was dead, Jason took at least a thousand men and launched an unexpected attack on the city. When the walls had been breached and the city was finally on the point of being taken, Menelaus took refuge in the Citadel. 6 Jason, however, made a pitiless slaughter of his fellow-citizens, oblivious of the fact that success against his own countrymen was the greatest of disasters, but rather picturing himself as winning trophies from some enemy, and not from his fellow-countrymen. 7 Even so, he did not manage to seize power; and, in the end, his machinations brought him nothing but shame, and he took refuge once more in Ammanitis. 8 His career of wickedness was thus brought to a halt: imprisoned by Aretas, the Arab despot, escaping from his town, hunted by everyone, detested for having overthrown the laws, abhorred as the butcher of his country and his countrymen, he drifted to Egypt. 9 He who had exiled so many from their fatherland, himself perished on foreign soil, having travelled to Sparta, hoping that, for kinship's sake, he might find harbour there. 10 So many carcases he had thrust out to lie unburied; now he himself had none to mourn him, no funeral rites, no place in the tomb of his ancestors.

11 When the king came to hear of what had happened, he concluded that Judaea was in revolt. He therefore marched from Egypt, raging like a wild beast, and began to storming the city. 12 He then ordered his soldiers to cut down without mercy everyone they encountered, and to butcher all who took refuge in their houses. 13 It was a massacre of young and old, a slaughter of women and children, a butchery of young girls and infants. 14 There were eighty thousand victims in the course of those three days, forty thousand dying by violence and as many again being sold into slavery. 15 e Not content with this, he had the audacity to enter the holiest Temple in the entire world, with Menelaus, that traitor to the laws and to his country, as his guide; 16 with impious hands he seized the sacred vessels; with impious hands he seized the offerings presented by other kings for the aggrandisement, glory and dignity of the holy place.

17 Holding so high an opinion of himself, Antiochus did not realise that the Lord was temporarily angry at the sins of the inhabitants of the city, hence his unconcern for the holy place. 18 Had they not been entangled in many sins,

not happened that they were involved in many sins, this man would have been flogged and turned back from his rash act as soon as he came forward, just as Heliodorus had been, whom King Seleucus sent to inspect the treasury. 19 But the Lord did not choose the nation for the sake of the holy place, but the place for the sake of the nation. 20 Therefore the place itself shared in the misfortunes that befell the nation and afterward participated in its benefits; and what was forsaken in the wrath of the Almighty was restored again in all its glory when the great Lord became reconciled.

21 So Antiochus carried off eighteen hundred talents from the temple, and hurried away to Antioch, thinking in his arrogance that he could sail on the land and walk on the sea, because his mind was elated. 22 He left governors to oppress the people: at Jerusalem, Philip, by birth a Phrygian and in character more barbarous than the man who appointed him; 23 and at Gerizim, Andronicus; and besides these Menelaus, who lorded it over his compatriots worse than the others did. In his malice toward the Jewish citizens,[v] 24 Antiochus[w] sent Apollonius, the captain of the Mysians, with an army of twenty-two thousand, and commanded him to kill all the grown men and to sell the women and boys as slaves. 25 When this man arrived in Jerusalem, he pretended to be peaceably disposed and waited until the holy sabbath day; then, finding the Jews not at work, he ordered his troops to parade under arms. 26 He put to the sword all those who came out to see them, then rushed into the city with his armed warriors and killed great numbers of people.

27 But Judas Maccabeus, with about nine others, got away to the wilderness, and kept himself and his companions alive in the mountains as wild animals do; they continued to live on what grew wild, so that they might not share in the defilement.

6 Not long after this, the king sent an Athenian[x] senator[y] to compel the Jews to forsake the laws of their ancestors and no longer to live by the laws of God; 2 also to pollute the temple in Jerusalem and to call it the temple of Olympian Zeus, and to call the one in Gerizim the temple of Zeus-the-Friend-of-Strangers, as did the people who lived in that place.

3 Harsh and utterly grievous was the onslaught of evil. 4 For the temple was filled with debauchery and reveling by the Gentiles, who dallied with prostitutes and had intercourse with women in the sacred precincts, and besides brought in things for sacrifice that were unfit. 5 The altar was covered with abominable offerings that were forbidden by the laws. 6 People could neither keep the sabbath, nor observe the festivals of their ancestors, nor so much as confess themselves to be Jews.

7 On the monthly celebration of the king's birthday, the Jews[z] were taken, under bitter constraint, to partake of the sacrifices; and when a festival of Dionysus was celebrated, they were compelled to wear wreathes of ivy and to walk in the procession in honor of Dionysus. 8 At the suggestion of the people of Ptolemais[a] a decree was issued to the neighboring Greek cities that they should adopt the same policy toward the Jews and make them partake of the sacrifices, 9 and should kill those who did not choose to change over to Greek customs. One could see, therefore, the misery that had come upon them. 10 For example, two women were

guilty of many sinful acts, Antiochus would have fared no better than Heliodorus, who was sent by King Seleucus to inspect the treasury; like him, he would have been flogged and his presumption foiled at once. 19 But the Lord did not choose the nation for the sake of the sanctuary; he chose the sanctuary for the sake of the nation. 20 That was why the sanctuary itself had its part in the misfortunes that befell the nation, and afterwards shared its good fortune; it was abandoned when the Almighty was roused to anger, but restored again in all its splendour when the great Master was reconciled with his people.

21 So Antiochus hastened back to Antioch, taking with him eighteen hundred talents from the temple. Carried away by arrogance he thought that he could make ships sail on dry land and men walk over the sea! 22 He left behind commissioners to oppress the people: in Jerusalem he left Philip, by race a Phrygian, by disposition more barbarous than the man who appointed him, 23 and in Mount Gerizim, Andronicus; and in addition to these there was Menelaus, who was more brutally overbearing to the citizens than the others. Further, such was the king's hostility towards the Jewish population 24 that he sent Apollonius, commander of the Mysian mercenaries, with an army of twenty-two thousand men; his orders were to slaughter all the adult males and to sell the women and children into slavery. 25 When Apollonius arrived at Jerusalem, he pretended he had come in peace; waiting until the holy sabbath day and finding the Jews abstaining from work, he paraded his troops under arms. 26 All who came out to witness the spectacle he put to the sword; then, charging into the city with his soldiers, he cut down an even greater number of the people.

27 But Judas, also called Maccabaeus, escaped with about nine others into the desert, where he and his companions lived in the mountains, fending for themselves like the wild animals, and all the while feeding on what vegetation they found there, so as to have no share in the pollution.

6 Not long afterwards King Antiochus sent an elderly Athenian to compel the Jews to give up their ancestral customs and to cease regulating their lives by the laws of God. 2 He was commissioned also to pollute the temple at Jerusalem and dedicate it to Olympian Zeus; the sanctuary on Mount Gerizim he was to dedicate to Zeus God of Hospitality, as requested by the local inhabitants.

3 This evil onslaught bore hard on the people and tried them grievously, 4 for the Gentiles filled the temple with licentious revelry: they took their pleasure with prostitutes and had intercourse with women in the sacred precincts. Moreover, they introduced things which the law forbade, 5 and heaped the altar with offerings prohibited as impure. 6 No one was allowed to observe the sabbath or to keep the traditional festivals or even to admit to being a Jew at all. 7 Each month during the celebration of the king's birthday, the Jews were forcibly compelled to eat the entrails of sacrificial victims, and on the feast of Dionysus to wear ivy-wreaths and join the procession in his honour. 8 At the instigation of the inhabitants of Ptolemais a royal decree was published in the neighbouring Greek cities to the effect that they should adopt the same policy of compelling the Jews to eat the entrails, 9 and that they should put to death everyone who refused to conform to Greek ways.

The miserable fate of the Jews was there for all to see.

---

[v] Or worse than the others did in his malice toward the Jewish citizens [w] Gk he [x] Other ancient authorities read Antiochian [y] Or Geron an Athenian [z] Gk they [a] Cn: Gk suggestion of the Ptolemies (or of Ptolemy)

6:8 At . . . Ptolemais: some witnesses read At the instigation of Ptolemaeus.

gled in so many sins, this man, like Heliodorus, who was sent by King Seleucus to inspect the treasury, would have been flogged and turned back from his presumptuous action as soon as he approached. 19 The LORD, however, had not chosen the people for the sake of the Place, but the Place for the sake of the people. 20 Therefore, the Place itself, having shared in the people's misfortunes, afterward participated in their good fortune; and what the Almighty had forsaken in his anger was restored in all its glory, once the great Sovereign became reconciled.

21 Antiochus carried off eighteen hundred talents from the temple, and hurried back to Antioch. In his arrogance he planned to make the land navigable and the sea passable on foot, so carried away was he with pride. 22 But he left governors to harass the nation: at Jerusalem, Philip, a Phrygian by birth, and in character more cruel than the man who appointed him; 23 at Mount Gerizim, Andronicus; and besides these, Menelaus, who lorded it over his fellow citizens worse than the others did. Out of hatred for the Jewish citizens, 24 the king sent Apollonius, commander of the Mysians, at the head of an army of twenty-two thousand men, with orders to kill all the grown men and sell the women and young men into slavery. 25 When this man arrived in Jerusalem, he pretended to be peacefully disposed and waited until the holy day of the sabbath; then, finding the Jews refraining from work, he ordered his men to parade fully armed. 26 All those who came out to watch, he massacred, and running through the city with armed men, he cut down a large number of people.

27 But Judas Maccabeus with about nine others withdrew to the wilderness where he and his companions lived like wild animals in the hills, continuing to eat what grew wild to avoid sharing the defilement.

Antiochus too, like Heliodorus when King Seleucus sent him to inspect the Treasury, would have been flogged the moment he arrived and checked in his presumption. 19 The Lord, however, had not chosen the people for the sake of the holy place, but the holy place for the sake of the people; 20 and so the holy place itself, having shared the disasters that befell the people, in due course also shared their good fortune; having been abandoned by the Almighty in his anger, once the great Sovereign was placated it was reinstated in all its glory.

21 Antiochus, having extracted eighteen hundred talents from the Temple, hurried back to Antioch; in his pride he would have undertaken to make the dry land navigable and the sea passable on foot, so high his arrogance soared. 22 But he left officials behind to plague the nation: in Jerusalem, Philip, a Phrygian by race, and by nature more barbarous than the man who appointed him; 23 on Mount Gerizim, Andronicus; and, besides these, Menelaus, who lorded it over his countrymen worse than all the others.

In his rooted hostility to the Jews, 24 the king also sent the Mysarch Apollonius at the head of an army twenty-two thousand strong, with orders to put to death all men in their prime and to sell the women and children. 25 Arriving in Jerusalem and posing as a man of peace, this man waited until the holy day of the Sabbath and then, taking advantage of the Jews as they rested from work, ordered his men to parade fully armed; 26 all those who came out to watch he put to the sword; then, rushing into the city with his armed troops, he cut down an immense number of people.

27 Judas, also known as Maccabaeus, however, with about nine others, withdrew into the desert. He lived like the wild animals in the hills with his companions, eating nothing but wild plants to avoid contracting defilement.

6 Not long after this the king sent an Athenian senator to force the Jews to abandon the customs of their ancestors and live no longer by the laws of God; 2 also to profane the temple in Jerusalem and dedicate it to Olympian Zeus, and that on Mount Gerizim to Zeus the Hospitable, as the inhabitants of the place requested. 3 This intensified the evil in an intolerable and utterly disgusting way. 4 The Gentiles filled the temple with debauchery and revelry; they amused themselves with prostitutes and had intercourse with women even in the sacred court. They also brought into the temple things that were forbidden, 5 so that the altar was covered with abominable offerings prohibited by the laws.

6 A man could not keep the sabbath or celebrate the traditional feasts, nor even admit that he was a Jew. 7 Moreover, at the monthly celebration of the king's birthday the Jews had, from bitter necessity, to partake of the sacrifices, and when the festival of Dionysus was celebrated, they were compelled to march in his procession, wearing wreaths of ivy.

8 At the suggestion of the citizens of Ptolemais, a decree was issued ordering the neighboring Greek cities to act in the same way against the Jews: oblige them to partake of the sacrifices, 9 and put to death those who would not consent to adopt the customs of the Greeks. It was obvious, therefore, that disaster impended. 10 Thus, two women who

6 f Shortly afterwards, the king sent Gerontes the Athenian to force the Jews to violate their ancestral customs and live no longer by the laws of God; 2 and to profane the Temple in Jerusalem and dedicate it to Olympian Zeus, and the one on Mount Gerizim to Zeus, Patron of Strangers, as the inhabitants of the latter place had requested. 3 The advent of these evils was painfully hard for all the people to bear. 4 The Temple was filled with revelling and debauchery by the gentiles, who took their pleasure with prostitutes and had intercourse with women in the sacred precincts, introducing other indecencies besides. 5 The altar of sacrifice was loaded with victims proscribed by the law as profane. 6 No one might either keep the Sabbath or observe the traditional feasts, or so much as admit to being a Jew. 7 People were driven by harsh compulsion to take part in the monthly ritual meal commemorating the king's birthday; and when a feast of Dionysus occurred, they were forced to wear ivy wreaths and walk in the Dionysiac procession. 8 A decree was issued at the instance of the people of Ptolemais for the neighbouring Greek cities, enforcing the same conduct on the Jews there, obliging them to share in the sacrificial meals, 9 and ordering the execution of those who would not voluntarily conform to Greek customs. So it became clear that disaster was imminent.

f 6 6:1seq. // 1 M 1:45–51, 60–61; 2:32–38.

brought in for having circumcised their children. They publicly paraded them around the city, with their babies hanging at their breasts, and then hurled them down headlong from the wall. 11 Others who had assembled in the caves nearby, in order to observe the seventh day secretly, were betrayed to Philip and were all burned together, because their piety kept them from defending themselves, in view of their regard for that most holy day.

12 Now I urge those who read this book not to be depressed by such calamities, but to recognize that these punishments were designed not to destroy but to discipline our people. 13 In fact, it is a sign of great kindness not to let the impious alone for long, but to punish them immediately. 14 For in the case of the other nations the Lord waits patiently to punish them until they have reached the full measure of their sins; but he does not deal in this way with us, 15 in order that he may not take vengeance on us afterward when our sins have reached their height. 16 Therefore he never withdraws his mercy from us. Although he disciplines us with calamities, he does not forsake his own people. 17 Let what we have said serve as a reminder; we must go on briefly with the story.

18 Eleazar, one of the scribes in high position, a man now advanced in age and of noble presence, was being forced to open his mouth to eat swine's flesh. 19 But he, welcoming death with honor rather than life with pollution, went up to the rack of his own accord, spitting out the flesh, 20 as all ought to go who have the courage to refuse things that it is not right to taste, even for the natural love of life.

21 Those who were in charge of that unlawful sacrifice took the man aside because of their long acquaintance with him, and privately urged him to bring meat of his own providing, proper for him to use, and to pretend that he was eating the flesh of the sacrificial meal that had been commanded by the king, 22 so that by doing this he might be saved from death, and be treated kindly on account of his old friendship with them. 23 But making a high resolve, worthy of his years and the dignity of his old age and the gray hairs that he had reached with distinction and his excellent life even from childhood, and moreover according to the holy God-given law, he declared himself quickly, telling them to send him to Hades.

24 "Such pretense is not worthy of our time of life," he said, "for many of the young might suppose that Eleazar in his ninetieth year had gone over to an alien religion, 25 and through my pretense, for the sake of living a brief moment longer, they would be led astray because of me, while I defile and disgrace my old age. 26 Even if for the present I would avoid the punishment of mortals, yet whether I live or die I shall not escape the hands of the Almighty. 27 Therefore, by bravely giving up my life now, I will show myself worthy of my old age 28 and leave to the young a noble example of how to die a good death willingly and nobly for the revered and holy laws."

When he had said this, he went*b* at once to the rack. 29 Those who a little before had acted toward him with goodwill now changed to ill will, because the words he had uttered were in their opinion sheer madness.*c* 30 When he was about to die under the blows, he groaned aloud and said: "It is clear to the Lord in his holy knowledge that, though I might have been saved from death, I am enduring terrible sufferings in my body under this beating, but in my soul I am glad to suffer these things because I fear him."

31 So in this way he died, leaving in his death an example of nobility and a memorial of courage, not only to the young but to the great body of his nation.

---

10 For instance, two women who had had their children circumcised were brought to trial; then, with their babies hanging at their breasts, they were paraded through the city and hurled headlong from the ramparts. 11 Other Jews, who had assembled secretly in nearby caves to observe the sabbath, were denounced to Philip and, since out of regard for the sanctity of the day they had scruples about defending themselves, they were burnt alive.

12 Now I beg my readers not to be disheartened by those tragic events, but to reflect that such penalties were inflicted for the discipline, not the destruction, of our race. 13 It is a sign of great benevolence that acts of impiety should not be overlooked for long but rather should meet their due recompense at once. 14 The Lord has not seen fit to deal with us as he does with other nations: with them he patiently holds his hand until they have reached the full extent of their sins, 15 but on us he inflicts retribution before our sins reach their limit. 16 So he never withdraws his mercy from us; although he may discipline his people by disaster, he does not desert them. 17 So much by way of reminder; I must now continue with my summary of events.

18 Eleazar, one of the leading teachers of the law, a man of great age and distinguished bearing, was being forced to open his mouth and eat pork; 19 but preferring death with honour to life with impiety, he spat it out and voluntarily submitted to the torture. 20 So should men act who have the courage to reject food which despite a natural desire to save their lives it is not lawful to eat. 21 Because of their long acquaintance with him, the officials in charge of this sacrilegious meal had a word with Eleazar in private; they urged him to bring meat which he was permitted to eat and had himself prepared; he need only pretend to comply with the king's order to eat the sacrificial meat. 22 In that way he would escape death by taking advantage of the clemency which their long-standing friendship merited. 23 But Eleazar made an honourable decision, one worthy of his years and the authority of old age, worthy of the grey hairs he had attained to and wore with such distinction, worthy of his faultless conduct from childhood, but above all worthy of the holy and God-given law; he replied at once: 'Send me to my grave! 24 If I went through with this pretence at my time of life, many of the young might believe that at the age of ninety Eleazar had turned apostate. 25 If I practised deceit for the sake of a brief moment of life, I should lead them astray and stain my old age with dishonour. 26 I might for the present avoid man's punishment, but alive or dead I should never escape the hand of the Almighty. 27 If I now die bravely, I shall show that I have deserved my long life 28 and leave to the young a noble example; I shall be teaching them how to die a good death, gladly and nobly, for our revered and holy laws.'

With these words he went straight to the torture, 29 while those who a short time before had shown him friendship now turned hostile because, to them, what he had said was madness. 30 When Eleazar was on the point of death from the blows he had received, he groaned aloud and said: 'To the Lord belongs all holy knowledge; he knows what terrible agony I endure in my body from this flogging, though I could have escaped death; yet he knows also that in my soul I suffer gladly, because I stand in awe of him.'

31 So he died; and by his death he left a noble example and a memorial of virtue, not only to the young but also to the great mass of his countrymen.

---

b Other ancient authorities read *was dragged*   *c* Meaning of Gk uncertain

were arrested for having circumcised their children were publicly paraded about the city with their babies hanging at their breasts and then thrown down from the top of the city wall. 11 Others, who had assembled in nearby caves to observe the sabbath in secret, were betrayed to Philip and all burned to death. In their respect for the holiness of that day, they had scruples about defending themselves.

12 Now I beg those who read this book not to be disheartened by these misfortunes, but to consider that these chastisements were meant not for the ruin but for the correction of our nation. 13 It is, in fact, a sign of great kindness to punish sinners promptly instead of letting them go for long. 14 Thus, in dealing with other nations, the LORD patiently waits until they reach the full measure of their sins before he punishes them; but with us he has decided to deal differently, 15 in order that he may not have to punish us more severely later, when our sins have reached their fullness. 16 He never withdraws his mercy from us. Although he disciplines us with misfortunes, he does not abandon his own people. 17 Let these words suffice for recalling this truth. Without further ado we must go on with our story.

18 Eleazar, one of the foremost scribes, a man of advanced age and noble appearance, was being forced to open his mouth to eat pork. 19 But preferring a glorious death to a life of defilement, he spat out the meat, and went forward of his own accord to the instrument of torture, 20 as men ought to do who have the courage to reject the food which it is unlawful to taste even for love of life. 21 Those in charge of that unlawful ritual meal took the man aside privately, because of their long acquaintance with him, and urged him to bring meat of his own providing, such as he could legitimately eat, and to pretend to be eating some of the meat of the sacrifice prescribed by the king; 22 in this way he would escape the death penalty, and be treated kindly because of their old friendship with him. 23 But he made up his mind in a noble manner, worthy of his years, the dignity of his advanced age, the merited distinction of his gray hair, and of the admirable life he had lived from childhood; and so he declared that above all he would be loyal to the holy laws given by God.

He told them to send him at once to the abode of the dead, explaining: 24 "At our age it would be unbecoming to make such a pretense; many young men would think the ninety-year-old Eleazar had gone over to an alien religion. 25 Should I thus dissimulate for the sake of a brief moment of life, they would be led astray by me, while I would bring shame and dishonor on my old age. 26 Even if, for the time being, I avoid the punishment of men, I shall never, whether alive or dead, escape the hands of the Almighty. 27 Therefore, by manfully giving up my life now, I will prove myself worthy of my old age, 28 and I will leave to the young a noble example of how to die willingly and generously for the revered and holy laws."

He spoke thus, and went immediately to the instrument of torture. 29 Those who shortly before had been kindly disposed, now became hostile toward him because what he had said seemed to them utter madness. 30 When he was about to die under the blows, he groaned and said: "The LORD in his holy knowledge knows full well that, although I could have escaped death, I am not only enduring terrible pain in my body from this scourging, but also suffering it with joy in my soul because of my devotion to him." 31 This is how he died, leaving in his death a model of courage and an unforgettable example of virtue not only for the young but for the whole nation.

10 For example, two women were charged with having circumcised their children. They were paraded publicly round the town, with their babies hung at their breasts, and then hurled over the city wall. 11 Other people, who had assembled in some near-by caves to keep the seventh day without attracting attention, were denounced to Philip, and were then all burnt to death together, since their consciences would not allow them to defend themselves, out of respect for the holiness of the day.

12 Now, I urge anyone who may read this book not to be dismayed at these calamities, but to reflect that such visitations are intended not to destroy our race but to discipline it. 13 Indeed, when evil-doers are not left for long to their own devices but incur swift retribution, it is a sign of great benevolence. 14 In the case of other nations, the Master waits patiently for them to attain the full measure of their sins before he punishes them, but with us he has decided to deal differently, 15 rather than have to punish us later, when our sins come to full measure. 16 And so he never entirely withdraws his mercy from us; he may discipline us by some disaster, but he does not desert his own people. 17 Let this be said simply by way of reminder; we must return to our story without more ado.

18 Eleazar, one of the foremost teachers of the Law, a man already advanced in years and of most noble appearance, had his mouth forced open, to make him eat a piece of pork. 19 But he, resolving to die with honour rather than to live disgraced, walked of his own accord to the torture of the wheel, 20 having spat the stuff out, as befits those with the courage to reject what is not lawful to taste, rather than live. 21 The people supervising the ritual meal, forbidden by the Law, because of the length of time for which they had known him, took him aside and privately urged him to have meat brought of a kind he could properly use, prepared by himself, and only pretend to eat the portions of sacrificial meat as prescribed by the king; 22 this action would enable him to escape death, by availing himself of an act of kindness prompted by their long friendship. 23 But having taken a noble decision worthy of his years and the dignity of his great age and the well-earned distinction of his grey hairs, worthy too of his impeccable conduct from boyhood, and above all of the holy legislation established by God himself, he answered accordingly, telling them to send him at once to Hades. 24 'Pretence', he said, 'does not befit our time of life; many young people would suppose that Eleazar at the age of ninety had conformed to the foreigners' way of life 25 and, because I had played this part for the sake of a paltry brief spell of life, might themselves be led astray on my account; I should only bring defilement and disgrace on my old age. 26 Even though for the moment I avoid execution by man, I can never, living or dead, elude the grasp of the Almighty. 27 Therefore if I am man enough to quit this life here and now, I shall prove myself worthy of my old age, 28 and I shall have left the young a noble example of how to make a good death, eagerly and generously, for the venerable and holy laws.'

So saying, he walked straight to the wheel, 29 while those who were escorting him, recently so well disposed towards him, turned against him after this declaration, which they regarded as sheer madness. 30 He for his part, just before he died under the blows, gave a sigh and said, 'The Lord whose knowledge is holy sees clearly that, though I might have escaped death, from awe of him I gladly endure these agonies of body under the lash, and that in my soul I am glad to suffer.'

31 This was how he died, leaving his death as an example of nobility and a record of virtue not only for the young but for the greater part of the nation.

NEW REVISED STANDARD VERSION

7 It happened also that seven brothers and their mother were arrested and were being compelled by the king, under torture with whips and thongs, to partake of unlawful swine's flesh. 2 One of them, acting as their spokesman, said, "What do you intend to ask and learn from us? For we are ready to die rather than transgress the laws of our ancestors."

3 The king fell into a rage, and gave orders to have pans and caldrons heated. 4 These were heated immediately, and he commanded that the tongue of their spokesman be cut out and that they scalp him and cut off his hands and feet, while the rest of the brothers and the mother looked on. 5 When he was utterly helpless, the king^d ordered them to take him to the fire, still breathing, and to fry him in a pan. The smoke from the pan spread widely, but the brothers^e and their mother encouraged one another to die nobly, saying, 6 "The Lord God is watching over us and in truth has compassion on us, as Moses declared in his song that bore witness against the people to their faces, when he said, 'And he will have compassion on his servants.' "^{f}

7 After the first brother had died in this way, they brought forward the second for their sport. They tore off the skin of his head with the hair, and asked him, "Will you eat rather than have your body punished limb by limb?" 8 He replied in the language of his ancestors and said to them, "No." Therefore he in turn underwent tortures as the first brother had done. 9 And when he was at his last breath, he said, "You accursed wretch, you dismiss us from this present life, but the King of the universe will raise us up to an everlasting renewal of life, because we have died for his laws."

10 After him, the third was the victim of their sport. When it was demanded, he quickly put out his tongue and courageously stretched forth his hands, 11 and said nobly, "I got these from Heaven, and because of his laws I disdain them, and from him I hope to get them back again." 12 As a result the king himself and those with him were astonished at the young man's spirit, for he regarded his sufferings as nothing.

13 After he too had died, they maltreated and tortured the fourth in the same way. 14 When he was near death, he said, "One cannot but choose to die at the hands of mortals and to cherish the hope God gives of being raised again by him. But for you there will be no resurrection to life!"

15 Next they brought forward the fifth and maltreated him. 16 But he looked at the king,^{g} and said, "Because you have authority among mortals, though you also are mortal, you do what you please. But do not think that God has forsaken our people. 17 Keep on, and see how his mighty power will torture you and your descendants!"

18 After him they brought forward the sixth. And when he was about to die, he said, "Do not deceive yourself in vain. For we are suffering these things on our own account, because of our sins against our own God. Therefore^h astounding things have happened. 19 But do not think that you will go unpunished for having tried to fight against God!"

20 The mother was especially admirable and worthy of honorable memory. Although she saw her seven sons perish within a single day, she bore it with good courage because of her hope in the Lord. 21 She encouraged each of them in the language of their ancestors. Filled with a noble spirit, she reinforced her woman's reasoning with a man's courage, and said to them, 22 "I do not know how you came into being in my womb. It was not I who gave you life and breath, nor I who set in order the elements within each of you. 23 Therefore the Creator of the world, who shaped the

REVISED ENGLISH BIBLE

7 Another incident concerned the arrest of seven brothers along with their mother. They were being tortured by the king with whips and thongs to force them to eat pork, contrary to the law. 2 But one of them, speaking for all, said: 'What do you expect to learn by interrogating us? Rather than break our ancestral laws we are prepared to die.' 3 In fury the king ordered great pans and cauldrons to be heated. 4 This was attended to without delay; meanwhile he gave orders that the spokesman's tongue should be cut out and that he should be scalped and mutilated before the eyes of his mother and six brothers. 5 A wreck of a man, but still breathing, he was taken at the king's direction to the fire and roasted in one of the pans. As the smoke from it streamed out, the mother and her sons encouraged each other to die nobly. 6 'The Lord God is looking on,' they said, 'and we may be sure he has compassion on us. Did not Moses say to Israel in the song plainly denouncing apostasy, "He will have compassion on his servants"?'

7 After the first brother had died in this way, the second was subjected to the same indignities. The skin and hair of his head were torn off, and he was asked: 'Will you eat, or must we tear you limb from limb?' 8 'Eat? Never!' he replied in his native language, and so he in turn underwent torture like the first. 9 With his final breath he said: 'Fiend though you are, you are setting us free from this present life, and the King of the universe will raise us up to a life everlastingly made new, since it is for his laws that we are dying.'

10 After him the third was tortured. When the question was put to him, he at once showed his tongue, courageously held out his hands, 11 and spoke nobly: 'The God of heaven gave these to me, but his laws mean far more to me than they do, and it is from him that I trust to receive them again.' 12 Both the king himself and those with him were astounded at the young man's spirit and his utter disregard for suffering.

13 When he too was dead, they tortured the fourth in the same cruel manner. 14 At the point of death, he uttered these words: 'Better to be killed by men and to cherish God's promise to raise us again! But for you there will be no resurrection.'

15 Next the fifth was dragged forward for torture. 16 Looking at the king, he said: 'Mortal as you are, you have authority among human beings and can do as you please. But do not imagine that God has abandoned our nation. 17 Wait, and you will see how his mighty power will torment you and your descendants!'

18 After him the sixth was brought and he, with his dying breath, said: 'Do not delude yourself: it is through our own fault that we suffer these things; we have sinned against our God and brought these appalling events on ourselves. 19 But do not suppose you yourself will escape the consequences of trying to contend with God.'

20 The mother was the most remarkable of all, and she deserves to be remembered with special honour. She watched her seven sons perish within the space of a single day, yet she bore it bravely, for she trusted in the Lord. 21 She encouraged each in turn in her native language; filled with noble resolution, her woman's thoughts fired by a manly spirit, she said to them: 22 'You appeared in my womb, I know not how; it was not I who gave you life and breath, not I who set in order the elements of your being.

---

^{d} Gk he ^{e} Gk they ^{f} Gk slaves ^{g} Gk at him ^{h} Lat: Other ancient authorities lack *Therefore*

7 It also happened that seven brothers with their mother were arrested and tortured with whips and scourges by the king, to force them to eat pork in violation of God's law. 2 One of the brothers, speaking for the others, said: "What do you expect to achieve by questioning us? We are ready to die rather than transgress the laws of our ancestors." 3 At that the king, in a fury, gave orders to have pans and caldrons heated. 4 While they were being quickly heated, he commanded his executioners to cut out the tongue of the one who had spoken for the others, to scalp him and cut off his hands and feet, while the rest of his brothers and his mother looked on. 5 When he was completely maimed but still breathing, the king ordered them to carry him to the fire and fry him. As a cloud of smoke spread from the pan, the brothers and their mother encouraged one another to die bravely, saying such words as these: 6 "The LORD God is looking on, and he truly has compassion on us, as Moses declared in his canticle, when he protested openly with the words, 'And he will have pity on his servants.' "

7 When the first brother had died in this manner, they brought the second to be made sport of. After tearing off the skin and hair of his head, they asked him, "Will you eat the pork rather than have your body tortured limb by limb?" 8 Answering in the language of his forefathers, he said, "Never!" So he too in turn suffered the same tortures as the first. 9 At the point of death he said: "You accursed fiend, you are depriving us of this present life, but the King of the world will raise us up to live again forever. It is for his laws that we are dying."

10 After him the third suffered their cruel sport. He put out his tongue at once when told to do so, and bravely held out his hands, 11 as he spoke these noble words: "It was from Heaven that I received these; for the sake of his laws I disdain them; from him I hope to receive them again." 12 Even the king and his attendants marveled at the young man's courage, because he regarded his sufferings as nothing.

13 After he had died, they tortured and maltreated the fourth brother in the same way. 14 When he was near death, he said, "It is my choice to die at the hands of men with the God-given hope of being restored to life by him; but for you, there will be no resurrection to life."

15 They next brought forward the fifth brother and maltreated him. 16 Looking at the king, he said: "Since you have power among men, mortal though you are, do what you please. But do not think that our nation is forsaken by God. 17 Only wait, and you will see how his great power will torment you and your descendants."

18 After him they brought the sixth brother. When he was about to die, he said: "Have no vain illusions. We suffer these things on our own account, because we have sinned against our God; that is why such astonishing things have happened to us. 19 Do not think, then, that you will go unpunished for having dared to fight against God."

20 Most admirable and worthy of everlasting remembrance was the mother, who saw her seven sons perish in a single day, yet bore it courageously because of her hope in the LORD. 21 Filled with a noble spirit that stirred her womanly heart with manly courage, she exhorted each of them in the language of their forefathers with these words: 22 "I do not know how you came into existence in my womb; it was not I who gave you the breath of life, nor was it I who set in order the elements of which each of you is composed.

7 It also happened that seven brothers were arrested with their mother. The king tried to force them to taste some pork, which the Law forbids, by torturing them with whips and scourges. 2 One of them, acting as spokesman for the others, said, 'What are you trying to find out from us? We are prepared to die rather than break the laws of our ancestors.' 3 The king, in a fury, ordered pans and cauldrons to be heated over a fire. 4 As soon as these were red-hot, he commanded that their spokesman should have his tongue cut out, his head scalped and his extremities cut off, while the other brothers and his mother looked on. 5 When he had been rendered completely helpless, the king gave orders for him to be brought, still breathing, to the fire and fried alive in a pan. As the smoke from the pan drifted about, his mother and the rest encouraged one another to die nobly, with such words as these, 6 'The Lord God is watching and certainly feels sorry for us, as Moses declared in his song, which clearly states that "he will take pity on his servants." '

7 When the first had left the world in this way, they brought the second forward to be tortured. After stripping the skin from his head, hair and all, they asked him, 'Will you eat some pork, before your body is tortured limb by limb?' 8 Replying in his ancestral tongue, he said, 'No!' So he too was put to the torture in his turn. 9 With his last breath he exclaimed, 'Cruel brute, you may discharge us from this present life, but the King of the world will raise us up, since we die for his laws, to live again for ever.'

10 After him, they tortured the third, who on being asked for his tongue promptly thrust it out and boldly held out his hands, 11 courageously saying, 'Heaven gave me these limbs; for the sake of his laws I have no concern for them; from him I hope to receive them again.' 12 The king and his attendants were astounded at the young man's courage and his utter indifference to suffering.

13 When this one was dead they subjected the fourth to the same torments and tortures. 14 When he neared his end he cried, 'Ours is the better choice, to meet death at men's hands, yet relying on God's promise that we shall be raised up by him; whereas for you there can be no resurrection to new life.'

15 Next they brought forward the fifth and began torturing him. 16 But he looked at the king and said, 'You have power over human beings, mortal as you are, and can act as you please. But do not think that our race has been deserted by God. 17 Only wait, and you will see in your turn how his mighty power will torment you and your descendants.'

18 After him, they led out the sixth, and his dying words were these, 'Do not delude yourself: we are suffering like this through our own fault, having sinned against our own God; hence, appalling things have befallen us— 19 but do not think you yourself will go unpunished for attempting to make war on God.'

20 But the mother was especially admirable and worthy of honourable remembrance, for she watched the death of seven sons in the course of a single day, and bravely endured it because of her hopes in the Lord. 21 Indeed she encouraged each of them in their ancestral tongue; filled with noble conviction, she reinforced her womanly argument with manly courage, saying to them, 22 'I do not know how you appeared in my womb; it was not I who endowed you with breath and life, I had not the shaping of your every part. 23 And hence, the Creator of the world, who made

beginning of humankind and devised the origin of all things, will in his mercy give life and breath back to you again, since you now forget yourselves for the sake of his laws."

24 Antiochus felt that he was being treated with contempt, and he was suspicious of her reproachful tone. The youngest brother being still alive, Antiochus[i] not only appealed to him in words, but promised with oaths that he would make him rich and enviable if he would turn from the ways of his ancestors, and that he would take him for his Friend and entrust him with public affairs. 25 Since the young man would not listen to him at all, the king called the mother to him and urged her to advise the youth to save himself. 26 After much urging on his part, she undertook to persuade her son. 27 But, leaning close to him, she spoke in their native language as follows, deriding the cruel tyrant: "My son, have pity on me. I carried you nine months in my womb, and nursed you for three years, and have reared you and brought you up to this point in your life, and have taken care of you.[j] 28 I beg you, my child, to look at the heaven and the earth and see everything that is in them, and recognize that God did not make them out of things that existed.[k] And in the same way the human race came into being. 29 Do not fear this butcher, but prove worthy of your brothers. Accept death, so that in God's mercy I may get you back again along with your brothers."

30 While she was still speaking, the young man said, "What are you[l] waiting for? I will not obey the king's command, but I obey the command of the law that was given to our ancestors through Moses. 31 But you,[m] who have contrived all sorts of evil against the Hebrews, will certainly not escape the hands of God. 32 For we are suffering because of our own sins. 33 And if our living Lord is angry for a little while, to rebuke and discipline us, he will again be reconciled with his own servants.[n] 34 But you, unholy wretch, you most defiled of all mortals, do not be elated in vain and puffed up by uncertain hopes, when you raise your hand against the children of heaven. 35 You have not yet escaped the judgment of the almighty, all-seeing God. 36 For our brothers after enduring a brief suffering have drunk[o] of ever-flowing life, under God's covenant; but you, by the judgment of God, will receive just punishment for your arrogance. 37 I, like my brothers, give up body and life for the laws of our ancestors, appealing to God to show mercy soon to our nation and by trials and plagues to make you confess that he alone is God, 38 and through me and my brothers to bring to an end the wrath of the Almighty that has justly fallen on our whole nation."

39 The king fell into a rage, and handled him worse than the others, being exasperated at his scorn. 40 So he died in his integrity, putting his whole trust in the Lord.

41 Last of all, the mother died, after her sons.

42 Let this be enough, then, about the eating of sacrifices and the extreme tortures.

8 Meanwhile Judas, who was also called Maccabeus, and his companions secretly entered the villages and summoned their kindred and enlisted those who had continued in the Jewish faith, and so they gathered about six thousand. 2 They implored the Lord to look upon the people who were oppressed by all; and to have pity on the temple that had been profaned by the godless; 3 to have mercy on the city that was being destroyed and about to be leveled to the ground; to hearken to the blood that cried out to him; 4 to

23 The Creator of the universe, who designed the beginning of mankind and devised the origin of all, will in his mercy give you back again breath and life, since now you put his laws above every thought of self.'

24 Antiochus felt that he was being treated with contempt and suspected an insult in her words. As the youngest brother was still left, the king, not content with appealing to him, even assured him on oath that once he abandoned his ancestral customs he would make him rich and enviable by enrolling him as a king's Friend and entrusting him with high office. 25 Since the youth paid no regard whatsoever, the king summoned the mother and urged her to advise her boy to save his life. 26 After much urging from the king, she agreed to persuade her son. 27 She leant towards him and, flouting the cruel tyrant, said in their native language: 'Son, take pity on me, who carried you nine months in the womb, nursed you for three years, reared you and brought you up to your present age. 28 I implore you, my child, to look at the heavens and the earth; consider all that is in them, and realize that God did not create them from what already existed and that a human being comes into existence in the same way. 29 Do not be afraid of this butcher; accept death willingly and prove yourself worthy of your brothers, so that by God's mercy I may receive back both you and them together.'

30 She had barely finished when the young man spoke out: 'What are you all waiting for? I will not submit to the king's command; I obey the command of the law given through Moses to our forefathers. 31 And you, King Antiochus, who have devised all manner of atrocities for the Hebrews, you will not escape God's hand. 32 It is for our own sins that we are suffering, 33 and, though to correct and discipline us our living Lord is angry for a brief time, yet he will be reconciled with his servants. 34 But you, impious creature, most villainous of the human race, do not let vain hopes buoy you up or empty delusions carry you away when you lay hands on Heaven's servants. 35 You are not yet safe from the judgement of the omnipotent, all-seeing God. 36 My brothers, after a short period of pain, have under God's covenant drunk of the waters of everlasting life; but you by God's verdict will pay the just penalty of your brutal insolence. 37 I, like my brothers, surrender my body and my life for our ancestral laws. I appeal to God to show favour speedily to his people and by whips and scourges to bring you to admit that he alone is God. 38 May the Almighty's anger, which has justly fallen on all our race, end with me and my brothers!'

39 Roused by this defiance, the king in his fury used him worse than the others, 40 and the young man, putting his whole trust in the Lord, died without having incurred defilement.

41 Last of all, after her sons, the mother died.

42 This then must conclude our account of the eating of the entrails and the monstrous tortures.

8 MEANWHILE Judas, who was called Maccabaeus, and his companions were making their way into the villages unobserved, summoning their kinsmen to their side and recruiting others who had remained faithful to the Jewish religion, until they had collected up to six thousand men. 2 They appealed to the Lord to look with compassion on his people whom all were trampling underfoot, to take pity on the temple now profaned by apostates, 3 and to have mercy on Jerusalem, which was being destroyed and would soon be levelled to the ground. They prayed him also to give ear to the blood that cried to him for vengeance, 4 to

---

[i] Gk he　[j] Or have borne the burden of your education　[k] Or God made them out of things that did not exist　[l] The Gk here for you is plural　[m] The Gk here for you is singular　[n] Gk slaves　[o] Cn: Gk fallen

7:36 drunk: prob. rdg; Gk fallen.

23 Therefore, since it is the Creator of the universe who shapes each man's beginning, as he brings about the origin of everything, he, in his mercy, will give you back both breath and life, because you now disregard yourselves for the sake of his law."

24 Antiochus, suspecting insult in her words, thought he was being ridiculed. As the youngest brother was still alive, the king appealed to him, not with mere words, but with promises on oath, to make him rich and happy if he would abandon his ancestral customs: he would make him his Friend and entrust him with high office. 25 When the youth paid no attention to him at all, the king appealed to the mother, urging her to advise her boy to save his life. 26 After he had urged her for a long time, she went through the motions of persuading her son. 27 In derision of the cruel tyrant, she leaned over close to her son and said in their native language: "Son, have pity on me, who carried you in my womb for nine months, nursed you for three years, brought you up, educated and supported you to your present age. 28 I beg you, child, to look at the heavens and the earth and see all that is in them; then you will know that God did not make them out of existing things; and in the same way the human race came into existence. 29 Do not be afraid of this executioner, but be worthy of your brothers and accept death, so that in the time of mercy I may receive you again with them."

30 She had scarcely finished speaking when the youth said: "What are you waiting for? I will not obey the king's command. I obey the command of the law given to our forefathers through Moses. 31 But you, who have contrived every kind of affliction for the Hebrews, will not escape the hands of God. 32 We, indeed, are suffering because of our sins. 33 Though our living LORD treats us harshly for a little while to correct us with chastisements, he will again be reconciled with his servants. 34 But you, wretch, vilest of all men! do not, in your insolence, concern yourself with unfounded hopes, as you raise your hand against the children of Heaven. 35 You have not yet escaped the judgment of the almighty and all-seeing God. 36 My brothers, after enduring brief pain, have drunk of never-failing life, under God's covenant, but you, by the judgment of God, shall receive just punishments for your arrogance. 37 Like my brothers, I offer up my body and my life for our ancestral laws, imploring God to show mercy soon to our nation, and by afflictions and blows to make you confess that he alone is God. 38 Through me and my brothers, may there be an end to the wrath of the Almighty that has justly fallen on our whole nation." 39 At that, the king became enraged and treated him even worse than the others, since he bitterly resented the boy's contempt. 40 Thus he too died undefiled, putting all his trust in the LORD. 41 The mother was last to die, after her sons.

42 Enough has been said about the sacrificial meals and the excessive cruelties.

8 Judas Maccabeus and his companions entered the villages secretly, summoned their kinsmen, and by also enlisting others who remained faithful to Judaism, assembled about six thousand men. 2 They implored the LORD to look kindly upon his people, who were being oppressed on all sides; to have pity on the temple, which was profaned by godless men; 3 to have mercy on the city, which was being destroyed and about to be leveled to the ground; to hearken to the blood that cried out to him; 4 to remember the criminal

everyone and ordained the origin of all things, will in his mercy give you back breath and life, since for the sake of his laws you have no concern for yourselves.'

24 Antiochus thought he was being ridiculed, suspecting insult in the tone of her voice; and as the youngest was still alive he appealed to him not with mere words but with promises on oath to make him both rich and happy if he would abandon the traditions of his ancestors; he would make him his Friend and entrust him with public office. 25 The young man took no notice at all, and so the king then appealed to the mother, urging her to advise the youth to save his life. 26 After a great deal of urging on his part she agreed to try persuasion on her son. 27 Bending over him, she fooled the cruel tyrant with these words, uttered in their ancestral tongue, 'My son, have pity on me; I carried you nine months in my womb and suckled you three years, fed you and reared you to the age you are now, and provided for you. 28 I implore you, my child, look at the earth and sky and everything in them, and consider how God made them out of what did not exist, and that human beings come into being in the same way. 29 Do not fear this executioner, but prove yourself worthy of your brothers and accept death, so that I may receive you back with them in the day of mercy.'

30 She had hardly finished, when the young man said, 'What are you all waiting for? I will not comply with the king's ordinance; I obey the ordinance of the Law given to our ancestors through Moses. 31 As for you, who have contrived every kind of evil against the Hebrews, you will certainly not escape the hands of God. 32 We are suffering for our own sins; 33 and if, to punish and discipline us, our living Lord is briefly angry with us, he will be reconciled with us in due course. 34 But you, unholy wretch and wickedest of villains, what cause have you for pride, nourishing vain hopes and raising your hand against his servants? — 35 for you have not yet escaped the judgement of God the almighty, the all-seeing. 36 Our brothers, having endured brief pain, for the sake of ever-flowing life have died for the covenant of God, while you, by God's judgement, will have to pay the just penalty for your arrogance. 37 I too, like my brothers, surrender my body and life for the laws of my ancestors, begging God quickly to take pity on our nation, and by trials and afflictions to bring you to confess that he alone is God, 38 so that with my brothers and myself there may be an end to the wrath of the Almighty, rightly let loose on our whole nation.'

39 The king fell into a rage and treated this one more cruelly than the others, for he was himself smarting from the young man's scorn. 40 And so the last brother met his end undefiled and with perfect trust in the Lord. 41 The mother was the last to die, after her sons.

42 But let this be sufficient account of the ritual meals and monstrous tortures.

8 Judas, otherwise known as Maccabaeus, and his companions made their way secretly among the villages, rallying their fellow-countrymen; they recruited those who remained loyal to Judaism and assembled about six thousand. 2 They called on the Lord to have regard for the people oppressed on all sides, to take pity on the Temple profaned by the godless, 3 to have mercy on the city now being destroyed and levelled to the ground, to hear the blood of the victims that cried aloud to him, 4 to remember too the crimi-

remember also the lawless destruction of the innocent babies and the blasphemies committed against his name; and to show his hatred of evil.

5 As soon as Maccabeus got his army organized, the Gentiles could not withstand him, for the wrath of the Lord had turned to mercy. 6 Coming without warning, he would set fire to towns and villages. He captured strategic positions and put to flight not a few of the enemy. 7 He found the nights most advantageous for such attacks. And talk of his valor spread everywhere.

8 When Philip saw that the man was gaining ground little by little, and that he was pushing ahead with more frequent successes, he wrote to Ptolemy, the governor of Coelesyria and Phoenicia, to come to the aid of the king's government. 9 Then Ptolemy*p* promptly appointed Nicanor son of Patroclus, one of the king's chief*q* Friends, and sent him, in command of no fewer than twenty thousand Gentiles of all nations, to wipe out the whole race of Judea. He associated with him Gorgias, a general and a man of experience in military service. 10 Nicanor determined to make up for the king the tribute due to the Romans, two thousand talents, by selling the captured Jews into slavery. 11 So he immediately sent to the towns on the seacoast, inviting them to buy Jewish slaves and promising to hand over ninety slaves for a talent, not expecting the judgment from the Almighty that was about to overtake him.

12 Word came to Judas concerning Nicanor's invasion; and when he told his companions of the arrival of the army, 13 those who were cowardly and distrustful of God's justice ran off and got away. 14 Others sold all their remaining property, and at the same time implored the Lord to rescue those who had been sold by the ungodly Nicanor before he ever met them, 15 if not for their own sake, then for the sake of the covenants made with their ancestors, and because he had called them by his holy and glorious name. 16 But Maccabeus gathered his forces together, to the number six thousand, and exhorted them not to be frightened by the enemy and not to fear the great multitude of Gentiles who were wickedly coming against them, but to fight nobly, 17 keeping before their eyes the lawless outrage that the Gentiles*r* had committed against the holy place, and the torture of the derided city, and besides, the overthrow of their ancestral way of life. 18 "For they trust to arms and acts of daring," he said, "but we trust in the Almighty God, who is able with a single nod to strike down those who are coming against us, and even, if necessary, the whole world."

19 Moreover, he told them of the occasions when help came to their ancestors; how, in the time of Sennacherib, when one hundred eighty-five thousand perished, 20 and the time of the battle against the Galatians that took place in Babylonia, when eight thousand Jews*s* fought along with four thousand Macedonians; yet when the Macedonians were hard pressed, the eight thousand, by the help that came to them from heaven, destroyed one hundred twenty thousand Galatians*t* and took a great amount of booty.

21 With these words he filled them with courage and made them ready to die for their laws and their country; then he divided his army into four parts. 22 He appointed his brothers also, Simon and Joseph and Jonathan, each to command a division, putting fifteen hundred men under each. 23 Besides, he appointed Eleazar to read aloud*u* from the holy book, and gave the watchword, "The help of God"; then, leading the first division himself, he joined battle with Nicanor.

keep in mind the infamous massacre of innocent children and the blasphemous deeds against his name, and to show his hatred of wickedness.

5 Once his band of partisans was organized, the Gentiles found Maccabaeus invincible, now that the Lord's anger had changed to mercy. 6 Maccabaeus came on towns and villages without warning and burnt them down; he recaptured strategic positions, and inflicted many reverses on the enemy, 7 choosing the night-time as being especially favourable for these attacks. Everywhere there was talk of his heroism.

8 When Philip realized that the gains made by Judas, though small, were occurring with increasing frequency, he wrote to Ptolemaeus, the governor of Coele-Syria and Phoenicia, asking for help in protecting the royal interests. 9 Ptolemaeus at once appointed Nicanor son of Patroclus, a member of the highest order of king's Friends, and sent him at the head of no fewer than twenty thousand troops of various nationalities to exterminate the whole population of Judaea; with him Ptolemaeus associated Gorgias, a general of wide military experience. 10 Nicanor purposed, by the sale of the Jews he would take prisoner, to pay off the two thousand talents due from the king as tribute to the Romans; 11 and he immediately made an offer of Jewish slaves to the coastal towns, undertaking to deliver them at the rate of ninety to the talent. But he had not reckoned with the punishment soon to overtake him from the Almighty.

12 When word of Nicanor's advance reached Judas, and his men were informed that the enemy was at hand, 13 the faint-hearted who doubted God's justice deserted and fled. 14 But the rest, disposing of their remaining possessions, joined in prayer to the Lord for deliverance from the godless Nicanor, who had put them up for sale even before any fighting took place; 15 and, if they could not ask this for their own merits, they did so on the ground of the covenants God had made with their forefathers, and because they bore his holy and majestic name.

16 Maccabaeus assembled his followers, six thousand in number, and urged them not to give way to panic in the face of the enemy nor to be afraid of the great horde of Gentiles coming against them without just cause. They should fight nobly, 17 keeping before their eyes the outrages committed by the Gentiles against the holy temple, the callous indignities inflicted on Jerusalem, and, moreover, the suppression of the traditional Jewish institutions. 18 'They rely on weapons and deeds of daring,' he said, 'but we put our trust in Almighty God, who is able with a nod to overthrow our present assailants and, if need be, the whole world.' 19 He went on to recount to them the occasions when God had come to the help of their ancestors: how, in Sennacherib's time, one hundred and eighty-five thousand of the enemy were destroyed, 20 and how, on the occasion of the battle in Babylonia against the Galatians, all the Jews engaged in the combat had numbered no more than eight thousand, with four thousand Macedonians yet, when the Macedonians were hard pressed, the eight thousand through Heaven's aid had destroyed one hundred and twenty thousand and taken much spoil.

21 His words put heart into his men and made them ready to die for their laws and their country. He divided the army into four, 22 putting each of his brothers, Simon, Josephus, and Jonathan, in command of a division of fifteen hundred men. 23 Besides this, Judas appointed Eleazar to read aloud from the holy book; then, giving the signal for battle with the cry 'God is our help' and taking command of the leading detachment, he joined battle with Nicanor. 24 With the Al-

---

p Gk he   *q* Gk one of the first   *r* Gk they   *s* Gk lacks Jews
t Gk lacks Galatians   *u* Meaning of Gk uncertain

8:23 **Besides ... book:** *prob. rdg; Gk obscure.*

slaughter of innocent children and the blasphemies uttered against his name; and to manifest his hatred of evil. 5 Once Maccabeus got his men organized, the Gentiles could not withstand him, for the LORD's wrath had now changed to mercy. 6 Coming unexpectedly upon towns and villages, he would set them on fire. He captured strategic positions, and put to flight a large number of the enemy. 7 He preferred the nights as being especially helpful for such attacks. Soon the fame of his valor spread everywhere.

8 When Philip saw that Judas was gaining ground little by little and that his successful advances were becoming more frequent, he wrote to Ptolemy, governor of Coelesyria and Phoenicia, to come to the aid of the king's government. 9 Ptolemy promptly selected Nicanor, son of Patroclus, one of the Chief Friends, and sent him at the head of at least twenty thousand armed men of various nations to wipe out the entire Jewish race. With him he associated Gorgias, a professional military commander, well-versed in the art of war. 10 Nicanor planned to raise the two thousand talents of tribute owed by the king to the Romans by selling captured Jews into slavery. 11 So he immediately sent word to the coastal cities, inviting them to buy Jewish slaves and promising to deliver ninety slaves for a talent—little did he dream of the punishment that was to fall upon him from the Almighty.

12 When Judas learned of Nicanor's advance and informed his companions about the approach of the army, 13 the cowardly and those who lacked faith in God's justice deserted and got away. 14 But the others sold everything they had left, and at the same time besought the LORD to deliver those whom the ungodly Nicanor had sold before even meeting them. 15 They begged the LORD to do this, if not for their sake, at least for the sake of the covenants made with their forefathers, and because they themselves bore his holy, glorious name. 16 Maccabeus assembled his men, six thousand strong, and exhorted them not to be panicstricken before the enemy, nor to fear the large number of the Gentiles attacking them unjustly, but to fight courageously, 17 keeping before their eyes the lawless outrage perpetrated by the Gentiles against the holy Place and the affliction of the humiliated city, as well as the subversion of their ancestral way of life. 18 "They trust in weapons and acts of daring," he said, "but we trust in almighty God, who can by a mere nod destroy not only those who attack us, but the whole world." 19 He went on to tell them of the times when help had been given their ancestors: both the time of Sennacherib, when a hundred and eighty-five thousand of his men were destroyed, 20 and the time of the battle in Babylonia against the Galatians, when only eight thousand Jews fought along with four thousand Macedonians; yet when the Macedonians were hard pressed, the eight thousand routed one hundred and twenty thousand and took a great quantity of booty, because of the help they received from Heaven. 21 With such words he encouraged them and made them ready to die for their laws and their country.

Then Judas divided his army into four, 22 placing his brothers, Simon, Joseph, and Jonathan, each over a division, assigning to each fifteen hundred men. 23 (There was also Eleazar.) After reading to them from the holy book and giving them the watchword, "The Help of God," he himself took charge of the first division and joined in battle with Nicanor. 24 With the Almighty as their ally, they killed

nal slaughter of innocent babies and to avenge the blasphemies perpetrated against his name. 5 As soon as Maccabaeus had an organised force, he at once proved invincible to the foreigners, the Lord's anger having turned into compassion. 6 Making surprise attacks on towns and villages, he fired them; he captured favourable positions and inflicted very heavy losses on the enemy, 7 generally availing himself of the cover of night for such enterprises. The fame of his valour spread far and wide.

8 g When Philip saw Judas was making steady progress and winning more and more frequent successes, he wrote to Ptolemy, the general officer commanding Coele-Syria and Phoenicia, asking for reinforcements in the royal interest. 9 Ptolemy chose Nicanor son of Patroclus, one of the king's First Friends, and sent him without delay at the head of an international force of at least twenty thousand men to exterminate the entire Jewish race. As his associate he appointed Gorgias, a professional general of wide military experience. 10 Nicanor for his part proposed, by the sale of Jewish prisoners of war, to raise the two thousand talents of tribute money owed by the king to the Romans. 11 He lost no time in sending the seaboard towns an invitation to come and buy Jewish manpower, promising delivery of ninety head for one talent; but he did not reckon on the judgement from the Almighty that was soon to overtake him.

12 When news reached Judas of Nicanor's advance, he warned his men of the enemy's approach, 13 whereupon the cowardly ones and those who lacked confidence in the justice of God took to their heels and ran away. 14 The rest sold all their remaining possessions, at the same time praying the Lord to deliver them from the godless Nicanor, who had sold them even in advance of any encounter— 15 if not for their own sakes, then at least out of consideration for the covenants made with their ancestors, and because they themselves bore his sacred and majestic name. 16 Maccabaeus marshalled his men, who numbered about six thousand, and exhorted them not to be dismayed at the enemy or discouraged at the vast horde of gentiles wickedly advancing against them, but to fight bravely, 17 keeping before their eyes the outrage committed by them against the holy place and the infamous and scornful treatment inflicted on the city, not to mention the destruction of their traditional way of life. 18 'They may put their trust in their weapons and their exploits,' he said, 'but our confidence is in almighty God, who is able with a single nod to overthrow both those marching on us and the whole world with them.' 19 He reminded them of the occasions on which their ancestors had received help: that time when, under Sennacherib, a hundred and eighty-five thousand men had perished;[h] 20 that time in Babylonia when in the battle with the Galatians the Jewish combatants numbered only eight thousand, with four thousand Macedonians, yet when the Macedonians were hard pressed, the eight thousand had destroyed a hundred and twenty thousand, thanks to the help they had received from Heaven, and had taken great booty as a result.

21 Having so roused their courage by these words that they were ready to die for the laws and their country, he then divided his army into four, 22 putting his brothers, Simon, Joseph and Jonathan in command of one division each, and assigning them fifteen hundred men apiece. 23 Next, he ordered Esdrias to read the Holy Book aloud and gave them their watchword 'Help from God'. Then, putting himself at the head of the first division, he attacked Nicanor. 24 With the Almighty for their ally they slaughtered

g 8 8:8seq. // 1 M 3:38—4:25.   h 8 2 K 19:35. The next incident is non-biblical.

24 With the Almighty as their ally, they killed more than nine thousand of the enemy, and wounded and disabled most of Nicanor's army, and forced them all to flee. 25 They captured the money of those who had come to buy them as slaves. After pursuing them for some distance, they were obliged to return because the hour was late. 26 It was the day before the sabbath, and for that reason they did not continue their pursuit. 27 When they had collected the arms of the enemy and stripped them of their spoils, they kept the sabbath, giving great praise and thanks to the Lord, who had preserved them for that day and allotted it to them as the beginning of mercy. 28 After the sabbath they gave some of the spoils to those who had been tortured and to the widows and orphans, and distributed the rest among themselves and their children. 29 When they had done this, they made common supplication and implored the merciful Lord to be wholly reconciled with his servants. *v*

30 In encounters with the forces of Timothy and Bacchides they killed more than twenty thousand of them and got possession of some exceedingly high strongholds, and they divided a very large amount of plunder, giving to those who had been tortured and to the orphans and widows, and also to the aged, shares equal to their own. 31 They collected the arms of the enemy, *w* and carefully stored all of them in strategic places; the rest of the spoils they carried to Jerusalem. 32 They killed the commander of Timothy's forces, a most wicked man, and one who had greatly troubled the Jews. 33 While they were celebrating the victory in the city of their ancestors, they burned those who had set fire to the sacred gates, Callisthenes and some others, who had fled into one little house; so these received the proper reward for their impiety. *x*

34 The thrice-accursed Nicanor, who had brought the thousand merchants to buy the Jews, 35 having been humbled with the help of the Lord by opponents whom he regarded as of the least account, took off his splendid uniform and made his way alone like a runaway slave across the country until he reached Antioch, having succeeded chiefly in the destruction of his own army! 36 So he who had undertaken to secure tribute for the Romans by the capture of the people of Jerusalem proclaimed that the Jews had a Defender, and that therefore the Jews were invulnerable, because they followed the laws ordained by him.

9 About that time, as it happened, Antiochus had retreated in disorder from the region of Persia. 2 He had entered the city called Persepolis and attempted to rob the temples and control the city. Therefore the people rushed to the rescue with arms, and Antiochus and his army were defeated, *y* with the result that Antiochus was put to flight by the inhabitants and beat a shameful retreat. 3 While he was in Ecbatana, news came to him of what had happened to Nicanor and the forces of Timothy. 4 Transported with rage, he conceived the idea of turning upon the Jews the injury done by those who had put him to flight; so he ordered his charioteer to drive without stopping until he completed the journey. But the judgment of heaven rode with him! For in his arrogance he said, "When I get there I will make Jerusalem a cemetery of Jews."

5 But the all-seeing Lord, the God of Israel, struck him with an incurable and invisible blow. As soon as he stopped speaking he was seized with a pain in his bowels, for which there was no relief, and with sharp internal tortures — 6 and that very justly, for he had tortured the bowels of others with many and strange inflictions. 7 Yet he did not in any

mighty fighting on their side they slaughtered over nine thousand of the enemy, wounded and disabled the greater part of Nicanor's forces, and routed them completely. 25 They also seized the money of those who had come to buy them as slaves. After chasing the enemy a considerable way, they were forced to break off because of the lateness of the hour; 26 it was the day before the sabbath, and for that reason they did not continue the pursuit. 27 They collected the enemy's weapons and stripped the dead, then turned to keep the sabbath, offering thanks and praises loud and long to the Lord who had kept the first drops of his mercy to shed on them that day. 28 When the sabbath was over, they distributed some of the spoils among the victims of persecution and among the widows and orphans; the remainder they divided among themselves and their children. 29 This done, all together made supplication to the merciful Lord, praying him to be fully reconciled with his servants.

30 The Jews now engaged the forces of Timotheus and Bacchides, killed over twenty thousand of them, and gained firm control of some of the high strongholds. They divided the immense booty, allocating to the victims of persecution, to the orphans and widows, as well as to the old, shares equal to their own. 31 All the enemy's weapons were carefully collected and stored at strategic points; the remainder of the spoils they brought into Jerusalem. 32 The officer commanding the bodyguard of Timotheus was put to death; he was an utterly godless man who had caused the Jews great suffering. 33 During the victory celebrations in their ancestral capital, they burnt alive the men who had set fire to the sacred gates, including Callisthenes, who had taken refuge in some small house; so he received the due reward of his impiety.

34 Thus Nicanor, that double-dyed villain who had brought along the thousand traders to buy the Jewish captives, 35 was with the Lord's help humiliated by the very people whom he had dismissed as of no consequence. He threw off his magnificent garment, and all alone made his escape across country like a runaway slave; he was, indeed, exceedingly fortunate to reach Antioch after the destruction of his army. 36 He who had undertaken to secure tribute for the Romans by taking prisoner the inhabitants of Jerusalem now proclaimed to the world that the Jews had a champion and were invulnerable, because they kept the laws this champion had given them.

9 It so happened that about this time Antiochus had returned in disorder from Persia. 2 He had entered the city called Persepolis and attempted to plunder its temples and gain control of the place. But the populace rose and resorted to arms, with the result that Antiochus was defeated by the inhabitants and forced into a humiliating withdrawal. 3 When he was near Ecbatana, a report reached him of what had befallen Nicanor and the forces of Timotheus, 4 and this so roused his anger that he proposed to make the Jews suffer for the injury inflicted by those who had routed him; to this end he ordered his charioteer not to stop until he reached his destination.

But riding with him was the divine judgement! In his arrogance he said: 'Once I reach Jerusalem, I will make it one big Jewish graveyard.' 5 But the all-seeing Lord, the God of Israel, dealt him a fatal, invisible blow. No sooner had he uttered the words than he was seized with incurable pains in his bowels and acute internal suffering— 6 a punishment entirely fitting for one who had inflicted many unheard-of torments on the bowels of others. 7 Still he did not

---

v Gk slaves   *w* Gk their arms   *x* Meaning of Gk uncertain
y Gk they were defeated

8:27 **kept . . . day:** *so some witnesses; others read* brought them safely to that day and had appointed it as the beginning of mercy for them.

more than nine thousand of the enemy, wounded and disabled the greater part of Nicanor's army, and put all of them to flight. 25 They also seized the money of those who had come to buy them as slaves. When they had pursued the enemy for some time, 26 they were obliged to return by reason of the late hour. It was the day before the sabbath, and for that reason they could not continue the pursuit. 27 They collected the enemy's arms and stripped them of their spoils, and then observed the sabbath with fervent praise and thanks to the LORD who kept them safe for that day on which he let descend on them the first dew of his mercy. 28 After the sabbath, they gave a share of the booty to the persecuted and to widows and orphans; the rest they divided among themselves and their children. 29 When this was done, they made supplication in common, imploring the merciful LORD to be completely reconciled with his servants.

30 They also challenged the forces of Timothy and Bacchides, killed more than twenty thousand of them, and captured some very high fortresses. They divided the enormous plunder, allotting half to themselves and the rest to the persecuted, to orphans, widows, and the aged. 31 They collected the enemies' weapons and carefully stored them in suitable places; the rest of the spoils they carried to Jerusalem. 32 They also killed the commander of Timothy's forces, a most wicked man, who had done great harm to the Jews. 33 While celebrating the victory in their ancestral city, they burned both those who had set fire to the sacred gates and Callisthenes, who had taken refuge in a little house; so he received the reward his wicked deeds deserved.

34 The accursed Nicanor, who had brought the thousand slave dealers to buy the Jews, 35 after being humbled through the LORD's help by those whom he had thought of no account, laid aside his fine clothes and fled alone across country like a runaway slave, until he reached Antioch. He was eminently successful in destroying his own army. 36 So he who had promised to provide tribute for the Romans by the capture of the people of Jerusalem testified that the Jews had a champion, and that they were invulnerable for the very reason that they followed the laws laid down by him.

9 About that time Antiochus retreated in disgrace from the region of Persia. 2 He had entered the city called Persepolis and attempted to rob the temple and gain control of the city. Thereupon the people had swift recourse to arms, and Antiochus' men were routed, so that in the end Antiochus was put to flight by the natives and forced to beat a shameful retreat. 3 On his arrival in Ecbatana, he learned what had happened to Nicanor and to Timothy's forces. 4 Overcome with anger, he planned to make the Jews suffer for the injury done by those who had put him to flight. Therefore he ordered his charioteer to drive without stopping until he finished the journey.

Yet the condemnation of Heaven rode with him, since he said in his arrogance, "I will make Jerusalem the common graveyard of the Jews as soon as I arrive there." 5 So the all-seeing LORD, the God of Israel, struck him down with an unseen but incurable blow; for scarcely had he uttered those words when he was seized with excruciating pains in his bowels and sharp internal torment, 6 a fit punishment for him who had tortured the bowels of others with many barbarous torments. 7 Far from giving up his insolence, he was all

over nine thousand of the enemy, wounded and crippled the greater part of Nicanor's army and put them all to flight. 25 The money of their prospective purchasers fell into their hands. After pursuing them for a good while, they turned back, since time was pressing: 26 it was the eve of the Sabbath, and for that reason they did not prolong their pursuit. 27 They collected the enemy's weapons and stripped them of their spoils, and because of the Sabbath even more heartily blessed and praised the Lord, who had saved them and who had chosen that day for the first manifestation of his compassion. 28 When the Sabbath was over, they distributed some of the booty among the victims of the persecution and the widows and orphans; the rest they divided among themselves and their children. 29 They then joined in public supplication, imploring the merciful Lord to be fully reconciled with his servants.

30 They also challenged the forces of Timotheus and Bacchides and destroyed over twenty thousand of them, gaining possession of several high fortresses. They divided their enormous booty into two equal shares, one for themselves, the other for the victims of the persecution and the orphans and widows, not forgetting the aged. 31 They carefully collected the enemy's weapons and stored them in suitable places. The rest of the spoils they took to Jerusalem. 32 They killed the tribal chieftain on Timotheus' staff, an extremely wicked man who had done great harm to the Jews. 33 In the course of their victory celebrations in Jerusalem, they burned the men who had fired the Holy Gates; with Callisthenes they had taken refuge in one small house; so these received a fitting reward for their sacrilege.

34 The triple-dyed scoundrel Nicanor, who had brought the thousand merchants to buy the Jews, 35 finding himself with the Lord's help humbled by men he had himself reckoned as of very little account, stripped off his robes of state, and made his way across country unaccompanied, like a runaway slave, reaching Antioch by a singular stroke of fortune, since his army had been destroyed. 36 Thus the man who had promised the Romans to make good their tribute money by selling the prisoners from Jerusalem, bore witness that the Jews had a defender and that they were in consequence invulnerable, since they followed the laws which that defender had ordained.

9 *i* At about the same time, Antiochus was beating a disorderly retreat from Persia. 2 He had entered the city called Persepolis, planning to rob the temple and occupy the city; but the population at once sprang to arms to defend themselves, with the result that Antiochus was routed by the inhabitants and forced to beat a humiliating retreat. 3 On his arrival in Ecbatana he learned what had happened to Nicanor and to Timotheus' forces. 4 Flying into a passion, he resolved to make the Jews pay for the disgrace inflicted by those who had routed him, and with this in mind he ordered his charioteer to drive without stopping and get the journey over. But the sentence of Heaven was already hanging over him. In his pride, he had said, 'When I reach Jerusalem, I shall turn it into a mass grave for the Jews.' 5 But the all-seeing Lord, the God of Israel, struck him with an incurable and unseen complaint. The words were hardly out of his mouth when he was seized with an incurable pain in his bowels and with excruciating internal torture; 6 and this was only right, since he had inflicted many barbaric tortures on the bowels of others. 7 Even so, he in no way diminished his

NEW REVISED STANDARD VERSION	REVISED ENGLISH BIBLE

NEW REVISED STANDARD VERSION

way stop his insolence, but was even more filled with arrogance, breathing fire in his rage against the Jews, and giving orders to drive even faster. And so it came about that he fell out of his chariot as it was rushing along, and the fall was so hard as to torture every limb of his body. 8 Thus he who only a little while before had thought in his superhuman arrogance that he could command the waves of the sea, and had imagined that he could weigh the high mountains in a balance, was brought down to earth and carried in a litter, making the power of God manifest to all. 9 And so the ungodly man's body swarmed with worms, and while he was still living in anguish and pain, his flesh rotted away, and because of the stench the whole army felt revulsion at his decay. 10 Because of his intolerable stench no one was able to carry the man who a little while before had thought that he could touch the stars of heaven. 11 Then it was that, broken in spirit, he began to lose much of his arrogance and to come to his senses under the scourge of God, for he was tortured with pain every moment. 12 And when he could not endure his own stench, he uttered these words, "It is right to be subject to God; mortals should not think that they are equal to God."z

13 Then the abominable fellow made a vow to the Lord, who would no longer have mercy on him, stating 14 that the holy city, which he was hurrying to level to the ground and to make a cemetery, he was now declaring to be free; 15 and the Jews, whom he had not considered worth burying but had planned to throw out with their children for the wild animals and for the birds to eat, he would make, all of them, equal to citizens of Athens; 16 and the holy sanctuary, which he had formerly plundered, he would adorn with the finest offerings; and all the holy vessels he would give back, many times over; and the expenses incurred for the sacrifices he would provide from his own revenues; 17 and in addition to all this he also would become a Jew and would visit every inhabited place to proclaim the power of God. 18 But when his sufferings did not in any way abate, for the judgment of God had justly come upon him, he gave up all hope for himself and wrote to the Jews the following letter, in the form of a supplication. This was its content:

19 "To his worthy Jewish citizens, Antiochus their king and general sends hearty greetings and good wishes for their health and prosperity. 20 If you and your children are well and your affairs are as you wish, I am glad. As my hope is in heaven, 21 I remember with affection your esteem and goodwill. On my way back from the region of Persia I suffered an annoying illness, and I have deemed it necessary to take thought for the general security of all. 22 I do not despair of my condition, for I have good hope of recovering from my illness, 23 but I observed that my father, on the occasions when he made expeditions into the upper country, appointed his successor, 24 so that, if anything unexpected happened or any unwelcome news came, the people throughout the realm would not be troubled, for they would know to whom the government was left. 25 Moreover, I understand how the princes along the borders and the neighbors of my kingdom keep watching for opportunities and waiting to see what will happen. So I have appointed my son Antiochus to be king, whom I have often entrusted and commended to most of you when I hurried off to the upper provinces; and I have written to him what is written here. 26 I therefore urge and beg you to remember the public and private services rendered to you and to maintain your present goodwill, each of you, toward me and my son.

REVISED ENGLISH BIBLE

in the least abate his insolence; more arrogant than ever and breathing fiery threats against the Jews, he gave orders for more speed on his journey. But as the chariot hurtled along he fell from it, and so violent was his fall that he suffered agony in every limb. 8 He, who in his pretension to be superhuman had been thinking that he could command the waves of the sea and weigh high mountains on the scales, was brought to the ground and had to be carried on a stretcher. The power of God was thus made manifest to all. 9 Worms swarmed from the body of this godless man and, while he was still alive and in agony, his flesh rotted off, and the whole army was overwhelmed by the stench of decay. 10 It was so unbearably offensive that no one was able to convey the man who only a short time before had seemed to reach to the stars in the heavens.

11 In this broken state, Antiochus began to moderate his monstrous arrogance; scourged by God and racked with incessant pain, he was coming to see things in their true light. 12 He was unable to endure his own stench and cried, 'It is right for mortals to submit to God and not claim equality with him.' 13 Though the Lord would spare him no longer, the villain made him a solemn promise: he vowed 14 that the Holy City, which he had been hurrying to level to the ground and transform into a graveyard, he would publicly declare to be free; 15 to all the Jews, a people he had considered not worthy of burial but fit only to be thrown out with their children as carrion for birds and beasts, he would now give privileges equal to those enjoyed by the citizens of Athens; 16 the holy temple, which he had earlier plundered, he would adorn with the most magnificent gifts, and would replace all the sacred vessels on a much more lavish scale, and he would meet the cost of the sacrifices from his own revenues. 17 In addition, he would even turn Jew and visit every inhabited place to proclaim God's might.

18 When his pain in no way abated, because the just judgement of God had befallen him, he was in despair and wrote to the Jews the following letter, as a kind of olive branch:

19 From Antiochus, King and Chief Magistrate, to my worthy citizens, the Jews.

Warm greetings and good wishes for your health and prosperity.

20 May you and your children flourish and your affairs progress as you wish. As I have my hope in Heaven, 21 I keep an affectionate remembrance of your respect and goodwill.

On my way back from Persia, I suffered a troublesome illness, and so I have judged it necessary to provide for the general security of all. 22 Not that I despair of my condition—on the contrary I have good hopes of recovery—23 but I observed that my father, whenever he undertook a campaign east of the Euphrates, nominated a successor, 24 so that, if anything unforeseen should happen or if some untoward report should spread, his subjects would not be disturbed, since they would know to whom the government had been entrusted. 25 Further, I am well aware that the neighbouring princes, those on the frontiers of my kingdom, are waiting on events and watching for their opportunity. I have therefore designated as king my son Antiochus, whom I frequently placed in your care and commended to most of you during my regular visits to the satrapies beyond the Euphrates. I have written to him and enclose a copy. 26 Wherefore most earnestly I urge each one of you to maintain your existing goodwill towards me and my son, remembering the services I have rendered to you, both as a community and as individuals. 27 I am confident my son will follow

NEW AMERICAN BIBLE

the more filled with arrogance. Breathing fire in his rage against the Jews, he gave orders to drive even faster. As a result he hurtled from the dashing chariot, and every part of his body was racked by the violent fall. 8 Thus he who previously, in his superhuman presumption, thought he could command the waves of the sea, and imagined he could weigh the mountaintops in his scales, was now thrown to the ground and had to be carried on a litter, clearly manifesting to all the power of God. 9 The body of this impious man swarmed with worms, and while he was still alive in hideous torments, his flesh rotted off, so that the entire army was sickened by the stench of his corruption. 10 Shortly before, he had thought that he could reach the stars of heaven, and now, no one could endure to transport the man because of this intolerable stench.

11 At last, broken in spirit, he began to give up his excessive arrogance, and to gain some understanding, under the scourge of God, for he was racked with pain unceasingly. 12 When he could no longer bear his own stench, he said, "It is right to be subject to God, and not to think one's mortal self divine." 13 Then this vile man vowed to the LORD, who would no longer have mercy on him, 14 that he would set free the holy city, toward which he had been hurrying with the intention of leveling it to the ground and making it a common graveyard; 15 he would put on perfect equality with the Athenians all the Jews, whom he had judged not even worthy of burial, but fit only to be thrown out with their children to be eaten by vultures and wild animals; 16 he would adorn with the finest offerings the holy temple which he had previously despoiled; he would restore all the sacred vessels many times over; and would provide from his own revenues the expenses required for the sacrifices. 17 Besides all this, he would become a Jew himself and visit every inhabited place to proclaim there the power of God. 18 But since God's punishment had justly come upon him, his sufferings were not lessened, so he lost hope for himself and wrote the following letter to the Jews in the form of a supplication. It read thus:

19 "To my esteemed Jewish citizens, Antiochus, their king and general, sends hearty greetings and best wishes for their health and happiness. 20 If you and your children are well and your affairs are going as you wish, I thank God very much, for my hopes are in heaven. 21 Now that I am ill, I recall with affection the esteem and good will you bear me. On returning from the regions of Persia, I fell victim to a troublesome illness; so I thought it necessary to form plans for the general welfare of all. 22 Actually, I do not despair about my health, since I have great hopes of recovering from my illness. 23 Nevertheless, I know that my father, whenever he went on campaigns in the hinterland, would name his successor, 24 so that, if anything unexpected happened or any unwelcome news came, the people throughout the realm would know to whom the government had been entrusted, and so not be disturbed. 25 I am also bearing in mind that the neighboring rulers, especially those on the borders of our kingdom, are on the watch for opportunities and waiting to see what will happen. I have therefore appointed as king my son Antiochus, whom I have often before entrusted and commended to most of you, when I made hurried visits to the outlying provinces. I have written to him the letter copied below. 26 Therefore I beg and entreat each of you to remember the general and individual benefits you have received, and to continue to show good will toward me and my son. 27 I am confident that, follow-

NEW JERUSALEM BIBLE

arrogance; still bursting with pride, breathing fire in his wrath against the Jews, he was in the act of ordering an even keener pace when the chariot gave a sudden lurch and out he fell and, in this serious fall, was dragged along, every joint of his body wrenched out of place. 8 He who only a little while before had thought in his superhuman boastfulness he could command the waves of the sea, he who had imagined he could weigh mountain peaks in a balance, found himself flat on the ground and then being carried in a litter, a visible demonstration to all of the power of God, 9 in that the very eyes of this godless man teemed with worms and his flesh rotted away while he lingered on in agonising pain, and the stench of his decay sickened the whole army. 10 A short while before, he had thought to grasp the stars of heaven; now no one could bring himself to act as his bearer, for the stench was intolerable.

11 Then and there, as a consequence, in his shattered state, he began to shed his excessive pride and come to his senses under the divine lash, spasms of pain overtaking him. 12 His stench being unbearable even to himself, he exclaimed, 'It is right to submit to God; no mortal should aspire to equality with the Godhead.' 13 The wretch began to pray to the Master, who would never take pity on him now, declaring 14 that the holy city, towards which he had been speeding to rase it to the ground and turn it into a mass grave, should be declared free; 15 as for the Jews, whom he had considered as not even worth burying, so much carrion to be thrown out with their children for birds and beasts to prey on, he would give them all equal rights with the Athenians; 16 the holy Temple which he had once plundered he would now adorn with the finest offerings; he would restore all the sacred vessels many times over; he would defray from his personal revenue the expenses incurred for the sacrifices; 17 and, to crown all, he would himself turn Jew and visit every inhabited place, proclaiming the power of God.

18 Finding no respite at all from his suffering, God's just sentence having overtaken him, he abandoned all hope for himself and wrote the Jews the letter transcribed below, which takes the form of an appeal in these terms:

19 'To the excellent Jews, to the citizens, Antiochus, king and commander-in-chief, sends hearty greetings, wishing them all health and prosperity.

20 'If you and your children are well and your affairs are as you would wish, we are profoundly thankful. 21 For my part, I cherish affectionate memories of you.

'On my return from the country of Persia I fell seriously ill, and thought it necessary to make provision for the common security of all. 22 Not that I despair of my condition, for I have great hope of shaking off the malady, 23 but considering how my father, whenever he was making an expedition into the uplands, would designate his successor 24 so that, in case of any unforeseen event or disquieting rumour, the people of the provinces might know to whom he had left the conduct of affairs, and thus remain undisturbed; 25 furthermore, being well aware that the sovereigns on our frontiers and the neighbours of our realm are watching for opportunities and waiting to see what will happen, I have designated as king my son Antiochus, whom I have more than once entrusted and commended to most of you when I was setting out for the upland satrapies; a transcript of my letter to him is appended hereto. 26 I therefore urge and require you, being mindful of the benefits both public and personal received from me, that you each persist in those sentiments of goodwill that you harbour towards me. 27 I am confident

| NEW REVISED STANDARD VERSION | REVISED ENGLISH BIBLE |

27 For I am sure that he will follow my policy and will treat you with moderation and kindness."

28 So the murderer and blasphemer, having endured the more intense suffering, such as he had inflicted on others, came to the end of his life by a most pitiable fate, among the mountains in a strange land. 29 And Philip, one of his courtiers, took his body home; then, fearing the son of Antiochus, he withdrew to Ptolemy Philometor in Egypt.

10 Now Maccabeus and his followers, the Lord leading them on, recovered the temple and the city; 2 they tore down the altars that had been built in the public square by the foreigners, and also destroyed the sacred precincts. 3 They purified the sanctuary, and made another altar of sacrifice; then, striking fire out of flint, they offered sacrifices, after a lapse of two years, and they offered incense and lighted lamps and set out the bread of the Presence. 4 When they had done this, they fell prostrate and implored the Lord that they might never again fall into such misfortunes, but that, if they should ever sin, they might be disciplined by him with forbearance and not be handed over to blasphemous and barbarous nations. 5 It happened that on the same day on which the sanctuary had been profaned by the foreigners, the purification of the sanctuary took place, that is, on the twenty-fifth day of the same month, which was Chislev. 6 They celebrated it for eight days with rejoicing, in the manner of the festival of booths, remembering how not long before, during the festival of booths, they had been wandering in the mountains and caves like wild animals. 7 Therefore, carrying ivy-wreathed wands and beautiful branches and also fronds of palm, they offered hymns of thanksgiving to him who had given success to the purifying of his own holy place. 8 They decreed by public edict, ratified by vote, that the whole nation of the Jews should observe these days every year.

9 Such then was the end of Antiochus, who was called Epiphanes.

10 Now we will tell what took place under Antiochus Eupator, who was the son of that ungodly man, and will give a brief summary of the principal calamities of the wars. 11 This man, when he succeeded to the kingdom, appointed one Lysias to have charge of the government and to be chief governor of Coelesyria and Phoenicia. 12 Ptolemy, who was called Macron, took the lead in showing justice to the Jews because of the wrong that had been done to them, and attempted to maintain peaceful relations with them. 13 As a result he was accused before Eupator by the king's Friends. He heard himself called a traitor at every turn, because he had abandoned Cyprus, which Philometor had entrusted to him, and had gone over to Antiochus Epiphanes. Unable to command the respect due his office,[a] he took poison and ended his life.

14 When Gorgias became governor of the region, he maintained a force of mercenaries, and at every turn kept attacking the Jews. 15 Besides this, the Idumeans, who had control of important strongholds, were harassing the Jews; they received those who were banished from Jerusalem, and endeavored to keep up the war. 16 But Maccabeus and his forces, after making solemn supplication and imploring God to fight on their side, rushed to the strongholds of the Idumeans. 17 Attacking them vigorously, they gained possession of the places, and beat off all who fought upon the wall, and slaughtered those whom they encountered, killing no fewer than twenty thousand.

18 When at least nine thousand took refuge in two very strong towers well equipped to withstand a siege, 19 Macca-

my policy of moderation and benevolence and will accommodate himself to your wishes.

28 So this murderer and blasphemer, suffering the greatest agony, such as he had made others suffer, met a pitiable end in the mountains of a foreign land. 29 His close friend Philip brought the body back, but being afraid of Antiochus's son he went over to Ptolemy Philometor in Egypt.

10 Under the Lord's guidance, Maccabeus and his followers recovered the temple and city of Jerusalem, 2 and demolished the altars erected by the heathen in the public square, together with their sacred precincts. 3 When they had purified the sanctuary, they made another altar, and striking fire with flints they offered sacrifice for the first time in two whole years; they restored the incense, the lamps, and the Bread of the Presence. 4 This done, they prostrated themselves and prayed to the Lord that he would never again allow them to fall into such disasters but, were they ever to sin, would discipline them himself with clemency rather than hand them over to blasphemous and barbarous Gentiles. 5 The sanctuary was purified on the twenty-fifth of Kislev, the same day of the same month as that on which foreigners had profaned it. 6 The joyful celebration lasted for eight days, like the feast of Tabernacles, and they recalled how, only a short time before, they had kept that feast while living like wild animals in the mountains and caves. 7 So carrying garlanded wands and flowering branches, as well as palm-fronds, they chanted hymns to the One who had so triumphantly achieved the purification of his own temple. 8 A decree was passed by the public assembly that every year the entire Jewish nation should keep these days holy.

9 We have already given an account of the end of Antiochus called Epiphanes. 10 Now we shall describe what transpired under that godless man's son, Antiochus Eupator, in a brief summary of the evils brought about by his wars. 11 At his accession, Eupator appointed as vicegerent a man called Lysias who had succeeded Ptolemaeus Macron as governor-general of Coele-Syria and Phoenicia. 12 Because of the injustice formerly done to the Jews, Ptolemaeus had taken the lead in treating them with justice and endeavoured to maintain amicable relations with them. 13 For this he was denounced to Eupator by the king's Friends; on every side he heard himself called traitor, because he had previously abandoned Cyprus, which had been entrusted to him by Philometor, and had gone over to Antiochus Epiphanes. He still enjoyed power, but no longer respect, and he ended his life by taking poison.

14 When Gorgias became governor of the region, he hired mercenaries and seized every opportunity of attacking the Jews. 15 At the same time the Idumaeans, who controlled strategic strongholds, were also harassing them; they harboured fugitives from Jerusalem and made every effort to foment hostilities. 16 But Maccabaeus and his men, after public prayers entreating God to fight on their side, launched an assault on the Idumaean strongholds. 17 They pressed the attack vigorously and captured them, driving off those who manned the walls and cutting down everyone they encountered. No less than twenty thousand of the enemy were killed.

18 But nine thousand or more took refuge in two exceedingly strong forts, which were fully equipped to withstand a siege. 19 Maccabaeus left Simon and Josephus behind with

[a] Cn: Meaning of Gk uncertain

ing my policy, he will treat you with mildness and kindness in his relations with you."

28 So this murderer and blasphemer, after extreme sufferings, such as he had inflicted on others, died a miserable death in the mountains of a foreign land. 29 His foster brother Philip brought the body home; but fearing Antiochus' son, he later withdrew into Egypt, to Ptolemy Philometor.

10 When Maccabeus and his companions, under the LORD's leadership, had recovered the temple and the city, 2 they destroyed the altars erected by the Gentiles in the marketplace and the sacred enclosures. 3 After purifying the temple, they made a new altar. Then, with fire struck from flint, they offered sacrifice for the first time in two years, burned incense, and lighted lamps. They also set out the showbread. 4 When they had done this, they prostrated themselves and begged the LORD that they might never again fall into such misfortunes, and that if they should sin at any time, he might chastise them with moderation and not hand them over to blasphemous and barbarous Gentiles. 5 On the anniversary of the day on which the temple had been profaned by the Gentiles, that is, the twenty-fifth of the same month Chislev, the purification of the temple took place. 6 The Jews celebrated joyfully for eight days as on the feast of Booths, remembering how, a little while before, they had spent the feast of Booths living like wild animals in caves on the mountains. 7 Carrying rods entwined with leaves, green branches and palms, they sang hymns of grateful praise to him who had brought about the purification of his own Place. 8 By public edict and decree they prescribed that the whole Jewish nation should celebrate these days every year.

9 Such was the end of Antiochus surnamed Epiphanes. 10 Now we shall relate what happened under Antiochus Eupator, the son of that godless man, and shall give a summary of the chief evils caused by the wars. 11 When Eupator succeeded to the kingdom, he put a certain Lysias in charge of the government as commander in chief of Coelesyria and Phoenicia. 12 Ptolemy, surnamed Macron, had taken the lead in treating the Jews fairly because of the previous injustice that had been done them, and he endeavored to have peaceful relations with them. 13 As a result, he was accused before Eupator by the King's Friends. In fact, on all sides he heard himself called a traitor for having abandoned Cyprus, which Philometor had entrusted to him, and for having gone over to Antiochus Epiphanes. Since he could not command the respect due to his high office, he ended his life by taking poison.

14 When Gorgias became governor of the region, he employed foreign troops and used every opportunity to attack the Jews. 15 At the same time the Idumeans, who held some important strongholds, were harassing the Jews; they welcomed fugitives from Jerusalem and endeavored to continue the war. 16 Maccabeus and his companions, after public prayers asking God to be their ally, moved quickly against the strongholds of the Idumeans. 17 Attacking vigorously, they gained control of the places, drove back all who manned the walls, and cut down those who opposed them, killing as many as twenty thousand men. 18 When at least nine thousand took refuge in two very strong towers, containing everything necessary to sustain a siege, 19 Macca-

that he will pursue my own policy with benevolence and humanity, and will prove accommodating to your interests.'

28 And so this murderer and blasphemer, having endured sufferings as terrible as those which he had made others endure, met his pitiable fate, and ended his life in the mountains far from his home. 29 His comrade Philip brought back his body, and then, fearing Antiochus' son, withdrew to Egypt, to the court of Ptolemy Philometor.

10 jMaccabaeus and his companions, under the Lord's guidance, restored the Temple and the city, 2 and pulled down the altars erected by the foreigners in the market place, as well as the shrines. 3 They purified the sanctuary and built another altar; then, striking fire from flints and using this fire, they offered the first sacrifice for two years, burning incense, lighting the lamps and setting out the loaves. 4 When they had done this, prostrating themselves on the ground, they implored the Lord never again to let them fall into such adversity, but if they should ever sin, to correct them with moderation and not to deliver them over to blasphemous and barbarous nations. 5 This day of the purification of the Temple fell on the very day on which the Temple had been profaned by the foreigners, the twenty-fifth of the same month, Chislev, 6 They kept eight festal days with rejoicing, in the manner of the feast of Shelters, remembering how, not long before at the time of the feast of Shelters, they had been living in the mountains and caverns like wild beasts. 7 Then, carrying thyrsuses, leafy boughs and palms, they offered hymns to him who had brought the cleansing of his own holy place to a happy outcome. 8 They also decreed by public edict, ratified by vote, that the whole Jewish nation should celebrate those same days every year.

9 Such were the circumstances attending the death of Antiochus styled Epiphanes. 10 Our task now is to unfold the history of Antiochus Eupator, son of that godless man, and briefly to relate the evil effects of the wars. 11 On coming to the throne, this prince put at the head of affairs a certain Lysias, the general officer commanding Coele-Syria and Phoenicia, 12 whereas Ptolemy, known as Macron, and the first person to govern the Jews justly, had done his best to govern them peacefully to make up for the wrongs inflicted on them in the past. 13 Denounced, in consequence, to Eupator by the Friends of the King, he heard himself called traitor at every turn: for having abandoned Cyprus, which had been entrusted to him by Philometer, for having gone over to Antiochus Epiphanes, and for having shed no lustre on his illustrious office: he committed suicide by poisoning himself.

14 Gorgias now became general of the area; he maintained a force of mercenaries and a continual state of war with the Jews.k 15 At the same time the Idumaeans, who controlled important fortresses, were harassing the Jews, welcoming outlaws from Jerusalem and endeavouring to maintain a state of war. 16 Maccabaeus and his men, after making public supplication to God, entreating him to support them, began operations against the Idumaean fortresses. 17 Vigorously pressing home their attack, they seized possession of these vantage points, beating off all who fought on the ramparts; they slaughtered all who fell into their hands, accounting for no fewer than twenty thousand. 18 Nine thousand at least took refuge in two exceptionally strong towers with everything they needed to withstand a siege, 19 where-

j 10 10:1seq. // 1 M 4:36–61.   k 10 // 1 M 5:1–8.

beus left Simon and Joseph, and also Zacchaeus and his troops, a force sufficient to besiege them; and he himself set off for places where he was more urgently needed. 20 But those with Simon, who were money-hungry, were bribed by some of those who were in the towers, and on receiving seventy thousand drachmas let some of them slip away. 21 When word of what had happened came to Maccabeus, he gathered the leaders of the people, and accused these men of having sold their kindred for money by setting their enemies free to fight against them. 22 Then he killed these men who had turned traitor, and immediately captured the two towers. 23 Having success at arms in everything he undertook, he destroyed more than twenty thousand in the two strongholds.

24 Now Timothy, who had been defeated by the Jews before, gathered a tremendous force of mercenaries and collected the cavalry from Asia in no small number. He came on, intending to take Judea by storm. 25 As he drew near, Maccabeus and his men sprinkled dust on their heads and girded their loins with sackcloth, in supplication to God. 26 Falling upon the steps before the altar, they implored him to be gracious to them and to be an enemy to their enemies and an adversary to their adversaries, as the law declares. 27 And rising from their prayer they took up their arms and advanced a considerable distance from the city; and when they came near the enemy they halted. 28 Just as dawn was breaking, the two armies joined battle, the one having as pledge of success and victory not only their valor but also their reliance on the Lord, while the other made rage their leader in the fight.

29 When the battle became fierce, there appeared to the enemy from heaven five resplendent men on horses with golden bridles, and they were leading the Jews. 30 Two of them took Maccabeus between them, and shielding him with their own armor and weapons, they kept him from being wounded. They showered arrows and thunderbolts on the enemy, so that, confused and blinded, they were thrown into disorder and cut to pieces. 31 Twenty thousand five hundred were slaughtered, besides six hundred cavalry.

32 Timothy himself fled to a stronghold called Gazara, especially well garrisoned, where Chaereas was commander. 33 Then Maccabeus and his men were glad, and they besieged the fort for four days. 34 The men within, relying on the strength of the place, kept blaspheming terribly and uttering wicked words. 35 But at dawn of the fifth day, twenty young men in the army of Maccabeus, fired with anger because of the blasphemies, bravely stormed the wall and with savage fury cut down everyone they met. 36 Others who came up in the same way wheeled around against the defenders and set fire to the towers; they kindled fires and burned the blasphemers alive. Others broke open the gates and let in the rest of the force, and they occupied the city. 37 They killed Timothy, who was hiding in a cistern, and his brother Chaereas, and Apollophanes. 38 When they had accomplished these things, with hymns and thanksgivings they blessed the Lord who shows great kindness to Israel and gives them the victory.

11 Very soon after this, Lysias, the king's guardian and kinsman, who was in charge of the government, being vexed at what had happened, 2 gathered about eighty thousand infantry and all his cavalry and came against the Jews. He intended to make the city a home for Greeks, 3 and to levy tribute on the temple as he did on the sacred places of the other nations, and to put up the high priesthood for sale every year. 4 He took no account what-

Zacchaeus and his troops in sufficient strength to besiege them, while he himself set out for areas which were being hard pressed. 20 But Simon's men were avaricious, and when they were offered seventy thousand drachmas by some of those in the forts, they accepted the bribe and let them slip through their lines. 21 On being informed of this, Maccabaeus denounced the men before the assembled leaders of the army for having sold their brothers for money by letting their enemies escape to fight again, 22 and he had them executed as traitors. He promptly reduced the two forts, 23 and his military operations were crowned with complete success. In the two strongholds he destroyed over twenty thousand of the enemy.

24 Timotheus, who had earlier suffered defeat at the hands of the Jews, now mustered a huge army of mercenaries and no small force of Asian cavalry, and marched on Judaea to take it by storm. 25 At his approach, Maccabaeus and his men made their prayer to God; they sprinkled dust on their heads and put sackcloth round their waists, 26 prostrated themselves on the altar-step and entreated God to show them favour — in the words of the law: 'to be an enemy of their enemies and an opponent of their opponents'.

27 After this prayer, they took up their weapons and, advancing a considerable distance from Jerusalem, halted near the enemy. 28 At first light the two armies came to grips. For the Jews success and victory were assured, not only because of their courage but still more because they had recourse to the Lord, whereas the other side had only their own fury to lead them into battle. 29 As the fighting grew fierce, there appeared to the enemy five magnificent figures in the sky, each riding a horse with a golden bridle. Placing themselves at the head of the Jews, 30 they formed a circle round Maccabaeus and kept him unharmed under the protection of their armour, while they launched arrows and thunderbolts at the enemy, who, confused and blinded, broke in complete disarray. 31 Twenty thousand five hundred of the infantry as well as six hundred cavalry were slain.

32 Timotheus himself fled to Gazara, a stoutly garrisoned stronghold under the command of Chaereas. 33 This outcome suited Maccabaeus and his men, and for four days they laid siege to the place. 34 The defenders, confident in the strength of their position, hurled horrible and wicked blasphemies at them 35 until, at dawn on the fifth day, twenty young men from the Maccabaean force, burning with rage at the blasphemy, bravely stormed the wall and in savage fury cut down all they encountered. 36 Under cover of this distraction others got up the same way and attacked the defenders, setting alight the towers and kindling fires on which they burnt the blasphemers alive. Others broke down the gates and let in the rest of the army, and thus the city was occupied. 37 Timotheus, who had hidden in a cistern, was killed along with his brother Chaereas and Apollophanes. 38 In celebration of their achievement, the Jews praised with hymns and thanksgivings the Lord who showers benefits on Israel and gives them the victory.

11 Very shortly afterwards, in anger at what had happened, the vicegerent Lysias, the king's guardian and Kinsman, 2 mustered about eighty thousand foot-soldiers, in addition to all his cavalry, and marched against the Jews. He planned to make Jerusalem a settlement for Gentiles, 3 with the temple subject to taxation like all gentile shrines and the high-priesthood up for auction each year.

NEW AMERICAN BIBLE

beus left Simon and Joseph, along with Zacchaeus and his men, in sufficient numbers to besiege them, while he himself went off to places where he was more urgently needed. 20 But some of the men in Simon's force who were money lovers let themselves be bribed by some of the men in the towers; on receiving seventy thousand drachmas, they allowed a number of them to escape. 21 When Maccabeus was told what had happened, he assembled the rulers of the people and accused those men of having sold their kinsmen for money by setting their enemies free to fight against them. 22 So he put them to death as traitors, and without delay captured the two towers. 23 As he was successful at arms in all his undertakings, he destroyed more than twenty thousand men in the two strongholds.

24 Timothy, who had previously been defeated by the Jews, gathered a tremendous force of foreign troops and collected a large number of cavalry from Asia; then he appeared in Judea, ready to conquer it by force. 25 At his approach, Maccabeus and his men made supplication to God, sprinkling earth upon their heads and girding their loins in sackcloth. 26 Lying prostrate at the foot of the altar, they begged him to be gracious to them, and to be an enemy to their enemies, and a foe to their foes, as the law declares.

27 After the prayer, they took up their arms and advanced a considerable distance from the city, halting when they were close to the enemy. 28 As soon as dawn broke, the armies joined battle, the one having as pledge of success and victory not only their valor but also their reliance on the LORD, and the other taking fury as their leader in the fight. 29 In the midst of the fierce battle, there appeared to the enemy from the heavens five majestic men riding on golden-bridled horses, who led the Jews on. 30 They surrounded Maccabeus, and shielding him with their own armor, kept him from being wounded. They shot arrows and hurled thunderbolts at the enemy, who were bewildered and blinded, thrown into confusion and routed. 31 Twenty-five hundred of their foot soldiers and six hundred of their horsemen were slain. 32 Timothy, however, fled to a well-fortified stronghold called Gazara, where Chaereas was in command. 33 For four days Maccabeus and his men eagerly besieged the fortress. 34 Those inside, relying on the strength of the place, kept repeating outrageous blasphemies and uttering abominable words. 35 When the fifth day dawned, twenty young men in the army of Maccabeus, angered over such blasphemies, bravely stormed the wall and with savage fury cut down everyone they encountered. 36 Others who climbed up the same way swung around on the defenders, taking the besieged in the rear; they put the towers to the torch, spread the fire and burned the blasphemers alive. Still others broke down the gates and let in the rest of the troops, who took possession of the city. 37 Timothy had hidden in a cistern, but they killed him, along with his brother Chaereas, and Apollophanes. 38 On completing these exploits, they blessed, with hymns of grateful praise, the LORD who shows great kindness to Israel and grants them victory.

11 Very soon afterward, Lysias, guardian and kinsman of the king and head of the government, being greatly displeased at what had happened, 2 mustered about eighty thousand infantry and all his cavalry and marched against the Jews. His plan was to make Jerusalem a Greek settlement; 3 to levy tribute on the temple, as he did on the sanctuaries of the other nations; and to put the high priesthood up for sale every year. 4 He did not take God's power

upon, Maccabaeus left Simon and Joseph, with Zacchaeus and his forces, in sufficient numbers to besiege them, and himself went off to other places requiring his attention. 20 But Simon's men were greedy for money and allowed themselves to be bribed by some of the men in the towers; accepting seventy thousand drachmas, they let a number of them escape. 21 When Maccabaeus was told what had happened, he summoned the people's commanders and accused the offenders of having sold their brothers for money by releasing their enemies to fight them. 22 Having executed them as traitors, he at once proceeded to capture both towers. 23 Successful in all that he undertook by force of arms, in these two fortresses he slaughtered more than twenty thousand men.

24 Timotheus, who had been beaten by the Jews once before, now assembled an enormous force of mercenaries, mustering cavalry from Asia in considerable numbers, and soon appeared in Judaea, expecting to conquer it by force of arms. 25 At his approach, Maccabaeus and his men made their supplications to God, sprinkling earth on their heads and putting sackcloth round their waists. 26 Prostrating themselves on the terrace before the altar, they begged him to support them and to show himself the enemy of their enemies, the adversary of their adversaries, as the Law clearly states.

27 After these prayers, they armed themselves and advanced a fair distance from the city, halting when they were close to the enemy. 28 As the first light of dawn began to spread, the two sides joined battle, the one having as their pledge of success and victory not only their own valour but their recourse to the Lord, the other making their own ardour their mainstay in the fight. 29 When the battle was at its height, the enemy saw five magnificent men appear from heaven on horses with golden bridles and put themselves at the head of the Jews; 30 surrounding Maccabaeus and screening him with their own armour, they kept him unscathed, while they rained arrows and thunderbolts on the enemy until, blinded and confused, they scattered in complete disorder. 31 Twenty thousand five hundred infantry and six hundred cavalry were slaughtered. 32 Timotheus himself fled to a strongly guarded citadel called Gezer, where Chaereas was in command. 33 For four days Maccabaeus and his men eagerly besieged the fortress, 34 while the defenders, confident in the security of the place, hurled fearful blasphemies and godless insults at them. 35 At daybreak on the fifth day, twenty young men of Maccabaeus' forces, fired with indignation at the blasphemies, manfully assaulted the wall, with wild courage cutting down everyone they encountered. 36 Others, in a similar scaling operation, took the defenders in the rear, and set fire to the towers, lighting pyres on which they burned the blasphemers alive. The first, meanwhile, breaking open the gates, let the rest of the army in and, at their head, captured the town. 37 Timotheus had hidden in a storage-well, but they killed him, with his brother Chaereas, and Apollophanes. 38 When all this was over, with hymns and thanksgiving they blessed the Lord, who had shown such great kindness to Israel and given them the victory.

11 1 Almost immediately afterwards, Lysias, the king's tutor and cousin, chief minister of the realm, much disturbed at the turn of events, 2 mustered about eighty thousand foot soldiers and his entire cavalry and advanced against the Jews, intending to make the city a place for Greeks to live in, 3 to levy a tax on the Temple as on other national shrines, and to put the office of high priest up for sale every year; 4 he took no account at all of the

1 11 11:1seq. // 1 M 4:26–35.

ever of the power of God, but was elated with his ten thousands of infantry, and his thousands of cavalry, and his eighty elephants. 5 Invading Judea, he approached Beth-zur, which was a fortified place about five stadia*b* from Jerusalem, and pressed it hard.

6 When Maccabeus and his men got word that Lysias*c* was besieging the strongholds, they and all the people, with lamentations and tears, prayed the Lord to send a good angel to save Israel. 7 Maccabeus himself was the first to take up arms, and he urged the others to risk their lives with him to aid their kindred. Then they eagerly rushed off together. 8 And there, while they were still near Jerusalem, a horseman appeared at their head, clothed in white and brandishing weapons of gold. 9 And together they all praised the merciful God, and were strengthened in heart, ready to assail not only humans but the wildest animals or walls of iron. 10 They advanced in battle order, having their heavenly ally, for the Lord had mercy on them. 11 They hurled themselves like lions against the enemy, and laid low eleven thousand of them and sixteen hundred cavalry, and forced all the rest to flee. 12 Most of them got away stripped and wounded, and Lysias himself escaped by disgraceful flight.

13 As he was not without intelligence, he pondered over the defeat that had befallen him, and realized that the Hebrews were invincible because the mighty God fought on their side. So he sent to them 14 and persuaded them to settle everything on just terms, promising that he would persuade the king, constraining him to be their friend.*b* 15 Maccabeus, having regard for the common good, agreed to all that Lysias urged. For the king granted every request in behalf of the Jews which Maccabeus delivered to Lysias in writing.

16 The letter written to the Jews by Lysias was to this effect:

"Lysias to the people of the Jews, greetings. 17 John and Absalom, who were sent by you, have delivered your signed communication and have asked about the matters indicated in it. 18 I have informed the king of everything that needed to be brought before him, and he has agreed to what was possible. 19 If you will maintain your goodwill toward the government, I will endeavor in the future to help promote your welfare. 20 And concerning such matters and their details, I have ordered these men and my representatives to confer with you. 21 Farewell. The one hundred forty-eighth year,*d* Dioscorinthius twenty-fourth."

22 The king's letter ran thus:

"King Antiochus to his brother Lysias, greetings. 23 Now that our father has gone on to the gods, we desire that the subjects of the kingdom be undisturbed in caring for their own affairs. 24 We have heard that the Jews do not consent to our father's change to Greek customs, but prefer their own way of living and ask that their own customs be allowed them. 25 Accordingly, since we choose that this nation also should be free from disturbance, our decision is that their temple be restored to them and that they shall live according to the customs of their ancestors. 26 You will do well, therefore, to send word to them and give them pledges of friendship, so that they may know our policy and be of good cheer and go on happily in the conduct of their own affairs."

4 Reckoning not at all with the might of God, he was carried away by the thought of his tens of thousands of infantry, his thousands of cavalry, his eighty elephants. 5 He invaded Judaea, and advancing on Bethsura, a fortified place about twenty miles distant from Jerusalem, he closely invested it.

6 When Maccabaeus and his men were informed that Lysias was besieging their strongholds, they and all the people, wailing and weeping, prayed the Lord to send a good angel to deliver Israel. 7 Maccabaeus himself was the first to take up arms, and he urged the others to share the danger with him and go to the rescue of their fellow-Jews. Readily they all set out together. 8 While they were still in the neighbourhood of Jerusalem, there appeared at their head a horseman arrayed in white and brandishing golden weapons. 9 With one voice they praised their merciful God and felt so strong in spirit that they could have attacked not only men but also the most savage animals, or even walls of iron. 10 Under the Lord's mercy and with their heavenly ally they came on in battle array. 11 Like lions they hurled themselves on the enemy, laid low eleven thousand foot-soldiers, as well as sixteen hundred cavalry, and put the remainder to flight. 12 Most of those who escaped had lost their weapons and were wounded, and Lysias himself saved his life, if not his honour, by ignominiously taking to his heels.

13 Yet Lysias was no fool, and as he took stock of the defeat he had suffered he realized that the Hebrews were invincible, because God in his power fought on their side. So he sent emissaries 14 to persuade the Jews to make a settlement on terms that were entirely acceptable, promising also to make the king well disposed towards them. 15 Out of regard for the general welfare, Maccabaeus agreed to all the proposals of Lysias, for the king had accepted whatever written terms Maccabaeus had forwarded to Lysias from the Jewish side.

16 Lysias's letter to the Jews ran as follows:

From Lysias to the Jewish community.
   Greeting.
17 Your representatives John and Absalom have laid before me the document a copy of which is attached, and have asked me to give my views on its contents. 18 Whatever required to be brought to the king's attention I have communicated to him, and what was within my own competence I have granted. 19 Provided, therefore, you maintain your goodwill towards the government, I for my part shall endeavour to promote your wellbeing for the future. 20 I have charged your representatives and mine to confer with you about the details. 21 Farewell.
   The twenty-fourth day of Dioscorus in the year 148.

22 The king's letter was as follows:

From King Antiochus to his brother Lysias.
   Greeting.
23 Now that our royal father has joined the company of the gods, we desire that our subjects shall be left undisturbed in the conduct of their own affairs. 24 It has been brought to our notice that the Jews are not prepared to accept our father's policy and adopt Greek ways; they prefer their own mode of life and request that they be allowed to observe their own laws. 25 It is our pleasure, therefore, that this nation like others shall continue undisturbed. We hereby decree that their temple be restored to them and that they be allowed to regulate their lives in accordance with their ancestral customs. 26 Have the goodness, therefore, to inform them of this and to ratify it, so that, apprised of our policy, they may be reassured and manage their affairs to their own satisfaction.

---

b Meaning of Gk uncertain   *c* Gk *he*   *d* 164 B.C.   11:21 **148:** *that is* 164 B.C.E.

into account at all, but felt exultant confidence in his myriads of foot soldiers, his thousands of horsemen, and his eighty elephants. 5 So he invaded Judea, and when he reached Beth-zur, a fortified place about twenty miles from Jerusalem, launched a strong attack against it. 6 When Maccabeus and his men learned that Lysias was besieging the strongholds, they and all the people begged the LORD with lamentations and tears to send a good angel to save Israel. 7 Maccabeus himself was the first to take up arms, and he exhorted the others to join him in risking their lives to help their kinsmen. Then they resolutely set out together. 8 Suddenly, while they were still near Jerusalem, a horseman appeared at their head, clothed in white garments and brandishing gold weapons. 9 Then all of them together thanked God for his mercy, and their hearts were filled with such courage that they were ready to assault not only men, but the most savage beasts, yes, even walls of iron. 10 Now that the LORD had shown his mercy toward them, they advanced in battle order with the aid of their heavenly ally. 11 Hurling themselves upon the enemy like lions, they laid low eleven thousand foot soldiers and sixteen hundred horsemen, and put all the rest to flight. 12 Most of those who got away were wounded and stripped of their arms, while Lysias himself escaped only by shameful flight.

13 But Lysias was not a stupid man. He reflected on the defeat he had suffered, and came to realize that the Hebrews were invincible because the mighty God was their ally. He therefore sent a message 14 persuading them to settle everything on just terms, and promising to persuade the king also, and to induce him to become their friend. 15 Maccabeus, solicitous for the common good, agreed to all that Lysias proposed; and the king, on his part, granted in behalf of the Jews all the written requests of Maccabeus to Lysias.

16 These are the terms of the letter which Lysias wrote to the Jews: "Lysias sends greetings to the Jewish people. 17 John and Absalom, your envoys, have presented your signed communication and asked about the matters contained in it. 18 Whatever had to be referred to the king I called to his attention, and the things that were acceptable he has granted. 19 If you maintain your loyalty to the government, I will endeavor to further your interests in the future. 20 On the details of these matters I have authorized my representatives, as well as your envoys, to confer with you. 21 Farewell." The year one hundred and forty-eight, the twenty-fourth of Dioscorinthius.

22 The king's letter read thus: "King Antiochus sends greetings to his brother Lysias. 23 Now that our father has taken his place among the gods, we wish the subjects of our kingdom to be undisturbed in conducting their own affairs. 24 We understand that the Jews do not agree with our father's policy concerning Greek customs but prefer their own way of life. They are petitioning us to let them retain their own customs. 25 Since we desire that this people too should be undisturbed, our decision is that their temple be restored to them and that they live in keeping with the customs of their ancestors. 26 Accordingly, please send them messengers to give them our assurances of friendship, so that, when they learn of our decision, they may have nothing to worry about but may contentedly go about their own business."

power of God, being sublimely confident in his tens of thousands of infantrymen, his thousands of cavalry, and his eighty elephants. 5 Invading Judaea, he approached Beth-Zur, a fortified position about twenty miles from Jerusalem, and began to subject it to strong pressure. 6 When Maccabaeus and his men learned that Lysias was besieging the fortresses, they and the populace with them begged the Lord with lamentation and tears to send a good angel to save Israel. 7 Maccabaeus himself was the first to take up his weapons, and he urged the rest to risk their lives with him in support of their brothers; so they sallied out resolutely, as one man. 8 They were still near Jerusalem when a rider attired in white appeared at their head, brandishing golden weapons. 9 With one accord they all blessed the God of mercy, and found themselves filled with such courage that they were ready to lay low not men only but the fiercest beasts and walls of iron. 10 They advanced in battle order with the aid of their celestial ally, the Lord having had mercy on them. 11 Charging like lions on the enemy, they laid low eleven thousand of the infantry and sixteen hundred horsemen, and routed all the rest. 12 Of those, the majority got away, wounded and weaponless. Lysias himself escaped only by ignominious flight.

13 m Now Lysias was not lacking in intelligence and, as he reflected on the reverse he had just suffered, he realised that the Hebrews were invincible because the mighty God fought for them. He therefore sent them a delegation 14 to persuade them to accept reasonable terms all round, and promised to compel the king to become their friend. 15 Maccabaeus, thinking only of the common good, agreed to all that Lysias proposed, and whatever Maccabaeus submitted to Lysias in writing concerning the Jews was granted by the king.

16 Here is the text of the letter Lysias wrote to the Jews:

'Lysias to the Jewish people, greetings.

17 'John and Absalom, your envoys, have delivered to me the communication transcribed below, requesting me to approve its provisions. 18 Anything requiring the king's attention I have put before him; whatever was possible, I have granted. 19 Provided you maintain your goodwill towards the interests of the State, I shall do my best in the future to promote your well-being. 20 As regards the details, I have given orders for your envoys and my own officials to discuss these with you. 21 May you prosper.

'The twenty-fourth day of Dioscorus, in the year one hundred and forty-eight.'

22 The king's letter ran as follows:

'King Antiochus to his brother Lysias, greetings.

23 'Now that our father has taken his place among the gods, our will is that the subjects of the realm be left undisturbed to attend to their own affairs. 24 We understand that the Jews do not approve our father's policy, the adoption of Greek customs, but prefer their own way of life and ask to be allowed to observe their own laws. 25 Accordingly, since we intend this people to be free from vexation like any other, our ruling is that the Temple be restored to them and that they conduct their affairs according to the customs of their ancestors.

26 'It will therefore be your concern to send them a mission of friendship, so that on learning our policy they may have confidence and happily go about their business.'

m 11 11:13seq. // 1 M 6:57.

27 To the nation the king's letter was as follows:
"King Antiochus to the senate of the Jews and to the other Jews, greetings. 28 If you are well, it is as we desire. We also are in good health. 29 Menelaus has informed us that you wish to return home and look after your own affairs. 30 Therefore those who go home by the thirtieth of Xanthicus will have our pledge of friendship and full permission 31 for the Jews to enjoy their own food and laws, just as formerly, and none of them shall be molested in any way for what may have been done in ignorance. 32 And I have also sent Menelaus to encourage you. 33 Farewell. The one hundred forty-eighth year,*e* Xanthicus fifteenth."

34 The Romans also sent them a letter, which read thus:
"Quintus Memmius and Titus Manius, envoys of the Romans, to the people of the Jews, greetings. 35 With regard to what Lysias the kinsman of the king has granted you, we also give consent. 36 But as to the matters that he decided are to be referred to the king, as soon as you have considered them, send some one promptly so that we may make proposals appropriate for you. For we are on our way to Antioch. 37 Therefore make haste and send messengers so that we may have your judgment. 38 Farewell. The one hundred forty-eighth year,*e* Xanthicus fifteenth."

12 When this agreement had been reached, Lysias returned to the king, and the Jews went about their farming.

2 But some of the governors in various places, Timothy and Apollonius son of Gennaeus, as well as Hieronymus and Demophon, and in addition to these Nicanor the governor of Cyprus, would not let them live quietly and in peace. 3 And the people of Joppa did so ungodly a deed as this: they invited the Jews who lived among them to embark, with their wives and children, on boats that they had provided, as though there were no ill will to the Jews;*f* 4 and this was done by public vote of the city. When they accepted, because they wished to live peaceably and suspected nothing, the people of Joppa*g* took them out to sea and drowned them, at least two hundred. 5 When Judas heard of the cruelty visited on his compatriots, he gave orders to his men 6 and, calling upon God, the righteous judge, attacked the murderers of his kindred. He set fire to the harbor by night, burned the boats, and massacred those who had taken refuge there. 7 Then, because the city's gates were closed, he withdrew, intending to come again and root out the whole community of Joppa. 8 But learning that the people in Jamnia meant in the same way to wipe out the Jews who were living among them, 9 he attacked the Jamnites by night and set fire to the harbor and the fleet, so that the glow of the light was seen in Jerusalem, thirty miles*h* distant.

10 When they had gone more than a mile*i* from there, on their march against Timothy, at least five thousand Arabs with five hundred cavalry attacked them. 11 After a hard fight, Judas and his companions, with God's help, were victorious. The defeated nomads begged Judas to grant them pledges of friendship, promising to give him livestock and to help his people*j* in all other ways. 12 Ju-

27 The king's letter to the people ran thus:
From King Antiochus to the Senate of the Jews and to the Jewish people.
Greeting.
28 We trust that all is well with you; we ourselves prosper. 29 Menelaus has made plain to us that it is your wish to return to your homes. 30 We therefore declare an amnesty for all who return before the thirtieth day of Xanthicus. 31 The Jews may follow their own food-laws as heretofore, and none of them will be in any way victimized for any previous offence committed in ignorance. 32 I am sending Menelaus to reassure you. 33 Farewell.
The fifteenth day of Xanthicus in the year 148.

34 The Romans also sent the Jews a letter. It read as follows:
From Quintus Memmius, Titus Manilius, and Manius Sergius, envoys of the Romans, to the Jewish people.
Greeting.
35 We give our assent to all the concessions that Lysias, the king's Kinsman, has granted you. 36 Be pleased to examine carefully the questions which he reserved for reference to the king; and then send someone without delay, so that we may make suitable proposals on your behalf, for we are proceeding to Antioch. 37 Send messengers immediately, therefore, so that we also may know what is your opinion. 38 Farewell.
The fifteenth day of Xanthicus in the year 148.

12 After the conclusion of these agreements, Lysias left and went to the king. The Jews busied themselves on their farms, 2 but they were prevented from leading stable and tranquil lives by some of the governors in the region, Timotheus and Apollonius son of Gennaeus, as well as Hieronymus and Demophon, and also by Nicanor, chief of the Cypriot mercenaries.

3 A DASTARDLY atrocity was perpetrated by the inhabitants of Joppa: they invited the Jews living among them to embark with their wives and children in boats they had provided, giving no indication of any animosity towards them. 4 As it was a public decision by the whole town and because they wished to live in peace and suspected nothing, the Jews accepted; but once out at sea the people of Joppa sank the boats, drowning no fewer than two hundred of the Jews. 5 As soon as Judas learnt of this brutal treatment of his fellow-countrymen he issued orders to his troops, 6 and, invoking God the just judge, he fell upon the murderers. Under cover of night he set the harbour of Joppa on fire, burnt the shipping, and put to the sword those who had taken refuge there. 7 But finding that the town was closed against him he withdrew, with the intention nevertheless of returning to wipe out the entire community. 8 When he learnt that the people of Jamnia planned to deal in the same way with the Jews living there, 9 he made a night attack on the town and set both harbour and fleet alight, so that the glow of the flames was visible at Jerusalem, thirty miles away.

10 When, in their advance against Timotheus, Judas and his men had marched more than a mile from Jamnia, they were set upon by not less than five thousand Arabs on foot, supported by five hundred horsemen. 11 Through God's help, the Jews were the victors in a hard-fought battle. The defeated nomads begged Judas to make an alliance with them, promising to supply cattle and to furnish the Jews with all other assistance. 12 Accepting that they could in-

e 164 B.C. *f* Gk to them *g* Gk they *h* Gk two hundred forty stadia *i* Gk nine stadia *j* Gk them

11:33 **148:** *that is* 164 B.C.E. 11:34 **Titus . . . Sergius:** *so some MSS; others* Titus Manius. 11:38 **148:** *that is* 164 B.C.E.

2544

27 The king's letter to the ...e was as follows: "King
Antiochus sends greetings ... Jewish senate and to the
rest of the Jews. 28 If you ...l, it is what we desire. We
too are in good health ...us has told us of your wish
to return home and at...r own affairs. 30 Therefore,
those who return b...l of Xanthicus will have our
assurance of full ...o observe their dietary laws
and other laws ...and none of the Jews shall be
molested in ...lts committed through ignorance. 32 I ...elaus to reassure you. 33 Farewell." In ...d and forty-eight, the fifteenth
of Xan...

...hem a letter as follows: "Quin-
...Ianius, legates of the Romans,
...ish people. 35 Whatever Lysias,
... granted you, we also approve.
34 ...ch he passed judgment should be
tus ... As soon as you have considered
...us with your decisions so that we
...r advantage, for we are on our way
...ste, then, to send us those who can
...tions. 38 Farewell." In the year one
...t, the fifteenth of Xanthicus.

hind an
sipater,
nd de-
con-
part
ed

12 After these agreements were made, Lysias returned
to the king, and the Jews went about their farming.
2 But some of the local governors, Timothy and Apollonius,
son of Gennaeus, as also Hieronymus and Demophon, to
say nothing of Nicanor, the commander of the Cyprians,
would not allow them to live in peace.
3 Some people of Joppa also committed this outrage: they
invited the Jews who lived among them, together with their
wives and children, to embark on boats which they had
provided. There was no hint of enmity toward them: 4 this
was done by public vote of the city. When the Jews, not
suspecting treachery and wishing to live on friendly terms,
accepted the invitation, the people of Joppa took them out
to sea and drowned at least two hundred of them.
5 As soon as Judas heard of the barbarous deed perpetrated against his countrymen, he summoned his men; 6 and
after calling upon God, the just judge, he marched against
the murderers of his kinsmen. In a night attack he set the
harbor on fire, burnt the boats, and put to the sword those
who had taken refuge there. 7 When the gates of the town
were shut, he withdrew, intending to come back later and
wipe out the entire population of Joppa.
8 On hearing that the men of Jamnia planned to give like
treatment to the Jews who lived among them, 9 he attacked
the Jamnian populace by night, setting fire to the harbor and
the fleet, so that the glow of the flames was visible as far
as Jerusalem, thirty miles away.
10 When the Jews had gone about a mile from there in the
campaign against Timothy, they were attacked by Arabs
numbering at least five thousand foot soldiers, and five
hundred horsemen. 11 After a hard fight, Judas and his companions, with God's help, were victorious. The defeated
nomads begged Judas to make friends with them and promised to supply the Jews with cattle and to help them in every
other way. 12 Realizing that they could indeed be useful in

27 The king's letter to the Jewish nation was in these terms:
'King Antiochus to the Jewish Senate and the rest of the
Jews, greetings.
28 'If you are well, that is as we would wish; we ourselves are in good health.
29 'Menelaus informs us that you wish to return home
and attend to your own affairs. 30 Accordingly, all those
who return before the thirtieth day of Xanthicus may rest
assured that they have nothing to fear. 31 The Jews may
make use of their own kind of food and their own laws
as formerly, and none of them is to be molested in any
way for any unwitting offences. 32 I am in fact sending
Menelaus to set your minds at rest. 33 Farewell.
'The fifteenth day of Xanthicus in the year one hundred and forty-eight.'
34 The Romans also sent the Jews a letter, which read as
follows:
'Quintus Memmius, Titus Manilius, Manius Sergius, legates of the Romans, to the people of the Jews, greetings.
35 'Whatever Lysias, the king's Cousin, has granted
you we also approve. 36 As for the matters he decided to
refer to the king, consider them carefully and send someone without delay, if we are to interpret them to your
advantage, because we are leaving for Antioch. 37 Lose
no time, therefore, in sending us those who can tell us
what your intentions are. 38 Farewell.
'The fifteenth day of Dioscorus in the year one hundred and forty-eight.'

12 These agreements once concluded, Lysias returned
to the king and the Jews went back to their farming.
2 Among the local generals, Timotheus and Apollonius son
of Gennaeus, as also Hieronymus and Demophon, and Nicanor the Cypriarch as well, would not allow the Jews to
live in peace and quiet.
3 The people of Joppa committed a particularly wicked
crime: they invited the Jews living among them to go aboard
some boats they had lying ready, taking their wives and
children. There was no hint of any intention to harm them;
4 there had been a public vote by the citizens, and the Jews
accepted, as well they might, being peaceable people with
no reason to suspect anything. But once out in the open sea
they were all sent to the bottom, a company of at least two
hundred.
5 When Judas heard of the cruel fate of his countrymen,
he issued his orders to his men 6 and after invoking God, the
just judge, he attacked his brothers' murderers. Under cover
of dark he set fire to the port, burned the boats and put to
the sword everyone who had taken refuge there. 7 As the
town gates were closed, he withdrew, intending to come
back and wipe out the whole community of Joppa. 8 But
hearing that the people of Jamnia were planning to treat
their resident Jews in the same way, 9 he made a night attack
on the Jamnites and fired the port with its fleet; the glow of
the flames was seen as far off as Jerusalem, thirty miles
away.
10 *n* When they had left the town barely a mile behind
them in their advance on Timotheus, Judas was attacked by
an Arab force of at least five thousand foot soldiers, with
five hundred cavalry. 11 A fierce engagement followed, and
with God's help Judas' men won the day; the defeated
nomads begged Judas to offer them the right hand of friendship, and promised to surrender their herds and make themselves generally useful to him. 12 Realising that they might

n **12** 12:10seq. // 1 M 5:24–54.

das, realizing that they might indeed be useful in many ways, agreed to make peace with them; and after receiving his pledges they went back to their tents.

13 He also attacked a certain town that was strongly fortified with earthworks[k] and walls, and inhabited by all sorts of Gentiles. Its name was Caspin. 14 Those who were within, relying on the strength of the walls and on their supply of provisions, behaved most insolently toward Judas and his men, railing at them and even blaspheming and saying unholy things. 15 But Judas and his men, calling against the great Sovereign of the world, who without battering-rams or engines of war overthrew Jericho in the days of Joshua, rushed furiously upon the walls. 16 They took the town by the will of God, and slaughtered untold numbers, so that the adjoining lake, a quarter of a mile[l] wide, appeared to be running over with blood.

17 When they had gone ninety-five miles[m] from there, they came to Charax, to the Jews who are called Toubiani. 18 They did not find Timothy in that region, for he had by then left there without accomplishing anything, though in one place he had left a very strong garrison. 19 Dositheus and Sosipater, who were captains under Maccabeus, marched out and destroyed those whom Timothy had left in the stronghold, more than ten thousand men. 20 But Maccabeus arranged his army in divisions, set men[n] in command of the divisions, and hurried after Timothy, who had with him one thousand twenty thousand infantry and two thousand five hundred cavalry. 21 When Timothy learned of the approach of Judas, he sent off the women and the children and also the baggage to a place called Carnaim; for that place was hard to besiege and difficult of access because of the narrowness of all the approaches. 22 But when Judas's first division appeared, terror and fear came over the enemy at the manifestation to them of him who sees all things. In their flight they rushed headlong in every direction, so that often they were injured by their own men and pierced by the points of their own swords. 23 Judas pressed the pursuit with the utmost vigor, putting the sinners to the sword, and destroyed as many as thirty thousand.

24 Timothy himself fell into the hands of Dositheus and Sosipater and their men. With great guile he begged them to let him go in safety, because he held the parents of most of them, and the brothers of some, to whom no consideration would be shown. 25 And when with many words he had confirmed his solemn promise to restore them unharmed, they let him go, for the sake of saving their kindred.

26 Then Judas[o] marched against Carnaim and the temple of Atargatis, and slaughtered twenty-five thousand people. 27 After the rout and destruction of these, he marched also against Ephron, a fortified town where Lysias lived with multitudes of people of all nationalities.[k] Stalwart young men took their stand before the walls and made a vigorous defense; and great stores of war engines and missiles were there. 28 But the Jews[p] called upon the Sovereign who with power shatters the might of his enemies, and they got the town into their hands, and killed as many as twenty-five thousand of those who were in it.

29 Setting out from there, they hastened to Scythopolis, which is seventy-five miles[q] from Jerusalem. 30 But when the Jews who lived there bore witness to the goodwill that the people of Scythopolis had shown them and their kind treatment of them in times of misfortune, 31 they thanked them and exhorted them to be well disposed to their race in the future also. Then they went up to Jerusalem, as the festival of weeks was close at hand.

deed be useful in many ways, ... agreed to make peace, and with assurances from ... went back to their tents.

13 Judas also attacked Caspin, a ... fied town inhabited by a mixe ... strongly forti- 14 Confident in the strength of the ... of Gentiles. of provisions, the defenders treated ... their stock insolence, abusing them and uttering ... with phemies. 15 But Judas's men invoked ... universe, who in the days of Joshua ... of Jericho without the aid of battering-r... then in a fierce onslaught they rushed the ... will of God, captured the town. The carnas... able; the nearby lake, a quarter of a mile w... be overflowing with blood.

17 From there they advanced about ninety-f... they reached Charax, which is inhabited by ... Jews, as they are called. 18 They did not catch ... for having had no success he had by that time ... from the district, though in one place he left ... exceedingly strong garrison. 19 Dositheus and S... Maccabaeus's generals, set out for the stronghold ... stroyed the garrison stationed there by Timotheus; i... sisted of over ten thousand men. 20 Maccabaeus for his... grouped his forces in a number of detachments, appoin... commanders for them, and hurried in pursuit of Timotheu... who had with him a hundred and twenty thousand infantry and two thousand five hundred cavalry. 21 When Timotheus learnt of Judas's approach, he sent on the women and children with the rest of the baggage train to a town called Carnaim, this being an inaccessible place, hard to storm because all the approaches to it were so narrow. 22 As soon as Judas's first detachment came into sight, panic seized the enemy, who were terrified at a hostile manifestation of the all-seeing One. In headlong flight they rushed in all directions, so that frequently they were injured by their own comrades and run through by the points of their swords. 23 Judas pressed the pursuit vigorously and cut down these wicked men, destroying up to thirty thousand of them. 24 Timotheus himself was taken prisoner by the troops of Dositheus and Sosipater, but with great cunning he begged them to let him go unmolested, pointing out that he held in his power the brothers of some of them and the parents of most of them, and it might well be that scant regard would be paid them. 25 On his repeated pledge to restore those hostages unharmed, they let him go in order to save their relatives.

26 Judas moved on Carnaim and the sanctuary of Atargatis, where he slaughtered twenty-five thousand people. 27 From this defeat and massacre of his enemies he marched on Ephron, a fortified town with a mixture of nationalities. Stalwart young men positioned themselves before the walls, where they put up a stout fight, while inside there was a great supply of engines of war and missiles. 28 But the Jews, invoking the Ruler whose might shatters the enemy's strength, made themselves masters of the town and laid low as many as twenty-five thousand of the defenders. 29 Leaving it behind, they pushed on to Scythopolis, some seventy-five miles from Jerusalem. 30 When the Jewish settlers there testified to the goodwill shown them by the people and the kindness with which they had been treated in times of misfortune, 31 Judas and his men thanked them, charging them to be no less friendly to the Jews in the future. Then, as the feast of Weeks was near, they proceeded to Jerusalem.

---

[k] Meaning of Gk uncertain   [l] Gk two stadia   [m] Gk seven hundred fifty stadia   [n] Gk them   [o] Gk he   [p] Gk they   [q] Gk six hundred stadia

12:27 **nationalities:** some witnesses add where Lysias had his headquarters.

many respects, Judas agreed to make peace with them. After the pledge of friendship had been exchanged, the Arabs withdrew to their tents.

13 He also attacked a certain city called Caspin, fortified with earthworks and ramparts and inhabited by a mixed population of Gentiles. 14 Relying on the strength of their walls and their supply of provisions, the besieged treated Judas and his men with contempt, insulting them and even uttering blasphemies and profanity. 15 But Judas and his men invoked the aid of the great Sovereign of the world, who, in the day of Joshua, overthrew Jericho without battering-ram or siege machine; then they furiously stormed the ramparts. 16 Capturing the city by the will of God, they inflicted such indescribable slaughter on it that the adjacent pool, which was about a quarter of a mile wide, seemed to be filled with the blood that flowed into it.

17 When they had gone on some ninety miles, they reached Charax, where there were certain Jews known as Toubiani. 18 But they did not find Timothy in that region, for he had already departed from there without having done anything except to leave behind in one place a very strong garrison. 19 But Dositheus and Sosipater, two of Maccabeus' captains, marched out and destroyed the force of more than ten thousand men that Timothy had left in the stronghold. 20 Meanwhile, Maccabeus divided his army into cohorts, with a commander over each cohort, and went in pursuit of Timothy, who had a force of a hundred and twenty thousand foot soldiers and twenty-five hundred horsemen. 21 When Timothy learned of the approach of Judas, he sent on ahead of him the women and children, as well as the baggage, to a place called Karnion, which was hard to besiege and even hard to reach because of the difficult terrain of that region. 22 But when Judas' first cohort appeared, the enemy was overwhelmed with fear and terror at the manifestation of the All-seeing. Scattering in every direction, they rushed away in such headlong flight that in many cases they wounded one another, pierced by the swords of their own men. 23 Judas pressed the pursuit vigorously, putting the sinners to the sword and destroying as many as thirty thousand men.

24 Timothy himself fell into the hands of the men under Dositheus and Sosipater; but with great cunning, he asked them to spare his life and let him go, because he had in his power the parents and relatives of many of them, and could make these suffer. 25 When he had fully confirmed his solemn pledge to restore them unharmed, they let him go for the sake of saving their brethren.

26 Judas then marched to Karnion and the shrine of Atargatis, where he killed twenty-five thousand people. 27 After the defeat and destruction of these, he moved his army to Ephron, a fortified city inhabited by people of many nationalities. Robust young men took up their posts in defense of the walls, from which they fought valiantly; inside were large supplies of machines and missiles. 28 But the Jews, invoking the Sovereign who forcibly shatters the might of his enemies, got possession of the city and slaughtered twenty-five thousand of the people in it. 29 Then they set out from there and hastened on to Scythopolis, seventy-five miles from Jerusalem. 30 But when the Jews who lived there testified to the good will shown by the Scythopolitans and to their kind treatment even in times of adversity, 31 Judas and his men thanked them and exhorted them to be well disposed to their race in the future also. Finally they arrived in Jerusalem, shortly before the feast of Weeks.

indeed prove valuable in many ways, Judas consented to make peace with them and after an exchange of pledges the Arabs withdrew to their tents.

13 Judas also attacked a certain fortified town, closed by ramparts and inhabited by a medley of races; its name was Caspin. 14 Confident in the strength of their walls and their stock of provisions, the besieged adopted an insolent attitude to Judas and his men, reinforcing their insults with blasphemies and profanity. 15 But Judas and his men invoked the great Sovereign of the world who without battering-ram or siege-engine had overthrown Jericho in the days of Joshua; they then made a fierce assault on the wall. 16 By God's will, having captured the town, they made such indescribable slaughter that the nearby lake, a quarter of a mile across, seemed filled to overflowing with blood.

17 o Ninety-five miles further on from there, they reached the Charax, in the country of Jews known as Tubians. 18 They did not find Timotheus himself in that neighbourhood; he had already left the district, having achieved nothing apart from leaving a very strong garrison at one point. 19 Dositheus and Sosipater, two of the Maccabaean generals, marched out and destroyed the force Timotheus had left behind in the fortress, amounting to more than ten thousand men. 20 Maccabaeus himself divided his army into cohorts to which he assigned commanders, and then hurried in pursuit of Timotheus, whose troops numbered one hundred and twenty thousand infantry and two thousand five hundred cavalry. 21 Timotheus' first move on learning of Judas' advance was to send away the women and children and the rest of the baggage train to the place called the Carnaim, since it was an impregnable position, difficult of access owing to the narrowness of all the approaches. 22 Judas' cohort came into sight first. The enemy, seized with fright and panic-stricken by the manifestation of the All-seeing, began to flee, one running this way, one running that, often wounding one another in consequence and running on the points of one another's swords. 23 Judas pursued them with a will, cutting the sinners to pieces and killing something like thirty thousand men. 24 Timotheus himself, having fallen into the hands of Dositheus and Sosipater and their men, very craftily pleaded with them to let him go with his life, on the grounds that he had the relatives and even the brothers of many of them in his power, and that these could otherwise expect short shrift. 25 When at long last he convinced them that he would honour his promise and return these people safe and sound, they let him go for the sake of saving their brothers.

26 Reaching the Carnaim and the Atargateion, Judas slaughtered twenty-five thousand men.

27 Having defeated and destroyed them, he led his army against Ephron, a fortified town, where Lysanias was living. Stalwart young men drawn up outside the walls offered vigorous resistance, while inside there were quantities of war-engines and missiles in reserve. 28 But the Jews, having invoked the Sovereign who by his power shatters enemies' defences, gained control of the town and cut down nearly twenty-five thousand of the people inside. 29 Moving off from there, they pressed on to Scythopolis, 30 seventy-five miles from Jerusalem. But as the Jews who had settled there assured Judas that the people of Scythopolis had always treated them well and had been particularly kind to them when times were at their worst, 31 he and his men thanked them and urged them to extend the same friendship to his race in the future.

They reached Jerusalem shortly before the feast of Weeks.

---

o 12 12:17seq. // 1 M 5:37–44.

32 After the festival called Pentecost, they hurried against Gorgias, the governor of Idumea, 33 who came out with three thousand infantry and four hundred cavalry. 34 When they joined battle, it happened that a few of the Jews fell. 35 But a certain Dositheus, one of Bacenor's men, who was on horseback and was a strong man, caught hold of Gorgias, and grasping his cloak was dragging him off by main strength, wishing to take the accursed man alive, when one of the Thracian cavalry bore down on him and cut off his arm; so Gorgias escaped and reached Marisa.

36 As Esdris and his men had been fighting for a long time and were weary, Judas called upon the Lord to show himself their ally and leader in the battle. 37 In the language of their ancestors he raised the battle cry, with hymns; then he charged against Gorgias's troops when they were not expecting it, and put them to flight.

38 Then Judas assembled his army and went to the city of Adullam. As the seventh day was coming on, they purified themselves according to the custom, and kept the sabbath there.

39 On the next day, as had now become necessary, Judas and his men went to take up the bodies of the fallen and to bring them back to lie with their kindred in the sepulchres of their ancestors. 40 Then under the tunic of each one of the dead they found sacred tokens of the idols of Jamnia, which the law forbids the Jews to wear. And it became clear to all that this was the reason these men had fallen. 41 So they all blessed the ways of the Lord, the righteous judge, who reveals the things that are hidden; 42 and they turned to supplication, praying that the sin that had been committed might be wholly blotted out. The noble Judas exhorted the people to keep themselves free from sin, for they had seen with their own eyes what had happened as the result of the sin of those who had fallen. 43 He also took up a collection, man by man, to the amount of two thousand drachmas of silver, and sent it to Jerusalem to provide for a sin offering. In doing this he acted very well and honorably, taking account of the resurrection. 44 For if he were not expecting that those who had fallen would rise again, it would have been superfluous and foolish to pray for the dead. 45 But if he was looking to the splendid reward that is laid up for those who fall asleep in godliness, it was a holy and pious thought. Therefore he made atonement for the dead, so that they might be delivered from their sin.

13 In the one hundred forty-ninth year^r word came to Judas and his men that Antiochus Eupator was coming with a great army against Judea, 2 and with him Lysias, his guardian, who had charge of the government. Each of them had a Greek force of one hundred ten thousand infantry, five thousand three hundred cavalry, twenty-two elephants, and three hundred chariots armed with scythes.

3 Menelaus also joined them and with utter hypocrisy urged Antiochus on, not for the sake of his country's welfare, but because he thought that he would be established in office. 4 But the King of kings aroused the anger of Antiochus against the scoundrel; and when Lysias informed him that this man was to blame for all the trouble, he ordered them to take him to Beroea and to put him to death by the method that is customary in that place. 5 For there is a tower there, fifty cubits high, full of ashes, and it has a rim running around it that on all sides inclines precipitously into the ashes. 6 There they all push to destruction anyone guilty of sacrilege or notorious for other crimes. 7 By such a fate it came about that Menelaus the lawbreaker died, without even burial in the earth. 8 And this was eminently just;

32 Immediately after celebrating Pentecost, as the feast is called, they marched against Gorgias, the general in charge of Idumaea, 33 who came out with three thousand infantry and four hundred cavalry. 34 Battle was joined and a small number of Jews fell. 35 But one of the Tubian Jews, Dositheus by name, a cavalryman of great strength, caught hold of Gorgias by his cloak and was dragging the villain away by main force, with the object of taking him alive, when a Thracian horseman bore down on Dositheus and chopped off his arm, and Gorgias escaped to Marisa.

36 As the troop under Esdrias were exhausted by the prolonged fighting, Judas appealed to the Lord to show himself their ally and leader in battle; 37 then, raising the battle cry with hymns in his native language, he launched a surprise attack and put Gorgias's army to flight. 38 Regrouping his forces, Judas led them to the town of Adullam, and since the seventh day was at hand they purified themselves according to custom and kept the sabbath there. 39 Next day they went to collect the bodies of the fallen, as by now had become necessary, in order to take them for burial with their kinsfolk in their family graves. 40 On each one of the dead they found under the tunic amulets sacred to the idols of Jamnia, objects forbidden to Jews by the law. It was evident to all that here was the reason these men had fallen. 41 So everyone praised the acts of the Lord, the just Judge and Revealer of secrets, 42 and turning to prayer they begged that every trace of this offence might be blotted out. The noble Judas exhorted the people to keep themselves free from wrongdoing, for they had seen with their own eyes what had happened because of the sin of those who had fallen. 43 He levied a contribution from each man, and sent to Jerusalem the total of two thousand silver drachmas to provide a sin-offering—a fit and proper act in which he took due account of the resurrection. 44 Had he not been expecting the fallen to rise again, it would have been superfluous and senseless to pray for the dead; 45 but since he had in view the splendid reward reserved for those who die a godly death, his purpose was holy and devout. That was why he offered the atoning sacrifice, to free the dead from their sin.

13 In the year 149, information reached Judas and those with him that Antiochus Eupator was advancing on Judaea with a large army; 2 he was accompanied by Lysias, his guardian and vicegerent, bringing in addition a Greek force consisting of one hundred and ten thousand infantry, five thousand three hundred cavalry, twenty-two elephants, and three hundred chariots fitted with scythes. 3 Menelaus, who had also joined them, kept egging Antiochus on. This he did most disingenuously, not for his country's good, but because he believed he would be established in office. 4 The King of kings, however, stirred up the anger of Antiochus against this wicked man, and when Lysias produced evidence that Menelaus was responsible for all the troubles, the king ordered him to be taken to Beroea and there executed in the manner customary at that place. 5 In Beroea there is a tower some seventy-five feet high, filled with ashes; it has a circular device sloping down sheer on all sides into the ashes. 6 This is where the citizens take anyone guilty of sacrilege or any other heinous crime, and thrust him to his doom; 7 and such was the fate of the renegade Menelaus, who, in accordance with his just deserts, was not even given burial in the earth. 8 Many a

12:43 **sin-offering:** or purification-offering.   13:1 **149:** that is 163 B.C.E.   13:5 **some . . . feet:** Gk fifty cubits.

32 After this feast called Pentecost, they lost no time in marching against Gorgias, governor of Idumea, 33 who opposed them with three thousand foot soldiers and four hundred horsemen. 34 In the ensuing battle, a few of the Jews were slain. 35 A man called Dositheus, a powerful horseman and one of Bacenor's men, caught hold of Gorgias, grasped his military cloak and dragged him along by main strength, intending to capture the vile wretch alive, when a Thracian horseman attacked Dositheus and cut off his arm at the shoulder. Then Gorgias fled to Marisa. 36 After Esdris and his men had been fighting for a long time and were weary, Judas called upon the LORD to show himself their ally and leader in the battle. 37 Then, raising a battle cry in his ancestral language, and with songs, he charged Gorgias' men when they were not expecting it and put them to flight. 38 Judas rallied his army and went to the city of Adullam. As the week was ending, they purified themselves according to custom and kept the sabbath there. 39 On the following day, since the task had now become urgent, Judas and his men went to gather up the bodies of the slain and bury them with their kinsmen in their ancestral tombs. 40 But under the tunic of each of the dead they found amulets sacred to the idols of Jamnia, which the law forbids the Jews to wear. So it was clear to all that this was why these men had been slain. 41 They all therefore praised the ways of the LORD, the just judge who brings to light the things that are hidden. 42 Turning to supplication, they prayed that the sinful deed might be fully blotted out. The noble Judas warned the soldiers to keep themselves free from sin, for they had seen with their own eyes what had happened because of the sin of those who had fallen. 43 He then took up a collection among all his soldiers, amounting to two thousand silver drachmas, which he sent to Jerusalem to provide for an expiatory sacrifice. In doing this he acted in a very excellent and noble way, inasmuch as he had the resurrection of the dead in view; 44 for if he were not expecting the fallen to rise again, it would have been useless and foolish to pray for them in death. 45 But if he did this with a view to the splendid reward that awaits those who had gone to rest in godliness, it was a holy and pious thought. 46 Thus he made atonement for the dead that they might be freed from this sin.

13 In the year one hundred and forty-nine, Judas and his men learned that Antiochus Eupator was invading Judea with a large force, 2 and that with him was Lysias, his guardian, who was in charge of the government. They led a Greek army of one hundred and ten thousand foot soldiers, fifty-three hundred horsemen, twenty-two elephants, and three hundred chariots armed with scythes. 3 Menelaus also joined them, and with great duplicity kept urging Antiochus on, not for the welfare of his country, but in the hope of being established in office. 4 But the King of kings aroused the anger of Antiochus against the scoundrel. When the king was shown by Lysias that Menelaus was to blame for all the trouble, he ordered him to be taken to Beroea and executed there in the customary local method. 5 There is at that place a tower seventy-five feet high, full of ashes, with a circular rim sloping down steeply on all sides toward the ashes. 6 A man guilty of sacrilege or notorious for certain other crimes is brought up there and then hurled down to destruction. 7 In such a manner was Menelaus, the transgressor of the law, fated to die; he was deprived even of decent burial. 8 It was altogether just that

32 After Pentecost, as it is called, they marched against Gorgias, the general commanding Idumaea. 33 He came out at the head of three thousand infantry and four hundred cavalry; 34 in the course of the ensuing battle a few Jews lost their lives. 35 A man called Dositheus, a horseman of the Tubian contingent, a valiant man, overpowered Gorgias and, gripping him by the cloak, was forcibly dragging him along, intending to take the accursed man alive, but one of the Thracian cavalry, hurling himself on Dositheus, slashed his shoulder, and Gorgias escaped to Marisa. 36 Meanwhile, since Esdrias and his men had been fighting for a long time and were exhausted, Judas called on the Lord to show himself their ally and leader in battle. 37 Then, chanting the battle cry and hymns at the top of his voice in his ancestral tongue, by a surprise attack he routed Gorgias' troops. 38 Judas then rallied his army and moved on to the town of Adullam where, as it was the seventh day of the week, they purified themselves according to custom and kept the Sabbath. 39 Next day, they came to find Judas (since the necessity was by now urgent) to have the bodies of the fallen taken up and laid to rest among their relatives in their ancestral tombs. 40 But when they found on each of the dead men, under their tunics, objects dedicated to the idols of Jamnia, which the Law prohibits to Jews, it became clear to everyone that this was why these men had lost their lives. 41 All then blessed the ways of the Lord, the upright judge who brings hidden things to light, 42 and gave themselves to prayer, begging that the sin committed might be completely forgiven. Next, the valiant Judas urged the soldiers to keep themselves free from all sin, having seen with their own eyes the effects of the sin of those who had fallen; 43 after this he took a collection from them individually, amounting to nearly two thousand drachmas, and sent it to Jerusalem to have a sacrifice for sin offered, an action altogether fine and noble, prompted by his belief in the resurrection. 44 For had he not expected the fallen to rise again, it would have been superfluous and foolish to pray for the dead, 45 whereas if he had in view the splendid recompense reserved for those who make a pious end, the thought was holy and devout. Hence, he had this expiatory sacrifice offered for the dead, so that they might be released from their sin.

13 In the year one hundred and forty-nine, Judas and his men discovered that Antiochus Eupator was advancing in force against Judaea, 2 and with him Lysias his tutor and chief minister; he had moreover a Greek force of one hundred and ten thousand infantry, five thousand three hundred cavalry, twenty-two elephants, and three hundred chariots fitted with scythes. 3 Menelaus, too, joined them and very craftily kept urging Antiochus on, not for the welfare of his own country but in the hope of being restored to office. 4 But the King of kings stirred up the anger of Antiochus against the guilty wretch, and when Lysias made it clear to the king that Menelaus was the cause of all the troubles, Antiochus gave orders for him to be taken to Beroea and there put to death by the local method of execution. 5 In that place there is a tower fifty cubits high, full of ash, with an internal lip all round overhanging the ashes. 6 If anyone is convicted of sacrilegious theft or of some other heinous crime, he is taken up to the top and pushed over to perish. 7 In such a manner was the renegade fated to die; Menelaus had not even the privilege of burial. 8 Deserved justice, this; since

| NEW REVISED STANDARD VERSION | REVISED ENGLISH BIBLE |

because he had committed many sins against the altar whose fire and ashes were holy, he met his death in ashes.

9 The king with barbarous arrogance was coming to show the Jews things far worse than those that had been done[s] in his father's time. 10 But when Judas heard of this, he ordered the people to call upon the Lord day and night, now if ever to help those who were on the point of being deprived of the law and their country and the holy temple, 11 and not to let the people who had just begun to revive fall into the hands of the blasphemous Gentiles. 12 When they had all joined in the same petition and had implored the merciful Lord with weeping and fasting and lying prostrate for three days without ceasing, Judas exhorted them and ordered them to stand ready.

13 After consulting privately with the elders, he determined to march out and decide the matter by the help of God before the king's army could enter Judea and get possession of the city. 14 So, committing the decision to the Creator of the world and exhorting his troops to fight bravely to the death for the laws, temple, city, country, and commonwealth, he pitched his camp near Modein. 15 He gave his troops the watchword, "God's victory," and with a picked force of the bravest young men, he attacked the king's pavilion at night and killed as many as two thousand men in the camp. He stabbed[t] the leading elephant and its rider. 16 In the end they filled the camp with terror and confusion and withdrew in triumph. 17 This happened, just as day was dawning, because the Lord's help protected him.

18 The king, having had a taste of the daring of the Jews, tried strategy in attacking their positions. 19 He advanced against Beth-zur, a strong fortress of the Jews, was turned back, attacked again,[u] and was defeated. 20 Judas sent in to the garrison whatever was necessary. 21 But Rhodocus, a man from the ranks of the Jews, gave secret information to the enemy; he was sought for, caught, and put in prison. 22 The king negotiated a second time with the people in Beth-zur, gave pledges, received theirs, withdrew, attacked Judas and his men, was defeated; 23 he got word that Philip, who had been left in charge of the government, had revolted in Antioch; he was dismayed, called in the Jews, yielded and swore to observe all their rights, settled with them and offered sacrifice, honored the sanctuary and showed generosity to the holy place. 24 He received Maccabeus, left Hegemonides as governor from Ptolemais to Gerar, 25 and went to Ptolemais. The people of Ptolemais were indignant over the treaty; in fact they were so angry that they wanted to annul its terms.[t] 26 Lysias took the public platform, made the best possible defense, convinced them, appeased them, gained their goodwill, and set out for Antioch. This is how the king's attack and withdrawal turned out.

time he had desecrated the sacred ashes of the altar-fire, and by ashes he met his death.

9 In savage arrogance the king came on, aiming to inflict sufferings on the Jews far worse than they had endured under his father. 10 When Judas learnt of this, he ordered the people to invoke the Lord day and night, and pray that now more than ever he would come to their aid, since law, country, and holy temple were all at risk; 11 and that he would not allow them, just when they had begun to revive, to fall into the hands of blaspheming Gentiles. 12 They all complied: for three days without respite they prayed to their merciful Lord, they wailed, they fasted, they prostrated themselves. Then, with many an exhortation, Judas called upon them to stand by him.

13 After a council of war with the elders, he decided not to wait for the king's army to invade Judaea and take Jerusalem, but to march out and with God's help put matters to the test. 14 He committed the outcome to the Lord of the universe, and exhorted his troops to fight nobly to the death for law, temple, and city, for their country and their way of life. He pitched camp near Modin, 15 and giving his men the watchword 'Victory with God!' he launched a night attack towards the royal tent with a picked force of his bravest young men. As many as two thousand in the enemy camp were killed, and Judas's men stabbed to death the leading elephant and its driver. 16 In the end they reduced the whole camp to panic and confusion, and then made a successful withdrawal. 17 Through the help and protection which Judas had received from the Lord it was all over by daybreak.

18 Now that he had had a taste of Jewish daring, the king resorted to stratagem in probing their positions. 19 He advanced on Bethsura, one of their strong forts, and was repulsed; he attacked again, and was defeated. 20 Judas meanwhile sent in supplies to the garrison. 21 A soldier in the Jewish ranks, Rhodocus by name, passed secret information to the enemy; but he was tracked down, caught, and put away. 22 A second time the king parleyed with the inhabitants of Bethsura; after giving and receiving guarantees he took his departure; he attacked Judas and his men, but had the worst of it. 23 He now received a report that Philip, who had been left in charge of affairs of state in Antioch, had made a mad bid for power. In consternation the king summoned the Jews, agreed to their terms, and took an oath to respect all their rights. After reaching this settlement he offered a sacrifice, paid honour to the sanctuary and its precincts, 24 and received Maccabeus in a friendly manner. He left Hegemonides as governor of the region from Ptolemais to Gerra, 25 while he himself went to Ptolemais, where the inhabitants resented the treaty he had made, and in their anger wanted to repudiate the terms. 26 Lysias mounted the rostrum and put forward the best defence he could. He won the people over, calmed them down, and, having thus gained their support, departed for Antioch.

Such was the course of the king's offensive and retreat.

14 Three years later, word came to Judas and his men that Demetrius son of Seleucus had sailed into the harbor of Tripolis with a strong army and a fleet, 2 and had taken possession of the country, having made away with Antiochus and his guardian Lysias.

14 AFTER three years had passed, information reached Judas and his followers that Demetrius son of Seleucus had sailed into the harbour at Tripolis with a powerful army and fleet, 2 and, having disposed of Antiochus and his guardian Lysias, had taken control of the country.

---

[s] Or the worst of the things that had been done   [t] Meaning of Gk uncertain   [u] Or faltered

13:15 **stabbed to death:** prob. rdg, based on one version.

he who had committed so many sins against the altar with its pure fire and ashes should meet his death in ashes.

9 The king was advancing, his mind full of savage plans for inflicting on the Jews worse things than those they suffered in his father's time. 10 When Judas learned of this, he urged the people to call upon the LORD night and day, to help them now, if ever, 11 when they were about to be deprived of their law, their country, and their holy temple; and not to allow this nation, which had just begun to revive, to be subjected again to blasphemous Gentiles. 12 When they had all joined in doing this, and had implored the merciful LORD continuously with weeping and fasting and prostrations for three days, Judas encouraged them and told them to stand ready. 13 After a private meeting with the elders, he decided that, before the king's army could invade Judea and take possession of the city, the Jews should march out and settle the matter with God's help. 14 Leaving the outcome to the Creator of the world, and exhorting his followers to fight nobly to death for the laws, the temple, the city, the country, and the government, he pitched his camp near Modein. 15 Giving his men the battle cry "God's Victory," he made a night attack on the king's pavilion with a picked force of the bravest young men and killed about two thousand in the camp. They also slew the lead elephant and its rider. 16 Finally they withdrew in triumph, having filled the camp with terror and confusion. 17 Day was just breaking when this was accomplished with the help and protection of the LORD.

18 The king, having had a taste of the Jews' daring, tried to take their positions by a stratagem. 19 So he marched against Beth-zur, a strong fortress of the Jews; but he was driven back, checked, and defeated. 20 Judas then sent supplies to the men inside, 21 but Rhodocus, of the Jewish army, betrayed military secrets to the enemy. He was found out, arrested, and imprisoned. 22 The king made a second attempt by negotiating with the men of Beth-zur. After giving them his pledge and receiving theirs, he withdrew 23 and attacked Judas and his men. But he was defeated. Next he heard that Philip, who was left in charge of the government in Antioch, had rebelled. Dismayed, he parleyed with the Jews, submitted to their terms, and swore to observe their rights. Having come to this agreement, he offered a sacrifice, and honored the temple with a generous donation. 24 He approved of Maccabeus and left him as military and civil governor of the territory from Ptolemais to the region of the Gerrenes. 25 When he came to Ptolemais, the people of that city angered by the peace treaty; in fact they were so indignant that they wanted to annul its provisions. 26 But Lysias took the platform, defended the treaty as well as he could, and won them over by persuasion. After calming them and gaining their good will, he returned to Antioch.

That is how the king's attack and withdrawal went.

he had committed many sins against the altar, the fire and ashes of which were holy, it was in ashes that he met his death.

9 The king, then, was advancing, his mind filled with barbarous designs, to give the Jews a demonstration of far worse things than anything that had happened under his father. 10 When Judas heard of this, he ordered the people day and night to call on the Lord as never before, to come to the help of those who were in peril of being deprived of the Law, their fatherland and the holy Temple, 11 and not to allow the people, just when they were beginning to breathe again, to fall into the power of ill-famed foreigners. 12 When they had all, with one voice, obeyed his instructions and had made their petitions to the merciful Lord, weeping, fasting and prostrating themselves for three days continuously, Judas spoke words of encouragement and told them to keep close to him. 13 After separate consultation with the elders, he resolved not to wait for the king's army to invade Judaea and take possession of the city, but to march out and settle the whole matter with the Lord's help.

14 Having thus committed the outcome to the Creator of the world, and having exhorted his soldiers to fight bravely to the death for the laws, the Temple, the city, their country and their way of life, he encamped his army near Modein. 15 Giving his men the password 'Victory from God', he made a night attack on the king's pavilion with a picked band of the bravest young men. Inside the camp he destroyed about two thousand, and his men cut down the largest of the elephants with its mahout; 16 having eventually filled the camp with terror and confusion, they successfully withdrew, 17 just as dawn was breaking. This was achieved, thanks to the protection which the Lord granted Judas.

18 p The king, having had a taste of Jewish daring, now tried to capture their positions by trickery. 19 He advanced on Beth-Zur, a strong fortress of the Jews, but was checked, overcome and so repulsed.

20 Judas supplied the garrison with what they needed, 21 but Rhodocus, of the Jewish army, supplied the enemy with secret information; the man was identified, arrested, and dealt with. 22 A second time, the king parleyed with the garrison of Beth-Zur; he offered and accepted pledges of friendship, retired, then attacked Judas and his men, but lost the battle. 23 He was then told that Philip, left in charge of affairs, had rebelled in Antioch. He was stunned by this, opened negotiations with the Jews, came to an agreement, and swore to abide by all reasonable conditions. Agreement reached, he offered a sacrifice, honoured the Temple, and made generous gifts to the holy place.

24 He received Maccabaeus kindly and, leaving Hegemonides to exercise command from Ptolemais to the territory of the Gerrenians, 25 went to Ptolemais. The inhabitants of the place disapproved of the treaty; they complained furiously and wanted to annul its provisions. 26 Lysias mounted the rostrum and made a convincing defence of the provisions which convinced and calmed them and won their goodwill. He then withdrew to Antioch.

So much for the episode of the king's offensive and retreat.

14 Three years later, Judas and his men learned that Demetrius, son of Seleucus, had sailed into the port of Tripolis with a powerful army and a fleet, 2 and that he had occupied the country, after doing away with Antiochus and his guardian Lysias.

14 q Three years after this, Judas and his men learned that Demetrius son of Seleucus had landed at the port of Tripolis with a strong army and a fleet, 2 and that he had occupied the country and had killed Antiochus and his tutor Lysias. 3 A certain Alcimus, a former high priest, had

| NEW REVISED STANDARD VERSION | REVISED ENGLISH BIBLE |

3 Now a certain Alcimus, who had formerly been high priest but had willfully defiled himself in the times of separation,*v* realized that there was no way for him to be safe or to have access again to the holy altar, 4 and went to King Demetrius in about the one hundred fifty-first year,*w* presenting to him a crown of gold and a palm, and besides these some of the customary olive branches from the temple. During that day he kept quiet. 5 But he found an opportunity that furthered his mad purpose when he was invited by Demetrius to a meeting of the council and was asked about the attitude and intentions of the Jews. He answered:

6 "Those of the Jews who are called Hasideans, whose leader is Judas Maccabeus, are keeping up war and stirring up sedition, and will not let the kingdom attain tranquility. 7 Therefore I have laid aside my ancestral glory—I mean the high priesthood—and have now come here, 8 first because I am genuinely concerned for the interests of the king, and second because I have regard also for my compatriots. For through the folly of those whom I have mentioned our whole nation is now in no small misfortune. 9 Since you are acquainted, O king, with the details of this matter, may it please you to take thought for our country and our hard-pressed nation with the gracious kindness that you show to all. 10 For as long as Judas lives, it is impossible for the government to find peace." 11 When he had said this, the rest of the king's Friends,*x* who were hostile to Judas, quickly inflamed Demetrius still more. 12 He immediately chose Nicanor, who had been in command of the elephants, appointed him governor of Judea, and sent him off 13 with orders to kill Judas and scatter his troops, and to install Alcimus as high priest of the great*y* temple. 14 And the Gentiles throughout Judea, who had fled before*z* Judas, flocked to join Nicanor, thinking that the misfortunes and calamities of the Jews would mean prosperity for themselves.

15 When the Jews*a* heard of Nicanor's coming and the gathering of the Gentiles, they sprinkled dust on their heads and prayed to him who established his own people forever and always upholds his own heritage by manifesting himself. 16 At the command of the leader, they*b* set out from there immediately and engaged them in battle at a village called Dessau.*z* 17 Simon, the brother of Judas, had encountered Nicanor, but had been temporarily*c* checked because of the sudden consternation created by the enemy. 18 Nevertheless Nicanor, hearing of the valor of Judas and his troops and their courage in battle for their country, shrank from deciding the issue by bloodshed. 19 Therefore he sent Posidonius, Theodotus, and Mattathias to give and receive pledges of friendship. 20 When the terms had been fully considered, and the leader had informed the people, and it had appeared that they were of one mind, they agreed to the covenant. 21 The leaders*d* set a day on which to meet by themselves. A chariot came forward from each army; seats of honor were set in place; 22 Judas posted armed men in readiness at key places to prevent sudden treachery on the part of the enemy; so they duly held the consultation.

23 Nicanor stayed on in Jerusalem and did nothing out of the way, but dismissed the flocks of people that had gathered. 24 And he kept Judas always in his presence; he was warmly attached to the man. 25 He urged him to marry and have children; so Judas*b* married, settled down, and shared the common life.

3 A certain Alcimus, who had formerly been high priest, had willingly submitted to defilement at the time of the revolt. Realizing now that there was no guarantee whatsoever of his safety, nor any possibility of access to the holy altar, 4 he went to King Demetrius about the year 151 and presented him with a gold crown and a palm, together with some of the customary olive branches from the temple. On that occasion he kept silent. 5 But when Demetrius summoned him to his council and questioned him about the attitude and aims of the Jews, he seized the opportunity to forward his own misguided scheme, and replied: 6 'Those Jews called Hasidaeans who are led by Judas Maccabeus are keeping the war alive and fomenting sedition; they refuse to let the kingdom have peace. 7 Thus, although I have been deprived of my hereditary dignity, by which I mean the high-priesthood, I have two motives in coming here today: 8 first, a genuine concern for the king's interests; and secondly, a regard for my fellow-citizens, since our whole race is suffering considerable hardship as a result of the senseless conduct of those people I have mentioned. 9 My advice to your majesty is to get to know the details of these matters and then, as befits your universal kindness and goodwill, make provision for our country and our beleaguered nation. 10 For as long as Judas remains alive there can be no peace for the state.'

11 No sooner had he spoken in this vein than the other Friends, who were hostile to Judas, added fresh fuel to Demetrius's anger. 12 There and then the king selected Nicanor, commander of the elephant corps, made him military governor of Judaea, and sent him 13 with a commission to make away with Judas and disperse his army, and to install Alcimus as high priest of the great temple. 14 The gentile population of Judaea, refugees from the attacks of Judas, now flocked to join Nicanor, supposing that defeat and misfortune for the Jews would spell prosperity for them.

15 When the Jews heard of Nicanor's offensive and the onset of the Gentiles, they sprinkled dust over themselves and prayed to him who has established his people for ever, who never fails to manifest himself and afford help when his chosen are in need. 16 At their leader's command, they moved forward immediately and made contact with the enemy at the village of Adasa. 17 Simon, the brother of Judas, had fought an engagement with Nicanor, but because the enemy came up unexpectedly he had suffered a slight reverse. 18 In spite of this, when Nicanor learnt how brave Judas and his troops were and how courageously they fought for their country, he shrank from deciding the issue by the sword; 19 so he sent Posidonius, Theodotus, and Mattathias to negotiate a settlement.

20 After a full consideration of the proposals Judas put them to his men, all of whom were in favour of accepting the terms. 21 On the day fixed for a private meeting of the leaders, a chariot advanced from each of the two lines, and seats were placed in position; 22 Judas posted armed men at strategic points ready to deal with any sudden treachery on the enemy's part. The discussion between the two leaders was harmonious. 23 Nicanor stayed some time in Jerusalem and behaved correctly. Dismissing the crowds that had flocked from round about, 24 he kept Judas close to himself at all times, for he had developed a real affection for him. 25 He urged him to marry and have children; so Judas married and settled down to the quiet life of an ordinary citizen.

---

v Other ancient authorities read *of mixing*   *w* 161 B.C.   *x* Gk *of the Friends*   *y* Gk *greatest*   *z* Meaning of Gk uncertain
a Gk *they*   *b* Gk *he*   *c* Other ancient authorities read *slowly*
d Gk *They*

14:4 **151:** *that is* 161 B.C.E.   14:16 **Adasa:** *prob. rdg; cp.*
1 Macc. 7:40.   14:17 **came up:** *prob. rdg, based on one version.*

3 A certain Alcimus, a former high priest, who had willfully incurred defilement at the time of the revolt, realized that there was no way for him to salvage his position and regain access to the holy altar. 4 So he went to King Demetrius in the year one hundred and fifty-one and presented him with a gold crown and a palm branch, as well as some of the customary olive branches from the temple. On that occasion he kept quiet. 5 But he found an opportunity to further his mad scheme when he was invited to the council by Demetrius and questioned about the dispositions and intentions of the Jews. He replied: 6 "Those Jews called Hasideans, led by Judas Maccabeus, are warmongers, who stir up sedition and keep the kingdom from enjoying peace and quiet. 7 For this reason, now that I am deprived of my ancestral dignity, that is to say, the high priesthood, I have come here— 8 first, out of my genuine concern for the king's interests, and secondly, out of consideration for my own countrymen, since our entire nation is suffering great affliction from the unreasonable conduct of the people just mentioned. 9 When you have informed yourself in detail on these matters, O king, act in the interest of our country and its hard-pressed people with the same gracious consideration that you show toward all. 10 As long as Judas is around, it is impossible for the state to have peace." 11 When he had said this, the other Friends who were hostile to Judas quickly added fuel to Demetrius' indignation.

12 The king immediately chose Nicanor, who had been in command of the elephants, and appointed him governor of Judea. He sent him off 13 with orders to put Judas to death, to disperse his followers, and to set up Alcimus as high priest of the great temple. 14 The Gentiles from Judea, who would have banished Judas, came flocking to Nicanor, thinking that the misfortunes and calamities of the Jews would mean prosperity for themselves. 15 When the Jews heard of Nicanor's coming, and that the Gentiles were rallying to him, they sprinkled themselves with earth and prayed to him who established his people forever, and who always comes to the aid of his heritage. 16 At their leader's command, they set out at once and came upon the enemy at the village of Adasa. 17 Judas' brother Simon had engaged Nicanor, but because of the sudden appearance of the enemy suffered a slight repulse. 18 However, when Nicanor heard of the valor of Judas and his men, and the great courage with which they fought for their country, he shrank from deciding the issue by bloodshed. 19 So he sent Posidonius, Theodotus and Mattathias to arrange an agreement. 20 After a long discussion of the terms, each leader communicated them to his troops; and when general agreement was expressed, they assented to the treaty. 21 A day was set on which the leaders would meet by themselves. From each side a chariot came forward and thrones were set in place. 22 Judas had posted armed men in readiness at suitable points for fear that the enemy might suddenly carry out some treacherous plan. But the conference was held in the proper way. 23 Nicanor stayed on in Jerusalem, where he did nothing out of place. He got rid of the throngs of ordinary people who gathered around him; 24 but he always kept Judas in his company, for he had a cordial affection for the man. 25 He urged him to marry and have children; so Judas married, settled down, and shared the common life.

wilfully incurred defilement at the time of the insurrection; realising that whichever way he turned there was no security for him, nor any further access to the holy altar, 4 he went to King Demetrius in about the year one hundred and fifty-one and presented him with a golden crown and a palm, together with the traditional olive branches from the Temple; there, for that day, he let the matter rest.

5 Presently he found an opportunity to further his mad plan. When Demetrius called him into his council and questioned him about the dispositions and intentions of the Jews, he replied, 6 'Those Jews called Hasidaeans, who are led by Judas Maccabaeus, are war-mongers and rebels who are preventing the kingdom from finding stability. 7 That is why, after being deprived of my hereditary dignity—I mean the high priesthood—I have come here now, 8 first out of genuine concern for the king's interests, and secondly, out of a regard for our own fellow-citizens, because the irresponsible behaviour of those I have mentioned has brought no slight misery on our entire race. 9 When your majesty has taken note of all these points, may it please you to make provision for the welfare of our country and our oppressed nation, as befits the gracious benevolence you extend to all; 10 for, as long as Judas remains alive, the State will never enjoy peace.'

11 No sooner had he spoken thus than the rest of the King's Friends, who were hostile to Judas' activities, stoked Demetrius' anger. 12 The latter at once selected Nicanor, then commander of the elephants, promoted him to the command of Judaea and despatched him 13 with instructions to dispose of Judas, disperse his followers and instal Alcimus as high priest of the greatest of temples. 14 The foreigners in Judaea, who had fled before Judas, flocked to join Nicanor, thinking that the misfortunes and troubles of the Jews would be to their own advantage.

15 When the Jews heard that Nicanor was coming and that the foreigners were about to attack, they sprinkled dust over themselves and made supplication to him who had established his people for ever and who never failed to support his own heritage by direct manifestations. 16 On their leader's orders, they at once left the place where they were and confronted the enemy at the village of Dessau. 17 Simon, brother of Judas, engaged Nicanor but, owing to the sudden arrival of the enemy, suffered a slight reverse. 18 Nicanor, however, had heard how brave Judas and his men were and how resolutely they always fought for their country, and he did not dare allow bloodshed to decide the issue. 19 And so he sent Posidonius, Theodotus and Mattathias to offer the Jews pledges of friendship and to accept theirs.

20 After careful consideration of his terms, the leader communicated them to his troops, and since they were all clearly of one mind they agreed to the treaty. 21 A day was fixed on which the respective leaders were to meet as individuals. A litter came out from either side and seats were set up. 22 Judas had posted armed men in strategic positions, in case of a sudden treacherous move by the enemy. The leaders held their conference and reached agreement. 23 Nicanor took up residence in Jerusalem and did nothing out of place there; indeed, he sent away the crowds that had flocked to join him. 24 He kept Judas constantly with him, becoming deeply attached to him 25 and encouraged him to marry and have children. Judas married, settled down and led a normal life.

26 But when Alcimus noticed their goodwill for one another, he took the covenant that had been made and went to Demetrius. He told him that Nicanor was disloyal to the government, since he had appointed that conspirator against the kingdom, Judas, to be his successor. 27 The king became excited and, provoked by the false accusations of that depraved man, wrote to Nicanor, stating that he was displeased with the covenant and commanding him to send Maccabeus to Antioch as a prisoner without delay.

28 When this message came to Nicanor, he was troubled and grieved that he had to annul their agreement when the man had done no wrong. 29 Since it was not possible to oppose the king, he watched for an opportunity to accomplish this by a stratagem. 30 But Maccabeus, noticing that Nicanor was more austere in his dealings with him and was meeting him more rudely than had been his custom, concluded that this austerity did not spring from the best motives. So he gathered not a few of his men, and went into hiding from Nicanor. 31 When the latter became aware that he had been cleverly outwitted by the man, he went to the great^e and holy temple while the priests were offering the customary sacrifices, and commanded them to hand the man over. 32 When they declared on oath that they did not know where the man was whom he wanted, 33 he stretched out his right hand toward the sanctuary, and swore this oath: "If you do not hand Judas over to me as a prisoner, I will level this shrine of God to the ground and tear down the altar, and build here a splendid temple to Dionysus."

34 Having said this, he went away. Then the priests stretched out their hands toward heaven and called upon the constant Defender of our nation, in these words: 35 "O Lord of all, though you have need of nothing, you were pleased that there should be a temple for your habitation among us; 36 so now, O holy One, Lord of all holiness, keep undefiled forever this house that has been so recently purified."

37 A certain Razis, one of the elders of Jerusalem, was denounced to Nicanor as a man who loved his compatriots and was very well thought of and for his goodwill was called father of the Jews. 38 In former times, when there was no mingling with the Gentiles, he had been accused of Judaism, and he had most zealously risked body and life for Judaism. 39 Nicanor, wishing to exhibit the enmity that he had for the Jews, sent more than five hundred soldiers to arrest him; 40 for he thought that by arresting^f him he would do them an injury. 41 When the troops were about to capture the tower and were forcing the door of the courtyard, they ordered that fire be brought and the doors burned. Being surrounded, Razis^g fell upon his own sword, 42 preferring to die nobly rather than to fall into the hands of sinners and suffer outrages unworthy of his noble birth. 43 But in the heat of the struggle he did not hit exactly, and the crowd was now rushing in through the doors. He courageously ran up on the wall, and bravely threw himself down into the crowd. 44 But as they quickly drew back, a space opened and he fell in the middle of the empty space. 45 Still alive and aflame with anger, he rose, and though his blood gushed forth and his wounds were severe he ran through the crowd; and standing upon a steep rock, 46 with his blood now completely drained from him, he tore out his entrails, took them in both hands and hurled them at the crowd, calling upon the Lord of life and spirit to give them back to him again. This was the manner of his death.

15 When Nicanor heard that Judas and his troops were in the region of Samaria, he made plans to attack them with complete safety on the day of rest. 2 When the

26 Alcimus, observing their friendliness, got hold of a copy of the agreement they had concluded, and went to Demetrius and claimed that Nicanor was pursuing a policy detrimental to the interests of the state by appointing Judas, a man guilty of conspiracy, as king's Friend designate. 27 Incensed by these villainous slanders, the king wrote angrily to Nicanor expressing his dissatisfaction with the terms agreed upon; he ordered him to arrest Maccabaeus and send him to Antioch at once. 28 The instructions dismayed Nicanor, and he took it hard that he should have to go back on his agreement when the man had committed no offence; 29 but since there was no gainsaying the king, he watched for an opportunity of carrying out the order by some stratagem. 30 Maccabaeus, on his part, noticed that Nicanor had become less friendly towards him and no longer showed him the same civility. He realized that this coolness boded ill for him, and collecting a good number of his followers he went into hiding.

31 Recognizing that he had been outmanoeuvred by the resolute action of Judas, Nicanor appeared before the great and holy temple at the time when the priests were offering the regular sacrifices, and ordered them to surrender Judas. 32 Though the priests declared on oath that they did not know the whereabouts of the wanted man, 33 Nicanor stretched out his right hand towards the shrine and swore this oath: 'Unless you surrender Judas to me in chains, I shall level this sanctuary of God to the ground and destroy the altar; on this spot I shall build a temple to Dionysus for all the world to see'; 34 and with those words he left. Then the priests, their hands uplifted to Heaven, prayed to the constant champion of our nation: 35 'Lord, you have no need of anything in the world, yet it was your pleasure that among us there should be a shrine for your dwelling-place; 36 now, holy Lord from whom all holiness comes, keep this house, so recently purified, free from defilement for ever.'

37 A man called Razis, a member of the Jerusalem senate, was denounced to Nicanor. He was a patriot and very highly spoken of, one who for his loyalty was known as Father of the Jews. 38 In the early days of the revolt he had stood trial for practising the Jewish religion, and with no hesitation had risked life and limb for that cause. 39 Nicanor, wishing to demonstrate his hostility towards the Jews, sent more than five hundred soldiers to arrest Razis; 40 he reckoned that this would be a severe blow to the Jews. 41 The tower of his house was on the point of being captured by this mob of soldiers, the outer gate was being forced, and there were calls for fire to burn down the inner doors, when Razis, beset on every side, turned his sword on himself; 42 he preferred to die nobly rather than fall into the hands of evil men and be subjected to gross humiliation. 43 With everything happening so quickly, he misjudged the stroke and, now that troops were pouring through the doorways, he ran up without hesitation on to the wall and heroically threw himself down into the crowd. 44 They hurriedly gave way and he fell to the ground in the space they left. 45 He was still breathing and still ablaze with courage; streaming with blood and severely wounded as he was, he picked himself up and dashed through the crowd. Finally, standing on a sheer rock, 46 and now completely drained of blood, he tore out his entrails and with both hands flung them at the crowd. And thus, invoking him who disposes of life and breath to give them back to him again, he died.

15 Nicanor, advised that Judas and his men were in the neighbourhood of Samaria, planned to attack them on their day of rest, when it could be done without risk. 2 Those Jews who were forced to accompany his army

^e Gk greatest   ^f Meaning of Gk uncertain   ^g Gk he

26 When Alcimus saw their friendship for each other, he took the treaty that had been made, went to Demetrius, and said that Nicanor was plotting against the state, and that he had appointed Judas, the conspirator against the kingdom, to be his successor. 27 Stirred up by the villain's calumnies, the king became enraged. He wrote to Nicanor, stating that he was displeased with the treaty, and ordering him to send Maccabeus as a prisoner to Antioch without delay. 28 When this message reached Nicanor he was dismayed, for he hated to break his agreement with a man who had done no wrong. 29 However, there was no way of opposing the king, so he watched for an opportunity to carry out this order by a stratagem. 30 But Maccabeus noticed that Nicanor was becoming cool in his dealings with him, and acting with unaccustomed rudeness when they met; he concluded that this coldness betokened no good. So he gathered together a large number of his men, and went into hiding from Nicanor.

31 When Nicanor realized that he had been disgracefully outwitted by the man, he went to the great and holy temple, at a time when the priests were offering the customary sacrifices, and ordered them to surrender Judas. 32 As they declared under oath that they did not know where the wanted man was, 33 he raised his right hand toward the temple and swore this oath: "If you do not hand Judas over to me as prisoner, I will level this shrine of God to the ground; I will tear down the altar, and erect here a splendid temple to Dionysus." 34 With these words he went away. The priests stretched out their hands toward heaven, calling upon the unfailing defender of our nation in these words: 35 "LORD of all, though you are in need of nothing, you have approved of a temple for your dwelling place among us. 36 Therefore, O holy One, LORD of all holiness, preserve forever undefiled this house, which has been so recently purified."

37 A certain Razis, one of the elders of Jerusalem, was denounced to Nicanor as a patriot. A man highly regarded, he was called a father of the Jews because of his love for them. 38 In the early days of the revolt, he had been convicted of Judaism, and had risked body and life in his ardent zeal for it. 39 Nicanor, to show his detestation of the Jews, sent more than five hundred soldiers to arrest him. 40 He thought that by arresting such a man he would deal the Jews a hard blow. 41 But when these troops, on the point of capturing the tower, were forcing the outer gate and calling for fire to set the door ablaze, Razis, now caught on all sides, turned his sword against himself, 42 preferring to die nobly rather than fall into the hands of vile men and suffer outrages unworthy of his noble birth. 43 In the excitement of the struggle he failed to strike exactly. So while the troops rushed in through the doors, he gallantly ran up to the top of the wall and with manly courage threw himself down into the crowd. 44 But as they quickly drew back and left an opening, he fell into the middle of the empty space. 45 Still breathing, and inflamed with anger, he got up and ran through the crowd, with blood gushing from his frightful wounds. 46 Then, standing on a steep rock, as he lost the last of his blood, he tore out his entrails and flung them with both hands into the crowd, calling upon the LORD of life and of spirit to give these back to him again. Such was the manner of his death.

15 When Nicanor learned that Judas and his companions were in the territory of Samaria, he decided to attack them in all safety on the day of rest. 2 The Jews who

26 When Alcimus saw how friendly the two men had become, he went to Demetrius with a copy of the treaty they had signed and told him that Nicanor was harbouring thoughts against the interests of the State, and was planning that Judas, an enemy of the realm, should fill the next vacancy among the Friends of the King.

27 The king flew into a rage; roused by the slanders of this villain, he wrote to Nicanor, telling him of his strong displeasure at these agreements and ordering him immediately to send Maccabaeus to Antioch in chains. 28 When the letter reached Nicanor, he was very much upset, for he disliked the prospect of breaking an agreement with a man who had done nothing wrong. 29 Since, however, there was no way of opposing the king, he waited for an opportunity to carry out the order by a stratagem. 30 Maccabaeus began to notice that Nicanor was treating him more sharply and that his manner of speaking to him was more abrupt than it had been, and he concluded that such sharpness could have no very good motive. He therefore collected a considerable number of his followers and got away from Nicanor. 31 The latter, realising that the man had well and truly outmanoeuvred him, went to the greatest and holiest of Temples when the priests were offering the customary sacrifices, and ordered them to surrender Judas. 32 When they protested on oath that they did not know where the wanted man could be, 33 he stretched out his right hand towards the Temple and swore this oath, 'If you do not hand Judas over to me as prisoner, I shall rase this dwelling of God to the ground, I shall demolish the altar, and on this very spot I shall erect a splendid temple to Dionysus.' 34 With these words he left them. The priests stretched out their hands to heaven, calling on him who has at all times done battle for our nation; this was their prayer: 35 'O Lord in need of nothing, it has pleased you that the Temple where you dwell should be here with us. 36 Now, therefore, holy Lord of all holiness, preserve for ever from all profanation this House, so newly purified.'

37 Now, a man called Razis, one of the elders of Jerusalem, was denounced to Nicanor. He was a man who loved his countrymen and stood high in their esteem, and he was known as the father of the Jews because of his kindness. 38 In the earlier days of the insurrection he had been convicted of Judaism, and he had risked both life and limb for Judaism with the utmost zeal. 39 Nicanor, by way of demonstrating the enmity he had for the Jews, sent over five hundred soldiers to arrest him, 40 reckoning that if he eliminated this man he would be dealing them a severe blow. 41 When the troops were on the point of capturing the tower and were forcing the outer door and calling for fire to set the doors alight, Razis, finding himself completely surrounded, fell on his own sword, 42 nobly resolving to die rather than fall into the clutches of these villains and suffer outrages unworthy of his noble birth. 43 But in the heat of conflict he missed his thrust, and while the troops swarmed in through the doorways, he ran nimbly upstairs to the parapet and manfully threw himself down among the troops. 44 But, as they immediately drew back, he fell into the middle of the empty space. 45 Still breathing, and blazing with anger, he struggled to his feet, blood spurting in all directions, and despite his terrible wounds ran right through the crowd; then, taking his stand on a steep rock, 46 although he had now lost every drop of blood, he tore out his entrails and taking them in both hands flung them down on the crowd, calling on the Master of his life and spirit to give them back to him one day. Thus he died.

15 Nicanor heard that Judas and his men were in the neighbourhood of Samaria, so he decided to attack them, at no risk to himself, on the day of rest. 2 Those Jews

Jews who were compelled to follow him said, "Do not destroy so savagely and barbarously, but show respect for the day that he who sees all things has honored and hallowed above other days," 3 the thrice-accursed wretch asked if there were a sovereign in heaven who had commanded the keeping of the sabbath day. 4 When they declared, "It is the living Lord himself, the Sovereign in heaven, who ordered us to observe the seventh day," 5 he replied, "But I am a sovereign also, on earth, and I command you to take up arms and finish the king's business." Nevertheless, he did not succeed in carrying out his abominable design.

6 This Nicanor in his utter boastfulness and arrogance had determined to erect a public monument of victory over Judas and his forces. 7 But Maccabeus did not cease to trust with all confidence that he would get help from the Lord. 8 He exhorted his troops not to fear the attack of the Gentiles, but to keep in mind the former times when help had come to them from heaven, and so to look for the victory that the Almighty would give them. 9 Encouraging them from the law and the prophets, and reminding them also of the struggles they had won, he made them the more eager. 10 When he had aroused their courage, he issued his orders, at the same time pointing out the perfidy of the Gentiles and their violation of oaths. 11 He armed each of them not so much with confidence in shields and spears as with the inspiration of brave words, and he cheered them all by relating a dream, a sort of vision,[h] which was worthy of belief.

12 What he saw was this: Onias, who had been high priest, a noble and good man, of modest bearing and gentle manner, one who spoke fittingly and had been trained from childhood in all that belongs to excellence, was praying with outstretched hands for the whole body of the Jews. 13 Then in the same fashion another appeared, distinguished by his gray hair and dignity, and of marvelous majesty and authority. 14 And Onias spoke, saying, "This is a man who loves the family of Israel and prays much for the people and the holy city — Jeremiah, the prophet of God." 15 Jeremiah stretched out his right hand and gave to Judas a golden sword, and as he gave it he addressed him thus: 16 "Take this holy sword, a gift from God, with which you will strike down your adversaries."

17 Encouraged by the words of Judas, so noble and so effective in arousing valor and awaking courage in the souls of the young, they determined not to carry on a campaign[i] but to attack bravely, and to decide the matter by fighting hand to hand with all courage, because the city and the sanctuary and the temple were in danger. 18 Their concern for wives and children, and also for brothers and sisters[j] and relatives, lay upon them less heavily; their greatest and first fear was for the consecrated sanctuary. 19 And those who had to remain in the city were in no little distress, being anxious over the encounter in the open country.

20 When all were now looking forward to the coming issue, and the enemy was already close at hand with their army drawn up for battle, the elephants[k] strategically stationed and the cavalry deployed on the flanks, 21 Maccabeus, observing the masses that were in front of him and the varied supply of arms and the savagery of the elephants, stretched out his hands toward heaven and called upon the Lord who works wonders; for he knew that it is not by arms, but as the Lord[l] decides, that he gains the victory for those who deserve it. 22 He called upon him in these words: "O Lord, you sent your angel in the time of King Hezekiah of Judea, and he killed fully one hundred eighty-five thousand in the camp of Sennacherib. 23 So now, O Sovereign

begged him not to carry out so savage and barbarous a massacre. 'Have regard for the day singled out and made holy by the all-seeing One,' they said. 3 The double-dyed villain retorted, 'Is there some ruler in the sky who has ordered the sabbath-day observance?' 4 The Jews declared, 'The living Lord himself is ruler in the sky, and he commanded the seventh day to be kept holy.' 5 'And I am a ruler on earth,' countered Nicanor; 'I order you to take up arms and do your duty to the king.' However, he did not succeed in carrying out this outrage he had planned.

6 In his pretentious and extravagant conceit, Nicanor had resolved to erect a public trophy from the spoils taken from Judas's army. 7 But Maccabaeus's confidence never wavered, and he had not the least doubt that he would obtain help from the Lord. 8 He urged his men to have no fear of the gentile attack, but to bear in mind the aid they had received from Heaven in the past and look with confidence to the Almighty for the victory he would send them on this occasion also. 9 He drew encouragement for them from the law and the prophets and, by reminding them of the struggles they had already come through, filled them with a fresh ardour. 10 When he had roused their courage, he issued his orders, reminding them at the same time of the Gentiles' broken faith and perjury. 11 He armed each one of them, not so much with shield and spear for protection, as with brave and reassuring words; and he cheered them all by recounting a dream he had had, a waking vision worthy of belief.

12 What he had seen was this: there had appeared to him the former high priest Onias, a good and noble man of modest bearing and mild disposition, a ready and apt speaker, an exemplar from childhood of every virtue; with uplifted hands Onias was praying for the whole Jewish community. 13 Next there appeared in the same attitude a figure of great age and dignity, whose wonderful air of authority marked him as a man of the utmost distinction. 14 Onias then spoke: 'This is God's prophet Jeremiah,' he said, 'one who loves his fellow-Jews and constantly offers prayers for the people and for the Holy City.' 15 Extending his right hand Jeremiah presented a golden sword to Judas, saying as he did so, 16 'Take this holy sword, a gift from God, and with it shatter the enemy.'

17 THE heroic words of Judas had the effect of evoking the bravery of everyone and of giving boys the courage of men. The Jews resolved not to undertake a long campaign, but nobly to go over to the offensive and decide the issue by fighting in close combat with all their courage. This they did because Jerusalem, their religion, and the temple were in peril. 18 Their fear was not chiefly for their wives and children, or for brothers and relatives, but first and foremost for the sacred shrine. 19 The distress of those shut up in Jerusalem was no less, for they were anxious about the outcome of a battle on open ground.

20 All were awaiting the decisive struggle which lay ahead. The enemy had already concentrated his forces: his army drawn up in battle order, the elephants strategically positioned, and the cavalry ranged on the flanks. 21 Maccabaeus observed the deployment of the troops, the variety of their weapons, and the ferocity of the elephants, and raising his hands towards heaven he invoked the Lord, the worker of miracles; he knew that God grants victory to those who deserve it, not because of their military strength but as he himself decides. 22 This was his prayer: 'Lord, in the days of King Hezekiah of Judah you sent your angel and he destroyed as many as a hundred and eighty-five thousand men in Sennacherib's camp. 23 Now, Ruler of heaven, send

---

[h] Meaning of Gk uncertain   [i] Or *to remain in camp*   [j] Gk *for brothers*   [k] Gk *animals*   [l] Gk *he*

were forced to follow him pleaded, "Do not massacre them in that way, like a savage barbarian, but show respect for the day which the All-seeing has exalted with holiness above all other days." 3 At this the thrice-sinful wretch asked if there was a ruler in heaven who prescribed the keeping of the sabbath day. 4 When they replied that there was indeed such a ruler in heaven, the living LORD himself, who commanded the observance of the sabbath day, 5 he said, "I, on my part, am ruler on earth, and my orders are that you take up arms and carry out the king's business." Nevertheless he did not succeed in carrying out his cruel plan.

6 In his utter boastfulness and arrogance Nicanor had determined to erect a public monument of victory over Judas and his men. 7 But Maccabeus remained confident, fully convinced that he would receive help from the LORD. 8 He urged his men not to fear the enemy, but mindful of the help they had received from Heaven in the past, to expect that now, too, victory would be given them by the Almighty. 9 By encouraging them with words from the law and the prophets, and by reminding them of the battles they had already won, he filled them with fresh enthusiasm. 10 Having stirred up their courage, he gave his orders and pointed out at the same time the perfidy of the Gentiles and their violation of oaths. 11 When he had armed each of them, not so much with the safety of shield and spear as with the encouragement of noble words, he cheered them all by relating a dream, a kind of vision, worthy of belief.

12 What he saw was this: Onias, the former high priest, a good and virtuous man, modest in appearance, gentle in manners, distinguished in speech, and trained from childhood in every virtuous practice, was praying with outstretched arms for the whole Jewish community. 13 Then in the same way another man appeared, distinguished by his white hair and dignity, and with an air about him of extraordinary, majestic authority. 14 Onias then said of him, "This is God's prophet Jeremiah, who loves his brethren and fervently prays for his people and their holy city." 15 Stretching out his right hand, Jeremiah presented a gold sword to Judas. As he gave it to him he said, 16 "Accept this holy sword as a gift from God; with it you shall crush your adversaries."

17 Encouraged by Judas' noble words, which had power to instill valor and stir young hearts to courage, the Jews determined not to delay, but to charge gallantly and decide the issue by hand-to-hand combat with the utmost courage, since their city and its temple with the sacred vessels were in danger. 18 They were not so much concerned about their wives and children or their brothers and kinsmen; their first and foremost fear was for the consecrated sanctuary. 19 Those who remained in the city suffered a like agony, anxious as they were about the battle in the open country. 20 Everyone now awaited the decisive moment. The enemy were already drawing near with their troops drawn up in battle line, their elephants placed in strategic positions, and their cavalry stationed on the flanks. 21 Maccabeus, contemplating the hosts before him, their elaborate equipment, and the fierceness of their elephants, stretched out his hands toward heaven and called upon the LORD who works miracles; for he knew that it is not through arms but through the LORD's decision that victory is won by those who deserve it. 22 He prayed to him thus: "You, O LORD, sent your angel in the days of King Hezekiah of Judea, and he slew a hundred and eighty-five thousand men of Sennacherib's army. 23 Sovereign of the heavens, send a good angel now

who had been compelled to follow him, said, 'Do not massacre them in such a savage, barbarous way. Respect the day on which the All-seeing has conferred a special holiness.' 3 At this the triple-dyed scoundrel asked if there were in heaven a sovereign who had ordered the keeping of the Sabbath day. 4 When they answered, 'The living Lord himself, the Heavenly Sovereign, has ordered the observance of the seventh day,' 5 he retorted, 'And I, as sovereign on earth, order you to take up arms and do the king's business.' For all that, he did not manage to carry out his wicked plan.

6 While Nicanor, in his unlimited boastfulness and pride, was planning to erect a general trophy with the spoils taken from Judas and his men, 7 Maccabaeus remained firm in his confident conviction that the Lord would stand by him. 8 He urged his men not to be dismayed by the foreigners' attacks but, keeping in mind the help that had come to them from Heaven in the past, to be confident that this time too victory would be theirs with the help of the Almighty. 9 He put fresh heart into them by citing the Law and the Prophets and, by stirring up memories of the battles they had already won, he filled them with new enthusiasm. 10 Having thus aroused their courage, he ended his exhortation by demonstrating the treachery of the foreigners and how they had violated their oaths.

11 Having armed each one of them not so much with the safety given by shield and lance as with that confidence which springs from noble language, he encouraged them all by describing to them a convincing dream — a vision, as it were. 12 What he had seen was this: Onias, the former high priest, that paragon of men, modest of bearing and gentle of manners, suitably eloquent and trained from boyhood in the practice of every virtue — Onias was stretching out his hands and praying for the whole Jewish community. 13 Next, there appeared a man equally remarkable for his great age and dignity and invested with a marvellous and impressive air of majesty. 14 Onias began to speak: 'This is a man', he said, 'who loves his brothers and prays much for the people and the holy city — Jeremiah, the prophet of God.' 15 Jeremiah then stretched out his right hand and presented Judas with a golden sword, saying as he gave it, 16 'Take this holy sword as a gift from God; with it you will shatter the enemy.'

17 Encouraged by the noble words of Judas, which had the power to inspire valour and give the young the spirit of mature men, they decided not to entrench themselves in a camp, but bravely to take the offensive and, in hand-to-hand fighting, to commit the result to the fortune of war, since the city, their holy religion and the Temple were in danger. 18 Their concern for their wives and children, their brothers and relatives, had shrunk to minute importance; their chief and greatest fear was for the consecrated Temple. 19 Those left behind in the city felt a similar anxiety, alarmed as they were about the forthcoming encounter in the open country. 20 Everyone now awaited the coming issue. The enemy had already concentrated their forces and stood formed up in order of battle, with the elephants drawn up in a strategic position and the cavalry disposed on the wings. 21 Maccabaeus took note of these masses confronting him, the glittering array of armour and the fierce aspect of the elephants; then, raising his hands to heaven, he called on the Lord who works miracles, in the knowledge that it is not by force of arms but as he sees fit to decide, that victory is granted by him to such as deserve it. 22 His prayer was worded thus: 'You, Master, sent your angel in the days of Hezekiah king of Judaea, and he destroyed no less than one hundred and eighty-five thousand of Sennacherib's army; 23 now, once again, Sovereign of heaven, send a good

of the heavens, send a good angel to spread terror and trembling before us. 24 By the might of your arm may these blasphemers who come against your holy people be struck down." With these words he ended his prayer.

25 Nicanor and his troops advanced with trumpets and battle songs, 26 but Judas and his troops met the enemy in battle with invocations to God and prayers. 27 So, fighting with their hands and praying to God in their hearts, they laid low at least thirty-five thousand, and were greatly gladdened by God's manifestation.

28 When the action was over and they were returning with joy, they recognized Nicanor, lying dead, in full armor. 29 Then there was shouting and tumult, and they blessed the Sovereign Lord in the language of their ancestors. 30 Then the man who was ever in body and soul the defender of his people, the man who maintained his youthful goodwill toward his compatriots, ordered them to cut off Nicanor's head and arm and carry them to Jerusalem. 31 When he arrived there and had called his compatriots together and stationed the priests before the altar, he sent for those who were in the citadel. 32 He showed them the vile Nicanor's head and that profane man's arm, which had been boastfully stretched out against the holy house of the Almighty. 33 He cut out the tongue of the ungodly Nicanor and said that he would feed it piecemeal to the birds and would hang up these rewards of his folly opposite the sanctuary. 34 And they all, looking to heaven, blessed the Lord who had manifested himself, saying, "Blessed is he who has kept his own place undefiled!" 35 Judas[m] hung Nicanor's head from the citadel, a clear and conspicuous sign to everyone of the help of the Lord. 36 And they all decreed by public vote never to let this day go unobserved, but to celebrate the thirteenth day of the twelfth month — which is called Adar in the Aramaic language — the day before Mordecai's day.

37 This, then, is how matters turned out with Nicanor, and from that time the city has been in the possession of the Hebrews. So I will here end my story.

38 If it is well told and to the point, that is what I myself desired; if it is poorly done and mediocre, that was the best I could do. 39 For just as it is harmful to drink wine alone, or, again, to drink water alone, while wine mixed with water is sweet and delicious and enhances one's enjoyment, so also the style of the story delights the ears of those who read the work. And here will be the end.

[m] Gk He

a good angel once again to go before us spreading fear and panic. 24 May these blasphemers who are coming to attack your holy people be struck down by your strong arm!' Such was his prayer.

25 Nicanor and his forces advanced to the sound of trumpets and war-songs, 26 but Judas and his men engaged the enemy with invocations and prayers on their lips. 27 Praying to God in their hearts and greatly cheered by his care, they killed no fewer than thirty-five thousand in hand-to-hand fighting.

28 The action over, they were joyfully disbanding, when they discovered Nicanor lying dead in full armour, 29 and with tumultuous shouts they praised the heavenly Ruler in their native language. 30 Judas their leader, who had always fought body and soul on behalf of his fellow-countrymen, without ever losing his youthful patriotism, ordered that Nicanor's head and whole arm should be cut off and taken to Jerusalem. 31 On arrival there he called together the people, stationed the priests before the altar, sent for the men in the citadel, 32 and put on display the head of that villainous Nicanor and the hand which the bragging blasphemer had stretched out against the Almighty's holy temple. 33 He cut out the godless Nicanor's tongue and swore he would feed it to the birds bit by bit; and he gave orders that the evidence of what Nicanor's folly had brought upon him should be hung up opposite the shrine. 34 All made the sky ring with the praises of the Lord who had shown his power: 'Praise to him who has preserved his own sanctuary from defilement!' 35 Judas hung Nicanor's head from the citadel, as a clear proof of the Lord's help for everyone to see. 36 It was unanimously decreed that this day should never pass unnoticed, but that the thirteenth of the twelfth month, called Adar in Aramaic, should be duly celebrated; it is the eve of Mordecai's Day. 37 Such, then, was the fate of Nicanor, and from that time Jerusalem has remained in the possession of the Hebrews.

At this point I shall bring my work to an end. 38 If it is found to be well written and aptly composed, that is what I myself aimed at; if superficial and mediocre, it was the best I could do. 39 For, just as it is disagreeable to drink wine by itself or water by itself, whereas the mixing of the two produces a pleasant and delightful taste, so too variety of style in a literary work charms the ear of the reader. Let this, then, be my final word.

to spread fear and dread before us. 24 By the might of your arm may those be struck down who have blasphemously come against your holy people!" With this he ended his prayer.

25 Nicanor and his men advanced to the sound of trumpets and battle songs. 26 But Judas and his men met the army with supplication and prayers. 27 Fighting with their hands and praying to God with their hearts, they laid low at least thirty-five thousand, and rejoiced greatly over this manifestation of God's power. 28 When the battle was over and they were joyfully departing, they discovered Nicanor lying there in all his armor; 29 so they raised tumultuous shouts in their native tongue in praise of the divine Sovereign.

30 Then Judas, who was ever in body and soul the chief defender of his fellow citizens, and had maintained from youth his affection for his countrymen, ordered Nicanor's head and whole right arm to be cut off and taken to Jerusalem. 31 When he arrived there, he assembled his countrymen, stationed the priests before the altar, and sent for those in the citadel. 32 He showed them the vile Nicanor's head and the wretched blasphemer's arm that had been boastfully stretched out against the holy dwelling of the Almighty. 33 He cut out the tongue of the godless Nicanor, saying he would feed it piecemeal to the birds and would hang up the other wages of his folly opposite the temple. 34 At this, everyone looked toward heaven and praised the LORD who manifests his divine power, saying, "Blessed be he who has kept his own Place undefiled!"

35 Judas hung up Nicanor's head on the wall of the citadel, a clear and evident proof to all of the Lord's help. 36 By public vote it was unanimously decreed never to let this day pass unobserved, but to celebrate it on the thirteenth day of the twelfth month, called Adar in Aramaic, the eve of Mordecai's Day.

37 Since Nicanor's doings ended in this way, with the city remaining in possession of the Hebrews from that time on, I will bring my own story to an end here too. 38 If it is well written and to the point, that is what I wanted; if it is poorly done and mediocre, that is the best I could do. 39 Just as it is harmful to drink wine alone or water alone, whereas mixing wine with water makes a more pleasant drink that increases delight, so a skillfully composed story delights the ears of those who read the work. Let this, then, be the end.

angel before us to spread terror and dismay. 24 May these men be struck down by the might of your arm, since they have come with blasphemy on their lips to attack your holy people.' And on these words he finished.

25 r Nicanor and his men advanced to the sound of trumpets and war songs, 26 but the men of Judas closed with the enemy uttering invocations and prayers. 27 Fighting with their hands and praying to God in their hearts, they cut down at least thirty-five thousand men and were greatly cheered by this manifestation of God. 28 When the engagement was over and they were withdrawing in triumph, they recognised Nicanor, lying dead in full armour.

29 With shouting and confusion all around, they blessed the sovereign Master in their ancestral tongue. 30 He who, as protagonist, had devoted himself, body and soul, to his fellow-citizens, and had preserved the love he felt even in youth for those of his own race, gave orders for Nicanor's head to be cut off, with his arm up to the shoulder, and taken to Jerusalem. 31 When he arrived there himself, he called his countrymen together, stationed the priests in front of the altar and then sent for the people from the Citadel. 32 He showed them the head of the abominable Nicanor, and the hand which this infamous man had stretched out so insolently against the holy House of the Almighty. 33 Then, cutting out godless Nicanor's tongue, he gave orders for it to be fed piecemeal to the birds, and for the salary of his folly to be hung up in front of the Temple. 34 At this, everyone sent blessings heavenwards to the glorious Lord, saying, 'Blessed be he who has preserved his holy place from pollution!'

35 He hung Nicanor's head from the Citadel, a clear and evident sign to all of the help of the Lord. 36 They all decreed by public vote never to let that day go by unobserved, but to celebrate the thirteenth day of the twelfth month, called Adar in Aramaic, the eve of what is called the Day of Mordecai.

37 So ends the episode of Nicanor, and as, since then, the city has remained in the possession of the Hebrews, I shall bring my own work to an end here too. 38 If it is well composed and to the point, that is just what I wanted. If it is worthless and mediocre, that is all I could manage. 39 Just as it is injurious to drink wine by itself, or again water alone, whereas wine mixed with water is pleasant and produces a delightful sense of well-being, so skill in presenting the incidents is what delights the understanding of those who read the book. And here I close.

r 15 15:25seq. // 1 M 7:43–50.

(b) The books from 1 Esdras through 3 Maccabees are recognized as Deuterocanonical Scripture by the Greek and the Russian Orthodox Churches. They are not so recognized by the Roman Catholic Church, but 1 Esdras and the Prayer of Manasseh (together with 2 Esdras) are placed in an appendix to the Latin Vulgate Bible.

1 Esdras is included only in the New Revised Standard Version and the Revised English Bible translations.

1 Esdras is included only in the New Revised Standard Version and the Revised English Bible translations.

1 Esdras

THE FIRST BOOK OF
Esdras

1 Josiah kept the passover to his Lord in Jerusalem; he killed the passover lamb on the fourteenth day of the first month, 2 having placed the priests according to their divisions, arrayed in their vestments, in the temple of the Lord. 3 He told the Levites, the temple servants of Israel, that they should sanctify themselves to the Lord and put the holy ark of the Lord in the house that King Solomon, son of David, had built; 4 and he said, "You need no longer carry it on your shoulders. Now worship the Lord your God and serve his people Israel; prepare yourselves by your families and kindred, 5 in accordance with the directions of King David of Israel and the magnificence of his son Solomon. Stand in order in the temple according to the groupings of the ancestral houses of you Levites, who minister before your kindred the people of Israel, 6 and kill the passover lamb and prepare the sacrifices for your kindred, and keep the passover according to the commandment of the Lord that was given to Moses."

7 To the people who were present Josiah gave thirty thousand lambs and kids, and three thousand calves; these were given from the king's possessions, as he promised, to the people and the priests and Levites. 8 Hilkiah, Zechariah, and Jehiel,[a] the chief officers of the temple, gave to the priests for the passover two thousand six hundred sheep and three hundred calves. 9 And Jeconiah and Shemaiah and his brother Nethanel, and Hashabiah and Ochiel and Joram, captains over thousands, gave the Levites for the passover five thousand sheep and seven hundred calves.

10 This is what took place. The priests and the Levites, having the unleavened bread, stood in proper order according to kindred 11 and the grouping of the ancestral houses, before the people, to make the offering to the Lord as it is written in the book of Moses; this they did in the morning. 12 They roasted the passover lamb with fire, as required; and they boiled the sacrifices in bronze pots and caldrons, with a pleasing odor, 13 and carried them to all the people. Afterward they prepared the passover for themselves and for their kindred the priests, the sons of Aaron, 14 because the priests were offering the fat until nightfall; so the Levites prepared it for themselves and for their kindred the priests, the sons of Aaron. 15 The temple singers, the sons of Asaph, were in their place according to the arrangement made by David, and also Asaph, Zechariah, and Eddinus, who represented the king. 16 The gatekeepers were at each gate; no one needed to interrupt his daily duties, for their kindred the Levites prepared the passover for them.

17 So the things that had to do with the sacrifices to the Lord were accomplished that day: the passover was kept 18 and the sacrifices were offered on the altar of the Lord, according to the command of King Josiah. 19 And the people of Israel who were present at that time kept the passover and the festival of unleavened bread seven days. 20 No passover like it had been kept in Israel since the times of the prophet Samuel; 21 none of the kings of Israel had kept such

1 Josiah celebrated the Passover to his Lord at Jerusalem, and the Passover victims were sacrificed on the fourteenth day of the first month. 2 He installed the priests, duly robed in their vestments, in the temple of the Lord according to the order of daily service. 3 He commanded the Levites, who served the temple in Israel, to purify themselves for the Lord, before placing the sacred Ark in the Lord's house, which King Solomon son of David built. 4 Josiah said to them, 'You shall not carry it about on your shoulders any longer. Now you are to serve the Lord your God and minister to his people Israel: prepare yourselves, family by family and clan by clan, 5 in the manner prescribed by King David of Israel and provided for so magnificently by his son Solomon. Stand in the holy place according to your family groups, you Levites who are in divisions to act for your brother Israelites. 6 Sacrifice the Passover victims, and prepare the sacrifices for your kinsmen. Keep the Passover according to the command given by the Lord to Moses.'

7 For those who were present Josiah contributed thirty thousand lambs and kids and three thousand calves; they were given from the king's own resources to the people and to the priests and Levites in fulfilment of his promise. 8 The temple wardens, Chelkias, Zacharias, and Esyelus, gave the priests two thousand six hundred sheep and three hundred calves for the Passover. 9 Jechonias, Samaeas, his brother Nathanael, Sabias, Ochielus, and Joram, high-ranking officers in the army, gave the Levites five thousand sheep and seven hundred calves for the Passover.

10 This was the procedure: the priests and the Levites, bearing the unleavened bread, stood in all their splendour by clans 11 and by family groups before the people, to make offerings to the Lord as is laid down in the book of Moses. This took place in the morning. 12 The Passover victims were roasted over the fire in the prescribed way and the sacrifices boiled with fragrant herbs in the bronze vessels and cauldrons; 13 then portions were carried round to the whole assembly. After that the Levites made preparations for themselves and for their kinsmen, the priests of Aaron's line. 14 It was because the priests were engaged until nightfall in offering up the fat portions that the Levites made the preparations both for themselves and for their kinsmen, the priests of Aaron's line. 15 The temple singers, the sons of Asaph, were in their places according to the ordinances of David, and Asaph, Zacharias, and Eddinous of the royal court; 16 the door-keepers were at each gateway. There was no need for any of them to leave their posts, for their kinsmen, the Levites, made the preparations for them.

17 Everything for the sacrifice to the Lord was completed that day: the celebration of the Passover 18 and the offering of the sacrifices on the Lord's altar, according to King Josiah's orders. 19 Israelites who were present at that time kept the Passover and the feast of Unleavened Bread for seven days. 20 No Passover like it had been celebrated in Israel since the time of the prophet Samuel; 21 none of the

[a] Gk Esyelus

a passover as was kept by Josiah and the priests and Levites and the people of Judah and all of Israel who were living in Jerusalem. 22 In the eighteenth year of the reign of Josiah this passover was kept.

23 And the deeds of Josiah were upright in the sight of the Lord, for his heart was full of godliness. 24 In ancient times the events of his reign have been recorded — concerning those who sinned and acted wickedly toward the Lord beyond any other people or kingdom, and how they grieved the Lord*b* deeply, so that the words of the Lord fell upon Israel.

25 After all these acts of Josiah, it happened that Pharaoh, king of Egypt, went to make war at Carchemish on the Euphrates, and Josiah went out against him. 26 And the king of Egypt sent word to him saying, "What have we to do with each other, O king of Judea? 27 I was not sent against you by the Lord God, for my war is at the Euphrates. And now the Lord is with me! The Lord is with me, urging me on! Stand aside, and do not oppose the Lord."

28 Josiah, however, did not turn back to his chariot, but tried to fight with him, and did not heed the words of the prophet Jeremiah from the mouth of the Lord. 29 He joined battle with him in the plain of Megiddo, and the commanders came down against King Josiah. 30 The king said to his servants, "Take me away from the battle, for I am very weak." And immediately his servants took him out of the line of battle. 31 He got into his second chariot; and after he was brought back to Jerusalem he died, and was buried in the tomb of his ancestors.

32 In all Judea they mourned for Josiah. The prophet Jeremiah lamented for Josiah, and the principal men, with the women,*c* have made lamentation for him to this day; it was ordained that this should always be done throughout the whole nation of Israel. 33 These things are written in the book of the histories of the kings of Judea; and every one of the acts of Josiah, and his splendor, and his understanding of the law of the Lord, and the things that he had done before, and these that are now told, are recorded in the book of the kings of Israel and Judah.

34 The men of the nation took Jeconiah*d* son of Josiah, who was twenty-three years old, and made him king in succession to his father Josiah. 35 He reigned three months in Judah and Jerusalem. Then the king of Egypt deposed him from reigning in Jerusalem, 36 and fined the nation one hundred talents of silver and one talent of gold. 37 The king of Egypt made his brother Jehoiakim king of Judea and Jerusalem. 38 Jehoiakim put the nobles in prison, and seized his brother Zarius and brought him back from Egypt.

39 Jehoiakim was twenty-five years old when he began to reign in Judea and Jerusalem; he did what was evil in the sight of the Lord. 40 King Nebuchadnezzar of Babylon came up against him; he bound him with a chain of bronze and took him away to Babylon. 41 Nebuchadnezzar also took some holy vessels of the Lord, and carried them away, and stored them in his temple in Babylon. 42 But the things that are reported about Jehoiakim,*b* and his uncleanness and impiety, are written in the annals of the kings.

43 His son Jehoiachin*e* became king in his place; when he was made king he was eighteen years old, 44 and he reigned three months and ten days in Jerusalem. He did what was evil in the sight of the Lord. 45 A year later Nebuchadnezzar sent and removed him to Babylon, with the holy vessels of the Lord, 46 and made Zedekiah king of Judea and Jerusalem.

Zedekiah was twenty-one years old, and he reigned eleven years. 47 He also did what was evil in the sight of the

kings of Israel had kept such a Passover as was kept by Josiah, with the priests, Levites, and men of Judah, and all the Israelites who happened to be resident in Jerusalem. 22 It was in the eighteenth year of Josiah's reign that this Passover was celebrated.

23 Josiah was deeply pious and his deeds were upright in the sight of his Lord. 24 The events of his reign are to be found among earlier records, records of sin and rebellion against the Lord graver than anything perpetrated by any other nation or kingdom, and of offences against him which brought down his judgement on Israel.

25 Some time after Josiah's act of worship had taken place, it happened that Pharaoh king of Egypt was advancing to open hostilities at Carchemish on the Euphrates. When Josiah marched out to confront him, 26 the Egyptian king sent him this message: 'What do you want with me, king of Judah? 27 It is not against you that the Lord God has sent me to fight; my campaign is on the Euphrates. On this occasion the Lord is with me. He is with me, speeding me on my way. Stand aside, and do not oppose the Lord.' 28 Josiah did not return to his chariot but set out to give battle, disregarding the words of the prophet Jeremiah, the spokesman of the Lord. 29 When he joined battle in the plain of Megiddo, Pharaoh's captains swept down on King Josiah. 30 'I am badly wounded,' the king said to his servants; 'take me out of the battle.' They took him out of the line at once, 31 and when he had been put into his second chariot, he was brought back to Jerusalem. There he died and was buried in the ancestral tomb.

32 Throughout Judah there was mourning for Josiah, and the prophet Jeremiah made lament for him. The lamentation for Josiah has been observed by the chief men and their wives from that day to this: an edict was issued to all the people of Israel that this should be done for all time. 33 These things are recorded in the annals of the kings of Judah; every deed of Josiah's which won him fame and showed his understanding of the law of the Lord, both what he did earlier and what is told of him here, is related in the book of the kings of Israel and Judah.

34 His fellow-countrymen took Jeconiah son of Josiah and made him king in succession to his father. He was twenty-three years old, 35 and he reigned over Judah and Jerusalem for three months. Then the king of Egypt deposed him, 36 fined the nation a hundred talents of silver and one talent of gold, 37 and replaced him by his brother Joakim as king of Judah and Jerusalem. 38 Joakim imprisoned the leading men and had his brother Zarius arrested and brought back from Egypt.

39 Joakim was twenty-five years old when he became king of Judah and Jerusalem. He did what was wrong in the eyes of the Lord, 40 and King Nebuchadnezzar of Babylon marched against him, put him in bronze fetters, and took him away to Babylon. 41 Nebuchadnezzar also seized some of the sacred vessels of the Lord; he carried them off and placed them in his own temple at Babylon. 42 The stories about Joakim, his depraved and impious conduct, are recorded in the chronicles of the kings.

43 He was succeeded by his son Joakim, who was eighteen years old when he came to the throne. 44 He reigned in Jerusalem for three months and ten days, and he too did what was wrong in the eyes of the Lord. 45 A year later Nebuchadnezzar sent and had him brought to Babylon together with the sacred vessels of the Lord, 46 and he made Zedekiah king of Judah and Jerusalem.

Zedekiah was twenty-one years old, and he reigned for eleven years. 47 He did what was wrong in the eyes of the

b Gk *him*   *c* Or *their wives*   *d* 2 Kings 23.30; 2 Chr 36.1 *Jehoahaz*
e Gk *Jehoiakim*

Lord, and did not heed the words that were spoken by the prophet Jeremiah from the mouth of the Lord. 48 Although King Nebuchadnezzar had made him swear by the name of the Lord, he broke his oath and rebelled; he stiffened his neck and hardened his heart and transgressed the laws of the Lord, the God of Israel. 49 Even the leaders of the people and of the priests committed many acts of sacrilege and lawlessness beyond all the unclean deeds of all the nations, and polluted the temple of the Lord in Jerusalem — the temple that God had made holy. 50 The God of their ancestors sent his messenger to call them back, because he would have spared them and his dwelling place. 51 But they mocked his messengers, and whenever the Lord spoke, they scoffed at his prophets, 52 until in his anger against his people because of their ungodly acts he gave command to bring against them the kings of the Chaldeans. 53 These killed their young men with the sword around their holy temple, and did not spare young man or young woman,*f* old man or child, for he gave them all into their hands. 54 They took all the holy vessels of the Lord, great and small, the treasure chests of the Lord, and the royal stores, and carried them away to Babylon. 55 They burned the house of the Lord, broke down the walls of Jerusalem, burned their towers with fire, 56 and utterly destroyed all its glorious things. The survivors he led away to Babylon with the sword, 57 and they were servants to him and to his sons until the Persians began to reign, in fulfillment of the word of the Lord by the mouth of Jeremiah, 58 saying, "Until the land has enjoyed its sabbaths, it shall keep sabbath all the time of its desolation until the completion of seventy years."

2 In the first year of Cyrus as king of the Persians, so that the word of the Lord by the mouth of Jeremiah might be accomplished — 2 the Lord stirred up the spirit of King Cyrus of the Persians, and he made a proclamation throughout all his kingdom and also put it in writing:

3 "Thus says Cyrus king of the Persians: The Lord of Israel, the Lord Most High, has made me king of the world, 4 and he has commanded me to build him a house at Jerusalem, which is in Judea. 5 If any of you, therefore, are of his people, may your Lord be with you; go up to Jerusalem, which is in Judea, and build the house of the Lord of Israel — he is the Lord who dwells in Jerusalem, 6 and let each of you, wherever you may live, be helped by the people of your place with gold and silver, 7 with gifts and with horses and cattle, besides the other things added as votive offerings for the temple of the Lord that is in Jerusalem."

8 Then arose the heads of families of the tribes of Judah and Benjamin, and the priests and the Levites, and all whose spirit the Lord had stirred to go up to build the house in Jerusalem for the Lord; 9 their neighbors helped them with everything, with silver and gold, with horses and cattle, and with a very great number of votive offerings from many whose hearts were stirred.

10 King Cyrus also brought out the holy vessels of the Lord that Nebuchadnezzar had carried away from Jerusalem and stored in his temple of idols. 11 When King Cyrus of the Persians brought these out, he gave them to Mithridates, his treasurer, 12 and by him they were given to Sheshbazzar,*g* the governor of Judea. 13 The number of these was: one thousand gold cups, one thousand silver cups, twenty-nine silver censers, thirty gold bowls, two thousand four hundred ten silver bowls, and one thousand other vessels. 14 All the vessels were handed over, gold and silver, five thousand four hundred sixty-nine, 15 and they were carried back by Sheshbazzar with the returning exiles from Babylon to Jerusalem.

Lord and disregarded the advice of the prophet Jeremiah, the spokesman of the Lord. 48 King Nebuchadnezzar had made him swear by the Lord an oath of allegiance, but he renounced his oath and rebelled. He was stubborn and obstinate, and broke the commandments of the Lord God of Israel.

49 The leaders of both people and priests committed many impious and lawless acts. They outdid even the heathen in their abominable practices, and defiled the Lord's temple which had been consecrated in Jerusalem. 50 The God of their fathers sent his messenger to reclaim them, because he wished to spare them and his dwelling-place. 51 But they held his messengers in derision: they were scoffing at his prophets on the very day when the Lord spoke. 52 At last his anger was so roused against his people on account of their impieties that he ordered the Chaldaean kings to attack them. 53 The Lord handed them all over to their enemies, who put their young men to the sword around the holy temple, and spared neither young man nor maiden, neither the old nor the infant. 54 All the sacred vessels of the Lord, large and small, the furnishings of the Ark of the Lord, and the royal treasures were taken as spoil to Babylon. 55 The Lord's house was burnt down, the walls of Jerusalem razed to the ground, its towers set ablaze, 56 and all its splendours brought to ruin. Nebuchadnezzar transported to Babylon those who escaped the sword, 57 and they remained slaves to him and his sons until his empire fell to the Persians. This fulfilled the word of the Lord spoken by Jeremiah 58 that, until the land should have run the full term of its sabbaths, it should keep sabbath all the time of its desolation till the end of the seventy years.

2 In the first year of King Cyrus of Persia the Lord, to fulfil his word spoken through Jeremiah, 2 moved the heart of the king so that throughout his kingdom the following proclamation was made and at the same time issued in writing:

3 The decree of King Cyrus of Persia.

The Lord of Israel, the Most High Lord, has made me king of the world 4 and has charged me to build him a house at Jerusalem in Judaea. 5 Whoever among you, therefore, belongs to his people, may his Lord be with him! Let him go up to Jerusalem in Judaea and build the house of the Lord of Israel, the Lord who dwells in Jerusalem. 6 Throughout the country let assistance be given to each man by his neighbours with gold and silver 7 and other gifts, with horses and pack-animals, together with anything else set aside as votive offerings for the temple of the Lord in Jerusalem.

8 Then the heads of the families of the tribes of Judah and Benjamin came forward, along with the priests, the Levites, and all who had been prompted by the Lord to go up and build his house in Jerusalem. 9 Their neighbours assisted with gifts of every kind, silver and gold, horses and pack-animals. Many were also moved to help with votive offerings in great quantity. 10 Moreover, the sacred vessels of the Lord which Nebuchadnezzar had removed from Jerusalem and placed in the temple of his idols were brought out by King Cyrus of Persia 11 and given into the charge of Mithradates his treasurer, 12 by whom they were handed over to Sanabassar, governor of Judaea. 13 Here is the list of them: a thousand gold cups, a thousand silver cups, twenty-nine silver censers, thirty gold bowls, two thousand four hundred and ten silver bowls, and a thousand other articles. 14 In all, five thousand four hundred and sixty-nine gold and silver vessels were sent back, 15 and they were brought by Sanabassar to Jerusalem from Babylon along with the exiles.

f Gk virgin   *g* Gk Sanabassaros

1:54 the furnishings of the Ark: in other MSS the treasure chests.

16 In the time of King Artaxerxes of the Persians, Bishlam, Mithridates, Tabeel, Rehum, Beltethmus, the scribe Shimshai, and the rest of their associates, living in Samaria and other places, wrote him the following letter, against those who were living in Judea and Jerusalem:

17 "To King Artaxerxes our lord, your servants the recorder Rehum and the scribe Shimshai and the other members of their council, and the judges in Coelesyria and Phoenicia: 18 Let it now be known to our lord the king that the Jews who came up from you to us have gone to Jerusalem and are building that rebellious and wicked city, repairing its market places and walls and laying the foundations for a temple. 19 Now if this city is built and the walls finished, they will not only refuse to pay tribute but will even resist kings. 20 Since the building of the temple is now going on, we think it best not to neglect such a matter, 21 but to speak to our lord the king, in order that, if it seems good to you, search may be made in the records of your ancestors. 22 You will find in the annals what has been written about them, and will learn that this city was rebellious, troubling both kings and other cities, 23 and that the Jews were rebels and kept setting up blockades in it from of old. That is why this city was laid waste. 24 Therefore we now make known to you, O lord and king, that if this city is built and its walls finished, you will no longer have access to Coelesyria and Phoenicia."

25 Then the king, in reply to the recorder Rehum, Beltethmus, the scribe Shimshai, and the others associated with them and living in Samaria and Syria and Phoenicia, wrote as follows:

26 "I have read the letter that you sent me. So I ordered search to be made, and it has been found that this city from of old has fought against kings, 27 that the people in it were given to rebellion and war, and that mighty and cruel kings ruled in Jerusalem and exacted tribute from Coelesyria and Phoenicia. 28 Therefore I have now issued orders to prevent these people from building the city and to take care that nothing more be done 29 and that such wicked proceedings go no further to the annoyance of kings."

30 Then, when the letter from King Artaxerxes was read, Rehum and the scribe Shimshai and their associates went quickly to Jerusalem, with cavalry and a large number of armed troops, and began to hinder the builders. And the building of the temple in Jerusalem stopped until the second year of the reign of King Darius of the Persians.

3 Now King Darius gave a great banquet for all that were under him, all that were born in his house, and all the nobles of Media and Persia, 2 and all the satraps and generals and governors that were under him in the hundred twenty-seven satrapies from India to Ethiopia. 3 They ate and drank, and when they were satisfied they went away, and King Darius went to his bedroom; he went to sleep, but woke up again.

4 Then the three young men of the bodyguard, who kept guard over the person of the king, said to one another, 5 "Let each of us state what one thing is strongest; and to the one whose statement seems wisest, King Darius will give rich gifts and great honors of victory. 6 He shall be clothed in purple, and drink from gold cups, and sleep on a gold bed, h and have a chariot with gold bridles, and a turban of fine linen, and a necklace around his neck; 7 and because of his wisdom he shall sit next to Darius and shall be called Kinsman of Darius."

16 But when Artaxerxes was king of Persia, Belemus, Mithradates, Tabellius, Rathymus, Beeltethmus, Semellius the secretary, and their colleagues in office in Samaria and elsewhere, wrote the king the following letter denouncing the inhabitants of Judaea and Jerusalem:

17 To our Sovereign Lord Artaxerxes your servants Rathymus the Recorder, Semellius the Secretary, the other members of their council, and the magistrates in Coele-Syria and Phoenicia. 18 Be it known to your majesty that the Jews who left you to come up here have arrived in Jerusalem, and are rebuilding that rebellious and wicked city, repairing its streets and walls and laying the foundation of a temple. 19 Once this city is rebuilt and the walls are completed, they will never submit to paying tribute but will even rebel against your royal house. 20 Since work on the temple is in hand, we have thought it well not to overlook such an important matter 21 but to bring it to your majesty's attention, in order that, if it please your majesty, search may be made in the records left by your predecessors. 22 You will discover in the archives references to these matters; you will learn that this has been a rebellious city, a source of trouble to kings and cities. 23 From earliest times it has been a centre of armed resistance by the Jews, and for that reason it was laid in ruins. 24 Therefore we now submit to your majesty that, if this city be rebuilt and its walls rise again, you will be denied access to Coele-Syria and Phoenicia.

25 The king sent this reply:
To Rathymus the Recorder, Beeltethmus, Semellius the Secretary, and their colleagues in office in Samaria, Syria, and Phoenicia.

26 Having read the letter you sent me, I ordered search to be made, and that city, it was discovered, has a long history of opposition to the royal house, 27 and its inhabitants have been given to rebellion and war. There have been powerful and ruthless kings ruling in Jerusalem who have exercised authority over Coele-Syria and Phoenicia and laid them under tribute. 28 I therefore command that the men of whom you write be prevented from rebuilding the city, and that measures be taken to enforce this order 29 and to check the spread of an evil likely to be troublesome to our royal house.

30 On receipt of the letter from King Artaxerxes, Rathymus, Semellius the secretary, and their colleagues hurried to Jerusalem with cavalry and a large body of other troops and stopped the builders. Work on the temple at Jerusalem remained at a standstill until the second year of the reign of King Darius of Persia.

3 KING Darius gave a great banquet for all his retainers, for all the members of his household, all the chief men of Media and Persia, 2 along with the whole body of satraps, commanders, and governors of his empire in the hundred and twenty-seven satrapies from India to Ethiopia. 3 After eating and drinking as much as they wanted, they withdrew. King Darius retired to his bedchamber, where he lay down and fell fast asleep.

4 Then the three young men of the king's personal bodyguard said among themselves: 5 'Let each of us name the thing he judges to be strongest, and to the one whose opinion appears wisest let King Darius give rich gifts and prizes: 6 he shall be robed in purple, drink from gold cups, and sleep on a golden bed; he shall have a chariot with gold-studded bridles, and a turban of fine linen, and a chain around his neck. 7 His wisdom shall give him the right to sit next to the king and to bear the title Kinsman of Darius.'

h Gk on gold

3:3 and fell fast asleep: prob. rdg; Gk sleepless.

8 Then each wrote his own statement, and they sealed them and put them under the pillow of King Darius, 9 and said, "When the king wakes, they will give him the writing; and to the one whose statement the king and the three nobles of Persia judge to be wisest the victory shall be given according to what is written." 10 The first wrote, "Wine is strongest." 11 The second wrote, "The king is strongest." 12 The third wrote, "Women are strongest, but above all things truth is victor."*i*

13 When the king awoke, they took the writing and gave it to him, and he read it. 14 Then he sent and summoned all the nobles of Persia and Media and the satraps and generals and governors and prefects, 15 and he took his seat in the council chamber, and the writing was read in their presence. 16 He said, "Call the young men, and they shall explain their statements." So they were summoned, and came in. 17 They said to them, "Explain to us what you have written."

Then the first, who had spoken of the strength of wine, began and said: 18 "Gentlemen, how is wine the strongest? It leads astray the minds of all who drink it. 19 It makes equal the mind of the king and the orphan, of the slave and the free, of the poor and the rich. 20 It turns every thought to feasting and mirth, and forgets all sorrow and debt. 21 It makes all hearts feel rich, forgets kings and satraps, and makes everyone talk in millions.*j* 22 When people drink they forget to be friendly with friends and kindred, and before long they draw their swords. 23 And when they recover from the wine, they do not remember what they have done. 24 Gentlemen, is not wine the strongest, since it forces people to do these things?" When he had said this, he stopped speaking.

4 Then the second, who had spoken of the strength of the king, began to speak: 2 "Gentlemen, are not men strongest, who rule over land and sea and all that is in them? 3 But the king is stronger; he is their lord and master, and whatever he says to them they obey. 4 If he tells them to make war on one another, they do it; and if he sends them out against the enemy, they go, and conquer mountains, walls, and towers. 5 They kill and are killed, and do not disobey the king's command; if they win the victory, they bring everything to the king — whatever spoil they take and everything else. 6 Likewise those who do not serve in the army or make war but till the soil; whenever they sow and reap, and bring some to the king; and they compel one another to pay taxes to the king. 7 And yet he is only one man! If he tells them to kill, they kill; if he tells them to release, they release; 8 if he tells them to attack, they attack; if he tells them to lay waste, they lay waste; if he tells them to build, they build; 9 if he tells them to cut down, they cut down; if he tells them to plant, they plant. 10 All his people and his armies obey him. Furthermore, he reclines, he eats and drinks and sleeps, 11 but they keep watch around him, and no one may go away to attend to his own affairs, nor do they disobey him. 12 Gentlemen, why is not the king the strongest, since he is to be obeyed in this fashion?" And he stopped speaking.

13 Then the third, who had spoken of women and truth (and this was Zerubbabel), began to speak: 14 "Gentlemen, is not the king great, and are not men many, and is not wine strong? Who is it, then, that rules them, or has the mastery over them? Is it not women? 15 Women gave birth to the king and to every people that rules over sea and land. 16 From women they came; and women brought up the very men who plant the vineyards from which comes wine. 17 Women make men's clothes; they bring men glory; men cannot exist without women. 18 If men gather gold and sil-

8 Each then put his opinion in writing, affixed his seal, and placed it under the king's pillow. 9 'When the king wakes,' they said, 'the writing will be given him, and the king and the three chief men of Persia shall judge whose opinion is wisest; the award will be made to that man on the evidence of what he has written.'

10 One wrote, 'Wine is strongest.' 11 The second wrote, 'The king is strongest.' 12 The third wrote, 'Women are strongest, but truth conquers all.' 13 When the king awoke, he was handed what they had written. Having read it 14 he summoned all the chief men of Persia and Media, satraps, commanders, governors, and chief officers, 15 and took his seat in the council-chamber. What each of the three had written was then read out before them. 16 'Call the young men,' said the king, 'and let them explain their opinions.' They were summoned and, on coming in, 17 were asked to clarify what they had written.

The first, who spoke about the strength of wine, began: 18 'Sirs, how true it is that wine is strongest! It bemuses the wits of all who drink it: 19 king and orphan, slave and free, poor and rich, on them all it has the same effect. 20 It turns all thoughts to revelry and mirth; it brings forgetfulness of grief and debt. 21 It makes everyone feel rich; it cares nothing for king or satrap, but sets all men talking in millions. 22 When they are in their cups, they forget to be friendly to friends and relations, and before long are drawing their swords; 23 and when they awake after their wine, they cannot remember what they have done. 24 Sirs, is not wine the strongest, seeing that it makes men behave in this way?' With that he ended his speech.

4 Then the second, he who spoke of the strength of the king, began: 2 'Sirs, is not man the strongest, man who subdues land and sea and everything in them? 3 But the strongest of men is the king; he is their lord and master, and they obey whatever command he gives them. 4 If he bids them make war on one another, they do so; if he dispatches them against his enemies, they march off and make their way over mountains and walls and towers. 5 They kill and are killed, but they never disobey the king's command. If they are victorious they bring everything, spoil and all else, to the king. 6 Again, take those who do not serve as soldiers or go to war, but work the land: they sow and reap, and lay the harvest before the king. They compel each other to pay him their tribute. 7 Though he is no more than one man, if he orders them to kill, they kill; if he orders them to release, they release. He orders them 8 to smite and they beat, to demolish and they demolish, to build and they build, 9 to cut down and they cut down, to plant and they plant. 10 People and troops all obey him. Further, while he himself is at table, whether he eats, drinks, or goes to sleep, 11 they stand in attendance round him and none can leave and see to his own affairs; in nothing whatever do they disobey. 12 Sirs, surely the king must be the strongest, when he commands such obedience!' With that he ended.

13 The third, he who spoke about women and truth, was Zerubbabel; he began: 14 'Sirs, it is true that the king is great, that men are many, and that wine is strong, but who rules over them? Who is the master? Women, surely! 15 The king and all his people, lords over land and sea, were born of women, 16 and from them they came. Women brought up the men who planted the vineyards which yield the wine. 17 They make the clothes men wear and they bring honour to men; without women men could not exist.

---

*i Or but truth is victor over all things   *j Gk talents

ver or any other beautiful thing, and then see a woman lovely in appearance and beauty, 19 they let all those things go, and gape at her, and with open mouths stare at her, and all prefer her to gold or silver or any other beautiful thing. 20 A man leaves his own father, who brought him up, and his own country, and clings to his wife. 21 With his wife he ends his days, with no thought of his father or his mother or his country. 22 Therefore you must realize that women rule over you!

"Do you not labor and toil, and bring everything and give it to women? 23 A man takes his sword, and goes out to travel and rob and steal and to sail the sea and rivers; 24 he faces lions, and he walks in darkness, and when he steals and robs and plunders, he brings it back to the woman he loves. 25 A man loves his wife more than his father or his mother. 26 Many men have lost their minds because of women, and have become slaves because of them. 27 Many have perished, or stumbled, or sinned because of women. 28 And now do you not believe me?

"Is not the king great in his power? Do not all lands fear to touch him? 29 Yet I have seen him with Apame, the king's concubine, the daughter of the illustrious Bartacus; she would sit at the king's right hand 30 and take the crown from the king's head and put it on her own, and slap the king with her left hand. 31 At this the king would gaze at her with mouth agape. If she smiles at him, he laughs; if she loses her temper with him, he flatters her, so that she may be reconciled to him. 32 Gentlemen, why are not women strong, since they do such things?"

33 Then the king and the nobles looked at one another; and he began to speak about truth: 34 "Gentlemen, are not women strong? The earth is vast, and heaven is high, and the sun is swift in its course, for it makes the circuit of the heavens and returns to its place in one day. 35 Is not the one who does these things great? But truth is great, and stronger than all things. 36 The whole earth calls upon truth, and heaven blesses her. All God's works[k] quake and tremble, and with him there is nothing unrighteous. 37 Wine is unrighteous, the king is unrighteous, women are unrighteous, all human beings are unrighteous, all their works are unrighteous, and all such things. There is no truth in them and in their unrighteousness they will perish. 38 But truth endures and is strong forever, and lives and prevails forever and ever. 39 With it there is no partiality or preference, but it does what is righteous instead of anything that is unrighteous or wicked. Everyone approves its deeds, 40 and there is nothing unrighteous in its judgment. To it belongs the strength and the kingship and the power and the majesty of all the ages. Blessed be the God of truth!" 41 When he stopped speaking, all the people shouted and said, "Great is truth, and strongest of all!"

42 Then the king said to him, "Ask what you wish, even beyond what is written, and we will give it to you, for you have been found to be the wisest. You shall sit next to me, and be called my Kinsman." 43 Then he said to the king, "Remember the vow that you made on the day when you became king, to build Jerusalem, 44 and to send back all the vessels that were taken from Jerusalem, which Cyrus set apart when he began[l] to destroy Babylon, and vowed to send them back there. 45 You also vowed to build the temple, which the Edomites burned when Judea was laid waste by the Chaldeans. 46 And now, O lord the king, this is what I ask and request of you, and this befits your greatness. I pray therefore that you fulfill the vow whose fulfillment you vowed to the King of heaven with your own lips."

18 'If men have amassed gold and silver and all manner of beautiful things, and then see a woman with a lovely face and figure, 19 they leave it all to gape and stare at her with open mouth, and every one of them will prefer her above gold and silver or any thing of beauty. 20 A man will abandon his father who brought him up, abandon even his country, and become one with his wife. 21 To the end of his days he stays with her, forgetful of father, mother, and country. 22 Here is the proof that women are your masters: do you not toil and sweat and then bring all you earn and give it to your wives? 23 A man will take his sword and sally forth to plunder and steal, to sail on sea and river; 24 he confronts lions, he goes about in the dark; and when he has stolen and robbed and looted, he brings the spoil home to his beloved.

25 'A man loves his wife above father or mother. 26 For women's sakes many men have been driven out of their minds, many have become slaves, 27 many have perished or come to grief or taken to evil ways. 28 Now do you believe me? Certainly the king wields great authority; no country dare lift a finger against him. 29 Yet I watched him with Apame, his favourite concubine, daughter of the celebrated Bartacus. She was sitting on the king's right, 30 and she took the diadem off his head and put it on her own. She was slapping his face with her left hand, 31 and all the king did was gape at her open-mouthed. When she laughed at him he laughed; when she was cross with him he coaxed her to make it up with him. 32 Sirs, if women do as well as this, how can their strength be denied?' 33 The king and the chief men looked at one another.

Zerubbabel then went on to speak about truth: 34 'Sirs, we have seen that women are strong. The earth is vast, the sky is lofty, yet the sun, swift in its course, moves through the circle of the sky and speeds home in a single day. 35 How great is the sun which can do this! But truth too is great; it is stronger than all else. 36 The whole earth calls on truth, and the sky praises her; all created things shake and tremble. With her there is no injustice. 37 There is injustice in wine, and in kings, and in women, injustice in all men and in all their works, whatever they may be. There is no truth in them, and in their injustice they shall perish. 38 But truth abides and remains strong for ever; she lives and is sovereign for ever and ever.

39 'There is no favouritism with her, no partiality; rather she exacts justice from everyone who is wicked or unjust. All approve what she does; 40 in her judgements there is no injustice. Hers are strength and royalty, the authority and majesty of all ages. Praise be to the God of truth!'

41 As Zerubbabel finished speaking, all the people shouted, 'Great is truth: truth is strongest!' 42 Then the king said to him, 'Ask what you will, even beyond what is laid down in the terms, and we shall grant it you. You have been proved to be the wisest, and you shall sit next to me and be called my Kinsman.' 43 Zerubbabel answered, 'Remember, O king, the vow you made on the day when you came to the throne: you promised to rebuild Jerusalem 44 and to send back all the vessels taken from there. Cyrus had set them aside, for when he vowed to destroy Babylon, at the same time he vowed to restore these vessels. 45 You also made a vow to rebuild the temple, burnt by the Edomites when Judaea had been ravaged by the Chaldaeans. 46 This is the favour I now beg of you, my lord king, this the magnanimous gesture I request: that you should perform the vow made by you to the King of heaven.'

[k] Gk *All the works*   [l] Cn: Gk *vowed*

47 Then King Darius got up and kissed him, and wrote letters for him to all the treasurers and governors and generals and satraps, that they should give safe conduct to him and to all who were going up with him to build Jerusalem. 48 And he wrote letters to all the governors in Coelesyria and Phoenicia and to those in Lebanon, to bring cedar timber from Lebanon to Jerusalem, and to help him build the city. 49 He wrote in behalf of all the Jews who were going up from his kingdom to Judea, in the interest of their freedom, that no officer or satrap or governor or treasurer should forcibly enter their doors; 50 that all the country that they would occupy should be theirs without tribute; that the Idumeans should give up the villages of the Jews that they held; 51 that twenty talents a year should be given for the building of the temple until it was completed, 52 and an additional ten talents a year for burnt offerings to be offered on the altar every day, in accordance with the commandment to make seventeen offerings; 53 and that all who came from Babylonia to build the city should have their freedom, they and their children and all the priests who came. 54 He wrote also concerning their support and the priests' vestments in which*m* they were to minister. 55 He wrote that the support for the Levites should be provided until the day when the temple would be finished and Jerusalem built. 56 He wrote that land and wages should be provided for all who guarded the city. 57 And he sent back from Babylon all the vessels that Cyrus had set apart; everything that Cyrus had ordered to be done, he also commanded to be done and to be sent to Jerusalem.

58 When the young man went out, he lifted up his face to heaven toward Jerusalem, and praised the King of heaven, saying, 59 "From you comes the victory; from you comes wisdom, and yours is the glory. I am your servant. 60 Blessed are you, who have given me wisdom; I give you thanks, O Lord of our ancestors."

61 So he took the letters, and went to Babylon and told this to all his kindred. 62 And they praised the God of their ancestors, because he had given them release and permission 63 to go up and build Jerusalem and the temple that is called by his name; and they feasted, with music and rejoicing, for seven days.

5 After this the heads of ancestral houses were chosen to go up, according to their tribes, with their wives and sons and daughters, and their male and female servants, and their livestock. 2 And Darius sent with them a thousand cavalry to take them back to Jerusalem in safety, with the music of drums and flutes; 3 all their kindred were making merry. And he made them go up with them.

4 These are the names of the men who went up, according to their ancestral houses in the tribes, over their groups: 5 the priests, the descendants of Phinehas son of Aaron; Jeshua son of Jozadak son of Seraiah and Joakim son of Zerubbabel son of Shealtiel, of the house of David, of the lineage of Phares, of the tribe of Judah, 6 who spoke wise words before King Darius of the Persians, in the second year of his reign, in the month of Nisan, the first month.

7 These are the Judeans who came up out of their sojourn in exile, whom King Nebuchadnezzar of Babylon had carried away to Babylon 8 and who returned to Jerusalem and the rest of Judea, each to his own town. They came with Zerubbabel and Jeshua, Nehemiah, Seraiah, Resaiah, Eneneus, Mordecai, Beelsarus, Aspharasus, Reeliah, Rehum, and Baanah, their leaders.

9 The number of those of the nation and their leaders: the descendants of Parosh, two thousand one hundred seventy-two. The descendants of Shephatiah, four hundred seventy-two. 10 The descendants of Arah, seven hundred

m Gk *in what priestly vestments*

47 King Darius stood up, embraced him, and wrote letters on his behalf, instructing all the treasurers, governors, commanders, and satraps to give safe conduct to him and to all those going up with him to rebuild Jerusalem. 48 He wrote also to all the governors in Coele-Syria and Phoenicia and to those in Lebanon ordering them to transport cedar-wood from Lebanon to Jerusalem and help Zerubbabel build the city. 49 He gave all Jews going up from his kingdom to Judaea a written assurance of their liberties: no one in authority, whether satrap, governor, or treasurer, was to molest them in their homes. 50 All land which they might acquire was to be exempt from taxation, and the Edomites were to surrender the villages they had seized from the Jews. 51 Each year twenty talents were to be contributed to the building of the temple until it was completed, 52 and a further ten talents annually for the seventeen whole-offerings to be sacrificed every day on the altar in accordance with their law. 53–54 All who were going from Babylonia to build the city were to enjoy freedom, they and their descendants after them. The king gave orders in writing that all the priests going there should also receive maintenance and the vestments in which they would officiate; 55 that the Levites too should receive maintenance, until that day when the temple should be completed and Jerusalem rebuilt; 56 and that all who guarded the city should be given land and pay. 57 He sent back from Babylon the vessels which Cyrus had set aside. He reaffirmed all that Cyrus had commanded, and gave orders that everything should be restored to Jerusalem.

58 When the young man, Zerubbabel, went out, he turned to face the direction of Jerusalem, and looking heavenwards praised the King of heaven, saying:

59 'From you come victory and wisdom;
    yours is the glory, and I am your servant.
60 All praise to you, for you have given me wisdom;
    to you, Lord of our fathers, I ascribe praise.'

61 He took the letters and set out for Babylon. There his fellow-Jews, on receiving his report, 62 praised the God of their fathers who had given them leave and liberty 63 to go up and rebuild Jerusalem and the temple which bore his name; and they feasted for seven days with music and rejoicing.

5 AFTER this the heads of families, tribe by tribe, were chosen to go up to Jerusalem with their sons and daughters, their male and female slaves, and their pack-animals. 2 Darius dispatched a thousand horsemen to escort them safely there, with a band of drums and flutes, 3 to which all their kinsmen danced. So he sent them off with their escort.

4 These are the names of the men who went up to Jerusalem, arranged according to their families and tribes and their allotted duties: 5 the priests, sons of Phineas son of Aaron, with Jeshua son of Josedek, son of Saraeas, and Joakim son of Zerubbabel, son of Salathiel, of the house of David of the line of Phares of the tribe of Judah; 6 it was Zerubbabel who spoke wise words before King Darius of Persia. This was in the second year of his reign, in Nisan the first month.

7 These are the men from Judaea who returned from captivity and exile, those whom King Nebuchadnezzar of Babylon had taken to Babylon. 8 Each of them returned to his own town, whether to Jerusalem or elsewhere in Judaea. They were led by Zerubbabel and Jeshua, Nehemiah, Zaraeas, Resaeas, Enenius, Mardochaeus, Beelsarus, Aspharasus, Reelias, Roimus, and Baana.

9 The number of those of the nation who returned with their leaders was: the line of Phoros two thousand one hundred and seventy-two; the line of Saphat four hundred and seventy-two; 10 the line of Ares seven hundred and fifty-six;

fifty-six. 11 The descendants of Pahath-moab, of the descendants of Jeshua and Joab, two thousand eight hundred twelve. 12 The descendants of Elam, one thousand two hundred fifty-four. The descendants of Zattu, nine hundred forty-five. The descendants of Chorbe, seven hundred five. The descendants of Bani, six hundred forty-eight. 13 The descendants of Bebai, six hundred twenty-three. The descendants of Azgad, one thousand three hundred twenty-two. 14 The descendants of Adonikam, six hundred sixty-seven. The descendants of Bigvai, two thousand sixty-six. The descendants of Adin, four hundred fifty-four. 15 The descendants of Ater, namely of Hezekiah, ninety-two. The descendants of Kilan and Azetas, sixty-seven. The descendants of Azaru, four hundred thirty-two. 16 The descendants of Annias, one hundred one. The descendants of Arom. The descendants of Bezai, three hundred twenty-three. The descendants of Arsiphurith, one hundred twelve. 17 The descendants of Baiterus, three thousand five. The descendants of Bethlomon, one hundred twenty-three. 18 Those from Netophah, fifty-five. Those from Anathoth, one hundred fifty-eight. Those from Bethasmoth, forty-two. 19 Those from Kiriatharim, twenty-five. Those from Chephirah and Beeroth, seven hundred forty-three. 20 The Chadiasans and Ammidians, four hundred twenty-two. Those from Kirama and Geba, six hundred twenty-one. 21 Those from Macalon, one hundred twenty-two. Those from Betolio, fifty-two. The descendants of Niphish, one hundred fifty-six. 22 The descendants of the other Calamolalus and Ono, seven hundred twenty-five. The descendants of Jerechus, three hundred forty-five. 23 The descendants of Senaah, three thousand three hundred thirty.

24 The priests: the descendants of Jedaiah son of Jeshua, of the descendants of Anasib, nine hundred seventy-two. The descendants of Immer, one thousand and fifty-two. 25 The descendants of Pashhur, one thousand two hundred forty-seven. The descendants of Charme, one thousand seventeen.

26 The Levites: the descendants of Jeshua and Kadmiel and Bannas and Sudias, seventy-four. 27 The temple singers: the descendants of Asaph, one hundred twenty-eight. 28 The gatekeepers: the descendants of Shallum, the descendants of Ater, the descendants of Talmon, the descendants of Akkub, the descendants of Hatita, the descendants of Shobai, in all one hundred thirty-nine.

29 The temple servants: the descendants of Esau, the descendants of Hasupha, the descendants of Tabbaoth, the descendants of Keros, the descendants of Sua, the descendants of Padon, the descendants of Lebanah, the descendants of Hagabah, 30 the descendants of Akkub, the descendants of Uthai, the descendants of Ketab, the descendants of Hagab, the descendants of Subai, the descendants of Hana, the descendants of Cathua, the descendants of Geddur, 31 the descendants of Jairus, the descendants of Daisan, the descendants of Noeba, the descendants of Chezib, the descendants of Gazera, the descendants of Uzza, the descendants of Phinoe, the descendants of Hasrah, the descendants of Basthai, the descendants of Asnah, the descendants of Maani, the descendants of Nephisim, the descendants of Acuph,[n] the descendants of Hakupha, the descendants of Asur, the descendants of Pharakim, the descendants of Bazluth, 32 the descendants of Mehida, the descendants of Cutha, the descendants of Charea, the descendants of Barkos, the descendants of Serar, the descendants of Temah, the descendants of Neziah, the descendants of Hatipha.

33 The descendants of Solomon's servants: the descendants of Assaphioth, the descendants of Peruda, the descendants of Jaalah, the descendants of Lozon, the descendants of Isdael, the descendants of Shephatiah, 34 the descendants

11 the line of Phaath-moab, belonging to the line of Jeshua and Joab, two thousand eight hundred and twelve; 12 the line of Olamus one thousand two hundred and fifty-four; the line of Zathui nine hundred and forty-five; the line of Chorbe seven hundred and five; the line of Banei six hundred and forty-eight; 13 the line of Bebae six hundred and twenty-three; the line of Argai one thousand three hundred and twenty-two; 14 the line of Adonikam six hundred and sixty-seven; the line of Bagoi two thousand and sixty-six; the line of Adinus four hundred and fifty-four; 15 the line of Ater son of Hezekias ninety-two; the line of Keilan and Azetas sixty-seven; the line of Azurus four hundred and thirty-two; 16 the line of Annias one hundred and one; the line of Arom and the line of Bassa three hundred and twenty-three; the line of Arsiphurith one hundred and twelve; 17 the line of Baeterus three thousand and five. The men of Bethlomon one hundred and twenty-three; 18 the men of Netophae fifty-five; the men of Anathoth one hundred and fifty-eight; the men of Bethasmoth forty-two; 19 the men of Cariathiarius twenty-five; the men of Caphira and Beroth seven hundred and forty-three; 20 the Chadiasans and Ammidaeans four hundred and twenty-two; the men of Kirama and Gabbes six hundred and twenty-one; 21 the men of Macalon one hundred and twenty-two; the men of Betolio fifty-two; the line of Niphis one hundred and fifty-six; 22 the line of Calamolalus and Onus seven hundred and twenty-five; the line of Jerechus three hundred and forty-five; 23 the line of Sanaas three thousand three hundred and thirty.

24 The priests: the line of Jeddu son of Jeshua, belonging to the line of Anasib, nine hundred and seventy-two; the line of Emmeruth one thousand and fifty-two; 25 the line of Phassurus one thousand two hundred and forty-seven; the line of Charme one thousand and seventeen.

26 The Levites: the line of Joshua, Cadmielus, Bannus, and Sudius seventy-four. 27 The temple singers: the line of Asaph one hundred and forty-eight.

28 The door-keepers: the line of Salum, of Atar, of Tolman, of Dacubi, of Ateta, of Sabi, in all one hundred and thirty-nine.

29 The temple servitors: the line of Esau, of Asipha, of Taboth, of Keras, of Soua, of Phaleas, of Labana, of Aggaba, 30 of Acud, of Uta, of Ketab, of Gaba, of Subai, of Anan, of Cathua, of Geddur, 31 of Jairus, of Desan, of Noeba, of Chaseba, of Gazera, of Ozius, of Phinoe, of Asara, of Basthae, of Asana, of Maani, of Naphisi, of Acum, of Achipha, of Asur, of Pharakim, of Baaloth, 32 of Meedda, of Coutha, of Charea, of Barchue, of Serar, of Thomi, of Nasith, of Atepha. 33 The descendants of Solomon's servants: the line of Asapphioth, of Pharida, of Jeeli, of Lozon, of Isdael, of Saphythi, 34 of Agia, of Pha-

n Other ancient authorities read Acub or Acum

of Agia, the descendants of Pochereth-hazzebaim, the descendants of Sarothie, the descendants of Masiah, the descendants of Gas, the descendants of Addus, the descendants of Subas, the descendants of Apherra, the descendants of Barodis, the descendants of Shaphat, the descendants of Allon.

35 All the temple servants and the descendants of Solomon's servants were three hundred seventy-two.

36 The following are those who came up from Telmelah and Tel-harsha, under the leadership of Cherub, Addan, and Immer, 37 though they could not prove by their ancestral houses or lineage that they belonged to Israel: the descendants of Delaiah son of Tobiah, and the descendants of Nekoda, six hundred fifty-two.

38 Of the priests the following had assumed the priesthood but were not found registered: the descendants of Habaiah, the descendants of Hakkoz, and the descendants of Jaddus who had married Agia, one of the daughters of Barzillai, and was called by his name. 39 When a search was made in the register and the genealogy of these men was not found, they were excluded from serving as priests. 40 And Nehemiah and Attharias* told them not to share in the holy things until a high priest should appear wearing Urim and Thummim. *p*

41 All those of Israel, twelve or more years of age, besides male and female servants, were forty-two thousand three hundred sixty; 42 their male and female servants were seven thousand three hundred thirty-seven; there were two hundred forty-five musicians and singers. 43 There were four hundred thirty-five camels, and seven thousand thirty-six horses, two hundred forty-five mules, and five thousand five hundred twenty-five donkeys.

44 Some of the heads of families, when they came to the temple of God that is in Jerusalem, vowed that, to the best of their ability, they would erect the house on its site, 45 and that they would give to the sacred treasury for the work a thousand minas of gold, five thousand minas of silver, and one hundred priests' vestments.

46 The priests, the Levites, and some of the people*q* settled in Jerusalem and its vicinity; and the temple singers, the gatekeepers, and all Israel in their towns.

47 When the seventh month came, and the Israelites were all in their own homes, they gathered with a single purpose in the square before the first gate toward the east. 48 Then Jeshua son of Jozadak, with his fellow priests, and Zerubbabel son of Shealtiel, with his kinsmen, took their places and prepared the altar of the God of Israel, 49 to offer burnt offerings upon it, in accordance with the directions in the book of Moses the man of God. 50 And some joined them from the other peoples of the land. And they erected the altar in its place, for all the peoples of the land were hostile to them and were stronger than they; and they offered sacrifices at the proper times and burnt offerings to the Lord morning and evening. 51 They kept the festival of booths, as it is commanded in the law, and offered the proper sacrifices every day, 52 and thereafter the regular offerings and sacrifices on sabbaths and at new moons and at all the consecrated feasts. 53 And all who had made any vow to God began to offer sacrifices to God, from the new moon of the seventh month, though the temple of God was not yet built. 54 They gave money to the masons and the carpenters, and food and drink 55 and carts*r* to the Sidonians and the Tyrians, to bring cedar logs from Lebanon and convey them in rafts to the harbor of Joppa, according to the decree that they had in writing from King Cyrus of the Persians.

careth, of Sabie, of Sarothie, of Masias, of Gas, of Addus, of Subas, of Apherra, of Barodis, of Saphat, of Allon. 35 The temple servitors and the descendants of Solomon's servants amounted to three hundred and seventy-two in all.

36 The following, who returned from Thermeleth and Thelsas with their leaders Chara, Athalar, and Alar, 37 were unable to prove by their families and descent that they were Israelites: the line of Dalan, the son of Tuban, and the line of Necodan amounting to six hundred and fifty-two.

38 From among the priests the claimants to the priesthood whose record could not be traced: the lines of Obdia, of Accos, and of Joddus who married Augia, one of the daughters of Pharzellaeus, and took his name. 39 When search was made for the record of their descent in the register it could not be traced, and so they were debarred from officiating. 40 Nehemiah the governor forbade them to partake of the sacred food until there should be a high priest wearing the breastpiece of Revelation and Truth.

41 They were in all: Israelites from twelve years old, not counting slaves male and female, forty-two thousand three hundred and sixty; 42 their slaves seven thousand three hundred and thirty-seven; musicians and singers two hundred and forty-five. 43 Their camels numbered four hundred and thirty-five, their horses seven thousand and thirty-six, their mules two hundred and forty-five, and their donkeys five thousand five hundred and twenty-five.

44 On their arrival at the temple of God in Jerusalem, certain of the heads of the families took a vow to put forth their best efforts to rebuild the house on its original site, 45 and to give to the sacred treasury one thousand minas of gold and five thousand minas of silver for the fabric and one hundred vestments for priests.

46 The priests, the Levites, and some of the people stayed in Jerusalem and its neighbourhood, while the temple musicians, the door-keepers, and all the rest of the Israelites lived in their villages.

47 WHEN it was the seventh month and the Israelites were settled in their homes, they came together with one accord in the broad square of the first gateway toward the east. 48 Jeshua son of Josedek and his fellow-priests, and Zerubbabel son of Salathiel and his colleagues set to work and made ready the altar of the God of Israel, 49 in order to offer on it whole-offerings as prescribed in the book of Moses, the man of God. 50 Other peoples of the land joined them, and they succeeded in setting up the altar on the original site; for in general the peoples in the land were hostile and too strong for them. Then they offered to the Lord sacrifices at the proper time and whole-offerings morning and evening. 51 They celebrated the feast of Tabernacles as decreed in the law, with the appropriate sacrifices each day, 52 and thereafter the regular offerings, and sacrifices on sabbaths, at new moons, and on all solemn feasts. 53 From the new moon of the seventh month, whoever had made a vow to God offered sacrifices to him, although the temple of God was not yet built. 54-55 Money was given to the stonemasons and carpenters; the Sidonians and Tyrians were supplied with food and drink, and with carts to bring cedar trees from the Lebanon, floating them down as rafts to the roadstead at Joppa. This was done on the written instructions of King Cyrus of Persia.

o Or the governor   *p* Gk Manifestation and Truth   *q* Or those who were of the people   *r* Meaning of Gk uncertain

5:40 the governor: prob. mng (cp. Ezra 2:63); Gk and Attharias.

56 In the second year after their coming to the temple of God in Jerusalem, in the second month, Zerubbabel son of Shealtiel and Jeshua son of Jozadak made a beginning, together with their kindred and the levitical priests and all who had come back to Jerusalem from exile; 57 and they laid the foundation of the temple of God on the new moon of the second month in the second year after they came to Judea and Jerusalem. 58 They appointed the Levites who were twenty or more years of age to have charge of the work of the Lord. And Jeshua arose, and his sons and kindred and his brother Kadmiel and the sons of Jeshua Emadabun and the sons of Joda son of Iliadun, with their sons and kindred, all the Levites, pressing forward the work on the house of God with a single purpose.

So the builders built the temple of the Lord. 59 And the priests stood arrayed in their vestments, with musical instruments and trumpets, and the Levites, the sons of Asaph, with cymbals, 60 praising the Lord and blessing him, according to the directions of King David of Israel; 61 they sang hymns, giving thanks to the Lord, "For his goodness and his glory are forever upon all Israel." 62 And all the people sounded trumpets and shouted with a great shout, praising the Lord for the erection of the house of the Lord. 63 Some of the levitical priests and heads of ancestral houses, old men who had seen the former house, came to the building of this one with outcries and loud weeping, 64 while many came with trumpets and a joyful noise, 65 so that the people could not hear the trumpets because of the weeping of the people.

For the multitude sounded the trumpets loudly, so that the sound was heard far away; 66 and when the enemies of the tribe of Judah and Benjamin heard it, they came to find out what the sound of the trumpets meant. 67 They learned that those who had returned from exile were building the temple for the Lord God of Israel. 68 So they approached Zerubbabel and Jeshua and the heads of the ancestral houses and said to them, "We will build with you. 69 For we obey your Lord just as you do and we have been sacrificing to him ever since the days of King Esar-haddon[s] of the Assyrians, who brought us here." 70 But Zerubbabel and Jeshua and the heads of the ancestral houses in Israel said to them, "You have nothing to do with us in building the house for the Lord our God, 71 for we alone will build it for the Lord of Israel, as Cyrus, the king of the Persians, has commanded us." 72 But the peoples of the land pressed hard[t] upon those in Judea, cut off their supplies, and hindered their building; 73 and by plots and demagoguery and uprisings they prevented the completion of the building as long as King Cyrus lived. They were kept from building for two years, until the reign of Darius.

6 Now in the second year of the reign of Darius, the prophets Haggai and Zechariah son of Iddo prophesied to the Jews who were in Judea and Jerusalem; they prophesied to them in the name of the Lord God of Israel. 2 Then Zerubbabel son of Shealtiel and Jeshua son of Jozadak began to build the house of the Lord that is in Jerusalem, with the help of the prophets of the Lord who were with them.

3 At the same time Sisinnes the governor of Syria and Phoenicia and Sathrabuzanes and their associates came to them and said, 4 "By whose order are you building this house and this roof and finishing all the other things? And who are the builders that are finishing these things?" 5 Yet the elders of the Jews were dealt with kindly, for the providence of the Lord was over the captives; 6 they were not prevented from building until word could be sent to Darius concerning them and a report made.

56 In the second month of the second year, Zerubbabel son of Salathiel came to the temple of God in Jerusalem and began the work. There were with him Jeshua son of Josedek, their kinsmen, the levitical priests, and all who had returned to Jerusalem from captivity; 57 and they laid the foundation of the temple of God. This was at the new moon, in the second month of the second year after the return to Judaea and Jerusalem. 58 Levites who were aged twenty and upwards were appointed to supervise the works of the Lord. Jeshua, his sons and his kinsmen, his brother Cadoel, the sons of Jeshua Emadabun, and the sons of Joda son of Iliadun with their sons and kinsmen, all the Levites who were supervising co-operated in the work on the house of God.

While the builders built the Lord's temple, 59 the priests in their vestments with musical instruments and trumpets, and the Levites the sons of Asaph with their cymbals, took their places 60 singing to the Lord and praising him in the manner prescribed by King David of Israel. 61 They sang psalms in praise of the Lord, 'for his goodness and glory towards all Israel endures for ever'. 62 The people all sounded their trumpets and raised a great shout, and they sang to the Lord as the building rose.

63 But those of the priests, Levites, and heads of families who were old enough to have seen the former house came to the building of this house with cries of lamentation. 64 Though many were shouting and sounding the trumpets loudly for joy — 65 so loudly as to be heard from afar — the people could not hear the trumpets for the noise of lamentation.

66 The enemies of Judah and Benjamin heard the sound of the trumpets and came to see what it meant. 67 When they found the returned exiles rebuilding the temple for the Lord God of Israel, 68 they approached Zerubbabel and Jeshua and the heads of the families. 'We will build with you,' they said, 69 'for like you we obey your Lord and have sacrificed to him ever since the days of King Abasareth of Assyria who brought us here.' 70 Zerubbabel, Jeshua, and the heads of the Israelite families replied: 'It is not for you to build the house for the Lord our God; 71 we alone shall build for the Lord of Israel, as King Cyrus of Persia commanded us.' 72 But the peoples of the land harassed and blockaded the men of Judaea, and interrupted the building. 73 By their plots, agitations, and riots they prevented its completion during the lifetime of King Cyrus. All building was held up for two years until Darius became king.

6 In the second year of the reign of Darius, the prophets Haggai and Zechariah son of Addo prophesied to the Jews in Judaea and Jerusalem, rebuking them in the name of the Lord God of Israel. 2 Then Zerubbabel son of Salathiel and Jeshua son of Josedek, with the prophets of the Lord at their side to help them, began at once to rebuild the Lord's house in Jerusalem. 3 Immediately Sisinnes, the governor-general of Syria and Phoenicia, together with Sathrabuzanes and their colleagues, came to them and asked, 4 'Who has given you authority to rebuild this house, to put on the roof and complete the whole work? Who are the builders engaged on this?' 5 But thanks to the Lord who protected the returned exiles, the elders of the Jews 6 were not prevented from building until such time as Darius should be informed and instructions issued.

---

s Gk Asbasareth   t Meaning of Gk uncertain   5:72 **harassed**: prob. rdg; Gk obscure.

7 A copy of the letter that Sisinnes the governor of Syria and Phoenicia, and Sathrabuzanes, and their associates the local rulers in Syria and Phoenicia, wrote and sent to Darius: 8 "To King Darius, greetings. Let it be fully known to our lord the king that, when we went to the country of Judea and entered the city of Jerusalem, we found the elders of the Jews, who had been in exile, 9 building in the city of Jerusalem a great new house for the Lord, of hewn stone, with costly timber laid in the walls. 10 These operations are going on rapidly, and the work is prospering in their hands and being completed with all splendor and care. 11 Then we asked these elders, 'At whose command are you building this house and laying the foundations of this structure?' 12 In order that we might inform you in writing who the leaders are, we questioned them and asked them for a list of the names of those who are at their head. 13 They answered us, 'We are the servants of the Lord who created the heaven and the earth. 14 The house was built many years ago by a king of Israel who was great and strong, and it was finished. 15 But when our ancestors sinned against the Lord of Israel who is in heaven, and provoked him, he gave them over into the hands of King Nebuchadnezzar of Babylon, king of the Chaldeans; 16 and they pulled down the house, and burned it, and carried the people away captive to Babylon. 17 But in the first year that Cyrus reigned over the country of Babylonia, King Cyrus wrote that this house should be rebuilt. 18 And the holy vessels of gold and of silver, which Nebuchadnezzar had taken out of the house in Jerusalem and stored in his own temple, these King Cyrus took out again from the temple in Babylon, and they were delivered to Zerubbabel and Sheshbazzar*u* the governor 19 with the command that he should take all these vessels back and put them in the temple at Jerusalem, and that this temple of the Lord should be rebuilt on its site. 20 Then this Sheshbazzar, after coming here, laid the foundations of the house of the Lord that is in Jerusalem. Although it has been in process of construction from that time until now, it has not yet reached completion.' 21 Now therefore, O king, if it seems wise to do so, let search be made in the royal archives of our lord*v* the king that are in Babylon; 22 if it is found that the building of the house of the Lord in Jerusalem was done with the consent of King Cyrus, and if it is approved by our lord the king, let him send us directions concerning these things."

23 Then Darius commanded that search be made in the royal archives that were deposited in Babylon. And in Ecbatana, the fortress that is in the country of Media, a scroll*w* was found in which this was recorded: 24 "In the first year of the reign of King Cyrus, he ordered the building of the house of the Lord in Jerusalem, where they sacrifice with perpetual fire; 25 its height to be sixty cubits and its width sixty cubits, with three courses of hewn stone and one course of new native timber; the cost to be paid from the treasury of King Cyrus; 26 and that the holy vessels of the house of the Lord, both of gold and of silver, which Nebuchadnezzar took out of the house in Jerusalem and carried away to Babylon, should be restored to the house in Jerusalem, to be placed where they had been."

27 So Darius*x* commanded Sisinnes the governor of Syria and Phoenicia, and Sathrabuzanes, and their associates, and those who were appointed as local rulers in Syria and Phoenicia, to keep away from the place, and to permit Zerubbabel, the servant of the Lord and governor of Judea, and the elders of the Jews to build this house of the Lord on its site. 28 "And I command that it be built completely, and

7 Here is a copy of the letter sent to Darius by Sisinnes, the governor-general of Syria and Phoenicia, with Sathrabuzanes and their colleagues the authorities in Syria and Phoenicia:

To King Darius.
    Greeting.
8 Be these matters fully known to our lord the king: we went to the province of Judaea and to Jerusalem, its city, and there we found the elders of the Jews returned from exile 9 building a great new house for their Lord with costly hewn stone and with beams set in the walls. 10 This work was carried on with all speed and the undertaking was making rapid headway under their direction; it was being executed in great splendour and with the utmost care. 11 We then enquired of these elders by whose authority they were building this house and laying such foundations. 12 We questioned them so that we could write and inform you who their leaders were, and we asked for a list of those in charge. 13 Their reply to us was: 'We are servants of the Lord who made heaven and earth. 14 This house was built and completed many years ago by a great and powerful king of Israel. 15 But when our fathers by their sin provoked the heavenly Lord of Israel to anger, he delivered them into the power of the Chaldaean monarch, King Nebuchadnezzar of Babylon. 16 The house was demolished and set on fire, and the people carried away captive to Babylon. 17 'But King Cyrus in the first year of his reign over Babylonia issued a decree that the house should be rebuilt. 18 He brought out again from the temple in Babylon the sacred vessels of gold and silver which Nebuchadnezzar had taken from the house at Jerusalem and set up in his own temple, and he handed them over to Zerubbabel and Sanabassar the governor, 19 with orders to take them all and restore them to the temple at Jerusalem, and to rebuild this temple of the Lord on its original site. 20 Then Sanabassar came and laid the foundations of the house of the Lord in Jerusalem; and from that time until now the rebuilding has continued and is still not completed.'

21 Now, therefore, if it please your majesty, let search be made in the Babylonian royal archives, 22 and if it is found that the building of the Lord's house in Jerusalem was done with the approval of King Cyrus, and if our lord the king should so decide, let directions be issued to us on this matter.

23 King Darius ordered search to be made in the archives deposited in Babylonia, and there was found in the citadel at Ecbatana in the province of Media a scroll containing the following memorandum:

24 In the first year of his reign King Cyrus gave orders for the rebuilding of the Lord's house at Jerusalem, where they sacrifice with perpetual fire. 25 Its height was to be sixty cubits and its breadth sixty cubits, with three courses of hewn stone to one of new local timber; the cost to be defrayed from the royal treasury. 26 The sacred vessels, both gold and silver, which Nebuchadnezzar carried away from the house of the Lord at Jerusalem and brought to Babylon, were to be restored to the house in Jerusalem and placed where they had been in former times.

27 Then Darius instructed Sisinnes, the governor-general of Syria and Phoenicia, with Sathrabuzanes, their colleagues, and the governors in office in Syria and Phoenicia, that they should see to it that the place was left unmolested and that the Lord's servant, Zerubbabel, governor of Judaea, and the elders of the Jews should be free to rebuild the house of the Lord on its original site. 28 'I have also issued instructions',

---

u Gk *Sanabassarus*   *v* Other ancient authorities read *of Cyrus*
w Other authorities read *passage*   *x* Gk *he*

that full effort be made to help those who have returned from the exile of Judea, until the house of the Lord is finished; 29 and that out of the tribute of Coelesyria and Phoenicia a portion be scrupulously given to these men, that is, to Zerubbabel the governor, for sacrifices to the Lord, for bulls and rams and lambs, 30 and likewise wheat and salt and wine and oil, regularly every year, without quibbling, for daily use as the priests in Jerusalem may indicate, 31 in order that libations may be made to the Most High God for the king and his children, and prayers be offered for their lives."

32 He commanded that if anyone should transgress or nullify any of the things herein written, y a beam should be taken out of the house of the perpetrator, who then shall be impaled upon it, and all property forfeited to the king.

33 "Therefore may the Lord, whose name is there called upon, destroy every king and nation that shall stretch out their hands to hinder or damage that house of the Lord in Jerusalem.

34 "I, King Darius, have decreed that it be done with all diligence as here prescribed."

7 Then Sisinnes the governor of Coelesyria and Phoenicia, and Sathrabuzanes, and their associates, following the orders of King Darius, 2 supervised the holy work with very great care, assisting the elders of the Jews and the chief officers of the temple. 3 The holy work prospered, while the prophets Haggai and Zechariah prophesied; 4 and they completed it by the command of the Lord God of Israel. So with the consent of Cyrus and Darius and Artaxerxes, kings of the Persians, 5 the holy house was finished by the twenty-third day of the month of Adar, in the sixth year of King Darius. 6 And the people of Israel, the priests, the Levites, and the rest of those who returned from exile who joined them, did according to what was written in the book of Moses. 7 They offered at the dedication of the temple of the Lord one hundred bulls, two hundred rams, four hundred lambs, 8 and twelve male goats for the sin of all Israel, according to the number of the twelve leaders of the tribes of Israel; 9 and the priests and the Levites stood arrayed in their vestments, according to kindred, for the services of the Lord God of Israel in accordance with the book of Moses; and the gatekeepers were at each gate.

10 The people of Israel who came from exile kept the passover on the fourteenth day of the first month, after the priests and the Levites were purified together. 11 Not all of the returned captives were purified, but the Levites were all purified together, z 12 and they sacrificed the passover lamb for all the returned captives and for their kindred the priests and for themselves. 13 The people of Israel who had returned from exile ate it, all those who had separated themselves from the abominations of the peoples of the land and sought the Lord. 14 They also kept the festival of unleavened bread seven days, rejoicing before the Lord, 15 because he had changed the will of the king of the Assyrians concerning them, to strengthen their hands for the service of the Lord God of Israel.

8 After these things, when Artaxerxes, the king of the Persians, was reigning, Ezra came, the son of Seraiah son of Azariah son of Hilkiah son of Shallum 2 son of Zadok son of Ahitub son of Amariah son of Uzzi son of Bukki son of Abishua son of Phineas son of Eleazar son of Aaron the high a priest. 3 This Ezra came up from Babylon as a scribe skilled in the law of Moses, which was given by the God of Israel; 4 and the king showed him honor, for he found favor

he went on, 'that it should be completely rebuilt, and that every effort be made to co-operate with the returned exiles in Judaea until the house of the Lord is finished. 29 From the tribute of Coele-Syria and Phoenicia a sufficient grant, payable to Zerubbabel the governor, is to be given to these men for sacrifices to the Lord, for bulls, rams, and lambs. 30 Similarly wheat, salt, wine, and olive oil as the priests in Jerusalem require to meet the needs of each day are to be provided regularly every year without question. 31 Let all this be expended in order that sacrifices and libations may be offered to the Most High God and intercession made for the king and his children.'

32 Darius further decreed: 'If anyone contravenes or fails to observe anything written herein, let a beam be taken from his own house and let him be hanged on it, and his property shall be forfeit to the king. 33 May the Lord himself, therefore, whose name is invoked in this temple, utterly destroy any king or people who lifts a finger to delay the work or damage the Lord's house in Jerusalem. 34 I, Darius, the king, have directed that these decrees shall be strictly obeyed.'

7 Then, in compliance with the orders of King Darius, Sisinnes, governor-general of Coele-Syria and Phoenicia, with Sathrabuzanes and their colleagues, 2 carefully supervised the sacred works, co-operating with the elders of the Jews and the temple officers. 3 Good progress was made with the sacred works, as the result of the prophecies of Haggai and Zechariah, 4 and they were finished as commanded by the Lord God of Israel and with the approval of Cyrus and Darius; 5 and the house was completed on the twenty-third of the month of Adar in the sixth year of King Darius.

6 The Israelites, priests, Levites, and the rest of the former exiles who had joined them carried out the directions in the book of Moses. 7 At the rededication of the temple of the Lord they offered one hundred bulls, two hundred rams, four hundred lambs, 8 and as a purification-offering for all Israel twelve he-goats corresponding to the number of the patriarchs of Israel. 9 The priests and the Levites robed in their vestments stood family by family to preside over the services of the Lord God of Israel according to the book of Moses, while the door-keepers were stationed at every gateway.

10 On the fourteenth day of the first month the Israelites who had returned from exile celebrated the Passover. The priests and the Levites were purified together; 11 not all the returned exiles were purified with the priests, but the Levites were. 12 They sacrificed the Passover victims for all the returned exiles, for their kinsmen the priests, and for themselves. 13 They were eaten by the Israelites who had returned from exile, and by all who had held aloof from the abominations of the peoples of the land and remained faithful to the Lord. 14 They celebrated the feast of Unleavened Bread for seven days, rejoicing before the Lord, 15 because he had changed the policy of the Assyrian king towards them so that he supported them in their work for the Lord God of Israel.

8 IT was after these events, when Artaxerxes was king of Persia, that Ezra came. He was the son of Saraeas son of Ezerias, son of Chelkias, son of Salemus, 2 son of Zadok, son of Ahitub, son of Amarias, son of Ezias, son of Mareroth, son of Zaraeas, son of Savia, son of Bocca, son of Abishua, son of Phineas, son of Eleazar, son of Aaron the chief priest. 3 Ezra had come up from Babylon. He was a scribe expert in the law of Moses that had been given by the God of Israel. 4 The king held him in high regard and looked

y Other authorities read stated above or added in writing
z Meaning of Gk uncertain   a Gk the first

7:8 **purification-offering:** or sin-offering.   7:11 **not all . . . but:** prob. rdg; Gk obscure; some witnesses omit not.   8:2 **son of Mareroth . . . Savia:** some MSS omit.

before the king*b* in all his requests. 5 There came up with him to Jerusalem some of the people of Israel and some of the priests and Levites and temple singers and gatekeepers and temple servants, 6 in the seventh year of the reign of Artaxerxes, in the fifth month (this was the king's seventh year); for they left Babylon on the new moon of the first month and arrived in Jerusalem on the new moon of the fifth month, by the prosperous journey that the Lord gave them.*c* 7 For Ezra possessed great knowledge, so that he omitted nothing from the law of the Lord or the commandments, but taught all Israel all the ordinances and judgments.

8 The following is a copy of the written commission from King Artaxerxes that was delivered to Ezra the priest and reader of the law of the Lord:

9 "King Artaxerxes to Ezra the priest and reader of the law of the Lord, greeting. 10 In accordance with my gracious decision, I have given orders that those of the Jewish nation and of the priests and Levites and others in our realm, those who freely choose to do so, may go with you to Jerusalem. 11 Let as many as are so disposed, therefore, leave with you, just as I and the seven Friends who are my counselors have decided, 12 in order to look into matters in Judea and Jerusalem, in accordance with what is in the law of the Lord, 13 and to carry to Jerusalem the gifts for the Lord of Israel that I and my Friends have vowed, and to collect for the Lord in Jerusalem all the gold and silver that may be found in the country of Babylonia, 14 together with what is given by the nation for the temple of their Lord that is in Jerusalem, both gold and silver for bulls and rams and lambs and what goes with them, 15 so as to offer sacrifices on the altar of their Lord that is in Jerusalem. 16 Whatever you and your kindred are minded to do with the gold and silver, perform it in accordance with the will of your God; 17 deliver the holy vessels of the Lord that are given you for the use of the temple of your God that is in Jerusalem. 18 And whatever else occurs to you as necessary for the temple of your God, you may provide out of the royal treasury.

19 "I, King Artaxerxes, have commanded the treasurers of Syria and Phoenicia that whatever Ezra the priest and reader of the law of the Most High God sends for, they shall take care to give him, 20 up to a hundred talents of silver, and likewise up to a hundred cors of wheat, a hundred baths of wine, and salt in abundance. 21 Let all things prescribed in the law of God be scrupulously fulfilled for the Most High God, so that wrath may not come upon the kingdom of the king and his sons. 22 You are also informed that no tribute or any other tax is to be laid on any of the priests or Levites or temple singers or gatekeepers or temple servants or persons employed in this temple, and that no one has authority to impose any tax on them.

23 "And you, Ezra, according to the wisdom of God, appoint judges and justices to judge all those who know the law of your God, throughout all Syria and Phoenicia; and you shall teach it to those who do not know it. 24 All who transgress the law of your God or the law of the kingdom shall be strictly punished, whether by death or some other punishment, either fine or imprisonment."

25 Then Ezra the scribe said,*d* "Blessed be the Lord alone, who put this into the heart of the king, to glorify his house that is in Jerusalem, 26 and who honored me in the sight of the king and his counselors and all his Friends and nobles. 27 I was encouraged by the help of the Lord my God, and I gathered men from Israel to go up with me."

with favour on all the requests he made.

5 He was accompanied to Jerusalem by a number of Israelites, priests, Levites, temple singers, door-keepers, and temple servitors 6 in the fifth month of the seventh year of Artaxerxes' reign. They left Babylon at the new moon in the first month and reached Jerusalem at the new moon in the fifth month, for the Lord gave them a good journey. 7 Ezra's knowledge of the law of the Lord and the commandments was full and exact, so that he was able to instruct all Israel in all the ordinances and judgements.

8 The following is a copy of the mandate from King Artaxerxes to Ezra the priest, doctor of the law of the Lord:

9 King Artaxerxes to Ezra the priest, doctor of the law of the Lord.
Greeting.
10 I have graciously decided, and now command, that throughout our kingdom any of the Jewish nation and of the priests and Levites who so desire, may go with you to Jerusalem. 11 I and my council of seven Friends have decreed that all who so choose may accompany you. 12 They are to consider the situation in Judaea and Jerusalem with regard to the law of your God. 13 They shall convey to Jerusalem for Israel's Lord the gifts which I and my Friends have vowed, together with all the gold and silver in Babylonia that may be found to belong to the Lord, 14 and the gifts provided by the nation for the temple of their Lord at Jerusalem. Let the gold and silver be expended on the purchase of bulls, rams, lambs, and the like, 15 so that sacrifices may be offered on the altar of their Lord in Jerusalem. 16 In whatever ways you and your colleagues may wish to use the gold and silver, let it be done in accordance with the will of your God. 17 You are to deliver the sacred vessels of the Lord which have been handed over for the service of the temple of your God in Jerusalem.

18 Any other expenses you may incur for the needs of the temple of your God you shall defray from the royal treasury.

19 I, Artaxerxes the king, hereby direct the treasurers of Syria and Phoenicia to supply exactly to Ezra the priest, doctor of the law of the Most High God, whatever he may request 20 up to one hundred talents of silver, and similarly up to one hundred sacks of wheat and one hundred casks of wine, and salt without limit. 21 Let all the requirements of God's law be diligently fulfilled in honour of the Most High God; otherwise wrath may befall the realm of the king and his sons. 22 You are also informed that no tribute or other impost is to be exacted from the priests, the Levites, the temple singers, the door-keepers, the temple servitors, or the lay officers of this temple; no one is authorized to impose any levy on them.

23 Under the wise guidance of God you, Ezra, are to appoint judges and magistrates throughout Syria and Phoenicia to administer justice for all who acknowledge the law of your God; you must instruct those who do not know it. 24 Whoever transgresses the law of your God or the law of the king shall be duly punished, whether he be put to death or sentenced to a fine or imprisonment.

25 Then Ezra the scribe said, 'Blessed is the Lord and he alone! He put this into the king's mind, to glorify his house in Jerusalem, 26 and has singled me out for honour in the eyes of the king and his counsellors, all his Friends and courtiers.

27 'Encouraged by the help of the Lord my God, I gathered men of Israel to go up with me. 28 These are the leaders

---

b Gk *him*   *c* Other authorities add *for him* or *upon him*   *d* Other ancient authorities lack *Then Ezra the scribe said*

28 These are the leaders, according to their ancestral houses and their groups, who went up with me from Babylon, in the reign of King Artaxerxes: 29 Of the descendants of Phineas, Gershom. Of the descendants of Ithamar, Gamael. Of the descendants of David, Hattush son of Shecaniah. 30 Of the descendants of Parosh, Zechariah, and with him a hundred fifty men enrolled. 31 Of the descendants of Pahath-moab, Eliehoenai son of Zerahiah, and with him two hundred men. 32 Of the descendants of Zattu, Shecaniah son of Jahaziel, and with him three hundred men. Of the descendants of Adin, Obed son of Jonathan, and with him two hundred fifty men. 33 Of the descendants of Elam, Jeshaiah son of Gotholiah, and with him seventy men. 34 Of the descendants of Shephatiah, Zeraiah son of Michael, and with him seventy men. 35 Of the descendants of Joab, Obadiah son of Jehiel, and with him two hundred twelve men. 36 Of the descendants of Bani, Shelomith son of Josiphiah, and with him a hundred sixty men. 37 Of the descendants of Bebai, Zechariah son of Bebai, and with him twenty-eight men. 38 Of the descendants of Azgad, Johanan son of Hakkatan, and with him a hundred ten men. 39 Of the descendants of Adonikam, the last ones, their names being Eliphelet, Jeuel, and Shemaiah, and with them seventy men. 40 Of the descendants of Bigvai, Uthai son of Istalcurus, and with him seventy men.

41 I assembled them at the river called Theras, and we encamped there three days, and I inspected them. 42 When I found there none of the descendants of the priests or of the Levites, 43 I sent word to Eliezar, Iduel, Maasmas, 44 Elnathan, Shemaiah, Jarib, Nathan, Elnathan, Zechariah, and Meshullam, who were leaders and men of understanding; 45 I told them to go to Iddo, who was the leading man at the place of the treasury, 46 and ordered them to tell Iddo and his kindred and the treasurers at that place to send us men to serve as priests in the house of our Lord. 47 And by the mighty hand of our Lord they brought us competent men of the descendants of Mahli son of Levi, son of Israel, namely Sherebiah[e] with his descendants and kinsmen, eighteen; 48 also Hashabiah and Annunus and his brother Jeshaiah, of the descendants of Hananiah, and their descendants, twenty men; 49 and of the temple servants, whom David and the leaders had given for the service of the Levites, two hundred twenty temple servants; the list of all their names was reported.

50 There I proclaimed a fast for the young men before our Lord, to seek from him a prosperous journey for ourselves and for our children and the livestock that were with us. 51 For I was ashamed to ask the king for foot soldiers and cavalry and an escort to keep us safe from our adversaries; 52 for we had said to the king, "The power of our Lord will be with those who seek him, and will support them in every way." 53 And again we prayed to our Lord about these things, and we found him very merciful.

54 Then I set apart twelve of the leaders of the priests, Sherebiah and Hashabiah, and ten of their kinsmen with them; 55 and I weighed out to them the silver and the gold and the holy vessels of the house of our Lord, which the king himself and his counselors and the nobles and all Israel had given. 56 I weighed and gave to them six hundred fifty talents of silver, and silver vessels worth a hundred talents, and a hundred talents of gold, 57 and twenty golden bowls, and twelve bronze vessels of fine bronze that glittered like gold. 58 And I said to them, "You are holy to the Lord, and the vessels are holy, and the silver and the gold are vowed to the Lord, the Lord of our ancestors. 59 Be watchful and

according to families and divisions who went up with me from Babylon in the reign of King Artaxerxes: 29 from the line of Phineas, Gershom; from the line of Ithamar, Gamael; from the line of David, Attus son of Sechenias; 30 from the line of Phoros, Zacharias and with him a hundred and fifty men according to the register; 31 from the line of Phaath-moab, Eliaonias son of Zaraeas and with him two hundred men; 32 from the line of Zathoe, Sechenias son of Jezelus and with him three hundred men; from the line of Adin, Obeth son of Jonathan and with him two hundred and fifty men; 33 from the line of Elam, Jessias son of Gotholias and with him seventy men; 34 from the line of Saphatias, Zaraeas son of Michael and with him seventy men; 35 from the line of Joab, Abadias son of Jezelus and with him two hundred and twelve men; 36 from the line of Banias, Salimoth son of Josaphias and with him a hundred and sixty men; 37 from the line of Babi, Zacharias son of Bebae and with him twenty-eight men; 38 from the line of Astath, Joannes son of Hacatan and with him a hundred and ten men; 39 last came those from the line of Adonikam, by name Eliphalatus, Jeuel, and Samaeas, and with them seventy men; 40 from the line of Bago, Uthi son of Istalcurus and with him seventy men.

41 'I assembled them by the river Theras, and we encamped there for three days. I checked them, 42 and finding no one there who was a priest or a Levite, 43 I sent to Eleazar, Iduelus, Maasmas, 44 Elnathan, Samaeas, Joribus, Nathan, Ennatas, Zacharias, and Mosollamus, who were prominent and discerning men, 45 and instructed them to go to Addaeus, the head of the treasury in the district. 46 I told them to speak with Addaeus and his colleagues and fellow-treasurers, asking that men should be sent to us to officiate in the house of our Lord. 47 Under the providence of our Lord they sent us discerning men from the line of Mooli son of Levi, son of Israel, Asebebias and his sons and brothers, eighteen men in all, 48 and Asebias and Annunus and his brother Hosaeas. Those of the line of Chanunaeus and their sons amounted to twenty men; 49 and those of the temple servitors whom David and the leading men appointed for the service of the Levites amounted to two hundred and twenty. A register of all those names was compiled.

50 'I made a vow there that the young men should fast before our Lord and ask from him a prosperous journey for ourselves, our children who accompanied us, and our pack-animals. 51 I was ashamed to apply to the king for an escort of infantry and cavalry to protect us against our enemies, 52 for we had told him that the might of our Lord would ensure a successful outcome for those who looked to him. 53 So once more we laid all these things before our Lord in prayer and found him gracious.

54 'Then I set apart twelve men from among the chiefs of the priestly families, Sarabias and Asamias and with them ten of their kinsmen. 55 I weighed out for them the silver and gold, and the sacred vessels for the house of our Lord which had been presented by the king, by his counsellors and courtiers, and by all Israel. 56 After weighing it, I handed over to them six hundred and fifty talents of silver, and silver vessels weighing a hundred talents, a hundred talents of gold, 57 and twenty gold dishes, and twelve vessels made of bronze so fine that it gleamed like gold. 58 I said, "Just as you are consecrated to the Lord, so too are the vessels; the silver and the gold are vowed to the Lord, the Lord of our fathers. 59 Guard them with all vigilance until you hand

[e] Gk Asbebias

on guard until you deliver them to the leaders of the priests and the Levites, and to the heads of the ancestral houses of Israel, in Jerusalem, in the chambers of the house of our Lord." 60 So the priests and the Levites who took the silver and the gold and the vessels that had been in Jerusalem carried them to the temple of the Lord.

61 We left the river Theras on the twelfth day of the first month; and we arrived in Jerusalem by the mighty hand of our Lord, which was upon us; he delivered us from every enemy on the way, and so we came to Jerusalem. 62 When we had been there three days, the silver and the gold were weighed and delivered in the house of our Lord to the priest Meremoth son of Uriah; 63 with him was Eleazar son of Phinehas, and with them were Jozabad son of Jeshua and Moeth son of Binnui,*f* the Levites. 64 The whole was counted and weighed, and the weight of everything was recorded at that very time. 65 And those who had returned from exile offered sacrifices to the Lord, the God of Israel, twelve bulls for all Israel, ninety-six rams, 66 seventy-two lambs, and as a thank offering twelve male goats — all as a sacrifice to the Lord. 67 They delivered the king's orders to the royal stewards and to the governors of Coelesyria and Phoenicia; and these officials*g* honored the people and the temple of the Lord.

68 After these things had been done, the leaders came to me and said, 69 "The people of Israel and the rulers and the priests and the Levites have not put away from themselves the alien peoples of the land and their pollutions, the Canaanites, the Hittites, the Perizzites, the Jebusites, the Moabites, the Egyptians, and the Edomites. 70 For they and their descendants have married the daughters of these people,*h* and the holy race has been mixed with the alien peoples of the land; and from the beginning of this matter the leaders and the nobles have been sharing in this iniquity."

71 As soon as I heard these things I tore my garments and my holy mantle, and pulled out hair from my head and beard, and sat down in anxiety and grief. 72 And all who were ever moved at*i* the word of the Lord of Israel gathered around me, as I mourned over this iniquity, and I sat grief-stricken until the evening sacrifice. 73 Then I rose from my fast, with my garments and my holy mantle torn, and kneeling down and stretching out my hands to the Lord 74 I said,

"O Lord, I am ashamed and confused before your face. 75 For our sins have risen higher than our heads, and our mistakes have mounted up to heaven 76 from the times of our ancestors, and we are in great sin to this day. 77 Because of our sins and the sins of our ancestors, we with our kindred and our kings and our priests were given over to the kings of the earth, to the sword and exile and plundering, in shame until this day. 78 And now in some measure mercy has come to us from you, O Lord, to leave to us a root and a name in your holy place, 79 and to uncover a light for us in the house of the Lord our God, and to give us food in the time of our servitude. 80 Even in our bondage we were not forsaken by our Lord, but he brought us into favor with the kings of the Persians, so that they have given us food 81 and glorified the temple of our Lord, and raised Zion from desolation, to give us a stronghold in Judea and Jerusalem.

82 "And now, O Lord, what shall we say, when we have these things? For we have transgressed your commandments, which you gave by your servants the prophets, saying, 83 'The land that you are entering to take possession of is a land polluted with the pollution of the aliens of the land, and they have filled it with their uncleanness.

them over at Jerusalem, in the priests' rooms in the house of our Lord, to the chiefs of the priestly and levitical families and to the leaders of the clans of Israel." 60 The priests and the Levites who had custody of the silver, the gold, and the vessels which had been in Jerusalem brought them to the temple of the Lord.

61 'On the twelfth day of the first month we struck camp at the river Theras and, under the powerful protection afforded by our Lord, who saved us from every enemy attack on the way, we reached Jerusalem. 62 On our fourth day there, the silver and gold were weighed and handed over in the house of our Lord to the priest Marmathi son of Uri, 63 with whom was Eleazar son of Phineas; present with them were the Levites Josabdus son of Jeshua and Moeth son of Sabannus. Everything was counted and weighed, 64 and every weight recorded then and there.

65 'Those who had returned from captivity offered sacrifices to the Lord, the God of Israel: twelve bulls for all Israel, with ninety-six rams 66 and seventy-two lambs, and also twelve goats for a shared-offering, the whole as a sacrifice to the Lord. 67 They delivered the king's orders to the royal treasurers and the governors of Coele-Syria and Phoenicia, thereby adding lustre to the nation and the temple of the Lord.

68 'Once this business was concluded, the leaders came to me and said: 69 "The people of Israel, including even the rulers, priests, and Levites, have not kept themselves apart from the alien population of the land with all their unclean practices, that is to say the Canaanites, Hittites, Perizzites, Jebusites, Moabites, Egyptians, and Edomites. 70 Both they and their sons have intermarried with the women of these peoples, so that the holy race has become mixed with the alien population of the land. From the very beginning, the leaders and principal men have shared in this violation of the law."

71 'At this news I rent my clothes and sacred vestment, I tore my hair and beard and sat appalled and grieving. 72 All who were moved by the word of the Lord of Israel gathered round me, and I sat grief-stricken over this failure to observe the law; and I sat in grief until the evening sacrifice. 73 Then with my clothes and sacred vestment torn I rose from my fast and, kneeling down, held out my hands in supplication to the Lord. 74 "O Lord," I said, "I am covered with shame and confusion in your presence. 75 Our sins tower above us and our offences have reached high heaven 76 ever since the time of our forefathers; and today we are as deep in sin as ever. 77 Because of our sins and the sins of our forefathers, we, together with our brothers, our kings, and our priests, have been given into the power of the earthly rulers to be killed, taken captive, pillaged, and humiliated, down to this very day. 78 Yet even now, Lord, how great is your mercy! For we still have a root and a name in this your holy place. 79 Our light has been rekindled in the house of our Lord, and we have been given sustenance in the time of our enslavement. 80 Even when we were slaves we were not forsaken by our Lord, but he secured for us the favour of the kings of Persia: they have provided our sustenance 81 and added lustre to the temple of our Lord and restored the ruins of Zion, establishing us securely in Judaea and Jerusalem.

82 'Now, Lord, in the face of this, what are we to say? For we have broken your commandments given through your servants the prophets. You said: 83 'The land which you are going to occupy is a land defiled with the pollution of its heathen population; they have filled it with their im-

84 Therefore do not give your daughters in marriage to their descendants, and do not take their daughters for your descendants; 85 do not seek ever to have peace with them, so that you may be strong and eat the good things of the land and leave it for an inheritance to your children forever.' 86 And all that has happened to us has come about because of our evil deeds and our great sins. For you, O Lord, lifted the burden of our sins 87 and gave us such a root as this; but we turned back again to transgress your law by mixing with the uncleanness of the peoples of the land. 88 Were you not angry enough with us to destroy us without leaving a root or seed or name? 89 O Lord of Israel, you are faithful; for we are left as a root to this day. 90 See, we are now before you in our iniquities; for we can no longer stand in your presence because of these things."

91 While Ezra was praying and making his confession, weeping and lying on the ground before the temple, there gathered around him a very great crowd of men and women and youths from Jerusalem; for there was great weeping among the multitude. 92 Then Shecaniah son of Jehiel, one of the men of Israel, called out, and said to Ezra, "We have sinned against the Lord, and have married foreign women from the peoples of the land; but even now there is hope for Israel. 93 Let us take an oath to the Lord about this, that we will put away all our foreign wives, with their children, 94 as seems good to you and to all who obey the law of the Lord. 95 Rise up*j* and take action, for it is your task, and we are with you to take strong measures." 96 Then Ezra rose up and made the leaders of the priests and Levites of all Israel swear that they would do this. And they swore to it.

9 Then Ezra set out and went from the court of the temple to the chamber of Jehohanan son of Eliashib, 2 and spent the night there; and he did not eat bread or drink water, for he was mourning over the great iniquities of the multitude. 3 And a proclamation was made throughout Judea and Jerusalem to all who had returned from exile that they should assemble at Jerusalem, 4 and that if any did not meet there within two or three days, in accordance with the decision of the ruling elders, their livestock would be seized for sacrifice and the men themselves*k* expelled from the multitude of those who had returned from the captivity.

5 Then the men of the tribe of Judah and Benjamin assembled at Jerusalem within three days; this was the ninth month, on the twentieth day of the month. 6 All the multitude sat in the open square before the temple, shivering because of the bad weather that prevailed. 7 Then Ezra stood up and said to them, "You have broken the law and married foreign women, and so have increased the sin of Israel. 8 Now then make confession and give glory to the Lord the God of our ancestors, 9 and do his will; separate yourselves from the peoples of the land and from your foreign wives."

10 Then all the multitude shouted and said with a loud voice, "We will do as you have said. 11 But the multitude is great and it is winter, and we are not able to stand in the open air. This is not a work we can do in one day or two, for we have sinned too much in these things. 12 So let the leaders of the multitude stay, and let all those in our settlements who have foreign wives come at the time appointed, 13 with the elders and judges of each place, until we are freed from the wrath of the Lord over this matter."

14 Jonathan son of Asahel and Jahzeiah son of Tikvah*l* undertook the matter on these terms, and Meshullam and Levi and Shabbethai served with them as judges. 15 And those who had returned from exile acted in accordance with all this.

pure ways. 84 Now therefore do not marry your daughters to their sons or take their daughters for your sons; 85 nor must you ever seek to be at peace with them. Only thus will you be strong and enjoy the good things of the land, and hand it on as an everlasting possession to your descendants.' 86 It is our evil deeds and great sins which have brought all our misfortunes on us. Although you, Lord, have lightened the burden of our sins 87 and given us firm roots in the land, yet we have fallen away again and broken your law by sharing in the impurity of the peoples of this land. 88 But you were not so angry with us as to destroy us, root, stock, and name. 89 O Lord of Israel, you are just; for we today are a root that is left. 90 In all our sin we are here before you; because of it we can no longer stand in your presence." '

91 While Ezra was praying and making confession, prostrate in tears before the temple, there gathered round him a vast throng from Jerusalem, men, women, and children, and there was widespread lamentation among the crowd. 92 One of the Israelites, Jechonias son of Jehiel, spoke up and said to Ezra: 'We have sinned against the Lord in taking foreign wives from the peoples of the land; yet there is still hope for Israel. 93 In this matter let us promise on oath to the Lord to get rid of our wives of foreign race together with their children, 94 in keeping with your judgement and the judgement of all who are obedient to the law of the Lord. 95 Get up and see to it; the matter is in your hands. Take strong action and we are with you!' 96 Ezra stood up and put the chiefs of the priestly and levitical families of all Israel on oath to act in this way.

9 Ezra then left the forecourt of the temple and went to the room of the priest Joanan grandson of Eliasib, 2 and there he stayed, eating no bread and drinking no water, for he was still mourning over the people's flagrant violations of the law. 3 A proclamation was issued throughout Judaea and Jerusalem that all the returned exiles were to assemble at Jerusalem. 4 If any failed to arrive within two or three days, as decided by the elders in office, they were to have their cattle confiscated for temple use and would themselves be excluded from the community of the exiles.

5 Three days later — it was the twentieth day of the ninth month — the men of Judah and Benjamin had assembled in Jerusalem, 6 where they all sat together in the broad space before the temple, shivering because winter had set in. 7 Ezra stood up and addressed them: 'In marrying foreign women you have broken the law and added to Israel's guilt. 8 Now acknowledge the majesty of the Lord God of our fathers: 9 do his will and cut yourselves off from the peoples of the land and from your foreign wives.'

10 The whole company assented loudly, 'We will do as you say! 11 But', they added, 'our numbers are great; it is the rainy season and we cannot stay out in the open. Besides, this is not the work of one or two days only, for the offence is rife amongst us. 12 Let the leaders of the community remain here, and let all members of our settlements who have foreign wives present themselves at a stated time 13 accompanied by the elders and judges for each place, until the Lord's anger at what has been done is averted from us.' 14 Jonathan son of Azael and Hezekias son of Thocanus took charge on these terms, and Mosollamus, Levi, and Sabbataeus were their assessors.

15 The returned exiles duly put all this into effect. 16 Ezra

---

j Other ancient authorities read *as seems good to you." And all who obeyed the law of the Lord rose and said to Ezra, "Rise up*
k Gk *he himself*   *l* Gk *Thocanos*

16 Ezra the priest chose for himself the leading men of their ancestral houses, all of them by name; and on the new moon of the tenth month they began their sessions to investigate the matter. 17 And the cases of the men who had foreign wives were brought to an end by the new moon of the first month.

18 Of the priests, those who were brought in and found to have foreign wives were: 19 of the descendants of Jeshua son of Jozadak and his kindred, Maaseiah, Eliezar, Jarib, and Jodan. 20 They pledged themselves to put away their wives, and to offer rams in expiation of their error. 21 Of the descendants of Immer: Hanani and Zebadiah and Maaseiah and Shemaiah and Jehiel and Azariah. 22 Of the descendants of Pashhur: Elioenai, Maaseiah, Ishmael, and Nathanael, and Gedaliah, and Salthas.

23 And of the Levites: Jozabad and Shimei and Kelaiah, who was Kelita, and Pethahiah and Judah and Jonah. 24 Of the temple singers: Eliashib and Zaccur.*m* 25 Of the gatekeepers: Shallum and Telem.*n*

26 Of Israel: of the descendants of Parosh: Ramiah, Izziah, Malchijah, Mijamin, and Eleazar, and Asibias, and Benaiah. 27 Of the descendants of Elam: Mattaniah and Zechariah, Jezrielus and Abdi, and Jeremoth and Elijah. 28 Of the descendants of Zamoth: Eliadas, Eliashib, Othoniah, Jeremoth, and Zabad and Zerdaiah. 29 Of the descendants of Bebai: Jehohanan and Hananiah and Zabbai and Emathis. 30 Of the descendants of Mani: Olamus, Mamuchus, Adaiah, Jashub, and Sheal and Jeremoth. 31 Of the descendants of Addi: Naathus and Moossias, Laccunus and Naidus, and Bescaspasmys and Sesthel, and Belnuus and Manasseas. 32 Of the descendants of Annan, Elionas and Asaias and Melchias and Sabbaias and Simon Chosamaeus. 33 Of the descendants of Hashum: Mattenai and Mattattah and Zabad and Eliphelet and Manasseh and Shimei. 34 Of the descendants of Bani: Jeremai, Momdius, Maerus, Joel, Mamdai and Bedeiah and Vaniah, Carabasion and Eliashib and Mamitanemus, Eliasis, Binnui, Elialis, Shimei, Shelemiah, Nethaniah. Of the descendants of Ezora: Shashai, Azarel, Azael, Samatus, Zambris, Joseph. 35 Of the descendants of Nooma: Mazitias, Zabad, Iddo, Joel, Benaiah. 36 All these had married foreign women, and they put them away together with their children.

37 The priests and the Levites and the Israelites settled in Jerusalem and in the country. On the new moon of the seventh month, when the people of Israel were in their settlements, 38 the whole multitude gathered with one accord in the open square before the east gate of the temple; 39 they told Ezra the chief priest and reader to bring the law of Moses that had been given by the Lord God of Israel. 40 So Ezra the chief priest brought the law, for all the multitude, men and women, and all the priests to hear the law, on the new moon of the seventh month. 41 He read aloud in the open square before the gate of the temple from early morning until midday, in the presence of both men and women; and all the multitude gave attention to the law. 42 Ezra the priest and reader of the law stood on the wooden platform that had been prepared; 43 and beside him stood Mattathiah, Shema, Ananias, Azariah, Uriah, Hezekiah, and Baalsamus on his right, 44 and on his left Pedaiah, Mishael, Malchijah, Lothasubus, Nabariah, and Zechariah. 45 Then Ezra took up the book of the law in the sight of the multitude, for he had the place of honor in the presence of all. 46 When he opened the law, they all stood erect. And Ezra blessed the Lord God Most High, the God of hosts, the Almighty, 47 and the multitude answered, "Amen." They lifted up their hands, and fell to the ground and worshiped the Lord. 48 Jeshua and Anniuth and Sherebiah, Jadinus,

the priest selected, each by name, certain men, chiefs of their clans. They met in session to investigate the matter at the new moon in the tenth month, 17 and by the new moon of the first month the affair of the men who had taken foreign wives was brought to a conclusion.

18 Among the priests, some of those who had come together were found to have married foreign women: 19 namely Mathelas, Eleazar, Joribus, and Joadanus of the line of Jeshua son of Josedek and his brothers. 20 They pledged themselves to dismiss their wives and to offer rams in expiation of their offence. 21 Of the line of Emmer: Ananias, Zabdaeus, Manes, Samaeus, Jereel, and Azarias; 22 of the line of Phaseus: Elionas, Massias, Ishmael, Nathanael, Okidelus, and Saloas. 23 Of the Levites: Jozabadus, Semis, Colius (this is Calitas), Phathaeus, Judah, and Jonas. 24 Of the temple singers: Eliasibus, Bacchurus. 25 Of the doorkeepers: Sallumus and Tolbanes.

26 Of the people of Israel there were, of the line of Phoros: Jermas, Jeddias, Melchias, Maelus, Eleazar, Asibias, and Bannaeas. 27 Of the line of Ela: Matthanias, Zacharias, Jezrielus, Oabdius, Jeremoth, and Aedias. 28 Of the line of Zamoth: Eliadas, Eliasimus, Othonias, Jarimoth, Sabathus, and Zardaeas. 29 Of the line of Bebae: Joannes, Ananias, Ozabadus, and Emathis. 30 Of the line of Mani: Olamus, Mamuchus, Jedaeus, Jasubus, Asaelus, and Jeremoth. 31 Of the line of Addi: Naathus, Moossias, Laccunus, Naidus, Matthanias, Sesthel, Balnuus, and Manasseas. 32 Of the line of Annas: Elionas, Asaeas, Melchias, Sabbaeas, and Simon Chosomaeus. 33 Of the line of Asom: Altannaeus, Mattathias, Bannaeus, Eliphalat, Manasses, and Semi. 34 Of the line of Baani: Jeremias, Momdis, Ismaerus, Juel, Mandae, Paedias, Anos, Carabasion, Enasibus, Mamnitanaemus, Eliasis, Bannus, Eliali, Somis, Selemias, and Nathanias. Of the line of Ezora: Sessis, Ezril, Azael, Samatus, Zambris, and Josephus. 35 Of the line of Nooma: Mazitias, Zabadaeas, Edaes, Juel, and Banaeas. 36 All these had married foreign women, whom they now dismissed together with their children.

37 The priests and Levites, with such Israelites as were in Jerusalem and its neighbourhood, settled down there. On the new moon of the seventh month, the other Israelites being now in their settlements, 38 the entire company assembled with one accord in the broad space in front of the east gateway of the temple precinct 39 and asked Ezra, priest and doctor of the law, to bring the law of Moses given by the Lord God of Israel. 40 At the new moon of the seventh month Ezra the high priest brought the law to the whole assembly, both men and women, and to all the priests, for them to hear it. 41 From daybreak until noon he read aloud from it in the square in front of the temple gateway, in the presence of both men and women, and all the company listened attentively to the law.

42 Ezra, priest and doctor of the law, stood on the wooden platform which had been made for this purpose. 43 Beside him stood Mattathias, Sammus, Ananias, Azarias, Urias, Hezekias, and Baalsamus on his right, 44 and on his left Phaldaeus, Misael, Melchias, Lothasubus, Nabarias, and Zacharias. 45 Then in front of the whole assembly, for he was seated in a prominent place where everyone could see him, Ezra took up the book of the law, 46 and when he opened it they all stood. Ezra praised the Lord God, the Most High God of Hosts, the Almighty, 47 and all the people cried 'Amen, Amen.' They raised their hands and prostrated themselves in worship before the Lord. 48 Jeshua,

---

m Gk *Bacchurus*   *n* Gk *Tolbanes*

Akkub, Shabbethai, Hodiah, Maiannas and Kelita, Azariah and Jozabad, Hanan, Pelaiah, the Levites, taught the law of the Lord,*o* at the same time explaining what was read. 49 Then Attharates*p* said to Ezra the chief priest and reader, and to the Levites who were teaching the multitude, and to all, 50 "This day is holy to the Lord" — now they were all weeping as they heard the law — 51 "so go your way, eat the fat and drink the sweet, and send portions to those who have none; 52 for the day is holy to the Lord; and do not be sorrowful, for the Lord will exalt you." 53 The Levites commanded all the people, saying, "This day is holy; do not be sorrowful." 54 Then they all went their way, to eat and drink and enjoy themselves, and to give portions to those who had none, and to make great rejoicing; 55 because they were inspired by the words which they had been taught. And they came together.*q*

o Other ancient authorities add *and read the law of the Lord to the multitude*   *p* Or *the governor*   *q* The Greek text ends abruptly: compare Neh 8.13

Annus, Sarabias, Jadinus, Jacubus, Sabbataeas, Autaeas, Maeannas, Calitas, Azarias, Jozabdus, Ananias, and Phiathas, the Levites, taught the law of the Lord. They read the law of the Lord to the people, at the same time instilling into their minds the sense of what was read.

49 The governor said to them all, to Ezra, high priest and doctor of the law, and to the Levites who taught the people: 50 'This day is holy to the Lord.' All were weeping as they listened to the law. 51 'Go, therefore,' he continued, 'feast yourselves on rich food and sweet drinks, and send a share to those who have none, 52 for the day is holy to the Lord. Let there be no sadness, for the Lord will give you glory.' 53 The Levites enjoined the people: 'This day is holy; let there be no sadness.' 54 So they all went away to eat and drink and make merry, and to distribute shares to those who had none. They held a great celebration, 55 because the teaching given them had been instilled into their minds.

So they held their assembly.

9:49 **The governor:** *cp. 5:40; Gk* Attharates.

The Prayer of Manasseh is included only in the New Revised Standard Version and the Revised English Bible translations.

The Prayer of Manasseh

1 O Lord Almighty,
  God of our ancestors,
  of Abraham and Isaac and Jacob
  and of their righteous offspring;
2 you who made heaven and earth
  with all their order;
3 who shackled the sea by your word of command,
  who confined the deep
  and sealed it with your terrible and glorious
    name;
4 at whom all things shudder,
  and tremble before your power,
5 for your glorious splendor cannot be borne,
  and the wrath of your threat to sinners is
    unendurable;
6 yet immeasurable and unsearchable
  is your promised mercy,
7 for you are the Lord Most High,
  of great compassion, long-suffering, and very
    merciful,
  and you relent at human suffering.
  O Lord, according to your great goodness
  you have promised repentance and forgiveness
  to those who have sinned against you,
  and in the multitude of your mercies
  you have appointed repentance for sinners,
  so that they may be saved.*a*
8 Therefore you, O Lord, God of the righteous,
  have not appointed repentance for the righteous,
  for Abraham and Isaac and Jacob, who did not
    sin against you,
  but you have appointed repentance for me, who
    am a sinner.
9 For the sins I have committed are more in
    number than the sand of the sea;
  my transgressions are multiplied, O Lord, they
    are multiplied!
  I am not worthy to look up and see the height of
    heaven
  because of the multitude of my iniquities.
10 I am weighted down with many an iron fetter,
  so that I am rejected*b* because of my sins,
  and I have no relief;
  for I have provoked your wrath
  and have done what is evil in your sight,
  setting up abominations and multiplying offenses.
11 And now I bend the knee of my heart,
  imploring you for your kindness.
12 I have sinned, O Lord, I have sinned,
  and I acknowledge my transgressions.
13 I earnestly implore you,
  forgive me, O Lord, forgive me!
  Do not destroy me with my transgressions!
  Do not be angry with me forever or store up evil
    for me;
  do not condemn me to the depths of the earth.

The Prayer of Manasseh is included only in the New Revised Standard Version and the Revised English Bible translations.

The Prayer of Manasseh

ALMIGHTY Lord,
  God of our fathers,
  of Abraham, Isaac, and Jacob, and of their
    righteous posterity,
2 who made heaven and earth in their manifold
    array,
3 who fettered the ocean by your word of command,
  who closed the abyss
  and sealed it with your fearful and glorious
    name —
4 before your power all things quake and tremble.
5 The majesty of your glory is more than can be
    borne;
  none can endure the threat of your wrath against
    sinners.
6 Your promised mercy is beyond measure and none
    can fathom it;
7 for you are Lord Most High,
  compassionate, patient, and of great mercy,
  relenting when men suffer for their sins.

Some witnesses add:

For out of your great goodness, Lord,
you have promised repentance and remission
to those who have sinned against you,
and in your boundless mercy you have appointed
repentance for sinners as the way to salvation.

---

8 Therefore, Lord God of the righteous,
  you appointed repentance not for Abraham, Isaac,
    and Jacob,
  who were righteous and did not sin against you,
  but for me, 9 whose sins outnumber the sands of
    the sea.
  My transgressions abound, Lord, my transgressions
    abound,
  and, because of the multitude of my wrongdoings,
  I am not worthy to look up and gaze at the height
    of heaven.
10 Bowed down with many an iron chain,
  I grieve over my sins and find no relief,
  because I have provoked your anger
  and done what is wrong in your eyes,
  setting up idols and so multiplying offences.
11 Now my heart submits to you, imploring your
    great goodness.
12 I have sinned, Lord, I have sinned,
  and I acknowledge my transgressions.
13 I beg and beseech you,
  spare me, Lord, spare me;
  destroy me not with my transgressions on my head,
  do not be angry with me for ever,
  or store up punishment for me.
  Do not condemn me to the depths of the earth,

---

a Other ancient authorities lack *O Lord, according . . . be saved*
b Other ancient authorities read *so that I cannot lift up my head*

7 **for their sins:** *In standard editions of the* Revised English Bible
the italicized lines that follow appear in a footnote.

For you, O Lord, are the God of those who
   repent,
14 and in me you will manifest your goodness;
   for, unworthy as I am, you will save me
      according to your great mercy,
15 and I will praise you continually all the days of
   my life.
For all the host of heaven sings your praise,
   and yours is the glory forever. Amen.

for you, Lord, are the God of the penitent.
14 You will show your goodness towards me,
   for, unworthy as I am, you will save me in your
      great mercy;
15 and I shall praise you continually all the days of
   my life.
The whole host of heaven sings your praise,
   and yours is the glory for ever. Amen.

Psalm 151 is included only in the New Revised
Standard Version translation.

Psalm 151

*This psalm is ascribed to David as his own composition
(though it is outside the number^a), after he had fought in
single combat with Goliath.*

1 I was small among my brothers,
   and the youngest in my father's house;
   I tended my father's sheep.

2 My hands made a harp;
   my fingers fashioned a lyre.

3 And who will tell my Lord?
   The Lord himself; it is he who hears.^b

4 It was he who sent his messenger^c
   and took me from my father's sheep,
   and anointed me with his anointing oil.

5 My brothers were handsome and tall,
   but the Lord was not pleased with them.

6 I went out to meet the Philistine,^d
   and he cursed me by his idols.

7 But I drew his own sword;
   I beheaded him, and took away disgrace from
      the people of Israel.

^aOther ancient authorities add *of the one hundred fifty* (psalms)
^bOther ancient authorities add *everything*; others add *me*; others read
who will hear me   ^cOr *angel*   ^dOr *foreigner*

3 Maccabees is included only in the New Revised Standard Version translation.

3 Maccabees

1 When Philopator learned from those who returned that the regions that he had controlled had been seized by Antiochus, he gave orders to all his forces, both infantry and cavalry, took with him his sister Arsinoë, and marched out to the region near Raphia, where the army of Antiochus was encamped. 2 But a certain Theodotus, determined to carry out the plot he had devised, took with him the best of the Ptolemaic arms that had been previously issued to him,[a] and crossed over by night to the tent of Ptolemy, intending single-handed to kill him and thereby end the war. 3 But Dositheus, known as the son of Drimylus, a Jew by birth who later changed his religion and apostatized from the ancestral traditions, had led the king away and arranged that a certain insignificant man should sleep in the tent; and so it turned out that this man incurred the vengeance meant for the king.[b] 4 When a bitter fight resulted, and matters were turning out rather in favor of Antiochus, Arsinoë went to the troops with wailing and tears, her locks all disheveled, and exhorted them to defend themselves and their children and wives bravely, promising to give them each two minas of gold if they won the battle. 5 And so it came about that the enemy was routed in the action, and many captives also were taken. 6 Now that he had foiled the plot, Ptolemy[c] decided to visit the neighboring cities and encourage them. 7 By doing this, and by endowing their sacred enclosures with gifts, he strengthened the morale of his subjects.

8 Since the Jews had sent some of their council and elders to greet him, to bring him gifts of welcome, and to congratulate him on what had happened, he was all the more eager to visit them as soon as possible. 9 After he had arrived in Jerusalem, he offered sacrifice to the supreme God[d] and made thank offerings and did what was fitting for the holy place.[e] Then, upon entering the place and being impressed by its excellence and its beauty, 10 he marveled at the good order of the temple, and conceived a desire to enter the sanctuary. 11 When they said that this was not permitted, because not even members of their own nation were allowed to enter, not even all of the priests, but only the high priest who was pre-eminent over all — and he only once a year — the king was by no means persuaded. 12 Even after the law had been read to him, he did not cease to maintain that he ought to enter, saying, "Even if those men are deprived of this honor, I ought not to be." 13 And he inquired why, when he entered every other temple,[f] no one there had stopped him. 14 And someone answered thoughtlessly that it was wrong to take that as a portent.[g] 15 "But since this has happened," the king[h] said, "why should not I at least enter, whether they wish it or not?"

16 Then the priests in all their vestments prostrated themselves and entreated the supreme God[d] to aid in the present situation and to avert the violence of this evil design, and they filled the temple with cries and tears; 17 those who remained behind in the city were agitated and hurried out, supposing that something mysterious was occurring. 18 Young women who had been secluded in their chambers rushed out with their mothers, sprinkled their hair with dust,[i] and filled the streets with groans and lamentations. 19 Those women who had recently been arrayed for marriage abandoned the bridal chambers[j] prepared for wedded union, and, neglecting proper modesty, in a disorderly rush flocked together in the city. 20 Mothers and nurses abandoned even newborn children here and there, some in houses and some in the streets, and without a backward look they crowded together at the most high temple. 21 Various were the supplications of those gathered there because of what the king was profanely plotting. 22 In addition, the bolder of the citizens would not tolerate the completion of his plans or the fulfillment of his intended purpose. 23 They shouted to their compatriots to take arms and die courageously for the ancestral law, and created a considerable disturbance in the holy place;[k] and being barely restrained by the old men and the elders,[l] they resorted to the same posture of supplication as the others. 24 Meanwhile the crowd, as before, was engaged in prayer, 25 while the elders near the king tried in various ways to change his arrogant mind from the plan that he had conceived. 26 But he, in his arrogance, took heed of nothing, and began now to approach, determined to bring the aforesaid plan to a conclusion. 27 When those who were around him observed this, they turned, together with our people, to call upon him who has all power to defend them in the present trouble and not to overlook this unlawful and haughty deed. 28 The continuous, vehement, and concerted cry of the crowds[m] resulted in an immense uproar; 29 for it seemed that not only the people but also the walls and the whole earth around echoed, because indeed all at that time[n] preferred death to the profanation of the place.

2 Then the high priest Simon, facing the sanctuary, bending his knees and extending his hands with calm dignity, prayed as follows:[o] 2 "Lord, Lord, king of the heavens, and sovereign of all creation, holy among the holy ones, the only ruler, almighty, give attention to us who are suffering grievously from an impious and profane man, puffed up in his audacity and power. 3 For you, the creator of all things and the governor of all, are a just Ruler, and you judge those who have done anything in insolence and arrogance. 4 You destroyed those who in the past committed injustice, among whom were even giants who trusted in their strength and boldness, whom you destroyed by bringing on them a boundless flood. 5 You consumed with fire and sulfur the people of Sodom who acted arrogantly, who were notorious for their vices;[p] and you made them an example to those who should come afterward. 6 You made known your mighty power by inflicting many and varied punishments on the audacious Pharaoh who had enslaved your holy people Israel. 7 And when he pursued them with chariots and a mass of troops, you overwhelmed him in the depths of the sea, but carried through safely those who had put their confidence in you, the Ruler over the whole creation. 8 And when they had seen works of your hands, they praised you, the Almighty. 9 You, O King, when you had created the boundless and immeasurable earth, chose this city and sanctified this place for your name, though you have no need of anything; and when you had glorified it by

---

[a] Or the best of the Ptolemaic soldiers previously put under his command   [b] Gk that one   [c] Gk he   [d] Gk the greatest God   [e] Gk the place   [f] Or entered the temple precincts   [g] Or to boast of this   [h] Gk he   [i] Other ancient authorities add and ashes

[j] Or the canopies   [k] Gk the place   [l] Other ancient authorities read priests   [m] Other ancient authorities read vehement cry of the assembled crowds   [n] Other ancient authorities lack at that time   [o] Other ancient authorities lack verse 1   [p] Other ancient authorities read secret in their vices

your magnificent manifestation,*q* you made it a firm foundation for the glory of your great and honored name. 10 And because you love the house of Israel, you promised that if we should have reverses and tribulation should overtake us, you would listen to our petition when we come to this place and pray. 11 And indeed you are faithful and true. 12 And because oftentimes when our fathers were oppressed you helped them in their humiliation, and rescued them from great evils, 13 see now, O holy King, that because of our many and great sins we are crushed with suffering, subjected to our enemies, and overtaken by helplessness. 14 In our downfall this audacious and profane man undertakes to violate the holy place on earth dedicated to your glorious name. 15 For your dwelling is the heaven of heavens, unapproachable by human beings. 16 But because you graciously bestowed your glory on your people Israel, you sanctified this place. 17 Do not punish us for the defilement committed by these men, or call us to account for this profanation, otherwise the transgressors will boast in their wrath and exult in the arrogance of their tongue, saying, 18 'We have trampled down the house of the sanctuary as the houses of the abominations are trampled down.' 19 Wipe away our sins and disperse our errors, and reveal your mercy at this hour. 20 Speedily let your mercies overtake us, and put praises in the mouth of those who are downcast and broken in spirit, and give us peace."

21 Thereupon God, who oversees all things, the first Father of all, holy among the holy ones, having heard the lawful supplication, scourged him who had exalted himself in insolence and audacity. 22 He shook him on this side and that as a reed is shaken by the wind, so that he lay helpless on the ground and, besides being paralyzed in his limbs, was unable even to speak, since he was smitten*r* by a righteous judgment. 23 Then both friends and bodyguards, seeing the severe punishment that had overtaken him, and fearing that he would lose his life, quickly dragged him out, panic-stricken in their exceedingly great fear. 24 After a while he recovered, and though he had been punished, he by no means repented, but went away uttering bitter threats.

25 When he arrived in Egypt, he increased in his deeds of malice, abetted by the previously mentioned drinking companions and comrades, who were strangers to everything just. 26 He was not content with his uncounted licentious deeds, but even continued with such audacity that he framed evil reports in the various localities; and many of his friends, intently observing the king's purpose, themselves also followed his will. 27 He proposed to inflict public disgrace on the Jewish community,*s* and he set up a stone*t* on the tower in the courtyard with this inscription: 28 "None of those who do not sacrifice shall enter their sanctuaries, and all Jews shall be subjected to a registration involving poll tax and to the status of slaves. Those who object to this are to be taken by force and put to death; 29 those who are registered are also to be branded on their bodies by fire with the ivy-leaf symbol of Dionysus, and they shall also be reduced to their former limited status." 30 In order that he might not appear to be an enemy of all, he inscribed below: "But if any of them prefer to join those who have been initiated into the mysteries, they shall have equal citizenship with the Alexandrians."

31 Now some, however, with an obvious abhorrence of the price to be exacted for maintaining the religion of their city,*u* readily gave themselves up, since they expected to enhance their reputation by their future association with the king. 32 But the majority acted firmly with a courageous spirit and did not abandon their religion; and by paying money in exchange for life they confidently attempted to save themselves from the registration. 33 They remained resolutely hopeful of obtaining help, and they abhorred those who separated themselves from them, considering them to be enemies of the Jewish nation,*v* and depriving them of companionship and mutual help.

3 When the impious king comprehended this situation, he became so infuriated that not only was he enraged against those Jews who lived in Alexandria, but was still more bitterly hostile toward those in the countryside; and he ordered that all should promptly be gathered into one place, and put to death by the most cruel means. 2 While these matters were being arranged, a hostile rumor was circulated against the Jewish nation by some who conspired to do them ill, a pretext being given by a report that they hindered others*w* from the observance of their customs. 3 The Jews, however, continued to maintain goodwill and unswerving loyalty toward the dynasty; 4 but because they worshiped God and conducted themselves by his law, they kept their separateness with respect to foods. For this reason they appeared hateful to some; 5 but since they adorned their style of life with the good deeds of upright people, they were established in good repute with everyone. 6 Nevertheless those of other races paid no heed to their good service to their nation, which was common talk among all; 7 instead they gossiped about the differences in worship and foods, alleging that these people were loyal neither to the king nor to his authorities, but were hostile and greatly opposed to his government. So they attached no ordinary reproach to them.

8 The Greeks in the city, though wronged in no way, when they saw an unexpected tumult around these people and the crowds that suddenly were forming, were not strong enough to help them, for they lived under tyranny. They did try to console them, being grieved at the situation, and expected that matters would change; 9 for such a great community ought not be left to its fate when it had committed no offense. 10 And already some of their neighbors and friends and business associates had taken some of them aside privately and were pledging to protect them and to exert more earnest efforts for their assistance.

11 Then the king, boastful of his present good fortune, and not considering the might of the supreme God,*x* but assuming that he would persevere constantly in his same purpose, wrote this letter against them:

12 "King Ptolemy Philopator to his generals and soldiers in Egypt and all its districts, greetings and good health:

13 "I myself and our government are faring well. 14 When our expedition took place in Asia, as you yourselves know, it was brought to conclusion, according to plan, by the gods' deliberate alliance with us in battle, 15 and we considered that we should not rule the nations inhabiting Coelesyria and Phoenicia by the power of the spear, but should cherish them with clemency and great benevolence, gladly treating them well. 16 And when we had granted very great revenues to the temples in the cities, we came on to Jerusalem also, and went up to honor the temple of those wicked people, who never cease from their folly. 17 They accepted our presence by word, but insincerely by deed, because when we proposed to enter their inner temple and honor it with magnificent and most beautiful offerings, 18 they were carried away by their traditional arrogance, and excluded us from entering; but they were spared the exercise of our power because of the benevolence that we have toward all. 19 By maintaining their manifest ill-will toward us, they become the only people among all nations who hold their heads high in defiance of kings and

---

q Or *epiphany*   *r* Other ancient authorities read *pierced*   *s* Gk *the nation*   *t* Gk *stele*   *u* Meaning of Gk uncertain   *v* Gk *the nation*   *w* Gk *them*   *x* Gk *the greatest God*

their own benefactors, and are unwilling to regard any action as sincere.

20 "But we, when we arrived in Egypt victorious, accommodated ourselves to their folly and did as was proper, since we treat all nations with benevolence. 21 Among other things, we made known to all our amnesty toward their compatriots here, both because of their alliance with us and the myriad affairs liberally entrusted to them from the beginning; and we ventured to make a change, by deciding both to deem them worthy of Alexandrian citizenship and to make them participants in our regular religious rites.*y* 22 But in their innate malice they took this in a contrary spirit, and disdained what is good. Since they incline constantly to evil, 23 they not only spurn the priceless citizenship, but also both by speech and by silence they abominate those few among them who are sincerely disposed toward us; in every situation, in accordance with their infamous way of life, they secretly suspect that we may soon alter our policy. 24 Therefore, fully convinced by these indications that they are ill-disposed toward us in every way, we have taken precautions so that, if a sudden disorder later arises against us, we shall not have these impious people behind our backs as traitors and barbarous enemies. 25 Therefore we have given orders that, as soon as this letter arrives, you are to send to us those who live among you, together with their wives and children, with insulting and harsh treatment, and bound securely with iron fetters, to suffer the sure and shameful death that befits enemies. 26 For when all of these have been punished, we are sure that for the remaining time the government will be established for ourselves in good order and in the best state. 27 But those who shelter any of the Jews, whether old people or children or even infants, will be tortured to death with the most hateful torments, together with their families. 28 Any who are willing to give information will receive the property of those who incur the punishment, and also two thousand drachmas from the royal treasury, and will be awarded their freedom.*z* 29 Every place detected sheltering a Jew is to be made unapproachable and burned with fire, and shall become useless for all time to any mortal creature." 30 The letter was written in the above form.

4 In every place, then, where this decree arrived, a feast at public expense was arranged for the Gentiles with shouts and gladness, for the inveterate enmity that had long ago been in their minds was now made evident and outspoken. 2 But among the Jews there was incessant mourning, lamentation, and tearful cries; everywhere their hearts were burning, and they groaned because of the unexpected destruction that had suddenly been decreed for them. 3 What district or city, or what habitable place at all, or what streets were not filled with mourning and wailing for them? 4 For with such a harsh and ruthless spirit were they being sent off, all together, by the generals in the several cities, that at the sight of their unusual punishments, even some of their enemies, perceiving the common object of pity before their eyes, reflected on the uncertainty of life and shed tears at the most miserable expulsion of these people. 5 For a multitude of gray-headed old men, sluggish and bent with age, was being led away, forced to march at a swift pace by the violence with which they were driven in such a shameful manner. 6 And young women who had just entered the bridal chamber*a* to share married life exchanged joy for wailing, their myrrh-perfumed hair sprinkled with ashes, and were carried away unveiled, all together raising a lament instead of a wedding song, as they were torn by the harsh treatment of the heathen.*b* 7 In bonds and in public

view they were violently dragged along as far as the place of embarkation. 8 Their husbands, in the prime of youth, their necks encircled with ropes instead of garlands, spent the remaining days of their marriage festival in lamentations instead of good cheer and youthful revelry, seeing death immediately before them.*c* 9 They were brought on board like wild animals, driven under the constraint of iron bonds; some were fastened by the neck to the benches of the boats, others had their feet secured by unbreakable fetters, 10 and in addition they were confined under a solid deck, so that, with their eyes in total darkness, they would undergo treatment befitting traitors during the whole voyage.

11 When these people had been brought to the place called Schedia, and the voyage was concluded as the king had decreed, he commanded that they should be enclosed in the hippodrome that had been built with a monstrous perimeter wall in front of the city, and that was well suited to make them an obvious spectacle to all coming back into the city and to those from the city*d* going out into the country, so that they could neither communicate with the king's forces nor in any way claim to be inside the circuit of the city.*e* 12 And when this had happened, the king, hearing that the Jews' compatriots from the city frequently went out in secret to lament bitterly the ignoble misfortune of their kindred, 13 ordered in his rage that these people be dealt with in precisely the same fashion as the others, not omitting any detail of their punishment. 14 The entire race was to be registered individually, not for the hard labor that has been briefly mentioned before, but to be tortured with the outrages that he had ordered, and at the end to be destroyed in the space of a single day. 15 The registration of these people was therefore conducted with bitter haste and zealous intensity from the rising of the sun until its setting, coming to an end after forty days but still uncompleted.

16 The king was greatly and continually filled with joy, organizing feasts in honor of all his idols, with a mind alienated from truth and with a profane mouth, praising speechless things that are not able even to communicate or to come to one's help, and uttering improper words against the supreme God.*f* 17 But after the previously mentioned interval of time the scribes declared to the king that they were no longer able to take the census of the Jews because of their immense number, 18 though most of them were still in the country, some still residing in their homes, and some at the place;*g* the task was impossible for all the generals in Egypt. 19 After he had threatened them severely, charging that they had been bribed to contrive a means of escape, he was clearly convinced about the matter 20 when they said and proved that both the paper*h* and the pens they used for writing had already given out. 21 But this was an act of the invincible providence of him who was aiding the Jews from heaven.

5 Then the king, completely inflexible, was filled with overpowering anger and wrath; so he summoned Hermon, keeper of the elephants, 2 and ordered him on the following day to drug all the elephants—five hundred in number—with large handfuls of frankincense and plenty of unmixed wine, and to drive them in, maddened by the lavish abundance of drink, so that the Jews might meet their doom. 3 When he had given these orders he returned to his feasting, together with those of his Friends and of the army who were especially hostile toward the Jews. 4 And Hermon, keeper of the elephants, proceeded faithfully to carry out the orders. 5 The servants in charge of the Jews*i* went out in the evening and bound the hands of the wretched

---

y Other ancient authorities read *partners of our regular priests*
z Gk *crowned with freedom*   *a* Or *the canopy*   *b* Other ancient authorities read *as though torn by heathen whelps*

c Gk *seeing Hades already lying at their feet*   *d* Gk *those of them*
e Or *claim protection of the walls*; meaning of Gk uncertain   *f* Gk *the greatest God*   *g* Other ancient authorities read *on the way*
h Or *paper factory*   *i* Gk *them*

people and arranged for their continued custody through the night, convinced that the whole nation would experience its final destruction. 6 For to the Gentiles it appeared that the Jews were left without any aid, 7 because in their bonds they were forcibly confined on every side. But with tears and a voice hard to silence they all called upon the Almighty Lord and Ruler of all power, their merciful God and Father, praying 8 that he avert with vengeance the evil plot against them and in a glorious manifestation rescue them from the fate now prepared for them. 9 So their entreaty ascended fervently to heaven.

10 Hermon, however, when he had drugged the pitiless elephants until they had been filled with a great abundance of wine and satiated with frankincense, presented himself at the courtyard early in the morning to report to the king about these preparations. 11 But the Lord[j] sent upon the king a portion of sleep, that beneficence that from the beginning, night and day, is bestowed by him who grants it to whomever he wishes. 12 And by the action of the Lord he was overcome by so pleasant and deep a sleep[k] that he quite failed in his lawless purpose and was completely frustrated in his inflexible plan. 13 Then the Jews, since they had escaped the appointed hour, praised their holy God and again implored him who is easily reconciled to show the might of his all-powerful hand to the arrogant Gentiles.

14 But now, since it was nearly the middle of the tenth hour, the person who was in charge of the invitations, seeing that the guests were assembled, approached the king and nudged him. 15 And when he had with difficulty roused him, he pointed out that the hour of the banquet was already slipping by, and he gave him an account of the situation. 16 The king, after considering this, returned to his drinking, and ordered those present for the banquet to recline opposite him. 17 When this was done he urged them to give themselves over to revelry and to make the present[l] portion of the banquet joyful by celebrating all the more. 18 After the party had been going on for some time, the king summoned Hermon and with sharp threats demanded to know why the Jews had been allowed to remain alive through the present day. 19 But when he, with the corroboration of his Friends, pointed out that while it was still night he had carried out completely the order given him, 20 the king,[j] possessed by a savagery worse than that of Phalaris, said that the Jews[m] were benefited by today's sleep, "but," he added, "tomorrow without delay prepare the elephants in the same way for the destruction of the lawless Jews!" 21 When the king had spoken, all those present readily and joyfully with one accord gave their approval, and all went to their own homes. 22 But they did not so much employ the duration of the night in sleep as in devising all sorts of insults for those they thought to be doomed.

23 Then, as soon as the cock had crowed in the early morning, Hermon, having equipped[n] the animals, began to move them along in the great colonnade. 24 The crowds of the city had been assembled for this most pitiful spectacle and they were eagerly waiting for daybreak. 25 But the Jews, at their last gasp — since the time had run out — stretched their hands toward heaven and with most tearful supplication and mournful dirges implored the supreme God[o] to help them again at once. 26 The rays of the sun were not yet shed abroad, and while the king was receiving his Friends, Hermon arrived and invited him to come out, indicating that what the king desired was ready for action. 27 But he, on receiving the report and being struck by the unusual invitation to come out — since he had been completely overcome by incomprehension — inquired what the

matter was for which this had been so zealously completed for him. 28 This was the act of God who rules over all things, for he had implanted in the king's mind a forgetfulness of the things he had previously devised. 29 Then Hermon and all the king's Friends[p] pointed out that the animals and the armed forces were ready, "O king, according to your eager purpose."[q] 30 But at these words he was filled with an overpowering wrath, because by the providence of God his whole mind had been deranged concerning these matters; and with a threatening look he said, 31 "If your parents or children were present, I would have prepared them to be a rich feast for the savage animals instead of the Jews, who give me no ground for complaint and have exhibited to an extraordinary degree a full and firm loyalty to my ancestors. 32 In fact you would have been deprived of life instead of these, if it were not for an affection arising from our nurture in common and your usefulness." 33 So Hermon suffered an unexpected and dangerous threat, and his eyes wavered and his face fell. 34 The king's Friends one by one sullenly slipped away and dismissed[r] the assembled people to their own occupations. 35 Then the Jews, on hearing what the king said, praised the manifest Lord God, King of kings, since this also was his aid that they had received.

36 The king, however, reconvened the party in the same manner and urged the guests to return to their celebrating. 37 After summoning Hermon he said in a threatening tone, "How many times, you poor wretch, must I give you orders about these things? 38 Equip[s] the elephants now once more for the destruction of the Jews tomorrow!" 39 But the officials who were at table with him, wondering at his instability of mind, remonstrated as follows: 40 "O king, how long will you put us to the test, as though we are idiots, ordering now for a third time that they be destroyed, and again revoking your decree in the matter?[t] 41 As a result the city is in a tumult because of its expectation; it is crowded with masses of people, and also in constant danger of being plundered."

42 At this the king, a Phalaris in everything and filled with madness, took no account of the changes of mind that had come about within him for the protection of the Jews, and he firmly swore an irrevocable oath that he would send them to death[u] without delay, mangled by the knees and feet of the animals, 43 and would also march against Judea and rapidly level it to the ground with fire and spear, and by burning to the ground the temple inaccessible to him[v] would quickly render it forever empty of those who offered sacrifices there. 44 Then the Friends and officers departed with great joy, and they confidently posted the armed forces at the places in the city most favorable for keeping guard.

45 Now when the animals had been brought virtually to a state of madness, so to speak, by the very fragrant draughts of wine mixed with frankincense and had been equipped with frightful devices, the elephant keeper 46 entered at about dawn into the courtyard — the city now being filled with countless masses of people crowding their way into the hippodrome — and urged the king on to the matter at hand. 47 So he, when he had filled his impious mind with a deep rage, rushed out in full force along with the animals, wishing to witness, with invulnerable heart and with his own eyes, the grievous and pitiful destruction of the aforementioned people.

48 When the Jews saw the dust raised by the elephants going out at the gate and by the following armed forces, as

well as by the trampling of the crowd, and heard the loud and tumultuous noise, 49 they thought that this was their last moment of life, the end of their most miserable suspense, and giving way to lamentation and groans they kissed each other, embracing relatives and falling into one another's arms*w* — parents and children, mothers and daughters, and others with babies at their breasts who were drawing their last milk. 50 Not only this, but when they considered the help that they had received before from heaven, they prostrated themselves with one accord on the ground, removing the babies from their breasts, 51 and cried out in a very loud voice, imploring the Ruler over every power to manifest himself and be merciful to them, as they stood now at the gates of death.*x*

6 Then a certain Eleazar, famous among the priests of the country, who had attained a ripe old age and throughout his life had been adorned with every virtue, directed the elders around him to stop calling upon the holy God, and he prayed as follows: 2 "King of great power, Almighty God Most High, governing all creation with mercy, 3 look upon the descendants of Abraham, O Father, upon the children of the sainted Jacob, a people of your consecrated portion who are perishing as foreigners in a foreign land. 4 Pharaoh with his abundance of chariots, the former ruler of this Egypt, exalted with lawless insolence and boastful tongue, you destroyed together with his arrogant army by drowning them in the sea, manifesting the light of your mercy on the nation of Israel. 5 Sennacherib exulting in his countless forces, oppressive king of the Assyrians, who had already gained control of the whole world by the spear and was lifted up against your holy city, speaking grievous words with boasting and insolence, you, O Lord, broke in pieces, showing your power to many nations. 6 The three companions in Babylon who had voluntarily surrendered their lives to the flames so as not to serve vain things, you rescued unharmed, even to a hair, moistening the fiery furnace with dew and turning the flame against all their enemies. 7 Daniel, who through envious slanders was thrown down into the ground to lions as food for wild animals, you brought up to the light unharmed. 8 And Jonah, wasting away in the belly of a huge, sea-born monster, you, Father, watched over and restored*y* unharmed to all his family. 9 And now, you who hate insolence, all-merciful and protector of all, reveal yourself quickly to those of the nation of Israel*z* — who are being outrageously treated by the abominable and lawless Gentiles.

10 "Even if our lives have become entangled in impieties in our exile, rescue us from the hand of the enemy, and destroy us, Lord, by whatever fate you choose. 11 Let not the vain-minded praise their vanities*a* at the destruction of your beloved people, saying, 'Not even their god has rescued them.' 12 But you, O Eternal One, who have all might and all power, watch over us now and have mercy on us who by the senseless insolence of the lawless are being deprived of life in the manner of traitors. 13 And let the Gentiles cower today in fear of your invincible might, O honored One, who have power to save the nation of Jacob. 14 The whole throng of infants and their parents entreat you with tears. 15 Let it be shown to all the Gentiles that you are with us, O Lord, and have not turned your face from us; but just as you have said, 'Not even when they were in the land of their enemies did I neglect them,' so accomplish it, O Lord."

16 Just as Eleazar was ending his prayer, the king arrived at the hippodrome with the animals and all the arrogance of his forces. 17 And when the Jews observed this they raised great cries to heaven so that even the nearby valleys resounded with them and brought an uncontrollable terror upon the army. 18 Then the most glorious, almighty, and true God revealed his holy face and opened the heavenly gates, from which two glorious angels of fearful aspect descended, visible to all but the Jews. 19 They opposed the forces of the enemy and filled them with confusion and terror, binding them with immovable shackles. 20 Even the king began to shudder bodily, and he forgot his sullen insolence. 21 The animals turned back upon the armed forces following them and began trampling and destroying them.

22 Then the king's anger was turned to pity and tears because of the things that he had devised beforehand. 23 For when he heard the shouting and saw them all fallen headlong to destruction, he wept and angrily threatened his Friends, saying, 24 "You are committing treason and surpassing tyrants in cruelty; and even me, your benefactor, you are now attempting to deprive of dominion and life by secretly devising acts of no advantage to the kingdom. 25 Who has driven from their homes those who faithfully kept our country's fortresses, and foolishly gathered every one of them here? 26 Who is it that has so lawlessly encompassed with outrageous treatment those who from the beginning differed from*b* all nations in their goodwill toward us and often have accepted willingly the worst of human dangers? 27 Loose and untie their unjust bonds! Send them back to their homes in peace, begging pardon for your former actions!*c* 28 Release the children of the almighty and living God of heaven, who from the time of our ancestors until now has granted an unimpeded and notable stability to our government." 29 These then were the things he said; and the Jews, immediately released, praised their holy God and Savior, since they now had escaped death.

30 Then the king, when he had returned to the city, summoned the official in charge of the revenues and ordered him to provide to the Jews both wines and everything else needed for a festival of seven days, deciding that they should celebrate their rescue with all joyfulness in that same place in which they had expected to meet their destruction. 31 Accordingly those disgracefully treated and near to death,*d* or rather, who stood at its gates, arranged for a banquet of deliverance instead of a bitter and lamentable death, and full of joy they apportioned to celebrants the place that had been prepared for their destruction and burial. 32 They stopped their chanting of dirges and took up the song of their ancestors, praising God, their Savior and worker of wonders.*e* Putting an end to all mourning and wailing, they formed choruses*f* as a sign of peaceful joy. 33 Likewise also the king, after convening a great banquet to celebrate these events, gave thanks to heaven unceasingly and lavishly for the unexpected rescue that he*g* had experienced. 34 Those who had previously believed that the Jews would be destroyed and become food for birds, and had joyfully registered them, groaned as they themselves were overcome by disgrace, and their fire-breathing boldness was ignominiously*h* quenched.

35 The Jews, as we have said before, arranged the aforementioned choral group*i* and passed the time in feasting to the accompaniment of joyous thanksgiving and psalms. 36 And when they had ordained a public rite for these things in their whole community and for their descendants, they instituted the observance of the aforesaid days as

---

w Gk *falling upon their necks*   *x* Gk *Hades*   *y* Other ancient authorities read *rescued and restored*; others, *mercifully restored*   *z* Other ancient authorities read *to the saints of Israel*   *a* Or *bless their vain gods*

b Or *excelled above*   *c* Other ancient authorities read *revoking your former commands*   *d* Gk *Hades*   *e* Other ancient authorities read *praising Israel and the wonder-working God*; or *praising Israel's Savior, the wonder-working God*   *f* Or *dances*   *g* Other ancient authorities read *they*   *h* Other ancient authorities read *completely*   *i* Or *dance*

a festival, not for drinking and gluttony, but because of the deliverance that had come to them through God. 37 Then they petitioned the king, asking for dismissal to their homes. 38 So their registration was carried out from the twenty-fifth of Pachon to the fourth of Epeiph,*j* for forty days; and their destruction was set for the fifth to the seventh of Epeiph,*k* the three days 39 on which the Lord of all most gloriously revealed his mercy and rescued them all together and unharmed. 40 Then they feasted, being provided with everything by the king, until the fourteenth day,*l* on which also they made the petition for their dismissal. 41 The king granted their request at once and wrote the following letter for them to the generals in the cities, magnanimously expressing his concern:

7 "King Ptolemy Philopator to the generals in Egypt and all in authority in his government, greetings and good health:

2 "We ourselves and our children are faring well, the great God guiding our affairs according to our desire. 3 Certain of our friends, frequently urging us with malicious intent, persuaded us to gather together the Jews of the kingdom in a body and to punish them with barbarous penalties as traitors; 4 for they declared that our government would never be firmly established until this was accomplished, because of the ill-will that these people had toward all nations. 5 They also led them out with harsh treatment as slaves, or rather as traitors and, girding themselves with a cruelty more savage than that of Scythian custom, they tried without any inquiry or examination to put them to death. 6 But we very severely threatened them for these acts, and in accordance with the clemency that we have toward all people we barely spared their lives. Since we have come to realize that the God of heaven surely defends the Jews, always taking their part as a father does for his children, 7 and since we have taken into account the friendly and firm goodwill that they had toward us and our ancestors, we justly have acquitted them of every charge of whatever kind. 8 We also have ordered all people to return to their own homes, with no one in any place*m* doing them harm at all or reproaching them for the irrational things that have happened. 9 For you should know that if we devise any evil against them or cause them any grief at all, we always shall have not a mortal but the Ruler over every power, the Most High God, in everything and inescapably as an antagonist to avenge such acts. Farewell."

10 On receiving this letter the Jews*n* did not immediately hurry to make their departure, but they requested of the king that at their own hands those of the Jewish nation who had willfully transgressed against the holy God and the law of God should receive the punishment they deserved. 11 They declared that those who for the belly's sake had transgressed the divine commandments would never be favorably disposed toward the king's government. 12 The king*o* then, admitting and approving the truth of what they said, granted them a general license so that freely, and without royal authority or supervision, they might destroy those everywhere in his kingdom who had transgressed the law of God. 13 When they had applauded him in fitting manner, their priests and the whole multitude shouted the Hallelujah and joyfully departed. 14 And so on their way they punished and put to a public and shameful death any whom they met of their compatriots who had become defiled. 15 In that day they put to death more than three hundred men; and they kept the day as a joyful festival, since they had destroyed the profaners. 16 But those who had held fast to God even to death and had received the full enjoyment of deliverance began their departure from the city, crowned with all sorts of very fragrant flowers, joyfully and loudly giving thanks to the one God of their ancestors, the eternal Savior*p* of Israel, in words of praise and all kinds of melodious songs.

17 When they had arrived at Ptolemais, called "rose-bearing" because of a characteristic of the place, the fleet waited for them, in accordance with the common desire, for seven days. 18 There they celebrated their deliverance,*q* for the king had generously provided all things to them for their journey until all of them arrived at their own houses. 19 And when they had all landed in peace with appropriate thanksgiving, there too in like manner they decided to observe these days as a joyous festival during the time of their stay. 20 Then, after inscribing them as holy on a pillar and dedicating a place of prayer at the site of the festival, they departed unharmed, free, and overjoyed, since at the king's command they had all of them been brought safely by land and sea and river to their own homes. 21 They also possessed greater prestige among their enemies, being held in honor and awe; and they were not subject at all to confiscation of their belongings by any one. 22 Besides, they all recovered all of their property, in accordance with the registration, so that those who held any of it restored it to them with extreme fear.*r* So the supreme God perfectly performed great deeds for their deliverance. 23 Blessed be the Deliverer of Israel through all times! Amen.

---

j July 7—August 15   *k* August 16—18   *l* August 25   *m* Other ancient authorities read *way*   *n* Gk *they*

o Gk *He*   *p* Other ancient authorities read *the holy Savior;* others, *the holy one*   *q* Gk *they made a cup of deliverance*   *r* Other ancient authorities read *with a very large supplement*

(c) The following book is included in the Slavonic Bible as 3 Esdras, but is not found in the Greek. It is included in the Appendix to the Latin Vulgate Bible as 4 Esdras.

2 Esdras is included only in the New Revised Standard Version and the Revised English Bible translations.

2 Esdras

Comprising what is sometimes called 5 Ezra (chapters 1–2), 4 Ezra (chapters 3–14), and 6 Ezra (chapters 15–16)

1 The book*a* of the prophet Ezra son of Seraiah son of Azariah son of Hilkiah son of Shallum son of Zadok son of Ahitub 2 son of Ahijah son of Phinehas son of Eli son of Amariah son of Azariah son of Meraimoth son of Arna son of Uzzi son of Borith son of Abishua son of Phinehas son of Eleazar 3 son of Aaron, of the tribe of Levi, who was a captive in the country of the Medes in the reign of Arta-xerxes, king of the Persians.*b*

4 The word of the Lord came to me, saying, 5 "Go, declare to my people their evil deeds, and to their children the iniquities that they have committed against me, so that they may tell*c* their children's children 6 that the sins of their parents have increased in them, for they have forgotten me and have offered sacrifices to strange gods. 7 Was it not I who brought them out of the land of Egypt, out of the house of bondage? But they have angered me and despised my counsels. 8 Now you, pull out the hair of your head and hurl*d* all evils upon them, for they have not obeyed my law—they are a rebellious people. 9 How long shall I en-dure them, on whom I have bestowed such great benefits? 10 For their sake I have overthrown many kings; I struck down Pharaoh with his servants and all his army. 11 I de-stroyed all nations before them, and scattered in the east the peoples of two provinces,*e* Tyre and Sidon; I killed all their enemies.

12 "But speak to them and say, Thus says the Lord: 13 Surely it was I who brought you through the sea, and made safe highways for you where there was no road; I gave you Moses as leader and Aaron as priest; 14 I provided light for you from a pillar of fire, and did great wonders among you. Yet you have forgotten me, says the Lord.

15 "Thus says the Lord Almighty:*f* The quails were a sign to you; I gave you camps for your protection, and in them you complained. 16 You have not exulted in my name at the destruction of your enemies, but to this day you still complain.*g* 17 Where are the benefits that I bestowed on you? When you were hungry and thirsty in the wilderness, did you not cry out to me, 18 saying, 'Why have you led us into this wilderness to kill us? It would have been better for us to serve the Egyptians than to die in this wilderness.' 19 I pitied your groanings and gave you manna for food; you ate the bread of angels. 20 When you were thirsty, did I not split the rock so that waters flowed in abundance? Because of the heat I clothed you with the leaves of trees.*h* 21 I divided

---

a Other ancient authorities read *The second book*   *b* Other ancient authorities, which place chapters 1 and 2 after 16.78, lack verses 1-3 and begin the chapter: *The word of the Lord that came to Ezra son of Chusi in the days of King Nebuchadnezzar, saying, "Go,*   *c* Other ancient authorities read *nourish*   *d* Other ancient authorities read *and shake out*   *e* Other ancient authorities read *Did I not destroy the city of Bethsaida because of you, and to the south burn two cities . . . ?*   *f* Other ancient authorities lack *Almighty*   *g* Other ancient authorities read verse 16, *Your pursuer with his army I sank in the sea, but still the people complain also concerning their own destruction.*   *h* Other ancient authorities read *I made for you trees with leaves*

---

2 Esdras is included only in the New Revised Standard Version and the Revised English Bible translations.

THE SECOND BOOK OF
Esdras

1 THE second book of the prophet Ezra son of Seraiah, son of Azariah, son of Hilkiah, son of Shallum, son of Zadok, son of Ahitub, 2 son of Ahijah, son of Phinehas, son of Eli, son of Amariah, son of Aziah, son of Marimoth, son of Arna, son of Uzzi, son of Borith, son of Abishua, son of Phinehas, son of Eleazar, 3 son of Aaron, of the tribe of Levi.

I, EZRA, was a captive in Media during the reign of King Artaxerxes of Persia 4 when this word of the Lord came to me: 5 Go to my people and proclaim their crimes; tell their children how they have sinned against me, and let them tell their children's children. 6 My people have sinned even more than their fathers, for they have forgotten me and sacrificed to alien gods. 7 Was it not I who brought them out of Egypt, out of the land where they were slaves? And yet they have aroused my anger and spurned my warnings.

8 But it is for you, Ezra, to tear out your hair and to let every calamity loose on those who have disobeyed my law. My people are beyond correction. 9 How much longer can I tolerate a people on whom I have lavished such great benefits? 10 Many are the kings I have overthrown for their sake; I struck down Pharaoh along with his court and his whole army. 11 Every nation that stood in their way I de-stroyed; in the east I routed the peoples of two provinces, Tyre and Sidon, and killed all Israel's enemies.

12 Say to them, 'These are the words of the Lord: 13 Was it not I who brought you through the sea, and made for you safe roads where no road had been? I gave you Moses as your leader, and Aaron as your priest; 14 I provided you with light from a pillar of fire; I performed great miracles among you. And yet you have forgotten me, says the Lord.

15-16 'These are the words of the Lord Almighty: The quails were a sign to you; I gave you a camp for your protection. Instead of celebrating the victory when I de-stroyed your enemies, all you did there was to grumble and complain, and from that day to this your complaints have never ceased. 17 Have you forgotten what benefits I con-ferred on you? When you were hungry and thirsty on your journey through the wilderness, you cried out: 18 "Why have you led us into this wilderness to kill us? Better for us to be slaves to the Egyptians than to perish here in this wilder-ness!" 19 Grieved at your complaints, I gave you manna for food; it was the bread of angels you were eating. 20 When you were thirsty, I split open the rock, and water flowed out in plenty. Against the summer heat I provided you with the shade of leafy trees. 21 I expelled those who opposed you,

fertile lands among you; I drove out the Canaanites, the Perizzites, and the Philistines[i] before you. What more can I do for you? says the Lord. 22 Thus says the Lord Almighty:[j] When you were in the wilderness, at the bitter stream, thirsty and blaspheming my name, 23 I did not send fire on you for your blasphemies, but threw a tree into the water and made the stream sweet.

24 "What shall I do to you, O Jacob? You, Judah, would not obey me. I will turn to other nations and will give them my name, so that they may keep my statutes. 25 Because you have forsaken me, I also will forsake you. When you beg mercy of me, I will show you no mercy. 26 When you call to me, I will not listen to you; for you have defiled your hands with blood, and your feet are swift to commit murder. 27 It is not as though you had forsaken me; you have forsaken yourselves, says the Lord.

28 "Thus says the Lord Almighty: Have I not entreated you as a father entreats his sons or a mother her daughters or a nurse her children, 29 so that you should be my people and I should be your God, and that you should be my children and I should be your father? 30 I gathered you as a hen gathers her chicks under her wings. But now, what shall I do to you? I will cast you out from my presence. 31 When you offer oblations to me, I will turn my face from you; for I have rejected your[k] festal days, and new moons, and circumcisions of the flesh.[l] 32 I sent you my servants the prophets, but you have taken and killed them and torn their bodies[m] in pieces; I will require their blood of you, says the Lord.[n]

33 "Thus says the Lord Almighty: Your house is desolate; I will drive you out as the wind drives straw; 34 and your sons will have no children, because with you[o] they have neglected my commandment and have done what is evil in my sight. 35 I will give your houses to a people that will come, who without having heard me will believe. Those to whom I have shown no signs will do what I have commanded. 36 They have seen no prophets, yet will recall their former state.[p] 37 I call to witness the gratitude of the people that is to come, whose children rejoice with gladness;[q] though they do not see me with bodily eyes, yet with the spirit they will believe the things I have said.

38 "And now, father,[r] look with pride and see the people coming from the east; 39 to them I will give as leaders Abraham, Isaac, and Jacob, and Hosea and Amos and Micah and Joel and Obadiah and Jonah 40 and Nahum and Habakkuk, Zephaniah, Haggai, Zechariah and Malachi, who is also called the messenger of the Lord.[s]

the Canaanites, Perizzites, and Philistines, and distributed their fertile lands among you. What more could I do for you? says the Lord.

22 'These are the words of the Lord Almighty: When you were in the wilderness, suffering thirst by the stream of bitter water and cursing me, 23 I did not bring fire down on you for your blasphemy; instead I cast a log into the stream and made the water sweet. 24 Jacob, what am I to do with you? You have refused to obey me, Judah! I shall turn to other nations and give them my name, and they will keep my statutes. 25 Because you have forsaken me, I shall forsake you; when you implore me for mercy, I shall show you none; 26 when you pray to me, I shall not listen. You have stained your hands with blood; you hasten hotfoot to commit murder. 27 It is not that you have forsaken me: you have forsaken yourselves, says the Lord.

28 'These are the words of the Lord Almighty: Have I not pleaded with you as a father with his sons, as a mother with her daughters, or as a nursemaid with her children, 29 that you should be my people and I should be your God, that you should be my sons and I should be your father? 30 I gathered you as a hen gathers her brood under her wing. But now, what am I to do with you? I shall cast you out from my presence. 31 When you offer me sacrifice, I shall turn from you, for I have rejected your feasts, your new moons, and your circumcisions. 32 I sent my servants the prophets to you, but you took them and killed them and mutilated their bodies. For their murder I shall call you to account, says the Lord.

33 'These are the words of the Lord Almighty: Your house is forsaken. I shall toss you away like straw before the wind. 34 Your children will have no posterity, because like you they have ignored my commandments and done what I have condemned. 35 I shall hand over your homes to a people yet to come: a people who will trust me, though they have not known me; who will do my bidding, though I gave them no signs; 36 who never saw the prophets, yet will keep in mind what the prophets taught of old. 37 I vow that this people yet to come shall have my favour; their little ones will jump for joy, and though they themselves have not seen me with their eyes, they will perceive by the spirit and believe what I have said.'

38 Now, father Ezra, look with pride at the nation coming from the east. 39 The leaders I shall give them are Abraham, Isaac, and Jacob, Hosea and Amos, Micah and Joel, Obadiah and Jonah, 40 Nahum, Habakkuk, and Zephaniah, Haggai and Zechariah, and Malachi, who is also called the Lord's messenger.

---

[i] Other ancient authorities read *Perizzites and their children*   [j] Other ancient authorities lack *Almighty*   [k] Other ancient authorities read *I have not commanded for you*   [l] Other ancient authorities lack *of the flesh*   [m] Other ancient authorities read *the bodies of the apostles*   [n] Other ancient authorities add *Thus says the Lord Almighty: Recently you also laid hands on me, crying out before the judge's seat for him to deliver me to you. You took me as a sinner, not as a father who freed you from slavery, and you delivered me to death by hanging me on the tree; these are the things you have done. Therefore, says the Lord, let my Father and his angels return and judge between you and me; if I have not kept the commandment of the Father, if I have not nourished you, if I have not done the things my Father commanded, I will contend in judgment with you, says the Lord.*   [o] Other ancient authorities lack *with you*   [p] Other ancient authorities read *their iniquities*   [q] Other ancient authorities read *The apostles bear witness to the coming people with joy*   [r] Other ancient authorities read *brother*   [s] Other ancient authorities read *and Jacob, Elijah and Enoch, Zechariah and Hosea, Amos, Joel, Micah, Obadiah, Zephaniah,* 40 *Nahum, Jonah, Mattia (or Mattathias), Habakkuk, and twelve angels with flowers*

|

2 "Thus says the Lord: I brought this people out of bondage, and I gave them commandments through my servants the prophets; but they would not listen to them, and made my counsels void. 2 The mother who bore them[r] says to them, 'Go, my children, because I am a widow and forsaken. 3 I brought you up with gladness; but with mourning and sorrow I have lost you, because you have sinned before the Lord God and have done what is evil in my sight. u 4 But now what can I do for you? For I am a widow and forsaken. Go, my children, and ask for mercy from the Lord.' 5 Now I call upon you, father, as a witness in addition to the mother of the children, because they would not keep my covenant, 6 so that you may bring confusion on them and bring their mother to ruin, so that they may have no offspring. 7 Let them be scattered among the nations; let their names be blotted out from the earth, because they despised my covenant.

8 "Woe to you, Assyria, who conceal the unrighteous within you! O wicked nation, remember what I did to Sodom and Gomorrah, 9 whose land lies in lumps of pitch and heaps of ashes. v That is what I will do to those who have not listened to me, says the Lord Almighty."

10 Thus says the Lord to Ezra: "Tell my people that I will give them the kingdom of Jerusalem, which I was going to give to Israel. 11 Moreover, I will take back to myself their glory, and will give to these others the everlasting habitations, which I had prepared for Israel. w 12 The tree of life shall give them fragrant perfume, and they shall neither toil nor become weary. 13 Go x and you will receive; pray that your days may be few, that they may be shortened. The kingdom is already prepared for you; be on the watch! 14 Call, O call heaven and earth to witness: I set aside evil and created good; for I am the Living One, says the Lord.

15 "Mother, embrace your children; bring them up with gladness, as does a dove; strengthen their feet, because I have chosen you, says the Lord. 16 And I will raise up the dead from their places, and bring them out from their tombs, because I recognize my name in them. 17 Do not fear, mother of children, for I have chosen you, says the Lord. 18 I will send you help, my servants Isaiah and Jeremiah. According to their counsel I have consecrated and prepared for you twelve trees loaded with various fruits, 19 and the same number of springs flowing with milk and honey, and seven mighty mountains on which roses and lilies grow; by these I will fill your children with joy.

20 "Guard the rights of the widow, secure justice for the ward, give to the needy, defend the orphan, clothe the naked, 21 care for the injured and the weak, do not ridicule the lame, protect the maimed, and let the blind have a vision of my splendor. 22 Protect the old and the young within your walls. 23 When you find any who are dead, commit them to the grave and mark it, y and I will give you the first place in my resurrection. 24 Pause and be quiet, my people, because your rest will come.

25 "Good nurse, nourish your children; strengthen their feet. 26 Not one of the servants z whom I have given you will perish, for I will require them from among your number. 27 Do not be anxious, for when the day of tribulation and anguish comes, others shall weep and be sorrowful, but you shall rejoice and have abundance. 28 The nations shall envy you, but they shall not be able to do anything against you, says the Lord. 29 My power will protect a you, so that your children may not see hell. b

2 These are the words of the Lord: I brought that people out of slavery and gave them commandments through my servants the prophets; but they shut their ears to the prophets, and allowed my precepts to become a dead letter. 2 The mother who bore them says: 'Go, my children; I am widowed and forsaken. 3 With joy I brought you up, but with mourning and sorrow I have lost you, because you have sinned against the Lord God and done what I have condemned. 4 But now, what can I do for you, widowed and forsaken as I am? Go, my children, ask the Lord for mercy.' 5 I call upon you, father Ezra, to add your testimony to hers that her children have refused to keep my covenant; 6 and let your words bring confusion on them. May their mother be despoiled, and may they themselves have no posterity. 7 Let them be dispersed among the nations and let their name vanish from the earth, because they have spurned my covenant.

8 Woe to you, Assyria, you harbourer of sinners! Remember, you evil nation, what I did to Sodom and Gomorrah: 9 their land lies buried under masses of pitch and heaps of ashes. So shall I deal with those who have disobeyed me, says the Lord Almighty.

10 These are the words of the Lord to Ezra: Tell my people that I shall give to them the kingdom of Jerusalem, which once I offered to Israel. 11 I shall also withdraw the splendour of my presence from Israel, and the home that was to be theirs for ever I shall give to my people. 12 The tree of life will spread its fragrance over them; they will neither toil nor grow weary. 13 Ask, and you will receive; pray that your short time of waiting may be cut shorter still. Even now the kingdom is ready for you; be vigilant! 14 I summon heaven and earth to witness: I have cancelled the evil and brought the good into being; for I am the Living One, says the Lord.

15 Mother, keep your children close to you. Rear them with gladness, as a dove rears her nestlings; teach them to walk without stumbling. You are my chosen one, says the Lord. 16 I shall raise up the dead from their resting-places and bring them out of their tombs, for I have acknowledged that they bear my name. 17 There is nothing to fear, mother of many children, for I have chosen you, says the Lord. 18 I shall send my servants Isaiah and Jeremiah to help you. As they prophesied, I have set you apart to be my people. I have made ready for you twelve trees laden with different kinds of fruit, 19 twelve fountains flowing with milk and honey, and seven great mountains covered with roses and lilies. There I shall fill your children with joy. 20 Champion the widow, defend the cause of the fatherless, give to the poor, protect the orphan, provide clothing for those who have none; 21 care for the weak and the helpless, and do not mock at the cripple; watch over the disabled, and bring the blind to the vision of my radiance. 22 Keep both old and young safe within your walls.

23 When you find the dead unburied, mark them with the sign and commit them to the tomb; and then, when I cause the dead to rise, I shall give you the chief place. 24 Be calm, my people; your time of rest will come. 25 Be a good nurse-maid to your children, and teach them to walk without stumbling. 26 Of servants whom I have given you, not one will be lost; I shall look for them from among your number. 27 Do not be anxious when the time of trouble and hardship comes; others will lament and be sad, but you will have happiness and plenty. 28 Though you become the envy of the nations, they will be powerless against you, says the Lord.

29 My power will protect you, and save your children from hell. 30 Be joyful, mother, you and your children, for

---

r Other ancient authorities read *They begat for themselves a mother who*   u Other ancient authorities read *in his sight*   v Other ancient authorities read *Gomorrah, whose land descends to hell*   w Lat *for those*   x Other ancient authorities read *Seek*   y Or *seal it; or mark them and commit them to the grave*   z Or *slaves*   a Lat *hands will cover*   b Lat *Gehenna*

30 "Rejoice, O mother, with your children, because I will deliver you, says the Lord. 31 Remember your children that sleep, because I will bring them out of the hiding places of the earth, and will show mercy to them; for I am merciful, says the Lord Almighty. 32 Embrace your children until I come, and proclaim mercy to them; because my springs run over, and my grace will not fail."

33 I, Ezra, received a command from the Lord on Mount Horeb to go to Israel. When I came to them they rejected me and refused the Lord's commandment. 34 Therefore I say to you, O nations that hear and understand, "Wait for your shepherd; he will give you everlasting rest, because he who will come at the end of the age is close at hand. 35 Be ready for the rewards of the kingdom, because perpetual light will shine on you forevermore. 36 Flee from the shadow of this age, receive the joy of your glory; I publicly call on my savior to witness.[c] 37 Receive what the Lord has entrusted to you and be joyful, giving thanks to him who has called you to the celestial kingdoms. 38 Rise, stand erect and see the number of those who have been sealed at the feast of the Lord. 39 Those who have departed from the shadow of this age have received glorious garments from the Lord. 40 Take again your full number, O Zion, and close the list of your people who are clothed in white, who have fulfilled the law of the Lord. 41 The number of your children, whom you desired, is now complete; implore the Lord's authority that your people, who have been called from the beginning, may be made holy."

42 I, Ezra, saw on Mount Zion a great multitude that I could not number, and they all were praising the Lord with songs. 43 In their midst was a young man of great stature, taller than any of the others, and on the head of each of them he placed a crown, but he was more exalted than they. And I was held spellbound. 44 Then I asked an angel, "Who are these, my lord?" 45 He answered and said to me, "These are they who have put off mortal clothing and have put on the immortal, and have confessed the name of God. Now they are being crowned, and receive palms." 46 Then I said to the angel, "Who is that young man who is placing crowns on them and putting palms in their hands?" 47 He answered and said to me, "He is the Son of God, whom they confessed in the world." So I began to praise those who had stood valiantly for the name of the Lord.[d] 48 Then the angel said to me, "Go, tell my people how great and how many are the wonders of the Lord God that you have seen."

3 In the thirtieth year after the destruction of the city, I was in Babylon—I, Salathiel, who am also called Ezra. I was troubled as I lay on my bed, and my thoughts welled up in my heart, 2 because I saw the desolation of Zion and the wealth of those who lived in Babylon. 3 My spirit was greatly agitated, and I began to speak anxious words to the Most High, and said, 4 "O sovereign Lord, did you not speak at the beginning when you planted[e] the earth—and that without help—and commanded the dust[f] 5 and it gave you Adam, a lifeless body? Yet he was the creation of your hands, and you breathed into him the breath of life, and he was made alive in your presence. 6 And you led him into the garden that your right hand had planted before the earth appeared. 7 And you laid upon him one commandment of yours; but he transgressed it, and immediately you appointed death for him and for his descendants. From him there sprang nations and tribes, peoples and clans without number. 8 And every nation walked after its own

I shall come to your rescue. 31 Remember your children who sleep in the grave; I shall bring them up from the depths of the earth, and show mercy to them; for I am merciful, says the Lord Almighty. 32 Keep your children close to you until I come; proclaim my mercy to them, for my grace which flows from gushing springs will never run dry.

33 I, Ezra, received on Mount Horeb a commission from the Lord to go to Israel; but when I came to them, they spurned me and rejected the Lord's command. 34 Therefore I say to you Gentiles, who hear and understand: 'Look forward to the coming of your shepherd; he who is to come at the end of the world is close at hand, and he will give you everlasting rest. 35 Be ready to receive the rewards of the kingdom, for light perpetual will shine on you throughout all time. 36 Flee from the shadow of this world, and receive the joy and splendour that await you. I bear witness openly to my Saviour. 37 It is he whom the Lord has appointed; receive him and be joyful, giving thanks to the One who has called you to the heavenly realms. 38 Arise, stand up and see the whole company of those who bear the Lord's mark and sit at his banquet. 39 They have moved out of the shadow of this world and have received shining robes from the Lord. 40 Take your full number, O Zion, and close the roll of those arrayed in white who have faithfully kept the law of the Lord. 41 The number of your children whom you so long desired is now complete. Pray that the Lord's kingdom may come, so that your people, whom he called when the world began, may be set apart as his own.'

42 I, Ezra, saw on Mount Zion a throng too vast to count, all singing hymns of praise to the Lord. 43 In the middle stood a young man. He was very tall, taller than any of the others, and was setting a crown on the head of each one of them; he towered above them all. Enthralled at the sight, 44 I asked the angel, 'My lord, who are these?' 45 He replied, 'They are those who have laid aside their mortal dress and put on the immortal, those who acknowledged the name of God. Now they are being given crowns and palms.' 46 I asked again, 'Who is the young man setting the crowns on their heads and giving them the palms?' 47 The angel replied, 'He is the Son of God, whom they acknowledged in this mortal life.' I began to praise those who had stood so valiantly for the Lord's name. 48 Then the angel said to me: 'Go and tell my people the many great and wonderful acts of the Lord God that you have seen.'

3 In the thirtieth year after the fall of Jerusalem, I, Salathiel (who am also Ezra), was in Babylon. Lying on my bed I was troubled and my mind filled with perplexity 2 as I reflected on the desolation of Zion and the prosperity of those who lived in Babylon. 3 I was deeply disturbed in spirit, and full of fear I addressed the Most High. 4 'My Master and Lord,' I said, 'was it not you alone who in the beginning spoke the word that formed the world? At your command the dust 5 brought forth Adam. His body was lifeless; yours were the hands that had moulded it, and you breathed the breath of life into it and he became a living person. 6 You led him into paradise, which you yourself had planted before the earth came into being. 7 You gave him your one commandment to obey; and when he disobeyed it, you made both him and his descendants subject to death.

'From him there sprang nations and tribes, peoples and families, too numerous to count. 8 Each nation went its own

[c] Other ancient authorities read *I testify that my savior has been commissioned by the Lord* [d] Other ancient authorities read *to praise and glorify the Lord* [e] Other ancient authorities read *formed* [f] Syr Ethiop: Lat *people* or *world*

will; they did ungodly things in your sight and rejected your commands, and you did not hinder them. 9 But again, in its time you brought the flood upon the inhabitants of the world and destroyed them. 10 And the same fate befell all of them: just as death came upon Adam, so the flood upon them. 11 But you left one of them, Noah with his household, and all the righteous who have descended from him.

12 "When those who lived on earth began to multiply, they produced children and peoples and many nations, and again they began to be more ungodly than were their ancestors. 13 And when they were committing iniquity in your sight, you chose for yourself one of them, whose name was Abraham; 14 you loved him, and to him alone you revealed the end of the times, secretly by night. 15 You made an everlasting covenant with him, and promised him that you would never forsake his descendants; and you gave him Isaac, and to Isaac you gave Jacob and Esau. 16 You set apart Jacob for yourself, but Esau you rejected; and Jacob became a great multitude. 17 And when you led his descendants out of Egypt, you brought them to Mount Sinai. 18 You bent down the heavens and shook g the earth, and moved the world, and caused the depths to tremble, and troubled the times. 19 Your glory passed through the four gates of fire and earthquake and wind and ice, to give the law to the descendants of Jacob, and your commandment to the posterity of Israel.

20 "Yet you did not take away their evil heart from them, so that your law might produce fruit in them. 21 For the first Adam, burdened with an evil heart, transgressed and was overcome, as were also all who were descended from him. 22 Thus the disease became permanent; the law was in the hearts of the people along with the evil root; but what was good departed, and the evil remained. 23 So the times passed and the years were completed, and you raised up for yourself a servant, named David. 24 You commanded him to build a city for your name, and there to offer you oblations from what is yours. 25 This was done for many years; but the inhabitants of the city transgressed, 26 in everything doing just as Adam and all his descendants had done, for they also had the evil heart. 27 So you handed over your city to your enemies.

28 "Then I said in my heart, Are the deeds of those who inhabit Babylon any better? Is that why it has gained dominion over Zion? 29 For when I came here I saw ungodly deeds without number, and my soul has seen many sinners during these thirty years. h And my heart failed me, 30 because I have seen how you endure those who sin, and have spared those who act wickedly, and have destroyed your people, and protected your enemies, 31 and have not shown to anyone how your way may be comprehended. i Are the deeds of Babylon better than those of Zion? 32 Or has another nation known you besides Israel? Or what tribes have so believed the covenants as these tribes of Jacob? 33 Yet their reward has not appeared and their labor has borne no fruit. For I have traveled widely among the nations and have seen that they abound in wealth, though they are unmindful of your commandments. 34 Now therefore weigh in a balance our iniquities and those of the inhabitants of the world; and it will be found which way the turn of the scale will incline. 35 When have the inhabitants of the earth not sinned in your sight? Or what nation has kept your commandments so well? 36 You may indeed find individuals who have kept your commandments, but nations you will not find."

4 Then the angel that had been sent to me, whose name was Uriel, answered 2 and said to me, "Your under-

way, sinning against you and treating you with scorn, and you did not stop them. 9 Then, in course of time, you brought the flood upon the inhabitants of the earth and destroyed them. 10 The same fate came upon all: death upon Adam, and the flood upon that generation. 11 But one man, Noah, you spared, together with his household and all the righteous descended from him.

12 'The population of the earth expanded; families and peoples increased, nation upon nation. But once again they began to sin, more wickedly than those before them. 13 When they sinned, you chose for yourself one of them; Abraham was his name. 14 Him you loved, and to him alone, secretly at dead of night, you disclosed how the world would end. 15 You made an everlasting covenant with him and promised never to abandon his descendants. 16 You gave him Isaac, and to Isaac you gave Jacob and Esau; of these you chose Jacob for yourself, and he grew to be a great nation; but Esau you rejected.

17 'You rescued Jacob's descendants from Egypt and led them to Mount Sinai. 18 There you made the heavens bow down, shook the earth, moved the world; you made the depths shudder and convulsed the whole creation. 19 Your glory passed through the four gates of fire and earthquake, wind and frost, in order to give the commandments of the law to the Israelites, the race of Jacob. 20 But you did not take away their evil heart and thus enable your law to bear fruit in them; 21 for the first man, Adam, burdened as he was with an evil heart, sinned and was overcome, and not only he but all who were descended from him. 22 So the weakness became inveterate, and although your law was in your people's hearts, a rooted wickedness was there too; thus the good came to nothing, and what was evil persisted.

23 'Years went by, and when the time came you raised up for yourself a servant, whose name was David. 24 You instructed him to build the city that bears your name and to offer to you there in sacrifice what was already your own. 25 This was done for many years, until the inhabitants of the city went astray, 26 behaving just like Adam and all his line; for they had the same evil heart. 27 And so you handed over your city into the power of your enemies.

28 'I had thought that perhaps those in Babylon lead better lives, and that is why Zion is in subjection. 29 But when I arrived here, I saw wickedness beyond reckoning, and with my own eyes I have seen evildoers in great numbers these thirty years. My heart sank 30 because I observed how you tolerate sinners and spare the godless, how you have destroyed your own people but preserved your enemies. You have given no indication 31 to anyone how your ways are to be understood. Is Babylon more virtuous than Zion? 32 Has any nation except Israel ever known you? What tribes have put their trust in your covenants as have the tribes of Jacob? 33 But they have seen no reward, no fruit for their labours. I have travelled far and wide among the nations and have seen how they prosper, heedless though they are of your commandments. 34 Now weigh our sins in the balance, therefore, against the sins of the rest of the world, and it will be clear which way the scale tips. 35 Has there ever been a time when the inhabitants of the earth did not sin against you? Has any nation ever kept your commandments like Israel? 36 You may indeed find a few individuals here and there who have done so, but nowhere a whole nation.'

4 Uriel, the angel who was sent to me, replied: 2 'You are completely at a loss to understand this world; can

standing has utterly failed regarding this world, and do you think you can comprehend the way of the Most High?" ³Then I said, "Yes, my lord." And he replied to me, "I have been sent to show you three ways, and to put before you three problems. ⁴If you can solve one of them for me, then I will show you the way you desire to see, and will teach you why the heart is evil."

5 I said, "Speak, my lord."

And he said to me, "Go, weigh for me the weight of fire, or measure for me a blast*j* of wind, or call back for me the day that is past."

6 I answered and said, "Who of those that have been born can do that, that you should ask me about such things?"

7 And he said to me, "If I had asked you, 'How many dwellings are in the heart of the sea, or how many streams are at the source of the deep, or how many streams are above the firmament, or which are the exits of Hades, or which are the entrances*k* of paradise?' ⁸perhaps you would have said to me, 'I never went down into the deep, nor as yet into Hades, neither did I ever ascend into heaven.' ⁹But now I have asked you only about fire and wind and the day — things that you have experienced and from which you cannot be separated, and you have given me no answer about them." ¹⁰He said to me, "You cannot understand the things with which you have grown up; ¹¹how then can your mind comprehend the way of the Most High? And how can one who is already worn out*l* by the corrupt world understand incorruption?"*m* When I heard this, I fell on my face*n* ¹²and said to him, "It would have been better for us not to be here than to come here and live in ungodliness, and to suffer and not understand why."

13 He answered me and said, "I went into a forest of trees of the plain, and they made a plan ¹⁴and said, 'Come, let us go and make war against the sea, so that it may recede before us and so that we may make for ourselves more forests.' ¹⁵In like manner the waves of the sea also made a plan and said, 'Come, let us go up and subdue the forest of the plain so that there also we may gain more territory for ourselves.' ¹⁶But the plan of the forest was in vain, for the fire came and consumed it; ¹⁷likewise also the plan of the waves of the sea was in vain,*o* for the sand stood firm and blocked it. ¹⁸If now you were a judge between them, which would you undertake to justify, and which to condemn?"

19 I answered and said, "Each made a foolish plan, for the land has been assigned to the forest, and the locale of the sea a place to carry its waves."

20 He answered me and said, "You have judged rightly, but why have you not judged so in your own case? ²¹For as the land has been assigned to the forest and the sea to its waves, so also those who inhabit the earth can understand only what is on the earth, and he who is*p* above the heavens can understand what is above the height of the heavens."

22 Then I answered and said, "I implore you, my lord, why*q* have I been endowed with the power of understanding? ²³For I did not wish to inquire about the ways above, but about those things that we daily experience: why Israel has been given over to the Gentiles in disgrace; why the people whom you loved has been given over to godless tribes, and the law of our ancestors has been brought to destruction and the written covenants no longer exist. ²⁴We

you then expect to understand the way of the Most High?' ³'Yes, my lord,' I said.

'I have been sent', he continued, 'to propound to you three of the ways of this world, to give you three illustrations; ⁴if you can explain to me any one of them, I shall show to you the way that you long to see and teach you why the heart is evil.'

⁵'Speak on, my lord,' I said. 'Come then, weigh me a pound of fire,' he said, 'or measure me a bushel of wind, or call back for me a day that has passed.'

⁶'How can you ask me to do that, something no man on earth can do?' I replied. ⁷Then said he, 'Suppose I had asked you, "How many dwellings are there in the heart of the sea? Or how many streams to feed the depths? Or how many paths above the vault of heaven? Or where are the ways out of the grave, or the roads into paradise?" ⁸You might have retorted, "I have not been down into the deep, I have not yet descended into the grave, or ever ascended into heaven." ⁹But, as it is, I have asked you only about fire, about wind, and about yesterday, things bound up with your experience and essential to your life; and yet you have failed to give me an answer. ¹⁰If then', he went on, 'you cannot understand things you have grown up with, ¹¹how can you with your limited mind grasp the way of the Most High? A man corrupted by the corrupt world can never know the way of the incorruptible.'

¹²At those words I fell prostrate, exclaiming: 'Better never to have come into existence than be born into a world of evil and suffering we cannot explain!' ¹³He replied, 'I went out into a wood, and the trees of the forest were devising a plot. ¹⁴They said, "Come, let us make war on the sea, force it to retreat, and so win ground for more woods." ¹⁵The waves of the sea had a similar plan: they said, "Come, let us attack and conquer the trees of the forest, and annex their territory." ¹⁶The plan made by the trees came to nothing, for fire broke out and burnt them up. ¹⁷So too the plot of the waves came to nothing, for the sand remained firm and blocked their way. ¹⁸If you had to judge between the two, which would you pronounce right, and which wrong?'

¹⁹'Both were wrong,' I answered; 'their plans were folly, for the land is assigned to the trees, and to the sea is allotted a place for its waves.'

²⁰'Yes,' he replied, 'you have judged rightly. Why then have you not done so with your own question? ²¹Just as the land belongs to the trees and the sea to the waves, so dwellers on earth can understand earthly things and nothing beyond; only he who lives above the heavens can understand the things high above the heavens.'

²²'But, my lord, please tell me,' I asked, 'why have I been given the faculty of understanding? ²³My question is not about the distant heavens, but about what happens every day before our eyes. Why has Israel been made a byword among the Gentiles? Why has the people you loved been put at the mercy of godless nations? Why has the law of our fathers been brought to nothing, and the written covenants made a dead letter? ²⁴We pass from the world like a flight

j Syr Ethiop Arab 1 Arab 2 Georg *a measure*   *k* Syr Compare Ethiop Arab 2 Arm: Lat lacks *of Hades, or which are the entrances* *l* Meaning of Lat uncertain   *m* Syr Ethiop *the way of the incorruptible?*   *n* Syr Ethiop Arab 1: Meaning of Lat uncertain *o* Lat lacks *was in vain*   *p* Or *those who are*   *q* Syr Ethiop Arm: Meaning of Lat uncertain

4:21 **he who lives:** *or* those who live.

pass from the world like locusts, and our life is like a mist,^{r} and we are not worthy to obtain mercy. 25 But what will he do for his^s name that is invoked over us? It is about these things that I have asked."

26 He answered me and said, "If you are alive, you will see, and if you live long,^{t} you will often marvel, because the age is hurrying swiftly to its end. 27 It will not be able to bring the things that have been promised to the righteous in their appointed times, because this age is full of sadness and infirmities. 28 For the evil about which^u you ask me has been sown, but the harvest of it has not yet come. 29 If therefore that which has been sown is not reaped, and if the place where the evil has been sown does not pass away, the field where the good has been sown will not come. 30 For a grain of evil seed was sown in Adam's heart from the beginning, and how much ungodliness it has produced until now —and will produce until the time of threshing comes! 31 Consider now for yourself how much fruit of ungodliness a grain of evil seed has produced. 32 When heads of grain without number are sown, how great a threshing floor they will fill!"

33 Then I answered and said, "How long?^{u} When will these things be? Why are our years few and evil?" 34 He answered me and said, "Do not be in a greater hurry than the Most High. You, indeed, are in a hurry for yourself,^{v} but the Highest is in a hurry on behalf of many. 35 Did not the souls of the righteous in their chambers ask about these matters, saying, 'How long are we to remain here?^{w} And when will the harvest of our reward come? 36 And the archangel Jeremiel answered and said, 'When the number of those like yourselves is completed;^{x} for he has weighed the age in the balance, 37 and measured the times by measure, and numbered the times by number; and he will not move or arouse them until that measure is fulfilled.' "

38 Then I answered and said, "But, O sovereign Lord, all of us also are full of ungodliness. 39 It is perhaps on account of us that the time of threshing is delayed for the righteous — on account of the sins of those who inhabit the earth."

40 He answered me and said, "Go and ask a pregnant woman whether, when her nine months have been completed, her womb can keep the fetus within her any longer."

41 And I said, "No, lord, it cannot."

He said to me, "In Hades the chambers of the souls are like the womb. 42 For just as a woman who is in labor makes haste to escape the pangs of birth, so also do these places hasten to give back those things that were committed to them from the beginning. 43 Then the things that you desire to see will be disclosed to you."

44 I answered and said, "If I have found favor in your sight, and if it is possible, and if I am worthy, 45 show me this also: whether more time is to come than has passed, or whether for us the greater part has gone by. 46 For I know what has gone by, but I do not know what is to come."

47 And he said to me, "Stand at my right side, and I will show you the interpretation of a parable."

48 So I stood and looked, and lo, a flaming furnace passed by before me, and when the flame had gone by I looked, and lo, the smoke remained. 49 And after this a cloud full of water passed before me and poured down a heavy and violent rain, and when the violent rainstorm had passed, drops still remained in the cloud.^{y}

of locusts, our life is but a vapour, and we are not worth the Lord's pity. 25 What then will he do for us who bear his name? Those are my questions.'

26 He answered: 'If you survive, you will see; if you live long enough, you will marvel. For this present age is passing away; 27 it is full of sorrow and weakness, too full to grasp what is promised in due time for the godly. 28 The evil about which you ask me has been sown, but the time for reaping is not yet. 29 Until the crop of evil has been reaped as well as sown, until the ground where it was sown has vanished, there will be no room for the field where the good is sown. 30 A grain of the evil seed was sown in the heart of Adam from the first; how much godlessness has it produced already! How much more will it produce before the harvest! 31 Reckon this up: if one grain of evil seed has produced so great a crop of godlessness, 32 how vast a harvest will there be when seeds beyond number have been sown!'

33 I asked, 'But when? How long have we to wait? Why are our lives short and miserable?' 34 He replied, 'Do not be in a greater hurry than the Most High himself. You are in a hurry for yourself alone; the Exalted One for many. 35 Are not these the very questions asked by the righteous in the storehouse of souls: "How long must we stay here? When will the harvest begin, the time when we get our reward?" 36 And the answer they got from the archangel Jeremiel was: "As soon as the tally of those like yourselves is complete. God has weighed the world in a balance, 37 he has measured and numbered the ages; he will move nothing, alter nothing, until the appointed measure is reached." '

38 'But, my master and lord,' I replied, 'we are all of us sinners through and through. 39 Can it be because of us, because of the sins of mankind, that the harvest and the reward of the just are delayed?' 40 'Go,' he said, 'ask a pregnant woman whether she can keep the child in her womb any longer once the nine months are up.' 41 'No, my lord, she cannot,' I said. He went on: 'The storehouses of souls in the world below are like the womb: 42 as a woman in labour is impatient to reach the end of the birth-pains, so they are impatient to give back all the souls entrusted to them since time began. 43 Then you will be shown all you wish to see.'

44 I said, 'If I have found favour with you and if it is possible for you to tell and for me to understand, 45 disclose to me one thing more: which is the longer—the future still to come, or the past that has gone by? 46 What is past I know, but not what is still to be.' 47 He said: 'Come, stand at my right hand, and I shall explain the vision you will see.'

48 I stood watching, and there passed before my eyes a blazing fire; when the flames had disappeared, there was still smoke left. 49 After that a dark rain-cloud passed before me; there was a heavy storm, and when it had gone over, there were still some raindrops left. 50 'Reflect on this,' said

---

^{r} Syr Ethiop Arab Georg: Lat *a trembling* ^{s} Ethiop adds *holy*
^{t} Syr: Lat *live* ^{u} Syr Ethiop: Meaning of Lat uncertain
^{v} Syr Ethiop Arab Arm: Meaning of Lat uncertain ^{w} Syr Ethiop
Arab 2 Georg: Lat *How long do I hope thus?* ^{x} Syr Ethiop Arab 2:
Lat *number of seeds is completed for you* ^{y} Lat *in it*

4:26 **if you live . . . marvel:** *so one Vs.; Lat*. live, you will often marvel.

50 He said to me, "Consider it for yourself; for just as the rain is more than the drops, and the fire is greater than the smoke, so the quantity that passed was far greater; but drops and smoke remained."

51 Then I prayed and said, "Do you think that I shall live until those days? Or who will be alive in those days?"

52 He answered me and said, "Concerning the signs about which you ask me, I can tell you in part; but I was not sent to tell you concerning your life, for I do not know.

5 "Now concerning the signs: lo, the days are coming when those who inhabit the earth shall be seized with great terror,*z* and the way of truth shall be hidden, and the land shall be barren of faith. 2 Unrighteousness shall be increased beyond what you yourself see, and beyond what you heard of formerly. 3 And the land that you now see ruling shall be a trackless waste, and people shall see it desolate. 4 But if the Most High grants that you live, you shall see it thrown into confusion after the third period;*a* and the sun shall suddenly begin to shine at
> night,
> and the moon during the day.
5 Blood shall drip from wood,
> and the stone shall utter its voice;
> the peoples shall be troubled,
> and the stars shall fall.*b*

6 And one shall reign whom those who inhabit the earth do not expect, and the birds shall fly away together; 7 and the Dead Sea*c* shall cast up fish; and one whom the many do not know shall make his voice heard by night, and all shall hear his voice.*d* 8 There shall be chaos also in many places, fire shall often break out, the wild animals shall roam beyond their haunts, and menstruous women shall bring forth monsters. 9 Salt waters shall be found in the sweet, and all friends shall conquer one another; then shall reason hide itself, and wisdom shall withdraw into its chamber, 10 and it shall be sought by many but shall not be found, and unrighteousness and unrestraint shall increase on earth. 11 One country shall ask its neighbor, 'Has righteousness, or anyone who does right, passed through you?' And it will answer, 'No.' 12 At that time people shall hope but not obtain; they shall labor, but their ways shall not prosper. 13 These are the signs that I am permitted to tell you, and if you pray again, and weep as you do now, and fast for seven days, you shall hear yet greater things than these."

14 Then I woke up, and my body shuddered violently, and my soul was so troubled that it fainted. 15 But the angel who had come and talked with me held me and strengthened me and set me on my feet.

16 Now on the second night Phaltiel, a chief of the people, came to me and said, "Where have you been? And why is your face sad? 17 Or do you not know that Israel has been entrusted to you in the land of their exile? 18 Rise therefore and eat some bread, and do not forsake us, like a shepherd who leaves the flock in the power of savage wolves."

19 Then I said to him, "Go away from me and do not come near me for seven days; then you may come to me."

He heard what I said and left me. 20 So I fasted seven days, mourning and weeping, as the angel Uriel had commanded me.

21 After seven days the thoughts of my heart were very grievous to me again. 22 Then my soul recovered the spirit

the angel. 'As the shower of rain filled a far greater space than the drops of water, and the fire more than the smoke, in the same way the past far exceeds the future in length; what remains is but raindrops and smoke.'

51 'Pray tell me,' I said, 'do you think that I shall live to see those days? Or in whose lifetime will they come?' 52 'If you ask me what signs will herald them,' he replied, 'I can tell you in part. But the length of your own life I am not commissioned to tell you; of that I know nothing.

5 'But to speak of the signs: a time is coming when the earth's inhabitants will be seized with great panic. The way of truth will be hidden from sight, and the land will be barren of faith. 2 Wickedness will increase beyond anything you yourself see or have ever heard of. 3 The country you now observe ruling the world will become a trackless desert, lying waste before men's eyes. 4 After the third period (if the Most High grants you a long enough life) you will see universal disorder. The sun will suddenly begin to shine at night, and the moon by day. 5 Trees will drip blood, stones will speak, nations will be in confusion, and the courses of the stars will be changed. 6 A king unwelcome to the earth's inhabitants will bear rule. The birds will all fly away, 7 the Dead Sea will cast up fish, and at night a voice will sound, unknown to the many but heard by all. 8 Chasms will open in many places and spurt out incessant flames. Wild beasts will range far from their haunts, menstruous women will give birth to monsters, 9 freshwater springs will run with brine, and everywhere friends will make war on one another. Then understanding will be hidden, and reason withdraw within her chamber. 10 Many will seek her, but not find her; the earth will overflow with wickedness and vice. 11 One country will ask another, "Has justice, justice in action, ever passed your way?" and the answer will be "No!" 12 In those days men will hope, but hope in vain; they will strive, but meet with no success.

13 'Those are the signs I am allowed to tell you. But turn once more to prayer, continue to weep and fast for seven days; then again you will hear of greater signs than those.'

14 I awoke with a start, trembling in every limb; my spirits faltered, and I was near to fainting. 15 But the angel who had come and talked to me held me and put strength into me, and raised me to my feet.

16 The next night Phaltiel, leader of the people, came to me and asked: 'Where have you been, and why that sad look? 17 Have you forgotten that Israel in exile has been entrusted to your care? 18 Rouse yourself; eat some food. Do not abandon us like a shepherd abandoning his flock to savage wolves.' 19 I replied: 'Leave me, and do not come near me for the next seven days; after that you may return.' On hearing this he went away.

20 For seven days I fasted with tears and lamentations, as commanded by the angel Uriel. 21 At the end of the seven days my mind was again deeply disturbed, 22 but I recov-

---

z Syr Ethiop: Meaning of Lat uncertain   *a* Literally *after the third*; Ethiop *after three months*; Arm *after the third vision*; Georg *after the third day*   *b* Ethiop Compare Syr and Arab: Meaning of Lat uncertain   *c* Lat *Sea of Sodom*   *d* Cn: Lat *fish; and it shall make its voice heard by night, which the many have not known, but all shall hear its voice.*

5:7 **Dead Sea:** *or* sea of Sodom.

of understanding, and I began once more to speak words in the presence of the Most High. 23 I said, "O sovereign Lord, from every forest of the earth and from all its trees you have chosen one vine, 24 and from all the lands of the world you have chosen for yourself one region, *e* and from all the flowers of the world you have chosen for yourself one lily, 25 and from all the depths of the sea you have filled for yourself one river, and from all the cities that have been built you have consecrated Zion for yourself, 26 and from all the birds that have been created you have named for yourself one dove, and from all the flocks that have been made you have provided for yourself one sheep, 27 and from all the multitude of peoples you have gotten for yourself one people; and to this people, whom you have loved, you have given the law that is approved by all. 28 And now, O Lord, why have you handed the one over to the many, and dishonored *f* the one root beyond the others, and scattered your only one among the many? 29 And those who opposed your promises have trampled on those who believed your covenants. 30 If you really hate your people, they should be punished at your own hands."

31 When I had spoken these words, the angel who had come to me on a previous night was sent to me. 32 He said to me, "Listen to me, and I will instruct you; pay attention to me, and I will tell you more."

33 Then I said, "Speak, my lord." And he said to me, "Are you greatly disturbed in mind over Israel? Or do you love him more than his Maker does?"

34 I said, "No, my lord, but because of my grief I have spoken; for every hour I suffer agonies of heart, while I strive to understand the way of the Most High and to search out some part of his judgment."

35 He said to me, "You cannot." And I said, "Why not, my lord? Why then was I born? Or why did not my mother's womb become my grave, so that I would not see the travail of Jacob and the exhaustion of the people of Israel?"

36 He said to me, "Count up for me those who have not yet come, and gather for me the scattered raindrops, and make the withered flowers bloom again for me; 37 open for me the closed chambers, and bring out for me the winds shut up in them, or show me the picture of a voice; and then I will explain to you the travail that you ask to understand." *g*

38 I said, "O sovereign Lord, who is able to know these things except the one whose dwelling is not with mortals? 39 As for me, I am without wisdom, and how can I speak concerning the things that you have asked me?"

40 He said to me, "Just as you cannot do one of the things that were mentioned, so you cannot discover my judgment, or the goal of the love that I have promised to my people."

41 I said, "Yet, O Lord, you have charge of those who are alive at the end, but what will those do who lived before me, or we, ourselves, or those who come after us?"

42 He said to me, "I shall liken my judgment to a circle; *h* just as for those who are last there is no slowness, so for those who are first there is no haste."

43 Then I answered and said, "Could you not have created at one time those who have been and those who are and those who will be, so that you might show your judgment the sooner?"

44 He replied to me and said, "The creation cannot move faster than the Creator, nor can the world hold at one time those who have been created in it."

ered the power of thought and began once more to address the Most High.

23 'My Master and Lord,' I said, 'out of all the forests on earth and all their trees, you have chosen one vine; 24 from all the lands in the whole world you have chosen one plot; and out of all the flowers in the world you have chosen one lily. 25 From all the depths of the sea you have filled one river for yourself, and of all the cities ever built you have set apart Zion as your own. 26 From all the birds that were created you have named for yourself one dove, and from all the animals that were fashioned you have taken one sheep. 27 Out of all the countless nations, you have adopted one for your own, and to this chosen people you have given a law approved above all others. 28 Why then, Lord, have you put this one people at the mercy of so many? Why have you humiliated this one stock more than all others, and dispersed your own people far and wide? 29 Those who reject your promises have trampled on the people who put their trust in your covenants. 30 If you are so deeply displeased with your people, yours should be the hand that punishes them.'

31 When I had finished speaking, there was sent to me the angel who had visited me that earlier night. 32 'Listen to me,' he said, 'and I shall instruct you; attend carefully, and I shall tell you more.' 33 'Speak on, my lord,' I replied.

He began: 'You are in great sorrow of heart for Israel's sake. Do you love Israel more than Israel's Maker does?' 34 'No, my lord,' I answered, 'but sorrow has compelled me to speak; my heart is tortured every hour as I strive to understand the ways of the Most High and to fathom even part of his judgement.'

35 'You cannot,' he said to me. 'Why not, my lord?' I asked. 'Why then was I born? Why could not my mother's womb have been my grave? Then I should never have seen Jacob's trials and the utter exhaustion of Israel's people.'

36 He said, 'Count me the days that are not yet come, collect the scattered raindrops for me, make the withered flowers bloom again for me, 37 unlock for me the storehouses and let loose the winds shut up there, or give visible form to a voice — then I shall answer your question about the trials of Israel.'

38 'My master and lord,' I argued, 'how can there be anyone with such knowledge except the One whose dwelling is not among men? 39 I am only a fool; how can I answer your questions?'

40 'Just as you cannot do any of the things I have put to you,' he replied, 'so you will not be able to find out my judgement or the ultimate purpose of the love I have promised to my people.'

41 'But surely,' I objected, 'your promise, lord, is for those who are alive at the end. What is to be the fate of those who lived before us, or of ourselves, or of those who come after us?'

42 He said, 'I shall compare my judgement to a circle: the latest will not be too late, nor the earliest too early.'

43 To this I replied, 'Could you not have made all men, past, present, and future, at one and the same time? Then you could have held your assize with less delay.' 44 His answer to me was: 'Creation may not proceed faster than the Creator, nor could the world support at the same time all those created to live in it.'

---

e Ethiop: Lat *pit*   *f* Syr Ethiop Arab: Lat *prepared*   *g* Lat *see*
h Or *crown*

5:41 **your promise:** *so one Vs.; Lat. obscure.*

45 I said, "How have you said to your servant that you[i] will certainly give life at one time to your creation? If therefore all creatures will live at one time[j] and the creation will sustain them, it might even now be able to support all of them present at one time."

46 He said to me, "Ask a woman's womb, and say to it, 'If you bear ten[k] children, why one after another?' Request it therefore to produce ten at one time."

47 I said, "Of course it cannot, but only each in its own time."

48 He said to me, "Even so I have given the womb of the earth to those who from time to time are sown in it. 49 For as an infant does not bring forth, and a woman who has become old does not bring forth any longer, so I have made the same rule for the world that I created."

50 Then I inquired and said, "Since you have now given me the opportunity, let me speak before you. Is our mother, of whom you have told me, still young? Or is she now approaching old age?"

51 He replied to me, "Ask a woman who bears children, and she will tell you. 52 Say to her, 'Why are those whom you have borne recently not like those whom you bore before, but smaller in stature?' 53 And she herself will answer you, 'Those born in the strength of youth are different from those born during the time of old age, when the womb is failing.' 54 Therefore you also should consider that you and your contemporaries are smaller in stature than those who were before you, 55 and those who come after you will be smaller than you, as born of a creation that already is aging and passing the strength of youth."

56 I said, "I implore you, O Lord, if I have found favor in your sight, show your servant through whom you will visit your creation."

6 He said to me, "At the beginning of the circle of the earth, before[l] the portals of the world were in place, and before the assembled winds blew, 2 and before the rumblings of thunder sounded, and before the flashes of lightning shone, and before the foundations of paradise were laid, 3 and before the beautiful flowers were seen, and before the powers of movements[m] were established, and before the innumerable hosts of angels were gathered together, 4 and before the heights of the air were lifted up, and before the measures of the firmaments were named, and before the footstool of Zion was established, 5 and before the present years were reckoned and before the imaginations of those who now sin were estranged, and before those who stored up treasures of faith were sealed— 6 then I planned these things, and they were made through me alone and not through another; just as the end shall come through me alone and not through another."

7 I answered and said, "What will be the dividing of the times? Or when will be the end of the first age and the beginning of the age that follows?"

8 He said to me, "From Abraham to Isaac,[n] because from him were born Jacob and Esau, for Jacob's hand held Esau's heel from the beginning. 9 Now Esau is the end of this age, and Jacob is the beginning of the age that follows. 10 The beginning of a person is the hand, and the end of a person is the heel;[o] seek for nothing else, Ezra, between the heel and the hand, Ezra!"

45 'My lord,' I pointed out, 'you have just told me that you will at one and the same time restore to life every creature you ever made; how can that be? If all of them are to be alive at the same time and the world is to support them all then, it could support all of them together now.' 46 He replied, 'Think of a woman's womb: say to a woman, "If you give birth to ten children, why do you do so at intervals? Why not give birth to ten at one and the same time?"' 47 'No,' I said, 'that would be impossible; the births must take place at intervals.' 48 'True,' he answered, 'and I have made the earth's womb to bring forth at intervals those conceived in it. 49 An infant cannot give birth, nor can a woman who is too old; and I have made the same rule for the world I have created.'

50 I continued my questioning. 'Since you have now opened the way for me,' I said, 'may I ask: is our mother that you speak of still young, or is she already approaching old age?' 51 He replied, 'For an answer, ask any mother; 52 ask why the children she has borne later are not like those born earlier, but smaller. 53 She will tell you that those who were born in the vigour of her youth are very different from those born in her old age, when her womb is beginning to fail. 54 Think of it, then, like this: if you are smaller than those born before you, 55 and those who follow you are smaller still, the reason is that creation is growing old and losing the strength of its youth.'

56 I said, 'If I have found favour with you, my lord, show me through whom you will judge your creation.'

6 1 He said to me, 'When the earth began, the gates of the world were not yet standing in place; no winds gathered and blew, 2 no thunder pealed, no lightning flashed; the foundations of paradise were not yet laid, 3 nor were its fair flowers there to see; the powers that move the stars were not established, nor the countless hosts of angels assembled, 4 nor the vast tracts of air lifted up on high; the divisions of the firmaments had not received their names. Zion had not yet been chosen as God's own footstool; 5 the present age had not been planned; the schemes of its sinners had not yet been outlawed, nor had God's seal yet been set on those who have laid up a treasure of faithfulness. 6 Then it was that I had my thought, and the whole world was created through me and through me alone; in the same way, through me and through me alone the end will be.'

7 'Tell me', I responded, 'about the interval that divides the ages. When will the first age end and the next begin?' 8 He said, 'The interval will be no bigger than that between Abraham and Abraham; for Jacob and Esau were his descendants, and Jacob's hand was grasping Esau's heel at the moment of their birth. 9 Esau's heel represents the end of the first age, and Jacob's hand the beginning of the next, 10 for the beginning of a man is his hand, and the end of a man is his heel; between the heel and the hand, Ezra, do not look for any interval.'

---

[i] Syr Ethiop Arab 1: Meaning of Lat uncertain   [j] Lat lacks If . . . one time   [k] Syr Ethiop Arab 2 Arm: Meaning of Lat uncertain
[l] Meaning of Lat uncertain: Compare Syr The beginning by the hand of humankind, but the end by my own hands. For as before the land of the world existed there, and before; Ethiop: At first by the Son of Man, and afterwards I myself. For before the earth and the lands were created, and before   [m] Or earthquakes   [n] Other ancient authorities read to Abraham   [o] Syr: Meaning of Lat uncertain

NEW REVISED STANDARD VERSION

11 I answered and said, "O sovereign Lord, if I have found favor in your sight, 12 show your servant the last of your signs of which you showed me a part on a previous night."

13 He answered and said to me, "Rise to your feet and you will hear a full, resounding voice. 14 And if the place where you are standing is greatly shaken 15 while the voice is speaking, do not be terrified; because the word concerns the end, and the foundations of the earth will understand 16 that the speech concerns them. They will tremble and be shaken, for they know that their end must be changed."

17 When I heard this, I got to my feet and listened; a voice was speaking, and its sound was like the sound of mighty*p* waters. 18 It said, "The days are coming when I draw near to visit the inhabitants of the earth, 19 and when I require from the doers of iniquity the penalty of their iniquity, and when the humiliation of Zion is complete. 20 When the seal is placed upon the age that is about to pass away, then I will show these signs: the books shall be opened before the face of the firmament, and all shall see my judgment*q* together. 21 Children a year old shall speak with their voices, and pregnant women shall give birth to premature children at three and four months, and these shall live and leap about. 22 Sown places shall suddenly appear unsown, and full storehouses shall suddenly be found to be empty; 23 the trumpet shall sound aloud, and when all hear it, they shall suddenly be terrified. 24 At that time friends shall make war on friends like enemies, the earth and those who inhabit it shall be terrified, and the springs of the fountains shall stand still, so that for three hours they shall not flow.

25 "It shall be that whoever remains after all that I have foretold to you shall be saved and shall see my salvation and the end of my world. 26 And they shall see those who were taken up, who from their birth have not tasted death; and the heart of the earth's*r* inhabitants shall be changed and converted to a different spirit. 27 For evil shall be blotted out, and deceit shall be quenched; 28 faithfulness shall flourish, and corruption shall be overcome, and the truth, which has been so long without fruit, shall be revealed."

29 While he spoke to me, little by little the place where I was standing began to rock to and fro. *s* 30 And he said to me, "I have come to show you these things this night.*t* 31 If therefore you will pray again and fast again for seven days, I will again declare to you greater things than these,*u* 32 because your voice has surely been heard by the Most High; for the Mighty One has seen your uprightness and has also observed the purity that you have maintained from your youth. 33 Therefore he sent me to show you all these things, and to say to you: 'Believe and do not be afraid! 34 Do not be quick to think vain thoughts concerning the former times; then you will not act hastily in the last times.'"

35 Now after this I wept again and fasted seven days in the same way as before, in order to complete the three weeks that had been prescribed for me. 36 Then on the eighth night my heart was troubled within me again, and I began to speak in the presence of the Most High. 37 My spirit was greatly aroused, and my soul was in distress. 38 I said, "O Lord, you spoke at the beginning of creation, and said on the first day, 'Let heaven and earth be made,' and your word accomplished the work. 39 Then the spirit was blowing, and darkness and silence embraced everything; the sound of human voices was not yet there.*v*

REVISED ENGLISH BIBLE

11 'My master and lord,' I said, 'if I have found favour with you, 12 make known to me the last of your signs, of which you showed me some part that former night.'

13 'Rise to your feet', he replied, 'and you will hear a voice, loud and resonant. 14–15 Do not be frightened if the place where you are standing shakes at the sound; it speaks of the end, and the earth's foundations will understand 16 that it is talking of them. They will tremble and shake, for they know that at the end they must be transformed.' 17 At this I stood up and listened. A voice began to speak, and the sound of it was like the sound of a mighty torrent. 18 The voice said: 'The time draws near when I shall come to judge earth's inhabitants, 19 the time when I shall enquire into the wickedness of wrongdoers, the time when Zion's humiliation will be over, 20 the time when a seal will be set on the age about to pass away. Then I shall perform these signs: the books will be opened out against the vault of heaven, and all will see my judgement at the same moment. 21 Children only one year old will be able to talk, and pregnant women will give birth prematurely at three and four months to babes who will survive and dance about. 22 Fields that were sown will suddenly prove unsown, and barns that were full will suddenly be found empty. 23 A loud trumpet-blast will sound, striking sudden terror into all who hear it. 24 At that time friends will make war on friends as though on foes; the earth and its inhabitants will be terrified. Running streams will stand still, and for three hours cease to flow.

25 'Whoever is left after all I have foretold will be saved and see the salvation that I bring and the end of this world of mine. 26 They will see the men who were taken up into heaven without ever tasting death. Then will earth's inhabitants have a change of heart and come to a better mind. 27 Wickedness will be blotted out and deceit destroyed, 28 but faithfulness will flourish, corruption be overcome, and truth, so long unfruitful, will be revealed.'

29 While the voice was speaking, the ground where I stood gradually moved to and fro. 30 Then the angel said to me, 'These are the revelations I have brought you this night. 31 If once again you pray and fast for seven days, then I shall return to tell you even greater things. 32 For be sure your voice has been heard by the Most High; the Mighty God has seen your integrity and the chastity you have observed all your life. 33 That is why he has sent me to you with all these revelations, and with this message: Be confident, and have no fear! 34 Do not rush too hurriedly into unprofitable thoughts about the past; then you will not act hastily when the last age comes.'

35 AFTER that I wept once more and I fasted for seven days as I did previously, thus completing the three weeks enjoined on me. 36 On the eighth night I was again troubled in mind, and began to address the Most High. 37 With spirit truly aflame and in agony of mind 38 I said: 'O Lord, at the beginning of creation you spoke the word. On the first day you said, "Let there be heaven and earth!" and your word accomplished its work. 39 At that time a wind was blowing, and there was encircling darkness with silence everywhere; there was as yet no sound of human voice. 40 Then you

p Lat *many*   *q* Syr: Lat lacks *my judgment*   *r* Syr Compare Ethiop Arab 1 Arm: Lat lacks *earth's*   *s* Syr Ethiop Compare Arab Arm: Meaning of Lat uncertain   *t* Syr Compare Ethiop: Meaning of Lat uncertain   *u* Syr Ethiop Arab 1 Arm: Lat adds *by day*
v Syr Ethiop: Lat *was not yet from you*

6:31 **greater things:** *Lat.* adds by day.

40 Then you commanded a ray of light to be brought out from your store-chambers, so that your works could be seen.

41 "Again, on the second day, you created the spirit of the firmament, and commanded it to divide and separate the waters, so that one part might move upward and the other part remain beneath.

42 "On the third day you commanded the waters to be gathered together in a seventh part of the earth; six parts you dried up and kept so that some of them might be planted and cultivated and be of service before you. 43 For your word went forth, and at once the work was done. 44 Immediately fruit came forth in endless abundance and of varied appeal to the taste, and flowers of inimitable color, and odors of inexpressible fragrance. These were made on the third day.

45 "On the fourth day you commanded the brightness of the sun, the light of the moon, and the arrangement of the stars to come into being; 46 and you commanded them to serve humankind, about to be formed.

47 "On the fifth day you commanded the seventh part, where the water had been gathered together, to bring forth living creatures, birds, and fishes; and so it was done. 48 The dumb and lifeless water produced living creatures, as it was commanded, so that therefore the nations might declare your wondrous works.

49 "Then you kept in existence two living creatures; w the one you called Behemoth x and the name of the other Leviathan. 50 And you separated one from the other, for the seventh part where the water had been gathered together could not hold them both. 51 And you gave Behemoth x one of the parts that had been dried up on the third day, to live in it, where there are a thousand mountains; 52 but to Leviathan you gave the seventh part, the watery part; and you have kept them to be eaten by whom you wish, and when you wish.

53 "On the sixth day you commanded the earth to bring forth before you cattle, wild animals, and creeping things; 54 and over these you placed Adam, as ruler over all the works that you had made; and from him we have all come, the people whom you have chosen.

55 "All this I have spoken before you, O Lord, because you have said that it was for us that you created this world. y 56 As for the other nations that have descended from Adam, you have said that they are nothing, and that they are like spittle, and you have compared their abundance to a drop from a bucket. 57 And now, O Lord, these nations, which are reputed to be as nothing, domineer over us and devour us. 58 But we your people, whom you have called your firstborn, only begotten, zealous for you, z and most dear, have been given into their hands. 59 If the world has indeed been created for us, why do we not possess our world as an inheritance? How long will this be so?"

7 When I had finished speaking these words, the angel who had been sent to me on the former nights was sent to me again. 2 He said to me, "Rise, Ezra, and listen to the words that I have come to speak to you."

3 I said, "Speak, my lord." And he said to me, "There is a sea set in a wide expanse so that it is deep and vast, 4 but it has an entrance set in a narrow place, so that it is like a river. 5 If there are those who wish to reach the sea, to look at it or to navigate it, how can they come to the broad part unless they pass through the narrow part? 6 Another example: There is a city built and set on a plain, and it is full of all good things; 7 but the entrance to it is narrow and set in a precipitous place, so that there is fire on the right hand and deep water on the left. 8 There is only one path lying be-

commanded a ray of light to be brought out of your treasure-chambers, to make your works visible from that time onwards.

41 'On the second day you created the angel of the firmament, and commanded him to make a barrier dividing the waters, so that one part of them should withdraw upwards and the other remain beneath.

42 'On the third day you ordered the waters to collect in a seventh part of the earth; the other six parts you made into dry land, and from it kept some to be sown and tilled for your service. 43 Your word went forth, and at once the work was done. 44 In an instant there appeared a vast profusion of fruits of every kind and taste that can be desired, with flowers of colours unsurpassed and scents mysterious in their fragrance. These were made on the third day.

45 'On the fourth day by your command were created the splendour of the sun, the light of the moon, and the stars in their appointed places; 46 and you ordered them to be at the service of mankind, whom you were about to create.

47 'On the fifth day you commanded the seventh part, where the water was collected, to bring forth living things, birds and fishes. At your command, 48 the dumb, lifeless water brought forth living creatures, and gave the nations cause to tell of your wonderful acts. 49 Then you set apart two creatures: to one you gave the name Behemoth and to the other Leviathan. 50 You put them in separate places, for the seventh part where the water was collected was not large enough to hold them both. 51 You assigned to Behemoth as his territory a part of the land which was made dry on the third day, a country of a thousand hills; 52 to Leviathan you gave the seventh part, the water. You have kept them to be food for whom you will and when you will.

53 'On the sixth day you ordered the earth to bring forth for you cattle, wild beasts, and creeping things. 54 To crown your work you created Adam, and gave him lordship over everything you had made. It is from Adam that we, your chosen people, are all descended.

55 'I have recited the whole story of the creation, O Lord, because you have said that it was for our sake you made this first world, 56 and that the rest of the nations descended from Adam are nothing, no better than spittle, and for all their numbers, no more than a drop from a bucket. 57 And yet, O Lord, those nations which count for nothing are today ruling over us and trampling us down. 58 We, your people, have been put into their power — your people, whom you have called your firstborn, your only son, your champion, and your best beloved. 59 Now if the world was made for us, why may we not take possession of our inheritance? How much longer must this go on?'

7 WHEN I had finished speaking, there was sent to me the same angel as on the previous nights. 2 He addressed me, 'Rise to your feet, Ezra, and listen to the message I have brought you.' 3 'Speak on, my lord,' I replied.

He said: 'Imagine a sea set in a vast open space and spreading far and wide, 4 but the entrance to it narrow like the gorge of a river. 5 If anyone wishes to reach this sea, whether to set eyes on it or to gain control of it, how can he arrive at its broad, open waters without passing through the narrow gorge? 6 Or again, imagine a city built in a plain, a city full of every good thing, 7 but the entrance to it narrow and steep, with fire to the right and deep water to the left.

---

w Syr Ethiop: Lat two souls   x Other Lat authorities read Enoch
y Syr Ethiop Arab 2: Lat the firstborn world Compare Arab 1 first
world   z Meaning of Lat uncertain

6:41 **angel**: lit. spirit. **firmament**: or vault of heaven.

tween them, that is, between the fire and the water, so that only one person can walk on the path. 9 If now the city is given to someone as an inheritance, how will the heir receive the inheritance unless by passing through the appointed danger?"

10 I said, "That is right, lord." He said to me, "So also is Israel's portion. 11 For I made the world for their sake, and when Adam transgressed my statutes, what had been made was judged. 12 And so the entrances of this world were made narrow and sorrowful and toilsome; they are few and evil, full of dangers and involved in great hardships. 13 But the entrances of the greater world are broad and safe, and yield the fruit of immortality. 14 Therefore unless the living pass through the difficult and futile experiences, they can never receive those things that have been reserved for them. 15 Now therefore why are you disturbed, seeing that you are to perish? Why are you moved, seeing that you are mortal? 16 Why have you not considered in your mind what is to come, rather than what is now present?"

17 Then I answered and said, "O sovereign Lord, you have ordained in your law that the righteous shall inherit these things, but that the ungodly shall perish. 18 The righteous, therefore, can endure difficult circumstances while hoping for easier ones; but those who have done wickedly have suffered the difficult circumstances and will never see the easier ones."

19 He said to me, "You are not a better judge than the Lord,*a* or wiser than the Most High! 20 Let many perish who are now living, rather than that the law of God that is set before them be disregarded! 21 For the Lord*b* strictly commanded those who came into the world, when they came, what they should do to live, and what they should observe to avoid punishment. 22 Nevertheless they were not obedient, and spoke against him;
    they devised for themselves vain thoughts,
23   and proposed to themselves wicked frauds;
    they even declared that the Most High does not exist,
    and they ignored his ways.
24 They scorned his law,
    and denied his covenants;
    they have been unfaithful to his statutes,
    and have not performed his works.
25 "That is the reason, Ezra, that empty things are for the empty, and full things are for the full.

26 "For indeed the time will come, when the signs that I have foretold to you will come to pass, that the city that now is not seen shall appear,*c* and the land that now is hidden shall be disclosed. 27 Everyone who has been delivered from the evils that I have foretold shall see my wonders. 28 For my son the Messiah*d* shall be revealed with those who are with him, and those who remain shall rejoice four hundred years. 29 After those years my son the Messiah shall die, and all who draw human breath.*e* 30 Then the world shall be turned back to primeval silence for seven days, as it was at the first beginnings, so that no one shall be left. 31 After seven days the world that is not yet awake shall be roused, and that which is corruptible shall perish. 32 The earth shall give up those who are asleep in it, and the dust those who rest there in silence; and the chambers shall give up the souls that have been committed to them. 33 The

8 Between the fire and the water there is only one path, and that wide enough for but one person at a time. 9 If someone has been given this city as a legacy, how can he take possession of his inheritance except by passing through this dangerous approach?" 10 I agreed: 'That is the only way, my lord.'

The angel said: 'Such is the lot of Israel. 11 It was for Israel that I made the world, and when Adam transgressed my decrees the creation came under judgement. 12 The entrances to the present world were made narrow, painful, and arduous, few and evil, full of perils and grinding hardship. 13 But the entrances to the greater world are broad and safe, and lead to immortality. 14 Everyone must therefore enter this narrow and futile existence; otherwise they can never attain the blessings in store. 15 Then why are you so disquieted and perturbed, Ezra, at the thought that you are mortal and must die? 16 Why have you not turned your mind from the present to the future?'

17 'My master and lord,' I replied, 'in your law you have laid it down that the just shall inherit these blessings, but the ungodly shall perish. 18 The just, therefore, can endure this narrow life and look for the spacious life hereafter; but those who have lived a wicked life will have gone through the narrows without ever reaching the open spaces.'

19 He said: 'You are not a better judge than God, nor wiser than the Most High. 20 Better that many now living should perish, than that the law which God has set before them should be despised! 21 God has given clear instructions to all when they come into this world, telling them how to attain life and how to avoid punishment. 22 But the ungodly have refused to obey him; they have adopted their own futile devices 23 and made deceit and wickedness their goal; they have even denied the existence of the Most High and ignored his ways. 24 They have rejected his law and repudiated his promises; they have neither put faith in his decrees nor done what he commands. 25 Therefore, Ezra, it is emptiness for the empty, fullness for the full!

26 'Listen! The time will come when the signs I have foretold will be seen; the city which is now invisible will appear and the country now hidden will be revealed. 27 Everyone who has been delivered from the calamities I have foretold will see for himself the wonderful things I shall do. 28 My son the Messiah will appear with his companions, bringing four hundred years of joy to all who survive. 29 At the end of that time my son the Messiah will die, and so will all mankind who draw breath. 30 Then the world will return to its original silence for seven days as at the beginning of creation; no one will be left alive. 31 After seven days the age which is not yet awake will be aroused, and the age which is corruptible will cease to be. 32 The earth will give up those who sleep in it, and the dust those who rest there in silence; and the storehouses will give back the souls entrusted to them. 33 The Most High will be seen on the

---

a Other ancient authorities read *God*; Ethiop Georg *the only One*
b Other ancient authorities read *God*   *c* Arm: Lat Syr *that the bride shall appear, even the city appearing*   *d* Syr Arab 1: Ethiop *my Messiah*; Arab 2 *the Messiah*; Arm *the Messiah of God*; Lat *my son Jesus*   *e* Arm *all who have continued in faith and in patience*

7:26 **the city . . . invisible:** *so some Vss.; Lat.* the city, the bride which is now seen.   7:28 **the Messiah:** *so some Vss.; Lat.* Jesus.

NEW REVISED STANDARD VERSION

REVISED ENGLISH BIBLE

Most High shall be revealed on the seat of judgment, and compassion shall pass away, and patience shall be withdrawn./ 34 Only judgment shall remain, truth shall stand, and faithfulness shall grow strong. 35 Recompense shall follow, and the reward shall be manifested; righteous deeds shall awake, and unrighteous deeds shall not sleep.g 36 The pith of torment shall appear, and opposite it shall be the place of rest; and the furnace of helli shall be disclosed, and opposite it the paradise of delight. 37 Then the Most High will say to the nations that have been raised from the dead, 'Look now, and understand whom you have denied, whom you have not served, whose commandments you have despised. 38 Look on this side and on that; here are delight and rest, and there are fire and torments.' Thus he willj speak to them on the day of judgment — 39 a day that has no sun or moon or stars, 40 or cloud or thunder or lightning, or wind or water or air, or darkness or evening or morning, 41 or summer or spring or heat or winterk or frost or cold, or hail or rain or dew, 42 or noon or night, or dawn or shining or brightness or light, but only the splendor of the glory of the Most High, by which all shall see what has been destined. 43 It will last as though for a week of years. 44 This is my judgment and its prescribed order; and to you alone I have shown these things."

45 I answered and said, "O sovereign Lord, I said then and/ I say now: Blessed are those who are alive and keep your commandments! 46 But what of those for whom I prayed? For who among the living is there that has not sinned, or who is there among mortals that has not transgressed your covenant? 47 And now I see that the world to come will bring delight to few, but torments to many. 48 For an evil heart has grown up in us, which has alienated us from God,m and has brought us into corruption and the ways of death, and has shown us the paths of perdition and removed us far from life — and that not merely for a few but for almost all who have been created."

49 He answered me and said, "Listen to me, Ezra,n and I will instruct you, and will admonish you once more. 50 For this reason the Most High has made not one world but two. 51 Inasmuch as you have said that the righteous are not many but few, while the ungodly abound, hear the explanation for this.

52 "If you have just a few precious stones, will you add to them lead and clay?"o 53 I said, "Lord, how could that be?" 54 And he said to me, "Not only that, but ask the earth and she will tell you; defer to her, and she will declare it to you. 55 Say to her, 'You produce gold and silver and bronze, and also iron and lead and clay; 56 but silver is more abundant than gold, and bronze than silver, and iron than bronze, and lead than iron, and clay than lead.' 57 Judge therefore which things are precious and desirable, those that are abundant or those that are rare?"

58 I said, "O sovereign Lord, what is plentiful is of less worth, for what is more rare is more precious."

59 He answered me and said, "Consider within yourselfp what you have thought, for the person who has what is hard to get rejoices more than the person who has what is plentiful. 60 So also will be the judgmentq that I have promised; for I will rejoice over the few who shall be saved, because it is they who have made my glory to prevail now, and through them my name has now been honored. 61 I will not

judgement-seat, and there will be an end of all pity and patience. 34 Judgement alone will remain, truth will stand firm, and faithfulness will be strong. 35 The work of each man will come forward and its recompense be made known; good deeds will awake and wicked deeds will not be allowed to sleep. (36) The place of torment will appear, and over against it the place of rest; the furnace of hell will be displayed, and on the opposite side the paradise of joy.

(37) 'Then the Most High will say to the nations that have been raised from the dead: "Look and understand who it is you have denied and refused to serve, whose commandments you have despised. (38) Look on this side, and on that: here are joy and rest, there fire and torments." That is how he will speak to them on the day of judgement.

(39) 'That day will be without sun, moon, or stars; (40) without cloud, thunder, or lightning; wind, water, or air; darkness, evening, or morning; (41) without summer, spring, or winter; without heat, frost, or cold; without hail, rain, or dew; (42) without noonday, night, or dawn; without brightness, light, or brilliance. There will be only the radiant glory of the Most High, by which all will see what lies before them. (43) That day will last for a week of years, as it were. (44) Such is the order that I have decreed for the judgement; but only to you have I given this revelation.'

(45) I replied: 'My lord, I repeat what I said before: "How blest are the living who obey your decrees!" (46) But as for those for whom I have been praying, has there ever lived a man who has not sinned, who has never transgressed your covenant? (47) I see now that only to the few will the next world bring joy, while to the many it will bring torment. (48) For an evil heart has grown strong in us; it has estranged us from God's decrees, brought us into corruption and the paths of death, opened up to us the way to ruin, and carried us far away from life. This it has done, not merely to a few, but to almost all who have been created.'

(49) The angel replied: 'Listen to me and I shall instruct and correct you yet further. (50) The Most High has made not one world but two, and for this reason: (51) there are, as you say, not many who are just, but only a few, whereas the wicked are very numerous; well then, listen to the explanation. (52) Suppose you had a very few precious stones; would you add to their number by putting common lead and clay among them?' (53) 'No, my lord,' I said, 'no one would do that.' (54) 'Look at it also in this way,' he continued: 'enquire of the earth, ask her humbly, and she will give you the answer. (55) Say to her, "You produce gold, silver, and copper, iron, lead, and clay. (56) There is more silver than gold, more copper than silver, more iron than copper, more lead than iron, more clay than lead." (57) Then judge for yourself which things are valuable and desirable — those which are plentiful, or those which are rare.' (58) 'My master and lord,' I said, 'what is plentiful is cheaper; the more rare is the more valuable.' (59) He replied, 'Consider then what follows from that: the owner of what is hard to get has more cause to be pleased than the owner of what is plentiful. (60) In the same way, when I fulfil my promise to the creation, I shall have joy in the few who are saved, because it is they who have made my glory prevail now, and through them my name has been made known. (61) I shall not grieve

---

/Lat *shall gather together* g The passage from verse 36 to verse 105, formerly missing, has been restored to the text h Syr Ethiop: Lat *place* i Lat Syr Ethiop *Gehenna* j Syr Ethiop Arab 1: Lat *you shall* k Or *storm* l Syr: Lat *And I answered, "I said then, O Lord, and* m Cn: Lat Syr Ethiop *from these* n Syr Arab 1 Georg: Lat Ethiop lack *Ezra* o Arab 1: Meaning of Lat Syr Ethiop uncertain p Syr Ethiop Arab 1: Meaning of Lat uncertain q Syr Arab 1: Lat *creation*

7:(36–105) *This passage, missing from the text of the Authorized (King James) Version, but found in ancient witnesses, has been restored.* 7:(48) **from . . . decrees:** *lit.* from these.

grieve over the great number of those who perish; for it is they who are now like a mist, and are similar to a flame and smoke — they are set on fire and burn hotly, and are extinguished."

62 I replied and said, "O earth, what have you brought forth, if the mind is made out of the dust like the other created things? 63For it would have been better if the dust itself had not been born, so that the mind might not have been made from it. 64But now the mind grows with us, and therefore we are tormented, because we perish and we know it. 65Let the human race lament, but let the wild animals of the field be glad; let all who have been born lament, but let the cattle and the flocks rejoice. 66It is much better with them than with us; for they do not look for a judgment, and they do not know of any torment or salvation promised to them after death. 67What does it profit us that we shall be preserved alive but cruelly tormented? 68For all who have been born are entangled in r iniquities, and are full of sins and burdened with transgressions. 69And if after death we were not to come into judgment, perhaps it would have been better for us."

70 He answered me and said, "When the Most High made the world and Adam and all who have come from him, he first prepared the judgment and the things that pertain to the judgment. 71But now, understand from your own words — for you have said that the mind grows with us. 72For this reason, therefore, those who live on earth shall be tormented, because though they had understanding, they committed iniquity; and though they received the commandments, they did not keep them; and though they obtained the law, they dealt unfaithfully with what they received. 73What, then, will they have to say in the judgment, or how will they answer in the last times? 74How long the Most High has been patient with those who inhabit the world! — and not for their sake, but because of the times that he has foreordained."

75 I answered and said, "If I have found favor in your sight, O Lord, show this also to your servant: whether after death, as soon as everyone of us yields up the soul, we shall be kept in rest until those times come when you will renew the creation, or whether we shall be tormented at once?"

76 He answered me and said, "I will show you that also, but do not include yourself with those who have shown scorn, or number yourself among those who are tormented. 77For you have a treasure of works stored up with the Most High, but it will not be shown to you until the last times. 78Now concerning death, the teaching is: When the decisive decree has gone out from the Most High that a person shall die, as the spirit leaves the body to return again to him who gave it, first of all it adores the glory of the Most High. 79If it is one of those who have shown scorn and have not kept the way of the Most High, who have despised his law and hated those who fear God — 80such spirits shall not enter into habitations, but shall immediately wander about in torments, always grieving and sad, in seven ways. 81The first way, because they have scorned the law of the Most High. 82The second way, because they cannot now make a good repentance so that they may live. 83The third way, they shall see the reward laid up for those who have trusted the covenants of the Most High. 84The fourth way, they shall consider the torment laid up for themselves in the last days. 85The fifth way, they shall see how the habitations of the others are guarded by angels in profound quiet. 86The sixth way, they shall see how some of them will cross over s into torments. 87The seventh way, which is worse t than all the

for the many who are lost, for even now they are no more than a vapour; they are like flame or smoke — they catch fire, blaze up, and then die out.'

(62)I said: 'Mother Earth, if the human mind, like the rest of creation, is but a product of the dust, why did you bring it forth? (63)It would have been better if the very dust had never come into being, for then the mind would never have been produced. (64)But, as it is, our mind grows up with us and we are tortured by it, for we realize we are doomed to die. (65)What sorrow for mankind; what happiness for the wild beasts! What sorrow for every mother's son; what joy for the cattle and flocks! (66)How much better their lot than ours! They have no judgement to expect, no knowledge of torment, no knowledge of salvation promised them after death. (67)What good to us is the promise of a future life if it is to be nothing but torture? (68)For everyone alive is burdened and defiled with wickedness, sinful through and through. (69)Would it not have been better for us if there had been no judgement awaiting us after death?'

(70)The angel replied: 'When the Most High was making the world and Adam and his descendants, he first of all planned the judgement and what goes with it. (71)Your own words, when you said that man's mind grows up with him, will give you the answer. (72)It was in spite of having a mind that the people of this world sinned, and that is why torment awaits them: they received the commandments, but did not keep them; they accepted the law, then violated it. (73)What defence will they be able to make at the judgement, what answer at the last day? (74)How patient the Most High has been with the inhabitants of this world, and for how long! — not for their own sake, but for the sake of the destined age to be.'

(75)'If I have found favour with you, my lord,' I said, 'make this also plain to me: at death, when each one of us gives back his soul, shall we be kept in peace until the time when you begin to create your new world, or does our torment begin at once?' (76)'That too I will explain to you,' he replied. 'Do not, however, include yourself among those who have despised my law, nor count yourself with those who are to be tormented. (77)You after all have a treasure of good works stored up with the Most High, though you will not be shown it until the last days. (78)But now to speak of death: when the Most High has pronounced final sentence for a person to die, the spirit leaves the body to return to the One who first gave it, that it may render adoration to the glory of the Most High. (79)As for those who have scornfully rejected the ways of the Most High, who have spurned his law, and who hate the godfearing, (80)their spirits enter no settled abode, but from then on must wander in torment, endless grief, and sorrow. And this for seven reasons. (81)First, they have held in contempt the law of the Most High. (82)Secondly, they have lost their chance of making a full repentance and so gaining life. (83)Thirdly, they can see the reward in store for those who have trusted the covenants of the Most High. (84)Fourthly, they begin to think of the torment that awaits them at the end. (85)Fifthly, they see that angels are guarding the abode of the other souls in undisturbed peace. (86)Sixthly, they see that they are soon to enter into torment. (87)The seventh cause for

---

r Syr defiled with   s Cn: Meaning of Lat uncertain   t Lat Syr
Ethiop greater

ways that have been mentioned, because they shall utterly waste away in confusion and be consumed with shame,[u] and shall wither with fear at seeing the glory of the Most High in whose presence they sinned while they were alive, and in whose presence they are to be judged in the last times.

88 "Now this is the order of those who have kept the ways of the Most High, when they shall be separated from their mortal body.[v] 89During the time that they lived in it,[w] they laboriously served the Most High, and withstood danger every hour so that they might keep the law of the Lawgiver perfectly. 90Therefore this is the teaching concerning them: 91First of all, they shall see with great joy the glory of him who receives them, for they shall have rest in seven orders. 92The first order, because they have striven with great effort to overcome the evil thought that was formed with them, so that it might not lead them astray from life into death. 93The second order, because they see the perplexity in which the souls of the ungodly wander and the punishment that awaits them. 94The third order, they see the witness that he who formed them bears concerning them, that throughout their life they kept the law with which they were entrusted. 95The fourth order, they understand the rest that they now enjoy, being gathered into their chambers and guarded by angels in profound quiet, and the glory waiting for them in the last days. 96The fifth order, they rejoice that they have now escaped what is corruptible and shall inherit what is to come; and besides they see the straits and toil[x] from which they have been delivered, and the spacious liberty that they are to receive and enjoy in immortality. 97The sixth order, when it is shown them how their face is to shine like the sun, and how they are to be made like the light of the stars, being incorruptible from then on. 98The seventh order, which is greater than all that have been mentioned, because they shall rejoice with boldness, and shall be confident without confusion, and shall be glad without fear, for they press forward to see the face of him whom they served in life and from whom they are to receive their reward when glorified. 99This is the order of the souls of the righteous, as henceforth is announced;[y] and the previously mentioned are the ways of torment that those who would not give heed shall suffer hereafter."

100 Then I answered and said, "Will time therefore be given to the souls, after they have been separated from the bodies, to see what you have described to me?"

101 He said to me, "They shall have freedom for seven days, so that during these seven days they may see the things of which you have been told, and afterwards they shall be gathered in their habitations."

102 I answered and said, "If I have found favor in your sight, show further to me, your servant, whether on the day of judgment the righteous will be able to intercede for the ungodly or to entreat the Most High for them— 103fathers for sons or sons for parents, brothers for brothers, relatives for their kindred, or friends for those who are most dear."

104 He answered me and said, "Since you have found favor in my sight, I will show you this also. The day of judgment is decisive[z] and displays to all the seal of truth. Just as now a father does not send his son, or a son his father, or a master his servant, or a friend his dearest friend, to be ill[a] or sleep or eat or be healed in his place, 105so no one shall ever pray for another on that day, neither shall anyone lay a burden on another;[b] for then all shall bear their own righteousness and unrighteousness."

grief, the greatest cause of all, is this: at the sight of the Most High in his glory they break down in shame, waste away in remorse, and shrivel with fear, remembering how they sinned against him in their lifetime and how they are soon to be brought before him for judgement on the last day.

(88) 'As for those who have kept to the ways of the Most High, this is what is appointed for them when their time comes to leave their mortal bodies. (89) During their stay on earth they served the Most High in spite of great hardship and constant danger, and kept to the last letter the law given them by the Lawgiver. (90) Therefore the decision is this: (91) they shall rejoice greatly to see the glory of God, who will receive them as his own, and they shall enter into rest through seven appointed stages. (92) The first stage is their victory in the long struggle against their innate impulse to evil, that it did not lead them astray from life into death. (93) The second is to see the souls of the wicked wandering endlessly and the punishment awaiting them. (94) The third is seeing the good report given of them by their Maker, that while they were alive they kept the law entrusted to them. (95) The fourth is to understand the rest which they are now to share in the storehouses, guarded by angels in undisturbed peace, and the glory awaiting them in the next age. (96) The fifth is the contrast between the corruptible world from which they have joyfully escaped and the future life that is to be their possession, between the cramped, arduous existence from which they have been set free and the spacious life which will soon be theirs to delight in for ever and ever. (97) The sixth will be the revelation that they are to shine like stars, never to fade or die, with faces radiant as the sun. (98) The seventh stage, the greatest of them all, will be the confident and joyful assurance which will be theirs, free from all fear and shame, as they press forward to see face to face the One whom they served in their lifetime, and from whom they are now to receive their reward in glory.

(99) 'What I have here set forth is the appointed destiny for the souls of the just; the torments I spoke of before are what the rebellious are to suffer!'

(100) I asked him: 'When souls are separated from their bodies, will they be given the opportunity to see what you have described to me?' (101) 'They will be allowed seven days,' he replied; 'for seven days they will be permitted to see the things I have told you, and after that they will join the other souls in their abodes.'

(102) 'If I have found favour with you, my lord,' I said, 'tell me one thing more: on the day of judgement will the just be able to plead for the wicked, or by prayer win pardon for them from the Most High? (103) Can fathers do so for their sons, or sons for their parents? Can brothers pray for brothers, relatives and friends for their nearest and dearest?'

(104) 'Since you have found favour with me,' the angel replied, 'this too I will tell you. The day of judgement is decisive and sets its seal on the truth for all to see. In the present age a father cannot send his son in his place, nor a son his father, nor a master his slave, nor a man his best friend, to be ill for him, or sleep, or eat, or be cured for him. (105) In like manner no one shall ever ask pardon for another; every individual will be held responsible for his own wickedness or goodness when that day comes.'

---

[u] Syr Ethiop: Meaning of Lat uncertain   [v] Lat *the corruptible vessel*
[w] Syr Ethiop: Meaning of Lat uncertain   [x] Syr Ethiop: Lat *fullness*
[y] Syr: Meaning of Lat uncertain   [z] Lat *bold*   [a] Syr Ethiop Arm:
Lat *to understand*   [b] Syr Ethiop: Lat lacks *on that . . . another*

7:(103) **friends:** *so some Vss.; Lat.* the faithful.

36 *106* I answered and said, "How then do we find that first Abraham prayed for the people of Sodom, and Moses for our ancestors who sinned in the desert, 37 *107* and Joshua after him for Israel in the days of Achan, 38 *108* and Samuel in the days of Saul, [c] and David for the plague, and Solomon for those at the dedication, 39 *109* and Elijah for those who received the rain, and for the one who was dead, that he might live, 40 *110* and Hezekiah for the people in the days of Sennacherib, and many others prayed for many? 41 *111* So if now, when corruption has increased and unrighteousness has multiplied, the righteous have prayed for the ungodly, why will it not be so then as well?"

42 *112* He answered me and said, "This present world is not the end; the full glory does not [d] remain in it; [e] therefore those who were strong prayed for the weak. 43 *113* But the day of judgment will be the end of this age and the beginning [f] of the immortal age to come, in which corruption has passed away, 44 *114* sinful indulgence has come to an end, unbelief has been cut off, and righteousness has increased and truth has appeared. 45 *115* Therefore no one will then be able to have mercy on someone who has been condemned in the judgment, or to harm [g] someone who is victorious."

46 *116* I answered and said, "This is my first and last comment: it would have been better if the earth had not produced Adam, or else, when it had produced him, had restrained him from sinning. 47 *117* For what good is it to all that they live in sorrow now and expect punishment after death? 48 *118* O Adam, what have you done? For though it was you who sinned, the fall was not yours alone, but ours also who are your descendants. 49 *119* For what good is it to us, if an immortal time has been promised to us, but we have done deeds that bring death? 50 *120* And what good is it that an everlasting hope has been promised to us, but we have miserably failed? 51 *121* Or that safe and healthful habitations have been reserved for us, but we have lived wickedly? 52 *122* Or that the glory of the Most High will defend those who have led a pure life, but we have walked in the most wicked ways? 53 *123* Or that a paradise shall be revealed, whose fruit remains unspoiled and in which are abundance and healing, but we shall not enter it 54 *124* because we have lived in perverse ways? [h] 55 *125* Or that the faces of those who practiced self-control shall shine more than the stars, but our faces shall be blacker than darkness? 56 *126* For while we lived and committed iniquity we did not consider what we should suffer after death."

57 *127* He answered and said, "This is the significance of the contest that all who are born on earth shall wage: 58 *128* if they are defeated they shall suffer what you have said, but if they are victorious they shall receive what I have said. [i] 59 *129* For this is the way of which Moses, while he was alive, spoke to the people, saying, 'Choose life for yourself, so that you may live!' 60 *130* But they did not believe him or the prophets after him, or even myself who have spoken to them. 61 *131* Therefore there shall not be [j] grief at their destruction, so much as joy over those to whom salvation is assured."

62 *132* I answered and said, "I know, O Lord, that the Most High is now called merciful, because he has mercy on those who have not yet come into the world; 63 *133* and gracious, because he is gracious to those who turn in repentance to his law; 64 *134* and patient, because he shows patience toward those who have sinned, since they are his own creatures; 65 *135* and bountiful, because he would rather give

36 (106) To this I replied: 'But how is it, then, that we read of intercessions in scripture? First, there is Abraham, who prayed for the people of Sodom; then Moses, who prayed for our ancestors when they sinned in the wilderness. 37 (107) Next, there is Joshua, who prayed for the Israelites in the time of Achan, 38 (108) as did Samuel in the time of Saul, David on account of the plague, and Solomon for those present at the dedication. 39 (109) Elijah prayed for rain for the people, and he prayed for one who had died, that he might be brought back to life. 40 (110) Hezekiah prayed for the nation in the time of Sennacherib; and there are many more besides. 41 (111) If, then, in an age when corruption had spread and wickedness increased, the just made entreaty for the wicked, why cannot it be the same on the day of judgement?'

42 (112) The answer he gave me was: 'The present world is not the end, and the glory of God does not stay in it continually. That is why the strong have prayed for the weak. 43 (113) But the day of judgement will be the end of the present world and the beginning of the eternal world to come, a world in which corruption will have disappeared, 44 (114) all excess will be abolished and unbelief eliminated, in which justice will be full-grown, and truth will have risen like the sun. 45 (115) On the day of judgement, therefore, there can be no mercy for those who have lost their case, no reversal for those who have won.'

46 (116) I replied, 'But this is my point, my first point and my last: how much better it would have been if the earth had never produced Adam at all, or, once it had done so, if he had been restrained from sinning! 47 (117) For what good does it do any of us to live in misery now and have nothing but punishment to expect after death? 48 (118) O Adam, what have you done? Though the sin was yours, the fall was not yours alone; it was ours also, the fall of all your descendants. 49 (119) What good is the promise of immortality to us, when we have committed mortal sins? 50 (120) What good is the hope of eternity, in the wretched and futile state to which we have come; 51 (121) or the prospect of dwelling in health and safety, when we have lived such wicked lives? 52 (122) You say that the glory of the Most High will guard those who have led pure lives; but what help is that to us who have walked in the most wicked ways? 53 (123) What good is the revelation to us of paradise and its imperishable fruit, the source of perfect satisfaction and healing? For we shall never enter it, 54 (124) since we have made depravity our home. 55 (125) You say that those who have practised self-discipline will shine with faces brighter than the stars; but what good is that to us whose faces are darker than night? 56 (126) During a lifetime of iniquity we have never given a thought to the sufferings in store for us after death.'

57 (127) The angel replied, 'This is the thought for every man on earth to keep in mind during the battle of life: 58 (128) if he is defeated, he must accept the sufferings you have mentioned, but if he is victorious, the rewards I have been describing will be his. 59 (129) That was the way which Moses in his time urged the people to take, when he said, "Choose life and live!" 60 (130) But they believed neither him, nor the prophets after him, no, nor me when I spoke to them. 61 (131) There will be no sorrow over their damnation; but there will be joy for the salvation of those who have believed.'

62 (132) 'My lord,' I said, 'I know that the Most High is now called compassionate, because he has compassion on those yet unborn; 63 (133) and merciful, because he shows mercy to those who repent and live by his law; 64 (134) and patient, because he shows patience to those who have sinned, his own creatures as they are; 65 (135) and Benefac-

---

[c] Syr Ethiop Arab 1: Lat Arab 2 Arm lack *in the days of Saul*
[d] Lat lacks *not*   [e] Or *the glory does not continuously abide in it*
[f] Syr Ethiop: Lat lacks *the beginning*   [g] Syr Ethiop: Lat *overwhelm*
[h] Cn: Lat Syr *places*   [i] Syr Ethiop Arab 1: Lat *what I say*
[j] Syr: Lat *there was not*

7:37 **Achan:** *Lat.* Achar.

than take away;*k* 66*136*and abundant in compassion, because he makes his compassions abound more and more to those now living and to those who are gone and to those yet to come— 67*137*for if he did not make them abound, the world with those who inhabit it would not have life— 68*138*and he is called the giver, because if he did not give out of his goodness so that those who have committed iniquities might be relieved of them, not one ten-thousandth of humankind could have life; 69*139*and the judge, because if he did not pardon those who were created by his word and blot out the multitude of their sins,*l* 70*140*there would probably be left only very few of the innumerable multitude."

8 He answered me and said, "The Most High made this world for the sake of many, but the world to come for the sake of only a few. 2But I tell you a parable, Ezra. Just as, when you ask the earth, it will tell you that it provides a large amount of clay from which earthenware is made, but only a little dust from which gold comes, so is the course of the present world. 3Many have been created, but only a few shall be saved."

4 I answered and said, "Then drink your fill of understanding,*m* O my soul, and drink wisdom, O my heart. 5For not of your own will did you come into the world,*n* and against your will you depart, for you have been given only a short time to live. 6O Lord above us, grant to your servant that we may pray before you, and give us a seed for our heart and cultivation of our understanding so that fruit may be produced, by which every mortal who bears the likeness*o* of a human being may be able to live. 7For you alone exist, and we are a work of your hands, as you have declared. 8And because you give life to the body that is now fashioned in the womb, and furnish it with members, what you have created is preserved amid fire and water, and for nine months the womb*p* endures your creature that has been created in it. 9But that which keeps and that which is kept shall both be kept by your keeping.*n* And when the womb gives up again what has been created in it, 10you have commanded that from the members themselves (that is, from the breasts) milk, the fruit of the breasts, should be supplied, 11so that what has been fashioned may be nourished for a time; and afterwards you will still guide it in your mercy. 12You have nurtured it in your righteousness, and instructed it in your law, and reproved it in your wisdom. 13You put it to death as your creation, and make it live as your work. 14If then you will suddenly and quickly*q* destroy what with so great labor was fashioned by your command, to what purpose was it made? 15And now I will speak out: About all humankind you know best; but I will speak about your people, for whom I am grieved, 16and about your inheritance, for whom I lament, and about Israel, for whom I am sad, and about the seed of Jacob, for whom I am troubled. 17Therefore I will pray before you for myself and for them, for I see the failings of us who inhabit the earth; 18and now also*r* I have heard of the swiftness of the judgment that is to come. 19Therefore hear my voice and understand my words, and I will speak before you."

The beginning of the words of Ezra's prayer,*s* before he was taken up. He said: 20"O Lord, you who inhabit eternity,*t* whose eyes are exalted*u* and whose upper chambers are in the air, 21whose throne is beyond measure and whose glory is beyond comprehension, before whom the hosts of angels stand trembling 22and at whose command they are

tor, because he would rather give than demand; 66 (136)and rich in forgiveness, because again and again he forgives sinners, past, present, and to come. 67 (137)Without his continued forgiveness there could be no hope of life for the world and its inhabitants. 68 (138)He is called generous, because without his generosity in releasing sinners from their sins, not one ten-thousandth part of mankind could hope to be given life; 69 (139)and he is also called Judge, for unless he grants pardon to those who have been created by his word, and blots out their countless offences, 70 (140)only a very few of the entire human race would, I suppose, be spared.'

8 The angel said to me, 'The Most High has made this world for many, the next world for but a few. 2Let me give you an illustration, Ezra: enquire of the earth, and it will tell you that it can produce an abundance of clay for making earthenware, but very little gold-dust. It is the same with the present world: 3many have been created, but only a few will be saved.'

4I SAID: 'My soul, drink deep of understanding and eat your fill of wisdom! 5Without your consent you came here, and against your will you depart; only a brief span of life is given you.

6'O Lord above, if I may be allowed to approach you in prayer, implant a seed in our hearts and minds, and make it grow until it bears fruit, so that fallen man may obtain life. 7For you alone are God, and by your hands we are all shaped in one mould, as your word declares. 8The body moulded in the womb receives from you life and limbs; that which you create is kept safe amid fire and water, and for nine months the body moulded by you bears what you have created in it. 9Both the womb which holds safely and that which is safely held will be kept safe only because you keep them so. And after the womb has delivered up what was created in it, 10then, at your command, from the breasts the human body itself supplies milk, the fruit of the breasts. 11For a certain time what has been made is nourished in that way; and afterwards in your mercy it is still cared for. 12You bring it up to know your justice, train it in your law, and correct it by your wisdom. 13It is your creature and you made it; you can put it to death or give it life, as you please. 14But if you should lightly destroy what was fashioned by your command with so much labour, to what purpose was it created?

15'And now let me say this: about mankind at large, you know best; but it is for your own people that I grieve, 16for your inheritance that I mourn; my sorrow is for Israel, my distress for the descendants of Jacob. 17For them and for myself, therefore, I shall address my prayer to you, since I perceive how low we have fallen, we who dwell in the land; 18and I have heard how quickly your judgement will follow. 19Hear, then, what I have to say, and consider the prayer which I make to you.'

This is the prayer offered by Ezra, before he was taken up to heaven: 20'O Lord, you inhabit eternity, to you the sky and the highest heavens belong; 21your throne is beyond imagining, your glory past conceiving; you are attended by the host of angels, trembling 22as they turn them-

---

k Or *he is ready to give according to requests*   *l* Lat *contempts*
m Syr: Lat *Then release understanding*   *n* Syr: Meaning of Lat uncertain   *o* Syr: Lat *place*   *p* Lat *what you have formed*
q Syr: Lat *will with a light command*   *r* Syr: Lat *but*
s Syr Ethiop; Lat *beginning of Ezra's words*   *t* Or *you who abide forever*   *u* Another Lat text reads *whose are the highest heavens*

changed to wind and fire,[v] whose word is sure and whose utterances are certain, whose command is strong and whose ordinance is terrible, 23 whose look dries up the depths and whose indignation makes the mountains melt away, and whose truth is established[w] forever— 24 hear, O Lord, the prayer of your servant, and give ear to the petition of your creature; attend to my words. 25 For as long as I live I will speak, and as long as I have understanding I will answer. 26 O do not look on the sins of your people, but on those who serve you in truth. 27 Do not take note of the endeavors of those who act wickedly, but of the endeavors of those who have kept your covenants amid afflictions. 28 Do not think of those who have lived wickedly in your sight, but remember those who have willingly acknowledged that you are to be feared. 29 Do not will the destruction of those who have the ways of cattle, but regard those who have gloriously taught your law.[x] 30 Do not be angry with those who are deemed worse than wild animals, but love those who have always put their trust in your glory. 31 For we and our ancestors have passed our lives in ways that bring death;[y] but it is because of us sinners that you are called merciful. 32 For if you have desired to have pity on us, who have no works of righteousness, then you will be called merciful. 33 For the righteous, who have many works laid up with you, shall receive their reward in consequence of their own deeds. 34 But what are mortals, that you are angry with them; or what is a corruptible race, that you are so bitter against it? 35 For in truth there is no one among those who have been born who has not acted wickedly; among those who have existed[z] there is no one who has not done wrong. 36 For in this, O Lord, your righteousness and goodness will be declared, when you are merciful to those who have no store of good works."

37 He answered me and said, "Some things you have spoken rightly, and it will turn out according to your words. 38 For indeed I will not concern myself about the fashioning of those who have sinned, or about their death, their judgment, or their destruction; 39 but I will rejoice over the creation of the righteous, over their pilgrimage also, and their salvation, and their receiving their reward. 40 As I have spoken, therefore, so it shall be.

41 "For just as the farmer sows many seeds in the ground and plants a multitude of seedlings, and yet not all that have been sown will come up[a] in due season, and not all that were planted will take root; so also those who have been sown in the world will not all be saved."

42 I answered and said, "If I have found favor in your sight, let me speak. 43 If the farmer's seed does not come up, because it has not received your rain in due season, or if it has been ruined by too much rain, it perishes.[b] 44 But people, who have been formed by your hands and are called your own image because they are made like you, and for whose sake you have formed all things—have you also made them like the farmer's seed? 45 Surely not, O Lord[c] above! But spare your people and have mercy on your inheritance, for you have mercy on your own creation."

46 He answered me and said, "Things that are present are for those who live now, and things that are future are for those who will live hereafter. 47 For you come far short of being able to love my creation more than I love it. But you have often compared yourself[d] to the unrighteous. Never do so! 48 But even in this respect you will be praiseworthy

selves into wind or fire at your bidding; your word is true, your declarations are constant, your commands mighty and terrible, 23 your glance dries up the depths, your anger melts the mountains, and your truth stands for ever: 24 hear, O Lord, the prayer of your servant, listen to my petition and attend to my words, for you it is who have fashioned me. 25 While I live, I must speak; while I have understanding, I must respond.

26 'Do not look upon the offences of your people, but rather look on those who have served you faithfully. 27 Pay heed not to the godless and their practices, but to those who have observed your covenant and suffered for it. 28 Do not think of those who all their lives have been untrue to you, but remember those who of their own will have acknowledged the fear due to you. 29 Do not destroy those who have lived like animals, but take account of those who have borne shining witness to your law. 30 Do not be angry with those considered worse than beasts, but show love to those who have put unfailing trust in your glory. 31 We and our fathers have lived evil lives, yet it is on account of us sinners that you are called merciful; 32 for if it is your desire to have mercy on us, sinners who have no just deeds to our credit, then indeed you will be called merciful. 33 The reward which will be given to the just, who have many good works stored up with you, will be no more than their own deeds have earned.

34 'What is man that you should be angry with him? Or the race of mortals that you should treat them so harshly? 35 The truth is, no one was ever born who did not sin, no one alive is innocent of offence. 36 Indeed, it is through your mercy shown towards those with no fund of good deeds to their name that your justice and kindness will be made known.'

37 In reply to me the angel said: 'Some part of what you have said is correct, and it will be as you say. 38 You may be sure that I shall not give thought to sinners, to their creation, death, judgement, or damnation; 39 but I shall have joy in the creation of the just, in their pilgrimage through this world, their salvation, and their final reward. 40 So I have said, and so it is. 41 The farmer sows many seeds in the ground and plants many plants, but not all the seeds come up safely in due season, nor do all the plants strike root. It is the same in the world of men: not all who are sown will be saved.'

42 To that I replied: 'If I have found favour with you, let me speak. 43 The farmer's seed may not come up, because you did not give it rain at the right time, or it may rot because of too much rain; 44 but man, who was fashioned by your hands and called your image because he is made like you, and for whose sake you formed everything, will you really compare him with seed sown by a farmer? 45 Do not be angry with us, Lord; but spare your people and show them pity, for it is your own creation you will be pitying.'

46 He answered: 'The present is for those now alive, the future for those yet to come. 47 It is not possible for you to love my creation with a love greater than mine—far from it! But never again rank yourself among the unjust, as so often you have done. 48 Yet the Most High approves 49 of the

---

v Syr: Lat *they whose service takes the form of wind and fire*
w Arab 2: Other authorities read *truth bears witness*   x Syr *have received the brightness of your law*   y Syr Ethiop: Meaning of Lat uncertain   z Syr: Meaning of Lat uncertain   a Syr Ethiop *will live*; Lat *will be saved*   b Cn: Compare Syr Arab 1 Arm Georg 2: Meaning of Lat uncertain   c Ethiop Arab Compare Syr: Lat lacks *O Lord*   d Syr Ethiop: Lat *brought yourself near*

before the Most High, 49 because you have humbled yourself, as is becoming for you, and have not considered yourself to be among the righteous. You will receive the greatest glory, 50 for many miseries will affect those who inhabit the world in the last times, because they have walked in great pride. 51 But think of your own case, and inquire concerning the glory of those who are like yourself, 52 because it is for you that paradise is opened, the tree of life is planted, the age to come is prepared, plenty is provided, a city is built, rest is appointed,e goodness is established and wisdom perfected beforehand. 53 The root of evil f is sealed up from you, illness is banished from you, and deathg is hidden; Hades has fled and corruption has been forgotten;h 54 sorrows have passed away, and in the end the treasure of immortality is made manifest. 55 Therefore do not ask any more questions about the great number of those who perish. 56 For when they had opportunity to choose, they despised the Most High, and were contemptuous of his law, and abandoned his ways. 57 Moreover, they have even trampled on his righteous ones, 58 and said in their hearts that there is no God—though they knew well that they must die. 59 For just as the things that I have predicted awaiti you, so the thirst and torment that are prepared await them. For the Most High did not intend that anyone should be destroyed; 60 but those who were created have themselves defiled the name of him who made them, and have been ungrateful to him who prepared life for them now. 61 Therefore my judgment is now drawing near; 62 I have not shown this to all people, but only to you and a few like you."

Then I answered and said, 63 "O Lord, you have already shown me a great number of the signs that you will do in the last times, but you have not shown me when you will do them."

9 He answered me and said, "Measure carefully in your mind, and when you see that some of the predicted signs have occurred, 2 then you will know that it is the very time when the Most High is about to visit the world that he has made. 3 So when there shall appear in the world earthquakes, tumult of peoples, intrigues of nations, wavering of leaders, confusion of princes, 4 then you will know that it was of these that the Most High spoke from the days that were of old, from the beginning. 5 For just as with everything that has occurred in the world, the beginning is evident,j and the end manifest; 6 so also are the times of the Most High: the beginnings are manifest in wonders and mighty works, and the end in penaltiesk and in signs.

7 It shall be that all who will be saved and will be able to escape on account of their works, or on account of the faith by which they have believed, 8 will survive the dangers that have been predicted, and will see my salvation in my land and within my borders, which I have sanctified for myself from the beginning. 9 Then those who have now abused my ways shall be amazed, and those who have rejected them with contempt shall live in torments. 10 For as many as did not acknowledge me in their lifetime, though they received my benefits, 11 and as many as scorned my law while they still had freedom, and did not understand but despised itl while an opportunity of repentance was still open to them, 12 these must in torment acknowledge itl after death. 13 Therefore, do not continue to be curious

proper modesty you have shown; you have not sought great glory by including yourself among the godly. 50 In the last days the inhabitants of the world will be punished for their arrogant lives by prolonged suffering. 51 But you should direct your thoughts to yourself and look to the glory awaiting those like you. 52 For all of you paradise lies open, the tree of life is planted, the age to come stands prepared, and rich abundance is in store; the city is already built, rest from toil is assured, goodness and wisdom are brought to perfection. 53 From you the root of evil has been cut off; for you disease is at an end and death abolished, hell is gone, and the corruption of the grave blotted out. 54 All sorrows are at an end, and the treasure of immortality has been finally revealed.

55 'Ask no more questions, therefore, about the many who are lost; 56 for when they were given freedom they used it to despise the Most High, to treat his law with contempt and abandon his ways. 57 What is more, they trampled on the godly. 58 "There is no God," they said to themselves, knowing full well that they must die. 59 Yours, then, will be the joys I have predicted, theirs the thirst and torments already prepared. It is not that the Most High has wanted any man to be destroyed, 60 but that those he created have themselves brought dishonour on their Creator's name, and shown ingratitude to the One who had put life within their reach. 61 That is why my judgement is now close at hand, 62 but I have not made this known to all—only to you and a few like you.'

63 'My lord,' I said, 'you have now revealed to me the many signs which you are to perform in the last days; but you have not shown me when that will be.'

9 The angel answered: 'Keep a careful check; when you see that some of the signs predicted have already passed, 2 then you will understand that the time has come for the Most High to begin to judge the world he created. 3 When the world becomes the scene of earthquakes, insurrections, plots among the nations, unstable government, and panic among rulers, 4 then you will recognize these as the events foretold by the Most High since first the world began. 5 Just as everything that is done on earth has its beginning and end clearly marked, 6 so it is with the times which the Most High has determined: the beginning is marked by portents and miracles, the end by manifestations of power.

7 'All who come safely through and escape destruction, thanks to their good deeds or the faith they have shown, 8 will survive the dangers I have foretold and witness the salvation I shall bring to my land, the territory I have set apart from all eternity as my own. 9 Then those who have neglected my ways will be taken by surprise; their utter contempt for my ways will bring them lasting torment. 10 All who in their lifetime failed to acknowledge me in spite of the benefits I brought them, 11 all who disdained my law while freedom still was theirs, who scornfully dismissed the idea of penitence while the way was still open— 12 all these must learn the truth through torments after death.

---

e Syr Ethiop: Lat allowed   f Lat lacks of evil   g Syr Ethiop Arm: Lat lacks death   h Syr: Lat Hades and corruption have fled into oblivion; or corruption has fled into Hades to be forgotten   i Syr: Lat will receive   j Syr: Ethiop is in the word; Meaning of Lat uncertain   k Syr: Ethiop in effects   l Or me

about how the ungodly will be punished; but inquire how the righteous will be saved, those to whom the age belongs and for whose sake the age was made."*m*

14 I answered and said, 15"I said before, and I say now, and will say it again: there are more who perish than those who will be saved, 16as a wave is greater than a drop of water."

17 He answered me and said, "As is the field, so is the seed; and as are the flowers, so are the colors; and as is the work, so is the product; and as is the farmer, so is the threshing floor. 18For there was a time in this age when I was preparing for those who now exist, before the world was made for them to live in, and no one opposed me then, for no one existed; 19but now those who have been created in this world, which is supplied both with an unfailing table and an inexhaustible pasture,*n* have become corrupt in their ways. 20So I considered my world, and saw that it was lost. I saw that my earth was in peril because of the devices of those who*o* had come into it. 21And I saw and spared some*p* with great difficulty, and saved for myself one grape out of a cluster, and one plant out of a great forest.*q* 22So let the multitude perish that has been born in vain, but let my grape and my plant be saved, because with much labor I have perfected them.

23 "Now, if you will let seven days more pass — do not, however, fast during them, 24but go into a field of flowers where no house has been built, and eat only of the flowers of the field, and taste no meat and drink no wine, but eat only flowers, 25and pray to the Most High continually. Then I will come and talk with you."

26 So I went, as he directed me, into the field that is called Ardat;*r* there I sat among the flowers and ate of the plants of the field, and the nourishment they afforded satisfied me. 27After seven days, while I lay on the grass, my heart was troubled again as it was before. 28Then my mouth was opened, and I began to speak before the Most High, and said, 29"O Lord, you showed yourself among us, to our ancestors in the wilderness when they came out from Egypt and when they came into the untrodden and unfruitful wilderness; 30and you said, 'Hear me, O Israel, and give heed to my words, O descendants of Jacob. 31For I sow my law in you, and it shall bring forth fruit in you, and you shall be glorified through it forever.' 32But though our ancestors received the law, they did not keep it and did not observe the*s* statutes; yet the fruit of the law did not perish — for it could not, because it was yours. 33Yet those who received it perished, because they did not keep what had been sown in them. 34Now this is the general rule that, when the ground has received seed, or the sea a ship, or any dish food or drink, and when it comes about that what was sown or what was launched or what was put in is destroyed, 35they are destroyed, but the things that held them remain; yet with us it has not been so. 36For we who have received the law and sinned will perish, as well as our hearts that received it; 37the law, however, does not perish but survives in its glory."

38 When I said these things in my heart, I looked around,*t* and on my right I saw a woman; she was mourning and weeping with a loud voice, and was deeply grieved at heart; her clothes were torn, and there were ashes on her head. 39Then I dismissed the thoughts with which I had been engaged, and turned to her 40and said to her, "Why are you weeping, and why are you grieved at heart?"

13Do not be curious any more, Ezra, to know how the godless will be tormented, but only how and when the just will be saved; the world is theirs and for their sake it exists.'

14I answered, 15'I repeat what I have said again and again: the lost outnumber the saved 16as a wave exceeds a drop of water.'

17The angel replied: 'The seed to be sown depends on the soil, the colour depends on the flower, the product on the craftsman, and the harvest on the farmer. There was a time 18before the world had been created for men to live in, and I was planning it for the sake of those who now exist. No one then disputed my plan, 19for no one existed. I supplied this world with unfailing food and a law not to be questioned; but those whom I created turned to corrupt ways of life. 20I looked at my world and there it lay spoilt, at my earth and it was in danger from men's wicked plans. 21I saw this and I was hard put to it to spare any at all; but I saved for myself one grape out of a cluster, one tree out of a large forest. 22So then let it be: destruction for the many who were born in vain, and salvation for my grape and my tree, which have cost me such labour to bring to perfection.

23 'You, however, must wait seven days more, Ezra. Do not fast this time, 24but go to a flowery field where no house stands, and eat only what grows there; taste no meat or wine, 25and pray to the Most High the whole time. I shall then come and talk with you.'

26I WENT out, as the angel told me, to a field called Ardat. There I sat among the flowers; my food was what grew in the field, and I ate to my heart's content. 27As I lay on the grass at the end of the seven days, I was troubled again in mind with all the same perplexities. 28I broke my silence and addressed the Most High: 29'Lord, you showed yourself to our fathers in the wilderness at the time of the exodus from Egypt, when they were travelling through a barren waste where no one ever trod, 30and you said, "Hear me, Israel, listen to my words, you descendants of Jacob: 31this is my law, which I am sowing among you to bear fruit and to bring you everlasting glory." 32But our fathers, though they received the law, did not observe it; they disobeyed its commandments. Not that the fruit of the law perished — that was impossible, for it was yours; 33rather, those who received it perished, because they failed to keep safe the seed that had been sown in them. 34Now the usual way of things is that when seed is put into the earth, or a ship on the sea, or food or drink into a jar, then if the seed, or the ship, 35or the contents of the jar should be destroyed, what held or contained them does not perish along with them. But with us sinners it is different: 36destruction will come upon us, the recipients of the law, and upon our hearts, the vessel that held the law. 37The law itself is not destroyed; it survives in all its glory.'

38While turning over these things in my mind, I looked round and on my right I saw a woman in great distress, mourning and lamenting loudly; her dress was torn, and she had ashes on her head. 39Breaking off my meditations, I turned to her 40and asked: 'Why are you weeping? What is troubling you?' 41'Sir,' she replied, 'please leave me to my

41 She said to me, "Let me alone, my lord, so that I may weep for myself and continue to mourn, for I am greatly embittered in spirit and deeply distressed."

42 I said to her, "What has happened to you? Tell me."

43 And she said to me, "Your servant was barren and had no child, though I lived with my husband for thirty years. 44 Every hour and every day during those thirty years I prayed to the Most High, night and day. 45 And after thirty years God heard your servant, and looked upon my low estate, and considered my distress, and gave me a son. I rejoiced greatly over him, I and my husband and all my neighbors;*u* and we gave great glory to the Mighty One. 46 And I brought him up with much care. 47 So when he grew up and I came to take a wife for him, I set a day for the marriage feast.

10 "But it happened that when my son entered his wedding chamber, he fell down and died. 2 So all of us put out our lamps, and all my neighbors*u* attempted to console me; I remained quiet until the evening of the second day. 3 But when all of them had stopped consoling me, encouraging me to be quiet, I got up in the night and fled, and I came to this field, as you see. 4 And now I intend not to return to the town, but to stay here; I will neither eat nor drink, but will mourn and fast continually until I die."

5 Then I broke off the reflections with which I was still engaged, and answered her in anger and said, 6 "You most foolish of women, do you not see our mourning, and what has happened to us? 7 For Zion, the mother of us all, is in deep grief and great distress. 8 It is most appropriate to mourn now, because we are all mourning, and to be sorrowful, because we are all sorrowing; you are sorrowing for one son, but we, the whole world, for our mother.*v* 9 Now ask the earth, and she will tell you that it is she who ought to mourn over so many who have come into being upon her. 10 From the beginning all have been born of her, and others will come; and, lo, almost all go*w* to perdition, and a multitude of them will come to doom. 11 Who then ought to mourn the more, she who lost so great a multitude, or you who are grieving for one alone? 12 But if you say to me, 'My lamentation is not like the earth's, for I have lost the fruit of my womb, which I brought forth in pain and bore in sorrow; 13 but it is with the earth according to the way of the earth—the multitude that is now in it goes as it came'; 14 then I say to you, 'Just as you brought forth in sorrow, so the earth also has from the beginning given her fruit, that is, humankind, to him who made her.' 15 Now, therefore, keep your sorrow to yourself, and bear bravely the troubles that have come upon you. 16 For if you acknowledge the decree of God to be just, you will receive your son back in due time, and will be praised among women. 17 Therefore go into the town to your husband."

18 She said to me, "I will not do so; I will not go into the city, but I will die here."

19 So I spoke again to her, and said, 20 "Do not do that, but let yourself be persuaded—for how many are the adversities of Zion?—and be consoled because of the sorrow of Jerusalem. 21 For you see how our sanctuary has been laid waste, our altar thrown down, our temple destroyed; 22 our

tears and my grief, for great is my bitterness of heart and great my affliction.' 42 'Tell me', I said, 'what has happened.' 43 'Sir, I was barren and childless throughout thirty years of marriage,' she replied; 44 'every hour of every day during those thirty years, night and day alike, I prayed to the Most High. 45 Then after thirty years God answered my prayer and had mercy on my affliction; he took note of my sorrow and granted me a son. What joy he brought to my husband and myself and to all our neighbours! What praise we gave to the Mighty God! 46 I took great pains over his upbringing, 47 and when he grew up I chose a wife for him and held a wedding feast.

10 'But when my son entered the bridal chamber, he fell down dead. 2 We put out all the lights, and my neighbours all came to comfort me; I controlled my feelings till the evening of the following day. 3 When everyone had stopped urging me to take comfort and control myself, I rose and stole away in the night, and came here, as you see, to this field. 4 I have made up my mind never to return to the city; I shall stay here, neither eating nor drinking, but mourning and fasting all the time until I die.'

5 At that I abandoned the reflections which occupied my mind and spoke sternly to the woman: 6 'You are the most foolish of women,' I said; 'are you blind to the mourning and sufferings of our nation? 7 It is for the anguish and affliction of Zion, the mother of us all, that you should mourn with such poignancy; 8 you should share in our common mourning and anguish. But your anguish is for your one son. 9 Ask the earth and she will tell you that she must mourn for the countless thousands who come to birth upon her. 10 In the beginning all sprang from her, and there are more still to come; yet almost all her children go to perdition, and vast numbers of them are wiped out. 11 Who, then, has the better right to be mourning—the earth, which has lost such vast numbers, or you, whose sorrow is for one only? 12 You may say to me, "But my lamentation is different from that of the earth; I have lost the fruit of my womb, which I brought to birth in pain and travail, 13 whereas it is only in the course of nature that the vast numbers now alive on earth should depart as they came." 14 My answer is: at the cost of pain you have been a mother, but in the same way the earth has always been the mother of mankind, bearing fruit to earth's Creator.

15 'Now, therefore, keep your sorrow to yourself, and bear your misfortunes bravely. 16 If you will accept God's decree as just, then in due time you will receive your son again and win an honoured name among women. 17 Go back, therefore, into the city to your husband.'

18 'No,' she replied, 'I will not. I will never go back; I shall die here.'

19 But I continued to argue with her. 20 'Do not do that,' I urged; 'let yourself be persuaded because of Zion's misfortunes, and take comfort from the sorrow of Jerusalem. 21 You see how our sanctuary has been laid waste, our altar demolished, our temple destroyed. 22 Our harps are un-

---

u Literally *all my citizens*   *v* Compare Syr: Meaning of Lat uncertain   *w* Literally *walk*

harp has been laid low, our song has been silenced, and our rejoicing has been ended; the light of our lampstand has been put out, the ark of our covenant has been plundered, our holy things have been polluted, and the name by which we are called has been almost profaned; our children*x* have suffered abuse, our priests have been burned to death, our Levites have gone into exile, our virgins have been defiled, and our wives have been ravished; our righteous men*y* have been carried off, our little ones have been cast out, our young men have been enslaved and our strong men made powerless. 23 And, worst of all, the seal of Zion has been deprived of its glory, and given over into the hands of those that hate us. 24 Therefore shake off your great sadness and lay aside your many sorrows, so that the Mighty One may be merciful to you again, and the Most High may give you rest, a respite from your troubles."

25 While I was talking to her, her face suddenly began to shine exceedingly; her countenance flashed like lightning, so that I was too frightened to approach her, and my heart was terrified. While*z* I was wondering what this meant, 26 she suddenly uttered a loud and fearful cry, so that the earth shook at the sound. 27 When I looked up, the woman was no longer visible to me, but a city was being built,*a* and a place of huge foundations showed itself. I was afraid, and cried with a loud voice and said, 28 "Where is the angel Uriel, who came to me at first? For it was he who brought me into this overpowering bewilderment; my end has become corruption, and my prayer a reproach."

29 While I was speaking these words, the angel who had come to me at first came to me, and when he saw me 30 lying there like a corpse, deprived of my understanding, he grasped my right hand and strengthened me and set me on my feet, and said to me, 31 "What is the matter with you? And why are you troubled? And why are your understanding and the thoughts of your mind troubled?"

32 I said, "It was because you abandoned me. I did as you directed, and went out into the field, and lo, what I have seen I saw, and can still see, I am unable to explain."

33 He said to me, "Stand up like a man, and I will instruct you."

34 I said, "Speak, my lord; only do not forsake me, so that I may not die before my time.*b* 35 For I have seen what I did not know, and I hear*c* what I do not understand 36 — or is my mind deceived, and my soul dreaming? 37 Now therefore I beg you to give your servant an explanation of this bewildering vision."

38 He answered me and said, "Listen to me, and I will teach you, and tell you about the things that you fear; for the Most High has revealed many secrets to you. 39 He has seen your righteous conduct, and that you have sorrowed continually for your people and mourned greatly over Zion. 40 This therefore is the meaning of the vision. 41 The woman who appeared to you a little while ago, whom you saw mourning and whom you began to console 42 (you do not now see the form of a woman, but there appeared to you a city being built)*d* 43 and who told you about the misfortune of her son — this is the interpretation: 44 The woman whom you saw is Zion, which you now behold as a city being built.*e* 45 And as for her telling you that she was barren for thirty years, the reason is that there were three thousand*f* years in the world before any offering was offered in it.*g*

strung, our hymns silenced, our shouts of joy cut short; the light of the sacred lamp has been extinguished, and the Ark of our covenant has been plundered; the holy vessels are defiled, and the name which God has conferred on us is disgraced; our leading men have been treated with violence, our priests burnt alive, and the Levites taken into captivity; our virgins have been ravished and our wives violated, our godfearing men carried off, and our children left abandoned; our young men have been enslaved, and our strong warriors reduced to impotence. 23 Worst of all, Zion, once sealed with God's own seal, has forfeited its glory and been delivered into the hands of those who hate us. 24 Then throw off your own heavy grief, and lay aside all your sorrows; may the Mighty God restore you to his favour, may the Most High give you rest and peace after your troubles!'

25 Suddenly, as I was still speaking to the woman, I saw her face begin to shine brightly. Her countenance flashed like lightning, and I shrank from her in fear, and wondered what this meant. 26 All at once she uttered a great cry of terror that shook the earth. 27 I looked up and saw no longer a woman but a city, built on massive foundations. I was terrified and cried aloud, 28 'Where is the angel Uriel who came to me before? It is his doing that I have reached this state of panic, that my end is to be bodily corruption, and my prayers are met by reproach.'

29 I was still speaking when there appeared the angel who had come previously. When he saw me 30 lying unconscious, in a dead faint, he grasped me by my right hand, put strength into me, and raised me to my feet. 31 'What is the matter?' he asked. 'Why are you overcome? What has so disturbed you and troubled your mind?' 32 'You abandoned me,' I replied. 'I did as you told me: I came out to the fields; and what I have seen here and can still see is beyond my power to explain.'

33 'Stand up like a man,' he said, 'and I shall enlighten you.'

34 'Speak on, my lord,' I replied; 'only do not abandon me and leave me to die to no purpose. 35 I have seen and heard things beyond my knowledge and understanding — 36 unless this is all an illusion and a dream. 37 My lord, explain this state, I beg you.'

38 'Listen to me,' replied the angel, 'while I expound the things that terrify you; for the Most High has revealed many secrets to you. 39 He has seen your upright life, your unceasing grief for your people, and your deep mourning over Zion.

40 'Here, then, is the meaning of the vision. 41 A little while ago you saw a woman mourning and tried to console her; 42 now you no longer see that woman, but a complete city has appeared to you. 43 She told you about losing her son, and this is the explanation. 44 The woman you saw is Zion, which you now see as a city complete with its buildings. 45 She told you she was childless for thirty years; that was because three thousand years passed before any sacrifices were offered in Zion. 46 But then, after the three thou-

---

x Ethiop *free men*   *y* Syr *our seers*   *z* Syr Ethiop Arab 1: Lat lacks *I was too . . . terrified. While*   *a* Lat: Syr Ethiop Arab 1 Arab 2 Arm *but there was an established city*   *b* Syr Ethiop Arab: Lat *die to no purpose*   *c* Other ancient authorities read *have heard* *d* Lat: Syr Ethiop Arab 1 Arab 2 Arm *an established city*   *e* Cn: Lat *an established city*   *f* Most Lat Mss read *three*   *g* Cn: Lat Syr Arab Arm *her*

46 And after three thousand[h] years Solomon built the city, and offered offerings; then it was that the barren woman bore a son. 47 And as for her telling you that she brought him up with much care, that was the period of residence in Jerusalem. 48 And as for her saying to you, 'My son died as he entered his wedding chamber,' and that misfortune had overtaken her,[i] this was the destruction that befell Jerusalem. 49 So you saw her likeness, how she mourned for her son, and you began to console her for what had happened.[j] 50 For now the Most High, seeing that you are sincerely grieved and profoundly distressed for her, has shown you the brilliance of her glory, and the loveliness of her beauty. 51 Therefore I told you to remain in the field where no house had been built, 52 for I knew that the Most High would reveal these things to you. 53 Therefore I told you to go into the field where there was no foundation of any building, 54 because no work of human construction could endure in a place where the city of the Most High was to be revealed.

55 "Therefore do not be afraid, and do not let your heart be terrified; but go in and see the splendor or[k] the vastness of the building, as far as it is possible for your eyes to see it, 56 and afterward you will hear as much as your ears can hear. 57 For you are more blessed than many, and you have been called to be with[l] the Most High as few have been. 58 But tomorrow night you shall remain here, 59 and the Most High will show you in those dream visions what the Most High will do to those who inhabit the earth in the last days."

So I slept that night and the following one, as he had told me.

11 On the second night I had a dream: I saw rising from the sea an eagle that had twelve feathered wings and three heads. 2 I saw it spread its wings over[m] the whole earth, and all the winds of heaven blew upon it, and the clouds were gathered around it.[n] 3 I saw that out of its wings there grew opposing wings; but they became little, puny wings. 4 But its heads were at rest; the middle head was larger than the other heads, but it too was at rest with them. 5 Then I saw that the eagle flew with its wings, and it reigned over the earth and over those who inhabit it. 6 And I saw how all things under heaven were subjected to it, and no one spoke against it — not a single creature that was on the earth. 7 Then I saw the eagle rise upon its talons, and it uttered a cry to its wings, saying, 8 "Do not all watch at the same time; let each sleep in its own place, and watch in its turn; 9 but let the heads be reserved for the last."

10 I looked again and saw that the voice did not come from its heads, but from the middle of its body. 11 I counted its rival wings, and there were eight of them. 12 As I watched, one wing on the right side rose up, and it reigned over all the earth. 13 And after a time its reign came to an end, and it disappeared, so that even its place was no longer visible. Then the next wing rose up and reigned, and it continued to reign a long time. 14 While it was reigning its end came also, so that it disappeared like the first. 15 And a voice sounded, saying to it, 16 "Listen to me, you who have ruled the earth all this time; I announce this to you before you disappear. 17 After you no one shall rule as long as you have ruled, not even half as long."

18 Then the third wing raised itself up, and held the rule as the earlier ones had done, and it also disappeared. 19 And so it went with all the wings; they wielded power one after another and then were never seen again. 20 I kept looking,

sand years, Solomon built the city and offered the sacrifices; that was when the childless woman bore a son. 47 She took great trouble, she said, over his upbringing; that was the period when Jerusalem was inhabited. 48 She told you of the loss she suffered, how her son had died on the day he entered his bridal chamber; that was the destruction which has overtaken Jerusalem. 49 Such then was the vision you saw — the woman mourning for her son — and you tried to comfort her in her sufferings; this was the revelation you had to receive. 50 Seeing the sincerity of your grief and how you feel for her with all your heart, the Most High is now showing you her radiant glory and her surpassing beauty. 51 That was why I told you to stay in a field where no house has been built, 52 for I knew that the Most High intended to send you this revelation. 53 I told you to come to this field, where no foundation had been laid for any building, 54 because in the place where the city of the Most High was to be revealed no building made by man could stand.

55 'Have no fear, then, and set your mind at rest; go into the city, and see the great buildings in all their splendour, so far as your eyes have power to see them. 56 After that you will hear as much as your ears have power to hear. 57 You are more blessed than most, and few have such a name with the Most High as you have. 58 Stay here till tomorrow night, 59 when the Most High will show you in dreams and visions what he will do to earth's inhabitants in the last days.' So, as I had been told, I slept there that night and the next.

11 ON the second night I had a vision in my sleep: there, rising out of the sea, appeared an eagle with twelve wings and three heads. 2 I saw it spread its wings over the whole earth; and all the winds of heaven blew upon it and clouds gathered about it. 3 Out of its wings I saw opposing wings sprout, which proved to be only small and stunted. 4 Its heads lay still; even the middle head, which was bigger than the others, lay still between them. 5 As I watched, the eagle rose on its wings to establish itself as ruler over the earth and its inhabitants. 6 I saw it bring into subjection everything under heaven; it encountered no protest at all from any creature on earth. 7 I saw the eagle stand erect on its talons and address its wings: 8 'Do not all wake together,' it said; 'sleep each of you in your place and wake up in your turn; 9 the heads are to be kept till the last.' 10 I saw that the sound was coming not from its heads but from the middle of its body. 11 I counted the opposing wings: there were eight of them.

12 As I watched, one of the wings on its right side rose and became ruler over the whole earth. 13 After a time its reign came to an end, and it disappeared, leaving no trace. Then the next arose and established its rule, holding sway for a long time. 14 When its reign was coming to an end and it was about to disappear like the first, 15 a voice could be heard addressing it: 16 'You have held the world in your grasp; now listen to my message before your time comes to disappear. 17 None of your successors will achieve a reign as long as yours, or even half as long.' 18 Then the third wing arose, exercised power for a time like its predecessors, and like them disappeared. 19 In the same way all the wings came to power one after the other, and in turn each disappeared.

---

h Syr Ethiop Arab Arm: Lat *three*   i Or *him*   j Most Lat Mss and Arab 1 add *these were the things to be opened to you*   k Other ancient authorities read *and*   l Or *been named by*   m Arab 2 Arm: Lat Syr Ethiop *in*   n Syr: Compare Ethiop Arab: Lat lacks *the clouds* and *around it*

11:2 **clouds:** *so some Vss.; Lat. omits.*

and in due time the wings that followed*o* also rose up on the right*p* side, in order to rule. There were some of them that ruled, yet disappeared suddenly; 21 and others of them rose up, but did not hold the rule.

22 And after this I looked and saw that the twelve wings and the two little wings had disappeared, 23 and nothing remained on the eagle's body except the three heads that were at rest and six little wings.

24 As I kept looking I saw that two little wings separated from the six and remained under the head that was on the right side; but four remained in their place. 25 Then I saw that these little wings*q* planned to set themselves up and hold the rule. 26 As I kept looking, one was set up, but suddenly disappeared; 27 a second also, and this disappeared more quickly than the first. 28 While I continued to look the two that remained were planning between themselves to reign together; 29 and while they were planning, one of the heads that were at rest (the one that was in the middle) suddenly awoke; it was greater than the other two heads. 30 And I saw how it allied the two heads with itself, 31 and how the head turned with those that were with it and devoured the two little wings*q* that were planning to reign. 32 Moreover this head gained control of the whole earth, and with much oppression dominated its inhabitants; it had greater power over the world than all the wings that had gone before.

33 After this I looked again and saw the head in the middle suddenly disappear, just as the wings had done. 34 But the two heads remained, which also in like manner ruled over the earth and its inhabitants. 35 And while I looked, I saw the head on the right side devour the one on the left.

36 Then I heard a voice saying to me, "Look in front of you and consider what you see." 37 When I looked, I saw what seemed to be a lion roused from the forest, roaring; and I heard how it uttered a human voice to the eagle, and spoke, saying, 38 "Listen and I will speak to you. The Most High says to you, 39 'Are you not the one that remains of the four beasts that I had made to reign in my world, so that the end of my times might come through them? 40 You, the fourth that has come, have conquered all the beasts that have gone before; and you have held sway over the world with great terror, and over all the earth with grievous oppression; and for so long you have lived on the earth with deceit.*r* 41 You have judged the earth, but not with truth, 42 for you have oppressed the meek and injured the peaceable; you have hated those who tell the truth, and have loved liars; you have destroyed the homes of those who brought forth fruit, and have laid low the walls of those who did you no harm. 43 Your insolence has come up before the Most High, and your pride to the Mighty One. 44 The Most High has looked at his times; now they have ended, and his ages have reached completion. 45 Therefore you, eagle, will surely disappear, you and your terrifying wings, your most evil little wings, your malicious heads, your most evil talons, and your whole worthless body, 46 so that the whole earth, freed from your violence, may be refreshed and relieved, and may hope for the judgment and mercy of him who made it.'"

12 While the lion was saying these words to the eagle, I looked 2 and saw that the remaining head had disappeared. The two wings that had gone over to it rose up and*s* set themselves up to reign, and their reign was brief and full of tumult. 3 When I looked again, they were already

20 As time went on, I saw the little wings on the right side also raise themselves up to seize power. Some achieved this, and at once passed from sight, 21 while others arose but never attained to power. 22 At this point I noticed that two of the little wings were, like the twelve large ones, no longer to be seen; 23 nothing was left on the eagle's body except the three motionless heads and six little wings. 24 As I watched, two of the six little wings separated from the rest and stationed themselves under the head on the right. The other four remained where they were, 25 and I saw them planning to rise up and seize power. 26 One rose, but disappeared immediately; 27 so too did the second, vanishing even more quickly than the first. 28 I saw the last two planning to make themselves the rulers; 29 but while they were still plotting, suddenly one of the heads woke from sleep, the one in the middle, the biggest of the three. 30 I saw how it joined with the other two heads, 31 and along with them turned and devoured the two little wings which were planning to become rulers. 32 This head got the whole earth into its grasp, establishing an oppressive regime over all its inhabitants and a world-wide kingdom mightier than any of the wings had governed. 33 But after that I saw the middle head vanish as suddenly as the wings had done. 34 There were two heads left, and they also made themselves rulers over the earth and its inhabitants, 35 but, as I watched, the head on the right devoured the head on the left.

36 Then I heard a voice saying to me: 'Look carefully at what you see in front of you.' 37 I looked, and saw what seemed to be a lion roused out of the forest and roaring as it came. I heard it address the eagle in a human voice. 38 'Listen, you, to what I tell you!' it said. 'The Most High says: 39 Are you not the sole survivor of the four beasts to which I gave the rule over my world, intending through them to bring to an end the times I fixed? 40–41 You are the fourth beast to come, and you have conquered all who went before, dominating the whole world and holding it in the grip of fear and harsh oppression. You have lived long in the world, governing it with deceit and with no regard for truth. 42 You have trodden underfoot the gentle and injured the peaceful, hating the truthful and loving liars; you have destroyed the homes of the prosperous, and razed to the ground the walls of those who had done you no harm. 43 Your insolence is known to the Most High, your pride to the Mighty One. 44 The Most High has surveyed the periods he has fixed: they are now at an end, and his ages have reached their completion. 45 Therefore, eagle, you must now disappear and be seen no more, you and your terrible great wings, your villainous small wings, your cruel heads, your grim talons, and your whole worthless carcass. 46 Then all the earth will be refreshed and relieved by being freed from your violence, and will look forward in hope to the judgement and mercy of its Creator.'

12 While the lion was still addressing the eagle, I looked 2 and saw the one remaining head disappear, and the two wings which had gone over to it arose and set themselves up as rulers. But their reign was short and troubled, 3 and when I looked they were already vanishing.

---

o Syr Arab 2 *the little wings*   *p* Some Ethiop Mss read *left*
q Syr: Lat *underwings*   *r* Syr Arab Arm: Lat Ethiop *The fourth came, however, and conquered . . . and held sway . . . and for so long lived*   *s* Ethiop: Lat lacks *rose up and*

vanishing. The whole body of the eagle was burned, and the earth was exceedingly terrified.

Then I woke up in great perplexity of mind and great fear, and I said to my spirit, 4"You have brought this upon me, because you search out the ways of the Most High. 5I am still weary in mind and very weak in my spirit, and not even a little strength is left in me, because of the great fear with which I have been terrified tonight. 6Therefore I will now entreat the Most High that he may strengthen me to the end."

7 Then I said, "O sovereign Lord, if I have found favor in your sight, and if I have been accounted righteous before you beyond many others, and if my prayer has indeed come up before your face, 8strengthen me and show me, your servant, the interpretation and meaning of this terrifying vision so that you may fully comfort my soul. 9For you have judged me worthy to be shown the end of the times and the last events of the times."

10 He said to me, "This is the interpretation of this vision that you have seen: 11The eagle that you saw coming up from the sea is the fourth kingdom that appeared in a vision to your brother Daniel. 12But it was not explained to him as I now explain to you or have explained it. 13The days are coming when a kingdom shall rise on earth, and it shall be more terrifying than all the kingdoms that have been before it. 14And twelve kings shall reign in it, one after another. 15But the second that is to reign shall hold sway for a longer time than any other one of the twelve. 16This is the interpretation of the twelve wings that you saw.

17 "As for your hearing a voice that spoke, coming not from the eagle's[t] heads but from the midst of its body, this is the interpretation: 18In the midst of[u] the time of that kingdom great struggles shall arise, and it shall be in danger of falling; nevertheless it shall not fall then, but shall regain its former power.[v] 19As for your seeing eight little wings[w] clinging to its wings, this is the interpretation: 20Eight kings shall arise in it, whose times shall be short and their years swift; 21two of them shall perish when the middle of its time draws near; and four shall be kept for the time when its end approaches, but two shall be kept until the end.

22 "As for your seeing three heads at rest, this is the interpretation: 23In its last days the Most High will raise up three kings,[x] and they[y] shall renew many things in it, and shall rule the earth 24and its inhabitants more oppressively than all who were before them. Therefore they are called the heads of the eagle, 25because it is they who shall sum up his wickedness and perform his last actions. 26As for your seeing that the large head disappeared, one of the kings[z] shall die in his bed, but in agonies. 27But as for the two who remained, the sword shall devour them. 28For the sword of one shall devour him who was with him; but he also shall fall by the sword in the last days.

29 As for your seeing two little wings[a] passing over to[b] the head which was on the right side, 30this is the interpretation: It is these whom the Most High has kept for the eagle's[t] end; this was the reign which was brief and full of tumult, as you have seen.

31 "And as for the lion whom you saw rousing up out of the forest and roaring and speaking to the eagle and reproving him for his unrighteousness, and as for all his words that you have heard, 32this is the Messiah[c] whom

Then the eagle's whole body burst into flames, filling the earth with terror.

So great was my agitation and alarm that I awoke. I said to myself: 4'See the result of the attempt to discover the ways of the Most High! 5I am weary of mind and utterly exhausted; the terrors I have experienced this night have bereft me of the last vestige of strength. 6I shall now pray, therefore, to the Most High to be given strength to the end.' 7I said: 'My Master and Lord, if I have found favour with you and am esteemed more just than most men, and if it is true that my prayers have reached your presence, 8then give me strength. Reveal to me, my Lord, the precise interpretation of this terrifying vision, and set my soul fully at ease, 9for you have already judged me worthy to be shown the end of the present age.'

10The angel answered: 'Here is the interpretation of your vision. 11The eagle you saw rising out of the sea represents the fourth kingdom in the vision seen by your brother Daniel. 12But he was not given the interpretation which I am now giving you or have already given you. 13The days are coming when the earth will be under an empire more terrible than any before. 14It will be ruled by twelve kings, one after another, 15the second to come to the throne having the longest reign of all the twelve. 16That is the meaning of the twelve wings you saw.

17'As for the voice which you heard speaking from the middle of the eagle's body, and not from its heads, this is what it means: 18after this second king's reign, great conflicts will arise, which will bring the empire into danger of collapse; yet it will not collapse then, but will be restored to its original power.

19'As for the eight lesser wings which you saw growing from the eagle's wings, this is what they mean: 20the empire will come under eight kings whose reigns will be brief and transient; 21two of them will come and go just before the middle of the period, four will be kept back until shortly before its end, and two will be left until the end itself.

22'As for the three heads which you saw sleeping, this is what they mean: 23in the last years of the empire, the Most High will bring to the throne three kings, who will restore much of its strength, and rule over the earth 24and its inhabitants more oppressively than any who preceded them. They are called the eagle's heads, 25because they will bring to a head and consummate its long series of wicked deeds. 26As for the greatest head, which you saw disappear, it signifies one of the kings; he will die in his bed, but in agony. 27The two that survived will be destroyed by the sword; 28one of them will fall victim to the sword of the other, who will himself fall by the sword in the last days.

29'As for the two little wings that went over to the head on the right side, 30this is what they mean: they are the ones whom the Most High has reserved until the last days, and their reign, as you saw, was short and troubled.

31'As for the lion which you saw coming out of the forest, roused from sleep and roaring, and which you heard addressing the eagle, taxing it with its wicked deeds and words, 32he is the Messiah whom the Most High has kept

---

[t] Lat *his* [u] Syr Arm: Lat *After* [v] Ethiop Arab 1 Arm: Lat Syr *its beginning* [w] Syr: Lat *underwings* [x] Syr Ethiop Arab Arm: Lat *kingdoms* [y] Syr Ethiop Arm: Lat *he* [z] Lat *them* [a] Arab 1: Lat *underwings* [b] Syr Ethiop: Lat lacks *to* [c] Literally *anointed one*

12:23 who . . . rule: *so some Vss.; Lat.* and he will restore . . . and they will rule.

the Most High has kept until the end of days, who will arise from the offspring of David, and will come and speak[d] with them. He will denounce them for their ungodliness and for their wickedness, and will display before them their contemptuous dealings. 33 For first he will bring them alive before his judgment seat, and when he has reproved them, then he will destroy them. 34 But in mercy he will set free the remnant of my people, those who have been saved throughout my borders, and he will make them joyful until the end comes, the day of judgment, of which I spoke to you at the beginning. 35 This is the dream that you saw, and this is its interpretation. 36 And you alone were worthy to learn this secret of the Most High. 37 Therefore write all these things that you have seen in a book, put it[e] in a hidden place; 38 and you shall teach them to the wise among your people, whose hearts you know are able to comprehend and keep these secrets. 39 But as for you, wait here seven days more, so that you may be shown whatever it pleases the Most High to show you." Then he left me.

40 When all the people heard that the seven days were past and I had not returned to the city, they all gathered together, from the least to the greatest, and came to me and spoke to me, saying, 41 "How have we offended you, and what harm have we done you, that you have forsaken us and sit in this place? 42 For of all the prophets you alone are left to us, like a cluster of grapes from the vintage, and like a lamp in a dark place, and like a haven for a ship saved from a storm. 43 Are not the disasters that have befallen us enough? 44 Therefore if you forsake us, how much better it would have been for us if we also had been consumed in the burning of Zion. 45 For we are no better than those who died there." And they wept with a loud voice.

Then I answered them and said, 46 "Take courage, O Israel; and do not be sorrowful, O house of Jacob; 47 for the Most High has you in remembrance, and the Mighty One has not forgotten you in your struggle. 48 As for me, I have neither forsaken you nor withdrawn from you; but I have come to this place to pray on account of the desolation of Zion, and to seek mercy on account of the humiliation of our[f] sanctuary. 49 Now go to your homes, every one of you, and after these days I will come to you." 50 So the people went into the city, as I told them to do. 51 But I sat in the field seven days, as the angel[g] had commanded me; and I ate only of the flowers of the field, and my food was of plants during those days.

13 After seven days I dreamed a dream in the night. 2 And lo, a wind arose from the sea and stirred up[h] all its waves. 3 As I kept looking the wind made something like the figure of a man come up out of the heart of the sea. And I saw[i] that this man flew[j] with the clouds of heaven; and wherever he turned his face to look, everything under his gaze trembled, 4 and whenever his voice issued from his mouth, all who heard his voice melted as wax melts[k] when it feels the fire.

5 After this I looked and saw that an innumerable multitude of people were gathered together from the four winds of heaven to make war against the man who came up out of the sea. 6 And I looked and saw that he carved out for himself a great mountain, and flew up on to it. 7 And I tried to see the region or place from which the mountain was carved, but I could not. 8 After this I looked and saw that all who had gathered together against him, to wage war with him, were filled with fear, and yet they dared to fight. 9 When he saw the

back until the end of the days; he will arise from the stock of David and will come and address those rulers, taxing them openly with their sins, their crimes, and their defiance. 33 First, he will bring them alive to judgement; then, after convicting them, he will destroy them. 34 But he will be merciful to the rest of my people, all who have survived in my land; he will set them free and give them joy, until the final day of judgement comes, about which I told you at the beginning.

35 'That is the vision you saw, and that its meaning. 36 It is the secret of the Most High, of which no one except yourself has proved worthy to be told. 37 You must therefore write in a book all you have seen, and deposit it in a hiding-place. 38 You must also disclose these secrets to those of your people whom you know to be wise enough to understand them and to keep them safe. 39 However, you must stay here for seven days more, to receive whatever revelation the Most High thinks fit to send you.' Then the angel left me.

40 When all the people heard that seven days had passed and I had not yet returned to the city, both high and low assembled and came to me and asked: 41 'What wrong or what injury have we done you, that you have abandoned us for good and settled in this place? 42 Out of all the prophets you are the only one left to us. You are like the last cluster in a vineyard, like a lamp in a dark place, or a safe harbour for a ship in a storm. 43 Have we not suffered enough already? 44 If you abandon us, we had far better have perished in the fire that destroyed Zion. 45 We are no better than those who died there.' And they wept aloud.

46 'Take courage, Israel,' I answered them; 'lay aside your grief, house of Jacob. 47 The Most High bears you in mind, the Mighty God has not forgotten you for ever. 48 I have not abandoned you, nor shall I leave you; I came here to pray for Zion in her desolation, and to beg for mercy for our sanctuary now fallen so low. 49 Go to your homes for the present, every one of you, and in a few days' time I shall come back to you.'

50 So the people returned to the city as I told them, 51 while I remained in the field. As commanded by the angel I stayed there for seven days, eating nothing but what grew in the field, and living on that for the whole of the time.

13 THE seven days passed; and the following night I had a dream. 2 In my dream, a wind arose from the sea and set all its waves in turmoil. 3 As I watched, the wind brought a figure like that of a man out of the depths, and he flew with the clouds of heaven. Wherever he turned his face, everything he looked at trembled, 4 and wherever the sound of his voice reached, everyone who heard it melted as wax at the touch of fire.

5 Next I saw a countless host of men gathering from the four winds of heaven to vanquish the man who had come up out of the sea. 6 I saw that the man hewed out for himself a great mountain, and flew on to it. 7 Though I tried to see from what region or place the mountain had been taken, I could not. 8 Then I saw that all who had gathered to fight against the man were greatly afraid, and yet they dared to fight. 9 When he saw the hordes advancing to the attack, he

---

[d] Syr: Lat lacks of days . . . and speak   [e] Ethiop Arab 1 Arab 2
Arm: Lat Syr them   [f] Syr Ethiop: Lat your   [g] Literally he
[h] Other ancient authorities read I saw a wind arise from the sea and stir up   [i] Syr: Lat lacks the wind . . . I saw   [j] Syr Ethiop Arab
Arm: Lat grew strong   [k] Syr: Lat burned as the earth rests

12:32 of the days . . . address: so one Vs.; Lat. defective.
13:3 the wind . . . depths: so other Vss.; Lat. defective.

·

onrush of the approaching multitude, he neither lifted his hand nor held a spear or any weapon of war; 10 but I saw only how he sent forth from his mouth something like a stream of fire, and from his lips a flaming breath, and from his tongue he shot forth a storm of sparks.*l* 11 All these were mingled together, the stream of fire and the flaming breath and the great storm, and fell on the onrushing multitude that was prepared to fight, and burned up all of them, so that suddenly nothing was seen of the innumerable multitude but only the dust of ashes and the smell of smoke. When I saw it, I was amazed.

12 After this I saw the same man come down from the mountain and call to himself another multitude that was peaceable. 13 Then many people*m* came to him, some of whom were joyful and some sorrowful; some of them were bound, and some were bringing others as offerings.

Then I woke up in great terror, and prayed to the Most High, and said, 14 "From the beginning you have shown your servant these wonders, and have deemed me worthy to have my prayer heard by you; 15 now show me the interpretation of this dream also. 16 For as I consider it in my mind, alas for those who will be left in those days! And still more, alas for those who are not left! 17 For those who are not left will be sad 18 because they understand the things that are reserved for the last days, but cannot attain them. 19 But alas for those also who are left, and for that very reason! For they shall see great dangers and much distress, as these dreams show. 20 Yet it is better*n* to come into these things,*o* though incurring peril, than to pass from the world like a cloud, and not to see what will happen in the last days."

He answered me and said, 21 "I will tell you the interpretation of the vision, and I will also explain to you the things that you have mentioned. 22 As for what you said about those who survive, and concerning those who do not survive,*p* this is the interpretation: 23 The one who brings the peril at that time will protect those who fall into peril, who have works and faith toward the Almighty. 24 Understand therefore that those who are left are more blessed than those who have died.

25 "This is the interpretation of the vision: As for your seeing a man come up from the heart of the sea, 26 this is he whom the Most High has been keeping for many ages, who will himself deliver his creation; and he will direct those who are left. 27 And as for your seeing wind and fire and a storm coming out of his mouth, 28 and as for his not holding a spear or weapon of war, yet destroying the onrushing multitude that came to conquer him, this is the interpretation: 29 The days are coming when the Most High will deliver those who are on the earth. 30 And bewilderment of mind shall come over those who inhabit the earth. 31 They shall plan to make war against one another, city against city, place against place, people against people, and kingdom against kingdom. 32 When these things take place and the signs occur that I showed you before, then my Son will be revealed, whom you saw as a man coming up from the sea.*q*

33 "Then, when all the nations hear his voice, all the nations shall leave their own lands and the warfare that they have against one another; 34 and an innumerable multitude shall be gathered together, as you saw, wishing to come and conquer him. 35 But he shall stand on the top of Mount Zion. 36 And Zion shall come and be made manifest to all people, prepared and built, as you saw the mountain carved out without hands. 37 Then he, my Son, will reprove the

did not so much as lift a finger against them. He had no spear in his hand, no weapon at all; 10 only, as I watched, he poured out what appeared to be a stream of fire from his mouth, a breath of flame from his lips with a storm of sparks from his tongue. 11 These, the stream of fire, the breath of flame, and the great storm, combined into one mass which fell on the host prepared for battle, and burnt them all up. Of that enormous multitude suddenly nothing was to be discerned but dust and ashes and a reek of smoke. I was astounded at the sight.

12 After that, I saw the man come down from the mountain and summon to himself a different, a peaceful company. 13 He was joined by great numbers of men, some with joy on their faces, others with sorrow, some coming from captivity, and some bringing others to him as an offering. I woke up overcome by terror, and I prayed to the Most High: 14 'O Lord, from first to last you have revealed those wonders to me, and judged me worthy to have my prayers answered. 15 Now show me the meaning of this dream also. 16 How terrible it will be, to my thinking, for all who survive to those days, but how much worse for those who do not! 17 Those who do not survive will have the sorrow 18 of knowing what the last days have in store, yet without attaining it. 19 Those who do survive are to be pitied for the terrible dangers and many trials which these visions show they will have to face. 20 But perhaps after all it is better to endure the dangers and reach the goal than to vanish from the world like a cloud and never see what will happen at the last.'

21 'Yes,' he replied, 'I shall disclose the meaning of the vision, and tell you what you ask. 22 To your question about those who survive, the answer is this: 23 the very person from whom danger will then come will protect those exposed to the danger if they have good deeds and faith laid up to their credit with God Most Mighty. 24 You may rest assured that those who survive are more blessed than those who have died.

25 'This is what the vision means: the man you saw coming up from the heart of the sea 26 is he whom the Most High has held in readiness during many ages; through him he will deliver the world he has made, and he will determine the destiny of those who survive. 27 As for the breath of flame, the fire, and the storm you saw issuing from the mouth of the man, 28 so that without spear or any other weapon in his hand he crushed the onslaught of the hordes advancing to fight against him, the meaning is this: 29 the day is near when the Most High will start bringing deliverance to those on earth. 30 Its panic-stricken inhabitants 31 will plot hostilities against one another, city against city, region against region, nation against nation, kingdom against kingdom. 32 When that happens, and all the signs that I have shown you take place, then my son will be revealed, he whom you saw as a man coming up out of the sea. 33 At the sound of his voice all nations will leave their own territories and their separate wars, 34 and unite as you saw in your vision in one large host past counting, all intent on overpowering him. 35 When he takes his stand on the summit of Mount Zion, 36 then Zion, completed and fully built, will come and appear before all people, corresponding to the mountain which you saw hewn out, though not by human hands. 37 My son

---

l Meaning of Lat uncertain   *m* Lat Syr Arab 2 literally *the faces of many people*   *n* Ethiop Compare Arab 2: Lat *easier*   *o* Syr: Lat *this*   *p* Syr Arab 1: Lat lacks *and . . . not survive*   *q* Syr and most Lat Mss lack *from the sea*

13:26 **him:** *so one Vs.; Lat.* himself.

| NEW REVISED STANDARD VERSION | REVISED ENGLISH BIBLE |

assembled nations for their ungodliness (this was symbolized by the storm), 38 and will reproach them to their face with their evil thoughts and the torments with which they are to be tortured (which were symbolized by the flames), and will destroy them without effort by means of the law[r] (which was symbolized by the fire).

39 "And as for your seeing him gather to himself another multitude that was peaceable, 40 these are the nine[s] tribes that were taken away from their own land into exile in the days of King Hoshea, whom Shalmaneser, king of the Assyrians, made captives; he took them across the river, and they were taken into another land. 41 But they formed this plan for themselves, that they would leave the multitude of the nations and go to a more distant region, where no human beings had ever lived, 42 so that there at least they might keep their statutes that they had not kept in their own land. 43 And they went in by the narrow passages of the Euphrates river. 44 For at that time the Most High performed signs for them, and stopped the channels of the river until they had crossed over. 45 Through that region there was a long way to go, a journey of a year and a half; and that country is called Arzareth.[t]

46 "Then they lived there until the last times; and now, when they are about to come again, 47 the Most High will stop[u] the channels of the river again, so that they may be able to cross over. Therefore you saw the multitude gathered together in peace. 48 But those who are left of your people, who are found within my holy borders, shall be saved.[v] 49 Therefore when he destroys the multitude of the nations that are gathered together, he will defend the people who remain. 50 And then he will show them very many wonders."

51 I said, "O sovereign Lord, explain this to me: Why did I see the man coming up from the heart of the sea?"

52 He said to me, "Just as no one can explore or know what is in the depths of the sea, so no one on earth can see my Son or those who are with him, except in the time of his day.[w] 53 This is the interpretation of the dream that you saw. And you alone have been enlightened about this, 54 because you have forsaken your own ways and have applied yourself to mine, and have searched out my law; 55 for you have devoted your life to wisdom, and called understanding your mother. 56 Therefore I have shown you these things; for there is a reward laid up with the Most High. For it will be that after three more days I will tell you other things, and explain weighty and wondrous matters to you."

57 Then I got up and walked in the field, giving great glory and praise to the Most High for the wonders that he does[x] from time to time, 58 and because he governs the times and whatever things come to pass in their seasons. And I stayed there three days.

14 On the third day, while I was sitting under an oak, suddenly a voice came out of a bush opposite me and said, "Ezra, Ezra!" 2 And I answered, "Here I am, Lord," and I rose to my feet. 3 Then he said to me, "I revealed myself in a bush and spoke to Moses when my people were in bondage in Egypt; 4 and I sent him and led[y] my people out of Egypt; and I led him up on Mount Sinai, where I kept him with me many days. 5 I told him many wondrous things, and showed him the secrets of the times and declared to him[z] the end of the times. Then I commanded him, saying, 6 'These words you shall publish openly, and these you shall keep secret.' 7 And now I say to

will convict of their godless deeds the nations that confront him; this will accord with the storm you saw. 38 He will reproach them to their face with their evil plotting and the torments they are soon to undergo; this is symbolized by the flame. And he will destroy them without effort by means of the law — and that is the fire.

39 'You saw him assemble a company which was different and peaceful. 40 They are the ten tribes that were taken into exile in the days of King Hoshea, whom King Shalmaneser of Assyria made captive. Carrying them off beyond the river Euphrates, he deported them to a foreign country. 41 But then they resolved to leave behind the gentile population and go to a more distant region never yet inhabited, 42 and there at least to be obedient to their laws, which in their own country they had failed to keep. 43 As they passed through the narrow passages of the Euphrates, 44 the Most High performed miracles for them, halting the flow of the river until they had crossed over. 45 Their long journey through that region called Arzareth took a year and a half. 46 They have lived there ever since, until this final age. Now they are on their way back, 47 and once more the Most High is halting the river to let them cross.

'That is the meaning of the peaceful company you saw assembled. 48 With them too are the survivors of your own people, all who are found inside my sacred borders. 49 When the time comes, therefore, for him to destroy the assembled nations, he will protect those of your people who are left, 50 and then display to them countless portents.'

51 'My master and lord,' I said, 'explain to me why the man I saw came up out of the heart of the sea.' 52 He replied: 'It is beyond the power of anyone to explore and discover what is in it; in the same way no one on earth can set eyes on my son and those who accompany him until the appointed day. 53 Such then is the meaning of your vision. This revelation has been given to you, and to you alone, 54 because you have laid aside your own affairs, and devoted yourself entirely to mine and to the study of my law. 55 You have taken wisdom as your guide in life, and you have called understanding your mother. 56 That is why I have given this revelation to you: there is a reward for you with the Most High. In three more days' time I shall speak with you again, and tell you of momentous and wonderful things.'

57 So I went away to the field, glorifying and praising the Most High for the wonders he performed from time to time 58 and for his providential control of the passing ages and what happens in them. There I remained for three days.

14 On the third day I was sitting under an oak tree, when there came a voice from a bush in front of me: 'Ezra, Ezra!' it called. 2 'Here I am, Lord,' I answered, rising to my feet. 3 The voice went on: 'When my people was in slavery in Egypt, I revealed myself in the bush and spoke to Moses, 4 sending him to lead Israel out of Egypt. I brought him to Mount Sinai, where for many days I kept him with me. 5 I explained many wonderful things to him, showing him the secrets of the ages and the end of time, and I instructed him 6 what to make public and what to keep hidden. 7 To you also I now say: 8 Store up in your mind the

---

[r] Syr: Lat *effort and the law*   [s] Other Lat Mss *ten*; Syr Ethiop Arab 1 Arm *nine and a half*   [t] That is *Another Land*   [u] Syr: Lat *stops*   [v] Syr: Lat lacks *shall be saved*   [w] Syr: Ethiop *except when his time and his day have come*. Lat lacks *his*   [x] Lat *did* [y] Syr Arab 1 Arab 2 *he led*   [z] Syr Ethiop Arab Arm: Lat lacks *declared to him*

you: 8 Lay up in your heart the signs that I have shown you, the dreams that you have seen, and the interpretations that you have heard; 9 for you shall be taken up from among humankind, and henceforth you shall live with my Son and with those who are like you, until the times are ended. 10 The age has lost its youth, and the times begin to grow old. 11 For the age is divided into twelve parts, and nine*a* of its parts have already passed, 12 as well as half of the tenth part; so two of its parts remain, besides half of the tenth part.*b* 13 Now therefore, set your house in order, and reprove your people; comfort the lowly among them, and instruct those that are wise.*c* And now renounce the life that is corruptible, 14 and put away from you mortal thoughts; cast away from you the burdens of humankind, and divest yourself now of your weak nature; 15 lay to one side the thoughts that are most grievous to you, and hurry to escape from these times. 16 For evils worse than those that you have now seen happen shall take place hereafter. 17 For the weaker the world becomes through old age, the more shall evils be increased upon its inhabitants. 18 Truth shall go farther away, and falsehood shall come near. For the eagle*d* that you saw in the vision is already hurrying to come."

19 Then I answered and said, "Let me speak*e* in your presence, Lord. 20 For I will go, as you have commanded me, and I will reprove the people who are now living; but who will warn those who will be born hereafter? For the world lies in darkness, and its inhabitants are without light. 21 For your law has been burned, and so no one knows the things which have been done or will be done by you. 22 If then I have found favor with you, send the holy spirit into me, and I will write everything that has happened in the world from the beginning, the things that were written in your law, so that people may be able to find the path, and that those who want to live in the last days may do so."

23 He answered me and said, "Go and gather the people, and tell them not to seek you for forty days. 24 But prepare for yourself many writing tablets, and take with you Sarea, Dabria, Selemia, Ethanus, and Asiel — these five, who are trained to write rapidly; 25 and you shall come here, and I will light in your heart the lamp of understanding, which shall not be put out until what you are about to write is finished. 26 And when you have finished, some things you shall make public, and some you shall deliver in secret to the wise; tomorrow at this hour you shall begin to write."

27 Then I went as he commanded me, and I gathered all the people together, and said, 28 "Hear these words, O Israel. 29 At first our ancestors lived as aliens in Egypt, and they were liberated from there 30 and received the law of life, which they did not keep, which you also have transgressed after them. 31 Then land was given to you for a possession in the land of Zion; but you and your ancestors committed iniquity and did not keep the ways that the Most High commanded you. 32 And since he is a righteous judge, in due time he took from you what he had given. 33 And now you are here, and your people*f* are farther in the interior.*g* 34 If you, then, will rule over your minds and discipline your hearts, you shall be kept alive, and after death you shall obtain mercy. 35 For after death the judgment will come, when we shall live again; and then the names of the righteous shall become manifest, and the deeds of the ungodly shall be disclosed. 36 But let no one come to me now, and let no one seek me for forty days."

signs I have shown you, the visions you have seen, and the interpretations you have heard. 9 You are about to be taken away from the world of men, and thereafter you will remain with my son and with those like you until the end of time. 10 The world has lost its youth, and time is growing old; 11 for the whole of time is in twelve divisions, of which nine divisions and half the tenth are already past; 12 so there remain only two and a half. 13 Now, therefore, set your house in order; admonish your nation, and give comfort to those of them who are lowly. Then take your leave of this corruptible life; 14 let go your earthly cares, and throw off your human burdens; shed your weak nature, 15 and put on one side the anxieties that vex you; then make haste to depart from this world of time. 16 However great the evils you have witnessed, there are worse to come. 17 As this ageing world grows ever more feeble, the more will evils increase for its inhabitants. 18 Truth will move farther away, and falsehood draw nearer. The eagle you saw in your vision is already on the wing.'

19 'Lord, if I may speak in your presence,' I replied, 20 'I am to depart, by your command, after admonishing those of my people who are now alive; but who will give a warning to those born hereafter? The world is shrouded in darkness and its inhabitants are without light. 21 Because your law was destroyed in the fire, no one can know what you have done or intend to do. 22 If, then, I have found favour with you, send into me your holy spirit, and I shall put in writing the whole story of the world from the very beginning, everything that was contained in your law, so that all may have the possibility of finding the right path, and, if they so choose, of obtaining life in the last days.'

23 'Go,' he answered, 'call the people together, and tell them not to look for you for forty days. 24 Prepare a large number of writing tablets, and bring with you Seraiah and Dabri, Shelemiah, Ethan, and Asiel, five men all trained to write quickly. 25 On your return here, I shall light in your mind a lamp of understanding which will not go out until you have finished what you are to write. 26 When it is complete, some of it you must make public; the rest you must give to wise men to keep hidden. Tomorrow at this time you shall begin writing.'

27 I went as I was ordered, called together all the people, and said: 28 'Israel, listen to what I say. 29 At first our ancestors lived as aliens in Egypt; from there they were rescued 30 and given the law which imparts life. But they disobeyed it, and you have followed their example. 31 You were given a land of your own, the land of Zion; but, like your ancestors, you sinned and abandoned the ways laid down for you by the Most High. 32 Being a just judge, he took back in due time what he had given you. 33 Now you are here, and your fellow-countrymen are still farther away. 34 If, therefore, you direct your understanding and instruct your minds, you will be kept safe in life and meet with mercy after death. 35 For after death will come the judgement: we shall be restored to life, and then the names of the just will be known and the deeds of the godless exposed. 36 But no one must come near me now or look for me during the next forty days.'

---

a Cn: Lat Ethiop *ten*   *b* Syr lacks verses 11, 12: Ethiop *For the world is divided into ten parts, and has come to the tenth, and half of the tenth remains. Now . . . c* Lat lacks *and . . . wise*
d Syr Ethiop Arab Arm: Meaning of Lat uncertain   *e* Most Lat Mss lack *Let me speak   f* Lat *brothers   g* Syr Ethiop Arm: Lat *are among you*

37 So I took the five men, as he commanded me, and we proceeded to the field, and remained there. 38 And on the next day a voice called me, saying, "Ezra, open your mouth and drink what I give you to drink." 39 So I opened my mouth, and a full cup was offered to me; it was full of something like water, but its color was like fire. 40 I took it and drank; and when I had drunk it, my heart poured forth understanding, and wisdom increased in my breast, for my spirit retained its memory, 41 and my mouth was opened and was no longer closed. 42 Moreover, the Most High gave understanding to the five men, and by turns they wrote what was dictated, using characters that they did not know.[h] They sat forty days; they wrote during the daytime, and ate their bread at night. 43 But as for me, I spoke in the daytime and was not silent at night. 44 So during the forty days, ninety-four[i] books were written. 45 And when the forty days were ended, the Most High spoke to me, saying, "Make public the twenty-four[j] books that you wrote first, and let the worthy and the unworthy read them; 46 but keep the seventy that were written last, in order to give them to the wise among your people. 47 For in them is the spring of understanding, the fountain of wisdom, and the river of knowledge." 48 And I did so.[k]

15 [l] Speak in the ears of my people the words of the prophecy that I will put in your mouth, says the Lord, 2 and cause them to be written on paper; for they are trustworthy and true. 3 Do not fear the plots against you, and do not be troubled by the unbelief of those who oppose you. 4 For all unbelievers shall die in their unbelief.[m]

5 Beware, says the Lord, I am bringing evils upon the world, the sword and famine, death and destruction, 6 because iniquity has spread throughout every land, and their harmful doings have reached their limit. 7 Therefore, says the Lord, 8 I will be silent no longer concerning their ungodly acts that they impiously commit, neither will I tolerate their wicked practices. Innocent and righteous blood cries out to me, and the souls of the righteous cry out continually. 9 I will surely avenge them, says the Lord, and will receive to myself all the innocent blood from among them. 10 See, my people are being led like a flock to the slaughter; I will not allow them to live any longer in the land of Egypt, 11 but I will bring them out with a mighty hand and with an uplifted arm, and will strike Egypt with plagues, as before, and will destroy all its land. 12 Let Egypt mourn, and its foundations, because of the plague of chastisement and castigation that the Lord will bring upon it. 13 Let the farmers that till the ground mourn, because their seed shall fail to grow[n] and their trees shall be ruined by blight and hail and by a terrible tempest. 14 Alas for the world and for those who live in it! 15 For the sword and misery draw near them, and nation shall rise up to fight against nation, with swords in their hands. 16 For there shall be unrest among people; growing strong against one another, they shall in their might have no respect for their king or the chief of their leaders. 17 For a person will desire to go into a city, and shall not be able to do so. 18 Because of their pride the cities shall be in confusion, the houses shall be destroyed, and people shall be afraid.

37 As instructed I took the five men with me, and we went out to the field and stayed there. 38 On the next day I heard a voice calling to me: 'Ezra, open your mouth and drink what I give you.' 39 I opened my mouth, and was handed a cup full of what seemed like water, except that its colour was the colour of fire. 40 I took it and drank, and, as soon as I had done so, understanding welled up in my mind, and wisdom increased within me. My memory remained fully active, 41 and I began to speak and went on without stopping. 42 The Most High gave understanding to the five men, who took turns at writing down what was said, using characters which they had not known before. They continued at work throughout the forty days, writing all day, and taking food only at night. 43 But as for me, I spoke all through the day, and even at night I did not break off. 44 In the forty days, ninety-four books were written down. 45 At the end of the time the Most High said to me: 'Make public the twenty-four books you wrote first; they are to be read by everyone, whether worthy to do so or not. 46 But the last seventy books are to be kept back, and given to none but the wise among your people; 47 they contain a stream of understanding, a fountain of wisdom, a flood of knowledge.' 48 And this I did.

15 Proclaim to my people the words of prophecy which I give you to speak, says the Lord; 2 have them written down, for they are trustworthy and true. 3 Do not be afraid of plots against you, and do not be troubled by the unbelief of your opponents; 4 for everyone who does not believe will die because of his unbelief.

5 Beware! says the Lord; I am letting loose over the earth terrible evils, sword and famine, death and destruction, 6 because evil men have spread their wickedness the whole world over, and it is filled to overflowing with their deeds of violence. 7 Therefore the Lord declares: 8 I shall no longer keep silent about their godless acts, nor shall I tolerate their wicked practices. See how the blood of innocent victims cries to me for vengeance, and the souls of the just never cease to plead with me! 9 I shall most surely avenge them, says the Lord, and give ear to the plea of all the innocent blood that has been shed. 10 My people are being led like sheep to the slaughter. I shall allow them to remain in Egypt no longer, 11 but shall rescue them with a strong hand and an outstretched arm; I shall strike the Egyptians with plagues, as I did once before, and bring ruin on their whole land. 12 Shaken to its very foundations, how Egypt will mourn when scourged and chastised by plagues from the Lord! 13 How workers on the land will mourn when seed fails to grow and their trees are devastated by blight and hail and terrible storm! 14 Woe to the world and its inhabitants: 15 the sword that will destroy them is not far distant! With blade unsheathed, nation will rise against nation. 16 Stable government will be at an end; as one faction prevails over another, they will in their day of power care nothing for king or magnate. 17 Anyone wishing to visit a city will find himself unable to do so, 18 for rival ambitions will have reduced cities to chaos, demolishing houses and inspiring widespread fear. 19 Sword in hand, a man will attack his

---

[h] Syr Compare Ethiop Arab 2 Arm: Meaning of Lat uncertain [i] Syr Ethiop Arab 1 Arm: Meaning of Lat uncertain [j] Syr Arab 1: Lat lacks *twenty-four* [k] Syr adds *in the seventh year of the sixth week, five thousand years and three months and twelve days after creation. At that time Ezra was caught up, and taken to the place of those who are like him, after he had written all these things. And he was called the scribe of the knowledge of the Most High for ever and ever.* Ethiop Arab 1 Arm have a similar ending [l] Chapters 15 and 16 (except 15.57-59, which has been found in Greek) are extant only in Lat [m] Other ancient authorities add *and all who believe shall be saved by their faith* [n] Lat lacks *to grow*

15:4 **because . . . unbelief:** *or* in his unbelief.

19 People shall have no pity for their neighbors, but shall make an assault upon*o* their houses with the sword, and plunder their goods, because of hunger for bread and because of great tribulation.

20 See how I am calling together all the kings of the earth to turn to me, says God, from the rising sun and from the south, from the east and from Lebanon; to turn and repay what they have given them. 21 Just as they have done to my elect until this day, so I will do, and will repay into their bosom. Thus says the Lord God: 22 My right hand will not spare the sinners, and my sword will not cease from those who shed innocent blood on earth. 23 And a fire went forth from his wrath, and consumed the foundations of the earth and the sinners, like burnt straw. 24 Alas for those who sin and do not observe my commandments, says the Lord; *p* 25 I will not spare them. Depart, you faithless children! Do not pollute my sanctuary. 26 For God*q* knows all who sin against him; therefore he will hand them over to death and slaughter. 27 Already calamities have come upon the whole earth, and you shall remain in them; God*q* will not deliver you, because you have sinned against him.

28 What a terrifying sight, appearing from the east! 29 The nations of the dragons of Arabia shall come out with many chariots, and from the day that they set out, their hissing shall spread over the earth, so that all who hear them will fear and tremble. 30 Also the Carmonians, raging in wrath, shall go forth like wild boars*r* from the forest, and with great power they shall come and engage them in battle, and with their tusks they shall devastate a portion of the land of the Assyrians with their teeth. 31 And then the dragons,*s* remembering their origin, shall become still stronger; and if they combine in great power and turn to pursue them, 32 then these shall be disorganized and silenced by their power, and shall turn and flee.*t* 33 And from the land of the Assyrians an enemy in ambush shall attack them and destroy one of them, and fear and trembling shall come upon their army, and indecision upon their kings.

34 See the clouds from the east, and from the north to the south! Their appearance is exceedingly threatening, full of wrath and storm. 35 They shall clash against one another and shall pour out a heavy tempest on the earth, and their own tempest;*u* and there shall be blood from the sword as high as a horse's belly 36 and a man's thigh and a camel's hock. 37 And there shall be fear and great trembling on the earth; those who see that wrath shall be horror-stricken, and they shall be seized with trembling. 38 After that, heavy storm clouds shall be stirred up from the south, and from the north, and another part from the west. 39 But the winds from the east shall prevail over the cloud that was*v* raised in wrath, and shall dispel it; and the tempest*u* that was to cause destruction by the east wind shall be driven violently toward the south and west. 40 Great and mighty clouds, full of wrath and tempest, shall rise and destroy all the earth and its inhabitants, and shall pour out upon every high and lofty place*w* a terrible tempest, 41 fire and hail and flying swords and floods of water, so that all the fields and all the streams shall be filled with the abundance of those waters. 42 They shall destroy cities and walls, mountains and hills, trees of the forests, and grass of the meadows, and their grain. 43 They shall go on steadily to Babylon and blot it out.

neighbour's house and plunder his possessions; when he is driven by famine and grinding misery, no pity will restrain him.

20 See how I summon all the kings of the earth, God says, from the sunrise and the south wind, from the east and the south, to turn and repay what has been given to them. 21 I shall do to them as they are doing to my chosen ones even to the present day; I shall pay them back in their own coin.

These are the words of the Lord God: 22 I shall show sinners no pity; the sword will not spare those murderers who stain the ground with innocent blood. 23 The Lord's anger has burst out in flame, scorching the earth to its foundations and consuming sinners like burning straw. 24 Woe to sinners who flout my commands! says the Lord; 25 I shall show them no mercy. Away from me, you rebels! Do not pollute my sanctuary with your presence. 26 The Lord well knows all who offend against him, and has consigned them to death and destruction. 27 Already calamities have spread over the world, and there is no escape for you; God will refuse to rescue you, because you have sinned against him.

28 How terrible is the vision that comes from the east! 29 Hordes of dragons from Arabia will sally forth with countless chariots, and from the first day of their advance their hissing is borne across the land, so that all who hear them will tremble in fear. 30 The Carmanians, beside themselves with fury, will rush like wild boars out of a thicket, advancing in full force to do battle with them; they will devastate whole tracts of Assyria with their tusks. 31 But then the dragons will summon up their native fury and prove the stronger. Massing all their forces, they will fall on the Carmanians with overwhelming might 32 until, routed and their power silenced, the Carmanians turn to flight. 33 Their way will be blocked by a lurking enemy from Assyria, and when one of them is killed, terror and trembling will spread in their army and confusion among their kings.

34 See the clouds stretching from east and north to south! Full of fury and tempest, their appearance is hideous. 35 They will clash together, letting loose a vast storm over the land; blood, shed by the sword, will reach as high as a horse's belly, 36 a man's thigh, or a camel's hock. 37 There will be terror and trembling throughout the world; those who see the fury rage will shudder, stricken with panic. 38 Then vast storm-clouds will approach from south and north, and others from the west. 39 But the winds from the east will be stronger still, and will hold in check the raging cloud and its leader; and the storm which was bent on destruction will be fiercely driven back to the south and west by the winds from the east. 40 Huge clouds, mighty and full of fury, will pile up and ravage the whole land and its inhabitants, and a terrible storm will sweep over all that is high and exalted, 41 with fire and hail and flying swords and a deluge of water which will flood all the plains and rivers. 42 They will flatten to the ground cities and walls, mountains and hills, trees in the woods and crops in the fields. 43 They will force their way to Babylon, and destroy her;

o Cn: Lat *shall empty*   *p* Other ancient authorities read *God*
q Other ancient authorities read *the Lord*   *r* Other ancient authorities
lack *like wild boars*   *s* Cn: Lat *dragon*   *t* Other ancient
authorities read *turn their face to the north*   *u* Meaning of Lat
uncertain   *v* Literally *that he*   *w* Or *eminent person*

44 They shall come to it and surround it; they shall pour out on it the tempest*x* and all its fury;*y* then the dust and smoke shall reach the sky, and all who are around it shall mourn for it. 45 And those who survive shall serve those who have destroyed it.

46 And you, Asia, who share in the splendor of Babylon and the glory of her person— 47 woe to you, miserable wretch! For you have made yourself like her; you have decked out your daughters for prostitution to please and glory in your lovers, who have always lusted after you. 48 You have imitated that hateful one in all her deeds and devices.*z* Therefore God*a* says, 49 I will send evils upon you: widowhood, poverty, famine, sword, and pestilence, bringing ruin to your houses, bringing destruction and death. 50 And the glory of your strength shall wither like a flower when the heat shall rise that is sent upon you. 51 You shall be weakened like a wretched woman who is beaten and wounded, so that you cannot receive your mighty lovers. 52 Would I have dealt with you so violently, says the Lord, 53 if you had not killed my chosen people continually, exulting and clapping your hands and talking about their death when you were drunk?

54 Beautify your face! 55 The reward of a prostitute is in your lap; therefore you shall receive your recompense. 56 As you will do to my chosen people, says the Lord, so God will do to you, and will hand you over to adversities. 57 Your children shall die of hunger, and you shall fall by the sword; your cities shall be wiped out, and all your people who are in the open country shall fall by the sword. 58 Those who are in the mountains and highlands*b* shall perish of hunger, and they shall eat their own flesh in hunger for bread and drink their own blood in thirst for water. 59 Unhappy above all others, you shall come and suffer fresh miseries. 60 As they pass by they shall crush the hateful*c* city, and shall destroy a part of your land and abolish a portion of your glory, when they return from devastated Babylon. 61 You shall be broken down by them like stubble,*d* and they shall be like fire to you. 62 They shall devour you and your cities, your land and your mountains; they shall burn with fire all your forests and your fruitful trees. 63 They shall carry your children away captive, plunder your wealth, and mar the glory of your countenance.

16 Woe to you, Babylon and Asia! Woe to you, Egypt and Syria! 2 Bind on sackcloth and cloth of goats' hair,*e* and wail for your children, and lament for them; for your destruction is at hand. 3 The sword has been sent upon you, and who is there to turn it back? 4 A fire has been sent upon you, and who is there to quench it? 5 Calamities have been sent upon you, and who is there to drive them away? 6 Can one drive off a hungry lion in the forest, or quench a fire in the stubble once it has started to burn?*f* 7 Can one turn back an arrow shot by a strong archer? 8 The Lord God sends calamities, and who will drive them away? 9 Fire will go forth from his wrath, and who is there to quench it? 10 He will flash lightning, and who will not be afraid? He will thunder, and who will not be terrified? 11 The Lord will threaten, and who will not be utterly shattered at his presence? 12 The earth and its foundations quake, the sea is churned up from the depths, and its waves and the fish with them shall be troubled at the presence of the Lord and the glory of his power. 13 For his right hand that bends the bow

44 for they will encompass her when they get there, and let loose a storm in all its fury. The dust and smoke will reach the sky, and all the neighbouring cities will mourn over her. 45 Any who survive in her will be enslaved by her destroyers.

46 And you, Asia, who have shared in the beauty and the glory of Babylon, 47 woe to you, miserable wretch! Like her you have dressed up your daughters as whores, to attract for your glorification the lovers who have always lusted for you. 48 You have imitated all the practices and schemes of that vile harlot. Therefore God says: 49 I shall unleash calamities on you—widowhood and poverty, famine, sword, and pestilence, to bring devastation to your homes with violence and death. 50 When the scorching heat bears down upon you, your strength and splendour will wither like a flower. 51 You will become a poor, weak woman, bruised, beaten, and wounded, unable any more to receive your wealthy lovers. 52 I should not be so fierce with you, says the Lord, 53 if you had not always killed my chosen ones, gloating over the blows you struck and hurling your drunken taunts at their corpses.

54 Paint your face; beautify yourself! 55 The prostitute's hire shall be yours; you will get what you have earned. 56 What you do to my chosen people, God will do to you, says the Lord; he will consign you to a terrible fate. 57 Your children will perish from hunger, you will fall by the sword, your cities will be reduced to rubble, and all your people will fall on the field of battle. 58 Those who are on the mountains will be dying of hunger: their hunger and thirst will drive them to gnaw their own flesh and drink their own blood. 59 You will be foremost in misery; and there will be more still to come. 60 As the victors go past on their way home from the sack of Babylon, they will reduce your peaceful city to dust, destroy a great part of your territory, and bring much of your splendour to an end. 61 They will destroy you—you will be stubble to their fire. 62 They will completely devour you and your cities, your land and your mountains, and will burn down all your woodlands and your fruit trees. 63 They will carry off your sons as captives and plunder your possessions; not a trace will be left of your splendid beauty.

16 Woe to you, Babylon and Asia! Woe to you, Egypt and Syria! 2 Put on sackcloth and hair shirt and raise a cry of lamentation over your people, for destruction is close at hand. 3 The sword is let loose against you, and who will turn it aside? 4 Fire is let loose upon you, and who will extinguish it? 5 Calamities have been let loose against you, and who is to avert them? 6 Can anyone drive off a hungry lion in the forest, or put out a fire among stubble once it has begun to blaze? 7 Can anyone ward off an arrow shot by a strong archer? 8 When the Lord God sends calamities, who can avert them? 9 When his anger bursts into flame, who can extinguish it? 10 When the lightning flashes, who will not tremble? When it thunders, who will not quake with dread? 11 When the Lord threatens, is there anyone who will not be crushed to the ground at his approach? 12 The earth is shaken to its very foundations, and the sea is churned up from the depths; its waves and all the fish are in turmoil before the presence of the Lord and the majesty of his power.

x Meaning of Lat uncertain   *y* Other ancient authorities add *until they destroy it to its foundations*   *z* Other ancient authorities add *you have followed after that one about to gratify her magnates and leaders so that you may be made proud and be pleased by her fornications*   *a* Other ancient authorities read *the Lord*   *b* Gk: Lat omits *and highlands*   *c* Another reading is *idle* or *unprofitable*   *d* Other ancient authorities read *like dry straw*   *e* Other ancient authorities lack *cloth of goats' hair*   *f* Other ancient authorities read *fire when dry straw has been set on fire*

is strong, and his arrows that he shoots are sharp and when they are shot to the ends of the world will not miss once. 14 Calamities are sent forth and shall not return until they come over the earth. 15 The fire is kindled, and shall not be put out until it consumes the foundations of the earth. 16 Just as an arrow shot by a mighty archer does not return, so the calamities that are sent upon the earth shall not return. 17 Alas for me! Alas for me! Who will deliver me in those days?

18 The beginning of sorrows, when there shall be much lamentation; the beginning of famine, when many shall perish; the beginning of wars, when the powers shall be terrified; the beginning of calamities, when all shall tremble. What shall they do, when the calamities come? 19 Famine and plague, tribulation and anguish are sent as scourges for the correction of humankind. 20 Yet for all this they will not turn from their iniquities, or ever be mindful of the scourges. 21 Indeed, provisions will be so cheap upon earth that people will imagine that peace is assured for them, and then calamities shall spring up on the earth — the sword, famine, and great confusion. 22 For many of those who live on the earth shall perish by famine; and those who survive the famine shall die by the sword. 23 And the dead shall be thrown out like dung, and there shall be no one to console them; for the earth shall be left desolate, and its cities shall be demolished. 24 No one shall be left to cultivate the earth or to sow it. 25 The trees shall bear fruit, but who will gather it? 26 The grapes shall ripen, but who will tread them? For in all places there shall be great solitude; 27 a person will long to see another human being, or even to hear a human voice. 28 For ten shall be left out of a city; and two, out of the field, those who have hidden themselves in thick groves and clefts in the rocks. 29 Just as in an olive orchard three or four olives may be left on every tree, 30 or just as when a vineyard is gathered, some clusters may be left g by those who search carefully through the vineyard, 31 so in those days three or four shall be left by those who search their houses with the sword. 32 The earth shall be left desolate, and its fields shall be plowed up, h and its roads and all its paths shall bring forth thorns, because no sheep will go along them. 33 Virgins shall mourn because they have no bridegrooms; women shall mourn because they have no husbands; their daughters shall mourn, because they have no help. 34 Their bridegrooms shall be killed in war, and their husbands shall perish of famine.

35 Listen now to these things, and understand them, you who are servants of the Lord. 36 This is word of the Lord; receive it and do not disbelieve what the Lord says. i 37 The calamities draw near, and are not delayed. 38 Just as a pregnant woman, in the ninth month when the time of her delivery draws near, has great pains around her womb for two or three hours beforehand, but when the child comes forth from the womb, there will not be a moment's delay, 39 so the calamities will not delay in coming upon the earth, and the world will groan, and pains will seize it on every side.

40 Hear my words, O my people; prepare for battle, and in the midst of the calamities be like strangers on the earth. 41 Let the one who sells be like one who will flee; let the one who buys be like one who will lose; 42 let the one who does business be like one who will not make a profit; and let the one who builds a house be like one who will not live in it; 43 let the one who sows be like one who will not reap; so also the one who prunes the vines, like one who will not gather the grapes; 44 those who marry, like those who will

13 Strong is his arm that bends the bow, and sharp the arrows he shoots; once they are on their way, nothing will stop them until they reach the ends of the earth. 14 Calamities are let loose, and will not turn back before they fetch up on earth. 15 The fire is alight and will not be put out until it has consumed earth's foundations. 16 An arrow shot by a powerful archer does not turn back; no more will the calamities let loose against the earth be recalled.

17 Alas, alas for me! Who will rescue me in those days? 18 At the onset of troubles, many will groan; at the onset of famine, many will die; at the onset of wars, empires will tremble; at the onset of bad times, all will be filled with terror. What will men do in the face of calamity? 19 Famine, plague, suffering, and hardship are scourges sent to teach them better ways; 20 but even so, they will not abandon their crimes or always keep the scourging in mind. 21 A time will come when food is so cheap that people will imagine peace and prosperity have arrived; but at that very moment the earth will become a hotbed of disasters — sword, famine, and anarchy. 22 Most of the inhabitants will die in the famine, while those who survive will be destroyed by the sword. 23 The dead will be thrown out like dung, and there will be no one to give them the last rites. The forsaken land will go to waste, and its cities to ruin; 24 no one will be left to cultivate the ground. 25 Trees will bear their fruits, but who will pick them? 26 Grapes will ripen, but who will tread them? There will be vast desolation everywhere. 27 A man will long to see a human face or hear a human voice, 28 for out of a whole city, only ten will survive, and in the countryside, only two will be left, hiding in the forest or in holes in the rocks. 29 As in an olive grove three or four olives might be left on each tree, 30 or as in a vineyard a few grapes might be overlooked by the sharp-eyed pickers, 31 so also in those days three or four will be overlooked by those who with sword in hand are searching the houses. 32 The forsaken land will go to waste and its fields be overrun with briars; thorns will grow over all the roads and paths, because there are no sheep to tread them. 33 Maidens will live in mourning with none to marry them; women will mourn because they have no husbands; their daughters will mourn because they have no one to support them. 34 The young men who should have been bridegrooms will have been killed in the war, and the men who were married will have been wiped out by the famine.

35 BUT you servants of the Lord, listen and learn. 36 This is the word of the Lord; take it to heart, and do not doubt what he says: 37 Calamities are close at hand, and will not be delayed. 38 When a woman is in the ninth month of her pregnancy and the moment of her child's birth is drawing near, there are two or three hours in which her womb suffers pangs of agony, and then the child comes from the womb without any further delay; 39 similarly, calamities will not defer their coming on the earth, and the world will groan under the pangs that beset it.

40 My people, listen to my words; get ready for battle, and when the calamities surround you, behave as though you were strangers on earth. 41 The seller must expect to have to run for his life, the buyer to lose what he buys; 42 the merchant must expect to make no profit, the builder never to live in the house he builds. 43 The sower must not expect to reap, nor should he who prunes the vine expect to harvest the grapes. 44 Those who marry must not look for children;

---

g Other ancient authorities read *a cluster may remain exposed*
h Other ancient authorities read *be for briers* i Cn: Lat *do not believe the gods of whom the Lord speaks*

NEW REVISED STANDARD VERSION

have no children; and those who do not marry, like those who are widowed. 45 Because of this those who labor, labor in vain; 46 for strangers shall gather their fruits, and plunder their goods, overthrow their houses, and take their children captive; for in captivity and famine they will produce their children. *j* 47 Those who conduct business, do so only to have it plundered; the more they adorn their cities, their houses and possessions, and their persons, 48 the more angry I will be with them for their sins, says the Lord. 49 Just as a respectable and virtuous woman abhors a prostitute, 50 so righteousness shall abhor iniquity, when she decks herself out, and shall accuse her to her face when he comes who will defend the one who searches out every sin on earth.

51 Therefore do not be like her or her works. 52 For in a very short time iniquity will be removed from the earth, and righteousness will reign over us. 53 Sinners must not say that they have not sinned;*k* for God*l* will burn coals of fire on the head of everyone who says, "I have not sinned before God and his glory." 54 The Lord*m* certainly knows everything that people do; he knows their imaginations and their thoughts and their hearts. 55 He said, "Let the earth be made," and it was made, and "Let the heaven be made," and it was made. 56 At his word the stars were fixed in their places, and he knows the number of the stars. 57 He searches the abyss and its treasures; he has measured the sea and its contents; 58 he has confined the sea in the midst of the waters;*n* and by his word he has suspended the earth over the water. 59 He has spread out the heaven like a dome and made it secure upon the waters; 60 he has put springs of water in the desert, and pools on the tops of the mountains, so as to send rivers from the heights to water the earth. 61 He formed human beings and put a heart in the midst of each body, and gave each person breath and life and understanding 62 and the spirit*o* of Almighty God, *p* who surely made all things and searches out hidden things in hidden places. 63 He knows your imaginations and what you think in your hearts! Woe to those who sin and want to hide their sins! 64 The Lord will strictly examine all their works, and will make a public spectacle of all of you. 65 You shall be put to shame when your sins come out before others, and your own iniquities shall stand as your accusers on that day. 66 What will you do? Or how will you hide your sins before the Lord and his glory? 67 Indeed, God*q* is the judge; fear him! Cease from your sins, and forget your iniquities, never to commit them again; so God*q* will lead you forth and deliver you from all tribulation.

68 The burning wrath of a great multitude is kindled over you; they shall drag some of you away and force you to eat what was sacrificed to idols. 69 And those who consent to eat shall be held in derision and contempt, and shall be trampled under foot. 70 For in many places*r* and in neighboring cities there shall be a great uprising against those who fear the Lord. 71 They shall*s* be like maniacs, sparing no one, but plundering and destroying those who continue to fear the Lord.*t* 72 For they shall destroy and plunder their goods, and drive them out of house and home. 73 Then the tested quality of my elect shall be manifest, like gold that is tested by fire.

j Other ancient authorities read *therefore those who are married may know that they will produce children for captivity and famine*
k Other ancient authorities add *or the unjust done injustice* *l* Lat *for he* *m* Other ancient authorities read *Lord God* *n* Other ancient authorities read *confined the world between the waters and the waters* *o* Or *breath* *p* Other ancient authorities read *of the Lord Almighty* *q* Other ancient authorities read *the Lord* *r* Meaning of Lat uncertain *s* Other ancient authorities read *For people, because of their misfortunes, shall* *t* Other ancient authorities read *fear God*

REVISED ENGLISH BIBLE

the unmarried must think of themselves as widowed. 45 For all who labour, labour in vain. 46 Their fruits will be gathered by foreigners, who will plunder their goods, pull down their houses, and take their sons captive, because only for captivity and famine will they bear children. 47 Any who make money do so only to have it plundered. The more care they lavish on their cities, houses, and property, and on their own persons, 48 the fiercer will be my indignation against their sins, says the Lord. 49 Like the indignation of a virtuous woman towards a prostitute, 50 so will be the indignation of justice towards wickedness decked out in finery; she will accuse her to her face, when the champion arrives to expose every sin on earth. 51 Therefore, do not imitate wickedness or her deeds; 52 in a very short time she will be swept away from the earth, and the reign of justice over us will begin.

53 Let not the sinner deny that he has sinned; he will only bring burning coals on his own head if he says, 'I have committed no sin against the majesty of God.' 54 Everything that men do is known to the Lord; he knows their plans, their schemes, their inmost thoughts. 55 He said, 'Let the earth be made,' and it was made; 'Let the heavens be made,' and they were made. 56 The stars were fixed in their places by his word, and he knows the number of the stars. 57 He looks into the depths with their treasures; by his word he has measured the sea and everything it contains. 58 By his word he confined the sea within the bounds of the waters and suspended the land above the water. 59 He spread out the sky like a vault, and fixed it firmly over the waters. 60 He provided springs in the desert, and pools on the mountaintops as the source of rivers flowing down to water the earth. 61 He created man, and put a heart in the middle of his body; he gave him breath, life, understanding, 62 and the very spirit of Almighty God who created all things and searches out secrets in secret places. 63 He knows well your plans and your inmost thoughts. Woe to sinners who try to conceal their sins! 64 The Lord will scrutinize all their deeds; he will call you all to account. 65 You will be covered with confusion, when your sins are brought into the open and your wicked deeds stand up to accuse you on that day. 66 What can you do? How will you hide your sins in the presence of God and his angels? 67 God is the judge; fear him! Abandon your sins, and have done with your wicked deeds for ever! Then God will set you free from all distress.

68 Fierce flames are being kindled to consume you. A great horde will descend on you; they will seize some of you and compel you to eat food sacrificed to idols. 69 Those who give in to them will be derided, taunted, and humiliated. 70 In place after place and throughout the neighbouring cities there will be a violent attack on those who fear the Lord. 71 Their enemies will be like maniacs, plundering and destroying without mercy all who still fear the Lord, 72 destroying and plundering their possessions, and ejecting them from their homes. 73 Then it will be seen that my chosen ones have stood the test like gold in the assayer's fire.

74 Listen, my elect ones, says the Lord; the days of tribulation are at hand, but I will deliver you from them. 75 Do not fear or doubt, for God[u] is your guide. 76 You who keep my commandments and precepts, says the Lord God, must not let your sins weigh you down, or your iniquities prevail over you. 77 Woe to those who are choked by their sins and overwhelmed by their iniquities! They are like a field choked with underbrush and its path[v] overwhelmed with thorns, so that no one can pass through. 78 It is shut off and given up to be consumed by fire.

[u] Other ancient authorities read *the Lord*   [v] Other ancient authorities read *seed*

74 Listen, you whom I have chosen, says the Lord: the days of harsh suffering are close at hand, but I shall rescue you from them. 75 Have done with fears and doubts! God is your guide. 76 As followers of my commandments and instructions, says the Lord God, you must not let your sins weigh you down or your wicked deeds gain the ascendancy. 77 Woe to those who are entangled in their sins and overrun with their wicked deeds! They are like a field where the path is entwined with bushes and brambles and there is no way through; 78 it is separated off in readiness for destruction by fire.

NEW REVISED STANDARD VERSION

(d) The following book appears in an appendix to the Greek Bible.

4 Maccabees is included only in the New Revised Standard Version translation.

4 Maccabees

1 The subject that I am about to discuss is most philosophical, that is, whether devout reason is sovereign over the emotions. So it is right for me to advise you to pay earnest attention to philosophy. 2 For the subject is essential to everyone who is seeking knowledge, and in addition it includes the praise of the highest virtue — I mean, of course, rational judgment. 3 If, then, it is evident that reason rules over those emotions that hinder self-control, namely, gluttony and lust, 4 it is also clear that it masters the emotions that hinder one from justice, such as malice, and those that stand in the way of courage, namely anger, fear, and pain. 5 Some might perhaps ask, "If reason rules the emotions, why is it not sovereign over forgetfulness and ignorance?" Their attempt at argument is ridiculous!*a* 6 For reason does not rule its own emotions, but those that are opposed to justice, courage, and self-control;*b* and it is not for the purpose of destroying them, but so that one may not give way to them.

7 I could prove to you from many and various examples that reason*c* is dominant over the emotions, 8 but I can demonstrate it best from the noble bravery of those who died for the sake of virtue, Eleazar and the seven brothers and their mother. 9 All of these, by despising sufferings that bring death, demonstrated that reason controls the emotions. 10 On this anniversary*d* it is fitting for me to praise for their virtues those who, with their mother, died for the sake of nobility and goodness, but I would also call them blessed for the honor in which they are held. 11 All people, even their torturers, marveled at their courage and endurance, and they became the cause of the downfall of tyranny over their nation. By their endurance they conquered the tyrant, and thus their native land was purified through them. 12 I shall shortly have an opportunity to speak of this; but, as my custom is, I shall begin by stating my main principle, and then I shall turn to their story, giving glory to the all-wise God.

13 Our inquiry, accordingly, is whether reason is sovereign over the emotions. 14 We shall decide just what reason is and what emotion is, how many kinds of emotions there are, and whether reason rules over all these. 15 Now reason is the mind that with sound logic prefers the life of wisdom. 16 Wisdom, next, is the knowledge of divine and human matters and the causes of these. 17 This, in turn, is education in the law, by which we learn divine matters reverently and human affairs to our advantage. 18 Now the kinds of wisdom are rational judgment, justice, courage, and self-control. 19 Rational judgment is supreme over all of these, since by means of it reason rules over the emotions. 20 The two most comprehensive types*e* of the emotions are pleasure and pain; and each of these is by nature concerned with both body and soul. 21 The emotions of both pleasure and pain have many consequences. 22 Thus desire precedes pleasure and delight follows it. 23 Fear precedes pain and sorrow comes after. 24 Anger, as a person will see by reflecting on this experience, is an emotion embracing pleasure and pain. 25 In pleasure there exists even a malevolent tendency, which is the most complex of all the emotions. 26 In the soul it is boastfulness, covetousness, thirst for honor, rivalry, and malice; 27 in the body, indiscriminate eating, gluttony, and solitary gormandizing.

28 Just as pleasure and pain are two plants growing from the body and the soul, so there are many offshoots of these plants,*f* 29 each of which the master cultivator, reason, weeds and prunes and ties up and waters and thoroughly irrigates, and so tames the jungle of habits and emotions. 30 For reason is the guide of the virtues, but over the emotions it is sovereign.

Observe now, first of all, that rational judgment is sovereign over the emotions by virtue of the restraining power of self-control. 31 Self-control, then, is dominance over the desires. 32 Some desires are mental, others are physical, and reason obviously rules over both. 33 Otherwise, how is it that when we are attracted to forbidden foods we abstain from the pleasure to be had from them? Is it not because reason is able to rule over appetites? I for one think so. 34 Therefore when we crave seafood and fowl and animals and all sorts of foods that are forbidden to us by the law, we abstain because of domination by reason. 35 For the emotions of the appetites are restrained, checked by the temperate mind, and all the impulses of the body are bridled by reason.

2 And why is it amazing that the desires of the mind for the enjoyment of beauty are rendered powerless? 2 It is for this reason, certainly, that the temperate Joseph is praised, because by mental effort*g* he overcame sexual desire. 3 For when he was young and in his prime for intercourse, by his reason he nullified the frenzy*h* of the passions. 4 Not only is reason proved to rule over the frenzied urge of sexual desire, but also over every desire.*i* 5 Thus the law says, "You shall not covet your neighbor's wife or anything that is your neighbor's." 6 In fact, since the law has told us not to covet, I could prove to you all the more that reason is able to control desires.

Just so it is with the emotions that hinder one from justice. 7 Otherwise how could it be that someone who is habitually a solitary gormandizer, a glutton, or even a drunkard can learn a better way, unless reason is clearly lord of the emotions? 8 Thus, as soon as one adopts a way of life in accordance with the law, even though a lover of money, one is forced to act contrary to natural ways and to lend without interest to the needy and to cancel the debt when the seventh year arrives. 9 If one is greedy, one is ruled by the law through reason so that one neither gleans the harvest nor gathers the last grapes from the vineyard.

In all other matters we can recognize that reason rules the emotions. 10 For the law prevails even over affection for parents, so that virtue is not abandoned for their sakes. 11 It is superior to love for one's wife, so that one rebukes her when she breaks the law. 12 It takes precedence over love for children, so that one punishes them for misdeeds. 13 It is sovereign over the relationship of friends, so that one rebukes friends when they act wickedly. 14 Do not consider it paradoxical when reason, through the law, can prevail even over enmity. The fruit trees of the enemy are not cut down, but one preserves the property of enemies

---

a Or *They are attempting to make my argument ridiculous!* *b* Other ancient authorities add *and rational judgment* *c* Other ancient authorities read *devout reason* *d* Gk *At this time* *e* Or *sources* *f* Other ancient authorities read *these emotions* *g* Other ancient authorities add *in reasoning* *h* Or *gadfly* *i* Or *all covetousness*

from marauders and helps raise up what has fallen.*j*

15 It is evident that reason rules even*k* the more violent emotions: lust for power, vainglory, boasting, arrogance, and malice. 16 For the temperate mind repels all these malicious emotions, just as it repels anger — for it is sovereign over even this. 17 When Moses was angry with Dathan and Abiram, he did nothing against them in anger, but controlled his anger by reason. 18 For, as I have said, the temperate mind is able to get the better of the emotions, to correct some, and to render others powerless. 19 Why else did Jacob, our most wise father, censure the households of Simeon and Levi for their irrational slaughter of the entire tribe of the Shechemites, saying, "Cursed be their anger"? 20 For if reason could not control anger, he would not have spoken thus. 21 Now when God fashioned human beings, he planted in them emotions and inclinations, 22 but at the same time he enthroned the mind among the senses as a sacred governor over them all. 23 To the mind he gave the law; and one who lives subject to this will rule a kingdom that is temperate, just, good, and courageous.

24 How is it then, one might say, that if reason is master of the emotions, it does not control forgetfulness and ignorance? 3 1 But this argument is entirely ridiculous; for it is evident that reason rules not over its own emotions, but over those of the body. 2 No one of us*l* can eradicate that kind of desire, but reason can provide a way for us not to be enslaved by desire. 3 No one of us can eradicate anger from the mind, but reason can help to deal with anger. 4 No one of us can eradicate malice, but reason can fight at our side so that we are not overcome by malice. 5 For reason does not uproot the emotions but is their antagonist.

6 Now this can be explained more clearly by the story of King David's thirst. 7 David had been attacking the Philistines all day long, and together with the soldiers of his nation had killed many of them. 8 Then when evening fell, he*m* came, sweating and quite exhausted, to the royal tent, around which the whole army of our ancestors had encamped. 9 Now all the rest were at supper, 10 but the king was extremely thirsty, and though springs were plentiful there, he could not satisfy his thirst from them. 11 But a certain irrational desire for the water in the enemy's territory tormented and inflamed him, undid and consumed him. 12 When his guards complained bitterly because of the king's craving, two staunch young soldiers, respecting*n* the king's desire, armed themselves fully, and taking a pitcher climbed over the enemy's ramparts. 13 Eluding the sentinels at the gates, they went searching throughout the enemy camp 14 and found the spring, and from it boldly brought the king a drink. 15 But David,*o* though he was burning with thirst, considered it an altogether fearful danger to his soul to drink what was regarded as equivalent to blood. 16 Therefore, opposing reason to desire, he poured out the drink as an offering to God. 17 For the temperate mind can conquer the drives of the emotions and quench the flames of frenzied desires; 18 it can overthrow bodily agonies even when they are extreme, and by nobility of reason spurn all domination by the emotions.

19 The present occasion now invites us to a narrative demonstration of temperate reason.

20 At a time when our ancestors were enjoying profound peace because of their observance of the law and were prospering, so that even Seleucus Nicanor, king of Asia, had both appropriated money to them for the temple service and recognized their commonwealth — 21 just at that time certain persons attempted a revolution against the

public harmony and caused many and various disasters.

4 Now there was a certain Simon, a political opponent of the noble and good man, Onias, who then held the high priesthood for life. When despite all manner of slander he was unable to injure Onias in the eyes of the nation, he fled the country with the purpose of betraying it. 2 So he came to Apollonius, governor of Syria, Phoenicia, and Cilicia, and said, 3 "I have come here because I am loyal to the king's government, to report that in the Jerusalem treasuries there are deposited tens of thousands in private funds, which are not the property of the temple but belong to King Seleucus." 4 When Apollonius learned the details of these things, he praised Simon for his service to the king and went up to Seleucus to inform him of the rich treasure. 5 On receiving authority to deal with this matter, he proceeded quickly to our country accompanied by the accursed Simon and a very strong military force. 6 He said that he had come with the king's authority to seize the private funds in the treasury. 7 The people indignantly protested his words, considering it outrageous that those who had committed deposits to the sacred treasury should be deprived of them, and did all that they could to prevent it. 8 But, uttering threats, Apollonius went on to the temple. 9 While the priests together with women and children were imploring God in the temple to shield the holy place that was being treated so contemptuously, 10 and while Apollonius was going up with his armed forces to seize the money, angels on horseback with lightning flashing from their weapons appeared from heaven, instilling in them great fear and trembling. 11 Then Apollonius fell down half dead in the temple area that was open to all, stretched out his hands toward heaven, and with tears begged the Hebrews to pray for him and propitiate the wrath of the heavenly army. 12 For he said that he had committed a sin deserving of death, and that if he were spared he would praise the blessedness of the holy place before all people. 13 Moved by these words, the high priest Onias, although otherwise he had scruples about doing so, prayed for him so that King Seleucus would not suppose that Apollonius had been overcome by human treachery and not by divine justice. 14 So Apollonius, *p* having been saved beyond all expectations, went away to report to the king what had happened to him.

15 When King Seleucus died, his son Antiochus Epiphanes succeeded to the throne, an arrogant and terrible man, 16 who removed Onias from the priesthood and appointed Onias's*q* brother Jason as high priest. 17 Jason*r* agreed that if the office were conferred on him he would pay the king three thousand six hundred sixty talents annually. 18 So the king appointed him high priest and ruler of the nation. 19 Jason*r* changed the nation's way of life and altered its form of government in complete violation of the law, 20 so that not only was a gymnasium constructed at the very citadel*s* of our native land, but also the temple service was abolished. 21 The divine justice was angered by these acts and caused Antiochus himself to make war on them. 22 For when he was warring against Ptolemy in Egypt, he heard that a rumor of his death had spread and that the people of Jerusalem had rejoiced greatly. He speedily marched against them, 23 and after he had plundered them he issued a decree that if any of them were found observing the ancestral law they should die. 24 When, by means of his decrees, he had not been able in any way to put an end to the people's observance of the law, but saw that all his threats and punishments were being disregarded 25 — even to the extent that women, because they had circumcised their sons, were thrown headlong from heights along with their infants, though they had known beforehand that they would suffer this — 26 when, I say, his decrees were despised by

---

j Or *the beasts that have fallen*   *k* Other ancient authorities read *through*   *l* Gk *you*   *m* Other ancient authorities read *he hurried and*   *n* Or *embarrassed because of*   *o* Gk *he*

p Gk *he*   *q* Gk *his*   *r* Gk *He*   *s* Or *high place*

the people, he himself tried through torture to compel everyone in the nation to eat defiling foods and to renounce Judaism.

5 The tyrant Antiochus, sitting in state with his counselors on a certain high place, and with his armed soldiers standing around him, 2 ordered the guards to seize each and every Hebrew and to compel them to eat pork and food sacrificed to idols. 3 If any were not willing to eat defiling food, they were to be broken on the wheel and killed. 4 When many persons had been rounded up, one man, Eleazar by name, leader of the flock, was brought[t] before the king. He was a man of priestly family, learned in the law, advanced in age, and known to many in the tyrant's court because of his philosophy.[u]

5 When Antiochus saw him he said, 6 "Before I begin to torture you, old man, I would advise you to save yourself by eating pork, 7 for I respect your age and your gray hairs. Although you have had them for so long a time, it does not seem to me that you are a philosopher when you observe the religion of the Jews. 8 When nature has granted it to us, why should you abhor eating the very excellent meat of this animal? 9 It is senseless not to enjoy delicious things that are not shameful, and wrong to spurn the gifts of nature. 10 It seems to me that you will do something even more senseless if, by holding a vain opinion concerning the truth, you continue to despise me to your own hurt. 11 Will you not awaken from your foolish philosophy, dispel your futile reasonings, adopt a mind appropriate to your years, philosophize according to the truth of what is beneficial, 12 and have compassion on your old age by honoring my humane advice? 13 For consider this: if there is some power watching over this religion of yours, it will excuse you from any transgression that arises out of compulsion."

14 When the tyrant urged him in this fashion to eat meat unlawfully, Eleazar asked to have a word. 15 When he had received permission to speak, he began to address the people as follows: 16 "We, O Antiochus, who have been persuaded to govern our lives by the divine law, think that there is no compulsion more powerful than our obedience to the law. 17 Therefore we consider that we should not transgress it in any respect. 18 Even if, as you suppose, our law were not truly divine and we had wrongly held it to be divine, not even so would it be right for us to invalidate our reputation for piety. 19 Therefore do not suppose that it would be a petty sin if we were to eat defiling food; 20 to transgress the law in matters either small or great is of equal seriousness, 21 for in either case the law is equally despised. 22 You scoff at our philosophy as though living by it were irrational, 23 but it teaches us self-control, so that we master all pleasures and desires, and it also trains us in courage, so that we endure any suffering willingly; 24 it instructs us in justice, so that in all our dealings we act impartially,[v] and it teaches us piety, so that with proper reverence we worship the only living God.

25 "Therefore we do not eat defiling food; for since we believe that the law was established by God, we know that in the nature of things the Creator of the world in giving us the law has shown sympathy toward us. 26 He has permitted us to eat what will be most suitable for our lives,[w] but he has forbidden us to eat meats that would be contrary to this. 27 It would be tyrannical for you to compel us not only to transgress the law, but also to eat in such a way that you may deride us for eating defiling foods, which are most hateful to us. 28 But you shall have no such occasion to laugh at me, 29 nor will I transgress the sacred oaths of my ancestors concerning the keeping of the law, 30 not even if

you gouge out my eyes and burn my entrails. 31 I am not so old and cowardly as not to be young in reason on behalf of piety. 32 Therefore get your torture wheels ready and fan the fire more vehemently! 33 I do not so pity my old age as to break the ancestral law by my own act. 34 I will not play false to you, O law that trained me, nor will I renounce you, beloved self-control. 35 I will not put you to shame, philosophical reason, nor will I reject you, honored priesthood and knowledge of the law. 36 You, O king,[x] shall not defile the honorable mouth of my old age, nor my long life lived lawfully. 37 My ancestors will receive me as pure, as one who does not fear your violence even to death. 38 You may tyrannize the ungodly, but you shall not dominate my religious principles, either by words or through deeds."

6 When Eleazar in this manner had made eloquent response to the exhortations of the tyrant, the guards who were standing by dragged him violently to the instruments of torture. 2 First they stripped the old man, though he remained adorned with the gracefulness of his piety. 3 After they had tied his arms on each side they flogged him, 4 while a herald who faced him cried out, "Obey the king's commands!" 5 But the courageous and noble man, like a true Eleazar, was unmoved, as though being tortured in a dream; 6 yet while the old man's eyes were raised to heaven, his flesh was being torn by scourges, his blood flowing, and his sides were being cut to pieces. 7 Although he fell to the ground because his body could not endure the agonies, he kept his reason upright and unswerving. 8 One of the cruel guards rushed at him and began to kick him in the side to make him get up again after he fell. 9 But he bore the pains and scorned the punishment and endured the tortures. 10 Like a noble athlete the old man, while being beaten, was victorious over his torturers; 11 in fact, with his face bathed in sweat, and gasping heavily for breath, he amazed even his torturers by his courageous spirit.

12 At that point, partly out of pity for his old age, 13 partly out of sympathy from their acquaintance with him, partly out of admiration for his endurance, some of the king's retinue came to him and said, 14 "Eleazar, why are you so irrationally destroying yourself through these evil things? 15 We will set before you some cooked meat; save yourself by pretending to eat pork."

16 But Eleazar, as though more bitterly tormented by this counsel, cried out: 17 "Never may we, the children of Abraham,[y] think so basely that out of cowardice we feign a role unbecoming to us! 18 For it would be irrational if having lived in accordance with truth up to old age and having maintained in accordance with the reputation of such a life, we should now change our course 19 and ourselves become a pattern of impiety to the young by setting them an example in the eating of defiling food. 20 It would be shameful if we should survive for a little while and during that time be a laughingstock to all for our cowardice, 21 and be despised by the tyrant as unmanly by not contending even to death for our divine law. 22 Therefore, O children of Abraham, die nobly for your religion! 23 And you, guards of the tyrant, why do you delay?"

24 When they saw that he was so courageous in the face of the afflictions, and that he had not been changed by their compassion, the guards brought him to the fire. 25 There they burned him with maliciously contrived instruments, threw him down, and poured stinking liquids into his nostrils. 26 When he was now burned to his very bones and about to expire, he lifted up his eyes to God and said, 27 "You know, O God, that though I might have saved myself, I am dying in burning torments for the sake of the law. 28 Be merciful to your people, and let our punishment suffice for them. 29 Make my blood their purification, and take

[t] Or was the first of the flock to be brought   [u] Other ancient authorities read his advanced age   [v] Or so that we hold in balance all our habitual inclinations   [w] Or souls

[x] Gk lacks O king   [y] Or O children of Abraham

my life in exchange for theirs." 30 After he said this, the holy man died nobly in his tortures; even in the tortures of death he resisted, by virtue of reason, for the sake of the law.

31 Admittedly, then, devout reason is sovereign over the emotions. 32 For if the emotions had prevailed over reason, we would have testified to their domination. 33 But now that reason has conquered the emotions, we properly attribute to it the power to govern. 34 It is right for us to acknowledge the dominance of reason when it masters even external agonies. It would be ridiculous to deny it.z 35 I have proved not only that reason has mastered agonies, but also that it masters pleasures and in no respect yields to them.

7 For like a most skillful pilot, the reason of our father Eleazar steered the ship of religion over the sea of the emotions, 2 and though buffeted by the stormings of the tyrant and overwhelmed by the mighty waves of tortures, 3 in no way did he turn the rudder of religion until he sailed into the haven of immortal victory. 4 No city besieged with many ingenious war machines has ever held out as did that most holy man. Although his sacred life was consumed by tortures and racks, he conquered the besiegers with the shield of his devout reason. 5 For in setting his mind firm like a jutting cliff, our father Eleazar broke the maddening waves of the emotions. 6 O priest, worthy of the priesthood, you neither defiled your sacred teeth nor profaned your stomach, which had room only for reverence and purity, by eating defiling foods. 7 O man in harmony with the law and philosopher of divine life! 8 Such should be those who are administrators of the law, shielding it with their own blood and noble sweat in sufferings even to death. 9 You, father, strengthened our loyalty to the law through your glorious endurance, and you did not abandon the holiness that you praised, but by your deeds you made your words of divinea philosophy credible. 10 O aged man, more powerful than tortures; O elder, fiercer than fire; O supreme king over the passions, Eleazar! 11 For just as our father Aaron, armed with the censer, ran through the multitude of the people and conquered the fieryb angel, 12 so the descendant of Aaron, Eleazar, though being consumed by the fire, remained unmoved in his reason. 13 Most amazing, indeed, though he was an old man, his body no longer tense and firm,c his muscles flabby, his sinews feeble, he became young again 14 in spirit through reason; and by reason like that of Isaac he rendered the many-headed rack ineffective. 15 O man of blessed age and of venerable gray hair and of law-abiding life, whom the faithful seal of death has perfected!

16 If, therefore, because of piety an aged man despised tortures even to death, most certainly devout reason is governor of the emotions. 17 Some perhaps might say, "Not all have full command of their emotions, because not all have prudent reason." 18 But as many as attend to religion with a whole heart, these alone are able to control the passions of the flesh, 19 since they believe that they, like our patriarchs Abraham and Isaac and Jacob, do not die to God, but live to God. 20 No contradiction therefore arises when some persons appear to be dominated by their emotions because of the weakness of their reason. 21 What person who lives as a philosopher by the whole rule of philosophy, and trusts in God, 22 and knows that it is blessed to endure any suffering for the sake of virtue, would not be able to overcome the emotions through godliness? 23 For only the wise and courageous are masters of their emotions.

8 For this is why even the very young, by following a philosophy in accordance with devout reason, have

prevailed over the most painful instruments of torture. 2 For when the tyrant was conspicuously defeated in his first attempt, being unable to compel an aged man to eat defiling foods, then in violent rage he commanded that others of the Hebrew captives be brought, and that any who ate defiling food would be freed after eating, but if any were to refuse, they would be tortured even more cruelly.

3 When the tyrant had given these orders, seven brothers — handsome, modest, noble, and accomplished in every way — were brought before him along with their aged mother. 4 When the tyrant saw them, grouped about their mother as though a chorus, he was pleased with them. And struck by their appearance and nobility, he smiled at them, and summoned them nearer and said, 5 "Young men, with favorable feelings I admire each and every one of you, and greatly respect the beauty and the number of such brothers. Not only do I advise you not to display the same madness as that of the old man who has just been tortured, but I also exhort you to yield to me and enjoy my friendship. 6 Just as I am able to punish those who disobey my orders, so I can be a benefactor to those who obey me. 7 Trust me, then, and you will have positions of authority in my government if you will renounce the ancestral tradition of your national life. 8 Enjoy your youth by adopting the Greek way of life and by changing your manner of living. 9 But if by disobedience you rouse my anger, you will compel me to destroy each and every one of you with dreadful punishments through tortures. 10 Therefore take pity on yourselves. Even I, your enemy, have compassion for your youth and handsome appearance. 11 Will you not consider this, that if you disobey, nothing remains for you but to die on the rack?"

12 When he had said these things, he ordered the instruments of torture to be brought forward so as to persuade them out of fear to eat the defiling food. 13 When the guards had placed before them wheels and joint-dislocators, rack and hooksd and catapultse and caldrons, braziers and thumbscrews and iron claws and wedges and bellows, the tyrant resumed speaking: 14 "Be afraid, young fellows; whatever justice you revere will be merciful to you when you transgress under compulsion."

15 But when they had heard the inducements and saw the dreadful devices, not only were they not afraid, but they also opposed the tyrant with their own philosophy, and by their right reasoning nullified his tyranny. 16 Let us consider, on the other hand, what arguments might have been used if some of them had been cowardly and unmanly. Would they not have been the following? 17 "O wretches that we are and so senseless! Since the king has summoned and exhorted us to accept kind treatment if we obey him, 18 why do we take pleasure in vain resolves and venture upon a disobedience that brings death? 19 O men and brothers, should we not fear the instruments of torture and consider the threats of torments, and give up this vain opinion and this arrogance that threatens to destroy us? 20 Let us take pity on our youth and have compassion on our mother's age; 21 and let us seriously consider that if we disobey we are dead! 22 Also, divine justice will excuse us for fearing the king when we are under compulsion. 23 Why do we banish ourselves from this most pleasant life and deprive ourselves of this delightful world? 24 Let us not struggle against compulsionf or take hollow pride in being put to the rack. 25 Not even the law itself would arbitrarily put us to death for fearing the instruments of torture. 26 Why does such contentiousness excite us and such a fatal stubbornness please us, when we can live in peace if we obey the king?"

27 But the youths, though about to be tortured, neither said any of these things nor even seriously considered them.

---

z Syr: Meaning of Gk uncertain   a Other ancient authorities lack divine   b Other ancient authorities lack fiery   c Gk the tautness of the body already loosed

d Meaning of Gk uncertain   e Here and elsewhere in 4 Macc an instrument of torture   f Or fate

28 For they were contemptuous of the emotions and sovereign over agonies, 29 so that as soon as the tyrant had ceased counseling them to eat defiling food, all with one voice together, as from one mind, said:

9 "Why do you delay, O tyrant? For we are ready to die rather than transgress our ancestral commandments; 2 we are obviously putting our forebears to shame unless we should practice ready obedience to the law and to Moses*g* our counselor. 3 Tyrant and counselor of lawlessness, in your hatred for us do not pity us more than we pity ourselves.*h* 4 For we consider this pity of yours, which insures our safety through transgression of the law, to be more grievous than death itself. 5 You are trying to terrify us by threatening us with death by torture, as though a short time ago you learned nothing from Eleazar. 6 And if the aged men of the Hebrews because of their religion lived piously*i* while enduring torture, it would be even more fitting that we young men should die despising your coercive tortures, which our aged instructor also overcame. 7 Therefore, tyrant, put us to the test; and if you take our lives because of our religion, do not suppose that you can injure us by torturing us. 8 For we, through this severe suffering and endurance, shall have the prize of virtue and shall be with God, on whose account we suffer; 9 but you, because of your bloodthirstiness toward us, will deservedly undergo from the divine justice eternal torment by fire."

10 When they had said these things, the tyrant was not only indignant, as at those who are disobedient, but also infuriated, as at those who are ungrateful. 11 Then at this command the guards brought forward the eldest, and having torn off his tunic, they bound his hands and arms with thongs on each side. 12 When they had worn themselves out beating him with scourges, without accomplishing anything, they placed him upon the wheel. 13 When the noble youth was stretched out around this, his limbs were dislocated, 14 and with every member disjointed he denounced the tyrant, saying, 15 "Most abominable tyrant, enemy of heavenly justice, savage of mind, you are mangling me in this manner, not because I am a murderer, or as one who acts impiously, but because I protect the divine law." 16 And when the guards said, "Agree to eat so that you may be released from the tortures," 17 he replied, "You abominable lackeys, your wheel is not so powerful as to strangle my reason. Cut my limbs, burn my flesh, and twist my joints; 18 through all these tortures I will convince you that children of the Hebrews alone are invincible where virtue is concerned." 19 While he was saying these things, they spread fire under him, and while fanning the flames*j* they tightened the wheel further. 20 The wheel was completely smeared with blood, and the heap of coals was being quenched by the drippings of gore, and pieces of flesh were falling off the axles of the machine. 21 Although the ligaments joining his bones were already severed, the courageous youth, worthy of Abraham, did not groan, 22 but as though transformed by fire into immortality, he nobly endured the rackings. 23 "Imitate me, brothers," he said. "Do not leave your post in my struggle*k* or renounce our courageous family ties. 24 Fight the sacred and noble battle for religion. Thereby the just Providence of our ancestors may become merciful to our nation and take vengeance on the accursed tyrant." 25 When he had said this, the saintly youth broke the thread of life.

26 While all were marveling at his courageous spirit, the guards brought in the next eldest, and after fitting themselves with iron gauntlets having sharp hooks, they bound him to the torture machine and catapult. 27 Before torturing him, they inquired if he were willing to eat, and they heard his noble decision.*l* 28 These leopard-like beasts tore out his sinews with the iron hands, flayed all his flesh up to his chin, and tore away his scalp. But he steadfastly endured this agony and said, 29 "How sweet is any kind of death for the religion of our ancestors!" 30 To the tyrant he said, "Do you not think, you most savage tyrant, that you are being tortured more than I, as you see the arrogant design of your tyranny being defeated by our endurance for the sake of religion? 31 I lighten my pain by the joys that come from virtue, 32 but you suffer torture by the threats that come from impiety. You will not escape, you most abominable tyrant, the judgments of the divine wrath."

10 When he too had endured a glorious death, the third was led in, and many repeatedly urged him to save himself by tasting the meat. 2 But he shouted, "Do you not know that the same father begot me as well as those who died, and the same mother bore me, and that I was brought up on the same teachings? 3 I do not renounce the noble kinship that binds me to my brothers."*m* 5 Enraged by the man's boldness, they disjointed his hands and feet with their instruments, dismembering him by prying his limbs from their sockets, 6 and breaking his fingers and arms and legs and elbows. 7 Since they were not able in any way to break his spirit,*n* they abandoned the instruments*o* and scalped him with their fingernails in a Scythian fashion. 8 They immediately brought him to the wheel, and while his vertebrae were being dislocated by this, he saw his own flesh torn all around and drops of blood flowing from his entrails. 9 When he was about to die, he said, 10 "We, most abominable tyrant, are suffering because of our godly training and virtue, 11 but you, because of your impiety and bloodthirstiness, will undergo unceasing torments."

12 When he too had died in a manner worthy of his brothers, they dragged in the fourth, saying, 13 "As for you, do not give way to the same insanity as your brothers, but obey the king and save yourself." 14 But he said to them, "You do not have a fire hot enough to make me play the coward. 15 No — by the blessed death of my brothers, by the eternal destruction of the tyrant, and by the everlasting life of the pious, I will not renounce our noble family ties. 16 Contrive tortures, tyrant, so that you may learn from them that I am a brother to those who have just now been tortured." 17 When he heard this, the bloodthirsty, murderous, and utterly abominable Antiochus gave orders to cut out his tongue. 18 But he said, "Even if you remove my organ of speech, God hears also those who are mute. 19 See, here is my tongue; cut it off, for in spite of this you will not make our reason speechless. 20 Gladly, for the sake of God, we let our bodily members be mutilated. 21 God will visit you swiftly, for you are cutting out a tongue that has been melodious with divine hymns."

11 When he too died, after being cruelly tortured, the fifth leaped up, saying, 2 "I will not refuse, tyrant, to be tortured for the sake of virtue. 3 I have come of my own accord, so that by murdering me you will incur punishment from the heavenly justice for even more crimes. 4 Hater of virtue, hater of humankind, for what act of ours are you destroying us in this way? 5 Is it because*p* we revere the Creator of all things and live according to his virtuous law? 6 But these deeds deserve honors, not tortures."*q*

---

g Other ancient authorities read *knowledge*   *h* Meaning of Gk uncertain   *i* Other ancient authorities read *died*   *j* Meaning of Gk uncertain   *k* Other ancient authorities read *post forever*   *l* Other ancient authorities read *having heard his noble decision, they tore him to shreds*   *m* Other ancient authorities add verse 4, *So if you have any instrument of torture, apply it to my body; for you cannot touch my soul, even if you wish.*   *n* Gk *to strangle him*   *o* Other ancient authorities read *they tore off his skin*   *p* Other ancient authorities read *Or does it seem evil to you that*   *q* Other ancient authorities add verses 7 and 8, *7 If you but understood human feelings and had hope of salvation from God— 8 but, as it is, you are a stranger to God and persecute those who serve him.*

9 While he was saying these things, the guards bound him and dragged him to the catapult; 10 they tied him to it on his knees, and fitting iron clamps on them, they twisted his back[r] around the wedge on the wheel,[s] so that he was completely curled back like a scorpion, and all his members were disjointed. 11 In this condition, gasping for breath and in anguish of body, 12 he said, "Tyrant, they are splendid favors that you grant us against your will, because through these noble sufferings you give us an opportunity to show our endurance for the law."

13 When he too had died, the sixth, a mere boy, was led in. When the tyrant inquired whether he was willing to eat and be released, he said, 14 "I am younger in age than my brothers, but I am their equal in mind. 15 Since to this end we were born and bred, we ought likewise to die for the same principles. 16 So if you intend to torture me for not eating defiling foods, go on torturing!" 17 When he had said this, they led him to the wheel. 18 He was carefully stretched tight upon it, his back was broken, and he was roasted[t] from underneath. 19 To his back they applied sharp spits that had been heated in the fire, and pierced his ribs so that his entrails were burned through. 20 While being tortured he said, "O contest befitting holiness, in which so many of us brothers have been summoned to an arena of sufferings for religion, and in which we have not been defeated! 21 For religious knowledge, O tyrant, is invincible. 22 I also, equipped with nobility, will die with my brothers, 23 and I myself will bring a great avenger upon you, you inventor of tortures and enemy of those who are truly devout. 24 We six boys have paralyzed your tyranny. 25 Since you have not been able to persuade us to change our mind or to force us to eat defiling foods, is not this your downfall? 26 Your fire is cold to us, and the catapults painless, and your violence powerless. 27 For it is not the guards of the tyrant but those of the divine law that are set over us; therefore, unconquered, we hold fast to reason."

12 When he too, thrown into the caldron, had died a blessed death, the seventh and youngest of all came forward. 2 Even though the tyrant had been vehemently reproached by the brothers, he felt strong compassion for this child when he saw that he was already in fetters. He summoned him to come nearer and tried to persuade him, saying, 3 "You see the result of your brothers' stupidity, for they died in torments because of their disobedience. 4 You too, if you do not obey, will be miserably tortured and die before your time, 5 but if you yield to persuasion you will be my friend and a leader in the government of the kingdom." 6 When he had thus appealed to him, he sent for the boy's mother to show compassion on her who had been bereaved of so many sons and to influence her to persuade the surviving son to obey and save himself. 7 But when his mother had exhorted him in the Hebrew language, as we shall tell a little later, 8 he said, "Let me loose, let me speak to the king and to all his friends that are with him." 9 Extremely pleased by the boy's declaration, they freed him at once. 10 Running to the nearest of the braziers, 11 he said, "You profane tyrant, most impious of all the wicked, since you have received good things and also your kingdom from God, were you not ashamed to murder his servants and torture on the wheel those who practice religion? 12 Because of this, justice has laid up for you intense and eternal fire and tortures, and these throughout all time[u] will never let you go. 13 As a man, were you not ashamed, you most savage beast, to cut out the tongues of men who have feelings like yours and are made of the same elements as you, and to maltreat and torture them in this way? 14 Surely they by dying nobly fulfilled their service to God, but you will wail bitterly for having killed without cause the contestants for virtue." 15 Then because he too was about to die, he said, 16 "I do not desert the excellent example[v] of my brothers, 17 and I call on the God of our ancestors to be merciful to our nation;[w] 18 but on you he will take vengeance both in this present life and when you are dead." 19 After he had uttered these imprecations, he flung himself into the braziers and so ended his life.[x]

13 Since, then, the seven brothers despised sufferings even unto death, everyone must concede that devout reason is sovereign over the emotions. 2 For if they had been slaves to their emotions and had eaten defiling food, we would say that they had been conquered by these emotions. 3 But in fact it was not so. Instead, by reason, which is praised before God, they prevailed over their emotions. 4 The supremacy of the mind over these cannot be overlooked, for the brothers[y] mastered both emotions and pains. 5 How then can one fail to confess the sovereignty of right reason over emotion in those who were not turned back by fiery agonies? 6 For just as towers jutting out over harbors hold back the threatening waves and make it calm for those who sail into the inner basin, 7 so the seven-towered right reason of the youths, by fortifying the harbor of religion, conquered the tempest of the emotions. 8 For they constituted a holy chorus of religion and encouraged one another, saying, 9 "Brothers, let us die like brothers for the sake of the law; let us imitate the three youths in Assyria who despised the same ordeal of the furnace. 10 Let us not be cowardly in the demonstration of our piety." 11 While one said, "Courage, brother," another said, "Bear up nobly," 12 and another reminded them, "Remember whence you came, and the father by whose hand Isaac would have submitted to being slain for the sake of religion." 13 Each of them and all of them together looking at one another, cheerful and undaunted, said, "Let us with all our hearts consecrate ourselves to God, who gave us our lives,[z] and let us use our bodies as a bulwark for the law. 14 Let us not fear him who thinks he is killing us, 15 for great is the struggle of the soul and the danger of eternal torment lying before those who transgress the commandment of God. 16 Therefore let us put on the full armor of self-control, which is divine reason. 17 For if we so die,[a] Abraham and Isaac and Jacob will welcome us, and all the fathers will praise us." 18 Those who were left behind said to each of the brothers who were being dragged away, "Do not put us to shame, brother, or betray the brothers who have died before us."

19 You are not ignorant of the affection of family ties, which the divine and all-wise Providence has bequeathed through the fathers to their descendants and which was implanted in the mother's womb. 20 There each of the brothers spent the same length of time and was shaped during the same period of time; and growing from the same blood and through the same life, they were brought to the light of day. 21 When they were born after an equal time of gestation, they drank milk from the same fountains. From such embraces brotherly-loving souls are nourished; 22 and they grow stronger from this common nurture and daily companionship, and from both general education and our discipline in the law of God.

23 Therefore, when sympathy and brotherly affection had been so established, the brothers were the more sympathetic to one another. 24 Since they had been educated by the same law and trained in the same virtues and brought up in right living, they loved one another all the more. 25 A common zeal for nobility strengthened their goodwill toward

---

[r] Gk loins   [s] Meaning of Gk uncertain   [t] Other ancient authorities add by fire   [u] Gk throughout the whole age   [v] Other ancient authorities read the witness   [w] Other ancient authorities read my race   [x] Gk and so gave up; other ancient authorities read gave up his spirit or his soul   [y] Gk they   [z] Or souls   [a] Other ancient authorities read suffer

one another, and their concord, 26 because they could make their brotherly love more fervent with the aid of their religion. 27 But although nature and companionship and virtuous habits had augmented the affection of family ties, those who were left endured for the sake of religion, while watching their brothers being maltreated and tortured to death.

14 Furthermore, they encouraged them to face the torture, so that they not only despised their agonies, but also mastered the emotions of brotherly love.

2 O reason,*b* more royal than kings and freer than the free! 3 O sacred and harmonious concord of the seven brothers on behalf of religion! 4 None of the seven youths proved coward or shrank from death, 5 but all of them, as though running the course toward immortality, hastened to death by torture. 6 Just as the hands and feet are moved in harmony with the guidance of the mind, so those holy youths, as though moved by an immortal spirit of devotion, agreed to go to death for its sake. 7 O most holy seven, brothers in harmony! For just as the seven days of creation move in choral dance around religion, 8 so these youths, forming a chorus, encircled the sevenfold fear of tortures and dissolved it. 9 Even now, we ourselves shudder as we hear of the suffering of these young men; they not only saw what was happening, not only heard the direct word of threat, but also bore the sufferings patiently, and in agonies of fire at that. 10 What could be more excruciatingly painful than this? For the power of fire is intense and swift, and it consumed their bodies quickly.

11 Do not consider it amazing that reason had full command over these men in their tortures, since the mind of woman despised even more diverse agonies, 12 for the mother of the seven young men bore up under the rackings of each one of her children.

13 Observe how complex is a mother's love for her children, which draws everything toward an emotion felt in her inmost parts. 14 Even unreasoning animals, as well as human beings, have a sympathy and parental love for their offspring. 15 For example, among birds, the ones that are tame protect their young by building on the housetops, 16 and the others, by building in precipitous chasms and in holes and tops of trees, hatch the nestlings and ward off the intruder. 17 If they are not able to keep the intruder*c* away, they do what they can to help their young by flying in circles around them in the anguish of love, warning them with their own calls. 18 And why is it necessary to demonstrate sympathy for children by the example of unreasoning animals, 19 since even bees at the time for making honeycombs defend themselves against intruders and, as though with an iron dart, sting those who approach their hive and defend it even to the death? 20 But sympathy for her children did not sway the mother of the young men; she was of the same mind as Abraham.

15 O reason of the children, tyrant over the emotions! O religion, more desirable to the mother than her children! 2 Two courses were open to this mother, that of religion, and that of preserving her seven sons for a time, as the tyrant had promised. 3 She loved religion more, the religion that preserves them for eternal life according to God's promise.*d* 4 In what manner might I express the emotions of parents who love their children? We impress upon the character of a small child a wondrous likeness both of mind and of form. Especially is this true of mothers, who because of their birth pangs have a deeper sympathy toward their offspring than do the fathers. 5 Considering that mothers are the weaker sex and give birth to many, they are more devoted to their children.*e* 6 The mother of the seven boys,

more than any other mother, loved her children. In seven pregnancies she had implanted in herself tender love toward them, 7 and because of the many pains she suffered with each of them she had sympathy for them; 8 yet because of the fear of God she disdained the temporary safety of her children. 9 Not only so, but also because of the nobility of her sons and their ready obedience to the law, she felt a greater tenderness toward them. 10 For they were righteous and self-controlled and brave and magnanimous, and loved their brothers and their mother, so that they obeyed her even to death in keeping the ordinances.

11 Nevertheless, though so many factors influenced the mother to suffer with them out of love for her children, in the case of none of them were the various tortures strong enough to pervert her reason. 12 But each child separately and all of them together the mother urged on to death for religion's sake. 13 O sacred nature and affection of parental love, yearning of parents toward offspring, nurture and indomitable suffering by mothers! 14 This mother, who saw them tortured and burned one by one, because of religion did not change her attitude. 15 She watched the flesh of her children being consumed by fire, their toes and fingers scattered*f* on the ground, and the flesh of the head to the chin exposed like masks.

16 O mother, tried now by more bitter pains than even the birth pangs you suffered for them! 17 O woman, who alone gave birth to such complete devotion! 18 When the firstborn breathed his last, it did not turn you aside, nor when the second in torments looked at you piteously nor when the third expired; 19 nor did you weep when you looked at the eyes of each one in his tortures gazing boldly at the same agonies, and saw in their nostrils the signs of the approach of death. 20 When you saw the flesh of children burned upon the flesh of other children, severed hands upon hands, scalped heads upon heads, and corpses fallen on other corpses, and when you saw the place filled with many spectators of the torturings, you did not shed tears. 21 Neither the melodies of sirens nor the songs of swans attract the attention of their hearers as did the voices of the children in torture calling to their mother. 22 How great and how many torments the mother suffered as her sons were tortured on the wheel and with the hot irons! 23 But devout reason, giving her heart a man's courage in the very midst of her emotions, strengthened her to disregard, for the time, her parental love.

24 Although she witnessed the destruction of seven children and the ingenious and various rackings, this noble mother disregarded all these*g* because of faith in God. 25 For as in the council chamber of her own soul she saw mighty advocates—nature, family, parental love, and the rackings of her children— 26 this mother held two ballots, one bearing death and the other deliverance for her children. 27 She did not approve the deliverance that would preserve the seven sons for a short time, 28 but as the daughter of God-fearing Abraham she remembered his fortitude.

29 O mother of the nation, vindicator of the law and champion of religion, who carried away the prize of the contest in your heart! 30 O more noble than males in steadfastness, and more courageous than men in endurance! 31 Just as Noah's ark, carrying the world in the universal flood, stoutly endured the waves, 32 so you, O guardian of the law, overwhelmed from every side by the flood of your emotions and the violent winds, the torture of your sons, endured nobly and withstood the wintry storms that assail religion.

16 If, then, a woman, advanced in years and mother of seven sons, endured seeing her children tortured to

---

b Or *O minds*   *c* Gk *it*   *d* Gk *according to God*   *e* Or *For to the degree that mothers are weaker and the more children they bear, the more they are devoted to their children.*

f Or *quivering*   *g* Other ancient authorities read *having bidden them farewell, surrendered them*

death, it must be admitted that devout reason is sovereign over the emotions. 2 Thus I have demonstrated not only that men have ruled over the emotions, but also that a woman has despised the fiercest tortures. 3 The lions surrounding Daniel were not so savage, nor was the raging fiery furnace of Mishael so intensely hot, as was her innate parental love, inflamed as she saw her seven sons tortured in such varied ways. 4 But the mother quenched so many and such great emotions by devout reason.

5 Consider this also: If this woman, though a mother, had been fainthearted, she would have mourned over them and perhaps spoken as follows: 6 "O how wretched am I and many times unhappy! After bearing seven children, I am now the mother of none! 7 O seven childbirths all in vain, seven profitless pregnancies, fruitless nurturings and wretched nursings! 8 In vain, my sons, I endured many birth pangs for you, and the more grievous anxieties of your upbringing. 9 Alas for my children, some unmarried, others married and without offspring.h I shall not see your children or have the happiness of being called grandmother. 10 Alas, I who had so many and beautiful children am a widow and alone, with many sorrows.i 11 And when I die, I shall have none of my sons to bury me."

12 Yet that holy and God-fearing mother did not wail with such a lament for any of them, nor did she dissuade any of them from dying, nor did she grieve as they were dying. 13 On the contrary, as though having a mind like adamant and giving rebirth for immortality to the whole number of her sons, she implored them and urged them on to death for the sake of religion. 14 O mother, soldier of God in the cause of religion, elder and woman! By steadfastness you have conquered even a tyrant, and in word and deed you have proved more powerful than a man. 15 For when you and your sons were arrested together, you stood and watched Eleazar being tortured, and said to your sons in the Hebrew language, 16 "My sons, noble is the contest to which you are called to bear witness for the nation. Fight zealously for our ancestral law. 17 For it would be shameful if, while an aged man endures such agonies for the sake of religion, you young men were to be terrified by tortures. 18 Remember that it is through God that you have had a share in the world and have enjoyed life, 19 and therefore you ought to endure any suffering for the sake of God. 20 For his sake also our father Abraham was zealous to sacrifice his son Isaac, the ancestor of our nation; and when Isaac saw his father's hand wielding a knifej and descending upon him, he did not cower. 21 Daniel the righteous was thrown to the lions, and Hananiah, Azariah, and Mishael were hurled into the fiery furnace and endured it for the sake of God. 22 You too must have the same faith in God and not be grieved. 23 It is unreasonable for people who have religious knowledge not to withstand pain."

24 By these words the mother of the seven encouraged and persuaded each of her sons to die rather than violate God's commandment. 25 They knew also that those who die for the sake of God live to God, as do Abraham and Isaac and Jacob and all the patriarchs.

17 Some of the guards said that when she also was about to be seized and put to death she threw herself into the flames so that no one might touch her body.

2 O mother, who with your seven sons nullified the violence of the tyrant, frustrated his evil designs, and showed the courage of your faith! 3 Nobly set like a roof on the pillars of your sons, you held firm and unswerving against the earthquake of the tortures. 4 Take courage, therefore, O holy-minded mother, maintaining firm an enduring hope in God. 5 The moon in heaven, with the stars, does not stand so august as you, who, after lighting the way of your star-

like seven sons to piety, stand in honor before God and are firmly set in heaven with them. 6 For your children were true descendants of father Abraham.k

7 If it were possible for us to paint the history of your religion as an artist might, would not those who first beheld it have shuddered as they saw the mother of the seven children enduring their varied tortures to death for the sake of religion? 8 Indeed it would be proper to inscribe on their tomb these words as a reminder to the people of our nation:l

9 "Here lie buried an aged priest and an aged woman and seven sons, because of the violence of the tyrant who wished to destroy the way of life of the Hebrews. 10 They vindicated their nation, looking to God and enduring torture even to death."

11 Truly the contest in which they were engaged was divine, 12 for on that day virtue gave the awards and tested them for their endurance. The prize was immortality in endless life. 13 Eleazar was the first contestant, the mother of the seven sons entered the competition, and the brothers contended. 14 The tyrant was the antagonist, and the world and the human race were the spectators. 15 Reverence for God was victor and gave the crown to its own athletes. 16 Who did not admire the athletes of the divinem legislation? Who were not amazed?

17 The tyrant himself and all his council marveled at theirn endurance, 18 because of which they now stand before the divine throne and live the life of eternal blessedness. 19 For Moses says, "All who are consecrated are under your hands." 20 These, then, who have been consecrated for the sake of God,o are honored, not only with this honor, but also by the fact that because of them our enemies did not rule over our nation, 21 the tyrant was punished, and the homeland purified — they having become, as it were, a ransom for the sin of our nation. 22 And through the blood of those devout ones and their death as an atoning sacrifice, divine Providence preserved Israel that previously had been mistreated.

23 For the tyrant Antiochus, when he saw the courage of their virtue and their endurance under the tortures, proclaimed them to his soldiers as an example for their own endurance, 24 and this made them brave and courageous for infantry battle and siege, and he ravaged and conquered all his enemies.

18 O Israelite children, offspring of the seed of Abraham, obey this law and exercise piety in every way, 2 knowing that devout reason is master of all emotions, not only of sufferings from within, but also of those from without.

3 Therefore those who gave over their bodies in suffering for the sake of religion were not only admired by mortals, but also were deemed worthy to share in a divine inheritance. 4 Because of them the nation gained peace, and by reviving observance of the law in the homeland they ravaged the enemy. 5 The tyrant Antiochus was both punished on earth and is being chastised after his death. Since in no way whatever was he able to compel the Israelites to become pagans and to abandon their ancestral customs, he left Jerusalem and marched against the Persians.

6 The mother of seven sons expressed also these principles to her children: 7 "I was a pure virgin and did not go outside my father's house; but I guarded the rib from which woman was made.p 8 No seducer corrupted me on a desert

k Gk For your childbearing was from Abraham the father; other ancient authorities read For . . . Abraham the servant   l Or as a memorial to the heroes of our people   m Other ancient authorities read true   n Other ancient authorities add virtue and   o Other ancient authorities lack for the sake of God   p Gk the rib that was built

h Gk without benefit   i Or much to be pitied   j Gk sword

plain, nor did the destroyer, the deceitful serpent, defile the purity of my virginity. 9 In the time of my maturity I remained with my husband, and when these sons had grown up their father died. A happy man was he, who lived out his life with good children, and did not have the grief of bereavement. 10 While he was still with you, he taught you the law and the prophets. 11 He read to you about Abel slain by Cain, and Isaac who was offered as a burnt offering, and about Joseph in prison. 12 He told you of the zeal of Phinehas, and he taught you about Hananiah, Azariah, and Mishael in the fire. 13 He praised Daniel in the den of the lions and blessed him. 14 He reminded you of the scripture of Isaiah, which says, 'Even though you go through the fire, the flame shall not consume you.' 15 He sang to you songs of the psalmist David, who said, 'Many are the afflictions of the righteous.' 16 He recounted to you Solomon's proverb, 'There is a tree of life for those who do his will.' 17 He confirmed the query of Ezekiel, 'Shall these dry bones

live?' 18 For he did not forget to teach you the song that Moses taught, which says, 19 'I kill and I make alive: this is your life and the length of your days.' "

20 O bitter was that day — and yet not bitter — when that bitter tyrant of the Greeks quenched fire with fire in his cruel caldrons, and in his burning rage brought those seven sons of the daughter of Abraham to the catapult and back again to more *q* tortures, 21 pierced the pupils of their eyes and cut out their tongues, and put them to death with various tortures. 22 For these crimes divine justice pursued and will pursue the accursed tyrant. 23 But the sons of Abraham with their victorious mother are gathered together into the chorus of the fathers, and have received pure and immortal *r* souls from God, 24 to whom be glory forever and ever. Amen.

q Other ancient authorities read *to all his*   *r* Other ancient authorities read *victorious*

The New Covenant Commonly Called

THE NEW TESTAMENT

THE GOSPEL ACCORDING TO

Matthew

THE GOSPEL ACCORDING TO

Matthew

1 An account of the genealogy^a of Jesus the Messiah,^b the son of David, the son of Abraham.

2 Abraham was the father of Isaac, and Isaac the father of Jacob, and Jacob the father of Judah and his brothers, 3 and Judah the father of Perez and Zerah by Tamar, and Perez the father of Hezron, and Hezron the father of Aram, 4 and Aram the father of Aminadab, and Aminadab the father of Nahshon, and Nahshon the father of Salmon, 5 and Salmon the father of Boaz by Rahab, and Boaz the father of Obed by Ruth, and Obed the father of Jesse, 6 and Jesse the father of King David.

And David was the father of Solomon by the wife of Uriah, 7 and Solomon the father of Rehoboam, and Rehoboam the father of Abijah, and Abijah the father of Asaph,^c 8 and Asaph^c the father of Jehoshaphat, and Jehoshaphat the father of Joram, and Joram the father of Uzziah, 9 and Uzziah the father of Jotham, and Jotham the father of Ahaz, and Ahaz the father of Hezekiah, 10 and Hezekiah the father of Manasseh, and Manasseh the father of Amos,^d and Amos^d the father of Josiah, 11 and Josiah the father of Jechoniah and his brothers, at the time of the deportation to Babylon.

12 And after the deportation to Babylon: Jechoniah was the father of Salathiel, and Salathiel the father of Zerubbabel, 13 and Zerubbabel the father of Abiud, and Abiud the father of Eliakim, and Eliakim the father of Azor, 14 and Azor the father of Zadok, and Zadok the father of Achim, and Achim the father of Eliud, 15 and Eliud the father of Eleazar, and Eleazar the father of Matthan, and Matthan the father of Jacob, 16 and Jacob the father of Joseph the husband of Mary, of whom Jesus was born, who is called the Messiah.^e

17 So all the generations from Abraham to David are fourteen generations; and from David to the deportation to Babylon, fourteen generations; and from the deportation to Babylon to the Messiah,^e fourteen generations.

18 Now the birth of Jesus the Messiah^b took place in this way. When his mother Mary had been engaged to Joseph, but before they lived together, she was found to be with child from the Holy Spirit. 19 Her husband Joseph, being a righteous man and unwilling to expose her to public disgrace, planned to dismiss her quietly. 20 But just when he

1 THE genealogy of Jesus Christ, son of David, son of Abraham.

2 Abraham was the father of Isaac, Isaac of Jacob, Jacob of Judah and his brothers, 3 Judah of Perez and Zarah (their mother was Tamar), Perez of Hezron, Hezron of Ram, 4 Ram of Amminadab, Amminadab of Nahshon, Nahshon of Salmon, 5 Salmon of Boaz (his mother was Rahab), Boaz of Obed (his mother was Ruth), Obed of Jesse; 6 and Jesse was the father of King David.

David was the father of Solomon (his mother had been the wife of Uriah), 7 Solomon of Rehoboam, Rehoboam of Abijah, Abijah of Asa, 8 Asa of Jehoshaphat, Jehoshaphat of Joram, Joram of Uzziah, 9 Uzziah of Jotham, Jotham of Ahaz, Ahaz of Hezekiah, 10 Hezekiah of Manasseh, Manasseh of Amon, Amon of Josiah; 11 and Josiah was the father of Jeconiah and his brothers at the time of the deportation to Babylon.

12 After the deportation Jeconiah was the father of Shealtiel, Shealtiel of Zerubbabel, 13 Zerubbabel of Abiud, Abiud of Eliakim, Eliakim of Azor, 14 Azor of Zadok, Zadok of Achim, Achim of Eliud, 15 Eliud of Eleazar, Eleazar of Matthan, Matthan of Jacob, 16 Jacob of Joseph, the husband of Mary, who gave birth to Jesus called Messiah.

17 There were thus fourteen generations in all from Abraham to David, fourteen from David until the deportation to Babylon, and fourteen from the deportation until the Messiah.

18 THIS is how the birth of Jesus Christ came about. His mother Mary was betrothed to Joseph; before their marriage she found she was going to have a child through the Holy Spirit. 19 Being a man of principle, and at the same time wanting to save her from exposure, Joseph made up his mind to have the marriage contract quietly set aside. 20 He

^a Or *birth*   ^b Or *Jesus Christ*   ^c Other ancient authorities read *Asa*
^d Other ancient authorities read *Amon*   ^e Or *the Christ*

THE GOSPEL ACCORDING TO
Matthew

1 The book of the genealogy of Jesus Christ, the son of David, the son of Abraham.

2 Abraham became the father of Isaac, Isaac the father of Jacob, Jacob the father of Judah and his brothers. 3 Judah became the father of Perez and Zerah, whose mother was Tamar. Perez became the father of Hezron, Hezron the father of Ram, 4 Ram the father of Amminadab. Amminadab became the father of Nahshon, Nahshon the father of Salmon, 5 Salmon the father of Boaz, whose mother was Rahab. Boaz became the father of Obed, whose mother was Ruth. Obed became the father of Jesse, 6 Jesse the father of David the king.

David became the father of Solomon, whose mother had been the wife of Uriah. 7 Solomon became the father of Rehoboam, Rehoboam the father of Abijah, Abijah the father of Asaph. 8 Asaph became the father of Jehoshaphat, Jehoshaphat the father of Joram, Joram the father of Uzziah. 9 Uzziah became the father of Jotham, Jotham the father of Ahaz, Ahaz the father of Hezekiah. 10 Hezekiah became the father of Manasseh, Manasseh the father of Amos, Amos the father of Josiah. 11 Josiah became the father of Jechoniah and his brothers at the time of the Babylonian exile.

12 After the Babylonian exile, Jechoniah became the father of Shealtiel, Shealtiel the father of Zerubbabel, 13 Zerubbabel the father of Abiud. Abiud became the father of Eliakim, Eliakim the father of Azor, 14 Azor the father of Zadok. Zadok became the father of Achim, Achim the father of Eliud, 15 Eliud the father of Eleazar. Eleazar became the father of Matthan, Matthan the father of Jacob, 16 Jacob the father of Joseph, the husband of Mary. Of her was born Jesus who is called the Messiah.

17 Thus the total number of generations from Abraham to David is fourteen generations; from David to the Babylonian exile, fourteen generations; from the Babylonian exile to the Messiah, fourteen generations.

18 Now this is how the birth of Jesus Christ came about. When his mother Mary was betrothed to Joseph, but before they lived together, she was found with child through the holy Spirit. 19 Joseph her husband, since he was a righteous man, yet unwilling to expose her to shame, decided to divorce her quietly. 20 Such was his intention when, behold,

THE GOSPEL ACCORDING TO
Matthew

1 Roll of the genealogy of Jesus Christ, son of David, son of Abraham:

2 Abraham fathered Isaac,
Isaac fathered Jacob,
Jacob fathered Judah and his brothers,
3 Judah fathered Perez and Zerah, whose mother was Tamar,
Perez fathered Hezron,
Hezron fathered Ram,
4 Ram fathered Amminadab,
Amminadab fathered Nahshon,
Nahshon fathered Salmon,
5 Salmon fathered Boaz, whose mother was Rahab,
Boaz fathered Obed, whose mother was Ruth,
Obed fathered Jesse;
6 and Jesse fathered King David.

David fathered Solomon, whose mother had been Uriah's wife,
7 Solomon fathered Rehoboam,
Rehoboam fathered Abijah,
Abijah fathered Asa,
8 Asa fathered Jehoshaphat,
Jehoshaphat fathered Joram,
Joram fathered Uzziah,
9 Uzziah fathered Jotham,
Jotham fathered Ahaz,
Ahaz fathered Hezekiah,
10 Hezekiah fathered Manasseh,
Manasseh fathered Amon,
Amon fathered Josiah;
11 and Josiah fathered Jechoniah and his brothers.
Then the deportation to Babylon took place.

12 After the deportation to Babylon:
Jechoniah fathered Shealtiel,
Shealtiel fathered Zerubbabel,
13 Zerubbabel fathered Abiud,
Abiud fathered Eliakim,
Eliakim fathered Azor,
14 Azor fathered Zadok,
Zadok fathered Achim,
Achim fathered Eliud,
15 Eliud fathered Eleazar,
Eleazar fathered Matthan,
Matthan fathered Jacob;
16 and Jacob fathered Joseph the husband of Mary;
of her was born Jesus who is called Christ.

17 The sum of generations is therefore: fourteen from Abraham to David; fourteen from David to the Babylonian deportation; and fourteen from the Babylonian deportation to Christ.

18 This is how Jesus Christ came to be born. His mother Mary was betrothed to Joseph; but before they came to live together she was found to be with child through the Holy Spirit. 19 Her husband Joseph, being an upright man and wanting to spare her disgrace, decided to divorce her informally. 20 He had made up his mind to do this when suddenly

NEW REVISED STANDARD VERSION

had resolved to do this, an angel of the Lord appeared to him in a dream and said, "Joseph, son of David, do not be afraid to take Mary as your wife, for the child conceived in her is from the Holy Spirit. 21 She will bear a son, and you are to name him Jesus, for he will save his people from their sins." 22 All this took place to fulfill what had been spoken by the Lord through the prophet:

23   "Look, the virgin shall conceive and bear a son,
     and they shall name him Emmanuel,"

which means, "God is with us." 24 When Joseph awoke from sleep, he did as the angel of the Lord commanded him; he took her as his wife, 25 but had no marital relations with her until she had borne a son;*f* and he named him Jesus.

2 In the time of King Herod, after Jesus was born in Bethlehem of Judea, wise men*g* from the East came to Jerusalem, 2 asking, "Where is the child who has been born king of the Jews? For we observed his star at its rising,*h* and have come to pay him homage." 3 When King Herod heard this, he was frightened, and all Jerusalem with him; 4 and calling together all the chief priests and scribes of the people, he inquired of them where the Messiah*i* was to be born. 5 They told him, "In Bethlehem of Judea; for so it has been written by the prophet:

6   'And you, Bethlehem, in the land of Judah,
    are by no means least among the rulers of
      Judah;
  for from you shall come a ruler
    who is to shepherd*j* my people Israel.'"

7 Then Herod secretly called for the wise men*g* and learned from them the exact time when the star had appeared. 8 Then he sent them to Bethlehem, saying, "Go and search diligently for the child; and when you have found him, bring me word so that I may also go and pay him homage." 9 When they had heard the king, they set out; and there, ahead of them, went the star that they had seen at its rising,*h* until it stopped over the place where the child was. 10 When they saw that the star had stopped,*k* they were overwhelmed with joy. 11 On entering the house, they saw the child with Mary his mother; and they knelt down and paid him homage. Then, opening their treasure chests, they offered him gifts of gold, frankincense, and myrrh. 12 And having been warned in a dream not to return to Herod, they left for their own country by another road.

13 Now after they had left, an angel of the Lord appeared to Joseph in a dream and said, "Get up, take the child and his mother, and flee to Egypt, and remain there until I tell you; for Herod is about to search for the child, to destroy him." 14 Then Joseph*l* got up, took the child and his mother by night, and went to Egypt, 15 and remained there until the death of Herod. This was to fulfill what had been spoken by the Lord through the prophet, "Out of Egypt I have called my son."

16 When Herod saw that he had been tricked by the wise men,*g* he was infuriated, and he sent and killed all the children in and around Bethlehem who were two years old or under, according to the time that he had learned from the wise men.*g* 17 Then was fulfilled what had been spoken through the prophet Jeremiah:

REVISED ENGLISH BIBLE

had resolved on this, when an angel of the Lord appeared to him in a dream and said, 'Joseph, son of David, do not be afraid to take Mary home with you to be your wife. It is through the Holy Spirit that she has conceived. 21 She will bear a son; and you shall give him the name Jesus, for he will save his people from their sins.' 22 All this happened in order to fulfil what the Lord declared through the prophet: 23 'A virgin will conceive and bear a son, and he shall be called Emmanuel,' a name which means 'God is with us'. 24 When he woke Joseph did as the angel of the Lord had directed him; he took Mary home to be his wife, 25 but had no intercourse with her until her son was born. And he named the child Jesus.

2 JESUS was born at Bethlehem in Judaea during the reign of Herod. After his birth astrologers from the east arrived in Jerusalem, 2 asking, 'Where is the new-born king of the Jews? We observed the rising of his star, and we have come to pay him homage.' 3 King Herod was greatly perturbed when he heard this, and so was the whole of Jerusalem. 4 He called together the chief priests and scribes of the Jews, and asked them where the Messiah was to be born. 5 'At Bethlehem in Judaea,' they replied, 'for this is what the prophet wrote: 6 "Bethlehem in the land of Judah, you are by no means least among the rulers of Judah; for out of you shall come a ruler to be the shepherd of my people Israel." '

7 Then Herod summoned the astrologers to meet him secretly, and ascertained from them the exact time when the star had appeared. 8 He sent them to Bethlehem, and said, 'Go and make a careful search for the child, and when you have found him, bring me word, so that I may go myself and pay him homage.' 9–10 After hearing what the king had to say they set out; there before them was the star they had seen rising, and it went ahead of them until it stopped above the place where the child lay. They were overjoyed at the sight of it 11 and, entering the house, they saw the child with Mary his mother and bowed low in homage to him; they opened their treasure chests and presented gifts to him: gold, frankincense, and myrrh. 12 Then they returned to their own country by another route, for they had been warned in a dream not to go back to Herod.

13 After they had gone, an angel of the Lord appeared to Joseph in a dream, and said, 'Get up, take the child and his mother and escape with them to Egypt, and stay there until I tell you; for Herod is going to search for the child to kill him.' 14 So Joseph got up, took mother and child by night, and sought refuge with them in Egypt, 15 where he stayed till Herod's death. This was to fulfil what the Lord had declared through the prophet: 'Out of Egypt I have called my son.'

16 When Herod realized that the astrologers had tricked him he flew into a rage, and gave orders for the massacre of all the boys aged two years or under, in Bethlehem and throughout the whole district, in accordance with the time he had ascertained from the astrologers. 17 So the words spoken through Jeremiah the prophet were fulfilled: 18 'A

---

f Other ancient authorities read *her firstborn son*   *g* Or *astrologers;*
Gk *magi*   *h* Or *in the East*   *i* Or *the Christ*   *j* Or *rule*
k Gk *saw the star*   *l* Gk *he*

1:21 **Jesus:** *that is* Saviour.

the angel of the Lord appeared to him in a dream and said, "Joseph, son of David, do not be afraid to take Mary your wife into your home. For it is through the holy Spirit that this child has been conceived in her. 21 She will bear a son and you are to name him Jesus, because he will save his people from their sins." 22 All this took place to fulfill what the Lord had said through the prophet:

23 "Behold, the virgin shall be with child and bear
    a son,
    and they shall name him Emmanuel,"

which means "God is with us." 24 When Joseph awoke, he did as the angel of the Lord had commanded him and took his wife into his home. 25 He had no relations with her until she bore a son, and he named him Jesus.

2 When Jesus was born in Bethlehem of Judea, in the days of King Herod, behold, magi from the east arrived in Jerusalem, 2 saying, "Where is the newborn king of the Jews? We saw his star at its rising and have come to do him homage." 3 When King Herod heard this, he was greatly troubled, and all Jerusalem with him. 4 Assembling all the chief priests and the scribes of the people, he inquired of them where the Messiah was to be born. 5 They said to him, "In Bethlehem of Judea, for thus it has been written through the prophet:

6 'And you, Bethlehem, land of Judah,
    are by no means least among the rulers of Judah;
  since from you shall come a ruler,
    who is to shepherd my people Israel.' "

7 Then Herod called the magi secretly and ascertained from them the time of the star's appearance. 8 He sent them to Bethlehem and said, "Go and search diligently for the child. When you have found him, bring me word, that I too may go and do him homage." 9 After their audience with the king they set out. And behold, the star that they had seen at its rising preceded them, until it came and stopped over the place where the child was. 10 They were overjoyed at seeing the star, 11 and on entering the house they saw the child with Mary his mother. They prostrated themselves and did him homage. Then they opened their treasures and offered him gifts of gold, frankincense, and myrrh. 12 And having been warned in a dream not to return to Herod, they departed for their country by another way.

13 When they had departed, behold, the angel of the Lord appeared to Joseph in a dream and said, "Rise, take the child and his mother, flee to Egypt, and stay there until I tell you. Herod is going to search for the child to destroy him." 14 Joseph rose and took the child and his mother by night and departed for Egypt. 15 He stayed there until the death of Herod, that what the Lord had said through the prophet might be fulfilled, "Out of Egypt I called my son."

16 When Herod realized that he had been deceived by the magi, he became furious. He ordered the massacre of all the boys in Bethlehem and its vicinity two years old and under, in accordance with the time he had ascertained from the magi. 17 Then was fulfilled what had been said through Jeremiah the prophet:

the angel of the Lord appeared to him in a dream and said, 'Joseph son of David, do not be afraid to take Mary home as your wife, because she has conceived what is in her by the Holy Spirit. 21 She will give birth to a son and you must name him Jesus, because he is the one who is to save his people from their sins.' 22 Now all this took place to fulfil what the Lord had spoken through the prophet:

23 Look! the virgin is with child and will give birth to
    a son
    whom they will call Immanuel,a

a name which means 'God-is-with-us'. 24 When Joseph woke up he did what the angel of the Lord had told him to do: he took his wife to his home; 25 he had not had intercourse with her when she gave birth to a son; and he named him Jesus.

2 After Jesus had been born at Bethlehem in Judaea during the reign of King Herod, suddenly some wise men came to Jerusalem from the east 2 asking, 'Where is the infant king of the Jews? We saw his star as it rose and have come to do him homage.' 3 When King Herod heard this he was perturbed, and so was the whole of Jerusalem. 4 He called together all the chief priests and the scribes of the people, and enquired of them where the Christ was to be born. 5 They told him, 'At Bethlehem in Judaea, for this is what the prophet wrote:

6 And you, Bethlehem, in the land of Judah,
    you are by no means the least among the leaders
      of Judah,
    for from you will come a leader
    who will shepherd my people Israel.'b

7 Then Herod summoned the wise men to see him privately. He asked them the exact date on which the star had appeared 8 and sent them on to Bethlehem with the words, 'Go and find out all about the child, and when you have found him, let me know, so that I too may go and do him homage.' 9 Having listened to what the king had to say, they set out. And suddenly the star they had seen rising went forward and halted over the place where the child was. 10 The sight of the star filled them with delight, 11 and going into the house they saw the child with his mother Mary, and falling to their knees they did him homage. Then, opening their treasures, they offered him gifts of gold and frankincense and myrrh. 12 But they were given a warning in a dream not to go back to Herod, and returned to their own country by a different way.

13 After they had left, suddenly the angel of the Lord appeared to Joseph in a dream and said, 'Get up, take the child and his mother with you, and escape into Egypt, and stay there until I tell you, because Herod intends to search for the child and do away with him.' 14 So Joseph got up and, taking the child and his mother with him, left that night for Egypt, 15 where he stayed until Herod was dead. This was to fulfil what the Lord had spoken through the prophet:

I called my son out of Egypt.c

16 Herod was furious on realising that he had been fooled by the wise men, and in Bethlehem and its surrounding district he had all the male children killed who were two years old or less, reckoning by the date he had been careful to ask the wise men. 17 Then were fulfilled the words spoken through the prophet Jeremiah:

a 1 Is 7:14.   b 2 Mi 5:1.   c 2 Nb 23:22.

18 "A voice was heard in Ramah,
    wailing and loud lamentation,
Rachel weeping for her children;
    she refused to be consoled, because they are no
        more."
19 When Herod died, an angel of the Lord suddenly appeared in a dream to Joseph in Egypt and said, 20 "Get up, take the child and his mother, and go to the land of Israel, for those who were seeking the child's life are dead." 21 Then Joseph[m] got up, took the child and his mother, and went to the land of Israel. 22 But when he heard that Archelaus was ruling over Judea in place of his father Herod, he was afraid to go there. And after being warned in a dream, he went away to the district of Galilee. 23 There he made his home in a town called Nazareth, so that what had been spoken through the prophets might be fulfilled, "He will be called a Nazorean."

3 In those days John the Baptist appeared in the wilderness of Judea, proclaiming, 2 "Repent, for the kingdom of heaven has come near."[n] 3 This is the one of whom the prophet Isaiah spoke when he said,
    "The voice of one crying out in the wilderness:
    'Prepare the way of the Lord,
        make his paths straight.'"
4 Now John wore clothing of camel's hair with a leather belt around his waist, and his food was locusts and wild honey. 5 Then the people of Jerusalem and all Judea were going out to him, and all the region along the Jordan, 6 and they were baptized by him in the river Jordan, confessing their sins.
7 But when he saw many Pharisees and Sadducees coming for baptism, he said to them, "You brood of vipers! Who warned you to flee from the wrath to come? 8 Bear fruit worthy of repentance. 9 Do not presume to say to yourselves, 'We have Abraham as our ancestor'; for I tell you, God is able from these stones to raise up children to Abraham. 10 Even now the ax is lying at the root of the trees; every tree therefore that does not bear good fruit is cut down and thrown into the fire.
11 "I baptize you with[o] water for repentance, but one who is more powerful than I is coming after me; I am not worthy to carry his sandals. He will baptize you with[o] the Holy Spirit and fire. 12 His winnowing fork is in his hand, and he will clear his threshing floor and will gather his wheat into the granary; but the chaff he will burn with unquenchable fire."
13 Then Jesus came from Galilee to John at the Jordan, to be baptized by him. 14 John would have prevented him, saying, "I need to be baptized by you, and do you come to me?" 15 But Jesus answered him, "Let it be so now; for it is proper for us in this way to fulfill all righteousness." Then he consented. 16 And when Jesus had been baptized, just as he came up from the water, suddenly the heavens were opened to him and he saw the Spirit of God descending like a dove and alighting on him. 17 And a voice from heaven said, "This is my Son, the Beloved,[p] with whom I am well pleased."

4 Then Jesus was led up by the Spirit into the wilderness to be tempted by the devil. 2 He fasted forty days and forty nights, and afterwards he was famished. 3 The tempter came and said to him, "If you are the Son of God, command these stones to become loaves of bread." 4 But he answered, "It is written,

voice was heard in Rama, sobbing in bitter grief; it was Rachel weeping for her children, and refusing to be comforted, because they were no more.'
19 After Herod's death an angel of the Lord appeared in a dream to Joseph in Egypt 20 and said to him, 'Get up, take the child and his mother, and go to the land of Israel, for those who threatened the child's life are dead.' 21 So he got up, took mother and child with him, and came to the land of Israel. 22 But when he heard that Archelaus had succeeded his father Herod as king of Judaea, he was afraid to go there. Directed by a dream, he withdrew to the region of Galilee, 23 where he settled in a town called Nazareth. This was to fulfil the words spoken through the prophets: 'He shall be called a Nazarene.'

3 In the course of time John the Baptist appeared in the Judaean wilderness, proclaiming this message: 2 'Repent, for the kingdom of Heaven is upon you!' 3 It was of him that the prophet Isaiah spoke when he said,

    A voice cries in the wilderness,
    'Prepare the way for the Lord;
    clear a straight path for him.'

4 John's clothing was a rough coat of camel's hair, with a leather belt round his waist, and his food was locusts and wild honey. 5 Everyone flocked to him from Jerusalem, Judaea, and the Jordan valley, 6 and they were baptized by him in the river Jordan, confessing their sins.
7 When he saw many of the Pharisees and Sadducees coming for baptism he said to them: 'Vipers' brood! Who warned you to escape from the wrath that is to come? 8 Prove your repentance by the fruit you bear; 9 and do not imagine you can say, "We have Abraham for our father." I tell you that God can make children for Abraham out of these stones. 10 The axe lies ready at the roots of the trees; every tree that fails to produce good fruit is cut down and thrown on the fire. 11 I baptize you with water, for repentance; but the one who comes after me is mightier than I am, whose sandals I am not worthy to remove. He will baptize you with the Holy Spirit and with fire. 12 His winnowing-shovel is ready in his hand and he will clear his threshing-floor; he will gather the wheat into his granary, but the chaff he will burn on a fire that can never be put out.'
13 Then Jesus arrived at the Jordan from Galilee, and came to John to be baptized by him. 14 John tried to dissuade him. 'Do you come to me?' he said. 'It is I who need to be baptized by you.' 15 Jesus replied, 'Let it be so for the present; it is right for us to do all that God requires.' Then John allowed him to come. 16 No sooner had Jesus been baptized and come up out of the water than the heavens were opened and he saw the Spirit of God descending like a dove to alight on him. 17 And there came a voice from heaven saying, 'This is my beloved Son, in whom I take delight.'

4 Jesus was then led by the Spirit into the wilderness, to be tempted by the devil. 2 For forty days and nights he fasted, and at the end of them he was famished. 3 The tempter approached him and said, 'If you are the Son of God, tell these stones to become bread.' 4 Jesus answered, 'Scripture says, "Man is not to

---

m Gk he   n Or is at hand   o Or in   p Or my beloved Son

3:17 This . . . Son: or This is my only Son.   4:1 tempted: or tested.

NEW AMERICAN BIBLE

18 "A voice was heard in Ramah,
sobbing and loud lamentation;
Rachel weeping for her children,
and she would not be consoled,
since they were no more."

19 When Herod had died, behold, the angel of the Lord appeared in a dream to Joseph in Egypt 20 and said, "Rise, take the child and his mother and go to the land of Israel, for those who sought the child's life are dead." 21 He rose, took the child and his mother, and went to the land of Israel. 22 But when he heard that Archelaus was ruling over Judea in place of his father Herod, he was afraid to go back there. And because he had been warned in a dream, he departed for the region of Galilee. 23 He went and dwelt in a town called Nazareth, so that what had been spoken through the prophets might be fulfilled, "He shall be called a Nazorean."

3 In those days John the Baptist appeared, preaching in the desert of Judea 2 [and] saying, "Repent, for the kingdom of heaven is at hand!" 3 It was of him that the prophet Isaiah had spoken when he said:

"A voice of one crying out in the desert,
'Prepare the way of the Lord,
make straight his paths.' "

4 John wore clothing made of camel's hair and had a leather belt around his waist. His food was locusts and wild honey. 5 At that time Jerusalem, all Judea, and the whole region around the Jordan were going out to him 6 and were being baptized by him in the Jordan River as they acknowledged their sins.

7 When he saw many of the Pharisees and Sadducees coming to his baptism, he said to them, "You brood of vipers! Who warned you to flee from the coming wrath? 8 Produce good fruit as evidence of your repentance. 9 And do not presume to say to yourselves, 'We have Abraham as our father.' For I tell you, God can raise up children to Abraham from these stones. 10 Even now the ax lies at the root of the trees. Therefore every tree that does not bear good fruit will be cut down and thrown into the fire. 11 I am baptizing you with water, for repentance, but the one who is coming after me is mightier than I. I am not worthy to carry his sandals. He will baptize you with the holy Spirit and fire. 12 His winnowing fan is in his hand. He will clear his threshing floor and gather his wheat into his barn, but the chaff he will burn with unquenchable fire."

13 Then Jesus came from Galilee to John at the Jordan to be baptized by him. 14 John tried to prevent him, saying, "I need to be baptized by you, and yet you are coming to me?" 15 Jesus said to him in reply, "Allow it now, for thus it is fitting for us to fulfill all righteousness." Then he allowed him. 16 After Jesus was baptized, he came up from the water and behold, the heavens were opened [for him], and he saw the Spirit of God descending like a dove [and] coming upon him. 17 And a voice came from the heavens, saying, "This is my beloved Son, with whom I am well pleased."

4 Then Jesus was led by the Spirit into the desert to be tempted by the devil. 2 He fasted for forty days and forty nights, and afterwards he was hungry. 3 The tempter approached and said to him, "If you are the Son of God, command that these stones become loaves of bread." 4 He said in reply, "It is written:

NEW JERUSALEM BIBLE

18 A voice is heard in Ramah,
lamenting and weeping bitterly:
it is Rachel weeping for her children,
refusing to be comforted
because they are no more. d

19 After Herod's death, suddenly the angel of the Lord appeared in a dream to Joseph in Egypt 20 and said, e 'Get up, take the child and his mother with you and go back to the land of Israel, for those who wanted to kill the child are dead.' 21 So Joseph got up and, taking the child and his mother with him, went back to the land of Israel. 22 But when he learnt that Archelaus had succeeded his father Herod as ruler of Judaea he was afraid to go there, and being warned in a dream he withdrew to the region of Galilee. 23 There he settled in a town called Nazareth. In this way the words spoken through the prophets were to be fulfilled:

He will be called a Nazarene.

3 In due course John the Baptist appeared; he proclaimed this message in the desert of Judaea, 2 'Repent, for the kingdom of Heaven is close at hand.' 3 This was the man spoken of by the prophet Isaiah when he said:

A voice of one that cries in the desert,
'Prepare a way for the Lord,
make his paths straight.' f

4 This man John wore a garment made of camel-hair with a leather loin-cloth round his waist, g and his food was locusts and wild honey. 5 Then Jerusalem and all Judaea and the whole Jordan district made their way to him, 6 and as they were baptised by him in the river Jordan they confessed their sins. 7 But when he saw a number of Pharisees and Sadducees coming for baptism he said to them, 'Brood of vipers, who warned you to flee from the coming retribution? 8 Produce fruit in keeping with repentance, 9 and do not presume to tell yourselves, "We have Abraham as our father," because, I tell you, God can raise children for Abraham from these stones. 10 Even now the axe is being laid to the root of the trees, so that any tree failing to produce good fruit will be cut down and thrown on the fire. 11 I baptise you in water for repentance, but the one who comes after me is more powerful than I, and I am not fit to carry his sandals; he will baptise you with the Holy Spirit and fire. 12 His winnowing-fan is in his hand; he will clear his threshing-floor and gather his wheat into his barn; but the chaff he will burn in a fire that will never go out.'

13 Then Jesus appeared: he came from Galilee to the Jordan to be baptised by John. 14 John tried to dissuade him, with the words, 'It is I who need baptism from you, and yet you come to me!' 15 But Jesus replied, 'Leave it like this for the time being; it is fitting that we should, in this way, do all that uprightness demands.' Then John gave in to him. 16 And when Jesus had been baptised he at once came up from the water, and suddenly the heavens opened and he saw the Spirit of God descending like a dove and coming down on him. 17 And suddenly there was a voice from heaven, 'This is my Son, the Beloved; my favour rests on him.' h

4 Then Jesus was led by the Spirit out into the desert to be put to the test by the devil. 2 He fasted for forty days and forty nights, after which he was hungry, 3 and the tester came and said to him, 'If you are Son of God, tell these stones to turn into loaves.' 4 But he replied, 'Scripture says:

d 2 In Jr 31:15 she weeps for the northern tribes. But traditionally she was buried near Bethlehem. e 2 cf. Ex. 4:19–20. There are several parallels with the stories of Moses' infancy. f 3 Is 40:3. g 3 As Elijah, 2 K 1:8. h 3 cf. Is 42:1.

'One does not live by bread alone,
but by every word that comes from the mouth
of God.' "

5 Then the devil took him to the holy city and placed
him on the pinnacle of the temple, 6 saying to him, "If you
are the Son of God, throw yourself down; for it is written,

'He will command his angels concerning you,'

and 'On their hands they will bear you up,

so that you will not dash your foot against a
stone.' "

7 Jesus said to him, "Again it is written, 'Do not put the
Lord your God to the test.' "

8 Again, the devil took him to a very high mountain and
showed him all the kingdoms of the world and their splendor; 9 and he said to him, "All these I will give you, if you
will fall down and worship me." 10 Jesus said to him,
"Away with you, Satan! for it is written,

'Worship the Lord your God,
and serve only him.' "

11 Then the devil left him, and suddenly angels came and
waited on him.

12 Now when Jesus*q* heard that John had been arrested,
he withdrew to Galilee. 13 He left Nazareth and made his
home in Capernaum by the sea, in the territory of Zebulun
and Naphtali, 14 so that what had been spoken through the
prophet Isaiah might be fulfilled:

15 "Land of Zebulun, land of Naphtali,
on the road by the sea, across the Jordan,
Galilee of the Gentiles —

16 the people who sat in darkness
have seen a great light,
and for those who sat in the region and shadow
of death
light has dawned."

17 From that time Jesus began to proclaim, "Repent, for the
kingdom of heaven has come near."*r*

18 As he walked by the Sea of Galilee, he saw two
brothers, Simon, who is called Peter, and Andrew his
brother, casting a net into the sea — for they were fishermen. 19 And he said to them, "Follow me, and I will make
you fish for people." 20 Immediately they left their nets and
followed him. 21 As he went from there, he saw two other
brothers, James son of Zebedee and his brother John, in the
boat with their father Zebedee, mending their nets, and he
called them. 22 Immediately they left the boat and their father, and followed him.

23 Jesus*s* went throughout Galilee, teaching in their
synagogues and proclaiming the good news*t* of the kingdom and curing every disease and every sickness among the
people. 24 So his fame spread throughout all Syria, and they
brought to him all the sick, those who were afflicted with
various diseases and pains, demoniacs, epileptics, and paralytics, and he cured them. 25 And great crowds followed
him from Galilee, the Decapolis, Jerusalem, Judea, and
from beyond the Jordan.

5 When Jesus*q* saw the crowds, he went up the mountain; and after he sat down, his disciples came to him.
2 Then he began to speak, and taught them, saying:

live on bread alone, but on every word that comes from the
mouth of God." '

5 The devil then took him to the Holy City and set him on
the parapet of the temple. 6 'If you are the Son of God,' he
said, 'throw yourself down; for scripture says, "He will put
his angels in charge of you, and they will support you in
their arms, for fear you should strike your foot against a
stone." ' 7 Jesus answered him, 'Scripture also says, "You
are not to put the Lord your God to the test." '

8 The devil took him next to a very high mountain, and
showed him all the kingdoms of the world in their glory.
9 'All these', he said, 'I will give you, if you will only fall
down and do me homage.' 10 But Jesus said, 'Out of my
sight, Satan! Scripture says, "You shall do homage to the
Lord your God and worship him alone." '

11 Then the devil left him; and angels came and attended
to his needs.

12 WHEN he heard that John had been arrested, Jesus withdrew to Galilee; 13 and leaving Nazareth he went and settled
at Capernaum on the sea of Galilee, in the district of Zebulun and Naphtali. 14 This was to fulfil the words of the
prophet Isaiah about 15 'the land of Zebulun, the land of
Naphtali, the road to the sea, the land beyond Jordan, Galilee of the Gentiles':

16 The people that lived in darkness
have seen a great light;
light has dawned on those
who lived in the land of death's dark shadow.

17 From that day Jesus began to proclaim the message: 'Repent, for the kingdom of Heaven is upon you.'

18 JESUS was walking by the sea of Galilee when he saw two
brothers, Simon called Peter and his brother Andrew, casting a net into the lake; for they were fishermen. 19 Jesus said
to them, 'Come with me, and I will make you fishers of
men.' 20 At once they left their nets and followed him.

21 Going on farther, he saw another pair of brothers,
James son of Zebedee and his brother John; they were in a
boat with their father Zebedee, mending their nets. He
called them, 22 and at once they left the boat and their father, and followed him.

23 He travelled throughout Galilee, teaching in the synagogues, proclaiming the good news of the kingdom, and
healing every kind of illness and infirmity among the people. 24 His fame spread throughout Syria; and they brought
to him sufferers from various diseases, those racked with
pain or possessed by demons, those who were epileptic or
paralysed, and he healed them all. 25 Large crowds followed
him, from Galilee and the Decapolis, from Jerusalem and
Judaea, and from Transjordan.

5 WHEN he saw the crowds he went up a mountain.
There he sat down, and when his disciples had gathered round him 2 he began to address them. And this is the
teaching he gave:

'One does not live by bread alone,
but by every word that comes forth
from the mouth of God.' "

5 Then the devil took him to the holy city, and made him stand on the parapet of the temple, 6 and said to him, "If you are the Son of God, throw yourself down. For it is written:

'He will command his angels concerning you'
and 'with their hands they will support you,
lest you dash your foot against a stone.' "

7 Jesus answered him, "Again it is written, 'You shall not put the Lord, your God, to the test.' " 8 Then the devil took him up to a very high mountain, and showed him all the kingdoms of the world in their magnificence, 9 and he said to him, "All these I shall give to you, if you will prostrate yourself and worship me." 10 At this, Jesus said to him, "Get away, Satan! It is written:

'The Lord, your God, shall you worship
and him alone shall you serve.' "

11 Then the devil left him and, behold, angels came and ministered to him.

12 When he heard that John had been arrested, he withdrew to Galilee. 13 He left Nazareth and went to live in Capernaum by the sea, in the region of Zebulun and Naphtali, 14 that what had been said through Isaiah the prophet might be fulfilled:

15 "Land of Zebulun and land of Naphtali,
the way to the sea, beyond the Jordan,
Galilee of the Gentiles,
16 the people who sit in darkness
have seen a great light,
on those dwelling in a land overshadowed by death
light has arisen."

17 From that time on, Jesus began to preach and say, "Repent, for the kingdom of heaven is at hand."

18 As he was walking by the Sea of Galilee, he saw two brothers, Simon who is called Peter, and his brother Andrew, casting a net into the sea; they were fishermen. 19 He said to them, "Come after me, and I will make you fishers of men." 20 At once they left their nets and followed him. 21 He walked along from there and saw two other brothers, James, the son of Zebedee, and his brother John. They were in a boat, with their father Zebedee, mending their nets. He called them, 22 and immediately they left their boat and their father and followed him.

23 He went around all of Galilee, teaching in their synagogues, proclaiming the gospel of the kingdom, and curing every disease and illness among the people. 24 His fame spread to all of Syria, and they brought to him all who were sick with various diseases and racked with pain, those who were possessed, lunatics, and paralytics, and he cured them. 25 And great crowds from Galilee, the Decapolis, Jerusalem, and Judea, and from beyond the Jordan followed him.

5 When he saw the crowds, he went up the mountain, and after he had sat down, his disciples came to him. 2 He began to teach them, saying:

Human beings live not on bread alone
but on every word that comes from the mouth of
God.' i

5 The devil then took him to the holy city and set him on the parapet of the Temple. 6 'If you are Son of God,' he said, 'throw yourself down; for scripture says:

He has given his angels orders about you,
and they will carry you in their arms
in case you trip over a stone.' j

7 Jesus said to him, 'Scripture also says:

Do not put the Lord your God to the test.' k

8 Next, taking him to a very high mountain, the devil showed him all the kingdoms of the world and their splendour. 9 And he said to him, 'I will give you all these, if you fall at my feet and do me homage.' 10 Then Jesus replied, 'Away with you, Satan! For scripture says:

The Lord your God is the one to whom you must
do homage,
him alone you must serve.' l

11 Then the devil left him, and suddenly angels appeared and looked after him.

12 Hearing that John had been arrested he withdrew to Galilee, 13 and leaving Nazara he went and settled in Capernaum, beside the lake, on the borders of Zebulun and Naphtali. 14 This was to fulfil what was spoken by the prophet Isaiah:

15 Land of Zebulun! Land of Naphtali!
Way of the sea beyond Jordan.
Galilee of the nations!
16 The people that lived in darkness
have seen a great light;
on those who lived in a country of shadow dark as
death
a light has dawned. m

17 From then onwards Jesus began his proclamation with the message, 'Repent, for the kingdom of Heaven is close at hand.'

18 As he was walking by the Lake of Galilee he saw two brothers, Simon, who was called Peter, and his brother Andrew; they were making a cast into the lake with their net, for they were fishermen. 19 And he said to them, 'Come after me and I will make you fishers of people.' 20 And at once they left their nets and followed him.

21 Going on from there he saw another pair of brothers, James son of Zebedee and his brother John; they were in their boat with their father Zebedee, mending their nets, and he called them. 22 And at once, leaving the boat and their father, they followed him.

23 He went round the whole of Galilee teaching in their synagogues, proclaiming the good news of the kingdom and curing all kinds of disease and illness among the people. 24 His fame spread throughout Syria, and those who were suffering from diseases and painful complaints of one kind or another, the possessed, epileptics, the paralysed, were all brought to him, and he cured them. 25 Large crowds followed him, coming from Galilee, the Decapolis, Jerusalem, Judaea and Transjordan.

5 n Seeing the crowds, he went onto the mountain. And when he was seated his disciples came to him. 2 Then he began to speak. This is what he taught them:

i 4 Dt 8:3.   j 4 Ps 91:10–12.   k 4 Dt 6:16.   l 4 Dt 6:13.
m 4 Is 8:23-9:1.   n 5 Lk 6:20–23.

NEW REVISED STANDARD VERSION

3 "Blessed are the poor in spirit, for theirs is the kingdom of heaven.

4 "Blessed are those who mourn, for they will be comforted.

5 "Blessed are the meek, for they will inherit the earth.

6 "Blessed are those who hunger and thirst for righteousness, for they will be filled.

7 "Blessed are the merciful, for they will receive mercy.

8 "Blessed are the pure in heart, for they will see God.

9 "Blessed are the peacemakers, for they will be called children of God.

10 "Blessed are those who are persecuted for righteousness' sake, for theirs is the kingdom of heaven.

11 "Blessed are you when people revile you and persecute you and utter all kinds of evil against you falsely[u] on my account. 12 Rejoice and be glad, for your reward is great in heaven, for in the same way they persecuted the prophets who were before you.

13 "You are the salt of the earth; but if salt has lost its taste, how can its saltiness be restored? It is no longer good for anything, but is thrown out and trampled under foot.

14 "You are the light of the world. A city built on a hill cannot be hid. 15 No one after lighting a lamp puts it under the bushel basket, but on the lampstand, and it gives light to all in the house. 16 In the same way, let your light shine before others, so that they may see your good works and give glory to your Father in heaven.

17 "Do not think that I have come to abolish the law or the prophets; I have come not to abolish but to fulfill. 18 For truly I tell you, until heaven and earth pass away, not one letter,[v] not one stroke of a letter, will pass from the law until all is accomplished. 19 Therefore, whoever breaks[w] one of the least of these commandments, and teaches others to do the same, will be called least in the kingdom of heaven; but whoever does them and teaches them will be called great in the kingdom of heaven. 20 For I tell you, unless your righteousness exceeds that of the scribes and Pharisees, you will never enter the kingdom of heaven.

21 "You have heard that it was said to those of ancient times, 'You shall not murder'; and 'whoever murders shall be liable to judgment.' 22 But I say to you that if you are angry with a brother or sister,[x] you will be liable to judgment; and if you insult[y] a brother or sister,[z] you will be liable to the council; and if you say, 'You fool,' you will be liable to the hell[a] of fire. 23 So when you are offering your gift at the altar, if you remember that your brother or sister[b] has something against you, 24 leave your gift there before the altar and go; first be reconciled to your brother or sister,[b] and then come and offer your gift. 25 Come to terms quickly with your accuser while you are on the way to court[c] with him, or your accuser may hand you over to the judge, and the judge to the guard, and you will be thrown into prison. 26 Truly I tell you, you will never get out until you have paid the last penny.

27 "You have heard that it was said, 'You shall not commit adultery.' 28 But I say to you that everyone who looks at a woman with lust has already committed adultery with her in his heart. 29 If your right eye causes you to sin, tear it out and throw it away; it is better for you to lose one of your members than for your whole body to be thrown into hell.[a] 30 And if your right hand causes you to sin, cut

REVISED ENGLISH BIBLE

3 'Blessed are the poor in spirit;
the kingdom of Heaven is theirs.
4 Blessed are the sorrowful;
they shall find consolation.
5 Blessed are the gentle;
they shall have the earth for their possession.
6 Blessed are those who hunger and thirst to see right prevail;
they shall be satisfied.
7 Blessed are those who show mercy;
mercy shall be shown to them.
8 Blessed are those whose hearts are pure;
they shall see God.
9 Blessed are the peacemakers;
they shall be called God's children.
10 Blessed are those who are persecuted in the cause of right;
the kingdom of Heaven is theirs.

11 'Blessed are you, when you suffer insults and persecution and calumnies of every kind for my sake. 12 Exult and be glad, for you have a rich reward in heaven; in the same way they persecuted the prophets before you.

13 'You are salt to the world. And if salt becomes tasteless, how is its saltness to be restored? It is good for nothing but to be thrown away and trodden underfoot.

14 'You are light for all the world. A town that stands on a hill cannot be hidden. 15 When a lamp is lit, it is not put under the meal-tub, but on the lampstand, where it gives light to everyone in the house. 16 Like the lamp, you must shed light among your fellows, so that, when they see the good you do, they may give praise to your Father in heaven.

17 'Do NOT suppose that I have come to abolish the law and the prophets; I did not come to abolish, but to complete. 18 Truly I tell you: so long as heaven and earth endure, not a letter, not a dot, will disappear from the law until all that must happen has happened. 19 Anyone therefore who sets aside even the least of the law's demands, and teaches others to do the same, will have the lowest place in the kingdom of Heaven, whereas anyone who keeps the law, and teaches others to do so, will rank high in the kingdom of Heaven. 20 I tell you, unless you show yourselves far better than the scribes and Pharisees, you can never enter the kingdom of Heaven.

21 'You have heard that our forefathers were told, "Do not commit murder; anyone who commits murder must be brought to justice." 22 But what I tell you is this: Anyone who nurses anger against his brother must be brought to justice. Whoever calls his brother "good for nothing" deserves the sentence of the court; whoever calls him "fool" deserves hell-fire. 23 So if you are presenting your gift at the altar and suddenly remember that your brother has a grievance against you, 24 leave your gift where it is before the altar. First go and make your peace with your brother; then come back and offer your gift. 25 If someone sues you, come to terms with him promptly while you are both on your way to court; otherwise he may hand you over to the judge, and the judge to the officer, and you will be thrown into jail. 26 Truly I tell you: once you are there you will not be let out until you have paid the last penny.

27 'You have heard that they were told, "Do not commit adultery." 28 But what I tell you is this: If a man looks at a woman with a lustful eye, he has already committed adultery with her in his heart. 29 If your right eye causes your downfall, tear it out and fling it away; it is better for you to lose one part of your body than for the whole of it to be thrown into hell. 30 If your right hand causes your downfall,

---

[u] Other ancient authorities lack *falsely*   [v] Gk *one iota*
[w] Or *annuls*   [x] Gk *a brother*; other ancient authorities add *without cause*   [y] Gk *say Raca to* (an obscure term of abuse)   [z] Gk *a brother*   [a] Gk *Gehenna*   [b] Gk *your brother*   [c] Gk lacks *to court*

5:6 **to . . . prevail**: *or* to do what is right.   5:18 **until . . . happened**: *or* before all that it stands for is achieved.

NEW AMERICAN BIBLE

NEW JERUSALEM BIBLE

3 "Blessed are the poor in spirit,
for theirs is the kingdom of heaven.
4 Blessed are they who mourn,
for they will be comforted.
5 Blessed are the meek,
for they will inherit the land.
6 Blessed are they who hunger and thirst
for righteousness,
for they will be satisfied.
7 Blessed are the merciful,
for they will be shown mercy.
8 Blessed are the clean of heart,
for they will see God.
9 Blessed are the peacemakers,
for they will be called children of God.
10 Blessed are they who are persecuted for the sake
of righteousness,
for theirs is the kingdom of heaven.

11 Blessed are you when they insult you and persecute you
and utter every kind of evil against you [falsely] because of
me. 12 Rejoice and be glad, for your reward will be great in
heaven. Thus they persecuted the prophets who were before
you.

13 "You are the salt of the earth. But if salt loses its taste,
with what can it be seasoned? It is no longer good for
anything but to be thrown out and trampled underfoot.
14 You are the light of the world. A city set on a mountain
cannot be hidden. 15 Nor do they light a lamp and then put
it under a bushel basket; it is set on a lampstand, where it
gives light to all in the house. 16 Just so, your light must
shine before others, that they may see your good deeds and
glorify your heavenly Father.

17 "Do not think that I have come to abolish the law or the
prophets. I have come not to abolish but to fulfill. 18 Amen,
I say to you, until heaven and earth pass away, not the
smallest letter or the smallest part of a letter will pass from
the law, until all things have taken place. 19 Therefore, whoever breaks one of the least of these commandments and
teaches others to do so will be called least in the kingdom
of heaven. But whoever obeys and teaches these commandments will be called greatest in the kingdom of heaven. 20 I
tell you, unless your righteousness surpasses that of the
scribes and Pharisees, you will not enter into the kingdom
of heaven.

21 "You have heard that it was said to your ancestors,
'You shall not kill; and whoever kills will be liable to judgment.' 22 But I say to you, whoever is angry with his brother
will be liable to judgment, and whoever says to his brother,
'Raqa,' will be answerable to the Sanhedrin, and whoever
says, 'You fool,' will be liable to fiery Gehenna. 23 Therefore, if you bring your gift to the altar, and there recall that
your brother has anything against you, 24 leave your gift
there at the altar, go first and be reconciled with your
brother, and then come and offer your gift. 25 Settle with
your opponent quickly while on the way to court with him.
Otherwise your opponent will hand you over to the judge,
and the judge will hand you over to the guard, and you will
be thrown into prison. 26 Amen, I say to you, you will not
be released until you have paid the last penny.

27 "You have heard that it was said, 'You shall not commit adultery.' 28 But I say to you, everyone who looks at a
woman with lust has already committed adultery with her in
his heart. 29 If your right eye causes you to sin, tear it out
and throw it away. It is better for you to lose one of your
members than to have your whole body thrown into Gehenna. 30 And if your right hand causes you to sin, cut it off

3 How blessed are the poor in spirit:
the kingdom of Heaven is theirs.
4 Blessed are *the gentle*:o
they shall have the earth as inheritance.p
5 Blessed are those who mourn:
they shall be comforted.
6 Blessed are those who hunger and thirst for
uprightness:
they shall have their fill.
7 Blessed are the merciful:
they shall have mercy shown them.
8 Blessed are the pure in heart:
they shall see God.
9 Blessed are the peacemakers:
they shall be recognised as children of God.
10 Blessed are those who are persecuted in the cause
of uprightness:
the kingdom of Heaven is theirs.

11 'Blessed are you when people abuse you and persecute
you and speak all kinds of calumny against you falsely on
my account. 12 Rejoice and be glad, for your reward will be
great in heaven; this is how they persecuted the prophets
before you.

13 'You are salt for the earth. But if salt loses its taste,
what can make it salty again? It is good for nothing, and can
only be thrown out to be trampled under people's feet.
14 'You are light for the world. A city built on a hill-top
cannot be hidden. 15 No one lights a lamp to put it under a
tub; they put it on the lamp-stand where it shines for everyone in the house. 16 In the same way your light must shine
in people's sight, so that, seeing your good works, they may
give praise to your Father in heaven.

17 'Do not imagine that I have come to abolish the Law
or the Prophets. I have come not to abolish but to complete
them. 18 In truth I tell you, till heaven and earth disappear,
not one dot, not one little stroke, is to disappear from the
Law until all its purpose is achieved. 19 Therefore, anyone
who infringes even one of the least of these commandments
and teaches others to do the same will be considered the
least in the kingdom of Heaven; but the person who keeps
them and teaches them will be considered great in the kingdom of Heaven.

20 'For I tell you, if your uprightness does not surpass that
of the scribes and Pharisees, you will never get into the
kingdom of Heaven.

21 'You have heard how it was said to our ancestors, *You
shall not kill;q* and if anyone does kill he must answer for
it before the court. 22 But I say this to you, anyone who is
angry with a brother will answer for it before the court;
anyone who calls a brother "Fool" will answer for it before
the Sanhedrin; and anyone who calls him "Traitor" will
answer for it in hell fire. 23 So then, if you are bringing your
offering to the altar and there remember that your brother
has something against you, 24 leave your offering there before the altar, go and be reconciled with your brother first,
and then come back and present your offering. 25 Come to
terms with your opponent in good time while you are still
on the way to the court with him, or he may hand you over
to the judge and the judge to the officer, and you will be
thrown into prison. 26 In truth I tell you, you will not get out
till you have paid the last penny.

27 'You have heard how it was said, *You shall not commit
adultery.r* 28 But I say this to you, if a man looks at a
woman lustfully, he has already committed adultery with
her in his heart. 29 If your right eye should be your downfall,
tear it out and throw it away; for it will do you less harm to
lose one part of yourself than to have your whole body
thrown into hell. 30 And if your right hand should be your

o 5 Ps 37:11.   p 5 Gn 13:15.   q 5 Ex 20:13.   r 5 Ex 20:14.

it off and throw it away; it is better for you to lose one of your members than for your whole body to go into hell.*d*
31 "It was also said, 'Whoever divorces his wife, let him give her a certificate of divorce.' 32 But I say to you that anyone who divorces his wife, except on the ground of unchastity, causes her to commit adultery; and whoever marries a divorced woman commits adultery.
33 "Again, you have heard that it was said to those of ancient times, 'You shall not swear falsely, but carry out the vows you have made to the Lord.' 34 But I say to you, Do not swear at all, either by heaven, for it is the throne of God, 35 or by the earth, for it is his footstool, or by Jerusalem, for it is the city of the great King. 36 And do not swear by your head, for you cannot make one hair white or black. 37 Let your word be 'Yes, Yes' or 'No, No'; anything more than this comes from the evil one.*e*
38 "You have heard that it was said, 'An eye for an eye and a tooth for a tooth.' 39 But I say to you, Do not resist an evildoer. But if anyone strikes you on the right cheek, turn the other also; 40 and if anyone wants to sue you and take your coat, give your cloak as well; 41 and if anyone forces you to go one mile, go also the second mile. 42 Give to everyone who begs from you, and do not refuse anyone who wants to borrow from you.
43 "You have heard that it was said, 'You shall love your neighbor and hate your enemy.' 44 But I say to you, Love your enemies and pray for those who persecute you, 45 so that you may be children of your Father in heaven; for he makes his sun rise on the evil and on the good, and sends rain on the righteous and on the unrighteous. 46 For if you love those who love you, what reward do you have? Do not even the tax collectors do the same? 47 And if you greet only your brothers and sisters,*f* what more are you doing than others? Do not even the Gentiles do the same? 48 Be perfect, therefore, as your heavenly Father is perfect.

6 "Beware of practicing your piety before others in order to be seen by them; for then you have no reward from your Father in heaven.
2 "So whenever you give alms, do not sound a trumpet before you, as the hypocrites do in the synagogues and in the streets, so that they may be praised by others. Truly I tell you, they have received their reward. 3 But when you give alms, do not let your left hand know what your right hand is doing, 4 so that your alms may be done in secret; and your Father who sees in secret will reward you.*g*
5 "And whenever you pray, do not be like the hypocrites; for they love to stand and pray in the synagogues and at the street corners, so that they may be seen by others. Truly I tell you, they have received their reward. 6 But whenever you pray, go into your room and shut the door and pray to your Father who is in secret; and your Father who sees in secret will reward you.*g*
7 "When you are praying, do not heap up empty phrases as the Gentiles do; for they think that they will be heard because of their many words. 8 Do not be like them, for your Father knows what you need before you ask him.
9 "Pray then in this way:

Our Father in heaven,
    hallowed be your name.
10   Your kingdom come.
    Your will be done,
        on earth as it is in heaven.
11   Give us this day our daily bread.*h*

cut it off and fling it away; it is better for you to lose one part of your body than for the whole of it to go to hell.
31 "They were told, "A man who divorces his wife must give her a certificate of dismissal." 32 But what I tell you is this: If a man divorces his wife for any cause other than unchastity he involves her in adultery; and whoever marries her commits adultery.
33 'Again, you have heard that our forefathers were told, "Do not break your oath," and "Oaths sworn to the Lord must be kept." 34 But what I tell you is this: You are not to swear at all — not by heaven, for it is God's throne, 35 nor by the earth, for it is his footstool, nor by Jerusalem, for it is the city of the great King, 36 nor by your own head, because you cannot turn one hair of it white or black. 37 Plain "Yes" or "No" is all you need to say; anything beyond that comes from the evil one.
38 'You have heard that they were told, "An eye for an eye, a tooth for a tooth." 39 But what I tell you is this: Do not resist those who wrong you. If anyone slaps you on the right cheek, turn and offer him the other also. 40 If anyone wants to sue you and takes your shirt, let him have your cloak as well. 41 If someone in authority presses you into service for one mile, go with him two. 42 Give to anyone who asks; and do not turn your back on anyone who wants to borrow.
43 'You have heard that they were told, "Love your neighbour and hate your enemy." 44 But what I tell you is this: Love your enemies and pray for your persecutors; 45 only so can you be children of your heavenly Father, who causes the sun to rise on good and bad alike, and sends the rain on the innocent and the wicked. 46 If you love only those who love you, what reward can you expect? Even the tax-collectors do as much as that. 47 If you greet only your brothers, what is there extraordinary about that? Even the heathen do as much. 48 There must be no limit to your goodness, as your heavenly Father's goodness knows no bounds.

6 'BE careful not to parade your religion before others; if you do, no reward awaits you with your Father in heaven.
2 'So, when you give alms, do not announce it with a flourish of trumpets, as the hypocrites do in synagogues and in the streets to win the praise of others. Truly I tell you: they have their reward already. 3 But when you give alms, do not let your left hand know what your right is doing; 4 your good deed must be secret, and your Father who sees what is done in secret will reward you.
5 'Again, when you pray, do not be like the hypocrites; they love to say their prayers standing up in synagogues and at street corners for everyone to see them. Truly I tell you: they have their reward already. 6 But when you pray, go into a room by yourself, shut the door, and pray to your Father who is in secret; and your Father who sees what is done in secret will reward you.
7 'In your prayers do not go babbling on like the heathen, who imagine that the more they say the more likely they are to be heard. 8 Do not imitate them, for your Father knows what your needs are before you ask him.
9 'This is how you should pray:

Our Father in heaven,
    may your name be hallowed;
10 your kingdom come,
    your will be done,
        on earth as in heaven.
11 Give us today our daily bread.

---

d Gk *Gehenna*   *e* Or *evil*   *f* Gk *your brothers*   *g* Other ancient authorities add *openly*   *h* Or *our bread for tomorrow*

6:11 **our . . . bread:** *or* our bread for the morrow.

NEW AMERICAN BIBLE

NEW JERUSALEM BIBLE

and throw it away. It is better for you to lose one of your members than to have your whole body go into Gehenna. 31 "It was also said, 'Whoever divorces his wife must give her a bill of divorce.' 32 But I say to you, whoever divorces his wife (unless the marriage is unlawful) causes her to commit adultery, and whoever marries a divorced woman commits adultery.

33 "Again you have heard that it was said to your ancestors, 'Do not take a false oath, but make good to the Lord all that you vow.' 34 But I say to you, do not swear at all; not by heaven, for it is God's throne; 35 nor by the earth, for it is his footstool; nor by Jerusalem, for it is the city of the great King. 36 Do not swear by your head, for you cannot make a single hair white or black. 37 Let your 'Yes' mean 'Yes,' and your 'No' mean 'No.' Anything more is from the evil one.

38 "You have heard that it was said, 'An eye for an eye and a tooth for a tooth.' 39 But I say to you, offer no resistance to one who is evil. When someone strikes you on [your] right cheek, turn the other one to him as well. 40 If anyone wants to go to law with you over your tunic, hand him your cloak as well. 41 Should anyone press you into service for one mile, go with him for two miles. 42 Give to the one who asks of you, and do not turn your back on one who wants to borrow.

43 "You have heard that it was said, 'You shall love your neighbor and hate your enemy.' 44 But I say to you, love your enemies, and pray for those who persecute you, 45 that you may be children of your heavenly Father, for he makes his sun rise on the bad and the good, and causes rain to fall on the just and the unjust. 46 For if you love those who love you, what recompense will you have? Do not the tax collectors do the same? 47 And if you greet your brothers only, what is unusual about that? Do not the pagans do the same? 48 So be perfect, just as your heavenly Father is perfect.

6 "[But] take care not to perform righteous deeds in order that people may see them; otherwise, you will have no recompense from your heavenly Father. 2 When you give alms, do not blow a trumpet before you, as the hypocrites do in the synagogues and in the streets to win the praise of others. Amen, I say to you, they have received their reward. 3 But when you give alms, do not let your left hand know what your right is doing, 4 so that your almsgiving may be secret. And your Father who sees in secret will repay you.

5 "When you pray, do not be like the hypocrites, who love to stand and pray in the synagogues and on street corners so that others may see them. Amen, I say to you, they have received their reward. 6 But when you pray, go to your inner room, close the door, and pray to your Father in secret. And your Father who sees in secret will repay you. 7 In praying, do not babble like the pagans, who think that they will be heard because of their many words. 8 Do not be like them. Your Father knows what you need before you ask him.

9 "This is how you are to pray:

Our Father in heaven,
  hallowed be your name,
10 your kingdom come,
  your will be done,
    on earth as in heaven.
11 Give us today our daily bread;

downfall, cut it off and throw it away; for it will do you less harm to lose one part of yourself than to have your whole body go to hell.

31 'It has also been said, *Anyone who divorces his wife must give her a writ of dismissal.* s 32 But I say this to you, everyone who divorces his wife, except for the case of an illicit marriage, t makes her an adulteress; and anyone who marries a divorced woman commits adultery.

33 'Again, you have heard how it was said to our ancestors, *You must not break your oath, but must fulfil your oaths to the Lord.u* 34 But I say this to you, do not swear at all, either by *heaven*, since that is *God's throne*; 35 or by *earth*, since that is *his footstool*; or by Jerusalem, since that is *the city of the great King.v* 36 Do not swear by your own head either, since you cannot turn a single hair white or black. 37 All you need say is "Yes" if you mean yes, "No" if you mean no; anything more than this comes from the Evil One.

38 'You have heard how it was said: *Eye for eye and tooth for tooth.w* 39 But I say this to you: offer no resistance to the wicked. On the contrary, if anyone hits you on the right cheek, offer him the other as well; 40 if someone wishes to go to law with you to get your tunic, let him have your cloak as well. 41 And if anyone requires you to go one mile, go two miles with him. 42 Give to anyone who asks you, and if anyone wants to borrow, do not turn away.

43 'You have heard how it was said, *You will love your neighbourx* and hate your enemy. 44 But I say to you, love your enemies and pray for those who persecute you; 45 so that you may be children of your Father in heaven, for he causes his sun to rise on the bad as well as the good, and sends down rain to fall on the upright and the wicked alike. 46 For if you love those who love you, what reward will you get? Do not even the tax collectors do as much? 47 And if you save your greetings for your brothers, are you doing anything exceptional? 48 Do not even the gentiles do as much? You must therefore be perfect, just as your heavenly Father is perfect.'

6 'Be careful not to parade your uprightness in public to attract attention; otherwise you will lose all reward from your Father in heaven. 2 So when you give alms, do not have it trumpeted before you; this is what the hypocrites do in the synagogues and in the streets to win human admiration. In truth I tell you, they have had their reward. 3 But when you give alms, your left hand must not know what your right is doing; 4 your almsgiving must be secret, and your Father who sees all that is done in secret will reward you.

5 'And when you pray, do not imitate the hypocrites: they love to say their prayers standing up in the synagogues and at the street corners for people to see them. In truth I tell you, they have had their reward. 6 But when you pray, *go to your private* room, shut yourself in, and so pray y to your Father who is in that secret place, and your Father who sees all that is done in secret will reward you.

7 'In your prayers do not babble as the gentiles do, for they think that by using many words they will make themselves heard. 8 Do not be like them; your Father knows what you need before you ask him. 9 So you should pray like this:

Our Father in heaven,
  may your name be held holy,
10 your kingdom come,
  your will be done,
    on earth as in heaven.
11 Give us today our daily bread.

s 5 Dt 24:1. t 5 Marriage within the Jewish forbidden degrees, allowed by the Romans but not in Christianity. u 5 Ex 20:7. v 5 Ps 48:2. w 5 Ex 21:24. x 5 Lv 19:18. The rest of the sentence is not from the OT. y 6 Is 26:20.

NEW REVISED STANDARD VERSION

12   And forgive us our debts,
          as we also have forgiven our debtors.
13   And do not bring us to the time of trial,[i]
          but rescue us from the evil one.[j]

14 For if you forgive others their trespasses, your heavenly Father will also forgive you; 15 but if you do not forgive others, neither will your Father forgive your trespasses.

16 "And whenever you fast, do not look dismal, like the hypocrites, for they disfigure their faces so as to show others that they are fasting. Truly I tell you, they have received their reward. 17 But when you fast, put oil on your head and wash your face, 18 so that your fasting may be seen not by others but by your Father who is in secret; and your Father who sees in secret will reward you.[k]

19 "Do not store up for yourselves treasures on earth, where moth and rust[l] consume and where thieves break in and steal; 20 but store up for yourselves treasures in heaven, where neither moth nor rust[l] consumes and where thieves do not break in and steal. 21 For where your treasure is, there your heart will be also.

22 "The eye is the lamp of the body. So, if your eye is healthy, your whole body will be full of light; 23 but if your eye is unhealthy, your whole body will be full of darkness. If then the light in you is darkness, how great is the darkness!

24 "No one can serve two masters; for a slave will either hate the one and love the other, or be devoted to the one and despise the other. You cannot serve God and wealth.[m]

25 "Therefore I tell you, do not worry about your life, what you will eat or what you will drink,[n] or about your body, what you will wear. Is not life more than food, and the body more than clothing? 26 Look at the birds of the air; they neither sow nor reap nor gather into barns, and yet your heavenly Father feeds them. Are you not of more value than they? 27 And can any of you by worrying add a single hour to your span of life?[o] 28 And why do you worry about clothing? Consider the lilies of the field, how they grow; they neither toil nor spin, 29 yet I tell you, even Solomon in all his glory was not clothed like one of these. 30 But if God so clothes the grass of the field, which is alive today and tomorrow is thrown into the oven, will he not much more clothe you—you of little faith? 31 Therefore do not worry, saying, 'What will we eat?' or 'What will we drink?' or 'What will we wear?' 32 For it is the Gentiles who strive for all these things; and indeed your heavenly Father knows that you need all these things. 33 But strive first for the kingdom of God[p] and his[q] righteousness, and all these things will be given to you as well.

34 "So do not worry about tomorrow, for tomorrow will bring worries of its own. Today's trouble is enough for today.

7 "Do not judge, so that you may not be judged. 2 For with the judgment you make you will be judged, and the measure you give will be the measure you get. 3 Why do you see the speck in your neighbor's[r] eye, but do not notice the log in your own eye? 4 Or how can you say to your neighbor,[s] 'Let me take the speck out of your eye,' while the log is in your own eye? 5 You hypocrite, first take the log out of your own eye, and then you will see clearly to take the speck out of your neighbor's[r] eye.

REVISED ENGLISH BIBLE

12 Forgive us the wrong we have done,
          as we have forgiven those who have wronged us.
13 And do not put us to the test,
          but save us from the evil one.

14 'For if you forgive others the wrongs they have done, your heavenly Father will also forgive you; 15 but if you do not forgive others, then your Father will not forgive the wrongs that you have done.

16 'So too when you fast, do not look gloomy like the hypocrites: they make their faces unsightly so that everybody may see that they are fasting. Truly I tell you: they have their reward already. 17 But when you fast, anoint your head and wash your face, 18 so that no one sees that you are fasting, but only your Father who is in secret; and your Father who sees what is done in secret will give you your reward.

19 'Do not store up for yourselves treasure on earth, where moth and rust destroy, and thieves break in and steal; 20 but store up treasure in heaven, where neither moth nor rust will destroy, nor thieves break in and steal. 21 For where your treasure is, there will your heart be also.

22 'The lamp of the body is the eye. If your eyes are sound, you will have light for your whole body; 23 if your eyes are bad, your whole body will be in darkness. If then the only light you have is darkness, how great a darkness that will be.

24 'No one can serve two masters; for either he will hate the first and love the second, or he will be devoted to the first and despise the second. You cannot serve God and Money.

25 'This is why I tell you not to be anxious about food and drink to keep you alive and about clothes to cover your body. Surely life is more than food, the body more than clothes. 26 Look at the birds in the sky; they do not sow and reap and store in barns, yet your heavenly Father feeds them. Are you not worth more than the birds? 27 Can anxious thought add a single day to your life? 28 And why be anxious about clothes? Consider how the lilies grow in the fields; they do not work, they do not spin; yet I tell you, even Solomon in all his splendour was not attired like one of them. 30 If that is how God clothes the grass in the fields, which is there today and tomorrow is thrown on the stove, will he not all the more clothe you? How little faith you have! 31 Do not ask anxiously, "What are we to eat? What are we to drink? What shall we wear?" 32 These are the things that occupy the minds of the heathen, but your heavenly Father knows that you need them all. 33 Set your mind on God's kingdom and his justice before everything else, and all the rest will come to you as well. 34 So do not be anxious about tomorrow; tomorrow will look after itself. Each day has troubles enough of its own.

7 'Do not judge, and you will not be judged. 2 For as you judge others, so you will yourselves be judged, and whatever measure you deal out to others will be dealt to you. 3 Why do you look at the speck of sawdust in your brother's eye, with never a thought for the plank in your own? 4 How can you say to your brother, "Let me take the speck out of your eye," when all the time there is a plank in your own? 5 You hypocrite! First take the plank out of your own eye, and then you will see clearly to take the speck out of your brother's.

---

[i] Or us into temptation   [j] Or from evil. Other ancient authorities add, in some form, For the kingdom and the power and the glory are yours forever. Amen.   [k] Other ancient authorities add openly [l] Gk eating   [m] Gk mammon   [n] Other ancient authorities lack or what you will drink   [o] Or add one cubit to your height   [p] Other ancient authorities lack of God   [q] Or its   [r] Gk brother's [s] Gk brother

6:13 **from the evil one:** or from evil. Some witnesses add For yours is the kingdom and the power and the glory, for ever. Amen. 6:27 **add . . . life:** or add one foot to your height.   6:28 **Consider . . . spin:** one witness reads Consider the lilies: they neither card, nor spin, nor work.

12 and forgive us our debts,
   as we forgive our debtors;
13 and do not subject us to the final test,
   but deliver us from the evil one.

14 If you forgive others their transgressions, your heavenly Father will forgive you. 15 But if you do not forgive others, neither will your Father forgive your transgressions.

16 "When you fast, do not look gloomy like the hypocrites. They neglect their appearance, so that they may appear to others to be fasting. Amen, I say to you, they have received their reward. 17 But when you fast, anoint your head and wash your face, 18 so that you may not appear to be fasting, except to your Father who is hidden. And your Father who sees what is hidden will repay you.

19 "Do not store up for yourselves treasures on earth, where moth and decay destroy, and thieves break in and steal. 20 But store up treasures in heaven, where neither moth nor decay destroy, nor thieves break in and steal. 21 For where your treasure is, there also will your heart be.

22 "The lamp of the body is the eye. If your eye is sound, your whole body will be filled with light; 23 but if your eye is bad, your whole body will be in darkness. And if the light in you is darkness, how great will the darkness be.

24 "No one can serve two masters. He will either hate one and love the other, or be devoted to one and despise the other. You cannot serve God and mammon.

25 "Therefore I tell you, do not worry about your life, what you will eat [or drink], or about your body, what you will wear. Is not life more than food and the body more than clothing? 26 Look at the birds in the sky; they do not sow or reap, they gather nothing into barns, yet your heavenly Father feeds them. Are not you more important than they? 27 Can any of you by worrying add a single moment to your life-span? 28 Why are you anxious about clothes? Learn from the way the wild flowers grow. They do not work or spin. 29 But I tell you that not even Solomon in all his splendor was clothed like one of them. 30 If God so clothes the grass of the field, which grows today and is thrown into the oven tomorrow, will he not much more provide for you, O you of little faith? 31 So do not worry and say, 'What are we to eat?' or 'What are we to drink?' or 'What are we to wear?' 32 All these things the pagans seek. Your heavenly Father knows that you need them all. 33 But seek first the kingdom [of God] and his righteousness, and all these things will be given you besides. 34 Do not worry about tomorrow; tomorrow will take care of itself. Sufficient for a day is its own evil.

7 "Stop judging, that you may not be judged. 2 For as you judge, so will you be judged, and the measure with which you measure will be measured out to you. 3 Why do you notice the splinter in your brother's eye, but do not perceive the wooden beam in your own eye? 4 How can you say to your brother, 'Let me remove that splinter from your eye,' while the wooden beam is in your eye? 5 You hypocrite, remove the wooden beam from your eye first; then you will see clearly to remove the splinter from your brother's eye.

12 And forgive us our debts,
   as we have forgiven those who are in debt to us.
13 And do not put us to the test,
   but save us from the Evil One. z

14 'Yes, if you forgive others their failings, your heavenly Father will forgive you yours; 15 but if you do not forgive others, your Father will not forgive your failings either.

16 'When you are fasting, do not put on a gloomy look as the hypocrites do: they go about looking unsightly to let people know they are fasting. In truth I tell you, they have had their reward. 17 But when you fast, put scent on your head and wash your face, 18 so that no one will know you are fasting except your Father who sees all that is done in secret; and your Father who sees all that is done in secret will reward you.

19 'Do not store up treasures for yourselves on earth, where moth and woodworm destroy them and thieves can break in and steal. 20 But store up treasures for yourselves in heaven, where neither moth nor woodworm destroys them and thieves cannot break in and steal. 21 For wherever your treasure is, there will your heart be too.

22 'The lamp of the body is the eye. It follows that if your eye is clear, your whole body will be filled with light. 23 But if your eye is diseased, your whole body will be darkness. If then, the light inside you is darkened, what darkness that will be!

24 'No one can be the slave of two masters: he will either hate the first and love the second, or be attached to the first and despise the second. You cannot be the slave both of God and of money.

25 'That is why I am telling you not to worry about your life and what you are to eat, nor about your body and what you are to wear. Surely life is more than food, and the body more than clothing! 26 Look at the birds in the sky. They do not sow or reap or gather into barns; yet your heavenly Father feeds them. Are you not worth much more than they are? 27 Can any of you, however much you worry, add one single cubit to your span of life? 28 And why worry about clothing? Think of the flowers growing in the fields; they never have to work or spin; 29 yet I assure you that not even Solomon in all his royal robes was clothed like one of these. 30 Now if that is how God clothes the wild flowers growing in the field which are there today and thrown into the furnace tomorrow, will he not much more look after you, you who have so little faith? 31 So do not worry; do not say, "What are we to eat? What are we to drink? What are we to wear?" 32 It is the gentiles who set their hearts on all these things. Your heavenly Father knows you need them all. 33 Set your hearts on his kingdom first, and on God's saving justice, and all these other things will be given you as well. 34 So do not worry about tomorrow: tomorrow will take care of itself. Each day has enough trouble of its own.'

7 'Do not judge, and you will not be judged; 2 because the judgements you give are the judgements you will get, and the standard you use will be the standard used for you. 3 Why do you observe the splinter in your brother's eye and never notice the great log in your own? 4 And how dare you say to your brother, "Let me take that splinter out of your eye," when, look, there is a great log in your own? 5 Hypocrite! Take the log out of your own eye first, and then you will see clearly enough to take the splinter out of your brother's eye.

z 6 Lk 11:2–4.

NEW REVISED STANDARD VERSION

6 "Do not give what is holy to dogs; and do not throw your pearls before swine, or they will trample them under foot and turn and maul you.

7 "Ask, and it will be given you; search, and you will find; knock, and the door will be opened for you. 8 For everyone who asks receives, and everyone who searches finds, and for everyone who knocks, the door will be opened. 9 Is there anyone among you who, if your child asks for bread, will give a stone? 10 Or if the child asks for a fish, will give a snake? 11 If you then, who are evil, know how to give good gifts to your children, how much more will your Father in heaven give good things to those who ask him!

12 "In everything do to others as you would have them do to you; for this is the law and the prophets.

13 "Enter through the narrow gate; for the gate is wide and the road is easy[t] that leads to destruction, and there are many who take it. 14 For the gate is narrow and the road is hard that leads to life, and there are few who find it.

15 "Beware of false prophets, who come to you in sheep's clothing but inwardly are ravenous wolves. 16 You will know them by their fruits. Are grapes gathered from thorns, or figs from thistles? 17 In the same way, every good tree bears good fruit, but the bad tree bears bad fruit. 18 A good tree cannot bear bad fruit, nor can a bad tree bear good fruit. 19 Every tree that does not bear good fruit is cut down and thrown into the fire. 20 Thus you will know them by their fruits.

21 "Not everyone who says to me, 'Lord, Lord,' will enter the kingdom of heaven, but only the one who does the will of my Father in heaven. 22 On that day many will say to me, 'Lord, Lord, did we not prophesy in your name, and cast out demons in your name, and do many deeds of power in your name?' 23 Then I will declare to them, 'I never knew you; go away from me, you evildoers.'

24 "Everyone then who hears these words of mine and acts on them will be like a wise man who built his house on rock. 25 The rain fell, the floods came, and the winds blew and beat on that house, but it did not fall, because it had been founded on rock. 26 And everyone who hears these words of mine and does not act on them will be like a foolish man who built his house on sand. 27 The rain fell, and the floods came, and the winds blew and beat against that house, and it fell — and great was its fall!"

28 Now when Jesus had finished saying these things, the crowds were astounded at his teaching, 29 for he taught them as one having authority, and not as their scribes.

8 When Jesus[u] had come down from the mountain, great crowds followed him; 2 and there was a leper[v] who came to him and knelt before him, saying, "Lord, if you choose, you can make me clean." 3 He stretched out his hand and touched him, saying, "I do choose. Be made clean!" Immediately his leprosy[v] was cleansed. 4 Then Jesus said to him, "See that you say nothing to anyone; but go, show yourself to the priest, and offer the gift that Moses commanded, as a testimony to them."

5 When he entered Capernaum, a centurion came to him, appealing to him 6 and saying, "Lord, my servant is lying at home paralyzed, in terrible distress." 7 And he said to him, "I will come and cure him." 8 The centurion answered, "Lord, I am not worthy to have you come under my roof; but only speak the word, and my servant will be healed. 9 For I also am a man under authority, with soldiers under me; and I say to one, 'Go,' and he goes, and to another, 'Come,' and he comes, and to my slave, 'Do this,'

REVISED ENGLISH BIBLE

6 'Do not give dogs what is holy; do not throw your pearls to the pigs: they will only trample on them, and turn and tear you to pieces.

7 'Ask, and you will receive; seek, and you will find; knock, and the door will be opened to you. 8 For everyone who asks receives, those who seek find, and to those who knock, the door will be opened.

9 'Would any of you offer his son a stone when he asks for bread, 10 or a snake when he asks for a fish? 11 If you, bad as you are, know how to give good things to your children, how much more will your heavenly Father give good things to those who ask him!

12 'Always treat others as you would like them to treat you: that is the law and the prophets.

13 'Enter by the narrow gate. Wide is the gate and broad the road that leads to destruction, and many enter that way; 14 narrow is the gate and constricted the road that leads to life, and those who find them are few.

15 'Beware of false prophets, who come to you dressed up as sheep while underneath they are savage wolves. 16 You will recognize them by their fruit. Can grapes be picked from briars, or figs from thistles? 17 A good tree always yields sound fruit, and a poor tree bad fruit. 18 A good tree cannot bear bad fruit, or a poor tree sound fruit. 19 A tree that does not yield sound fruit is cut down and thrown on the fire. 20 That is why I say you will recognize them by their fruit.

21 'Not everyone who says to me, "Lord, Lord" will enter the kingdom of Heaven, but only those who do the will of my heavenly Father. 22 When the day comes, many will say to me, "Lord, Lord, did we not prophesy in your name, drive out demons in your name, and in your name perform many miracles?" 23 Then I will tell them plainly, "I never knew you. Out of my sight; your deeds are evil!"

24 'So whoever hears these words of mine and acts on them is like a man who had the sense to build his house on rock. 25 The rain came down, the floods rose, the winds blew and beat upon that house; but it did not fall, because its foundations were on rock. 26 And whoever hears these words of mine and does not act on them is like a man who was foolish enough to build his house on sand. 27 The rain came down, the floods rose, the winds blew and battered against that house; and it fell with a great crash.'

28 When Jesus had finished this discourse the people were amazed at his teaching; 29 unlike their scribes he taught with a note of authority.

8 When he came down from the mountain great crowds followed him. 2 And now a leper approached him, bowed before him, and said, 'Sir, if only you will, you can make me clean.' 3 Jesus stretched out his hand and touched him, saying, 'I will; be clean.' And his leprosy was cured immediately. 4 Then Jesus said to him, 'See that you tell nobody; but go and show yourself to the priest, and make the offering laid down by Moses to certify the cure.'

5 As Jesus entered Capernaum a centurion came up to ask his help. 6 'Sir,' he said, 'my servant is lying at home paralysed and racked with pain.' 7 Jesus said, 'I will come and cure him.' 8 But the centurion replied, 'Sir, I am not worthy to have you under my roof. You need only say the word and my servant will be cured. 9 I know, for I am myself under orders, with soldiers under me. I say to one, "Go," and he goes; to another, "Come here," and he comes; and to my servant, "Do this," and he does it.' 10 Jesus heard him with

---

[t] Other ancient authorities read *for the road is wide and easy*
[u] Gk *he*　[v] The terms *leper* and *leprosy* can refer to several diseases

6 "Do not give what is holy to dogs, or throw your pearls before swine, lest they trample them underfoot, and turn and tear you to pieces.

7 "Ask and it will be given to you; seek and you will find; knock and the door will be opened to you. 8 For everyone who asks, receives; and the one who seeks, finds; and to the one who knocks, the door will be opened. 9 Which one of you would hand his son a stone when he asks for a loaf of bread, 10 or a snake when he asks for a fish? 11 If you then, who are wicked, know how to give good gifts to your children, how much more will your heavenly Father give good things to those who ask him.

12 "Do to others whatever you would have them do to you. This is the law and the prophets.

13 "Enter through the narrow gate; for the gate is wide and the road broad that leads to destruction, and those who enter through it are many. 14 How narrow the gate and constricted the road that leads to life. And those who find it are few.

15 "Beware of false prophets, who come to you in sheep's clothing, but underneath are ravenous wolves. 16 By their fruits you will know them. Do people pick grapes from thornbushes, or figs from thistles? 17 Just so, every good tree bears good fruit, and a rotten tree bears bad fruit. 18 A good tree cannot bear bad fruit, nor can a rotten tree bear good fruit. 19 Every tree that does not bear good fruit will be cut down and thrown into the fire. 20 So by their fruits you will know them.

21 "Not everyone who says to me, 'Lord, Lord,' will enter the kingdom of heaven, but only the one who does the will of my Father in heaven. 22 Many will say to me on that day, 'Lord, Lord, did we not prophesy in your name? Did we not drive out demons in your name? Did we not do mighty deeds in your name?' 23 Then I will declare to them solemnly, 'I never knew you. Depart from me, you evildoers.'

24 "Everyone who listens to these words of mine and acts on them will be like a wise man who built his house on rock. 25 The rain fell, the floods came, and the winds blew and buffeted the house. But it did not collapse; it had been set solidly on rock. 26 And everyone who listens to these words of mine but does not act on them will be like a fool who built his house on sand. 27 The rain fell, the floods came, and the winds blew and buffeted the house. And it collapsed and was completely ruined."

28 When Jesus finished these words, the crowds were astonished at his teaching, 29 for he taught them as one having authority, and not as their scribes.

8 When Jesus came down from the mountain, great crowds followed him. 2 And then a leper approached, did him homage, and said, "Lord, if you wish, you can make me clean." 3 He stretched out his hand, touched him, and said, "I will do it. Be made clean." His leprosy was cleansed immediately. 4 Then Jesus said to him, "See that you tell no one, but go show yourself to the priest, and offer the gift that Moses prescribed; that will be proof for them."

5 When he entered Capernaum, a centurion approached him and appealed to him, 6 saying, "Lord, my servant is lying at home paralyzed, suffering dreadfully." 7 He said to him, "I will come and cure him." 8 The centurion said in reply, "Lord, I am not worthy to have you enter under my roof; only say the word and my servant will be healed. 9 For I too am a person subject to authority, with soldiers subject to me. And I say to one, 'Go,' and he goes; and to another, 'Come here,' and he comes; and to my slave, 'Do this,' and

6 'Do not give dogs what is holy; and do not throw your pearls in front of pigs, or they may trample them and then turn on you and tear you to pieces.

7 'Ask, and it will be given to you; search, and you will find; knock, and the door will be opened to you. 8 Everyone who asks receives; everyone who searches finds; everyone who knocks will have the door opened. 9 Is there anyone among you who would hand his son a stone when he asked for bread? 10 Or would hand him a snake when he asked for a fish? 11 If you, then, evil as you are, know how to give your children what is good, how much more will your Father in heaven give good things to those who ask him!

12 'So always treat others as you would like them to treat you; that is the Law and the Prophets.

13 'Enter by the narrow gate, since the road that leads to destruction is wide and spacious, and many take it; 14 but it is a narrow gate and a hard road that leads to life, and only a few find it.

15 'Beware of false prophets who come to you disguised as sheep but underneath are ravenous wolves. 16 You will be able to tell them by their fruits. Can people pick grapes from thorns, or figs from thistles? 17 In the same way, a sound tree produces good fruit but a rotten tree bad fruit. 18 A sound tree cannot bear bad fruit, nor a rotten tree bear good fruit. 19 Any tree that does not produce good fruit is cut down and thrown on the fire. 20 I repeat, you will be able to tell them by their fruits.

21 'It is not anyone who says to me, "Lord, Lord," who will enter the kingdom of Heaven, but the person who does the will of my Father in heaven. 22 When the day comes many will say to me, "Lord, Lord, did we not prophesy in your name, drive out demons in your name, work many miracles in your name?" 23 Then I shall tell them to their faces: I have never known you; *away from me, all evil doers!*[a]

24 'Therefore, everyone who listens to these words of mine and acts on them will be like a sensible man who built his house on rock. 25 Rain came down, floods rose, gales blew and hurled themselves against that house, and it did not fall: it was founded on rock. 26 But everyone who listens to these words of mine and does not act on them will be like a stupid man who built his house on sand. 27 Rain came down, floods rose, gales blew and struck that house, and it fell; and what a fall it had!'

28 Jesus had now finished what he wanted to say, and his teaching made a deep impression on the people 29 because he taught them with authority, unlike their own scribes.

8 After he had come down from the mountain large crowds followed him. 2 Suddenly a man with a virulent skin-disease came up and bowed low in front of him, saying, 'Lord, if you are willing, you can cleanse me.' 3 Jesus stretched out his hand and touched him saying, 'I am willing. Be cleansed.' And his skin-disease was cleansed at once. 4 Then Jesus said to him, 'Mind you tell no one, but go and show yourself to the priest and make the offering prescribed by Moses,[b] as evidence to them.'

5 When he went into Capernaum a centurion came up and pleaded with him. 6 'Sir,' he said, 'my servant is lying at home paralysed and in great pain.' 7 Jesus said to him, 'I will come myself and cure him.' 8 The centurion replied, 'Sir, I am not worthy to have you under my roof; just give the word and my servant will be cured. 9 For I am under authority myself and have soldiers under me; and I say to one man, "Go," and he goes; to another, "Come here," and he comes; to my servant, "Do this," and he does it.'

a 7 Ps 6:8.   b 8 Lv 14:1–32.

NEW REVISED STANDARD VERSION

REVISED ENGLISH BIBLE

and the slave does it." 10 When Jesus heard him, he was amazed and said to those who followed him, "Truly I tell you, in no one*w* in Israel have I found such faith. 11 I tell you, many will come from east and west and will eat with Abraham and Isaac and Jacob in the kingdom of heaven, 12 while the heirs of the kingdom will be thrown into the outer darkness, where there will be weeping and gnashing of teeth." 13 And to the centurion Jesus said, "Go; let it be done for you according to your faith." And the servant was healed in that hour.

14 When Jesus entered Peter's house, he saw his mother-in-law lying in bed with a fever; 15 he touched her hand, and the fever left her, and she got up and began to serve him. 16 That evening they brought to him many who were possessed with demons; and he cast out the spirits with a word, and cured all who were sick. 17 This was to fulfill what had been spoken through the prophet Isaiah, "He took our infirmities and bore our diseases."

18 Now when Jesus saw great crowds around him, he gave orders to go over to the other side. 19 A scribe then approached and said, "Teacher, I will follow you wherever you go." 20 And Jesus said to him, "Foxes have holes, and birds of the air have nests; but the Son of Man has nowhere to lay his head." 21 Another of his disciples said to him, "Lord, first let me go and bury my father." 22 But Jesus said to him, "Follow me, and let the dead bury their own dead."

23 And when he got into the boat, his disciples followed him. 24 A windstorm arose on the sea, so great that the boat was being swamped by the waves; but he was asleep. 25 And they went and woke him up, saying, "Lord, save us! We are perishing!" 26 And he said to them, "Why are you afraid, you of little faith?" Then he got up and rebuked the winds and the sea; and there was a dead calm. 27 They were amazed, saying, "What sort of man is this, that even the winds and the sea obey him?"

28 When he came to the other side, to the country of the Gadarenes,*x* two demoniacs coming out of the tombs met him. They were so fierce that no one could pass that way. 29 Suddenly they shouted, "What have you to do with us, Son of God? Have you come here to torment us before the time?" 30 Now a large herd of swine was feeding at some distance from them. 31 The demons begged him, "If you cast us out, send us into the herd of swine." 32 And he said to them, "Go!" So they came out and entered the swine; and suddenly, the whole herd rushed down the steep bank into the sea and perished in the water. 33 The swineherds ran off, and on going into the town, they told the whole story about what had happened to the demoniacs. 34 Then the whole town came out to meet Jesus; and when they saw him, they 9 begged him to leave their neighborhood. 1 And after getting into a boat he crossed the sea and came to his own town.

2 And just then some people were carrying a paralyzed man lying on a bed. When Jesus saw their faith, he said to the paralytic, "Take heart, son; your sins are forgiven." 3 Then some of the scribes said to themselves, "This man is blaspheming." 4 But Jesus, perceiving their thoughts, said, "Why do you think evil in your hearts? 5 For which is easier, to say, 'Your sins are forgiven,' or to say, 'Stand up and walk'? 6 But so that you may know that the Son of Man has authority on earth to forgive sins"—he then said to the paralytic—"Stand up, take your bed and go to your home." 7 And he stood up and went to his home. 8 When the crowds saw it, they were filled with awe, and they glorified God, who had given such authority to human beings.

astonishment, and said to the people who were following him, 'Truly I tell you: nowhere in Israel have I found such faith. 11 Many, I tell you, will come from east and west to sit with Abraham, Isaac, and Jacob at the banquet in the kingdom of Heaven. 12 But those who were born to the kingdom will be thrown out into the dark, where there will be wailing and grinding of teeth.' 13 Then Jesus said to the centurion, 'Go home; as you have believed, so let it be.' At that very moment the boy recovered.

14 Jesus then went to Peter's house and found Peter's mother-in-law in bed with fever. 15 So he took her by the hand; the fever left her, and she got up and attended to his needs.

16 That evening they brought to him many who were possessed by demons; and he drove the spirits out with a word and healed all who were sick, 17 to fulfil the prophecy of Isaiah: 'He took our illnesses from us and carried away our diseases.'

18 AT the sight of the crowd surrounding him Jesus gave word to cross to the other side of the lake. 19 A scribe came up and said to him, 'Teacher, I will follow you wherever you go.' 20 Jesus replied, 'Foxes have their holes and birds their roosts; but the Son of Man has nowhere to lay his head.' 21 Another man, one of his disciples, said to him, 'Lord, let me go and bury my father first.' 22 Jesus replied, 'Follow me, and leave the dead to bury their dead.'

23 Jesus then got into the boat, and his disciples followed. 24 All at once a great storm arose on the lake, till the waves were breaking right over the boat; but he went on sleeping. 25 So they came and woke him, saying: 'Save us, Lord; we are sinking!' 26 'Why are you such cowards?' he said. 'How little faith you have!' With that he got up and rebuked the wind and the sea, and there was a dead calm. 27 The men were astonished at what had happened, and exclaimed, 'What sort of man is this? Even the wind and the sea obey him.'

28 When he reached the country of the Gadarenes on the other side, two men came to meet him from among the tombs; they were possessed by demons, and so violent that no one dared pass that way. 29 'Son of God,' they shouted, 'what do you want with us? Have you come here to torment us before our time?' 30 In the distance a large herd of pigs was feeding; 31 and the demons begged him: 'If you drive us out, send us into that herd of pigs.' 32 'Go!' he said. Then they came out and went into the pigs, and the whole herd rushed over the edge into the lake, and perished in the water. 33 The men in charge of them took to their heels, and made for the town, where they told the whole story, and what had happened to the madmen. 34 Then the whole town came out to meet Jesus; and when they saw him they begged 9 him to leave the district. 1 So he got into the boat and crossed over, and came to his own town.

2 Some men appeared, bringing to Jesus a paralysed man on a bed. When he saw their faith Jesus said to the man, 'Take heart, my son; your sins are forgiven.' 3 At this some of the scribes said to themselves, 'This man is blaspheming!' 4 Jesus realized what they were thinking, and said, 'Why do you harbour evil thoughts? 5 Is it easier to say, "Your sins are forgiven," or to say, "Stand up and walk"? 6 But to convince you that the Son of Man has authority on earth to forgive sins'—he turned to the paralysed man—'stand up, take your bed, and go home.' 7 And he got up and went off home. 8 The people were filled with awe at the sight, and praised God for granting such authority to men.

---

w Other ancient authorities read *Truly I tell you, not even* *x* Other ancient authorities read *Gergesenes*; others, *Gerasenes*

NEW AMERICAN BIBLE

he does it." 10 When Jesus heard this, he was amazed and said to those following him, "Amen, I say to you, in no one in Israel have I found such faith. 11 I say to you, many will come from the east and the west, and will recline with Abraham, Isaac, and Jacob at the banquet in the kingdom of heaven, 12 but the children of the kingdom will be driven out into the outer darkness, where there will be wailing and grinding of teeth." 13 And Jesus said to the centurion, "You may go; as you have believed, let it be done for you." And at that very hour [his] servant was healed.

14 Jesus entered the house of Peter, and saw his mother-in-law lying in bed with a fever. 15 He touched her hand, the fever left her, and she rose and waited on him.

16 When it was evening, they brought him many who were possessed by demons, and he drove out the spirits by a word and cured all the sick, 17 to fulfill what had been said by Isaiah the prophet:

"He took away our infirmities
and bore our diseases."

18 When Jesus saw a crowd around him, he gave orders to cross to the other side. 19 A scribe approached and said to him, "Teacher, I will follow you wherever you go." 20 Jesus answered him, "Foxes have dens and birds of the sky have nests, but the Son of Man has nowhere to rest his head." 21 Another of [his] disciples said to him, "Lord, let me go first and bury my father." 22 But Jesus answered him, "Follow me, and let the dead bury their dead."

23 He got into a boat and his disciples followed him. 24 Suddenly a violent storm came up on the sea, so that the boat was being swamped by waves; but he was asleep. 25 They came and woke him, saying, "Lord, save us! We are perishing!" 26 He said to them, "Why are you terrified, O you of little faith?" Then he got up, rebuked the winds and the sea, and there was great calm. 27 The men were amazed and said, "What sort of man is this, whom even the winds and the sea obey?"

28 When he came to the other side, to the territory of the Gadarenes, two demoniacs who were coming from the tombs met him. They were so savage that no one could travel by that road. 29 They cried out, "What have you to do with us, Son of God? Have you come here to torment us before the appointed time?" 30 Some distance away a herd of many swine was feeding. 31 The demons pleaded with him, "If you drive us out, send us into the herd of swine." 32 And he said to them, "Go then!" They came out and entered the swine, and the whole herd rushed down the steep bank into the sea where they drowned. 33 The swineherds ran away, and when they came to the town they reported everything, including what had happened to the demoniacs. 34 Thereupon the whole town came out to meet Jesus, and when they saw him they begged him to leave their district.

9 He entered a boat, made the crossing, and came into his own town. 2 And there people brought to him a paralytic lying on a stretcher. When Jesus saw their faith, he said to the paralytic, "Courage, child, your sins are forgiven." 3 At that, some of the scribes said to themselves, "This man is blaspheming." 4 Jesus knew what they were thinking, and said, "Why do you harbor evil thoughts? 5 Which is easier, to say, 'Your sins are forgiven,' or to say, 'Rise and walk'? 6 But that you may know that the Son of Man has authority on earth to forgive sins"—he then said to the paralytic, "Rise, pick up your stretcher, and go home." 7 He rose and went home. 8 When the crowds saw this they were struck with awe and glorified God who had given such authority to human beings.

NEW JERUSALEM BIBLE

10 When Jesus heard this he was astonished and said to those following him, 'In truth I tell you, in no one in Israel have I found faith as great as this. 11 And I tell you that many will come from east and west and sit down with Abraham and Isaac and Jacob at the feast in the kingdom of Heaven; 12 but the children of the kingdom will be thrown out into the darkness outside, where there will be weeping and grinding of teeth.' 13 And to the centurion Jesus said, 'Go back, then; let this be done for you, as your faith demands.' And the servant was cured at that moment.

14 And going into Peter's house Jesus found Peter's mother-in-law in bed and feverish. 15 He touched her hand and the fever left her, and she got up and began to serve him.

16 That evening they brought him many who were possessed by devils. He drove out the spirits with a command and cured all who were sick. 17 This was to fulfil what was spoken by the prophet Isaiah:

*He himself bore our sicknesses away and carried
our diseases.*c

18 When Jesus saw the crowd all about him he gave orders to leave for the other side. 19 One of the scribes then came up and said to him, 'Master, I will follow you wherever you go.' 20 Jesus said, 'Foxes have holes and the birds of the air have nests, but the Son of man has nowhere to lay his head.' 21 Another man, one of the disciples, said to him, 'Lord, let me go and bury my father first.' 22 But Jesus said, 'Follow me, and leave the dead to bury their dead.'

23 Then he got into the boat followed by his disciples. 24 Suddenly a storm broke over the lake, so violent that the boat was being swamped by the waves. But he was asleep. 25 So they went to him and woke him saying, 'Save us, Lord, we are lost!' 26 And he said to them, 'Why are you so frightened, you who have so little faith?' And then he stood up and rebuked the winds and the sea; and there was a great calm. 27 They were astounded and said, 'Whatever kind of man is this, that even the winds and the sea obey him?'

28 When he reached the territory of the Gadarenes on the other side, two demoniacs came towards him out of the tombs—they were so dangerously violent that nobody could use that path. 29 Suddenly they shouted, 'What do you want with us, Son of God? Have you come here to torture us before the time?' 30 Now some distance away there was a large herd of pigs feeding, 31 and the devils pleaded with Jesus, 'If you drive us out, send us into the herd of pigs.' 32 And he said to them, 'Go then,' and they came out and made for the pigs; and at that the whole herd charged down the cliff into the lake and perished in the water. 33 The herdsmen ran off and made for the city, where they told the whole story, including what had happened to the demoniacs. 34 Suddenly the whole city set out to meet Jesus; and as soon as they saw him they implored him to leave their neighbourhood.

9 He got back in the boat, crossed the water and came to his home town. 2 And suddenly some people brought him a paralytic stretched out on a bed. Seeing their faith, Jesus said to the paralytic, 'Take comfort, my child, your sins are forgiven.' 3 And now some scribes said to themselves, 'This man is being blasphemous.' 4 Knowing what was in their minds Jesus said, 'Why do you have such wicked thoughts in your hearts? 5 Now, which of these is easier: to say, "Your sins are forgiven," or to say, "Get up and walk"? 6 But to prove to you that the Son of man has authority on earth to forgive sins,'—then he said to the paralytic—'get up, pick up your bed and go off home.' 7 And the man got up and went home. 8 A feeling of awe came over the crowd when they saw this, and they praised God for having given such authority to human beings.

c **8** Is 53:4.

NEW REVISED STANDARD VERSION

9 As Jesus was walking along, he saw a man called Matthew sitting at the tax booth; and he said to him, "Follow me." And he got up and followed him.

10 And as he sat at dinner ᵞ in the house, many tax collectors and sinners came and were sitting ᶻ with him and his disciples. 11 When the Pharisees saw this, they said to his disciples, "Why does your teacher eat with tax collectors and sinners?" 12 But when he heard this, he said, "Those who are well have no need of a physician, but those who are sick. 13 Go and learn what this means, 'I desire mercy, not sacrifice.' For I have come to call not the righteous but sinners."

14 Then the disciples of John came to him, saying, "Why do we and the Pharisees fast often, ᵃ but your disciples do not fast?" 15 And Jesus said to them, "The wedding guests cannot mourn as long as the bridegroom is with them, can they? The days will come when the bridegroom is taken away from them, and then they will fast. 16 No one sews a piece of unshrunk cloth on an old cloak, for the patch pulls away from the cloak, and a worse tear is made. 17 Neither is new wine put into old wineskins; otherwise, the skins burst, and the wine is spilled, and the skins are destroyed; but new wine is put into fresh wineskins, and so both are preserved."

18 While he was saying these things to them, suddenly a leader of the synagogue ᵇ came in and knelt before him, saying, "My daughter has just died; but come and lay your hand on her, and she will live." 19 And Jesus got up and followed him, with his disciples. 20 Then suddenly a woman who had been suffering from hemorrhages for twelve years came up behind him and touched the fringe of his cloak, 21 for she said to herself, "If I only touch his cloak, I will be made well." 22 Jesus turned, and seeing her he said, "Take heart, daughter; your faith has made you well." And instantly the woman was made well. 23 When Jesus came to the leader's house and saw the flute players and the crowd making a commotion, 24 he said, "Go away; for the girl is not dead but sleeping." And they laughed at him. 25 But when the crowd had been put outside, he went in and took her by the hand, and the girl got up. 26 And the report of this spread throughout that district.

27 As Jesus went on from there, two blind men followed him, crying loudly, "Have mercy on us, Son of David!" 28 When he entered the house, the blind men came to him; and Jesus said to them, "Do you believe that I am able to do this?" They said to him, "Yes, Lord." 29 Then he touched their eyes and said, "According to your faith let it be done to you." 30 And their eyes were opened. Then Jesus sternly ordered them, "See that no one knows of this." 31 But they went away and spread the news about him throughout that district.

32 After they had gone away, a demoniac who was mute was brought to him. 33 And when the demon had been cast out, the one who had been mute spoke; and the crowds were amazed and said, "Never has anything like this been seen in Israel." 34 But the Pharisees said, "By the ruler of the demons he casts out the demons." ᶜ

35 Then Jesus went about all the cities and villages, teaching in their synagogues, and proclaiming the good news of the kingdom, and curing every disease and every sickness. 36 When he saw the crowds, he had compassion for them, because they were harassed and helpless, like sheep without a shepherd. 37 Then he said to his disciples, "The harvest is plentiful, but the laborers are few; 38 therefore ask the Lord of the harvest to send out laborers into his harvest."

ᵞ Gk reclined   ᶻ Gk were reclining   ᵃ Other ancient authorities lack often   ᵇ Gk lacks of the synagogue   ᶜ Other ancient authorities lack this verse

REVISED ENGLISH BIBLE

9 As HE went on from there Jesus saw a man named Matthew at his seat in the custom-house, and said to him, 'Follow me'; and Matthew rose and followed him.

10 When Jesus was having a meal in the house, many tax-collectors and sinners were seated with him and his disciples. 11 Noticing this, the Pharisees said to his disciples, 'Why is it that your teacher eats with tax-collectors and sinners?' 12 Hearing this he said, 'It is not the healthy who need a doctor, but the sick. 13 Go and learn what this text means, "I require mercy, not sacrifice." I did not come to call the virtuous, but sinners.'

14 Then John's disciples came to him with the question: 'Why is it that we and the Pharisees fast but your disciples do not?' 15 Jesus replied, 'Can you expect the bridegroom's friends to be sad while the bridegroom is with them? The time will come when the bridegroom will be taken away from them; then they will fast.

16 'No one puts a patch of unshrunk cloth on an old garment; for then the patch tears away from the garment, and leaves a bigger hole. 17 Nor do people put new wine into old wineskins; if they do, the skins burst, and then the wine runs out and the skins are ruined. No, they put new wine into fresh skins; then both are preserved.'

18 EVEN as he spoke, an official came up, who bowed before him and said, 'My daughter has just died; but come and lay your hand on her, and she will live.' 19 Jesus rose and went with him, and so did his disciples.

20 Just then a woman who had suffered from haemorrhages for twelve years came up from behind, and touched the edge of his cloak; 21 for she said to herself, 'If I can only touch his cloak, I shall be healed.' 22 But Jesus turned and saw her, and said, 'Take heart, my daughter; your faith has healed you.' And from that moment she recovered.

23 When Jesus arrived at the official's house and saw the flute-players and the general commotion, 24 he said, 'Go away! The girl is not dead: she is asleep'; and they laughed at him. 25 After turning them all out, he went into the room and took the girl by the hand, and she got up. 26 The story became the talk of the whole district.

27 As he went on from there Jesus was followed by two blind men, shouting, 'Have pity on us, Son of David!' 28 When he had gone indoors they came to him, and Jesus asked, 'Do you believe that I have the power to do what you want?' 'We do,' they said. 29 Then he touched their eyes, and said, 'As you have believed, so let it be'; 30 and their sight was restored. Jesus said to them sternly, 'See that no one hears about this.' 31 But as soon as they had gone out they talked about him all over the region.

32 They were on their way out when a man was brought to him, who was dumb and possessed by a demon; 33 the demon was driven out and the dumb man spoke. The crowd was astonished and said, 'Nothing like this has ever been seen in Israel.'

35 So JESUS went round all the towns and villages teaching in their synagogues, proclaiming the good news of the kingdom, and curing every kind of illness and infirmity. 36 The sight of the crowds moved him to pity: they were like sheep without a shepherd, harassed and helpless. 37 Then he said to his disciples, 'The crop is heavy, but the labourers too few; 38 you must ask the owner to send labourers to bring in the harvest.'

9:20 edge: or tassel.   9:33 in Israel: some witnesses add 34 But the Pharisees said, 'He drives out devils by the prince of devils.'

9 As Jesus passed on from there, he saw a man named Matthew sitting at the customs post. He said to him, "Follow me." And he got up and followed him. 10 While he was at table in his house, many tax collectors and sinners came and sat with Jesus and his disciples. 11 The Pharisees saw this and said to his disciples, "Why does your teacher eat with tax collectors and sinners?" 12 He heard this and said, "Those who are well do not need a physician, but the sick do. 13 Go and learn the meaning of the words, 'I desire mercy, not sacrifice.' I did not come to call the righteous but sinners."

14 Then the disciples of John approached him and said, "Why do we and the Pharisees fast [much], but your disciples do not fast?" 15 Jesus answered them, "Can the wedding guests mourn as long as the bridegroom is with them? The days will come when the bridegroom is taken away from them, and then they will fast. 16 No one patches an old cloak with a piece of unshrunken cloth, for its fullness pulls away from the cloak and the tear gets worse. 17 People do not put new wine into old wineskins. Otherwise the skins burst, the wine spills out, and the skins are ruined. Rather, they pour new wine into fresh wineskins, and both are preserved."

18 While he was saying these things to them, an official came forward, knelt down before him, and said, "My daughter has just died. But come, lay your hand on her, and she will live." 19 Jesus rose and followed him, and so did his disciples. 20 A woman suffering hemorrhages for twelve years came up behind him and touched the tassel on his cloak. 21 She said to herself, "If only I can touch his cloak, I shall be cured." 22 Jesus turned around and saw her, and said, "Courage, daughter! Your faith has saved you." And from that hour the woman was cured.

23 When Jesus arrived at the official's house and saw the flute players and the crowd who were making a commotion, 24 he said, "Go away! The girl is not dead but sleeping." And they ridiculed him. 25 When the crowd was put out, he came and took her by the hand, and the little girl arose. 26 And news of this spread throughout all that land.

27 And as Jesus passed on from there, two blind men followed [him], crying out, "Son of David, have pity on us!" 28 When he entered the house, the blind men approached him and Jesus said to them, "Do you believe that I can do this?" "Yes, Lord," they said to him. 29 Then he touched their eyes and said, "Let it be done for you according to your faith." 30 And their eyes were opened. Jesus warned them sternly, "See that no one knows about this." 31 But they went out and spread word of him through all that land.

32 As they were going out, a demoniac who could not speak was brought to him, 33 and when the demon was driven out the mute person spoke. The crowds were amazed and said, "Nothing like this has ever been seen in Israel." 34 But the Pharisees said, "He drives out demons by the prince of demons."

35 Jesus went around to all the towns and villages, teaching in their synagogues, proclaiming the gospel of the kingdom, and curing every disease and illness. 36 At the sight of the crowds, his heart was moved with pity for them because they were troubled and abandoned, like sheep without a shepherd. 37 Then he said to his disciples, "The harvest is abundant but the laborers are few; 38 so ask the master of the harvest to send out laborers for his harvest."

9 As Jesus was walking on from there he saw a man named Matthew sitting at the tax office, and he said to him, 'Follow me.' And he got up and followed him.

10 Now while he was at table in the house it happened that a number of tax collectors and sinners came to sit at the table with Jesus and his disciples. 11 When the Pharisees saw this, they said to his disciples, 'Why does your master eat with tax collectors and sinners?' 12 When he heard this he replied, 'It is not the healthy who need the doctor, but the sick. 13 Go and learn the meaning of the words: *Mercy is what pleases me, not sacrifice.* d And indeed I came to call not the upright, but sinners.'

14 Then John's disciples came to him and said, 'Why is it that we and the Pharisees fast, but your disciples do not?' 15 Jesus replied, 'Surely the bridegroom's attendants cannot mourn as long as the bridegroom is still with them? But the time will come when the bridegroom is taken away from them, and then they will fast. 16 No one puts a piece of unshrunken cloth onto an old cloak, because the patch pulls away from the cloak and the tear gets worse. 17 Nor do people put new wine into old wineskins; otherwise, the skins burst, the wine runs out, and the skins are lost. No; they put new wine in fresh skins and both are preserved.'

18 While he was speaking to them, suddenly one of the officials came up, who bowed low in front of him and said, 'My daughter has just died, but come and lay your hand on her and her life will be saved.' 19 Jesus rose and, with his disciples, followed him.

20 Then suddenly from behind him came a woman, who had been suffering from a haemorrhage for twelve years, and she touched the fringe of his cloak, 21 for she was thinking, 'If only I can touch his cloak I shall be saved.' 22 Jesus turned round and saw her; and he said to her, 'Courage, my daughter, your faith has saved you.' And from that moment the woman was saved.

23 When Jesus reached the official's house and saw the flute-players, with the crowd making a commotion, he said, 24 'Get out of here; the little girl is not dead; she is asleep.' And they ridiculed him. 25 But when the people had been turned out he went inside and took her by the hand; and she stood up. 26 And the news of this spread all round the countryside.

27 As Jesus went on his way two blind men followed him shouting, 'Take pity on us, son of David.' 28 And when Jesus reached the house the blind men came up to him and he said to them, 'Do you believe I can do this?' They said, 'Lord, we do.' 29 Then he touched their eyes saying, 'According to your faith, let it be done to you.' 30 And their sight returned. Then Jesus sternly warned them, 'Take care that no one learns about this.' 31 But when they had gone away, they talked about him all over the countryside.

32 They had only just left when suddenly a man was brought to him, a dumb demoniac. 33 And when the devil was driven out, the dumb man spoke and the people were amazed and said, 'Nothing like this has ever been seen in Israel.' 34 But the Pharisees said, 'It is through the prince of devils that he drives out devils.'

35 Jesus made a tour through all the towns and villages, teaching in their synagogues, proclaiming the good news of the kingdom and curing all kinds of disease and all kinds of illness.

36 And when he saw the crowds he felt sorry for them because they were harassed and dejected, like sheep without a shepherd. 37 Then he said to his disciples, 'The harvest is rich but the labourers are few, so ask the Lord of the harvest to send out labourers to his harvest.'

d 9 Ho 6:6.

NEW REVISED STANDARD VERSION	REVISED ENGLISH BIBLE

10 Then Jesus[d] summoned his twelve disciples and gave them authority over unclean spirits, to cast them out, and to cure every disease and every sickness. 2 These are the names of the twelve apostles: first, Simon, also known as Peter, and his brother Andrew; James son of Zebedee, and his brother John; 3 Philip and Bartholomew; Thomas and Matthew the tax collector; James son of Alphaeus, and Thaddaeus;[e] 4 Simon the Cananaean, and Judas Iscariot, the one who betrayed him.

5 These twelve Jesus sent out with the following instructions: "Go nowhere among the Gentiles, and enter no town of the Samaritans, 6 but go rather to the lost sheep of the house of Israel. 7 As you go, proclaim the good news, 'The kingdom of heaven has come near.'[f] 8 Cure the sick, raise the dead, cleanse the lepers,[g] cast out demons. You received without payment; give without payment. 9 Take no gold, or silver, or copper in your belts, 10 no bag for your journey, or two tunics, or sandals, or a staff; for laborers deserve their food. 11 Whatever town or village you enter, find out who in it is worthy, and stay there until you leave. 12 As you enter the house, greet it. 13 If the house is worthy, let your peace come upon it; but if it is not worthy, let your peace return to you. 14 If anyone will not welcome you or listen to your words, shake off the dust from your feet as you leave that house or town. 15 Truly I tell you, it will be more tolerable for the land of Sodom and Gomorrah on the day of judgment than for that town.

16 "See, I am sending you out like sheep into the midst of wolves; so be wise as serpents and innocent as doves. 17 Beware of them, for they will hand you over to councils and flog you in their synagogues; 18 and you will be dragged before governors and kings because of me, as a testimony to them and the Gentiles. 19 When they hand you over, do not worry about how you are to speak or what you are to say; for what you are to say will be given to you at that time; 20 for it is not you who speak, but the Spirit of your Father speaking through you. 21 Brother will betray brother to death, and a father his child, and children will rise against parents and have them put to death; 22 and you will be hated by all because of my name. But the one who endures to the end will be saved. 23 When they persecute you in one town, flee to the next; for truly I tell you, you will not have gone through all the towns of Israel before the Son of Man comes.

24 "A disciple is not above the teacher, nor a slave above the master; 25 it is enough for the disciple to be like the teacher, and the slave like the master. If they have called the master of the house Beelzebul, how much more will they malign those of his household!

26 "So have no fear of them; for nothing is covered up that will not be uncovered, and nothing secret that will not become known. 27 What I say to you in the dark, tell in the light; and what you hear whispered, proclaim from the housetops. 28 Do not fear those who kill the body but cannot kill the soul; rather fear him who can destroy both soul and body in hell.[h] 29 Are not two sparrows sold for a penny? Yet not one of them will fall to the ground apart from your Father. 30 And even the hairs of your head are all counted. 31 So do not be afraid; you are of more value than many sparrows.

10 THEN he called his twelve disciples to him and gave them authority to drive out unclean spirits and to cure every kind of illness and infirmity.

2 These are the names of the twelve apostles: first Simon, also called Peter, and his brother Andrew; James son of Zebedee, and his brother John; 3 Philip and Bartholomew, Thomas and Matthew the tax-collector, James son of Alphaeus, Thaddaeus, 4 Simon the Zealot, and Judas Iscariot, the man who betrayed him.

5 These twelve Jesus sent out with the following instructions: 'Do not take the road to gentile lands, and do not enter any Samaritan town; 6 but go rather to the lost sheep of the house of Israel. 7 And as you go proclaim the message: "The kingdom of Heaven is upon you." 8 Heal the sick, raise the dead, cleanse lepers, drive out demons. You received without cost; give without charge.

9 'Take no gold, silver, or copper in your belts, 10 no pack for the road, no second coat, no sandals, no stick; the worker deserves his keep.

11 'Whatever town or village you enter, look for some suitable person in it, and stay with him until you leave. 12 Wish the house peace as you enter it; 13 if it is welcoming, let your peace descend on it, and if it is not, let your peace come back to you. 14 If anyone will not receive you or listen to what you say, then as you leave that house or that town shake the dust of it off your feet. 15 Truly I tell you: on the day of judgement it will be more bearable for the land of Sodom and Gomorrah than for that town.

16 'I send you out like sheep among wolves; be wary as serpents, innocent as doves.

17 'Be on your guard, for you will be handed over to the courts, they will flog you in their synagogues, 18 and you will be brought before governors and kings on my account, to testify before them and the Gentiles. 19 But when you are arrested, do not worry about what you are to say, for when the time comes, the words you need will be given you; 20 it will not be you speaking, but the Spirit of your Father speaking in you.

21 'Brother will hand over brother to death, and a father his child; children will turn against their parents and send them to their death. 22 Everyone will hate you for your allegiance to me, but whoever endures to the end will be saved. 23 When you are persecuted in one town, take refuge in another; truly I tell you: before you have gone through all the towns of Israel the Son of Man will have come.

24 'No pupil ranks above his teacher, no servant above his master. 25 The pupil should be content to share his teacher's lot, the servant to share his master's. If the master has been called Beelzebul, how much more his household!

26 'So do not be afraid of them. There is nothing covered up that will not be uncovered, nothing hidden that will not be made known. 27 What I say to you in the dark you must repeat in broad daylight; what you hear whispered you must shout from the housetops. 28 Do not fear those who kill the body, but cannot kill the soul. Fear him rather who is able to destroy both soul and body in hell.

29 'Are not two sparrows sold for a penny? Yet without your Father's knowledge not one of them can fall to the ground. 30 As for you, even the hairs of your head have all been counted. 31 So do not be afraid; you are worth more than any number of sparrows.

---

d Gk he   e Other ancient authorities read *Lebbaeus*, or *Lebbaeus called Thaddaeus*   f Or *is at hand*   g The terms *leper* and *leprosy* can refer to several diseases   h Gk *Gehenna*

10:3 **Thaddaeus:** *some witnesses read* Lebbaeus.

10 Then he summoned his twelve disciples and gave them authority over unclean spirits to drive them out and to cure every disease and every illness. 2 The names of the twelve apostles are these: first, Simon called Peter, and his brother Andrew; James, the son of Zebedee, and his brother John; 3 Philip and Bartholomew, Thomas and Matthew the tax collector; James, the son of Alphaeus, and Thaddeus; 4 Simon the Cananean, and Judas Iscariot who betrayed him.

5 Jesus sent out these twelve after instructing them thus, "Do not go into pagan territory or enter a Samaritan town. 6 Go rather to the lost sheep of the house of Israel. 7 As you go, make this proclamation: 'The kingdom of heaven is at hand.' 8 Cure the sick, raise the dead, cleanse lepers, drive out demons. Without cost you have received; without cost you are to give. 9 Do not take gold or silver or copper for your belts; 10 no sack for the journey, or a second tunic, or sandals, or walking stick. The laborer deserves his keep. 11 Whatever town or village you enter, look for a worthy person in it, and stay there until you leave. 12 As you enter a house, wish it peace. 13 If the house is worthy, let your peace come upon it; if not, let your peace return to you. 14 Whoever will not receive you or listen to your words — go outside that house or town and shake the dust from your feet. 15 Amen, I say to you, it will be more tolerable for the land of Sodom and Gomorrah on the day of judgment than for that town.

16 "Behold, I am sending you like sheep in the midst of wolves; so be shrewd as serpents and simple as doves. 17 But beware of people, for they will hand you over to courts and scourge you in their synagogues, 18 and you will be led before governors and kings for my sake as a witness before them and the pagans. 19 When they hand you over, do not worry about how you are to speak or what you are to say. You will be given at that moment what you are to say. 20 For it will not be you who speak but the Spirit of your Father speaking through you. 21 Brother will hand over brother to death, and the father his child; children will rise up against parents and have them put to death. 22 You will be hated by all because of my name, but whoever endures to the end will be saved. 23 When they persecute you in one town, flee to another. Amen, I say to you, you will not finish the towns of Israel before the Son of Man comes. 24 No disciple is above his teacher, no slave above his master. 25 It is enough for the disciple that he become like his teacher, for the slave that he become like his master. If they have called the master of the house Beelzebul, how much more those of his household!

26 "Therefore do not be afraid of them. Nothing is concealed that will not be revealed, nor secret that will not be known. 27 What I say to you in the darkness, speak in the light; what you hear whispered, proclaim on the housetops. 28 And do not be afraid of those who kill the body but cannot kill the soul; rather, be afraid of the one who can destroy both soul and body in Gehenna. 29 Are not two sparrows sold for a small coin? Yet not one of them falls to the ground without your Father's knowledge. 30 Even all the hairs of your head are counted. 31 So do not be afraid; you are worth more than many sparrows. 32 Everyone who ac-

10 He summoned his twelve disciples[e] and gave them authority over unclean spirits with power to drive them out and to cure all kinds of disease and all kinds of illness.

2 These are the names of the twelve apostles: first, Simon who is known as Peter, and his brother Andrew; James the son of Zebedee, and his brother John; 3 Philip and Bartholomew; Thomas, and Matthew the tax collector; James the son of Alphaeus, and Thaddaeus; 4 Simon the Zealot and Judas Iscariot, who was also his betrayer. 5 These twelve Jesus sent out, instructing them as follows:

'Do not make your way to gentile territory, and do not enter any Samaritan town; 6 go instead to the lost sheep of the House of Israel. 7 And as you go, proclaim that the kingdom of Heaven is close at hand. 8 Cure the sick, raise the dead, cleanse those suffering from virulent skin-diseases, drive out devils. You received without charge, give without charge. 9 Provide yourselves with no gold or silver, not even with coppers for your purses, 10 with no haversack for the journey or spare tunic or footwear or a staff, for the labourer deserves his keep.

11 'Whatever town or village you go into, seek out someone worthy and stay with him until you leave. 12 As you enter his house, salute it, 13 and if the house deserves it, may your peace come upon it; if it does not, may your peace come back to you. 14 And if anyone does not welcome you or listen to what you have to say, as you walk out of the house or town shake the dust from your feet. 15 In truth I tell you, on the Day of Judgement it will be more bearable for Sodom and Gomorrah than for that town. 16 Look, I am sending you out like sheep among wolves; so be cunning as snakes and yet innocent as doves.

17 'Be prepared for people to hand you over to sanhedrins and scourge you in their synagogues. 18 You will be brought before governors and kings for my sake, as evidence to them and to the gentiles. 19 But when you are handed over, do not worry about how to speak or what to say; what you are to say will be given to you when the time comes, 20 because it is not you who will be speaking; the Spirit of your Father will be speaking in you.

21 'Brother will betray brother to death, and a father his child; children will come forward against their parents and have them put to death. 22 You will be universally hated on account of my name; but anyone who stands firm to the end will be saved. 23 If they persecute you in one town, take refuge in the next; and if they persecute you in that, take refuge in another. In truth I tell you, you will not have gone the round of the towns of Israel before the Son of man comes.

24 'Disciple is not superior to teacher, nor slave to master. 25 It is enough for disciple to grow to be like teacher, and slave like master. If they have called the master of the house "Beelzebul", how much more the members of his household?

26 'So do not be afraid of them. Everything now covered up will be uncovered, and everything now hidden will be made clear. 27 What I say to you in the dark, tell in the daylight; what you hear in whispers, proclaim from the housetops.

28 'Do not be afraid of those who kill the body but cannot kill the soul; fear him rather who can destroy both body and soul in hell. 29 Can you not buy two sparrows for a penny? And yet not one falls to the ground without your Father knowing. 30 Why, every hair on your head has been counted. 31 So there is no need to be afraid; you are worth more than many sparrows.

e **10** Mk 3:14–19; Lk 6:13–16; the order and even some of the names vary in the different lists.

32 "Everyone therefore who acknowledges me before others, I also will acknowledge before my Father in heaven; 33 but whoever denies me before others, I also will deny before my Father in heaven.

34 "Do not think that I have come to bring peace to the earth; I have not come to bring peace, but a sword.

35 For I have come to set a man against his father,
　　and a daughter against her mother,
　　and a daughter-in-law against her mother-in-law;
36 　and one's foes will be members of one's own
　　household.

37 Whoever loves father or mother more than me is not worthy of me; and whoever loves son or daughter more than me is not worthy of me; 38 and whoever does not take up the cross and follow me is not worthy of me. 39 Those who find their life will lose it, and those who lose their life for my sake will find it.

40 "Whoever welcomes you welcomes me, and whoever welcomes me welcomes the one who sent me. 41 Whoever welcomes a prophet in the name of a prophet will receive a prophet's reward; and whoever welcomes a righteous person in the name of a righteous person will receive the reward of the righteous; 42 and whoever gives even a cup of cold water to one of these little ones in the name of a disciple — truly I tell you, none of these will lose their reward."

11 Now when Jesus had finished instructing his twelve disciples, he went on from there to teach and proclaim his message in their cities.

2 When John heard in prison what the Messiah[i] was doing, he sent word by his[j] disciples 3 and said to him, "Are you the one who is to come, or are we to wait for another?" 4 Jesus answered them, "Go and tell John what you hear and see: 5 the blind receive their sight, the lame walk, the lepers[k] are cleansed, the deaf hear, the dead are raised, and the poor have good news brought to them. 6 And blessed is anyone who takes no offense at me."

7 As they went away, Jesus began to speak to the crowds about John: "What did you go out into the wilderness to look at? A reed shaken by the wind? 8 What then did you go out to see? Someone[l] dressed in soft robes? Look, those who wear soft robes are in royal palaces. 9 What then did you go out to see? A prophet?[m] Yes, I tell you, and more than a prophet. 10 This is the one about whom it is written,

'See, I am sending my messenger ahead of you,
　who will prepare your way before you.'

11 Truly I tell you, among those born of women no one has arisen greater than John the Baptist; yet the least in the kingdom of heaven is greater than he. 12 From the days of John the Baptist until now the kingdom of heaven has suffered violence,[n] and the violent take it by force. 13 For all the prophets and the law prophesied until John came; 14 and if you are willing to accept it, he is Elijah who is to come. 15 Let anyone with ears[o] listen!

16 "But to what will I compare this generation? It is like children sitting in the marketplaces and calling to one another,

17 'We played the flute for you, and you did not
　　dance;
we wailed, and you did not mourn.'

---

32 'Whoever will acknowledge me before others, I will acknowledge before my Father in heaven; 33 and whoever disowns me before others, I will disown before my Father in heaven.

34 'You must not think that I have come to bring peace to the earth; I have not come to bring peace, but a sword. 35 I have come to set a man against his father, a daughter against her mother, a daughter-in-law against her mother-in-law; 36 and a man will find his enemies under his own roof.

37 'No one is worthy of me who cares more for father or mother than for me; no one is worthy of me who cares more for son or daughter; 38 no one is worthy of me who does not take up his cross and follow me. 39 Whoever gains his life will lose it; whoever loses his life for my sake will gain it.

40 'To receive you is to receive me, and to receive me is to receive the One who sent me. 41 Whoever receives a prophet because he is a prophet will be given a prophet's reward, and whoever receives a good man because he is a good man will be given a good man's reward. 42 Truly I tell you: anyone who gives so much as a cup of cold water to one of these little ones because he is a disciple of mine, will certainly not go unrewarded.'

11 When Jesus had finished giving instructions to his twelve disciples, he went from there to teach and preach in the neighbouring towns.

2 JOHN, who was in prison, heard what Christ was doing, and sent his own disciples 3 to put this question to him: 'Are you the one who is to come, or are we to expect someone else?' 4 Jesus answered, 'Go and report to John what you hear and see: 5 the blind recover their sight, the lame walk, lepers are made clean, the deaf hear, the dead are raised to life, the poor are brought good news — 6 and blessed are those who do not find me an obstacle to faith.'

7 When the messengers were on their way back, Jesus began to speak to the crowds about John: 'What was the spectacle that drew you to the wilderness? A reed swaying in the wind? 8 No? Then what did you go out to see? A man dressed in finery? Fine clothes are to be found in palaces. 9 But why did you go out? To see a prophet? Yes indeed, and far more than a prophet. 10 He is the man of whom scripture says,

Here is my herald, whom I send ahead of you,
　and he will prepare your way before you.

11 'Truly I tell you: among all who have ever been born, no one has been greater than John the Baptist, and yet the least in the kingdom of Heaven is greater than he.

12 'Since the time of John the Baptist the kingdom of Heaven has been subjected to violence and violent men are taking it by force. 13 For until John, all the prophets and the law foretold things to come; 14 and John is the destined Elijah, if you will but accept it. 15 If you have ears, then hear.

16 'How can I describe this generation? They are like children sitting in the market-place and calling to each other,

17 We piped for you and you would not dance.
　We lamented, and you would not mourn.

---

i Or the Christ 　j Other ancient authorities read two of his
k The terms leper and leprosy can refer to several diseases
l Or Why then did you go out? To see someone 　m Other ancient authorities read Why then did you go out? To see a prophet?
n Or has been coming violently 　o Other ancient authorities add to hear

11:12 has been . . . force: or has been forcing its way forward, and men of force are seizing it.

knowledges me before others I will acknowledge before my heavenly Father. 33 But whoever denies me before others, I will deny before my heavenly Father.

34 "Do not think that I have come to bring peace upon the earth. I have come to bring not peace but the sword. 35 For I have come to set

a man 'against his father,
a daughter against her mother,
and a daughter-in-law against her mother-in-law;
36   and one's enemies will be those of
his household.'

37 "Whoever loves father or mother more than me is not worthy of me, and whoever loves son or daughter more than me is not worthy of me; 38 and whoever does not take up his cross and follow after me is not worthy of me. 39 Whoever finds his life will lose it, and whoever loses his life for my sake will find it.

40 "Whoever receives you receives me, and whoever receives me receives the one who sent me. 41 Whoever receives a prophet because he is a prophet will receive a prophet's reward, and whoever receives a righteous man because he is righteous will receive a righteous man's reward. 42 And whoever gives only a cup of cold water to one of these little ones to drink because he is a disciple — amen, I say to you, he will surely not lose his reward."

11 When Jesus finished giving these commands to his twelve disciples, he went away from that place to teach and to preach in their towns.

2 When John heard in prison of the works of the Messiah, he sent his disciples to him 3 with this question, "Are you the one who is to come, or should we look for another?" 4 Jesus said to them in reply, "Go and tell John what you hear and see: 5 the blind regain their sight, the lame walk, lepers are cleansed, the deaf hear, the dead are raised, and the poor have the good news proclaimed to them. 6 And blessed is the one who takes no offense at me."

7 As they were going off, Jesus began to speak to the crowds about John, "What did you go out to the desert to see? A reed swayed by the wind? 8 Then what did you go out to see? Someone dressed in fine clothing? Those who wear fine clothing are in royal palaces. 9 Then why did you go out? To see a prophet? Yes, I tell you, and more than a prophet. 10 This is the one about whom it is written:

'Behold, I am sending my messenger ahead of you;
he will prepare your way before you.'

11 Amen, I say to you, among those born of women there has been none greater than John the Baptist; yet the least in the kingdom of heaven is greater than he. 12 From the days of John the Baptist until now, the kingdom of heaven suffers violence, and the violent are taking it by force. 13 All the prophets and the law prophesied up to the time of John. 14 And if you are willing to accept it, he is Elijah, the one who is to come. 15 Whoever has ears ought to hear.

16 "To what shall I compare this generation? It is like children who sit in marketplaces and call to one another, 17 'We played the flute for you, but you did not dance, we sang a dirge but you did not mourn.' 18 For John came

32 "So if anyone declares himself for me in the presence of human beings, I will declare myself for him in the presence of my Father in heaven. 33 But the one who disowns me in the presence of human beings, I will disown in the presence of my Father in heaven.

34 'Do not suppose that I have come to bring peace to the earth: it is not peace I have come to bring, but a sword. 35 For I have come to set son against *father, daughter against mother, daughter-in-law against mother-in-law;* 36 *a person's enemies will be the members of his own household.f*

37 'No one who prefers father or mother to me is worthy of me. No one who prefers son or daughter to me is worthy of me. 38 Anyone who does not take his cross and follow in my footsteps is not worthy of me. 39 Anyone who finds his life will lose it; anyone who loses his life for my sake will find it.

40 'Anyone who welcomes you welcomes me; and anyone who welcomes me welcomes the one who sent me.

41 'Anyone who welcomes a prophet because he is a prophet will have a prophet's reward; and anyone who welcomes an upright person because he is upright will have the reward of an upright person.

42 'If anyone gives so much as a cup of cold water to one of these little ones because he is a disciple, then in truth I tell you, he will most certainly not go without his reward.'

11 When Jesus had finished instructing his twelve disciples he moved on from there to teach and preach in their towns.

2 Now John had heard in prison what Christ was doing and he sent his disciples to ask him, 3 'Are you the one who is to come, or are we to expect someone else?' 4 Jesus answered, 'Go back and tell John what you hear and see; 5 the blind see again, and the lame walk, those suffering from virulent skin-diseases are cleansed, and the deaf hear, the dead are raised to life and the good news is proclaimed to the poor;g 6 and blessed is anyone who does not find me a cause of falling.'

7 As the men were leaving, Jesus began to talk to the people about John, 'What did you go out into the desert to see? A reed swaying in the breeze? No? 8 Then what did you go out to see? A man wearing fine clothes? Look, those who wear fine clothes are to be found in palaces. 9 Then what did you go out for? To see a prophet? Yes, I tell you, and much more than a prophet: 10 he is the one of whom scripture says:

Look, I am going to send my messenger in front of
you
to prepare your way before you.*h*

11 'In truth I tell you, of all the children born to women, there has never been anyone greater than John the Baptist; yet the least in the kingdom of Heaven is greater than he. 12 Since John the Baptist came, up to this present time, the kingdom of Heaven has been subjected to violence and the violent are taking it by storm. 13 Because it was towards John that all the prophecies of the prophets and of the Law were leading; 14 and he, if you will believe me, is the Elijah who was to return. 15 Anyone who has ears should listen!

16 'What comparison can I find for this generation? It is like children shouting to each other as they sit in the market place:

17 We played the pipes for you,
and you wouldn't dance;
we sang dirges,
and you wouldn't be mourners.

f 10 Mi 7:6.   g 11 cf. Is 35:5; 61:1.   h 11 Ml 3:1.

NEW REVISED STANDARD VERSION

REVISED ENGLISH BIBLE

18 For John came neither eating nor drinking, and they say, 'He has a demon'; 19 the Son of Man came eating and drinking, and they say, 'Look, a glutton and a drunkard, a friend of tax collectors and sinners!' Yet wisdom is vindicated by her deeds."*p*

20 Then he began to reproach the cities in which most of his deeds of power had been done, because they did not repent. 21 "Woe to you, Chorazin! Woe to you, Bethsaida! For if the deeds of power done in you had been done in Tyre and Sidon, they would have repented long ago in sackcloth and ashes. 22 But I tell you, on the day of judgment it will be more tolerable for Tyre and Sidon than for you. 23 And you, Capernaum,

will you be exalted to heaven?
No, you will be brought down to Hades.

For if the deeds of power done in you had been done in Sodom, it would have remained until this day. 24 But I tell you that on the day of judgment it will be more tolerable for the land of Sodom than for you."

25 At that time Jesus said, "I thank*q* you, Father, Lord of heaven and earth, because you have hidden these things from the wise and the intelligent and have revealed them to infants; 26 yes, Father, for such was your gracious will.*r* 27 All things have been handed over to me by my Father; and no one knows the Son except the Father, and no one knows the Father except the Son and anyone to whom the Son chooses to reveal him.

28 "Come to me, all you that are weary and are carrying heavy burdens, and I will give you rest. 29 Take my yoke upon you, and learn from me; for I am gentle and humble in heart, and you will find rest for your souls. 30 For my yoke is easy, and my burden is light."

12 At that time Jesus went through the grainfields on the sabbath; his disciples were hungry, and they began to pluck heads of grain and to eat. 2 When the Pharisees saw it, they said to him, "Look, your disciples are doing what is not lawful to do on the sabbath." 3 He said to them, "Have you not read what David did when he and his companions were hungry? 4 He entered the house of God and ate the bread of the Presence, which it was not lawful for him or his companions to eat, but only for the priests. 5 Or have you not read in the law that on the sabbath the priests in the temple break the sabbath and yet are guiltless? 6 I tell you, something greater than the temple is here. 7 But if you had known what this means, 'I desire mercy and not sacrifice,' you would not have condemned the guiltless. 8 For the Son of Man is lord of the sabbath."

9 He left that place and entered their synagogue; 10 a man was there with a withered hand, and they asked him, "Is it lawful to cure on the sabbath?" so that they might accuse him. 11 He said to them, "Suppose one of you has only one sheep and it falls into a pit on the sabbath; will you not lay hold of it and lift it out? 12 How much more valuable is a human being than a sheep! So it is lawful to do good on the sabbath." 13 Then he said to the man, "Stretch out your hand." He stretched it out, and it was restored, as sound as the other. 14 But the Pharisees went out and conspired against him, how to destroy him.

15 When Jesus became aware of this, he departed. Many crowds*s* followed him, and he cured all of them, 16 and he ordered them not to make him known. 17 This was to fulfill what had been spoken through the prophet Isaiah:

18 'For John came, neither eating nor drinking, and people say, "He is possessed"; 19 the Son of Man came, eating and drinking, and they say, "Look at him! A glutton and a drinker, a friend of tax-collectors and sinners!" Yet God's wisdom is proved right by its results.'

20 THEN he spoke of the towns in which most of his miracles had been performed, and denounced them for their impenitence. 21 'Alas for you, Chorazin!' he said. 'Alas for you, Bethsaida! If the miracles performed in you had taken place in Tyre and Sidon, they would have repented long ago in sackcloth and ashes. 22 But it will be more bearable, I tell you, for Tyre and Sidon on the day of judgement than for you. 23 As for you, Capernaum, will you be exalted to heaven? No, you will be brought down to Hades! For if the miracles performed in you had taken place in Sodom, Sodom would be standing to this day. 24 But it will be more bearable, I tell you, for the land of Sodom on the day of judgement than for you.'

25 At that time Jesus spoke these words: 'I thank you, Father, Lord of heaven and earth, for hiding these things from the learned and wise, and revealing them to the simple. 26 Yes, Father, such was your choice. 27 Everything is entrusted to me by my Father; and no one knows the Son but the Father, and no one knows the Father but the Son and those to whom the Son chooses to reveal him.

28 'Come to me, all who are weary and whose load is heavy; I will give you rest. 29 Take my yoke upon you, and learn from me, for I am gentle and humble-hearted; and you will find rest for your souls. 30 For my yoke is easy to wear, my load is light.'

12 ABOUT that time Jesus was going through the cornfields on the sabbath; and his disciples, feeling hungry, began to pluck some ears of corn and eat them. 2 When the Pharisees saw this, they said to him, 'Look, your disciples are doing what is forbidden on the sabbath.' 3 He answered, 'Have you not read what David did when he and his men were hungry? 4 He went into the house of God and ate the sacred bread, though neither he nor his men had a right to eat it, but only the priests. 5 Or have you not read in the law that on the sabbath the priests in the temple break the sabbath and they are not held to be guilty? 6 But I tell you, there is something greater than the temple here. 7 If you had known what this text means, "It is mercy I require, not sacrifice," you would not have condemned the innocent. 8 For the Son of Man is lord of the sabbath.'

9 He went on to another place, and entered their synagogue. 10 A man was there with a withered arm, and they asked Jesus, 'Is it permitted to heal on the sabbath?' (They wanted to bring a charge against him.) 11 But he said to them, 'Suppose you had one sheep, and it fell into a ditch on the sabbath; is there a single one of you who would not catch hold of it and lift it out? 12 Surely a man is worth far more than a sheep! It is therefore permitted to do good on the sabbath.' 13 Then he said to the man, 'Stretch out your arm.' He stretched it out, and it was made sound again like the other. 14 But the Pharisees, on leaving the synagogue, plotted to bring about Jesus's death.

15 Jesus was aware of it and withdrew, and many followed him. He healed all who were ill, 16 and gave strict instructions that they were not to make him known. 17 This was to fulfil Isaiah's prophecy:

---

p Other ancient authorities read *children* *q* Or *praise* *r* Or *for so it was well-pleasing in your sight* *s* Other ancient authorities lack *crowds*

11:26 **Yes . . . such:** *or* Yes, I thank you, Father, that such.

neither eating nor drinking, and they said, 'He is possessed by a demon.' 19 The Son of Man came eating and drinking and they said, 'Look, he is a glutton and a drunkard, a friend of tax collectors and sinners.' But wisdom is vindicated by her works."

20 Then he began to reproach the towns where most of his mighty deeds had been done, since they had not repented. 21 "Woe to you, Chorazin! Woe to you, Bethsaida! For if the mighty deeds done in your midst had been done in Tyre and Sidon, they would long ago have repented in sackcloth and ashes. 22 But I tell you, it will be more tolerable for Tyre and Sidon on the day of judgment than for you. 23 And as for you, Capernaum:

'Will you be exalted to heaven?
    You will go down to the netherworld.'

For if the mighty deeds done in your midst had been done in Sodom, it would have remained until this day. 24 But I tell you, it will be more tolerable for the land of Sodom on the day of judgment than for you."

25 At that time Jesus said in reply, "I give praise to you, Father, Lord of heaven and earth, for although you have hidden these things from the wise and the learned you have revealed them to the childlike. 26 Yes, Father, such has been your gracious will. 27 All things have been handed over to me by my Father. No one knows the Son except the Father, and no one knows the Father except the Son and anyone to whom the Son wishes to reveal him.

28 "Come to me, all you who labor and are burdened, and I will give you rest. 29 Take my yoke upon you and learn from me, for I am meek and humble of heart; and you will find rest for yourselves. 30 For my yoke is easy, and my burden light."

12 At that time Jesus was going through a field of grain on the sabbath. His disciples were hungry and began to pick the heads of grain and eat them. 2 When the Pharisees saw this, they said to him, "See, your disciples are doing what is unlawful to do on the sabbath." 3 He said to them, "Have you not read what David did when he and his companions were hungry, 4 how he went into the house of God and ate the bread of offering, which neither he nor his companions but only the priests could lawfully eat? 5 Or have you not read in the law that on the sabbath the priests serving in the temple violate the sabbath and are innocent? 6 I say to you, something greater than the temple is here. 7 If you knew what this meant, 'I desire mercy, not sacrifice,' you would not have condemned these innocent men. 8 For the Son of Man is Lord of the sabbath."

9 Moving on from there, he went into their synagogue. 10 And behold, there was a man there who had a withered hand. They questioned him, "Is it lawful to cure on the sabbath?" so that they might accuse him. 11 He said to them, "Which one of you who has a sheep that falls into a pit on the sabbath will not take hold of it and lift it out? 12 How much more valuable a person is than a sheep. So it is lawful to do good on the sabbath." 13 Then he said to the man, "Stretch out your hand." He stretched it out, and it was restored as sound as the other. 14 But the Pharisees went out and took counsel against him to put him to death.

15 When Jesus realized this, he withdrew from that place. Many [people] followed him, and he cured them all, 16 but he warned them not to make him known. 17 This was to fulfill what had been spoken through Isaiah the prophet:

18 'For John came, neither eating nor drinking, and they say, "He is possessed." 19 The Son of man came, eating and drinking, and they say, "Look, a glutton and a drunkard, a friend of tax collectors and sinners." Yet wisdom is justified by her deeds.'

20 Then he began to reproach the towns in which most of his miracles had been worked, because they refused to repent. 21 'Alas for you, Chorazin! Alas for you, Bethsaida! For if the miracles done in you had been done in Tyre and Sidon, they would have repented long ago in sackcloth and ashes. 22 Still, I tell you that it will be more bearable for Tyre and Sidon on Judgement Day than for you. 23 And as for you, Capernaum, did you want to be *raised as high as heaven? You shall be flung down to hell.*[i] For if the miracles done in you had been done in Sodom, it would have been standing yet. 24 Still, I tell you that it will be more bearable for Sodom on Judgement Day than for you.'

25 At that time Jesus exclaimed, 'I bless you, Father, Lord of heaven and of earth, for hiding these things from the learned and the clever and revealing them to little children. 26 Yes, Father, for that is what it pleased you to do. 27 Everything has been entrusted to me by my Father; and no one knows the Son except the Father, just as no one knows the Father except the Son and those to whom the Son chooses to reveal him.

28 'Come to me, all you who labour and are overburdened, and I will give you rest. 29 Shoulder my yoke and learn from me, for I am gentle and humble in heart, *and you will find rest for your souls.*[j] 30 Yes, my yoke is easy and my burden light.'

12 At that time Jesus went through the cornfields one Sabbath day. His disciples were hungry and began to pick ears of corn and eat them. 2 The Pharisees noticed it and said to him, 'Look, your disciples are doing something that is forbidden on the Sabbath.' 3 But he said to them, 'Have you not read what David did when he and his followers were hungry — 4 how he went into the house of God and they ate the loaves of the offering although neither he nor his followers were permitted to eat them, but only the priests? 5 Or again, have you not read in the Law that on the Sabbath day the Temple priests break the Sabbath without committing any fault? 6 Now here, I tell you, is something greater than the Temple. 7 And if you had understood the meaning of the words: *Mercy is what pleases me, not sacrifice,*[k] you would not have condemned the blameless. 8 For the Son of man is master of the Sabbath.'

9 He moved on from there and went to their synagogue; 10 now a man was there with a withered hand. They asked him, 'Is it permitted to cure somebody on the Sabbath day?' hoping for something to charge him with. 11 But he said to them, 'If any one of you here had only one sheep and it fell down a hole on the Sabbath day, would he not get hold of it and lift it out? 12 Now a man is far more important than a sheep, so it follows that it is permitted on the Sabbath day to do good.' 13 Then he said to the man, 'Stretch out your hand.' He stretched it out and his hand was restored, as sound as the other one. 14 At this the Pharisees went out and began to plot against him, discussing how to destroy him.

15 Jesus knew this and withdrew from the district. Many followed him and he cured them all 16 but warned them not to make him known. 17 This was to fulfil what was spoken by the prophet Isaiah:

i 11 Is 14:13, 15.   *j* 11 Jr 6:16.   *k* 12 Ho 6:6.

18 "Here is my servant, whom I have chosen,
  my beloved, with whom my soul is well
    pleased.
  I will put my Spirit upon him,
    and he will proclaim justice to the Gentiles.
19 He will not wrangle or cry aloud,
    nor will anyone hear his voice in the streets.
20 He will not break a bruised reed
    or quench a smoldering wick
  until he brings justice to victory."
21 And in his name the Gentiles will hope."

22 Then they brought to him a demoniac who was blind and mute; and he cured him, so that the one who had been mute could speak and see. 23 All the crowds were amazed and said, "Can this be the Son of David?" 24 But when the Pharisees heard it, they said, "It is only by Beelzebul, the ruler of the demons, that this fellow casts out the demons." 25 He knew what they were thinking and said to them, "Every kingdom divided against itself is laid waste, and no city or house divided against itself will stand. 26 If Satan casts out Satan, he is divided against himself; how then will his kingdom stand? 27 If I cast out demons by Beelzebul, by whom do your own exorcists⸍ cast them out? Therefore they will be your judges. 28 But if it is by the Spirit of God that I cast out demons, then the kingdom of God has come to you. 29 Or how can one enter a strong man's house and plunder his property, without first tying up the strong man? Then indeed the house can be plundered. 30 Whoever is not with me is against me, and whoever does not gather with me scatters. 31 Therefore I tell you, people will be forgiven for every sin and blasphemy, but blasphemy against the Spirit will not be forgiven. 32 Whoever speaks a word against the Son of Man will be forgiven, but whoever speaks against the Holy Spirit will not be forgiven, either in this age or in the age to come.

33 "Either make the tree good, and its fruit good; or make the tree bad, and its fruit bad; for the tree is known by its fruit. 34 You brood of vipers! How can you speak good things, when you are evil? For out of the abundance of the heart the mouth speaks. 35 The good person brings good things out of a good treasure, and the evil person brings evil things out of an evil treasure. 36 I tell you, on the day of judgment you will have to give an account for every careless word you utter; 37 for by your words you will be justified, and by your words you will be condemned."

38 Then some of the scribes and Pharisees said to him, "Teacher, we wish to see a sign from you." 39 But he answered them, "An evil and adulterous generation asks for a sign, but no sign will be given to it except the sign of the prophet Jonah. 40 For just as Jonah was three days and three nights in the belly of the sea monster, so for three days and three nights the Son of Man will be in the heart of the earth. 41 The people of Nineveh will rise up at the judgment with this generation and condemn it, because they repented at the proclamation of Jonah, and see, something greater than Jonah is here! 42 The queen of the South will rise up at the judgment with this generation and condemn it, because she came from the ends of the earth to listen to the wisdom of Solomon, and see, something greater than Solomon is here!

18 Here is my servant, whom I have chosen,
  my beloved, in whom I take delight;
  I will put my Spirit upon him,
    and he will proclaim justice among the nations.
19 He will not strive, he will not shout,
    nor will his voice be heard in the streets.
20 He will not snap off a broken reed,
    nor snuff out a smouldering wick,
  until he leads justice on to victory.
21 In him the nations shall put their hope.

22 THEN they brought him a man who was possessed by a demon; he was blind and dumb, and Jesus cured him, restoring both speech and sight. 23 The bystanders were all amazed, and the word went round: 'Can this be the Son of David?' 24 But when the Pharisees heard it they said, 'It is only by Beelzebul prince of devils that this man drives the devils out.'

25 Knowing what was in their minds, he said to them, 'Every kingdom divided against itself is laid waste; and no town or household that is divided against itself can stand. 26 And if it is Satan who drives out Satan, he is divided against himself; how then can his kingdom stand? 27 If it is by Beelzebul that I drive out devils, by whom do your own people drive them out? If this is your argument, they themselves will refute you. 28 But if it is by the Spirit of God that I drive out the devils, then be sure the kingdom of God has already come upon you.

29 'Or again, how can anyone break into a strong man's house and make off with his goods, unless he has first tied up the strong man? Then he can ransack the house.

30 'He who is not with me is against me, and he who does not gather with me scatters.

31 'So I tell you this: every sin and every slander can be forgiven, except slander spoken against the Spirit; that will not be forgiven. 32 Anyone who speaks a word against the Son of Man will be forgiven; but if anyone speaks against the Holy Spirit, for him there will be no forgiveness, either in this age or in the age to come.

33 'Get a good tree and its fruit will be good; get a bad tree and its fruit will be bad. You can tell a tree by its fruit. 34 Vipers' brood! How can your words be good when you yourselves are evil? It is from the fullness of the heart that the mouth speaks. 35 Good people from their store of good produce good; and evil people from their store of evil produce evil.

36 'I tell you this: every thoughtless word you speak you will have to account for on the day of judgement. 37 For out of your own mouth you will be acquitted; out of your own mouth you will be condemned.'

38 At this some of the scribes and the Pharisees said, 'Teacher, we would like you to show us a sign.' 39 He answered: 'It is a wicked, godless generation that asks for a sign, and the only sign that will be given it is the sign of the prophet Jonah. 40 Just as Jonah was in the sea monster's belly for three days and three nights, so the Son of Man will be three days and three nights in the bowels of the earth. 41 The men of Nineveh will appear in court when this generation is on trial, and ensure its condemnation, for they repented at the preaching of Jonah; and what is here is greater than Jonah. 42 The queen of the south will appear in court when this generation is on trial, and ensure its condemnation; for she came from the ends of the earth to listen to the wisdom of Solomon, and what is here is greater than Solomon.

12:41 will appear . . . trial: or will rise again with this generation at the judgement.   12:42 The queen . . . trial: or The queen of the south will be raised to life with this generation at the judgement.

⸍Gk sons

18 "Behold, my servant whom I have chosen,
　my beloved in whom I delight;
I shall place my spirit upon him,
　and he will proclaim justice to the Gentiles.
19 He will not contend or cry out,
　nor will anyone hear his voice in the streets.
20 A bruised reed he will not break,
　a smoldering wick he will not quench,
　until he brings justice to victory.
21 And in his name the Gentiles will hope."

22 Then they brought to him a demoniac who was blind and mute. He cured the mute person so that he could speak and see. 23 All the crowd was astounded, and said, "Could this perhaps be the Son of David?" 24 But when the Pharisees heard this, they said, "This man drives out demons only by the power of Beelzebul, the prince of demons." 25 But he knew what they were thinking and said to them, "Every kingdom divided against itself will be laid waste, and no town or house divided against itself will stand. 26 And if Satan drives out Satan, he is divided against himself; how, then, will his kingdom stand? 27 And if I drive out demons by Beelzebul, by whom do your own people drive them out? Therefore they will be your judges. 28 But if it is by the Spirit of God that I drive out demons, then the kingdom of God has come upon you. 29 How can anyone enter a strong man's house and steal his property, unless he first ties up the strong man? Then he can plunder his house. 30 Whoever is not with me is against me, and whoever does not gather with me scatters. 31 Therefore, I say to you, every sin and blasphemy will be forgiven people, but blasphemy against the Spirit will not be forgiven. 32 And whoever speaks a word against the Son of Man will be forgiven; but whoever speaks against the holy Spirit will not be forgiven, either in this age or in the age to come.

33 "Either declare the tree good and its fruit is good, or declare the tree rotten and its fruit is rotten, for a tree is known by its fruit. 34 You brood of vipers, how can you say good things when you are evil? For from the fullness of the heart the mouth speaks. 35 A good person brings forth good out of a store of goodness, but an evil person brings forth evil out of a store of evil. 36 I tell you, on the day of judgment people will render an account for every careless word they speak. 37 By your words you will be acquitted, and by your words you will be condemned."

38 Then some of the scribes and Pharisees said to him, "Teacher, we wish to see a sign from you." 39 He said to them in reply, "An evil and unfaithful generation seeks a sign, but no sign will be given it except the sign of Jonah the prophet. 40 Just as Jonah was in the belly of the whale three days and three nights, so will the Son of Man be in the heart of the earth three days and three nights. 41 At the judgment, the men of Nineveh will arise with this generation and condemn it, because they repented at the preaching of Jonah; and there is something greater than Jonah here. 42 At the judgment the queen of the south will arise with this generation and condemn it, because she came from the ends of the earth to hear the wisdom of Solomon; and there is something greater than Solomon here.

18 Look! My servant whom I have chosen,
　my beloved, in whom my soul delights,
I will send my Spirit upon him,
　and he will present judgement to the nations;
19 he will not brawl or cry out,
　his voice is not heard in the streets,
20 he will not break the crushed reed,
　or snuff the faltering wick,
21 until he has made judgement victorious;
　in him the nations will put their hope.[l]

22 Then they brought to him a blind and dumb demoniac; and he cured him, so that the dumb man could speak and see. 23 All the people were astounded and said, 'Can this be the son of David?' 24 But when the Pharisees heard this they said, 'The man drives out devils only through Beelzebul, the chief of the devils.' 25 Knowing what was in their minds he said to them, 'Every kingdom divided against itself is heading for ruin; and no town, no household divided against itself can last. 26 Now if Satan drives out Satan, he is divided against himself; so how can his kingdom last? 27 And if it is through Beelzebul that I drive devils out, through whom do your own experts drive them out? They shall be your judges, then. 28 But if it is through the Spirit of God that I drive out devils, then be sure that the kingdom of God has caught you unawares.

29 'Or again, how can anyone make his way into a strong man's house and plunder his property unless he has first tied up the strong man? Only then can he plunder his house.

30 'Anyone who is not with me is against me, and anyone who does not gather in with me throws away. 31 And so I tell you, every human sin and blasphemy will be forgiven, but blasphemy against the Spirit will not be forgiven. 32 And anyone who says a word against the Son of man will be forgiven; but no one who speaks against the Holy Spirit will be forgiven either in this world or in the next.

33 'Make a tree sound and its fruit will be sound; make a tree rotten and its fruit will be rotten. For the tree can be told by its fruit. 34 You brood of vipers, how can your speech be good when you are evil? For words flow out of what fills the heart. 35 Good people draw good things from their store of goodness; bad people draw bad things from their store of badness. 36 So I tell you this, that for every unfounded word people utter they will answer on Judgement Day, 37 since it is by your words you will be justified, and by your words condemned.'

38 Then some of the scribes and Pharisees spoke up. 'Master,' they said, 'we should like to see a sign from you.' 39 He replied, 'It is an evil and unfaithful generation that asks for a sign! The only sign it will be given is the sign of the prophet Jonah. 40 For as Jonah remained in the belly of the sea-monster for three days and three nights,[m] so will the Son of man be in the heart of the earth for three days and three nights. 41 On Judgement Day the men of Nineveh will appear against this generation and they will be its condemnation, because when Jonah preached they repented; and look, there is something greater than Jonah here. 42 On Judgement Day the Queen of the South will appear against this generation and be its condemnation, because she came from the ends of the earth to hear the wisdom of Solomon; and look, there is something greater than Solomon here.

l 12 Is 42:1–4.　　m 12 Jon 2:1.

NEW REVISED STANDARD VERSION

43 "When the unclean spirit has gone out of a person, it wanders through waterless regions looking for a resting place, but it finds none. 44 Then it says, 'I will return to my house from which I came.' When it comes, it finds it empty, swept, and put in order. 45 Then it goes and brings along seven other spirits more evil than itself, and they enter and live there; and the last state of that person is worse than the first. So will it be also with this evil generation."

46 While he was still speaking to the crowds, his mother and his brothers were standing outside, wanting to speak to him. 47 Someone told him, "Look, your mother and your brothers are standing outside, wanting to speak to you."u 48 But to the one who had told him this, Jesusv replied, "Who is my mother, and who are my brothers?" 49 And pointing to his disciples, he said, "Here are my mother and my brothers! 50 For whoever does the will of my Father in heaven is my brother and sister and mother."

13 That same day Jesus went out of the house and sat beside the sea. 2 Such great crowds gathered around him that he got into a boat and sat there, while the whole crowd stood on the beach. 3 And he told them many things in parables, saying: "Listen! A sower went out to sow. 4 And as he sowed, some seeds fell on the path, and the birds came and ate them up. 5 Other seeds fell on rocky ground, where they did not have much soil, and they sprang up quickly, since they had no depth of soil. 6 But when the sun rose, they were scorched; and since they had no root, they withered away. 7 Other seeds fell among thorns, and the thorns grew up and choked them. 8 Other seeds fell on good soil and brought forth grain, some a hundredfold, some sixty, some thirty. 9 Let anyone with earsw listen!"

10 Then the disciples came and asked him, "Why do you speak to them in parables?" 11 He answered, "To you it has been given to know the secretsx of the kingdom of heaven, but to them it has not been given. 12 For to those who have, more will be given, and they will have an abundance; but from those who have nothing, even what they have will be taken away. 13 The reason I speak to them in parables is that 'seeing they do not perceive, and hearing they do not listen, nor do they understand.' 14 With them indeed is fulfilled the prophecy of Isaiah that says:

'You will indeed listen, but never understand,
    and you will indeed look, but never perceive.
15 For this people's heart has grown dull,
    and their ears are hard of hearing,
        and they have shut their eyes;
        so that they might not look with their eyes,
    and listen with their ears,
    and understand with their heart and turn —
        and I would heal them.'

16 But blessed are your eyes, for they see, and your ears, for they hear. 17 Truly I tell you, many prophets and righteous people longed to see what you see, but did not see it, and to hear what you hear, but did not hear it.

18 "Hear then the parable of the sower. 19 When anyone hears the word of the kingdom and does not understand it, the evil one comes and snatches away what is sown in the heart; this is what was sown on the path. 20 As for what was sown on rocky ground, this is the one who hears the word and immediately receives it with joy; 21 yet such a person

REVISED ENGLISH BIBLE

43 'When an unclean spirit comes out of someone it wanders over the desert sands seeking a resting-place, and finds none. 44 Then it says, "I will go back to the home I left." So it returns and finds the house unoccupied, swept clean, and tidy. 45 It goes off and collects seven other spirits more wicked than itself, and they all come in and settle there; and in the end that person's plight is worse than before. That is how it will be with this wicked generation.'

46 He was still speaking to the crowd when his mother and brothers appeared; they stood outside, wanting to speak to him. 47 Someone said, 'Your mother and your brothers are standing outside; they want to speak to you.' 48 Jesus turned to the man who brought the message, and said, 'Who is my mother? Who are my brothers?' 49 and pointing to his disciples, he said, 'Here are my mother and my brothers. 50 Whoever does the will of my heavenly Father is my brother and sister and mother.'

13 That same day Jesus went out and sat by the lakeside, 2 where so many people gathered round him that he had to get into a boat. He sat there, and all the people stood on the shore. 3 He told them many things in parables.

He said: 'A sower went out to sow. 4 And as he sowed, some of the seed fell along the footpath; and the birds came and ate it up. 5 Some fell on rocky ground, where it had little soil, and it sprouted quickly because it had no depth of earth; 6 but when the sun rose it was scorched, and as it had no root it withered away. 7 Some fell among thistles; and the thistles grew up and choked it. 8 And some of the seed fell on good soil, where it produced a crop, some a hundredfold, some sixtyfold, and some thirtyfold. 9 If you have ears, then hear.'

10 The disciples came to him and asked, 'Why do you speak to them in parables?' 11 He replied, 'To you it has been granted to know the secrets of the kingdom of Heaven, but not to them. 12 For those who have will be given more, till they have enough and to spare; and those who have not will forfeit even what they have. 13 That is why I speak to them in parables; for they look without seeing, and listen without hearing or understanding. 14 The prophecy of Isaiah is being fulfilled in them: "You may listen and listen, but you will never understand; you may look and look, but you will never see. 15 For this people's mind has become dull; they have stopped their ears and shut their eyes. Otherwise, their eyes might see, their ears hear, and their mind understand, and then they might turn to me, and I would heal them."

16 'But happy are your eyes because they see, and your ears because they hear! 17 Truly I tell you: many prophets and saints longed to see what you now see, yet never saw it; to hear what you hear, yet never heard it.

18 'Hear then the parable of the sower. 19 When anyone hears the word that tells of the Kingdom, but fails to understand it, the evil one comes and carries off what has been sown in his heart; that is the seed sown along the footpath. 20 The seed sown on rocky ground stands for the person who hears the word and accepts it at once with joy; 21 it strikes

uOther ancient authorities lack verse 47   vGk he   wOther ancient authorities add to hear   xOr mysteries

NEW AMERICAN BIBLE

NEW JERUSALEM BIBLE

43 "When an unclean spirit goes out of a person it roams through arid regions searching for rest but finds none. 44 Then it says, 'I will return to my home from which I came.' But upon returning, it finds it empty, swept clean, and put in order. 45 Then it goes and brings back with itself seven other spirits more evil than itself, and they move in and dwell there; and the last condition of that person is worse than the first. Thus it will be with this evil generation."

46 While he was still speaking to the crowds, his mother and his brothers appeared outside, wishing to speak with him. [47 Someone told him, "Your mother and your brothers are standing outside, asking to speak with you."] 48 But he said in reply to the one who told him, "Who is my mother? Who are my brothers?" 49 And stretching out his hand toward his disciples, he said, "Here are my mother and my brothers. 50 For whoever does the will of my heavenly Father is my brother, and sister, and mother."

13 On that day, Jesus went out of the house and sat down by the sea. 2 Such large crowds gathered around him that he got into a boat and sat down, and the whole crowd stood along the shore. 3 And he spoke to them at length in parables, saying: "A sower went out to sow. 4 And as he sowed, some seed fell on the path, and birds came and ate it up. 5 Some fell on rocky ground, where it had little soil. It sprang up at once because the soil was not deep, 6 and when the sun rose it was scorched, and it withered for lack of roots. 7 Some seed fell among thorns, and the thorns grew up and choked it. 8 But some seed fell on rich soil, and produced fruit, a hundred or sixty or thirtyfold. 9 Whoever has ears ought to hear."

10 The disciples approached him and said, "Why do you speak to them in parables?" 11 He said to them in reply, "Because knowledge of the mysteries of the kingdom of heaven has been granted to you, but to them it has not been granted. 12 To anyone who has, more will be given and he will grow rich; from anyone who has not, even what he has will be taken away. 13 This is why I speak to them in parables, because 'they look but do not see and hear but do not listen or understand.' 14 Isaiah's prophecy is fulfilled in them, which says:

'You shall indeed hear but not understand,
    you shall indeed look but never see.
15 Gross is the heart of this people,
    they will hardly hear with their ears,
    they have closed their eyes,
    lest they see with their eyes
    and hear with their ears
and understand with their heart and be converted
    and I heal them.'

16 "But blessed are your eyes, because they see, and your ears, because they hear. 17 Amen, I say to you, many prophets and righteous people longed to see what you see but did not see it, and to hear what you hear but did not hear it.

18 "Hear then the parable of the sower. 19 The seed sown on the path is the one who hears the word of the kingdom without understanding it, and the evil one comes and steals away what was sown in his heart. 20 The seed sown on rocky ground is the one who hears the word and receives it at once with joy. 21 But he has no root and lasts only for a

43 'When an unclean spirit goes out of someone it wanders through waterless country looking for a place to rest, and cannot find one. 44 Then it says, "I will return to the home I came from." But on arrival, finding it unoccupied, swept and tidied, 45 it then goes off and collects seven other spirits more wicked than itself, and they go in and set up house there, and so that person ends up worse off than before. That is what will happen to this wicked generation.'

46 He was still speaking to the crowds when suddenly his mother and his brothers[n] were standing outside and were anxious to have a word with him. [47][o] 48 But to the man who told him this Jesus replied, 'Who is my mother? Who are my brothers?' 49 And stretching out his hand towards his disciples he said, 'Here are my mother and my brothers. 50 Anyone who does the will of my Father in heaven is my brother and sister and mother.'

13 That same day, Jesus left the house and sat by the lakeside, 2 but such large crowds gathered round him that he got into a boat and sat there. The people all stood on the shore, 3 and he told them many things in parables.

He said, 'Listen, a sower went out to sow. 4 As he sowed, some seeds fell on the edge of the path, and the birds came and ate them up. 5 Others fell on patches of rock where they found little soil and sprang up at once, because there was no depth of earth; 6 but as soon as the sun came up they were scorched and, not having any roots, they withered away. 7 Others fell among thorns, and the thorns grew up and choked them. 8 Others fell on rich soil and produced their crop, some a hundredfold, some sixty, some thirty. 9 Anyone who has ears should listen!'

10 Then the disciples went up to him and asked, 'Why do you talk to them in parables?' 11 In answer, he said, 'Because to you is granted to understand the mysteries of the kingdom of Heaven, but to them it is not granted. 12 Anyone who has will be given more and will have more than enough; but anyone who has not will be deprived even of what he has. 13 The reason I talk to them in parables is that they look without seeing and listen without hearing or understanding. 14 So in their case what was spoken by the prophet Isaiah is being fulfilled:

Listen and listen, but never understand!
Look and look, but never perceive!
15 *This people's heart has grown coarse,*
    their ears dulled, they have shut their eyes tight
to avoid using their eyes to see, their ears to hear,
    their heart to understand,
changing their ways and being healed by me.[p]

16 'But blessed are your eyes because they see, your ears because they hear! 17 In truth I tell you, many prophets and upright people longed to see what you see, and never saw it; to hear what you hear, and never heard it.

18 'So pay attention to the parable of the sower. 19 When anyone hears the word of the kingdom without understanding, the Evil One comes and carries off what was sown in his heart: this is the seed sown on the edge of the path. 20 The seed sown on patches of rock is someone who hears the word and welcomes it at once with joy. 21 But such a

n 12 Not necessarily Mary's children. The Hebr. and Aram. word includes cousins and close relations. o 12 v. 47 ('Someone said to him: Your mother and brothers are standing outside and want to speak to you') is omitted by some important textual witnesses. It is probably a restatement of v. 46 modelled on Mk and Lk. p 13 Is 6:9–10.

12, 47: This verse is omitted in some important textual witnesses, including Codex Sinaiticus (original reading) and Codex Vaticanus.

has no root, but endures only for a while, and when trouble or persecution arises on account of the word, that person immediately falls away.*y* 22 As for what was sown among thorns, this is the one who hears the word, but the cares of the world and the lure of wealth choke the word, and it yields nothing. 23 But as for what was sown on good soil, this is the one who hears the word and understands it, who indeed bears fruit and yields, in one case a hundredfold, in another sixty, and in another thirty."

24 He put before them another parable: "The kingdom of heaven may be compared to someone who sowed good seed in his field; 25 but while everybody was asleep, an enemy came and sowed weeds among the wheat, and then went away. 26 So when the plants came up and bore grain, then the weeds appeared as well. 27 And the slaves of the householder came and said to him, 'Master, did you not sow good seed in your field? Where, then, did these weeds come from?' 28 He answered, 'An enemy has done this.' The slaves said to him, 'Then do you want us to go and gather them?' 29 But he replied, 'No; for in gathering the weeds you would uproot the wheat along with them. 30 Let both of them grow together until the harvest; and at harvest time I will tell the reapers, Collect the weeds first and bind them in bundles to be burned, but gather the wheat into my barn.' "

31 He put before them another parable: "The kingdom of heaven is like a mustard seed that someone took and sowed in his field; 32 it is the smallest of all the seeds, but when it has grown it is the greatest of shrubs and becomes a tree, so that the birds of the air come and make nests in its branches."

33 He told them another parable: "The kingdom of heaven is like yeast that a woman took and mixed in with*z* three measures of flour until all of it was leavened."

34 Jesus told the crowds all these things in parables; without a parable he told them nothing. 35 This was to fulfill what had been spoken through the prophet:*a*

"I will open my mouth to speak in parables;
I will proclaim what has been hidden from the foundation of the world."*b*

36 Then he left the crowds and went into the house. And his disciples approached him, saying, "Explain to us the parable of the weeds of the field." 37 He answered, "The one who sows the good seed is the Son of Man; 38 the field is the world, and the good seed are the children of the kingdom; the weeds are the children of the evil one, 39 and the enemy who sowed them is the devil; the harvest is the end of the age, and the reapers are angels. 40 Just as the weeds are collected and burned up with fire, so will it be at the end of the age. 41 The Son of Man will send his angels, and they will collect out of his kingdom all causes of sin and all evildoers, 42 and they will throw them into the furnace of fire, where there will be weeping and gnashing of teeth. 43 Then the righteous will shine like the sun in the kingdom of their Father. Let anyone with ears*c* listen!

44 "The kingdom of heaven is like treasure hidden in a field, which someone found and hid; then in his joy he goes and sells all that he has and buys that field.

45 "Again, the kingdom of heaven is like a merchant in search of fine pearls; 46 on finding one pearl of great value, he went and sold all that he had and bought it.

47 "Again, the kingdom of heaven is like a net that was thrown into the sea and caught fish of every kind; 48 when it was full, they drew it ashore, sat down, and put the good into baskets but threw out the bad. 49 So it will be at the end

no root in him and he has no staying-power; when there is trouble or persecution on account of the word he quickly loses faith. 22 The seed sown among thistles represents the person who hears the word, but worldly cares and the false glamour of wealth choke it, and it proves barren. 23 But the seed sown on good soil is the person who hears the word and understands it; he does bear fruit and yields a hundredfold, or sixtyfold, or thirtyfold.'

24 Here is another parable he gave them: 'The kingdom of Heaven is like this. A man sowed his field with good seed; 25 but while everyone was asleep his enemy came, sowed darnel among the wheat, and made off. 26 When the corn sprouted and began to fill out, the darnel could be seen among it. 27 The farmer's men went to their master and said, "Sir, was it not good seed that you sowed in your field? So where has the darnel come from?" 28 "This is an enemy's doing," he replied. "Well then," they said, "shall we go and gather the darnel?" 29 "No," he answered; "in gathering it you might pull up the wheat at the same time. 30 Let them both grow together till harvest; and at harvest time I will tell the reapers, 'Gather the darnel first, and tie it in bundles for burning; then collect the wheat into my barn.' " '

31 This is another parable he gave them: 'The kingdom of Heaven is like a mustard seed, which a man took and sowed in his field. 32 Mustard is smaller than any other seed, but when it has grown it is taller than other plants; it becomes a tree, big enough for the birds to come and roost among its branches.'

33 He told them also this parable: 'The kingdom of Heaven is like yeast, which a woman took and mixed with three measures of flour till it was all leavened.'

34 In all this teaching to the crowds Jesus spoke in parables; indeed he never spoke to them except in parables. 35 This was to fulfil the saying of the prophet:

I will open my mouth in parables;
I will utter things kept secret since the world was made.

36 Then he sent the people away, and went into the house, where his disciples came to him and said, 'Explain to us the parable of the darnel in the field.' 37 He replied, 'The sower of the good seed is the Son of Man. 38 The field is the world; the good seed stands for the children of the Kingdom, the darnel for the children of the evil one, 39 and the enemy who sowed the darnel is the devil. The harvest is the end of time, and the reapers are angels. 40 As the darnel is gathered up and burnt, so at the end of time 41 the Son of Man will send his angels, who will gather out of his kingdom every cause of sin, and all whose deeds are evil; 42 these will be thrown into the blazing furnace, where there will be wailing and grinding of teeth. 43 Then the righteous will shine like the sun in the kingdom of their Father. If you have ears, then hear.

44 'The kingdom of Heaven is like treasure which a man found buried in a field. He buried it again, and in joy went and sold everything he had, and bought the field.

45 'Again, the kingdom of Heaven is like this. A merchant looking out for fine pearls 46 found one of very special value; so he went and sold everything he had and bought it.

47 'Again the kingdom of Heaven is like a net cast into the sea, where it caught fish of every kind. 48 When it was full, it was hauled ashore. Then the men sat down and collected the good fish into baskets and threw the worthless away. 49 That is how it will be at the end of time. The angels will

---

y Gk *stumbles* *z* Gk *hid in* *a* Other ancient authorities read *the prophet Isaiah* *b* Other ancient authorities lack *of the world* *c* Other ancient authorities add *to hear*

13:35 **prophet:** *some witnesses add* Isaiah.

time. When some tribulation or persecution comes because of the word, he immediately falls away. 22 The seed sown among thorns is the one who hears the word, but then worldly anxiety and the lure of riches choke the word and it bears no fruit. 23 But the seed sown on rich soil is the one who hears the word and understands it, who indeed bears fruit and yields a hundred or sixty or thirtyfold."

24 He proposed another parable to them. "The kingdom of heaven may be likened to a man who sowed good seed in his field. 25 While everyone was asleep his enemy came and sowed weeds all through the wheat, and then went off. 26 When the crop grew and bore fruit, the weeds appeared as well. 27 The slaves of the householder came to him and said, 'Master, did you not sow good seed in your field? Where have the weeds come from?' 28 He answered, 'An enemy has done this.' His slaves said to him, 'Do you want us to go and pull them up?' 29 He replied, 'No, if you pull up the weeds you might uproot the wheat along with them. 30 Let them grow together until harvest; then at harvest time I will say to the harvesters, "First collect the weeds and tie them in bundles for burning; but gather the wheat into my barn." ' "

31 He proposed another parable to them. "The kingdom of heaven is like a mustard seed that a person took and sowed in a field. 32 It is the smallest of all the seeds, yet when full-grown it is the largest of plants. It becomes a large bush, and the 'birds of the sky come and dwell in its branches.' "

33 He spoke to them another parable. "The kingdom of heaven is like yeast that a woman took and mixed with three measures of wheat flour until the whole batch was leavened."

34 All these things Jesus spoke to the crowds in parables. He spoke to them only in parables, 35 to fulfill what had been said through the prophet:

"I will open my mouth in parables,
    I will announce what has lain hidden from
        the foundation [of the world]."

36 Then, dismissing the crowds, he went into the house. His disciples approached him and said, "Explain to us the parable of the weeds in the field." 37 He said in reply, "He who sows good seed is the Son of Man, 38 the field is the world, the good seed the children of the kingdom. The weeds are the children of the evil one, 39 and the enemy who sows them is the devil. The harvest is the end of the age, and the harvesters are angels. 40 Just as weeds are collected and burned [up] with fire, so will it be at the end of the age. 41 The Son of Man will send his angels, and they will collect out of his kingdom all who cause others to sin and all evildoers. 42 They will throw them into the fiery furnace, where there will be wailing and grinding of teeth. 43 Then the righteous will shine like the sun in the kingdom of their Father. Whoever has ears ought to hear.

44 "The kingdom of heaven is like a treasure buried in a field, which a person finds and hides again, and out of joy goes and sells all that he has and buys that field. 45 Again, the kingdom of heaven is like a merchant searching for fine pearls. 46 When he finds a pearl of great price, he goes and sells all that he has and buys it. 47 Again, the kingdom of heaven is like a net thrown into the sea, which collects fish of every kind. 48 When it is full they haul it ashore and sit down to put what is good into buckets. What is bad they throw away. 49 Thus it will be at the end of the age. The

person has no root deep down and does not last; should some trial come, or some persecution on account of the word, at once he falls away. 22 The seed sown in thorns is someone who hears the word, but the worry of the world and the lure of riches choke the word and so it produces nothing. 23 And the seed sown in rich soil is someone who hears the word and understands it; this is the one who yields a harvest and produces now a hundredfold, now sixty, now thirty.'

24 He put another parable before them, 'The kingdom of Heaven may be compared to a man who sowed good seed in his field. 25 While everybody was asleep his enemy came, sowed darnel all among the wheat, and made off. 26 When the new wheat sprouted and ripened, then the darnel appeared as well. 27 The owner's labourers went to him and said, "Sir, was it not good seed that you sowed in your field? If so, where does the darnel come from?" 28 He said to them, "Some enemy has done this." And the labourers said, "Do you want us to go and weed it out?" 29 But he said, "No, because when you weed out the darnel you might pull up the wheat with it. 30 Let them both grow till the harvest; and at harvest time I shall say to the reapers: First collect the darnel and tie it in bundles to be burnt, then gather the wheat into my barn." '

31 He put another parable before them, 'The kingdom of Heaven is like a mustard seed which a man took and sowed in his field. 32 It is the smallest of all the seeds, but when it has grown it is the biggest of shrubs and becomes a tree, so that the birds of the air can come and shelter in its branches.'

33 He told them another parable, 'The kingdom of Heaven is like the yeast a woman took and mixed in with three measures of flour till it was leavened all through.'

34 In all this Jesus spoke to the crowds in parables; indeed, he would never speak to them except in parables. 35 This was to fulfil what was spoken by the prophet:

I will speak to you in parables,
    unfold what has been hidden since the foundation
        of the world. q

36 Then, leaving the crowds, he went to the house; and his disciples came to him and said, 'Explain to us the parable about the darnel in the field.' 37 He said in reply, 'The sower of the good seed is the Son of man. 38 The field is the world; the good seed is the subjects of the kingdom; the darnel, the subjects of the Evil One; 39 the enemy who sowed it, the devil; the harvest is the end of the world; the reapers are the angels. 40 Well then, just as the darnel is gathered up and burnt in the fire, so it will be at the end of time. 41 The Son of man will send his angels and they will gather out of his kingdom all causes of falling and all who do evil, 42 and throw them into the blazing furnace, where there will be weeping and grinding of teeth. 43 Then the upright will shine like the sun in the kingdom of their Father. Anyone who has ears should listen!

44 'The kingdom of Heaven is like treasure hidden in a field which someone has found; he hides it again, goes off in his joy, sells everything he owns and buys the field.

45 'Again, the kingdom of Heaven is like a merchant looking for fine pearls; 46 when he finds one of great value he goes and sells everything he owns and buys it.

47 'Again, the kingdom of Heaven is like a dragnet that is cast in the sea and brings in a haul of all kinds of fish. 48 When it is full, the fishermen bring it ashore; then, sitting down, they collect the good ones in baskets and throw away those that are no use. 49 This is how it will be at the end of

of the age. The angels will come out and separate the evil from the righteous ⁵⁰ and throw them into the furnace of fire, where there will be weeping and gnashing of teeth.

51 "Have you understood all this?" They answered, "Yes." ⁵² And he said to them, "Therefore every scribe who has been trained for the kingdom of heaven is like the master of a household who brings out of his treasure what is new and what is old." ⁵³ When Jesus had finished these parables, he left that place.

54 He came to his hometown and began to teach the people*d* in their synagogue, so that they were astounded and said, "Where did this man get this wisdom and these deeds of power? ⁵⁵ Is not this the carpenter's son? Is not his mother called Mary? And are not his brothers James and Joseph and Simon and Judas? ⁵⁶ And are not all his sisters with us? Where then did this man get all this?" ⁵⁷ And they took offense at him. But Jesus said to them, "Prophets are not without honor except in their own country and in their own house." ⁵⁸ And he did not do many deeds of power there, because of their unbelief.

14 At that time Herod the ruler*e* heard reports about Jesus; ² and he said to his servants, "This is John the Baptist; he has been raised from the dead, and for this reason these powers are at work in him." ³ For Herod had arrested John, bound him, and put him in prison on account of Herodias, his brother Philip's wife,*f* ⁴ because John had been telling him, "It is not lawful for you to have her." ⁵ Though Herod*g* wanted to put him to death, he feared the crowd, because they regarded him as a prophet. ⁶ But when Herod's birthday came, the daughter of Herodias danced before the company, and she pleased Herod ⁷ so much that he promised on oath to grant her whatever she might ask. ⁸ Prompted by her mother, she said, "Give me the head of John the Baptist here on a platter." ⁹ The king was grieved, yet out of regard for his oaths and for the guests, he commanded it to be given; ¹⁰ he sent and had John beheaded in the prison. ¹¹ The head was brought on a platter and given to the girl, who brought it to her mother. ¹² His disciples came and took the body and buried it; then they went and told Jesus.

13 Now when Jesus heard this, he withdrew from there in a boat to a deserted place by himself. But when the crowds heard it, they followed him on foot from the towns. ¹⁴ When he went ashore, he saw a great crowd; and he had compassion for them and cured their sick. ¹⁵ When it was evening, the disciples came to him and said, "This is a deserted place, and the hour is now late; send the crowds away so that they may go into the villages and buy food for themselves." ¹⁶ Jesus said to them, "They need not go away; you give them something to eat." ¹⁷ They replied, "We have nothing here but five loaves and two fish." ¹⁸ And he said, "Bring them here to me." ¹⁹ Then he ordered the crowds to sit down on the grass. Taking the five loaves and the two fish, he looked up to heaven, and blessed and broke the loaves, and gave them to the disciples, and the disciples gave them to the crowds. ²⁰ And all ate and were filled; and they took up what was left over of the broken pieces, twelve baskets full. ²¹ And those who ate were about five thousand men, besides women and children.

22 Immediately he made the disciples get into the boat and go on ahead to the other side, while he dismissed the crowds. ²³ And after he had dismissed the crowds, he went up the mountain by himself to pray. When evening came, he was there alone, ²⁴ but by this time the boat, battered by the waves, was far from the land,*h* for the wind was against them. ²⁵ And early in the morning he came walking toward

go out, and they will separate the wicked from the good, ⁵⁰ and throw them into the blazing furnace, where there will be wailing and grinding of teeth.

51 'Have you understood all this?' he asked; and they answered, 'Yes.' ⁵² So he said to them, 'When, therefore, a teacher of the law has become a learner in the kingdom of Heaven, he is like a householder who can produce from his store things new and old.'

53 When Jesus had finished these parables he left that place, ⁵⁴ and came to his home town, where he taught the people in their synagogue. In amazement they asked, 'Where does he get this wisdom from, and these miraculous powers? ⁵⁵ Is he not the carpenter's son? Is not his mother called Mary, his brothers James, Joseph, Simon, and Judas? ⁵⁶ And are not all his sisters here with us? Where does he get all this from?' ⁵⁷ So they turned against him. Jesus said to them, 'A prophet never lacks honour, except in his home town and in his own family.' ⁵⁸ And he did not do many miracles there, such was their want of faith.

14 It was at that time that reports about Jesus reached Herod the tetrarch. ² 'This is John the Baptist,' he said to his attendants; 'he has been raised from the dead, and that is why these miraculous powers are at work in him.'

3 Now Herod had arrested John, put him in chains, and thrown him into prison, on account of Herodias, his brother Philip's wife; ⁴ for John had told him: 'You have no right to her.' ⁵ Herod would have liked to put him to death, but he was afraid of the people, in whose eyes John was a prophet. ⁶ But at his birthday celebrations the daughter of Herodias danced before the guests, and Herod was so delighted ⁷ that he promised on oath to give her anything she asked for. ⁸ Prompted by her mother, she said, 'Give me here on a dish the head of John the Baptist.' ⁹ At this the king was distressed, but because of his oath and his guests, he ordered the request to be granted, ¹⁰ and had John beheaded in prison. ¹¹ The head was brought on a dish and given to the girl; and she carried it to her mother. ¹² Then John's disciples came and took away the body, and buried it; and they went and told Jesus.

13 When he heard what had happened Jesus withdrew privately by boat to a remote place; but large numbers of people heard of it, and came after him on foot from the towns. ¹⁴ When he came ashore and saw a large crowd, his heart went out to them, and he healed those who were sick. ¹⁵ As evening drew on, the disciples came up to him and said, 'This is a remote place and the day has gone; send the people off to the villages to buy themselves food.' ¹⁶ Jesus answered, 'There is no need for them to go; give them something to eat yourselves.' ¹⁷ 'All we have here', they said, 'is five loaves and two fish.' ¹⁸ 'Bring them to me,' he replied. ¹⁹ So he told the people to sit down on the grass; then, taking the five loaves and the two fish, he looked up to heaven, said the blessing, broke the loaves, and gave them to the disciples; and the disciples gave them to the people. ²⁰ They all ate and were satisfied; and twelve baskets were filled with what was left over. ²¹ Some five thousand men shared in this meal, not counting women and children.

22 As soon as they had finished, he made the disciples embark and cross to the other side ahead of him, while he dismissed the crowd; ²³ then he went up the hill by himself to pray. It had grown late, and he was there alone. ²⁴ The boat was already some distance from the shore, battling with a head wind and a rough sea. ²⁵ Between three and six

---

d Gk *them* *e* Gk *tetrarch* *f* Other ancient authorities read *his*
brother's wife *g* Gk *he* *h* Other ancient authorities read *was out*
on the sea

NEW AMERICAN BIBLE | NEW JERUSALEM BIBLE

angels will go out and separate the wicked from the righteous 50 and throw them into the fiery furnace, where there will be wailing and grinding of teeth.

51 "Do you understand all these things?" They answered, "Yes." 52 And he replied, "Then every scribe who has been instructed in the kingdom of heaven is like the head of a household who brings from his storeroom both the new and the old." 53 When Jesus finished these parables, he went away from there.

54 He came to his native place and taught the people in their synagogue. They were astonished and said, "Where did this man get such wisdom and mighty deeds? 55 Is he not the carpenter's son? Is not his mother named Mary and his brothers James, Joseph, Simon, and Judas? 56 Are not his sisters all with us? Where did this man get all this?" 57 And they took offense at him. But Jesus said to them, "A prophet is not without honor except in his native place and in his own house." 58 And he did not work many mighty deeds there because of their lack of faith.

14 At that time Herod the tetrarch heard of the reputation of Jesus 2 and said to his servants, "This man is John the Baptist. He has been raised from the dead; that is why mighty powers are at work in him."

3 Now Herod had arrested John, bound [him], and put him in prison on account of Herodias, the wife of his brother Philip, 4 for John had said to him, "It is not lawful for you to have her." 5 Although he wanted to kill him, he feared the people, for they regarded him as a prophet. 6 But at a birthday celebration for Herod, the daughter of Herodias performed a dance before the guests and delighted Herod 7 so much that he swore to give her whatever she might ask for. 8 Prompted by her mother, she said, "Give me here on a platter the head of John the Baptist." 9 The king was distressed, but because of his oaths and the guests who were present, he ordered that it be given, 10 and he had John beheaded in the prison. 11 His head was brought in on a platter and given to the girl, who took it to her mother. 12 His disciples came and took away the corpse and buried him; and they went and told Jesus.

13 When Jesus heard of it, he withdrew in a boat to a deserted place by himself. The crowds heard of this and followed him on foot from their towns. 14 When he disembarked and saw the vast crowd, his heart was moved with pity for them, and he cured their sick. 15 When it was evening, the disciples approached him and said, "This is a deserted place and it is already late; dismiss the crowds so that they can go to the villages and buy food for themselves." 16 [Jesus] said to them, "There is no need for them to go away; give them some food yourselves." 17 But they said to him, "Five loaves and two fish are all we have here." 18 Then he said, "Bring them here to me," 19 and he ordered the crowds to sit down on the grass. Taking the five loaves and the two fish, and looking up to heaven, he said the blessing, broke the loaves, and gave them to the disciples, who in turn gave them to the crowds. 20 They all ate and were satisfied, and they picked up the fragments left over — twelve wicker baskets full. 21 Those who ate were about five thousand men, not counting women and children.

22 Then he made the disciples get into the boat and precede him to the other side, while he dismissed the crowds. 23 After doing so, he went up on the mountain by himself to pray. When it was evening he was there alone. 24 Meanwhile the boat, already a few miles offshore, was being tossed about by the waves, for the wind was against it. 25 During the fourth watch of the night, he came toward

time: the angels will appear and separate the wicked from the upright, 50 to throw them into the blazing furnace, where there will be weeping and grinding of teeth.

51 'Have you understood all these?' They said, 'Yes.' 52 And he said to them, 'Well then, every scribe who becomes a disciple of the kingdom of Heaven is like a householder who brings out from his storeroom new things as well as old.'

53 When Jesus had finished these parables he left the district; 54 and, coming to his home town, he taught the people in their synagogue in such a way that they were astonished and said, 'Where did the man get this wisdom and these miraculous powers? 55 This is the carpenter's son, surely? Is not his mother the woman called Mary, and his brothers James and Joseph and Simon and Jude? 56 His sisters, too, are they not all here with us? So where did the man get it all?' 57 And they would not accept him. But Jesus said to them, 'A prophet is despised only in his own country and in his own house,' 58 and he did not work many miracles there because of their lack of faith.

14 At that time Herod the tetrarch heard about the reputation of Jesus 2 and said to his court, 'This is John the Baptist himself; he has risen from the dead, and that is why miraculous powers are at work in him.'

3 Now it was Herod who had arrested John, chained him up and put him in prison because of Herodias, his brother Philip's wife. 4 For John had told him, 'It is against the Law for you to have her.' 5 He had wanted to kill him but was afraid of the people, who regarded John as a prophet. 6 Then, during the celebrations for Herod's birthday, the daughter of Herodias danced before the company and so delighted Herod 7 that he promised on oath to give her anything she asked. 8 Prompted by her mother she said, 'Give me John the Baptist's head, here, on a dish.' 9 The king was distressed but, thinking of the oaths he had sworn and of his guests, he ordered it to be given her, 10 and sent and had John beheaded in the prison. 11 The head was brought in on a dish and given to the girl, who took it to her mother. 12 John's disciples came and took the body and buried it; then they went off to tell Jesus.

13 When Jesus received this news he withdrew by boat to a lonely place where they could be by themselves. But the crowds heard of this and, leaving the towns, went after him on foot. 14 So as he stepped ashore he saw a large crowd; and he took pity on them and healed their sick. 15 When evening came, the disciples went to him and said, 'This is a lonely place, and time has slipped by; so send the people away, and they can go to the villages to buy themselves some food.' 16 Jesus replied, 'There is no need for them to go: give them something to eat yourselves.' 17 But they answered, 'All we have with us is five loaves and two fish.' 18 So he said, 'Bring them here to me.' 19 He gave orders that the people were to sit down on the grass; then he took the five loaves and the two fish, raised his eyes to heaven and said the blessing. And breaking the loaves he handed them to his disciples, who gave them to the crowds. 20 They all ate as much as they wanted, and they collected the scraps left over, twelve baskets full. 21 Now about five thousand men had eaten, to say nothing of women and children. r

22 And at once he made the disciples get into the boat and go on ahead to the other side while he sent the crowds away. 23 After sending the crowds away he went up into the hills by himself to pray. When evening came, he was there alone, 24 while the boat, by now some furlongs from land, was hard pressed by rough waves, for there was a headwind. 25 In the fourth watch of the night he came towards

r 14 This and 15:32–39 are probably varying accounts of the same incident. This one echoes 2 K 4:42.

NEW REVISED STANDARD VERSION	REVISED ENGLISH BIBLE

them on the sea. 26 But when the disciples saw him walking on the sea, they were terrified, saying, "It is a ghost!" And they cried out in fear. 27 But immediately Jesus spoke to them and said, "Take heart, it is I; do not be afraid."

28 Peter answered him, "Lord, if it is you, command me to come to you on the water." 29 He said, "Come." So Peter got out of the boat, started walking on the water, and came toward Jesus. 30 But when he noticed the strong wind,*i* he became frightened, and beginning to sink, he cried out, "Lord, save me!" 31 Jesus immediately reached out his hand and caught him, saying to him, "You of little faith, why did you doubt?" 32 When they got into the boat, the wind ceased. 33 And those in the boat worshiped him, saying, "Truly you are the Son of God."

34 When they had crossed over, they came to land at Gennesaret. 35 After the people of that place recognized him, they sent word throughout the region and brought all who were sick to him, 36 and begged him that they might touch even the fringe of his cloak; and all who touched it were healed.

15 Then Pharisees and scribes came to Jesus from Jerusalem and said, 2 "Why do your disciples break the tradition of the elders? For they do not wash their hands before they eat." 3 He answered them, "And why do you break the commandment of God for the sake of your tradition? 4 For God said,*j* 'Honor your father and your mother,' and, 'Whoever speaks evil of father or mother must surely die.' 5 But you say that whoever tells father or mother, 'Whatever support you might have had from me is given to God,'*k* then that person need not honor the father.*l* 6 So, for the sake of your tradition, you make void the word*m* of God. 7 You hypocrites! Isaiah prophesied rightly about you when he said:
8 	'This people honors me with their lips,
	but their hearts are far from me;
9 	in vain do they worship me,
	teaching human precepts as doctrines.' "
10 Then he called the crowd to him and said to them, "Listen and understand: 11 it is not what goes into the mouth that defiles a person, but it is what comes out of the mouth that defiles." 12 Then the disciples approached and said to him, "Do you know that the Pharisees took offense when they heard what you said?" 13 He answered, "Every plant that my heavenly Father has not planted will be uprooted. 14 Let them alone; they are blind guides of the blind.*n* And if one blind person guides another, both will fall into a pit." 15 But Peter said to him, "Explain this parable to us." 16 Then he said, "Are you also still without understanding? 17 Do you not see that whatever goes into the mouth enters the stomach, and goes out into the sewer? 18 But what comes out of the mouth proceeds from the heart, and this is what defiles. 19 For out of the heart come evil intentions, murder, adultery, fornication, theft, false witness, slander. 20 These are what defile a person, but to eat with unwashed hands does not defile."

21 Jesus left that place and went away to the district of Tyre and Sidon. 22 Just then a Canaanite woman from that region came out and started shouting, "Have mercy on me, Lord, Son of David; my daughter is tormented by a demon." 23 But he did not answer her at all. And his disciples came and urged him, saying, "Send her away, for she keeps shouting after us." 24 He answered, "I was sent only to the

in the morning he came towards them, walking across the lake. 26 When the disciples saw him walking on the lake they were so shaken that they cried out in terror: 'It is a ghost!' 27 But at once Jesus spoke to them: 'Take heart! It is I; do not be afraid.'

28 Peter called to him: 'Lord, if it is you, tell me to come to you over the water.' 29 'Come,' said Jesus. Peter got down out of the boat, and walked over the water towards Jesus. 30 But when he saw the strength of the gale he was afraid; and beginning to sink, he cried, 'Save me, Lord!' 31 Jesus at once reached out and caught hold of him. 'Why did you hesitate?' he said. 'How little faith you have!' 32 Then they climbed into the boat; and the wind dropped. 33 And the men in the boat fell at his feet, exclaiming, 'You must be the Son of God.'

34 So they completed the crossing and landed at Gennesaret. 35 The people there recognized Jesus and sent word to all the country round. They brought to him all who were ill 36 and begged him to let them simply touch the edge of his cloak; and all who touched it were completely cured.

15 THEN Jesus was approached by a group of Pharisees and scribes from Jerusalem, with the question: 2 'Why do your disciples break the ancient tradition? They do not wash their hands before eating.' 3 He answered them: 'And what about you? Why do you break God's commandment in the interest of your tradition? 4 For God said, "Honour your father and mother," and "Whoever curses his father or mother shall be put to death." 5 But you say, "Whoever says to his father or mother, 'Anything I have which might have been used for your benefit is set apart for God,' 6 must not honour his father or his mother." You have made God's law null and void out of regard for your tradition. 7 What hypocrites! How right Isaiah was when he prophesied about you: 8 "This people pays me lip-service, but their heart is far from me; 9 they worship me in vain, for they teach as doctrines the commandments of men." '

10 He called the crowd and said to them, 'Listen and understand! 11 No one is defiled by what goes into his mouth; only by what comes out of it.'

12 Then the disciples came to him and said, 'Do you know that the Pharisees have taken great offence at what you have been saying?' 13 He answered: 'Any plant that is not of my heavenly Father's planting will be rooted up. 14 Leave them alone; they are blind guides, and if one blind man guides another they will both fall into the ditch.'

15 Then Peter said, 'Tell us what that parable means.' 16 Jesus said, 'Are you still as dull as the rest? 17 Do you not see that whatever goes in by the mouth passes into the stomach and so is discharged into the drain? 18 But what comes out of the mouth has its origins in the heart; and that is what defiles a person. 19 Wicked thoughts, murder, adultery, fornication, theft, perjury, slander—these all proceed from the heart; 20 and these are the things that defile a person; but to eat without first washing his hands, that cannot defile him.'

21 JESUS then withdrew to the region of Tyre and Sidon. 22 And a Canaanite woman from those parts came to meet him crying, 'Son of David! Have pity on me; my daughter is tormented by a devil.' 23 But he said not a word in reply. His disciples came and urged him: 'Send her away! See how she comes shouting after us.' 24 Jesus replied, 'I was sent to

---

i Other ancient authorities read *the wind* *j* Other ancient authorities read *commanded, saying* *k* Or *is an offering* *l* Other ancient authorities add *or the mother* *m* Other ancient authorities read *law*; others, *commandment* *n* Other ancient authorities lack *of the blind*

14:36 **edge**: *or* tassel.   15:14 **blind guides**: *some witnesses add* of blind men.

them, walking on the sea. 26 When the disciples saw him walking on the sea they were terrified. "It is a ghost," they said, and they cried out in fear. 27 At once [Jesus] spoke to them, "Take courage, it is I; do not be afraid." 28 Peter said to him in reply, "Lord, if it is you, command me to come to you on the water." 29 He said, "Come." Peter got out of the boat and began to walk on the water toward Jesus. 30 But when he saw how [strong] the wind was he became frightened; and, beginning to sink, he cried out, "Lord, save me!" 31 Immediately Jesus stretched out his hand and caught him, and said to him, "O you of little faith, why did you doubt?" 32 After they got into the boat, the wind died down. 33 Those who were in the boat did him homage, saying, "Truly, you are the Son of God."

34 After making the crossing, they came to land at Gennesaret. 35 When the men of that place recognized him, they sent word to all the surrounding country. People brought to him all those who were sick 36 and begged him that they might touch only the tassel on his cloak, and as many as touched it were healed.

15 Then Pharisees and scribes came to Jesus from Jerusalem and said, 2 "Why do your disciples break the tradition of the elders? They do not wash [their] hands when they eat a meal." 3 He said to them in reply, "And why do you break the commandment of God for the sake of your tradition? 4 For God said, 'Honor your father and your mother,' and 'Whoever curses father or mother shall die.' 5 But you say, 'Whoever says to father or mother, "Any support you might have had from me is dedicated to God," 6 need not honor his father.' You have nullified the word of God for the sake of your tradition. 7 Hypocrites, well did Isaiah prophesy about you when he said:

> 8 'This people honors me with their lips,
>   but their hearts are far from me;
> 9 in vain do they worship me,
>   teaching as doctrines human precepts.'"

10 He summoned the crowd and said to them, "Hear and understand. 11 It is not what enters one's mouth that defiles that person; but what comes out of the mouth is what defiles one." 12 Then his disciples approached and said to him, "Do you know that the Pharisees took offense when they heard what you said?" 13 He said in reply, "Every plant that my heavenly Father has not planted will be uprooted. 14 Let them alone; they are blind guides [of the blind]. If a blind person leads a blind person, both will fall into a pit." 15 Then Peter said to him in reply, "Explain [this] parable to us." 16 He said to them, "Are even you still without understanding? 17 Do you not realize that everything that enters the mouth passes into the stomach and is expelled into the latrine? 18 But the things that come out of the mouth come from the heart, and they defile. 19 For from the heart come evil thoughts, murder, adultery, unchastity, theft, false witness, blasphemy. 20 These are what defile a person, but to eat with unwashed hands does not defile."

21 Then Jesus went from that place and withdrew to the region of Tyre and Sidon. 22 And behold, a Canaanite woman of that district came and called out, "Have pity on me, Lord, Son of David! My daughter is tormented by a demon." 23 But he did not say a word in answer to her. His disciples came and asked him, "Send her away, for she keeps calling out after us." 24 He said in reply, "I was sent

them, walking on the sea, 26 and when the disciples saw him walking on the sea they were terrified. 'It is a ghost,' they said, and cried out in fear. 27 But at once Jesus called out to them, saying, 'Courage! It's me! Don't be afraid.' 28 It was Peter who answered. 'Lord,' he said, 'if it is you, tell me to come to you across the water.' 29 Jesus said, 'Come.' Then Peter got out of the boat and started walking towards Jesus across the water, 30 but then noticing the wind, he took fright and began to sink. 'Lord,' he cried, 'save me!' 31 Jesus put out his hand at once and held him. 'You have so little faith,' he said, 'why did you doubt?' 32 And as they got into the boat the wind dropped. 33 The men in the boat bowed down before him and said, 'Truly, you are the Son of God.'

34 Having made the crossing, they came to land at Gennesaret. 35 When the local people recognised him they spread the news through the whole neighbourhood and took all that were sick to him, 36 begging him just to let them touch the fringe of his cloak. And all those who touched it were saved.

15 Then Pharisees and scribes from Jerusalem came to Jesus and said, 2 'Why do your disciples break away from the tradition of the elders? They eat without washing their hands.' 3 He answered, 'And why do you break away from the commandment of God for the sake of your tradition? 4 For God said, *"Honour your father and your mother"* and *"Anyone who curses his father or mother will be put to death."* [s] 5 But you say, "If anyone says to his father or mother: Anything I might have used to help you is dedicated to God, 6 he is rid of his duty to father or mother." In this way you have made God's word ineffective by means of your tradition. 7 Hypocrites! How rightly Isaiah prophesied about you when he said:

> 8 *This people honours me only with lip-service,*
>   *while their hearts are far from me.*
> 9 *Their reverence of me is worthless;*
>   *the lessons they teach are nothing but human*
>   *commandments.'* [t]

10 He called the people to him and said, 'Listen, and understand. 11 What goes into the mouth does not make anyone unclean; it is what comes out of the mouth that makes someone unclean.'

12 Then the disciples came to him and said, 'Do you know that the Pharisees were shocked when they heard what you said?' 13 He replied, 'Any plant my heavenly Father has not planted will be pulled up by the roots. 14 Leave them alone. They are blind leaders of the blind; and if one blind person leads another, both will fall into a pit.'

15 At this, Peter said to him, 'Explain the parable for us.' 16 Jesus replied, 'Even you—don't you yet understand? 17 Can't you see that whatever goes into the mouth passes through the stomach and is discharged into the sewer? 18 But whatever comes out of the mouth comes from the heart, and it is this that makes someone unclean. 19 For from the heart come evil intentions: murder, adultery, fornication, theft, perjury, slander. 20 These are the things that make a person unclean. But eating with unwashed hands does not make anyone unclean.'

21 Jesus left that place and withdrew to the region of Tyre and Sidon. 22 And suddenly out came a Canaanite woman from that district and started shouting, 'Lord, Son of David, take pity on me. My daughter is tormented by a devil.' 23 But he said not a word in answer to her. And his disciples went and pleaded with him, saying, 'Give her what she wants, because she keeps shouting after us.' 24 He said in

s 15 Ex 20:12 and 21:17.   t 15 Is 29:13.

NEW REVISED STANDARD VERSION

lost sheep of the house of Israel." 25 But she came and knelt before him, saying, "Lord, help me." 26 He answered, "It is not fair to take the children's food and throw it to the dogs." 27 She said, "Yes, Lord, yet even the dogs eat the crumbs that fall from their masters' table." 28 Then Jesus answered her, "Woman, great is your faith! Let it be done for you as you wish." And her daughter was healed instantly.

29 After Jesus had left that place, he passed along the Sea of Galilee, and he went up the mountain, where he sat down. 30 Great crowds came to him, bringing with them the lame, the maimed, the blind, the mute, and many others. They put them at his feet, and he cured them, 31 so that the crowd was amazed when they saw the mute speaking, the maimed whole, the lame walking, and the blind seeing. And they praised the God of Israel.

32 Then Jesus called his disciples to him and said, "I have compassion for the crowd, because they have been with me now for three days and have nothing to eat; and I do not want to send them away hungry, for they might faint on the way." 33 The disciples said to him, "Where are we to get enough bread in the desert to feed so great a crowd?" 34 Jesus asked them, "How many loaves have you?" They said, "Seven, and a few small fish." 35 Then ordering the crowd to sit down on the ground, 36 he took the seven loaves and the fish; and after giving thanks he broke them and gave them to the disciples, and the disciples gave them to the crowds. 37 And all of them ate and were filled; and they took up the broken pieces left over, seven baskets full. 38 Those who had eaten were four thousand men, besides women and children. 39 After sending away the crowds, he got into the boat and went to the region of Magadan.o

16 The Pharisees and Sadducees came, and to test Jesus p they asked him to show them a sign from heaven. 2 He answered them, "When it is evening, you say, 'It will be fair weather, for the sky is red.' 3 And in the morning, 'It will be stormy today, for the sky is red and threatening.' You know how to interpret the appearance of the sky, but you cannot interpret the signs of the times.q 4 An evil and adulterous generation asks for a sign, but no sign will be given to it except the sign of Jonah." Then he left and went away.

5 When the disciples reached the other side, they had forgotten to bring any bread. 6 Jesus said to them, "Watch out, and beware of the yeast of the Pharisees and Sadducees." 7 They said to one another, "It is because we have brought no bread." 8 And becoming aware of it, Jesus said, "You of little faith, why are you talking about having no bread? 9 Do you still not perceive? Do you not remember the five loaves for the five thousand, and how many baskets you gathered? 10 Or the seven loaves for the four thousand, and how many baskets you gathered? 11 How could you fail to perceive that I was not speaking about bread? Beware of the yeast of the Pharisees and Sadducees!" 12 Then they understood that he had not told them to beware of the yeast of bread, but of the teaching of the Pharisees and Sadducees.

13 Now when Jesus came into the district of Caesarea Philippi, he asked his disciples, "Who do people say that the Son of Man is?" 14 And they said, "Some say John the Baptist, but others Elijah, and still others Jeremiah or one of the prophets." 15 He said to them, "But who do you say that I am?" 16 Simon Peter answered, "You are the Mes-

REVISED ENGLISH BIBLE

the lost sheep of the house of Israel, and to them alone.' 25 But the woman came and fell at his feet and cried, 'Help me, sir.' 26 Jesus replied, 'It is not right to take the children's bread and throw it to the dogs.' 27 'True, sir,' she answered, 'and yet the dogs eat the scraps that fall from their master's table.' 28 Hearing this Jesus replied, 'What faith you have! Let it be as you wish!' And from that moment her daughter was restored to health.

29 After leaving that region Jesus took the road by the sea of Galilee, where he climbed a hill and sat down. 30 Crowds flocked to him, bringing with them the lame, blind, dumb, and crippled, and many other sufferers; they put them down at his feet, and he healed them. 31 Great was the amazement of the people when they saw the dumb speaking, the crippled made strong, the lame walking, and the blind with their sight restored; and they gave praise to the God of Israel.

32 Jesus called his disciples and said to them, 'My heart goes out to these people; they have been with me now for three days and have nothing to eat. I do not want to send them away hungry; they might faint on the way.' 33 The disciples replied, 'Where in this remote place can we find bread enough to feed such a crowd?' 34 'How many loaves have you?' Jesus asked. 'Seven,' they replied, 'and a few small fish.' 35 So he ordered the people to sit down on the ground; 36 then he took the seven loaves and the fish, and after giving thanks to God he broke them and gave them to the disciples, and the disciples gave them to the people. 37 They all ate and were satisfied; and seven baskets were filled with what was left over. 38 Those who were fed numbered four thousand men, not counting women and children. 39 After dismissing the crowd, he got into a boat and went to the neighbourhood of Magadan.

16 The Pharisees and Sadducees came, and to test him they asked him to show them a sign from heaven. 2 He answered: 4 'It is a wicked, godless generation that asks for a sign; and the only sign that will be given it is the sign of Jonah.' With that he left them and went away.

5 In crossing to the other side the disciples had forgotten to take any bread. 6 So when Jesus said to them, 'Take care; be on your guard against the leaven of the Pharisees and Sadducees,' 7 they began to say to one another, 'We have brought no bread!' 8 Knowing what they were discussing, Jesus said, 'Why are you talking about having no bread? Where is your faith? 9 Do you still not understand? Have you forgotten the five loaves for the five thousand, and how many basketfuls you picked up? 10 Or the seven loaves for the four thousand, and how many basketfuls you picked up? 11 How can you fail to see that I was not talking about bread? Be on your guard, I said, against the leaven of the Pharisees and Sadducees.' 12 Then they understood: they were to be on their guard, not against baker's leaven, but against the teaching of the Pharisees and Sadducees.

13 WHEN he came to the territory of Caesarea Philippi, Jesus asked his disciples, 'Who do people say that the Son of Man is?' 14 They answered, 'Some say John the Baptist, others Elijah, others Jeremiah, or one of the prophets.' 15 'And you,' he asked, 'who do you say I am?' 16 Simon Peter

16:2 **He answered:** *some witnesses here insert* 'In the evening you say, "It will be fine weather, for the sky is red"; 3 and in the morning you say, "It will be stormy today; the sky is red and lowering." You know how to interpret the appearance of the sky; can you not interpret the signs of the times?'

o Other ancient authorities read *Magdala* or *Magdalan*   p Gk *him*
q Other ancient authorities lack 2 *When it is . . . of the times*

NEW AMERICAN BIBLE

only to the lost sheep of the house of Israel." 25 But the woman came and did him homage, saying, "Lord, help me." 26 He said in reply, "It is not right to take the food of the children and throw it to the dogs." 27 She said, "Please, Lord, for even the dogs eat the scraps that fall from the table of their masters." 28 Then Jesus said to her in reply, "O woman, great is your faith! Let it be done for you as you wish." And her daughter was healed from that hour.

29 Moving on from there Jesus walked by the Sea of Galilee, went up on the mountain, and sat down there. 30 Great crowds came to him, having with them the lame, the blind, the deformed, the mute, and many others. They placed them at his feet, and he cured them. 31 The crowds were amazed when they saw the mute speaking, the deformed made whole, the lame walking, and the blind able to see, and they glorified the God of Israel.

32 Jesus summoned his disciples and said, "My heart is moved with pity for the crowd, for they have been with me now for three days and have nothing to eat. I do not want to send them away hungry, for fear they may collapse on the way." 33 The disciples said to him, "Where could we ever get enough bread in this deserted place to satisfy such a crowd?" 34 Jesus said to them, "How many loaves do you have?" "Seven," they replied, "and a few fish." 35 He ordered the crowd to sit down on the ground. 36 Then he took the seven loaves and the fish, gave thanks, broke the loaves, and gave them to the disciples, who in turn gave them to the crowds. 37 They all ate and were satisfied. They picked up the fragments left over — seven baskets full. 38 Those who ate were four thousand men, not counting women and children. 39 And when he had dismissed the crowds, he got into the boat and came to the district of Magadan.

16 The Pharisees and Sadducees came and, to test him, asked him to show them a sign from heaven. 2 He said to them in reply, "[In the evening you say, 'Tomorrow will be fair, for the sky is red'; 3 and, in the morning, 'Today will be stormy, for the sky is red and threatening.' You know how to judge the appearance of the sky, but you cannot judge the signs of the times.] 4 An evil and unfaithful generation seeks a sign, but no sign will be given it except the sign of Jonah." Then he left them and went away.

5 In coming to the other side of the sea, the disciples had forgotten to bring bread. 6 Jesus said to them, "Look out, and beware of the leaven of the Pharisees and Sadducees." 7 They concluded among themselves, saying, "It is because we have brought no bread." 8 When Jesus became aware of this he said, "You of little faith, why do you conclude among yourselves that it is because you have no bread? 9 Do you not yet understand, and do you not remember the five loaves for the five thousand, and how many wicker baskets you took up? 10 Or the seven loaves for the four thousand, and how many baskets you took up? 11 How do you not comprehend that I was not speaking to you about bread? Beware of the leaven of the Pharisees and Sadducees." 12 Then they understood that he was not telling them to beware of the leaven of bread, but of the teaching of the Pharisees and Sadducees.

13 When Jesus went into the region of Caesarea Philippi he asked his disciples, "Who do people say that the Son of Man is?" 14 They replied, "Some say John the Baptist, others Elijah, still others Jeremiah or one of the prophets." 15 He said to them, "But who do you say that I am?" 16 Si-

NEW JERUSALEM BIBLE

reply, 'I was sent only to the lost sheep of the House of Israel.' 25 But the woman had come up and was bowing low before him. 'Lord,' she said, 'help me.' 26 He replied, 'It is not fair to take the children's food and throw it to little dogs.' 27 She retorted, 'Ah yes, Lord; but even little dogs eat the scraps that fall from their masters' table.' 28 Then Jesus answered her, 'Woman, you have great faith. Let your desire be granted.' And from that moment her daughter was well again.

29 Jesus went on from there and reached the shores of the Lake of Galilee, and he went up onto the mountain. He took his seat, 30 and large crowds came to him bringing the lame, the crippled, the blind, the dumb and many others; these they put down at his feet, and he cured them. 31 The crowds were astonished to see the dumb speaking, the cripples whole again, the lame walking and the blind with their sight, and they praised the God of Israel.

32 But Jesus called his disciples to him and said, 'I feel sorry for all these people; they have been with me for three days now and have nothing to eat. I do not want to send them off hungry, or they might collapse on the way.' 33 The disciples said to him, 'Where in a deserted place could we get sufficient bread for such a large crowd to have enough to eat?' 34 Jesus said to them, 'How many loaves have you?' They said, 'Seven, and a few small fish.' 35 Then he instructed the crowd to sit down on the ground, 36 and he took the seven loaves and the fish, and after giving thanks he broke them and began handing them to the disciples, who gave them to the crowds. 37 They all ate as much as they wanted, and they collected what was left of the scraps, seven baskets full. 38 Now four thousand men had eaten, to say nothing of women and children. 39 And when he had sent the crowds away he got into the boat and went to the territory of Magadan.

16 The Pharisees and Sadducees came, and to put him to the test they asked if he would show them a sign from heaven. 2 He replied, 'In the evening you say, "It will be fine; there's a red sky," 3 and in the morning, "Stormy weather today; the sky is red and overcast." You know how to read the face of the sky, but you cannot read the signs of the times. 4 It is an evil and unfaithful generation asking for a sign, and the only sign it will be given is the sign of Jonah.' And he left them and went off.

5 The disciples, having crossed to the other side, had forgotten to take any food. 6 Jesus said to them, 'Keep your eyes open, and be on your guard against the yeast of the Pharisees and Sadducees.' 7 And they said among themselves, 'It is because we have not brought any bread.' 8 Jesus knew it, and he said, 'You have so little faith, why are you talking among yourselves about having no bread? 9 Do you still not understand? Do you not remember the five loaves for the five thousand and the number of baskets you collected? 10 Or the seven loaves for the four thousand and the number of baskets you collected? 11 How could you fail to understand that I was not talking about bread? What I said was: Beware of the yeast of the Pharisees and Sadducees.' 12 Then they understood that he was telling them to be on their guard, not against yeast for making bread, but against the teaching of the Pharisees and Sadducees.

13 When Jesus came to the region of Caesarea Philippi he put this question to his disciples, 'Who do people say the Son of man is?' 14 And they said, 'Some say John the Baptist, some Elijah, and others Jeremiah or one of the prophets.' 15 'But you,' he said, 'who do you say I am?' 16 Then

16, 2–3: The answer of Jesus in these verses is omitted in many important textual witnesses, and it is very uncertain that it is an original part of this gospel. It resembles Lk 12, 54–56 and may have been inserted from there.

NEW REVISED STANDARD VERSION

REVISED ENGLISH BIBLE

siah,*r* the Son of the living God." 17 And Jesus answered him, "Blessed are you, Simon son of Jonah! For flesh and blood has not revealed this to you, but my Father in heaven. 18 And I tell you, you are Peter,*s* and on this rock*t* I will build my church, and the gates of Hades will not prevail against it. 19 I will give you the keys of the kingdom of heaven, and whatever you bind on earth will be bound in heaven, and whatever you loose on earth will be loosed in heaven." 20 Then he sternly ordered the disciples not to tell anyone that he was*u* the Messiah.*r*

21 From that time on, Jesus began to show his disciples that he must go to Jerusalem and undergo great suffering at the hands of the elders and chief priests and scribes, and be killed, and on the third day be raised. 22 And Peter took him aside and began to rebuke him, saying, "God forbid it, Lord! This must never happen to you." 23 But he turned and said to Peter, "Get behind me, Satan! You are a stumbling block to me; for you are setting your mind not on divine things but on human things."

24 Then Jesus told his disciples, "If any want to become my followers, let them deny themselves and take up their cross and follow me. 25 For those who want to save their life will lose it, and those who lose their life for my sake will find it. 26 For what will it profit them if they gain the whole world but forfeit their life? Or what will they give in return for their life?

27 "For the Son of Man is to come with his angels in the glory of his Father, and then he will repay everyone for what has been done. 28 Truly I tell you, there are some standing here who will not taste death before they see the Son of Man coming in his kingdom."

17 Six days later, Jesus took with him Peter and James and his brother John and led them up a high mountain, by themselves. 2 And he was transfigured before them, and his face shone like the sun, and his clothes became dazzling white. 3 Suddenly there appeared to them Moses and Elijah, talking with him. 4 Then Peter said to Jesus, "Lord, it is good for us to be here; if you wish, I*v* will make three dwellings*w* here, one for you, one for Moses, and one for Elijah." 5 While he was still speaking, suddenly a bright cloud overshadowed them, and from the cloud a voice said, "This is my Son, the Beloved;*x* with him I am well pleased; listen to him!" 6 When the disciples heard this, they fell to the ground and were overcome by fear. 7 But Jesus came and touched them, saying, "Get up and do not be afraid." 8 And when they looked up, they saw no one except Jesus himself alone.

9 As they were coming down the mountain, Jesus ordered them, "Tell no one about the vision until after the Son of Man has been raised from the dead." 10 And the disciples asked him, "Why, then, do the scribes say that Elijah must come first?" 11 He replied, "Elijah is indeed coming and will restore all things; 12 but I tell you that Elijah has already come, and they did not recognize him, but they did to him whatever they pleased. So also the Son of Man is about to suffer at their hands." 13 Then the disciples understood that he was speaking to them about John the Baptist.

14 When they came to the crowd, a man came to him, knelt before him, 15 and said, "Lord, have mercy on my son, for he is an epileptic and he suffers terribly; he often falls into the fire and often into the water. 16 And I brought him to your disciples, but they could not cure him." 17 Jesus answered, "You faithless and perverse generation, how much longer must I be with you? How much longer must I put up with you? Bring him here to me." 18 And Jesus

answered: 'You are the Messiah, the Son of the living God.' 17 Then Jesus said: 'Simon son of Jonah, you are favoured indeed! You did not learn that from any human being; it was revealed to you by my heavenly Father. 18 And I say to you: you are Peter, the Rock; and on this rock I will build my church, and the powers of death shall never conquer it. 19 I will give you the keys of the kingdom of Heaven; what you forbid on earth shall be forbidden in heaven, and what you allow on earth shall be allowed in heaven.' 20 He then gave his disciples strict orders not to tell anyone that he was the Messiah.

21 From that time Jesus began to make it clear to his disciples that he had to go to Jerusalem, and endure great suffering at the hands of the elders, chief priests, and scribes; to be put to death, and to be raised again on the third day. 22 At this Peter took hold of him and began to rebuke him: 'Heaven forbid!' he said. 'No, Lord, this shall never happen to you.' 23 Then Jesus turned and said to Peter, 'Out of my sight, Satan; you are a stumbling block to me. You think as men think, not as God thinks.'

24 Jesus then said to his disciples, 'Anyone who wishes to be a follower of mine must renounce self; he must take up his cross and follow me. 25–26 Whoever wants to save his life will lose it, but whoever loses his life for my sake will find it. What will anyone gain by winning the whole world at the cost of his life? Or what can he give to buy his life back? 27 For the Son of Man is to come in the glory of his Father with his angels, and then he will give everyone his due reward. 28 Truly I tell you: there are some of those standing here who will not taste death before they have seen the Son of Man coming in his kingdom.'

17 Six days later Jesus took Peter, James, and John the brother of James, and led them up a high mountain by themselves. 2 And in their presence he was transfigured; his face shone like the sun, and his clothes became a brilliant white. 3 And they saw Moses and Elijah appear, talking with him. 4 Then Peter spoke: 'Lord,' he said, 'it is good that we are here. Would you like me to make three shelters here, one for you, one for Moses, and one for Elijah?' 5 While he was still speaking, a bright cloud suddenly cast its shadow over them, and a voice called from the cloud: 'This is my beloved Son, in whom I take delight; listen to him.' 6 At the sound of the voice the disciples fell on their faces in terror. 7 Then Jesus came up to them, touched them, and said, 'Stand up; do not be afraid.' 8 And when they raised their eyes there was no one but Jesus to be seen.

9 On their way down the mountain, Jesus commanded them not to tell anyone of the vision until the Son of Man had been raised from the dead. 10 The disciples put a question to him: 'Why then do the scribes say that Elijah must come first?' 11 He replied, 'Elijah is to come and set everything right. 12 But I tell you that Elijah has already come, and they failed to recognize him, and did to him as they wanted; in the same way the Son of Man is to suffer at their hands.' 13 Then the disciples understood that he meant John the Baptist.

14 When they returned to the crowd, a man came up to Jesus, fell on his knees before him, and said, 15 'Have pity, sir, on my son: he is epileptic and has bad fits; he keeps falling into the fire or into the water. 16 I brought him to your disciples, but they could not cure him.' 17 Jesus answered, 'What an unbelieving and perverse generation! How long shall I be with you? How long must I endure you? Bring him here to me.' 18 Then Jesus spoke sternly to him;

r Or *the Christ*   *s* Gk *Petros*   *t* Gk *petra*   *u* Other ancient authorities add *Jesus*   *v* Other ancient authorities read *we*   *w* Or *tents*   *x* Or *my beloved Son*

16:18 **powers of death:** lit. gates of Hades.   17:5 **This . . . Son:** or This is my only Son.

mon Peter said in reply, "You are the Messiah, the Son of the living God." 17 Jesus said to him in reply, "Blessed are you, Simon son of Jonah. For flesh and blood has not revealed this to you, but my heavenly Father. 18 And so I say to you, you are Peter, and upon this rock I will build my church, and the gates of the netherworld shall not prevail against it. 19 I will give you the keys to the kingdom of heaven. Whatever you bind on earth shall be bound in heaven; and whatever you loose on earth shall be loosed in heaven." 20 Then he strictly ordered his disciples to tell no one that he was the Messiah.

21 From that time on, Jesus began to show his disciples that he must go to Jerusalem and suffer greatly from the elders, the chief priests, and the scribes, and be killed and on the third day be raised. 22 Then Peter took him aside and began to rebuke him, "God forbid, Lord! No such thing shall ever happen to you." 23 He turned and said to Peter, "Get behind me, Satan! You are an obstacle to me. You are thinking not as God does, but as human beings do."

24 Then Jesus said to his disciples, "Whoever wishes to come after me must deny himself, take up his cross, and follow me. 25 For whoever wishes to save his life will lose it, but whoever loses his life for my sake will find it. 26 What profit would there be for one to gain the whole world and forfeit his life? Or what can one give in exchange for his life? 27 For the Son of Man will come with his angels in his Father's glory, and then he will repay everyone according to his conduct. 28 Amen, I say to you, there are some standing here who will not taste death until they see the Son of Man coming in his kingdom."

17 After six days Jesus took Peter, James, and John his brother, and led them up a high mountain by themselves. 2 And he was transfigured before them; his face shone like the sun and his clothes became white as light. 3 And behold, Moses and Elijah appeared to them, conversing with him. 4 Then Peter said to Jesus in reply, "Lord, it is good that we are here. If you wish, I will make three tents here, one for you, one for Moses, and one for Elijah." 5 While he was still speaking, behold, a bright cloud cast a shadow over them, then from the cloud came a voice that said, "This is my beloved Son, with whom I am well pleased; listen to him." 6 When the disciples heard this, they fell prostrate and were very much afraid. 7 But Jesus came and touched them, saying, "Rise, and do not be afraid." 8 And when the disciples raised their eyes, they saw no one else but Jesus alone.

9 As they were coming down from the mountain, Jesus charged them, "Do not tell the vision to anyone until the Son of Man has been raised from the dead." 10 Then the disciples asked him, "Why do the scribes say that Elijah must come first?" 11 He said in reply, "Elijah will indeed come and restore all things; 12 but I tell you that Elijah has already come, and they did not recognize him but did to him whatever they pleased. So also will the Son of Man suffer at their hands." 13 Then the disciples understood that he was speaking to them of John the Baptist.

14 When they came to the crowd a man approached, knelt down before him, 15 and said, "Lord, have pity on my son, for he is a lunatic and suffers severely; often he falls into fire, and often into water. 16 I brought him to your disciples, but they could not cure him." 17 Jesus said in reply, "O faithless and perverse generation, how long will I be with you? How long will I endure you? Bring him here to me." 18 Jesus rebuked him and the demon came out of him,

Simon Peter spoke up and said, 'You are the Christ, the Son of the living God.' 17 Jesus replied, 'Simon son of Jonah, you are a blessed man! Because it was no human agency that revealed this to you but my Father in heaven. 18 So I now say to you: You are Peter[u] and on this rock I will build my community. And the gates of the underworld can never overpower it. 19 I will give you the keys of the kingdom of Heaven: whatever you bind on earth will be bound in heaven; whatever you loose on earth will be loosed in heaven.' 20 Then he gave the disciples strict orders not to say to anyone that he was the Christ.

21 From then onwards Jesus began to make it clear to his disciples that he was destined to go to Jerusalem and suffer grievously at the hands of the elders and chief priests and scribes and to be put to death and to be raised up on the third day. 22 Then, taking him aside, Peter started to rebuke him. 'Heaven preserve you, Lord,' he said, 'this must not happen to you.' 23 But he turned and said to Peter, 'Get behind me, Satan! You are an obstacle in my path, because you are thinking not as God thinks but as human beings do.'

24 Then Jesus said to his disciples, 'If anyone wants to be a follower of mine, let him renounce himself and take up his cross and follow me. 25 Anyone who wants to save his life will lose it; but anyone who loses his life for my sake will find it. 26 What, then, will anyone gain by winning the whole world and forfeiting his life? Or what can anyone offer in exchange for his life?

27 'For the Son of man is going to come in the glory of his Father with his angels, and then he will reward each one according to his behaviour. 28 In truth I tell you, there are some standing here who will not taste death before they see the Son of man coming with his kingdom.'

17 Six days later, Jesus took with him Peter and James and his brother John and led them up a high mountain by themselves. 2 There in their presence he was transfigured: his face shone like the sun and his clothes became as dazzling as light. 3 And suddenly Moses and Elijah appeared to them; they were talking with him. 4 Then Peter spoke to Jesus. 'Lord,' he said, 'it is wonderful for us to be here; if you want me to, I will make three shelters here, one for you, one for Moses and one for Elijah.' 5 He was still speaking when suddenly a bright cloud[v] covered them with shadow, and suddenly from the cloud there came a voice which said, 'This is my Son, the Beloved; he enjoys my favour. Listen to him.'[w] 6 When they heard this, the disciples fell on their faces, overcome with fear. 7 But Jesus came up and touched them, saying, 'Stand up, do not be afraid.' 8 And when they raised their eyes they saw no one but Jesus.

9 As they came down from the mountain Jesus gave them this order, 'Tell no one about this vision until the Son of man has risen from the dead.' 10 And the disciples put this question to him, 'Why then do the scribes say that Elijah must come first?' 11 He replied, 'Elijah is indeed coming, and he will set everything right again; 12 however, I tell you that Elijah has come already and they did not recognise him but treated him as they pleased; and the Son of man will suffer similarly at their hands.' 13 Then the disciples understood that he was speaking of John the Baptist.

14 As they were rejoining the crowd a man came up to him and went down on his knees before him. 15 'Lord,' he said, 'take pity on my son: he is demented and in a wretched state; he is always falling into fire and into water. 16 I took him to your disciples and they were unable to cure him.' 17 In reply, Jesus said, 'Faithless and perverse generation! How much longer must I be with you? How much longer must I put up with you? Bring him here to me.' 18 And when

---

u 16 The name means 'rock'. v 17 cf. Ex 13:22.
w 17 Dt 18:15, 19; Is 42:1.

| NEW REVISED STANDARD VERSION | REVISED ENGLISH BIBLE |

rebuked the demon,*y* and it*z* came out of him, and the boy was cured instantly. 19 Then the disciples came to Jesus privately and said, "Why could we not cast it out?" 20 He said to them, "Because of your little faith. For truly I tell you, if you have faith the size of a*a* mustard seed, you will say to this mountain, 'Move from here to there,' and it will move; and nothing will be impossible for you."*b*

22 As they were gathering*c* in Galilee, Jesus said to them, "The Son of Man is going to be betrayed into human hands, 23 and they will kill him, and on the third day he will be raised." And they were greatly distressed.

24 When they reached Capernaum, the collectors of the temple tax*d* came to Peter and said, "Does your teacher not pay the temple tax?"*d* 25 He said, "Yes, he does." And when he came home, Jesus spoke of it first, asking, "What do you think, Simon? From whom do kings of the earth take toll or tribute? From their children or from others?" 26 When Peter*e* said, "From others," Jesus said to him, "Then the children are free. 27 However, so that we do not give offense to them, go to the sea and cast a hook; take the first fish that comes up; and when you open its mouth, you will find a coin;*f* take that and give it to them for you and me."

18 At that time the disciples came to Jesus and asked, "Who is the greatest in the kingdom of heaven?" 2 He called a child, whom he put among them, 3 and said, "Truly I tell you, unless you change and become like children, you will never enter the kingdom of heaven. 4 Whoever becomes humble like this child is the greatest in the kingdom of heaven. 5 Whoever welcomes one such child in my name welcomes me.

6 "If any of you put a stumbling block before one of these little ones who believe in me, it would be better for you if a great millstone were fastened around your neck and you were drowned in the depth of the sea. 7 Woe to the world because of stumbling blocks! Occasions for stumbling are bound to come, but woe to the one by whom the stumbling block comes!

8 "If your hand or your foot causes you to stumble, cut it off and throw it away; it is better for you to enter life maimed or lame than to have two hands or two feet and to be thrown into the eternal fire. 9 And if your eye causes you to stumble, tear it out and throw it away; it is better for you to enter life with one eye than to have two eyes and to be thrown into the hell*g* of fire.

10 "Take care that you do not despise one of these little ones; for, I tell you, in heaven their angels continually see the face of my Father in heaven.*h* 12 What do you think? If a shepherd has a hundred sheep, and one of them has gone astray, does he not leave the ninety-nine on the mountains and go in search of the one that went astray? 13 And if he finds it, truly I tell you, he rejoices over it more than over the ninety-nine that never went astray. 14 So it is not the will of your*i* Father in heaven that one of these little ones should be lost.

15 "If another member of the church*j* sins against you,*k* go and point out the fault when the two of you are alone. If the member listens to you, you have regained that one.*l* 16 But if you are not listened to, take one or two

the demon left the boy, and from that moment he was cured.

19 Afterwards the disciples came to Jesus and asked him privately, 'Why could we not drive it out?' 'Your faith is too small. Truly I tell you: if you have faith no bigger than a mustard seed, you will say to this mountain, "Move from here to there!" and it will move; nothing will be impossible for you.'

22 THEY were going about together in Galilee when Jesus said to them, 'The Son of Man is to be handed over into the power of men, 23 and they will kill him; then on the third day he will be raised again.' And they were filled with grief.

24 On their arrival at Capernaum the collectors of the temple tax came up to Peter and asked, 'Does your master not pay temple tax?' 25 'He does,' said Peter. When he went indoors Jesus forestalled him by asking, 'Tell me, Simon, from whom do earthly monarchs collect tribute money? From their own people, or from aliens?' 26 'From aliens,' said Peter. 'Yes,' said Jesus, 'and their own people are exempt. 27 But as we do not want to cause offence, go and cast a line in the lake; take the first fish you catch, open its mouth, and you will find a silver coin; take that and pay the tax for us both.'

18 AT that time the disciples came to Jesus and asked, 'Who is the greatest in the kingdom of Heaven?' 2 He called a child, set him in front of them, 3 and said, 'Truly I tell you: unless you turn round and become like children, you will never enter the kingdom of Heaven. 4 Whoever humbles himself and becomes like this child will be the greatest in the kingdom of Heaven, 5 and whoever receives one such child in my name receives me. 6 But if anyone causes the downfall of one of these little ones who believe in me, it would be better for him to have a millstone hung round his neck and be drowned in the depths of the sea. 7 Alas for the world that any of them should be made to fall! Such things must happen, but alas for the one through whom they happen!

8 'If your hand or your foot causes your downfall, cut it off and fling it away; it is better for you to enter into life maimed or lame, than to keep two hands or two feet and be thrown into the eternal fire. 9 And if your eye causes your downfall, tear it out and fling it away; it is better to enter into life with one eye than to keep both eyes and be thrown into the fires of hell.

10 'See that you do not despise one of these little ones; I tell you, they have their angels in heaven, who look continually on the face of my heavenly Father.

12 'What do you think? Suppose someone has a hundred sheep, and one of them strays, does he not leave the other ninety-nine on the hillside and go in search of the one that strayed? 13 Truly I tell you: if he should find it, he is more delighted over that sheep than over the ninety-nine that did not stray. 14 In the same way, it is not your heavenly Father's will that one of these little ones should be lost.

15 'If your brother does wrong, go and take the matter up with him, strictly between yourselves. If he listens to you, you have won your brother over. 16 But if he will not listen,

---

y Gk *it* or *him*   *z* Gk *the demon*   *a* Gk *faith as a grain of*
b Other ancient authorities add verse 21, *But this kind does not come out except by prayer and fasting*   *c* Other ancient authorities read *living*   *d* Gk *didrachma*   *e* Gk *he*   *f* Gk *stater*; the stater was worth two didrachmas   *g* Gk *Gehenna*   *h* Other ancient authorities add verse 11, *For the Son of Man came to save the lost*
i Other ancient authorities read *my*   *j* Gk *If your brother*   *k* Other ancient authorities lack *against you*   *l* Gk *the brother*

17:20 **impossible for you:** *some witnesses add* 21 But there is no means of driving out this sort but prayer and fasting.
18:10 **Father:** *some witnesses add* 11 For the Son of Man came to save the lost.   18:15 **wrong:** *some witnesses add* to you.

NEW AMERICAN BIBLE

NEW JERUSALEM BIBLE

and from that hour the boy was cured. 19 Then the disciples approached Jesus in private and said, "Why could we not drive it out?" 20 He said to them, "Because of your little faith. Amen, I say to you, if you have faith the size of a mustard seed, you will say to this mountain, 'Move from here to there,' and it will move. Nothing will be impossible for you." [21]

22 As they were gathering in Galilee, Jesus said to them, "The Son of Man is to be handed over to men, 23 and they will kill him, and he will be raised on the third day." And they were overwhelmed with grief.

24 When they came to Capernaum, the collectors of the temple tax approached Peter and said, "Doesn't your teacher pay the temple tax?" 25 "Yes," he said. When he came into the house, before he had time to speak, Jesus asked him, "What is your opinion, Simon? From whom do the kings of the earth take tolls or census tax? From their subjects or from foreigners?" 26 When he said, "From foreigners," Jesus said to him, "Then the subjects are exempt. 27 But that we may not offend them, go to the sea, drop in a hook, and take the first fish that comes up. Open its mouth and you will find a coin worth twice the temple tax. Give that to them for me and for you."

18 At that time the disciples approached Jesus and said, "Who is the greatest in the kingdom of heaven?" 2 He called a child over, placed it in their midst, 3 and said, "Amen, I say to you, unless you turn and become like children, you will not enter the kingdom of heaven. 4 Whoever humbles himself like this child is the greatest in the kingdom of heaven. 5 And whoever receives one child such as this in my name receives me.

6 "Whoever causes one of these little ones who believe in me to sin, it would be better for him to have a great millstone hung around his neck and to be drowned in the depths of the sea. 7 Woe to the world because of things that cause sin! Such things must come, but woe to the one through whom they come! 8 If your hand or foot causes you to sin, cut it off and throw it away. It is better for you to enter into life maimed or crippled than with two hands or two feet to be thrown into eternal fire. 9 And if your eye causes you to sin, tear it out and throw it away. It is better for you to enter into life with one eye than with two eyes to be thrown into fiery Gehenna.

10 "See that you do not despise one of these little ones, for I say to you that their angels in heaven always look upon the face of my heavenly Father. [11] 12 What is your opinion? If a man has a hundred sheep and one of them goes astray, will he not leave the ninety-nine in the hills and go in search of the stray? 13 And if he finds it, amen, I say to you, he rejoices more over it than over the ninety-nine that did not stray. 14 In just the same way, it is not the will of your heavenly Father that one of these little ones be lost.

15 "If your brother sins [against you], go and tell him his fault between you and him alone. If he listens to you, you have won over your brother. 16 If he does not listen, take

Jesus rebuked it the devil came out of the boy, who was cured from that moment.

19 Then the disciples came privately to Jesus. 'Why were we unable to drive it out?' they asked. 20 He answered, 'Because you have so little faith. In truth I tell you, if your faith is the size of a mustard seed you will say to this mountain, "Move from here to there," and it will move; nothing will be impossible for you.' [21]x

22 When they were together in Galilee, Jesus said to them, 'The Son of man is going to be delivered into the power of men; 23 they will put him to death, and on the third day he will be raised up again.' And a great sadness came over them.

24 When they reached Capernaum, the collectors of the half-shekely came to Peter and said, 'Does your master not pay the half-shekel?' 25 'Yes,' he replied, and went into the house. But before he could speak, Jesus said, 'Simon, what is your opinion? From whom do earthly kings take toll or tribute? From their sons or from foreigners?' 26 And when he replied, 'From foreigners,' Jesus said, 'Well then, the sons are exempt. 27 However, so that we shall not be the downfall of others, go to the lake and cast a hook; take the first fish that rises, open its mouth and there you will find a shekel; take it and give it to them for me and for yourself.'

18 At this time the disciples came to Jesus and said, 'Who is the greatest in the kingdom of Heaven?' 2 So he called a little child to him whom he set among them. 3 Then he said, 'In truth I tell you, unless you change and become like little children you will never enter the kingdom of Heaven. 4 And so, the one who makes himself as little as this little child is the greatest in the kingdom of Heaven.

5 'Anyone who welcomes one little child like this in my name welcomes me. 6 But anyone who is the downfall of one of these little ones who have faith in me would be better drowned in the depths of the sea with a great millstone round his neck. 7 Alas for the world that there should be such causes of falling! Causes of falling indeed there must be, but alas for anyone who provides them!

8 'If your hand or your foot should be your downfall, cut it off and throw it away: it is better for you to enter into life crippled or lame, than to have two hands or two feet and be thrown into eternal fire. 9 And if your eye should be your downfall, tear it out and throw it away: it is better for you to enter into life with one eye, than to have two eyes and be thrown into the hell of fire.

10 'See that you never despise any of these little ones, for I tell you that their angels in heaven are continually in the presence of my Father in heaven. [11]z

12 'Tell me. Suppose a man has a hundred sheep and one of them strays; will he not leave the ninety-nine on the hillside and go in search of the stray? 13 In truth I tell you, if he finds it, it gives him more joy than do the ninety-nine that did not stray at all. 14 Similarly, it is never the will of your Father in heaven that one of these little ones should be lost.

15 'If your brother does something wrong, go and have it out with him alone, between your two selves. If he listens to you, you have won back your brother. 16 If he does not

---

17, 21: Some manuscripts add, "But this kind does not come out except by prayer and fasting"; this is a variant of the better reading of Mk 9, 29.   18, 11: Some manuscripts add, "For the Son of Man has come to save what was lost"; cf 9, 13. This is practically identical with Lk 19, 10 and is probably a copyist's addition from that source.   18, 15: The bracketed words, against you, are widely attested but they are not in the important codices Sinaiticus and Vaticanus or in some other textual witnesses. Their omission broadens the type of sin in question.

x 17 Some authorities add v. 21, 'As for this kind, it is cast out only by prayer and fasting.' cf. Mk 9:29.   y 17 A yearly tax on all Jews for the upkeep of the Temple.   z 18 Some authorities add v. 11, 'For the Son of man has come to save what was lost.' cf. Lk 19:10.

others along with you, so that every word may be confirmed by the evidence of two or three witnesses. 17 If the member refuses to listen to them, tell it to the church; and if the offender refuses to listen even to the church, let such a one be to you as a Gentile and a tax collector. 18 Truly I tell you, whatever you bind on earth will be bound in heaven, and whatever you loose on earth will be loosed in heaven. 19 Again, truly I tell you, if two of you agree on earth about anything you ask, it will be done for you by my Father in heaven. 20 For where two or three are gathered in my name, I am there among them."

21 Then Peter came and said to him, "Lord, if another member of the church*m* sins against me, how often should I forgive? As many as seven times?" 22 Jesus said to him, "Not seven times, but, I tell you, seventy-seven*n* times.

23 "For this reason the kingdom of heaven may be compared to a king who wished to settle accounts with his slaves. 24 When he began the reckoning, one who owed him ten thousand talents*o* was brought to him; 25 and, as he could not pay, his lord ordered him to be sold, together with his wife and children and all his possessions, and payment to be made. 26 So the slave fell on his knees before him, saying, 'Have patience with me, and I will pay you everything.' 27 And out of pity for him, the lord of that slave released him and forgave him the debt. 28 But that same slave, as he went out, came upon one of his fellow slaves who owed him a hundred denarii; *p* and seizing him by the throat, he said, 'Pay what you owe.' 29 Then his fellow slave fell down and pleaded with him, 'Have patience with me, and I will pay you.' 30 But he refused; then he went and threw him into prison until he would pay the debt. 31 When his fellow slaves saw what had happened, they were greatly distressed, and they went and reported to their lord all that had taken place. 32 Then his lord summoned him and said to him, 'You wicked slave! I forgave you all that debt because you pleaded with me. 33 Should you not have had mercy on your fellow slave, as I had mercy on you?' 34 And in anger his lord handed him over to be tortured until he would pay his entire debt. 35 So my heavenly Father will also do to every one of you, if you do not forgive your brother or sister *q* from your heart."

19 When Jesus had finished saying these things, he left Galilee and went to the region of Judea beyond the Jordan. 2 Large crowds followed him, and he cured them there.

3 Some Pharisees came to him, and to test him they asked, "Is it lawful for a man to divorce his wife for any cause?" 4 He answered, "Have you not read that the one who made them at the beginning 'made them male and female,' 5 and said, 'For this reason a man shall leave his father and mother and be joined to his wife, and the two shall become one flesh'? 6 So they are no longer two, but one flesh. Therefore what God has joined together, let no one separate." 7 They said to him, "Why then did Moses command us to give a certificate of dismissal and to divorce her?" 8 He said to them, "It was because you were so hard-hearted that Moses allowed you to divorce your wives, but from the beginning it was not so. 9 And I say to you, who-

take one or two others with you, so that every case may be settled on the evidence of two or three witnesses. 17 If he refuses to listen to them, report the matter to the congregation; and if he will not listen even to the congregation, then treat him as you would a pagan or a tax-collector.

18 'Truly I tell you: whatever you forbid on earth shall be forbidden in heaven, and whatever you allow on earth shall be allowed in heaven.

19 'And again I tell you: if two of you agree on earth about any request you have to make, that request will be granted by my heavenly Father. 20 For where two or three meet together in my name, I am there among them.'

21 Then Peter came to him and asked, 'Lord, how often am I to forgive my brother if he goes on wronging me? As many as seven times?' 22 Jesus replied, 'I do not say seven times but seventy times seven.

23 'The kingdom of Heaven, therefore, should be thought of in this way: There was once a king who decided to settle accounts with the men who served him. 24 At the outset there appeared before him a man who owed ten thousand talents. 25 Since he had no means of paying, his master ordered him to be sold, with his wife, his children, and everything he had, to meet the debt. 26 The man fell at his master's feet. "Be patient with me," he implored, "and I will pay you in full"; 27 and the master was so moved with pity that he let the man go and cancelled the debt. 28 But no sooner had the man gone out than he met a fellow-servant who owed him a hundred denarii; he took hold of him, seizing him by the throat, and said, "Pay me what you owe." 29 The man fell at his fellow-servant's feet, and begged him, "Be patient with me, and I will pay you"; 30 but he refused, and had him thrown into jail until he should pay the debt. 31 The other servants were deeply distressed when they saw what had happened, and they went to their master and told him the whole story. 32 Then he sent for the man and said, "You scoundrel! I cancelled the whole of your debt when you appealed to me; 33 ought you not to have shown mercy to your fellow-servant just as I showed mercy to you?" 34 And so angry was the master that he condemned the man to be tortured until he should pay the debt in full. 35 That is how my heavenly Father will deal with you, unless you each forgive your brother from your hearts.'

19 When Jesus had finished this discourse he left Galilee and came into the region of Judaea on the other side of the Jordan. 2 Great crowds followed him, and he healed them there.

3 Some Pharisees came and tested him by asking, 'Is it lawful for a man to divorce his wife for any cause he pleases?' 4 He responded by asking, 'Have you never read that in the beginning the Creator made them male and female?' 5 and he added, 'That is why a man leaves his father and mother, and is united to his wife, and the two become one flesh. 6 It follows that they are no longer two individuals: they are one flesh. Therefore what God has joined together, man must not separate.' 7 'Then why,' they objected, 'did Moses lay it down that a man might divorce his wife by a certificate of dismissal?' 8 He answered, 'It was because of your stubbornness that Moses gave you permission to divorce your wives; but it was not like that at the beginning. 9 I tell you, if a man divorces his wife for any

---

m Gk *if my brother*   *n* Or *seventy times seven*   *o* A talent was worth more than fifteen years' wages of a laborer   *p* The denarius was the usual day's wage for a laborer   *q* Gk *brother*

18:22 **seventy times seven:** or seventy-seven times.
18:24 **talents:** *see p. xxix.*   18:28 **denarii:** *see p. xxix.*

NEW AMERICAN BIBLE | NEW JERUSALEM BIBLE

one or two others along with you, so that 'every fact may be established on the testimony of two or three witnesses.' 17 If he refuses to listen to them, tell the church. If he refuses to listen even to the church, then treat him as you would a Gentile or a tax collector. 18 Amen, I say to you, whatever you bind on earth shall be bound in heaven, and whatever you loose on earth shall be loosed in heaven. 19 Again, [amen,] I say to you, if two of you agree on earth about anything for which they are to pray, it shall be granted to them by my heavenly Father. 20 For where two or three are gathered together in my name, there am I in the midst of them."

21 Then Peter approaching asked him, "Lord, if my brother sins against me, how often must I forgive him? As many as seven times?" 22 Jesus answered, "I say to you, not seven times but seventy-seven times. 23 That is why the kingdom of heaven may be likened to a king who decided to settle accounts with his servants. 24 When he began the accounting, a debtor was brought before him who owed him a huge amount. 25 Since he had no way of paying it back, his master ordered him to be sold, along with his wife, his children, and all his property, in payment of the debt. 26 At that, the servant fell down, did him homage, and said, 'Be patient with me, and I will pay you back in full.' 27 Moved with compassion the master of that servant let him go and forgave him the loan. 28 When that servant had left, he found one of his fellow servants who owed him a much smaller amount. He seized him and started to choke him, demanding, 'Pay back what you owe.' 29 Falling to his knees, his fellow servant begged him, 'Be patient with me, and I will pay you back.' 30 But he refused. Instead, he had him put in prison until he paid back the debt. 31 Now when his fellow servants saw what had happened, they were deeply disturbed, and went to their master and reported the whole affair. 32 His master summoned him and said to him, 'You wicked servant! I forgave you your entire debt because you begged me to. 33 Should you not have had pity on your fellow servant, as I had pity on you?' 34 Then in anger his master handed him over to the torturers until he should pay back the whole debt. 35 So will my heavenly Father do to you, unless each of you forgives his brother from his heart."

19 When Jesus finished these words, he left Galilee and went to the district of Judea across the Jordan. 2 Great crowds followed him, and he cured them there. 3 Some Pharisees approached him, and tested him, saying, "Is it lawful for a man to divorce his wife for any cause whatever?" 4 He said in reply, "Have you not read that from the beginning the Creator 'made them male and female' 5 and said, 'For this reason a man shall leave his father and mother and be joined to his wife, and the two shall become one flesh'? 6 So they are no longer two, but one flesh. Therefore, what God has joined together, no human being must separate." 7 They said to him, "Then why did Moses command that the man give the woman a bill of divorce and dismiss [her]?" 8 He said to them, "Because of the hardness of your hearts Moses allowed you to divorce your wives, but from the beginning it was not so. 9 I say to you, whoever

listen, take one or two others along with you: *whatever the misdemeanour, the evidence of two or three witnesses is required to sustain the charge.*[a] 17 But if he refuses to listen to these, report it to the community; and if he refuses to listen to the community, treat him like a gentile or a tax collector.

18 'In truth I tell you, whatever you bind on earth will be bound in heaven; whatever you loose on earth will be loosed in heaven.

19 'In truth I tell you once again, if two of you on earth agree to ask anything at all, it will be granted to you by my Father in heaven. 20 For where two or three meet in my name, I am there among them.'

21 Then Peter went up to him and said, 'Lord, how often must I forgive my brother if he wrongs me? As often as seven times?' 22 Jesus answered, 'Not seven, I tell you, but seventy-seven times.

23 'And so the kingdom of Heaven may be compared to a king who decided to settle his accounts with his servants. 24 When the reckoning began, they brought him a man who owed ten thousand talents; 25 he had no means of paying, so his master gave orders that he should be sold, together with his wife and children and all his possessions, to meet the debt. 26 At this, the servant threw himself down at his master's feet, with the words, "Be patient with me and I will pay the whole sum." 27 And the servant's master felt so sorry for him that he let him go and cancelled the debt. 28 Now as this servant went out, he happened to meet a fellow-servant who owed him one hundred denarii;[b] and he seized him by the throat and began to throttle him, saying, "Pay what you owe me." 29 His fellow-servant fell at his feet and appealed to him, saying, "Be patient with me and I will pay you." 30 But the other would not agree; on the contrary, he had him thrown into prison till he should pay the debt. 31 His fellow-servants were deeply distressed when they saw what had happened, and they went to their master and reported the whole affair to him. 32 Then the master sent for the man and said to him, "You wicked servant, I cancelled all that debt of yours when you appealed to me. 33 Were you not bound, then, to have pity on your fellow-servant just as I had pity on you?" 34 And in his anger the master handed him over to the torturers till he should pay all his debt. 35 And that is how my heavenly Father will deal with you unless you each forgive your brother from your heart.'

19 Jesus had now finished what he wanted to say, and he left Galilee and came into the territory of Judaea on the far side of the Jordan. 2 Large crowds followed him and he healed them there.

3 Some Pharisees approached him, and to put him to the test they said, 'Is it against the Law for a man to divorce his wife on any pretext whatever?' 4 He answered, 'Have you not read that the Creator from the beginning *made them male and female* 5 and that he said: *This is why a man leaves his father and mother and becomes attached to his wife, and the two become one flesh?*[c] 6 They are no longer two, therefore, but one flesh. So then, what God has united, human beings must not divide.'

7 They said to him, 'Then why did Moses command that a writ of dismissal should be given in cases of divorce?'[d] 8 He said to them, 'It was because you were so hard hearted, that Moses allowed you to divorce your wives, but it was not like this from the beginning. 9 Now I say this to you:

---

a **18** Dt 19:15.   b **18** About $200, contrasted with the other debt of over $60 million.   c **19** Gn 1:17; 2:24.   d **19** Dt 24:1. On Mt's exception in v. 9, *see* 5:32.

NEW REVISED STANDARD VERSION

ever divorces his wife, except for unchastity, and marries another commits adultery."r

10 His disciples said to him, "If such is the case of a man with his wife, it is better not to marry." 11 But he said to them, "Not everyone can accept this teaching, but only those to whom it is given. 12 For there are eunuchs who have been so from birth, and there are eunuchs who have been made eunuchs by others, and there are eunuchs who have made themselves eunuchs for the sake of the kingdom of heaven. Let anyone accept this who can."

13 Then little children were being brought to him in order that he might lay his hands on them and pray. The disciples spoke sternly to those who brought them; 14 but Jesus said, "Let the little children come to me, and do not stop them; for it is to such as these that the kingdom of heaven belongs." 15 And he laid his hands on them and went on his way.

16 Then someone came to him and said, "Teacher, what good deed must I do to have eternal life?" 17 And he said to him, "Why do you ask me about what is good? There is only one who is good. If you wish to enter into life, keep the commandments." 18 He said to him, "Which ones?" And Jesus said, "You shall not murder; You shall not commit adultery; You shall not steal; You shall not bear false witness; 19 Honor your father and mother; also, You shall love your neighbor as yourself." 20 The young man said to him, "I have kept all these;s what do I still lack?" 21 Jesus said to him, "If you wish to be perfect, go, sell your possessions, and give the moneyt to the poor, and you will have treasure in heaven; then come, follow me." 22 When the young man heard this word, he went away grieving, for he had many possessions.

23 Then Jesus said to his disciples, "Truly I tell you, it will be hard for a rich person to enter the kingdom of heaven. 24 Again I tell you, it is easier for a camel to go through the eye of a needle than for someone who is rich to enter the kingdom of God." 25 When the disciples heard this, they were greatly astounded and said, "Then who can be saved?" 26 But Jesus looked at them and said, "For mortals it is impossible, but for God all things are possible."

27 Then Peter said in reply, "Look, we have left everything and followed you. What then will we have?" 28 Jesus said to them, "Truly I tell you, at the renewal of all things, when the Son of Man is seated on the throne of his glory, you who have followed me will also sit on twelve thrones, judging the twelve tribes of Israel. 29 And everyone who has left houses or brothers or sisters or father or mother or children or fields, for my name's sake, will receive a hundredfold,u and will inherit eternal life. 30 But many who are first will be last, and the last will be first.

20 "For the kingdom of heaven is like a landowner who went out early in the morning to hire laborers for his vineyard. 2 After agreeing with the laborers for the usual daily wage,v he sent them into his vineyard. 3 When he went out about nine o'clock, he saw others standing idle in the marketplace; 4 and he said to them, 'You also go into the vineyard, and I will pay you whatever is right.' So they went. 5 When he went out again about noon and about three o'clock, he did the same. 6 And about five o'clock he went out and found others standing around; and he said to them, 'Why are you standing here idle all day?' 7 They said to him, 'Because no one has hired us.' He said to them, 'You also go into the vineyard.' 8 When evening came, the owner

REVISED ENGLISH BIBLE

cause other than unchastity, and marries another, he commits adultery.'

10 The disciples said to him, 'If that is how things stand for a man with a wife, it is better not to marry.' 11 To this he replied, 'That is a course not everyone can accept, but only those for whom God has appointed it. 12 For while some are incapable of marriage because they were born so, or were made so by men, there are others who have renounced marriage for the sake of the kingdom of Heaven. Let those accept this who can.'

13 They brought children for him to lay his hands on them with prayer. The disciples rebuked them, 14 but Jesus said, 'Let the children come to me; do not try to stop them; for the kingdom of Heaven belongs to such as these.' 15 And he laid his hands on the children, and went on his way.

16 A man came up and asked him, 'Teacher, what good must I do to gain eternal life?' 17 'Good?' said Jesus. 'Why do you ask me about that? One alone is good. But if you wish to enter into life, keep the commandments.' 18 'Which commandments?' he asked. Jesus answered, 'Do not murder; do not commit adultery; do not steal; do not give false evidence; 19 honour your father and mother; and love your neighbour as yourself.' 20 The young man answered, 'I have kept all these. What do I still lack?' 21 Jesus said to him, 'If you wish to be perfect, go, sell your possessions, and give to the poor, and you will have treasure in heaven; then come and follow me.' 22 When the young man heard this, he went away with a heavy heart; for he was a man of great wealth.

23 Jesus said to his disciples, 'Truly I tell you: a rich man will find it hard to enter the kingdom of Heaven. 24 I repeat, it is easier for a camel to pass through the eye of a needle than for a rich man to enter the kingdom of God.' 25 The disciples were astonished when they heard this, and exclaimed, 'Then who can be saved?' 26 Jesus looked at them and said, 'For men this is impossible; but everything is possible for God.'

27 Then Peter said, 'What about us? We have left everything to follow you. How shall we fare?' 28 Jesus replied, 'Truly I tell you: in the world that is to be, when the Son of Man is seated on his glorious throne, you also will sit on twelve thrones, judging the twelve tribes of Israel. 29 And anyone who has left houses, or brothers or sisters, or father or mother, or children, or land for the sake of my name will be repaid many times over, and gain eternal life. 30 But many who are first will be last, and the last first.

20 'The kingdom of Heaven is like this. There was once a landowner who went out early one morning to hire labourers for his vineyard; 2 and after agreeing to pay them the usual day's wage he sent them off to work. 3 Three hours later he went out again and saw some more men standing idle in the market-place. 4 "Go and join the others in the vineyard," he said, "and I will pay you a fair wage"; so off they went. 5 At midday he went out again, and at three in the afternoon, and made the same arrangement as before. 6 An hour before sunset he went out and found another group standing there; so he said to them, "Why are you standing here all day doing nothing?" 7 "Because no one has hired us," they replied; so he told them, "Go and join the others in the vineyard." 8 When evening fell, the owner

---

r Other ancient authorities read except on the ground of unchastity, causes her to commit adultery; others add at the end of the verse and he who marries a divorced woman commits adultery   s Other ancient authorities add from my youth   t Gk lacks the money   u Other ancient authorities read manifold   v Gk a denarius

19:9 adultery: some witnesses add And the man who marries a woman so divorced commits adultery.   20:2 the . . . wage: lit. one denarius for the day.

divorces his wife (unless the marriage is unlawful) and marries another commits adultery." ¹⁰[His] disciples said to him, "If that is the case of a man with his wife, it is better not to marry." ¹¹He answered, "Not all can accept [this] word, but only those to whom that is granted. ¹²Some are incapable of marriage because they were born so; some, because they were made so by others; some, because they have renounced marriage for the sake of the kingdom of heaven. Whoever can accept this ought to accept it."

¹³Then children were brought to him that he might lay his hands on them and pray. The disciples rebuked them, ¹⁴but Jesus said, "Let the children come to me, and do not prevent them; for the kingdom of heaven belongs to such as these." ¹⁵After he placed his hands on them, he went away.

¹⁶Now someone approached him and said, "Teacher, what good must I do to gain eternal life?" ¹⁷He answered him, "Why do you ask me about the good? There is only One who is good. If you wish to enter into life, keep the commandments." ¹⁸He asked him, "Which ones?" And Jesus replied, " 'You shall not kill; you shall not commit adultery; you shall not steal; you shall not bear false witness; ¹⁹honor your father and your mother'; and 'you shall love your neighbor as yourself.' " ²⁰The young man said to him, "All of these I have observed. What do I still lack?" ²¹Jesus said to him, "If you wish to be perfect, go, sell what you have and give to [the] poor, and you will have treasure in heaven. Then come, follow me." ²²When the young man heard this statement, he went away sad, for he had many possessions. ²³Then Jesus said to his disciples, "Amen, I say to you, it will be hard for one who is rich to enter the kingdom of heaven. ²⁴Again I say to you, it is easier for a camel to pass through the eye of a needle than for one who is rich to enter the kingdom of God." ²⁵When the disciples heard this, they were greatly astonished and said, "Who then can be saved?" ²⁶Jesus looked at them and said, "For human beings this is impossible, but for God all things are possible." ²⁷Then Peter said to him in reply, "We have given up everything and followed you. What will there be for us?" ²⁸Jesus said to them, "Amen, I say to you that you who have followed me, in the new age, when the Son of Man is seated on his throne of glory, will yourselves sit on twelve thrones, judging the twelve tribes of Israel. ²⁹And everyone who has given up houses or brothers or sisters or father or mother or children or lands for the sake of my name will receive a hundred times more, and will inherit eternal life. ³⁰But many who are first will be last, and the last will be first.

20 "The kingdom of heaven is like a landowner who went out at dawn to hire laborers for his vineyard. ²After agreeing with them for the usual daily wage, he sent them into his vineyard. ³Going out about nine o'clock, he saw others standing idle in the marketplace, ⁴and he said to them, 'You too go into my vineyard, and I will give you what is just.' ⁵So they went off. [And] he went out again around noon, and around three o'clock, and did likewise. ⁶Going out about five o'clock, he found others standing around, and said to them, 'Why do you stand here idle all day?' ⁷They answered, 'Because no one has hired us.' He said to them, 'You too go into my vineyard.' ⁸When it was

anyone who divorces his wife—I am not speaking of an illicit marriage—and marries another, is guilty of adultery.' ¹⁰The disciples said to him, 'If that is how things are between husband and wife, it is advisable not to marry.' ¹¹But he replied, 'It is not everyone who can accept what I have said, but only those to whom it is granted. ¹²There are eunuchs born so from their mother's womb, there are eunuchs made so by human agency and there are eunuchs who have made themselves so for the sake of the kingdom of Heaven. Let anyone accept this who can.'

¹³Then people brought little children to him, for him to lay his hands on them and pray. The disciples scolded them, ¹⁴but Jesus said, 'Let the little children alone, and do not stop them from coming to me; for it is to such as these that the kingdom of Heaven belongs.' ¹⁵Then he laid his hands on them and went on his way.

¹⁶And now a man came to him and asked, 'Master, what good deed must I do to possess eternal life?' ¹⁷Jesus said to him, 'Why do you ask me about what is good? There is one alone who is good. But if you wish to enter into life, keep the commandments.' ¹⁸He said, 'Which ones?' Jesus replied, 'These: *You shall not kill. You shall not commit adultery. You shall not steal. You shall not give false witness.* ¹⁹*Honour your father and your mother. You shall love your neighbour as yourself.'ᵉ* ²⁰The young man said to him, 'I have kept all these. What more do I need to do?' ²¹Jesus said, 'If you wish to be perfect, go and sell your possessions and give the money to the poor, and you will have treasure in heaven; then come, follow me.' ²²But when the young man heard these words he went away sad, for he was a man of great wealth.

²³Then Jesus said to his disciples, 'In truth I tell you, it is hard for someone rich to enter the kingdom of Heaven. ²⁴Yes, I tell you again, it is easier for a camel to pass through the eye of a needle than for someone rich to enter the kingdom of Heaven.' ²⁵When the disciples heard this they were astonished. 'Who can be saved, then?' they said. ²⁶Jesus gazed at them. 'By human resources', he told them, 'this is impossible; for God everything is possible.'

²⁷Then Peter answered and said, 'Look, we have left everything and followed you. What are we to have, then?' ²⁸Jesus said to them, 'In truth I tell you, when everything is made new again and the Son of man is seated on his throne of glory, you yourselves will sit on twelve thrones to judge the twelve tribes of Israel. ²⁹And everyone who has left houses, brothers, sisters, father, mother, children or land for the sake of my name will receive a hundred times as much, and also inherit eternal life.

³⁰'Many who are first will be last, and the last, first.'

20 'Now the kingdom of Heaven is like a landowner going out at daybreak to hire workers for his vineyard. ²He made an agreement with the workers for one denarius a day and sent them to his vineyard. ³Going out at about the third hour he saw others standing idle in the market place ⁴and said to them, "You go to my vineyard too and I will give you a fair wage." ⁵So they went. At about the sixth hour and again at about the ninth hour, he went out and did the same. ⁶Then at about the eleventh hour he went out and found more men standing around, and he said to them, "Why have you been standing here idle all day?" ⁷"Because no one has hired us," they answered. He said to them, "You go into my vineyard too." ⁸In the evening, the

ᵉ **19** Ex 20:12–16.

NEW REVISED STANDARD VERSION

of the vineyard said to his manager, 'Call the laborers and give them their pay, beginning with the last and then going to the first.' 9 When those hired about five o'clock came, each of them received the usual daily wage. *w* 10 Now when the first came, they thought they would receive more; but each of them also received the usual daily wage. *w* 11 And when they received it, they grumbled against the landowner, 12 saying, 'These last worked only one hour, and you have made them equal to us who have borne the burden of the day and the scorching heat.' 13 But he replied to one of them, 'Friend, I am doing you no wrong; did you not agree with me for the usual daily wage? *w* 14 Take what belongs to you and go; I choose to give to this last the same as I give to you. 15 Am I not allowed to do what I choose with what belongs to me? Or are you envious because I am generous?' *x* 16 So the last will be first, and the first will be last.' *y*

17 While Jesus was going up to Jerusalem, he took the twelve disciples aside by themselves, and said to them on the way, 18 "See, we are going up to Jerusalem, and the Son of Man will be handed over to the chief priests and scribes, and they will condemn him to death; 19 then they will hand him over to the Gentiles to be mocked and flogged and crucified; and on the third day he will be raised."

20 Then the mother of the sons of Zebedee came to him with her sons, and kneeling before him, she asked a favor of him. 21 And he said to her, "What do you want?" She said to him, "Declare that these two sons of mine will sit, one at your right hand and one at your left, in your kingdom." 22 But Jesus answered, "You do not know what you are asking. Are you able to drink the cup that I am about to drink?" *z* They said to him, "We are able." 23 He said to them, "You will indeed drink my cup, but to sit at my right hand and at my left, this is not mine to grant, but it is for those for whom it has been prepared by my Father."

24 When the ten heard it, they were angry with the two brothers. 25 But Jesus called them to him and said, "You know that the rulers of the Gentiles lord it over them, and their great ones are tyrants over them. 26 It will not be so among you; but whoever wishes to be great among you must be your servant, 27 and whoever wishes to be first among you must be your slave; 28 just as the Son of Man came not to be served but to serve, and to give his life a ransom for many."

29 As they were leaving Jericho, a large crowd followed him. 30 There were two blind men sitting by the roadside. When they heard that Jesus was passing by, they shouted, "Lord, *a* have mercy on us, Son of David!" 31 The crowd sternly ordered them to be quiet; but they shouted even more loudly, "Have mercy on us, Lord, Son of David!" 32 Jesus stood still and called them, saying, "What do you want me to do for you?" 33 They said to him, "Lord, let our eyes be opened." 34 Moved with compassion, Jesus touched their eyes. Immediately they regained their sight and followed him.

21 When they had come near Jerusalem and had reached Bethphage, at the Mount of Olives, Jesus sent two disciples, 2 saying to them, "Go into the village ahead of you, and immediately you will find a donkey tied, and a colt with her; untie them and bring them to me. 3 If anyone says anything to you, just say this, 'The Lord needs them.' And he will send them immediately. *b* 4 This took place to fulfill what had been spoken through the prophet, saying,

REVISED ENGLISH BIBLE

of the vineyard said to the overseer, "Call the labourers and give them their pay, beginning with those who came last and ending with the first." 9 Those who had started work an hour before sunset came forward, and were paid the full day's wage. 10 When it was the turn of the men who had come first, they expected something extra, but were paid the same as the others. 11 As they took it, they grumbled at their employer: 12 "These latecomers did only one hour's work, yet you have treated them on a level with us, who have sweated the whole day long in the blazing sun!" 13 The owner turned to one of them and said, "My friend, I am not being unfair to you. You agreed on the usual wage for the day, did you not? 14 Take your pay and go home. I choose to give the last man the same as you. 15 Surely I am free to do what I like with my own money? Why be jealous because I am generous?" 16 So the last will be first, and the first last.'

17 JESUS was journeying towards Jerusalem, and on the way he took the Twelve aside and said to them, 18 'We are now going up to Jerusalem, and the Son of Man will be handed over to the chief priests and the scribes; they will condemn him to death 19 and hand him over to the Gentiles, to be mocked and flogged and crucified; and on the third day he will be raised to life again.'

20 The mother of Zebedee's sons then approached him with her sons. She bowed before him and begged a favour. 21 'What is it you want?' asked Jesus. She replied, 'Give orders that in your kingdom these two sons of mine may sit next to you, one at your right hand and the other at your left.' 22 Jesus turned to the brothers and said, 'You do not understand what you are asking. Can you drink the cup that I am to drink?' 'We can,' they replied. 23 'You shall indeed drink my cup,' he said; 'but to sit on my right or on my left is not for me to grant; that honour is for those to whom it has already been assigned by my Father.'

24 When the other ten heard this, they were indignant with the two brothers. 25 So Jesus called them to him and said, 'You know that, among the Gentiles, rulers lord it over their subjects, and the great make their authority felt. 26 It shall not be so with you; among you, whoever wants to be great must be your servant, 27 and whoever wants to be first must be the slave of all — 28 just as the Son of Man did not come to be served but to serve, and to give his life as a ransom for many.'

29 As they were leaving Jericho he was followed by a huge crowd. 30 At the roadside sat two blind men. When they heard that Jesus was passing by they shouted, 'Have pity on us, Son of David.' 31 People told them to be quiet, but they shouted all the more, 'Sir, have pity on us; have pity on us, Son of David.' 32 Jesus stopped and called the men. 'What do you want me to do for you?' 33 he asked. 'Sir,' they answered, 'open our eyes.' 34 Jesus was deeply moved, and touched their eyes. At once they recovered their sight and followed him.

21 THEY were approaching Jerusalem, and when they reached Bethphage at the mount of Olives Jesus sent off two disciples, 2 and told them: 'Go into the village opposite, where you will at once find a donkey tethered with her foal beside her. Untie them, and bring them to me. 3 If anyone says anything to you, answer, "The Master needs them"; and he will let you have them at once.' 4 This was to fulfil the prophecy which says, 5 'Tell the daughter

---

w Gk *a denarius*   *x* Gk *is your eye evil because I am good?*
y Other ancient authorities add *for many are called but few are chosen*
z Other ancient authorities add *or to be baptized with the baptism that I am baptized with?*   *a* Other ancient authorities lack *Lord*
b Or *'The Lord needs them and will send them back immediately.'*

20:9 **the . . . wage:** *lit.* one denarius each.   20:13 **You . . . day:** *lit.* You agreed on a denarius.   21:3 **The Master . . . once:** *or* "The Master needs them and will send them back without delay."

evening the owner of the vineyard said to his foreman, 'Summon the laborers and give them their pay, beginning with the last and ending with the first.' 9 When those who had started about five o'clock came, each received the usual daily wage. 10 So when the first came, they thought that they would receive more, but each of them also got the usual wage. 11 And on receiving it they grumbled against the landowner, 12 saying, 'These last ones worked only one hour, and you have made them equal to us, who bore the day's burden and the heat.' 13 He said to one of them in reply, 'My friend, I am not cheating you. Did you not agree with me for the usual daily wage? 14 Take what is yours and go. What if I wish to give this last one the same as you? 15 [Or] am I not free to do as I wish with my own money? Are you envious because I am generous?' 16 Thus, the last will be first, and the first will be last."

17 As Jesus was going up to Jerusalem, he took the twelve [disciples] aside by themselves, and said to them on the way, 18 "Behold, we are going up to Jerusalem, and the Son of Man will be handed over to the chief priests and the scribes, and they will condemn him to death, 19 and hand him over to the Gentiles to be mocked and scourged and crucified, and he will be raised on the third day."

20 Then the mother of the sons of Zebedee approached him with her sons and did him homage, wishing to ask him for something. 21 He said to her, "What do you wish?" She answered him, "Command that these two sons of mine sit, one at your right and the other at your left, in your kingdom." 22 Jesus said in reply, "You do not know what you are asking. Can you drink the cup that I am going to drink?" They said to him, "We can." 23 He replied, "My cup you will indeed drink, but to sit at my right and at my left [, this] is not mine to give but is for those for whom it has been prepared by my Father." 24 When the ten heard this, they became indignant at the two brothers. 25 But Jesus summoned them and said, "You know that the rulers of the Gentiles lord it over them, and the great ones make their authority over them felt. 26 But it shall not be so among you. Rather, whoever wishes to be great among you shall be your servant; 27 whoever wishes to be first among you shall be your slave. 28 Just so, the Son of Man did not come to be served but to serve and to give his life as a ransom for many."

29 As they left Jericho, a great crowd followed him. 30 Two blind men were sitting by the roadside, and when they heard that Jesus was passing by, they cried out, "[Lord,] Son of David, have pity on us!" 31 The crowd warned them to be silent, but they called out all the more, "Lord, Son of David, have pity on us!" 32 Jesus stopped and called them and said, "What do you want me to do for you?" 33 They answered him, "Lord, let our eyes be opened." 34 Moved with pity, Jesus touched their eyes. Immediately they received their sight, and followed him.

21 When they drew near Jerusalem and came to Bethphage on the Mount of Olives, Jesus sent two disciples, 2 saying to them, "Go into the village opposite you, and immediately you will find an ass tethered, and a colt with her. Untie them and bring here to me. 3 And if anyone should say anything to you, reply, 'The master has need of them.' Then he will send them at once." 4 This happened so that what had been spoken through the prophet might be fulfilled:

owner of the vineyard said to his bailiff, "Call the workers and pay them their wages, starting with the last arrivals and ending with the first." 9 So those who were hired at about the eleventh hour came forward and received one denarius each. 10 When the first came, they expected to get more, but they too received one denarius each. 11 They took it, but grumbled at the landowner saying, 12 "The men who came last have done only one hour, and you have treated them the same as us, though we have done a heavy day's work in all the heat." 13 He answered one of them and said, "My friend, I am not being unjust to you; did we not agree on one denarius? 14 Take your earnings and go. I choose to pay the lastcomer as much as I pay you. 15 Have I no right to do what I like with my own? Why should you be envious because I am generous?" 16 Thus the last will be first, and the first, last.'

17 Jesus was going up to Jerusalem, and on the road he took the Twelve aside by themselves and said to them, 18 'Look, we are going up to Jerusalem, and the Son of man is about to be handed over to the chief priests and scribes. They will condemn him to death 19 and will hand him over to the gentiles to be mocked and scourged and crucified; and on the third day he will be raised up again.'

20 Then the mother of Zebedee's sons came with her sons to make a request of him, and bowed low; 21 and he said to her, 'What is it you want?' She said to him, 'Promise that these two sons of mine may sit one at your right hand and the other at your left in your kingdom.' 22 Jesus answered, 'You do not know what you are asking. Can you drink the cup that I am going to drink?' They replied, 'We can.' 23 He said to them, 'Very well; you shall drink my cup, but as for seats at my right hand and my left, these are not mine to grant; they belong to those to whom they have been allotted by my Father.'

24 When the other ten heard this they were indignant with the two brothers. 25 But Jesus called them to him and said, 'You know that among the gentiles the rulers lord it over them, and great men make their authority felt. 26 Among you this is not to happen. No; anyone who wants to become great among you must be your servant, 27 and anyone who wants to be first among you must be your slave, 28 just as the Son of man came not to be served but to serve, and to give his life as a ransom for many.'

29 As they left Jericho a large crowd followed him. 30 And now there were two blind men sitting at the side of the road. When they heard that it was Jesus who was passing by, they shouted, 'Lord! Have pity on us, son of David.' 31 And the crowd scolded them and told them to keep quiet, but they only shouted the louder, 'Lord! Have pity on us, son of David.' 32 Jesus stopped, called them over and said, 'What do you want me to do for you?' 33 They said to him, 'Lord, let us have our sight back.' 34 Jesus felt pity for them and touched their eyes, and at once their sight returned and they followed him.

21 When they were near Jerusalem and had come to Bethphage on the Mount of Olives, then Jesus sent two disciples, 2 saying to them, 'Go to the village facing you, and you will at once find a tethered donkey and a colt with her. Untie them and bring them to me. 3 If anyone says anything to you, you are to say, "The Master needs them and will send them back at once." ' 4 This was to fulfil what was spoken by the prophet:

20, 30: [*Lord*]: some important textual witnesses omit this, but that may be because copyists assimilated this verse to 9, 27.

5 "Tell the daughter of Zion,
Look, your king is coming to you,
humble, and mounted on a donkey,
and on a colt, the foal of a donkey."
6 The disciples went and did as Jesus had directed them;
7 they brought the donkey and the colt, and put their cloaks
on them, and he sat on them. 8 A very large crowd[c] spread
their cloaks on the road, and others cut branches from the
trees and spread them on the road. 9 The crowds that went
ahead of him and that followed were shouting,
"Hosanna to the Son of David!
Blessed is the one who comes in the name of
the Lord!
Hosanna in the highest heaven!"
10 When he entered Jerusalem, the whole city was in turmoil, asking, "Who is this?" 11 The crowds were saying,
"This is the prophet Jesus from Nazareth in Galilee."

12 Then Jesus entered the temple[d] and drove out all
who were selling and buying in the temple, and he overturned the tables of the money changers and the seats of
those who sold doves. 13 He said to them, "It is written,
'My house shall be called a house of prayer';
but you are making it a den of robbers."

14 The blind and the lame came to him in the temple,
and he cured them. 15 But when the chief priests and the
scribes saw the amazing things that he did, and heard[e] the
children crying out in the temple, "Hosanna to the Son of
David," they became angry 16 and said to him, "Do you hear
what these are saying?" Jesus said to them, "Yes; have you
never read,
'Out of the mouths of infants and nursing babies
you have prepared praise for yourself'?"
17 He left them, went out of the city to Bethany, and spent
the night there.

18 In the morning, when he returned to the city, he was
hungry. 19 And seeing a fig tree by the side of the road, he
went to it and found nothing at all on it but leaves. Then he
said to it, "May no fruit ever come from you again!" And
the fig tree withered at once. 20 When the disciples saw it,
they were amazed, saying, "How did the fig tree wither at
once?" 21 Jesus answered them, "Truly I tell you, if you
have faith and do not doubt, not only will you do what has
been done to the fig tree, but even if you say to this mountain, 'Be lifted up and thrown into the sea,' it will be done.
22 Whatever you ask for in prayer with faith, you will receive."

23 When he entered the temple, the chief priests and the
elders of the people came to him as he was teaching, and
said, "By what authority are you doing these things, and
who gave you this authority?" 24 Jesus said to them, "I will
also ask you one question; if you tell me the answer, then
I will also tell you by what authority I do these things.
25 Did the baptism of John come from heaven, or was it of
human origin?" And they argued with one another, "If we
say, 'From heaven,' he will say to us, 'Why then did you
not believe him?' 26 But if we say, 'Of human origin,' we
are afraid of the crowd; for all regard John as a prophet."
27 So they answered Jesus, "We do not know." And he said
to them, "Neither will I tell you by what authority I am
doing these things.

28 "What do you think? A man had two sons; he went
to the first and said, 'Son, go and work in the vineyard
today.' 29 He answered, 'I will not'; but later he changed his
mind and went. 30 The father[f] went to the second and said

of Zion, "Here is your king, who comes to you in gentleness, riding on a donkey, on the foal of a beast of burden." '
6 The disciples went and did as Jesus had directed, 7 and
brought the donkey and her foal; they laid their cloaks on
them and Jesus mounted. 8 Crowds of people carpeted the
road with their cloaks, and some cut branches from the trees
to spread in his path. 9 Then the crowds in front and behind
raised the shout: 'Hosanna to the Son of David! Blessed is
he who comes in the name of the Lord! Hosanna in the
heavens!'
10 When he entered Jerusalem the whole city went wild
with excitement. 'Who is this?' people asked, 11 and the
crowds replied, 'This is the prophet Jesus, from Nazareth in
Galilee.'

12 Jesus went into the temple and drove out all who were
buying and selling in the temple precincts; he upset the
tables of the money-changers and the seats of the dealers in
pigeons, 13 and said to them, 'Scripture says, "My house
shall be called a house of prayer"; but you are making it a
bandits' cave.'

14 In the temple the blind and the crippled came to him,
and he healed them. 15 When the chief priests and scribes
saw the wonderful things he did, and heard the boys in the
temple shouting, 'Hosanna to the Son of David!' they were
indignant 16 and asked him, 'Do you hear what they are
saying?' Jesus answered, 'I do. Have you never read the
text, "You have made children and babes at the breast sound
your praise aloud"?' 17 Then he left them and went out of
the city to Bethany, where he spent the night.

18 Next morning on his way to the city he felt hungry;
19 and seeing a fig tree at the roadside he went up to it, but
found nothing on it but leaves. He said to the tree, 'May you
never bear fruit again!' and at once the tree withered away.
20 The disciples were amazed at the sight. 'How is it', they
asked, 'that the tree has withered so suddenly?' 21 Jesus
answered them, 'Truly I tell you: if only you have faith and
have no doubts, you will do what has been done to the fig
tree. And more than that: you need only say to this mountain, "Be lifted from your place and hurled into the sea,"
and what you say will be done. 22 Whatever you pray for in
faith you will receive.'

23 He entered the temple, and, as he was teaching, the
chief priests and elders of the nation came up to him and
asked: 'By what authority are you acting like this? Who
gave you this authority?' 24 Jesus replied, 'I also have a
question for you. If you answer it, I will tell you by what
authority I act. 25 The baptism of John: was it from God, or
from men?' This set them arguing among themselves: 'If we
say, "From God," he will say, "Then why did you not
believe him?" 26 But if we say, "From men," we are afraid
of the people's reaction, for they all take John for a prophet.' 27 So they answered, 'We do not know.' And Jesus said:
'Then I will not tell you either by what authority I act.

28 'But what do you think about this? There was a man
who had two sons. He went to the first, and said, "My son,
go and work today in the vineyard." 29 "I will, sir," the boy
replied; but he did not go. 30 The father came to the second

5 "Say to daughter Zion,
'Behold, your king comes to you,
meek and riding on an ass,
and on a colt, the foal of a beast of burden.' "

6 The disciples went and did as Jesus had ordered them. 7 They brought the ass and the colt and laid their cloaks over them, and he sat upon them. 8 The very large crowd spread their cloaks on the road, while others cut branches from the trees and strewed them on the road. 9 The crowds preceding him and those following kept crying out and saying:

"Hosanna to the Son of David;
blessed is he who comes in the name of
the Lord;
hosanna in the highest."

10 And when he entered Jerusalem the whole city was shaken and asked, "Who is this?" 11 And the crowds replied, "This is Jesus the prophet, from Nazareth in Galilee." 12 Jesus entered the temple area and drove out all those engaged in selling and buying there. He overturned the tables of the money changers and the seats of those who were selling doves. 13 And he said to them, "It is written:

'My house shall be a house of prayer,'
but you are making it a den of thieves."

14 The blind and the lame approached him in the temple area, and he cured them. 15 When the chief priests and the scribes saw the wondrous things he was doing, and the children crying out in the temple area, "Hosanna to the Son of David," they were indignant 16 and said to him, "Do you hear what they are saying?" Jesus said to them, "Yes; and have you never read the text, 'Out of the mouths of infants and nurslings you have brought forth praise'?" 17 And leaving them, he went out of the city to Bethany, and there he spent the night.

18 When he was going back to the city in the morning, he was hungry. 19 Seeing a fig tree by the road, he went over to it, but found nothing on it except leaves. And he said to it, "May no fruit ever come from you again." And immediately the fig tree withered. 20 When the disciples saw this, they were amazed and said, "How was it that the fig tree withered immediately?" 21 Jesus said to them in reply, "Amen, I say to you, if you have faith and do not waver, not only will you do what has been done to the fig tree, but even if you say to this mountain, 'Be lifted up and thrown into the sea,' it will be done. 22 Whatever you ask for in prayer with faith, you will receive."

23 When he had come into the temple area, the chief priests and the elders of the people approached him as he was teaching and said, "By what authority are you doing these things? And who gave you this authority?" 24 Jesus said to them in reply, "I shall ask you one question, and if you answer it for me, then I shall tell you by what authority I do these things. 25 Where was John's baptism from? Was it of heavenly or of human origin?" They discussed this among themselves and said, "If we say 'Of heavenly origin,' he will say to us, 'Then why did you not believe him?' 26 But if we say, 'Of human origin,' we fear the crowd, for they all regard John as a prophet." 27 So they said to Jesus in reply, "We do not know." He himself said to them, "Neither shall I tell you by what authority I do these things.

28 "What is your opinion? A man had two sons. He came to the first and said, 'Son, go out and work in the vineyard today.' 29 He said in reply, 'I will not,' but afterwards he changed his mind and went. 30 The man came to the other

5 Say to the daughter of Zion:
Look, your king is approaching,
humble and riding on a donkey
and on a colt, the foal of a beast of burden. f

6 So the disciples went and did as Jesus had told them. 7 They brought the donkey and the colt, then they laid their cloaks on their backs and he took his seat on them. 8 Great crowds of people spread their cloaks on the road, while others were cutting branches from the trees and spreading them in his path. 9 The crowds who went in front of him and those who followed were all shouting:

Hosanna to the son of David!
Blessed is he who is coming in the name of the
Lord! g
Hosanna in the highest heavens!

10 And when he entered Jerusalem, the whole city was in turmoil as people asked, 'Who is this?' 11 and the crowds answered, 'This is the prophet Jesus from Nazareth in Galilee.' 12 Jesus then went into the Temple and drove out all those who were selling and buying there; he upset the tables of the money changers and the seats of the dove sellers. 13 He said to them, 'According to scripture, my house will be called a house of prayer; but you are turning it into a bandits' den.' h 14 There were also blind and lame people who came to him in the Temple, and he cured them. 15 At the sight of the wonderful things he did and of the children shouting, 'Hosanna to the son of David' in the Temple, the chief priests and the scribes were indignant and said to him, 16 'Do you hear what they are saying?' Jesus answered, 'Yes. Have you never read this:

By the mouths of children, babes in arms,
you have made sure of praise?' i

17 With that he left them and went out of the city to Bethany, where he spent the night.

18 As he was returning to the city in the early morning, he felt hungry. 19 Seeing a fig tree by the road, he went up to it and found nothing on it but leaves. And he said to it, 'May you never bear fruit again,' and instantly the fig tree withered. 20 The disciples were amazed when they saw it and said, 'How is it that the fig tree withered instantly?' 21 Jesus answered, 'In truth I tell you, if you have faith and do not doubt at all, not only will you do what I have done to the fig tree, but even if you say to this mountain, "Be pulled up and thrown into the sea," it will be done. 22 And if you have faith, everything you ask for in prayer, you will receive.'

23 He had gone into the Temple and was teaching, when the chief priests and the elders of the people came to him and said, 'What authority have you for acting like this? And who gave you this authority?' 24 In reply Jesus said to them, 'And I will ask you a question, just one; if you tell me the answer to it, then I will tell you my authority for acting like this. 25 John's baptism: what was its origin, heavenly or human?' And they argued this way among themselves, 'If we say heavenly, he will retort to us, "Then why did you refuse to believe him?"; 26 but if we say human, we have the people to fear, for they all hold that John was a prophet.' 27 So their reply to Jesus was, 'We do not know.' And he retorted to them, 'Nor will I tell you my authority for acting like this.'

28 'What is your opinion? A man had two sons. He went and said to the first, "My boy, go and work in the vineyard today." 29 He answered, "I will not go," but afterwards thought better of it and went. 30 The man then went and said

f **21** Zc 9:9.　　g **21** Ps 118:26.　　h **21** Is 56:7; Jr 7:11.　　i **21** Ps 8:2.

NEW REVISED STANDARD VERSION | REVISED ENGLISH BIBLE

the same; and he answered, 'I go, sir'; but he did not go. 31 Which of the two did the will of his father?" They said, "The first." Jesus said to them, "Truly I tell you, the tax collectors and the prostitutes are going into the kingdom of God ahead of you. 32 For John came to you in the way of righteousness and you did not believe him, but the tax collectors and the prostitutes believed him; and even after you saw it, you did not change your minds and believe him.

33 "Listen to another parable. There was a landowner who planted a vineyard, put a fence around it, dug a wine press in it, and built a watchtower. Then he leased it to tenants and went to another country. 34 When the harvest time had come, he sent his slaves to the tenants to collect his produce. 35 But the tenants seized his slaves and beat one, killed another, and stoned another. 36 Again he sent other slaves, more than the first; and they treated them in the same way. 37 Finally he sent his son to them, saying, 'They will respect my son.' 38 But when the tenants saw the son, they said to themselves, 'This is the heir; come, let us kill him and get his inheritance.' 39 So they seized him, threw him out of the vineyard, and killed him. 40 Now when the owner of the vineyard comes, what will he do to those tenants?" 41 They said to him, "He will put those wretches to a miserable death, and lease the vineyard to other tenants who will give him the produce at the harvest time."

42 Jesus said to them, "Have you never read in the scriptures:

'The stone that the builders rejected
     has become the cornerstone;g
this was the Lord's doing,
     and it is amazing in our eyes'?

43 Therefore I tell you, the kingdom of God will be taken away from you and given to a people that produces the fruits of the kingdom. h 44 The one who falls on this stone will be broken to pieces; and it will crush anyone on whom it falls." i

45 When the chief priests and the Pharisees heard his parables, they realized that he was speaking about them. 46 They wanted to arrest him, but they feared the crowds, because they regarded him as a prophet.

22 Once more Jesus spoke to them in parables, saying: 2 "The kingdom of heaven may be compared to a king who gave a wedding banquet for his son. 3 He sent his slaves to call those who had been invited to the wedding banquet, but they would not come. 4 Again he sent other slaves, saying, 'Tell those who have been invited: Look, I have prepared my dinner, my oxen and my fat calves have been slaughtered, and everything is ready; come to the wedding banquet.' 5 But they made light of it and went away, one to his farm, another to his business, 6 while the rest seized his slaves, mistreated them, and killed them. 7 The king was enraged. He sent his troops, destroyed those murderers, and burned their city. 8 Then he said to his slaves, 'The wedding is ready, but those invited were not worthy. 9 Go therefore into the main streets, and invite everyone you find to the wedding banquet.' 10 Those slaves went out into the streets and gathered all whom they found, both good and bad; so the wedding hall was filled with guests.

11 "But when the king came in to see the guests, he noticed a man there who was not wearing a wedding robe, 12 and he said to him, 'Friend, how did you get in here without a wedding robe?' And he was speechless. 13 Then the king said to the attendants, 'Bind him hand and foot, and throw him into the outer darkness, where there will be weeping and gnashing of teeth.' 14 For many are called, but few are chosen."

and said the same. "I will not," he replied; but afterwards he changed his mind and went. 31 Which of the two did what his father wanted?' 'The second,' they replied. Then Jesus said, 'Truly I tell you: tax-collectors and prostitutes are entering the kingdom of God ahead of you. 32 For when John came to show you the right way to live, you did not believe him, but the tax-collectors and prostitutes did; and even when you had seen that, you did not change your minds and believe him.

33 'Listen to another parable. There was a landowner who planted a vineyard: he put a wall round it, hewed out a winepress, and built a watch-tower; then he let it out to vine-growers and went abroad. 34 When the harvest season approached, he sent his servants to the tenants to collect the produce due to him. 35 But they seized his servants, thrashed one, killed another, and stoned a third. 36 Again, he sent other servants, this time a larger number; and they treated them in the same way. 37 Finally he sent his son. "They will respect my son," he said. 38 But when they saw the son the tenants said to one another, "This is the heir; come on, let us kill him, and get his inheritance." 39 So they seized him, flung him out of the vineyard, and killed him. 40 When the owner of the vineyard comes, how do you think he will deal with those tenants?' 41 'He will bring those bad men to a bad end,' they answered, 'and hand the vineyard over to other tenants, who will give him his share of the crop when the season comes.' 42 Jesus said to them, 'Have you never read in the scriptures: "The stone which the builders rejected has become the main corner-stone. This is the Lord's doing, and it is wonderful in our eyes"? 43 Therefore, I tell you, the kingdom of God will be taken away from you, and given to a nation that yields the proper fruit.'

45 When the chief priests and Pharisees heard his parables, they saw that he was referring to them. 46 They wanted to arrest him, but were afraid of the crowds, who looked on Jesus as a prophet.

22 JESUS spoke to them again in parables: 2 'The kingdom of Heaven is like this. There was a king who arranged a banquet for his son's wedding; 3 but when he sent his servants to summon the guests he had invited, they refused to come. 4 Then he sent other servants, telling them to say to the guests, "Look! I have prepared this banquet for you. My bullocks and fatted beasts have been slaughtered, and everything is ready. Come to the wedding." 5 But they took no notice; one went off to his farm, another to his business, 6 and the others seized the servants, attacked them brutally, and killed them. 7 The king was furious; he sent troops to put those murderers to death and set their town on fire. 8 Then he said to his servants, "The wedding banquet is ready; but the guests I invited did not deserve the honour. 9 Go out therefore to the main thoroughfares, and invite everyone you can find to the wedding." 10 The servants went out into the streets, and collected everyone they could find, good and bad alike. So the hall was packed with guests.

11 'When the king came in to watch them feasting, he observed a man who was not dressed for a wedding. 12 "My friend," said the king, "how do you come to be here without wedding clothes?" But he had nothing to say. 13 The king then said to his attendants, "Bind him hand and foot; fling him out into the dark, the place of wailing and grinding of teeth." 14 For many are invited, but few are chosen.'

g Or keystone   h Gk the fruits of it   i Other ancient authorities lack verse 44

21:43 **proper fruit:** *some witnesses add* 44 Any man who falls on this stone will be dashed to pieces; and if it falls on a man he will be crushed by it.

son and gave the same order. He said in reply, 'Yes, sir,' but did not go. 31 Which of the two did his father's will?" They answered, "The first." Jesus said to them, "Amen, I say to you, tax collectors and prostitutes are entering the kingdom of God before you. 32 When John came to you in the way of righteousness, you did not believe him; but tax collectors and prostitutes did. Yet even when you saw that, you did not later change your minds and believe him.

33 "Hear another parable. There was a landowner who planted a vineyard, put a hedge around it, dug a wine press in it, and built a tower. Then he leased it to tenants and went on a journey. 34 When vintage time drew near, he sent his servants to the tenants to obtain his produce. 35 But the tenants seized the servants and one they beat, another they killed, and a third they stoned. 36 Again he sent other servants, more numerous than the first ones, but they treated them in the same way. 37 Finally, he sent his son to them, thinking, 'They will respect my son.' 38 But when the tenants saw the son, they said to one another, 'This is the heir. Come, let us kill him and acquire his inheritance.' 39 They seized him, threw him out of the vineyard, and killed him. 40 What will the owner of the vineyard do to those tenants when he comes?" 41 They answered him, "He will put those wretched men to a wretched death and lease his vineyard to other tenants who will give him the produce at the proper times." 42 Jesus said to them, "Did you never read in the scriptures:

'The stone that the builders rejected
    has become the cornerstone;
by the Lord has this been done,
    and it is wonderful in our eyes'?

43 Therefore, I say to you, the kingdom of God will be taken away from you and given to a people that will produce its fruit. [44 The one who falls on this stone will be dashed to pieces; and it will crush anyone on whom it falls.]" 45 When the chief priests and the Pharisees heard his parables, they knew that he was speaking about them. 46 And although they were attempting to arrest him, they feared the crowds, for they regarded him as a prophet.

22 Jesus again in reply spoke to them in parables, saying, 2 "The kingdom of heaven may be likened to a king who gave a wedding feast for his son. 3 He dispatched his servants to summon the invited guests to the feast, but they refused to come. 4 A second time he sent other servants, saying, 'Tell those invited: "Behold, I have prepared my banquet, my calves and fattened cattle are killed, and everything is ready; come to the feast." ' 5 Some ignored the invitation and went away, one to his farm, another to his business. 6 The rest laid hold of his servants, mistreated them, and killed them. 7 The king was enraged and sent his troops, destroyed those murderers, and burned their city. 8 Then he said to his servants, 'The feast is ready, but those who were invited were not worthy to come. 9 Go out, therefore, into the main roads and invite to the feast whomever you find.' 10 The servants went out into the streets and gathered all they found, bad and good alike, and the hall was filled with guests. 11 But when the king came in to meet the guests he saw a man there not dressed in a wedding garment. 12 He said to him, 'My friend, how is it that you came in here without a wedding garment?' But he was reduced to silence. 13 Then the king said to his attendants, 'Bind his hands and feet, and cast him into the darkness outside, where there will be wailing and grinding of teeth.' 14 Many are invited, but few are chosen."

the same thing to the second who answered, "Certainly, sir," but did not go. 31 Which of the two did the father's will?' They said, 'The first.' Jesus said to them, 'In truth I tell you, tax collectors and prostitutes are making their way into the kingdom of God before you. 32 For John came to you, showing the way of uprightness, but you did not believe him, and yet the tax collectors and prostitutes did. Even after seeing that, you refused to think better of it and believe in him.

33 'Listen to another parable. There was a man, a landowner, who planted a vineyard; he fenced it round, dug a winepress in it and built a tower; then he leased it to tenants and went abroad. 34 When vintage time drew near he sent his servants to the tenants to collect his produce. 35 But the tenants seized his servants, thrashed one, killed another and stoned a third. 36 Next he sent some more servants, this time a larger number, and they dealt with them in the same way. 37 Finally he sent his son to them thinking, "They will respect my son." 38 But when the tenants saw the son, they said to each other, "This is the heir. Come on, let us kill him and take over his inheritance." 39 So they seized him and threw him out of the vineyard and killed him. 40 Now when the owner of the vineyard comes, what will he do to those tenants?' 41 They answered, 'He will bring those wretches to a wretched end and lease the vineyard to other tenants who will deliver the produce to him at the proper time.' 42 Jesus said to them, 'Have you never read in the scriptures:

The stone which the builders rejected
has become the cornerstone;
this is the Lord's doing
and we marvel at it? j

43 'I tell you, then, that the kingdom of God will be taken from you and given to a people who will produce its fruit.' [44] k

45 When they heard his parables, the chief priests and the scribes realised he was speaking about them, 46 but though they would have liked to arrest him they were afraid of the crowds, who looked on him as a prophet.

22 Jesus began to speak to them in parables once again, 2 'The kingdom of Heaven may be compared to a king who gave a feast for his son's wedding. 3 He sent his servants to call those who had been invited, but they would not come. 4 Next he sent some more servants with the words, "Tell those who have been invited: Look, my banquet is all prepared, my oxen and fattened cattle have been slaughtered, everything is ready. Come to the wedding." 5 But they were not interested: one went off to his farm, another to his business, 6 and the rest seized his servants, maltreated them and killed them. 7 The king was furious. He despatched his troops, destroyed those murderers and burnt their town. 8 Then he said to his servants, "The wedding is ready; but as those who were invited proved to be unworthy, 9 go to the main crossroads and invite everyone you can find to come to the wedding." 10 So these servants went out onto the roads and collected together everyone they could find, bad and good alike; and the wedding hall was filled with guests. 11 When the king came in to look at the guests he noticed one man who was not wearing a wedding garment, 12 and said to him, "How did you get in here, my friend, without a wedding garment?" And the man was silent. 13 Then the king said to the attendants, "Bind him hand and foot and throw him into the darkness outside, where there will be weeping and grinding of teeth." 14 For many are invited but not all are chosen.'

21, 44: The majority of textual witnesses omit this verse. It is probably an early addition to Mt from Lk 20, 18 with which it is practically identical.

j 21 Ps 118:22–23.   k 21 Some authorities add v. 44, taken from Lk 20:18.

NEW REVISED STANDARD VERSION

15 Then the Pharisees went and plotted to entrap him in what he said. 16 So they sent their disciples to him, along with the Herodians, saying, "Teacher, we know that you are sincere, and teach the way of God in accordance with truth, and show deference to no one; for you do not regard people with partiality. 17 Tell us, then, what you think. Is it lawful to pay taxes to the emperor, or not?" 18 But Jesus, aware of their malice, said, "Why are you putting me to the test, you hypocrites? 19 Show me the coin used for the tax." And they brought him a denarius. 20 Then he said to them, "Whose head is this, and whose title?" 21 They answered, "The emperor's." Then he said to them, "Give therefore to the emperor the things that are the emperor's, and to God the things that are God's." 22 When they heard this, they were amazed; and they left him and went away.

23 The same day some Sadducees came to him, saying there is no resurrection; *j* and they asked him a question, saying, 24 "Teacher, Moses said, 'If a man dies childless, his brother shall marry the widow, and raise up children for his brother.' 25 Now there were seven brothers among us; the first married, and died childless, leaving the widow to his brother. 26 The second did the same, so also the third, down to the seventh. 27 Last of all, the woman herself died. 28 In the resurrection, then, whose wife of the seven will she be? For all of them had married her."

29 Jesus answered them, "You are wrong, because you know neither the scriptures nor the power of God. 30 For in the resurrection they neither marry nor are given in marriage, but are like angels *k* in heaven. 31 And as for the resurrection of the dead, have you not read what was said to you by God, 32 'I am the God of Abraham, the God of Isaac, and the God of Jacob'? He is God not of the dead, but of the living." 33 And when the crowd heard it, they were astounded at his teaching.

34 When the Pharisees heard that he had silenced the Sadducees, they gathered together, 35 and one of them, a lawyer, asked him a question to test him. 36 "Teacher, which commandment in the law is the greatest?" 37 He said to him, " 'You shall love the Lord your God with all your heart, and with all your soul, and with all your mind.' 38 This is the greatest and first commandment. 39 And a second is like it: 'You shall love your neighbor as yourself.' 40 On these two commandments hang all the law and the prophets."

41 Now while the Pharisees were gathered together, Jesus asked them this question: 42 "What do you think of the Messiah? *l* Whose son is he?" They said to him, "The son of David." 43 He said to them, "How is it then that David by the Spirit *m* calls him Lord, saying,

44 'The Lord said to my Lord,
"Sit at my right hand,
  until I put your enemies under your feet" '?
45 If David thus calls him Lord, how can he be his son?" 46 No one was able to give him an answer, nor from that day did anyone dare to ask him any more questions.

23 Then Jesus said to the crowds and to his disciples, 2 "The scribes and the Pharisees sit on Moses' seat; 3 therefore, do whatever they teach you and follow it; but do not do as they do, for they do not practice what they teach. 4 They tie up heavy burdens, hard to bear, *n* and lay them on the shoulders of others; but they themselves are unwilling to lift a finger to move them. 5 They do all their deeds to be

REVISED ENGLISH BIBLE

15 THEN the Pharisees went away and agreed on a plan to trap him in argument. 16 They sent some of their followers to him, together with members of Herod's party. 'Teacher,' they said, 'we know you are a sincere man; you teach in all sincerity the way of life that God requires, courting no man's favour, whoever he may be. 17 Give us your ruling on this: are we or are we not permitted to pay taxes to the Roman emperor?' 18 Jesus was aware of their malicious intention and said, 'You hypocrites! Why are you trying to catch me out? 19 Show me the coin used for the tax.' They handed him a silver piece. 20 Jesus asked, 'Whose head is this, and whose inscription?' 21 'Caesar's,' they replied. He said to them, 'Then pay to Caesar what belongs to Caesar, and to God what belongs to God.' 22 Taken aback by this reply, they went away and left him alone.

23 The same day Sadducees, who maintain that there is no resurrection, came to him and asked: 24 'Teacher, Moses said that if a man dies childless, his brother shall marry the widow and provide an heir for his brother. 25 We know a case involving seven brothers. The first married and died, and as he was without issue his wife was left to his brother. 26 The same thing happened with the second, and the third, and so on with all seven. 27 Last of all the woman died. 28 At the resurrection, then, whose wife will she be, since they had all married her?' 29 Jesus answered: 'How far you are from the truth! You know neither the scriptures nor the power of God. 30 In the resurrection men and women do not marry; they are like angels in heaven.

31 'As for the resurrection of the dead, have you never read what God himself said to you: 32 "I am the God of Abraham, the God of Isaac, the God of Jacob"? God is not God of the dead but of the living.' 33 When the crowds heard this, they were amazed at his teaching.

34 Hearing that he had silenced the Sadducees, the Pharisees came together in a body, 35 and one of them tried to catch him out with this question: 36 'Teacher, which is the greatest commandment in the law?' 37 He answered, ' "Love the Lord your God with all your heart, with all your soul, and with all your mind." 38 That is the greatest, the first commandment. 39 The second is like it: "Love your neighbour as yourself." 40 Everything in the law and the prophets hangs on these two commandments.'

41 Turning to the assembled Pharisees Jesus asked them, 42 'What is your opinion about the Messiah? Whose son is he?' 'The son of David,' they replied. 43 'Then how is it', he asked, 'that David by inspiration calls him "Lord"? For he says, 44 "The Lord said to my Lord, 'Sit at my right hand until I put your enemies under your feet.' " 45 If then David calls him "Lord", how can he be David's son?' 46 Nobody was able to give him an answer; and from that day no one dared to put any more questions to him.

23 JESUS then addressed the crowds and his disciples 2 in these words: 'The scribes and the Pharisees occupy Moses' seat; 3 so be careful to do whatever they tell you. But do not follow their practice; for they say one thing and do another. 4 They make up heavy loads and pile them on the shoulders of others, but will not themselves lift a finger to ease the burden. 5 Whatever they do is done for

---

j Other ancient authorities read *who say that there is no resurrection*
k Other ancient authorities add *of God*   *l* Or *Christ*   *m* Gk *in spirit*
n Other ancient authorities lack *hard to bear*

22:35 **one of them:** *some witnesses add* an expert in the law.

15 Then the Pharisees went off and plotted how they might entrap him in speech. 16 They sent their disciples to him, with the Herodians, saying, "Teacher, we know that you are a truthful man and that you teach the way of God in accordance with the truth. And you are not concerned with anyone's opinion, for you do not regard a person's status. 17 Tell us, then, what is your opinion: Is it lawful to pay the census tax to Caesar or not?" 18 Knowing their malice, Jesus said, "Why are you testing me, you hypocrites? 19 Show me the coin that pays the census tax." Then they handed him the Roman coin. 20 He said to them, "Whose image is this and whose inscription?" 21 They replied, "Caesar's." At that he said to them, "Then repay to Caesar what belongs to Caesar and to God what belongs to God." 22 When they heard this they were amazed, and leaving him they went away.

23 On that day Sadducees approached him, saying that there is no resurrection. They put this question to him, 24 saying, "Teacher, Moses said, 'If a man dies without children, his brother shall marry his wife and raise up descendants for his brother.' 25 Now there were seven brothers among us. The first married and died and, having no descendants, left his wife to his brother. 26 The same happened with the second and the third, through all seven. 27 Finally the woman died. 28 Now at the resurrection, of the seven, whose wife will she be? For they all had been married to her." 29 Jesus said to them in reply, "You are misled because you do not know the scriptures or the power of God. 30 At the resurrection they neither marry nor are given in marriage but are like the angels in heaven. 31 And concerning the resurrection of the dead, have you not read what was said to you by God, 32 'I am the God of Abraham, the God of Isaac, and the God of Jacob'? He is not the God of the dead but of the living." 33 When the crowds heard this, they were astonished at his teaching.

34 When the Pharisees heard that he had silenced the Sadducees, they gathered together, 35 and one of them [a scholar of the law] tested him by asking, 36 "Teacher, which commandment in the law is the greatest?" 37 He said to him, "You shall love the Lord, your God, with all your heart, with all your soul, and with all your mind. 38 This is the greatest and the first commandment. 39 The second is like it: You shall love your neighbor as yourself. 40 The whole law and the prophets depend on these two commandments."

41 While the Pharisees were gathered together, Jesus questioned them, 42 saying, "What is your opinion about the Messiah? Whose son is he?" They replied, "David's." 43 He said to them, "How, then, does David, inspired by the Spirit, call him 'lord,' saying:

44 'The Lord said to my lord,
  "Sit at my right hand
  until I place your enemies under your feet" '?

45 If David calls him 'lord,' how can he be his son?" 46 No one was able to answer him a word, nor from that day on did anyone dare to ask him any more questions.

23 Then Jesus spoke to the crowds and to his disciples, 2 saying, "The scribes and the Pharisees have taken their seat on the chair of Moses. 3 Therefore, do and observe all things whatsoever they tell you, but do not follow their example. For they preach but they do not practice. 4 They tie up heavy burdens [hard to carry] and lay them on people's shoulders, but they will not lift a finger to move them.

15 Then the Pharisees went away to work out between them how to trap him in what he said. 16 And they sent their disciples to him, together with some Herodians, to say, 'Master, we know that you are an honest man and teach the way of God in all honesty, and that you are not afraid of anyone, because human rank means nothing to you. 17 Give us your opinion, then. Is it permissible to pay taxes to Caesar or not?' 18 But Jesus was aware of their malice and replied, 'You hypocrites! Why are you putting me to the test? 19 Show me the money you pay the tax with.' They handed him a denarius, 20 and he said, 'Whose portrait is this? Whose title?' 21 They replied, 'Caesar's.' Then he said to them, 'Very well, pay Caesar what belongs to Caesar — and God what belongs to God.' 22 When they heard this they were amazed; they left him alone and went away.

23 That day some Sadducees — who deny that there is a resurrection — approached him and they put this question to him, 24 'Master, Moses said[l] that if a man dies childless, his brother is to marry the widow, his sister-in-law, to raise children for his brother. 25 Now we had a case involving seven brothers; the first married and then died without children, leaving his wife to his brother; 26 the same thing happened with the second and third and so on to the seventh, 27 and then last of all the woman herself died. 28 Now at the resurrection, whose wife among the seven will she be, since she had been married to them all?' 29 Jesus answered them, 'You are wrong, because you understand neither the scriptures nor the power of God. 30 For at the resurrection men and women do not marry; no, they are like the angels in heaven. 31 And as for the resurrection of the dead, have you never read what God himself said to you: 32 I am the God of Abraham, the God of Isaac and the God of Jacob?[m] He is God, not of the dead, but of the living.' 33 And his teaching made a deep impression on the people who heard it.

34 But when the Pharisees heard that he had silenced the Sadducees they got together 35 and, to put him to the test, one of them put a further question, 36 'Master, which is the greatest commandment of the Law?' 37 Jesus said to him, 'You must love the Lord your God with all your heart, with all your soul, and with all your mind. 38 This is the greatest and the first commandment. 39 The second resembles it: You must love your neighbour as yourself.[n] 40 On these two commandments hang the whole Law, and the Prophets too.'

41 While the Pharisees were gathered round, Jesus put to them this question, 42 'What is your opinion about the Christ? Whose son is he?' They told him, 'David's.' 43 He said to them, 'Then how is it that David, moved by the Spirit, calls him Lord, where he says:

44 The Lord declared to my Lord,
  take your seat at my right hand,
  till I have made your enemies
  your footstool?[o]

45 'If David calls him Lord, how then can he be his son?' 46 No one could think of anything to say in reply, and from that day no one dared to ask him any further questions.

23 Then addressing the crowds and his disciples Jesus said, 2 'The scribes and the Pharisees occupy the chair of Moses. 3 You must therefore do and observe what they tell you; but do not be guided by what they do, since they do not practise what they preach. 4 They tie up heavy burdens and lay them on people's shoulders, but will they lift a finger to move them? Not they! 5 Everything they do

22, 35: [A scholar of the law]: meaning "scribe." Although this reading is supported by the vast majority of textual witnesses, it is the only time that the Greek word so translated occurs in Mt. It is relatively frequent in Lk, and there is reason to think that it may have been added here by a copyist since it occurs in the Lucan parallel (10, 25–28).

l 22 Dt 25:5–6.　　m 22 Ex 3:6.　　n 22 Dt 6:5 combined with Lv 19:18.　　o 22 Ps 110:1.

seen by others; for they make their phylacteries broad and their fringes long. 6 They love to have the place of honor at banquets and the best seats in the synagogues, 7 and to be greeted with respect in the marketplaces, and to have people call them rabbi. 8 But you are not to be called rabbi, for you have one teacher, and you are all students. *o* 9 And call no one your father on earth, for you have one Father — the one in heaven. 10 Nor are you to be called instructors, for you have one instructor, the Messiah. *p* 11 The greatest among you will be your servant. 12 All who exalt themselves will be humbled, and all who humble themselves will be exalted.

13 "But woe to you, scribes and Pharisees, hypocrites! For you lock people out of the kingdom of heaven. For you do not go in yourselves, and when others are going in, you stop them. *q* 15 Woe to you, scribes and Pharisees, hypocrites! For you cross sea and land to make a single convert, and you make the new convert twice as much a child of hell *r* as yourselves.

16 "Woe to you, blind guides, who say, 'Whoever swears by the sanctuary is bound by nothing, but whoever swears by the gold of the sanctuary is bound by the oath.' 17 You blind fools! For which is greater, the gold or the sanctuary that has made the gold sacred? 18 And you say, 'Whoever swears by the altar is bound by nothing, but whoever swears by the gift that is on the altar is bound by the oath.' 19 How blind you are! For which is greater, the gift or the altar that makes the gift sacred? 20 So whoever swears by the altar, swears by it and by everything on it; 21 and whoever swears by the sanctuary, swears by it and by the one who dwells in it; 22 and whoever swears by heaven, swears by the throne of God and by the one who is seated upon it.

23 "Woe to you, scribes and Pharisees, hypocrites! For you tithe mint, dill, and cummin, and have neglected the weightier matters of the law: justice and mercy and faith. It is these you ought to have practiced without neglecting the others. 24 You blind guides! You strain out a gnat but swallow a camel!

25 "Woe to you, scribes and Pharisees, hypocrites! For you clean the outside of the cup and of the plate, but inside they are full of greed and self-indulgence. 26 You blind Pharisee! First clean the inside of the cup, *s* so that the outside also may become clean.

27 "Woe to you, scribes and Pharisees, hypocrites! For you are like whitewashed tombs, which on the outside look beautiful, but inside they are full of the bones of the dead and of all kinds of filth. 28 So you also on the outside look righteous to others, but inside you are full of hypocrisy and lawlessness.

29 "Woe to you, scribes and Pharisees, hypocrites! For you build the tombs of the prophets and decorate the graves of the righteous, 30 and you say, 'If we had lived in the days of our ancestors, we would not have taken part with them in shedding the blood of the prophets.' 31 Thus you testify against yourselves that you are descendants of those who murdered the prophets. 32 Fill up, then, the measure of your ancestors. 33 You snakes, you brood of vipers! How can you escape being sentenced to hell? *r* 34 Therefore I send you prophets, sages, and scribes, some of whom you will kill and crucify, and some you will flog in your synagogues and pursue from town to town, 35 so that upon you may come all

show. They go about wearing broad phylacteries and with large tassels on their robes; 6 they love to have the place of honour at feasts and the chief seats in synagogues, 7 to be greeted respectfully in the street, and to be addressed as "rabbi".

8 'But you must not be called "rabbi", for you have one Rabbi, and you are all brothers. 9 Do not call any man on earth "father", for you have one Father, and he is in heaven. 10 Nor must you be called "teacher"; you have one Teacher, the Messiah. 11 The greatest among you must be your servant. 12 Whoever exalts himself will be humbled; and whoever humbles himself will be exalted.

13 'Alas for you, scribes and Pharisees, hypocrites! You shut the door of the kingdom of Heaven in people's faces; you do not enter yourselves, and when others try to enter, you stop them.

15 'Alas for you, scribes and Pharisees, hypocrites! You travel over sea and land to win one convert; and when you have succeeded you make him twice as fit for hell as you are yourselves.

16 'Alas for you, blind guides! You say, "If someone swears by the sanctuary, that is nothing; but if he swears by the gold in the sanctuary, he is bound by his oath." 17 Blind fools! Which is the more important, the gold, or the sanctuary which sanctifies the gold? 18 Or you say, "If someone swears by the altar, that is nothing; but if he swears by the offering that lies on the altar, he is bound by his oath." 19 What blindness! Which is the more important, the offering, or the altar which sanctifies it? 20 To swear by the altar, then, is to swear both by the altar and by whatever lies on it; 21 to swear by the sanctuary is to swear both by the sanctuary and by him who dwells there; 22 and to swear by Heaven is to swear both by the throne of God and by him who sits upon it.

23 'Alas for you, scribes and Pharisees, hypocrites! You pay tithes of mint and dill and cummin; but you have overlooked the weightier demands of the law — justice, mercy, and good faith. It is these you should have practised, without neglecting the others. 24 Blind guides! You strain off a midge, yet gulp down a camel!

25 'Alas for you, scribes and Pharisees, hypocrites! You clean the outside of a cup or a dish, and leave the inside full of greed and self-indulgence! 26 Blind Pharisee! Clean the inside of the cup first; then the outside will be clean also.

27 'Alas for you, scribes and Pharisees, hypocrites! You are like tombs covered with whitewash; they look fine on the outside, but inside they are full of dead men's bones and of corruption. 28 So it is with you: outwardly you look like honest men, but inside you are full of hypocrisy and lawlessness.

29 'Alas for you, scribes and Pharisees, hypocrites! You build up the tombs of the prophets and embellish the monuments of the saints, 30 and you say, "If we had been living in the time of our forefathers, we should never have taken part with them in the murder of the prophets." 31 So you acknowledge that you are the sons of those who killed the prophets. 32 Go on then, finish off what your fathers began! 33 Snakes! Vipers' brood! How can you escape being condemned to hell?

34 'I am sending you therefore prophets and wise men and teachers of the law; some of them you will kill and crucify, others you will flog in your synagogues and hound from city to city. 35 So on you will fall the guilt of all the innocent

---

o Gk *brothers*   *p* Or *the Christ*   *q* Other authorities add here (or after verse 12) verse 14, *Woe to you, scribes and Pharisees, hypocrites! For you devour widows' houses and for the sake of appearance you make long prayers; therefore you will receive the greater condemnation*   *r* Gk *Gehenna*   *s* Other ancient authorities add *and of the plate*

23:13 **you stop them:** *some witnesses add* 14 Alas for you, scribes and Pharisees, hypocrites! You eat up the property of widows, while for appearance' sake you say long prayers. You will receive the severest sentence.   23:32 **Go on . . . began:** *or* You too must come up to your fathers' standards.

5 All their works are performed to be seen. They widen their phylacteries and lengthen their tassels. 6 They love places of honor at banquets, seats of honor in synagogues, 7 greetings in marketplaces, and the salutation 'Rabbi.' 8 As for you, do not be called 'Rabbi.' You have but one teacher, and you are all brothers. 9 Call no one on earth your father; you have but one Father in heaven. 10 Do not be called 'Master'; you have but one master, the Messiah. 11 The greatest among you must be your servant. 12 Whoever exalts himself will be humbled; but whoever humbles himself will be exalted.

13 "Woe to you, scribes and Pharisees, you hypocrites. You lock the kingdom of heaven before human beings. You do not enter yourselves, nor do you allow entrance to those trying to enter. [14]

15 "Woe to you, scribes and Pharisees, you hypocrites. You traverse sea and land to make one convert, and when that happens you make him a child of Gehenna twice as much as yourselves.

16 "Woe to you, blind guides, who say, 'If one swears by the temple, it means nothing, but if one swears by the gold of the temple, one is obligated.' 17 Blind fools, which is greater, the gold, or the temple that made the gold sacred? 18 And you say, 'If one swears by the altar, it means nothing, but if one swears by the gift on the altar, one is obligated.' 19 You blind ones, which is greater, the gift, or the altar that makes the gift sacred? 20 One who swears by the altar swears by it and all that is upon it; 21 one who swears by the temple swears by it and by him who dwells in it; 22 one who swears by heaven swears by the throne of God and by him who is seated on it.

23 "Woe to you, scribes and Pharisees, you hypocrites. You pay tithes of mint and dill and cummin, and have neglected the weightier things of the law: judgment and mercy and fidelity. [But] these you should have done, without neglecting the others. 24 Blind guides, who strain out the gnat and swallow the camel!

25 "Woe to you, scribes and Pharisees, you hypocrites. You cleanse the outside of cup and dish, but inside they are full of plunder and self-indulgence. 26 Blind Pharisee, cleanse first the inside of the cup, so that the outside also may be clean.

27 "Woe to you, scribes and Pharisees, you hypocrites. You are like whitewashed tombs, which appear beautiful on the outside, but inside are full of dead men's bones and every kind of filth. 28 Even so, on the outside you appear righteous, but inside you are filled with hypocrisy and evildoing.

29 "Woe to you, scribes and Pharisees, you hypocrites. You build the tombs of the prophets and adorn the memorials of the righteous, 30 and you say, 'If we had lived in the days of our ancestors, we would not have joined them in shedding the prophets' blood.' 31 Thus you bear witness against yourselves that you are the children of those who murdered the prophets; 32 now fill up what your ancestors measured out! 33 You serpents, you brood of vipers, how can you flee from the judgment of Gehenna? 34 Therefore, behold, I send to you prophets and wise men and scribes; some of them you will kill and crucify, some of them you will scourge in your synagogues and pursue from town to town, 35 so that there may come upon you all the righteous

is done to attract attention, like wearing broader headbands and longer tassels, 6 like wanting to take the place of honour at banquets and the front seats in the synagogues, 7 being greeted respectfully in the market squares and having people call them Rabbi.

8 'You, however, must not allow yourselves to be called Rabbi, since you have only one Master, and you are all brothers. 9 You must call no one on earth your father, since you have only one Father, and he is in heaven. 10 Nor must you allow yourselves to be called teachers, for you have only one Teacher, the Christ. 11 The greatest among you must be your servant. 12 Anyone who raises himself up will be humbled, and anyone who humbles himself will be raised up.

13 'Alas for you, scribes and Pharisees, you hypocrites! You shut up the kingdom of Heaven in people's faces, neither going in yourselves nor allowing others to go in who want to. [14]p

15 'Alas for you, scribes and Pharisees, you hypocrites! You travel over sea and land to make a single proselyte, and anyone who becomes one you make twice as fit for hell as you are.

16 'Alas for you, blind guides! You say, "If anyone swears by the Temple, it has no force; but anyone who swears by the gold of the Temple is bound." 17 Fools and blind! For which is of greater value, the gold or the Temple that makes the gold sacred? 18 Again, "If anyone swears by the altar it has no force; but anyone who swears by the offering on the altar, is bound." 19 You blind men! For which is of greater worth, the offering or the altar that makes the offering sacred? 20 Therefore, someone who swears by the altar is swearing by that and by everything on it. 21 And someone who swears by the Temple is swearing by that and by the One who dwells in it. 22 And someone who swears by heaven is swearing by the throne of God and by the One who is seated there.

23 'Alas for you, scribes and Pharisees, you hypocrites! You pay your tithe of mint and dill and cummin and have neglected the weightier matters of the Law — justice, mercy, good faith! These you should have practised, those not neglected. 24 You blind guides, straining out gnats and swallowing camels!

25 'Alas for you, scribes and Pharisees, you hypocrites! You clean the outside of cup and dish and leave the inside full of extortion and intemperance. 26 Blind Pharisee! Clean the inside of cup and dish first so that it and the outside are both clean.

27 'Alas for you, scribes and Pharisees, you hypocrites! You are like whitewashed tombs that look handsome on the outside, but inside are full of the bones of the dead and every kind of corruption. 28 In just the same way, from the outside you look upright, but inside you are full of hypocrisy and lawlessness.

29 'Alas for you, scribes and Pharisees, you hypocrites! You build the sepulchres of the prophets and decorate the tombs of the upright, 30 saying, "We would never have joined in shedding the blood of the prophets, had we lived in our ancestors' day." 31 So! Your own evidence tells against you! You are the children of those who murdered the prophets! 32 Very well then, finish off the work that your ancestors began.

33 'You serpents, brood of vipers, how can you escape being condemned to hell? 34 This is why — look — I am sending you prophets and wise men and scribes; some you will slaughter and crucify, some you will scourge in your synagogues and hunt from town to town; 35 and so you will

---

23, 14: Some manuscripts add a verse here or after v 12, "Woe to you, scribes and Pharisees, you hypocrites. You devour the houses of widows and, as a pretext, recite lengthy prayers. Because of this, you will receive a very severe condemnation."

p 23 Some authorities add v. 14, taken from Mk 12:40.

NEW REVISED STANDARD VERSION | REVISED ENGLISH BIBLE

the righteous blood shed on earth, from the blood of righteous Abel to the blood of Zechariah son of Barachiah, whom you murdered between the sanctuary and the altar. 36 Truly I tell you, all this will come upon this generation.

37 "Jerusalem, Jerusalem, the city that kills the prophets and stones those who are sent to it! How often have I desired to gather your children together as a hen gathers her brood under her wings, and you were not willing! 38 See, your house is left to you, desolate.*t* 39 For I tell you, you will not see me again until you say, 'Blessed is the one who comes in the name of the Lord.'"

24 As Jesus came out of the temple and was going away, his disciples came to point out to him the buildings of the temple. 2 Then he asked them, "You see all these, do you not? Truly I tell you, not one stone will be left here upon another; all will be thrown down."

3 When he was sitting on the Mount of Olives, the disciples came to him privately, saying, "Tell us, when will this be, and what will be the sign of your coming and of the end of the age?" 4 Jesus answered them, "Beware that no one leads you astray. 5 For many will come in my name, saying, 'I am the Messiah!'*u* and they will lead many astray. 6 And you will hear of wars and rumors of wars; see that you are not alarmed; for this must take place, but the end is not yet. 7 For nation will rise against nation, and kingdom against kingdom, and there will be famines*v* and earthquakes in various places: 8 all this is but the beginning of the birth pangs.

9 "Then they will hand you over to be tortured and will put you to death, and you will be hated by all nations because of my name. 10 Then many will fall away,*w* and they will betray one another and hate one another. 11 And many false prophets will arise and lead many astray. 12 And because of the increase of lawlessness, the love of many will grow cold. 13 But the one who endures to the end will be saved. 14 And this good news*x* of the kingdom will be proclaimed throughout the world, as a testimony to all the nations; and then the end will come.

15 "So when you see the desolating sacrilege standing in the holy place, as was spoken of by the prophet Daniel (let the reader understand), 16 then those in Judea must flee to the mountains; 17 the one on the housetop must not go down to take what is in the house; 18 the one in the field must not turn back to get a coat. 19 Woe to those who are pregnant and to those who are nursing infants in those days! 20 Pray that your flight may not be in winter or on a sabbath. 21 For at that time there will be great suffering, such as has not been from the beginning of the world until now, no, and never will be. 22 And if those days had not been cut short, no one would be saved; but for the sake of the elect those days will be cut short. 23 Then if anyone says to you, 'Look! Here is the Messiah!'*u* or 'There he is!'—do not believe it. 24 For false messiahs*y* and false prophets will appear and produce great signs and omens, to lead astray, if possible, even the elect. 25 Take note, I have told you beforehand. 26 So, if they say to you, 'Look! He is in the wilderness,' do not go out. If they say, 'Look! He is in the inner rooms,' do not believe it. 27 For as the lightning comes from the east and flashes as far as the west, so will be the coming of the

---

blood spilt on the ground, from the blood of innocent Abel to the blood of Zechariah son of Berachiah, whom you murdered between the sanctuary and the altar. 36 Truly I tell you: this generation will bear the guilt of it all.

37 'O Jerusalem, Jerusalem, city that murders the prophets and stones the messengers sent to her! How often have I longed to gather your children, as a hen gathers her brood under her wings; but you would not let me. 38 Look! There is your temple, forsaken by God and laid waste. 39 I tell you, you will not see me until the time when you say, "Blessed is he who comes in the name of the Lord!" '

24 JESUS left the temple and was walking away when his disciples came and pointed to the temple buildings. 2 He answered, 'Yes, look at it all. Truly I tell you: not one stone will be left upon another; they will all be thrown down.'

3 As he sat on the mount of Olives the disciples came to speak to him privately. 'Tell us,' they said, 'when will this happen? And what will be the sign of your coming and the end of the age?'

4 Jesus replied: 'Take care that no one misleads you. 5 For many will come claiming my name and saying, "I am the Messiah," and many will be misled by them. 6 The time is coming when you will hear of wars and rumours of wars. See that you are not alarmed. Such things are bound to happen; but the end is still to come. 7 For nation will go to war against nation, kingdom against kingdom; there will be famines and earthquakes in many places. 8 All these things are the first birth-pangs of the new age.

9 'You will then be handed over for punishment and execution; all nations will hate you for your allegiance to me. 10 At that time many will fall from their faith; they will betray one another and hate one another. 11 Many false prophets will arise, and will mislead many; 12 and as lawlessness spreads, the love of many will grow cold. 13 But whoever endures to the end will be saved. 14 And this gospel of the kingdom will be proclaimed throughout the earth as a testimony to all nations; and then the end will come.

15 'So when you see "the abomination of desolation", of which the prophet Daniel spoke, standing in the holy place (let the reader understand), 16 then those who are in Judaea must take to the hills. 17 If anyone is on the roof, he must not go down to fetch his goods from the house; 18 if anyone is in the field, he must not turn back for his coat. 19 Alas for women with child in those days, and for those who have children at the breast! 20 Pray that it may not be winter or a sabbath when you have to make your escape. 21 It will be a time of great distress, such as there has never been before since the beginning of the world, and will never be again. 22 If that time of troubles were not cut short, no living thing could survive; but for the sake of God's chosen it will be cut short.

23 'If anyone says to you then, "Look, here is the Messiah," or "There he is," do not believe it. 24 Impostors will come claiming to be messiahs or prophets, and they will produce great signs and wonders to mislead, if possible, even God's chosen. 25 See, I have forewarned you. 26 If therefore they tell you, "He is there in the wilderness," do not go out; or if they say, "He is there in the inner room," do not believe it. 27 Like a lightning-flash, that lights the sky from east to west, will be the coming of the Son of Man.

---

t Other ancient authorities lack *desolate*   *u* Or *the Christ*   *v* Other ancient authorities add *and pestilences*   *w* Or *stumble*   *x* Or *gospel*   *y* Or *christs*

23:38 *Some witnesses omit* and laid waste.

blood shed upon earth, from the righteous blood of Abel to the blood of Zechariah, the son of Barachiah, whom you murdered between the sanctuary and the altar. 36 Amen, I say to you, all these things will come upon this generation.

37 "Jerusalem, Jerusalem, you who kill the prophets and stone those sent to you, how many times I yearned to gather your children together, as a hen gathers her young under her wings, but you were unwilling! 38 Behold, your house will be abandoned, desolate. 39 I tell you, you will not see me again until you say, 'Blessed is he who comes in the name of the Lord.' "

24 Jesus left the temple area and was going away, when his disciples approached him to point out the temple buildings. 2 He said to them in reply, "You see all these things, do you not? Amen, I say to you, there will not be left here a stone upon another stone that will not be thrown down."

3 As he was sitting on the Mount of Olives, the disciples approached him privately and said, "Tell us, when will this happen, and what sign will there be of your coming, and of the end of the age?" 4 Jesus said to them in reply, "See that no one deceives you. 5 For many will come in my name, saying, 'I am the Messiah,' and they will deceive many. 6 You will hear of wars and reports of wars; see that you are not alarmed, for these things must happen, but it will not yet be the end. 7 Nation will rise against nation, and kingdom against kingdom; there will be famines and earthquakes from place to place. 8 All these are the beginning of the labor pains. 9 Then they will hand you over to persecution, and they will kill you. You will be hated by all nations because of my name. 10 And then many will be led into sin; they will betray and hate one another. 11 Many false prophets will arise and deceive many; 12 and because of the increase of evildoing, the love of many will grow cold. 13 But the one who perseveres to the end will be saved. 14 And this gospel of the kingdom will be preached throughout the world as a witness to all nations, and then the end will come.

15 "When you see the desolating abomination spoken of through Daniel the prophet standing in the holy place (let the reader understand), 16 then those in Judea must flee to the mountains, 17 a person on the housetop must not go down to get things out of his house, 18 a person in the field must not return to get his cloak. 19 Woe to pregnant women and nursing mothers in those days. 20 Pray that your flight not be in winter or on the sabbath, 21 for at that time there will be great tribulation, such as has not been since the beginning of the world until now, nor ever will be. 22 And if those days had not been shortened, no one would be saved; but for the sake of the elect they will be shortened. 23 If anyone says to you then, 'Look, here is the Messiah!' or, 'There he is!' do not believe it. 24 False messiahs and false prophets will arise, and they will perform signs and wonders so great as to deceive, if that were possible, even the elect. 25 Behold, I have told it to you beforehand. 26 So if they say to you, 'He is in the desert,' do not go out there; if they say, 'He is in the inner rooms,' do not believe it. 27 For just as lightning comes from the east and is seen as far as the west, so will the coming of the Son of Man be.

draw down on yourselves the blood of every upright person that has been shed on earth, from the blood of Abel the holy to the blood of Zechariah son of Barachiah whom you murdered between the sanctuary and the altar. 36 In truth I tell you, it will all recoil on this generation.

37 'Jerusalem, Jerusalem, you that kill the prophets and stone those who are sent to you! How often have I longed to gather your children together, as a hen gathers her chicks under her wings, and you refused! 38 Look! Your house will be deserted, 39 for, I promise, you shall not see me any more until you are saying:

> *Blessed is he who is coming in the name of the Lord!'* q

24 r Jesus left the Temple, and as he was going away his disciples came up to draw his attention to the Temple buildings. 2 He said to them in reply, 'You see all these? In truth I tell you, not a single stone here will be left on another: everything will be pulled down.' 3 And while he was sitting on the Mount of Olives the disciples came and asked him when they were by themselves, 'Tell us, when is this going to happen, and what sign will there be of your coming and of the end of the world?'

4 And Jesus answered them, 'Take care that no one deceives you, 5 because many will come using my name and saying, "I am the Christ," and they will deceive many. 6 You will hear of wars and rumours of wars; see that you are not alarmed, for this is something that must happen, but the end will not be yet. 7 For nation will fight against nation, and kingdom against kingdom. There will be famines and earthquakes in various places. 8 All this is only the beginning of the birthpangs.

9 'Then you will be handed over to be tortured and put to death; and you will be hated by all nations on account of my name. 10 And then many will fall away; people will betray one another and hate one another. 11 Many false prophets will arise; they will deceive many, 12 and with the increase of lawlessness, love in most people will grow cold; 13 but anyone who stands firm to the end will be saved.

14 'This good news of the kingdom will be proclaimed to the whole world as evidence to the nations. And then the end will come.

15 'So when you see *the appalling abomination,* s of which the prophet Daniel spoke, set up in the holy place (let the reader understand), 16 then those in Judaea must escape to the mountains; 17 if anyone is on the housetop, he must not come down to collect his belongings from the house; 18 if anyone is in the fields, he must not turn back to fetch his cloak. 19 Alas for those with child, or with babies at the breast, when those days come! 20 Pray that you will not have to make your escape in winter or on a Sabbath. 21 For then there will be *great distress, unparalleled since t* the world began, and such as will never be again. 22 And if that time had not been shortened, no human being would have survived; but shortened that time shall be, for the sake of those who are chosen.

23 'If anyone says to you then, "Look, here is the Christ," or "Over here," do not believe it; 24 for false Christs and false prophets will arise and provide great signs and portents, enough to deceive even the elect, if that were possible. 25 Look! I have given you warning.

26 'If, then, they say to you, "Look, he is in the desert," do not go there; "Look, he is in some hiding place," do not believe it; 27 because the coming of the Son of man will be like lightning striking in the east and flashing far into the

q 23 Ps 118:26.　r 24 In this discourse on the future of Christ's community, Mt links the destruction of Jerusalem in AD 70 to the final coming of Christ.　s 24 Dn 9:27; 11:31; 12:11.　t 24 Dn 12:1.

NEW REVISED STANDARD VERSION	REVISED ENGLISH BIBLE

Son of Man. 28 Wherever the corpse is, there the vultures will gather.

29 "Immediately after the suffering of those days
the sun will be darkened,
and the moon will not give its light;
the stars will fall from heaven,
and the powers of heaven will be shaken.
30 Then the sign of the Son of Man will appear in heaven, and then all the tribes of the earth will mourn, and they will see 'the Son of Man coming on the clouds of heaven' with power and great glory. 31 And he will send out his angels with a loud trumpet call, and they will gather his elect from the four winds, from one end of heaven to the other.

32 "From the fig tree learn its lesson: as soon as its branch becomes tender and puts forth its leaves, you know that summer is near. 33 So also, when you see all these things, you know that he z is near, at the very gates. 34 Truly I tell you, this generation will not pass away until all these things have taken place. 35 Heaven and earth will pass away, but my words will not pass away.

36 "But about that day and hour no one knows, neither the angels of heaven, nor the Son, a but only the Father. 37 For as the days of Noah were, so will be the coming of the Son of Man. 38 For as in those days before the flood they were eating and drinking, marrying and giving in marriage, until the day Noah entered the ark, 39 and they knew nothing until the flood came and swept them all away, so too will be the coming of the Son of Man. 40 Then two will be in the field; one will be taken and one will be left. 41 Two women will be grinding meal together; one will be taken and one will be left. 42 Keep awake therefore, for you do not know on what day b your Lord is coming. 43 But understand this: if the owner of the house had known in what part of the night the thief was coming, he would have stayed awake and would not have let his house be broken into. 44 Therefore you also must be ready, for the Son of Man is coming at an unexpected hour.

45 "Who then is the faithful and wise slave, whom his master has put in charge of his household, to give the other slaves c their allowance of food at the proper time? 46 Blessed is that slave whom his master will find at work when he arrives. 47 Truly I tell you, he will put that one in charge of all his possessions. 48 But if that wicked slave says to himself, 'My master is delayed,' 49 and he begins to beat his fellow slaves, and eats and drinks with drunkards, 50 the master of that slave will come on a day when he does not expect him and at an hour that he does not know. 51 He will cut him in pieces d and put him with the hypocrites, where there will be weeping and gnashing of teeth.

25 "Then the kingdom of heaven will be like this. Ten bridesmaids e took their lamps and went to meet the bridegroom. f 2 Five of them were foolish, and five were wise. 3 When the foolish took their lamps, they took no oil with them; 4 but the wise took flasks of oil with their lamps. 5 As the bridegroom was delayed, all of them became drowsy and slept. 6 But at midnight there was a shout, 'Look! Here is the bridegroom! Come out to meet him.' 7 Then all those bridesmaids e got up and trimmed their lamps. 8 The foolish said to the wise, 'Give us some of your oil, for our lamps are going out.' 9 But the wise replied, 'No! there will not be enough for you and for us; you had better go to the dealers and buy some for yourselves.'

28 'Wherever the carcass is, there will the vultures gather.
29 'As soon as that time of distress has passed,

the sun will be darkened,
the moon will not give her light;
the stars will fall from the sky,
the celestial powers will be shaken.

30 'Then will appear in heaven the sign that heralds the Son of Man. All the peoples of the world will make lamentation, and they will see the Son of Man coming on the clouds of heaven with power and great glory. 31 With a trumpet-blast he will send out his angels, and they will gather his chosen from the four winds, from the farthest bounds of heaven on every side.

32 'Learn a lesson from the fig tree. When its tender shoots appear and are breaking into leaf, you know that summer is near. 33 In the same way, when you see all these things, you may know that the end is near, at the very door. 34 Truly I tell you: the present generation will live to see it all. 35 Heaven and earth will pass away, but my words will never pass away.

36 'Yet about that day and hour no one knows, not even the angels in heaven, not even the Son; no one but the Father alone.

37 'As it was in the days of Noah, so will it be when the Son of Man comes. 38 In the days before the flood they ate and drank and married, until the day that Noah went into the ark, 39 and they knew nothing until the flood came and swept them all away. That is how it will be when the Son of Man comes. 40 Then there will be two men in the field: one will be taken, the other left; 41 two women grinding at the mill: one will be taken, the other left.

42 'Keep awake, then, for you do not know on what day your Lord will come. 43 Remember, if the householder had known at what time of night the burglar was coming, he would have stayed awake and not let his house be broken into. 44 Hold yourselves ready, therefore, because the Son of Man will come at the time you least expect him.

45 'Who is the faithful and wise servant, charged by his master to manage his household and supply them with food at the proper time? 46 Happy that servant if his master comes home and finds him at work! 47 Truly I tell you: he will be put in charge of all his master's property. 48 But if he is a bad servant and says to himself, "The master is a long time coming," 49 and begins to bully the other servants and to eat and drink with his drunken friends, 50 then the master will arrive on a day when the servant does not expect him, at a time he has not been told. 51 He will cut him in pieces and assign him a place among the hypocrites, where there is wailing and grinding of teeth.

25 'When the day comes, the kingdom of Heaven will be like this. There were ten girls, who took their lamps and went out to meet the bridegroom. 2 Five of them were foolish, and five prudent; 3 when the foolish ones took their lamps, they took no oil with them, 4 but the others took flasks of oil with their lamps. 5 As the bridegroom was a long time in coming, they all dozed off to sleep. 6 But at midnight there came a shout: "Here is the bridegroom! Come out to meet him." 7 Then the girls all got up and trimmed their lamps. 8 The foolish said to the prudent, "Our lamps are going out; give us some of your oil." 9 "No," they answered; "there will never be enough for all of us. You had better go to the dealers and buy some for yourselves."

---

z Or it   a Other ancient authorities lack nor the Son   b Other ancient authorities read at what hour   c Gk to give them   d Or cut him off   e Gk virgins   f Other ancient authorities add and the bride

24:33 that . . . near: or that he is near.

28 Wherever the corpse is, there the vultures will gather. 29 "Immediately after the tribulation of those days,

the sun will be darkened,
and the moon will not give its light,
and the stars will fall from the sky,
and the powers of the heavens will be shaken.

30 And then the sign of the Son of Man will appear in heaven, and all the tribes of the earth will mourn, and they will see the Son of Man coming upon the clouds of heaven with power and great glory. 31 And he will send out his angels with a trumpet blast, and they will gather his elect from the four winds, from one end of the heavens to the other.

32 "Learn a lesson from the fig tree. When its branch becomes tender and sprouts leaves, you know that summer is near. 33 In the same way, when you see all these things, know that he is near, at the gates. 34 Amen, I say to you, this generation will not pass away until all these things have taken place. 35 Heaven and earth will pass away, but my words will not pass away.

36 "But of that day and hour no one knows, neither the angels of heaven, nor the Son, but the Father alone. 37 For as it was in the days of Noah, so it will be at the coming of the Son of Man. 38 In [those] days before the flood, they were eating and drinking, marrying and giving in marriage, up to the day that Noah entered the ark. 39 They did not know until the flood came and carried them all away. So will it be [also] at the coming of the Son of Man. 40 Two men will be out in the field; one will be taken, and one will be left. 41 Two women will be grinding at the mill; one will be taken, and one will be left. 42 Therefore, stay awake! For you do not know on which day your Lord will come. 43 Be sure of this: if the master of the house had known the hour of night when the thief was coming, he would have stayed awake and not let his house be broken into. 44 So too, you also must be prepared, for at an hour you do not expect, the Son of Man will come.

45 "Who, then, is the faithful and prudent servant, whom the master has put in charge of his household to distribute to them their food at the proper time? 46 Blessed is that servant whom his master on his arrival finds doing so. 47 Amen, I say to you, he will put him in charge of all his property. 48 But if that wicked servant says to himself, 'My master is long delayed,' 49 and begins to beat his fellow servants, and eat and drink with drunkards, 50 the servant's master will come on an unexpected day and at an unknown hour 51 and will punish him severely and assign him a place with the hypocrites, where there will be wailing and grinding of teeth.

25 "Then the kingdom of heaven will be like ten virgins who took their lamps and went out to meet the bridegroom. 2 Five of them were foolish and five were wise. 3 The foolish ones, when taking their lamps, brought no oil with them, 4 but the wise brought flasks of oil with their lamps. 5 Since the bridegroom was long delayed, they all became drowsy and fell asleep. 6 At midnight, there was a cry, 'Behold, the bridegroom! Come out to meet him!' 7 Then all those virgins got up and trimmed their lamps. 8 The foolish ones said to the wise, 'Give us some of your oil, for our lamps are going out.' 9 But the wise ones replied, 'No, for there may not be enough for us and you. Go instead to the merchants and buy some for yourselves.'

west. 28 Wherever the corpse is, that is where the vultures will gather.

29 'Immediately after the distress of those days the sun will be darkened,ᵘ the moon will not give its light, the stars will fall from the sky and the powers of the heavens will be shaken. 30 And then the sign of the Son of man will appear in heaven; then, too, all the peoples of the earth will beat their breasts; and they will see the *Son of man coming on the clouds of heaven* with power and great glory.ᵛ 31 And he will send his angels with a loud trumpet to gather his elect from the four winds, from one end of heaven to the other.

32 'Take the fig tree as a parable: as soon as its twigs grow supple and its leaves come out, you know that summer is near. 33 So with you when you see all these things: know that he is near, right at the gates. 34 In truth I tell you, before this generation has passed away, all these things will have taken place. 35 Sky and earth will pass away, but my words will never pass away. 36 But as for that day and hour, nobody knows it, neither the angels of heaven, nor the Son, no one but the Father alone.

37 'As it was in Noah's day, so will it be when the Son of man comes. 38 For in those days before the Flood people were eating, drinking, taking wives, taking husbands, right up to the day Noah went into the ark,ʷ 39 and they suspected nothing till the Flood came and swept them all away. This is what it will be like when the Son of man comes. 40 Then of two men in the fields, one is taken, one left; 41 of two women grinding at the mill, one is taken, one left.

42 'So stay awake, because you do not know the day when your master is coming. 43 You may be quite sure of this, that if the householder had known at what time of the night the burglar would come, he would have stayed awake and would not have allowed anyone to break through the wall of his house. 44 Therefore, you too must stand ready because the Son of man is coming at an hour you do not expect.

45 'Who, then, is the wise and trustworthy servant whom the master placed over his household to give them their food at the proper time? 46 Blessed that servant if his master's arrival finds him doing exactly that. 47 In truth I tell you, he will put him in charge of everything he owns. 48 But if the servant is dishonest and says to himself, "My master is taking his time," 49 and sets about beating his fellow-servants and eating and drinking with drunkards, 50 his master will come on a day he does not expect and at an hour he does not know. 51 The master will cut him off and send him to the same fate as the hypocrites, where there will be weeping and grinding of teeth.'

25 'Then the kingdom of Heaven will be like this: Ten wedding attendants took their lamps and went to meet the bridegroom. 2 Five of them were foolish and five were sensible: 3 the foolish ones, though they took their lamps, took no oil with them, 4 whereas the sensible ones took flasks of oil as well as their lamps. 5 The bridegroom was late, and they all grew drowsy and fell asleep. 6 But at midnight there was a cry, "Look! The bridegroom! Go out and meet him." 7 Then all those wedding attendants woke up and trimmed their lamps, 8 and the foolish ones said to the sensible ones, "Give us some of your oil: our lamps are going out." 9 But they replied, "There may not be enough for us and for you; you had better go to those who sell it and buy some for yourselves." 10 They had gone off to buy it

| NEW REVISED STANDARD VERSION | REVISED ENGLISH BIBLE |

10 And while they went to buy it, the bridegroom came, and those who were ready went with him into the wedding banquet; and the door was shut. 11 Later the other brides-maids*g* came also, saying, 'Lord, lord, open to us.' 12 But he replied, 'Truly I tell you, I do not know you.' 13 Keep awake therefore, for you know neither the day nor the hour.*h*

14 "For it is as if a man, going on a journey, summoned his slaves and entrusted his property to them; 15 to one he gave five talents,*i* to another two, to another one, to each according to his ability. Then he went away. 16 The one who had received the five talents went off at once and traded with them, and made five more talents. 17 In the same way, the one who had the two talents made two more talents. 18 But the one who had received the one talent went off and dug a hole in the ground and hid his master's money. 19 After a long time the master of those slaves came and settled accounts with them. 20 Then the one who had received the five talents came forward, bringing five more talents, saying, 'Master, you handed over to me five talents; see, I have made five more talents.' 21 His master said to him, 'Well done, good and trustworthy slave; you have been trustworthy in a few things, I will put you in charge of many things; enter into the joy of your master.' 22 And the one with the two talents also came forward, saying, 'Master, you handed over to me two talents; see, I have made two more talents.' 23 His master said to him, 'Well done, good and trustworthy slave; you have been trustworthy in a few things, I will put you in charge of many things; enter into the joy of your master.' 24 Then the one who had received the one talent also came forward, saying, 'Master, I knew that you were a harsh man, reaping where you did not sow, and gathering where you did not scatter seed; 25 so I was afraid, and I went and hid your talent in the ground. Here you have what is yours.' 26 But his master replied, 'You wicked and lazy slave! You knew, did you, that I reap where I did not sow, and gather where I did not scatter? 27 Then you ought to have invested my money with the bankers, and on my return I would have received what was my own with interest. 28 So take the talent from him, and give it to the one with the ten talents. 29 For to all those who have, more will be given, and they will have an abundance; but from those who have nothing, even what they have will be taken away. 30 As for this worthless slave, throw him into the outer darkness, where there will be weeping and gnashing of teeth.'

31 "When the Son of Man comes in his glory, and all the angels with him, then he will sit on the throne of his glory. 32 All the nations will be gathered before him, and he will separate people one from another as a shepherd separates the sheep from the goats, 33 and he will put the sheep at his right hand and the goats at the left. 34 Then the king will say to those at his right hand, 'Come, you that are blessed by my Father, inherit the kingdom prepared for you from the foundation of the world; 35 for I was hungry and you gave me food, I was thirsty and you gave me something to drink, I was a stranger and you welcomed me, 36 I was naked and you gave me clothing, I was sick and you took care of me, I was in prison and you visited me.' 37 Then the righteous will answer him, 'Lord, when was it that we saw you hungry and gave you food, or thirsty and gave you something to drink? 38 And when was it that we saw you a stranger and welcomed you, or naked and gave you clothing? 39 And when was it that we saw you sick or in prison and visited you?' 40 And the king will answer them, 'Truly I tell you, just as you did it to one of the least of these who are members of my family,*j* you did it to me.' 41 Then he

10 While they were away the bridegroom arrived; those who were ready went in with him to the wedding banquet; and the door was shut. 11 Later the others came back. "Sir, sir, open the door for us," they cried. 12 But he answered, "Truly I tell you: I do not know you." 13 Keep awake then, for you know neither the day nor the hour.

14 'It is like a man going abroad, who called his servants and entrusted his capital to them; 15 to one he gave five bags of gold, to another two, to another one, each according to his ability. Then he left the country. 16 The man who had the five bags went at once and employed them in business, and made a profit of five bags, 17 and the man who had the two bags made two. 18 But the man who had been given one bag of gold went off and dug a hole in the ground, and hid his master's money. 19 A long time afterwards their master returned, and proceeded to settle accounts with them. 20 The man who had been given the five bags of gold came and produced the five he had made: "Master," he said, "you left five bags with me; look, I have made five more." 21 "Well done, good and faithful servant!" said the master. "You have proved trustworthy in a small matter; I will now put you in charge of something big. Come and share your master's joy." 22 The man with the two bags then came and said, "Master, you left two bags with me; look, I have made two more." 23 "Well done, good and faithful servant!" said the master. "You have proved trustworthy in a small matter; I will now put you in charge of something big. Come and share your master's joy." 24 Then the man who had been given one bag came and said, "Master, I knew you to be a hard man: you reap where you have not sown, you gather where you have not scattered; 25 so I was afraid, and I went and hid your gold in the ground. Here it is — you have what belongs to you." 26 "You worthless, lazy servant!" said the master. "You knew, did you, that I reap where I have not sown, and gather where I have not scattered? 27 Then you ought to have put my money on deposit, and on my return I should have got it back with interest. 28 Take the bag of gold from him, and give it to the one with the ten bags. 29 For everyone who has will be given more, till he has enough and to spare; and everyone who has nothing will forfeit even what he has. 30 As for the useless servant, throw him out into the dark, where there will be wailing and grinding of teeth!"

31 'When the Son of Man comes in his glory and all the angels with him, he will sit on his glorious throne, 32 with all the nations gathered before him. He will separate people into two groups, as a shepherd separates the sheep from the goats; 33 he will place the sheep on his right hand and the goats on his left. 34 Then the king will say to those on his right, "You have my Father's blessing; come, take possession of the kingdom that has been ready for you since the world was made. 35 For when I was hungry, you gave me food; when thirsty, you gave me drink; when I was a stranger, you took me into your home; 36 when naked, you clothed me; when I was ill, you came to my help; when in prison, you visited me." 37 Then the righteous will reply, "Lord, when was it that we saw you hungry and fed you, or thirsty and gave you drink, 38 a stranger and took you home, or naked and clothed you? 39 When did we see you ill or in prison, and come to visit you?" 40 And the king will answer, "Truly I tell you: anything you did for one of my brothers here, however insignificant, you did for me." 41 Then he

g Gk *virgins*   *h* Other ancient authorities add *in which the Son of Man is coming*   *i* A talent was worth more than fifteen years' wages of a laborer   *j* Gk *these my brothers*

NEW AMERICAN BIBLE

10 While they went off to buy it, the bridegroom came and those who were ready went into the wedding feast with him. Then the door was locked. 11 Afterwards the other virgins came and said, 'Lord, Lord, open the door for us!' 12 But he said in reply, 'Amen, I say to you, I do not know you.' 13 Therefore, stay awake, for you know neither the day nor the hour.

14 "It will be as when a man who was going on a journey called in his servants and entrusted his possessions to them. 15 To one he gave five talents; to another, two; to a third, one — to each according to his ability. Then he went away. Immediately 16 the one who received five talents went and traded with them, and made another five. 17 Likewise, the one who received two made another two. 18 But the man who received one went off and dug a hole in the ground and buried his master's money. 19 After a long time the master of those servants came back and settled accounts with them. 20 The one who had received five talents came forward bringing the additional five. He said, 'Master, you gave me five talents. See, I have made five more.' 21 His master said to him, 'Well done, my good and faithful servant. Since you were faithful in small matters, I will give you great responsibilities. Come, share your master's joy.' 22 [Then] the one who had received two talents also came forward and said, 'Master, you gave me two talents. See, I have made two more.' 23 His master said to him, 'Well done, my good and faithful servant. Since you were faithful in small matters, I will give you great responsibilities. Come, share your master's joy.' 24 Then the one who had received the one talent came forward and said, 'Master, I knew you were a demanding person, harvesting where you did not plant and gathering where you did not scatter; 25 so out of fear I went off and buried your talent in the ground. Here it is back.' 26 His master said to him in reply, 'You wicked, lazy servant! So you knew that I harvest where I did not plant and gather where I did not scatter? 27 Should you not then have put my money in the bank so that I could have got it back with interest on my return? 28 Now then! Take the talent from him and give it to the one with ten. 29 For to everyone who has, more will be given and he will grow rich; but from the one who has not, even what he has will be taken away. 30 And throw this useless servant into the darkness outside, where there will be wailing and grinding of teeth.'

31 "When the Son of Man comes in his glory, and all the angels with him, he will sit upon his glorious throne, 32 and all the nations will be assembled before him. And he will separate them one from another, as a shepherd separates the sheep from the goats. 33 He will place the sheep on his right and the goats on his left. 34 Then the king will say to those on his right, 'Come, you who are blessed by my Father. Inherit the kingdom prepared for you from the foundation of the world. 35 For I was hungry and you gave me food, I was thirsty and you gave me drink, a stranger and you welcomed me, 36 naked and you clothed me, ill and you cared for me, in prison and you visited me.' 37 Then the righteous will answer him and say, 'Lord, when did we see you hungry and feed you, or thirsty and give you drink? 38 When did we see you a stranger and welcome you, or naked and clothe you? 39 When did we see you ill or in prison, and visit you?' 40 And the king will say to them in reply, 'Amen, I say to you, whatever you did for one of these least brothers of mine, you did for me.' 41 Then he will say to those on his

NEW JERUSALEM BIBLE

when the bridegroom arrived. Those who were ready went in with him to the wedding hall and the door was closed. 11 The other attendants arrived later. "Lord, Lord," they said, "open the door for us." 12 But he replied, "In truth I tell you, I do not know you." 13 So stay awake, because you do not know either the day or the hour.

14 'It is like a man about to go abroad who summoned his servants and entrusted his property to them. 15 To one he gave five talents, to another two, to a third one, each in proportion to his ability. Then he set out on his journey. 16 The man who had received the five talents promptly went and traded with them and made five more. 17 The man who had received two made two more in the same way. 18 But the man who had received one went off and dug a hole in the ground and hid his master's money. 19 Now a long time afterwards, the master of those servants came back and went through his accounts with them. 20 The man who had received the five talents came forward bringing five more. "Sir," he said, "you entrusted me with five talents; here are five more that I have made." 21 His master said to him, "Well done, good and trustworthy servant; you have shown you are trustworthy in small things; I will trust you with greater; come and join in your master's happiness." 22 Next the man with the two talents came forward. "Sir," he said, "you entrusted me with two talents; here are two more that I have made." 23 His master said to him, "Well done, good and trustworthy servant; you have shown you are trustworthy in small things; I will trust you with greater; come and join in your master's happiness." 24 Last came forward the man who had the single talent. "Sir," said he, "I had heard you were a hard man, reaping where you had not sown and gathering where you had not scattered; 25 so I was afraid, and I went off and hid your talent in the ground. Here it is; it was yours, you have it back." 26 But his master answered him, "You wicked and lazy servant! So you knew that I reap where I have not sown and gather where I have not scattered? 27 Well then, you should have deposited my money with the bankers, and on my return I would have got my money back with interest. 28 So now, take the talent from him and give it to the man who has the ten talents. 29 For to everyone who has will be given more, and he will have more than enough; but anyone who has not, will be deprived even of what he has. 30 As for this good-for-nothing servant, throw him into the darkness outside, where there will be weeping and grinding of teeth."

31 'When the Son of man comes in his glory, escorted by all the angels, then he will take his seat on his throne of glory. 32 All nations will be assembled before him and he will separate people one from another as the shepherd separates sheep from goats. 33 He will place the sheep on his right hand and the goats on his left. 34 Then the King will say to those on his right hand, "Come, you whom my Father has blessed, take as your heritage the kingdom prepared for you since the foundation of the world. 35 For I was hungry and you gave me food, I was thirsty and you gave me drink, I was a stranger and you made me welcome, 36 lacking clothes and you clothed me, sick and you visited me, in prison and you came to see me." 37 Then the upright will say to him in reply, "Lord, when did we see you hungry and feed you, or thirsty and give you drink? 38 When did we see you a stranger and make you welcome, lacking clothes and clothe you? 39 When did we find you sick or in prison and go to see you?" 40 And the King will answer, "In truth I tell you, in so far as you did this to one of the least of these brothers of mine, you did it to me." 41 Then he will say to

NEW REVISED STANDARD VERSION

will say to those at his left hand, 'You that are accursed, depart from me into the eternal fire prepared for the devil and his angels; 42 for I was hungry and you gave me no food, I was thirsty and you gave me nothing to drink, 43 I was a stranger and you did not welcome me, naked and you did not give me clothing, sick and in prison and you did not visit me.' 44 Then they also will answer, 'Lord, when was it that we saw you hungry or thirsty or a stranger or naked or sick or in prison, and did not take care of you?' 45 Then he will answer them, 'Truly I tell you, just as you did not do it to one of the least of these, you did not do it to me.' 46 And these will go away into eternal punishment, but the righteous into eternal life."

26 When Jesus had finished saying all these things, he said to his disciples, 2 "You know that after two days the Passover is coming, and the Son of Man will be handed over to be crucified."

3 Then the chief priests and the elders of the people gathered in the palace of the high priest, who was called Caiaphas, 4 and they conspired to arrest Jesus by stealth and kill him. 5 But they said, "Not during the festival, or there may be a riot among the people."

6 Now while Jesus was at Bethany in the house of Simon the leper,^k 7 a woman came to him with an alabaster jar of very costly ointment, and she poured it on his head as he sat at the table. 8 But when the disciples saw it, they were angry and said, "Why this waste? 9 For this ointment could have been sold for a large sum, and the money given to the poor." 10 But Jesus, aware of this, said to them, "Why do you trouble the woman? She has performed a good service for me. 11 For you always have the poor with you, but you will not always have me. 12 By pouring this ointment on my body she has prepared me for burial. 13 Truly I tell you, wherever this good news^l is proclaimed in the whole world, what she has done will be told in remembrance of her."

14 Then one of the twelve, who was called Judas Iscariot, went to the chief priests 15 and said, "What will you give me if I betray him to you?" They paid him thirty pieces of silver. 16 And from that moment he began to look for an opportunity to betray him.

17 On the first day of Unleavened Bread the disciples came to Jesus, saying, "Where do you want us to make the preparations for you to eat the Passover?" 18 He said, "Go into the city to a certain man, and say to him, 'The Teacher says, My time is near; I will keep the Passover at your house with my disciples.' " 19 So the disciples did as Jesus had directed them, and they prepared the Passover meal.

20 When it was evening, he took his place with the twelve;^m 21 and while they were eating, he said, "Truly I tell you, one of you will betray me." 22 And they became greatly distressed and began to say to him one after another, "Surely not I, Lord?" 23 He answered, "The one who has dipped his hand into the bowl with me will betray me. 24 The Son of Man goes as it is written of him, but woe to that one by whom the Son of Man is betrayed! It would have been better for that one not to have been born." 25 Judas, who betrayed him, said, "Surely not I, Rabbi?" He replied, "You have said so."

26 While they were eating, Jesus took a loaf of bread, and after blessing it he broke it, gave it to the disciples, and said, "Take, eat; this is my body." 27 Then he took a cup, and after giving thanks he gave it to them, saying, "Drink from it, all of you; 28 for this is my blood of the^n covenant, which is poured out for many for the forgiveness of sins. 29 I

REVISED ENGLISH BIBLE

will say to those on his left, "A curse is on you; go from my sight to the eternal fire that is ready for the devil and his angels. 42 For when I was hungry, you gave me nothing to eat; when thirsty, nothing to drink; 43 when I was a stranger, you did not welcome me; when I was naked, you did not clothe me; when I was ill and in prison, you did not come to my help." 44 And they in their turn will reply, "Lord, when was it that we saw you hungry or thirsty or a stranger or naked or ill or in prison, and did nothing for you?" 45 And he will answer, "Truly I tell you: anything you failed to do for one of these, however insignificant, you failed to do for me." 46 And they will go away to eternal punishment, but the righteous will enter eternal life.'

26 When Jesus had finished all these discourses he said to his disciples, 2 'You know that in two days' time it will be Passover, when the Son of Man will be handed over to be crucified.'

3 Meanwhile the chief priests and the elders of the people met in the house of the high priest, Caiaphas, 4 and discussed a scheme to seize Jesus and put him to death. 5 'It must not be during the festival,' they said, 'or there may be rioting among the people.'

6 Jesus was at Bethany in the house of Simon the leper, 7 when a woman approached him with a bottle of very costly perfume; and she began to pour it over his head as he sat at table. 8 The disciples were indignant when they saw it. 'Why this waste?' they said. 9 'It could have been sold for a large sum and the money given to the poor.' 10 Jesus noticed, and said to them, 'Why make trouble for the woman? It is a fine thing she has done for me. 11 You have the poor among you always, but you will not always have me. 12 When she poured this perfume on my body it was her way of preparing me for burial. 13 Truly I tell you: wherever this gospel is proclaimed throughout the world, what she has done will be told as her memorial.'

14 Then one of the Twelve, the man called Judas Iscariot, went to the chief priests 15 and said, 'What will you give me to betray him to you?' They weighed him out thirty silver pieces. 16 From that moment he began to look for an opportunity to betray him.

17 On the first day of Unleavened Bread the disciples came and asked Jesus, 'Where would you like us to prepare the Passover for you?' 18 He told them to go to a certain man in the city with this message: 'The Teacher says, "My appointed time is near; I shall keep the Passover with my disciples at your house." ' 19 The disciples did as Jesus directed them and prepared the Passover.

20 In the evening he sat down with the twelve disciples; 21 and during supper he said, 'Truly I tell you: one of you will betray me.' 22 Greatly distressed at this, they asked him one by one, 'Surely you do not mean me, Lord?' 23 He answered, 'One who has dipped his hand into the bowl with me will betray me. 24 The Son of Man is going the way appointed for him in the scriptures; but alas for that man by whom the Son of Man is betrayed! It would be better for that man if he had never been born.' 25 Then Judas spoke, the one who was to betray him: 'Rabbi, surely you do not mean me?' Jesus replied, 'You have said it.'

26 During supper Jesus took bread, and having said the blessing he broke it and gave it to the disciples with the words: 'Take this and eat; this is my body.' 27 Then he took a cup, and having offered thanks to God he gave it to them with the words: 'Drink from it, all of you. 28 For this is my blood, the blood of the covenant, shed for many for the forgiveness of sins. 29 I tell you, never again shall I drink

---

^k The terms *leper* and *leprosy* can refer to several diseases
^l Or *gospel*   ^m Other ancient authorities add *disciples*   ^n Other ancient authorities add *new*

NEW AMERICAN BIBLE

NEW JERUSALEM BIBLE

left, 'Depart from me, you accursed, into the eternal fire prepared for the devil and his angels. 42 For I was hungry and you gave me no food, I was thirsty and you gave me no drink, 43 a stranger and you gave me no welcome, naked and you gave me no clothing, ill and in prison, and you did not care for me.' 44 Then they will answer and say, 'Lord, when did we see you hungry or thirsty or a stranger or naked or ill or in prison, and not minister to your needs?' 45 He will answer them, 'Amen, I say to you, what you did not do for one of these least ones, you did not do for me.' 46 And these will go off to eternal punishment, but the righteous to eternal life."

26 When Jesus finished all these words, he said to his disciples, 2 "You know that in two days' time it will be Passover, and the Son of Man will be handed over to be crucified." 3 Then the chief priests and the elders of the people assembled in the palace of the high priest, who was called Caiaphas, 4 and they consulted together to arrest Jesus by treachery and put him to death. 5 But they said, "Not during the festival, that there may not be a riot among the people."

6 Now when Jesus was in Bethany in the house of Simon the leper, 7 a woman came up to him with an alabaster jar of costly perfumed oil, and poured it on his head while he was reclining at table. 8 When the disciples saw this, they were indignant and said, "Why this waste? 9 It could have been sold for much, and the money given to the poor." 10 Since Jesus knew this, he said to them, "Why do you make trouble for the woman? She has done a good thing for me. 11 The poor you will always have with you; but you will not always have me. 12 In pouring this perfumed oil upon my body, she did it to prepare me for burial. 13 Amen, I say to you, wherever this gospel is proclaimed in the whole world, what she has done will be spoken of, in memory of her."

14 Then one of the Twelve, who was called Judas Iscariot, went to the chief priests 15 and said, "What are you willing to give me if I hand him over to you?" They paid him thirty pieces of silver, 16 and from that time on he looked for an opportunity to hand him over.

17 On the first day of the Feast of Unleavened Bread, the disciples approached Jesus and said, "Where do you want us to prepare for you to eat the Passover?" 18 He said, "Go into the city to a certain man and tell him, 'The teacher says, "My appointed time draws near; in your house I shall celebrate the Passover with my disciples." ' " 19 The disciples then did as Jesus had ordered, and prepared the Passover.

20 When it was evening, he reclined at table with the Twelve. 21 And while they were eating, he said, "Amen, I say to you, one of you will betray me." 22 Deeply distressed at this, they began to say to him one after another, "Surely it is not I, Lord?" 23 He said in reply, "He who has dipped his hand into the dish with me is the one who will betray me. 24 The Son of Man indeed goes, as it is written of him, but woe to that man by whom the Son of Man is betrayed. It would be better for that man if he had never been born." 25 Then Judas, his betrayer, said in reply, "Surely it is not I, Rabbi?" He answered, "You have said so."

26 While they were eating, Jesus took bread, said the blessing, broke it, and giving it to his disciples said, "Take and eat; this is my body." 27 Then he took a cup, gave thanks, and gave it to them, saying, "Drink from it, all of you, 28 for this is my blood of the covenant, which will be shed on behalf of many for the forgiveness of sins. 29 I tell

those on his left hand, "Go away from me, with your curse upon you, to the eternal fire prepared for the devil and his angels. 42 For I was hungry and you never gave me food, I was thirsty and you never gave me anything to drink, 43 I was a stranger and you never made me welcome, lacking clothes and you never clothed me, sick and in prison and you never visited me." 44 Then it will be their turn to ask, "Lord, when did we see you hungry or thirsty, a stranger or lacking clothes, sick or in prison, and did not come to your help?" 45 Then he will answer, "In truth I tell you, in so far as you neglected to do this to one of the least of these, you neglected to do it to me." 46 And they will go away to eternal punishment, and the upright to eternal life.'

26 Jesus had now finished all he wanted to say, and he told his disciples, 2 'It will be Passover, as you know, in two days' time, and the Son of man will be handed over to be crucified.'

3 Then the chief priests and the elders of the people assembled in the palace of the high priest, whose name was Caiaphas, 4 and made plans to arrest Jesus by some trick and have him put to death. 5 They said, however, 'It must not be during the festivities; there must be no disturbance among the people.'

6 Jesus was at Bethany in the house of Simon, a man who had suffered from a virulent skin-disease, when 7 a woman came to him with an alabaster jar of very expensive ointment, and poured it on his head as he was at table. 8 When they saw this, the disciples said indignantly, 'Why this waste? 9 This could have been sold for a high price and the money given the poor.' 10 But Jesus noticed this and said, 'Why are you upsetting the woman? What she has done for me is indeed a good work! 11 You have the poor with you always, but you will not always have me. 12 When she poured this ointment on my body, she did it to prepare me for burial. 13 In truth I tell you, wherever in all the world this gospel is proclaimed, what she has done will be told as well, in remembrance of her.'

14 Then one of the Twelve, the man called Judas Iscariot, went to the chief priests 15 and said, 'What are you prepared to give me if I hand him over to you?' They paid him thirty silver pieces, 16 and from then onwards he began to look for an opportunity to betray him.

17 Now on the first day of Unleavened Bread the disciples came to Jesus to say, 'Where do you want us to make the preparations for you to eat the Passover?' 18 He said, 'Go to a certain man in the city and say to him, "The Master says: My time is near. It is at your house that I am keeping Passover with my disciples." ' 19 The disciples did what Jesus told them and prepared the Passover.

20 When evening came he was at table with the Twelve. 21 And while they were eating he said, 'In truth I tell you, one of you is about to betray me.' 22 They were greatly distressed and started asking him in turn, 'Not me, Lord, surely?' 23 He answered, 'Someone who has dipped his hand into the dish with me will betray me. 24 The Son of man is going to his fate, as the scriptures say he will, but alas for that man by whom the Son of man is betrayed! Better for that man if he had never been born!' 25 Judas, who was to betray him, asked in his turn, 'Not me, Rabbi, surely?' Jesus answered, 'It is you who say it.'

26 Now as they were eating, Jesus took bread, and when he had said the blessing he broke it and gave it to the disciples. 'Take it and eat,' he said, 'this is my body.' 27 Then he took a cup, and when he had given thanks he handed it to them saying, 'Drink from this, all of you, 28 for this is my blood, the blood of the covenant, poured out for many for the forgiveness of sins. 29 From now on, I tell you,

NEW REVISED STANDARD VERSION

tell you, I will never again drink of this fruit of the vine until that day when I drink it new with you in my Father's kingdom."

30 When they had sung the hymn, they went out to the Mount of Olives.

31 Then Jesus said to them, "You will all become deserters because of me this night; for it is written,

'I will strike the shepherd,
and the sheep of the flock will be scattered.'

32 But after I am raised up, I will go ahead of you to Galilee." 33 Peter said to him, "Though all become deserters because of you, I will never desert you." 34 Jesus said to him, "Truly I tell you, this very night, before the cock crows, you will deny me three times." 35 Peter said to him, "Even though I must die with you, I will not deny you." And so said all the disciples.

36 Then Jesus went with them to a place called Gethsemane; and he said to his disciples, "Sit here while I go over there and pray." 37 He took with him Peter and the two sons of Zebedee, and began to be grieved and agitated. 38 Then he said to them, "I am deeply grieved, even to death; remain here, and stay awake with me." 39 And going a little farther, he threw himself on the ground and prayed, "My Father, if it is possible, let this cup pass from me; yet not what I want but what you want." 40 Then he came to the disciples and found them sleeping; and he said to Peter, "So, could you not stay awake with me one hour? 41 Stay awake and pray that you may not come into the time of trial;*o* the spirit indeed is willing, but the flesh is weak." 42 Again he went away for the second time and prayed, "My Father, if this cannot pass unless I drink it, your will be done." 43 Again he came and found them sleeping, for their eyes were heavy. 44 So leaving them again, he went away and prayed for the third time, saying the same words. 45 Then he came to the disciples and said to them, "Are you still sleeping and taking your rest? See, the hour is at hand, and the Son of Man is betrayed into the hands of sinners. 46 Get up, let us be going. See, my betrayer is at hand."

47 While he was still speaking, Judas, one of the twelve, arrived; with him was a large crowd with swords and clubs, from the chief priests and the elders of the people. 48 Now the betrayer had given them a sign, saying, "The one I will kiss is the man; arrest him." 49 At once he came up to Jesus and said, "Greetings, Rabbi!" and kissed him. 50 Jesus said to him, "Friend, do what you are here to do." Then they came and laid hands on Jesus and arrested him. 51 Suddenly, one of those with Jesus put his hand on his sword, drew it, and struck the slave of the high priest, cutting off his ear. 52 Then Jesus said to him, "Put your sword back into its place; for all who take the sword will perish by the sword. 53 Do you think that I cannot appeal to my Father, and he will at once send me more than twelve legions of angels? 54 But how then would the scriptures be fulfilled, which say it must happen in this way?" 55 At that hour Jesus said to the crowds, "Have you come out with swords and clubs to arrest me as though I were a bandit? Day after day I sat in the temple teaching, and you did not arrest me. 56 But all this has taken place, so that the scriptures of the prophets may be fulfilled." Then all the disciples deserted him and fled.

57 Those who had arrested Jesus took him to Caiaphas the high priest, in whose house the scribes and the elders had gathered. 58 But Peter was following him at a distance, as far as the courtyard of the high priest; and going inside, he sat with the guards in order to see how this would end.

REVISED ENGLISH BIBLE

from this fruit of the vine until that day when I drink it new with you in the kingdom of my Father.'

30 After singing the Passover hymn, they went out to the mount of Olives. 31 Then Jesus said to them, 'Tonight you will all lose faith because of me; for it is written: "I will strike the shepherd and the sheep of his flock will be scattered." 32 But after I am raised, I shall go ahead of you into Galilee.' 33 Peter replied, 'Everyone else may lose faith because of you, but I never will.' 34 Jesus said to him, 'Truly I tell you: tonight before the cock crows you will disown me three times.' 35 Peter said, 'Even if I have to die with you, I will never disown you.' And all the disciples said the same.

36 Jesus then came with his disciples to a place called Gethsemane, and he said to them, 'Sit here while I go over there to pray.' 37 He took with him Peter and the two sons of Zebedee. Distress and anguish overwhelmed him, 38 and he said to them, 'My heart is ready to break with grief. Stop here, and stay awake with me.' 39 Then he went on a little farther, threw himself down, and prayed, 'My Father, if it is possible, let this cup pass me by. Yet not my will but yours.'

40 He came back to the disciples and found them asleep; and he said to Peter, 'What! Could none of you stay awake with me for one hour? 41 Stay awake, and pray that you may be spared the test. The spirit is willing, but the flesh is weak.'

42 He went away a second time and prayed: 'My Father, if it is not possible for this cup to pass me by without my drinking it, your will be done.' 43 He came again and found them asleep, for their eyes were heavy. 44 So he left them and went away again and prayed a third time, using the same words as before.

45 Then he came to the disciples and said to them, 'Still asleep? Still resting? The hour has come! The Son of Man is betrayed into the hands of sinners. 46 Up, let us go! The traitor is upon us.'

47 He was still speaking when Judas, one of the Twelve, appeared, and with him a great crowd armed with swords and cudgels, sent by the chief priests and the elders of the nation. 48 The traitor had given them this sign: 'The one I kiss is your man; seize him.' 49 Going straight up to Jesus, he said, 'Hail, Rabbi!' and kissed him. 50 Jesus replied, 'Friend, do what you are here to do.' Then they came forward, seized Jesus, and held him fast.

51 At that moment one of those with Jesus reached for his sword and drew it, and struck the high priest's servant, cutting off his ear. 52 But Jesus said to him, 'Put up your sword. All who take the sword die by the sword. 53 Do you suppose that I cannot appeal for help to my Father, and at once be sent more than twelve legions of angels? 54 But how then would the scriptures be fulfilled, which say that this must happen?'

55 Then Jesus spoke to the crowd: 'Do you take me for a bandit, that you have come out with swords and cudgels to arrest me? Day after day I sat teaching in the temple, and you did not lay hands on me. 56 But this has all happened to fulfil what the prophets wrote.'

Then the disciples all deserted him and ran away.

57 Jesus was led away under arrest to the house of Caiaphas the high priest, where the scribes and elders were assembled. 58 Peter followed him at a distance till he came to the high priest's courtyard; he went in and sat down among the attendants, to see how it would all end.

---

o Or into temptation

you, from now on I shall not drink this fruit of the vine until the day when I drink it with you new in the kingdom of my Father." 30 Then, after singing a hymn, they went out to the Mount of Olives.

31 Then Jesus said to them, "This night all of you will have your faith in me shaken, for it is written:

'I will strike the shepherd,
    and the sheep of the flock will be dispersed';

32 but after I have been raised up, I shall go before you to Galilee." 33 Peter said to him in reply, "Though all may have their faith in you shaken, mine will never be." 34 Jesus said to him, "Amen, I say to you, this very night before the cock crows, you will deny me three times." 35 Peter said to him, "Even though I should have to die with you, I will not deny you." And all the disciples spoke likewise.

36 Then Jesus came with them to a place called Gethsemane, and he said to his disciples, "Sit here while I go over there and pray." 37 He took along Peter and the two sons of Zebedee, and began to feel sorrow and distress. 38 Then he said to them, "My soul is sorrowful even to death. Remain here and keep watch with me." 39 He advanced a little and fell prostrate in prayer, saying, "My Father, if it is possible, let this cup pass from me; yet, not as I will, but as you will." 40 When he returned to his disciples he found them asleep. He said to Peter, "So you could not keep watch with me for one hour? 41 Watch and pray that you may not undergo the test. The spirit is willing, but the flesh is weak." 42 Withdrawing a second time, he prayed again, "My Father, if it is not possible that this cup pass without my drinking it, your will be done!" 43 Then he returned once more and found them asleep, for they could not keep their eyes open. 44 He left them and withdrew again and prayed a third time, saying the same thing again. 45 Then he returned to his disciples and said to them, "Are you still sleeping and taking your rest? Behold, the hour is at hand when the Son of Man is to be handed over to sinners. 46 Get up, let us go. Look, my betrayer is at hand."

47 While he was still speaking, Judas, one of the Twelve, arrived, accompanied by a large crowd, with swords and clubs, who had come from the chief priests and the elders of the people. 48 His betrayer had arranged a sign with them, saying, "The man I shall kiss is the one; arrest him." 49 Immediately he went over to Jesus and said, "Hail, Rabbi!" and he kissed him. 50 Jesus answered him, "Friend, do what you have come for." Then stepping forward they laid hands on Jesus and arrested him. 51 And behold, one of those who accompanied Jesus put his hand to his sword, drew it, and struck the high priest's servant, cutting off his ear. 52 Then Jesus said to him, "Put your sword back into its sheath, for all who take the sword will perish by the sword. 53 Do you think that I cannot call upon my Father and he will not provide me at this moment with more than twelve legions of angels? 54 But then how would the scriptures be fulfilled which say that it must come to pass in this way?" 55 At that hour Jesus said to the crowds, "Have you come out as against a robber, with swords and clubs to seize me? Day after day I sat teaching in the temple area, yet you did not arrest me. 56 But all this has come to pass that the writings of the prophets may be fulfilled." Then all the disciples left him and fled.

57 Those who had arrested Jesus led him away to Caiaphas the high priest, where the scribes and the elders were assembled. 58 Peter was following him at a distance as far as the high priest's courtyard, and going inside he sat down with the servants to see the outcome. 59 The chief priests

I shall never again drink wine until the day I drink the new wine with you in the kingdom of my Father.'

30 After the psalms had been sung they left for the Mount of Olives. 31 Then Jesus said to them, 'You will all fall away from me tonight, for the scripture says: *I shall strike the shepherd and the sheep of the flock will be scattered,*x 32 but after my resurrection I shall go ahead of you to Galilee.' 33 At this, Peter said to him, 'Even if all fall away from you, I will never fall away.' 34 Jesus answered him, 'In truth I tell you, this very night, before the cock crows, you will have disowned me three times.' 35 Peter said to him, 'Even if I have to die with you, I will never disown you.' And all the disciples said the same.

36 Then Jesus came with them to a plot of land called Gethsemane; and he said to his disciples, 'Stay here while I go over there to pray.' 37 He took Peter and the two sons of Zebedee with him. And he began to feel sadness and anguish. 38 Then he said to them, 'My soul is sorrowful to the point of death. Wait here and stay awake with me.' 39 And going on a little further he fell on his face and prayed. 'My Father,' he said, 'if it is possible, let this cup pass me by. Nevertheless, let it be as you, not I, would have it.' 40 He came back to the disciples and found them sleeping, and he said to Peter, 'So you had not the strength to stay awake with me for one hour? 41 Stay awake, and pray not to be put to the test. The spirit is willing enough, but human nature is weak.' 42 Again, a second time, he went away and prayed: 'My Father,' he said, 'if this cup cannot pass by, but I must drink it, your will be done!'y 43 And he came back again and found them sleeping, their eyes were so heavy. 44 Leaving them there, he went away again and prayed for the third time, repeating the same words. 45 Then he came back to the disciples and said to them, 'You can sleep on now and have your rest. Look, the hour has come when the Son of man is to be betrayed into the hands of sinners. 46 Get up! Let us go! Look, my betrayer is not far away.'

47 And suddenly while he was still speaking, Judas, one of the Twelve, appeared, and with him a large number of men armed with swords and clubs, sent by the chief priests and elders of the people. 48 Now the traitor had arranged a sign with them saying, 'The one I kiss, he is the man. Arrest him.' 49 So he went up to Jesus at once and said, 'Greetings, Rabbi,' and kissed him. 50 Jesus said to him, 'My friend, do what you are here for.' Then they came forward, seized Jesus and arrested him. 51 And suddenly, one of the followers of Jesus grasped his sword and drew it; he struck the high priest's servant and cut off his ear. 52 Jesus then said, 'Put your sword back, for all who draw the sword will die by the sword. 53 Or do you think that I cannot appeal to my Father, who would promptly send more than twelve legions of angels to my defence? 54 But then, how would the scriptures be fulfilled that say this is the way it must be?' 55 It was at this time that Jesus said to the crowds, 'Am I a bandit, that you had to set out to capture me with swords and clubs? I sat teaching in the Temple day after day and you never laid a hand on me.' 56 Now all this happened to fulfil the prophecies in scripture. Then all the disciples deserted him and ran away.

57 The men who had arrested Jesus led him off to the house of Caiaphas the high priest, where the scribes and the elders were assembled. 58 Peter followed him at a distance right to the high priest's palace, and he went in and sat down with the attendants to see what the end would be.

x **26** Zc 13:7.   y **26** = 6:10.

NEW REVISED STANDARD VERSION

59 Now the chief priests and the whole council were looking for false testimony against Jesus so that they might put him to death, 60 but they found none, though many false witnesses came forward. At last two came forward 61 and said, "This fellow said, 'I am able to destroy the temple of God and to build it in three days.' " 62 The high priest stood up and said, "Have you no answer? What is it that they testify against you?" 63 But Jesus was silent. Then the high priest said to him, "I put you under oath before the living God, tell us if you are the Messiah,p the Son of God." 64 Jesus said to him, "You have said so. But I tell you,

From now on you will see the Son of Man
    seated at the right hand of Power
    and coming on the clouds of heaven."

65 Then the high priest tore his clothes and said, "He has blasphemed! Why do we still need witnesses? You have now heard his blasphemy. 66 What is your verdict?" They answered, "He deserves death." 67 Then they spat in his face and struck him; and some slapped him, 68 saying, "Prophesy to us, you Messiah!p Who is it that struck you?"

69 Now Peter was sitting outside in the courtyard. A servant-girl came to him and said, "You also were with Jesus the Galilean." 70 But he denied it before all of them, saying, "I do not know what you are talking about." 71 When he went out to the porch, another servant-girl saw him, and she said to the bystanders, "This man was with Jesus of Nazareth."q 72 Again he denied it with an oath, "I do not know the man." 73 After a little while the bystanders came up and said to Peter, "Certainly you are also one of them, for your accent betrays you." 74 Then he began to curse, and he swore an oath, "I do not know the man!" At that moment the cock crowed. 75 Then Peter remembered what Jesus had said: "Before the cock crows, you will deny me three times." And he went out and wept bitterly.

27 When morning came, all the chief priests and the elders of the people conferred together against Jesus in order to bring about his death. 2 They bound him, led him away, and handed him over to Pilate the governor.

3 When Judas, his betrayer, saw that Jesusr was condemned, he repented and brought back the thirty pieces of silver to the chief priests and the elders. 4 He said, "I have sinned by betraying innocents blood." But they said, "What is that to us? See to it yourself." 5 Throwing down the pieces of silver in the temple, he departed; and he went and hanged himself. 6 But the chief priests, taking the pieces of silver, said, "It is not lawful to put them into the treasury, since they are blood money." 7 After conferring together, they used them to buy the potter's field as a place to bury foreigners. 8 For this reason that field has been called the Field of Blood to this day. 9 Then was fulfilled what had been spoken through the prophet Jeremiah,t "And they tooku the thirty pieces of silver, the price of the one on whom a price had been set,v on whom some of the people of Israel had set a price, 10 and they gavew them for the potter's field, as the Lord commanded me."

11 Now Jesus stood before the governor; and the governor asked him, "Are you the King of the Jews?" Jesus said, "You say so." 12 But when he was accused by the chief priests and elders, he did not answer. 13 Then Pilate said to him, "Do you not hear how many accusations they make against you?" 14 But he gave him no answer, not even to a single charge, so that the governor was greatly amazed.

REVISED ENGLISH BIBLE

59 The chief priests and the whole Council tried to find some allegation against Jesus that would warrant a death sentence; 60 but they failed to find one, though many came forward with false evidence. Finally two men 61 alleged that he had said, 'I can pull down the temple of God, and rebuild it in three days.' 62 At this the high priest rose and said to him, 'Have you no answer to the accusations that these witnesses bring against you?' 63 But Jesus remained silent. The high priest then said, 'By the living God I charge you to tell us: are you the Messiah, the Son of God?' 64 Jesus replied, 'The words are yours. But I tell you this: from now on you will see the Son of Man seated at the right hand of the Almighty and coming on the clouds of heaven.' 65 At these words the high priest tore his robes and exclaimed, 'This is blasphemy! Do we need further witnesses? You have just heard the blasphemy. 66 What is your verdict?' 'He is guilty,' they answered; 'he should die.'

67 Then they spat in his face and struck him with their fists; some said, as they beat him, 68 'Now, Messiah, if you are a prophet, tell us who hit you.'

69 Meanwhile Peter was sitting outside in the courtyard when a servant-girl accosted him; 'You were with Jesus the Galilean,' she said. 70 Peter denied it in front of them all. 'I do not know what you are talking about,' he said. 71 He then went out to the gateway, where another girl, seeing him, said to the people there, 'He was with Jesus of Nazareth.' 72 Once again he denied it, saying with an oath, 'I do not know the man.' 73 Shortly afterwards the bystanders came up and said to Peter, 'You must be one of them; your accent gives you away!' 74 At this he started to curse and declared with an oath: 'I do not know the man.' At that moment a cock crowed; 75 and Peter remembered how Jesus had said, 'Before the cock crows you will disown me three times.' And he went outside, and wept bitterly.

27 When morning came, the chief priests and the elders of the nation all met together to plan the death of Jesus. 2 They bound him and led him away, to hand him over to Pilate, the Roman governor.

3 When Judas the traitor saw that Jesus had been condemned, he was seized with remorse, and returned the thirty silver pieces to the chief priests and elders. 4 'I have sinned,' he said; 'I have brought an innocent man to his death.' But they said, 'What is that to us? It is your concern.' 5 So he threw the money down in the temple and left; he went away and hanged himself.

6 The chief priests took up the money, but they said, 'This cannot be put into the temple fund; it is blood-money.' 7 So after conferring they used it to buy the Potter's Field, as a burial-place for foreigners. 8 This explains the name Blood Acre, by which that field has been known ever since; 9 and in this way fulfilment was given to the saying of the prophet Jeremiah: 'They took the thirty silver pieces, the price set on a man's head (for that was his price among the Israelites), 10 and gave the money for the potter's field, as the Lord directed me.'

11 Jesus was now brought before the governor; 'Are you the king of the Jews?' the governor asked him. 'The words are yours,' said Jesus; 12 and when the chief priests and elders brought charges against him he made no reply. 13 Then Pilate said to him, 'Do you not hear all this evidence they are bringing against you?' 14 but to the governor's great astonishment he refused to answer a single word.

---

p Or Christ   q Gk the Nazorean   r Gk he   s Other ancient authorities read righteous   t Other ancient authorities read Zechariah or Isaiah   u Or I took   v Or the price of the precious One   w Other ancient authorities read I gave

26:64 **The words are yours:** or It is as you say.   27:9 **They took:** or I took.   27:11 **The words are yours:** or It is as you say.

NEW AMERICAN BIBLE | NEW JERUSALEM BIBLE

and the entire Sanhedrin kept trying to obtain false testimony against Jesus in order to put him to death, 60 but they found none, though many false witnesses came forward. Finally two came forward 61 who stated, "This man said, 'I can destroy the temple of God and within three days rebuild it.' " 62 The high priest rose and addressed him, "Have you no answer? What are these men testifying against you?" 63 But Jesus was silent. Then the high priest said to him, "I order you to tell us under oath before the living God whether you are the Messiah, the Son of God." 64 Jesus said to him in reply, "You have said so. But I tell you:

> From now on you will see 'the Son of Man
> seated at the right hand of the Power'
> and 'coming on the clouds of heaven.' "

65 Then the high priest tore his robes and said, "He has blasphemed! What further need have we of witnesses? You have now heard the blasphemy; 66 what is your opinion?" They said in reply, "He deserves to die!" 67 Then they spat in his face and struck him, while some slapped him, 68 saying, "Prophesy for us, Messiah: who is it that struck you?"

69 Now Peter was sitting outside in the courtyard. One of the maids came over to him and said, "You too were with Jesus the Galilean." 70 But he denied it in front of everyone, saying, "I do not know what you are talking about!" 71 As he went out to the gate, another girl saw him and said to those who were there, "This man was with Jesus the Nazorean." 72 Again he denied it with an oath, "I do not know the man!" 73 A little later the bystanders came over and said to Peter, "Surely you too are one of them; even your speech gives you away." 74 At that he began to curse and to swear, "I do not know the man." And immediately a cock crowed. 75 Then Peter remembered the word that Jesus had spoken: "Before the cock crows you will deny me three times." He went out and began to weep bitterly.

27 When it was morning, all the chief priests and the elders of the people took counsel against Jesus to put him to death. 2 They bound him, led him away, and handed him over to Pilate, the governor.

3 Then Judas, his betrayer, seeing that Jesus had been condemned, deeply regretted what he had done. He returned the thirty pieces of silver to the chief priests and elders, 4 saying, "I have sinned in betraying innocent blood." They said, "What is that to us? Look to it yourself." 5 Flinging the money into the temple, he departed and went off and hanged himself. 6 The chief priests gathered up the money, but said, "It is not lawful to deposit this in the temple treasury, for it is the price of blood." 7 After consultation, they used it to buy the potter's field as a burial place for foreigners. 8 That is why that field even today is called the Field of Blood. 9 Then was fulfilled what had been said through Jeremiah the prophet, "And they took the thirty pieces of silver, the value of a man with a price on his head, a price set by some of the Israelites, 10 and they paid it out for the potter's field just as the Lord had commanded me."

11 Now Jesus stood before the governor, and he questioned him, "Are you the king of the Jews?" Jesus said, "You say so." 12 And when he was accused by the chief priests and elders, he made no answer. 13 Then Pilate said to him, "Do you not hear how many things they are testifying against you?" 14 But he did not answer him one word, so that the governor was greatly amazed.

59 The chief priests and the whole Sanhedrin z were looking for evidence against Jesus, however false, on which they might have him executed. 60 But they could not find any, though several lying witnesses came forward. Eventually two came forward 61 and made a statement, 'This man said, "I have power to destroy the Temple of God and in three days build it up." ' 62 The high priest then rose and said to him, 'Have you no answer to that? What is this evidence these men are bringing against you?' 63 But Jesus was silent. And the high priest said to him, 'I put you on oath by the living God to tell us if you are the Christ, the Son of God.' 64 Jesus answered him, 'It is you who say it. But, I tell you that from this time onward you will see the *Son of man seated at the right hand of the Power* and *coming on the clouds of heaven.'a* 65 Then the high priest tore his clothes and said, 'He has blasphemed. What need of witnesses have we now? There! You have just heard the blasphemy. 66 What is your opinion?' They answered, 'He deserves to die.'

67 Then they spat in his face and hit him with their fists; others said as they struck him, 68 'Prophesy to us, Christ! Who hit you then?'

69 Meanwhile Peter was sitting outside in the courtyard, and a servant-girl came up to him saying, 'You, too, were with Jesus the Galilean.' 70 But he denied it in front of them all. 'I do not know what you are talking about,' he said. 71 When he went out to the gateway another servant-girl saw him and said to the people there, 'This man was with Jesus the Nazarene.' 72 And again, with an oath, he denied it, 'I do not know the man.' 73 A little later the bystanders came up and said to Peter, 'You are certainly one of them too! Why, your accentb gives you away.' 74 Then he started cursing and swearing, 'I do not know the man.' And at once the cock crowed, 75 and Peter remembered what Jesus had said, 'Before the cock crows you will have disowned me three times.' And he went outside and wept bitterly.

27 When morning came, all the chief priests and the elders of the people met in council to bring about the death of Jesus. 2 They had him bound and led him away to hand him over to Pilate, the governor.

3 When he found that Jesus had been condemned, then Judas, his betrayer, was filled with remorse and took the thirty silver pieces back to the chief priests and elders 4 saying, 'I have sinned. I have betrayed innocent blood.' They replied, 'What is that to us? That is your concern.' 5 And flinging down the silver pieces in the sanctuary he made off, and went and hanged himself. 6 The chief priests picked up the silver pieces and said, 'It is against the Law to put this into the treasury; it is blood-money.' 7 So they discussed the matter and with it bought the potter's field as a graveyard for foreigners, 8 and this is why the field is still called the Field of Blood. 9 The word spoken through the prophet Jeremiah was then fulfilled: *And they took the thirty silver pieces, the sum at which the precious One was priced by the children of Israel,* 10 *and they gave them for the potter's field, just as the Lord directed me.c*

11 Jesus, then, was brought before the governor, and the governor put to him this question, 'Are you the king of the Jews?' Jesus replied, 'It is you who say it.' 12 But when he was accused by the chief priests and the elders he refused to answer at all. 13 Pilate then said to him, 'Do you not hear how many charges they have made against you?' 14 But to the governor's amazement, he offered not a word in answer to any of the charges.

---

z **26** The gospels differ: Lk and Jn mention an interrogation at night and a Sanhedrin session in the morning. Mt and Mk place this morning session in the night.   a **26** Ps 110:1 and Dn 7:13.
b **26** Presumably Galileans had a local accent.   c **27** Zc 11:12–13.

NEW REVISED STANDARD VERSION

15 Now at the festival the governor was accustomed to release a prisoner for the crowd, anyone whom they wanted. 16 At that time they had a notorious prisoner, called Jesus[x] Barabbas. 17 So after they had gathered, Pilate said to them, "Whom do you want me to release for you, Jesus[x] Barabbas or Jesus who is called the Messiah?"[y] 18 For he realized that it was out of jealousy that they had handed him over. 19 While he was sitting on the judgment seat, his wife sent word to him, "Have nothing to do with that innocent man, for today I have suffered a great deal because of a dream about him." 20 Now the chief priests and the elders persuaded the crowds to ask for Barabbas and to have Jesus killed. 21 The governor again said to them, "Which of the two do you want me to release for you?" And they said, "Barabbas." 22 Pilate said to them, "Then what should I do with Jesus who is called the Messiah?"[y] All of them said, "Let him be crucified!" 23 Then he asked, "Why, what evil has he done?" But they shouted all the more, "Let him be crucified!"

24 So when Pilate saw that he could do nothing, but rather that a riot was beginning, he took some water and washed his hands before the crowd, saying, "I am innocent of this man's blood;[z] see to it yourselves." 25 Then the people as a whole answered, "His blood be on us and on our children!" 26 So he released Barabbas for them; and after flogging Jesus, he handed him over to be crucified.

27 Then the soldiers of the governor took Jesus into the governor's headquarters,[a] and they gathered the whole cohort around him. 28 They stripped him and put a scarlet robe on him, 29 and after twisting some thorns into a crown, they put it on his head. They put a reed in his right hand and knelt before him and mocked him, saying, "Hail, King of the Jews!" 30 They spat on him, and took the reed and struck him on the head. 31 After mocking him, they stripped him of the robe and put his own clothes on him. Then they led him away to crucify him.

32 As they went out, they came upon a man from Cyrene named Simon; they compelled this man to carry his cross. 33 And when they came to a place called Golgotha (which means Place of a Skull), 34 they offered him wine to drink, mixed with gall; but when he tasted it, he would not drink it. 35 And when they had crucified him, they divided his clothes among themselves by casting lots;[b] 36 then they sat down there and kept watch over him. 37 Over his head they put the charge against him, which read, "This is Jesus, the King of the Jews."

38 Then two bandits were crucified with him, one on his right and one on his left. 39 Those who passed by derided[c] him, shaking their heads 40 and saying, "You who would destroy the temple and build it in three days, save yourself! If you are the Son of God, come down from the cross." 41 In the same way the chief priests also, along with the scribes and elders, were mocking him, saying, 42 "He saved others; he cannot save himself.[d] He is the King of Israel; let him come down from the cross now, and we will believe in him. 43 He trusts in God; let God deliver him now, if he wants to; for he said, 'I am God's Son.'" 44 The bandits who were crucified with him also taunted him in the same way.

45 From noon on, darkness came over the whole land[e] until three in the afternoon. 46 And about three o'clock Jesus cried with a loud voice, "Eli, Eli, lema sabachthani?" that is, "My God, my God, why have you forsaken me?"

REVISED ENGLISH BIBLE

15 At the festival season it was customary for the governor to release one prisoner chosen by the people. 16 There was then in custody a man of some notoriety, called Jesus Barabbas. 17 When the people assembled Pilate said to them, 'Which would you like me to release to you—Jesus Barabbas, or Jesus called Messiah?' 18 For he knew it was out of malice that Jesus had been handed over to him.

19 While Pilate was sitting in court a message came to him from his wife: 'Have nothing to do with that innocent man; I was much troubled on his account in my dreams last night.'

20 Meanwhile the chief priests and elders had persuaded the crowd to ask for the release of Barabbas and to have Jesus put to death. 21 So when the governor asked, 'Which of the two would you like me to release to you?' they said, 'Barabbas.' 22 'Then what am I to do with Jesus called Messiah?' asked Pilate; and with one voice they answered, 'Crucify him!' 23 'Why, what harm has he done?' asked Pilate; but they shouted all the louder, 'Crucify him!'

24 When Pilate saw that he was getting nowhere, and that there was danger of a riot, he took water and washed his hands in full view of the crowd. 'My hands are clean of this man's blood,' he declared. 'See to that yourselves.' 25 With one voice the people cried, 'His blood be on us and on our children.' 26 He then released Barabbas to them; but he had Jesus flogged, and then handed him over to be crucified.

27 Then the soldiers of the governor took Jesus into his residence, the Praetorium, where they collected the whole company round him. 28 They stripped him and dressed him in a scarlet cloak; 29 and plaiting a crown of thorns they placed it on his head, and a stick in his right hand. Falling on their knees before him they jeered at him: 'Hail, king of the Jews!' 30 They spat on him, and used the stick to beat him about the head. 31 When they had finished mocking him, they stripped off the cloak and dressed him in his own clothes.

Then they led him away to be crucified. 32 On their way out they met a man from Cyrene, Simon by name, and pressed him into service to carry his cross.

33 Coming to a place called Golgotha (which means 'Place of a Skull'), 34 they offered him a drink of wine mixed with gall; but after tasting it he would not drink. 35 When they had crucified him they shared out his clothes by casting lots, 36 and then sat down there to keep watch. 37 Above his head was placed the inscription giving the charge against him: 'This is Jesus, the king of the Jews.' 38 Two bandits were crucified with him, one on his right and the other on his left.

39 The passers-by wagged their heads and jeered at him, 40 crying, 'So you are the man who was to pull down the temple and rebuild it in three days! If you really are the Son of God, save yourself and come down from the cross.' 41 The chief priests with the scribes and elders joined in the mockery: 42 'He saved others,' they said, 'but he cannot save himself. King of Israel, indeed! Let him come down now from the cross, and then we shall believe him. 43 He trusted in God, did he? Let God rescue him, if he wants him—for he said he was God's Son.' 44 Even the bandits who were crucified with him taunted him in the same way.

45 From midday a darkness fell over the whole land, which lasted until three in the afternoon; 46 and about three Jesus cried aloud, 'Eli, Eli, lema sabachthani?' which means, 'My God, my God, why have you forsaken me?'

---

[x] Other ancient authorities lack *Jesus*   [y] Or *the Christ*   [z] Other ancient authorities read *this righteous blood,* or *this righteous man's blood*   [a] Gk *the praetorium*   [b] Other ancient authorities add *in order that what had been spoken through the prophet might be fulfilled, "They divided my clothes among themselves, and for my clothing they cast lots."*   [c] Or *blasphemed*   [d] Or *is he unable to save himself?*   [e] Or *earth*

27:16,17 **Jesus Barabbas:** *many witnesses omit* Jesus *in both verses.*

NEW AMERICAN BIBLE

15 Now on the occasion of the feast the governor was accustomed to release to the crowd one prisoner whom they wished. 16 And at that time they had a notorious prisoner called [Jesus] Barabbas. 17 So when they had assembled, Pilate said to them, "Which one do you want me to release to you, [Jesus] Barabbas, or Jesus called Messiah?" 18 For he knew that it was out of envy that they had handed him over. 19 While he was still seated on the bench, his wife sent him a message, "Have nothing to do with that righteous man. I suffered much in a dream today because of him." 20 The chief priests and the elders persuaded the crowds to ask for Barabbas but to destroy Jesus. 21 The governor said to them in reply, "Which of the two do you want me to release to you?" They answered, "Barabbas!" 22 Pilate said to them, "Then what shall I do with Jesus called Messiah?" They all said, "Let him be crucified!" 23 But he said, "Why? What evil has he done?" They only shouted the louder, "Let him be crucified!" 24 When Pilate saw that he was not succeeding at all, but that a riot was breaking out instead, he took water and washed his hands in the sight of the crowd, saying, "I am innocent of this man's blood. Look to it yourselves." 25 And the whole people said in reply, "His blood be upon us and upon our children." 26 Then he released Barabbas to them, but after he had Jesus scourged, he handed him over to be crucified.

27 Then the soldiers of the governor took Jesus inside the praetorium and gathered the whole cohort around him. 28 They stripped off his clothes and threw a scarlet military cloak about him. 29 Weaving a crown out of thorns, they placed it on his head, and a reed in his right hand. And kneeling before him, they mocked him, saying, "Hail, King of the Jews!" 30 They spat upon him and took the reed and kept striking him on the head. 31 And when they had mocked him, they stripped him of the cloak, dressed him in his own clothes, and led him off to crucify him.

32 As they were going out, they met a Cyrenian named Simon; this man they pressed into service to carry his cross.

33 And when they came to a place called Golgotha (which means Place of the Skull), 34 they gave Jesus wine to drink mixed with gall. But when he had tasted it, he refused to drink. 35 After they had crucified him, they divided his garments by casting lots; 36 then they sat down and kept watch over him there. 37 And they placed over his head the written charge against him: This is Jesus, the King of the Jews. 38 Two revolutionaries were crucified with him, one on his right and the other on his left. 39 Those passing by reviled him, shaking their heads 40 and saying, "You who would destroy the temple and rebuild it in three days, save yourself, if you are the Son of God, [and] come down from the cross!" 41 Likewise the chief priests with the scribes and elders mocked him and said, 42 "He saved others; he cannot save himself. So he is the king of Israel! Let him come down from the cross now, and we will believe in him. 43 He trusted in God; let him deliver him now if he wants him. For he said, 'I am the Son of God.' " 44 The revolutionaries who were crucified with him also kept abusing him in the same way.

45 From noon onward, darkness came over the whole land until three in the afternoon. 46 And about three o'clock Jesus cried out in a loud voice, "Eli, Eli, lema sabachthani?" which means, "My God, my God, why have you forsaken

NEW JERUSALEM BIBLE

15 At festival time it was the governor's practice to release a prisoner for the people, anyone they chose. 16 Now there was then a notorious prisoner whose name was Barabbas. 17 So when the crowd gathered, Pilate said to them, 'Which do you want me to release for you: Barabbas, or Jesus who is called Christ?' 18 For Pilate knew it was out of jealousy that they had handed him over.

19 Now as he was seated in the chair of judgement, his wife sent him a message, 'Have nothing to do with that upright man; I have been extremely upset today by a dream that I had about him.'

20 The chief priests and the elders, however, had persuaded the crowd to demand the release of Barabbas and the execution of Jesus. 21 So when the governor spoke and asked them, 'Which of the two do you want me to release for you?' they said, 'Barabbas.' 22 Pilate said to them, 'But in that case, what am I to do with Jesus who is called Christ?' They all said, 'Let him be crucified!' 23 He asked, 'But what harm has he done?' But they shouted all the louder, 'Let him be crucified!' 24 Then Pilate saw that he was making no impression, that in fact a riot was imminent. So he took some water, washed his hands in front of the crowd and said, 'I am innocent of this man's blood. It is your concern.' 25 And the people, every one of them, shouted back, 'Let his blood be on us and on our children!' 26 Then he released Barabbas for them. After having Jesus scourged he handed him over to be crucified.

27 Then the governor's soldiers took Jesus with them into the Praetorium and collected the whole cohort round him. 28 And they stripped him and put a scarlet cloak round him, 29 and having twisted some thorns into a crown they put this on his head and placed a reed in his right hand. To make fun of him they knelt to him saying, 'Hail, king of the Jews!' 30 And they spat on him and took the reed and struck him on the head with it. 31 And when they had finished making fun of him, they took off the cloak and dressed him in his own clothes and led him away to crucifixion.

32 On their way out, they came across a man from Cyrene, called Simon, and enlisted him to carry his cross. 33 When they had reached a place called Golgotha, that is, the place of the skull, 34 they gave him wine to drink mixed with gall, d which he tasted but refused to drink. 35 When they had finished crucifying him they shared out his clothing by casting lots, 36 and then sat down and stayed there keeping guard over him.

37 Above his head was placed the charge against him; it read: 'This is Jesus, the King of the Jews.' 38 Then two bandits were crucified with him, one on the right and one on the left.

39 The passers-by jeered at him; they shook their heads 40 and said, 'So you would destroy the Temple and in three days rebuild it! Then save yourself if you are God's son and come down from the cross!' 41 The chief priests with the scribes and elders mocked him in the same way, 42 with the words, 'He saved others; he cannot save himself. He is the king of Israel; let him come down from the cross now, and we will believe in him. 43 He has put his trust in God; now let God rescue him if he wants him. For he did say, "I am God's son." e ' 44 Even the bandits who were crucified with him taunted him in the same way.

45 From the sixth hour there was darkness over all the land until the ninth hour. 46 And about the ninth hour, Jesus cried out in a loud voice, 'Eli, eli, lama sabachthani?' that is, 'My God, my God, why have you forsaken me?' f

27, 16–17: [*Jesus*] *Barabbas:* it is possible that the double name is the original reading; *Jesus* was a common Jewish name. This reading is found in only a few textual witnesses, although its absence in the majority can be explained as an omission of *Jesus* made for reverential reasons. That name is bracketed because of its uncertain textual attestation.

d 27 cf. Ps 69:21.   e 27 cf. Ws 2:18–20.   f 27 Ps 22:1.

NEW REVISED STANDARD VERSION	REVISED ENGLISH BIBLE

47 When some of the bystanders heard it, they said, "This man is calling for Elijah." 48 At once one of them ran and got a sponge, filled it with sour wine, put it on a stick, and gave it to him to drink. 49 But the others said, "Wait, let us see whether Elijah will come to save him."*f* 50 Then Jesus cried again with a loud voice and breathed his last.*g* 51 At that moment the curtain of the temple was torn in two, from top to bottom. The earth shook, and the rocks were split. 52 The tombs also were opened, and many bodies of the saints who had fallen asleep were raised. 53 After his resurrection they came out of the tombs and entered the holy city and appeared to many. 54 Now when the centurion and those with him, who were keeping watch over Jesus, saw the earthquake and what took place, they were terrified and said, "Truly this man was God's Son!"*h*

55 Many women were also there, looking on from a distance; they had followed Jesus from Galilee and had provided for him. 56 Among them were Mary Magdalene, and Mary the mother of James and Joseph, and the mother of the sons of Zebedee.

57 When it was evening, there came a rich man from Arimathea, named Joseph, who was also a disciple of Jesus. 58 He went to Pilate and asked for the body of Jesus; then Pilate ordered it to be given to him. 59 So Joseph took the body and wrapped it in a clean linen cloth 60 and laid it in his own new tomb, which he had hewn in the rock. He then rolled a great stone to the door of the tomb and went away. 61 Mary Magdalene and the other Mary were there, sitting opposite the tomb.

62 The next day, that is, after the day of Preparation, the chief priests and the Pharisees gathered before Pilate 63 and said, "Sir, we remember what that impostor said while he was still alive, 'After three days I will rise again.' 64 Therefore command the tomb to be made secure until the third day; otherwise his disciples may come and steal him away, and tell the people, 'He has been raised from the dead,' and the last deception would be worse than the first." 65 Pilate said to them, "You have a guard*i* of soldiers; go, make it as secure as you can."*j* 66 So they went with the guard and made the tomb secure by sealing the stone.

28 After the sabbath, as the first day of the week was dawning, Mary Magdalene and the other Mary went to see the tomb. 2 And suddenly there was a great earthquake; for an angel of the Lord, descending from heaven, came and rolled back the stone and sat on it. 3 His appearance was like lightning, and his clothing white as snow. 4 For fear of him the guards shook and became like dead men. 5 But the angel said to the women, "Do not be afraid; I know that you are looking for Jesus who was crucified. 6 He is not here; for he has been raised, as he said. Come, see the place where he*k* lay. 7 Then go quickly and tell his disciples, 'He has been raised from the dead,*l* and indeed he is going ahead of you to Galilee; there you will see him.' This is my message for you." 8 So they left the tomb quickly with fear and great joy, and ran to tell his disciples. 9 Suddenly Jesus met them and said, "Greetings!" And they came to him, took hold of his feet, and worshiped him. 10 Then Jesus said to them, "Do not be afraid; go and tell my brothers to go to Galilee; there they will see me."

11 While they were going, some of the guard went into the city and told the chief priests everything that had happened. 12 After the priests*m* had assembled with the elders,

47 Hearing this, some of the bystanders said, 'He is calling Elijah.' 48 One of them ran at once and fetched a sponge, which he soaked in sour wine and held to his lips on the end of a stick. 49 But the others said, 'Let us see if Elijah will come to save him.'

50 Jesus again cried aloud and breathed his last. 51 At that moment the curtain of the temple was torn in two from top to bottom. The earth shook, rocks split, 52 and graves opened; many of God's saints were raised from sleep, 53 and coming out of their graves after his resurrection entered the Holy City, where many saw them. 54 And when the centurion and his men who were keeping watch over Jesus saw the earthquake and all that was happening, they were filled with awe and said, 'This must have been a son of God.'

55 A NUMBER of women were also present, watching from a distance; they had followed Jesus from Galilee and looked after him. 56 Among them were Mary of Magdala, Mary the mother of James and Joseph, and the mother of the sons of Zebedee.

57 When evening fell, a wealthy man from Arimathaea, Joseph by name, who had himself become a disciple of Jesus, 58 approached Pilate and asked for the body of Jesus; and Pilate gave orders that he should have it. 59 Joseph took the body, wrapped it in a clean linen sheet, 60 and laid it in his own unused tomb, which he had cut out of the rock. He then rolled a large stone against the entrance, and went away. 61 Mary of Magdala was there, and the other Mary, sitting opposite the grave.

62 Next day, the morning after the day of preparation, the chief priests and the Pharisees came in a body to Pilate. 63 'Your excellency,' they said, 'we recall how that impostor said while he was still alive, "I am to be raised again after three days." 64 We request you to give orders for the grave to be made secure until the third day. Otherwise his disciples may come and steal the body, and then tell the people that he has been raised from the dead; and the final deception will be worse than the first.' 65 'You may have a guard,' said Pilate; 'go and make the grave as secure as you can.' 66 So they went and made it secure by sealing the stone and setting a guard.

28 ABOUT daybreak on the first day of the week, when the sabbath was over, Mary of Magdala and the other Mary came to look at the grave. 2 Suddenly there was a violent earthquake; an angel of the Lord descended from heaven and came and rolled away the stone, and sat down on it. 3 His face shone like lightning; his garments were white as snow. 4 At the sight of him the guards shook with fear and fell to the ground as though dead.

5 The angel spoke to the women: 'You', he said, 'have nothing to fear. I know you are looking for Jesus who was crucified. 6 He is not here; he has been raised, as he said he would be. Come and see the place where he was laid, 7 and then go quickly and tell his disciples: "He has been raised from the dead and is going ahead of you into Galilee; there you will see him." That is what I came to tell you.'

8 They hurried away from the tomb in awe and great joy, and ran to bring the news to the disciples. 9 Suddenly Jesus was there in their path, greeting them. They came up and clasped his feet, kneeling before him. 10 'Do not be afraid,' Jesus said to them. 'Go and take word to my brothers that they are to leave for Galilee. They will see me there.'

11 While the women were on their way, some of the guard went into the city and reported to the chief priests everything that had happened. 12 After meeting and conferring

f Other ancient authorities add *And another took a spear and pierced his side, and out came water and blood*   *g* Or *gave up his spirit*
h Or *a son of God*   *i* Or *Take a guard*   *j* Gk *you know how*
k Other ancient authorities read *the Lord*   *l* Other ancient authorities lack *from the dead*   *m* Gk *they*

27:54 **a son of God:** *or* the Son of God.

me?" 47 Some of the bystanders who heard it said, "This one is calling for Elijah." 48 Immediately one of them ran to get a sponge; he soaked it in wine, and putting it on a reed, gave it to him to drink. 49 But the rest said, "Wait, let us see if Elijah comes to save him." 50 But Jesus cried out again in a loud voice, and gave up his spirit. 51 And behold, the veil of the sanctuary was torn in two from top to bottom. The earth quaked, rocks were split, 52 tombs were opened, and the bodies of many saints who had fallen asleep were raised. 53 And coming forth from their tombs after his resurrection, they entered the holy city and appeared to many. 54 The centurion and the men with him who were keeping watch over Jesus feared greatly when they saw the earthquake and all that was happening, and they said, "Truly, this was the Son of God!" 55 There were many women there, looking on from a distance, who had followed Jesus from Galilee, ministering to him. 56 Among them were Mary Magdalene and Mary the mother of James and Joseph, and the mother of the sons of Zebedee.

57 When it was evening, there came a rich man from Arimathea named Joseph, who was himself a disciple of Jesus. 58 He went to Pilate and asked for the body of Jesus; then Pilate ordered it to be handed over. 59 Taking the body, Joseph wrapped it [in] clean linen 60 and laid it in his new tomb that he had hewn in the rock. Then he rolled a huge stone across the entrance to the tomb and departed. 61 But Mary Magdalene and the other Mary remained sitting there, facing the tomb.

62 The next day, the one following the day of preparation, the chief priests and the Pharisees gathered before Pilate 63 and said, "Sir, we remember that this impostor while still alive said, 'After three days I will be raised up.' 64 Give orders, then, that the grave be secured until the third day, lest his disciples come and steal him and say to the people, 'He has been raised from the dead.' This last imposture would be worse than the first." 65 Pilate said to them, "The guard is yours; go secure it as best you can." 66 So they went and secured the tomb by fixing a seal to the stone and setting the guard.

28 After the sabbath, as the first day of the week was dawning, Mary Magdalene and the other Mary came to see the tomb. 2 And behold, there was a great earthquake; for an angel of the Lord descended from heaven, approached, rolled back the stone, and sat upon it. 3 His appearance was like lightning and his clothing was white as snow. 4 The guards were shaken with fear of him and became like dead men. 5 Then the angel said to the women in reply, "Do not be afraid! I know that you are seeking Jesus the crucified. 6 He is not here, for he has been raised just as he said. Come and see the place where he lay. 7 Then go quickly and tell his disciples, 'He has been raised from the dead, and he is going before you to Galilee; there you will see him.' Behold, I have told you." 8 Then they went away quickly from the tomb, fearful yet overjoyed, and ran to announce this to his disciples. 9 And behold, Jesus met them on their way and greeted them. They approached, embraced his feet, and did him homage. 10 Then Jesus said to them, "Do not be afraid. Go tell my brothers to go to Galilee, and there they will see me."

11 While they were going, some of the guard went into the city and told the chief priests all that had happened. 12 They

47 When some of those who stood there heard this, they said, 'The man is calling on Elijah,' 48 and one of them quickly ran to get a sponge which he filled with vinegar and, putting it on a reed, gave it to him to drink. 49 But the rest of them said, 'Wait! And see if Elijah will come to save him.' 50 But Jesus, again crying out in a loud voice, yielded up his spirit.

51 And suddenly, the veil of the Sanctuary was torn in two from top to bottom, the earth quaked, the rocks were split, 52 the tombs opened and the bodies of many holy people rose from the dead, 53 and these, after his resurrection, came out of the tombs, entered the holy city and appeared to a number of people. 54 The centurion, together with the others guarding Jesus, had seen the earthquake and all that was taking place, and they were terrified and said, 'In truth this man was son of God.'

55 And many women were there, watching from a distance, the same women who had followed Jesus from Galilee and looked after him. 56 Among them were Mary of Magdala, Mary the mother of James and Joseph, and the mother of Zebedee's sons.

57 When it was evening, there came a rich man of Arimathaea, called Joseph, who had himself become a disciple of Jesus. 58 This man went to Pilate and asked for the body of Jesus. Then Pilate ordered it to be handed over. 59 So Joseph took the body, wrapped it in a clean shroud 60 and put it in his own new tomb which he had hewn out of the rock. He then rolled a large stone across the entrance of the tomb and went away. 61 Now Mary of Magdala and the other Mary were there, sitting opposite the sepulchre.

62 Next day, that is, when Preparation Day was over, the chief priests and the Pharisees went in a body to Pilate 63 and said to him, 'Your Excellency, we recall that this impostor said, while he was still alive, "After three days I shall rise again." 64 Therefore give the order to have the sepulchre kept secure until the third day, for fear his disciples come and steal him away and tell the people, "He has risen from the dead." This last piece of fraud would be worse than what went before.' 65 Pilate said to them, 'You may have your guard; go and make all as secure as you know how.' 66 So they went and made the sepulchre secure, putting seals on the stone and mounting a guard.

28 After the Sabbath, and towards dawn on the first day of the week, Mary of Magdala and the other Mary went to visit the sepulchre. 2 And suddenly there was a violent earthquake, for an angel of the Lord, descending from heaven, came and rolled away the stone and sat on it. 3 His face was like lightning, his robe white as snow. 4 The guards were so shaken by fear of him that they were like dead men. 5 But the angel spoke; and he said to the women, 'There is no need for you to be afraid. I know you are looking for Jesus, who was crucified. 6 He is not here, for he has risen, as he said he would. Come and see the place where he lay, 7 then go quickly and tell his disciples, "He has risen from the dead and now he is going ahead of you to Galilee; that is where you will see him." Look! I have told you.' 8 Filled with awe and great joy the women came quickly away from the tomb and ran to tell his disciples.

9 And suddenly, coming to meet them, was Jesus. 'Greetings,' he said. And the women came up to him and, clasping his feet, they did him homage. 10 Then Jesus said to them, 'Do not be afraid; go and tell my brothers that they must leave for Galilee; there they will see me.'

11 Now while they were on their way, some of the guards went off into the city to tell the chief priests all that had happened. 12 These held a meeting with the elders and, after

they devised a plan to give a large sum of money to the soldiers, 13 telling them, "You must say, 'His disciples came by night and stole him away while we were asleep.' 14 If this comes to the governor's ears, we will satisfy him and keep you out of trouble." 15 So they took the money and did as they were directed. And this story is still told among the Jews to this day.

16 Now the eleven disciples went to Galilee, to the mountain to which Jesus had directed them. 17 When they saw him, they worshiped him; but some doubted. 18 And Jesus came and said to them, "All authority in heaven and on earth has been given to me. 19 Go therefore and make disciples of all nations, baptizing them in the name of the Father and of the Son and of the Holy Spirit, 20 and teaching them to obey everything that I have commanded you. And remember, I am with you always, to the end of the age."[n]

n Other ancient authorities add *Amen*

with the elders, the chief priests offered the soldiers a substantial bribe 13 and told them to say, 'His disciples came during the night and stole the body while we were asleep.' 14 They added, 'If this should reach the governor's ears, we will put matters right with him and see you do not suffer.' 15 So they took the money and did as they were told. Their story became widely known, and is current in Jewish circles to this day.

16 The eleven disciples made their way to Galilee, to the mountain where Jesus had told them to meet him. 17 When they saw him, they knelt in worship, though some were doubtful. 18 Jesus came near and said to them: 'Full authority in heaven and on earth has been committed to me. 19 Go therefore to all nations and make them my disciples; baptize them in the name of the Father and the Son and the Holy Spirit, 20 and teach them to observe all that I have commanded you. I will be with you always, to the end of time.'

assembled with the elders and took counsel; then they gave a large sum of money to the soldiers, 13 telling them, "You are to say, 'His disciples came by night and stole him while we were asleep.' 14 And if this gets to the ears of the governor, we will satisfy [him] and keep you out of trouble." 15 The soldiers took the money and did as they were instructed. And this story has circulated among the Jews to the present [day].

16 The eleven disciples went to Galilee, to the mountain to which Jesus had ordered them. 17 When they saw him, they worshiped, but they doubted. 18 Then Jesus approached and said to them, "All power in heaven and on earth has been given to me. 19 Go, therefore, and make disciples of all nations, baptizing them in the name of the Father, and of the Son, and of the holy Spirit, 20 teaching them to observe all that I have commanded you. And behold, I am with you always, until the end of the age."

some discussion, handed a considerable sum of money to the soldiers 13 with these instructions, 'This is what you must say, "His disciples came during the night and stole him away while we were asleep." 14 And should the governor come to hear of this, we undertake to put things right with him ourselves and to see that you do not get into trouble.' 15 So they took the money and carried out their instructions, and to this day that is the story among the Jews.

16 Meanwhile the eleven disciples set out for Galilee, to the mountain where Jesus had arranged to meet them. 17 When they saw him they fell down before him, though some hesitated. 18 Jesus came up and spoke to them. He said, 'All authority in heaven and on earth has been given to me. g 19 Go, therefore, make disciples of all nations; baptise them in the name of the Father and of the Son and of the Holy Spirit, 20 and teach them to observe all the commands I gave you. And look, I am with you always; yes, to the end of time.'

g 28 cf. Dn 7:14.

THE GOSPEL ACCORDING TO

Mark

THE GOSPEL ACCORDING TO

Mark

1 The beginning of the good news[a] of Jesus Christ, the Son of God.[b] 2 As it is written in the prophet Isaiah,[c]

"See, I am sending my messenger ahead of
  you,[d]
who will prepare your way;
3 the voice of one crying out in the wilderness:
'Prepare the way of the Lord,
  make his paths straight,' "

4 John the baptizer appeared[e] in the wilderness, proclaiming a baptism of repentance for the forgiveness of sins. 5 And people from the whole Judean countryside and all the people of Jerusalem were going out to him, and were baptized by him in the river Jordan, confessing their sins. 6 Now John was clothed with camel's hair, with a leather belt around his waist, and he ate locusts and wild honey. 7 He proclaimed, "The one who is more powerful than I is coming after me; I am not worthy to stoop down and untie the thong of his sandals. 8 I have baptized you with[f] water; but he will baptize you with[f] the Holy Spirit."

9 In those days Jesus came from Nazareth of Galilee and was baptized by John in the Jordan. 10 And just as he was coming up out of the water, he saw the heavens torn apart and the Spirit descending like a dove on him. 11 And a voice came from heaven, "You are my Son, the Beloved;[g] with you I am well pleased."

12 And the Spirit immediately drove him out into the wilderness. 13 He was in the wilderness forty days, tempted by Satan; and he was with the wild beasts; and the angels waited on him.

14 Now after John was arrested, Jesus came to Galilee, proclaiming the good news[a] of God,[h] 15 and saying, "The time is fulfilled, and the kingdom of God has come near;[i] repent, and believe in the good news."[a]

16 As Jesus passed along the Sea of Galilee, he saw Simon and his brother Andrew casting a net into the sea— for they were fishermen. 17 And Jesus said to them, "Follow me and I will make you fish for people." 18 And immediately they left their nets and followed him. 19 As he went a little farther, he saw James son of Zebedee and his brother John, who were in their boat mending the nets. 20 Immediately he called them; and they left their father Zebedee in the boat with the hired men, and followed him.

21 They went to Capernaum; and when the sabbath came, he entered the synagogue and taught. 22 They were astounded at his teaching, for he taught them as one having authority, and not as the scribes. 23 Just then there was in their synagogue a man with an unclean spirit, 24 and he cried out, "What have you to do with us, Jesus of Nazareth? Have you come to destroy us? I know who you are, the Holy One of God." 25 But Jesus rebuked him, saying, "Be silent, and come out of him!" 26 And the unclean spirit, convulsing him and crying with a loud voice, came out of him. 27 They were

1 THE beginning of the gospel of Jesus Christ the Son of God.

2 IN the prophet Isaiah it stands written:

I am sending my herald ahead of you;
he will prepare your way.
3 A voice cries in the wilderness,
'Prepare the way for the Lord;
clear a straight path for him.'

4 John the Baptist appeared in the wilderness proclaiming a baptism in token of repentance, for the forgiveness of sins; 5 and everyone flocked to him from the countryside of Judaea and the city of Jerusalem, and they were baptized by him in the river Jordan, confessing their sins. 6 John was dressed in a rough coat of camel's hair, with a leather belt round his waist, and he fed on locusts and wild honey. 7 He proclaimed: 'After me comes one mightier than I am, whose sandals I am not worthy to stoop down and unfasten. 8 I have baptized you with water; he will baptize you with the Holy Spirit.'

9 It was at this time that Jesus came from Nazareth in Galilee and was baptized in the Jordan by John. 10 As he was coming up out of the water, he saw the heavens break open and the Spirit descend on him, like a dove. 11 And a voice came from heaven: 'You are my beloved Son; in you I take delight.'

12 At once the Spirit drove him out into the wilderness, 13 and there he remained for forty days tempted by Satan. He was among the wild beasts; and angels attended to his needs.

14 AFTER John had been arrested, Jesus came into Galilee proclaiming the gospel of God: 15 'The time has arrived; the kingdom of God is upon you. Repent, and believe the gospel.'

16 Jesus was walking by the sea of Galilee when he saw Simon and his brother Andrew at work with casting-nets in the lake; for they were fishermen. 17 Jesus said to them, 'Come, follow me, and I will make you fishers of men.' 18 At once they left their nets and followed him.

19 Going a little farther, he saw James son of Zebedee and his brother John in a boat mending their nets. 20 At once he called them; and they left their father Zebedee in the boat with the hired men and followed him.

21 They came to Capernaum, and on the sabbath he went to the synagogue and began to teach. 22 The people were amazed at his teaching, for, unlike the scribes, he taught with a note of authority. 23 Now there was a man in their synagogue possessed by an unclean spirit. He shrieked at him: 24 'What do you want with us, Jesus of Nazareth? Have you come to destroy us? I know who you are—the Holy One of God.' 25 Jesus rebuked him: 'Be silent,' he said, 'and come out of him.' 26 The unclean spirit threw the man into convulsions and with a loud cry left him. 27 They were

---

a Or *gospel*   b Other ancient authorities lack *the Son of God*
c Other ancient authorities read *in the prophets*   d Gk *before your
face*   e Other ancient authorities read *John was baptizing*   f Or *in*
g Or *my beloved Son*   h Other ancient authorities read *of the
kingdom*   i Or *is at hand*

1:1 *Some witnesses omit* the Son of God.   1:11 **You are ... Son:**
or You are my only Son.   1:24 **Have you:** *or* You have.

THE GOSPEL ACCORDING TO
Mark

1 The beginning of the gospel of Jesus Christ [the Son of God].
² As it is written in Isaiah the prophet:

> "Behold, I am sending my messenger ahead
> of you;
> he will prepare your way.
> ³ A voice of one crying out in the desert:
> 'Prepare the way of the Lord,
> make straight his paths.' "

⁴ John [the] Baptist appeared in the desert proclaiming a baptism of repentance for the forgiveness of sins. ⁵ People of the whole Judean countryside and all the inhabitants of Jerusalem were going out to him and were being baptized by him in the Jordan River as they acknowledged their sins. ⁶ John was clothed in camel's hair, with a leather belt around his waist. He fed on locusts and wild honey. ⁷ And this is what he proclaimed: "One mightier than I is coming after me. I am not worthy to stoop and loosen the thongs of his sandals. ⁸ I have baptized you with water; he will baptize you with the holy Spirit."

⁹ It happened in those days that Jesus came from Nazareth of Galilee and was baptized in the Jordan by John. ¹⁰ On coming up out of the water he saw the heavens being torn open and the Spirit, like a dove, descending upon him. ¹¹ And a voice came from the heavens, "You are my beloved Son; with you I am well pleased."

¹² At once the Spirit drove him out into the desert, ¹³ and he remained in the desert for forty days, tempted by Satan. He was among wild beasts, and the angels ministered to him.

¹⁴ After John had been arrested, Jesus came to Galilee proclaiming the gospel of God: ¹⁵ "This is the time of fulfillment. The kingdom of God is at hand. Repent, and believe in the gospel."

¹⁶ As he passed by the Sea of Galilee, he saw Simon and his brother Andrew casting their nets into the sea; they were fishermen. ¹⁷ Jesus said to them, "Come after me, and I will make you fishers of men." ¹⁸ Then they left their nets and followed him. ¹⁹ He walked along a little farther and saw James, the son of Zebedee, and his brother John. They too were in a boat mending their nets. ²⁰ Then he called them. So they left their father Zebedee in the boat along with the hired men and followed him.

²¹ Then they came to Capernaum, and on the sabbath he entered the synagogue and taught. ²² The people were astonished at his teaching, for he taught them as one having authority and not as the scribes. ²³ In their synagogue was a man with an unclean spirit; ²⁴ he cried out, "What have you to do with us, Jesus of Nazareth? Have you come to destroy us? I know who you are — the Holy One of God!" ²⁵ Jesus rebuked him and said, "Quiet! Come out of him!" ²⁶ The unclean spirit convulsed him and with a loud cry came out of him. ²⁷ All were amazed and asked one another,

THE GOSPEL ACCORDING TO
Mark

1 The beginning of the gospel about Jesus Christ, the Son of God. ² It is written in the prophet Isaiah:

> *Look, I am going to send my messenger in front of*
> *you*
> *to prepare your way before you.*ᵃ

> ³ *A voice of one that cries in the desert:*
> *Prepare a way for the Lord,*
> *make his paths straight.*

⁴ John the Baptist was in the desert, proclaiming a baptism of repentance for the forgiveness of sins. ⁵ All Judaea and all the people of Jerusalem made their way to him, and as they were baptised by him in the river Jordan they confessed their sins. ⁶ John wore a garment of camel-skin, and he lived on locusts and wild honey. ⁷ In the course of his preaching he said, 'After me is coming someone who is more powerful than me, and I am not fit to kneel down and undo the strap of his sandals. ⁸ I have baptised you with water, but he will baptise you with the Holy Spirit.'

⁹ It was at this time that Jesus came from Nazareth in Galilee and was baptised in the Jordan by John. ¹⁰ And at once, as he was coming up out of the water, he saw the heavens torn apart and the Spirit, like a dove, descending on him. ¹¹ And a voice came from heaven, 'You are my Son, the Beloved; my favour rests on you.'

¹² And at once the Spirit drove him into the desert ¹³ and he remained there for forty days, and was put to the test by Satan. He was with the wild animals, and the angels looked after him.

¹⁴ After John had been arrested, Jesus went into Galilee. There he proclaimed the gospel from God saying, ¹⁵ 'The time is fulfilled, and the kingdom of God is close at hand. Repent, and believe the gospel.'

¹⁶ As he was walking along by the Lake of Galilee he saw Simon and Simon's brother Andrew casting a net in the lake — for they were fishermen. ¹⁷ And Jesus said to them, 'Come after me and I will make you into fishers of people.' ¹⁸ And at once they left their nets and followed him. ¹⁹ Going on a little further, he saw James son of Zebedee and his brother John; they too were in their boat, mending the nets. ²⁰ At once he called them and, leaving their father Zebedee in the boat with the men he employed, they went after him.

²¹ They went as far as Capernaum, and at once on the Sabbath he went into the synagogue and began to teach. ²² And his teaching made a deep impression on them because, unlike the scribes, he taught them with authority. ²³ And at once in their synagogue there was a man with an unclean spirit, and he shouted, ²⁴ 'What do you want with us, Jesus of Nazareth? Have you come to destroy us? I know who you are: the Holy One of God.' ²⁵ But Jesus rebuked it saying, 'Be quiet! Come out of him!' ²⁶ And the unclean spirit threw the man into convulsions and with a loud cry went out of him. ²⁷ The people were so astonished

---

1, 1: *The gospel of Jesus Christ [the Son of God]:* some important manuscripts here omit *the Son of God.*

ᵃ **1** Ml 3:1 followed by Is 40:3.

all amazed, and they kept on asking one another, "What is this? A new teaching—with authority! He *j* commands even the unclean spirits, and they obey him." 28 At once his fame began to spread throughout the surrounding region of Galilee.

29 As soon as they *k* left the synagogue, they entered the house of Simon and Andrew, with James and John. 30 Now Simon's mother-in-law was in bed with a fever, and they told him about her at once. 31 He came and took her by the hand and lifted her up. Then the fever left her, and she began to serve them.

32 That evening, at sundown, they brought to him all who were sick or possessed with demons. 33 And the whole city was gathered around the door. 34 And he cured many who were sick with various diseases, and cast out many demons; and he would not permit the demons to speak, because they knew him.

35 In the morning, while it was still very dark, he got up and went out to a deserted place, and there he prayed. 36 And Simon and his companions hunted for him. 37 When they found him, they said to him, "Everyone is searching for you." 38 He answered, "Let us go on to the neighboring towns, so that I may proclaim the message there also; for that is what I came out to do." 39 And he went throughout Galilee, proclaiming the message in their synagogues and casting out demons.

40 A leper *l* came to him begging him, and kneeling *m* he said to him, "If you choose, you can make me clean." 41 Moved with pity, *n* Jesus *o* stretched out his hand and touched him, and said to him, "I do choose. Be made clean!" 42 Immediately the leprosy *l* left him, and he was made clean. 43 After sternly warning him he sent him away at once, 44 saying to him, "See that you say nothing to anyone; but go, show yourself to the priest, and offer for your cleansing what Moses commanded, as a testimony to them." 45 But he went out and began to proclaim it freely, and to spread the word, so that Jesus *o* could no longer go into a town openly, but stayed out in the country; and people came to him from every quarter.

2 When he returned to Capernaum after some days, it was reported that he was at home. 2 So many gathered around that there was no longer room for them, not even in front of the door; and he was speaking the word to them. 3 Then some people *p* came, bringing to him a paralyzed man, carried by four of them. 4 And when they could not bring him to Jesus because of the crowd, they removed the roof above him; and after having dug through it, they let down the mat on which the paralytic lay. 5 When Jesus saw their faith, he said to the paralytic, "Son, your sins are forgiven." 6 Now some of the scribes were sitting there, questioning in their hearts, 7 "Why does this fellow speak in this way? It is blasphemy! Who can forgive sins but God alone?" 8 At once Jesus perceived in his spirit that they were discussing these questions among themselves; and he said to them, "Why do you raise such questions in your hearts? 9 Which is easier, to say to the paralytic, 'Your sins are forgiven,' or to say, 'Stand up and take your mat and walk'? 10 But so that you may know that the Son of Man has authority on earth to forgive sins"—he said to the paralytic— 11 "I say to you, stand up, take your mat and go to your home." 12 And he stood up, and immediately took the mat and went out before all of them; so that they were all amazed and glorified God, saying, "We have never seen anything like this!"

all amazed and began to ask one another, 'What is this? A new kind of teaching! He speaks with authority. When he gives orders, even the unclean spirits obey.' 28 His fame soon spread far and wide throughout Galilee.

29 On leaving the synagogue, they went straight to the house of Simon and Andrew; and James and John went with them. 30 Simon's mother-in-law was in bed with a fever. As soon as they told him about her, 31 Jesus went and took hold of her hand, and raised her to her feet. The fever left her, and she attended to their needs.

32 That evening after sunset they brought to him all who were ill or possessed by demons; 33 and the whole town was there, gathered at the door. 34 He healed many who suffered from various diseases, and drove out many demons. He would not let the demons speak, because they knew who he was.

35 Very early next morning he got up and went out. He went away to a remote spot and remained there in prayer. 36 But Simon and his companions went in search of him, 37 and when they found him, they said, 'Everybody is looking for you.' 38 He answered, 'Let us move on to the neighbouring towns, so that I can proclaim my message there as well, for that is what I came out to do.' 39 So he went through the whole of Galilee, preaching in their synagogues and driving out demons.

40 On one occasion he was approached by a leper, who knelt before him and begged for help. 'If only you will,' said the man, 'you can make me clean.' 41 Jesus was moved to anger; he stretched out his hand, touched him, and said, 'I will; be clean.' 42 The leprosy left him immediately, and he was clean. 43 Then he dismissed him with this stern warning: 44 'See that you tell nobody, but go and show yourself to the priest, and make the offering laid down by Moses for your cleansing; that will certify the cure.' 45 But the man went away and made the whole story public, spreading it far and wide, until Jesus could no longer show himself in any town. He stayed outside in remote places; yet people kept coming to him from all quarters.

2 After some days he returned to Capernaum, and news went round that he was at home; 2 and such a crowd collected that there was no room for them even in the space outside the door. While he was proclaiming the message to them, 3 a man was brought who was paralysed. Four men were carrying him, 4 but because of the crowd they could not get him near. So they made an opening in the roof over the place where Jesus was, and when they had broken through they lowered the bed on which the paralysed man was lying. 5 When he saw their faith, Jesus said to the man, 'My son, your sins are forgiven.'

6 Now there were some scribes sitting there, thinking to themselves, 7 'How can the fellow talk like that? It is blasphemy! Who but God can forgive sins?' 8 Jesus knew at once what they were thinking, and said to them, 'Why do you harbour such thoughts? 9 Is it easier to say to this paralysed man, "Your sins are forgiven," or to say, "Stand up, take your bed, and walk"? 10 But to convince you that the Son of Man has authority on earth to forgive sins'—he turned to the paralysed man—11 'I say to you, stand up, take your bed, and go home.' 12 And he got up, and at once took his bed and went out in full view of them all, so that they were astounded and praised God. 'Never before', they said, 'have we seen anything like this.'

---

j Or *A new teaching! With authority he* read *he*   *k* Other ancient authorities read *he*   *l* The terms *leper* and *leprosy* can refer to several diseases *m* Other ancient authorities lack *kneeling*   *n* Other ancient authorities read *anger*   *o* Gk *he*   *p* Gk *they*

1:41 **to anger:** *many witnesses read* with pity.

"What is this? A new teaching with authority. He commands even the unclean spirits and they obey him." 28 His fame spread everywhere throughout the whole region of Galilee.

29 On leaving the synagogue he entered the house of Simon and Andrew with James and John. 30 Simon's mother-in-law lay sick with a fever. They immediately told him about her. 31 He approached, grasped her hand, and helped her up. Then the fever left her and she waited on them. 32 When it was evening, after sunset, they brought to him all who were ill or possessed by demons. 33 The whole town was gathered at the door. 34 He cured many who were sick with various diseases, and he drove out many demons, not permitting them to speak because they knew him.

35 Rising very early before dawn, he left and went off to a deserted place, where he prayed. 36 Simon and those who were with him pursued him 37 and on finding him said, "Everyone is looking for you." 38 He told them, "Let us go on to the nearby villages that I may preach there also. For this purpose have I come." 39 So he went into their synagogues, preaching and driving out demons throughout the whole of Galilee.

40 A leper came to him [and kneeling down] begged him and said, "If you wish, you can make me clean." 41 Moved with pity, he stretched out his hand, touched him, and said to him, "I do will it. Be made clean." 42 The leprosy left him immediately, and he was made clean. 43 Then, warning him sternly, he dismissed him at once. 44 Then he said to him, "See that you tell no one anything, but go, show yourself to the priest and offer for your cleansing what Moses prescribed; that will be proof for them." 45 The man went away and began to publicize the whole matter. He spread the report abroad so that it was impossible for Jesus to enter a town openly. He remained outside in deserted places, and people kept coming to him from everywhere.

2 When Jesus returned to Capernaum after some days, it became known that he was at home. 2 Many gathered together so that there was no longer room for them, not even around the door, and he preached the word to them. 3 They came bringing to him a paralytic carried by four men. 4 Unable to get near Jesus because of the crowd, they opened up the roof above him. After they had broken through, they let down the mat on which the paralytic was lying. 5 When Jesus saw their faith, he said to the paralytic, "Child, your sins are forgiven." 6 Now some of the scribes were sitting there asking themselves, 7 "Why does this man speak that way? He is blaspheming. Who but God alone can forgive sins?" 8 Jesus immediately knew in his mind what they were thinking to themselves, so he said, "Why are you thinking such things in your hearts? 9 Which is easier, to say to the paralytic, 'Your sins are forgiven,' or to say, 'Rise, pick up your mat and walk'? 10 But that you may know that the Son of Man has authority to forgive sins on earth" — 11 he said to the paralytic, "I say to you, rise, pick up your mat, and go home." 12 He rose, picked up his mat at once, and went away in the sight of everyone. They were all astounded and glorified God, saying, "We have never seen anything like this."

that they started asking one another what it all meant, saying, 'Here is a teaching that is new, and with authority behind it: he gives orders even to unclean spirits and they obey him.' 28 And his reputation at once spread everywhere, through all the surrounding Galilean countryside.

29 And at once on leaving the synagogue, he went with James and John straight to the house of Simon and Andrew. 30 Now Simon's mother-in-law was in bed and feverish, and at once they told him about her. 31 He went in to her, took her by the hand and helped her up. And the fever left her and she began to serve them.

32 That evening, after sunset, they brought to him all who were sick and those who were possessed by devils. 33 The whole town came crowding round the door, 34 and he cured many who were sick with diseases of one kind or another; he also drove out many devils, but he would not allow them to speak, because they knew who he was.

35 In the morning, long before dawn, he got up and left the house and went off to a lonely place and prayed there. 36 Simon and his companions set out in search of him, 37 and when they found him they said, 'Everybody is looking for you.' 38 He answered, 'Let us go elsewhere, to the neighbouring country towns, so that I can proclaim the message there too, because that is why I came.' 39 And he went all through Galilee, preaching in their synagogues and driving out devils.

40 A man suffering from a virulent skin-disease came to him and pleaded on his knees saying, 'If you are willing, you can cleanse me.' 41 Feeling sorry for him, Jesus stretched out his hand, touched him and said to him, 'I am willing. Be cleansed.' 42 And at once the skin-disease left him and he was cleansed. 43 And at once Jesus sternly sent him away and said to him, 44 'Mind you tell no one anything, but go and show yourself to the priest, and make the offering for your cleansing prescribed by Moses as evidence to them.' 45 The man went away, but then started freely proclaiming and telling the story everywhere, so that Jesus could no longer go openly into any town, but stayed outside in deserted places. Even so, people from all around kept coming to him.

2 When he returned to Capernaum, some time later word went round that he was in the house; 2 and so many people collected that there was no room left, even in front of the door. He was preaching the word to them 3 when some people came bringing him a paralytic carried by four men, 4 but as they could not get the man to him through the crowd, they stripped the roof over the place where Jesus was; and when they had made an opening, they lowered the stretcher on which the paralytic lay. 5 Seeing their faith, Jesus said to the paralytic, 'My child, your sins are forgiven.' 6 Now some scribes were sitting there, and they thought to themselves, 7 'How can this man talk like that? He is being blasphemous. Who but God can forgive sins?' 8 And at once, Jesus, inwardly aware that this is what they were thinking, said to them, 'Why do you have these thoughts in your hearts? 9 Which of these is easier: to say to the paralytic, "Your sins are forgiven" or to say, "Get up, pick up your stretcher and walk"? 10 But to prove to you that the Son of man has authority to forgive sins on earth' — 11 he said to the paralytic — 'I order you: get up, pick up your stretcher, and go off home.' 12 And the man got up, and at once picked up his stretcher and walked out in front of everyone, so that they were all astonished and praised God saying, 'We have never seen anything like this.'

NEW REVISED STANDARD VERSION

13 Jesus*q* went out again beside the sea; the whole crowd gathered around him, and he taught them. 14 As he was walking along, he saw Levi son of Alphaeus sitting at the tax booth, and he said to him, "Follow me." And he got up and followed him.

15 And as he sat at dinner*r* in Levi's*s* house, many tax collectors and sinners were also sitting*t* with Jesus and his disciples — for there were many who followed him. 16 When the scribes of*u* the Pharisees saw that he was eating with sinners and tax collectors, they said to his disciples, "Why does he eat*v* with tax collectors and sinners?" 17 When Jesus heard this, he said to them, "Those who are well have no need of a physician, but those who are sick; I have come to call not the righteous but sinners."

18 Now John's disciples and the Pharisees were fasting; and people*w* came and said to him, "Why do John's disciples and the disciples of the Pharisees fast, but your disciples do not fast?" 19 Jesus said to them, "The wedding guests cannot fast while the bridegroom is with them, can they? As long as they have the bridegroom with them, they cannot fast. 20 The days will come when the bridegroom is taken away from them, and then they will fast on that day.

21 "No one sews a piece of unshrunk cloth on an old cloak; otherwise, the patch pulls away from it, the new from the old, and a worse tear is made. 22 And no one puts new wine into old wineskins; otherwise, the wine will burst the skins, and the wine is lost, and so are the skins; but one puts new wine into fresh wineskins."*x*

23 One sabbath he was going through the grainfields; and as they made their way his disciples began to pluck heads of grain. 24 The Pharisees said to him, "Look, why are they doing what is not lawful on the sabbath?" 25 And he said to them, "Have you never read what David did when he and his companions were hungry and in need of food? 26 He entered the house of God, when Abiathar was high priest, and ate the bread of the Presence, which it is not lawful for any but the priests to eat, and he gave some to his companions." 27 Then he said to them, "The sabbath was made for humankind, and not humankind for the sabbath; 28 so the Son of Man is lord even of the sabbath."

3 Again he entered the synagogue, and a man was there who had a withered hand. 2 They watched him to see whether he would cure him on the sabbath, so that they might accuse him. 3 And he said to the man who had the withered hand, "Come forward." 4 Then he said to them, "Is it lawful to do good or to do harm on the sabbath, to save life or to kill?" But they were silent. 5 He looked around at them with anger; he was grieved at their hardness of heart and said to the man, "Stretch out your hand." He stretched it out, and his hand was restored. 6 The Pharisees went out and immediately conspired with the Herodians against him, how to destroy him.

7 Jesus departed with his disciples to the sea, and a great multitude from Galilee followed him; 8 hearing all that he was doing, they came to him in great numbers from Judea, Jerusalem, Idumea, beyond the Jordan, and the region around Tyre and Sidon. 9 He told his disciples to have a boat ready for him because of the crowd, so that they would not crush him; 10 for he had cured many, so that all who had diseases pressed upon him to touch him. 11 Whenever the unclean spirits saw him, they fell down before him and shouted, "You are the Son of God!" 12 But he sternly ordered them not to make him known.

REVISED ENGLISH BIBLE

13 Once more he went out to the lakeside. All the crowd came to him there, and he taught them. 14 As he went along, he saw Levi son of Alphaeus at his seat in the custom-house, and said to him, 'Follow me'; and he rose and followed him.

15 When Jesus was having a meal in his house, many tax-collectors and sinners were seated with him and his disciples, for there were many of them among his followers. 16 Some scribes who were Pharisees, observing the company in which he was eating, said to his disciples, 'Why does he eat with tax-collectors and sinners?' 17 Hearing this, Jesus said to them, 'It is not the healthy who need a doctor, but the sick; I did not come to call the virtuous, but sinners.'

18 Once, when John's disciples and the Pharisees were keeping a fast, some people came and asked him, 'Why is it that John's disciples and the disciples of the Pharisees are fasting, but yours are not?' 19 Jesus replied, 'Can you expect the bridegroom's friends to fast while the bridegroom is with them? As long as he is with them, there can be no fasting. 20 But the time will come when the bridegroom will be taken away from them; that will be the time for them to fast.

21 'No one sews a patch of unshrunk cloth on to an old garment; if he does, the patch tears away from it, the new from the old, and leaves a bigger hole. 22 No one puts new wine into old wineskins; if he does, the wine will burst the skins, and then wine and skins are both lost. New wine goes into fresh skins.'

23 One sabbath he was going through the cornfields; and as they went along his disciples began to pluck ears of corn. 24 The Pharisees said to him, 'Why are they doing what is forbidden on the sabbath?' 25 He answered, 'Have you never read what David did when he and his men were hungry and had nothing to eat? 26 He went into the house of God, in the time of Abiathar the high priest, and ate the sacred bread, though no one but a priest is allowed to eat it, and even gave it to his men.'

27 He also said to them, 'The sabbath was made for man, not man for the sabbath: 28 so the Son of Man is lord even of the sabbath.'

3 On another occasion when he went to synagogue, there was a man in the congregation who had a withered arm; 2 and they were watching to see whether Jesus would heal him on the sabbath, so that they could bring a charge against him. 3 He said to the man with the withered arm, 'Come and stand out here.' 4 Then he turned to them: 'Is it permitted to do good or to do evil on the sabbath, to save life or to kill?' They had nothing to say; 5 and, looking round at them with anger and sorrow at their obstinate stupidity, he said to the man, 'Stretch out your arm.' He stretched it out and his arm was restored. 6 Then the Pharisees, on leaving the synagogue, at once began plotting with the men of Herod's party to bring about Jesus's death.

7 Jesus went away to the lakeside with his disciples. Great numbers from Galilee, Judaea 8 and Jerusalem, Idumaea and Transjordan, and the neighbourhood of Tyre and Sidon, heard what he was doing and came to him. 9 So he told his disciples to have a boat ready for him, to save him from being crushed by the crowd. 10 For he healed so many that the sick all came crowding round to touch him. 11 The unclean spirits too, when they saw him, would fall at his feet and cry aloud, 'You are the Son of God'; 12 but he insisted that they should not make him known.

---

q Gk *He*   *r* Gk *reclined*   *s* Gk *his*   *t* Gk *reclining*   *u* Other ancient authorities read *and*   *v* Other ancient authorities add *and drink*   *w* Gk *they*   *x* Other ancient authorities lack *but one puts new wine into fresh wineskins*

13 Once again he went out along the sea. All the crowd came to him and he taught them. 14 As he passed by, he saw Levi, son of Alphaeus, sitting at the customs post. He said to him, "Follow me." And he got up and followed him. 15 While he was at table in his house, many tax collectors and sinners sat with Jesus and his disciples; for there were many who followed him. 16 Some scribes who were Pharisees saw that he was eating with sinners and tax collectors and said to his disciples, "Why does he eat with tax collectors and sinners?" 17 Jesus heard this and said to them [that], "Those who are well do not need a physician, but the sick do. I did not come to call the righteous but sinners."

18 The disciples of John and of the Pharisees were accustomed to fast. People came to him and objected, "Why do the disciples of John and the disciples of the Pharisees fast, but your disciples do not fast?" 19 Jesus answered them, "Can the wedding guests fast while the bridegroom is with them? As long as they have the bridegroom with them they cannot fast. 20 But the days will come when the bridegroom is taken away from them, and then they will fast on that day. 21 No one sews a piece of unshrunken cloth on an old cloak. If he does, its fullness pulls away, the new from the old, and the tear gets worse. 22 Likewise, no one pours new wine into old wineskins. Otherwise, the wine will burst the skins, and both the wine and the skins are ruined. Rather, new wine is poured into fresh wineskins."

23 As he was passing through a field of grain on the sabbath, his disciples began to make a path while picking the heads of grain. 24 At this the Pharisees said to him, "Look, why are they doing what is unlawful on the sabbath?" 25 He said to them, "Have you never read what David did when he was in need and he and his companions were hungry? 26 How he went into the house of God when Abiathar was high priest and ate the bread of offering that only the priests could lawfully eat, and shared it with his companions?" 27 Then he said to them, "The sabbath was made for man, not man for the sabbath. 28 That is why the Son of Man is lord even of the sabbath."

3 Again he entered the synagogue. There was a man there who had a withered hand. 2 They watched him closely to see if he would cure him on the sabbath so that they might accuse him. 3 He said to the man with the withered hand, "Come up here before us." 4 Then he said to them, "Is it lawful to do good on the sabbath rather than to do evil, to save life rather than to destroy it?" But they remained silent. 5 Looking around at them with anger and grieved at their hardness of heart, he said to the man, "Stretch out your hand." He stretched it out and his hand was restored. 6 The Pharisees went out and immediately took counsel with the Herodians against him to put him to death.

7 Jesus withdrew toward the sea with his disciples. A large number of people [followed] from Galilee and from Judea. 8 Hearing what he was doing, a large number of people came to him also from Jerusalem, from Idumea, from beyond the Jordan, and from the neighborhood of Tyre and Sidon. 9 He told his disciples to have a boat ready for him because of the crowd, so that they would not crush him. 10 He had cured many and, as a result, those who had diseases were pressing upon him to touch him. 11 And whenever unclean spirits saw him they would fall down before him and shout, "You are the Son of God." 12 He warned them sternly not to make him known.

13 He went out again to the shore of the lake; and all the people came to him, and he taught them. 14 As he was walking along he saw Levi the son of Alphaeus sitting at the tax office, and he said to him, 'Follow me.' And he got up and followed him. 15 When Jesus was at dinner in his house, a number of tax collectors and sinners were also sitting at table with Jesus and his disciples; for there were many of them among his followers. 16 When the scribes of the Pharisee party saw him eating with sinners and tax collectors, they said to his disciples, 'Why does he eat with tax collectors and sinners?' 17 When Jesus heard this he said to them, 'It is not the healthy who need the doctor, but the sick. I came to call not the upright, but sinners.'

18 John's disciples and the Pharisees were keeping a fast, when some people came to him and said to him, 'Why is it that John's disciples and the disciples of the Pharisees fast, but your disciples do not?' 19 Jesus replied, 'Surely the bridegroom's attendants cannot fast while the bridegroom is still with them? As long as they have the bridegroom with them, they cannot fast. 20 But the time will come when the bridegroom is taken away from them, and then, on that day, they will fast. 21 No one sews a piece of unshrunken cloth on an old cloak; otherwise, the patch pulls away from it, the new from the old, and the tear gets worse. 22 And nobody puts new wine into old wineskins; otherwise, the wine will burst the skins, and the wine is lost and the skins too. No! New wine into fresh skins!'

23 It happened that one Sabbath day he was taking a walk through the cornfields, and his disciples began to make a path by plucking ears of corn. 24 And the Pharisees said to him, 'Look, why are they doing something on the Sabbath day that is forbidden?' 25 And he replied, 'Have you never read what David did in his time of need when he and his followers were hungry — 26 how he went into the house of God when Abiathar[b] was high priest, and ate the loaves of the offering which only the priests are allowed to eat, and how he also gave some to the men with him?'

27 And he said to them, 'The Sabbath was made for man, not man for the Sabbath; 28 so the Son of man is master even of the Sabbath.'

3 Another time he went into the synagogue, and there was a man present whose hand was withered. 2 And they were watching him to see if he would cure him on the Sabbath day, hoping for something to charge him with. 3 He said to the man with the withered hand, 'Get up and stand in the middle!' 4 Then he said to them, 'Is it permitted on the Sabbath day to do good, or to do evil; to save life, or to kill?' But they said nothing. 5 Then he looked angrily round at them, grieved to find them so obstinate, and said to the man, 'Stretch out your hand.' He stretched it out and his hand was restored. 6 The Pharisees went out and began at once to plot with the Herodians[c] against him, discussing how to destroy him.

7 Jesus withdrew with his disciples to the lakeside, and great crowds from Galilee followed him. From Judaea, 8 and from Jerusalem, from Idumaea and Transjordan and the region of Tyre and Sidon, great numbers who had heard of all he was doing came to him. 9 And he asked his disciples to have a boat ready for him because of the crowd, to keep him from being crushed. 10 For he had cured so many that all who were afflicted in any way were crowding forward to touch him. 11 And the unclean spirits, whenever they saw him, would fall down before him and shout, 'You are the Son of God!' 12 But he warned them strongly not to make him known.

b 2 In fact his father, Ahimelech, was high priest, 1 S 21:1–7.
c 3 Supporters of the Herodian dynasty, campaigning for the return of all Palestine to their rule.

NEW REVISED STANDARD VERSION

REVISED ENGLISH BIBLE

13 He went up the mountain and called to him those whom he wanted, and they came to him. 14 And he appointed twelve, whom he also named apostles,*y* to be with him, and to be sent out to proclaim the message, 15 and to have authority to cast out demons. 16 So he appointed the twelve:*z* Simon (to whom he gave the name Peter); 17 James son of Zebedee and John the brother of James (to whom he gave the name Boanerges, that is, Sons of Thunder); 18 and Andrew, and Philip, and Bartholomew, and Matthew, and Thomas, and James son of Alphaeus, and Thaddaeus, and Simon the Cananaean, 19 and Judas Iscariot, who betrayed him.

Then he went home; 20 and the crowd came together again, so that they could not even eat. 21 When his family heard it, they went out to restrain him, for people were saying, "He has gone out of his mind." 22 And the scribes who came down from Jerusalem said, "He has Beelzebul, and by the ruler of the demons he casts out demons." 23 And he called them to him, and spoke to them in parables, "How can Satan cast out Satan? 24 If a kingdom is divided against itself, that kingdom cannot stand. 25 And if a house is divided against itself, that house will not be able to stand. 26 And if Satan has risen up against himself and is divided, he cannot stand, but his end has come. 27 But no one can enter a strong man's house and plunder his property without first tying up the strong man; then indeed the house can be plundered.

28 "Truly I tell you, people will be forgiven for their sins and whatever blasphemies they utter; 29 but whoever blasphemes against the Holy Spirit can never have forgiveness, but is guilty of an eternal sin" — 30 for they had said, "He has an unclean spirit."

31 Then his mother and his brothers came; and standing outside, they sent to him and called him. 32 A crowd was sitting around him; and they said to him, "Your mother and your brothers and sisters*a* are outside, asking for you." 33 And he replied, "Who are my mother and my brothers?" 34 And looking at those who sat around him, he said, "Here are my mother and my brothers! 35 Whoever does the will of God is my brother and sister and mother."

4 Again he began to teach beside the sea. Such a very large crowd gathered around him that he got into a boat on the sea and sat there, while the whole crowd was beside the sea on the land. 2 He began to teach them many things in parables, and in his teaching he said to them: 3 "Listen! A sower went out to sow. 4 And as he sowed, some seed fell on the path, and the birds came and ate it up. 5 Other seed fell on rocky ground, where it did not have much soil, and it sprang up quickly, since it had no depth of soil. 6 And when the sun rose, it was scorched; and since it had no root, it withered away. 7 Other seed fell among thorns, and the thorns grew up and choked it, and it yielded no grain. 8 Other seed fell into good soil and brought forth grain, growing up and increasing and yielding thirty and sixty and a hundredfold." 9 And he said, "Let anyone with ears to hear listen!"

10 When he was alone, those who were around him along with the twelve asked him about the parables. 11 And he said to them, "To you has been given the secret*b* of the kingdom of God, but for those outside, everything comes in parables; 12 in order that

'they may indeed look, but not perceive,
and may indeed listen, but not understand;
so that they may not turn again and be
forgiven.' "

13 Then he went up into the hill-country and summoned the men he wanted; and they came and joined him. 14 He appointed twelve to be his companions, and to be sent out to proclaim the gospel, 15 with authority to drive out demons. 16 The Twelve he appointed were: Simon, whom he named Peter; 17 the sons of Zebedee, James and his brother John, whom he named Boanerges, Sons of Thunder; 18 Andrew, Philip, Bartholomew, Matthew, Thomas, James son of Alphaeus, Thaddaeus, Simon the Zealot, 19 and Judas Iscariot, the man who betrayed him.

He entered a house, 20 and once more such a crowd collected round them that they had no chance even to eat. 21 When his family heard about it they set out to take charge of him. 'He is out of his mind,' they said.

22 The scribes, too, who had come down from Jerusalem said, 'He is possessed by Beelzebul,' and, 'He drives out demons by the prince of demons.' 23 So he summoned them, and spoke to them in parables: 'How can Satan drive out Satan? 24 If a kingdom is divided against itself, that kingdom cannot stand; 25 if a household is divided against itself, that house cannot stand; 26 and if Satan is divided and rebels against himself, he cannot stand, and that is the end of him.

27 'On the other hand, no one can break into a strong man's house and make off with his goods unless he has first tied up the strong man; then he can ransack the house. 28 'Truly I tell you: every sin and every slander can be forgiven; 29 but whoever slanders the Holy Spirit can never be forgiven; he is guilty of an eternal sin.' 30 He said this because they had declared that he was possessed by an unclean spirit.

31 Then his mother and his brothers arrived; they stayed outside and sent in a message asking him to come out to them. 32 A crowd was sitting round him when word was brought that his mother and brothers were outside asking for him. 33 'Who are my mother and my brothers?' he replied. 34 And looking round at those who were sitting in the circle about him he said, 'Here are my mother and my brothers. 35 Whoever does the will of God is my brother and sister and mother.'

4 On another occasion he began to teach by the lakeside. The crowd that gathered round him was so large that he had to get into a boat on the lake and sit there, with the whole crowd on the beach right down to the water's edge. 2 And he taught them many things by parables.

As he taught he said:

3 'Listen! A sower went out to sow. 4 And it happened that as he sowed, some of the seed fell along the footpath; and the birds came and ate it up. 5 Some fell on rocky ground, where it had little soil, and it sprouted quickly because it had no depth of earth; 6 but when the sun rose it was scorched, and as it had no root it withered away. 7 Some fell among thistles; and the thistles grew up and choked the corn, and it produced no crop. 8 And some of the seed fell into good soil, where it came up and grew, and produced a crop; and the yield was thirtyfold, sixtyfold, even a hundredfold.' 9 He added, 'If you have ears to hear, then hear.'

10 When Jesus was alone with the Twelve and his other companions they questioned him about the parables. 11 He answered, 'To you the secret of the kingdom of God has been given; but to those who are outside, everything comes by way of parables, 12 so that (as scripture says) they may look and look, but see nothing; they may listen and listen, but understand nothing; otherwise they might turn to God and be forgiven.'

13 He went up the mountain and summoned those whom he wanted and they came to him. 14 He appointed twelve [whom he also named apostles] that they might be with him and he might send them forth to preach 15 and to have authority to drive out demons: 16 [he appointed the twelve:] Simon, whom he named Peter; 17 James, son of Zebedee, and John the brother of James, whom he named Boanerges, that is, sons of thunder; 18 Andrew, Philip, Bartholomew, Matthew, Thomas, James the son of Alphaeus; Thaddeus, Simon the Cananean, 19 and Judas Iscariot who betrayed him.

20 He came home. Again [the] crowd gathered, making it impossible for them even to eat. 21 When his relatives heard of this they set out to seize him, for they said, "He is out of his mind." 22 The scribes who had come from Jerusalem said, "He is possessed by Beelzebul," and "By the prince of demons he drives out demons."

23 Summoning them, he began to speak to them in parables, "How can Satan drive out Satan? 24 If a kingdom is divided against itself, that kingdom cannot stand. 25 And if a house is divided against itself, that house will not be able to stand. 26 And if Satan has risen up against himself and is divided, he cannot stand; that is the end of him. 27 But no one can enter a strong man's house to plunder his property unless he first ties up the strong man. Then he can plunder his house. 28 Amen, I say to you, all sins and all blasphemies that people utter will be forgiven them. 29 But whoever blasphemes against the holy Spirit will never have forgiveness, but is guilty of an everlasting sin." 30 For they had said, "He has an unclean spirit."

31 His mother and his brothers arrived. Standing outside they sent word to him and called him. 32 A crowd seated around him told him, "Your mother and your brothers [and your sisters] are outside asking for you." 33 But he said to them in reply, "Who are my mother and [my] brothers?" 34 And looking around at those seated in the circle he said, "Here are my mother and my brothers. 35 [For] whoever does the will of God is my brother and sister and mother."

4 On another occasion he began to teach by the sea. A very large crowd gathered around him so that he got into a boat on the sea and sat down. And the whole crowd was beside the sea on land. 2 And he taught them at length in parables, and in the course of his instruction he said to them, 3 "Hear this! A sower went out to sow. 4 And as he sowed, some seed fell on the path, and the birds came and ate it up. 5 Other seed fell on rocky ground where it had little soil. It sprang up at once because the soil was not deep. 6 And when the sun rose, it was scorched and it withered for lack of roots. 7 Some seed fell among thorns, and the thorns grew up and choked it and it produced no grain. 8 And some seed fell on rich soil and produced fruit. It came up and grew and yielded thirty, sixty, and a hundredfold." 9 He added, "Whoever has ears to hear ought to hear."

10 And when he was alone, those present along with the Twelve questioned him about the parables. 11 He answered them, "The mystery of the kingdom of God has been granted to you. But to those outside everything comes in parables, 12 so that

'they may look and see but not perceive,
and hear and listen but not understand,
in order that they may not be converted and
be forgiven.'"

13 He now went up onto the mountain and summoned those he wanted. So they came to him 14 and he appointed twelve; they were to be his companions and to be sent out to proclaim the message, 15 with power to drive out devils. 16 And so he appointed the Twelve, Simon to whom he gave the name Peter, 17 James the son of Zebedee and John the brother of James, to whom he gave the name Boanerges or 'Sons of Thunder'; 18 Andrew, Philip, Bartholomew, Matthew, Thomas, James the son of Alphaeus, Thaddaeus, Simon the Zealot 19 and Judas Iscariot, the man who was to betray him.

20 He went home again, and once more such a crowd collected that they could not even have a meal. 21 When his relations heard of this, they set out to take charge of him; they said, 'He is out of his mind.'

22 The scribes who had come down from Jerusalem were saying, 'Beelzebul is in him,' and, 'It is through the prince of devils that he drives devils out.' 23 So he called them to him and spoke to them in parables, 24 'How can Satan drive out Satan? If a kingdom is divided against itself, that kingdom cannot last. 25 And if a household is divided against itself, that household can never last. 26 Now if Satan has rebelled against himself and is divided, he cannot last either — it is the end of him. 27 But no one can make his way into a strong man's house and plunder his property unless he has first tied up the strong man. Only then can he plunder his house.

28 'In truth I tell you, all human sins will be forgiven, and all the blasphemies ever uttered; 29 but anyone who blasphemes against the Holy Spirit will never be forgiven, but is guilty of an eternal sin.' 30 This was because they were saying, 'There is an unclean spirit in him.'

31 Now his mother and his brothers arrived and, standing outside, sent in a message asking for him. 32 A crowd was sitting round him at the time the message was passed to him, 'Look, your mother and brothers and sisters are outside asking for you.' 33 He replied, 'Who are my mother and my brothers?' 34 And looking at those sitting in a circle round him, he said, 'Here are my mother and my brothers. 35 Anyone who does the will of God, that person is my brother and sister and mother.'

4 Again he began to teach them by the lakeside, but such a huge crowd gathered round him that he got into a boat on the water and sat there. The whole crowd were at the lakeside on land. 2 He taught them many things in parables, and in the course of his teaching he said to them, 3 'Listen! Imagine a sower going out to sow. 4 Now it happened that, as he sowed, some of the seed fell on the edge of the path, and the birds came and ate it up. 5 Some fell on rocky ground where it found little soil and at once sprang up, because there was no depth of earth; 6 and when the sun came up it was scorched and, not having any roots, it withered away. 7 Some seed fell into thorns, and the thorns grew up and choked it, and it produced no crop. 8 And some seeds fell into rich soil, grew tall and strong, and produced a good crop; the yield was thirty, sixty, even a hundredfold.' 9 And he said, 'Anyone who has ears for listening should listen!'

10 When he was alone, the Twelve, together with the others who formed his company, asked what the parables meant. 11 He told them, 'To you is granted the secret of the kingdom of God, but to those who are outside everything comes in parables,

12 so that *they may look and look, but never perceive;*
listen and listen, but never understand;
to avoid changing their ways and being healed.'[d]

d 4 Is 6:9–10.

NEW REVISED STANDARD VERSION	REVISED ENGLISH BIBLE

13 And he said to them, "Do you not understand this parable? Then how will you understand all the parables? 14 The sower sows the word. 15 These are the ones on the path where the word is sown: when they hear, Satan immediately comes and takes away the word that is sown in them. 16 And these are the ones sown on rocky ground: when they hear the word, they immediately receive it with joy. 17 But they have no root, and endure only for a while; then, when trouble or persecution arises on account of the word, immediately they fall away.*c* 18 And others are those sown among the thorns: these are the ones who hear the word, 19 but the cares of the world, and the lure of wealth, and the desire for other things come in and choke the word, and it yields nothing. 20 And these are the ones sown on the good soil: they hear the word and accept it and bear fruit, thirty and sixty and a hundredfold."

21 He said to them, "Is a lamp brought in to be put under the bushel basket, or under the bed, and not on the lampstand? 22 For there is nothing hidden, except to be disclosed; nor is anything secret, except to come to light. 23 Let anyone with ears to hear listen!" 24 And he said to them, "Pay attention to what you hear; the measure you give will be the measure you get, and still more will be given you. 25 For to those who have, more will be given; and from those who have nothing, even what they have will be taken away."

26 He also said, "The kingdom of God is as if someone would scatter seed on the ground, 27 and would sleep and rise night and day, and the seed would sprout and grow, he does not know how. 28 The earth produces of itself, first the stalk, then the head, then the full grain in the head. 29 But when the grain is ripe, at once he goes in with his sickle, because the harvest has come."

30 He also said, "With what can we compare the kingdom of God, or what parable will we use for it? 31 It is like a mustard seed, which, when sown upon the ground, is the smallest of all the seeds on earth; 32 yet when it is sown it grows up and becomes the greatest of all shrubs, and puts forth large branches, so that the birds of the air can make nests in its shade."

33 With many such parables he spoke the word to them, as they were able to hear it; 34 he did not speak to them except in parables, but he explained everything in private to his disciples.

35 On that day, when evening had come, he said to them, "Let us go across to the other side." 36 And leaving the crowd behind, they took him with them in the boat, just as he was. Other boats were with him. 37 A great windstorm arose, and the waves beat into the boat, so that the boat was already being swamped. 38 But he was in the stern, asleep on the cushion; and they woke him up and said to him, "Teacher, do you not care that we are perishing?" 39 He woke up and rebuked the wind, and said to the sea, "Peace! Be still!" Then the wind ceased, and there was a dead calm. 40 He said to them, "Why are you afraid? Have you still no faith?" 41 And they were filled with great awe and said to one another, "Who then is this, that even the wind and the sea obey him?"

5 They came to the other side of the sea, to the country of the Gerasenes.*d* 2 And when he had stepped out of the boat, immediately a man out of the tombs with an unclean spirit met him. 3 He lived among the tombs; and no one could restrain him any more, even with a chain; 4 for he had often been restrained with shackles and chains, but the chains he wrenched apart, and the shackles he broke in pieces; and no one had the strength to subdue him. 5 Night

13 He went on: 'Do you not understand this parable? How then are you to understand any parable? 14 The sower sows the word. 15 With some the seed falls along the footpath; no sooner have they heard it than Satan comes and carries off the word which has been sown in them. 16 With others the seed falls on rocky ground; as soon as they hear the word, they accept it with joy, 17 but it strikes no root in them; they have no staying-power, and when there is trouble or persecution on account of the word, they quickly lose faith. 18 With others again the seed falls among thistles; they hear the word, 19 but worldly cares and the false glamour of wealth and evil desires of all kinds come in and choke the word, and it proves barren. 20 But there are some with whom the seed is sown on good soil; they accept the word when they hear it, and they bear fruit thirtyfold, sixtyfold, or a hundredfold.'

21 He said to them, 'Is a lamp brought in to be put under the measuring bowl or under the bed? No, it is put on the lampstand. 22 Nothing is hidden except to be disclosed, and nothing concealed except to be brought into the open. 23 If you have ears to hear, then hear.'

24 He also said to them, 'Take note of what you hear; the measure you give is the measure you will receive, with something more besides. 25 For those who have will be given more, and those who have not will forfeit even what they have.'

26 He said, 'The kingdom of God is like this. A man scatters seed on the ground; 27 he goes to bed at night and gets up in the morning, and meanwhile the seed sprouts and grows — how, he does not know. 28 The ground produces a crop by itself, first the blade, then the ear, then full grain in the ear; 29 but as soon as the crop is ripe, he starts reaping, because harvest time has come.'

30 He said, 'How shall we picture the kingdom of God, or what parable shall we use to describe it? 31 It is like a mustard seed; when sown in the ground it is smaller than any other seed, 32 but once sown, it springs up and grows taller than any other plant, and forms branches so large that birds can roost in its shade.'

33 With many such parables he used to give them his message, so far as they were able to receive it. 34 He never spoke to them except in parables; but privately to his disciples he explained everything.

35 THAT day, in the evening, he said to them, 'Let us cross over to the other side of the lake.' 36 So they left the crowd and took him with them in the boat in which he had been sitting; and some other boats went with him. 37 A fierce squall blew up and the waves broke over the boat until it was all but swamped. 38 Now he was in the stern asleep on a cushion; they roused him and said, 'Teacher, we are sinking! Do you not care?' 39 He awoke and rebuked the wind, and said to the sea, 'Silence! Be still!' The wind dropped and there was a dead calm. 40 He said to them, 'Why are you such cowards? Have you no faith even now?' 41 They were awestruck and said to one another, 'Who can this be? Even the wind and the sea obey him.'

5 So they came to the country of the Gerasenes on the other side of the lake. 2 As he stepped ashore, a man possessed by an unclean spirit came up to him from among the tombs 3 where he had made his home. Nobody could control him any longer; even chains were useless, 4 for he had often been fettered and chained up, but had snapped his chains and broken the fetters. No one was strong enough to master him. 5 Unceasingly, night and day, he would cry

c Or *stumble* *d* Other ancient authorities read *Gergesenes*; others, *Gadarenes*

NEW AMERICAN BIBLE

NEW JERUSALEM BIBLE

13 Jesus said to them, "Do you not understand this parable? Then how will you understand any of the parables? 14 The sower sows the word. 15 These are the ones on the path where the word is sown. As soon as they hear, Satan comes at once and takes away the word sown in them. 16 And these are the ones sown on rocky ground who, when they hear the word, receive it at once with joy. 17 But they have no root; they last only for a time. Then when tribulation or persecution comes because of the word, they quickly fall away. 18 Those sown among thorns are another sort. They are the people who hear the word, 19 but worldly anxiety, the lure of riches, and the craving for other things intrude and choke the word, and it bears no fruit. 20 But those sown on rich soil are the ones who hear the word and accept it and bear fruit thirty and sixty and a hundredfold."

21 He said to them, "Is a lamp brought in to be placed under a bushel basket or under a bed, and not to be placed on a lampstand? 22 For there is nothing hidden except to be made visible; nothing is secret except to come to light. 23 Anyone who has ears to hear ought to hear." 24 He also told them, "Take care what you hear. The measure with which you measure will be measured out to you, and still more will be given to you. 25 To the one who has, more will be given; from the one who has not, even what he has will be taken away."

26 He said, "This is how it is with the kingdom of God; it is as if a man were to scatter seed on the land 27 and would sleep and rise night and day and the seed would sprout and grow, he knows not how. 28 Of its own accord the land yields fruit, first the blade, then the ear, then the full grain in the ear. 29 And when the grain is ripe, he wields the sickle at once, for the harvest has come."

30 He said, "To what shall we compare the kingdom of God, or what parable can we use for it? 31 It is like a mustard seed that, when it is sown in the ground, is the smallest of all the seeds on the earth. 32 But once it is sown, it springs up and becomes the largest of plants and puts forth large branches, so that the birds of the sky can dwell in its shade." 33 With many such parables he spoke the word to them as they were able to understand it. 34 Without parables he did not speak to them, but to his own disciples he explained everything in private.

35 On that day, as evening drew on, he said to them, "Let us cross to the other side." 36 Leaving the crowd, they took him with them in the boat just as he was. And other boats were with him. 37 A violent squall came up and waves were breaking over the boat, so that it was already filling up. 38 Jesus was in the stern, asleep on a cushion. They woke him and said to him, "Teacher, do you not care that we are perishing?" 39 He woke up, rebuked the wind, and said to the sea, "Quiet! Be still!" The wind ceased and there was great calm. 40 Then he asked them, "Why are you terrified? Do you not yet have faith?" 41 They were filled with great awe and said to one another, "Who then is this whom even wind and sea obey?"

5 They came to the other side of the sea, to the territory of the Gerasenes. 2 When he got out of the boat, at once a man from the tombs who had an unclean spirit met him. 3 The man had been dwelling among the tombs, and no one could restrain him any longer, even with a chain. 4 In fact, he had frequently been bound with shackles and chains, but the chains had been pulled apart by him and the shackles smashed, and no one was strong enough to subdue him. 5 Night and day among the tombs and on the hillsides

13 He said to them, 'Do you not understand this parable? Then how will you understand any of the parables? 14 What the sower is sowing is the word. 15 Those on the edge of the path where the word is sown are people who have no sooner heard it than Satan at once comes and carries away the word that was sown in them. 16 Similarly, those who are sown on patches of rock are people who, when first they hear the word, welcome it at once with joy. 17 But they have no root deep down and do not last; should some trial come, or some persecution on account of the word, at once they fall away. 18 Then there are others who are sown in thorns. These have heard the word, 19 but the worries of the world, the lure of riches and all the other passions come in to choke the word, and so it produces nothing. 20 And there are those who have been sown in rich soil; they hear the word and accept it and yield a harvest, thirty, sixty, and a hundredfold.'

21 He also said to them, 'Is a lamp brought in to be put under a tub or under the bed? Surely to be put on the lamp-stand? 22 For there is nothing hidden, but it must be disclosed, nothing kept secret except to be brought to light. 23 Anyone who has ears for listening should listen!'

24 He also said to them, 'Take notice of what you are hearing. The standard you use will be used for you — and you will receive more besides; 25 anyone who has, will be given more; anyone who has not, will be deprived even of what he has.'

26 He also said, 'This is what the kingdom of God is like. A man scatters seed on the land. 27 Night and day, while he sleeps, when he is awake, the seed is sprouting and growing; how, he does not know. 28 Of its own accord the land produces first the shoot, then the ear, then the full grain in the ear. 29 And when the crop is ready, at once he starts to reap because the harvest has come.'

30 He also said, 'What can we say that the kingdom is like? What parable can we find for it? 31 It is like a mustard seed which, at the time of its sowing, is the smallest of all the seeds on earth. 32 Yet once it is sown it grows into the biggest shrub of them all and puts out big branches so that the birds of the air can shelter in its shade.'

33 Using many parables like these, he spoke the word to them, so far as they were capable of understanding it. 34 He would not speak to them except in parables, but he explained everything to his disciples when they were by themselves.

35 With the coming of evening that same day, he said to them, 'Let us cross over to the other side.' 36 And leaving the crowd behind they took him, just as he was, in the boat; and there were other boats with him. 37 Then it began to blow a great gale and the waves were breaking into the boat so that it was almost swamped. 38 But he was in the stern, his head on the cushion, asleep. 39 They woke him and said to him, 'Master, do you not care? We are lost!' And he woke up and rebuked the wind and said to the sea, 'Quiet now! Be calm!' And the wind dropped, and there followed a great calm. 40 Then he said to them, 'Why are you so frightened? Have you still no faith?' 41 They were overcome with awe and said to one another, 'Who can this be? Even the wind and the sea obey him.'

5 They reached the territory of the Gerasenes on the other side of the lake, 2 and when he disembarked, a man with an unclean spirit at once came out from the tombs towards him. 3 The man lived in the tombs and no one could secure him any more, even with a chain, 4 because he had often been secured with fetters and chains but had snapped the chains and broken the fetters, and no one had the strength to control him. 5 All night and all day, among the

and day among the tombs and on the mountains he was always howling and bruising himself with stones. 6 When he saw Jesus from a distance, he ran and bowed down before him; 7 and he shouted at the top of his voice, "What have you to do with me, Jesus, Son of the Most High God? I adjure you by God, do not torment me." 8 For he had said to him, "Come out of the man, you unclean spirit!" 9 Then Jesus*e* asked him, "What is your name?" He replied, "My name is Legion; for we are many." 10 He begged him earnestly not to send them out of the country. 11 Now there on the hillside a great herd of swine was feeding; 12 and the unclean spirits*f* begged him, "Send us into the swine; let us enter them." 13 So he gave them permission. And the unclean spirits came out and entered the swine; and the herd, numbering about two thousand, rushed down the steep bank into the sea, and were drowned in the sea.

14 The swineherds ran off and told it in the city and in the country. Then people came to see what it was that had happened. 15 They came to Jesus and saw the demoniac sitting there, clothed and in his right mind, the very man who had had the legion; and they were afraid. 16 Those who had seen what had happened to the demoniac and to the swine reported it. 17 Then they began to beg Jesus*g* to leave their neighborhood. 18 As he was getting into the boat, the man who had been possessed by demons begged him that he might be with him. 19 But Jesus*e* refused, and said to him, "Go home to your friends, and tell them how much the Lord has done for you, and what mercy he has shown you." 20 And he went away and began to proclaim in the Decapolis how much Jesus had done for him; and everyone was amazed.

21 When Jesus had crossed again in the boat*h* to the other side, a great crowd gathered around him; and he was by the sea. 22 Then one of the leaders of the synagogue named Jairus came and, when he saw him, fell at his feet 23 and begged him repeatedly, "My little daughter is at the point of death. Come and lay your hands on her, so that she may be made well, and live." 24 So he went with him.

And a large crowd followed him and pressed in on him. 25 Now there was a woman who had been suffering from hemorrhages for twelve years. 26 She had endured much under many physicians, and had spent all that she had; and she was no better, but rather grew worse. 27 She had heard about Jesus, and came up behind him in the crowd and touched his cloak, 28 for she said, "If I but touch his clothes, I will be made well." 29 Immediately her hemorrhage stopped; and she felt in her body that she was healed of her disease. 30 Immediately aware that power had gone forth from him, Jesus turned about in the crowd and said, "Who touched my clothes?" 31 And his disciples said to him, "You see the crowd pressing in on you; how can you say, 'Who touched me?' " 32 He looked all around to see who had done it. 33 But the woman, knowing what had happened to her, came in fear and trembling, fell down before him, and told him the whole truth. 34 He said to her, "Daughter, your faith has made you well; go in peace, and be healed of your disease."

35 While he was still speaking, some people came from the leader's house to say, "Your daughter is dead. Why trouble the teacher any further?" 36 But overhearing*i* what they said, Jesus said to the leader of the synagogue, "Do not fear, only believe." 37 He allowed no one to follow him except Peter, James, and John, the brother of James. 38 When they came to the house of the leader of the synagogue, he saw a commotion, people weeping and wailing

aloud among the tombs and on the hillsides and gash himself with stones. 6 When he saw Jesus in the distance, he ran up and flung himself down before him, 7 shouting at the top of his voice, 'What do you want with me, Jesus, son of the Most High God? In God's name do not torment me.' 8 For Jesus was already saying to him, 'Out, unclean spirit, come out of the man!' 9 Jesus asked him, 'What is your name?' 'My name is Legion,' he said, 'there are so many of us.' 10 And he implored Jesus not to send them out of the district. 11 There was a large herd of pigs nearby, feeding on the hillside, 12 and the spirits begged him, 'Send us among the pigs; let us go into them.' 13 He gave them leave; and the unclean spirits came out and went into the pigs; and the herd, of about two thousand, rushed over the edge into the lake and were drowned.

14 The men in charge of them took to their heels and carried the news to the town and countryside; and the people came out to see what had happened. 15 When they came to Jesus and saw the madman who had been possessed by the legion of demons, sitting there clothed and in his right mind, they were afraid. 16 When eyewitnesses told them what had happened to the madman and what had become of the pigs, 17 they begged Jesus to leave the district. 18 As he was getting into the boat, the man who had been possessed begged to go with him. 19 But Jesus would not let him. 'Go home to your own people,' he said, 'and tell them what the Lord in his mercy has done for you.' 20 The man went off and made known throughout the Decapolis what Jesus had done for him; and everyone was amazed.

21 As soon as Jesus had returned by boat to the other shore, a large crowd gathered round him. While he was by the lakeside, 22 there came a synagogue president named Jairus; and when he saw him, he threw himself down at his feet 23 and pleaded with him. 'My little daughter is at death's door,' he said. 'I beg you to come and lay your hands on her so that her life may be saved.' 24 So Jesus went with him, accompanied by a great crowd which pressed round him.

25 Among them was a woman who had suffered from haemorrhages for twelve years; 26 and in spite of long treatment by many doctors, on which she had spent all she had, she had become worse rather than better. 27 She had heard about Jesus, and came up behind him in the crowd and touched his cloak; 28 for she said, 'If I touch even his clothes, I shall be healed.' 29 And there and then the flow of blood dried up and she knew in herself that she was cured of her affliction. 30 Aware at once that power had gone out of him, Jesus turned round in the crowd and asked, 'Who touched my clothes?' 31 His disciples said to him, 'You see the crowd pressing round you and yet you ask, "Who touched me?" ' 32 But he kept looking around to see who had done it. 33 Then the woman, trembling with fear because she knew what had happened to her, came and fell at his feet and told him the whole truth. 34 He said to her, 'Daughter, your faith has healed you. Go in peace, free from your affliction.'

35 While he was still speaking, a message came from the president's house, 'Your daughter has died; why trouble the teacher any more?' 36 But Jesus, overhearing the message as it was delivered, said to the president of the synagogue, 'Do not be afraid; simply have faith.' 37 Then he allowed no one to accompany him except Peter and James and James's brother John. 38 They came to the president's house, where he found a great commotion, with loud crying and wailing.

e Gk he   *f* Gk they   *g* Gk him   *h* Other ancient authorities lack *in the boat*   *i* Or *ignoring*; other ancient authorities read *hearing*

he was always crying out and bruising himself with stones. 6 Catching sight of Jesus from a distance, he ran up and prostrated himself before him, 7 crying out in a loud voice, "What have you to do with me, Jesus, Son of the Most High God? I adjure you by God, do not torment me!" 8 (He had been saying to him, "Unclean spirit, come out of the man!") 9 He asked him, "What is your name?" He replied, "Legion is my name. There are many of us." 10 And he pleaded earnestly with him not to drive them away from that territory.

11 Now a large herd of swine was feeding there on the hillside. 12 And they pleaded with him, "Send us into the swine. Let us enter them." 13 And he let them, and the unclean spirits came out and entered the swine. The herd of about two thousand rushed down a steep bank into the sea, where they were drowned. 14 The swineherds ran away and reported the incident in the town and throughout the countryside. And people came out to see what had happened. 15 As they approached Jesus, they caught sight of the man who had been possessed by Legion, sitting there clothed and in his right mind. And they were seized with fear. 16 Those who witnessed the incident explained to them what had happened to the possessed man and to the swine. 17 Then they began to beg him to leave their district. 18 As he was getting into the boat, the man who had been possessed pleaded to remain with him. 19 But he would not permit him but told him instead, "Go home to your family and announce to them all that the Lord in his pity has done for you." 20 Then the man went off and began to proclaim in the Decapolis what Jesus had done for him; and all were amazed.

21 When Jesus had crossed again [in the boat] to the other side, a large crowd gathered around him, and he stayed close to the sea. 22 One of the synagogue officials, named Jairus, came forward. Seeing him he fell at his feet 23 and pleaded earnestly with him, saying, "My daughter is at the point of death. Please, come lay your hands on her that she may get well and live." 24 He went off with him, and a large crowd followed him and pressed upon him.

25 There was a woman afflicted with hemorrhages for twelve years. 26 She had suffered greatly at the hands of many doctors and had spent all that she had. Yet she was not helped but only grew worse. 27 She had heard about Jesus and came up behind him in the crowd and touched his cloak. 28 She said, "If I but touch his clothes, I shall be cured." 29 Immediately her flow of blood dried up. She felt in her body that she was healed of her affliction. 30 Jesus, aware at once that power had gone out from him, turned around in the crowd and asked, "Who has touched my clothes?" 31 But his disciples said to him, "You see how the crowd is pressing upon you, and yet you ask, 'Who touched me?'" 32 And he looked around to see who had done it. 33 The woman, realizing what had happened to her, approached in fear and trembling. She fell down before Jesus and told him the whole truth. 34 He said to her, "Daughter, your faith has saved you. Go in peace and be cured of your affliction."

35 While he was still speaking, people from the synagogue official's house arrived and said, "Your daughter has died; why trouble the teacher any longer?" 36 Disregarding the message that was reported, Jesus said to the synagogue official, "Do not be afraid; just have faith." 37 He did not allow anyone to accompany him inside except Peter, James, and John, the brother of James. 38 When they arrived at the house of the synagogue official, he caught sight of a commotion, people weeping and wailing loudly. 39 So he went

tombs and in the mountains, he would howl and gash himself with stones. 6 Catching sight of Jesus from a distance, he ran up and fell at his feet 7 and shouted at the top of his voice, 'What do you want with me, Jesus, son of the Most High God? In God's name do not torture me!' 8 For Jesus had been saying to him, 'Come out of the man, unclean spirit.' 9 Then he asked, 'What is your name?' He answered, 'My name is Legion, for there are many of us.' 10 And he begged him earnestly not to send them out of the district. 11 Now on the mountainside there was a great herd of pigs feeding, 12 and the unclean spirits begged him, 'Send us to the pigs, let us go into them.' 13 So he gave them leave. With that, the unclean spirits came out and went into the pigs, and the herd of about two thousand pigs charged down the cliff into the lake, and there they were drowned. 14 The men looking after them ran off and told their story in the city and in the country round about; and the people came to see what had really happened. 15 They came to Jesus and saw the demoniac sitting there — the man who had had the legion in him — properly dressed and in his full senses, and they were afraid. 16 And those who had witnessed it reported what had happened to the demoniac and what had become of the pigs. 17 Then they began to implore Jesus to leave their neighbourhood. 18 As he was getting into the boat, the man who had been possessed begged to be allowed to stay with him. 19 Jesus would not let him but said to him, 'Go home to your people and tell them all that the Lord in his mercy has done for you.' 20 So the man went off and proceeded to proclaim in the Decapolis all that Jesus had done for him. And everyone was amazed.

21 When Jesus had crossed again in the boat to the other side, a large crowd gathered round him and he stayed by the lake. 22 Then the president of the synagogue came up, named Jairus, and seeing him, fell at his feet 23 and begged him earnestly, saying, 'My little daughter is desperately sick. Do come and lay your hands on her that she may be saved and may live.' 24 Jesus went with him and a large crowd followed him; they were pressing all round him.

25 Now there was a woman who had suffered from a haemorrhage for twelve years; 26 after long and painful treatment under various doctors, she had spent all she had without being any the better for it; in fact, she was getting worse. 27 She had heard about Jesus, and she came up through the crowd and touched his cloak from behind, thinking, 28 'If I can just touch his clothes, I shall be saved.' 29 And at once the source of the bleeding dried up, and she felt in herself that she was cured of her complaint. 30 And at once aware of the power that had gone out from him, Jesus turned round in the crowd and said, 'Who touched my clothes?' 31 His disciples said to him, 'You see how the crowd is pressing round you; how can you ask, "Who touched me?"' 32 But he continued to look all round to see who had done it. 33 Then the woman came forward, frightened and trembling because she knew what had happened to her, and she fell at his feet and told him the whole truth. 34 'My daughter,' he said, 'your faith has restored you to health; go in peace and be free of your complaint.'

35 While he was still speaking some people arrived from the house of the president of the synagogue to say, 'Your daughter is dead; why put the Master to any further trouble?' 36 But Jesus overheard what they said and he said to the president of the synagogue, 'Do not be afraid; only have faith.' 37 And he allowed no one to go with him except Peter and James and John the brother of James. 38 So they came to the house of the president of the synagogue, and Jesus noticed all the commotion, with people weeping and wailing unrestrainedly. 39 He went in and said to them, 'Why all

loudly. 39 When he had entered, he said to them, "Why do you make a commotion and weep? The child is not dead but sleeping." 40 And they laughed at him. Then he put them all outside, and took the child's father and mother and those who were with him, and went in where the child was. 41 He took her by the hand and said to her, "Talitha cum," which means, "Little girl, get up!" 42 And immediately the girl got up and began to walk about (she was twelve years of age). At this they were overcome with amazement. 43 He strictly ordered them that no one should know this, and told them to give her something to eat.

6 He left that place and came to his hometown, and his disciples followed him. 2 On the sabbath he began to teach in the synagogue, and many who heard him were astounded. They said, "Where did this man get all this? What is this wisdom that has been given to him? What deeds of power are being done by his hands! 3 Is not this the carpenter, the son of Mary^j and brother of James and Joses and Judas and Simon, and are not his sisters here with us?" And they took offense^k at him. 4 Then Jesus said to them, "Prophets are not without honor, except in their hometown, and among their own kin, and in their own house." 5 And he could do no deed of power there, except that he laid his hands on a few sick people and cured them. 6 And he was amazed at their unbelief.

Then he went about among the villages teaching. 7 He called the twelve and began to send them out two by two, and gave them authority over the unclean spirits. 8 He ordered them to take nothing for their journey except a staff; no bread, no bag, no money in their belts; 9 but to wear sandals and not to put on two tunics. 10 He said to them, "Wherever you enter a house, stay there until you leave the place. 11 If any place will not welcome you and they refuse to hear you, as you leave, shake off the dust that is on your feet as a testimony against them." 12 So they went out and proclaimed that all should repent. 13 They cast out many demons, and anointed with oil many who were sick and cured them.

14 King Herod heard of it, for Jesus'^{l} name had become known. Some were^m saying, "John the baptizer has been raised from the dead; and for this reason these powers are at work in him." 15 But others said, "It is Elijah." And others said, "It is a prophet, like one of the prophets of old." 16 But when Herod heard of it, he said, "John, whom I beheaded, has been raised."

17 For Herod himself had sent men who arrested John, bound him, and put him in prison on account of Herodias, his brother Philip's wife, because Herod^n had married her. 18 For John had been telling Herod, "It is not lawful for you to have your brother's wife." 19 And Herodias had a grudge against him, and wanted to kill him. But she could not, 20 for Herod feared John, knowing that he was a righteous and holy man, and he protected him. When he heard him, he was greatly perplexed;^{o} and yet he liked to listen to him. 21 But an opportunity came when Herod on his birthday gave a banquet for his courtiers and officers and for the leaders of Galilee. 22 When his daughter Herodias^p came in and danced, she pleased Herod and his guests; and the king said to the girl, "Ask me for whatever you wish, and I will give it." 23 And he solemnly swore to her, "Whatever you ask me, I will give you, even half of my kingdom." 24 She went out and said to her mother, "What should I ask for?" She replied, "The head of John the baptizer." 25 Immediately she rushed back to the king and requested, "I want you to give me at once the head of John the Baptist on a platter."

39 So he went in and said to them, 'Why this crying and commotion? The child is not dead: she is asleep'; 40 and they laughed at him. After turning everyone out, he took the child's father and mother and his own companions into the room where the child was. 41 Taking hold of her hand, he said to her, 'Talitha cum,' which means, 'Get up, my child.' 42 Immediately the girl got up and walked about— she was twelve years old. They were overcome with amazement; 43 but he gave them strict instructions not to let anyone know about it, and told them to give her something to eat.

6 From there he went to his home town accompanied by his disciples. 2 When the sabbath came he began to teach in the synagogue; and the large congregation who heard him asked in amazement, 'Where does he get it from? What is this wisdom he has been given? How does he perform such miracles? 3 Is he not the carpenter, the son of Mary, the brother of James and Joses and Judas and Simon? Are not his sisters here with us?' So they turned against him. 4 Jesus said to them, 'A prophet never lacks honour except in his home town, among his relations and his own family.' 5 And he was unable to do any miracle there, except that he put his hands on a few sick people and healed them; 6 and he was astonished at their want of faith.

AS HE went round the villages teaching, 7 he summoned the Twelve and sent them out two by two with authority over unclean spirits. 8 He instructed them to take nothing for the journey except a stick—no bread, no pack, no money in their belts. 9 They might wear sandals, but not a second coat. 10 'When you enter a house,' he told them, 'stay there until you leave that district. 11 At any place where they will not receive you or listen to you, shake the dust off your feet as you leave, as a solemn warning.' 12 So they set out and proclaimed the need for repentance; 13 they drove out many demons, and anointed many sick people with oil and cured them.

14 Now King Herod heard of Jesus, for his fame had spread, and people were saying, 'John the Baptist has been raised from the dead, and that is why these miraculous powers are at work in him.' 15 Others said, 'It is Elijah.' Others again, 'He is a prophet like one of the prophets of old.' 16 But when Herod heard of it, he said, 'This is John, whom I beheaded, raised from the dead.'

17 It was this Herod who had sent men to arrest John and put him in prison at the instance of his brother Philip's wife, Herodias, whom he had married. 18 John had told him, 'You have no right to take your brother's wife.' 19 Herodias nursed a grudge against John and would willingly have killed him, but she could not, 20 for Herod went in awe of him, knowing him to be a good and holy man; so he gave him his protection. He liked to listen to him, although what he heard left him greatly disturbed. 21 Herodias found her opportunity when Herod on his birthday gave a banquet to his chief officials and commanders and the leading men of Galilee. 22 Her daughter came in and danced, and so delighted Herod and his guests that the king said to the girl, 'Ask me for anything you like and I will give it to you.' 23 He even said on oath: 'Whatever you ask I will give you, up to half my kingdom.' 24 She went out and said to her mother, 'What shall I ask for?' She replied, 'The head of John the Baptist.' 25 The girl hurried straight back to the king with her request: 'I want you to give me, here and now, on a dish, the head of John the Baptist.'

---

^{j} Other ancient authorities read *son of the carpenter and of Mary*
^{k} Or *stumbled* ^{l} Gk *his* ^{m} Other ancient authorities read *He was*
^{n} Gk *he* ^{o} Other ancient authorities read *he did many things*
^{p} Other ancient authorities read *the daughter of Herodias herself*

6:3 **the carpenter . . . Mary:** *some witnesses read* the son of the carpenter and Mary. 6:14 **and . . . saying:** *some witnesses read* and he said.

NEW AMERICAN BIBLE

in and said to them, "Why this commotion and weeping? The child is not dead but asleep." 40 And they ridiculed him. Then he put them all out. He took along the child's father and mother and those who were with him and entered the room where the child was. 41 He took the child by the hand and said to her, "*Talitha koum,*" which means, "Little girl, I say to you, arise!" 42 The girl, a child of twelve, arose immediately and walked around. [At that] they were utterly astounded. 43 He gave strict orders that no one should know this and said that she should be given something to eat.

6 He departed from there and came to his native place, accompanied by his disciples. 2 When the sabbath came he began to teach in the synagogue, and many who heard him were astonished. They said, "Where did this man get all this? What kind of wisdom has been given him? What mighty deeds are wrought by his hands! 3 Is he not the carpenter, the son of Mary, and the brother of James and Joses and Judas and Simon? And are not his sisters here with us?" And they took offense at him. 4 Jesus said to them, "A prophet is not without honor except in his native place and among his own kin and in his own house." 5 So he was not able to perform any mighty deed there, apart from curing a few sick people by laying his hands on them. 6 He was amazed at their lack of faith.

He went around to the villages in the vicinity teaching. 7 He summoned the Twelve and began to send them out two by two and gave them authority over unclean spirits. 8 He instructed them to take nothing for the journey but a walking stick — no food, no sack, no money in their belts. 9 They were, however, to wear sandals but not a second tunic. 10 He said to them, "Wherever you enter a house, stay there until you leave from there. 11 Whatever place does not welcome you or listen to you, leave there and shake the dust of your feet in testimony against them." 12 So they went off and preached repentance. 13 They drove out many demons, and they anointed with oil many who were sick and cured them.

14 King Herod heard about it, for his fame had become widespread, and people were saying, "John the Baptist has been raised from the dead; that is why mighty powers are at work in him." 15 Others were saying, "He is Elijah"; still others, "He is a prophet like any of the prophets." 16 But when Herod learned of it, he said, "It is John whom I beheaded. He has been raised up."

17 Herod was the one who had John arrested and bound in prison on account of Herodias, the wife of his brother Philip, whom he had married. 18 John had said to Herod, "It is not lawful for you to have your brother's wife." 19 Herodias harbored a grudge against him and wanted to kill him but was unable to do so. 20 Herod feared John, knowing him to be a righteous and holy man, and kept him in custody. When he heard him speak he was very much perplexed, yet he liked to listen to him. 21 She had an opportunity one day when Herod, on his birthday, gave a banquet for his courtiers, his military officers, and the leading men of Galilee. 22 Herodias's own daughter came in and performed a dance that delighted Herod and his guests. The king said to the girl, "Ask of me whatever you wish and I will grant it to you." 23 He even swore [many things] to her, "I will grant you whatever you ask of me, even to half of my kingdom." 24 She went out and said to her mother, "What shall I ask for?" She replied, "The head of John the Baptist." 25 The girl hurried back to the king's presence and made her request, "I want you to give me at once on a platter the head of John the Baptist." 26 The king was deeply distressed, but

NEW JERUSALEM BIBLE

this commotion and crying? The child is not dead, but asleep.' 40 But they ridiculed him. So he turned them all out and, taking with him the child's father and mother and his own companions, he went into the place where the child lay. 41 And taking the child by the hand he said to her, '*Talitha kum!*' which means, 'Little girl, I tell you to get up.' 42 The little girl got up at once and began to walk about, for she was twelve years old. At once they were overcome with astonishment, 43 and he gave them strict orders not to let anyone know about it, and told them to give her something to eat.

6 Leaving that district, he went to his home town, and his disciples accompanied him. 2 With the coming of the Sabbath he began teaching in the synagogue, and most of them were astonished when they heard him. They said, 'Where did the man get all this? What is this wisdom that has been granted him, and these miracles that are worked through him? 3 This is the carpenter, surely, the son of Mary, the brother of James and Joset and Jude and Simon? His sisters, too, are they not here with us?' And they would not accept him. 4 And Jesus said to them, 'A prophet is despised only in his own country, among his own relations and in his own house'; 5 and he could work no miracle there, except that he cured a few sick people by laying his hands on them. 6 He was amazed at their lack of faith.

He made a tour round the villages, teaching. 7 Then he summoned the Twelve and began to send them out in pairs, giving them authority over unclean spirits. 8 And he instructed them to take nothing for the journey except a staff — no bread, no haversack, no coppers for their purses. 9 They were to wear sandals but, he added, 'Don't take a spare tunic.' 10 And he said to them, 'If you enter a house anywhere, stay there until you leave the district. 11 And if any place does not welcome you and people refuse to listen to you, as you walk away shake off the dust under your feet as evidence to them.' 12 So they set off to proclaim repentance; 13 and they cast out many devils, and anointed many sick people with oil and cured them.

14 King Herod had heard about him, since by now his name was well known. Some were saying, 'John the Baptist has risen from the dead, and that is why miraculous powers are at work in him.' 15 Others said, 'He is Elijah,' others again, 'He is a prophet, like the prophets we used to have.' 16 But when Herod heard this he said, 'It is John whose head I cut off; he has risen from the dead.'

17 Now it was this same Herod who had sent to have John arrested, and had had him chained up in prison because of Herodias, his brother Philip's wife whom he had married. 18 For John had told Herod, 'It is against the law for you to have your brother's wife.' 19 As for Herodias, she was furious with him and wanted to kill him, but she was not able to do so, 20 because Herod was in awe of John, knowing him to be a good and upright man, and gave him his protection. When he had heard him speak he was greatly perplexed, and yet he liked to listen to him. 21 An opportunity came on Herod's birthday when he gave a banquet for the nobles of his court, for his army officers and for the leading figures in Galilee. 22 When the daughter of this same Herodias came in and danced, she delighted Herod and his guests; so the king said to the girl, 'Ask me anything you like and I will give it you.' 23 And he swore her an oath, 'I will give you anything you ask, even half my kingdom.' 24 She went out and said to her mother, 'What shall I ask for?' She replied, 'The head of John the Baptist.' 25 The girl at once rushed back to the king and made her request, 'I want you to give me John the Baptist's head, immediately, on a dish.' 26 The king was deeply dis-

NEW REVISED STANDARD VERSION

REVISED ENGLISH BIBLE

26 The king was deeply grieved; yet out of regard for his oaths and for the guests, he did not want to refuse her. 27 Immediately the king sent a soldier of the guard with orders to bring John's*q* head. He went and beheaded him in the prison, 28 brought his head on a platter, and gave it to the girl. Then the girl gave it to her mother. 29 When his disciples heard about it, they came and took his body, and laid it in a tomb.

30 The apostles gathered around Jesus, and told him all that they had done and taught. 31 He said to them, "Come away to a deserted place all by yourselves and rest a while." For many were coming and going, and they had no leisure even to eat. 32 And they went away in the boat to a deserted place by themselves. 33 Now many saw them going and recognized them, and they hurried there on foot from all the towns and arrived ahead of them. 34 As he went ashore, he saw a great crowd; and he had compassion for them, because they were like sheep without a shepherd; and he began to teach them many things. 35 When it grew late, his disciples came to him and said, "This is a deserted place, and the hour is now very late; 36 send them away so that they may go into the surrounding country and villages and buy something for themselves to eat." 37 But he answered them, "You give them something to eat." They said to him, "Are we to go and buy two hundred denarii*r* worth of bread, and give it to them to eat?" 38 And he said to them, "How many loaves have you? Go and see." When they had found out, they said, "Five, and two fish." 39 Then he ordered them to get all the people to sit down in groups on the green grass. 40 So they sat down in groups of hundreds and of fifties. 41 Taking the five loaves and the two fish, he looked up to heaven, and blessed and broke the loaves, and gave them to his disciples to set before the people; and he divided the two fish among them all. 42 And all ate and were filled; 43 and they took up twelve baskets full of broken pieces and of the fish. 44 Those who had eaten the loaves numbered five thousand men.

45 Immediately he made his disciples get into the boat and go on ahead to the other side, to Bethsaida, while he dismissed the crowd. 46 After saying farewell to them, he went up on the mountain to pray.

47 When evening came, the boat was out on the sea, and he was alone on the land. 48 When he saw that they were straining at the oars against an adverse wind, he came towards them early in the morning, walking on the sea. He intended to pass them by. 49 But when they saw him walking on the sea, they thought it was a ghost and cried out; 50 for they all saw him and were terrified. But immediately he spoke to them and said, "Take heart, it is I; do not be afraid." 51 Then he got into the boat with them and the wind ceased. And they were utterly astounded, 52 for they did not understand about the loaves, but their hearts were hardened.

53 When they had crossed over, they came to land at Gennesaret and moored the boat. 54 When they got out of the boat, people at once recognized him, 55 and rushed about that whole region and began to bring the sick on mats to wherever they heard he was. 56 And wherever he went, into villages or cities or farms, they laid the sick in the marketplaces, and begged him that they might touch even the fringe of his cloak; and all who touched it were healed.

7 Now when the Pharisees and some of the scribes who had come from Jerusalem gathered around him, 2 they noticed that some of his disciples were eating with defiled hands, that is, without washing them. 3 (For the Pharisees,

26 The king was greatly distressed, yet because of his oath and his guests he could not bring himself to refuse her. 27 He sent a soldier of the guard with orders to bring John's head; and the soldier went to the prison and beheaded him; 28 then he brought the head on a dish, and gave it to the girl; and she gave it to her mother.

29 When John's disciples heard the news, they came and took his body away and laid it in a tomb.

30 THE apostles rejoined Jesus and reported to him all that they had done and taught. 31 He said to them, 'Come with me, by yourselves, to some remote place and rest a little.' With many coming and going they had no time even to eat. 32 So they set off by boat privately for a remote place. 33 But many saw them leave and recognized them, and people from all the towns hurried round on foot and arrived there first. 34 When he came ashore and saw a large crowd, his heart went out to them, because they were like sheep without a shepherd; and he began to teach them many things. 35 It was already getting late, and his disciples came to him and said, 'This is a remote place and it is already very late; 36 send the people off to the farms and villages round about, to buy themselves something to eat.' 37 'Give them something to eat yourselves,' he answered. They replied, 'Are we to go and spend two hundred denarii to provide them with food?' 38 'How many loaves have you?' he asked. 'Go and see.' They found out and told him, 'Five, and two fish.' 39 He ordered them to make the people sit down in groups on the green grass, 40 and they sat down in rows, in companies of fifty and a hundred. 41 Then, taking the five loaves and the two fish, he looked up to heaven, said the blessing, broke the loaves, and gave them to the disciples to distribute. He also divided the two fish among them. 42 They all ate and were satisfied; 43 and twelve baskets were filled with what was left of the bread and the fish. 44 Those who ate the loaves numbered five thousand men.

45 As soon as they had finished, he made his disciples embark and cross to Bethsaida ahead of him, while he himself dismissed the crowd. 46 After taking leave of them, he went up the hill to pray. 47 It was now late and the boat was already well out on the water, while he was alone on the land. 48 Somewhere between three and six in the morning, seeing them labouring at the oars against a head wind, he came towards them, walking on the lake. He was going to pass by them; 49 but when they saw him walking on the lake, they thought it was a ghost and cried out; 50 for they all saw him and were terrified. But at once he spoke to them: 'Take heart! It is I; do not be afraid.' 51 Then he climbed into the boat with them, and the wind dropped. At this they were utterly astounded, 52 for they had not understood the incident of the loaves; their minds were closed.

53 So they completed the crossing and landed at Gennesaret, where they made fast. 54 When they came ashore, he was recognized at once; 55 and the people scoured the whole countryside and brought the sick on their beds to any place where he was reported to be. 56 Wherever he went, to village or town or farm, they laid the sick in the market-place and begged him to let them simply touch the edge of his cloak; and all who touched him were healed.

7 A GROUP of Pharisees, with some scribes who had come from Jerusalem, met him 2 and noticed that some of his disciples were eating their food with defiled hands — in other words, without washing them. 3 (For Pharisees and

---

q Gk *his*   *r* The denarius was the usual day's wage for a laborer   6:37 **denarii:** *see p. xxix.*   6:56 **edge:** *or* tassel.

NEW AMERICAN BIBLE

because of his oaths and the guests he did not wish to break his word to her. 27 So he promptly dispatched an executioner with orders to bring back his head. He went off and beheaded him in the prison. 28 He brought in the head on a platter and gave it to the girl. The girl in turn gave it to her mother. 29 When his disciples heard about it, they came and took his body and laid it in a tomb.

30 The apostles gathered together with Jesus and reported all they had done and taught. 31 He said to them, "Come away by yourselves to a deserted place and rest a while." People were coming and going in great numbers, and they had no opportunity even to eat. 32 So they went off in the boat by themselves to a deserted place. 33 People saw them leaving and many came to know about it. They hastened there on foot from all the towns and arrived at the place before them.

34 When he disembarked and saw the vast crowd, his heart was moved with pity for them, for they were like sheep without a shepherd; and he began to teach them many things. 35 By now it was already late and his disciples approached him and said, "This is a deserted place and it is already very late. 36 Dismiss them so that they can go to the surrounding farms and villages and buy themselves something to eat." 37 He said to them in reply, "Give them some food yourselves." But they said to him, "Are we to buy two hundred days' wages worth of food and give it to them to eat?" 38 He asked them, "How many loaves do you have? Go and see." And when they had found out they said, "Five loaves and two fish." 39 So he gave orders to have them sit down in groups on the green grass. 40 The people took their places in rows by hundreds and by fifties. 41 Then, taking the five loaves and the two fish and looking up to heaven, he said the blessing, broke the loaves, and gave them to [his] disciples to set before the people; he also divided the two fish among them all. 42 They all ate and were satisfied. 43 And they picked up twelve wicker baskets full of fragments and what was left of the fish. 44 Those who ate [of the loaves] were five thousand men.

45 Then he made his disciples get into the boat and precede him to the other side toward Bethsaida, while he dismissed the crowd. 46 And when he had taken leave of them, he went off to the mountain to pray. 47 When it was evening, the boat was far out on the sea and he was alone on shore. 48 Then he saw that they were tossed about while rowing, for the wind was against them. About the fourth watch of the night, he came towards them walking on the sea. He meant to pass by them. 49 But when they saw him walking on the sea, they thought it was a ghost and cried out. 50 They had all seen him and were terrified. But at once he spoke with them, "Take courage, it is I, do not be afraid!" 51 He got into the boat with them and the wind died down. They were [completely] astounded. 52 They had not understood the incident of the loaves. On the contrary, their hearts were hardened.

53 After making the crossing, they came to land at Gennesaret and tied up there. 54 As they were leaving the boat, people immediately recognized him. 55 They scurried about the surrounding country and began to bring in the sick on mats to wherever they heard he was. 56 Whatever villages or towns or countryside he entered, they laid the sick in the marketplaces and begged him that they might touch only the tassel on his cloak; and as many as touched it were healed.

7 Now when the Pharisees with some scribes who had come from Jerusalem gathered around him, 2 they observed that some of his disciples ate their meals with unclean, that is, unwashed, hands. 3 (For the Pharisees and, in

NEW JERUSALEM BIBLE

tressed but, thinking of the oaths he had sworn and of his guests, he was reluctant to break his word to her. 27 At once the king sent one of the bodyguard with orders to bring John's head. 28 The man went off and beheaded him in the prison; then he brought the head on a dish and gave it to the girl, and the girl gave it to her mother. 29 When John's disciples heard about this, they came and took his body and laid it in a tomb.

30 The apostles rejoined Jesus and told him all they had done and taught. 31 And he said to them, 'Come away to some lonely place all by yourselves and rest for a while'; for there were so many coming and going that there was no time for them even to eat. 32 So they went off in the boat to a lonely place where they could be by themselves. 33 But people saw them going, and many recognised them; and from every town they all hurried to the place on foot and reached it before them. 34 So as he stepped ashore he saw a large crowd; and he took pity on them because they were like sheep without a shepherd, and he set himself to teach them at some length. 35 By now it was getting very late, and his disciples came up to him and said, 'This is a lonely place and it is getting very late, 36 so send them away, and they can go to the farms and villages round about, to buy themselves something to eat.' 37 He replied, 'Give them something to eat yourselves.' They answered, 'Are we to go and spend two hundred denarii on bread for them to eat?' 38 He asked, 'How many loaves have you? Go and see.' And when they had found out they said, 'Five, and two fish.' 39 Then he ordered them to get all the people to sit down in groups on the green grass, 40 and they sat down on the ground in squares of hundreds and fifties. 41 Then he took the five loaves and the two fish, raised his eyes to heaven and said the blessing; then he broke the loaves and began handing them to his disciples to distribute among the people. He also shared out the two fish among them all. 42 They all ate as much as they wanted. 43 They collected twelve basketfuls of scraps of bread and pieces of fish. 44 Those who had eaten the loaves numbered five thousand men.

45 And at once he made his disciples get into the boat and go on ahead to the other side near Bethsaida, while he himself sent the crowd away. 46 After saying goodbye to them he went off into the hills to pray. 47 When evening came, the boat was far out on the sea, and he was alone on the land. 48 He could see that they were hard pressed in their rowing, for the wind was against them; and about the fourth watch of the night he came towards them, walking on the sea. He was going to pass them by, 49 but when they saw him walking on the sea they thought it was a ghost and cried out; 50 for they had all seen him and were terrified. But at once he spoke to them and said, 'Courage! It's me! Don't be afraid.' 51 Then he got into the boat with them and the wind dropped. They were utterly and completely dumbfounded, 52 because they had not seen what the miracle of the loaves meant; their minds were closed.

53 Having made the crossing, they came to land at Gennesaret and moored there. 54 When they disembarked people at once recognised him, 55 and started hurrying all through the countryside and brought the sick on stretchers to wherever they heard he was. 56 And wherever he went, to village or town or farm, they laid down the sick in the open spaces, begging him to let them touch even the fringe of his cloak. And all those who touched him were saved.

7 The Pharisees and some of the scribes who had come from Jerusalem gathered round him, 2 and they noticed that some of his disciples were eating with unclean hands, that is, without washing them. 3 For the Pharisees, and all

NEW REVISED STANDARD VERSION	REVISED ENGLISH BIBLE

and all the Jews, do not eat unless they thoroughly wash their hands,[s] thus observing the tradition of the elders; 4and they do not eat anything from the market unless they wash it;[t] and there are also many other traditions that they observe, the washing of cups, pots, and bronze kettles.[u] 5So the Pharisees and the scribes asked him, "Why do your disciples not live[v] according to the tradition of the elders, but eat with defiled hands?" 6He said to them, "Isaiah prophesied rightly about you hypocrites, as it is written,

'This people honors me with their lips,
　　but their hearts are far from me;
7 in vain do they worship me,
　　teaching human precepts as doctrines.'

8You abandon the commandment of God and hold to human tradition."

9　Then he said to them, "You have a fine way of rejecting the commandment of God in order to keep your tradition! 10For Moses said, 'Honor your father and your mother'; and, 'Whoever speaks evil of father or mother must surely die.' 11But you say that if anyone tells father or mother, 'Whatever support you might have had from me is Corban' (that is, an offering to God[w]) — 12then you no longer permit doing anything for a father or mother, 13thus making void the word of God through your tradition that you have handed on. And you do many things like this."

14　Then he called the crowd again and said to them, "Listen to me, all of you, and understand: 15there is nothing outside a person that by going in can defile, but the things that come out are what defile."[x]

17　When he had left the crowd and entered the house, his disciples asked him about the parable. 18He said to them, "Then do you also fail to understand? Do you not see that whatever goes into a person from outside cannot defile, 19since it enters, not the heart but the stomach, and goes out into the sewer?" (Thus he declared all foods clean.) 20And he said, "It is what comes out of a person that defiles. 21For it is from within, from the human heart, that evil intentions come: fornication, theft, murder, 22adultery, avarice, wickedness, deceit, licentiousness, envy, slander, pride, folly. 23All these evil things come from within, and they defile a person."

24　From there he set out and went away to the region of Tyre.[y] He entered a house and did not want anyone to know he was there. Yet he could not escape notice, 25but a woman whose little daughter had an unclean spirit immediately heard about him, and she came and bowed down at his feet. 26Now the woman was a Gentile, of Syrophoenician origin. She begged him to cast the demon out of her daughter. 27He said to her, "Let the children be fed first, for it is not fair to take the children's food and throw it to the dogs." 28But she answered him, "Sir,[z] even the dogs under the table eat the children's crumbs." 29Then he said to her, "For saying that, you may go — the demon has left your daughter." 30So she went home, found the child lying on the bed, and the demon gone.

31　Then he returned from the region of Tyre, and went by way of Sidon towards the Sea of Galilee, in the region of the Decapolis. 32They brought to him a deaf man who

Jews in general never eat without washing their hands, in obedience to ancient tradition; 4and on coming from the market-place they never eat without first washing. And there are many other points on which they maintain traditional rules, for example in the washing of cups and jugs and copper bowls.) 5These Pharisees and scribes questioned Jesus: 'Why do your disciples not conform to the ancient tradition, but eat their food with defiled hands?' 6He answered, 'How right Isaiah was when he prophesied about you hypocrites in these words: "This people pays me lip-service, but their heart is far from me: 7they worship me in vain, for they teach as doctrines the commandments of men." 8You neglect the commandment of God, in order to maintain the tradition of men.'

9He said to them, 'How clever you are at setting aside the commandment of God in order to maintain your tradition! 10Moses said, "Honour your father and your mother," and again, "Whoever curses his father or mother shall be put to death." 11But you hold that if someone says to his father or mother, "Anything I have which might have been used for your benefit is Corban," ' (that is, set apart for God) 12'he is no longer allowed to do anything for his father or mother. 13In this way by your tradition, handed down among you, you make God's word null and void. And you do many other things just like that.'

14On another occasion he called the people and said to them, 'Listen to me, all of you, and understand this: 15nothing that goes into a person from outside can defile him; no, it is the things that come out of a person that defile him.'

17When he had left the people and gone indoors, his disciples questioned him about the parable. 18He said to them, 'Are you as dull as the rest? Do you not see that nothing that goes into a person from outside can defile him, 19because it does not go into the heart but into the stomach, and so goes out into the drain?' By saying this he declared all foods clean. 20He went on, 'It is what comes out of a person that defiles him. 21From inside, from the human heart, come evil thoughts, acts of fornication, theft, murder, 22adultery, greed, and malice; fraud, indecency, envy, slander, arrogance, and folly; 23all these evil things come from within, and they are what defile a person.'

24He moved on from there into the territory of Tyre. He found a house to stay in, and would have liked to remain unrecognized, but that was impossible. 25Almost at once a woman whose small daughter was possessed by an unclean spirit heard of him and came and fell at his feet. 26(The woman was a Gentile, a Phoenician of Syria by nationality.) She begged him to drive the demon out of her daughter. 27He said to her, 'Let the children be satisfied first; it is not right to take the children's bread and throw it to the dogs.' 28'Sir,' she replied, 'even the dogs under the table eat the children's scraps.' 29He said to her, 'For saying that, go, and you will find the demon has left your daughter.' 30And when she returned home, she found the child lying in bed; the demon had left her.

31On his journey back from Tyrian territory he went by way of Sidon to the sea of Galilee, well within the territory of the Decapolis. 32They brought to him a man who was

---

[s]Meaning of Gk uncertain 　[t]Other ancient authorities read and when they come from the marketplace, they do not eat unless they purify themselves 　[u]Other ancient authorities add and beds [v]Gk walk 　[w]Gk lacks to God 　[x]Other ancient authorities add verse 16, "Let anyone with ears to hear listen" 　[y]Other ancient authorities add and Sidon 　[z]Or Lord; other ancient authorities prefix Yes

7:3 **washing their hands:** some witnesses add with the fist; others add frequently; or thoroughly. 　7:9 **maintain:** some witnesses read establish. 　7:15 **that defile him:** some witnesses here add 16If you have ears to hear, then hear.

fact, all Jews, do not eat without carefully washing their hands, keeping the tradition of the elders. 4 And on coming from the marketplace they do not eat without purifying themselves. And there are many other things that they have traditionally observed, the purification of cups and jugs and kettles [and beds].) 5 So the Pharisees and scribes questioned him, "Why do your disciples not follow the tradition of the elders but instead eat a meal with unclean hands?" 6 He responded, "Well did Isaiah prophesy about you hypocrites, as it is written:

'This people honors me with their lips,
  but their hearts are far from me;
7 In vain do they worship me,
  teaching as doctrines human precepts.'

8 You disregard God's commandment but cling to human tradition." 9 He went on to say, "How well you have set aside the commandment of God in order to uphold your tradition! 10 For Moses said, 'Honor your father and your mother,' and 'Whoever curses father or mother shall die.' 11 Yet you say, 'If a person says to father or mother, "Any support you might have had from me is qorban"' (meaning, dedicated to God), 12 you allow him to do nothing more for his father or mother. 13 You nullify the word of God in favor of your tradition that you have handed on. And you do many such things." 14 He summoned the crowd again and said to them, "Hear me, all of you, and understand. 15 Nothing that enters one from outside can defile that person; but the things that come out from within are what defile."[16]

17 When he got home away from the crowd his disciples questioned him about the parable. 18 He said to them, "Are even you likewise without understanding? Do you not realize that everything that goes into a person from outside cannot defile, 19 since it enters not the heart but the stomach and passes out into the latrine?" (Thus he declared all foods clean.) 20 "But what comes out of a person, that is what defiles. 21 From within people, from their hearts, come evil thoughts, unchastity, theft, murder, 22 adultery, greed, malice, deceit, licentiousness, envy, blasphemy, arrogance, folly. 23 All these evils come from within and they defile."

24 From that place he went off to the district of Tyre. He entered a house and wanted no one to know about it, but he could not escape notice. 25 Soon a woman whose daughter had an unclean spirit heard about him. She came and fell at his feet. 26 The woman was a Greek, a Syrophoenician by birth, and she begged him to drive the demon out of her daughter. 27 He said to her, "Let the children be fed first. For it is not right to take the food of the children and throw it to the dogs." 28 She replied and said to him, "Lord, even the dogs under the table eat the children's scraps." 29 Then he said to her, "For saying this, you may go. The demon has gone out of your daughter." 30 When the woman went home, she found the child lying in bed and the demon gone.

31 Again he left the district of Tyre and went by way of Sidon to the Sea of Galilee, into the district of the Decapolis. 32 And people brought to him a deaf man who had a

the Jews, keep the tradition of the elders and never eat without washing their arms as far as the elbow; 4 and on returning from the market place they never eat without first sprinkling themselves. There are also many other observances which have been handed down to them to keep, concerning the washing of cups and pots and bronze dishes. 5 So the Pharisees and scribes asked him, 'Why do your disciples not respect the tradition of the elders but eat their food with unclean hands?' 6 He answered, 'How rightly Isaiah prophesied about you hypocrites in the passage of scripture:

This people honours me
  only with lip-service,
  while their hearts are far from me.
7 Their reverence of me is worthless;
  the lessons they teach
  are nothing but human commandments.e

8 You put aside the commandment of God to observe human traditions.' 9 And he said to them, 'How ingeniously you get round the commandment of God in order to preserve your own tradition! 10 For Moses said: Honour your father and your mother, and, Anyone who curses father or mother must be put to death.f 11 But you say, "If a man says to his father or mother: Anything I have that I might have used to help you is Korbang (that is, dedicated to God)," 12 then he is forbidden from that moment to do anything for his father or mother. 13 In this way you make God's word ineffective for the sake of your tradition which you have handed down. And you do many other things like this.'

14 He called the people to him again and said, 'Listen to me, all of you, and understand. 15 Nothing that goes into someone from outside can make that person unclean; it is the things that come out of someone that make that person unclean. 16 Anyone who has ears for listening should listen!'

17 When he had gone into the house, away from the crowd, his disciples questioned him about the parable. 18 He said to them, 'Even you — don't you understand? Can't you see that nothing that goes into someone from outside can make that person unclean, 19 because it goes not into the heart but into the stomach and passes into the sewer?' (Thus he pronounced all foods clean.) 20 And he went on, 'It is what comes out of someone that makes that person unclean. 21 For it is from within, from the heart, that evil intentions emerge: fornication, theft, murder, 22 adultery, avarice, malice, deceit, indecency, envy, slander, pride, folly. 23 All these evil things come from within and make a person unclean.'

24 He left that place and set out for the territory of Tyre. There he went into a house and did not want anyone to know he was there; but he could not pass unrecognised. 25 At once a woman whose little daughter had an unclean spirit heard about him and came and fell at his feet. 26 Now this woman was a gentile, by birth a Syro-Phoenician, and she begged him to drive the devil out of her daughter. 27 And he said to her, 'The children should be fed first, because it is not fair to take the children's food and throw it to little dogs.' 28 But she spoke up, 'Ah yes, sir,' she replied, 'but little dogs under the table eat the scraps from the children.' 29 And he said to her, 'For saying this you may go home happy; the devil has gone out of your daughter.' 30 So she went off home and found the child lying on the bed and the devil gone.

31 Returning from the territory of Tyre, he went by way of Sidon towards the Lake of Galilee, right through the Decapolis territory. 32 And they brought him a deaf man

---

7, 16: Verse 16, "Anyone who has ears to hear ought to hear," is omitted because it is lacking in some of the best Greek manuscripts and was probably transferred here by scribes from 4, (9).23.

e 7 Is 29:13.   f 7 Ex 20:12; 21:17.   g 7 Nothing Korban could be used for anyone else — a convenient legal fiction.

had an impediment in his speech; and they begged him to lay his hand on him. 33 He took him aside in private, away from the crowd, and put his fingers into his ears, and he spat and touched his tongue. 34 Then looking up to heaven, he sighed and said to him, "Ephphatha," that is, "Be opened." 35 And immediately his ears were opened, his tongue was released, and he spoke plainly. 36 Then Jesus*a* ordered them to tell no one; but the more he ordered them, the more zealously they proclaimed it. 37 They were astounded beyond measure, saying, "He has done everything well; he even makes the deaf to hear and the mute to speak."

8 In those days when there was again a great crowd without anything to eat, he called his disciples and said to them, 2 "I have compassion for the crowd, because they have been with me now for three days and have nothing to eat. 3 If I send them away hungry to their homes, they will faint on the way — and some of them have come from a great distance." 4 His disciples replied, "How can one feed these people with bread here in the desert?" 5 He asked them, "How many loaves do you have?" They said, "Seven." 6 Then he ordered the crowd to sit down on the ground; and he took the seven loaves, and after giving thanks he broke them and gave them to his disciples to distribute; and they distributed them to the crowd. 7 They had also a few small fish; and after blessing them, he ordered that these too should be distributed. 8 They ate and were filled; and they took up the broken pieces left over, seven baskets full. 9 Now there were about four thousand people. And he sent them away. 10 And immediately he got into the boat with his disciples and went to the district of Dalmanutha.*b*

11 The Pharisees came and began to argue with him, asking him for a sign from heaven, to test him. 12 And he sighed deeply in his spirit and said, "Why does this generation ask for a sign? Truly I tell you, no sign will be given to this generation." 13 And he left them, and getting into the boat again, he went across to the other side.

14 Now the disciples*c* had forgotten to bring any bread; and they had only one loaf with them in the boat. 15 And he cautioned them, saying, "Watch out — beware of the yeast of the Pharisees and the yeast of Herod."*d* 16 They said to one another, "It is because we have no bread." 17 And becoming aware of it, Jesus said to them, "Why are you talking about having no bread? Do you still not perceive or understand? Are your hearts hardened? 18 Do you have eyes, and fail to see? Do you have ears, and fail to hear? And do you not remember? 19 When I broke the five loaves for the five thousand, how many baskets full of broken pieces did you collect?" They said to him, "Twelve." 20 "And the seven for the four thousand, how many baskets full of broken pieces did you collect?" And they said to him, "Seven." 21 Then he said to them, "Do you not yet understand?"

22 They came to Bethsaida. Some people*e* brought a blind man to him and begged him to touch him. 23 He took the blind man by the hand and led him out of the village; and when he had put saliva on his eyes and laid his hands on him, he asked him, "Can you see anything?" 24 And the man*a* looked up and said, "I can see people, but they look like trees, walking." 25 Then Jesus*a* laid his hands on his eyes again; and he looked intently and his sight was restored, and he saw everything clearly. 26 Then he sent him away to his home, saying, "Do not even go into the village."*f*

deaf and had an impediment in his speech, and begged Jesus to lay his hand on him. 33 He took him aside, away from the crowd; then he put his fingers in the man's ears, and touched his tongue with spittle. 34 Looking up to heaven, he sighed, and said to him, 'Ephphatha,' which means 'Be opened.' 35 With that his hearing was restored, and at the same time the impediment was removed and he spoke clearly. 36 Jesus forbade them to tell anyone; but the more he forbade them, the more they spread it abroad. 37 Their astonishment knew no bounds: 'All that he does, he does well,' they said; 'he even makes the deaf hear and the dumb speak.'

8 THERE was another occasion about this time when a huge crowd had collected, and, as they had no food, Jesus called his disciples and said to them, 2 'My heart goes out to these people; they have been with me now for three days and have nothing to eat. 3 If I send them home hungry, they will faint on the way, and some of them have a long way to go.' 4 His disciples answered, 'How can anyone provide these people with bread in this remote place?' 5 'How many loaves have you?' he asked; and they answered, 'Seven.' 6 So he ordered the people to sit down on the ground; then he took the seven loaves, and after giving thanks to God he broke the bread and gave it to his disciples to distribute; and they distributed it to the people. 7 They had also a few small fish, which he blessed and ordered them to distribute. 8 They ate and were satisfied, and seven baskets were filled with what was left over. 9 The people numbered about four thousand. Then he dismissed them, 10 and at once got into the boat with his disciples and went to the district of Dalmanutha.

11 Then the Pharisees came out and began to argue with him. To test him they asked him for a sign from heaven. 12 He sighed deeply and said, 'Why does this generation ask for a sign? Truly I tell you: no sign shall be given to this generation.' 13 With that he left them, re-embarked, and made for the other shore.

14 Now they had forgotten to take bread with them, and had only one loaf in the boat. 15 He began to warn them: 'Beware,' he said, 'be on your guard against the leaven of the Pharisees and the leaven of Herod.' 16 So they began to talk among themselves about having no bread. 17 Knowing this, he said to them, 'Why are you talking about having no bread? Have you no inkling yet? Do you still not understand? Are your minds closed? 18 You have eyes: can you not see? You have ears: can you not hear? Have you forgotten? 19 When I broke the five loaves among five thousand, how many basketfuls of pieces did you pick up?' 'Twelve,' they said. 20 'And how many when I broke the seven loaves among four thousand?' 'Seven,' they answered. 21 He said to them, 'Do you still not understand?'

22 They arrived at Bethsaida. There the people brought a blind man to Jesus and begged him to touch him. 23 He took the blind man by the hand and led him out of the village. Then he spat on his eyes, laid his hands upon him, and asked whether he could see anything. 24 The man's sight began to come back, and he said, 'I see people — they look like trees, but they are walking about.' 25 Jesus laid his hands on his eyes again; he looked hard, and now he was cured and could see everything clearly. 26 Then Jesus sent him home, saying, 'Do not even go into the village.'

---

a Gk *he*　　*b* Other ancient authorities read *Mageda* or *Magdala*
c Gk *they*　　*d* Other ancient authorities read *the Herodians*
e Gk *They*　　*f* Other ancient authorities add *or tell anyone in the village*

8:10 **Dalmanutha:** *some witnesses read* Magedan; *others read* Magdala.　　8:26 **Do . . . village:** *some witnesses read* Do not tell anyone in the village.

speech impediment and begged him to lay his hand on him. ³³He took him off by himself away from the crowd. He put his finger into the man's ears and, spitting, touched his tongue; ³⁴then he looked up to heaven and groaned, and said to him, *"Ephphatha!"* (that is, "Be opened!") ³⁵And [immediately] the man's ears were opened, his speech impediment was removed, and he spoke plainly. ³⁶He ordered them not to tell anyone. But the more he ordered them not to, the more they proclaimed it. ³⁷They were exceedingly astonished and they said, "He has done all things well. He makes the deaf hear and [the] mute speak."

8 In those days when there again was a great crowd without anything to eat, he summoned the disciples and said, ²"My heart is moved with pity for the crowd, because they have been with me now for three days and have nothing to eat. ³If I send them away hungry to their homes, they will collapse on the way, and some of them have come a great distance." ⁴His disciples answered him, "Where can anyone get enough bread to satisfy them here in this deserted place?" ⁵Still he asked them, "How many loaves do you have?" "Seven," they replied. ⁶He ordered the crowd to sit down on the ground. Then, taking the seven loaves he gave thanks, broke them, and gave them to his disciples to distribute, and they distributed them to the crowd. ⁷They also had a few fish. He said the blessing over them and ordered them distributed also. ⁸They ate and were satisfied. They picked up the fragments left over—seven baskets. ⁹There were about four thousand people.

He dismissed them ¹⁰and got into the boat with his disciples and came to the region of Dalmanutha.

¹¹The Pharisees came forward and began to argue with him, seeking from him a sign from heaven to test him. ¹²He sighed from the depth of his spirit and said, "Why does this generation seek a sign? Amen, I say to you, no sign will be given to this generation." ¹³Then he left them, got into the boat again, and went off to the other shore.

¹⁴They had forgotten to bring bread, and they had only one loaf with them in the boat. ¹⁵He enjoined them, "Watch out, guard against the leaven of the Pharisees and the leaven of Herod." ¹⁶They concluded among themselves that it was because they had no bread. ¹⁷When he became aware of this he said to them, "Why do you conclude that it is because you have no bread? Do you not yet understand or comprehend? Are your hearts hardened? ¹⁸Do you have eyes and not see, ears and not hear? And do you not remember, ¹⁹when I broke the five loaves for the five thousand, how many wicker baskets full of fragments you picked up?" They answered him, "Twelve." ²⁰"When I broke the seven loaves for the four thousand, how many full baskets of fragments did you pick up?" They answered [him], "Seven." ²¹He said to them, "Do you still not understand?"

²²When they arrived at Bethsaida, they brought to him a blind man and begged him to touch him. ²³He took the blind man by the hand and led him outside the village. Putting spittle on his eyes he laid his hands on him and asked, "Do you see anything?" ²⁴Looking up he replied, "I see people looking like trees and walking." ²⁵Then he laid hands on his eyes a second time and he saw clearly; his sight was restored and he could see everything distinctly. ²⁶Then he sent him home and said, "Do not even go into the village."

who had an impediment in his speech; and they asked him to lay his hand on him. ³³He took him aside to be by themselves, away from the crowd, put his fingers into the man's ears and touched his tongue with spittle. ³⁴Then looking up to heaven he sighed; and he said to him, 'Ephphatha,' that is, 'Be opened.' ³⁵And his ears were opened, and at once the impediment of his tongue was loosened and he spoke clearly. ³⁶And Jesus ordered them to tell no one about it, but the more he insisted, the more widely they proclaimed it. ³⁷Their admiration was unbounded, and they said, 'Everything he does is good, he makes the deaf hear and the dumb speak.'

8 And now once again a great crowd had gathered, and they had nothing to eat. So he called his disciples to him and said to them, ²'I feel sorry for all these people; they have been with me for three days now and have nothing to eat. ³If I send them off home hungry they will collapse on the way; some have come a great distance.' ⁴His disciples replied, 'Where could anyone get these people enough bread to eat in a deserted place?' ⁵He asked them, 'How many loaves have you?' And they said to him, 'Seven.' ⁶Then he instructed the crowd to sit down on the ground, and he took the seven loaves, and after giving thanks he broke them and began handing them to his disciples to distribute; and they distributed them among the crowd. ⁷They had a few small fishes as well, and over these he said a blessing and ordered them to be distributed too. ⁸They ate as much as they wanted, and they collected seven basketfuls of the scraps left over. ⁹Now there had been about four thousand people. He sent them away ¹⁰and at once, getting into the boat with his disciples, went to the region of Dalmanutha.

¹¹The Pharisees came up and started a discussion with him; they demanded of him a sign from heaven, to put him to the test. ¹²And with a profound sigh he said, 'Why does this generation demand a sign? In truth I tell you, no sign shall be given to this generation.' ¹³And, leaving them again, he re-embarked and went away to the other side.

¹⁴The disciples had forgotten to take any bread and they had only one loaf with them in the boat. ¹⁵Then he gave them this warning, 'Keep your eyes open; look out for the yeast of the Pharisees and the yeast of Herod.' ¹⁶And they said to one another, 'It is because we have no bread.' ¹⁷And Jesus knew it, and he said to them, 'Why are you talking about having no bread? Do you still not understand, still not realise? Are your minds closed? ¹⁸Have you *eyes and do not see, ears and do not hear?* ^h Or do you not remember? ¹⁹When I broke the five loaves for the five thousand, how many baskets full of scraps did you collect?' They answered, 'Twelve.' ²⁰'And when I broke the seven loaves for the four thousand, how many baskets full of scraps did you collect?' And they answered, 'Seven.' ²¹Then he said to them, 'Do you still not realise?'

²²They came to Bethsaida, and some people brought to him a blind man whom they begged him to touch. ²³He took the blind man by the hand and led him outside the village. Then, putting spittle on his eyes and laying his hands on him, he asked, 'Can you see anything?' ²⁴The man, who was beginning to see, replied, 'I can see people; they look like trees as they walk around.' ²⁵Then he laid his hands on the man's eyes again and he saw clearly; he was cured, and he could see everything plainly and distinctly. ²⁶And Jesus sent him home, saying, 'Do not even go into the village.'

h 8 Jr 5:21; Ezk 12:2.

NEW REVISED STANDARD VERSION

27 Jesus went on with his disciples to the villages of Caesarea Philippi; and on the way he asked his disciples, "Who do people say that I am?" 28 And they answered him, "John the Baptist; and others, Elijah; and still others, one of the prophets." 29 He asked them, "But who do you say that I am?" Peter answered him, "You are the Messiah."g 30 And he sternly ordered them not to tell anyone about him.

31 Then he began to teach them that the Son of Man must undergo great suffering, and be rejected by the elders, the chief priests, and the scribes, and be killed, and after three days rise again. 32 He said all this quite openly. And Peter took him aside and began to rebuke him. 33 But turning and looking at his disciples, he rebuked Peter and said, "Get behind me, Satan! For you are setting your mind not on divine things but on human things."

34 He called the crowd with his disciples, and said to them, "If any want to become my followers, let them deny themselves and take up their cross and follow me. 35 For those who want to save their life will lose it, and those who lose their life for my sake, and for the sake of the gospel,h will save it. 36 For what will it profit them to gain the whole world and forfeit their life? 37 Indeed, what can they give in return for their life? 38 Those who are ashamed of me and of my wordsi in this adulterous and sinful generation, of them the Son of Man will also be ashamed when he comes in the glory of his Father with the holy angels." 1 And he said to them, "Truly I tell you, there are some standing here who will not taste death until they see that the kingdom of God has come withj power."

2 Six days later, Jesus took with him Peter and James and John, and led them up a high mountain apart, by themselves. And he was transfigured before them, 3 and his clothes became dazzling white, such as no onek on earth could bleach them. 4 And there appeared to them Elijah with Moses, who were talking with Jesus. 5 Then Peter said to Jesus, "Rabbi, it is good for us to be here; let us make three dwellings,l one for you, one for Moses, and one for Elijah." 6 He did not know what to say, for they were terrified. 7 Then a cloud overshadowed them, and from the cloud there came a voice, "This is my Son, the Beloved;m listen to him!" 8 Suddenly when they looked around, they saw no one with them any more, but only Jesus.

9 As they were coming down the mountain, he ordered them to tell no one about what they had seen, until after the Son of Man had risen from the dead. 10 So they kept the matter to themselves, questioning what this rising from the dead could mean. 11 Then they asked him, "Why do the scribes say that Elijah must come first?" 12 He said to them, "Elijah is indeed coming first to restore all things. How then is it written about the Son of Man, that he is to go through many sufferings and be treated with contempt? 13 But I tell you that Elijah has come, and they did to him whatever they pleased, as it is written about him."

14 When they came to the disciples, they saw a great crowd around them, and some scribes arguing with them. 15 When the whole crowd saw him, they were immediately overcome with awe, and they ran forward to greet him. 16 He asked them, "What are you arguing about with them?" 17 Someone from the crowd answered him, "Teacher, I brought you my son; he has a spirit that makes him unable to speak; 18 and whenever it seizes him, it dashes him down; and he foams and grinds his teeth and becomes rigid; and I asked your disciples to cast it out, but they could not do so."

REVISED ENGLISH BIBLE

27 JESUS and his disciples set out for the villages of Caesarea Philippi, and on the way he asked his disciples, 'Who do people say I am?' 28 They answered, 'Some say John the Baptist, others Elijah, others one of the prophets.' 29 'And you,' he asked, 'who do you say I am?' Peter replied: 'You are the Messiah.' 30 Then he gave them strict orders not to tell anyone about him; 31 and he began to teach them that the Son of Man had to endure great suffering, and to be rejected by the elders, chief priests, and scribes; to be put to death, and to rise again three days afterwards. 32 He spoke about it plainly. At this Peter took hold of him and began to rebuke him. 33 But Jesus, turning and looking at his disciples, rebuked Peter. 'Out of my sight, Satan!' he said. 'You think as men think, not as God thinks.'

34 Then he called the people to him, as well as his disciples, and said to them, 'Anyone who wants to be a follower of mine must renounce self; he must take up his cross and follow me. 35 Whoever wants to save his life will lose it, but whoever loses his life for my sake and for the gospel's will save it. 36 What does anyone gain by winning the whole world at the cost of his life? 37 What can he give to buy his life back? 38 If anyone is ashamed of me and my words in this wicked and godless age, the Son of Man will be ashamed of him, when he comes in the glory of his Father with the holy angels.'

9 He said to them, 'Truly I tell you: there are some of those standing here who will not taste death before they have seen the kingdom of God come with power.'

2 Six days later Jesus took Peter, James, and John with him and led them up a high mountain by themselves. And in their presence he was transfigured; 3 his clothes became dazzling white, with a whiteness no bleacher on earth could equal. 4 They saw Elijah appear and Moses with him, talking with Jesus. 5 Then Peter spoke: 'Rabbi,' he said, 'it is good that we are here! Shall we make three shelters, one for you, one for Moses, and one for Elijah?' 6 For he did not know what to say; they were so terrified. 7 Then a cloud appeared, casting its shadow over them, and out of the cloud came a voice: 'This is my beloved Son; listen to him.' 8 And suddenly, when they looked around, only Jesus was with them; there was no longer anyone else to be seen.

9 On their way down the mountain, he instructed them not to tell anyone what they had seen until the Son of Man had risen from the dead. 10 They seized upon those words, and discussed among themselves what this 'rising from the dead' could mean. 11 And they put a question to him: 'Why do the scribes say that Elijah must come first?' 12 He replied, 'Elijah does come first to set everything right. How is it, then, that the scriptures say of the Son of Man that he is to endure great suffering and be treated with contempt? 13 However, I tell you, Elijah has already come and they have done to him what they wanted, as the scriptures say of him.'

14 When they came back to the disciples they saw a large crowd surrounding them and scribes arguing with them. 15 As soon as they saw Jesus the whole crowd were overcome with awe and ran forward to welcome him. 16 He asked them, 'What is this argument about?' 17 A man in the crowd spoke up: 'Teacher, I brought my son for you to cure. He is possessed by a spirit that makes him dumb. 18 Whenever it attacks him, it flings him to the ground, and he foams at the mouth, grinds his teeth, and goes rigid. I asked your disciples to drive it out, but they could not.'

---

g Or the Christ   h Other ancient authorities read lose their life for the sake of the gospel   i Other ancient authorities read and of mine   j Or in   k Gk no fuller   l Or tents   m Or my beloved Son

8:38 me and my words: some witnesses read me and mine. Father . . . angels: some witnesses read Father and of the holy angels.
9:7 This . . . Son: or This is my only Son.

27 Now Jesus and his disciples set out for the villages of Caesarea Philippi. Along the way he asked his disciples, "Who do people say that I am?" 28 They said in reply, "John the Baptist, others Elijah, still others one of the prophets." 29 And he asked them, "But who do you say that I am?" Peter said to him in reply, "You are the Messiah." 30 Then he warned them not to tell anyone about him.

31 He began to teach them that the Son of Man must suffer greatly and be rejected by the elders, the chief priests, and the scribes, and be killed, and rise after three days. 32 He spoke this openly. Then Peter took him aside and began to rebuke him. 33 At this he turned around and, looking at his disciples, rebuked Peter and said, "Get behind me, Satan. You are thinking not as God does, but as human beings do."

34 He summoned the crowd with his disciples and said to them, "Whoever wishes to come after me must deny himself, take up his cross, and follow me. 35 For whoever wishes to save his life will lose it, but whoever loses his life for my sake and that of the gospel will save it. 36 What profit is there for one to gain the whole world and forfeit his life? 37 What could one give in exchange for his life? 38 Whoever is ashamed of me and of my words in this faithless and sinful generation, the Son of Man will be ashamed of when he comes in his Father's glory with the holy angels."

9 He also said to them, "Amen, I say to you, there are some standing here who will not taste death until they see that the kingdom of God has come in power."

2 After six days Jesus took Peter, James, and John and led them up a high mountain apart by themselves. And he was transfigured before them, 3 and his clothes became dazzling white, such as no fuller on earth could bleach them. 4 Then Elijah appeared to them along with Moses, and they were conversing with Jesus. 5 Then Peter said to Jesus in reply, "Rabbi, it is good that we are here! Let us make three tents: one for you, one for Moses, and one for Elijah." 6 He hardly knew what to say, they were so terrified. 7 Then a cloud came, casting a shadow over them; then from the cloud came a voice, "This is my beloved Son. Listen to him." 8 Suddenly, looking around, they no longer saw anyone but Jesus alone with them.

9 As they were coming down from the mountain, he charged them not to relate what they had seen to anyone, except when the Son of Man had risen from the dead. 10 So they kept the matter to themselves, questioning what rising from the dead meant. 11 Then they asked him, "Why do the scribes say that Elijah must come first?" 12 He told them, "Elijah will indeed come first and restore all things, yet how is it written regarding the Son of Man that he must suffer greatly and be treated with contempt? 13 But I tell you that Elijah has come and they did to him whatever they pleased, as it is written of him."

14 When they came to the disciples, they saw a large crowd around them and scribes arguing with them. 15 Immediately on seeing him, the whole crowd was utterly amazed. They ran up to him and greeted him. 16 He asked them, "What are you arguing about with them?" 17 Someone from the crowd answered him, "Teacher, I have brought to you my son possessed by a mute spirit. 18 Wherever it seizes him, it throws him down; he foams at the mouth, grinds his teeth, and becomes rigid. I asked your disciples to drive it out, but they were unable to do so." 19 He said to them in

27 Jesus and his disciples left for the villages round Caesarea Philippi. On the way he put this question to his disciples, 'Who do people say I am?' 28 And they told him, 'John the Baptist, others Elijah, others again, one of the prophets.' 29 'But you,' he asked, 'who do you say I am?' Peter spoke up and said to him, 'You are the Christ.' 30 And he gave them strict orders not to tell anyone about him.

31 Then he began to teach them that the Son of man was destined to suffer grievously, and to be rejected by the elders and the chief priests and the scribes, and to be put to death, and after three days to rise again; 32 and he said all this quite openly. Then, taking him aside, Peter tried to rebuke him. 33 But, turning and seeing his disciples, he rebuked Peter and said to him, 'Get behind me, Satan! You are thinking not as God thinks, but as human beings do.'

34 He called the people and his disciples to him and said, 'If anyone wants to be a follower of mine, let him renounce himself and take up his cross and follow me. 35 Anyone who wants to save his life will lose it; but anyone who loses his life for my sake, and for the sake of the gospel, will save it. 36 What gain, then, is it for anyone to win the whole world and forfeit his life? 37 And indeed what can anyone offer in exchange for his life? 38 For if anyone in this sinful and adulterous generation is ashamed of me and of my words, the Son of man will also be ashamed of him when he comes in the glory of his Father with the holy angels.'

9 And he said to them, 'In truth I tell you, there are some standing here who will not taste death before they see the kingdom of God come with power.'

2 Six days later, Jesus took with him Peter and James and John and led them up a high mountain on their own by themselves. There in their presence he was transfigured: 3 his clothes became brilliantly white, whiter than any earthly bleacher could make them. 4 Elijah appeared to them with Moses; and they were talking to Jesus. 5 Then Peter spoke to Jesus, 'Rabbi,' he said, 'it is wonderful for us to be here; so let us make three shelters, one for you, one for Moses and one for Elijah.' 6 He did not know what to say; they were so frightened. 7 And a cloud came, covering them in shadow; and from the cloud there came a voice, 'This is my Son, the Beloved. Listen to him.' 8 Then suddenly, when they looked round, they saw no one with them any more but only Jesus.

9 As they were coming down from the mountain he warned them to tell no one what they had seen, until after the Son of man had risen from the dead. 10 They observed the warning faithfully, though among themselves they discussed what 'rising from the dead' could mean. 11 And they put this question to him, 'Why do the scribes say that Elijah must come first?' 12 He said to them, 'Elijah is indeed first coming to set everything right again; yet how is it that the scriptures say about the Son of man that he must suffer grievously and be treated with contempt? 13 But I tell you that Elijah has come and they have treated him as they pleased, just as the scriptures say about him.'

14 As they were rejoining the disciples they saw a large crowd round them and some scribes arguing with them. 15 At once, when they saw him, the whole crowd were struck with amazement and ran to greet him. 16 And he asked them, 'What are you arguing about with them?' 17 A man answered him from the crowd, 'Master, I have brought my son to you; there is a spirit of dumbness in him, 18 and when it takes hold of him it throws him to the ground, and he foams at the mouth and grinds his teeth and goes rigid. And I asked your disciples to drive it out and they were

NEW REVISED STANDARD VERSION

19 He answered them, "You faithless generation, how much longer must I be among you? How much longer must I put up with you? Bring him to me." 20 And they brought the boy[n] to him. When the spirit saw him, immediately it convulsed the boy,[n] and he fell on the ground and rolled about, foaming at the mouth. 21 Jesus[o] asked the father, "How long has this been happening to him?" And he said, "From childhood. 22 It has often cast him into the fire and into the water, to destroy him; but if you are able to do anything, have pity on us and help us." 23 Jesus said to him, "If you are able! — All things can be done for the one who believes." 24 Immediately the father of the child cried out,[p] "I believe; help my unbelief!" 25 When Jesus saw that a crowd came running together, he rebuked the unclean spirit, saying to it, "You spirit that keeps this boy from speaking and hearing, I command you, come out of him, and never enter him again!" 26 After crying out and convulsing him terribly, it came out, and the boy was like a corpse, so that most of them said, "He is dead." 27 But Jesus took him by the hand and lifted him up, and he was able to stand. 28 When he had entered the house, his disciples asked him privately, "Why could we not cast it out?" 29 He said to them, "This kind can come out only through prayer."[q]

30 They went on from there and passed through Galilee. He did not want anyone to know it; 31 for he was teaching his disciples, saying to them, "The Son of Man is to be betrayed into human hands, and they will kill him, and three days after being killed, he will rise again." 32 But they did not understand what he was saying and were afraid to ask him.

33 Then they came to Capernaum; and when he was in the house he asked them, "What were you arguing about on the way?" 34 But they were silent, for on the way they had argued with one another who was the greatest. 35 He sat down, called the twelve, and said to them, "Whoever wants to be first must be last of all and servant of all." 36 Then he took a little child and put it among them; and taking it in his arms, he said to them, 37 "Whoever welcomes one such child in my name welcomes me, and whoever welcomes me welcomes not me but the one who sent me."

38 John said to him, "Teacher, we saw someone[r] casting out demons in your name, and we tried to stop him, because he was not following us." 39 But Jesus said, "Do not stop him; for no one who does a deed of power in my name will be able soon afterward to speak evil of me. 40 Whoever is not against us is for us. 41 For truly I tell you, whoever gives you a cup of water to drink because you bear the name of Christ will by no means lose the reward.

42 "If any of you put a stumbling block before one of these little ones who believe in me,[s] it would be better for you if a great millstone were hung around your neck and you were thrown into the sea. 43 If your hand causes you to stumble, cut it off; it is better for you to enter life maimed than to have two hands and to go to hell,[t] to the unquenchable fire.[u] 45 And if your foot causes you to stumble, cut it off; it is better for you to enter life lame than to have two feet and to be thrown into hell.[t,u] 47 And if your eye causes you to stumble, tear it out; it is better for you to enter the kingdom of God with one eye than to have two eyes and to be thrown into hell,[t] 48 where their worm never dies, and the fire is never quenched. 49 "For everyone will be salted with fire.[v] 50 Salt is

REVISED ENGLISH BIBLE

19 Jesus answered: 'What an unbelieving generation! How long shall I be with you? How long must I endure you? Bring him to me.' 20 So they brought the boy to him; and as soon as the spirit saw him it threw the boy into convulsions, and he fell on the ground and rolled about foaming at the mouth. 21 Jesus asked his father, 'How long has he been like this?' 'From childhood,' he replied; 22 'it has often tried to destroy him by throwing him into the fire or into water. But if it is at all possible for you, take pity on us and help us.' 23 'If it is possible!' said Jesus. 'Everything is possible to one who believes.' 24 At once the boy's father cried: 'I believe; help my unbelief.' 25 When Jesus saw that the crowd was closing in on them, he spoke sternly to the unclean spirit. 'Deaf and dumb spirit,' he said, 'I command you, come out of him and never go back!' 26 It shrieked aloud and threw the boy into repeated convulsions, and then came out, leaving him looking like a corpse; in fact, many said, 'He is dead.' 27 But Jesus took hold of his hand and raised him to his feet, and he stood up.

28 Then Jesus went indoors, and his disciples asked him privately, 'Why could we not drive it out?' 29 He said, 'This kind cannot be driven out except by prayer.'

30 THEY left that district and made their way through Galilee. Jesus did not want anyone to know, 31 because he was teaching his disciples, and telling them, 'The Son of Man is now to be handed over into the power of men, and they will kill him; and three days after being killed he will rise again.' 32 But they did not understand what he said, and were afraid to ask.

33 So they came to Capernaum; and when he had gone indoors, he asked them, 'What were you arguing about on the way?' 34 They were silent, because on the way they had been discussing which of them was the greatest. 35 So he sat down, called the Twelve, and said to them, 'If anyone wants to be first, he must make himself last of all and servant of all.' 36 Then he took a child, set him in front of them, and put his arm round him. 37 'Whoever receives a child like this in my name,' he said, 'receives me; and whoever receives me, receives not me but the One who sent me.'

38 John said to him, 'Teacher, we saw someone driving out demons in your name, and as he was not one of us, we tried to stop him.' 39 Jesus said, 'Do not stop him, for no one who performs a miracle in my name will be able the next moment to speak evil of me. 40 He who is not against us is on our side. 41 Truly I tell you: whoever gives you a cup of water to drink because you are followers of the Messiah will certainly not go unrewarded.

42 'If anyone causes the downfall of one of these little ones who believe, it would be better for him to be thrown into the sea with a millstone round his neck. 43 If your hand causes your downfall, cut it off; it is better for you to enter into life maimed than to keep both hands and go to hell, to the unquenchable fire. 45 If your foot causes your downfall, cut it off; it is better to enter into life crippled than to keep both your feet and be thrown into hell. 47 And if your eye causes your downfall, tear it out; it is better to enter into the kingdom of God with one eye than to keep both eyes and be thrown into hell, 48 where the devouring worm never dies and the fire is never quenched. 49 'Everyone will be salted with fire.

---

[n] Gk him   [o] Gk He   [p] Other ancient authorities add with tears
[q] Other ancient authorities add and fasting   [r] Other ancient authorities add who does not follow us   [s] Other ancient authorities lack in me   [t] Gk Gehenna   [u] Verses 44 and 46 (which are identical with verse 48) are lacking in the best ancient authorities
[v] Other ancient authorities either add or substitute and every sacrifice will be salted with salt

9:29 by prayer: some witnesses add and fasting.
9:43 unquenchable fire: some witnesses add 44 where the devouring worm never dies and the fire is never quenched.   9:45 into hell: some witnesses add 46 where the devouring worm never dies and the fire is never quenched.

reply, "O faithless generation, how long will I be with you? How long will I endure you? Bring him to me." 20 They brought the boy to him. And when he saw him, the spirit immediately threw the boy into convulsions. As he fell to the ground, he began to roll around and foam at the mouth. 21 Then he questioned his father, "How long has this been happening to him?" He replied, "Since childhood. 22 It has often thrown him into fire and into water to kill him. But if you can do anything, have compassion on us and help us." 23 Jesus said to him, " 'If you can!' Everything is possible to one who has faith." 24 Then the boy's father cried out, "I do believe, help my unbelief!" 25 Jesus, on seeing a crowd rapidly gathering, rebuked the unclean spirit and said to it, "Mute and deaf spirit, I command you: come out of him and never enter him again!" 26 Shouting and throwing the boy into convulsions, it came out. He became like a corpse, which caused many to say, "He is dead!" 27 But Jesus took him by the hand, raised him, and he stood up. 28 When he entered the house, his disciples asked him in private, "Why could we not drive it out?" 29 He said to them, "This kind can only come out through prayer."

30 They left from there and began a journey through Galilee, but he did not wish anyone to know about it. 31 He was teaching his disciples and telling them, "The Son of Man is to be handed over to men and they will kill him, and three days after his death he will rise." 32 But they did not understand the saying, and they were afraid to question him.

33 They came to Capernaum and, once inside the house, he began to ask them, "What were you arguing about on the way?" 34 But they remained silent. They had been discussing among themselves on the way who was the greatest. 35 Then he sat down, called the Twelve, and said to them, "If anyone wishes to be first, he shall be the last of all and the servant of all." 36 Taking a child he placed it in their midst, and putting his arms around it he said to them, 37 "Whoever receives one child such as this in my name, receives me; and whoever receives me, receives not me but the One who sent me."

38 John said to him, "Teacher, we saw someone driving out demons in your name, and we tried to prevent him because he does not follow us." 39 Jesus replied, "Do not prevent him. There is no one who performs a mighty deed in my name who can at the same time speak ill of me. 40 For whoever is not against us is for us. 41 Anyone who gives you a cup of water to drink because you belong to Christ, amen, I say to you, will surely not lose his reward.

42 "Whoever causes one of these little ones who believe [in me] to sin, it would be better for him if a great millstone were put around his neck and he were thrown into the sea. 43 If your hand causes you to sin, cut it off. It is better for you to enter into life maimed than with two hands to go into Gehenna, into the unquenchable fire. [44] 45 And if your foot causes you to sin, cut if off. It is better for you to enter into life crippled than with two feet to be thrown into Gehenna. [46] 47 And if your eye causes you to sin, pluck it out. Better for you to enter into the kingdom of God with one eye than with two eyes to be thrown into Gehenna, 48 where 'their worm does not die, and the fire is not quenched.'

49 "Everyone will be salted with fire. 50 Salt is good, but

unable to.' 19 In reply he said to them, 'Faithless generation, how much longer must I be among you? How much longer must I put up with you? Bring him to me.' 20 They brought the boy to him, and at once the spirit of dumbness threw the boy into convulsions, and he fell to the ground and lay writhing there, foaming at the mouth. 21 Jesus asked the father, 'How long has this been happening to him?' 'From childhood,' he said, 22 'and it has often thrown him into fire and into water, in order to destroy him. 23 But if you can do anything, have pity on us and help us.' 24 'If you can?' retorted Jesus. 'Everything is possible for one who has faith.' At once the father of the boy cried out, 'I have faith. Help my lack of faith!' 25 And when Jesus saw that a crowd was gathering, he rebuked the unclean spirit. 'Deaf and dumb spirit,' he said, 'I command you: come out of him and never enter him again.' 26 Then it threw the boy into violent convulsions and came out shouting, and the boy lay there so like a corpse that most of them said, 'He is dead.' 27 But Jesus took him by the hand and helped him up, and he was able to stand. 28 When he had gone indoors, his disciples asked him when they were by themselves, 'Why were we unable to drive it out?' 29 He answered, 'This is the kind that can be driven out only by prayer.'

30 After leaving that place they made their way through Galilee; and he did not want anyone to know, 31 because he was instructing his disciples; he was telling them, 'The Son of man will be delivered into the power of men; they will put him to death; and three days after he has been put to death he will rise again.' 32 But they did not understand what he said and were afraid to ask him.

33 They came to Capernaum, and when he got into the house he asked them, 'What were you arguing about on the road?' 34 They said nothing, because on the road they had been arguing which of them was the greatest. 35 So he sat down, called the Twelve to him and said, 'If anyone wants to be first, he must make himself last of all and servant of all.' 36 He then took a little child whom he set among them and embraced, and he said to them, 37 'Anyone who welcomes a little child such as this in my name, welcomes me; and anyone who welcomes me, welcomes not me but the one who sent me.'

38 John said to him, 'Master, we saw someone who is not one of us driving out devils in your name, and because he was not one of us we tried to stop him.' 39 But Jesus said, 'You must not stop him; no one who works a miracle in my name could soon afterwards speak evil of me. 40 Anyone who is not against us is for us.

41 'If anyone gives you a cup of water to drink because you belong to Christ, then in truth I tell you, he will most certainly not lose his reward.

42 'But anyone who is the downfall of one of these little ones who have faith, would be better thrown into the sea with a great millstone hung round his neck. 43 And if your hand should be your downfall, cut it off; it is better for you to enter into life crippled, than to have two hands and go to hell, into the fire that can never be put out. [44]i 45 And if your foot should be your downfall, cut it off; it is better for you to enter into life lame, than to have two feet and be thrown into hell. [46]j 47 And if your eye should be your downfall, tear it out; it is better for you to enter into the kingdom of God with one eye, than to have two eyes and be thrown into hell 48 where *their worm will never die nor their fire be put out*.k 49 For everyone will be salted with

---

9, 44.46: These verses, lacking in some important early manuscripts, are here omitted as scribal additions. They simply repeat v 48, itself a modified citation of Is 66, 24.

i 9 Omitting, with the best MSS, vv. 44 and 46 (Vulg.), as repetitions of v. 48. j 9 See i 9 above. k 9 Is 66:24. The word for hell is 'Gehenna', the rubbish-dump of Jerusalem, with its perpetual fires.

NEW REVISED STANDARD VERSION

good; but if salt has lost its saltiness, how can you season it?*w* Have salt in yourselves, and be at peace with one another."

10 He left that place and went to the region of Judea and*x* beyond the Jordan. And crowds again gathered around him; and, as was his custom, he again taught them.

2 Some Pharisees came, and to test him they asked, "Is it lawful for a man to divorce his wife?" 3 He answered them, "What did Moses command you?" 4 They said, "Moses allowed a man to write a certificate of dismissal and to divorce her." 5 But Jesus said to them, "Because of your hardness of heart he wrote this commandment for you. 6 But from the beginning of creation, 'God made them male and female.' 7 'For this reason a man shall leave his father and mother and be joined to his wife,*y* 8 and the two shall become one flesh.' So they are no longer two, but one flesh. 9 Therefore what God has joined together, let no one separate."

10 Then in the house the disciples asked him again about this matter. 11 He said to them, "Whoever divorces his wife and marries another commits adultery against her; 12 and if she divorces her husband and marries another, she commits adultery."

13 People were bringing little children to him in order that he might touch them; and the disciples spoke sternly to them. 14 But when Jesus saw this, he was indignant and said to them, "Let the little children come to me; do not stop them; for it is to such as these that the kingdom of God belongs. 15 Truly I tell you, whoever does not receive the kingdom of God as a little child will never enter it." 16 And he took them up in his arms, laid his hands on them, and blessed them.

17 As he was setting out on a journey, a man ran up and knelt before him, and asked him, "Good Teacher, what must I do to inherit eternal life?" 18 Jesus said to him, "Why do you call me good? No one is good but God alone. 19 You know the commandments: 'You shall not murder; You shall not commit adultery; You shall not steal; You shall not bear false witness; You shall not defraud; Honor your father and mother.' " 20 He said to him, "Teacher, I have kept all these since my youth." 21 Jesus, looking at him, loved him and said, "You lack one thing; go, sell what you own, and give the money*z* to the poor, and you will have treasure in heaven; then come, follow me." 22 When he heard this, he was shocked and went away grieving, for he had many possessions.

23 Then Jesus looked around and said to his disciples, "How hard it will be for those who have wealth to enter the kingdom of God!" 24 And the disciples were perplexed at these words. But Jesus said to them again, "Children, how hard it is*a* to enter the kingdom of God! 25 It is easier for a camel to go through the eye of a needle than for someone who is rich to enter the kingdom of God." 26 They were greatly astounded and said to one another,*b* "Then who can be saved?" 27 Jesus looked at them and said, "For mortals it is impossible, but not for God; for God all things are possible."

28 Peter began to say to him, "Look, we have left everything and followed you." 29 Jesus said, "Truly I tell you, there is no one who has left house or brothers or sisters or mother or father or children or fields, for my sake and for the sake of the good news,*c* 30 who will not receive a hun-

REVISED ENGLISH BIBLE

50 'Salt is good; but if the salt loses its saltness, how will you season it?

'You must have salt within yourselves, and be at peace with one another.'

10 ON leaving there he came into the regions of Judaea and Transjordan. Once again crowds gathered round him, and he taught them as was his practice. 2 He was asked: 'Is it lawful for a man to divorce his wife?' This question was put to test him. 3 He responded by asking, 'What did Moses command you?' 4 They answered, 'Moses permitted a man to divorce his wife by a certificate of dismissal.' 5 Jesus said to them, 'It was because of your stubbornness that he made this rule for you. 6 But in the beginning, at the creation, "God made them male and female." 7 "That is why a man leaves his father and mother, and is united to his wife, 8 and the two become one flesh." It follows that they are no longer two individuals: they are one flesh. 9 Therefore what God has joined together, man must not separate.'

10 When they were indoors again, the disciples questioned him about this. 11 He said to them, 'Whoever divorces his wife and remarries commits adultery against her; 12 so too, if she divorces her husband and remarries, she commits adultery.'

13 They brought children for him to touch. The disciples rebuked them, 14 but when Jesus saw it he was indignant, and said to them, 'Let the children come to me; do not try to stop them; for the kingdom of God belongs to such as these. 15 Truly I tell you: whoever does not accept the kingdom of God like a child will never enter it.' 16 And he put his arms round them, laid his hands on them, and blessed them.

17 As he was starting out on a journey, a stranger ran up and, kneeling before him, asked, 'Good Teacher, what must I do to win eternal life?' 18 Jesus said to him, 'Why do you call me good? No one is good except God alone. 19 You know the commandments: "Do not murder; do not commit adultery; do not steal; do not give false evidence; do not defraud; honour your father and mother." ' 20 'But Teacher,' he replied, 'I have kept all these since I was a boy.' 21 As Jesus looked at him, his heart warmed to him. 'One thing you lack,' he said. 'Go, sell everything you have, and give to the poor, and you will have treasure in heaven; then come and follow me.' 22 At these words his face fell and he went away with a heavy heart; for he was a man of great wealth.

23 Jesus looked round at his disciples and said to them, 'How hard it will be for the wealthy to enter the kingdom of God!' 24 They were amazed that he should say this, but Jesus insisted, 'Children, how hard it is to enter the kingdom of God! 25 It is easier for a camel to pass through the eye of a needle than for a rich man to enter the kingdom of God.' 26 They were more astonished than ever, and said to one another, 'Then who can be saved?' 27 Jesus looked at them and said, 'For men it is impossible, but not for God; everything is possible for God.'

28 'What about us?' said Peter. 'We have left everything to follow you.' 29 Jesus said, 'Truly I tell you: there is no one who has given up home, brothers or sisters, mother, father or children, or land, for my sake and for the gospel, 30 who will not receive in this age a hundred times as

---

w Or *how can you restore its saltiness?*   *x* Other ancient authorities lack *and*   *y* Other ancient authorities lack *and be joined to his wife*   *z* Gk lacks *the money*   *a* Other ancient authorities add *for those who trust in riches*   *b* Other ancient authorities read *to him*   *c* Or *gospel*

10:2 **He was asked:** *some witnesses read* Pharisees approached and asked him.   10:24 **how hard it is:** *some witnesses add* for those who trust in riches.

if salt becomes insipid, with what will you restore its flavor? Keep salt in yourselves and you will have peace with one another."

10 He set out from there and went into the district of Judea [and] across the Jordan. Again crowds gathered around him and, as was his custom, he again taught them. 2 The Pharisees approached and asked, "Is it lawful for a husband to divorce his wife?" They were testing him. 3 He said to them in reply, "What did Moses command you?" 4 They replied, "Moses permitted him to write a bill of divorce and dismiss her." 5 But Jesus told them, "Because of the hardness of your hearts he wrote you this commandment. 6 But from the beginning of creation, 'God made them male and female. 7 For this reason a man shall leave his father and mother [and be joined to his wife], 8 and the two shall become one flesh.' So they are no longer two but one flesh. 9 Therefore what God has joined together, no human being must separate." 10 In the house the disciples again questioned him about this. 11 He said to them, "Whoever divorces his wife and marries another commits adultery against her; 12 and if she divorces her husband and marries another, she commits adultery."

13 And people were bringing children to him that he might touch them, but the disciples rebuked them. 14 When Jesus saw this he became indignant and said to them, "Let the children come to me; do not prevent them, for the kingdom of God belongs to such as these. 15 Amen, I say to you, whoever does not accept the kingdom of God like a child will not enter it." 16 Then he embraced them and blessed them, placing his hands on them.

17 As he was setting out on a journey, a man ran up, knelt down before him, and asked him, "Good teacher, what must I do to inherit eternal life?" 18 Jesus answered him, "Why do you call me good? No one is good but God alone. 19 You know the commandments: 'You shall not kill; you shall not commit adultery; you shall not steal; you shall not bear false witness; you shall not defraud; honor your father and your mother.'" 20 He replied and said to him, "Teacher, all of these I have observed from my youth." 21 Jesus, looking at him, loved him and said to him, "You are lacking in one thing. Go, sell what you have, and give to [the] poor and you will have treasure in heaven; then come, follow me." 22 At that statement his face fell, and he went away sad, for he had many possessions.

23 Jesus looked around and said to his disciples, "How hard it is for those who have wealth to enter the kingdom of God!" 24 The disciples were amazed at his words. So Jesus again said to them in reply, "Children, how hard it is to enter the kingdom of God! 25 It is easier for a camel to pass through [the] eye of [a] needle than for one who is rich to enter the kingdom of God." 26 They were exceedingly astonished and said among themselves, "Then who can be saved?" 27 Jesus looked at them and said, "For human beings it is impossible, but not for God. All things are possible for God." 28 Peter began to say to him, "We have given up everything and followed you." 29 Jesus said, "Amen, I say to you, there is no one who has given up house or brothers or sisters or mother or father or children or lands for my sake and for the sake of the gospel 30 who will not receive

fire. 50 Salt is a good thing, but if salt has become insipid, how can you make it salty again? Have salt in yourselves and be at peace with one another.'

10 After leaving there, he came into the territory of Judaea and Transjordan. And again crowds gathered round him, and again he taught them, as his custom was. 2 Some Pharisees approached him and asked, 'Is it lawful for a man to divorce his wife?' They were putting him to the test. 3 He answered them, 'What did Moses command you?' 4 They replied, 'Moses allowed us to draw up a writ of dismissal in cases of divorce.'[l] 5 Then Jesus said to them, 'It was because you were so hard hearted that he wrote this commandment for you. 6 But from the beginning of creation *he made them male and female.* 7 *This is why a man leaves his father and mother,* 8 *and the two become one flesh.*[m] They are no longer two, therefore, but one flesh. 9 So then, what God has united, human beings must not divide.' 10 Back in the house the disciples questioned him again about this, 11 and he said to them, 'Whoever divorces his wife and marries another is guilty of adultery against her. 12 And if a woman divorces her husband and marries another she is guilty of adultery too.'

13 People were bringing little children to him, for him to touch them. The disciples scolded them, 14 but when Jesus saw this he was indignant and said to them, 'Let the little children come to me; do not stop them; for it is to such as these that the kingdom of God belongs. 15 In truth I tell you, anyone who does not welcome the kingdom of God like a little child will never enter it.' 16 Then he embraced them, laid his hands on them and gave them his blessing.

17 He was setting out on a journey when a man ran up, knelt before him and put this question to him, 'Good master, what must I do to inherit eternal life?' 18 Jesus said to him, 'Why do you call me good? No one is good but God alone. 19 You know the commandments: *You shall not kill; You shall not commit adultery; You shall not steal; You shall not give false witness; You shall not defraud; Honour your father and mother.'*[n] 20 And he said to him, 'Master, I have kept all these since my earliest days.' 21 Jesus looked steadily at him and he was filled with love for him, and he said, 'You need to do one thing more. Go and sell what you own and give the money to the poor, and you will have treasure in heaven; then come, follow me.' 22 But his face fell at these words and he went away sad, for he was a man of great wealth.

23 Jesus looked round and said to his disciples, 'How hard it is for those who have riches to enter the kingdom of God!' 24 The disciples were astounded by these words, but Jesus insisted, 'My children,' he said to them, 'how hard it is to enter the kingdom of God! 25 It is easier for a camel to pass through the eye of a needle than for someone rich to enter the kingdom of God.' 26 They were more astonished than ever, saying to one another, 'In that case, who can be saved?' 27 Jesus gazed at them and said, 'By human resources it is impossible, but not for God: because for God everything is possible.'

28 Peter took this up. 'Look,' he said to him, 'we have left everything and followed you.' 29 Jesus said, 'In truth I tell you, there is no one who has left house, brothers, sisters, mother, father, children or land for my sake and for the sake of the gospel 30 who will not receive a hundred times as

---

l **10** Dt 24:1.　*m* **10** Gn 1:27; 2:24.　*n* **10** Ex 20:12–16.

NEW REVISED STANDARD VERSION

dredfold now in this age — houses, brothers and sisters, mothers and children, and fields with persecutions — and in the age to come eternal life. 31 But many who are first will be last, and the last will be first."

32 They were on the road, going up to Jerusalem, and Jesus was walking ahead of them; they were amazed, and those who followed were afraid. He took the twelve aside again and began to tell them what was to happen to him, 33 saying, "See, we are going up to Jerusalem, and the Son of Man will be handed over to the chief priests and the scribes, and they will condemn him to death; then they will hand him over to the Gentiles; 34 they will mock him, and spit upon him, and flog him, and kill him; and after three days he will rise again."

35 James and John, the sons of Zebedee, came forward to him and said to him, "Teacher, we want you to do for us whatever we ask of you." 36 And he said to them, "What is it you want me to do for you?" 37 And they said to him, "Grant us to sit, one at your right hand and one at your left, in your glory." 38 But Jesus said to them, "You do not know what you are asking. Are you able to drink the cup that I drink, or be baptized with the baptism that I am baptized with?" 39 They replied, "We are able." Then Jesus said to them, "The cup that I drink you will drink; and with the baptism with which I am baptized, you will be baptized; 40 but to sit at my right hand or at my left is not mine to grant, but it is for those for whom it has been prepared."

41 When the ten heard this, they began to be angry with James and John. 42 So Jesus called them and said to them, "You know that among the Gentiles those whom they recognize as their rulers lord it over them, and their great ones are tyrants over them. 43 But it is not so among you; but whoever wishes to become great among you must be your servant, 44 and whoever wishes to be first among you must be slave of all. 45 For the Son of Man came not to be served but to serve, and to give his life a ransom for many."

46 They came to Jericho. As he and his disciples and a large crowd were leaving Jericho, Bartimaeus son of Timaeus, a blind beggar, was sitting by the roadside. 47 When he heard that it was Jesus of Nazareth, he began to shout out and say, "Jesus, Son of David, have mercy on me!" 48 Many sternly ordered him to be quiet, but he cried out even more loudly, "Son of David, have mercy on me!" 49 Jesus stood still and said, "Call him here." And they called the blind man, saying to him, "Take heart; get up, he is calling you." 50 So throwing off his cloak, he sprang up and came to Jesus. 51 Then Jesus said to him, "What do you want me to do for you?" The blind man said to him, "My teacher,*d* let me see again." 52 Jesus said to him, "Go; your faith has made you well." Immediately he regained his sight and followed him on the way.

11 When they were approaching Jerusalem, at Bethphage and Bethany, near the Mount of Olives, he sent two of his disciples 2 and said to them, "Go into the village ahead of you, and immediately as you enter it, you will find tied there a colt that has never been ridden; untie it and bring it. 3 If anyone says to you, 'Why are you doing this?' just say this, 'The Lord needs it and will send it back here immediately.' " 4 They went away and found a colt tied near a door, outside in the street. As they were untying it, 5 some of the bystanders said to them, "What are you doing, untying the colt?" 6 They told them what Jesus had said; and they allowed them to take it. 7 Then they brought the colt to Jesus and threw their cloaks on it; and he sat on it. 8 Many people spread their cloaks on the road, and others spread leafy branches that they had cut in the fields. 9 Then those

REVISED ENGLISH BIBLE

much — houses, brothers and sisters, mothers and children, and land — and persecutions besides; and in the age to come eternal life. 31 But many who are first will be last, and the last first.'

32 THEY were on the road going up to Jerusalem, and Jesus was leading the way; and the disciples were filled with awe, while those who followed behind were afraid. Once again he took the Twelve aside and began to tell them what was to happen to him. 33 'We are now going up to Jerusalem,' he said, 'and the Son of Man will be handed over to the chief priests and the scribes; they will condemn him to death and hand him over to the Gentiles. 34 He will be mocked and spat upon, and flogged and killed; and three days afterwards, he will rise again.'

35 James and John, the sons of Zebedee, approached him and said, 'Teacher, we should like you to do us a favour.' 36 'What is it you want me to do for you?' he asked. 37 They answered, 'Allow us to sit with you in your glory, one at your right hand and the other at your left.' 38 Jesus said to them, 'You do not understand what you are asking. Can you drink the cup that I drink, or be baptized with the baptism I am baptized with?' 39 'We can,' they answered. Jesus said, 'The cup that I drink you shall drink, and the baptism I am baptized with shall be your baptism; 40 but to sit on my right or on my left is not for me to grant; that honour is for those to whom it has already been assigned.'

41 When the other ten heard this, they were indignant with James and John. 42 Jesus called them to him and said, 'You know that among the Gentiles the recognized rulers lord it over their subjects, and the great make their authority felt. 43 It shall not be so with you; among you, whoever wants to be great must be your servant, 44 and whoever wants to be first must be the slave of all. 45 For the Son of Man did not come to be served but to serve, and to give his life as a ransom for many.'

46 They came to Jericho; and as he was leaving the town, with his disciples and a large crowd, Bartimaeus (that is, son of Timaeus), a blind beggar, was seated at the roadside. 47 Hearing that it was Jesus of Nazareth, he began to shout, 'Son of David, Jesus, have pity on me!' 48 Many of the people told him to hold his tongue; but he shouted all the more, 'Son of David, have pity on me.' 49 Jesus stopped and said, 'Call him'; so they called the blind man: 'Take heart,' they said. 'Get up; he is calling you.' 50 At that he threw off his cloak, jumped to his feet, and came to Jesus. 51 Jesus said to him, 'What do you want me to do for you?' 'Rabbi,' the blind man answered, 'I want my sight back.' 52 Jesus said to him, 'Go; your faith has healed you.' And at once he recovered his sight and followed him on the road.

11 THEY were now approaching Jerusalem, and when they reached Bethphage and Bethany, close by the mount of Olives, he sent off two of his disciples. 2 'Go into the village opposite,' he told them, 'and just as you enter you will find tethered there a colt which no one has yet ridden. Untie it and bring it here. 3 If anyone asks why you are doing this, say, "The Master needs it, and will send it back here without delay." ' 4 So they went off, and found the colt outside in the street, tethered beside a door. As they were untying it, 5 some of the bystanders asked, 'What are you doing, untying that colt?' 6 They answered as Jesus had told them, and were then allowed to take it. 7 So they brought the colt to Jesus, and when they had spread their cloaks on it he mounted it. 8 Many people carpeted the road with their cloaks, while others spread greenery which they

---

d Aramaic *Rabbouni*

11:3 **The Master:** *or* Its owner.

a hundred times more now in this present age: houses and brothers and sisters and mothers and children and lands, with persecutions, and eternal life in the age to come. 31 But many that are first will be last, and [the] last will be first."

32 They were on the way, going up to Jerusalem, and Jesus went ahead of them. They were amazed, and those who followed were afraid. Taking the Twelve aside again, he began to tell them what was going to happen to him. 33 "Behold, we are going up to Jerusalem, and the Son of Man will be handed over to the chief priests and the scribes, and they will condemn him to death and hand him over to the Gentiles 34 who will mock him, spit upon him, scourge him, and put him to death, but after three days he will rise."

35 Then James and John, the sons of Zebedee, came to him and said to him, "Teacher, we want you to do for us whatever we ask of you." 36 He replied, "What do you wish [me] to do for you?" 37 They answered him, "Grant that in your glory we may sit one at your right and the other at your left." 38 Jesus said to them, "You do not know what you are asking. Can you drink the cup that I drink or be baptized with the baptism with which I am baptized?" 39 They said to him, "We can." Jesus said to them, "The cup that I drink, you will drink, and with the baptism with which I am baptized, you will be baptized; 40 but to sit at my right or at my left is not mine to give but is for those for whom it has been prepared." 41 When the ten heard this, they became indignant at James and John. 42 Jesus summoned them and said to them, "You know that those who are recognized as rulers over the Gentiles lord it over them, and their great ones make their authority over them felt. 43 But it shall not be so among you. Rather, whoever wishes to be great among you will be your servant; 44 whoever wishes to be first among you will be the slave of all. 45 For the Son of Man did not come to be served but to serve and to give his life as a ransom for many."

46 They came to Jericho. And as he was leaving Jericho with his disciples and a sizable crowd, Bartimaeus, a blind man, the son of Timaeus, sat by the roadside begging. 47 On hearing that it was Jesus of Nazareth, he began to cry out and say, "Jesus, son of David, have pity on me." 48 And many rebuked him, telling him to be silent. But he kept calling out all the more, "Son of David, have pity on me." 49 Jesus stopped and said, "Call him." So they called the blind man, saying to him, "Take courage; get up, he is calling you." 50 He threw aside his cloak, sprang up, and came to Jesus. 51 Jesus said to him in reply, "What do you want me to do for you?" The blind man replied to him, "Master, I want to see." 52 Jesus told him, "Go your way; your faith has saved you." Immediately he received his sight and followed him on the way.

11 When they drew near to Jerusalem, to Bethphage and Bethany at the Mount of Olives, he sent two of his disciples 2 and said to them, "Go into the village opposite you, and immediately on entering it, you will find a colt tethered on which no one has ever sat. Untie it and bring it here. 3 If anyone should say to you, 'Why are you doing this?' reply, 'The Master has need of it and will send it back here at once.'" 4 So they went off and found a colt tethered at a gate outside on the street, and they untied it. 5 Some of the bystanders said to them, "What are you doing, untying the colt?" 6 They answered them just as Jesus had told them to, and they permitted them to do it. 7 So they brought the colt to Jesus and put their cloaks over it. And he sat on it. 8 Many people spread their cloaks on the road, and others spread leafy branches that they had cut from the

much, houses, brothers, sisters, mothers, children and land — and persecutions too — now in this present time and, in the world to come, eternal life. 31 Many who are first will be last, and the last, first.'

32 They were on the road, going up to Jerusalem; Jesus was walking on ahead of them; they were in a daze, and those who followed were apprehensive. Once more taking the Twelve aside he began to tell them what was going to happen to him, 33 'Now we are going up to Jerusalem, and the Son of man is about to be handed over to the chief priests and the scribes. They will condemn him to death and will hand him over to the gentiles, 34 who will mock him and spit at him and scourge him and put him to death; and after three days he will rise again.'

35 James and John, the sons of Zebedee, approached him. 'Master,' they said to him, 'We want you to do us a favour.' 36 He said to them, 'What is it you want me to do for you?' 37 They said to him, 'Allow us to sit one at your right hand and the other at your left in your glory.' 38 But Jesus said to them, 'You do not know what you are asking. Can you drink the cup that I shall drink, or be baptised with the baptism with which I shall be baptised?' 39 They replied, 'We can.' Jesus said to them, 'The cup that I shall drink you shall drink, and with the baptism with which I shall be baptised you shall be baptised, 40 but as for seats at my right hand or my left, these are not mine to grant; they belong to those to whom they have been allotted.'

41 When the other ten heard this they began to feel indignant with James and John, 42 so Jesus called them to him and said to them, 'You know that among the gentiles those they call their rulers lord it over them, and their great men make their authority felt. 43 Among you this is not to happen. No; anyone who wants to become great among you must be your servant, 44 and anyone who wants to be first among you must be slave to all. 45 For the Son of man himself came not to be served but to serve, and to give his life as a ransom for many.'

46 They reached Jericho; and as he left Jericho with his disciples and a great crowd, Bartimaeus — that is, the son of Timaeus — a blind beggar, was sitting at the side of the road. 47 When he heard that it was Jesus of Nazareth, he began to shout and cry out, 'Son of David, Jesus, have pity on me.' 48 And many of them scolded him and told him to keep quiet, but he only shouted all the louder, 'Son of David, have pity on me.' 49 Jesus stopped and said, 'Call him here.' So they called the blind man over. 'Courage,' they said, 'get up; he is calling you.' 50 So throwing off his cloak, he jumped up and went to Jesus. 51 Then Jesus spoke, 'What do you want me to do for you?' The blind man said to him, 'Rabbuni, let me see again.' 52 Jesus said to him, 'Go; your faith has saved you.' And at once his sight returned and he followed him along the road.

11 When they were approaching Jerusalem, at Bethphage and Bethany, close by the Mount of Olives, he sent two of his disciples 2 and said to them, 'Go to the village facing you, and as you enter it you will at once find a tethered colt that no one has yet ridden. Untie it and bring it here. 3 If anyone says to you, "What are you doing?" say, "The Master needs it and will send it back here at once."' 4 They went off and found a colt tethered near a door in the open street. As they untied it, 5 some men standing there said, 'What are you doing, untying that colt?' 6 They gave the answer Jesus had told them, and the men let them go. 7 Then they took the colt to Jesus and threw their cloaks on its back, and he mounted it. 8 Many people spread their cloaks on the road, and others greenery which they had cut

who went ahead and those who followed were shouting,
"Hosanna!
> Blessed is the one who comes in the name of
> the Lord!
10   Blessed is the coming kingdom of our ancestor
> David!
Hosanna in the highest heaven!"

11 Then he entered Jerusalem and went into the temple;
and when he had looked around at everything, as it was
already late, he went out to Bethany with the twelve.

12 On the following day, when they came from Bethany, he was hungry. 13 Seeing in the distance a fig tree in
leaf, he went to see whether perhaps he would find anything
on it. When he came to it, he found nothing but leaves; for
it was not the season for figs. 14 He said to it, "May no one
ever eat fruit from you again." And his disciples heard it.

15 Then they came to Jerusalem. And he entered the
temple and began to drive out those who were selling and
those who were buying in the temple, and he overturned the
tables of the money changers and the seats of those who
sold doves; 16 and he would not allow anyone to carry anything through the temple. 17 He was teaching and saying, "Is
it not written,

> 'My house shall be called a house of prayer for
> all the nations'?
But you have made it a den of robbers."

18 And when the chief priests and the scribes heard it, they
kept looking for a way to kill him; for they were afraid of
him, because the whole crowd was spellbound by his teaching. 19 And when evening came, Jesus and his disciples*e*
went out of the city.

20 In the morning as they passed by, they saw the fig
tree withered away to its roots. 21 Then Peter remembered
and said to him, "Rabbi, look! The fig tree that you cursed
has withered." 22 Jesus answered them, "Have*f* faith in
God. 23 Truly I tell you, if you say to this mountain, 'Be
taken up and thrown into the sea,' and if you do not doubt
in your heart, but believe that what you say will come to
pass, it will be done for you. 24 So I tell you, whatever you
ask for in prayer, believe that you have received*g* it, and it
will be yours.

25 "Whenever you stand praying, forgive, if you have
anything against anyone; so that your Father in heaven may
also forgive you your trespasses."*h*

27 Again they came to Jerusalem. As he was walking in
the temple, the chief priests, the scribes, and the elders
came to him 28 and said, "By what authority are you doing
these things? Who gave you this authority to do them?"
29 Jesus said to them, "I will ask you one question; answer
me, and I will tell you by what authority I do these things.
30 Did the baptism of John come from heaven, or was it of
human origin? Answer me." 31 They argued with one another, "If we say, 'From heaven,' he will say, 'Why then
did you not believe him?' 32 But shall we say, 'Of human
origin'?"—they were afraid of the crowd, for all regarded
John as truly a prophet. 33 So they answered Jesus, "We do
not know." And Jesus said to them, "Neither will I tell you
by what authority I am doing these things."

12 Then he began to speak to them in parables. "A
man planted a vineyard, put a fence around it, dug
a pit for the wine press, and built a watchtower; then he
leased it to tenants and went to another country. 2 When the
season came, he sent a slave to the tenants to collect from
them his share of the produce of the vineyard. 3 But they

had cut in the fields; 9 and those in front and those behind
shouted, 'Hosanna! Blessed is he who comes in the name of
the Lord! 10 Blessed is the kingdom of our father David
which is coming! Hosanna in the heavens!'

11 He entered Jerusalem and went into the temple. He
looked round at everything; then, as it was already late, he
went out to Bethany with the Twelve.

12 On the following day, as they left Bethany, he felt
hungry, 13 and, noticing in the distance a fig tree in leaf, he
went to see if he could find anything on it. But when he
reached it he found nothing but leaves; for it was not the
season for figs. 14 He said to the tree, 'May no one ever
again eat fruit from you!' And his disciples were listening.

15 So they came to Jerusalem, and he went into the temple
and began to drive out those who bought and sold there. He
upset the tables of the money-changers and the seats of the
dealers in pigeons; 16 and he would not allow anyone to
carry goods through the temple court. 17 Then he began to
teach them, and said, 'Does not scripture say, "My house
shall be called a house of prayer for all nations"? But you
have made it a robbers' cave.' 18 The chief priests and the
scribes heard of this and looked for a way to bring about his
death; for they were afraid of him, because the whole crowd
was spellbound by his teaching. 19 And when evening came
they went out of the city.

20 Early next morning, as they passed by, they saw that
the fig tree had withered from the roots up; 21 and Peter,
recalling what had happened, said to him, 'Rabbi, look, the
fig tree which you cursed has withered.' 22 Jesus answered
them, 'Have faith in God. 23 Truly I tell you: if anyone says
to this mountain, "Be lifted from your place and hurled into
the sea," and has no inward doubts, but believes that what
he says will happen, it will be done for him. 24 I tell you,
then, whatever you ask for in prayer, believe that you have
received it and it will be yours.

25 'And when you stand praying, if you have a grievance
against anyone, forgive him, so that your Father in heaven
may forgive you the wrongs you have done.'

27 THEY came once more to Jerusalem. And as he was walking in the temple court the chief priests, scribes, and elders
came to him 28 and said, 'By what authority are you acting
like this? Who gave you authority to act in this way?'
29 Jesus said to them, 'I also have a question for you, and
if you give me an answer, I will tell you by what authority
I act. 30 The baptism of John: was it from God, or from
men? Answer me.' 31 This set them arguing among themselves: 'What shall we say? If we say, "From God," he will
say, "Then why did you not believe him?" 32 Shall we say,
"From men"?'—but they were afraid of the people, for all
held that John was in fact a prophet. 33 So they answered,
'We do not know.' And Jesus said to them, 'Then I will not
tell you either by what authority I act.'

12 He went on to speak to them in parables: 'A man
planted a vineyard and put a wall round it, hewed
out a winepress, and built a watch-tower; then he let it out
to vine-growers and went abroad. 2 When the season came,
he sent a servant to the tenants to collect from them his
share of the produce. 3 But they seized him, thrashed him,

---

e Gk *they*: other ancient authorities read *he*   *f* Other ancient
authorities read *"If you have*   *g* Other ancient authorities read *are
receiving*   *h* Other ancient authorities add verse 26, *"But if you do
not forgive, neither will your Father in heaven forgive your
trespasses."*

11:25 **wrongs you have done:** *some witnesses add* 26 But if you do
not forgive others, then the wrongs you have done will not be
forgiven by your Father in heaven.

NEW AMERICAN BIBLE

fields. 9 Those preceding him as well as those following kept crying out:

"Hosanna!
Blessed is he who comes in the name of the Lord!
10 Blessed is the kingdom of our father David that is to come!
Hosanna in the highest!"

11 He entered Jerusalem and went into the temple area. He looked around at everything and, since it was already late, went out to Bethany with the Twelve.

12 The next day as they were leaving Bethany he was hungry. 13 Seeing from a distance a fig tree in leaf, he went over to see if he could find anything on it. When he reached it he found nothing but leaves; it was not the time for figs. 14 And he said to it in reply, "May no one ever eat of your fruit again!" And his disciples heard it.

15 They came to Jerusalem, and on entering the temple area he began to drive out those selling and buying there. He overturned the tables of the money changers and the seats of those who were selling doves. 16 He did not permit anyone to carry anything through the temple area. 17 Then he taught them saying, "Is it not written:

'My house shall be called a house of prayer for all peoples'?
But you have made it a den of thieves."

18 The chief priests and the scribes came to hear of it and were seeking a way to put him to death, yet they feared him because the whole crowd was astonished at his teaching. 19 When evening came, they went out of the city.

20 Early in the morning, as they were walking along, they saw the fig tree withered to its roots. 21 Peter remembered and said to him, "Rabbi, look! The fig tree that you cursed has withered." 22 Jesus said to them in reply, "Have faith in God. 23 Amen, I say to you, whoever says to this mountain, 'Be lifted up and thrown into the sea,' and does not doubt in his heart but believes that what he says will happen, it shall be done for him. 24 Therefore I tell you, all that you ask for in prayer, believe that you will receive it and it shall be yours. 25 When you stand to pray, forgive anyone against whom you have a grievance, so that your heavenly Father may in turn forgive you your transgressions. [26]"

27 They returned once more to Jerusalem. As he was walking in the temple area, the chief priests, the scribes, and the elders approached him 28 and said to him, "By what authority are you doing these things? Or who gave you this authority to do them?" 29 Jesus said to them, "I shall ask you one question. Answer me, and I will tell you by what authority I do these things. 30 Was John's baptism of heavenly or of human origin? Answer me." 31 They discussed this among themselves and said, "If we say, 'Of heavenly origin,' he will say, '[Then] why did you not believe him?' 32 But shall we say, 'Of human origin'?" — they feared the crowd, for they all thought John really was a prophet. 33 So they said to Jesus in reply, "We do not know." Then Jesus said to them, "Neither shall I tell you by what authority I do these things."

12 He began to speak to them in parables. "A man planted a vineyard, put a hedge around it, dug a wine press, and built a tower. Then he leased it to tenant farmers and left on a journey. 2 At the proper time he sent a servant to the tenants to obtain from them some of the produce of the vineyard. 3 But they seized him, beat him,

NEW JERUSALEM BIBLE

in the fields. 9 And those who went in front and those who followed were all shouting, 'Hosanna! Blessed is he who is coming in the name of the Lord!o 10 Blessed is the coming kingdom of David our father!p Hosanna in the highest heavens!' 11 He entered Jerusalem and went into the Temple; and when he had surveyed it all, as it was late by now, he went out to Bethany with the Twelve.

12 Next day as they were leaving Bethany, he felt hungry. 13 Seeing a fig tree in leaf some distance away, he went to see if he could find any fruit on it, but when he came up to it he found nothing but leaves; for it was not the season for figs. 14 And he addressed the fig tree, 'May no one ever eat fruit from you again.' And his disciples heard him say this.

15 So they reached Jerusalem and he went into the Temple and began driving out the men selling and buying there; he upset the tables of the money changers and the seats of the dove sellers. 16 Nor would he allow anyone to carry anything through the Temple. 17 And he taught them, 'Does not scripture say: My house will be called a house of prayer for all peoples? But you have turned it into a bandits' den.'q 18 This came to the ears of the chief priests and the scribes, and they tried to find some way of doing away with him; they were afraid of him because the people were carried away by his teaching. 19 And when evening came he went out of the city.

20 Next morning, as they passed by, they saw the fig tree withered to the roots. 21 Peter remembered. 'Look, Rabbi,' he said to Jesus, 'the fig tree that you cursed has withered away.' 22 Jesus answered, 'Have faith in God. 23 In truth I tell you, if anyone says to this mountain, "Be pulled up and thrown into the sea," with no doubt in his heart, but believing that what he says will happen, it will be done for him. 24 I tell you, therefore, everything you ask and pray for, believe that you have it already, and it will be yours. 25 And when you stand in prayer, forgive whatever you have against anybody, so that your Father in heaven may forgive your failings too.' [26]r

27 They came to Jerusalem again, and as Jesus was walking in the Temple, the chief priests and the scribes and the elders came to him, 28 and they said to him, 'What authority have you for acting like this? Or who gave you authority to act like this?' 29 Jesus said to them, 'And I will ask you a question, just one; answer me and I will tell you my authority for acting like this. 30 John's baptism, what was its origin, heavenly or human? Answer me that.' 31 And they argued this way among themselves, 'If we say heavenly, he will say, "Then why did you refuse to believe him?" 32 But dare we say human?' — they had the people to fear, for everyone held that John had been a real prophet. 33 So their reply to Jesus was, 'We do not know.' And Jesus said to them, 'Nor will I tell you my authority for acting like this.'

12 He went on to speak to them in parables, 'A man planted a vineyard; he fenced it round, dug out a trough for the winepress and built a tower; then he leased it to tenants and went abroad. 2 When the time came, he sent a servant to the tenants to collect from them his share of the produce of the vineyard. 3 But they seized the man, thrashed

---

11, 26: This verse, which reads, "But if you do not forgive, neither will your heavenly Father forgive your transgressions," is omitted in the best manuscripts. It was probably added by copyists under the influence of Mt 6, 15.

o **11** Ps 118:25–26. p **11** 2 S 7:16. q **11** Is 56:7 followed by Jr 7:11. r **11** Some authorities add a v. borrowed from Mt 6:15.

seized him, and beat him, and sent him away empty-handed. 4 And again he sent another slave to them; this one they beat over the head and insulted. 5 Then he sent another, and that one they killed. And so it was with many others; some they beat, and others they killed. 6 He had still one other, a beloved son. Finally he sent him to them, saying, 'They will respect my son.' 7 But those tenants said to one another, 'This is the heir; come, let us kill him, and the inheritance will be ours.' 8 So they seized him, killed him, and threw him out of the vineyard. 9 What then will the owner of the vineyard do? He will come and destroy the tenants and give the vineyard to others. 10 Have you not read this scripture:

'The stone that the builders rejected
    has become the cornerstone;*i*
11 this was the Lord's doing,
    and it is amazing in our eyes'?"

12 When they realized that he had told this parable against them, they wanted to arrest him, but they feared the crowd. So they left him and went away.

13 Then they sent to him some Pharisees and some Herodians to trap him in what he said. 14 And they came and said to him, "Teacher, we know that you are sincere, and show deference to no one; for you do not regard people with partiality, but teach the way of God in accordance with truth. Is it lawful to pay taxes to the emperor, or not? 15 Should we pay them, or should we not?" But knowing their hypocrisy, he said to them, "Why are you putting me to the test? Bring me a denarius and let me see it." 16 And they brought one. Then he said to them, "Whose head is this, and whose title?" They answered, "The emperor's." 17 Jesus said to them, "Give to the emperor the things that are the emperor's, and to God the things that are God's." And they were utterly amazed at him.

18 Some Sadducees, who say there is no resurrection, came to him and asked him a question, saying, 19 "Teacher, Moses wrote for us that if a man's brother dies, leaving a wife but no child, the man*j* shall marry the widow and raise up children for his brother. 20 There were seven brothers; the first married and, when he died, left no children; 21 and the second married her and died, leaving no children; and the third likewise; 22 none of the seven left children. Last of all the woman herself died. 23 In the resurrection*k* whose wife will she be? For the seven had married her."

24 Jesus said to them, "Is not this the reason you are wrong, that you know neither the scriptures nor the power of God? 25 For when they rise from the dead, they neither marry nor are given in marriage, but are like angels in heaven. 26 And as for the dead being raised, have you not read in the book of Moses, in the story about the bush, how God said to him, 'I am the God of Abraham, the God of Isaac, and the God of Jacob'? 27 He is God not of the dead, but of the living; you are quite wrong."

28 One of the scribes came near and heard them disputing with one another, and seeing that he answered them well, he asked him, "Which commandment is the first of all?" 29 Jesus answered, "The first is, 'Hear, O Israel: the Lord our God, the Lord is one; 30 you shall love the Lord your God with all your heart, and with all your soul, and with all your mind, and with all your strength.' 31 The second is this, 'You shall love your neighbor as yourself.' There is no other commandment greater than these." 32 Then the scribe said to him, "You are right, Teacher; you have truly said that 'he is one, and besides him there is no other'; 33 and 'to love him with all the heart, and with all the

and sent him away empty-handed. 4 Again, he sent them another servant, whom they beat about the head and treated outrageously, 5 and then another, whom they killed. He sent many others and they thrashed some and killed the rest. 6 He had now no one left to send except his beloved son, and in the end he sent him. "They will respect my son," he said; 7 but the tenants said to one another, "This is the heir; come on, let us kill him, and the inheritance will be ours." 8 So they seized him and killed him, and flung his body out of the vineyard. 9 What will the owner of the vineyard do? He will come and put the tenants to death and give the vineyard to others.

10 'Have you never read this text: "The stone which the builders rejected has become the main corner-stone. 11 This is the Lord's doing, and it is wonderful in our eyes"?'

12 They saw that the parable was aimed at them and wanted to arrest him; but they were afraid of the people, so they left him alone and went away.

13 A NUMBER of Pharisees and men of Herod's party were sent to trap him with a question. 14 They came and said, 'Teacher, we know you are a sincere man and court no one's favour, whoever he may be; you teach in all sincerity the way of life that God requires. Are we or are we not permitted to pay taxes to the Roman emperor? 15 Shall we pay or not?' He saw through their duplicity, and said, 'Why are you trying to catch me out? Fetch me a silver piece, and let me look at it.' 16 They brought one, and he asked them, 'Whose head is this, and whose inscription?' 'Caesar's,' they replied. 17 Then Jesus said, 'Pay Caesar what belongs to Caesar, and God what belongs to God.' His reply left them completely taken aback.

18 Next Sadducees, who maintain that there is no resurrection, came to him and asked: 19 'Teacher, Moses laid it down for us that if there are brothers, and one dies leaving a wife but no child, then the next should marry the widow and provide an heir for his brother. 20 Now there were seven brothers. The first took a wife and died without issue. 21 Then the second married her, and he too died without issue; so did the third; 22 none of the seven left any issue. Finally the woman died. 23 At the resurrection, when they rise from the dead, whose wife will she be, since all seven had married her?' 24 Jesus said to them, 'How far you are from the truth! You know neither the scriptures nor the power of God. 25 When they rise from the dead, men and women do not marry; they are like angels in heaven.

26 'As for the resurrection of the dead, have you not read in the book of Moses, in the story of the burning bush, how God spoke to him and said, "I am the God of Abraham, the God of Isaac, the God of Jacob"? 27 He is not God of the dead but of the living. You are very far from the truth.'

28 Then one of the scribes, who had been listening to these discussions and had observed how well Jesus answered, came forward and asked him, 'Which is the first of all the commandments?' 29 He answered, 'The first is, "Hear, O Israel: the Lord our God is the one Lord, 30 and you must love the Lord your God with all your heart, with all your soul, with all your mind, and with all your strength." 31 The second is this: "You must love your neighbour as yourself." No other commandment is greater than these.' 32 The scribe said to him, 'Well said, Teacher. You are right in saying that God is one and beside him there is no other. 33 And to love him with all your heart, all your

---

i Or keystone   *j* Gk his brother   *k* Other ancient authorities add when they rise

12:6 **his beloved son:** or his only son.

and sent him away empty-handed. 4 Again he sent them another servant. And that one they beat over the head and treated shamefully. 5 He sent yet another whom they killed. So, too, many others; some they beat, others they killed. 6 He had one other to send, a beloved son. He sent him to them last of all, thinking, 'They will respect my son.' 7 But those tenants said to one another, 'This is the heir. Come, let us kill him, and the inheritance will be ours.' 8 So they seized him and killed him, and threw him out of the vineyard. 9 What [then] will the owner of the vineyard do? He will come, put the tenants to death, and give the vineyard to others. 10 Have you not read this scripture passage:

'The stone that the builders rejected
    has become the cornerstone;
11 by the Lord has this been done,
    and it is wonderful in our eyes'?"

12 They were seeking to arrest him, but they feared the crowd, for they realized that he had addressed the parable to them. So they left him and went away.

13 They sent some Pharisees and Herodians to him to ensnare him in his speech. 14 They came and said to him, "Teacher, we know that you are a truthful man and that you are not concerned with anyone's opinion. You do not regard a person's status but teach the way of God in accordance with the truth. Is it lawful to pay the census tax to Caesar or not? Should we pay or should we not pay?" 15 Knowing their hypocrisy he said to them, "Why are you testing me? Bring me a denarius to look at." 16 They brought one to him and he said to them, "Whose image and inscription is this?" They replied to him, "Caesar's." 17 So Jesus said to them, "Repay to Caesar what belongs to Caesar and to God what belongs to God." They were utterly amazed at him.

18 Some Sadducees, who say there is no resurrection, came to him and put this question to him, 19 saying, "Teacher, Moses wrote for us, 'If someone's brother dies, leaving a wife but no child, his brother must take the wife and raise up descendants for his brother.' 20 Now there were seven brothers. The first married a woman and died, leaving no descendants. 21 So the second married her and died, leaving no descendants, and the third likewise. 22 And the seven left no descendants. Last of all the woman also died. 23 At the resurrection [when they arise] whose wife will she be? For all seven had been married to her." 24 Jesus said to them, "Are you not misled because you do not know the scriptures or the power of God? 25 When they rise from the dead, they neither marry nor are given in marriage, but they are like the angels in heaven. 26 As for the dead being raised, have you not read in the Book of Moses, in the passage about the bush, how God told him, 'I am the God of Abraham, [the] God of Isaac, and [the] God of Jacob'? 27 He is not God of the dead but of the living. You are greatly misled."

28 One of the scribes, when he came forward and heard them disputing and saw how well he had answered them, asked him, "Which is the first of all the commandments?" 29 Jesus replied, "The first is this: 'Hear, O Israel! The Lord our God is Lord alone! 30 You shall love the Lord your God with all your heart, with all your soul, with all your mind, and with all your strength.' 31 The second is this: 'You shall love your neighbor as yourself.' There is no other commandment greater than these." 32 The scribe said to him, "Well said, teacher. You are right in saying, 'He is One and there is no other than he.' 33 And 'to love him with all your

him and sent him away empty handed. 4 Next he sent another servant to them; him they beat about the head and treated shamefully. 5 And he sent another and him they killed; then a number of others, and they thrashed some and killed the rest. 6 He had still someone left: his beloved son. He sent him to them last of all, thinking, "They will respect my son." 7 But those tenants said to each other, "This is the heir. Come on, let us kill him, and the inheritance will be ours." 8 So they seized him and killed him and threw him out of the vineyard. 9 Now what will the owner of the vineyard do? He will come and make an end of the tenants and give the vineyard to others. 10 Have you not read this text of scripture:

The stone which the builders rejected
    has become the cornerstone;
11 this is the Lord's doing,
    and we marvel at it?'s

12 And they would have liked to arrest him, because they realised that the parable was aimed at them, but they were afraid of the crowds. So they left him alone and went away.

13 Next they sent to him some Pharisees and some Herodians to catch him out in what he said. 14 These came and said to him, 'Master, we know that you are an honest man, that you are not afraid of anyone, because human rank means nothing to you, and that you teach the way of God in all honesty. Is it permissible to pay taxes to Caesar or not? Should we pay or not?' 15 Recognising their hypocrisy he said to them, 'Why are you putting me to the test? Hand me a denarius and let me see it.' 16 They handed him one and he said to them, 'Whose portrait is this? Whose title?' They said to him, 'Caesar's.' 17 Jesus said to them, 'Pay Caesar what belongs to Caesar—and God what belongs to God.' And they were amazed at him.

18 Then some Sadducees—who deny that there is a resurrection—came to him and they put this question to him, 19 'Master, Moses prescribed for us that if a man's brother dies leaving a wife but no child, the man must marry the widow to raise up children for his brother. 20 Now there were seven brothers; the first married a wife and then died leaving no children. 21 The second married the widow, and he too died leaving no children; with the third it was the same, 22 and none of the seven left any children. Last of all the woman herself died. 23 Now at the resurrection, when they rise again, whose wife will she be, since she had been married to all seven?'

24 Jesus said to them, 'Surely the reason why you are wrong is that you understand neither the scriptures nor the power of God. 25 For when they rise from the dead, men and women do not marry; no, they are like the angels in heaven. 26 Now about the dead rising again, have you never read in the Book of Moses, in the passage about the bush, how God spoke to him and said: I am the God of Abraham, the God of Isaac and the God of Jacob?t 27 He is God, not of the dead, but of the living. You are very much mistaken.'

28 One of the scribes who had listened to them debating appreciated that Jesus had given a good answer and put a further question to him, 'Which is the first of all the commandments?' 29 Jesus replied, 'This is the first:u Listen, Israel, the Lord our God is the one, only Lord, 30 and you must love the Lord your God with all your heart, with all your soul, with all your mind and with all your strength. 31 The second is this:v You must love your neighbour as yourself. There is no commandment greater than these.' 32 The scribe said to him, 'Well spoken, Master; what you have said is true, that he is one and there is no other. 33 To

s 12 Ps 118:22–23.   t 12 Ex 3:6.   u 12 Dt 6:4–5.
v 12 Lv 19:18.

2737

understanding, and with all the strength,' and 'to love one's neighbor as oneself,' — this is much more important than all whole burnt offerings and sacrifices." 34 When Jesus saw that he answered wisely, he said to him, "You are not far from the kingdom of God." After that no one dared to ask him any question.

35 While Jesus was teaching in the temple, he said, "How can the scribes say that the Messiah*l* is the son of David? 36 David himself, by the Holy Spirit, declared,

'The Lord said to my Lord,
"Sit at my right hand,
    until I put your enemies under your feet." '

37 David himself calls him Lord; so how can he be his son?" And the large crowd was listening to him with delight.

38 As he taught, he said, "Beware of the scribes, who like to walk around in long robes, and to be greeted with respect in the marketplaces, 39 and to have the best seats in the synagogues and places of honor at banquets! 40 They devour widows' houses and for the sake of appearance say long prayers. They will receive the greater condemnation."

41 He sat down opposite the treasury, and watched the crowd putting money into the treasury. Many rich people put in large sums. 42 A poor widow came and put in two small copper coins, which are worth a penny. 43 Then he called his disciples and said to them, "Truly I tell you, this poor widow has put in more than all those who are contributing to the treasury. 44 For all of them have contributed out of their abundance; but she out of her poverty has put in everything she had, all she had to live on."

13 As he came out of the temple, one of his disciples said to him, "Look, Teacher, what large stones and what large buildings!" 2 Then Jesus asked him, "Do you see these great buildings? Not one stone will be left here upon another; all will be thrown down."

3 When he was sitting on the Mount of Olives opposite the temple, Peter, James, John, and Andrew asked him privately, 4 "Tell us, when will this be, and what will be the sign that all these things are about to be accomplished?" 5 Then Jesus began to say to them, "Beware that no one leads you astray. 6 Many will come in my name and say, 'I am he!'*m* and they will lead many astray. 7 When you hear of wars and rumors of wars, do not be alarmed; this must take place, but the end is still to come. 8 For nation will rise against nation, and kingdom against kingdom; there will be earthquakes in various places; there will be famines. This is but the beginning of the birth pangs.

9 "As for yourselves, beware; for they will hand you over to councils; and you will be beaten in synagogues; and you will stand before governors and kings because of me, as a testimony to them. 10 And the good news*n* must first be proclaimed to all nations. 11 When they bring you to trial and hand you over, do not worry beforehand about what you are to say; but say whatever is given you at that time, for it is not you who speak, but the Holy Spirit. 12 Brother will betray brother to death, and a father his child, and children will rise against parents and have them put to death; 13 and you will be hated by all because of my name. But the one who endures to the end will be saved.

14 "But when you see the desolating sacrilege set up where it ought not to be (let the reader understand), then those in Judea must flee to the mountains; 15 the one on the

understanding, and all your strength, and to love your neighbour as yourself — that means far more than any whole-offerings and sacrifices.' 34 When Jesus saw how thoughtfully he answered, he said to him, 'You are not far from the kingdom of God.' After that nobody dared put any more questions to him.

35 As he taught in the temple, Jesus went on to say, 'How can the scribes maintain that the Messiah is a son of David? 36 It was David himself who said, when inspired by the Holy Spirit, "The Lord said to my Lord, 'Sit at my right hand until I put your enemies under your feet.' " 37 David himself calls him "Lord"; how can he be David's son?'

There was a large crowd listening eagerly. 38 As he taught them, he said, 'Beware of the scribes, who love to walk up and down in long robes and be greeted respectfully in the street, 39 to have the chief seats in synagogues and places of honour at feasts. 40 Those who eat up the property of widows, while for appearance' sake they say long prayers, will receive a sentence all the more severe.'

41 As he was sitting opposite the temple treasury, he watched the people dropping their money into the chest. Many rich people were putting in large amounts. 42 Presently there came a poor widow who dropped in two tiny coins, together worth a penny. 43 He called his disciples to him and said, 'Truly I tell you: this poor widow has given more than all those giving to the treasury; 44 for the others who have given had more than enough, but she, with less than enough, has given all that she had to live on.'

13 As he was leaving the temple, one of his disciples exclaimed, 'Look, Teacher, what huge stones! What fine buildings!' 2 Jesus said to him, 'You see these great buildings? Not one stone will be left upon another; they will all be thrown down.'

3 As he sat on the mount of Olives opposite the temple he was questioned privately by Peter, James, John, and Andrew. 4 'Tell us,' they said, 'when will this happen? What will be the sign that all these things are about to be fulfilled?'

5 Jesus began: 'Be on your guard; let no one mislead you. 6 Many will come claiming my name, and saying, "I am he"; and many will be misled by them. 7 When you hear of wars and rumours of wars, do not be alarmed. Such things are bound to happen; but the end is still to come. 8 For nation will go to war against nation, kingdom against kingdom; there will be earthquakes in many places; there will be famines. These are the first birth-pangs of the new age.

9 'As for you, be on your guard. You will be handed over to the courts; you will be beaten in synagogues; you will be summoned to appear before governors and kings on my account to testify in their presence. 10 Before the end the gospel must be proclaimed to all nations. 11 So when you are arrested and put on trial do not worry beforehand about what you will say, but when the time comes say whatever is given you to say, for it is not you who will be speaking, but the Holy Spirit. 12 Brother will hand over brother to death, and a father his child; children will turn against their parents and send them to their death. 13 Everyone will hate you for your allegiance to me, but whoever endures to the end will be saved.

14 'But when you see "the abomination of desolation" usurping a place which is not his (let the reader understand), then those who are in Judaea must take to the hills. 15 If

heart, with all your understanding, with all your strength, and to love your neighbor as yourself' is worth more than all burnt offerings and sacrifices." 34 And when Jesus saw that [he] answered with understanding, he said to him, "You are not far from the kingdom of God." And no one dared to ask him any more questions.

35 As Jesus was teaching in the temple area he said, "How do the scribes claim that the Messiah is the son of David? 36 David himself, inspired by the holy Spirit, said:

'The Lord said to my lord,
"Sit at my right hand
until I place your enemies under your feet." '

37 David himself calls him 'lord'; so how is he his son?" [The] great crowd heard this with delight.

38 In the course of his teaching he said, "Beware of the scribes, who like to go around in long robes and accept greetings in the marketplaces, 39 seats of honor in synagogues, and places of honor at banquets. 40 They devour the houses of widows and, as a pretext, recite lengthy prayers. They will receive a very severe condemnation."

41 He sat down opposite the treasury and observed how the crowd put money into the treasury. Many rich people put in large sums. 42 A poor widow also came and put in two small coins worth a few cents. 43 Calling his disciples to himself, he said to them, "Amen, I say to you, this poor widow put in more than all the other contributors to the treasury. 44 For they have all contributed from their surplus wealth, but she, from her poverty, has contributed all she had, her whole livelihood."

13 As he was making his way out of the temple area one of his disciples said to him, "Look, teacher, what stones and what buildings!" 2 Jesus said to him, "Do you see these great buildings? There will not be one stone left upon another that will not be thrown down."

3 As he was sitting on the Mount of Olives opposite the temple area, Peter, James, John, and Andrew asked him privately, 4 "Tell us, when will this happen, and what sign will there be when all these things are about to come to an end?" 5 Jesus began to say to them, "See that no one deceives you. 6 Many will come in my name saying, 'I am he,' and they will deceive many. 7 When you hear of wars and reports of wars do not be alarmed; such things must happen, but it will not yet be the end. 8 Nation will rise against nation and kingdom against kingdom. There will be earthquakes from place to place and there will be famines. These are the beginnings of the labor pains.

9 "Watch out for yourselves. They will hand you over to the courts. You will be beaten in synagogues. You will be arraigned before governors and kings because of me, as a witness before them. 10 But the gospel must first be preached to all nations. 11 When they lead you away and hand you over, do not worry beforehand about what you are to say. But say whatever will be given to you at that hour. For it will not be you who are speaking but the holy Spirit. 12 Brother will hand over brother to death, and the father his child; children will rise up against parents and have them put to death. 13 You will be hated by all because of my name. But the one who perseveres to the end will be saved.

14 "When you see the desolating abomination standing where he should not (let the reader understand), then those in Judea must flee to the mountains, 15 [and] a person on a

---

love him with all your heart, with all your understanding and strength, and to *love your neighbour as yourself,* this is far more important than any burnt offering or sacrifice.' 34 Jesus, seeing how wisely he had spoken, said, 'You are not far from the kingdom of God.' And after that no one dared to question him any more.

35 While teaching in the Temple, Jesus said, 'How can the scribes maintain that the Christ is the son of David? 36 David himself, moved by the Holy Spirit, said:

The Lord declared to my Lord,
take your seat at my right hand
till I have made your enemies
your footstool. w

37 David himself calls him Lord; in what way then can he be his son?' And the great crowd listened to him with delight.

38 In his teaching he said, 'Beware of the scribes who like to walk about in long robes, to be greeted respectfully in the market squares, 39 to take the front seats in the synagogues and the places of honour at banquets; 40 these are the men who devour the property of widows and for show offer long prayers. The more severe will be the sentence they receive.'

41 He sat down opposite the treasury and watched the people putting money into the treasury, and many of the rich put in a great deal. 42 A poor widow came and put in two small coins, the equivalent of a penny. 43 Then he called his disciples and said to them, 'In truth I tell you, this poor widow has put more in than all who have contributed to the treasury; 44 for they have all put in money they could spare, but she in her poverty has put in everything she possessed, all she had to live on.'

13 x As he was leaving the Temple one of his disciples said to him, 'Master, look at the size of those stones! Look at the size of those buildings!' 2 And Jesus said to him, 'You see these great buildings? Not a single stone will be left on another; everything will be pulled down.'

3 And while he was sitting on the Mount of Olives, facing the Temple, Peter, James, John and Andrew questioned him when they were by themselves, 4 'Tell us, when is this going to happen, and what sign will there be that it is all about to take place?'

5 Then Jesus began to tell them, 'Take care that no one deceives you. 6 Many will come using my name and saying, "I am he," and they will deceive many. 7 When you hear of wars and rumours of wars, do not be alarmed; this is something that must happen, but the end will not be yet. 8 For nation will fight against nation, and kingdom against kingdom. There will be earthquakes in various places; there will be famines. This is the beginning of the birth-pangs.

9 'Be on your guard: you will be handed over to sanhedrins; you will be beaten in synagogues; and you will be brought before governors and kings for my sake, as evidence to them, 10 since the gospel must first be proclaimed to all nations.

11 'And when you are taken to be handed over, do not worry beforehand about what to say; no, say whatever is given to you when the time comes, because it is not you who will be speaking; it is the Holy Spirit. 12 Brother will betray brother to death, and a father his child; children will come forward against their parents and have them put to death. 13 You will be universally hated on account of my name; but anyone who stands firm to the end will be saved.

14 'When you see *the appalling abomination* set up where it ought not to be (let the reader understand), then those in Judaea must escape to the mountains; 15 if a man is

---

w **12** Ps 110:1.   x **13** By contrast with Mt 24—25, Mk's eschatological discourse concerns only the destruction of Jerusalem as an act of God delivering his people.   y **13** Dn 9:27; 11:31; 12:11.

housetop must not go down or enter the house to take anything away; 16 the one in the field must not turn back to get a coat. 17 Woe to those who are pregnant and to those who are nursing infants in those days! 18 Pray that it may not be in winter. 19 For in those days there will be suffering, such as has not been from the beginning of the creation that God created until now, no, and never will be. 20 And if the Lord had not cut short those days, no one would be saved; but for the sake of the elect, whom he chose, he has cut short those days. 21 And if anyone says to you at that time, 'Look! Here is the Messiah!'o or 'Look! There he is!'—do not believe it. 22 False messiahs p and false prophets will appear and produce signs and omens, to lead astray, if possible, the elect. 23 But be alert; I have already told you everything.

24 "But in those days, after that suffering,
    the sun will be darkened,
        and the moon will not give its light,
25 and the stars will be falling from heaven,
        and the powers in the heavens will be shaken.
26 Then they will see 'the Son of Man coming in clouds' with great power and glory. 27 Then he will send out the angels, and gather his elect from the four winds, from the ends of the earth to the ends of heaven.

28 "From the fig tree learn its lesson: as soon as its branch becomes tender and puts forth its leaves, you know that summer is near. 29 So also, when you see these things taking place, you know that he q is near, at the very gates. 30 Truly I tell you, this generation will not pass away until all these things have taken place. 31 Heaven and earth will pass away, but my words will not pass away.

32 "But about that day or hour no one knows, neither the angels in heaven, nor the Son, but only the Father. 33 Beware, keep alert; r for you do not know when the time will come. 34 It is like a man going on a journey, when he leaves home and puts his slaves in charge, each with his work, and commands the doorkeeper to be on the watch. 35 Therefore, keep awake—for you do not know when the master of the house will come, in the evening, or at midnight, or at cockcrow, or at dawn, 36 or else he may find you asleep when he comes suddenly. 37 And what I say to you I say to all: Keep awake."

14 It was two days before the Passover and the festival of Unleavened Bread. The chief priests and the scribes were looking for a way to arrest Jesus s by stealth and kill him; 2 for they said, "Not during the festival, or there may be a riot among the people."

3 While he was at Bethany in the house of Simon the leper, t as he sat at the table, a woman came with an alabaster jar of very costly ointment of nard, and she broke open the jar and poured the ointment on his head. 4 But some were there who said to one another in anger, "Why was the ointment wasted in this way? 5 For this ointment could have been sold for more than three hundred denarii, u and the money given to the poor." And they scolded her. 6 But Jesus said, "Let her alone; why do you trouble her? She has performed a good service for me. 7 For you always have the poor with you, and you can show kindness to them whenever you wish; but you will not always have me. 8 She has done what she could; she has anointed my body beforehand for its burial. 9 Truly I tell you, wherever the good news v is proclaimed in the whole world, what she has done will be told in remembrance of her."

anyone is on the roof, he must not go down into the house to fetch anything out; 16 if anyone is in the field, he must not turn back for his coat. 17 Alas for women with child in those days, and for those who have children at the breast! 18 Pray that it may not come in winter. 19 For those days will bring distress such as there has never been before since the beginning of the world which God created, and will never be again. 20 If the Lord had not cut short that time of troubles, no living thing could survive. However, for the sake of his own, whom he has chosen, he has cut short the time.

21 'If anyone says to you then, "Look, here is the Messiah," or, "Look, there he is," do not believe it. 22 Impostors will come claiming to be messiahs or prophets, and they will produce signs and wonders to mislead, if possible, God's chosen. 23 Be on your guard; I have forewarned you of it all.

24 'But in those days, after that distress,
    the sun will be darkened,
        the moon will not give her light;
25 the stars will come falling from the sky,
        the celestial powers will be shaken.
26 'Then they will see the Son of Man coming in the clouds with great power and glory, 27 and he will send out the angels and gather his chosen from the four winds, from the farthest bounds of earth to the farthest bounds of heaven.

28 'Learn a lesson from the fig tree. When its tender shoots appear and are breaking into leaf, you know that summer is near. 29 In the same way, when you see all this happening, you may know that the end is near, at the very door. 30 Truly I tell you: the present generation will live to see it all. 31 Heaven and earth will pass away, but my words will never pass away.

32 'Yet about that day or hour no one knows, not even the angels in heaven, not even the Son; no one but the Father. 33 'Be on your guard, keep watch. You do not know when the moment is coming. 34 It is like a man away from home: he has left his house and put his servants in charge, each with his own work to do, and he has ordered the door-keeper to stay awake. 35 Keep awake, then, for you do not know when the master of the house will come. Evening or midnight, cock-crow or early dawn—36 if he comes suddenly, do not let him find you asleep. 37 And what I say to you, I say to everyone: Keep awake.'

14 It was two days before the festival of Passover and Unleavened Bread, and the chief priests and the scribes were trying to devise some scheme to seize him and put him to death. 2 'It must not be during the festival,' they said, 'or we should have rioting among the people.'

3 Jesus was at Bethany, in the house of Simon the leper. As he sat at table, a woman came in carrying a bottle of very costly perfume, pure oil of nard. She broke it open and poured the oil over his head. 4 Some of those present said indignantly to one another, 'Why this waste? 5 The perfume might have been sold for more than three hundred denarii and the money given to the poor'; and they began to scold her. 6 But Jesus said, 'Leave her alone. Why make trouble for her? It is a fine thing she has done for me. 7 You have the poor among you always, and you can help them whenever you like; but you will not always have me. 8 She has done what lay in her power; she has anointed my body in anticipation of my burial. 9 Truly I tell you: wherever the gospel is proclaimed throughout the world, what she has done will be told as her memorial.'

o Or the Christ   p Or christs   q Or it   r Other ancient authorities add and pray   s Gk him   t The terms leper and leprosy can refer to several diseases   u The denarius was the usual day's wage for a laborer   v Or gospel

13:29 the end is near: or he is near.   13:33 keep watch: some witnesses add and pray.   14:5 denarii: see p. xxix.

housetop must not go down or enter to get anything out of his house, 16 and a person in a field must not return to get his cloak. 17 Woe to pregnant women and nursing mothers in those days. 18 Pray that this does not happen in winter. 19 For those times will have tribulation such as has not been since the beginning of God's creation until now, nor ever will be. 20 If the Lord had not shortened those days, no one would be saved; but for the sake of the elect whom he chose, he did shorten the days. 21 If anyone says to you then, 'Look, here is the Messiah! Look, there he is!' do not believe it. 22 False messiahs and false prophets will arise and will perform signs and wonders in order to mislead, if that were possible, the elect. 23 Be watchful! I have told it all to you beforehand.

24 "But in those days after that tribulation

the sun will be darkened,
  and the moon will not give its light,
25 and the stars will be falling from the sky,
  and the powers in the heavens will be shaken.

26 And then they will see 'the Son of Man coming in the clouds' with great power and glory, 27 and then he will send out the angels and gather [his] elect from the four winds, from the end of the earth to the end of the sky.

28 "Learn a lesson from the fig tree. When its branch becomes tender and sprouts leaves, you know that summer is near. 29 In the same way, when you see these things happening, know that he is near, at the gates. 30 Amen, I say to you, this generation will not pass away until all these things have taken place. 31 Heaven and earth will pass away, but my words will not pass away.

32 "But of that day or hour, no one knows, neither the angels in heaven, nor the Son, but only the Father. 33 Be watchful! Be alert! You do not know when the time will come. 34 It is like a man traveling abroad. He leaves home and places his servants in charge, each with his work, and orders the gatekeeper to be on the watch. 35 Watch, therefore; you do not know when the lord of the house is coming, whether in the evening, or at midnight, or at cockcrow, or in the morning. 36 May he not come suddenly and find you sleeping. 37 What I say to you, I say to all: 'Watch!' "

on the housetop, he must not come down or go inside to collect anything from his house; 16 if a man is in the fields, he must not turn back to fetch his cloak. 17 Alas for those with child, or with babies at the breast, when those days come! 18 Pray that this may not be in winter. 19 For in those days there will be *great distress, unparalleled since z* God created the world, and such as will never be again. 20 And if the Lord had not shortened that time, no human being would have survived; but he did shorten the time, for the sake of the elect whom he chose.

21 'And if anyone says to you then, "Look, here is the Christ" or, "Look, he is there," do not believe it; 22 for false Christs and false prophets will arise and produce signs and portents to deceive the elect, if that were possible. 23 You, therefore, must be on your guard. I have given you full warning.

24 'But in those days, after that time of distress, the sun will be darkened, the moon will not give its light, 25 the stars will come falling out of the sky and the powers in the heavens will be shaken. 26 And then they will see the *Son of man coming in the clouds* with great power and glory. a 27 And then he will send the angels to gather his elect from the four winds, from the ends of the world to the ends of the sky. b

28 'Take the fig tree as a parable: as soon as its twigs grow supple and its leaves come out, you know that summer is near. 29 So with you when you see these things happening: know that he is near, right at the gates. 30 In truth I tell you, before this generation has passed away all these things will have taken place. 31 Sky and earth will pass away, but my words will not pass away.

32 'But as for that day or hour, nobody knows it, neither the angels in heaven, nor the Son; no one but the Father. 33 'Be on your guard, stay awake, because you never know when the time will come. 34 It is like a man travelling abroad: he has gone from his home, and left his servants in charge, each with his own work to do; and he has told the doorkeeper to stay awake. 35 So stay awake, because you do not know when the master of the house is coming, evening, midnight, cockcrow or dawn; 36 if he comes unexpectedly, he must not find you asleep. 37 And what I am saying to you I say to all: Stay awake!'

14 The Passover and the Feast of Unleavened Bread were to take place in two days' time. So the chief priests and the scribes were seeking a way to arrest him by treachery and put him to death. 2 They said, "Not during the festival, for fear that there may be a riot among the people."

3 When he was in Bethany reclining at table in the house of Simon the leper, a woman came with an alabaster jar of perfumed oil, costly genuine spikenard. She broke the alabaster jar and poured it on his head. 4 There were some who were indignant. "Why has there been this waste of perfumed oil? 5 It could have been sold for more than three hundred days' wages and the money given to the poor." They were infuriated with her. 6 Jesus said, "Let her alone. Why do you make trouble for her? She has done a good thing for me. 7 The poor you will always have with you, and whenever you wish you can do good to them, but you will not always have me. 8 She has done what she could. She has anticipated anointing my body for burial. 9 Amen, I say to you, wherever the gospel is proclaimed to the whole world, what she has done will be told in memory of her."

14 It was two days before the Passover and the feast of Unleavened Bread, and the chief priests and the scribes were looking for a way to arrest Jesus by some trick and have him put to death. 2 For they said, 'It must not be during the festivities, or there will be a disturbance among the people.'

3 He was at Bethany in the house of Simon, a man who had suffered from a virulent skin-disease; he was at table when a woman came in with an alabaster jar of very costly ointment, pure nard. She broke the jar and poured the ointment on his head. 4 Some who were there said to one another indignantly, 'Why this waste of ointment? 5 Ointment like this could have been sold for over three hundred denarii and the money given to the poor'; and they were angry with her. 6 But Jesus said, 'Leave her alone. Why are you upsetting her? What she has done for me is a good work. 7 You have the poor with you always, and you can be kind to them whenever you wish, but you will not always have me. 8 She has done what she could: she has anointed my body beforehand for its burial. 9 In truth I tell you, wherever throughout all the world the gospel is proclaimed, what she has done will be told as well, in remembrance of her.'

---

10 Then Judas Iscariot, who was one of the twelve, went to the chief priests in order to betray him to them. 11 When they heard it, they were greatly pleased, and promised to give him money. So he began to look for an opportunity to betray him.

12 On the first day of Unleavened Bread, when the Passover lamb is sacrificed, his disciples said to him, "Where do you want us to go and make the preparations for you to eat the Passover?" 13 So he sent two of his disciples, saying to them, "Go into the city, and a man carrying a jar of water will meet you; follow him, 14 and wherever he enters, say to the owner of the house, 'The Teacher asks, Where is my guest room where I may eat the Passover with my disciples?' 15 He will show you a large room upstairs, furnished and ready. Make preparations for us there." 16 So the disciples set out and went to the city, and found everything as he had told them; and they prepared the Passover meal.

17 When it was evening, he came with the twelve. 18 And when they had taken their places and were eating, Jesus said, "Truly I tell you, one of you will betray me, one who is eating with me." 19 They began to be distressed and to say to him one after another, "Surely, not I?" 20 He said to them, "It is one of the twelve, one who is dipping bread^w into the bowl^x with me. 21 For the Son of Man goes as it is written of him, but woe to that one by whom the Son of Man is betrayed! It would have been better for that one not to have been born."

22 While they were eating, he took a loaf of bread, and after blessing it he broke it, gave it to them, and said, "Take; this is my body." 23 Then he took a cup, and after giving thanks he gave it to them, and all of them drank from it. 24 He said to them, "This is my blood of the^y covenant, which is poured out for many. 25 Truly I tell you, I will never again drink of the fruit of the vine until that day when I drink it new in the kingdom of God."

26 When they had sung the hymn, they went out to the Mount of Olives. 27 And Jesus said to them, "You will all become deserters; for it is written,

'I will strike the shepherd,
and the sheep will be scattered.'

28 But after I am raised up, I will go before you to Galilee." 29 Peter said to him, "Even though all become deserters, I will not." 30 Jesus said to him, "Truly I tell you, this day, this very night, before the cock crows twice, you will deny me three times." 31 But he said vehemently, "Even though I must die with you, I will not deny you." And all of them said the same.

32 They went to a place called Gethsemane; and he said to his disciples, "Sit here while I pray." 33 He took with him Peter and James and John, and began to be distressed and agitated. 34 And he said to them, "I am deeply grieved, even to death; remain here, and keep awake." 35 And going a little farther, he threw himself on the ground and prayed that, if it were possible, the hour might pass from him. 36 He said, "Abba,^z Father, for you all things are possible; remove this cup from me; yet, not what I want, but what you want." 37 He came and found them sleeping; and he said to Peter, "Simon, are you asleep? Could you not keep awake one hour? 38 Keep awake and pray that you may not come into the time of trial;^a the spirit indeed is willing, but the flesh is weak." 39 And again he went away and prayed, saying the same words. 40 And once more he came and found them sleeping, for their eyes were very heavy; and they did not know what to say to him. 41 He came a third

10 Then Judas Iscariot, one of the Twelve, went to the chief priests to betray him to them. 11 When they heard what he had come for, they were glad and promised him money; and he began to look for an opportunity to betray him.

12 Now ON the first day of Unleavened Bread, when the Passover lambs were being slaughtered, his disciples said to him, 'Where would you like us to go and prepare the Passover for you?' 13 So he sent off two of his disciples with these instructions: 'Go into the city, and a man will meet you carrying a jar of water. Follow him, 14 and when he enters a house give this message to the householder: "The Teacher says, 'Where is the room in which I am to eat the Passover with my disciples?' " 15 He will show you a large upstairs room, set out in readiness. Make the preparations for us there.' 16 Then the disciples went off, and when they came into the city they found everything just as he had told them. So they prepared the Passover.

17 In the evening he came to the house with the Twelve. 18 As they sat at supper Jesus said, 'Truly I tell you: one of you will betray me — one who is eating with me.' 19 At this they were distressed; and one by one they said to him, 'Surely you do not mean me?' 20 'It is one of the Twelve', he said, 'who is dipping into the bowl with me. 21 The Son of Man is going the way appointed for him in the scriptures; but alas for that man by whom the Son of Man is betrayed! It would be better for that man if he had never been born.'

22 During supper he took bread, and having said the blessing he broke it and gave it to them, with the words: 'Take this; this is my body.' 23 Then he took a cup, and having offered thanks to God he gave it to them; and they all drank from it. 24 And he said to them, 'This is my blood, the blood of the covenant, shed for many. 25 Truly I tell you: never again shall I drink from the fruit of the vine until that day when I drink it new in the kingdom of God.'

26 After singing the Passover hymn, they went out to the mount of Olives. 27 And Jesus said to them, 'You will all lose faith; for it is written: "I will strike the shepherd and the sheep will be scattered." 28 Nevertheless, after I am raised I shall go ahead of you into Galilee.' 29 Peter answered, 'Everyone else may lose faith, but I will not.' 30 Jesus said to him, 'Truly I tell you: today, this very night, before the cock crows twice, you yourself will disown me three times.' 31 But Peter insisted: 'Even if I have to die with you, I will never disown you.' And they all said the same.

32 WHEN they reached a place called Gethsemane, he said to his disciples, 'Sit here while I pray.' 33 And he took Peter and James and John with him. Horror and anguish overwhelmed him, 34 and he said to them, 'My heart is ready to break with grief; stop here, and stay awake.' 35 Then he went on a little farther, threw himself on the ground, and prayed that if it were possible this hour might pass him by. 36 'Abba, Father,' he said, 'all things are possible to you; take this cup from me. Yet not my will but yours.'

37 He came back and found them asleep; and he said to Peter, 'Asleep, Simon? Could you not stay awake for one hour? 38 Stay awake, all of you; and pray that you may be spared the test. The spirit is willing, but the flesh is weak.' 39 Once more he went away and prayed. 40 On his return he found them asleep again, for their eyes were heavy; and they did not know how to answer him.

14:39 **prayed:** *some witnesses add* using the same words.

10 Then Judas Iscariot, one of the Twelve, went off to the chief priests to hand him over to them. 11 When they heard him they were pleased and promised to pay him money. Then he looked for an opportunity to hand him over.

12 On the first day of the Feast of Unleavened Bread, when they sacrificed the Passover lamb, his disciples said to him, "Where do you want us to go and prepare for you to eat the Passover?" 13 He sent two of his disciples and said to them, "Go into the city and a man will meet you, carrying a jar of water. Follow him. 14 Wherever he enters, say to the master of the house, 'The Teacher says, "Where is my guest room where I may eat the Passover with my disciples?"' 15 Then he will show you a large upper room furnished and ready. Make the preparations for us there." 16 The disciples then went off, entered the city, and found it just as he had told them; and they prepared the Passover.

17 When it was evening, he came with the Twelve. 18 And as they reclined at table and were eating, Jesus said, "Amen, I say to you, one of you will betray me, one who is eating with me." 19 They began to be distressed and to say to him, one by one, "Surely it is not I?" 20 He said to them, "One of the Twelve, the one who dips with me into the dish. 21 For the Son of Man indeed goes, as it is written of him, but woe to that man by whom the Son of Man is betrayed. It would be better for that man if he had never been born."

22 While they were eating, he took bread, said the blessing, broke it, and gave it to them, and said, "Take it; this is my body." 23 Then he took a cup, gave thanks, and gave it to them, and they all drank from it. 24 He said to them, "This is my blood of the covenant, which will be shed for many. 25 Amen, I say to you, I shall not drink again the fruit of the vine until the day when I drink it new in the kingdom of God." 26 Then, after singing a hymn, they went out to the Mount of Olives.

27 Then Jesus said to them, "All of you will have your faith shaken, for it is written:

'I will strike the shepherd,
    and the sheep will be dispersed.'

28 But after I have been raised up, I shall go before you to Galilee." 29 Peter said to him, "Even though all should have their faith shaken, mine will not be." 30 Then Jesus said to him, "Amen, I say to you, this very night before the cock crows twice you will deny me three times." 31 But he vehemently replied, "Even though I should have to die with you, I will not deny you." And they all spoke similarly.

32 Then they came to a place named Gethsemane, and he said to his disciples, "Sit here while I pray." 33 He took with him Peter, James, and John, and began to be troubled and distressed. 34 Then he said to them, "My soul is sorrowful even to death. Remain here and keep watch." 35 He advanced a little and fell to the ground and prayed that if it were possible the hour might pass by him; 36 he said, "Abba, Father, all things are possible to you. Take this cup away from me, but not what I will but what you will." 37 When he returned he found them asleep. He said to Peter, "Simon, are you asleep? Could you not keep watch for one hour? 38 Watch and pray that you may not undergo the test. The spirit is willing but the flesh is weak." 39 Withdrawing again, he prayed, saying the same thing. 40 Then he returned once more and found them asleep, for they could not keep their eyes open and did not know what to answer him. 41 He

10 Judas Iscariot, one of the Twelve, approached the chief priests with an offer to hand Jesus over to them. 11 They were delighted to hear it, and promised to give him money; and he began to look for a way of betraying him when the opportunity should occur.

12 On the first day of Unleavened Bread, when the Passover lamb was sacrificed, his disciples said to him, 'Where do you want us to go and make the preparations for you to eat the Passover?' 13 So he sent two of his disciples, saying to them, 'Go into the city and you will meet a man carrying a pitcher of water. Follow him, 14 and say to the owner of the house which he enters, "The Master says: Where is the room for me to eat the Passover with my disciples?" 15 He will show you a large upper room furnished with couches, all prepared. Make the preparations for us there.' 16 The disciples set out and went to the city and found everything as he had told them, and prepared the Passover.

17 When evening came he arrived with the Twelve. 18 And while they were at table eating, Jesus said, 'In truth I tell you, one of you is about to betray me, one of you eating with me.'c 19 They were distressed and said to him, one after another, 'Not me, surely?' 20 He said to them, 'It is one of the Twelve, one who is dipping into the same dish with me. 21 Yes, the Son of man is going to his fate, as the scriptures say he will, but alas for that man by whom the Son of man is betrayed! Better for that man if he had never been born.'

22 And as they were eating he took bread, and when he had said the blessing he broke it and gave it to them. 'Take it,' he said, 'this is my body.' 23 Then he took a cup, and when he had given thanks he handed it to them, and all drank from it, 24 and he said to them, 'This is my blood, the blood of the covenant, poured out for many. 25 In truth I tell you, I shall never drink wine any more until the day I drink the new wine in the kingdom of God.'

26 After the psalms had been sung they left for the Mount of Olives. 27 And Jesus said to them, 'You will all fall away, for the scripture says: I shall strike the shepherd and the sheep will be scattered;d 28 however, after my resurrection I shall go before you into Galilee.' 29 Peter said, 'Even if all fall away, I will not.' 30 And Jesus said to him, 'In truth I tell you, this day, this very night, before the cock crows twice, you will have disowned me three times.' 31 But he repeated still more earnestly, 'If I have to die with you, I will never disown you.' And they all said the same.

32 They came to a plot of land called Gethsemane, and he said to his disciples, 'Stay here while I pray.' 33 Then he took Peter and James and John with him. 34 And he began to feel terror and anguish. And he said to them, 'My soul is sorrowful to the point of death. Wait here, and stay awake.' 35 And going on a little further he threw himself on the ground and prayed that, if it were possible, this hour might pass him by. 36 'Abba,e Father!' he said, 'For you everything is possible. Take this cup away from me. But let it be as you, not I, would have it.' 37 He came back and found them sleeping, and he said to Peter, 'Simon, are you asleep? Had you not the strength to stay awake one hour? 38 Stay awake and pray not to be put to the test. The spirit is willing enough, but human nature is weak.' 39 Again he went away and prayed, saying the same words. 40 And once more he came back and found them sleeping, their eyes were so heavy; and they could find no answer for him. 41 He

---

c 14 Ps 41:9.   d 14 Zc 13:7.   e 14 An affectionate Aramaic word, address of child to father.

time and said to them, "Are you still sleeping and taking your rest? Enough! The hour has come; the Son of Man is betrayed into the hands of sinners. 42 Get up, let us be going. See, my betrayer is at hand."

43 Immediately, while he was still speaking, Judas, one of the twelve, arrived; and with him there was a crowd with swords and clubs, from the chief priests, the scribes, and the elders. 44 Now the betrayer had given them a sign, saying, "The one I will kiss is the man; arrest him and lead him away under guard." 45 So when he came, he went up to him at once and said, "Rabbi!" and kissed him. 46 Then they laid hands on him and arrested him. 47 But one of those who stood near drew his sword and struck the slave of the high priest, cutting off his ear. 48 Then Jesus said to them, "Have you come out with swords and clubs to arrest me as though I were a bandit? 49 Day after day I was with you in the temple teaching, and you did not arrest me. But let the scriptures be fulfilled." 50 All of them deserted him and fled.

51 A certain young man was following him, wearing nothing but a linen cloth. They caught hold of him, 52 but he left the linen cloth and ran off naked.

53 They took Jesus to the high priest; and all the chief priests, the elders, and the scribes were assembled. 54 Peter had followed him at a distance, right into the courtyard of the high priest; and he was sitting with the guards, warming himself at the fire. 55 Now the chief priests and the whole council were looking for testimony against Jesus to put him to death; but they found none. 56 For many gave false testimony against him, and their testimony did not agree. 57 Some stood up and gave false testimony against him, saying, 58 "We will destroy this temple that is made with hands, and in three days I will build another, not made with hands.' " 59 But even on this point their testimony did not agree. 60 Then the high priest stood up before them and asked Jesus, "Have you no answer? What is it that they testify against you?" 61 But he was silent and did not answer. Again the high priest asked him, "Are you the Messiah,[b] the Son of the Blessed One?" 62 Jesus said, "I am; and

'you will see the Son of Man
    seated at the right hand of the Power,'
and 'coming with the clouds of heaven.' "
63 Then the high priest tore his clothes and said, "Why do we still need witnesses? 64 You have heard his blasphemy! What is your decision?" All of them condemned him as deserving death. 65 Some began to spit on him, to blindfold him, and to strike him, saying to him, "Prophesy!" The guards also took him over and beat him.

66 While Peter was below in the courtyard, one of the servant-girls of the high priest came by. 67 When she saw Peter warming himself, she stared at him and said, "You also were with Jesus, the man from Nazareth." 68 But he denied it, saying, "I do not know or understand what you are talking about." And he went out into the forecourt.[c] Then the cock crowed.[d] 69 And the servant-girl, on seeing him, began again to say to the bystanders, "This man is one of them." 70 But again he denied it. Then after a little while the bystanders again said to Peter, "Certainly you are one of them; for you are a Galilean." 71 But he began to curse, and he swore an oath, "I do not know this man you are talking about." 72 At that moment the cock crowed for the second

41 He came a third time and said to them, 'Still asleep? Still resting? Enough! The hour has come. The Son of Man is betrayed into the hands of sinners. 42 Up, let us go! The traitor is upon us.'

43 He was still speaking when Judas, one of the Twelve, appeared, and with him a crowd armed with swords and cudgels, sent by the chief priests, scribes, and elders. 44 Now the traitor had agreed with them on a signal: 'The one I kiss is your man; seize him and get him safely away.' 45 When he reached the spot, he went straight up to him and said, 'Rabbi,' and kissed him. 46 Then they seized him and held him fast.

47 One of the bystanders drew his sword, and struck the high priest's servant, cutting off his ear. 48 Then Jesus spoke: 'Do you take me for a robber, that you have come out with swords and cudgels to arrest me? 49 Day after day I have been among you teaching in the temple, and you did not lay hands on me. But let the scriptures be fulfilled.' 50 Then the disciples all deserted him and ran away.

51 Among those who had followed Jesus was a young man with nothing on but a linen cloth. They tried to seize him; 52 but he slipped out of the linen cloth and ran away naked.

53 THEN they led Jesus away to the high priest's house, where the chief priests, elders, and scribes were all assembling. 54 Peter followed him at a distance right into the high priest's courtyard; and there he remained, sitting among the attendants and warming himself at the fire.

55 The chief priests and the whole Council tried to find evidence against Jesus that would warrant a death sentence, but failed to find any. 56 Many gave false evidence against him, but their statements did not tally. 57 Some stood up and gave false evidence against him to this effect: 58 'We heard him say, "I will pull down this temple, made with human hands, and in three days I will build another, not made with hands." ' 59 But even on this point their evidence did not agree.

60 Then the high priest rose to his feet and questioned Jesus: 'Have you no answer to the accusations that these witnesses bring against you?' 61 But he remained silent and made no reply.

Again the high priest questioned him: 'Are you the Messiah, the Son of the Blessed One?' 62 'I am,' said Jesus; 'and you will see the Son of Man seated at the right hand of the Almighty and coming with the clouds of heaven.' 63 Then the high priest tore his robes and said, 'Do we need further witnesses? 64 You have heard the blasphemy. What is your decision?' Their judgement was unanimous: that he was guilty and should be put to death.

65 Some began to spit at him; they blindfolded him and struck him with their fists, crying out, 'Prophesy!' And the attendants slapped him in the face.

66 Meanwhile Peter was still below in the courtyard. One of the high priest's servant-girls came by 67 and saw him there warming himself. She looked closely at him and said, 'You were with this man from Nazareth, this Jesus.' 68 But he denied it: 'I know nothing,' he said; 'I have no idea what you are talking about,' and he went out into the forecourt. 69 The servant-girl saw him there and began to say again to the bystanders, 'He is one of them'; 70 and again he denied it.

Again, a little later, the bystanders said to Peter, 'You must be one of them; you are a Galilean.' 71 At this he started to curse, and declared with an oath, 'I do not know this man you are talking about.' 72 At that moment the cock

14:41 **Enough:** *the meaning of the Greek cannot be confidently decided.* 14:65 **Prophesy:** *some witnesses add* Who hit you? *as in Matthew and Luke.* 14:68 **into the forecourt:** *some witnesses add* and a cock crowed.

[b] Or *the Christ* [c] Or *gateway* [d] Other ancient authorities lack *Then the cock crowed*

returned a third time and said to them, "Are you still sleep-ing and taking your rest? It is enough. The hour has come. Behold, the Son of Man is to be handed over to sinners. 42 Get up, let us go. See, my betrayer is at hand."

43 Then, while he was still speaking, Judas, one of the Twelve, arrived, accompanied by a crowd with swords and clubs who had come from the chief priests, the scribes, and the elders. 44 His betrayer had arranged a signal with them, saying, "The man I shall kiss is the one; arrest him and lead him away securely." 45 He came and immediately went over to him and said, "Rabbi." And he kissed him. 46 At this they laid hands on him and arrested him. 47 One of the bystanders drew his sword, struck the high priest's servant, and cut off his ear. 48 Jesus said to them in reply, "Have you come out as against a robber, with swords and clubs, to seize me? 49 Day after day I was with you teaching in the temple area, yet you did not arrest me; but that the scriptures may be fulfilled." 50 And they all left him and fled. 51 Now a young man followed him wearing nothing but a linen cloth about his body. They seized him, 52 but he left the cloth behind and ran off naked.

53 They led Jesus away to the high priest, and all the chief priests and the elders and the scribes came together. 54 Peter followed him at a distance into the high priest's courtyard and was seated with the guards, warming himself at the fire. 55 The chief priests and the entire Sanhedrin kept trying to obtain testimony against Jesus in order to put him to death, but they found none. 56 Many gave false witness against him, but their testimony did not agree. 57 Some took the stand and testified falsely against him, alleging, 58 "We heard him say, 'I will destroy this temple made with hands and within three days I will build another not made with hands.' " 59 Even so their testimony did not agree. 60 The high priest rose before the assembly and questioned Jesus, saying, "Have you no answer? What are these men testify-ing against you?" 61 But he was silent and answered noth-ing. Again the high priest asked him and said to him, "Are you the Messiah, the son of the Blessed One?" 62 Then Jesus answered, "I am;

and 'you will see the Son of Man
seated at the right hand of the Power
and coming with the clouds of heaven.' "

63 At that the high priest tore his garments and said, "What further need have we of witnesses? 64 You have heard the blasphemy. What do you think?" They all condemned him as deserving to die. 65 Some began to spit on him. They blindfolded him and struck him and said to him, "Proph-esy!" And the guards greeted him with blows.

66 While Peter was below in the courtyard, one of the high priest's maids came along. 67 Seeing Peter warming himself, she looked intently at him and said, "You too were with the Nazarene, Jesus." 68 But he denied it saying, "I neither know nor understand what you are talking about." So he went out into the outer court. [Then the cock crowed.] 69 The maid saw him and began again to say to the bystand-ers, "This man is one of them." 70 Once again he denied it. A little later the bystanders said to Peter once more, "Surely you are one of them; for you too are a Galilean." 71 He began to curse and to swear, "I do not know this man about whom you are talking." 72 And immediately a cock crowed

came back a third time and said to them, 'You can sleep on now and have your rest. It is all over. The hour has come. Now the Son of man is to be betrayed into the hands of sinners. 42 Get up! Let us go! My betrayer is not far away.'

43 And at once, while he was still speaking, Judas, one of the Twelve, came up and with him a number of men armed with swords and clubs, sent by the chief priests, the scribes and the elders. 44 Now the traitor had arranged a signal with them saying, 'The one I kiss, he is the man. Arrest him, and see he is well guarded when you lead him away.' 45 So when the traitor came, he went up to Jesus at once and said, 'Rabbi!' and kissed him. 46 The others seized him and arrested him. 47 Then one of the bystanders drew his sword and struck out at the high priest's servant and cut off his ear.

48 Then Jesus spoke. 'Am I a bandit,' he said, 'that you had to set out to capture me with swords and clubs? 49 I was among you teaching in the Temple day after day and you never laid a hand on me. But this is to fulfil the scriptures.' 50 And they all deserted him and ran away. 51 A young man followed with nothing on but a linen cloth. They caught hold of him, 52 but he left the cloth in their hands and ran away naked.

53 They led Jesus off to the high priest; and all the chief priests and the elders and the scribes assembled there. 54 Pe-ter had followed him at a distance, right into the high priest's palace, and was sitting with the attendants warming himself at the fire.

55 The chief priests and the whole Sanhedrin were looking for evidence against Jesus in order to have him executed. But they could not find any. 56 Several, indeed, brought false witness against him, but their evidence was conflict-ing. 57 Some stood up and submitted this false evidence against him, 58 'We heard him say, "I am going to destroy this Temple made by human hands, and in three days build another, not made by human hands." ' 59 But even on this point their evidence was conflicting. 60 The high priest then rose before the whole assembly and put this question to Jesus, 'Have you no answer to that? What is this evidence these men are bringing against you?' 61 But he was silent and made no answer at all. The high priest put a second question to him saying, 'Are you the Christ, the Son of the Blessed One?' 62 'I am,' said Jesus, 'and you will see the *Son of man seated at the right hand of the Power and coming with the clouds of heaven.'* f 63 The high priest tore his robes and said, 'What need of witnesses have we now? 64 You heard the blasphemy. What is your finding?' Their verdict was unanimous: he deserved to die.

65 Some of them started spitting at his face, hitting him and saying, 'Play the prophet!' And the attendants struck him too.

66 While Peter was down below in the courtyard, one of the high priest's servant-girls came up. 67 She saw Peter warming himself there, looked closely at him and said, 'You too were with Jesus, the man from Nazareth.' 68 But he denied it. 'I do not know, I do not understand what you are talking about,' he said. And he went out into the fore-court, and a cock crowed. 69 The servant-girl saw him and again started telling the bystanders, 'This man is one of them.' 70 But again he denied it. A little later the bystanders themselves said to Peter, 'You are certainly one of them! Why, you are a Galilean.' 71 But he started cursing and swearing, 'I do not know the man you speak of.' 72 And at

---

14, 68: [*Then the cock crowed*]: found in most manuscripts, perhaps in view of vv 30 and 72, but omitted in others.

f **14** Dn 7:13; Ps 110:1.

NEW REVISED STANDARD VERSION

time. Then Peter remembered that Jesus had said to him, "Before the cock crows twice, you will deny me three times." And he broke down and wept.

15 As soon as it was morning, the chief priests held a consultation with the elders and scribes and the whole council. They bound Jesus, led him away, and handed him over to Pilate. 2 Pilate asked him, "Are you the King of the Jews?" He answered him, "You say so." 3 Then the chief priests accused him of many things. 4 Pilate asked him again, "Have you no answer? See how many charges they bring against you." 5 But Jesus made no further reply, so that Pilate was amazed.

6 Now at the festival he used to release a prisoner for them, anyone for whom they asked. 7 Now a man called Barabbas was in prison with the rebels who had committed murder during the insurrection. 8 So the crowd came and began to ask Pilate to do for them according to his custom. 9 Then he answered them, "Do you want me to release for you the King of the Jews?" 10 For he realized that it was out of jealousy that the chief priests had handed him over. 11 But the chief priests stirred up the crowd to have him release Barabbas for them instead. 12 Pilate spoke to them again, "Then what do you wish me to do*e* with the man you call *f* the King of the Jews?" 13 They shouted back, "Crucify him!" 14 Pilate asked them, "Why, what evil has he done?" But they shouted all the more, "Crucify him!" 15 So Pilate, wishing to satisfy the crowd, released Barabbas for them; and after flogging Jesus, he handed him over to be crucified.

16 Then the soldiers led him into the courtyard of the palace (that is, the governor's headquarters*g*); and they called together the whole cohort. 17 And they clothed him in a purple cloak; and after twisting some thorns into a crown, they put it on him. 18 And they began saluting him, "Hail, King of the Jews!" 19 They struck his head with a reed, spat upon him, and knelt down in homage to him. 20 After mocking him, they stripped him of the purple cloak and put his own clothes on him. Then they led him out to crucify him.

21 They compelled a passer-by, who was coming in from the country, to carry his cross; it was Simon of Cyrene, the father of Alexander and Rufus. 22 Then they brought Jesus*h* to the place called Golgotha (which means the place of a skull). 23 And they offered him wine mixed with myrrh; but he did not take it. 24 And they crucified him, and divided his clothes among them, casting lots to decide what each should take.

25 It was nine o'clock in the morning when they crucified him. 26 The inscription of the charge against him read, "The King of the Jews." 27 And with him they crucified two bandits, one on his right and one on his left.*i* 29 Those who passed by derided *j* him, shaking their heads and saying, "Aha! You who would destroy the temple and build it in three days, 30 save yourself, and come down from the cross!" 31 In the same way the chief priests, along with the scribes, were also mocking him among themselves and saying, "He saved others; he cannot save himself. 32 Let the Messiah,*k* the King of Israel, come down from the cross now, so that we may see and believe." Those who were crucified with him also taunted him.

33 When it was noon, darkness came over the whole land*l* until three in the afternoon. 34 At three o'clock Jesus

REVISED ENGLISH BIBLE

crowed for the second time; and Peter remembered how Jesus had said to him, 'Before the cock crows twice, you will disown me three times.' And he burst into tears.

15 As soon as morning came, the whole Council, chief priests, elders, and scribes, made their plans. They bound Jesus and led him away to hand him over to Pilate. 2 'Are you the king of the Jews?' Pilate asked him. 'The words are yours,' he replied. 3 And the chief priests brought many charges against him. 4 Pilate questioned him again: 'Have you nothing to say in your defence? You see how many charges they are bringing against you.' 5 But, to Pilate's astonishment, Jesus made no further reply.

6 At the festival season the governor used to release one prisoner requested by the people. 7 As it happened, a man known as Barabbas was then in custody with the rebels who had committed murder in the rising. 8 When the crowd appeared and began asking for the usual favour, 9 Pilate replied, 'Would you like me to release the king of the Jews?' 10 For he knew it was out of malice that Jesus had been handed over to him. 11 But the chief priests incited the crowd to ask instead for the release of Barabbas. 12 Pilate spoke to them again: 'Then what shall I do with the man you call king of the Jews?' 13 They shouted back, 'Crucify him!' 14 'Why, what wrong has he done?' Pilate asked; but they shouted all the louder, 'Crucify him!' 15 So Pilate, in his desire to satisfy the mob, released Barabbas to them; and he had Jesus flogged, and then handed him over to be crucified.

16 The soldiers took him inside the governor's residence, the Praetorium, and called the whole company together. 17 They dressed him in purple and, plaiting a crown of thorns, placed it on his head. 18 Then they began to salute him: 'Hail, king of the Jews!' 19 They beat him about the head with a stick and spat at him, and then knelt and paid homage to him. 20 When they had finished their mockery, they stripped off the purple robe and dressed him in his own clothes.

THEN they led him out to crucify him. 21 A man called Simon, from Cyrene, the father of Alexander and Rufus, was passing by on his way in from the country, and they pressed him into service to carry his cross.

22 They brought Jesus to the place called Golgotha, which means 'Place of a Skull', 23 and they offered him drugged wine, but he did not take it. 24 Then they fastened him to the cross. They shared out his clothes, casting lots to decide what each should have.

25 It was nine in the morning when they crucified him; 26 and the inscription giving the charge against him read, 'The King of the Jews'. 27 Two robbers were crucified with him, one on his right and the other on his left.

29 The passers-by wagged their heads and jeered at him: 'Bravo!' they cried, 'So you are the man who was to pull down the temple, and rebuild it in three days! 30 Save yourself and come down from the cross.' 31 The chief priests and scribes joined in, jesting with one another: 'He saved others,' they said, 'but he cannot save himself. 32 Let the Messiah, the king of Israel, come down now from the cross. If we see that, we shall believe.' Even those who were crucified with him taunted him.

33 At midday a darkness fell over the whole land, which lasted till three in the afternoon; 34 and at three Jesus cried

---

e Other ancient authorities read *what should I do*   *f* Other ancient authorities lack *the man you call*   *g* Gk *the praetorium*   *h* Gk *him*   *i* Other ancient authorities add verse 28, *And the scripture was fulfilled that says, "And he was counted among the lawless."*   *j* Or *blasphemed*   *k* Or *the Christ*   *l* Or *earth*

15:2 **The words are yours:** *or* It is as you say.   15:8 **appeared:** *some witnesses read* shouted.   15:27 **on his left:** *some witnesses add* 28 So was fulfilled the text of scripture which says, 'He was reckoned among criminals.'

a second time. Then Peter remembered the word that Jesus had said to him, "Before the cock crows twice you will deny me three times." He broke down and wept.

15 As soon as morning came, the chief priests with the elders and the scribes, that is, the whole Sanhedrin, held a council. They bound Jesus, led him away, and handed him over to Pilate. 2 Pilate questioned him, "Are you the king of the Jews?" He said to him in reply, "You say so." 3 The chief priests accused him of many things. 4 Again Pilate questioned him, "Have you no answer? See how many things they accuse you of." 5 Jesus gave him no further answer, so that Pilate was amazed.

6 Now on the occasion of the feast he used to release to them one prisoner whom they requested. 7 A man called Barabbas was then in prison along with the rebels who had committed murder in a rebellion. 8 The crowd came forward and began to ask him to do for them as he was accustomed. 9 Pilate answered, "Do you want me to release to you the king of the Jews?" 10 For he knew that it was out of envy that the chief priests had handed him over. 11 But the chief priests stirred up the crowd to have him release Barabbas for them instead. 12 Pilate again said to them in reply, "Then what [do you want] me to do with [the man you call] the king of the Jews?" 13 They shouted again, "Crucify him." 14 Pilate said to them, "Why? What evil has he done?" They only shouted the louder, "Crucify him." 15 So Pilate, wishing to satisfy the crowd, released Barabbas to them and, after he had Jesus scourged, handed him over to be crucified.

16 The soldiers led him away inside the palace, that is, the praetorium, and assembled the whole cohort. 17 They clothed him in purple and, weaving a crown of thorns, placed it on him. 18 They began to salute him with, "Hail, King of the Jews!" 19 and kept striking his head with a reed and spitting upon him. They knelt before him in homage. 20 And when they had mocked him, they stripped him of the purple cloak, dressed him in his own clothes, and led him out to crucify him.

21 They pressed into service a passer-by, Simon, a Cyrenian, who was coming in from the country, the father of Alexander and Rufus, to carry his cross.

22 They brought him to the place of Golgotha (which is translated Place of the Skull). 23 They gave him wine drugged with myrrh, but he did not take it. 24 Then they crucified him and divided his garments by casting lots for them to see what each should take. 25 It was nine o'clock in the morning when they crucified him. 26 The inscription of the charge against him read, "The King of the Jews." 27 With him they crucified two revolutionaries, one on his right and one on his left. [28] 29 Those passing by reviled him, shaking their heads and saying, "Aha! You who would destroy the temple and rebuild it in three days, 30 save yourself by coming down from the cross." 31 Likewise the chief priests, with the scribes, mocked him among themselves and said, "He saved others; he cannot save himself. 32 Let the Messiah, the King of Israel, come down now from the cross that we may see and believe." Those who were crucified with him also kept abusing him.

33 At noon darkness came over the whole land until three in the afternoon. 34 And at three o'clock Jesus cried out in

once the cock crowed for the second time, and Peter recalled what Jesus had said to him, 'Before the cock crows twice, you will have disowned me three times.' And he burst into tears.

15 First thing in the morning, the chief priests, together with the elders and scribes and the rest of the Sanhedrin, had their plan ready. They had Jesus bound and took him away and handed him over to Pilate.

2 Pilate put to him this question, 'Are you the king of the Jews?' He replied, 'It is you who say it.' 3 And the chief priests brought many accusations against him. 4 Pilate questioned him again, 'Have you no reply at all? See how many accusations they are bringing against you!' 5 But, to Pilate's surprise, Jesus made no further reply.

6 At festival time Pilate used to release a prisoner for them, any one they asked for. 7 Now a man called Barabbas was then in prison with the rebels who had committed murder during the uprising. 8 When the crowd went up and began to ask Pilate the customary favour, 9 Pilate answered them, 'Do you want me to release for you the king of the Jews?' 10 For he realised it was out of jealousy that the chief priests had handed Jesus over. 11 The chief priests, however, had incited the crowd to demand that he should release Barabbas for them instead. 12 Then Pilate spoke again, 'But in that case, what am I to do with the man you call king of the Jews?' 13 They shouted back, 'Crucify him!' 14 Pilate asked them, 'What harm has he done?' But they shouted all the louder, 'Crucify him!' 15 So Pilate, anxious to placate the crowd, released Barabbas for them and, after having Jesus scourged, he handed him over to be crucified.

16 The soldiers led him away to the inner part of the palace, that is, the Praetorium, and called the whole cohort together. 17 They dressed him up in purple, twisted some thorns into a crown and put it on him. 18 And they began saluting him, 'Hail, king of the Jews!' 19 They struck his head with a reed and spat on him; and they went down on their knees to do him homage. 20 And when they had finished making fun of him, they took off the purple and dressed him in his own clothes.

They led him out to crucify him. 21 They enlisted a passer-by, Simon of Cyrene, father of Alexander and Rufus,*g* who was coming in from the country, to carry his cross. 22 They brought Jesus to the place called Golgotha, which means the place of the skull.

23 They offered him wine mixed with myrrh, but he refused it. 24 Then they crucified him, and shared out his clothing, casting lots to decide what each should get. 25 It was the third hour when they crucified him. 26 The inscription giving the charge against him read, 'The King of the Jews'. 27 And they crucified two bandits with him, one on his right and one on his left. [28]*h* 29 The passers-by jeered at him; they shook their heads and said, 'Aha! So you would destroy the Temple and rebuild it in three days! 30 Then save yourself; come down from the cross!' 31 The chief priests and the scribes mocked him among themselves in the same way with the words, 'He saved others, he cannot save himself. 32 Let the Christ, the king of Israel, come down from the cross now, for us to see it and believe.' Even those who were crucified with him taunted him.

33 When the sixth hour came there was darkness over the whole land until the ninth hour. 34 And at the ninth hour

---

15, 28: This verse, "And the scripture was fulfilled that says, 'And he was counted among the wicked,'" is omitted in the earliest and best manuscripts. It contains a citation from Is 53, 12, and was probably introduced from Lk 22, 37.

g **15** cf. Rm 16:13.   *h* **15** Some authorities add a verse similar to Lk 22:37.

NEW REVISED STANDARD VERSION

cried out with a loud voice, "Eloi, Eloi, lema sabachthani?" which means, "My God, my God, why have you forsaken me?"*m* 35 When some of the bystanders heard it, they said, "Listen, he is calling for Elijah." 36 And someone ran, filled a sponge with sour wine, put it on a stick, and gave it to him to drink, saying, "Wait, let us see whether Elijah will come to take him down." 37 Then Jesus gave a loud cry and breathed his last. 38 And the curtain of the temple was torn in two, from top to bottom. 39 Now when the centurion, who stood facing him, saw that in this way he*n* breathed his last, he said, "Truly this man was God's Son!"*o*

40 There were also women looking on from a distance; among them were Mary Magdalene, and Mary the mother of James the younger and of Joses, and Salome. 41 These used to follow him and provided for him when he was in Galilee; and there were many other women who had come up with him to Jerusalem.

42 When evening had come, and since it was the day of Preparation, that is, the day before the sabbath, 43 Joseph of Arimathea, a respected member of the council, who was also himself waiting expectantly for the kingdom of God, went boldly to Pilate and asked for the body of Jesus. 44 Then Pilate wondered if he were already dead; and summoning the centurion, he asked him whether he had been dead for some time. 45 When he learned from the centurion that he was dead, he granted the body to Joseph. 46 Then Joseph*p* bought a linen cloth, and taking down the body,*q* wrapped it in the linen cloth, and laid it in a tomb that had been hewn out of the rock. He then rolled a stone against the door of the tomb. 47 Mary Magdalene and Mary the mother of Joses saw where the body*q* was laid.

16 When the sabbath was over, Mary Magdalene, and Mary the mother of James, and Salome bought spices, so that they might go and anoint him. 2 And very early on the first day of the week, when the sun had risen, they went to the tomb. 3 They had been saying to one another, "Who will roll away the stone for us from the entrance to the tomb?" 4 When they looked up, they saw that the stone, which was very large, had already been rolled back. 5 As they entered the tomb, they saw a young man, dressed in a white robe, sitting on the right side; and they were alarmed. 6 But he said to them, "Do not be alarmed; you are looking for Jesus of Nazareth, who was crucified. He has been raised; he is not here. Look, there is the place they laid him. 7 But go, tell his disciples and Peter that he is going ahead of you to Galilee; there you will see him, just as he told you." 8 So they went out and fled from the tomb, for terror and amazement had seized them; and they said nothing to anyone, for they were afraid.*r*

THE SHORTER ENDING OF MARK

[And all that had been commanded them they told briefly to those around Peter. And afterward Jesus himself sent out through them, from east to west, the sacred and imperishable proclamation of eternal salvation.*s*]

m Other ancient authorities read *made me a reproach*   *n* Other ancient authorities add *cried out and*   *o* Or *a son of God*   *p* Gk *he*   *q* Gk *it*   *r* Some of the most ancient authorities bring the book to a close at the end of verse 8. One authority concludes the book with the shorter ending; others include the shorter ending and then continue with verses 9-20. In most authorities verses 9-20 follow immediately after verse 8, though in some of these authorities the passage is marked as being doubtful.   *s* Other ancient authorities add *Amen*

REVISED ENGLISH BIBLE

aloud, 'Eloï, Eloï, lema sabachthani?' which means, 'My God, my God, why have you forsaken me?' 35 Hearing this, some of the bystanders said, 'Listen! He is calling Elijah.' 36 Someone ran and soaked a sponge in sour wine and held it to his lips on the end of a stick. 'Let us see', he said, 'if Elijah will come to take him down.' 37 Then Jesus gave a loud cry and died; 38 and the curtain of the temple was torn in two from top to bottom. 39 When the centurion who was standing opposite him saw how he died, he said, 'This man must have been a son of God.'

40 A NUMBER of women were also present, watching from a distance. Among them were Mary of Magdala, Mary the mother of James the younger and of Joses, and Salome, 41 who had all followed him and looked after him when he was in Galilee, and there were many others who had come up to Jerusalem with him.

42 By this time evening had come; and as it was the day of preparation (that is, the day before the sabbath), 43 Joseph of Arimathaea, a respected member of the Council, a man who looked forward to the kingdom of God, bravely went in to Pilate and asked for the body of Jesus. 44 Pilate was surprised to hear that he had died so soon, and sent for the centurion to make sure that he was already dead. 45 And when he heard the centurion's report, he gave Joseph leave to take the body. 46 So Joseph bought a linen sheet, took him down from the cross, and wrapped him in the sheet. Then he laid him in a tomb cut out of the rock, and rolled a stone against the entrance. 47 And Mary of Magdala and Mary the mother of Joses were watching and saw where he was laid.

16 WHEN the sabbath was over, Mary of Magdala, Mary the mother of James, and Salome bought aromatic oils, intending to go and anoint him; 2 and very early on the first day of the week, just after sunrise, they came to the tomb. 3 They were wondering among themselves who would roll away the stone for them from the entrance to the tomb, 4 when they looked up and saw that the stone, huge as it was, had been rolled back already. 5 They went into the tomb, where they saw a young man sitting on the right-hand side, wearing a white robe; and they were dumbfounded. 6 But he said to them, 'Do not be alarmed; you are looking for Jesus of Nazareth, who was crucified. He has been raised; he is not here. Look, there is the place where they laid him. 7 But go and say to his disciples and to Peter: "He is going ahead of you into Galilee: there you will see him, as he told you." ' 8 Then they went out and ran away from the tomb, trembling with amazement. They said nothing to anyone, for they were afraid.

[AND they delivered all these instructions briefly to Peter and his companions. Afterwards Jesus himself sent out by them, from east to west, the sacred and imperishable message of eternal salvation.]

15:39 **a son of God:** *or* the Son of God.   16:1 **When . . . Salome:** *some witnesses omit, reading* And they went and bought . . .   16:8 **afraid:** *at this point some of the most ancient witnesses bring the book to a close.* **And they delivered . . . salvation:** *some witnesses add this passage, which in one of them is the conclusion of the book.*

a loud voice, *"Eloi, Eloi, lema sabachthani?"* which is translated, "My God, my God, why have you forsaken me?" 35 Some of the bystanders who heard it said, "Look, he is calling Elijah." 36 One of them ran, soaked a sponge with wine, put it on a reed, and gave it to him to drink, saying, "Wait, let us see if Elijah comes to take him down." 37 Jesus gave a loud cry and breathed his last. 38 The veil of the sanctuary was torn in two from top to bottom. 39 When the centurion who stood facing him saw how he breathed his last he said, "Truly this man was the Son of God!" 40 There were also women looking on from a distance. Among them were Mary Magdalene, Mary the mother of the younger James and of Joses, and Salome. 41 These women had followed him when he was in Galilee and ministered to him. There were also many other women who had come up with him to Jerusalem.

42 When it was already evening, since it was the day of preparation, the day before the sabbath, 43 Joseph of Arimathea, a distinguished member of the council, who was himself awaiting the kingdom of God, came and courageously went to Pilate and asked for the body of Jesus. 44 Pilate was amazed that he was already dead. He summoned the centurion and asked him if Jesus had already died. 45 And when he learned of it from the centurion, he gave the body to Joseph. 46 Having bought a linen cloth, he took him down, wrapped him in the linen cloth and laid him in a tomb that had been hewn out of the rock. Then he rolled a stone against the entrance to the tomb. 47 Mary Magdalene and Mary the mother of Joses watched where he was laid.

16 When the sabbath was over, Mary Magdalene, Mary, the mother of James, and Salome bought spices so that they might go and anoint him. 2 Very early when the sun had risen, on the first day of the week, they came to the tomb. 3 They were saying to one another, "Who will roll back the stone for us from the entrance to the tomb?" 4 When they looked up, they saw that the stone had been rolled back; it was very large. 5 On entering the tomb they saw a young man sitting on the right side, clothed in a white robe, and they were utterly amazed. 6 He said to them, "Do not be amazed! You seek Jesus of Nazareth, the crucified. He has been raised; he is not here. Behold, the place where they laid him. 7 But go and tell his disciples and Peter, 'He is going before you to Galilee; there you will see him, as he told you.' " 8 Then they went out and fled from the tomb, seized with trembling and bewilderment. They said nothing to anyone, for they were afraid.

‡ The Shorter Ending: see below ‡

Jesus cried out in a loud voice, *'Eloi, eloi,i lama sabachthani?'* which means, *'My God, my God, why have you forsaken me?'* 35 When some of those who stood by heard this, they said, 'Listen, he is calling on Elijah.' 36 Someone ran and soaked a sponge in vinegar and, putting it on a reed, gave it to him to drink saying, 'Wait! And see if Elijah will come to take him down.' 37 But Jesus gave a loud cry and breathed his last. 38 And the veil of the Sanctuary was torn in two from top to bottom. 39 The centurion, who was standing in front of him, had seen how he had died, and he said, 'In truth this man was Son of God.'

40 There were some women watching from a distance. Among them were Mary of Magdala, Mary who was the mother of James the younger and Joset, and Salome. 41 These used to follow him and look after him when he was in Galilee. And many other women were there who had come up to Jerusalem with him.

42 It was now evening, and since it was Preparation Day —that is, the day before the Sabbath— 43 Joseph of Arimathaea, a prominent member of the Council, who himself lived in the hope of seeing the kingdom of God, and he boldly went to Pilate and asked for the body of Jesus. 44 Pilate, astonished that he should have died so soon, summoned the centurion and enquired if he had been dead for some time. 45 Having been assured of this by the centurion, he granted the corpse to Joseph 46 who bought a shroud, took Jesus down from the cross, wrapped him in the shroud and laid him in a tomb which had been hewn out of the rock. He then rolled a stone against the entrance to the tomb. 47 Mary of Magdala and Mary the mother of Joset took note of where he was laid.

16 When the Sabbath was over, Mary of Magdala, Mary the mother of James, and Salome, bought spices with which to go and anoint him. 2 And very early in the morning on the first day of the week they went to the tomb when the sun had risen.

3 They had been saying to one another, 'Who will roll away the stone for us from the entrance to the tomb?' 4 But when they looked they saw that the stone —which was very big— had already been rolled back. 5 On entering the tomb they saw a young man in a white robe seated on the right-hand side, and they were struck with amazement. 6 But he said to them, 'There is no need to be so amazed. You are looking for Jesus of Nazareth, who was crucified: he has risen, he is not here. See, here is the place where they laid him. 7 But you must go and tell his disciples and Peter, "He is going ahead of you to Galilee; that is where you will see him, just as he told you." ' 8 And the women came out and ran away from the tomb because they were frightened out of their wits; and they said nothing to anyone, for they were afraid.j

‡ A shorter ending: see below in footnote *k* ‡

i 15 This Aramaic form cf. Ps 22:1, explains the soldiers' pun about Elijah better than Mt's Hebr form *eli*.   *j* 16 Originally Mk probably ended abruptly on this note of awe and wonder. The next 12 vv., missing in some MSS, are a summary of material gathered from other NT writings.

THE LONGER ENDING OF MARK

9 ⟦Now after he rose early on the first day of the week, he appeared first to Mary Magdalene, from whom he had cast out seven demons. 10 She went out and told those who had been with him, while they were mourning and weeping. 11 But when they heard that he was alive and had been seen by her, they would not believe it.

12 After this he appeared in another form to two of them, as they were walking into the country. 13 And they went back and told the rest, but they did not believe them.

14 Later he appeared to the eleven themselves as they were sitting at the table; and he upbraided them for their lack of faith and stubbornness, because they had not believed those who saw him after he had risen.*t* 15 And he said to them, "Go into all the world and proclaim the good news*u* to the whole creation. 16 The one who believes and is baptized will be saved; but the one who does not believe will be condemned. 17 And these signs will accompany those who believe: by using my name they will cast out demons; they will speak in new tongues; 18 they will pick up snakes in their hands,*v* and if they drink any deadly thing, it will not hurt them; they will lay their hands on the sick, and they will recover."

19 So then the Lord Jesus, after he had spoken to them, was taken up into heaven and sat down at the right hand of God. 20 And they went out and proclaimed the good news everywhere, while the Lord worked with them and confirmed the message by the signs that accompanied it.*w*⟧

[9 WHEN he had risen from the dead, early on the first day of the week, he appeared first to Mary of Magdala, from whom he had driven out seven demons. 10 She went and carried the news to his mourning and sorrowful followers, 11 but when they were told that he was alive and that she had seen him they did not believe it.

12 Later he appeared in a different form to two of them while they were on their way into the country. 13 These also went and took the news to the others, but again no one believed them.

14 Still later he appeared to the eleven while they were at table, and reproached them for their incredulity and dullness, because they had not believed those who had seen him after he was raised from the dead. 15 Then he said to them: 'Go to every part of the world, and proclaim the gospel to the whole creation. 16 Those who believe it and receive baptism will be saved; those who do not believe will be condemned. 17 Faith will bring with it these miracles: believers will drive out demons in my name and speak in strange tongues; 18 if they handle snakes or drink any deadly poison, they will come to no harm; and the sick on whom they lay their hands will recover.'

19 So after talking with them the Lord Jesus was taken up into heaven and took his seat at the right hand of God; 20 but they went out to proclaim their message far and wide, and the Lord worked with them and confirmed their words by the miracles that followed.]

---

t Other ancient authorities add, in whole or in part, And they excused themselves, saying, "This age of lawlessness and unbelief is under Satan, who does not allow the truth and power of God to prevail over the unclean things of the spirits. Therefore reveal your righteousness now"—thus they spoke to Christ. And Christ replied to them, "The term of years of Satan's power has been fulfilled, but other terrible things draw near. And for those who have sinned I was handed over to death, that they may return to the truth and sin no more, that they may inherit the spiritual and imperishable glory of righteousness that is in heaven." u Or gospel v Other ancient authorities lack in their hands w Other ancient authorities add Amen

16:9–20 *Some witnesses give these verses either instead of, or in addition to, the passage And they delivered . . . salvation (here printed before verse 9), and so bring the book to a close. Others insert further additional matter.*

NEW AMERICAN BIBLE

NEW JERUSALEM BIBLE

THE LONGER ENDING

[9 When he had risen, early on the first day of the week, he appeared first to Mary Magdalene, out of whom he had driven seven demons. 10 She went and told his companions who were mourning and weeping. 11 When they heard that he was alive and had been seen by her, they did not believe.

12 After this he appeared in another form to two of them walking along on their way to the country. 13 They returned and told the others; but they did not believe them either.

14 [But] later, as the eleven were at table, he appeared to them and rebuked them for their unbelief and hardness of heart because they had not believed those who saw him after he had been raised. 15 He said to them, "Go into the whole world and proclaim the gospel to every creature. 16 Whoever believes and is baptized will be saved; whoever does not believe will be condemned. 17 These signs will accompany those who believe: in my name they will drive out demons, they will speak new languages. 18 They will pick up serpents [with their hands], and if they drink any deadly thing, it will not harm them. They will lay hands on the sick, and they will recover."

19 So then the Lord Jesus, after he spoke to them, was taken up into heaven and took his seat at the right hand of God. 20 But they went forth and preached everywhere, while the Lord worked with them and confirmed the word through accompanying signs.]

THE SHORTER ENDING

[And they reported all the instructions briefly to Peter's companions. Afterwards Jesus himself, through them, sent forth from east to west the sacred and imperishable proclamation of eternal salvation. Amen.]

16, 9–20: This passage, termed the Longer Ending to the Marcan gospel by comparison with a much briefer conclusion found in some less important manuscripts, has traditionally been accepted as a canonical part of the gospel and was defined as such by the Council of Trent.

The Shorter Ending: Found after v 8 before the Longer Ending in four seventh-to-ninth-century Greek manuscripts as well as in one Old Latin version, where it appears alone without the Longer Ending.

The Freer Logion: Found after v 14 in a fourth-fifth century manuscript preserved in the Freer Gallery of Art, Washington, DC, this ending was known to Jerome in the fourth century. It reads: "And they excused themselves, saying, 'This age of lawlessness and unbelief is under Satan, who does not allow the truth and power of God to prevail over the unclean things dominated by the spirits [or, does not allow the unclean things dominated by the spirits to grasp the truth and power of God]. Therefore reveal your righteousness now.' They spoke to Christ. And Christ responded to them, 'The limit of the years of Satan's power is completed, but other terrible things draw near. And for those who sinned I was handed over to death, that they might return to the truth and no longer sin, in order that they might inherit the spiritual and incorruptible heavenly glory of righteousness. But . . . .'"

9 k Having risen in the morning on the first day of the week, he appeared first to Mary of Magdala from whom he had cast out seven devils. 10 She then went to those who had been his companions, and who were mourning and in tears, and told them. 11 But they did not believe her when they heard her say that he was alive and that she had seen him.

12 After this, he showed himself under another form to two of them as they were on their way into the country. 13 These went back and told the others, who did not believe them either.

14 Lastly, he showed himself to the Eleven themselves while they were at table. He reproached them for their incredulity and obstinacy, because they had refused to believe those who had seen him after he had risen. 15 And he said to them, 'Go out to the whole world; proclaim the gospel to all creation. 16 Whoever believes and is baptised will be saved; whoever does not believe will be condemned. 17 These are the signs that will be associated with believers: in my name they will cast out devils; they will have the gift of tongues; 18 they will pick up snakes in their hands and be unharmed should they drink deadly poison; they will lay their hands on the sick, who will recover.'

19 And so the Lord Jesus, after he had spoken to them, was taken up into heaven; there at the right hand of God he took his place, 20 while they, going out, preached everywhere, the Lord working with them and confirming the word by the signs that accompanied it.

k 16 The 'longer ending' of Mk. vv. 9–20, is included in the canonically accepted body of inspired scripture, although some important MSS (including Vat. and Sin.) omit it, and it does not seem to be by Mk. It is in a different style, and is little more than a summary of the appearances of the risen Christ, with other material, all of which could be derived from various NT writings. One MS gives instead a shorter ending after v. 8: 'They reported briefly to Peter's companions what they had been told. Then Jesus himself through their agency broadcast from east to west the sacred and incorruptible message of eternal salvation.' Four MSS give the shorter ending and add the longer to it. One MS has the longer ending with the following insertion between vv. 14 and 15: 'And they defended themselves thus, "This age of lawlessness and unbelief is under the sway of Satan, who does not allow those under the yoke of unclean spirits to understand God's truth and power. Now, therefore, reveal your uprightness." This is what they said to Christ, and Christ answered, "The number of years allowed for Satan's authority has been reached, but other terrible things draw near. I was handed over to be killed for those who have sinned, so that they might turn to the truth and sin no more, and so inherit the spiritual and incorruptible glory of uprightness which is in heaven . . ."'

One explanation of this diversity is that Mk's original ending was lost. More probably Mk intended to finish his Gospel at v. 8; but comparison with the other gospels made the first Christian generation feel that this ending was incomplete (and also stylistically somewhat harsh). This led them to add the 'longer ending'.

THE GOSPEL ACCORDING TO
Luke

1 Since many have undertaken to set down an orderly account of the events that have been fulfilled among us, 2 just as they were handed on to us by those who from the beginning were eyewitnesses and servants of the word, 3 I too decided, after investigating everything carefully from the very first,*a* to write an orderly account for you, most excellent Theophilus, 4 so that you may know the truth concerning the things about which you have been instructed.

5 In the days of King Herod of Judea, there was a priest named Zechariah, who belonged to the priestly order of Abijah. His wife was a descendant of Aaron, and her name was Elizabeth. 6 Both of them were righteous before God, living blamelessly according to all the commandments and regulations of the Lord. 7 But they had no children, because Elizabeth was barren, and both were getting on in years.

8 Once when he was serving as priest before God and his section was on duty, 9 he was chosen by lot, according to the custom of the priesthood, to enter the sanctuary of the Lord and offer incense. 10 Now at the time of the incense offering, the whole assembly of the people was praying outside. 11 Then there appeared to him an angel of the Lord, standing at the right side of the altar of incense. 12 When Zechariah saw him, he was terrified; and fear overwhelmed him. 13 But the angel said to him, "Do not be afraid, Zechariah, for your prayer has been heard. Your wife Elizabeth will bear you a son, and you will name him John. 14 You will have joy and gladness, and many will rejoice at his birth, 15 for he will be great in the sight of the Lord. He must never drink wine or strong drink; even before his birth he will be filled with the Holy Spirit. 16 He will turn many of the people of Israel to the Lord their God. 17 With the spirit and power of Elijah he will go before him, to turn the hearts of parents to their children, and the disobedient to the wisdom of the righteous, to make ready a people prepared for the Lord." 18 Zechariah said to the angel, "How will I know that this is so? For I am an old man, and my wife is getting on in years." 19 The angel replied, "I am Gabriel. I stand in the presence of God, and I have been sent to speak to you and to bring you this good news. 20 But now, because you did not believe my words, which will be fulfilled in their time, you will become mute, unable to speak, until the day these things occur."

21 Meanwhile the people were waiting for Zechariah, and wondered at his delay in the sanctuary. 22 When he did come out, he could not speak to them, and they realized that he had seen a vision in the sanctuary. He kept motioning to them and remained unable to speak. 23 When his time of service was ended, he went to his home.

24 After those days his wife Elizabeth conceived, and for five months she remained in seclusion. She said, 25 "This is what the Lord has done for me when he looked favorably on me and took away the disgrace I have endured among my people."

26 In the sixth month the angel Gabriel was sent by God to a town in Galilee called Nazareth, 27 to a virgin engaged to a man whose name was Joseph, of the house of David. The virgin's name was Mary. 28 And he came to her and said, "Greetings, favored one! The Lord is with you."*b*

THE GOSPEL ACCORDING TO
Luke

1 To THEOPHILUS : Many writers have undertaken to draw up an account of the events that have taken place among us, 2 following the traditions handed down to us by the original eyewitnesses and servants of the gospel. 3 So I in my turn, as one who has investigated the whole course of these events in detail, have decided to write an orderly narrative for you, your excellency, 4 so as to give you authentic knowledge about the matters of which you have been informed.

5 IN the reign of Herod king of Judaea there was a priest named Zechariah, of the division of the priesthood called after Abijah. His wife, whose name was Elizabeth, was also of priestly descent. 6 Both of them were upright and devout, blamelessly observing all the commandments and ordinances of the Lord. 7 But they had no children, for Elizabeth was barren, and both were well on in years.

8 Once, when it was the turn of his division and he was there to take part in the temple service, 9 he was chosen by lot, by priestly custom, to enter the sanctuary of the Lord and offer the incense; 10 and at the hour of the offering the people were all assembled at prayer outside. 11 There appeared to him an angel of the Lord, standing on the right of the altar of incense. 12 At this sight, Zechariah was startled and overcome by fear. 13 But the angel said to him, 'Do not be afraid, Zechariah; your prayer has been heard: your wife Elizabeth will bear you a son, and you are to name him John. 14 His birth will fill you with joy and delight, and will bring gladness to many; 15 for he will be great in the eyes of the Lord. He is never to touch wine or strong drink. From his very birth he will be filled with the Holy Spirit; 16 and he will bring back many Israelites to the Lord their God. 17 He will go before him as forerunner, possessed by the spirit and power of Elijah, to reconcile father and child, to convert the rebellious to the ways of the righteous, to prepare a people that shall be fit for the Lord.' 18 Zechariah said to the angel, 'How can I be sure of this? I am an old man and my wife is well on in years.'

19 The angel replied, 'I am Gabriel; I stand in attendance on God, and I have been sent to speak to you and bring you this good news. 20 But now, because you have not believed me, you will lose all power of speech and remain silent until the day when these things take place; at their proper time my words will be proved true.'

21 Meanwhile the people were waiting for Zechariah, surprised that he was staying so long inside the sanctuary. 22 When he did come out he could not speak to them, and they realized that he had had a vision. He stood there making signs to them, and remained dumb.

23 When his period of duty was completed Zechariah returned home. 24 His wife Elizabeth conceived, and for five months she lived in seclusion, thinking, 25 'This is the Lord's doing; now at last he has shown me favour and taken away from me the disgrace of childlessness.'

26 In the sixth month the angel Gabriel was sent by God to Nazareth, a town in Galilee, 27 with a message for a girl betrothed to a man named Joseph, a descendant of David; the girl's name was Mary. 28 The angel went in and said to her, 'Greetings, most favoured one! The Lord is with you.'

---

a Or *for a long time*   *b* Other ancient authorities add *Blessed are*
you among women

THE GOSPEL ACCORDING TO
Luke

1 Since many have undertaken to compile a narrative of the events that have been fulfilled among us, 2 just as those who were eyewitnesses from the beginning and ministers of the word have handed them down to us, 3 I too have decided, after investigating everything accurately anew, to write it down in an orderly sequence for you, most excellent Theophilus, 4 so that you may realize the certainty of the teachings you have received.

5 In the days of Herod, King of Judea, there was a priest named Zechariah of the priestly division of Abijah; his wife was from the daughters of Aaron, and her name was Elizabeth. 6 Both were righteous in the eyes of God, observing all the commandments and ordinances of the Lord blamelessly. 7 But they had no child, because Elizabeth was barren and both were advanced in years. 8 Once when he was serving as priest in his division's turn before God, 9 according to the practice of the priestly service, he was chosen by lot to enter the sanctuary of the Lord to burn incense. 10 Then, when the whole assembly of the people was praying outside at the hour of the incense offering, 11 the angel of the Lord appeared to him, standing at the right of the altar of incense. 12 Zechariah was troubled by what he saw, and fear came upon him. 13 But the angel said to him, "Do not be afraid, Zechariah, because your prayer has been heard. Your wife Elizabeth will bear you a son, and you shall name him John. 14 And you will have joy and gladness, and many will rejoice at his birth, 15 for he will be great in the sight of [the] Lord. He will drink neither wine nor strong drink. He will be filled with the holy Spirit even from his mother's womb, 16 and he will turn many of the children of Israel to the Lord their God. 17 He will go before him in the spirit and power of Elijah to turn the hearts of fathers toward children and the disobedient to the understanding of the righteous, to prepare a people fit for the Lord." 18 Then Zechariah said to the angel, "How shall I know this? For I am an old man, and my wife is advanced in years." 19 And the angel said to him in reply, "I am Gabriel, who stand before God. I was sent to speak to you and to announce to you this good news. 20 But now you will be speechless and unable to talk until the day these things take place, because you did not believe my words, which will be fulfilled at their proper time."

21 Meanwhile the people were waiting for Zechariah and were amazed that he stayed so long in the sanctuary. 22 But when he came out, he was unable to speak to them, and they realized that he had seen a vision in the sanctuary. He was gesturing to them but remained mute. 23 Then, when his days of ministry were completed, he went home. 24 After this time his wife Elizabeth conceived, and she went into seclusion for five months, saying, 25 "So has the Lord done for me at a time when he has seen fit to take away my disgrace before others."

26 In the sixth month, the angel Gabriel was sent from God to a town of Galilee called Nazareth, 27 to a virgin betrothed to a man named Joseph, of the house of David, and the virgin's name was Mary. 28 And coming to her, he said, "Hail, favored one! The Lord is with you." 29 But she

THE GOSPEL ACCORDING TO
Luke

1 Seeing that many others have undertaken to draw up accounts of the events that have reached their fulfilment among us, 2 as these were handed down to us by those who from the outset were eyewitnesses and ministers of the word, 3 I in my turn, after carefully going over the whole story from the beginning, have decided to write an ordered account for you, Theophilus,*a* 4 so that your Excellency may learn how well founded the teaching is that you have received.

5 In the days of King Herod of Judaea there lived a priest called Zechariah who belonged to the Abijah section of the priesthood, and he had a wife, Elizabeth by name, who was a descendant of Aaron. 6 Both were upright in the sight of God and impeccably carried out all the commandments and observances of the Lord. 7 But they were childless: Elizabeth was barren and they were both advanced in years.

8 Now it happened that it was the turn of his section to serve, and he was exercising his priestly office before God 9 when it fell to him by lot, as the priestly custom was, to enter the Lord's sanctuary and burn incense there. 10 And at the hour of incense all the people were outside, praying.

11 Then there appeared to him the angel of the Lord, standing on the right of the altar of incense. 12 The sight disturbed Zechariah and he was overcome with fear. 13 But the angel said to him, 'Zechariah, do not be afraid, for your prayer has been heard. Your wife Elizabeth is to bear you a son and you shall name him John. 14 He will be your joy and delight and many will rejoice at his birth, 15 for he will be great in the sight of the Lord; he must drink no wine, no strong drink;*b* even from his mother's womb he will be filled with the Holy Spirit, 16 and he will bring back many of the Israelites to the Lord their God. 17 With the spirit and power of Elijah, he will go before him *to reconcile fathers to their children*c and the disobedient to the good sense of the upright, preparing for the Lord a people fit for him.' 18 Zechariah said to the angel, '*How can I know this*?*d* I am an old man and my wife is getting on in years.' 19 The angel replied, 'I am Gabriel, who stand in God's presence, and I have been sent to speak to you and bring you this good news. 20 Look! Since you did not believe my words, which will come true at their appointed time, you will be silenced and have no power of speech until this has happened.' 21 Meanwhile the people were waiting for Zechariah and were surprised that he stayed in the sanctuary so long. 22 When he came out he could not speak to them, and they realised that he had seen a vision in the sanctuary. But he could only make signs to them and remained dumb.

23 When his time of service came to an end he returned home. 24 Some time later his wife Elizabeth conceived and for five months she kept to herself, saying, 25 'The Lord has done this for me, now that it has pleased him to take away the humiliation I suffered in public.'

26 In the sixth month the angel Gabriel was sent by God to a town in Galilee called Nazareth, 27 to a virgin betrothed to a man named Joseph, of the House of David; and the virgin's name was Mary. 28 He went in and said to her, 'Rejoice, you who enjoy God's favour! The Lord is with

---

a **1** Theophilus (= 'God-lover') may be real or imaginary.
b **1** cf. Nb 6:2–3.　　*c* **1** Ml 3:23–24.　　*d* **1** Gn 15:8.

29 But she was much perplexed by his words and pondered what sort of greeting this might be. 30 The angel said to her, "Do not be afraid, Mary, for you have found favor with God. 31 And now, you will conceive in your womb and bear a son, and you will name him Jesus. 32 He will be great, and will be called the Son of the Most High, and the Lord God will give to him the throne of his ancestor David. 33 He will reign over the house of Jacob forever, and of his kingdom there will be no end." 34 Mary said to the angel, "How can this be, since I am a virgin?"*c* 35 The angel said to her, "The Holy Spirit will come upon you, and the power of the Most High will overshadow you; therefore the child to be born*d* will be holy; he will be called Son of God. 36 And now, your relative Elizabeth in her old age has also conceived a son; and this is the sixth month for her who was said to be barren. 37 For nothing will be impossible with God." 38 Then Mary said, "Here am I, the servant of the Lord; let it be with me according to your word." Then the angel departed from her.

39 In those days Mary set out and went with haste to a Judean town in the hill country, 40 where she entered the house of Zechariah and greeted Elizabeth. 41 When Elizabeth heard Mary's greeting, the child leaped in her womb. And Elizabeth was filled with the Holy Spirit 42 and exclaimed with a loud cry, "Blessed are you among women, and blessed is the fruit of your womb. 43 And why has this happened to me, that the mother of my Lord comes to me? 44 For as soon as I heard the sound of your greeting, the child in my womb leaped for joy. 45 And blessed is she who believed that there would be*e* a fulfillment of what was spoken to her by the Lord."

46 And Mary*f* said,
"My soul magnifies the Lord,
47 and my spirit rejoices in God my Savior,
48 for he has looked with favor on the lowliness of
   his servant.
   Surely, from now on all generations will call
   me blessed;
49 for the Mighty One has done great things for me,
   and holy is his name.
50 His mercy is for those who fear him
   from generation to generation.
51 He has shown strength with his arm;
   he has scattered the proud in the thoughts of
   their hearts.
52 He has brought down the powerful from their
   thrones,
   and lifted up the lowly;
53 he has filled the hungry with good things,
   and sent the rich away empty.
54 He has helped his servant Israel,
   in remembrance of his mercy,
55 according to the promise he made to our
   ancestors,
   to Abraham and to his descendants forever."

56 And Mary remained with her about three months and then returned to her home.

57 Now the time came for Elizabeth to give birth, and she bore a son. 58 Her neighbors and relatives heard that the Lord had shown his great mercy to her, and they rejoiced with her.

59 On the eighth day they came to circumcise the child, and they were going to name him Zechariah after his father. 60 But his mother said, "No; he is to be called John." 61 They said to her, "None of your relatives has this name." 62 Then

29 But she was deeply troubled by what he said and wondered what this greeting could mean. 30 Then the angel said to her, 'Do not be afraid, Mary, for God has been gracious to you; 31 you will conceive and give birth to a son, and you are to give him the name Jesus. 32 He will be great, and will be called Son of the Most High. The Lord God will give him the throne of his ancestor David, 33 and he will be king over Israel for ever; his reign shall never end.' 34 'How can this be?' said Mary. 'I am still a virgin.' 35 The angel answered, 'The Holy Spirit will come upon you, and the power of the Most High will overshadow you; for that reason the holy child to be born will be called Son of God. 36 Moreover your kinswoman Elizabeth has herself conceived a son in her old age; and she who is reputed barren is now in her sixth month, 37 for God's promises can never fail.' 38 'I am the Lord's servant,' said Mary; 'may it be as you have said.' Then the angel left her.

39 Soon afterwards Mary set out and hurried away to a town in the uplands of Judah. 40 She went into Zechariah's house and greeted Elizabeth. 41 And when Elizabeth heard Mary's greeting, the baby stirred in her womb. Then Elizabeth was filled with the Holy Spirit 42 and exclaimed in a loud voice, 'God's blessing is on you above all women, and his blessing is on the fruit of your womb. 43 Who am I, that the mother of my Lord should visit me? 44 I tell you, when your greeting sounded in my ears, the baby in my womb leapt for joy. 45 Happy is she who has had faith that the Lord's promise to her would be fulfilled!'

46 And Mary said:

'My soul tells out the greatness of the Lord,
47 my spirit has rejoiced in God my Saviour;
48 for he has looked with favour on his servant,
   lowly as she is.
   From this day forward
   all generations will count me blessed,
49 for the Mighty God has done great things for me.
   His name is holy,
50 his mercy sure from generation to generation
   toward those who fear him.
51 He has shown the might of his arm,
   he has routed the proud and all their schemes;
52 he has brought down monarchs from their thrones,
   and raised on high the lowly.
53 He has filled the hungry with good things,
   and sent the rich away empty.
54–55 He has come to the help of Israel his servant,
   as he promised to our forefathers;
   he has not forgotten to show mercy
   to Abraham and his children's children for ever.'

56 Mary stayed with Elizabeth about three months and then returned home.

57 WHEN the time came for Elizabeth's child to be born, she gave birth to a son. 58 Her neighbours and relatives heard what great kindness the Lord had shown her, and they shared her delight. 59 On the eighth day they came to circumcise the child; and they were going to name him Zechariah after his father, 60 but his mother spoke up: 'No!' she said. 'He is to be called John.' 61 'But', they said, 'there is nobody in your family who has that name.' 62 They en-

---

c Gk *I do not know a man*   *d* Other ancient authorities add *of you*
e Or *believed, for there will be*   *f* Other ancient authorities read *Elizabeth*

1:33 **Israel:** *lit.* the house of Jacob.   1:35 **the holy child . . . God:** *or* the child to be born will be called holy, Son of God.
1:37 **for God's . . . fail:** *some witnesses read* for with God nothing will prove impossible.   1:46 **Mary:** *a few witnesses read* Elizabeth.

was greatly troubled at what was said and pondered what sort of greeting this might be. 30 Then the angel said to her, "Do not be afraid, Mary, for you have found favor with God. 31 Behold, you will conceive in your womb and bear a son, and you shall name him Jesus. 32 He will be great and will be called Son of the Most High, and the Lord God will give him the throne of David his father, 33 and he will rule over the house of Jacob forever, and of his kingdom there will be no end." 34 But Mary said to the angel, "How can this be, since I have no relations with a man?" 35 And the angel said to her in reply, "The holy Spirit will come upon you, and the power of the Most High will overshadow you. Therefore the child to be born will be called holy, the Son of God. 36 And behold, Elizabeth, your relative, has also conceived a son in her old age, and this is the sixth month for her who was called barren; 37 for nothing will be impossible for God." 38 Mary said, "Behold, I am the handmaid of the Lord. May it be done to me according to your word." Then the angel departed from her.

39 During those days Mary set out and traveled to the hill country in haste to a town of Judah, 40 where she entered the house of Zechariah and greeted Elizabeth. 41 When Elizabeth heard Mary's greeting, the infant leaped in her womb, and Elizabeth, filled with the holy Spirit, 42 cried out in a loud voice and said, "Most blessed are you among women, and blessed is the fruit of your womb. 43 And how does this happen to me, that the mother of my Lord should come to me? 44 For at the moment the sound of your greeting reached my ears, the infant in my womb leaped for joy. 45 Blessed are you who believed that what was spoken to you by the Lord would be fulfilled."

46 And Mary said:

"My soul proclaims the greatness of the Lord;
47   my spirit rejoices in God my savior.
48 For he has looked upon his handmaid's lowliness;
      behold, from now on will all ages call
         me blessed.
49 The Mighty One has done great things for me,
      and holy is his name.
50 His mercy is from age to age
      to those who fear him.
51 He has shown might with his arm,
      dispersed the arrogant of mind and heart.
52 He has thrown down the rulers from their thrones
      but lifted up the lowly.
53 The hungry he has filled with good things;
      the rich he has sent away empty.
54 He has helped Israel his servant,
      remembering his mercy,
55 according to his promise to our fathers,
      to Abraham and to his descendants forever."

56 Mary remained with her about three months and then returned to her home.

57 When the time arrived for Elizabeth to have her child she gave birth to a son. 58 Her neighbors and relatives heard that the Lord had shown his great mercy toward her, and they rejoiced with her. 59 When they came on the eighth day to circumcise the child, they were going to call him Zechariah after his father, 60 but his mother said in reply, "No. He will be called John." 61 But they answered her, "There is no one among your relatives who has this name." 62 So they

you.' 29 She was deeply disturbed by these words and asked herself what this greeting could mean, 30 but the angel said to her, 'Mary, do not be afraid; you have won God's favour. 31 Look! You are to conceive in your womb and bear a son, and you must name him Jesus. 32 He will be great and will be called Son of the Most High. The Lord God will give him the throne of his ancestor David; 33 he will rule over the House of Jacob for ever and his reign will have no end.'e 34 Mary said to the angel, 'But how can this come about, since I have no knowledge of man?' 35 The angel answered, 'The Holy Spirit will come upon you, and the power of the Most High will cover you with its shadow. And so the child will be holy and will be called Son of God. 36 And I tell you this too: your cousin Elizabeth also, in her old age, has conceived a son, and she whom people called barren is now in her sixth month, 37 for nothing is impossible to God.'f 38 Mary said, 'You see before you the Lord's servant, let it happen to me as you have said.' And the angel left her.

39 Mary set out at that time and went as quickly as she could into the hill country to a town in Judah. 40 She went into Zechariah's house and greeted Elizabeth. 41 Now it happened that as soon as Elizabeth heard Mary's greeting, the child leapt in her womb and Elizabeth was filled with the Holy Spirit. 42 She gave a loud cry and said, 'Of all women you are the most blessed, and blessed is the fruit of your womb. 43 Why should I be honoured with a visit from the mother of my Lord? 44 Look, the moment your greeting reached my ears, the child in my womb leapt for joy. 45 Yes, blessed is she who believed that the promise made her by the Lord would be fulfilled.'

46 And Mary said:g

My soul proclaims the greatness of the Lord
47 and my spirit rejoices in God my Saviour;
48 because he has looked upon the humiliation of his
      servant.
   Yes, from now onwards all generations will call
         me blessed,
49 for the Almighty has done great things for me.
   Holy is his name,
50 and his faithful love extends age after age to those
         who fear him.
51 He has used the power of his arm,
   he has routed the arrogant of heart.
52 He has pulled down princes from their thrones and
      raised high the lowly.
53 He has filled the starving with good things, sent
      the rich away empty.
54 He has come to the help of Israel his servant,
      mindful of his faithful love
55 — according to the promise he made to our
         ancestors —
   of his mercy to Abraham and to his descendants
      for ever.

56 Mary stayed with her some three months and then went home.

57 The time came for Elizabeth to have her child, and she gave birth to a son; 58 and when her neighbours and relations heard that the Lord had lavished on her his faithful love, they shared her joy.

59 Now it happened that on the eighth day they came to circumcise the child; they were going to call him Zechariah after his father, 60 but his mother spoke up. 'No,' she said, 'he is to be called John.' 61 They said to her, 'But no one in your family has that name,' 62 and made signs to his father

e 1 cf. 2 S 7:12–16.   f 1 Gn 18:14.   g 1 Mary's canticle echoes Hannah's 1 S 2:1–10, and also 1 S 1:11; Ps 103:17; 111:9; Jb 5:11; 12:19; Ps 98:2; 107:9; Is 41:8–9.

they began motioning to his father to find out what name he wanted to give him. 63 He asked for a writing tablet and wrote, "His name is John." And all of them were amazed. 64 Immediately his mouth was opened and his tongue freed, and he began to speak, praising God. 65 Fear came over all their neighbors, and all these things were talked about throughout the entire hill country of Judea. 66 All who heard them pondered them and said, "What then will this child become?" For, indeed, the hand of the Lord was with him.

67 Then his father Zechariah was filled with the Holy Spirit and spoke this prophecy:

68 "Blessed be the Lord God of Israel,
        for he has looked favorably on his people and
            redeemed them.
69 He has raised up a mighty savior*g* for us
        in the house of his servant David,
70 as he spoke through the mouth of his holy
            prophets from of old,
71 that we would be saved from our enemies and
        from the hand of all who hate us.
72 Thus he has shown the mercy promised to our
            ancestors,
        and has remembered his holy covenant,
73 the oath that he swore to our ancestor Abraham,
        to grant us 74 that we, being rescued from the
            hands of our enemies,
    might serve him without fear, 75 in holiness and
            righteousness
        before him all our days.
76 And you, child, will be called the prophet of the
            Most High;
        for you will go before the Lord to prepare his
            ways,
77 to give knowledge of salvation to his people
        by the forgiveness of their sins.
78 By the tender mercy of our God,
        the dawn from on high will break upon*h* us,
79 to give light to those who sit in darkness and in
            the shadow of death,
        to guide our feet into the way of peace."

80 The child grew and became strong in spirit, and he was in the wilderness until the day he appeared publicly to Israel.

2 In those days a decree went out from Emperor Augustus that all the world should be registered. 2 This was the first registration and was taken while Quirinius was governor of Syria. 3 All went to their own towns to be registered. 4 Joseph also went from the town of Nazareth in Galilee to Judea, to the city of David called Bethlehem, because he was descended from the house and family of David. 5 He went to be registered with Mary, to whom he was engaged and who was expecting a child. 6 While they were there, the time came for her to deliver her child. 7 And she gave birth to her firstborn son and wrapped him in bands of cloth, and laid him in a manger, because there was no place for them in the inn.

8 In that region there were shepherds living in the fields, keeping watch over their flock by night. 9 Then an angel of the Lord stood before them, and the glory of the Lord shone around them, and they were terrified. 10 But the angel said to them, "Do not be afraid; for see—I am bringing you good news of great joy for all the people: 11 to you is born

quired of his father by signs what he would like him to be called. 63 He asked for a writing tablet and to everybody's astonishment wrote, 'His name is John.' 64 Immediately his lips and tongue were freed and he began to speak, praising God. 65 All the neighbours were overcome with awe, and throughout the uplands of Judaea the whole story became common talk. 66 All who heard it were deeply impressed and said, 'What will this child become?' For indeed the hand of the Lord was upon him.

67 And Zechariah his father was filled with the Holy Spirit and uttered this prophecy:

68 'Praise to the Lord, the God of Israel!
        For he has turned to his people and set them free.
69 He has raised for us a strong deliverer
        from the house of his servant David.
70 'So he promised: age after age he proclaimed
        by the lips of his holy prophets,
71 that he would deliver us from our enemies,
        out of the hands of all who hate us;
72 that, calling to mind his solemn covenant,
        he would deal mercifully with our fathers.
73 'This was the oath he swore to our father
            Abraham,
74 to rescue us from enemy hands and set us free
            from fear,
        so that we might worship 75 in his presence
    in holiness and righteousness our whole life long.
76 'And you, my child, will be called Prophet of the
            Most High,
        for you will be the Lord's forerunner, to prepare
            his way
77 and lead his people to a knowledge of salvation
        through the forgiveness of their sins:
78 for in the tender compassion of our God
        the dawn from heaven will break upon us,
79 to shine on those who live in darkness, under the
            shadow of death,
        and to guide our feet into the way of peace.'

80 As the child grew up he became strong in spirit; he lived out in the wilderness until the day when he appeared publicly before Israel.

2 IN those days a decree was issued by the emperor Augustus for a census to be taken throughout the Roman world. 2 This was the first registration of its kind; it took place when Quirinius was governor of Syria. 3 Everyone made his way to his own town to be registered. 4-5 Joseph went up to Judaea from the town of Nazareth in Galilee, to register in the city of David called Bethlehem, because he was of the house of David by descent; and with him went Mary, his betrothed, who was expecting her child. 6 While they were there the time came for her to have her baby, 7 and she gave birth to a son, her firstborn. She wrapped him in swaddling clothes, and laid him in a manger, because there was no room for them at the inn.

8 Now in this same district there were shepherds out in the fields, keeping watch through the night over their flock. 9 Suddenly an angel of the Lord appeared to them, and the glory of the Lord shone round them. They were terrified, 10 but the angel said, 'Do not be afraid; I bring you good news, news of great joy for the whole nation. 11 Today there

---

g Gk *a horn of salvation*   *h* Other ancient authorities read *has broken upon*

2:2 registration . . . Quirinius: *or* registration carried out while Quirinius.   2:7 no . . . inn: *or* no other space in their lodging.

made signs, asking his father what he wished him to be called. 63 He asked for a tablet and wrote, "John is his name," and all were amazed. 64 Immediately his mouth was opened, his tongue freed, and he spoke blessing God. 65 Then fear came upon all their neighbors, and all these matters were discussed throughout the hill country of Judea. 66 All who heard these things took them to heart, saying, "What, then, will this child be?" For surely the hand of the Lord was with him.

67 Then Zechariah his father, filled with the holy Spirit, prophesied, saying:

68 "Blessed be the Lord, the God of Israel,
 for he has visited and brought redemption to
  his people.
69 He has raised up a horn for our salvation
 within the house of David his servant,
70 even as he promised through the mouth of his holy
  prophets from of old:
71 salvation from our enemies and from the hand
   of all who hate us,
72 to show mercy to our fathers
 and to be mindful of his holy covenant
73 and of the oath he swore to Abraham our father,
 and to grant us that, 74 rescued from the hand
  of enemies,
 without fear we might worship him 75 in holiness
  and righteousness
 before him all our days.
76 And you, child, will be called prophet of the
  Most High,
 for you will go before the Lord to prepare
  his ways,
77 to give his people knowledge of salvation
 through the forgiveness of their sins,
78 because of the tender mercy of our God
 by which the daybreak from on high will visit us
79 to shine on those who sit in darkness and
  death's shadow,
 to guide our feet into the path of peace."

80 The child grew and became strong in spirit, and he was in the desert until the day of his manifestation to Israel.

2 In those days a decree went out from Caesar Augustus that the whole world should be enrolled. 2 This was the first enrollment, when Quirinius was governor of Syria. 3 So all went to be enrolled, each to his own town. 4 And Joseph too went up from Galilee from the town of Nazareth to Judea, to the city of David that is called Bethlehem, because he was of the house and family of David, 5 to be enrolled with Mary, his betrothed, who was with child. 6 While they were there, the time came for her to have her child, 7 and she gave birth to her firstborn son. She wrapped him in swaddling clothes and laid him in a manger, because there was no room for them in the inn.

8 Now there were shepherds in that region living in the fields and keeping the night watch over their flock. 9 The angel of the Lord appeared to them and the glory of the Lord shone around them, and they were struck with great fear. 10 The angel said to them, "Do not be afraid; for behold, I proclaim to you good news of great joy that will be for all

to find out what he wanted him called. 63 The father asked for a writing-tablet and wrote, 'His name is John.' And they were all astonished. 64 At that instant his power of speech returned and he spoke and praised God. 65 All their neighbours were filled with awe and the whole affair was talked about throughout the hill country of Judaea. 66 All those who heard of it treasured it in their hearts. 'What will this child turn out to be?' they wondered. And indeed the hand of the Lord was with him.

67 His father Zechariah was filled with the Holy Spirit and spoke this prophecy: h

68 Blessed be the Lord, the God of Israel,
 for he has visited his people, he has set them free,
69 and he has established for us a saving power
 in the House of his servant David,
70 just as he proclaimed,
 by the mouth of his holy prophets from ancient
  times,
71 that he would save us from our enemies
 and from the hands of all those who hate us,
72 and show faithful love to our ancestors,
 and so keep in mind his holy covenant.
73 This was the oath he swore
 to our father Abraham,
74 that he would grant us, free from fear,
 to be delivered from the hands of our enemies,
75 to serve him in holiness and uprightness
 in his presence, all our days.
76 And you, little child,
 you shall be called Prophet of the Most High,
 for you will go before the Lord
 to prepare a way for him,
77 to give his people knowledge of salvation
 through the forgiveness of their sins,
78 because of the faithful love of our God
 in which the rising Sun has come from on high to
  visit us,
79 to give light to those who live
 in darkness and the shadow dark as death,
 and to guide our feet
 into the way of peace.

80 Meanwhile the child grew up and his spirit grew strong. And he lived in the desert until the day he appeared openly to Israel.

2 Now it happened that at this time Caesar Augustus issued a decree that a census should be made of the whole inhabited world. 2 This census — the first — took place while Quirinius was governor of Syria, 3 and everyone went to be registered, each to his own town. 4 So Joseph set out from the town of Nazareth in Galilee for Judaea, to David's town called Bethlehem, since he was of David's House and line, 5 in order to be registered together with Mary, his betrothed, who was with child. 6 Now it happened that, while they were there, the time came for her to have her child, 7 and she gave birth to a son, her first-born. She wrapped him in swaddling clothes and laid him in a manger because there was no room for them in the living-space. 8 In the countryside close by there were shepherds out in the fields keeping guard over their sheep during the watches of the night. 9 An angel of the Lord stood over them and the glory of the Lord shone round them. They were terrified, 10 but the angel said, 'Do not be afraid. Look, I bring you news of great joy, a joy to be shared by the whole people.

h 1 The canticle uses Ps 41:13; 111:9; Lv 26:42; Is 9:1.

this day in the city of David a Savior, who is the Messiah,[i] the Lord. 12 This will be a sign for you: you will find a child wrapped in bands of cloth and lying in a manger." 13 And suddenly there was with the angel a multitude of the heavenly host,[j] praising God and saying,

14 "Glory to God in the highest heaven,
and on earth peace among those whom he favors!"[k]

15 When the angels had left them and gone into heaven, the shepherds said to one another, "Let us go now to Bethlehem and see this thing that has taken place, which the Lord has made known to us." 16 So they went with haste and found Mary and Joseph, and the child lying in the manger. 17 When they saw this, they made known what had been told them about this child; 18 and all who heard it were amazed at what the shepherds told them. 19 But Mary treasured all these words and pondered them in her heart. 20 The shepherds returned, glorifying and praising God for all they had heard and seen, as it had been told them.

21 After eight days had passed, it was time to circumcise the child; and he was called Jesus, the name given by the angel before he was conceived in the womb.

22 When the time came for their purification according to the law of Moses, they brought him up to Jerusalem to present him to the Lord 23 (as it is written in the law of the Lord, "Every firstborn male shall be designated as holy to the Lord"), 24 and they offered a sacrifice according to what is stated in the law of the Lord, "a pair of turtledoves or two young pigeons."

25 Now there was a man in Jerusalem whose name was Simeon;[l] this man was righteous and devout, looking forward to the consolation of Israel, and the Holy Spirit rested on him. 26 It had been revealed to him by the Holy Spirit that he would not see death before he had seen the Lord's Messiah.[m] 27 Guided by the Spirit, Simeon[n] came into the temple; and when the parents brought in the child Jesus, to do for him what was customary under the law, 28 Simeon[o] took him in his arms and praised God, saying,

29 "Master, now you are dismissing your servant[p] in peace,
according to your word;
30 for my eyes have seen your salvation,
31 which you have prepared in the presence of all peoples,
32 a light for revelation to the Gentiles
and for glory to your people Israel."

33 And the child's father and mother were amazed at what was being said about him. 34 Then Simeon[l] blessed them and said to his mother Mary, "This child is destined for the falling and the rising of many in Israel, and to be a sign that will be opposed 35 so that the inner thoughts of many will be revealed — and a sword will pierce your own soul too."

36 There was also a prophet, Anna[q] the daughter of Phanuel, of the tribe of Asher. She was of a great age, having lived with her husband seven years after her marriage, 37 then as a widow to the age of eighty-four. She never left the temple but worshiped there with fasting and prayer night and day. 38 At that moment she came, and began to praise God and to speak about the child[r] to all who were looking for the redemption of Jerusalem.

39 When they had finished everything required by the law of the Lord, they returned to Galilee, to their own town of Nazareth. 40 The child grew and became strong, filled with wisdom; and the favor of God was upon him.

has been born to you in the city of David a deliverer — the Messiah, the Lord. 12 This will be the sign for you: you will find a baby wrapped in swaddling clothes, and lying in a manger.' 13 All at once there was with the angel a great company of the heavenly host, singing praise to God:

14 'Glory to God in highest heaven,
and on earth peace to all in whom he delights.'

15 After the angels had left them and returned to heaven the shepherds said to one another, 'Come, let us go straight to Bethlehem and see this thing that has happened, which the Lord has made known to us.' 16 They hurried off and found Mary and Joseph, and the baby lying in the manger. 17 When they saw the child, they related what they had been told about him; 18 and all who heard were astonished at what the shepherds said. 19 But Mary treasured up all these things and pondered over them. 20 The shepherds returned glorifying and praising God for what they had heard and seen; it had all happened as they had been told.

21 Eight days later the time came to circumcise him, and he was given the name Jesus, the name given by the angel before he was conceived.

22 Then, after the purification had been completed in accordance with the law of Moses, they brought him up to Jerusalem to present him to the Lord 23 (as prescribed in the law of the Lord: 'Every firstborn male shall be deemed to belong to the Lord'), 24 and also to make the offering as stated in the law: 'a pair of turtle-doves or two young pigeons'.

25 There was at that time in Jerusalem a man called Simeon. This man was upright and devout, one who watched and waited for the restoration of Israel, and the Holy Spirit was upon him. 26 It had been revealed to him by the Holy Spirit that he would not see death until he had seen the Lord's Messiah. 27 Guided by the Spirit he came into the temple; and when the parents brought in the child Jesus to do for him what the law required, 28 he took him in his arms, praised God, and said:

29 'Now, Lord, you are releasing your servant in peace,
according to your promise.
30 For I have seen with my own eyes
the deliverance 31 you have made ready in full view of all nations:
32 a light that will bring revelation to the Gentiles
and glory to your people Israel.'

33 The child's father and mother were full of wonder at what was being said about him. 34–35 Simeon blessed them and said to Mary his mother, 'This child is destined to be a sign that will be rejected; and you too will be pierced to the heart. Many in Israel will stand or fall because of him; and so the secret thoughts of many will be laid bare.'

36 There was also a prophetess, Anna the daughter of Phanuel, of the tribe of Asher. She was a very old woman, who had lived seven years with her husband after she was first married, 37 and then alone as a widow to the age of eighty-four. She never left the temple, but worshipped night and day with fasting and prayer. 38 Coming up at that very moment, she gave thanks to God; and she talked about the child to all who were looking for the liberation of Jerusalem.

39 When they had done everything prescribed in the law of the Lord, they returned to Galilee to their own town of Nazareth. 40 The child grew big and strong and full of wisdom; and God's favour was upon him.

---

[i] Or the Christ [j] Gk army [k] Other ancient authorities read peace, goodwill among people [l] Gk Symeon [m] Or the Lord's Christ [n] Gk In the Spirit, he [o] Gk he [p] Gk slave [q] Gk Hanna [r] Gk him

2:11 **the Messiah, the Lord:** *some witnesses read* the Lord's Messiah.

the people. 11 For today in the city of David a savior has been born for you who is Messiah and Lord. 12 And this will be a sign for you: you will find an infant wrapped in swaddling clothes and lying in a manger." 13 And suddenly there was a multitude of the heavenly host with the angel, praising God and saying:

14 "Glory to God in the highest
and on earth peace to those on whom his
favor rests."

15 When the angels went away from them to heaven, the shepherds said to one another, "Let us go, then, to Bethlehem to see this thing that has taken place, which the Lord has made known to us." 16 So they went in haste and found Mary and Joseph, and the infant lying in the manger. 17 When they saw this, they made known the message that had been told them about this child. 18 All who heard it were amazed by what had been told them by the shepherds. 19 And Mary kept all these things, reflecting on them in her heart. 20 Then the shepherds returned, glorifying and praising God for all they had heard and seen, just as it had been told to them.

21 When eight days were completed for his circumcision, he was named Jesus, the name given him by the angel before he was conceived in the womb.

22 When the days were completed for their purification according to the law of Moses, they took him up to Jerusalem to present him to the Lord, 23 just as it is written in the law of the Lord, "Every male that opens the womb shall be consecrated to the Lord," 24 and to offer the sacrifice of "a pair of turtledoves or two young pigeons," in accordance with the dictate in the law of the Lord.

25 Now there was a man in Jerusalem whose name was Simeon. This man was righteous and devout, awaiting the consolation of Israel, and the holy Spirit was upon him. 26 It had been revealed to him by the holy Spirit that he should not see death before he had seen the Messiah of the Lord. 27 He came in the Spirit into the temple; and when the parents brought in the child Jesus to perform the custom of the law in regard to him, 28 he took him into his arms and blessed God, saying:

29 "Now, Master, you may let your servant go
in peace, according to your word,
30 for my eyes have seen your salvation,
31   which you prepared in sight of all the peoples,
32 a light for revelation to the Gentiles,
and glory for your people Israel."

33 The child's father and mother were amazed at what was said about him; 34 and Simeon blessed them and said to Mary his mother, "Behold, this child is destined for the fall and rise of many in Israel, and to be a sign that will be contradicted 35 (and you yourself a sword will pierce) so that the thoughts of many hearts may be revealed." 36 There was also a prophetess, Anna, the daughter of Phanuel, of the tribe of Asher. She was advanced in years, having lived seven years with her husband after her marriage, 37 and then as a widow until she was eighty-four. She never left the temple, but worshiped night and day with fasting and prayer. 38 And coming forward at that very time, she gave thanks to God and spoke about the child to all who were awaiting the redemption of Jerusalem.

39 When they had fulfilled all the prescriptions of the law of the Lord, they returned to Galilee, to their own town of Nazareth. 40 The child grew and became strong, filled with wisdom; and the favor of God was upon him.

11 Today in the town of David a Saviour has been born to you; he is Christ the Lord. 12 And here is a sign for you: you will find a baby wrapped in swaddling clothes and lying in a manger.' 13 And all at once with the angel there was a great throng of the hosts of heaven, praising God with the words:

14 Glory to God in the highest heaven,
and on earth peace for those he favours.

15 Now it happened that when the angels had gone from them into heaven, the shepherds said to one another, 'Let us go to Bethlehem and see this event which the Lord has made known to us.' 16 So they hurried away and found Mary and Joseph, and the baby lying in the manger. 17 When they saw the child they repeated what they had been told about him, 18 and everyone who heard it was astonished at what the shepherds said to them. 19 As for Mary, she treasured all these things and pondered them in her heart. 20 And the shepherds went back glorifying and praising God for all they had heard and seen, just as they had been told.

21 When the eighth day came and the child was to be circumcised, they gave him the name Jesus, the name the angel had given him before his conception.

22 And when the day came for them to be purified in keeping with the Law of Moses, they took him up to Jerusalem to present him to the Lord — 23 observing what is written in the Law of the Lord: *Every first-born male must be consecrated to the Lord* — *i* 24 and also to offer in sacrifice, in accordance with what is prescribed in the Law of the Lord, *a pair of turtledoves or two young pigeons. j* 25 Now in Jerusalem there was a man named Simeon. He was an upright and devout man; he looked forward to the restoration of Israel and the Holy Spirit rested on him. 26 It had been revealed to him by the Holy Spirit that he would not see death until he had set eyes on the Christ of the Lord. 27 Prompted by the Spirit he came to the Temple; and when the parents brought in the child Jesus to do for him what the Law required, 28 he took him into his arms and blessed God; and he said:

29 Now, Master, you are letting your servant go in
peace
as you promised;
30 for my eyes have seen the salvation
31 which you have made ready in the sight of the
nations;
32 a light of revelation for the gentiles
and glory for your people Israel.

33 As the child's father and mother were wondering at the things that were being said about him, 34 Simeon blessed them and said to Mary his mother, 'Look, he is destined for the fall and for the rise of many in Israel, destined to be a sign that is opposed — 35 and a sword will pierce your soul too — so that the secret thoughts of many may be laid bare.'

36 There was a prophetess, too, Anna the daughter of Phanuel, of the tribe of Asher. She was well on in years. Her days of girlhood over, she had been married for seven years 37 before becoming a widow. She was now eighty-four years old and never left the Temple, serving God night and day with fasting and prayer. 38 She came up just at that moment and began to praise God; and she spoke of the child to all who looked forward to the deliverance of Jerusalem.

39 When they had done everything the Law of the Lord required, they went back to Galilee, to their own town of Nazareth. 40 And as the child grew to maturity, he was filled with wisdom; and God's favour was with him.

i 2 Ex 13:2.   *j* 2 Lv 5:7.

NEW REVISED STANDARD VERSION

41 Now every year his parents went to Jerusalem for the festival of the Passover. 42 And when he was twelve years old, they went up as usual for the festival. 43 When the festival was ended and they started to return, the boy Jesus stayed behind in Jerusalem, but his parents did not know it. 44 Assuming that he was in the group of travelers, they went a day's journey. Then they started to look for him among their relatives and friends. 45 When they did not find him, they returned to Jerusalem to search for him. 46 After three days they found him in the temple, sitting among the teachers, listening to them and asking them questions. 47 And all who heard him were amazed at his understanding and his answers. 48 When his parents*s* saw him they were astonished; and his mother said to him, "Child, why have you treated us like this? Look, your father and I have been searching for you in great anxiety." 49 He said to them, "Why were you searching for me? Did you not know that I must be in my Father's house?"*t* 50 But they did not understand what he said to them. 51 Then he went down with them and came to Nazareth, and was obedient to them. His mother treasured all these things in her heart.

52 And Jesus increased in wisdom and in years,*u* and in divine and human favor.

3 In the fifteenth year of the reign of Emperor Tiberius, when Pontius Pilate was governor of Judea, and Herod was ruler*v* of Galilee, and his brother Philip ruler*v* of the region of Ituraea and Trachonitis, and Lysanias ruler*v* of Abilene, 2 during the high priesthood of Annas and Caiaphas, the word of God came to John son of Zechariah in the wilderness. 3 He went into all the region around the Jordan, proclaiming a baptism of repentance for the forgiveness of sins, 4 as it is written in the book of the words of the prophet Isaiah,

"The voice of one crying out in the wilderness:
 'Prepare the way of the Lord,
  make his paths straight.
5 Every valley shall be filled,
  and every mountain and hill shall be made low,
  and the crooked shall be made straight,
  and the rough ways made smooth;
6 and all flesh shall see the salvation of God.' "

7 John said to the crowds that came out to be baptized by him, "You brood of vipers! Who warned you to flee from the wrath to come? 8 Bear fruits worthy of repentance. Do not begin to say to yourselves, 'We have Abraham as our ancestor'; for I tell you, God is able from these stones to raise up children to Abraham. 9 Even now the ax is lying at the root of the trees; every tree therefore that does not bear good fruit is cut down and thrown into the fire."

10 And the crowds asked him, "What then should we do?" 11 In reply he said to them, "Whoever has two coats must share with anyone who has none; and whoever has food must do likewise." 12 Even tax collectors came to be baptized, and they asked him, "Teacher, what should we do?" 13 He said to them, "Collect no more than the amount prescribed for you." 14 Soldiers also asked him, "And we, what should we do?" He said to them, "Do not extort money from anyone by threats or false accusation, and be satisfied with your wages."

15 As the people were filled with expectation, and all were questioning in their hearts concerning John, whether he might be the Messiah,*w* 16 John answered all of them by saying, "I baptize you with water; but one who is more powerful than I is coming; I am not worthy to untie the thong of his sandals. He will baptize you with*x* the Holy Spirit and fire. 17 His winnowing fork is in his hand, to clear

REVISED ENGLISH BIBLE

41 Now it was the practice of his parents to go to Jerusalem every year for the Passover festival; 42 and when he was twelve, they made the pilgrimage as usual. 43 When the festive season was over and they set off for home, the boy Jesus stayed behind in Jerusalem. His parents did not know of this; 44 but supposing that he was with the party they travelled for a whole day, and only then did they begin looking for him among their friends and relations. 45 When they could not find him they returned to Jerusalem to look for him; 46 and after three days they found him sitting in the temple surrounded by the teachers, listening to them and putting questions; 47 and all who heard him were amazed at his intelligence and the answers he gave. 48 His parents were astonished to see him there, and his mother said to him, 'My son, why have you treated us like this? Your father and I have been anxiously searching for you.' 49 'Why did you search for me?' he said. 'Did you not know that I was bound to be in my Father's house?' 50 But they did not understand what he meant. 51 Then he went back with them to Nazareth, and continued to be under their authority; his mother treasured up all these things in her heart. 52 As Jesus grew he advanced in wisdom and in favour with God and men.

3 In the fifteenth year of the emperor Tiberius, when Pontius Pilate was governor of Judaea, when Herod was tetrarch of Galilee, his brother Philip prince of Ituraea and Trachonitis, and Lysanias prince of Abilene, 2 during the high-priesthood of Annas and Caiaphas, the word of God came to John son of Zechariah in the wilderness. 3 And he went all over the Jordan valley proclaiming a baptism in token of repentance for the forgiveness of sins, 4 as it is written in the book of the prophecies of Isaiah:

A voice cries in the wilderness,
 'Prepare the way for the Lord;
  clear a straight path for him.
5 Every ravine shall be filled in,
  and every mountain and hill levelled;
  winding paths shall be straightened,
  and rough ways made smooth;
6 and all mankind shall see God's deliverance.'

7 Crowds of people came out to be baptized by him, and he said to them: 'Vipers' brood! Who warned you to escape from the wrath that is to come? 8 Prove your repentance by the fruit you bear; and do not begin saying to yourselves, "We have Abraham for our father." I tell you that God can make children for Abraham out of these stones. 9 Already the axe is laid to the roots of the trees; and every tree that fails to produce good fruit is cut down and thrown on the fire.'

10 The people asked him, 'Then what are we to do?' 11 He replied, 'Whoever has two shirts must share with him who has none, and whoever has food must do the same.' 12 Among those who came to be baptized were tax-collectors, and they said to him, 'Teacher, what are we to do?' 13 He told them, 'Exact no more than the assessment.' 14 Some soldiers also asked him, 'And what of us?' To them he said, 'No bullying; no blackmail; make do with your pay!'

15 The people were all agog, wondering about John, whether perhaps he was the Messiah, 16 but he spoke out and said to them all: 'I baptize you with water; but there is one coming who is mightier than I am. I am not worthy to unfasten the straps of his sandals. He will baptize you with the Holy Spirit and with fire. 17 His winnowing-shovel is

---

s Gk *they*   *t* Or *be about my Father's interests?*   *u* Or *in stature*
v Gk *tetrarch*   *w* Or *the Christ*   *x* Or *in*

2:49 **in . . . house:** *or* about my Father's business.

41 Each year his parents went to Jerusalem for the feast of Passover, 42 and when he was twelve years old, they went up according to festival custom. 43 After they had completed its days, as they were returning, the boy Jesus remained behind in Jerusalem, but his parents did not know it. 44 Thinking that he was in the caravan, they journeyed for a day and looked for him among their relatives and acquaintances, 45 but not finding him, they returned to Jerusalem to look for him. 46 After three days they found him in the temple, sitting in the midst of the teachers, listening to them and asking them questions, 47 and all who heard him were astounded at his understanding and his answers. 48 When his parents saw him, they were astonished, and his mother said to him, "Son, why have you done this to us? Your father and I have been looking for you with great anxiety." 49 And he said to them, "Why were you looking for me? Did you not know that I must be in my Father's house?" 50 But they did not understand what he said to them. 51 He went down with them and came to Nazareth, and was obedient to them; and his mother kept all these things in her heart. 52 And Jesus advanced [in] wisdom and age and favor before God and man.

3 In the fifteenth year of the reign of Tiberius Caesar, when Pontius Pilate was governor of Judea, and Herod was tetrarch of Galilee, and his brother Philip tetrarch of the region of Ituraea and Trachonitis, and Lysanias was tetrarch of Abilene, 2 during the high priesthood of Annas and Caiaphas, the word of God came to John the son of Zechariah in the desert. 3 He went throughout [the] whole region of the Jordan, proclaiming a baptism of repentance for the forgiveness of sins, 4 as it is written in the book of the words of the prophet Isaiah:

"A voice of one crying out in the desert:
'Prepare the way of the Lord,
   make straight his paths.
5 Every valley shall be filled
   and every mountain and hill shall be made low.
The winding roads shall be made straight,
   and the rough ways shall be made smooth,
6 and all flesh shall see the salvation of God.' "

7 He said to the crowds who came out to be baptized by him, "You brood of vipers! Who warned you to flee from the coming wrath? 8 Produce good fruits as evidence of your repentance; and do not begin to say to yourselves, 'We have Abraham as our father,' for I tell you, God can raise up children to Abraham from these stones. 9 Even now the ax lies at the root of the trees. Therefore every tree that does not produce good fruit will be cut down and thrown into the fire."

10 And the crowds asked him, "What then should we do?" 11 He said to them in reply, "Whoever has two cloaks should share with the person who has none. And whoever has food should do likewise." 12 Even tax collectors came to be baptized and they said to him, "Teacher, what should we do?" 13 He answered them, "Stop collecting more than what is prescribed." 14 Soldiers also asked him, "And what is it that we should do?" He told them, "Do not practice extortion, do not falsely accuse anyone, and be satisfied with your wages."

15 Now the people were filled with expectation, and all were asking in their hearts whether John might be the Messiah. 16 John answered them all, saying, "I am baptizing you with water, but one mightier than I is coming. I am not worthy to loosen the thongs of his sandals. He will baptize you with the holy Spirit and fire. 17 His winnowing fan is in

41 Every year his parents used to go to Jerusalem for the feast of the Passover. 42 When he was twelve years old, they went up for the feast as usual. 43 When the days of the feast were over and they set off home, the boy Jesus stayed behind in Jerusalem without his parents knowing it. 44 They assumed he was somewhere in the party, and it was only after a day's journey that they went to look for him among their relations and acquaintances. 45 When they failed to find him they went back to Jerusalem looking for him everywhere.

46 It happened that, three days later, they found him in the Temple, sitting among the teachers, listening to them, and asking them questions; 47 and all those who heard him were astounded at his intelligence and his replies. 48 They were overcome when they saw him, and his mother said to him, 'My child, why have you done this to us? See how worried your father and I have been, looking for you.' 49 He replied, 'Why were you looking for me? Did you not know that I must be in my Father's house?' 50 But they did not understand what he meant.

51 He went down with them then and came to Nazareth and lived under their authority. His mother stored up all these things in her heart. 52 And Jesus increased in wisdom, in stature, and in favour with God and with people.

3 In the fifteenth year of Tiberius Caesar's reign, when Pontius Pilate was governor of Judaea, Herod tetrarch of Galilee, his brother Philip tetrarch of the territories of Ituraea and Trachonitis, Lysanias tetrarch of Abilene, 2 and while the high-priesthood was held by Annas and Caiaphas, the word of God came to John the son of Zechariah, in the desert. 3 He went through the whole Jordan area proclaiming a baptism of repentance for the forgiveness of sins, 4 as it is written in the book of the sayings of Isaiah the prophet:

*A voice of one that cries in the desert:
Prepare a way for the Lord,
   make his paths straight!
5 Let every valley be filled in,
   every mountain and hill be levelled,
winding ways be straightened
   and rough roads made smooth,
6 and all humanity will see the salvation of God.* k

7 He said, therefore, to the crowds who came to be baptised by him, 'Brood of vipers, who warned you to flee from the coming retribution? 8 Produce fruit in keeping with repentance, and do not start telling yourselves, "We have Abraham as our father," because, I tell you, God can raise children for Abraham from these stones. 9 Yes, even now the axe is being laid to the root of the trees, so that any tree failing to produce good fruit will be cut down and thrown on the fire.'

10 When all the people asked him, 'What must we do, then?' 11 he answered, 'Anyone who has two tunics must share with the one who has none, and anyone with something to eat must do the same.' 12 There were tax collectors, too, who came for baptism, and these said to him, 'Master, what must we do?' 13 He said to them, 'Exact no more than the appointed rate.' 14 Some soldiers asked him in their turn, 'What about us? What must we do?' He said to them, 'No intimidation! No extortion! Be content with your pay!'

15 A feeling of expectancy had grown among the people, who were beginning to wonder whether John might be the Christ, 16 so John declared before them all, 'I baptise you with water, but someone is coming, who is more powerful than me, and I am not fit to undo the strap of his sandals; he will baptise you with the Holy Spirit and fire. 17 His

k 3 Is 40:3–5.

his threshing floor and to gather the wheat into his granary; but the chaff he will burn with unquenchable fire."

18 So, with many other exhortations, he proclaimed the good news to the people. 19 But Herod the ruler,y who had been rebuked by him because of Herodias, his brother's wife, and because of all the evil things that Herod had done, 20 added to them all by shutting up John in prison.

21 Now when all the people were baptized, and when Jesus also had been baptized and was praying, the heaven was opened, 22 and the Holy Spirit descended upon him in bodily form like a dove. And a voice came from heaven, "You are my Son, the Beloved;z with you I am well pleased."a

23 Jesus was about thirty years old when he began his work. He was the son (as was thought) of Joseph son of Heli, 24 son of Matthat, son of Levi, son of Melchi, son of Jannai, son of Joseph, 25 son of Mattathias, son of Amos, son of Nahum, son of Esli, son of Naggai, 26 son of Maath, son of Mattathias, son of Semein, son of Josech, son of Joda, 27 son of Joanan, son of Rhesa, son of Zerubbabel, son of Shealtiel,b son of Neri, 28 son of Melchi, son of Addi, son of Cosam, son of Elmadam, son of Er, 29 son of Joshua, son of Eliezer, son of Jorim, son of Matthat, son of Levi, 30 son of Simeon, son of Judah, son of Joseph, son of Jonam, son of Eliakim, 31 son of Melea, son of Menna, son of Mattatha, son of Nathan, son of David, 32 son of Jesse, son of Obed, son of Boaz, son of Sala,c son of Nahshon, 33 son of Amminadab, son of Admin, son of Arni,d son of Hezron, son of Perez, son of Judah, 34 son of Jacob, son of Isaac, son of Abraham, son of Terah, son of Nahor, 35 son of Serug, son of Reu, son of Peleg, son of Eber, son of Shelah, 36 son of Cainan, son of Arphaxad, son of Shem, son of Noah, son of Lamech, 37 son of Methuselah, son of Enoch, son of Jared, son of Mahalaleel, son of Cainan, 38 son of Enos, son of Seth, son of Adam, son of God.

4 Jesus, full of the Holy Spirit, returned from the Jordan and was led by the Spirit in the wilderness, 2 where for forty days he was tempted by the devil. He ate nothing at all during those days, and when they were over, he was famished. 3 The devil said to him, "If you are the Son of God, command this stone to become a loaf of bread." 4 Jesus answered him, "It is written, 'One does not live by bread alone.'"

5 Then the devile led him up and showed him in an instant all the kingdoms of the world. 6 And the devile said to him, "To you I will give their glory and all this authority; for it has been given over to me, and I give it to anyone I please. 7 If you, then, will worship me, it will all be yours." 8 Jesus answered him, "It is written,

'Worship the Lord your God,
    and serve only him.'"

9 Then the devile took him to Jerusalem, and placed him on the pinnacle of the temple, saying to him, "If you are the Son of God, throw yourself down from here, 10 for it is written,

'He will command his angels concerning you,
    to protect you,'

ready in his hand, to clear his threshing-floor and gather the wheat into his granary; but the chaff he will burn on a fire that can never be put out.'

18 In this and many other ways he made his appeal to the people and announced the good news. 19 But Herod the tetrarch, when he was rebuked by him over the affair of his brother's wife Herodias and all his other misdeeds, 20 crowned them all by shutting John up in prison.

21 DURING a general baptism of the people, when Jesus too had been baptized and was praying, heaven opened 22 and the Holy Spirit descended on him in bodily form like a dove, and there came a voice from heaven, 'You are my beloved Son; in you I delight.'

23 When Jesus began his work he was about thirty years old, the son, as people thought, of Joseph son of Heli, 24 son of Matthat, son of Levi, son of Melchi, son of Jannai, son of Joseph, 25 son of Mattathias, son of Amos, son of Nahum, son of Esli, son of Naggai, 26 son of Maath, son of Mattathias, son of Semein, son of Josech, son of Joda, 27 son of Johanan, son of Rhesa, son of Zerubbabel, son of Shealtiel, son of Neri, 28 son of Melchi, son of Addi, son of Cosam, son of Elmadam, son of Er, 29 son of Joshua, son of Eliezer, son of Jorim, son of Matthat, son of Levi, 30 son of Symeon, son of Judah, son of Joseph, son of Jonam, son of Eliakim, 31 son of Melea, son of Menna, son of Mattatha, son of Nathan, son of David, 32 son of Jesse, son of Obed, son of Boaz, son of Salma, son of Nahshon, 33 son of Amminadab, son of Arni, son of Hezron, son of Perez, son of Judah, 34 son of Jacob, son of Isaac, son of Abraham, son of Terah, son of Nahor, 35 son of Serug, son of Reu, son of Peleg, son of Eber, son of Shelah, 36 son of Cainan, son of Arphaxad, son of Shem, son of Noah, son of Lamech, 37 son of Methuselah, son of Enoch, son of Jared, son of Mahalaleel, son of Cainan, 38 son of Enosh, son of Seth, son of Adam, son of God.

4 1-2 FULL of the Holy Spirit, Jesus returned from the Jordan, and for forty days he wandered in the wilderness, led by the Spirit and tempted by the devil.

During that time he ate nothing, and at the end of it he was famished. 3 The devil said to him, 'If you are the Son of God, tell this stone to become bread.' 4 Jesus answered, 'Scripture says, "Man is not to live on bread alone."'

5 Next the devil led him to a height and showed him in a flash all the kingdoms of the world. 6 'All this dominion will I give to you,' he said, 'and the glory that goes with it; for it has been put in my hands and I can give it to anyone I choose. 7 You have only to do homage to me and it will all be yours.' 8 Jesus answered him, 'Scripture says, "You shall do homage to the Lord your God and worship him alone."'

9 The devil took him to Jerusalem and set him on the parapet of the temple. 'If you are the Son of God,' he said, 'throw yourself down from here; 10 for scripture says, "He will put his angels in charge of you," 11 and again, "They

y Gk tetrarch   z Or my beloved Son   a Other ancient authorities read You are my Son, today I have begotten you   b Gk Salathiel   c Other ancient authorities read Salmon   d Other ancient authorities read Amminadab, son of Aram; others vary widely   e Gk he

3:22 You are . . . Son: or You are my only Son. You are . . . delight: some witnesses read You are my Son; this day I have begotten you.   3:33 Amminadab: some witnesses add son of Admin.

his hand to clear his threshing floor and to gather the wheat into his barn, but the chaff he will burn with unquenchable fire." 18 Exhorting them in many other ways, he preached good news to the people. 19 Now Herod the tetrarch, who had been censured by him because of Herodias, his brother's wife, and because of all the evil deeds Herod had committed, 20 added still another to these by [also] putting John in prison.

21 After all the people had been baptized and Jesus also had been baptized and was praying, heaven was opened 22 and the holy Spirit descended upon him in bodily form like a dove. And a voice came from heaven, "You are my beloved Son; with you I am well pleased."

23 When Jesus began his ministry he was about thirty years of age. He was the son, as was thought, of Joseph, the son of Heli, 24 the son of Matthat, the son of Levi, the son of Melchi, the son of Jannai, the son of Joseph, 25 the son of Mattathias, the son of Amos, the son of Nahum, the son of Esli, the son of Naggai, 26 the son of Maath, the son of Mattathias, the son of Semein, the son of Josech, the son of Joda, 27 the son of Joanan, the son of Rhesa, the son of Zerubbabel, the son of Shealtiel, the son of Neri, 28 the son of Melchi, the son of Addi, the son of Cosam, the son of Elmadam, the son of Er, 29 the son of Joshua, the son of Eliezer, the son of Jorim, the son of Matthat, the son of Levi, 30 the son of Simeon, the son of Judah, the son of Joseph, the son of Jonam, the son of Eliakim, 31 the son of Melea, the son of Menna, the son of Mattatha, the son of Nathan, the son of David, 32 the son of Jesse, the son of Obed, the son of Boaz, the son of Sala, the son of Nahshon, 33 the son of Amminadab, the son of Admin, the son of Arni, the son of Hezron, the son of Perez, the son of Judah, 34 the son of Jacob, the son of Isaac, the son of Abraham, the son of Terah, the son of Nahor, 35 the son of Serug, the son of Reu, the son of Peleg, the son of Eber, the son of Shelah, 36 the son of Cainan, the son of Arphaxad, the son of Shem, the son of Noah, the son of Lamech, 37 the son of Methuselah, the son of Enoch, the son of Jared, the son of Mahalaleel, the son of Cainan, 38 the son of Enos, the son of Seth, the son of Adam, the son of God.

4 Filled with the holy Spirit, Jesus returned from the Jordan and was led by the Spirit into the desert 2 for forty days, to be tempted by the devil. He ate nothing during those days, and when they were over he was hungry. 3 The devil said to him, "If you are the Son of God, command this stone to become bread." 4 Jesus answered him, "It is written, 'One does not live by bread alone.'" 5 Then he took him up and showed him all the kingdoms of the world in a single instant. 6 The devil said to him, "I shall give to you all this power and their glory; for it has been handed over to me, and I may give it to whomever I wish. 7 All this will be yours, if you worship me." 8 Jesus said to him in reply, "It is written:

'You shall worship the Lord, your God,
and him alone shall you serve.'"

9 Then he led him to Jerusalem, made him stand on the parapet of the temple, and said to him, "If you are the Son of God, throw yourself down from here, 10 for it is written:
'He will command his angels concerning you,
to guard you,'

winnowing-fan is in his hand, to clear his threshing-floor and to gather the wheat into his barn; but the chaff he will burn in a fire that will never go out.' 18 And he proclaimed the good news to the people with many other exhortations too.

19 But Herod the tetrarch, censured by John for his relations with his brother's wife Herodias and for all the other crimes he had committed, 20 added a further crime to all the rest by shutting John up in prison.

21 Now it happened that when all the people had been baptised and while Jesus after his own baptism was at prayer, heaven opened 22 and the Holy Spirit descended on him in a physical form, like a dove. And a voice came from heaven, 'You are my Son; today have I fathered you.' l

23 When he began, Jesus was about thirty years old, being the son, as it was thought, of Joseph son of Heli, 24 son of Matthat, son of Levi, son of Melchi, son of Jannai, son of Joseph, 25 son of Mattathias, son of Amos, son of Nahum, son of Esli, son of Naggai, 26 son of Maath, son of Mattathias, son of Semein, son of Josech, son of Joda, 27 son of Joanan, son of Rhesa, son of Zerubbabel, son of Shealtiel, son of Neri, 28 son of Melchi, son of Addi, son of Cosam, son of Elmadam, son of Er, 29 son of Jesus, son of Eliezer, son of Jorim, son of Matthat, son of Levi, 30 son of Symeon, son of Judah, son of Joseph, son of Jonam, son of Eliakim, 31 son of Melea, son of Menna, son of Mattatha, son of Nathan, son of David, 32 son of Jesse, son of Obed, son of Boaz, son of Sala, son of Nahshon, 33 son of Amminadab, son of Admin, son of Arni, son of Hezron, son of Perez, son of Judah, 34 son of Jacob, son of Isaac, son of Abraham, son of Terah, son of Nahor, 35 son of Serug, son of Reu, son of Peleg, son of Eber, son of Shelah, 36 son of Cainan, son of Arphaxad, son of Shem, son of Noah, son of Lamech, 37 son of Methuselah, son of Enoch, son of Jared, son of Mahalaleel, son of Cainan, 38 son of Enos, son of Seth, son of Adam, son of God.

4 Filled with the Holy Spirit, Jesus left the Jordan and was led by the Spirit into the desert, 2 for forty days being put to the test by the devil. During that time he ate nothing and at the end he was hungry. 3 Then the devil said to him, 'If you are Son of God, tell this stone to turn into a loaf.' 4 But Jesus replied, 'Scripture says:

Human beings live not on bread alone.' m

5 Then leading him to a height, the devil showed him in a moment of time all the kingdoms of the world 6 and said to him, 'I will give you all this power and their splendour, for it has been handed over to me, for me to give it to anyone I choose. 7 Do homage, then, to me, and it shall all be yours.' 8 But Jesus answered him, 'Scripture says:

You must do homage to the Lord your God, him
alone you must serve.' n

9 Then he led him to Jerusalem and set him on the parapet of the Temple. 'If you are Son of God,' he said to him, 'throw yourself down from here, 10 for scripture says:

He has given his angels orders about you, to guard
you,

l 3 Ps 2:7.   m 4 Dt 8:3.   n 4 Dt 6:13.

11 and

'On their hands they will bear you up,
    so that you will not dash your foot against a
        stone.' "
12 Jesus answered him, "It is said, 'Do not put the Lord your God to the test.' " 13 When the devil had finished every test, he departed from him until an opportune time.

14 Then Jesus, filled with the power of the Spirit, returned to Galilee, and a report about him spread through all the surrounding country. 15 He began to teach in their synagogues and was praised by everyone.

16 When he came to Nazareth, where he had been brought up, he went to the synagogue on the sabbath day, as was his custom. He stood up to read, 17 and the scroll of the prophet Isaiah was given to him. He unrolled the scroll and found the place where it was written:

18 "The Spirit of the Lord is upon me,
    because he has anointed me
        to bring good news to the poor.
He has sent me to proclaim release to the
        captives
    and recovery of sight to the blind,
        to let the oppressed go free,
19 to proclaim the year of the Lord's favor."

20 And he rolled up the scroll, gave it back to the attendant, and sat down. The eyes of all in the synagogue were fixed on him. 21 Then he began to say to them, "Today this scripture has been fulfilled in your hearing." 22 All spoke well of him and were amazed at the gracious words that came from his mouth. They said, "Is not this Joseph's son?" 23 He said to them, "Doubtless you will quote to me this proverb, 'Doctor, cure yourself!' And you will say, 'Do here also in your hometown the things that we have heard you did at Capernaum.' " 24 And he said, "Truly I tell you, no prophet is accepted in the prophet's hometown. 25 But the truth is, there were many widows in Israel in the time of Elijah, when the heaven was shut up three years and six months, and there was a severe famine over all the land; 26 yet Elijah was sent to none of them except to a widow at Zarephath in Sidon. 27 There were also many lepers *f* in Israel in the time of the prophet Elisha, and none of them was cleansed except Naaman the Syrian." 28 When they heard this, all in the synagogue were filled with rage. 29 They got up, drove him out of the town, and led him to the brow of the hill on which their town was built, so that they might hurl him off the cliff. 30 But he passed through the midst of them and went on his way.

31 He went down to Capernaum, a city in Galilee, and was teaching them on the sabbath. 32 They were astounded at his teaching, because he spoke with authority. 33 In the synagogue there was a man who had the spirit of an unclean demon, and he cried out with a loud voice, 34 "Let us alone! What have you to do with us, Jesus of Nazareth? Have you come to destroy us? I know who you are, the Holy One of God." 35 But Jesus rebuked him, saying, "Be silent, and come out of him!" When the demon had thrown him down before them, he came out of him without having done him any harm. 36 They were all amazed and kept saying to one another, "What kind of utterance is this? For with authority and power he commands the unclean spirits, and out they come!" 37 And a report about him began to reach every place in the region.

will support you in their arms for fear you should strike your foot against a stone." ' 12 Jesus answered him, 'It has been said, "You are not to put the Lord your God to the test." ' 13 So, having come to the end of all these temptations, the devil departed, biding his time.

14 Then Jesus, armed with the power of the Spirit, returned to Galilee; and reports about him spread through the whole countryside. 15 He taught in their synagogues and everyone sang his praises.

16 He came to Nazareth, where he had been brought up, and went to the synagogue on the sabbath day as he regularly did. He stood up to read the lesson 17 and was handed the scroll of the prophet Isaiah. He opened the scroll and found the passage which says,

18 'The spirit of the Lord is upon me
    because he has anointed me;
he has sent me to announce good news to the poor,
    to proclaim release for prisoners
    and recovery of sight for the blind;
        to let the broken victims go free,
19 to proclaim the year of the Lord's favour.'

20 He rolled up the scroll, gave it back to the attendant, and sat down; and all eyes in the synagogue were fixed on him. 21 He began to address them: 'Today', he said, 'in your hearing this text has come true.' 22 There was general approval; they were astonished that words of such grace should fall from his lips. 'Is not this Joseph's son?' they asked. 23 Then Jesus said, 'No doubt you will quote to me the proverb, "Physician, heal yourself!" and say, "We have heard of all your doings at Capernaum; do the same here in your own home town." 24 Truly I tell you,' he went on: 'no prophet is recognized in his own country. 25 There were indeed many widows in Israel in Elijah's time, when for three and a half years the skies never opened, and famine lay hard over the whole country; 26 yet it was to none of these that Elijah was sent, but to a widow at Sarepta in the territory of Sidon. 27 Again, in the time of the prophet Elisha there were many lepers in Israel, and not one of them was healed, but only Naaman, the Syrian.' 28 These words roused the whole congregation to fury; 29 they leapt up, drove him out of the town, and took him to the brow of the hill on which it was built, meaning to hurl him over the edge. 30 But he walked straight through the whole crowd, and went away.

31 Coming down to Capernaum, a town in Galilee, he taught the people on the sabbath, 32 and they were amazed at his teaching, for what he said had the note of authority. 33 Now there was a man in the synagogue possessed by a demon, an unclean spirit. He shrieked at the top of his voice, 34 'What do you want with us, Jesus of Nazareth? Have you come to destroy us? I know who you are—the Holy One of God.' 35 Jesus rebuked him: 'Be silent', he said, 'and come out of him.' Then the demon, after throwing the man down in front of the people, left him without doing him any injury. 36 Amazement fell on them all and they said to one another: 'What is there in this man's words? He gives orders to the unclean spirits with authority and power, and they go.' 37 So the news spread, and he was the talk of the whole district.

---

f The terms *leper* and *leprosy* can refer to several diseases

4:34 **Have you:** *or* You have.

11 and:

> 'With their hands they will support you,
> lest you dash your foot against a stone.' "

12 Jesus said to him in reply, "It also says, 'You shall not put the Lord, your God, to the test.' " 13 When the devil had finished every temptation, he departed from him for a time.

14 Jesus returned to Galilee in the power of the Spirit, and news of him spread throughout the whole region. 15 He taught in their synagogues and was praised by all.

16 He came to Nazareth, where he had grown up, and went according to his custom into the synagogue on the sabbath day. He stood up to read 17 and was handed a scroll of the prophet Isaiah. He unrolled the scroll and found the passage where it was written:

> 18 "The Spirit of the Lord is upon me,
> because he has anointed me
> to bring glad tidings to the poor.
> He has sent me to proclaim liberty to captives
> and recovery of sight to the blind,
> to let the oppressed go free,
> 19 and to proclaim a year acceptable to the Lord."

20 Rolling up the scroll, he handed it back to the attendant and sat down, and the eyes of all in the synagogue looked intently at him. 21 He said to them, "Today this scripture passage is fulfilled in your hearing." 22 And all spoke highly of him and were amazed at the gracious words that came from his mouth. They also asked, "Isn't this the son of Joseph?" 23 He said to them, "Surely you will quote me this proverb, 'Physician, cure yourself,' and say, 'Do here in your native place the things that we heard were done in Capernaum.' " 24 And he said, "Amen, I say to you, no prophet is accepted in his own native place. 25 Indeed, I tell you, there were many widows in Israel in the days of Elijah when the sky was closed for three and a half years and a severe famine spread over the entire land. 26 It was to none of these that Elijah was sent, but only to a widow in Zarephath in the land of Sidon. 27 Again, there were many lepers in Israel during the time of Elisha the prophet; yet not one of them was cleansed, but only Naaman the Syrian." 28 When the people in the synagogue heard this, they were all filled with fury. 29 They rose up, drove him out of the town, and led him to the brow of the hill on which their town had been built, to hurl him down headlong. 30 But he passed through the midst of them and went away.

31 Jesus then went down to Capernaum, a town of Galilee. He taught them on the sabbath, 32 and they were astonished at his teaching because he spoke with authority. 33 In the synagogue there was a man with the spirit of an unclean demon, and he cried out in a loud voice, 34 "Ha! What have you to do with us, Jesus of Nazareth? Have you come to destroy us? I know who you are — the Holy One of God!" 35 Jesus rebuked him and said, "Be quiet! Come out of him!" Then the demon threw the man down in front of them and came out of him without doing him any harm. 36 They were all amazed and said to one another, "What is there about his word? For with authority and power he commands the unclean spirits, and they come out." 37 And news of him spread everywhere in the surrounding region.

and again:

> 11 They will carry you in their arms in case you trip
> over a stone.' o

12 But Jesus answered him, 'Scripture says:

> Do not put the Lord your God to the test.' p

13 Having exhausted every way of putting him to the test, the devil left him, until the opportune moment.

14 Jesus, with the power of the Spirit in him, returned to Galilee; and his reputation spread throughout the countryside. 15 He taught in their synagogues and everyone glorified him.

16 He came to Nazara, where he had been brought up, and went into the synagogue on the Sabbath day as he usually did. He stood up to read, 17 and they handed him the scroll of the prophet Isaiah. Unrolling the scroll he found the place where it is written:

> 18 The spirit of the Lord is on me,
> for he has anointed me
> to bring the good news to the afflicted.
> He has sent me to proclaim liberty to captives,
> sight to the blind,
> to let the oppressed go free,
> 19 to proclaim a year of favour from the Lord. q

20 He then rolled up the scroll, gave it back to the assistant and sat down. And all eyes in the synagogue were fixed on him. 21 Then he began to speak to them, 'This text is being fulfilled today even while you are listening.' 22 And he won the approval of all, and they were astonished by the gracious words that came from his lips.

They said, 'This is Joseph's son, surely?' 23 But he replied, 'No doubt you will quote me the saying, "Physician, heal yourself," and tell me, "We have heard all that happened in Capernaum, do the same here in your own country." ' 24 And he went on, 'In truth I tell you, no prophet is ever accepted in his own country.

25 'There were many widows in Israel, I can assure you, in Elijah's day, when heaven remained shut for three years and six months and a great famine raged throughout the land, 26 but Elijah was not sent to any one of these: he was sent to a widow at Zarephath, a town in Sidonia. r 27 And in the prophet Elisha's time there were many suffering from virulent skin-diseases in Israel, but none of these was cured — only Naaman the Syrian.' s

28 When they heard this everyone in the synagogue was enraged. 29 They sprang to their feet and hustled him out of the town; and they took him up to the brow of the hill their town was built on, intending to throw him off the cliff, 30 but he passed straight through the crowd and walked away.

31 He went down to Capernaum, a town in Galilee, and taught them on the Sabbath. 32 And his teaching made a deep impression on them because his word carried authority.

33 In the synagogue there was a man possessed by the spirit of an unclean devil, and he shouted at the top of his voice, 34 'Ha! What do you want with us, Jesus of Nazareth? Have you come to destroy us? I know who you are: the Holy One of God.' 35 But Jesus rebuked it, saying, 'Be quiet! Come out of him!' And the devil, throwing the man into the middle, went out of him without hurting him at all. 36 Astonishment seized them and they were all saying to one another, 'What is it in his words? He gives orders to unclean spirits with authority and power and they come out.' 37 And the news of him travelled all through the surrounding countryside.

o 4 Ps 91:11–12.   p 4 Dt 6:16.   q 4 Is 61:1–2.   r 4 1 K 17:9.
s 4 2 K 5:14.

NEW REVISED STANDARD VERSION

38 After leaving the synagogue he entered Simon's house. Now Simon's mother-in-law was suffering from a high fever, and they asked him about her. 39 Then he stood over her and rebuked the fever, and it left her. Immediately she got up and began to serve them.

40 As the sun was setting, all those who had any who were sick with various kinds of diseases brought them to him; and he laid his hands on each of them and cured them. 41 Demons also came out of many, shouting, "You are the Son of God!" But he rebuked them and would not allow them to speak, because they knew that he was the Messiah. g

42 At daybreak he departed and went into a deserted place. And the crowds were looking for him; and when they reached him, they wanted to prevent him from leaving them. 43 But he said to them, "I must proclaim the good news of the kingdom of God to the other cities also; for I was sent for this purpose." 44 So he continued proclaiming the message in the synagogues of Judea. h

5 Once while Jesus i was standing beside the lake of Gennesaret, and the crowd was pressing in on him to hear the word of God, 2 he saw two boats there at the shore of the lake; the fishermen had gone out of them and were washing their nets. 3 He got into one of the boats, the one belonging to Simon, and asked him to put out a little way from the boat. Then he sat down and taught the crowds from the boat. 4 When he had finished speaking, he said to Simon, "Put out into the deep water and let down your nets for a catch." 5 Simon answered, "Master, we have worked all night long but have caught nothing. Yet if you say so, I will let down the nets." 6 When they had done this, they caught so many fish that their nets were beginning to break. 7 So they signaled their partners in the other boat to come and help them. And they came and filled both boats, so that they began to sink. 8 But when Simon Peter saw it, he fell down at Jesus' knees, saying, "Go away from me, Lord, for I am a sinful man!" 9 For he and all who were with him were amazed at the catch of fish that they had taken; 10 and so also were James and John, sons of Zebedee, who were partners with Simon. Then Jesus said to Simon, "Do not be afraid; from now on you will be catching people." 11 When they had brought their boats to shore, they left everything and followed him.

12 Once, when he was in one of the cities, there was a man covered with leprosy. j When he saw Jesus, he bowed with his face to the ground and begged him, "Lord, if you choose, you can make me clean." 13 Then Jesus i stretched out his hand, touched him, and said, "I do choose. Be made clean." Immediately the leprosy j left him. 14 Then he ordered him to tell no one. "Go," he said, "and show yourself to the priest, and, as Moses commanded, make an offering for your cleansing, for a testimony to them." 15 But now more than ever the word about Jesus k spread abroad; many crowds would gather to hear him and to be cured of their diseases. 16 But he would withdraw to deserted places and pray.

17 One day, while he was teaching, Pharisees and teachers of the law were sitting near by (they had come from every village of Galilee and Judea and from Jerusalem); and the power of the Lord was with him to heal. l 18 Just then some men came, carrying a paralyzed man on a bed. They were trying to bring him in and lay him before Jesus; k

REVISED ENGLISH BIBLE

38 On leaving the synagogue he went to Simon's house. Simon's mother-in-law was in the grip of a high fever; and they asked him to help her. 39 He stood over her and rebuked the fever. It left her, and she got up at once and attended to their needs.

40 At sunset all who had friends ill with diseases of one kind or another brought them to him; and he laid his hands on them one by one and healed them. 41 Demons also came out of many of them, shouting, 'You are the Son of God.' But he rebuked them and forbade them to speak, because they knew he was the Messiah.

42 When day broke he went out and made his way to a remote spot. But the crowds went in search of him, and when they came to where he was they pressed him not to leave them. 43 But he said, 'I must give the good news of the kingdom of God to the other towns also, for that is what I was sent to do.' 44 So he proclaimed the gospel in the synagogues of Judaea.

5 One day as he stood by the lake of Gennesaret, with people crowding in on him to listen to the word of God, 2 he noticed two boats lying at the water's edge; the fishermen had come ashore and were washing their nets. 3 He got into one of the boats, which belonged to Simon, and asked him to put out a little way from the shore; then he went on teaching the crowds as he sat in the boat. 4 When he had finished speaking, he said to Simon, 'Put out into deep water and let down your nets for a catch.' 5 Simon answered, 'Master, we were hard at work all night and caught nothing; but if you say so, I will let down the nets.' 6 They did so and made such a huge catch of fish that their nets began to split. 7 So they signalled to their partners in the other boat to come and help them. They came, and loaded both boats to the point of sinking. 8 When Simon saw what had happened he fell at Jesus's knees and said, 'Go, Lord, leave me, sinner that I am!' 9 For he and all his companions were amazed at the catch they had made; 10 so too were his partners James and John, Zebedee's sons. 'Do not be afraid,' said Jesus to Simon; 'from now on you will be catching people.' 11 As soon as they had brought the boats to land, they left everything and followed him.

12 He was once in a certain town where there was a man covered with leprosy; when he saw Jesus, he threw himself to the ground and begged his help. 'Sir,' he said, 'if only you will, you can make me clean.' 13 Jesus stretched out his hand and touched him, saying, 'I will; be clean.' The leprosy left him immediately. 14 Jesus then instructed him not to tell anybody. 'But go,' he said, 'show yourself to the priest, and make the offering laid down by Moses for your cleansing; that will certify the cure.' 15 But the talk about him spread ever wider, so that great crowds kept gathering to hear him and to be cured of their ailments. 16 And from time to time he would withdraw to remote places for prayer.

17 One day as he was teaching, Pharisees and teachers of the law were sitting round him. People had come from every village in Galilee and from Judaea and Jerusalem, and the power of the Lord was with him to heal the sick. 18 Some men appeared carrying a paralysed man on a bed, and tried to bring him in and set him down in front of Jesus.

---

g Or the Christ h Other ancient authorities read Galilee i Gk he
j The terms leper and leprosy can refer to several diseases
k Gk him l Other ancient authorities read was present to heal them

5:17 Pharisees . . . Jerusalem: some witnesses read Pharisees and teachers of the law, who had come from every village in Galilee and from Judaea and Jerusalem, were sitting round him.

38 After he left the synagogue, he entered the house of Simon. Simon's mother-in-law was afflicted with a severe fever, and they interceded with him about her. 39 He stood over her, rebuked the fever, and it left her. She got up immediately and waited on them.

40 At sunset, all who had people sick with various diseases brought them to him. He laid his hands on each of them and cured them. 41 And demons also came out from many, shouting, "You are the Son of God." But he rebuked them and did not allow them to speak because they knew that he was the Messiah.

42 At daybreak, Jesus left and went to a deserted place. The crowds went looking for him, and when they came to him, they tried to prevent him from leaving them. 43 But he said to them, "To the other towns also I must proclaim the good news of the kingdom of God, because for this purpose I have been sent." 44 And he was preaching in the synagogues of Judea.

5 While the crowd was pressing in on Jesus and listening to the word of God, he was standing by the Lake of Gennesaret. 2 He saw two boats there alongside the lake; the fishermen had disembarked and were washing their nets. 3 Getting into one of the boats, the one belonging to Simon, he asked him to put out a short distance from the shore. Then he sat down and taught the crowds from the boat. 4 After he had finished speaking, he said to Simon, "Put out into deep water and lower your nets for a catch." 5 Simon said in reply, "Master, we have worked hard all night and have caught nothing, but at your command I will lower the nets." 6 When they had done this, they caught a great number of fish and their nets were tearing. 7 They signaled to their partners in the other boat to come to help them. They came and filled both boats so that they were in danger of sinking. 8 When Simon Peter saw this, he fell at the knees of Jesus and said, "Depart from me, Lord, for I am a sinful man." 9 For astonishment at the catch of fish they had made seized him and all those with him, 10 and likewise James and John, the sons of Zebedee, who were partners of Simon. Jesus said to Simon, "Do not be afraid; from now on you will be catching men." 11 When they brought their boats to the shore, they left everything and followed him.

12 Now there was a man full of leprosy in one of the towns where he was; and when he saw Jesus, he fell prostrate, pleaded with him, and said, "Lord, if you wish, you can make me clean." 13 Jesus stretched out his hand, touched him, and said, "I do will it. Be made clean." And the leprosy left him immediately. 14 Then he ordered him not to tell anyone, but "Go, show yourself to the priest and offer for your cleansing what Moses prescribed; that will be proof for them." 15 The report about him spread all the more, and great crowds assembled to listen to him and to be cured of their ailments, 16 but he would withdraw to deserted places to pray.

17 One day as Jesus was teaching, Pharisees and teachers of the law were sitting there who had come from every village of Galilee and Judea and Jerusalem, and the power of the Lord was with him for healing. 18 And some men brought on a stretcher a man who was paralyzed; they were trying to bring him in and set [him] in his presence. 19 But

38 Leaving the synagogue he went to Simon's house. Now Simon's mother-in-law was in the grip of a high fever and they asked him to do something for her. 39 Standing over her he rebuked the fever and it left her. And she immediately got up and began to serve them.

40 At sunset all those who had friends suffering from diseases of one kind or another brought them to him, and laying his hands on each he cured them. 41 Devils too came out of many people, shouting, 'You are the Son of God.' But he warned them and would not allow them to speak because they knew that he was the Christ.

42 When daylight came he left the house and made his way to a lonely place. The crowds went to look for him, and when they had caught up with him they wanted to prevent him leaving them, 43 but he answered, 'I must proclaim the good news of the kingdom of God to the other towns too, because that is what I was sent to do.' 44 And he continued his proclamation in the synagogues of Judaea.

5 Now it happened that he was standing one day by the Lake of Gennesaret, with the crowd pressing round him listening to the word of God, 2 when he caught sight of two boats at the water's edge. The fishermen had got out of them and were washing their nets. 3 He got into one of the boats—it was Simon's—and asked him to put out a little from the shore. Then he sat down and taught the crowds from the boat.

4 When he had finished speaking he said to Simon, 'Put out into deep water and pay out your nets for a catch.' 5 Simon replied, 'Master, we worked hard all night long and caught nothing, but if you say so, I will pay out the nets.' 6 And when they had done this they netted such a huge number of fish that their nets began to tear, 7 so they signalled to their companions in the other boat to come and help them; when these came, they filled both boats to sinking point.

8 When Simon Peter saw this he fell at the knees of Jesus saying, 'Leave me, Lord; I am a sinful man.' 9 For he and all his companions were completely awestruck at the catch they had made; 10 so also were James and John, sons of Zebedee, who were Simon's partners. But Jesus said to Simon, 'Do not be afraid; from now on it is people you will be catching.' 11 Then, bringing their boats back to land they left everything and followed him.

12 Now it happened that Jesus was in one of the towns when suddenly a man appeared, covered with a skin-disease. Seeing Jesus he fell on his face and implored him saying, 'Sir, if you are willing you can cleanse me.' 13 He stretched out his hand, and touched him saying, 'I am willing. Be cleansed.' At once the skin-disease left him. 14 He ordered him to tell no one, 'But go and show yourself to the priest and make the offering for your cleansing just as Moses prescribed, as evidence to them.'

15 But the news of him kept spreading, and large crowds would gather to hear him and to have their illnesses cured, 16 but he would go off to some deserted place and pray.

17 Now it happened that he was teaching one day, and Pharisees and teachers of the Law, who had come from every village in Galilee, from Judaea and from Jerusalem, were sitting there. And the power of the Lord was there so that he should heal. 18 And now some men appeared, bringing on a bed a paralysed man whom they were trying to bring in and lay down in front of him. 19 But as they could

NEW REVISED STANDARD VERSION

19 but finding no way to bring him in because of the crowd, they went up on the roof and let him down with his bed through the tiles into the middle of the crowd*m* in front of Jesus. 20 When he saw their faith, he said, "Friend,*n* your sins are forgiven you." 21 Then the scribes and the Pharisees began to question, "Who is this who is speaking blasphemies? Who can forgive sins but God alone?" 22 When Jesus perceived their questionings, he answered them, "Why do you raise such questions in your hearts? 23 Which is easier, to say, 'Your sins are forgiven you,' or to say, 'Stand up and walk'? 24 But so that you may know that the Son of Man has authority on earth to forgive sins" — he said to the one who was paralyzed — "I say to you, stand up and take your bed and go to your home." 25 Immediately he stood up before them, took what he had been lying on, and went to his home, glorifying God. 26 Amazement seized all of them, and they glorified God and were filled with awe, saying, "We have seen strange things today."

27 After this he went out and saw a tax collector named Levi, sitting at the tax booth; and he said to him, "Follow me." 28 And he got up, left everything, and followed him.

29 Then Levi gave a great banquet for him in his house; and there was a large crowd of tax collectors and others sitting at the table*o* with them. 30 The Pharisees and their scribes were complaining to his disciples, saying, "Why do you eat and drink with tax collectors and sinners?" 31 Jesus answered, "Those who are well have no need of a physician, but those who are sick; 32 I have come to call not the righteous but sinners to repentance."

33 Then they said to him, "John's disciples, like the disciples of the Pharisees, frequently fast and pray, but your disciples eat and drink." 34 Jesus said to them, "You cannot make wedding guests fast while the bridegroom is with them, can you? 35 The days will come when the bridegroom will be taken away from them, and then they will fast in those days." 36 He also told them a parable: "No one tears a piece from a new garment and sews it on an old garment; otherwise the new will be torn, and the piece from the new will not match the old. 37 And no one puts new wine into old wineskins; otherwise the new wine will burst the skins and will be spilled, and the skins will be destroyed. 38 But new wine must be put into fresh wineskins. 39 And no one after drinking old wine desires new wine, but says, 'The old is good.' "*p*

6 One sabbath*q* while Jesus*r* was going through the grainfields, his disciples plucked some heads of grain, rubbed them in their hands, and ate them. 2 But some of the Pharisees said, "Why are you doing what is not lawful*s* on the sabbath?" 3 Jesus answered, "Have you not read what David did when he and his companions were hungry? 4 He entered the house of God and took and ate the bread of the Presence, which it is not lawful for any but the priests to eat, and gave some to his companions?" 5 Then he said to them, "The Son of Man is lord of the sabbath."

6 On another sabbath he entered the synagogue and taught, and there was a man there whose right hand was withered. 7 The scribes and the Pharisees watched him to see whether he would cure on the sabbath, so that they might find an accusation against him. 8 Even though he knew what they were thinking, he said to the man who had the withered hand, "Come and stand here." He got up and stood there. 9 Then Jesus said to them, "I ask you, is it

REVISED ENGLISH BIBLE

19 Finding no way to do so because of the crowd, they went up onto the roof and let him down through the tiling, bed and all, into the middle of the company in front of Jesus. 20 When Jesus saw their faith, he said to the man, 'Your sins are forgiven you.'

21 The scribes and Pharisees began asking among themselves, 'Who is this fellow with his blasphemous talk? Who but God alone can forgive sins?' 22 But Jesus knew what they were thinking and answered them: 'Why do you harbour these thoughts? 23 Is it easier to say, "Your sins are forgiven you," or to say, "Stand up and walk"? 24 But to convince you that the Son of Man has the right on earth to forgive sins' — he turned to the paralysed man — 'I say to you, stand up, take your bed, and go home.' 25 At once the man rose to his feet before their eyes, took up the bed he had been lying on, and went home praising God. 26 They were all lost in amazement and praised God; filled with awe they said, 'The things we have seen today are beyond belief!'

27 Later, when he went out, he saw a tax-collector, Levi by name, at his seat in the custom-house, and said to him, 'Follow me.' 28 Leaving everything, he got up and followed him.

29 Afterwards Levi held a big reception in his house for Jesus; among the guests was a large party of tax-collectors and others. 30 The Pharisees, some of whom were scribes, complained to his disciples: 'Why', they said, 'do you eat and drink with tax-collectors and sinners?' 31 Jesus answered them: 'It is not the healthy that need a doctor, but the sick; 32 I have not come to call the virtuous but sinners to repentance.'

33 Then they said to him, 'John's disciples are much given to fasting and the practice of prayer, and so are the disciples of the Pharisees; but yours eat and drink.' 34 Jesus replied, 'Can you make the bridegroom's friends fast while the bridegroom is with them? 35 But the time will come when the bridegroom will be taken away from them; that will be the time for them to fast.'

36 He told them this parable also: 'No one tears a piece from a new garment to patch an old one; if he does, he will have made a hole in the new garment, and the patch taken from the new will not match the old. 37 No one puts new wine into old wineskins; if he does, the new wine will burst the skins, the wine will spill out, and the skins be ruined. 38 New wine goes into fresh skins! 39 And no one after drinking old wine wants new; for he says, "The old wine is good." '

6 One sabbath he was going through the cornfields, and his disciples were plucking the ears of corn, rubbing them in their hands, and eating them. 2 Some Pharisees said, 'Why are you doing what is forbidden on the sabbath?' 3 Jesus answered, 'Have you not read what David did when he and his men were hungry? 4 He went into the house of God and took the sacred bread to eat and gave it to his men, though only the priests are allowed to eat it.' 5 He also said to them, 'The Son of Man is master of the sabbath.'

6 On another sabbath he had gone to synagogue and was teaching. There was a man in the congregation whose right arm was withered; 7 and the scribes and Pharisees were on the watch to see whether Jesus would heal him on the sabbath, so that they could find a charge to bring against him. 8 But he knew what was in their minds and said to the man with the withered arm, 'Stand up and come out here.' So he stood up and came out. 9 Then Jesus said to them, 'I put this

---

m Gk *into the midst* *n* Gk *Man* *o* Gk *reclining* *p* Other ancient authorities read *better*; others lack verse 39 *q* Other ancient authorities read *On the second first sabbath* *r* Gk *he* *s* Other ancient authorities add *to do*

not finding a way to bring him in because of the crowd, they went up on the roof and lowered him on the stretcher through the tiles into the middle in front of Jesus. 20 When he saw their faith, he said, "As for you, your sins are forgiven." 21 Then the scribes and Pharisees began to ask themselves, "Who is this who speaks blasphemies? Who but God alone can forgive sins?" 22 Jesus knew their thoughts and said to them in reply, "What are you thinking in your hearts? 23 Which is easier, to say, 'Your sins are forgiven,' or to say, 'Rise and walk'? 24 But that you may know that the Son of Man has authority on earth to forgive sins" — he said to the man who was paralyzed, "I say to you, rise, pick up your stretcher, and go home." 25 He stood up immediately before them, picked up what he had been lying on, and went home, glorifying God. 26 Then astonishment seized them all and they glorified God, and, struck with awe, they said, "We have seen incredible things today."

27 After this he went out and saw a tax collector named Levi sitting at the customs post. He said to him, "Follow me." 28 And leaving everything behind, he got up and followed him. 29 Then Levi gave a great banquet for him in his house, and a large crowd of tax collectors and others were at table with them. 30 The Pharisees and their scribes complained to his disciples, saying, "Why do you eat and drink with tax collectors and sinners?" 31 Jesus said to them in reply, "Those who are healthy do not need a physician, but the sick do. 32 I have not come to call the righteous to repentance but sinners."

33 And they said to him, "The disciples of John fast often and offer prayers, and the disciples of the Pharisees do the same; but yours eat and drink." 34 Jesus answered them, "Can you make the wedding guests fast while the bridegroom is with them? 35 But the days will come, and when the bridegroom is taken away from them, then they will fast in those days." 36 And he also told them a parable. "No one tears a piece from a new cloak to patch an old one. Otherwise, he will tear the new and the piece from it will not match the old cloak. 37 Likewise, no one pours new wine into old wineskins. Otherwise, the new wine will burst the skins, and it will be spilled, and the skins will be ruined. 38 Rather, new wine must be poured into fresh wineskins. 39 [And] no one who has been drinking old wine desires new, for he says, 'The old is good.' "

6 While he was going through a field of grain on a sabbath, his disciples were picking the heads of grain, rubbing them in their hands, and eating them. 2 Some Pharisees said, "Why are you doing what is unlawful on the sabbath?" 3 Jesus said to them in reply, "Have you not read what David did when he and those [who were] with him were hungry? 4 [How] he went into the house of God, took the bread of offering, which only the priests could lawfully eat, ate of it, and shared it with his companions." 5 Then he said to them, "The Son of Man is lord of the sabbath."

6 On another sabbath he went into the synagogue and taught, and there was a man there whose right hand was withered. 7 The scribes and the Pharisees watched him closely to see if he would cure on the sabbath so that they might discover a reason to accuse him. 8 But he realized their intentions and said to the man with the withered hand, "Come up and stand before us." And he rose and stood there. 9 Then Jesus said to them, "I ask you, is it lawful to

find no way of getting the man through the crowd, they went up onto the top of the house and lowered him and his stretcher down through the tiles into the middle of the gathering, in front of Jesus. 20 Seeing their faith he said, 'My friend, your sins are forgiven you.' 21 The scribes and the Pharisees began to think this over. 'Who is this man, talking blasphemy? Who but God alone can forgive sins?' 22 But Jesus, aware of their thoughts, made them this reply, 'What are these thoughts you have in your hearts? 23 Which of these is easier: to say, "Your sins are forgiven you," or to say, "Get up and walk"? 24 But to prove to you that the Son of man has authority on earth to forgive sins,' — he said to the paralysed man — 'I order you: get up, and pick up your stretcher and go home.' 25 And immediately before their very eyes he got up, picked up what he had been lying on and went home praising God.

26 They were all astounded and praised God and were filled with awe, saying, 'We have seen strange things today.'

27 When he went out after this, he noticed a tax collector, Levi by name, sitting at the tax office, and said to him, 'Follow me.' 28 And leaving everything Levi got up and followed him.

29 In his honour Levi held a great reception in his house, and with them at table was a large gathering of tax collectors and others. 30 The Pharisees and their scribes complained to his disciples and said, 'Why do you eat and drink with tax collectors and sinners?' 31 Jesus said to them in reply, 'It is not those that are well who need the doctor, but the sick. 32 I have come to call not the upright but sinners to repentance.'

33 They then said to him, 'John's disciples are always fasting and saying prayers, and the disciples of the Pharisees, too, but yours go on eating and drinking.' 34 Jesus replied, 'Surely you cannot make the bridegroom's attendants fast while the bridegroom is still with them? 35 But the time will come when the bridegroom is taken away from them; then, in those days, they will fast.'

36 He also told them a parable, 'No one tears a piece from a new cloak to put it on an old cloak; otherwise, not only will the new one be torn, but the piece taken from the new will not match the old.

37 'And nobody puts new wine in old wineskins; otherwise, the new wine will burst the skins and run to waste, and the skins will be ruined. 38 No; new wine must be put in fresh skins. 39 And nobody who has been drinking old wine wants new. "The old is good," he says.'

6 It happened that one Sabbath he was walking through the cornfields, and his disciples were picking ears of corn, rubbing them in their hands and eating them. 2 Some of the Pharisees said, 'Why are you doing something that is forbidden on the Sabbath day?' 3 Jesus answered them, 'So you have not read what David did* when he and his followers were hungry — 4 how he went into the house of God and took the loaves of the offering and ate them and gave them to his followers, loaves which the priests alone are allowed to eat?' 5 And he said to them, 'The Son of man is master of the Sabbath.'

6 Now on another Sabbath he went into the synagogue and began to teach, and a man was present, and his right hand was withered. 7 The scribes and the Pharisees were watching him to see if he would cure somebody on the Sabbath, hoping to find something to charge him with. 8 But he knew their thoughts; and he said to the man with the withered hand, 'Get up and stand out in the middle!' And he came forward and stood there. 9 Then Jesus said to them,

lawful to do good or to do harm on the sabbath, to save life or to destroy it?" ¹⁰ After looking around at all of them, he said to him, "Stretch out your hand." He did so, and his hand was restored. ¹¹ But they were filled with fury and discussed with one another what they might do to Jesus.

12 Now during those days he went out to the mountain to pray; and he spent the night in prayer to God. ¹³ And when day came, he called his disciples and chose twelve of them, whom he also named apostles: ¹⁴ Simon, whom he named Peter, and his brother Andrew, and James, and John, and Philip, and Bartholomew, ¹⁵ and Matthew, and Thomas, and James son of Alphaeus, and Simon, who was called the Zealot, ¹⁶ and Judas son of James, and Judas Iscariot, who became a traitor.

17 He came down with them and stood on a level place, with a great crowd of his disciples and a great multitude of people from all Judea, Jerusalem, and the coast of Tyre and Sidon. ¹⁸ They had come to hear him and to be healed of their diseases; and those who were troubled with unclean spirits were cured. ¹⁹ And all in the crowd were trying to touch him, for power came out from him and healed all of them.

20 Then he looked up at his disciples and said:
"Blessed are you who are poor,
    for yours is the kingdom of God.
21 "Blessed are you who are hungry now,
    for you will be filled.
"Blessed are you who weep now,
    for you will laugh.
22 "Blessed are you when people hate you, and when they exclude you, revile you, and defame you[t] on account of the Son of Man. ²³ Rejoice in that day and leap for joy, for surely your reward is great in heaven; for that is what their ancestors did to the prophets.
24 "But woe to you who are rich,
    for you have received your consolation.
25 "Woe to you who are full now,
    for you will be hungry.
"Woe to you who are laughing now,
    for you will mourn and weep.
26 "Woe to you when all speak well of you, for that is what their ancestors did to the false prophets.

27 "But I say to you that listen, Love your enemies, do good to those who hate you, ²⁸ bless those who curse you, pray for those who abuse you. ²⁹ If anyone strikes you on the cheek, offer the other also; and from anyone who takes away your coat do not withhold even your shirt. ³⁰ Give to everyone who begs from you; and if anyone takes away your goods, do not ask for them again. ³¹ Do to others as you would have them do to you.

32 "If you love those who love you, what credit is that to you? For even sinners love those who love them. ³³ If you do good to those who do good to you, what credit is that to you? For even sinners do the same. ³⁴ If you lend to those from whom you hope to receive, what credit is that to you? Even sinners lend to sinners, to receive as much again. ³⁵ But love your enemies, do good, and lend, expecting nothing in return.[u] Your reward will be great, and you will be children of the Most High; for he is kind to the ungrateful and the wicked. ³⁶ Be merciful, just as your Father is merciful.

37 "Do not judge, and you will not be judged; do not condemn, and you will not be condemned. Forgive, and you will be forgiven; ³⁸ give, and it will be given to you. A

question to you: is it permitted to do good or to do evil on the sabbath, to save life or to destroy it?' ¹⁰ He looked round at them all, and then he said to the man, 'Stretch out your arm.' He did so, and his arm was restored. ¹¹ But they totally failed to understand, and began to discuss with one another what they could do to Jesus.

12 During this time he went out one day into the hill-country to pray, and spent the night in prayer to God. ¹³ When day broke he called his disciples to him, and from among them he chose twelve and named them apostles: ¹⁴ Simon, to whom he gave the name Peter, and Andrew his brother, James and John, Philip and Bartholomew, ¹⁵ Matthew and Thomas, James son of Alphaeus, and Simon who was called the Zealot, ¹⁶ Judas son of James, and Judas Iscariot who turned traitor.

17 He came down the hill with them and stopped on some level ground where a large crowd of his disciples had gathered, and with them great numbers of people from Jerusalem and all Judaea and from the coastal region of Tyre and Sidon, who had come to listen to him, and to be cured of their diseases. ¹⁸ Those who were troubled with unclean spirits were healed; ¹⁹ and everyone in the crowd was trying to touch him, because power went out from him and cured them all.

20 TURNING to his disciples he began to speak:
'Blessed are you who are in need;
    the kingdom of God is yours.
21 Blessed are you who now go hungry;
    you will be satisfied.
Blessed are you who weep now;
    you will laugh.
22 'Blessed are you when people hate you and ostracize you, when they insult you and slander your very name, because of the Son of Man. ²³ On that day exult and dance for joy, for you have a rich reward in heaven; that is how their fathers treated the prophets.
24 'But alas for you who are rich;
    you have had your time of happiness.
25 Alas for you who are well fed now;
    you will go hungry.
Alas for you who laugh now;
    you will mourn and weep.
26 Alas for you when all speak well of you;
    that is how their fathers treated the false prophets.

27 'But to you who are listening I say: Love your enemies; do good to those who hate you; ²⁸ bless those who curse you; pray for those who treat you spitefully. ²⁹ If anyone hits you on the cheek, offer the other also; if anyone takes your coat, let him have your shirt as well. ³⁰ Give to everyone who asks you; if anyone takes what is yours, do not demand it back.

31 'Treat others as you would like them to treat you. ³² If you love only those who love you, what credit is that to you? Even sinners love those who love them. ³³ Again, if you do good only to those who do good to you, what credit is there in that? Even sinners do as much. ³⁴ And if you lend only where you expect to be repaid, what credit is there in that? Even sinners lend to each other to be repaid in full. ³⁵ But you must love your enemies and do good, and lend without expecting any return; and you will have a rich reward: you will be sons of the Most High, because he himself is kind to the ungrateful and the wicked. ³⁶ Be compassionate, as your Father is compassionate.

37 'Do not judge, and you will not be judged; do not condemn, and you will not be condemned; pardon, and you will be pardoned; ³⁸ give, and gifts will be given you. Good

---

[t] Gk *cast out your name as evil*   [u] Other ancient authorities read *despairing of no one*

do good on the sabbath rather than to do evil, to save life rather than to destroy it?" 10 Looking around at them all, he then said to him, "Stretch out your hand." He did so and his hand was restored. 11 But they became enraged and discussed together what they might do to Jesus.

12 In those days he departed to the mountain to pray, and he spent the night in prayer to God. 13 When day came, he called his disciples to himself, and from them he chose Twelve, whom he also named apostles: 14 Simon, whom he named Peter, and his brother Andrew, James, John, Philip, Bartholomew, 15 Matthew, Thomas, James the son of Alphaeus, Simon who was called a Zealot, 16 and Judas the son of James, and Judas Iscariot, who became a traitor.

17 And he came down with them and stood on a stretch of level ground. A great crowd of his disciples and a large number of the people from all Judea and Jerusalem and the coastal region of Tyre and Sidon 18 came to hear him and to be healed of their diseases; and even those who were tormented by unclean spirits were cured. 19 Everyone in the crowd sought to touch him because power came forth from him and healed them all.

20 And raising his eyes toward his disciples he said:

"Blessed are you who are poor,
  for the kingdom of God is yours.
21 Blessed are you who are now hungry,
  for you will be satisfied.
Blessed are you who are now weeping,
  for you will laugh.
22 Blessed are you when people hate you,
  and when they exclude and insult you,
  and denounce your name as evil
  on account of the Son of Man.

23 Rejoice and leap for joy on that day! Behold, your reward will be great in heaven. For their ancestors treated the prophets in the same way.

24 But woe to you who are rich,
  for you have received your consolation.
25 But woe to you who are filled now,
  for you will be hungry.
Woe to you who laugh now,
  for you will grieve and weep.
26 Woe to you when all speak well of you,
  for their ancestors treated the false prophets in
    this way.

27 "But to you who hear I say, love your enemies, do good to those who hate you, 28 bless those who curse you, pray for those who mistreat you. 29 To the person who strikes you on one cheek, offer the other one as well, and from the person who takes your cloak, do not withhold even your tunic. 30 Give to everyone who asks of you, and from the one who takes what is yours do not demand it back. 31 Do to others as you would have them do to you. 32 For if you love those who love you, what credit is that to you? Even sinners love those who love them. 33 And if you do good to those who do good to you, what credit is that to you? Even sinners do the same. 34 If you lend money to those from whom you expect repayment, what credit [is] that to you? Even sinners lend to sinners, and get back the same amount. 35 But rather, love your enemies and do good to them, and lend expecting nothing back; then your reward will be great and you will be children of the Most High, for he himself is kind to the ungrateful and the wicked. 36 Be merciful, just as [also] your Father is merciful.

37 "Stop judging and you will not be judged. Stop condemning and you will not be condemned. Forgive and you will be forgiven. 38 Give and gifts will be given to you; a

'I put it to you: is it permitted on the Sabbath to do good, or to do evil; to save life, or to destroy it?' 10 Then he looked round at them all and said to the man, 'Stretch out your hand.' He did so, and his hand was restored. 11 But they were furious and began to discuss the best way of dealing with Jesus.

12 Now it happened in those days that he went onto the mountain to pray; and he spent the whole night in prayer to God. 13 When day came he summoned his disciples and picked out twelve of them; he called them 'apostles': 14 Simon whom he called Peter, and his brother Andrew, James, John, Philip, Bartholomew, 15 Matthew, Thomas, James son of Alphaeus, Simon called the Zealot, 16 Judas son of James, and Judas Iscariot who became a traitor.

17 He then came down with them and stopped at a piece of level ground where there was a large gathering of his disciples, with a great crowd of people from all parts of Judaea and Jerusalem and the coastal region of Tyre and Sidon 18 who had come to hear him and to be cured of their diseases. People tormented by unclean spirits were also cured, 19 and everyone in the crowd was trying to touch him because power came out of him that cured them all.

20 Then fixing his eyes on his disciples he said: u

How blessed are you who are poor: the kingdom of
    God is yours.
21 Blessed are you who are hungry now: you shall
    have your fill.
Blessed are you who are weeping now: you shall
    laugh.

22 'Blessed are you when people hate you, drive you out, abuse you, denounce your name as criminal, on account of the Son of man. 23 Rejoice when that day comes and dance for joy, look! — your reward will be great in heaven. This was the way their ancestors treated the prophets.

24 But alas for you who are rich: you are having your
    consolation now.
25 Alas for you who have plenty to eat now: you shall
    go hungry.
Alas for you who are laughing now: you shall
    mourn and weep.

26 'Alas for you when everyone speaks well of you! This was the way their ancestors treated the false prophets.

27 'But I say this to you who are listening: Love your enemies, do good to those who hate you, 28 bless those who curse you, pray for those who treat you badly. 29 To anyone who slaps you on one cheek, present the other cheek as well; to anyone who takes your cloak from you, do not refuse your tunic. 30 Give to everyone who asks you, and do not ask for your property back from someone who takes it. 31 Treat others as you would like people to treat you. 32 If you love those who love you, what credit can you expect? Even sinners love those who love them. 33 And if you do good to those who do good to you, what credit can you expect? For even sinners do that much. 34 And if you lend to those from whom you hope to get money back, what credit can you expect? Even sinners lend to sinners to get back the same amount. 35 Instead, love your enemies and do good to them, and lend without any hope of return. You will have a great reward, and you will be children of the Most High, for he himself is kind to the ungrateful and the wicked.

36 'Be compassionate just as your Father is compassionate. 37 Do not judge, and you will not be judged; do not condemn, and you will not be condemned; forgive, and you will be forgiven. 38 Give, and there will be gifts for you: a

u 6 Mt 5:1.

NEW REVISED STANDARD VERSION	REVISED ENGLISH BIBLE

good measure, pressed down, shaken together, running over, will be put into your lap; for the measure you give will be the measure you get back."

39 He also told them a parable: "Can a blind person guide a blind person? Will not both fall into a pit? 40 A disciple is not above the teacher, but everyone who is fully qualified will be like the teacher. 41 Why do you see the speck in your neighbor's^v eye, but do not notice the log in your own eye? 42 Or how can you say to your neighbor,^{w} 'Friend,^{w} let me take out the speck in your eye,' when you yourself do not see the log in your own eye? You hypocrite, first take the log out of your own eye, and then you will see clearly to take the speck out of your neighbor's^v eye.

43 "No good tree bears bad fruit, nor again does a bad tree bear good fruit; 44 for each tree is known by its own fruit. Figs are not gathered from thorns, nor are grapes picked from a bramble bush. 45 The good person out of the good treasure of the heart produces good, and the evil person out of evil treasure produces evil; for it is out of the abundance of the heart that the mouth speaks.

46 "Why do you call me 'Lord, Lord,' and do not do what I tell you? 47 I will show you what someone is like who comes to me, hears my words, and acts on them. 48 That one is like a man building a house, who dug deeply and laid the foundation on rock; when a flood arose, the river burst against that house but could not shake it, because it had been well built.^{x} 49 But the one who hears and does not act is like a man who built a house on the ground without a foundation. When the river burst against it, immediately it fell, and great was the ruin of that house."

7 After Jesus^y had finished all his sayings in the hearing of the people, he entered Capernaum. 2 A centurion there had a slave whom he valued highly, and who was ill and close to death. 3 When he heard about Jesus, he sent some Jewish elders to him, asking him to come and heal his slave. 4 When they came to Jesus, they appealed to him earnestly, saying, "He is worthy of having you do this for him, 5 for he loves our people, and it is he who built our synagogue for us." 6 And Jesus went with them, but when he was not far from the house, the centurion sent friends to say to him, "Lord, do not trouble yourself, for I am not worthy to have you come under my roof; 7 therefore I did not presume to come to you. But only speak the word, and let my servant be healed. 8 For I also am a man set under authority, with soldiers under me; and I say to one, 'Go,' and he goes, and to another, 'Come,' and he comes, and to my slave, 'Do this,' and the slave does it." 9 When Jesus heard this he was amazed at him, and turning to the crowd that followed him, he said, "I tell you, not even in Israel have I found such faith." 10 When those who had been sent returned to the house, they found the slave in good health.

11 Soon afterwards^z he went to a town called Nain, and his disciples and a large crowd went with him. 12 As he approached the gate of the town, a man who had died was being carried out. He was his mother's only son, and she was a widow; and with her was a large crowd from the town. 13 When the Lord saw her, he had compassion for her and said to her, "Do not weep." 14 Then he came forward and touched the bier, and the bearers stood still. And he said, "Young man, I say to you, rise!" 15 The dead man sat up and began to speak, and Jesus^y gave him to his mother. 16 Fear seized all of them; and they glorified God, saying, "A great prophet has risen among us!" and "God has looked

measure, pressed and shaken down and running over, will be poured into your lap; for whatever measure you deal out to others will be dealt to you in turn.'

39 He also spoke to them in a parable: 'Can one blind man guide another? Will not both fall into the ditch? 40 No pupil ranks above his teacher; fully trained he can but reach his teacher's level.

41 'Why do you look at the speck in your brother's eye, with never a thought for the plank in your own? 42 How can you say to your brother, "Brother, let me take the speck out of your eye," when you are blind to the plank in your own? You hypocrite! First take the plank out of your own eye, and then you will see clearly to take the speck out of your brother's.

43 'There is no such thing as a good tree producing bad fruit, nor yet a bad tree producing good fruit. 44 Each tree is known by its own fruit: you do not gather figs from brambles or pick grapes from thistles. 45 Good people produce good from the store of good within themselves; and evil people produce evil from the evil within them. For the words that the mouth utters come from the overflowing of the heart.

46 'Why do you call me "Lord, Lord"—and never do what I tell you? 47 Everyone who comes to me and hears my words and acts on them—I will show you what he is like. 48 He is like a man building a house, who dug deep and laid the foundations on rock. When the river was in flood, it burst upon that house, but could not shift it, because it had been soundly built. 49 But he who hears and does not act is like a man who built his house on the soil without foundations. As soon as the river burst upon it, the house collapsed, and fell with a great crash.'

7 WHEN he had finished addressing the people, he entered Capernaum. 2 A centurion there had a servant whom he valued highly, but the servant was ill and near to death. 3 Hearing about Jesus, he sent some Jewish elders to ask him to come and save his servant's life. 4 They approached Jesus and made an urgent appeal to him: 'He deserves this favour from you,' they said, 5 'for he is a friend of our nation and it is he who built us our synagogue.' 6 Jesus went with them; but when he was not far from the house, the centurion sent friends with this message: 'Do not trouble further, sir; I am not worthy to have you come under my roof, 7 and that is why I did not presume to approach you in person. But say the word and my servant will be cured. 8 I know, for I am myself under orders, with soldiers under me. I say to one, "Go," and he goes; to another, "Come here," and he comes; and to my servant, "Do this," and he does it.' 9 When Jesus heard this, he was astonished, and, turning to the crowd that was following him, he said, 'I tell you, not even in Israel have I found such faith.' 10 When the messengers returned to the house, they found the servant in good health.

11 Afterwards Jesus went to a town called Nain, accompanied by his disciples and a large crowd. 12 As he approached the gate of the town he met a funeral. The dead man was the only son of his widowed mother; and many of the townspeople were there with her. 13 When the Lord saw her his heart went out to her, and he said, 'Do not weep.' 14 He stepped forward and laid his hand on the bier; and the bearers halted. Then he spoke: 'Young man, I tell you to get up.' 15 The dead man sat up and began to speak; and Jesus restored him to his mother. 16 Everyone was filled with awe and praised God. 'A great prophet has arisen among us,' they said; 'God has shown his care for his people.' 17 The

---

^{v} Gk brother's ^{w} Gk brother ^{x} Other ancient authorities read *founded upon the rock* ^{y} Gk he ^{z} Other ancient authorities read *Next day*

NEW AMERICAN BIBLE	NEW JERUSALEM BIBLE

good measure, packed together, shaken down, and overflowing, will be poured into your lap. For the measure with which you measure will in return be measured out to you." 39 And he told them a parable, "Can a blind person guide a blind person? Will not both fall into a pit? 40 No disciple is superior to the teacher; but when fully trained, every disciple will be like his teacher. 41 Why do you notice the splinter in your brother's eye, but do not perceive the wooden beam in your own? 42 How can you say to your brother, 'Brother, let me remove that splinter in your eye,' when you do not even notice the wooden beam in your own eye? You hypocrite! Remove the wooden beam from your eye first; then you will see clearly to remove the splinter in your brother's eye.

43 "A good tree does not bear rotten fruit, nor does a rotten tree bear good fruit. 44 For every tree is known by its own fruit. For people do not pick figs from thornbushes, nor do they gather grapes from brambles. 45 A good person out of the store of goodness in his heart produces good, but an evil person out of a store of evil produces evil; for from the fullness of the heart the mouth speaks.

46 "Why do you call me, 'Lord, Lord,' but not do what I command? 47 I will show you what someone is like who comes to me, listens to my words, and acts on them. 48 That one is like a person building a house, who dug deeply and laid the foundation on rock; when the flood came, the river burst against that house but could not shake it because it had been well built. 49 But the one who listens and does not act is like a person who built a house on the ground without a foundation. When the river burst against it, it collapsed at once and was completely destroyed."

7 When he had finished all his words to the people, he entered Capernaum. 2 A centurion there had a slave who was ill and about to die, and he was valuable to him. 3 When he heard about Jesus, he sent elders of the Jews to him, asking him to come and save the life of his slave. 4 They approached Jesus and strongly urged him to come, saying, "He deserves to have you do this for him, 5 for he loves our nation and he built the synagogue for us." 6 And Jesus went with them, but when he was only a short distance from the house, the centurion sent friends to tell him, "Lord, do not trouble yourself, for I am not worthy to have you enter under my roof. 7 Therefore, I did not consider myself worthy to come to you; but say the word and let my servant be healed. 8 For I too am a person subject to authority, with soldiers subject to me. And I say to one, 'Go,' and he goes; and to another, 'Come here,' and he comes; and to my slave, 'Do this,' and he does it." 9 When Jesus heard this he was amazed at him and, turning, said to the crowd following him, "I tell you, not even in Israel have I found such faith." 10 When the messengers returned to the house, they found the slave in good health.

11 Soon afterward he journeyed to a city called Nain, and his disciples and a large crowd accompanied him. 12 As he drew near to the gate of the city, a man who had died was being carried out, the only son of his mother, and she was a widow. A large crowd from the city was with her. 13 When the Lord saw her, he was moved with pity for her and said to her, "Do not weep." 14 He stepped forward and touched the coffin; at this the bearers halted, and he said, "Young man, I tell you, arise!" 15 The dead man sat up and began to speak, and Jesus gave him to his mother. 16 Fear seized them all, and they glorified God, exclaiming, "A great prophet has arisen in our midst," and "God has visited

full measure, pressed down, shaken together, and overflowing, will be poured into your lap; because the standard you use will be the standard used for you.'

39 He also told them a parable, 'Can one blind person guide another? Surely both will fall into a pit? 40 Disciple is not superior to teacher; but fully trained disciple will be like teacher. 41 Why do you observe the splinter in your brother's eye and never notice the great log in your own? 42 How can you say to your brother, "Brother, let me take out that splinter in your eye," when you cannot see the great log in your own? Hypocrite! Take the log out of your own eye first, and then you will see clearly enough to take out the splinter in your brother's eye.

43 'There is no sound tree that produces rotten fruit, nor again a rotten tree that produces sound fruit. 44 Every tree can be told by its own fruit: people do not pick figs from thorns, nor gather grapes from brambles. 45 Good people draw what is good from the store of goodness in their hearts; bad people draw what is bad from the store of badness. For the words of the mouth flow out of what fills the heart.

46 'Why do you call me, "Lord, Lord" and not do what I say?

47 'Everyone who comes to me and listens to my words and acts on them — I will show you what such a person is like. 48 Such a person is like the man who, when he built a house, dug, and dug deep, and laid the foundations on rock; when the river was in flood it bore down on that house but could not shake it, it was so well built. 49 But someone who listens and does nothing is like the man who built a house on soil, with no foundations; as soon as the river bore down on it, it collapsed; and what a ruin that house became!'

7 When he had come to the end of all he wanted the people to hear, he went into Capernaum. 2 A centurion there had a servant, a favourite of his, who was sick and near death. 3 Having heard about Jesus he sent some Jewish elders to him to ask him to come and heal his servant. 4 When they came to Jesus they pleaded earnestly with him saying, 'He deserves this of you, 5 because he is well disposed towards our people; he built us our synagogue himself.' 6 So Jesus went with them, and was not very far from the house when the centurion sent word to him by some friends to say to him, 'Sir, do not put yourself to any trouble because I am not worthy to have you under my roof; 7 and that is why I did not presume to come to you myself; let my boy be cured by your giving the word. 8 For I am under authority myself, and have soldiers under me; and I say to one man, "Go," and he goes; to another, "Come here," and he comes; to my servant, "Do this," and he does it.' 9 When Jesus heard these words he was astonished at him and, turning round, said to the crowd following him, 'I tell you, not even in Israel have I found faith as great as this.' 10 And when the messengers got back to the house they found the servant in perfect health.

11 It happened that soon afterwards he went to a town called Nain, accompanied by his disciples and a great number of people. 12 Now when he was near the gate of the town there was a dead man being carried out, the only son of his mother, and she was a widow. And a considerable number of the townspeople was with her. 13 When the Lord saw her he felt sorry for her and said to her, 'Don't cry.' 14 Then he went up and touched the bier and the bearers stood still, and he said, 'Young man, I tell you: get up.' 15 And the dead man sat up and began to talk, and Jesus *gave him to his mother.*v 16 Everyone was filled with awe and glorified God saying, 'A great prophet has risen up among us; God

v 7 1 K 17:23.

favorably on his people!" 17 This word about him spread throughout Judea and all the surrounding country.

18 The disciples of John reported all these things to him. So John summoned two of his disciples 19 and sent them to the Lord to ask, "Are you the one who is to come, or are we to wait for another?" 20 When the men had come to him, they said, "John the Baptist has sent us to you to ask, 'Are you the one who is to come, or are we to wait for another?' " 21 Jesus a had just then cured many people of diseases, plagues, and evil spirits, and had given sight to many who were blind. 22 And he answered them, "Go and tell John what you have seen and heard: the blind receive their sight, the lame walk, the lepers b are cleansed, the deaf hear, the dead are raised, the poor have good news brought to them. 23 And blessed is anyone who takes no offense at me."

24 When John's messengers had gone, Jesus c began to speak to the crowds about John: d "What did you go out into the wilderness to look at? A reed shaken by the wind? 25 What then did you go out to see? Someone e dressed in soft robes? Look, those who put on fine clothing and live in luxury are in royal palaces. 26 What then did you go out to see? A prophet? Yes, I tell you, and more than a prophet. 27 This is the one about whom it is written,

'See, I am sending my messenger ahead of you,
who will prepare your way before you.'

28 I tell you, among those born of women no one is greater than John; yet the least in the kingdom of God is greater than he." 29 (And all the people who heard this, including the tax collectors, acknowledged the justice of God, f because they had been baptized with John's baptism. 30 But by refusing to be baptized by him, the Pharisees and the lawyers rejected God's purpose for themselves.)

31 "To what then will I compare the people of this generation, and what are they like? 32 They are like children sitting in the marketplace and calling to one another,

'We played the flute for you, and you did not
dance;
we wailed, and you did not weep.'

33 For John the Baptist has come eating no bread and drinking no wine, and you say, 'He has a demon'; 34 the Son of Man has come eating and drinking, and you say, 'Look, a glutton and a drunkard, a friend of tax collectors and sinners!' 35 Nevertheless, wisdom is vindicated by all her children."

36 One of the Pharisees asked Jesus d to eat with him, and he went into the Pharisee's house and took his place at the table. 37 And a woman in the city, who was a sinner, having learned that he was eating in the Pharisee's house, brought an alabaster jar of ointment. 38 She stood behind him at his feet, weeping, and began to bathe his feet with her tears and to dry them with her hair. Then she continued kissing his feet and anointing them with the ointment. 39 Now when the Pharisee who had invited him saw it, he said to himself, "If this man were a prophet, he would have known who and what kind of woman this is who is touching him—that she is a sinner." 40 Jesus spoke up and said to him, "Simon, I have something to say to you." "Teacher," he replied, "Speak." 41 "A certain creditor had two debtors; one owed five hundred denarii, g and the other fifty. 42 When they could not pay, he canceled the debts for both of them. Now which of them will love him more?" 43 Simon

story of what he had done spread through the whole of Judaea and all the region around.

18 When John was informed of all this by his disciples, 19 he summoned two of them and sent them to the Lord with this question: 'Are you the one who is to come, or are we to expect someone else?' 20 The men made their way to Jesus and said, 'John the Baptist has sent us to ask you, "Are you the one who is to come, or are we to expect someone else?" ' 21 There and then he healed many sufferers from diseases, plagues, and evil spirits; and on many blind people he bestowed sight. 22 Then he gave them this answer: 'Go and tell John what you have seen and heard: the blind regain their sight, the lame walk, lepers are made clean, the deaf hear, the dead are raised to life, the poor are brought good news—23 and happy is he who does not find me an obstacle to faith.'

24 After John's messengers had left, Jesus began to speak about him to the crowds: 'What did you go out into the wilderness to see? A reed swaying in the wind? 25 No? Then what did you go out to see? A man dressed in finery? Grand clothes and luxury are to be found in palaces. 26 But what did you go out to see? A prophet? Yes indeed, and far more than a prophet. 27 He is the man of whom scripture says,

Here is my herald, whom I send ahead of you,
and he will prepare your way before you.

28 'I tell you, among all who have been born, no one has been greater than John; yet the least in the kingdom of God is greater than he is.'

29 When they heard him, all the people, including the tax-collectors, acknowledged the goodness of God, for they had accepted John's baptism; 30 but the Pharisees and lawyers, who had refused his baptism, rejected God's purpose for themselves.

31 'How can I describe the people of this generation? What are they like? 32 They are like children sitting in the market-place and calling to each other,

We piped for you and you would not dance.
We lamented, and you would not mourn.

33 'For John the Baptist came, neither eating bread nor drinking wine, and you say, "He is possessed." 34 The Son of Man came, eating and drinking, and you say, "Look at him! A glutton and a drinker, a friend of tax-collectors and sinners!" 35 And yet God's wisdom is proved right by all who are her children.'

36 One of the Pharisees invited Jesus to a meal; he went to the Pharisee's house and took his place at table. 37 A woman who was living an immoral life in the town had learned that Jesus was a guest in the Pharisee's house and had brought oil of myrrh in a small flask. 38 She took her place behind him, by his feet, weeping. His feet were wet with her tears and she wiped them with her hair, kissing them and anointing them with the myrrh. 39 When his host the Pharisee saw this he said to himself, 'If this man were a real prophet, he would know who this woman is and what a bad character she is.' 40 Jesus took him up: 'Simon,' he said, 'I have something to say to you.' 'What is it, Teacher?' he asked. 41 'Two men were in debt to a moneylender: one owed him five hundred silver pieces, the other fifty. 42 As they did not have the means to pay he cancelled both debts. Now, which will love him more?'

---

a Gk He   b The terms leper and leprosy can refer to several diseases
c Gk he   d Gk him   e Or Why then did you go out? To see
someone   f Or praised God   g The denarius was the usual day's
wage for a laborer

his people." 17 This report about him spread through the whole of Judea and in all the surrounding region.

18 The disciples of John told him about all these things. John summoned two of his disciples 19 and sent them to the Lord to ask, "Are you the one who is to come, or should we look for another?" 20 When the men came to him, they said, "John the Baptist has sent us to you to ask, 'Are you the one who is to come, or should we look for another?' " 21 At that time he cured many of their diseases, sufferings, and evil spirits; he also granted sight to many who were blind. 22 And he said to them in reply, "Go and tell John what you have seen and heard: the blind regain their sight, the lame walk, lepers are cleansed, the deaf hear, the dead are raised, the poor have the good news proclaimed to them. 23 And blessed is the one who takes no offense at me."

24 When the messengers of John had left, Jesus began to speak to the crowds about John. "What did you go out to the desert to see — a reed swayed by the wind? 25 Then what did you go out to see? Someone dressed in fine garments? Those who dress luxuriously and live sumptuously are found in royal palaces. 26 Then what did you go out to see? A prophet? Yes, I tell you, and more than a prophet. 27 This is the one about whom scripture says:

'Behold, I am sending my messenger ahead
    of you,
  he will prepare your way before you.'

28 I tell you, among those born of women, no one is greater than John; yet the least in the kingdom of God is greater than he." 29 (All the people who listened, including the tax collectors, and who were baptized with the baptism of John, acknowledged the righteousness of God; 30 but the Pharisees and scholars of the law, who were not baptized by him, rejected the plan of God for themselves.)

31 "Then to what shall I compare the people of this generation? What are they like? 32 They are like children who sit in the marketplace and call to one another,

'We played the flute for you, but you did
    not dance.
  We sang a dirge, but you did not weep.'

33 For John the Baptist came neither eating food nor drinking wine, and you said, 'He is possessed by a demon.' 34 The Son of Man came eating and drinking and you said, 'Look, he is a glutton and a drunkard, a friend of tax collectors and sinners.' 35 But wisdom is vindicated by all her children."

36 A Pharisee invited him to dine with him, and he entered the Pharisee's house and reclined at table. 37 Now there was a sinful woman in the city who learned that he was at table in the house of the Pharisee. Bringing an alabaster flask of ointment, 38 she stood behind him at his feet weeping and began to bathe his feet with her tears. Then she wiped them with her hair, kissed them, and anointed them with the ointment. 39 When the Pharisee who had invited him saw this he said to himself, "If this man were a prophet, he would know who and what sort of woman this is who is touching him, that she is a sinner." 40 Jesus said to him in reply, "Simon, I have something to say to you." "Tell me, teacher," he said. 41 "Two people were in debt to a certain creditor; one owed five hundred days' wages and the other owed fifty. 42 Since they were unable to repay the debt, he forgave it for both. Which of them will love him more?"

has visited his people.' 17 And this view of him spread throughout Judaea and all over the countryside.

18 The disciples of John gave him all this news, and John, summoning two of his disciples, 19 sent them to the Lord to ask, 'Are you the one who is to come, or are we to expect someone else?' 20 When the men reached Jesus they said, 'John the Baptist has sent us to you to ask, "Are you the one who is to come or are we to expect someone else?" ' 21 At that very time he cured many people of diseases and afflictions and of evil spirits, and gave the gift of sight to many who were blind. 22 Then he gave the messengers their answer, 'Go back and tell John what you have seen and heard: the blind see again, the lame walk, those suffering from virulent skin-diseases are cleansed, and the deaf hear, the dead are raised to life, the good news is proclaimed to the poor; 23 and blessed is anyone who does not find me a cause of falling.'

24 When John's messengers had gone he began to talk to the people about John, 25 'What did you go out into the desert to see? A reed swaying in the breeze? No! Then what did you go out to see? A man dressed in fine clothes? Look, those who go in magnificent clothes and live luxuriously are to be found at royal courts! 26 Then what did you go out to see? A prophet? Yes, I tell you, and much more than a prophet: 27 he is the one of whom scripture says:

Look, I am going to send my messenger in front of
*   you*
* to prepare your way before you.* w

28 'I tell you, of all the children born to women, there is no one greater than John; yet the least in the kingdom of God is greater than he.' 29 All the people who heard him, and the tax collectors too, acknowledged God's saving justice by accepting baptism from John; 30 but by refusing baptism from him the Pharisees and the lawyers thwarted God's plan for them.

31 'What comparison, then, can I find for the people of this generation? What are they like? 32 They are like children shouting to one another while they sit in the market place:

  We played the pipes for you,
    and you wouldn't dance;
  we sang dirges,
    and you wouldn't cry.

33 'For John the Baptist has come, not eating bread, not drinking wine, and you say, "He is possessed." 34 The Son of man has come, eating and drinking, and you say, "Look, a glutton and a drunkard, a friend of tax collectors and sinners." 35 Yet wisdom is justified by all her children.'

36 One of the Pharisees invited him to a meal. When he arrived at the Pharisee's house and took his place at table, 37 suddenly a woman came in, who had a bad name in the town. She had heard he was dining with the Pharisee and had brought with her an alabaster jar of ointment. 38 She waited behind him at his feet, weeping, and her tears fell on his feet, and she wiped them away with her hair; then she covered his feet with kisses and anointed them with the ointment.

39 When the Pharisee who had invited him saw this, he said to himself, 'If this man were a prophet, he would know who this woman is and what sort of person it is who is touching him and what a bad name she has.' 40 Then Jesus took him up and said, 'Simon, I have something to say to you.' He replied, 'Say on, Master.' 41 'There was once a creditor who had two men in his debt; one owed him five hundred denarii, the other fifty. 42 They were unable to pay, so he let them both off. Which of them will love him more?'

w 7 Ml 3:1.

NEW REVISED STANDARD VERSION

answered, "I suppose the one for whom he canceled the greater debt." And Jesus[h] said to him, "You have judged rightly." 44 Then turning toward the woman, he said to Simon, "Do you see this woman? I entered your house; you gave me no water for my feet, but she has bathed my feet with her tears and dried them with her hair. 45 You gave me no kiss, but from the time I came in she has not stopped kissing my feet. 46 You did not anoint my head with oil, but she has anointed my feet with ointment. 47 Therefore, I tell you, her sins, which were many, have been forgiven; hence she has shown great love. But the one to whom little is forgiven, loves little." 48 Then he said to her, "Your sins are forgiven." 49 But those who were at the table with him began to say among themselves, "Who is this who even forgives sins?" 50 And he said to the woman, "Your faith has saved you; go in peace."

8 Soon afterwards he went on through cities and villages, proclaiming and bringing the good news of the kingdom of God. The twelve were with him, 2 as well as some women who had been cured of evil spirits and infirmities: Mary, called Magdalene, from whom seven demons had gone out, 3 and Joanna, the wife of Herod's steward Chuza, and Susanna, and many others, who provided for them[i] out of their resources.

4 When a great crowd gathered and people from town after town came to him, he said in a parable: 5 "A sower went out to sow his seed; and as he sowed, some fell on the path and was trampled on, and the birds of the air ate it up. 6 Some fell on the rock; and as it grew up, it withered for lack of moisture. 7 Some fell among thorns, and the thorns grew with it and choked it. 8 Some fell into good soil, and when it grew, it produced a hundredfold." As he said this, he called out, "Let anyone with ears to hear listen!"

9 Then his disciples asked him what this parable meant. 10 He said, "To you it has been given to know the secrets[j] of the kingdom of God; but to others I speak[k] in parables, so that

'looking they may not perceive,
and listening they may not understand.'

11 "Now the parable is this: The seed is the word of God. 12 The ones on the path are those who have heard; then the devil comes and takes away the word from their hearts, so that they may not believe and be saved. 13 The ones on the rock are those who, when they hear the word, receive it with joy. But these have no root; they believe only for a while and in a time of testing fall away. 14 As for what fell among the thorns, these are the ones who hear; but as they go on their way, they are choked by the cares and riches and pleasures of life, and their fruit does not mature. 15 But as for that in the good soil, these are the ones who, when they hear the word, hold it fast in an honest and good heart, and bear fruit with patient endurance.

16 "No one after lighting a lamp hides it under a jar, or puts it under a bed, but puts it on a lampstand, so that those who enter may see the light. 17 For nothing is hidden that will not be disclosed, nor is anything secret that will not become known and come to light. 18 Then pay attention to how you listen; for to those who have, more will be given; and from those who do not have, even what they seem to have will be taken away."

19 Then his mother and his brothers came to him, but they could not reach him because of the crowd. 20 And he was told, "Your mother and your brothers are standing outside, wanting to see you." 21 But he said to them, "My

REVISED ENGLISH BIBLE

43 Simon replied, 'I should think the one that was let off more.' 'You are right,' said Jesus. 44 Then turning to the woman, he said to Simon, 'You see this woman? I came to your house: you provided no water for my feet; but this woman has made my feet wet with her tears and wiped them with her hair. 45 You gave me no kiss; but she has been kissing my feet ever since I came in. 46 You did not anoint my head with oil; but she has anointed my feet with myrrh. 47 So, I tell you, her great love proves that her many sins have been forgiven; where little has been forgiven, little love is shown.' 48 Then he said to her, 'Your sins are forgiven.' 49 The other guests began to ask themselves, 'Who is this, that he can forgive sins?' 50 But he said to the woman, 'Your faith has saved you; go in peace.'

8 AFTER this he went journeying from town to town and village to village, proclaiming the good news of the kingdom of God. With him were the Twelve 2 and a number of women who had been set free from evil spirits and infirmities: Mary, known as Mary of Magdala, from whom seven demons had come out, 3 Joanna, the wife of Chuza a steward of Herod's, Susanna, and many others. These women provided for them out of their own resources.

4 People were now gathering in large numbers, and as they made their way to him from one town after another, he said in a parable: 5 'A sower went out to sow his seed. And as he sowed, some of the seed fell along the footpath, where it was trampled on, and the birds ate it up. 6 Some fell on rock and, after coming up, it withered for lack of moisture. 7 Some fell among thistles, and the thistles grew up with it and choked it. 8 And some of the seed fell into good soil, and grew, and yielded a hundredfold.' As he said this he called out, 'If you have ears to hear, then hear.'

9 His disciples asked him what this parable meant, 10 and he replied, 'It has been granted to you to know the secrets of the kingdom of God; but the others have only parables, so that they may look but see nothing, hear but understand nothing.

11 'This is what the parable means. The seed is the word of God. 12 The seed along the footpath stands for those who hear it, and then the devil comes and carries off the word from their hearts for fear they should believe and be saved. 13 The seed sown on rock stands for those who receive the word with joy when they hear it, but have no root; they are believers for a while, but in the time of testing they give up. 14 That which fell among thistles represents those who hear, but their growth is choked by cares and wealth and pleasures of life, and they bring nothing to maturity. 15 But the seed in good soil represents those who bring a good and honest heart to the hearing of the word, hold it fast, and by their perseverance yield a harvest.

16 'Nobody lights a lamp and then covers it with a basin or puts it under the bed. You put it on a lampstand so that those who come in may see the light. 17 For there is nothing hidden that will not be disclosed, nothing concealed that will not be made known and brought into the open.

18 'Take care, then, how you listen; for those who have will be given more, and those who have not will forfeit even what they think they have.'

19 His mother and his brothers arrived but could not get to him for the crowd. 20 He was told, 'Your mother and brothers are standing outside, and want to see you.' 21 He replied,

---

[h] Gk he [i] Other ancient authorities read him [j] Or mysteries
[k] Gk lacks I speak

7:47 her great . . . have been forgiven: or her sins, which are many, have been forgiven because she has loved much.

43 Simon said in reply, "The one, I suppose, whose larger debt was forgiven." He said to him, "You have judged rightly." 44 Then he turned to the woman and said to Simon, "Do you see this woman? When I entered your house, you did not give me water for my feet, but she has bathed them with her tears and wiped them with her hair. 45 You did not give me a kiss, but she has not ceased kissing my feet since the time I entered. 46 You did not anoint my head with oil, but she anointed my feet with ointment. 47 So I tell you, her many sins have been forgiven; hence, she has shown great love. But the one to whom little is forgiven, loves little." 48 He said to her, "Your sins are forgiven." 49 The others at table said to themselves, "Who is this who even forgives sins?" 50 But he said to the woman, "Your faith has saved you; go in peace."

8 Afterward he journeyed from one town and village to another, preaching and proclaiming the good news of the kingdom of God. Accompanying him were the Twelve 2 and some women who had been cured of evil spirits and infirmities, Mary, called Magdalene, from whom seven demons had gone out, 3 Joanna, the wife of Herod's steward Chuza, Susanna, and many others who provided for them out of their resources.

4 When a large crowd gathered, with people from one town after another journeying to him, he spoke in a parable. 5 "A sower went out to sow his seed. And as he sowed, some seed fell on the path and was trampled, and the birds of the sky ate it up. 6 Some seed fell on rocky ground, and when it grew, it withered for lack of moisture. 7 Some seed fell among thorns, and the thorns grew with it and choked it. 8 And some seed fell on good soil, and when it grew, it produced fruit a hundredfold." After saying this, he called out, "Whoever has ears to hear ought to hear."

9 Then his disciples asked him what the meaning of this parable might be. 10 He answered, "Knowledge of the mysteries of the kingdom of God has been granted to you; but to the rest, they are made known through parables so that 'they may look but not see, and hear but not understand.' 11 "This is the meaning of the parable. The seed is the word of God. 12 Those on the path are the ones who have heard, but the devil comes and takes away the word from their hearts that they may not believe and be saved. 13 Those on rocky ground are the ones who, when they hear, receive the word with joy, but they have no root; they believe only for a time and fall away in time of trial. 14 As for the seed that fell among thorns, they are the ones who have heard, but as they go along, they are choked by the anxieties and riches and pleasures of life, and they fail to produce mature fruit. 15 But as for the seed that fell on rich soil, they are the ones who, when they have heard the word, embrace it with a generous and good heart, and bear fruit through perseverance.

16 "No one who lights a lamp conceals it with a vessel or sets it under a bed; rather, he places it on a lampstand so that those who enter may see the light. 17 For there is nothing hidden that will not become visible, and nothing secret that will not be known and come to light. 18 Take care, then, how you hear. To anyone who has, more will be given, and from the one who has not, even what he seems to have will be taken away."

19 Then his mother and his brothers came to him but were unable to join him because of the crowd. 20 He was told, "Your mother and your brothers are standing outside and they wish to see you." 21 He said to them in reply, "My

43 Simon answered, 'The one who was let off more, I suppose.' Jesus said, 'You are right.'

44 Then he turned to the woman and said to Simon, 'You see this woman? I came into your house, and you poured no water over my feet, but she has poured out her tears over my feet and wiped them away with her hair. 45 You gave me no kiss, but she has been covering my feet with kisses ever since I came in. 46 You did not anoint my head with oil, but she has anointed my feet with ointment. 47 For this reason I tell you that her sins, many as they are, have been forgiven her, because she has shown such great love. x It is someone who is forgiven little who shows little love.' 48 Then he said to her, 'Your sins are forgiven.' 49 Those who were with him at table began to say to themselves, 'Who is this man, that even forgives sins?' 50 But he said to the woman, 'Your faith has saved you; go in peace.'

8 Now it happened that after this he made his way through towns and villages preaching and proclaiming the good news of the kingdom of God. With him went the Twelve, 2 as well as certain women who had been cured of evil spirits and ailments: Mary surnamed the Magdalene, from whom seven demons had gone out, 3 Joanna the wife of Herod's steward Chuza, Susanna, and many others who provided for them out of their own resources.

4 With a large crowd gathering and people from every town finding their way to him, he told this parable:

5 'A sower went out to sow his seed. Now as he sowed, some fell on the edge of the path and was trampled on; and the birds of the air ate it up. 6 Some seed fell on rock, and when it came up it withered away, having no moisture. 7 Some seed fell in the middle of thorns and the thorns grew with it and choked it. 8 And some seed fell into good soil and grew and produced its crop a hundredfold.' Saying this he cried, 'Anyone who has ears for listening should listen!'

9 His disciples asked him what this parable might mean, 10 and he said, 'To you is granted to understand the secrets of the kingdom of God; for the rest it remains in parables, so that

they may look but not perceive,
listen but not understand.y

11 'This, then, is what the parable means: the seed is the word of God. 12 Those on the edge of the path are people who have heard it, and then the devil comes and carries away the word from their hearts in case they should believe and be saved. 13 Those on the rock are people who, when they first hear it, welcome the word with joy. But these have no root; they believe for a while, and in time of trial they give up. 14 As for the part that fell into thorns, this is people who have heard, but as they go on their way they are choked by the worries and riches and pleasures of life and never produce any crops. 15 As for the part in the rich soil, this is people with a noble and generous heart who have heard the word and take it to themselves and yield a harvest through their perseverance.

16 'No one lights a lamp to cover it with a bowl or to put it under a bed. No, it is put on a lamp-stand so that people may see the light when they come in. 17 For nothing is hidden but it will be made clear, nothing secret but it will be made known and brought to light. 18 So take care how you listen; anyone who has, will be given more; anyone who has not, will be deprived even of what he thinks he has.'

19 His mother and his brothers came looking for him, but they could not get to him because of the crowd. 20 He was told, 'Your mother and brothers are standing outside and want to see you.' 21 But he said in answer, 'My mother and

x 7 In most of the story love wins forgiveness, but in vv. 40–43 and 47a, forgiveness nourishes love. y 8 Is 6:9.

mother and my brothers are those who hear the word of God and do it."

22 One day he got into a boat with his disciples, and he said to them, "Let us go across to the other side of the lake." So they put out, 23 and while they were sailing he fell asleep. A windstorm swept down on the lake, and the boat was filling with water, and they were in danger. 24 They went to him and woke him up, shouting, "Master, Master, we are perishing!" And he woke up and rebuked the wind and the raging waves; they ceased, and there was a calm. 25 He said to them, "Where is your faith?" They were afraid and amazed, and said to one another, "Who then is this, that he commands even the winds and the water, and they obey him?"

26 Then they arrived at the country of the Gerasenes,*l* which is opposite Galilee. 27 As he stepped out on land, a man of the city who had demons met him. For a long time he had worn*m* no clothes, and he did not live in a house but in the tombs. 28 When he saw Jesus, he fell down before him and shouted at the top of his voice, "What have you to do with me, Jesus, Son of the Most High God? I beg you, do not torment me" — 29 for Jesus*n* had commanded the unclean spirit to come out of the man. (For many times it had seized him; he was kept under guard and bound with chains and shackles, but he would break the bonds and be driven by the demon into the wilds.) 30 Jesus then asked him, "What is your name?" He said, "Legion"; for many demons had entered him. 31 They begged him not to order them to go back into the abyss.

32 Now there on the hillside a large herd of swine was feeding; and the demons*o* begged Jesus*p* to let them enter these. So he gave them permission. 33 Then the demons came out of the man and entered the swine, and the herd rushed down the steep bank into the lake and was drowned.

34 When the swineherds saw what had happened, they ran off and told it in the city and in the country. 35 Then people came out to see what had happened, and when they came to Jesus, they found the man from whom the demons had gone sitting at the feet of Jesus, clothed and in his right mind. And they were afraid. 36 Those who had seen it told them how the one who had been possessed by demons had been healed. 37 Then all the people of the surrounding country of the Gerasenes*l* asked Jesus*p* to leave them; for they were seized with great fear. So he got into the boat and returned. 38 The man from whom the demons had gone begged that he might be with him; but Jesus*n* sent him away, saying, 39 "Return to your home, and declare how much God has done for you." So he went away, proclaiming throughout the city how much Jesus had done for him.

40 Now when Jesus returned, the crowd welcomed him, for they were all waiting for him. 41 Just then there came a man named Jairus, a leader of the synagogue. He fell at Jesus' feet and begged him to come to his house, 42 for he had an only daughter, about twelve years old, who was dying.

As he went, the crowds pressed in on him. 43 Now there was a woman who had been suffering from hemorrhages for twelve years; and though she had spent all she had on physicians,*q* no one could cure her. 44 She came up behind him and touched the fringe of his clothes, and immediately her hemorrhage stopped. 45 Then Jesus asked, "Who touched me?" When all denied it, Peter*r* said, "Master, the crowds surround you and press in on you." 46 But Jesus said,

'My mother and my brothers are those who hear the word of God and act upon it.'

22 One day he got into a boat with his disciples and said to them, 'Let us cross over to the other side of the lake.' So they put out; 23 and as they sailed along he fell asleep. Then a heavy squall struck the lake; they began to ship water and were in grave danger. 24 They came and roused him: 'Master, Master, we are sinking!' they cried. He awoke, and rebuked the wind and the turbulent waters. The storm subsided and there was calm. 25 'Where is your faith?' he asked. In fear and astonishment they said to one another, 'Who can this be? He gives his orders to the wind and the waves, and they obey him.'

26 So they landed in the country of the Gerasenes, which is opposite Galilee. 27 As he stepped ashore he was met by a man from the town who was possessed by demons. For a long time he had neither worn clothes nor lived in a house, but stayed among the tombs. 28 When he saw Jesus he cried out, and fell at his feet. 'What do you want with me, Jesus, Son of the Most High God?' he shouted. 'I implore you, do not torment me.' 29 For Jesus was already ordering the unclean spirit to come out of the man. Many a time it had seized him, and then, for safety's sake, they would secure him with chains and fetters; but each time he broke loose and was driven by the demon out into the wilds.

30 Jesus asked him, 'What is your name?' 'Legion,' he replied. This was because so many demons had taken possession of him. 31 And they begged him not to banish them to the abyss.

32 There was a large herd of pigs nearby, feeding on the hillside; and the demons begged him to let them go into these pigs. He gave them leave; 33 the demons came out of the man and went into the pigs, and the herd rushed over the edge into the lake and were drowned.

34 When the men in charge of them saw what had happened, they took to their heels and carried the news to the town and countryside; 35 and the people came out to see what had happened. When they came to Jesus, and found the man from whom the demons had gone out sitting at his feet clothed and in his right mind, they were afraid. 36 Eye-witnesses told them how the madman had been cured. 37 Then the whole population of the Gerasene district was overcome by fear and asked Jesus to go away. So he got into the boat and went away. 38 The man from whom the demons had gone out begged to go with him; but Jesus sent him away: 39 'Go back home,' he said, 'and tell them what God has done for you.' The man went all over the town proclaiming what Jesus had done for him.

40 When Jesus returned, the people welcomed him, for they were all expecting him. 41 Then a man appeared — Jairus was his name and he was president of the synagogue. Throwing himself down at Jesus's feet he begged him to come to his house, 42 because his only daughter, who was about twelve years old, was dying.

While Jesus was on his way he could hardly breathe for the crowds. 43 Among them was a woman who had suffered from haemorrhages for twelve years; and nobody had been able to cure her. 44 She came up from behind and touched the edge of his cloak, and at once her haemorrhage stopped. 45 Jesus said, 'Who was it who touched me?' All disclaimed it, and Peter said, 'Master, the crowds are hemming you in and pressing upon you!' 46 But Jesus said, 'Someone did

---

l Other ancient authorities read *Gadarenes*; others, *Gergesenes*
m Other ancient authorities read *a man of the city who had had demons for a long time met him. He wore* *n* Gk *he* *o* Gk *they*
p Gk *him* *q* Other ancient authorities lack *and had spent all she had on physicians* *r* Other ancient authorities add *and those who were with him*

8:26 **Gerasenes:** *some witnesses read* Gergesenes; *others read* Gadarenes. 8:37 **Gerasene:** *some witnesses read* Gergesene; *others read* Gadarene. 8:43 **years; and:** *some witnesses add* though she had spent all she had on doctors. 8:44 **edge:** *or* tassel.

mother and my brothers are those who hear the word of God and act on it."

22 One day he got into a boat with his disciples and said to them, "Let us cross to the other side of the lake." So they set sail, 23 and while they were sailing he fell asleep. A squall blew over the lake, and they were taking in water and were in danger. 24 They came and woke him saying, "Master, master, we are perishing!" He awakened, rebuked the wind and the waves, and they subsided and there was a calm. 25 Then he asked them, "Where is your faith?" But they were filled with awe and amazed and said to one another, "Who then is this, who commands even the winds and the sea, and they obey him?"

26 Then they sailed to the territory of the Gerasenes, which is opposite Galilee. 27 When he came ashore a man from the town who was possessed by demons met him. For a long time he had not worn clothes; he did not live in a house, but lived among the tombs. 28 When he saw Jesus, he cried out and fell down before him; in a loud voice he shouted, "What have you to do with me, Jesus, son of the Most High God? I beg you, do not torment me!" 29 For he had ordered the unclean spirit to come out of the man. (It had taken hold of him many times, and he used to be bound with chains and shackles as a restraint, but he would break his bonds and be driven by the demon into deserted places.) 30 Then Jesus asked him, "What is your name?" He replied, "Legion," because many demons had entered him. 31 And they pleaded with him not to order them to depart to the abyss.

32 A herd of many swine was feeding there on the hillside, and they pleaded with him to allow them to enter those swine; and he let them. 33 The demons came out of the man and entered the swine, and the herd rushed down the steep bank into the lake and was drowned. 34 When the swineherds saw what had happened, they ran away and reported the incident in the town and throughout the countryside. 35 People came out to see what had happened and, when they approached Jesus, they discovered the man from whom the demons had come out sitting at his feet. He was clothed and in his right mind, and they were seized with fear. 36 Those who witnessed it told them how the possessed man had been saved. 37 The entire population of the region of the Gerasenes asked Jesus to leave them because they were seized with great fear. So he got into a boat and returned. 38 The man from whom the demons had come out begged to remain with him, but he sent him away, saying, 39 "Return home and recount what God has done for you." The man went off and proclaimed throughout the whole town what Jesus had done for him.

40 When Jesus returned, the crowd welcomed him, for they were all waiting for him. 41 And a man named Jairus, an official of the synagogue, came forward. He fell at the feet of Jesus and begged him to come to his house, 42 because he had an only daughter, about twelve years old, and she was dying. As he went, the crowds almost crushed him. 43 And a woman afflicted with hemorrhages for twelve years, who [had spent her whole livelihood on doctors and] was unable to be cured by anyone, 44 came up behind him and touched the tassel on his cloak. Immediately her bleeding stopped. 45 Jesus then asked, "Who touched me?" While all were denying it, Peter said, "Master, the crowds are pushing and pressing in upon you." 46 But Jesus said,

my brothers are those who hear the word of God and put it into practice.'

22 It happened that one day he got into a boat with his disciples and said to them, 'Let us cross over to the other side of the lake.' So they set out, 23 and as they sailed he fell asleep. When a squall of wind came down on the lake the boat started shipping water and they found themselves in danger. 24 So they went to rouse him saying, 'Master! Master! We are lost!' Then he woke up and rebuked the wind and the rough water; and they subsided and it was calm again. 25 He said to them, 'Where is your faith?' They were awestruck and astounded and said to one another, 'Who can this be, that gives orders even to winds and waves and they obey him?'

26 They came to land in the territory of the Gerasenes, which is opposite Galilee. 27 He was stepping ashore when a man from the city who was possessed by devils came towards him; for a long time the man had been living with no clothes on, not in a house, but in the tombs. 28 Catching sight of Jesus he gave a shout, fell at his feet and cried out at the top of his voice, 'What do you want with me, Jesus, son of the Most High God? I implore you, do not torture me.' 29 For Jesus had been telling the unclean spirit to come out of the man. It had seized on him a great many times, and then they used to secure him with chains and fetters to restrain him, but he would always break the fastenings, and the devil would drive him out into the wilds. 30 Jesus asked him, 'What is your name?' He said, 'Legion' —because many devils had gone into him. 31 And these begged him not to order them to depart into the Abyss.

32 Now there was a large herd of pigs feeding there on the mountain, and the devils begged him to let them go into these. So he gave them leave. 33 The devils came out of the man and went into the pigs, and the herd charged down the cliff into the lake and was drowned.

34 When the swineherds saw what had happened they ran off and told their story in the city and in the country round about; 35 and the people went out to see what had happened. When they came to Jesus they found the man from whom the devils had gone out sitting at the feet of Jesus, wearing clothes and in his right mind; and they were afraid. 36 Those who had witnessed it told them how the man who had been possessed came to be saved. 37 The entire population of the Gerasene territory was in great fear and asked Jesus to leave them. So he got into the boat and went back.

38 The man from whom the devils had gone out asked to be allowed to stay with him, but he sent him away, saying, 39 'Go back home and report all that God has done for you.' So the man went off and proclaimed throughout the city all that Jesus had done for him.

40 On his return Jesus was welcomed by the crowd, for they were all there waiting for him. 41 And suddenly there came a man named Jairus, who was president of the synagogue. He fell at Jesus' feet and pleaded with him to come to his house, 42 because he had an only daughter about twelve years old, who was dying. And the crowds were almost stifling Jesus as he went.

43 Now there was a woman suffering from a haemorrhage for the past twelve years, whom no one had been able to cure. 44 She came up behind him and touched the fringe of his cloak; and the haemorrhage stopped at that very moment. 45 Jesus said, 'Who was it that touched me?' When they all denied it, Peter said, 'Master, it is the crowds round

"Someone touched me; for I noticed that power had gone out from me." 47 When the woman saw that she could not remain hidden, she came trembling; and falling down before him, she declared in the presence of all the people why she had touched him, and how she had been immediately healed. 48 He said to her, "Daughter, your faith has made you well; go in peace."

49 While he was still speaking, someone came from the leader's house to say, "Your daughter is dead; do not trouble the teacher any longer." 50 When Jesus heard this, he replied, "Do not fear. Only believe, and she will be saved." 51 When he came to the house, he did not allow anyone to enter with him, except Peter, John, and James, and the child's father and mother. 52 They were all weeping and wailing for her; but he said, "Do not weep; for she is not dead but sleeping." 53 And they laughed at him, knowing that she was dead. 54 But he took her by the hand and called out, "Child, get up!" 55 Her spirit returned, and she got up at once. Then he directed them to give her something to eat. 56 Her parents were astounded; but he ordered them to tell no one what had happened.

9 Then Jesus*s* called the twelve together and gave them power and authority over all demons and to cure diseases, 2 and he sent them out to proclaim the kingdom of God and to heal. 3 He said to them, "Take nothing for your journey, no staff, nor bag, nor bread, nor money — not even an extra tunic. 4 Whatever house you enter, stay there, and leave from there. 5 Wherever they do not welcome you, as you are leaving that town shake the dust off your feet as a testimony against them." 6 They departed and went through the villages, bringing the good news and curing diseases everywhere.

7 Now Herod the ruler*t* heard about all that had taken place, and he was perplexed, because it was said by some that John had been raised from the dead, 8 by some that Elijah had appeared, and by others that one of the ancient prophets had arisen. 9 Herod said, "John I beheaded; but who is this about whom I hear such things?" And he tried to see him.

10 On their return the apostles told Jesus*u* all they had done. He took them with him and withdrew privately to a city called Bethsaida. 11 When the crowds found out about it, they followed him; and he welcomed them, and spoke to them about the kingdom of God, and healed those who needed to be cured.

12 The day was drawing to a close, and the twelve came to him and said, "Send the crowd away, so that they may go into the surrounding villages and countryside, to lodge and get provisions; for we are here in a deserted place." 13 But he said to them, "You give them something to eat." They said, "We have no more than five loaves and two fish — unless we are to go and buy food for all these people." 14 For there were about five thousand men. And he said to his disciples, "Make them sit down in groups of about fifty each." 15 They did so and made them all sit down. 16 And taking the five loaves and the two fish, he looked up to heaven, and blessed and broke them, and gave them to the disciples to set before the crowd. 17 And all ate and were filled. What was left over was gathered up, twelve baskets of broken pieces.

18 Once when Jesus*s* was praying alone, with only the disciples near him, he asked them, "Who do the crowds say that I am?" 19 They answered, "John the Baptist; but others, Elijah; and still others, that one of the ancient prophets has arisen." 20 He said to them, "But who do you say that I am?" Peter answered, "The Messiah*v* of God."

touch me, for I felt that power had gone out from me.' 47 Then the woman, seeing that she was detected, came trembling and fell at his feet. Before all the people she explained why she had touched him and how she had been cured instantly. 48 He said to her, 'Daughter, your faith has healed you. Go in peace.'

49 While he was still speaking, a man came from the president's house with the message, 'Your daughter is dead; do not trouble the teacher any more.' 50 But Jesus heard, and said, 'Do not be afraid; simply have faith and she will be well again.' 51 When he arrived at the house he allowed no one to go in with him except Peter, John, and James, and the child's father and mother. 52 Everyone was weeping and lamenting for her. He said, 'Stop your weeping; she is not dead: she is asleep'; 53 and they laughed at him, well knowing that she was dead. 54 But Jesus took hold of her hand and called to her: 'Get up, my child.' 55 Her spirit returned, she stood up immediately, and he told them to give her something to eat. 56 Her parents were astounded; but he forbade them to tell anyone what had happened.

9 CALLING the Twelve together he gave them power and authority to overcome all demons and to cure diseases, 2 and sent them out to proclaim the kingdom of God and to heal the sick. 3 'Take nothing for the journey,' he told them, 'neither stick nor pack, neither bread nor money; nor are you to have a second coat. 4 When you enter a house, stay there until you leave that place. 5 As for those who will not receive you, when you leave their town shake the dust off your feet as a warning to them.' 6 So they set out and travelled from village to village, and everywhere they announced the good news and healed the sick.

7 Now Herod the tetrarch heard of all that was happening, and did not know what to make of it; for some were saying that John had been raised from the dead, 8 others that Elijah had appeared, others again that one of the prophets of old had come back to life. 9 Herod said, 'As for John, I beheaded him; but who is this I hear so much about?' And he was anxious to see him.

10 On their return the apostles gave Jesus an account of all they had done. Then he took them with him and withdrew privately to a town called Bethsaida, 11 but the crowds found out and followed. He welcomed them, and spoke to them about the kingdom of God, and cured those who were in need of healing. 12 When evening was drawing on, the Twelve came to him and said, 'Send the people off, so that they can go into the villages and farms round about to find food and lodging, for this is a remote place we are in.' 13 'Give them something to eat yourselves,' he replied. But they said, 'All we have is five loaves and two fish, nothing more — or do you intend us to go and buy food for all these people?' 14 For there were about five thousand men. Then he said to his disciples, 'Make them sit down in groups of about fifty.' 15 They did so and got them all seated. 16 Then, taking the five loaves and the two fish, he looked up to heaven, said the blessing over them, broke them, and gave them to the disciples to distribute to the people. 17 They all ate and were satisfied; and the scraps they left were picked up and filled twelve baskets.

18 One day, when he had been praying by himself in the company of his disciples, he asked them, 'Who do the people say I am?' 19 They answered, 'Some say John the Baptist, others Elijah, others that one of the prophets of old has come back to life.' 20 'And you,' he said, 'who do you say I am?' Peter answered, 'God's Messiah.' 21 Then he

"Someone has touched me; for I know that power has gone out from me." 47 When the woman realized that she had not escaped notice, she came forward trembling. Falling down before him, she explained in the presence of all the people why she had touched him and how she had been healed immediately. 48 He said to her, "Daughter, your faith has saved you; go in peace."

49 While he was still speaking, someone from the synagogue official's house arrived and said, "Your daughter is dead; do not trouble the teacher any longer." 50 On hearing this, Jesus answered him, "Do not be afraid; just have faith and she will be saved." 51 When he arrived at the house he allowed no one to enter with him except Peter and John and James, and the child's father and mother. 52 All were weeping and mourning for her, when he said, "Do not weep any longer, for she is not dead, but sleeping." 53 And they ridiculed him, because they knew that she was dead. 54 But he took her by the hand and called to her, "Child, arise!" 55 Her breath returned and she immediately arose. He then directed that she should be given something to eat. 56 Her parents were astounded, and he instructed them to tell no one what had happened.

9 He summoned the Twelve and gave them power and authority over all demons and to cure diseases, 2 and he sent them to proclaim the kingdom of God and to heal [the sick]. 3 He said to them, "Take nothing for the journey, neither walking stick, nor sack, nor food, nor money, and let no one take a second tunic. 4 Whatever house you enter, stay there and leave from there. 5 And as for those who do not welcome you, when you leave that town, shake the dust from your feet in testimony against them." 6 Then they set out and went from village to village proclaiming the good news and curing diseases everywhere.

7 Herod the tetrarch heard about all that was happening, and he was greatly perplexed because some were saying, "John has been raised from the dead"; 8 others were saying, "Elijah has appeared"; still others, "One of the ancient prophets has arisen." 9 But Herod said, "John I beheaded. Who then is this about whom I hear such things?" And he kept trying to see him.

10 When the apostles returned, they explained to him what they had done. He took them and withdrew in private to a town called Bethsaida. 11 The crowds, meanwhile, learned of this and followed him. He received them and spoke to them about the kingdom of God, and he healed those who needed to be cured. 12 As the day was drawing to a close, the Twelve approached him and said, "Dismiss the crowd so that they can go to the surrounding villages and farms and find lodging and provisions; for we are in a deserted place here." 13 He said to them, "Give them some food yourselves." They replied, "Five loaves and two fish are all we have, unless we ourselves go and buy food for all these people." 14 Now the men there numbered about five thousand. Then he said to his disciples, "Have them sit down in groups of [about] fifty." 15 They did so and made them all sit down. 16 Then taking the five loaves and the two fish, and looking up to heaven, he said the blessing over them, broke them, and gave them to the disciples to set before the crowd. 17 They all ate and were satisfied. And when the leftover fragments were picked up, they filled twelve wicker baskets.

18 Once when Jesus was praying in solitude, and the disciples were with him, he asked them, "Who do the crowds say that I am?" 19 They said in reply, "John the Baptist; others, Elijah; still others, 'One of the ancient prophets has arisen.' " 20 Then he said to them, "But who do you say that I am?" Peter said in reply, "The Messiah of God." 21 He

you, pushing.' 46 But Jesus said, 'Somebody touched me. I felt that power had gone out from me.' 47 Seeing herself discovered, the woman came forward trembling, and falling at his feet explained in front of all the people why she had touched him and how she had been cured at that very moment. 48 'My daughter,' he said, 'your faith has saved you; go in peace.'

49 While he was still speaking, someone arrived from the house of the president of the synagogue to say, 'Your daughter has died. Do not trouble the Master any further.' 50 But Jesus heard this, and he spoke to the man, 'Do not be afraid, only have faith and she will be saved.' 51 When he came to the house he allowed no one to go in with him except Peter and John and James, and the child's father and mother. 52 They were all crying and mourning for her, but Jesus said, 'Stop crying; she is not dead, but asleep.' 53 But they ridiculed him, knowing she was dead. 54 But taking her by the hand himself he spoke to her, 'Child, get up.' 55 And her spirit returned and she got up at that very moment. Then he told them to give her something to eat. 56 Her parents were astonished, but he ordered them not to tell anyone what had happened.

9 He called the Twelve together and gave them power and authority over all devils and to cure diseases, 2 and he sent them out to proclaim the kingdom of God and to heal. 3 He said to them, 'Take nothing for the journey: neither staff, nor haversack, nor bread, nor money; and do not have a spare tunic. 4 Whatever house you enter, stay there; and when you leave your departure be from there. 5 As for those who do not welcome you, when you leave their town shake the dust from your feet as evidence against them.' 6 So they set out and went from village to village proclaiming the good news and healing everywhere.

7 Meanwhile Herod the tetrarch had heard about all that was going on; and he was puzzled, because some people were saying that John had risen from the dead, 8 others that Elijah had reappeared, still others that one of the ancient prophets had come back to life. 9 But Herod said, 'John? I beheaded him. So who is this I hear such reports about?' And he was anxious to see him.

10 On their return the apostles gave him an account of all they had done. Then he took them with him and withdrew towards a town called Bethsaida where they could be by themselves. 11 But the crowds got to know and they went after him. He made them welcome and talked to them about the kingdom of God; and he cured those who were in need of healing.

12 It was late afternoon when the Twelve came up to him and said, 'Send the people away, and they can go to the villages and farms round about to find lodging and food; for we are in a lonely place here.' 13 He replied, 'Give them something to eat yourselves.' But they said, 'We have no more than five loaves and two fish, unless we are to go ourselves and buy food for all these people.' 14 For there were about five thousand men. But he said to his disciples, 'Get them to sit down in parties of about fifty.' 15 They did so and made them all sit down. 16 Then he took the five loaves and the two fish, raised his eyes to heaven, and said the blessing over them; then he broke them and handed them to his disciples to distribute among the crowd. 17 They all ate as much as they wanted, and when the scraps left over were collected they filled twelve baskets.

18 Now it happened that he was praying alone, and his disciples came to him and he put this question to them, 'Who do the crowds say I am?' 19 And they answered, 'Some say John the Baptist; others Elijah; others again one of the ancient prophets come back to life.' 20 'But you,' he said to them, 'who do you say I am?' It was Peter who spoke up. 'The Christ of God,' he said. 21 But he gave them

NEW REVISED STANDARD VERSION

21 He sternly ordered and commanded them not to tell anyone, 22 saying, "The Son of Man must undergo great suffering, and be rejected by the elders, chief priests, and scribes, and be killed, and on the third day be raised."

23 Then he said to them all, "If any want to become my followers, let them deny themselves and take up their cross daily and follow me. 24 For those who want to save their life will lose it, and those who lose their life for my sake will save it. 25 What does it profit them if they gain the whole world, but lose or forfeit themselves? 26 Those who are ashamed of me and of my words, of them the Son of Man will be ashamed when he comes in his glory and the glory of the Father and of the holy angels. 27 But truly I tell you, there are some standing here who will not taste death before they see the kingdom of God."

28 Now about eight days after these sayings Jesus[w] took with him Peter and John and James, and went up on the mountain to pray. 29 And while he was praying, the appearance of his face changed, and his clothes became dazzling white. 30 Suddenly they saw two men, Moses and Elijah, talking to him. 31 They appeared in glory and were speaking of his departure, which he was about to accomplish at Jerusalem. 32 Now Peter and his companions were weighed down with sleep; but since they had stayed awake,[x] they saw his glory and the two men who stood with him. 33 Just as they were leaving him, Peter said to Jesus, "Master, it is good for us to be here; let us make three dwellings,[y] one for you, one for Moses, and one for Elijah" — not knowing what he said. 34 While he was saying this, a cloud came and overshadowed them; and they were terrified as they entered the cloud. 35 Then from the cloud came a voice that said, "This is my Son, my Chosen;[z] listen to him!" 36 When the voice had spoken, Jesus was found alone. And they kept silent and in those days told no one any of the things they had seen.

37 On the next day, when they had come down from the mountain, a great crowd met him. 38 Just then a man from the crowd shouted, "Teacher, I beg you to look at my son; he is my only child. 39 Suddenly a spirit seizes him, and all at once he[a] shrieks. It convulses him until he foams at the mouth; it mauls him and will scarcely leave him. 40 I begged your disciples to cast it out, but they could not." 41 Jesus answered, "You faithless and perverse generation, how much longer must I be with you and bear with you? Bring your son here." 42 While he was coming, the demon dashed him to the ground in convulsions. But Jesus rebuked the unclean spirit, healed the boy, and gave him back to his father. 43 And all were astounded at the greatness of God.

While everyone was amazed at all that he was doing, he said to his disciples, 44 "Let these words sink into your ears: The Son of Man is going to be betrayed into human hands." 45 But they did not understand this saying; its meaning was concealed from them, so that they could not perceive it. And they were afraid to ask him about this saying.

46 An argument arose among them as to which one of them was the greatest. 47 But Jesus, aware of their inner thoughts, took a little child and put it by his side, 48 and said to them, "Whoever welcomes this child in my name welcomes me, and whoever welcomes me welcomes the one who sent me; for the least among all of you is the greatest."

REVISED ENGLISH BIBLE

gave them strict orders not to tell this to anyone. 22 And he said, 'The Son of Man has to endure great sufferings, and to be rejected by the elders, chief priests, and scribes, to be put to death, and to be raised again on the third day.'

23 To everybody he said, 'Anyone who wants to be a follower of mine must renounce self; day after day he must take up his cross, and follow me. 24 Whoever wants to save his life will lose it, but whoever loses his life for my sake will save it. 25 What does anyone gain by winning the whole world at the cost of destroying himself? 26 If anyone is ashamed of me and my words, the Son of Man will be ashamed of him, when he comes in his glory and the glory of the Father and the holy angels. 27 In truth I tell you: there are some of those standing here who will not taste death before they have seen the kingdom of God.'

28 About a week after this he took Peter, John, and James and went up a mountain to pray. 29 And while he was praying the appearance of his face changed and his clothes became dazzling white. 30 Suddenly there were two men talking with him — Moses and Elijah — 31 who appeared in glory and spoke of his departure, the destiny he was to fulfil in Jerusalem. 32 Peter and his companions had been overcome by sleep; but when they awoke, they saw his glory and the two men who stood beside him. 33 As these two were moving away from Jesus, Peter said to him, 'Master, it is good that we are here. Shall we make three shelters, one for you, one for Moses, and one for Elijah?' but he spoke without knowing what he was saying. 34 As he spoke there came a cloud which cast its shadow over them; they were afraid as they entered the cloud, 35 and from it a voice spoke: 'This is my Son, my Chosen; listen to him.' 36 After the voice had spoken, Jesus was seen to be alone. The disciples kept silence and did not at that time say a word to anyone of what they had seen.

37 Next day when they came down from the mountain a large crowd came to meet him. 38 A man in the crowd called out: 'Teacher, I implore you to look at my son, my only child. 39 From time to time a spirit seizes him and with a sudden scream throws him into convulsions so that he foams at the mouth; it keeps on tormenting him and can hardly be made to let him go. 40 I begged your disciples to drive it out, but they could not.' 41 Jesus answered, 'What an unbelieving and perverse generation! How long shall I be with you and endure you? Bring your son here.' 42 But before the boy could reach him the demon dashed him to the ground and threw him into convulsions. Jesus spoke sternly to the unclean spirit, cured the boy, and gave him back to his father. 43 And they were all struck with awe at the greatness of God.

Amid the general astonishment at all he was doing, Jesus said to his disciples, 44 'Listen to what I have to tell you. The Son of Man is to be given up into the power of men.' 45 But they did not understand what he said; its meaning had been hidden from them, so that they could not grasp it, and they were afraid to ask him about it.

46 An argument started among them as to which of them was the greatest. 47 Jesus, who knew what was going on in their minds, took a child, stood him by his side, 48 and said, 'Whoever receives this child in my name receives me; and whoever receives me receives the one who sent me. For the least among you all is the greatest.'

---

[w] Gk *he*   [x] Or *but when they were fully awake*   [y] Or *tents*
[z] Other ancient authorities read *my Beloved*   [a] Or *it*

9:26 **me and my words:** *some witnesses read* me and mine.
9:31 **departure:** *lit.* exodus.

rebuked them and directed them not to tell this to anyone.
²² He said, "The Son of Man must suffer greatly and be rejected by the elders, the chief priests, and the scribes, and be killed and on the third day be raised."
²³ Then he said to all, "If anyone wishes to come after me, he must deny himself and take up his cross daily and follow me. ²⁴ For whoever wishes to save his life will lose it, but whoever loses his life for my sake will save it. ²⁵ What profit is there for one to gain the whole world yet lose or forfeit himself? ²⁶ Whoever is ashamed of me and of my words, the Son of Man will be ashamed of when he comes in his glory and in the glory of the Father and of the holy angels. ²⁷ Truly I say to you, there are some standing here who will not taste death until they see the kingdom of God."
²⁸ About eight days after he said this, he took Peter, John, and James and went up the mountain to pray. ²⁹ While he was praying his face changed in appearance and his clothing became dazzling white. ³⁰ And behold, two men were conversing with him, Moses and Elijah, ³¹ who appeared in glory and spoke of his exodus that he was going to accomplish in Jerusalem. ³² Peter and his companions had been overcome by sleep, but becoming fully awake, they saw his glory and the two men standing with him. ³³ As they were about to part from him, Peter said to Jesus, "Master, it is good that we are here; let us make three tents, one for you, one for Moses, and one for Elijah." But he did not know what he was saying. ³⁴ While he was still speaking, a cloud came and cast a shadow over them, and they became frightened when they entered the cloud. ³⁵ Then from the cloud came a voice that said, "This is my chosen Son; listen to him." ³⁶ After the voice had spoken, Jesus was found alone. They fell silent and did not at that time tell anyone what they had seen.
³⁷ On the next day, when they came down from the mountain, a large crowd met him. ³⁸ There was a man in the crowd who cried out, "Teacher, I beg you, look at my son; he is my only child. ³⁹ For a spirit seizes him and he suddenly screams and it convulses him until he foams at the mouth; it releases him only with difficulty, wearing him out. ⁴⁰ I begged your disciples to cast it out but they could not." ⁴¹ Jesus said in reply, "O faithless and perverse generation, how long will I be with you and endure you? Bring your son here." ⁴² As he was coming forward, the demon threw him to the ground in a convulsion; but Jesus rebuked the unclean spirit, healed the boy, and returned him to his father. ⁴³ And all were astonished by the majesty of God.
While they were all amazed at his every deed, he said to his disciples, ⁴⁴ "Pay attention to what I am telling you. The Son of Man is to be handed over to men." ⁴⁵ But they did not understand this saying; its meaning was hidden from them so that they should not understand it, and they were afraid to ask him about this saying.
⁴⁶ An argument arose among the disciples about which of them was the greatest. ⁴⁷ Jesus realized the intention of their hearts and took a child and placed it by his side ⁴⁸ and said to them, "Whoever receives this child in my name receives me, and whoever receives me receives the one who sent me. For the one who is least among all of you is the one who is the greatest."

strict orders and charged them not to say this to anyone.
²² He said, 'The Son of man is destined to suffer grievously, to be rejected by the elders and chief priests and scribes and to be put to death, and to be raised up on the third day.'
²³ Then, speaking to all, he said, 'If anyone wants to be a follower of mine, let him renounce himself and take up his cross every day and follow me. ²⁴ Anyone who wants to save his life will lose it; but anyone who loses his life for my sake, will save it. ²⁵ What benefit is it to anyone to win the whole world and forfeit or lose his very self? ²⁶ For if anyone is ashamed of me and of my words, of him the Son of man will be ashamed when he comes in his own glory and in the glory of the Father and the holy angels.
²⁷ 'I tell you truly, there are some standing here who will not taste death before they see the kingdom of God.'
²⁸ Now about eight days after this had been said, he took with him Peter, John and James and went up the mountain to pray. ²⁹ And it happened that, as he was praying, the aspect of his face was changed and his clothing became sparkling white. ³⁰ And suddenly there were two men talking to him; they were Moses and Elijah ³¹ appearing in glory, and they were speaking of his passing which he was to accomplish in Jerusalem. ³² Peter and his companions were heavy with sleep, but they woke up and saw his glory and the two men standing with him. ³³ As these were leaving him, Peter said to Jesus, 'Master, it is wonderful for us to be here; so let us make three shelters, one for you, one for Moses and one for Elijah.' He did not know what he was saying. ³⁴ As he was saying this, a cloud came and covered them with shadow; and when they went into the cloud the disciples were afraid. ³⁵ And a voice came from the cloud saying, 'This is my Son, the Chosen One. Listen to him.'ᶻ ³⁶ And after the voice had spoken, Jesus was found alone. The disciples kept silence and, at that time, told no one what they had seen.
³⁷ Now it happened that on the following day when they were coming down from the mountain a large crowd came to meet him. ³⁸ And suddenly a man in the crowd cried out. 'Master,' he said, 'I implore you to look at my son: he is my only child. ³⁹ A spirit will suddenly take hold of him, and all at once it gives a sudden cry and throws the boy into convulsions with foaming at the mouth; it is slow to leave him, but when it does, it leaves the boy worn out. ⁴⁰ I begged your disciples to drive it out, and they could not.' ⁴¹ In reply Jesus said, 'Faithless and perverse generation! How much longer must I be among you and put up with you? Bring your son here.' ⁴² Even while the boy was coming, the devil threw him to the ground in convulsions. But Jesus rebuked the unclean spirit and cured the boy and gave him back to his father, ⁴³ and everyone was awestruck by the greatness of God.
But while everyone was full of admiration for all he did, he said to his disciples, ⁴⁴ 'For your part, you must have these words constantly in mind: The Son of man is going to be delivered into the power of men.' ⁴⁵ But they did not understand what he said; it was hidden from them so that they should not see the meaning of it, and they were afraid to ask him about it.
⁴⁶ An argument started between them about which of them was the greatest. ⁴⁷ Jesus knew what thoughts were going through their minds, and he took a little child whom he set by his side ⁴⁸ and then he said to them, 'Anyone who welcomes this little child in my name welcomes me; and anyone who welcomes me, welcomes the one who sent me. The least among you all is the one who is the greatest.'

ᶻ**9** Dt 18:15, 19; Is 42:1.

NEW REVISED STANDARD VERSION

49 John answered, "Master, we saw someone casting out demons in your name, and we tried to stop him, because he does not follow with us." 50 But Jesus said to him, "Do not stop him; for whoever is not against you is for you."

51 When the days drew near for him to be taken up, he set his face to go to Jerusalem. 52 And he sent messengers ahead of him. On their way they entered a village of the Samaritans to make ready for him; 53 but they did not receive him, because his face was set toward Jerusalem. 54 When his disciples James and John saw it, they said, "Lord, do you want us to command fire to come down from heaven and consume them?"b 55 But he turned and rebuked them. 56 Thenc they went on to another village.

57 As they were going along the road, someone said to him, "I will follow you wherever you go." 58 And Jesus said to him, "Foxes have holes, and birds of the air have nests; but the Son of Man has nowhere to lay his head." 59 To another he said, "Follow me." But he said, "Lord, first let me go and bury my father." 60 But Jesusd said to him, "Let the dead bury their own dead; but as for you, go and proclaim the kingdom of God." 61 Another said, "I will follow you, Lord; but let me first say farewell to those at my home." 62 Jesus said to him, "No one who puts a hand to the plow and looks back is fit for the kingdom of God."

10 After this the Lord appointed seventye others and sent them on ahead of him in pairs to every town and place where he himself intended to go. 2 He said to them, "The harvest is plentiful, but the laborers are few; therefore ask the Lord of the harvest to send out laborers into his harvest. 3 Go on your way. See, I am sending you out like lambs into the midst of wolves. 4 Carry no purse, no bag, no sandals; and greet no one on the road. 5 Whatever house you enter, first say, 'Peace to this house!' 6 And if anyone is there who shares in peace, your peace will rest on that person; but if not, it will return to you. 7 Remain in the same house, eating and drinking whatever they provide, for the laborer deserves to be paid. Do not move about from house to house. 8 Whenever you enter a town and its people welcome you, eat what is set before you; 9 cure the sick who are there, and say to them, 'The kingdom of God has come near to you.'f 10 But whenever you enter a town and they do not welcome you, go out into its streets and say, 11 'Even the dust of your town that clings to our feet, we wipe off in protest against you. Yet know this: the kingdom of God has come near.'g 12 I tell you, on that day it will be more tolerable for Sodom than for that town.

13 "Woe to you, Chorazin! Woe to you, Bethsaida! For if the deeds of power done in you had been done in Tyre and Sidon, they would have repented long ago, sitting in sackcloth and ashes. 14 But at the judgment it will be more tolerable for Tyre and Sidon than for you. 15 And you, Capernaum,

will you be exalted to heaven?
No, you will be brought down to Hades.

16 "Whoever listens to you listens to me, and whoever rejects you rejects me, and whoever rejects me rejects the one who sent me."

17 The seventye returned with joy, saying, "Lord, in your name even the demons submit to us!" 18 He said to them, "I watched Satan fall from heaven like a flash of lightning. 19 See, I have given you authority to tread on

REVISED ENGLISH BIBLE

49 'Master,' said John, 'we saw someone driving out demons in your name, but as he is not one of us we tried to stop him.' 50 Jesus said to him, 'Do not stop him, for he who is not against you is on your side.'

51 As the time approached when he was to be taken up to heaven, he set his face resolutely towards Jerusalem, 52 and sent messengers ahead. They set out and went into a Samaritan village to make arrangements for him; 53 but the villagers would not receive him because he was on his way to Jerusalem. 54 When the disciples James and John saw this they said, 'Lord, do you want us to call down fire from heaven to consume them?' 55 But he turned and rebuked them, 56 and they went on to another village.

57 As they were going along the road a man said to him, 'I will follow you wherever you go.' 58 Jesus answered, 'Foxes have their holes and birds their roosts; but the Son of Man has nowhere to lay his head.' 59 To another he said, 'Follow me,' but the man replied, 'Let me first go and bury my father.' 60 Jesus said, 'Leave the dead to bury their dead; you must go and announce the kingdom of God.' 61 Yet another said, 'I will follow you, sir; but let me first say goodbye to my people at home.' 62 To him Jesus said, 'No one who sets his hand to the plough and then looks back is fit for the kingdom of God.'

10 After this the Lord appointed a further seventy-two and sent them on ahead in pairs to every town and place he himself intended to visit. 2 He said to them: 'The crop is heavy, but the labourers are few. Ask the owner therefore to send labourers to bring in the harvest. 3 Be on your way; I am sending you like lambs among wolves. 4 Carry no purse or pack, and travel barefoot. Exchange no greetings on the road. 5 When you go into a house, let your first words be, "Peace to this house." 6 If there is a man of peace there, your peace will rest on him; if not, it will return to you. 7 Stay in that house, sharing their food and drink; for the worker deserves his pay. Do not move around from house to house. 8 When you enter a town and you are made welcome, eat the food provided for you; 9 heal the sick there, and say, "The kingdom of God has come upon you." 10 But when you enter a town and you are not made welcome, go out into its streets and say, 11 "The very dust of your town that clings to our feet we wipe off to your shame. Only take note of this: the kingdom of God has come." 12 I tell you, on the day of judgement the fate of Sodom will be more bearable than the fate of that town.

13 'Alas for you, Chorazin! Alas for you, Bethsaida! If the miracles performed in you had taken place in Tyre and Sidon, they would have repented long ago, sitting in sackcloth and ashes. 14 But it will be more bearable for Tyre and Sidon at the judgement than for you. 15 As for you, Capernaum, will you be exalted to heaven? No, you will be brought down to Hades!

16 'Whoever listens to you listens to me; whoever rejects you rejects me. And whoever rejects me rejects the One who sent me.'

17 The seventy-two came back jubilant. 'In your name, Lord,' they said, 'even the demons submit to us.' 18 He replied, 'I saw Satan fall, like lightning, from heaven. 19 And I have given you the power to tread underfoot snakes

---

b Other ancient authorities add as Elijah did   c Other ancient authorities read rebuked them, and said, "You do not know what spirit you are of, 56for the Son of Man has not come to destroy the lives of human beings but to save them." Then   d Gk he   e Other ancient authorities read seventy-two   f Or is at hand for you   g Or is at hand

9:54 consume them: some witnesses add as Elijah did.
9:55 rebuked them: some witnesses add 'You do not know', he said, 'to what spirit you belong; (56)for the Son of Man did not come to destroy men's lives but to save them.'   10:1 seventy-two: some witnesses read seventy.   10:9 come upon you: or come close to you.   10:11 has come: or has come close.
10:17 seventy-two: some witnesses read seventy.

NEW AMERICAN BIBLE

49 Then John said in reply, "Master, we saw someone casting out demons in your name and we tried to prevent him because he does not follow in our company." 50 Jesus said to him, "Do not prevent him, for whoever is not against you is for you."

51 When the days for his being taken up were fulfilled, he resolutely determined to journey to Jerusalem, 52 and he sent messengers ahead of him. On the way they entered a Samaritan village to prepare for his reception there, 53 but they would not welcome him because the destination of his journey was Jerusalem. 54 When the disciples James and John saw this they asked, "Lord, do you want us to call down fire from heaven to consume them?" 55 Jesus turned and rebuked them, 56 and they journeyed to another village.

57 As they were proceeding on their journey someone said to him, "I will follow you wherever you go." 58 Jesus answered him, "Foxes have dens and birds of the sky have nests, but the Son of Man has nowhere to rest his head." 59 And to another he said, "Follow me." But he replied, "[Lord,] let me go first and bury my father." 60 But he answered him, "Let the dead bury their dead. But you, go and proclaim the kingdom of God." 61 And another said, "I will follow you, Lord, but first let me say farewell to my family at home." 62 [To him] Jesus said, "No one who sets a hand to the plow and looks to what was left behind is fit for the kingdom of God."

10 After this the Lord appointed seventy[-two] others whom he sent ahead of him in pairs to every town and place he intended to visit. 2 He said to them, "The harvest is abundant but the laborers are few; so ask the master of the harvest to send out laborers for his harvest. 3 Go on your way; behold, I am sending you like lambs among wolves. 4 Carry no money bag, no sack, no sandals; and greet no one along the way. 5 Into whatever house you enter, first say, 'Peace to this household.' 6 If a peaceful person lives there, your peace will rest on him; but if not, it will return to you. 7 Stay in the same house and eat and drink what is offered to you, for the laborer deserves his payment. Do not move about from one house to another. 8 Whatever town you enter and they welcome you, eat what is set before you, 9 cure the sick in it and say to them, 'The kingdom of God is at hand for you.' 10 Whatever town you enter and they do not receive you, go out into the streets and say, 11 'The dust of your town that clings to our feet, even that we shake off against you.' Yet know this: the kingdom of God is at hand. 12 I tell you, it will be more tolerable for Sodom on that day than for that town.

13 "Woe to you, Chorazin! Woe to you, Bethsaida! For if the mighty deeds done in your midst had been done in Tyre and Sidon, they would long ago have repented, sitting in sackcloth and ashes. 14 But it will be more tolerable for Tyre and Sidon at the judgment than for you. 15 And as for you, Capernaum, 'Will you be exalted to heaven? You will go down to the netherworld.' " 16 Whoever listens to you listens to me. Whoever rejects you rejects me. And whoever rejects me rejects the one who sent me."

17 The seventy[-two] returned rejoicing, and said, "Lord, even the demons are subject to us because of your name." 18 Jesus said, "I have observed Satan fall like lightning from the sky. 19 Behold, I have given you the power 'to tread

NEW JERUSALEM BIBLE

49 John spoke up. 'Master,' he said, 'we saw someone driving out devils in your name, and because he is not with us we tried to stop him.' 50 But Jesus said to him, 'You must not stop him: anyone who is not against you is for you.'

51 Now it happened that as the time drew near for him to be taken up, he resolutely turned his face towards Jerusalem 52 and sent messengers ahead of him. These set out, and they went into a Samaritan village to make preparations for him, 53 but the people would not receive him because he was making for Jerusalem. 54 Seeing this, the disciples James and John said, 'Lord, do you want us to call down fire from heaven to burn them up?' 55 But he turned and rebuked them, 56 and they went on to another village.

57 As they travelled along they met a man on the road who said to him, 'I will follow you wherever you go.' 58 Jesus answered, 'Foxes have holes and the birds of the air have nests, but the Son of man has nowhere to lay his head.' 59 Another to whom he said, 'Follow me,' replied, 'Let me go and bury my father first.' 60 But he answered, 'Leave the dead to bury their dead; your duty is to go and spread the news of the kingdom of God.' 61 Another said, 'I will follow you, sir, but first let me go and say good-bye to my people at home.' 62 Jesus said to him, 'Once the hand is laid on the plough, no one who looks back is fit for the kingdom of God.'

10 After this the Lord appointed seventy-two others and sent them out ahead of him in pairs, to all the towns and places he himself would be visiting. 2 And he said to them, 'The harvest is rich but the labourers are few, so ask the Lord of the harvest to send labourers to do his harvesting. 3 Start off now, but look, I am sending you out like lambs among wolves. 4 Take no purse with you, no haversack, no sandals. Salute no one on the road. 5 Whatever house you enter, let your first words be, "Peace to this house!" 6 And if a man of peace lives there, your peace will go and rest on him; if not, it will come back to you. 7 Stay in the same house, taking what food and drink they have to offer, for the labourer deserves his wages; do not move from house to house. 8 Whenever you go into a town where they make you welcome, eat what is put before you. 9 Cure those in it who are sick, and say, "The kingdom of God is very near to you." 10 But whenever you enter a town and they do not make you welcome, go out into its streets and say, 11 "We wipe off the very dust of your town that clings to our feet, and leave it with you. Yet be sure of this: the kingdom of God is very near." 12 I tell you, on the great Day it will be more bearable for Sodom than for that town.

13 'Alas for you, Chorazin! Alas for you, Bethsaida! For if the miracles done in you had been done in Tyre and Sidon, they would have repented long ago, sitting in sackcloth and ashes. 14 And still, it will be more bearable for Tyre and Sidon at the Judgement than for you. 15 And as for you, Capernaum, did you want to be *raised high as heaven? You shall be flung down to hell.* a

16 'Anyone who listens to you listens to me; anyone who rejects you rejects me, and those who reject me reject the one who sent me.'

17 The seventy-two came back rejoicing. 'Lord,' they said, 'even the devils submit to us when we use your name.' 18 He said to them, 'I watched Satan fall like lightning from heaven. 19 Look, I have given you power to tread down

---

10, 1: *Seventy*[*-two*]: important representatives of the Alexandrian and Caesarean text types read "seventy," while other important Alexandrian texts and Western readings have "seventy-two."

a 10 Is 14:13–15.

NEW REVISED STANDARD VERSION	REVISED ENGLISH BIBLE

NEW REVISED STANDARD VERSION

snakes and scorpions, and over all the power of the enemy; and nothing will hurt you. 20 Nevertheless, do not rejoice at this, that the spirits submit to you, but rejoice that your names are written in heaven."

21 At that same hour Jesus[h] rejoiced in the Holy Spirit[i] and said, "I thank[j] you, Father, Lord of heaven and earth, because you have hidden these things from the wise and the intelligent and have revealed them to infants; yes, Father, for such was your gracious will.[k] 22 All things have been handed over to me by my Father; and no one knows who the Son is except the Father, or who the Father is except the Son and anyone to whom the Son chooses to reveal him."

23 Then turning to the disciples, Jesus[h] said to them privately, "Blessed are the eyes that see what you see! 24 For I tell you that many prophets and kings desired to see what you see, but did not see it, and to hear what you hear, but did not hear it."

25 Just then a lawyer stood up to test Jesus.[l] "Teacher," he said, "what must I do to inherit eternal life?" 26 He said to him, "What is written in the law? What do you read there?" 27 He answered, "You shall love the Lord your God with all your heart, and with all your soul, and with all your strength, and with all your mind; and your neighbor as yourself." 28 And he said to him, "You have given the right answer; do this, and you will live."

29 But wanting to justify himself, he asked Jesus, "And who is my neighbor?" 30 Jesus replied, "A man was going down from Jerusalem to Jericho, and fell into the hands of robbers, who stripped him, beat him, and went away, leaving him half dead. 31 Now by chance a priest was going down that road; and when he saw him, he passed by on the other side. 32 So likewise a Levite, when he came to the place and saw him, passed by on the other side. 33 But a Samaritan while traveling came near him; and when he saw him, he was moved with pity. 34 He went to him and bandaged his wounds, having poured oil and wine on them. Then he put him on his own animal, brought him to an inn, and took care of him. 35 The next day he took out two denarii,[m] gave them to the innkeeper, and said, 'Take care of him; and when I come back, I will repay you whatever more you spend.' 36 Which of these three, do you think, was a neighbor to the man who fell into the hands of the robbers?" 37 He said, "The one who showed him mercy." Jesus said to him, "Go and do likewise."

38 Now as they went on their way, he entered a certain village, where a woman named Martha welcomed him into her home. 39 She had a sister named Mary, who sat at the Lord's feet and listened to what he was saying. 40 But Martha was distracted by her many tasks; so she came to him and asked, "Lord, do you not care that my sister has left me to do all the work by myself? Tell her then to help me." 41 But the Lord answered her, "Martha, Martha, you are worried and distracted by many things; 42 there is need of only one thing.[n] Mary has chosen the better part, which will not be taken away from her."

11 He was praying in a certain place, and after he had finished, one of his disciples said to him, "Lord, teach us to pray, as John taught his disciples." 2 He said to them, "When you pray, say:

REVISED ENGLISH BIBLE

and scorpions and all the forces of the enemy. Nothing will ever harm you. 20 Nevertheless, do not rejoice that the spirits submit to you, but that your names are enrolled in heaven.'

21 At that moment Jesus exulted in the Holy Spirit and said, 'I thank you, Father, Lord of heaven and earth, for hiding these things from the learned and wise, and revealing them to the simple. Yes, Father, such was your choice. 22 Everything is entrusted to me by my Father; no one knows who the Son is but the Father, or who the Father is but the Son, and those to whom the Son chooses to reveal him.'

23 When he was alone with his disciples he turned to them and said, 'Happy the eyes that see what you are seeing! 24 I tell you, many prophets and kings wished to see what you now see, yet never saw it; to hear what you hear, yet never heard it.'

25 A LAWYER once came forward to test him by asking: 'Teacher, what must I do to inherit eternal life?' 26 Jesus said, 'What is written in the law? What is your reading of it?' 27 He replied, 'Love the Lord your God with all your heart, and with all your soul, with all your strength, and with all your mind; and your neighbour as yourself.' 28 'That is the right answer,' said Jesus; 'do that and you will have life.'

29 Wanting to justify his question, he asked, 'But who is my neighbour?' 30 Jesus replied, 'A man was on his way from Jerusalem down to Jericho when he was set upon by robbers, who stripped and beat him, and went off leaving him half dead. 31 It so happened that a priest was going down by the same road, and when he saw him, he went past on the other side. 32 So too a Levite came to the place, and when he saw him went past on the other side. 33 But a Samaritan who was going that way came upon him, and when he saw him he was moved to pity. 34 He went up and bandaged his wounds, bathing them with oil and wine. Then he lifted him on to his own beast, brought him to an inn, and looked after him. 35 Next day he produced two silver pieces and gave them to the innkeeper, and said, "Look after him; and if you spend more, I will repay you on my way back." 36 Which of these three do you think was neighbour to the man who fell into the hands of the robbers?' 37 He answered, 'The one who showed him kindness.' Jesus said to him, 'Go and do as he did.'

38 While they were on their way Jesus came to a village where a woman named Martha made him welcome. 39 She had a sister, Mary, who seated herself at the Lord's feet and stayed there listening to his words. 40 Now Martha was distracted by her many tasks, so she came to him and said, 'Lord, do you not care that my sister has left me to get on with the work by myself? Tell her to come and give me a hand.' 41 But the Lord answered, 'Martha, Martha, you are fretting and fussing about so many things; 42 only one thing is necessary. Mary has chosen what is best; it shall not be taken away from her.'

11 At one place after Jesus had been praying, one of his disciples said, 'Lord, teach us to pray, as John taught his disciples.' 2 He answered, 'When you pray, say,

[h] Gk he   [i] Other authorities read in the spirit   [j] Or praise
[k] Or for so it was well-pleasing in your sight   [l] Gk him
[m] The denarius was the usual day's wage for a laborer   [n] Other ancient authorities read few things are necessary, or only one

10:21 Holy Spirit: some witnesses omit Holy. Yes . . . such: or Yes, I thank you, Father, that such.   10:42 only . . . necessary: some witnesses read only few things are necessary, or rather, one alone.

upon serpents' and scorpions and upon the full force of the enemy and nothing will harm you. 20 Nevertheless, do not rejoice because the spirits are subject to you, but rejoice because your names are written in heaven."

21 At that very moment he rejoiced [in] the holy Spirit and said, "I give you praise, Father, Lord of heaven and earth, for although you have hidden these things from the wise and the learned you have revealed them to the childlike. Yes, Father, such has been your gracious will. 22 All things have been handed over to me by my Father. No one knows who the Son is except the Father, and who the Father is except the Son and anyone to whom the Son wishes to reveal him."

23 Turning to the disciples in private he said, "Blessed are the eyes that see what you see. 24 For I say to you, many prophets and kings desired to see what you see, but did not see it, and to hear what you hear, but did not hear it."

25 There was a scholar of the law who stood up to test him and said, "Teacher, what must I do to inherit eternal life?" 26 Jesus said to him, "What is written in the law? How do you read it?" 27 He said in reply, "You shall love the Lord, your God, with all your heart, with all your being, with all your strength, and with all your mind, and your neighbor as yourself." 28 He replied to him, "You have answered correctly; do this and you will live."

29 But because he wished to justify himself, he said to Jesus, "And who is my neighbor?" 30 Jesus replied, "A man fell victim to robbers as he went down from Jerusalem to Jericho. They stripped and beat him and went off leaving him half-dead. 31 A priest happened to be going down that road, but when he saw him, he passed by on the opposite side. 32 Likewise a Levite came to the place, and when he saw him, he passed by on the opposite side. 33 But a Samaritan traveler who came upon him was moved with compassion at the sight. 34 He approached the victim, poured oil and wine over his wounds and bandaged them. Then he lifted him up on his own animal, took him to an inn and cared for him. 35 The next day he took out two silver coins and gave them to the innkeeper with the instruction, 'Take care of him. If you spend more than what I have given you, I shall repay you on my way back.' 36 Which of these three, in your opinion, was neighbor to the robbers' victim?" 37 He answered, "The one who treated him with mercy." Jesus said to him, "Go and do likewise."

38 As they continued their journey he entered a village where a woman whose name was Martha welcomed him. 39 She had a sister named Mary [who] sat beside the Lord at his feet listening to him speak. 40 Martha, burdened with much serving, came to him and said, "Lord, do you not care that my sister has left me by myself to do the serving? Tell her to help me." 41 The Lord said to her in reply, "Martha, Martha, you are anxious and worried about many things. 42 There is need of only one thing. Mary has chosen the better part and it will not be taken from her."

11 He was praying in a certain place, and when he had finished, one of his disciples said to him, "Lord, teach us to pray just as John taught his disciples." 2 He said to them, "When you pray, say:

serpents and scorpions and the whole strength of the enemy; nothing shall ever hurt you. 20 Yet do not rejoice that the spirits submit to you; rejoice instead that your names are written in heaven.'

21 Just at this time, filled with joy by the Holy Spirit, he said, 'I bless you, Father, Lord of heaven and of earth, for hiding these things from the learned and the clever and revealing them to little children. Yes, Father, for that is what it has pleased you to do. 22 Everything has been entrusted to me by my Father; and no one knows who the Son is except the Father, and who the Father is except the Son and those to whom the Son chooses to reveal him.'

23 Then turning to his disciples he spoke to them by themselves, 'Blessed are the eyes that see what you see, 24 for I tell you that many prophets and kings wanted to see what you see, and never saw it; to hear what you hear, and never heard it.'

25 And now a lawyer stood up and, to test him, asked, 'Master, what must I do to inherit eternal life?' 26 He said to him, 'What is written in the Law? What is your reading of it?' 27 He replied, '*You must love the Lord your God with all your heart, with all your soul, with all your strength,* and with all your mind, *and your neighbour as yourself.*' [b] 28 Jesus said to him, 'You have answered right, do this and life is yours.'

29 But the man was anxious to justify himself and said to Jesus, 'And who is my neighbour?' 30 In answer Jesus said, 'A man was once on his way down from Jerusalem to Jericho and fell into the hands of bandits; they stripped him, beat him and then made off, leaving him half dead. 31 Now a priest happened to be travelling down the same road, but when he saw the man, he passed by on the other side. 32 In the same way a Levite who came to the place saw him, and passed by on the other side. 33 But a Samaritan traveller who came on him was moved with compassion when he saw him. 34 He went up to him and bandaged his wounds, pouring oil and wine on them. He then lifted him onto his own mount and took him to an inn and looked after him. 35 Next day, he took out two denarii and handed them to the innkeeper and said, "Look after him, and on my way back I will make good any extra expense you have." 36 Which of these three, do you think, proved himself a neighbour to the man who fell into the bandits' hands?' 37 He replied, 'The one who showed pity towards him.' Jesus said to him, 'Go, and do the same yourself.'

38 In the course of their journey he came to a village, and a woman named Martha welcomed him into her house. 39 She had a sister called Mary, who sat down at the Lord's feet and listened to him speaking. 40 Now Martha, who was distracted with all the serving, came to him and said, 'Lord, do you not care that my sister is leaving me to do the serving all by myself? Please tell her to help me.' 41 But the Lord answered, 'Martha, Martha,' he said, 'you worry and fret about so many things, 42 and yet few are needed, indeed only one. It is Mary who has chosen the better part, and it is not to be taken from her.'

11 Now it happened that he was in a certain place praying, and when he had finished, one of his disciples said, 'Lord, teach us to pray, as John taught his disciples.' 2 He said to them, 'When you pray, this is what to say:

b **10** Dt 6:5 and Lv 19:18.

NEW REVISED STANDARD VERSION

Father,*o* hallowed be your name.
Your kingdom come.*p*
3 Give us each day our daily bread.*q*
4 And forgive us our sins,
for we ourselves forgive everyone indebted
to us.
And do not bring us to the time of trial."*r*

5 And he said to them, "Suppose one of you has a friend, and you go to him at midnight and say to him, 'Friend, lend me three loaves of bread; 6 for a friend of mine has arrived, and I have nothing to set before him.' 7 And he answers from within, 'Do not bother me; the door has already been locked, and my children are with me in bed; I cannot get up and give you anything.' 8 I tell you, even though he will not get up and give him anything because he is his friend, at least because of his persistence he will get up and give him whatever he needs.

9 "So I say to you, Ask, and it will be given you; search, and you will find; knock, and the door will be opened for you. 10 For everyone who asks receives, and everyone who searches finds, and for everyone who knocks, the door will be opened. 11 Is there anyone among you who, if your child asks for*s* a fish, will give a snake instead of a fish? 12 Or if the child asks for an egg, will give a scorpion? 13 If you then, who are evil, know how to give good gifts to your children, how much more will the heavenly Father give the Holy Spirit*t* to those who ask him!"

14 Now he was casting out a demon that was mute; when the demon had gone out, the one who had been mute spoke, and the crowds were amazed. 15 But some of them said, "He casts out demons by Beelzebul, the ruler of the demons." 16 Others, to test him, kept demanding from him a sign from heaven. 17 But he knew what they were thinking and said to them, "Every kingdom divided against itself becomes a desert, and house falls on house. 18 If Satan also is divided against himself, how will his kingdom stand? —for you say that I cast out the demons by Beelzebul. 19 Now if I cast out the demons by Beelzebul, by whom do your exorcists*u* cast them out? Therefore they will be your judges. 20 But if it is by the finger of God that I cast out the demons, then the kingdom of God has come to you. 21 When a strong man, fully armed, guards his castle, his property is safe. 22 But when one stronger than he attacks him and overpowers him, he takes away his armor in which he trusted and divides his plunder. 23 Whoever is not with me is against me, and whoever does not gather with me scatters.

24 "When the unclean spirit has gone out of a person, it wanders through waterless regions looking for a resting place, but not finding any, it says, 'I will return to my house from which I came.' 25 When it comes, it finds it swept and put in order. 26 Then it goes and brings seven other spirits more evil than itself, and they enter and live there; and the last state of that person is worse than the first."

27 While he was saying this, a woman in the crowd raised her voice and said to him, "Blessed is the womb that bore you and the breasts that nursed you!" 28 But he said, "Blessed rather are those who hear the word of God and obey it!"

REVISED ENGLISH BIBLE

Father, may your name be hallowed;
your kingdom come.
3 Give us each day our daily bread.
4 And forgive us our sins,
for we too forgive all who have done us wrong.
And do not put us to the test.'

5 Then he said to them, 'Suppose one of you has a friend who comes to him in the middle of the night and says, "My friend, lend me three loaves, 6 for a friend of mine on a journey has turned up at my house, and I have nothing to offer him"; 7 and he replies from inside, "Do not bother me. The door is shut for the night; my children and I have gone to bed; and I cannot get up and give you what you want." 8 I tell you that even if he will not get up and provide for him out of friendship, his very persistence will make the man get up and give him all he needs. 9 So I say to you, ask, and you will receive; seek, and you will find; knock, and the door will be opened to you. 10 For everyone who asks receives, those who seek find, and to those who knock, the door will be opened.

11 'Would any father among you offer his son a snake when he asks for a fish, 12 or a scorpion when he asks for an egg? 13 If you, bad as you are, know how to give good things to your children, how much more will the heavenly Father give the Holy Spirit to those who ask him!'

14 HE was driving out a demon which was dumb; and when the demon had come out, the dumb man began to speak. The people were astonished, 15 but some of them said, 'It is by Beelzebul prince of demons that he drives the demons out.' 16 Others, by way of a test, demanded of him a sign from heaven. 17 But he knew what was in their minds, and said, 'Every kingdom divided against itself is laid waste, and a divided household falls. 18 And if Satan is divided against himself, how can his kingdom stand—since, as you claim, I drive out the demons by Beelzebul? 19 If it is by Beelzebul that I drive out demons, by whom do your own people drive them out? If this is your argument, they themselves will refute you. 20 But if it is by the finger of God that I drive out the demons, then be sure the kingdom of God has already come upon you.

21 'When a strong man fully armed is on guard over his palace, his possessions are safe. 22 But when someone stronger attacks and overpowers him, he carries off the arms and armour on which the man had relied and distributes the spoil.

23 'He who is not with me is against me, and he who does not gather with me scatters.

24 'When an unclean spirit comes out of someone it wanders over the desert sands seeking a resting-place; and if it finds none, it says, "I will go back to the home I left." 25 So it returns and finds the house swept clean and tidy. 26 It goes off and collects seven other spirits more wicked than itself, and they all come in and settle there; and in the end that person's plight is worse than before.'

27 While he was speaking thus, a woman in the crowd called out, 'Happy the womb that carried you and the breasts that suckled you!' 28 He rejoined, 'No, happy are those who hear the word of God and keep it.'

---

o Other ancient authorities read *Our Father in heaven*   *p* A few ancient authorities read *Your Holy Spirit come upon us and cleanse us.* Other ancient authorities add *Your will be done, on earth as in heaven*   *q* Or *our bread for tomorrow*   *r* Or *us into temptation.* Other ancient authorities add *but rescue us from the evil one* (or *from evil*)   *s* Other ancient authorities add *bread, will give a stone; or if your child asks for*   *t* Other ancient authorities read *the Father give the Holy Spirit from heaven*   *u* Gk *sons*

11:2 **Father:** *some witnesses read* Our Father in heaven. **your kingdom come:** *one witness reads* your kingdom come upon us; *some others have* your Holy Spirit come upon us and cleanse us; *some add* your will be done, on earth as in heaven.   11:3 **daily bread:** *or* bread for the morrow.   11:4 **to the test:** *some witnesses add* but save us from the evil one (*or* from evil).   11:11 **offer his son:** *some witnesses add* a stone when he asks for bread, or.

Father, hallowed be your name,
your kingdom come.
3 Give us each day our daily bread
4 and forgive us our sins
for we ourselves forgive everyone in debt to us,
and do not subject us to the final test."

5 And he said to them, "Suppose one of you has a friend to whom he goes at midnight and says, 'Friend, lend me three loaves of bread, 6 for a friend of mine has arrived at my house from a journey and I have nothing to offer him,' 7 and he says in reply from within, 'Do not bother me; the door has already been locked and my children and I are already in bed. I cannot get up to give you anything.' 8 I tell you, if he does not get up to give him the loaves because of their friendship, he will get up to give him whatever he needs because of his persistence.

9 "And I tell you, ask and you will receive; seek and you will find; knock and the door will be opened to you. 10 For everyone who asks, receives; and the one who seeks, finds; and to the one who knocks, the door will be opened. 11 What father among you would hand his son a snake when he asks for a fish? 12 Or hand him a scorpion when he asks for an egg? 13 If you then, who are wicked, know how to give good gifts to your children, how much more will the Father in heaven give the holy Spirit to those who ask him?"

14 He was driving out a demon [that was] mute, and when the demon had gone out, the mute person spoke and the crowds were amazed. 15 Some of them said, "By the power of Beelzebul, the prince of demons, he drives out demons." 16 Others, to test him, asked him for a sign from heaven. 17 But he knew their thoughts and said to them, "Every kingdom divided against itself will be laid waste and house will fall against house. 18 And if Satan is divided against himself, how will his kingdom stand? For you say that it is by Beelzebul that I drive out demons. 19 If I, then, drive out demons by Beelzebul, by whom do your own people drive them out? Therefore they will be your judges. 20 But if it is by the finger of God that [I] drive out demons, then the kingdom of God has come upon you. 21 When a strong man fully armed guards his palace, his possessions are safe. 22 But when one stronger than he attacks and overcomes him, he takes away the armor on which he relied and distributes the spoils. 23 Whoever is not with me is against me, and whoever does not gather with me scatters.

24 "When an unclean spirit goes out of someone, it roams through arid regions searching for rest but, finding none, it says, 'I shall return to my home from which I came.' 25 But upon returning, it finds it swept clean and put in order. 26 Then it goes and brings back seven other spirits more wicked than itself who move in and dwell there, and the last condition of that person is worse than the first."

27 While he was speaking, a woman from the crowd called out and said to him, "Blessed is the womb that carried you and the breasts at which you nursed." 28 He replied, "Rather, blessed are those who hear the word of God and observe it."

Father, may your name be held holy,
your kingdom come;
3 give us each day our daily bread,
and forgive us our sins,
4 for we ourselves forgive each one who is in debt to us.
And do not put us to the test.' c

5 He also said to them, 'Suppose one of you has a friend and goes to him in the middle of the night to say, "My friend, lend me three loaves, 6 because a friend of mine on his travels has just arrived at my house and I have nothing to offer him;" 7 and the man answers from inside the house, "Do not bother me. The door is bolted now, and my children are with me in bed; I cannot get up to give it to you." 8 I tell you, if the man does not get up and give it to him for friendship's sake, persistence will make him get up and give his friend all he wants.

9 'So I say to you: Ask, and it will be given to you; search, and you will find; knock, and the door will be opened to you. 10 For everyone who asks receives; everyone who searches finds; everyone who knocks will have the door opened. 11 What father among you, if his son asked for a fish, would hand him a snake? 12 Or if he asked for an egg, hand him a scorpion? 13 If you then, evil as you are, know how to give your children what is good, how much more will the heavenly Father give the Holy Spirit to those who ask him!'

14 He was driving out a devil and it was dumb; and it happened that when the devil had gone out the dumb man spoke, and the people were amazed. 15 But some of them said, 'It is through Beelzebul, the prince of devils, that he drives devils out.' 16 Others asked him, as a test, for a sign from heaven; 17 but, knowing what they were thinking, he said to them, 'Any kingdom which is divided against itself is heading for ruin, and house collapses against house. 18 So, too, with Satan: if he is divided against himself, how can his kingdom last? — since you claim that it is through Beelzebul that I drive devils out. 19 Now if it is through Beelzebul that I drive devils out, through whom do your own sons drive them out? They shall be your judges, then. 20 But if it is through the finger of God that I drive devils out, then the kingdom of God has indeed caught you unawares. 21 So long as a strong man fully armed guards his own home, his goods are undisturbed; 22 but when someone stronger than himself attacks and defeats him, the stronger man takes away all the weapons he relied on and shares out his spoil.

23 'Anyone who is not with me is against me; and anyone who does not gather in with me throws away.

24 'When an unclean spirit goes out of someone it wanders through waterless country looking for a place to rest, and not finding one it says, "I will go back to the home I came from." 25 But on arrival, finding it swept and tidied, 26 it then goes off and brings seven other spirits more wicked than itself, and they go in and set up house there, and so that person ends up worse off than before.'

27 It happened that as he was speaking, a woman in the crowd raised her voice and said, 'Blessed the womb that bore you and the breasts that fed you!' 28 But he replied, 'More blessed still are those who hear the word of God and keep it!'

29 When the crowds were increasing, he began to say, "This generation is an evil generation; it asks for a sign, but no sign will be given to it except the sign of Jonah. 30 For just as Jonah became a sign to the people of Nineveh, so the Son of Man will be to this generation. 31 The queen of the South will rise at the judgment with the people of this generation and condemn them, because she came from the ends of the earth to listen to the wisdom of Solomon, and see, something greater than Solomon is here! 32 The people of Nineveh will rise up at the judgment with this generation and condemn it, because they repented at the proclamation of Jonah, and see, something greater than Jonah is here!

33 "No one after lighting a lamp puts it in a cellar,ᵛ but on the lampstand so that those who enter may see the light. 34 Your eye is the lamp of your body. If your eye is healthy, your whole body is full of light; but if it is not healthy, your body is full of darkness. 35 Therefore consider whether the light in you is not darkness. 36 If then your whole body is full of light, with no part of it in darkness, it will be as full of light as when a lamp gives you light with its rays."

37 While he was speaking, a Pharisee invited him to dine with him; so he went in and took his place at the table. 38 The Pharisee was amazed to see that he did not first wash before dinner. 39 Then the Lord said to him, "Now you Pharisees clean the outside of the cup and of the dish, but inside you are full of greed and wickedness. 40 You fools! Did not the one who made the outside make the inside also? 41 So give for alms those things that are within; and see, everything will be clean for you.

42 "But woe to you Pharisees! For you tithe mint and rue and herbs of all kinds, and neglect justice and the love of God; it is these you ought to have practiced, without neglecting the others. 43 Woe to you Pharisees! For you love to have the seat of honor in the synagogues and to be greeted with respect in the marketplaces. 44 Woe to you! For you are like unmarked graves, and people walk over them without realizing it."

45 One of the lawyers answered him, "Teacher, when you say these things, you insult us too." 46 And he said, "Woe also to you lawyers! For you load people with burdens hard to bear, and you yourselves do not lift a finger to ease them. 47 Woe to you! For you build the tombs of the prophets whom your ancestors killed. 48 So you are witnesses and approve of the deeds of your ancestors; for they killed them, and you build their tombs. 49 Therefore also the Wisdom of God said, 'I will send them prophets and apostles, some of whom they will kill and persecute,' 50 so that this generation may be charged with the blood of all the prophets shed since the foundation of the world, 51 from the blood of Abel to the blood of Zechariah, who perished between the altar and the sanctuary. Yes, I tell you, it will be charged against this generation. 52 Woe to you lawyers! For you have taken away the key of knowledge; you did not enter yourselves, and you hindered those who were entering."

53 When he went outside, the scribes and the Pharisees began to be very hostile toward him and to cross-examine him about many things, 54 lying in wait for him, to catch him in something he might say.

29 With the crowds swarming round him he went on to say: 'This is a wicked generation. It demands a sign, and the only sign that will be given it is the sign of Jonah. 30 For just as Jonah was a sign to the Ninevites, so will the Son of Man be to this generation. 31 The queen of the south will appear in court when the men of this generation are on trial, and ensure their condemnation; for she came from the ends of the earth to listen to the wisdom of Solomon, and what is here is greater than Solomon. 32 The men of Nineveh will appear in court when this generation is on trial, and ensure its condemnation; for they repented at the preaching of Jonah; and what is here is greater than Jonah.

33 'No one lights a lamp and puts it in a cellar, but on the lampstand so that those who come in may see the light. 34 The lamp of your body is the eye. When your eyes are sound, you have light for your whole body; but when they are bad, your body is in darkness. 35 See to it then that the light you have is not darkness. 36 If you have light for your whole body with no trace of darkness, it will all be full of light, as when the light of a lamp shines on you.'

37 WHEN he had finished speaking, a Pharisee invited him to a meal, and he came in and sat down. 38 The Pharisee noticed with surprise that he had not begun by washing before the meal. 39 But the Lord said to him, 'You Pharisees clean the outside of cup and plate; but inside you are full of greed and wickedness. 40 You fools! Did not he who made the outside make the inside too? 41 But let what is inside be given in charity, and all is clean.

42 'Alas for you Pharisees! You pay tithes of mint and rue and every garden herb, but neglect justice and the love of God. It is these you should have practised, without overlooking the others.

43 'Alas for you Pharisees! You love to have the chief seats in synagogues, and to be greeted respectfully in the street.

44 'Alas, alas, you are like unmarked graves which people walk over unawares.'

45 At this one of the lawyers said, 'Teacher, when you say things like this you are insulting us too.' 46 Jesus rejoined: 'Alas for you lawyers also! You load men with intolerable burdens, and will not lift a finger to lighten the load.

47 'Alas, you build monuments to the prophets whom your fathers murdered, 48 and so testify that you approve of the deeds your fathers did; they committed the murders and you provide the monuments.

49 'This is why the Wisdom of God said, "I will send them prophets and messengers; and some of these they will persecute and kill"; 50 so that this generation will have to answer for the blood of all the prophets shed since the foundation of the world; 51 from the blood of Abel to the blood of Zechariah who met his death between the altar and the sanctuary. I tell you, this generation will have to answer for it all.

52 'Alas for you lawyers! You have taken away the key of knowledge. You did not go in yourselves, and those who were trying to go in, you prevented.'

53 After he had left the house, the scribes and Pharisees began to assail him fiercely and to ply him with a host of questions, 54 laying snares to catch him with his own words.

11:31 **will appear . . . trial:** or will be raised to life at the judgement together with the men of this generation.   11:32 **The men . . . ensure:** or At the judgement the men of Nineveh will rise again together with this generation and will ensure.   11:33 **in a cellar:** some witnesses add or under the measuring bowl.

ᵛ Other ancient authorities add or under the bushel basket

29 While still more people gathered in the crowd, he said to them, "This generation is an evil generation; it seeks a sign, but no sign will be given it, except the sign of Jonah. 30 Just as Jonah became a sign to the Ninevites, so will the Son of Man be to this generation. 31 At the judgment the queen of the south will rise with the men of this generation and she will condemn them, because she came from the ends of the earth to hear the wisdom of Solomon, and there is something greater than Solomon here. 32 At the judgment the men of Nineveh will arise with this generation and condemn it, because at the preaching of Jonah they repented, and there is something greater than Jonah here.

33 "No one who lights a lamp hides it away or places it [under a bushel basket], but on a lampstand so that those who enter might see the light. 34 The lamp of the body is your eye. When your eye is sound, then your whole body is filled with light, but when it is bad, then your body is in darkness. 35 Take care, then, that the light in you not become darkness. 36 If your whole body is full of light, and no part of it is in darkness, then it will be as full of light as a lamp illuminating you with its brightness."

37 After he had spoken, a Pharisee invited him to dine at his home. He entered and reclined at table to eat. 38 The Pharisee was amazed to see that he did not observe the prescribed washing before the meal. 39 The Lord said to him, "Oh you Pharisees! Although you cleanse the outside of the cup and the dish, inside you are filled with plunder and evil. 40 You fools! Did not the maker of the outside also make the inside? 41 But as to what is within, give alms, and behold, everything will be clean for you. 42 Woe to you Pharisees! You pay tithes of mint and of rue and of every garden herb, but you pay no attention to judgment and to love for God. These you should have done, without overlooking the others. 43 Woe to you Pharisees! You love the seat of honor in synagogues and greetings in marketplaces. 44 Woe to you! You are like unseen graves over which people unknowingly walk."

45 Then one of the scholars of the law said to him in reply, "Teacher, by saying this you are insulting us too." 46 And he said, "Woe also to you scholars of the law! You impose on people burdens hard to carry, but you yourselves do not lift one finger to touch them. 47 Woe to you! You build the memorials of the prophets whom your ancestors killed. 48 Consequently, you bear witness and give consent to the deeds of your ancestors, for they killed them and you do the building. 49 Therefore, the wisdom of God said, 'I will send to them prophets and apostles; some of them they will kill and persecute' 50 in order that this generation might be charged with the blood of all the prophets shed since the foundation of the world, 51 from the blood of Abel to the blood of Zechariah who died between the altar and the temple building. Yes, I tell you, this generation will be charged with their blood! 52 Woe to you, scholars of the law! You have taken away the key of knowledge. You yourselves did not enter and you stopped those trying to enter." 53 When he left, the scribes and Pharisees began to act with hostility toward him and to interrogate him about many things, 54 for they were plotting to catch him at something he might say.

29 The crowds got even bigger and he addressed them, 'This is an evil generation; it is asking for a sign. The only sign it will be given is the sign of Jonah. 30 For just as Jonah became a sign to the people of Nineveh, so will the Son of man be a sign to this generation. 31 On Judgement Day the Queen of the South will stand up against the people of this generation and be their condemnation, because she came from the ends of the earth to hear the wisdom of Solomon;d and, look, there is something greater than Solomon here. 32 On Judgement Day the men of Nineveh will appear against this generation and be its condemnation, because when Jonah preached they repented; and, look, there is something greater than Jonah here.

33 'No one lights a lamp and puts it in some hidden place or under a tub; they put it on the lamp-stand so that people may see the light when they come in. 34 The lamp of the body is your eye. When your eye is clear, your whole body, too, is filled with light; but when it is diseased your body, too, will be darkened. 35 See to it then that the light inside you is not darkness. 36 If, therefore, your whole body is filled with light, and not darkened at all, it will be light entirely, as when the lamp shines on you with its rays.'

37 He had just finished speaking when a Pharisee invited him to dine at his house. He went in and sat down at table. 38 The Pharisee saw this and was surprised that he had not first washed before the meal. 39 But the Lord said to him, 'You Pharisees! You clean the outside of cup and plate, while inside yourselves you are filled with extortion and wickedness. 40 Fools! Did not he who made the outside make the inside too? 41 Instead, give alms from what you have and, look, everything will be clean for you. 42 But alas for you Pharisees, because you pay your tithe of mint and rue and all sorts of garden herbs and neglect justice and the love of God! These you should have practised, without neglecting the others. 43 Alas for you Pharisees, because you like to take the seats of honour in the synagogues and to be greeted respectfully in the market squares! 44 Alas for you, because you are like the unmarked tombs that people walk on without knowing it!'

45 A lawyer then spoke up. 'Master,' he said, 'when you speak like this you insult us too.' 46 But he said, 'Alas for you lawyers as well, because you load on people burdens that are unendurable, burdens that you yourselves do not touch with your fingertips.

47 'Alas for you because you build tombs for the prophets, the people your ancestors killed! 48 In this way you both witness to what your ancestors did and approve it; they did the killing, you do the building.

49 'And that is why the Wisdom of God said, "I will send them prophets and apostles; some they will slaughter and persecute, 50 so that this generation will have to answer for every prophet's blood that has been shed since the foundation of the world, 51 from the blood of Abel to the blood of Zechariah, who perished between the altar and the Temple." Yes, I tell you, this generation will have to answer for it all.

52 'Alas for you lawyers who have taken away the key of knowledge! You have not gone in yourselves and have prevented others from going in who wanted to.'

53 When he left there, the scribes and the Pharisees began a furious attack on him and tried to force answers from him on innumerable questions, 54 lying in wait to catch him out in something he might say.

d 11 1 K 10:1–10.

NEW REVISED STANDARD VERSION

12 Meanwhile, when the crowd gathered by the thousands, so that they trampled on one another, he began to speak first to his disciples, "Beware of the yeast of the Pharisees, that is, their hypocrisy. 2 Nothing is covered up that will not be uncovered, and nothing secret that will not become known. 3 Therefore whatever you have said in the dark will be heard in the light, and what you have whispered behind closed doors will be proclaimed from the housetops.

4 "I tell you, my friends, do not fear those who kill the body, and after that can do nothing more. 5 But I will warn you whom to fear: fear him who, after he has killed, has authority[w] to cast into hell.[x] Yes, I tell you, fear him! 6 Are not five sparrows sold for two pennies? Yet not one of them is forgotten in God's sight. 7 But even the hairs of your head are all counted. Do not be afraid; you are of more value than many sparrows.

8 "And I tell you, everyone who acknowledges me before others, the Son of Man also will acknowledge before the angels of God; 9 but whoever denies me before others will be denied before the angels of God. 10 And everyone who speaks a word against the Son of Man will be forgiven; but whoever blasphemes against the Holy Spirit will not be forgiven. 11 When they bring you before the synagogues, the rulers, and the authorities, do not worry about how[y] you are to defend yourselves or what you are to say; 12 for the Holy Spirit will teach you at that very hour what you ought to say."

13 Someone in the crowd said to him, "Teacher, tell my brother to divide the family inheritance with me." 14 But he said to him, "Friend, who set me to be a judge or arbitrator over you?" 15 And he said to them, "Take care! Be on your guard against all kinds of greed; for one's life does not consist in the abundance of possessions." 16 Then he told them a parable: "The land of a rich man produced abundantly. 17 And he thought to himself, 'What should I do, for I have no place to store my crops?' 18 Then he said, 'I will do this: I will pull down my barns and build larger ones, and there I will store all my grain and my goods. 19 And I will say to my soul, 'Soul, you have ample goods laid up for many years; relax, eat, drink, be merry.' 20 But God said to him, 'You fool! This very night your life is being demanded of you. And the things you have prepared, whose will they be?' 21 So it is with those who store up treasures for themselves but are not rich toward God."

22 He said to his disciples, "Therefore I tell you, do not worry about your life, what you will eat, or about your body, what you will wear. 23 For life is more than food, and the body more than clothing. 24 Consider the ravens: they neither sow nor reap, they have neither storehouse nor barn, and yet God feeds them. Of how much more value are you than the birds! 25 And can any of you by worrying add a single hour to your span of life?[z] 26 If then you are not able to do so small a thing as that, why do you worry about the rest? 27 Consider the lilies, how they grow: they neither toil nor spin;[a] yet I tell you, even Solomon in all his glory was not clothed like one of these. 28 But if God so clothes the grass of the field, which is alive today and tomorrow is thrown into the oven, how much more will he clothe you— you of little faith! 29 And do not keep striving for what you are to eat and what you are to drink, and do not keep worrying. 30 For it is the nations of the world that strive after all these things, and your Father knows that you need them. 31 Instead, strive for his[b] kingdom, and these things will be given to you as well.

[w] Or power   [x] Gk Gehenna   [y] Other ancient authorities add or what   [z] Or add a cubit to your stature   [a] Other ancient authorities read Consider the lilies; they neither spin nor weave   [b] Other ancient authorities read God's

REVISED ENGLISH BIBLE

12 MEANWHILE, when a crowd of many thousands had gathered, packed so close that they were trampling on one another, he began to speak first to his disciples: 'Be on your guard against the leaven of the Pharisees—I mean their hypocrisy. 2 There is nothing covered up that will not be uncovered, nothing hidden that will not be made known. 3 Therefore everything you have said in the dark will be heard in broad daylight, and what you have whispered behind closed doors will be shouted from the housetops.

4 'To you who are my friends I say: do not fear those who kill the body and after that have nothing more they can do. 5 I will show you whom to fear: fear him who, after he has killed, has authority to cast into hell. Believe me, he is the one to fear.

6 'Are not five sparrows sold for twopence? Yet not one of them is overlooked by God. 7 More than that, even the hairs of your head have all been counted. Do not be afraid; you are worth more than any number of sparrows.

8 'I tell you this: whoever acknowledges me before others, the Son of Man will acknowledge before the angels of God; 9 but whoever disowns me before others will be disowned before the angels of God.

10 'Anyone who speaks a word against the Son of Man will be forgiven; but for him who slanders the Holy Spirit there will be no forgiveness.

11 'When you are brought before synagogues and state authorities, do not worry about how you will conduct your defence or what you will say. 12 When the time comes the Holy Spirit will instruct you what to say.'

13 Someone in the crowd said to him, 'Teacher, tell my brother to divide the family property with me.' 14 He said to the man, 'Who set me over you to judge or arbitrate?' 15 Then to the people he said, 'Beware! Be on your guard against greed of every kind, for even when someone has more than enough, his possessions do not give him life.' 16 And he told them this parable: 'There was a rich man whose land yielded a good harvest. 17 He debated with himself: "What am I to do? I have not the space to store my produce. 18 This is what I will do," said he: "I will pull down my barns and build them bigger. I will collect in them all my grain and other goods, 19 and I will say to myself, 'You have plenty of good things laid by, enough for many years to come: take life easy, eat, drink, and enjoy yourself.' " 20 But God said to him, "You fool, this very night you must surrender your life; and the money you have made, who will get it now?" 21 That is how it is with the man who piles up treasure for himself and remains a pauper in the sight of God.'

22 To his disciples he said, 'This is why I tell you not to worry about food to keep you alive or clothes to cover your body. 23 Life is more than food, the body more than clothes. 24 Think of the ravens: they neither sow nor reap; they have no storehouse or barn; yet God feeds them. You are worth far more than the birds! 25 Can anxious thought add a day to your life? 26 If, then, you cannot do even a very little thing, why worry about the rest?

27 'Think of the lilies: they neither spin nor weave; yet I tell you, even Solomon in all his splendour was not attired like one of them. 28 If that is how God clothes the grass, which is growing in the field today, and tomorrow is thrown on the stove, how much more will he clothe you! How little faith you have! 29 Do not set your minds on what you are to eat or drink; do not be anxious. 30 These are all things that occupy the minds of the Gentiles, but your Father knows that you need them. 31 No, set your minds on his kingdom, and the rest will come to you as well.

12:25 **a day . . . life:** or a foot to your height.

12 Meanwhile, so many people were crowding together that they were trampling one another underfoot. He began to speak, first to his disciples, "Beware of the leaven — that is, the hypocrisy — of the Pharisees. 2 "There is nothing concealed that will not be revealed, nor secret that will not be known. 3 Therefore whatever you have said in the darkness will be heard in the light, and what you have whispered behind closed doors will be proclaimed on the housetops. 4 I tell you, my friends, do not be afraid of those who kill the body but after that can do no more. 5 I shall show you whom to fear. Be afraid of the one who after killing has the power to cast into Gehenna; yes, I tell you, be afraid of that one. 6 Are not five sparrows sold for two small coins? Yet not one of them has escaped the notice of God. 7 Even the hairs of your head have all been counted. Do not be afraid. You are worth more than many sparrows. 8 I tell you, everyone who acknowledges me before others the Son of Man will acknowledge before the angels of God. 9 But whoever denies me before others will be denied before the angels of God.

10 "Everyone who speaks a word against the Son of Man will be forgiven, but the one who blasphemes against the holy Spirit will not be forgiven. 11 When they take you before synagogues and before rulers and authorities, do not worry about how or what your defense will be or about what you are to say. 12 For the holy Spirit will teach you at that moment what you should say."

13 Someone in the crowd said to him, "Teacher, tell my brother to share the inheritance with me." 14 He replied to him, "Friend, who appointed me as your judge and arbitrator?" 15 Then he said to the crowd, "Take care to guard against all greed, for though one may be rich, one's life does not consist of possessions."

16 Then he told them a parable. "There was a rich man whose land produced a bountiful harvest. 17 He asked himself, 'What shall I do, for I do not have space to store my harvest?' 18 And he said, 'This is what I shall do: I shall tear down my barns and build larger ones. There I shall store all my grain and other goods 19 and I shall say to myself, "Now as for you, you have so many good things stored up for many years, rest, eat, drink, be merry!" ' 20 But God said to him, 'You fool, this night your life will be demanded of you; and the things you have prepared, to whom will they belong?' 21 Thus will it be for the one who stores up treasure for himself but is not rich in what matters to God."

22 He said to [his] disciples, "Therefore I tell you, do not worry about your life and what you will eat, or about your body and what you will wear. 23 For life is more than food and the body more than clothing. 24 Notice the ravens: they do not sow or reap; they have neither storehouse nor barn, yet God feeds them. How much more important are you than birds! 25 Can any of you by worrying add a moment to your life-span? 26 If even the smallest things are beyond your control, why are you anxious about the rest? 27 Notice how the flowers grow. They do not toil or spin. But I tell you, not even Solomon in all his splendor was dressed like one of them. 28 If God so clothes the grass in the field that grows today and is thrown into the oven tomorrow, will he not much more provide for you, O you of little faith? 29 As for you, do not seek what you are to eat and what you are to drink, and do not worry anymore. 30 All the nations of the world seek for these things, and your Father knows that you need them. 31 Instead, seek his kingdom, and these other

12 Meanwhile the people had gathered in their thousands so that they were treading on one another. And he began to speak, first of all to his disciples. 'Be on your guard against the yeast of the Pharisees — their hypocrisy. 2 Everything now covered up will be uncovered, and everything now hidden will be made clear. 3 For this reason, whatever you have said in the dark will be heard in the daylight, and what you have whispered in hidden places will be proclaimed from the housetops.

4 'To you my friends I say: Do not be afraid of those who kill the body and after that can do no more. 5 I will tell you whom to fear: fear him who, after he has killed, has the power to cast into hell. Yes, I tell you, he is the one to fear. 6 Can you not buy five sparrows for two pennies? And yet not one is forgotten in God's sight. 7 Why, every hair on your head has been counted. There is no need to be afraid: you are worth more than many sparrows.

8 'I tell you, if anyone openly declares himself for me in the presence of human beings, the Son of man will declare himself for him in the presence of God's angels. 9 But anyone who disowns me in the presence of human beings will be disowned in the presence of God's angels.

10 'Everyone who says a word against the Son of man will be forgiven, but no one who blasphemes against the Holy Spirit will be forgiven.

11 'When they take you before synagogues and magistrates and authorities, do not worry about how to defend yourselves or what to say, 12 because when the time comes, the Holy Spirit will teach you what you should say.'

13 A man in the crowd said to him, 'Master, tell my brother to give me a share of our inheritance.' 14 He said to him, 'My friend, who appointed me your judge, or the arbitrator of your claims?' 15 Then he said to them, 'Watch, and be on your guard against avarice of any kind, for life does not consist in possessions, even when someone has more than he needs.'

16 Then he told them a parable, 'There was once a rich man who, having had a good harvest from his land, 17 thought to himself, "What am I to do? I have not enough room to store my crops." 18 Then he said, "This is what I will do: I will pull down my barns and build bigger ones, and store all my grain and my goods in them, 19 and I will say to my soul: My soul, you have plenty of good things laid by for many years to come; take things easy, eat, drink, have a good time." 20 But God said to him, "Fool! This very night the demand will be made for your soul; and this hoard of yours, whose will it be then?" 21 So it is when someone stores up treasure for himself instead of becoming rich in the sight of God.'

22 Then he said to his disciples, 'That is why I am telling you not to worry about your life and what you are to eat, nor about your body and how you are to clothe it. 23 For life is more than food, and the body more than clothing. 24 Think of the ravens. They do not sow or reap; they have no storehouses and no barns; yet God feeds them. And how much more are you worth than the birds! 25 Can any of you, however much you worry, add a single cubit to your span of life? 26 If a very small thing is beyond your powers, why worry about the rest? 27 Think how the flowers grow; they never have to spin or weave; yet, I assure you, not even Solomon in all his royal robes was clothed like one of them. 28 Now if that is how God clothes a flower which is growing wild today and is thrown into the furnace tomorrow, how much more will he look after you, who have so little faith! 29 But you must not set your hearts on things to eat and things to drink; nor must you worry. 30 It is the gentiles of this world who set their hearts on all these things. Your Father well knows you need them. 31 No; set your hearts on his kingdom, and these other things will be given you as well.

NEW REVISED STANDARD VERSION

32 "Do not be afraid, little flock, for it is your Father's good pleasure to give you the kingdom. 33 Sell your possessions, and give alms. Make purses for yourselves that do not wear out, an unfailing treasure in heaven, where no thief comes near and no moth destroys. 34 For where your treasure is, there your heart will be also.

35 "Be dressed for action and have your lamps lit; 36 be like those who are waiting for their master to return from the wedding banquet, so that they may open the door for him as soon as he comes and knocks. 37 Blessed are those slaves whom the master finds alert when he comes; truly I tell you, he will fasten his belt and have them sit down to eat, and he will come and serve them. 38 If he comes during the middle of the night, or near dawn, and finds them so, blessed are those slaves.

39 "But know this: if the owner of the house had known at what hour the thief was coming, he*c* would not have let his house be broken into. 40 You also must be ready, for the Son of Man is coming at an unexpected hour."

41 Peter said, "Lord, are you telling this parable for us or for everyone?" 42 And the Lord said, "Who then is the faithful and prudent manager whom his master will put in charge of his slaves, to give them their allowance of food at the proper time? 43 Blessed is that slave whom his master will find at work when he arrives. 44 Truly I tell you, he will put that one in charge of all his possessions. 45 But if that slave says to himself, 'My master is delayed in coming,' and if he begins to beat the other slaves, men and women, and to eat and drink and get drunk, 46 the master of that slave will come on a day when he does not expect him and at an hour that he does not know, and will cut him in pieces, *d* and put him with the unfaithful. 47 That slave who knew what his master wanted, but did not prepare himself or do what was wanted, will receive a severe beating. 48 But the one who did not know and did what deserved a beating will receive a light beating. From everyone to whom much has been given, much will be required; and from the one to whom much has been entrusted, even more will be demanded.

49 "I came to bring fire to the earth, and how I wish it were already kindled! 50 I have a baptism with which to be baptized, and what stress I am under until it is completed! 51 Do you think that I have come to bring peace to the earth? No, I tell you, but rather division! 52 From now on five in one household will be divided, three against two and two against three; 53 they will be divided:

father against son
    and son against father,
mother against daughter
    and daughter against mother,
mother-in-law against her daughter-in-law
    and daughter-in-law against mother-in-law."

54 He also said to the crowds, "When you see a cloud rising in the west, you immediately say, 'It is going to rain'; and so it happens. 55 And when you see the south wind blowing, you say, 'There will be scorching heat'; and it happens. 56 You hypocrites! You know how to interpret the appearance of earth and sky, but why do you not know how to interpret the present time?

57 "And why do you not judge for yourselves what is right? 58 Thus, when you go with your accuser before a magistrate, on the way make an effort to settle the case, *e* or you may be dragged before the judge, and the judge hand you over to the officer, and the officer throw you in prison. 59 I tell you, you will never get out until you have paid the very last penny."

REVISED ENGLISH BIBLE

32 'Have no fear, little flock; for your Father has chosen to give you the kingdom. 33 Sell your possessions and give to charity. Provide for yourselves purses that do not wear out, and never-failing treasure in heaven, where no thief can get near it, no moth destroy it. 34 For where your treasure is, there will your heart be also.

35 'Be ready for action, with your robes hitched up and your lamps alight. 36 Be like people who wait for their master's return from a wedding party, ready to let him in the moment he arrives and knocks. 37 Happy are those servants whom the master finds awake when he comes. Truly I tell you: he will hitch up his robe, seat them at table, and come and wait on them. 38 If it is the middle of the night or before dawn when he comes and he still finds them awake, then are they happy indeed. 39 Remember, if the householder had known at what time the burglar was coming he would not have let his house be broken into. 40 So hold yourselves in readiness, because the Son of Man will come at the time you least expect him.'

41 Peter said, 'Lord, do you intend this parable specially for us or is it for everyone?' 42 The Lord said, 'Who is the trusty and sensible man whom his master will appoint as his steward, to manage his servants and issue their rations at the proper time? 43 Happy that servant if his master comes home and finds him at work! 44 I tell you this: he will be put in charge of all his master's property. 45 But if that servant says to himself, "The master is a long time coming," and begins to bully the menservants and maids, and to eat and drink and get drunk, 46 then the master will arrive on a day when the servant does not expect him, at a time he has not been told. He will cut him in pieces and assign him a place among the faithless.

47 'The servant who knew his master's wishes, yet made no attempt to carry them out, will be flogged severely. 48 But one who did not know them and earned a beating will be flogged less severely. Where someone has been given much, much will be expected of him; and the more he has had entrusted to him the more will be demanded of him.

49 'I have come to set fire to the earth, and how I wish it were already kindled! 50 I have a baptism to undergo, and what constraint I am under until it is over! 51 Do you suppose I came to establish peace on the earth? No indeed, I have come to bring dissension. 52 From now on, a family of five will be divided, three against two and two against three; 53 father against son and son against father, mother against daughter and daughter against mother, mother-in-law against daughter-in-law and daughter-in-law against mother-in-law.'

54 He also said to the people, 'When you see clouds gathering in the west, you say at once, "It is going to rain," and rain it does. 55 And when the wind is from the south, you say, "It will be hot," and it is. 56 What hypocrites you are! You know how to interpret the appearance of earth and sky, but cannot interpret this fateful hour.

57 'Why can you not judge for yourselves what is right? 58 When you are going with your opponent to court, make an effort to reach a settlement with him while you are still on the way; otherwise he may drag you before the judge, and the judge hand you over to the officer, and the officer throw you into jail. 59 I tell you, you will not be let out until you have paid the very last penny.'

---

c Other ancient authorities add *would have watched and*   *d* Or cut *him off*   *e* Gk *settle with him*

things will be given you besides. 32 Do not be afraid any longer, little flock, for your Father is pleased to give you the kingdom. 33 Sell your belongings and give alms. Provide money bags for yourselves that do not wear out, an inexhaustible treasure in heaven that no thief can reach nor moth destroy. 34 For where your treasure is, there also will your heart be.

35 "Gird your loins and light your lamps 36 and be like servants who await their master's return from a wedding, ready to open immediately when he comes and knocks. 37 Blessed are those servants whom the master finds vigilant on his arrival. Amen, I say to you, he will gird himself, have them recline at table, and proceed to wait on them. 38 And should he come in the second or third watch and find them prepared in this way, blessed are those servants. 39 Be sure of this: if the master of the house had known the hour when the thief was coming, he would not have let his house be broken into. 40 You also must be prepared, for at an hour you do not expect, the Son of Man will come."

41 Then Peter said, "Lord, is this parable meant for us or for everyone?" 42 And the Lord replied, "Who, then, is the faithful and prudent steward whom the master will put in charge of his servants to distribute [the] food allowance at the proper time? 43 Blessed is that servant whom his master on arrival finds doing so. 44 Truly, I say to you, he will put him in charge of all his property. 45 But if that servant says to himself, 'My master is delayed in coming,' and begins to beat the menservants and the maidservants, to eat and drink and get drunk, 46 then that servant's master will come on an unexpected day and at an unknown hour and will punish him severely and assign him a place with the unfaithful. 47 That servant who knew his master's will but did not make preparations nor act in accord with his will shall be beaten severely; 48 and the servant who was ignorant of his master's will but acted in a way deserving of a severe beating shall be beaten only lightly. Much will be required of the person entrusted with much, and still more will be demanded of the person entrusted with more.

49 "I have come to set the earth on fire, and how I wish it were already blazing! 50 There is a baptism with which I must be baptized, and how great is my anguish until it is accomplished! 51 Do you think that I have come to establish peace on the earth? No, I tell you, but rather division. 52 From now on a household of five will be divided, three against two and two against three; 53 a father will be divided against his son and a son against his father, a mother against her daughter and a daughter against her mother, a mother-in-law against her daughter-in-law and a daughter-in-law against her mother-in-law."

54 He also said to the crowds, "When you see [a] cloud rising in the west you say immediately that it is going to rain — and so it does; 55 and when you notice that the wind is blowing from the south you say that it is going to be hot — and so it is. 56 You hypocrites! You know how to interpret the appearance of th earth and the sky; why do you not know how to interpret the present time?

57 "Why do you not judge for yourselves what is right? 58 If you are to go with your opponent before a magistrate, make an effort to settle the matter on the way; otherwise your opponent will turn you over to the judge, and the judge hand you over to the constable, and the constable throw you into prison. 59 I say to you, you will not be released until you have paid the last penny."

32 'There is no need to be afraid, little flock, for it has pleased your Father to give you the kingdom.

33 'Sell your possessions and give to those in need. Get yourselves purses that do not wear out, treasure that will not fail you, in heaven where no thief can reach it and no moth destroy it. 34 For wherever your treasure is, that is where your heart will be too.

35 'See that you have your belts done up and your lamps lit. 36 Be like people waiting for their master to return from the wedding feast, ready to open the door as soon as he comes and knocks. 37 Blessed those servants whom the master finds awake when he comes. In truth I tell you, he will do up his belt, sit them down at table and wait on them. 38 It may be in the second watch that he comes, or in the third, but blessed are those servants if he finds them ready. 39 You may be quite sure of this, that if the householder had known at what time the burglar would come, he would not have let anyone break through the wall of his house. 40 You too must stand ready, because the Son of man is coming at an hour you do not expect.'

41 Peter said, 'Lord, do you mean this parable for us, or for everyone?' 42 The Lord replied, 'Who, then, is the wise and trustworthy steward whom the master will place over his household to give them at the proper time their allowance of food? 43 Blessed that servant if his master's arrival finds him doing exactly that. 44 I tell you truly, he will put him in charge of everything that he owns. 45 But if the servant says to himself, "My master is taking his time coming," and sets about beating the menservants and the servant-girls, and eating and drinking and getting drunk, 46 his master will come on a day he does not expect and at an hour he does not know. The master will cut him off and send him to the same fate as the unfaithful.

47 'The servant who knows what his master wants, but has got nothing ready and done nothing in accord with those wishes, will be given a great many strokes of the lash. 48 The one who did not know, but has acted in such a way that he deserves a beating, will be given fewer strokes. When someone is given a great deal, a great deal will be demanded of that person; when someone is entrusted with a great deal, of that person even more will be expected.

49 'I have come to bring fire to the earth, and how I wish it were blazing already! 50 There is a baptism I must still receive, and what constraint I am under until it is completed!

51 'Do you suppose that I am here to bring peace on earth? No, I tell you, but rather division. 52 For from now on, a household of five will be divided: three against two and two against three; 53 father opposed to son, son to father, mother to daughter, daughter to mother, mother-in-law to daughter-in-law, daughter-in-law to mother-in-law.'e

54 He said again to the crowds, 'When you see a cloud looming up in the west you say at once that rain is coming, and so it does. 55 And when the wind is from the south you say it's going to be hot, and so it does. 56 Hypocrites! You know how to interpret the face of the earth and the sky. How is it you do not know how to interpret these times?

57 'Why not judge for yourselves what is upright? 58 For example: when you are going to court with your opponent, make an effort to settle with him on the way, or he may drag you before the judge and the judge hand you over to the officer and the officer have you thrown into prison. 59 I tell you, you will not get out till you have paid the very last penny.'

13 At that very time there were some present who told him about the Galileans whose blood Pilate had mingled with their sacrifices. 2 He asked them, "Do you think that because these Galileans suffered in this way they were worse sinners than all other Galileans? 3 No, I tell you; but unless you repent, you will all perish as they did. 4 Or those eighteen who were killed when the tower of Siloam fell on them—do you think that they were worse offenders than all the others living in Jerusalem? 5 No, I tell you; but unless you repent, you will all perish just as they did."

6 Then he told this parable: "A man had a fig tree planted in his vineyard; and he came looking for fruit on it and found none. 7 So he said to the gardener, 'See here! For three years I have come looking for fruit on this fig tree, and still I find none. Cut it down! Why should it be wasting the soil?' 8 He replied, 'Sir, let it alone for one more year, until I dig around it and put manure on it. 9 If it bears fruit next year, well and good; but if not, you can cut it down.'"

10 Now he was teaching in one of the synagogues on the sabbath. 11 And just then there appeared a woman with a spirit that had crippled her for eighteen years. She was bent over and was quite unable to stand up straight. 12 When Jesus saw her, he called her over and said, "Woman, you are set free from your ailment." 13 When he laid his hands on her, immediately she stood up straight and began praising God. 14 But the leader of the synagogue, indignant because Jesus had cured on the sabbath, kept saying to the crowd, "There are six days on which work ought to be done; come on those days and be cured, and not on the sabbath day." 15 But the Lord answered him and said, "You hypocrites! Does not each of you on the sabbath untie his ox or his donkey from the manger, and lead it away to give it water? 16 And ought not this woman, a daughter of Abraham whom Satan bound for eighteen long years, be set free from this bondage on the sabbath day?" 17 When he said this, all his opponents were put to shame; and the entire crowd was rejoicing at all the wonderful things that he was doing.

18 He said therefore, "What is the kingdom of God like? And to what should I compare it? 19 It is like a mustard seed that someone took and sowed in the garden; it grew and became a tree, and the birds of the air made nests in its branches."

20 And again he said, "To what should I compare the kingdom of God? 21 It is like yeast that a woman took and mixed in with *f* three measures of flour until all of it was leavened."

22 Jesus *g* went through one town and village after another, teaching as he made his way to Jerusalem. 23 Someone asked him, "Lord, will only a few be saved?" He said to them, 24 "Strive to enter through the narrow door; for many, I tell you, will try to enter and will not be able. 25 When once the owner of the house has got up and shut the door, and you begin to stand outside and to knock at the door, saying, 'Lord, open to us,' then in reply he will say to you, 'I do not know where you come from.' 26 Then you will begin to say, 'We ate and drank with you, and you taught in our streets.' 27 But he will say, 'I do not know where you come from; go away from me, all you evildoers!' 28 There will be weeping and gnashing of teeth when you see Abraham and Isaac and Jacob and all the prophets in the kingdom of God, and you yourselves thrown out. 29 Then people will come from east and west, from north and south,

13 AT that time some people came and told him about the Galileans whose blood Pilate had mixed with their sacrifices. 2 He answered them: 'Do you suppose that, because these Galileans suffered this fate, they must have been greater sinners than anyone else in Galilee? 3 No, I tell you; but unless you repent, you will all of you come to the same end. 4 Or the eighteen people who were killed when the tower fell on them at Siloam—do you imagine they must have been more guilty than all the other people living in Jerusalem? 5 No, I tell you; but unless you repent, you will all come to an end like theirs.'

6 He told them this parable: 'A man had a fig tree growing in his vineyard, and he came looking for fruit on it, but found none. 7 So he said to the vine-dresser, "For the last three years I have come looking for fruit on this fig tree without finding any. Cut it down. Why should it go on taking goodness from the soil?" 8 But he replied, "Leave it, sir, for this one year, while I dig round it and manure it. 9 And if it bears next season, well and good; if not, you shall have it down."'

10 He was teaching in one of the synagogues on the sabbath, 11 and there was a woman there possessed by a spirit that had crippled her for eighteen years. She was bent double and quite unable to stand up straight. 12 When Jesus saw her he called her and said, 'You are rid of your trouble,' 13 and he laid his hands on her. Immediately she straightened up and began to praise God. 14 But the president of the synagogue, indignant with Jesus for healing on the sabbath, intervened and said to the congregation, 'There are six working days: come and be cured on one of them, and not on the sabbath.' 15 The Lord gave him this answer: 'What hypocrites you are!' he said. 'Is there a single one of you who does not loose his ox or his donkey from its stall and take it out to water on the sabbath? 16 And here is this woman, a daughter of Abraham, who has been bound by Satan for eighteen long years: was it not right for her to be loosed from her bonds on the sabbath?' 17 At these words all his opponents were covered with confusion, while the mass of the people were delighted at all the wonderful things he was doing.

18 'What is the kingdom of God like?' he continued. 'To what shall I compare it? 19 It is like a mustard seed which a man took and sowed in his garden; and it grew to be a tree and the birds came to roost among its branches.'

20 Again he said, 'To what shall I compare the kingdom of God? 21 It is like yeast which a woman took and mixed with three measures of flour till it was all leavened.'

22 HE continued his journey through towns and villages, teaching as he made his way towards Jerusalem. 23 Someone asked him, 'Sir, are only a few to be saved?' His answer was: 24 'Make every effort to enter through the narrow door; for I tell you that many will try to enter but will not succeed.

25 'When once the master of the house has got up and locked the door, you may stand outside and knock, and say, "Sir, let us in!" but he will only answer, "I do not know where you come from." 26 Then you will protest, "We used to eat and drink with you, and you taught in our streets." 27 But he will repeat, "I tell you, I do not know where you come from. Out of my sight, all of you, and your wicked ways!" 28 There will be wailing and grinding of teeth there, when you see Abraham, Isaac, Jacob, and all the prophets, in the kingdom of God, and you yourselves are driven away. 29 From east and west, from north and south, people will come and take their places at the banquet

13 At that time some people who were present there told him about the Galileans whose blood Pilate had mingled with the blood of their sacrifices. 2 He said to them in reply, "Do you think that because these Galileans suffered in this way they were greater sinners than all other Galileans? 3 By no means! But I tell you, if you do not repent, you will all perish as they did! 4 Or those eighteen people who were killed when the tower at Siloam fell on them — do you think they were more guilty than everyone else who lived in Jerusalem? 5 By no means! But I tell you, if you do not repent, you will all perish as they did!"

6 And he told them this parable: "There once was a person who had a fig tree planted in his orchard, and when he came in search of fruit on it but found none, 7 he said to the gardener, 'For three years now I have come in search of fruit on this fig tree but have found none. [So] cut it down. Why should it exhaust the soil?' 8 He said to him in reply, "Sir, leave it for this year also, and I shall cultivate the ground around it and fertilize it; 9 it may bear fruit in the future. If not you can cut it down.' "

10 He was teaching in a synagogue on the sabbath. 11 And a woman was there who for eighteen years had been crippled by a spirit; she was bent over, completely incapable of standing erect. 12 When Jesus saw her, he called to her and said, "Woman, you are set free of your infirmity." 13 He laid his hands on her, and she at once stood up straight and glorified God. 14 But the leader of the synagogue, indignant that Jesus had cured on the sabbath, said to the crowd in reply, "There are six days when work should be done. Come on those days to be cured, not on the sabbath day." 15 The Lord said to him in reply, "Hypocrites! Does not each one of you on the sabbath untie his ox or his ass from the manger and lead it out for watering? 16 This daughter of Abraham, whom Satan has bound for eighteen years now, ought she not to have been set free on the sabbath day from this bondage?" 17 When he said this, all his adversaries were humiliated; and the whole crowd rejoiced at all the splendid deeds done by him.

18 Then he said, "What is the kingdom of God like? To what can I compare it? 19 It is like a mustard seed that a person took and planted in the garden. When it was fully grown, it became a large bush and 'the birds of the sky dwelt in its branches.' "

20 Again he said, "To what shall I compare the kingdom of God? 21 It is like yeast that a woman took and mixed [in] with three measures of wheat flour until the whole batch of dough was leavened."

22 He passed through towns and villages, teaching as he went and making his way to Jerusalem. 23 Someone asked him, "Lord, will only a few people be saved?" He answered them, 24 "Strive to enter through the narrow gate, for many, I tell you, will attempt to enter but will not be strong enough. 25 After the master of the house has arisen and locked the door, then will you stand outside knocking and saying, 'Lord, open the door for us.' He will say to you in reply, 'I do not know where you are from.' 26 And you will say, 'We ate and drank in your company and you taught in our streets.' 27 Then he will say to you, 'I do not know where [you] are from. Depart from me, all you evildoers!' 28 And there will be wailing and grinding of teeth when you see Abraham, Isaac, and Jacob and all the prophets in the kingdom of God and you yourselves cast out. 29 And people will come from the east and the west and from the north and the south and will recline at table in the kingdom of God.

13 It was just about this time that some people arrived and told him about the Galileans whose blood Pilate had mingled with that of their sacrifices. At this he said to them, 2 'Do you suppose that these Galileans were worse sinners than any others, that this should have happened to them? 3 They were not, I tell you. No; but unless you repent you will all perish as they did. 4 Or those eighteen on whom the tower at Siloam fell, killing them all? Do you suppose that they were more guilty than all the other people living in Jerusalem? 5 They were not, I tell you. No; but unless you repent you will all perish as they did.'

6 He told this parable, 'A man had a fig tree planted in his vineyard, and he came looking for fruit on it but found none. 7 He said to his vinedresser, "For three years now I have been coming to look for fruit on this fig tree and finding none. Cut it down: why should it be taking up the ground?" 8 "Sir," the man replied, "leave it one more year and give me time to dig round it and manure it: 9 it may bear fruit next year; if not, then you can cut it down." '

10 One Sabbath day he was teaching in one of the synagogues, 11 and there before him was a woman who for eighteen years had been possessed by a spirit that crippled her; she was bent double and quite unable to stand upright. 12 When Jesus saw her he called her over and said, 'Woman, you are freed from your disability,' 13 and he laid his hands on her. And at once she straightened up, and she glorified God.

14 But the president of the synagogue was indignant because Jesus had healed on the Sabbath, and he addressed all those present saying, 'There are six days when work is to be done. Come and be healed on one of those days and not on the Sabbath.' 15 But the Lord answered him and said, 'Hypocrites! Is there one of you who does not untie his ox or his donkey from the manger on the Sabbath and take it out for watering? 16 And this woman, a daughter of Abraham whom Satan has held bound these eighteen years — was it not right to untie this bond on the Sabbath day?' 17 When he said this, all his adversaries were covered with confusion, and all the people were overjoyed at all the wonders he worked.

18 He went on to say, 'What is the kingdom of God like? What shall I compare it with? 19 It is like a mustard seed which a man took and threw into his garden: it grew and became a tree, and the birds of the air sheltered in its branches.'

20 Again he said, 'What shall I compare the kingdom of God with? 21 It is like the yeast a woman took and mixed in with three measures of flour till it was leavened all through.'

22 Through towns and villages he went teaching, making his way to Jerusalem. 23 Someone said to him, 'Sir, will there be only a few saved?' He said to them, 24 'Try your hardest to enter by the narrow door, because, I tell you, many will try to enter and will not succeed.

25 'Once the master of the house has got up and locked the door, you may find yourself standing outside knocking on the door, saying, "Lord, open to us," but he will answer, "I do not know where you come from." 26 Then you will start saying, "We once ate and drank in your company; you taught in our streets," 27 but he will reply, "I do not know where you come from; *away from me, all evil doers!"* f

28 'Then there will be weeping and grinding of teeth, when you see Abraham and Isaac and Jacob and all the prophets in the kingdom of God, and yourselves thrown out. 29 And people from east and west, from north and south, will come and sit down at the feast in the kingdom of God.

f 13 Ps 6:8.

NEW REVISED STANDARD VERSION

and will eat in the kingdom of God. 30 Indeed, some are last who will be first, and some are first who will be last."

31 At that very hour some Pharisees came and said to him, "Get away from here, for Herod wants to kill you." 32 He said to them, "Go and tell that fox for me,*h* 'Listen, I am casting out demons and performing cures today and tomorrow, and on the third day I finish my work. 33 Yet today, tomorrow, and the next day I must be on my way, because it is impossible for a prophet to be killed outside of Jerusalem.' 34 Jerusalem, Jerusalem, the city that kills the prophets and stones those who are sent to it! How often have I desired to gather your children together as a hen gathers her brood under her wings, and you were not willing! 35 See, your house is left to you. And I tell you, you will not see me until the time comes when*i* you say, 'Blessed is the one who comes in the name of the Lord.'"

14 On one occasion when Jesus*j* was going to the house of a leader of the Pharisees to eat a meal on the sabbath, they were watching him closely. 2 Just then, in front of him, there was a man who had dropsy. 3 And Jesus asked the lawyers and Pharisees, "Is it lawful to cure people on the sabbath, or not?" 4 But they were silent. So Jesus*j* took him and healed him, and sent him away. 5 Then he said to them, "If one of you has a child*k* or an ox that has fallen into a well, will you not immediately pull it out on a sabbath day?" 6 And they could not reply to this.

7 When he noticed how the guests chose the places of honor, he told them a parable. 8 "When you are invited by someone to a wedding banquet, do not sit down at the place of honor, in case someone more distinguished than you has been invited by your host; 9 and the host who invited both of you may come and say to you, 'Give this person your place,' and then in disgrace you would start to take the lowest place. 10 But when you are invited, go and sit down at the lowest place, so that when your host comes, he may say to you, 'Friend, move up higher'; then you will be honored in the presence of all who sit at the table with you. 11 For all who exalt themselves will be humbled, and those who humble themselves will be exalted."

12 He said also to the one who had invited him, "When you give a luncheon or a dinner, do not invite your friends or your brothers or your relatives or rich neighbors, in case they may invite you in return, and you would be repaid. 13 But when you give a banquet, invite the poor, the crippled, the lame, and the blind. 14 And you will be blessed, because they cannot repay you, for you will be repaid at the resurrection of the righteous."

15 One of the dinner guests, on hearing this, said to him, "Blessed is anyone who will eat bread in the kingdom of God!" 16 Then Jesus*j* said to him, "Someone gave a great dinner and invited many. 17 At the time for the dinner he sent his slave to say to those who had been invited, 'Come; for everything is ready now.' 18 But they all alike began to make excuses. The first said to him, 'I have bought a piece of land, and I must go out and see it; please accept my regrets.' 19 Another said, 'I have bought five yoke of oxen, and I am going to try them out; please accept my regrets.' 20 Another said, 'I have just been married, and therefore I cannot come.' 21 So the slave returned and reported this to his master. Then the owner of the house became angry and said to his slave, 'Go out at once into the streets and lanes of the town and bring in the poor, the crippled, the blind, and the lame.' 22 And the slave said,

REVISED ENGLISH BIBLE

in the kingdom of God. 30 Yes, and some who are now last will be first, and some who are first will be last.'

31 At that time a number of Pharisees came and warned him, 'Leave this place and be on your way; Herod wants to kill you.' 32 He replied, 'Go and tell that fox, "Listen: today and tomorrow I shall be driving out demons and working cures; on the third day I reach my goal." 33 However, I must go on my way today and tomorrow and the next day, because it is unthinkable for a prophet to meet his death anywhere but in Jerusalem.

34 'O Jerusalem, Jerusalem, city that murders the prophets and stones the messengers sent to her! How often have I longed to gather your children, as a hen gathers her brood under her wings; but you would not let me. 35 Look! There is your temple, forsaken by God. I tell you, you will not see me until the time comes when you say, "Blessings on him who comes in the name of the Lord!"'

14 ONE sabbath he went to have a meal in the house of one of the leading Pharisees; and they were watching him closely. 2 There, in front of him, was a man suffering from dropsy. 3 and Jesus asked the lawyers and the Pharisees: 'Is it permitted to heal people on the sabbath or not?' 4 They said nothing. So he took the man, cured him, and sent him away. 5 Then he turned to them and said, 'If one of you has a son or an ox that falls into a well, will he hesitate to pull him out on the sabbath day?' 6 To this they could find no reply.

7 When he noticed how the guests were trying to secure the places of honour, he spoke to them in a parable: 8 'When somebody asks you to a wedding feast, do not sit down in the place of honour. It may be that some person more distinguished than yourself has been invited; 9 and the host will come to say to you, "Give this man your seat." Then you will look foolish as you go to take the lowest place. 10 No, when you receive an invitation, go and sit down in the lowest place, so that when your host comes he will say, "Come up higher, my friend." Then all your fellow-guests will see the respect in which you are held. 11 For everyone who exalts himself will be humbled; and whoever humbles himself will be exalted.'

12 Then he said to his host, 'When you are having guests for lunch or supper, do not invite your friends, your brothers or other relations, or your rich neighbours; they will only ask you back again and so you will be repaid. 13 But when you give a party, ask the poor, the crippled, the lame, and the blind. 14 That is the way to find happiness, because they have no means of repaying you. You will be repaid on the day when the righteous rise from the dead.'

15 Hearing this one of the company said to him, 'Happy are those who will sit at the feast in the kingdom of God!' 16 Jesus answered, 'A man was giving a big dinner party and had sent out many invitations. 17 At dinner-time he sent his servant to tell his guests, "Come please, everything is now ready." 18 One after another they all sent excuses. The first said, "I have bought a piece of land, and I must go and inspect it; please accept my apologies." 19 The second said, "I have bought five yoke of oxen, and I am on my way to try them out; please accept my apologies." 20 The next said, "I cannot come; I have just got married." 21 When the servant came back he reported this to his master. The master of the house was furious and said to him, "Go out quickly into the streets and alleys of the town, and bring in the poor, the crippled, the blind, and the lame." 22 When the servant

---

h Gk lacks *for me* *when*   *j* Gk *he*

i Other ancient authorities lack *the time comes*

k Other ancient authorities read *a donkey*

14:5 **son:** *some witnesses read* donkey.

30 For behold, some are last who will be first, and some are first who will be last."

31 At that time some Pharisees came to him and said, "Go away, leave this area because Herod wants to kill you." 32 He replied, "Go and tell that fox, 'Behold, I cast out demons and I perform healings today and tomorrow, and on the third day I accomplish my purpose. 33 Yet I must continue on my way today, tomorrow, and the following day, for it is impossible that a prophet should die outside of Jerusalem.'

34 "Jerusalem, Jerusalem, you who kill the prophets and stone those sent to you, how many times I yearned to gather your children together as a hen gathers her brood under her wings, but you were unwilling! 35 Behold, your house will be abandoned. [But] I tell you, you will not see me until [the time comes when] you say, 'Blessed is he who comes in the name of the Lord.' "

14 On a sabbath he went to dine at the home of one of the leading Pharisees, and the people there were observing him carefully. 2 In front of him there was a man suffering from dropsy. 3 Jesus spoke to the scholars of the law and Pharisees in reply, asking, "Is it lawful to cure on the sabbath or not?" 4 But they kept silent; so he took the man and, after he had healed him, dismissed him. 5 Then he said to them, "Who among you, if your son or ox falls into a cistern, would not immediately pull him out on the sabbath day?" 6 But they were unable to answer his question.

7 He told a parable to those who had been invited, noticing how they were choosing the places of honor at the table. 8 "When you are invited by someone to a wedding banquet, do not recline at table in the place of honor. A more distinguished guest than you may have been invited by him, 9 and the host who invited both of you may approach you and say, 'Give your place to this man," and then you would proceed with embarrassment to take the lowest place. 10 Rather, when you are invited, go and take the lowest place so that when the host comes to you he may say, 'My friend, move up to a higher position.' Then you will enjoy the esteem of your companions at the table. 11 For everyone who exalts himself will be humbled, but the one who humbles himself will be exalted." 12 Then he said to the host who invited him, "When you hold a lunch or a dinner, do not invite your friends or your brothers or your relatives or your wealthy neighbors, in case they may invite you back and you have repayment. 13 Rather, when you hold a banquet, invite the poor, the crippled, the lame, the blind; 14 blessed indeed will you be because of their inability to repay you. For you will be repaid at the resurrection of the righteous."

15 One of his fellow guests on hearing this said to him, "Blessed is the one who will dine in the kingdom of God." 16 He replied to him, "A man gave a great dinner to which he invited many. 17 When the time for the dinner came, he dispatched his servant to say to those invited, 'Come, everything is now ready.' 18 But one by one, they all began to excuse themselves. The first said to him, 'I have purchased a field and must go to examine it; I ask you, consider me excused.' 19 And another said, 'I have purchased five yoke of oxen and am on my way to evaluate them; I ask you, consider me excused.' 20 And another said, 'I have just married a woman, and therefore I cannot come.' 21 The servant went and reported this to his master. Then the master of the house in a rage commanded his servant, 'Go out quickly into the streets and alleys of the town and bring in here the poor and the crippled, the blind and the lame.'

30 'Look, there are those now last who will be first, and those now first who will be last.'

31 Just at this time some Pharisees came up. 'Go away,' they said. 'Leave this place, because Herod g means to kill you.' 32 He replied, 'You may go and give that fox this message: Look! Today and tomorrow I drive out devils and heal, and on the third day I attain my end. 33 But for today and tomorrow and the next day I must go on, since it would not be right for a prophet to die outside Jerusalem.

34 'Jerusalem, Jerusalem, you that kill the prophets and stone those who are sent to you! How often have I longed to gather your children together, as a hen gathers her brood under her wings, and you refused! 35 Look! Your house will be left to you. Yes, I promise you, you shall not see me till the time comes when you are saying:

Blessed is he who is coming in the name of the Lord!' h

14 Now it happened that on a Sabbath day he had gone to share a meal in the house of one of the leading Pharisees; and they watched him closely. 2 Now there in front of him was a man with dropsy, 3 and Jesus addressed the lawyers and Pharisees with the words, 'Is it against the law to cure someone on the Sabbath, or not?' 4 But they remained silent, so he took the man and cured him and sent him away. 5 Then he said to them, 'Which of you here, if his son falls into a well, or his ox, will not pull him out on a Sabbath day without any hesitation?' 6 And to this they could find no answer.

7 He then told the guests a parable, because he had noticed how they picked the places of honour. He said this, 8 'When someone invites you to a wedding feast, do not take your seat in the place of honour. A more distinguished person than you may have been invited, 9 and the person who invited you both may come and say, "Give up your place to this man." And then, to your embarrassment, you will have to go and take the lowest place. 10 No; when you are a guest, make your way to the lowest place and sit there, so that, when your host comes, he may say, "My friend, move up higher." Then, everyone with you at the table will see you honoured. 11 For everyone who raises himself up will be humbled, and the one who humbles himself will be raised up.'

12 Then he said to his host, 'When you give a lunch or a dinner, do not invite your friends or your brothers or your relations or rich neighbours, in case they invite you back and so repay you. 13 No; when you have a party, invite the poor, the crippled, the lame, the blind; 14 then you will be blessed, for they have no means to repay you and so you will be repaid when the upright rise again.'

15 On hearing this, one of those gathered round the table said to him, 'Blessed is anyone who will share the meal in the kingdom of God!' 16 But he said to him, 'There was a man who gave a great banquet, and he invited a large number of people. 17 When the time for the banquet came, he sent his servant to say to those who had been invited, "Come along: everything is ready now." 18 But all alike started to make excuses. The first said, "I have bought a piece of land and must go and see it. Please accept my apologies." 19 Another said, "I have bought five yoke of oxen and am on my way to try them out. Please accept my apologies." 20 Yet another said, "I have just got married and so am unable to come." 21 'The servant returned and reported this to his master. Then the householder, in a rage, said to his servant, "Go out quickly into the streets and alleys of the town and bring in here the poor, the crippled, the blind and the lame."

g 13 Herod Antipas, son of Herod the Great.   h 13 Ps 118:26.

'Sir, what you ordered has been done, and there is still room.' 23 Then the master said to the slave, 'Go out into the roads and lanes, and compel people to come in, so that my house may be filled. 24 For I tell you,*l* none of those who were invited will taste my dinner.' "

25 Now large crowds were traveling with him; and he turned and said to them, 26 "Whoever comes to me and does not hate father and mother, wife and children, brothers and sisters, yes, and even life itself, cannot be my disciple. 27 Whoever does not carry the cross and follow me cannot be my disciple. 28 For which of you, intending to build a tower, does not first sit down and estimate the cost, to see whether he has enough to complete it? 29 Otherwise, when he has laid a foundation and is not able to finish, all who see it will begin to ridicule him, 30 saying, 'This fellow began to build and was not able to finish.' 31 Or what king, going out to wage war against another king, will not sit down first and consider whether he is able with ten thousand to oppose the one who comes against him with twenty thousand? 32 If he cannot, then, while the other is still far away, he sends a delegation and asks for the terms of peace. 33 So therefore, none of you can become my disciple if you do not give up all your possessions.

34 "Salt is good; but if salt has lost its taste, how can its saltiness be restored?*m* 35 It is fit neither for the soil nor for the manure pile; they throw it away. Let anyone with ears to hear listen!"

15 Now all the tax collectors and sinners were coming near to listen to him. 2 And the Pharisees and the scribes were grumbling and saying, "This fellow welcomes sinners and eats with them."

3 So he told them this parable: 4 "Which one of you, having a hundred sheep and losing one of them, does not leave the ninety-nine in the wilderness and go after the one that is lost until he finds it? 5 When he has found it, he lays it on his shoulders and rejoices. 6 And when he comes home, he calls together his friends and neighbors, saying to them, 'Rejoice with me, for I have found my sheep that was lost.' 7 Just so, I tell you, there will be more joy in heaven over one sinner who repents than over ninety-nine righteous persons who need no repentance.

8 "Or what woman having ten silver coins,*n* if she loses one of them, does not light a lamp, sweep the house, and search carefully until she finds it? 9 When she has found it, she calls together her friends and neighbors, saying, 'Rejoice with me, for I have found the coin that I had lost.' 10 Just so, I tell you, there is joy in the presence of the angels of God over one sinner who repents."

11 Then Jesus*o* said, "There was a man who had two sons. 12 The younger of them said to his father, 'Father, give me the share of the property that will belong to me.' So he divided his property between them. 13 A few days later the younger son gathered all he had and traveled to a distant country, and there he squandered his property in dissolute living. 14 When he had spent everything, a severe famine took place throughout that country, and he began to be in need. 15 So he went and hired himself out to one of the citizens of that country, who sent him to his fields to feed the pigs. 16 He would gladly have filled himself with*p* the pods that the pigs were eating; and no one gave him anything. 17 But when he came to himself he said, 'How many

informed him that his orders had been carried out and there was still room, 23 his master replied, "Go out on the highways and along the hedgerows and compel them to come in; I want my house full. 24 I tell you, not one of those who were invited shall taste my banquet." '

25 Once when great crowds were accompanying him, he turned to them and said: 26 'If anyone comes to me and does not hate his father and mother, wife and children, brothers and sisters, even his own life, he cannot be a disciple of mine. 27 No one who does not carry his cross and come with me can be a disciple of mine. 28 Would any of you think of building a tower without first sitting down and calculating the cost, to see whether he could afford to finish it? 29 Otherwise, if he has laid its foundation and then is unable to complete it, everyone who sees it will laugh at him. 30 "There goes the man", they will say, "who started to build and could not finish." 31 Or what king will march to battle against another king, without first sitting down to consider whether with ten thousand men he can face an enemy coming to meet him with twenty thousand? 32 If he cannot, then, long before the enemy approaches, he sends envoys and asks for terms. 33 So also, if you are not prepared to leave all your possessions behind, you cannot be my disciples.

34 'Salt is good; but if salt itself becomes tasteless, how will it be seasoned? 35 It is useless either on the land or on the dungheap; it can only be thrown away. If you have ears to hear, then hear.'

15 ANOTHER time, the tax-collectors and sinners were all crowding in to listen to him; 2 and the Pharisees and scribes began murmuring their disapproval: 'This fellow', they said, 'welcomes sinners and eats with them.' 3 He answered them with this parable: 4 'If one of you has a hundred sheep and loses one of them, does he not leave the ninety-nine in the wilderness and go after the one that is missing until he finds it? 5 And when he does, he lifts it joyfully on to his shoulders, 6 and goes home to call his friends and neighbours together. "Rejoice with me!" he cries. "I have found my lost sheep." 7 In the same way, I tell you, there will be greater joy in heaven over one sinner who repents than over ninety-nine righteous people who do not need to repent.

8 'Or again, if a woman has ten silver coins and loses one of them, does she not light the lamp, sweep out the house, and look in every corner till she finds it? 9 And when she does, she calls her friends and neighbours together, and says, "Rejoice with me! I have found the coin that I lost." 10 In the same way, I tell you, there is joy among the angels of God over one sinner who repents.'

11 Again he said: 'There was once a man who had two sons; 12 and the younger said to his father, "Father, give me my share of the property." So he divided his estate between them. 13 A few days later the younger son turned the whole of his share into cash and left home for a distant country, where he squandered it in dissolute living. 14 He had spent it all, when a severe famine fell upon that country and he began to be in need. 15 So he went and attached himself to one of the local landowners, who sent him on to his farm to mind the pigs. 16 He would have been glad to fill his belly with the pods that the pigs were eating, but no one gave him anything. 17 Then he came to his senses: "How many of my

---

l The Greek word for *you* here is plural   *m* Or *how can it be used for seasoning?*   *n* Gk *drachmas*, each worth about a day's wage for a laborer   *o* Gk *he*   *p* Other ancient authorities read *filled his stomach with*

22 The servant reported, 'Sir, your orders have been carried out and still there is room.' 23 The master then ordered the servant, 'Go out to the highways and hedgerows and make people come in that my home may be filled. 24 For, I tell you, none of those men who were invited will taste my dinner.' "

25 Great crowds were traveling with him, and he turned and addressed them, 26 "If anyone comes to me without hating his father and mother, wife and children, brothers and sisters, and even his own life, he cannot be my disciple. 27 Whoever does not carry his own cross and come after me cannot be my disciple. 28 Which of you wishing to construct a tower does not first sit down and calculate the cost to see if there is enough for its completion? 29 Otherwise, after laying the foundation and finding himself unable to finish the work the onlookers should laugh at him 30 and say, 'This one began to build but did not have the resources to finish.' 31 Or what king marching into battle would not first sit down and decide whether with ten thousand troops he can successfully oppose another king advancing upon him with twenty thousand troops? 32 But if not, while he is still far away, he will send a delegation to ask for peace terms. 33 In the same way, everyone of you who does not renounce all his possessions cannot be my disciple.

34 "Salt is good, but if salt itself loses its taste, with what can its flavor be restored? 35 It is fit neither for the soil nor for the manure pile; it is thrown out. Whoever has ears to hear ought to hear."

15 The tax collectors and sinners were all drawing near to listen to him, 2 but the Pharisees and scribes began to complain, saying, "This man welcomes sinners and eats with them." 3 So to them he addressed this parable. 4 "What man among you having a hundred sheep and losing one of them would not leave the ninety-nine in the desert and go after the lost one until he finds it? 5 And when he does find it, he sets it on his shoulders with great joy 6 and, upon his arrival home, he calls together his friends and neighbors and says to them, 'Rejoice with me because I have found my lost sheep.' 7 I tell you, in just the same way there will be more joy in heaven over one sinner who repents than over ninety-nine righteous people who have no need of repentance.

8 "Or what woman having ten coins and losing one would not light a lamp and sweep the house, searching carefully until she finds it? 9 And when she does find it, she calls together her friends and neighbors and says to them, 'Rejoice with me because I have found the coin that I lost.' 10 In just the same way, I tell you, there will be rejoicing among the angels of God over one sinner who repents."

11 Then he said, "A man had two sons, 12 and the younger son said to his father, 'Father, give me the share of your estate that should come to me.' So the father divided the property between them. 13 After a few days, the younger son collected all his belongings and set off to a distant country where he squandered his inheritance on a life of dissipation. 14 When he had freely spent everything, a severe famine struck that country, and he found himself in dire need. 15 So he hired himself out to one of the local citizens who sent him to his farm to tend the swine. 16 And he longed to eat his fill of the pods on which the swine fed, but nobody gave him any. 17 Coming to his senses he

22 "Sir," said the servant, "your orders have been carried out and there is still room." 23 Then the master said to his servant, "Go to the open roads and the hedgerows and press people to come in, to make sure my house is full; 24 because, I tell you, not one of those who were invited shall have a taste of my banquet." ' "

25 Great crowds accompanied him on his way and he turned and spoke to them. 26 'Anyone who comes to me without hating father, mother, wife, children, brothers, sisters, yes and his own life too, cannot be my disciple. 27 No one who does not carry his cross and come after me can be my disciple.

28 'And indeed, which of you here, intending to build a tower, would not first sit down and work out the cost to see if he had enough to complete it? 29 Otherwise, if he laid the foundation and then found himself unable to finish the work, anyone who saw it would start making fun of him and saying, 30 "Here is someone who started to build and was unable to finish." 31 Or again, what king marching to war against another king would not first sit down and consider whether with ten thousand men he could stand up to the other who was advancing against him with twenty thousand? 32 If not, then while the other king was still a long way off, he would send envoys to sue for peace. 33 So in the same way, none of you can be my disciple without giving up all that he owns.

34 'Salt is a good thing. But if salt itself loses its taste, what can make it salty again? 35 It is good for neither soil nor manure heap. People throw it away. Anyone who has ears for listening should listen!'

15 The tax collectors and sinners, however, were all crowding round to listen to him, 2 and the Pharisees and scribes complained saying, 'This man welcomes sinners and eats with them.' 3 So he told them this parable: 4 'Which one of you with a hundred sheep, if he lost one, would fail to leave the ninety-nine in the desert and go after the missing one till he found it? 5 And when he found it, would he not joyfully take it on his shoulders 6 and then, when he got home, call together his friends and neighbours, saying to them, "Rejoice with me, I have found my sheep that was lost." 7 In the same way, I tell you, there will be more rejoicing in heaven over one sinner repenting than over ninety-nine upright people who have no need of repentance.

8 'Or again, what woman with ten drachmas would not, if she lost one, light a lamp and sweep out the house and search thoroughly till she found it? 9 And then, when she had found it, call together her friends and neighbours, saying to them, "Rejoice with me, I have found the drachma I lost." 10 In the same way, there is rejoicing among the angels of God over one repentant sinner.'

11 Then he said, 'There was a man who had two sons. 12 The younger one said to his father, "Father, let me have the share of the estate that will come to me." So the father divided the property between them. 13 A few days later, the younger son got together everything he had and left for a distant country where he squandered his money on a life of debauchery.

14 'When he had spent it all, that country experienced a severe famine, and now he began to feel the pinch; 15 so he hired himself out to one of the local inhabitants who put him on his farm to feed the pigs. 16 And he would willingly have filled himself with the husks the pigs were eating but no one would let him have them. 17 Then he came to his senses and

NEW REVISED STANDARD VERSION

of my father's hired hands have bread enough and to spare, but here I am dying of hunger! 18 I will get up and go to my father, and I will say to him, "Father, I have sinned against heaven and before you; 19 I am no longer worthy to be called your son; treat me like one of your hired hands." ' 20 So he set off and went to his father. But while he was still far off, his father saw him and was filled with compassion; he ran and put his arms around him and kissed him. 21 Then the son said to him, 'Father, I have sinned against heaven and before you; I am no longer worthy to be called your son.' q 22 But the father said to his slaves, 'Quickly, bring out a robe — the best one — and put it on him; put a ring on his finger and sandals on his feet. 23 And get the fatted calf and kill it, and let us eat and celebrate; 24 for this son of mine was dead and is alive again; he was lost and is found!' And they began to celebrate.

25 "Now his elder son was in the field; and when he came and approached the house, he heard music and dancing. 26 He called one of the slaves and asked what was going on. 27 He replied, 'Your brother has come, and your father has killed the fatted calf, because he has got him back safe and sound.' 28 Then he became angry and refused to go in. His father came out and began to plead with him. 29 But he answered his father, 'Listen! For all these years I have been working like a slave for you, and I have never disobeyed your command; yet you have never given me even a young goat so that I might celebrate with my friends. 30 But when this son of yours came back, who has devoured your property with prostitutes, you killed the fatted calf for him!' 31 Then the father r said to him, 'Son, you are always with me, and all that is mine is yours. 32 But we had to celebrate and rejoice, because this brother of yours was dead and has come to life; he was lost and has been found.' "

16 Then Jesus r said to the disciples, "There was a rich man who had a manager, and charges were brought to him that this man was squandering his property. 2 So he summoned him and said to him, 'What is this that I hear about you? Give me an accounting of your management, because you cannot be my manager any longer.' 3 Then the manager said to himself, 'What will I do, now that my master is taking the position away from me? I am not strong enough to dig, and I am ashamed to beg. 4 I have decided what to do so that, when I am dismissed as manager, people may welcome me into their homes.' 5 So, summoning his master's debtors one by one, he asked the first, 'How much do you owe my master?' 6 He answered, 'A hundred jugs of olive oil.' He said to him, 'Take your bill, sit down quickly, and make it fifty.' 7 Then he asked another, 'And how much do you owe?' He replied, 'A hundred containers of wheat.' He said to him, 'Take your bill and make it eighty.' 8 And his master commended the dishonest manager because he had acted shrewdly; for the children of this age are more shrewd in dealing with their own generation than are the children of light. 9 And I tell you, make friends for yourselves by means of dishonest wealth s so that when it is gone, they may welcome you into the eternal homes. t

10 "Whoever is faithful in a very little is faithful also in much; and whoever is dishonest in a very little is dishonest also in much. 11 If then you have not been faithful with the dishonest wealth, s who will entrust to you the true riches? 12 And if you have not been faithful with what belongs to another, who will give you what is your own? 13 No slave can serve two masters; for a slave will either hate the one and love the other, or be devoted to the one and despise the other. You cannot serve God and wealth." s

REVISED ENGLISH BIBLE

father's hired servants have more food than they can eat," he said, "and here am I, starving to death! 18 I will go at once to my father, and say to him, 'Father, I have sinned against God and against you; 19 I am no longer fit to be called your son; treat me as one of your hired servants.' " 20 So he set out for his father's house. But while he was still a long way off his father saw him, and his heart went out to him; he ran to meet him, flung his arms round him, and kissed him. 21 The son said, "Father, I have sinned against God and against you; I am no longer fit to be called your son." 22 But the father said to his servants, "Quick! Fetch a robe, the best we have, and put it on him; put a ring on his finger and sandals on his feet. 23 Bring the fatted calf and kill it, and let us celebrate with a feast. 24 For this son of mine was dead and has come back to life; he was lost and is found." And the festivities began.

25 'Now the elder son had been out on the farm; and on his way back, as he approached the house, he heard music and dancing. 26 He called one of the servants and asked what it meant. 27 The servant told him, "Your brother has come home, and your father has killed the fatted calf because he has him back safe and sound." 28 But he was angry and refused to go in. His father came out and pleaded with him; 29 but he retorted, "You know how I have slaved for you all these years; I never once disobeyed your orders; yet you never gave me so much as a kid, to celebrate with my friends. 30 But now that this son of yours turns up, after running through your money with his women, you kill the fatted calf for him." 31 "My boy," said the father, "you are always with me, and everything I have is yours. 32 How could we fail to celebrate this happy day? Your brother here was dead and has come back to life; he was lost and has been found." '

16 He said to his disciples, 'There was a rich man who had a steward, and he received complaints that this man was squandering the property. 2 So he sent for him, and said, "What is this that I hear about you? Produce your accounts, for you cannot be steward any longer." 3 The steward said to himself, "What am I to do now that my master is going to dismiss me from my post? I am not strong enough to dig, and I am too proud to beg. 4 I know what I must do, to make sure that, when I am dismissed, there will be people who will take me into their homes." 5 He summoned his master's debtors one by one. To the first he said, "How much do you owe my master?" 6 He replied, "A hundred jars of olive oil." He said, "Here is your account. Sit down and make it fifty, and be quick about it." 7 Then he said to another, "And you, how much do you owe?" He said, "A hundred measures of wheat," and was told, "Here is your account; make it eighty." 8 And the master applauded the dishonest steward for acting so astutely. For in dealing with their own kind the children of this world are more astute than the children of light.

9 'So I say to you, use your worldly wealth to win friends for yourselves, so that when money is a thing of the past you may be received into an eternal home.

10 'Anyone who can be trusted in small matters can be trusted also in great; and anyone who is dishonest in small matters is dishonest also in great. 11 If, then, you have not proved trustworthy with the wealth of this world, who will trust you with the wealth that is real? 12 And if you have proved untrustworthy with what belongs to another, who will give you anything of your own?

13 'No slave can serve two masters; for either he will hate the first and love the second, or he will be devoted to the first and despise the second. You cannot serve God and Money.'

---

q Other ancient authorities add *treat me as one of your hired servants*
r Gk *he*   s Gk *mammon*   t Gk *tents*

thought, 'How many of my father's hired workers have more than enough food to eat, but here am I, dying from hunger. 18 I shall get up and go to my father and I shall say to him, "Father, I have sinned against heaven and against you. 19 I no longer deserve to be called your son; treat me as you would treat one of your hired workers." ' 20 So he got up and went back to his father. While he was still a long way off, his father caught sight of him, and was filled with compassion. He ran to his son, embraced him and kissed him. 21 His son said to him, 'Father, I have sinned against heaven and against you; I no longer deserve to be called your son.' 22 But his father ordered his servants, 'Quickly bring the finest robe and put it on him; put a ring on his finger and sandals on his feet. 23 Take the fattened calf and slaughter it. Then let us celebrate with a feast, 24 because this son of mine was dead, and has come to life again; he was lost, and has been found.' Then the celebration began. 25 Now the older son had been out in the field and, on his way back, as he neared the house, he heard the sound of music and dancing. 26 He called one of the servants and asked what this might mean. 27 The servant said to him, 'Your brother has returned and your father has slaughtered the fattened calf because he has him back safe and sound.' 28 He became angry, and when he refused to enter the house, his father came out and pleaded with him. 29 He said to his father in reply, 'Look, all these years I served you and not once did I disobey your orders; yet you never gave me even a young goat to feast on with my friends. 30 But when your son returns who swallowed up your property with prostitutes, for him you slaughter the fattened calf.' 31 He said to him, 'My son, you are here with me always; everything I have is yours. 32 But now we must celebrate and rejoice, because your brother was dead and has come to life again; he was lost and has been found.' "

16 Then he also said to his disciples, "A rich man had a steward who was reported to him for squandering his property. 2 He summoned him and said, 'What is this I hear about you? Prepare a full account of your stewardship, because you can no longer be my steward.' 3 The steward said to himself, 'What shall I do, now that my master is taking the position of steward away from me? I am not strong enough to dig and I am ashamed to beg. 4 I know what I shall do so that, when I am removed from the stewardship, they may welcome me into their homes.' 5 He called in his master's debtors one by one. To the first he said, 'How much do you owe my master?' 6 He replied, 'One hundred measures of olive oil.' He said to him, 'Here is your promissory note. Sit down and quickly write one for fifty.' 7 Then to another he said, 'And you, how much do you owe?' He replied, 'One hundred kors of wheat.' He said to him, 'Here is your promissory note; write one for eighty.' 8 And the master commended that dishonest steward for acting prudently.

"For the children of this world are more prudent in dealing with their own generation than are the children of light. 9 I tell you, make friends for yourselves with dishonest wealth, so that when it fails, you will be welcomed into eternal dwellings. 10 The person who is trustworthy in very small matters is also trustworthy in great ones; and the person who is dishonest in very small matters is also dishonest in great ones. 11 If, therefore, you are not trustworthy with dishonest wealth, who will trust you with true wealth? 12 If you are not trustworthy with what belongs to another, who will give you what is yours? 13 No servant can serve two masters. He will either hate one and love the other, or be devoted to one and despise the other. You cannot serve God and mammon."

said, "How many of my father's hired men have all the food they want and more, and here am I dying of hunger! 18 I will leave this place and go to my father and say: Father, I have sinned against heaven and against you; 19 I no longer deserve to be called your son; treat me as one of your hired men." 20 So he left the place and went back to his father.

'While he was still a long way off, his father saw him and was moved with pity. He ran to the boy, clasped him in his arms and kissed him. 21 Then his son said, "Father, I have sinned against heaven and against you. I no longer deserve to be called your son." 22 But the father said to his servants, "Quick! Bring out the best robe and put it on him; put a ring on his finger and sandals on his feet. 23 Bring the calf we have been fattening, and kill it; we will celebrate by having a feast, 24 because this son of mine was dead and has come back to life; he was lost and is found." And they began to celebrate.

25 'Now the elder son was out in the fields, and on his way back, as he drew near the house, he could hear music and dancing. 26 Calling one of the servants he asked what it was all about. 27 The servant told him, "Your brother has come, and your father has killed the calf we had been fattening because he has got him back safe and sound." 28 He was angry then and refused to go in, and his father came out and began to urge him to come in; 29 but he retorted to his father, "All these years I have slaved for you and never once disobeyed any orders of yours, yet you never offered me so much as a kid for me to celebrate with my friends. 30 But, for this son of yours, when he comes back after swallowing up your property — he and his loose women — you kill the calf we had been fattening."

31 'The father said, "My son, you are with me always and all I have is yours. 32 But it was only right we should celebrate and rejoice, because your brother here was dead and has come to life; he was lost and is found." '

16 He also said to his disciples, 'There was a rich man and he had a steward who was denounced to him for being wasteful with his property. 2 He called for the man and said, "What is this I hear about you? Draw me up an account of your stewardship because you are not to be my steward any longer." 3 Then the steward said to himself, "Now that my master is taking the stewardship from me, what am I to do? Dig? I am not strong enough. Go begging? I should be too ashamed. 4 Ah, I know what I will do to make sure that when I am dismissed from office there will be some to welcome me into their homes."

5 'Then he called his master's debtors one by one. To the first he said, "How much do you owe my master?" 6 "One hundred measures of oil," he said. The steward said, "Here, take your bond; sit down and quickly write fifty." 7 To another he said, "And you, sir, how much do you owe?" "One hundred measures of wheat," he said. The steward said, "Here, take your bond and write eighty."

8 'The master praised the dishonest steward for his astuteness. For the children of this world are more astute in dealing with their own kind than are the children of light.'

9 'And so I tell you this: use money, tainted as it is, to win you friends, and thus make sure that when it fails you, they will welcome you into eternal dwellings. 10 Anyone who is trustworthy in little things is trustworthy in great; anyone who is dishonest in little things is dishonest in great. 11 If then you are not trustworthy with money, that tainted thing, who will trust you with genuine riches? 12 And if you are not trustworthy with what is not yours, who will give you what is your very own?

13 'No servant can be the slave of two masters: he will either hate the first and love the second, or be attached to the first and despise the second. You cannot be the slave both of God and of money.'

NEW REVISED STANDARD VERSION

14 The Pharisees, who were lovers of money, heard all this, and they ridiculed him. 15 So he said to them, "You are those who justify yourselves in the sight of others; but God knows your hearts; for what is prized by human beings is an abomination in the sight of God.

16 "The law and the prophets were in effect until John came; since then the good news of the kingdom of God is proclaimed, and everyone tries to enter it by force. *u* 17 But it is easier for heaven and earth to pass away, than for one stroke of a letter in the law to be dropped.

18 "Anyone who divorces his wife and marries another commits adultery, and whoever marries a woman divorced from her husband commits adultery.

19 "There was a rich man who was dressed in purple and fine linen and who feasted sumptuously every day. 20 And at his gate lay a poor man named Lazarus, covered with sores, 21 who longed to satisfy his hunger with what fell from the rich man's table; even the dogs would come and lick his sores. 22 The poor man died and was carried away by the angels to be with Abraham. *v* The rich man also died and was buried. 23 In Hades, where he was being tormented, he looked up and saw Abraham far away with Lazarus by his side. *w* 24 He called out, 'Father Abraham, have mercy on me, and send Lazarus to dip the tip of his finger in water and cool my tongue; for I am in agony in these flames.' 25 But Abraham said, 'Child, remember that during your lifetime you received your good things, and Lazarus in like manner evil things; but now he is comforted here, and you are in agony. 26 Besides all this, between you and us a great chasm has been fixed, so that those who might want to pass from here to you cannot do so, and no one can cross from there to us.' 27 He said, 'Then, father, I beg you to send him to my father's house — 28 for I have five brothers — that he may warn them, so that they will not also come into this place of torment.' 29 Abraham replied, 'They have Moses and the prophets; they should listen to them.' 30 He said, 'No, father Abraham; but if someone goes to them from the dead, they will repent.' 31 He said to him, 'If they do not listen to Moses and the prophets, neither will they be convinced even if someone rises from the dead.'"

17 Jesus*x* said to his disciples, "Occasions for stumbling are bound to come, but woe to anyone by whom they come! 2 It would be better for you if a millstone were hung around your neck and you were thrown into the sea than for you to cause one of these little ones to stumble. 3 Be on your guard! If another disciple*y* sins, you must rebuke the offender, and if there is repentance, you must forgive. 4 And if the same person sins against you seven times a day, and turns back to you seven times and says, 'I repent,' you must forgive."

5 The apostles said to the Lord, "Increase our faith!" 6 The Lord replied, "If you had faith the size of a*z* mustard seed, you could say to this mulberry tree, 'Be uprooted and planted in the sea,' and it would obey you.

7 "Who among you would say to your slave who has just come in from plowing or tending sheep in the field, 'Come here at once and take your place at the table'? 8 Would you not rather say to him, 'Prepare supper for me, put on your apron and serve me while I eat and drink; later you may eat and drink'? 9 Do you thank the slave for doing what was commanded? 10 So you also, when you have done all that you were ordered to do, say, 'We are worthless slaves; we have done only what we ought to have done!'"

u Or everyone is strongly urged to enter it   *v* Gk to Abraham's bosom   *w* Gk in his bosom   *x* Gk He   *y* Gk your brother   *z* Gk faith as a grain of

REVISED ENGLISH BIBLE

14 The Pharisees, who loved money, heard all this and scoffed at him. 15 He said to them, 'You are the people who impress others with your righteousness; but God sees through you; for what is considered admirable in human eyes is detestable in the sight of God.

16 'The law and the prophets were until John: since then, the good news of the kingdom of God is proclaimed, and everyone forces a way in.

17 'It is easier for heaven and earth to come to an end than for one letter of the law to lose its force.

18 'A man who divorces his wife and marries another commits adultery; and anyone who marries a woman divorced from her husband commits adultery.

19 'There was a rich man, who used to dress in purple and the finest linen, and feasted sumptuously every day. 20 At his gate lay a poor man named Lazarus, who was covered with sores. 21 He would have been glad to satisfy his hunger with the scraps from the rich man's table. Dogs used to come and lick his sores. 22 One day the poor man died and was carried away by the angels to be with Abraham. The rich man also died and was buried. 23 In Hades, where he was in torment, he looked up and there, far away, was Abraham with Lazarus close beside him. 24 "Abraham, my father," he called out, "take pity on me! Send Lazarus to dip the tip of his finger in water, to cool my tongue, for I am in agony in this fire." 25 But Abraham said, "My child, remember that the good things fell to you in your lifetime, and the bad to Lazarus. Now he has his consolation here and it is you who are in agony. 26 But that is not all: there is a great gulf fixed between us; no one can cross it from our side to reach you, and none may pass from your side to us." 27 "Then, father," he replied, "will you send him to my father's house, 28 where I have five brothers, to warn them, so that they may not come to this place of torment?" 29 But Abraham said, "They have Moses and the prophets; let them listen to them." 30 "No, father Abraham," he replied, "but if someone from the dead visits them, they will repent." 31 Abraham answered, "If they do not listen to Moses and the prophets they will pay no heed even if someone should rise from the dead."'

17 He said to his disciples, 'There are bound to be causes of stumbling; but woe betide the person through whom they come. 2 It would be better for him to be thrown into the sea with a millstone round his neck than to cause the downfall of one of these little ones. 3 So be on your guard.

'If your brother does wrong, reprove him; and if he repents, forgive him. 4 Even if he wrongs you seven times in a day and comes back to you seven times saying, "I am sorry," you are to forgive him.'

5 The apostles said to the Lord, 'Increase our faith'; 6 and the Lord replied, 'If you had faith no bigger than a mustard seed, you could say to this mulberry tree, "Be rooted up and planted in the sea"; and it would obey you.

7 'Suppose one of you has a servant ploughing or minding sheep. When he comes in from the fields, will the master say, "Come and sit down straight away"? 8 Will he not rather say, "Prepare my supper; hitch up your robe, and wait on me while I have my meal. You can have yours afterwards"? 9 Is he grateful to the servant for carrying out his orders? 10 So with you: when you have carried out all you have been ordered to do, you should say, "We are servants and deserve no credit; we have only done our duty."'

14 The Pharisees, who loved money, heard all these things and sneered at him. 15 And he said to them, "You justify yourselves in the sight of others, but God knows your hearts; for what is of human esteem is an abomination in the sight of God.

16 "The law and the prophets lasted until John; but from then on the kingdom of God is proclaimed, and everyone who enters does so with violence. 17 It is easier for heaven and earth to pass away than for the smallest part of a letter of the law to become invalid.

18 "Everyone who divorces his wife and marries another commits adultery, and the one who marries a woman divorced from her husband commits adultery.

19 "There was a rich man who dressed in purple garments and fine linen and dined sumptuously each day. 20 And lying at his door was a poor man named Lazarus, covered with sores, 21 who would gladly have eaten his fill of the scraps that fell from the rich man's table. Dogs even used to come and lick his sores. 22 When the poor man died, he was carried away by angels to the bosom of Abraham. The rich man also died and was buried, 23 and from the netherworld, where he was in torment, he raised his eyes and saw Abraham far off and Lazarus at his side. 24 And he cried out, 'Father Abraham, have pity on me. Send Lazarus to dip the tip of his finger in water and cool my tongue, for I am suffering torment in these flames.' 25 Abraham replied, 'My child, remember that you received what was good during your lifetime while Lazarus likewise received what was bad; but now he is comforted here, whereas you are tormented. 26 Moreover, between us and you a great chasm is established to prevent anyone from crossing who might wish to go from our side to yours or from your side to ours.' 27 He said, 'Then I beg you, father, send him to my father's house, 28 for I have five brothers, so that he may warn them, lest they too come to this place of torment.' 29 But Abraham replied, 'They have Moses and the prophets. Let them listen to them.' 30 He said, 'Oh no, father Abraham, but if someone from the dead goes to them, they will repent.' 31 Then Abraham said, 'If they will not listen to Moses and the prophets, neither will they be persuaded if someone should rise from the dead.' "

17 He said to his disciples, "Things that cause sin will inevitably occur, but woe to the person through whom they occur. 2 It would be better for him if a millstone were put around his neck and he be thrown into the sea than for him to cause one of these little ones to sin. 3 Be on your guard! If your brother sins, rebuke him; and if he repents, forgive him. 4 And if he wrongs you seven times in one day and returns to you seven times saying, 'I am sorry,' you should forgive him."

5 And the apostles said to the Lord, "Increase our faith." 6 The Lord replied, "If you have faith the size of a mustard seed, you would say to [this] mulberry tree, 'Be uprooted and planted in the sea,' and it would obey you.

7 "Who among you would say to your servant who has just come in from plowing or tending sheep in the field, 'Come here immediately and take your place at table'? 8 Would he not rather say to him, 'Prepare something for me to eat. Put on your apron and wait on me while I eat and drink. You may eat and drink when I am finished'? 9 Is he grateful to that servant because he did what was commanded? 10 So should it be with you. When you have done all you have been commanded, say, 'We are unprofitable servants; we have done what we were obliged to do.' "

14 The Pharisees, who loved money, heard all this and jeered at him. 15 He said to them, 'You are the very ones who pass yourselves off as upright in people's sight, but God knows your hearts. For what is highly esteemed in human eyes is loathsome in the sight of God.

16 'Up to the time of John it was the Law and the Prophets; from then onwards, the kingdom of God has been preached, and everyone is forcing their way into it.

17 'It is easier for heaven and earth to disappear than for one little stroke to drop out of the Law.

18 'Everyone who divorces his wife and marries another is guilty of adultery, and the man who marries a woman divorced by her husband commits adultery.

19 'There was a rich man who used to dress in purple and fine linen and feast magnificently every day. 20 And at his gate there used to lie a poor man called Lazarus, covered with sores, 21 who longed to fill himself with what fell from the rich man's table. Even dogs came and licked his sores. 22 Now it happened that the poor man died and was carried away by the angels into Abraham's embrace. The rich man also died and was buried.

23 'In his torment in Hades he looked up and saw Abraham a long way off with Lazarus in his embrace. 24 So he cried out, "Father Abraham, pity me and send Lazarus to dip the tip of his finger in water and cool my tongue, for I am in agony in these flames." 25 Abraham said, "My son, remember that during your life you had your fill of good things, just as Lazarus his fill of bad. Now he is being comforted here while you are in agony. 26 But that is not all: between us and you a great gulf has been fixed, to prevent those who want to cross from our side to yours or from your side to ours."

27 'So he said, "Father, I beg you then to send Lazarus to my father's house, 28 since I have five brothers, to give them warning so that they do not come to this place of torment too." 29 Abraham said, "They have Moses and the prophets, let them listen to them." 30 The rich man replied, "Ah no, father Abraham, but if someone comes to them from the dead, they will repent." 31 Then Abraham said to him, "If they will not listen either to Moses or to the prophets, they will not be convinced even if someone should rise from the dead." '

17 He said to his disciples, 'Causes of falling are sure to come, but alas for the one through whom they occur! 2 It would be better for such a person to be thrown into the sea with a millstone round the neck than to be the downfall of a single one of these little ones. 3 Keep watch on yourselves.

'If your brother does something wrong, rebuke him and, if he is sorry, forgive him. 4 And if he wrongs you seven times a day and seven times comes back to you and says, "I am sorry," you must forgive him.'

5 The apostles said to the Lord, 'Increase our faith.' 6 The Lord replied, 'If you had faith like a mustard seed you could say to this mulberry tree, "Be uprooted and planted in the sea," and it would obey you.

7 'Which of you, with a servant ploughing or minding sheep, would say to him when he returned from the fields, "Come and have your meal at once"? 8 Would he not be more likely to say, "Get my supper ready; fasten your belt and wait on me while I eat and drink. You yourself can eat and drink afterwards"? 9 Must he be grateful to the servant for doing what he was told? 10 So with you: when you have done all you have been told to do, say, "We are useless servants: we have done no more than our duty." '

NEW REVISED STANDARD VERSION

11 On the way to Jerusalem Jesus*a* was going through the region between Samaria and Galilee. 12 As he entered a village, ten lepers*b* approached him. Keeping their distance, 13 they called out, saying, "Jesus, Master, have mercy on us!" 14 When he saw them, he said to them, "Go and show yourselves to the priests." And as they went, they were made clean. 15 Then one of them, when he saw that he was healed, turned back, praising God with a loud voice. 16 He prostrated himself at Jesus'*c* feet and thanked him. And he was a Samaritan. 17 Then Jesus asked, "Were not ten made clean? But the other nine, where are they? 18 Was none of them found to return and give praise to God except this foreigner?" 19 Then he said to him, "Get up and go on your way; your faith has made you well."

20 Once Jesus*a* was asked by the Pharisees when the kingdom of God was coming, and he answered, "The kingdom of God is not coming with things that can be observed; 21 nor will they say, 'Look, here it is!' or 'There it is!' For, in fact, the kingdom of God is among*d* you."

22 Then he said to the disciples, "The days are coming when you will long to see one of the days of the Son of Man, and you will not see it. 23 They will say to you, 'Look there!' or 'Look here!' Do not go, do not set off in pursuit. 24 For as the lightning flashes and lights up the sky from one side to the other, so will the Son of Man be in his day.*e* 25 But first he must endure much suffering and be rejected by this generation. 26 Just as it was in the days of Noah, so too it will be in the days of the Son of Man. 27 They were eating and drinking, and marrying and being given in marriage, until the day Noah entered the ark, and the flood came and destroyed all of them. 28 Likewise, just as it was in the days of Lot: they were eating and drinking, buying and selling, planting and building, 29 but on the day that Lot left Sodom, it rained fire and sulfur from heaven and destroyed all of them 30 — it will be like that on the day that the Son of Man is revealed. 31 On that day, anyone on the housetop who has belongings in the house must not come down to take them away; and likewise anyone in the field must not turn back. 32 Remember Lot's wife. 33 Those who try to make their life secure will lose it, but those who lose their life will keep it. 34 I tell you, on that night there will be two in one bed; one will be taken and the other left. 35 There will be two women grinding meal together; one will be taken and the other left."*f* 37 Then they asked him, "Where, Lord?" He said to them, "Where the corpse is, there the vultures will gather."

18 Then Jesus*a* told them a parable about their need to pray always and not to lose heart. 2 He said, "In a certain city there was a judge who neither feared God nor had respect for people. 3 In that city there was a widow who kept coming to him and saying, 'Grant me justice against my opponent.' 4 For a while he refused; but later he said to himself, 'Though I have no fear of God and no respect for anyone, 5 yet because this widow keeps bothering me, I will grant her justice, so that she may not wear me out by continually coming.' "*g* 6 And the Lord said, "Listen to what the unjust judge says. 7 And will not God grant justice to his chosen ones who cry to him day and night? Will he delay long in helping them? 8 I tell you, he will quickly grant justice to them. And yet, when the Son of Man comes, will he find faith on earth?"

REVISED ENGLISH BIBLE

11 In the course of his journey to Jerusalem he was travelling through the borderlands of Samaria and Galilee. 12 As he was entering a village he was met by ten men with leprosy. They stood some way off 13 and called out to him, 'Jesus, Master, take pity on us.' 14 When he saw them he said, 'Go and show yourselves to the priests'; and while they were on their way, they were made clean. 15 One of them, finding himself cured, turned back with shouts of praise to God. 16 He threw himself down at Jesus's feet and thanked him. And he was a Samaritan. 17 At this Jesus said: 'Were not all ten made clean? The other nine, where are they? 18 Was no one found returning to give praise to God except this foreigner?' 19 And he said to the man, 'Stand up and go on your way; your faith has cured you.'

20 THE Pharisees asked him, 'When will the kingdom of God come?' He answered, 'You cannot tell by observation when the kingdom of God comes. 21 You cannot say, "Look, here it is," or "There it is!" For the kingdom of God is among you!'

22 He said to the disciples, 'The time will come when you will long to see one of the days of the Son of Man and will not see it. 23 They will say to you, "Look! There!" and "Look! Here!" Do not go running off in pursuit. 24 For like a lightning-flash, that lights up the earth from end to end, will the Son of Man be in his day. 25 But first he must endure much suffering and be rejected by this generation. 26 'As it was in the days of Noah, so will it be in the days of the Son of Man. 27 They ate and drank and married, until the day that Noah went into the ark and the flood came and made an end of them all. 28 So too in the days of Lot, they ate and drank, they bought and sold, they planted and built; 29 but on the day that Lot left Sodom, fire and sulphur rained from the sky and made an end of them all. 30 It will be like that on the day when the Son of Man is revealed. 31 'On that day if anyone is on the roof while his belongings are in the house, he must not go down to fetch them; and if anyone is in the field, he must not turn back. 32 Remember Lot's wife. 33 Whoever seeks to preserve his life will lose it; and whoever loses his life will gain it. 34 'I tell you, on that night there will be two people in one bed: one will be taken, the other left. 35 There will be two women together grinding corn: one will be taken, the other left.' 37 When they heard this they asked, 'Where, Lord?' He said, 'Where the carcass is, there will the vultures gather.'

18 HE told them a parable to show that they should keep on praying and never lose heart: 2 'In a certain city there was a judge who had no fear of God or respect for man, 3 and in the same city there was a widow who kept coming before him to demand justice against her opponent. 4 For a time he refused; but in the end he said to himself, "Although I have no fear of God or respect for man, 5 yet this widow is so great a nuisance that I will give her justice before she wears me out with her persistence." ' 6 The Lord said, 'You hear what the unjust judge says. 7 Then will not God give justice to his chosen, to whom he listens patiently while they cry out to him day and night? 8 I tell you, he will give them justice soon enough. But when the Son of Man comes, will he find faith on earth?'

---

a Gk *he*   *b* The terms *leper* and *leprosy* can refer to several diseases   *c* Gk *his*   *d* Or *within*   *e* Other ancient authorities lack *in his day*   *f* Other ancient authorities add verse 36, *"Two will be in the field; one will be taken and the other left."*   *g* Or *so that she may not finally come and slap me in the face*

17.21 **For ... among you!:** *or* For the kingdom of God is within you! *or* For the kingdom of God is within your grasp! *or* For suddenly the kingdom of God will be among you.   17.35 **the other left:** *some witnesses add* 36 'There will be two men in the fields: one will be taken, the other left.'

11 As he continued his journey to Jerusalem, he traveled through Samaria and Galilee. 12 As he was entering a village, ten lepers met [him]. They stood at a distance from him 13 and raised their voice, saying, "Jesus, Master! Have pity on us!" 14 And when he saw them, he said, "Go show yourselves to the priests." As they were going they were cleansed. 15 And one of them, realizing he had been healed, returned, glorifying God in a loud voice; 16 and he fell at the feet of Jesus and thanked him. He was a Samaritan. 17 Jesus said in reply, "Ten were cleansed, were they not? Where are the other nine? 18 Has none but this foreigner returned to give thanks to God?" 19 Then he said to him, "Stand up and go; your faith has saved you."

20 Asked by the Pharisees when the kingdom of God would come, he said in reply, "The coming of the kingdom of God cannot be observed, 21 and no one will announce, 'Look, here it is,' or, 'There it is.' For behold, the kingdom of God is among you."

22 Then he said to his disciples, "The days will come when you will long to see one of the days of the Son of Man, but you will not see it. 23 There will be those who will say to you, 'Look, there he is,' [or] 'Look, here he is.' Do not go off, do not run in pursuit. 24 For just as lightning flashes and lights up the sky from one side to the other, so will the Son of Man be [in his day]. 25 But first he must suffer greatly and be rejected by this generation. 26 As it was in the days of Noah, so it will be in the days of the Son of Man; 27 they were eating and drinking, marrying and giving in marriage up to the day that Noah entered the ark, and the flood came and destroyed them all. 28 Similarly, as it was in the days of Lot: they were eating, drinking, buying, selling, planting, building; 29 on the day when Lot left Sodom, fire and brimstone rained from the sky to destroy them all. 30 So it will be on the day the Son of Man is revealed. 31 On that day, a person who is on the housetop and whose belongings are in the house must not go down to get them, and likewise a person in the field must not return to what was left behind. 32 Remember the wife of Lot. 33 Whoever seeks to preserve his life will lose it, but whoever loses it will save it. 34 I tell you, on that night there will be two people in one bed; one will be taken, the other left. 35 And there will be two women grinding meal together; one will be taken, the other left. [36] 37 They said to him in reply, "Where, Lord?" He said to them, "Where the body is, there also the vultures will gather."

18 Then he told them a parable about the necessity for them to pray always without becoming weary. He said, 2 "There was a judge in a certain town who neither feared God nor respected any human being. 3 And a widow in that town used to come to him and say, 'Render a just decision for me against my adversary.' 4 For a long time the judge was unwilling, but eventually he thought, 'While it is true that I neither fear God nor respect any human being, 5 because this widow keeps bothering me I shall deliver a just decision for her lest she finally come and strike me.'" 6 The Lord said, "Pay attention to what the dishonest judge says. 7 Will not God then secure the rights of his chosen ones who call out to him day and night? Will he be slow to answer them? 8 I tell you, he will see to it that justice is done for them speedily. But when the Son of Man comes, will he find faith on earth?"

11 Now it happened that on the way to Jerusalem he was travelling in the borderlands of Samaria and Galilee. 12 As he entered one of the villages, ten men suffering from a virulent skin-disease came to meet him. They stood some way off 13 and called to him, 'Jesus! Master! Take pity on us.' 14 When he saw them he said, 'Go and show yourselves to the priests.' Now as they were going away they were cleansed. 15 Finding himself cured, one of them turned back praising God at the top of his voice 16 and threw himself prostrate at the feet of Jesus and thanked him. The man was a Samaritan. 17 This led Jesus to say, 'Were not all ten made clean? The other nine, where are they? 18 It seems that no one has come back to give praise to God, except this foreigner.' 19 And he said to the man, 'Stand up and go on your way. Your faith has saved you.'

20 Asked by the Pharisees when the kingdom of God was to come, he gave them this answer, 'The coming of the kingdom of God does not admit of observation 21 and there will be no one to say, "Look, it is here! Look, it is there!" For look, the kingdom of God is among you.'

22 He said to the disciples, 'A time will come when you will long to see one of the days of the Son of man and will not see it. 23 They will say to you, "Look, it is there!" or, "Look, it is here!" Make no move; do not set off in pursuit; 24 for as the lightning flashing from one part of heaven lights up the other, so will the Son of man be when his Day comes. 25 But first he is destined to suffer grievously and be rejected by this generation.

26 'As it was in Noah's day, so will it also be in the days of the Son of man. 27 People were eating and drinking, marrying wives and husbands, right up to the day Noah went into the ark, and the Flood came and destroyed them all. 28 It will be the same as it was in Lot's day: people were eating and drinking, buying and selling, planting and building, 29 but the day Lot left Sodom, it rained fire and brimstone from heaven and it destroyed them all. 30 It will be the same when the day comes for the Son of man to be revealed.

31 'When that Day comes, no one on the housetop, with his possessions in the house, must come down to collect them, nor must anyone in the fields turn back. 32 Remember Lot's wife. 33 Anyone who tries to preserve his life will lose it; and anyone who loses it will keep it safe. 34 I tell you, on that night, when two are in one bed, one will be taken, the other left; 35 when two women are grinding corn together, one will be taken, the other left.' [36]i 37 The disciples spoke up and asked, 'Where, Lord?' He said, 'Where the body is, there too will the vultures gather.'

18 Then he told them a parable about the need to pray continually and never lose heart. 2 'There was a judge in a certain town,' he said, 'who had neither fear of God nor respect for anyone. 3 In the same town there was also a widow who kept on coming to him and saying, "I want justice from you against my enemy!" 4 For a long time he refused, but at last he said to himself, "Even though I have neither fear of God nor respect for any human person, 5 I must give this widow her just rights since she keeps pestering me, or she will come and slap me in the face."' 6 And the Lord said, 'You notice what the unjust judge has to say? 7 Now, will not God see justice done to his elect if they keep calling to him day and night even though he still delays to help them? 8 I promise you, he will see justice done to them, and done speedily. But when the Son of man comes, will he find any faith on earth?'

17, 36: The inclusion of v 36, "There will be two men in the field; one will be taken, the other left behind," in some Western manuscripts appears to be a scribal assimilation to Mt 24, 40.

i 17 Add. v. 36, 'There will be two men in the fields; one will be taken, the other left,' cf. Mt 24:40.

NEW REVISED STANDARD VERSION	REVISED ENGLISH BIBLE

9 He also told this parable to some who trusted in themselves that they were righteous and regarded others with contempt: 10 "Two men went up to the temple to pray, one a Pharisee and the other a tax collector. 11 The Pharisee, standing by himself, was praying thus, 'God, I thank you that I am not like other people: thieves, rogues, adulterers, or even like this tax collector. 12 I fast twice a week; I give a tenth of all my income.' 13 But the tax collector, standing far off, would not even look up to heaven, but was beating his breast and saying, 'God, be merciful to me, a sinner!' 14 I tell you, this man went down to his home justified rather than the other; for all who exalt themselves will be humbled, but all who humble themselves will be exalted."

15 People were bringing even infants to him that he might touch them; and when the disciples saw it, they sternly ordered them not to do it. 16 But Jesus called for them and said, "Let the little children come to me, and do not stop them; for it is to such as these that the kingdom of God belongs. 17 Truly I tell you, whoever does not receive the kingdom of God as a little child will never enter it."

18 A certain ruler asked him, "Good Teacher, what must I do to inherit eternal life?" 19 Jesus said to him, "Why do you call me good? No one is good but God alone. 20 You know the commandments: 'You shall not commit adultery; You shall not murder; You shall not steal; You shall not bear false witness; Honor your father and mother.'" 21 He replied, "I have kept all these since my youth." 22 When Jesus heard this, he said to him, "There is still one thing lacking. Sell all that you own and distribute the money*h* to the poor, and you will have treasure in heaven; then come, follow me." 23 But when he heard this, he became sad; for he was very rich. 24 Jesus looked at him and said, "How hard it is for those who have wealth to enter the kingdom of God! 25 Indeed, it is easier for a camel to go through the eye of a needle than for someone who is rich to enter the kingdom of God."

26 Those who heard it said, "Then who can be saved?" 27 He replied, "What is impossible for mortals is possible for God."

28 Then Peter said, "Look, we have left our homes and followed you." 29 And he said to them, "Truly I tell you, there is no one who has left house or wife or brothers or parents or children, for the sake of the kingdom of God, 30 who will not get back very much more in this age, and in the age to come eternal life."

31 Then he took the twelve aside and said to them, "See, we are going up to Jerusalem, and everything that is written about the Son of Man by the prophets will be accomplished. 32 For he will be handed over to the Gentiles; and he will be mocked and insulted and spat upon. 33 After they have flogged him, they will kill him, and on the third day he will rise again." 34 But they understood nothing about all these things; in fact, what he said was hidden from them, and they did not grasp what was said.

35 As he approached Jericho, a blind man was sitting by the roadside begging. 36 When he heard a crowd going by, he asked what was happening. 37 They told him, "Jesus of Nazareth*i* is passing by." 38 Then he shouted, "Jesus, Son of David, have mercy on me!" 39 Those who were in front sternly ordered him to be quiet; but he shouted even more loudly, "Son of David, have mercy on me!" 40 Jesus stood still and ordered the man to be brought to him; and when he came near, he asked him, 41 "What do you want me to do for you?" He said, "Lord, let me see again." 42 Jesus said to him, "Receive your sight; your faith has saved you." 43 Im-

9 Here is another parable that he told; it was aimed at those who were sure of their own goodness and looked down on everyone else. 10 'Two men went up to the temple to pray, one a Pharisee and the other a tax-collector. 11 The Pharisee stood up and prayed this prayer: "I thank you, God, that I am not like the rest of mankind—greedy, dishonest, adulterous—or, for that matter, like this tax-collector. 12 I fast twice a week; I pay tithes on all that I get." 13 But the other kept his distance and would not even raise his eyes to heaven, but beat upon his breast, saying, "God, have mercy on me, sinner that I am." 14 It was this man, I tell you, and not the other, who went home acquitted of his sins. For everyone who exalts himself will be humbled; and whoever humbles himself will be exalted.'

15 They brought babies for him to touch, and when the disciples saw them they rebuked them. 16 But Jesus called for the children and said, 'Let the children come to me; do not try to stop them; for the kingdom of God belongs to such as these. 17 Truly I tell you: whoever does not accept the kingdom of God like a child will never enter it.'

18 One of the rulers put this question to him: 'Good Teacher, what must I do to win eternal life?' 19 Jesus said to him, 'Why do you call me good? No one is good except God alone. 20 You know the commandments: "Do not commit adultery; do not murder; do not steal; do not give false evidence; honour your father and mother."' 21 The man answered, 'I have kept all these since I was a boy.' 22 On hearing this Jesus said, 'There is still one thing you lack: sell everything you have and give to the poor, and you will have treasure in heaven; then come and follow me.' 23 When he heard this his heart sank, for he was a very rich man. 24 When Jesus saw it he said, 'How hard it is for the wealthy to enter the kingdom of God! 25 It is easier for a camel to go through the eye of a needle than for a rich man to enter the kingdom of God.' 26 Those who heard asked, 'Then who can be saved?' 27 He answered, 'What is impossible for men is possible for God.'

28 Peter said, 'What about us? We left all we had to follow you.' 29 Jesus said to them, 'Truly I tell you: there is no one who has given up home, or wife, brothers, parents, or children, for the sake of the kingdom of God, 30 who will not be repaid many times over in this age, and in the age to come eternal life.'

31 He took the Twelve aside and said, 'We are now going up to Jerusalem; and everything that was written by the prophets will find its fulfilment in the Son of Man. 32 He will be handed over to the Gentiles. He will be mocked, maltreated, and spat upon; 33 they will flog him and kill him; and on the third day he will rise again.' 34 But they did not understand this at all or grasp what he was talking about; its meaning was concealed from them.

35 As he approached Jericho a blind man sat at the roadside begging. 36 Hearing a crowd going past, he asked what was happening, 37 and was told that Jesus of Nazareth was passing by. 38 Then he called out, 'Jesus, Son of David, have pity on me.' 39 The people in front told him to hold his tongue; but he shouted all the more, 'Son of David, have pity on me.' 40 Jesus stopped and ordered the man to be brought to him. When he came up Jesus asked him, 41 'What do you want me to do for you?' 'Sir, I want my sight back,' he answered. 42 Jesus said to him, 'Have back your sight; your faith has healed you.' 43 He recovered his

h Gk lacks *the money*   *i* Gk *the Nazorean*

2808

9 He then addressed this parable to those who were convinced of their own righteousness and despised everyone else. 10 "Two people went up to the temple area to pray; one was a Pharisee and the other was a tax collector. 11 The Pharisee took up his position and spoke this prayer to himself, 'O God, I thank you that I am not like the rest of humanity — greedy, dishonest, adulterous — or even like this tax collector. 12 I fast twice a week, and I pay tithes on my whole income.' 13 But the tax collector stood off at a distance and would not even raise his eyes to heaven but beat his breast and prayed, 'O God, be merciful to me a sinner.' 14 I tell you, the latter went home justified, not the former; for everyone who exalts himself will be humbled, and the one who humbles himself will be exalted."

15 People were bringing even infants to him that he might touch them, and when the disciples saw this, they rebuked them. 16 Jesus, however, called the children to himself and said, "Let the children come to me and do not prevent them; for the kingdom of God belongs to such as these. 17 Amen, I say to you, whoever does not accept the kingdom of God like a child will not enter it."

18 An official asked him this question, "Good teacher, what must I do to inherit eternal life?" 19 Jesus answered him, "Why do you call me good? No one is good but God alone. 20 You know the commandments, 'You shall not commit adultery; you shall not kill; you shall not steal; you shall not bear false witness; honor your father and your mother.'" 21 And he replied, "All of these I have observed from my youth." 22 When Jesus heard this he said to him, "There is still one thing left for you: sell all that you have and distribute it to the poor, and you will have a treasure in heaven. Then come, follow me." 23 But when he heard this he became quite sad, for he was very rich.

24 Jesus looked at him [now sad] and said, "How hard it is for those who have wealth to enter the kingdom of God! 25 For it is easier for a camel to pass through the eye of a needle than for a rich person to enter the kingdom of God." 26 Those who heard this said, "Then who can be saved?" 27 And he said, "What is impossible for human beings is possible for God." 28 Then Peter said, "We have given up our possessions and followed you." 29 He said to them, "Amen, I say to you, there is no one who has given up house or wife or brothers or parents or children for the sake of the kingdom of God 30 who will not receive [back] an overabundant return in this present age and eternal life in the age to come."

31 Then he took the Twelve aside and said to them, "Behold, we are going up to Jerusalem and everything written by the prophets about the Son of Man will be fulfilled. 32 He will be handed over to the Gentiles and he will be mocked and insulted and spat upon; 33 and after they have scourged him they will kill him, but on the third day he will rise." 34 But they understood nothing of this; the word remained hidden from them and they failed to comprehend what he said.

35 Now as he approached Jericho a blind man was sitting by the roadside begging, 36 and hearing a crowd going by, he inquired what was happening. 37 They told him, "Jesus of Nazareth is passing by." 38 He shouted, "Jesus, Son of David, have pity on me!" 39 The people walking in front rebuked him, telling him to be silent, but he kept calling out all the more, "Son of David, have pity on me!" 40 Then Jesus stopped and ordered that he be brought to him; and when he came near, Jesus asked him, 41 "What do you want me to do for you?" He replied, "Lord, please let me see." 42 Jesus told him, "Have sight; your faith has saved you." 43 He immediately received his sight and followed him, giv-

9 He spoke the following parable to some people who prided themselves on being upright and despised everyone else, 10 'Two men went up to the Temple to pray, one a Pharisee, the other a tax collector. 11 The Pharisee stood there and said this prayer to himself, "I thank you, God, that I am not grasping, unjust, adulterous like everyone else, and particularly that I am not like this tax collector here. 12 I fast twice a week; I pay tithes on all I get." 13 The tax collector stood some distance away, not daring even to raise his eyes to heaven; but he beat his breast and said, "God, be merciful to me, a sinner." 14 This man, I tell you, went home again justified; the other did not. For everyone who raises himself up will be humbled, but anyone who humbles himself will be raised up.'

15 People even brought babies to him, for him to touch them; but when the disciples saw this they scolded them. 16 But Jesus called the children to him and said, 'Let the little children come to me, and do not stop them; for it is to such as these that the kingdom of God belongs. 17 In truth I tell you, anyone who does not welcome the kingdom of God like a little child will never enter it.'

18 One of the rulers put this question to him, 'Good Master, what shall I do to inherit eternal life?' 19 Jesus said to him, 'Why do you call me good? No one is good but God alone. 20 You know the commandments: *You shall not commit adultery; You shall not kill; You shall not steal; You shall not give false witness; Honour your father and your mother.*[j] 21 He replied, 'I have kept all these since my earliest days.' 22 And when Jesus heard this he said, 'There is still one thing you lack. Sell everything you own and distribute the money to the poor, and you will have treasure in heaven; then come, follow me.' 23 But when he heard this he was overcome with sadness, for he was very rich.

24 Jesus looked at him and said, 'How hard it is for those who have riches to make their way into the kingdom of God! 25 Yes, it is easier for a camel to pass through the eye of a needle than for someone rich to enter the kingdom of God.' 26 Those who were listening said, 'In that case, who can be saved?' 27 He replied, 'Things that are impossible by human resources, are possible for God.'

28 But Peter said, 'Look, we left all we had to follow you.' 29 He said to them, 'In truth I tell you, there is no one who has left house, wife, brothers, parents or children for the sake of the kingdom of God 30 who will not receive many times as much in this present age and, in the world to come, eternal life.'

31 Then taking the Twelve aside he said to them, 'Look, we are going up to Jerusalem, and everything that is written by the prophets about the Son of man is to come true. 32 For he will be handed over to the gentiles and will be mocked, maltreated and spat on, 33 and when they have scourged him they will put him to death; and on the third day he will rise again.' 34 But they could make nothing of this; what he said was quite obscure to them, they did not understand what he was telling them.

35 Now it happened that as he drew near to Jericho there was a blind man sitting at the side of the road begging. 36 When he heard the crowd going past he asked what it was all about, 37 and they told him that Jesus the Nazarene was passing by. 38 So he called out, 'Jesus, Son of David, have pity on me.' 39 The people in front scolded him and told him to keep quiet, but he only shouted all the louder, 'Son of David, have pity on me.' 40 Jesus stopped and ordered them to bring the man to him, and when he came up, asked him, 41 'What do you want me to do for you?' 'Sir,' he replied, 'let me see again.' 42 Jesus said to him, 'Receive your sight. Your faith has saved you.' 43 And instantly his sight re-

mediately he regained his sight and followed him, glorifying God; and all the people, when they saw it, praised God.

19 He entered Jericho and was passing through it. 2 A man was there named Zacchaeus; he was a chief tax collector and was rich. 3 He was trying to see who Jesus was, but on account of the crowd he could not, because he was short in stature. 4 So he ran ahead and climbed a sycamore tree to see him, because he was going to pass that way. 5 When Jesus came to the place, he looked up and said to him, "Zacchaeus, hurry and come down; for I must stay at your house today." 6 So he hurried down and was happy to welcome him. 7 All who saw it began to grumble and said, "He has gone to be the guest of one who is a sinner." 8 Zacchaeus stood there and said to the Lord, "Look, half of my possessions, Lord, I will give to the poor; and if I have defrauded anyone of anything, I will pay back four times as much." 9 Then Jesus said to him, "Today salvation has come to this house, because he too is a son of Abraham. 10 For the Son of Man came to seek out and to save the lost."

11 As they were listening to this, he went on to tell a parable, because he was near Jerusalem, and because they supposed that the kingdom of God was to appear immediately. 12 So he said, "A nobleman went to a distant country to get royal power for himself and then return. 13 He summoned ten of his slaves, and gave them ten pounds, *j* and said to them, 'Do business with these until I come back.' 14 But the citizens of his country hated him and sent a delegation after him, saying, 'We do not want this man to rule over us.' 15 When he returned, having received royal power, he ordered these slaves, to whom he had given the money, to be summoned so that he might find out what they had gained by trading. 16 The first came forward and said, 'Lord, your pound has made ten more pounds.' 17 He said to him, 'Well done, good slave! Because you have been trustworthy in a very small thing, take charge of ten cities.' 18 Then the second came, saying, 'Lord, your pound has made five pounds.' 19 He said to him, 'And you, rule over five cities.' 20 Then the other came, saying, 'Lord, here is your pound. I wrapped it up in a piece of cloth, 21 for I was afraid of you, because you are a harsh man; you take what you did not deposit, and reap what you did not sow.' 22 He said to him, 'I will judge you by your own words, you wicked slave! You knew, did you, that I was a harsh man, taking what I did not deposit and reaping what I did not sow? 23 Why then did you not put my money into the bank? Then when I returned, I could have collected it with interest.' 24 He said to the bystanders, 'Take the pound from him and give it to the one who has ten pounds.' 25 (And they said to him, 'Lord, he has ten pounds!') 26 'I tell you, to all those who have, more will be given; but from those who have nothing, even what they have will be taken away. 27 But as for these enemies of mine who did not want me to be king over them — bring them here and slaughter them in my presence.' "

28 After he had said this, he went on ahead, going up to Jerusalem.

29 When he had come near Bethphage and Bethany, at the place called the Mount of Olives, he sent two of the disciples, 30 saying, "Go into the village ahead of you, and as you enter it you will find tied there a colt that has never been ridden. Untie it and bring it here. 31 If anyone asks you, 'Why are you untying it?' just say this, 'The Lord needs it.' " 32 So those who were sent departed and found it as he had told them. 33 As they were untying the colt, its

19 Entering Jericho he made his way through the city. 2 There was a man there named Zacchaeus; he was superintendent of taxes and very rich. 3 He was eager to see what Jesus looked like; but, being a little man, he could not see him for the crowd. 4 So he ran on ahead and climbed a sycomore tree in order to see him, for he was to pass that way. 5 When Jesus came to the place, he looked up and said, 'Zacchaeus, be quick and come down, for I must stay at your house today.' 6 He climbed down as quickly as he could and welcomed him gladly. 7 At this there was a general murmur of disapproval. 'He has gone in to be the guest of a sinner,' they said. 8 But Zacchaeus stood there and said to the Lord, 'Here and now, sir, I give half my possessions to charity; and if I have defrauded anyone, I will repay him four times over.' 9 Jesus said to him, 'Today salvation has come to this house — for this man too is a son of Abraham. 10 The Son of Man has come to seek and to save what is lost.'

11 While they were listening to this, he went on to tell them a parable, because he was now close to Jerusalem and they thought the kingdom of God might dawn at any moment. 12 He said, 'A man of noble birth went on a long journey abroad, to have himself appointed king and then return. 13 But first he called ten of his servants and gave them each a sum of money, saying, "Trade with this while I am away." 14 His fellow-citizens hated him and sent a delegation after him to say, "We do not want this man as our king." 15 He returned however as king, and sent for the servants to whom he had given the money, to find out what profit each had made. 16 The first came and said, "Your money, sir, has increased tenfold." 17 "Well done," he replied; "you are a good servant. Because you have shown yourself trustworthy in a very small matter, you shall have charge of ten cities." 18 The second came and said, "Your money, sir, has increased fivefold"; 19 and he was told, "You shall be in charge of five cities." 20 The third came and said, "Here is your money, sir; I kept it wrapped up in a handkerchief. 21 I was afraid of you, because you are a hard man: you draw out what you did not put in and reap what you did not sow." 22 "You scoundrel!" he replied. "I will condemn you out of your own mouth. You knew me to be a hard man, did you, drawing out what I never put in, and reaping what I did not sow? 23 Then why did you not put my money on deposit, and I could have claimed it with interest when I came back?" 24 Turning to his attendants he said, "Take the money from him and give it to the man with the most." 25 "But, sir," they replied, "he has ten times as much already." 26 "I tell you," he said, "everyone who has will be given more; but whoever has nothing will forfeit even what he has. 27 But as for those enemies of mine who did not want me for their king, bring them here and slaughter them in my presence." '

28 WITH that Jesus set out on the ascent to Jerusalem. 29 As he approached Bethphage and Bethany at the hill called Olivet, he sent off two of the disciples, 30 telling them: 'Go into the village opposite; as you enter it you will find tethered there a colt which no one has yet ridden. Untie it and bring it here. 31 If anyone asks why you are untying it, say, "The Master needs it." ' 32 The two went on their errand and found everything just as he had told them. 33 As they were

---

j The mina, rendered here by *pound,* was about three months' wages for a laborer

ing glory to God. When they saw this, all the people gave praise to God.

19 He came to Jericho and intended to pass through the town. ²Now a man there named Zacchaeus, who was a chief tax collector and also a wealthy man, ³ was seeking to see who Jesus was; but he could not see him because of the crowd, for he was short in stature. ⁴ So he ran ahead and climbed a sycamore tree in order to see Jesus, who was about to pass that way. ⁵ When he reached the place, Jesus looked up and said to him, "Zacchaeus, come down quickly, for today I must stay at your house." ⁶ And he came down quickly and received him with joy. ⁷ When they all saw this, they began to grumble, saying, "He has gone to stay at the house of a sinner." ⁸ But Zacchaeus stood there and said to the Lord, "Behold, half of my possessions, Lord, I shall give to the poor, and if I have extorted anything from anyone I shall repay it four times over." ⁹ And Jesus said to him, "Today salvation has come to this house because this man too is a descendant of Abraham. ¹⁰ For the Son of Man has come to seek and to save what was lost."

¹¹ While they were listening to him speak, he proceeded to tell a parable because he was near Jerusalem and they thought that the kingdom of God would appear there immediately. ¹² So he said, "A nobleman went off to a distant country to obtain the kingship for himself and then to return. ¹³ He called ten of his servants and gave them ten gold coins and told them, 'Engage in trade with these until I return.' ¹⁴ His fellow citizens, however, despised him and sent a delegation after him to announce, 'We do not want this man to be our king.' ¹⁵ But when he returned after obtaining the kingship, he had the servants called, to whom he had given the money, to learn what they had gained by trading. ¹⁶ The first came forward and said, 'Sir, your gold coin has earned ten additional ones.' ¹⁷ He replied, 'Well done, good servant! You have been faithful in this very small matter; take charge of ten cities.' ¹⁸ Then the second came and reported, 'Your gold coin, sir, has earned five more.' ¹⁹ And to this servant too he said, 'You, take charge of five cities.' ²⁰ Then the other servant came and said, 'Sir, here is your gold coin; I kept it stored away in a handkerchief, ²¹ for I was afraid of you, because you are a demanding person; you take up what you did not lay down and you harvest what you did not plant.' ²² He said to him, 'With your own words I shall condemn you, you wicked servant. You knew I was a demanding person, taking up what I did not lay down and harvesting what I did not plant; ²³ why did you not put my money in a bank? Then on my return I would have collected it with interest.' ²⁴ And to those standing by he said, 'Take the gold coin from him and give it to the servant who has ten.' ²⁵ But they said to him, 'Sir, he has ten gold coins.' ²⁶ 'I tell you, to everyone who has, more will be given, but from the one who has not, even what he has will be taken away. ²⁷ Now as for those enemies of mine who did not want me as their king, bring them here and slay them before me.' "

²⁸ After he had said this, he proceeded on his journey up to Jerusalem. ²⁹ As he drew near to Bethphage and Bethany at the place called the Mount of Olives, he sent two of his disciples. ³⁰ He said, "Go into the village opposite you, and as you enter it you will find a colt tethered on which no one has ever sat. Untie it and bring it here. ³¹ And if anyone should ask you, 'Why are you untying it?' you will answer, 'The Master has need of it.' " ³² So those who had been sent went off and found everything just as he had told them.

turned and he followed him praising God, and all the people who saw it gave praise to God.

19 He entered Jericho and was going through the town ²and suddenly a man whose name was Zacchaeus made his appearance; he was one of the senior tax collectors and a wealthy man. ³ He kept trying to see which Jesus was, but he was too short and could not see him for the crowd; ⁴ so he ran ahead and climbed a sycamore tree to catch a glimpse of Jesus who was to pass that way. ⁵ When Jesus reached the spot he looked up and spoke to him, 'Zacchaeus, come down. Hurry, because I am to stay at your house today.' ⁶ And he hurried down and welcomed him joyfully. ⁷ They all complained when they saw what was happening. 'He has gone to stay at a sinner's house,' they said. ⁸ But Zacchaeus stood his ground and said to the Lord, 'Look, sir, I am going to give half my property to the poor, and if I have cheated anybody I will pay him back four times the amount.' ⁹ And Jesus said to him, 'Today salvation has come to this house, because this man too is a son of Abraham; ¹⁰ for the Son of man has come to seek out and save what was lost.'

¹¹ While the people were listening to this he went on to tell a parable, because he was near Jerusalem and they thought that the kingdom of God was going to show itself then and there. ¹² Accordingly he said, 'A man of noble birth went to a distant country to be appointed king and then return. ¹³ He summoned ten of his servants and gave them ten pounds, telling them, "Trade with these, until I get back." ¹⁴ But his compatriots detested him and sent a delegation to follow him with this message, "We do not want this man to be our king."

¹⁵ 'Now it happened that on his return, having received his appointment as king, he sent for those servants to whom he had given the money, to find out what profit each had made by trading. ¹⁶ The first came in, "Sir," he said, "your one pound has brought in ten." ¹⁷ He replied, "Well done, my good servant! Since you have proved yourself trustworthy in a very small thing, you shall have the government of ten cities." ¹⁸ Then came the second, "Sir," he said, "your one pound has made five." ¹⁹ To this one also he said, "And you shall be in charge of five cities." ²⁰ Next came the other, "Sir," he said, "here is your pound. I put it away safely wrapped up in a cloth ²¹ because I was afraid of you; for you are an exacting man: you gather in what you have not laid out and reap what you have not sown." ²² He said to him, "You wicked servant! Out of your own mouth I condemn you. So you knew that I was an exacting man, gathering in what I have not laid out and reaping what I have not sown? ²³ Then why did you not put my money in the bank? On my return I could have drawn it out with interest." ²⁴ And he said to those standing by, "Take the pound from him and give it to the man who has ten pounds." ²⁵ And they said to him, "But, sir, he has ten pounds . . ." ²⁶ "I tell you, to everyone who has will be given more; but anyone who has not will be deprived even of what he has.

²⁷ 'As for my enemies who did not want me for their king, bring them here and execute them in my presence." '

²⁸ When he had said this he went on ahead, going up to Jerusalem. ²⁹ Now it happened that when he was near Bethphage and Bethany, close by the Mount of Olives as it is called, he sent two of the disciples, saying, ³⁰ 'Go to the village opposite, and as you enter it you will find a tethered colt that no one has ever yet ridden. Untie it and bring it here. ³¹ If anyone asks you, "Why are you untying it?" you are to say this, "The Master needs it." ' ³² The messengers went off and found everything just as he had told them.

NEW REVISED STANDARD VERSION	REVISED ENGLISH BIBLE

owners asked them, "Why are you untying the colt?" ³⁴ They said, "The Lord needs it." ³⁵ Then they brought it to Jesus; and after throwing their cloaks on the colt, they set Jesus on it. ³⁶ As he rode along, people kept spreading their cloaks on the road. ³⁷ As he was now approaching the path down from the Mount of Olives, the whole multitude of the disciples began to praise God joyfully with a loud voice for all the deeds of power that they had seen, ³⁸ saying,

"Blessed is the king
who comes in the name of the Lord!
Peace in heaven,
and glory in the highest heaven!"

³⁹ Some of the Pharisees in the crowd said to him, "Teacher, order your disciples to stop." ⁴⁰ He answered, "I tell you, if these were silent, the stones would shout out."

⁴¹ As he came near and saw the city, he wept over it, ⁴² saying, "If you, even you, had only recognized on this day the things that make for peace! But now they are hidden from your eyes. ⁴³ Indeed, the days will come upon you, when your enemies will set up ramparts around you and surround you, and hem you in on every side. ⁴⁴ They will crush you to the ground, you and your children within you, and they will not leave within you one stone upon another; because you did not recognize the time of your visitation from God."ᵏ

⁴⁵ Then he entered the temple and began to drive out those who were selling things there; ⁴⁶ and he said, "It is written,

'My house shall be a house of prayer';
but you have made it a den of robbers."

⁴⁷ Every day he was teaching in the temple. The chief priests, the scribes, and the leaders of the people kept looking for a way to kill him; ⁴⁸ but they did not find anything they could do, for all the people were spellbound by what they heard.

20 One day, as he was teaching the people in the temple and telling the good news, the chief priests and the scribes came with the elders ² and said to him, "Tell us, by what authority are you doing these things? Who is it who gave you this authority?" ³ He answered them, "I will also ask you a question, and you tell me: ⁴ Did the baptism of John come from heaven, or was it of human origin?" ⁵ They discussed it with one another, saying, "If we say, 'From heaven,' he will say, 'Why did you not believe him?' ⁶ But if we say, 'Of human origin,' all the people will stone us; for they are convinced that John was a prophet." ⁷ So they answered that they did not know where it came from. ⁸ Then Jesus said to them, "Neither will I tell you by what authority I am doing these things."

⁹ He began to tell the people this parable: "A man planted a vineyard, and leased it to tenants, and went to another country for a long time. ¹⁰ When the season came, he sent a slave to the tenants in order that they might give him his share of the produce of the vineyard; but the tenants beat him and sent him away empty-handed. ¹¹ Next he sent another slave; that one also they beat and insulted and sent away empty-handed. ¹² And he sent still a third; this one also they wounded and threw out. ¹³ Then the owner of the vineyard said, 'What shall I do? I will send my beloved son; perhaps they will respect him.' ¹⁴ But when the tenants saw him, they discussed it among themselves and said, 'This is the heir; let us kill him so that the inheritance may be ours.' ¹⁵ So they threw him out of the vineyard and killed him. What then will the owner of the vineyard do to them? ¹⁶ He

untying the colt, its owners asked, 'Why are you untying that colt?' ³⁴ They answered, 'The Master needs it.'

³⁵ So they brought the colt to Jesus, and threw their cloaks on it for Jesus to mount. ³⁶ As he went along people laid their cloaks on the road. ³⁷ And when he reached the descent from the mount of Olives, the whole company of his disciples in their joy began to sing aloud the praises of God for all the great things they had seen:

³⁸ 'Blessed is he who comes as king in the name of the Lord!
Peace in heaven, glory in highest heaven!'

³⁹ Some Pharisees in the crowd said to him, 'Teacher, restrain your disciples.' ⁴⁰ He answered, 'I tell you, if my disciples are silent the stones will shout aloud.'

⁴¹ When he came in sight of the city, he wept over it ⁴² and said, 'If only you had known this day the way that leads to peace! But no; it is hidden from your sight. ⁴³ For a time will come upon you, when your enemies will set up siege-works against you; they will encircle you and hem you in at every point; ⁴⁴ they will bring you to the ground, you and your children within your walls, and not leave you one stone standing on another, because you did not recognize the time of God's visitation.'

⁴⁵ Then he went into the temple and began driving out the traders, ⁴⁶ with these words: 'Scripture says, "My house shall be a house of prayer"; but you have made it a bandits' cave.'

⁴⁷ Day by day he taught in the temple. The chief priests and scribes, with the support of the leading citizens, wanted to bring about his death, ⁴⁸ but found they were helpless, because the people all hung on his words.

20 One day, as he was teaching the people in the temple and telling them the good news, the chief priests and scribes, accompanied by the elders, confronted him. ² 'Tell us', they said, 'by what authority you are acting like this; who gave you this authority?' ³ He answered them, 'I also have a question for you: tell me, ⁴ was the baptism of John from God or from man?' ⁵ This set them arguing among themselves: 'If we say, "From God," he will say, "Why did you not believe him?" ⁶ And if we say, "From man," the people will all stone us, for they are convinced that John was a prophet.' ⁷ So they answered that they could not tell. ⁸ And Jesus said to them, 'Then neither will I tell you by what authority I act.'

⁹ He went on to tell the people this parable: 'A man planted a vineyard, let it out to vine-growers, and went abroad for a long time. ¹⁰ When the season came, he sent a servant to the tenants to collect from them his share of the produce; but the tenants thrashed him and sent him away empty-handed. ¹¹ He tried again and sent a second servant; but they thrashed him too, treated him outrageously, and sent him away empty-handed. ¹² He tried once more and sent a third; him too they wounded and flung out. ¹³ Then the owner of the vineyard said, "What am I to do? I will send my beloved son; perhaps they will respect him." ¹⁴ But when the tenants saw him they discussed what they should do. "This is the heir," they said; "let us kill him so that the inheritance may come to us." ¹⁵ So they flung him out of the vineyard and killed him. What, therefore, will the owner of

ᵏ Gk lacks *from God*

20:13 **my beloved son:** *or* my only son.

33 And as they were untying the colt, its owners said to them, "Why are you untying this colt?" 34 They answered, "The Master has need of it." 35 So they brought it to Jesus, threw their cloaks over the colt, and helped Jesus to mount. 36 As he rode along, the people were spreading their cloaks on the road; 37 and now as he was approaching the slope of the Mount of Olives, the whole multitude of his disciples began to praise God aloud with joy for all the mighty deeds they had seen. 38 They proclaimed:

"Blessed is the king who comes
    in the name of the Lord.
Peace in heaven
    and glory in the highest."

39 Some of the Pharisees in the crowd said to him, "Teacher, rebuke your disciples." 40 He said in reply, "I tell you, if they keep silent, the stones will cry out!"

41 As he drew near, he saw the city and wept over it, 42 saying, "If this day you only knew what makes for peace —but now it is hidden from your eyes. 43 For the days are coming upon you when your enemies will raise a palisade against you; they will encircle you and hem you in on all sides. 44 They will smash you to the ground and your children within you, and they will not leave one stone upon another within you because you did not recognize the time of your visitation."

45 Then Jesus entered the temple area and proceeded to drive out those who were selling things, 46 saying to them, "It is written, 'My house shall be a house of prayer, but you have made it a den of thieves.'" 47 And every day he was teaching in the temple area. The chief priests, the scribes, and the leaders of the people, meanwhile, were seeking to put him to death, 48 but they could find no way to accomplish their purpose because all the people were hanging on his words.

20 One day as he was teaching the people in the temple area and proclaiming the good news, the chief priests and scribes, together with the elders, approached him 2 and said to him, "Tell us, by what authority are you doing these things? Or who is the one who gave you this authority?" 3 He said to them in reply, "I shall ask you a question. Tell me, 4 was John's baptism of heavenly or of human origin?" 5 They discussed this among themselves, and said, "If we say, 'Of heavenly origin,' he will say, 'Why did you not believe him?' 6 But if we say, 'Of human origin,' then all the people will stone us, for they are convinced that John was a prophet." 7 So they answered that they did not know from where it came. 8 Then Jesus said to them, "Neither shall I tell you by what authority I do these things."

9 Then he proceeded to tell the people this parable. "[A] man planted a vineyard, leased it to tenant farmers, and then went on a journey for a long time. 10 At harvest time he sent a servant to the tenant farmers to receive some of the produce of the vineyard. But they beat the servant and sent him away empty-handed. 11 So he proceeded to send another servant, but him also they beat and insulted and sent away empty-handed. 12 Then he proceeded to send a third, but this one too they wounded and threw out. 13 The owner of the vineyard said, 'What shall I do? I shall send my beloved son; maybe they will respect him.' 14 But when the tenant farmers saw him they said to one another, 'This is the heir. Let us kill him that the inheritance may become ours.' 15 So they threw him out of the vineyard and killed him. What will the owner of the vineyard do to them? 16 He will come

33 As they were untying the colt, its owners said, 'Why are you untying it?' 34 and they answered, 'The Master needs it.'

35 So they took the colt to Jesus and, throwing their cloaks on its back, they lifted Jesus on to it. 36 As he moved off, they spread their cloaks in the road, 37 and now, as he was approaching the downward slope of the Mount of Olives, the whole group of disciples joyfully began to praise God at the top of their voices for all the miracles they had seen. 38 They cried out:

*Blessed is he who is coming
as King* in the name of the Lord!*k*
Peace in heaven
and glory in the highest heavens!

39 Some Pharisees in the crowd said to him, 'Master, reprove your disciples,' 40 but he answered, 'I tell you, if these keep silence, the stones will cry out.'

41 As he drew near and came in sight of the city he shed tears over it 42 and said, 'If you too had only recognised on this day the way to peace! But in fact it is hidden from your eyes! 43 Yes, a time is coming when your enemies will raise fortifications all round you, when they will encircle you and hem you in on every side; 44 they will dash you and the children inside your walls to the ground; they will leave not one stone standing on another within you, because you did not recognise the moment of your visitation.'

45 Then he went into the Temple and began driving out those who were busy trading, saying to them, 46 'According to scripture, *my house shall be a house of prayer* but you have turned it into *a bandits' den*.'*l*

47 He taught in the Temple every day. The chief priests and the scribes, in company with the leading citizens, tried to do away with him, 48 but they could not find a way to carry this out because the whole people hung on his words.

20 Now it happened that one day while he was teaching the people in the Temple and proclaiming the good news, the chief priests and the scribes came up, together with the elders, 2 and spoke to him. 'Tell us,' they said, 'what authority have you for acting like this? Or who gives you this authority?' 3 In reply he said to them, 'And I will ask you a question, just one. Tell me: 4 John's baptism: what was its origin, heavenly or human?' 5 And they debated this way among themselves, 'If we say heavenly, he will retort, "Why did you refuse to believe him?"; 6 and if we say human, the whole people will stone us, for they are convinced that John was a prophet.' 7 So their reply was that they did not know where it came from. 8 And Jesus said to them, 'Nor will I tell you my authority for acting like this.'

9 And he went on to tell the people this parable, 'A man planted a vineyard and leased it to tenants, and went abroad for a long while. 10 When the right time came, he sent a servant to the tenants to get his share of the produce of the vineyard. But the tenants thrashed him, and sent him away empty-handed. 11 But he went on to send a second servant; they thrashed him too and treated him shamefully and sent him away empty-handed. 12 He still went on to send a third; they wounded this one too, and threw him out. 13 Then the owner of the vineyard thought, "What am I to do? I will send them my own beloved son. Perhaps they will respect him." 14 But when the tenants saw him they put their heads together saying, "This is the heir, let us kill him so that the inheritance will be ours." 15 So they threw him out of the vineyard and killed him.

'Now what will the owner of the vineyard do to them?

k 19 Ps 118:26.   *l* 19 Is 56:7 and Jr 7:11.

will come and destroy those tenants and give the vineyard to others." When they heard this, they said, "Heaven forbid!" 17 But he looked at them and said, "What then does this text mean:

'The stone that the builders rejected
has become the cornerstone'?[l]

18 Everyone who falls on that stone will be broken to pieces; and it will crush anyone on whom it falls." 19 When the scribes and chief priests realized that he had told this parable against them, they wanted to lay hands on him at that very hour, but they feared the people.

20 So they watched him and sent spies who pretended to be honest, in order to trap him by what he said, so as to hand him over to the jurisdiction and authority of the governor. 21 So they asked him, "Teacher, we know that you are right in what you say and teach, and you show deference to no one, but teach the way of God in accordance with truth. 22 Is it lawful for us to pay taxes to the emperor, or not?" 23 But he perceived their craftiness and said to them, 24 "Show me a denarius. Whose head and whose title does it bear?" They said, "The emperor's." 25 He said to them, "Then give to the emperor the things that are the emperor's, and to God the things that are God's." 26 And they were not able in the presence of the people to trap him by what he said; and being amazed by his answer, they became silent.

27 Some Sadducees, those who say there is no resurrection, came to him 28 and asked him a question, "Teacher, Moses wrote for us that if a man's brother dies, leaving a wife but no children, the man[m] shall marry the widow and raise up children for his brother. 29 Now there were seven brothers; the first married, and died childless; 30 then the second 31 and the third married her, and so in the same way all seven died childless. 32 Finally the woman also died. 33 In the resurrection, therefore, whose wife will the woman be? For the seven had married her."

34 Jesus said to them, "Those who belong to this age marry and are given in marriage; 35 but those who are considered worthy of a place in that age and in the resurrection from the dead neither marry nor are given in marriage. 36 Indeed they cannot die anymore, because they are like angels and are children of God, being children of the resurrection. 37 And the fact that the dead are raised Moses himself showed, in the story about the bush, where he speaks of the Lord as the God of Abraham, the God of Isaac, and the God of Jacob. 38 Now he is God not of the dead, but of the living; for to him all of them are alive." 39 Then some of the scribes answered, "Teacher, you have spoken well." 40 For they no longer dared to ask him another question.

41 Then he said to them, "How can they say that the Messiah[n] is David's son? 42 For David himself says in the book of Psalms,

'The Lord said to my Lord,
"Sit at my right hand,
43 until I make your enemies your footstool."'

44 David thus calls him Lord; so how can he be his son?"

45 In the hearing of all the people he said to the[o] disciples, 46 "Beware of the scribes, who like to walk around in long robes, and love to be greeted with respect in the marketplaces, and to have the best seats in the synagogues and places of honor at banquets. 47 They devour widows' houses and for the sake of appearance say long prayers. They will receive the greater condemnation."

the vineyard do to them? 16 He will come and put those tenants to death and give the vineyard to others.'

When they heard this, they said, 'God forbid!' 17 But he looked straight at them and said, 'Then what does this text of scripture mean: "The stone which the builders rejected has become the main corner-stone"? 18 Everyone who falls on that stone will be dashed to pieces; anyone on whom it falls will be crushed.'

19 The scribes and chief priests wanted to seize him there and then, for they saw that this parable was aimed at them; but they were afraid of the people. 20 So they watched their opportunity and sent agents in the guise of honest men, to seize on some word of his that they could use as a pretext for handing him over to the authority and jurisdiction of the governor. 21 They put a question to him: 'Teacher,' they said, 'we know that what you speak and teach is sound; you pay deference to no one, but teach in all sincerity the way of life that God requires. 22 Are we or are we not permitted to pay taxes to the Roman emperor?' 23 He saw through their trick and said, 24 'Show me a silver piece. Whose head does it bear, and whose inscription?' 'Caesar's,' they replied. 25 'Very well then,' he said, 'pay to Caesar what belongs to Caesar, and to God what belongs to God.' 26 Thus their attempt to catch him out in public failed, and, taken aback by his reply, they fell silent.

27 Then some Sadducees, who deny that there is a resurrection, came forward and asked: 28 'Teacher, Moses laid it down for us that if there are brothers, and one dies leaving a wife but no child, then the next should marry the widow and provide an heir for his brother. 29 Now, there were seven brothers: the first took a wife and died childless; 30 then the second married her, 31 then the third. In this way the seven of them died leaving no children. 32 Last of all the woman also died. 33 At the resurrection, therefore, whose wife is she to be, since all seven had married her?' 34 Jesus said to them, 'The men and women of this world marry; 35 but those who have been judged worthy of a place in the other world, and of the resurrection from the dead, do not marry, 36 for they are no longer subject to death. They are like angels; they are children of God, because they share in the resurrection. 37 That the dead are raised to life again is shown by Moses himself in the story of the burning bush, when he calls the Lord "the God of Abraham, the God of Isaac, the God of Jacob". 38 God is not God of the dead but of the living; in his sight all are alive.'

39 At this some of the scribes said, 'Well spoken, Teacher.' 40 And nobody dared put any further question to him.

41 He said to them, 'How can they say that the Messiah is David's son? 42 For David himself says in the book of Psalms: "The Lord said to my Lord, 'Sit at my right hand 43 until I make your enemies your footstool.' " 44 Thus David calls him "Lord"; how then can he be David's son?'

45 In the hearing of all the people Jesus said to his disciples: 46 'Beware of the scribes, who like to walk up and down in long robes, and love to be greeted respectfully in the street, to have the chief seats in synagogues and places of honour at feasts. 47 These are the men who eat up the property of widows, while for appearance' sake they say long prayers; the sentence they receive will be all the more severe.'

---

[l] Or keystone   [m] Gk his brother   [n] Or the Christ   [o] Other ancient authorities read his

and put those tenant farmers to death and turn over the vineyard to others." When the people heard this, they exclaimed, "Let it not be so!" 17 But he looked at them and asked, "What then does this scripture passage mean:

'The stone which the builders rejected
has become the cornerstone'?

18 Everyone who falls on that stone will be dashed to pieces; and it will crush anyone on whom it falls." 19 The scribes and chief priests sought to lay their hands on him at that very hour, but they feared the people, for they knew that he had addressed this parable to them.

20 They watched him closely and sent agents pretending to be righteous who were to trap him in speech, in order to hand him over to the authority and power of the governor. 21 They posed this question to him, "Teacher, we know that what you say and teach is correct, and you show no partiality, but teach the way of God in accordance with the truth. 22 Is it lawful for us to pay tribute to Caesar or not?" 23 Recognizing their craftiness he said to them, 24 "Show me a denarius; whose image and name does it bear?" They replied, "Caesar's." 25 So he said to them, "Then repay to Caesar what belongs to Caesar and to God what belongs to God." 26 They were unable to trap him by something he might say before the people, and so amazed were they at his reply that they fell silent.

27 Some Sadducees, those who deny that there is a resurrection, came forward and put this question to him, 28 saying, "Teacher, Moses wrote for us, 'If someone's brother dies leaving a wife but no child, his brother must take the wife and raise up descendants for his brother.' 29 Now there were seven brothers; the first married a woman but died childless. 30 Then the second 31 and the third married her, and likewise all the seven died childless. 32 Finally the woman also died. 33 Now at the resurrection whose wife will that woman be? For all seven had been married to her." 34 Jesus said to them, "The children of this age marry and remarry; 35 but those who are deemed worthy to attain to the coming age and to the resurrection of the dead neither marry nor are given in marriage. 36 They can no longer die, for they are like angels; and they are the children of God because they are the ones who will rise. 37 That the dead will rise even Moses made known in the passage about the bush, when he called 'Lord' the God of Abraham, the God of Isaac, and the God of Jacob; 38 and he is not God of the dead, but of the living, for to him all are alive." 39 Some of the scribes said in reply, "Teacher, you have answered well." 40 And they no longer dared to ask him anything.

41 Then he said to them, "How do they claim that the Messiah is the Son of David? 42 For David himself in the Book of Psalms says:

'The Lord said to my lord,
"Sit at my right hand
43   till I make your enemies your footstool."'

44 Now if David calls him 'lord,' how can he be his son?"

45 Then, within the hearing of all the people, he said to [his] disciples, 46 "Be on guard against the scribes, who like to go around in long robes and love greetings in marketplaces, seats of honor in synagogues, and places of honor at banquets. 47 They devour the houses of widows and, as a pretext, recite lengthy prayers. They will receive a very severe condemnation."

16 He will come and make an end of these tenants and give the vineyard to others.' Hearing this they said, 'God forbid!' 17 But he looked hard at them and said, 'Then what does this text in the scriptures mean:

*The stone which the builders rejected
has become the cornerstone?* m

18 Anyone who falls on that stone will be dashed to pieces; anyone it falls on will be crushed.'

19 And the scribes and the chief priests would have liked to lay hands on him that very moment, because they realised that this parable was aimed at them, but they were afraid of the people.

20 So they awaited their opportunity and sent agents to pose as upright men, and to catch him out in something he might say and so enable them to hand him over to the jurisdiction and authority of the governor. 21 They put to him this question, 'Master, we know that you say and teach what is right; you favour no one, but teach the way of God in all honesty. 22 Is it permissible for us to pay taxes to Caesar or not?' 23 But he was aware of their cunning and said, 24 'Show me a denarius. Whose portrait and title are on it?' They said, 'Caesar's.' 25 He said to them, 'Well then, pay Caesar what belongs to Caesar — and God what belongs to God.'

26 They were unable to catch him out in anything he had to say in public; they were amazed at his answer and were silenced.

27 Some Sadducees — those who argue that there is no resurrection — approached him and they put this question to him, 28 'Master, Moses prescribed for us, if a man's married brother dies childless, the man must marry the widow to raise up children for his brother. 29 Well then, there were seven brothers; the first, having married a wife, died childless. 30 The second 31 and then the third married the widow. And the same with all seven, they died leaving no children. 32 Finally the woman herself died. 33 Now, at the resurrection, whose wife will she be, since she had been married to all seven?'

34 Jesus replied, 'The children of this world take wives and husbands, 35 but those who are judged worthy of a place in the other world and in the resurrection from the dead do not marry 36 because they can no longer die, for they are the same as the angels, and being children of the resurrection they are children of God. 37 And Moses himself implies that the dead rise again, in the passage about the bush where he calls the Lord *the God of Abraham, the God of Isaac and the God of Jacob.* n 38 Now he is God, not of the dead, but of the living; for to him everyone is alive.'

39 Some scribes then spoke up. They said, 'Well put, Master.' 40 They did not dare to ask him any more questions.

41 He then said to them, 'How can people maintain that the Christ is son of David? 42 Why, David himself says in the Book of Psalms:

*The Lord declared to my Lord,
take your seat at my right hand,
43 till I have made your enemies
your footstool.* o

44 David here calls him Lord; how then can he be his son?'

45 While all the people were listening he said to the disciples, 46 'Beware of the scribes who like to walk about in long robes and love to be greeted respectfully in the market squares, to take the front seats in the synagogues and the places of honour at banquets, 47 who devour the property of widows, and for show offer long prayers. The more severe will be the sentence they receive.'

m 20 Ps 118:22.   n 20 Ex 3:6.   o 20 Ps 110:1.

NEW REVISED STANDARD VERSION

21 He looked up and saw rich people putting their gifts into the treasury; 2 he also saw a poor widow put in two small copper coins. 3 He said, "Truly I tell you, this poor widow has put in more than all of them; 4 for all of them have contributed out of their abundance, but she out of her poverty has put in all she had to live on."

5 When some were speaking about the temple, how it was adorned with beautiful stones and gifts dedicated to God, he said, 6 "As for these things that you see, the days will come when not one stone will be left upon another; all will be thrown down."

7 They asked him, "Teacher, when will this be, and what will be the sign that this is about to take place?" 8 And he said, "Beware that you are not led astray; for many will come in my name and say, 'I am he!'p and, 'The time is near!'q Do not go after them.

9 "When you hear of wars and insurrections, do not be terrified; for these things must take place first, but the end will not follow immediately." 10 Then he said to them, "Nation will rise against nation, and kingdom against kingdom; 11 there will be great earthquakes, and in various places famines and plagues; and there will be dreadful portents and great signs from heaven.

12 "But before all this occurs, they will arrest you and persecute you; they will hand you over to synagogues and prisons, and you will be brought before kings and governors because of my name. 13 This will give you an opportunity to testify. 14 So make up your minds not to prepare your defense in advance; 15 for I will give you wordsr and a wisdom that none of your opponents will be able to withstand or contradict. 16 You will be betrayed even by parents and brothers, by relatives and friends; and they will put some of you to death. 17 You will be hated by all because of my name. 18 But not a hair of your head will perish. 19 By your endurance you will gain your souls.

20 "When you see Jerusalem surrounded by armies, then know that its desolation has come near.s 21 Then those in Judea must flee to the mountains, and those inside the city must leave it, and those out in the country must not enter it; 22 for these are days of vengeance, as a fulfillment of all that is written. 23 Woe to those who are pregnant and to those who are nursing infants in those days! For there will be great distress on the earth and wrath against this people; 24 they will fall by the edge of the sword and be taken away as captives among all nations; and Jerusalem will be trampled on by the Gentiles, until the times of the Gentiles are fulfilled.

25 "There will be signs in the sun, the moon, and the stars, and on the earth distress among nations confused by the roaring of the sea and the waves. 26 People will faint from fear and foreboding of what is coming upon the world, for the powers of the heavens will be shaken. 27 Then they will see 'the Son of Man coming in a cloud' with power and great glory. 28 Now when these things begin to take place, stand up and raise your heads, because your redemption is drawing near."

29 Then he told them a parable: "Look at the fig tree and all the trees; 30 as soon as they sprout leaves you can see for yourselves and know that summer is already near. 31 So also, when you see these things taking place, you know that the kingdom of God is near. 32 Truly I tell you, this generation will not pass away until all things have taken place. 33 Heaven and earth will pass away, but my words will not pass away.

34 "Be on guard so that your hearts are not weighed down with dissipation and drunkenness and the worries of this life, and that day catch you unexpectedly, 35 like a trap.

REVISED ENGLISH BIBLE

21 As Jesus looked up and saw rich people dropping their gifts into the chest of the temple treasury, 2 he noticed a poor widow putting in two tiny coins. 3 'I tell you this,' he said: 'this poor widow has given more than any of them; 4 for those others who have given had more than enough, but she, with less than enough, has given all she had to live on.'

5 Some people were talking about the temple and the beauty of its fine stones and ornaments. He said, 6 'These things you are gazing at—the time will come when not one stone will be left upon another; they will all be thrown down.' 7 'Teacher,' they asked, 'when will that be? What will be the sign that these things are about to happen?'

8 He said, 'Take care that you are not misled. For many will come claiming my name and saying, "I am he," and, "The time has come." Do not follow them. 9 And when you hear of wars and insurrections, do not panic. These things are bound to happen first; but the end does not follow at once.' 10 Then he added, 'Nation will go to war against nation, kingdom against kingdom; 11 there will be severe earthquakes, famines and plagues in many places, and in the sky terrors and great portents.

12 'But before all this happens they will seize you and persecute you. You will be handed over to synagogues and put in prison; you will be haled before kings and governors for your allegiance to me. 13 This will be your opportunity to testify. 14 So resolve not to prepare your defence beforehand, 15 because I myself will give you such words and wisdom as no opponent can resist or refute. 16 Even your parents and brothers, your relations and friends, will betray you. Some of you will be put to death; 17 and everyone will hate you for your allegiance to me. 18 But not a hair of your head will be lost. 19 By standing firm you will win yourselves life.

20 'But when you see Jerusalem encircled by armies, then you may be sure that her devastation is near. 21 Then those who are in Judaea must take to the hills; those who are in the city itself must leave it, and those who are out in the country must not return; 22 because this is the time of retribution, when all that stands written is to be fulfilled. 23 Alas for women with child in those days, and for those who have children at the breast! There will be great distress in the land and a terrible judgement on this people. 24 They will fall by the sword; they will be carried captive into all countries; and Jerusalem will be trampled underfoot by Gentiles until the day of the Gentiles has run its course.

25 'Portents will appear in sun and moon and stars. On earth nations will stand helpless, not knowing which way to turn from the roar and surge of the sea. 26 People will faint with terror at the thought of all that is coming upon the world; for the celestial powers will be shaken. 27 Then they will see the Son of Man coming in a cloud with power and great glory. 28 When all this begins to happen, stand upright and hold your heads high, because your liberation is near.'

29 He told them a parable: 'Look at the fig tree, or at any other tree. 30 As soon as it buds, you can see for yourselves that summer is near. 31 In the same way, when you see all this happening, you may know that the kingdom of God is near.

32 'Truly I tell you: the present generation will live to see it all. 33 Heaven and earth will pass away, but my words will never pass away.

34 'Be on your guard; do not let your minds be dulled by dissipation and drunkenness and worldly cares so that the great day catches you suddenly 35 like a trap; for that day

21 When he looked up he saw some wealthy people putting their offerings into the treasury 2 and he noticed a poor widow putting in two small coins. 3 He said, "I tell you truly, this poor widow put in more than all the rest; 4 for those others have all made offerings from their surplus wealth, but she, from her poverty, has offered her whole livelihood."

5 While some people were speaking about how the temple was adorned with costly stones and votive offerings, he said, 6 "All that you see here — the days will come when there will not be left a stone upon another stone that will not be thrown down."

7 Then they asked him, "Teacher, when will this happen? And what sign will there be when all these things are about to happen?" 8 He answered, "See that you not be deceived, for many will come in my name, saying, 'I am he,' and 'The time has come.' Do not follow them! 9 When you hear of wars and insurrections, do not be terrified; for such things must happen first, but it will not immediately be the end." 10 Then he said to them, "Nation will rise against nation, and kingdom against kingdom. 11 There will be powerful earthquakes, famines, and plagues from place to place; and awesome sights and mighty signs will come from the sky.

12 "Before all this happens, however, they will seize and persecute you, they will hand you over to the synagogues and to prisons, and they will have you led before kings and governors because of my name. 13 It will lead to your giving testimony. 14 Remember, you are not to prepare your defense beforehand, 15 for I myself shall give you a wisdom in speaking that all your adversaries will be powerless to resist or refute. 16 You will even be handed over by parents, brothers, relatives, and friends, and they will put some of you to death. 17 You will be hated by all because of my name, 18 but not a hair on your head will be destroyed. 19 By your perseverance you will secure your lives.

20 "When you see Jerusalem surrounded by armies, know that its desolation is at hand. 21 Then those in Judea must flee to the mountains. Let those within the city escape from it, and let those in the countryside not enter the city, 22 for these days are the time of punishment when all the scriptures are fulfilled. 23 Woe to pregnant women and nursing mothers in those days, for a terrible calamity will come upon the earth and a wrathful judgment upon this people. 24 They will fall by the edge of the sword and be taken as captives to all the Gentiles; and Jerusalem will be trampled underfoot by the Gentiles until the times of the Gentiles are fulfilled.

25 "There will be signs in the sun, the moon, and the stars, and on earth nations will be in dismay, perplexed by the roaring of the sea and the waves. 26 People will die of fright in anticipation of what is coming upon the world, for the powers of the heavens will be shaken. 27 And then they will see the Son of Man coming in a cloud with power and great glory. 28 But when these signs begin to happen, stand erect and raise your heads because your redemption is at hand."

29 He taught them a lesson. "Consider the fig tree and all the other trees. 30 When their buds burst open, you see for yourselves and know that summer is now near; 31 in the same way, when you see these things happening, know that the kingdom of God is near. 32 Amen, I say to you, this generation will not pass away until all these things have taken place. 33 Heaven and earth will pass away, but my words will not pass away.

34 "Beware that your hearts do not become drowsy from carousing and drunkenness and the anxieties of daily life, and that day catch you by surprise 35 like a trap. For that day

21 Looking up, he saw rich people putting their offerings into the treasury; 2 and he noticed a poverty-stricken widow putting in two small coins, 3 and he said, 'I tell you truly, this poor widow has put in more than any of them; 4 for these have all put in money they could spare, but she in her poverty has put in all she had to live on.'

5 When some were talking about the Temple, remarking how it was adorned with fine stonework and votive offerings, he said, 6 'All these things you are staring at now — the time will come when not a single stone will be left on another; everything will be destroyed.' 7 And they put to him this question, 'Master,' they said, 'when will this happen, then, and what sign will there be that it is about to take place?'

8 But he said, 'Take care not to be deceived, because many will come using my name and saying, "I am the one" and "The time is near at hand." Refuse to join them. 9 And when you hear of wars and revolutions, do not be terrified, for this is something that must happen first, but the end will not come at once.' 10 Then he said to them, 'Nation will fight against nation, and kingdom against kingdom. 11 There will be great earthquakes and plagues and famines in various places; there will be terrifying events and great signs from heaven.

12 'But before all this happens, you will be seized and persecuted; you will be handed over to the synagogues and to imprisonment, and brought before kings and governors for the sake of my name 13 — and that will be your opportunity to bear witness. 14 Make up your minds not to prepare your defence, 15 because I myself shall give you an eloquence and a wisdom that none of your opponents will be able to resist or contradict. 16 You will be betrayed even by parents and brothers, relations and friends; and some of you will be put to death. 17 You will be hated universally on account of my name, 18 but not a hair of your head will be lost. 19 Your perseverance will win you your lives.

20 'When you see Jerusalem surrounded by armies, then you must realise that it will soon be laid desolate. 21 Then those in Judaea must escape to the mountains, those inside the city must leave it, and those in country districts must not take refuge in it. 22 For this is the time of retribution when all that scripture says must be fulfilled. 23 Alas for those with child, or with babies at the breast, when those days come!

24 'For great misery will descend on the land and retribution on this people. They will fall by the edge of the sword and be led captive to every gentile country; and Jerusalem will be trampled down by the gentiles until their time is complete.

25 'There will be signs in the sun and moon and stars; on earth nations in agony, bewildered by the turmoil of the ocean and its waves; 26 men fainting away with terror and fear at what menaces the world, for the powers of heaven will be shaken. 27 And then they will see the *Son of man coming in a cloud* with power and great glory.p 28 When these things begin to take place, stand erect, hold your heads high, because your liberation is near at hand.'

29 And he told them a parable, 'Look at the fig tree and indeed every tree. 30 As soon as you see them bud, you can see for yourselves that summer is now near. 31 So with you when you see these things happening: know that the kingdom of God is near. 32 In truth I tell you, before this generation has passed away all will have taken place. 33 Sky and earth will pass away, but my words will never pass away.

34 'Watch yourselves, or your hearts will be coarsened by debauchery and drunkenness and the cares of life, and that day will come upon you unexpectedly, 35 like a trap. For it

For it will come upon all who live on the face of the whole earth. 36 Be alert at all times, praying that you may have the strength to escape all these things that will take place, and to stand before the Son of Man."

37 Every day he was teaching in the temple, and at night he would go out and spend the night on the Mount of Olives, as it was called. 38 And all the people would get up early in the morning to listen to him in the temple.

22 Now the festival of Unleavened Bread, which is called the Passover, was near. 2 The chief priests and the scribes were looking for a way to put Jesus[t] to death, for they were afraid of the people.

3 Then Satan entered into Judas called Iscariot, who was one of the twelve; 4 he went away and conferred with the chief priests and officers of the temple police about how he might betray him to them. 5 They were greatly pleased and agreed to give him money. 6 So he consented and began to look for an opportunity to betray him to them when no crowd was present.

7 Then came the day of Unleavened Bread, on which the Passover lamb had to be sacrificed. 8 So Jesus[u] sent Peter and John, saying, "Go and prepare the Passover meal for us that we may eat it." 9 They asked him, "Where do you want us to make preparations for it?" 10 "Listen," he said to them, "when you have entered the city, a man carrying a jar of water will meet you; follow him into the house he enters 11 and say to the owner of the house, 'The teacher asks you, "Where is the guest room, where I may eat the Passover with my disciples?" ' 12 He will show you a large room upstairs, already furnished. Make preparations for us there." 13 So they went and found everything as he had told them; and they prepared the Passover meal.

14 When the hour came, he took his place at the table, and the apostles with him. 15 He said to them, "I have eagerly desired to eat this Passover with you before I suffer; 16 for I tell you, I will not eat it[v] until it is fulfilled in the kingdom of God." 17 Then he took a cup, and after giving thanks he said, "Take this and divide it among yourselves; 18 for I tell you that from now on I will not drink of the fruit of the vine until the kingdom of God comes." 19 Then he took a loaf of bread, and when he had given thanks, he broke it and gave it to them, saying, "This is my body, which is given for you. Do this in remembrance of me." 20 And he did the same with the cup after supper, saying, "This cup that is poured out for you is the new covenant in my blood.[w] 21 But see, the one who betrays me is with me, and his hand is on the table. 22 For the Son of Man is going as it has been determined, but woe to that one by whom he is betrayed!" 23 Then they began to ask one another, which one of them it could be who would do this.

24 A dispute also arose among them as to which one of them was to be regarded as the greatest. 25 But he said to them, "The kings of the Gentiles lord it over them; and those in authority over them are called benefactors. 26 But not so with you; rather the greatest among you must become like the youngest, and the leader like one who serves. 27 For who is greater, the one who is at the table or the one who serves? Is it not the one at the table? But I am among you as one who serves.

28 "You are those who have stood by me in my trials; 29 and I confer on you, just as my Father has conferred on me, a kingdom, 30 so that you may eat and drink at my table in my kingdom, and you will sit on thrones judging the twelve tribes of Israel.

will come on everyone, the whole world over. 36 Be on the alert, praying at all times for strength to pass safely through all that is coming and to stand in the presence of the Son of Man.'

37 His days were given to teaching in the temple; every evening he would leave the city and spend the night on the hill called Olivet. 38 And in the early morning the people flocked to listen to him in the temple.

22 THE festival of Unleavened Bread, known as Passover, was approaching, 2 and the chief priests and the scribes were trying to devise some means of doing away with him; for they were afraid of the people.

3 Then Satan entered into Judas, who was called Iscariot, one of the Twelve; 4 and he went to the chief priests and temple guards to discuss ways of betraying Jesus to them. 5 They were glad and undertook to pay him a sum of money. 6 He agreed, and began to look for an opportunity to betray him to them without collecting a crowd.

7 Then came the day of Unleavened Bread, on which the Passover lambs had to be slaughtered, 8 and Jesus sent off Peter and John, saying, 'Go and prepare the Passover supper for us.' 9 'Where would you like us to make the preparations?' they asked. 10 He replied, 'As soon as you set foot in the city a man will meet you carrying a jar of water. Follow him into the house that he enters 11 and give this message to the householder: "The Teacher says, 'Where is the room in which I am to eat the Passover with my disciples?' " 12 He will show you a large room upstairs all set out: make the preparations there.' 13 They went and found everything as he had said. So they prepared for Passover.

14 When the hour came he took his place at table, and the apostles with him; 15 and he said to them, 'How I have longed to eat this Passover with you before my death! 16 For I tell you, never again shall I eat it until the time when it finds its fulfilment in the kingdom of God.'

17 Then he took a cup, and after giving thanks he said, 'Take this and share it among yourselves; 18 for I tell you, from this moment I shall not drink the fruit of the vine until the time when the kingdom of God comes.' 19 Then he took bread, and after giving thanks he broke it, and gave it to them with the words: 'This is my body.'

21 'Even now my betrayer is here, his hand with mine on the table. 22 For the Son of Man is going his appointed way; but alas for that man by whom he is betrayed!' 23 At that they began to ask among themselves which of them it could possibly be who was to do this.

24 Then a dispute began as to which of them should be considered the greatest. 25 But he said, 'Among the Gentiles, kings lord it over their subjects; and those in authority are given the title Benefactor. 26 Not so with you: on the contrary, the greatest among you must bear himself like the youngest, the one who rules like one who serves. 27 For who is greater—the one who sits at table or the servant who waits on him? Surely the one who sits at table. Yet I am among you like a servant.

28 'You have stood firmly by me in my times of trial; 29 and I now entrust to you the kingdom which my Father entrusted to me; 30 in my kingdom you shall eat and drink at my table and sit on thrones as judges of the twelve tribes of Israel.

21:38 in the temple: some witnesses here insert John 7:53—8:11.
22:16 For . . . shall I: some witnesses read But I tell you, I shall not.
22:19 my body: some witnesses add, in whole or in part, and with various arrangements, the following: 'which is given for you; do this as a memorial of me.' 20 In the same way he took the cup after supper, and said, 'This cup, poured out for you, is the new covenant sealed by my blood.' 22:29–30 and I now . . . and sit: or and as my Father gave me the right to reign, so I give you the right to eat and to drink at my table in my kingdom and to sit.

[t] Gk him   [u] Gk he   [v] Other ancient authorities read never eat it again   [w] Other ancient authorities lack, in whole or in part, verses 19b-20 (which is given . . . in my blood)

NEW AMERICAN BIBLE

will assault everyone who lives on the face of the earth. 36 Be vigilant at all times and pray that you have the strength to escape the tribulations that are imminent and to stand before the Son of Man."

37 During the day, Jesus was teaching in the temple area, but at night he would leave and stay at the place called the Mount of Olives. 38 And all the people would get up early each morning to listen to him in the temple area.

22 Now the feast of Unleavened Bread, called the Passover, was drawing near, 2 and the chief priests and the scribes were seeking a way to put him to death, for they were afraid of the people. 3 Then Satan entered into Judas, the one surnamed Iscariot, who was counted among the Twelve, 4 and he went to the chief priests and temple guards to discuss a plan for handing him over to them. 5 They were pleased and agreed to pay him money. 6 He accepted their offer and sought a favorable opportunity to hand him over to them in the absence of a crowd.

7 When the day of the feast of Unleavened Bread arrived, the day for sacrificing the Passover lamb, 8 he sent out Peter and John, instructing them, "Go and make preparations for us to eat the Passover." 9 They asked him, "Where do you want us to make the preparations?" 10 And he answered them, "When you go into the city, a man will meet you carrying a jar of water. Follow him into the house that he enters 11 and say to the master of the house, 'The teacher says to you, "Where is the guest room where I may eat the Passover with my disciples?" ' 12 He will show you a large upper room that is furnished. Make the preparations there." 13 Then they went off and found everything exactly as he had told them, and there they prepared the Passover.

14 When the hour came, he took his place at table with the apostles. 15 He said to them, "I have eagerly desired to eat this Passover with you before I suffer, 16 for, I tell you, I shall not eat it [again] until there is fulfillment in the kingdom of God." 17 Then he took a cup, gave thanks, and said, "Take this and share it among yourselves; 18 for I tell you [that] from this time on I shall not drink of the fruit of the vine until the kingdom of God comes." 19 Then he took the bread, said the blessing, broke it, and gave it to them, saying, "This is my body, which will be given for you; do this in memory of me." 20 And likewise the cup after they had eaten, saying, "This cup is the new covenant in my blood, which will be shed for you.

21 "And yet behold, the hand of the one who is to betray me is with me on the table; 22 for the Son of Man indeed goes as it has been determined; but woe to that man by whom he is betrayed." 23 And they began to debate among themselves who among them would do such a deed.

24 Then an argument broke out among them about which of them should be regarded as the greatest. 25 He said to them, "The kings of the Gentiles lord it over them and those in authority over them are addressed as 'Benefactors'; 26 but among you it shall not be so. Rather, let the greatest among you be as the youngest, and the leader as the servant. 27 For who is greater: the one seated at table or the one who serves? Is it not the one seated at table? I am among you as the one who serves. 28 It is you who have stood by me in my trials; 29 and I confer a kingdom on you, just as my Father has conferred one on me, 30 that you may eat and drink at my table in my kingdom; and you will sit on thrones judging the twelve tribes of Israel.

NEW JERUSALEM BIBLE

will come down on all those living on the face of the earth. 36 Stay awake, praying at all times for the strength to survive all that is going to happen, and to hold your ground before the Son of man.'

37 All day long he would be in the Temple teaching, but would spend the night in the open on the hill called the Mount of Olives. 38 And from early morning the people thronged to him in the Temple to listen to him.

22 q The feast of Unleavened Bread, called the Passover, was now drawing near, 2 and the chief priests and the scribes were looking for some way of doing away with him, because they were afraid of the people. 3 Then Satan entered into Judas, surnamed Iscariot, who was one of the Twelve. 4 He approached the chief priests and the officers of the guard to discuss some way of handing Jesus over to them. 5 They were delighted and agreed to give him money. 6 He accepted and began to look for an opportunity to betray him to them without people knowing about it.

7 The day of Unleavened Bread came round, on which the Passover had to be sacrificed, 8 and he sent Peter and John, saying, 'Go and make the preparations for us to eat the Passover.' 9 They asked him, 'Where do you want us to prepare it?' 10 He said to them, 'Look, as you go into the city you will meet a man carrying a pitcher of water. Follow him into the house he enters 11 and tell the owner of the house, "The Master says this to you: Where is the room for me to eat the Passover with my disciples?" 12 The man will show you a large upper room furnished with couches. Make the preparations there.' 13 They set off and found everything as he had told them and prepared the Passover.

14 When the time came he took his place at table, and the apostles with him. 15 And he said to them, 'I have ardently longed to eat this Passover with you before I suffer; 16 because, I tell you, I shall not eat it until it is fulfilled in the kingdom of God.' 17 Then, taking a cup, he gave thanks and said, 'Take this and share it among you, 18 because from now on, I tell you, I shall never again drink wine until the kingdom of God comes.'

19 Then he took bread, and when he had given thanks, he broke it and gave it to them, saying, 'This is my body given for you; do this in remembrance of me.' 20 He did the same with the cup after supper, and said, 'This cup is the new covenant in my blood poured out for you.

21 'But look, here with me on the table is the hand of the man who is betraying me. 22 The Son of man is indeed on the path which was decreed, but alas for that man by whom he is betrayed!' 23 And they began to ask one another which of them it could be who was to do this.

24 An argument also began between them about who should be reckoned the greatest; 25 but he said to them, 'Among the gentiles it is the kings who lord it over them, and those who have authority over them are given the title Benefactor. 26 With you this must not happen. No; the greatest among you must behave as if he were the youngest, the leader as if he were the one who serves. 27 For who is the greater: the one at table or the one who serves? The one at table, surely? Yet here am I among you as one who serves!

28 'You are the men who have stood by me faithfully in my trials; 29 and now I confer a kingdom on you, just as my Father conferred one on me: 30 you will eat and drink at my table in my kingdom, and you will sit on thrones to judge the twelve tribes of Israel.

22, 19c–20: *Which will be given . . . do this in memory of me:* these words are omitted in some important Western text manuscripts and a few Syriac manuscripts. Other ancient text types, including the oldest papyrus manuscript of Lk dating from the late second or early third century, contain the longer reading presented here.

q 22 For this section Lk has a good deal of information which he does not share with Mt and Mk. It is often close to Jn.

31 "Simon, Simon, listen! Satan has demanded[x] to sift all of you like wheat, 32 but I have prayed for you that your own faith may not fail; and you, when once you have turned back, strengthen your brothers." 33 And he said to him, "Lord, I am ready to go with you to prison and to death!" 34 Jesus[y] said, "I tell you, Peter, the cock will not crow this day, until you have denied three times that you know me."

35 He said to them, "When I sent you out without a purse, bag, or sandals, did you lack anything?" They said, "No, not a thing." 36 He said to them, "But now, the one who has a purse must take it, and likewise a bag. And the one who has no sword must sell his cloak and buy one. 37 For I tell you, this scripture must be fulfilled in me, 'And he was counted among the lawless'; and indeed what is written about me is being fulfilled." 38 They said, "Lord, look, here are two swords." He replied, "It is enough."

39 He came out and went, as was his custom, to the Mount of Olives; and the disciples followed him. 40 When he reached the place, he said to them, "Pray that you may not come into the time of trial."[z] 41 Then he withdrew from them about a stone's throw, knelt down, and prayed, 42 "Father, if you are willing, remove this cup from me; yet, not my will but yours be done." [[43 Then an angel from heaven appeared to him and gave him strength. 44 In his anguish he prayed more earnestly, and his sweat became like great drops of blood falling down on the ground.]][a] 45 When he got up from prayer, he came to the disciples and found them sleeping because of grief, 46 and he said to them, "Why are you sleeping? Get up and pray that you may not come into the time of trial."[z]

47 While he was still speaking, suddenly a crowd came, and the one called Judas, one of the twelve, was leading them. He approached Jesus to kiss him; 48 but Jesus said to him, "Judas, is it with a kiss that you are betraying the Son of Man?" 49 When those who were around him saw what was coming, they asked, "Lord, should we strike with the sword?" 50 Then one of them struck the slave of the high priest and cut off his right ear. 51 But Jesus said, "No more of this!" And he touched his ear and healed him. 52 Then Jesus said to the chief priests, the officers of the temple police, and the elders who had come for him, "Have you come out with swords and clubs as if I were a bandit? 53 When I was with you day after day in the temple, you did not lay hands on me. But this is your hour, and the power of darkness!"

54 Then they seized him and led him away, bringing him into the high priest's house. But Peter was following at a distance. 55 When they had kindled a fire in the middle of the courtyard and sat down together, Peter sat among them. 56 Then a servant-girl, seeing him in the firelight, stared at him and said, "This man also was with him." 57 But he denied it, saying, "Woman, I do not know him." 58 A little later someone else, on seeing him, said, "You also are one of them." But Peter said, "Man, I am not!" 59 Then about an hour later still another kept insisting, "Surely this man also was with him; for he is a Galilean." 60 But Peter said, "Man, I do not know what you are talking about!" At that moment, while he was still speaking, the cock crowed. 61 The Lord turned and looked at Peter. Then Peter remembered the word of the Lord, how he had said to him, "Before the cock crows today, you will deny me three times." 62 And he went out and wept bitterly.

63 Now the men who were holding Jesus began to mock him and beat him; 64 they also blindfolded him and kept

31 'Simon, Simon, take heed: Satan has been given leave to sift all of you like wheat; 32 but I have prayed for you, Simon, that your faith may not fail; and when you are restored, give strength to your brothers.' 33 'Lord,' he replied, 'I am ready to go with you to prison and to death.' 34 Jesus said, 'I tell you, Peter, the cock will not crow tonight until you have denied three times over that you know me.'

35 He said to them, 'When I sent you out barefoot without purse or pack, were you ever short of anything?' 'No,' they answered. 36 'It is different now,' he said; 'whoever has a purse had better take it with him, and his pack too; and if he has no sword, let him sell his cloak to buy one. 37 For scripture says, "And he was reckoned among transgressors," and this, I tell you, must be fulfilled in me; indeed, all that is written of me is reaching its fulfilment.' 38 'Lord,' they said, 'we have two swords here.' 'Enough!' he replied.

39 THEN he went out and made his way as usual to the mount of Olives, accompanied by the disciples. 40 When he reached the place he said to them, 'Pray that you may be spared the test.' 41 He himself withdrew from them about a stone's throw, knelt down, and began to pray: 42 'Father, if it be your will, take this cup from me. Yet not my will but yours be done.'

43 And now there appeared to him an angel from heaven bringing him strength, 44 and in anguish of spirit he prayed the more urgently; and his sweat was like drops of blood falling to the ground.

45 When he rose from prayer and came to the disciples he found them asleep, worn out by grief. 46 'Why are you sleeping?' he said. 'Rise and pray that you may be spared the test.'

47 WHILE he was still speaking a crowd appeared with the man called Judas, one of the Twelve, at their head. He came up to Jesus to kiss him; 48 but Jesus said, 'Judas, would you betray the Son of Man with a kiss?'

49 When his followers saw what was coming, they said, 'Lord, shall we use our swords?' 50 And one of them struck at the high priest's servant, cutting off his right ear. 51 But Jesus answered, 'Stop! No more of that!' Then he touched the man's ear and healed him.

52 Turning to the chief priests, the temple guards, and the elders, who had come to seize him, he said, 'Do you take me for a robber, that you have come out with swords and cudgels? 53 Day after day, I have been with you in the temple, and you did not raise a hand against me. But this is your hour—when darkness reigns.'

54 Then they arrested him and led him away. They brought him to the high priest's house, and Peter followed at a distance. 55 They lit a fire in the middle of the courtyard and sat round it, and Peter sat among them. 56 A serving-maid who saw him sitting in the firelight stared at him and said, 'This man was with him too.' 57 But he denied it: 'I do not know him,' he said. 58 A little later a man noticed him and said, 'You also are one of them.' But Peter said to him, 'No, I am not.' 59 About an hour passed and someone else spoke more strongly still: 'Of course he was with him. He must have been; he is a Galilean.' 60 But Peter said, 'I do not know what you are talking about.' At that moment, while he was still speaking, a cock crowed; 61 and the Lord turned and looked at Peter. Peter remembered the Lord's words, 'Tonight before the cock crows you will disown me three times.' 62 And he went outside, and wept bitterly.

63 The men who were guarding Jesus mocked him. They beat him, 64 they blindfolded him, and kept asking him, 'If

---

x Or has obtained permission   y Gk He   z Or into temptation
a Other ancient authorities lack verses 43 and 44

22:43–44 Some witnesses omit And now . . . ground.
22:51 Stop! No more of that: or Let them have their way.

31 "Simon, Simon, behold Satan has demanded to sift all of you like wheat, 32 but I have prayed that your own faith may not fail; and once you have turned back, you must strengthen your brothers." 33 He said to him, "Lord, I am prepared to go to prison and to die with you." 34 But he replied, "I tell you, Peter, before the cock crows this day, you will deny three times that you know me."

35 He said to them, "When I sent you forth without a money bag or a sack or sandals, were you in need of anything?" "No, nothing," they replied. 36 He said to them, "But now one who has a money bag should take it, and likewise a sack, and one who does not have a sword should sell his cloak and buy one. 37 For I tell you that this scripture must be fulfilled in me, namely, 'He was counted among the wicked'; and indeed what is written about me is coming to fulfillment." 38 Then they said, "Lord, look, there are two swords here." But he replied, "It is enough!"

39 Then going out he went, as was his custom, to the Mount of Olives, and the disciples followed him. 40 When he arrived at the place he said to them, "Pray that you may not undergo the test." 41 After withdrawing about a stone's throw from them and kneeling, he prayed, 42 saying, "Father, if you are willing, take this cup away from me; still, not my will but yours be done." [43 And to strengthen him an angel from heaven appeared to him. 44 He was in such agony and he prayed so fervently that his sweat became like drops of blood falling on the ground.] 45 When he rose from prayer and returned to his disciples, he found them sleeping from grief. 46 He said to them, "Why are you sleeping? Get up and pray that you may not undergo the test."

47 While he was still speaking, a crowd approached and in front was one of the Twelve, a man named Judas. He went up to Jesus to kiss him. 48 Jesus said to him, "Judas, are you betraying the Son of Man with a kiss?" 49 His disciples realized what was about to happen, and they asked, "Lord, shall we strike with a sword?" 50 And one of them struck the high priest's servant and cut off his right ear. 51 But Jesus said in reply, "Stop, no more of this!" Then he touched the servant's ear and healed him. 52 And Jesus said to the chief priests and temple guards and elders who had come for him, "Have you come out as against a robber, with swords and clubs? 53 Day after day I was with you in the temple area, and you did not seize me; but this is your hour, the time for the power of darkness."

54 After arresting him they led him away and took him into the house of the high priest; Peter was following at a distance. 55 They lit a fire in the middle of the courtyard and sat around it, and Peter sat down with them. 56 When a maid saw him seated in the light, she looked intently at him and said, "This man too was with him." 57 But he denied it saying, "Woman, I do not know him." 58 A short while later someone else saw him and said, "You too are one of them"; but Peter answered, "My friend, I am not." 59 About an hour later, still another insisted, "Assuredly, this man too was with him, for he also is a Galilean." 60 But Peter said, "My friend, I do not know what you are talking about." Just as he was saying this, the cock crowed, 61 and the Lord turned and looked at Peter; and Peter remembered the word of the Lord, how he had said to him, "Before the cock crows today, you will deny me three times." 62 He went out and began to weep bitterly. 63 The men who held Jesus in custody were ridiculing and beating him. 64 They blindfolded him and questioned him, saying, "Prophesy! Who is it that

31 'Simon, Simon! Look, Satan has got his wish to sift you all like wheat; 32 but I have prayed for you, Simon, that your faith may not fail, and once you have recovered, you in your turn must strengthen your brothers.' 33 'Lord,' he answered, 'I would be ready to go to prison with you, and to death.' 34 Jesus replied, 'I tell you, Peter, by the time the cock crows today you will have denied three times that you know me.'

35 He said to them, 'When I sent you out without purse or haversack or sandals, were you short of anything?' 36 'No, nothing,' they said. He said to them, 'But now if you have a purse, take it, and the same with a haversack; if you have no sword, sell your cloak and buy one, 37 because I tell you these words of scripture are destined to be fulfilled in me: *He was counted as one of the rebellious.*r Yes, what it says about me is even now reaching its fulfilment.' 38 They said, 'Lord, here are two swords.' He said to them, 'That is enough!'

39 He then left to make his way as usual to the Mount of Olives, with the disciples following. 40 When he reached the place he said to them, 'Pray not to be put to the test.' 41 Then he withdrew from them, about a stone's throw away, and knelt down and prayed. 42 'Father,' he said, 'if you are willing, take this cup away from me. Nevertheless, let your will be done, not mine.' 43 Then an angel appeared to him, coming from heaven to give him strength. 44 In his anguish he prayed even more earnestly, and his sweat fell to the ground like great drops of blood.

45 When he rose from prayer he went to the disciples and found them sleeping for sheer grief. 46 And he said to them, 'Why are you asleep? Get up and pray not to be put to the test.'

47 Suddenly, while he was still speaking, a number of men appeared, and at the head of them the man called Judas, one of the Twelve, who went up to Jesus to kiss him. 48 Jesus said, 'Judas, are you betraying the Son of man with a kiss?' 49 His followers, seeing what was about to happen, said, 'Lord, shall we use our swords?' 50 And one of them struck the high priest's servant and cut off his right ear. 51 But at this Jesus said, 'That is enough.' And touching the man's ear he healed him. 52 Then Jesus said to the chief priests and captains of the Temple guard and elders who had come for him, 'Am I a bandit, that you had to set out with swords and clubs? 53 When I was among you in the Temple day after day you never made a move to lay hands on me. But this is your hour; this is the reign of darkness.'

54 They seized him then and led him away, and they took him to the high priest's house. Peter followed at a distance. 55 They had lit a fire in the middle of the courtyard and Peter sat down among them, 56 and as he was sitting there by the blaze a servant-girl saw him, peered at him, and said, 'This man was with him too.' 57 But he denied it. 'Woman, I do not know him,' he said. 58 Shortly afterwards someone else saw him and said, 'You are one of them too.' But Peter replied, 'I am not, my friend.' 59 About an hour later another man insisted, saying, 'This fellow was certainly with him. Why, he is a Galilean.' 60 Peter said, 'My friend, I do not know what you are talking about.' At that instant, while he was still speaking, the cock crowed, 61 and the Lord turned and looked straight at Peter, and Peter remembered the Lord's words when he had said to him, 'Before the cock crows today, you will have disowned me three times.' 62 And he went outside and wept bitterly.

63 Meanwhile the men who guarded Jesus were mocking and beating him. 64 They blindfolded him and questioned

22, 43–44: These verses, though very ancient, were probably not part of the original text of Lk. They are absent from the oldest papyrus manuscripts of Lk and from manuscripts of wide geographical distribution.

r 22 Is 53:12.

asking him, "Prophesy! Who is it that struck you?" 65 They kept heaping many other insults on him.

66 When day came, the assembly of the elders of the people, both chief priests and scribes, gathered together, and they brought him to their council. 67 They said, "If you are the Messiah,*b* tell us." He replied, "If I tell you, you will not believe; 68 and if I question you, you will not answer. 69 But from now on the Son of Man will be seated at the right hand of the power of God." 70 All of them asked, "Are you, then, the Son of God?" He said to them, "You say that I am." 71 Then they said, "What further testimony do we need? We have heard it ourselves from his own lips!"

23 Then the assembly rose as a body and brought Jesus*c* before Pilate. 2 They began to accuse him, saying, "We found this man perverting our nation, forbidding us to pay taxes to the emperor, and saying that he himself is the Messiah, a king."*d* 3 Then Pilate asked him, "Are you the king of the Jews?" He answered, "You say so." 4 Then Pilate said to the chief priests and the crowds, "I find no basis for an accusation against this man." 5 But they were insistent and said, "He stirs up the people by teaching throughout all Judea, from Galilee where he began even to this place."

6 When Pilate heard this, he asked whether the man was a Galilean. 7 And when he learned that he was under Herod's jurisdiction, he sent him off to Herod, who was himself in Jerusalem at that time. 8 When Herod saw Jesus, he was very glad, for he had been wanting to see him for a long time, because he had heard about him and was hoping to see him perform some sign. 9 He questioned him at some length, but Jesus*e* gave him no answer. 10 The chief priests and the scribes stood by, vehemently accusing him. 11 Even Herod with his soldiers treated him with contempt and mocked him; then he put an elegant robe on him, and sent him back to Pilate. 12 That same day Herod and Pilate became friends with each other; before this they had been enemies.

13 Pilate then called together the chief priests, the leaders, and the people, 14 and said to them, "You brought me this man as one who was perverting the people; and here I have examined him in your presence and have not found this man guilty of any of your charges against him. 15 Neither has Herod, for he sent him back to us. Indeed, he has done nothing to deserve death. 16 I will therefore have him flogged and release him."*f*

18 Then they all shouted out together, "Away with this fellow! Release Barabbas for us!" 19 (This was a man who had been put in prison for an insurrection that had taken place in the city, and for murder.) 20 Pilate, wanting to release Jesus, addressed them again; 21 but they kept shouting, "Crucify, crucify him!" 22 A third time he said to them, "Why, what evil has he done? I have found in him no ground for the sentence of death; I will therefore have him flogged and then release him." 23 But they kept urgently demanding with loud shouts that he should be crucified; and their voices prevailed. 24 So Pilate gave his verdict that their demand should be granted. 25 He released the man they asked for, the one who had been put in prison for insurrection and murder, and he handed Jesus over as they wished.

26 As they led him away, they seized a man, Simon of Cyrene, who was coming from the country, and they laid the cross on him, and made him carry it behind Jesus. 27 A great number of the people followed him, and among them were women who were beating their breasts and wailing for him. 28 But Jesus turned to them and said, "Daughters of Jerusalem, do not weep for me, but weep for yourselves and

you are a prophet, tell us who hit you.' 65 And so they went on heaping insults upon him.

66 AS SOON as it was day, the elders of the people, chief priests, and scribes assembled, and he was brought before their Council. 67 'Tell us,' they said, 'are you the Messiah?' 'If I tell you,' he replied, 'you will not believe me; 68 and if I ask questions, you will not answer. 69 But from now on, the Son of Man will be seated at the right hand of Almighty God.' 70 'You are the Son of God, then?' they all said, and he replied, 'It is you who say I am.' 71 At that they said, 'What further evidence do we need? We have heard this ourselves from his own lips.'

23 With that the whole assembly rose and brought him before Pilate. 2 They opened the case against him by saying, 'We found this man subverting our nation, opposing the payment of taxes to Caesar, and claiming to be Messiah, a king.' 3 Pilate asked him, 'Are you the king of the Jews?' He replied, 'The words are yours.' 4 Pilate then said to the chief priests and the crowd, 'I find no case for this man to answer.' 5 But they insisted: 'His teaching is causing unrest among the people all over Judea. It started from Galilee and now has spread here.'

6 When Pilate heard this, he asked if the man was a Galilean, 7 and on learning that he belonged to Herod's jurisdiction he remitted the case to him, for Herod was also in Jerusalem at that time. 8 When Herod saw Jesus he was greatly pleased; he had heard about him and had long been wanting to see him in the hope of witnessing some miracle performed by him. 9 He questioned him at some length without getting any reply; 10 but the chief priests and scribes appeared and pressed the case against him vigorously. 11 Then Herod and his troops treated him with contempt and ridicule, and sent him back to Pilate dressed in a gorgeous robe. 12 That same day Herod and Pilate became friends; till then there had been a feud between them.

13 Pilate now summoned the chief priests, councillors, and people, 14 and said to them, 'You brought this man before me on a charge of subversion. But, as you see, I have myself examined him in your presence and found nothing in him to support your charges. 15 No more did Herod, for he has referred him back to us. Clearly he has done nothing to deserve death. 16 I therefore propose to flog him and let him go.' 18 But there was a general outcry. 'Away with him! Set Barabbas free!' 19 (Now Barabbas had been put in prison for his part in a rising in the city and for murder.) 20 Pilate addressed them again, in his desire to release Jesus, 21 but they shouted back, 'Crucify him, crucify him!' 22 For the third time he spoke to them: 'Why, what wrong has he done? I have not found him guilty of any capital offence. I will therefore flog him and let him go.' 23 But they persisted with their demand, shouting that Jesus should be crucified. Their shouts prevailed, 24 and Pilate decided that they should have their way. 25 He released the man they asked for, the man who had been put in prison for insurrection and murder, and gave Jesus over to their will.

26 AS THEY led him away to execution they took hold of a man called Simon, from Cyrene, on his way in from the country; putting the cross on his back they made him carry it behind Jesus.

27 Great numbers of people followed, among them many women who mourned and lamented over him. 28 Jesus turned to them and said, 'Daughters of Jerusalem, do not weep for me; weep for yourselves and your children. 29 For

---

b Or *the Christ*   *c* Gk *him*   *d* Or *is an anointed king*   *e* Gk *he*
f Here, or after verse 19, other ancient authorities add verse 17, *Now he was obliged to release someone for them at the festival*

22:69 **of Almighty God:** *lit.* of the Power of God.   22:70 **It is . . . I am:** *or* You are right, for I am.   23:3 **The words are yours:** *or* It is as you say.   23:18 **But there was:** *some witnesses read* 17At festival time he was obliged to release one person for them; 18and now there was.

struck you?" 65 And they reviled him in saying many other things against him.

66 When day came the council of elders of the people met, both chief priests and scribes, and they brought him before their Sanhedrin. 67 They said, "If you are the Messiah, tell us," but he replied to them, "If I tell you, you will not believe, 68 and if I question, you will not respond. 69 But from this time on the Son of Man will be seated at the right hand of the power of God." 70 They all asked, "Are you then the Son of God?" He replied to them, "You say that I am." 71 Then they said, "What further need have we for testimony? We have heard it from his own mouth."

23 Then the whole assembly of them arose and brought him before Pilate. 2 They brought charges against him, saying, "We found this man misleading our people; he opposes the payment of taxes to Caesar and maintains that he is the Messiah, a king." 3 Pilate asked him, "Are you the king of the Jews?" He said to him in reply, "You say so." 4 Pilate then addressed the chief priests and the crowds, "I find this man not guilty." 5 But they were adamant and said, "He is inciting the people with his teaching throughout all Judea, from Galilee where he began even to here."

6 On hearing this Pilate asked if the man was a Galilean; 7 and upon learning that he was under Herod's jurisdiction, he sent him to Herod who was in Jerusalem at that time. 8 Herod was very glad to see Jesus; he had been wanting to see him for a long time, for he had heard about him and had been hoping to see him perform some sign. 9 He questioned him at length, but he gave him no answer. 10 The chief priests and scribes, meanwhile, stood by accusing him harshly. 11 [Even] Herod and his soldiers treated him contemptuously and mocked him, and after clothing him in resplendent garb, he sent him back to Pilate. 12 Herod and Pilate became friends that very day, even though they had been enemies formerly. 13 Pilate then summoned the chief priests, the rulers, and the people 14 and said to them, "You brought this man to me and accused him of inciting the people to revolt. I have conducted my investigation in your presence and have not found this man guilty of the charges you have brought against him, 15 nor did Herod, for he sent him back to us. So no capital crime has been committed by him. 16 Therefore I shall have him flogged and then release him." [17]

18 But all together they shouted out, "Away with this man! Release Barabbas to us." 19 (Now Barabbas had been imprisoned for a rebellion that had taken place in the city and for murder.) 20 Again Pilate addressed them, still wishing to release Jesus, 21 but they continued their shouting, "Crucify him! Crucify him!" 22 Pilate addressed them a third time, "What evil has this man done? I found him guilty of no capital crime. Therefore I shall have him flogged and then release him." 23 With loud shouts, however, they persisted in calling for his crucifixion, and their voices prevailed. 24 The verdict of Pilate was that their demand should be granted. 25 So he released the man who had been imprisoned for rebellion and murder, for whom they asked, and he handed Jesus over to them to deal with as they wished.

26 As they led him away they took hold of a certain Simon, a Cyrenian, who was coming in from the country; and after laying the cross on him, they made him carry it behind Jesus. 27 A large crowd of people followed Jesus, including many women who mourned and lamented him. 28 Jesus turned to them and said, "Daughters of Jerusalem, do not weep for me; weep instead for yourselves and for your children, 29 for indeed, the days are coming when people

him, saying, 'Prophesy! Who hit you then?' 65 And they heaped many other insults on him.

66 When day broke there was a meeting of the elders of the people, the chief priests and scribes. He was brought before their council, 67 and they said to him, 'If you are the Christ, tell us.' He replied, 'If I tell you, you will not believe, 68 and if I question you, you will not answer. 69 But from now on, the Son of man will be seated at the right hand of the Power of God.'s 70 They all said, 'So you are the Son of God then?' He answered, 'It is you who say I am.' 71 Then they said, 'Why do we need any evidence? We have heard it for ourselves from his own lips.'

23 The whole assembly then rose, and they brought him before Pilate.

2 They began their accusation by saying, 'We found this man inciting our people to revolt, opposing payment of the tribute to Caesar, and claiming to be Christ, a king.' 3 Pilate put to him this question, 'Are you the king of the Jews?' He replied, 'It is you who say it.' 4 Pilate then said to the chief priests and the crowd, 'I find no case against this man.' 5 But they persisted, 'He is inflaming the people with his teaching all over Judaea and all the way from Galilee, where he started, down to here.' 6 When Pilate heard this, he asked if the man were a Galilean; 7 and finding that he came under Herod's jurisdiction, he passed him over to Herod, who was also in Jerusalem at that time.

8 Herod was delighted to see Jesus; he had heard about him and had been wanting for a long time to set eyes on him; moreover, he was hoping to see some miracle worked by him. 9 So he questioned him at some length, but without getting any reply. 10 Meanwhile the chief priests and the scribes were there, vigorously pressing their accusations. 11 Then Herod, together with his guards, treated him with contempt and made fun of him; he put a rich cloak on him and sent him back to Pilate. 12 And though Herod and Pilate had been enemies before, they were reconciled that same day.

13 Pilate then summoned the chief priests and the leading men and the people. 14 He said to them, 'You brought this man before me as a popular agitator. Now I have gone into the matter myself in your presence and found no grounds in the man for any of the charges you bring against him. 15 Nor has Herod either, since he has sent him back to us. As you can see, the man has done nothing that deserves death, 16 so I shall have him flogged and then let him go.' [17]t 18 But as one man they howled, 'Away with him! Give us Barabbas!' 19 (This man had been thrown into prison because of a riot in the city and murder.)

20 In his desire to set Jesus free, Pilate addressed them again, 21 but they shouted back, 'Crucify him! Crucify him!' 22 And for the third time he spoke to them, 'But what harm has this man done? I have found no case against him that deserves death, so I shall have him flogged and then let him go.' 23 But they kept on shouting at the top of their voices, demanding that he should be crucified. And their shouts kept growing louder.

24 Pilate then gave his verdict: their demand was to be granted. 25 He released the man they asked for, who had been imprisoned because of rioting and murder, and handed Jesus over to them to deal with as they pleased.

26 As they were leading him away they seized on a man, Simon from Cyrene, who was coming in from the country, and made him shoulder the cross and carry it behind Jesus. 27 Large numbers of people followed him, and women too, who mourned and lamented for him. 28 But Jesus turned to them and said, 'Daughters of Jerusalem, do not weep for me; weep rather for yourselves and for your children. 29 For

23, 17: This verse, "He was obliged to release one prisoner for them at the festival," is not part of the original text of Lk. It is an explanatory gloss from Mk 15, 6 (also Mt 27, 15). It is not found in many early and important Greek manuscripts.

s 22 Ps 110:1.   t 23 Some authorities add v. 17, borrowed from Mt 27:15.

NEW REVISED STANDARD VERSION

for your children. 29 For the days are surely coming when they will say, 'Blessed are the barren, and the wombs that never bore, and the breasts that never nursed.' 30 Then they will begin to say to the mountains, 'Fall on us'; and to the hills, 'Cover us.' 31 For if they do this when the wood is green, what will happen when it is dry?"

32 Two others also, who were criminals, were led away to be put to death with him. 33 When they came to the place that is called The Skull, they crucified Jesus*g* there with the criminals, one on his right and one on his left. [[34 Then Jesus said, "Father, forgive them; for they do not know what they are doing."]]*h* And they cast lots to divide his clothing. 35 And the people stood by, watching; but the leaders scoffed at him, saying, "He saved others; let him save himself if he is the Messiah*i* of God, his chosen one!" 36 The soldiers also mocked him, coming up and offering him sour wine, 37 and saying, "If you are the King of the Jews, save yourself!" 38 There was also an inscription over him,*j* "This is the King of the Jews."

39 One of the criminals who were hanged there kept deriding*k* him and saying, "Are you not the Messiah?*i* Save yourself and us!" 40 But the other rebuked him, saying, "Do you not fear God, since you are under the same sentence of condemnation? 41 And we indeed have been condemned justly, for we are getting what we deserve for our deeds, but this man has done nothing wrong." 42 Then he said, "Jesus, remember me when you come into*l* your kingdom." 43 He replied, "Truly I tell you, today you will be with me in Paradise."

44 It was now about noon, and darkness came over the whole land*m* until three in the afternoon, 45 while the sun's light failed;*n* and the curtain of the temple was torn in two. 46 Then Jesus, crying with a loud voice, said, "Father, into your hands I commend my spirit." Having said this, he breathed his last. 47 When the centurion saw what had taken place, he praised God and said, "Certainly this man was innocent."*o* 48 And when all the crowds who had gathered there for this spectacle saw what had taken place, they returned home, beating their breasts. 49 But all his acquaintances, including the women who had followed him from Galilee, stood at a distance, watching these things.

50 Now there was a good and righteous man named Joseph, who, though a member of the council, 51 had not agreed to their plan and action. He came from the Jewish town of Arimathea, and he was waiting expectantly for the kingdom of God. 52 This man went to Pilate and asked for the body of Jesus. 53 Then he took it down, wrapped it in a linen cloth, and laid it in a rock-hewn tomb where no one had ever been laid. 54 It was the day of Preparation, and the sabbath was beginning.*p* 55 The women who had come with him from Galilee followed, and they saw the tomb and how his body was laid. 56 Then they returned, and prepared spices and ointments.

On the sabbath they rested according to the commandment.

24 But on the first day of the week, at early dawn, they came to the tomb, taking the spices that they had prepared. 2 They found the stone rolled away from the tomb, 3 but when they went in, they did not find the body.*q*

REVISED ENGLISH BIBLE

the days are surely coming when people will say, "Happy are the barren, the wombs that never bore a child, the breasts that never fed one." 30 Then they will begin to say to the mountains, "Fall on us," and to the hills, "Cover us." 31 For if these things are done when the wood is green, what will happen when it is dry?'

32 There were two others with him, criminals who were being led out to execution; 33 and when they reached the place called The Skull, they crucified him there, and the criminals with him, one on his right and the other on his left. 34 Jesus said, 'Father, forgive them; they do not know what they are doing.'

They shared out his clothes by casting lots. 35 The people stood looking on, and their rulers jeered at him: 'He saved others: now let him save himself, if this is God's Messiah, his Chosen.' 36 The soldiers joined in the mockery and came forward offering him sour wine. 37 'If you are the king of the Jews,' they said, 'save yourself.' 38 There was an inscription above his head which ran: 'This is the king of the Jews.'

39 One of the criminals hanging there taunted him: 'Are not you the Messiah? Save yourself, and us.' 40 But the other rebuked him: 'Have you no fear of God? You are under the same sentence as he is. 41 In our case it is plain justice; we are paying the price for our misdeeds. But this man has done nothing wrong.' 42 And he said, 'Jesus, remember me when you come to your throne.' 43 Jesus answered, 'Truly I tell you: today you will be with me in Paradise.'

44 By now it was about midday and a darkness fell over the whole land, which lasted until three in the afternoon: 45 the sun's light failed. And the curtain of the temple was torn in two. 46 Then Jesus uttered a loud cry and said, 'Father, into your hands I commit my spirit'; and with these words he died. 47 When the centurion saw what had happened, he gave praise to God. 'Beyond all doubt', he said, 'this man was innocent.'

48 The crowd who had assembled for the spectacle, when they saw what had happened, went home beating their breasts.

49 His friends had all been standing at a distance; the women who had accompanied him from Galilee stood with them and watched it all.

50 Now there was a man called Joseph, a member of the Council, a good and upright man, 51 who had dissented from their policy and the action they had taken. He came from the Judaean town of Arimathaea, and he was one who looked forward to the kingdom of God. 52 This man now approached Pilate and asked for the body of Jesus. 53 Taking it down from the cross, he wrapped it in a linen sheet, and laid it in a tomb cut out of the rock, in which no one had been laid before. 54 It was the day of preparation, and the sabbath was about to begin.

55 The women who had accompanied Jesus from Galilee followed; they took note of the tomb and saw his body laid in it. 56 Then they went home and prepared spices and perfumes; and on the sabbath they rested in obedience to the commandment.

24 But very early on the first day of the week they came to the tomb bringing the spices they had prepared. 2 They found that the stone had been rolled away from the tomb, 3 but when they went inside, they did not find the body of the Lord Jesus. 4 While they stood utterly

---

g Gk *him* *h* Other ancient authorities lack the sentence *Then Jesus . . . what they are doing* *i* Or *the Christ* *j* Other ancient authorities add *written in Greek and Latin and Hebrew* (that is, *Aramaic*) *k* Or *blaspheming* *l* Other ancient authorities read *in* *m* Or *earth* *n* Or *the sun was eclipsed*. Other ancient authorities read *the sun was darkened* *o* Or *righteous* *p* Gk *was dawning* *q* Other ancient authorities add *of the Lord Jesus*

23:34 *Some witnesses omit* Jesus said, 'Father . . . doing.'

will say, 'Blessed are the barren, the wombs that never bore and the breasts that never nursed.' 30 At that time people will say to the mountains, 'Fall upon us!' and to the hills, 'Cover us!' 31 for if these things are done when the wood is green what will happen when it is dry?" 32 Now two others, both criminals, were led away with him to be executed.

33 When they came to the place called the Skull, they crucified him and the criminals there, one on his right, the other on his left. 34 [Then Jesus said, "Father, forgive them, they know not what they do."] They divided his garments by casting lots. 35 The people stood by and watched; the rulers, meanwhile, sneered at him and said, "He saved others, let him save himself if he is the chosen one, the Messiah of God." 36 Even the soldiers jeered at him. As they approached to offer him wine 37 they called out, "If you are King of the Jews, save yourself." 38 Above him there was an inscription that read, "This is the King of the Jews."

39 Now one of the criminals hanging there reviled Jesus, saying, "Are you not the Messiah? Save yourself and us." 40 The other, however, rebuking him, said in reply, "Have you no fear of God, for you are subject to the same condemnation? 41 And indeed, we have been condemned justly, for the sentence we received corresponds to our crimes, but this man has done nothing criminal." 42 Then he said, "Jesus, remember me when you come into your kingdom." 43 He replied to him, "Amen, I say to you, today you will be with me in Paradise."

44 It was now about noon and darkness came over the whole land until three in the afternoon 45 because of an eclipse of the sun. Then the veil of the temple was torn down the middle. 46 Jesus cried out in a loud voice, "Father, into your hands I commend my spirit"; and when he had said this he breathed his last. 47 The centurion who witnessed what had happened glorified God and said, "This man was innocent beyond doubt." 48 When all the people who had gathered for this spectacle saw what had happened, they returned home beating their breasts; 49 but all his acquaintances stood at a distance, including the women who had followed him from Galilee and saw these events.

50 Now there was a virtuous and righteous man named Joseph who, though he was a member of the council, 51 had not consented to their plan of action. He came from the Jewish town of Arimathea and was awaiting the kingdom of God. 52 After he had taken the body down, he wrapped it in a linen cloth and laid him in a rock-hewn tomb in which no one had yet been buried. 54 It was the day of preparation, and the sabbath was about to begin. 55 The women who had come from Galilee with him followed behind, and when they had seen the tomb and the way in which his body was laid in it, 56 they returned and prepared spices and perfumed oils. Then they rested on the sabbath according to the commandment.

24 But at daybreak on the first day of the week they took the spices they had prepared and went to the tomb. 2 They found the stone rolled away from the tomb; 3 but when they entered, they did not find the body of the Lord Jesus. 4 While they were puzzling over this, behold,

look, the days are surely coming when people will say, "Blessed are those who are barren, the wombs that have never borne children, the breasts that have never suckled!" 30 Then they will begin to say to the mountains, "Fall on us!"; to the hills, "Cover us!" u 31 For if this is what is done to green wood, what will be done when the wood is dry?' 32 Now they were also leading out two others, criminals, to be executed with him.

33 When they reached the place called The Skull, there they crucified him and the two criminals, one on his right, the other on his left. 34 Jesus said, 'Father, forgive them; they do not know what they are doing.' Then they cast lots to share out his clothing.

35 The people stayed there watching. As for the leaders, they jeered at him with the words, 'He saved others, let him save himself if he is the Christ of God, the Chosen One.' 36 The soldiers mocked him too, coming up to him, offering him vinegar, 37 and saying, 'If you are the king of the Jews, save yourself.' 38 Above him there was an inscription: 'This is the King of the Jews'.

39 One of the criminals hanging there abused him: 'Are you not the Christ? Save yourself and us as well.' 40 But the other spoke up and rebuked him. 'Have you no fear of God at all?' he said. 'You got the same sentence as he did, 41 but in our case we deserved it: we are paying for what we did. But this man has done nothing wrong.' 42 Then he said, 'Jesus, remember me when you come into your kingdom.' 43 He answered him, 'In truth I tell you, today you will be with me in paradise.'

44 It was now about the sixth hour and the sun's light failed, so that darkness came over the whole land until the ninth hour. 45 The veil of the Sanctuary was torn right down the middle. 46 Jesus cried out in a loud voice saying, 'Father, into your hands I commit my spirit.' v With these words he breathed his last.

47 When the centurion saw what had taken place, he gave praise to God and said, 'Truly, this was an upright man.' 48 And when all the crowds who had gathered for the spectacle saw what had happened, they went home beating their breasts.

49 All his friends stood at a distance; so also did the women who had accompanied him from Galilee and saw all this happen.

50 And now a member of the Council arrived, a good and upright man named Joseph. 51 He had not consented to what the others had planned and carried out. He came from Arimathaea, a Jewish town, and he lived in the hope of seeing the kingdom of God. 52 This man went to Pilate and asked for the body of Jesus. 53 He then took it down, wrapped it in a shroud and put it in a tomb which was hewn in stone and which had never held a body. 54 It was Preparation day and the Sabbath was beginning to grow light.

55 Meanwhile the women who had come from Galilee with Jesus were following behind. They took note of the tomb and how the body had been laid.

56 Then they returned and prepared spices and ointments. And on the Sabbath day they rested, as the Law required.

24 On the first day of the week, at the first sign of dawn, they went to the tomb with the spices they had prepared. 2 They found that the stone had been rolled away from the tomb, 3 but on entering they could not find the body of the Lord Jesus. 4 As they stood there puzzled

---

23, 34a: [*Then Jesus said, "Father, forgive them, they know not what they do."*]: this portion of v 34 does not occur in the oldest papyrus manuscript of Lk and in other early Greek manuscripts and ancient versions of wide geographical distribution.

u **23** Ho 10:8.   v **23** Ps 31:5.

4 While they were perplexed about this, suddenly two men in dazzling clothes stood beside them. 5 The women*r* were terrified and bowed their faces to the ground, but the men*s* said to them, "Why do you look for the living among the dead? He is not here, but has risen.*t* 6 Remember how he told you, while he was still in Galilee, 7 that the Son of Man must be handed over to sinners, and be crucified, and on the third day rise again." 8 Then they remembered his words, 9 and returning from the tomb, they told all this to the eleven and to all the rest. 10 Now it was Mary Magdalene, Joanna, Mary the mother of James, and the other women with them who told this to the apostles. 11 But these words seemed to them an idle tale, and they did not believe them. 12 But Peter got up and ran to the tomb; stooping and looking in, he saw the linen cloths by themselves; then he went home, amazed at what had happened.*u*

13 Now on that same day two of them were going to a village called Emmaus, about seven miles*v* from Jerusalem, 14 and talking with each other about all these things that had happened. 15 While they were talking and discussing, Jesus himself came near and went with them, 16 but their eyes were kept from recognizing him. 17 And he said to them, "What are you discussing with each other while you walk along?" They stood still, looking sad.*w* 18 Then one of them, whose name was Cleopas, answered him, "Are you the only stranger in Jerusalem who does not know the things that have taken place there in these days?" 19 He asked them, "What things?" They replied, "The things about Jesus of Nazareth,*x* who was a prophet mighty in deed and word before God and all the people, 20 and how our chief priests and leaders handed him over to be condemned to death and crucified him. 21 But we had hoped that he was the one to redeem Israel.*y* Yes, and besides all this, it is now the third day since these things took place. 22 Moreover, some women of our group astounded us. They were at the tomb early this morning, 23 and when they did not find his body there, they came back and told us that they had indeed seen a vision of angels who said that he was alive. 24 Some of those who were with us went to the tomb and found it just as the women had said; but they did not see him." 25 Then he said to them, "Oh, how foolish you are, and how slow of heart to believe all that the prophets have declared! 26 Was it not necessary that the Messiah*z* should suffer these things and then enter into his glory?" 27 Then beginning with Moses and all the prophets, he interpreted to them the things about himself in all the scriptures.

28 As they came near the village to which they were going, he walked ahead as if he were going on. 29 But they urged him strongly, saying, "Stay with us, because it is almost evening and the day is now nearly over." So he went in to stay with them. 30 When he was at the table with them, he took bread, blessed and broke it, and gave it to them. 31 Then their eyes were opened, and they recognized him; and he vanished from their sight. 32 They said to each other, "Were not our hearts burning within us*a* while he was talking to us on the road, while he was opening the scriptures to us?" 33 That same hour they got up and returned to Jerusalem; and they found the eleven and their companions gathered together. 34 They were saying, "The Lord has risen indeed, and he has appeared to Simon!" 35 Then they told what had happened on the road, and how he had been made known to them in the breaking of the bread.

at a loss, suddenly two men in dazzling garments were at their side. 5 They were terrified, and stood with eyes cast down, but the men said, 'Why search among the dead for one who is alive? 6 Remember how he told you, while he was still in Galilee, 7 that the Son of Man must be given into the power of sinful men and be crucified, and must rise again on the third day.' 8 Then they recalled his words 9 and, returning from the tomb, they reported everything to the eleven and all the others.

10 The women were Mary of Magdala, Joanna, and Mary the mother of James, and they, with the other women, told these things to the apostles. 11 But the story appeared to them to be nonsense, and they would not believe them.

13 THAT same day two of them were on their way to a village called Emmaus, about seven miles from Jerusalem, 14 talking together about all that had happened. 15 As they talked and argued, Jesus himself came up and walked with them; 16 but something prevented them from recognizing him. 17 He asked them, 'What is it you are debating as you walk?' They stood still, their faces full of sadness, 18 and one, called Cleopas, answered, 'Are you the only person staying in Jerusalem not to have heard the news of what has happened there in the last few days?' 19 'What news?' he said. 'About Jesus of Nazareth,' they replied, 'who, by deeds and words of power, proved himself a prophet in the sight of God and the whole people; 20 and how our chief priests and rulers handed him over to be sentenced to death, and crucified him. 21 But we had been hoping that he was to be the liberator of Israel. What is more, this is the third day since it happened, 22 and now some women of our company have astounded us: they went early to the tomb, 23 but failed to find his body, and returned with a story that they had seen a vision of angels who told them he was alive. 24 Then some of our people went to the tomb and found things just as the women had said; but him they did not see.'

25 'How dull you are!' he answered. 'How slow to believe all that the prophets said! 26 Was not the Messiah bound to suffer in this way before entering upon his glory?' 27 Then, starting from Moses and all the prophets, he explained to them in the whole of scripture the things that referred to himself.

28 By this time they had reached the village to which they were going, and he made as if to continue his journey. 29 But they pressed him: 'Stay with us, for evening approaches, and the day is almost over.' So he went in to stay with them. 30 And when he had sat down with them at table, he took bread and said the blessing; he broke the bread, and offered it to them. 31 Then their eyes were opened, and they recognized him; but he vanished from their sight. 32 They said to one another, 'Were not our hearts on fire as he talked with us on the road and explained the scriptures to us?'

33 Without a moment's delay they set out and returned to Jerusalem. There they found that the eleven and the rest of the company had assembled, 34 and were saying, 'It is true: the Lord has risen; he has appeared to Simon.' 35 Then they described what had happened on their journey and told how he had made himself known to them in the breaking of the bread.

---

two men in dazzling garments appeared to them. 5 They were terrified and bowed their faces to the ground. They said to them, "Why do you seek the living one among the dead? 6 He is not here, but he has been raised. Remember what he said to you while he was still in Galilee, 7 that the Son of Man must be handed over to sinners and be crucified, and rise on the third day." 8 And they remembered his words. 9 Then they returned from the tomb and announced all these things to the eleven and to all the others. 10 The women were Mary Magdalene, Joanna, and Mary the mother of James; the others who accompanied them also told this to the apostles, 11 but their story seemed like nonsense and they did not believe them. 12 But Peter got up and ran to the tomb, bent down, and saw the burial cloths alone; then he went home amazed at what had happened.

13 Now that very day two of them were going to a village seven miles from Jerusalem called Emmaus, 14 and they were conversing about all the things that had occurred. 15 And it happened that while they were conversing and debating, Jesus himself drew near and walked with them, 16 but their eyes were prevented from recognizing him. 17 He asked them, "What are you discussing as you walk along?" They stopped, looking downcast. 18 One of them, named Cleopas, said to him in reply, "Are you the only visitor to Jerusalem who does not know of the things that have taken place there in these days?" 19 And he replied to them, "What sort of things?" They said to him, "The things that happened to Jesus the Nazarene, who was a prophet mighty in deed and word before God and all the people, 20 how our chief priests and rulers both handed him over to a sentence of death and crucified him. 21 But we were hoping that he would be the one to redeem Israel; and besides all this, it is now the third day since this took place. 22 Some women from our group, however, have astounded us: they were at the tomb early in the morning 23 and did not find his body; they came back and reported that they had indeed seen a vision of angels who announced that he was alive. 24 Then some of those with us went to the tomb and found things just as the women had described, but him they did not see." 25 And he said to them, "Oh, how foolish you are! How slow of heart to believe all that the prophets spoke! 26 Was it not necessary that the Messiah should suffer these things and enter into his glory?" 27 Then beginning with Moses and all the prophets, he interpreted to them what referred to him in all the scriptures. 28 As they approached the village to which they were going, he gave the impression that he was going on farther. 29 But they urged him, "Stay with us, for it is nearly evening and the day is almost over." So he went in to stay with them. 30 And it happened that, while he was with them at table, he took bread, said the blessing, broke it, and gave it to them. 31 With that their eyes were opened and they recognized him, but he vanished from their sight. 32 Then they said to each other, "Were not our hearts burning [within us] while he spoke to us on the way and opened the scriptures to us?" 33 So they set out at once and returned to Jerusalem where they found gathered together the eleven and those with them 34 who were saying, "The Lord has truly been raised and has appeared to Simon!" 35 Then the two recounted what had taken place on the way and how he was made known to them in the breaking of the bread.

about this, two men in brilliant clothes suddenly appeared at their side. 5 Terrified, the women bowed their heads to the ground. But the two said to them, 'Why look among the dead for someone who is alive? 6 He is not here; he has risen. Remember what he told you when he was still in Galilee: 7 that the Son of man was destined to be handed over into the power of sinful men and be crucified, and rise again on the third day.' 8 And they remembered his words.

9 And they returned from the tomb and told all this to the Eleven and to all the others. 10 The women were Mary of Magdala, Joanna, and Mary the mother of James. And the other women with them also told the apostles, 11 but this story of theirs seemed pure nonsense, and they did not believe them.

12 Peter, however, went off to the tomb, running. He bent down and looked in and saw the linen cloths but nothing else; he then went back home, amazed at what had happened.

13 Now that very same day, two of them were on their way to a village called Emmaus, seven miles from Jerusalem, 14 and they were talking together about all that had happened. 15 And it happened that as they were talking together and discussing it, Jesus himself came up and walked by their side; 16 but their eyes were prevented from recognising him. 17 He said to them, 'What are all these things that you are discussing as you walk along?' They stopped, their faces downcast.

18 Then one of them, called Cleopas, answered him, 'You must be the only person staying in Jerusalem who does not know the things that have been happening there these last few days.' 19 He asked, 'What things?' They answered, 'All about Jesus of Nazareth, who showed himself a prophet powerful in action and speech before God and the whole people; 20 and how our chief priests and our leaders handed him over to be sentenced to death, and had him crucified. 21 Our own hope had been that he would be the one to set Israel free. And this is not all: two whole days have now gone by since it all happened; 22 and some women from our group have astounded us: they went to the tomb in the early morning, 23 and when they could not find the body, they came back to tell us they had seen a vision of angels who declared he was alive. 24 Some of our friends went to the tomb and found everything exactly as the women had reported, but of him they saw nothing.'

25 Then he said to them, 'You foolish men! So slow to believe all that the prophets have said! 26 Was it not necessary that the Christ should suffer before entering into his glory?' 27 Then, starting with Moses and going through all the prophets, he explained to them the passages throughout the scriptures that were about himself.

28 When they drew near to the village to which they were going, he made as if to go on; 29 but they pressed him to stay with them saying, 'It is nearly evening, and the day is almost over.' So he went in to stay with them. 30 Now while he was with them at table, he took the bread and said the blessing; then he broke it and handed it to them. 31 And their eyes were opened and they recognised him; but he had vanished from their sight. 32 Then they said to each other, 'Did not our hearts burn within us as he talked to us on the road and explained the scriptures to us?'

33 They set out that instant and returned to Jerusalem. There they found the Eleven assembled together with their companions, 34 who said to them, 'The Lord has indeed risen and has appeared to Simon.' 35 Then they told their story of what had happened on the road and how they had recognised him at the breaking of bread.

24, 12: This verse is missing from the Western textual tradition but is found in the best and oldest manuscripts of other text types.

36 While they were talking about this, Jesus himself stood among them and said to them, "Peace be with you."[b] 37 They were startled and terrified, and thought that they were seeing a ghost. 38 He said to them, "Why are you frightened, and why do doubts arise in your hearts? 39 Look at my hands and my feet; see that it is I myself. Touch me and see; for a ghost does not have flesh and bones as you see that I have." 40 And when he had said this, he showed them his hands and his feet.[c] 41 While in their joy they were disbelieving and still wondering, he said to them, "Have you anything here to eat?" 42 They gave him a piece of broiled fish, 43 and he took it and ate in their presence.

44 Then he said to them, "These are my words that I spoke to you while I was still with you — that everything written about me in the law of Moses, the prophets, and the psalms must be fulfilled." 45 Then he opened their minds to understand the scriptures, 46 and he said to them, "Thus it is written, that the Messiah[d] is to suffer and to rise from the dead on the third day, 47 and that repentance and forgiveness of sins is to be proclaimed in his name to all nations,[e] beginning from Jerusalem. 48 You are witnesses of these things. 49 And see, I am sending upon you what my Father promised; so stay here in the city until you have been clothed with power from on high."

50 Then he led them out as far as Bethany, and, lifting up his hands, he blessed them. 51 While he was blessing them, he withdrew from them and was carried up into heaven.[f] 52 And they worshiped him, and[g] returned to Jerusalem with great joy; 53 and they were continually in the temple blessing God.[h]

[b] Other ancient authorities lack *and said to them, "Peace be with you."* [c] Other ancient authorities lack verse 40 [d] Or *the Christ* [e] Or *nations. Beginning from Jerusalem you are witnesses* [f] Other ancient authorities lack *and was carried up into heaven* [g] Other ancient authorities lack *worshiped him, and* [h] Other ancient authorities add *Amen*

36 As they were talking about all this, there he was, standing among them. 37 Startled and terrified, they thought they were seeing a ghost. 38 But he said, 'Why are you so perturbed? Why do doubts arise in your minds? 39 Look at my hands and feet. It is I myself. Touch me and see; no ghost has flesh and bones as you can see that I have.' 41 They were still incredulous, still astounded, for it seemed too good to be true. So he asked them, 'Have you anything here to eat?' 42 They offered him a piece of fish they had cooked, 43 which he took and ate before their eyes.

44 And he said to them, 'This is what I meant by saying, while I was still with you, that everything written about me in the law of Moses and in the prophets and psalms was bound to be fulfilled.' 45 Then he opened their minds to understand the scriptures. 46 'So you see', he said, 'that scripture foretells the sufferings of the Messiah and his rising from the dead on the third day, 47 and declares that in his name repentance bringing the forgiveness of sins is to be proclaimed to all nations beginning from Jerusalem. 48 You are to be witnesses to it all. 49 I am sending on you the gift promised by my Father; wait here in this city until you are armed with power from above.'

50 Then he led them out as far as Bethany, and blessed them with uplifted hands; 51 and in the act of blessing he parted from them. 52 And they returned to Jerusalem full of joy, 53 and spent all their time in the temple praising God.

24:36 **among them:** *some witnesses add* And he said to them, 'Peace be with you!' 24:39 **I have:** *some witnesses add* 40 After saying this he showed them his hands and feet. 24:51 **parted from them:** *some witnesses add* and was carried up into heaven. 24:52 **And they:** *some witnesses add* worshiped him and.

NEW AMERICAN BIBLE

36 While they were still speaking about this, he stood in their midst and said to them, "Peace be with you." 37 But they were startled and terrified and thought that they were seeing a ghost. 38 Then he said to them, "Why are you troubled? And why do questions arise in your hearts? 39 Look at my hands and my feet, that it is I myself. Touch me and see, because a ghost does not have flesh and bones as you can see I have." 40 And as he said this, he showed them his hands and his feet. 41 While they were still incredulous for joy and were amazed, he asked them, "Have you anything here to eat?" 42 They gave him a piece of baked fish; 43 he took it and ate it in front of them.

44 He said to them, "These are my words that I spoke to you while I was still with you, that everything written about me in the law of Moses and in the prophets and psalms must be fulfilled." 45 Then he opened their minds to understand the scriptures. 46 And he said to them, "Thus it is written that the Messiah would suffer and rise from the dead on the third day 47 and that repentance, for the forgiveness of sins, would be preached in his name to all the nations, beginning from Jerusalem. 48 You are witnesses of these things. 49 And [behold] I am sending the promise of my Father upon you; but stay in the city until you are clothed with power from on high."

50 Then he led them [out] as far as Bethany, raised his hands, and blessed them. 51 As he blessed them he parted from them and was taken up to heaven. 52 They did him homage and then returned to Jerusalem with great joy, 53 and they were continually in the temple praising God.

NEW JERUSALEM BIBLE

36 They were still talking about all this when he himself stood among them and said to them, 'Peace be with you!' 37 In a state of alarm and fright, they thought they were seeing a ghost. 38 But he said, 'Why are you so agitated, and why are these doubts stirring in your hearts? 39 See by my hands and my feet that it is I myself. Touch me and see for yourselves; a ghost has no flesh and bones as you can see I have.' 40 And as he said this he showed them his hands and his feet. 41 Their joy was so great that they still could not believe it, as they were dumbfounded; so he said to them, 'Have you anything here to eat?' 42 And they offered him a piece of grilled fish, 43 which he took and ate before their eyes.

44 Then he told them, 'This is what I meant when I said, while I was still with you, that everything written about me in the Law of Moses, in the Prophets and in the Psalms, was destined to be fulfilled.' 45 He then opened their minds to understand the scriptures, 46 and he said to them, 'So it is written that the Christ would suffer and on the third day rise from the dead, 47 and that, in his name, repentance for the forgiveness of sins would be preached to all nations, beginning from Jerusalem. 48 You are witnesses to this.

49 'And now I am sending upon you what the Father has promised. Stay in the city, then, until you are clothed with the power from on high.'

50 Then he took them out as far as the outskirts of Bethany, and raising his hands he blessed them. 51 Now as he blessed them, he withdrew from them and was carried up to heaven. 52 They worshipped him and then went back to Jerusalem full of joy; 53 and they were continually in the Temple praising God.

THE GOSPEL ACCORDING TO

John

1 In the beginning was the Word, and the Word was with God, and the Word was God. 2 He was in the beginning with God. 3 All things came into being through him, and without him not one thing came into being. What has come into being 4 in him was life,*a* and the life was the light of all people. 5 The light shines in the darkness, and the darkness did not overcome it.

6 There was a man sent from God, whose name was John. 7 He came as a witness to testify to the light, so that all might believe through him. 8 He himself was not the light, but he came to testify to the light. 9 The true light, which enlightens everyone, was coming into the world.*b*

10 He was in the world, and the world came into being through him; yet the world did not know him. 11 He came to what was his own,*c* and his own people did not accept him. 12 But to all who received him, who believed in his name, he gave power to become children of God, 13 who were born, not of blood or of the will of the flesh or of the will of man, but of God.

14 And the Word became flesh and lived among us, and we have seen his glory, the glory as of a father's only son,*d* full of grace and truth. 15 (John testified to him and cried out, "This was he of whom I said, 'He who comes after me ranks ahead of me because he was before me.' ") 16 From his fullness we have all received, grace upon grace. 17 The law indeed was given through Moses; grace and truth came through Jesus Christ. 18 No one has ever seen God. It is God the only Son,*e* who is close to the Father's heart,*f* who has made him known.

THE GOSPEL ACCORDING TO

John

1 IN the beginning the Word already was. The Word was in God's presence, and what God was, the Word was. 2 He was with God at the beginning, 3 and through him all things came to be; without him no created thing came into being. 4 In him was life, and that life was the light of mankind. 5 The light shines in the darkness, and the darkness has never mastered it.

6 There appeared a man named John. He was sent from God, 7 and came as a witness to testify to the light, so that through him all might become believers. 8 He was not himself the light; he came to bear witness to the light. 9 The true light which gives light to everyone was even then coming into the world.

10 He was in the world; but the world, though it owed its being to him, did not recognize him. 11 He came to his own, and his own people would not accept him. 12 But to all who did accept him, to those who put their trust in him, he gave the right to become children of God, 13 born not of human stock, by the physical desire of a human father, but of God. 14 So the Word became flesh; he made his home among us, and we saw his glory, such glory as befits the Father's only Son, full of grace and truth.

15 John bore witness to him and proclaimed: 'This is the man of whom I said, "He comes after me, but ranks ahead of me"; before I was born, he already was.'

16 From his full store we have all received grace upon grace; 17 for the law was given through Moses, but grace and truth came through Jesus Christ. 18 No one has ever seen God; God's only Son, he who is nearest to the Father's heart, has made him known.

---

a Or 3through him. And without him not one thing came into being that has come into being. 4In him was life *b Or He was the true light that enlightens everyone coming into the world* *c Or to his own home* *d Or the Father's only Son* *e Other ancient authorities read It is an only Son, God, or It is the only Son* *f Gk bosom*

1:3–4 **through him . . . was life:** *or* without him no single thing was created. All that came to be was alive with his life. 1:9 **The true . . . world:** *or* The true light was in being, which gives light to everyone entering the world. 1:18 **God's only Son:** *some witnesses read* the only begotten God.

THE GOSPEL ACCORDING TO

John

1 In the beginning was the Word,
and the Word was with God,
and the Word was God.
² He was in the beginning with God.
³ All things came to be through him,
and without him nothing came to be.
What came to be ⁴ through him was life,
and this life was the light of the human race;
⁵ the light shines in the darkness,
and the darkness has not overcome it.

⁶ A man named John was sent from God. ⁷ He came for testimony, to testify to the light, so that all might believe through him. ⁸ He was not the light, but came to testify to the light. ⁹ The true light, which enlightens everyone, was coming into the world.

¹⁰ He was in the world,
and the world came to be through him,
but the world did not know him.
¹¹ He came to what was his own,
but his own people did not accept him.

¹² But to those who did accept him he gave power to become children of God, to those who believe in his name, ¹³ who were born not by natural generation nor by human choice nor by a man's decision but of God.

¹⁴ And the Word became flesh
and made his dwelling among us,
and we saw his glory,
the glory as of the Father's only Son,
full of grace and truth.

¹⁵ John testified to him and cried out, saying, "This was he of whom I said, 'The one who is coming after me ranks ahead of me because he existed before me.'" ¹⁶ From his fullness we have all received, grace in place of grace, ¹⁷ because while the law was given through Moses, grace and truth came through Jesus Christ. ¹⁸ No one has ever seen God. The only Son, God, who is at the Father's side, has revealed him.

THE GOSPEL ACCORDING TO

John

1 In the beginning was the Word:ᵃ
the Word was with God
and the Word was God.
² He was with God in the beginning.
³ Through him all things came into being,
not one thing came into being except through him.
⁴ What has come into being in him was life,
life that was the light of men;
⁵ and light shines in darkness,
and darkness could not overpower it.

⁶ A man came, sent by God.
His name was John.
⁷ He came as a witness,
to bear witness to the light,
so that everyone might believe through him.
⁸ He was not the light,
he was to bear witness to the light.

⁹ The Word was the real light
that gives light to everyone;
he was coming into the world.
¹⁰ He was in the world
that had come into being through him,
and the world did not recognise him.
¹¹ He came to his own
and his own people did not accept him.
¹² But to those who did accept him
he gave power to become children of God,
to those who believed in his name
¹³ who wereᵇ born not from human stock
or human desire
or human will
but from God himself.
¹⁴ The Word became flesh,
he lived among us,
and we saw his glory,
the glory that he has from the Father as only Son
of the Father,
full of grace and truth.

¹⁵ John witnesses to him. He proclaims:
'This is the one of whom I said:
He who comes after me
has passed ahead of me
because he existed before me.'

¹⁶ Indeed, from his fullness we have, all of us,
received—
one gift replacing another,
¹⁷ for the Law was given through Moses,
grace and truth have come through Jesus Christ.
¹⁸ No one has ever seen God;
it is the only Son, who is close to the Father's
heart,
who has made him known.

ᵃ 1 In the OT the Word or Wisdom of God is present with God before the world existed and reveals God to the world. Jn sees this Word-Wisdom in the person of Jesus.   ᵇ 1 Some MSS have the singular 'was', which would refer to Jesus' divine origin.

19 This is the testimony given by John when the Jews sent priests and Levites from Jerusalem to ask him, "Who are you?" 20 He confessed and did not deny it, but confessed, "I am not the Messiah."ᵍ 21 And they asked him, "What then? Are you Elijah?" He said, "I am not." "Are you the prophet?" He answered, "No." 22 Then they said to him, "Who are you? Let us have an answer for those who sent us. What do you say about yourself?" 23 He said,

"I am the voice of one crying out in the wilderness,
'Make straight the way of the Lord,'"
as the prophet Isaiah said.

24 Now they had been sent from the Pharisees. 25 They asked him, "Why then are you baptizing if you are neither the Messiah,ᵍ nor Elijah, nor the prophet?" 26 John answered them, "I baptize with water. Among you stands one whom you do not know, 27 the one who is coming after me; I am not worthy to untie the thong of his sandal." 28 This took place in Bethany across the Jordan where John was baptizing.

29 The next day he saw Jesus coming toward him and declared, "Here is the Lamb of God who takes away the sin of the world! 30 This is he of whom I said, 'After me comes a man who ranks ahead of me because he was before me.' 31 I myself did not know him; but I came baptizing with water for this reason, that he might be revealed to Israel." 32 And John testified, "I saw the Spirit descending from heaven like a dove, and it remained on him. 33 I myself did not know him, but the one who sent me to baptize with water said to me, 'He on whom you see the Spirit descend and remain is the one who baptizes with the Holy Spirit.' 34 And I myself have seen and have testified that this is the Son of God."ʰ

35 The next day John again was standing with two of his disciples, 36 and as he watched Jesus walk by, he exclaimed, "Look, here is the Lamb of God!" 37 The two disciples heard him say this, and they followed Jesus. 38 When Jesus turned and saw them following, he said to them, "What are you looking for?" They said to him, "Rabbi" (which translated means Teacher), "where are you staying?" 39 He said to them, "Come and see." They came and saw where he was staying, and they remained with him that day. It was about four o'clock in the afternoon. 40 One of the two who heard John speak and followed him was Andrew, Simon Peter's brother. 41 He first found his brother Simon and said to him, "We have found the Messiah" (which is translated Anointedⁱ). 42 He brought Simonʲ to Jesus, who looked at him and said, "You are Simon son of John. You are to be called Cephas" (which is translated Peterᵏ).

43 The next day Jesus decided to go to Galilee. He found Philip and said to him, "Follow me." 44 Now Philip was from Bethsaida, the city of Andrew and Peter. 45 Philip found Nathanael and said to him, "We have found him about whom Moses in the law and also the prophets wrote, Jesus son of Joseph from Nazareth." 46 Nathanael said to him, "Can anything good come out of Nazareth?" Philip said to him, "Come and see." 47 When Jesus saw Nathanael coming toward him, he said of him, "Here is truly an Israelite in whom there is no deceit!" 48 Nathanael asked him, "Where did you get to know me?" Jesus answered, "I saw you under the fig tree before Philip called you." 49 Nathanael replied, "Rabbi, you are the Son of God! You are the King of Israel!" 50 Jesus answered, "Do you believe because I told you that I saw you under the fig tree? You will see greater things than these." 51 And he said to him, "Very

19 THIS is the testimony John gave when the Jews of Jerusalem sent a deputation of priests and Levites to ask him who he was. 20 He readily acknowledged, 'I am not the Messiah.' 21 'What then? Are you Elijah?' 'I am not,' he replied. 'Are you the Prophet?' 'No,' he said. 22 'Then who are you?' they asked. 'We must give an answer to those who sent us. What account do you give of yourself?' 23 He answered in the words of the prophet Isaiah: 'I am a voice crying in the wilderness, "Make straight the way for the Lord."'

24 Some Pharisees who were in the deputation 25 asked him, 'If you are not the Messiah, nor Elijah, nor the Prophet, then why are you baptizing?' 26 'I baptize in water,' John replied, 'but among you, though you do not know him, stands the one 27 who is to come after me. I am not worthy to unfasten the strap of his sandal.' 28 This took place at Bethany beyond Jordan, where John was baptizing.

29 The next day he saw Jesus coming towards him. 'There is the Lamb of God,' he said, 'who takes away the sin of the world. 30 He it is of whom I said, "After me there comes a man who ranks ahead of me"; before I was born, he already was. 31 I did not know who he was; but the reason why I came, baptizing in water, was that he might be revealed to Israel.'

32 John testified again: 'I saw the Spirit come down from heaven like a dove and come to rest on him. 33 I did not know him; but he who sent me to baptize in water had told me, "The man on whom you see the Spirit come down and rest is the one who is to baptize in Holy Spirit." 34 I have seen it and have borne witness: this is God's Chosen One.'

35 The next day again, John was standing with two of his disciples 36 when Jesus passed by. John looked towards him and said, 'There is the Lamb of God!' 37 When the two disciples heard what he said, they followed Jesus. 38 He turned and saw them following; 'What are you looking for?' he asked. They said, 'Rabbi,' (which means 'Teacher') 'where are you staying?' 39 'Come and see,' he replied. So they went and saw where he was staying, and spent the rest of the day with him. It was about four in the afternoon.

40 One of the two who followed Jesus after hearing what John said was Andrew, Simon Peter's brother. 41 The first thing he did was to find his brother Simon and say to him, 'We have found the Messiah' (which is the Hebrew for Christ). 42 He brought Simon to Jesus, who looked at him and said, 'You are Simon son of John; you shall be called Cephas' (that is, Peter, 'the Rock').

43-44 The next day Jesus decided to leave for Galilee. He met Philip, who, like Andrew and Peter, came from Bethsaida, and said to him, 'Follow me.' 45 Philip went to find Nathanael and told him, 'We have found the man of whom Moses wrote in the law, the man foretold by the prophets: it is Jesus son of Joseph, from Nazareth.' 46 'Nazareth!' Nathanael exclaimed. 'Can anything good come from Nazareth?' Philip said, 'Come and see.' 47 When Jesus saw Nathanael coming towards him, he said, 'Here is an Israelite worthy of the name; there is nothing false in him.' 48 Nathanael asked him, 'How is it you know me?' Jesus replied, 'I saw you under the fig tree before Philip spoke to you.' 49 'Rabbi,' said Nathanael, 'you are the Son of God; you are king of Israel.' 50 Jesus answered, 'Do you believe this because I told you I saw you under the fig tree? You will see greater things than that.' 51 Then he added, 'In very truth I

ᵍ Or the Christ   ʰ Other ancient authorities read is God's chosen one   ⁱ Or Christ   ʲ Gk him   ᵏ From the word for rock in Aramaic (kepha) and Greek (petra), respectively

1:34 this . . . One: some witnesses read this is the Son of God.

NEW AMERICAN BIBLE

19 And this is the testimony of John. When the Jews from Jerusalem sent priests and Levites [to him] to ask him, "Who are you?" 20 he admitted and did not deny it, but admitted, "I am not the Messiah." 21 So they asked him, "What are you then? Are you Elijah?" And he said, "I am not." "Are you the Prophet?" He answered, "No." 22 So they said to him, "Who are you, so we can give an answer to those who sent us? What do you have to say for yourself?" 23 He said:

"I am 'the voice of one crying out in the desert,
"Make straight the way of the Lord," '

as Isaiah the prophet said." 24 Some Pharisees were also sent. 25 They asked him, "Why then do you baptize if you are not the Messiah or Elijah or the Prophet?" 26 John answered them, "I baptize with water; but there is one among you whom you do not recognize, 27 the one who is coming after me, whose sandal strap I am not worthy to untie." 28 This happened in Bethany across the Jordan, where John was baptizing.

29 The next day he saw Jesus coming toward him and said, "Behold, the Lamb of God, who takes away the sin of the world. 30 He is the one of whom I said, 'A man is coming after me who ranks ahead of me because he existed before me.' 31 I did not know him, but the reason why I came baptizing with water was that he might be made known to Israel." 32 John testified further, saying, "I saw the Spirit come down like a dove from the sky and remain upon him. 33 I did not know him, but the one who sent me to baptize with water told me, 'On whomever you see the Spirit come down and remain, he is the one who will baptize with the holy Spirit.' 34 Now I have seen and testified that he is the Son of God."

35 The next day John was there again with two of his disciples, 36 and as he watched Jesus walk by, he said, "Behold, the Lamb of God." 37 The two disciples heard what he said and followed Jesus. 38 Jesus turned and saw them following him and said to them, "What are you looking for?" They said to him, "Rabbi" (which translated means Teacher), "where are you staying?" 39 He said to them, "Come, and you will see." So they went and saw where he was staying, and they stayed with him that day. It was about four in the afternoon. 40 Andrew, the brother of Simon Peter, was one of the two who heard John and followed Jesus. 41 He first found his own brother Simon and told him, "We have found the Messiah" (which is translated Anointed). 42 Then he brought him to Jesus. Jesus looked at him and said, "You are Simon the son of John; you will be called Kephas" (which is translated Peter).

43 The next day he decided to go to Galilee, and he found Philip. And Jesus said to him, "Follow me." 44 Now Philip was from Bethsaida, the town of Andrew and Peter. 45 Philip found Nathanael and told him, "We have found the one about whom Moses wrote in the law, and also the prophets, Jesus son of Joseph, from Nazareth." 46 But Nathanael said to him, "Can anything good come from Nazareth?" Philip said to him, "Come and see." 47 Jesus saw Nathanael coming toward him and said of him, "Here is a true Israelite. There is no duplicity in him." 48 Nathanael said to him, "How do you know me?" Jesus answered and said to him, "Before Philip called you, I saw you under the fig tree." 49 Nathanael answered him, "Rabbi, you are the Son of God; you are the King of Israel." 50 Jesus answered and said to him, "Do you believe because I told you that I saw you under the fig tree? You will see greater things than this." 51 And he said to him, "Amen, amen, I say to you,

19 This was the witness of John, when the Jews sent to him priests and Levites from Jerusalem to ask him, 'Who are you?' 20 He declared, he did not deny but declared, 'I am not the Christ.' 21 So they asked, 'Then are you Elijah?' He replied, 'I am not.' 'Are you the Prophet?' He answered, 'No.' 22 So they said to him, 'Who are you? We must take back an answer to those who sent us. What have you to say about yourself?' 23 So he said, 'I am, as Isaiah prophesied:

A voice of one that cries in the desert:
Prepare a way for the Lord.
Make his paths straight! c

24 Now those who had been sent were Pharisees, 25 and they put this question to him, 'Why are you baptising if you are not the Christ, and not Elijah, and not the Prophet?' 26 John answered them, 'I baptise with water; but standing among you — unknown to you — 27 is the one who is coming after me; and I am not fit to undo the strap of his sandal.' 28 This happened at Bethany, on the far side of the Jordan, where John was baptising.

29 The next day, he saw Jesus coming towards him and said, 'Look, there is the lamb of God that takes away the sin of the world. 30 It was of him that I said, "Behind me comes one who has passed ahead of me because he existed before me." 31 I did not know him myself, and yet my purpose in coming to baptise with water was so that he might be revealed to Israel.' 32 And John declared, 'I saw the Spirit come down on him like a dove from heaven and rest on him. 33 I did not know him myself, but he who sent me to baptise with water had said to me, "The man on whom you see the Spirit come down and rest is the one who is to baptise with the Holy Spirit." 34 I have seen and I testify that he is the Chosen One of God.'

35 The next day as John stood there again with two of his disciples, Jesus went past, 36 and John looked towards him and said, 'Look, there is the lamb of God.' 37 And the two disciples heard what he said and followed Jesus. 38 Jesus turned round, saw them following and said, 'What do you want?' They answered, 'Rabbi' — which means Teacher — 'where do you live?' 39 He replied, 'Come and see'; so they went and saw where he lived, and stayed with him that day. It was about the tenth hour.

40 One of these two who became followers of Jesus after hearing what John had said was Andrew, the brother of Simon Peter. 41 The first thing Andrew did was to find his brother and say to him, 'We have found the Messiah' — which means the Christ — 42 and he took Simon to Jesus. Jesus looked at him and said, 'You are Simon son of John; you are to be called Cephas' — which means Rock.

43 The next day, after Jesus had decided to leave for Galilee, he met Philip and said, 'Follow me.' 44 Philip came from the same town, Bethsaida, as Andrew and Peter. 45 Philip found Nathanael and said to him, 'We have found him of whom Moses in the Law and the prophets wrote, Jesus son of Joseph, from Nazareth.' 46 Nathanael said to him, 'From Nazareth? Can anything good come from that place?' Philip replied, 'Come and see.' 47 When Jesus saw Nathanael coming he said of him, 'There, truly, is an Israelite in whom there is no deception.' 48 Nathanael asked, 'How do you know me?' Jesus replied, 'Before Philip came to call you, I saw you under the fig tree.' 49 Nathanael answered, 'Rabbi, you are the Son of God, you are the king of Israel.' 50 Jesus replied, 'You believe that just because I said: I saw you under the fig tree. You are going to see greater things than that.' 51 And then he added, 'In all truth

c 1 Is 40:3.

NEW REVISED STANDARD VERSION

REVISED ENGLISH BIBLE

truly, I tell you,*l* you will see heaven opened and the angels of God ascending and descending upon the Son of Man."

2 On the third day there was a wedding in Cana of Galilee, and the mother of Jesus was there. 2 Jesus and his disciples had also been invited to the wedding. 3 When the wine gave out, the mother of Jesus said to him, "They have no wine." 4 And Jesus said to her, "Woman, what concern is that to you and to me? My hour has not yet come." 5 His mother said to the servants, "Do whatever he tells you." 6 Now standing there were six stone water jars for the Jewish rites of purification, each holding twenty or thirty gallons. 7 Jesus said to them, "Fill the jars with water." And they filled them up to the brim. 8 He said to them, "Now draw some out, and take it to the chief steward." So they took it. 9 When the steward tasted the water that had become wine, and did not know where it came from (though the servants who had drawn the water knew), the steward called the bridegroom 10 and said to him, "Everyone serves the good wine first, and then the inferior wine after the guests have become drunk. But you have kept the good wine until now." 11 Jesus did this, the first of his signs, in Cana of Galilee, and revealed his glory; and his disciples believed in him.

12 After this he went down to Capernaum with his mother, his brothers, and his disciples; and they remained there a few days.

13 The Passover of the Jews was near, and Jesus went up to Jerusalem. 14 In the temple he found people selling cattle, sheep, and doves, and the money changers seated at their tables. 15 Making a whip of cords, he drove all of them out of the temple, both the sheep and the cattle. He also poured out the coins of the money changers and overturned their tables. 16 He told those who were selling the doves, "Take these things out of here! Stop making my Father's house a marketplace!" 17 His disciples remembered that it was written, "Zeal for your house will consume me." 18 The Jews then said to him, "What sign can you show us for doing this?" 19 Jesus answered them, "Destroy this temple, and in three days I will raise it up." 20 The Jews then said, "This temple has been under construction for forty-six years, and will you raise it up in three days?" 21 But he was speaking of the temple of his body. 22 After he was raised from the dead, his disciples remembered that he had said this; and they believed the scripture and the word that Jesus had spoken.

23 When he was in Jerusalem during the Passover festival, many believed in his name because they saw the signs that he was doing. 24 But Jesus on his part would not entrust himself to them, because he knew all people 25 and needed no one to testify about anyone; for he himself knew what was in everyone.

3 Now there was a Pharisee named Nicodemus, a leader of the Jews. 2 He came to Jesus*m* by night and said to him, "Rabbi, we know that you are a teacher who has come from God; for no one can do these signs that you do apart from the presence of God." 3 Jesus answered him, "Very truly, I tell you, no one can see the kingdom of God without being born from above."*n* 4 Nicodemus said to him, "How can anyone be born after having grown old? Can one enter a second time into the mother's womb and be born?" 5 Jesus answered, "Very truly, I tell you, no one can enter the kingdom of God without being born of water and Spirit.

tell you all: you will see heaven wide open and God's angels ascending and descending upon the Son of Man.'

2 TWO DAYS later there was a wedding at Cana-in-Galilee. The mother of Jesus was there, 2 and Jesus and his disciples were also among the guests. 3 The wine gave out, so Jesus's mother said to him, 'They have no wine left.' 4 He answered, 'That is no concern of mine. My hour has not yet come.' 5 His mother said to the servants, 'Do whatever he tells you.' 6 There were six stone water-jars standing near, of the kind used for Jewish rites of purification; each held from twenty to thirty gallons. 7 Jesus said to the servants, 'Fill the jars with water,' and they filled them to the brim. 8 'Now draw some off,' he ordered, 'and take it to the master of the feast'; and they did so. 9 The master tasted the water now turned into wine, not knowing its source, though the servants who had drawn the water knew. He hailed the bridegroom 10 and said, 'Everyone else serves the best wine first, and the poorer only when the guests have drunk freely; but you have kept the best wine till now.'

11 So Jesus performed at Cana-in-Galilee the first of the signs which revealed his glory and led his disciples to believe in him.

12 AFTER this he went down to Capernaum with his mother, his brothers, and his disciples, and they stayed there a few days. 13 As it was near the time of the Jewish Passover, Jesus went up to Jerusalem. 14 In the temple precincts he found the dealers in cattle, sheep, and pigeons, and the money-changers seated at their tables. 15 He made a whip of cords and drove them out of the temple, sheep, cattle, and all. He upset the tables of the money-changers, scattering their coins. 16 Then he turned on the dealers in pigeons: 'Take them out of here,' he said; 'do not turn my Father's house into a market.' 17 His disciples recalled the words of scripture: 'Zeal for your house will consume me.' 18 The Jews challenged Jesus: 'What sign can you show to justify your action?' 19 'Destroy this temple,' Jesus replied, 'and in three days I will raise it up again.' 20 The Jews said, 'It has taken forty-six years to build this temple. Are you going to raise it up again in three days?' 21 But the temple he was speaking of was his body. 22 After his resurrection his disciples recalled what he had said, and they believed the scripture and the words that Jesus had spoken.

23 WHILE he was in Jerusalem for Passover many put their trust in him when they saw the signs that he performed. 24 But Jesus for his part would not trust himself to them. He knew them all, 25 and had no need of evidence from others about anyone, for he himself could tell what was in people.

3 ONE of the Pharisees, called Nicodemus, a member of the Jewish Council, 2 came to Jesus by night. 'Rabbi,' he said, 'we know that you are a teacher sent by God; no one could perform these signs of yours unless God were with him.' 3 Jesus answered, 'In very truth I tell you, no one can see the kingdom of God unless he has been born again.' 4 'But how can someone be born when he is old?' asked Nicodemus. 'Can he enter his mother's womb a second time and be born?' 5 Jesus answered, 'In very truth I tell you, no one can enter the kingdom of God without being born from water and spirit. 6 Flesh can give birth only to flesh; it is

---

l Both instances of the Greek word for *you* in this verse are plural
m Gk *him* *n* Or *born anew*

you will see the sky opened and the angels of God ascending and descending on the Son of Man."

2 On the third day there was a wedding in Cana in Galilee, and the mother of Jesus was there. 2 Jesus and his disciples were also invited to the wedding. 3 When the wine ran short, the mother of Jesus said to him, "They have no wine." 4 [And] Jesus said to her, "Woman, how does your concern affect me? My hour has not yet come." 5 His mother said to the servers, "Do whatever he tells you." 6 Now there were six stone water jars there for Jewish ceremonial washings, each holding twenty to thirty gallons. 7 Jesus told them, "Fill the jars with water." So they filled them to the brim. 8 Then he told them, "Draw some out now and take it to the headwaiter." So they took it. 9 And when the headwaiter tasted the water that had become wine, without knowing where it came from (although the servers who had drawn the water knew), the headwaiter called the bridegroom 10 and said to him, "Everyone serves good wine first, and then when people have drunk freely, an inferior one; but you have kept the good wine until now." 11 Jesus did this as the beginning of his signs in Cana in Galilee and so revealed his glory, and his disciples began to believe in him.

12 After this, he and his mother, [his] brothers, and his disciples went down to Capernaum and stayed there only a few days.

13 Since the Passover of the Jews was near, Jesus went up to Jerusalem. 14 He found in the temple area those who sold oxen, sheep, and doves, as well as the money-changers seated there. 15 He made a whip out of cords and drove them all out of the temple area, with the sheep and oxen, and spilled the coins of the money-changers and overturned their tables, 16 and to those who sold doves he said, "Take these out of here, and stop making my Father's house a marketplace." 17 His disciples recalled the words of scripture, "Zeal for your house will consume me." 18 At this the Jews answered and said to him, "What sign can you show us for doing this?" 19 Jesus answered and said to them, "Destroy this temple and in three days I will raise it up." 20 The Jews said, "This temple has been under construction for forty-six years, and you will raise it up in three days?" 21 But he was speaking about the temple of his body. 22 Therefore, when he was raised from the dead, his disciples remembered that he had said this, and they came to believe the scripture and the word Jesus had spoken.

23 While he was in Jerusalem for the feast of Passover, many began to believe in his name when they saw the signs he was doing. 24 But Jesus would not trust himself to them because he knew them all, 25 and did not need anyone to testify about human nature. He himself understood it well.

3 Now there was a Pharisee named Nicodemus, a ruler of the Jews. 2 He came to Jesus at night and said to him, "Rabbi, we know that you are a teacher who has come from God, for no one can do these signs that you are doing unless God is with him." 3 Jesus answered and said to him, "Amen, amen, I say to you, no one can see the kingdom of God without being born from above." 4 Nicodemus said to him, "How can a person once grown old be born again? Surely he cannot reenter his mother's womb and be born again, can he?" 5 Jesus answered, "Amen, amen, I say to you, no one can enter the kingdom of God without being born of water and Spirit. 6 What is born of flesh is flesh and

I tell you, you will see heaven open and the angels of God ascending and descending over the Son of man.'

2 On the third day there was a wedding at Cana in Galilee. The mother of Jesus was there, 2 and Jesus and his disciples had also been invited. 3 And they ran out of wine, since the wine provided for the feast had all been used, and the mother of Jesus said to him, 'They have no wine.' 4 Jesus said, 'Woman, what do you want from me? My hour has not come yet.' 5 His mother said to the servants, 'Do whatever he tells you.' d 6 There were six stone water jars standing there, meant for the ablutions that are customary among the Jews: each could hold twenty or thirty gallons. 7 Jesus said to the servants, 'Fill the jars with water,' and they filled them to the brim. 8 Then he said to them, 'Draw some out now and take it to the president of the feast.' 9 They did this; the president tasted the water, and it had turned into wine. Having no idea where it came from — though the servants who had drawn the water knew — the president of the feast called the bridegroom 10 and said, 'Everyone serves good wine first and the worse wine when the guests are well wined; but you have kept the best wine till now.'

11 This was the first of Jesus' signs: it was at Cana in Galilee. He revealed his glory, and his disciples believed in him. 12 After this he went down to Capernaum with his mother and his brothers and his disciples, but they stayed there only a few days.

13 When the time of the Jewish Passover was near Jesus went up to Jerusalem, 14 and in the Temple he found people selling cattle and sheep and doves, and the money changers sitting there. 15 Making a whip out of cord, he drove all out of the Temple, sheep and cattle as well, scattered the money changers' coins, knocked their tables over 16 and said to the dove sellers, 'Take all this out of here and stop using my Father's house as a market.' 17 Then his disciples remembered the words of scripture: *I am eaten up with zeal for your house.* e 18 The Jews intervened and said, 'What sign can you show us that you should act like this?' 19 Jesus answered, 'Destroy this Temple, and in three days I will raise it up.' 20 The Jews replied, 'It has taken forty-six years to build this Temple: f are you going to raise it up again in three days?' 21 But he was speaking of the Temple that was his body, 22 and when Jesus rose from the dead, his disciples remembered that he had said this, and they believed the scripture and what he had said.

23 During his stay in Jerusalem for the feast of the Passover many believed in his name when they saw the signs that he did, 24 but Jesus knew all people and did not trust himself to them; 25 he never needed evidence about anyone; he could tell what someone had within.

3 There was one of the Pharisees called Nicodemus, a leader of the Jews, 2 who came to Jesus by night and said, 'Rabbi, we know that you have come from God as a teacher; for no one could perform the signs that you do unless God were with him.' 3 Jesus answered:

In all truth I tell you,
no one can see the kingdom of God
without being born from above.

4 Nicodemus said, 'How can anyone who is already old be born? Is it possible to go back into the womb again and be born?' 5 Jesus replied:

In all truth I tell you,
no one can enter the kingdom of God
without being born through water and the Spirit;

d 2 Gn 41:55.   e 2 Ps 69:9.   f 2 Reconstruction work began in 19 BC, so this is Passover AD 28.

6 What is born of the flesh is flesh, and what is born of the Spirit is spirit.*o* 7 Do not be astonished that I said to you, 'You*p* must be born from above.'*q* 8 The wind*o* blows where it chooses, and you hear the sound of it, but you do not know where it comes from or where it goes. So it is with everyone who is born of the Spirit." 9 Nicodemus said to him, "How can these things be?" 10 Jesus answered him, "Are you a teacher of Israel, and yet you do not understand these things?

11 "Very truly, I tell you, we speak of what we know and testify to what we have seen; yet you*r* do not receive our testimony. 12 If I have told you about earthly things and you do not believe, how can you believe if I tell you about heavenly things? 13 No one has ascended into heaven except the one who descended from heaven, the Son of Man,*s* 14 And just as Moses lifted up the serpent in the wilderness, so must the Son of Man be lifted up, 15 that whoever believes in him may have eternal life.*t*

16 "For God so loved the world that he gave his only Son, so that everyone who believes in him may not perish but may have eternal life.

17 "Indeed, God did not send the Son into the world to condemn the world, but in order that the world might be saved through him. 18 Those who believe in him are not condemned; but those who do not believe are condemned already, because they have not believed in the name of the only Son of God. 19 And this is the judgment, that the light has come into the world, and people loved darkness rather than light because their deeds were evil. 20 For all who do evil hate the light and do not come to the light, so that their deeds may not be exposed. 21 But those who do what is true come to the light, so that it may be clearly seen that their deeds have been done in God."*t*

22 After this Jesus and his disciples went into the Judean countryside, and he spent some time there with them and baptized. 23 John also was baptizing at Aenon near Salim because water was abundant there; and people kept coming and were being baptized 24 — John, of course, had not yet been thrown into prison.

25 Now a discussion about purification arose between John's disciples and a Jew.*u* 26 They came to John and said to him, "Rabbi, the one who was with you across the Jordan, to whom you testified, here he is baptizing, and all are going to him." 27 John answered, "No one can receive anything except what has been given from heaven. 28 You yourselves are my witnesses that I said, 'I am not the Messiah,*v* but I have been sent ahead of him.' 29 He who has the bride

spirit that gives birth to spirit. 7 You ought not to be astonished when I say, "You must all be born again." 8 The wind blows where it wills; you hear the sound of it, but you do not know where it comes from or where it is going. So it is with everyone who is born from the Spirit.'

9 'How is this possible?' asked Nicodemus. 10 'You a teacher of Israel and ignorant of such things!' said Jesus. 11 'In very truth I tell you, we speak of what we know, and testify to what we have seen, and yet you all reject our testimony. 12 If you do not believe me when I talk to you about earthly things, how are you to believe if I should talk about the things of heaven?

13 'No one has gone up into heaven except the one who came down from heaven, the Son of Man who is in heaven. 14 Just as Moses lifted up the serpent in the wilderness, so the Son of Man must be lifted up, 15 in order that everyone who has faith may in him have eternal life.

16 'God so loved the world that he gave his only Son, that everyone who has faith in him may not perish but have eternal life. 17 It was not to judge the world that God sent his Son into the world, but that through him the world might be saved.

18 'No one who puts his faith in him comes under judgement; but the unbeliever has already been judged because he has not put his trust in God's only Son. 19 This is the judgement: the light has come into the world, but people preferred darkness to light because their deeds were evil. 20 Wrongdoers hate the light and avoid it, for fear their misdeeds should be exposed. 21 Those who live by the truth come to the light so that it may be clearly seen that God is in all they do.'

22 After this Jesus went with his disciples into Judaea; he remained there with them and baptized. 23 John too was baptizing at Aenon, near Salim, because water was plentiful in that region; and all the time people were coming for baptism. 24 This was before John's imprisonment.

25 John's disciples were engaged in a debate with some Jews about purification; 26 so they came to John and said, 'Rabbi, there was a man with you on the other side of the Jordan, to whom you bore your witness. Now he is baptizing, and everyone is flocking to him.' 27 John replied: 'One can have only what is given one from Heaven. 28 You yourselves can testify that I said, "I am not the Messiah; I have been sent as his forerunner." 29 It is the bridegroom who

---

o The same Greek word means both *wind* and *spirit* *p* The Greek word for *you* here is plural *q* Or *anew* *r* The Greek word for *you* here and in verse 12 is plural *s* Other ancient authorities add *who is in heaven* *t* Some interpreters hold that the quotation concludes with verse 15 *u* Other ancient authorities read *the Jews* *v* Or *the Christ*

3:8 *wind* and *spirit* are translations of the same Greek word, which has both meanings. 3:13 *Some witnesses omit* who is in heaven. 3:25 *some Jews: some witnesses read* a Jew.

what is born of spirit is spirit. 7 Do not be amazed that I told you, 'You must be born from above.' 8 The wind blows where it wills, and you can hear the sound it makes, but you do not know where it comes from or where it goes; so it is with everyone who is born of the Spirit." 9 Nicodemus answered and said to him, "How can this happen?" 10 Jesus answered and said to him, "You are the teacher of Israel and you do not understand this? 11 Amen, amen, I say to you, we speak of what we know and we testify to what we have seen, but you people do not accept our testimony. 12 If I tell you about earthly things and you do not believe, how will you believe if I tell you about heavenly things? 13 No one has gone up to heaven except the one who has come down from heaven, the Son of Man. 14 And just as Moses lifted up the serpent in the desert, so must the Son of Man be lifted up, 15 so that everyone who believes in him may have eternal life."

16 For God so loved the world that he gave his only Son, so that everyone who believes in him might not perish but might have eternal life. 17 For God did not send his Son into the world to condemn the world, but that the world might be saved through him. 18 Whoever believes in him will not be condemned, but whoever does not believe has already been condemned, because he has not believed in the name of the only Son of God. 19 And this is the verdict, that the light came into the world, but people preferred darkness to light, because their works were evil. 20 For everyone who does wicked things hates the light and does not come toward the light, so that his works might not be exposed. 21 But whoever lives the truth comes to the light, so that his works may be clearly seen as done in God.

22 After this, Jesus and his disciples went into the region of Judea, where he spent some time with them baptizing. 23 John was also baptizing in Aenon near Salim, because there was an abundance of water there, and people came to be baptized, 24 for John had not yet been imprisoned. 25 Now a dispute arose between the disciples of John and a Jew about ceremonial washings. 26 So they came to John and said to him, "Rabbi, the one who was with you across the Jordan, to whom you testified, here he is baptizing and everyone is coming to him." 27 John answered and said, "No one can receive anything except what has been given him from heaven. 28 You yourselves can testify that I said [that] I am not the Messiah, but that I was sent before him.

6 what is born of human nature is human;
  what is born of the Spirit is spirit.
7 Do not be surprised when I say:
  You must be born from above.
8 The wind blows where it pleases;
  you can hear its sound,
  but you cannot tell where it comes from or where
    it is going.
  So it is with everyone who is born of the Spirit.

9 'How is that possible?' asked Nicodemus. 10 Jesus replied, 'You are the Teacher of Israel, and you do not know these things!

11 'In all truth I tell you,
  we speak only about what we know
  and witness only to what we have seen
  and yet you people reject our evidence.
12 If you do not believe me
  when I speak to you about earthly things,
  how will you believe me
  when I speak to you about heavenly things?
13 No one has gone up to heaven
  except the one who came down from heaven,
  the Son of man;
14 as Moses lifted up the snake in the desert,
  so must the Son of man be lifted up
15 so that everyone who believes may have eternal
    life in him.
16 For this is how God loved the world:
  he gave his only Son,
  so that everyone who believes in him may not
    perish
  but may have eternal life.
17 For God sent his Son into the world
  not to judge the world,
  but so that through him the world might be saved.
18 No one who believes in him will be judged;
  but whoever does not believe is judged already,
  because that person does not believe
  in the Name of God's only Son.
19 And the judgement is this:
  though the light has come into the world
  people have preferred
  darkness to the light
  because their deeds were evil.
20 And indeed, everybody who does wrong
  hates the light and avoids it,
  to prevent his actions from being shown up;
21 but whoever does the truth
  comes out into the light,
  so that what he is doing may plainly appear as
    done in God.'

22 After this, Jesus went with his disciples into the Judaean countryside and stayed with them there and baptised. 23 John also was baptising at Aenon near Salim, where there was plenty of water, and people were going there and were being baptised. 24 For John had not yet been put in prison. 25 Now a discussion arose between some of John's disciples and a Jew about purification, 26 so they went to John and said, 'Rabbi, the man who was with you on the far side of the Jordan, the man to whom you bore witness, is baptising now, and everyone is going to him.' 27 John replied:

'No one can have anything
  except what is given him from heaven.

28 'You yourselves can bear me out. I said, "I am not the Christ; I am the one who has been sent to go in front of him."

is the bridegroom. The friend of the bridegroom, who stands and hears him, rejoices greatly at the bridegroom's voice. For this reason my joy has been fulfilled. 30 He must increase, but I must decrease."*w*

31 The one who comes from above is above all; the one who is of the earth belongs to the earth and speaks about earthly things. The one who comes from heaven is above all. 32 He testifies to what he has seen and heard, yet no one accepts his testimony. 33 Whoever has accepted his testimony has certified*x* this, that God is true. 34 He whom God has sent speaks the words of God, for he gives the Spirit without measure. 35 The Father loves the Son and has placed all things in his hands. 36 Whoever believes in the Son has eternal life; whoever disobeys the Son will not see life, but must endure God's wrath.

4 Now when Jesus*y* learned that the Pharisees had heard, "Jesus is making and baptizing more disciples than John" 2 — although it was not Jesus himself but his disciples who baptized — 3 he left Judea and started back to Galilee. 4 But he had to go through Samaria. 5 So he came to a Samaritan city called Sychar, near the plot of ground that Jacob had given to his son Joseph. 6 Jacob's well was there, and Jesus, tired out by his journey, was sitting by the well. It was about noon.

7 A Samaritan woman came to draw water, and Jesus said to her, "Give me a drink." 8 (His disciples had gone to the city to buy food.) 9 The Samaritan woman said to him, "How is it that you, a Jew, ask a drink of me, a woman of Samaria?" (Jews do not share things in common with Samaritans.)*z* 10 Jesus answered her, "If you knew the gift of God, and who it is that is saying to you, 'Give me a drink,' you would have asked him, and he would have given you living water." 11 The woman said to him, "Sir, you have no bucket, and the well is deep. Where do you get that living water? 12 Are you greater than our ancestor Jacob, who gave us the well, and with his sons and his flocks drank from it?" 13 Jesus said to her, "Everyone who drinks of this water will be thirsty again, 14 but those who drink of the water that I will give them will never be thirsty. The water that I will give will become in them a spring of water gushing up to eternal life." 15 The woman said to him, "Sir, give me this water, so that I may never be thirsty or have to keep coming here to draw water."

16 Jesus said to her, "Go, call your husband, and come back." 17 The woman answered him, "I have no husband." Jesus said to her, "You are right in saying, 'I have no husband'; 18 for you have had five husbands, and the one you have now is not your husband. What you have said is true!" 19 The woman said to him, "Sir, I see that you are a prophet. 20 Our ancestors worshiped on this mountain, but

marries the bride. The bridegroom's friend, who stands by and listens to him, is overjoyed at hearing the bridegroom's voice. This is my joy and now it is complete. 30 He must grow greater; I must become less.'

31 He who comes from above is above all others; he who is from the earth belongs to the earth and uses earthly speech. He who comes from heaven 32 bears witness to what he has seen and heard, even though no one accepts his witness. 33 To accept his witness is to affirm that God speaks the truth; 34 for he whom God sent utters the words of God, so measureless is God's gift of the Spirit. 35 The Father loves the Son and has entrusted him with complete authority. 36 Whoever puts his faith in the Son has eternal life. Whoever disobeys the Son will not see that life; God's wrath rests upon him.

4 1-2 NEWS now reached the Pharisees that Jesus was winning and baptizing more disciples than John; although, in fact, it was his disciples who were baptizing, not Jesus himself. When Jesus heard this, 3 he left Judaea and set out once more for Galilee. 4 He had to pass through Samaria, 5 and on his way came to a Samaritan town called Sychar, near the plot of ground which Jacob gave to his son Joseph; 6 Jacob's well was there. It was about noon, and Jesus, tired after his journey, was sitting by the well.

8 His disciples had gone into the town to buy food. 7 Meanwhile a Samaritan woman came to draw water, and Jesus said to her, 'Give me a drink.' 9 The woman said, 'What! You, a Jew, ask for a drink from a Samaritan woman?' (Jews do not share drinking vessels with Samaritans.) 10 Jesus replied, 'If only you knew what God gives, and who it is that is asking you for a drink, you would have asked him and he would have given you living water.' 11 'Sir,' the woman said, 'you have no bucket and the well is deep, so where can you get "living water"? 12 Are you greater than Jacob our ancestor who gave us the well and drank from it himself, he and his sons and his cattle too?' 13 Jesus answered, 'Everyone who drinks this water will be thirsty again; 14 but whoever drinks the water I shall give will never again be thirsty. The water that I shall give will be a spring of water within him, welling up and bringing eternal life.' 15 'Sir,' said the woman, 'give me this water, and then I shall not be thirsty, nor have to come all this way to draw water.'

16 'Go and call your husband,' said Jesus, 'and come back here.' 17 She answered, 'I have no husband.' Jesus said, 'You are right in saying that you have no husband, 18 for though you have had five husbands, the man you are living with now is not your husband. You have spoken the truth!' 19 'Sir,' replied the woman, 'I can see you are a prophet. 20 Our fathers worshipped on this mountain, but

---

w Some interpreters hold that the quotation continues through verse 36
x Gk *set a seal to*   *y* Other ancient authorities read *the Lord*
z Other ancient authorities lack this sentence

3:31 **from heaven:** *some witnesses add* is above all and.
4:9 **Jews . . . Samaritans:** *some witnesses omit these words.*

29 The one who has the bride is the bridegroom; the best man, who stands and listens for him, rejoices greatly at the bridegroom's voice. So this joy of mine has been made complete. 30 He must increase; I must decrease."

31 The one who comes from above is above all. The one who is of the earth is earthly and speaks of earthly things. But the one who comes from heaven [is above all]. 32 He testifies to what he has seen and heard, but no one accepts his testimony. 33 Whoever does accept his testimony certifies that God is trustworthy. 34 For the one whom God sent speaks the words of God. He does not ration his gift of the Spirit. 35 The Father loves the Son and has given everything over to him. 36 Whoever believes in the Son has eternal life, but whoever disobeys the Son will not see life, but the wrath of God remains upon him.

4 Now when Jesus learned that the Pharisees had heard that Jesus was making and baptizing more disciples than John 2 (although Jesus himself was not baptizing, just his disciples), 3 he left Judea and returned to Galilee. 4 He had to pass through Samaria. 5 So he came to a town of Samaria called Sychar, near the plot of land that Jacob had given to his son Joseph. 6 Jacob's well was there. Jesus, tired from his journey, sat down there at the well. It was about noon.

7 A woman of Samaria came to draw water. Jesus said to her, "Give me a drink." 8 His disciples had gone into the town to buy food. 9 The Samaritan woman said to him, "How can you, a Jew, ask me, a Samaritan woman, for a drink?" (For Jews use nothing in common with Samaritans.) 10 Jesus answered and said to her, "If you knew the gift of God and who is saying to you, 'Give me a drink,' you would have asked him and he would have given you living water." 11 [The woman] said to him, "Sir, you do not even have a bucket and the cistern is deep; where then can you get this living water? 12 Are you greater than our father Jacob, who gave us this cistern and drank from it himself with his children and his flocks?" 13 Jesus answered and said to her, "Everyone who drinks this water will be thirsty again; 14 but whoever drinks the water I shall give will never thirst; the water I shall give will become in him a spring of water welling up to eternal life." 15 The woman said to him, "Sir, give me this water, so that I may not be thirsty or have to keep coming here to draw water."

16 Jesus said to her, "Go call your husband and come back." 17 The woman answered and said to him, "I do not have a husband." Jesus answered her, "You are right in saying, 'I do not have a husband.' 18 For you have had five husbands, and the one you have now is not your husband. What you have said is true." 19 The woman said to him, "Sir, I can see that you are a prophet. 20 Our ancestors

29 'It is the bridegroom who has the bride;
and yet the bridegroom's friend,
who stands there and listens to him,
is filled with joy at the bridegroom's voice.
This is the joy I feel, and it is complete.
30 He must grow greater,
I must grow less.
31 He who comes from above
is above all others;
he who is of the earth
is earthly himself and speaks in an earthly way.
He who comes from heaven
32 bears witness to the things he has seen and heard,
but his testimony is not accepted by anybody;
33 though anyone who does accept his testimony
is attesting that God is true,
34 since he whom God has sent
speaks God's own words,
for God gives him the Spirit without reserve.
35 The Father loves the Son
and has entrusted everything to his hands.
36 Anyone who believes in the Son has eternal life,
but anyone who refuses to believe in the Son will
never see life:
God's retribution hangs over him.'

4 When Jesus heard that the Pharisees had found out that he was making and baptising more disciples than John — 2 though in fact it was his disciples who baptised, not Jesus himself — 3 he left Judaea and went back to Galilee. 4 He had to pass through Samaria. 5 On the way he came to the Samaritan town called Sychar near the land that Jacob gave to his son Joseph. 6 Jacob's well was there and Jesus, tired by the journey, sat down by the well. It was about the sixth hour. 7 When a Samaritan woman came to draw water, Jesus said to her, 'Give me something to drink.' 8 His disciples had gone into the town to buy food. 9 The Samaritan woman said to him, 'You are a Jew. How is it that you ask me, a Samaritan, for something to drink?' — Jews, of course, do not associate with Samaritans. 10 Jesus replied to her:

If you only knew what God is offering
and who it is that is saying to you,
'Give me something to drink,'
you would have been the one to ask,
and he would have given you living water.

11 'You have no bucket, sir,' she answered, 'and the well is deep: how do you get this living water? 12 Are you a greater man than our father Jacob, who gave us this well and drank from it himself with his sons and his cattle?' 13 Jesus replied:

Whoever drinks this water
will be thirsty again;
14 but no one who drinks the water that I shall give
will ever be thirsty again:
the water that I shall give
will become a spring of water within, welling up
for eternal life.

15 'Sir,' said the woman, 'give me some of that water, so that I may never be thirsty or come here again to draw water.' 16 'Go and call your husband,' said Jesus to her, 'and come back here.' 17 The woman answered, 'I have no husband.' Jesus said to her, 'You are right to say, "I have no husband"; 18 for although you have had five, the one you now have is not your husband. You spoke the truth there.' 19 'I see you are a prophet, sir,' said the woman. 20 'Our

you*a* say that the place where people must worship is in Jerusalem." 21 Jesus said to her, "Woman, believe me, the hour is coming when you will worship the Father neither on this mountain nor in Jerusalem. 22 You worship what you do not know; we worship what we know, for salvation is from the Jews. 23 But the hour is coming, and is now here, when the true worshipers will worship the Father in spirit and truth, for the Father seeks such as these to worship him. 24 God is spirit, and those who worship him must worship in spirit and truth." 25 The woman said to him, "I know that Messiah is coming" (who is called Christ). "When he comes, he will proclaim all things to us." 26 Jesus said to her, "I am he,*b* the one who is speaking to you."

27 Just then his disciples came. They were astonished that he was speaking with a woman, but no one said, "What do you want?" or, "Why are you speaking with her?" 28 Then the woman left her water jar and went back to the city. She said to the people, 29 "Come and see a man who told me everything I have ever done! He cannot be the Messiah,*c* can he?" 30 They left the city and were on their way to him.

31 Meanwhile the disciples were urging him, "Rabbi, eat something." 32 But he said to them, "I have food to eat that you do not know about." 33 So the disciples said to one another, "Surely no one has brought him something to eat?" 34 Jesus said to them, "My food is to do the will of him who sent me and to complete his work. 35 Do you not say, 'Four months more, then comes the harvest'? But I tell you, look around you, and see how the fields are ripe for harvesting. 36 The reaper is already receiving*d* wages and is gathering fruit for eternal life, so that sower and reaper may rejoice together. 37 For here the saying holds true, 'One sows and another reaps.' 38 I sent you to reap that for which you did not labor. Others have labored, and you have entered into their labor."

39 Many Samaritans from that city believed in him because of the woman's testimony, "He told me everything I have ever done." 40 So when the Samaritans came to him, they asked him to stay with them; and he stayed there two days. 41 And many more believed because of his word. 42 They said to the woman, "It is no longer because of what you said that we believe, for we have heard for ourselves, and we know that this is truly the Savior of the world."

43 When the two days were over, he went from that place to Galilee 44 (for Jesus himself had testified that a prophet has no honor in the prophet's own country).

you Jews say that the place where God must be worshipped is in Jerusalem.' 21 'Believe me,' said Jesus, 'the time is coming when you will worship the Father neither on this mountain nor in Jerusalem. 22 You Samaritans worship you know not what; we worship what we know. It is from the Jews that salvation comes. 23 But the time is coming, indeed it is already here, when true worshippers will worship the Father in spirit and in truth. These are the worshippers the Father wants. 24 God is spirit, and those who worship him must worship in spirit and in truth.' 25 The woman answered, 'I know that Messiah' (that is, Christ) 'is coming. When he comes he will make everything clear to us.' 26 Jesus said to her, 'I am he, I who am speaking to you.'

27 At that moment his disciples returned, and were astonished to find him talking with a woman; but none of them said, 'What do you want?' or, 'Why are you talking with her?' 28 The woman left her water-jar and went off to the town, where she said to the people, 29 'Come and see a man who has told me everything I ever did. Could this be the Messiah?' 30 They left the town and made their way towards him.

31 MEANWHILE the disciples were urging him, 'Rabbi, have something to eat.' 32 But he said, 'I have food to eat of which you know nothing.' 33 At this the disciples said to one another, 'Can someone have brought him food?' 34 But Jesus said, 'For me it is meat and drink to do the will of him who sent me until I have finished his work.

35 'Do you not say, "Four months more and then comes harvest"? But look, I tell you, look around at the fields: they are already white, ripe for harvesting. 36 The reaper is drawing his pay and harvesting a crop for eternal life, so that sower and reaper may rejoice together. 37 That is how the saying comes true: "One sows, another reaps." 38 I sent you to reap a crop for which you have not laboured. Others laboured and you have come in for the harvest of their labour.'

39 Many Samaritans of that town came to believe in him because of the woman's testimony: 'He told me everything I ever did.' 40 So when these Samaritans came to him they pressed him to stay with them; and he stayed there two days. 41 Many more became believers because of what they heard from his own lips. 42 They told the woman, 'It is no longer because of what you said that we believe, for we have heard him ourselves; and we are convinced that he is the Saviour of the world.'

43 WHEN the two days were over Jesus left for Galilee; 44 for he himself had declared that a prophet is without honour in his own country. 45 On his arrival the Galileans made him

---

a The Greek word for *you* here and in verses 21 and 22 is plural
b Gk *I am*   *c* Or *the Christ*   *d* Or 35. . . *the fields are already ripe for harvesting.* 36 *The reaper is receiving*

worshiped on this mountain; but you people say that the place to worship is in Jerusalem." 21 Jesus said to her, "Believe me, woman, the hour is coming when you will worship the Father neither on this mountain nor in Jerusalem. 22 You people worship what you do not understand; we worship what we understand, because salvation is from the Jews. 23 But the hour is coming, and is now here, when true worshipers will worship the Father in Spirit and truth; and indeed the Father seeks such people to worship him. 24 God is Spirit, and those who worship him must worship in Spirit and truth." 25 The woman said to him, "I know that the Messiah is coming, the one called the Anointed; when he comes, he will tell us everything." 26 Jesus said to her, "I am he, the one who is speaking with you."

27 At that moment his disciples returned, and were amazed that he was talking with a woman, but still no one said, "What are you looking for?" or "Why are you talking with her?" 28 The woman left her water jar and went into the town and said to the people, 29 "Come see a man who told me everything I have done. Could he possibly be the Messiah?" 30 They went out of the town and came to him. 31 Meanwhile, the disciples urged him, "Rabbi, eat." 32 But he said to them, "I have food to eat of which you do not know." 33 So the disciples said to one another, "Could someone have brought him something to eat?" 34 Jesus said to them, "My food is to do the will of the one who sent me and to finish his work. 35 Do you not say, 'In four months the harvest will be here'? I tell you, look up and see the fields ripe for the harvest. 36 The reaper is already receiving his payment and gathering crops for eternal life, so that the sower and reaper can rejoice together. 37 For here the saying is verified that 'One sows and another reaps.' 38 I sent you to reap what you have not worked for; others have done the work, and you are sharing the fruits of their work."

39 Many of the Samaritans of that town began to believe in him because of the word of the woman who testified, "He told me everything I have done." 40 When the Samaritans came to him, they invited him to stay with them; and he stayed there two days. 41 Many more began to believe in him because of his word, 42 and they said to the woman, "We no longer believe because of your word; for we have heard for ourselves, and we know that this is truly the savior of the world."

43 After the two days, he left there for Galilee. 44 For Jesus himself testified that a prophet has no honor in his native place. 45 When he came into Galilee, the Galileans

fathers worshipped on this mountain, g though you say that Jerusalem is the place where one ought to worship.' 21 Jesus said:

Believe me, woman, the hour is coming
when you will worship the Father
neither on this mountain nor in Jerusalem.
22 You worship what you do not know;
we worship what we do know;
for salvation comes from the Jews.
23 But the hour is coming — indeed is already here —
when true worshippers will worship the Father in
spirit and truth:
that is the kind of worshipper
the Father seeks.
24 God is spirit,
and those who worship
must worship in spirit and truth.

25 The woman said to him, 'I know that Messiah — that is, Christ — is coming; and when he comes he will explain everything.' 26 Jesus said, 'That is who I am, I who speak to you.'

27 At this point his disciples returned and were surprised to find him speaking to a woman, though none of them asked, 'What do you want from her?' or, 'What are you talking to her about?' 28 The woman put down her water jar and hurried back to the town to tell the people, 29 'Come and see a man who has told me everything I have done; could this be the Christ?' 30 This brought people out of the town and they made their way towards him.

31 Meanwhile, the disciples were urging him, 'Rabbi, do have something to eat'; 32 but he said, 'I have food to eat that you do not know about.' 33 So the disciples said to one another, 'Has someone brought him food?' 34 But Jesus said:

My food
is to do the will of the one who sent me,
and to complete his work.
35 Do you not have a saying:
Four months and then the harvest?
Well, I tell you,
look around you, look at the fields;
already they are white, ready for harvest!
36 Already the reaper is being paid his wages,
already he is bringing in the grain for eternal life,
so that sower and reaper can rejoice together.
37 For here the proverb holds true:
one sows, another reaps;
38 I sent you to reap
a harvest you have not laboured for.
Others have laboured for it;
and you have come into the rewards of their
labour.

39 Many Samaritans of that town believed in him on the strength of the woman's words of testimony, 'He told me everything I have done.' 40 So, when the Samaritans came up to him, they begged him to stay with them. He stayed for two days, and 41 many more came to believe on the strength of the words he spoke to them; 42 and they said to the woman, 'Now we believe no longer because of what you told us; we have heard him ourselves and we know that he is indeed the Saviour of the world.'

43 When the two days were over Jesus left for Galilee. 44 He himself had declared that a prophet is not honoured in his own home town. 45 On his arrival the Galileans received

g 4 Gerizim, where there had been a Temple rivalling Jerusalem's. To Jesus both are provisional.

| NEW REVISED STANDARD VERSION | REVISED ENGLISH BIBLE |

NEW REVISED STANDARD VERSION

45 When he came to Galilee, the Galileans welcomed him, since they had seen all that he had done in Jerusalem at the festival; for they too had gone to the festival.

46 Then he came again to Cana in Galilee where he had changed the water into wine. Now there was a royal official whose son lay ill in Capernaum. 47 When he heard that Jesus had come from Judea to Galilee, he went and begged him to come down and heal his son, for he was at the point of death. 48 Then Jesus said to him, "Unless you*e* see signs and wonders you will not believe." 49 The official said to him, "Sir, come down before my little boy dies." 50 Jesus said to him, "Go; your son will live." The man believed the word that Jesus spoke to him and started on his way. 51 As he was going down, his slaves met him and told him that his child was alive. 52 So he asked them the hour when he began to recover, and they said to him, "Yesterday at one in the afternoon the fever left him." 53 The father realized that this was the hour when Jesus had said to him, "Your son will live." So he himself believed, along with his whole household. 54 Now this was the second sign that Jesus did after coming from Judea to Galilee.

5 After this there was a festival of the Jews, and Jesus went up to Jerusalem.

2 Now in Jerusalem by the Sheep Gate there is a pool, called in Hebrew*f* Beth-zatha,*g* which has five porticoes. 3 In these lay many invalids — blind, lame, and paralyzed.*h* 5 One man was there who had been ill for thirty-eight years. 6 When Jesus saw him lying there and knew that he had been there a long time, he said to him, "Do you want to be made well?" 7 The sick man answered him, "Sir, I have no one to put me into the pool when the water is stirred up; and while I am making my way, someone else steps down ahead of me." 8 Jesus said to him, "Stand up, take your mat and walk." 9 At once the man was made well, and he took up his mat and began to walk.

Now that day was a sabbath. 10 So the Jews said to the man who had been cured, "It is the sabbath; it is not lawful for you to carry your mat." 11 But he answered them, "The man who made me well said to me, 'Take up your mat and walk.'" 12 They asked him, "Who is the man who said to you, 'Take it up and walk'?" 13 Now the man who had been healed did not know who it was, for Jesus had disappeared in*i* the crowd that was there. 14 Later Jesus found him in the temple and said to him, "See, you have been made well! Do not sin any more, so that nothing worse happens to you." 15 The man went away and told the Jews that it was Jesus who had made him well. 16 Therefore the Jews started persecuting Jesus, because he was doing such things on the sabbath. 17 But Jesus answered them, "My Father is still working, and I also am working." 18 For this reason the Jews were seeking all the more to kill him, because he was not only breaking the sabbath, but was also calling God his own Father, thereby making himself equal to God.

19 Jesus said to them, "Very truly, I tell you, the Son can do nothing on his own, but only what he sees the Father doing; for whatever the Father*j* does, the Son does likewise. 20 The Father loves the Son and shows him all that he himself is doing; and he will show him greater works than these, so that you will be astonished. 21 Indeed, just as the

REVISED ENGLISH BIBLE

welcome, because they had seen all he did at the festival in Jerusalem; they had been at the festival themselves.

46 Once again he visited Cana-in-Galilee, where he had turned the water into wine. An officer in the royal service was there, whose son was lying ill at Capernaum. 47 When he heard that Jesus had come from Judaea into Galilee, he went to him and begged him to go down and cure his son, who was at the point of death. 48 Jesus said to him, 'Will none of you ever believe without seeing signs and portents?' 49 The officer pleaded with him, 'Sir, come down before my boy dies.' 50 'Return home,' said Jesus; 'your son will live.' The man believed what Jesus said and started for home. 51 While he was on his way down his servants met him with the news that his child was going to live. 52 So he asked them at what time he had begun to recover, and they told him, 'It was at one o'clock yesterday afternoon that the fever left him.' 53 The father realized that this was the time at which Jesus had said to him, 'Your son will live,' and he and all his household became believers.

54 This was the second sign which Jesus performed after coming from Judaea into Galilee.

5 Some time later, Jesus went up to Jerusalem for one of the Jewish festivals. 2 Now at the Sheep Gate in Jerusalem there is a pool whose Hebrew name is Bethesda. It has five colonnades 3 and in them lay a great number of sick people, blind, lame, and paralysed. 5 Among them was a man who had been crippled for thirty-eight years. 6 Jesus saw him lying there, and knowing that he had been ill a long time he asked him, 'Do you want to get well?' 7 'Sir,' he replied, 'I have no one to put me in the pool when the water is disturbed; while I am getting there, someone else steps into the pool before me.' 8 Jesus answered, 'Stand up, take your bed and walk.' 9 The man recovered instantly; he took up his bed, and began to walk.

That day was a sabbath. 10 So the Jews said to the man who had been cured, 'It is the sabbath. It is against the law for you to carry your bed.' 11 He answered, 'The man who cured me, he told me, "Take up your bed and walk."' 12 They asked him, 'Who is this man who told you to take it up and walk?' 13 But the man who had been cured did not know who it was; for the place was crowded and Jesus had slipped away. 14 A little later Jesus found him in the temple and said to him, 'Now that you are well, give up your sinful ways, or something worse may happen to you.' 15 The man went off and told the Jews that it was Jesus who had cured him.

16 It was for doing such things on the sabbath that the Jews began to take action against Jesus. 17 He defended himself by saying, 'My Father continues to work, and I must work too.' 18 This made the Jews all the more determined to kill him, because not only was he breaking the sabbath but, by calling God his own Father, he was claiming equality with God.

19 To this charge Jesus replied, 'In very truth I tell you, the Son can do nothing by himself; he does only what he sees the Father doing: whatever the Father does, the Son does. 20 For the Father loves the Son and shows him all that he himself is doing, and will show him even greater deeds, to fill you with wonder. 21 As the Father raises the dead and

---

e Both instances of the Greek word for *you* in this verse are plural *f* That is, *Aramaic*   *g* Other ancient authorities read *Bethesda*, others *Bethsaida*   *h* Other ancient authorities add, wholly or in part, *waiting for the stirring of the water;* 4*for an angel of the Lord went down at certain seasons into the pool, and stirred up the water; whoever stepped in first after the stirring of the water was made well from whatever disease that person had.*   *i* Or *had left because of*   *j* Gk *that one*

5:3 **paralysed:** *some witnesses add* waiting for the disturbance of the water; *some also add* 4for from time to time an angel came down into the pool and stirred up the water. The first to plunge in after this disturbance recovered from whatever disease had afflicted him.

NEW AMERICAN BIBLE

NEW JERUSALEM BIBLE

welcomed him, since they had seen all he had done in Jerusalem at the feast; for they themselves had gone to the feast. 46 Then he returned to Cana in Galilee, where he had made the water wine. Now there was a royal official whose son was ill in Capernaum. 47 When he heard that Jesus had arrived in Galilee from Judea, he went to him and asked him to come down and heal his son, who was near death. 48 Jesus said to him, "Unless you people see signs and wonders, you will not believe." 49 The royal official said to him, "Sir, come down before my child dies." 50 Jesus said to him, "You may go; your son will live." The man believed what Jesus said and left. 51 While he was on his way back, his slaves met him and told him that his boy would live. 52 He asked them when he began to recover. They told him, "The fever left him yesterday, about one in the afternoon." 53 The father realized that just at that time Jesus had said to him, "Your son will live," and he and his whole household came to believe. 54 [Now] this was the second sign Jesus did when he came to Galilee from Judea.

5 After this, there was a feast of the Jews, and Jesus went up to Jerusalem. 2 Now there is in Jerusalem at the Sheep [Gate] a pool called in Hebrew Bethesda, with five porticoes. 3 In these lay a large number of ill, blind, lame, and crippled. [4] 5 One man was there who had been ill for thirty-eight years. 6 When Jesus saw him lying there and knew that he had been ill for a long time, he said to him, "Do you want to be well?" 7 The sick man answered him, "Sir, I have no one to put me into the pool when the water is stirred up; while I am on my way, someone else gets down there before me." 8 Jesus said to him, "Rise, take up your mat, and walk." 9 Immediately the man became well, took up his mat, and walked.

Now that day was a sabbath. 10 So the Jews said to the man who was cured, "It is the sabbath, and it is not lawful for you to carry your mat." 11 He answered them, "The man who made me well told me, 'Take up your mat and walk.'" 12 They asked him, "Who is the man who told you, 'Take it up and walk'?" 13 The man who was healed did not know who it was, for Jesus had slipped away, since there was a crowd there. 14 After this Jesus found him in the temple area and said to him, "Look, you are well; do not sin any more, so that nothing worse may happen to you." 15 The man went and told the Jews that Jesus was the one who had made him well. 16 Therefore, the Jews began to persecute Jesus because he did this on a sabbath. 17 But Jesus answered them, "My Father is at work until now, so I am at work." 18 For this reason the Jews tried all the more to kill him, because he not only broke the sabbath but he also called God his own father, making himself equal to God.

19 Jesus answered and said to them, "Amen, amen, I say to you, a son cannot do anything on his own, but only what he sees his father doing; for what he does, his son will do also. 20 For the Father loves his Son and shows him everything that he himself does, and he will show him greater works than these, so that you may be amazed. 21 For just as

him well, having seen all that he had done at Jerusalem during the festival which they too had attended. 46 He went again to Cana in Galilee, where he had changed the water into wine. And there was a royal official whose son was ill at Capernaum; 47 hearing that Jesus had arrived in Galilee from Judaea, he went and asked him to come and cure his son, as he was at the point of death. 48 Jesus said to him, 'Unless you see signs and portents you will not believe!' 49 'Sir,' answered the official, 'come down before my child dies.' 50 'Go home,' said Jesus, 'your son will live.' The man believed what Jesus had said and went on his way home; 51 and while he was still on the way his servants met him with the news that his boy was alive. 52 He asked them when the boy had begun to recover. They replied, 'The fever left him yesterday at the seventh hour.' 53 The father realised that this was exactly the time when Jesus had said, 'Your son will live'; and he and all his household believed. 54 This new sign, the second, Jesus performed on his return from Judaea to Galilee.

5 After this there was a Jewish festival, and Jesus went up to Jerusalem. 2 Now in Jerusalem next to the Sheep Pool there is a pool called Bethesda in Hebrew, which has five porticos; 3 and under these were crowds of sick people, blind, lame, paralysed. h 5 One man there had an illness which had lasted thirty-eight years, 6 and when Jesus saw him lying there and knew he had been in that condition for a long time, he said, 'Do you want to be well again?' 7 'Sir,' replied the sick man, 'I have no one to put me into the pool when the water is disturbed; and while I am still on the way, someone else gets down there before me.' 8 Jesus said, 'Get up, pick up your sleeping-mat and walk around.' 9 The man was cured at once, and he picked up his mat and started to walk around.

Now that day happened to be the Sabbath, 10 so the Jews said to the man who had been cured, 'It is the Sabbath; you are not allowed to carry your sleeping-mat.' 11 He replied, 'But the man who cured me told me, "Pick up your sleeping-mat and walk around."' 12 They asked, 'Who is the man who said to you, "Pick up your sleeping-mat and walk around"?' 13 The man had no idea who it was, since Jesus had disappeared, as the place was crowded. 14 After a while Jesus met him in the Temple and said, 'Now you are well again, do not sin any more, or something worse may happen to you.' 15 The man went back and told the Jews that it was Jesus who had cured him. 16 It was because he did things like this on the Sabbath that the Jews began to harass Jesus. 17 His answer to them was, 'My Father still goes on working, and I am at work, too.' 18 But that only made the Jews even more intent on killing him, because not only was he breaking the Sabbath, but he spoke of God as his own Father and so made himself God's equal.

19 To this Jesus replied:

In all truth I tell you,
by himself the Son can do nothing;
he can do only what he sees the Father doing:
and whatever the Father does the Son does too.
20 For the Father loves the Son
and shows him everything he himself does,
and he will show him even greater things than
these,
works that will astonish you.

5, 4: Toward the end of the second century in the West and among the fourth-century Greek Fathers, an additional verse was known: "For [from time to time] an angel of the Lord used to come down into the pool; and the water was stirred up, so the first one to get in [after the stirring of the water] was healed of whatever disease afflicted him." This verse is missing from all early Greek manuscripts and the earliest versions, including the original Vulgate.

h 5 Some ancient MSS add: 'waiting for the water to move; 4 for at intervals the angel of the Lord came down into the pool, and the water was disturbed, and the first person to enter the water after this disturbance was cured of any ailment from which he was suffering'.

Father raises the dead and gives them life, so also the Son gives life to whomever he wishes. 22 The Father judges no one but has given all judgment to the Son, 23 so that all may honor the Son just as they honor the Father. Anyone who does not honor the Son does not honor the Father who sent him. 24 Very truly, I tell you, anyone who hears my word and believes him who sent me has eternal life, and does not come under judgment, but has passed from death to life.

25 "Very truly, I tell you, the hour is coming, and is now here, when the dead will hear the voice of the Son of God, and those who hear will live. 26 For just as the Father has life in himself, so he has granted the Son also to have life in himself; 27 and he has given him authority to execute judgment, because he is the Son of Man. 28 Do not be astonished at this; for the hour is coming when all who are in their graves will hear his voice 29 and will come out — those who have done good, to the resurrection of life, and those who have done evil, to the resurrection of condemnation.

30 "I can do nothing on my own. As I hear, I judge; and my judgment is just, because I seek to do not my own will but the will of him who sent me.

31 "If I testify about myself, my testimony is not true. 32 There is another who testifies on my behalf, and I know that his testimony to me is true. 33 You sent messengers to John, and he testified to the truth. 34 Not that I accept such human testimony, but I say these things so that you may be saved. 35 He was a burning and shining lamp, and you were willing to rejoice for a while in his light. 36 But I have a testimony greater than John's. The works that the Father has given me to complete, the very works that I am doing, testify on my behalf that the Father has sent me. 37 And the Father who sent me has himself testified on my behalf. You have never heard his voice or seen his form, 38 and you do not have his word abiding in you, because you do not believe him whom he has sent.

39 "You search the scriptures because you think that in them you have eternal life; and it is they that testify on my behalf. 40 Yet you refuse to come to me to have life. 41 I do not accept glory from human beings. 42 But I know that you do not have the love of God in*k* you. 43 I have come in my

gives them life, so the Son gives life as he chooses. 22 Again, the Father does not judge anyone, but has given full jurisdiction to the Son; 23 it is his will that all should pay the same honour to the Son as to the Father. To deny honour to the Son is to deny it to the Father who sent him.

24 'In very truth I tell you, whoever heeds what I say and puts his trust in him who sent me has eternal life; he does not come to judgement, but has already passed from death to life. 25 In very truth I tell you, the time is coming, indeed it is already here, when the dead shall hear the voice of the Son of God, and those who hear shall come to life. 26 For as the Father has life in himself, so by his gift the Son also has life in himself.

27 'As Son of Man he has also been given authority to pass judgement. 28 Do not be surprised at this, because the time is coming when all who are in the grave shall hear his voice 29 and come out: those who have done right will rise to life; those who have done wrong will rise to judgement. 30 I cannot act by myself; I judge as I am bidden, and my sentence is just, because I seek to do not my own will, but the will of him who sent me.

31 'If I testify on my own behalf, that testimony is not valid. 32 There is another who bears witness for me, and I know that his testimony about me is valid. 33 You sent messengers to John, and he has testified to the truth. 34 Not that I rely on human testimony, but I remind you of it for your own salvation. 35 John was a brightly burning lamp, and for a time you were ready to exult in his light. 36 But I rely on a testimony higher than John's: the work my Father has given me to do and to finish, the very work I have in hand, testifies that the Father has sent me. 37 And the Father who has sent me has borne witness on my behalf. His voice you have never heard, his form you have never seen; 38 his word has found no home in you, because you do not believe the one whom he sent. 39 You study the scriptures diligently, supposing that in having them you have eternal life; their testimony points to me, 40 yet you refuse to come to me to receive that life.

41 'I do not look to men for honour. 42 But I know that with you it is different, for you have no love of God in you.

the Father raises the dead and gives life, so also does the Son give life to whomever he wishes. 22 Nor does the Father judge anyone, but he has given all judgment to his Son, 23 so that all may honor the Son just as they honor the Father. Whoever does not honor the Son does not honor the Father who sent him. 24 Amen, amen, I say to you, whoever hears my word and believes in the one who sent me has eternal life and will not come to condemnation, but has passed from death to life. 25 Amen, amen, I say to you, the hour is coming and is now here when the dead will hear the voice of the Son of God, and those who hear will live. 26 For just as the Father has life in himself, so also he gave to his Son the possession of life in himself. 27 And he gave him power to exercise judgment, because he is the Son of Man. 28 Do not be amazed at this, because the hour is coming in which all who are in the tombs will hear his voice 29 and will come out, those who have done good deeds to the resurrection of life, but those who have done wicked deeds to the resurrection of condemnation.

30 "I cannot do anything on my own; I judge as I hear, and my judgment is just, because I do not seek my own will but the will of the one who sent me.

31 "If I testify on my own behalf, my testimony cannot be verified. 32 But there is another who testifies on my behalf, and I know that the testimony he gives on my behalf is true. 33 You sent emissaries to John, and he testified to the truth. 34 I do not accept testimony from a human being, but I say this so that you may be saved. 35 He was a burning and shining lamp, and for a while you were content to rejoice in his light. 36 But I have testimony greater than John's. The works that the Father gave me to accomplish, these works that I perform testify on my behalf that the Father has sent me. 37 Moreover, the Father who sent me has testified on my behalf. But you have never heard his voice nor seen his form, 38 and you do not have his word remaining in you, because you do not believe in the one whom he has sent. 39 You search the scriptures, because you think you have eternal life through them; even they testify on my behalf. 40 But you do not want to come to me to have life.

41 "I do not accept human praise; 42 moreover, I know that you do not have the love of God in you. 43 I came in the

21 Thus, as the Father raises the dead and gives them life,
so the Son gives life to anyone he chooses;
22 for the Father judges no one;
he has entrusted all judgement to the Son,
23 so that all may honour the Son
as they honour the Father.
Whoever refuses honour to the Son
refuses honour to the Father who sent him.
24 In all truth I tell you,
whoever listens to my words,
and believes in the one who sent me,
has eternal life;
without being brought to judgement
such a person has passed from death to life.
25 In all truth I tell you,
the hour is coming — indeed it is already here —
when the dead will hear the voice of the Son of God,
and all who hear it will live.
26 For as the Father has life in himself,
so he has granted the Son also to have life in himself;
27 and, because he is the Son of man,
has granted him power to give judgement.
28 Do not be surprised at this,
for the hour is coming
when the dead will leave their graves
at the sound of his voice:
29 those who did good
will come forth to life;
and those who did evil will come forth to judgement.
30 By myself I can do nothing;
I can judge only as I am told to judge,
and my judging is just,
because I seek to do not my own will
but the will of him who sent me.
31 Were I to testify on my own behalf,
my testimony would not be true;
32 but there is another witness who speaks on my behalf,
and I know that his testimony is true.
33 You sent messengers to John,
and he gave his testimony to the truth —
34 not that I depend on human testimony;
no, it is for your salvation that I mention it.
35 John was a lamp lit and shining
and for a time you were content to enjoy the light that he gave.
36 But my testimony is greater than John's:
the deeds my Father has given me to perform,
these same deeds of mine
testify that the Father has sent me.
37 Besides, the Father who sent me
bears witness to me himself.
You have never heard his voice,
you have never seen his shape,
38 and his word finds no home in you
because you do not believe
in the one whom he has sent.

39 You pore over the scriptures,
believing that in them you can find eternal life;
it is these scriptures that testify to me,
40 and yet you refuse to come to me to receive life!
41 Human glory means nothing to me.
42 Besides, I know you too well:
you have no love of God in you.

NEW REVISED STANDARD VERSION

Father's name, and you do not accept me; if another comes in his own name, you will accept him. 44 How can you believe when you accept glory from one another and do not seek the glory that comes from the one who alone is God? 45 Do not think that I will accuse you before the Father; your accuser is Moses, on whom you have set your hope. 46 If you believed Moses, you would believe me, for he wrote about me. 47 But if you do not believe what he wrote, how will you believe what I say?"

6 After this Jesus went to the other side of the Sea of Galilee, also called the Sea of Tiberias.¹ 2 A large crowd kept following him, because they saw the signs that he was doing for the sick. 3 Jesus went up the mountain and sat down there with his disciples. 4 Now the Passover, the festival of the Jews, was near. 5 When he looked up and saw a large crowd coming toward him, Jesus said to Philip, "Where are we to buy bread for these people to eat?" 6 He said this to test him, for he himself knew what he was going to do. 7 Philip answered him, "Six months' wages*m* would not buy enough bread for each of them to get a little." 8 One of his disciples, Andrew, Simon Peter's brother, said to him, 9 "There is a boy here who has five barley loaves and two fish. But what are they among so many people?" 10 Jesus said, "Make the people sit down." Now there was a great deal of grass in the place; so they*n* sat down, about five thousand in all. 11 Then Jesus took the loaves, and when he had given thanks, he distributed them to those who were seated; so also the fish, as much as they wanted. 12 When they were satisfied, he told his disciples, "Gather up the fragments left over, so that nothing may be lost." 13 So they gathered them up, and from the fragments of the five barley loaves, left by those who had eaten, they filled twelve baskets. 14 When the people saw the sign that he had done, they began to say, "This is indeed the prophet who is to come into the world."

15 When Jesus realized that they were about to come and take him by force to make him king, he withdrew again to the mountain by himself.

16 When evening came, his disciples went down to the sea, 17 got into a boat, and started across the sea to Capernaum. It was now dark, and Jesus had not yet come to them. 18 The sea became rough because a strong wind was blowing. 19 When they had rowed about three or four miles,*o* they saw Jesus walking on the sea and coming near the boat, and they were terrified. 20 But he said to them, "It is I;*p* do not be afraid." 21 Then they wanted to take him into the boat, and immediately the boat reached the land toward which they were going.

22 The next day the crowd that had stayed on the other side of the sea saw that there had been only one boat there. They also saw that Jesus had not got into the boat with his disciples, but that his disciples had gone away alone. 23 Then some boats from Tiberias came near the place where they had eaten the bread after the Lord had given thanks.*q* 24 So when the crowd saw that neither Jesus nor his disciples were there, they themselves got into the boats and went to Capernaum looking for Jesus.

REVISED ENGLISH BIBLE

43 I have come accredited by my Father, and you have no welcome for me; but let someone self-accredited come, and you will give him a welcome. 44 How can you believe when you accept honour from one another, and care nothing for the honour that comes from him who alone is God? 45 Do not imagine that I shall be your accuser at the Father's tribunal. Your accuser is Moses, the very Moses on whom you have set your hope. 46 If you believed him you would believe me, for it was of me that he wrote. 47 But if you do not believe what he wrote, how are you to believe what I say?'

6 SOME time later Jesus withdrew to the farther shore of the sea of Galilee (or Tiberias), 2 and a large crowd of people followed him because they had seen the signs he performed in healing the sick. 3 Jesus went up the hillside and sat down with his disciples. 4 It was near the time of Passover, the great Jewish festival. 5 Looking up and seeing a large crowd coming towards him, Jesus said to Philip, 'Where are we to buy bread to feed these people?' 6 He said this to test him; Jesus himself knew what he meant to do. 7 Philip replied, 'We would need two hundred denarii to buy enough bread for each of them to have a little.' 8 One of his disciples, Andrew, the brother of Simon Peter, said to him, 9 'There is a boy here who has five barley loaves and two fish; but what is that among so many?' 10 Jesus said, 'Make the people sit down.' There was plenty of grass there, so the men sat down, about five thousand of them. 11 Then Jesus took the loaves, gave thanks, and distributed them to the people as they sat there. He did the same with the fish, and they had as much as they wanted. 12 When everyone had had enough, he said to his disciples, 'Gather up the pieces left over, so that nothing is wasted.' 13 They gathered them up, and filled twelve baskets with the pieces of the five barley loaves that were left uneaten.

14 When the people saw the sign Jesus had performed, the word went round, 'Surely this must be the Prophet who was to come into the world.' 15 Jesus, realizing that they meant to come and seize him to proclaim him king, withdrew again to the hills by himself.

16 At nightfall his disciples went down to the sea, 17 and set off by boat to cross to Capernaum. Though darkness had fallen, Jesus had not yet joined them; 18 a strong wind was blowing and the sea grew rough. 19 When they had rowed about three or four miles they saw Jesus walking on the sea and approaching the boat. They were terrified, 20 but he called out, 'It is I; do not be afraid.' 21 With that they were ready to take him on board, and immediately the boat reached the land they were making for.

22 NEXT morning the crowd was still on the opposite shore. They had seen only one boat there, and Jesus, they knew, had not embarked with his disciples, who had set off by themselves. 23 Boats from Tiberias, however, had come ashore near the place where the people had eaten the bread over which the Lord gave thanks. 24 When the crowd saw that Jesus had gone as well as his disciples, they went on board these boats and made for Capernaum in search of him. 25 They found him on the other side. 'Rabbi,' they

---

¹ Gk *of Galilee of Tiberias*   *m* Gk *Two hundred denarii*; the denarius was the usual day's wage for a laborer   *n* Gk *the men*
o Gk *about twenty-five or thirty stadia*   *p* Gk *I am*   *q* Other ancient authorities lack *after the Lord had given thanks*

6:7 **denarii:** *see p. xxix.*   6:23 *Some witnesses omit* over which the Lord gave thanks.

name of my Father, but you do not accept me; yet if another comes in his own name, you will accept him. 44 How can you believe, when you accept praise from one another and do not seek the praise that comes from the only God? 45 Do not think that I will accuse you before the Father: the one who will accuse you is Moses, in whom you have placed your hope. 46 For if you had believed Moses, you would have believed me, because he wrote about me. 47 But if you do not believe his writings, how will you believe my words?"

6 After this, Jesus went across the Sea of Galilee [of Tiberias]. 2 A large crowd followed him, because they saw the signs he was performing on the sick. 3 Jesus went up on the mountain, and there he sat down with his disciples. 4 The Jewish feast of Passover was near. 5 When Jesus raised his eyes and saw that a large crowd was coming to him, he said to Philip, "Where can we buy enough food for them to eat?" 6 He said this to test him, because he himself knew what he was going to do. 7 Philip answered him, "Two hundred days' wages worth of food would not be enough for each of them to have a little [bit]." 8 One of his disciples, Andrew, the brother of Simon Peter, said to him, 9 "There is a boy here who has five barley loaves and two fish; but what good are these for so many?" 10 Jesus said, "Have the people recline." Now there was a great deal of grass in that place. So the men reclined, about five thousand in number. 11 Then Jesus took the loaves, gave thanks, and distributed them to those who were reclining, and also as much of the fish as they wanted. 12 When they had had their fill, he said to his disciples, "Gather the fragments left over, so that nothing will be wasted." 13 So they collected them, and filled twelve wicker baskets with fragments from the five barley loaves that had been more than they could eat. 14 When the people saw the sign he had done, they said, "This is truly the Prophet, the one who is to come into the world." 15 Since Jesus knew that they were going to come and carry him off to make him king, he withdrew again to the mountain alone.

16 When it was evening, his disciples went down to the sea, 17 embarked in a boat, and went across the sea to Capernaum. It had already grown dark, and Jesus had not yet come to them. 18 The sea was stirred up because a strong wind was blowing. 19 When they had rowed about three or four miles, they saw Jesus walking on the sea and coming near the boat, and they began to be afraid. 20 But he said to them, "It is I. Do not be afraid." 21 They wanted to take him into the boat, but the boat immediately arrived at the shore to which they were heading.

22 The next day, the crowd that remained across the sea saw that there had been only one boat there, and that Jesus had not gone along with his disciples in the boat, but only his disciples had left. 23 Other boats came from Tiberias near the place where they had eaten the bread when the Lord gave thanks. 24 When the crowd saw that neither Jesus nor his disciples were there, they themselves got into boats and came to Capernaum looking for Jesus. 25 And when they

43 I have come in the name of my Father
and you refuse to accept me;
if someone else should come in his own name
you would accept him.
44 How can you believe,
since you look to each other for glory
and are not concerned
with the glory that comes from the one God?
45 Do not imagine that I am going to accuse you
before the Father:
you have placed your hopes on Moses,
and Moses will be the one who accuses you.
46 If you really believed him
you would believe me too,
since it was about me that he was writing;
47 but if you will not believe what he wrote,
how can you believe what I say?

6 After this, Jesus crossed the Sea of Galilee — or of Tiberias — 2 and a large crowd followed him, impressed by the signs he had done in curing the sick. 3 Jesus climbed the hillside and sat down there with his disciples. 4 The time of the Jewish Passover was near. 5 Looking up, Jesus saw the crowds approaching and said to Philip, 'Where can we buy some bread for these people to eat?' 6 He said this only to put Philip to the test; he himself knew exactly what he was going to do. 7 Philip answered, 'Two hundred denarii would not buy enough to give them a little piece each.' 8 One of his disciples, Andrew, Simon Peter's brother, said, 9 'Here is a small boy with five barley loaves and two fish; but what is that among so many?' 10 Jesus said to them, 'Make the people sit down.' There was plenty of grass there, and as many as five thousand men sat down. 11 Then Jesus took the loaves, gave thanks, and distributed them to those who were sitting there; he then did the same with the fish, distributing as much as they wanted. 12 When they had eaten enough he said to the disciples, 'Pick up the pieces left over, so that nothing is wasted.' 13 So they picked them up and filled twelve large baskets with scraps left over from the meal of five barley loaves. 14 Seeing the sign that he had done, the people said, 'This is indeed the prophet who is to come into the world.' 15 Jesus, as he realised they were about to come and take him by force and make him king, fled back to the hills alone.

16 That evening the disciples went down to the shore of the sea 17 and got into a boat to make for Capernaum on the other side of the sea. It was getting dark by now and Jesus had still not rejoined them. 18 The wind was strong, and the sea was getting rough. 19 They had rowed three or four miles when they saw Jesus walking on the sea and coming towards the boat. They were afraid, 20 but he said, 'It's me. Don't be afraid.' 21 They were ready to take him into the boat, and immediately it reached the shore at the place they were making for.

22 Next day, the crowd that had stayed on the other side saw that only one boat had been there, and that Jesus had not got into the boat with his disciples, but that the disciples had set off by themselves. 23 Other boats, however, had put in from Tiberias, near the place where the bread had been eaten. 24 When the people saw that neither Jesus nor his disciples were there, they got into those boats and crossed to Capernaum to look for Jesus. 25 When they found him on

---

6, 1: [*Of Tiberias*]: the awkward apposition represents a later name of the Sea of Galilee. It was probably originally a marginal gloss.

25 When they found him on the other side of the sea, they said to him, "Rabbi, when did you come here?" 26 Jesus answered them, "Very truly, I tell you, you are looking for me, not because you saw signs, but because you ate your fill of the loaves. 27 Do not work for the food that perishes, but for the food that endures for eternal life, which the Son of Man will give you. For it is on him that God the Father has set his seal." 28 Then they said to him, "What must we do to perform the works of God?" 29 Jesus answered them, "This is the work of God, that you believe in him whom he has sent." 30 So they said to him, "What sign are you going to give us then, so that we may see it and believe you? What work are you performing? 31 Our ancestors ate the manna in the wilderness; as it is written, 'He gave them bread from heaven to eat.'" 32 Then Jesus said to them, "Very truly, I tell you, it was not Moses who gave you the bread from heaven, but it is my Father who gives you the true bread from heaven. 33 For the bread of God is that which[r] comes down from heaven and gives life to the world." 34 They said to him, "Sir, give us this bread always."

35 Jesus said to them, "I am the bread of life. Whoever comes to me will never be hungry, and whoever believes in me will never be thirsty. 36 But I said to you that you have seen me and yet do not believe. 37 Everything that the Father gives me will come to me, and anyone who comes to me I will never drive away; 38 for I have come down from heaven, not to do my own will, but the will of him who sent me. 39 And this is the will of him who sent me, that I should lose nothing of all that he has given me, but raise it up on the last day. 40 This is indeed the will of my Father, that all who see the Son and believe in him may have eternal life; and I will raise them up on the last day."

41 Then the Jews began to complain about him because he said, "I am the bread that came down from heaven." 42 They were saying, "Is not this Jesus, the son of Joseph, whose father and mother we know? How can he now say, 'I have come down from heaven'?" 43 Jesus answered them, "Do not complain among yourselves. 44 No one can come to me unless drawn by the Father who sent me; and I will raise that person up on the last day. 45 It is written in the prophets,

asked, 'when did you come here?' 26 Jesus replied, 'In very truth I tell you, it is not because you saw signs that you came looking for me, but because you ate the bread and your hunger was satisfied. 27 You should work, not for this perishable food, but for the food that lasts, the food of eternal life.

'This food the Son of Man will give you, for on him God the Father has set the seal of his authority.' 28 'Then what must we do', they asked, 'if our work is to be the work of God?' 29 Jesus replied, 'This is the work that God requires: to believe in the one whom he has sent.'

30 They asked, 'What sign can you give us, so that we may see it and believe you? What is the work you are doing? 31 Our ancestors had manna to eat in the desert; as scripture says, "He gave them bread from heaven to eat."' 32 Jesus answered, 'In very truth I tell you, it was not Moses who gave you the bread from heaven; it is my Father who gives you the true bread from heaven. 33 The bread that God gives comes down from heaven and brings life to the world.' 34 'Sir,' they said, 'give us this bread now and always.' 35 Jesus said to them, 'I am the bread of life. Whoever comes to me will never be hungry, and whoever believes in me will never be thirsty. 36 But you, as I said, have seen and yet you do not believe. 37 All that the Father gives me will come to me, and anyone who comes to me I will never turn away. 38 I have come down from heaven, to do not my own will, but the will of him who sent me. 39 It is his will that I should not lose even one of those he has given me, but should raise them all up on the last day. 40 For it is my Father's will that everyone who sees the Son and has faith in him should have eternal life; and I will raise them up on the last day.'

41 At this the Jews began to grumble because he said, 'I am the bread which came down from heaven.' 42 They said, 'Surely this is Jesus, Joseph's son! We know his father and mother. How can he say, "I have come down from heaven"?' 43 'Stop complaining among yourselves,' Jesus told them. 44 'No one can come to me unless he is drawn by the Father who sent me; and I will raise him up on the last day.

found him across the sea they said to him, "Rabbi, when did you get here?" 26 Jesus answered them and said, "Amen, amen, I say to you, you are looking for me not because you saw signs but because you ate the loaves and were filled. 27 Do not work for food that perishes but for the food that endures for eternal life, which the Son of Man will give you. For on him the Father, God, has set his seal." 28 So they said to him, "What can we do to accomplish the works of God?" 29 Jesus answered and said to them, "This is the work of God, that you believe in the one he sent." 30 So they said to him, "What sign can you do, that we may see and believe in you? What can you do? 31 Our ancestors ate manna in the desert, as it is written:

'He gave them bread from heaven to eat.' "

32 So Jesus said to them, "Amen, amen, I say to you, it was not Moses who gave the bread from heaven; my Father gives you the true bread from heaven. 33 For the bread of God is that which comes down from heaven and gives life to the world."

34 So they said to him, "Sir, give us this bread always." 35 Jesus said to them, "I am the bread of life; whoever comes to me will never hunger, and whoever believes in me will never thirst. 36 But I told you that although you have seen [me], you do not believe. 37 Everything that the Father gives me will come to me, and I will not reject anyone who comes to me, 38 because I came down from heaven not to do my own will but the will of the one who sent me. 39 And this is the will of the one who sent me, that I should not lose anything of what he gave me, but that I should raise it [on] the last day. 40 For this is the will of my Father, that everyone who sees the Son and believes in him may have eternal life, and I shall raise him [on] the last day."

41 The Jews murmured about him because he said, "I am the bread that came down from heaven," 42 and they said, "Is this not Jesus, the son of Joseph? Do we not know his father and mother? Then how can he say, 'I have come down from heaven'?" 43 Jesus answered and said to them, "Stop murmuring among yourselves. 44 No one can come to me unless the Father who sent me draw him, and I will raise him on the last day. 45 It is written in the prophets:

---

the other side, they said to him, 'Rabbi, when did you come here?' 26 Jesus answered:

In all truth I tell you,
you are looking for me
not because you have seen the signs
but because you had all the bread you wanted to
    eat.
27 Do not work for food that goes bad,
but work for food that endures for eternal life,
which the Son of man will give you,
for on him the Father, God himself, has set his
    seal.

28 Then they said to him, 'What must we do if we are to carry out God's work?' 29 Jesus gave them this answer, 'This is carrying out God's work: you must believe in the one he has sent.' 30 So they said, 'What sign will you yourself do, the sight of which will make us believe in you? What work will you do? 31 Our fathers ate manna in the desert; as scripture says: *He gave them bread from heaven to eat.*' i

32 Jesus answered them:

In all truth I tell you,
it was not Moses who gave you the bread from
    heaven,
it is my Father who gives you the bread from
    heaven,
the true bread;
33 for the bread of God
is the bread which comes down from heaven
and gives life to the world.

34 'Sir,' they said, 'give us that bread always.' 35 Jesus answered them:

I am the bread of life.
No one who comes to me will ever hunger;
no one who believes in me will ever thirst.
36 But, as I have told you,
you can see me and still you do not believe.
37 Everyone whom the Father gives me will come to
    me;
I will certainly not reject
anyone who comes to me,
38 because I have come from heaven,
not to do my own will,
but to do the will of him who sent me.
39 Now the will of him who sent me
is that I should lose nothing
of all that he has given to me,
but that I should raise it up on the last day.
40 It is my Father's will
that whoever sees the Son and believes in him
should have eternal life,
and that I should raise that person up on the last
    day.

41 Meanwhile the Jews were complaining to each other about him, because he had said, 'I am the bread that has come down from heaven.' 42 They were saying, 'Surely this is Jesus son of Joseph, whose father and mother we know. How can he now say, "I have come down from heaven?"' 43 Jesus said in reply to them, 'Stop complaining to each other.

44 'No one can come to me
unless drawn by the Father who sent me,
and I will raise that person up on the last day.

i 6 Ps 78:24. 'Bread from heaven' is commented vv. 32–48 and 'to eat' vv. 49–58.

'And they shall all be taught by God.' Everyone who has heard and learned from the Father comes to me. 46 Not that anyone has seen the Father except the one who is from God; he has seen the Father. 47 Very truly, I tell you, whoever believes has eternal life. 48 I am the bread of life. 49 Your ancestors ate the manna in the wilderness, and they died. 50 This is the bread that comes down from heaven, so that one may eat of it and not die. 51 I am the living bread that came down from heaven. Whoever eats of this bread will live forever; and the bread that I will give for the life of the world is my flesh."

52 The Jews then disputed among themselves, saying, "How can this man give us his flesh to eat?" 53 So Jesus said to them, "Very truly, I tell you, unless you eat the flesh of the Son of Man and drink his blood, you have no life in you. 54 Those who eat my flesh and drink my blood have eternal life, and I will raise them up on the last day; 55 for my flesh is true food and my blood is true drink. 56 Those who eat my flesh and drink my blood abide in me, and I in them. 57 Just as the living Father sent me, and I live because of the Father, so whoever eats me will live because of me. 58 This is the bread that came down from heaven, not like that which your ancestors ate, and they died. But the one who eats this bread will live forever." 59 He said these things while he was teaching in the synagogue at Capernaum.

60 When many of his disciples heard it, they said, "This teaching is difficult; who can accept it?" 61 But Jesus, being aware that his disciples were complaining about it, said to them, "Does this offend you? 62 Then what if you were to see the Son of Man ascending to where he was before? 63 It is the spirit that gives life; the flesh is useless. The words that I have spoken to you are spirit and life. 64 But among you there are some who do not believe." For Jesus knew from the first who were the ones that did not believe, and who was the one that would betray him. 65 And he said, "For this reason I have told you that no one can come to me unless it is granted by the Father."

66 Because of this many of his disciples turned back and no longer went about with him. 67 So Jesus asked the twelve, "Do you also wish to go away?" 68 Simon Peter answered him, "Lord, to whom can we go? You have the words of eternal life. 69 We have come to believe and know that you are the Holy One of God."*s* 70 Jesus answered them, "Did I not choose you, the twelve? Yet one of you is a devil." 71 He was speaking of Judas son of Simon Iscar-

45 It is written in the prophets: "They will all be taught by God." Everyone who has listened to the Father and learned from him comes to me.

46 'I do not mean that anyone has seen the Father; he who has come from God has seen the Father, and he alone. 47 In very truth I tell you, whoever believes has eternal life. 48 I am the bread of life. 49 Your ancestors ate manna in the wilderness, yet they are dead. 50 I am speaking of the bread that comes down from heaven; whoever eats it will never die. 51 I am the living bread that has come down from heaven; if anyone eats this bread, he will live for ever. The bread which I shall give is my own flesh, given for the life of the world.'

52 This led to a fierce dispute among the Jews. 'How can this man give us his flesh to eat?' they protested. 53 Jesus answered them, 'In very truth I tell you, unless you eat the flesh of the Son of Man and drink his blood you can have no life in you. 54 Whoever eats my flesh and drinks my blood has eternal life, and I will raise him up on the last day. 55 My flesh is real food; my blood is real drink. 56 Whoever eats my flesh and drinks my blood dwells in me and I in him. 57 As the living Father sent me, and I live because of the Father, so whoever eats me will live because of me. 58 This is the bread which came down from heaven; it is not like the bread which our fathers ate; they are dead, but whoever eats this bread will live for ever.'

59 JESUS said these things in the synagogue as he taught in Capernaum. 60 On hearing them, many of his disciples exclaimed, 'This is more than we can stand! How can anyone listen to such talk?' 61 Jesus was aware that his disciples were grumbling about it and asked them, 'Does this shock you? 62 Then what if you see the Son of Man ascending to where he was before? 63 It is the spirit that gives life; the flesh can achieve nothing; the words I have spoken to you are both spirit and life. 64 Yet there are some of you who have no faith.' For Jesus knew from the outset who were without faith and who was to betray him. 65 So he said, 'This is why I told you that no one can come to me unless it has been granted to him by the Father.'

66 From that moment many of his disciples drew back and no longer went about with him. 67 So Jesus asked the Twelve, 'Do you also want to leave?' 68 Simon Peter answered him, 'Lord, to whom shall we go? Your words are words of eternal life. 69 We believe and know that you are God's Holy One.' 70 Jesus answered, 'Have I not chosen the twelve of you? Yet one of you is a devil.' 71 He meant Judas

---

s Other ancient authorities read *the Christ, the Son of the living God*

'They shall all be taught by God.'
Everyone who listens to my Father and learns from him
comes to me. 46 Not that anyone has seen the Father except
the one who is from God; he has seen the Father. 47 Amen,
amen, I say to you, whoever believes has eternal life. 48 I
am the bread of life. 49 Your ancestors ate the manna in the
desert, but they died; 50 this is the bread that comes down
from heaven so that one may eat it and not die. 51 I am the
living bread that came down from heaven; whoever eats this
bread will live forever; and the bread that I will give is my
flesh for the life of the world."

52 The Jews quarreled among themselves, saying, "How
can this man give us [his] flesh to eat?" 53 Jesus said to
them, "Amen, amen, I say to you, unless you eat the flesh
of the Son of Man and drink his blood, you do not have life
within you. 54 Whoever eats my flesh and drinks my blood
has eternal life, and I will raise him on the last day. 55 For
my flesh is true food, and my blood is true drink. 56 Whoever eats my flesh and drinks my blood remains in me and
I in him. 57 Just as the living Father sent me and I have life
because of the Father, so also the one who feeds on me will
have life because of me. 58 This is the bread that came down
from heaven. Unlike your ancestors who ate and still died,
whoever eats this bread will live forever." 59 These things
he said while teaching in the synagogue in Capernaum.

60 Then many of his disciples who were listening said,
"This saying is hard; who can accept it?" 61 Since Jesus
knew that his disciples were murmuring about this, he said
to them, "Does this shock you? 62 What if you were to see
the Son of Man ascending to where he was before? 63 It is
the spirit that gives life, while the flesh is of no avail. The
words I have spoken to you are spirit and life. 64 But there
are some of you who do not believe." Jesus knew from the
beginning the ones who would not believe and the one who
would betray him. 65 And he said, "For this reason I have
told you that no one can come to me unless it is granted him
by my Father."

66 As a result of this, many [of] his disciples returned to
their former way of life and no longer accompanied him.
67 Jesus then said to the Twelve, "Do you also want to
leave?" 68 Simon Peter answered him, "Master, to whom
shall we go? You have the words of eternal life. 69 We have
come to believe and are convinced that you are the Holy
One of God." 70 Jesus answered them, "Did I not choose
you twelve? Yet is not one of you a devil?" 71 He was

45 It is written in the prophets:
They will all be taught by God; j
everyone who has listened to the Father,
    and learnt from him,
comes to me.
46 Not that anybody has seen the Father,
except him who has his being from God:
he has seen the Father.
47 In all truth I tell you,
everyone who believes has eternal life.
48 I am the bread of life.
49 Your fathers ate manna in the desert
    and they are dead;
50 but this is the bread which comes down from
        heaven,
so that a person may eat it and not die.
51 I am the living bread which has come down from
        heaven.
Anyone who eats this bread will live for ever;
and the bread that I shall give
is my flesh, for the life of the world.'

52 Then the Jews started arguing among themselves,
'How can this man give us his flesh to eat?' 53 Jesus replied
to them:

In all truth I tell you,
if you do not eat the flesh of the Son of man
    and drink his blood,
you have no life in you.
54 Anyone who does eat my flesh and drink my blood
has eternal life,
and I shall raise that person up on the last day.
55 For my flesh is real food
and my blood is real drink.
56 Whoever eats my flesh and drinks my blood
lives in me
and I live in that person.
57 As the living Father sent me
and I draw life from the Father,
so whoever eats me will also draw life from me.
58 This is the bread which has come down from
        heaven;
it is not like the bread our ancestors ate:
they are dead,
but anyone who eats this bread will live for ever.

59 This is what he taught at Capernaum in the synagogue.
60 After hearing it, many of his followers said, 'This is
intolerable language. How could anyone accept it?' 61 Jesus
was aware that his followers were complaining about it and
said, 'Does this disturb you? 62 What if you should see the
Son of man ascend to where he was before?

63 'It is the spirit that gives life,
the flesh has nothing to offer.
The words I have spoken to you are spirit
and they are life.

64 'But there are some of you who do not believe.' For
Jesus knew from the outset who did not believe and who
was to betray him. 65 He went on, 'This is why I told you
that no one could come to me except by the gift of the
Father.' 66 After this, many of his disciples went away and
accompanied him no more.

67 Then Jesus said to the Twelve, 'What about you, do
you want to go away too?' 68 Simon Peter answered, 'Lord,
to whom shall we go? You have the message of eternal life,
69 and we believe; we have come to know that you are the
Holy One of God.' 70 Jesus replied to them, 'Did I not
choose the Twelve of you? Yet one of you is a devil.' 71 He

j 6 Is 54:13.

iot,ᵗ for he, though one of the twelve, was going to betray him.

7 After this Jesus went about in Galilee. He did not wishᵘ to go about in Judea because the Jews were looking for an opportunity to kill him. 2 Now the Jewish festival of Boothsᵛ was near. 3 So his brothers said to him, "Leave here and go to Judea so that your disciples also may see the works you are doing; 4 for no one who wantsʷ to be widely known acts in secret. If you do these things, show yourself to the world." 5 (For not even his brothers believed in him.) 6 Jesus said to them, "My time has not yet come, but your time is always here. 7 The world cannot hate you, but it hates me because I testify against it that its works are evil. 8 Go to the festival yourselves. I am notˣ going to this festival, for my time has not yet fully come." 9 After saying this, he remained in Galilee.

10 But after his brothers had gone to the festival, then he also went, not publicly but as it wereʸ in secret. 11 The Jews were looking for him at the festival and saying, "Where is he?" 12 And there was considerable complaining about him among the crowds. While some were saying, "He is a good man," others were saying, "No, he is deceiving the crowd." 13 Yet no one would speak openly about him for fear of the Jews.

14 About the middle of the festival Jesus went up into the temple and began to teach. 15 The Jews were astonished at it, saying, "How does this man have such learning,ᶻ when he has never been taught?" 16 Then Jesus answered them, "My teaching is not mine but his who sent me. 17 Anyone who resolves to do the will of God will know whether the teaching is from God or whether I am speaking on my own. 18 Those who speak on their own seek their own glory; but the one who seeks the glory of him who sent him is true, and there is nothing false in him. 19 "Did not Moses give you the law? Yet none of you keeps the law. Why are you looking for an opportunity to kill me?" 20 The crowd answered, "You have a demon! Who is trying to kill you?" 21 Jesus answered them, "I performed one work, and all of you are astonished. 22 Moses gave you circumcision (it is, of course, not from Moses, but from the patriarchs), and you circumcise a man on the sabbath. 23 If a man receives circumcision on the sabbath in order that the law of Moses may not be broken, are you angry with me because I healed a man's whole body on the sabbath? 24 Do not judge by appearances, but judge with right judgment."

25 Now some of the people of Jerusalem were saying, "Is not this the man whom they are trying to kill? 26 And here he is, speaking openly, but they say nothing to him! Can it be that the authorities really know that this is the Messiah?ᵃ 27 Yet we know where this man is from; but when the Messiahᵃ comes, no one will know where he is from." 28 Then Jesus cried out as he was teaching in the temple, "You know me, and you know where I am from. I have not come on my own. But the one who sent me is true, and you do not know him. 29 I know him, because I am from him, and he sent me." 30 Then they tried to arrest him, but

son of Simon Iscariot. It was he who would betray him, and he was one of the Twelve.

7 AFTER that Jesus travelled around within Galilee; he decided to avoid Judaea because the Jews were looking for a chance to kill him. 2 But when the Jewish feast of Tabernacles was close at hand, 3 his brothers said to him, 'You should leave here and go into Judaea, so that your disciples may see the great things you are doing. 4 No one can hope for recognition if he works in obscurity. If you can really do such things as these, show yourself to the world.' 5 For even his brothers had no faith in him. 6 Jesus answered: 'The right time for me has not yet come, but any time is right for you. 7 The world cannot hate you; but it hates me for exposing the wickedness of its ways. 8 Go up to the festival yourselves. I am not going to this festival, because the right time for me has not yet come.' 9 So saying he stayed behind in Galilee.

10 Later, when his brothers had gone to the festival, he went up too, not openly, but in secret. 11 At the festival the Jews were looking for him and asking where he was, 12 and there was much murmuring about him in the crowds. 'He is a good man,' said some. 'No,' said others, 'he is leading the people astray.' 13 No one talked freely about him, however, for fear of the Jews.

14 WHEN the festival was already half over, Jesus went up to the temple and began to teach. 15 The Jews were astonished: 'How is it', they said, 'that this untrained man has such learning?' 16 Jesus replied, 'My teaching is not my own but his who sent me. 17 Whoever chooses to do the will of God will know whether my teaching comes from him or is merely my own. 18 Anyone whose teaching is merely his own seeks his own glory; but if anyone seeks the glory of him who sent him, he is sincere and there is nothing false in him.

19 'Did not Moses give you the law? Yet not one of you keeps it. Why are you trying to kill me?' 20 The crowd answered, 'You are possessed! Who wants to kill you?' 21 Jesus replied, 'I did one good deed, and you are all taken aback. 22 But consider: Moses gave you the law of circumcision (not that it originated with Moses, but with the patriarchs) and you circumcise even on the sabbath. 23 Well then, if someone can be circumcised on the sabbath to avoid breaking the law of Moses, why are you indignant with me for making someone's whole body well on the sabbath? 24 Stop judging by appearances; be just in your judgements.'

25 This prompted some of the people of Jerusalem to say, 'Is not this the man they want to put to death? 26 Yet here he is, speaking in public, and they say not one word to him. Can it be that our rulers have decided that this is the Messiah? 27 Yet we know where this man comes from; when the Messiah appears no one is to know where he comes from.' 28 Jesus responded to this as he taught in the temple: 'Certainly you know me,' he declared, 'and you know where I come from. Yet I have not come of my own accord; I was sent by one who is true, and him you do not know. 29 I know him because I come from him, and he it is who sent me.'

ᵗ Other ancient authorities read *Judas Iscariot son of Simon;* others, *Judas son of Simon from Karyot* (Kerioth)   ᵘ Other ancient authorities read *was not at liberty*   ᵛ Or *Tabernacles*   ʷ Other ancient authorities read *wants it*   ˣ Other ancient authorities add *yet*   ʸ Other ancient authorities lack *as it were*   ᶻ Or *this man know his letters*   ᵃ Or *the Christ*

7:8 **not going:** *some witnesses read* not yet going.
7:28 **Certainly . . . come from:** *or* Do you know me? And do you know where I come from?

referring to Judas, son of Simon the Iscariot; it was he who would betray him, one of the Twelve.

7 After this, Jesus moved about within Galilee; but he did not wish to travel in Judea, because the Jews were trying to kill him. 2 But the Jewish feast of Tabernacles was near. 3 So his brothers said to him, "Leave here and go to Judea, so that your disciples also may see the works you are doing. 4 No one works in secret if he wants to be known publicly. If you do these things, manifest yourself to the world." 5 For his brothers did not believe in him. 6 So Jesus said to them, "My time is not yet here, but the time is always right for you. 7 The world cannot hate you, but it hates me, because I testify to it that its works are evil. 8 You go up to the feast. I am not going up to this feast, because my time has not yet been fulfilled." 9 After he had said this, he stayed on in Galilee.

10 But when his brothers had gone up to the feast, he himself also went up, not openly but [as it were] in secret. 11 The Jews were looking for him at the feast and saying, "Where is he?" 12 And there was considerable murmuring about him in the crowds. Some said, "He is a good man," [while] others said, "No; on the contrary, he misleads the crowd." 13 Still, no one spoke openly about him because they were afraid of the Jews.

14 When the feast was already half over, Jesus went up into the temple area and began to teach. 15 The Jews were amazed and said, "How does he know scripture without having studied?" 16 Jesus answered them and said, "My teaching is not my own but is from the one who sent me. 17 Whoever chooses to do his will shall know whether my teaching is from God or whether I speak on my own. 18 Whoever speaks on his own seeks his own glory, but whoever seeks the glory of the one who sent him is truthful, and there is no wrong in him. 19 Did not Moses give you the law? Yet none of you keeps the law. Why are you trying to kill me?" 20 The crowd answered, "You are possessed! Who is trying to kill you?" 21 Jesus answered and said to them, "I performed one work and all of you are amazed 22 because of it. Moses gave you circumcision—not that it came from Moses but rather from the patriarchs—and you circumcise a man on the sabbath. 23 If a man can receive circumcision on a sabbath so that the law of Moses may not be broken, are you angry with me because I made a whole person well on a sabbath? 24 Stop judging by appearances, but judge justly."

25 So some of the inhabitants of Jerusalem said, "Is he not the one they are trying to kill? 26 And look, he is speaking openly and they say nothing to him. Could the authorities have realized that he is the Messiah? 27 But we know where he is from. When the Messiah comes, no one will know where he is from." 28 So Jesus cried out in the temple area as he was teaching and said, "You know me and also know where I am from. Yet I did not come on my own, but the one who sent me, whom you do not know, is true. 29 I know him, because I am from him, and he sent me." 30 So they

meant Judas son of Simon Iscariot, since this was the man, one of the Twelve, who was to betray him.

7 After this Jesus travelled round Galilee; he could not travel round Judaea, because the Jews were seeking to kill him.

2 As the Jewish feast of Shelters drew near, 3 his brothers said to him, 'Leave this place and go to Judaea, so that your disciples, too, can see the works you are doing; 4 no one who wants to be publicly known acts in secret; if this is what you are doing, you should reveal yourself to the world.' 5 Not even his brothers had faith in him. 6 Jesus answered, 'For me the right time has not come yet, but for you any time is the right time. 7 The world cannot hate you, but it does hate me, because I give evidence that its ways are evil. 8 Go up to the festival yourselves: I am not going to this festival, because for me the time is not ripe yet.' 9 Having said that, he stayed behind in Galilee.

10 However, after his brothers had left for the festival, he went up as well, not publicly but secretly. 11 At the festival the Jews were on the look-out for him: 'Where is he?' they said. 12 There was a great deal of talk about him in the crowds. Some said, 'He is a good man'; others, 'No, he is leading the people astray.' 13 Yet no one spoke about him openly, for fear of the Jews.

14 When the festival was half over, Jesus went to the Temple and began to teach. 15 The Jews were astonished and said, 'How did he learn to read? He has not been educated.' 16 Jesus answered them:

'My teaching is not from myself:
it comes from the one who sent me;
17 anyone who is prepared to do his will,
will know whether my teaching is from God
or whether I speak on my own account.
18 When someone speaks on his own account,
he is seeking honour for himself;
but when he is seeking the honour of the person
who sent him,
then he is true
and altogether without dishonesty.
19 Did not Moses give you the Law?
And yet not one of you keeps the Law!

'Why do you want to kill me?' 20 The crowd replied, 'You are mad! Who wants to kill you?' 21 Jesus answered, 'One work I did, and you are all amazed at it. 22 Moses ordered you to practise circumcision—not that it began with him, it goes back to the patriarchs—and you circumcise on the Sabbath. 23 Now if someone can be circumcised on the Sabbath so that the Law of Moses is not broken, why are you angry with me for making someone completely healthy on a Sabbath? 24 Do not keep judging according to appearances; let your judgement be according to what is right.'

25 Meanwhile some of the people of Jerusalem were saying, 'Isn't this the man they want to kill? 26 And here he is, speaking openly, and they have nothing to say to him! Can it be true the authorities have recognised that he is the Christ? 27 Yet we all know where he comes from; but when the Christ appears no one will know where he comes from.'

28 Then, as Jesus was teaching in the Temple, he cried out:

You know me and you know where I came from.
Yet I have not come of my own accord:
but he who sent me is true;
You do not know him,
29 but I know him
because I have my being from him
and it was he who sent me.

no one laid hands on him, because his hour had not yet come. 31 Yet many in the crowd believed in him and were saying, "When the Messiah*b* comes, will he do more signs than this man has done?"*c*

32 The Pharisees heard the crowd muttering such things about him, and the chief priests and Pharisees sent temple police to arrest him. 33 Jesus then said, "I will be with you a little while longer, and then I am going to him who sent me. 34 You will search for me, but you will not find me; and where I am, you cannot come." 35 The Jews said to one another, "Where does this man intend to go that we will not find him? Does he intend to go to the Dispersion among the Greeks and teach the Greeks? 36 What does he mean by saying, 'You will search for me and you will not find me' and 'Where I am, you cannot come'?"

37 On the last day of the festival, the great day, while Jesus was standing there, he cried out, "Let anyone who is thirsty come to me, 38 and let the one who believes in me drink. As*d* the scripture has said, 'Out of the believer's heart*e* shall flow rivers of living water.' " 39 Now he said this about the Spirit, which believers in him were to receive; for as yet there was no Spirit,*f* because Jesus was not yet glorified.

40 When they heard these words, some in the crowd said, "This is really the prophet." 41 Others said, "This is the Messiah."*b* But some asked, "Surely the Messiah*b* does not come from Galilee, does he? 42 Has not the scripture said that the Messiah*b* is descended from David and comes from Bethlehem, the village where David lived?" 43 So there was a division in the crowd because of him. 44 Some of them wanted to arrest him, but no one laid hands on him.

45 Then the temple police went back to the chief priests and Pharisees, who asked them, "Why did you not arrest him?" 46 The police answered, "Never has anyone spoken like this!" 47 Then the Pharisees replied, "Surely you have not been deceived too, have you? 48 Has any one of the authorities or of the Pharisees believed in him? 49 But this crowd, which does not know the law — they are accursed." 50 Nicodemus, who had gone to Jesus*g* before, and who was one of them, asked, 51 "Our law does not judge people without first giving them a hearing to find out what they are doing, does it?" 52 They replied, "Surely you are not also from Galilee, are you? Search and you will see that no prophet is to arise from Galilee."

30 At this they tried to seize him, but no one could lay hands on him because his appointed hour had not yet come. 31 Among the people many believed in him. 'When the Messiah comes,' they said, 'is it likely that he will perform more signs than this man?'

32 The Pharisees overheard these mutterings about him among the people, so the chief priests and the Pharisees sent temple police to arrest him. 33 Then Jesus said, 'For a little longer I shall be with you; then I am going away to him who sent me. 34 You will look for me, but you will not find me; and where I am, you cannot come.' 35 So the Jews said to one another, 'Where does he intend to go, that we should not be able to find him? Will he go to the Dispersion among the Gentiles, and teach Gentiles? 36 What does he mean by saying, "You will look for me, but you will not find me; and where I am, you cannot come"?'

37 On the last and greatest day of the festival Jesus stood and declared, 'If anyone is thirsty, let him come to me and drink. 38 Whoever believes in me, as scripture says, "Streams of living water shall flow from within him." ' 39 He was speaking of the Spirit which believers in him would later receive; for the Spirit had not yet been given, because Jesus had not yet been glorified.

40 On hearing his words some of the crowd said, 'This must certainly be the Prophet.' 41 Others said, 'This is the Messiah.' But others argued, 'Surely the Messiah is not to come from Galilee? 42 Does not scripture say that the Messiah is to be of the family of David, from David's village of Bethlehem?' 43 Thus he was the cause of a division among the people. 44 Some were for arresting him, but no one laid hands on him.

45 The temple police went back to the chief priests and Pharisees, who asked them, 'Why have you not brought him?' 46 'No one ever spoke as this man speaks,' they replied. 47 The Pharisees retorted, 'Have you too been misled? 48 Has a single one of our rulers believed in him, or any of the Pharisees? 49 As for this rabble, which cares nothing for the law, a curse is on them.' 50 Then one of their number, Nicodemus (the man who once visited Jesus), intervened. 51 'Does our law', he asked them, 'permit us to pass judgement on someone without first giving him a hearing and learning the facts?' 52 'Are you a Galilean too?' they retorted. 'Study the scriptures and you will find that the Prophet does not come from Galilee.'

8 [53 Then each of them went home, 1 while Jesus went to the Mount of Olives. 2 Early in the morning he came again to the temple. All the people came to him and he sat

8 [53 AND they all went home, 1 while Jesus went to the mount of Olives. 2 At daybreak he appeared again in the temple, and all the people gathered round him. He had taken his seat and was engaged in teaching them 3 when the

7:37–38 **If anyone . . . within him:** *or* If anyone is thirsty, let him come to me; whoever believes in me, let him drink. As scripture says, "Streams of living water shall flow from within him."
7:52 **the Prophet does not:** *most witnesses read* the prophets do not.
7:53 – 8:11 *This passage, which in most editions of the New Testament is printed in the text of John, 7:53 – 8:11, has no fixed place in our witnesses. Some of them do not contain it at all. Some place it after Luke 21:38, others after John 7:36, or 7:52, or 21:24.*

b Or *the Christ*   *c* Other ancient authorities read *is doing*
d Or *come to me and drink.* 38 *The one who believes in me, as*
e Gk *out of his belly*   *f* Other ancient authorities read *for as yet the Spirit* (others, *Holy Spirit*) *had not been given*   *g* Gk *him*

tried to arrest him, but no one laid a hand upon him, because his hour had not yet come. 31 But many of the crowd began to believe in him, and said, "When the Messiah comes, will he perform more signs than this man has done?"

32 The Pharisees heard the crowd murmuring about him to this effect, and the chief priests and the Pharisees sent guards to arrest him. 33 So Jesus said, "I will be with you only a little while longer, and then I will go to the one who sent me. 34 You will look for me but not find [me], and where I am you cannot come." 35 So the Jews said to one another, "Where is he going that we will not find him? Surely he is not going to the dispersion among the Greeks to teach the Greeks, is he? 36 What is the meaning of his saying, 'You will look for me and not find [me], and where I am you cannot come'?"

37 On the last and greatest day of the feast, Jesus stood up and exclaimed, "Let anyone who thirsts come to me and drink. 38 Whoever believes in me, as scripture says:

'Rivers of living water will flow from
within him.' "

39 He said this in reference to the Spirit that those who came to believe in him were to receive. There was, of course, no Spirit yet, because Jesus had not yet been glorified. 40 Some in the crowd who heard these words said, "This is truly the Prophet." 41 Others said, "This is the Messiah." But others said, "The Messiah will not come from Galilee, will he? 42 Does not scripture say that the Messiah will be of David's family and come from Bethlehem, the village where David lived?" 43 So a division occurred in the crowd because of him. 44 Some of them even wanted to arrest him, but no one laid hands on him.

45 So the guards went to the chief priests and Pharisees, who asked them, "Why did you not bring him?" 46 The guards answered, "Never before has anyone spoken like this one." 47 So the Pharisees answered them, "Have you also been deceived? 48 Have any of the authorities or the Pharisees believed in him? 49 But this crowd, which does not know the law, is accursed." 50 Nicodemus, one of their members who had come to him earlier, said to them, 51 "Does our law condemn a person before it first hears him and finds out what he is doing?" 52 They answered and said to him, "You are not from Galilee also, are you? Look and see that no prophet arises from Galilee."

8 [53 Then each went to his own house, 1 while Jesus went to the Mount of Olives. 2 But early in the morning he arrived again in the temple area, and all the people started coming to him, and he sat down and taught them.

30 They wanted to arrest him then, but because his hour had not yet come no one laid a hand on him. 31 There were many people in the crowds, however, who believed in him; they were saying, 'When the Christ comes, will he give more signs than this man has?' 32 Hearing that talk like this about him was spreading among the people, the Pharisees sent the Temple guards to arrest him. 33 Then Jesus said:

For a short time I am with you still;
then I shall go back to the one who sent me.
34 You will look for me and will not find me;
where I am
you cannot come.

35 So the Jews said to one another, 'Where is he intending to go that we shall not be able to find him? Is he intending to go abroad to the people who are dispersed among the Greeks and to teach the Greeks? 36 What does he mean when he says:

"You will look for me and will not find me;
where I am,
you cannot come?" '

37 On the last day, the great day of the festival, Jesus stood and cried out:

'Let anyone who is thirsty come to me!
38 Let anyone who believes in me come and drink!

As scripture says, "From his heart shall flow streams of living water." '
39 He was speaking of the Spirit which those who believed in him were to receive; for there was no Spirit as yet because Jesus had not yet been glorified. 40 Some of the crowd who had been listening said, 'He is indeed the prophet,' 41 and some said, 'He is the Christ,' but others said, 'Would the Christ come from Galilee? 42 Does not scripture say that the Christ must be descended from David and come from Bethlehem, the village where David was?' 43 So the people could not agree about him. 44 Some wanted to arrest him, but no one actually laid a hand on him.

45 The guards went back to the chief priests and Pharisees who said to them, 'Why haven't you brought him?' 46 The guards replied, 'No one has ever spoken like this man.' 47 'So,' the Pharisees answered, 'you, too, have been led astray? 48 Have any of the authorities come to believe in him? Any of the Pharisees? 49 This rabble knows nothing about the Law—they are damned.' 50 One of them, Nicodemus—the same man who had come to Jesus earlier—said to them, 51 'But surely our Law does not allow us to pass judgement on anyone without first giving him a hearing and discovering what he is doing?' 52 To this they answered, 'Are you a Galilean too? Go into the matter, and see for yourself: prophets do not arise in Galilee.'

8 53 k They all went home, 1 and Jesus went to the Mount of Olives.
2 At daybreak he appeared in the Temple again; and as all the people came to him, he sat down and began to teach them.

7, 53—8, 11: The story of the woman caught in adultery is a later insertion here, missing from all early Greek manuscripts. A Western text-type insertion, attested mainly in Old Latin translations, it is found in different places in different manuscripts: here, or after 7, 36, or at the end of this gospel, or after Lk 21, 38, or at the end of that gospel.

k 7 Many ancient MSS omit 7:53—8:11.

down and began to teach them. 3 The scribes and the Pharisees brought a woman who had been caught in adultery; and making her stand before all of them, 4 they said to him, "Teacher, this woman was caught in the very act of committing adultery. 5 Now in the law Moses commanded us to stone such women. Now what do you say?" 6 They said this to test him, so that they might have some charge to bring against him. Jesus bent down and wrote with his finger on the ground. 7 When they kept on questioning him, he straightened up and said to them, "Let anyone among you who is without sin be the first to throw a stone at her." 8 And once again he bent down and wrote on the ground. *h* 9 When they heard it, they went away, one by one, beginning with the elders; and Jesus was left alone with the woman standing before him. 10 Jesus straightened up and said to her, "Woman, where are they? Has no one condemned you?" 11 She said, "No one, sir." *i* And Jesus said, "Neither do I condemn you. Go your way, and from now on do not sin again." *j*

12 Again Jesus spoke to them, saying, "I am the light of the world. Whoever follows me will never walk in darkness but will have the light of life." 13 Then the Pharisees said to him, "You are testifying on your own behalf; your testimony is not valid." 14 Jesus answered, "Even if I testify on my own behalf, my testimony is valid because I know where I have come from and where I am going, but you do not know where I come from or where I am going. 15 You judge by human standards; *k* I judge no one. 16 Yet even if I do judge, my judgment is valid; for it is not I alone who judge, but I and the Father *l* who sent me. 17 In your law it is written that the testimony of two witnesses is valid. 18 I testify on my own behalf, and the Father who sent me testifies on my behalf." 19 Then they said to him, "Where is your Father?" Jesus answered, "You know neither me nor my Father. If you knew me, you would know my Father also." 20 He spoke these words while he was teaching in the treasury of the temple, but no one arrested him, because his hour had not yet come.

21 Again he said to them, "I am going away, and you will search for me, but you will die in your sin. Where I am going, you cannot come." 22 Then the Jews said, "Is he going to kill himself? Is that what he means by saying, 'Where I am going, you cannot come'?" 23 He said to them, "You are from below, I am from above; you are of this world, I am not of this world. 24 I told you that you would

scribes and the Pharisees brought in a woman caught committing adultery. Making her stand in the middle 4 they said to him, 'Teacher, this woman was caught in the very act of adultery. 5 In the law Moses has laid down that such women are to be stoned. What do you say about it?' 6 They put the question as a test, hoping to frame a charge against him. Jesus bent down and wrote with his finger on the ground. 7 When they continued to press their question he sat up straight and said, 'Let whichever of you is free from sin throw the first stone at her.' 8 Then once again he bent down and wrote on the ground. 9 When they heard what he said, one by one they went away, the eldest first; and Jesus was left alone, with the woman still standing there. 10 Jesus again sat up and said to the woman, 'Where are they? Has no one condemned you?' 11 She answered, 'No one, sir.' 'Neither do I condemn you,' Jesus said. 'Go; do not sin again.']

12 ONCE again Jesus addressed the people: 'I am the light of the world. No follower of mine shall walk in darkness; he shall have the light of life.' 13 The Pharisees said to him, 'You are witness in your own cause; your testimony is not valid.' 14 Jesus replied, 'My testimony is valid, even though I do testify on my own behalf; because I know where I come from, and where I am going. But you know neither where I come from nor where I am going. 15 You judge by worldly standards; I pass judgement on no one. 16 If I do judge, my judgement is valid because it is not I alone who judge, but I and he who sent me. 17 In your own law it is written that the testimony of two witnesses is valid. 18 I am a witness in my own cause, and my other witness is the Father who sent me.' 19 'Where is your father?' they asked him. Jesus replied, 'You do not know me or my Father; if you knew me you would know my Father too.'

20 Jesus was teaching near the treasury in the temple when he said this; but no one arrested him, because his hour had not yet come.

21 Again he said to them, 'I am going away. You will look for me, but you will die in your sin; where I am going, you cannot come.' 22 At this the Jews said, 'Perhaps he will kill himself: is that what he means when he says, "Where I am going, you cannot come"?' 23 Jesus continued, 'You belong to this world below, I to the world above. Your home is in this world, mine is not. 24 That is why I told you

---

h Other ancient authorities add *the sins of each of them* *i* Or *Lord*
j The most ancient authorities lack 7.53—8.11; other authorities add the passage here or after 7.36 or after 21.25 or after Luke 21.38, with variations of text; some mark the passage as doubtful.
k Gk *according to the flesh* *l* Other ancient authorities read *he*

8:9 **they went away:** *some witnesses add* convicted by their conscience.

3 Then the scribes and the Pharisees brought a woman who had been caught in adultery and made her stand in the middle. 4 They said to him, "Teacher, this woman was caught in the very act of committing adultery. 5 Now in the law, Moses commanded us to stone such women. So what do you say?" 6 They said this to test him, so that they could have some charge to bring against him. Jesus bent down and began to write on the ground with his finger. 7 But when they continued asking him, he straightened up and said to them, "Let the one among you who is without sin be the first to throw a stone at her." 8 Again he bent down and wrote on the ground. 9 And in response, they went away one by one, beginning with the elders. So he was left alone with the woman before him. 10 Then Jesus straightened up and said to her, "Woman, where are they? Has no one condemned you?" 11 She replied, "No one, sir." Then Jesus said, "Neither do I condemn you. Go, [and] from now on do not sin any more."]

12 Jesus spoke to them again, saying, "I am the light of the world. Whoever follows me will not walk in darkness, but will have the light of life." 13 So the Pharisees said to him, "You testify on your own behalf, so your testimony cannot be verified." 14 Jesus answered and said to them, "Even if I do testify on my own behalf, my testimony can be verified, because I know where I came from and where I am going. But you do not know where I come from or where I am going. 15 You judge by appearances, but I do not judge anyone. 16 And even if I should judge, my judgment is valid, because I am not alone, but it is I and the Father who sent me. 17 Even in your law it is written that the testimony of two men can be verified. 18 I testify on my behalf and so does the Father who sent me." 19 So they said to him, "Where is your father?" Jesus answered, "You know neither me nor my Father. If you knew me, you would know my Father also." 20 He spoke these words while teaching in the treasury in the temple area. But no one arrested him, because his hour had not yet come.

21 He said to them again, "I am going away and you will look for me, but you will die in your sin. Where I am going you cannot come." 22 So the Jews said, "He is not going to kill himself, is he, because he said, 'Where I am going you cannot come'?" 23 He said to them, "You belong to what is below, I belong to what is above. You belong to this world, but I do not belong to this world. 24 That is why I told you

3 The scribes and Pharisees brought a woman along who had been caught committing adultery; and making her stand there in the middle 4 they said to Jesus, 'Master, this woman was caught in the very act of committing adultery, 5 and in the Law Moses has ordered us to stone women of this kind. What have you got to say?' 6 They asked him this as a test, looking for an accusation to use against him. But Jesus bent down and started writing on the ground with his finger. 7 As they persisted with their question, he straightened up and said, 'Let the one among you who is guiltless be the first to throw a stone at her.' 8 Then he bent down and continued writing on the ground. 9 When they heard this they went away one by one, beginning with the eldest, until the last one had gone and Jesus was left alone with the woman, who remained in the middle. 10 Jesus again straightened up and said, 'Woman, where are they? Has no one condemned you?' 11 'No one, sir,' she replied. 'Neither do I condemn you,' said Jesus. 'Go away, and from this moment sin no more.'

12 When Jesus spoke to the people again, he said:

I am the light of the world;
anyone who follows me will not be walking in the dark,
but will have the light of life.

13 At this the Pharisees said to him, 'You are testifying on your own behalf; your testimony is not true.' 14 Jesus replied:

Even though I am testifying on my own behalf,
my testimony is still true,
because I know
where I have come from and where I am going;
but you do not know
where I come from or where I am going.
15 You judge by human standards;
I judge no one,
16 but if I judge,
my judgement will be true,
because I am not alone:
the one who sent me is with me;
17 and in your Law it is written
that the testimony of two witnesses is true.
18 I testify on my own behalf,
but the Father who sent me testifies on my behalf, too.

19 They asked him, 'Where is your Father then?' Jesus answered:

You do not know me, nor do you know my Father;
if you did know me, you would know my Father as well.

20 He spoke these words in the Treasury, while teaching in the Temple. No one arrested him, because his hour had not yet come.
21 Again he said to them:

I am going away; you will look for me
and you will die in your sin.
Where I am going, you cannot come.

22 So the Jews said to one another, 'Is he going to kill himself, that he says, "Where I am going, you cannot come?" ' 23 Jesus went on:

You are from below;
I am from above.
You are of this world;
I am not of this world.

die in your sins, for you will die in your sins unless you believe that I am he."*m* 25 They said to him, "Who are you?" Jesus said to them, "Why do I speak to you at all?*n* 26 I have much to say about you and much to condemn; but the one who sent me is true, and I declare to the world what I have heard from him." 27 They did not understand that he was speaking to them about the Father. 28 So Jesus said, "When you have lifted up the Son of Man, then you will realize that I am he,*m* and that I do nothing on my own, but I speak these things as the Father instructed me. 29 And the one who sent me is with me; he has not left me alone, for I always do what is pleasing to him." 30 As he was saying these things, many believed in him.

31 Then Jesus said to the Jews who had believed in him, "If you continue in my word, you are truly my disciples; 32 and you will know the truth, and the truth will make you free." 33 They answered him, "We are descendants of Abraham and have never been slaves to anyone. What do you mean by saying, 'You will be made free'?"

34 Jesus answered them, "Very truly, I tell you, everyone who commits sin is a slave to sin. 35 The slave does not have a permanent place in the household; the son has a place there forever. 36 So if the Son makes you free, you will be free indeed. 37 I know that you are descendants of Abraham; yet you look for an opportunity to kill me, because there is no place in you for my word. 38 I declare what I have seen in the Father's presence; as for you, you should do what you have heard from the Father."*o*

39 They answered him, "Abraham is our father." Jesus said to them, "If you were Abraham's children, you would be doing*p* what Abraham did, 40 but now you are trying to kill me, a man who has told you the truth that I heard from God. This is not what Abraham did. 41 You are indeed doing what your father does." They said to him, "We are not illegitimate children; we have one father, God himself." 42 Jesus said to them, "If God were your Father, you would love me, for I came from God and now I am here. I did not come on my own, but he sent me. 43 Why do you not understand what I say? It is because you cannot accept my word.

that you would die in your sins; and you will die in your sins unless you believe that I am what I am.' 25 'And who are you?' they asked him. Jesus answered, 'What I have told you all along. 26 I have much to say about you—and in judgement. But he who sent me speaks the truth, and what I heard from him I report to the world.'

27 They did not understand that he was speaking to them about the Father. 28 So Jesus said to them, 'When you have lifted up the Son of Man you will know that I am what I am. I do nothing on my own authority, but in all I say, I have been taught by my Father. 29 He who sent me is present with me, and has not left me on my own; for I always do what is pleasing to him.' 30 As he said this, many put their faith in him.

31 Turning to the Jews who had believed him, Jesus said, 'If you stand by my teaching, you are truly my disciples; 32 you will know the truth, and the truth will set you free.' 33 'We are Abraham's descendants,' they replied; 'we have never been in slavery to anyone. What do you mean by saying, "You will become free"?' 34 'In very truth I tell you', said Jesus, 'that everyone who commits sin is a slave. 35 The slave has no permanent standing in the household, but the son belongs to it for ever. 36 If then the Son sets you free, you will indeed be free.

37 'I know that you are descended from Abraham, yet you are bent on killing me because my teaching makes no headway with you. 38 I tell what I have seen in my Father's presence; you do what you have learned from your father.' 39 They retorted, 'Abraham is our father.' 'If you were Abraham's children', Jesus replied, 'you would do as Abraham did. 40 As it is, you are bent on killing me, because I have told you the truth, which I heard from God. That is not how Abraham acted. 41 You are doing your own father's work.'

They said, 'We are not illegitimate; God is our father, and God alone.' 42 Jesus said to them, 'If God were your father, you would love me, for God is the source of my being, and from him I come. I have not come of my own accord; he sent me. 43 Why do you not understand what I am saying? It is because my teaching is beyond your grasp.

---

m Gk *I am*   *n* Or *What I have told you from the beginning*
o Other ancient authorities read *you do what you have heard from your father*   *p* Other ancient authorities read *If you are Abraham's children, then do*

8:25 **What . . . along:** or *Why should I speak to you at all?*

that you will die in your sins. For if you do not believe that I AM, you will die in your sins." 25 So they said to him, "Who are you?" Jesus said to them, "What I told you from the beginning. 26 I have much to say about you in condemnation. But the one who sent me is true, and what I heard from him I tell the world." 27 They did not realize that he was speaking to them of the Father. 28 So Jesus said [to them], "When you lift up the Son of Man, then you will realize that I AM, and that I do nothing on my own, but I say only what the Father taught me. 29 The one who sent me is with me. He has not left me alone, because I always do what is pleasing to him." 30 Because he spoke this way, many came to believe in him.

31 Jesus then said to those Jews who believed in him, "If you remain in my word, you will truly be my disciples, 32 and you will know the truth, and the truth will set you free." 33 They answered him, "We are descendants of Abraham and have never been enslaved to anyone. How can you say, 'You will become free'?" 34 Jesus answered them, "Amen, amen, I say to you, everyone who commits sin is a slave of sin. 35 A slave does not remain in a household forever, but a son always remains. 36 So if a son frees you, then you will truly be free. 37 I know that you are descendants of Abraham. But you are trying to kill me, because my word has no room among you. 38 I tell you what I have seen in the Father's presence; then do what you have heard from the Father."

39 They answered and said to him, "Our father is Abraham." Jesus said to them, "If you were Abraham's children, you would be doing the works of Abraham. 40 But now you are trying to kill me, a man who has told you the truth that I heard from God; Abraham did not do this. 41 You are doing the works of your father!" [So] they said to him, "We are not illegitimate. We have one Father, God." 42 Jesus said to them, "If God were your Father, you would love me, for I came from God and am here; I did not come on my own, but he sent me. 43 Why do you not understand what I am saying? Because you cannot bear to hear my word.

---

24 I have told you already: You will die in your sins. Yes, if you do not believe that I am He,[i] you will die in your sins.

25 So they said to him, 'Who are you?' Jesus answered:

> What I have told you from the outset.
> 26 About you I have much to say
> and much to judge;
> but the one who sent me is true,
> and what I declare to the world
> I have learnt from him.

27 They did not recognise that he was talking to them about the Father. 28 So Jesus said:

> When you have lifted up the Son of man,
> then you will know that I am He
> and that I do nothing of my own accord.
> What I say
> is what the Father has taught me;
> 29 he who sent me is with me,
> and has not left me to myself,
> for I always do what pleases him.

30 As he was saying this, many came to believe in him. 31 To the Jews who believed in him Jesus said:

> If you make my word your home
> you will indeed be my disciples;
> 32 you will come to know the truth,
> and the truth will set you free.

33 They answered, 'We are descended from Abraham and we have never been the slaves of anyone; what do you mean, "You will be set free?" ' 34 Jesus replied:

> In all truth I tell you,
> everyone who commits sin is a slave.
> 35 Now a slave has no permanent standing in the household,
> but a son belongs to it for ever.
> 36 So if the Son sets you free,
> you will indeed be free.
> 37 I know that you are descended from Abraham;
> but you want to kill me
> because my word finds no place in you.
> 38 What I speak of
> is what I have seen at my Father's side,
> and you too put into action
> the lessons you have learnt from your father.

39 They repeated, 'Our father is Abraham.' Jesus said to them:

> If you are Abraham's children,
> do as Abraham did.
> 40 As it is, you want to kill me,
> a man who has told you the truth
> as I have learnt it from God;
> that is not what Abraham did.
> 41 You are doing your father's work.

They replied, 'We were not born illegitimate, the only father we have is God.' 42 Jesus answered:

> If God were your father, you would love me,
> since I have my origin in God and have come from him;
> I did not come of my own accord,
> but he sent me.
> 43 Why do you not understand what I say?
> Because you cannot bear to listen to my words.

_i_ **8** Here and in vv. 28, 58 Jesus appropriates the divine name revealed to Moses in Ex 3:14.

NEW REVISED STANDARD VERSION

44 You are from your father the devil, and you choose to do your father's desires. He was a murderer from the beginning and does not stand in the truth, because there is no truth in him. When he lies, he speaks according to his own nature, for he is a liar and the father of lies. 45 But because I tell the truth, you do not believe me. 46 Which of you convicts me of sin? If I tell the truth, why do you not believe me? 47 Whoever is from God hears the words of God. The reason you do not hear them is that you are not from God."

48 The Jews answered him, "Are we not right in saying that you are a Samaritan and have a demon?" 49 Jesus answered, "I do not have a demon; but I honor my Father, and you dishonor me. 50 Yet I do not seek my own glory; there is one who seeks it and he is the judge. 51 Very truly, I tell you, whoever keeps my word will never see death." 52 The Jews said to him, "Now we know that you have a demon. Abraham died, and so did the prophets; yet you say, 'Whoever keeps my word will never taste death.' 53 Are you greater than our father Abraham, who died? The prophets also died. Who do you claim to be?" 54 Jesus answered, "If I glorify myself, my glory is nothing. It is my Father who glorifies me, he of whom you say, 'He is our God,' 55 though you do not know him. But I know him; if I would say that I do not know him, I would be a liar like you. But I do know him and I keep his word. 56 Your ancestor Abraham rejoiced that he would see my day; he saw it and was glad." 57 Then the Jews said to him, "You are not yet fifty years old, and have you seen Abraham?"*q* 58 Jesus said to them, "Very truly, I tell you, before Abraham was, I am." 59 So they picked up stones to throw at him, but Jesus hid himself and went out of the temple.

9 As he walked along, he saw a man blind from birth. 2 His disciples asked him, "Rabbi, who sinned, this man or his parents, that he was born blind?" 3 Jesus answered, "Neither this man nor his parents sinned; he was born blind so that God's works might be revealed in him. 4 We*r* must work the works of him who sent me*s* while it is day; night is coming when no one can work. 5 As long as I am in the world, I am the light of the world." 6 When he

REVISED ENGLISH BIBLE

44 Your father is the devil and you choose to carry out your father's desires. He was a murderer from the beginning, and is not rooted in the truth; there is no truth in him. When he tells a lie he is speaking his own language, for he is a liar and the father of lies. 45 But because I speak the truth, you do not believe me. 46 Which of you can convict me of sin? If what I say is true, why do you not believe me? 47 He who has God for his father listens to the words of God. You are not God's children, and that is why you do not listen.'

48 The Jews answered, 'Are we not right in saying that you are a Samaritan, and that you are possessed?' 49 'I am not possessed,' said Jesus; 'I am honouring my Father, but you dishonour me. 50 I do not care about my own glory; there is one who does care, and he is judge. 51 In very truth I tell you, if anyone obeys my teaching he will never see death.'

52 The Jews said, 'Now we are certain that you are possessed. Abraham is dead and so are the prophets; yet you say, "If anyone obeys my teaching he will never taste death." 53 Are you greater than our father Abraham? He is dead and the prophets too are dead. Who do you claim to be?'

54 Jesus replied, 'If I glorify myself, that glory of mine is worthless. It is the Father who glorifies me, he of whom you say, "He is our God," 55 though you do not know him. But I know him; if I were to say that I did not know him I should be a liar like you. I do know him and I obey his word. 56 Your father Abraham was overjoyed to see my day; he saw it and was glad.' 57 The Jews protested, 'You are not yet fifty years old. How can you have seen Abraham?' 58 Jesus said, 'In very truth I tell you, before Abraham was born, I am.' 59 They took up stones to throw at him, but he was not to be seen; and he left the temple.

9 As he went on his way Jesus saw a man who had been blind from birth. 2 His disciples asked him, 'Rabbi, why was this man born blind? Who sinned, this man or his parents?' 3 'It is not that he or his parents sinned,' Jesus answered; 'he was born blind so that God's power might be displayed in curing him. 4 While daylight lasts we must carry on the work of him who sent me; night is coming, when no one can work. 5 While I am in the world I am the light of the world.'

---

q Other ancient authorities read *has Abraham seen you?*   *r* Other ancient authorities read *I*   *s* Other ancient authorities read *us*

9:4 we: *some witnesses read* I.

44 You belong to your father the devil and you willingly carry out your father's desires. He was a murderer from the beginning and does not stand in truth, because there is no truth in him. When he tells a lie, he speaks in character, because he is a liar and the father of lies. 45 But because I speak the truth, you do not believe me. 46 Can any of you charge me with sin? If I am telling the truth, why do you not believe me? 47 Whoever belongs to God hears the words of God; for this reason you do not listen, because you do not belong to God."

48 The Jews answered and said to him, "Are we not right in saying that you are a Samaritan and are possessed?" 49 Jesus answered, "I am not possessed; I honor my Father, but you dishonor me. 50 I do not seek my own glory; there is one who seeks it and he is the one who judges. 51 Amen, amen, I say to you, whoever keeps my word will never see death." 52 [So] the Jews said to him, "Now we are sure that you are possessed. Abraham died, as did the prophets, yet you say, 'Whoever keeps my word will never taste death.' 53 Are you greater than our father Abraham, who died? Or the prophets, who died? Who do you make yourself out to be?" 54 Jesus answered, "If I glorify myself, my glory is worth nothing; but it is my Father who glorifies me, of whom you say, 'He is our God.' 55 You do not know him, but I know him. And if I should say that I do not know him, I would be like you a liar. But I do know him and I keep his word. 56 Abraham your father rejoiced to see my day; he saw it and was glad. 57 So the Jews said to him, "You are not yet fifty years old and you have seen Abraham?" 58 Jesus said to them, "Amen, amen, I say to you, before Abraham came to be, I AM." 59 So they picked up stones to throw at him; but Jesus hid and went out of the temple area.

9 As he passed by he saw a man blind from birth. 2 His disciples asked him, "Rabbi, who sinned, this man or his parents, that he was born blind?" 3 Jesus answered, "Neither he nor his parents sinned; it is so that the works of God might be made visible through him. 4 We have to do the works of the one who sent me while it is day. Night is coming when no one can work. 5 While I am in the world, I am the light of the world." 6 When he had said this, he spat

---

44 You are from your father, the devil,
and you prefer to do
what your father wants.
He was a murderer from the start;
he was never grounded in the truth;
there is no truth in him at all.
When he lies
he is speaking true to his nature,
because he is a liar, and the father of lies.
45 But it is because I speak the truth
that you do not believe me.
46 Can any of you convict me of sin?
If I speak the truth, why do you not believe me?
47 Whoever comes from God
listens to the words of God;
the reason why you do not listen
is that you are not from God.

48 The Jews replied, 'Are we not right in saying that you are a Samaritan and possessed by a devil?' Jesus answered:

49 I am not possessed;
but I honour my Father,
and you deny me honour.
50 I do not seek my own glory;
there is someone who does seek it and is the judge of it.
51 In all truth I tell you,
whoever keeps my word
will never see death.

52 The Jews said, 'Now we know that you are possessed. Abraham is dead, and the prophets are dead, and yet you say, "Whoever keeps my word will never know the taste of death." 53 Are you greater than our father Abraham, who is dead? The prophets are dead too. Who are you claiming to be?' 54 Jesus answered:

If I were to seek my own glory
my glory would be worth nothing;
in fact, my glory is conferred by the Father,
by the one of whom you say, 'He is our God,'
55 although you do not know him.
But I know him,
and if I were to say, 'I do not know him,'
I should be a liar, as you yourselves are.
But I do know him, and I keep his word.
56 Your father Abraham rejoiced
to think that he would see my Day;
he saw it and was glad.

57 The Jews then said, 'You are not fifty yet, and you have seen Abraham!' 58 Jesus replied:

In all truth I tell you,
before Abraham ever was,
I am.

59 At this they picked up stones to throw at him; but Jesus hid himself and left the Temple.

9 As he went along, he saw a man who had been blind from birth. 2 His disciples asked him, 'Rabbi, who sinned, this man or his parents, that he should have been born blind?' 3 'Neither he nor his parents sinned,' Jesus answered, 'he was born blind so that the works of God might be revealed in him.

4 'As long as day lasts
we must carry out the work of the one who sent me;
the night will soon be here when no one can work.
5 As long as I am in the world
I am the light of the world.'

had said this, he spat on the ground and made mud with the saliva and spread the mud on the man's eyes, 7 saying to him, "Go, wash in the pool of Siloam" (which means Sent). Then he went and washed and came back able to see. 8 The neighbors and those who had seen him before as a beggar began to ask, "Is this not the man who used to sit and beg?" 9 Some were saying, "It is he." Others were saying, "No, but it is someone like him." He kept saying, "I am the man." 10 But they kept asking him, "Then how were your eyes opened?" 11 He answered, "The man called Jesus made mud, spread it on my eyes, and said to me, 'Go to Siloam and wash.' Then I went and washed and received my sight." 12 They said to him, "Where is he?" He said, "I do not know."

13 They brought to the Pharisees the man who had formerly been blind. 14 Now it was a sabbath day when Jesus made the mud and opened his eyes. 15 Then the Pharisees also began to ask him how he had received his sight. He said to them, "He put mud on my eyes. Then I washed, and now I see." 16 Some of the Pharisees said, "This man is not from God, for he does not observe the sabbath." But others said, "How can a man who is a sinner perform such signs?" And they were divided. 17 So they said again to the blind man, "What do you say about him? It was your eyes he opened." He said, "He is a prophet."

18 The Jews did not believe that he had been blind and had received his sight until they called the parents of the man who had received his sight 19 and asked them, "Is this your son, who you say was born blind? How then does he now see?" 20 His parents answered, "We know that this is our son, and that he was born blind; 21 but we do not know how it is that now he sees, nor do we know who opened his eyes. Ask him; he is of age. He will speak for himself." 22 His parents said this because they were afraid of the Jews; for the Jews had already agreed that anyone who confessed Jesus[t] to be the Messiah[u] would be put out of the synagogue. 23 Therefore his parents said, "He is of age; ask him."

24 So for the second time they called the man who had been blind, and they said to him, "Give glory to God! We know that this man is a sinner." 25 He answered, "I do not know whether he is a sinner. One thing I do know, that though I was blind, now I see." 26 They said to him, "What did he do to you? How did he open your eyes?" 27 He answered them, "I have told you already, and you would not listen. Why do you want to hear it again? Do you also want to become his disciples?" 28 Then they reviled him, saying, "You are his disciple, but we are disciples of Moses. 29 We know that God has spoken to Moses, but as for this man, we do not know where he comes from." 30 The man answered, "Here is an astonishing thing! You do not know where he comes from, and yet he opened my eyes. 31 We know that God does not listen to sinners, but he does listen to one who worships him and obeys his will. 32 Never since the world began has it been heard that anyone opened the eyes of a person born blind. 33 If this man were not from God, he could do nothing." 34 They answered him, "You were born entirely in sins, and are you trying to teach us?" And they drove him out.

35 Jesus heard that they had driven him out, and when he found him, he said, "Do you believe in the Son of Man?"[v] 36 He answered, "And who is he, sir?[w] Tell me, so that I may believe in him." 37 Jesus said to him, "You have seen him, and the one speaking with you is he." 38 He said, "Lord,[w] I believe." And he worshiped him. 39 Jesus said, "I

6 With these words he spat on the ground and made a paste with the spittle; he spread it on the man's eyes, 7 and said to him, 'Go and wash in the pool of Siloam.' (The name means 'Sent'.) The man went off and washed, and came back able to see.

8 His neighbours and those who were accustomed to see him begging said, 'Is not this the man who used to sit and beg?' 9 Some said, 'Yes, it is.' Others said, 'No, but it is someone like him.' He himself said, 'I am the man.' 10 They asked him, 'How were your eyes opened?' 11 He replied, 'The man called Jesus made a paste and smeared my eyes with it, and told me to go to Siloam and wash. So I went and washed, and found I could see.' 12 'Where is he?' they asked. 'I do not know,' he said.

13 The man who had been blind was brought before the Pharisees. 14 As it was a sabbath day when Jesus made the paste and opened his eyes, 15 the Pharisees too asked him how he had gained his sight. The man told them, 'He spread a paste on my eyes; then I washed, and now I can see.' 16 Some of the Pharisees said, 'This man cannot be from God; he does not keep the sabbath.' Others said, 'How could such signs come from a sinful man?' So they took different sides. 17 Then they continued to question him: 'What have you to say about him? It was your eyes he opened.' He answered, 'He is a prophet.'

18 The Jews would not believe that the man had been blind and had gained his sight, until they had summoned his parents 19 and questioned them: 'Is this your son? Do you say that he was born blind? How is it that he can see now?' 20 The parents replied, 'We know that he is our son, and that he was born blind. 21 But how it is that he can now see, or who opened his eyes, we do not know. Ask him; he is of age; let him speak for himself.' 22 His parents gave this answer because they were afraid of the Jews; for the Jewish authorities had already agreed that anyone who acknowledged Jesus as Messiah should be banned from the synagogue. 23 That is why the parents said, 'He is of age; ask him.'

24 So for the second time they summoned the man who had been blind, and said, 'Speak the truth before God. We know that this man is a sinner.' 25 'Whether or not he is a sinner, I do not know,' the man replied. 'All I know is this: I was blind and now I can see.' 26 'What did he do to you?' they asked. 'How did he open your eyes?' 27 'I have told you already,' he retorted, 'but you took no notice. Why do you want to hear it again? Do you also want to become his disciples?' 28 Then they became abusive. 'You are that man's disciple,' they said, 'but we are disciples of Moses. 29 We know that God spoke to Moses, but as for this man, we do not know where he comes from.'

30 The man replied, 'How extraordinary! Here is a man who has opened my eyes, yet you do not know where he comes from! 31 We know that God does not listen to sinners; he listens to anyone who is devout and obeys his will. 32 To open the eyes of a man born blind—that is unheard of since time began. 33 If this man was not from God he could do nothing.' 34 'Who are you to lecture us?' they retorted. 'You were born and bred in sin.' Then they turned him out.

35 Hearing that they had turned him out, Jesus found him and asked, 'Have you faith in the Son of Man?' 36 The man answered, 'Tell me who he is, sir, that I may put my faith in him.' 37 'You have seen him,' said Jesus; 'indeed, it is he who is speaking to you.' 38 'Lord, I believe,' he said, and fell on his knees before him.

---

[t] Gk him   [u] Or the Christ   [v] Other ancient authorities read the Son of God   [w] Sir and Lord translate the same Greek word

9:35 **Son of Man:** some witnesses read Son of God.

on the ground and made clay with the saliva, and smeared the clay on his eyes, 7 and said to him, "Go wash in the Pool of Siloam" (which means Sent). So he went and washed, and came back able to see.

8 His neighbors and those who had seen him earlier as a beggar said, "Isn't this the one who used to sit and beg?" 9 Some said, "It is," but others said, "No, he just looks like him." He said, "I am." 10 So they said to him, "[So] how were your eyes opened?" 11 He replied, "The man called Jesus made clay and anointed my eyes and told me, 'Go to Siloam and wash.' So I went there and washed and was able to see." 12 And they said to him, "Where is he?" He said, "I don't know."

13 They brought the one who was once blind to the Pharisees. 14 Now Jesus had made clay and opened his eyes on a sabbath. 15 So then the Pharisees also asked him how he was able to see. He said to them, "He put clay on my eyes, and I washed, and now I can see." 16 So some of the Pharisees said, "This man is not from God, because he does not keep the sabbath." [But] others said, "How can a sinful man do such signs?" And there was a division among them. 17 So they said to the blind man again, "What do you have to say about him, since he opened your eyes?" He said, "He is a prophet."

18 Now the Jews did not believe that he had been blind and gained his sight until they summoned the parents of the one who had gained his sight. 19 They asked them, "Is this your son, who you say was born blind? How does he now see?" 20 His parents answered and said, "We know that this is our son and that he was born blind. 21 We do not know how he sees now, nor do we know who opened his eyes. Ask him, he is of age; he can speak for himself." 22 His parents said this because they were afraid of the Jews, for the Jews had already agreed that if anyone acknowledged him as the Messiah, he would be expelled from the synagogue. 23 For this reason his parents said, "He is of age; question him."

24 So a second time they called the man who had been blind and said to him, "Give God the praise! We know that this man is a sinner." 25 He replied, "If he is a sinner, I do not know. One thing I do know is that I was blind and now I see." 26 So they said to him, "What did he do to you? How did he open your eyes?" 27 He answered them, "I told you already and you did not listen. Why do you want to hear it again? Do you want to become his disciples, too?" 28 They ridiculed him and said, "You are that man's disciple; we are disciples of Moses! 29 We know that God spoke to Moses, but we do not know where this one is from." 30 The man answered and said to them, "This is what is so amazing, that you do not know where he is from, yet he opened my eyes. 31 We know that God does not listen to sinners, but if one is devout and does his will, he listens to him. 32 It is unheard of that anyone ever opened the eyes of a person born blind. 33 If this man were not from God, he would not be able to do anything." 34 They answered and said to him, "You were born totally in sin, and are you trying to teach us?" Then they threw him out.

35 When Jesus heard that they had thrown him out, he found him and said, "Do you believe in the Son of Man?" 36 He answered and said, "Who is he, sir, that I may believe in him?" 37 Jesus said to him, "You have seen him and the one speaking with you is he." 38 He said, "I do believe, Lord," and he worshiped him. 39 Then Jesus said, "I came

6 Having said this, he spat on the ground, made a paste with the spittle, put this over the eyes of the blind man, 7 and said to him, 'Go and wash in the Pool of Siloam' (the name means 'one who has been sent'). So he went off and washed and came back able to see.

8 His neighbours and the people who used to see him before (for he was a beggar) said, 'Isn't this the man who used to sit and beg?' 9 Some said, 'Yes, it is the same one.' Others said, 'No, but he looks just like him.' The man himself said, 'Yes, I am the one.' 10 So they said to him, 'Then how is it that your eyes were opened?' 11 He answered, 'The man called Jesus made a paste, daubed my eyes with it and said to me, "Go off and wash at Siloam"; so I went, and when I washed I gained my sight.' 12 They asked, 'Where is he?' He answered, 'I don't know.'

13 They brought to the Pharisees the man who had been blind. 14 It had been a Sabbath day when Jesus made the paste and opened the man's eyes, 15 so when the Pharisees asked him how he had gained his sight, he said, 'He put a paste on my eyes, and I washed, and I can see.' 16 Then some of the Pharisees said, 'That man cannot be from God: he does not keep the Sabbath.' Others said, 'How can a sinner produce signs like this?' And there was division among them. 17 So they spoke to the blind man again, 'What have you to say about him yourself, now that he has opened your eyes?' The man answered, 'He is a prophet.'

18 However, the Jews would not believe that the man had been blind without first sending for the parents of the man who had gained his sight and 19 asking them, 'Is this man really the son of yours who you say was born blind? If so, how is it that he is now able to see?' 20 His parents answered, 'We know he is our son and we know he was born blind, 21 but how he can see, we don't know, nor who opened his eyes. Ask him. He is old enough: let him speak for himself.' 22 His parents spoke like this out of fear of the Jews, who had already agreed to ban from the synagogue anyone who should acknowledge Jesus as the Christ. 23 This was why his parents said, 'He is old enough; ask him.'

24 So the Jews sent for the man again and said to him, 'Give glory to God! We are satisfied that this man is a sinner.' 25 The man answered, 'Whether he is a sinner I don't know; all I know is that I was blind and now I can see.' 26 They said to him, 'What did he do to you? How did he open your eyes?' 27 He replied, 'I have told you once and you wouldn't listen. Why do you want to hear it all again? Do you want to become his disciples yourselves?' 28 At this they hurled abuse at him, 'It is you who are his disciple, we are disciples of Moses: 29 we know that God spoke to Moses, but as for this man, we don't know where he comes from.' 30 The man replied, 'That is just what is so amazing! You don't know where he comes from and he has opened my eyes! 31 We know that God doesn't listen to sinners, but God does listen to people who are devout and do his will. 32 Ever since the world began it is unheard of for anyone to open the eyes of someone born blind; 33 if this man were not from God, he wouldn't have been able to do anything.' 34 They retorted, 'Are you trying to teach us, and you a sinner through and through ever since you were born!' And they ejected him.

35 Jesus heard they had ejected him, and when he found him he said to him, 'Do you believe in the Son of man?' 36 'Sir,' the man replied, 'tell me who he is so that I may believe in him.' 37 Jesus said, 'You have seen him; he is speaking to you.' 38 The man said, 'Lord, I believe,' and worshipped him.

came into this world for judgment so that those who do not see may see, and those who do see may become blind." 40 Some of the Pharisees near him heard this and said to him, "Surely we are not blind, are we?" 41 Jesus said to them, "If you were blind, you would not have sin. But now that you say, 'We see,' your sin remains.

10 "Very truly, I tell you, anyone who does not enter the sheepfold by the gate but climbs in by another way is a thief and a bandit. 2 The one who enters by the gate is the shepherd of the sheep. 3 The gatekeeper opens the gate for him, and the sheep hear his voice. He calls his own sheep by name and leads them out. 4 When he has brought out all his own, he goes ahead of them, and the sheep follow him because they know his voice. 5 They will not follow a stranger, but they will run from him because they do not know the voice of strangers." 6 Jesus used this figure of speech with them, but they did not understand what he was saying to them.

7 So again Jesus said to them, "Very truly, I tell you, I am the gate for the sheep. 8 All who came before me are thieves and bandits; but the sheep did not listen to them. 9 I am the gate. Whoever enters by me will be saved, and will come in and go out and find pasture. 10 The thief comes only to steal and kill and destroy. I came that they may have life, and have it abundantly.

11 "I am the good shepherd. The good shepherd lays down his life for the sheep. 12 The hired hand, who is not the shepherd and does not own the sheep, sees the wolf coming and leaves the sheep and runs away — and the wolf snatches them and scatters them. 13 The hired hand runs away because a hired hand does not care for the sheep. 14 I am the good shepherd. I know my own and my own know me, 15 just as the Father knows me and I know the Father. And I lay down my life for the sheep. 16 I have other sheep that do not belong to this fold. I must bring them also, and they will listen to my voice. So there will be one flock, one shepherd. 17 For this reason the Father loves me, because I lay down my life in order to take it up again. 18 No one

39 Jesus said, 'It is for judgement that I have come into this world — to give sight to the sightless and to make blind those who see.' 40 Some Pharisees who were present asked, 'Do you mean that we are blind?' 41 'If you were blind,' said Jesus, 'you would not be guilty, but because you claim to see, your guilt remains.

10 'In very truth I tell you, the man who does not enter the sheepfold by the door, but climbs in some other way, is nothing but a thief and a robber. 2 He who enters by the door is the shepherd in charge of the sheep. 3 The door-keeper admits him, and the sheep hear his voice; he calls his own sheep by name, and leads them out. 4 When he has brought them all out, he goes ahead of them and the sheep follow, because they know his voice. 5 They will not follow a stranger; they will run away from him, because they do not recognize the voice of strangers.'

6 This was a parable that Jesus told them, but they did not understand what he meant by it.

7 So Jesus spoke again: 'In very truth I tell you, I am the door of the sheepfold. 8 The sheep paid no heed to any who came before me, for they were all thieves and robbers. 9 I am the door; anyone who comes into the fold through me will be safe. He will go in and out and find pasture.

10 'A thief comes only to steal, kill, and destroy; I have come that they may have life, and may have it in all its fullness. 11 I am the good shepherd; the good shepherd lays down his life for the sheep. 12 The hired man, when he sees the wolf coming, abandons the sheep and runs away, because he is not the shepherd and the sheep are not his. Then the wolf harries the flock and scatters the sheep. 13 The man runs away because he is a hired man and cares nothing for the sheep.

14 'I am the good shepherd; I know my own and my own know me, 15 as the Father knows me and I know the Father; and I lay down my life for the sheep. 16 But there are other sheep of mine, not belonging to this fold; I must lead them as well, and they too will listen to my voice. There will then be one flock, one shepherd. 17 The Father loves me because I lay down my life, to receive it back again. 18 No one takes

NEW AMERICAN BIBLE

into this world for judgment, so that those who do not see might see, and those who do see might become blind."

⁴⁰Some of the Pharisees who were with him heard this and said to him, "Surely we are not also blind, are we?" ⁴¹Jesus said to them, "If you were blind, you would have no sin; but now you are saying, 'We see,' so your sin remains.

10 "Amen, amen, I say to you, whoever does not enter a sheepfold through the gate but climbs over elsewhere is a thief and a robber. ²But whoever enters through the gate is the shepherd of the sheep. ³The gatekeeper opens it for him, and the sheep hear his voice, as he calls his own sheep by name and leads them out. ⁴When he has driven out all his own, he walks ahead of them, and the sheep follow him, because they recognize his voice. ⁵But they will not follow a stranger; they will run away from him, because they do not recognize the voice of strangers." ⁶Although Jesus used this figure of speech, they did not realize what he was trying to tell them.

⁷So Jesus said again, "Amen, amen, I say to you, I am the gate for the sheep. ⁸All who came [before me] are thieves and robbers, but the sheep did not listen to them. ⁹I am the gate. Whoever enters through me will be saved, and will come in and go out and find pasture. ¹⁰A thief comes only to steal and slaughter and destroy; I came so that they might have life and have it more abundantly. ¹¹I am the good shepherd. A good shepherd lays down his life for the sheep. ¹²A hired man, who is not a shepherd and whose sheep are not his own, sees a wolf coming and leaves the sheep and runs away, and the wolf catches and scatters them. ¹³This is because he works for pay and has no concern for the sheep. ¹⁴I am the good shepherd, and I know mine and mine know me, ¹⁵just as the Father knows me and I know the Father; and I will lay down my life for the sheep. ¹⁶I have other sheep that do not belong to this fold. These also I must lead, and they will hear my voice, and there will be one flock, one shepherd. ¹⁷This is why the Father loves me, because I lay down my life in order to take it up again.

NEW JERUSALEM BIBLE

³⁹Jesus said:

It is for judgement
that I have come into this world,
so that those without sight may see
and those with sight may become blind.

⁴⁰Hearing this, some Pharisees who were present said to him, 'So we are blind, are we?' ⁴¹Jesus replied:

If you were blind,
you would not be guilty,
but since you say, 'We can see,'
your guilt remains.

10 ᵐ'In all truth I tell you, anyone who does not enter the sheepfold through the gate, but climbs in some other way, is a thief and a bandit. ²He who enters through the gate is the shepherd of the flock; ³the gatekeeper lets him in, the sheep hear his voice, one by one he calls his own sheep and leads them out. ⁴When he has brought out all those that are his, he goes ahead of them, and the sheep follow because they know his voice. ⁵They will never follow a stranger, but will run away from him because they do not recognise the voice of strangers.'

⁶Jesus told them this parable but they failed to understand what he was saying to them.

⁷So Jesus spoke to them again:

In all truth I tell you,
I am the gate of the sheepfold.
⁸All who have come before me
are thieves and bandits,
but the sheep took no notice of them.
⁹I am the gate.
Anyone who enters through me will be safe:
such a one will go in and out
and will find pasture.
¹⁰The thief comes
only to steal and kill and destroy.
I have come
so that they may have life
and have it to the full.
¹¹I am the good shepherd:
the good shepherd lays down his life for his sheep.
¹²The hired man, since he is not the shepherd
and the sheep do not belong to him,
abandons the sheep
as soon as he sees a wolf coming, and runs away,
and then the wolf attacks and scatters the sheep;
¹³he runs away because he is only a hired man
and has no concern for the sheep.
¹⁴I am the good shepherd;
I know my own
and my own know me,
¹⁵just as the Father knows me
and I know the Father;
and I lay down my life for my sheep.
¹⁶And there are other sheep I have
that are not of this fold,
and I must lead these too.
They too will listen to my voice,
and there will be only one flock,
one shepherd.
¹⁷The Father loves me,
because I lay down my life
in order to take it up again.

10, 8: [*Before me*]: these words are omitted in many good early manuscripts and versions.

ᵐ**10** cf. Jr 23; Ezk 34.

takes*x* it from me, but I lay it down of my own accord. I have power to lay it down, and I have power to take it up again. I have received this command from my Father."

19 Again the Jews were divided because of these words. 20 Many of them were saying, "He has a demon and is out of his mind. Why listen to him?" 21 Others were saying, "These are not the words of one who has a demon. Can a demon open the eyes of the blind?"

22 At that time the festival of the Dedication took place in Jerusalem. It was winter, 23 and Jesus was walking in the temple, in the portico of Solomon. 24 So the Jews gathered around him and said to him, "How long will you keep us in suspense? If you are the Messiah,*y* tell us plainly." 25 Jesus answered, "I have told you, and you do not believe. The works that I do in my Father's name testify to me; 26 but you do not believe, because you do not belong to my sheep. 27 My sheep hear my voice. I know them, and they follow me. 28 I give them eternal life, and they will never perish. No one will snatch them out of my hand. 29 What my Father has given me is greater than all else, and no one can snatch it out of the Father's hand.*z* 30 The Father and I are one."

31 The Jews took up stones again to stone him. 32 Jesus replied, "I have shown you many good works from the Father. For which of these are you going to stone me?" 33 The Jews answered, "It is not for a good work that we are going to stone you, but for blasphemy, because you, though only a human being, are making yourself God." 34 Jesus answered, "Is it not written in your law,*a* 'I said, you are gods'? 35 If those to whom the word of God came were called 'gods'—and the scripture cannot be annulled— 36 can you say that the one whom the Father has sanctified and sent into the world is blaspheming because I said, 'I am God's Son'? 37 If I am not doing the works of my Father, then do not believe me. 38 But if I do them, even though you do not believe me, believe the works, so that you may know and understand*b* that the Father is in me and I am in the Father." 39 Then they tried to arrest him again, but he escaped from their hands.

40 He went away again across the Jordan to the place where John had been baptizing earlier, and he remained there. 41 Many came to him, and they were saying, "John performed no sign, but everything that John said about this man was true." 42 And many believed in him there.

it away from me; I am laying it down of my own free will. I have the right to lay it down, and I have the right to receive it back again; this charge I have received from my Father.'

19 These words once again caused a division among the Jews. 20 Many of them said, 'He is possessed, he is out of his mind. Why listen to him?' 21 Others said, 'No one possessed by a demon could speak like this. Could a demon open the eyes of the blind?'

22 It was winter, and the festival of the Dedication was being held in Jerusalem. 23 As Jesus was walking in the temple precincts, in Solomon's Portico, 24 the Jews gathered round him and asked: 'How long are you going to keep us in suspense? Tell us plainly: are you the Messiah?' 25 'I have told you,' said Jesus, 'and you do not believe. My deeds done in my Father's name are my credentials, 26 but because you are not sheep of my flock you do not believe. 27 My own sheep listen to my voice; I know them and they follow me. 28 I give them eternal life and they will never perish; no one will snatch them from my care. 29 My Father who has given them to me is greater than all, and no one can snatch them out of the Father's care. 30 The Father and I are one.'

31 Once again the Jews picked up stones to stone him. 32 At this Jesus said to them, 'By the Father's power I have done many good deeds before your eyes; for which of these are you stoning me?' 33 'We are not stoning you for any good deed,' the Jews replied, 'but for blasphemy: you, a man, are claiming to be God.' 34 Jesus answered, 'Is it not written in your law, "I said: You are gods"? 35 It is those to whom God's word came who are called gods—and scripture cannot be set aside. 36 Then why do you charge me with blasphemy for saying, "I am God's son," I whom the Father consecrated and sent into the world?

37 'If my deeds are not the deeds of my Father, do not believe me. 38 But if they are, then even if you do not believe me, believe the deeds, so that you may recognize and know that the Father is in me, and I in the Father.' 39 This provoked them to make another attempt to seize him, but he escaped from their clutches.

40 Jesus withdrew again across the Jordan, to the place where John had been baptizing earlier, and stayed there 41 while crowds came to him. 'John gave us no miraculous sign,' they said, 'but all that he told us about this man was true.' 42 And many came to believe in him there.

---

x Other ancient authorities read *has taken*   *y* Or *the Christ*
z Other ancient authorities read *My Father who has given them to me is greater than all, and no one can snatch them out of the Father's hand*   *a* Other ancient authorities read *in the law*   *b* Other ancient authorities lack *and understand*; others read *and believe*

10:29 **My Father . . . snatch them:** *some witnesses read* That which my Father has given me is greater than all, and no one can snatch it.
10:33 **claiming . . . God:** *or* claiming to be a god.

18 No one takes it from me, but I lay it down on my own. I have power to lay it down, and power to take it up again. This command I have received from my Father."

19 Again there was a division among the Jews because of these words. 20 Many of them said, "He is possessed and out of his mind; why listen to him?" 21 Others said, "These are not the words of one possessed; surely a demon cannot open the eyes of the blind, can he?"

22 The feast of the Dedication was then taking place in Jerusalem. It was winter. 23 And Jesus walked about in the temple area on the Portico of Solomon. 24 So the Jews gathered around him and said to him, "How long are you going to keep us in suspense? If you are the Messiah, tell us plainly." 25 Jesus answered them, "I told you and you do not believe. The works I do in my Father's name testify to me. 26 But you do not believe, because you are not among my sheep. 27 My sheep hear my voice; I know them, and they follow me. 28 I give them eternal life, and they shall never perish. No one can take them out of my hand. 29 My Father, who has given them to me, is greater than all, and no one can take them out of the Father's hand. 30 The Father and I are one."

31 The Jews again picked up rocks to stone him. 32 Jesus answered them, "I have shown you many good works from my Father. For which of these are you trying to stone me?" 33 The Jews answered him, "We are not stoning you for a good work but for blasphemy. You, a man, are making yourself God." 34 Jesus answered them, "Is it not written in your law, 'I said, "You are gods"'? 35 If it calls them gods to whom the word of God came, and scripture cannot be set aside, 36 can you say that the one whom the Father has consecrated and sent into the world blasphemes because I said, 'I am the Son of God'? 37 If I do not perform my Father's works, do not believe me; 38 but if I perform them, even if you do not believe me, believe the works, so that you may realize [and understand] that the Father is in me and I am in the Father." 39 [Then] they tried again to arrest him; but he escaped from their power.

40 He went back across the Jordan to the place where John first baptized, and there he remained. 41 Many came to him and said, "John performed no sign, but everything John said about this man was true." 42 And many there began to believe in him.

18 No one takes it from me;
  I lay it down of my own free will,
  and as I have power to lay it down,
  so I have power to take it up again;
  and this is the command I have received from my
    Father.

19 These words caused a fresh division among the Jews. 20 Many said, 'He is possessed, he is raving; why do you listen to him?' 21 Others said, 'These are not the words of a man possessed by a devil: could a devil open the eyes of the blind?'

22 It was the time of the feast of Dedication in Jerusalem. It was winter, 23 and Jesus was in the Temple walking up and down in the Portico of Solomon. 24 The Jews gathered round him and said, 'How much longer are you going to keep us in suspense? If you are the Christ, tell us openly.' 25 Jesus replied:

I have told you, but you do not believe.
  The works I do in my Father's name are my
    witness;
26 but you do not believe,
  because you are no sheep of mine.
27 The sheep that belong to me listen to my voice;
  I know them and they follow me.
28 I give them eternal life;
  they will never be lost
  and no one will ever steal them from my hand.
29 The Father, for what he has given me, is greater
    than anyone,
  and no one can steal anything from the Father's
    hand.
30 The Father and I are one.

31 The Jews fetched stones to stone him, 32 so Jesus said to them, 'I have shown you many good works from my Father; for which of these are you stoning me?' 33 The Jews answered him, 'We are stoning you, not for doing a good work, but for blasphemy; though you are only a man, you claim to be God.' 34 Jesus answered:

Is it not written in your Law:
  I said, you are gods? n
35 So it uses the word 'gods'
  of those people to whom the word of God was
    addressed
  —and scripture cannot be set aside.
36 Yet to someone whom the Father has consecrated
  and sent into the world you say,
  'You are blaspheming'
  because I said, 'I am Son of God.'
37 If I am not doing my Father's work,
  there is no need to believe me;
38 but if I am doing it,
  then even if you refuse to believe in me,
  at least believe in the work I do;
  then you will know for certain
  that the Father is in me and I am in the Father.

39 They again wanted to arrest him then, but he eluded their clutches.
40 He went back again to the far side of the Jordan to the district where John had been baptising at first and he stayed there. 41 Many people who came to him said, 'John gave no signs, but all he said about this man was true'; 42 and many of them believed in him.

n 10 Ps 82:6.

11 Now a certain man was ill, Lazarus of Bethany, the village of Mary and her sister Martha. 2 Mary was the one who anointed the Lord with perfume and wiped his feet with her hair; her brother Lazarus was ill. 3 So the sisters sent a message to Jesus,c "Lord, he whom you love is ill." 4 But when Jesus heard it, he said, "This illness does not lead to death; rather it is for God's glory, so that the Son of God may be glorified through it." 5 Accordingly, though Jesus loved Martha and her sister and Lazarus, 6 after having heard that Lazarusd was ill, he stayed two days longer in the place where he was.

7 Then after this he said to the disciples, "Let us go to Judea again." 8 The disciples said to him, "Rabbi, the Jews were just now trying to stone you, and are you going there again?" 9 Jesus answered, "Are there not twelve hours of daylight? Those who walk during the day do not stumble, because they see the light of this world. 10 But those who walk at night stumble, because the light is not in them." 11 After saying this, he told them, "Our friend Lazarus has fallen asleep, but I am going there to awaken him." 12 The disciples said to him, "Lord, if he has fallen asleep, he will be all right." 13 Jesus, however, had been speaking about his death, but they thought that he was referring merely to sleep. 14 Then Jesus told them plainly, "Lazarus is dead. 15 For your sake I am glad I was not there, so that you may believe. But let us go to him." 16 Thomas, who was called the Twin,e said to his fellow disciples, "Let us also go, that we may die with him."

17 When Jesus arrived, he found that Lazarusd had already been in the tomb four days. 18 Now Bethany was near Jerusalem, some two milesf away, 19 and many of the Jews had come to Martha and Mary to console them about their brother. 20 When Martha heard that Jesus was coming, she went and met him, while Mary stayed at home. 21 Martha said to Jesus, "Lord, if you had been here, my brother would not have died. 22 But even now I know that God will give you whatever you ask of him." 23 Jesus said to her, "Your brother will rise again." 24 Martha said to him, "I know that he will rise again in the resurrection on the last day." 25 Jesus said to her, "I am the resurrection and the life.g Those who believe in me, even though they die, will live, 26 and everyone who lives and believes in me will never die. Do you believe this?" 27 She said to him, "Yes, Lord, I believe that you are the Messiah,h the Son of God, the one coming into the world."

28 When she had said this, she went back and called her sister Mary, and told her privately, "The Teacher is here and is calling for you." 29 And when she heard it, she got up quickly and went to him. 30 Now Jesus had not yet come to the village, but was still at the place where Martha had met him. 31 The Jews who were with her in the house, consoling her, saw Mary get up quickly and go out. They followed her because they thought that she was going to the tomb to weep there. 32 When Mary came where Jesus was and saw him, she knelt at his feet and said to him, "Lord, if you had been here, my brother would not have died." 33 When Jesus saw her weeping, and the Jews who came with her also weeping, he was greatly disturbed in spirit and deeply moved. 34 He said, "Where have you laid him?" They said to him, "Lord, come and see." 35 Jesus began to weep. 36 So the Jews said, "See how he loved him!" 37 But some of them said, "Could not he who opened the eyes of the blind man have kept this man from dying?"

38 Then Jesus, again greatly disturbed, came to the tomb. It was a cave, and a stone was lying against it.

11 There was a man named Lazarus who had fallen ill. His home was at Bethany, the village of Mary and her sister Martha. 2 This Mary, whose brother Lazarus had fallen ill, was the woman who anointed the Lord with ointment and wiped his feet with her hair. 3 The sisters sent a message to him: 'Sir, you should know that your friend lies ill.' 4 When Jesus heard this he said, 'This illness is not to end in death; through it God's glory is to be revealed and the Son of God glorified.' 5 Therefore, though he loved Martha and her sister and Lazarus, 6 he stayed where he was for two days after hearing of Lazarus's illness.

7 He then said to his disciples, 'Let us go back to Judaea.' 8 'Rabbi,' his disciples said, 'it is not long since the Jews there were wanting to stone you. Are you going there again?' 9 Jesus replied, 'Are there not twelve hours of daylight? Anyone can walk in the daytime without stumbling, because he has this world's light to see by. 10 But if he walks after nightfall he stumbles, because the light fails him.'

11 After saying this he added, 'Our friend Lazarus has fallen asleep, but I shall go and wake him.' 12 The disciples said, 'Master, if he is sleeping he will recover.' 13 Jesus had been speaking of Lazarus's death, but they thought that he meant natural sleep. 14 Then Jesus told them plainly: 'Lazarus is dead. 15 I am glad for your sake that I was not there; for it will lead you to believe. But let us go to him.' 16 Thomas, called 'the Twin', said to his fellow-disciples, 'Let us also go and die with him.'

17 On his arrival Jesus found that Lazarus had already been four days in the tomb. 18 Bethany was just under two miles from Jerusalem, 19 and many of the Jews had come from the city to visit Martha and Mary and condole with them about their brother. 20 As soon as Martha heard that Jesus was on his way, she went to meet him, and left Mary sitting at home. 21 Martha said to Jesus, 'Lord, if you had been here my brother would not have died. 22 Even now I know that God will grant you whatever you ask of him.' 23 Jesus said, 'Your brother will rise again.' 24 'I know that he will rise again', said Martha, 'at the resurrection on the last day.' 25 Jesus said, 'I am the resurrection and the life. Whoever has faith in me shall live, even though he dies; 26 and no one who lives and has faith in me shall ever die. Do you believe this?' 27 'I do, Lord,' she answered; 'I believe that you are the Messiah, the Son of God who was to come into the world.'

28 So saying she went to call her sister Mary and, taking her aside, she said, 'The Master is here and is asking for you.' 29 As soon as Mary heard this she rose and went to him. 30 Jesus had not yet entered the village, but was still at the place where Martha had met him. 31 When the Jews who were in the house condoling with Mary saw her hurry out, they went after her, assuming that she was going to the tomb to weep there.

32 Mary came to the place where Jesus was, and as soon as she saw him she fell at his feet and said, 'Lord, if you had been here my brother would not have died.' 33 When Jesus saw her weeping and the Jews who had come with her weeping, he was moved with indignation and deeply distressed. 34 'Where have you laid him?' he asked. They replied, 'Come and see.' 35 Jesus wept. 36 The Jews said, 'How dearly he must have loved him!' 37 But some of them said, 'Could not this man, who opened the blind man's eyes, have done something to keep Lazarus from dying?'

38 Jesus, again deeply moved, went to the tomb. It was a cave, with a stone placed against it. 39 Jesus said, 'Take

---

cGk him dGk he eGk Didymus fGk fifteen stadia
gOther ancient authorities lack and the life hOr the Christ

11:25 Some witnesses omit and the life.

11 Now a man was ill, Lazarus from Bethany, the village of Mary and her sister Martha. 2 Mary was the one who had anointed the Lord with perfumed oil and dried his feet with her hair; it was her brother Lazarus who was ill. 3 So the sisters sent word to him, saying, "Master, the one you love is ill." 4 When Jesus heard this he said, "This illness is not to end in death, but is for the glory of God, that the Son of God may be glorified through it." 5 Now Jesus loved Martha and her sister and Lazarus. 6 So when he heard that he was ill, he remained for two days in the place where he was. 7 Then after this he said to his disciples, "Let us go back to Judea." 8 The disciples said to him, "Rabbi, the Jews were just trying to stone you, and you want to go back there?" 9 Jesus answered, "Are there not twelve hours in a day? If one walks during the day, he does not stumble, because he sees the light of this world. 10 But if one walks at night, he stumbles, because the light is not in him." 11 He said this, and then told them, "Our friend Lazarus is asleep, but I am going to awaken him." 12 So the disciples said to him, "Master, if he is asleep, he will be saved." 13 But Jesus was talking about his death, while they thought that he meant ordinary sleep. 14 So then Jesus said to them clearly, "Lazarus has died. 15 And I am glad for you that I was not there, that you may believe. Let us go to him." 16 So Thomas, called Didymus, said to his fellow disciples, "Let us also go to die with him."

17 When Jesus arrived, he found that Lazarus had already been in the tomb for four days. 18 Now Bethany was near Jerusalem, only about two miles away. 19 And many of the Jews had come to Martha and Mary to comfort them about their brother. 20 When Martha heard that Jesus was coming, she went to meet him; but Mary sat at home. 21 Martha said to Jesus, "Lord, if you had been here, my brother would not have died. 22 [But] even now I know that whatever you ask of God, God will give you." 23 Jesus said to her, "Your brother will rise." 24 Martha said to him, "I know he will rise, in the resurrection on the last day." 25 Jesus told her, "I am the resurrection and the life; whoever believes in me, even if he dies, will live, 26 and everyone who lives and believes in me will never die. Do you believe this?" 27 She said to him, "Yes, Lord. I have come to believe that you are the Messiah, the Son of God, the one who is coming into the world."

28 When she had said this, she went and called her sister Mary secretly, saying, "The teacher is here and is asking for you." 29 As soon as she heard this, she rose quickly and went to him. 30 For Jesus had not yet come into the village, but was still where Martha had met him. 31 So when the Jews who were with her in the house comforting her saw Mary get up quickly and go out, they followed her, presuming that she was going to the tomb to weep there. 32 When Mary came to where Jesus was and saw him, she fell at his feet and said to him, "Lord, if you had been here, my brother would not have died." 33 When Jesus saw her weeping and the Jews who had come with her weeping, he became perturbed and deeply troubled, 34 and said, "Where have you laid him?" They said to him, "Sir, come and see." 35 And Jesus wept. 36 So the Jews said, "See how he loved him." 37 But some of them said, "Could not the one who opened the eyes of the blind man have done something so that this man would not have died?"

38 So Jesus, perturbed again, came to the tomb. It was a cave, and a stone lay across it. 39 Jesus said, "Take away the

11 There was a man named Lazarus of Bethany, the village of Mary and her sister, Martha, and he was ill. 2 It was the same Mary, the sister of the sick man Lazarus, who anointed the Lord with ointment and wiped his feet with her hair. 3 The sisters sent this message to Jesus, 'Lord, the man you love is ill.' 4 On receiving the message, Jesus said, 'This sickness will not end in death, but it is for God's glory so that through it the Son of God may be glorified.' 5 Jesus loved Martha and her sister and Lazarus, 6 yet when he heard that he was ill he stayed where he was for two more days 7 before saying to the disciples, 'Let us go back to Judaea.' 8 The disciples said, 'Rabbi, it is not long since the Jews were trying to stone you; are you going back there again?' 9 Jesus replied:

Are there not twelve hours in the day?
No one who walks in the daytime stumbles,
    having the light of this world to see by;
10 anyone who walks around at night stumbles,
    having no light as a guide.

11 He said that and then added, 'Our friend Lazarus is at rest; I am going to wake him.' 12 The disciples said to him, 'Lord, if he is at rest he will be saved.' 13 Jesus was speaking of the death of Lazarus, but they thought that by 'rest' he meant 'sleep'; 14 so Jesus put it plainly, 'Lazarus is dead; 15 and for your sake I am glad I was not there because now you will believe. But let us go to him.' 16 Then Thomas — known as the Twin — said to the other disciples, 'Let us also go to die with him.'

17 On arriving, Jesus found that Lazarus had been in the tomb for four days already. 18 Bethany is only about two miles from Jerusalem, 19 and many Jews had come to Martha and Mary to comfort them about their brother. 20 When Martha heard that Jesus was coming she went to meet him. Mary remained sitting in the house. 21 Martha said to Jesus, 'Lord, if you had been here, my brother would not have died, 22 but even now I know that God will grant whatever you ask of him.' 23 Jesus said to her, 'Your brother will rise again.' 24 Martha said, 'I know he will rise again at the resurrection on the last day.' 25 Jesus said:

I am the resurrection.
Anyone who believes in me, even though that
        person dies, will live,
26 and whoever lives and believes in me
    will never die.
Do you believe this?

27 'Yes, Lord,' she said, 'I believe that you are the Christ, the Son of God, the one who was to come into this world.' 28 When she had said this, she went and called her sister Mary, saying in a low voice, 'The Master is here and wants to see you.' 29 Hearing this, Mary got up quickly and went to him. 30 Jesus had not yet come into the village; he was still at the place where Martha had met him. 31 When the Jews who were in the house comforting Mary saw her get up so quickly and go out, they followed her, thinking that she was going to the tomb to weep there.

32 Mary went to Jesus, and as soon as she saw him she threw herself at his feet, saying, 'Lord, if you had been here, my brother would not have died.' 33 At the sight of her tears, and those of the Jews who had come with her, Jesus was greatly distressed, and with a profound sigh he said, 34 'Where have you put him?' They said, 'Lord, come and see.' 35 Jesus wept; 36 and the Jews said, 'See how much he loved him!' 37 But there were some who remarked, 'He opened the eyes of the blind man. Could he not have prevented this man's death?' 38 Sighing again, Jesus reached the tomb: it was a cave with a stone to close the opening.

NEW REVISED STANDARD VERSION

39 Jesus said, "Take away the stone." Martha, the sister of the dead man, said to him, "Lord, already there is a stench because he has been dead four days." 40 Jesus said to her, "Did I not tell you that if you believed, you would see the glory of God?" 41 So they took away the stone. And Jesus looked upward and said, "Father, I thank you for having heard me. 42 I knew that you always hear me, but I have said this for the sake of the crowd standing here, so that they may believe that you sent me." 43 When he had said this, he cried with a loud voice, "Lazarus, come out!" 44 The dead man came out, his hands and feet bound with strips of cloth, and his face wrapped in a cloth. Jesus said to them, "Unbind him, and let him go."

45 Many of the Jews therefore, who had come with Mary and had seen what Jesus did, believed in him. 46 But some of them went to the Pharisees and told them what he had done. 47 So the chief priests and the Pharisees called a meeting of the council, and said, "What are we to do? This man is performing many signs. 48 If we let him go on like this, everyone will believe in him, and the Romans will come and destroy both our holy place[i] and our nation." 49 But one of them, Caiaphas, who was high priest that year, said to them, "You know nothing at all! 50 You do not understand that it is better for you to have one man die for the people than to have the whole nation destroyed." 51 He did not say this on his own, but being high priest that year he prophesied that Jesus was about to die for the nation, 52 and not for the nation only, but to gather into one the dispersed children of God. 53 So from that day on they planned to put him to death.

54 Jesus therefore no longer walked about openly among the Jews, but went from there to a town called Ephraim in the region near the wilderness; and he remained there with the disciples.

55 Now the Passover of the Jews was near, and many went up from the country to Jerusalem before the Passover to purify themselves. 56 They were looking for Jesus and were asking one another as they stood in the temple, "What do you think? Surely he will not come to the festival, will he?" 57 Now the chief priests and the Pharisees had given orders that anyone who knew where Jesus[j] was should let them know, so that they might arrest him.

12 Six days before the Passover Jesus came to Bethany, the home of Lazarus, whom he had raised from the dead. 2 There they gave a dinner for him. Martha served, and Lazarus was one of those at the table with him. 3 Mary took a pound of costly perfume made of pure nard, anointed Jesus' feet, and wiped them[k] with her hair. The house was filled with the fragrance of the perfume. 4 But Judas Iscariot, one of his disciples (the one who was about to betray him), said, 5 "Why was this perfume not sold for three hundred denarii[l] and the money given to the poor?" 6 (He said this not because he cared about the poor, but because he was a thief; he kept the common purse and used to steal what was put into it.) 7 Jesus said, "Leave her alone. She bought it[m] so that she might keep it for the day of my burial. 8 You always have the poor with you, but you do not always have me."

9 When the great crowd of the Jews learned that he was there, they came not only because of Jesus but also to see Lazarus, whom he had raised from the dead. 10 So the chief priests planned to put Lazarus to death as well, 11 since it

REVISED ENGLISH BIBLE

away the stone.' Martha, the dead man's sister, said to him, 'Sir, by now there will be a stench; he has been there four days.' 40 Jesus said, 'Did I not tell you that if you have faith you will see the glory of God?' 41 Then they removed the stone.

Jesus looked upwards and said, 'Father, I thank you for hearing me. 42 I know that you always hear me, but I have spoken for the sake of the people standing round, that they may believe it was you who sent me.'

43 Then he raised his voice in a great cry: 'Lazarus, come out.' 44 The dead man came out, his hands and feet bound with linen bandages, his face wrapped in a cloth. Jesus said, 'Loose him; let him go.'

45 MANY of the Jews who had come to visit Mary, and had seen what Jesus did, put their faith in him. 46 But some of them went off to the Pharisees and reported what he had done.

47 Thereupon the chief priests and the Pharisees convened a meeting of the Council. 'This man is performing many signs,' they said, 'and what action are we taking? 48 If we let him go on like this the whole populace will believe in him, and then the Romans will come and sweep away our temple and our nation.' 49 But one of them, Caiaphas, who was high priest that year, said, 'You have no grasp of the situation at all; 50 you do not realize that it is more to your interest that one man should die for the people, than that the whole nation should be destroyed.' 51 He did not say this of his own accord, but as the high priest that year he was prophesying that Jesus would die for the nation, 52 and not for the nation alone but to gather together the scattered children of God. 53 So from that day on they plotted his death.

54 Accordingly Jesus no longer went about openly among the Jews, but withdrew to a town called Ephraim, in the country bordering on the desert, and stayed there with his disciples.

55 THE Jewish Passover was now at hand, and many people went up from the country to Jerusalem to purify themselves before the festival. 56 They looked out for Jesus, and as they stood in the temple they asked one another, 'What do you think? Perhaps he is not coming to the festival.' 57 Now the chief priests and the Pharisees had given orders that anyone who knew where he was must report it, so that they might arrest him.

12 Six days before the Passover festival Jesus came to Bethany, the home of Lazarus whom he had raised from the dead. 2 They gave a supper in his honour, at which Martha served, and Lazarus was among the guests with Jesus. 3 Then Mary brought a pound of very costly perfume, pure oil of nard, and anointed Jesus's feet and wiped them with her hair, till the house was filled with the fragrance. 4 At this, Judas Iscariot, one of his disciples — the one who was to betray him — protested, 5 'Could not this perfume have been sold for three hundred denarii and the money given to the poor?' 6 He said this, not out of any concern for the poor, but because he was a thief; he had charge of the common purse and used to pilfer the money kept in it. 7 'Leave her alone,' said Jesus. 'Let her keep it for the day of my burial. 8 The poor you have always among you, but you will not always have me.'

9 Learning he was there the Jews came in large numbers, not only because of Jesus but also to see Lazarus whom he had raised from the dead. 10 The chief priests then resolved to do away with Lazarus as well, 11 since on his account

---

[i] Or our temple; Greek our place   [j] Gk he   [k] Gk his feet
[l] Three hundred denarii would be nearly a year's wages for a laborer
[m] Gk lacks She bought it

12:5 **denarii:** see p. xxix.   12:8 Some witnesses omit The poor . . . have me.

stone." Martha, the dead man's sister, said to him, "Lord, by now there will be a stench; he has been dead for four days." 40 Jesus said to her, "Did I not tell you that if you believe you will see the glory of God?" 41 So they took away the stone. And Jesus raised his eyes and said, "Father, I thank you for hearing me. 42 I know that you always hear me; but because of the crowd here I have said this, that they may believe that you sent me." 43 And when he had said this, he cried out in a loud voice, "Lazarus, come out!" 44 The dead man came out, tied hand and foot with burial bands, and his face was wrapped in a cloth. So Jesus said to them, "Untie him and let him go."

45 Now many of the Jews who had come to Mary and seen what he had done began to believe in him. 46 But some of them went to the Pharisees and told them what Jesus had done. 47 So the chief priests and the Pharisees convened the Sanhedrin and said, "What are we going to do? This man is performing many signs. 48 If we leave him alone, all will believe in him, and the Romans will come and take away both our land and our nation." 49 But one of them, Caiaphas, who was high priest that year, said to them, "You know nothing, 50 nor do you consider that it is better for you that one man should die instead of the people, so that the whole nation may not perish." 51 He did not say this on his own, but since he was high priest for that year, he prophesied that Jesus was going to die for the nation, 52 and not only for the nation, but also to gather into one the dispersed children of God. 53 So from that day on they planned to kill him.

54 So Jesus no longer walked about in public among the Jews, but he left for the region near the desert, to a town called Ephraim, and there he remained with his disciples.

55 Now the Passover of the Jews was near, and many went up from the country to Jerusalem before Passover to purify themselves. 56 They looked for Jesus and said to one another as they were in the temple area, "What do you think? That he will not come to the feast?" 57 For the chief priests and the Pharisees had given orders that if anyone knew where he was, he should inform them, so that they might arrest him.

12 Six days before Passover Jesus came to Bethany, where Lazarus was, whom Jesus had raised from the dead. 2 They gave a dinner for him there, and Martha served, while Lazarus was one of those reclining at table with him. 3 Mary took a liter of costly perfumed oil made from genuine aromatic nard and anointed the feet of Jesus and dried them with her hair; the house was filled with the fragrance of the oil. 4 Then Judas the Iscariot, one [of] his disciples, and the one who would betray him, said, 5 "Why was this oil not sold for three hundred days' wages and given to the poor?" 6 He said this not because he cared about the poor but because he was a thief and held the money bag and used to steal the contributions. 7 So Jesus said, "Leave her alone. Let her keep this for the day of my burial. 8 You always have the poor with you, but you do not always have me."

9 [The] large crowd of the Jews found out that he was there and came, not only because of Jesus, but also to see Lazarus, whom he had raised from the dead. 10 And the chief priests plotted to kill Lazarus too, 11 because many of

---

39 Jesus said, 'Take the stone away.' Martha, the dead man's sister, said to him, 'Lord, by now he will smell; this is the fourth day since he died.' 40 Jesus replied, 'Have I not told you that if you believe you will see the glory of God?' 41 So they took the stone away. Then Jesus lifted up his eyes and said:

Father, I thank you for hearing my prayer.
42 I myself knew that you hear me always,
but I speak
for the sake of all these who are standing around me,
so that they may believe it was you who sent me.

43 When he had said this, he cried in a loud voice, 'Lazarus, come out!' 44 The dead man came out, his feet and hands bound with strips of material, and a cloth over his face. Jesus said to them, 'Unbind him, let him go free.'

45 Many of the Jews who had come to visit Mary, and had seen what he did, believed in him, 46 but some of them went to the Pharisees to tell them what Jesus had done. 47 Then the chief priests and Pharisees called a meeting. 'Here is this man working all these signs,' they said, 'and what action are we taking? 48 If we let him go on in this way everybody will believe in him, and the Romans will come and suppress the Holy Place and our nation.' 49 One of them, Caiaphas, the high priest that year, said, 'You do not seem to have grasped the situation at all; 50 you fail to see that it is to your advantage that one man should die for the people, rather than that the whole nation should perish.' 51 He did not speak in his own person, but as high priest of that year he was prophesying that Jesus was to die for the nation — 52 and not for the nation only, but also to gather together into one the scattered children of God. 53 From that day onwards they were determined to kill him. 54 So Jesus no longer went about openly among the Jews, but left the district for a town called Ephraim, in the country bordering on the desert, and stayed there with his disciples.

55 The Jewish Passover was drawing near, and many of the country people who had gone up to Jerusalem before the Passover to purify themselves 56 were looking out for Jesus, saying to one another as they stood about in the Temple, 'What do you think? Will he come to the festival or not?' 57 The chief priests and Pharisees had by now given their orders: anyone who knew where he was must inform them so that they could arrest him.

12 Six days before the Passover, Jesus went to Bethany, where Lazarus was, whom he had raised from the dead. 2 They gave a dinner for him there; Martha waited on them and Lazarus was among those at table. 3 Mary brought in a pound of very costly ointment, pure nard, and with it anointed the feet of Jesus, wiping them with her hair; the house was filled with the scent of the ointment. 4 Then Judas Iscariot — one of his disciples, the man who was to betray him — said, 5 'Why was this ointment not sold for three hundred denarii and the money given to the poor?' 6 He said this, not because he cared about the poor, but because he was a thief; he was in charge of the common fund and used to help himself to the contents. 7 So Jesus said, 'Leave her alone; let her keep it for the day of my burial. 8 You have the poor with you always, you will not always have me.'

9 Meanwhile a large number of Jews heard that he was there and came not only on account of Jesus but also to see Lazarus whom he had raised from the dead. 10 Then the chief priests decided to kill Lazarus as well, 11 since it was

was on account of him that many of the Jews were deserting and were believing in Jesus.

12 The next day the great crowd that had come to the festival heard that Jesus was coming to Jerusalem. 13 So they took branches of palm trees and went out to meet him, shouting,

"Hosanna!
Blessed is the one who comes in the name
of the Lord—
the King of Israel!"

14 Jesus found a young donkey and sat on it; as it is written:

15 "Do not be afraid, daughter of Zion.
Look, your king is coming,
sitting on a donkey's colt!"

16 His disciples did not understand these things at first; but when Jesus was glorified, then they remembered that these things had been written of him and had been done to him. 17 So the crowd that had been with him when he called Lazarus out of the tomb and raised him from the dead continued to testify.[n] 18 It was also because they heard that he had performed this sign that the crowd went to meet him. 19 The Pharisees then said to one another, "You see, you can do nothing. Look, the world has gone after him!"

20 Now among those who went up to worship at the festival were some Greeks. 21 They came to Philip, who was from Bethsaida in Galilee, and said to him, "Sir, we wish to see Jesus." 22 Philip went and told Andrew; then Andrew and Philip went and told Jesus. 23 Jesus answered them, "The hour has come for the Son of Man to be glorified. 24 Very truly, I tell you, unless a grain of wheat falls into the earth and dies, it remains just a single grain; but if it dies, it bears much fruit. 25 Those who love their life lose it, and those who hate their life in this world will keep it for eternal life. 26 Whoever serves me must follow me, and where I am, there will my servant be also. Whoever serves me, the Father will honor.

27 "Now my soul is troubled. And what should I say— 'Father, save me from this hour'? No, it is for this reason that I have come to this hour. 28 Father, glorify your name." Then a voice came from heaven, "I have glorified it, and I will glorify it again." 29 The crowd standing there heard it and said that it was thunder. Others said, "An angel has spoken to him." 30 Jesus answered, "This voice has come for your sake, not for mine. 31 Now is the judgment of this world; now the ruler of this world will be driven out. 32 And I, when I am lifted up from the earth, will draw all people[o] to myself." 33 He said this to indicate the kind of death he was to die. 34 The crowd answered him, "We have heard from the law that the Messiah[p] remains forever. How can you say that the Son of Man must be lifted up? Who is this Son of Man?" 35 Jesus said to them, "The light is with you

many Jews were going over to Jesus and putting their faith in him.

12 THE next day the great crowd of pilgrims who had come for the festival, hearing that Jesus was on the way to Jerusalem, 13 went out to meet him with palm branches in their hands, shouting, 'Hosanna! Blessed is he who comes in the name of the Lord! Blessed is the king of Israel!' 14 Jesus found a donkey and mounted it, in accordance with the words of scripture: 15 'Fear no more, daughter of Zion; see, your king is coming, mounted on a donkey's colt.' 16 At the time his disciples did not understand this, but after Jesus had been glorified they remembered that this had been written about him, and that it had happened to him.

17 The people who were present when he called Lazarus out of the tomb and raised him from the dead kept telling what they had seen and heard. 18 That is why the crowd went to meet him: they had heard of this sign that he had performed. 19 The Pharisees said to one another, 'You can see we are getting nowhere; all the world has gone after him!'

20 AMONG those who went up to worship at the festival were some Gentiles. 21 They approached Philip, who was from Bethsaida in Galilee, and said to him, 'Sir, we should like to see Jesus.' 22 Philip went and told Andrew, and the two of them went to tell Jesus. 23 Jesus replied: 'The hour has come for the Son of Man to be glorified. 24 In very truth I tell you, unless a grain of wheat falls into the ground and dies, it remains that and nothing more; but if it dies, it bears a rich harvest. 25 Whoever loves himself is lost, but he who hates himself in this world will be kept safe for eternal life. 26 If anyone is to serve me, he must follow me; where I am, there will my servant be. Whoever serves me will be honoured by the Father.

27 'Now my soul is in turmoil, and what am I to say? "Father, save me from this hour"? No, it was for this that I came to this hour. 28 Father, glorify your name.' A voice came from heaven: 'I have glorified it, and I will glorify it again.' 29 The crowd standing by said it was thunder they heard, while others said, 'An angel has spoken to him.' 30 Jesus replied, 'This voice spoke for your sake, not mine. 31 Now is the hour of judgement for this world; now shall the prince of this world be driven out. 32 And when I am lifted up from the earth I shall draw everyone to myself.' 33 This he said to indicate the kind of death he was to die.

34 The people answered, 'Our law teaches us that the Messiah remains for ever. What do you mean by saying that the Son of Man must be lifted up? What Son of Man is this?' 35 Jesus answered them: 'The light is among you still,

---

[n] Other ancient authorities read with him began to testify that he had called . . . from the dead   [o] Other ancient authorities read all things
[p] Or the Christ

the Jews were turning away and believing in Jesus because of him.

12 On the next day, when the great crowd that had come to the feast heard that Jesus was coming to Jerusalem, 13 they took palm branches and went out to meet him, and cried out:

"Hosanna!
Blessed is he who comes in the name of the Lord,
[even] the king of Israel."

14 Jesus found an ass and sat upon it, as is written:

15 "Fear no more, O daughter Zion;
see, your king comes, seated upon an
ass's colt."

16 His disciples did not understand this at first, but when Jesus had been glorified they remembered that these things were written about him and that they had done this for him. 17 So the crowd that was with him when he called Lazarus from the tomb and raised him from death continued to testify. 18 This was [also] why the crowd went to meet him, because they heard that he had done this sign. 19 So the Pharisees said to one another, "You see that you are gaining nothing. Look, the whole world has gone after him."

20 Now there were some Greeks among those who had come up to worship at the feast. 21 They came to Philip, who was from Bethsaida in Galilee, and asked him, "Sir, we would like to see Jesus." 22 Philip went and told Andrew; then Andrew and Philip went and told Jesus. 23 Jesus answered them, "The hour has come for the Son of Man to be glorified. 24 Amen, amen, I say to you, unless a grain of wheat falls to the ground and dies, it remains just a grain of wheat; but if it dies, it produces much fruit. 25 Whoever loves his life loses it, and whoever hates his life in this world will preserve it for eternal life. 26 Whoever serves me must follow me, and where I am, there also will my servant be. The Father will honor whoever serves me.

27 "I am troubled now. Yet what should I say? 'Father, save me from this hour'? But it was for this purpose that I came to this hour. 28 Father, glorify your name." Then a voice came from heaven, "I have glorified it and will glorify it again." 29 The crowd there heard it and said it was thunder; but others said, "An angel has spoken to him." 30 Jesus answered and said, "This voice did not come for my sake but for yours. 31 Now is the time of judgment on this world; now the ruler of this world will be driven out. 32 And when I am lifted up from the earth, I will draw everyone to myself." 33 He said this indicating the kind of death he would die. 34 So the crowd answered him, "We have heard from the law that the Messiah remains forever. Then how can you say that the Son of Man must be lifted up? Who is this Son of Man?" 35 Jesus said to them, "The light will be

on his account that many of the Jews were leaving them and believing in Jesus.

12 The next day the great crowd of people who had come up for the festival heard that Jesus was on his way to Jerusalem. 13 They took branches of palm and went out to receive him, shouting:

'Hosanna!
Blessed is he who is coming in the name of the
Lord,o
the king of Israel.'

14 Jesus found a young donkey and mounted it — as scripture says:

15 Do not be afraid, daughter of Zion;
look, your king is approaching,
riding on the foal of a donkey.p

16 At first his disciples did not understand this, but later, after Jesus had been glorified, they remembered that this had been written about him and that this was what had happened to him. 17 The crowd who had been with him when he called Lazarus out of the tomb and raised him from the dead kept bearing witness to it; 18 this was another reason why the crowd came out to receive him: they had heard that he had given this sign. 19 Then the Pharisees said to one another, 'You see, you are making no progress; look, the whole world has gone after him!'

20 Among those who went up to worship at the festival were some Greeks. 21 These approached Philip, who came from Bethsaida in Galilee, and put this request to him, 'Sir, we should like to see Jesus.' 22 Philip went to tell Andrew, and Andrew and Philip together went to tell Jesus.

23 Jesus replied to them:

Now the hour has come
for the Son of man to be glorified.
24 In all truth I tell you,
unless a wheat grain falls into the earth and dies,
it remains only a single grain;
but if it dies
it yields a rich harvest.
25 Anyone who loves his life loses it;
anyone who hates his life in this world
will keep it for eternal life.
26 Whoever serves me, must follow me,
and my servant will be with me wherever I am.
If anyone serves me, my Father will honour him.
27 Now my soul is troubled.
What shall I say:
Father, save me from this hour?q
But it is for this very reason that I have come to
this hour.
28 Father, glorify your name!

A voice came from heaven, 'I have glorified it, and I will again glorify it.'

29 The crowd standing by, who heard this, said it was a clap of thunder; others said, 'It was an angel speaking to him.' 30 Jesus answered, 'It was not for my sake that this voice came, but for yours.

31 'Now sentence is being passed on this world;
now the prince of this world is to be driven out.
32 And when I am lifted up from the earth,
I shall draw all people to myself.'

33 By these words he indicated the kind of death he would die. 34 The crowd answered, 'The Law has taught us that the Christ will remain for ever. So how can you say, "The Son of man must be lifted up"? Who is this Son of man?'

o 12 Ps 118:25–26.   p 12 Zc 9:9–10.   q 12 cf. Lk 22:40–46par.

NEW REVISED STANDARD VERSION

for a little longer. Walk while you have the light, so that the darkness may not overtake you. If you walk in the darkness, you do not know where you are going. 36 While you have the light, believe in the light, so that you may become children of light."

After Jesus had said this, he departed and hid from them. 37 Although he had performed so many signs in their presence, they did not believe in him. 38 This was to fulfill the word spoken by the prophet Isaiah:

"Lord, who has believed our message,
and to whom has the arm of the Lord been revealed?"

39 And so they could not believe, because Isaiah also said,
40 "He has blinded their eyes
and hardened their heart,
so that they might not look with their eyes,
and understand with their heart and turn—
and I would heal them."

41 Isaiah said this because*q* he saw his glory and spoke about him. 42 Nevertheless many, even of the authorities, believed in him. But because of the Pharisees they did not confess it, for fear that they would be put out of the synagogue; 43 for they loved human glory more than the glory that comes from God.

44 Then Jesus cried aloud: "Whoever believes in me believes not in me but in him who sent me. 45 And whoever sees me sees him who sent me. 46 I have come as light into the world, so that everyone who believes in me should not remain in the darkness. 47 I do not judge anyone who hears my words and does not keep them, for I came not to judge the world, but to save the world. 48 The one who rejects me and does not receive my word has a judge; on the last day the word that I have spoken will serve as judge, 49 for I have not spoken on my own, but the Father who sent me has himself given me a commandment about what to say and what to speak. 50 And I know that his commandment is eternal life. What I speak, therefore, I speak just as the Father has told me."

REVISED ENGLISH BIBLE

but not for long. Go on your way while you have the light, so that darkness may not overtake you. He who journeys in the dark does not know where he is going. 36 Trust to the light while you have it, so that you may become children of light.' After these words Jesus went away from them into hiding.'

37 IN spite of the many signs which Jesus had performed in their presence they would not believe in him, 38 for the prophet Isaiah's words had to be fulfilled: 'Lord, who has believed what we reported, and to whom has the power of the Lord been revealed?' 39 And there is another saying of Isaiah which explains why they could not believe: 40 'He has blinded their eyes and dulled their minds, lest they should see with their eyes, and perceive with their minds, and turn to me to heal them.' 41 Isaiah said this because he saw his glory and spoke about him.

42 For all that, even among those in authority many believed in him, but would not acknowledge him on account of the Pharisees, for fear of being banned from the synagogue. 43 For they valued human reputation rather than the honour which comes from God.

44 JESUS proclaimed: 'To believe in me, is not to believe in me but in him who sent me; 45 to see me, is to see him who sent me. 46 I have come into the world as light, so that no one who has faith in me should remain in darkness. 47 But if anyone hears my words and disregards them, I am not his judge; I have not come to judge the world, but to save the world. 48 There is a judge for anyone who rejects me and does not accept my words; the word I have spoken will be his judge on the last day. 49 I do not speak on my own authority, but the Father who sent me has himself commanded me what to say and how to speak. 50 I know that his commands are eternal life. What the Father has said to me, therefore—that is what I speak.'

13 Now before the festival of the Passover, Jesus knew that his hour had come to depart from this world and go to the Father. Having loved his own who were in the world, he loved them to the end. 2 The devil had already put it into the heart of Judas son of Simon Iscariot to betray him. And during supper 3 Jesus, knowing that the Father had given all things into his hands, and that he had come from God and was going to God, 4 got up from the table,*r*

13 IT was before the Passover festival, and Jesus knew that his hour had come and that he must leave this world and go to the Father. He had always loved his own who were in the world, and he loved them to the end. 2 The devil had already put it into the mind of Judas son of Simon Iscariot to betray him. During supper, 3 Jesus, well aware that the Father had entrusted everything to him, and that he had come from God and was going back to God,

q Other ancient witnesses read *when*　*r* Gk *from supper*

NEW AMERICAN BIBLE

among you only a little while. Walk while you have the light, so that darkness may not overcome you. Whoever walks in the dark does not know where he is going. 36 While you have the light, believe in the light, so that you may become children of the light."

After he had said this, Jesus left and hid from them. 37 Although he had performed so many signs in their presence they did not believe in him, 38 in order that the word which Isaiah the prophet spoke might be fulfilled:

"Lord, who has believed our preaching,
to whom has the might of the Lord
been revealed?"

39 For this reason they could not believe, because again Isaiah said:

40 "He blinded their eyes
and hardened their heart,
so that they might not see with their eyes
and understand with their heart and
be converted,
and I would heal them."

41 Isaiah said this because he saw his glory and spoke about him. 42 Nevertheless, many, even among the authorities, believed in him, but because of the Pharisees they did not acknowledge it openly in order not to be expelled from the synagogue. 43 For they preferred human praise to the glory of God.

44 Jesus cried out and said, "Whoever believes in me believes not only in me but also in the one who sent me, 45 and whoever sees me sees the one who sent me. 46 I came into the world as light, so that everyone who believes in me might not remain in darkness. 47 And if anyone hears my words and does not observe them, I do not condemn him, for I did not come to condemn the world but to save the world. 48 Whoever rejects me and does not accept my words has something to judge him: the word that I spoke, it will condemn him on the last day, 49 because I did not speak on my own, but the Father who sent me commanded me what to say and speak. 50 And I know that his commandment is eternal life. So what I say, I say as the Father told me."

NEW JERUSALEM BIBLE

35 Jesus then said:

The light will be with you only a little longer now.
Go on your way while you have the light,
or darkness will overtake you,
and nobody who walks in the dark knows where he
is going.
36 While you still have the light,
believe in the light
so that you may become children of light.

Having said this, Jesus left them and was hidden from their sight.

37 Though they had been present when he gave so many signs, they did not believe in him; 38 this was to fulfil the words of the prophet Isaiah:

*Lord, who has given credence to what they have
heard from us,
and who has seen in it a revelation of the Lord's
arm?* r

39 Indeed, they were unable to believe because, as Isaiah says again:

40 *He has blinded their eyes,
he has hardened their heart,
to prevent them from using their eyes to see,
using their heart to understand,
changing their ways and being healed by me.* s

41 Isaiah said this because he saw his glory, and his words referred to Jesus.

42 And yet there were many who did believe in him, even among the leading men, but they did not admit it, because of the Pharisees and for fear of being banned from the synagogue: 43 they put human glory before God's glory.

44 Jesus declared publicly:

Whoever believes in me
believes not in me
but in the one who sent me,
45 and whoever sees me,
sees the one who sent me.
46 I have come into the world as light,
to prevent anyone who believes in me
from staying in the dark any more.
47 If anyone hears my words and does not keep them
faithfully,
it is not I who shall judge such a person,
since I have come not to judge the world,
but to save the world:
48 anyone who rejects me and refuses my words
has his judge already:
the word itself that I have spoken
will be his judge on the last day.
49 For I have not spoken of my own accord;
but the Father who sent me
commanded me what to say and what to speak,
50 and I know that his commands mean eternal life.
And therefore what the Father has told me
is what I speak.

13 Before the feast of Passover, Jesus knew that his hour had come to pass from this world to the Father. He loved his own in the world and he loved them to the end. 2 The devil had already induced Judas, son of Simon the Iscariot, to hand him over. So, during supper, 3 fully aware that the Father had put everything into his power and that he had come from God and was returning to

13 Before the festival of the Passover, Jesus, knowing that his hour had come to pass from this world to the Father, having loved those who were his in the world, loved them to the end.

2 They were at supper, and the devil had already put it into the mind of Judas Iscariot son of Simon, to betray him. 3 Jesus knew that the Father had put everything into his hands, and that he had come from God and was returning

r **12** Is 53:1.   s **12** Is 6:10.

NEW REVISED STANDARD VERSION

took off his outer robe, and tied a towel around himself. 5 Then he poured water into a basin and began to wash the disciples' feet and to wipe them with the towel that was tied around him. 6 He came to Simon Peter, who said to him, "Lord, are you going to wash my feet?" 7 Jesus answered, "You do not know now what I am doing, but later you will understand." 8 Peter said to him, "You will never wash my feet." Jesus answered, "Unless I wash you, you have no share with me." 9 Simon Peter said to him, "Lord, not my feet only but also my hands and my head!" 10 Jesus said to him, "One who has bathed does not need to wash, except for the feet,s but is entirely clean. And your are clean, though not all of you." 11 For he knew who was to betray him; for this reason he said, "Not all of you are clean."

12 After he had washed their feet, had put on his robe, and had returned to the table, he said to them, "Do you know what I have done to you? 13 You call me Teacher and Lord — and you are right, for that is what I am. 14 So if I, your Lord and Teacher, have washed your feet, you also ought to wash one another's feet. 15 For I have set you an example, that you also should do as I have done to you. 16 Very truly, I tell you, servantsu are not greater than their master, nor are messengers greater than the one who sent them. 17 If you know these things, you are blessed if you do them. 18 I am not speaking of all of you; I know whom I have chosen. But it is to fulfill the scripture, 'The one who ate my breadv has lifted his heel against me.' 19 I tell you this now, before it occurs, so that when it does occur, you may believe that I am he.w 20 Very truly, I tell you, whoever receives one whom I send receives me; and whoever receives me receives him who sent me."

21 After saying this Jesus was troubled in spirit, and declared, "Very truly, I tell you, one of you will betray me." 22 The disciples looked at one another, uncertain of whom he was speaking. 23 One of his disciples — the one whom Jesus loved — was reclining next to him; 24 Simon Peter therefore motioned to him to ask Jesus of whom he was speaking. 25 So while reclining next to Jesus, he asked him, "Lord, who is it?" 26 Jesus answered, "It is the one to whom I give this piece of bread when I have dipped it in the dish."x So when he had dipped the piece of bread, he gave it to Judas son of Simon Iscariot.y 27 After he received the piece of bread,z Satan entered into him. Jesus said to him, "Do quickly what you are going to do." 28 Now no one at the table knew why he said this to him. 29 Some thought that, because Judas had the common purse, Jesus was telling him, "Buy what we need for the festival"; or, that he should give something to the poor. 30 So, after receiving the piece of bread, he immediately went out. And it was night.

31 When he had gone out, Jesus said, "Now the Son of Man has been glorified, and God has been glorified in him. 32 If God has been glorified in him,a God will also glorify him in himself and will glorify him at once. 33 Little chil-

REVISED ENGLISH BIBLE

4 rose from the supper table, took off his outer garment and, taking a towel, tied it round him. 5 Then he poured water into a basin, and began to wash his disciples' feet and to wipe them with the towel.

6 When he came to Simon Peter, Peter said to him, 'You, Lord, washing my feet?' 7 Jesus replied, 'You do not understand now what I am doing, but one day you will.' 8 Peter said, 'I will never let you wash my feet.' 'If I do not wash you,' Jesus replied, 'you have no part with me.' 9 'Then, Lord,' said Simon Peter, 'not my feet only; wash my hands and head as well!'

10 Jesus said to him, 'Anyone who has bathed needs no further washing; he is clean all over; and you are clean, though not every one of you.' 11 He added the words 'not every one of you' because he knew who was going to betray him.

12 After washing their feet he put on his garment and sat down again. 'Do you understand what I have done for you?' he asked. 13 'You call me Teacher and Lord, and rightly so, for that is what I am. 14 Then if I, your Lord and Teacher, have washed your feet, you also ought to wash one another's feet. 15 I have set you an example: you are to do as I have done for you. 16 In very truth I tell you, a servant is not greater than his master, nor a messenger than the one who sent him. 17 If you know this, happy are you if you act upon it.

18 'I am not speaking about all of you; I know whom I have chosen. But there is a text of scripture to be fulfilled: "He who eats bread with me has turned against me." 19 I tell you this now, before the event, so that when it happens you may believe that I am what I am. 20 In very truth I tell you, whoever receives any messenger of mine receives me; and receiving me, he receives the One who sent me.'

21 After saying this, Jesus exclaimed in deep distress, 'In very truth I tell you, one of you is going to betray me.' 22 The disciples looked at one another in bewilderment: which of them could he mean? 23 One of them, the disciple he loved, was reclining close beside Jesus. 24 Simon Peter signalled to him to find out which one he meant. 25 That disciple leaned back close to Jesus and asked, 'Lord, who is it?' 26 Jesus replied, 'It is the one to whom I give this piece of bread when I have dipped it in the dish.' Then he took it, dipped it in the dish, and gave it to Judas son of Simon Iscariot. 27 As soon as Judas had received it Satan entered him. Jesus said to him, 'Do quickly what you have to do.' 28 No one at the table understood what he meant by this. 29 Some supposed that, as Judas was in charge of the common purse, Jesus was telling him to buy what was needed for the festival, or to make some gift to the poor. 30 As soon as Judas had received the bread he went out. It was night.

31 WHEN he had gone out, Jesus said, 'Now the Son of Man is glorified, and in him God is glorified. 32 If God is glorified in him, God will also glorify him in himself; and he will glorify him now. 33 My children, I am to be with you

---

s Other ancient authorities lack *except for the feet* t The Greek word for *you* here is plural u Gk *slaves* v Other ancient authorities read *ate bread with me* w Gk *I am* x Gk *dipped it* y Other ancient authorities read *Judas Iscariot son of Simon*; others, *Judas son of Simon from Karyot* (Kerioth) z Gk *After the piece of bread* a Other ancient authorities lack *If God has been glorified in him*

13:10 **needs ... washing:** *some witnesses read* needs only to wash his feet. 13:32 *Some witnesses omit* If God . . . in him.

God, 4 he rose from supper and took off his outer garments. He took a towel and tied it around his waist. 5 Then he poured water into a basin and began to wash the disciples' feet and dry them with the towel around his waist. 6 He came to Simon Peter, who said to him, "Master, are you going to wash my feet?" 7 Jesus answered and said to him, "What I am doing, you do not understand now, but you will understand later." 8 Peter said to him, "You will never wash my feet." Jesus answered him, "Unless I wash you, you will have no inheritance with me." 9 Simon Peter said to him, "Master, then not only my feet, but my hands and head as well." 10 Jesus said to him, "Whoever has bathed has no need except to have his feet washed, for he is clean all over; so you are clean, but not all." 11 For he knew who would betray him; for this reason, he said, "Not all of you are clean."

12 So when he had washed their feet [and] put his garments back on and reclined at table again, he said to them, "Do you realize what I have done for you? 13 You call me 'teacher' and 'master,' and rightly so, for indeed I am. 14 If I, therefore, the master and teacher, have washed your feet, you ought to wash one another's feet. 15 I have given you a model to follow, so that as I have done for you, you should also do. 16 Amen, amen, I say to you, no slave is greater than his master nor any messenger greater than the one who sent him. 17 If you understand this, blessed are you if you do it. 18 I am not speaking of all of you. I know those whom I have chosen. But so that the scripture might be fulfilled, 'The one who ate my food has raised his heel against me.' 19 From now on I am telling you before it happens, so that when it happens you may believe that I AM. 20 Amen, amen, I say to you, whoever receives the one I send receives me, and whoever receives me receives the one who sent me."

21 When he had said this, Jesus was deeply troubled and testified, "Amen, amen, I say to you, one of you will betray me." 22 The disciples looked at one another, at a loss as to whom he meant. 23 One of his disciples, the one whom Jesus loved, was reclining at Jesus' side. 24 So Simon Peter nodded to him to find out whom he meant. 25 He leaned back against Jesus' chest and said to him, "Master, who is it?" 26 Jesus answered, "It is the one to whom I hand the morsel after I have dipped it." So he dipped the morsel and [took it and] handed it to Judas, son of Simon the Iscariot. 27 After he took the morsel, Satan entered him. So Jesus said to him, "What you are going to do, do quickly." 28 [Now] none of those reclining at table realized why he said this to him. 29 Some thought that since Judas kept the money bag, Jesus had told him, "Buy what we need for the feast," or to give something to the poor. 30 So he took the morsel and left at once. And it was night.

31 When he had left, Jesus said, "Now is the Son of Man glorified, and God is glorified in him. 32 [If God is glorified in him,] God will also glorify him in himself, and he will glorify him at once. 33 My children, I will be with you only

to God, 4 and he got up from table, removed his outer garments and, taking a towel, wrapped it round his waist; 5 he then poured water into a basin and began to wash the disciples' feet and to wipe them with the towel he was wearing.

6 He came to Simon Peter, who said to him, 'Lord, are you going to wash my feet?' 7 Jesus answered, 'At the moment you do not know what I am doing, but later you will understand.' 8 'Never!' said Peter. 'You shall never wash my feet.' Jesus replied, 'If I do not wash you, you can have no share with me.' Simon Peter said, 9 'Well then, Lord, not only my feet, but my hands and my head as well!' 10 Jesus said, 'No one who has had a bath needs washing, such a person is clean all over. You too are clean, though not all of you are.' 11 He knew who was going to betray him, and that was why he said, 'though not all of you are'.

12 When he had washed their feet and put on his outer garments again he went back to the table. 'Do you understand', he said, 'what I have done to you? 13 You call me Master and Lord, and rightly; so I am. 14 If I, then, the Lord and Master, have washed your feet, you must wash each other's feet. 15 I have given you an example so that you may copy what I have done to you.

16 'In all truth I tell you,
no servant is greater than his master,
no messenger is greater than the one who sent him.

17 'Now that you know this, blessed are you if you behave accordingly. 18 I am not speaking about all of you: I know the ones I have chosen; but what scripture says must be fulfilled:

'He who shares my table
takes advantage of me.[t]
19 I tell you this now, before it happens,
so that when it does happen
you may believe that I am He.
20 In all truth I tell you,
whoever welcomes the one I send, welcomes me,
and whoever welcomes me, welcomes the one who
sent me.'

21 Having said this, Jesus was deeply disturbed and declared, 'In all truth I tell you, one of you is going to betray me.' 22 The disciples looked at each other, wondering whom he meant. 23 The disciple Jesus loved was reclining next to Jesus; 24 Simon Peter signed to him and said, 'Ask who it is he means,' 25 so leaning back close to Jesus' chest he said, 'Who is it, Lord?' 26 Jesus answered, 'It is the one to whom I give the piece of bread that I dip in the dish.' And when he had dipped the piece of bread he gave it to Judas son of Simon Iscariot. 27 At that instant, after Judas had taken the bread, Satan entered him. Jesus then said, 'What you are going to do, do quickly.' 28 None of the others at table understood why he said this. 29 Since Judas had charge of the common fund, some of them thought Jesus was telling him, 'Buy what we need for the festival,' or telling him to give something to the poor. 30 As soon as Judas had taken the piece of bread he went out. It was night.

31 u When he had gone, Jesus said:

Now has the Son of man been glorified,
and in him God has been glorified.
32 If God has been glorified in him,
God will in turn glorify him in himself,
and will glorify him very soon.

t 13 Ps 41:9.   u 13 The farewell discourses in v. 31 seq. contain teaching given also on other occasions, and perhaps in different versions. Ch. 16 may be another version of ch. 14, and ch. 17 yet another.

NEW REVISED STANDARD VERSION

dren, I am with you only a little longer. You will look for me; and as I said to the Jews so now I say to you, 'Where I am going, you cannot come.' 34 I give you a new commandment, that you love one another. Just as I have loved you, you also should love one another. 35 By this everyone will know that you are my disciples, if you have love for one another."

36 Simon Peter said to him, "Lord, where are you going?" Jesus answered, "Where I am going, you cannot follow me now; but you will follow afterward." 37 Peter said to him, "Lord, why can I not follow you now? I will lay down my life for you." 38 Jesus answered, "Will you lay down your life for me? Very truly, I tell you, before the cock crows, you will have denied me three times.

14 "Do not let your hearts be troubled. Believe[b] in God, believe also in me. 2 In my Father's house there are many dwelling places. If it were not so, would I have told you that I go to prepare a place for you?[c] 3 And if I go and prepare a place for you, I will come again and will take you to myself, so that where I am, there you may be also. 4 And you know the way to the place where I am going."[d] 5 Thomas said to him, "Lord, we do not know where you are going. How can we know the way?" 6 Jesus said to him, "I am the way, and the truth, and the life. No one comes to the Father except through me. 7 If you know me, you will know[e] my Father also. From now on you do know him and have seen him."

8 Philip said to him, "Lord, show us the Father, and we will be satisfied." 9 Jesus said to him, "Have I been with you all this time, Philip, and you still do not know me? Whoever has seen me has seen the Father. How can you say, 'Show us the Father'? 10 Do you not believe that I am in the Father and the Father is in me? The words that I say to you I do not speak on my own; but the Father who dwells in me does his works. 11 Believe me that I am in the Father and the Father is in me; but if you do not, then believe me because of the works themselves. 12 Very truly, I tell you, the one who believes in me will also do the works that I do and, in fact, will do greater works than these, because I am going to the Father. 13 I will do whatever you ask in my name, so that the Father may be glorified in the Son. 14 If in my name you ask me[f] for anything, I will do it.

15 "If you love me, you will keep[g] my commandments. 16 And I will ask the Father, and he will give you another Advocate,[h] to be with you forever. 17 This is the

REVISED ENGLISH BIBLE

for a little longer; then you will look for me, and, as I told the Jews, I tell you now: where I am going you cannot come. 34 I give you a new commandment: love one another; as I have loved you, so you are to love one another. 35 If there is this love among you, then everyone will know that you are my disciples.'

36 Simon Peter said to him, 'Lord, where are you going?' Jesus replied, 'I am going where you cannot follow me now, but one day you will.' 37 Peter said, 'Lord, why cannot I follow you now? I will lay down my life for you.' 38 Jesus answered, 'Will you really lay down your life for me? In very truth I tell you, before the cock crows you will have denied me three times.

14 'Set your troubled hearts at rest. Trust in God always; trust also in me. 2 There are many dwelling-places in my Father's house; if it were not so I should have told you; for I am going to prepare a place for you. 3 And if I go and prepare a place for you, I shall come again and take you to myself, so that where I am you may be also; 4 and you know the way I am taking.' 5 Thomas said, 'Lord, we do not know where you are going, so how can we know the way?' 6 Jesus replied, 'I am the way, the truth, and the life; no one comes to the Father except by me.

7 'If you knew me you would know my Father too. From now on you do know him; you have seen him.' 8 Philip said to him, 'Lord, show us the Father; we ask no more.' 9 Jesus answered, 'Have I been all this time with you, Philip, and still you do not know me? Anyone who has seen me has seen the Father. Then how can you say, "Show us the Father"? 10 Do you not believe that I am in the Father, and the Father in me? I am not myself the source of the words I speak to you: it is the Father who dwells in me doing his own work. 11 Believe me when I say that I am in the Father and the Father in me; or else accept the evidence of the deeds themselves. 12 In very truth I tell you, whoever has faith in me will do what I am doing; indeed he will do greater things still because I am going to the Father. 13 Anything you ask in my name I will do, so that the Father may be glorified in the Son. 14 If you ask anything in my name I will do it.

15 'If you love me you will obey my commands; 16 and I will ask the Father, and he will give you another to be your advocate, who will be with you for ever — 17 the Spirit of

---

b Or *You believe*   *c* Or *If it were not so, I would have told you; for I go to prepare a place for you*   *d* Other ancient authorities read *Where I am going you know, and the way you know*   *e* Other ancient authorities read *If you had known me, you would have known*   *f* Other ancient authorities lack *me*   *g* Other ancient authorities read *me, keep*   *h* Or *Helper*

14:3 **also:** *some witnesses add* you know where I am going. 14:7 **If you . . . too:** *some witnesses read* If you know me you will know my Father too.   14:14 **If you ask:** *some witnesses add* me.

a little while longer. You will look for me, and as I told the Jews, 'Where I go you cannot come,' so now I say it to you. 34 I give you a new commandment: love one another. As I have loved you, so you also should love one another. 35 This is how all will know that you are my disciples, if you have love for one another."

36 Simon Peter said to him, "Master, where are you going?" Jesus answered [him], "Where I am going, you cannot follow me now, though you will follow later." 37 Peter said to him, "Master, why can't I follow you now? I will lay down my life for you." 38 Jesus answered, "Will you lay down your life for me? Amen, amen, I say to you, the cock will not crow before you deny me three times."

14 "Do not let your hearts be troubled. You have faith in God; have faith also in me. 2 In my Father's house there are many dwelling places. If there were not, would I have told you that I am going to prepare a place for you? 3 And if I go and prepare a place for you, I will come back again and take you to myself, so that where I am you also may be. 4 Where [I] am going you know the way." 5 Thomas said to him, "Master, we do not know where you are going; how can we know the way?" 6 Jesus said to him, "I am the way and the truth and the life. No one comes to the Father except through me. 7 If you know me, then you will also know my Father. From now on you do know him and have seen him." 8 Philip said to him, "Master, show us the Father, and that will be enough for us." 9 Jesus said to him, "Have I been with you for so long a time and you still do not know me, Philip? Whoever has seen me has seen the Father. How can you say, 'Show us the Father'? 10 Do you not believe that I am in the Father and the Father is in me? The words that I speak to you I do not speak on my own. The Father who dwells in me is doing his works. 11 Believe me that I am in the Father and the Father is in me, or else, believe because of the works themselves. 12 Amen, amen, I say to you, whoever believes in me will do the works that I do, and will do greater ones than these, because I am going to the Father. 13 And whatever you ask in my name, I will do, so that the Father may be glorified in the Son. 14 If you ask anything of me in my name, I will do it.

15 "If you love me, you will keep my commandments. 16 And I will ask the Father, and he will give you another Advocate to be with you always, 17 the Spirit of truth, which

33 Little children,
I shall be with you only a little longer.
You will look for me,
and, as I told the Jews,
where I am going,
you cannot come.
34 I give you a new commandment:
love one another;
you must love one another
just as I have loved you.
35 It is by your love for one another,
that everyone will recognise you
as my disciples.

36 Simon Peter said, 'Lord, where are you going?' Jesus replied, 'Now you cannot follow me where I am going, but later you shall follow me.' 37 Peter said to him, 'Why can I not follow you now? I will lay down my life for you.' 38 'Lay down your life for me?' answered Jesus. 'In all truth I tell you, before the cock crows you will have disowned me three times.'

14 Do not let your hearts be troubled.
You trust in God, trust also in me.
2 In my Father's house there are many places to live in;
otherwise I would have told you.
I am going now to prepare a place for you,
3 and after I have gone and prepared you a place,
I shall return to take you to myself,
so that you may be with me
where I am.
4 You know the way to the place where I am going.

5 Thomas said, 'Lord, we do not know where you are going, so how can we know the way?' 6 Jesus said:

I am the Way; I am Truth and Life.
No one can come to the Father except through me.
7 If you know me, you will know my Father too.
From this moment you know him and have seen him.

8 Philip said, 'Lord, show us the Father and then we shall be satisfied.' Jesus said to him, 9 'Have I been with you all this time, Philip, and you still do not know me?

'Anyone who has seen me has seen the Father,
so how can you say, "Show us the Father"?
10 Do you not believe
that I am in the Father and the Father is in me?
What I say to you I do not speak of my own accord:
it is the Father, living in me, who is doing his works.
11 You must believe me when I say
that I am in the Father and the Father is in me;
or at least believe it on the evidence of these works.
12 In all truth I tell you,
whoever believes in me
will perform the same works as I do myself,
and will perform even greater works,
because I am going to the Father.
13 Whatever you ask in my name I will do,
so that the Father may be glorified in the Son.
14 If you ask me anything in my name,
I will do it.
15 If you love me you will keep my commandments.
16 I shall ask the Father,
and he will give you another Paraclete v
to be with you for ever,

v **14** The Gk word means 'advocate', 'counsellor', 'protector'.

NEW REVISED STANDARD VERSION

Spirit of truth, whom the world cannot receive, because it neither sees him nor knows him. You know him, because he abides with you, and he will be in[i] you. 18 "I will not leave you orphaned; I am coming to you. 19 In a little while the world will no longer see me, but you will see me; because I live, you also will live. 20 On that day you will know that I am in my Father, and you in me, and I in you. 21 They who have my commandments and keep them are those who love me; and those who love me will be loved by my Father, and I will love them and reveal myself to them." 22 Judas (not Iscariot) said to him, "Lord, how is it that you will reveal yourself to us, and not to the world?" 23 Jesus answered him, "Those who love me will keep my word, and my Father will love them, and we will come to them and make our home with them. 24 Whoever does not love me does not keep my words; and the word that you hear is not mine, but is from the Father who sent me.

25 "I have said these things to you while I am still with you. 26 But the Advocate,[j] the Holy Spirit, whom the Father will send in my name, will teach you everything, and remind you of all that I have said to you. 27 Peace I leave with you; my peace I give to you. I do not give to you as the world gives. Do not let your hearts be troubled, and do not let them be afraid. 28 You heard me say to you, 'I am going away, and I am coming to you.' If you loved me, you would rejoice that I am going to the Father, because the Father is greater than I. 29 And now I have told you this before it occurs, so that when it does occur, you may believe. 30 I will no longer talk much with you, for the ruler of this world is coming. He has no power over me; 31 but I do as the Father has commanded me, so that the world may know that I love the Father. Rise, let us be on our way.

15 "I am the true vine, and my Father is the vine-grower. 2 He removes every branch in me that bears no fruit. Every branch that bears fruit he prunes[k] to make it bear more fruit. 3 You have already been cleansed[k] by the word that I have spoken to you. 4 Abide in me as I abide in you. Just as the branch cannot bear fruit by itself unless it abides in the vine, neither can you unless you abide in me.

REVISED ENGLISH BIBLE

truth. The world cannot accept him, because the world neither sees nor knows him; but you know him, because he dwells with you and will be in you. 18 I will not leave you bereft; I am coming back to you. 19 In a little while the world will see me no longer, but you will see me; because I live, you too will live. 20 When that day comes you will know that I am in my Father, and you in me and I in you. 21 Anyone who has received my commands and obeys them — he it is who loves me; and he who loves me will be loved by my Father; and I will love him and disclose myself to him.'

22 Judas said — the other Judas, not Iscariot — 'Lord, how has it come about that you mean to disclose yourself to us and not to the world?' 23 Jesus replied, 'Anyone who loves me will heed what I say; then my Father will love him, and we will come to him and make our dwelling with him; 24 but whoever does not love me does not heed what I say. And the word you hear is not my own: it is the word of the Father who sent me. 25 I have told you these things while I am still with you; 26 but the advocate, the Holy Spirit whom the Father will send in my name, will teach you everything and remind you of all that I have told you.

27 'Peace is my parting gift to you, my own peace, such as the world cannot give. Set your troubled hearts at rest, and banish your fears. 28 You heard me say, "I am going away, and I am coming back to you." If you loved me you would be glad that I am going to the Father; for the Father is greater than I am. 29 I have told you now, before it happens, so that when it does happen you may have faith.

30 'I shall not talk much longer with you, for the prince of this world approaches. He has no rights over me; 31 but the world must be shown that I love the Father and am doing what he commands; come, let us go!

15 'I AM the true vine, and my Father is the gardener. 2 Any branch of mine that is barren he cuts away; and any fruiting branch he prunes clean, to make it more fruitful still. 3 You are already clean because of the word I have spoken to you. 4 Dwell in me, as I in you. No branch can bear fruit by itself, but only if it remains united with the vine; no more can you bear fruit, unless you remain united with me.

---

[i] Or among   [j] Or Helper   [k] The same Greek root refers to pruning and cleansing

14:17 will be: some witnesses read is.

the world cannot accept, because it neither sees nor knows it. But you know it, because it remains with you, and will be in you. ¹⁸ I will not leave you orphans; I will come to you. ¹⁹ In a little while the world will no longer see me, but you will see me, because I live and you will live. ²⁰ On that day you will realize that I am in my Father and you are in me and I in you. ²¹ Whoever has my commandments and observes them is the one who loves me. And whoever loves me will be loved by my Father, and I will love him and reveal myself to him." ²² Judas, not the Iscariot, said to him, "Master, [then] what happened that you will reveal yourself to us and not to the world?" ²³ Jesus answered and said to him, "Whoever loves me will keep my word, and my Father will love him, and we will come to him and make our dwelling with him. ²⁴ Whoever does not love me does not keep my words; yet the word you hear is not mine but that of the Father who sent me.

²⁵ "I have told you this while I am with you. ²⁶ The Advocate, the holy Spirit that the Father will send in my name — he will teach you everything and remind you of all that [I] told you. ²⁷ Peace I leave with you; my peace I give to you. Not as the world gives do I give it to you. Do not let your hearts be troubled or afraid. ²⁸ You heard me tell you, 'I am going away and I will come back to you.' If you loved me, you would rejoice that I am going to the Father; for the Father is greater than I. ²⁹ And now I have told you this before it happens, so that when it happens you may believe. ³⁰ I will no longer speak much with you, for the ruler of the world is coming. He has no power over me, ³¹ but the world must know that I love the Father and that I do just as the Father has commanded me. Get up, let us go.

15 "I am the true vine, and my Father is the vine grower. ² He takes away every branch in me that does not bear fruit, and everyone that does he prunes so that it bears more fruit. ³ You are already pruned because of the word that I spoke to you. ⁴ Remain in me, as I remain in you. Just as a branch cannot bear fruit on its own unless it remains on the vine, so neither can you unless you remain

---

¹⁷ the Spirit of truth
  whom the world can never accept
  since it neither sees nor knows him;
  but you know him,
  because he is with you, he is in you.
¹⁸ I shall not leave you orphans;
  I shall come to you.
¹⁹ In a short time the world will no longer see me;
  but you will see that I live
  and you also will live.
²⁰ On that day
  you will know that I am in my Father
  and you in me and I in you.
²¹ Whoever holds to my commandments and keeps
    them
  is the one who loves me;
  and whoever loves me will be loved by my Father,
  and I shall love him and reveal myself to him.'

²² Judas — not Judas Iscariot — said to him, 'Lord, what has happened, that you intend to show yourself to us and not to the world?' ²³ Jesus replied:

Anyone who loves me will keep my word,
  and my Father will love him,
  and we shall come to him
  and make a home in him.
²⁴ Anyone who does not love me does not keep my
    words.
  And the word that you hear is not my own:
  it is the word of the Father who sent me.
²⁵ I have said these things to you
  while still with you;
²⁶ but the Paraclete, the Holy Spirit,
  whom the Father will send in my name,
  will teach you everything
  and remind you of all I have said to you.
²⁷ Peace I bequeath to you,
  my own peace I give you,
  a peace which the world cannot give, this is my
    gift to you.
  Do not let your hearts be troubled or afraid.
²⁸ You heard me say:
  I am going away and shall return.
  If you loved me you would be glad that I am going
    to the Father,
  for the Father is greater than I.
²⁹ I have told you this now, before it happens,
  so that when it does happen you may believe.
³⁰ I shall not talk to you much longer,
  because the prince of this world is on his way.
  He has no power over me,
³¹ but the world must recognise that I love the Father
  and that I act just as the Father commanded.
  Come now, let us go.

15 I am the true vine,ʷ
  and my Father is the vinedresser.
² Every branch in me that bears no fruit
  he cuts away,
  and every branch that does bear fruit he prunes
  to make it bear even more.
³ You are clean already,
  by means of the word that I have spoken to you.
⁴ Remain in me, as I in you.
  As a branch cannot bear fruit all by itself,
  unless it remains part of the vine,
  neither can you unless you remain in me.

ʷ **15** cf. Is 5:1–7; Mk 12:1–12.

5 I am the vine, you are the branches. Those who abide in me and I in them bear much fruit, because apart from me you can do nothing. 6 Whoever does not abide in me is thrown away like a branch and withers; such branches are gathered, thrown into the fire, and burned. 7 If you abide in me, and my words abide in you, ask for whatever you wish, and it will be done for you. 8 My Father is glorified by this, that you bear much fruit and become*l* my disciples. 9 As the Father has loved me, so I have loved you; abide in my love. 10 If you keep my commandments, you will abide in my love, just as I have kept my Father's commandments and abide in his love. 11 I have said these things to you so that my joy may be in you, and that your joy may be complete.

12 "This is my commandment, that you love one another as I have loved you. 13 No one has greater love than this, to lay down one's life for one's friends. 14 You are my friends if you do what I command you. 15 I do not call you servants*m* any longer, because the servant*n* does not know what the master is doing; but I have called you friends, because I have made known to you everything that I have heard from my Father. 16 You did not choose me but I chose you. And I appointed you to go and bear fruit, fruit that will last, so that the Father will give you whatever you ask him in my name. 17 I am giving you these commands so that you may love one another.

18 "If the world hates you, be aware that it hated me before it hated you. 19 If you belonged to the world,*o* the world would love you as its own. Because you do not belong to the world, but I have chosen you out of the world—therefore the world hates you. 20 Remember the word that I said to you, 'Servants*p* are not greater than their master.' If they persecuted me, they will persecute you; if they kept my word, they will keep yours also. 21 But they will do all these things to you on account of my name, because they do not know him who sent me. 22 If I had not

5 'I am the vine; you are the branches. Anyone who dwells in me, as I dwell in him, bears much fruit; apart from me you can do nothing. 6 Anyone who does not dwell in me is thrown away like a withered branch. The withered branches are gathered up, thrown on the fire, and burnt.

7 'If you dwell in me, and my words dwell in you, ask whatever you want, and you shall have it. 8 This is how my Father is glorified: you are to bear fruit in plenty and so be my disciples. 9 As the Father has loved me, so I have loved you. Dwell in my love. 10 If you heed my commands, you will dwell in my love, as I have heeded my Father's commands and dwell in his love.

11 'I have spoken thus to you, so that my joy may be in you, and your joy complete. 12 This is my commandment: love one another, as I have loved you. 13 There is no greater love than this, that someone should lay down his life for his friends. 14 You are my friends, if you do what I command you. 15 No longer do I call you servants, for a servant does not know what his master is about. I have called you friends, because I have disclosed to you everything that I heard from my Father. 16 You did not choose me: I chose you. I appointed you to go on and bear fruit, fruit that will last; so that the Father may give you whatever you ask in my name. 17 This is my commandment to you: love one another.

18 'If the world hates you, it hated me first, as you know well. 19 If you belonged to the world, the world would love its own; but you do not belong to the world, now that I have chosen you out of the world, and for that reason the world hates you. 20 Remember what I said: "A servant is not greater than his master." If they persecuted me, they will also persecute you; if they have followed my teaching, they will follow yours. 21 All this will they do to you on my account, because they do not know the One who sent me.

15:18 **it hated . . . well:** *or bear in mind that it hated me first.*

in me. 5 I am the vine, you are the branches. Whoever remains in me and I in him will bear much fruit, because without me you can do nothing. 6 Anyone who does not remain in me will be thrown out like a branch and wither; people will gather them and throw them into a fire and they will be burned. 7 If you remain in me and my words remain in you, ask for whatever you want and it will be done for you. 8 By this is my Father glorified, that you bear much fruit and become my disciples. 9 As the Father loves me, so I also love you. Remain in my love. 10 If you keep my commandments, you will remain in my love, just as I have kept my Father's commandments and remain in his love.

11 "I have told you this so that my joy might be in you and your joy might be complete. 12 This is my commandment: love one another as I love you. 13 No one has greater love than this, to lay down one's life for one's friends. 14 You are my friends if you do what I command you. 15 I no longer call you slaves, because a slave does not know what his master is doing. I have called you friends, because I have told you everything I have heard from my Father. 16 It was not you who chose me, but I who chose you and appointed you to go and bear fruit that will remain, so that whatever you ask the Father in my name he may give you. 17 This I command you: love one another.

18 "If the world hates you, realize that it hated me first. 19 If you belonged to the world, the world would love its own; but because you do not belong to the world, and I have chosen you out of the world, the world hates you. 20 Remember the word I spoke to you, 'No slave is greater than his master.' If they persecuted me, they will also persecute you. If they kept my word, they will also keep yours. 21 And they will do all these things to you on account of my name, because they do not know the one who sent me. 22 If I had

5 I am the vine,
you are the branches.
Whoever remains in me, with me in him,
bears fruit in plenty;
for cut off from me you can do nothing.
6 Anyone who does not remain in me
is thrown away like a branch
— and withers;
these branches are collected and thrown on the fire
and are burnt.
7 If you remain in me
and my words remain in you,
you may ask for whatever you please
and you will get it.
8 It is to the glory of my Father that you should bear
much fruit
and be my disciples.
9 I have loved you
just as the Father has loved me.
Remain in my love.
10 If you keep my commandments
you will remain in my love,
just as I have kept my Father's commandments
and remain in his love.
11 I have told you this
so that my own joy may be in you
and your joy be complete.
12 This is my commandment:
love one another,
as I have loved you.
13 No one can have greater love
than to lay down his life for his friends.
14 You are my friends,
if you do what I command you.
15 I shall no longer call you servants,
because a servant does not know
the master's business;
I call you friends,
because I have made known to you
everything I have learnt from my Father.
16 You did not choose me,
no, I chose you;
and I commissioned you
to go out and to bear fruit,
fruit that will last;
so that the Father will give you
anything you ask him in my name.
17 My command to you
is to love one another.
18 If the world hates you,
you must realise that it hated me before it hated
you.
19 If you belonged to the world,
the world would love you as its own;
but because you do not belong to the world,
because my choice of you has drawn you out of
the world,
that is why the world hates you.
20 Remember the words I said to you:
A servant is not greater than his master.
If they persecuted me,
they will persecute you too;
if they kept my word,
they will keep yours as well.
21 But it will be on my account that they will do all
this to you,
because they do not know the one who sent me.

| NEW REVISED STANDARD VERSION | REVISED ENGLISH BIBLE |

come and spoken to them, they would not have sin; but now they have no excuse for their sin. 23 Whoever hates me hates my Father also. 24 If I had not done among them the works that no one else did, they would not have sin. But now they have seen and hated both me and my Father. 25 It was to fulfill the word that is written in their law, 'They hated me without a cause.'

26 "When the Advocate*q* comes, whom I will send to you from the Father, the Spirit of truth who comes from the Father, he will testify on my behalf. 27 You also are to testify because you have been with me from the beginning.

16 "I have said these things to you to keep you from stumbling. 2 They will put you out of the synagogues. Indeed, an hour is coming when those who kill you will think that by doing so they are offering worship to God. 3 And they will do this because they have not known the Father or me. 4 But I have said these things to you so that when their hour comes you may remember that I told you about them.

"I did not say these things to you from the beginning, because I was with you. 5 But now I am going to him who sent me; yet none of you asks me, 'Where are you going?' 6 But because I have said these things to you, sorrow has filled your hearts. 7 Nevertheless I tell you the truth: it is to your advantage that I go away, for if I do not go away, the Advocate*q* will not come to you; but if I go, I will send him to you. 8 And when he comes, he will prove the world wrong about*r* sin and righteousness and judgment: 9 about sin, because they do not believe in me; 10 about righteousness, because I am going to the Father and you will see me no longer; 11 about judgment, because the ruler of this world has been condemned.

12 "I still have many things to say to you, but you cannot bear them now. 13 When the Spirit of truth comes, he will guide you into all the truth; for he will not speak on his own, but will speak whatever he hears, and he will declare to you the things that are to come. 14 He will glorify me, because he will take what is mine and declare it to you.

22 'If I had not come and spoken to them, they would not be guilty of sin; but now they have no excuse for their sin: 23 whoever hates me, hates my Father also. 24 If I had not done such deeds among them as no one else has ever done, they would not be guilty of sin; but now they have seen and hated both me and my Father. 25 This text in their law had to come true: "They hated me without reason."

26 'When the advocate has come, whom I shall send you from the Father — the Spirit of truth that issues from the Father — he will bear witness to me. 27 And you also are my witnesses, because you have been with me from the first.

16 'I have told you all this to guard you against the breakdown of your faith. 2 They will ban you from the synagogue; indeed, the time is coming when anyone who kills you will suppose that he is serving God. 3 They will do these things because they did not know either the Father or me. 4 I have told you all this so that when the time comes for it to happen you may remember my warning. I did not tell you this at first, because then I was with you; 5 but now I am going away to him who sent me. None of you asks me, "Where are you going?" 6 Yet you are plunged into grief at what I have told you. 7 Nevertheless I assure you that it is in your interest that I am leaving you. If I do not go, the advocate will not come, whereas if I go, I will send him to you. 8 When he comes, he will prove the world wrong about sin, justice, and judgement: 9 about sin, because they refuse to believe in me; 10 about justice, because I go to the Father when I pass from your sight; 11 about judgement, because the prince of this world stands condemned.

12 'There is much more that I could say to you, but the burden would be too great for you now. 13 However, when the Spirit of truth comes, he will guide you into all the truth; for he will not speak on his own authority, but will speak only what he hears; and he will make known to you what is to come. 14 He will glorify me, for he will take what is mine and make it known to you. 15 All that the Father has is mine,

not come and spoken to them, they would have no sin; but as it is they have no excuse for their sin. 23 Whoever hates me also hates my Father. 24 If I had not done works among them that no one else ever did, they would not have sin; but as it is, they have seen and hated both me and my Father. 25 But in order that the word written in their law might be fulfilled, 'They hated me without cause.'

26 "When the Advocate comes whom I will send you from the Father, the Spirit of truth that proceeds from the Father, he will testify to me. 27 And you also testify, because you have been with me from the beginning.

16 "I have told you this so that you may not fall away. 2 They will expel you from the synagogues; in fact, the hour is coming when everyone who kills you will think he is offering worship to God. 3 They will do this because they have not known either the Father or me. 4 I have told you this so that when their hour comes you may remember that I told you.

"I did not tell you this from the beginning, because I was with you. 5 But now I am going to the one who sent me, and not one of you asks me, 'Where are you going?' 6 But because I told you this, grief has filled your hearts. 7 But I tell you the truth, it is better for you that I go. For if I do not go, the Advocate will not come to you. But if I go, I will send him to you. 8 And when he comes he will convict the world in regard to sin and righteousness and condemnation: 9 sin, because they do not believe in me; 10 righteousness, because I am going to the Father and you will no longer see me; 11 condemnation, because the ruler of this world has been condemned.

12 "I have much more to tell you, but you cannot bear it now. 13 But when he comes, the Spirit of truth, he will guide you to all truth. He will not speak on his own, but he will speak what he hears, and will declare to you the things that are coming. 14 He will glorify me, because he will take from what is mine and declare it to you. 15 Everything that

22 If I had not come,
  if I had not spoken to them,
  they would have been blameless;
  but as it is they have no excuse for their sin.
23 Anyone who hates me hates my Father.
24 If I had not performed such works among them
  as no one else has ever done,
  they would be blameless;
  but as it is, in spite of what they have seen,
  they hate both me and my Father.
25 But all this was only to fulfil the words written in
    their Law:
    They hated me without reason. x
26 When the Paraclete comes,
  whom I shall send to you from the Father,
  the Spirit of truth who issues from the Father,
  he will be my witness.
27 And you too will be witnesses,
  because you have been with me from the
    beginning.

16 I have told you all this
  so that you may not fall away.
2 They will expel you from the synagogues,
  and indeed the time is coming
  when anyone who kills you will think he is doing a
    holy service to God.
3 They will do these things
  because they have never known either the Father or
    me.
4 But I have told you all this,
  so that when the time for it comes
  you may remember that I told you.
  I did not tell you this from the beginning,
  because I was with you;
5 but now I am going to the one who sent me.
  Not one of you asks, 'Where are you going?'
6 Yet you are sad at heart because I have told you
    this.
7 Still, I am telling you the truth:
  it is for your own good that I am going,
  because unless I go,
  the Paraclete will not come to you;
  but if I go,
  I will send him to you.
8 And when he comes,
  he will show the world how wrong it was,
  about sin,
  and about who was in the right,
  and about judgement:
9 about sin:
  in that they refuse to believe in me;
10 about who was in the right:
  in that I am going to the Father
  and you will see me no more;
11 about judgement:
  in that the prince of this world is already
    condemned.
12 I still have many things to say to you
  but they would be too much for you to bear now.
13 However, when the Spirit of truth comes
  he will lead you to the complete truth,
  since he will not be speaking of his own accord,
  but will say only what he has been told;
  and he will reveal to you the things to come.
14 He will glorify me,
  since all he reveals to you
  will be taken from what is mine.

x **15** Ps 69:4.

15 All that the Father has is mine. For this reason I said that he will take what is mine and declare it to you.

16 "A little while, and you will no longer see me, and again a little while, and you will see me." 17 Then some of his disciples said to one another, "What does he mean by saying to us, 'A little while, and you will no longer see me, and again a little while, and you will see me'; and 'Because I am going to the Father'?" 18 They said, "What does he mean by this 'a little while'? We do not know what he is talking about." 19 Jesus knew that they wanted to ask him, so he said to them, "Are you discussing among yourselves what I meant when I said, 'A little while, and you will no longer see me, and again a little while, and you will see me'? 20 Very truly, I tell you, you will weep and mourn, but the world will rejoice; you will have pain, but your pain will turn into joy. 21 When a woman is in labor, she has pain, because her hour has come. But when her child is born, she no longer remembers the anguish because of the joy of having brought a human being into the world. 22 So you have pain now; but I will see you again, and your hearts will rejoice, and no one will take your joy from you. 23 On that day you will ask nothing of me.^{s} Very truly, I tell you, if you ask anything of the Father in my name, he will give it to you.^{t} 24 Until now you have not asked for anything in my name. Ask and you will receive, so that your joy may be complete.

25 "I have said these things to you in figures of speech. The hour is coming when I will no longer speak to you in figures, but will tell you plainly of the Father. 26 On that day you will ask in my name. I do not say to you that I will ask the Father on your behalf; 27 for the Father himself loves you, because you have loved me and have believed that I came from God.^{u} 28 I came from the Father and have come into the world; again, I am leaving the world and am going to the Father."

29 His disciples said, "Yes, now you are speaking plainly, not in any figure of speech! 30 Now we know that you know all things, and do not need to have anyone question you; by this we believe that you came from God." 31 Jesus answered them, "Do you now believe? 32 The hour

and that is why I said, "He will take what is mine and make it known to you."

16 'A LITTLE while, and you see me no more; again a little while, and you will see me.' 17 Some of his disciples said to one another, 'What does he mean by this: "A little while, and you will not see me, and again a little while, and you will see me," and by this: "Because I am going to the Father"?' 18 So they asked, 'What is this "little while" that he is talking about? We do not know what he means.' 19 Jesus knew that they were wanting to question him, and said, 'Are you discussing that saying of mine: "A little while, and you will not see me, and again a little while, and you will see me"? 20 In very truth I tell you, you will weep and mourn, but the world will be glad. But though you will be plunged in grief, your grief will be turned to joy. 21 A woman in labour is in pain because her time has come; but when her baby is born she forgets the anguish in her joy that a child has been born into the world. 22 So it is with you: for the moment you are sad; but I shall see you again, and then you will be joyful, and no one shall rob you of your joy. 23 When that day comes you will ask me nothing more. In very truth I tell you, if you ask the Father for anything in my name, he will give it you. 24 So far you have asked nothing in my name. Ask and you will receive, that your joy may be complete.

25 'Till now I have been using figures of speech; a time is coming when I shall no longer use figures, but tell you of the Father in plain words. 26 When that day comes you will make your request in my name, and I do not say that I shall pray to the Father for you, 27 for the Father loves you himself, because you have loved me and believed that I came from God. 28 I came from the Father and have come into the world; and now I am leaving the world again and going to the Father.' 29 His disciples said, 'Now you are speaking plainly, not in figures of speech! 30 We are certain now that you know everything, and do not need to be asked; because of this we believe that you have come from God.'

31 Jesus answered, 'Do you now believe? 32 I warn you,

---

^{s} Or will ask me no question ^{t} Other ancient authorities read *Father, he will give it to you in my name* ^{u} Other ancient authorities read *the Father*

16:23 **if you ask . . . you:** *some witnesses read* if you ask the Father for anything, he will give it you in my name.

the Father has is mine; for this reason I told you that he will take from what is mine and declare it to you.

16 "A little while and you will no longer see me, and again a little while later and you will see me." 17 So some of his disciples said to one another, "What does this mean that he is saying to us, 'A little while and you will not see me, and again a little while and you will see me,' and 'Because I am going to the Father'?" 18 So they said, "What is this 'little while' [of which he speaks]? We do not know what he means." 19 Jesus knew that they wanted to ask him, so he said to them, "Are you discussing with one another what I said, 'A little while and you will not see me, and again a little while and you will see me'? 20 Amen, amen, I say to you, you will weep and mourn, while the world rejoices; you will grieve, but your grief will become joy. 21 When a woman is in labor, she is in anguish because her hour has arrived; but when she has given birth to a child, she no longer remembers the pain because of her joy that a child has been born into the world. 22 So you also are now in anguish. But I will see you again, and your hearts will rejoice, and no one will take your joy away from you. 23 On that day you will not question me about anything. Amen, amen, I say to you, whatever you ask the Father in my name he will give you. 24 Until now you have not asked anything in my name; ask and you will receive, so that your joy may be complete.

25 "I have told you this in figures of speech. The hour is coming when I will no longer speak to you in figures but I will tell you clearly about the Father. 26 On that day you will ask in my name, and I do not tell you that I will ask the Father for you. 27 For the Father himself loves you, because you have loved me and have come to believe that I came from God. 28 I came from the Father and have come into the world. Now I am leaving the world and going back to the Father." 29 His disciples said, "Now you are talking plainly, and not in any figure of speech. 30 Now we realize that you know everything and that you do not need to have anyone question you. Because of this we believe that you came from God." 31 Jesus answered them, "Do you believe now?

15 Everything the Father has is mine;
   that is why I said:
   all he reveals to you
   will be taken from what is mine.
16 In a short time you will no longer see me,
   and then a short time later you will see me again.

17 Then some of his disciples said to one another, 'What does he mean, "In a short time you will no longer see me, and then a short time later you will see me again," and, "I am going to the Father"? 18 What is this "short time"? We don't know what he means.' 19 Jesus knew that they wanted to question him, so he said, 'You are asking one another what I meant by saying, "In a short time you will no longer see me, and then a short time later you will see me again."

20 'In all truth I tell you,
   you will be weeping and wailing
   while the world will rejoice;
   you will be sorrowful,
   but your sorrow will turn to joy.
21 A woman in childbirth suffers,
   because her time has come;
   but when she has given birth to the child she
      forgets the suffering
   in her joy that a human being has been born into
      the world.
22 So it is with you: you are sad now,
   but I shall see you again, and your hearts will be
      full of joy,
   and that joy no one shall take from you.
23 When that day comes,
   you will not ask me any questions.
   In all truth I tell you,
   anything you ask from the Father
   he will grant in my name.
24 Until now you have not asked anything in my
      name.
   Ask and you will receive,
   and so your joy will be complete.
25 I have been telling you these things in veiled
      language.
   The hour is coming
   when I shall no longer speak to you in veiled
      language
   but tell you about the Father in plain words.
26 When that day comes
   you will ask in my name;
   and I do not say that I shall pray to the Father for
      you,
27 because the Father himself loves you
   for loving me,
   and believing that I came from God.
28 I came from the Father and have come into the
      world
   and now I am leaving the world to go to the
      Father.'

29 His disciples said, 'Now you are speaking plainly and not using veiled language. 30 Now we see that you know everything and need not wait for questions to be put into words; because of this we believe that you came from God.' 31 Jesus answered them:

   Do you believe at last?

NEW REVISED STANDARD VERSION

REVISED ENGLISH BIBLE

is coming, indeed it has come, when you will be scattered, each one to his home, and you will leave me alone. Yet I am not alone because the Father is with me. 33 I have said this to you, so that in me you may have peace. In the world you face persecution. But take courage; I have conquered the world!"

17 After Jesus had spoken these words, he looked up to heaven and said, "Father, the hour has come; glorify your Son so that the Son may glorify you, 2 since you have given him authority over all people,^{v} to give eternal life to all whom you have given him. 3 And this is eternal life, that they may know you, the only true God, and Jesus Christ whom you have sent. 4 I glorified you on earth by finishing the work that you gave me to do. 5 So now, Father, glorify me in your own presence with the glory that I had in your presence before the world existed.

6 "I have made your name known to those whom you gave me from the world. They were yours, and you gave them to me, and they have kept your word. 7 Now they know that everything you have given me is from you; 8 for the words that you gave to me I have given to them, and they have received them and know in truth that I came from you; and they have believed that you sent me. 9 I am asking on their behalf; I am not asking on behalf of the world, but on behalf of those whom you gave me, because they are yours. 10 All mine are yours, and yours are mine; and I have been glorified in them. 11 And now I am no longer in the world, but they are in the world, and I am coming to you. Holy Father, protect them in your name that you have given me, so that they may be one, as we are one. 12 While I was with them, I protected them in your name that^w you have given me. I guarded them, and not one of them was lost except the one destined to be lost,^{x} so that the scripture might be fulfilled. 13 But now I am coming to you, and I speak these things in the world so that they may have my joy made complete in themselves.^{y} 14 I have given them your word, and the world has hated them because they do not belong to the world, just as I do not belong to the world.

the hour is coming, has indeed already come, when you are to be scattered, each to his own home, leaving me alone. Yet I am not alone, for the Father is with me. 33 I have told you all this so that in me you may find peace. In the world you will have suffering. But take heart! I have conquered the world.'

17 THEN Jesus looked up to heaven and said: 'Father, the hour has come. Glorify your Son, that the Son may glorify you. 2 For you have made him sovereign over all mankind, to give eternal life to all whom you have given him. 3 This is eternal life: to know you the only true God, and Jesus Christ whom you have sent. 4 I have glorified you on earth by finishing the work which you gave me to do; 5 and now, Father, glorify me in your own presence with the glory which I had with you before the world began.

6 'I have made your name known to the men whom you gave me out of the world. They were yours and you gave them to me, and they have obeyed your command. 7 Now they know that all you gave me has come from you; 8 for I have taught them what I learned from you, and they have received it: they know with certainty that I came from you, and they have believed that you sent me.

9 'I pray for them; I am not praying for the world but for those whom you have given me, because they belong to you. 10 All that is mine is yours, and what is yours is mine; and through them is my glory revealed.

11 'I am no longer in the world; they are still in the world, but I am coming to you. Holy Father, protect them by the power of your name, the name you have given me, that they may be one, as we are one. 12 While I was with them, I protected them by the power of your name which you gave me, and kept them safe. Not one of them is lost except the man doomed to be lost, for scripture has to be fulfilled.

13 'Now I am coming to you; but while I am still in the world I speak these words, so that they may have my joy within them in full measure. 14 I have delivered your word to them, and the world hates them because they are strang-

---

^{v} Gk *flesh* ^{w} Other ancient authorities read *protected in your name* *those whom* ^{x} Gk *except the son of destruction* ^{y} Or *among* *themselves*

17:11 **protect . . . given me:** *some witnesses read* protect by the power of your name those whom you have given me.
17:12 **protected . . . gave me:** *some witnesses read* protected by the power of your name those whom you have given me.

32 Behold, the hour is coming and has arrived when each of you will be scattered to his own home and you will leave me alone. But I am not alone, because the Father is with me. 33 I have told you this so that you might have peace in me. In the world you will have trouble, but take courage, I have conquered the world."

17 When Jesus had said this, he raised his eyes to heaven and said, "Father, the hour has come. Give glory to your son, so that your son may glorify you, 2 just as you gave him authority over all people, so that he may give eternal life to all you gave him. 3 Now this is eternal life, that they should know you, the only true God, and the one whom you sent, Jesus Christ. 4 I glorified you on earth by accomplishing the work that you gave me to do. 5 Now glorify me, Father, with you, with the glory that I had with you before the world began.

6 "I revealed your name to those whom you gave me out of the world. They belonged to you, and you gave them to me, and they have kept your word. 7 Now they know that everything you gave me is from you, 8 because the words you gave to me I have given to them, and they accepted them and truly understood that I came from you, and they have believed that you sent me. 9 I pray for them. I do not pray for the world but for the ones you have given me, because they are yours, 10 and everything of mine is yours and everything of yours is mine, and I have been glorified in them. 11 And now I will no longer be in the world, but they are in the world, while I am coming to you. Holy Father, keep them in your name that you have given me, so that they may be one just as we are. 12 When I was with them I protected them in your name that you gave me, and I guarded them, and none of them was lost except the son of destruction, in order that the scripture might be fulfilled. 13 But now I am coming to you. I speak this in the world so that they may share my joy completely. 14 I gave them your word, and the world hated them, because they do not belong to the world any more than I belong to the world. 15 I do not

32 Listen; the time will come—indeed it has come
   already—
when you are going to be scattered, each going his
   own way
and leaving me alone.
And yet I am not alone,
because the Father is with me.
33 I have told you all this
so that you may find peace in me.
In the world you will have hardship,
but be courageous:
I have conquered the world.

17 After saying this, Jesus raised his eyes to heaven
   and said:

Father, the hour has come:
glorify your Son
so that your Son may glorify you;
2 so that, just as you have given him power over all
   humanity,
he may give eternal life to all those you have
   entrusted to him.
3 And eternal life is this:
to know you,
the only true God,
and Jesus Christ whom you have sent.
4 I have glorified you on earth
by finishing the work
that you gave me to do.
5 Now, Father, glorify me
with that glory I had with you
before the world existed.
6 I have revealed your name
to those whom you took from the world to give
   me.
They were yours and you gave them to me,
and they have kept your word.
7 Now at last they have recognised
that all you have given me comes from you
8 for I have given them
the teaching you gave to me,
and they have indeed accepted it
and know for certain that I came from you,
and have believed that it was you who sent me.
9 It is for them that I pray.
I am not praying for the world
but for those you have given me,
because they belong to you.
10 All I have is yours
and all you have is mine,
and in them I am glorified.
11 I am no longer in the world,
but they are in the world,
and I am coming to you.
Holy Father,
keep those you have given me true to your name,
so that they may be one like us.
12 While I was with them,
I kept those you had given me true to your name.
I have watched over them and not one is lost
except one who was destined to be lost,
and this was to fulfil the scriptures.
13 But now I am coming to you
and I say these things in the world
to share my joy with them to the full.
14 I passed your word on to them,
and the world hated them,
because they belong to the world
no more than I belong to the world.

NEW REVISED STANDARD VERSION

REVISED ENGLISH BIBLE

15 I am not asking you to take them out of the world, but I ask you to protect them from the evil one.*z* 16 They do not belong to the world, just as I do not belong to the world. 17 Sanctify them in the truth; your word is truth. 18 As you have sent me into the world, so I have sent them into the world. 19 And for their sakes I sanctify myself, so that they also may be sanctified in truth.

20 "I ask not only on behalf of these, but also on behalf of those who will believe in me through their word, 21 that they may all be one. As you, Father, are in me and I am in you, may they also be in us,*a* so that the world may believe that you have sent me. 22 The glory that you have given me I have given them, so that they may be one, as we are one, 23 I in them and you in me, that they may become completely one, so that the world may know that you have sent me and have loved them even as you have loved me. 24 Father, I desire that those also, whom you have given me, may be with me where I am, to see my glory, which you have given me because you loved me before the foundation of the world.

25 "Righteous Father, the world does not know you, but I know you; and these know that you have sent me. 26 I made your name known to them, and I will make it known, so that the love with which you have loved me may be in them, and I in them."

ers in the world, as I am. 15 I do not pray you to take them out of the world, but to keep them from the evil one. 16 They are strangers in the world, as I am. 17 Consecrate them by the truth; your word is truth. 18 As you sent me into the world, I have sent them into the world, 19 and for their sake I consecrate myself, that they too may be consecrated by the truth.

20 'It is not for these alone that I pray, but for those also who through their words put their faith in me. 21 May they all be one; as you, Father, are in me, and I in you, so also may they be in us, that the world may believe that you sent me. 22 The glory which you gave me I have given to them, that they may be one, as we are one; 23 I in them and you in me, may they be perfectly one. Then the world will know that you sent me, and that you loved them as you loved me.

24 'Father, they are your gift to me; and my desire is that they may be with me where I am, so that they may look upon my glory, which you have given me because you loved me before the world began. 25 Righteous Father, although the world does not know you, I know you, and they know that you sent me. 26 I made your name known to them, and will make it known, so that the love you had for me may be in them, and I in them.'

---

18 After Jesus had spoken these words, he went out with his disciples across the Kidron valley to a place where there was a garden, which he and his disciples entered. 2 Now Judas, who betrayed him, also knew the place, because Jesus often met there with his disciples. 3 So Judas brought a detachment of soldiers together with police from the chief priests and the Pharisees, and they came there with lanterns and torches and weapons. 4 Then Jesus, knowing all that was to happen to him, came forward and asked them, "Whom are you looking for?" 5 They answered, "Jesus of Nazareth."*b* Jesus replied, "I am he."*c* Judas, who betrayed him, was standing with them. 6 When Jesus*d* said to them, "I am he,"*c* they stepped back and fell to the ground. 7 Again he asked them, "Whom are you looking for?" And they said, "Jesus of Nazareth."*b* 8 Jesus answered, "I told you that I am he.*c* So if you are looking for me, let these men go." 9 This was to fulfill the word that he had spoken, "I did not lose a single one of those whom you gave me." 10 Then Simon Peter, who had a sword, drew it, struck the high priest's slave, and cut off his right ear. The slave's name was Malchus. 11 Jesus said to Peter, "Put

18 AFTER this prayer, Jesus went out with his disciples across the Kedron ravine. There was a garden there, and he and his disciples went into it. 2 The place was known to Judas, his betrayer, because Jesus had often met there with his disciples. 3 So Judas made his way there with a detachment of soldiers, and with temple police provided by the chief priests and the Pharisees; they were equipped with lanterns, torches, and weapons. 4 Jesus, knowing everything that was to happen to him, stepped forward and asked them, 'Who is it you want?' 5 'Jesus of Nazareth,' they answered. Jesus said, 'I am he.' And Judas the traitor was standing there with them. 6 When Jesus said, 'I am he,' they drew back and fell to the ground. 7 Again he asked, 'Who is it you want?' 'Jesus of Nazareth,' they repeated. 8 'I have told you that I am he,' Jesus answered. 'If I am the man you want, let these others go.' 9 (This was to make good his words, 'I have not lost one of those you gave me.') 10 Thereupon Simon Peter drew the sword he was wearing and struck at the high priest's servant, cutting off his right ear. The servant's name was Malchus. 11 Jesus said to Peter,

---

z Or *from evil*   *a* Other ancient authorities read *be one in us*
b Gk *the Nazorean*   *c* Gk *I am*   *d* Gk *he*

|

ask that you take them out of the world but that you keep them from the evil one. 16 They do not belong to the world any more than I belong to the world. 17 Consecrate them in the truth. Your word is truth. 18 As you sent me into the world, so I sent them into the world. 19 And I consecrate myself for them, so that they also may be consecrated in truth.

20 "I pray not only for them, but also for those who will believe in me through their word, 21 so that they may all be one, as you, Father, are in me and I in you, that they also may be in us, that the world may believe that you sent me. 22 And I have given them the glory you gave me, so that they may be one, as we are one, 23 I in them and you in me, that they may be brought to perfection as one, that the world may know that you sent me, and that you loved them even as you loved me. 24 Father, they are your gift to me. I wish that where I am they also may be with me, that they may see my glory that you gave me, because you loved me before the foundation of the world. 25 Righteous Father, the world also does not know you, but I know you, and they know that you sent me. 26 I made known to them your name and I will make it known, that the love with which you loved me may be in them and I in them."

18 When he had said this, Jesus went out with his disciples across the Kidron valley to where there was a garden, into which he and his disciples entered. 2 Judas his betrayer also knew the place, because Jesus had often met there with his disciples. 3 So Judas got a band of soldiers and guards from the chief priests and the Pharisees and went there with lanterns, torches, and weapons. 4 Jesus, knowing everything that was going to happen to him, went out and said to them, "Whom are you looking for?" 5 They answered him, "Jesus the Nazorean." He said to them, "I AM." Judas his betrayer was also with them. 6 When he said to them, "I AM," they turned away and fell to the ground. 7 So he again asked them, "Whom are you looking for?" They said, "Jesus the Nazorean." 8 Jesus answered, "I told you that I AM. So if you are looking for me, let these men go." 9 This was to fulfill what he had said, "I have not lost any of those you gave me." 10 Then Simon Peter, who had a sword, drew it, struck the high priest's slave, and cut off his right ear. The slave's name was Malchus. 11 Jesus said

15 I am not asking you to remove them from the
  world,
  but to protect them from the Evil One.
16 They do not belong to the world
  any more than I belong to the world.
17 Consecrate them in the truth;
  your word is truth.
18 As you sent me into the world,
  I have sent them into the world,
19 and for their sake I consecrate myself
  so that they too may be consecrated in truth.
20 I pray not only for these
  but also for those
  who through their teaching will come to believe in
  me.
21 May they all be one,
  just as, Father, you are in me and I am in you,
  so that they also may be in us,
  so that the world may believe it was you who sent
  me.
22 I have given them the glory you gave to me,
  that they may be one as we are one.
23 With me in them and you in me,
  may they be so perfected in unity
  that the world will recognise that it was you who
  sent me
  and that you have loved them as you have loved
  me."
24 Father,
  I want those you have given me
  to be with me where I am,
  so that they may always see my glory
  which you have given me
  because you loved me
  before the foundation of the world.
25 Father, Upright One,
  the world has not known you,
  but I have known you,
  and these have known
  that you have sent me.
26 I have made your name known to them
  and will continue to make it known,
  so that the love with which you loved me may be
  in them,
  and so that I may be in them.'

18 After he had said all this, Jesus left with his disciples and crossed the Kidron valley where there was a garden into which he went with his disciples. 2 Judas the traitor knew the place also, since Jesus had often met his disciples there, 3 so Judas brought the cohort to this place together with guards sent by the chief priests and the Pharisees, all with lanterns and torches and weapons. 4 Knowing everything that was to happen to him, Jesus came forward and said, 'Who are you looking for?' 5 They answered, 'Jesus the Nazarene.' He said, 'I am he.' Now Judas the traitor was standing among them. 6 When Jesus said to them, 'I am he,' they moved back and fell on the ground. 7 He asked them a second time, 'Who are you looking for?' They said, 'Jesus the Nazarene.' 8 Jesus replied, 'I have told you that I am he. If I am the one you are looking for, let these others go.' 9 This was to fulfil the words he had spoken, 'Not one of those you gave me have I lost.' 10 Simon Peter, who had a sword, drew it and struck the high priest's servant, cutting off his right ear. The servant's name was Malchus. 11 Jesus said to Peter, 'Put your sword

NEW REVISED STANDARD VERSION

your sword back into its sheath. Am I not to drink the cup that the Father has given me?"

12 So the soldiers, their officer, and the Jewish police arrested Jesus and bound him. 13 First they took him to Annas, who was the father-in-law of Caiaphas, the high priest that year. 14 Caiaphas was the one who had advised the Jews that it was better to have one person die for the people.

15 Simon Peter and another disciple followed Jesus. Since that disciple was known to the high priest, he went with Jesus into the courtyard of the high priest, 16 but Peter was standing outside at the gate. So the other disciple, who was known to the high priest, went out, spoke to the woman who guarded the gate, and brought Peter in. 17 The woman said to Peter, "You are not also one of this man's disciples, are you?" He said, "I am not." 18 Now the slaves and the police had made a charcoal fire because it was cold, and they were standing around it and warming themselves. Peter also was standing with them and warming himself.

19 Then the high priest questioned Jesus about his disciples and about his teaching. 20 Jesus answered, "I have spoken openly to the world; I have always taught in synagogues and in the temple, where all the Jews come together. I have said nothing in secret. 21 Why do you ask me? Ask those who heard what I said to them; they know what I said." 22 When he had said this, one of the police standing nearby struck Jesus on the face, saying, "Is that how you answer the high priest?" 23 Jesus answered, "If I have spoken wrongly, testify to the wrong. But if I have spoken rightly, why do you strike me?" 24 Then Annas sent him bound to Caiaphas the high priest.

25 Now Simon Peter was standing and warming himself. They asked him, "You are not also one of his disciples, are you?" He denied it and said, "I am not." 26 One of the slaves of the high priest, a relative of the man whose ear Peter had cut off, asked, "Did I not see you in the garden with him?" 27 Again Peter denied it, and at that moment the cock crowed.

28 Then they took Jesus from Caiaphas to Pilate's headquarters.*e* It was early in the morning. They themselves did not enter the headquarters,*e* so as to avoid ritual defilement and to be able to eat the Passover. 29 So Pilate went out to them and said, "What accusation do you bring against this man?" 30 They answered, "If this man were not a criminal, we would not have handed him over to you." 31 Pilate said to them, "Take him yourselves and judge him according to your law." The Jews replied, "We are not permitted to put anyone to death." 32 (This was to fulfill what Jesus had said when he indicated the kind of death he was to die.)

33 Then Pilate entered the headquarters*e* again, summoned Jesus, and asked him, "Are you the King of the Jews?" 34 Jesus answered, "Do you ask this on your own, or did others tell you about me?" 35 Pilate replied, "I am not a Jew, am I? Your own nation and the chief priests have handed you over to me. What have you done?" 36 Jesus answered, "My kingdom is not from this world. If my kingdom were from this world, my followers would be fighting to keep me from being handed over to the Jews. But as it is, my kingdom is not from here." 37 Pilate asked him, "So you are a king?" Jesus answered, "You say that I am a king. For this I was born, and for this I came into the world, to testify to the truth. Everyone who belongs to the truth listens to my voice." 38 Pilate asked him, "What is truth?"

After he had said this, he went out to the Jews again and told them, "I find no case against him. 39 But you have a custom that I release someone for you at the Passover. Do you want me to release for you the King of the Jews?"

REVISED ENGLISH BIBLE

'Put away your sword. This is the cup the Father has given me; shall I not drink it?'

12 THE troops with their commander, and the Jewish police, now arrested Jesus and secured him. 13 They took him first to Annas, father-in-law of Caiaphas, the high priest for that year — 14 the same Caiaphas who had advised the Jews that it would be to their interest if one man died for the people. 15 Jesus was followed by Simon Peter and another disciple. This disciple, who was known to the high priest, went with Jesus into the high priest's courtyard, 16 but Peter stayed outside at the door. So the other disciple, the high priest's acquaintance, went back and spoke to the girl on duty at the door, and brought Peter in. 17 The girl said to Peter, 'Are you another of this man's disciples?' 'I am not,' he said. 18 As it was cold, the servants and the police had made a charcoal fire, and were standing round it warming themselves. Peter too was standing with them, sharing the warmth.

19 The high priest questioned Jesus about his disciples and about his teaching. 20 Jesus replied, 'I have spoken openly for all the world to hear; I have always taught in synagogues or in the temple, where all Jews congregate; I have said nothing in secret. 21 Why are you questioning me? Question those who heard me; they know what I said.' 22 When he said this, one of the police standing near him struck him on the face. 'Is that the way to answer the high priest?' he demanded. 23 Jesus replied, 'If I was wrong to speak what I did, produce evidence to prove it; if I was right, why strike me?'

24 So Annas sent him bound to Caiaphas the high priest.

25 Meanwhile, as Simon Peter stood warming himself, he was asked, 'Are you another of his disciples?' But he denied it: 'I am not,' he said. 26 One of the high priest's servants, a relation of the man whose ear Peter had cut off, insisted, 'Did I not see you with him in the garden?' 27 Once again Peter denied it; and at that moment a cock crowed.

28 FROM Caiaphas Jesus was led into the governor's headquarters. It was now early morning, and the Jews themselves stayed outside the headquarters to avoid defilement, so that they could eat the Passover meal. 29 So Pilate came out to them and asked, 'What charge do you bring against this man?' 30 'If he were not a criminal', they replied, 'we would not have brought him before you.' 31 Pilate said, 'Take him yourselves and try him by your own law.' The Jews answered, 'We are not allowed to put anyone to death.' 32 Thus they ensured the fulfilment of the words by which Jesus had indicated the kind of death he was to die.

33 Pilate then went back into his headquarters and summoned Jesus. 'So you are the king of the Jews?' he said. 34 Jesus replied, 'Is that your own question, or have others suggested it to you?' 35 'Am I a Jew?' said Pilate. 'Your own nation and their chief priests have brought you before me. What have you done?' 36 Jesus replied, 'My kingdom does not belong to this world. If it did, my followers would be fighting to save me from the clutches of the Jews. My kingdom belongs elsewhere.' 37 'You are a king, then?' said Pilate. Jesus answered, ' "King" is your word. My task is to bear witness to the truth. For this I was born; for this I came into the world, and all who are not deaf to truth listen to my voice.' 38 Pilate said, 'What is truth?' With those words he went out again to the Jews and said, 'For my part I find no case against him. 39 But you have a custom that I release one prisoner for you at Passover. Would you like me

---

e Gk *the praetorium*

to Peter, "Put your sword into its scabbard. Shall I not drink the cup that the Father gave me?"

12 So the band of soldiers, the tribune, and the Jewish guards seized Jesus, bound him, 13 and brought him to Annas first. He was the father-in-law of Caiaphas, who was high priest that year. 14 It was Caiaphas who had counseled the Jews that it was better that one man should die rather than the people.

15 Simon Peter and another disciple followed Jesus. Now the other disciple was known to the high priest, and he entered the courtyard of the high priest with Jesus. 16 But Peter stood at the gate outside. So the other disciple, the acquaintance of the high priest, went out and spoke to the gatekeeper and brought Peter in. 17 Then the maid who was the gatekeeper said to Peter, "You are not one of this man's disciples, are you?" He said, "I am not." 18 Now the slaves and the guards were standing around a charcoal fire that they had made, because it was cold, and were warming themselves. Peter was also standing there keeping warm.

19 The high priest questioned Jesus about his disciples and about his doctrine. 20 Jesus answered him, "I have spoken publicly to the world. I have always taught in a synagogue or in the temple area where all the Jews gather, and in secret I have said nothing. 21 Why ask me? Ask those who heard me what I said to them. They know what I said." 22 When he had said this, one of the temple guards standing there struck Jesus and said, "Is this the way you answer the high priest?" 23 Jesus answered him, "If I have spoken wrongly, testify to the wrong; but if I have spoken rightly, why do you strike me?" 24 Then Annas sent him bound to Caiaphas the high priest.

25 Now Simon Peter was standing there keeping warm. And they said to him, "You are not one of his disciples, are you?" He denied it and said, "I am not." 26 One of the slaves of the high priest, a relative of the one whose ear Peter had cut off, said, "Didn't I see you in the garden with him?" 27 Again Peter denied it. And immediately the cock crowed.

28 Then they brought Jesus from Caiaphas to the praetorium. It was morning. And they themselves did not enter the praetorium, in order not to be defiled so that they could eat the Passover. 29 So Pilate came out to them and said, "What charge do you bring [against] this man?" 30 They answered and said to him, "If he were not a criminal, we would not have handed him over to you." 31 At this, Pilate said to them, "Take him yourselves, and judge him according to your law." The Jews answered him, "We do not have the right to execute anyone," 32 in order that the word of Jesus might be fulfilled that he said indicating the kind of death he would die. 33 So Pilate went back into the praetorium and summoned Jesus and said to him, "Are you the King of the Jews?" 34 Jesus answered, "Do you say this on your own or have others told you about me?" 35 Pilate answered, "I am not a Jew, am I? Your own nation and the chief priests handed you over to me. What have you done?" 36 Jesus answered, "My kingdom does not belong to this world. If my kingdom did belong to this world, my attendants [would] be fighting to keep me from being handed over to the Jews. But as it is, my kingdom is not here." 37 So Pilate said to him, "Then you are a king?" Jesus answered, "You say I am a king. For this I was born and for this I came into the world, to testify to the truth. Everyone who belongs to the truth listens to my voice." 38 Pilate said to him, "What is truth?"

When he had said this, he again went out to the Jews and said to them, "I find no guilt in him. 39 But you have a custom that I release one prisoner to you at Passover. Do you want me to release to you the King of the Jews?"

back in its scabbard; am I not to drink the cup that the Father has given me?'

12 The cohort and its tribune and the Jewish guards seized Jesus and bound him. 13 They took him first to Annas, because Annas was the father-in-law of Caiaphas, who was high priest that year. 14 It was Caiaphas who had counselled the Jews, 'It is better for one man to die for the people.'

15 Simon Peter, with another disciple, followed Jesus. This disciple, who was known to the high priest, went with Jesus into the high priest's palace, 16 but Peter stayed outside the door. So the other disciple, the one known to the high priest, went out, spoke to the doorkeeper and brought Peter in. 17 The girl on duty at the door said to Peter, 'Aren't you another of that man's disciples?' He answered, 'I am not.' 18 Now it was cold, and the servants and guards had lit a charcoal fire and were standing there warming themselves; so Peter stood there too, warming himself with the others.

19 The high priest questioned Jesus about his disciples and his teaching. 20 Jesus answered, 'I have spoken openly for all the world to hear; I have always taught in the synagogue and in the Temple where all the Jews meet together; I have said nothing in secret. 21 Why ask me? Ask my hearers what I taught; they know what I said.' 22 At these words, one of the guards standing by gave Jesus a slap in the face, saying, 'Is that the way you answer the high priest?' 23 Jesus replied, 'If there is some offence in what I said, point it out; but if not, why do you strike me?' 24 Then Annas sent him, bound, to Caiaphas the high priest.y

25 As Simon Peter stood there warming himself, someone said to him, 'Aren't you another of his disciples?' He denied it saying, 'I am not.' 26 One of the high priest's servants, a relation of the man whose ear Peter had cut off, said, 'Didn't I see you in the garden with him?' 27 Again Peter denied it; and at once a cock crowed.

28 They then led Jesus from the house of Caiaphas to the Praetorium. It was now morning. They did not go into the Praetorium themselves to avoid becoming defiled and unable to eat the Passover. 29 So Pilate came outside to them and said, 'What charge do you bring against this man?' They replied, 30 'If he were not a criminal, we should not have handed him over to you.' 31 Pilate said, 'Take him yourselves, and try him by your own Law.' The Jews answered, 'We are not allowed to put anyone to death.' 32 This was to fulfil the words Jesus had spoken indicating the way he was going to die.

33 So Pilate went back into the Praetorium and called Jesus to him and asked him, 'Are you the king of the Jews?' 34 Jesus replied, 'Do you ask this of your own accord, or have others said it to you about me?' 35 Pilate answered, 'Am I a Jew? It is your own people and the chief priests who have handed you over to me: what have you done?' 36 Jesus replied, 'Mine is not a kingdom of this world; if my kingdom were of this world, my men would have fought to prevent my being surrendered to the Jews. As it is, my kingdom does not belong here.' 37 Pilate said, 'So, then you are a king?' Jesus answered, 'It is you who say that I am a king. I was born for this, I came into the world for this, to bear witness to the truth; and all who are on the side of truth listen to my voice.' 38 'Truth?' said Pilate. 'What is that?' And so saying he went out again to the Jews and said, 'I find no case against him. 39 But according to a custom of yours I should release one prisoner at the Passover; would you like me, then, to release for you the king of the Jews?'

---

y 18 Jn has no Sanhedrin session as the other gospels have, only a private interrogation at night.

NEW REVISED STANDARD VERSION	REVISED ENGLISH BIBLE

NEW REVISED STANDARD VERSION

40 They shouted in reply, "Not this man, but Barabbas!" Now Barabbas was a bandit.

19 Then Pilate took Jesus and had him flogged. 2 And the soldiers wove a crown of thorns and put it on his head, and they dressed him in a purple robe. 3 They kept coming up to him, saying, "Hail, King of the Jews!" and striking him on the face. 4 Pilate went out again and said to them, "Look, I am bringing him out to you to let you know that I find no case against him." 5 So Jesus came out, wearing the crown of thorns and the purple robe. Pilate said to them, "Here is the man!" 6 When the chief priests and the police saw him, they shouted, "Crucify him! Crucify him!" Pilate said to them, "Take him yourselves and crucify him; I find no case against him." 7 The Jews answered him, "We have a law, and according to that law he ought to die because he has claimed to be the Son of God."

8 Now when Pilate heard this, he was more afraid than ever. 9 He entered his headquarters *f* again and asked Jesus, "Where are you from?" But Jesus gave him no answer. 10 Pilate therefore said to him, "Do you refuse to speak to me? Do you not know that I have power to release you, and power to crucify you?" 11 Jesus answered him, "You would have no power over me unless it had been given you from above; therefore the one who handed me over to you is guilty of a greater sin." 12 From then on Pilate tried to release him, but the Jews cried out, "If you release this man, you are no friend of the emperor. Everyone who claims to be a king sets himself against the emperor."

13 When Pilate heard these words, he brought Jesus outside and sat *g* on the judge's bench at a place called The Stone Pavement, or in Hebrew *h* Gabbatha. 14 Now it was the day of Preparation for the Passover; and it was about noon. He said to the Jews, "Here is your King!" 15 They cried out, "Away with him! Away with him! Crucify him!" Pilate asked them, "Shall I crucify your King?" The chief priests answered, "We have no king but the emperor." 16 Then he handed him over to them to be crucified.

So they took Jesus; 17 and carrying the cross by himself, he went out to what is called The Place of the Skull, which in Hebrew *h* is called Golgotha. 18 There they crucified him, and with him two others, one on either side, with Jesus between them. 19 Pilate also had an inscription written and put on the cross. It read, "Jesus of Nazareth,*i* the King of the Jews." 20 Many of the Jews read this inscription, because the place where Jesus was crucified was near the city; and it was written in Hebrew,*h* in Latin, and in Greek. 21 Then the chief priests of the Jews said to Pilate, "Do not write, 'The King of the Jews,' but, 'This man said, I am King of the Jews.' " 22 Pilate answered, "What I have written I have written." 23 When the soldiers had crucified Jesus, they took his clothes and divided them into four parts, one for each soldier. They also took his tunic; now the tunic was seamless, woven in one piece from the top. 24 So they said to one another, "Let us not tear it, but cast lots for it to see who will get it." This was to fulfill what the scripture says,

"They divided my clothes among themselves,
and for my clothing they cast lots."

25 And that is what the soldiers did.

Meanwhile, standing near the cross of Jesus were his mother, and his mother's sister, Mary the wife of Clopas, and Mary Magdalene. 26 When Jesus saw his mother and the disciple whom he loved standing beside her, he said to his mother, "Woman, here is your son." 27 Then he said to the disciple, "Here is your mother." And from that hour the disciple took her into his own home.

REVISED ENGLISH BIBLE

to release the king of the Jews?' 40 At this they shouted back: 'Not him; we want Barabbas!' Barabbas was a bandit.

19 Pilate now took Jesus and had him flogged; 2 and the soldiers plaited a crown of thorns and placed it on his head, and robed him in a purple cloak. 3 Then one after another they came up to him, crying, 'Hail, king of the Jews!' and struck him on the face.

4 Once more Pilate came out and said to the Jews, 'Here he is; I am bringing him out to let you know that I find no case against him'; 5 and Jesus came out, wearing the crown of thorns and the purple cloak. 'Here is the man,' said Pilate. 6 At the sight of him the chief priests and the temple police shouted, 'Crucify! Crucify!' 'Take him yourselves and crucify him,' said Pilate; 'for my part I find no case against him.' 7 The Jews answered, 'We have a law; and according to that law he ought to die, because he has claimed to be God's Son.'

8 When Pilate heard that, he was more afraid than ever, 9 and going back into his headquarters he asked Jesus, 'Where have you come from?' But Jesus gave him no answer. 10 'Do you refuse to speak to me?' said Pilate. 'Surely you know that I have authority to release you, and authority to crucify you?' 11 'You would have no authority at all over me', Jesus replied, 'if it had not been granted you from above; and therefore the deeper guilt lies with the one who handed me over to you.'

12 From that moment Pilate tried hard to release him; but the Jews kept shouting, 'If you let this man go, you are no friend to Caesar; anyone who claims to be a king is opposing Caesar.' 13 When Pilate heard what they were saying, he brought Jesus out and took his seat on the tribunal at the place known as The Pavement (in Hebrew, 'Gabbatha'). 14 It was the day of preparation for the Passover, about noon. Pilate said to the Jews, 'Here is your king.' 15 They shouted, 'Away with him! Away with him! Crucify him!' 'Am I to crucify your king?' said Pilate. 'We have no king but Caesar,' replied the chief priests. 16 Then at last, to satisfy them, he handed Jesus over to be crucified.

JESUS was taken away, 17 and went out, carrying the cross himself, to the place called The Skull (in Hebrew, 'Golgotha'); 18 there they crucified him, and with him two others, one on either side, with Jesus in between.

19 Pilate had an inscription written and fastened to the cross; it read, 'Jesus of Nazareth, King of the Jews'. 20 This inscription, in Hebrew, Latin, and Greek, was read by many Jews, since the place where Jesus was crucified was not far from the city. 21 So the Jewish chief priests said to Pilate, 'You should not write "King of the Jews", but rather "He claimed to be king of the Jews".' 22 Pilate replied, 'What I have written, I have written.'

23 When the soldiers had crucified Jesus they took his clothes and, leaving aside the tunic, divided them into four parts, one for each soldier. The tunic was seamless, woven in one piece throughout; 24 so they said to one another, 'We must not tear this; let us toss for it.' Thus the text of scripture came true: 'They shared my garments among them, and cast lots for my clothing.'

That is what the soldiers did. 25 Meanwhile near the cross on which Jesus hung, his mother was standing with her sister, Mary wife of Clopas, and Mary of Magdala. 26 Seeing his mother, with the disciple whom he loved standing beside her, Jesus said to her, 'Mother, there is your son'; 27 and to the disciple, 'There is your mother'; and from that moment the disciple took her into his home.

---

f Gk *the praetorium* *g* Or *seated him* *h* That is, *Aramaic*
i Gk *the Nazorean*

19:14 **It was ... Passover:** *or* It was Friday in Passover.

40 They cried out again, "Not this one but Barabbas!" Now Barabbas was a revolutionary.

19 Then Pilate took Jesus and had him scourged. 2 And the soldiers wove a crown out of thorns and placed it on his head, and clothed him in a purple cloak, 3 and they came to him and said, "Hail, King of the Jews!" And they struck him repeatedly. 4 Once more Pilate went out and said to them, "Look, I am bringing him out to you, so that you may know that I find no guilt in him." 5 So Jesus came out, wearing the crown of thorns and the purple cloak. And he said to them, "Behold, the man!" 6 When the chief priests and the guards saw him they cried out, "Crucify him, crucify him!" Pilate said to them, "Take him yourselves and crucify him. I find no guilt in him." 7 The Jews answered, "We have a law, and according to that law he ought to die, because he made himself the Son of God." 8 Now when Pilate heard this statement, he became even more afraid, 9 and went back into the praetorium and said to Jesus, "Where are you from?" Jesus did not answer him. 10 So Pilate said to him, "Do you not speak to me? Do you not know that I have power to release you and I have power to crucify you?" 11 Jesus answered [him], "You would have no power over me if it had not been given to you from above. For this reason the one who handed me over to you has the greater sin." 12 Consequently, Pilate tried to release him; but the Jews cried out, "If you release him, you are not a Friend of Caesar. Everyone who makes himself a king opposes Caesar."

13 When Pilate heard these words he brought Jesus out and seated him on the judge's bench in the place called Stone Pavement, in Hebrew, Gabbatha. 14 It was preparation day for Passover, and it was about noon. And he said to the Jews, "Behold, your king!" 15 They cried out, "Take him away, take him away! Crucify him!" Pilate said to them, "Shall I crucify your king?" The chief priests answered, "We have no king but Caesar." 16 Then he handed him over to them to be crucified.

So they took Jesus, 17 and carrying the cross himself he went out to what is called the Place of the Skull, in Hebrew, Golgotha. 18 There they crucified him, and with him two others, one on either side, with Jesus in the middle. 19 Pilate also had an inscription written and put on the cross. It read, "Jesus the Nazorean, the King of the Jews." 20 Now many of the Jews read this inscription, because the place where Jesus was crucified was near the city; and it was written in Hebrew, Latin, and Greek. 21 So the chief priests of the Jews said to Pilate, "Do not write 'The King of the Jews,' but that he said, 'I am the King of the Jews.'" 22 Pilate answered, "What I have written, I have written."

23 When the soldiers had crucified Jesus, they took his clothes and divided them into four shares, a share for each soldier. They also took his tunic, but the tunic was seamless, woven in one piece from the top down. 24 So they said to one another, "Let's not tear it, but cast lots for it to see whose it will be," in order that the passage of scripture might be fulfilled [that says]:

"They divided my garments among them,
and for my vesture they cast lots."

This is what the soldiers did. 25 Standing by the cross of Jesus were his mother and his mother's sister, Mary the wife of Clopas, and Mary of Magdala. 26 When Jesus saw his mother and the disciple there whom he loved, he said to his mother, "Woman, behold, your son." 27 Then he said to the disciple, "Behold, your mother." And from that hour the disciple took her into his home.

40 At this they shouted, 'Not this man,' they said, 'but Barabbas.' Barabbas was a bandit.

19 Pilate then had Jesus taken away and scourged; 2 and after this, the soldiers twisted some thorns into a crown and put it on his head and dressed him in a purple robe. 3 They kept coming up to him and saying, 'Hail, king of the Jews!' and slapping him in the face.

4 Pilate came outside again and said to them, 'Look, I am going to bring him out to you to let you see that I find no case against him.' 5 Jesus then came outside wearing the crown of thorns and the purple robe. Pilate said, 'Here is the man.' 6 When they saw him, the chief priests and the guards shouted, 'Crucify him! Crucify him!' Pilate said, 'Take him yourselves and crucify him: I find no case against him.' 7 The Jews replied, 'We have a Law, and according to that Law he ought to be put to death, because he has claimed to be Son of God.'

8 When Pilate heard them say this his fears increased. 9 Re-entering the Praetorium, he said to Jesus, 'Where do you come from?' But Jesus made no answer. 10 Pilate then said to him, 'Are you refusing to speak to me? Surely you know I have power to release you and I have power to crucify you?' 11 Jesus replied, 'You would have no power over me at all if it had not been given you from above; that is why the man who handed me over to you has the greater guilt.'

12 From that moment Pilate was anxious to set him free, but the Jews shouted, 'If you set him free you are no friend of Caesar's; anyone who makes himself king is defying Caesar.' 13 Hearing these words, Pilate had Jesus brought out, and seated him on the chair of judgement at a place called the Pavement, in Hebrew Gabbatha. 14 It was the Day of Preparation, about the sixth hour. 'Here is your king,' said Pilate to the Jews. 15 But they shouted, 'Away with him, away with him, crucify him.' Pilate said, 'Shall I crucify your king?' The chief priests answered, 'We have no king except Caesar.' 16 So at that Pilate handed him over to them to be crucified.

They then took charge of Jesus, 17 and carrying his own cross he went out to the Place of the Skull or, as it is called in Hebrew, Golgotha, 18 where they crucified him with two others, one on either side, Jesus being in the middle. 19 Pilate wrote out a notice and had it fixed to the cross; it ran: 'Jesus the Nazarene, King of the Jews'. 20 This notice was read by many of the Jews, because the place where Jesus was crucified was near the city, and the writing was in Hebrew, Latin and Greek. 21 So the Jewish chief priests said to Pilate, 'You should not write "King of the Jews", but that the man said, "I am King of the Jews".' 22 Pilate answered, 'What I have written, I have written.'

23 When the soldiers had finished crucifying Jesus they took his clothing and divided it into four shares, one for each soldier. His undergarment was seamless, woven in one piece from neck to hem; 24 so they said to one another, 'Instead of tearing it, let's throw dice to decide who is to have it.' In this way the words of scripture were fulfilled:

*They divide my garments among them
and cast lots for my clothes.z*

That is what the soldiers did.

25 Near the cross of Jesus stood his mother and his mother's sister, Mary the wife of Clopas, and Mary of Magdala. 26 Seeing his mother and the disciple whom he loved standing near her, Jesus said to his mother, 'Woman, this is your son.' 27 Then to the disciple he said, 'This is your mother.' And from that hour the disciple took her into his home.

z **19** Ps 22:18.

28 After this, when Jesus knew that all was now finished, he said (in order to fulfill the scripture), "I am thirsty." 29 A jar full of sour wine was standing there. So they put a sponge full of the wine on a branch of hyssop and held it to his mouth. 30 When Jesus had received the wine, he said, "It is finished." Then he bowed his head and gave up his spirit.

31 Since it was the day of Preparation, the Jews did not want the bodies left on the cross during the sabbath, especially because that sabbath was a day of great solemnity. So they asked Pilate to have the legs of the crucified men broken and the bodies removed. 32 Then the soldiers came and broke the legs of the first and of the other who had been crucified with him. 33 But when they came to Jesus and saw that he was already dead, they did not break his legs. 34 Instead, one of the soldiers pierced his side with a spear, and at once blood and water came out. 35 (He who saw this has testified so that you also may believe. His testimony is true, and he knows j that he tells the truth.) 36 These things occurred so that the scripture might be fulfilled, "None of his bones shall be broken." 37 And again another passage of scripture says, "They will look on the one whom they have pierced."

38 After these things, Joseph of Arimathea, who was a disciple of Jesus, though a secret one because of his fear of the Jews, asked Pilate to let him take away the body of Jesus. Pilate gave him permission; so he came and removed his body. 39 Nicodemus, who had at first come to Jesus by night, also came, bringing a mixture of myrrh and aloes, weighing about a hundred pounds. 40 They took the body of Jesus and wrapped it with the spices in linen cloths, according to the burial custom of the Jews. 41 Now there was a garden in the place where he was crucified, and in the garden there was a new tomb in which no one had ever been laid. 42 And so, because it was the Jewish day of Preparation, and the tomb was nearby, they laid Jesus there.

20 Early on the first day of the week, while it was still dark, Mary Magdalene came to the tomb and saw that the stone had been removed from the tomb. 2 So she ran and went to Simon Peter and the other disciple, the one whom Jesus loved, and said to them, "They have taken the Lord out of the tomb, and we do not know where they have laid him." 3 Then Peter and the other disciple set out and went toward the tomb. 4 The two were running together, but the other disciple outran Peter and reached the tomb first. 5 He bent down to look in and saw the linen wrappings lying there, but he did not go in. 6 Then Simon Peter came, following him, and went into the tomb. He saw the linen wrappings lying there, 7 and the cloth that had been on Jesus' head, not lying with the linen wrappings but rolled up in a place by itself. 8 Then the other disciple, who reached the tomb first, also went in, and he saw and believed; 9 for as yet they did not understand the scripture, that he must rise from the dead. 10 Then the disciples returned to their homes.

11 But Mary stood weeping outside the tomb. As she wept, she bent over to look k into the tomb; 12 and she saw two angels in white, sitting where the body of Jesus had been lying, one at the head and the other at the feet. 13 They said to her, "Woman, why are you weeping?" She said to them, "They have taken away my Lord, and I do not know where they have laid him." 14 When she had said this, she

28 After this, Jesus, aware that all had now come to its appointed end, said in fulfilment of scripture, 'I am thirsty.' 29 A jar stood there full of sour wine; so they soaked a sponge with the wine, fixed it on hyssop, and held it up to his lips. 30 Having received the wine, he said, 'It is accomplished!' Then he bowed his head and gave up his spirit.

31 Because it was the eve of the sabbath, the Jews were anxious that the bodies should not remain on the crosses, since that sabbath was a day of great solemnity; so they requested Pilate to have the legs broken and the bodies taken down. 32 The soldiers accordingly came to the men crucified with Jesus and broke the legs of each in turn, 33 but when they came to Jesus and found he was already dead, they did not break his legs. 34 But one of the soldiers thrust a lance into his side, and at once there was a flow of blood and water. 35 This is vouched for by an eyewitness, whose evidence is to be trusted. He knows that he speaks the truth, so that you too may believe; 36 for this happened in fulfilment of the text of scripture: 'No bone of his shall be broken.' 37 And another text says, 'They shall look on him whom they pierced.'

38 After that, Joseph of Arimathaea, a disciple of Jesus, but a secret disciple for fear of the Jews, asked Pilate for permission to remove the body of Jesus. He consented; so Joseph came and removed the body. 39 He was joined by Nicodemus (the man who had visited Jesus by night), who brought with him a mixture of myrrh and aloes, more than half a hundredweight. 40 They took the body of Jesus and following Jewish burial customs they wrapped it, with the spices, in strips of linen cloth. 41 Near the place where he had been crucified there was a garden, and in the garden a new tomb, not yet used for burial; 42 and there, since it was the eve of the Jewish sabbath and the tomb was near at hand, they laid Jesus.

20 Early on the first day of the week, while it was still dark, Mary of Magdala came to the tomb. She saw that the stone had been moved away from the entrance, 2 and ran to Simon Peter and the other disciple, the one whom Jesus loved. 'They have taken the Lord out of the tomb,' she said, 'and we do not know where they have laid him.' 3 So Peter and the other disciple set out and made their way to the tomb. 4 They ran together, but the other disciple ran faster than Peter and reached the tomb first. 5 He peered in and saw the linen wrappings lying there, but he did not enter. 6 Then Simon Peter caught up with him and went into the tomb. He saw the linen wrappings lying there, 7 and the napkin which had been round his head, not with the wrappings but rolled up in a place by itself. 8 Then the disciple who had reached the tomb first also went in, and he saw and believed; 9 until then they had not understood the scriptures, which showed that he must rise from the dead.

10 So the disciples went home again; 11 but Mary stood outside the tomb weeping. And as she wept, she peered into the tomb, 12 and saw two angels in white sitting there, one at the head, and one at the feet, where the body of Jesus had lain. 13 They asked her, 'Why are you weeping?' She answered, 'They have taken my Lord away, and I do not know where they have laid him.' 14 With these words she turned

---

j Or there is one who knows   k Gk lacks to look   19:29 hyssop: one witness reads a javelin.

28 After this, aware that everything was now finished, in order that the scripture might be fulfilled, Jesus said, "I thirst." 29 There was a vessel filled with common wine. So they put a sponge soaked in wine on a sprig of hyssop and put it up to his mouth. 30 When Jesus had taken the wine, he said, "It is finished." And bowing his head, he handed over the spirit.

31 Now since it was preparation day, in order that the bodies might not remain on the cross on the sabbath, for the sabbath day of that week was a solemn one, the Jews asked Pilate that their legs be broken and they be taken down. 32 So the soldiers came and broke the legs of the first and then of the other one who was crucified with Jesus. 33 But when they came to Jesus and saw that he was already dead, they did not break his legs, 34 but one soldier thrust his lance into his side, and immediately blood and water flowed out. 35 An eyewitness has testified, and his testimony is true; he knows that he is speaking the truth, so that you also may [come to] believe. 36 For this happened so that the scripture passage might be fulfilled:

"Not a bone of it will be broken."

37 And again another passage says:

"They will look upon him whom they
have pierced."

38 After this, Joseph of Arimathea, secretly a disciple of Jesus for fear of the Jews, asked Pilate if he could remove the body of Jesus. And Pilate permitted it. So he came and took his body. 39 Nicodemus, the one who had first come to him at night, also came bringing a mixture of myrrh and aloes weighing about one hundred pounds. 40 They took the body of Jesus and bound it with burial cloths along with the spices, according to the Jewish burial custom. 41 Now in the place where he had been crucified there was a garden, and in the garden a new tomb, in which no one had yet been buried. 42 So they laid Jesus there because of the Jewish preparation day; for the tomb was close by.

20 On the first day of the week, Mary of Magdala came to the tomb early in the morning, while it was still dark, and saw the stone removed from the tomb. 2 So she ran and went to Simon Peter and to the other disciple whom Jesus loved, and told them, "They have taken the Lord from the tomb, and we don't know where they put him." 3 So Peter and the other disciple went out and came to the tomb. 4 They both ran, but the other disciple ran faster than Peter and arrived at the tomb first; 5 he bent down and saw the burial cloths there, but did not go in. 6 When Simon Peter arrived after him, he went into the tomb and saw the burial cloths there, 7 and the cloth that had covered his head, not with the burial cloths but rolled up in a separate place. 8 Then the other disciple also went in, the one who had arrived at the tomb first, and he saw and believed. 9 For they did not yet understand the scripture that he had to rise from the dead. 10 Then the disciples returned home.

11 But Mary stayed outside the tomb weeping. And as she wept, she bent over into the tomb 12 and saw two angels in white sitting there, one at the head and one at the feet where the body of Jesus had been. 13 And they said to her, "Woman, why are you weeping?" She said to them, "They have taken my Lord, and I don't know where they laid him." 14 When she had said this, she turned around and saw

28 After this, Jesus knew that everything had now been completed and, so that the scripture should be completely fulfilled, he said:

I am thirsty.ᵃ

29 A jar full of sour wine stood there; so, putting a sponge soaked in the wine on a hyssop stick, they held it up to his mouth. 30 After Jesus had taken the wine he said, 'It is fulfilled'; and bowing his head he gave up his spirit.

31 It was the Day of Preparation, and to avoid the bodies' remaining on the cross during the Sabbath — since that Sabbath was a day of special solemnity — the Jews asked Pilate to have the legs broken and the bodies taken away. 32 Consequently the soldiers came and broke the legs of the first man who had been crucified with him and then of the other. 33 When they came to Jesus, they saw he was already dead, and so instead of breaking his legs 34 one of the soldiers pierced his side with a lance; and immediately there came out blood and water. 35 This is the evidence of one who saw it — true evidence, and he knows that what he says is true — and he gives it so that you may believe as well. 36 Because all this happened to fulfil the words of scripture:

Not one bone of his will be broken;ᵇ

37 and again, in another place scripture says:

*They will look to the one whom they have
pierced.ᶜ*

38 After this, Joseph of Arimathaea, who was a disciple of Jesus — though a secret one because he was afraid of the Jews — asked Pilate to let him remove the body of Jesus. Pilate gave permission, so they came and took it away. 39 Nicodemus came as well — the same one who had first come to Jesus at night-time — and he brought a mixture of myrrh and aloes, weighing about a hundred pounds. 40 They took the body of Jesus and bound it in linen cloths with the spices, following the Jewish burial custom. 41 At the place where he had been crucified there was a garden, and in this garden a new tomb in which no one had yet been buried. 42 Since it was the Jewish Day of Preparation and the tomb was nearby, they laid Jesus there.

20 It was very early on the first day of the week and still dark, when Mary of Magdala came to the tomb. She saw that the stone had been moved away from the tomb 2 and came running to Simon Peter and the other disciple, the one whom Jesus loved. 'They have taken the Lord out of the tomb,' she said, 'and we don't know where they have put him.'

3 So Peter set out with the other disciple to go to the tomb. 4 They ran together, but the other disciple, running faster than Peter, reached the tomb first; 5 he bent down and saw the linen cloths lying on the ground, but did not go in. 6 Simon Peter, following him, also came up, went into the tomb, saw the linen cloths lying on the ground 7 and also the cloth that had been over his head; this was not with the linen cloths but rolled up in a place by itself. 8 Then the other disciple who had reached the tomb first also went in; he saw and he believed. 9 Till this moment they had still not understood the scripture, that he must rise from the dead. 10 The disciples then went back home.

11 But Mary was standing outside near the tomb, weeping. Then, as she wept, she stooped to look inside, 12 and saw two angels in white sitting where the body of Jesus had been, one at the head, the other at the feet. 13 They said, 'Woman, why are you weeping?' 'They have taken my Lord away,' she replied, 'and I don't know where they have put him.' 14 As she said this she turned round and saw Jesus

ᵃ 19 Ps 69:21.   ᵇ 19 Ex 12:46 and Ps 34:20.   ᶜ 19 Zc 12:10.

turned around and saw Jesus standing there, but she did not know that it was Jesus. 15 Jesus said to her, "Woman, why are you weeping? Whom are you looking for?" Supposing him to be the gardener, she said to him, "Sir, if you have carried him away, tell me where you have laid him, and I will take him away." 16 Jesus said to her, "Mary!" She turned and said to him in Hebrew,*l* "Rabbouni!" (which means Teacher). 17 Jesus said to her, "Do not hold on to me, because I have not yet ascended to the Father. But go to my brothers and say to them, 'I am ascending to my Father and your Father, to my God and your God.'" 18 Mary Magdalene went and announced to the disciples, "I have seen the Lord"; and she told them that he had said these things to her.

19 When it was evening on that day, the first day of the week, and the doors of the house where the disciples had met were locked for fear of the Jews, Jesus came and stood among them and said, "Peace be with you." 20 After he said this, he showed them his hands and his side. Then the disciples rejoiced when they saw the Lord. 21 Jesus said to them again, "Peace be with you. As the Father has sent me, so I send you." 22 When he had said this, he breathed on them and said to them, "Receive the Holy Spirit. 23 If you forgive the sins of any, they are forgiven them; if you retain the sins of any, they are retained."

24 But Thomas (who was called the Twin*m*), one of the twelve, was not with them when Jesus came. 25 So the other disciples told him, "We have seen the Lord." But he said to them, "Unless I see the mark of the nails in his hands, and put my finger in the mark of the nails and my hand in his side, I will not believe."

26 A week later his disciples were again in the house, and Thomas was with them. Although the doors were shut, Jesus came and stood among them and said, "Peace be with you." 27 Then he said to Thomas, "Put your finger here and see my hands. Reach out your hand and put it in my side. Do not doubt but believe." 28 Thomas answered him, "My Lord and my God!" 29 Jesus said to him, "Have you believed because you have seen me? Blessed are those who have not seen and yet have come to believe."

30 Now Jesus did many other signs in the presence of his disciples, which are not written in this book. 31 But these are written so that you may come to believe*n* that Jesus is the Messiah,*o* the Son of God, and that through believing you may have life in his name.

21 After these things Jesus showed himself again to the disciples by the Sea of Tiberias; and he showed himself in this way. 2 Gathered there together were Simon Peter, Thomas called the Twin,*m* Nathanael of Cana in Galilee, the sons of Zebedee, and two others of his disciples. 3 Simon Peter said to them, "I am going fishing." They said to him, "We will go with you." They went out and got into the boat, but that night they caught nothing.

4 Just after daybreak, Jesus stood on the beach; but the disciples did not know that it was Jesus. 5 Jesus said to them, "Children, you have no fish, have you?" They answered him, "No." 6 He said to them, "Cast the net to the

round and saw Jesus standing there, but she did not recognize him. 15 Jesus asked her, 'Why are you weeping? Who are you looking for?' Thinking it was the gardener, she said, 'If it is you, sir, who removed him, tell me where you have laid him, and I will take him away.' 16 Jesus said, 'Mary!' She turned and said to him, 'Rabbuni!' (which is Hebrew for 'Teacher'). 17 'Do not cling to me,' said Jesus, 'for I have not yet ascended to the Father. But go to my brothers, and tell them that I am ascending to my Father and your Father, to my God and your God.' 18 Mary of Magdala went to tell the disciples. 'I have seen the Lord!' she said, and gave them his message.

19 Late that same day, the first day of the week, when the disciples were together behind locked doors for fear of the Jews, Jesus came and stood among them. 'Peace be with you!' he said; 20 then he showed them his hands and his side. On seeing the Lord the disciples were overjoyed. 21 Jesus said again, 'Peace be with you! As the Father sent me, so I send you.' 22 Then he breathed on them, saying, 'Receive the Holy Spirit! 23 If you forgive anyone's sins, they are forgiven; if you pronounce them unforgiven, unforgiven they remain.'

24 One of the Twelve, Thomas the Twin, was not with the rest when Jesus came. 25 So the others kept telling him, 'We have seen the Lord.' But he said, 'Unless I see the mark of the nails on his hands, unless I put my finger into the place where the nails were, and my hand into his side, I will never believe it.'

26 A week later his disciples were once again in the room, and Thomas was with them. Although the doors were locked, Jesus came and stood among them, saying, 'Peace be with you!' 27 Then he said to Thomas, 'Reach your finger here; look at my hands. Reach your hand here and put it into my side. Be unbelieving no longer, but believe.' 28 Thomas said, 'My Lord and my God!' 29 Jesus said to him, 'Because you have seen me you have found faith. Happy are they who find faith without seeing me.'

30 There were indeed many other signs that Jesus performed in the presence of his disciples, which are not recorded in this book. 31 Those written here have been recorded in order that you may believe that Jesus is the Christ, the Son of God, and that through this faith you may have life by his name.

21 SOME time later, Jesus showed himself to his disciples once again, by the sea of Tiberias. This is how it happened. 2 Simon Peter was with Thomas the Twin, Nathanael from Cana-in-Galilee, the sons of Zebedee, and two other disciples. 3 'I am going out fishing,' said Simon Peter. 'We will go with you,' said the others. So they set off and got into the boat; but that night they caught nothing.

4 Morning came, and Jesus was standing on the beach, but the disciples did not know that it was Jesus. 5 He called out to them, 'Friends, have you caught anything?' 'No,' they answered. 6 He said, 'Throw out the net to starboard,

---

l That is, Aramaic *m* Gk Didymus *n* Other ancient authorities read *may continue to believe* *o* Or *the Christ*

20:31 **believe**: *witnesses read different tenses, some implying* continue to believe, *others* come to believe.

Jesus there, but did not know it was Jesus. 15 Jesus said to her, "Woman, why are you weeping? Whom are you looking for?" She thought it was the gardener and said to him, "Sir, if you carried him away, tell me where you laid him, and I will take him." 16 Jesus said to her, "Mary!" She turned and said to him in Hebrew, "Rabbouni," which means Teacher. 17 Jesus said to her, "Stop holding on to me, for I have not yet ascended to the Father. But go to my brothers and tell them, 'I am going to my Father and your Father, to my God and your God.'" 18 Mary of Magdala went and announced to the disciples, "I have seen the Lord," and what he told her.

19 On the evening of that first day of the week, when the doors were locked, where the disciples were, for fear of the Jews, Jesus came and stood in their midst and said to them, "Peace be with you." 20 When he had said this, he showed them his hands and his side. The disciples rejoiced when they saw the Lord. 21 [Jesus] said to them again, "Peace be with you. As the Father has sent me, so I send you." 22 And when he had said this, he breathed on them and said to them, "Receive the holy Spirit. 23 Whose sins you forgive are forgiven them, and whose sins you retain are retained."

24 Thomas, called Didymus, one of the Twelve, was not with them when Jesus came. 25 So the other disciples said to him, "We have seen the Lord." But he said to them, "Unless I see the mark of the nails in his hands and put my finger into the nailmarks and put my hand into his side, I will not believe." 26 Now a week later his disciples were again inside and Thomas was with them. Jesus came, although the doors were locked, and stood in their midst and said, "Peace be with you." 27 Then he said to Thomas, "Put your finger here and see my hands, and bring your hand and put it into my side, and do not be unbelieving, but believe." 28 Thomas answered and said to him, "My Lord and my God!" 29 Jesus said to him, "Have you come to believe because you have seen me? Blessed are those who have not seen and have believed."

30 Now Jesus did many other signs in the presence of [his] disciples that are not written in this book. 31 But these are written that you may [come to] believe that Jesus is the Messiah, the Son of God, and that through this belief you may have life in his name.

21 After this, Jesus revealed himself again to his disciples at the Sea of Tiberias. He revealed himself in this way. 2 Together were Simon Peter, Thomas called Didymus, Nathanael from Cana in Galilee, Zebedee's sons, and two others of his disciples. 3 Simon Peter said to them, "I am going fishing." They said to him, "We also will come with you." So they went out and got into the boat, but that night they caught nothing. 4 When it was already dawn, Jesus was standing on the shore; but the disciples did not realize that it was Jesus. 5 Jesus said to them, "Children, have you caught anything to eat?" They answered him, "No." 6 So he said to them, "Cast the net over the right side

standing there, though she did not realise that it was Jesus. 15 Jesus said to her, 'Woman, why are you weeping? Who are you looking for?' Supposing him to be the gardener, she said, 'Sir, if you have taken him away, tell me where you have put him, and I will go and remove him.' 16 Jesus said, 'Mary!' She turned round then and said to him in Hebrew, 'Rabbuni!' — which means Master. 17 Jesus said to her, 'Do not cling to me, because I have not yet ascended to the Father. But go to the brothers, and tell them: I am ascending to my Father and your Father, to my God and your God.' 18 So Mary of Magdala told the disciples, 'I have seen the Lord,' and that he had said these things to her.

19 In the evening of that same day, the first day of the week, the doors were closed in the room where the disciples were, for fear of the Jews. Jesus came and stood among them. He said to them, 'Peace be with you,' 20 and, after saying this, he showed them his hands and his side. The disciples were filled with joy at seeing the Lord, 21 and he said to them again, 'Peace be with you.

> 'As the Father sent me,
> so am I sending you.'

22 After saying this he breathed on them and said:

> Receive the Holy Spirit.
> 23 If you forgive anyone's sins,
>   they are forgiven;
>   if you retain anyone's sins,
>   they are retained.

24 Thomas, called the Twin, who was one of the Twelve, was not with them when Jesus came. 25 So the other disciples said to him, 'We have seen the Lord,' but he answered, 'Unless I can see the holes that the nails made in his hands and can put my finger into the holes they made, and unless I can put my hand into his side, I refuse to believe.' 26 Eight days later the disciples were in the house again and Thomas was with them. The doors were closed, but Jesus came in and stood among them. 'Peace be with you,' he said. 27 Then he spoke to Thomas, 'Put your finger here; look, here are my hands. Give me your hand; put it into my side. Do not be unbelieving any more but believe.' 28 Thomas replied, 'My Lord and my God!' 29 Jesus said to him:

> You believe because you can see me.
> Blessed are those who have not seen and yet
>   believe.

30 There were many other signs that Jesus worked in the sight of the disciples, but they are not recorded in this book. 31 These are recorded so that you may believe that Jesus is the Christ, the Son of God, and that believing this you may have life through his name.

21 d Later on, Jesus revealed himself again to the disciples. It was by the Sea of Tiberias, and it happened like this: 2 Simon Peter, Thomas called the Twin, Nathanael from Cana in Galilee, the sons of Zebedee and two other disciples were together. 3 Simon Peter said, 'I'm going fishing.' They replied, 'We'll come with you.' They went out and got into the boat but caught nothing that night.

4 When it was already light, there stood Jesus on the shore, though the disciples did not realise that it was Jesus. 5 Jesus called out, 'Haven't you caught anything, friends?' And when they answered, 'No,' 6 he said, 'Throw the net

---

20, 31: While many manuscripts read *come to believe,* possibly implying a missionary purpose for John's gospel, a small number of quite early ones read "continue to believe," suggesting that the audience consists of Christians whose faith is to be deepened by the book; cf 19, 35.

d 21 Added by the evangelist or one of his disciples.

right side of the boat, and you will find some." So they cast it, and now they were not able to haul it in because there were so many fish. 7 That disciple whom Jesus loved said to Peter, "It is the Lord!" When Simon Peter heard that it was the Lord, he put on some clothes, for he was naked, and jumped into the sea. 8 But the other disciples came in the boat, dragging the net full of fish, for they were not far from the land, only about a hundred yards *p* off.

9 When they had gone ashore, they saw a charcoal fire there, with fish on it, and bread. 10 Jesus said to them, "Bring some of the fish that you have just caught." 11 So Simon Peter went aboard and hauled the net ashore, full of large fish, a hundred fifty-three of them; and though there were so many, the net was not torn. 12 Jesus said to them, "Come and have breakfast." Now none of the disciples dared to ask him, "Who are you?" because they knew it was the Lord. 13 Jesus came and took the bread and gave it to them, and did the same with the fish. 14 This was now the third time that Jesus appeared to the disciples after he was raised from the dead.

15 When they had finished breakfast, Jesus said to Simon Peter, "Simon son of John, do you love me more than these?" He said to him, "Yes, Lord; you know that I love you." Jesus said to him, "Feed my lambs." 16 A second time he said to him, "Simon son of John, do you love me?" He said to him, "Yes, Lord; you know that I love you." Jesus said to him, "Tend my sheep." 17 He said to him the third time, "Simon son of John, do you love me?" Peter felt hurt because he said to him the third time, "Do you love me?" And he said to him, "Lord, you know everything; you know that I love you." Jesus said to him, "Feed my sheep. 18 Very truly, I tell you, when you were younger, you used to fasten your own belt and to go wherever you wished. But when you grow old, you will stretch out your hands, and someone else will fasten a belt around you and take you where you do not wish to go." 19 (He said this to indicate the kind of death by which he would glorify God.) After this he said to him, "Follow me."

20 Peter turned and saw the disciple whom Jesus loved following them; he was the one who had reclined next to Jesus at the supper and had said, "Lord, who is it that is going to betray you?" 21 When Peter saw him, he said to Jesus, "Lord, what about him?" 22 Jesus said to him, "If it is my will that he remain until I come, what is that to you? Follow me!" 23 So the rumor spread in the community *q* that this disciple would not die. Yet Jesus did not say to him that he would not die, but, "If it is my will that he remain until I come, what is that to you?" *r*

24 This is the disciple who is testifying to these things and has written them, and we know that his testimony is true. 25 But there are also many other things that Jesus did; if every one of them were written down, I suppose that the world itself could not contain the books that would be written.

p Gk *two hundred cubits*   *q* Gk *among the brothers*   *r* Other ancient authorities lack *what is that to you*

---

and you will make a catch.' They did so, and found they could not haul the net on board, there were so many fish in it. 7 Then the disciple whom Jesus loved said to Peter, 'It is the Lord!' As soon as Simon Peter heard him say, 'It is the Lord,' he fastened his coat about him (for he had stripped) and plunged into the sea. 8 The rest of them came on in the boat, towing the net full of fish. They were only about a hundred yards from land.

9 When they came ashore, they saw a charcoal fire there with fish laid on it, and some bread. 10 Jesus said, 'Bring some of the fish you have caught.' 11 Simon Peter went on board and hauled the net to land; it was full of big fish, a hundred and fifty-three in all; and yet, many as they were, the net was not torn. 12 Jesus said, 'Come and have breakfast.' None of the disciples dared to ask 'Who are you?' They knew it was the Lord. 13 Jesus came, took the bread and gave it to them, and the fish in the same way. 14 This makes the third time that Jesus appeared to his disciples after his resurrection from the dead.

15 After breakfast Jesus said to Simon Peter, 'Simon son of John, do you love me more than these others?' 'Yes, Lord,' he answered, 'you know that I love you.' 'Then feed my lambs,' he said. 16 A second time he asked, 'Simon son of John, do you love me?' 'Yes, Lord, you know I love you.' 'Then tend my sheep.' 17 A third time he said, 'Simon son of John, do you love me?' Peter was hurt that he asked him a third time, 'Do you love me?' 'Lord,' he said, 'you know everything; you know I love you.' Jesus said, 'Then feed my sheep.

18 'In very truth I tell you: when you were young you fastened your belt about you and walked where you chose; but when you are old you will stretch out your arms, and a stranger will bind you fast, and carry you where you have no wish to go.' 19 He said this to indicate the manner of death by which Peter was to glorify God. Then he added, 'Follow me.'

20 Peter looked round, and saw the disciple whom Jesus loved following—the one who at supper had leaned back close to him to ask the question, 'Lord, who is it that will betray you?' 21 When he saw him, Peter asked, 'Lord, what about him?' 22 Jesus said, 'If it should be my will that he stay until I come, what is it to you? Follow me.'

23 That saying of Jesus became current among his followers, and was taken to mean that that disciple would not die. But in fact Jesus did not say he would not die; he only said, 'If it should be my will that he stay until I come, what is it to you?'

24 It is this same disciple who vouches for what has been written here. He it is who wrote it, and we know that his testimony is true.

25 There is much else that Jesus did. If it were all to be recorded in detail, I suppose the world could not hold the books that would be written.

21:24 **is true:** *some witnesses here insert the passage printed on pp. 2854, 2856 (7:53–8:11).*

of the boat and you will find something." So they cast it, and were not able to pull it in because of the number of fish. 7 So the disciple whom Jesus loved said to Peter, "It is the Lord." When Simon Peter heard that it was the Lord, he tucked in his garment, for he was lightly clad, and jumped into the sea. 8 The other disciples came in the boat, for they were not far from shore, only about a hundred yards, dragging the net with the fish. 9 When they climbed out on shore, they saw a charcoal fire with fish on it and bread. 10 Jesus said to them, "Bring some of the fish you just caught." 11 So Simon Peter went over and dragged the net ashore full of one hundred fifty-three large fish. Even though there were so many, the net was not torn. 12 Jesus said to them, "Come, have breakfast." And none of the disciples dared to ask him, "Who are you?" because they realized it was the Lord. 13 Jesus came over and took the bread and gave it to them, and in like manner the fish. 14 This was now the third time Jesus was revealed to his disciples after being raised from the dead.

15 When they had finished breakfast, Jesus said to Simon Peter, "Simon, son of John, do you love me more than these?" He said to him, "Yes, Lord, you know that I love you." He said to him, "Feed my lambs." 16 He then said to him a second time, "Simon, son of John, do you love me?" He said to him, "Yes, Lord, you know that I love you." He said to him, "Tend my sheep." 17 He said to him the third time, "Simon, son of John, do you love me?" Peter was distressed that he had said to him a third time, "Do you love me?" and he said to him, "Lord, you know everything; you know that I love you." [Jesus] said to him, "Feed my sheep. 18 Amen, amen, I say to you, when you were younger, you used to dress yourself and go where you wanted; but when you grow old, you will stretch out your hands, and someone else will dress you and lead you where you do not want to go." 19 He said this signifying by what kind of death he would glorify God. And when he had said this, he said to him, "Follow me."

20 Peter turned and saw the disciple following whom Jesus loved, the one who had also reclined upon his chest during the supper and had said, "Master, who is the one who will betray you?" 21 When Peter saw him, he said to Jesus, "Lord, what about him?" 22 Jesus said to him, "What if I want him to remain until I come? What concern is it of yours? You follow me." 23 So the word spread among the brothers that that disciple would not die. But Jesus had not told him that he would not die, just "What if I want him to remain until I come? [What concern is it of yours?]"

24 It is this disciple who testifies to these things and has written them, and we know that his testimony is true. 25 There are also many other things that Jesus did, but if these were to be described individually, I do not think the whole world would contain the books that would be written.

out to starboard and you'll find something.' So they threw the net out and could not haul it in because of the quantity of fish. 7 The disciple whom Jesus loved said to Peter, 'It is the Lord.' At these words, 'It is the Lord,' Simon Peter tied his outer garment round him (for he had nothing on) and jumped into the water. 8 The other disciples came on in the boat, towing the net with the fish; they were only about a hundred yards from land.

9 As soon as they came ashore they saw that there was some bread there and a charcoal fire with fish cooking on it. 10 Jesus said, 'Bring some of the fish you have just caught.' 11 Simon Peter went aboard and dragged the net ashore, full of big fish, one hundred and fifty-three of them; and in spite of there being so many the net was not broken. 12 Jesus said to them, 'Come and have breakfast.' None of the disciples was bold enough to ask, 'Who are you?'. They knew quite well it was the Lord. 13 Jesus then stepped forward, took the bread and gave it to them, and the same with the fish. 14 This was the third time that Jesus revealed himself to the disciples after rising from the dead.

15 When they had eaten, Jesus said to Simon Peter, 'Simon son of John, do you love me more than these others do?' He answered, 'Yes, Lord, you know I love you.' Jesus said to him, 'Feed my lambs.' 16 A second time he said to him, 'Simon son of John, do you love me?' He replied, 'Yes, Lord, you know I love you.' Jesus said to him, 'Look after my sheep.' 17 Then he said to him a third time, 'Simon son of John, do you love me?' Peter was hurt that he asked him a third time, 'Do you love me?' and said, 'Lord, you know everything; you know I love you.' Jesus said to him, 'Feed my sheep.

18 In all truth I tell you,
when you were young
you put on your own belt
and walked where you liked;
but when you grow old
you will stretch out your hands,
and somebody else will put a belt round you
and take you where you would rather not go.'

19 In these words he indicated the kind of death by which Peter would give glory to God. After this he said, 'Follow me.'

20 Peter turned and saw the disciple whom Jesus loved[e] following them — the one who had leant back close to his chest at the supper and had said to him, 'Lord, who is it that will betray you?' 21 Seeing him, Peter said to Jesus, 'What about him, Lord?' 22 Jesus answered, 'If I want him to stay behind till I come, what does it matter to you? You are to follow me.' 23 The rumour then went out among the brothers that this disciple would not die. Yet Jesus had not said to Peter, 'He will not die,' but, 'If I want him to stay behind till I come.'

24 This disciple is the one who vouches for these things and has written them down, and we know that his testimony is true.

25 There was much else that Jesus did; if it were written down in detail, I do not suppose the world itself would hold all the books that would be written.

e 21 The source of Jn's tradition; but his identity is uncertain.

The Acts

OF THE APOSTLES

1 In the first book, Theophilus, I wrote about all that Jesus did and taught from the beginning 2 until the day when he was taken up to heaven, after giving instructions through the Holy Spirit to the apostles whom he had chosen. 3 After his suffering he presented himself alive to them by many convincing proofs, appearing to them during forty days and speaking about the kingdom of God. 4 While staying*a* with them, he ordered them not to leave Jerusalem, but to wait there for the promise of the Father. "This," he said, "is what you have heard from me; 5 for John baptized with water, but you will be baptized with*b* the Holy Spirit not many days from now."

6 So when they had come together, they asked him, "Lord, is this the time when you will restore the kingdom to Israel?" 7 He replied, "It is not for you to know the times or periods that the Father has set by his own authority. 8 But you will receive power when the Holy Spirit has come upon you; and you will be my witnesses in Jerusalem, in all Judea and Samaria, and to the ends of the earth." 9 When he had said this, as they were watching, he was lifted up, and a cloud took him out of their sight. 10 While he was going and they were gazing up toward heaven, suddenly two men in white robes stood by them. 11 They said, "Men of Galilee, why do you stand looking up toward heaven? This Jesus, who has been taken up from you into heaven, will come in the same way as you saw him go into heaven."

12 Then they returned to Jerusalem from the mount called Olivet, which is near Jerusalem, a sabbath day's journey away. 13 When they had entered the city, they went to the room upstairs where they were staying, Peter, and John, and James, and Andrew, Philip and Thomas, Bartholomew and Matthew, James son of Alphaeus, and Simon the Zealot, and Judas son of*c* James. 14 All these were constantly devoting themselves to prayer, together with certain women, including Mary the mother of Jesus, as well as his brothers.

15 In those days Peter stood up among the believers*d* (together the crowd numbered about one hundred twenty persons) and said, 16 "Friends,*e* the scripture had to be fulfilled, which the Holy Spirit through David foretold concerning Judas, who became a guide for those who arrested Jesus— 17 for he was numbered among us and was allotted his share in this ministry." 18 (Now this man acquired a field with the reward of his wickedness; and falling headlong,*f* he burst open in the middle and all his bowels gushed out. 19 This became known to all the residents of Jerusalem, so that the field was called in their language Hakeldama, that is, Field of Blood.) 20 "For it is written in the book of Psalms,

'Let his homestead become desolate,
    and let there be no one to live in it';

and

'Let another take his position of overseer.'

21 So one of the men who have accompanied us during all the time that the Lord Jesus went in and out among us, 22 beginning from the baptism of John until the day when he was taken up from us — one of these must become a witness with us to his resurrection." 23 So they proposed two, Jo-

Acts

of the Apostles

1 In the first part of my work, Theophilus, I gave an account of all that Jesus did and taught from the beginning 2 until the day when he was taken up to heaven, after giving instructions through the Holy Spirit to the apostles whom he had chosen. 3 To these men he showed himself after his death and gave ample proof that he was alive: he was seen by them over a period of forty days and spoke to them about the kingdom of God. 4 While he was in their company he directed them not to leave Jerusalem. 'You must wait', he said, 'for the gift promised by the Father, of which I told you; 5 John, as you know, baptized with water, but within the next few days you will be baptized with the Holy Spirit.'

6 When they were all together, they asked him, 'Lord, is this the time at which you are to restore sovereignty to Israel?' 7 He answered, 'It is not for you to know about dates or times which the Father has set within his own control. 8 But you will receive power when the Holy Spirit comes upon you; and you will bear witness for me in Jerusalem, and throughout all Judaea and Samaria, and even in the farthest corners of the earth.'

9 After he had said this, he was lifted up before their very eyes, and a cloud took him from their sight. 10 They were gazing intently into the sky as he went, and all at once there stood beside them two men robed in white, 11 who said, 'Men of Galilee, why stand there looking up into the sky? This Jesus who has been taken from you up to heaven will come in the same way as you have seen him go.'

12 THEY then returned to Jerusalem from the hill called Olivet, which is near the city, no farther than a sabbath day's journey. 13 On their arrival they went to the upstairs room where they were lodging: Peter and John and James and Andrew, Philip and Thomas, Bartholomew and Matthew, James son of Alphaeus, Simon the Zealot, and Judas son of James. 14 All these with one accord were constantly at prayer, together with a group of women, and Mary the mother of Jesus, and his brothers.

15 It was during this time that Peter stood up before the assembled brotherhood, about one hundred and twenty in all, and said: 16 'My friends, the prophecy in scripture, which the Holy Spirit uttered concerning Judas through the mouth of David, was bound to come true; Judas acted as guide to those who arrested Jesus— 17 he was one of our number and had his place in this ministry.' 18 (After buying a plot of land with the price of his villainy, this man fell headlong and burst open so that all his entrails spilled out; 19 everyone in Jerusalem came to hear of this, and in their own language they named the plot Akeldama, which means 'Blood Acre'.) 20 'The words I have in mind', Peter continued, 'are in the book of Psalms: "Let his homestead fall desolate; let there be none to inhabit it." And again, "Let his charge be given to another." 21 Therefore one of those who bore us company all the while the Lord Jesus was going about among us, 22 from his baptism by John until the day when he was taken up from us — one of those must now join us as a witness to his resurrection.'

---

a Or *eating*   *b* Or *by*   *c* Or *the brother of*   *d* Gk *brothers*
e Gk *Men, brothers*   *f* Or *swelling up*

The Acts
of the Apostles

1 In the first book, Theophilus, I dealt with all that Jesus did and taught ²until the day he was taken up, after giving instructions through the holy Spirit to the apostles whom he had chosen. ³He presented himself alive to them by many proofs after he had suffered, appearing to them during forty days and speaking about the kingdom of God. ⁴While meeting with them, he enjoined them not to depart from Jerusalem, but to wait for "the promise of the Father about which you have heard me speak; ⁵for John baptized with water, but in a few days you will be baptized with the holy Spirit."

⁶When they had gathered together they asked him, "Lord, are you at this time going to restore the kingdom to Israel?" ⁷He answered them, "It is not for you to know the times or seasons that the Father has established by his own authority. ⁸But you will receive power when the holy Spirit comes upon you, and you will be my witnesses in Jerusalem, throughout Judea and Samaria, and to the ends of the earth." ⁹When he had said this, as they were looking on, he was lifted up, and a cloud took him from their sight. ¹⁰While they were looking intently at the sky as he was going, suddenly two men dressed in white garments stood beside them. ¹¹They said, "Men of Galilee, why are you standing there looking at the sky? This Jesus who has been taken up from you into heaven will return in the same way as you have seen him going into heaven." ¹²Then they returned to Jerusalem from the mount called Olivet, which is near Jerusalem, a sabbath day's journey away.

¹³When they entered the city they went to the upper room where they were staying, Peter and John and James and Andrew, Philip and Thomas, Bartholomew and Matthew, James son of Alphaeus, Simon the Zealot, and Judas son of James. ¹⁴All these devoted themselves with one accord to prayer, together with some women, and Mary the mother of Jesus, and his brothers.

¹⁵During those days Peter stood up in the midst of the brothers (there was a group of about one hundred and twenty persons in the one place). He said, ¹⁶"My brothers, the scripture had to be fulfilled which the holy Spirit spoke beforehand through the mouth of David, concerning Judas, who was the guide for those who arrested Jesus. ¹⁷He was numbered among us and was allotted a share in this ministry. ¹⁸He bought a parcel of land with the wages of his iniquity, and falling headlong, he burst open in the middle, and all his insides spilled out. ¹⁹This became known to everyone who lived in Jerusalem, so that the parcel of land was called in their language 'Akeldama,' that is, Field of Blood. ²⁰For it is written in the Book of Psalms:

'Let his encampment become desolate,
  and may no one dwell in it.'

And:

'May another take his office.'

²¹Therefore, it is necessary that one of the men who accompanied us the whole time the Lord Jesus came and went among us, ²²beginning from the baptism of John until the day on which he was taken up from us, become with us a witness to his resurrection." ²³So they proposed two, Jo-

Acts
OF THE APOSTLES

1 In my earlier work, Theophilus, I dealt with everything Jesus had done and taught from the beginning ²until the day he gave his instructions to the apostles he had chosen through the Holy Spirit, and was taken up to heaven. ³He had shown himself alive to them after his Passion by many demonstrations: for forty days he had continued to appear to them and tell them about the kingdom of God. ⁴While at table with them, he had told them not to leave Jerusalem, but to wait there for what the Father had promised. 'It is', he had said, 'what you have heard me speak about: ⁵John baptised with water but, not many days from now, you are going to be baptised with the Holy Spirit.'

⁶Now having met together, they asked him, 'Lord, has the time come for you to restore the kingdom to Israel?' ⁷He replied, 'It is not for you to know times or dates that the Father has decided by his own authority, ⁸but you will receive the power of the Holy Spirit which will come on you, and then you will be my witnesses not only in Jerusalem but throughout Judaea and Samaria, and indeed to earth's remotest end.'

⁹As he said this he was lifted up while they looked on, and a cloud took him from their sight. ¹⁰They were still staring into the sky as he went, when suddenly two men in white were standing beside them, ¹¹and they said, 'Why are you Galileans standing here looking into the sky? This Jesus who has been taken up from you into heaven will come back in the same way as you have seen him go to heaven.'

¹²So from the Mount of Olives, as it is called, they went back to Jerusalem, a short distance away, no more than a Sabbath walk; ¹³and when they reached the city they went to the upper room where they were staying; there were Peter and John, James and Andrew, Philip and Thomas, Bartholomew and Matthew, James son of Alphaeus and Simon the Zealot, and Jude son of James. ¹⁴With one heart all these joined constantly in prayer, together with some women, including Mary the mother of Jesus, and with his brothers.

¹⁵One day Peter stood up to speak to the brothers — there were about a hundred and twenty people in the congregation, ¹⁶'Brothers,' he said, 'the passage of scripture had to be fulfilled in which the Holy Spirit, speaking through David, foretells the fate of Judas, who acted as guide to the men who arrested Jesus — ¹⁷after being one of our number and sharing our ministry. ¹⁸As you know, he bought a plot of land with the money he was paid for his crime. He fell headlong and burst open, and all his entrails poured out.ᵃ ¹⁹Everybody in Jerusalem heard about it and the plot came to be called "Bloody Acre", in their language Hakeldama. ²⁰Now in the Book of Psalms it says:

*Reduce his encampment to ruin
and leave his tent unoccupied.*

And again:

Let someone else take over his office.

²¹'Out of the men who have been with us the whole time that the Lord Jesus was living with us, ²²from the time when John was baptising until the day when he was taken up from us, one must be appointed to serve with us as a witness to his resurrection.'

ᵃ **1** cf. Ws 4:19. Ps 69:5; 109:8 are also used.

seph called Barsabbas, who was also known as Justus, and Matthias. 24 Then they prayed and said, "Lord, you know everyone's heart. Show us which one of these two you have chosen 25 to take the place*g* in this ministry and apostleship from which Judas turned aside to go to his own place." 26 And they cast lots for them, and the lot fell on Matthias; and he was added to the eleven apostles.

2 When the day of Pentecost had come, they were all together in one place. 2 And suddenly from heaven there came a sound like the rush of a violent wind, and it filled the entire house where they were sitting. 3 Divided tongues, as of fire, appeared among them, and a tongue rested on each of them. 4 All of them were filled with the Holy Spirit and began to speak in other languages, as the Spirit gave them ability.

5 Now there were devout Jews from every nation under heaven living in Jerusalem. 6 And at this sound the crowd gathered and was bewildered, because each one heard them speaking in the native language of each. 7 Amazed and astonished, they asked, "Are not all these who are speaking Galileans? 8 And how is it that we hear, each of us, in our own native language? 9 Parthians, Medes, Elamites, and residents of Mesopotamia, Judea and Cappadocia, Pontus and Asia, 10 Phrygia and Pamphylia, Egypt and the parts of Libya belonging to Cyrene, and visitors from Rome, both Jews and proselytes, 11 Cretans and Arabs — in our own languages we hear them speaking about God's deeds of power." 12 All were amazed and perplexed, saying to one another, "What does this mean?" 13 But others sneered and said, "They are filled with new wine."

14 But Peter, standing with the eleven, raised his voice and addressed them, "Men of Judea and all who live in Jerusalem, let this be known to you, and listen to what I say. 15 Indeed, these are not drunk, as you suppose, for it is only nine o'clock in the morning. 16 No, this is what was spoken through the prophet Joel:

17 'In the last days it will be, God declares,
that I will pour out my Spirit upon all flesh,
    and your sons and your daughters shall
        prophesy,
and your young men shall see visions,
    and your old men shall dream dreams.
18 Even upon my slaves, both men and women,
    in those days I will pour out my Spirit;
        and they shall prophesy.
19 And I will show portents in the heaven above
    and signs on the earth below,
        blood, and fire, and smoky mist.
20 The sun shall be turned to darkness
    and the moon to blood,
        before the coming of the Lord's great and
            glorious day.
21 Then everyone who calls on the name of the Lord
    shall be saved.'

22 "You that are Israelites,*h* listen to what I have to say: Jesus of Nazareth,*i* a man attested to you by God with deeds of power, wonders, and signs that God did through him among you, as you yourselves know — 23 this man, handed over to you according to the definite plan and foreknowledge of God, you crucified and killed by the hands of those outside the law. 24 But God raised him up, having freed him from death,*j* because it was impossible for him to be held in its power. 25 For David says concerning him,

23 Two names were put forward: Joseph, who was known as Barsabbas and bore the added name of Justus, and Matthias. 24 Then they prayed and said, 'You know the hearts of everyone, Lord; declare which of these two you have chosen 25 to receive this office of ministry and apostleship which Judas abandoned to go where he belonged.' 26 They drew lots, and the lot fell to Matthias; so he was elected to be an apostle with the other eleven.

2 THE day of Pentecost had come, and they were all together in one place. 2 Suddenly there came from the sky what sounded like a strong, driving wind, a noise which filled the whole house where they were sitting. 3 And there appeared to them flames like tongues of fire distributed among them and coming to rest on each one. 4 They were all filled with the Holy Spirit and began to talk in other tongues, as the Spirit gave them power of utterance.

5 Now there were staying in Jerusalem devout Jews drawn from every nation under heaven. 6 At this sound a crowd of them gathered, and were bewildered because each one heard his own language spoken; 7 they were amazed and in astonishment exclaimed, 'Surely these people who are speaking are all Galileans! 8 How is it that each of us can hear them in his own native language? 9 Parthians, Medes, Elamites; inhabitants of Mesopotamia, of Judaea and Cappadocia, of Pontus and Asia, 10 of Phrygia and Pamphylia, of Egypt and the districts of Libya around Cyrene; visitors from Rome, both Jews and proselytes; 11 Cretans and Arabs — all of us hear them telling in our own tongues the great things God has done.' 12 They were all amazed and perplexed, saying to one another, 'What can this mean?' 13 Others said contemptuously, 'They have been drinking!'

14 But Peter stood up with the eleven, and in a loud voice addressed the crowd: 'Fellow-Jews, and all who live in Jerusalem, listen and take note of what I say. 15 These people are not drunk, as you suppose; it is only nine in the morning! 16 No, this is what the prophet Joel spoke of: 17 "In the last days, says God, I will pour out my Spirit on all mankind; and your sons and daughters shall prophesy; your young men shall see visions, and your old men shall dream dreams. 18 Yes, on my servants and my handmaids I will pour out my Spirit in those days, and they shall prophesy. 19 I will show portents in the sky above, and signs on the earth below — blood and fire and a pall of smoke. 20 The sun shall be turned to darkness, and the moon to blood, before that great, resplendent day, the day of the Lord, shall come. 21 Everyone who calls on the name of the Lord on that day shall be saved."

22 'Men of Israel, hear me: I am speaking of Jesus of Nazareth, singled out by God and made known to you through miracles, portents, and signs, which God worked among you through him, as you well know. 23 By the deliberate will and plan of God he was given into your power, and you killed him, using heathen men to crucify him. 24 But God raised him to life again, setting him free from the pangs of death, because it could not be that death should keep him in its grip.
25 'For David says of him:

g Other ancient authorities read *the share*   *h* Gk *Men, Israelites*
i Gk *the Nazorean*   *j* Gk *the pains of death*

seph called Barsabbas, who was also known as Justus, and Matthias. 24 Then they prayed, "You, Lord, who know the hearts of all, show which one of these two you have chosen 25 to take the place in this apostolic ministry from which Judas turned away to go to his own place." 26 Then they gave lots to them, and the lot fell upon Matthias, and he was counted with the eleven apostles.

2 When the time for Pentecost was fulfilled, they were all in one place together. 2 And suddenly there came from the sky a noise like a strong driving wind, and it filled the entire house in which they were. 3 Then there appeared to them tongues as of fire, which parted and came to rest on each one of them. 4 And they were all filled with the holy Spirit and began to speak in different tongues, as the Spirit enabled them to proclaim.

5 Now there were devout Jews from every nation under heaven staying in Jerusalem. 6 At this sound, they gathered in a large crowd, but they were confused because each one heard them speaking in his own language. 7 They were astounded, and in amazement they asked, "Are not all these people who are speaking Galileans? 8 Then how does each of us hear them in his own native language? 9 We are Parthians, Medes, and Elamites, inhabitants of Mesopotamia, Judea and Cappadocia, Pontus and Asia, 10 Phrygia and Pamphylia, Egypt and the districts of Libya near Cyrene, as well as travelers from Rome, 11 both Jews and converts to Judaism, Cretans and Arabs, yet we hear them speaking in our own tongues of the mighty acts of God." 12 They were all astounded and bewildered, and said to one another, "What does this mean?" 13 But others said, scoffing, "They have had too much new wine."

14 Then Peter stood up with the Eleven, raised his voice, and proclaimed to them, "You who are Jews, indeed all of you staying in Jerusalem. Let this be known to you, and listen to my words. 15 These people are not drunk, as you suppose, for it is only nine o'clock in the morning. 16 No, this is what was spoken through the prophet Joel:

17 'It will come to pass in the last days,' God says,
  'that I will pour out a portion of my spirit
    upon all flesh.
  Your sons and your daughters shall prophesy,
    your young men shall see visions,
    your old men shall dream dreams.
18 Indeed, upon my servants and my handmaids
    I will pour out a portion of my spirit in
      those days,
    and they shall prophesy.
19 And I will work wonders in the heavens above
    and signs on the earth below:
      blood, fire, and a cloud of smoke.
20 The sun shall be turned to darkness,
    and the moon to blood,
      before the coming of the great and splendid
        day of the Lord,
21 and it shall be that everyone shall be saved who
    calls on the name of the Lord.'

22 You who are Israelites, hear these words. Jesus the Nazorean was a man commended to you by God with mighty deeds, wonders, and signs, which God worked through him in your midst, as you yourselves know. 23 This man, delivered up by the set plan and foreknowledge of God, you killed, using lawless men to crucify him. 24 But God raised him up, releasing him from the throes of death, because it was impossible for him to be held by it. 25 For David says of him:

23 Having nominated two candidates, Joseph known as Barsabbas, whose surname was Justus, and Matthias, 24 they prayed, 'Lord, you can read everyone's heart; show us therefore which of these two you have chosen 25 to take over this ministry and apostolate, which Judas abandoned to go to his proper place.' 26 They then drew lots for them, and as the lot fell to Matthias, he was listed as one of the twelve apostles.

2 When Pentecost day came round, they had all met together, 2 when suddenly there came from heaven a sound as of a violent wind which filled the entire house in which they were sitting; 3 and there appeared to them tongues as of fire; these separated and came to rest on the head of each of them. 4 They were all filled with the Holy Spirit and began to speak different languages as the Spirit gave them power to express themselves.

5 Now there were devout men living in Jerusalem from every nation under heaven, 6 and at this sound they all assembled, and each one was bewildered to hear these men speaking his own language. 7 They were amazed and astonished. 'Surely,' they said, 'all these men speaking are Galileans? 8 How does it happen that each of us hears them in his own native language? 9 Parthians, Medes and Elamites; people from Mesopotamia, Judaea and Cappadocia, Pontus and Asia, 10 Phrygia and Pamphylia, Egypt and the parts of Libya round Cyrene; residents of Rome— 11 Jews and proselytes alike— Cretans and Arabs, we hear them preaching in our own language about the marvels of God.' 12 Everyone was amazed and perplexed; they asked one another what it all meant. 13 Some, however, laughed it off. 'They have been drinking too much new wine,' they said.

14 Then Peter stood up with the Eleven and addressed them in a loud voice:
'Men of Judaea, and all you who live in Jerusalem, make no mistake about this, but listen carefully to what I say. 15 These men are not drunk, as you imagine; why, it is only the third hour of the day. 16 On the contrary, this is what the prophet was saying:

17 In the last days—the Lord declares—
    I shall pour out my Spirit on all humanity.
    Your sons and daughters shall prophesy,
    your young people shall see visions,
    your old people dream dreams.
18 Even on the slaves, men and women,
    shall I pour out my Spirit.
19 I will show portents in the sky above
    and signs on the earth below:
20 The sun will be turned into darkness
    and the moon into blood
    before the day of the Lord comes,
    that great and terrible Day.
21 And all who call on the name of the Lord will be
    saved. b

22 'Men of Israel, listen to what I am going to say: Jesus the Nazarene was a man commended to you by God by the miracles and portents and signs that God worked through him when he was among you, as you know. 23 This man, who was put into your power by the deliberate intention and foreknowledge of God, you took and had crucified and killed by men outside the Law. 24 But God raised him to life, freeing him from the pangs of Hades; for it was impossible for him to be held in its power since, 25 as David says of him:

b 2 Jl 3:1–5.

NEW REVISED STANDARD VERSION

'I saw the Lord always before me,
　for he is at my right hand so that I will not be
　　shaken;
26 therefore my heart was glad, and my tongue
　　rejoiced;
　moreover my flesh will live in hope.
27 For you will not abandon my soul to Hades,
　or let your Holy One experience corruption.
28 You have made known to me the ways of life;
　you will make me full of gladness with your
　　presence.'

29 "Fellow Israelites,[k] I may say to you confidently of our ancestor David that he both died and was buried, and his tomb is with us to this day. 30 Since he was a prophet, he knew that God had sworn with an oath to him that he would put one of his descendants on his throne. 31 Foreseeing this, David[l] spoke of the resurrection of the Messiah,[m] saying,

'He was not abandoned to Hades,
　nor did his flesh experience corruption.'

32 This Jesus God raised up, and of that all of us are witnesses. 33 Being therefore exalted at[n] the right hand of God, and having received from the Father the promise of the Holy Spirit, he has poured out this that you both see and hear. 34 For David did not ascend into the heavens, but he himself says,

'The Lord said to my Lord,
　"Sit at my right hand,
35　until I make your enemies your footstool." '

36 Therefore let the entire house of Israel know with certainty that God has made him both Lord and Messiah,[o] this Jesus whom you crucified."

37 Now when they heard this, they were cut to the heart and said to Peter and to the other apostles, "Brothers,[k] what should we do?" 38 Peter said to them, "Repent, and be baptized every one of you in the name of Jesus Christ so that your sins may be forgiven; and you will receive the gift of the Holy Spirit. 39 For the promise is for you, for your children, and for all who are far away, everyone whom the Lord our God calls to him." 40 And he testified with many other arguments and exhorted them, saying, "Save yourselves from this corrupt generation." 41 So those who welcomed his message were baptized, and that day about three thousand persons were added. 42 They devoted themselves to the apostles' teaching and fellowship, to the breaking of bread and the prayers.

43 Awe came upon everyone, because many wonders and signs were being done by the apostles. 44 All who believed were together and had all things in common; 45 they would sell their possessions and goods and distribute the proceeds[p] to all, as any had need. 46 Day by day, as they spent much time together in the temple, they broke bread at home[q] and ate their food with glad and generous[r] hearts, 47 praising God and having the goodwill of all the people. And day by day the Lord added to their number those who were being saved.

3 One day Peter and John were going up to the temple at the hour of prayer, at three o'clock in the afternoon. 2 And a man lame from birth was being carried in. People would lay him daily at the gate of the temple called the Beautiful Gate so that he could ask for alms from those entering the temple. 3 When he saw Peter and John about to

REVISED ENGLISH BIBLE

I foresaw that the Lord would be with me for ever,
　with him at my right hand I cannot be shaken;
26 therefore my heart is glad
　and my tongue rejoices,
　moreover, my flesh shall dwell in hope,
27 for you will not abandon me to death,
　nor let your faithful servant suffer corruption.
28 You have shown me the paths of life;
　your presence will fill me with joy.

29 'My friends, nobody can deny that the patriarch David died and was buried; we have his tomb here to this very day. 30 It is therefore clear that he spoke as a prophet who knew that God had sworn to him that one of his own direct descendants should sit on his throne; 31 and when he said he was not abandoned to death, and his flesh never saw corruption, he spoke with foreknowledge of the resurrection of the Messiah. 32 Now Jesus has been raised by God, and of this we are all witnesses. 33 Exalted at God's right hand he received from the Father the promised Holy Spirit, and all that you now see and hear flows from him. 34 For it was not David who went up to heaven; his own words are: "The Lord said to my Lord, 'Sit at my right hand 35 until I make your enemies your footstool.' " 36 Let all Israel then accept as certain that God has made this same Jesus, whom you crucified, both Lord and Messiah.'

37 When they heard this they were cut to the heart, and said to Peter and the other apostles, 'Friends, what are we to do?' 38 'Repent', said Peter, 'and be baptized, every one of you, in the name of Jesus the Messiah; then your sins will be forgiven and you will receive the gift of the Holy Spirit. 39 The promise is to you and to your children and to all who are far away, to everyone whom the Lord our God may call.'

40 He pressed his case with many other arguments and pleaded with them: 'Save yourselves from this crooked age.' 41 Those who accepted what he said were baptized, and some three thousand were added to the number of believers that day. 42 They met constantly to hear the apostles teach and to share the common life, to break bread, and to pray.

43 A sense of awe was felt by everyone, and many portents and signs were brought about through the apostles. 44 All the believers agreed to hold everything in common: 45 they began to sell their property and possessions and distribute to everyone according to his need. 46 One and all they kept up their daily attendance at the temple, and, breaking bread in their homes, they shared their meals with unaffected joy, 47 as they praised God and enjoyed the favour of the whole people. And day by day the Lord added new converts to their number.

3 ONE day at three in the afternoon, the hour of prayer, Peter and John were on their way up to the temple. 2 Now a man who had been a cripple from birth used to be carried there and laid every day by the temple gate called Beautiful to beg from people as they went in. 3 When he saw

---

[k] Gk Men, brothers　[l] Gk he　[m] Or the Christ　[n] Or by
[o] Or Christ　[p] Gk them　[q] Or from house to house　[r] Or sincere　2:33 at: or by.

NEW AMERICAN BIBLE

'I saw the Lord ever before me,
   with him at my right hand I shall not
      be disturbed.
26 Therefore my heart has been glad and my tongue
      has exulted;
   my flesh, too, will dwell in hope,
27 because you will not abandon my soul to the
      nether world,
   nor will you suffer your holy one to
      see corruption.
28 You have made known to me the paths of life;
   you will fill me with joy in your presence.'

29 My brothers, one can confidently say to you about the patriarch David that he died and was buried, and his tomb is in our midst to this day. 30 But since he was a prophet and knew that God had sworn an oath to him that he would set one of his descendants upon his throne, 31 he foresaw and spoke of the resurrection of the Messiah, that neither was he abandoned to the netherworld nor did his flesh see corruption. 32 God raised this Jesus; of this we are all witnesses. 33 Exalted at the right hand of God, he received the promise of the holy Spirit from the Father and poured it forth, as you [both] see and hear. 34 For David did not go up into heaven, but he himself said:

'The Lord said to my Lord,
   "Sit at my right hand
35   until I make your enemies your footstool." '

36 Therefore let the whole house of Israel know for certain that God has made him both Lord and Messiah, this Jesus whom you crucified."

37 Now when they heard this, they were cut to the heart, and they asked Peter and the other apostles, "What are we to do, my brothers?" 38 Peter [said] to them, "Repent and be baptized, every one of you, in the name of Jesus Christ for the forgiveness of your sins; and you will receive the gift of the holy Spirit. 39 For the promise is made to you and to your children and to all those far off, whomever the Lord our God will call." 40 He testified with many other arguments, and was exhorting them, "Save yourselves from this corrupt generation." 41 Those who accepted his message were baptized, and about three thousand persons were added that day.

42 They devoted themselves to the teaching of the apostles and to the communal life, to the breaking of the bread and to the prayers. 43 Awe came upon everyone, and many wonders and signs were done through the apostles. 44 All who believed were together and had all things in common; 45 they would sell their property and possessions and divide them among all according to each one's need. 46 Every day they devoted themselves to meeting together in the temple area and to breaking bread in their homes. They ate their meals with exultation and sincerity of heart, 47 praising God and enjoying favor with all the people. And every day the Lord added to their number those who were being saved.

3 Now Peter and John were going up to the temple area for the three o'clock hour of prayer. 2 And a man crippled from birth was carried and placed at the gate of the temple called "the Beautiful Gate" every day to beg for alms from the people who entered the temple. 3 When he saw

NEW JERUSALEM BIBLE

I kept the Lord before my sight always,
   for with him at my right hand nothing can shake
      me.
26 So my heart rejoiced
   my tongue delighted;
   my body, too, will rest secure,
27 for you will not abandon me to Hades
   or allow your holy one to see corruption.
28 You have taught me the way of life,
   you will fill me with joy in your presence.c

29 'Brothers, no one can deny that the patriarch David himself is dead and buried: his tomb is still with us. 30 But since he was a prophet, and knew that God had sworn him an oath to make one of his descendants succeed him on the throne, 31 he spoke with foreknowledge about the resurrection of the Christ: he is the one who was not abandoned to Hades, and whose body did not see corruption. 32 God raised this man Jesus to life, and of that we are all witnesses. 33 Now raised to the heights by God's right hand, he has received from the Father the Holy Spirit, who was promised, and what you see and hear is the outpouring of that Spirit. 34 For David himself never went up to heaven, but yet he said:

The Lord declared to my Lord,
   take your seat at my right hand,
35 till I have made your enemies
   your footstool.d

36 'For this reason the whole House of Israel can be certain that the Lord and Christ whom God has made is this Jesus whom you crucified.'

37 Hearing this, they were cut to the heart and said to Peter and the other apostles, 'What are we to do, brothers?' 38 'You must repent,' Peter answered, 'and every one of you must be baptised in the name of Jesus Christ for the forgiveness of your sins, and you will receive the gift of the Holy Spirit. 39 The promise that was made is for you and your children, and for all those who are far away, for all those whom the Lord our God is calling to himself.'e 40 He spoke to them for a long time using many other arguments, and he urged them, 'Save yourselves from this perverse generation.' 41 They accepted what he said and were baptised. That very day about three thousand were added to their number.

42 These remained faithful to the teaching of the apostles, to the brotherhood, to the breaking of bread and to the prayers.

43 And everyone was filled with awe; the apostles worked many signs and miracles.

44 And all who shared the faith owned everything in common; 45 they sold their goods and possessions and distributed the proceeds among themselves according to what each one needed.

46 Each day, with one heart, they regularly went to the Temple but met in their houses for the breaking of bread; they shared their food gladly and generously; 47 they praised God and were looked up to by everyone. Day by day the Lord added to their community those destined to be saved.

3 Once, when Peter and John were going up to the Temple for the prayers at the ninth hour, 2 it happened that there was a man being carried along.f He was a cripple from birth; and they used to put him down every day near the Temple entrance called the Beautiful Gate so that he could beg from the people going in. 3 When this man saw

c 2 Ps 16:8–11 LXX.   d 2 Ps 110:1.   e 2 Ps 57:19.
f 3 cf. Ac 14:8–10; Lk 8:51.

NEW REVISED STANDARD VERSION	REVISED ENGLISH BIBLE

NEW REVISED STANDARD VERSION

go into the temple, he asked them for alms. 4 Peter looked intently at him, as did John, and said, "Look at us." 5 And he fixed his attention on them, expecting to receive something from them. 6 But Peter said, "I have no silver or gold, but what I have I give you; in the name of Jesus Christ of Nazareth,*s* stand up and walk." 7 And he took him by the right hand and raised him up; and immediately his feet and ankles were made strong. 8 Jumping up, he stood and began to walk, and he entered the temple with them, walking and leaping and praising God. 9 All the people saw him walking and praising God, 10 and they recognized him as the one who used to sit and ask for alms at the Beautiful Gate of the temple; and they were filled with wonder and amazement at what had happened to him.

11 While he clung to Peter and John, all the people ran together to them in the portico called Solomon's Portico, utterly astonished. 12 When Peter saw it, he addressed the people, "You Israelites,*t* why do you wonder at this, or why do you stare at us, as though by our own power or piety we had made him walk? 13 The God of Abraham, the God of Isaac, and the God of Jacob, the God of our ancestors has glorified his servant*u* Jesus, whom you handed over and rejected in the presence of Pilate, though he had decided to release him. 14 But you rejected the Holy and Righteous One and asked to have a murderer given to you, 15 and you killed the Author of life, whom God raised from the dead. To this we are witnesses. 16 And by faith in his name, his name itself has made this man strong, whom you see and know; and the faith that is through Jesus*v* has given him this perfect health in the presence of all of you.

17 "And now, friends,*w* I know that you acted in ignorance, as did also your rulers. 18 In this way God fulfilled what he had foretold through all the prophets, that his Messiah*x* would suffer. 19 Repent therefore, and turn to God so that your sins may be wiped out, 20 so that times of refreshing may come from the presence of the Lord, and that he may send the Messiah*y* appointed for you, that is, Jesus, 21 who must remain in heaven until the time of universal restoration that God announced long ago through his holy prophets. 22 Moses said, 'The Lord your God will raise up for you from your own people*w* a prophet like me. You must listen to whatever he tells you. 23 And it will be that everyone who does not listen to that prophet will be utterly rooted out of the people.' 24 And all the prophets, as many as have spoken, from Samuel and those after him, also predicted these days. 25 You are the descendants of the prophets and of the covenant that God gave to your ancestors, saying to Abraham, 'And in your descendants all the families of the earth shall be blessed.' 26 When God raised up his servant,*u* he sent him first to you, to bless you by turning each of you from your wicked ways."

4 While Peter and John*z* were speaking to the people, the priests, the captain of the temple, and the Sadducees came to them, 2 much annoyed because they were teaching the people and proclaiming that in Jesus there is the resurrection of the dead. 3 So they arrested them and put them in custody until the next day, for it was already evening. 4 But many of those who heard the word believed; and they numbered about five thousand.

5 The next day their rulers, elders, and scribes assembled in Jerusalem, 6 with Annas the high priest, Caiaphas, John,*a* and Alexander, and all who were of the high-priestly family. 7 When they had made the prisoners*b* stand

REVISED ENGLISH BIBLE

Peter and John on their way into the temple, he asked for alms. 4 They both fixed their eyes on him, and Peter said, 'Look at us.' 5 Expecting a gift from them, the man was all attention. 6 Peter said, 'I have no silver or gold; but what I have I give you: in the name of Jesus Christ of Nazareth, get up and walk.' 7 Then, grasping him by the right hand he helped him up; and at once his feet and ankles grew strong; 8 he sprang to his feet, and started to walk. He entered the temple with them, leaping and praising God as he went. 9 Everyone saw him walking and praising God, 10 and when they recognized him as the man who used to sit begging at Beautiful Gate they were filled with wonder and amazement at what had happened to him.

11 While he still clung to Peter and John all the people came running in astonishment towards them in Solomon's Portico, as it is called. 12 Peter saw them coming and met them with these words: 'Men of Israel, why be surprised at this? Why stare at us as if we had made this man walk by some power or godliness of our own? 13–14 The God of Abraham, Isaac, and Jacob, the God of our fathers, has given the highest honour to his servant Jesus, whom you handed over for trial and disowned in Pilate's court—disowned the holy and righteous one when Pilate had decided to release him. You asked for the reprieve of a murderer, 15 and killed the Prince of life. But God raised him from the dead; of that we are witnesses. 16 The name of Jesus, by awakening faith, has given strength to this man whom you see and know, and this faith has made him completely well as you can all see.

17 'Now, my friends, I know quite well that you acted in ignorance, as did your rulers; 18 but this is how God fulfilled what he had foretold through all the prophets: that his Messiah would suffer. 19 Repent, therefore, and turn to God, so that your sins may be wiped out. Then the Lord may grant you a time of recovery 20 and send the Messiah appointed for you, that is, Jesus. 21 He must be received into heaven until the time comes for the universal restoration of which God has spoken through his holy prophets from the beginning. 22 Moses said, "The Lord God will raise up for you a prophet like me from among yourselves. Listen to everything he says to you, 23 for anyone who refuses to listen to that prophet must be cut off from the people." 24 From Samuel onwards, every prophet who spoke predicted this present time.

25 'You are the heirs of the prophets, and of that covenant which God made with your fathers when he said to Abraham, "And in your offspring all the families on earth shall find blessing." 26 When God raised up his servant, he sent him to you first, to bring you blessing by turning every one of you from your wicked ways.'

4 They were still addressing the people when the chief priests, together with the controller of the temple and the Sadducees, broke in on them, 2 annoyed because they were proclaiming the resurrection from the dead by teaching the people about Jesus. 3 They were arrested and, as it was already evening, put in prison for the night. 4 But many of those who had heard the message became believers, bringing the number of men to about five thousand.

5 Next day the Jewish rulers, elders, and scribes met in Jerusalem. 6 There were present Annas the high priest, Caiaphas, John, Alexander, and all who were of the high-priestly family. 7 They brought the apostles before the court

---

s Gk *the Nazorean*   *t* Gk *Men, Israelites*   *u* Or *child*   *v* Gk *him*
w Gk *brothers*   *x* Or *his Christ*   *y* Or *the Christ*   *z* Gk *While they*   *a* Other ancient authorities read *Jonathan*   *b* Gk *them*

3:22 **a prophet like me:** *or* a prophet as he raised up me.   4:1 **the chief priests:** *some witnesses omit* chief.   4:6 **John:** *some witnesses read* Jonathan.

Peter and John about to go into the temple, he asked for alms. 4 But Peter looked intently at him, as did John, and said, "Look at us." 5 He paid attention to them, expecting to receive something from them. 6 Peter said, "I have neither silver nor gold, but what I do have I give you: in the name of Jesus Christ the Nazorean, [rise and] walk." 7 Then Peter took him by the right hand and raised him up, and immediately his feet and ankles grew strong. 8 He leaped up, stood, and walked around, and went into the temple with them, walking and jumping and praising God. 9 When all the people saw him walking and praising God, 10 they recognized him as the one who used to sit begging at the Beautiful Gate of the temple, and they were filled with amazement and astonishment at what had happened to him.

11 As he clung to Peter and John, all the people hurried in amazement toward them in the portico called "Solomon's Portico." 12 When Peter saw this, he addressed the people, "You Israelites, why are you amazed at this, and why do you look so intently at us as if we had made him walk by our own power or piety? 13 The God of Abraham, [the God] of Isaac, and [the God] of Jacob, the God of our ancestors, has glorified his servant Jesus whom you handed over and denied in Pilate's presence, when he had decided to release him. 14 You denied the Holy and Righteous One and asked that a murderer be released to you. 15 The author of life you put to death, but God raised him from the dead; of this we are witnesses. 16 And by faith in his name, this man, whom you see and know, his name has made strong, and the faith that comes through it has given him this perfect health, in the presence of all of you. 17 Now I know, brothers, that you acted out of ignorance, just as your leaders did; 18 but God has thus brought to fulfillment what he had announced beforehand through the mouth of all the prophets, that his Messiah would suffer. 19 Repent, therefore, and be converted, that your sins may be wiped away, 20 and that the Lord may grant you times of refreshment and send you the Messiah already appointed for you, Jesus, 21 whom heaven must receive until the times of universal restoration of which God spoke through the mouth of his holy prophets from of old. 22 For Moses said:

'A prophet like me will the Lord, your God, raise up for you
from among your own kinsmen;
to him you shall listen in all that he may say to you.
23 Everyone who does not listen to that prophet
will be cut off from the people.'

24 Moreover, all the prophets who spoke, from Samuel and those afterwards, also announced these days. 25 You are the children of the prophets and of the covenant that God made with your ancestors when he said to Abraham, 'In your offspring all the families of the earth shall be blessed.' 26 For you first, God raised up his servant and sent him to bless you by turning each of you from your evil ways."

4 While they were still speaking to the people, the priests, the captain of the temple guard, and the Sadducees confronted them, 2 disturbed that they were teaching the people and proclaiming in Jesus the resurrection of the dead. 3 They laid hands on them and put them in custody until the next day, since it was already evening. 4 But many of those who heard the word came to believe and [the] number of men grew to [about] five thousand.

5 On the next day, their leaders, elders, and scribes were assembled in Jerusalem, 6 with Annas the high priest, Caiaphas, John, Alexander, and all who were of the high-priestly class. 7 They brought them into their presence and

Peter and John on their way into the Temple he begged from them. 4 Peter, and John too, looked straight at him and said, 'Look at us.' 5 He turned to them expectantly, hoping to get something from them, 6 but Peter said, 'I have neither silver nor gold, but I will give you what I have: in the name of Jesus Christ the Nazarene, walk!' 7 Then he took him by the right hand and helped him to stand up. Instantly his feet and ankles became firm, 8 he jumped up, stood, and began to walk, and he went with them into the Temple, walking and jumping and praising God. 9 Everyone could see him walking and praising God, 10 and they recognised him as the man who used to sit begging at the Beautiful Gate of the Temple. They were all astonished and perplexed at what had happened to him.

11 Everyone came running towards them in great excitement, to the Portico of Solomon, as it is called, where the man was still clinging to Peter and John. 12 When Peter saw the people he addressed them, 'Men of Israel, why are you so surprised at this? Why are you staring at us as though we had made this man walk by our own power or holiness? 13 It is *the God of Abraham, Isaac and Jacob, the God of our ancestors, who has glorified his servant* Jesus whom you handed over and then disowned in the presence of Pilate after he had given his verdict to release him. 14 It was you who accused the Holy and Upright One, you who demanded that a murderer should be released to you 15 while you killed the prince of life. God, however, raised him from the dead, and to that fact we are witnesses; 16 and it is the name of Jesus which, through faith in him, has brought back the strength of this man whom you see here and who is well known to you. It is faith in him that has restored this man to health, as you can all see.

17 'Now I know, brothers, that neither you nor your leaders had any idea what you were really doing; 18 but this was the way God carried out what he had foretold, when he said through all his prophets that his Christ would suffer. 19 Now you must repent and turn to God, so that your sins may be wiped out, 20 and so that the Lord may send the time of comfort. Then he will send you the Christ he has predestined, that is Jesus, 21 whom heaven must keep till the universal restoration comes which God proclaimed, speaking through his holy prophets. 22 Moses, for example, said, *"From among your brothers the Lord God will raise up for you a prophet like me; you will listen to whatever he tells you. 23 Anyone who refuses to listen to that prophet shall be cut off from the people."* h 24 In fact, all the prophets that have ever spoken, from Samuel onwards, have predicted these days.

25 'You are the heirs of the prophets, the heirs of the covenant God made with your ancestors when he told Abraham, *"All the nations of the earth will be blessed in your descendants".* i 26 It was for you in the first place that God raised up his servant and sent him to bless you as every one of you turns from his wicked ways.'

4 While they were still talking to the people the priests came up to them, accompanied by the captain of the Temple and the Sadducees. 2 They were extremely annoyed at their teaching the people the resurrection from the dead by proclaiming the resurrection of Jesus. 3 They arrested them, and, as it was already late, they kept them in prison till the next day. 4 But many of those who had listened to their message became believers; the total number of men had now risen to something like five thousand.

5 It happened that the next day the rulers, elders and scribes held a meeting in Jerusalem 6 with Annas the high priest, Caiaphas, Jonathan, Alexander and all the members of the high-priestly families. 7 They made the prisoners

g 3 Ex 3:6 with Is 52:13.   h 3 Dt 18:15, 19.   i 3 Gn 22:18.

in their midst, they inquired, "By what power or by what name did you do this?" 8 Then Peter, filled with the Holy Spirit, said to them, "Rulers of the people and elders, 9 if we are questioned today because of a good deed done to someone who was sick and are asked how this man has been healed, 10 let it be known to all of you, and to all the people of Israel, that this man is standing before you in good health by the name of Jesus Christ of Nazareth, *c* whom you crucified, whom God raised from the dead. 11 This Jesus *d* is

'the stone that was rejected by you, the builders;
    it has become the cornerstone.' *e*

12 There is salvation in no one else, for there is no other name under heaven given among mortals by which we must be saved."

13 Now when they saw the boldness of Peter and John and realized that they were uneducated and ordinary men, they were amazed and recognized them as companions of Jesus. 14 When they saw the man who had been cured standing beside them, they had nothing to say in opposition. 15 So they ordered them to leave the council while they discussed the matter with one another. 16 They said, "What will we do with them? For it is obvious to all who live in Jerusalem that a notable sign has been done through them; we cannot deny it. 17 But to keep it from spreading further among the people, let us warn them to speak no more to anyone in this name." 18 So they called them and ordered them not to speak or teach at all in the name of Jesus. 19 But Peter and John answered them, "Whether it is right in God's sight to listen to you rather than to God, you must judge; 20 for we cannot keep from speaking about what we have seen and heard." 21 After threatening them again, they let them go, finding no way to punish them because of the people, for all of them praised God for what had happened. 22 For the man on whom this sign of healing had been performed was more than forty years old.

23 After they were released, they went to their friends *f* and reported what the chief priests and the elders had said to them. 24 When they heard it, they raised their voices together to God and said, "Sovereign Lord, who made the heaven and the earth, the sea, and everything in them, 25 it is you who said by the Holy Spirit through our ancestor David, your servant: *g*

'Why did the Gentiles rage,
    and the peoples imagine vain things?
26 The kings of the earth took their stand,
    and the rulers have gathered together
        against the Lord and against his Messiah.' *h*

27 For in this city, in fact, both Herod and Pontius Pilate, with the Gentiles and the peoples of Israel, gathered together against your holy servant *g* Jesus, whom you anointed, 28 to do whatever your hand and your plan had predestined to take place. 29 And now, Lord, look at their threats, and grant to your servants *i* to speak your word with all boldness, 30 while you stretch out your hand to heal, and signs and wonders are performed through the name of your holy servant *g* Jesus." 31 When they had prayed, the place in which they were gathered together was shaken; and they were all filled with the Holy Spirit and spoke the word of God with boldness.

32 Now the whole group of those who believed were of one heart and soul, and no one claimed private ownership of any possessions, but everything they owned was held in common. 33 With great power the apostles gave their testimony to the resurrection of the Lord Jesus, and great grace was upon them all. 34 There was not a needy person among

and began to interrogate them. 'By what power', they asked, 'or by what name have such men as you done this?' 8 Then Peter, filled with the Holy Spirit, answered, 'Rulers of the people and elders, 9 if it is about help given to a sick man that we are being questioned today, and the means by which he was cured, 10 this is our answer to all of you and to all the people of Israel: it was by the name of Jesus Christ of Nazareth, whom you crucified, and whom God raised from the dead; through him this man stands here before you fit and well. 11 This Jesus is the stone, rejected by you the builders, which has become the corner-stone. 12 There is no salvation through anyone else; in all the world no other name has been granted to mankind by which we can be saved.'

13 Observing that Peter and John were uneducated laymen, they were astonished at their boldness and took note that they had been companions of Jesus; 14 but with the man who had been cured standing in full view beside them, they had nothing to say in reply. 15 So they ordered them to leave the court, and then conferred among themselves. 16 'What are we to do with these men?' they said. 'It is common knowledge in Jerusalem that a notable miracle has come about through them; and we cannot deny it. 17 But to stop this from spreading farther among the people, we had better caution them never again to speak to anyone in this name.' 18 They then called them in and ordered them to refrain from all public speaking and teaching in the name of Jesus.

19 But Peter and John replied: 'Is it right in the eyes of God for us to obey you rather than him? Judge for yourselves. 20 We cannot possibly give up speaking about what we have seen and heard.'

21 With a repeated caution the court discharged them. They could not see how they were to punish them, because the people were all giving glory to God for what had happened. 22 The man upon whom this miracle of healing had been performed was over forty years old.

23 As soon as they were discharged the apostles went back to their friends and told them everything that the chief priests and elders had said. 24 When they heard it, they raised their voices with one accord and called upon God.

'Sovereign Lord, Maker of heaven and earth and sea and of everything in them, 25 you said by the Holy Spirit, through the mouth of David your servant,

Why did the Gentiles rage
    and the peoples hatch their futile plots?
26 The kings of the earth took their stand
    and the rulers made common cause
        against the Lord and against his Messiah.

27 'They did indeed make common cause in this very city against your holy servant Jesus whom you anointed as Messiah. Herod and Pontius Pilate conspired with the Gentiles and with the peoples of Israel 28 to do all the things which, under your hand and by your decree, were foreordained. 29 And now, O Lord, mark their threats, and enable those who serve you to speak your word with all boldness. 30 Stretch out your hand to heal and cause signs and portents to be done through the name of your holy servant Jesus.'

31 When they had ended their prayer, the building where they were assembled rocked, and all were filled with the Holy Spirit and spoke God's word with boldness.

32 THE whole company of believers was united in heart and soul. Not one of them claimed any of his possessions as his own; everything was held in common. 33 With great power the apostles bore witness to the resurrection of the Lord Jesus, and all were held in high esteem. 34 There was never

---

c Gk *the Nazorean*   *d* Gk *This*   *e* Or *keystone*   *f* Gk *their own*
g Or *child*   *h* Or *his Christ*   *i* Gk *slaves*

4:33 **all . . . esteem:** or grace was strongly at work in them all.

questioned them, "By what power or by what name have you done this?" 8 Then Peter, filled with the holy Spirit, answered them, "Leaders of the people and elders: 9 If we are being examined today about a good deed done to a cripple, namely, by what means he was saved, 10 then all of you and all the people of Israel should know that it was in the name of Jesus Christ the Nazorean whom you crucified, whom God raised from the dead; in his name this man stands before you healed. 11 He is 'the stone rejected by you, the builders, which has become the cornerstone.' 12 There is no salvation through anyone else, nor is there any other name under heaven given to the human race by which we are to be saved."

13 Observing the boldness of Peter and John and perceiving them to be uneducated, ordinary men, they were amazed, and they recognized them as the companions of Jesus. 14 Then when they saw the man who had been cured standing there with them, they could say nothing in reply. 15 So they ordered them to leave the Sanhedrin, and conferred with one another, saying, 16 "What are we to do with these men? Everyone living in Jerusalem knows that a remarkable sign was done through them, and we cannot deny it. 17 But so that it may not be spread any further among the people, let us give them a stern warning never again to speak to anyone in this name."

18 So they called them back and ordered them not to speak or teach at all in the name of Jesus. 19 Peter and John, however, said to them in reply, "Whether it is right in the sight of God for us to obey you rather than God, you be the judges. 20 It is impossible for us not to speak about what we have seen and heard." 21 After threatening them further, they released them, finding no way to punish them, on account of the people who were all praising God for what had happened. 22 For the man on whom this sign of healing had been done was over forty years old.

23 After their release they went back to their own people and reported what the chief priests and elders had told them. 24 And when they heard it, they raised their voices to God with one accord and said, "Sovereign Lord, maker of heaven and earth and the sea and all that is in them, 25 you said by the holy Spirit through the mouth of our father David, your servant:

'Why did the Gentiles rage
    and the peoples entertain folly?
26 The kings of the earth took their stand
    and the princes gathered together
        against the Lord and against his anointed.'

27 Indeed they gathered in this city against your holy servant Jesus whom you anointed, Herod and Pontius Pilate, together with the Gentiles and the peoples of Israel, 28 to do what your hand and [your] will had long ago planned to take place. 29 And now, Lord, take note of their threats, and enable your servants to speak your word with all boldness, 30 as you stretch forth [your] hand to heal, and signs and wonders are done through the name of your holy servant Jesus." 31 As they prayed, the place where they were gathered shook, and they were all filled with the holy Spirit and continued to speak the word of God with boldness.

32 The community of believers was of one heart and mind, and no one claimed that any of his possessions was his own, but they had everything in common. 33 With great power the apostles bore witness to the resurrection of the Lord Jesus, and great favor was accorded them all. 34 There

stand in the middle and began to interrogate them, 'By what power, and by whose name have you men done this?' 8 Then Peter, filled with the Holy Spirit, addressed them, 'Rulers of the people, and elders! 9 If you are questioning us today about an act of kindness to a cripple and asking us how he was healed, 10 you must know, all of you, and the whole people of Israel, that it is by the name of Jesus Christ the Nazarene, whom you crucified, and God raised from the dead, by this name and by no other that this man stands before you cured. 11 This is *the stone which* you, *the builders, rejected* but which *has become the cornerstone. j* Only in him is there salvation; 12 for of all the names in the world given to men, this is the only one by which we can be saved.'

13 They were astonished at the fearlessness shown by Peter and John, considering that they were uneducated laymen; and they recognised them as associates of Jesus; 14 but when they saw the man who had been cured standing by their side, they could find no answer. 15 So they ordered them to stand outside while the Sanhedrin had a private discussion. 16 'What are we going to do with these men?' they asked. 'It is obvious to everybody in Jerusalem that a notable miracle has been worked through them, and we cannot deny it. 17 But to stop the whole thing spreading any further among the people, let us threaten them against ever speaking to anyone in this name again.'

18 So they called them in and gave them a warning on no account to make statements or to teach in the name of Jesus. 19 But Peter and John retorted, 'You must judge whether in God's eyes it is right to listen to you and not to God. 20 We cannot stop proclaiming what we have seen and heard.' 21 The court repeated the threats and then released them; they could not think of any way to punish them, since all the people were giving glory to God for what had happened. 22 The man who had been miraculously cured was over forty years old.

23 As soon as they were released they went to the community and told them everything the chief priests and elders had said to them. 24 When they heard it they lifted up their voice to God with one heart. 'Master,' they prayed, 'it is you who made sky and earth and sea, and everything in them; 25 it is you who said through the Holy Spirit and speaking through our ancestor David, your servant:

Why this uproar among the nations,
    this impotent muttering of the peoples?
26 *Kings on earth take up position,*
    princes plot together
        against the Lord and his Anointed. k

27 'This is what has come true: in this very city Herod and Pontius Pilate *plotted together* with the gentile *nations* and the *peoples* of Israel, against your holy servant Jesus whom you *anointed*, 28 to bring about the very thing that you in your strength and your wisdom had predetermined should happen. 29 And now, Lord, take note of their threats and help your servants to proclaim your message with all fearlessness, 30 by stretching out your hand to heal and to work miracles and marvels through the name of your holy servant Jesus.' 31 As they prayed, the house where they were assembled rocked. From this time they were all filled with the Holy Spirit and began to proclaim the word of God fearlessly.

32 The whole group of believers was united, heart and soul; no one claimed private ownership of any possessions, as everything they owned was held in common.

33 The apostles continued to testify to the resurrection of the Lord Jesus with great power, and they were all accorded great respect.

j 4 Ps 118:22.   *k* 4 Ps 2:1–2.

them, for as many as owned lands or houses sold them and brought the proceeds of what was sold. 35 They laid it at the apostles' feet, and it was distributed to each as any had need. 36 There was a Levite, a native of Cyprus, Joseph, to whom the apostles gave the name Barnabas (which means "son of encouragement"). 37 He sold a field that belonged to him, then brought the money, and laid it at the apostles' feet.

5 But a man named Ananias, with the consent of his wife Sapphira, sold a piece of property; 2 with his wife's knowledge, he kept back some of the proceeds, and brought only a part and laid it at the apostles' feet. 3 "Ananias," Peter asked, "why has Satan filled your heart to lie to the Holy Spirit and to keep back part of the proceeds of the land? 4 While it remained unsold, did it not remain your own? And after it was sold, were not the proceeds at your disposal? How is it that you have contrived this deed in your heart? You did not lie to us *j* but to God!" 5 Now when Ananias heard these words, he fell down and died. And great fear seized all who heard of it. 6 The young men came and wrapped up his body, *k* then carried him out and buried him.

7 After an interval of about three hours his wife came in, not knowing what had happened. 8 Peter said to her, "Tell me whether you and your husband sold the land for such and such a price." And she said, "Yes, that was the price." 9 Then Peter said to her, "How is it that you have agreed together to put the Spirit of the Lord to the test? Look, the feet of those who have buried your husband are at the door, and they will carry you out." 10 Immediately she fell down at his feet and died. When the young men came in they found her dead, so they carried her out and buried her beside her husband. 11 And great fear seized the whole church and all who heard of these things.

12 Now many signs and wonders were done among the people through the apostles. And they were all together in Solomon's Portico. 13 None of the rest dared to join them, but the people held them in high esteem. 14 Yet more than ever believers were added to the Lord, great numbers of both men and women, 15 so that they even carried out the sick into the streets, and laid them on cots and mats, in order that Peter's shadow might fall on some of them as he came by. 16 A great number of people would also gather from the towns around Jerusalem, bringing the sick and those tormented by unclean spirits, and they were all cured.

17 Then the high priest took action; he and all who were with him (that is, the sect of the Sadducees), being filled with jealousy, 18 arrested the apostles and put them in the public prison. 19 But during the night an angel of the Lord opened the prison doors, brought them out, and said, 20 "Go, stand in the temple and tell the people the whole message about this life." 21 When they heard this, they entered the temple at daybreak and went on with their teaching.

When the high priest and those with him arrived, they called together the council and the whole body of the elders of Israel, and sent to the prison to have them brought. 22 But when the temple police went there, they did not find them in the prison; so they returned and reported, 23 "We found the prison securely locked and the guards standing at the doors, but when we opened them, we found no one inside." 24 Now when the captain of the temple and the chief priests heard these words, they were perplexed about them, wondering what might be going on. 25 Then someone arrived and announced, "Look, the men whom you put in prison are standing in the temple and teaching the people!" 26 Then the

a needy person among them, because those who had property in land or houses would sell it, bring the proceeds of the sale, 35 and lay them at the feet of the apostles, to be distributed to any who were in need. 36 For instance Joseph, surnamed by the apostles Barnabas (which means 'Son of Encouragement'), a Levite and by birth a Cypriot, 37 sold an estate which he owned; he brought the money and laid it at the apostles' feet.

5 But a man called Ananias sold a property, 2 and with the connivance of his wife Sapphira kept back some of the proceeds, and brought part only to lay at the apostles' feet. 3 Peter said, 'Ananias, how was it that Satan so possessed your mind that you lied to the Holy Spirit by keeping back part of the price of the land? 4 While it remained unsold, did it not remain yours? Even after it was turned into money, was it not still at your own disposal? What made you think of doing this? You have lied not to men but to God.' 5 When Ananias heard these words he dropped dead; and all who heard were awestruck. 6 The younger men rose and covered his body, then carried him out and buried him.

7 About three hours passed, and his wife came in, unaware of what had happened. 8 Peter asked her, 'Tell me, were you paid such and such a price for the land?' 'Yes,' she replied, 'that was the price.' 9 Peter said, 'Why did the two of you conspire to put the Spirit of the Lord to the test? Those who buried your husband are there at the door, and they will carry you away.' 10 At once she dropped dead at his feet. When the young men came in, they found her dead; and they carried her out and buried her beside her husband.

11 Great awe fell on the whole church and on all who heard of this. 12 Many signs and wonders were done among the people by the apostles. All the believers used to meet by common consent in Solomon's Portico; 13 no one from outside their number ventured to join them, yet people in general spoke highly of them. 14 An ever-increasing number of men and women who believed in the Lord were added to their ranks. 15 As a result the sick were carried out into the streets and laid there on beds and stretchers, so that at least Peter's shadow might fall on one or another as he passed by; 16 and the people from the towns round Jerusalem flocked in, bringing those who were ill or harassed by unclean spirits, and all were cured.

17 Then the high priest and his colleagues, the Sadducean party, were goaded by jealousy 18 to arrest the apostles and put them in official custody. 19 But during the night, an angel of the Lord opened the prison doors, led them out, and said, 20 'Go, stand in the temple and tell the people all about this new life.' 21 Accordingly they entered the temple at daybreak and went on with their teaching.

When the high priest arrived with his colleagues they summoned the Sanhedrin, the full Council of the Israelite nation, and sent to the jail for the prisoners. 22 The officers who went to the prison failed to find them there, so they returned and reported, 23 'We found the jail securely locked at every point, with the warders at their posts by the doors, but on opening them we found no one inside.' 24 When they heard this, the controller of the temple and the chief priests were at a loss to know what could have become of them, 25 until someone came and reported: 'The men you put in prison are standing in the temple teaching the people.'

was no needy person among them, for those who owned property or houses would sell them, bring the proceeds of the sale, 35 and put them at the feet of the apostles, and they were distributed to each according to need.

36 Thus Joseph, also named by the apostles Barnabas (which is translated "son of encouragement"), a Levite, a Cypriot by birth, 37 sold a piece of property that he owned, then brought the money and put it at the feet of the apostles.

5 A man named Ananias, however, with his wife Sapphira, sold a piece of property. 2 He retained for himself, with his wife's knowledge, some of the purchase price, took the remainder, and put it at the feet of the apostles. 3 But Peter said, "Ananias, why has Satan filled your heart so that you lied to the holy Spirit and retained part of the price of the land? 4 While it remained unsold, did it not remain yours? And when it was sold, was it not still under your control? Why did you contrive this deed? You have lied not to human beings, but to God." 5 When Ananias heard these words, he fell down and breathed his last, and great fear came upon all who heard of it. 6 The young men came and wrapped him up, then carried him out and buried him.

7 After an interval of about three hours, his wife came in, unaware of what had happened. 8 Peter said to her, "Tell me, did you sell the land for this amount?" She answered, "Yes, for that amount." 9 Then Peter said to her, "Why did you agree to test the Spirit of the Lord? Listen, the footsteps of those who have buried your husband are at the door, and they will carry you out." 10 At once, she fell down at his feet and breathed her last. When the young men entered they found her dead, so they carried her out and buried her beside her husband. 11 And great fear came upon the whole church and upon all who heard of these things.

12 Many signs and wonders were done among the people at the hands of the apostles. They were all together in Solomon's portico. 13 None of the others dared to join them, but the people esteemed them. 14 Yet more than ever, believers in the Lord, great numbers of men and women, were added to them. 15 Thus they even carried the sick out into the streets and laid them on cots and mats so that when Peter came by, at least his shadow might fall on one or another of them. 16 A large number of people from the towns in the vicinity of Jerusalem also gathered, bringing the sick and those disturbed by unclean spirits, and they were all cured.

17 Then the high priest rose up and all his companions, that is, the party of the Sadducees, and, filled with jealousy, 18 laid hands upon the apostles and put them in the public jail. 19 But during the night, the angel of the Lord opened the doors of the prison, led them out, and said, 20 "Go and take your place in the temple area, and tell the people everything about this life." 21 When they heard this, they went to the temple early in the morning and taught. When the high priest and his companions arrived, they convened the Sanhedrin, the full senate of the Israelites, and sent to the jail to have them brought in. 22 But the court officers who went did not find them in the prison, so they came back and reported, 23 "We found the jail securely locked and the guards stationed outside the doors, but when we opened them, we found no one inside." 24 When they heard this report, the captain of the temple guard and the chief priests were at a loss about them, as to what this would come to. 25 Then someone came in and reported to them, "The men whom you put in prison are in the temple area and are teaching the people." 26 Then the captain and the court offi-

34 None of their members was ever in want, as all those who owned land or houses would sell them, and bring the money from the sale of them, 35 to present it to the apostles; it was then distributed to any who might be in need.

36 There was a Levite of Cypriot origin called Joseph whom the apostles surnamed Barnabas (which means 'son of encouragement'). 37 He owned a piece of land and he sold it and brought the money and presented it to the apostles.

5 There was also a man called Ananias. He and his wife, Sapphira, agreed to sell a property; 2 but with his wife's connivance he kept back part of the price and brought the rest and presented it to the apostles. 3 Peter said, 'Ananias, how can Satan have so possessed you that you should lie to the Holy Spirit and keep back part of the price of the land? 4 While you still owned the land, wasn't it yours to keep, and after you had sold it wasn't the money yours to do with as you liked? What put this scheme into your mind? You have been lying not to men, but to God.' 5 When he heard this Ananias fell down dead. And a great fear came upon everyone present. 6 The younger men got up, wrapped up the body, carried it out and buried it.

7 About three hours later his wife came in, not knowing what had taken place. 8 Peter challenged her, 'Tell me, was this the price you sold the land for?' 'Yes,' she said, 'that was the price.' 9 Peter then said, 'Why did you and your husband agree to put the Spirit of the Lord to the test? Listen! At the door are the footsteps of those who have buried your husband; they will carry you out, too.' 10 Instantly she dropped dead at his feet. When the young men came in they found she was dead, and they carried her out and buried her by the side of her husband. 11 And a great fear came upon the whole church and on all who heard of it.

12 The apostles worked many signs and miracles among the people. One in heart, they all used to meet in the Portico of Solomon. 13 No one else dared to join them, but the people were loud in their praise 14 and the numbers of men and women who came to believe in the Lord increased steadily. Many signs and wonders were worked among the people at the hands of the apostles 15 so that the sick were even taken out into the streets and laid on beds and sleeping-mats in the hope that at least the shadow of Peter might fall across some of them as he went past. 16 People even came crowding in from the towns round about Jerusalem, bringing with them their sick and those tormented by unclean spirits, and all of them were cured.

17 ¹ Then the high priest intervened with all his supporters from the party of the Sadducees. Filled with jealousy, 18 they arrested the apostles and had them put in the public gaol.

19 But at night the angel of the Lord opened the prison gates and said as he led them out, 20 'Go and take up position in the Temple, and tell the people all about this new Life.' 21 They did as they were told; they went into the Temple at dawn and began to preach.

When the high priest arrived, he and his supporters convened the Sanhedrin — this was the full Senate of Israel — and sent to the gaol for them to be brought. 22 But when the officials arrived at the prison they found they were not inside, so they went back and reported, 23 'We found the gaol securely locked and the warders on duty at the gates, but when we unlocked the door we found no one inside.' 24 When the captain of the Temple and the chief priests heard this news they wondered what could be happening. 25 Then a man arrived with fresh news. 'Look!' he said, 'the men you imprisoned are in the Temple. They are standing there preaching to the people.' 26 The captain went with his

¹5 cf. 12:6–11; 16:26–27.

captain went with the temple police and brought them, but without violence, for they were afraid of being stoned by the people.

27 When they had brought them, they had them stand before the council. The high priest questioned them, 28 saying, "We gave you strict orders not to teach in this name,*l* yet here you have filled Jerusalem with your teaching and you are determined to bring this man's blood on us." 29 But Peter and the apostles answered, "We must obey God rather than any human authority.*m* 30 The God of our ancestors raised up Jesus, whom you had killed by hanging him on a tree. 31 God exalted him at his right hand as Leader and Savior that he might give repentance to Israel and forgiveness of sins. 32 And we are witnesses to these things, and so is the Holy Spirit whom God has given to those who obey him."

33 When they heard this, they were enraged and wanted to kill them. 34 But a Pharisee in the council named Gamaliel, a teacher of the law, respected by all the people, stood up and ordered the men to be put outside for a short time. 35 Then he said to them, "Fellow Israelites,*n* consider carefully what you propose to do to these men. 36 For some time ago Theudas rose up, claiming to be somebody, and a number of men, about four hundred, joined him; but he was killed, and all who followed him were dispersed and disappeared. 37 After him Judas the Galilean rose up at the time of the census and got people to follow him; he also perished, and all who followed him were scattered. 38 So in the present case, I tell you, keep away from these men and let them alone; because if this plan or this undertaking is of human origin, it will fail; 39 but if it is of God, you will not be able to overthrow them — in that case you may even be found fighting against God!"

They were convinced by him, 40 and when they had called in the apostles, they had them flogged. Then they ordered them not to speak in the name of Jesus, and let them go. 41 As they left the council, they rejoiced that they were considered worthy to suffer dishonor for the sake of the name. 42 And every day in the temple and at home*o* they did not cease to teach and proclaim Jesus as the Messiah.*p*

6 Now during those days, when the disciples were increasing in number, the Hellenists complained against the Hebrews because their widows were being neglected in the daily distribution of food. 2 And the twelve called together the whole community of the disciples and said, "It is not right that we should neglect the word of God in order to wait on tables.*q* 3 Therefore, friends,*r* select from among yourselves seven men of good standing, full of the Spirit and of wisdom, whom we may appoint to this task, 4 while we, for our part, will devote ourselves to prayer and to serving the word." 5 What they said pleased the whole community, and they chose Stephen, a man full of faith and the Holy Spirit, together with Philip, Prochorus, Nicanor, Timon, Parmenas, and Nicolaus, a proselyte of Antioch. 6 They had these men stand before the apostles, who prayed and laid their hands on them.

7 The word of God continued to spread; the number of the disciples increased greatly in Jerusalem, and a great many of the priests became obedient to the faith.

8 Stephen, full of grace and power, did great wonders and signs among the people. 9 Then some of those who

26 Then the controller went off with the officers and fetched them, but without use of force, for fear of being stoned by the people.

27 When they had been brought in and made to stand before the Council, the high priest began his examination. 28 'We gave you explicit orders', he said, 'to stop teaching in that name; and what has happened? You have filled Jerusalem with your teaching, and you are trying to hold us responsible for that man's death.' 29 Peter replied for the apostles: 'We must obey God rather than men. 30 The God of our fathers raised up Jesus; after you had put him to death by hanging him on a gibbet, 31 God exalted him at his right hand as leader and saviour, to grant Israel repentance and forgiveness of sins. 32 And we are witnesses to all this, as is the Holy Spirit who is given by God to those obedient to him.'

33 This touched them on the raw, and they wanted to put them to death. 34 But a member of the Council rose to his feet, a Pharisee called Gamaliel, a teacher of the law held in high regard by all the people. He had the men put outside for a while, 35 and then said, 'Men of Israel, be very careful in deciding what to do with these men. 36 Some time ago Theudas came forward, making claims for himself, and a number of our people, about four hundred, joined him. But he was killed and his whole movement was destroyed and came to nothing. 37 After him came Judas the Galilean at the time of the census; he induced some people to revolt under his leadership, but he too perished and his whole movement was broken up. 38 Now, my advice to you is this: keep clear of these men; let them alone. For if what is being planned and done is human in origin, it will collapse; 39 but if it is from God, you will never be able to stamp it out, and you risk finding yourselves at war with God.'

40 Convinced by this, they sent for the apostles and had them flogged; then they ordered them to give up speaking in the name of Jesus, and discharged them. 41 The apostles went out from the Council rejoicing that they had been found worthy to suffer humiliation for the sake of the name. 42 And every day they went steadily on with their teaching in the temple and in private houses, telling the good news of Jesus the Messiah.

6 DURING this period, when disciples were growing in number, a grievance arose on the part of those who spoke Greek, against those who spoke the language of the Jews; they complained that their widows were being overlooked in the daily distribution. 2 The Twelve called the whole company of disciples together and said, 'It would not be fitting for us to neglect the word of God in order to assist in the distribution. 3 Therefore, friends, pick seven men of good repute from your number, men full of the Spirit and of wisdom, and we will appoint them for this duty; 4 then we can devote ourselves to prayer and to the ministry of the word.' 5 This proposal proved acceptable to the whole company. They elected Stephen, a man full of faith and of the Holy Spirit, along with Philip, Prochorus, Nicanor, Timon, Parmenas, and Nicolas of Antioch, who had been a convert to Judaism, 6 and presented them to the apostles, who prayed and laid their hands on them.

7 The word of God spread more and more widely; the number of disciples in Jerusalem was increasing rapidly, and very many of the priests adhered to the faith.

8 Stephen, full of grace and power, began to do great wonders and signs among the people. 9 Some members of

---

l Other ancient authorities read *Did we not give you strict orders not to teach in this name?*   *m* Gk *than men*   *n* Gk *Men, Israelites*
o Or *from house to house*   *p* Or *the Christ*   *q* Or *keep accounts*
r Gk *brothers*

5:31 **at his right hand:** *or* with his right hand.   6:1 **those who spoke Greek:** *lit.* the Hellenists. **those who spoke the language of the Jews:** *lit.* the Hebrews.

cers went and brought them in, but without force, because they were afraid of being stoned by the people.

27 When they had brought them in and made them stand before the Sanhedrin, the high priest questioned them, 28 "We gave you strict orders [did we not?] to stop teaching in that name. Yet you have filled Jerusalem with your teaching and want to bring this man's blood upon us." 29 But Peter and the apostles said in reply, "We must obey God rather than men. 30 The God of our ancestors raised Jesus, though you had him killed by hanging him on a tree. 31 God exalted him at his right hand as leader and savior to grant Israel repentance and forgiveness of sins. 32 We are witnesses of these things, as is the holy Spirit that God has given to those who obey him."

33 When they heard this, they became infuriated and wanted to put them to death. 34 But a Pharisee in the Sanhedrin named Gamaliel, a teacher of the law, respected by all the people, stood up, ordered the men to be put outside for a short time, 35 and said to them, "Fellow Israelites, be careful what you are about to do to these men. 36 Some time ago, Theudas appeared, claiming to be someone important, and about four hundred men joined him, but he was killed, and all those who were loyal to him were disbanded and came to nothing. 37 After him came Judas the Galilean at the time of the census. He also drew people after him, but he too perished and all who were loyal to him were scattered. 38 So now I tell you, have nothing to do with these men, and let them go. For if this endeavor or this activity is of human origin, it will destroy itself. 39 But if it comes from God, you will not be able to destroy them; you may even find yourselves fighting against God." They were persuaded by him. 40 After recalling the apostles, they had them flogged, ordered them to stop speaking in the name of Jesus, and dismissed them. 41 So they left the presence of the Sanhedrin, rejoicing that they had been found worthy to suffer dishonor for the sake of the name. 42 And all day long, both at the temple and in their homes, they did not stop teaching and proclaiming the Messiah, Jesus.

6 At that time, as the number of disciples continued to grow, the Hellenists complained against the Hebrews because their widows were being neglected in the daily distribution. 2 So the Twelve called together the community of the disciples and said, "It is not right for us to neglect the word of God to serve at table. 3 Brothers, select from among you seven reputable men, filled with the Spirit and wisdom, whom we shall appoint to this task, 4 whereas we shall devote ourselves to prayer and to the ministry of the word." 5 The proposal was acceptable to the whole community, so they chose Stephen, a man filled with faith and the holy Spirit, also Philip, Prochorus, Nicanor, Timon, Parmenas, and Nicholas of Antioch, a convert to Judaism. 6 They presented these men to the apostles who prayed and laid hands on them. 7 The word of God continued to spread, and the number of the disciples in Jerusalem increased greatly; even a large group of priests were becoming obedient to the faith.

8 Now Stephen, filled with grace and power, was working great wonders and signs among the people. 9 Certain mem-

men and fetched them — though not by force, for they were afraid that the people might stone them.

27 When they had brought them in to face the Sanhedrin, the high priest demanded an explanation. 28 'We gave you a strong warning', he said, 'not to preach in this name, and what have you done? You have filled Jerusalem with your teaching, and seem determined to fix the guilt for this man's death on us.' 29 In reply Peter and the apostles said, 'Obedience to God comes before obedience to men; 30 it was the God of our ancestors who raised up Jesus, whom you executed by hanging on a tree. 31 By his own right hand God has now raised him up to be leader and Saviour, to give repentance and forgiveness of sins through him to Israel. 32 We are witnesses to this, we and the Holy Spirit whom God has given to those who obey him.' 33 This so infuriated them that they wanted to put them to death.

34 One member of the Sanhedrin, however, a Pharisee called Gamaliel, who was a teacher of the Law respected by the whole people, stood up and asked to have the men taken outside for a time. 35 Then he addressed the Sanhedrin, 'Men of Israel, be careful how you deal with these people. 36 Some time ago there arose Theudas. He claimed to be someone important, and collected about four hundred followers; but when he was killed, all his followers scattered and that was the end of them. 37 And then there was Judas the Galilean, at the time of the census, who attracted crowds of supporters; but he was killed too, and all his followers dispersed. 38 What I suggest, therefore, is that you leave these men alone and let them go. If this enterprise, this movement of theirs, is of human origin it will break up of its own accord; 39 but if it does in fact come from God you will be unable to destroy them. Take care not to find yourselves fighting against God.'

His advice was accepted; 40 and they had the apostles called in, gave orders for them to be flogged, warned them not to speak in the name of Jesus and released them. 41 And so they left the presence of the Sanhedrin, glad to have had the honour of suffering humiliation for the sake of the name.

42 Every day they went on ceaselessly teaching and proclaiming the good news of Christ Jesus, both in the temple and in private houses.

6 About this time, when the number of disciples was increasing, the Hellenists*m* made a complaint against the Hebrews: in the daily distribution their own widows were being overlooked. 2 So the Twelve called a full meeting of the disciples and addressed them, 'It would not be right for us to neglect the word of God so as to give out food; 3 you, brothers, must select from among yourselves seven men of good reputation, filled with the Spirit and with wisdom, to whom we can hand over this duty. 4 We ourselves will continue to devote ourselves to prayer and to the service of the word.' 5 The whole assembly approved of this proposal and elected Stephen, a man full of faith and of the Holy Spirit, together with Philip, Prochorus, Nicanor, Timon, Parmenas, and Nicolaus of Antioch, a convert to Judaism. 6 They presented these to the apostles, and after prayer they laid their hands on them.

7 The word of the Lord continued to spread: the number of disciples in Jerusalem was greatly increased, and a large group of priests made their submission to the faith.

8 Stephen was filled with grace and power and began to work miracles and great signs among the people. 9 Then

m 6 Jews from outside Palestine, or Gk-speakers.

belonged to the synagogue of the Freedmen (as it was called), Cyrenians, Alexandrians, and others of those from Cilicia and Asia, stood up and argued with Stephen. 10 But they could not withstand the wisdom and the Spirit[s] with which he spoke. 11 Then they secretly instigated some men to say, "We have heard him speak blasphemous words against Moses and God." 12 They stirred up the people as well as the elders and the scribes; then they suddenly confronted him, seized him, and brought him before the council. 13 They set up false witnesses who said, "This man never stops saying things against this holy place and the law; 14 for we have heard him say that this Jesus of Nazareth[t] will destroy this place and will change the customs that Moses handed on to us." 15 And all who sat in the council looked intently at him, and they saw that his face was like the face of an angel.

7 Then the high priest asked him, "Are these things so?" 2 And Stephen replied:

"Brothers[u] and fathers, listen to me. The God of glory appeared to our ancestor Abraham when he was in Mesopotamia, before he lived in Haran, 3 and said to him, 'Leave your country and your relatives and go to the land that I will show you.' 4 Then he left the country of the Chaldeans and settled in Haran. After his father died, God had him move from there to this country in which you are now living. 5 He did not give him any of it as a heritage, not even a foot's length, but promised to give it to him as his possession and to his descendants after him, even though he had no child. 6 And God spoke in these terms, that his descendants would be resident aliens in a country belonging to others, who would enslave them and mistreat them during four hundred years. 7 'But I will judge the nation that they serve,' said God, 'and after that they shall come out and worship me in this place.' 8 Then he gave him the covenant of circumcision. And so Abraham[v] became the father of Isaac and circumcised him on the eighth day; and Isaac became the father of Jacob, and Jacob of the twelve patriarchs.

9 "The patriarchs, jealous of Joseph, sold him into Egypt; but God was with him, 10 and rescued him from all his afflictions, and enabled him to win favor and to show wisdom when he stood before Pharaoh, king of Egypt, who appointed him ruler over Egypt and over all his household. 11 Now there came a famine throughout Egypt and Canaan, and great suffering, and our ancestors could find no food. 12 But when Jacob heard that there was grain in Egypt, he sent our ancestors there on their first visit. 13 On the second visit Joseph made himself known to his brothers, and Joseph's family became known to Pharaoh. 14 Then Joseph sent and invited his father Jacob and all his relatives to come to him, seventy-five in all; 15 so Jacob went down to Egypt. He himself died there as well as our ancestors, 16 and their bodies[w] were brought back to Shechem and laid in the tomb that Abraham had bought for a sum of silver from the sons of Hamor in Shechem.

17 "But as the time drew near for the fulfillment of the promise that God had made to Abraham, our people in Egypt increased and multiplied 18 until another king who had not known Joseph ruled over Egypt. 19 He dealt craftily with our race and forced our ancestors to abandon their infants so that they would die. 20 At this time Moses was born, and he was beautiful before God. For three months he was brought up in his father's house; 21 and when he was abandoned, Pharaoh's daughter adopted him and brought him up as her own son. 22 So Moses was instructed in all the wisdom of the Egyptians and was powerful in his words and deeds.

the synagogue called the Synagogue of Freedmen, comprising Cyrenians and Alexandrians and people from Cilicia and Asia, came forward and argued with Stephen, 10 but could not hold their own against the inspired wisdom with which he spoke. 11 They then put up men to allege that they had heard him make blasphemous statements against Moses and against God. 12 They stirred up the people and the elders and scribes, set upon him and seized him, and brought him before the Council. 13 They produced false witnesses who said, 'This fellow is for ever saying things against this holy place and against the law. 14 For we have heard him say this Jesus of Nazareth will destroy this place and alter the customs handed down to us by Moses.' 15 All who were sitting in the Council fixed their eyes on him, and his face seemed to them like the face of an angel.

7 Then the high priest asked him, 'Is this true?' 2 He replied, 'My brothers, fathers of this nation, listen to me. The God of glory appeared to Abraham our ancestor while he was in Mesopotamia, before he had settled in Harran, 3 and said: "Leave your country and your kinsfolk, and come away to a land that I will show you." 4 Thereupon he left the land of the Chaldaeans and settled in Harran. From there, after his father's death, God led him to migrate to this land where you now live. 5 He gave him no foothold in it, nothing to call his own, but promised to give it as a possession for ever to him and to his descendants after him, though he was then childless. 6 This is what God said: "Abraham's descendants shall live as aliens in a foreign land, held in slavery and oppression for four hundred years. 7 And I will pass judgement", he said, "on the nation whose slaves they are; and after that they shall escape and worship me in this place." 8 God gave Abraham the covenant of circumcision, and so, when his son Isaac was born, he circumcised him on the eighth day; and Isaac was the father of Jacob, and Jacob of the twelve patriarchs.

9 'The patriarchs out of jealousy sold Joseph into slavery in Egypt, but God was with him 10 and rescued him from all his troubles. He gave him wisdom which so commended him to Pharaoh king of Egypt that he appointed him governor of Egypt and of the whole royal household.

11 'When famine struck all Egypt and Canaan, causing great distress, and our ancestors could find nothing to eat, 12 Jacob heard that there was food in Egypt and sent our fathers there. This was their first visit. 13 On the second visit Joseph made himself known to his brothers, and his ancestry was disclosed to Pharaoh. 14 Joseph sent for his father Jacob and the whole family, seventy-five persons in all; 15 and Jacob went down into Egypt. There he and our fathers ended their days. 16 Their remains were later removed to Shechem and buried in the tomb for which Abraham paid a sum of money to the sons of Hamor at Shechem.

17 'Now as the time approached for God to fulfil the promise he had made to Abraham, our people in Egypt grew and increased in numbers. 18 At length another king, who knew nothing of Joseph, ascended the throne of Egypt. 19 He employed cunning to harm our race, and forced our ancestors to expose their children so that they should not survive. 20 It was at this time that Moses was born. He was a fine child, and pleasing to God. For three months he was nursed in his father's house; 21 then when he was exposed, Pharaoh's daughter adopted him and brought him up as her own son. 22 So Moses was trained in all the wisdom of the Egyptians, a powerful speaker and a man of action.

---

[s] Or spirit   [t] Gk the Nazorean   [u] Gk Men, brothers   [v] Gk he
[w] Gk they

NEW AMERICAN BIBLE

bers of the so-called Synagogue of Freedmen, Cyrenians, and Alexandrians, and people from Cilicia and Asia, came forward and debated with Stephen, 10 but they could not withstand the wisdom and the spirit with which he spoke. 11 Then they instigated some men to say, "We have heard him speaking blasphemous words against Moses and God." 12 They stirred up the people, the elders, and the scribes, accosted him, seized him, and brought him before the Sanhedrin. 13 They presented false witnesses who testified, "This man never stops saying things against [this] holy place and the law. 14 For we have heard him claim that this Jesus the Nazorean will destroy this place and change the customs that Moses handed down to us." 15 All those who sat in the Sanhedrin looked intently at him and saw that his face was like the face of an angel.

7 Then the high priest asked, "Is this so?" 2 And he replied, "My brothers and fathers, listen. The God of glory appeared to our father Abraham while he was in Mesopotamia, before he had settled in Haran, 3 and said to him, 'Go forth from your land and [from] your kinsfolk to the land that I will show you.' 4 So he went forth from the land of the Chaldeans and settled in Haran. And from there, after his father died, he made him migrate to this land where you now dwell. 5 Yet he gave him no inheritance in it, not even a foot's length, but he did promise to give it to him and his descendants as a possession, even though he was childless. 6 And God spoke thus, 'His descendants shall be aliens in a land not their own, where they shall be enslaved and oppressed for four hundred years; 7 but I will bring judgment on the nation they serve,' God said, 'and after that they will come out and worship me in this place.' 8 Then he gave him the covenant of circumcision, and so he became the father of Isaac, and circumcised him on the eighth day, as Isaac did Jacob, and Jacob the twelve patriarchs.

9 "And the patriarchs, jealous of Joseph, sold him into slavery in Egypt; but God was with him 10 and rescued him from all his afflictions. He granted him favor and wisdom before Pharaoh, the king of Egypt, who put him in charge of Egypt and [of] his entire household. 11 Then a famine and great affliction struck all Egypt and Canaan, and our ancestors could find no food; 12 but when Jacob heard that there was grain in Egypt, he sent our ancestors there a first time. 13 The second time, Joseph made himself known to his brothers, and Joseph's family became known to Pharaoh. 14 Then Joseph sent for his father Jacob, inviting him and his whole clan, seventy-five persons; 15 and Jacob went down to Egypt. And he and our ancestors died 16 and were brought back to Shechem and placed in the tomb that Abraham had purchased for a sum of money from the sons of Hamor at Shechem.

17 "When the time drew near for the fulfillment of the promise that God pledged to Abraham, the people had increased and become very numerous in Egypt, 18 until another king who knew nothing of Joseph came to power [in Egypt]. 19 He dealt shrewdly with our people and oppressed [our] ancestors by forcing them to expose their infants, that they might not survive. 20 At this time Moses was born, and he was extremely beautiful. For three months he was nursed in his father's house; 21 but when he was exposed, Pharaoh's daughter adopted him and brought him up as her own son. 22 Moses was educated [in] all the wisdom of the Egyptians and was powerful in his words and deeds.

certain people came forward to debate with Stephen, some from Cyrene and Alexandria who were members of the synagogue called the Synagogue of Freedmen, and others from Cilicia and Asia. 10 They found they could not stand up against him because of his wisdom, and the Spirit that prompted what he said. 11 So they procured some men to say, 'We heard him using blasphemous language against Moses and against God.' 12 Having turned the people against him as well as the elders and scribes, they took Stephen by surprise, and arrested him and brought him before the Sanhedrin. 13 There they put up false witnesses to say, 'This man is always making speeches against this Holy Place and the Law. 14 We have heard him say that Jesus, this Nazarene, is going to destroy this Place and alter the traditions that Moses handed down to us.' 15 The members of the Sanhedrin all looked intently at Stephen, and his face appeared to them like the face of an angel.

7 The high priest asked, 'Is this true?' 2 He replied, 'My brothers, my fathers, listen to what I have to say.*n* The God of glory appeared to our ancestor Abraham, while he was in Mesopotamia before settling in Haran, 3 and *said to him, "Leave your country, your kindred and your father's house for this country which I shall show you."* 4 So he left Chaldaea and settled in Haran; and after his father died God made him leave that place and come to this land where you are living today. 5 God did not give him any property in this land or even a foothold, yet he promised to *give it to him and after him to his descendants, childless* though he was. 6 The actual words God used when he spoke to him are that *his descendants would be exiles in a land not their own, where they would be enslaved and oppressed for four hundred years.* 7 *"But I will bring judgement on the nation that enslaves them,"* God said, *"and after this they will leave, and worship me in this place."* 8 Then he made the *covenant of circumcision* with him: and so when his son Isaac was born Abraham *circumcised him on the eighth day;* similarly Isaac circumcised Jacob, and Jacob the twelve patriarchs.

9 'The patriarchs were *jealous of Joseph and sold him into slavery in Egypt.* But *God was with him,* 10 and rescued him from all his miseries by making him so wise that he *won the favour* of Pharaoh king of Egypt, who *made him governor of Egypt* and *put him in charge of his household.* 11 *Then a famine set in* that caused much suffering *throughout Egypt and Canaan,* and our ancestors could find nothing to eat. 12 When Jacob *heard that there were supplies in Egypt,* he sent our ancestors there on a first visit; 13 and on the second *Joseph made himself known to his brothers,* and Pharaoh came to know his origin. 14 Joseph then sent for his father Jacob and his whole family, a total of *seventy-five people.* 15 Jacob went down into Egypt and after he and our ancestors had died there, 16 their bodies were brought back to Shechem and buried in the tomb that Abraham had bought for money from the sons of Hamor, the father of Shechem.

17 'As the time drew near for God to fulfil the promise he had solemnly made to Abraham, our nation in Egypt *became very powerful and numerous,* 18 *there came to power in Egypt a new king who had never heard of Joseph.* 19 *He took precautions and wore down* our race, forcing our ancestors to expose their babies rather than *letting them live.* 20 It was at this time that Moses was born, *a fine child before God.* He was looked after for *three months in his* father's house, 21 and after he had been exposed, *Pharaoh's daughter adopted* him and brought him up *like a son.* 22 So Moses was taught all the wisdom of the Egyptians and became a man with power both in his speech and in his actions.

n 7 A survey using chiefly Gn and Ex.

23 "When he was forty years old, it came into his heart to visit his relatives, the Israelites.ˣ 24 When he saw one of them being wronged, he defended the oppressed man and avenged him by striking down the Egyptian. 25 He supposed that his kinsfolk would understand that God through him was rescuing them, but they did not understand. 26 The next day he came to some of them as they were quarreling and tried to reconcile them, saying, 'Men, you are brothers; why do you wrong each other?' 27 But the man who was wronging his neighbor pushed Mosesʸ aside, saying, 'Who made you a ruler and a judge over us? 28 Do you want to kill me as you killed the Egyptian yesterday?' 29 When he heard this, Moses fled and became a resident alien in the land of Midian. There he became the father of two sons.

30 "Now when forty years had passed, an angel appeared to him in the wilderness of Mount Sinai, in the flame of a burning bush. 31 When Moses saw it, he was amazed at the sight; and as he approached to look, there came the voice of the Lord: 32 'I am the God of your ancestors, the God of Abraham, Isaac, and Jacob.' Moses began to tremble and did not dare to look. 33 Then the Lord said to him, 'Take off the sandals from your feet, for the place where you are standing is holy ground. 34 I have surely seen the mistreatment of my people who are in Egypt and have heard their groaning, and I have come down to rescue them. Come now, I will send you to Egypt.'

35 "It was this Moses whom they rejected when they said, 'Who made you a ruler and a judge?' and whom God now sent as both ruler and liberator through the angel who appeared to him in the bush. 36 He led them out, having performed wonders and signs in Egypt, at the Red Sea, and in the wilderness for forty years. 37 This is the Moses who said to the Israelites, 'God will raise up a prophet for you from your own peopleᶻ as he raised me up.' 38 He is the one who was in the congregation in the wilderness with the angel who spoke to him at Mount Sinai, and with our ancestors; and he received living oracles to give to us. 39 Our ancestors were unwilling to obey him; instead, they pushed him aside, and in their hearts they turned back to Egypt, 40 saying to Aaron, 'Make gods for us who will lead the way for us; as for this Moses who led us out from the land of Egypt, we do not know what has happened to him.' 41 At that time they made a calf, offered a sacrifice to the idol, and reveled in the works of their hands. 42 But God turned away from them and handed them over to worship the host of heaven, as it is written in the book of the prophets:

'Did you offer to me slain victims and sacrifices
      forty years in the wilderness, O house of
      Israel?
43 No; you took along the tent of Moloch,
      and the star of your god Rephan,
      the images that you made to worship;
    so I will remove you beyond Babylon.'

44 "Our ancestors had the tent of testimony in the wilderness, as Godᵃ directed when he spoke to Moses, ordering him to make it according to the pattern he had seen. 45 Our ancestors in turn brought it in with Joshua when they dispossessed the nations that God drove out before our ancestors. And it was there until the time of David, 46 who found favor with God and asked that he might find a dwelling place for the house of Jacob.ᵇ 47 But it was Solomon who built a house for him. 48 Yet the Most High does not dwell in houses made with human hands;ᶜ as the prophet says,

23 'He was approaching the age of forty, when it occurred to him to visit his fellow-countrymen the Israelites. 24 Seeing one of them being ill-treated, he went to his aid, and avenged the victim by striking down the Egyptian. 25 He thought his countrymen would understand that God was offering them deliverance through him, but they did not understand. 26 The next day he came upon two of them fighting, and tried to persuade them to make up their quarrel. "Men, you are brothers!" he said. "Why are you ill-treating one another?" 27 But the man who was at fault pushed him away. "Who made you ruler and judge over us?" he said. 28 "Are you going to kill me as you killed the Egyptian yesterday?" 29 At this Moses fled the country and settled in Midianite territory. There two sons were born to him.

30 'After forty years had passed, an angel appeared to him in the flame of a burning bush in the desert near Mount Sinai. 31 Moses was amazed at the sight, and as he approached to look more closely, the voice of the Lord came to him: 32 "I am the God of your fathers, the God of Abraham, Isaac, and Jacob." Moses was terrified and did not dare to look. 33 Then the Lord said to him, "Take off your sandals; the place where you are standing is holy ground. 34 I have indeed seen how my people are oppressed in Egypt and have heard their groans; and I have come down to rescue them. Come now, I will send you to Egypt."

35 'This Moses, whom they had rejected with the words, "Who made you ruler and judge?"—this very man was commissioned as ruler and liberator by God himself, speaking through the angel who appeared to him in the bush. 36 It was Moses who led them out, doing signs and wonders in Egypt, at the Red Sea, and for forty years in the desert. 37 It was he who said to the Israelites, "God will raise up for you from among yourselves a prophet like me." 38 It was he again who, in the assembly in the desert, kept company with the angel, who spoke to him on Mount Sinai, and with our forefathers, and received the living utterances of God to pass on to us.

39 'Our forefathers would not accept his leadership but thrust him aside. They wished themselves back in Egypt, 40 and said to Aaron, "Make us gods to go before us. As for this fellow Moses, who brought us out of Egypt, we do not know what has become of him." 41 That was when they made the bull-calf and offered sacrifice to the idol, and held festivities in honour of what their hands had made. 42 So God turned away from them and gave them over to the worship of the host of heaven, as it stands written in the book of the prophets: "Did you bring me victims and offerings those forty years in the desert, you people of Israel? 43 No, you carried aloft the shrine of Moloch and the star of the god Rephan, the images which you had made for your adoration. I will banish you beyond Babylon."

44 'Our forefathers had the Tent of the Testimony in the desert, as God commanded when he told Moses to make it after the pattern which he had seen. 45 In the next generation, our fathers under Joshua brought it with them when they dispossessed the nations whom God drove out before them, and so it was until the time of David. 46 David found favour with God and begged leave to provide a dwelling-place for the God of Jacob; 47 but it was Solomon who built him a house. 48 However, the Most High does not live in houses made by men; as the prophet says: 49 "Heaven is my

---

ˣ Gk his brothers, the sons of Israel   ʸ Gk him   ᶻ Gk your brothers   ᵃ Gk he   ᵇ Other ancient authorities read for the God of Jacob   ᶜ Gk with hands

7:37 like me: or as he raised up me.   7:46 for . . . Jacob: some witnesses read for the house of Jacob.

23 "When he was forty years old, he decided to visit his kinsfolk, the Israelites. 24 When he saw one of them treated unjustly, he defended and avenged the oppressed man by striking down the Egyptian. 25 He assumed [his] kinsfolk would understand that God was offering them deliverance through him, but they did not understand. 26 The next day he appeared to them as they were fighting and tried to reconcile them peacefully, saying, 'Men, you are brothers. Why are you harming one another?' 27 Then the one who was harming his neighbor pushed him aside, saying, 'Who appointed you ruler and judge over us? 28 Are you thinking of killing me as you killed the Egyptian yesterday?' 29 Moses fled when he heard this and settled as an alien in the land of Midian, where he became the father of two sons.

30 "Forty years later, an angel appeared to him in the desert near Mount Sinai in the flame of a burning bush. 31 When Moses saw it, he was amazed at the sight, and as he drew near to look at it, the voice of the Lord came, 32 'I am the God of your fathers, the God of Abraham, of Isaac, and of Jacob.' Then Moses, trembling, did not dare to look at it. 33 But the Lord said to him, 'Remove the sandals from your feet, for the place where you stand is holy ground. 34 I have witnessed the affliction of my people in Egypt and have heard their groaning, and I have come down to rescue them. Come now, I will send you to Egypt.' 35 This Moses, whom they had rejected with the words, 'Who appointed you ruler and judge?' God sent as [both] ruler and deliverer, through the angel who appeared to him in the bush. 36 This man led them out, performing wonders and signs in the land of Egypt, at the Red Sea, and in the desert for forty years. 37 It was this Moses who said to the Israelites, 'God will raise up for you, from among your own kinsfolk, a prophet like me.' 38 It was he who, in the assembly in the desert, was with the angel who spoke to him on Mount Sinai and with our ancestors, and he received living utterances to hand on to us.

39 "Our ancestors were unwilling to obey him; instead, they pushed him aside and in their hearts turned back to Egypt, 40 saying to Aaron, 'Make us gods who will be our leaders. As for that Moses who led us out of the land of Egypt, we do not know what has happened to him.' 41 So they made a calf in those days, offered sacrifice to the idol, and reveled in the works of their hands. 42 Then God turned and handed them over to worship the host of heaven, as it is written in the book of the prophets:

'Did you bring me sacrifices and offerings
for forty years in the desert, O house of Israel?
43 No, you took up the tent of Moloch
and the star of [your] god Rephan,
the images that you made to worship.
So I shall take you into exile beyond Babylon.'

44 "Our ancestors had the tent of testimony in the desert just as the One who spoke to Moses directed him to make it according to the pattern he had seen. 45 Our ancestors who inherited it brought it with Joshua when they dispossessed the nations that God drove out from before our ancestors, up to the time of David, 46 who found favor in the sight of God and asked that he might find a dwelling place for the house of Jacob. 47 But Solomon built a house for him. 48 Yet the Most High does not dwell in houses made by human hands. As the prophet says:

23 'At the age of forty he decided to visit *his kinsmen, the Israelites*. 24 When he saw one of them being ill-treated he went to his defence and rescued the man by *killing the Egyptian*. 25 He thought his brothers would realise that through him God would liberate them, but they did not. 26 The next day, when he came across some of them fighting, he tried to reconcile them, and said, "Friends, you are brothers; why are you hurting each other?" 27 But *the man who was attacking his kinsman* pushed him aside, saying, "*And who appointed you to be prince over us and judge?* 28 *Do you intend to kill me as you killed the Egyptian yesterday?*" 29 Moses fled when he heard this and *he went to dwell in the land of Midian*, where he fathered two sons.

30 'When forty years were fulfilled, *in the desert near Mount Sinai, an angel appeared to him in a flame blazing from a bush* that was on fire. 31 Moses was amazed by what he saw. *As he went nearer to look at it, the voice of the Lord was* heard, 32 "I am the God of your ancestors, the God of Abraham, Isaac and Jacob." Moses trembled and *was afraid to look*. 33 The Lord said to him, "*Take off your sandals*, for the place where you are standing is holy ground. 34 *I have seen the misery of my people in Egypt, I have heard them crying for help, and I have come down to rescue them. So come here; I am sending you into Egypt.*"

35 'It was the same Moses that they had disowned when they said, "*Who appointed you to be our leader and judge?*" whom God sent to be both leader and redeemer through the angel who had appeared to him in the bush. 36 It was this man who led them out, after performing *miracles and signs in Egypt* and at the Red Sea and *in the desert for forty years.* 37 It was this Moses who told the sons of Israel, "*From among your own brothers God will raise up a prophet like me.*" 38 When they held the assembly in the desert it was he who was with our ancestors and the angel who had spoken to him on Mount Sinai; it was he who was entrusted with words of life to hand on to us. 39 This is the man that our ancestors refused to listen to; they pushed him aside, *went back to Egypt* in their thoughts, 40 *and said to Aaron, "Make us a god to go at our head; for that Moses, the man who brought us out from Egypt, we do not know what has become of him."* 41 It was then that *they made the statue of a calf and offered sacrifice* to the idol. They were perfectly happy with something they had made for themselves. 42 God turned away from them and abandoned them to the worship of the army of heaven, as scripture says in the book of the prophets:

Did you bring me sacrifices and oblations
those forty years in the desert, House of Israel?
43 *No, you carried the tent of Moloch on your*
shoulders
and the star of the god Rephan,
the idols you made for yourselves to adore,
and so now I am about to drive you into captivity
beyond Babylon. *o*

44 'While they were in the desert our ancestors possessed the Tent of Testimony that had been constructed according to the instructions God gave Moses, telling him to *work to the design* he had been shown. 45 It was handed down from one ancestor of ours to another until Joshua brought it into the country that had belonged to the nations which were driven out by God before us. Here it stayed until the time of David. 46 He won God's favour and asked permission *to find a dwelling for* the House of *Jacob,* 47 though it was *Solomon* who actually *built a house for God.* 48 Even so the Most High does not live in a house that human hands have built: for as the prophet says:

o 7 Am 5:25–27.

49 'Heaven is my throne,
and the earth is my footstool.
What kind of house will you build for me, says
the Lord,
or what is the place of my rest?
50 Did not my hand make all these things?'

51 "You stiff-necked people, uncircumcised in heart and ears, you are forever opposing the Holy Spirit, just as your ancestors used to do. 52 Which of the prophets did your ancestors not persecute? They killed those who foretold the coming of the Righteous One, and now you have become his betrayers and murderers. 53 You are the ones that received the law as ordained by angels, and yet you have not kept it."

54 When they heard these things, they became enraged and ground their teeth at Stephen.d 55 But filled with the Holy Spirit, he gazed into heaven and saw the glory of God and Jesus standing at the right hand of God. 56 "Look," he said, "I see the heavens opened and the Son of Man standing at the right hand of God!" 57 But they covered their ears, and with a loud shout all rushed together against him. 58 Then they dragged him out of the city and began to stone him; and the witnesses laid their coats at the feet of a young man named Saul. 59 While they were stoning Stephen, he prayed, "Lord Jesus, receive my spirit." 60 Then he knelt down and cried out in a loud voice, "Lord, do not hold this sin against them." When he had said this, he died.e

8 1 And Saul approved of their killing him.

That day a severe persecution began against the church in Jerusalem, and all except the apostles were scattered throughout the countryside of Judea and Samaria. 2 Devout men buried Stephen and made loud lamentation over him. 3 But Saul was ravaging the church by entering house after house; dragging off both men and women, he committed them to prison.

4 Now those who were scattered went from place to place, proclaiming the word. 5 Philip went down to the cityf of Samaria and proclaimed the Messiahg to them. 6 The crowds with one accord listened eagerly to what was said by Philip, hearing and seeing the signs that he did, 7 for unclean spirits, crying with loud shrieks, came out of many who were possessed; and many others who were paralyzed or lame were cured. 8 So there was great joy in that city.

9 Now a certain man named Simon had previously practiced magic in the city and amazed the people of Samaria, saying that he was someone great. 10 All of them, from the least to the greatest, listened to him eagerly, saying, "This man is the power of God that is called Great." 11 And they listened eagerly to him because for a long time he had amazed them with his magic. 12 But when they believed Philip, who was proclaiming the good news about the kingdom of God and the name of Jesus Christ, they were baptized, both men and women. 13 Even Simon himself believed. After being baptized, he stayed constantly with Philip and was amazed when he saw the signs and great miracles that took place.

14 Now when the apostles at Jerusalem heard that Samaria had accepted the word of God, they sent Peter and John to them. 15 The two went down and prayed for them that they might receive the Holy Spirit 16 (for as yet the Spirit had not comeh upon any of them; they had only been baptized in the name of the Lord Jesus). 17 Then Peter and Johni laid their hands on them, and they received the Holy Spirit. 18 Now when Simon saw that the Spirit was given through the laying on of the apostles' hands, he offered them money, 19 saying, "Give me also this power so that

throne and earth my footstool. What kind of house will you build for me, says the Lord; where shall my resting-place be? 50 Are not all these things of my own making?"

51 'How stubborn you are, heathen still at heart and deaf to the truth! You always resist the Holy Spirit. You are just like your fathers! 52 Was there ever a prophet your fathers did not persecute? They killed those who foretold the coming of the righteous one, and now you have betrayed him and murdered him. 53 You received the law given by God's angels and yet you have not kept it.'

54 This touched them on the raw, and they ground their teeth with fury. 55 But Stephen, filled with the Holy Spirit, and gazing intently up to heaven, saw the glory of God, and Jesus standing at God's right hand. 56 'Look!' he said. 'I see the heavens opened and the Son of Man standing at the right hand of God.' 57 At this they gave a great shout, and stopped their ears; they made a concerted rush at him, 58 threw him out of the city, and set about stoning him. The witnesses laid their coats at the feet of a young man named Saul. 59 As they stoned him Stephen called out, 'Lord Jesus, receive my spirit.' 60 He fell on his knees and cried aloud, 'Lord, do not hold this sin against them,' and with that he

8 died. 1 Saul was among those who approved of his execution.

That day was the beginning of a time of violent persecution for the church in Jerusalem; and all except the apostles were scattered over the country districts of Judaea and Samaria. 2 Stephen was given burial by devout men, who made a great lamentation for him. 3 Saul, meanwhile, was harrying the church; he entered house after house, seizing men and women and sending them to prison.

4 As for those who had been scattered, they went through the country preaching the word. 5 Philip came down to a city in Samaria and began proclaiming the Messiah there. 6 As the crowds heard Philip and saw the signs he performed, everyone paid close attention to what he had to say. 7 In many cases of possession the unclean spirits came out with a loud cry, and many paralysed and crippled folk were cured; 8 and there was great rejoicing in that city.

9 A man named Simon had been in the city for some time and had captivated the Samaritans with his magical arts, making large claims for himself. 10 Everybody, high and low, listened intently to him. 'This man', they said, 'is that power of God which is called "The Great Power".' 11 They listened because they had for so long been captivated by his magic. 12 But when they came to believe Philip, with his good news about the kingdom of God and the name of Jesus Christ, men and women alike were baptized. 13 Even Simon himself believed, and after his baptism was constantly in Philip's company. He was captivated when he saw the powerful signs and miracles that were taking place.

14 When the apostles in Jerusalem heard that Samaria had accepted the word of God, they sent off Peter and John, 15 who went down there and prayed for the converts, asking that they might receive the Holy Spirit. 16 Until then the Spirit had not come upon any of them; they had been baptized into the name of the Lord Jesus, that and nothing more. 17 So Peter and John laid their hands on them, and they received the Holy Spirit.

18 When Simon observed that the Spirit was bestowed through the laying on of the apostles' hands, he offered them money 19 and said, 'Give me too the same power, so

---

d Gk him   e Gk fell asleep   f Other ancient authorities read a city
g Or the Christ   h Gk fallen   i Gk they

49 'The heavens are my throne,
    the earth is my footstool.
What kind of house can you build for me?
    says the Lord,
      or what is to be my resting place?
50 Did not my hand make all these things?'

51 "You stiff-necked people, uncircumcised in heart and ears, you always oppose the holy Spirit; you are just like your ancestors. 52 Which of the prophets did your ancestors not persecute? They put to death those who foretold the coming of the righteous one, whose betrayers and murderers you have now become. 53 You received the law as transmitted by angels, but you did not observe it."

54 When they heard this, they were infuriated, and they ground their teeth at him. 55 But he, filled with the holy Spirit, looked up intently to heaven and saw the glory of God and Jesus standing at the right hand of God, 56 and he said, "Behold, I see the heavens opened and the Son of Man standing at the right hand of God." 57 But they cried out in a loud voice, covered their ears, and rushed upon him together. 58 They threw him out of the city, and began to stone him. The witnesses laid down their cloaks at the feet of a young man named Saul. 59 As they were stoning Stephen, he called out, "Lord Jesus, receive my spirit." 60 Then he fell to his knees and cried out in a loud voice, "Lord, do not hold this sin against them"; and when he said this, he fell asleep.

8 Now Saul was consenting to his execution.
On that day, there broke out a severe persecution of the church in Jerusalem, and all were scattered throughout the countryside of Judea and Samaria, except the apostles. 2 Devout men buried Stephen and made a loud lament over him. 3 Saul, meanwhile, was trying to destroy the church; entering house after house and dragging out men and women, he handed them over for imprisonment.

4 Now those who had been scattered went about preaching the word. 5 Thus Philip went down to [the] city of Samaria and proclaimed the Messiah to them. 6 With one accord, the crowds paid attention to what was said by Philip when they heard it and saw the signs he was doing. 7 For unclean spirits, crying out in a loud voice, came out of many possessed people, and many paralyzed and crippled people were cured. 8 There was great joy in that city.

9 A man named Simon used to practice magic in the city and astounded the people of Samaria, claiming to be someone great. 10 All of them, from the least to the greatest, paid attention to him, saying, "This man is the 'Power of God' that is called 'Great.' " 11 They paid attention to him because he had astounded them by his magic for a long time, 12 but once they began to believe Philip as he preached the good news about the kingdom of God and the name of Jesus Christ, men and women alike were baptized. 13 Even Simon himself believed and, after being baptized, became devoted to Philip; and when he saw the signs and mighty deeds that were occurring, he was astounded.

14 Now when the apostles in Jerusalem heard that Samaria had accepted the word of God, they sent them Peter and John, 15 who went down and prayed for them, that they might receive the holy Spirit, 16 for it had not yet fallen upon any of them; they had only been baptized in the name of the Lord Jesus. 17 Then they laid hands on them and they received the holy Spirit.

18 When Simon saw that the Spirit was conferred by the laying on of the apostles' hands, he offered them money

49 With heaven my throne
    and earth my footstool,
    what house could you build me, says the Lord,
    what place for me to rest,
50 when all these things were made by me? p

51 'You stubborn people, with uncircumcised hearts and ears. You are always resisting the Holy Spirit, just as your ancestors used to do. 52 Can you name a single prophet your ancestors never persecuted? They killed those who foretold the coming of the Upright One, and now you have become his betrayers, his murderers. 53 In spite of being given the Law through angels, you have not kept it.'

54 They were infuriated when they heard this, and ground their teeth at him. 55 But Stephen, filled with the Holy Spirit, gazed into heaven and saw the glory of God, and Jesus standing at God's right hand. 56 'Look! I can see heaven thrown open,' he said, 'and the Son of man standing at the right hand of God.' 57 All the members of the council shouted out and stopped their ears with their hands; then they made a concerted rush at him, 58 thrust him out of the city and stoned him. The witnesses put down their clothes at the feet of a young man called Saul. 59 As they were stoning him, Stephen said in invocation, 'Lord Jesus, receive my spirit.' 60 Then he knelt down and said aloud, 'Lord, do not hold this sin against them.' And with these words he fell asleep.

8 Saul approved of the killing.
That day a bitter persecution started against the church in Jerusalem, and everyone except the apostles scattered to the country districts of Judaea and Samaria. 2 There were some devout people, however, who buried Stephen and made great mourning for him.

3 Saul then began doing great harm to the church; he went from house to house arresting both men and women and sending them to prison.

4 Once they had scattered, they went from place to place preaching the good news. 5 And Philip went to a Samaritan town and proclaimed the Christ to them. 6 The people unanimously welcomed the message Philip preached, because they had heard of the miracles he worked and because they saw them for themselves. 7 For unclean spirits came shrieking out of many who were possessed, and several paralytics and cripples were cured. 8 As a result there was great rejoicing in that town.

9 Now a man called Simon had for some time been practising magic arts in the town and astounded the Samaritan people. He had given it out that he was someone momentous, 10 and everyone believed in him; eminent citizens and ordinary people alike had declared, 'He is the divine power that is called Great.' 11 He had this following because for a considerable period they had been astounded by his wizardry. 12 But when they came to accept Philip's preaching of the good news about the kingdom of God and the name of Jesus Christ, they were baptised, both men and women, 13 and even Simon himself became a believer. After his baptism Simon went round constantly with Philip and was astonished when he saw the wonders and great miracles that took place.

14 When the apostles in Jerusalem heard that Samaria had accepted the word of God, they sent Peter and John to them, 15 and they went down there and prayed for them to receive the Holy Spirit, 16 for as yet he had not come down on any of them: they had only been baptised in the name of the Lord Jesus. 17 Then they laid hands on them, and they received the Holy Spirit.

18 When Simon saw that the Spirit was given through the laying on of the apostles' hands, he offered them money,

p 7 Is 66:1–2.

NEW REVISED STANDARD VERSION

anyone on whom I lay my hands may receive the Holy Spirit." 20 But Peter said to him, "May your silver perish with you, because you thought you could obtain God's gift with money! 21 You have no part or share in this, for your heart is not right before God. 22 Repent therefore of this wickedness of yours, and pray to the Lord that, if possible, the intent of your heart may be forgiven you. 23 For I see that you are in the gall of bitterness and the chains of wickedness." 24 Simon answered, "Pray for me to the Lord, that nothing of what you*j* have said may happen to me."

25 Now after Peter and John*k* had testified and spoken the word of the Lord, they returned to Jerusalem, proclaiming the good news to many villages of the Samaritans.

26 Then an angel of the Lord said to Philip, "Get up and go toward the south*l* to the road that goes down from Jerusalem to Gaza." (This is a wilderness road.) 27 So he got up and went. Now there was an Ethiopian eunuch, a court official of the Candace, queen of the Ethiopians, in charge of her entire treasury. He had come to Jerusalem to worship 28 and was returning home; seated in his chariot, he was reading the prophet Isaiah. 29 Then the Spirit said to Philip, "Go over to this chariot and join it." 30 So Philip ran up to it and heard him reading the prophet Isaiah. He asked, "Do you understand what you are reading?" 31 He replied, "How can I, unless someone guides me?" And he invited Philip to get in and sit beside him. 32 Now the passage of the scripture that he was reading was this:

"Like a sheep he was led to the slaughter,
    and like a lamb silent before its shearer,
        so he does not open his mouth.
33 In his humiliation justice was denied him.
    Who can describe his generation?
        For his life is taken away from the earth."

34 The eunuch asked Philip, "About whom, may I ask you, does the prophet say this, about himself or about someone else?" 35 Then Philip began to speak, and starting with this scripture, he proclaimed to him the good news about Jesus. 36 As they were going along the road, they came to some water; and the eunuch said, "Look, here is water! What is to prevent me from being baptized?"*m* 38 He commanded the chariot to stop, and both of them, Philip and the eunuch, went down into the water, and Philip*n* baptized him. 39 When they came up out of the water, the Spirit of the Lord snatched Philip away; the eunuch saw him no more, and went on his way rejoicing. 40 But Philip found himself at Azotus, and as he was passing through the region, he proclaimed the good news to all the towns until he came to Caesarea.

9 Meanwhile Saul, still breathing threats and murder against the disciples of the Lord, went to the high priest 2 and asked him for letters to the synagogues at Damascus, so that if he found any who belonged to the Way, men or women, he might bring them bound to Jerusalem. 3 Now as he was going along and approaching Damascus, suddenly a light from heaven flashed around him. 4 He fell to the ground and heard a voice saying to him, "Saul, Saul, why do you persecute me?" 5 He asked, "Who are you, Lord?" The reply came, "I am Jesus, whom you are persecuting. 6 But get up and enter the city, and you will be told what you are to do." 7 The men who were traveling with him stood speechless because they heard the voice but saw no one. 8 Saul got up from the ground, and though his eyes

REVISED ENGLISH BIBLE

that anyone I lay my hands on will receive the Holy Spirit.' 20 Peter replied, 'You thought God's gift was for sale? Your money can go with you to damnation! 21 You have neither part nor share in this, for you are corrupt in the eyes of God. 22 Repent of this wickedness of yours and pray the Lord to forgive you for harbouring such a thought. 23 I see that bitter gall and the chains of sin will be your fate.' 24 Simon said to them, 'Pray to the Lord for me, and ask that none of the things you have spoken of may befall me.'

25 After giving their testimony and speaking the word of the Lord, they took the road back to Jerusalem, bringing the good news to many Samaritan villages on the way.

26 Then the angel of the Lord said to Philip, 'Start out and go south to the road that leads down from Jerusalem to Gaza.' (This is the desert road.) 27 He set out and was on his way when he caught sight of an Ethiopian. This man was a eunuch, a high official of the Kandake, or queen, of Ethiopia, in charge of all her treasure; he had been to Jerusalem on a pilgrimage 28 and was now returning home, sitting in his carriage and reading aloud from the prophet Isaiah. 29 The Spirit said to Philip, 'Go and meet the carriage.' 30 When Philip ran up he heard him reading from the prophet Isaiah and asked, 'Do you understand what you are reading?' 31 He said, 'How can I without someone to guide me?' and invited Philip to get in and sit beside him.

32 The passage he was reading was this: 'He was led like a sheep to the slaughter; like a lamb that is dumb before the shearer, he does not open his mouth. 33 He has been humiliated and has no redress. Who will be able to speak of his posterity? For he is cut off from the world of the living.'

34 'Please tell me', said the eunuch to Philip, 'who it is that the prophet is speaking about here: himself or someone else?' 35 Then Philip began and, starting from this passage, he told him the good news of Jesus. 36 As they were going along the road, they came to some water. 'Look,' said the eunuch, 'here is water: what is to prevent my being baptized?' 38 and he ordered the carriage to stop. Then they both went down into the water, Philip and the eunuch, and he baptized him. 39 When they came up from the water the Spirit snatched Philip away; the eunuch did not see him again, but went on his way rejoicing. 40 Philip appeared at Azotus, and toured the country, preaching in all the towns till he reached Caesarea.

9 SAUL, still breathing murderous threats against the Lord's disciples, went to the high priest 2 and applied for letters to the synagogues at Damascus authorizing him to arrest any followers of the new way whom he found, men or women, and bring them to Jerusalem. 3 While he was still on the road and nearing Damascus, suddenly a light from the sky flashed all around him. 4 He fell to the ground and heard a voice saying, 'Saul, Saul, why are you persecuting me?' 5 'Tell me, Lord,' he said, 'who you are.' The voice answered, 'I am Jesus, whom you are persecuting. 6 But now get up and go into the city, and you will be told what you have to do.' 7 Meanwhile the men who were travelling with him stood speechless; they heard the voice but could see no one. 8 Saul got up from the ground, but when he

---

j The Greek word for *you* and the verb *pray* are plural   *k* Gk *after they*   *l* Or *go at noon*   *m* Other ancient authorities add all or most of verse 37, *And Philip said, "If you believe with all your heart, you may." And he replied, "I believe that Jesus is the Son of God."*   *n* Gk *he*

8:36 **baptized:** *some witnesses add* 37 Philip said, 'If you wholeheartedly believe, it is permitted.' He replied, 'I believe that Jesus Christ is the Son of God.'

19 and said, "Give me this power too, so that anyone upon whom I lay my hands may receive the holy Spirit." 20 But Peter said to him, "May your money perish with you, because you thought that you could buy the gift of God with money. 21 You have no share or lot in this matter, for your heart is not upright before God. 22 Repent of this wickedness of yours and pray to the Lord that, if possible, your intention may be forgiven. 23 For I see that you are filled with bitter gall and are in the bonds of iniquity." 24 Simon said in reply, "Pray for me to the Lord, that nothing of what you have said may come upon me." 25 So when they had testified and proclaimed the word of the Lord, they returned to Jerusalem and preached the good news to many Samaritan villages.

26 Then the angel of the Lord spoke to Philip, "Get up and head south on the road that goes down from Jerusalem to Gaza, the desert route." 27 So he got up and set out. Now there was an Ethiopian eunuch, a court official of the Candace, that is, the queen of the Ethiopians, in charge of her entire treasury, who had come to Jerusalem to worship, 28 and was returning home. Seated in his chariot, he was reading the prophet Isaiah. 29 The Spirit said to Philip, "Go and join up with that chariot." 30 Philip ran up and heard him reading Isaiah the prophet and said, "Do you understand what you are reading?" 31 He replied, "How can I, unless someone instructs me?" So he invited Philip to get in and sit with him. 32 This was the scripture passage he was reading:

"Like a sheep he was led to the slaughter,
and as a lamb before its shearer is silent,
so he opened not his mouth.
33 In [his] humiliation justice was denied him.
Who will tell of his posterity?
For his life is taken from the earth."

34 Then the eunuch said to Philip in reply, "I beg you, about whom is the prophet saying this? About himself, or about someone else?" 35 Then Philip opened his mouth and, beginning with this scripture passage, he proclaimed Jesus to him. 36 As they traveled along the road they came to some water, and the eunuch said, "Look, there is water. What is to prevent my being baptized?"

[37] 38 Then he ordered the chariot to stop, and Philip and the eunuch both went down into the water, and he baptized him. 39 When they came out of the water, the Spirit of the Lord snatched Philip away, and the eunuch saw him no more, but continued on his way rejoicing. 40 Philip came to Azotus, and went about proclaiming the good news to all the towns until he reached Caesarea.

9 Now Saul, still breathing murderous threats against the disciples of the Lord, went to the high priest 2 and asked him for letters to the synagogues in Damascus, that, if he should find any men or women who belonged to the Way, he might bring them back to Jerusalem in chains. 3 On his journey, as he was nearing Damascus, a light from the sky suddenly flashed around him. 4 He fell to the ground and heard a voice saying to him, "Saul, Saul, why are you persecuting me?" 5 He said, "Who are you, sir?" The reply came, "I am Jesus, whom you are persecuting. 6 Now get up and go into the city and you will be told what you must do." 7 The men who were traveling with him stood speechless, for they heard the voice but could see no one. 8 Saul got up

19 with the words, 'Give me the same power so that anyone I lay my hands on will receive the Holy Spirit.' 20 Peter answered, 'May your silver be lost for ever, and you with it, for thinking that money could buy what God has given for nothing! 21 You have no share, no part, in this: God can see how your heart is warped. 22 Repent of this wickedness of yours, and pray to the Lord that this scheme of yours may be forgiven; 23 it is plain to me that you are held in the bitterness of gall and the chains of sin.' 24 Simon replied, 'Pray to the Lord for me yourselves so that none of the things you have spoken about may happen to me.'

25 Having given their testimony and proclaimed the word of the Lord, they went back to Jerusalem, preaching the good news to a number of Samaritan villages.

26 The angel of the Lord spoke to Philip saying, 'Set out at noon and go along the road that leads from Jerusalem down to Gaza, the desert road.' 27 So he set off on his journey. Now an Ethiopian had been on pilgrimage to Jerusalem; he was a eunuch and an officer at the court of the kandake, or queen, of Ethiopia; he was her chief treasurer. 28 He was now on his way home; and as he sat in his chariot he was reading the prophet Isaiah. 29 The Spirit said to Philip, 'Go up and join that chariot.' 30 When Philip ran up, he heard him reading Isaiah the prophet and asked, 'Do you understand what you are reading?' 31 He replied, 'How could I, unless I have someone to guide me?' So he urged Philip to get in and sit by his side. 32 Now the passage of scripture he was reading was this:

Like a lamb led to the slaughter-house,
like a sheep dumb in front of its shearers,
he never opens his mouth.
33 In his humiliation fair judgement was denied him.
Who will ever talk about his descendants,
since his life on earth has been cut short? q

34 The eunuch addressed Philip and said, 'Tell me, is the prophet referring to himself or someone else?' 35 Starting, therefore, with this text of scripture Philip proceeded to explain the good news of Jesus to him.

36 Further along the road they came to some water, and the eunuch said, 'Look, here is some water; is there anything to prevent my being baptised?' [37] r 38 He ordered the chariot to stop, then Philip and the eunuch both went down into the water and he baptised him. 39 But after they had come up out of the water again Philip was taken away by the Spirit of the Lord, and the eunuch never saw him again but went on his way rejoicing. 40 Philip appeared in Azotus and continued his journey, proclaiming the good news in every town as far as Caesarea.

9 5 Meanwhile Saul was still breathing threats to slaughter the Lord's disciples. He went to the high priest 2 and asked for letters addressed to the synagogues in Damascus, that would authorise him to arrest and take to Jerusalem any followers of the Way, men or women, that he might find.

3 It happened that while he was travelling to Damascus and approaching the city, suddenly a light from heaven shone all round him. 4 He fell to the ground, and then he heard a voice saying, 'Saul, Saul, why are you persecuting me?' 5 'Who are you, Lord?' he asked, and the answer came, 'I am Jesus, whom you are persecuting. 6 Get up and go into the city, and you will be told what you are to do.' 7 The men travelling with Saul stood there speechless, for though they heard the voice they could see no one. 8 Saul

---

8, 37: The oldest and best manuscripts of Acts omit this verse, which is a Western text reading: "And Philip said, 'If you believe with all your heart, you may.' And he said in reply, 'I believe that Jesus Christ is the Son of God.'"

q 8 Is 53:7–8.　r 8 v. 37, omitted here, is a very ancient gloss: 'And Philip said, "If you believe with all your heart, you may." And he replied, "I believe that Jesus is the Son of God." '　s 9 = 22; 26; cf. 2 M 3.

were open, he could see nothing; so they led him by the hand and brought him into Damascus. 9 For three days he was without sight, and neither ate nor drank.

10 Now there was a disciple in Damascus named Ananias. The Lord said to him in a vision, "Ananias." He answered, "Here I am, Lord." 11 The Lord said to him, "Get up and go to the street called Straight, and at the house of Judas look for a man of Tarsus named Saul. At this moment he is praying, 12 and he has seen in a vision^o a man named Ananias come in and lay his hands on him so that he might regain his sight." 13 But Ananias answered, "Lord, I have heard from many about this man, how much evil he has done to your saints in Jerusalem; 14 and here he has authority from the chief priests to bind all who invoke your name." 15 But the Lord said to him, "Go, for he is an instrument whom I have chosen to bring my name before Gentiles and kings and before the people of Israel; 16 I myself will show him how much he must suffer for the sake of my name." 17 So Ananias went and entered the house. He laid his hands on Saul^p and said, "Brother Saul, the Lord Jesus, who appeared to you on your way here, has sent me so that you may regain your sight and be filled with the Holy Spirit." 18 And immediately something like scales fell from his eyes, and his sight was restored. Then he got up and was baptized, 19 and after taking some food, he regained his strength.

For several days he was with the disciples in Damascus, 20 and immediately he began to proclaim Jesus in the synagogues, saying, "He is the Son of God." 21 All who heard him were amazed and said, "Is not this the man who made havoc in Jerusalem among those who invoked this name? And has he not come here for the purpose of bringing them bound before the chief priests?" 22 Saul became increasingly more powerful and confounded the Jews who lived in Damascus by proving that Jesus^q was the Messiah.^{r}

23 After some time had passed, the Jews plotted to kill him, 24 but their plot became known to Saul. They were watching the gates day and night so that they might kill him; 25 but his disciples took him by night and let him down through an opening in the wall,^{s} lowering him in a basket.

26 When he had come to Jerusalem, he attempted to join the disciples; and they were all afraid of him, for they did not believe that he was a disciple. 27 But Barnabas took him, brought him to the apostles, and described for them how on the road he had seen the Lord, who had spoken to him, and how in Damascus he had spoken boldly in the name of Jesus. 28 So he went in and out among them in Jerusalem, speaking boldly in the name of the Lord. 29 He spoke and argued with the Hellenists; but they were attempting to kill him. 30 When the believers^t learned of it, they brought him down to Caesarea and sent him off to Tarsus.

31 Meanwhile the church throughout Judea, Galilee, and Samaria had peace and was built up. Living in the fear of the Lord and in the comfort of the Holy Spirit, it increased in numbers.

32 Now as Peter went here and there among all the believers,^{u} he came down also to the saints living in Lydda. 33 There he found a man named Aeneas, who had been bedridden for eight years, for he was paralyzed. 34 Peter said to him, "Aeneas, Jesus Christ heals you; get up and make your bed!" And immediately he got up. 35 And all the residents of Lydda and Sharon saw him and turned to the Lord.

opened his eyes he could not see; they led him by the hand and brought him into Damascus. 9 He was blind for three days, and took no food or drink.

10 There was in Damascus a disciple named Ananias. He had a vision in which he heard the Lord say: 'Ananias!' 'Here I am, Lord,' he answered. 11 The Lord said to him, 'Go to Straight Street, to the house of Judas, and ask for a man from Tarsus named Saul. You will find him at prayer; 12 he has had a vision of a man named Ananias coming in and laying hands on him to restore his sight.' 13 Ananias answered, 'Lord, I have often heard about this man and all the harm he has done your people in Jerusalem. 14 Now he is here with authority from the chief priests to arrest all who invoke your name.' 15 But the Lord replied, 'You must go, for this man is my chosen instrument to bring my name before the nations and their kings, and before the people of Israel. 16 I myself will show him all that he must go through for my name's sake.'

17 So Ananias went and, on entering the house, laid his hands on him and said, 'Saul, my brother, the Lord Jesus, who appeared to you on your way here, has sent me so that you may recover your sight and be filled with the Holy Spirit.' 18 Immediately it was as if scales had fallen from his eyes, and he regained his sight. He got up and was baptized, 19 and when he had eaten his strength returned.

He stayed some time with the disciples in Damascus. 20 Without delay he proclaimed Jesus publicly in the synagogues, declaring him to be the Son of God. 21 All who heard were astounded. 'Is not this the man', they said, 'who was in Jerusalem hunting down those who invoke this name? Did he not come here for the sole purpose of arresting them and taking them before the chief priests?' 22 But Saul went from strength to strength, and confounded the Jews of Damascus with his cogent proofs that Jesus was the Messiah.

23 When some time had passed, the Jews hatched a plot against his life; 24 but their plans became known to Saul. They kept watch on the city gates day and night so that they might murder him; 25 but one night some disciples took him and, lowering him in a basket, let him down over the wall.

26 On reaching Jerusalem he tried to join the disciples, but they were all afraid of him, because they did not believe that he really was a disciple. 27 Barnabas, however, took him and introduced him to the apostles; he described to them how on his journey Saul had seen the Lord and heard his voice, and how at Damascus he had spoken out boldly in the name of Jesus. 28 Saul now stayed with them, moving about freely in Jerusalem. 29 He spoke out boldly and openly in the name of the Lord, talking and debating with the Greek-speaking Jews. But they planned to murder him, 30 and when the brethren discovered this they escorted him down to Caesarea and sent him away to Tarsus.

31 MEANWHILE the church, throughout Judaea, Galilee, and Samaria, was left in peace to build up its strength, and to live in the fear of the Lord. Encouraged by the Holy Spirit, it grew in numbers.

32 In the course of a tour Peter was making throughout the region he went down to visit God's people at Lydda. 33 There he found a man named Aeneas who had been bedridden with paralysis for eight years. 34 Peter said to him, 'Aeneas, Jesus Christ cures you; get up and make your bed!' and immediately he stood up. 35 All who lived in Lydda and Sharon saw him; and they turned to the Lord.

---

^{o} Other ancient authorities lack *in a vision* ^{p} Gk *him* ^{q} Gk *that*
this ^{r} Or *the Christ* ^{s} Gk *through the wall* ^{t} Gk *brothers*
^{u} Gk *all of them*

9:29 **Greek-speaking Jews:** *lit.* Hellenists.

from the ground, but when he opened his eyes he could see nothing; so they led him by the hand and brought him to Damascus. 9 For three days he was unable to see, and he neither ate nor drank.

10 There was a disciple in Damascus named Ananias, and the Lord said to him in a vision, "Ananias." He answered, "Here I am, Lord." 11 The Lord said to him, "Get up and go to the street called Straight and ask at the house of Judas for a man from Tarsus named Saul. He is there praying, 12 and [in a vision] he has seen a man named Ananias come in and lay [his] hands on him, that he may regain his sight." 13 But Ananias replied, "Lord, I have heard from many sources about this man, what evil things he has done to your holy ones in Jerusalem. 14 And here he has authority from the chief priests to imprison all who call upon your name." 15 But the Lord said to him, "Go, for this man is a chosen instrument of mine to carry my name before Gentiles, kings, and Israelites, 16 and I will show him what he will have to suffer for my name." 17 So Ananias went and entered the house; laying his hands on him, he said, "Saul, my brother, the Lord has sent me, Jesus who appeared to you on the way by which you came, that you may regain your sight and be filled with the holy Spirit." 18 Immediately things like scales fell from his eyes and he regained his sight. He got up and was baptized, 19 and when he had eaten, he recovered his strength.

He stayed some days with the disciples in Damascus, 20 and he began at once to proclaim Jesus in the synagogues, that he is the Son of God. 21 All who heard him were astounded and said, "Is not this the man who in Jerusalem ravaged those who call upon this name, and came here expressly to take them back in chains to the chief priests?" 22 But Saul grew all the stronger and confounded [the] Jews who lived in Damascus, proving that this is the Messiah.

23 After a long time had passed, the Jews conspired to kill him, 24 but their plot became known to Saul. Now they were keeping watch on the gates day and night so as to kill him, 25 but his disciples took him one night and let him down through an opening in the wall, lowering him in a basket.

26 When he arrived in Jerusalem he tried to join the disciples, but they were all afraid of him, not believing that he was a disciple. 27 Then Barnabas took charge of him and brought him to the apostles, and he reported to them how on the way he had seen the Lord and that he had spoken to him, and how in Damascus he had spoken out boldly in the name of Jesus. 28 He moved about freely with them in Jerusalem, and spoke out boldly in the name of the Lord. 29 He also spoke and debated with the Hellenists, but they tried to kill him. 30 And when the brothers learned of this, they took him down to Caesarea and sent him on his way to Tarsus.

31 The church throughout all Judea, Galilee, and Samaria was at peace. It was being built up and walked in the fear of the Lord, and with the consolation of the holy Spirit it grew in numbers.

32 As Peter was passing through every region, he went down to the holy ones living in Lydda. 33 There he found a man named Aeneas, who had been confined to bed for eight years, for he was paralyzed. 34 Peter said to him, "Aeneas, Jesus Christ heals you. Get up and make your bed." He got up at once. 35 And all the inhabitants of Lydda and Sharon saw him, and they turned to the Lord.

got up from the ground, but when he opened his eyes he could see nothing at all, and they had to lead him into Damascus by the hand. 9 For three days he was without his sight and took neither food nor drink.

10 There was a disciple in Damascus called Ananias, and he had a vision in which the Lord said to him, 'Ananias!' When he replied, 'Here I am, Lord,' 11 the Lord said, 'Get up and go to Straight Street and ask at the house of Judas for someone called Saul, who comes from Tarsus. At this moment he is praying, 12 and has seen a man called Ananias coming in and laying hands on him to give him back his sight.'

13 But in response, Ananias said, 'Lord, I have heard from many people about this man and all the harm he has been doing to your holy people in Jerusalem. 14 He has come here with a warrant from the chief priests to arrest everybody who invokes your name.' 15 The Lord replied, 'Go, for this man is my chosen instrument to bring my name before gentiles and kings and before the people of Israel; 16 I myself will show him how much he must suffer for my name.' 17 Then Ananias went. He entered the house, and laid his hands on Saul and said, 'Brother Saul, I have been sent by the Lord Jesus, who appeared to you on your way here, so that you may recover your sight and be filled with the Holy Spirit.' 18 It was as though scales fell away from his eyes and immediately he was able to see again. So he got up and was baptised, 19 and after taking some food he regained his strength.

After he had spent only a few days with the disciples in Damascus, 20 he began preaching in the synagogues, 'Jesus is the Son of God.' 21 All his hearers were amazed, and said, 'Surely, this is the man who did such damage in Jerusalem to the people who invoke this name, and who came here for the sole purpose of arresting them to have them tried by the chief priests?' 22 Saul's power increased steadily, and he was able to throw the Jewish colony at Damascus into complete confusion by the way he demonstrated that Jesus was the Christ.

23 Some time passed, and the Jews worked out a plot to kill him, 24 but news of it reached Saul. They were keeping watch at the gates day and night in order to kill him, 25 but the disciples took him by night and let him down from the wall, lowering him in a basket.

26 When he got to Jerusalem[r] he tried to join the disciples, but they were all afraid of him: they could not believe he was really a disciple. 27 Barnabas, however, took charge of him, introduced him to the apostles, and explained how the Lord had appeared to him and spoken to him on his journey, and how he had preached fearlessly at Damascus in the name of Jesus. 28 Saul now started to go round with them in Jerusalem, preaching fearlessly in the name of the Lord. 29 But after he had spoken to the Hellenists and argued with them, they became determined to kill him. 30 When the brothers got to know of this, they took him to Caesarea and sent him off from there to Tarsus.

31 The churches throughout Judaea, Galilee and Samaria were now left in peace, building themselves up and living in the fear of the Lord; encouraged by the Holy Spirit, they continued to grow.

32 It happened that Peter visited one place after another and eventually came to God's holy people living down in Lydda. 33 There he found a man called Aeneas, a paralytic who had been bedridden for eight years. 34 Peter said to him, 'Aeneas, Jesus Christ cures you: get up and make your bed.' Aeneas got up immediately; 35 everybody who lived in Lydda and Sharon saw him, and they were converted to the Lord.

r 9 // Ga 1:18–19?

36 Now in Joppa there was a disciple whose name was Tabitha, which in Greek is Dorcas. *v* She was devoted to good works and acts of charity. 37 At that time she became ill and died. When they had washed her, they laid her in a room upstairs. 38 Since Lydda was near Joppa, the disciples, who heard that Peter was there, sent two men to him with the request, "Please come to us without delay." 39 So Peter got up and went with them; and when he arrived, they took him to the room upstairs. All the widows stood beside him, weeping and showing tunics and other clothing that Dorcas had made while she was with them. 40 Peter put all of them outside, and then he knelt down and prayed. He turned to the body and said, "Tabitha, get up." Then she opened her eyes, and seeing Peter, she sat up. 41 He gave her his hand and helped her up. Then calling the saints and widows, he showed her to be alive. 42 This became known throughout Joppa, and many believed in the Lord. 43 Meanwhile he stayed in Joppa for some time with a certain Simon, a tanner.

10 In Caesarea there was a man named Cornelius, a centurion of the Italian Cohort, as it was called. 2 He was a devout man who feared God with all his household; he gave alms generously to the people and prayed constantly to God. 3 One afternoon at about three o'clock he had a vision in which he clearly saw an angel of God coming in and saying to him, "Cornelius." 4 He stared at him in terror and said, "What is it, Lord?" He answered, "Your prayers and your alms have ascended as a memorial before God. 5 Now send men to Joppa for a certain Simon who is called Peter; 6 he is lodging with Simon, a tanner, whose house is by the seaside." 7 When the angel who spoke to him had left, he called two of his slaves and a devout soldier from the ranks of those who served him, 8 and after telling them everything, he sent them to Joppa.

9 About noon the next day, as they were on their journey and approaching the city, Peter went up on the roof to pray. 10 He became hungry and wanted something to eat; and while it was being prepared, he fell into a trance. 11 He saw the heaven opened and something like a large sheet coming down, being lowered to the ground by its four corners. 12 In it were all kinds of four-footed creatures and reptiles and birds of the air. 13 Then he heard a voice saying, "Get up, Peter; kill and eat." 14 But Peter said, "By no means, Lord; for I have never eaten anything that is profane or unclean." 15 The voice said to him again, a second time, "What God has made clean, you must not call profane." 16 This happened three times, and the thing was suddenly taken up to heaven.

17 Now while Peter was greatly puzzled about what to make of the vision that he had seen, suddenly the men sent by Cornelius appeared. They were asking for Simon's house and were standing by the gate. 18 They called out to ask whether Simon, who was called Peter, was staying there. 19 While Peter was still thinking about the vision, the Spirit said to him, "Look, three *w* men are searching for you. 20 Now get up, go down, and go with them without hesitation; for I have sent them." 21 So Peter went down to the men and said, "I am the one you are looking for; what is the reason for your coming?" 22 They answered, "Cornelius, a centurion, an upright and God-fearing man, who is well spoken of by the whole Jewish nation, was directed by a holy angel to send for you to come to his house and to hear what you have to say." 23 So Peter *x* invited them in and gave them lodging.

36 In Joppa there was a disciple named Tabitha (in Greek, Dorcas, meaning 'Gazelle'), who filled her days with acts of kindness and charity. 37 At that time she fell ill and died; and they washed her body and laid it in a room upstairs. 38 As Lydda was near Joppa, the disciples, who had heard that Peter was there, sent two men to him with the urgent request, 'Please come over to us without delay.' 39 At once Peter went off with them. When he arrived he was taken up to the room, and all the widows came and stood round him in tears, showing him the shirts and coats that Dorcas used to make while she was with them. 40 Peter sent them all outside, and knelt down and prayed; then, turning towards the body, he said, 'Tabitha, get up.' She opened her eyes, saw Peter, and sat up. 41 He gave her his hand and helped her to her feet. Then he called together the members of the church and the widows and showed her to them alive. 42 News of it spread all over Joppa, and many came to believe in the Lord. 43 Peter stayed on in Joppa for some time at the house of a tanner named Simon.

10 At Caesarea there was a man named Cornelius, a centurion in the Italian Cohort, as it was called. 2 He was a devout man, and he and his whole family joined in the worship of God; he gave generously to help the Jewish people, and was regular in his prayers to God. 3 One day about three in the afternoon he had a vision in which he clearly saw an angel of God come into his room and say, 'Cornelius!' 4 Cornelius stared at him in terror. 'What is it, my lord?' he asked. The angel said, 'Your prayers and acts of charity have gone up to heaven to speak for you before God. 5 Now send to Joppa for a man named Simon, also called Peter: 6 he is lodging with another Simon, a tanner, whose house is by the sea.' 7 When the angel who spoke to him had gone, he summoned two of his servants and a military orderly who was a religious man, 8 told them the whole story, and ordered them to Joppa.

9 Next day about noon, while they were still on their way and approaching the city, Peter went up on the roof to pray. 10 He grew hungry and wanted something to eat, but while they were getting it ready, he fell into a trance. 11 He saw heaven opened, and something coming down that looked like a great sheet of sailcloth; it was slung by the four corners and was being lowered to the earth, 12 and in it he saw creatures of every kind, four-footed beasts, reptiles, and birds. 13 There came a voice which said to him, 'Get up, Peter, kill and eat.' 14 But Peter answered, 'No, Lord! I have never eaten anything profane or unclean.' 15 The voice came again, a second time: 'It is not for you to call profane what God counts clean.' 16 This happened three times, and then the thing was taken up into heaven.

17 While Peter was still puzzling over the meaning of the vision he had seen, the messengers from Cornelius had been asking the way to Simon's house, and now arrived at the entrance. 18 They called out and asked if Simon Peter was lodging there. 19 Peter was thinking over the vision, when the Spirit said to him, 'Some men are here looking for you; 20 get up and go downstairs. You may go with them without any misgiving, for it was I who sent them.' 21 Peter came down to the men and said, 'You are looking for me? Here I am. What brings you here?' 22 'We are from the centurion Cornelius,' they replied, 'a good and religious man, acknowledged as such by the whole Jewish nation. He was directed by a holy angel to send for you to his house and hear what you have to say.' 23 So Peter asked them in and gave them a night's lodging.

---

v The name Tabitha in Aramaic and the name Dorcas in Greek mean *a gazelle* *w* One ancient authority reads *two*; others lack the word *x* Gk *he*

NEW AMERICAN BIBLE

36 Now in Joppa there was a disciple named Tabitha (which translated means Dorcas). She was completely occupied with good deeds and almsgiving. 37 Now during those days she fell sick and died, so after washing her, they laid [her] out in a room upstairs. 38 Since Lydda was near Joppa, the disciples, hearing that Peter was there, sent two men to him with the request, "Please come to us without delay." 39 So Peter got up and went with them. When he arrived, they took him to the room upstairs where all the widows came to him weeping and showing him the tunics and cloaks that Dorcas had made while she was with them. 40 Peter sent them all out and knelt down and prayed. Then he turned to her body and said, "Tabitha, rise up." She opened her eyes, saw Peter, and sat up. 41 He gave her his hand and raised her up, and when he had called the holy ones and the widows, he presented her alive. 42 This became known all over Joppa, and many came to believe in the Lord. 43 And he stayed a long time in Joppa with Simon, a tanner.

10 Now in Caesarea there was a man named Cornelius, a centurion of the Cohort called the Italica, 2 devout and God-fearing along with his whole household, who used to give alms generously to the Jewish people and pray to God constantly. 3 One afternoon about three o'clock, he saw plainly in a vision an angel of God come in to him and say to him, "Cornelius." 4 He looked intently at him and, seized with fear, said, "What is it, sir?" He said to him, "Your prayers and almsgiving have ascended as a memorial offering before God. 5 Now send some men to Joppa and summon one Simon who is called Peter. 6 He is staying with another Simon, a tanner, who has a house by the sea." 7 When the angel who spoke to him had left, he called two of his servants and a devout soldier from his staff, 8 explained everything to them, and sent them to Joppa.

9 The next day, while they were on their way and nearing the city, Peter went up to the roof terrace to pray at about noontime. 10 He was hungry and wished to eat, and while they were making preparations he fell into a trance. 11 He saw heaven opened and something resembling a large sheet coming down, lowered to the ground by its four corners. 12 In it were all the earth's four-legged animals and reptiles and the birds of the sky. 13 A voice said to him, "Get up, Peter. Slaughter and eat." 14 But Peter said, "Certainly not, sir. For never have I eaten anything profane and unclean." 15 The voice spoke to him again, a second time, "What God has made clean, you are not to call profane." 16 This happened three times, and then the object was taken up into the sky.

17 While Peter was in doubt about the meaning of the vision he had seen, the men sent by Cornelius asked for Simon's house and arrived at the entrance. 18 They called out inquiring whether Simon, who is called Peter, was staying there. 19 As Peter was pondering the vision, the Spirit said [to him], "There are three men here looking for you. 20 So get up, go downstairs, and accompany them without hesitation, because I have sent them." 21 Then Peter went down to the men and said, "I am the one you are looking for. What is the reason for your being here?" 22 They answered, "Cornelius, a centurion, an upright and God-fearing man, respected by the whole Jewish nation, was directed by a holy angel to summon you to his house and to hear what you have to say." 23 So he invited them in and showed them hospitality.

NEW JERUSALEM BIBLE

36 At Jaffa there was a disciple called Tabitha, or in Greek, Dorcas, who never tired of doing good or giving to those in need. 37 But it happened that at this time she became ill and died, and they washed her and laid her out in an upper room. 38 Lydda is not far from Jaffa, so when the disciples heard that Peter was there, they sent two men to urge him, 'Come to us without delay.' 39 Peter went back with them immediately, and on his arrival they took him to the upper room, where all the widows stood round him in tears, showing him tunics and other clothes Dorcas had made when she was with them. 40 Peter sent everyone out of the room and knelt down and prayed. Then he turned to the dead woman and said, 'Tabitha, stand up.' She opened her eyes, looked at Peter and sat up. 41 Peter helped her to her feet, then he called in the members of the congregation and widows and showed them she was alive. 42 The whole of Jaffa heard about it and many believed in the Lord. 43 Peter stayed on some time in Jaffa, lodging with a leather-tanner called Simon.

10 One of the centurions of the Italica cohort stationed in Caesarea was called Cornelius. 2 He and the whole of his household were devout and God-fearing, and he gave generously to Jewish causes and prayed constantly to God. 3 One day at about the ninth hour he had a vision in which he distinctly saw the angel of God come into his house and call out to him, 'Cornelius!' 4 He stared at the vision in terror and exclaimed, 'What is it, Lord?' The angel answered, 'Your prayers and charitable gifts have been accepted by God. 5 Now you must send some men to Jaffa and fetch a man called Simon, known as Peter, 6 who is lodging with Simon the tanner whose house is by the sea.' 7 When the angel who said this had gone, Cornelius called two of the slaves and a devout soldier of his staff, 8 told them all that had happened, and sent them off to Jaffa.

9 Next day, while they were still on their journey and had only a short distance to go before reaching the town, Peter went to the housetop at about the sixth hour to say his prayers. 10 He felt hungry and was looking forward to his meal, but before it was ready he fell into a trance 11 and saw heaven thrown open and something like a big sheet being let down to earth by its four corners; 12 it contained every kind of animal, reptile and bird. 13 A voice then said to him, 'Now, Peter, kill and eat!' 14 But Peter answered, 'Certainly not, Lord; I have never yet eaten anything profane or unclean.' 15 Again, a second time, the voice spoke to him, 'What God has made clean, you have no right to call profane.' 16 This was repeated three times, and then suddenly the container was drawn up to heaven again.

17 Peter was still at a loss over the meaning of the vision he had seen, when the men sent by Cornelius arrived. They had asked where Simon's house was and they were now standing at the door, 18 calling out to know if the Simon known as Peter was lodging there. 19 While Peter's mind was still on the vision, the Spirit told him, 'Look! Some men have come to see you. 20 Hurry down, and do not hesitate to return with them; it was I who told them to come.' 21 Peter went down and said to them, 'I am the man you are looking for; why have you come?' 22 They said, 'The centurion Cornelius, who is an upright and God-fearing man, highly regarded by the entire Jewish people, was told by God through a holy angel to send for you and bring you to his house and to listen to what you have to say.' 23 So Peter asked them in and gave them lodging.

NEW REVISED STANDARD VERSION

The next day he got up and went with them, and some of the believers*y* from Joppa accompanied him. 24 The following day they came to Caesarea. Cornelius was expecting them and had called together his relatives and close friends. 25 On Peter's arrival Cornelius met him, and falling at his feet, worshiped him. 26 But Peter made him get up, saying, "Stand up; I am only a mortal." 27 And as he talked with him, he went in and found that many had assembled; 28 and he said to them, "You yourselves know that it is unlawful for a Jew to associate with or to visit a Gentile; but God has shown me that I should not call anyone profane or unclean. 29 So when I was sent for, I came without objection. Now may I ask why you sent for me?"

30 Cornelius replied, "Four days ago at this very hour, at three o'clock, I was praying in my house when suddenly a man in dazzling clothes stood before me. 31 He said, 'Cornelius, your prayer has been heard and your alms have been remembered before God. 32 Send therefore to Joppa and ask for Simon, who is called Peter; he is staying in the home of Simon, a tanner, by the sea.' 33 Therefore I sent for you immediately, and you have been kind enough to come. So now all of us are here in the presence of God to listen to all that the Lord has commanded you to say."

34 Then Peter began to speak to them: "I truly understand that God shows no partiality, 35 but in every nation anyone who fears him and does what is right is acceptable to him. 36 You know the message he sent to the people of Israel, preaching peace by Jesus Christ—he is Lord of all. 37 That message spread throughout Judea, beginning in Galilee after the baptism that John announced: 38 how God anointed Jesus of Nazareth with the Holy Spirit and with power; how he went about doing good and healing all who were oppressed by the devil, for God was with him. 39 We are witnesses to all that he did both in Judea and in Jerusalem. They put him to death by hanging him on a tree; 40 but God raised him on the third day and allowed him to appear, 41 not to all the people but to us who were chosen by God as witnesses, and who ate and drank with him after he rose from the dead. 42 He commanded us to preach to the people and to testify that he is the one ordained by God as judge of the living and the dead. 43 All the prophets testify about him that everyone who believes in him receives forgiveness of sins through his name."

44 While Peter was still speaking, the Holy Spirit fell upon all who heard the word. 45 The circumcised believers who had come with Peter were astounded that the gift of the Holy Spirit had been poured out even on the Gentiles, 46 for they heard them speaking in tongues and extolling God. Then Peter said, 47 "Can anyone withhold the water for baptizing these people who have received the Holy Spirit just as we have?" 48 So he ordered them to be baptized in the name of Jesus Christ. Then they invited him to stay for several days.

11 Now the apostles and the believers*y* who were in Judea heard that the Gentiles had also accepted the word of God. 2 So when Peter went up to Jerusalem, the circumcised believers*z* criticized him, 3 saying, "Why did you go to uncircumcised men and eat with them?" 4 Then Peter began to explain it to them, step by step, saying, 5 "I

REVISED ENGLISH BIBLE

Next day he set out with them, accompanied by some members of the congregation at Joppa, 24 and on the following day arrived at Caesarea. Cornelius was expecting them and had called together his relatives and close friends. 25 When Peter arrived, Cornelius came to meet him, and bowed to the ground in deep reverence. 26 But Peter raised him to his feet and said, 'Stand up; I am only a man like you.' 27 Still talking with him he went in and found a large gathering. 28 He said to them, 'I need not tell you that a Jew is forbidden by his religion to visit or associate with anyone of another race. Yet God has shown me clearly that I must not call anyone profane or unclean; 29 that is why I came here without demur when you sent for me. May I ask what was your reason for doing so?'

30 Cornelius said, 'Three days ago, just about this time, I was in the house here saying the afternoon prayers, when suddenly a man in shining robes stood before me. 31 He said: "Cornelius, your prayer has been heard and your acts of charity have spoken for you before God. 32 Send to Simon Peter at Joppa, and ask him to come; he is lodging in the house of Simon the tanner, by the sea." 33 I sent to you there and then, and you have been good enough to come. So now we are all met here before God, to listen to everything that the Lord has instructed you to say.'

34 Peter began: 'I now understand how true it is that God has no favourites, 35 but that in every nation those who are god-fearing and do what is right are acceptable to him. 36 He sent his word to the Israelites and gave the good news of peace through Jesus Christ, who is Lord of all. 37 I need not tell you what has happened lately all over the land of the Jews, starting from Galilee after the baptism proclaimed by John. 38 You know how God anointed Jesus of Nazareth with the Holy Spirit and with power. Because God was with him he went about doing good and healing all who were oppressed by the devil. 39 And we can bear witness to all that he did in the Jewish countryside and in Jerusalem. They put him to death, hanging him on a gibbet; 40 but God raised him to life on the third day, and allowed him to be clearly seen, 41 not by the whole people, but by witnesses whom God had chosen in advance—by us, who ate and drank with him after he rose from the dead. 42 He commanded us to proclaim him to the people, and affirm that he is the one designated by God as judge of the living and the dead. 43 It is to him that all the prophets testify, declaring that everyone who trusts in him receives forgiveness of sins through his name.'

44 Peter was still speaking when the Holy Spirit came upon all who were listening to the message. 45 The believers who had come with Peter, men of Jewish birth, were amazed that the gift of the Holy Spirit should have been poured out even on Gentiles, 46 for they could hear them speaking in tongues of ecstasy and acclaiming the greatness of God. Then Peter spoke: 47 'Is anyone prepared to withhold the water of baptism from these persons, who have received the Holy Spirit just as we did?' 48 Then he ordered them to be baptized in the name of Jesus Christ. After that they asked him to stay on with them for a time.

11 News came to the apostles and the members of the church in Judaea that Gentiles too had accepted the word of God; 2 and when Peter came up to Jerusalem those who were of Jewish birth took issue with him. 3 'You have been visiting men who are uncircumcised,' they said, 'and sitting at table with them!' 4 Peter began by laying before them the facts as they had happened.

The next day he got up and went with them, and some of the brothers from Joppa went with him. 24 On the following day he entered Caesarea. Cornelius was expecting them and had called together his relatives and close friends. 25 When Peter entered, Cornelius met him and, falling at his feet, paid him homage. 26 Peter, however, raised him up, saying, "Get up. I myself am also a human being." 27 While he conversed with him, he went in and found many people gathered together 28 and said to them, "You know that it is unlawful for a Jewish man to associate with, or visit, a Gentile, but God has shown me that I should not call any person profane or unclean. 29 And that is why I came without objection when sent for. May I ask, then, why you summoned me?"

30 Cornelius replied, "Four days ago at this hour, three o'clock in the afternoon, I was at prayer in my house when suddenly a man in dazzling robes stood before me and said, 31 'Cornelius, your prayer has been heard and your almsgiving remembered before God. 32 Send therefore to Joppa and summon Simon, who is called Peter. He is a guest in the house of Simon, a tanner, by the sea.' 33 So I sent for you immediately, and you were kind enough to come. Now therefore we are all here in the presence of God to listen to all that you have been commanded by the Lord."

34 Then Peter proceeded to speak and said, "In truth, I see that God shows no partiality. 35 Rather, in every nation whoever fears him and acts uprightly is acceptable to him. 36 You know the word [that] he sent to the Israelites as he proclaimed peace through Jesus Christ, who is Lord of all, 37 what has happened all over Judea, beginning in Galilee after the baptism that John preached, 38 how God anointed Jesus of Nazareth with the holy Spirit and power. He went about doing good and healing all those oppressed by the devil, for God was with him. 39 We are witnesses of all that he did both in the country of the Jews and [in] Jerusalem. They put him to death by hanging him on a tree. 40 This man God raised [on] the third day and granted that he be visible, 41 not to all the people, but to us, the witnesses chosen by God in advance, who ate and drank with him after he rose from the dead. 42 He commissioned us to preach to the people and testify that he is the one appointed by God as judge of the living and the dead. 43 To him all the prophets bear witness, that everyone who believes in him will receive forgiveness of sins through his name."

44 While Peter was still speaking these things, the holy Spirit fell upon all who were listening to the word. 45 The circumcised believers who had accompanied Peter were astounded that the gift of the holy Spirit should have been poured out on the Gentiles also, 46 for they could hear them speaking in tongues and glorifying God. Then Peter responded, 47 "Can anyone withhold the water for baptizing these people, who have received the holy Spirit even as we have?" 48 He ordered them to be baptized in the name of Jesus Christ. 49 Then they invited him to stay for a few days.

11 Now the apostles and the brothers who were in Judea heard that the Gentiles too had accepted the word of God. 2 So when Peter went up to Jerusalem the circumcised believers confronted him, 3 saying, "You entered the house of uncircumcised people and ate with them." 4 Peter began and explained it to them step by step,

Next day, he was ready to go off with them, accompanied by some of the brothers from Jaffa. 24 They reached Caesarea the following day, and Cornelius was waiting for them. He had asked his relations and close friends to be there, 25 and as Peter reached the house Cornelius went out to meet him, fell at his feet and did him reverence. 26 But Peter helped him up. 'Stand up,' he said, 'after all, I am only a man!' 27 Talking together they went in to meet all the people assembled there, 28 and Peter said to them, 'You know it is forbidden for Jews to mix with people of another race and visit them; but God has made it clear to me that I must not call anyone profane or unclean. 29 That is why I made no objection to coming when I was sent for; but I should like to know exactly why you sent for me.' 30 Cornelius replied, 'At this time three days ago I was in my house saying the prayers for the ninth hour, when I suddenly saw a man in front of me in shining robes. 31 He said, "Cornelius, your prayer has been heard and your charitable gifts have not been forgotten by God; 32 so now you must send to Jaffa and fetch Simon known as Peter who is lodging in the house of Simon the tanner, by the sea." 33 So I sent for you at once, and you have been kind enough to come. Here we all are, assembled in front of you to hear all the instructions God has given you.'

34 Then Peter addressed them, 'I now really understand', he said, 'that God has no favourites, 35 but that anybody of any nationality who fears him and does what is right is acceptable to him.

36 'God sent his word to the people of Israel, and it was to them that *the good news of peace was brought*[u] by Jesus Christ — he is the Lord of all. 37 You know what happened all over Judaea, how Jesus of Nazareth began in Galilee, after John had been preaching baptism. 38 *God had anointed him with the Holy Spirit* and with power, and because God was with him, Jesus went about doing good and curing all who had fallen into the power of the devil. 39 Now we are witnesses to everything he did throughout the countryside of Judaea and in Jerusalem itself: and they killed him by hanging him on a tree, 40 yet on the third day God raised him to life and allowed him to be seen, 41 not by the whole people but only by certain witnesses that God had chosen beforehand. Now we are those witnesses — we have eaten and drunk with him after his resurrection from the dead — 42 and he has ordered us to proclaim this to his people and to bear witness that God has appointed him to judge everyone, alive or dead. 43 It is to him that all the prophets bear this witness: that all who believe in Jesus will have their sins forgiven through his name.'

44 While Peter was still speaking the Holy Spirit came down[v] on all the listeners. 45 Jewish believers who had accompanied Peter were all astonished that the gift of the Holy Spirit should be poured out on gentiles too, 46 since they could hear them speaking strange languages and proclaiming the greatness of God. Peter himself then said, 47 'Could anyone refuse the water of baptism to these people, now they have received the Holy Spirit just as we have?' 48 He then gave orders for them to be baptised in the name of Jesus Christ. Afterwards they begged him to stay on for some days.

11 The apostles and the brothers in Judaea heard that gentiles too had accepted the word of God, 2 and when Peter came up to Jerusalem the circumcised believers protested to him 3 and said, 'So you have been visiting the uncircumcised and eating with them!' 4 Peter in reply gave them the details point by point, 5 'One day, when I was in

was in the city of Joppa praying, and in a trance I saw a vision. There was something like a large sheet coming down from heaven, being lowered by its four corners; and it came close to me. 6 As I looked at it closely I saw four-footed animals, beasts of prey, reptiles, and birds of the air. 7 I also heard a voice saying to me, 'Get up, Peter; kill and eat.' 8 But I replied, 'By no means, Lord; for nothing profane or unclean has ever entered my mouth.' 9 But a second time the voice answered from heaven, 'What God has made clean, you must not call profane.' 10 This happened three times; then everything was pulled up again to heaven. 11 At that very moment three men, sent to me from Caesarea, arrived at the house where we were. 12 The Spirit told me to go with them and not to make a distinction between them and us. *a* These six brothers also accompanied me, and we entered the man's house. 13 He told us how he had seen the angel standing in his house and saying, 'Send to Joppa and bring Simon, who is called Peter; 14 he will give you a message by which you and your entire household will be saved.' 15 And as I began to speak, the Holy Spirit fell upon them just as it had upon us at the beginning. 16 And I remembered the word of the Lord, how he had said, 'John baptized with water, but you will be baptized with the Holy Spirit.' 17 If then God gave them the same gift that he gave us when we believed in the Lord Jesus Christ, who was I that I could hinder God?" 18 When they heard this, they were silenced. And they praised God, saying, "Then God has given even to the Gentiles the repentance that leads to life."

19 Now those who were scattered because of the persecution that took place over Stephen traveled as far as Phoenicia, Cyprus, and Antioch, and they spoke the word to no one except Jews. 20 But among them were some men of Cyprus and Cyrene who, on coming to Antioch, spoke to the Hellenists*b* also, proclaiming the Lord Jesus. 21 The hand of the Lord was with them, and a great number became believers and turned to the Lord. 22 News of this came to the ears of the church in Jerusalem, and they sent Barnabas to Antioch. 23 When he came and saw the grace of God, he rejoiced, and he exhorted them all to remain faithful to the Lord with steadfast devotion; 24 for he was a good man, full of the Holy Spirit and of faith. And a great many people were brought to the Lord. 25 Then Barnabas went to Tarsus to look for Saul, 26 and when he had found him, he brought him to Antioch. So it was that for an entire year they met with*c* the church and taught a great many people, and it was in Antioch that the disciples were first called "Christians."

27 At that time prophets came down from Jerusalem to Antioch. 28 One of them named Agabus stood up and predicted by the Spirit that there would be a severe famine over all the world; and this took place during the reign of Claudius. 29 The disciples determined that according to their ability, each would send relief to the believers*d* living in Judea; 30 this they did, sending it to the elders by Barnabas and Saul.

5 'I was at prayer in the city of Joppa,' he said, 'and while in a trance I had a vision: I saw something coming down that looked like a great sheet of sailcloth, slung by the four corners and lowered from heaven till it reached me. 6 I looked intently to make out what was in it and I saw four-footed beasts, wild animals, reptiles, and birds. 7 Then I heard a voice saying to me, "Get up, Peter, kill and eat." 8 But I said, "No, Lord! Nothing profane or unclean has ever entered my mouth." 9 A voice from heaven came a second time: "It is not for you to call profane what God counts clean." 10 This happened three times, and then they were all drawn up again into heaven. 11 At that very moment three men who had been sent to me from Caesarea arrived at the house where I was staying; 12 and the Spirit told me to go with them. My six companions here came with me and we went into the man's house. 13 He told us how he had seen an angel standing in his house who said, "Send to Joppa for Simon Peter. 14 He will speak words that will bring salvation to you and all your household." 15 Hardly had I begun speaking, when the Holy Spirit came upon them, just as upon us at the beginning, 16 and I recalled what the Lord had said: "John baptized with water, but you will be baptized with the Holy Spirit." 17 God gave them no less a gift than he gave us when we came to believe in the Lord Jesus Christ. How could I stand in God's way?'

18 When they heard this their doubts were silenced, and they gave praise to God. 'This means', they said, 'that God has granted life-giving repentance to the Gentiles also.'

19 MEANWHILE those who had been scattered after the persecution that arose over Stephen made their way to Phoenicia, Cyprus, and Antioch, bringing the message to Jews only and to no others. 20 But there were some natives of Cyprus and Cyrene among them, and these, when they arrived at Antioch, began to speak to Gentiles as well, telling them the good news of the Lord Jesus. 21 The power of the Lord was with them, and a great many became believers and turned to the Lord.

22 The news reached the ears of the church in Jerusalem; and they sent Barnabas to Antioch. 23 When he arrived and saw the divine grace at work, he rejoiced and encouraged them all to hold fast to the Lord with resolute hearts, 24 for he was a good man, full of the Holy Spirit and of faith. And large numbers were won over to the Lord.

25 He then went off to Tarsus to look for Saul; 26 and when he had found him, he brought him to Antioch. For a whole year the two of them lived in fellowship with the church there, and gave instruction to large numbers. It was in Antioch that the disciples first got the name of Christians.

27 During this period some prophets came down from Jerusalem to Antioch, 28 and one of them, Agabus by name, was inspired to stand up and predict a severe and world-wide famine, which in fact occurred in the reign of Claudius. 29 So the disciples agreed to make a contribution, each according to his means, for the relief of their fellow-Christians in Judaea. 30 This they did, and sent it off to the elders, entrusting it to Barnabas and Saul.

12 About that time King Herod laid violent hands upon some who belonged to the church. 2 He had James, the brother of John, killed with the sword. 3 After he saw that it pleased the Jews, he proceeded to arrest Peter also. (This was during the festival of Unleavened Bread.) 4 When

12 IT was about this time that King Herod launched an attack on certain members of the church. 2 He beheaded James, the brother of John, 3 and, when he saw that the Jews approved, proceeded to arrest Peter also. This happened during the festival of Unleavened Bread. 4 Having

---

a Or *not to hesitate* *b* Other ancient authorities read *Greeks*
c Or *were guests of* *d* Gk *brothers*

11:11 **I was:** *some witnesses read* we were. 11:12 **with them:** *some witnesses add* making no distinctions; *others add* without any misgiving, *as in 10:20.*

saying, 5 "I was at prayer in the city of Joppa when in a trance I had a vision, something resembling a large sheet coming down, lowered from the sky by its four corners, and it came to me. 6 Looking intently into it, I observed and saw the four-legged animals of the earth, the wild beasts, the reptiles, and the birds of the sky. 7 I also heard a voice say to me, 'Get up, Peter. Slaughter and eat.' 8 But I said, 'Certainly not, sir, because nothing profane or unclean has ever entered my mouth.' 9 But a second time a voice from heaven answered, 'What God has made clean, you are not to call profane.' 10 This happened three times, and then everything was drawn up again into the sky. 11 Just then three men appeared at the house where we were, who had been sent to me from Caesarea. 12 The Spirit told me to accompany them without discriminating. These six brothers also went with me, and we entered the man's house. 13 He related to us how he had seen [the] angel standing in his house, saying, 'Send someone to Joppa and summon Simon, who is called Peter, 14 who will speak words to you by which you and all your household will be saved.' 15 As I began to speak, the holy Spirit fell upon them as it had upon us at the beginning, 16 and I remembered the word of the Lord, how he had said, 'John baptized with water but you will be baptized with the holy Spirit.' 17 If then God gave them the same gift he gave to us when we came to believe in the Lord Jesus Christ, who was I to be able to hinder God?" 18 When they heard this, they stopped objecting and glorified God, saying, "God has then granted life-giving repentance to the Gentiles too."

19 Now those who had been scattered by the persecution that arose because of Stephen went as far as Phoenicia, Cyprus, and Antioch, preaching the word to no one but Jews. 20 There were some Cypriots and Cyrenians among them, however, who came to Antioch and began to speak to the Greeks as well, proclaiming the Lord Jesus. 21 The hand of the Lord was with them and a great number who believed turned to the Lord. 22 The news about them reached the ears of the church in Jerusalem, and they sent Barnabas [to go] to Antioch. 23 When he arrived and saw the grace of God, he rejoiced and encouraged them all to remain faithful to the Lord in firmness of heart, 24 for he was a good man, filled with the holy Spirit and faith. And a large number of people was added to the Lord. 25 Then he went to Tarsus to look for Saul, 26 and when he had found him he brought him to Antioch. For a whole year they met with the church and taught a large number of people, and it was in Antioch that the disciples were first called Christians.

27 At that time some prophets came down from Jerusalem to Antioch, 28 and one of them named Agabus stood up and predicted by the Spirit that there would be a severe famine all over the world, and it happened under Claudius. 29 So the disciples determined that, according to ability, each should send relief to the brothers who lived in Judea. 30 This they did, sending it to the presbyters in care of Barnabas and Saul.

12 About that time King Herod laid hands upon some members of the church to harm them. 2 He had James, the brother of John, killed by the sword, 3 and when he saw that this was pleasing to the Jews he proceeded to arrest Peter also. (It was [the] feast of Unleavened Bread.)

the town of Jaffa,' he began, 'I fell into a trance as I was praying and had a vision of something like a big sheet being let down from heaven by its four corners. This sheet came right down beside me. 6 I looked carefully into it and saw four-footed animals of the earth, wild beasts, reptiles, and birds of heaven. 7 Then I heard a voice that said to me, "Now, Peter, kill and eat!" 8 But I answered, "Certainly not, Lord; nothing profane or unclean has ever crossed my lips." 9 And a second time the voice spoke from heaven, "What God has made clean, you have no right to call profane." 10 This was repeated three times, before the whole of it was drawn up to heaven again.

11 'Just at that moment, three men stopped outside the house where we were staying; they had been sent from Caesarea to fetch me, 12 and the Spirit told me to have no hesitation about going back with them. The six brothers here came with me as well, and we entered the man's house. 13 He told us he had seen an angel standing in his house who said, "Send to Jaffa and fetch Simon known as Peter; 14 he has a message for you that will save you and your entire household."

15 'I had scarcely begun to speak when the Holy Spirit came down on them in the same way as it came on us at the beginning, 16 and I remembered that the Lord had said, "John baptised with water, but you will be baptised with the Holy Spirit." 17 I realised then that God was giving them the identical gift he gave to us when we believed in the Lord Jesus Christ; and who was I to stand in God's way?'

18 This account satisfied them, and they gave glory to God, saying, 'God has clearly granted to the gentiles too the repentance that leads to life.'

19 Those who had scattered because of the persecution that arose over Stephen travelled as far as Phoenicia and Cyprus and Antioch, but they proclaimed the message only to Jews. 20 Some of them, however, who came from Cyprus and Cyrene, went to Antioch where they started preaching also to the Greeks, proclaiming the good news of the Lord Jesus to them. 21 The Lord helped them, and a great number believed and were converted to the Lord.

22 The news of them came to the ears of the church in Jerusalem and they sent Barnabas out to Antioch. 23 There he was glad to see for himself that God had given grace, and he urged them all to remain faithful to the Lord with heartfelt devotion; 24 for he was a good man, filled with the Holy Spirit and with faith. And a large number of people were won over to the Lord.

25 Barnabas then left for Tarsus to look for Saul, 26 and when he found him he brought him to Antioch. And it happened that they stayed together in that church a whole year, instructing a large number of people. It was at Antioch that the disciples were first called 'Christians'.

27 While they were there some prophets came down to Antioch from Jerusalem, 28 and one of them whose name was Agabus, seized by the Spirit, stood up and predicted that a severe and universal famine was going to happen. This in fact happened while Claudius was emperor. 29 The disciples decided to send relief, each to contribute what he could afford, to the brothers living in Judaea. 30 They did this and delivered their contributions to the elders through the agency of Barnabas and Saul.

12 It was about this time that King Herod started persecuting certain members of the church. 2 He had James the brother of John beheaded, 3 and when he saw that this pleased the Jews he went on to arrest Peter as well. 4 As

NEW REVISED STANDARD VERSION

he had seized him, he put him in prison and handed him over to four squads of soldiers to guard him, intending to bring him out to the people after the Passover. 5 While Peter was kept in prison, the church prayed fervently to God for him.

6 The very night before Herod was going to bring him out, Peter, bound with two chains, was sleeping between two soldiers, while guards in front of the door were keeping watch over the prison. 7 Suddenly an angel of the Lord appeared and a light shone in the cell. He tapped Peter on the side and woke him, saying, "Get up quickly." And the chains fell off his wrists. 8 The angel said to him, "Fasten your belt and put on your sandals." He did so. Then he said to him, "Wrap your cloak around you and follow me." 9 Peter*e* went out and followed him; he did not realize that what was happening with the angel's help was real; he thought he was seeing a vision. 10 After they had passed the first and the second guard, they came before the iron gate leading into the city. It opened for them of its own accord, and they went outside and walked along a lane, when suddenly the angel left him. 11 Then Peter came to himself and said, "Now I am sure that the Lord has sent his angel and rescued me from the hands of Herod and from all that the Jewish people were expecting."

12 As soon as he realized this, he went to the house of Mary, the mother of John whose other name was Mark, where many had gathered and were praying. 13 When he knocked at the outer gate, a maid named Rhoda came to answer. 14 On recognizing Peter's voice, she was so overjoyed that, instead of opening the gate, she ran in and announced that Peter was standing at the gate. 15 They said to her, "You are out of your mind!" But she insisted that it was so. They said, "It is his angel." 16 Meanwhile Peter continued knocking; and when they opened the gate, they saw him and were amazed. 17 He motioned to them with his hand to be silent, and described for them how the Lord had brought him out of the prison. And he added, "Tell this to James and to the believers."*f* Then he left and went to another place.

18 When morning came, there was no small commotion among the soldiers over what had become of Peter. 19 When Herod had searched for him and could not find him, he examined the guards and ordered them to be put to death. Then he went down from Judea to Caesarea and stayed there.

20 Now Herod*g* was angry with the people of Tyre and Sidon. So they came to him in a body; and after winning over Blastus, the king's chamberlain, they asked for a reconciliation, because their country depended on the king's country for food. 21 On an appointed day Herod put on his royal robes, took his seat on the platform, and delivered a public address to them. 22 The people kept shouting, "The voice of a god, and not of a mortal!" 23 And immediately, because he had not given the glory to God, an angel of the Lord struck him down, and he was eaten by worms and died.

24 But the word of God continued to advance and gain adherents. 25 Then after completing their mission Barnabas and Saul returned to*h* Jerusalem and brought with them John, whose other name was Mark.

13 Now in the church at Antioch there were prophets and teachers: Barnabas, Simeon who was called Niger, Lucius of Cyrene, Manaen a member of the court of Herod the ruler,*i* and Saul. 2 While they were worshiping the Lord and fasting, the Holy Spirit said, "Set apart for me Barnabas and Saul for the work to which I have called

REVISED ENGLISH BIBLE

secured him, he put him in prison under a military guard, four squads of four men each, meaning to produce him in public after Passover. 5 So, while Peter was held in prison, the church kept praying fervently to God for him.

6 On the very night before Herod had planned to produce him, Peter was asleep between two soldiers, secured by two chains, while outside the doors sentries kept guard over the prison. 7 All at once an angel of the Lord stood there, and the cell was ablaze with light. He tapped Peter on the shoulder to wake him. 'Quick! Get up!' he said, and the chains fell away from Peter's wrists. 8 The angel said, 'Do up your belt and put on your sandals.' He did so. 'Now wrap your cloak round you and follow me.' 9 Peter followed him out, with no idea that the angel's intervention was real: he thought it was just a vision. 10 They passed the first guardpost, then the second, and reached the iron gate leading out into the city. This opened for them of its own accord; they came out and had walked the length of one street when suddenly the angel left him.

11 Then Peter came to himself. 'Now I know it is true,' he said: 'the Lord has sent his angel and rescued me from Herod's clutches and from all that the Jewish people were expecting.' 12 Once he had realized this, he made for the house of Mary, the mother of John Mark, where a large company was at prayer. 13 He knocked at the outer door and a maidservant called Rhoda came to answer it. 14 She recognized Peter's voice and was so overjoyed that instead of opening the door she ran in and announced that Peter was standing outside. 15 'You are crazy,' they told her; but she insisted that it was so. Then they said, 'It must be his angel.'

16 Peter went on knocking, and when they opened the door and saw him, they were astounded. 17 He motioned to them with his hand to keep quiet, and described to them how the Lord had brought him out of prison. 'Tell James and the members of the church,' he said. Then he left the house and went off elsewhere.

18 When morning came, there was consternation among the soldiers: what could have become of Peter? 19 Herod made careful search, but failed to find him, so he interrogated the guards and ordered their execution.

Afterwards Herod left Judaea to reside for a while at Caesarea. 20 He had for some time been very angry with the people of Tyre and Sidon, who now by common agreement presented themselves at his court. There they won over Blastus the royal chamberlain, and sued for peace, because their country drew its supplies from the king's territory. 21 On an appointed day Herod, attired in his royal robes and seated on the rostrum, addressed the populace; 22 they responded, 'It is a god speaking, not a man!' 23 Instantly an angel of the Lord struck him down, because he had usurped the honour due to God; he was eaten up with worms and so died.

24 Meanwhile the word of God continued to grow and spread; 25 and Barnabas and Saul, their task fulfilled, returned from Jerusalem, taking John Mark with them.

13 THERE were in the church at Antioch certain prophets and teachers: Barnabas, Simeon called Niger, Lucius of Cyrene, Manaen, a close friend of Prince Herod, and Saul. 2 While they were offering worship to the Lord and fasting, the Holy Spirit said, 'Set Barnabas and Saul apart for me, to do the work to which I have called them.'

NEW AMERICAN BIBLE

NEW JERUSALEM BIBLE

4 He had him taken into custody and put in prison under the guard of four squads of four soldiers each. He intended to bring him before the people after Passover. 5 Peter thus was being kept in prison, but prayer by the church was fervently being made to God on his behalf.

6 On the very night before Herod was to bring him to trial, Peter, secured by double chains, was sleeping between two soldiers, while outside the door guards kept watch on the prison. 7 Suddenly the angel of the Lord stood by him and a light shone in the cell. He tapped Peter on the side and awakened him, saying, "Get up quickly." The chains fell from his wrists. 8 The angel said to him, "Put on your belt and your sandals." He did so. Then he said to him, "Put on your cloak and follow me." 9 So he followed him out, not realizing that what was happening through the angel was real; he thought he was seeing a vision. 10 They passed the first guard, then the second, and came to the iron gate leading out to the city, which opened for them by itself. They emerged and made their way down an alley, and suddenly the angel left him. 11 Then Peter recovered his senses and said, "Now I know for certain that [the] Lord sent his angel and rescued me from the hand of Herod and from all that the Jewish people had been expecting." 12 When he realized this, he went to the house of Mary, the mother of John who is called Mark, where there were many people gathered in prayer. 13 When he knocked on the gateway door, a maid named Rhoda came to answer it. 14 She was so overjoyed when she recognized Peter's voice that, instead of opening the gate, she ran in and announced that Peter was standing at the gate. 15 They told her, "You are out of your mind," but she insisted that it was so. But they kept saying, "It is his angel." 16 But Peter continued to knock, and when they opened it, they saw him and were astounded. 17 He motioned to them with his hand to be quiet and explained [to them] how the Lord had led him out of the prison, and said, "Report this to James and the brothers." Then he left and went to another place. 18 At daybreak there was no small commotion among the soldiers over what had become of Peter. 19 Herod, after instituting a search but not finding him, ordered the guards tried and executed. Then he left Judea to spend some time in Caesarea.

20 He had long been very angry with the people of Tyre and Sidon, who now came to him in a body. After winning over Blastus, the king's chamberlain, they sued for peace because their country was supplied with food from the king's territory. 21 On an appointed day, Herod, attired in royal robes, [and] seated on the rostrum, addressed them publicly. 22 The assembled crowd cried out, "This is the voice of a god, not of a man." 23 At once the angel of the Lord struck him down because he did not ascribe the honor to God, and he was eaten by worms and breathed his last. 24 But the word of God continued to spread and grow.

25 After Barnabas and Saul completed their relief mission, they returned to Jerusalem, taking with them John, who is called Mark.

it was during the days of Unleavened Bread that he had arrested him, he put him in prison, assigning four sections of four soldiers each to guard him, meaning to try him in public after the Passover. 5 All the time Peter was under guard the church prayed to God for him unremittingly.

6 On the night before Herod was to try him, Peter was sleeping between two soldiers, fastened with two chains, while guards kept watch at the main entrance to the prison. 7 Then suddenly an angel of the Lord stood there, and the cell was filled with light. He tapped Peter on the side and woke him. 'Get up!' he said, 'Hurry!'—and the chains fell from his hands. 8 The angel then said, 'Put on your belt and sandals.' After he had done this, the angel next said, 'Wrap your cloak round you and follow me.' 9 He followed him out, but had no idea that what the angel did was all happening in reality; he thought he was seeing a vision. 10 They passed through the first guard post and then the second and reached the iron gate leading to the city. This opened of its own accord; they went through it and had walked the whole length of one street when suddenly the angel left him. 11 It was only then that Peter came to himself. And he said, 'Now I know it is all true. The Lord really did send his angel and save me from Herod and from all that the Jewish people were expecting.'

12 As soon as he had realised this he went straight to the house of Mary the mother of John Mark, where a number of people had assembled and were praying. 13 He knocked at the outside door and a servant called Rhoda came to answer it. 14 She recognised Peter's voice and was so overcome with joy that, instead of opening the door, she ran inside with the news that Peter was standing at the main entrance. 15 They said to her, 'You are out of your mind,' but she insisted that it was true. Then they said, 'It must be his angel!' 16 Peter, meanwhile, was still knocking. When they opened the door, they were amazed to see that it really was Peter himself. 17 He raised his hand for silence and described to them how the Lord had led him out of prison. He added, 'Tell James and the brothers.' Then he left and went elsewhere.

18 When daylight came there was a great commotion among the soldiers, who could not imagine what had become of Peter. 19 Herod put out an unsuccessful search for him; he had the guards questioned, and before leaving Judaea to take up residence in Caesarea he gave orders for their execution.

20 w Now Herod was on bad terms with the Tyrians and Sidonians. Yet they sent a joint deputation which managed to enlist the support of Blastus, the king's chamberlain, and through him negotiated a treaty, since their country depended for its food supply on the king's territory. 21 A day was fixed, and Herod, wearing his robes of state and seated on a throne, began to make a speech to them. 22 The people acclaimed him with, 'It is a god speaking, not a man!' 23 and at that moment the angel of the Lord struck him down, because he had not given the glory to God. He was eaten away by worms and died.

24 The word of God continued to spread and to gain followers.

25 Barnabas and Saul completed their task at Jerusalem and came back, bringing John Mark with them.

13 Now there were in the church at Antioch prophets and teachers: Barnabas, Symeon who was called Niger, Lucius of Cyrene, Manaen who was a close friend of Herod the tetrarch, and Saul. 2 While they were worshiping the Lord and fasting, the holy Spirit said, "Set apart for me Barnabas and Saul for the work to which I have called

13 In the church at Antioch the following were prophets and teachers: Barnabas, Simeon called Niger, and Lucius of Cyrene, Manaen, who had been brought up with Herod the tetrarch, and Saul. 2 One day while they were offering worship to the Lord and keeping a fast, the Holy Spirit said, 'I want Barnabas and Saul set apart for the work to which I have called them.' 3 So it was that after

w 12 cf. 2 M 9:5–28.

them." 3 Then after fasting and praying they laid their hands on them and sent them off.

4 So, being sent out by the Holy Spirit, they went down to Seleucia; and from there they sailed to Cyprus. 5 When they arrived at Salamis, they proclaimed the word of God in the synagogues of the Jews. And they had John also to assist them. 6 When they had gone through the whole island as far as Paphos, they met a certain magician, a Jewish false prophet, named Bar-Jesus. 7 He was with the proconsul, Sergius Paulus, an intelligent man, who summoned Barnabas and Saul and wanted to hear the word of God. 8 But the magician Elymas (for that is the translation of his name) opposed them and tried to turn the proconsul away from the faith. 9 But Saul, also known as Paul, filled with the Holy Spirit, looked intently at him 10 and said, "You son of the devil, you enemy of all righteousness, full of all deceit and villainy, will you not stop making crooked the straight paths of the Lord? 11 And now listen — the hand of the Lord is against you, and you will be blind for a while, unable to see the sun." Immediately mist and darkness came over him, and he went about groping for someone to lead him by the hand. 12 When the proconsul saw what had happened, he believed, for he was astonished at the teaching about the Lord.

13 Then Paul and his companions set sail from Paphos and came to Perga in Pamphylia. John, however, left them and returned to Jerusalem; 14 but they went on from Perga and came to Antioch in Pisidia. And on the sabbath day they went into the synagogue and sat down. 15 After the reading of the law and the prophets, the officials of the synagogue sent them a message, saying, "Brothers, if you have any word of exhortation for the people, give it." 16 So Paul stood up and with a gesture began to speak:

"You Israelites, *j* and others who fear God, listen. 17 The God of this people Israel chose our ancestors and made the people great during their stay in the land of Egypt, and with uplifted arm he led them out of it. 18 For about forty years he put up with*k* them in the wilderness. 19 After he had destroyed seven nations in the land of Canaan, he gave them their land as an inheritance 20 for about four hundred fifty years. After that he gave them judges until the time of the prophet Samuel. 21 Then they asked for a king; and God gave them Saul son of Kish, a man of the tribe of Benjamin, who reigned for forty years. 22 When he had removed him, he made David their king. In his testimony about him he said, 'I have found David, son of Jesse, to be a man after my heart, who will carry out all my wishes.' 23 Of this man's posterity God has brought to Israel a Savior, Jesus, as he promised; 24 before his coming John had already proclaimed a baptism of repentance to all the people of Israel. 25 And as John was finishing his work, he said, 'What do you suppose that I am? I am not he. No, but one is coming after me; I am not worthy to untie the thong of the sandals*l* on his feet.'

26 "My brothers, you descendants of Abraham's family, and others who fear God, to us*m* the message of this salvation has been sent. 27 Because the residents of Jerusalem and their leaders did not recognize him or understand the words of the prophets that are read every sabbath, they fulfilled those words by condemning him. 28 Even though they found no cause for a sentence of death, they asked Pilate to have him killed. 29 When they had carried out everything that was written about him, they took him down from the tree and laid him in a tomb. 30 But God raised him from the dead; 31 and for many days he appeared to those

3 Then, after further fasting and prayer, they laid their hands on them and sent them on their way.

4 These two, sent out on their mission by the Holy Spirit, came down to Seleucia, and from there sailed to Cyprus. 5 Arriving at Salamis, they declared the word of God in the Jewish synagogues; they had John with them as their assistant. 6 They went through the whole island as far as Paphos, and there they came upon a sorcerer, a Jew who posed as a prophet, Barjesus by name. 7 He was in the retinue of the governor, Sergius Paulus, a learned man, who had sent for Barnabas and Saul and wanted to hear the word of God. 8 This Elymas the sorcerer (so his name may be translated) opposed them, trying to turn the governor away from the faith. 9 But Saul, also known as Paul, filled with the Holy Spirit, fixed his eyes on him 10 and said, 'You are a swindler, an out-and-out fraud! You son of the devil and enemy of all goodness, will you never stop perverting the straight ways of the Lord? 11 Look now, the hand of the Lord strikes: you shall be blind, and for a time you shall not see the light of the sun.' At once mist and darkness came over his eyes, and he groped about for someone to lead him by the hand. 12 When the governor saw what had happened he became a believer, deeply impressed by what he learnt about the Lord.

13 Sailing from Paphos, Paul and his companions went to Perga in Pamphylia; John, however, left them and returned to Jerusalem. 14 From Perga they continued their journey as far as Pisidian Antioch. On the sabbath they went to synagogue and took their seats; 15 and after the readings from the law and the prophets, the officials of the synagogue sent this message to them: 'Friends, if you have anything to say to the people by way of exhortation, let us hear it.' 16 Paul stood up, raised his hand for silence, and began.

'Listen, men of Israel and you others who worship God! 17 The God of this people, Israel, chose our forefathers. When they were still living as aliens in Egypt, he made them into a great people and, with arm outstretched, brought them out of that country. 18 For some forty years he bore with their conduct in the desert. 19 Then in the Canaanite country, after overthrowing seven nations, whose lands he gave them to be their heritage 20 for some four hundred and fifty years, he appointed judges for them until the time of the prophet Samuel.

21 'It was then that they asked for a king, and God gave them Saul son of Kish, a man of the tribe of Benjamin. He reigned for forty years 22 before God removed him and appointed David as their king, with this commendation: "I have found David the son of Jesse to be a man after my own heart; he will carry out all my purposes." 23 This is the man from whose descendants God, as he promised, has brought Israel a saviour, Jesus. 24 John had made ready for his coming by proclaiming a baptism in token of repentance to the whole people of Israel; 25 and, nearing the end of his earthly course, John said, "I am not the one you think I am. No, after me comes one whose sandals I am not worthy to unfasten."

26 'My brothers, who come of Abraham's stock, and others among you who worship God, we are the people to whom this message of salvation has been sent. 27 The people of Jerusalem and their rulers did not recognize Jesus, or understand the words of the prophets which are read sabbath by sabbath; indeed, they fulfilled them by condemning him. 28 Though they failed to find grounds for the sentence of death, they asked Pilate to have him executed. 29 When they had carried out all that the scriptures said about him, they took him down from the gibbet and laid him in a tomb. 30 But God raised him from the dead; 31 and over a period of

---

j Gk *Men, Israelites*   *k* Other ancient authorities read *cared for*
l Gk *untie the sandals*   *m* Other ancient authorities read *you*

13:18 **he . . . conduct:** *some witnesses read* he sustained them.

them." 3 Then, completing their fasting and prayer, they laid hands on them and sent them off.

4 So they, sent forth by the holy Spirit, went down to Seleucia and from there sailed to Cyprus. 5 When they arrived in Salamis, they proclaimed the word of God in the Jewish synagogues. They had John also as their assistant. 6 When they had traveled through the whole island as far as Paphos, they met a magician named Bar-Jesus who was a Jewish false prophet. 7 He was with the proconsul Sergius Paulus, a man of intelligence, who had summoned Barnabas and Saul and wanted to hear the word of God. 8 But Elymas the magician (for that is what his name means) opposed them in an attempt to turn the proconsul away from the faith. 9 But Saul, also known as Paul, filled with the holy Spirit, looked intently at him 10 and said, "You son of the devil, you enemy of all that is right, full of every sort of deceit and fraud. Will you not stop twisting the straight paths of [the] Lord? 11 Even now the hand of the Lord is upon you. You will be blind, and unable to see the sun for a time." Immediately a dark mist fell upon him, and he went about seeking people to lead him by the hand. 12 When the proconsul saw what had happened, he came to believe, for he was astonished by the teaching about the Lord.

13 From Paphos, Paul and his companions set sail and arrived at Perga in Pamphylia. But John left them and returned to Jerusalem. 14 They continued on from Perga and reached Antioch in Pisidia. On the sabbath they entered [into] the synagogue and took their seats. 15 After the reading of the law and the prophets, the synagogue officials sent word to them, "My brothers, if one of you has a word of exhortation for the people, please speak."

16 So Paul got up, motioned with his hand, and said, "Fellow Israelites and you others who are God-fearing, listen. 17 The God of this people Israel chose our ancestors and exalted the people during their sojourn in the land of Egypt. With uplifted arms he led them out of it 18 and for about forty years he put up with them in the desert. 19 When he had destroyed seven nations in the land of Canaan, he gave them their land as an inheritance 20 at the end of about four hundred and fifty years. After these things he provided judges up to Samuel [the] prophet. 21 Then they asked for a king. God gave them Saul, son of Kish, a man from the tribe of Benjamin, for forty years. 22 Then he removed him and raised up David as their king; of him he testified, 'I have found David, son of Jesse, a man after my own heart; he will carry out my every wish.' 23 From this man's descendants God, according to his promise, has brought to Israel a savior, Jesus. 24 John heralded his coming by proclaiming a baptism of repentance to all the people of Israel; 25 and as John was completing his course, he would say, 'What do you suppose that I am? I am not he. Behold, one is coming after me; I am not worthy to unfasten the sandals of his feet.'

26 "My brothers, children of the family of Abraham, and those others among you who are God-fearing, to us this word of salvation has been sent. 27 The inhabitants of Jerusalem and their leaders failed to recognize him, and by condemning him they fulfilled the oracles of the prophets that are read sabbath after sabbath. 28 For even though they found no grounds for a death sentence, they asked Pilate to have him put to death, 29 and when they had accomplished all that was written about him, they took him down from the tree and placed him in a tomb. 30 But God raised him from the dead, 31 and for many days he appeared to those who

fasting and prayer they laid their hands on them and sent them off.

4 So these two, sent on their mission by the Holy Spirit, went down to Seleucia and from there set sail for Cyprus. 5 They landed at Salamis and proclaimed the word of God in the synagogues of the Jews; John acted as their assistant. 6 They travelled the whole length of the island, and at Paphos they came in contact with a Jewish magician and false prophet called Bar-Jesus. 7 He was one of the attendants of the proconsul Sergius Paulus, who was an extremely intelligent man. The proconsul summoned Barnabas and Saul and asked to hear the word of God, 8 but Elymas the magician (this is what his name means in Greek) tried to stop them so as to prevent the proconsul's conversion to the faith. 9 Then Saul, whose other name is Paul, filled with the Holy Spirit, looked at him intently 10 and said, 'You utter fraud, you impostor, you son of the devil, you enemy of all uprightness, will you not stop twisting the straightforward ways of the Lord? 11 Now watch how the hand of the Lord will strike you: you will be blind, and for a time you will not see the sun.' That instant, everything went misty and dark for him, and he groped about to find someone to lead him by the hand. 12 The proconsul, who had watched everything, became a believer, being much struck by what he had learnt about the Lord.

13 Paul and his companions went by sea from Paphos to Perga in Pamphylia where John left them to go back to Jerusalem. 14 The others carried on from Perga till they reached Antioch in Pisidia. Here they went to synagogue on the Sabbath and took their seats. 15 After the passages from the Law and the Prophets had been read, the presidents of the synagogue sent them a message, 'Brothers, if you would like to address some words of encouragement to the congregation, please do so.' 16 Paul stood up, raised his hand for silence and began to speak: x

'Men of Israel, and fearers of God, listen! 17 The God of our nation Israel chose our ancestors and made our people great when they were living in Egypt, a land not their own; then by divine power he led them out 18 and for about forty years *took care of* them in the desert. 19 *When he had destroyed seven nations in Canaan, he put them in possession* of their land 20 for about four hundred and fifty years. After this he gave them judges, down to the prophet Samuel. 21 Then they demanded a king, and God gave them Saul son of Kish, a man of the tribe of Benjamin. After forty years, 22 he deposed him and raised up David to be king, whom he attested in these words, "*I have found David son of Jesse, a man after my own heart, who will perform my entire will.*" 23 To keep his promise, God has raised up for Israel one of David's descendants, Jesus, as Saviour, 24 whose coming was heralded by John when he proclaimed a baptism of repentance for the whole people of Israel. 25 Before John ended his course he said, "I am not the one you imagine me to be; there is someone coming after me whose sandal I am not fit to undo."

26 'My brothers, sons of Abraham's race, and all you godfearers, this message of salvation is meant for you. 27 What the people of Jerusalem and their rulers did, though they did not realise it, was in fact to fulfil the prophecies read on every Sabbath. 28 Though they found nothing to justify his execution, they condemned him and asked Pilate to have him put to death. 29 When they had carried out everything that scripture foretells about him they took him down from the tree and buried him in a tomb. 30 But God raised him from the dead, 31 and for many days he appeared

x 13 Paul uses Dt 1:31; 7:1; Ps 89:14; 2:7; Is 55:3; Ps 16:9; Hab 1:5.

who came up with him from Galilee to Jerusalem, and they are now his witnesses to the people. 32 And we bring you the good news that what God promised to our ancestors 33 he has fulfilled for us, their children, by raising Jesus; as also it is written in the second psalm,

'You are my Son;
today I have begotten you.'

34 As to his raising him from the dead, no more to return to corruption, he has spoken in this way,

'I will give you the holy promises made to David.'

35 Therefore he has also said in another psalm,

'You will not let your Holy One experience corruption.'

36 For David, after he had served the purpose of God in his own generation, died,*n* was laid beside his ancestors, and experienced corruption; 37 but he whom God raised up experienced no corruption. 38 Let it be known to you therefore, my brothers, that through this man forgiveness of sins is proclaimed to you; 39 by this Jesus*o* everyone who believes is set free from all those sins*p* from which you could not be freed by the law of Moses. 40 Beware, therefore, that what the prophets said does not happen to you:

41   'Look, you scoffers!
        Be amazed and perish,
    for in your days I am doing a work,
        a work that you will never believe, even if
            someone tells you.' "

42   As Paul and Barnabas*q* were going out, the people urged them to speak about these things again the next sabbath. 43 When the meeting of the synagogue broke up, many Jews and devout converts to Judaism followed Paul and Barnabas, who spoke to them and urged them to continue in the grace of God.

44   The next sabbath almost the whole city gathered to hear the word of the Lord.*r* 45 But when the Jews saw the crowds, they were filled with jealousy; and blaspheming, they contradicted what was spoken by Paul. 46 Then both Paul and Barnabas spoke out boldly, saying, "It was necessary that the word of God should be spoken first to you. Since you reject it and judge yourselves to be unworthy of eternal life, we are now turning to the Gentiles. 47 For so the Lord has commanded us, saying,

'I have set you to be a light for the Gentiles,
    so that you may bring salvation to the ends of
        the earth.' "

48   When the Gentiles heard this, they were glad and praised the word of the Lord; and as many as had been destined for eternal life became believers. 49 Thus the word of the Lord spread throughout the region. 50 But the Jews incited the devout women of high standing and the leading men of the city, and stirred up persecution against Paul and Barnabas, and drove them out of their region. 51 So they shook the dust off their feet in protest against them, and went to Iconium. 52 And the disciples were filled with joy and with the Holy Spirit.

14   The same thing occurred in Iconium, where Paul and Barnabas*q* went into the Jewish synagogue and spoke in such a way that a great number of both Jews and Greeks became believers. 2 But the unbelieving Jews stirred up the Gentiles and poisoned their minds against the brothers. 3 So they remained for a long time, speaking boldly for the Lord, who testified to the word of his grace by granting signs and wonders to be done through them. 4 But the resi-

many days he appeared to those who had come up with him from Galilee to Jerusalem, and they are now his witnesses before our people.

32 'We are here to give you the good news that God, who made the promise to the fathers, 33 has fulfilled it for the children by raising Jesus from the dead, as indeed it stands written in the second Psalm: "You are my son; this day I have begotten you." 34 Again, that he raised him from the dead, never to be subjected to corruption, he declares in these words: "I will give you the blessings promised to David, holy and sure." 35 This is borne out by another passage: "You will not let your faithful servant suffer corruption." 36 As for David, when he had served the purpose of God in his own generation, he died and was gathered to his fathers, and suffered corruption; 37 but the one whom God raised up did not suffer corruption. 38 You must understand, my brothers, it is through him that forgiveness of sins is now being proclaimed to you. 39 It is through him that everyone who has faith is acquitted of everything for which there was no acquittal under the law of Moses. 40 Beware, then, lest you bring down upon yourselves the doom proclaimed by the prophets: 41 "See this, you scoffers, marvel, and begone; for I am doing a deed in your days, a deed which you will never believe when you are told of it." '

42 As they were leaving the synagogue they were asked to come again and speak on these subjects next sabbath; 43 and after the congregation had dispersed, many Jews and gentile worshippers went with Paul and Barnabas, who spoke to them and urged them to hold fast to the grace of God.

44 On the following sabbath almost the whole city gathered to hear the word of God. 45 When the Jews saw the crowds, they were filled with jealous resentment, and contradicted what Paul had said with violent abuse. 46 But Paul and Barnabas were outspoken in their reply. 'It was necessary', they said, 'that the word of God should be declared to you first. But since you reject it and judge yourselves unworthy of eternal life, we now turn to the Gentiles. 47 For these are our instructions from the Lord: "I have appointed you to be a light for the Gentiles, and a means of salvation to earth's farthest bounds." ' 48 When the Gentiles heard this, they were overjoyed and thankfully acclaimed the word of the Lord, and those who were marked out for eternal life became believers. 49 Thus the word of the Lord spread throughout the region. 50 But the Jews stirred up feeling among those worshippers who were women of standing, and among the leading men of the city; a campaign of persecution was started against Paul and Barnabas, and they were expelled from the district. 51 They shook the dust off their feet in protest against them and went to Iconium. 52 And the disciples were filled with joy and with the Holy Spirit.

14   At Iconium they went together into the Jewish synagogue and spoke to such purpose that Jews and Greeks in large numbers became believers. 2 But the unconverted Jews stirred up the Gentiles and poisoned their minds against the Christians. 3 So Paul and Barnabas stayed on for some time, and spoke boldly and openly in reliance on the Lord, who confirmed the message of his grace by enabling them to work signs and miracles. 4 The populace was divid-

---

n Gk *fell asleep*   *o* Gk *this*   *p* Gk *all*   *q* Gk *they*   *r* Other ancient authorities read *God*

13:33 **for the children:** *some witnesses read* for our children; *others read* for us their children.

had come up with him from Galilee to Jerusalem. These are [now] his witnesses before the people. 32 We ourselves are proclaiming this good news to you that what God promised our ancestors 33 he has brought to fulfillment for us, [their] children, by raising up Jesus, as it is written in the second psalm, 'You are my son; this day I have begotten you.' 34 And that he raised him from the dead never to return to corruption he declared in this way, 'I shall give you the benefits assured to David.' 35 That is why he also says in another psalm, 'You will not suffer your holy one to see corruption.' 36 Now David, after he had served the will of God in his lifetime, fell asleep, was gathered to his ancestors, and did see corruption. 37 But the one whom God raised up did not see corruption. 38 You must know, my brothers, that through him forgiveness of sins is being proclaimed to you, [and] in regard to everything from which you could not be justified under the law of Moses, 39 in him every believer is justified. 40 Be careful, then, that what was said in the prophets not come about:

41 'Look on, you scoffers,
be amazed and disappear.
For I am doing a work in your days,
a work that you will never believe even if someone
tells you.' "

42 As they were leaving, they invited them to speak on these subjects the following sabbath. 43 After the congregation had dispersed, many Jews and worshipers who were converts to Judaism followed Paul and Barnabas, who spoke to them and urged them to remain faithful to the grace of God.

44 On the following sabbath almost the whole city gathered to hear the word of the Lord. 45 When the Jews saw the crowds, they were filled with jealousy and with violent abuse contradicted what Paul said. 46 Both Paul and Barnabas spoke out boldly and said, "It was necessary that the word of God be spoken to you first, but since you reject it and condemn yourselves as unworthy of eternal life, we now turn to the Gentiles. 47 For so the Lord has commanded us, 'I have made you a light to the Gentiles, that you may be an instrument of salvation to the ends of the earth.' "

48 The Gentiles were delighted when they heard this and glorified the word of the Lord. All who were destined for eternal life came to believe, 49 and the word of the Lord continued to spread through the whole region. 50 The Jews, however, incited the women of prominence who were worshipers and the leading men of the city, stirred up a persecution against Paul and Barnabas, and expelled them from their territory. 51 So they shook the dust from their feet in protest against them and went to Iconium. 52 The disciples were filled with joy and the holy Spirit.

14 In Iconium they entered the Jewish synagogue together and spoke in such a way that a great number of both Jews and Greeks came to believe, 2 although the disbelieving Jews stirred up and poisoned the minds of the Gentiles against the brothers. 3 So they stayed for a considerable period, speaking out boldly for the Lord, who confirmed the word about his grace by granting signs and wonders to occur through their hands. 4 The people of the city

to those who had accompanied him from Galilee to Jerusalem: and it is these same companions of his who are now his witnesses before our people.

32 'We have come here to tell you the good news that the promise made to our ancestors has come about. 33 God has fulfilled it to their children by raising Jesus from the dead. As scripture says in the psalms: *You are my son: today I have fathered you.* 34 The fact that God raised him from the dead, never to return to corruption, is no more than what he had declared: *To you I shall give the holy things promised to David which can be relied upon.* 35 This is also why it says in another text: *You will not allow your Holy One to see corruption.* 36 Now when David in his own time had served God's purposes he died; he was buried with his ancestors and has certainly *seen corruption.* 37 The one whom God has raised up, however, has not *seen corruption.*

38 'My brothers, I want you to realise that it is through him that forgiveness of sins is being proclaimed to you. Through him justification from all sins from which the Law of Moses was unable to justify 39 is being offered to every believer.

40 'So be careful — or what the prophets say will happen to you.

41 *Cast your eyes around you, mockers;
be amazed, and perish!
For I am doing something in your own days
that you would never believe if you were told of it.'*

42 As they left they were urged to continue this preaching the following Sabbath. 43 When the meeting broke up many Jews and devout converts followed Paul and Barnabas, and in their talks with them Paul and Barnabas urged them to remain faithful to the grace God had given them.

44 The next Sabbath almost the whole town assembled to hear the word of God. 45 When they saw the crowds, the Jews, filled with jealousy, used blasphemies to contradict everything Paul said. 46 Then Paul and Barnabas spoke out fearlessly. 'We had to proclaim the word of God to you first, but since you have rejected it, since you do not think yourselves worthy of eternal life, here and now we turn to the gentiles. 47 For this is what the Lord commanded us to do when he said:

*I have made you a light to the nations,
so that my salvation may reach the remotest parts
of the earth.'y*

48 It made the gentiles very happy to hear this and they gave thanks to the Lord for his message; all who were destined for eternal life became believers. 49 Thus the word of the Lord spread through the whole countryside.

50 But the Jews worked on some of the devout women of the upper classes and the leading men of the city; they stirred up a persecution against Paul and Barnabas and expelled them from their territory. 51 So they shook the dust from their feet in protest against them and went off to Iconium; but the converts were filled with joy and the Holy Spirit.

14 It happened that at Iconium they went to the Jewish synagogue, in the same way, and they spoke so effectively that a great many Jews and Greeks became believers.

2 (However, the Jews who refused to believe stirred up the gentiles against the brothers and set them in opposition.)

3 Accordingly Paul and Barnabas stayed on for some time, preaching fearlessly in the Lord; and he attested all they said about his gift of grace, allowing signs and wonders to be performed by them.

y **13** Is 49:6; cf. 18:6; 28:25.

NEW REVISED STANDARD VERSION

dents of the city were divided; some sided with the Jews, and some with the apostles. 5 And when an attempt was made by both Gentiles and Jews, with their rulers, to mistreat them and to stone them, 6 the apostles*s* learned of it and fled to Lystra and Derbe, cities of Lycaonia, and to the surrounding country; 7 and there they continued proclaiming the good news.

8 In Lystra there was a man sitting who could not use his feet and had never walked, for he had been crippled from birth. 9 He listened to Paul as he was speaking. And Paul, looking at him intently and seeing that he had faith to be healed, 10 said in a loud voice, "Stand upright on your feet." And the man*t* sprang up and began to walk. 11 When the crowds saw what Paul had done, they shouted in the Lycaonian language, "The gods have come down to us in human form!" 12 Barnabas they called Zeus, and Paul they called Hermes, because he was the chief speaker. 13 The priest of Zeus, whose temple was just outside the city,*u* brought oxen and garlands to the gates; he and the crowds wanted to offer sacrifice. 14 When the apostles Barnabas and Paul heard of it, they tore their clothes and rushed out into the crowd, shouting, 15 "Friends,*v* why are you doing this? We are mortals just like you, and we bring you good news, that you should turn from these worthless things to the living God, who made the heaven and the earth and the sea and all that is in them. 16 In past generations he allowed all the nations to follow their own ways; 17 yet he has not left himself without a witness in doing good — giving you rains from heaven and fruitful seasons, and filling you with food and your hearts with joy." 18 Even with these words, they scarcely restrained the crowds from offering sacrifice to them.

19 But Jews came there from Antioch and Iconium and won over the crowds. Then they stoned Paul and dragged him out of the city, supposing that he was dead. 20 But when the disciples surrounded him, he got up and went into the city. The next day he went on with Barnabas to Derbe.

21 After they had proclaimed the good news to that city and had made many disciples, they returned to Lystra, then on to Iconium and Antioch. 22 There they strengthened the souls of the disciples and encouraged them to continue in the faith, saying, "It is through many persecutions that we must enter the kingdom of God." 23 And after they had appointed elders for them in each church, with prayer and fasting they entrusted them to the Lord in whom they had come to believe.

24 Then they passed through Pisidia and came to Pamphylia. 25 When they had spoken the word in Perga, they went down to Attalia. 26 From there they sailed back to Antioch, where they had been commended to the grace of God for the work*w* that they had completed. 27 When they arrived, they called the church together and related all that God had done with them, and how he had opened a door of faith for the Gentiles. 28 And they stayed there with the disciples for some time.

15 Then certain individuals came down from Judea and were teaching the brothers, "Unless you are circumcised according to the custom of Moses, you cannot be saved." 2 And after Paul and Barnabas had no small dissension and debate with them, Paul and Barnabas and some of the others were appointed to go up to Jerusalem to discuss this question with the apostles and the elders. 3 So

REVISED ENGLISH BIBLE

ed, some siding with the Jews, others with the apostles. 5 A move was made by Gentiles and Jews together, with the connivance of the city authorities, to maltreat them and stone them, 6 and when they became aware of this, they made their escape to the Lycaonian cities of Lystra and Derbe and the surrounding country. 7 There they continued to spread the good news.

8 At Lystra a cripple, lame from birth, who had never walked in his life, 9 sat listening to Paul as he spoke. Paul fixed his eyes on him and, seeing that he had the faith to be cured, 10 said in a loud voice, 'Stand up straight on your feet'; and he sprang up and began to walk. 11 When the crowds saw what Paul had done, they shouted, in their native Lycaonian, 'The gods have come down to us in human form!' 12 They called Barnabas Zeus, and Paul they called Hermes, because he was the spokesman. 13 The priest of Zeus, whose temple was just outside the city, brought oxen and garlands to the gates, and he and the people were about to offer sacrifice.

14 But when the apostles Barnabas and Paul heard of it, they tore their clothes and rushed into the crowd shouting, 15 'Men, why are you doing this? We are human beings, just like you. The good news we bring tells you to turn from these follies to the living God, who made heaven and earth and sea and everything in them. 16 In past ages he has allowed all nations to go their own way; 17 and yet he has not left you without some clue to his nature, in the benefits he bestows: he sends you rain from heaven and the crops in their seasons, and gives you food in plenty and keeps you in good heart.' 18 Even with these words they barely managed to prevent the crowd from offering sacrifice to them.

19 Then Jews from Antioch and Iconium came on the scene and won over the crowds. They stoned Paul, and dragged him out of the city, thinking him dead. 20 The disciples formed a ring round him, and he got to his feet and went into the city. Next day he left with Barnabas for Derbe.

21 After bringing the good news to that town and gaining many converts, they returned to Lystra, then to Iconium, and then to Antioch, 22 strengthening the disciples and encouraging them to be true to the faith. They warned them that to enter the kingdom of God we must undergo many hardships. 23 They also appointed for them elders in each congregation, and with prayer and fasting committed them to the Lord in whom they had put their trust.

24 They passed through Pisidia and came into Pamphylia. 25 When they had delivered the message at Perga, they went down to Attalia, 26 and from there sailed to Antioch, where they had originally been commended to the grace of God for the task which they had now completed. 27 On arrival there, they called the congregation together and reported all that God had accomplished through them, and how he had thrown open the gates of faith to the Gentiles. 28 And they stayed for some time with the disciples there.

15 SOME people who had come down from Judaea began to teach the brotherhood that those who were not circumcised in accordance with Mosaic practice could not be saved. 2 That brought them into fierce dissension and controversy with Paul and Barnabas, and it was arranged that these two and some others from Antioch should go up to Jerusalem to see the apostles and elders about this question.

s Gk *they*   *t* Gk *he*   *u* Or *The priest of Zeus-Outside-the-City*
v Gk *Men*   *w* Or *committed in the grace of God to the work*

were divided: some were with the Jews; others, with the apostles. 5 When there was an attempt by both the Gentiles and the Jews, together with their leaders, to attack and stone them, 6 they realized it and fled to the Lycaonian cities of Lystra and Derbe and to the surrounding countryside, 7 where they continued to proclaim the good news.

8 At Lystra there was a crippled man, lame from birth, who had never walked. 9 He listened to Paul speaking, who looked intently at him, saw that he had the faith to be healed, 10 and called out in a loud voice, "Stand up straight on your feet." He jumped up and began to walk about. 11 When the crowds saw what Paul had done, they cried out in Lycaonian, "The gods have come down to us in human form." 12 They called Barnabas "Zeus" and Paul "Hermes," because he was the chief speaker. 13 And the priest of Zeus, whose temple was at the entrance to the city, brought oxen and garlands to the gates, for he together with the people intended to offer sacrifice.

14 The apostles Barnabas and Paul tore their garments when they heard this and rushed out into the crowd, shouting, 15 "Men, why are you doing this? We are of the same nature as you, human beings. We proclaim to you good news that you should turn from these idols to the living God, 'who made heaven and earth and sea and all that is in them.' 16 In past generations he allowed all Gentiles to go their own ways; 17 yet, in bestowing his goodness, he did not leave himself without witness, for he gave you rains from heaven and fruitful seasons, and filled you with nourishment and gladness for your hearts." 18 Even with these words, they scarcely restrained the crowds from offering sacrifice to them.

19 However, some Jews from Antioch and Iconium arrived and won over the crowds. They stoned Paul and dragged him out of the city, supposing that he was dead. 20 But when the disciples gathered around him, he got up and entered the city. On the following day he left with Barnabas for Derbe.

21 After they had proclaimed the good news to that city and made a considerable number of disciples, they returned to Lystra and to Iconium and to Antioch. 22 They strengthened the spirits of the disciples and exhorted them to persevere in the faith, saying, "It is necessary for us to undergo many hardships to enter the kingdom of God." 23 They appointed presbyters for them in each church and, with prayer and fasting, commended them to the Lord in whom they had put their faith. 24 Then they traveled through Pisidia and reached Pamphylia. 25 After proclaiming the word at Perga they went down to Attalia. 26 From there they sailed to Antioch, where they had been commended to the grace of God for the work they had now accomplished. 27 And when they arrived, they called the church together and reported what God had done with them and how he had opened the door of faith to the Gentiles. 28 Then they spent no little time with the disciples.

15 Some who had come down from Judea were instructing the brothers, "Unless you are circumcised according to the Mosaic practice, you cannot be saved." 2 Because there arose no little dissension and debate by Paul and Barnabas with them, it was decided that Paul, Barnabas, and some of the others should go up to Jerusalem to the apostles and presbyters about this question. 3 They were

4 The people in the city were divided; some supported the Jews, others the apostles, 5 but eventually with the connivance of the authorities a move was made by gentiles as well as Jews to make attacks on them and to stone them. 6 When they came to hear of this, they went off for safety to Lycaonia where, in the towns of Lystra and Derbe and in the surrounding country, 7 they preached the good news.

8 There was a man sitting there who had never walked in his life, because his feet were crippled from birth; 9 he was listening to Paul preaching, and Paul looked at him intently and saw that he had the faith to be cured. 10 Paul said in a loud voice, 'Get to your feet — stand up,' and the cripple jumped up and began to walk.

11 When the crowds saw what Paul had done they shouted in the language of Lycaonia, 'The gods have come down to us in human form.' 12 They addressed Barnabas as Zeus, and since Paul was the principal speaker they called him Hermes. 13 The priests of Zeus-outside-the-Gate, proposing that all the people should offer sacrifice with them, brought garlanded oxen to the gates. 14 When the apostles Barnabas and Paul heard what was happening they tore their clothes, and rushed into the crowd, shouting, 15 'Friends, what do you think you are doing? We are only human beings, mortal like yourselves. We have come with good news to make you turn from these empty idols to the living God who made sky and earth and the sea and all that these hold. 16 In the past he allowed all the nations to go their own way; 17 but even then he did not leave you without evidence of himself in the good things he does for you: he sends you rain from heaven and seasons of fruitfulness; he fills you with food and your hearts with merriment.' 18 With this speech they just managed to prevent the crowd from offering them sacrifice.

19 Then some Jews arrived from Antioch and Iconium and turned the people against them. They stoned Paul and dragged him outside the town, thinking he was dead. 20 The disciples came crowding round him but, as they did so, he stood up and went back to the town. The next day he and Barnabas left for Derbe.

21 Having preached the good news in that town and made a considerable number of disciples, they went back through Lystra, Iconium and Antioch. 22 They put fresh heart into the disciples, encouraging them to persevere in the faith, saying, 'We must all experience many hardships before we enter the kingdom of God.' 23 In each of these churches they appointed elders, and with prayer and fasting they commended them to the Lord in whom they had come to believe.

24 They passed through Pisidia and reached Pamphylia. 25 Then after proclaiming the word at Perga they went down to Attalia 26 and from there sailed for Antioch, where they had originally been commended to the grace of God for the work they had now completed.

27 On their arrival they assembled the church and gave an account of all that God had done with them, and how he had opened the door of faith to the gentiles. 28 They stayed there with the disciples for some time.

15 Then some men came down from Judaea and taught the brothers, 'Unless you have yourselves circumcised in the tradition of Moses you cannot be saved.' 2 This led to disagreement, and after Paul and Barnabas had had a long argument with these men it was decided that Paul and Barnabas and others of the church should go up to Jerusalem and discuss the question with the apostles and elders.

they were sent on their way by the church, and as they passed through both Phoenicia and Samaria, they reported the conversion of the Gentiles, and brought great joy to all the believers.*x* 4 When they came to Jerusalem, they were welcomed by the church and the apostles and the elders, and they reported all that God had done with them. 5 But some believers who belonged to the sect of the Pharisees stood up and said, "It is necessary for them to be circumcised and ordered to keep the law of Moses."

6 The apostles and the elders met together to consider this matter. 7 After there had been much debate, Peter stood up and said to them, "My brothers,*y* you know that in the early days God made a choice among you, that I should be the one through whom the Gentiles would hear the message of the good news and become believers. 8 And God, who knows the human heart, testified to them by giving them the Holy Spirit, just as he did to us; 9 and in cleansing their hearts by faith he has made no distinction between them and us. 10 Now therefore why are you putting God to the test by placing on the neck of the disciples a yoke that neither our ancestors nor we have been able to bear? 11 On the contrary, we believe that we will be saved through the grace of the Lord Jesus, just as they will."

12 The whole assembly kept silence, and listened to Barnabas and Paul as they told of all the signs and wonders that God had done through them among the Gentiles. 13 After they finished speaking, James replied, "My brothers,*y* listen to me. 14 Simeon has related how God first looked favorably on the Gentiles, to take from among them a people for his name. 15 This agrees with the words of the prophets, as it is written,

16 'After this I will return,
and I will rebuild the dwelling of David, which
has fallen;
from its ruins I will rebuild it,
and I will set it up,
17 so that all other peoples may seek the Lord—
even all the Gentiles over whom my name has
been called.
Thus says the Lord, who has been making
these things 18 known from long ago.'*z*

19 Therefore I have reached the decision that we should not trouble those Gentiles who are turning to God, 20 but we should write to them to abstain only from things polluted by idols and from fornication and from whatever has been strangled*a* and from blood. 21 For in every city, for generations past, Moses has had those who proclaim him, for he has been read aloud every sabbath in the synagogues."

22 Then the apostles and the elders, with the consent of the whole church, decided to choose men from among their members*b* and to send them to Antioch with Paul and Barnabas. They sent Judas called Barsabbas, and Silas, leaders among the brothers, 23 with the following letter: "The brothers, both the apostles and the elders, to the believers*x* of Gentile origin in Antioch and Syria and Cilicia, greetings. 24 Since we have heard that certain persons who have gone out from us, though with no instructions from us, have said things to disturb you and have unsettled your minds,*c* 25 we have decided unanimously to choose representatives*d* and send them to you, along with our beloved Barnabas and Paul, 26 who have risked their lives for the sake of our Lord Jesus Christ. 27 We have therefore sent Judas and Silas, who themselves will tell you the same things by word of mouth. 28 For it has seemed good to the Holy Spirit and to us to

3 They were sent on their way by the church, and travelled through Phoenicia and Samaria, telling the full story of the conversion of the Gentiles, and causing great rejoicing among all the Christians.

4 When they reached Jerusalem they were welcomed by the church and the apostles and elders, and they reported all that God had accomplished through them. 5 But some of the Pharisaic party who had become believers came forward and declared, 'Those Gentiles must be circumcised and told to keep the law of Moses.'

6 The apostles and elders met to look into this matter, 7 and, after a long debate, Peter rose to address them. 'My friends,' he said, 'in the early days, as you yourselves know, God made his choice among you: from my lips the Gentiles were to hear and believe the message of the gospel. 8 And God, who can read human hearts, showed his approval by giving the Holy Spirit to them as he did to us. 9 He made no difference between them and us; for he purified their hearts by faith. 10 Then why do you now try God's patience by laying on the shoulders of these converts a yoke which neither we nor our forefathers were able to bear? 11 For our belief is that we are saved in the same way as they are: by the grace of the Lord Jesus.'

12 At that the whole company fell silent and listened to Barnabas and Paul as they described all the signs and portents that God had worked among the Gentiles through them.

13 When they had finished speaking, James summed up: 'My friends,' he said, 'listen to me. 14 Simon has described how it first happened that God, in his providence, chose from among the Gentiles a people to bear his name. 15 This agrees with the words of the prophets: as scripture has it,

16 Thereafter I will return and rebuild the fallen house
of David;
I will rebuild its ruins and set it up again,
17 that the rest of mankind may seek the Lord,
all the Gentiles whom I have claimed for my own.
Thus says the Lord, who is doing this
18 as he made known long ago.

19 'In my judgement, therefore, we should impose no irksome restrictions on those of the Gentiles who are turning to God; 20 instead we should instruct them by letter to abstain from things polluted by contact with idols, from fornication, from anything that has been strangled, and from blood. 21 Moses, after all, has never lacked spokesmen in every town for generations past; he is read in the synagogues sabbath by sabbath.'

22 Then, with the agreement of the whole church, the apostles and elders resolved to choose representatives and send them to Antioch with Paul and Barnabas. They chose two leading men in the community, Judas Barsabbas and Silas, 23 and gave them this letter to deliver:

From the apostles and elders to our brothers of gentile origin in Antioch, Syria, and Cilicia. Greetings! 24 We have heard that some of our number, without any instructions from us, have disturbed you with their talk and unsettled your minds. 25 In consequence, we have resolved unanimously to send to you our chosen representatives with our well-beloved Barnabas and Paul, 26 who have given up their lives to the cause of our Lord Jesus Christ; 27 so we are sending Judas and Silas, who will, by word of mouth, confirm what is written in this letter. 28 It is the decision of the Holy Spirit, and our

x Gk *brothers*   *y* Gk *Men, brothers*   *z* Other ancient authorities read *things.* 18 *Known to God from of old are all his works.'*
a Other ancient authorities lack *and from whatever has been strangled*
b Gk *from among them*   *c* Other ancient authorities add *saying, 'You must be circumcised and keep the law,'*   *d* Gk *men*

15:14 **Simon:** *Gk* Simeon.   15:20 **from fornication . . . blood:** *some witnesses omit* from fornication; *others omit* from anything that has been strangled; *some add (after* blood) and to refrain from doing to others what they would not like done to themselves.

sent on their journey by the church, and passed through Phoenicia and Samaria telling of the conversion of the Gentiles, and brought great joy to all the brothers. 4 When they arrived in Jerusalem, they were welcomed by the church, as well as by the apostles and the presbyters, and they reported what God had done with them. 5 But some from the party of the Pharisees who had become believers stood up and said, "It is necessary to circumcise them and direct them to observe the Mosaic law."

6 The apostles and the presbyters met together to see about this matter. 7 After much debate had taken place, Peter got up and said to them, "My brothers, you are well aware that from early days God made his choice among you that through my mouth the Gentiles would hear the word of the gospel and believe. 8 And God, who knows the heart, bore witness by granting them the holy Spirit just as he did us. 9 He made no distinction between us and them, for by faith he purified their hearts. 10 Why, then, are you now putting God to the test by placing on the shoulders of the disciples a yoke that neither our ancestors nor we have been able to bear? 11 On the contrary, we believe that we are saved through the grace of the Lord Jesus, in the same way as they." 12 The whole assembly fell silent, and they listened while Paul and Barnabas described the signs and wonders God had worked among the Gentiles through them.

13 After they had fallen silent, James responded, "My brothers, listen to me. 14 Symeon has described how God first concerned himself with acquiring from among the Gentiles a people for his name. 15 The words of the prophets agree with this, as is written:

16 'After this I shall return
    and rebuild the fallen hut of David;
from its ruins I shall rebuild it
    and raise it up again,
17 so that the rest of humanity may seek out the Lord,
    even all the Gentiles on whom my name
        is invoked.
Thus says the Lord who accomplishes these things,
18   known from of old.'

19 It is my judgment, therefore, that we ought to stop troubling the Gentiles who turn to God, 20 but tell them by letter to avoid pollution from idols, unlawful marriage, the meat of strangled animals, and blood. 21 For Moses, for generations now, has had those who proclaim him in every town, as he has been read in the synagogues every sabbath."

22 Then the apostles and presbyters, in agreement with the whole church, decided to choose representatives and to send them to Antioch with Paul and Barnabas. The ones chosen were Judas, who was called Barsabbas, and Silas, leaders among the brothers. 23 This is the letter delivered by them: "The apostles and the presbyters, your brothers, to the brothers in Antioch, Syria, and Cilicia of Gentile origin: greetings. 24 Since we have heard that some of our number [who went out] without any mandate from us have upset you with their teachings and disturbed your peace of mind, 25 we have with one accord decided to choose representatives and to send them to you along with our beloved Barnabas and Paul, 26 who have dedicated their lives to the name of our Lord Jesus Christ. 27 So we are sending Judas and Silas who will also convey this same message by word of mouth: 28 'It is the decision of the holy Spirit and of us not

3 The members of the church saw them off, and as they passed through Phoenicia and Samaria they told how the gentiles had been converted, and this news was received with the greatest satisfaction by all the brothers. 4 When they arrived in Jerusalem they were welcomed by the church and by the apostles and elders, and gave an account of all that God had done through them.

5 But certain members of the Pharisees' party who had become believers objected, insisting that gentiles should be circumcised and instructed to keep the Law of Moses. 6 The apostles and elders metᶻ to look into the matter, 7 and after a long discussion, Peter stood up and addressed them.

'My brothers,' he said, 'you know perfectly well that in the early days God made his choice among you: the gentiles were to learn the good news from me and so become believers. 8 And God, who can read everyone's heart, showed his approval of them by giving the Holy Spirit to them just as he had to us. 9 God made no distinction between them and us, since he purified their hearts by faith. 10 Why do you put God to the test now by imposing on the disciples the very burden that neither our ancestors nor we ourselves were strong enough to support? 11 But we believe that we are saved in the same way as they are: through the grace of the Lord Jesus.'

12 The entire assembly fell silent, and they listened to Barnabas and Paul describing all the signs and wonders God had worked through them among the gentiles.

13 When they had finished it was James who spoke. 'My brothers,' he said, 'listen to me. 14 Simeon has described how God first arranged to enlist a people for his name out of the gentiles. 15 This is entirely in harmony with the words of the prophets, since the scriptures say:

16 After that I shall return
    and rebuild the fallen hut of David;
I shall make good the gaps in it
    and restore it.
17 Then the rest of humanity,
    and of all the nations once called mine,
    will look for the Lord,
    says the Lord who made this 18 known so long
        ago.ᵃ

19 'My verdict is, then, that instead of making things more difficult for gentiles who turn to God, 20 we should send them a letter telling them merely to abstain from anything polluted by idols, from illicit marriages, from the meat of strangled animals and from blood. 21 For Moses has always had his preachers in every town and is read aloud in the synagogues every Sabbath.'

22 Then the apostles and elders, with the whole church, decided to choose delegates from among themselves to send to Antioch with Paul and Barnabas. They chose Judas, known as Barsabbas, and Silas, both leading men in the brotherhood, 23 and gave them this letter to take with them:

'The apostles and elders, your brothers, send greetings to the brothers of gentile birth in Antioch, Syria and Cilicia. 24 We hear that some people coming from here, but acting without any authority from ourselves, have disturbed you with their demands and have unsettled your minds; 25 and so we have decided unanimously to elect delegates and to send them to you with our well-beloved Barnabas and Paul, 26 who have committed their lives to the name of our Lord Jesus Christ. 27 Accordingly we are sending you Judas and Silas, who will confirm by word of mouth what we have written. 28 It has been decided by the Holy Spirit

---

ᶻ 15 Two disputes are combined: Peter's speech concerns obligations of gentiles to keep the Jewish Law, James' concerns social contact.
ᵃ 15 Am 9:11–12.

impose on you no further burden than these essentials: 29 that you abstain from what has been sacrificed to idols and from blood and from what is strangled*e* and from fornication. If you keep yourselves from these, you will do well. Farewell."

30 So they were sent off and went down to Antioch. When they gathered the congregation together, they delivered the letter. 31 When its members*f* read it, they rejoiced at the exhortation. 32 Judas and Silas, who were themselves prophets, said much to encourage and strengthen the believers.*g* 33 After they had been there for some time, they were sent off in peace by the believers*g* to those who had sent them.*h* 35 But Paul and Barnabas remained in Antioch, and there, with many others, they taught and proclaimed the word of the Lord.

36 After some days Paul said to Barnabas, "Come, let us return and visit the believers*g* in every city where we proclaimed the word of the Lord and see how they are doing." 37 Barnabas wanted to take with them John called Mark. 38 But Paul decided not to take with them one who had deserted them in Pamphylia and had not accompanied them in the work. 39 The disagreement became so sharp that they parted company; Barnabas took Mark with him and sailed away to Cyprus. 40 But Paul chose Silas and set out, the believers*g* commending him to the grace of the Lord. 41 He went through Syria and Cilicia, strengthening the churches.

16 Paul*i* went on also to Derbe and to Lystra, where there was a disciple named Timothy, the son of a Jewish woman who was a believer; but his father was a Greek. 2 He was well spoken of by the believers*g* in Lystra and Iconium. 3 Paul wanted Timothy to accompany him; and he took him and had him circumcised because of the Jews who were in those places, for they all knew that his father was a Greek. 4 As they went from town to town, they delivered to them for observance the decisions that had been reached by the apostles and elders who were in Jerusalem. 5 So the churches were strengthened in the faith and increased in numbers daily.

6 They went through the region of Phrygia and Galatia, having been forbidden by the Holy Spirit to speak the word in Asia. 7 When they had come opposite Mysia, they attempted to go into Bithynia, but the Spirit of Jesus did not allow them; 8 so, passing by Mysia, they went down to Troas. 9 During the night Paul had a vision: there stood a man of Macedonia pleading with him and saying, "Come over to Macedonia and help us." 10 When he had seen the vision, we immediately tried to cross over to Macedonia, being convinced that God had called us to proclaim the good news to them.

11 We set sail from Troas and took a straight course to Samothrace, the following day to Neapolis, 12 and from there to Philippi, which is a leading city of the district*j* of Macedonia and a Roman colony. We remained in this city for some days. 13 On the sabbath day we went outside the gate by the river, where we supposed there was a place of prayer; and we sat down and spoke to the women who had gathered there. 14 A certain woman named Lydia, a wor-

decision, to lay no further burden upon you beyond these essentials: 29 you are to abstain from meat that has been offered to idols, from blood, from anything that has been strangled, and from fornication. If you keep yourselves free from these things you will be doing well. Farewell.

30 So they took their leave and travelled down to Antioch, where they called the congregation together and delivered the letter. 31 When it was read, all rejoiced at the encouragement it brought, 32 and Judas and Silas, who were themselves prophets, said much to encourage and strengthen the members. 33 After spending some time there, they took their leave with the good wishes of the brethren, to return to those who had sent them. 35 But Paul and Barnabas stayed on at Antioch, where, along with many others, they taught and preached the word of the Lord.

36 AFTER a while Paul said to Barnabas, 'Let us go back and see how our brothers are getting on in the various towns where we proclaimed the word of the Lord.' 37 Barnabas wanted to take John Mark with them; 38 but Paul insisted that the man who had deserted them in Pamphylia and had not gone on to share in their work was not the man to take with them now. 39 The dispute was so sharp that they parted company. Barnabas took Mark with him and sailed for Cyprus. 40 Paul chose Silas and started on his journey, commended by the brothers to the grace of the Lord. 41 He travelled through Syria and Cilicia bringing new strength to the churches.

16 He went on to Derbe and then to Lystra, where he found a disciple named Timothy, the son of a Jewish Christian mother and a gentile father, 2 well spoken of by the Christians at Lystra and Iconium. 3 Paul wanted to take him with him when he left, so he had him circumcised out of consideration for the Jews who lived in those parts, for they all knew that his father was a Gentile. 4 As they made their way from town to town they handed on the decisions taken by the apostles and elders in Jerusalem and enjoined their observance. 5 So, day by day, the churches grew stronger in faith and increased in numbers.

6 They travelled through the Phrygian and Galatian region, prevented by the Holy Spirit from delivering the message in the province of Asia. 7 When they approached the Mysian border they tried to enter Bithynia, but, as the Spirit of Jesus would not allow them, 8 they passed through Mysia and reached the coast at Troas. 9 During the night a vision came to Paul: a Macedonian stood there appealing to him, 'Cross over to Macedonia and help us.' 10 As soon as he had seen this vision, we set about getting a passage to Macedonia, convinced that God had called us to take the good news there.

11 We sailed from Troas and made a straight run to Samothrace, the next day to Neapolis, 12 and from there to Philippi, a leading city in that district of Macedonia and a Roman colony. Here we stayed for some days, 13 and on the sabbath we went outside the city gate by the riverside, where we thought there would be a place of prayer; we sat down and talked to the women who had gathered there. 14 One of

15:29 **from anything . . . fornication:** *some witnesses omit* from anything that has been strangled; *some omit* and from fornication; *and some witnesses add* and refrain from doing to others what you would not like done to yourselves. 15:33 **sent them:** *some witnesses add* 34But Silas decided to remain there. 16:6 **through . . . region:** *or* through Phrygia and the Galatian region. 16:13 **where . . . prayer:** *some witnesses read* where there was a recognized place of prayer.

e Other ancient authorities lack *and from what is strangled* *f* Gk When they *g* Gk *brothers* *h* Other ancient authorities add verse 34, *But it seemed good to Silas to remain there* *i* Gk *He* *j* Other authorities read *a city of the first district*

to place on you any burden beyond these necessities, 29 namely, to abstain from meat sacrificed to idols, from blood, from meats of strangled animals, and from unlawful marriage. If you keep free of these, you will be doing what is right. Farewell.' "

30 And so they were sent on their journey. Upon their arrival in Antioch they called the assembly together and delivered the letter. 31 When the people read it, they were delighted with the exhortation. 32 Judas and Silas, who were themselves prophets, exhorted and strengthened the brothers with many words. 33 After they had spent some time there, they were sent off with greetings of peace from the brothers to those who had commissioned them. [34] 35 But Paul and Barnabas remained in Antioch, teaching and proclaiming with many others the word of the Lord.

36 After some time, Paul said to Barnabas, "Come, let us make a return visit to see how the brothers are getting on in all the cities where we proclaimed the word of the Lord." 37 Barnabas wanted to take with them also John, who was called Mark, 38 but Paul insisted that they should not take with them someone who had deserted them at Pamphylia and who had not continued with them in their work. 39 So sharp was their disagreement that they separated. Barnabas took Mark and sailed to Cyprus. 40 But Paul chose Silas and departed after being commended by the brothers to the grace of the Lord. 41 He traveled through Syria and Cilicia bringing strength to the churches.

16 He reached [also] Derbe and Lystra where there was a disciple named Timothy, the son of a Jewish woman who was a believer, but his father was a Greek. 2 The brothers in Lystra and Iconium spoke highly of him, 3 and Paul wanted him to come along with him. On account of the Jews of that region, Paul had him circumcised, for they all knew that his father was a Greek. 4 As they traveled from city to city, they handed on to the people for observance the decisions reached by the apostles and presbyters in Jerusalem. 5 Day after day the churches grew stronger in faith and increased in number.

6 They traveled through the Phrygian and Galatian territory because they had been prevented by the holy Spirit from preaching the message in the province of Asia. 7 When they came to Mysia, they tried to go on into Bithynia, but the Spirit of Jesus did not allow them, 8 so they crossed through Mysia and came down to Troas. 9 During [the] night Paul had a vision. A Macedonian stood before him and implored him with these words, "Come over to Macedonia and help us." 10 When he had seen the vision, we sought passage to Macedonia at once, concluding that God had called us to proclaim the good news to them.

11 We set sail from Troas, making a straight run for Samothrace, and on the next day to Neapolis, 12 and from there to Philippi, a leading city in that district of Macedonia and a Roman colony. We spent some time in that city. 13 On the sabbath we went outside the city gate along the river where we thought there would be a place of prayer. We sat and spoke with the women who had gathered there. 14 One of

and by ourselves not to impose on you any burden beyond these essentials: 29 you are to abstain from food sacrificed to idols, from blood, from the meat of strangled animals and from illicit marriages. Avoid these, and you will do what is right. Farewell.'

30 The party left and went down to Antioch, where they summoned the whole community and delivered the letter. 31 The community read it and were delighted with the encouragement it gave them. 32 Judas and Silas, being themselves prophets, spoke for a long time, encouraging and strengthening the brothers. 33 These two spent some time there, and then the brothers wished them peace and they went back to those who had sent them. [34] b 35 Paul and Barnabas, however, stayed on in Antioch, and there with many others they taught and proclaimed the good news, the word of the Lord.

36 On a later occasion Paul said to Barnabas, 'Let us go back and visit the brothers in all the towns where we preached the word of the Lord, so that we can see how they are doing.' 37 Barnabas suggested taking John Mark, 38 but Paul was not in favour of taking along the man who had deserted them in Pamphylia and had refused to share in their work.

39 There was sharp disagreement so that they parted company, and Barnabas sailed off with Mark to Cyprus. 40 Before Paul left, he chose Silas to accompany him and was commended by the brothers to the grace of God.

41 He travelled through Syria and Cilicia, consolidating the churches.

16 From there he went to Derbe, and then on to Lystra, where there was a disciple called Timothy, whose mother was Jewish and had become a believer; but his father was a Greek. 2 The brothers at Lystra and Iconium spoke well of him, 3 and Paul, who wanted to have him as a travelling companion, had him circumcised. This was on account of the Jews in the locality where everyone knew his father was a Greek.

4 As they visited one town after another, they passed on the decisions reached by the apostles and elders in Jerusalem, with instructions to observe them.

5 So the churches grew strong in the faith, as well as growing daily in numbers.

6 They travelled through Phrygia and the Galatian country, because they had been told by the Holy Spirit not to preach the word in Asia. 7 When they reached the frontier of Mysia they tried to go into Bithynia, but as the Spirit of Jesus would not allow them, 8 they went through Mysia and came down to Troas.

9 One night Paul had a vision: a Macedonian appeared and kept urging him in these words, 'Come across to Macedonia and help us.' 10 Once he had seen this vision we lost no time in arranging a passage to Macedonia, convinced that God had called us to bring them the good news.

11 Sailing from Troas we made a straight run for Samothrace; the next day for Neapolis, 12 and from there for Philippi, a Roman colony and the principal city of that district of Macedonia. 13 After a few days in this city we went outside the gates beside a river as it was the Sabbath and this was a customary place for prayer. We sat down and preached to the women who had come to the meeting.

15, 34: Some manuscripts add, in various wordings, "But Silas decided to remain there."

b **15** Some MSS add v. 34 'But Silas decided to stay there'.

NEW REVISED STANDARD VERSION

shiper of God, was listening to us; she was from the city of Thyatira and a dealer in purple cloth. The Lord opened her heart to listen eagerly to what was said by Paul. 15 When she and her household were baptized, she urged us, saying, "If you have judged me to be faithful to the Lord, come and stay at my home." And she prevailed upon us.

16 One day, as we were going to the place of prayer, we met a slave-girl who had a spirit of divination and brought her owners a great deal of money by fortune-telling. 17 While she followed Paul and us, she would cry out, "These men are slaves of the Most High God, who proclaim to you*k* a way of salvation." 18 She kept doing this for many days. But Paul, very much annoyed, turned and said to the spirit, "I order you in the name of Jesus Christ to come out of her." And it came out that very hour.

19 But when her owners saw that their hope of making money was gone, they seized Paul and Silas and dragged them into the marketplace before the authorities. 20 When they had brought them before the magistrates, they said, "These men are disturbing our city; they are Jews 21 and are advocating customs that are not lawful for us as Romans to adopt or observe." 22 The crowd joined in attacking them, and the magistrates had them stripped of their clothing and ordered them to be beaten with rods. 23 After they had given them a severe flogging, they threw them into prison and ordered the jailer to keep them securely. 24 Following these instructions, he put them in the innermost cell and fastened their feet in the stocks.

25 About midnight Paul and Silas were praying and singing hymns to God, and the prisoners were listening to them. 26 Suddenly there was an earthquake, so violent that the foundations of the prison were shaken; and immediately all the doors were opened and everyone's chains were unfastened. 27 When the jailer woke up and saw the prison doors wide open, he drew his sword and was about to kill himself, since he supposed that the prisoners had escaped. 28 But Paul shouted in a loud voice, "Do not harm yourself, for we are all here." 29 The jailer*l* called for lights, and rushing in, he fell down trembling before Paul and Silas. 30 Then he brought them outside and said, "Sirs, what must I do to be saved?" 31 They answered, "Believe on the Lord Jesus, and you will be saved, you and your household." 32 They spoke the word of the Lord*m* to him and to all who were in his house. 33 At the same hour of the night he took them and washed their wounds; then he and his entire family were baptized without delay. 34 He brought them up into the house and set food before them; and he and his entire household rejoiced that he had become a believer in God.

35 When morning came, the magistrates sent the police, saying, "Let those men go." 36 And the jailer reported the message to Paul, saying, "The magistrates sent word to let you go; therefore come out now and go in peace." 37 But Paul replied, "They have beaten us in public, uncondemned, men who are Roman citizens, and have thrown us into prison; and now are they going to discharge us in secret? Certainly not! Let them come and take us out themselves." 38 The police reported these words to the magistrates, and they were afraid when they heard that they were Roman citizens; 39 so they came and apologized to them. And they took them out and asked them to leave the city. 40 After leaving the prison they went to Lydia's home; and when they had seen and encouraged the brothers and sisters*n* there, they departed.

17 After Paul and Silas*o* had passed through Amphipolis and Apollonia, they came to Thessalonica, where there was a synagogue of the Jews. 2 And Paul went

REVISED ENGLISH BIBLE

those listening was called Lydia, a dealer in purple fabric, who came from the city of Thyatira; she was a worshipper of God, and the Lord opened her heart to respond to what Paul said. 15 She was baptized, and her household with her, and then she urged us, 'Now that you have accepted me as a believer in the Lord, come and stay at my house.' And she insisted on our going.

16 Once, on our way to the place of prayer, we met a slave-girl who was possessed by a spirit of divination and brought large profits to her owners by telling fortunes. 17 She followed Paul and the rest of us, shouting, 'These men are servants of the Most High God, and are declaring to you a way of salvation.' 18 She did this day after day, until, in exasperation, Paul rounded on the spirit. 'I command you in the name of Jesus Christ to come out of her,' he said, and it came out instantly.

19 When the girl's owners saw that their hope of profit had gone, they seized Paul and Silas and dragged them to the city authorities in the main square; 20 bringing them before the magistrates, they alleged, 'These men are causing a disturbance in our city; they are Jews, 21 and they are advocating practices which it is illegal for us Romans to adopt and follow.' 22 The mob joined in the attack; and the magistrates had the prisoners stripped and gave orders for them to be flogged. 23 After a severe beating they were flung into prison and the jailer was ordered to keep them under close guard. 24 In view of these orders, he put them into the inner prison and secured their feet in the stocks.

25 About midnight Paul and Silas, at their prayers, were singing praises to God, and the other prisoners were listening, 26 when suddenly there was such a violent earthquake that the foundations of the jail were shaken; the doors burst open and all the prisoners found their fetters unfastened. 27 The jailer woke up to see the prison doors wide open and, assuming that the prisoners had escaped, drew his sword intending to kill himself. 28 But Paul shouted, 'Do yourself no harm; we are all here.' 29 The jailer called for lights, rushed in, and threw himself down before Paul and Silas, trembling with fear. 30 He then escorted them out and said, 'Sirs, what must I do to be saved?' 31 They answered, 'Put your trust in the Lord Jesus, and you will be saved, you and your household,' 32 and they imparted the word of the Lord to him and to everyone in his house. 33 At that late hour of the night the jailer took them and washed their wounds, and there and then he and his whole family were baptized. 34 He brought them up into his house, set out a meal, and rejoiced with his whole household in his new-found faith in God.

35 When daylight came, the magistrates sent their officers with the order, 'Release those men.' 36 The jailer reported these instructions to Paul: 'The magistrates have sent an order for your release. Now you are free to go in peace.' 37 But Paul said to the officers: 'We are Roman citizens! They gave us a public flogging and threw us into prison without trial. Are they now going to smuggle us out by stealth? No indeed! Let them come in person and escort us out.' 38 The officers reported his words to the magistrates. Alarmed to hear that they were Roman citizens, 39 they came and apologized to them, and then escorted them out and requested them to go away from the city. 40 On leaving the prison, they went to Lydia's house, where they met their fellow-Christians and spoke words of encouragement to them, and then they took their departure.

17 THEY now travelled by way of Amphipolis and Apollonia and came to Thessalonica, where there was a Jewish synagogue. 2 Following his usual practice Paul

---

k Other ancient authorities read *to us*   *l* Gk *He*   *m* Other ancient authorities read *word of God*   *n* Gk *brothers*   *o* Gk *they*

them, a woman named Lydia, a dealer in purple cloth, from the city of Thyatira, a worshiper of God, listened, and the Lord opened her heart to pay attention to what Paul was saying. 15 After she and her household had been baptized, she offered us an invitation, "If you consider me a believer in the Lord, come and stay at my home," and she prevailed on us.

16 As we were going to the place of prayer, we met a slave girl with an oracular spirit, who used to bring a large profit to her owners through her fortune-telling. 17 She began to follow Paul and us, shouting, "These people are slaves of the Most High God, who proclaim to you a way of salvation." 18 She did this for many days. Paul became annoyed, turned, and said to the spirit, "I command you in the name of Jesus Christ to come out of her." Then it came out at that moment.

19 When her owners saw that their hope of profit was gone, they seized Paul and Silas and dragged them to the public square before the local authorities. 20 They brought them before the magistrates and said, "These people are Jews and are disturbing our city 21 and are advocating customs that are not lawful for us Romans to adopt or practice." 22 The crowd joined in the attack on them, and the magistrates had them stripped and ordered them to be beaten with rods. 23 After inflicting many blows on them, they threw them into prison and instructed the jailer to guard them securely. 24 When he received these instructions, he put them in the innermost cell and secured their feet to a stake.

25 About midnight, while Paul and Silas were praying and singing hymns to God as the prisoners listened, 26 there was suddenly such a severe earthquake that the foundations of the jail shook; all the doors flew open, and the chains of all were pulled loose. 27 When the jailer woke up and saw the prison doors wide open, he drew [his] sword and was about to kill himself, thinking that the prisoners had escaped. 28 But Paul shouted out in a loud voice, "Do no harm to yourself; we are all here." 29 He asked for a light and rushed in and, trembling with fear, he fell down before Paul and Silas. 30 Then he brought them out and said, "Sirs, what must I do to be saved?" 31 And they said, "Believe in the Lord Jesus and you and your household will be saved." 32 So they spoke the word of the Lord to him and to everyone in his house. 33 He took them in at that hour of the night and bathed their wounds; then he and all his family were baptized at once. 34 He brought them up into his house and provided a meal and with his household rejoiced at having come to faith in God.

35 But when it was day, the magistrates sent the lictors with the order, "Release those men." 36 The jailer reported the[se] words to Paul, "The magistrates have sent orders that you be released. Now, then, come out and go in peace." 37 But Paul said to them, "They have beaten us publicly, even though we are Roman citizens and have not been tried, and have thrown us into prison. And now, are they going to release us secretly? By no means. Let them come themselves and lead us out." 38 The lictors reported these words to the magistrates, and they became alarmed when they heard that they were Roman citizens. 39 So they came and placated them, and led them out and asked that they leave the city. 40 When they had come out of the prison, they went to Lydia's house where they saw and encouraged the brothers, and then they left.

17 When they took the road through Amphipolis and Apollonia, they reached Thessalonica, where there was a synagogue of the Jews. 2 Following his usual custom,

14 One of these women was called Lydia, a woman from the town of Thyatira who was in the purple-dye trade, and who revered God. She listened to us, and the Lord opened her heart to accept what Paul was saying. 15 After she and her household had been baptised she kept urging us, 'If you judge me a true believer in the Lord,' she said, 'come and stay with us.' And she would take no refusal.

16 It happened one day that as we were going to prayer, we were met by a slave-girl who was a soothsayer and made a lot of money for her masters by foretelling the future. 17 This girl started following Paul and the rest of us and shouting, 'Here are the servants of the Most High God; they have come to tell you how to be saved!' 18 She did this day after day until Paul was exasperated and turned round and said to the spirit, 'I order you in the name of Jesus Christ to leave that woman.' The spirit went out of her then and there.

19 When her masters saw that there was no hope of making any more money out of her, they seized Paul and Silas and dragged them into the market place before the authorities. 20 Taking them before the magistrates they said, 'These people are causing a disturbance in our city. They are Jews 21 and are advocating practices which it is unlawful for us as Romans to accept or follow.' 22 The crowd joined in and showed its hostility to them, so the magistrates had them stripped and ordered them to be flogged. 23 They were given many lashes and then thrown into prison, and the gaoler was told to keep a close watch on them. 24 So, following such instructions, he threw them into the inner prison and fastened their feet in the stocks.

25 In the middle of the night Paul and Silas were praying and singing God's praises, while the other prisoners listened. 26 Suddenly there was an earthquake that shook the prison to its foundations. All the doors flew open and the chains fell from all the prisoners. 27 When the gaoler woke and saw the doors wide open he drew his sword and was about to commit suicide, presuming that the prisoners had escaped. 28 But Paul shouted at the top of his voice, 'Do yourself no harm; we are all here.'

29 He called for lights, then rushed in, threw himself trembling at the feet of Paul and Silas, 30 and escorted them out, saying, 'Sirs, what must I do to be saved?' 31 They told him, 'Become a believer in the Lord Jesus, and you will be saved, and your household too.' 32 Then they preached the word of the Lord to him and to all his household. 33 Late as it was, he took them to wash their wounds, and was baptised then and there with all his household. 34 Afterwards he took them into his house and gave them a meal, and the whole household celebrated their conversion to belief in God.

35 When it was daylight the magistrates sent the lictors with the order: 'Release those men.' 36 The gaoler reported the message to Paul, 'The magistrates have sent an order for your release; you can go now and be on your way.' 37 'What!' Paul replied. 'Without trial they gave us a public flogging, though we are Roman citizens, and threw us into prison, and now they want to send us away on the quiet! Oh no! They must come and escort us out themselves.'

38 The lictors reported this to the magistrates, who were terrified when they heard they were Roman citizens. 39 They came and urged them to leave the town. 40 From the prison they went to Lydia's house where they saw all the brothers and gave them some encouragement; then they left.

17 Passing through Amphipolis and Apollonia, they eventually reached Thessalonica, where there was a Jewish synagogue. 2 Paul as usual went in and for three

in, as was his custom, and on three sabbath days argued with them from the scriptures, 3 explaining and proving that it was necessary for the Messiah p to suffer and to rise from the dead, and saying, "This is the Messiah, p Jesus whom I am proclaiming to you." 4 Some of them were persuaded and joined Paul and Silas, as did a great many of the devout Greeks and not a few of the leading women. 5 But the Jews became jealous, and with the help of some ruffians in the marketplaces they formed a mob and set the city in an uproar. While they were searching for Paul and Silas to bring them out to the assembly, they attacked Jason's house. 6 When they could not find them, they dragged Jason and some believers q before the city authorities, r shouting, "These people who have been turning the world upside down have come here also, 7 and Jason has entertained them as guests. They are all acting contrary to the decrees of the emperor, saying that there is another king named Jesus." 8 The people and the city officials were disturbed when they heard this, 9 and after they had taken bail from Jason and the others, they let them go.

10 That very night the believers q sent Paul and Silas off to Beroea; and when they arrived, they went to the Jewish synagogue. 11 These Jews were more receptive than those in Thessalonica, for they welcomed the message very eagerly and examined the scriptures every day to see whether these things were so. 12 Many of them therefore believed, including not a few Greek women and men of high standing. 13 But when the Jews of Thessalonica learned that the word of God had been proclaimed by Paul in Beroea as well, they came there too, to stir up and incite the crowds. 14 Then the believers q immediately sent Paul away to the coast, but Silas and Timothy remained behind. 15 Those who conducted Paul brought him as far as Athens; and after receiving instructions to have Silas and Timothy join him as soon as possible, they left him.

16 While Paul was waiting for them in Athens, he was deeply distressed to see that the city was full of idols. 17 So he argued in the synagogue with the Jews and the devout persons, and also in the marketplace s every day with those who happened to be there. 18 Also some Epicurean and Stoic philosophers debated with him. Some said, "What does this babbler want to say?" Others said, "He seems to be a proclaimer of foreign divinities." (This was because he was telling the good news about Jesus and the resurrection.) 19 So they took him and brought him to the Areopagus and asked him, "May we know what this new teaching is that you are presenting? 20 It sounds rather strange to us, so we would like to know what it means." 21 Now all the Athenians and the foreigners living there would spend their time in nothing but telling or hearing something new.

22 Then Paul stood in front of the Areopagus and said, "Athenians, I see how extremely religious you are in every way. 23 For as I went through the city and looked carefully at the objects of your r worship, I found among them an altar with the inscription, 'To an unknown god.' What therefore you worship as unknown, this I proclaim to you. 24 The God who made the world and everything in it, he who is Lord of heaven and earth, does not live in shrines made by human hands, 25 nor is he served by human hands, as though he needed anything, since he himself gives to all mortals life and breath and all things. 26 From one ancestor t he made all nations to inhabit the whole earth, and he allotted the times of their existence and the boundaries of the places where they would live, 27 so that they would search for

went to their meetings; and for the next three sabbaths he argued with them, quoting texts of scripture 3 which he expounded and applied to show that the Messiah had to suffer and rise from the dead. 'And this Jesus', he said, 'whom I am proclaiming to you is the Messiah.' 4 Some of them were convinced and joined Paul and Silas, as did a great number of godfearing Gentiles and a good many influential women.

5 The Jews in their jealousy recruited some ruffians from the dregs of society to gather a mob. They put the city in an uproar, and made for Jason's house with the intention of bringing Paul and Silas before the town assembly. 6 Failing to find them, they dragged Jason himself and some members of the congregation before the magistrates, shouting, 'The men who have made trouble the whole world over have now come here, 7 and Jason has harboured them. All of them flout the emperor's laws, and assert there is a rival king, Jesus.' 8 These words alarmed the mob and the magistrates also, 9 who took security from Jason and the others before letting them go.

10 As soon as darkness fell, the members of the congregation sent Paul and Silas off to Beroea; and, on arrival, they made their way to the synagogue. 11 The Jews here were more fair-minded than those at Thessalonica: they received the message with great eagerness, studying the scriptures every day to see whether it was true. 12 Many of them therefore became believers, and so did a fair number of Gentiles, women of standing as well as men. 13 But when the Thessalonian Jews learnt that the word of God had now been proclaimed by Paul in Beroea, they followed him there to stir up trouble and rouse the rabble. 14 At once the members of the congregation sent Paul down to the coast, while Silas and Timothy both stayed behind. 15 Paul's escort brought him as far as Athens, and came away with instructions for Silas and Timothy to rejoin him with all speed.

16 While Paul was waiting for them at Athens, he was outraged to see the city so full of idols. 17 He argued in the synagogue with the Jews and gentile worshippers, and also in the city square every day with casual passers-by. 18 Moreover, some of the Epicurean and Stoic philosophers joined issue with him. Some said, 'What can this charlatan be trying to say?' and others, 'He would appear to be a propagandist for foreign deities' — this because he was preaching about Jesus and the Resurrection. 19 They brought him to the Council of the Areopagus and asked, 'May we know what this new doctrine is that you propound? 20 You are introducing ideas that sound strange to us, and we should like to know what they mean.' 21 Now, all the Athenians and the resident foreigners had time for nothing except talking or hearing about the latest novelty.

22 Paul stood up before the Council of the Areopagus and began: 'Men of Athens, I see that in everything that concerns religion you are uncommonly scrupulous. 23 As I was going round looking at the objects of your worship, I noticed among other things an altar bearing the inscription "To an Unknown God". What you worship but do not know — this is what I now proclaim.

24 'The God who created the world and everything in it, and who is Lord of heaven and earth, does not live in shrines made by human hands. 25 It is not because he lacks anything that he accepts service at our hands, for he is himself the universal giver of life and breath — indeed of everything. 26 He created from one stock every nation of men to inhabit the whole earth's surface. He determined their eras in history and the limits of their territory. 27 They

---

p Or the Christ   q Gk brothers   r Gk politarchs   s Or civic
center; Gk agora   t Gk From one; other ancient authorities read
From one blood

17:19 to ... Areopagus: or to Mars' Hill.   17:22 before ...
Areopagus: or in the middle of Mars' Hill.   17:26 determined
... history: or fixed the ordered seasons.

Paul joined them, and for three sabbaths he entered into discussions with them from the scriptures, 3 expounding and demonstrating that the Messiah had to suffer and rise from the dead, and that "This is the Messiah, Jesus, whom I proclaim to you." 4 Some of them were convinced and joined Paul and Silas; so, too, a great number of Greeks who were worshipers, and not a few of the prominent women. 5 But the Jews became jealous and recruited some worthless men loitering in the public square, formed a mob, and set the city in turmoil. They marched on the house of Jason, intending to bring them before the people's assembly. 6 When they could not find them, they dragged Jason and some of the brothers before the city magistrates, shouting, "These people who have been creating a disturbance all over the world have now come here, 7 and Jason has welcomed them. They all act in opposition to the decrees of Caesar and claim instead that there is another king, Jesus." 8 They stirred up the crowd and the city magistrates who, upon hearing these charges, 9 took a surety payment from Jason and the others before releasing them.

10 The brothers immediately sent Paul and Silas to Beroea during the night. Upon arrival they went to the synagogue of the Jews. 11 These Jews were more fair-minded than those in Thessalonica, for they received the word with all willingness and examined the scriptures daily to determine whether these things were so. 12 Many of them became believers, as did not a few of the influential Greek women and men. 13 But when the Jews of Thessalonica learned that the word of God had now been proclaimed by Paul in Beroea also, they came there too to cause a commotion and stir up the crowds. 14 So the brothers at once sent Paul on his way to the seacoast, while Silas and Timothy remained behind. 15 After Paul's escorts had taken him to Athens, they came away with instructions for Silas and Timothy to join him as soon as possible.

16 While Paul was waiting for them in Athens, he grew exasperated at the sight of the city full of idols. 17 So he debated in the synagogue with the Jews and with the worshipers, and daily in the public square with whoever happened to be there. 18 Even some of the Epicurean and Stoic philosophers engaged him in discussion. Some asked, "What is this scavenger trying to say?" Others said, "He sounds like a promoter of foreign deities," because he was preaching about 'Jesus' and 'Resurrection.' 19 They took him and led him to the Areopagus and said, "May we learn what this new teaching is that you speak of? 20 For you bring some strange notions to our ears; we should like to know what these things mean.' 21 Now all the Athenians as well as the foreigners residing there used their time for nothing else but telling or hearing something new.

22 Then Paul stood up at the Areopagus and said: "You Athenians, I see that in every respect you are very religious. 23 For as I walked around looking carefully at your shrines, I even discovered an altar inscribed, 'To an Unknown God.' What therefore you unknowingly worship, I proclaim to you. 24 The God who made the world and all that is in it, the Lord of heaven and earth, does not dwell in sanctuaries made by human hands, 25 nor is he served by human hands because he needs anything. Rather it is he who gives to everyone life and breath and everything. 26 He made from one the whole human race to dwell on the entire surface of the earth, and he fixed the ordered seasons and the boundaries of their regions, 27 so that people might seek

consecutive Sabbaths developed the arguments from scripture for them, 3 explaining and proving how it was ordained that the Christ should suffer and rise from the dead. 'And the Christ', he said, 'is this Jesus whom I am proclaiming to you.' 4 Some of them were convinced and joined Paul and Silas, and so did a great many godfearing people and Greeks, as well as a number of the leading women.

5 The Jews, full of resentment, enlisted the help of a gang from the market place, stirred up a crowd, and soon had the whole city in an uproar. They made for Jason's house, hoping to bring them before the People's Assembly; 6 however, they found only Jason and some of the brothers, and these they dragged before the city council, shouting, 'The people who have been turning the whole world upside down have come here now; 7 they have been staying at Jason's. They have broken Caesar's edicts by claiming that there is another king, Jesus.' 8 Hearing this, the citizens and the city councillors were alarmed, 9 and they made Jason and the rest give security before setting them free.

10 When it was dark the brothers immediately sent Paul and Silas away to Beroea, where they went to the Jewish synagogue as soon as they arrived. 11 Here the Jews were more noble-minded than those in Thessalonica, and they welcomed the word very readily; every day they studied the scriptures to check whether it was true. 12 Many of them became believers, and so did many Greek women of high standing and a number of the men.

13 When the Jews of Thessalonica came to learn that the word of God was being preached by Paul in Beroea as well, they went there to make trouble and stir up the people. 14 So the brothers arranged for Paul to go immediately as far as the coast, leaving Silas and Timothy behind. 15 Paul's escort took him as far as Athens, and went back with instructions for Silas and Timothy to rejoin Paul as soon as they could.

16 Paul waited for them in Athens and there his whole soul was revolted at the sight of a city given over to idolatry. 17 In the synagogue he debated with the Jews and the godfearing, and in the market place he debated every day with anyone whom he met. 18 Even a few Epicurean and Stoic philosophers argued with him. Some said, 'What can this parrot mean?' And, because he was preaching about Jesus and Resurrection, others said, 'He seems to be a propagandist for some outlandish gods.'

19 They got him to accompany them to the Areopagus, where they said to him, 'Can we know what this new doctrine is that you are teaching? 20 Some of the things you say seemed startling to us and we would like to find out what they mean.' 21 The one amusement the Athenians and the foreigners living there seem to have is to discuss and listen to the latest ideas.

22 So Paul stood before the whole council of the Areopagus and made this speech:

'Men of Athens, I have seen for myself how extremely scrupulous you are in all religious matters, 23 because, as I strolled round looking at your sacred monuments, I noticed among other things an altar inscribed: To An Unknown God. In fact, the unknown God you revere is the one I proclaim to you.

24 'Since the God who made the world and everything in it is himself Lord of heaven and earth, he does not make his home in shrines made by human hands. 25 Nor is he in need of anything, that he should be served by human hands; on the contrary, it is he who gives everything—including life and breath—to everyone. 26 From one single principle he not only created the whole human race so that they could occupy the entire earth, but he decreed the times and limits of their habitation. 27 And he did this so that they might seek

NEW REVISED STANDARD VERSION

God*u* and perhaps grope for him and find him — though indeed he is not far from each one of us. 28 For 'In him we live and move and have our being'; as even some of your own poets have said,

'For we too are his offspring.'

29 Since we are God's offspring, we ought not to think that the deity is like gold, or silver, or stone, an image formed by the art and imagination of mortals. 30 While God has overlooked the times of human ignorance, now he commands all people everywhere to repent, 31 because he has fixed a day on which he will have the world judged in righteousness by a man whom he has appointed, and of this he has given assurance to all by raising him from the dead."

32 When they heard of the resurrection of the dead, some scoffed; but others said, "We will hear you again about this." 33 At that point Paul left them. 34 But some of them joined him and became believers, including Dionysius the Areopagite and a woman named Damaris, and others with them.

18 After this Paul*v* left Athens and went to Corinth. 2 There he found a Jew named Aquila, a native of Pontus, who had recently come from Italy with his wife Priscilla, because Claudius had ordered all Jews to leave Rome. Paul*w* went to see them, 3 and, because he was of the same trade, he stayed with them, and they worked together — by trade they were tentmakers. 4 Every sabbath he would argue in the synagogue and would try to convince Jews and Greeks.

5 When Silas and Timothy arrived from Macedonia, Paul was occupied with proclaiming the word,*x* testifying to the Jews that the Messiah*y* was Jesus. 6 When they opposed and reviled him, in protest he shook the dust from his clothes*z* and said to them, "Your blood be on your own heads! I am innocent. From now on I will go to the Gentiles." 7 Then he left the synagogue*a* and went to the house of a man named Titus*b* Justus, a worshiper of God; his house was next door to the synagogue. 8 Crispus, the official of the synagogue, became a believer in the Lord, together with all his household; and many of the Corinthians who heard Paul became believers and were baptized. 9 One night the Lord said to Paul in a vision, "Do not be afraid, but speak and do not be silent; 10 for I am with you, and no one will lay a hand on you to harm you, for there are many in this city who are my people." 11 He stayed there a year and six months, teaching the word of God among them.

12 But when Gallio was proconsul of Achaia, the Jews made a united attack on Paul and brought him before the tribunal. 13 They said, "This man is persuading people to worship God in ways that are contrary to the law." 14 Just as Paul was about to speak, Gallio said to the Jews, "If it were a matter of crime or serious villainy, I would be justified in accepting the complaint of you Jews; 15 but since it is a matter of questions about words and names and your own law, see to it yourselves; I do not wish to be a judge of these matters." 16 And he dismissed them from the tribunal. 17 Then all of them*c* seized Sosthenes, the official of the synagogue, and beat him in front of the tribunal. But Gallio paid no attention to any of these things.

18 After staying there for a considerable time, Paul said farewell to the believers*d* and sailed for Syria, accompanied by Priscilla and Aquila. At Cenchreae he had his hair cut, for he was under a vow. 19 When they reached Ephesus,

REVISED ENGLISH BIBLE

were to seek God in the hope that, groping after him, they might find him; though indeed he is not far from each one of us, 28 for in him we live and move, in him we exist; as some of your own poets have said, "We are also his offspring." 29 Being God's offspring, then, we ought not to suppose that the deity is like an image in gold or silver or stone, shaped by human craftsmanship and design. 30 God has overlooked the age of ignorance; but now he commands men and women everywhere to repent, 31 because he has fixed the day on which he will have the world judged, and justly judged, by a man whom he has designated; of this he has given assurance to all by raising him from the dead.'

32 When they heard about the raising of the dead, some scoffed; others said, 'We will hear you on this subject some other time.' 33 So Paul left the assembly. 34 Some men joined him and became believers, including Dionysius, a member of the Council of the Areopagus; and also a woman named Damaris, with others besides.

18 After this he left Athens and went to Corinth. 2 There he met a Jew named Aquila, a native of Pontus, and his wife Priscilla; they had recently arrived from Italy because Claudius had issued an edict that all Jews should leave Rome. Paul approached them 3 and, because he was of the same trade, he made his home with them; they were tentmakers and Paul worked with them. 4 He also held discussions in the synagogue sabbath by sabbath, trying to convince both Jews and Gentiles.

5 Then Silas and Timothy came down from Macedonia, and Paul devoted himself entirely to preaching, maintaining before the Jews that the Messiah is Jesus. 6 When, however, they opposed him and resorted to abuse, he shook out the folds of his cloak and declared, 'Your blood be on your own heads! My conscience is clear! From now on I shall go to the Gentiles.' 7 With that he left, and went to the house of a worshipper of God named Titus Justus, who lived next door to the synagogue. 8 Crispus, the president of the synagogue, became a believer in the Lord, as did all his household; and a number of Corinthians who heard him believed and were baptized. 9 One night in a vision the Lord said to Paul, 'Have no fear: go on with your preaching and do not be silenced. 10 I am with you, and no attack shall harm you, for I have many in this city who are my people.' 11 So he settled there for eighteen months, teaching the word of God among them.

12 But when Gallio was proconsul of Achaia, the Jews made a concerted attack on Paul and brought him before the court. 13 'This man', they said, 'is inducing people to worship God in ways that are against the law.' 14 Paul was just about to speak when Gallio declared, 'If it had been a question of crime or grave misdemeanour, I should, of course, have given you Jews a patient hearing, 15 but if it is some bickering about words and names and your Jewish law, you may settle it yourselves. I do not intend to be a judge of these matters.' 16 And he dismissed them from the court. 17 Then they all attacked Sosthenes, the president of the synagogue, and beat him up in full view of the tribunal. But all this left Gallio quite unconcerned.

18 Paul stayed on at Corinth for some time, and then took leave of the congregation. Accompanied by Priscilla and Aquila, he sailed for Syria, having had his hair cut off at Cenchreae in fulfilment of a vow. 19 They put in at Ephesus,

---

u Other ancient authorities read *the Lord*   *v* Gk *he*   *w* Gk *He*
x Gk *with the word*   *y* Or *the Christ*   *z* Gk *reviled him, he shook out his clothes*   *a* Gk *left there*   *b* Other ancient authorities read *Titus*   *c* Other ancient authorities read *all the Greeks*
d Gk *brothers*

NEW AMERICAN BIBLE

God, even perhaps grope for him and find him, though indeed he is not far from any one of us. 28 For 'In him we live and move and have our being,' as even some of your poets have said, 'For we too are his offspring.' 29 Since therefore we are the offspring of God, we ought not to think that the divinity is like an image fashioned from gold, silver, or stone by human art and imagination. 30 God has overlooked the times of ignorance, but now he demands that all people everywhere repent 31 because he has established a day on which he will 'judge the world with justice' through a man he has appointed, and he has provided confirmation for all by raising him from the dead."

32 When they heard about resurrection of the dead, some began to scoff, but others said, "We should like to hear you on this some other time." 33 And so Paul left them. 34 But some did join him, and became believers. Among them were Dionysius, a member of the Court of the Areopagus, a woman named Damaris, and others with them.

18 After this he left Athens and went to Corinth. 2 There he met a Jew named Aquila, a native of Pontus, who had recently come from Italy with his wife Priscilla because Claudius had ordered all the Jews to leave Rome. He went to visit them 3 and, because he practiced the same trade, stayed with them and worked, for they were tentmakers by trade. 4 Every sabbath, he entered into discussions in the synagogue, attempting to convince both Jews and Greeks.

5 When Silas and Timothy came down from Macedonia, Paul began to occupy himself totally with preaching the word, testifying to the Jews that the Messiah was Jesus. 6 When they opposed him and reviled him, he shook out his garments and said to them, "Your blood be on your heads! I am clear of responsibility. From now on I will go to the Gentiles." 7 So he left there and went to a house belonging to a man named Titus Justus, a worshiper of God; his house was next to a synagogue. 8 Crispus, the synagogue official, came to believe in the Lord along with his entire household, and many of the Corinthians who heard believed and were baptized. 9 One night in a vision the Lord said to Paul, "Do not be afraid. Go on speaking, and do not be silent, 10 for I am with you. No one will attack and harm you, for I have many people in this city." 11 He settled there for a year and a half and taught the word of God among them.

12 But when Gallio was proconsul of Achaia, the Jews rose up together against Paul and brought him to the tribunal, 13 saying, "This man is inducing people to worship God contrary to the law." 14 When Paul was about to reply, Gallio spoke to the Jews, "If it were a matter of some crime or malicious fraud, I should with reason hear the complaint of you Jews; 15 but since it is a question of arguments over doctrine and titles and your own law, see to it yourselves. I do not wish to be a judge of such matters." 16 And he drove them away from the tribunal. 17 They all seized Sosthenes, the synagogue official, and beat him in full view of the tribunal. But none of this was of concern to Gallio.

18 Paul remained for quite some time, and after saying farewell to the brothers he sailed for Syria, together with Priscilla and Aquila. At Cenchreae he had his hair cut because he had taken a vow. 19 When they reached Ephesus,

NEW JERUSALEM BIBLE

the deity and, by feeling their way towards him, succeed in finding him; and indeed he is not far from any of us, 28 since it is in him that we live, and move, and exist, c as indeed some of your own writers have said:

We are all his children. d

29 'Since we are the children of God, we have no excuse for thinking that the deity looks like anything in gold, silver or stone that has been carved and designed by a man.

30 'But now, overlooking the times of ignorance, God is telling everyone everywhere that they must repent, 31 because he has fixed a day when the whole world will be judged in uprightness by a man he has appointed. And God has publicly proved this by raising him from the dead.'

32 At this mention of rising from the dead, some of them burst out laughing; others said, 'We would like to hear you talk about this another time.' 33 After that Paul left them, 34 but there were some who attached themselves to him and became believers, among them Dionysius the Areopagite and a woman called Damaris, and others besides.

18 After this Paul left Athens and went to Corinth, 2 where he met a Jew called Aquila whose family came from Pontus. He and his wife Priscilla had recently left Italy because an edict of Claudius had expelled all the Jews from Rome. Paul went to visit them, 3 and when he found they were tentmakers, of the same trade as himself, he lodged with them, and they worked together. 4 Every Sabbath he used to hold debates in the synagogues, trying to convert Jews as well as Greeks.

5 After Silas and Timothy had arrived from Macedonia, Paul devoted all his time to preaching, declaring to the Jews that Jesus was the Christ. 6 When they turned against him and started to insult him, he took his cloak and shook it out in front of them, e saying, 'Your blood be on your own heads; from now on I will go to the gentiles with a clear conscience.' 7 Then he left the synagogue and moved to the house next door that belonged to a worshipper of God called Justus. 8 Crispus, president of the synagogue, and his whole household, all became believers in the Lord. Many Corinthians when they heard this became believers and were baptised. 9 One night the Lord spoke to Paul in a vision, 'Be fearless; speak out and do not keep silence: 10 I am with you. I have so many people that belong to me in this city that no one will attempt to hurt you.' 11 So Paul stayed there preaching the word of God among them for eighteen months.

12 But while Gallio was proconsul of Achaia, the Jews made a concerted attack on Paul and brought him before the tribunal, saying, 13 'We accuse this man of persuading people to worship God in a way that breaks the Law.' 14 Before Paul could open his mouth, Gallio said to the Jews, 'Listen, you Jews. If this were a misdemeanour or a crime, it would be in order for me to listen to your plea; 15 but if it is only quibbles about words and names, and about your own Law, then you must deal with it yourselves — I have no intention of making legal decisions about these things.' 16 Then he began to hustle them out of the court, 17 and at once they all turned on Sosthenes, the synagogue president, and beat him in front of the tribunal. Gallio refused to take any notice at all.

18 After staying on for some time, Paul took leave of the brothers and sailed for Syria, accompanied by Priscilla and Aquila. At Cenchreae he had his hair cut off, because of a vow he had made.

c 17 From the Gk poet Epimenides.   d 17 The Gk philosopher Aratus.   e 18 cf. 13:47; 28:25.

| NEW REVISED STANDARD VERSION | REVISED ENGLISH BIBLE |

he left them there, but first he himself went into the synagogue and had a discussion with the Jews. 20 When they asked him to stay longer, he declined; 21 but on taking leave of them, he said, "I*e* will return to you, if God wills." Then he set sail from Ephesus.

22 When he had landed at Caesarea, he went up to Jerusalem*f* and greeted the church, and then went down to Antioch. 23 After spending some time there he departed and went from place to place through the region of Galatia*g* and Phrygia, strengthening all the disciples.

24 Now there came to Ephesus a Jew named Apollos, a native of Alexandria. He was an eloquent man, well-versed in the scriptures. 25 He had been instructed in the Way of the Lord; and he spoke with burning enthusiasm and taught accurately the things concerning Jesus, though he knew only the baptism of John. 26 He began to speak boldly in the synagogue; but when Priscilla and Aquila heard him, they took him aside and explained the Way of God to him more accurately. 27 And when he wished to cross over to Achaia, the believers*h* encouraged him and wrote to the disciples to welcome him. On his arrival he greatly helped those who through grace had become believers, 28 for he powerfully refuted the Jews in public, showing by the scriptures that the Messiah*i* is Jesus.

19 While Apollos was in Corinth, Paul passed through the interior regions and came to Ephesus, where he found some disciples. 2 He said to them, "Did you receive the Holy Spirit when you became believers?" They replied, "No, we have not even heard that there is a Holy Spirit." 3 Then he said, "Into what then were you baptized?" They answered, "Into John's baptism." 4 Paul said, "John baptized with the baptism of repentance, telling the people to believe in the one who was to come after him, that is, in Jesus." 5 On hearing this, they were baptized in the name of the Lord Jesus. 6 When Paul had laid his hands on them, the Holy Spirit came upon them, and they spoke in tongues and prophesied— 7 altogether there were about twelve of them.

8 He entered the synagogue and for three months spoke out boldly, and argued persuasively about the kingdom of God. 9 When some stubbornly refused to believe and spoke evil of the Way before the congregation, he left them, taking the disciples with him, and argued daily in the lecture hall of Tyrannus.*j* 10 This continued for two years, so that all the residents of Asia, both Jews and Greeks, heard the word of the Lord.

11 God did extraordinary miracles through Paul, 12 so that when the handkerchiefs or aprons that had touched his skin were brought to the sick, their diseases left them, and the evil spirits came out of them. 13 Then some itinerant Jewish exorcists tried to use the name of the Lord Jesus over those who had evil spirits, saying, "I adjure you by the Jesus whom Paul proclaims." 14 Seven sons of a Jewish high priest named Sceva were doing this. 15 But the evil spirit said to them in reply, "Jesus I know, and Paul I know; but who are you?" 16 Then the man with the evil spirit leaped on them, mastered them all, and so overpowered them that they fled out of the house naked and wounded. 17 When this became known to all residents of Ephesus, both Jews and Greeks, everyone was awestruck; and the name of the Lord Jesus was praised. 18 Also many of those who became believers confessed and disclosed their practices. 19 A number

where he parted from his companions; he himself went into the synagogue and held a discussion with the Jews. 20 He was asked to stay longer, but he declined 21 and set sail from Ephesus, promising, as he took leave of them, 'I shall come back to you if it is God's will.' 22 On landing at Caesarea, he went up and greeted the church; and then went down to Antioch. 23 After some time there he set out again on a journey through the Galatian country and then through Phrygia, bringing new strength to all the disciples.

24 THERE arrived at Ephesus a Jew named Apollos, an Alexandrian by birth, an eloquent man, powerful in his use of the scriptures. 25 He had been instructed in the way of the Lord and was full of spiritual fervour; and in his discourses he taught accurately the facts about Jesus, though the only baptism he knew was John's. 26 He now began to speak boldly in the synagogue, where Priscilla and Aquila heard him; they took him in hand and expounded the way to him in greater detail. 27 Finding that he wanted to go across to Achaia, the congregation gave him their support, and wrote to the disciples there to make him welcome. From the time of his arrival, he was very helpful to those who had by God's grace become believers, 28 for he strenuously confuted the Jews, demonstrating publicly from the scriptures that the Messiah is Jesus.

19 While Apollos was at Corinth, Paul travelled through the inland regions till he came to Ephesus, where he found a number of disciples. 2 When he asked them, 'Did you receive the Holy Spirit when you became believers?' they replied, 'No, we were not even told that there is a Holy Spirit.' 3 He asked, 'Then what baptism were you given?' 'John's baptism,' they answered. 4 Paul said, 'The baptism that John gave was a baptism in token of repentance, and he told the people to put their trust in one who was to come after him, that is, in Jesus.' 5 On hearing this they were baptized into the name of the Lord Jesus; 6 and when Paul had laid his hands on them, the Holy Spirit came upon them and they spoke in tongues of ecstasy and prophesied. 7 There were about a dozen men in all.

8 During the next three months he attended the synagogue and with persuasive argument spoke boldly about the kingdom of God. 9 When some proved obdurate and would not believe, speaking evil of the new way before the congregation, he withdrew from them, taking the disciples with him, and continued to hold discussions daily in the lecture hall of Tyrannus. 10 This went on for two years, with the result that the whole population of the province of Asia, both Jews and Gentiles, heard the word of the Lord. 11 God worked extraordinary miracles through Paul: 12 when handkerchiefs and scarves which had been in contact with his skin were carried to the sick, they were cured of their diseases, and the evil spirits came out of them.

13 Some itinerant Jewish exorcists tried their hand at using the name of the Lord Jesus on those possessed by evil spirits; they would say, 'I adjure you by Jesus whom Paul proclaims.' 14 There were seven sons of Sceva, a Jewish chief priest, who were doing this, 15 when the evil spirit responded, 'Jesus I recognize, Paul I know, but who are you?' 16 The man with the evil spirit flew at them, overpowered them all, and handled them with such violence that they ran out of the house battered and naked. 17 Everybody in Ephesus, Jew and Gentile alike, got to know of it, and all were awestruck, while the name of the Lord Jesus gained in honour. 18 Moreover many of those who had become believers came and openly confessed that they had been using magical spells. 19 A good many of those who formerly prac-

---

e Other ancient authorities read *I must at all costs keep the approaching festival in Jerusalem, but I* *f* Gk *went up* *g* Gk *the Galatian region* *h* Gk *brothers* *i* Or *the Christ* *j* Other ancient authorities read *of a certain Tyrannus, from eleven o'clock in the morning to four in the afternoon*

18:24 **an eloquent man:** *or* a learned man. 18:26 **the way:** *some witnesses read* the way of God.

NEW AMERICAN BIBLE

he left them there, while he entered the synagogue and held discussions with the Jews. 20 Although they asked him to stay for a longer time, he did not consent, 21 but as he said farewell he promised, "I shall come back to you again, God willing." Then he set sail from Ephesus. 22 Upon landing at Caesarea, he went up and greeted the church and then went down to Antioch. 23 After staying there some time, he left and traveled in orderly sequence through the Galatian country and Phrygia, bringing strength to all the disciples.

24 A Jew named Apollos, a native of Alexandria, an eloquent speaker, arrived in Ephesus. He was an authority on the scriptures. 25 He had been instructed in the Way of the Lord and, with ardent spirit, spoke and taught accurately about Jesus, although he knew only the baptism of John. 26 He began to speak boldly in the synagogue; but when Priscilla and Aquila heard him, they took him aside and explained to him the Way [of God] more accurately. 27 And when he wanted to cross to Achaia, the brothers encouraged him and wrote to the disciples there to welcome him. After his arrival he gave great assistance to those who had come to believe through grace. 28 He vigorously refuted the Jews in public, establishing from the scriptures that the Messiah is Jesus.

19 While Apollos was in Corinth, Paul traveled through the interior of the country and came [down] to Ephesus where he found some disciples. 2 He said to them, "Did you receive the holy Spirit when you became believers?" They answered him, "We have never even heard that there is a holy Spirit." 3 He said, "How were you baptized?" They replied, "With the baptism of John." 4 Paul then said, "John baptized with a baptism of repentance, telling the people to believe in the one who was to come after him, that is, in Jesus." 5 When they heard this, they were baptized in the name of the Lord Jesus. 6 And when Paul laid [his] hands on them, the holy Spirit came upon them, and they spoke in tongues and prophesied. 7 Altogether there were about twelve men.

8 He entered the synagogue, and for three months debated boldly with persuasive arguments about the kingdom of God. 9 But when some in their obstinacy and disbelief disparaged the Way before the assembly, he withdrew and took his disciples with him and began to hold daily discussions in the lecture hall of Tyrannus. 10 This continued for two years with the result that all the inhabitants of the province of Asia heard the word of the Lord, Jews and Greeks alike. 11 So extraordinary were the mighty deeds God accomplished at the hands of Paul 12 that when face cloths or aprons that touched his skin were applied to the sick, their diseases left them and the evil spirits came out of them. 13 Then some itinerant Jewish exorcists tried to invoke the name of the Lord Jesus over those with evil spirits, saying, "I adjure you by the Jesus whom Paul preaches." 14 When the seven sons of Sceva, a Jewish high priest, tried to do this, 15 the evil spirit said to them in reply, "Jesus I recognize, Paul I know, but who are you?" 16 The person with the evil spirit then sprang at them and subdued them all. He so overpowered them that they fled naked and wounded from that house. 17 When this became known to all the Jews and Greeks who lived in Ephesus, fear fell upon them all, and the name of the Lord Jesus was held in great esteem. 18 Many of those who had become believers came forward and openly acknowledged their former practices. 19 More-

NEW JERUSALEM BIBLE

19 When they reached Ephesus, he left them, but first he went alone to the synagogue to debate with the Jews. 20 They asked him to stay longer, but he declined, 21 though when he took his leave he said, 'I will come back another time, God willing.' Then he sailed from Ephesus. 22 He landed at Caesarea and went up to greet the church. Then he came down to Antioch 23 where he spent a short time before continuing his journey through the Galatian country and then through Phrygia, encouraging all the followers.

24 An Alexandrian Jew named Apollos *f* now arrived in Ephesus. He was an eloquent man, with a sound knowledge of the scriptures, and yet, 25 though he had been given instruction in the Way of the Lord and preached with great spiritual fervour and was accurate in all the details he taught about Jesus, he had experienced only the baptism of John. 26 He began to teach fearlessly in the synagogue and, when Priscilla and Aquila heard him, they attached themselves to him and gave him more detailed instruction about the Way. 27 When Apollos thought of crossing over to Achaia, the brothers encouraged him and wrote asking the disciples to welcome him. When he arrived there he was able by God's grace to help the believers considerably 28 by the energetic way he refuted the Jews in public, demonstrating from the scriptures that Jesus was the Christ.

19 It happened that while Apollos was in Corinth, Paul made his way overland as far as Ephesus, where he found a number of disciples. 2 When he asked, 'Did you receive the Holy Spirit when you became believers?' they answered, 'No, we were never even told there was such a thing as a Holy Spirit.' 3 He asked, 'Then how were you baptised?' They replied, 'With John's baptism.' 4 Paul said, 'John's baptism was a baptism of repentance; but he insisted that the people should believe in the one who was to come after him—namely Jesus.' 5 When they heard this, they were baptised in the name of the Lord Jesus, 6 and the moment Paul had laid hands on them the Holy Spirit came down on them, and they began to speak with tongues and to prophesy. 7 There were about twelve of these men in all.

8 He began by going to the synagogue, where he spoke out fearlessly and argued persuasively about the kingdom of God. He did this for three months, 9 till the attitude of some of the congregation hardened into unbelief. As soon as they began attacking the Way in public, he broke with them and took his disciples apart to hold daily discussions in the lecture room of Tyrannus. 10 This went on for two years, with the result that all the inhabitants of Asia, both Jews and Greeks, were able to hear the word of the Lord. 11 So remarkable were the miracles worked by God at Paul's hands 12 that handkerchiefs or aprons which had touched him were taken to the sick, and they were cured of their illnesses, and the evil spirits came out of them. 13 But some itinerant Jewish exorcists too tried pronouncing the name of the Lord Jesus over people who were possessed by evil spirits; they used to say, 'I adjure you by the Jesus whose spokesman is Paul.' 14 Among those who did this were seven sons of Sceva, a Jewish chief priest. 15 The evil spirit replied, 'Jesus I recognise, and Paul I know, but who are you?' 16 and the man with the evil spirit hurled himself at them and overpowered first one and then another, and handled them so violently that they fled from that house stripped of clothing and badly mauled. 17 Everybody in Ephesus, both Jews and Greeks, heard about this episode; everyone was filled with awe, and the name of the Lord Jesus came to be held in great honour. 18 Some believers, too, came forward to admit in detail how they had used spells 19 and a number of them who had

---

18, 26: *The Way [of God]:* other manuscripts here read "the Way of the Lord," "the word of the Lord," or simply "the Way."

f **18** cf. 1 Co 1:12; 3:4–11.

NEW REVISED STANDARD VERSION

REVISED ENGLISH BIBLE

of those who practiced magic collected their books and burned them publicly; when the value of these books*k* was calculated, it was found to come to fifty thousand silver coins. 20 So the word of the Lord grew mightily and prevailed.

21 Now after these things had been accomplished, Paul resolved in the Spirit to go through Macedonia and Achaia, and then to go on to Jerusalem. He said, "After I have gone there, I must also see Rome." 22 So he sent two of his helpers, Timothy and Erastus, to Macedonia, while he himself stayed for some time longer in Asia.

23 About that time no little disturbance broke out concerning the Way. 24 A man named Demetrius, a silversmith who made silver shrines of Artemis, brought no little business to the artisans. 25 These he gathered together, with the workers of the same trade, and said, "Men, you know that we get our wealth from this business. 26 You also see and hear that not only in Ephesus but in almost the whole of Asia this Paul has persuaded and drawn away a considerable number of people by saying that gods made with hands are not gods. 27 And there is danger not only that this trade of ours may come into disrepute but also that the temple of the great goddess Artemis will be scorned, and she will be deprived of her majesty that brought all Asia and the world to worship her."

28 When they heard this, they were enraged and shouted, "Great is Artemis of the Ephesians!" 29 The city was filled with the confusion; and people*l* rushed together to the theater, dragging with them Gaius and Aristarchus, Macedonians who were Paul's travel companions. 30 Paul wished to go into the crowd, but the disciples would not let him; 31 even some officials of the province of Asia,*m* who were friendly to him, sent him a message urging him not to venture into the theater. 32 Meanwhile, some were shouting one thing, some another; for the assembly was in confusion, and most of them did not know why they had come together. 33 Some of the crowd gave instructions to Alexander, whom the Jews had pushed forward. And Alexander motioned for silence and tried to make a defense before the people. 34 But when they recognized that he was a Jew, for about two hours all of them shouted in unison, "Great is Artemis of the Ephesians!" 35 But when the town clerk had quieted the crowd, he said, "Citizens of Ephesus, who is there that does not know that the city of the Ephesians is the temple keeper of the great Artemis and of the statue that fell from heaven?*n* 36 Since these things cannot be denied, you ought to be quiet and do nothing rash. 37 You have brought these men here who are neither temple robbers nor blasphemers of our*o* goddess. 38 If therefore Demetrius and the artisans with him have a complaint against anyone, the courts are open, and there are proconsuls; let them bring charges there against one another. 39 If there is anything further*p* you want to know, it must be settled in the regular assembly. 40 For we are in danger of being charged with rioting today, since there is no cause that we can give to justify this commotion." 41 When he had said this, he dismissed the assembly.

20 After the uproar had ceased, Paul sent for the disciples; and after encouraging them and saying farewell, he left for Macedonia. 2 When he had gone through

tised magic collected their books and burnt them publicly, and when the total value was reckoned up it came to fifty thousand pieces of silver. 20 In such ways the word of the Lord showed its power, spreading more and more widely and effectively.

21 When matters had reached this stage, Paul made up his mind to visit Macedonia and Achaia and then go on to Jerusalem. 'After I have been there,' he said, 'I must see Rome also.' 22 He sent two of his assistants, Timothy and Erastus, to Macedonia, while he himself stayed some time longer in the province of Asia.

23 It was about this time that the Christian movement gave rise to a serious disturbance. 24 There was a man named Demetrius, a silversmith who made silver shrines of Artemis, and provided considerable employment for the craftsmen. 25 He called a meeting of them and of the workers in allied trades, and addressed them: 'As you men know, our prosperity depends on this industry. 26 But this fellow Paul, as you can see and hear for yourselves, has perverted crowds of people with his propaganda, not only at Ephesus but also in practically the whole of the province of Asia; he tells them that gods made by human hands are not gods at all. 27 There is danger for us here; it is not only that our line of business will be discredited, but also that the sanctuary of the great goddess Artemis will cease to command respect; and then it will not be long before she who is worshipped by all Asia and the civilized world is brought down from her divine pre-eminence.'

28 On hearing this, they were enraged, and began to shout, 'Great is Artemis of the Ephesians!' 29 The whole city was in an uproar; they made a concerted rush into the theatre, hustling along with them Paul's travelling companions, the Macedonians Gaius and Aristarchus. 30 Paul wanted to appear before the assembly but the other Christians would not let him. 31 Even some of the dignitaries of the province, who were friendly towards him, sent a message urging him not to venture into the theatre. 32 Meanwhile some were shouting one thing, some another, for the assembly was in an uproar and most of them did not know what they had all come for. 33 Some of the crowd explained the trouble to Alexander, whom the Jews had pushed to the front, and he, motioning for silence, attempted to make a defence before the assembly. 34 But when they recognized that he was a Jew, one shout arose from them all: 'Great is Artemis of the Ephesians!' and they kept it up for about two hours.

35 The town clerk, however, quietened the crowd. 'Citizens of Ephesus,' he said, 'all the world knows that our city of Ephesus is temple warden of the great Artemis and of that image of her which fell from heaven. 36 Since these facts are beyond dispute, your proper course is to keep calm and do nothing rash. 37 These men whom you have brought here as offenders have committed no sacrilege and uttered no blasphemy against our goddess. 38 If, therefore, Demetrius and his craftsmen have a case against anyone, there are assizes and there are proconsuls; let the parties bring their charges and countercharges. 39 But if it is a larger question you are raising, it will be dealt with in the statutory assembly. 40 We certainly run the risk of being charged with riot for this day's work. There is no justification for it, and it would be impossible for us to give any explanation of this turmoil.' 41 With that he dismissed the assembly.

20 When the disturbance was over, Paul sent for the disciples and, after encouraging them, said goodbye and set out on his journey to Macedonia. 2 He travelled

k Gk *them*   *l* Gk *they*   *m* Gk *some of the Asiarchs*   *n* Meaning of Gk uncertain   *o* Other ancient authorities read *your*   *p* Other ancient authorities read *about other matters*

over, a large number of those who had practiced magic collected their books and burned them in public. They calculated their value and found it to be fifty thousand silver pieces. 20 Thus did the word of the Lord continue to spread with influence and power.

21 When this was concluded, Paul made up his mind to travel through Macedonia and Achaia, and then to go on to Jerusalem, saying, "After I have been there, I must visit Rome also." 22 Then he sent to Macedonia two of his assistants, Timothy and Erastus, while he himself stayed for a while in the province of Asia.

23 About that time a serious disturbance broke out concerning the Way. 24 There was a silversmith named Demetrius who made miniature silver shrines of Artemis and provided no little work for the craftsmen. 25 He called a meeting of these and other workers in related crafts and said, "Men, you know well that our prosperity derives from this work. 26 As you can now see and hear, not only in Ephesus but throughout most of the province of Asia this Paul has persuaded and misled a great number of people by saying that gods made by hands are not gods at all. 27 The danger grows, not only that our business will be discredited, but also that the temple of the great goddess Artemis will be of no account, and that she whom the whole province of Asia and all the world worship will be stripped of her magnificence."

28 When they heard this, they were filled with fury and began to shout, "Great is Artemis of the Ephesians!" 29 The city was filled with confusion, and the people rushed with one accord into the theater, seizing Gaius and Aristarchus, the Macedonians, Paul's traveling companions. 30 Paul wanted to go before the crowd, but the disciples would not let him, 31 and even some of the Asiarchs who were friends of his sent word to him advising him not to venture into the theater. 32 Meanwhile, some were shouting one thing, others something else; the assembly was in chaos, and most of the people had no idea why they had come together. 33 Some of the crowd prompted Alexander, as the Jews pushed him forward, and Alexander signaled with his hand that he wished to explain something to the gathering. 34 But when they recognized that he was a Jew, they all shouted in unison, for about two hours, "Great is Artemis of the Ephesians!" 35 Finally the town clerk restrained the crowd and said, "You Ephesians, what person is there who does not know that the city of the Ephesians is the guardian of the temple of the great Artemis and of her image that fell from the sky? 36 Since these things are undeniable, you must calm yourselves and not do anything rash. 37 The men you brought here are not temple robbers, nor have they insulted our goddess. 38 If Demetrius and his fellow craftsmen have a complaint against anyone, courts are in session, and there are proconsuls. Let them bring charges against one another. 39 If you have anything further to investigate, let the matter be settled in the lawful assembly, 40 for, as it is, we are in danger of being charged with rioting because of today's conduct. There is no cause for it. We shall [not] be able to give a reason for this demonstration." With these words he dismissed the assembly.

20 When the disturbance was over, Paul had the disciples summoned and, after encouraging them, he bade them farewell and set out on his journey to Macedonia.

practised magic collected their books and made a bonfire of them in public. The value of these was calculated to be fifty thousand silver pieces.

20 In this powerful way the word of the Lord spread more and more widely and successfully.

21 When all this was over Paul made up his mind to go back to Jerusalem through Macedonia and Achaia. 'After I have been there,' he said, 'I must go on to see Rome as well.' 22 So he sent two of his helpers, Timothy and Erastus, ahead of him to Macedonia, while he remained for a time in Asia.

23 It was during this time that a serious disturbance broke out in connection with the Way. 24 A silversmith called Demetrius, who provided work for a large number of craftsmen making silver shrines of Diana, 25 called a general meeting of them with others in the same trade. 'As you know,' he said, 'it is on this industry that we depend for our prosperity. 26 Now you must have seen and heard how, not just in Ephesus but nearly everywhere in Asia, this man Paul has persuaded and converted a great number of people with his argument that gods made by hand are not gods at all. 27 This threatens not only to discredit our trade, but also to reduce the sanctuary of the great goddess Diana to unimportance. It could end up by taking away the prestige of a goddess venerated all over Asia, and indeed all over the world.' 28 This speech roused them to fury, and they started to shout, 'Great is Diana of the Ephesians!' 29 The whole town was filled with the uproar and the mob made a concerted rush to the theatre, dragging along two of Paul's Macedonian travelling companions, Gaius and Aristarchus. 30 Paul wanted to make an appeal to the people, but the disciples refused to let him; 31 in fact, some of the Asiarchs, who were friends of his, sent messages urging him not to take the risk of going into the theatre.

32 By now everybody was shouting different things, till the assembly itself had no idea what was going on; most of them did not even know why they had gathered together. 33 Some of the crowd prevailed upon Alexander, whom the Jews pushed forward; he raised his hand for silence with the intention of explaining things to the people. 34 As soon as they realised he was a Jew, they all started shouting in unison, 'Great is Diana of the Ephesians!' and they kept this up for two hours. 35 When the town clerk eventually succeeded in calming the crowd, he said, 'Citizens of Ephesus! Is there anybody who does not know that the city of the Ephesians is the guardian of the temple of great Diana and of her statue that fell from heaven? 36 Nobody can contradict this and there is no need for you to get excited or do anything rash. 37 These men you have brought here are not guilty of any sacrilege or blasphemy against our goddess. 38 If Demetrius and the craftsmen he has with him want to complain about anyone, there are the assizes and the proconsuls; let them take the case to court. 39 And if you want to ask any more questions you must raise them in the regular assembly. 40 We could easily be charged with rioting for today's happenings: there is no ground for it all, and we can give no justification for this gathering.' When he had finished this speech he dismissed the assembly.

20 When the disturbance was over, Paul sent for the disciples and, after speaking words of encouragement to them, said good-bye and set out for Macedonia.

19, 40: Some manuscripts omit the negative in [not] be able, making the meaning, "There is no cause for which we shall be able to give a reason for this demonstration."

NEW REVISED STANDARD VERSION

those regions and had given the believers*q* much encouragement, he came to Greece, 3 where he stayed for three months. He was about to set sail for Syria when a plot was made against him by the Jews, and so he decided to return through Macedonia. 4 He was accompanied by Sopater son of Pyrrhus from Beroea, by Aristarchus and Secundus from Thessalonica, by Gaius from Derbe, and by Timothy, as well as by Tychicus and Trophimus from Asia. 5 They went ahead and were waiting for us in Troas; 6 but we sailed from Philippi after the days of Unleavened Bread, and in five days we joined them in Troas, where we stayed for seven days.

7 On the first day of the week, when we met to break bread, Paul was holding a discussion with them; since he intended to leave the next day, he continued speaking until midnight. 8 There were many lamps in the room upstairs where we were meeting. 9 A young man named Eutychus, who was sitting in the window, began to sink off into a deep sleep while Paul talked still longer. Overcome by sleep, he fell to the ground three floors below and was picked up dead. 10 But Paul went down, and bending over him took him in his arms, and said, "Do not be alarmed, for his life is in him." 11 Then Paul went upstairs, and after he had broken bread and eaten, he continued to converse with them until dawn; then he left. 12 Meanwhile they had taken the boy away alive and were not a little comforted.

13 We went ahead to the ship and set sail for Assos, intending to take Paul on board there; for he had made this arrangement, intending to go by land himself. 14 When he met us in Assos, we took him on board and went to Mitylene. 15 We sailed from there, and on the following day we arrived opposite Chios. The next day we touched at Samos, and*r* the day after that we came to Miletus. 16 For Paul had decided to sail past Ephesus, so that he might not have to spend time in Asia; he was eager to be in Jerusalem, if possible, on the day of Pentecost.

17 From Miletus he sent a message to Ephesus, asking the elders of the church to meet him. 18 When they came to him, he said to them:

"You yourselves know how I lived among you the entire time from the first day that I set foot in Asia, 19 serving the Lord with all humility and with tears, enduring the trials that came to me through the plots of the Jews. 20 I did not shrink from doing anything helpful, proclaiming the message to you and teaching you publicly and from house to house, 21 as I testified to both Jews and Greeks about repentance toward God and faith toward our Lord Jesus. 22 And now, as a captive to the Spirit,*s* I am on my way to Jerusalem, not knowing what will happen to me there, 23 except that the Holy Spirit testifies to me in every city that imprisonment and persecutions are waiting for me. 24 But I do not count my life of any value to myself, if only I may finish my course and the ministry that I received from the Lord Jesus, to testify to the good news of God's grace.

25 "And now I know that none of you, among whom I have gone about proclaiming the kingdom, will ever see my face again. 26 Therefore I declare to you this day that I am not responsible for the blood of any of you, 27 for I did not shrink from declaring to you the whole purpose of God. 28 Keep watch over yourselves and over all the flock, of which the Holy Spirit has made you overseers, to shepherd the church of God*t* that he obtained with the blood of his own Son.*u* 29 I know that after I have gone, savage wolves will come in among you, not sparing the flock. 30 Some

through that region, constantly giving encouragement to the Christians, and finally reached Greece. 3 When he had spent three months there and was on the point of embarking for Syria, a plot was laid against him by the Jews, so he decided to return by way of Macedonia. 4 He was accompanied by Sopater son of Pyrrhus from Beroea, Aristarchus and Secundus from Thessalonica, Gaius of Derbe, and Timothy, and from Asia Tychicus and Trophimus. 5 These went ahead and waited for us at Troas; 6 we ourselves sailed from Philippi after the Passover season, and five days later rejoined them at Troas, where we spent a week.

7 On the Saturday night, when we gathered for the breaking of bread, Paul, who was to leave next day, addressed the congregation and went on speaking until midnight. 8 Now there were many lamps in the upstairs room where we were assembled, 9 and a young man named Eutychus, who was sitting on the window-ledge, grew more and more drowsy as Paul went on talking, until, completely overcome by sleep, he fell from the third storey to the ground, and was picked up dead. 10 Paul went down, threw himself upon him, and clasped him in his arms. 'Do not distress yourselves,' he said to them; 'he is alive.' 11 He then went upstairs, broke bread and ate, and after much conversation, which lasted until dawn, he departed. 12 And they took the boy home, greatly relieved that he was alive.

13 We went on ahead to the ship and embarked for Assos, where we were to take Paul aboard; this was the arrangement he had made, since he was going to travel by road. 14 When he met us at Assos, we took him aboard and proceeded to Mitylene. 15 We sailed from there and next day arrived off Chios. On the second day we made Samos, and the following day we reached Miletus. 16 Paul had decided to bypass Ephesus and so avoid having to spend time in the province of Asia; he was eager to be in Jerusalem on the day of Pentecost, if that were possible. 17 He did, however, send from Miletus to Ephesus and summon the elders of the church. 18 When they joined him, he spoke to them as follows.

'You know how, from the day that I first set foot in the province of Asia, I spent my whole time with you, 19 serving the Lord in all humility amid the sorrows and trials that came upon me through the intrigues of the Jews. 20 You know that I kept back nothing that was for your good: I delivered the message to you, and taught you, in public and in your homes; 21 with Jews and Gentiles alike I insisted on repentance before God and faith in our Lord Jesus. 22 Now, as you see, I am constrained by the Spirit to go to Jerusalem. I do not know what will befall me there, 23 except that in city after city the Holy Spirit assures me that imprisonment and hardships await me. 24 For myself, I set no store by life; all I want is to finish the race, and complete the task which the Lord Jesus assigned to me, that of bearing my testimony to the gospel of God's grace.

25 'One thing more: I have gone about among you proclaiming the kingdom, but now I know that none of you will ever see my face again. 26 That being so, I here and now declare that no one's fate can be laid at my door; I have kept back nothing; 27 I have disclosed to you the whole purpose of God. 28 Keep guard over yourselves and over all the flock of which the Holy Spirit has given you charge, as shepherds of the church of the Lord, which he won for himself by his own blood. 29 I know that when I am gone, savage wolves will come in among you and will not spare the flock.

---

q Gk *given them*   *r* Other ancient authorities add *after remaining at Trogyllium*   *s* Or *And now, bound in the spirit*   *t* Other ancient authorities read *of the Lord*   *u* Or *with his own blood*; Gk *with the blood of his Own*

20:6 **after . . . season:** *lit.* after the days of Unleavened Bread.
20:28 **of the Lord . . . blood:** *some witnesses read* of God, which he won for himself by the blood of his Own.

2 As he traveled throughout those regions, he provided many words of encouragement for them. Then he arrived in Greece, 3 where he stayed for three months. But when a plot was made against him by the Jews as he was about to set sail for Syria, he decided to return by way of Macedonia.

4 Sopater, the son of Pyrrhus, from Beroea, accompanied him, as did Aristarchus and Secundus from Thessalonica, Gaius from Derbe, Timothy, and Tychicus and Trophimus from Asia 5 who went on ahead and waited for us at Troas. 6 We sailed from Philippi after the feast of Unleavened Bread, and rejoined them five days later in Troas, where we spent a week.

7 On the first day of the week when we gathered to break bread, Paul spoke to them because he was going to leave on the next day, and he kept on speaking until midnight. 8 There were many lamps in the upstairs room where we were gathered, 9 and a young man named Eutychus who was sitting on the window sill was sinking into a deep sleep as Paul talked on and on. Once overcome by sleep, he fell down from the third story and when he was picked up, he was dead. 10 Paul went down, threw himself upon him, and said as he embraced him, "Don't be alarmed; there is life in him." 11 Then he returned upstairs, broke the bread, and ate; after a long conversation that lasted until daybreak, he departed. 12 And they took the boy away alive and were immeasurably comforted.

13 We went ahead to the ship and set sail for Assos where we were to take Paul on board, as he had arranged, since he was going overland. 14 When he met us in Assos, we took him aboard and went on to Mitylene. 15 We sailed away from there on the next day and reached a point off Chios, and a day later we reached Samos, and on the following day we arrived at Miletus. 16 Paul had decided to sail past Ephesus in order not to lose time in the province of Asia, for he was hurrying to be in Jerusalem, if at all possible, for the day of Pentecost.

17 From Miletus he had the presbyters of the church at Ephesus summoned. 18 When they came to him, he addressed them, "You know how I lived among you the whole time from the day I first came to the province of Asia. 19 I served the Lord with all humility and with the tears and trials that came to me because of the plots of the Jews, 20 and I did not at all shrink from telling you what was for your benefit, or from teaching you in public or in your homes. 21 I earnestly bore witness for both Jews and Greeks to repentance before God and to faith in our Lord Jesus. 22 But now, compelled by the Spirit, I am going to Jerusalem. What will happen to me there I do not know, 23 except that in one city after another the holy Spirit has been warning me that imprisonment and hardships await me. 24 Yet I consider life of no importance to me, if only I may finish my course and the ministry that I received from the Lord Jesus, to bear witness to the gospel of God's grace.

25 "But now I know that none of you to whom I preached the kingdom during my travels will ever see my face again. 26 And so I solemnly declare to you this day that I am not responsible for the blood of any of you, 27 for I did not shrink from proclaiming to you the entire plan of God. 28 Keep watch over yourselves and over the whole flock of which the holy Spirit has appointed you overseers, in which you tend the church of God that he acquired with his own blood. 29 I know that after my departure savage wolves will come among you, and they will not spare the flock. 30 And

2 On his way through those areas he said many words of encouragement to them and then made his way into Greece, 3 where he spent three months. He was leaving by ship for Syria when a plot organised against him by the Jews made him decide to go back by way of Macedonia. 4 He was accompanied by Sopater, son of Pyrrhus, who came from Beroea; Aristarchus and Secundus who came from Thessalonica; Gaius from Derbe, and Timothy, as well as Tychicus and Trophimus who were from Asia. 5 They all went on to Troas where they waited for us. 6 We ourselves left Philippi by ship after the days of Unleavened Bread and joined them five days later at Troas, where we stayed for a week.

7 On the first day of the week we met for the breaking of bread. Paul was due to leave the next day, and he preached a sermon that went on till the middle of the night. 8 A number of lamps were lit in the upstairs room where we were assembled, 9 and as Paul went on and on, a young man called Eutychus who was sitting on the window-sill grew drowsy and was overcome by sleep and fell to the ground three floors below. He was picked up dead. 10 Paul went down and stooped to clasp the boy to him, saying, 'There is no need to worry, there is still life in him.' 11 Then he went back upstairs where he broke the bread and ate and carried on talking till he left at daybreak. 12 They took the boy away alive, and were greatly encouraged.

13 We were now to go on ahead by sea, so we set sail for Assos, where we were to take Paul on board; this was what he had arranged, for he wanted to go overland. 14 When he rejoined us at Assos we took Paul aboard and went on to Mitylene. 15 The next day we sailed from there and arrived opposite Chios. The second day we touched at Samos and, after stopping at Trogyllium, made Miletus the next day. 16 Paul had decided to pass wide of Ephesus so as to avoid spending time in Asia, since he was anxious to be in Jerusalem, if possible, for the day of Pentecost.

17 From Miletus he sent for the elders of the church of Ephesus. 18 When they arrived he addressed these words to them:

'You know what my way of life has been ever since the first day I set foot among you in Asia, 19 how I have served the Lord in all humility, with all the sorrows and trials that came to me through the plots of the Jews. 20 I have not hesitated to do anything that would be helpful to you; I have preached to you and instructed you both in public and in your homes, 21 urging both Jews and Greeks to turn to God and to believe in our Lord Jesus.

22 'And now you see me on my way to Jerusalem in captivity to the Spirit; I have no idea what will happen to me there, 23 except that the Holy Spirit, in town after town, has made it clear to me that imprisonment and persecution await me. 24 But I do not place any value on my own life, provided that I complete the mission the Lord Jesus gave me — to bear witness to the good news of God's grace.

25 'I now feel sure that none of you among whom I have gone about proclaiming the kingdom will ever see my face again. 26 And so on this very day I swear that my conscience is clear as far as all of you are concerned, 27 for I have without faltering put before you the whole of God's purpose.

28 'Be on your guard for yourselves and for all the flock of which the Holy Spirit has made you the guardians, to feed the Church of God which he bought with the blood of his own Son.

29 'I know quite well that when I have gone fierce wolves will invade you and will have no mercy on the flock.

NEW REVISED STANDARD VERSION

REVISED ENGLISH BIBLE

even from your own group will come distorting the truth in order to entice the disciples to follow them. 31 Therefore be alert, remembering that for three years I did not cease night or day to warn everyone with tears. 32 And now I commend you to God and to the message of his grace, a message that is able to build you up and to give you the inheritance among all who are sanctified. 33 I coveted no one's silver or gold or clothing. 34 You know for yourselves that I worked with my own hands to support myself and my companions. 35 In all this I have given you an example that by such work we must support the weak, remembering the words of the Lord Jesus, for he himself said, 'It is more blessed to give than to receive.'"

36 When he had finished speaking, he knelt down with them all and prayed. 37 There was much weeping among them all; they embraced Paul and kissed him, 38 grieving especially because of what he had said, that they would not see him again. Then they brought him to the ship.

21 When we had parted from them and set sail, we came by a straight course to Cos, and the next day to Rhodes, and from there to Patara.ᵛ 2 When we found a ship bound for Phoenicia, we went on board and set sail. 3 We came in sight of Cyprus; and leaving it on our left, we sailed to Syria and landed at Tyre, because the ship was to unload its cargo there. 4 We looked up the disciples and stayed there for seven days. Through the Spirit they told Paul not to go on to Jerusalem. 5 When our days there were ended, we left and proceeded on our journey; and all of them, with wives and children, escorted us outside the city. There we knelt down on the beach and prayed 6 and said farewell to one another. Then we went on board the ship, and they returned home.

7 When we had finishedʷ the voyage from Tyre, we arrived at Ptolemais; and we greeted the believersˣ and stayed with them for one day. 8 The next day we left and came to Caesarea; and we went into the house of Philip the evangelist, one of the seven, and stayed with him. 9 He had four unmarried daughtersʸ who had the gift of prophecy. 10 While we were staying there for several days, a prophet named Agabus came down from Judea. 11 He came to us and took Paul's belt, bound his own feet and hands with it, and said, "Thus says the Holy Spirit, 'This is the way the Jews in Jerusalem will bind the man who owns this belt and will hand him over to the Gentiles.'" 12 When we heard this, we and the people there urged him not to go up to Jerusalem. 13 Then Paul answered, "What are you doing, weeping and breaking my heart? For I am ready not only to be bound but even to die in Jerusalem for the name of the Lord Jesus." 14 Since he would not be persuaded, we remained silent except to say, "The Lord's will be done."

15 After these days we got ready and started to go up to Jerusalem. 16 Some of the disciples from Caesarea also came along and brought us to the house of Mnason of Cyprus, an early disciple, with whom we were to stay.

17 When we arrived in Jerusalem, the brothers welcomed us warmly. 18 The next day Paul went with us to visit James; and all the elders were present. 19 After greeting them, he related one by one the things that God had done among the Gentiles through his ministry. 20 When they heard it, they praised God. Then they said to him, "You see, brother, how many thousands of believers there are among the Jews, and they are all zealous for the law.

30 Even from your own number men will arise who will distort the truth in order to get the disciples to break away and follow them. 31 So be on the alert; remember how with tears I never ceased to warn each one of you night and day for three years.

32 'And now I commend you to God and to the word of his grace, which has power to build you up and give you your heritage among all those whom God has made his own. 33 I have not wanted anyone's money or clothes for myself; 34 you all know that these hands of mine earned enough for the needs of myself and my companions. 35 All along I showed you that it is our duty to help the weak in this way, by hard work, and that we should keep in mind the words of the Lord Jesus, who himself said, "Happiness lies more in giving than in receiving." '

36 As he finished speaking, he knelt down with them all and prayed. 37 There were loud cries of sorrow from them all, as they folded Paul in their arms and kissed him; 38 what distressed them most was his saying that they would never see his face again. Then they escorted him to the ship.

21 We tore ourselves away from them and, putting to sea, made a straight run and came to Cos; next day to Rhodes, and thence to Patara. 2 There we found a ship bound for Phoenicia, so we went aboard and sailed in her. 3 We came in sight of Cyprus and, leaving it to port, we continued our voyage to Syria and put in at Tyre, where the ship was to unload her cargo. 4 We sought out the disciples and stayed there a week. Warned by the Spirit, they urged Paul to abandon his visit to Jerusalem. 5 But when our time ashore was ended, we left and continued our journey; and they and their wives and children all escorted us out of the city. We knelt down on the beach and prayed, 6 and then bade each other goodbye; we went on board, and they returned home.

7 We made the passage from Tyre and reached Ptolemais, where we greeted the brotherhood and spent a day with them. 8 Next day we left and came to Caesarea, where we went to the home of Philip the evangelist, who was one of the Seven, and stayed with him. 9 He had four unmarried daughters, who possessed the gift of prophecy. 10 When we had been there several days, a prophet named Agabus arrived from Judaea. 11 He came to us, took Paul's belt, bound his own feet and hands with it, and said, 'These are the words of the Holy Spirit: Thus will the Jews in Jerusalem bind the man to whom this belt belongs, and hand him over to the Gentiles.' 12 When we heard this, we and the local people begged and implored Paul to abandon his visit to Jerusalem. 13 Then Paul gave his answer: 'Why all these tears? Why are you trying to weaken my resolution? I am ready, not merely to be bound, but even to die at Jerusalem for the name of the Lord Jesus.' 14 So, as he would not be dissuaded, we gave up and said, 'The Lord's will be done.'

15 At the end of our stay we packed our baggage and took the road up to Jerusalem. 16 Some of the disciples from Caesarea came along with us, to direct us to a Cypriot named Mnason, a Christian from the early days, with whom we were to spend the night. 17 On our arrival at Jerusalem, the congregation welcomed us gladly.

18 Next day Paul paid a visit to James; we accompanied him, and all the elders were present. 19 After greeting them, he described in detail all that God had done among the Gentiles by means of his ministry. 20 When they heard this, they gave praise to God. Then they said to Paul: 'You observe, brother, how many thousands of converts we have among the Jews, all of them staunch upholders of the law.

ᵛOther ancient authorities add and Myra   ʷOr continued
ˣGk brothers   ʸGk four daughters, virgins,

NEW AMERICAN BIBLE

NEW JERUSALEM BIBLE

from your own group, men will come forward perverting the truth to draw the disciples away after them. 31 So be vigilant and remember that for three years, night and day, I unceasingly admonished each of you with tears. 32 And now I commend you to God and to that gracious word of his that can build you up and give you the inheritance among all who are consecrated. 33 I have never wanted anyone's silver or gold or clothing. 34 You know well that these very hands have served my needs and my companions. 35 In every way I have shown you that by hard work of that sort we must help the weak, and keep in mind the words of the Lord Jesus who himself said, 'It is more blessed to give than to receive.'"

36 When he had finished speaking he knelt down and prayed with them all. 37 They were all weeping loudly as they threw their arms around Paul and kissed him, 38 for they were deeply distressed that he had said that they would never see his face again. Then they escorted him to the ship.

21 When we had taken leave of them we set sail, made a straight run for Cos, and on the next day for Rhodes, and from there to Patara. 2 Finding a ship crossing to Phoenicia, we went on board and put out to sea. 3 We caught sight of Cyprus but passed by it on our left and sailed on toward Syria and put in at Tyre where the ship was to unload cargo. 4 There we sought out the disciples and stayed for a week. They kept telling Paul through the Spirit not to embark for Jerusalem. 5 At the end of our stay we left and resumed our journey. All of them, women and children included, escorted us out of the city, and after kneeling on the beach to pray, 6 we bade farewell to one another. Then we boarded the ship, and they returned home.

7 We continued the voyage and came from Tyre to Ptolemais, where we greeted the brothers and stayed a day with them. 8 On the next day we resumed the trip and came to Caesarea, where we went to the house of Philip the evangelist, who was one of the Seven, and stayed with him. 9 He had four virgin daughters gifted with prophecy. 10 We had been there several days when a prophet named Agabus came down from Judea. 11 He came up to us, took Paul's belt, bound his own feet and hands with it, and said, "Thus says the holy Spirit: This is the way the Jews will bind the owner of this belt in Jerusalem, and they will hand him over to the Gentiles." 12 When we heard this, we and the local residents begged him not to go up to Jerusalem. 13 Then Paul replied, "What are you doing, weeping and breaking my heart? I am prepared not only to be bound but even to die in Jerusalem for the name of the Lord Jesus." 14 Since he would not be dissuaded we let the matter rest, saying, "The Lord's will be done."

15 After these days we made preparations for our journey, then went up to Jerusalem. 16 Some of the disciples from Caesarea came along to lead us to the house of Mnason, a Cypriot, a disciple of long standing, with whom we were to stay. 17 When we reached Jerusalem the brothers welcomed us warmly. 18 The next day, Paul accompanied us on a visit to James, and all the presbyters were present. 19 He greeted them, then proceeded to tell them in detail what God had accomplished among the Gentiles through his ministry. 20 They praised God when they heard it but said to him, "Brother, you see how many thousands of believers there are from among the Jews, and they are all zealous observers of the law. 21 They have been informed that you are teach-

30 Even from your own ranks there will be men coming forward with a travesty of the truth on their lips to induce the disciples to follow them. 31 So be on your guard, remembering how night and day for three years I never slackened in counselling each one of you with tears. 32 And now I commend you to God and to the word of his grace that has power to build you up and to give you your inheritance among all the sanctified.

33 'I have never asked anyone for money or clothes; 34 you know for yourselves that these hands of mine earned enough to meet my needs and those of my companions. 35 By every means I have shown you that we must exert ourselves in this way to support the weak, remembering the words of the Lord Jesus, who himself said, "There is more happiness in giving than in receiving." ' g

36 When he had finished speaking he knelt down with them all and prayed. 37 By now they were all in tears; they put their arms round Paul's neck and kissed him; 38 what saddened them most was his saying they would never see his face again. Then they escorted him to the ship.

21 When we had at last torn ourselves away from them and put to sea, we set a straight course and arrived at Cos; the next day we reached Rhodes, and from there went on to Patara. 2 Here we found a ship bound for Phoenicia, so we went on board and sailed in her. 3 After sighting Cyprus and leaving it to port, we sailed to Syria and put in at Tyre, since the ship was to unload her cargo there. 4 We sought out the disciples and stayed there a week. Speaking in the Spirit, they kept telling Paul not to go on to Jerusalem, 5 but when our time was up we set off. Together with the women and children they all escorted us on our way till we were out of the town. When we reached the beach, we knelt down and prayed; 6 then, after saying good-bye to each other, we went aboard and they returned home.

7 The end of our voyage from Tyre came when we landed at Ptolemais, where we greeted the brothers and stayed one day with them. 8 The next day we left and came to Caesarea. Here we called on Philip the evangelist, one of the Seven, and stayed with him. 9 He had four unmarried daughters who were prophets. 10 When we had been there several days a prophet called Agabus arrived from Judaea. 11 He came up to us, took Paul's belt and tied up his own feet and hands, and said, 'This is what the Holy Spirit says, "The man to whom this girdle belongs will be tied up like this by the Jews in Jerusalem and handed over to the gentiles." ' 12 When we heard this, we and all the local people urged Paul not to go on to Jerusalem. 13 To this he replied, 'What are you doing, weeping and breaking my heart? For my part, I am ready not only to be bound but even to die in Jerusalem for the name of the Lord Jesus.' 14 And so, as he would not be persuaded, we gave up the attempt, saying, 'The Lord's will be done.'

15 After this we made our preparations and went on up to Jerusalem. 16 Some of the disciples from Caesarea accompanied us and took us to the house of a Cypriot with whom we were to lodge; he was called Mnason and had been one of the earliest disciples.

17 On our arrival in Jerusalem the brothers gave us a very warm welcome. 18 The next day Paul went with us to visit James, and all the elders were present. 19 After greeting them he gave a detailed account of all that God had done among the gentiles through his ministry. 20 They gave glory to God when they heard this. Then they said, 'You see, brother, how thousands of Jews have now become believers, all of them staunch upholders of the Law; 21 and what

g **20** This saying does not occur in the gospels.

21 They have been told about you that you teach all the Jews living among the Gentiles to forsake Moses, and that you tell them not to circumcise their children or observe the customs. 22 What then is to be done? They will certainly hear that you have come. 23 So do what we tell you. We have four men who are under a vow. 24 Join these men, go through the rite of purification with them, and pay for the shaving of their heads. Thus all will know that there is nothing in what they have been told about you, but that you yourself observe and guard the law. 25 But as for the Gentiles who have become believers, we have sent a letter with our judgment that they should abstain from what has been sacrificed to idols and from blood and from what is strangled*z* and from fornication." 26 Then Paul took the men, and the next day, having purified himself, he entered the temple with them, making public the completion of the days of purification when the sacrifice would be made for each of them.

27 When the seven days were almost completed, the Jews from Asia, who had seen him in the temple, stirred up the whole crowd. They seized him, 28 shouting, "Fellow Israelites, help! This is the man who is teaching everyone everywhere against our people, our law, and this place; more than that, he has actually brought Greeks into the temple and has defiled this holy place." 29 For they had previously seen Trophimus the Ephesian with him in the city, and they supposed that Paul had brought him into the temple. 30 Then all the city was aroused, and the people rushed together. They seized Paul and dragged him out of the temple, and immediately the doors were shut. 31 While they were trying to kill him, word came to the tribune of the cohort that all Jerusalem was in an uproar. 32 Immediately he took soldiers and centurions and ran down to them. When they saw the tribune and the soldiers, they stopped beating Paul. 33 Then the tribune came, arrested him, and ordered him to be bound with two chains; he inquired who he was and what he had done. 34 Some in the crowd shouted one thing, some another; and as he could not learn the facts because of the uproar, he ordered him to be brought into the barracks. 35 When Paul*a* came to the steps, the violence of the mob was so great that he had to be carried by the soldiers. 36 The crowd that followed kept shouting, "Away with him!"

37 Just as Paul was about to be brought into the barracks, he said to the tribune, "May I say something to you?" The tribune*b* replied, "Do you know Greek? 38 Then you are not the Egyptian who recently stirred up a revolt and led the four thousand assassins out into the wilderness?" 39 Paul replied, "I am a Jew, from Tarsus in Cilicia, a citizen of an important city; I beg you, let me speak to the people." 40 When he had given him permission, Paul stood on the steps and motioned to the people for silence; and when there was a great hush, he addressed them in the Hebrew*c* language, saying:

22 "Brothers and fathers, listen to the defense that I now make before you."

2 When they heard him addressing them in Hebrew,*c* they became even more quiet. Then he said:

3 "I am a Jew, born in Tarsus in Cilicia, but brought up in this city at the feet of Gamaliel, educated strictly according to our ancestral law, being zealous for God, just as all of you are today. 4 I persecuted this Way up to the point of death by binding both men and women and putting them in prison, 5 as the high priest and the whole council of elders

21 Now they have been given certain information about you: it is said that you teach all the Jews in the gentile world to turn their backs on Moses, and tell them not to circumcise their children or follow our way of life. 22 What is to be done, then? They are sure to hear that you have arrived. 23 Our proposal is this: we have four men here who are under a vow; 24 take them with you and go through the ritual of purification together, and pay their expenses, so that they may have their heads shaved; then everyone will know that there is nothing in the reports they have heard about you, but that you are yourself a practising Jew and observe the law. 25 As for the gentile converts, we sent them our decision that they should abstain from meat that has been offered to idols, from blood, from anything that has been strangled, and from fornication.' 26 So Paul took the men, and next day, after going through the ritual of purification with them, he went into the temple to give notice of the date when the period of purification would end and the offering be made for each of them.

27 BUT just before the seven days were up, the Jews from the province of Asia saw him in the temple. They stirred up all the crowd and seized him, 28 shouting, 'Help us, men of Israel! This is the fellow who attacks our people, our law, and this sanctuary, and spreads his teaching the whole world over. What is more, he has brought Gentiles into the temple and profaned this holy place.' 29 They had previously seen Trophimus the Ephesian with him in the city, and assumed that Paul had brought him into the temple.

30 The whole city was in a turmoil, and people came running from all directions. They seized Paul and dragged him out of the temple, and at once the doors were shut. 31 They were bent on killing him, but word came to the officer commanding the cohort that all Jerusalem was in an uproar. 32 He immediately took a force of soldiers with their centurions and came down at the double to deal with the riot. When the crowd saw the commandant and his troops, they stopped beating Paul. 33 As soon as the commandant could reach Paul, he arrested him and ordered him to be shackled with two chains; he enquired who he was and what he had been doing. 34 Some in the crowd shouted one thing, some another, and as the commandant could not get at the truth because of the hubbub, he ordered him to be taken to the barracks. 35 When Paul reached the steps, he found himself carried up by the soldiers because of the violence of the mob; 36 for the whole crowd was at their heels yelling, 'Kill him!'

37 Just before he was taken into the barracks Paul said to the commandant, 'May I have a word with you?' The commandant said, 'So you speak Greek? 38 Then you are not the Egyptian who started a revolt some time ago and led a force of four thousand terrorists out into the desert?' 39 Paul replied, 'I am a Jew from Tarsus in Cilicia, a citizen of no mean city. May I have your permission to speak to the people?' 40 When this was given, Paul stood on the steps and raised his hand to call for the attention of the people. As soon as quiet was restored, he addressed them in the Jewish language:

22 'Brothers and fathers, give me a hearing while I put my case to you.' 2 When they heard him speaking to them in their own language, they listened more quietly. 3 'I am a true-born Jew,' he began, 'a native of Tarsus in Cilicia. I was brought up in this city, and as a pupil of Gamaliel I was thoroughly trained in every point of our ancestral law. I have always been ardent in God's service, as you all are today. 4 And so I persecuted this movement to the death, arresting its followers, men and women alike, and committing them to prison, 5 as the high priest and the whole Coun-

ing all the Jews who live among the Gentiles to abandon Moses and that you are telling them not to circumcise their children or to observe their customary practices. 22 What is to be done? They will surely hear that you have arrived. 23 So do what we tell you. We have four men who have taken a vow. 24 Take these men and purify yourself with them, and pay their expenses that they may have their heads shaved. In this way everyone will know that there is nothing to the reports they have been given about you but that you yourself live in observance of the law. 25 As for the Gentiles who have come to believe, we sent them our decision that they abstain from meat sacrificed to idols, from blood, from the meat of strangled animals, and from unlawful marriage." 26 So Paul took the men, and on the next day after purifying himself together with them entered the temple to give notice of the day when the purification would be completed and the offering made for each of them.

27 When the seven days were nearly completed, the Jews from the province of Asia noticed him in the temple, stirred up the whole crowd, and laid hands on him, 28 shouting, "Fellow Israelites, help us. This is the man who is teaching everyone everywhere against the people and the law and this place, and what is more, he has even brought Greeks into the temple and defiled this sacred place." 29 For they had previously seen Trophimus the Ephesian in the city with him and supposed that Paul had brought him into the temple. 30 The whole city was in turmoil with people rushing together. They seized Paul and dragged him out of the temple, and immediately the gates were closed. 31 While they were trying to kill him, a report reached the cohort commander that all Jerusalem was rioting. 32 He immediately took soldiers and centurions and charged down on them. When they saw the commander and the soldiers they stopped beating Paul. 33 The cohort commander came forward, arrested him, and ordered him to be secured with two chains; he tried to find out who he might be and what he had done. 34 Some in the mob shouted one thing, others something else; so, since he was unable to ascertain the truth because of the uproar, he ordered Paul to be brought into the compound. 35 When he reached the steps, he was carried by the soldiers because of the violence of the mob, 36 for a crowd of people followed and shouted, "Away with him!"

37 Just as Paul was about to be taken into the compound, he said to the cohort commander, "May I say something to you?" He replied, "Do you speak Greek? 38 So then you are not the Egyptian who started a revolt some time ago and led the four thousand assassins into the desert?" 39 Paul answered, "I am a Jew, of Tarsus in Cilicia, a citizen of no mean city; I request you to permit me to speak to the people." 40 When he had given his permission, Paul stood on the steps and motioned with his hand to the people; and when all was quiet he addressed them in Hebrew.

22 "My brothers and fathers, listen to what I am about to say to you in my defense." 2 When they heard him addressing them in Hebrew they became all the more quiet. And he continued, 3 "I am a Jew, born in Tarsus in Cilicia, but brought up in this city. At the feet of Gamaliel I was educated strictly in our ancestral law and was zealous for God, just as all of you are today. 4 I persecuted this Way to death, binding both men and women and delivering them to prison. 5 Even the high priest and the whole council of

they have heard about you is that you instruct all Jews living among the gentiles to break away from Moses, authorising them not to circumcise their children or to follow the customary practices. 22 What is to be done? A crowd is sure to gather, for they will hear that you have come. 23 So this is what we suggest that you should do; we have four men here who are under a vow; 24 take these men along and be purified with them and pay all the expenses connected with the shaving of their heads. This will let everyone know there is no truth in the reports they have heard about you, and that you too observe the Law by your way of life. 25 About the gentiles who have become believers, we have written giving them our decision that they must abstain from things sacrificed to idols, from blood, from the meat of strangled animals and from illicit marriages.'

26 So the next day Paul took the men along and was purified with them, and he visited the Temple to give notice of the time when the period of purification would be over and the offering would have to be presented on behalf of each of them.

27 The seven days were nearly over when some Jews from Asia caught sight of him in the Temple and stirred up the crowd and seized him, 28 shouting, 'Men of Israel, help! This is the man who preaches to everyone everywhere against our people, against the Law and against this place. He has even profaned this Holy Place by bringing Greeks into the Temple.' 29 They had, in fact, previously seen Trophimus the Ephesian in the city with him and thought that Paul had brought him into the Temple.

30 This roused the whole city; people came running from all sides; they seized Paul and dragged him out of the Temple, and the gates were closed behind them. 31 While they were setting about killing him, word reached the tribune of the cohort that there was tumult all over Jerusalem. 32 He immediately called out soldiers and centurions and charged down on the crowd, who stopped beating Paul when they saw the tribune and the soldiers. 33 When the tribune came up he took Paul into custody, had him bound with two chains and enquired who he was and what he had done. 34 People in the crowd called out different things, and since the noise made it impossible for him to get any positive information, the tribune ordered Paul to be taken into the fortress. 35 When Paul reached the steps, the crowd became so violent that he had to be carried by the soldiers; 36 and indeed the whole mob was after them, shouting, 'Do away with him!'

37 Just as Paul was being taken into the fortress, he asked the tribune if he could have a word with him. The tribune said, 'You speak Greek, then? 38 Aren't you the Egyptian who started the recent revolt and led those four thousand cut-throats out into the desert?' 39 'I?' said Paul, 'I am a Jew and a citizen of the well-known city of Tarsus in Cilicia. Please give me permission to speak to the people.' 40 The man gave his consent and Paul, standing at the top of the steps, raised his hand to the people for silence. A profound silence followed, and he started speaking to them in Hebrew.

22 'My brothers, my fathers, listen to what I have to say to you in my defence.' 2 When they realised he was speaking in Hebrew, the silence was even greater than before. 3 'I am a Jew,' Paul said, 'and was born at Tarsus in Cilicia. I was brought up here in this city. It was under Gamaliel that I studied and was taught the exact observance of the Law of our ancestors. In fact, I was as full of duty towards God as you all are today. 4 I even persecuted this Way to the death and sent women as well as men to prison in chains 5 as the high priest and the whole council of elders

can testify about me. From them I also received letters to the brothers in Damascus, and I went there in order to bind those who were there and to bring them back to Jerusalem for punishment.

6 "While I was on my way and approaching Damascus, about noon a great light from heaven suddenly shone about me. 7 I fell to the ground and heard a voice saying to me, 'Saul, Saul, why are you persecuting me?' 8 I answered, 'Who are you, Lord?' Then he said to me, 'I am Jesus of Nazareth[d] whom you are persecuting.' 9 Now those who were with me saw the light but did not hear the voice of the one who was speaking to me. 10 I asked, 'What am I to do, Lord?' The Lord said to me, 'Get up and go to Damascus; there you will be told everything that has been assigned for you to do.' 11 Since I could not see because of the brightness of that light, those who were with me took my hand and led me to Damascus.

12 "A certain Ananias, who was a devout man according to the law and well spoken of by all the Jews living there, 13 came to me; and standing beside me, he said, 'Brother Saul, regain your sight!' In that very hour I regained my sight and saw him. 14 Then he said, 'The God of our ancestors has chosen you to know his will, to see the Righteous One and to hear his own voice; 15 for you will be his witness to all the world of what you have seen and heard. 16 And now why do you delay? Get up, be baptized, and have your sins washed away, calling on his name.'

17 "After I had returned to Jerusalem and while I was praying in the temple, I fell into a trance 18 and saw Jesus[e] saying to me, 'Hurry and get out of Jerusalem quickly, because they will not accept your testimony about me.' 19 And I said, 'Lord, they themselves know that in every synagogue I imprisoned and beat those who believed in you. 20 And while the blood of your witness Stephen was shed, I myself was standing by, approving and keeping the coats of those who killed him.' 21 Then he said to me, 'Go, for I will send you far away to the Gentiles.' "

22 Up to this point they listened to him, but then they shouted, "Away with such a fellow from the earth! For he should not be allowed to live." 23 And while they were shouting, throwing off their cloaks, and tossing dust into the air, 24 the tribune directed that he was to be brought into the barracks, and ordered him to be examined by flogging, to find out the reason for this outcry against him. 25 But when they had tied him up with thongs,[f] Paul said to the centurion who was standing by, "Is it legal for you to flog a Roman citizen who is uncondemned?" 26 When the centurion heard that, he went to the tribune and said to him, "What are you about to do? This man is a Roman citizen." 27 The tribune came and asked Paul,[e] "Tell me, are you a Roman citizen?" And he said, "Yes." 28 The tribune answered, "It cost me a large sum of money to get my citizenship." Paul said, "But I was born a citizen." 29 Immediately those who were about to examine him drew back from him; and the tribune also was afraid, for he realized that Paul was a Roman citizen and that he had bound him.

30 Since he wanted to find out what Paul[g] was being accused of by the Jews, the next day he released him and ordered the chief priests and the entire council to meet. He brought Paul down and had him stand before them.

23 While Paul was looking intently at the council he said, "Brothers,[h] up to this day I have lived my life with a clear conscience before God." 2 Then the high priest Ananias ordered those standing near him to strike him on the mouth. 3 At this Paul said to him, "God will strike you,

cil of Elders can testify. It was they who gave me letters to our fellow-Jews at Damascus, and I was on my way to make arrests there also and bring the prisoners to Jerusalem for punishment. 6 What happened to me on my journey was this: when I was nearing Damascus, about midday, a great light suddenly flashed from the sky all around me. 7 I fell to the ground, and heard a voice saying: "Saul, Saul, why do you persecute me?" 8 I answered, "Tell me, Lord, who you are." "I am Jesus of Nazareth, whom you are persecuting," he said. 9 My companions saw the light, but did not hear the voice that spoke to me. 10 "What shall I do, Lord?" I asked, and he replied, "Get up, and go on to Damascus; there you will be told all that you are appointed to do." 11 As I had been blinded by the brilliance of that light, my companions led me by the hand, and so I came to Damascus.

12 'There a man called Ananias, a devout observer of the law and well spoken of by all the Jews who lived there, 13 came and stood beside me, and said, "Saul, my brother, receive your sight again!" Instantly I recovered my sight and saw him. 14 He went on: "The God of our fathers appointed you to know his will and to see the Righteous One and to hear him speak, 15 because you are to be his witness to tell the world what you have seen and heard. 16 Do not delay. Be baptized at once and wash away your sins, calling on his name."

17 'After my return to Jerusalem, as I was praying in the temple I fell into a trance 18 and saw him there, speaking to me. "Make haste", he said, "and leave Jerusalem quickly, for they will not accept your testimony about me." 19 "But surely, Lord," I answered, "they know that I imprisoned those who believe in you and flogged them in every synagogue; 20 when the blood of Stephen your witness was shed I stood by, approving, and I looked after the clothes of those who killed him." 21 He said to me, "Go, for I mean to send you far away to the Gentiles." '

22 Up to this point the crowd had given him a hearing; but now they began to shout, 'Down with the scoundrel! He is not fit to be alive!' 23 And as they were yelling and waving their cloaks and flinging dust in the air, 24 the commandant ordered him to be brought into the barracks, and gave instructions that he should be examined under the lash, to find out what reason there was for such an outcry against him. 25 But when they tied him up for the flogging, Paul said to the centurion who was standing there, 'Does the law allow you to flog a Roman citizen, and an unconvicted one at that?' 26 When the centurion heard this, he went and reported to the commandant: 'What are you about? This man is a Roman citizen.' 27 The commandant came to Paul and asked, 'Tell me, are you a Roman citizen?' 'Yes,' said he. 28 The commandant rejoined, 'Citizenship cost me a large sum of money.' Paul said, 'It was mine by birth.' 29 Then those who were about to examine him promptly withdrew; and the commandant himself was alarmed when he realized that Paul was a Roman citizen and that he had put him in irons.

30 THE following day, wishing to be quite sure what charge the Jews were bringing against Paul, he released him and ordered the chief priests and the entire Council to assemble. He then brought Paul down to stand before them.

23 With his eyes steadily fixed on the Council, Paul said, 'My brothers, all my life to this day I have lived with a perfectly clear conscience before God.' 2 At this the high priest Ananias ordered his attendants to strike him on the mouth. 3 Paul retorted, 'God will strike you, you

---

[d] Gk *the Nazorean* [e] Gk *him* [f] Or *up for the lashes* [g] Gk *he*
[h] Gk *Men, brothers*

elders can testify on my behalf. For from them I even received letters to the brothers and set out for Damascus to bring back to Jerusalem in chains for punishment those there as well.

6 "On that journey as I drew near to Damascus, about noon a great light from the sky suddenly shone around me. 7 I fell to the ground and heard a voice saying to me, 'Saul, Saul, why are you persecuting me?' 8 I replied, 'Who are you, sir?' And he said to me, 'I am Jesus the Nazorean whom you are persecuting.' 9 My companions saw the light but did not hear the voice of the one who spoke to me. 10 I asked, 'What shall I do, sir?' The Lord answered me, 'Get up and go into Damascus, and there you will be told about everything appointed for you to do.' 11 Since I could see nothing because of the brightness of that light, I was led by hand by my companions and entered Damascus.

12 "A certain Ananias, a devout observer of the law, and highly spoken of by all the Jews who lived there, 13 came to me and stood there and said, 'Saul, my brother, regain your sight.' And at that very moment I regained my sight and saw him. 14 Then he said, 'The God of our ancestors designated you to know his will, to see the Righteous One, and to hear the sound of his voice; 15 for you will be his witness before all to what you have seen and heard. 16 Now, why delay? Get up and have yourself baptized and your sins washed away, calling upon his name.'

17 "After I had returned to Jerusalem and while I was praying in the temple, I fell into a trance 18 and saw the Lord saying to me, 'Hurry, leave Jerusalem at once, because they will not accept your testimony about me.' 19 But I replied, 'Lord, they themselves know that from synagogue to synagogue I used to imprison and beat those who believed in you. 20 And when the blood of your witness Stephen was being shed, I myself stood by giving my approval and keeping guard over the cloaks of his murderers.' 21 Then he said to me, 'Go, I shall send you far away to the Gentiles.' "

22 They listened to him until he said this, but then they raised their voices and shouted, "Take such a one as this away from the earth. It is not right that he should live." 23 And as they were yelling and throwing off their cloaks and flinging dust into the air, 24 the cohort commander ordered him to be brought into the compound and gave instruction that he be interrogated under the lash to determine the reason why they were making such an outcry against him. 25 But when they had stretched him out for the whips, Paul said to the centurion on duty, "Is it lawful for you to scourge a man who is a Roman citizen and has not been tried?" 26 When the centurion heard this, he went to the cohort commander and reported it, saying, "What are you going to do? This man is a Roman citizen." 27 Then the commander came and said to him, "Tell me, are you a Roman citizen?" "Yes," he answered. 28 The commander replied, "I acquired this citizenship for a large sum of money." Paul said, "But I was born one." 29 At once those who were going to interrogate him backed away from him, and the commander became alarmed when he realized that he was a Roman citizen and that he had had him bound.

30 The next day, wishing to determine the truth about why he was being accused by the Jews, he freed him and ordered the chief priests and the whole Sanhedrin to convene. Then he brought Paul down and made him stand before them.

23 Paul looked intently at the Sanhedrin and said, "My brothers, I have conducted myself with a perfectly clear conscience before God to this day." 2 The high priest Ananias ordered his attendants to strike his mouth. 3 Then

can testify. I even received letters from them to the brothers in Damascus, which I took with me when I set off to bring prisoners back from there to Jerusalem for punishment.

6 'It happened[h] that I was on that journey and nearly at Damascus when in the middle of the day a bright light from heaven suddenly shone round me. 7 I fell to the ground and heard a voice saying, "Saul, Saul, why are you persecuting me?" 8 I answered, "Who are you, Lord?" and he said to me, "I am Jesus the Nazarene, whom you are persecuting." 9 The people with me saw the light but did not hear the voice which spoke to me. 10 I said, "What am I to do, Lord?" The Lord answered, "Get up and go into Damascus, and there you will be told what you have been appointed to do." 11 Since the light had been so dazzling that I was blind, I got to Damascus only because my companions led me by the hand.

12 'Someone called Ananias, a devout follower of the Law and highly thought of by all the Jews living there, 13 came to see me; he stood beside me and said, "Brother Saul, receive your sight." Instantly my sight came back and I was able to see him. 14 Then he said, "The God of our ancestors has chosen you to know his will, to see the Upright One and hear his own voice speaking, 15 because you are to be his witness before all humanity, testifying to what you have seen and heard. 16 And now why delay? Hurry and be baptised and wash away your sins, calling on his name."

17 'It happened that, when I got back to Jerusalem, and was praying in the Temple, I fell into a trance 18 and then I saw him. "Hurry," he said, "leave Jerusalem at once; they will not accept the testimony you are giving about me." 19 "Lord," I answered, "they know that I used to go from synagogue to synagogue, imprisoning and flogging those who believed in you; 20 and that when the blood of your witness Stephen was being shed, I, too, was standing by, in full agreement with his murderers, and in charge of their clothes." 21 Then he said to me, "Go! I am sending you out to the gentiles far away." '

22 So far they had listened to him, but at these words they began to shout, 'Rid the earth of the man! He is not fit to live!' 23 They were yelling, waving their cloaks and throwing dust into the air, 24 and so the tribune had him brought into the fortress and ordered him to be examined under the lash, to find out the reason for the outcry against him. 25 But when they had strapped him down Paul said to the centurion on duty, 'Is it legal for you to flog a man who is a Roman citizen and has not been brought to trial?' 26 When he heard this the centurion went and told the tribune; 'Do you realise what you are doing?' he said. 'This man is a Roman citizen.' 27 So the tribune came and asked him, 'Tell me, are you a Roman citizen?' Paul answered 'Yes'. 28 To this the tribune replied, 'It cost me a large sum to acquire this citizenship.' 'But I was born to it,' said Paul. 29 Then those who were about to examine him hurriedly withdrew, and the tribune himself was alarmed when he realised that he had put a Roman citizen in chains.

30 The next day, since he wanted to know for sure what charge the Jews were bringing, he freed Paul and gave orders for a meeting of the chief priests and the entire Sanhedrin; then he brought Paul down and set him in front of them.

23 Paul looked steadily at the Sanhedrin and began to speak, 'My brothers, to this day I have conducted myself before God with a perfectly clear conscience.' 2 At this the high priest Ananias ordered his attendants to strike him on the mouth. 3 Then Paul said to him, 'God will surely

h 22 = 9; 26.

you whitewashed wall! Are you sitting there to judge me according to the law, and yet in violation of the law you order me to be struck?" 4 Those standing nearby said, "Do you dare to insult God's high priest?" 5 And Paul said, "I did not realize, brothers, that he was high priest; for it is written, 'You shall not speak evil of a leader of your people.' "

6 When Paul noticed that some were Sadducees and others were Pharisees, he called out in the council, "Brothers, I am a Pharisee, a son of Pharisees. I am on trial concerning the hope of the resurrection^i of the dead." 7 When he said this, a dissension began between the Pharisees and the Sadducees, and the assembly was divided. 8 (The Sadducees say that there is no resurrection, or angel, or spirit; but the Pharisees acknowledge all three.) 9 Then a great clamor arose, and certain scribes of the Pharisees' group stood up and contended, "We find nothing wrong with this man. What if a spirit or an angel has spoken to him?" 10 When the dissension became violent, the tribune, fearing that they would tear Paul to pieces, ordered the soldiers to go down, take him by force, and bring him into the barracks.

11 That night the Lord stood near him and said, "Keep up your courage! For just as you have testified for me in Jerusalem, so you must bear witness also in Rome."

12 In the morning the Jews joined in a conspiracy and bound themselves by an oath neither to eat nor drink until they had killed Paul. 13 There were more than forty who joined in this conspiracy. 14 They went to the chief priests and elders and said, "We have strictly bound ourselves by an oath to taste no food until we have killed Paul. 15 Now then, you and the council must notify the tribune to bring him down to you, on the pretext that you want to make a more thorough examination of his case. And we are ready to do away with him before he arrives."

16 Now the son of Paul's sister heard about the ambush; so he went and gained entrance to the barracks and told Paul. 17 Paul called one of the centurions and said, "Take this young man to the tribune, for he has something to report to him." 18 So he took him, brought him to the tribune, and said, "The prisoner Paul called me and asked me to bring this young man to you; he has something to tell you." 19 The tribune took him by the hand, drew him aside privately, and asked, "What is it that you have to report to me?" 20 He answered, "The Jews have agreed to ask you to bring Paul down to the council tomorrow, as though they were going to inquire more thoroughly into his case. 21 But do not be persuaded by them, for more than forty of their men are lying in ambush for him. They have bound themselves by an oath neither to eat nor drink until they kill him. They are ready now and are waiting for your consent." 22 So the tribune dismissed the young man, ordering him, "Tell no one that you have informed me of this."

23 Then he summoned two of the centurions and said, "Get ready to leave by nine o'clock tonight for Caesarea with two hundred soldiers, seventy horsemen, and two hundred spearmen. 24 Also provide mounts for Paul to ride, and take him safely to Felix the governor." 25 He wrote a letter to this effect:

26 "Claudius Lysias to his Excellency the governor Felix, greetings. 27 This man was seized by the Jews and was about to be killed by them, but when I had learned that he was a Roman citizen, I came with the guard and rescued him. 28 Since I wanted to know the charge for which they accused him, I had him brought to their council. 29 I found that he was accused concerning questions of their law, but was charged with nothing deserving death or imprisonment.

whitewashed wall! You sit there to judge me in accordance with the law; then, in defiance of the law, you order me to be struck!' 4 The attendants said, 'Would you insult God's high priest?' 5 'Brothers,' said Paul, 'I had no idea he was high priest; scripture, I know, says: "You shall not abuse the ruler of your people." '

6 Well aware that one section of them were Sadducees and the other Pharisees, Paul called out in the Council, 'My brothers, I am a Pharisee, a Pharisee born and bred; and the issue in this trial is our hope of the resurrection of the dead.' 7 At these words the Pharisees and Sadducees fell out among themselves, and the assembly was divided. 8 (The Sadducees deny that there is any resurrection or angel or spirit, but the Pharisees believe in all three.) 9 A great uproar ensued; and some of the scribes belonging to the Pharisaic party openly took sides and declared, 'We find no fault with this man; perhaps an angel or spirit has spoken to him.' 10 In the mounting dissension, the commandant was afraid that Paul would be torn to pieces, so he ordered the troops to go down, pull him out of the crowd, and bring him into the barracks.

11 The following night the Lord appeared to him and said, 'Keep up your courage! You have affirmed the truth about me in Jerusalem, and you must do the same in Rome.'

12 When day broke, the Jews banded together and took an oath not to eat or drink until they had killed Paul. 13 There were more than forty in the conspiracy; 14 they went to the chief priests and elders and said, 'We have bound ourselves by a solemn oath not to taste food until we have killed Paul. 15 It is now up to you and the rest of the Council to apply to the commandant to have him brought down to you on the pretext of a closer investigation of his case; we have arranged to make away with him before he reaches you.'

16 The son of Paul's sister, however, learnt of the plot and, going to the barracks, obtained entry, and reported it to Paul, 17 who called one of the centurions and said, 'Take this young man to the commandant; he has something to report.' 18 The centurion brought him to the commandant and explained, 'The prisoner Paul sent for me and asked me to bring this young man to you; he has something to tell you.' 19 The commandant took him by the arm, drew him aside, and asked him, 'What is it you have to report?' 20 He replied, 'The Jews have agreed on a plan: they will request you to bring Paul down to the Council tomorrow on the pretext of obtaining more precise information about him. 21 Do not listen to them; for a party more than forty strong are lying in wait for him, and they have sworn not to eat or drink until they have done away with him. They are now ready, waiting only for your consent.' 22 The commandant dismissed the young man, with orders not to let anyone know that he had given him this information.

23 He then summoned two of his centurions and gave them these orders: 'Have two hundred infantry ready to proceed to Caesarea, together with seventy cavalrymen and two hundred light-armed troops; parade them three hours after sunset, 24 and provide mounts for Paul so that he may be conducted under safe escort to Felix the governor.' 25 And he wrote a letter to this effect:

26 From Claudius Lysias to His Excellency the Governor Felix. Greeting.

27 This man was seized by the Jews and was on the point of being murdered when I intervened with the troops, and, on discovering that he was a Roman citizen, I removed him to safety. 28 As I wished to ascertain the ground of their charge against him, I brought him down to their Council. 29 I found that their case had to do with controversial matters of their law, but there was no charge against him which merited death or imprisonment.

---

^{i} Gk concerning hope and resurrection

NEW AMERICAN BIBLE

NEW JERUSALEM BIBLE

Paul said to him, "God will strike you, you whitewashed wall. Do you indeed sit in judgment upon me according to the law and yet in violation of the law order me to be struck?" 4 The attendants said, "Would you revile God's high priest?" 5 Paul answered, "Brothers, I did not realize he was the high priest. For it is written, 'You shall not curse a ruler of your people.' "

6 Paul was aware that some were Sadducees and some Pharisees, so he called out before the Sanhedrin, "My brothers, I am a Pharisee, the son of Pharisees; [I] am on trial for hope in the resurrection of the dead." 7 When he said this, a dispute broke out between the Pharisees and Sadducees, and the group became divided. 8 For the Sadducees say that there is no resurrection or angels or spirits, while the Pharisees acknowledge all three. 9 A great uproar occurred, and some scribes belonging to the Pharisee party stood up and sharply argued, "We find nothing wrong with this man. Suppose a spirit or an angel has spoken to him?" 10 The dispute was so serious that the commander, afraid that Paul would be torn to pieces by them, ordered his troops to go down and rescue him from their midst and take him into the compound. 11 The following night the Lord stood by him and said, "Take courage. For just as you have borne witness to my cause in Jerusalem, so you must also bear witness in Rome."

12 When day came, the Jews made a plot and bound themselves by oath not to eat or drink until they had killed Paul. 13 There were more than forty who formed this conspiracy. 14 They went to the chief priests and elders and said, "We have bound ourselves by a solemn oath to taste nothing until we have killed Paul. 15 You, together with the Sanhedrin, must now make an official request to the commander to have him bring him down to you, as though you meant to investigate his case more thoroughly. We on our part are prepared to kill him before he arrives." 16 The son of Paul's sister, however, heard about the ambush; so he went and entered the compound and reported it to Paul. 17 Paul then called one of the centurions and requested, "Take this young man to the commander; he has something to report to him." 18 So he took him and brought him to the commander and explained, "The prisoner Paul called me and asked that I bring this young man to you; he has something to say to you." 19 The commander took him by the hand, drew him aside, and asked him privately, "What is it you have to report to me?" 20 He replied, "The Jews have conspired to ask you to bring Paul down to the Sanhedrin tomorrow, as though they meant to inquire about him more thoroughly, 21 but do not believe them. More than forty of them are lying in wait for him; they have bound themselves by oath not to eat or drink until they have killed him. They are now ready and only wait for your consent." 22 As the commander dismissed the young man he directed him, "Tell no one that you gave me this information."

23 Then he summoned two of the centurions and said, "Get two hundred soldiers ready to go to Caesarea by nine o'clock tonight, along with seventy horsemen and two hundred auxiliaries. 24 Provide mounts for Paul to ride and give him safe conduct to Felix the governor." 25 Then he wrote a letter with this content: 26 "Claudius Lysias to his excellency the governor Felix, greetings. 27 This man, seized by the Jews and about to be murdered by them, I rescued after intervening with my troops when I learned that he was a Roman citizen. 28 I wanted to learn the reason for their accusations against him so I brought him down to their Sanhedrin. 29 I discovered that he was accused in matters of controversial questions of their law and not of any charge deserving death or imprisonment. 30 Since it was brought to

strike you, you whitewashed wall! How can you sit there to judge me according to the Law, and then break the Law by ordering a man to strike me?' 4 The attendants said, 'Are you insulting the high priest of God?' 5 Paul answered, 'Brothers, I did not realise it was the high priest; certainly scripture says, *You will not curse your people's leader.*' [i]

6 Now Paul was well aware that one party was made up of Sadducees and the other of Pharisees, so he called out in the Sanhedrin, 'Brothers, I am a Pharisee and the son of Pharisees. It is for our hope in the resurrection of the dead that I am on trial.' 7 As soon as he said this, a dispute broke out between the Pharisees and Sadducees, and the assembly was split between the two parties. 8 For the Sadducees say there is neither resurrection, nor angel, nor spirit, while the Pharisees accept all three. 9 The shouting grew louder, and some of the scribes from the Pharisees' party stood up and protested strongly, 'We find nothing wrong with this man. Suppose a spirit has spoken to him, or an angel?' 10 Feeling was running high, and the tribune, afraid that they would tear Paul to pieces, ordered his troops to go down and haul him out and bring him into the fortress.

11 Next night, the Lord appeared to him and said, 'Courage! You have borne witness for me in Jerusalem, now you must do the same in Rome.'

12 When it was day, the Jews held a secret meeting at which they made a vow not to eat or drink until they had killed Paul. 13 More than forty of them entered this pact, 14 and they went to the chief priests and elders and told them, 'We have made a solemn vow to let nothing pass our lips until we have killed Paul. 15 Now it is up to you and the Sanhedrin together to apply to the tribune to bring him down to you, as though you meant to examine his case more closely; we, on our side, are prepared to dispose of him before he reaches you.'

16 But the son of Paul's sister heard of the ambush they were laying and made his way into the fortress and told Paul, 17 who called one of the centurions and said, 'Take this young man to the tribune; he has something to tell him.' 18 So the man took him to the tribune, and reported, 'The prisoner Paul summoned me and requested me to bring this young man to you; he has something to tell you.' 19 Then the tribune took him by the hand and drew him aside and questioned him in private, 'What is it you have to tell me?' 20 He replied, 'The Jews have made a plan to ask you to take Paul down to the Sanhedrin tomorrow, as though they meant to enquire more closely into his case. 21 Do not believe them. There are more than forty of them lying in wait for him, and they have vowed not to eat or drink until they have got rid of him. They are ready now and only waiting for your order to be given.' 22 The tribune let the young man go with this order, 'Tell no one that you have given me this information.'

23 Then he summoned two of the centurions and said, 'Get two hundred soldiers ready to leave for Caesarea by the third hour of the night with seventy cavalry and two hundred auxiliaries; 24 provide horses for Paul, and deliver him unharmed to Felix the governor.' 25 He also wrote a letter in these terms:

26 'Claudius Lysias to his Excellency the governor Felix, greetings. 27 This man had been seized by the Jews and would have been murdered by them; but I came on the scene with my troops and got him away, having discovered that he was a Roman citizen. 28 Wanting to find out what charge they were making against him, I brought him before their Sanhedrin. 29 I found that the accusation concerned disputed points of their Law, but that there was no charge deserving death or imprisonment. 30 Acting on

i 23 Ex 22:27. Ananias became high priest in AD 47.

NEW REVISED STANDARD VERSION

30 When I was informed that there would be a plot against the man, I sent him to you at once, ordering his accusers also to state before you what they have against him. *j* "

31 So the soldiers, according to their instructions, took Paul and brought him during the night to Antipatris. 32 The next day they let the horsemen go on with him, while they returned to the barracks. 33 When they came to Caesarea and delivered the letter to the governor, they presented Paul also before him. 34 On reading the letter, he asked what province he belonged to, and when he learned that he was from Cilicia, 35 he said, "I will give you a hearing when your accusers arrive." Then he ordered that he be kept under guard in Herod's headquarters. *k*

24 Five days later the high priest Ananias came down with some elders and an attorney, a certain Tertullus, and they reported their case against Paul to the governor. 2 When Paul *l* had been summoned, Tertullus began to accuse him, saying:

"Your Excellency, *m* because of you we have long enjoyed peace, and reforms have been made for this people because of your foresight. 3 We welcome this in every way and everywhere with utmost gratitude. 4 But, to detain you no further, I beg you to hear us briefly with your customary graciousness. 5 We have, in fact, found this man a pestilent fellow, an agitator among all the Jews throughout the world, and a ringleader of the sect of the Nazarenes. *n* 6 He even tried to profane the temple, and so we seized him. *o* 8 By examining him yourself you will be able to learn from him concerning everything of which we accuse him."

9 The Jews also joined in the charge by asserting that all this was true.

10 When the governor motioned to him to speak, Paul replied:

"I cheerfully make my defense, knowing that for many years you have been a judge over this nation. 11 As you can find out, it is not more than twelve days since I went up to worship in Jerusalem. 12 They did not find me disputing with anyone in the temple or stirring up a crowd either in the synagogues or throughout the city. 13 Neither can they prove to you the charge that they now bring against me. 14 But this I admit to you, that according to the Way, which they call a sect, I worship the God of our ancestors, believing everything laid down according to the law or written in the prophets. 15 I have a hope in God — a hope that they themselves also accept — that there will be a resurrection of both *p* the righteous and the unrighteous. 16 Therefore I do my best always to have a clear conscience toward God and all people. 17 Now after some years I came to bring alms to my nation and to offer sacrifices. 18 While I was doing this, they found me in the temple, completing the rite of purification, without any crowd or disturbance. 19 But there were some Jews from Asia — they ought to be here before you to make an accusation, if they have anything against me. 20 Or let these men here tell what crime they had found when I stood before the council, 21 unless it was this one sentence that I called out while standing before them, 'It is about the resurrection of the dead that I am on trial before you today.'"

22 But Felix, who was rather well informed about the Way, adjourned the hearing with the comment, "When Lys-

REVISED ENGLISH BIBLE

30 Information, however, has now been brought to my notice of an attempt to be made on the man's life, so I am sending him to you without delay, and have instructed his accusers to state their case against him before you.

31 Acting on their orders, the infantry took custody of Paul and brought him by night to Antipatris. 32 Next day they returned to their barracks, leaving the cavalry to escort him the rest of the way. 33 When the cavalry reached Caesarea, they delivered the letter to the governor, and handed Paul over to him. 34 He read the letter, and asked him what province he was from; and learning that he was from Cilicia 35 he said, 'I will hear your case when your accusers arrive.' He ordered him to be held in custody at his headquarters in Herod's palace.

24 FIVE days later the high priest Ananias came down, accompanied by some of the elders and an advocate named Tertullus, to lay before the governor their charge against Paul. 2-3 When the prisoner was called, Tertullus opened the case.

'Your excellency,' he said to Felix, 'we owe it to you that we enjoy unbroken peace, and it is due to your provident care that, in all kinds of ways and in all sorts of places, improvements are being made for the good of this nation. We appreciate this, and are most grateful to you. 4 And now, not to take up too much of your time, I crave your indulgence for a brief statement of our case. 5 We have found this man to be a pest, a fomenter of discord among the Jews all over the world, a ringleader of the sect of the Nazarenes. 6 He made an attempt to profane the temple and we arrested him. 8 If you examine him yourself you can ascertain the truth of all the charges we bring against him.' 9 The Jews supported the charge, alleging that the facts were as he stated.

10 The governor then motioned to Paul to speak, and he replied as follows: 'Knowing as I do that for many years you have administered justice to this nation, I make my defence with confidence. 11 As you can ascertain for yourself, it is not more than twelve days since I went up to Jerusalem on a pilgrimage. 12 They did not find me in the temple arguing with anyone or collecting a crowd, or in the synagogues or anywhere else in the city; 13 and they cannot make good the charges they now bring against me. 14 But this much I will admit: I am a follower of the new way (the "sect" they speak of), and it is in that manner that I worship the God of our fathers; for I believe all that is written in the law and the prophets, 15 and in reliance on God I hold the hope, which my accusers too accept, that there is to be a resurrection of good and wicked alike. 16 Accordingly I, no less than they, train myself to keep at all times a clear conscience before God and man.

17 'After an absence of several years I came to bring charitable gifts to my nation and to offer sacrifices. 18 I was ritually purified and engaged in this service when they found me in the temple; I had no crowd with me, and there was no disturbance. But some Jews from the province of Asia were there, 19 and if they had any charge against me, it is they who ought to have been in court to state it. 20 Failing that, it is for these persons here present to say what crime they discovered when I was brought before the Council, 21 apart from this one declaration which I made as I stood there: "The issue in my trial before you today is the resurrection of the dead." '

22 Then Felix, who was well informed about the new way, adjourned the hearing. 'I will decide your case when

---

j Other ancient authorities add *Farewell*   *k* Gk *praetorium*
l Gk *he*   *m* Gk lacks *Your Excellency*   *n* Gk *Nazoreans*   *o* Other ancient authorities add *and we would have judged him according to our law.* *7 But the chief captain Lysias came and with great violence took him out of our hands,* *8 commanding his accusers to come before you.*   *p* Other ancient authorities read *of the dead, both of*

24:6 **arrested him:** *some witnesses add* It was our intention to try him under our law; 7 but Lysias the commandant intervened and forcibly removed him out of our hands, (8) ordering his accusers to come before you.

my attention that there will be a plot against the man, I am sending him to you at once, and have also notified his accusers to state [their case] against him before you."

31 So the soldiers, according to their orders, took Paul and escorted him by night to Antipatris. 32 The next day they returned to the compound, leaving the horsemen to complete the journey with him. 33 When they arrived in Caesarea they delivered the letter to the governor and presented Paul to him. 34 When he had read it and asked to what province he belonged, and learned that he was from Cilicia, 35 he said, "I shall hear your case when your accusers arrive." Then he ordered that he be held in custody in Herod's praetorium.

24 Five days later the high priest Ananias came down with some elders and an advocate, a certain Tertullus, and they presented formal charges against Paul to the governor. 2 When he was called, Tertullus began to accuse him, saying, "Since we have attained much peace through you, and reforms have been accomplished in this nation through your provident care, 3 we acknowledge this in every way and everywhere, most excellent Felix, with all gratitude. 4 But in order not to detain you further, I ask you to give us a brief hearing with your customary graciousness. 5 We found this man to be a pest; he creates dissension among Jews all over the world and is a ringleader of the sect of the Nazoreans. 6 He even tried to desecrate our temple, but we arrested him. [7] 8 If you examine him you will be able to learn from him for yourself about everything of which we are accusing him." 9 The Jews also joined in the attack and asserted that these things were so.

10 Then the governor motioned to him to speak and Paul replied, "I know that you have been a judge over this nation for many years and so I am pleased to make my defense before you. 11 As you can verify, not more than twelve days have passed since I went up to Jerusalem to worship. 12 Neither in the temple, nor in the synagogues, nor anywhere in the city did they find me arguing with anyone or instigating a riot among the people. 13 Nor can they prove to you the accusations they are now making against me. 14 But this I do admit to you, that according to the Way, which they call a sect, I worship the God of our ancestors and I believe everything that is in accordance with the law and written in the prophets. 15 I have the same hope in God as they themselves have that there will be a resurrection of the righteous and the unrighteous. 16 Because of this, I always strive to keep my conscience clear before God and man. 17 After many years, I came to bring alms for my nation and offerings. 18 While I was so engaged, they found me, after my purification, in the temple without a crowd or disturbance. 19 But some Jews from the province of Asia, who should be here before you to make whatever accusation they might have against me — 20 or let these men themselves state what crime they discovered when I stood before the Sanhedrin, 21 unless it was my one outcry as I stood among them, that 'I am on trial before you today for the resurrection of the dead.'"

22 Then Felix, who was accurately informed about the Way, postponed the trial, saying, "When Lysias the com-

information that there was a conspiracy against the man, I hasten to send him to you, and have notified his accusers that they must state their case against him in your presence.'

31 The soldiers carried out their orders; they took Paul and escorted him by night to Antipatris. 32 Next day they left the mounted escort to go on with him and returned to the fortress. 33 On arriving at Caesarea the escort delivered the letter to the governor and handed Paul over to him. 34 When he had read it, he asked Paul what province he came from. Learning that he was from Cilicia he said, 35 'I will hear your case as soon as your accusers are here too.' Then he ordered him to be held in Herod's praetorium.

24 Five days later the high priest Ananias came down with some of the elders and an advocate named Tertullus, and they laid information against Paul before the governor. 2 Paul was called, and Tertullus opened for the prosecution, 'Your Excellency, Felix, the unbroken peace we enjoy and the reforms this nation owes to your foresight 3 are matters we accept, always and everywhere, with all gratitude. 4 I do not want to take up too much of your time, but I urge you in your graciousness to give us a brief hearing. 5 We have found this man a perfect pest; he stirs up trouble among Jews the world over and is a ringleader of the Nazarene sect. 6 He has even attempted to profane the Temple. We placed him under arrest.j [7] 8 If you ask him you can find out for yourself the truth of all our accusations against this man.' 9 The Jews supported him, asserting that these were the facts.

10 When the governor motioned him to speak, Paul answered:

'I know that you have administered justice over this nation for many years, and I can therefore speak with confidence in my defence. 11 As you can verify for yourself, it is no more than twelve days since I went up to Jerusalem on pilgrimage, 12 and it is not true that they ever found me arguing with anyone or stirring up the mob, either in the Temple, in the synagogues, or about the town; 13 neither can they give you any proof of the accusations they are making against me now.

14 'What I do admit to you is this: it is according to the Way, which they describe as a sect, that I worship the God of my ancestors, retaining my belief in all points of the Law and in what is written in the prophets; 15 and I hold the same hope in God as they do that there will be a resurrection of the upright and the wicked alike. 16 In these things, I, as much as they, do my best to keep a clear conscience at all times before God and everyone.

17 'After several years I came to bring relief-money to my nationk and to make offerings; 18 it was in connection with these that they found me in the Temple; I had been purified, and there was no crowd involved, and no disturbance. 19 But some Jews from Asia — these are the ones who should have appeared before you and accused me of whatever they had against me. 20 At least let those who are present say what crime they held against me when I stood before the Sanhedrin, 21 unless it were to do with this single claim, when I stood up among them and called out, "It is about the resurrection of the dead that I am on trial before you today." '

22 At this, Felix, who was fairly well informed about the Way, adjourned the case, saying, 'When Lysias the tribune

---

24, 7: The Western text has added here a verse (really 6b-8a) that is not found in the best Greek manuscripts. It reads, "and would have judged him according to our own law, but the cohort commander Lysias came and violently took him out of our hands and ordered his accusers to come before you."

j 24 Several witnesses add 'intending to judge him according to our Law, [7] but the tribune Lysias intervened and took him out of our hands by force, [8] ordering the accusers to appear before you'.
k 24 cf. 1 Co 16:1.

NEW REVISED STANDARD VERSION

ias the tribune comes down, I will decide your case." 23 Then he ordered the centurion to keep him in custody, but to let him have some liberty and not to prevent any of his friends from taking care of his needs.

24 Some days later when Felix came with his wife Drusilla, who was Jewish, he sent for Paul and heard him speak concerning faith in Christ Jesus. 25 And as he discussed justice, self-control, and the coming judgment, Felix became frightened and said, "Go away for the present; when I have an opportunity, I will send for you." 26 At the same time he hoped that money would be given him by Paul, and for that reason he used to send for him very often and converse with him.

27 After two years had passed, Felix was succeeded by Porcius Festus; and since he wanted to grant the Jews a favor, Felix left Paul in prison.

25 Three days after Festus had arrived in the province, he went up from Caesarea to Jerusalem 2 where the chief priests and the leaders of the Jews gave him a report against Paul. They appealed to him 3 and requested, as a favor to them against Paul,*q* to have him transferred to Jerusalem. They were, in fact, planning an ambush to kill him along the way. 4 Festus replied that Paul was being kept at Caesarea, and that he himself intended to go there shortly. 5 "So," he said, "let those of you who have the authority come down with me, and if there is anything wrong about the man, let them accuse him."

6 After he had stayed among them not more than eight or ten days, he went down to Caesarea; the next day he took his seat on the tribunal and ordered Paul to be brought. 7 When he arrived, the Jews who had gone down from Jerusalem surrounded him, bringing many serious charges against him, which they could not prove. 8 Paul said in his defense, "I have in no way committed an offense against the law of the Jews, or against the temple, or against the emperor." 9 But Festus, wishing to do the Jews a favor, asked Paul, "Do you wish to go up to Jerusalem and be tried there before me on these charges?" 10 Paul said, "I am appealing to the emperor's tribunal; this is where I should be tried. I have done no wrong to the Jews, as you very well know. 11 Now if I am in the wrong and have committed something for which I deserve to die, I am not trying to escape death; but if there is nothing to their charges against me, no one can turn me over to them. I appeal to the emperor." 12 Then Festus, after he had conferred with his council, replied, "You have appealed to the emperor; to the emperor you will go."

13 After several days had passed, King Agrippa and Bernice arrived at Caesarea to welcome Festus. 14 Since they were staying there several days, Festus laid Paul's case before the king, saying, "There is a man here who was left in prison by Felix. 15 When I was in Jerusalem, the chief priests and the elders of the Jews informed me about him and asked for a sentence against him. 16 I told them that it was not the custom of the Romans to hand over anyone before the accused had met the accusers face to face and had been given an opportunity to make a defense against the charge. 17 So when they met here, I lost no time, but on the next day took my seat on the tribunal and ordered the man to be brought. 18 When the accusers stood up, they did not charge him with any of the crimes*r* that I was expecting. 19 Instead they had certain points of disagreement with him about their own religion and about a certain Jesus, who had died, but whom Paul asserted to be alive. 20 Since I was at a loss how to investigate these questions, I asked whether he wished to go to Jerusalem and be tried there on these charges.*s* 21 But when Paul had appealed to be kept in

REVISED ENGLISH BIBLE

Lysias the commanding officer comes down,' he said. 23 He gave orders to the centurion to keep Paul under open arrest and not to prevent any of his friends from making themselves useful to him.

24 Some days later Felix came with his wife Drusilla, who was a Jewess, and sent for Paul. He let him talk to him about faith in Christ Jesus, 25 but when the discourse turned to questions of morals, self-control, and the coming judgement, Felix became alarmed and exclaimed, 'Enough for now! When I find it convenient I will send for you again.' 26 He also had hopes of a bribe from Paul, so he sent for him frequently and talked with him. 27 When two years had passed, Felix was succeeded by Porcius Festus. Wishing to curry favour with the Jews, Felix left Paul in custody.

25 THREE days after taking up his appointment, Festus went up from Caesarea to Jerusalem, 2 where the chief priests and the Jewish leaders laid before him their charge against Paul. 3 They urged Festus to support them in their case and have Paul sent to Jerusalem, for they were plotting to kill him on the way. 4 Festus, however, replied, 'Paul is in safe custody at Caesarea, and I shall be leaving Jerusalem shortly myself; 5 so let your leading men come down with me, and if the man is at fault in any way, let them prosecute him.'

6 After spending eight or ten days at most in Jerusalem, he went down to Caesarea, and next day he took his seat in court and ordered Paul to be brought before him. 7 When he appeared, the Jews who had come down from Jerusalem stood round bringing many grave charges, which they were unable to prove. 8 Paul protested: 'I have committed no offence against the Jewish law, or against the temple, or against the emperor.' 9 Festus, anxious to ingratiate himself with the Jews, turned to Paul and asked, 'Are you willing to go up to Jerusalem and stand trial on these charges before me there?' 10 But Paul said, 'I am now standing before the emperor's tribunal; that is where I ought to be tried. I have committed no offence against the Jews, as you very well know. 11 If I am guilty of any capital crime, I do not ask to escape the death penalty; if, however, there is no substance in the charges which these men bring against me, it is not open to anyone to hand me over to them. I appeal to Caesar!' 12 Then Festus, after conferring with his advisers, replied, 'You have appealed to Caesar: to Caesar you shall go!'

13 Some days later King Agrippa and Bernice arrived at Caesarea on a courtesy visit to Festus. 14 They spent some time there, and during their stay Festus raised Paul's case with the king. 'There is a man here', he said, 'left in custody by Felix; 15 and when I was in Jerusalem the chief priests and elders of the Jews brought a charge against him, demanding his condemnation. 16 I replied that it was not Roman practice to hand a man over before he had been confronted with his accusers and given an opportunity of answering the charge. 17 So when they had come here with me I lost no time, but took my seat in court the very next day and ordered the man to be brought before me. 18 When his accusers rose to speak, they brought none of the charges I was expecting; 19 they merely had certain points of disagreement with him about their religion, and about someone called Jesus, a dead man whom Paul alleged to be alive. 20 Finding myself out of my depth in such discussions, I asked if he was willing to go to Jerusalem and stand trial there on these issues. 21 But Paul appealed to be remanded

q Gk him   *r* Other ancient authorities read *with anything*   *s* Gk on them

mander comes down, I shall decide your case." 23 He gave orders to the centurion that he should be kept in custody but have some liberty, and that he should not prevent any of his friends from caring for his needs.

24 Several days later Felix came with his wife Drusilla, who was Jewish. He had Paul summoned and listened to him speak about faith in Christ Jesus. 25 But as he spoke about righteousness and self-restraint and the coming judgment, Felix became frightened and said, "You may go for now; when I find an opportunity I shall summon you again." 26 At the same time he hoped that a bribe would be offered him by Paul, and so he sent for him very often and conversed with him.

27 Two years passed and Felix was succeeded by Porcius Festus. Wishing to ingratiate himself with the Jews, Felix left Paul in prison.

25 Three days after his arrival in the province, Festus went up from Caesarea to Jerusalem 2 where the chief priests and Jewish leaders presented him their formal charges against Paul. They asked him 3 as a favor to have him sent to Jerusalem, for they were plotting to kill him along the way. 4 Festus replied that Paul was being held in custody in Caesarea and that he himself would be returning there shortly. 5 He said, "Let your authorities come down with me, and if this man has done something improper, let them accuse him."

6 After spending no more than eight or ten days with them, he went down to Caesarea, and on the following day took his seat on the tribunal and ordered that Paul be brought in. 7 When he appeared, the Jews who had come down from Jerusalem surrounded him and brought many serious charges against him, which they were unable to prove. 8 In defending himself Paul said, "I have committed no crime either against the Jewish law or against the temple or against Caesar." 9 Then Festus, wishing to ingratiate himself with the Jews, said to Paul in reply, "Are you willing to go up to Jerusalem and there stand trial before me on these charges?" 10 Paul answered, "I am standing before the tribunal of Caesar; this is where I should be tried. I have committed no crime against the Jews, as you very well know. 11 If I have committed a crime or done anything deserving death, I do not seek to escape the death penalty; but if there is no substance to the charges they are bringing against me, then no one has the right to hand me over to them. I appeal to Caesar." 12 Then Festus, after conferring with his council, replied, "You have appealed to Caesar. To Caesar you will go."

13 When a few days had passed, King Agrippa and Bernice arrived in Caesarea on a visit to Festus. 14 Since they spent several days there, Festus referred Paul's case to the king, saying, "There is a man here left in custody by Felix. 15 When I was in Jerusalem the chief priests and the elders of the Jews brought charges against him and demanded his condemnation. 16 I answered them that it was not Roman practice to hand over an accused person before he has faced his accusers and had the opportunity to defend himself against their charge. 17 So when [they] came together here, I made no delay; the next day I took my seat on the tribunal and ordered the man to be brought in. 18 His accusers stood around him, but did not charge him with any of the crimes I suspected. 19 Instead they had some issues with him about their own religion and about a certain Jesus who had died but who Paul claimed was alive. 20 Since I was at a loss how to investigate this controversy, I asked if he were willing to go to Jerusalem and there stand trial on these charges.

comes down I will give judgement about your case.' 23 He then gave orders to the centurion that Paul should be kept under arrest but free from restriction, and that none of his own people should be prevented from seeing to his needs.

24 Some days later Felix came with his wife Drusilla who was a Jewess. He sent for Paul and gave him a hearing on the subject of faith in Christ Jesus. 25 But when Paul began to treat of uprightness, self-control and the coming Judgement, Felix took fright and said, 'You may go for the present; I will send for you when I find it convenient.' 26 At the same time he had hopes of receiving money from Paul, and for this reason he sent for him frequently and had talks with him.

27 When two years came to an end, Felix was succeeded by Porcius Festus and, being anxious to gain favour with the Jews, Felix left Paul in custody.

25 Three days after his arrival in the province, Festus went up to Jerusalem from Caesarea. 2 The chief priests and leaders of the Jews informed him of the case against Paul, 3 urgently asking him to support them against him, and to have him transferred to Jerusalem. They were preparing an ambush to murder him on the way. 4 But Festus replied that Paul was in custody in Caesarea, and that he would be going back there shortly himself. 5 'Let your authorities come down with me, and if there is anything wrong about the man, they can bring a charge against him.'

6 After staying with them for eight or ten days at the most, he went down to Caesarea and the next day he took his seat on the tribunal and had Paul brought in. 7 As soon as Paul appeared, the Jews who had come down from Jerusalem surrounded him, making many serious accusations which they were unable to substantiate. 8 Paul's defence was this, 'I have committed no offence whatever against either Jewish law, or the Temple, or Caesar.' 9 Festus was anxious to gain favour with the Jews, so he said to Paul, 'Are you willing to go up to Jerusalem and be tried on these charges before me there?' 10 But Paul replied, 'I am standing before the tribunal of Caesar and this is where I should be tried. I have done the Jews no wrong, as you very well know. 11 If I am guilty of committing any capital crime, I do not ask to be spared the death penalty. But if there is no substance in the accusations these persons bring against me, no one has a right to surrender me to them. I appeal to Caesar.' 12 Then Festus conferred with his advisers and replied, 'You have appealed to Caesar; to Caesar you shall go.'

13 Some days later King Agrippa and Bernice arrived in Caesarea and paid their respects to Festus. 14 Their visit lasted several days, and Festus put Paul's case before the king, saying, 'There is a man here whom Felix left behind in custody, 15 and while I was in Jerusalem the chief priests and elders of the Jews laid information against him, demanding his condemnation. 16 But I told them that Romans are not in the habit of surrendering any man, until the accused confronts his accusers and is given an opportunity to defend himself against the charge. 17 So they came here with me, and I wasted no time but took my seat on the tribunal the very next day and had the man brought in. 18 When confronted with him, his accusers did not charge him with any of the crimes I had expected; 19 but they had some argument or other with him about their own religion and about a dead man called Jesus whom Paul alleged to be alive. 20 Not feeling qualified to deal with questions of this sort, I asked him if he would be willing to go to Jerusalem to be tried there on this issue. 21 But Paul put in an appeal

NEW REVISED STANDARD VERSION

custody for the decision of his Imperial Majesty, I ordered him to be held until I could send him to the emperor. 22 Agrippa said to Festus, "I would like to hear the man myself." "Tomorrow," he said, "you will hear him."

23 So on the next day Agrippa and Bernice came with great pomp, and they entered the audience hall with the military tribunes and the prominent men of the city. Then Festus gave the order and Paul was brought in. 24 And Festus said, "King Agrippa and all here present with us, you see this man about whom the whole Jewish community petitioned me, both in Jerusalem and here, shouting that he ought not to live any longer. 25 But I found that he had done nothing deserving death; and when he appealed to his Imperial Majesty, I decided to send him. 26 But I have nothing definite to write to our sovereign about him. Therefore I have brought him before all of you, and especially before you, King Agrippa, so that, after we have examined him, I may have something to write — 27 for it seems to me unreasonable to send a prisoner without indicating the charges against him."

26 Agrippa said to Paul, "You have permission to speak for yourself." Then Paul stretched out his hand and began to defend himself:

2 "I consider myself fortunate that it is before you, King Agrippa, I am to make my defense today against all the accusations of the Jews; 3 because you are especially familiar with all the customs and controversies of the Jews; therefore I beg of you to listen to me patiently.

4 "All the Jews know my way of life from my youth, a life spent from the beginning among my own people and in Jerusalem. 5 They have known for a long time, if they are willing to testify, that I have belonged to the strictest sect of our religion and lived as a Pharisee. 6 And now I stand here on trial on account of my hope in the promise made by God to our ancestors, 7 a promise that our twelve tribes hope to attain, as they earnestly worship day and night. It is for this hope, your Excellency,[t] that I am accused by Jews! 8 Why is it thought incredible by any of you that God raises the dead?

9 "Indeed, I myself was convinced that I ought to do many things against the name of Jesus of Nazareth.[u] 10 And that is what I did in Jerusalem; with authority received from the chief priests, I not only locked up many of the saints in prison, but I also cast my vote against them when they were being condemned to death. 11 By punishing them often in all the synagogues I tried to force them to blaspheme; and since I was so furiously enraged at them, I pursued them even to foreign cities.

12 "With this in mind, I was traveling to Damascus with the authority and commission of the chief priests, 13 when at midday along the road, your Excellency,[t] I saw a light from heaven, brighter than the sun, shining around me and my companions. 14 When we had all fallen to the ground, I heard a voice saying to me in the Hebrew[v] language, 'Saul, Saul, why are you persecuting me? It hurts you to kick against the goads.' 15 I asked, 'Who are you, Lord?' The Lord answered, 'I am Jesus whom you are persecuting. 16 But get up and stand on your feet; for I have appeared to you for this purpose, to appoint you to serve and testify to the things in which you have seen me[w] and to those in which I will appear to you. 17 I will rescue you from your people and from the Gentiles — to whom I am sending you 18 to open their eyes so that they may turn from darkness to light and from the power of Satan to God, so that they may receive forgiveness of sins and a place among those who are sanctified by faith in me.'

REVISED ENGLISH BIBLE

in custody for his imperial majesty's decision, and I ordered him to be detained until I could send him to the emperor.' 22 Agrippa said to Festus, 'I should rather like to hear the man myself.' 'You shall hear him tomorrow,' he answered.

23 Next day Agrippa and Bernice came in full state and entered the audience-chamber accompanied by high-ranking officers and prominent citizens; and on the orders of Festus, Paul was brought in. 24 Then Festus said, 'King Agrippa, and all you who are in attendance, you see this man: the whole body of the Jews approached me both in Jerusalem and here, loudly insisting that he had no right to remain alive. 25 It was clear to me, however, that he had committed no capital crime, and when he himself appealed to his imperial majesty, I decided to send him. 26 As I have nothing definite about him to put in writing for our sovereign, I have brought him before you all and particularly before you, King Agrippa, so that as a result of this preliminary enquiry I may have something to report. 27 There is no sense, it seems to me, in sending on a prisoner without indicating the charges against him.'

26 Agrippa said to Paul: 'You have our permission to give an account of yourself.' Then Paul stretched out his hand and began his defence.

2 'I consider myself fortunate, King Agrippa, that it is before you I am to make my defence today on all the charges brought against me by the Jews, 3 particularly as you are expert in all our Jewish customs and controversies. I beg you therefore to give me a patient hearing.

4 'My life from my youth up, a life spent from the first among my nation and in Jerusalem, is familiar to all Jews. 5 Indeed they have known me long enough to testify, if they would, that I belonged to the strictest group in our religion: I was a Pharisee. 6 It is the hope based on the promise God made to our forefathers that has led to my being on trial today. 7 Our twelve tribes worship with intense devotion night and day in the hope of seeing the fulfilment of that promise; and for this very hope I am accused, your majesty, and accused by Jews. 8 Why should Jews find it incredible that God should raise the dead?

9 'I myself once thought it my duty to work actively against the name of Jesus of Nazareth; 10 and I did so in Jerusalem. By authority obtained from the chief priests, I sent many of God's people to prison, and when they were condemned to death, my vote was cast against them. 11 In all the synagogues I tried by repeated punishment to make them commit blasphemy; indeed my fury rose to such a pitch that I extended my persecution to foreign cities.

12 'On one such occasion I was travelling to Damascus with authority and commission from the chief priests; 13 and as I was on my way, your majesty, at midday I saw a light from the sky, more brilliant than the sun, shining all around me and my companions. 14 We all fell to the ground, and I heard a voice saying to me in the Jewish language, "Saul, Saul, why do you persecute me? It hurts to kick like this against the goad." 15 I said, "Tell me, Lord, who you are," and the Lord replied, "I am Jesus, whom you are persecuting. 16 But now, get to your feet. I have appeared to you for a purpose: to appoint you my servant and witness, to tell what you have seen and what you shall yet see of me. 17 I will rescue you from your own people and from the Gentiles to whom I am sending you. 18 You are to open their eyes and to turn them from darkness to light, from the dominion of Satan to God, so that they may obtain forgiveness of sins and a place among those whom God has made his own through faith in me."

---

t Gk *O king*   *u* Gk *the Nazorean*   *v* That is, *Aramaic*   *w* Other ancient authorities read *the things that you have seen*

21 And when Paul appealed that he be held in custody for the Emperor's decision, I ordered him held until I could send him to Caesar." 22 Agrippa said to Festus, "I too should like to hear this man." He replied, "Tomorrow you will hear him."

23 The next day Agrippa and Bernice came with great ceremony and entered the audience hall in the company of cohort commanders and the prominent men of the city and, by command of Festus, Paul was brought in. 24 And Festus said, "King Agrippa and all you here present with us, look at this man about whom the whole Jewish populace petitioned me here and in Jerusalem, clamoring that he should live no longer. 25 I found, however, that he had done nothing deserving death, and so when he appealed to the Emperor, I decided to send him. 26 But I have nothing definite to write about him to our sovereign; therefore I have brought him before all of you, and particularly before you, King Agrippa, so that I may have something to write as a result of this investigation. 27 For it seems senseless to me to send up a prisoner without indicating the charges against him."

26 Then Agrippa said to Paul, "You may now speak on your own behalf." So Paul stretched out his hand and began his defense. 2 "I count myself fortunate, King Agrippa, that I am to defend myself before you today against all the charges made against me by the Jews, 3 especially since you are an expert in all the Jewish customs and controversies. And therefore I beg you to listen patiently. 4 My manner of living from my youth, a life spent from the beginning among my people and in Jerusalem, all [the] Jews know. 5 They have known about me from the start, if they are willing to testify, that I have lived my life as a Pharisee, the strictest party of our religion. 6 But now I am standing trial because of my hope in the promise made by God to our ancestors. 7 Our twelve tribes hope to attain to that promise as they fervently worship God day and night; and on account of this hope I am accused by Jews, O king. 8 Why is it thought unbelievable among you that God raises the dead? 9 I myself once thought that I had to do many things against the name of Jesus the Nazorean, 10 and I did so in Jerusalem. I imprisoned many of the holy ones with the authorization I received from the chief priests, and when they were to be put to death I cast my vote against them. 11 Many times, in synagogue after synagogue, I punished them in an attempt to force them to blaspheme; I was so enraged against them that I pursued them even to foreign cities.

12 "On one such occasion I was traveling to Damascus with the authorization and commission of the chief priests. 13 At midday, along the way, O king, I saw a light from the sky, brighter than the sun, shining around me and my traveling companions. 14 We all fell to the ground and I heard a voice saying to me in Hebrew, 'Saul, Saul, why are you persecuting me? It is hard for you to kick against the goad.' 15 And I said, 'Who are you, sir?' And the Lord replied, 'I am Jesus whom you are persecuting. 16 Get up now, and stand on your feet. I have appeared to you for this purpose, to appoint you as a servant and witness of what you have seen [of me] and what you will be shown. 17 I shall deliver you from this people and from the Gentiles to whom I send you, 18 to open their eyes that they may turn from darkness to light and from the power of Satan to God, so that they may obtain forgiveness of sins and an inheritance among those who have been consecrated by faith in me.'

for his case to be reserved for the judgement of the emperor, so I ordered him to be remanded until I could send him to Caesar.' 22 Agrippa said to Festus, 'I should like to hear the man myself.' He answered, 'Tomorrow you shall hear him.'

23 So the next day Agrippa and Bernice arrived in great state and entered the audience chamber attended by the tribunes and the city notables; and Festus ordered Paul to be brought in. 24 Then Festus said, 'King Agrippa, and all here present with us, you see before you the man about whom the whole Jewish community has petitioned me, both in Jerusalem and here, loudly protesting that he ought not to be allowed to remain alive. 25 For my own part I am satisfied that he has committed no capital crime, but when he himself appealed to the emperor I decided to send him. 26 But I have nothing definite that I can write to his Imperial Majesty about him; that is why I have produced him before you all, and before you in particular, King Agrippa, so that after the examination I may have something to write. 27 It seems to me pointless to send a prisoner without indicating the charges against him.'

26 Then Agrippa said to Paul, 'You have leave to speak on your own behalf.' And Paul held up his hand and began his defence:

2 'I consider myself fortunate, King Agrippa, in that it is before you I am to answer today all the charges made against me by the Jews, 3 the more so because you are an expert in matters of custom and controversy among the Jews. So I beg you to listen to me patiently.

4 'My manner of life from my youth, a life spent from the beginning among my own people and in Jerusalem, is common knowledge among the Jews. 5 They have known me for a long time and could testify, if they would, that I followed the strictest party in our religion and lived as a Pharisee. 6 And now it is for my hope in the promise made by God to our ancestors that I am on trial, 7 the promise that our twelve tribes, constant in worship night and day, hope to attain. For that hope, Your Majesty, I am actually put on trial by Jews! 8 Why does it seem incredible to you that God should raise the dead?

9 'As for me, I once thought it was my duty to use every means to oppose the name of Jesus the Nazarene. 10 This I did in Jerusalem; I myself threw many of God's holy people into prison, acting on authority from the chief priests, and when they were being sentenced to death I cast my vote against them. 11 I often went round the synagogues inflicting penalties, trying in this way to force them to renounce their faith; my fury against them was so extreme that I even pursued them into foreign cities.

12 'On such an expedition I was going to Damascus, armed with full powers and a commission from the chief priests,*l* 13 and in the middle of the day as I was on my way, Your Majesty, I saw a light from heaven shining more brilliantly than the sun round me and my fellow-travellers. 14 We all fell to the ground, and I heard a voice saying to me in Hebrew, "Saul, Saul, why are you persecuting me? It is hard for you, kicking against the goad." 15 Then I said, "Who are you, Lord?" And the Lord answered, "I am Jesus, whom you are persecuting. 16 But get up and stand on your feet, for I have appeared to you for this reason: to appoint you as my servant and as witness of this vision in which you have seen me, and of others in which I shall appear to you. 17 *I shall rescue you* from the people and from *the nations to whom I send you* 18 *to open their eyes*, so that they may turn *from darkness to light,m* from the dominion of Satan to God, and receive, through faith in me, forgiveness of their sins and a share in the inheritance of the sanctified."

l **26** = 9; 22. *m* **26** Jr 1:5–8 followed by Is 42:16.

NEW REVISED STANDARD VERSION | REVISED ENGLISH BIBLE

19 "After that, King Agrippa, I was not disobedient to the heavenly vision, 20 but declared first to those in Damascus, then in Jerusalem and throughout the countryside of Judea, and also to the Gentiles, that they should repent and turn to God and do deeds consistent with repentance. 21 For this reason the Jews seized me in the temple and tried to kill me. 22 To this day I have had help from God, and so I stand here, testifying to both small and great, saying nothing but what the prophets and Moses said would take place: 23 that the Messiah*x* must suffer, and that, by being the first to rise from the dead, he would proclaim light both to our people and to the Gentiles."

24 While he was making this defense, Festus exclaimed, "You are out of your mind, Paul! Too much learning is driving you insane!" 25 But Paul said, "I am not out of my mind, most excellent Festus, but I am speaking the sober truth. 26 Indeed the king knows about these things, and to him I speak freely; for I am certain that none of these things has escaped his notice, for this was not done in a corner. 27 King Agrippa, do you believe the prophets? I know that you believe." 28 Agrippa said to Paul, "Are you so quickly persuading me to become a Christian?"*y* 29 Paul replied, "Whether quickly or not, I pray to God that not only you but also all who are listening to me today might become such as I am — except for these chains."

30 Then the king got up, and with him the governor and Bernice and those who had been seated with them; 31 and as they were leaving, they said to one another, "This man is doing nothing to deserve death or imprisonment." 32 Agrippa said to Festus, "This man could have been set free if he had not appealed to the emperor."

27 When it was decided that we were to sail for Italy, they transferred Paul and some other prisoners to a centurion of the Augustan Cohort, named Julius. 2 Embarking on a ship of Adramyttium that was about to set sail to the ports along the coast of Asia, we put to sea, accompanied by Aristarchus, a Macedonian from Thessalonica. 3 The next day we put in at Sidon; and Julius treated Paul kindly, and allowed him to go to his friends to be cared for. 4 Putting out to sea from there, we sailed under the lee of Cyprus, because the winds were against us. 5 After we had sailed across the sea that is off Cilicia and Pamphylia, we came to Myra in Lycia. 6 There the centurion found an Alexandrian ship bound for Italy and put us on board. 7 We sailed slowly for a number of days and arrived with difficulty off Cnidus, and as the wind was against us, we sailed under the lee of Crete off Salmone. 8 Sailing past it with difficulty, we came to a place called Fair Havens, near the city of Lasea.

9 Since much time had been lost and sailing was now dangerous, because even the Fast had already gone by, Paul advised them, 10 saying, "Sirs, I can see that the voyage will be with danger and much heavy loss, not only of the cargo and the ship, but also of our lives." 11 But the centurion paid more attention to the pilot and to the owner of the ship than to what Paul said. 12 Since the harbor was not suitable for spending the winter, the majority was in favor of putting to sea from there, on the chance that somehow they could reach Phoenix, where they could spend the winter. It was a harbor of Crete, facing southwest and northwest.

13 When a moderate south wind began to blow, they thought they could achieve their purpose; so they weighed anchor and began to sail past Crete, close to the shore. 14 But soon a violent wind, called the northeaster, rushed down from Crete.*z* 15 Since the ship was caught and could

19 'So, King Agrippa, I did not disobey the heavenly vision. 20 I preached first to the inhabitants of Damascus, and then to Jerusalem and all the country of Judaea, and to the Gentiles, calling on them to repent and turn to God, and to prove their repentance by their deeds. 21 That is why the Jews seized me in the temple and tried to do away with me. 22 But I have had God's help to this very day, and here I stand bearing witness to the great and to the lowly. I assert nothing beyond what was foretold by the prophets and by Moses: 23 that the Messiah would suffer and that, as the first to rise from the dead, he would announce the dawn both to the Jewish people and to the Gentiles.'

24 While Paul was thus making his defence, Festus shouted at the top of his voice, 'Paul, you are raving; too much study is driving you mad.' 25 'I am not mad, your excellency,' said Paul; 'what I am asserting is sober truth. 26 The king is well versed in these matters, and I can speak freely to him. I do not believe that he can be unaware of any of these facts, for this has been no hole-and-corner business. 27 King Agrippa, do you believe the prophets? I know you do.' 28 Agrippa said to Paul, 'With a little more of your persuasion you will make a Christian of me.' 29 'Little or much,' said Paul, 'I wish to God that not only you, but all those who are listening to me today, might become what I am — apart from these chains!'

30 With that the king rose, and with him the governor, Bernice, and the rest of the company, 31 and after they had withdrawn they talked it over. 'This man', they agreed, 'is doing nothing that deserves death or imprisonment.' 32 Agrippa said to Festus, 'The fellow could have been discharged, if he had not appealed to the emperor.'

27 WHEN it was decided that we should sail for Italy, Paul and some other prisoners were handed over to a centurion named Julius, of the Augustan Cohort. 2 We embarked in a ship of Adramyttium, bound for ports in the province of Asia, and put out to sea. Aristarchus, a Macedonian from Thessalonica, came with us. 3 Next day we landed at Sidon, and Julius very considerately allowed Paul to go to his friends to be cared for. 4 Leaving Sidon we sailed under the lee of Cyprus because of the head winds, 5 then across the open sea off the coast of Cilicia and Pamphylia, and so reached Myra in Lycia.

6 There the centurion found an Alexandrian vessel bound for Italy and put us on board. 7 For a good many days we made little headway, and we were hard put to it to reach Cnidus. Then, as the wind continued against us, off Salmone we began to sail under the lee of Crete, 8 and, hugging the coast, struggled on to a place called Fair Havens, not far from the town of Lasea.

9 By now much time had been lost, and with the Fast already over, it was dangerous to go on with the voyage. So Paul gave them this warning: 10 'I can see, gentlemen, that this voyage will be disastrous; it will mean heavy loss, not only of ship and cargo but also of life.' 11 But the centurion paid more attention to the captain and to the owner of the ship than to what Paul said; 12 and as the harbour was unsuitable for wintering, the majority was in favour of putting to sea, hoping, if they could get so far, to winter at Phoenix, a Cretan harbour facing south-west and north-west. 13 When a southerly breeze sprang up, they thought that their purpose was as good as achieved, and, weighing anchor, they sailed along the coast of Crete hugging the land. 14 But before very long a violent wind, the Northeaster as they call it, swept down from the landward side. 15 It

x Or *the Christ*   *y* Or *Quickly you will persuade me to play the Christian*   *z* Gk *it*

19 "And so, King Agrippa, I was not disobedient to the heavenly vision. 20 On the contrary, first to those in Damascus and in Jerusalem and throughout the whole country of Judea, and then to the Gentiles, I preached the need to repent and turn to God, and to do works giving evidence of repentance. 21 That is why the Jews seized me [when I was] in the temple and tried to kill me. 22 But I have enjoyed God's help to this very day, and so I stand here testifying to small and great alike, saying nothing different from what the prophets and Moses foretold, 23 that the Messiah must suffer and that, as the first to rise from the dead, he would proclaim light both to our people and to the Gentiles."

24 While Paul was so speaking in his defense, Festus said in a loud voice, "You are mad, Paul; much learning is driving you mad." 25 But Paul replied, "I am not mad, most excellent Festus; I am speaking words of truth and reason. 26 The king knows about these matters and to him I speak boldly, for I cannot believe that [any] of this has escaped his notice; this was not done in a corner. 27 King Agrippa, do you believe the prophets? I know you believe." 28 Then Agrippa said to Paul, "You will soon persuade me to play the Christian." 29 Paul replied, "I would pray to God that sooner or later not only you but all who listen to me today might become as I am except for these chains."

30 Then the king rose, and with him the governor and Bernice and the others who sat with them. 31 And after they had withdrawn they said to one another, "This man is doing nothing [at all] that deserves death or imprisonment." 32 And Agrippa said to Festus, "This man could have been set free if he had not appealed to Caesar."

27 When it was decided that we should sail to Italy, they handed Paul and some other prisoners over to a centurion named Julius of the Cohort Augusta. 2 We went on board a ship from Adramyttium bound for ports in the province of Asia and set sail. Aristarchus, a Macedonian from Thessalonica, was with us. 3 On the following day we put in at Sidon where Julius was kind enough to allow Paul to visit his friends who took care of him. 4 From there we put out to sea and sailed around the sheltered side of Cyprus because of the headwinds, 5 and crossing the open sea off the coast of Cilicia and Pamphylia we came to Myra in Lycia.

6 There the centurion found an Alexandrian ship that was sailing to Italy and put us on board. 7 For many days we made little headway, arriving at Cnidus only with difficulty, and because the wind would not permit us to continue our course we sailed for the sheltered side of Crete off Salmone. 8 We sailed past it with difficulty and reached a place called Fair Havens, near which was the city of Lasea.

9 Much time had now passed and sailing had become hazardous because the time of the fast had already gone by, so Paul warned them, 10 "Men, I can see that this voyage will result in severe damage and heavy loss not only to the cargo and the ship, but also to our lives." 11 The centurion, however, paid more attention to the pilot and to the owner of the ship than to what Paul said. 12 Since the harbor was unfavorably situated for spending the winter, the majority planned to put out to sea from there in the hope of reaching Phoenix, a port in Crete facing west-northwest, there to spend the winter.

13 A south wind blew gently, and thinking they had attained their objective, they weighed anchor and sailed along close to the coast of Crete. 14 Before long an offshore wind of hurricane force called a "Northeaster" struck. 15 Since the

19 'After that, King Agrippa, I could not disobey the heavenly vision. 20 On the contrary I started preaching, first to the people of Damascus, then to those of Jerusalem and all Judaean territory, and also to the gentiles, urging them to repent and turn to God, proving their change of heart by their deeds. 21 This was why the Jews laid hands on me in the Temple and tried to do away with me. 22 But I was blessed with God's help, and so I have stood firm to this day, testifying to great and small alike, saying nothing more than what the prophets and Moses himself said would happen: 23 that the Christ was to suffer and that, as the first to rise from the dead, he was to proclaim a light for our people and for the gentiles.'

24 He had reached this point in his defence when Festus shouted out, 'Paul, you are out of your mind; all that learning of yours is driving you mad.' 25 But Paul answered, 'Festus, your Excellency, I am not mad: I am speaking words of sober truth and good sense. 26 The king understands these matters, and to him I now speak fearlessly. I am confident that nothing of all this comes as a surprise to him; after all, these things were not done in a corner. 27 King Agrippa, do you believe in the prophets? I know you do.' 28 At this Agrippa said to Paul, 'A little more, and your arguments would make a Christian of me.' 29 Paul replied, 'Little or much, I wish before God that not only you but all who are listening to me today were to come to be as I am — except for these chains.'

30 At this the king rose to his feet, with the governor and Bernice and those who sat there with them. 31 When they had retired they talked together and agreed, 'This man is doing nothing that deserves death or imprisonment.' 32 And Agrippa remarked to Festus, 'The man could have been set free if he had not appealed to Caesar.'

27 When it had been decided that we should sail to Italy, Paul and some other prisoners were handed over to a centurion called Julius, of the Augustan cohort. 2 We boarded a vessel from Adramyttium bound for ports on the Asiatic coast and put to sea; we had Aristarchus with us, a Macedonian of Thessalonica. 3 Next day we put in at Sidon, and Julius was considerate enough to allow Paul to go to his friends to be looked after.

4 From there we put to sea again, but as the winds were against us we sailed under the lee of Cyprus, 5 then across the open sea off Cilicia and Pamphylia, taking a fortnight to reach Myra in Lycia. 6 There the centurion found an Alexandrian ship leaving for Italy and put us aboard.

7 For some days we made little headway, and we had difficulty in making Cnidus. The wind would not allow us to touch there, so we sailed under the lee of Crete off Cape Salmone 8 and struggled along the coast until we came to a place called Fair Havens, near the town of Lasea.

9 A great deal of time had been lost, and navigation was already hazardous, since it was now well after the time of the Fast, so Paul gave them this warning, 10 'Friends, I can see this voyage will be dangerous and that we will run considerable risk of losing not only the cargo and the ship but also our lives as well.' 11 But the centurion took more notice of the captain and the ship's owner than of what Paul was saying; 12 and since the harbour was unsuitable for wintering, the majority were for putting out from there in the hope of wintering at Phoenix — a harbour in Crete, facing south-west and north-west.

13 A southerly breeze sprang up and, thinking their objective as good as reached, they weighed anchor and began to sail past Crete, close inshore. 14 But it was not long before a hurricane, the 'north-easter' as they call it, burst on them from across the island. 15 The ship was caught and could not

not be turned head-on into the wind, we gave way to it and were driven. 16 By running under the lee of a small island called Cauda*a* we were scarcely able to get the ship's boat under control. 17 After hoisting it up they took measures*b* to undergird the ship; then, fearing that they would run on the Syrtis, they lowered the sea anchor and so were driven. 18 We were being pounded by the storm so violently that on the next day they began to throw the cargo overboard, 19 and on the third day with their own hands they threw the ship's tackle overboard. 20 When neither sun nor stars appeared for many days, and no small tempest raged, all hope of our being saved was at last abandoned.

21 Since they had been without food for a long time, Paul then stood up among them and said, "Men, you should have listened to me and not have set sail from Crete and thereby avoided this damage and loss. 22 I urge you now to keep up your courage, for there will be no loss of life among you, but only of the ship. 23 For last night there stood by me an angel of the God to whom I belong and whom I worship, 24 and he said, 'Do not be afraid, Paul; you must stand before the emperor; and indeed, God has granted safety to all those who are sailing with you.' 25 So keep up your courage, men, for I have faith in God that it will be exactly as I have been told. 26 But we will have to run aground on some island."

27 When the fourteenth night had come, as we were drifting across the sea of Adria, about midnight the sailors suspected that they were nearing land. 28 So they took soundings and found twenty fathoms; a little farther on they took soundings again and found fifteen fathoms. 29 Fearing that we might run on the rocks, they let down four anchors from the stern and prayed for day to come. 30 But when the sailors tried to escape from the ship and had lowered the boat into the sea, on the pretext of putting out anchors from the bow, 31 Paul said to the centurion and the soldiers, "Unless these men stay in the ship, you cannot be saved." 32 Then the soldiers cut away the ropes of the boat and set it adrift.

33 Just before daybreak, Paul urged all of them to take some food, saying, "Today is the fourteenth day that you have been in suspense and remaining without food, having eaten nothing. 34 Therefore I urge you to take some food, for it will help you survive; for none of you will lose a hair from your heads." 35 After he had said this, he took bread; and giving thanks to God in the presence of all, he broke it and began to eat. 36 Then all of them were encouraged and took food for themselves. 37 (We were in all two hundred seventy-six*c* persons in the ship.) 38 After they had satisfied their hunger, they lightened the ship by throwing the wheat into the sea.

39 In the morning they did not recognize the land, but they noticed a bay with a beach, on which they planned to run the ship ashore, if they could. 40 So they cast off the anchors and left them in the sea. At the same time they loosened the ropes that tied the steering-oars; then hoisting the foresail to the wind, they made for the beach. 41 But striking a reef,*d* they ran the ship aground; the bow stuck and remained immovable, but the stern was being broken up by the force of the waves. 42 The soldiers' plan was to kill the prisoners, so that none might swim away and escape; 43 but the centurion, wishing to save Paul, kept them from carrying out their plan. He ordered those who could swim to jump overboard first and make for the land, 44 and the rest to follow, some on planks and others on pieces of the ship. And so it was that all were brought safely to land.

caught the ship and, as it was impossible to keep head to wind, we had to give way and run before it. 16 As we passed under the lee of a small island called Cauda, we managed with a struggle to get the ship's boat under control. 17 When they had hoisted it on board, they made use of tackle to brace the ship. Then, afraid of running on to the sandbanks of Syrtis, they put out a sea-anchor and let her drift. 18 Next day, as we were making very heavy weather, they began to lighten the ship; 19 and on the third day they jettisoned the ship's gear with their own hands. 20 For days on end there was no sign of either sun or stars, the storm was raging unabated, and our last hopes of coming through alive began to fade.

21 When they had gone for a long time without food, Paul stood up among them and said, 'You should have taken my advice, gentlemen, not to put out from Crete: then you would have avoided this damage and loss. 22 But now I urge you not to lose heart; not a single life will be lost, only the ship. 23 Last night there stood by me an angel of the God whose I am and whom I worship. 24 "Do not be afraid, Paul," he said; "it is ordained that you shall appear before Caesar; and, be assured, God has granted you the lives of all who are sailing with you." 25 So take heart, men! I trust God: it will turn out as I have been told; 26 we are to be cast ashore on an island.'

27 The fourteenth night came and we were still drifting in the Adriatic Sea. At midnight the sailors felt that land was getting nearer, 28 so they took a sounding and found twenty fathoms. Sounding again after a short interval they found fifteen fathoms; 29 then, fearing that we might be cast ashore on a rugged coast, they let go four anchors from the stern and prayed for daylight to come. 30 The sailors tried to abandon ship; they had already lowered the ship's boat, pretending they were going to lay out anchors from the bows, 31 when Paul said to the centurion and the soldiers, 'Unless these men stay on board you cannot reach safety.' 32 At that the soldiers cut the ropes of the boat and let it drop away.

33 Shortly before daybreak Paul urged them all to take some food. 'For the last fourteen days', he said, 'you have lived in suspense and gone hungry; you have eaten nothing. 34 So have something to eat, I beg you; your lives depend on it. Remember, not a hair of your heads will be lost.' 35 With these words, he took bread, gave thanks to God in front of them all, broke it, and began eating. 36 Then they plucked up courage, and began to take food themselves. 37 All told there were on board two hundred and seventy-six of us. 38 After they had eaten as much as they wanted, they lightened the ship by dumping the grain into the sea.

39 When day broke, they did not recognize the land, but they sighted a bay with a sandy beach, on which they decided, if possible, to run ashore. 40 So they slipped the anchors and let them go; at the same time they loosened the lashings of the steering-paddles, set the foresail to the wind, and let her drive to the beach. 41 But they found themselves caught between cross-currents and ran the ship aground, so that the bow stuck fast and remained immovable, while the stern was being pounded to pieces by the breakers. 42 The soldiers thought they had better kill the prisoners for fear that any should swim away and escape; 43 but the centurion was determined to bring Paul safely through, and prevented them from carrying out their plan. He gave orders that those who could swim should jump overboard first and get to land; 44 the rest were to follow, some on planks, some on parts of the ship. And thus it was that all came safely to land.

a Other ancient authorities read *Clauda*   *b* Gk *helps*   *c* Other ancient authorities read *seventy-six*; others, *about seventy-six*
d Gk *place of two seas*

27:17 **put . . . sea-anchor:** *or* lowered the mainsail.

ship was caught up in it and could not head into the wind we gave way and let ourselves be driven. 16 We passed along the sheltered side of an island named Cauda and managed only with difficulty to get the dinghy under control. 17 They hoisted it aboard, then used cables to undergird the ship. Because of their fear that they would run aground on the shoal of Syrtis, they lowered the drift anchor and were carried along in this way. 18 We were being pounded by the storm so violently that the next day they jettisoned some cargo, 19 and on the third day with their own hands they threw even the ship's tackle overboard. 20 Neither the sun nor the stars were visible for many days, and no small storm raged. Finally, all hope of our surviving was taken away.

21 When many would no longer eat, Paul stood among them and said, "Men, you should have taken my advice and not have set sail from Crete and you would have avoided this disastrous loss. 22 I urge you now to keep up your courage; not one of you will be lost, only the ship. 23 For last night an angel of the God to whom [I] belong and whom I serve stood by me 24 and said, 'Do not be afraid, Paul. You are destined to stand before Caesar; and behold, for your sake, God has granted safety to all who are sailing with you.' 25 Therefore, keep up your courage, men; I trust in God that it will turn out as I have been told. 26 We are destined to run aground on some island."

27 On the fourteenth night, as we were still being driven about on the Adriatic Sea, toward midnight the sailors began to suspect that they were nearing land. 28 They took soundings and found twenty fathoms; a little farther on, they again took soundings and found fifteen fathoms. 29 Fearing that we would run aground on a rocky coast, they dropped four anchors from the stern and prayed for day to come. 30 The sailors then tried to abandon ship; they lowered the dinghy to the sea on the pretext of going to lay out anchors from the bow. 31 But Paul said to the centurion and the soldiers, "Unless these men stay with the ship, you cannot be saved." 32 So the soldiers cut the ropes of the dinghy and set it adrift.

33 Until the day began to dawn, Paul kept urging all to take some food. He said, "Today is the fourteenth day that you have been waiting, going hungry and eating nothing. 34 I urge you, therefore, to take some food; it will help you survive. Not a hair of the head of anyone of you will be lost." 35 When he said this, he took bread, gave thanks to God in front of them all, broke it, and began to eat. 36 They were all encouraged, and took some food themselves. 37 In all, there were two hundred seventy-six of us on the ship. 38 After they had eaten enough, they lightened the ship by throwing the wheat into the sea.

39 When day came they did not recognize the land, but made out a bay with a beach. They planned to run the ship ashore on it, if they could. 40 So they cast off the anchors and abandoned them to the sea, and at the same time they unfastened the lines of the rudders, and hoisting the foresail into the wind, they made for the beach. 41 But they struck a sandbar and ran the ship aground. The bow was wedged in and could not be moved, but the stern began to break up under the pounding [of the waves]. 42 The soldiers planned to kill the prisoners so that none might swim away and escape, 43 but the centurion wanted to save Paul and so kept them from carrying out their plan. He ordered those who could swim to jump overboard first and get to the shore, 44 and then the rest, some on planks, others on debris from the ship. In this way, all reached shore safely.

keep head to wind, so we had to give way to the wind and let ourselves be driven. 16 We ran under the lee of a small island called Cauda and managed with some difficulty to bring the ship's boat under control. 17 Having hauled it up they used it to undergird the ship; then, afraid of running aground on the Syrtis banks, they floated out the sea-anchor and so let themselves drift. 18 As we were thoroughly storm-bound, the next day they began to jettison the cargo, 19 and the third day they threw the ship's gear overboard with their own hands. 20 For a number of days both the sun and the stars were invisible and the storm raged unabated until at last we gave up all hope of surviving.

21 Then, when they had been without food for a long time, Paul stood up among the men. 'Friends,' he said, 'you should have listened to me and not put out from Crete. You would have spared yourselves all this damage and loss. 22 But now I ask you not to give way to despair. There will be no loss of life at all, only of the ship. 23 Last night there appeared beside me an angel of the God to whom I belong and whom I serve, 24 and he said, "Do not be afraid, Paul. You are destined to appear before Caesar, and God grants you the safety of all who are sailing with you." 25 So take courage, friends; I trust in God that things will turn out just as I was told; 26 but we are to be stranded on some island.'

27 On the fourteenth night we were being driven one way and another in the Adriatic, when about midnight the crew sensed that land of some sort was near. 28 They took soundings and found twenty fathoms; after a short interval they sounded again and found fifteen fathoms. 29 Then, afraid that we might run aground somewhere on a reef, they dropped four anchors from the stern and prayed for daylight. 30 When the crew tried to escape from the ship and lowered the ship's boat into the sea as though they meant to lay out anchors from the bows, Paul said to the centurion and his men, 31 'Unless those men stay on board you cannot hope to be saved.' 32 So the soldiers cut the boat's ropes and let it drop away.

33 Just before daybreak Paul urged them all to have something to eat. 'For fourteen days', he said, 'you have been in suspense, going hungry and eating nothing. 34 I urge you to have something to eat; your safety depends on it. Not a hair of any of your heads will be lost.' 35 With these words he took some bread, gave thanks to God in view of them all, broke it and began to eat. 36 They all plucked up courage and took something to eat themselves. 37 In all we were two hundred and seventy-six souls on board that ship. 38 When they had eaten what they wanted they lightened the ship by throwing the corn overboard into the sea.

39 When day came they did not recognise the land, but they could make out a bay with a beach; they planned to run the ship aground on this if they could. 40 They slipped the anchors and let them fall into the sea, and at the same time loosened the lashings of the rudders; then, hoisting the fore-sail to the wind, they headed for the beach. 41 But the cross-currents carried them into a shoal and the vessel ran aground. The bows were wedged in and stuck fast, while the stern began to break up with the pounding of the waves.

42 The soldiers planned to kill the prisoners for fear that any should swim off and escape. 43 But the centurion was determined to bring Paul safely through and would not let them carry out their plan. He gave orders that those who could swim should jump overboard first and so get ashore, 44 and the rest follow either on planks or on pieces of wreckage. In this way it happened that all came safe and sound to land.

28 After we had reached safety, we then learned that the island was called Malta. 2 The natives showed us unusual kindness. Since it had begun to rain and was cold, they kindled a fire and welcomed all of us around it. 3 Paul had gathered a bundle of brushwood and was putting it on the fire, when a viper, driven out by the heat, fastened itself on his hand. 4 When the natives saw the creature hanging from his hand, they said to one another, "This man must be a murderer; though he has escaped from the sea, justice has not allowed him to live." 5 He, however, shook off the creature into the fire and suffered no harm. 6 They were expecting him to swell up or drop dead, but after they had waited a long time and saw that nothing unusual had happened to him, they changed their minds and began to say that he was a god.

7 Now in the neighborhood of that place were lands belonging to the leading man of the island, named Publius, who received us and entertained us hospitably for three days. 8 It so happened that the father of Publius lay sick in bed with fever and dysentery. Paul visited him and cured him by praying and putting his hands on him. 9 After this happened, the rest of the people on the island who had diseases also came and were cured. 10 They bestowed many honors on us, and when we were about to sail, they put on board all the provisions we needed.

11 Three months later we set sail on a ship that had wintered at the island, an Alexandrian ship with the Twin Brothers as its figurehead. 12 We put in at Syracuse and stayed there for three days; 13 then we weighed anchor and came to Rhegium. After one day there a south wind sprang up, and on the second day we came to Puteoli. 14 There we found believers*e* and were invited to stay with them for seven days. And so we came to Rome. 15 The believers*e* from there, when they heard of us, came as far as the Forum of Appius and Three Taverns to meet us. On seeing them, Paul thanked God and took courage.

16 When we came into Rome, Paul was allowed to live by himself, with the soldier who was guarding him.

17 Three days later he called together the local leaders of the Jews. When they had assembled, he said to them, "Brothers, though I had done nothing against our people or the customs of our ancestors, yet I was arrested in Jerusalem and handed over to the Romans. 18 When they had examined me, the Romans*f* wanted to release me, because there was no reason for the death penalty in my case. 19 But when the Jews objected, I was compelled to appeal to the emperor —even though I had no charge to bring against my nation. 20 For this reason therefore I have asked to see you and speak with you,*g* since it is for the sake of the hope of Israel that I am bound with this chain." 21 They replied, "We have received no letters from Judea about you, and none of the brothers coming here has reported or spoken anything evil about you. 22 But we would like to hear from you what you think, for with regard to this sect we know that everywhere it is spoken against."

23 After they had set a day to meet with him, they came to him at his lodgings in great numbers. From morning until evening he explained the matter to them, testifying to the kingdom of God and trying to convince them about Jesus both from the law of Moses and from the prophets. 24 Some were convinced by what he had said, while others refused to believe. 25 So they disagreed with each other; and as they were leaving, Paul made one further statement: "The Holy Spirit was right in saying to your ancestors through the prophet Isaiah,

28 Once we had made our way to safety, we identified the island as Malta. 2 The natives treated us with uncommon kindness: because it had started to rain and was cold they lit a bonfire and made us all welcome. 3 Paul had got together an armful of sticks and put them on the fire, when a viper, driven out by the heat, fastened on his hand. 4 The natives, seeing the snake hanging on to his hand, said to one another, 'The man must be a murderer; he may have escaped from the sea, but divine justice would not let him live.' 5 Paul, however, shook off the snake into the fire and was none the worse. 6 They still expected him to swell up or suddenly drop down dead, but after waiting a long time without seeing anything out of the way happen to him, they changed their minds and said, 'He is a god.'

7 In that neighbourhood there were lands belonging to the chief magistrate of the island, whose name was Publius. He took us in and entertained us hospitably for three days. 8 It so happened that this man's father was in bed suffering from recurrent bouts of fever and dysentery. Paul visited him and, after prayer, laid his hands on him and healed him; 9 whereupon the other sick people on the island came and were cured. 10 They honoured us with many marks of respect, and when we were leaving they put on board the supplies we needed.

11 Three months had passed when we put to sea in a ship which had wintered in the island; she was the *Castor and Pollux* of Alexandria. 12 We landed at Syracuse and spent three days there; 13 then we sailed up the coast and arrived at Rhegium. Next day a south wind sprang up and we reached Puteoli in two days. 14 There we found fellow-Christians and were invited to stay a week with them. And so to Rome. 15 The Christians there had had news of us and came out to meet us as far as Appii Forum and the Three Taverns, and when Paul saw them, he gave thanks to God and took courage.

16 WHEN we entered Rome Paul was allowed to lodge privately, with a soldier in charge of him. 17 Three days later he called together the local Jewish leaders, and when they were assembled, he said to them: 'My brothers, I never did anything against our people or against the customs of our forefathers; yet I was arrested in Jerusalem and handed over to the Romans. 18 They examined me and would have liked to release me because there was no capital charge against me; 19 but the Jews objected, and I had no option but to appeal to Caesar; not that I had any accusation to bring against my own people. 20 This is why I have asked to see and talk to you; it is for loyalty to the hope of Israel that I am in these chains.' 21 They replied, 'We have had no communication about you from Judaea, nor has any countryman of ours arrived with any report or gossip to your discredit. 22 We should like to hear from you what your views are; all we know about this sect is that no one has a good word to say for it.'

23 So they fixed a day, and came in large numbers to his lodging. From dawn to dusk he put his case to them; he spoke urgently of the kingdom of God and sought to convince them about Jesus by appealing to the law of Moses and the prophets. 24 Some were won over by his arguments; others remained unconvinced. 25 Without reaching any agreement among themselves they began to disperse, but not before Paul had spoken this final word: 'How well the Holy Spirit spoke to your fathers through the prophet Isaiah

---

e Gk *brothers*   *f* Gk *they*   *g* Or *I have asked you to see me and speak with me*

28 Once we had reached safety we learned that the island was called Malta. 2 The natives showed us extraordinary hospitality; they lit a fire and welcomed all of us because it had begun to rain and was cold. 3 Paul had gathered a bundle of brushwood and was putting it on the fire when a viper, escaping from the heat, fastened on his hand. 4 When the natives saw the snake hanging from his hand, they said to one another, "This man must certainly be a murderer; though he escaped the sea, Justice has not let him remain alive." 5 But he shook the snake off into the fire and suffered no harm. 6 They were expecting him to swell up or suddenly to fall down dead but, after waiting a long time and seeing nothing unusual happen to him, they changed their minds and began to say that he was a god. 7 In the vicinity of that place were lands belonging to a man named Publius, the chief of the island. He welcomed us and received us cordially as his guests for three days. 8 It so happened that the father of Publius was sick with a fever and dysentery. Paul visited him and, after praying, laid his hands on him and healed him. 9 After this had taken place, the rest of the sick on the island came to Paul and were cured. 10 They paid us great honor and when we eventually set sail they brought us the provisions we needed.

11 Three months later we set sail on a ship that had wintered at the island. It was an Alexandrian ship with the Dioscuri as its figurehead. 12 We put in at Syracuse and stayed there three days, 13 and from there we sailed round the coast and arrived at Rhegium. After a day, a south wind came up and in two days we reached Puteoli. 14 There we found some brothers and were urged to stay with them for seven days. And thus we came to Rome. 15 The brothers from there heard about us and came as far as the Forum of Appius and Three Taverns to meet us. On seeing them, Paul gave thanks to God and took courage. 16 When he entered Rome, Paul was allowed to live by himself, with the soldier who was guarding him.

17 Three days later he called together the leaders of the Jews. When they had gathered he said to them, "My brothers, although I had done nothing against our people or our ancestral customs, I was handed over to the Romans as a prisoner from Jerusalem. 18 After trying my case the Romans wanted to release me, because they found nothing against me deserving the death penalty. 19 But when the Jews objected, I was obliged to appeal to Caesar, even though I had no accusation to make against my own nation. 20 This is the reason, then, I have requested to see you and to speak with you, for it is on account of the hope of Israel that I wear these chains." 21 They answered him, "We have received no letters from Judea about you, nor has any of the brothers arrived with a damaging report or rumor about you. 22 But we should like to hear you present your views, for we know that this sect is denounced everywhere."

23 So they arranged a day with him and came to his lodgings in great numbers. From early morning until evening, he expounded his position to them, bearing witness to the kingdom of God and trying to convince them about Jesus from the law of Moses and the prophets. 24 Some were convinced by what he had said, while others did not believe. 25 Without reaching any agreement among themselves they began to leave; then Paul made one final statement. "Well did the holy Spirit speak to your ancestors through the prophet Isaiah, saying:

28 Once we had come safely through, we discovered that the island was called Malta. 2 The inhabitants treated us with unusual kindness. They made us all welcome by lighting a huge fire because it had started to rain and the weather was cold. 3 Paul had collected a bundle of sticks and was putting them on the fire when a viper brought out by the heat attached itself to his hand. 4 When the inhabitants saw the creature hanging from his hand they said to one another, 'That man must be a murderer; he may have escaped the sea, but divine justice would not let him live.' 5 However, he shook the creature off into the fire and came to no harm, 6 although they were expecting him at any moment to swell up or drop dead on the spot. After they had waited a long time without seeing anything out of the ordinary happen to him, they changed their minds and began to say he was a god.

7 In that neighbourhood there were estates belonging to the chief man of the island, whose name was Publius. He received us and entertained us hospitably for three days. 8 It happened that Publius' father was in bed, suffering from fever and dysentery. Paul went in to see him, and after a prayer he laid his hands on the man and healed him. 9 When this happened, the other sick people on the island also came and were cured; 10 they honoured us with many marks of respect, and when we sailed they put on board the provisions we needed.

11 At the end of three months we set sail in a ship that had wintered in the island; she came from Alexandria and her figurehead was the Twins. 12 We put in at Syracuse and spent three days there; 13 from there we followed the coast up to Rhegium. After one day there a south wind sprang up and on the second day we made Puteoli, 14 where we found some brothers and had the great encouragement of staying a week with them. And so we came to Rome.

15 When the brothers there heard about us they came to meet us, as far as the Forum of Appius and the Three Taverns. When Paul saw them he thanked God and took courage. 16 On our arrival in Rome Paul was allowed to stay in lodgings of his own with the soldier who guarded him.

17 After three days he called together the leading Jews. When they had assembled, he said to them, 'Brothers, although I have done nothing against our people or the customs of our ancestors, I was arrested in Jerusalem and handed over to the Romans. 18 They examined me and would have set me free, since they found me guilty of nothing involving the death penalty; 19 but the Jews lodged an objection, and I was forced to appeal to Caesar, though not because I had any accusation to make against my own nation. 20 That is why I have urged you to see me and have a discussion with me, for it is on account of the hope of Israel that I wear this chain.'

21 They answered, 'We have received no letters from Judaea about you, nor has any of the brothers arrived here with any report or story of anything to your discredit. 22 We think it would be as well to hear your own account of your position; all we know about this sect is that it encounters opposition everywhere.'

23 So they arranged a day with him and a large number of them visited him at his lodgings. He put his case to them, testifying to the kingdom of God and trying to persuade them about Jesus, arguing from the Law of Moses and the prophets from early morning until evening; 24 and some were convinced by what he said, while the rest were sceptical. 25 So they disagreed among themselves and, as they went away, Paul had one last thing to say to them, 'How aptly the Holy Spirit spoke when he told your ancestors through the prophet Isaiah:

26 'Go to this people and say,
    You will indeed listen, but never understand,
        and you will indeed look, but never perceive.
27 For this people's heart has grown dull,
        and their ears are hard of hearing,
            and they have shut their eyes;
        so that they might not look with their eyes,
        and listen with their ears,
    and understand with their heart and turn —
        and I would heal them.'

28 Let it be known to you then that this salvation of God has been sent to the Gentiles; they will listen."[h]

30 He lived there two whole years at his own expense[i] and welcomed all who came to him, 31 proclaiming the kingdom of God and teaching about the Lord Jesus Christ with all boldness and without hindrance.

[h] Other ancient authorities add verse 29, *And when he had said these words, the Jews departed, arguing vigorously among themselves*
[i] Or *in his own hired dwelling*

26 when he said, "Go to this people and say: You may listen and listen, but you will never understand; you may look and look, but you will never see. 27 For this people's mind has become dull; they have stopped their ears and closed their eyes. Otherwise, their eyes might see, their ears hear, and their mind understand, and then they might turn again, and I would heal them." 28 Therefore take note that this salvation of God has been sent to the Gentiles; the Gentiles will listen.'

30 He stayed there two full years at his own expense, with a welcome for all who came to him; 31 he proclaimed the kingdom of God and taught the facts about the Lord Jesus Christ quite openly and without hindrance.

28:28 **listen:** *some witnesses add* 29 After he had spoken, the Jews went away, arguing vigorously among themselves.

NEW AMERICAN BIBLE

26 'Go to this people and say:
You shall indeed hear but not understand.
You shall indeed look but never see.
27 Gross is the heart of this people;
they will not hear with their ears;
they have closed their eyes,
so they may not see with their eyes
and hear with their ears
and understand with their heart and be converted,
and I heal them.'

28 Let it be known to you that this salvation of God has been sent to the Gentiles; they will listen." [29]

30 He remained for two full years in his lodgings. He received all who came to him, 31 and with complete assurance and without hindrance he proclaimed the kingdom of God and taught about the Lord Jesus Christ.

28, 29: The Western text has added here a verse that is not found in the best Greek manuscripts: "And when he had said this, the Jews left, seriously arguing among themselves."

NEW JERUSALEM BIBLE

26 *Go and say to this people:*
Listen and listen but never understand!
Look and look but never perceive!
27 *This people's heart is torpid,*
their ears dulled, they have shut their eyes tight,
to avoid using their eyes to see, their ears to hear,
using their heart to understand,
changing their ways and being healed by me. n

28 'You must realise, then, that this salvation of God has been sent to the gentiles; and they will listen to it.' [29]o

30 He spent the whole of the two years in his own rented lodging. He welcomed all who came to visit him, 31 proclaiming the kingdom of God and teaching the truth about the Lord Jesus Christ with complete fearlessness and without any hindrance from anyone.

n **28** Is 6:9–10; cf. 13:47; 18:6.   o **28** Some MSS add v. 29 'And when he had said this, the Jews left, arguing hotly among themselves.'

THE LETTER OF PAUL TO THE

Romans

THE LETTER OF PAUL TO THE

Romans

1 Paul, a servant*a* of Jesus Christ, called to be an apostle, set apart for the gospel of God, 2 which he promised beforehand through his prophets in the holy scriptures, 3 the gospel concerning his Son, who was descended from David according to the flesh 4 and was declared to be Son of God with power according to the spirit*b* of holiness by resurrection from the dead, Jesus Christ our Lord, 5 through whom we have received grace and apostleship to bring about the obedience of faith among all the Gentiles for the sake of his name, 6 including yourselves who are called to belong to Jesus Christ,

7 To all God's beloved in Rome, who are called to be saints:

Grace to you and peace from God our Father and the Lord Jesus Christ.

8 First, I thank my God through Jesus Christ for all of you, because your faith is proclaimed throughout the world. 9 For God, whom I serve with my spirit by announcing the gospel*c* of his Son, is my witness that without ceasing I remember you always in my prayers, 10 asking that by God's will I may somehow at last succeed in coming to you. 11 For I am longing to see you so that I may share with you some spiritual gift to strengthen you— 12 or rather so that we may be mutually encouraged by each other's faith, both yours and mine. 13 I want you to know, brothers and sisters,*d* that I have often intended to come to you (but thus far have been prevented), in order that I may reap some harvest among you as I have among the rest of the Gentiles. 14 I am a debtor both to Greeks and to barbarians, both to the wise and to the foolish 15 — hence my eagerness to proclaim the gospel to you also who are in Rome.

16 For I am not ashamed of the gospel; it is the power of God for salvation to everyone who has faith, to the Jew first and also to the Greek. 17 For in it the righteousness of God is revealed through faith for faith; as it is written, "The one who is righteous will live by faith."*e*

18 For the wrath of God is revealed from heaven against all ungodliness and wickedness of those who by their wickedness suppress the truth. 19 For what can be known about God is plain to them, because God has shown it to them. 20 Ever since the creation of the world his eternal power and divine nature, invisible though they are, have been understood and seen through the things he has made. So they are without excuse; 21 for though they knew God, they did not honor him as God or give thanks to him, but they became futile in their thinking, and their senseless minds were darkened. 22 Claiming to be wise, they became fools; 23 and they exchanged the glory of the immortal God for images resembling a mortal human being or birds or four-footed animals or reptiles.

24 Therefore God gave them up in the lusts of their hearts to impurity, to the degrading of their bodies among themselves, 25 because they exchanged the truth about God for a lie and worshiped and served the creature rather than the Creator, who is blessed forever! Amen.

1 FROM Paul, servant of Christ Jesus, called by God to be an apostle and set apart for the service of his gospel. 2 This gospel God announced beforehand in sacred scriptures through his prophets. 3–4 It is about his Son: on the human level he was a descendant of David, but on the level of the spirit—the Holy Spirit—he was proclaimed Son of God by an act of power that raised him from the dead: it is about Jesus Christ our Lord. 5 Through him I received the privilege of an apostolic commission to bring people of all nations to faith and obedience in his name, 6 including you who have heard the call and belong to Jesus Christ.

7 I send greetings to all of you in Rome, who are loved by God and called to be his people. Grace and peace to you from God our Father and the Lord Jesus Christ.

8 Let me begin by thanking my God, through Jesus Christ, for you all, because the story of your faith is being told all over the world. 9 God is my witness, to whom I offer the service of my spirit by preaching the gospel of his Son: God knows that I make mention of you in my prayers continually, 10 and am always asking that by his will I may, somehow or other, at long last succeed in coming to visit you. 11 For I long to see you; I want to bring you some spiritual gift to make you strong; 12 or rather, I want us to be encouraged by one another's faith when I am with you, I by yours and you by mine.

13 Brothers and sisters, I should like you to know that I have often planned to come, though so far without success, in the hope of achieving something among you, as I have in the rest of the gentile world. 14 I have an obligation to Greek and non-Greek, to learned and simple; 15 hence my eagerness to declare the gospel to you in Rome as well. 16 For I am not ashamed of the gospel. It is the saving power of God for everyone who has faith—the Jew first, but the Greek also—17 because in it the righteousness of God is seen at work, beginning in faith and ending in faith; as scripture says, 'Whoever is justified through faith shall gain life.'

18 DIVINE retribution is to be seen at work, falling from heaven on all the impiety and wickedness of men and women who in their wickedness suppress the truth. 19 For all that can be known of God lies plain before their eyes; indeed God himself has disclosed it to them. 20 Ever since the world began his invisible attributes, that is to say his everlasting power and deity, have been visible to the eye of reason, in the things he has made. Their conduct, therefore, is indefensible; 21 knowing God, they have refused to honour him as God, or to render him thanks. Hence all their thinking has ended in futility, and their misguided minds are plunged in darkness. 22 They boast of their wisdom, but they have made fools of themselves, 23 exchanging the glory of the immortal God for an image shaped like mortal man, even for images like birds, beasts, and reptiles.

24 For this reason God has given them up to their own vile desires, and the consequent degradation of their bodies. 25 They have exchanged the truth of God for a lie, and have offered reverence and worship to created things instead of to the Creator. Blessed is he for ever, Amen. 26 As a result

---

a Gk *slave*   *b* Or *Spirit*   *c* Gk *my spirit in the gospel*
d Gk *brothers*   *e* Or *The one who is righteous through faith will live*

1:3–4 **Son of God . . . dead:** *or* Son of God with full power at his resurrection from the dead.   1:17 **Whoever . . . life:** *or* The righteous shall live by faith.

The Letter to the Romans

1 Paul, a slave of Christ Jesus, called to be an apostle and set apart for the gospel of God, 2 which he promised previously through his prophets in the holy scriptures, 3 the gospel about his Son, descended from David according to the flesh, 4 but established as Son of God in power according to the spirit of holiness through resurrection from the dead, Jesus Christ our Lord. 5 Through him we have received the grace of apostleship, to bring about the obedience of faith, for the sake of his name, among all the Gentiles, 6 among whom are you also, who are called to belong to Jesus Christ; 7 to all the beloved of God in Rome, called to be holy. Grace to you and peace from God our Father and the Lord Jesus Christ.

8 First, I give thanks to my God through Jesus Christ for all of you, because your faith is heralded throughout the world. 9 God is my witness, whom I serve with my spirit in proclaiming the gospel of his Son, that I remember you constantly, 10 always asking in my prayers that somehow by God's will I may at last find my way clear to come to you. 11 For I long to see you, that I may share with you some spiritual gift so that you may be strengthened, 12 that is, that you and I may be mutually encouraged by one another's faith, yours and mine. 13 I do not want you to be unaware, brothers, that I often planned to come to you, though I was prevented until now, that I might harvest some fruit among you, too, as among the rest of the Gentiles. 14 To Greeks and non-Greeks alike, to the wise and the ignorant, I am under obligation; 15 that is why I am eager to preach the gospel also to you in Rome.

16 For I am not ashamed of the gospel. It is the power of God for the salvation of everyone who believes: for Jew first, and then Greek. 17 For in it is revealed the righteousness of God from faith to faith; as it is written, "The one who is righteous by faith will live."

18 The wrath of God is indeed being revealed from heaven against every impiety and wickedness of those who suppress the truth by their wickedness. 19 For what can be known about God is evident to them, because God made it evident to them. 20 Ever since the creation of the world, his invisible attributes of eternal power and divinity have been able to be understood and perceived in what he has made. As a result, they have no excuse; 21 for although they knew God they did not accord him glory as God or give him thanks. Instead, they became vain in their reasoning, and their senseless minds were darkened. 22 While claiming to be wise, they became fools 23 and exchanged the glory of the immortal God for the likeness of an image of mortal man or of birds or of four-legged animals or of snakes.

24 Therefore, God handed them over to impurity through the lusts of their hearts for the mutual degradation of their bodies. 25 They exchanged the truth of God for a lie and revered and worshiped the creature rather than the creator, who is blessed forever. Amen. 26 Therefore, God handed

Romans

THE LETTER OF PAUL TO THE CHURCH IN ROME

1 From Paul, a servant of Christ Jesus, called to be an apostle, 2 set apart for the service of the gospel that God promised long ago through his prophets in the holy scriptures.

3 This is the gospel concerning his Son who, in terms of human nature 4 was born a descendant of David and who, in terms of the Spirit and of holiness, was designated Son of God in power by resurrection from the dead: Jesus Christ, our Lord, 5 through whom we have received grace and our apostolic mission of winning the obedience of faith among all the nations for the honour of his name. 6 You are among these, and by his call you belong to Jesus Christ. 7 To you all, God's beloved in Rome, called to be his holy people. Grace and peace to you from God our Father and the Lord Jesus Christ.

8 First I give thanks to my God through Jesus Christ for all of you because your faith is talked of all over the world. 9 God, whom I serve with my spirit in preaching the gospel of his Son, is my witness that I continually mention you in my prayers, 10 asking always that by some means I may at long last be enabled to visit you, if it is God's will. 11 For I am longing to see you so that I can convey to you some spiritual gift that will be a lasting strength, 12 or rather that we may be strengthened together through our mutual faith, yours and mine. 13 I want you to be quite certain too, brothers, that I have often planned to visit you — though up to the present I have always been prevented — in the hope that I might work as fruitfully among you as I have among the gentiles elsewhere. 14 I have an obligation to Greeks as well as barbarians, to the educated as well as the ignorant, 15 and hence the eagerness on my part to preach the gospel to you in Rome too.

16 For I see no reason to be ashamed of the gospel; it is God's power for the salvation of everyone who has faith — Jews first, but Greeks as well — 17 for in it is revealed the saving justice of God: a justice based on faith and addressed to faith. As it says in scripture: *Anyone who is upright through faith will live.* a

18 The retribution of God from heaven is being revealed against the ungodliness and injustice of human beings who in their injustice hold back the truth. 19 For what can be known about God is perfectly plain to them, since God has made it plain to them: 20 ever since the creation of the world, the invisible existence of God and his everlasting power have been clearly seen by the mind's understanding of created things. And so these people have no excuse: 21 they knew God and yet they did not honour him as God or give thanks to him, but their arguments became futile and their uncomprehending minds were darkened. 22 While they claimed to be wise, in fact they were growing so stupid 23 that *they exchanged the glory* of the immortal God *for an imitation,* b for the image of a mortal human being, or of birds, or animals, or crawling things.

24 That is why God abandoned them in their inmost cravings to filthy practices of dishonouring their own bodies — 25 because they *exchanged God's truth* for a lie and have worshipped and served the creature instead of the Creator, who is blessed for ever. Amen.

---

a 1 Hab 2:4 LXX.   b 1 Jr 2:11.

NEW REVISED STANDARD VERSION

REVISED ENGLISH BIBLE

26 For this reason God gave them up to degrading passions. Their women exchanged natural intercourse for unnatural, 27 and in the same way also the men, giving up natural intercourse with women, were consumed with passion for one another. Men committed shameless acts with men and received in their own persons the due penalty for their error.

28 And since they did not see fit to acknowledge God, God gave them up to a debased mind and to things that should not be done. 29 They were filled with every kind of wickedness, evil, covetousness, malice. Full of envy, murder, strife, deceit, craftiness, they are gossips, 30 slanderers, God-haters, *f* insolent, haughty, boastful, inventors of evil, rebellious toward parents, 31 foolish, faithless, heartless, ruthless. 32 They know God's decree, that those who practice such things deserve to die — yet they not only do them but even applaud others who practice them.

2 Therefore you have no excuse, whoever you are, when you judge others; for in passing judgment on another you condemn yourself, because you, the judge, are doing the very same things. 2 You say, *g* "We know that God's judgment on those who do such things is in accordance with truth." 3 Do you imagine, whoever you are, that when you judge those who do such things and yet do them yourself, you will escape the judgment of God? 4 Or do you despise the riches of his kindness and forbearance and patience? Do you not realize that God's kindness is meant to lead you to repentance? 5 But by your hard and impenitent heart you are storing up wrath for yourself on the day of wrath, when God's righteous judgment will be revealed. 6 For he will repay according to each one's deeds: 7 to those who by patiently doing good seek for glory and honor and immortality, he will give eternal life; 8 while for those who are self-seeking and who obey not the truth but wickedness, there will be wrath and fury. 9 There will be anguish and distress for everyone who does evil, the Jew first and also the Greek, 10 but glory and honor and peace for everyone who does good, the Jew first and also the Greek. 11 For God shows no partiality.

12 All who have sinned apart from the law will also perish apart from the law, and all who have sinned under the law will be judged by the law. 13 For it is not the hearers of the law who are righteous in God's sight, but the doers of the law who will be justified. 14 When Gentiles, who do not possess the law, do instinctively what the law requires, these, though not having the law, are a law to themselves. 15 They show that what the law requires is written on their hearts, to which their own conscience also bears witness; and their conflicting thoughts will accuse or perhaps excuse them 16 on the day when, according to my gospel, God, through Jesus Christ, will judge the secret thoughts of all.

17 But if you call yourself a Jew and rely on the law and boast of your relation to God 18 and know his will and determine what is best because you are instructed in the law, 19 and if you are sure that you are a guide to the blind, a light to those who are in darkness, 20 a corrector of the foolish, a teacher of children, having in the law the embodiment of knowledge and truth, 21 you, then, that teach others, will you not teach yourself? While you preach against stealing, do you steal? 22 You that forbid adultery, do you commit adultery? You that abhor idols, do you rob temples? 23 You that boast in the law, do you dishonor God by break-

God has given them up to shameful passions. Among them women have exchanged natural intercourse for unnatural, 27 and men too, giving up natural relations with women, burn with lust for one another; males behave indecently with males, and are paid in their own persons the fitting wage of such perversion.

28 Thus, because they have not seen fit to acknowledge God, he has given them up to their own depraved way of thinking, and this leads them to break all rules of conduct. 29 They are filled with every kind of wickedness, villainy, greed, and malice; they are one mass of envy, murder, rivalry, treachery, and malevolence; gossips 30 and scandalmongers; and blasphemers, insolent, arrogant, and boastful; they invent new kinds of vice, they show no respect to parents, 31 they are without sense or fidelity, without natural affection or pity. 32 They know well enough the just decree of God, that those who behave like this deserve to die; yet they not only do these things themselves but approve such conduct in others.

2 You have no defence, then, whoever you may be, when you sit in judgement — for in judging others you condemn yourself, since you, the judge, are equally guilty. 2 We all know that God's judgement on those who commit such crimes is just; 3 and do you imagine — you that pass judgement on the guilty while committing the same crimes yourself — do you imagine that you, any more than they, will escape the judgement of God? 4 Or do you despise his wealth of kindness and tolerance and patience, failing to see that God's kindness is meant to lead you to repentance? 5 In the obstinate impenitence of your heart you are laying up for yourself a store of retribution against the day of retribution, when God's just judgement will be revealed, 6 and he will pay everyone for what he has done. 7 To those who pursue glory, honour, and immortality by steady persistence in well-doing, he will give eternal life; 8 but the retribution of his wrath awaits those who are governed by selfish ambition, who refuse obedience to truth and take evil for their guide. 9 There will be affliction and distress for every human being who is a wrongdoer, for the Jew first and for the Greek also; 10 but for everyone who does right there will be glory, honour, and peace, for the Jew first and also for the Greek. 11 God has no favourites.

12 Those who have sinned outside the pale of the law of Moses will perish outside the law, and all who have sinned under that law will be judged by it. 13 None will be justified before God by hearing the law, but by doing it. 14 When Gentiles who do not possess the law carry out its precepts by the light of nature, then, although they have no law, they are their own law; 15 they show that what the law requires is inscribed on their hearts, and to this their conscience gives supporting witness, since their own thoughts argue the case, sometimes against them, sometimes even for them. 16 So it will be on the day when, according to my gospel, God will judge the secrets of human hearts through Christ Jesus.

17 BUT as for you who bear the name of Jew and rely on the law: you take pride in your God; 18 you know his will; taught by the law, you know what really matters; 19 you are confident that you are a guide to the blind, a light to those in darkness, 20 an instructor of the foolish, and a teacher of the immature, because you possess in the law the embodiment of knowledge and truth. 21 You teach others, then; do you not teach yourself? You proclaim, 'Do not steal'; but are you yourself a thief? 22 You say, 'Do not commit adultery'; but are you an adulterer? You abominate false gods; but do you rob shrines? 23 While you take pride in the law, you dishonour God by breaking it. 24 As scripture says,

them over to degrading passions. Their females exchanged natural relations for unnatural, 27 and the males likewise gave up natural relations with females and burned with lust for one another. Males did shameful things with males and thus received in their own persons the due penalty for their perversity. 28 And since they did not see fit to acknowledge God, God handed them over to their undiscerning mind to do what is improper. 29 They are filled with every form of wickedness, evil, greed, and malice; full of envy, murder, rivalry, treachery, and spite. They are gossips 30 and scandalmongers and they hate God. They are insolent, haughty, boastful, ingenious in their wickedness, and rebellious toward their parents. 31 They are senseless, faithless, heartless, ruthless. 32 Although they know the just decree of God that all who practice such things deserve death, they not only do them but give approval to those who practice them.

2 Therefore, you are without excuse, every one of you who passes judgment. For by the standard by which you judge another you condemn yourself, since you, the judge, do the very same things. 2 We know that the judgment of God on those who do such things is true. 3 Do you suppose, then, you who judge those who engage in such things and yet do them yourself, that you will escape the judgment of God? 4 Or do you hold his priceless kindness, forbearance, and patience in low esteem, unaware that the kindness of God would lead you to repentance? 5 By your stubbornness and impenitent heart, you are storing up wrath for yourself for the day of wrath and revelation of the just judgment of God, 6 who will repay everyone according to his works: 7 eternal life to those who seek glory, honor, and immortality through perseverance in good works, 8 but wrath and fury to those who selfishly disobey the truth and obey wickedness. 9 Yes, affliction and distress will come upon every human being who does evil, Jew first and then Greek. 10 But there will be glory, honor, and peace for everyone who does good, Jew first and then Greek. 11 There is no partiality with God.

12 All who sin outside the law will also perish without reference to it, and all who sin under the law will be judged in accordance with it. 13 For it is not those who hear the law who are just in the sight of God; rather, those who observe the law will be justified. 14 For when the Gentiles who do not have the law by nature observe the prescriptions of the law, they are a law for themselves even though they do not have the law. 15 They show that the demands of the law are written in their hearts, while their conscience also bears witness and their conflicting thoughts accuse or even defend them 16 on the day when, according to my gospel, God will judge people's hidden works through Christ Jesus.

17 Now if you call yourself a Jew and rely on the law and boast of God 18 and know his will and are able to discern what is important since you are instructed from the law, 19 and if you are confident that you are a guide for the blind and a light for those in darkness, 20 that you are a trainer of the foolish and teacher of the simple, because in the law you have the formulation of knowledge and truth— 21 then you who teach another, are you failing to teach yourself? You who preach against stealing, do you steal? 22 You who forbid adultery, do you commit adultery? You who detest idols, do you rob temples? 23 You who boast of the law, do you dishonor God by breaking the law? 24 For, as it is writ-

26 That is why God abandoned them to degrading passions: 27 why their women have exchanged natural intercourse for unnatural practices; and the men, in a similar fashion, too, giving up normal relations with women, are consumed with passion for each other, men doing shameful things with men and receiving in themselves due reward for their perversion.

28 In other words, since they would not consent to acknowledge God, God abandoned them to their unacceptable thoughts and indecent behaviour. 29 And so now they are steeped in all sorts of injustice, rottenness, greed and malice; full of envy, murder, wrangling, treachery and spite, 30 libellers, slanderers, enemies of God, rude, arrogant and boastful, enterprising in evil, rebellious to parents, 31 without brains, honour, love or pity. 32 They are well aware of God's ordinance: that those who behave like this deserve to die — yet they not only do it, but even applaud others who do the same.

2 So no matter who you are, if you pass judgement you have no excuse. It is yourself that you condemn when you judge others, since you behave in the same way as those you are condemning. 2 We are well aware that people who behave like that are justly condemned by God. 3 But you — when you judge those who behave like this while you are doing the same yourself — do you think you will escape God's condemnation? 4 Or are you not disregarding his abundant goodness, tolerance and patience, failing to realise that this generosity of God is meant to bring you to repentance? 5 Your stubborn refusal to repent is only storing up retribution for yourself on that Day of retribution when God's just verdicts will be made known. 6 He will repay everyone as their deeds deserve.c 7 For those who aimed for glory and honour and immortality by persevering in doing good, there will be eternal life; 8 but for those who out of jealousy have taken for their guide not truth but injustice, there will be the fury of retribution. 9 Trouble and distress will come to every human being who does evil — Jews first, but Greeks as well; 10 glory and honour and peace will come to everyone who does good — Jews first, but Greeks as well. 11 There is no favouritism with God.d

12 All those who have sinned without the Law will perish without the Law; and those under the Law who have sinned will be judged by the Law. 13 For the ones that God will justify are not those who have heard the Law but those who have kept the Law. 14 So, when gentiles, not having the Law, still through their own innate sense behave as the Law commands, then, even though they have no Law, they are a law for themselves. 15 They can demonstrate the effect of the Law engraved on their hearts, to which their own conscience bears witness; since they are aware of various considerations, some of which accuse them, while others provide them with a defence . . . on the day when, 16 according to the gospel that I preach, God, through Jesus Christ, judges all human secrets.

17 If you can call yourself a Jew, and you really trust in the Law, and are proud of your God, 18 and know his will, and tell right from wrong because you have been taught by the Law; 19 if you are confident that you are a guide to the blind and a beacon to those in the dark, 20 that you can teach the ignorant and instruct the unlearned because the Law embodies all knowledge and all truth— 21 so then, in teaching others, do you teach yourself as well? You preach that there is to be no stealing, but do you steal? 22 You say that adultery is forbidden, but do you commit adultery? You detest the worship of objects, but do you desecrate holy things yourself? 23 If, while you are boasting of the Law, you disobey it, then you are bringing God into contempt.

c 2 Ps 62:12.   d 2 Dt 10:17.

| NEW REVISED STANDARD VERSION | REVISED ENGLISH BIBLE |

ing the law? 24 For, as it is written, "The name of God is blasphemed among the Gentiles because of you."

25 Circumcision indeed is of value if you obey the law; but if you break the law, your circumcision has become uncircumcision. 26 So, if those who are uncircumcised keep the requirements of the law, will not their uncircumcision be regarded as circumcision? 27 Then those who are physically uncircumcised but keep the law will condemn you that have the written code and circumcision but break the law. 28 For a person is not a Jew who is one outwardly, nor is true circumcision something external and physical. 29 Rather, a person is a Jew who is one inwardly, and real circumcision is a matter of the heart—it is spiritual and not literal. Such a person receives praise not from others but from God.

3 Then what advantage has the Jew? Or what is the value of circumcision? 2 Much, in every way. For in the first place the Jews*h* were entrusted with the oracles of God. 3 What if some were unfaithful? Will their faithlessness nullify the faithfulness of God? 4 By no means! Although everyone is a liar, let God be proved true, as it is written,
"So that you may be justified in your words,
    and prevail in your judging."*i*
5 But if our injustice serves to confirm the justice of God, what should we say? That God is unjust to inflict wrath on us? (I speak in a human way.) 6 By no means! For then how could God judge the world? 7 But if through my falsehood God's truthfulness abounds to his glory, why am I still being condemned as a sinner? 8 And why not say (as some people slander us by saying that we say), "Let us do evil so that good may come"? Their condemnation is deserved!

9 What then? Are we any better off?*j* No, not at all; for we have already charged that all, both Jews and Greeks, are under the power of sin, 10 as it is written:
"There is no one who is righteous, not even one;
11   there is no one who has understanding,
        there is no one who seeks God.
12 All have turned aside, together they have become
        worthless;
    there is no one who shows kindness,
        there is not even one."
13 "Their throats are opened graves;
    they use their tongues to deceive."
"The venom of vipers is under their lips."
14   "Their mouths are full of cursing and
        bitterness."
15 "Their feet are swift to shed blood;
16   ruin and misery are in their paths,
17   and the way of peace they have not known."
18   "There is no fear of God before their eyes."
19 Now we know that whatever the law says, it speaks to those who are under the law, so that every mouth may be silenced, and the whole world may be held accountable to God. 20 For "no human being will be justified in his sight" by deeds prescribed by the law, for through the law comes the knowledge of sin.

21 But now, apart from law, the righteousness of God has been disclosed, and is attested by the law and the prophets, 22 the righteousness of God through faith in Jesus Christ*k* for all who believe. For there is no distinction, 23 since all have sinned and fall short of the glory of God;

'Because of you the name of God is profaned among the Gentiles.'

25 Circumcision has value, provided you keep the law; but if you break the law, then your circumcision is as if it had never been. 26 Equally, if an uncircumcised man keeps the precepts of the law, will he not count as circumcised? 27 He may be physically uncircumcised, but by fulfilling the law he will pass judgement on you who break it, for all your written code and your circumcision. 28 It is not externals that make a Jew, nor an external mark in the flesh that makes circumcision. 29 The real Jew is one who is inwardly a Jew, and his circumcision is of the heart, spiritual not literal; he receives his commendation not from men but from God.

3 Then what advantage has the Jew? What is the value of circumcision? 2 Great, in every way. In the first place, the Jews were entrusted with the oracles of God. 3 What if some of them were unfaithful? Will their faithlessness cancel the faithfulness of God? 4 Certainly not! God must be true though all men be proved liars; for we read in scripture, 'When you speak you will be vindicated; when you are accused, you will win the case.'

5 Another question: if our injustice serves to confirm God's justice, what are we to say? Is it unjust of God (I speak of him in human terms) to bring retribution upon us? 6 Certainly not! If God were unjust, how could he judge the world?

7 Again, if the truth of God is displayed to his greater glory through my falsehood, why should I any longer be condemned as a sinner? 8 Why not indeed 'do evil that good may come', as some slanderously report me as saying? To condemn such men as these is surely just.

9 Well then, are we Jews any better off? No, not at all! For we have already drawn up the indictment that all, Jews and Greeks alike, are under the power of sin. 10 Scripture says:

There is no one righteous; no, not one;
11 no one who understands, no one who seeks God.
12 All have swerved aside, all alike have become
        debased;
    there is no one to show kindness: no, not one.

13 Their throats are open tombs,
    they use their tongues for treachery,
    adders' venom is on their lips,
14 and their mouths are full of bitter curses.
15 Their feet hasten to shed blood,
16 ruin and misery mark their tracks,
17 they are strangers to the path of peace,
18 and reverence for God does not enter their
        thoughts.

19 Now all the words of the law are addressed, as we know, to those who are under the law, so that no one may have anything to say in self-defence, and the whole world may be exposed to God's judgement. 20 For no human being can be justified in the sight of God by keeping the law: law brings only the consciousness of sin.

21 But now, quite independently of law, though with the law and the prophets bearing witness to it, the righteousness of God has been made known; 22 it is effective through faith in Christ for all who have such faith—all, without distinction. 23 For all alike have sinned, and are deprived of the divine glory; 24 and all are justified by God's free grace

---

h Gk *they* *i* Gk *when you are being judged* *j* Or *at any
disadvantage?* *k* Or *through the faith of Jesus Christ*

3:9 **No, not at all:** or Not altogether.

NEW AMERICAN BIBLE

NEW JERUSALEM BIBLE

ten, "Because of you the name of God is reviled among the Gentiles."

25 Circumcision, to be sure, has value if you observe the law; but if you break the law, your circumcision has become uncircumcision. 26 Again, if an uncircumcised man keeps the precepts of the law, will he not be considered circumcised? 27 Indeed, those who are physically uncircumcised but carry out the law will pass judgment on you, with your written law and circumcision, who break the law. 28 One is not a Jew outwardly. True circumcision is not outward, in the flesh. 29 Rather, one is a Jew inwardly, and circumcision is of the heart, in the spirit, not the letter; his praise is not from human beings but from God.

3 What advantage is there then in being a Jew? Or what is the value of circumcision? 2 Much, in every respect. [For] in the first place, they were entrusted with the utterances of God. 3 What if some were unfaithful? Will their infidelity nullify the fidelity of God? 4 Of course not! God must be true, though every human being is a liar, as it is written:

"That you may be justified in your words,
    and conquer when you are judged."

5 But if our wickedness provides proof of God's righteousness, what can we say? Is God unjust, humanly speaking, to inflict his wrath? 6 Of course not! For how else is God to judge the world? 7 But if God's truth redounds to his glory through my falsehood, why am I still being condemned as a sinner? 8 And why not say — as we are accused and as some claim we say — that we should do evil that good may come of it? Their penalty is what they deserve.

9 Well, then, are we better off? Not entirely, for we have already brought the charge against Jews and Greeks alike that they are all under the domination of sin, 10 as it is written:

"There is no one just, not one,
11   there is no one who understands,
        there is no one who seeks God.
12 All have gone astray; all alike are worthless;
        there is not one who does good,
        [there is not] even one.
13 Their throats are open graves;
        they deceive with their tongues;
    the venom of asps is on their lips;
14   their mouths are full of bitter cursing.
15 Their feet are quick to shed blood;
16   ruin and misery in their ways,
17 and the way of peace they know not.
18   There is no fear of God before their eyes."

19 Now we know that what the law says is addressed to those under the law, so that every mouth may be silenced and the whole world stand accountable to God, 20 since no human being will be justified in his sight by observing the law; for through the law comes consciousness of sin.

21 But now the righteousness of God has been manifested apart from the law, though testified to by the law and the prophets, 22 the righteousness of God through faith in Jesus Christ for all who believe. For there is no distinction; 23 all have sinned and are deprived of the glory of God. 24 They

24 As scripture says: *It is your fault that the name of God is held in contempt among the nations.* e

25 Circumcision has its value if you keep the Law; but if you go on breaking the Law, you are no more circumcised than the uncircumcised. 26 And if an uncircumcised man keeps the commands of the Law, will not his uncircumcised state count as circumcision? 27 More, the man who, in his native uncircumcised state, keeps the Law, is a condemnation of you, who, by your concentration on the letter and on circumcision, actually break the Law. 28 Being a Jew is not only having the outward appearance of a Jew, and circumcision is not only a visible physical operation. 29 The real Jew is the one who is inwardly a Jew, and real circumcision is in the heart, a thing not of the letter but of the spirit. He may not be praised by any human being, but he will be praised by God.

3 Is there any benefit, then, in being a Jew? Is there any advantage in being circumcised? 2 A great deal, in every way. First of all, it was to the Jews that the message of God was entrusted. 3 What if some of them were unfaithful? Do you think their lack of faith could cancel God's faithfulness? 4 Out of the question! God will always be true even if *no human being can be relied on.* f As scripture says: *That you may show your saving justice when you pass sentence and your victory may appear when you give judgement.* 5 But if our injustice serves to bring God's saving justice into view, can we say that God is unjust when — to use human terms — he brings his retribution down on us? 6 Out of the question! It would mean that God could not be the judge of the world. 7 You might as well say that if my untruthfulness makes God demonstrate his truthfulness, to his greater glory, then I should not be judged to be a sinner at all. 8 In this case, the slanderous report some people are spreading would be true, that we teach that one should do evil that good may come of it. In fact such people are justly condemned.

9 Well: are we any better off? Not at all: we have already indicted Jews and Greeks as being all alike under the dominion of sin. 10 As scripture says:

    Not one of them is upright, not a single one,
11 *not a single one is wise,
    not a single one seeks God.*
12 *All have turned away, all alike turned sour,
    not one of them does right, not a single one.*
13 *Their throats are wide-open graves,
    their tongues seductive.
    Viper's venom behind their lips;*
14 *their speech is full of cursing and bitterness.*
15 *Their feet quick to shed innocent blood,*
16 *wherever they go there is havoc and ruin.*
17 *They do not know the way of peace,*
18 *there is no fear of God before their eyes.*

19 Now we are well aware that whatever the Law says is said for those who are subject to the Law, so that every mouth may be silenced, and the whole world brought under the judgement of God. 20 So then, *no human being can be found upright at the tribunal* of God by keeping the Law; all that the Law does is to tell us what is sinful.

21 God's saving justice was witnessed by the Law and the Prophets, but now it has been revealed altogether apart from law: 22 God's saving justice given through faith in Jesus Christ to all who believe. 23 No distinction is made: all have sinned and lack God's glory, 24 and all are justified by the

---

e 2 Ezk 36:20.   f 3 In vv. 4–20 Paul uses numerous quotations from the Pss and Is 59:7–8.

NEW REVISED STANDARD VERSION

24they are now justified by his grace as a gift, through the redemption that is in Christ Jesus, 25whom God put forward as a sacrifice of atonement*l* by his blood, effective through faith. He did this to show his righteousness, because in his divine forbearance he had passed over the sins previously committed; 26it was to prove at the present time that he himself is righteous and that he justifies the one who has faith in Jesus.*m*

27 Then what becomes of boasting? It is excluded. By what law? By that of works? No, but by the law of faith. 28For we hold that a person is justified by faith apart from works prescribed by the law. 29Or is God the God of Jews only? Is he not the God of Gentiles also? Yes, of Gentiles also, 30since God is one; and he will justify the circumcised on the ground of faith and the uncircumcised through that same faith. 31Do we then overthrow the law by this faith? By no means! On the contrary, we uphold the law.

4 What then are we to say was gained by*n* Abraham, our ancestor according to the flesh? 2For if Abraham was justified by works, he has something to boast about, but not before God. 3For what does the scripture say? "Abraham believed God, and it was reckoned to him as righteousness." 4Now to one who works, wages are not reckoned as a gift but as something due. 5But to one who without works trusts him who justifies the ungodly, such faith is reckoned as righteousness. 6So also David speaks of the blessedness of those to whom God reckons righteousness apart from works:

7 "Blessed are those whose iniquities are forgiven,
      and whose sins are covered;
8 blessed is the one against whom the Lord will not
      reckon sin."

9 Is this blessedness, then, pronounced only on the circumcised, or also on the uncircumcised? We say, "Faith was reckoned to Abraham as righteousness." 10How then was it reckoned to him? Was it before or after he had been circumcised? It was not after, but before he was circumcised. 11He received the sign of circumcision as a seal of the righteousness that he had by faith while he was still uncircumcised. The purpose was to make him the ancestor of all who believe without being circumcised and who thus have righteousness reckoned to them, 12and likewise the ancestor of the circumcised who are not only circumcised but who also follow the example of the faith that our ancestor Abraham had before he was circumcised.

13 For the promise that he would inherit the world did not come to Abraham or to his descendants through the law but through the righteousness of faith. 14If it is the adherents of the law who are to be the heirs, faith is null and the promise is void. 15For the law brings wrath; but where there is no law, neither is there violation.

16 For this reason it depends on faith, in order that the promise may rest on grace and be guaranteed to all his descendants, not only to the adherents of the law but also to those who share the faith of Abraham (for he is the father of all of us, 17as it is written, "I have made you the father of many nations") — in the presence of the God in whom he believed, who gives life to the dead and calls into existence the things that do not exist. 18Hoping against hope, he

REVISED ENGLISH BIBLE

alone, through his act of liberation in the person of Christ Jesus. 25For God designed him to be the means of expiating sin by his death, effective through faith. God meant by this to demonstrate his justice, because in his forbearance he had overlooked the sins of the past — 26to demonstrate his justice now in the present, showing that he is himself just and also justifies anyone who puts his faith in Jesus.

27What room then is left for human pride? It is excluded. And on what principle? The keeping of the law would not exclude it, but faith does. 28For our argument is that people are justified by faith quite apart from any question of keeping the law.

29Do you suppose God is the God of the Jews alone? Is he not the God of Gentiles also? Certainly, of Gentiles also. 30For if the Lord is indeed one, he will justify the circumcised by their faith and the uncircumcised through their faith. 31Does this mean that we are using faith to undermine the law? By no means: we are upholding the law.

4 WHAT, then, are we to say about Abraham, our ancestor by natural descent? 2If Abraham was justified by anything he did, then he has grounds for pride. But not in the eyes of God! 3For what does scripture say? 'Abraham put his faith in God, and that faith was counted to him as righteousness.'

4Now if someone does a piece of work, his wages are not 'counted' to be a gift; they are paid as his due. 5But if someone without any work to his credit simply puts his faith in him who acquits the wrongdoer, then his faith is indeed 'counted as righteousness'. 6In the same sense David speaks of the happiness of the man whom God 'counts' as righteous, apart from any good works: 7'Happy are they', he says, 'whose lawless deeds are forgiven, whose sins are blotted out; 8happy is the man whose sin the Lord does not count against him.'

9Is this happiness confined to the circumcised, or is it for the uncircumcised also? We have just been saying: 'Abraham's faith was counted as righteousness.' 10In what circumstances was it so counted? Was he circumcised at the time, or not? He was not yet circumcised, but uncircumcised; 11he received circumcision later as the sign and hallmark of that righteousness which faith had given him while he was still uncircumcised. It follows that he is the father of all who have faith when uncircumcised, and so have righteousness 'counted' to them; 12and at the same time he is the father of the circumcised, provided they are not merely circumcised, but also follow that path of faith which our father Abraham trod while he was still uncircumcised.

13It was not through law that Abraham and his descendants were given the promise that the world should be their inheritance, but through righteousness that came from faith. 14If the heirs are those who hold by the law, then faith becomes pointless and the promise goes for nothing; 15law can bring only retribution, and where there is no law there can be no breach of law. 16The promise was made on the ground of faith in order that it might be a matter of sheer grace, and that it might be valid for all Abraham's descendants, not only for those who hold by the law, but also for those who have Abraham's faith. For he is the father of us all, 17as scripture says: 'I have appointed you to be father of many nations.' In the presence of God, the God who makes the dead live and calls into being things that are not, Abraham had faith. 18When hope seemed hopeless, his

---

l Or *a place of atonement*   *m* Or *who has the faith of Jesus*
n Other ancient authorities read *say about*

3:25 **designed him to be:** *or* set him forth as.

are justified freely by his grace through the redemption in Christ Jesus, 25 whom God set forth as an expiation, through faith, by his blood, to prove his righteousness because of the forgiveness of sins previously committed, 26 through the forbearance of God — to prove his righteousness in the present time, that he might be righteous and justify the one who has faith in Jesus.

27 What occasion is there then for boasting? It is ruled out. On what principle, that of works? No, rather on the principle of faith. 28 For we consider that a person is justified by faith apart from works of the law. 29 Does God belong to Jews alone? Does he not belong to Gentiles, too? Yes, also to Gentiles, 30 for God is one and will justify the circumcised on the basis of faith and the uncircumcised through faith. 31 Are we then annulling the law by this faith? Of course not! On the contrary, we are supporting the law.

4 What then can we say that Abraham found, our ancestor according to the flesh? 2 Indeed, if Abraham was justified on the basis of his works, he has reason to boast; but this was not so in the sight of God. 3 For what does the scripture say? "Abraham believed God, and it was credited to him as righteousness." 4 A worker's wage is credited not as a gift, but as something due. 5 But when one does not work, yet believes in the one who justifies the ungodly, his faith is credited as righteousness. 6 So also David declares the blessedness of the person to whom God credits righteousness apart from works:

7 "Blessed are they whose iniquities are forgiven
and whose sins are covered.
8 Blessed is the man whose sin the Lord does
not record."

9 Does this blessedness apply only to the circumcised, or to the uncircumcised as well? Now we assert that "faith was credited to Abraham as righteousness." 10 Under what circumstances was it credited? Was he circumcised or not? He was not circumcised, but uncircumcised. 11 And he received the sign of circumcision as a seal on the righteousness received through faith while he was uncircumcised. Thus he was to be the father of all the uncircumcised who believe, so that to them [also] righteousness might be credited, 12 as well as the father of the circumcised who not only are circumcised but also follow the path of faith that our father Abraham walked while still uncircumcised.

13 It was not through the law that the promise was made to Abraham and his descendants that he would inherit the world, but through the righteousness that comes from faith. 14 For if those who adhere to the law are the heirs, faith is null and the promise is void. 15 For the law produces wrath; but where there is no law, neither is there violation. 16 For this reason, it depends on faith, so that it may be a gift, and the promise may be guaranteed to all his descendants, not to those who only adhere to the law but to those who follow the faith of Abraham, who is the father of all of us, 17 as it is written, "I have made you father of many nations." He is our father in the sight of God, in whom he believed, who gives life to the dead and calls into being what does not exist. 18 He believed, hoping against hope, that he would

free gift of his grace through being set free in Christ Jesus. 25 God appointed him as a sacrifice for reconciliation, through faith, by the shedding of his blood, and so showed his justness; first for the past, when sins went unpunished because he held his hand; 26 and now again for the present age, to show how he is just and justifies everyone who has faith in Jesus.

27 So what becomes of our boasts? There is no room for them. On what principle — that only actions count? No; that faith is what counts, 28 since, as we see it, a person is justified by faith and not by doing what the Law tells him to do. 29 Do you think God is the God only of the Jews, and not of gentiles too? Most certainly of gentiles too, 30 since there is only one God; he will justify the circumcised by their faith, and he will justify the uncircumcised through their faith. 31 Are we saying that the Law has been made pointless by faith? Out of the question; we are placing the Law on its true footing.

4 Then what do we say about Abraham, the ancestor from whom we are descended physically? 2 If Abraham had been justified because of what he had done, then he would have had something to boast about. But not before God: 3 does our scripture say: *Abraham put his faith in God and this was reckoned to him as uprightness?* g 4 Now, when someone works, the wages for this are not considered as a favour but as due; 5 however, when someone, without working, puts faith in the one who justifies the godless, it is this faith that is reckoned as uprightness. 6 David, too, says the same: he calls someone blessed if God attributes uprightness to that person, apart from any action undertaken:

7 *How blessed are those whose offence is forgiven,*
whose sin is blotted out.
8 *How blessed are those to whom the Lord imputes*
no guilt. h

9 Is this blessing only for the circumcised, or is it said of the uncircumcised as well? Well, we said of Abraham that *his faith was reckoned to him as uprightness.* 10 Now how did this come about? When he was already circumcised, or before he had been circumcised? Not when he had been circumcised, but while he was still uncircumcised; 11 and *circumcision* i was given to him later, *as a sign* and a guarantee that the faith which he had while still uncircumcised was reckoned to him as uprightness. In this way, Abraham was to be the ancestor of all believers who are uncircumcised, so that they might be reckoned as upright; 12 as well as the ancestor of those of the circumcision who not only have their circumcision but who also follow our ancestor Abraham along the path of faith that he trod before he was circumcised.

13 For the promise to Abraham and his descendants that he should inherit the world was not through the Law, but through the uprightness of faith. 14 For if it is those who live by the Law who will gain the inheritance, faith is worthless and the promise is without force; 15 for the Law produces nothing but God's retribution, and it is only where there is no Law that it is possible to live without breaking the Law. 16 That is why the promise is to faith, so that it comes as a free gift and is secure for all the descendants, not only those who rely on the Law but all those others who rely on the faith of Abraham, the ancestor of us all 17 (as scripture says: *I have made you the father of many nations*). Abraham is our father in the eyes of God, in whom he put his faith, and who brings the dead to life and calls into existence what does not yet exist.

18 Though there seemed no hope, he hoped and believed

g 4 Gn 15:6.   h 4 Ps 32:1–2.   i 4 Quotations about Abraham from Gn (17:10; 17:5; 15:5; 17:17).

NEW REVISED STANDARD VERSION	REVISED ENGLISH BIBLE

believed that he would become "the father of many nations," according to what was said, "So numerous shall your descendants be." 19 He did not weaken in faith when he considered his own body, which was already*o* as good as dead (for he was about a hundred years old), or when he considered the barrenness of Sarah's womb. 20 No distrust made him waver concerning the promise of God, but he grew strong in his faith as he gave glory to God, 21 being fully convinced that God was able to do what he had promised. 22 Therefore his faith*p* "was reckoned to him as righteousness." 23 Now the words, "it was reckoned to him," were written not for his sake alone, 24 but for ours also. It will be reckoned to us who believe in him who raised Jesus our Lord from the dead, 25 who was handed over to death for our trespasses and was raised for our justification.

5 Therefore, since we are justified by faith, we*q* have peace with God through our Lord Jesus Christ, 2 through whom we have obtained access*r* to this grace in which we stand; and we*s* boast in our hope of sharing the glory of God. 3 And not only that, but we*s* also boast in our sufferings, knowing that suffering produces endurance, 4 and endurance produces character, and character produces hope, 5 and hope does not disappoint us, because God's love has been poured into our hearts through the Holy Spirit that has been given to us.

6 For while we were still weak, at the right time Christ died for the ungodly. 7 Indeed, rarely will anyone die for a righteous person—though perhaps for a good person someone might actually dare to die. 8 But God proves his love for us in that while we still were sinners Christ died for us. 9 Much more surely then, now that we have been justified by his blood, will we be saved through him from the wrath of God.*t* 10 For if while we were enemies, we were reconciled to God through the death of his Son, much more surely, having been reconciled, will we be saved by his life. 11 But more than that, we even boast in God through our Lord Jesus Christ, through whom we have now received reconciliation.

12 Therefore, just as sin came into the world through one man, and death came through sin, and so death spread to all because all have sinned— 13 sin was indeed in the world before the law, but sin is not reckoned when there is no law. 14 Yet death exercised dominion from Adam to Moses, even over those whose sins were not like the transgression of Adam, who is a type of the one who was to come.

15 But the free gift is not like the trespass. For if the many died through the one man's trespass, much more surely have the grace of God and the free gift in the grace of the one man, Jesus Christ, abounded for the many. 16 And the free gift is not like the effect of the one man's sin. For the judgment following one trespass brought condemnation, but the free gift following many trespasses brings justification. 17 If, because of the one man's trespass, death exercised dominion through that one, much more surely will those who receive the abundance of grace and the free gift of righteousness exercise dominion in life through the one man, Jesus Christ.

18 Therefore just as one man's trespass led to condemnation for all, so one man's act of righteousness leads to justification and life for all. 19 For just as by the one man's disobedience the many were made sinners, so by the one man's obedience the many will be made righteous. 20 But

faith was such that he became 'father of many nations', in fulfilment of the promise, 'So shall your descendants be.' 19 His faith did not weaken when he considered his own body, which was as good as dead (for he was about a hundred years old), and the deadness of Sarah's womb; 20 no distrust made him doubt God's promise, but, strong in faith, he gave glory to God, 21 convinced that what he had promised he was able to do. 22 And that is why Abraham's faith was 'counted to him as righteousness'.

23 The words 'counted to him' were meant to apply not only to Abraham 24 but to us; our faith too is to be 'counted', the faith in the God who raised Jesus our Lord from the dead; 25 for he was given up to death for our misdeeds, and raised to life for our justification.

5 THEREFORE, now that we have been justified through faith, we are at peace with God through our Lord Jesus Christ, 2 who has given us access to that grace in which we now live; and we exult in the hope of the divine glory that is to be ours. 3 More than this: we even exult in our present sufferings, because we know that suffering is a source of endurance, 4 endurance of approval, and approval of hope. 5 Such hope is no fantasy; through the Holy Spirit he has given us, God's love has flooded our hearts.

6 It was while we were still helpless that, at the appointed time, Christ died for the wicked. 7 Even for a just man one of us would hardly die, though perhaps for a good man one might actually brave death; 8 but Christ died for us while we were yet sinners, and that is God's proof of his love towards us. 9 And so, since we have now been justified by Christ's sacrificial death, we shall all the more certainly be saved through him from final retribution. 10 For if, when we were God's enemies, we were reconciled to him through the death of his Son, how much more, now that we have been reconciled, shall we be saved by his life! 11 But that is not all: we also exult in God through our Lord Jesus, through whom we have now been granted reconciliation.

12 What does this imply? It was through one man that sin entered the world, and through sin death, and thus death pervaded the whole human race, inasmuch as all have sinned. 13 For sin was already in the world before there was law; and although in the absence of law no reckoning is kept of sin, 14 death held sway from Adam to Moses, even over those who had not sinned as Adam did, by disobeying a direct command—and Adam foreshadows the man who was to come. 15 But God's act of grace is out of all proportion to Adam's wrongdoing. For if the wrongdoing of that one man brought death upon so many, its effect is vastly exceeded by the grace of God and the gift that came to so many by the grace of the one man, Jesus Christ. 16 And again, the gift of God is not to be compared in its effect with that one man's sin; for the judicial action, following on the one offence, resulted in a verdict of condemnation, but the act of grace, following on so many misdeeds, resulted in a verdict of acquittal. 17 If, by the wrongdoing of one man, death established its reign through that one man, much more shall those who in far greater measure receive grace and the gift of righteousness live and reign through the one man, Jesus Christ.

18 It follows, then, that as the result of one misdeed was condemnation for all people, so the result of one righteous act is acquittal and life for all. 19 For as through the disobedience of one man many were made sinners, so through the obedience of one man many will be made righteous.

---

o Other ancient authorities lack *already* *p* Gk *Therefore it* *q* Other ancient authorities read *let us* *r* Other ancient authorities add *by faith* *s* Or *let us* *t* Gk *the wrath*

5:1 **we are at peace:** *some witnesses read* let us continue at peace.
5:2 **we exult:** *or* let us exult.   5:3 **we even exult:** *or* let us even exult.

become "the father of many nations," according to what was said, "Thus shall your descendants be." 19 He did not weaken in faith when he considered his own body as [already] dead (for he was almost a hundred years old) and the dead womb of Sarah. 20 He did not doubt God's promise in unbelief; rather, he was empowered by faith and gave glory to God 21 and was fully convinced that what he had promised he was also able to do. 22 That is why "it was credited to him as righteousness." 23 But it was not for him alone that it was written that "it was credited to him"; 24 it was also for us, to whom it will be credited, who believe in the one who raised Jesus our Lord from the dead, 25 who was handed over for our transgressions and was raised for our justification.

5 Therefore, since we have been justified by faith, we have peace with God through our Lord Jesus Christ, 2 through whom we have gained access [by faith] to this grace in which we stand, and we boast in hope of the glory of God. 3 Not only that, but we even boast of our afflictions, knowing that affliction produces endurance, 4 and endurance, proven character, and proven character, hope, 5 and hope does not disappoint, because the love of God has been poured out into our hearts through the holy Spirit that has been given to us. 6 For Christ, while we were still helpless, yet died at the appointed time for the ungodly. 7 Indeed, only with difficulty does one die for a just person, though perhaps for a good person one might even find courage to die. 8 But God proves his love for us in that while we were still sinners Christ died for us. 9 How much more then, since we are now justified by his blood, will we be saved through him from the wrath. 10 Indeed, if, while we were enemies, we were reconciled to God through the death of his Son, how much more, once reconciled, will we be saved by his life. 11 Not only that, but we also boast of God through our Lord Jesus Christ, through whom we have now received reconciliation.

12 Therefore, just as through one person sin entered the world, and through sin, death, and thus death came to all, inasmuch as all sinned— 13 for up to the time of the law, sin was in the world, though sin is not accounted when there is no law. 14 But death reigned from Adam to Moses, even over those who did not sin after the pattern of the trespass of Adam, who is the type of the one who was to come. 15 But the gift is not like the transgression. For if by that one person's transgression the many died, how much more did the grace of God and the gracious gift of the one person Jesus Christ overflow for the many. 16 And the gift is not like the result of the one person's sinning. For after one sin there was the judgment that brought condemnation; but the gift, after many transgressions, brought acquittal. 17 For if, by the transgression of one person, death came to reign through that one, how much more will those who receive the abundance of grace and of the gift of justification come to reign in life through the one person Jesus Christ. 18 In conclusion, just as through one transgression condemnation came upon all, so through one righteous act acquittal and life came to all. 19 For just as through the disobedience of one person the many were made sinners, so through the obedience of one the many will be made righteous. 20 The

that he was to become *father of many nations* in fulfilment of the promise: *Just so will your descendants be.* 19 Even the thought that his body was as good as dead — he was about a hundred years old — and that Sarah's womb was dead too did not shake his faith. 20 Counting on the promise of God,[#] he did not doubt or disbelieve, but drew strength from faith and gave glory to God, 21 fully convinced that whatever God promised he has the power to perform. 22 This is the faith that was *reckoned to him as uprightness.* 23 And the word 'reckoned' in scripture applies not only to him; 24 it is there for our sake too — our faith, too, will be 'reckoned' 25 because we believe in him who raised from the dead our Lord Jesus who was *handed over to death for our sins*[j] and raised to life for our justification.

5 So then, now that we have been justified by faith, we are at peace with God through our Lord Jesus Christ; 2 it is through him, by faith, that we have been admitted into God's favour in which we are living, and look forward exultantly to God's glory. 3 Not only that; let us exult, too, in our hardships, understanding that hardship develops perseverance, 4 and perseverance develops a tested character, something that gives us hope, 5 and a hope which will not let us down, because the love of God has been poured into our hearts by the Holy Spirit which has been given to us. 6 When we were still helpless, at the appointed time, Christ died for the godless. 7 You could hardly find anyone ready to die even for someone upright; though it is just possible that, for a really good person, someone might undertake to die. 8 So it is proof of God's own love for us, that Christ died for us while we were still sinners. 9 How much more can we be sure, therefore, that, now that we have been justified by his death, we shall be saved through him from the retribution of God. 10 For if, while we were enemies, we were reconciled to God through the death of his Son, how much more can we be sure that, being now reconciled, we shall be saved by his life. 11 What is more, we are filled with exultant trust in God, through our Lord Jesus Christ, through whom we have already gained our reconciliation.

12 Well then; it was through one man that sin *came into the world*,[k] and through sin death, and thus death has spread through the whole human race because everyone has sinned. 13 Sin already existed in the world before there was any law, even though sin is not reckoned when there is no law. 14 Nonetheless death reigned over all from Adam to Moses, even over those whose sin was not the breaking of a commandment, as Adam's was. He prefigured the One who was to come . . .

15 There is no comparison between the free gift and the offence. If death came to many through the offence of one man, how much greater an effect the grace of God has had, coming to so many and so plentifully as a free gift through the one man Jesus Christ! 16 Again, there is no comparison between the gift and the offence of one man. One single offence brought condemnation, but now, after many offences, have come the free gift and so acquittal! 17 It was by one man's offence that death came to reign over all, but how much greater the reign in life of those who receive the fullness of grace and the gift of saving justice, through the one man, Jesus Christ. 18 One man's offence brought condemnation on all humanity; and one man's good act has brought justification and life to all humanity. 19 Just as by one man's disobedience many were made sinners, so by one man's obedience are many to be made upright. 20 When law

j 4 Is 53:6.   *k* 5 Ws 2:24.

NEW REVISED STANDARD VERSION

REVISED ENGLISH BIBLE

law came in, with the result that the trespass multiplied; but where sin increased, grace abounded all the more, 21 so that, just as sin exercised dominion in death, so grace might also exercise dominion through justification*u* leading to eternal life through Jesus Christ our Lord.

6 What then are we to say? Should we continue in sin in order that grace may abound? 2 By no means! How can we who died to sin go on living in it? 3 Do you not know that all of us who have been baptized into Christ Jesus were baptized into his death? 4 Therefore we have been buried with him by baptism into death, so that, just as Christ was raised from the dead by the glory of the Father, so we too might walk in newness of life.

5 For if we have been united with him in a death like his, we will certainly be united with him in a resurrection like his. 6 We know that our old self was crucified with him so that the body of sin might be destroyed, and we might no longer be enslaved to sin. 7 For whoever has died is freed from sin. 8 But if we have died with Christ, we believe that we will also live with him. 9 We know that Christ, being raised from the dead, will never die again; death no longer has dominion over him. 10 The death he died, he died to sin, once for all; but the life he lives, he lives to God. 11 So you also must consider yourselves dead to sin and alive to God in Christ Jesus.

12 Therefore, do not let sin exercise dominion in your mortal bodies, to make you obey their passions. 13 No longer present your members to sin as instruments*v* of wickedness, but present yourselves to God as those who have been brought from death to life, and present your members to God as instruments*v* of righteousness. 14 For sin will have no dominion over you, since you are not under law but under grace.

15 What then? Should we sin because we are not under law but under grace? By no means! 16 Do you not know that if you present yourselves to anyone as obedient slaves, you are slaves of the one whom you obey, either of sin, which leads to death, or of obedience, which leads to righteousness? 17 But thanks be to God that you, having once been slaves of sin, have become obedient from the heart to the form of teaching to which you were entrusted, 18 and that you, having been set free from sin, have become slaves of righteousness. 19 I am speaking in human terms because of your natural limitations.*w* For just as you once presented your members as slaves to impurity and to greater and greater iniquity, so now present your members as slaves to righteousness for sanctification.

20 When you were slaves of sin, you were free in regard to righteousness. 21 So what advantage did you then get from the things of which you now are ashamed? The end of those things is death. 22 But now that you have been freed from sin and enslaved to God, the advantage you get is sanctification. The end is eternal life. 23 For the wages of sin is death, but the free gift of God is eternal life in Christ Jesus our Lord.

7 Do you not know, brothers and sisters*x*—for I am speaking to those who know the law—that the law is binding on a person only during that person's lifetime? 2 Thus a married woman is bound by the law to her husband as long as he lives; but if her husband dies, she is discharged from the law concerning the husband. 3 Accordingly, she

20 Law intruded into this process to multiply law-breaking. But where sin was multiplied, grace immeasurably exceeded it, 21 in order that, as sin established its reign by way of death, so God's grace might establish its reign in righteousness, and result in eternal life through Jesus Christ our Lord.

6 WHAT are we to say, then? Shall we persist in sin, so that there may be all the more grace? 2 Certainly not! We died to sin: how can we live in it any longer? 3 Have you forgotten that when we were baptized into union with Christ Jesus we were baptized into his death? 4 By that baptism into his death we were buried with him, in order that, as Christ was raised from the dead by the glorious power of the Father, so also we might set out on a new life.

5 For if we have become identified with him in his death, we shall also be identified with him in his resurrection. 6 We know that our old humanity has been crucified with Christ, for the destruction of the sinful self, so that we may no longer be slaves to sin, 7 because death cancels the claims of sin. 8 But if we thus died with Christ, we believe that we shall also live with him, 9 knowing as we do that Christ, once raised from the dead, is never to die again: he is no longer under the dominion of death. 10 When he died, he died to sin, once for all, and now that he lives, he lives to God. 11 In the same way you must regard yourselves as dead to sin and alive to God, in union with Christ Jesus.

12 Therefore sin must no longer reign in your mortal body, exacting obedience to the body's desires. 13 You must no longer put any part of it at sin's disposal, as an implement for doing wrong. Put yourselves instead at the disposal of God; think of yourselves as raised from death to life, and yield your bodies to God as implements for doing right. 14 Sin shall no longer be your master, for you are no longer under law, but under grace.

15 What then? Are we to sin, because we are not under law but under grace? Of course not! 16 You know well enough that if you bind yourselves to obey a master, you are slaves of the master you obey; and this is true whether the master is sin and the outcome death, or obedience and the outcome righteousness. 17 Once you were slaves of sin, but now, thank God, you have yielded wholehearted obedience to that pattern of teaching to which you were made subject; 18 emancipated from sin, you have become slaves of righteousness 19 (to use language that suits your human weakness). As you once yielded your bodies to the service of impurity and lawlessness, making for moral anarchy, so now you must yield them to the service of righteousness, making for a holy life.

20 When you were slaves of sin, you were free from the control of righteousness. 21 And what gain did that bring you? Things that now make you ashamed, for their end is death. 22 But now, freed from the commands of sin and bound to the service of God, you have gains that lead to holiness, and the end is eternal life. 23 For sin pays a wage, and the wage is death, but God gives freely, and his gift is eternal life in union with Christ Jesus our Lord.

7 YOU must be aware, my friends—I am sure you have some knowledge of law—that a person is subject to the law only so long as he is alive. 2 For example, a married woman is by law bound to her husband while he lives; but if the husband dies, she is released from the marriage bond.

---

u Or *righteousness*   *v* Or *weapons*   *w* Gk *the weakness of your flesh*   *x* Gk *brothers*

6:17 **to which . . . subject:** *or* which was handed on to you.

NEW AMERICAN BIBLE

NEW JERUSALEM BIBLE

law entered in so that transgression might increase but, where sin increased, grace overflowed all the more, 21 so that, as sin reigned in death, grace also might reign through justification for eternal life through Jesus Christ our Lord.

6 What then shall we say? Shall we persist in sin that grace may abound? Of course not! 2 How can we who died to sin yet live in it? 3 Or are you unaware that we who were baptized into Christ Jesus were baptized into his death? 4 We were indeed buried with him through baptism into death, so that, just as Christ was raised from the dead by the glory of the Father, we too might live in newness of life.

5 For if we have grown into union with him through a death like his, we shall also be united with him in the resurrection. 6 We know that our old self was crucified with him, so that our sinful body might be done away with, that we might no longer be in slavery to sin. 7 For a dead person has been absolved from sin. 8 If, then, we have died with Christ, we believe that we shall also live with him. 9 We know that Christ, raised from the dead, dies no more; death no longer has power over him. 10 As to his death, he died to sin once and for all; as to his life, he lives for God. 11 Consequently, you too must think of yourselves as [being] dead to sin and living for God in Christ Jesus.

12 Therefore, sin must not reign over your mortal bodies so that you obey their desires. 13 And do not present the parts of your bodies to sin as weapons for wickedness, but present yourselves to God as raised from the dead to life and the parts of your bodies to God as weapons for righteousness. 14 For sin is not to have any power over you, since you are not under the law but under grace.

15 What then? Shall we sin because we are not under the law but under grace? Of course not! 16 Do you not know that if you present yourselves to someone as obedient slaves, you are slaves of the one you obey, either of sin, which leads to death, or of obedience, which leads to righteousness? 17 But thanks be to God that, although you were once slaves of sin, you have become obedient from the heart to the pattern of teaching to which you were entrusted. 18 Freed from sin, you have become slaves of righteousness. 19 I am speaking in human terms because of the weakness of your nature. For just as you presented the parts of your bodies as slaves to impurity and to lawlessness for lawlessness, so now present them as slaves to righteousness for sanctification. 20 For when you were slaves of sin, you were free from righteousness. 21 But what profit did you get then from the things of which you are now ashamed? For the end of those things is death. 22 But now that you have been freed from sin and have become slaves of God, the benefit that you have leads to sanctification, and its end is eternal life. 23 For the wages of sin is death, but the gift of God is eternal life in Christ Jesus our Lord.

7 Are you unaware, brothers (for I am speaking to people who know the law), that the law has jurisdiction over one as long as one lives? 2 Thus a married woman is bound by law to her living husband; but if her husband dies, she is released from the law in respect to her husband.

came on the scene, it was to multiply the offences. But however much sin increased, grace was always greater; 21 so that as sin's reign brought death, so grace was to rule through saving justice that leads to eternal life through Jesus Christ our Lord.

6 What should we say then? Should we remain in sin so that grace may be given the more fully? 2 Out of the question! We have died to sin; how could we go on living in it? 3 You cannot have forgotten that all of us, when we were baptised into Christ Jesus, were baptised into his death. 4 So by our baptism into his death we were buried with him, so that as Christ was raised from the dead by the Father's glorious power, we too should begin living a new life. 5 If we have been joined to him by dying a death like his, so we shall be by a resurrection like his; 6 realising that our former self was crucified with him, so that the self which belonged to sin should be destroyed and we should be freed from the slavery of sin. 7 Someone who has died, of course, no longer has to answer for sin.

8 But we believe that, if we died with Christ, then we shall live with him too. 9 We know that Christ has been raised from the dead and will never die again. Death has no power over him any more. 10 For by dying, he is dead to sin once and for all, and now the life that he lives is life with God. 11 In the same way, you must see yourselves as being dead to sin but alive for God in Christ Jesus.

12 That is why you must not allow sin to reign over your mortal bodies and make you obey their desires; 13 or give any parts of your bodies over to sin to be used as instruments of evil. Instead, give yourselves to God, as people brought to life from the dead, and give every part of your bodies to God to be instruments of uprightness; 14 and then sin will no longer have any power over you — you are living not under law, but under grace.

15 What is the implication? That we are free to sin, now that we are not under law but under grace? Out of the question! 16 You know well that if you undertake to be somebody's slave and obey him, you are the slave of him you obey: you can be the slave either of sin which leads to death, or of obedience which leads to saving justice. 17 Once you were slaves of sin, but thank God you have given whole-hearted obedience to the pattern of teaching to which you were introduced; 18 and so, being freed from serving sin, you took uprightness as your master. 19 I am putting it in human terms because you are still weak human beings: as once you surrendered yourselves as servants to immorality and to a lawlessness which results in more lawlessness, now you have to surrender yourselves to uprightness which is to result in sanctification.

20 When you were the servants of sin, you felt no obligation to uprightness, 21 and what did you gain from living like that? Experiences of which you are now ashamed, for that sort of behaviour ends in death. 22 But, now you are set free from sin and bound to the service of God, your gain will be sanctification and the end will be eternal life. 23 For the wage paid by sin is death; the gift freely given by God is eternal life in Christ Jesus our Lord.

7 As people who are familiar with the Law, brothers, you cannot have forgotten that the law can control a person only during that person's lifetime. 2 A married woman, for instance, is bound to her husband by law, as long as he lives, but when her husband dies all her legal obligation to him as husband is ended. 3 So if she were to

NEW REVISED STANDARD VERSION

will be called an adulteress if she lives with another man while her husband is alive. But if her husband dies, she is free from that law, and if she marries another man, she is not an adulteress.

4 In the same way, my friends,ʸ you have died to the law through the body of Christ, so that you may belong to another, to him who has been raised from the dead in order that we may bear fruit for God. 5 While we were living in the flesh, our sinful passions, aroused by the law, were at work in our members to bear fruit for death. 6 But now we are discharged from the law, dead to that which held us captive, so that we are slaves not under the old written code but in the new life of the Spirit.

7 What then should we say? That the law is sin? By no means! Yet, if it had not been for the law, I would not have known sin. I would not have known what it is to covet if the law had not said, "You shall not covet." 8 But sin, seizing an opportunity in the commandment, produced in me all kinds of covetousness. Apart from the law sin lies dead. 9 I was once alive apart from the law, but when the commandment came, sin revived 10 and I died, and the very commandment that promised life proved to be death to me. 11 For sin, seizing an opportunity in the commandment, deceived me and through it killed me. 12 So the law is holy, and the commandment is holy and just and good.

13 Did what is good, then, bring death to me? By no means! It was sin, working death in me through what is good, in order that sin might be shown to be sin, and through the commandment might become sinful beyond measure.

14 For we know that the law is spiritual; but I am of the flesh, sold into slavery under sin.ᶻ 15 I do not understand my own actions. For I do not do what I want, but I do the very thing I hate. 16 Now if I do what I do not want, I agree that the law is good. 17 But in fact it is no longer I that do it, but sin that dwells within me. 18 For I know that nothing good dwells within me, that is, in my flesh. I can will what is right, but I cannot do it. 19 For I do not do the good I want, but the evil I do not want is what I do. 20 Now if I do what I do not want, it is no longer I that do it, but sin that dwells within me.

21 So I find it to be a law that when I want to do what is good, evil lies close at hand. 22 For I delight in the law of God in my inmost self, 23 but I see in my members another law at war with the law of my mind, making me captive to the law of sin that dwells in my members. 24 Wretched man that I am! Who will rescue me from this body of death? 25 Thanks be to God through Jesus Christ our Lord!

So then, with my mind I am a slave to the law of God, but with my flesh I am a slave to the law of sin.

8 There is therefore now no condemnation for those who are in Christ Jesus. 2 For the law of the Spiritᵃ of life in Christ Jesus has set youᵇ free from the law of sin and of death. 3 For God has done what the law, weakened by the flesh, could not do: by sending his own Son in the likeness of sinful flesh, and to deal with sin,ᶜ he condemned sin in the flesh, 4 so that the just requirement of the law might be fulfilled in us, who walk not according to the flesh but according to the Spirit.ᵃ 5 For those who live according to

---

REVISED ENGLISH BIBLE

3 If, therefore, in her husband's lifetime she gives herself to another man, she will be held to be an adulteress; but if the husband dies, she is free of the law and she does not commit adultery by giving herself to another man. 4 So too, my friends, through the body of Christ you died to the law and were set free to give yourselves to another, to him who rose from the dead so that we may bear fruit for God. 5 While we lived on the level of mere human nature, the sinful passions evoked by the law were active in our bodies, and bore fruit for death. 6 But now, having died to that which held us bound, we are released from the law, to serve God in a new way, the way of the spirit in contrast to the old way of a written code.

7 What follows? Is the law identical with sin? Of course not! Yet had it not been for the law I should never have become acquainted with sin. For example, I should never have known what it was to covet, if the law had not said, 'You shall not covet.' 8 Through that commandment sin found its opportunity, and produced in me all kinds of wrong desires. In the absence of law, sin is devoid of life. 9 There was a time when, in the absence of law, I was fully alive; but when the commandment came, sin sprang to life and I died. 10 The commandment which should have led to life proved in my experience to lead to death, 11 because in the commandment sin found its opportunity to seduce me, and through the commandment killed me. 12 So then, the law in itself is holy and the commandment is holy and just and good.

13 Are we therefore to say that this good thing caused my death? Of course not! It was sin that killed me, and thereby sin exposed its true character: it used a good thing to bring about my death, and so, through the commandment, sin became more sinful than ever. 14 We know that the law is spiritual; but I am not: I am unspiritual, sold as a slave to sin. 15 I do not even acknowledge my own actions as mine, for what I do is not what I want to do, but what I detest. 16 But if what I do is against my will, then clearly I agree with the law and hold it to be admirable. 17 This means that it is no longer I who perform the action, but sin that dwells in me. 18 For I know that nothing good dwells in me—my unspiritual self, I mean—for though the will to do good is there, the ability to effect it is not. 19 The good which I want to do, I fail to do; but what I do is the wrong which is against my will; 20 and if what I do is against my will, clearly it is no longer I who am the agent, but sin that has its dwelling in me.

21 I discover this principle, then: that when I want to do right, only wrong is within my reach. 22 In my inmost self I delight in the law of God, 23 but I perceive in my outward actions a different law, fighting against the law that my mind approves, and making me a prisoner under the law of sin which controls my conduct. 24 Wretched creature that I am, who is there to rescue me from this state of death? 25 Who but God? Thanks be to him through Jesus Christ our Lord! To sum up then: left to myself I serve God's law with my mind, but with my unspiritual nature I serve the law of sin.

8 It follows that there is now no condemnation for those who are united with Christ Jesus. 2 In Christ Jesus the life-giving law of the Spirit has set you free from the law of sin and death. 3 What the law could not do, because human weakness robbed it of all potency, God has done: by sending his own Son in the likeness of our sinful nature and to deal with sin, he has passed judgement against sin within that very nature, 4 so that the commandment of the law may find fulfilment in us, whose conduct is no longer controlled by the old nature, but by the Spirit.

ʸ Gk brothers ᶻ Gk sold under sin ᵃ Or spirit ᵇ Here the Greek word you is singular number; other ancient authorities read me or us ᶜ Or and as a sin offering

8:3 **and to deal with sin:** or and as a sacrifice for sin.

³Consequently, while her husband is alive she will be called an adulteress if she consorts with another man. But if her husband dies she is free from that law, and she is not an adulteress if she consorts with another man.

⁴In the same way, my brothers, you also were put to death to the law through the body of Christ, so that you might belong to another, to the one who was raised from the dead in order that we might bear fruit for God. ⁵For when we were in the flesh, our sinful passions, awakened by the law, worked in our members to bear fruit for death. ⁶But now we are released from the law, dead to what held us captive, so that we may serve in the newness of the spirit and not under the obsolete letter.

⁷What then can we say? That the law is sin? Of course not! Yet I did not know sin except through the law, and I did not know what it is to covet except that the law said, "You shall not covet." ⁸But sin, finding an opportunity in the commandment, produced in me every kind of covetousness. Apart from the law sin is dead. ⁹I once lived outside the law, but when the commandment came, sin became alive; ¹⁰then I died, and the commandment that was for life turned out to be death for me. ¹¹For sin, seizing an opportunity in the commandment, deceived me and through it put me to death. ¹²So then the law is holy, and the commandment is holy and righteous and good.

¹³Did the good, then, become death for me? Of course not! Sin, in order that it might be shown to be sin, worked death in me through the good, so that sin might become sinful beyond measure through the good. ¹⁴We know that the law is spiritual; but I am carnal, sold into slavery to sin. ¹⁵What I do, I do not understand. For I do not do what I want, but I do what I hate. ¹⁶Now if I do what I do not want, I concur that the law is good. ¹⁷So now it is no longer I who do it, but sin that dwells in me. ¹⁸For I know that good does not dwell in me, that is, in my flesh. The willing is ready at hand, but doing the good is not. ¹⁹For I do not do the good I want, but I do the evil I do not want. ²⁰Now if [I] do what I do not want, it is no longer I who do it, but sin that dwells in me. ²¹So, then, I discover the principle that when I want to do right, evil is at hand. ²²For I take delight in the law of God, in my inner self, ²³but I see in my members another principle at war with the law of my mind, taking me captive to the law of sin that dwells in my members. ²⁴Miserable one that I am! Who will deliver me from this mortal body? ²⁵Thanks be to God through Jesus Christ our Lord. Therefore, I myself, with my mind, serve the law of God but, with my flesh, the law of sin.

8 Hence, now there is no condemnation for those who are in Christ Jesus. ²For the law of the spirit of life in Christ Jesus has freed you from the law of sin and death. ³For what the law, weakened by the flesh, was powerless to do, this God has done: by sending his own Son in the likeness of sinful flesh and for the sake of sin, he condemned sin in the flesh, ⁴so that the righteous decree of the law might be fulfilled in us, who live not according to the flesh but according to the spirit. ⁵For those who live accord-

have relations with another man while her husband was still alive, she would be termed an adulteress; but if her husband dies, her legal obligation comes to an end and if she then has relations with another man, that does not make her an adulteress. ⁴In the same way you, my brothers, through the body of Christ have become dead to the Law and so you are able to belong to someone else, that is, to him who was raised from the dead to make us live fruitfully for God. ⁵While we were still living by our natural inclinations, the sinful passions aroused by the Law were working in all parts of our bodies to make us live lives which were fruitful only for death. ⁶But now we are released from the Law, having died to what was binding us, and so we are in a new service, that of the spirit, and not in the old service of a written code.

⁷What should we say, then? That the Law itself is sin? Out of the question! All the same, if it had not been for the Law, I should not have known what sin was; for instance, I should not have known what it meant to covet if the Law had not said: *You are not to covet.*ˡ ⁸But, once it found the opportunity through that commandment, sin produced in me all kinds of covetousness; as long as there is no Law, sin is dead.

⁹Once, when there was no Law, I used to be alive; but when the commandment came, sin came to life ¹⁰and I died. The commandment was meant to bring life but I found it brought death, ¹¹because sin, finding its opportunity by means of the commandment, *beguiled*ᵐ me and, by means of it, killed me.

¹²So then, the Law is holy, and what it commands is holy and upright and good. ¹³Does that mean that something good resulted in my dying? Out of the question! But sin, in order to be identified as sin, caused my death through that good thing, and so it is by means of the commandment that sin shows its unbounded sinful power.

¹⁴We are well aware that the Law is spiritual: but I am a creature of flesh and blood sold as a slave to sin. ¹⁵I do not understand my own behaviour; I do not act as I mean to, but I do things that I hate. ¹⁶While I am acting as I do not want to, I still acknowledge the Law as good, ¹⁷so it is not myself acting, but the sin which lives in me. ¹⁸And really, I know of nothing good living in me — in my natural self, that is — for though the will to do what is good is in me, the power to do it is not: ¹⁹the good thing I want to do, I never do; the evil thing which I do not want — that is what I do. ²⁰But every time I do what I do not want to, then it is not myself acting, but the sin that lives in me.

²¹So I find this rule: that for me, where I want to do nothing but good, evil is close at my side. ²²In my inmost self I dearly love God's law, ²³but I see that acting on my body there is a different law which battles against the law in my mind. So I am brought to be a prisoner of that law of sin which lives inside my body.

²⁴What a wretched man I am! Who will rescue me from this body doomed to death? ²⁵God — thanks be to him — through Jesus Christ our Lord.

So it is that I myself with my mind obey the law of God, but in my disordered nature I obey the law of sin.

8 Thus, condemnation will never come to those who are in Christ Jesus, ²because the law of the Spirit which gives life in Christ Jesus has set you free from the law of sin and death. ³What the Law could not do because of the weakness of human nature, God did, sending his own Son in the same human nature as any sinner to be a sacrifice for sin, and condemning sin in that human nature. ⁴This was so that the Law's requirements might be fully satisfied in us as we direct our lives not by our natural inclinations but by the Spirit. ⁵Those who are living by their natural inclinations

the flesh set their minds on the things of the flesh, but those who live according to the Spirit*d* set their minds on the things of the Spirit. *d* 6 To set the mind on the flesh is death, but to set the mind on the Spirit*d* is life and peace. 7 For this reason the mind that is set on the flesh is hostile to God; it does not submit to God's law — indeed it cannot, 8 and those who are in the flesh cannot please God.

9 But you are not in the flesh; you are in the Spirit,*d* since the Spirit of God dwells in you. Anyone who does not have the Spirit of Christ does not belong to him. 10 But if Christ is in you, though the body is dead because of sin, the Spirit*d* is life because of righteousness. 11 If the Spirit of him who raised Jesus from the dead dwells in you, he who raised Christ*e* from the dead will give life to your mortal bodies also through*f* his Spirit that dwells in you.

12 So then, brothers and sisters,*g* we are debtors, not to the flesh, to live according to the flesh — 13 for if you live according to the flesh, you will die; but if by the Spirit you put to death the deeds of the body, you will live. 14 For all who are led by the Spirit of God are children of God. 15 For you did not receive a spirit of slavery to fall back into fear, but you have received a spirit of adoption. When we cry, "Abba!*h* Father!" 16 it is that very Spirit bearing witness*i* with our spirit that we are children of God, 17 and if children, then heirs, heirs of God and joint heirs with Christ — if, in fact, we suffer with him so that we may also be glorified with him.

18 I consider that the sufferings of this present time are not worth comparing with the glory about to be revealed to us. 19 For the creation waits with eager longing for the revealing of the children of God; 20 for the creation was subjected to futility, not of its own will but by the will of the one who subjected it, in hope 21 that the creation itself will be set free from its bondage to decay and will obtain the freedom of the glory of the children of God. 22 We know that the whole creation has been groaning in labor pains until now; 23 and not only the creation, but we ourselves, who have the first fruits of the Spirit, groan inwardly while we wait for adoption, the redemption of our bodies. 24 For in *j* hope we were saved. Now hope that is seen is not hope. For who hopes*k* for what is seen? 25 But if we hope for what we do not see, we wait for it with patience.

26 Likewise the Spirit helps us in our weakness; for we do not know how to pray as we ought, but that very Spirit intercedes*l* with sighs too deep for words. 27 And God,*m* who searches the heart, knows what is the mind of the Spirit, because the Spirit*n* intercedes for the saints according to the will of God.*o*

28 We know that all things work together for good *p* for those who love God, who are called according to his purpose. 29 For those whom he foreknew he also predestined to be conformed to the image of his Son, in order that he might be the firstborn within a large family.*q* 30 And those whom he predestined he also called; and those whom he called he also justified; and those whom he justified he also glorified.

31 What then are we to say about these things? If God is for us, who is against us? 32 He who did not withhold his own Son, but gave him up for all of us, will he not with him also give us everything else? 33 Who will bring any charge against God's elect? It is God who justifies. 34 Who is to

5–6 Those who live on the level of the old nature have their outlook formed by it, and that spells death; but those who live on the level of the spirit have the spiritual outlook, and that is life and peace. 7 For the outlook of the unspiritual nature is enmity with God; it is not subject to the law of God and indeed it cannot be; 8 those who live under its control cannot please God.

9 But you do not live like that. You live by the spirit, since God's Spirit dwells in you; and anyone who does not possess the Spirit of Christ does not belong to Christ. 10 But if Christ is in you, then although the body is dead because of sin, yet the Spirit is your life because you have been justified. 11 Moreover, if the Spirit of him who raised Jesus from the dead dwells in you, then the God who raised Christ Jesus from the dead will also give new life to your mortal bodies through his indwelling Spirit.

12 It follows, my friends, that our old nature has no claim on us; we are not obliged to live in that way. 13 If you do so, you must die. But if by the Spirit you put to death the base pursuits of the body, then you will live.

14 For all who are led by the Spirit of God are sons of God. 15 The Spirit you have received is not a spirit of slavery, leading you back into a life of fear, but a Spirit of adoption, enabling us to cry 'Abba! Father!' 16 The Spirit of God affirms to our spirit that we are God's children; 17 and if children, then heirs, heirs of God and fellow-heirs with Christ; but we must share his sufferings if we are also to share his glory.

18 For I reckon that the sufferings we now endure bear no comparison with the glory, as yet unrevealed, which is in store for us. 19 The created universe is waiting with eager expectation for God's sons to be revealed. 20 It was made subject to frustration, not of its own choice but by the will of him who subjected it, yet with the hope 21 that the universe itself is to be freed from the shackles of mortality and is to enter upon the glorious liberty of the children of God. 22 Up to the present, as we know, the whole created universe in all its parts groans as if in the pangs of childbirth. 23 What is more, we also, to whom the Spirit is given as the firstfruits of the harvest to come, are groaning inwardly while we look forward eagerly to our adoption, our liberation from mortality. 24 It was with this hope that we were saved. Now to see something is no longer to hope: why hope for what is already seen? 25 But if we hope for something we do not yet see, then we look forward to it eagerly and with patience.

26 In the same way the Spirit comes to the aid of our weakness. We do not even know how we ought to pray, but through our inarticulate groans the Spirit himself is pleading for us, 27 and God who searches our inmost being knows what the Spirit means, because he pleads for God's people as God himself wills; 28 and in everything, as we know, he co-operates for good with those who love God and are called according to his purpose. 29 For those whom God knew before ever they were, he also ordained to share the likeness of his Son, so that he might be the eldest among a large family of brothers; 30 and those whom he foreordained, he also called, and those whom he called he also justified, and those whom he justified he also glorified.

31 With all this in mind, what are we to say? If God is on our side, who is against us? 32 He did not spare his own Son, but gave him up for us all; how can he fail to lavish every other gift upon us? 33 Who will bring a charge against those whom God has chosen? Not God, who acquits! 34 Who will

---

ing to the flesh are concerned with the things of the flesh, but those who live according to the spirit with the things of the spirit. 6 The concern of the flesh is death, but the concern of the spirit is life and peace. 7 For the concern of the flesh is hostility toward God; it does not submit to the law of God, nor can it; 8 and those who are in the flesh cannot please God. 9 But you are not in the flesh; on the contrary, you are in the spirit, if only the Spirit of God dwells in you. Whoever does not have the Spirit of Christ does not belong to him. 10 But if Christ is in you, although the body is dead because of sin, the spirit is alive because of righteousness. 11 If the Spirit of the one who raised Jesus from the dead dwells in you, the one who raised Christ from the dead will give life to your mortal bodies also, through his Spirit that dwells in you. 12 Consequently, brothers, we are not debtors to the flesh, to live according to the flesh. 13 For if you live according to the flesh, you will die, but if by the spirit you put to death the deeds of the body, you will live.

14 For those who are led by the Spirit of God are children of God. 15 For you did not receive a spirit of slavery to fall back into fear, but you received a spirit of adoption, through which we cry, "Abba, Father!" 16 The Spirit itself bears witness with our spirit that we are children of God, 17 and if children, then heirs, heirs of God and joint heirs with Christ, if only we suffer with him so that we may also be glorified with him.

18 I consider that the sufferings of this present time are as nothing compared with the glory to be revealed for us. 19 For creation awaits with eager expectation the revelation of the children of God; 20 for creation was made subject to futility, not of its own accord but because of the one who subjected it, in hope 21 that creation itself would be set free from slavery to corruption and share in the glorious freedom of the children of God. 22 We know that all creation is groaning in labor pains even until now; 23 and not only that, but we ourselves, who have the firstfruits of the Spirit, we also groan within ourselves as we wait for adoption, the redemption of our bodies. 24 For in hope we were saved. Now hope that sees for itself is not hope. For who hopes for what one sees? 25 But if we hope for what we do not see, we wait with endurance.

26 In the same way, the Spirit too comes to the aid of our weakness; for we do not know how to pray as we ought, but the Spirit itself intercedes with inexpressible groanings. 27 And the one who searches hearts knows what is the intention of the Spirit, because it intercedes for the holy ones according to God's will.

28 We know that all things work for good for those who love God, who are called according to his purpose. 29 For those he foreknew he also predestined to be conformed to the image of his Son, so that he might be the firstborn among many brothers. 30 And those he predestined he also called; and those he called he also justified; and those he justified he also glorified.

31 What then shall we say to this? If God is for us, who can be against us? 32 He who did not spare his own Son but handed him over for us all, how will he not also give us everything else along with him? 33 Who will bring a charge against God's chosen ones? It is God who acquits us.

have their minds on the things human nature desires; those who live in the Spirit have their minds on spiritual things. 6 And human nature has nothing to look forward to but death, while the Spirit looks forward to life and peace, 7 because the outlook of disordered human nature is opposed to God, since it does not submit to God's Law, and indeed it cannot, 8 and those who live by their natural inclinations can never be pleasing to God. 9 You, however, live not by your natural inclinations, but by the Spirit, since the Spirit of God has made a home in you. Indeed, anyone who does not have the Spirit of Christ does not belong to him. 10 But when Christ is in you, the body is dead because of sin but the spirit is alive because you have been justified; 11 and if the Spirit of him who raised Jesus from the dead has made his home in you, then he who raised Christ Jesus from the dead will give life to your own mortal bodies through his Spirit living in you.

12 So then, my brothers, we have no obligation to human nature to be dominated by it. 13 If you do live in that way, you are doomed to die; but if by the Spirit you put to death the habits originating in the body, you will have life.

14 All who are guided by the Spirit of God are sons of God; 15 for what you received was not the spirit of slavery to bring you back into fear; you received the Spirit of adoption, enabling us to cry out, 'Abba, Father!' 16 The Spirit himself joins with our spirit to bear witness that we are children of God. 17 And if we are children, then we are heirs, heirs of God and joint-heirs with Christ, provided that we share his suffering, so as to share his glory.

18 In my estimation, all that we suffer in the present time is nothing in comparison with the glory which is destined to be disclosed for us, 19 for the whole creation is waiting with eagerness for the children of God to be revealed. 20 It was not for its own purposes that creation had frustration imposed on it, but for the purposes of him who imposed it— 21 with the intention that the whole creation itself might be freed from its slavery to corruption and brought into the same glorious freedom as the children of God. 22 We are well aware that the whole creation, until this time, has been groaning in labour pains. 23 And not only that: we too, who have the first-fruits of the Spirit, even we are groaning inside ourselves, waiting with eagerness for our bodies to be set free. 24 In hope, we already have salvation; in hope, not visibly present, or we should not be hoping—nobody goes on hoping for something which is already visible. 25 But having this hope for what we cannot yet see, we are able to wait for it with persevering confidence.

26 And as well as this, the Spirit too comes to help us in our weakness, for, when we do not know how to pray properly, then the Spirit personally makes our petitions for us in groans that cannot be put into words; 27 and he who can see into all hearts knows what the Spirit means because the prayers that the Spirit makes for God's holy people are always in accordance with the mind of God.

28 We are well aware that God works with those who love him, those who have been called in accordance with his purpose, and turns everything to their good. 29 He decided beforehand who were the ones destined to be moulded to the pattern of his Son, so that he should be the eldest of many brothers; 30 it was those so destined that he called; those that he called, he justified, and those that he has justified he has brought into glory.

31 After saying this, what can we add? If God is for us, who can be against us? 32 Since he did not spare his own Son, but gave him up for the sake of all of us, then can we not expect that with him he will freely give us all his gifts? 33 Who can bring any accusation against those that God has chosen? When God grants saving justice 34 who can con-

condemn? It is Christ Jesus, who died, yes, who was raised, who is at the right hand of God, who indeed intercedes for us.[r] 35 Who will separate us from the love of Christ? Will hardship, or distress, or persecution, or famine, or nakedness, or peril, or sword? 36 As it is written,

"For your sake we are being killed all day long;
  we are accounted as sheep to be slaughtered."

37 No, in all these things we are more than conquerors through him who loved us. 38 For I am convinced that neither death, nor life, nor angels, nor rulers, nor things present, nor things to come, nor powers, 39 nor height, nor depth, nor anything else in all creation, will be able to separate us from the love of God in Christ Jesus our Lord.

9 I am speaking the truth in Christ—I am not lying; my conscience confirms it by the Holy Spirit— 2 I have great sorrow and unceasing anguish in my heart. 3 For I could wish that I myself were accursed and cut off from Christ for the sake of my own people,[s] my kindred according to the flesh. 4 They are Israelites, and to them belong the adoption, the glory, the covenants, the giving of the law, the worship, and the promises; 5 to them belong the patriarchs, and from them, according to the flesh, comes the Messiah,[t] who is over all, God blessed forever.[u] Amen.

6 It is not as though the word of God had failed. For not all Israelites truly belong to Israel, 7 and not all of Abraham's children are his true descendants; but "It is through Isaac that descendants shall be named for you." 8 This means that it is not the children of the flesh who are the children of God, but the children of the promise are counted as descendants. 9 For this is what the promise said, "About this time I will return and Sarah shall have a son." 10 Nor is that all; something similar happened to Rebecca when she had conceived children by one husband, our ancestor Isaac. 11 Even before they had been born or had done anything good or bad (so that God's purpose of election might continue, 12 not by works but by his call) she was told, "The elder shall serve the younger." 13 As it is written,

"I have loved Jacob,
  but I have hated Esau."

14 What then are we to say? Is there injustice on God's part? By no means! 15 For he says to Moses,

"I will have mercy on whom I have mercy,
  and I will have compassion on whom I have
    compassion."

16 So it depends not on human will or exertion, but on God who shows mercy. 17 For the scripture says to Pharaoh, "I have raised you up for the very purpose of showing my power in you, so that my name may be proclaimed in all the earth." 18 So then he has mercy on whomever he chooses, and he hardens the heart of whomever he chooses.

19 You will say to me then, "Why then does he still find fault? For who can resist his will?" 20 But who indeed are you, a human being, to argue with God? Will what is molded say to the one who molds it, "Why have you made me like this?" 21 Has the potter no right over the clay, to make out of the same lump one object for special use and another for ordinary use? 22 What if God, desiring to show

pronounce judgement? Not Christ, who died, or rather rose again; not Christ, who is at God's right hand and pleads our cause! 35 Then what can separate us from the love of Christ? Can affliction or hardship? Can persecution, hunger, nakedness, danger, or sword? 36 'We are being done to death for your sake all day long,' as scripture says; 'we have been treated like sheep for slaughter'—37 and yet, throughout it all, overwhelming victory is ours through him who loved us. 38 For I am convinced that there is nothing in death or life, in the realm of spirits or superhuman powers, in the world as it is or the world as it shall be, in the forces of the universe, 39 in heights or depths—nothing in all creation that can separate us from the love of God in Christ Jesus our Lord.

9 I AM speaking the truth as a Christian; my conscience, enlightened by the Holy Spirit, assures me that I do not lie when I tell you 2 that there is great grief and unceasing sorrow in my heart. 3 I would even pray to be an outcast myself, cut off from Christ, if it would help my brothers, my kinsfolk by natural descent. 4 They are descendants of Israel, chosen to be God's sons; theirs is the glory of the divine presence, theirs the covenants, the law, the temple worship, and the promises. 5 The patriarchs are theirs, and from them by natural descent came the Messiah. May God, supreme above all, be blessed for ever! Amen.

6 It cannot be that God's word has proved false. Not all the offspring of Israel are truly Israel, 7 nor does being Abraham's descendants make them all his true children; but, in the words of scripture, 'It is through the line of Isaac's descendants that your name will be traced.' 8 That is to say, it is not the children of Abraham by natural descent who are children of God; it is the children born through God's promise who are reckoned as Abraham's descendants. 9 For the promise runs: 'In due season I will come, and Sarah shall have a son.'

10 And that is not all: Rebecca's children had one and the same father, our ancestor Isaac; 11 yet, even before they were born, when they as yet had done nothing, whether good or ill, in order that the purpose of God, which is a matter of his choice, might stand firm, based not on human deeds but on the call of God, 12 she was told, 'The elder shall be servant to the younger.' 13 That accords with the text of scripture, 'Jacob I loved and Esau I hated.'

14 What shall we say to that? Is God to be charged with injustice? Certainly not! 15 He says to Moses, 'I will show mercy to whom I will show mercy, and have pity on whom I will have pity.' 16 Thus it does not depend on human will or effort, but on God's mercy. 17 For in scripture Pharaoh is told, 'I have raised you up for this very purpose, to exhibit my power in my dealings with you, and to spread my fame over all the earth.' 18 Thus he not only shows mercy as he chooses, but also makes stubborn as he chooses.

19 You will say, 'Then why does God find fault, if no one can resist his will?' 20 Who do you think you are to answer God back? Can the pot say to the potter, 'Why did you make me like this?'? 21 Surely the potter can do what he likes with the clay. Is he not free to make two vessels out of the same lump, one to be treasured, the other for common use?

9:5 **Messiah**: Gk Christ. **Messiah . . . for ever:** or Messiah, who is God, supreme above all and blessed for ever; or Messiah, who is supreme above all. Blessed be God for ever!   9:7 **all . . . children:** or all children of God.

[r] Or Is it Christ Jesus . . . for us?   [s] Gk my brothers   [t] Or the Christ   [u] Or Messiah, who is God over all, blessed forever; or Messiah. May he who is God over all be blessed forever

34 Who will condemn? It is Christ [Jesus] who died, rather, was raised, who also is at the right hand of God, who indeed intercedes for us. 35 What will separate us from the love of Christ? Will anguish, or distress, or persecution, or famine, or nakedness, or peril, or the sword? 36 As it is written:

"For your sake we are being slain all the day;
    we are looked upon as sheep to be slaughtered."

37 No, in all these things we conquer overwhelmingly through him who loved us. 38 For I am convinced that neither death, nor life, nor angels, nor principalities, nor present things, nor future things, nor powers, 39 nor height, nor depth, nor any other creature will be able to separate us from the love of God in Christ Jesus our Lord.

9 I speak the truth in Christ, I do not lie; my conscience joins with the holy Spirit in bearing me witness 2 that I have great sorrow and constant anguish in my heart. 3 For I could wish that I myself were accursed and separated from Christ for the sake of my brothers, my kin according to the flesh. 4 They are Israelites; theirs the adoption, the glory, the covenants, the giving of the law, the worship, and the promises; 5 theirs the patriarchs, and from them, according to the flesh, is the Messiah. God who is over all be blessed forever. Amen.

6 But it is not that the word of God has failed. For not all who are of Israel are Israel, 7 nor are they all children of Abraham because they are his descendants; but "It is through Isaac that descendants shall bear your name." 8 This means that it is not the children of the flesh who are the children of God, but the children of the promise are counted as descendants. 9 For this is the wording of the promise, "About this time I shall return and Sarah will have a son." 10 And not only that, but also when Rebecca had conceived children by one husband, our father Isaac — 11 before they had yet been born or had done anything, good or bad, in order that God's elective plan might continue, 12 not by works but by his call — she was told, "The older shall serve the younger." 13 As it is written:

"I loved Jacob
    but hated Esau."

14 What then are we to say? Is there injustice on the part of God? Of course not! 15 For he says to Moses:

"I will show mercy to whom I will,
    I will take pity on whom I will."

16 So it depends not upon a person's will or exertion, but upon God, who shows mercy. 17 For the scripture says to Pharaoh, "This is why I have raised you up, to show my power through you that my name may be proclaimed throughout the earth." 18 Consequently, he has mercy upon whom he wills, and he hardens whom he wills.

19 You will say to me then, "Why [then] does he still find fault? For who can oppose his will?" 20 But who indeed are you, a human being, to talk back to God? Will what is made say to its maker, "Why have you created me so?" 21 Or does not the potter have a right over the clay, to make out of the same lump one vessel for a noble purpose and another for an ignoble one? 22 What if God, wishing to show his wrath

demn?[n] Are we not sure that it is Christ Jesus, who died — yes and more, who was raised from the dead and is at God's right hand — and who is adding his plea for us? 35 Can anything cut us off from the love of Christ — can hardships or distress, or persecution, or lack of food and clothing, or threats or violence; 36 as scripture says:

For your sake we are being massacred all day
    long,
treated as sheep to be slaughtered?[o]

37 No; we come through all these things triumphantly victorious, by the power of him who loved us. 38 For I am certain of this: neither death nor life, nor angels, nor principalities, nothing already in existence and nothing still to come, nor any power, 39 nor the heights nor the depths, nor any created thing whatever, will be able to come between us and the love of God, known to us in Christ Jesus our Lord.

9 [p]This is the truth and I am speaking in Christ, without pretence, as my conscience testifies for me in the Holy Spirit; 2 there is great sorrow and unremitting agony in my heart: 3 I could pray that I myself might be accursed and cut off from Christ, if this could benefit the brothers who are my own flesh and blood. 4 They are Israelites; it was they who were adopted as children, the glory was theirs and the covenants; to them were given the Law and the worship of God and the promises. 5 To them belong the fathers and out of them, so far as physical descent is concerned, came Christ who is above all, God, blessed for ever. Amen.

6 It is not that God's promise has failed. Not all born Israelites belong to Israel, 7 and not all the descendants of Abraham count as his children, for

Isaac is the one through whom your Name will be
    carried on.

8 That is, it is not by being children through physical descent that people become children of God; it is the children of the promise that are counted as the heirs. 9 The actual words of the promise were: *I shall come back to you at this season, and Sarah will have a son.* 10 Even more to the point is what was said to Rebecca when she was pregnant by our ancestor, Isaac, 11 before her children were born, so that neither had yet done anything either good or bad, in order that it should be God's choice which prevailed 12 — not human merit, but his call — she was told: *the elder one will serve the younger.* 13 Or as scripture says elsewhere: *I loved Jacob but hated Esau.*

14 What should we say, then? That God is unjust? Out of the question! 15 For speaking to Moses, he said: *I am gracious to those to whom I am gracious and I take pity on those on whom I take pity.* 16 So it is not a matter of what any person wants or what any person does, but only of God having mercy. 17 Scripture says to Pharaoh: *I raised you up for this reason,* to display my power in you and to have my name talked of throughout the world. 18 In other words, if God wants to show mercy on someone, he does so, and if he wants to harden someone's heart, he does so.

19 Then you will ask me, 'How then can he ever blame anyone, since no one can oppose his will?' 20 But you — who do you think you, a human being, are, to answer back to God? *Something that was made, can it say to its maker: why did you make me* this shape? 21 A potter surely has the right over his clay to make out of the same lump either a pot for special use or one for ordinary use.

---

n **8** Is 50:8.   o **8** Ps 44:22.   p **9** The quotations in chh. 9—11 are too frequent to be placed.

NEW REVISED STANDARD VERSION

his wrath and to make known his power, has endured with much patience the objects of wrath that are made for destruction; 23 and what if he has done so in order to make known the riches of his glory for the objects of mercy, which he has prepared beforehand for glory — 24 including us whom he has called, not from the Jews only but also from the Gentiles? 25 As indeed he says in Hosea,

"Those who were not my people I will call 'my people,'
and her who was not beloved I will call 'beloved.' "

26 "And in the very place where it was said to them, 'You are not my people,' there they shall be called children of the living God."

27 And Isaiah cries out concerning Israel, "Though the number of the children of Israel were like the sand of the sea, only a remnant of them will be saved; 28 for the Lord will execute his sentence on the earth quickly and decisively."^{v} 29 And as Isaiah predicted,

"If the Lord of hosts had not left survivors^w to us,
we would have fared like Sodom
and been made like Gomorrah."

30 What then are we to say? Gentiles, who did not strive for righteousness, have attained it, that is, righteousness through faith; 31 but Israel, who did strive for the righteousness that is based on the law, did not succeed in fulfilling that law. 32 Why not? Because they did not strive for it on the basis of faith, but as if it were based on works. They have stumbled over the stumbling stone, 33 as it is written,

"See, I am laying in Zion a stone that will make people stumble, a rock that will make them fall,
and whoever believes in him^x will not be put to shame."

10 Brothers and sisters,^{y} my heart's desire and prayer to God for them is that they may be saved. 2 I can testify that they have a zeal for God, but it is not enlightened. 3 For, being ignorant of the righteousness that comes from God, and seeking to establish their own, they have not submitted to God's righteousness. 4 For Christ is the end of the law so that there may be righteousness for everyone who believes.

5 Moses writes concerning the righteousness that comes from the law, that "the person who does these things will live by them." 6 But the righteousness that comes from faith says, "Do not say in your heart, 'Who will ascend into heaven?' " (that is, to bring Christ down) 7 "or 'Who will descend into the abyss?' " (that is, to bring Christ up from the dead). 8 But what does it say?

"The word is near you,
on your lips and in your heart"

(that is, the word of faith that we proclaim); 9 because^z if you confess with your lips that Jesus is Lord and believe in your heart that God raised him from the dead, you will be saved. 10 For one believes with the heart and so is justified, and one confesses with the mouth and so is saved. 11 The scripture says, "No one who believes in him will be put to shame." 12 For there is no distinction between Jew and Greek; the same Lord is Lord of all and is generous to all who call on him. 13 For, "Everyone who calls on the name of the Lord shall be saved."

REVISED ENGLISH BIBLE

22 But if it is indeed God's purpose to display his retribution and to make his power known, can it be that he has with great patience tolerated vessels that were objects of retribution due for destruction, 23 precisely in order to make known the full wealth of his glory on vessels that were objects of mercy, prepared from the first for glory?

24 We are those objects of mercy, whom he has called from among Jews and Gentiles alike, 25 as he says in Hosea: 'Those who were not my people I will call my people, and the unloved I will call beloved. 26 In the very place where they were told, "You are no people of mine," they shall be called sons of the living God.' 27 But about Israel Isaiah makes this proclamation: 'Though the Israelites be countless as the sands of the sea, only a remnant shall be saved, 28 for the Lord's sentence on the land will be summary and final'; 29 as also he said previously, 'If the Lord of Hosts had not left us descendants, we should have become like Sodom, and no better than Gomorrah.'

30 Then what are we to say? That Gentiles, who made no effort after righteousness, nevertheless achieved it, a righteousness based on faith; 31 whereas Israel made great efforts after a law of righteousness, but never attained to it. 32 Why was this? Because their efforts were not based on faith but, mistakenly, on deeds. They tripped over the 'stone' 33 mentioned in scripture: 'Here I lay in Zion a stone to trip over, a rock to stumble against; but he who has faith in it will not be put to shame.'

10 Friends, my heart's desire and my prayer to God is for their salvation. 2 To their zeal for God I can testify; but it is an ill-informed zeal. 3 For they ignore God's way of righteousness, and try to set up their own, and therefore they have not submitted themselves to God's righteousness; 4 for Christ is the end of the law and brings righteousness for everyone who has faith.

5 Of righteousness attained through the law Moses writes, 'Anyone who keeps it shall have life by it.' 6 But the righteousness that comes by faith says, 'Do not say to yourself, "Who can go up to heaven?" ' (that is, to bring Christ down) 7 'or, "Who can go down to the abyss?" ' (to bring Christ up from the dead). 8 And what does it say next? 'The word is near you: it is on your lips and in your heart'; and that means the word of faith which we proclaim. 9 If the confession 'Jesus is Lord' is on your lips, and the faith that God raised him from the dead is in your heart, you will find salvation. 10 For faith in the heart leads to righteousness, and confession on the lips leads to salvation.

11 Scripture says, 'No one who has faith in him will be put to shame': 12 there is no distinction between Jew and Greek, because the same Lord is Lord of all, and has riches enough for all who call on him. 13 For 'Everyone who calls on the name of the Lord will be saved.' 14 But how could

---

^{v} Other ancient authorities read *for he will finish his work and cut it short in righteousness, because the Lord will make the sentence shortened on the earth* ^{w} Or *descendants*; Gk *seed* ^{x} Or *trusts in it* ^{y} Gk *Brothers* ^{z} Or *namely, that*

NEW AMERICAN BIBLE

and make known his power, has endured with much patience the vessels of wrath made for destruction? 23 This was to make known the riches of his glory to the vessels of mercy, which he has prepared previously for glory, 24 namely, us whom he has called, not only from the Jews but also from the Gentiles.

25 As indeed he says in Hosea:
"Those who were not my people I will call
'my people,'
and her who was not beloved I will
call 'beloved.'
26 And in the very place where it was said to them,
'You are not my people,'
there they shall be called children of the
living God."

27 And Isaiah cries out concerning Israel, "Though the number of the Israelites were like the sand of the sea, only a remnant will be saved; 28 for decisively and quickly will the Lord execute sentence upon the earth." 29 And as Isaiah predicted:
"Unless the Lord of hosts had left us descendants,
we would have become like Sodom
and have been made like Gomorrah."

30 What then shall we say? That Gentiles, who did not pursue righteousness, have achieved it, that is, righteousness that comes from faith; 31 but that Israel, who pursued the law of righteousness, did not attain to that law? 32 Why not? Because they did it not by faith, but as if it could be done by works. They stumbled over the stone that causes stumbling, 33 as it is written:
"Behold, I am laying a stone in Zion
that will make people stumble
and a rock that will make them fall,
and whoever believes in him shall not be put
to shame."

10 Brothers, my heart's desire and prayer to God on their behalf is for salvation. 2 I testify with regard to them that they have zeal for God, but it is not discerning. 3 For, in their unawareness of the righteousness that comes from God and their attempt to establish their own [righteousness], they did not submit to the righteousness of God. 4 For Christ is the end of the law for the justification of everyone who has faith.

5 Moses writes about the righteousness that comes from [the] law, "The one who does these things will live by them." 6 But the righteousness that comes from faith says, "Do not say in your heart, 'Who will go up into heaven?' (that is, to bring Christ down) 7 or 'Who will go down into the abyss?' (that is, to bring Christ up from the dead)." 8 But what does it say?
"The word is near you,
in your mouth and in your heart"
(that is, the word of faith that we preach), 9 for, if you confess with your mouth that Jesus is Lord and believe in your heart that God raised him from the dead, you will be saved. 10 For one believes with the heart and so is justified, and one confesses with the mouth and so is saved. 11 For the scripture says, "No one who believes in him will be put to shame." 12 For there is no distinction between Jew and Greek; the same Lord is Lord of all, enriching all who call upon him. 13 For "everyone who calls on the name of the Lord will be saved."

NEW JERUSALEM BIBLE

22 But suppose that God, although all the time he wanted to reveal his retribution and demonstrate his power, has with great patience gone on putting up with those who are the instruments of his retribution and designed to be destroyed; 23 so that he may make known the glorious riches ready for the people who are the instruments of his faithful love and were long ago prepared for that glory. 24 We are that people, called by him not only out of the Jews but out of the gentiles too.

25 Just as he says in the book of Hosea: *I shall tell those who were not my people, 'You are my people,' and I shall take pity on those on whom I had no pity.* 26 *And in the very place where they were told, 'You are not my people,' they will be told that they are 'children of the living God'.* 27 And about Israel, this is what Isaiah cried out: *Though the people of Israel are like the sand of the sea, only a remnant will be saved;* 28 *for without hesitation or delay the Lord will execute his sentence on the earth.* 29 As Isaiah foretold: *Had the Lord Sabaoth not left us a few survivors, we should be like Sodom, we should be the same as Gomorrah.*

30 What should we say, then? That the gentiles, although they were not looking for saving justice, found it, and this was the saving justice that comes of faith; 31 while Israel, looking for saving justice by law-keeping, did not succeed in fulfilling the Law. 32 And why? Because they were trying to find it in actions and not in faith, and so they stumbled over the *stumbling-stone* — 33 as it says in scripture: *Now I am laying in Zion a stumbling-stone, a rock to trip people up; but he who relies on this will not be brought to disgrace.*

10 Brothers, my dearest wish and my prayer to God is for them, that they may be saved. 2 I readily testify to their fervour for God, but it is misguided. 3 Not recognising God's saving justice they have tried to establish their own, instead of submitting to the saving justice of God. 4 But the Law has found its fulfilment in Christ so that all who have faith will be justified.

5 Moses writes of the saving justice that comes by the Law and says that *whoever complies with it will find life in it.* 6 But the saving justice of faith says this: *Do not think in your heart, 'Who will go up to heaven?'* — 7 that is to bring Christ down; or *'Who will go down to the depths?'* — that is to bring Christ back from the dead. 8 What does it say, then? *The word is very near to you; it is in your mouth and in your heart,* that is, the word of faith, the faith which we preach, 9 that if you declare with your mouth that Jesus is Lord, and if you believe with your heart that God raised him from the dead, then you will be saved. 10 It is by believing with the heart that you are justified, and by making the declaration with your lips that you are saved. 11 When scripture says: *No one who relies on this will be brought to disgrace,* 12 it makes no distinction between Jew and Greek: the same Lord is the Lord of all, and his generosity is offered to all who appeal to him, 13 for *all who call on the name of the Lord will be saved.*

14 But how are they to call on one in whom they have not believed? And how are they to believe in one of whom they have never heard? And how are they to hear without someone to proclaim him? 15 And how are they to proclaim him unless they are sent? As it is written, "How beautiful are the feet of those who bring good news!" 16 But not all have obeyed the good news; *a* for Isaiah says, "Lord, who has believed our message?" 17 So faith comes from what is heard, and what is heard comes through the word of Christ. *b*

18 But I ask, have they not heard? Indeed they have; for
"Their voice has gone out to all the earth,
 and their words to the ends of the world."
19 Again I ask, did Israel not understand? First Moses says,
"I will make you jealous of those who are not a
 nation;
 with a foolish nation I will make you angry."
20 Then Isaiah is so bold as to say,
"I have been found by those who did not seek
 me;
 I have shown myself to those who did not ask
 for me."
21 But of Israel he says, "All day long I have held out my hands to a disobedient and contrary people."

11 I ask, then, has God rejected his people? By no means! I myself am an Israelite, a descendant of Abraham, a member of the tribe of Benjamin. 2 God has not rejected his people whom he foreknew. Do you not know what the scripture says of Elijah, how he pleads with God against Israel? 3 "Lord, they have killed your prophets, they have demolished your altars; I alone am left, and they are seeking my life." 4 But what is the divine reply to him? "I have kept for myself seven thousand who have not bowed the knee to Baal." 5 So too at the present time there is a remnant, chosen by grace. 6 But if it is by grace, it is no longer on the basis of works, otherwise grace would no longer be grace. *c*

7 What then? Israel failed to obtain what it was seeking. The elect obtained it, but the rest were hardened, 8 as it is written,
"God gave them a sluggish spirit,
 eyes that would not see
 and ears that would not hear,
 down to this very day."
9 And David says,
"Let their table become a snare and a trap,
 a stumbling block and a retribution for them;
 10 let their eyes be darkened so that they cannot see,
 and keep their backs forever bent."

11 So I ask, have they stumbled so as to fall? By no means! But through their stumbling *d* salvation has come to the Gentiles, so as to make Israel *e* jealous. 12 Now if their stumbling *d* means riches for the world, and if their defeat means riches for Gentiles, how much more will their full inclusion mean!

13 Now I am speaking to you Gentiles. Inasmuch then as I am an apostle to the Gentiles, I glorify my ministry 14 in order to make my own people *f* jealous, and thus save some of them. 15 For if their rejection is the reconciliation of the world, what will their acceptance be but life from the dead! 16 If the part of the dough offered as first fruits is holy, then the whole batch is holy; and if the root is holy, then the branches also are holy.

they call on him without having faith in him? And how could they have faith without having heard of him? And how could they hear without someone to spread the news? 15 And how could anyone spread the news without being sent? As scripture says, 'How welcome are the feet of the messengers of good news!' 16 It is true that not all have responded to the good news; as Isaiah says, 'Lord, who believed when they heard us?' 17 So then faith does come from hearing, and hearing through the word of Christ.

18 I ask, then: Can it be that they never heard? Of course they did: 'Their voice has sounded all over the world, and their words to the ends of the earth.' 19 I ask again: Can it be that Israel never understood? Listen first to Moses: 'I will use a nation that is no nation to stir you to envy, and a foolish nation to rouse your anger.' 20 Isaiah is still more daring: 'I was found,' he says, 'by those who were not looking for me; I revealed myself to those who never asked about me'; 21 while of Israel he says, 'All day long I have stretched out my hands to a disobedient and defiant people.'

11 I ASK, then: Has God rejected his people? Of course not! I am an Israelite myself, of the stock of Abraham, of the tribe of Benjamin. 2 God has not rejected the people he acknowledged of old as his own. Surely you know what scripture says in the story of Elijah—how he pleads with God against Israel: 3 'Lord, they have killed your prophets, they have torn down your altars, and I alone am left, and they are seeking my life.' 4 But what was the divine word to him? 'I have left myself seven thousand men who have not knelt to Baal.' 5 In just the same way at the present time a 'remnant' has come into being, chosen by the grace of God. 6 But if it is by grace, then it does not rest on deeds, or grace would cease to be grace.

7 What follows? What Israel sought, Israel has not attained, but the chosen few have attained it. The rest were hardened, 8 as it stands written: 'God has dulled their senses; he has given them blind eyes and deaf ears, and so it is to this day.' 9 Similarly David says:
May their table be a snare and a trap,
 their downfall and their retribution!
10 May their eyes become darkened and blind!
 Bow down their backs unceasingly!

11 I ask, then: When they stumbled, was their fall final? Far from it! Through a false step on their part salvation has come to the Gentiles, and this in turn will stir them to envy. 12 If their false step means the enrichment of the world, if their falling short means the enrichment of the Gentiles, how much more will their coming to full strength mean!

13 It is to you Gentiles that I am speaking. As an apostle to the Gentiles, I make much of that ministry, 14 yet always in the hope of stirring those of my own race to envy, and so saving some of them. 15 For if their rejection has meant the reconciliation of the world, what will their acceptance mean? Nothing less than life from the dead! 16 If the first loaf is holy, so is the whole batch. If the root is holy, so are the branches. 17 But if some of the branches have been

---

a Or *gospel*   *b* Or *about Christ*; other ancient authorities read *of God*
c Other ancient authorities add *But if it is by works, it is no longer on the basis of grace, otherwise work would no longer be work*
d Gk *transgression*   *e* Gk *them*   *f* Gk *my flesh*

NEW AMERICAN BIBLE

NEW JERUSALEM BIBLE

14 But how can they call on him in whom they have not believed? And how can they believe in him of whom they have not heard? And how can they hear without someone to preach? 15 And how can people preach unless they are sent? As it is written, "How beautiful are the feet of those who bring [the] good news!" 16 But not everyone has heeded the good news; for Isaiah says, "Lord, who has believed what was heard from us?" 17 Thus faith comes from what is heard, and what is heard comes through the word of Christ. 18 But I ask, did they not hear? Certainly they did; for

"Their voice has gone forth to all the earth,
    and their words to the ends of the world."

19 But I ask, did not Israel understand? First Moses says:

"I will make you jealous of those who are not
    a nation;
with a senseless nation I will make you angry."

20 Then Isaiah speaks boldly and says:

"I was found [by] those who were not seeking me;
    I revealed myself to those who were not asking
        for me."

21 But regarding Israel he says, "All day long I stretched out my hands to a disobedient and contentious people."

11 I ask, then, has God rejected his people? Of course not! For I too am an Israelite, a descendant of Abraham, of the tribe of Benjamin. 2 God has not rejected his people whom he foreknew. Do you not know what the scripture says about Elijah, how he pleads with God against Israel? 3 "Lord, they have killed your prophets, they have torn down your altars, and I alone am left, and they are seeking my life." 4 But what is God's response to him? "I have left for myself seven thousand men who have not knelt to Baal." 5 So also at the present time there is a remnant, chosen by grace. 6 But if by grace, it is no longer because of works; otherwise grace would no longer be grace. 7 What then? What Israel was seeking it did not attain, but the elect attained it; the rest were hardened, 8 as it is written:

"God gave them a spirit of deep sleep,
    eyes that should not see
    and ears that should not hear,
down to this very day."

9 And David says:

"Let their table become a snare and a trap,
    a stumbling block and a retribution for them;
10 let their eyes grow dim so that they may not see,
    and keep their backs bent forever."

11 Hence I ask, did they stumble so as to fall? Of course not! But through their transgression salvation has come to the Gentiles, so as to make them jealous. 12 Now if their transgression is enrichment for the world, and if their diminished number is enrichment for the Gentiles, how much more their full number.

13 Now I am speaking to you Gentiles. Inasmuch then as I am the apostle to the Gentiles, I glory in my ministry 14 in order to make my race jealous and thus save some of them. 15 For if their rejection is the reconciliation of the world, what will their acceptance be but life from the dead? 16 If the firstfruits are holy, so is the whole batch of dough; and if the root is holy, so are the branches.

14 How then are they to call on him if they have not come to believe in him? And how can they believe in him if they have never heard of him? And how will they hear of him unless there is a preacher for them? 15 And how will there be preachers if they are not sent? As scripture says: *How beautiful are the feet of the messenger of good news.*

16 But in fact they have not all responded to the good news. As Isaiah says: *Lord, who has given credence to what they have heard from us?* 17 But it is in that way faith comes, from hearing, and that means hearing the word of Christ.

18 Well then, I say, is it possible that they have not heard? Indeed they have: *in the entire earth their voice stands out, their message reaches the whole world.* 19 Well, another question, then: is it possible that Israel did not understand? In the first place Moses said: *I shall rouse you to jealousy with a non-people, I shall exasperate you with a stupid nation.* 20 And Isaiah is even bold enough to say: *I have let myself be found by those who did not seek me; I have let myself be seen by those who did not consult me;* 21 and referring to Israel, he says: *All day long I have been stretching out my hands to a disobedient and rebellious people.*

11 What I am saying is this: is it possible that *God abandoned his people*? Out of the question! I too am an Israelite, descended from Abraham, of the tribe of Benjamin. 2 God never abandoned his own people to whom, ages ago, he had given recognition. Do you not remember what scripture says about Elijah and how he made a complaint to God against Israel: 3 *Lord, they have put your prophets to the sword, torn down your altars. I am the only one left, and now they want to kill me?* 4 And what was the prophetic answer given? *I have spared* for myself *seven thousand men that have not bent the knee to Baal.* 5 In the same way, then, in our own time, there is a remnant, set aside by grace. 6 And since it is by grace, it cannot now be by good actions, or grace would not be grace at all!

7 What follows? Israel failed to find what it was seeking; only those who were chosen found it and the rest had their minds hardened; 8 just as it says in scripture: *God has infused them with a spirit of lethargy; until today they have not eyes to see or ears to hear.* 9 David too says: *May their own table prove a trap for them, a pitfall and a snare; let that be their retribution.* 10 *May their eyes grow so dim they cannot see, and their backs be bent for ever.*

11 What I am saying is this: Was this stumbling to lead to their final downfall? Out of the question! On the contrary, their failure has brought salvation for the gentiles, in order to stir them to envy. 12 And if their fall has proved a great gain to the world, and their loss has proved a great gain to the gentiles — how much greater a gain will come when all is restored to them!

13 Let me say then to you gentiles that, as far as I am an apostle to the gentiles, I take pride in this work of service; 14 and I want it to be the means of rousing to envy the people who are my own blood-relations and so of saving some of them. 15 Since their rejection meant the reconciliation of the world, do you know what their re-acceptance will mean? Nothing less than life from the dead!

16 When the first-fruits are made holy, so is the whole batch; and if the root is holy, so are the branches. 17 Now

NEW REVISED STANDARD VERSION

17 But if some of the branches were broken off, and you, a wild olive shoot, were grafted in their place to share the rich root*g* of the olive tree, 18 do not boast over the branches. If you do boast, remember that it is not you that support the root, but the root that supports you. 19 You will say, "Branches were broken off so that I might be grafted in." 20 That is true. They were broken off because of their unbelief, but you stand only through faith. So do not become proud, but stand in awe. 21 For if God did not spare the natural branches, perhaps he will not spare you.*h* 22 Note then the kindness and the severity of God: severity toward those who have fallen, but God's kindness toward you, provided you continue in his kindness; otherwise you also will be cut off. 23 And even those of Israel,*i* if they do not persist in unbelief, will be grafted in, for God has the power to graft them in again. 24 For if you have been cut from what is by nature a wild olive tree and grafted, contrary to nature, into a cultivated olive tree, how much more will these natural branches be grafted back into their own olive tree.

25 So that you may not claim to be wiser than you are, brothers and sisters,*j* I want you to understand this mystery: a hardening has come upon part of Israel, until the full number of the Gentiles has come in. 26 And so all Israel will be saved; as it is written,

"Out of Zion will come the Deliverer;
    he will banish ungodliness from Jacob."
27 "And this is my covenant with them,
    when I take away their sins."

28 As regards the gospel they are enemies of God*k* for your sake; but as regards election they are beloved, for the sake of their ancestors; 29 for the gifts and the calling of God are irrevocable. 30 Just as you were once disobedient to God but have now received mercy because of their disobedience, 31 so they have now been disobedient in order that, by the mercy shown to you, they too may now*l* receive mercy. 32 For God has imprisoned all in disobedience so that he may be merciful to all.

33 O the depth of the riches and wisdom and knowledge of God! How unsearchable are his judgments and how inscrutable his ways!
34   "For who has known the mind of the Lord?
        Or who has been his counselor?"
35   "Or who has given a gift to him,
        to receive a gift in return?"
36 For from him and through him and to him are all things. To him be the glory forever. Amen.

12 I appeal to you therefore, brothers and sisters,*j* by the mercies of God, to present your bodies as a living sacrifice, holy and acceptable to God, which is your spiritual*m* worship. 2 Do not be conformed to this world,*n* but be transformed by the renewing of your minds, so that you may discern what is the will of God — what is good and acceptable and perfect.*o*

3 For by the grace given to me I say to everyone among you not to think of yourself more highly than you ought to think, but to think with sober judgment, each according to the measure of faith that God has assigned. 4 For as in one body we have many members, and not all the members have

REVISED ENGLISH BIBLE

lopped off, and you, a wild olive, have been grafted in among them, and have come to share the same root and sap as the olive, 18 do not make yourself superior to the branches. If you do, remember that you do not sustain the root: the root sustains you.

19 You will say, 'Branches were lopped off so that I might be grafted in.' 20 Very well: they were lopped off for lack of faith, and by faith you hold your place. Put away your pride, and be on your guard; 21 for if God did not spare the natural branches, no more will he spare you. 22 Observe the kindness and the severity of God — severity to those who fell away, divine kindness to you provided that you remain within its scope; otherwise you too will be cut off, 23 whereas they, if they do not continue faithless, will be grafted in, since it is in God's power to graft them in again. 24 For if you were cut from your native wild olive and against nature grafted into the cultivated olive, how much more readily will they, the natural olive branches, be grafted into their native stock!

25 There is a divine secret here, my friends, which I want to share with you, to keep you from thinking yourselves wise: this partial hardening has come on Israel only until the Gentiles have been admitted in full strength; 26 once that has happened, the whole of Israel will be saved, in accordance with scripture:

From Zion shall come the Deliverer;
    he shall remove wickedness from Jacob.
27 And this is the covenant I will grant them,
    when I take away their sins.

28 Judged by their response to the gospel, they are God's enemies for your sake; but judged by his choice, they are dear to him for the sake of the patriarchs; 29 for the gracious gifts of God and his calling are irrevocable. 30 Just as formerly you were disobedient to God, but now have received mercy because of their disobedience, 31 so now, because of the mercy shown to you, they have proved disobedient, but only in order that they too may receive mercy. 32 For in shutting all mankind in the prison of their disobedience, God's purpose was to show mercy to all mankind.

33 How deep are the wealth
    and the wisdom and the knowledge of God!
    How inscrutable his judgements,
    how unsearchable his ways!
34 'Who knows the mind of the Lord?
    Who has been his counsellor?'
35 'Who has made a gift to him first,
    and earned a gift in return?'
36 From him and through him and for him all things exist —
    to him be glory for ever! Amen.

12 THEREFORE, my friends, I implore you by God's mercy to offer your very selves to him: a living sacrifice, dedicated and fit for his acceptance, the worship offered by mind and heart. 2 Conform no longer to the pattern of this present world, but be transformed by the renewal of your minds. Then you will be able to discern the will of God, and to know what is good, acceptable, and perfect.

3 By authority of the grace God has given me I say to everyone among you: do not think too highly of yourself, but form a sober estimate based on the measure of faith that God has dealt to each of you. 4 For just as in a single human body there are many limbs and organs, all with different

---

g Other ancient authorities read *the richness*   *h* Other ancient authorities read *neither will he spare you*   *i* Gk lacks *of Israel*   *j* Gk *brothers*   *k* Gk lacks *of God*   *l* Other ancient authorities lack *now*   *m* Or *reasonable*   *n* Gk *age*   *o* Or *what is the good and acceptable and perfect will of God*

NEW AMERICAN BIBLE

NEW JERUSALEM BIBLE

17 But if some of the branches were broken off, and you, a wild olive shoot, were grafted in their place and have come to share in the rich root of the olive tree, 18 do not boast against the branches. If you do boast, consider that you do not support the root; the root supports you. 19 Indeed you will say, "Branches were broken off so that I might be grafted in." 20 That is so. They were broken off because of unbelief, but you are there because of faith. So do not become haughty, but stand in awe. 21 For if God did not spare the natural branches, [perhaps] he will not spare you either. 22 See, then, the kindness and severity of God: severity toward those who fell, but God's kindness to you, provided you remain in his kindness; otherwise you too will be cut off. 23 And they also, if they do not remain in unbelief, will be grafted in, for God is able to graft them in again. 24 For if you were cut from what is by nature a wild olive tree, and grafted, contrary to nature, into a cultivated one, how much more will they who belong to it by nature be grafted back into their own olive tree.

25 I do not want you to be unaware of this mystery, brothers, so that you will not become wise [in] your own estimation: a hardening has come upon Israel in part, until the full number of the Gentiles comes in, 26 and thus all Israel will be saved, as it is written:

"The deliverer will come out of Zion,
  he will turn away godlessness from Jacob;
27 and this is my covenant with them
  when I take away their sins."

28 In respect to the gospel, they are enemies on your account; but in respect to election, they are beloved because of the patriarchs. 29 For the gifts and the call of God are irrevocable. 30 Just as you once disobeyed God but have now received mercy because of their disobedience, 31 so they have now disobeyed in order that, by virtue of the mercy shown to you, they too may [now] receive mercy. 32 For God delivered all to disobedience, that he might have mercy upon all.

33 Oh, the depth of the riches and wisdom and knowledge of God! How inscrutable are his judgments and how unsearchable his ways!

34 "For who has known the mind of the Lord
  or who has been his counselor?"
35 "Or who has given him anything
  that he may be repaid?"

36 For from him and through him and for him are all things. To him be glory forever. Amen.

12 I urge you therefore, brothers, by the mercies of God, to offer your bodies as a living sacrifice, holy and pleasing to God, your spiritual worship. 2 Do not conform yourself to this age but be transformed by the renewal of your mind, that you may discern what is the will of God, what is good and pleasing and perfect.

3 For by the grace given to me I tell everyone among you not to think of himself more highly than one ought to think, but to think soberly, each according to the measure of faith that God has apportioned. 4 For as in one body we have many parts, and all the parts do not have the same function,

suppose that some branches were broken off, and you are wild olive, grafted among the rest to share with the others the rich sap of the olive tree; 18 then it is not for you to consider yourself superior to the other branches; and if you start feeling proud, think: it is not you that sustain the root, but the root that sustains you. 19 You will say, 'Branches were broken off on purpose for me to be grafted in.' True; 20 they through their unbelief were broken off, and you are established through your faith. So it is not pride that you should have, but fear: 21 if God did not spare the natural branches, he might not spare you either. 22 Remember God's severity as well as his goodness: his severity to those who fell, and his goodness to you as long as you persevere in it; if not, you too will be cut off. 23 And they, if they do not persevere in their unbelief, will be grafted in; for it is within the power of God to graft them back again. 24 After all, if you, cut off from what was by nature a wild olive, could then be grafted unnaturally on to a cultivated olive, how much easier will it be for them, the branches that naturally belong there, to be grafted on to the olive tree which is their own.

25 I want you to be quite certain, brothers, of this mystery, to save you from *congratulating yourselves on your own good sense*: part of Israel had its mind hardened, but only until the gentiles have wholly come in; 26 and this is how all Israel will be saved. As scripture says:

From Zion will come the Redeemer,
  he will remove godlessness from Jacob.
27 *And this will be my covenant with them,*
  when I take their sins away.

28 As regards the gospel, they are enemies, but for your sake; but as regards those who are God's choice, they are still well loved for the sake of their ancestors. 29 There is no change of mind on God's part about the gifts he has made or of his choice.

30 Just as you were in the past disobedient to God but now you have been shown mercy, through their disobedience; 31 so in the same way they are disobedient now, so that through the mercy shown to you they too will receive mercy. 32 God has imprisoned all human beings in their own disobedience only to show mercy to them all.

33 How rich and deep are the wisdom and the knowledge of God! We cannot reach to the root of his decisions or his ways. 34 *Who has ever known the mind of the Lord? Who has ever been his adviser?* 35 *Who has given anything to him, so that his presents come only as a debt returned?* 36 Everything there is comes from him and is caused by him and exists for him. To him be glory for ever! Amen.

12 I urge you, then, brothers, remembering the mercies of God, to offer your bodies as a living sacrifice, dedicated and acceptable to God; that is the kind of worship for you, as sensible people. 2 Do not model your behaviour on the contemporary world, but let the renewing of your minds transform you, so that you may discern for yourselves what is the will of God — what is good and acceptable and mature.

3 And through the grace that I have been given, I say this to every one of you: never pride yourself on being better than you really are, but think of yourself dispassionately, recognising that God has given to each one his measure of faith. 4 Just as each of us has various parts in one body, and the parts do not all have the same function: 5 in the same

NEW REVISED STANDARD VERSION

the same function, 5 so we, who are many, are one body in Christ, and individually we are members one of another. 6 We have gifts that differ according to the grace given to us: prophecy, in proportion to faith; 7 ministry, in ministering; the teacher, in teaching; 8 the exhorter, in exhortation; the giver, in generosity; the leader, in diligence; the compassionate, in cheerfulness.

9 Let love be genuine; hate what is evil, hold fast to what is good; 10 love one another with mutual affection; outdo one another in showing honor. 11 Do not lag in zeal, be ardent in spirit, serve the Lord.ᵖ 12 Rejoice in hope, be patient in suffering, persevere in prayer. 13 Contribute to the needs of the saints; extend hospitality to strangers.

14 Bless those who persecute you; bless and do not curse them. 15 Rejoice with those who rejoice, weep with those who weep. 16 Live in harmony with one another; do not be haughty, but associate with the lowly; q do not claim to be wiser than you are. 17 Do not repay anyone evil for evil, but take thought for what is noble in the sight of all. 18 If it is possible, so far as it depends on you, live peaceably with all. 19 Beloved, never avenge yourselves, but leave room for the wrath of God;ʳ for it is written, "Vengeance is mine, I will repay, says the Lord." 20 No, "if your enemies are hungry, feed them; if they are thirsty, give them something to drink; for by doing this you will heap burning coals on their heads." 21 Do not be overcome by evil, but overcome evil with good.

13 Let every person be subject to the governing authorities; for there is no authority except from God, and those authorities that exist have been instituted by God. 2 Therefore whoever resists authority resists what God has appointed, and those who resist will incur judgment. 3 For rulers are not a terror to good conduct, but to bad. Do you wish to have no fear of the authority? Then do what is good, and you will receive its approval; 4 for it is God's servant for your good. But if you do what is wrong, you should be afraid, for the authorityˢ does not bear the sword in vain! It is the servant of God to execute wrath on the wrongdoer. 5 Therefore one must be subject, not only because of wrath but also because of conscience. 6 For the same reason you also pay taxes, for the authorities are God's servants, busy with this very thing. 7 Pay to all what is due them — taxes to whom taxes are due, revenue to whom revenue is due, respect to whom respect is due, honor to whom honor is due.

8 Owe no one anything, except to love one another; for the one who loves another has fulfilled the law. 9 The commandments, "You shall not commit adultery; You shall not murder; You shall not steal; You shall not covet"; and any other commandment, are summed up in this word, "Love your neighbor as yourself." 10 Love does no wrong to a neighbor; therefore, love is the fulfilling of the law.

11 Besides this, you know what time it is, how it is now the moment for you to wake from sleep. For salvation is nearer to us now than when we became believers; 12 the

REVISED ENGLISH BIBLE

functions, 5 so we who are united with Christ, though many, form one body, and belong to one another as its limbs and organs.

6 Let us use the different gifts allotted to each of us by God's grace: the gift of inspired utterance, for example, let us use in proportion to our faith; 7 the gift of administration to administer, the gift of teaching to teach, 8 the gift of counselling to counsel. If you give to charity, give without grudging; if you are a leader, lead with enthusiasm; if you help others in distress, do it cheerfully.

9 Love in all sincerity, loathing evil and holding fast to the good. 10 Let love of the Christian community show itself in mutual affection. Esteem others more highly than yourself.

11 With unflagging zeal, aglow with the Spirit, serve the Lord. 12 Let hope keep you joyful; in trouble stand firm; persist in prayer; 13 contribute to the needs of God's people, and practise hospitality. 14 Call down blessings on your persecutors — blessings, not curses. 15 Rejoice with those who rejoice, weep with those who weep. 16 Live in agreement with one another. Do not be proud, but be ready to mix with humble people. Do not keep thinking how wise you are.

17 Never pay back evil for evil. Let your aims be such as all count honourable. 18 If possible, so far as it lies with you, live at peace with all. 19 My dear friends, do not seek revenge, but leave a place for divine retribution; for there is a text which reads, 'Vengeance is mine, says the Lord, I will repay.' 20 But there is another text: 'If your enemy is hungry, feed him; if he is thirsty, give him a drink; by doing this you will heap live coals on his head.' 21 Do not let evil conquer you, but use good to conquer evil.

13 Every person must submit to the authorities in power, for all authority comes from God, and the existing authorities are instituted by him. 2 It follows that anyone who rebels against authority is resisting a divine institution, and those who resist have themselves to thank for the punishment they will receive. 3 Governments hold no terrors for the law-abiding but only for the criminal. You wish to have no fear of the authorities? Then continue to do right and you will have their approval, 4 for they are God's agents working for your good. But if you are doing wrong, then you will have cause to fear them; it is not for nothing that they hold the power of the sword, for they are God's agents of punishment bringing retribution on the offender. 5 That is why you are obliged to submit. It is an obligation imposed not merely by fear of retribution but by conscience. 6 That is also why you pay taxes. The authorities are in God's service and it is to this they devote their energies.

7 Discharge your obligations to everyone; pay tax and levy, reverence and respect, to those to whom they are due. 8 Leave no debt outstanding, but remember the debt of love you owe one another. He who loves his neighbour has met every requirement of the law. 9 The commandments, 'You shall not commit adultery, you shall not commit murder, you shall not steal, you shall not covet,' and any other commandment there may be, are all summed up in the one rule, 'Love your neighbour as yourself.' 10 Love cannot wrong a neighbour; therefore love is the fulfilment of the law.

11 Always remember that this is the hour of crisis: it is high time for you to wake out of sleep, for deliverance is nearer to us now than it was when we first believed. 12 It is

---

ᵖ Other ancient authorities read *serve the opportune time*   q Or give *yourselves to humble tasks*   ʳ Gk *the wrath*   ˢ Gk *it*

13:10 **the fulfilment of the law:** *or* the whole content of the law.

5 so we, though many, are one body in Christ and individually parts of one another. 6 Since we have gifts that differ according to the grace given to us, let us exercise them: if prophecy, in proportion to the faith; 7 if ministry, in ministering; if one is a teacher, in teaching; 8 if one exhorts, in exhortation; if one contributes, in generosity; if one is over others, with diligence; if one does acts of mercy, with cheerfulness.

9 Let love be sincere; hate what is evil, hold on to what is good; 10 love one another with mutual affection; anticipate one another in showing honor. 11 Do not grow slack in zeal, be fervent in spirit, serve the Lord. 12 Rejoice in hope, endure in affliction, persevere in prayer. 13 Contribute to the needs of the holy ones, exercise hospitality. 14 Bless those who persecute [you], bless and do not curse them. 15 Rejoice with those who rejoice, weep with those who weep. 16 Have the same regard for one another; do not be haughty but associate with the lowly; do not be wise in your own estimation. 17 Do not repay anyone evil for evil; be concerned for what is noble in the sight of all. 18 If possible, on your part, live at peace with all. 19 Beloved, do not look for revenge but leave room for the wrath; for it is written, "Vengeance is mine, I will repay, says the Lord." 20 Rather, "if your enemy is hungry, feed him; if he is thirsty, give him something to drink; for by so doing you will heap burning coals upon his head." 21 Do not be conquered by evil but conquer evil with good.

13 Let every person be subordinate to the higher authorities, for there is no authority except from God, and those that exist have been established by God. 2 Therefore, whoever resists authority opposes what God has appointed, and those who oppose it will bring judgment upon themselves. 3 For rulers are not a cause of fear to good conduct, but to evil. Do you wish to have no fear of authority? Then do what is good and you will receive approval from it, 4 for it is a servant of God for your good. But if you do evil, be afraid, for it does not bear the sword without purpose; it is the servant of God to inflict wrath on the evildoer. 5 Therefore, it is necessary to be subject not only because of the wrath but also because of conscience. 6 This is why you also pay taxes, for the authorities are ministers of God, devoting themselves to this very thing. 7 Pay to all their dues, taxes to whom taxes are due, toll to whom toll is due, respect to whom respect is due, honor to whom honor is due.

8 Owe nothing to anyone, except to love one another; for the one who loves another has fulfilled the law. 9 The commandments, "You shall not commit adultery; you shall not kill; you shall not steal; you shall not covet," and whatever other commandment there may be, are summed up in this saying, [namely] "You shall love your neighbor as yourself." 10 Love does no evil to the neighbor; hence, love is the fulfillment of the law.

11 And do this because you know the time; it is the hour now for you to awake from sleep. For our salvation is nearer now than when we first believed; 12 the night is advanced,

way, all of us, though there are so many of us, make up one body in Christ, and as different parts we are all joined to one another. 6 Then since the gifts that we have differ according to the grace that was given to each of us: if it is a gift of prophecy, we should prophesy as much as our faith tells us; 7 if it is a gift of practical service, let us devote ourselves to serving; if it is teaching, to teaching; 8 if it is encouraging, to encouraging. When you give, you should give generously from the heart; if you are put in charge, you must be conscientious; if you do works of mercy, let it be because you enjoy doing them. 9 Let love be without any pretence. Avoid what is evil; stick to what is good. 10 In brotherly love let your feelings of deep affection for one another come to expression and regard others as more important than yourself. 11 In the service of the Lord, work not halfheartedly but with conscientiousness and an eager spirit. 12 Be joyful in hope, persevere in hardship; keep praying regularly; 13 share with any of God's holy people who are in need; look for opportunities to be hospitable.

14 Bless your persecutors; never curse them, bless them. 15 Rejoice with others when they rejoice, and be sad with those in sorrow. 16 Give the same consideration to all others alike. Pay no regard to social standing, but meet humble people on their own terms. *Do not congratulate yourself on your own wisdom.q* 17 Never pay back evil with evil, but *bear in mind the ideals that all regard with respect.* 18 As much as possible, and to the utmost of your ability, be at peace with everyone. 19 Never try to get revenge: leave that, my dear friends, to the Retribution. As scripture says: *Vengeance is mine — I will pay them back,* the Lord promises. 20 And more: *If your enemy is hungry, give him something to eat; if thirsty, something to drink. By this, you will be heaping red-hot coals on his head.* 21 Do not be mastered by evil, but master evil with good.

13 Everyone is to obey the governing authorities, because there is no authority except from God and so whatever authorities exist have been appointed by God. 2 So anyone who disobeys an authority is rebelling against God's ordinance; and rebels must expect to receive the condemnation they deserve. 3 Magistrates bring fear not to those who do good, but to those who do evil. So if you want to live with no fear of authority, live honestly and you will have its approval; 4 it is there to serve God for you and for your good. But if you do wrong, then you may well be afraid; because it is not for nothing that the symbol of authority is the sword: it is there to serve God, too, as his avenger, to bring retribution to wrongdoers. 5 You must be obedient, therefore, not only because of this retribution, but also for conscience's sake. 6 And this is why you should pay taxes, too, because the authorities are all serving God as his agents, even while they are busily occupied with that particular task. 7 Pay to each one what is due to each: taxes to the one to whom tax is due, tolls to the one to whom tolls are due, respect to the one to whom respect is due, honour to the one to whom honour is due.

8 The only thing you should owe to anyone is love for one another, for to love the other person is to fulfil the law. 9 All these: *You shall not commit adultery, You shall not kill, You shall not steal, You shall not covet,* and all the other commandments that there are, are summed up in this single phrase: *You must love your neighbour as yourself.r* 10 Love can cause no harm to your neighbour, and so love is the fulfilment of the Law.

11 Besides, you know the time has come; the moment is here for you to stop sleeping and wake up, because by now our salvation is nearer than when we first began to believe.

---

q 12 Pr 3:7, followed by Lv 19:18; Pr 25:21–22.
r 13 Ex 20:13–17 summed up in Lv 19:18.

night is far gone, the day is near. Let us then lay aside the works of darkness and put on the armor of light; 13 let us live honorably as in the day, not in reveling and drunkenness, not in debauchery and licentiousness, not in quarreling and jealousy. 14 Instead, put on the Lord Jesus Christ, and make no provision for the flesh, to gratify its desires.

14 Welcome those who are weak in faith,*t* but not for the purpose of quarreling over opinions. 2 Some believe in eating anything, while the weak eat only vegetables. 3 Those who eat must not despise those who abstain, and those who abstain must not pass judgment on those who eat; for God has welcomed them. 4 Who are you to pass judgment on servants of another? It is before their own lord that they stand or fall. And they will be upheld, for the Lord*u* is able to make them stand.

5 Some judge one day to be better than another, while others judge all days to be alike. Let all be fully convinced in their own minds. 6 Those who observe the day, observe it in honor of the Lord. Also those who eat, eat in honor of the Lord, since they give thanks to God; while those who abstain, abstain in honor of the Lord and give thanks to God.

7 We do not live to ourselves, and we do not die to ourselves. 8 If we live, we live to the Lord, and if we die, we die to the Lord; so then, whether we live or whether we die, we are the Lord's. 9 For to this end Christ died and lived again, so that he might be Lord of both the dead and the living.

10 Why do you pass judgment on your brother or sister?*v* Or you, why do you despise your brother or sister?*v* For we will all stand before the judgment seat of God.*w* 11 For it is written,

"As I live, says the Lord, every knee shall bow to me,
  and every tongue shall give praise to*x* God."

12 So then, each of us will be accountable to God.*y*

13 Let us therefore no longer pass judgment on one another, but resolve instead never to put a stumbling block or hindrance in the way of another.*z* 14 I know and am persuaded in the Lord Jesus that nothing is unclean in itself; but it is unclean for anyone who thinks it unclean. 15 If your brother or sister*v* is being injured by what you eat, you are no longer walking in love. Do not let what you eat cause the ruin of one for whom Christ died. 16 So do not let your good be spoken of as evil. 17 For the kingdom of God is not food and drink but righteousness and peace and joy in the Holy Spirit. 18 The one who thus serves Christ is acceptable to God and has human approval. 19 Let us then pursue what makes for peace and for mutual upbuilding. 20 Do not, for the sake of food, destroy the work of God. Everything is indeed clean, but it is wrong for you to make others fall by what you eat; 21 it is good not to eat meat or drink wine or do anything that makes your brother or sister*v* stumble.*a* 22 The faith that you have, have as your own conviction before God. Blessed are those who have no reason to condemn themselves because of what they approve. 23 But those who have doubts are condemned if they eat, because they do not act from faith;*t* for whatever does not proceed from faith*t* is sin.*b*

far on in the night; day is near. Let us therefore throw off the deeds of darkness and put on the armour of light. 13 Let us behave with decency as befits the day: no drunken orgies, no debauchery or vice, no quarrels or jealousies! 14 Let Christ Jesus himself be the armour that you wear; give your unspiritual nature no opportunity to satisfy its desires.

14 ACCEPT anyone who is weak in faith without debate about his misgivings. 2 For instance, one person may have faith strong enough to eat all kinds of food, while another who is weaker eats only vegetables. 3 Those who eat meat must not look down on those who do not, and those who do not eat meat must not pass judgement on those who do; for God has accepted them. 4 Who are you to pass judgement on someone else's servant? Whether he stands or falls is his own Master's business; and stand he will, because his Master has power to enable him to stand.

5 Again, some make a distinction between this day and that; others regard all days alike. Everyone must act on his own convictions. 6 Those who honour the day honour the Lord, and those who eat meat also honour the Lord, since when they eat they give thanks to God; and those who abstain have the Lord in mind when abstaining, since they too give thanks to God.

7 For none of us lives, and equally none of us dies, for himself alone. 8 If we live, we live for the Lord; and if we die, we die for the Lord. So whether we live or die, we belong to the Lord. 9 This is why Christ died and lived again, to establish his lordship over both dead and living. 10 You, then, why do you pass judgement on your fellow-Christian? And you, why do you look down on your fellow-Christian? We shall all stand before God's tribunal; 11 for we read in scripture, 'As I live, says the Lord, to me every knee shall bow and every tongue acknowledge God.' 12 So, you see, each of us will be answerable to God.

13 Let us therefore cease judging one another, but rather make up our minds to place no obstacle or stumbling block in a fellow-Christian's way. 14 All that I know of the Lord Jesus convinces me that nothing is impure in itself; only, if anyone considers something impure, then for him it is impure. 15 If your fellow-Christian is outraged by what you eat, then you are no longer guided by love. Do not by your eating be the ruin of one for whom Christ died! 16 You must not let what you think good be brought into disrepute; 17 for the kingdom of God is not eating and drinking, but justice, peace, and joy, inspired by the Holy Spirit. 18 Everyone who shows himself a servant of Christ in this way is acceptable to God and approved by men.

19 Let us, then, pursue the things that make for peace and build up the common life. 20 Do not destroy the work of God for the sake of food. Everything is pure in itself, but it is wrong to eat if by eating you cause another to stumble. 21 It is right to abstain from eating meat or drinking wine or from anything else which causes a fellow-Christian to stumble. 22 If you have some firm conviction, keep it between yourself and God. Anyone who can make his decision without misgivings is fortunate. 23 But anyone who has misgivings and yet eats is guilty, because his action does not arise from conviction, and anything which does not arise from conviction is sin.

t Or conviction   *u* Other ancient authorities read *for God*
v Gk *brother*   *w* Other ancient authorities read *of Christ*
x Or *confess*   *y* Other ancient authorities lack *to God*   *z* Gk *of a brother*   *a* Other ancient authorities add *or be upset or be weakened*   *b* Other authorities, some ancient, add here 16.25-27

14:23 *See note on* 16:27.

NEW AMERICAN BIBLE

NEW JERUSALEM BIBLE

the day is at hand. Let us then throw off the works of darkness [and] put on the armor of light; 13 let us conduct ourselves properly as in the day, not in orgies and drunkenness, not in promiscuity and licentiousness, not in rivalry and jealousy. 14 But put on the Lord Jesus Christ, and make no provision for the desires of the flesh.

14 Welcome anyone who is weak in faith, but not for disputes over opinions. 2 One person believes that one may eat anything, while the weak person eats only vegetables. 3 The one who eats must not despise the one who abstains, and the one who abstains must not pass judgment on the one who eats; for God has welcomed him. 4 Who are you to pass judgment on someone else's servant? Before his own master he stands or falls. And he will be upheld, for the Lord is able to make him stand. 5 [For] one person considers one day more important than another, while another person considers all days alike. Let everyone be fully persuaded in his own mind. 6 Whoever observes the day, observes it for the Lord. Also whoever eats, eats for the Lord, since he gives thanks to God; while whoever abstains, abstains for the Lord and gives thanks to God. 7 None of us lives for oneself, and no one dies for oneself. 8 For if we live, we live for the Lord, and if we die, we die for the Lord; so then, whether we live or die, we are the Lord's. 9 For this is why Christ died and came to life, that he might be Lord of both the dead and the living. 10 Why then do you judge your brother? Or you, why do you look down on your brother? For we shall all stand before the judgment seat of God; 11 for it is written:

"As I live, says the Lord, every knee shall bend before me,
and every tongue shall give praise to God."

12 So [then] each of us shall give an account of himself [to God].

13 Then let us no longer judge one another, but rather resolve never to put a stumbling block or hindrance in the way of a brother. 14 I know and am convinced in the Lord Jesus that nothing is unclean in itself; still, it is unclean for someone who thinks it unclean. 15 If your brother is being hurt by what you eat, your conduct is no longer in accord with love. Do not because of your food destroy him for whom Christ died. 16 So do not let your good be reviled. 17 For the kingdom of God is not a matter of food and drink, but of righteousness, peace, and joy in the holy Spirit; 18 whoever serves Christ in this way is pleasing to God and approved by others. 19 Let us then pursue what leads to peace and to building up one another. 20 For the sake of food, do not destroy the work of God. Everything is indeed clean, but it is wrong for anyone to become a stumbling block by eating; 21 it is good not to eat meat or drink wine or do anything that causes your brother to stumble. 22 Keep the faith [that] you have to yourself in the presence of God; blessed is the one who does not condemn himself for what he approves. 23 But whoever has doubts is condemned if he eats, because this is not from faith; for whatever is not from faith is sin.

12 The night is nearly over, daylight is on the way; so let us throw off everything that belongs to the darkness and equip ourselves for the light. 13 Let us live decently, as in the light of day; with no orgies or drunkenness, no promiscuity or licentiousness, and no wrangling or jealousy. 14 Let your armour be the Lord Jesus Christ, and stop worrying about how your disordered natural inclinations may be fulfilled.

14 Give a welcome to anyone whose faith is not strong, but do not get into arguments about doubtful points. 2 One person may have faith enough to eat any kind of food; another, less strong, will eat only vegetables. 3 Those who feel free to eat freely are not to condemn those who are unwilling to eat freely; nor must the person who does not eat freely pass judgement on the one who does — because God has welcomed him. 4 And who are you, to sit in judgement over somebody else's servant? Whether he deserves to be upheld or to fall is for his own master to decide; and he shall be upheld, for the Lord has power to uphold him. 5 One person thinks that some days are holier than others, and another thinks them all equal. Let each of them be fully convinced in his own mind. 6 The one who makes special observance of a particular day observes it in honour of the Lord. So the one who eats freely, eats in honour of the Lord, making his thanksgiving to God; and the one who does not, abstains from eating in honour of the Lord and makes his thanksgiving to God. 7 For none of us lives for himself and none of us dies for himself; 8 while we are alive, we are living for the Lord, and when we die, we die for the Lord: and so, alive or dead, we belong to the Lord. 9 It was for this purpose that Christ both died and came to life again: so that he might be Lord of both the dead and the living. 10 Why, then, does one of you make himself judge over his brother, and why does another among you despise his brother? All of us will have to stand in front of the judgement-seat of God: 11 as scripture says: *By my own life* says the Lord, *every knee shall bow before me, every tongue shall give glory to God.* ᶳ 12 It is to God, then, that each of us will have to give an account of himself.

13 Let us each stop passing judgement, therefore, on one another and decide instead that none of us will place obstacles in any brother's way, or anything that can bring him down. 14 I am sure, and quite convinced in the Lord Jesus, that no food is unclean in itself; it is only if someone classifies any kind of food as unclean, then for him it is unclean. 15 And indeed, if through any kind of food you are causing offence to a brother, then you are no longer being guided by love. You are not to let the food that you eat cause the ruin of anyone for whom Christ died. 16 A privilege of yours must not be allowed to give rise to harmful talk; 17 for it is not eating and drinking that make the kingdom of God, but the saving justice, the peace and the joy brought by the Holy Spirit. 18 It is the person who serves Christ in these things that will be approved by God and respected by everyone. 19 So then, let us be always seeking the ways which lead to peace and the ways in which we can support one another. 20 Do not wreck God's work for the sake of food. Certainly all foods are clean; but all the same, any kind can be evil for someone to whom it is an offence to eat it. 21 It is best to abstain from eating any meat, or drinking any wine, or from any other activity which might cause a brother to fall away, or to be scandalised, or to weaken.

22 Within yourself, before God, hold on to what you already believe. Blessed is the person whose principles do not condemn his practice. 23 But anyone who eats with qualms of conscience is condemned, because this eating does not spring from faith — and every action which does not spring from faith is sin.

ᶳ **14** Is 45:23.

15 We who are strong ought to put up with the failings of the weak, and not to please ourselves. 2 Each of us must please our neighbor for the good purpose of building up the neighbor. 3 For Christ did not please himself; but, as it is written, "The insults of those who insult you have fallen on me." 4 For whatever was written in former days was written for our instruction, so that by steadfastness and by the encouragement of the scriptures we might have hope. 5 May the God of steadfastness and encouragement grant you to live in harmony with one another, in accordance with Christ Jesus, 6 so that together you may with one voice glorify the God and Father of our Lord Jesus Christ.

7 Welcome one another, therefore, just as Christ has welcomed you, for the glory of God. 8 For I tell you that Christ has become a servant of the circumcised on behalf of the truth of God in order that he might confirm the promises given to the patriarchs, 9 and in order that the Gentiles might glorify God for his mercy. As it is written,

"Therefore I will confess*c* you among the
         Gentiles,
      and sing praises to your name";

10 and again he says,

      "Rejoice, O Gentiles, with his people";

11 and again,

      "Praise the Lord, all you Gentiles,
         and let all the peoples praise him";

12 and again Isaiah says,

      "The root of Jesse shall come,
         the one who rises to rule the Gentiles;
      in him the Gentiles shall hope."

13 May the God of hope fill you with all joy and peace in believing, so that you may abound in hope by the power of the Holy Spirit.

14 I myself feel confident about you, my brothers and sisters,*d* that you yourselves are full of goodness, filled with all knowledge, and able to instruct one another. 15 Nevertheless on some points I have written to you rather boldly by way of reminder, because of the grace given me by God 16 to be a minister of Christ Jesus to the Gentiles in the priestly service of the gospel of God, so that the offering of the Gentiles may be acceptable, sanctified by the Holy Spirit. 17 In Christ Jesus, then, I have reason to boast of my work for God. 18 For I will not venture to speak of anything except what Christ has accomplished*e* through me to win obedience from the Gentiles, by word and deed, 19 by the power of signs and wonders, by the power of the Spirit of God,*f* so that from Jerusalem and as far around as Illyricum I have fully proclaimed the good news*g* of Christ. 20 Thus I make it my ambition to proclaim the good news,*g* not where Christ has already been named, so that I do not build on someone else's foundation, 21 but as it is written,

      "Those who have never been told of him shall
         see,
      and those who have never heard of him shall
         understand."

22 This is the reason that I have so often been hindered from coming to you. 23 But now, with no further place for me in these regions, I desire, as I have for many years, to come to you 24 when I go to Spain. For I do hope to see you on my journey and to be sent on by you, once I have enjoyed your company for a little while. 25 At present, however, I am going to Jerusalem in a ministry to the saints; 26 for Macedonia and Achaia have been pleased to share their resources with the poor among the saints at Jerusalem.

15 1 Those of us who are strong must accept as our own burden the tender scruples of the weak, and not just please ourselves. 2 Each of us must consider his neighbour and think what is for his good and will build up the common life. 3 Christ too did not please himself; to him apply the words of scripture, 'The reproaches of those who reproached you fell on me.' 4 The scriptures written long ago were all written for our instruction, in order that through the encouragement they give us we may maintain our hope with perseverance. 5 And may God, the source of all perseverance and all encouragement, grant that you may agree with one another after the manner of Christ Jesus, 6 and so with one mind and one voice may praise the God and Father of our Lord Jesus Christ.

7 In a word, accept one another as Christ accepted us, to the glory of God. 8 Remember that Christ became a servant of the Jewish people to maintain the faithfulness of God by making good his promises to the patriarchs, 9 and by giving the Gentiles cause to glorify God for his mercy. As scripture says, 'Therefore I will praise you among the Gentiles and sing hymns to your name'; 10 and again, 'Gentiles, join in celebration with his people'; 11 and yet again, 'All Gentiles, praise the Lord; let all peoples praise him.' 12 Once again, Isaiah says, 'The Scion of Jesse shall come, a ruler who rises to govern the Gentiles; on him shall they set their hope.' 13 And may God, who is the ground of hope, fill you with all joy and peace as you lead the life of faith until, by the power of the Holy Spirit, you overflow with hope.

14 My friends, I have no doubt in my own mind that you yourselves are full of goodness and equipped with knowledge of every kind, well able to give advice to one another; 15 nevertheless I have written to refresh your memory, and written somewhat boldly at times, in virtue of the gift I have from God. 16 His grace has made me a minister of Christ Jesus to the Gentiles; and in the service of the gospel of God it is my priestly task to offer the Gentiles to him as an acceptable sacrifice, consecrated by the Holy Spirit.

17 In Christ Jesus I have indeed grounds for pride in the service of God. 18 I will venture to speak only of what Christ has done through me to bring the Gentiles into his allegiance, by word and deed, 19 by the power of signs and portents, and by the power of the Holy Spirit. I have completed the preaching of the gospel of Christ from Jerusalem as far round as Illyricum. 20 But I have always made a point of taking the gospel to places where the name of Christ has not been heard, not wanting to build on another man's foundation; 21 as scripture says,

      Those who had no news of him shall see,
      and those who never heard of him shall
            understand.

22 That is why I have been prevented all this time from coming to you. 23 But now I have no further scope in these parts, and I have been longing for many years to visit you 24 on my way to Spain; for I hope to see you in passing, and to be sent on my way there with your support after having enjoyed your company for a while. 25 But at the moment I am on my way to Jerusalem, on an errand to God's people there. 26 For Macedonia and Achaia have resolved to raise a fund for the benefit of the poor among God's people at

---

c Or *thank*   *d* Gk *brothers*   *e* Gk *speak of those things that Christ has not accomplished*   *f* Other ancient authorities read *of the Spirit* or *of the Holy Spirit*   *g* Or *gospel*

15 We who are strong ought to put up with the failings of the weak and not to please ourselves; 2 let each of us please our neighbor for the good, for building up. 3 For Christ did not please himself; but, as it is written, "The insults of those who insult you fall upon me." 4 For whatever was written previously was written for our instruction, that by endurance and by the encouragement of the scriptures we might have hope. 5 May the God of endurance and encouragement grant you to think in harmony with one another, in keeping with Christ Jesus, 6 that with one accord you may with one voice glorify the God and Father of our Lord Jesus Christ.

7 Welcome one another, then, as Christ welcomed you, for the glory of God. 8 For I say that Christ became a minister of the circumcised to show God's truthfulness, to confirm the promises to the patriarchs, 9 but so that the Gentiles might glorify God for his mercy. As it is written:

"Therefore, I will praise you among the Gentiles
and sing praises to your name."

10 And again it says:

"Rejoice, O Gentiles, with his people."

11 And again:

"Praise the Lord, all you Gentiles,
and let all the peoples praise him."

12 And again Isaiah says:

"The root of Jesse shall come,
raised up to rule the Gentiles;
in him shall the Gentiles hope."

13 May the God of hope fill you with all joy and peace in believing, so that you may abound in hope by the power of the holy Spirit.

14 I myself am convinced about you, my brothers, that you yourselves are full of goodness, filled with all knowledge, and able to admonish one another. 15 But I have written to you rather boldly in some respects to remind you, because of the grace given me by God 16 to be a minister of Christ Jesus to the Gentiles in performing the priestly service of the gospel of God, so that the offering up of the Gentiles may be acceptable, sanctified by the holy Spirit. 17 In Christ Jesus, then, I have reason to boast in what pertains to God. 18 For I will not dare to speak of anything except what Christ has accomplished through me to lead the Gentiles to obedience by word and deed, 19 by the power of signs and wonders, by the power of the Spirit [of God], so that from Jerusalem all the way around to Illyricum I have finished preaching the gospel of Christ. 20 Thus I aspire to proclaim the gospel not where Christ has already been named, so that I do not build on another's foundation, 21 but as it is written:

"Those who have never been told of him shall see,
and those who have never heard of him
shall understand."

22 That is why I have so often been prevented from coming to you. 23 But now, since I no longer have any opportunity in these regions and since I have desired to come to you for many years, 24 I hope to see you in passing as I go to Spain and to be sent on my way there by you, after I have enjoyed being with you for a time. 25 Now, however, I am going to Jerusalem to minister to the holy ones. 26 For Macedonia and Achaia have decided to make some contribution for the poor among the holy ones in Jerusalem; 27 they de-

15 It is for us who are strong to bear with the susceptibilities of the weaker ones, and not please ourselves. 2 Each of us must consider his neighbour's good, so that we support one another. 3 Christ did not indulge his own feelings, either; indeed, as scripture says: *The insults of those who insult you fall on me.*[t] 4 And all these things which were written so long ago were written so that we, learning perseverance and the encouragement which the scriptures give, should have hope. 5 Now the God of perseverance and encouragement give you all the same purpose, following the example of Christ Jesus, 6 so that you may together give glory to the God and Father of our Lord Jesus Christ with one heart.

7 Accept one another, then, for the sake of God's glory, as Christ accepted you. 8 I tell you that Christ's work was to serve the circumcised, fulfilling the truthfulness of God by carrying out the promises made to the fathers, 9 and his work was also for the gentiles, so that they should give glory to God for his faithful love; as scripture says: *For this I shall praise you among the nations and sing praise to your name.*[u] 10 And in another place it says: *Nations, rejoice, with his people,* 11 and in another place again: *Praise the Lord, all nations, extol him, all peoples.* 12 And in Isaiah, it says: *The root of Jesse will appear, he who rises up to rule the nations, and in him the nations will put their hope.*

13 May the God of hope fill you with all joy and peace in your faith, so that in the power of the Holy Spirit you may be rich in hope.

14 My brothers, I am quite sure that you, in particular, are full of goodness, fully instructed and capable of correcting each other. 15 But I have special confidence in writing on some points to you, to refresh your memories, because of the grace that was given to me by God. 16 I was given grace to be a minister of Christ Jesus to the gentiles, dedicated to offer them the gospel of God, so that gentiles might become an acceptable offering, sanctified by the Holy Spirit.

17 So I can be proud, in Christ Jesus, of what I have done for God. 18 Of course I can dare to speak only of the things which Christ has done through me to win the allegiance of the gentiles, using what I have said and done, 19 by the power of signs and wonders, by the power of the Spirit of God. In this way, from Jerusalem all round, even as far as Illyricum, I have fully carried out the preaching of the gospel of Christ; 20 and what is more, it has been my rule to preach the gospel only where the name of Christ has not already been heard, for I do not build on another's foundations; 21 in accordance with scripture: *Those who have never been told about him will see him, and those who have never heard about him will understand.*[v]

22 That is why I have been so often prevented from coming to see you; 23 now, however, as there is nothing more to keep me in these parts, I hope, after longing for many years past to visit you, to see you when I am on the way to Spain— 24 and after enjoying at least something of your company, to be sent on my way with your support. 25 But now I have undertaken to go to Jerusalem in the service of the holy people of God there, 26 since Macedonia and Achaia have chosen to make a generous contribution to the poor among God's holy people at Jerusalem.

t 15 Ps 69:9.   *u* 15 Ps 18:49, followed by Dt 32:43; Ps 117:1; Is 11:10.   *v* 15 Is 52:15.

3007

| NEW REVISED STANDARD VERSION | REVISED ENGLISH BIBLE |

27 They were pleased to do this, and indeed they owe it to them; for if the Gentiles have come to share in their spiritual blessings, they ought also to be of service to them in material things. 28 So, when I have completed this, and have delivered to them what has been collected,*h* I will set out by way of you to Spain; 29 and I know that when I come to you, I will come in the fullness of the blessing*i* of Christ.

30 I appeal to you, brothers and sisters,*j* by our Lord Jesus Christ and by the love of the Spirit, to join me in earnest prayer to God on my behalf, 31 that I may be rescued from the unbelievers in Judea, and that my ministry*k* to Jerusalem may be acceptable to the saints, 32 so that by God's will I may come to you with joy and be refreshed in your company. 33 The God of peace be with all of you.*l* Amen.

16 I commend to you our sister Phoebe, a deacon*m* of the church at Cenchreae, 2 so that you may welcome her in the Lord as is fitting for the saints, and help her in whatever she may require from you, for she has been a benefactor of many and of myself as well.

3 Greet Prisca and Aquila, who work with me in Christ Jesus, 4 and who risked their necks for my life, to whom not only I give thanks, but also all the churches of the Gentiles. 5 Greet also the church in their house. Greet my beloved Epaenetus, who was the first convert*n* in Asia for Christ. 6 Greet Mary, who has worked very hard among you. 7 Greet Andronicus and Junia,*o* my relatives*p* who were in prison with me; they are prominent among the apostles, and they were in Christ before I was. 8 Greet Ampliatus, my beloved in the Lord. 9 Greet Urbanus, our co-worker in Christ, and my beloved Stachys. 10 Greet Apelles, who is approved in Christ. Greet those who belong to the family of Aristobulus. 11 Greet my relative*q* Herodion. Greet those in the Lord who belong to the family of Narcissus. 12 Greet those workers in the Lord, Tryphaena and Tryphosa. Greet the beloved Persis, who has worked hard in the Lord. 13 Greet Rufus, chosen in the Lord; and greet his mother — a mother to me also. 14 Greet Asyncritus, Phlegon, Hermes, Patrobas, Hermas, and the brothers and sisters*j* who are with them. 15 Greet Philologus, Julia, Nereus and his sister, and Olympas, and all the saints who are with them. 16 Greet one another with a holy kiss. All the churches of Christ greet you.

17 I urge you, brothers and sisters,*j* to keep an eye on those who cause dissensions and offenses, in opposition to the teaching that you have learned; avoid them. 18 For such people do not serve our Lord Christ, but their own appetites,*r* and by smooth talk and flattery they deceive the hearts of the simple-minded. 19 For while your obedience is known to all, so that I rejoice over you, I want you to be wise in what is good and guileless in what is evil. 20 The God of peace will shortly crush Satan under your feet. The grace of our Lord Jesus Christ be with you.*s*

21 Timothy, my co-worker, greets you; so do Lucius and Jason and Sosipater, my relatives.*p*

22 I Tertius, the writer of this letter, greet you in the Lord.*t*

Jerusalem. 27 They have resolved to do so, and indeed they are under an obligation to them. For if the Jewish Christians shared their spiritual treasures with the Gentiles, the Gentiles have a clear duty to contribute to their material needs. 28 So when I have finished this business and seen the proceeds safely delivered to them, I shall set out for Spain and visit you on the way; 29 I am sure that when I come it will be with a full measure of the blessing of Christ.

30 I implore you by our Lord Jesus Christ and by the love that the Spirit inspires, be my allies in the fight; pray to God for me 31 that I may be saved from unbelievers in Judaea and that my errand to Jerusalem may find acceptance with God's people, 32 in order that by his will I may come to you in a happy frame of mind and enjoy a time of rest with you. 33 The God of peace be with you all. Amen.

16 I COMMEND to you Phoebe, a fellow-Christian who is a minister in the church at Cenchreae. 2 Give her, in the fellowship of the Lord, a welcome worthy of God's people, and support her in any business in which she may need your help, for she has herself been a good friend to many, including myself.

3 Give my greetings to Prisca and Aquila, my fellow-workers in Christ Jesus. 4 They risked their necks to save my life, and not I alone but all the gentile churches are grateful to them. 5 Greet also the church that meets at their house.

Give my greetings to my dear friend Epaenetus, the first convert to Christ in Asia, 6 and to Mary, who worked so hard for you. 7 Greet Andronicus and Junia, my fellow-countrymen and comrades in captivity, who are eminent among the apostles and were Christians before I was.

8 Greetings to Ampliatus, my dear friend in the fellowship of the Lord, 9 to Urban my comrade in Christ, and to my dear Stachys. 10 My greetings to Apelles, well proved in Christ's service, to the household of Aristobulus, 11 to my countryman Herodion, and to those of the household of Narcissus who are in the Lord's fellowship. 12 Greet Tryphaena and Tryphosa, who work hard in the Lord's service, and dear Persis who has worked hard in his service for so long. 13 Give my greetings to Rufus, an outstanding follower of the Lord, and to his mother, whom I call mother too. 14 Greet Asyncritus, Phlegon, Hermes, Patrobas, Hermas, and any other Christians who are with them. 15 Greet Philologus and Julia, Nereus and his sister, and Olympas, and all God's people who are with them.

16 Greet one another with the kiss of peace. All Christ's churches send you their greetings.

17 I implore you, my friends, keep an eye on those who stir up quarrels and lead others astray, contrary to the teaching you received. Avoid them; 18 such people are servants not of Christ our Lord but of their own appetites, and they seduce the minds of simple people with smooth and specious words. 19 The fame of your obedience has spread everywhere, and this makes me happy about you. I want you to be expert in goodness, but innocent of evil, 20 and the God of peace will soon crush Satan beneath your feet. The grace of our Lord Jesus be with you!

21 Greetings to you from my colleague Timothy, and from Lucius, Jason, and Sosipater my fellow-countrymen. 22 (I Tertius, who took this letter down, add my Christian

h Gk *have sealed to them this fruit*   *i* Other ancient authorities add *of the gospel*   *j* Gk *brothers*   *k* Other ancient authorities read *my bringing of a gift*   *l* One ancient authority adds 16.25-27 here   *m* Gk *minister*   *n* Gk *first fruits*   *o* Or *Junias;* other ancient authorities read *Julia*   *p* Or *compatriots*   *q* Or *compatriot*   *r* Gk *their own belly*   *s* Other ancient authorities lack this sentence   *t* Or *I Tertius, writing this letter in the Lord, greet you*

15:33 *See note on* 16:27.   16:1 **minister:** *or* deacon.   16:7 **Junia:** *or* Junias.   16:15 **Julia:** *or* Julias.   16:20 **The grace . . . with you:** *These words are omitted at this point in some witnesses; in some, these or similar words are given as verse 24, and in some others after verse 27.*

cided to do it, and in fact they are indebted to them, for if the Gentiles have come to share in their spiritual blessings, they ought also to serve them in material blessings. 28 So when I have completed this and safely handed over this contribution to them, I shall set out by way of you to Spain; 29 and I know that in coming to you I shall come in the fullness of Christ's blessing.

30 I urge you, [brothers,] by our Lord Jesus Christ and by the love of the Spirit, to join me in the struggle by your prayers to God on my behalf, 31 that I may be delivered from the disobedient in Judea, and that my ministry for Jerusalem may be acceptable to the holy ones, 32 so that I may come to you with joy by the will of God and be refreshed together with you. 33 The God of peace be with all of you. Amen.

16 I commend to you Phoebe our sister, who is [also] a minister of the church at Cenchreae, 2 that you may receive her in the Lord in a manner worthy of the holy ones, and help her in whatever she may need from you, for she has been a benefactor to many and to me as well.

3 Greet Prisca and Aquila, my co-workers in Christ Jesus, 4 who risked their necks for my life, to whom not only I am grateful but also all the churches of the Gentiles; 5 greet also the church at their house. Greet my beloved Epaenetus, who was the firstfruits in Asia for Christ. 6 Greet Mary, who has worked hard for you. 7 Greet Andronicus and Junia, my relatives and my fellow prisoners; they are prominent among the apostles and they were in Christ before me. 8 Greet Ampliatus, my beloved in the Lord. 9 Greet Urbanus, our co-worker in Christ, and my beloved Stachys. 10 Greet Apelles, who is approved in Christ. Greet those who belong to the family of Aristobulus. 11 Greet my relative Herodion. Greet those in the Lord who belong to the family of Narcissus. 12 Greet those workers in the Lord, Tryphaena and Tryphosa. Greet the beloved Persis, who has worked hard in the Lord. 13 Greet Rufus, chosen in the Lord, and his mother and mine. 14 Greet Asyncritus, Phlegon, Hermes, Patrobas, Hermas, and the brothers who are with them. 15 Greet Philologus, Julia, Nereus and his sister, and Olympas, and all the holy ones who are with them. 16 Greet one another with a holy kiss. All the churches of Christ greet you.

17 I urge you, brothers, to watch out for those who create dissensions and obstacles, in opposition to the teaching that you learned; avoid them. 18 For such people do not serve our Lord Christ but their own appetites, and by fair and flattering speech they deceive the hearts of the innocent. 19 For while your obedience is known to all, so that I rejoice over you, I want you to be wise as to what is good, and simple as to what is evil; 20 then the God of peace will quickly crush Satan under your feet. The grace of our Lord Jesus be with you.

21 Timothy, my co-worker, greets you; so do Lucius and Jason and Sosipater, my relatives. 22 I, Tertius, the writer of this letter, greet you in the Lord. 23 Gaius, who is host to me

27 Yes, they chose to; not that they did not owe it to them. For if the gentiles have been given a share in their spiritual possessions, then in return to give them help with material possessions is repaying a debt to them. 28 So when I have done this, and given this harvest into their possession, I shall visit you on the way to Spain. 29 I am sure that, when I do come to you, I shall come with the fullest blessing of Christ.

30 Meanwhile I urge you, brothers, by our Lord Jesus Christ and by the love of the Spirit, that in your prayers to God for me you exert yourselves to help me; 31 praying that I may escape the unbelievers in Judaea, and that the aid I am carrying to Jerusalem will be acceptable to God's holy people. 32 Then I shall come to you, if God wills, for a happy time of relaxation in your company. w 33 The God of peace be with you all. Amen.

16 x I commend to you our sister Phoebe, a deaconess of the church at Cenchreae; 2 give her, in the Lord, a welcome worthy of God's holy people, and help her with whatever she needs from you — she herself has come to the help of many people, including myself.

3 My greetings to Prisca and Aquila, my fellow-workers in Christ Jesus, 4 who risked their own necks to save my life; to them, thanks not only from me, but from all the churches among the gentiles; 5 and my greetings to the church at their house.

Greetings to my dear friend Epaenetus, the first of Asia's offerings to Christ. 6 Greetings to Mary, who worked so hard for you. 7 Greetings to those outstanding apostles, Andronicus and Junias, my kinsmen and fellow-prisoners, who were in Christ before me. 8 Greetings to Ampliatus, my dear friend in the Lord. 9 Greetings to Urban, my fellow-worker in Christ, and to my dear friend Stachys. 10 Greetings to Apelles, proved servant of Christ. Greetings to all the household of Aristobulus. 11 Greetings to my kinsman, Herodion, and greetings to those who belong to the Lord in the household of Narcissus. 12 Greetings to Tryphaena and Tryphosa who work hard in the Lord; greetings to my dear friend Persis, also a very hard worker in the Lord. 13 Greetings to Rufus, chosen servant of the Lord, and to his mother — a mother to me too. 14 Greetings to Asyncritus, Phlegon, Hermes, Patrobas, Hermas, and the brothers who are with them. 15 Greetings to Philologus and Julia, Nereus and his sister, and Olympas and all God's holy people who are with them. 16 Greet each other with the holy kiss. All the churches of Christ send their greetings.

17 I urge you, brothers, be on your guard against the people who are out to stir up disagreements and bring up difficulties against the teaching which you learnt. Avoid them. 18 People of that sort are servants not of our Lord Christ, but of their own greed; and with talk that sounds smooth and reasonable they deceive the minds of the unwary. 19 Your obedience has become known to everyone, and I am very pleased with you for it; but I should want you to be learned only in what is good, and unsophisticated about all that is evil. 20 The God of peace will soon crush Satan under your feet. The grace of our Lord Jesus Christ be with you.

21 Timothy, who is working with me, sends greetings to you, and so do my kinsmen Lucius, Jason and Sosipater. 22 I, Tertius, who am writing this letter, greet you in the

---

w **15** We do not know whether Paul completed this journey.
x **16** vv. 1–23 possibly formed no part of the original letter.

| NEW REVISED STANDARD VERSION | REVISED ENGLISH BIBLE |

23 Gaius, who is host to me and to the whole church, greets you. Erastus, the city treasurer, and our brother Quartus, greet you. [u]

25 Now to God[v] who is able to strengthen you according to my gospel and the proclamation of Jesus Christ, according to the revelation of the mystery that was kept secret for long ages [26] but is now disclosed, and through the prophetic writings is made known to all the Gentiles, according to the command of the eternal God, to bring about the obedience of faith— [27] to the only wise God, through Jesus Christ, to whom[w] be the glory forever! Amen.[x]

[u] Other ancient authorities add verse 24, *The grace of our Lord Jesus Christ be with all of you. Amen.*   [v] Gk *the one*   [w] Other ancient authorities lack *to whom*. The verse then reads, *to the only wise God be the glory through Jesus Christ forever. Amen.*   [x] Other ancient authorities lack 16.25-27 or include it after 14.23 or 15.33; others put verse 24 after verse 27

greetings.) [23] Greetings also from Gaius, my host and host of the whole congregation, and from Erastus, treasurer of this city, and our brother Quartus.

[25] To him who has power to make you stand firm, according to my gospel and the proclamation of Jesus Christ, according to the revelation of that divine secret kept in silence for long ages [26] but now disclosed, and by the eternal God's command made known to all nations through prophetic scriptures, to bring them to faith and obedience— [27] to the only wise God through Jesus Christ be glory for endless ages! Amen.

16:23 *After this verse some witnesses add* [24] The grace of our Lord Jesus Christ be with you all! Amen.   16:27 *After this verse some witnesses add* The grace of our Lord Jesus Christ be with you! *Some witnesses place verses 25–27 at the end of chapter 14, one other places them at the end of chapter 15, and others omit them altogether.*

and to the whole church, greets you. Erastus, the city treasurer, and our brother Quartus greet you.[24]

[25 Now to him who can strengthen you, according to my gospel and the proclamation of Jesus Christ, according to the revelation of the mystery kept secret for long ages 26 but now manifested through the prophetic writings and, according to the command of the eternal God, made known to all nations to bring about the obedience of faith, 27 to the only wise God, through Jesus Christ be glory forever and ever. Amen.]

16, 24: Some manuscripts add, similarly to v 20, "The grace of our Lord Jesus Christ be with you all. Amen." 16, 25–27: This doxology is assigned variously to the end of chs 14, 15, and 16 in the manuscript tradition. Some manuscripts omit it entirely.

Lord. 23 Greetings to you from Gaius, my host here, and host of the whole church. Erastus, the city treasurer, sends greetings to you, and our brother Quartus.[24]y

25 zAnd now to him who can make you strong
  in accordance with the gospel that I preach
  and the proclamation of Jesus Christ,
  in accordance with that mystery
  which for endless ages was kept secret
26 but now (as the prophets wrote) is revealed,
  as the eternal God commanded,
  to be made known to all the nations,
  so that they obey in faith:
27 to him, the only wise God,
  give glory through Jesus Christ
  for ever and ever. Amen.

y 16 Some authorities add v. 24, 'The grace . . . with you' as in v. 20.
z 16 A solemn summary, placed by some authorities after 15:33.

THE FIRST LETTER OF PAUL TO THE
Corinthians

1 Paul, called to be an apostle of Christ Jesus by the will of God, and our brother Sosthenes,

2 To the church of God that is in Corinth, to those who are sanctified in Christ Jesus, called to be saints, together with all those who in every place call on the name of our Lord Jesus Christ, both their Lord*a* and ours:

3 Grace to you and peace from God our Father and the Lord Jesus Christ.

4 I give thanks to my*b* God always for you because of the grace of God that has been given you in Christ Jesus, 5 for in every way you have been enriched in him, in speech and knowledge of every kind — 6 just as the testimony of*c* Christ has been strengthened among you — 7 so that you are not lacking in any spiritual gift as you wait for the revealing of our Lord Jesus Christ. 8 He will also strengthen you to the end, so that you may be blameless on the day of our Lord Jesus Christ. 9 God is faithful; by him you were called into the fellowship of his Son, Jesus Christ our Lord.

10 Now I appeal to you, brothers and sisters,*d* by the name of our Lord Jesus Christ, that all of you be in agreement and that there be no divisions among you, but that you be united in the same mind and the same purpose. 11 For it has been reported to me by Chloe's people that there are quarrels among you, my brothers and sisters.*e* 12 What I mean is that each of you says, "I belong to Paul," or "I belong to Apollos," or "I belong to Cephas," or "I belong to Christ." 13 Has Christ been divided? Was Paul crucified for you? Or were you baptized in the name of Paul? 14 I thank God*f* that I baptized none of you except Crispus and Gaius, 15 so that no one can say that you were baptized in my name. 16 (I did baptize also the household of Stephanas; beyond that, I do not know whether I baptized anyone else.) 17 For Christ did not send me to baptize but to proclaim the gospel, and not with eloquent wisdom, so that the cross of Christ might not be emptied of its power.

18 For the message about the cross is foolishness to those who are perishing, but to us who are being saved it is the power of God. 19 For it is written,

"I will destroy the wisdom of the wise,
    and the discernment of the discerning I will thwart."

20 Where is the one who is wise? Where is the scribe? Where is the debater of this age? Has not God made foolish the wisdom of the world? 21 For since, in the wisdom of God, the world did not know God through wisdom, God decided, through the foolishness of our proclamation, to save those who believe. 22 For Jews demand signs and Greeks desire wisdom, 23 but we proclaim Christ crucified, a stumbling block to Jews and foolishness to Gentiles, 24 but to those who are the called, both Jews and Greeks, Christ the power of God and the wisdom of God. 25 For God's foolishness is wiser than human wisdom, and God's weakness is stronger than human strength.

26 Consider your own call, brothers and sisters:*d* not many of you were wise by human standards,*g* not many were powerful, not many were of noble birth. 27 But God

THE FIRST LETTER OF PAUL TO THE
Corinthians

1 FROM Paul, apostle of Christ Jesus by God's call and by his will, together with our colleague Sosthenes, 2 to God's church at Corinth, dedicated to him in Christ Jesus, called to be his people, along with all who invoke the name of our Lord Jesus Christ wherever they may be — their Lord as well as ours.

3 Grace and peace to you from God our Father and the Lord Jesus Christ.

4 I am always thanking God for you. I thank him for his grace given to you in Christ Jesus; 5 I thank him for all the enrichment that has come to you in Christ. You possess full knowledge and you can give full expression to it, 6 because what we testified about Christ has been confirmed in your experience. 7 There is indeed no single gift you lack, while you wait expectantly for our Lord Jesus Christ to reveal himself. 8 He will keep you firm to the end, without reproach on the day of our Lord Jesus. 9 It is God himself who called you to share in the life of his Son Jesus Christ our Lord; and God keeps faith.

10 I APPEAL to you, my friends, in the name of our Lord Jesus Christ: agree among yourselves, and avoid divisions; let there be complete unity of mind and thought. 11 My friends, it has been brought to my notice by Chloe's people that there are quarrels among you. 12 What I mean is this: each of you is saying, 'I am for Paul,' or 'I am for Apollos'; 'I am for Cephas,' or 'I am for Christ.' 13 Surely Christ has not been divided! Was it Paul who was crucified for you? Was it in Paul's name that you were baptized? 14 Thank God, I never baptized any of you, except Crispus and Gaius; 15 no one can say you were baptized in my name. 16 I did of course baptize the household of Stephanas; I cannot think of anyone else. 17 Christ did not send me to baptize, but to proclaim the gospel; and to do it without recourse to the skills of rhetoric, lest the cross of Christ be robbed of its effect.

18 The message of the cross is sheer folly to those on the way to destruction, but to us, who are on the way to salvation, it is the power of God. 19 Scripture says, 'I will destroy the wisdom of the wise, and bring to nothing the cleverness of the clever.' 20 Where is your wise man now, your man of learning, your subtle debater of this present age? God has made the wisdom of this world look foolish! 21 As God in his wisdom ordained, the world failed to find him by its wisdom, and he chose by the folly of the gospel to save those who have faith. 22 Jews demand signs, Greeks look for wisdom, 23 but we proclaim Christ nailed to the cross; and though this is an offence to Jews and folly to Gentiles, 24 yet to those who are called, Jews and Greeks alike, he is the power of God and the wisdom of God.

25 The folly of God is wiser than human wisdom, and the weakness of God stronger than human strength. 26 My friends, think what sort of people you are, whom God has called. Few of you are wise by any human standard, few powerful or of noble birth. 27 Yet, to shame the wise, God

---

a Gk *theirs* *b* Other ancient authorities lack *my* *c* Or *to*
d Gk *brothers* *e* Gk *my brothers* *f* Other ancient authorities read
I am thankful *g* Gk *according to the flesh*

The First Letter to the Corinthians

1 Paul, called to be an apostle of Christ Jesus by the will of God, and Sosthenes our brother, ²to the church of God that is in Corinth, to you who have been sanctified in Christ Jesus, called to be holy, with all those everywhere who call upon the name of our Lord Jesus Christ, their Lord and ours. ³Grace to you and peace from God our Father and the Lord Jesus Christ.

⁴I give thanks to my God always on your account for the grace of God bestowed on you in Christ Jesus, ⁵that in him you were enriched in every way, with all discourse and all knowledge, ⁶as the testimony to Christ was confirmed among you, ⁷so that you are not lacking in any spiritual gift as you wait for the revelation of our Lord Jesus Christ. ⁸He will keep you firm to the end, irreproachable on the day of our Lord Jesus [Christ]. ⁹God is faithful, and by him you were called to fellowship with his Son, Jesus Christ our Lord.

¹⁰I urge you, brothers, in the name of our Lord Jesus Christ, that all of you agree in what you say, and that there be no divisions among you, but that you be united in the same mind and in the same purpose. ¹¹For it has been reported to me about you, my brothers, by Chloe's people, that there are rivalries among you. ¹²I mean that each of you is saying, "I belong to Paul," or "I belong to Apollos," or "I belong to Kephas," or "I belong to Christ." ¹³Is Christ divided? Was Paul crucified for you? Or were you baptized in the name of Paul? ¹⁴I give thanks [to God] that I baptized none of you except Crispus and Gaius, ¹⁵so that no one can say you were baptized in my name. ¹⁶(I baptized the household of Stephanas also; beyond that I do not know whether I baptized anyone else.) ¹⁷For Christ did not send me to baptize but to preach the gospel, and not with the wisdom of human eloquence, so that the cross of Christ might not be emptied of its meaning.

¹⁸The message of the cross is foolishness to those who are perishing, but to us who are being saved it is the power of God. ¹⁹For it is written:

> "I will destroy the wisdom of the wise,
> and the learning of the learned I will set aside."

²⁰Where is the wise one? Where is the scribe? Where is the debater of this age? Has not God made the wisdom of the world foolish? ²¹For since in the wisdom of God the world did not come to know God through wisdom, it was the will of God through the foolishness of the proclamation to save those who have faith. ²²For Jews demand signs and Greeks look for wisdom, ²³but we proclaim Christ crucified, a stumbling block to Jews and foolishness to Gentiles, ²⁴but to those who are called, Jews and Greeks alike, Christ the power of God and the wisdom of God. ²⁵For the foolishness of God is wiser than human wisdom, and the weakness of God is stronger than human strength.

²⁶Consider your own calling, brothers. Not many of you were wise by human standards, not many were powerful, not many were of noble birth. ²⁷Rather, God chose the

1 Corinthians

THE FIRST LETTER OF PAUL TO THE CHURCH AT CORINTH

1 Paul, called by the will of God to be an apostle of Christ Jesus, and Sosthenes, our brother, ²to the church of God in Corinth, to those who have been consecrated in Christ Jesus and called to be God's holy people, with all those everywhere who call on the name of our Lord Jesus Christ, their Lord as well as ours. ³Grace to you and peace from God our Father and the Lord Jesus Christ.

⁴I am continually thanking God about you, for the grace of God which you have been given in Christ Jesus; ⁵in him you have been richly endowed in every kind of utterance and knowledge; ⁶so firmly has witness to Christ taken root in you. ⁷And so you are not lacking in any gift as you wait for our Lord Jesus Christ to be revealed; ⁸he will continue to give you strength till the very end, so that you will be irreproachable on the Day of our Lord Jesus Christ. ⁹You can rely on God, who has called you to be partners with his Son Jesus Christ our Lord.

¹⁰Brothers, I urge you, in the name of our Lord Jesus Christ, not to have factions among yourselves but all to be in agreement in what you profess; so that you are perfectly united in your beliefs and judgements. ¹¹From what Chloe's people have been telling me about you, brothers, it is clear that there are serious differences among you. ¹²What I mean is this: every one of you is declaring, 'I belong to Paul,' or 'I belong to Apollos,' or 'I belong to Cephas,'ᵃ or 'I belong to Christ.' ¹³Has Christ been split up? Was it Paul that was crucified for you, or was it in Paul's name that you were baptised? ¹⁴I am thankful I did not baptise any of you, except Crispus and Gaius, ¹⁵so that no one can say that you were baptised in my name. ¹⁶Yes, I did baptise the family of Stephanas, too; but besides these I do not think I baptised anyone.

¹⁷After all, Christ sent me not to baptise, but to preach the gospel; and not by means of wisdom of language, wise words which would make the cross of Christ pointless. ¹⁸The message of the cross is folly for those who are on the way to ruin, but for those of us who are on the road to salvation it is the power of God. ¹⁹As scripture says: *I am going to destroy the wisdom of the wise and bring to nothing the understanding of any who understand.* ²⁰*Where are the philosophers? Where are the experts?*ᵇ And where are the debaters of this age? Do you not see how God has shown up human wisdom as folly? ²¹Since in the wisdom of God the world was unable to recognise God through wisdom, it was God's own pleasure to save believers through the folly of the gospel. ²²While the Jews demand miracles and the Greeks look for wisdom, ²³we are preaching a crucified Christ: to the Jews an obstacle they cannot get over, to the gentiles foolishness, ²⁴but to those who have been called, whether they are Jews or Greeks, a Christ who is both the power of God and the wisdom of God. ²⁵God's folly is wiser than human wisdom, and God's weakness is stronger than human strength. ²⁶Consider, brothers, how you were called; not many of you are wise by human standards, not many influential, not many from noble families. ²⁷No, God

a 1 *Cephas* is the Aramaic word for 'Peter'. For Apollos *see* Ac 18:24.
b 1 Is 29:14; 19:12.

NEW REVISED STANDARD VERSION	REVISED ENGLISH BIBLE

chose what is foolish in the world to shame the wise; God chose what is weak in the world to shame the strong; 28 God chose what is low and despised in the world, things that are not, to reduce to nothing things that are, 29 so that no one[h] might boast in the presence of God. 30 He is the source of your life in Christ Jesus, who became for us wisdom from God, and righteousness and sanctification and redemption, 31 in order that, as it is written, "Let the one who boasts, boast in[i] the Lord."

2 When I came to you, brothers and sisters,[j] I did not come proclaiming the mystery[k] of God to you in lofty words or wisdom. 2 For I decided to know nothing among you except Jesus Christ, and him crucified. 3 And I came to you in weakness and in fear and in much trembling. 4 My speech and my proclamation were not with plausible words of wisdom,[l] but with a demonstration of the Spirit and of power, 5 so that your faith might rest not on human wisdom but on the power of God.

6 Yet among the mature we do speak wisdom, though it is not a wisdom of this age or of the rulers of this age, who are doomed to perish. 7 But we speak God's wisdom, secret and hidden, which God decreed before the ages for our glory. 8 None of the rulers of this age understood this; for if they had, they would not have crucified the Lord of glory. 9 But, as it is written,

"What no eye has seen, nor ear heard,
nor the human heart conceived,
what God has prepared for those who love
him"—

10 these things God has revealed to us through the Spirit; for the Spirit searches everything, even the depths of God. 11 For what human being knows what is truly human except the human spirit that is within? So also no one comprehends what is truly God's except the Spirit of God. 12 Now we have received not the spirit of the world, but the Spirit that is from God, so that we may understand the gifts bestowed on us by God. 13 And we speak of these things in words not taught by human wisdom but taught by the Spirit, interpreting spiritual things to those who are spiritual.[m]

14 Those who are unspiritual[n] do not receive the gifts of God's Spirit, for they are foolishness to them, and they are unable to understand them because they are spiritually discerned. 15 Those who are spiritual discern all things, and they are themselves subject to no one else's scrutiny. 16 "For who has known the mind of the Lord
so as to instruct him?"
But we have the mind of Christ.

3 And so, brothers and sisters,[j] I could not speak to you as spiritual people, but rather as people of the flesh, as infants in Christ. 2 I fed you with milk, not solid food, for you were not ready for solid food. Even now you are still not ready, 3 for you are still of the flesh. For as long as there is jealousy and quarreling among you, are you not of the flesh, and behaving according to human inclinations? 4 For when one says, "I belong to Paul," and another, "I belong to Apollos," are you not merely human?

5 What then is Apollos? What is Paul? Servants through whom you came to believe, as the Lord assigned to each. 6 I planted, Apollos watered, but God gave the growth. 7 So neither the one who plants nor the one who waters is anything, but only God who gives the growth. 8 The one who

has chosen what the world counts folly, and to shame what is strong, God has chosen what the world counts weakness. 28 He has chosen things without rank or standing in the world, mere nothings, to overthrow the existing order. 29 So no place is left for any human pride in the presence of God. 30 By God's act you are in Christ Jesus; God has made him our wisdom, and in him we have our righteousness, our holiness, our liberation. 31 Therefore, in the words of scripture, 'If anyone must boast, let him boast of the Lord.'

2 So it was, my friends, that I came to you, without any pretensions to eloquence or wisdom in declaring the truth about God. 2 I resolved that while I was with you I would not claim to know anything but Jesus Christ—Christ nailed to the cross. 3 I came before you in weakness, in fear, in great trepidation. 4 The word I spoke, the gospel I proclaimed, did not sway you with clever arguments; it carried conviction by spiritual power, 5 so that your faith might be built not on human wisdom but on the power of God.

6 Among the mature I do speak words of wisdom, though not a wisdom belonging to this present age or to its governing powers, already in decline; 7 I speak God's hidden wisdom, his secret purpose framed from the very beginning to bring us to our destined glory. 8 None of the powers that rule the world has known that wisdom; if they had, they would not have crucified the Lord of glory. 9 Scripture speaks of 'things beyond our seeing, things beyond our hearing, things beyond our imagining, all prepared by God for those who love him'; 10 and these are what God has revealed to us through the Spirit. For the Spirit explores everything, even the depths of God's own nature. 11 Who knows what a human being is but the human spirit within him? In the same way, only the Spirit of God knows what God is. 12 And we have received this Spirit from God, not the spirit of the world, so that we may know all that God has lavished on us; 13 and, because we are interpreting spiritual truths to those who have the Spirit, we speak of these gifts of God in words taught us not by our human wisdom but by the Spirit. 14 An unspiritual person refuses what belongs to the Spirit of God; it is folly to him; he cannot grasp it, because it needs to be judged in the light of the Spirit. 15 But a spiritual person can judge the worth of everything, yet is not himself subject to judgement by others. 16 Scripture indeed asks, 'Who can know the mind of the Lord or be his counsellor?' Yet we possess the mind of Christ.

3 BUT I could not talk to you, my friends, as people who have the Spirit; I had to deal with you on the natural plane, as infants in Christ. 2 I fed you on milk, instead of solid food, for which you were not yet ready. Indeed, you are still not ready for it; 3 you are still on the merely natural plane. Can you not see that as long as there is jealousy and strife among you, you are unspiritual, living on the purely human level? 4 When one declares, 'I am for Paul,' and another, 'I am for Apollos,' are you not all too human?

5 After all, what is Apollos? What is Paul? Simply God's agents in bringing you to faith. Each of us performed the task which the Lord assigned to him: 6 I planted the seed, and Apollos watered it; but God made it grow. 7 It is not the gardeners with their planting and watering who count, but God who makes it grow. 8 Whether they plant or water, they

foolish of the world to shame the wise, and God chose the weak of the world to shame the strong, 28 and God chose the lowly and despised of the world, those who count for nothing, to reduce to nothing those who are something, 29 so that no human being might boast before God. 30 It is due to him that you are in Christ Jesus, who became for us wisdom from God, as well as righteousness, sanctification, and redemption, 31 so that, as it is written, "Whoever boasts, should boast in the Lord."

2 When I came to you, brothers, proclaiming the mystery of God, I did not come with sublimity of words or of wisdom. 2 For I resolved to know nothing while I was with you except Jesus Christ, and him crucified. 3 I came to you in weakness and fear and much trembling, 4 and my message and my proclamation were not with persuasive [words of] wisdom, but with a demonstration of spirit and power, 5 so that your faith might rest not on human wisdom but on the power of God.

6 Yet we do speak a wisdom to those who are mature, but not a wisdom of this age, nor of the rulers of this age who are passing away. 7 Rather we speak God's wisdom, mysterious, hidden, which God predetermined before the ages for our glory, 8 and which none of the rulers of this age knew, for if they had known it, they would not have crucified the Lord of glory. 9 But as it is written:

"What eye has not seen, and ear has not heard,
    and what has not entered the human heart,
    what God has prepared for those who love him,"

10 this God has revealed to us through the Spirit.

For the Spirit scrutinizes everything, even the depths of God. 11 Among human beings, who knows what pertains to a person except the spirit of the person that is within? Similarly, no one knows what pertains to God except the Spirit of God. 12 We have not received the spirit of the world but the Spirit that is from God, so that we may understand the things freely given us by God. 13 And we speak about them not with words taught by human wisdom, but with words taught by the Spirit, describing spiritual realities in spiritual terms.

14 Now the natural person does not accept what pertains to the Spirit of God, for to him it is foolishness, and he cannot understand it, because it is judged spiritually. 15 The spiritual person, however, can judge everything but is not subject to judgment by anyone.

16 For "who has known the mind of the Lord, so as to counsel him?" But we have the mind of Christ.

3 My brothers, I could not talk to you as spiritual people, but as fleshly people, as infants in Christ. 2 I fed you milk, not solid food, because you were unable to take it. Indeed, you are still not able, even now, 3 for you are still of the flesh. While there is jealousy and rivalry among you, are you not of the flesh and behaving in an ordinary human way? 4 Whenever someone says, "I belong to Paul," and another, "I belong to Apollos," are you not merely human?

5 What is Apollos, after all, and what is Paul? Ministers through whom you became believers, just as the Lord assigned each one. 6 I planted, Apollos watered, but God caused the growth. 7 Therefore, neither the one who plants nor the one who waters is anything, but only God, who causes the growth. 8 The one who plants and the one who

chose those who by human standards are fools to shame the wise; he chose those who by human standards are weak to shame the strong, 28 those who by human standards are common and contemptible — indeed those who count for nothing — to reduce to nothing all those that do count for something, 29 so that no human being might feel boastful before God. 30 It is by him that you exist in Christ Jesus, who for us was made wisdom from God, and saving justice and holiness and redemption. 31 As scripture says: If anyone wants to boast, let him boast of the Lord.c

2 Now when I came to you, brothers, I did not come with any brilliance of oratory or wise argument to announce to you the mystery of God. 2 I was resolved that the only knowledge I would have while I was with you was knowledge of Jesus, and of him as the crucified Christ. 3 I came among you in weakness, in fear and great trembling 4 and what I spoke and proclaimed was not meant to convince by philosophical argument, but to demonstrate the convincing power of the Spirit, 5 so that your faith should depend not on human wisdom but on the power of God.

6 But still, to those who have reached maturity, we do talk of a wisdom, not, it is true, a philosophy of this age or of the rulers of this age, who will not last long now. 7 It is of the mysterious wisdom of God that we talk, the wisdom that was hidden, which God predestined to be for our glory before the ages began. 8 None of the rulers of the age recognised it; for if they had recognised it, they would not have crucified the Lord of glory; 9 but it is as scripture says: What no eye has seen and no ear has heard, what the mind of man cannot visualise; all that God has prepared for those who love him;d 10 to us, though, God has given revelation through the Spirit, for the Spirit explores the depths of everything, even the depths of God. 11 After all, is there anyone who knows the qualities of anyone except his own spirit, within him; and in the same way, nobody knows the qualities of God except the Spirit of God. 12 Now, the Spirit we have received is not the spirit of the world but God's own Spirit, so that we may understand the lavish gifts God has given us. 13 And these are what we speak of, not in the terms learnt from human philosophy, but in terms learnt from the Spirit, fitting spiritual language to spiritual things. 14 The natural person has no room for the gifts of God's Spirit; to him they are folly; he cannot recognise them, because their value can be assessed only in the Spirit. 15 The spiritual person, on the other hand, can assess the value of everything, and that person's value cannot be assessed by anybody else. 16 For: who has ever known the mind of the Lord? Who has ever been his adviser?e But we are those who have the mind of Christ.

3 And so, brothers, I was not able to talk to you as spiritual people; I had to talk to you as people still living by your natural inclinations, still infants in Christ; 2 I fed you with milk and not solid food, for you were not yet able to take it — and even now, you are still not able to, 3 for you are still living by your natural inclinations. As long as there are jealousy and rivalry among you, that surely means that you are still living by your natural inclinations and by merely human principles. 4 While there is one that says, 'I belong to Paul' and another that says, 'I belong to Apollos' are you not being only too human?

5 For what is Apollos and what is Paul? The servants through whom you came to believe, and each has only what the Lord has given him. 6 I did the planting, Apollos did the watering, but God gave growth. 7 In this, neither the planter nor the waterer counts for anything; only God, who gives growth. 8 It is all one who does the planting and who does

2, 4: Among many manuscript readings here the best is either "not with the persuasion of wisdom" or "not with persuasive words of wisdom," which differ only by a nuance.

c 1 cf. Jr 9:22–23.   d 2 A free combination of Is 64:3 and Jr 3:16.
e 2 Is 40:13.

plants and the one who waters have a common purpose, and each will receive wages according to the labor of each. 9 For we are God's servants, working together; you are God's field, God's building.

10 According to the grace of God given to me, like a skilled master builder I laid a foundation, and someone else is building on it. Each builder must choose with care how to build on it. 11 For no one can lay any foundation other than the one that has been laid; that foundation is Jesus Christ. 12 Now if anyone builds on the foundation with gold, silver, precious stones, wood, hay, straw — 13 the work of each builder will become visible, for the Day will disclose it, because it will be revealed with fire, and the fire will test what sort of work each has done. 14 If what has been built on the foundation survives, the builder will receive a reward. 15 If the work is burned up, the builder will suffer loss; the builder will be saved, but only as through fire.

16 Do you not know that you are God's temple and that God's Spirit dwells in you?ₒ 17 If anyone destroys God's temple, God will destroy that person. For God's temple is holy, and you are that temple.

18 Do not deceive yourselves. If you think that you are wise in this age, you should become fools so that you may become wise. 19 For the wisdom of this world is foolishness with God. For it is written,

"He catches the wise in their craftiness,"

20 and again,

"The Lord knows the thoughts of the wise,
    that they are futile."

21 So let no one boast about human leaders. For all things are yours, 22 whether Paul or Apollos or Cephas or the world or life or death or the present or the future — all belong to you, 23 and you belong to Christ, and Christ belongs to God.

4 Think of us in this way, as servants of Christ and stewards of God's mysteries. 2 Moreover, it is required of stewards that they be found trustworthy. 3 But with me it is a very small thing that I should be judged by you or by any human court. I do not even judge myself. 4 I am not aware of anything against myself, but I am not thereby acquitted. It is the Lord who judges me. 5 Therefore do not pronounce judgment before the time, before the Lord comes, who will bring to light the things now hidden in darkness and will disclose the purposes of the heart. Then each one will receive commendation from God.

6 I have applied all this to Apollos and myself for your benefit, brothers and sisters,ₚ so that you may learn through us the meaning of the saying, "Nothing beyond what is written," so that none of you will be puffed up in favor of one against another. 7 For who sees anything different in you?ₚ What do you have that you did not receive? And if you received it, why do you boast as if it were not a gift?

8 Already you have all you want! Already you have become rich! Quite apart from us you have become kings! Indeed, I wish that you had become kings, so that we might be kings with you! 9 For I think that God has exhibited us apostles as last of all, as though sentenced to death, because we have become a spectacle to the world, to angels and to mortals. 10 We are fools for the sake of Christ, but you are wise in Christ. We are weak, but you are strong. You are held in honor, but we in disrepute. 11 To the present hour we are hungry and thirsty, we are poorly clothed and beaten and homeless, 12 and we grow weary from the work of our own hands. When reviled, we bless; when persecuted, we endure; 13 when slandered, we speak kindly. We have be-

work as a team, though each will get his own pay for his own labour. 9 We are fellow-workers in God's service; and you are God's garden.

Or again, you are God's building. 10 God gave me the privilege of laying the foundation like a skilled master builder; others put up the building. Let each take care how he builds. 11 There can be no other foundation than the one already laid: I mean Jesus Christ himself. 12 If anyone builds on that foundation with gold, silver, and precious stones, or with wood, hay, and straw, 13 the work that each does will at last be brought to light; the day of judgement will expose it. For that day dawns in fire, and the fire will test the worth of each person's work. 14 If anyone's building survives, he will be rewarded; 15 if it burns down, he will have to bear the loss; yet he will escape with his life, though only by passing through the fire. 16 Surely you know that you are God's temple, where the Spirit of God dwells. 17 Anyone who destroys God's temple will himself be destroyed by God, because the temple of God is holy; and you are that temple.

18 Make no mistake about this: if there is anyone among you who fancies himself wise — wise, I mean, by the standards of this age — he must become a fool if he is to be truly wise. 19 For the wisdom of this world is folly in God's sight. Scripture says, 'He traps the wise in their own cunning,' 20 and again, 'The Lord knows that the arguments of the wise are futile.' 21 So never make any human being a cause for boasting. For everything belongs to you — 22 Paul, Apollos, and Cephas, the world, life, and death, the present and the future, all are yours — 23 and you belong to Christ, and Christ to God.

4 We are to be regarded as Christ's subordinates and as stewards of the secrets of God. 2 Now stewards are required to show themselves trustworthy. 3 To me it matters not at all if I am called to account by you or by any human court. Nor do I pass judgement on myself, 4 for I have nothing on my conscience; but that does not prove me innocent. My judge is the Lord. 5 So pass no premature judgement; wait until the Lord comes. He will bring to light what darkness hides and disclose our inward motives; then will be the time for each to receive commendation from God.

6 My friends, I have applied all this to Apollos and myself for your benefit, so that you may take our case as an example, and learn the true meaning of 'nothing beyond what stands written', and may not be inflated with pride as you take sides in support of one against another. 7 My friend, who makes you so important? What do you possess that was not given you? And if you received it as a gift, why take the credit to yourself?

8 No doubt you already have all you could desire; you have come into your fortune already! Without us you have come into your kingdom. How I wish you had indeed come into your kingdom; then you might share it with us! 9 For it seems to me God has made us apostles the last act in the show, like men condemned to death in the arena, a spectacle to the whole universe — to angels as well as men. 10 We are fools for Christ's sake, while you are sensible Christians! We are weak; you are powerful! You are honoured; we are in disgrace! 11 To this day we go hungry and thirsty and in rags; we are beaten up; we wander from place to place; 12 we wear ourselves out earning a living with our own hands. People curse us, and we bless; they persecute us, and we submit; 13 they slander us, and we try to be

ₒ In verses 16 and 17 the Greek word for you is plural
ₚ Gk brothers   ₚ Or Who makes you different from another?

3:9 We . . . service: or We are God's fellow-workers.

waters are equal, and each will receive wages in proportion to his labor. 9 For we are God's co-workers; you are God's field, God's building.

10 According to the grace of God given to me, like a wise master builder I laid a foundation, and another is building upon it. But each one must be careful how he builds upon it, 11 for no one can lay a foundation other than the one that is there, namely, Jesus Christ. 12 If anyone builds on this foundation with gold, silver, precious stones, wood, hay, or straw, 13 the work of each will come to light, for the Day will disclose it. It will be revealed with fire, and the fire [itself] will test the quality of each one's work. 14 If the work stands that someone built upon the foundation, that person will receive a wage. 15 But if someone's work is burned up, that one will suffer loss; the person will be saved, but only as through fire. 16 Do you not know that you are the temple of God, and that the Spirit of God dwells in you? 17 If anyone destroys God's temple, God will destroy that person; for the temple of God, which you are, is holy.

18 Let no one deceive himself. If anyone among you considers himself wise in this age, let him become a fool so as to become wise. 19 For the wisdom of this world is foolishness in the eyes of God, for it is written:

"He catches the wise in their own ruses,"

20 and again:

"The Lord knows the thoughts of the wise, that
they are vain."

21 So let no one boast about human beings, for everything belongs to you, 22 Paul or Apollos or Kephas, or the world or life or death, or the present or the future: all belong to you, 23 and you to Christ, and Christ to God.

4 Thus should one regard us: as servants of Christ and stewards of the mysteries of God. 2 Now it is of course required of stewards that they be found trustworthy. 3 It does not concern me in the least that I be judged by you or any human tribunal; I do not even pass judgment on myself; 4 I am not conscious of anything against me, but I do not thereby stand acquitted; the one who judges me is the Lord. 5 Therefore, do not make any judgment before the appointed time, until the Lord comes, for he will bring to light what is hidden in darkness and will manifest the motives of our hearts, and then everyone will receive praise from God.

6 I have applied these things to myself and Apollos for your benefit, brothers, so that you may learn from us not to go beyond what is written, so that none of you will be inflated with pride in favor of one person over against another. 7 Who confers distinction upon you? What do you possess that you have not received? But if you have received it, why are you boasting as if you did not receive it? 8 You are already satisfied; you have already grown rich; you have become kings without us! Indeed, I wish that you had become kings, so that we also might become kings with you.

9 For as I see it, God has exhibited us apostles as the last of all, like people sentenced to death, since we have become a spectacle to the world, to angels and human beings alike. 10 We are fools on Christ's account, but you are wise in Christ; we are weak, but you are strong; you are held in honor, but we in disrepute. 11 To this very hour we go hungry and thirsty, we are poorly clad and roughly treated, we wander about homeless 12 and we toil, working with our own hands. When ridiculed, we bless; when persecuted, we endure; 13 when slandered, we respond gently. We have

the watering, and each will have the proper pay for the work that he has done. 9 After all, we do share in God's work; you are God's farm, God's building.

10 By the grace of God which was given to me, I laid the foundations like a trained master-builder, and someone else is building on them. Now each one must be careful how he does the building. 11 For nobody can lay down any other foundation than the one which is there already, namely Jesus Christ. 12 On this foundation, different people may build in gold, silver, jewels, wood, hay or straw 13 but each person's handiwork will be shown for what it is. The Day which dawns in fire will make it clear and the fire itself will test the quality of each person's work. 14 The one whose work stands up to it will be given his wages; 15 the one whose work is burnt down will suffer the loss of it, though he himself will be saved; he will be saved as someone might expect to be saved from a fire.

16 Do you not realise that you are a temple of God with the Spirit of God living in you? 17 If anybody should destroy the temple of God, God will destroy that person, because God's temple is holy; and you are that temple.

18 There is no room for self-delusion. Any one of you who thinks he is wise by worldly standards must learn to be a fool in order to be really wise. 19 For the wisdom of the world is folly to God. As scripture says: *He traps the crafty in the snare of their own cunning* 20 and again: *The Lord knows the plans of the wise and how insipid they are.* ƒ 21 So there is to be no boasting about human beings: everything belongs to you, 22 whether it is Paul, or Apollos, or Cephas, the world, or life or death, the present or the future — all belong to you; 23 but you belong to Christ and Christ belongs to God.

4 People should think of us as Christ's servants, stewards entrusted with the mysteries of God. 2 In such a matter, what is expected of stewards is that each one should be found trustworthy. 3 It is of no importance to me how you or any other human court may judge me: I will not even be the judge of my own self. 4 It is true that my conscience does not reproach me, but that is not enough to justify me: it is the Lord who is my judge. 5 For that reason, do not judge anything before the due time, until the Lord comes; he will bring to light everything that is hidden in darkness and reveal the designs of all hearts. Then everyone will receive from God the appropriate commendation.

6 I have applied all this to myself and Apollos for your sakes, so that you can learn how the saying, 'Nothing beyond what is written' is true of us: no individual among you must become filled with his own importance and make comparisons, to another's detriment. 7 Who made you so important? What have you got that was not given to you? And if it was given to you, why are you boasting as though it were your own? 8 You already have everything — you are rich already — you have come into your kingdom, without any help from us! Well, I wish you were kings and we could be kings with you! 9 For it seems to me that God has put us apostles on show right at the end, like men condemned to death: we have been exhibited as a spectacle to the whole universe, both angelic and human. 10 Here we are, fools for Christ's sake, while you are the clever ones in Christ; we are weak, while you are strong; you are honoured, while we are disgraced. 11 To this day, we go short of food and drink and clothes, we are beaten up and we have no homes; 12 we earn our living by labouring with our own hands; when we are cursed, we answer with a blessing; when we are hounded, we endure it passively; 13 when we are insulted,

ƒ **3** Jb 5:13 followed by Ps 94:11.

3017

come like the rubbish of the world, the dregs of all things, to this very day.

14 I am not writing this to make you ashamed, but to admonish you as my beloved children. 15 For though you might have ten thousand guardians in Christ, you do not have many fathers. Indeed, in Christ Jesus I became your father through the gospel. 16 I appeal to you, then, be imitators of me. 17 For this reason I sent[r] you Timothy, who is my beloved and faithful child in the Lord, to remind you of my ways in Christ Jesus, as I teach them everywhere in every church. 18 But some of you, thinking that I am not coming to you, have become arrogant. 19 But I will come to you soon, if the Lord wills, and I will find out not the talk of these arrogant people but their power. 20 For the kingdom of God depends not on talk but on power. 21 What would you prefer? Am I to come to you with a stick, or with love in a spirit of gentleness?

5 It is actually reported that there is sexual immorality among you, and of a kind that is not found even among pagans; for a man is living with his father's wife. 2 And you are arrogant! Should you not rather have mourned, so that he who has done this would have been removed from among you?

3 For though absent in body, I am present in spirit; and as if present I have already pronounced judgment 4 in the name of the Lord Jesus on the man who has done such a thing.[s] When you are assembled, and my spirit is present with the power of our Lord Jesus, 5 you are to hand this man over to Satan for the destruction of the flesh, so that his spirit may be saved in the day of the Lord.[t]

6 Your boasting is not a good thing. Do you not know that a little yeast leavens the whole batch of dough? 7 Clean out the old yeast so that you may be a new batch, as you really are unleavened. For our paschal lamb, Christ, has been sacrificed. 8 Therefore, let us celebrate the festival, not with the old yeast, the yeast of malice and evil, but with the unleavened bread of sincerity and truth.

9 I wrote to you in my letter not to associate with sexually immoral persons — 10 not at all meaning the immoral of this world, or the greedy and robbers, or idolaters, since you would then need to go out of the world. 11 But now I am writing to you not to associate with anyone who bears the name of brother or sister[u] who is sexually immoral or greedy, or is an idolater, reviler, drunkard, or robber. Do not even eat with such a one. 12 For what have I to do with judging those outside? Is it not those who are inside that you are to judge? 13 God will judge those outside. "Drive out the wicked person from among you."

6 When any of you has a grievance against another, do you dare to take it to court before the unrighteous, instead of taking it before the saints? 2 Do you not know that the saints will judge the world? And if the world is to be judged by you, are you incompetent to try trivial cases? 3 Do you not know that we are to judge angels — to say nothing of ordinary matters? 4 If you have ordinary cases, then, do you appoint as judges those who have no standing in the

conciliatory. To this day we are treated as the scum of the earth, as the dregs of humanity.

14 I am not writing this to shame you, but to bring you to reason; for you are my dear children. 15 You may have thousands of tutors in Christ, but you have only one father; for in Christ Jesus I am your offspring, and mine alone, through the preaching of the gospel. 16 I appeal to you therefore to follow my example. 17 That is why I have sent Timothy, who is a dear son to me and a trustworthy Christian, to remind you of my way of life in Christ, something I teach everywhere in all the churches. 18 There are certain persons who are filled with self-importance because they think I am not coming to Corinth. 19 I shall come very soon, if it is the Lord's will; and then I shall take the measure of these self-important people, not by what they say, but by what they can do, 20 for the kingdom of God is not a matter of words, but of power. 21 Choose, then: am I to come to you with a rod in my hand, or with love and a gentle spirit?

5 I ACTUALLY hear reports of sexual immorality among you, immorality such as even pagans do not tolerate: the union of a man with his stepmother. 2 And you are proud of yourselves! You ought to have gone into mourning; anyone who behaves like that should be turned out of your community. 3 For my part, though I am absent in body, I am present in spirit, and have already reached my judgement on the man who did this thing, as if I were indeed present: 4 when you are all assembled in the name of our Lord Jesus, and I am with you in spirit, through the power of our Lord Jesus you are 5 to consign this man to Satan for the destruction of his body, so that his spirit may be saved on the day of the Lord.

6 Your self-satisfaction ill becomes you. Have you never heard the saying, 'A little leaven leavens all the dough'? 7 Get rid of the old leaven and then you will be a new batch of unleavened dough. Indeed you already are, because Christ our Passover lamb has been sacrificed. 8 So we who observe the festival must not use the old leaven, the leaven of depravity and wickedness, but only the unleavened bread which is sincerity and truth.

9 In my letter I wrote that you must have nothing to do with those who are sexually immoral. 10 I was not, of course, referring to people in general who are immoral or extortioners or swindlers or idolaters; to avoid them you would have to withdraw from society altogether. 11 I meant that you must have nothing to do with any so-called Christian who leads an immoral life, or is extortionate, idolatrous, a slanderer, a drunkard, or a swindler; with anyone like that you should not even eat. 12–13 What business of mine is it to judge outsiders? God is their judge. But within the fellowship, you are the judges: 'Root out the wrongdoer from your community.'

6 IF one of your number has a dispute with another, does he have the face to go to law before a pagan court instead of before God's people? 2 It is God's people who are to judge the world; surely you know that. And if the world is subject to your judgement, are you not competent to deal with these trifling cases? 3 Are you not aware that we are to judge angels, not to mention day to day affairs? 4 If therefore you have such everyday disputes, how can you entrust jurisdiction to outsiders with no standing in the church? 5 I

---

[r] Or *am sending* [s] Or *on the man who has done such a thing in the name of the Lord Jesus* [t] Other ancient authorities add *Jesus*
[u] Gk *brother*

become like the world's rubbish, the scum of all, to this very moment. 14 I am writing you this not to shame you, but to admonish you as my beloved children. 15 Even if you should have countless guides to Christ, yet you do not have many fathers, for I became your father in Christ Jesus through the gospel. 16 Therefore, I urge you, be imitators of me. 17 For this reason I am sending you Timothy, who is my beloved and faithful son in the Lord; he will remind you of my ways in Christ [Jesus], just as I teach them everywhere in every church.

18 Some have become inflated with pride, as if I were not coming to you. 19 But I will come to you soon, if the Lord is willing, and I shall ascertain not the talk of these inflated people but their power. 20 For the kingdom of God is not a matter of talk but of power. 21 Which do you prefer? Shall I come to you with a rod, or with love and a gentle spirit?

5 It is widely reported that there is immorality among you, and immorality of a kind not found even among pagans—a man living with his father's wife. 2 And you are inflated with pride. Should you not rather have been sorrowful? The one who did this deed should be expelled from your midst. 3 I, for my part, although absent in body but present in spirit, have already, as if present, pronounced judgment on the one who has committed this deed, 4 in the name of [our] Lord Jesus: when you have gathered together and I am with you in spirit with the power of the Lord Jesus, 5 you are to deliver this man to Satan for the destruction of his flesh, so that his spirit may be saved on the day of the Lord.

6 Your boasting is not appropriate. Do you not know that a little yeast leavens all the dough? 7 Clear out the old yeast, so that you may become a fresh batch of dough, inasmuch as you are unleavened. For our paschal lamb, Christ, has been sacrificed. 8 Therefore, let us celebrate the feast, not with the old yeast, the yeast of malice and wickedness, but with the unleavened bread of sincerity and truth.

9 I wrote you in my letter not to associate with immoral people, 10 not at all referring to the immoral of this world or the greedy and robbers or idolaters; for you would then have to leave the world. 11 But I now write to you not to associate with anyone named a brother, if he is immoral, greedy, an idolater, a slanderer, a drunkard, or a robber, not even to eat with such a person. 12 For why should I be judging outsiders? Is it not your business to judge those within? 13 God will judge those outside. "Purge the evil person from your midst."

6 How can any one of you with a case against another dare to bring it to the unjust for judgment instead of to the holy ones? 2 Do you not know that the holy ones will judge the world? If the world is to be judged by you, are you unqualified for the lowest law courts? 3 Do you not know that we will judge angels? Then why not everyday matters? 4 If, therefore, you have courts for everyday matters, do you seat as judges people of no standing in the church? 5 I say

we give a courteous answer. We are treated even now as the dregs of the world, the very lowest scum.

14 I am writing all this not to make you ashamed but simply to remind you, as my dear children; 15 for even though you might have ten thousand slaves to look after you in Christ, you still have no more than one father, and it was I who fathered you in Christ Jesus, by the gospel. 16 That is why I urge you to take me as your pattern 17 and why I have sent you Timothy, a dear and faithful son to me in the Lord, who will remind you of my principles of conduct in Christ, as I teach them everywhere in every church.

18 On the assumption that I was not coming to you, some of you have become filled with your own self-importance; 19 but I shall be coming to you soon, the Lord willing, and then I shall find out not what these self-important people say, but what power they have. 20 For the kingdom of God consists not in spoken words but in power. 21 What do you want then? Am I to come to you with a stick in my hand or in love, and with a spirit of gentleness?

5 It is widely reported that there is sexual immorality among you, immorality of a kind that is not found even among gentiles: that one of you is living with his step-mother.g 2 And you so filled with your own self-importance! It would have been better if you had been grieving bitterly, so that the man who has done this thing were turned out of the community. 3 For my part, however distant I am physically, I am present in spirit and have already condemned the man who behaved in this way, just as though I were present in person. 4 When you have gathered together in the name of our Lord Jesus, with the presence of my spirit, and in the power of our Lord Jesus, 5 hand such a man over to Satan, to be destroyed as far as natural life is concerned, so that on the Day of the Lord his spirit may be saved.

6 Your self-satisfaction is ill founded. Do you not realise that only a little yeast leavens the whole batch of dough? 7 Throw out the old yeast so that you can be the fresh dough, unleavened as you are. For our Passover has been sacrificed, that is, Christ; 8 let us keep the feast, then, with none of the old yeast and no leavening of evil and wickedness, but only the unleavened bread of sincerity and truth.

9 In my letter, I wrote to you that you should have nothing to do with people living immoral lives. 10 I was not including everybody in this present world who is sexually immoral, or everybody who is greedy, or dishonest or worships false gods—that would mean you would have to cut yourselves off completely from the world. 11 In fact what I meant was that you were not to have anything to do with anyone going by the name of brother who is sexually immoral, or is greedy, or worships false gods, or is a slanderer or a drunkard or dishonest; never even have a meal with anybody of that kind. 12 It is no concern of mine to judge outsiders. It is for you to judge those who are inside, is it not? 13 But outsiders are for God to judge.

You must banish this evil-doer from among you.h

6 Is one of you with a complaint against another so brazen as to seek judgement from sinners and not from God's holy people? 2 Do you not realise that the holy people of God are to be the judges of the world? And if the world is to be judged by you, are you not competent for petty cases? 3 Do you not realise that we shall be the judges of angels?—then quite certainly over matters of this life. 4 But when you have matters of this life to be judged, you bring them before those who are of no account in the Church! 5 I

g 5 Against OT and Roman law, but seemingly not Corinthian law, it was forbidden by the Jerusalem decision (Ac 15:20).   h 5 Dt 13:6.

NEW REVISED STANDARD VERSION

REVISED ENGLISH BIBLE

church? 5 I say this to your shame. Can it be that there is no one among you wise enough to decide between one believer[v] and another, 6 but a believer[v] goes to court against a believer[v] — and before unbelievers at that?

7 In fact, to have lawsuits at all with one another is already a defeat for you. Why not rather be wronged? Why not rather be defrauded? 8 But you yourselves wrong and defraud — and believers[w] at that.

9 Do you not know that wrongdoers will not inherit the kingdom of God? Do not be deceived! Fornicators, idolaters, adulterers, male prostitutes, sodomites, 10 thieves, the greedy, drunkards, revilers, robbers — none of these will inherit the kingdom of God. 11 And this is what some of you used to be. But you were washed, you were sanctified, you were justified in the name of the Lord Jesus Christ and in the Spirit of our God.

12 "All things are lawful for me," but not all things are beneficial. "All things are lawful for me," but I will not be dominated by anything. 13 "Food is meant for the stomach and the stomach for food,"[x] and God will destroy both one and the other. The body is meant not for fornication but for the Lord, and the Lord for the body. 14 And God raised the Lord and will also raise us by his power. 15 Do you not know that your bodies are members of Christ? Should I therefore take the members of Christ and make them members of a prostitute? Never! 16 Do you not know that whoever is united to a prostitute becomes one body with her? For it is said, "The two shall be one flesh." 17 But anyone united to the Lord becomes one spirit with him. 18 Shun fornication! Every sin that a person commits is outside the body; but the fornicator sins against the body itself. 19 Or do you not know that your body is a temple[y] of the Holy Spirit within you, which you have from God, and that you are not your own? 20 For you were bought with a price; therefore glorify God in your body.

7 Now concerning the matters about which you wrote: "It is well for a man not to touch a woman." 2 But because of cases of sexual immorality, each man should have his own wife and each woman her own husband. 3 The husband should give to his wife her conjugal rights, and likewise the wife to her husband. 4 For the wife does not have authority over her own body, but the husband does; likewise the husband does not have authority over his own body, but the wife does. 5 Do not deprive one another except perhaps by agreement for a set time, to devote yourselves to prayer, and then come together again, so that Satan may not tempt you because of your lack of self-control. 6 This I say by way of concession, not of command. 7 I wish that all were as I myself am. But each has a particular gift from God, one having one kind and another a different kind.

8 To the unmarried and the widows I say that it is well for them to remain unmarried as I am. 9 But if they are not practicing self-control, they should marry. For it is better to marry than to be aflame with passion.

10 To the married I give this command — not I but the Lord — that the wife should not separate from her husband 11 (but if she does separate, let her remain unmarried or else be reconciled to her husband), and that the husband should not divorce his wife.

12 To the rest I say — I and not the Lord — that if any believer[v] has a wife who is an unbeliever, and she consents

write this to shame you. Can it be that there is not among you a single person wise enough to give a decision in a fellow-Christian's cause? 6 Must Christian go to law with Christian — and before unbelievers at that? 7 Indeed, you suffer defeat by going to law with one another at all. Why not rather submit to wrong? Why not let yourself be defrauded? 8 But instead, it is you who are wronging and defrauding, and fellow-Christians at that! 9 Surely you know that wrongdoers will never possess the kingdom of God. Make no mistake: no fornicator or idolater, no adulterer or sexual pervert, 10 no thief, extortioner, drunkard, slanderer, or swindler will possess the kingdom of God. 11 Such were some of you; but you have been washed clean, you have been dedicated to God, you have been justified through the name of the Lord Jesus and through the Spirit of our God.

12 'I am free to do anything,' you say. Yes, but not everything does good. No doubt I am free to do anything, but I for one will not let anything make free with me. 13 'Food is for the belly and the belly for food,' you say. True; and one day God will put an end to both. But the body is not for fornication; it is for the Lord — and the Lord for the body. 14 God not only raised our Lord from the dead; he will also raise us by his power. 15 Do you not know that your bodies are limbs and organs of Christ? Shall I then take parts of Christ's body and make them over to a prostitute? Never! 16 You surely know that anyone who joins himself to a prostitute becomes physically one with her, for scripture says, 'The two shall become one flesh'; 17 but anyone who joins himself to the Lord is one with him spiritually. 18 Have nothing to do with fornication. Every other sin that one may commit is outside the body; but the fornicator sins against his own body. 19 Do you not know that your body is a temple of the indwelling Holy Spirit, and the Spirit is God's gift to you? You do not belong to yourselves; 20 you were bought at a price. Then honour God in your body.

7 Now for the matters you wrote about. You say, 'It is a good thing for a man not to have intercourse with a woman.' 2 Rather, in the face of so much immorality, let each man have his own wife and each woman her own husband. 3 The husband must give the wife what is due to her, and equally the wife must give the husband his due. 4 The wife cannot claim her body as her own; it is her husband's. Equally, the husband cannot claim his body as his own; it is his wife's. 5 Do not deny yourselves to one another, except when you agree to devote yourselves to prayer for a time, and to come together again afterwards; otherwise, through lack of self-control, you may be tempted by Satan. 6 I say this by way of concession, not command. 7 I should like everyone to be as I myself am; but each person has the gift God has granted him, one this gift and another that.

8 To the unmarried and to widows I say this: it is a good thing if like me they stay as they are; 9 but if they do not have self-control, they should marry. It is better to be married than burn with desire.

10 To the married I give this ruling, which is not mine but the Lord's: a wife must not separate herself from her husband — 11 if she does, she must either remain unmarried or be reconciled to her husband — and the husband must not divorce his wife.

12 To the rest I say this, as my own word, not as the Lord's: if a Christian has a wife who is not a believer, and

---

[v] Gk brother   [w] Gk brothers   [x] The quotation may extend to the word other   [y] Or sanctuary

NEW AMERICAN BIBLE

NEW JERUSALEM BIBLE

this to shame you. Can it be that there is not one among you wise enough to be able to settle a case between brothers? 6 But rather brother goes to court against brother, and that before unbelievers?

7 Now indeed [then] it is, in any case, a failure on your part that you have lawsuits against one another. Why not rather put up with injustice? Why not rather let yourselves be cheated? 8 Instead, you inflict injustice and cheat, and this to brothers. 9 Do you not know that the unjust will not inherit the kingdom of God? Do not be deceived; neither fornicators nor idolaters nor adulterers nor boy prostitutes nor practicing homosexuals 10 nor thieves nor the greedy nor drunkards nor slanderers nor robbers will inherit the kingdom of God. 11 That is what some of you used to be; but now you have had yourselves washed, you were sanctified, you were justified in the name of the Lord Jesus Christ and in the Spirit of our God.

12 "Everything is lawful for me," but not everything is beneficial. "Everything is lawful for me," but I will not let myself be dominated by anything. 13 "Food for the stomach and the stomach for food," but God will do away with both the one and the other. The body, however, is not for immorality, but for the Lord, and the Lord is for the body; 14 God raised the Lord and will also raise us by his power.

15 Do you not know that your bodies are members of Christ? Shall I then take Christ's members and make them the members of a prostitute? Of course not! 16 [Or] do you not know that anyone who joins himself to a prostitute becomes one body with her? For "the two," it says, "will become one flesh." 17 But whoever is joined to the Lord becomes one spirit with him. 18 Avoid immorality. Every other sin a person commits is outside the body, but the immoral person sins against his own body. 19 Do you not know that your body is a temple of the holy Spirit within you, whom you have from God, and that you are not your own? 20 For you have been purchased at a price. Therefore glorify God in your body.

7 Now in regard to the matters about which you wrote: "It is a good thing for a man not to touch a woman," 2 but because of cases of immorality every man should have his own wife, and every woman her own husband. 3 The husband should fulfill his duty toward his wife, and likewise the wife toward her husband. 4 A wife does not have authority over her own body, but rather her husband, and similarly a husband does not have authority over his own body, but rather his wife. 5 Do not deprive each other, except perhaps by mutual consent for a time, to be free for prayer, but then return to one another, so that Satan may not tempt you through your lack of self-control. 6 This I say by way of concession, however, not as a command. 7 Indeed, I wish everyone to be as I am, but each has a particular gift from God, one of one kind and one of another.

8 Now to the unmarried and to widows I say: It is a good thing for them to remain as they are, as I do, 9 but if they cannot exercise self-control they should marry, for it is better to marry than to be on fire. 10 To the married, however, I give this instruction (not I, but the Lord): A wife should not separate from her husband 11 — and if she does separate she must either remain single or become reconciled to her husband — and a husband should not divorce his wife.

12 To the rest I say (not the Lord): If any brother has a wife who is an unbeliever, and she is willing to go on living

say this to make you ashamed of yourselves. Can it really be that it is impossible to find in the community one sensible person capable of deciding questions between brothers, 6 and that this is why brother goes to law against brother, and that before unbelievers? 7 No; it is a fault in you, by itself, that one of you should go to law against another at all: why do you not prefer to suffer injustice, why not prefer to be defrauded? 8 And here you are, doing the injustice and the defrauding, and to your own brothers.

9 Do you not realise that people who do evil will never inherit the kingdom of God? Make no mistake — the sexually immoral, idolaters, adulterers, the self-indulgent, sodomites, 10 thieves, misers, drunkards, slanderers and swindlers, none of these will inherit the kingdom of God. 11 Some of you used to be of that kind: but you have been washed clean, you have been sanctified, and you have been justified in the name of the Lord Jesus Christ and through the Spirit of our God.

12 'For me everything is permissible'; i maybe, but not everything does good. True, for me everything is permissible, but I am determined not to be dominated by anything. 13 Foods are for the stomach, and the stomach is for foods; and God will destroy them both. But the body is not for sexual immorality; 14 it is for the Lord, and the Lord is for the body. God raised up the Lord and he will raise us up too by his power. 15 Do you not realise that your bodies are members of Christ's body; do you think one can take parts of Christ's body and join them to the body of a prostitute? Out of the question! 16 Or do you not realise that anyone who attaches himself to a prostitute is one body with her, since the two, as it is said, become one flesh.j 17 But anyone who attaches himself to the Lord is one spirit with him.

18 Keep away from sexual immorality. All other sins that people may commit are done outside the body; but the sexually immoral person sins against his own body. 19 Do you not realise that your body is the temple of the Holy Spirit, who is in you and whom you received from God? 20 You are not your own property, then; you have been bought at a price. So use your body for the glory of God.

7 Now for the questions about which you wrote. Yes, it is a good thing for a man not to touch a woman; 2 yet to avoid immorality every man should have his own wife and every woman her own husband. 3 The husband must give to his wife what she has a right to expect, and so too the wife to her husband. 4 The wife does not have authority over her own body, but the husband; and in the same way, the husband does not have authority over his own body, but the wife does. 5 You must not deprive each other, except by mutual consent for a limited time, to leave yourselves free for prayer, and to come together again afterwards; otherwise Satan may take advantage of any lack of self-control to put you to the test. 6 I am telling you this as a concession, not an order. 7 I should still like everyone to be as I am myself; but everyone has his own gift from God, one this kind and the next something different.

8 To the unmarried and to widows I say: it is good for them to stay as they are, like me. 9 But if they cannot exercise self-control, let them marry, since it is better to be married than to be burnt up.

10 To the married I give this ruling, and this is not mine but the Lord's: a wife must not be separated from her husband — 11 or if she has already left him, she must remain unmarried or else be reconciled to her husband — and a husband must not divorce his wife.

12 For other cases these instructions are my own, not the Lord's. If one of the brothers has a wife who is not a

i 6 Perhaps a saying of Paul now (and 10:23) quoted against him.
j 6 Gn 2:24.

to live with him, he should not divorce her. 13 And if any woman has a husband who is an unbeliever, and he consents to live with her, she should not divorce him. 14 For the unbelieving husband is made holy through his wife, and the unbelieving wife is made holy through her husband. Otherwise, your children would be unclean, but as it is, they are holy. 15 But if the unbelieving partner separates, let it be so; in such a case the brother or sister is not bound. It is to peace that God has called you.*z* 16 Wife, for all you know, you might save your husband. Husband, for all you know, you might save your wife.

17 However that may be, let each of you lead the life that the Lord has assigned, to which God called you. This is my rule in all the churches. 18 Was anyone at the time of his call already circumcised? Let him not seek to remove the marks of circumcision. Was anyone at the time of his call uncircumcised? Let him not seek circumcision. 19 Circumcision is nothing, and uncircumcision is nothing; but obeying the commandments of God is everything. 20 Let each of you remain in the condition in which you were called.

21 Were you a slave when called? Do not be concerned about it. Even if you can gain your freedom, make use of your present condition now more than ever.*a* 22 For whoever was called in the Lord as a slave is a freed person belonging to the Lord, just as whoever was free when called is a slave of Christ. 23 You were bought with a price; do not become slaves of human masters. 24 In whatever condition you were called, brothers and sisters,*b* there remain with God.

25 Now concerning virgins, I have no command of the Lord, but I give my opinion as one who by the Lord's mercy is trustworthy. 26 I think that, in view of the impending*c* crisis, it is well for you to remain as you are. 27 Are you bound to a wife? Do not seek to be free. Are you free from a wife? Do not seek a wife. 28 But if you marry, you do not sin, and if a virgin marries, she does not sin. Yet those who marry will experience distress in this life,*d* and I would spare you that. 29 I mean, brothers and sisters,*b* the appointed time has grown short; from now on, let even those who have wives be as though they had none, 30 and those who mourn as though they were not mourning, and those who rejoice as though they were not rejoicing, and those who buy as though they had no possessions, 31 and those who deal with the world as though they had no dealings with it. For the present form of this world is passing away.

32 I want you to be free from anxieties. The unmarried man is anxious about the affairs of the Lord, how to please the Lord; 33 but the married man is anxious about the affairs of the world, how to please his wife, 34 and his interests are divided. And the unmarried woman and the virgin are anxious about the affairs of the Lord, so that they may be holy in body and spirit; but the married woman is anxious about the affairs of the world, how to please her husband. 35 I say

she is willing to live with him, he must not divorce her; 13 and if a woman has a husband who is not a believer, and he is willing to live with her, she must not divorce him. 14 For the husband now belongs to God through his Christian wife, and the wife through her Christian husband. Otherwise your children would not belong to God, whereas in fact they do. 15 If however the unbelieving partner wishes for a separation, it should be granted; in such cases the Christian husband or wife is not bound by the marriage. God's call is a call to live in peace. 16 But remember: a wife may save her husband; and a husband may save his wife.

17 However that may be, each one should accept the lot which the Lord has assigned him and continue as he was when God called him. That is the rule I give in all the churches. 18 Was a man called with the marks of circumcision on him? Let him not remove them. Was he uncircumcised when he was called? Let him not be circumcised. 19 Circumcision or uncircumcision is neither here nor there; what matters is to keep God's commands. 20 Everyone should remain in the condition in which he was called. 21 Were you a slave when you were called? Do not let that trouble you; though if a chance of freedom should come, by all means take it. 22 Anyone who received his call to be a Christian while a slave is the Lord's freedman; and, equally, every free man who has received the call is a slave in the service of Christ. 23 You were bought at a price; do not become slaves of men. 24 So, my friends, everyone is to remain before God in the condition in which he received his call.

25 About the unmarried, I have no instructions from the Lord, but I give my opinion as one who by the Lord's mercy is fit to be trusted. 26 I think the best way for a man to live in a time of stress like the present is this—to remain as he is. 27 Are you bound in marriage? Do not seek a dissolution. Has your marriage been dissolved? Do not seek a wife. 28 But if you do marry, you are not doing anything wrong, nor does a girl if she marries; it is only that those who marry will have hardships to endure, and my aim is to spare you.

29 What I mean, my friends, is this: the time we live in will not last long. While it lasts, married men should be as if they had no wives; 30 mourners should be as if they had nothing to grieve them, the joyful as if they did not rejoice; those who buy should be as if they possessed nothing, 31 and those who use the world's wealth as if they did not have full use of it. For the world as we know it is passing away.

32 I want you to be free from anxious care. An unmarried man is concerned with the Lord's business; his aim is to please the Lord. 33 But a married man is concerned with worldly affairs; his aim is to please his wife, 34 and he is pulled in two directions. The unmarried woman or girl is concerned with the Lord's business; her aim is to be dedicated to him in body as in spirit. But the married woman is concerned with worldly affairs; her aim is to please her husband.

35 In saying this I am thinking simply of your own good.

7:21 **though if . . . take it:** *or* but even if a chance of freedom should come, choose rather to make good use of your servitude.
7:33–34 **his wife . . . girl is concerned:** *some witnesses read* his wife. 34 There is this difference between the wife and the virgin; the unmarried woman is concerned.

z Other ancient authorities read *us*   *a* Or *avail yourself of the opportunity*   *b* Gk *brothers*   *c* Or *present*   *d* Gk *in the flesh*

with him, he should not divorce her; 13 and if any woman has a husband who is an unbeliever, and he is willing to go on living with her, she should not divorce her husband. 14 For the unbelieving husband is made holy through his wife, and the unbelieving wife is made holy through the brother. Otherwise your children would be unclean, whereas in fact they are holy.

15 If the unbeliever separates, however, let him separate. The brother or sister is not bound in such cases; God has called you to peace. 16 For how do you know, wife, whether you will save your husband; or how do you know, husband, whether you will save your wife?

17 Only, everyone should live as the Lord has assigned, just as God called each one. I give this order in all the churches. 18 Was someone called after he had been circumcised? He should not try to undo his circumcision. Was an uncircumcised person called? He should not be circumcised. 19 Circumcision means nothing, and uncircumcision means nothing; what matters is keeping God's commandments. 20 Everyone should remain in the state in which he was called.

21 Were you a slave when you were called? Do not be concerned but, rather, even if you can gain your freedom, make the most of it. 22 For the slave called in the Lord is a freed person in the Lord, just as the free person who has been called is a slave of Christ. 23 You have been purchased at a price. Do not become slaves to human beings. 24 Brothers, everyone should continue before God in the state in which he was called.

25 Now in regard to virgins I have no commandment from the Lord, but I give my opinion as one who by the Lord's mercy is trustworthy. 26 So this is what I think best because of the present distress: that it is a good thing for a person to remain as he is. 27 Are you bound to a wife? Do not seek a separation. Are you free of a wife? Then do not look for a wife. 28 If you marry, however, you do not sin, nor does an unmarried woman sin if she marries; but such people will experience affliction in their earthly life, and I would like to spare you that.

29 I tell you, brothers, the time is running out. From now on, let those having wives act as not having them, 30 those weeping as not weeping, those rejoicing as not rejoicing, those buying as not owning, 31 those using the world as not using it fully. For the world in its present form is passing away.

32 I should like you to be free of anxieties. An unmarried man is anxious about the things of the Lord, how he may please the Lord. 33 But a married man is anxious about the things of the world, how he may please his wife, 34 and he is divided. An unmarried woman or a virgin is anxious about the things of the Lord, so that she may be holy in both body and spirit. A married woman, on the other hand, is anxious about the things of the world, how she may please her husband. 35 I am telling you this for your own benefit,

believer, and she is willing to stay with him, he should not divorce her; 13 and if a woman has a husband who is not a believer and he is willing to stay with her, she should not divorce her husband. 14 You see, the unbelieving husband is sanctified through his wife and the unbelieving wife is sanctified through the brother. If this were not so, your children would be unclean, whereas in fact they are holy. 15 But if the unbeliever chooses to leave, then let the separation take place: in these circumstances, the brother or sister is no longer tied. But God has called you to live in peace: 16 as a wife, how can you tell whether you are to be the salvation of your husband; as a husband, how can you tell whether you are to be the salvation of your wife?

17 Anyway let everyone continue in the part which the Lord has allotted to him, as he was when God called him. This is the rule that I give to all the churches. 18 If a man who is called has already been circumcised, then he must stay circumcised; when an uncircumcised man is called, he may not be circumcised. 19 To be circumcised is of no importance, and to be uncircumcised is of no importance; what is important is the keeping of God's commandments. 20 Everyone should stay in whatever state he was in when he was called. 21 So, if when you were called, you were a slave, do not think it matters — even if you have a chance of freedom, you should prefer to make full use of your condition as a slave. 22 You see, anyone who was called in the Lord while a slave, is a freeman of the Lord; and in the same way, anyone who was free when called, is a slave of Christ. 23 You have been bought at a price; do not be slaves now to any human being. 24 Each one of you, brothers, is to stay before God in the state in which you were called.

25 About people remaining virgin, I have no directions from the Lord, but I give my own opinion as a person who has been granted the Lord's mercy to be faithful. 26 Well then, because of the stress which is weighing upon us, the right thing seems to be this: it is good for people to stay as they are. 27 If you are joined to a wife, do not seek to be released; if you are freed of a wife, do not look for a wife. 28 However, if you do get married, that is not a sin, and it is not sinful for a virgin to enter upon marriage. But such people will have the hardships consequent on human nature, and I would like you to be without that.

29 What I mean, brothers, is that the time has become limited, and from now on, those who have spouses should live as though they had none; 30 and those who mourn as though they were not mourning; those who enjoy life as though they did not enjoy it; those who have been buying property as though they had no possessions; 31 and those who are involved with the world as though they were people not engrossed in it. Because this world as we know it is passing away.

32 I should like you to have your minds free from all worry. The unmarried man gives his mind to the Lord's affairs and to how he can please the Lord; 33 but the man who is married gives his mind to the affairs of this world and to how he can please his wife, and he is divided in mind. 34 So, too, the unmarried woman, and the virgin, gives her mind to the Lord's affairs and to being holy in body and spirit; but the married woman gives her mind to the affairs of this world and to how she can please her husband. 35 I am saying this only to help you, not to put a

| NEW REVISED STANDARD VERSION | REVISED ENGLISH BIBLE |

this for your own benefit, not to put any restraint upon you, but to promote good order and unhindered devotion to the Lord.

36 If anyone thinks that he is not behaving properly toward his fiancée,*e* if his passions are strong, and so it has to be, let him marry as he wishes; it is no sin. Let them marry. 37 But if someone stands firm in his resolve, being under no necessity but having his own desire under control, and has determined in his own mind to keep her as his fiancée,*e* he will do well. 38 So then, he who marries his fiancée*e* does well; and he who refrains from marriage will do better.

39 A wife is bound as long as her husband lives. But if the husband dies,*f* she is free to marry anyone she wishes, only in the Lord. 40 But in my judgment she is more blessed if she remains as she is. And I think that I too have the Spirit of God.

8 Now concerning food sacrificed to idols: we know that "all of us possess knowledge." Knowledge puffs up, but love builds up. 2 Anyone who claims to know something does not yet have the necessary knowledge; 3 but anyone who loves God is known by him.

4 Hence, as to the eating of food offered to idols, we know that "no idol in the world really exists," and that "there is no God but one." 5 Indeed, even though there may be so-called gods in heaven or on earth — as in fact there are many gods and many lords — 6 yet for us there is one God, the Father, from whom are all things and for whom we exist, and one Lord, Jesus Christ, through whom are all things and through whom we exist.

7 It is not everyone, however, who has this knowledge. Since some have become so accustomed to idols until now, they still think of the food they eat as food offered to an idol; and their conscience, being weak, is defiled. 8 "Food will not bring us close to God."*g* We are no worse off if we do not eat, and no better off if we do. 9 But take care that this liberty of yours does not somehow become a stumbling block to the weak. 10 For if others see you, who possess knowledge, eating in the temple of an idol, might they not, since their conscience is weak, be encouraged to the point of eating food sacrificed to idols? 11 So by your knowledge those weak believers for whom Christ died are destroyed.*h* 12 But when you thus sin against members of your family,*i* and wound their conscience when it is weak, you sin against Christ. 13 Therefore, if food is a cause of their falling,*j* I will never eat meat, so that I may not cause one of them*k* to fall.

9 Am I not free? Am I not an apostle? Have I not seen Jesus our Lord? Are you not my work in the Lord? 2 If

I have no wish to keep you on a tight rein; I only want you to be beyond criticism and be free from distraction in your devotion to the Lord. 36 But if a man feels that he is not behaving properly towards the girl to whom he is betrothed, if his passions are strong and something must be done, let him carry out his intention by getting married; there is nothing wrong in it. 37 But if a man is steadfast in his purpose and under no obligation, if he is free to act at his own discretion, and has decided in his own mind to respect her virginity, he will do well. 38 Thus he who marries his betrothed does well, and he who does not marry does better.

39 A wife is bound to her husband as long as he lives. But if the husband dies, she is free to marry whom she will, provided the marriage is within the Lord's fellowship. 40 But she is better off as she is; that is my opinion, and I believe that I too have the Spirit of God.

8 Now ABOUT meat consecrated to heathen deities. Of course 'We all have knowledge,' as you say. 'Knowledge' inflates a man, whereas love builds him up. 2 If anyone fancies that he has some kind of knowledge, he does not yet know in the true sense of knowing. 3 But if anyone loves God, he is known by God.

4 Well then, about eating this consecrated meat: of course, as you say, 'A false god has no real existence, and there is no god but one.' 5 Even though there be so-called gods, whether in heaven or on earth — and indeed there are many such gods and many such lords — 6 yet for us there is one God, the Father, from whom are all things, and we exist for him; there is one Lord, Jesus Christ, through whom are all things, and we exist through him.

7 But not everyone possesses this knowledge. There are some who have been so accustomed to idolatry that they still think of this meat as consecrated to the idol, and their conscience, being weak, is defiled by eating it. 8 Certainly food will not bring us into God's presence: if we do not eat, we are none the worse, and if we do eat, we are none the better. 9 But be careful that this liberty of yours does not become a pitfall for the weak. 10 If one of them sees you sitting down to a meal in a heathen temple — you with your 'knowledge' — will not his conscience be emboldened to eat meat consecrated to the heathen deity? 11 This 'knowledge' of yours destroys the weak, the fellow-Christian for whom Christ died. 12 In sinning against your brothers and sisters in this way and wounding their conscience, weak as it is, you sin against Christ. 13 Therefore, if food be the downfall of a fellow-Christian, I will never eat meat again, for I will not be the cause of a fellow-Christian's downfall.

9 Am I not free? Am I not an apostle? Have I not seen Jesus our Lord? Are not you my own handiwork in the

---

e Gk *virgin*   *f* Gk *falls asleep*   *g* The quotation may extend to the end of the verse   *h* Gk *the weak brother . . . is destroyed*
i Gk *against the brothers*   *j* Gk *my brother's falling*   *k* Gk *cause my brother*

7:36–38 **But if . . . better:** *or* But if a man feels open to criticism about his daughter, because she has reached puberty and the normal course ought to be followed, he may do as he wishes: let the marriage take place; there is nothing wrong in it. 37 But if a man is steadfast in his purpose and under no obligation, if he is free to act at his own discretion, and has decided in his own mind to keep the girl unmarried, he will do well. 38 Thus he who gives his daughter in marriage does well, and he who does not does better. *Or* But if a man has a partner in celibacy and feels that he is not behaving properly towards her, if, that is, his instincts are too strong for him, and something must be done, let him do what he wishes: let them marry; there is nothing wrong in it. 37 But if a man is steadfast in his purpose and under no obligation, if he is free to act at his own discretion, and has decided in his own mind to keep his partner in her virginity, he will do well. 38 Thus he who marries his partner does well, and he who does not marry her does better.   8:12 *some witnesses omit* weak as it is.

not to impose a restraint upon you, but for the sake of propriety and adherence to the Lord without distraction. ³⁶ If anyone thinks he is behaving improperly toward his virgin, and if a critical moment has come and so it has to be, let him do as he wishes. He is committing no sin; let them get married. ³⁷ The one who stands firm in his resolve, however, who is not under compulsion but has power over his own will, and has made up his mind to keep his virgin, will be doing well. ³⁸ So then, the one who marries his virgin does well; the one who does not marry her will do better.

³⁹ A wife is bound to her husband as long as he lives. But if her husband dies, she is free to be married to whomever she wishes, provided that it be in the Lord. ⁴⁰ She is more blessed, though, in my opinion, if she remains as she is, and I think that I too have the Spirit of God.

8 Now in regard to meat sacrificed to idols: we realize that "all of us have knowledge"; knowledge inflates with pride, but love builds up. ² If anyone supposes he knows something, he does not yet know as he ought to know. ³ But if one loves God, one is known by him.

⁴ So about the eating of meat sacrificed to idols: we know that "there is no idol in the world," and that "there is no God but one." ⁵ Indeed, even though there are so-called gods in heaven and on earth (there are, to be sure, many "gods" and many "lords"), ⁶ yet for us there is

one God, the Father,
    from whom all things are and for whom
        we exist,
and one Lord, Jesus Christ,
    through whom all things are and through whom
        we exist.

⁷ But not all have this knowledge. There are some who have been so used to idolatry up until now that, when they eat meat sacrificed to idols, their conscience, which is weak, is defiled. ⁸ Now food will not bring us closer to God. We are no worse off if we do not eat, nor are we better off if we do. ⁹ But make sure that this liberty of yours in no way becomes a stumbling block to the weak. ¹⁰ If someone sees you, with your knowledge, reclining at table in the temple of an idol, may not his conscience too, weak as it is, be "built up" to eat the meat sacrificed to idols? ¹¹ Thus through your knowledge, the weak person is brought to destruction, the brother for whom Christ died. ¹² When you sin in this way against your brothers and wound their consciences, weak as they are, you are sinning against Christ. ¹³ Therefore, if food causes my brother to sin, I will never eat meat again, so that I may not cause my brother to sin.

9 Am I not free? Am I not an apostle? Have I not seen Jesus our Lord? Are you not my work in the Lord?

bridle on you, but so that everything is as it should be, and you are able to give your undivided attention to the Lord. ³⁶ If someone with strong passions thinks that he is behaving badly towards his fiancée and that things should take their due course, he should follow his desires. There is no sin in it; they should marry. ³⁷ But if he stands firm in his resolution, without any compulsion but with full control of his own will, and decides to let her remain as his fiancée, then he is acting well. ³⁸ In other words, he who marries his fiancée is doing well, and he who does not, better still.

³⁹ A wife is tied as long as her husband is alive. But if the husband dies, she is free to marry anybody she likes, only it must be in the Lord. ⁴⁰ She would be happier if she stayed as she is, to my way of thinking — and I believe that I too have the Spirit of God.

8 Now about food which has been dedicated to false gods.ᵏ We are well aware that all of us have knowledge; but while knowledge puffs up, love is what builds up. ² Someone may think that he has full knowledge of something and yet not know it as well as he should; ³ but someone who loves God is known by God. ⁴ On the subject of eating foods dedicated to false gods, we are well aware that none of the false gods exists in reality and that there is no God other than the One. ⁵ Though there are so-called gods, in the heavens or on earth — and there are plenty of gods and plenty of lords — ⁶ yet for us there is only one God, the Father from whom all things come and for whom we exist, and one Lord, Jesus Christ, through whom all things come and through whom we exist.

⁷ However, not everybody has this knowledge. There are some in whose consciences false gods still play such a part that they take the food as though it had been dedicated to a god; then their conscience, being vulnerable, is defiled. ⁸ But of course food cannot make us acceptable to God; we lose nothing by not eating it, we gain nothing by eating it. ⁹ Only be careful that this freedom of yours does not in any way turn into an obstacle to trip those who are vulnerable. ¹⁰ Suppose someone sees you, who have the knowledge, sitting eating in the temple of some false god, do you not think that his conscience, vulnerable as it is, may be encouraged to eat foods dedicated to false gods? ¹¹ And then it would be through your knowledge that this brother for whom Christ died, vulnerable as he is, has been lost. ¹² So, sinning against your brothers and wounding their vulnerable consciences, you would be sinning against Christ. ¹³ That is why, if food can be the cause of a brother's downfall, I will never eat meat any more, rather than cause my brother's downfall.

9 Am I not free? Am I not an apostle? Have I not seen Jesus our Lord? Are you not my work in the Lord?

ᵏ **8** Food, especially meat, left over from sacrifices, was offered for sale cheap in the markets.

I am not an apostle to others, at least I am to you; for you are the seal of my apostleship in the Lord.

3 This is my defense to those who would examine me. 4 Do we not have the right to our food and drink? 5 Do we not have the right to be accompanied by a believing wife,[l] as do the other apostles and the brothers of the Lord and Cephas? 6 Or is it only Barnabas and I who have no right to refrain from working for a living? 7 Who at any time pays the expenses for doing military service? Who plants a vineyard and does not eat any of its fruit? Or who tends a flock and does not get any of its milk?

8 Do I say this on human authority? Does not the law also say the same? 9 For it is written in the law of Moses, "You shall not muzzle an ox while it is treading out the grain." Is it for oxen that God is concerned? 10 Or does he not speak entirely for our sake? It was indeed written for our sake, for whoever plows should plow in hope and whoever threshes should thresh in hope of a share in the crop. 11 If we have sown spiritual good among you, is it too much if we reap your material benefits? 12 If others share this rightful claim on you, do not we still more?

Nevertheless, we have not made use of this right, but we endure anything rather than put an obstacle in the way of the gospel of Christ. 13 Do you not know that those who are employed in the temple service get their food from the temple, and those who serve at the altar share in what is sacrificed on the altar? 14 In the same way, the Lord commanded that those who proclaim the gospel should get their living by the gospel.

15 But I have made no use of any of these rights, nor am I writing this so that they may be applied in my case. Indeed, I would rather die than that — no one will deprive me of my ground for boasting! 16 If I proclaim the gospel, this gives me no ground for boasting, for an obligation is laid on me, and woe to me if I do not proclaim the gospel! 17 For if I do this of my own will, I have a reward; but if not of my own will, I am entrusted with a commission. 18 What then is my reward? Just this: that in my proclamation I may make the gospel free of charge, so as not to make full use of my rights in the gospel.

19 For though I am free with respect to all, I have made myself a slave to all, so that I might win more of them. 20 To the Jews I became as a Jew, in order to win Jews. To those under the law I became as one under the law (though I myself am not under the law) so that I might win those under the law. 21 To those outside the law I became as one outside the law (though I am not free from God's law but am under Christ's law) so that I might win those outside the law. 22 To the weak I became weak, so that I might win the weak. I have become all things to all people, that I might by all means save some. 23 I do it all for the sake of the gospel, so that I may share in its blessings.

24 Do you not know that in a race the runners all compete, but only one receives the prize? Run in such a way that you may win it. 25 Athletes exercise self-control in all things; they do it to receive a perishable wreath, but we an imperishable one. 26 So I do not run aimlessly, nor do I box as though beating the air; 27 but I punish my body and enslave it, so that after proclaiming to others I myself should not be disqualified.

10 I do not want you to be unaware, brothers and sisters,[m] that our ancestors were all under the cloud, and all passed through the sea, 2 and all were baptized into Moses in the cloud and in the sea, 3 and all ate the same spiritual food, 4 and all drank the same spiritual drink. For they drank from the spiritual rock that followed them, and

Lord? 2 If others do not accept me as an apostle, you at least are bound to do so, for in the Lord you are the very seal of my apostleship.

3 To those who would call me to account, this is my defence: 4 Have I no right to eat and drink? 5 Have I not the right to take a Christian wife about with me, like the rest of the apostles and the Lord's brothers and Cephas? 6 Are only Barnabas and I bound to work for our living? 7 Did you ever hear of a man serving in the army at his own expense? Or planting a vineyard without eating the fruit? Or tending a flock without using the milk? 8 My case does not rest on these human analogies, for the law says the same; 9 in the law of Moses we read, 'You shall not muzzle an ox while it is treading out the grain.' Do you suppose God's concern is with oxen? 10 Must not the saying refer to us? Of course it does: the ploughman should plough and the thresher thresh in hope of sharing the produce. 11 If we have sown a spiritual crop for you, is it too much to expect from you a material harvest? 12 If you allow others those rights, have not we a stronger claim?

But I have never availed myself of any such right. On the contrary, I put up with all that comes my way rather than offer any hindrance to the gospel of Christ. 13 You must know that those who are engaged in temple service eat the temple offerings, and those who officiate at the altar claim their share of the sacrifice. 14 In the same way the Lord gave instructions that those who preach the gospel should get their living by the gospel. 15 But I have never taken advantage of any such right, nor do I intend to claim it in this letter. I had rather die! No one shall make my boast an empty boast. 16 Even if I preach the gospel, I can claim no credit for it; I cannot help myself; it would be agony for me not to preach. 17 If I did it of my own choice, I should be earning my pay; but since I have no choice, I am simply discharging a trust. 18 Then what is my pay? It is the satisfaction of preaching the gospel without expense to anyone; in other words, of waiving the rights my preaching gives me.

19 I am free and own no master; but I have made myself everyone's servant, to win over as many as possible. 20 To Jews I behaved like a Jew, to win Jews; that is, to win those under the law I behaved as if under the law, though not myself subject to the law. 21 To win those outside that law, I behaved as if outside the law, though not myself outside God's law, but subject to the law of Christ. 22 To the weak I became weak, to win the weak. To them all I have become everything in turn, so that in one way or another I may save some. 23 All this I do for the sake of the gospel, to have a share in its blessings.

24 At the games, as you know, all the runners take part, though only one wins the prize. You also must run to win. 25 Every athlete goes into strict training. They do it to win a fading garland; we, to win a garland that never fades. 26 For my part, I am no aimless runner; I am not a boxer who beats the air. 27 I do not spare my body, but bring it under strict control, for fear that after preaching to others I should find myself disqualified.

10 Let me remind you, my friends, that our ancestors were all under the cloud, and all of them passed through the Red Sea; 2 so they all received baptism into the fellowship of Moses in cloud and sea. 3 They all ate the same supernatural food, 4 and all drank the same supernatural drink; for they drank from the supernatural rock that

---

[l] Gk *a sister as wife* [m] Gk *brothers*

2 Although I may not be an apostle for others, certainly I am for you, for you are the seal of my apostleship in the Lord. 3 My defense against those who would pass judgment on me is this. 4 Do we not have the right to eat and drink? 5 Do we not have the right to take along a Christian wife, as do the rest of the apostles, and the brothers of the Lord, and Kephas? 6 Or is it only myself and Barnabas who do not have the right not to work? 7 Who ever serves as a soldier at his own expense? Who plants a vineyard without eating its produce? Or who shepherds a flock without using some of the milk from the flock? 8 Am I saying this on human authority, or does not the law also speak of these things? 9 It is written in the law of Moses, "You shall not muzzle an ox while it is treading out the grain." Is God concerned about oxen, 10 or is he not really speaking for our sake? It was written for our sake, because the plowman should plow in hope, and the thresher in hope of receiving a share. 11 If we have sown spiritual seed for you, is it a great thing that we reap a material harvest from you? 12 If others share this rightful claim on you, do not we still more?

Yet we have not used this right. On the contrary, we endure everything so as not to place an obstacle to the gospel of Christ. 13 Do you not know that those who perform the temple services eat [what] belongs to the temple, and those who minister at the altar share in the sacrificial offerings? 14 In the same way, the Lord ordered that those who preach the gospel should live by the gospel.

15 I have not used any of these rights, however, nor do I write this that it be done so in my case. I would rather die. Certainly no one is going to nullify my boast. 16 If I preach the gospel, this is no reason for me to boast, for an obligation has been imposed on me, and woe to me if I do not preach it! 17 If I do so willingly, I have a recompense, but if unwillingly, then I have been entrusted with a stewardship. 18 What then is my recompense? That, when I preach, I offer the gospel free of charge so as not to make full use of my right in the gospel.

19 Although I am free in regard to all, I have made myself a slave to all so as to win over as many as possible. 20 To the Jews I became like a Jew to win over Jews; to those under the law I became like one under the law—though I myself am not under the law—to win over those under the law. 21 To those outside the law I became like one outside the law—though I am not outside God's law but within the law of Christ—to win over those outside the law. 22 To the weak I became weak, to win over the weak. I have become all things to all, to save at least some. 23 All this I do for the sake of the gospel, so that I too may have a share in it.

24 Do you not know that the runners in the stadium all run in the race, but only one wins the prize? Run so as to win. 25 Every athlete exercises discipline in every way. They do it to win a perishable crown, but we an imperishable one. 26 Thus I do not run aimlessly; I do not fight as if I were shadowboxing. 27 No, I drive my body and train it, for fear that, after having preached to others, I myself should be disqualified.

10 I do not want you to be unaware, brothers, that our ancestors were all under the cloud and all passed through the sea, 2 and all of them were baptized into Moses in the cloud and in the sea. 3 All ate the same spiritual food, 4 and all drank the same spiritual drink, for they drank from

2 Even if to others I am not an apostle, to you at any rate I am, for you are the seal of my apostolate in the Lord. 3 To those who want to interrogate me, this is my answer. 4 Have we not every right to eat and drink? 5 And every right to be accompanied by a Christian wife, like the other apostles, like the brothers of the Lord, and like Cephas? 6 Are Barnabas and I the only ones who have no right to stop working? 7 What soldier would ever serve in the army at his own expense? And who is there who would plant a vineyard and never eat the fruit from it; or would keep a flock and not feed on the milk from his flock? 8 Do not think that this is merely worldly wisdom. Does not the Law say exactly the same? It is written in the Law of Moses: 9 *You must not muzzle an ox when it is treading out the corn.*[1] Is it about oxen that God is concerned here, 10 or is it not said entirely for our sake? Clearly it was written for our sake, because it is right that whoever ploughs should plough with the expectation of having his share, and whoever threshes should thresh with the expectation of having his share. 11 If we have sown the seed of spiritual things in you, is it too much to ask that we should receive from you a crop of material things? 12 Others have been given such rights over you and do we not deserve more? In fact, we have never exercised this right; on the contrary, we have put up with anything rather than obstruct the gospel of Christ in any way. 13 Do you not realise that the ministers in the Temple get their food from the Temple, and those who serve at the altar can claim their share from the altar? 14 In the same way, the Lord gave the instruction that those who preach the gospel should get their living from the gospel.

15 However, I have never availed myself of any rights of this kind; and I have not written this to secure such treatment for myself; I would rather die than that . . . No one shall take from me this ground of boasting. 16 In fact, preaching the gospel gives me nothing to boast of, for I am under compulsion and I should be in trouble if I failed to do it. 17 If I did it on my own initiative I would deserve a reward; but if I do it under compulsion I am simply accepting a task entrusted to me. 18 What reward do I have, then? That in my preaching I offer the gospel free of charge to avoid using the rights which the gospel allows me.

19 So though I was not a slave to any human being, I put myself in slavery to all people, to win as many as I could. 20 To the Jews I made myself as a Jew, to win the Jews; to those under the Law as one under the Law (though I am not), in order to win those under the Law; 21 to those outside the Law as one outside the Law, though I am not outside the Law but under Christ's law, to win those outside the Law. 22 To the weak, I made myself weak, to win the weak. I accommodated myself to people in all kinds of different situations, so that by all possible means I might bring some to salvation. 23 All this I do for the sake of the gospel, that I may share its benefits with others.

24 Do you not realise that, though all the runners in the stadium take part in the race, only one of them gets the prize? Run like that—to win. 25 Every athlete concentrates completely on training, and this is to win a wreath that will wither, whereas ours will never wither. 26 So that is how I run, not without a clear goal; and how I box, not wasting blows on air. 27 I punish my body and bring it under control, to avoid any risk that, having acted as herald for others, I myself may be disqualified.

10 I want you to be quite certain, brothers, that our ancestors all had the cloud over them and all passed through the sea. 2 In the cloud and in the sea they were all baptised into Moses; 3 all ate the same spiritual food 4 and all drank the same spiritual drink, since they drank from the

NEW REVISED STANDARD VERSION	REVISED ENGLISH BIBLE

the rock was Christ. 5 Nevertheless, God was not pleased with most of them, and they were struck down in the wilderness.

6 Now these things occurred as examples for us, so that we might not desire evil as they did. 7 Do not become idolaters as some of them did; as it is written, "The people sat down to eat and drink, and they rose up to play." 8 We must not indulge in sexual immorality as some of them did, and twenty-three thousand fell in a single day. 9 We must not put Christ[n] to the test, as some of them did, and were destroyed by serpents. 10 And do not complain as some of them did, and were destroyed by the destroyer. 11 These things happened to them to serve as an example, and they were written down to instruct us, on whom the ends of the ages have come. 12 So if you think you are standing, watch out that you do not fall. 13 No testing has overtaken you that is not common to everyone. God is faithful, and he will not let you be tested beyond your strength, but with the testing he will also provide the way out so that you may be able to endure it.

14 Therefore, my dear friends,[o] flee from the worship of idols. 15 I speak as to sensible people; judge for yourselves what I say. 16 The cup of blessing that we bless, is it not a sharing in the blood of Christ? The bread that we break, is it not a sharing in the body of Christ? 17 Because there is one bread, we who are many are one body, for we all partake of the one bread. 18 Consider the people of Israel;[p] are not those who eat the sacrifices partners in the altar? 19 What do I imply then? That food sacrificed to idols is anything, or that an idol is anything? 20 No, I imply that what pagans sacrifice, they sacrifice to demons and not to God. I do not want you to be partners with demons. 21 You cannot drink the cup of the Lord and the cup of demons. You cannot partake of the table of the Lord and the table of demons. 22 Or are we provoking the Lord to jealousy? Are we stronger than he?

23 "All things are lawful," but not all things are beneficial. "All things are lawful," but not all things build up. 24 Do not seek your own advantage, but that of the other. 25 Eat whatever is sold in the meat market without raising any question on the ground of conscience, 26 for "the earth and its fullness are the Lord's." 27 If an unbeliever invites you to a meal and you are disposed to go, eat whatever is set before you without raising any question on the ground of conscience. 28 But if someone says to you, "This has been offered in sacrifice," then do not eat it, out of consideration for the one who informed you, and for the sake of conscience — 29 I mean the other's conscience, not your own. For why should my liberty be subject to the judgment of someone else's conscience? 30 If I partake with thankfulness, why should I be denounced because of that for which I give thanks?

31 So, whether you eat or drink, or whatever you do, do everything for the glory of God. 32 Give no offense to Jews or to Greeks or to the church of God, 33 just as I try to please everyone in everything I do, not seeking my own advantage, but that of many, so that they may be saved.

11

1 Be imitators of me, as I am of Christ.

accompanied their travels — and that rock was Christ. 5 Yet most of them were not accepted by God, for the wilderness was strewn with their corpses.

6 These events happened as warnings to us not to set our desires on evil things as they did. 7 Do not be idolaters, like some of them; as scripture says, 'The people sat down to feast and rose up to revel.' 8 Let us not commit fornication; some of them did, and twenty-three thousand died in one day. 9 Let us not put the Lord to the test as some of them did; they were destroyed by the snakes. 10 Do not grumble as some of them did; they were destroyed by the Destroyer.

11 All these things that happened to them were symbolic, and were recorded as a warning for us, upon whom the end of the ages has come. 12 If you think you are standing firm, take care, or you may fall. 13 So far you have faced no trial beyond human endurance; God keeps faith and will not let you be tested beyond your powers, but when the test comes he will at the same time provide a way out and so enable you to endure.

14 So THEN, my dear friends, have nothing to do with idolatry. 15 I appeal to you as sensible people; form your own judgement on what I say. 16 When we bless the cup of blessing, is it not a means of sharing in the blood of Christ? When we break the bread, is it not a means of sharing in the body of Christ? 17 Because there is one loaf, we, though many, are one body; for it is one loaf of which we all partake.

18 Consider Jewish practice: are not those who eat the sacrificial meal partners in the altar? 19 What do I imply by this? That meat consecrated to an idol is anything more than meat, or that an idol is anything more than an idol? 20 No, I mean that pagan sacrifices are offered (in the words of scripture) 'to demons and to that which is not God'; and I will not have you become partners with demons. 21 You cannot drink the cup of the Lord and the cup of demons. You cannot partake of the Lord's table and the table of demons. 22 Are we to provoke the Lord? Are we stronger than he is?

23 'We are free to do anything,' you say. Yes, but not everything is good for us. We are free to do anything, but not everything builds up the community. 24 You should each look after the interests of others, not your own.

25 You may eat anything sold in the meat market without raising questions of conscience; 26 'for the earth is the Lord's and all that is in it'.

27 If an unbeliever invites you to a meal and you accept, eat whatever is put before you, without raising questions of conscience. 28 But if somebody says to you, 'This food has been offered in sacrifice,' then, out of consideration for him and for conscience' sake, do not eat it — 29 not your conscience, I mean, but his.

'What?' you say. 'Is my freedom to be called in question by another's conscience? 30 If I partake with thankfulness, why am I blamed for eating food over which I have said grace?' 31 You may eat or drink, or do anything else, provided it is all done to the glory of God; 32 give no offence to Jews, or Greeks, or to the church of God. 33 For my part I always try to be considerate to everyone, not seeking my own good but the good of the many, so that they may be

11

saved. 1 Follow my example as I follow Christ's.

---

[n] Other ancient authorities read the Lord   [o] Gk my beloved
[p] Gk Israel according to the flesh

10:9 the Lord: some witnesses read Christ.   10:17 Because . . .
body: or For we, many as we are, are one loaf, one body.

a spiritual rock that followed them, and the rock was the Christ. 5 Yet God was not pleased with most of them, for they were struck down in the desert.

6 These things happened as examples for us, so that we might not desire evil things, as they did. 7 And do not become idolaters, as some of them did, as it is written, "The people sat down to eat and drink, and rose up to revel." 8 Let us not indulge in immorality as some of them did, and twenty-three thousand fell within a single day. 9 Let us not test Christ as some of them did, and suffered death by serpents. 10 Do not grumble as some of them did, and suffered death by the destroyer. 11 These things happened to them as an example, and they have been written down as a warning to us, upon whom the end of the ages has come. 12 Therefore whoever thinks he is standing secure should take care not to fall. 13 No trial has come to you but what is human. God is faithful and will not let you be tried beyond your strength; but with the trial he will also provide a way out, so that you may be able to bear it.

14 Therefore, my beloved, avoid idolatry. 15 I am speaking as to sensible people; judge for yourselves what I am saying. 16 The cup of blessing that we bless, is it not a participation in the blood of Christ? The bread that we break, is it not a participation in the body of Christ? 17 Because the loaf of bread is one, we, though many, are one body, for we all partake of the one loaf.

18 Look at Israel according to the flesh; are not those who eat the sacrifices participants in the altar? 19 So what am I saying? That meat sacrificed to idols is anything? Or that an idol is anything? 20 No, I mean that what they sacrifice, [they sacrifice] to demons, not to God, and I do not want you to become participants with demons. 21 You cannot drink the cup of the Lord and also the cup of demons. You cannot partake of the table of the Lord and of the table of demons. 22 Or are we provoking the Lord to jealous anger? Are we stronger than he?

23 "Everything is lawful," but not everything is beneficial. "Everything is lawful," but not everything builds up. 24 No one should seek his own advantage, but that of his neighbor. 25 Eat anything sold in the market, without raising questions on grounds of conscience, 26 for "the earth and its fullness are the Lord's." 27 If an unbeliever invites you and you want to go, eat whatever is placed before you, without raising questions on grounds of conscience. 28 But if someone says to you, "This was offered in sacrifice," do not eat it on account of the one who called attention to it and on account of conscience; 29 I mean not your own conscience, but the other's. For why should my freedom be determined by someone else's conscience? 30 If I partake thankfully, why am I reviled for that over which I give thanks?

31 So whether you eat or drink, or whatever you do, do everything for the glory of God. 32 Avoid giving offense, whether to Jews or Greeks or the church of God, 33 just as I try to please everyone in every way, not seeking my own benefit but that of the many, that they may be saved.

11 1 Be imitators of me, as I am of Christ.

spiritual rock which followed them, m and that rock was Christ. 5 In spite of this, God was not pleased with most of them, and their corpses *were scattered over the desert*. n 6 Now these happenings were examples, for our benefit, so that we should never set our hearts, as they did, on evil things; 7 nor are you to worship false gods, as some of them did, as it says in scripture: *The people sat down to eat and drink, and afterwards got up to amuse themselves*. o 8 Nor, again, are we to fall into sexual immorality; some of them did this, and twenty-three thousand met their downfall in one day. 9 And we are not to put the Lord to the test; some of them put him to the test, and they were killed by snakes. 10 Never complain; some of them complained, and they were killed by the Destroyer. 11 Now all these things happened to them by way of example, and they were described in writing to be a lesson for us, to whom it has fallen to live in the last days of the ages. 12 Everyone, no matter how firmly he thinks he is standing, must be careful he does not fall. 13 None of the trials which have come upon you is more than a human being can stand. You can trust that God will not let you be put to the test beyond your strength, but with any trial will also provide a way out by enabling you to put up with it.

14 For that reason, my dear friends, have nothing to do with the worship of false gods. 15 I am talking to you as sensible people; weigh up for yourselves what I have to say. 16 The blessing-cup, which we bless, is it not a sharing in the blood of Christ; and the loaf of bread which we break, is it not a sharing in the body of Christ? 17 And as there is one loaf, so we, although there are many of us, are one single body, for we all share in the one loaf. 18 Now compare the natural people of Israel: is it not true that those who eat the sacrifices share the altar? 19 What does this mean? That the dedication of food to false gods amounts to anything? Or that false gods themselves amount to anything? 20 No, it does not; simply that when pagans sacrifice, *what is sacrificed by them is sacrificed to demons who are not God*. p I do not want you to share with demons. 21 You cannot drink the cup of the Lord and the cup of demons as well; you cannot have a share in the Lord's table and the demons' table as well. 22 Do we really want to arouse the Lord's jealousy; are we stronger than he is?

23 'Everything is permissible'; maybe so, but not everything does good. True, everything is permissible, but not everything builds people up. 24 Nobody should be looking for selfish advantage, but everybody for someone else's. 25 Eat anything that is sold in butchers' shops; there is no need to ask questions for conscience's sake, 26 since *To the Lord belong the earth and all it contains*. q 27 If an unbeliever invites you to a meal, go if you want to, and eat whatever is put before you; you need not ask questions of conscience first. 28 But if someone says to you, 'This food has been offered in sacrifice,' do not eat it, out of consideration for the person that told you, for conscience's sake — 29 not your own conscience, I mean, but the other person's. Why should my freedom be governed by somebody else's conscience? 30 Provided that I accept it with gratitude, why should I be blamed for eating food for which I give thanks? 31 Whatever you eat, then, or drink, and whatever else you do, do it all for the glory of God. 32 Never be a cause of offence, either to Jews or to Greeks or to the Church of God, 33 just as I try to accommodate everybody in everything, not looking for my own advantage, but for the advantage of everybody else, so that they may be saved.

11 Take me as your pattern, just as I take Christ for mine.

---

m **10** In rabbinic tradition the rock of Nb 20:8 followed them.
n **10** Nb 14:16.   o **10** Ex 32:6.   p **10** Dt 32:17.   q **10** Ps 24:1.

2 I commend you because you remember me in everything and maintain the traditions just as I handed them on to you. 3 But I want you to understand that Christ is the head of every man, and the husband*q* is the head of his wife,*r* and God is the head of Christ. 4 Any man who prays or prophesies with something on his head disgraces his head, 5 but any woman who prays or prophesies with her head unveiled disgraces her head—it is one and the same thing as having her head shaved. 6 For if a woman will not veil herself, then she should cut off her hair; but if it is disgraceful for a woman to have her hair cut off or to be shaved, she should wear a veil. 7 For a man ought not to have his head veiled, since he is the image and reflection*s* of God; but woman is the reflection*s* of man. 8 Indeed, man was not made from woman, but woman from man. 9 Neither was man created for the sake of woman, but woman for the sake of man. 10 For this reason a woman ought to have a symbol of*t* authority on her head,*u* because of the angels. 11 Nevertheless, in the Lord woman is not independent of man or man independent of woman. 12 For just as woman came from man, so man comes through woman; but all things come from God. 13 Judge for yourselves: is it proper for a woman to pray to God with her head unveiled? 14 Does not nature itself teach you that if a man wears long hair, it is degrading to him, 15 but if a woman has long hair, it is her glory? For her hair is given to her for a covering. 16 But if anyone is disposed to be contentious—we have no such custom, nor do the churches of God.

17 Now in the following instructions I do not commend you, because when you come together it is not for the better but for the worse. 18 For, to begin with, when you come together as a church, I hear that there are divisions among you; and to some extent I believe it. 19 Indeed, there have to be factions among you, for only so will it become clear who among you are genuine. 20 When you come together, it is not really to eat the Lord's supper. 21 For when the time comes to eat, each of you goes ahead with your own supper, and one goes hungry and another becomes drunk. 22 What! Do you not have homes to eat and drink in? Or do you show contempt for the church of God and humiliate those who have nothing? What should I say to you? Should I commend you? In this matter I do not commend you!

23 For I received from the Lord what I also handed on to you, that the Lord Jesus on the night when he was betrayed took a loaf of bread, 24 and when he had given thanks, he broke it and said, "This is my body that is for*v* you. Do this in remembrance of me." 25 In the same way he took the cup also, after supper, saying, "This cup is the new covenant in my blood. Do this, as often as you drink it, in remembrance of me." 26 For as often as you eat this bread and drink the cup, you proclaim the Lord's death until he comes.

27 Whoever, therefore, eats the bread or drinks the cup of the Lord in an unworthy manner will be answerable for the body and blood of the Lord. 28 Examine yourselves, and only then eat of the bread and drink of the cup. 29 For all who eat and drink*w* without discerning the body,*x* eat and drink judgment against themselves. 30 For this reason many of you are weak and ill, and some have died.*y* 31 But if we judged ourselves, we would not be judged. 32 But when we are judged by the Lord, we are disciplined*z* so that we may not be condemned along with the world.

2 I COMMEND you for always keeping me in mind, and maintaining the tradition I handed on to you. 3 But I wish you to understand that, while every man has Christ for his head, a woman's head is man, as Christ's head is God. 4 A man who keeps his head covered when he prays or prophesies brings shame on his head; 5 but a woman brings shame on her head if she prays or prophesies bareheaded; it is as bad as if her head were shaved. 6 If a woman does not cover her head she might as well have her hair cut off; but if it is a disgrace for her to be cropped and shaved, then she should cover her head. 7 A man must not cover his head, because man is the image of God, and the mirror of his glory, whereas a woman reflects the glory of man. 8 For man did not originally spring from woman, but woman was made out of man; 9 and man was not created for woman's sake, but woman for the sake of man; 10 and therefore a woman must have the sign of her authority on her head, out of regard for the angels. 11 Yet in the Lord's fellowship woman is as essential to man as man to woman. 12 If woman was made out of man, it is through woman that man now comes to be; and God is the source of all.

13 Judge for yourselves: is it fitting for a woman to pray to God bareheaded? 14 Does not nature herself teach you that while long hair disgraces a man, 15 it is a woman's glory? For her hair was given as a covering.

16 And if anyone still insists on arguing, there is no such custom among us, or in any of the congregations of God's people.

17 In giving you these instructions I come to something I cannot commend: your meetings tend to do more harm than good. 18 To begin with, I am told that when you meet as a congregation you fall into sharply divided groups. I believe there is some truth in it, 19 for divisions are bound to arise among you if only to show which of your members are genuine. 20 The result is that when you meet as a congregation, it is not the Lord's Supper you eat; when it comes to eating, 21 each of you takes his own supper, one goes hungry and another has too much to drink. 22 Have you no homes of your own to eat and drink? Or are you so contemptuous of the church of God that you shame its poorer members? What am I to say? Can I commend you? On this point, certainly not!

23 For the tradition which I handed on to you came to me from the Lord himself: that on the night of his arrest the Lord Jesus took bread, 24 and after giving thanks to God broke it and said: 'This is my body, which is for you; do this in memory of me.' 25 In the same way, he took the cup after supper, and said: 'This cup is the new covenant sealed by my blood. Whenever you drink it, do this in memory of me.' 26 For every time you eat this bread and drink the cup, you proclaim the death of the Lord, until he comes.

27 It follows that anyone who eats the bread or drinks the cup of the Lord unworthily will be guilty of offending against the body and blood of the Lord. 28 Everyone must test himself before eating from the bread and drinking from the cup. 29 For he who eats and drinks eats and drinks judgement on himself if he does not discern the body. 30 That is why many of you are feeble and sick, and a number have died. 31 But if we examined ourselves, we should not fall under judgement. 32 When, however, we do fall under the Lord's judgement, he is disciplining us to save us from being condemned with the rest of the world.

---

q The same Greek word means *man* or *husband*   *r* Or *head of the woman*   *s* Or *glory*   *t* Gk lacks *a symbol of choice regarding her head*   *u* Or *have freedom of choice regarding her head*   *v* Other ancient authorities read *is broken for*   *w* Other ancient authorities add *in an unworthy manner,*   *x* Other ancient authorities read *the Lord's body*   *y* Gk *fallen asleep*   *z* Or *When we are judged, we are being disciplined by the Lord*

11:3 **is man:** *or* is her husband.   11:7 **a woman . . . man:** *or* a woman reflects her husband's glory.

NEW AMERICAN BIBLE

2 I praise you because you remember me in everything and hold fast to the traditions, just as I handed them on to you.

3 But I want you to know that Christ is the head of every man, and a husband the head of his wife, and God the head of Christ. 4 Any man who prays or prophesies with his head covered brings shame upon his head. 5 But any woman who prays or prophesies with her head unveiled brings shame upon her head, for it is one and the same thing as if she had had her head shaved. 6 For if a woman does not have her head veiled, she may as well have her hair cut off. But if it is shameful for a woman to have her hair cut off or her head shaved, then she should wear a veil.

7 A man, on the other hand, should not cover his head, because he is the image and glory of God, but woman is the glory of man. 8 For man did not come from woman, but woman from man; 9 nor was man created for woman, but woman for man; 10 for this reason a woman should have a sign of authority on her head, because of the angels. 11 Woman is not independent of man or man of woman in the Lord. 12 For just as woman came from man, so man is born of woman; but all things are from God.

13 Judge for yourselves: is it proper for a woman to pray to God with her head unveiled? 14 Does not nature itself teach you that if a man wears his hair long it is a disgrace to him, 15 whereas if a woman has long hair it is her glory, because long hair has been given [her] for a covering? 16 But if anyone is inclined to be argumentative, we do not have such a custom, nor do the churches of God.

17 In giving this instruction, I do not praise the fact that your meetings are doing more harm than good. 18 First of all, I hear that when you meet as a church there are divisions among you, and to a degree I believe it; 19 there have to be factions among you in order that [also] those who are approved among you may become known. 20 When you meet in one place, then, it is not to eat the Lord's supper, 21 for in eating, each one goes ahead with his own supper, and one goes hungry while another gets drunk. 22 Do you not have houses in which you can eat and drink? Or do you show contempt for the church of God and make those who have nothing feel ashamed? What can I say to you? Shall I praise you? In this matter I do not praise you.

23 For I received from the Lord what I also handed on to you, that the Lord Jesus, on the night he was handed over, took bread, 24 and, after he had given thanks, broke it and said, "This is my body that is for you. Do this in remembrance of me." 25 In the same way also the cup, after supper, saying, "This cup is the new covenant in my blood. Do this, as often as you drink it, in remembrance of me." 26 For as often as you eat this bread and drink the cup, you proclaim the death of the Lord until he comes.

27 Therefore whoever eats the bread or drinks the cup of the Lord unworthily will have to answer for the body and blood of the Lord. 28 A person should examine himself, and so eat the bread and drink the cup. 29 For anyone who eats and drinks without discerning the body, eats and drinks judgment on himself. 30 That is why many among you are ill and infirm, and a considerable number are dying. 31 If we discerned ourselves, we would not be under judgment; 32 but since we are judged by [the] Lord, we are being disciplined so that we may not be condemned along with the world.

NEW JERUSALEM BIBLE

2 I congratulate you for remembering me so consistently and for maintaining the traditions exactly as I passed them on to you. 3 But I should like you to understand that the head of every man is Christ, the head of woman is man, and the head of Christ is God. 4 For any man to pray or to prophesy with his head covered shows disrespect for his head. 5 And for a woman to pray or prophesy with her head uncovered shows disrespect for her head; it is exactly the same as if she had had her hair shaved off. 6 Indeed, if a woman does go without a veil, she should have her hair cut off too; but if it is a shameful thing for a woman to have her hair cut off or shaved off, then she should wear a veil.

7 But for a man it is not right to have his head covered, since he is the image of God and reflects God's glory; but woman is the reflection of man's glory. 8 For man did not come from woman; no, woman came from man; 9 nor was man created for the sake of woman, but woman for the sake of man: 10 and this is why it is right for a woman to wear on her head a sign of the authority over her, because of the angels. 11 However, in the Lord, though woman is nothing without man, man is nothing without woman; 12 and though woman came from man, so does every man come from a woman, and everything comes from God.

13 Decide for yourselves: does it seem fitting that a woman should pray to God without a veil? 14 Does not nature itself teach you that if a man has long hair, it is a disgrace to him, 15 but when a woman has long hair, it is her glory? After all, her hair was given to her to be a covering. 16 If anyone wants to be contentious, I say that we have no such custom, nor do any of the churches of God.

17 Now that I am on the subject of instructions, I cannot congratulate you on the meetings you hold; they do more harm than good. 18 In the first place, I hear that when you all come together in your assembly, there are separate factions among you, and to some extent I believe it. 19 It is no bad thing, either, that there should be differing groups among you so that those who are to be trusted among you can be clearly recognised. 20 So, when you meet together, it is not the Lord's Supper that you eat; 21 for when the eating begins, each one of you has his own supper first, and there is one going hungry while another is getting drunk. 22 Surely you have homes for doing your eating and drinking in? Or have you such disregard for God's assembly that you can put to shame those who have nothing? What am I to say to you? Congratulate you? On this I cannot congratulate you.

23 For the tradition I received[r] from the Lord and also handed on to you is that on the night he was betrayed, the Lord Jesus took some bread, 24 and after he had given thanks, he broke it, and he said, 'This is my body, which is for you; do this in remembrance of me.' 25 And in the same way, with the cup after supper, saying, 'This cup is the new covenant in my blood. Whenever you drink it, do this as a memorial of me.' 26 Whenever you eat this bread, then, and drink this cup, you are proclaiming the Lord's death until he comes. 27 Therefore anyone who eats the bread or drinks the cup of the Lord unworthily is answerable for the body and blood of the Lord.

28 Everyone is to examine himself and only then eat of the bread or drink from the cup; 29 because a person who eats and drinks without recognising the body is eating and drinking his own condemnation. 30 That is why many of you are weak and ill and a good number have died. 31 If we were critical of ourselves we would not be condemned, 32 but when we are judged by the Lord, we are corrected by the Lord to save us from being condemned along with the world.

r 11 cf. 15:3.

33 So then, my brothers and sisters,*a* when you come together to eat, wait for one another. 34 If you are hungry, eat at home, so that when you come together, it will not be for your condemnation. About the other things I will give instructions when I come.

12 Now concerning spiritual gifts,*b* brothers and sisters,*a* I do not want you to be uninformed. 2 You know that when you were pagans, you were enticed and led astray to idols that could not speak. 3 Therefore I want you to understand that no one speaking by the Spirit of God ever says "Let Jesus be cursed!" and no one can say "Jesus is Lord" except by the Holy Spirit.

4 Now there are varieties of gifts, but the same Spirit; 5 and there are varieties of services, but the same Lord; 6 and there are varieties of activities, but it is the same God who activates all of them in everyone. 7 To each is given the manifestation of the Spirit for the common good. 8 To one is given through the Spirit the utterance of wisdom, and to another the utterance of knowledge according to the same Spirit, 9 to another faith by the same Spirit, to another gifts of healing by the one Spirit, 10 to another the working of miracles, to another prophecy, to another the discernment of spirits, to another various kinds of tongues, to another the interpretation of tongues. 11 All these are activated by one and the same Spirit, who allots to each one individually just as the Spirit chooses.

12 For just as the body is one and has many members, and all the members of the body, though many, are one body, so it is with Christ. 13 For in the one Spirit we were all baptized into one body—Jews or Greeks, slaves or free—and we were all made to drink of one Spirit.

14 Indeed, the body does not consist of one member but of many. 15 If the foot would say, "Because I am not a hand, I do not belong to the body," that would not make it any less a part of the body. 16 And if the ear would say, "Because I am not an eye, I do not belong to the body," that would not make it any less a part of the body. 17 If the whole body were an eye, where would the hearing be? If the whole body were hearing, where would the sense of smell be? 18 But as it is, God arranged the members in the body, each one of them, as he chose. 19 If all were a single member, where would the body be? 20 As it is, there are many members, yet one body. 21 The eye cannot say to the hand, "I have no need of you," nor again the head to the feet, "I have no need of you." 22 On the contrary, the members of the body that seem to be weaker are indispensable, 23 and those members of the body that we think less honorable we clothe with greater honor, and our less respectable members are treated with greater respect; 24 whereas our more respectable members do not need this. But God has so arranged the body, giving the greater honor to the inferior member, 25 that there may be no dissension within the body, but the members may have the same care for one another. 26 If one member suffers, all suffer together with it; if one member is honored, all rejoice together with it.

27 Now you are the body of Christ and individually members of it. 28 And God has appointed in the church first apostles, second prophets, third teachers; then deeds of power, then gifts of healing, forms of assistance, forms of leadership, various kinds of tongues. 29 Are all apostles? Are all prophets? Are all teachers? Do all work miracles? 30 Do all possess gifts of healing? Do all speak in tongues? Do all interpret? 31 But strive for the greater gifts. And I will show you a still more excellent way.

33 Therefore, my friends, when you meet for this meal, wait for one another. 34 If you are hungry, eat at home, so that in meeting together you may not fall under judgement. The other matters I will settle when I come.

12 ABOUT gifts of the Spirit, my friends, I want there to be no misunderstanding.

2 You know how, in the days when you were still pagan, you used to be carried away by some impulse or other to those dumb heathen gods. 3 For this reason I must impress upon you that no one who says 'A curse on Jesus!' can be speaking under the influence of the Spirit of God; and no one can say 'Jesus is Lord!' except under the influence of the Holy Spirit.

4 There are varieties of gifts, but the same Spirit. 5 There are varieties of service, but the same Lord. 6 There are varieties of activity, but in all of them and in everyone the same God is active. 7 In each of us the Spirit is seen to be at work for some useful purpose. 8 One, through the Spirit, has the gift of wise speech, while another, by the power of the same Spirit, can put the deepest knowledge into words. 9 Another, by the same Spirit, is granted faith; another, by the one Spirit, gifts of healing, 10 and another miraculous powers; another has the gift of prophecy, and another the ability to distinguish true spirits from false; yet another has the gift of tongues of various kinds, and another the ability to interpret them. 11 But all these gifts are the activity of one and the same Spirit, distributing them to each individual at will.

12 Christ is like a single body with its many limbs and organs, which, many as they are, together make up one body; 13 for in the one Spirit we were all brought into one body by baptism, whether Jews or Greeks, slaves or free; we were all given that one Spirit to drink.

14 A body is not a single organ, but many. 15 Suppose the foot were to say, 'Because I am not a hand, I do not belong to the body,' it belongs to the body none the less. 16 Suppose the ear were to say, 'Because I am not an eye, I do not belong to the body,' it still belongs to the body. 17 If the body were all eye, how could it hear? If the body were all ear, how could it smell? 18 But, in fact, God appointed each limb and organ to its own place in the body as he chose. 19 If the whole were a single organ, there would not be a body at all; 20 in fact, however, there are many different organs, but one body. 21 The eye cannot say to the hand, 'I do not need you,' or the head to the feet, 'I do not need you.' 22 Quite the contrary: those parts of the body which seem to be more frail than others are indispensable, 23 and those parts of the body which we regard as less honourable are treated with special honour. The parts we are modest about are treated with special respect, 24 whereas our respectable parts have no such need. But God has combined the various parts of the body, giving special honour to the humbler parts, 25 so that there might be no division in the body, but that all its parts might feel the same concern for one another. 26 If one part suffers, all suffer together; if one flourishes, all rejoice together.

27 Now you are Christ's body, and each of you a limb or organ of it. 28 Within our community God has appointed in the first place apostles, in the second place prophets, thirdly teachers; then miracle-workers, then those who have gifts of healing, or ability to help others or power to guide them, or the gift of tongues of various kinds. 29 Are all apostles? All prophets? All teachers? Do all work miracles? 30 Do all have gifts of healing? Do all speak in tongues of ecstasy? Can all interpret them? 31 The higher gifts are those you should prize.

But I can show you an even better way.

---

a Gk brothers   *b* Or *spiritual persons*

NEW AMERICAN BIBLE

NEW JERUSALEM BIBLE

33 Therefore, my brothers, when you come together to eat, wait for one another. 34 If anyone is hungry, he should eat at home, so that your meetings may not result in judgment. The other matters I shall set in order when I come.

12 Now in regard to spiritual gifts, brothers, I do not want you to be unaware. 2 You know how, when you were pagans, you were constantly attracted and led away to mute idols. 3 Therefore, I tell you that nobody speaking by the spirit of God says, "Jesus be accursed." And no one can say, "Jesus is Lord," except by the holy Spirit.

4 There are different kinds of spiritual gifts but the same Spirit; 5 there are different forms of service but the same Lord; 6 there are different workings but the same God who produces all of them in everyone. 7 To each individual the manifestation of the Spirit is given for some benefit. 8 To one is given through the Spirit the expression of wisdom; to another the expression of knowledge according to the same Spirit; 9 to another faith by the same Spirit; to another gifts of healing by the one Spirit; 10 to another mighty deeds; to another prophecy; to another discernment of spirits; to another varieties of tongues; to another interpretation of tongues. 11 But one and the same Spirit produces all of these, distributing them individually to each person as he wishes.

12 As a body is one though it has many parts, and all the parts of the body, though many, are one body, so also Christ. 13 For in one Spirit we were all baptized into one body, whether Jews or Greeks, slaves or free persons, and we were all given to drink of one Spirit.

14 Now the body is not a single part, but many. 15 If a foot should say, "Because I am not a hand I do not belong to the body," it does not for this reason belong any less to the body. 16 Or if an ear should say, "Because I am not an eye I do not belong to the body," it does not for this reason belong any less to the body. 17 If the whole body were an eye, where would the hearing be? If the whole body were hearing, where would the sense of smell be? 18 But as it is, God placed the parts, each one of them, in the body as he intended. 19 If they were all one part, where would the body be? 20 But as it is, there are many parts, yet one body. 21 The eye cannot say to the hand, "I do not need you," nor again the head to the feet, "I do not need you." 22 Indeed, the parts of the body that seem to be weaker are all the more necessary, 23 and those parts of the body that we consider less honorable we surround with greater honor, and our less presentable parts are treated with greater propriety, 24 whereas our more presentable parts do not need this. But God has so constructed the body as to give greater honor to a part that is without it, 25 so that there may be no division in the body, but that the parts may have the same concern for one another. 26 If [one] part suffers, all the parts suffer with it; if one part is honored, all the parts share its joy.

27 Now you are Christ's body, and individually parts of it. 28 Some people God has designated in the church to be, first, apostles; second, prophets; third, teachers; then, mighty deeds; then gifts of healing, assistance, administration, and varieties of tongues. 29 Are all apostles? Are all prophets? Are all teachers? Do all work mighty deeds? 30 Do all have gifts of healing? Do all speak in tongues? Do all interpret? 31 Strive eagerly for the greatest spiritual gifts.

But I shall show you a still more excellent way.

33 So then, my brothers, when you meet for the Meal, wait for each other; 34 anyone who is hungry should eat at home. Then your meeting will not bring your condemnation. The other matters I shall arrange when I come.

12 About the gifts of the Spirit, brothers, I want you to be quite certain. 2 You remember that, when you were pagans, you were irresistibly drawn to inarticulate heathen gods. 3 Because of that, I want to make it quite clear to you that no one who says 'A curse on Jesus' can be speaking in the Spirit of God, and nobody is able to say, 'Jesus is Lord' except in the Holy Spirit.

4 There are many different gifts, but it is always the same Spirit; 5 there are many different ways of serving, but it is always the same Lord. 6 There are many different forms of activity, but in everybody it is the same God who is at work in them all. 7 The particular manifestation of the Spirit granted to each one is to be used for the general good. 8 To one is given from the Spirit the gift of utterance expressing wisdom; to another the gift of utterance expressing knowledge, in accordance with the same Spirit; 9 to another, faith, from the same Spirit; and to another, the gifts of healing, through this one Spirit; 10 to another, the working of miracles; to another, prophecy; to another, the power of distinguishing spirits; to one, the gift of different tongues and to another, the interpretation of tongues. 11 But at work in all these is one and the same Spirit, distributing them at will to each individual.

12 For as with the human body which is a unity although it has many parts — all the parts of the body, though many, still making up one single body — so it is with Christ. 13 We were baptised into one body in a single Spirit, Jews as well as Greeks, slaves as well as free men, and we were all given the same Spirit to drink. 14 And indeed the body consists not of one member but of many. 15 If the foot were to say, 'I am not a hand and so I do not belong to the body,' it does not belong to the body any the less for that. 16 Or if the ear were to say, 'I am not an eye, and so I do not belong to the body,' that would not stop its belonging to the body. 17 If the whole body were just an eye, how would there be any hearing? If the whole body were hearing, how would there be any smelling?

18 As it is, God has put all the separate parts into the body as he chose. 19 If they were all the same part, how could it be a body? 20 As it is, the parts are many but the body is one. 21 The eye cannot say to the hand, 'I have no need of you,' and nor can the head say to the feet, 'I have no need of you.'

22 What is more, it is precisely the parts of the body that seem to be the weakest which are the indispensable ones. 23 It is the parts of the body which we consider least dignified that we surround with the greatest dignity; and our less presentable parts are given greater presentability 24 which our presentable parts do not need. God has composed the body so that greater dignity is given to the parts which were without it, 25 and so that there may not be disagreements inside the body but each part may be equally concerned for all the others. 26 If one part is hurt, all the parts share its pain. And if one part is honoured, all the parts share its joy.

27 Now Christ's body is yourselves, each of you with a part to play in the whole. 28 And those whom God has appointed in the Church are, first apostles, secondly prophets, thirdly teachers; after them, miraculous powers, then gifts of healing, helpful acts, guidance, various kinds of tongues. 29 Are all of them apostles? Or all prophets? Or all teachers? Or all miracle-workers? 30 Do all have the gifts of healing? Do all of them speak in tongues and all interpret them?

31 Set your mind on the higher gifts. And now I am going to put before you the best way of all.

13 If I speak in the tongues of mortals and of angels, but do not have love, I am a noisy gong or a clanging cymbal. 2 And if I have prophetic powers, and understand all mysteries and all knowledge, and if I have all faith, so as to remove mountains, but do not have love, I am nothing. 3 If I give away all my possessions, and if I hand over my body so that I may boast,c but do not have love, I gain nothing.

4 Love is patient; love is kind; love is not envious or boastful or arrogant 5 or rude. It does not insist on its own way; it is not irritable or resentful; 6 it does not rejoice in wrongdoing, but rejoices in the truth. 7 It bears all things, believes all things, hopes all things, endures all things.

8 Love never ends. But as for prophecies, they will come to an end; as for tongues, they will cease; as for knowledge, it will come to an end. 9 For we know only in part, and we prophesy only in part; 10 but when the complete comes, the partial will come to an end. 11 When I was a child, I spoke like a child, I thought like a child, I reasoned like a child; when I became an adult, I put an end to childish ways. 12 For now we see in a mirror, dimly,d but then we will see face to face. Now I know only in part; then I will know fully, even as I have been fully known. 13 And now faith, hope, and love abide, these three; and the greatest of these is love.

14 Pursue love and strive for the spiritual gifts, and especially that you may prophesy. 2 For those who speak in a tongue do not speak to other people but to God; for nobody understands them, since they are speaking mysteries in the Spirit. 3 On the other hand, those who prophesy speak to other people for their upbuilding and encouragement and consolation. 4 Those who speak in a tongue build up themselves, but those who prophesy build up the church. 5 Now I would like all of you to speak in tongues, but even more to prophesy. One who prophesies is greater than one who speaks in tongues, unless someone interprets, so that the church may be built up.

6 Now, brothers and sisters,e if I come to you speaking in tongues, how will I benefit you unless I speak to you in some revelation or knowledge or prophecy or teaching? 7 It is the same way with lifeless instruments that produce sound, such as the flute or the harp. If they do not give distinct notes, how will anyone know what is being played? 8 And if the bugle gives an indistinct sound, who will get ready for battle? 9 So with yourselves; if in a tongue you utter speech that is not intelligible, how will anyone know what is being said? For you will be speaking into the air. 10 There are doubtless many different kinds of sounds in the world, and nothing is without sound. 11 If then I do not know the meaning of a sound, I will be a foreigner to the speaker and the speaker a foreigner to me. 12 So with yourselves; since you are eager for spiritual gifts, strive to excel in them for building up the church.

13 Therefore, one who speaks in a tongue should pray for the power to interpret. 14 For if I pray in a tongue, my spirit prays but my mind is unproductive. 15 What should I do then? I will pray with the spirit, but I will pray with the mind also; I will sing praise with the spirit, but I will sing praise with the mind also. 16 Otherwise, if you say a bless-

13 I may speak in tongues of men or of angels, but if I have no love, I am a sounding gong or a clanging cymbal. 2 I may have the gift of prophecy and the knowledge of every hidden truth; I may have faith enough to move mountains; but if I have no love, I am nothing. 3 I may give all I possess to the needy, I may give my body to be burnt, but if I have no love, I gain nothing by it.

4 Love is patient and kind. Love envies no one, is never boastful, never conceited, 5 never rude; love is never selfish, never quick to take offence. Love keeps no score of wrongs, 6 takes no pleasure in the sins of others, but delights in the truth. 7 There is nothing love cannot face; there is no limit to its faith, its hope, its endurance.

8 Love will never come to an end. Prophecies will cease; tongues of ecstasy will fall silent; knowledge will vanish. 9 For our knowledge and our prophecy alike are partial, 10 and the partial vanishes when wholeness comes. 11 When I was a child I spoke like a child, thought like a child, reasoned like a child; but when I grew up I finished with childish things. 12 At present we see only puzzling reflections in a mirror, but one day we shall see face to face. My knowledge now is partial; then it will be whole, like God's knowledge of me. 13 There are three things that last for ever: faith, hope, and love; and the greatest of the three is love.

14 Make love your aim; then be eager for the gifts of the Spirit, above all for prophecy. 2 If anyone speaks in tongues he is talking with God, not with men and women; no one understands him, for he speaks divine mysteries in the Spirit. 3 On the other hand, if anyone prophesies, he is talking to men and women, and his words have power to build; they stimulate and they encourage. 4 Speaking in tongues may build up the speaker himself, but it is prophecy that builds up a Christian community. 5 I am happy for you all to speak in tongues, but happier still for you to prophesy. The prophet is worth more than one who speaks in tongues—unless indeed he can explain its meaning, and so help to build up the community. 6 Suppose, my friends, that when I come to you I speak in tongues: what good shall I do you unless what I say contains something by way of revelation, or enlightenment, or prophecy, or instruction?

7 Even with inanimate things that produce sounds—a flute, say, or a lyre—unless their notes are distinct, how can you tell what tune is being played? 8 Or again, if the trumpet-call is not clear, who will prepare for battle? 9 In the same way, if what you say in tongues yields no precise meaning, how can anyone tell what is being said? You will be talking to empty air. 10 There are any number of different languages in the world; nowhere is without language. 11 If I do not know the speaker's language, his words will be gibberish to me, and mine to him. 12 You are, I know, eager for gifts of the Spirit; then aspire above all to excel in those which build up the church.

13 Anyone who speaks in tongues should pray for the ability to interpret. 14 If I use such language in prayer, my spirit prays, but my mind is barren. 15 What then? I will pray with my spirit, but also with my mind; I will sing hymns with my spirit, but with my mind as well. 16 Suppose

---

c Other ancient authorities read *body to be burned* d Gk *in a riddle*
e Gk *brothers*

13:3 **give my ... burnt:** *some witnesses read* seek glory by self-sacrifice.

13 If I speak in human and angelic tongues, but do not have love, I am a resounding gong or a clashing cymbal. 2 And if I have the gift of prophecy and comprehend all mysteries and all knowledge; if I have all faith so as to move mountains, but do not have love, I am nothing. 3 If I give away everything I own, and if I hand my body over so that I may boast but do not have love, I gain nothing.

4 Love is patient, love is kind. It is not jealous, [love] is not pompous, it is not inflated, 5 it is not rude, it does not seek its own interests, it is not quick-tempered, it does not brood over injury, 6 it does not rejoice over wrongdoing but rejoices with the truth. 7 It bears all things, believes all things, hopes all things, endures all things.

8 Love never fails. If there are prophecies, they will be brought to nothing; if tongues, they will cease; if knowledge, it will be brought to nothing. 9 For we know partially and we prophesy partially, 10 but when the perfect comes, the partial will pass away. 11 When I was a child, I used to talk as a child, think as a child, reason as a child; when I became a man, I put aside childish things. 12 At present we see indistinctly, as in a mirror, but then face to face. At present I know partially; then I shall know fully, as I am fully known. 13 So faith, hope, love remain, these three; but the greatest of these is love.

14 Pursue love, but strive eagerly for the spiritual gifts, above all that you may prophesy. 2 For one who speaks in a tongue does not speak to human beings but to God, for no one listens; he utters mysteries in spirit. 3 On the other hand, one who prophesies does speak to human beings, for their building up, encouragement, and solace. 4 Whoever speaks in a tongue builds himself up, but whoever prophesies builds up the church. 5 Now I should like all of you to speak in tongues, but even more to prophesy. One who prophesies is greater than one who speaks in tongues, unless he interprets, so that the church may be built up.

6 Now, brothers, if I should come to you speaking in tongues, what good will I do you if I do not speak to you by way of revelation, or knowledge, or prophecy, or instruction? 7 Likewise, if inanimate things that produce sound, such as flute or harp, do not give out the tones distinctly, how will what is being played on flute or harp be recognized? 8 And if the bugle gives an indistinct sound, who will get ready for battle? 9 Similarly, if you, because of speaking in tongues, do not utter intelligible speech, how will anyone know what is being said? For you will be talking to the air. 10 It happens that there are many different languages in the world, and none is meaningless; 11 but if I do not know the meaning of a language, I shall be a foreigner to one who speaks it, and one who speaks it a foreigner to me. 12 So with yourselves: since you strive eagerly for spirits, seek to have an abundance of them for building up the church.

13 Therefore, one who speaks in a tongue should pray to be able to interpret. 14 [For] if I pray in a tongue, my spirit is at prayer but my mind is unproductive. 15 So what is to be done? I will pray with the spirit, but I will also pray with the mind. I will sing praise with the spirit, but I will also sing praise with the mind. 16 Otherwise, if you pronounce a

13 Though I command languages both human and angelic — if I speak without love, I am no more than a gong booming or a cymbal clashing. 2 And though I have the power of prophecy, to penetrate all mysteries and knowledge, and though I have all the faith necessary to move mountains — if I am without love, I am nothing. 3 Though I should give away to the poor all that I possess, and even give up my body to be burned — if I am without love, it will do me no good whatever.

4 Love is always patient and kind; love is never jealous; love is not boastful or conceited, 5 it is never rude and never seeks its own advantage, it does not take offence or store up grievances. 6 Love does not rejoice at wrongdoing, but finds its joy in the truth. 7 It is always ready to make allowances, to trust, to hope and to endure whatever comes.

8 Love never comes to an end. But if there are prophecies, they will be done away with; if tongues, they will fall silent; and if knowledge, it will be done away with. 9 For we know only imperfectly, and we prophesy imperfectly; 10 but once perfection comes, all imperfect things will be done away with. 11 When I was a child, I used to talk like a child, and see things as a child does, and think like a child; but now that I have become an adult, I have finished with all childish ways. 12 Now we see only reflections in a mirror, mere riddles, but then we shall be seeing face to face. Now I can know only imperfectly; but then I shall know just as fully as I am myself known.

13 As it is, these remain: faith, hope and love, the three of them; and the greatest of them is love.

14 Make love your aim; but be eager, too, for spiritual gifts, and especially for prophesying. 2 Those who speak in a tongue speak to God, but not to other people, because nobody understands them; they are speaking in the Spirit and the meaning is hidden. 3 On the other hand, someone who prophesies speaks to other people, building them up and giving them encouragement and reassurance. 4 Those who speak in a tongue may build themselves up, but those who prophesy build up the community. 5 While I should like you all to speak in tongues, I would much rather you could prophesy; since those who prophesy are of greater importance than those who speak in tongues, unless they can interpret what they say so that the church is built up by it.

6 Now suppose, brothers, I come to you and speak in tongues, what good shall I do you if my speaking provides no revelation or knowledge or prophecy or instruction? 7 It is the same with an inanimate musical instrument. If it does not make any distinction between notes, how can one recognise what is being played on flute or lyre? 8 If the trumpet sounds a call which is unrecognisable, who is going to get ready for the attack? 9 It is the same with you: if you do not use your tongue to produce speech that can be readily understood, how can anyone know what you are saying? You will be talking to the air. 10 However many the languages used in the world, all of them use sound; 11 but if I do not understand the meaning of the sound, I am a barbarian[s] to the person who is speaking, and the speaker is a barbarian to me. 12 So with you, as you are eager to have spiritual powers, aim to be rich in those which build up the community.

13 That is why anybody who speaks in a tongue must pray that he may be given the interpretation. 14 For if I pray in a tongue, my spirit may be praying but my mind derives no fruit from it. 15 What then? I shall pray with the spirit, but I shall pray with the mind as well; I shall sing praises with the spirit and I shall sing praises with the mind as well.

s 14 i.e. someone who does not understand Gk.

ing with the spirit, how can anyone in the position of an outsider say the "Amen" to your thanksgiving, since the outsider does not know what you are saying? 17 For you may give thanks well enough, but the other person is not built up. 18 I thank God that I speak in tongues more than all of you; 19 nevertheless, in church I would rather speak five words with my mind, in order to instruct others also, than ten thousand words in a tongue.

20 Brothers and sisters,*f* do not be children in your thinking; rather, be infants in evil, but in thinking be adults. 21 In the law it is written,

"By people of strange tongues
 and by the lips of foreigners
I will speak to this people;
 yet even then they will not listen to me,"

says the Lord. 22 Tongues, then, are a sign not for believers but for unbelievers, while prophecy is not for unbelievers but for believers. 23 If, therefore, the whole church comes together and all speak in tongues, and outsiders or unbelievers enter, will they not say that you are out of your mind? 24 But if all prophesy, an unbeliever or outsider who enters is reproved by all and called to account by all. 25 After the secrets of the unbeliever's heart are disclosed, that person will bow down before God and worship him, declaring, "God is really among you."

26 What should be done then, my friends?*f* When you come together, each one has a hymn, a lesson, a revelation, a tongue, or an interpretation. Let all things be done for building up. 27 If anyone speaks in a tongue, let there be only two or at most three, and each in turn; and let one interpret. 28 But if there is no one to interpret, let them be silent in church and speak to themselves and to God. 29 Let two or three prophets speak, and let the others weigh what is said. 30 If a revelation is made to someone else sitting nearby, let the first person be silent. 31 For you can all prophesy one by one, so that all may learn and all be encouraged. 32 And the spirits of prophets are subject to the prophets, 33 for God is a God not of disorder but of peace.

(As in all the churches of the saints, 34 women should be silent in the churches. For they are not permitted to speak, but should be subordinate, as the law also says. 35 If there is anything they desire to know, let them ask their husbands at home. For it is shameful for a woman to speak in church.*g* 36 Or did the word of God originate with you? Or are you the only ones it has reached?)

37 Anyone who claims to be a prophet, or to have spiritual powers, must acknowledge that what I am writing to you is a command of the Lord. 38 Anyone who does not recognize this is not to be recognized. 39 So, my friends,*h* be eager to prophesy, and do not forbid speaking in tongues; 40 but all things should be done decently and in order.

15 Now I would remind you, brothers and sisters,*f* of the good news*i* that I proclaimed to you, which you in turn received, in which also you stand, 2 through which also you are being saved, if you hold firmly to the message that I proclaimed to you — unless you have come to believe in vain.

3 For I handed on to you as of first importance what I in turn had received: that Christ died for our sins in accordance with the scriptures, 4 and that he was buried, and that

you are praising God with the spirit alone: how will an ordinary person who is present be able to say 'Amen' to your thanksgiving, when he does not know what you are saying? 17 Your prayer of thanksgiving may be splendid, but it is no help to the other person. 18 Thank God, I am more gifted in tongues than any of you, 19 but in the congregation I would rather speak five intelligible words, for the benefit of others as well as myself, than thousands of words in the language of ecstasy.

20 Do not be children in your thinking, my friends; be infants in evil, but in your thinking be grown-up. 21 We read in the law: 'I will speak to this people through strange tongues, and by the lips of foreigners; and even so they will not heed me, says the Lord.' 22 Clearly then these 'strange tongues' are not intended as a sign for believers, but for unbelievers, whereas prophecy is designed not for unbelievers but for believers. 23 So if the whole congregation is assembled and all are using the 'strange tongues' of ecstasy, and some uninstructed persons or unbelievers should enter, will they not think you are mad? 24 But if all are uttering prophecies, the visitor, when he enters, hears from everyone something that searches his conscience and brings conviction, 25 and the secrets of his heart are laid bare. So he will fall down and worship God, declaring, 'God is certainly among you!'

26 To sum up, my friends: when you meet for worship, each of you contributing a hymn, some instruction, a revelation, an ecstatic utterance, or its interpretation, see that all of these aim to build up the church. 27 If anyone speaks in tongues, only two should speak, or at most three, one at a time, and someone must interpret. 28 If there is no interpreter, they should keep silent and speak to themselves and to God. 29 Of the prophets, two or three may speak, while the rest exercise their judgement upon what is said. 30 If someone else present receives a revelation, let the first speaker stop. 31 You can all prophesy, one at a time, so that all may receive instruction and encouragement. 32 It is for prophets to control prophetic inspiration, 33 for God is not a God of disorder but of peace.

As in all congregations of God's people, 34 women should keep silent at the meeting. They have no permission to talk, but should keep their place as the law directs. 35 If there is something they want to know, they can ask their husbands at home. It is a shocking thing for a woman to talk at the meeting.

36 Did the word of God originate with you? Or are you the only people to whom it came? 37 If anyone claims to be inspired or a prophet, let him recognize that what I write has the Lord's authority. 38 If he does not acknowledge this, his own claim cannot be acknowledged.

39 In short, my friends, be eager to prophesy; do not forbid speaking in tongues; 40 but let all be done decently and in order.

15 AND now, my friends, I must remind you of the gospel that I preached to you; the gospel which you received, on which you have taken your stand, 2 and which is now bringing you salvation. Remember the terms in which I preached the gospel to you — for I assume that you hold it fast and that your conversion was not in vain.

3 First and foremost, I handed on to you the tradition I had received: that Christ died for our sins, in accordance with the scriptures; 4 that he was buried; that he was raised to life

---

f Gk *brothers* *g* Other ancient authorities put verses 34-35 after verse 40 *h* Gk *my brothers* *i* Or *gospel*

14:38 **If . . . acknowledged:** *some witnesses read* If he refuses to recognize this, let him refuse!

NEW AMERICAN BIBLE

NEW JERUSALEM BIBLE

blessing [with] the spirit, how shall one who holds the place of the uninstructed say the "Amen" to your thanksgiving, since he does not know what you are saying? 17 For you may be giving thanks very well, but the other is not built up. 18 I give thanks to God that I speak in tongues more than any of you, 19 but in the church I would rather speak five words with my mind, so as to instruct others also, than ten thousand words in a tongue.

20 Brothers, stop being childish in your thinking. In respect to evil be like infants, but in your thinking be mature. 21 It is written in the law:

"By people speaking strange tongues
and by the lips of foreigners
I will speak to this people,
and even so they will not listen to me,

says the Lord." 22 Thus, tongues are a sign not for those who believe but for unbelievers, whereas prophecy is not for unbelievers but for those who believe.

23 So if the whole church meets in one place and everyone speaks in tongues, and then uninstructed people or unbelievers should come in, will they not say that you are out of your minds? 24 But if everyone is prophesying, and an unbeliever or uninstructed person should come in, he will be convinced by everyone and judged by everyone, 25 and the secrets of his heart will be disclosed, and so he will fall down and worship God, declaring, "God is really in your midst."

26 So what is to be done, brothers? When you assemble, one has a psalm, another an instruction, a revelation, a tongue, or an interpretation. Everything should be done for building up. 27 If anyone speaks in a tongue, let it be two or at most three, and each in turn, and one should interpret. 28 But if there is no interpreter, the person should keep silent in the church and speak to himself and to God.

29 Two or three prophets should speak, and the others discern. 30 But if a revelation is given to another person sitting there, the first one should be silent. 31 For you can all prophesy one by one, so that all may learn and all be encouraged. 32 Indeed, the spirits of prophets are under the prophets' control, 33 since he is not the God of disorder but of peace.

As in all the churches of the holy ones, 34 women should keep silent in the churches, for they are not allowed to speak, but should be subordinate, as even the law says. 35 But if they want to learn anything, they should ask their husbands at home. For it is improper for a woman to speak in the church. 36 Or did the word of God go forth from you? Or has it come to you alone?

37 If anyone thinks that he is a prophet or a spiritual person, he should recognize that what I am writing to you is a commandment of the Lord. 38 If anyone does not acknowledge this, he is not acknowledged. 39 So, [my] brothers, strive eagerly to prophesy, and do not forbid speaking in tongues, 40 but everything must be done properly and in order.

15 Now I am reminding you, brothers, of the gospel I preached to you, which you indeed received and in which you also stand. 2 Through it you are also being saved, if you hold fast to the word I preached to you, unless you believed in vain. 3 For I handed on to you as of first importance what I also received: that Christ died for our sins in accordance with the scriptures; 4 that he was buried; that he

16 Otherwise, if you say your blessing only with the spirit, how is the uninitiated person going to answer 'Amen' to your thanksgiving, without understanding what you are saying? 17 You may be making your thanksgiving well, but the other person is not built up at all. 18 I thank God that I speak with tongues more than any of you; 19 all the same, when I am in the assembly I would rather say five words with my mind, to instruct others as well, than ten thousand words in a tongue.

20 Brothers, do not remain children in your thinking; infants in wickedness — agreed, but in your thinking grown-ups. 21 It says in the written Law: *In strange tongues and in a foreign language I will talk to this nation, and even so they will refuse to listen,*[t] says the Lord. 22 So then, strange languages are significant not for believers, but for unbelievers; whereas on the other hand, prophesying is not for unbelievers, but for believers. 23 Suppose that, if the whole congregation were meeting and all of them speaking in tongues, and some uninitiated people or unbelievers were to come in, don't you think they would say that you were all raving? 24 But if you were all prophesying when an unbeliever or someone uninitiated came in, he would find himself put to the test by all and judged by all 25 and the secrets of his heart revealed; and so he would fall down on his face and worship God, declaring that *God is indeed among you.*[u]

26 Then what should it be like, brothers? When you come together each of you brings a psalm or some instruction or a revelation, or speaks in a tongue or gives an interpretation. Let all these things be done in a way that will build up the community. 27 If there are to be any people speaking in a tongue, then let there be only two, or at the most three, and those one at a time, and let one of these interpret. 28 If there is no interpreter, then let each of them be quiet in the assembly, and speak only to himself and God. 29 Let two prophets, or three, speak while the rest weigh their words; 30 and if a revelation comes to someone else who is sitting by, the speaker should stop speaking. 31 You can all prophesy, but one at a time, then all will learn something and all receive encouragement. 32 The prophetic spirit is to be under the prophets' control, 33 for God is a God not of disorder but of peace.

As in all the churches of God's holy people, 34 women are to remain quiet in the assemblies, since they have no permission to speak: theirs is a subordinate part, as the Law itself says. 35 If there is anything they want to know, they should ask their husbands at home: it is shameful for a woman to speak in the assembly.

36 Do you really think that you are the source of the word of God? Or that you are the only people to whom it has come? 37 Anyone who claims to be a prophet, or to have any spiritual powers must recognise that what I am writing to you is a commandment from the Lord. 38 If anyone does not recognise this, it is because that person is not recognised himself.

39 So, my brothers, be eager to prophesy, and do not suppress the gift of speaking in tongues. 40 But make sure that everything is done in a proper and orderly fashion.

15 I want to make quite clear to you, brothers, what the message of the gospel that I preached to you is; you accepted it and took your stand on it, 2 and you are saved by it, if you keep to the message I preached to you; otherwise your coming to believe was in vain. 3 The tradition I handed on to you in the first place, a tradition which I had myself received,[v] was that Christ died for our sins, in accordance with the scriptures, 4 and that he was buried;

---

t **14** Is 28:11–12.   *u* **14** Is 45:14.   *v* **15** cf. 11:23.

NEW REVISED STANDARD VERSION

he was raised on the third day in accordance with the scriptures, 5 and that he appeared to Cephas, then to the twelve. 6 Then he appeared to more than five hundred brothers and sisters*j* at one time, most of whom are still alive, though some have died.*k* 7 Then he appeared to James, then to all the apostles. 8 Last of all, as to one untimely born, he appeared also to me. 9 For I am the least of the apostles, unfit to be called an apostle, because I persecuted the church of God. 10 But by the grace of God I am what I am, and his grace toward me has not been in vain. On the contrary, I worked harder than any of them—though it was not I, but the grace of God that is with me. 11 Whether then it was I or they, so we proclaim and so you have come to believe.

12　Now if Christ is proclaimed as raised from the dead, how can some of you say there is no resurrection of the dead? 13 If there is no resurrection of the dead, then Christ has not been raised; 14 and if Christ has not been raised, then our proclamation has been in vain and your faith has been in vain. 15 We are even found to be misrepresenting God, because we testified of God that he raised Christ—whom he did not raise if it is true that the dead are not raised. 16 For if the dead are not raised, then Christ has not been raised. 17 If Christ has not been raised, your faith is futile and you are still in your sins. 18 Then those also who have died*k* in Christ have perished. 19 If for this life only we have hoped in Christ, we are of all people most to be pitied.

20　But in fact Christ has been raised from the dead, the first fruits of those who have died.*k* 21 For since death came through a human being, the resurrection of the dead has also come through a human being; 22 for as all die in Adam, so all will be made alive in Christ. 23 But each in his own order: Christ the first fruits, then at his coming those who belong to Christ. 24 Then comes the end,*l* when he hands over the kingdom to God the Father, after he has destroyed every ruler and every authority and power. 25 For he must reign until he has put all his enemies under his feet. 26 The last enemy to be destroyed is death. 27 For "God*m* has put all things in subjection under his feet." But when it says, "All things are put in subjection," it is plain that this does not include the one who put all things in subjection under him. 28 When all things are subjected to him, then the Son himself will also be subjected to the one who put all things in subjection under him, so that God may be all in all.

29　Otherwise, what will those people do who receive baptism on behalf of the dead? If the dead are not raised at all, why are people baptized on their behalf?

30　And why are we putting ourselves in danger every hour? 31 I die every day! That is as certain, brothers and sisters,*j* as my boasting of you—a boast that I make in Christ Jesus our Lord. 32 If with merely human hopes I fought with wild animals at Ephesus, what would I have gained by it? If the dead are not raised,

"Let us eat and drink,
　　for tomorrow we die."
33 Do not be deceived:

"Bad company ruins good morals."

34 Come to a sober and right mind, and sin no more; for some people have no knowledge of God. I say this to your shame.

35　But someone will ask, "How are the dead raised? With what kind of body do they come?" 36 Fool! What you sow does not come to life unless it dies. 37 And as for what you sow, you do not sow the body that is to be, but a bare seed, perhaps of wheat or of some other grain. 38 But God

REVISED ENGLISH BIBLE

on the third day, in accordance with the scriptures; 5 and that he appeared to Cephas, and afterwards to the Twelve. 6 Then he appeared to over five hundred of our brothers at once, most of whom are still alive, though some have died. 7 Then he appeared to James, and afterwards to all the apostles.

8 Last of all he appeared to me too; it was like a sudden, abnormal birth. 9 For I am the least of the apostles, indeed not fit to be called an apostle, because I had persecuted the church of God. 10 However, by God's grace I am what I am, and his grace to me has not proved vain; in my labours I have outdone them all—not I, indeed, but the grace of God working with me. 11 But no matter whether it was I or they! This is what we all proclaim, and this is what you believed.

12 Now if this is what we proclaim, that Christ was raised from the dead, how can some of you say there is no resurrection of the dead? 13 If there is no resurrection, then Christ was not raised; 14 and if Christ was not raised, then our gospel is null and void, and so too is your faith; 15 and we turn out to have given false evidence about God, because we bore witness that he raised Christ to life, whereas, if the dead are not raised, he did not raise him. 16 For if the dead are not raised, it follows that Christ was not raised; 17 and if Christ was not raised, your faith has nothing to it and you are still in your old state of sin. 18 It follows also that those who have died within Christ's fellowship are utterly lost. 19 If it is for this life only that Christ has given us hope, we of all people are most to be pitied.

20 But the truth is, Christ was raised to life—the firstfruits of the harvest of the dead. 21 For since it was a man who brought death into the world, a man also brought resurrection of the dead. 22 As in Adam all die, so in Christ all will be brought to life; 23 but each in proper order: Christ the firstfruits, and afterwards, at his coming, those who belong to Christ. 24 Then comes the end, when he delivers up the kingdom to God the Father, after deposing every sovereignty, authority, and power. 25 For he is destined to reign until God has put all enemies under his feet; 26 and the last enemy to be deposed is death. 27 Scripture says, 'He has put all things in subjection under his feet.' But in saying 'all things', it clearly means to exclude God who made all things subject to him; 28 and when all things are subject to him, then the Son himself will also be made subject to God who made all things subject to him, and thus God will be all in all.

29 Again, there are those who receive baptism on behalf of the dead. What do you suppose they are doing? If the dead are not raised to life at all, what do they mean by being baptized on their behalf?

30 And why do we ourselves face danger hour by hour? 31 Every day I die: I swear it by my pride in you, my friends—for in Christ Jesus our Lord I am proud of you. 32 With no more than human hopes, what would have been the point of my fighting those wild beasts at Ephesus? If the dead are never raised to life, 'Let us eat and drink, for tomorrow we die.'

33 Make no mistake: 'Bad company ruins good character.' 34 Wake up, be sober, and stop sinning: some of you have no knowledge of God—to your shame I say it.

35 But, you may ask, how are the dead raised? In what kind of body? 36 What stupid questions! The seed you sow does not come to life unless it has first died; 37 and what you sow is not the body that shall be, but a bare grain, of wheat perhaps, or something else; 38 and God gives it the body of

---

j Gk *brothers*　　*k* Gk *fallen asleep*　　*l* Or *Then come the rest*
m Gk *he*

NEW AMERICAN BIBLE

was raised on the third day in accordance with the scriptures; 5 that he appeared to Kephas, then to the Twelve. 6 After that, he appeared to more than five hundred brothers at once, most of whom are still living, though some have fallen asleep. 7 After that he appeared to James, then to all the apostles. 8 Last of all, as to one born abnormally, he appeared to me. 9 For I am the least of the apostles, not fit to be called an apostle, because I persecuted the church of God. 10 But by the grace of God I am what I am, and his grace to me has not been ineffective. Indeed, I have toiled harder than all of them; not I, however, but the grace of God [that is] with me. 11 Therefore, whether it be I or they, so we preach and so you believed.

12 But if Christ is preached as raised from the dead, how can some among you say there is no resurrection of the dead? 13 If there is no resurrection of the dead, then neither has Christ been raised. 14 And if Christ has not been raised, then empty [too] is our preaching; empty, too, your faith. 15 Then we are also false witnesses to God, because we testified against God that he raised Christ, whom he did not raise if in fact the dead are not raised. 16 For if the dead are not raised, neither has Christ been raised, 17 and if Christ has not been raised, your faith is vain; you are still in your sins. 18 Then those who have fallen asleep in Christ have perished. 19 If for this life only we have hoped in Christ, we are the most pitiable people of all.

20 But now Christ has been raised from the dead, the firstfruits of those who have fallen asleep. 21 For since death came through a human being, the resurrection of the dead came also through a human being. 22 For just as in Adam all die, so too in Christ shall all be brought to life, 23 but each one in proper order: Christ the firstfruits; then, at his coming, those who belong to Christ; 24 then comes the end, when he hands over the kingdom to his God and Father, when he has destroyed every sovereignty and every authority and power. 25 For he must reign until he has put all his enemies under his feet. 26 The last enemy to be destroyed is death, 27 for "he subjected everything under his feet." But when it says that everything has been subjected, it is clear that it excludes the one who subjected everything to him. 28 When everything is subjected to him, then the Son himself will [also] be subjected to the one who subjected everything to him, so that God may be all in all.

29 Otherwise, what will people accomplish by having themselves baptized for the dead? If the dead are not raised at all, then why are they having themselves baptized for them? 30 Moreover, why are we endangering ourselves all the time? 31 Every day I face death; I swear it by the pride in you [brothers] that I have in Christ Jesus our Lord. 32 If at Ephesus I fought with beasts, so to speak, what benefit was it to me? If the dead are not raised:

"Let us eat and drink,
    for tomorrow we die."

33 Do not be led astray:

"Bad company corrupts good morals."

34 Become sober as you ought and stop sinning. For some have no knowledge of God; I say this to your shame.

35 But someone may say, "How are the dead raised? With what kind of body will they come back?" 36 You fool! What you sow is not brought to life unless it dies. 37 And what you sow is not the body that is to be but a bare kernel of wheat, perhaps, or of some other kind;

NEW JERUSALEM BIBLE

and that on the third day, he was raised to life, in accordance with the scriptures; 5 and that he appeared to Cephas; and later to the Twelve; 6 and next he appeared to more than five hundred of the brothers at the same time, most of whom are still with us, though some have fallen asleep; 7 then he appeared to James, and then to all the apostles. 8 Last of all he appeared to me too, as though I was a child born abnormally.

9 For I am the least of the apostles and am not really fit to be called an apostle, because I had been persecuting the Church of God; 10 but what I am now, I am through the grace of God, and the grace which was given to me has not been wasted. Indeed, I have worked harder than all the others — not I, but the grace of God which is with me. 11 Anyway, whether it was they or I, this is what we preach and what you believed.

12 Now if Christ is proclaimed as raised from the dead, how can some of you be saying that there is no resurrection of the dead? 13 If there is no resurrection of the dead, then Christ cannot have been raised either, 14 and if Christ has not been raised, then our preaching is without substance, and so is your faith. 15 What is more, we have proved to be false witnesses to God, for testifying against God that he raised Christ to life when he did not raise him — if it is true that the dead are not raised. 16 For, if the dead are not raised, neither is Christ; 17 and if Christ has not been raised, your faith is pointless and you have not, after all, been released from your sins. 18 In addition, those who have fallen asleep in Christ are utterly lost. 19 If our hope in Christ has been for this life only, we are of all people the most pitiable.

20 In fact, however, Christ has been raised from the dead, as the first-fruits of all who have fallen asleep. 21 As it was by one man that death came, so through one man has come the resurrection of the dead. 22 Just as all die in Adam, so in Christ all will be brought to life; 23 but all of them in their proper order: Christ the first-fruits, and next, at his coming, those who belong to him. 24 After that will come the end, when he will hand over the kingdom to God the Father, having abolished every principality, every ruling force and power. 25 For he is to be king *until he has made* his enemies his footstool, 26 and the last of the enemies to be done away with is death, for *he has put all things under his feet.*w 27 But when it is said everything is subjected, this obviously cannot include the One who subjected everything to him. 28 When everything has been subjected to him, then the Son himself will be subjected to the One who has subjected everything to him, so that God may be all in all.

29 Otherwise, what are people up to who have themselves baptised on behalf of the dead? If the dead are not raised at all, what is the point of being baptised on their behalf? 30 And what about us? Why should we endanger ourselves every hour of our lives? 31 I swear by the pride that I take in you, in Christ Jesus our Lord, that I face death every day. 32 If I fought wild animals at Ephesus in a purely human perspective, what had I to gain by it? 33 If the dead are not going to be raised, then *Let us eat and drink, for tomorrow we shall be dead.*x 34 So do not let anyone lead you astray, 'Bad company corrupts good ways.'y Wake up from your stupor as you should and leave sin alone; some of you have no understanding of God; I tell you this to instil some shame in you.

35 Someone may ask: How are dead people raised, and what sort of body do they have when they come? 36 How foolish! What you sow must die before it is given new life; 37 and what you sow is not the body that is to be, but only a bare grain, of wheat I dare say, or some other kind; 38 it

w 15 Ps 110:1.   x 15 Is 22:13.   y 15 A proverb found also in Menander's *Thais.*

3039

gives it a body as he has chosen, and to each kind of seed its own body. 39 Not all flesh is alike, but there is one flesh for human beings, another for animals, another for birds, and another for fish. 40 There are both heavenly bodies and earthly bodies, but the glory of the heavenly is one thing, and that of the earthly is another. 41 There is one glory of the sun, and another glory of the moon, and another glory of the stars; indeed, star differs from star in glory.

42 So it is with the resurrection of the dead. What is sown is perishable, what is raised is imperishable. 43 It is sown in dishonor, it is raised in glory. It is sown in weakness, it is raised in power. 44 It is sown a physical body, it is raised a spiritual body. If there is a physical body, there is also a spiritual body. 45 Thus it is written, "The first man, Adam, became a living being"; the last Adam became a life-giving spirit. 46 But it is not the spiritual that is first, but the physical, and then the spiritual. 47 The first man was from the earth, a man of dust; the second man is[n] from heaven. 48 As was the man of dust, so are those who are of the dust; and as is the man of heaven, so are those who are of heaven. 49 Just as we have borne the image of the man of dust, we will[o] also bear the image of the man of heaven.

50 What I am saying, brothers and sisters,[p] is this: flesh and blood cannot inherit the kingdom of God, nor does the perishable inherit the imperishable. 51 Listen, I will tell you a mystery! We will not all die,[q] but we will all be changed, 52 in a moment, in the twinkling of an eye, at the last trumpet. For the trumpet will sound, and the dead will be raised imperishable, and we will be changed. 53 For this perishable body must put on imperishability, and this mortal body must put on immortality. 54 When this perishable body puts on imperishability, and this mortal body puts on immortality, then the saying that is written will be fulfilled: "Death has been swallowed up in victory."
55 "Where, O death, is your victory?
     Where, O death, is your sting?"
56 The sting of death is sin, and the power of sin is the law. 57 But thanks be to God, who gives us the victory through our Lord Jesus Christ.

58 Therefore, my beloved,[r] be steadfast, immovable, always excelling in the work of the Lord, because you know that in the Lord your labor is not in vain.

16 Now concerning the collection for the saints: you should follow the directions I gave to the churches of Galatia. 2 On the first day of every week, each of you is to put aside and save whatever extra you earn, so that collections need not be taken when I come. 3 And when I arrive, I will send any whom you approve with letters to take your gift to Jerusalem. 4 If it seems advisable that I should go also, they will accompany me.

5 I will visit you after passing through Macedonia—for I intend to pass through Macedonia— 6 and perhaps I will stay with you or even spend the winter, so that you may send me on my way, wherever I go. 7 I do not want to see you now just in passing, for I hope to spend some time with you, if the Lord permits. 8 But I will stay in Ephesus until Pentecost, 9 for a wide door for effective work has opened to me, and there are many adversaries.

10 If Timothy comes, see that he has nothing to fear among you, for he is doing the work of the Lord just as I am; 11 therefore let no one despise him. Send him on his way in peace, so that he may come to me; for I am expecting him with the brothers.

his choice, each seed its own particular body. 39 All flesh is not the same: there is human flesh, flesh of beasts, of birds, and of fishes—all different. 40 There are heavenly bodies and earthly bodies; and the splendour of the heavenly bodies is one thing, the splendour of the earthly another. 41 The sun has a splendour of its own, the moon another splendour, and the stars yet another; and one star differs from another in brightness. 42 So it is with the resurrection of the dead: what is sown as a perishable thing is raised imperishable. 43 Sown in humiliation, it is raised in glory; sown in weakness, it is raised in power; 44 sown a physical body, it is raised a spiritual body.

If there is such a thing as a physical body, there is also a spiritual body. 45 It is in this sense that scripture says, 'The first man, Adam, became a living creature,' whereas the last Adam has become a life-giving spirit. 46 Observe, the spiritual does not come first; the physical body comes first, and then the spiritual. 47 The first man is from earth, made of dust: the second man is from heaven. 48 The man made of dust is the pattern of all who are made of dust, and the heavenly man is the pattern of all the heavenly. 49 As we have worn the likeness of the man made of dust, so we shall wear the likeness of the heavenly man.

50 What I mean, my friends, is this: flesh and blood can never possess the kingdom of God, the perishable cannot possess the imperishable. 51 Listen! I will unfold a mystery: we shall not all die, but we shall all be changed 52 in a flash, in the twinkling of an eye, at the last trumpet-call. For the trumpet will sound, and the dead will rise imperishable, and we shall be changed. 53 This perishable body must be clothed with the imperishable, and what is mortal with immortality. 54 And when this perishable body has been clothed with the imperishable and our mortality has been clothed with immortality, then the saying of scripture will come true: 'Death is swallowed up; victory is won!' 55 'O Death, where is your victory? O Death, where is your sting?' 56 The sting of death is sin, and sin gains its power from the law. 57 But thanks be to God! He gives us victory through our Lord Jesus Christ.

58 Therefore, my dear friends, stand firm and immovable, and work for the Lord always, work without limit, since you know that in the Lord your labour cannot be lost.

16 Now ABOUT the collection in aid of God's people: you should follow the instructions I gave to our churches in Galatia. 2 Every Sunday each of you is to put aside and keep by him whatever he can afford, so that there need be no collecting when I come. 3 When I arrive, I will give letters of introduction to persons approved by you, and send them to carry your gift to Jerusalem. 4 If it seems right for me to go as well, they can travel with me.

5 I shall come to Corinth after passing through Macedonia—for I am travelling by way of Macedonia—6 and I may stay some time with you, perhaps even for the whole winter; and then you can help me on my way wherever I go next. 7 I do not want this to be a flying visit; I hope to spend some time with you, if the Lord permits. 8 But I shall remain at Ephesus until Pentecost, 9 for a great opportunity has opened for effective work, and there is much opposition.

10 If Timothy comes, see that you put him at his ease; for it is the Lord's work that he is engaged on, as I am myself; 11 so no one must slight him. Speed him on his way with your blessing; for he is to join me, and I am waiting for him

---

[n] Other ancient authorities add the Lord   [o] Other ancient authorities read let us   [p] Gk brothers   [q] Gk fall asleep   [r] Gk beloved brothers

15:54 Some witnesses omit this perishable body has been clothed with the imperishable and.

38 but God gives it a body as he chooses, and to each of the seeds its own body. 39 Not all flesh is the same, but there is one kind for human beings, another kind of flesh for animals, another kind of flesh for birds, and another for fish. 40 There are both heavenly bodies and earthly bodies, but the brightness of the heavenly is one kind and that of the earthly another. 41 The brightness of the sun is one kind, the brightness of the moon another, and the brightness of the stars another. For star differs from star in brightness.

42 So also is the resurrection of the dead. It is sown corruptible; it is raised incorruptible. 43 It is sown dishonorable; it is raised glorious. It is sown weak; it is raised powerful. 44 It is sown a natural body; it is raised a spiritual body. If there is a natural body, there is also a spiritual one.

45 So, too, it is written, "The first man, Adam, became a living being," the last Adam a life-giving spirit. 46 But the spiritual was not first; rather the natural and then the spiritual. 47 The first man was from the earth, earthly; the second man, from heaven. 48 As was the earthly one, so also are the earthly, and as is the heavenly one, so also are the heavenly. 49 Just as we have borne the image of the earthly one, we shall also bear the image of the heavenly one.

50 This I declare, brothers: flesh and blood cannot inherit the kingdom of God, nor does corruption inherit incorruption. 51 Behold, I tell you a mystery. We shall not all fall asleep, but we will all be changed, 52 in an instant, in the blink of an eye, at the last trumpet. For the trumpet will sound, the dead will be raised incorruptible, and we shall be changed. 53 For this which is corruptible must clothe itself with incorruptibility, and this which is mortal must clothe itself with immortality. 54 And when this which is corruptible clothes itself with incorruptibility and this which is mortal clothes itself with immortality, then the word that is written shall come about:

> "Death is swallowed up in victory.
> 55 Where, O death, is your victory?
> Where, O death, is your sting?"

56 The sting of death is sin, and the power of sin is the law. 57 But thanks be to God who gives us the victory through our Lord Jesus Christ.

58 Therefore, my beloved brothers, be firm, steadfast, always fully devoted to the work of the Lord, knowing that in the Lord your labor is not in vain.

16 Now in regard to the collection for the holy ones, you also should do as I ordered the churches of Galatia. 2 On the first day of the week each of you should set aside and save whatever one can afford, so that collections will not be going on when I come. 3 And when I arrive, I shall send those whom you have approved with letters of recommendation to take your gracious gift to Jerusalem. 4 If it seems fitting that I should go also, they will go with me.

5 I shall come to you after I pass through Macedonia (for I am going to pass through Macedonia), 6 and perhaps I shall stay or even spend the winter with you, so that you may send me on my way wherever I may go. 7 For I do not wish to see you now just in passing, but I hope to spend some time with you, if the Lord permits. 8 I shall stay in Ephesus until Pentecost, 9 because a door has opened for me wide and productive for work, but there are many opponents.

10 If Timothy comes, see that he is without fear in your company, for he is doing the work of the Lord just as I am. 11 Therefore, no one should disdain him. Rather, send him on his way in peace that he may come to me, for I am expecting him with the brothers. 12 Now in regard to our

is God who gives it the sort of body that he has chosen for it, and for each kind of seed its own kind of body.

39 Not all flesh is the same flesh: there is human flesh; animals have another kind of flesh, birds another and fish yet another. 40 Then there are heavenly bodies and earthly bodies; the heavenly have a splendour of their own, and the earthly a different splendour. 41 The sun has its own splendour, the moon another splendour, and the stars yet another splendour; and the stars differ among themselves in splendour. 42 It is the same too with the resurrection of the dead: what is sown is perishable, but what is raised is imperishable; 43 what is sown is contemptible but what is raised is glorious; what is sown is weak, but what is raised is powerful; 44 what is sown is a natural body, and what is raised is a spiritual body.

If there is a natural body, there is a spiritual body too. 45 So the first *man*, Adam, as scripture says, *became a living soul*;[z] and the last Adam has become a life-giving spirit. 46 But first came the natural body, not the spiritual one; that came only afterwards. 47 The first man, being made of earth, is earthly by nature; the second man is from heaven. 48 The earthly man is the pattern for earthly people, the heavenly man for heavenly ones. 49 And as we have borne the likeness of the earthly man, so we shall bear the likeness of the heavenly one.

50 What I am saying, brothers, is that mere human nature cannot inherit the kingdom of God: what is perishable cannot inherit what is imperishable. 51 Now I am going to tell you a mystery: we are not all going to fall asleep, 52 but we are all going to be changed, instantly, in the twinkling of an eye, when the last trumpet sounds. The trumpet is going to sound, and then the dead will be raised imperishable, and we shall be changed, 53 because this perishable nature of ours must put on imperishability, this mortal nature must put on immortality.

54 And after this perishable nature has put on imperishability and this mortal nature has put on immortality, then will the words of scripture come true: *Death is swallowed up in victory. 55 Death, where is your victory? Death, where is your sting?*[a] 56 The sting of death is sin, and the power of sin comes from the Law. 57 Thank God, then, for giving us the victory through Jesus Christ our Lord.

58 So, my dear brothers, keep firm and immovable, always abounding in energy for the Lord's work, being sure that in the Lord none of your labours is wasted.

16 Now about the collection for God's holy people;[b] you are to do the same as I prescribed for the churches in Galatia. 2 On the first day of the week, each of you should put aside and reserve as much as each can spare; do not delay the collection till I arrive. 3 When I come, I will send to Jerusalem with letters of introduction those people you approve to deliver your gift; 4 if it is worth my going too, they can travel with me.

5 In any case, I shall be coming to you after I have passed through Macedonia, as I have to go through Macedonia; 6 and I may be staying some time with you, perhaps wintering, so that you can start me on my next journey, wherever I may be going. 7 I do not want to make only a passing visit to you, and I am hoping to spend quite a time with you, the Lord permitting. 8 But I shall remain at Ephesus until Pentecost, 9 for a very promising door is standing wide open to me and there are many against us.

10 If Timothy comes, make sure that he has nothing to fear from you; he is doing the Lord's work, just as I am, 11 and nobody is to underrate him. Start him off in peace on his journey to come on to me: the brothers and I are waiting

---

z **15** Gn 2:7.   a **15** A free version of Is 25:8 and Hos 13:14.
b **16** cf. Ac 24:17; 2 Co 8–9.

12 Now concerning our brother Apollos, I strongly urged him to visit you with the other brothers, but he was not at all willing[s] to come now. He will come when he has the opportunity.

13 Keep alert, stand firm in your faith, be courageous, be strong. 14 Let all that you do be done in love.

15 Now, brothers and sisters,[t] you know that members of the household of Stephanas were the first converts in Achaia, and they have devoted themselves to the service of the saints; 16 I urge you to put yourselves at the service of such people, and of everyone who works and toils with them. 17 I rejoice at the coming of Stephanas and Fortunatus and Achaicus, because they have made up for your absence; 18 for they refreshed my spirit as well as yours. So give recognition to such persons.

19 The churches of Asia send greetings. Aquila and Prisca, together with the church in their house, greet you warmly in the Lord. 20 All the brothers and sisters[t] send greetings. Greet one another with a holy kiss.

21 I, Paul, write this greeting with my own hand. 22 Let anyone be accursed who has no love for the Lord. Our Lord, come![u] 23 The grace of the Lord Jesus be with you. 24 My love be with all of you in Christ Jesus.[v]

[s] Or it was not at all God's will for him   [t] Gk brothers
[u] Gk Marana tha. These Aramaic words can also be read Maran atha, meaning Our Lord has come   [v] Other ancient authorities add Amen

with our friends. 12 As for our friend Apollos, I urged him strongly to go to Corinth with the others, but he was quite determined not to go at present; he will go when the time is right.

13 Be on the alert; stand firm in the faith; be valiant, be strong. 14 Let everything you do be done in love.

15 One thing more, my friends. You know that the Stephanas family were the first converts in Achaia, and have devoted themselves to the service of God's people. 16 I urge you to accept the leadership of people like them, of anyone who labours hard at our common task. 17 It is a great pleasure to me that Stephanas, Fortunatus, and Achaicus have arrived, because they have done what you had no chance to do; 18 they have raised my spirits—and no doubt yours too. Such people deserve recognition.

19 Greetings from the churches of Asia. Many greetings in the Lord from Aquila and Prisca and the church that meets in their house. 20 Greetings from the whole brotherhood. Greet one another with the kiss of peace.

21 This greeting is in my own hand—Paul. 22 If anyone does not love the Lord, let him be outcast. Marana tha—Come, Lord! 23 The grace of the Lord Jesus be with you. 24 My love to you all in Christ Jesus.

16:12 but . . . not to go: or but it was clearly not the will of God that he should go.

brother Apollos, I urged him strongly to go to you with the brothers, but it was not at all his will that he go now. He will go when he has an opportunity.

13 Be on your guard, stand firm in the faith, be courageous, be strong. 14 Your every act should be done with love.

15 I urge you, brothers — you know that the household of Stephanas is the firstfruits of Achaia and that they have devoted themselves to the service of the holy ones — 16 be subordinate to such people and to everyone who works and toils with them. 17 I rejoice in the arrival of Stephanas, Fortunatus, and Achaicus, because they made up for your absence, 18 for they refreshed my spirit as well as yours. So give recognition to such people.

19 The churches of Asia send you greetings. Aquila and Prisca together with the church at their house send you many greetings in the Lord. 20 All the brothers greet you. Greet one another with a holy kiss.

21 I, Paul, write you this greeting in my own hand. 22 If anyone does not love the Lord, let him be accursed. *Marana tha.* 23 The grace of the Lord Jesus be with you. 24 My love to all of you in Christ Jesus.

for him. 12 As for our brother Apollos, I urged him earnestly to come to you with the brothers, but he was quite firm that he did not want to go yet, and he will come when he finds an opportunity.

13 Be vigilant, stay firm in the faith, be brave and strong. 14 Let everything you do be done in love.

15 There is something else I must urge you to do, brothers. You know how Stephanas' family have been the firstfruits of Achaia and have devoted themselves to the service of God's holy people; 16 I ask you in turn to put yourselves at the service of people like this and all that work with them in this arduous task. 17 I am delighted that Stephanas and Fortunatus and Achaicus have arrived; they have made up for your not being here. 18 They have set my mind at rest, just as they did yours; you should appreciate people like them.

19 The churches of Asia send their greetings. Aquila and Prisca send their best wishes in the Lord, together with the church that meets in their house. 20 All the brothers send their greetings. Greet one another with the holy kiss.

21 This greeting is in my own hand — PAUL. 22 If there is anyone who does not love the Lord, a curse on such a one. *Maran atha.* c

23 The grace of the Lord Jesus Christ be with you.

24 My love is with you all in Christ Jesus.

c **16** Aram. 'The Lord is coming' (or perhaps 'Lord, come').

THE SECOND LETTER OF PAUL TO THE
Corinthians

1 Paul, an apostle of Christ Jesus by the will of God, and Timothy our brother,

To the church of God that is in Corinth, including all the saints throughout Achaia:

2 Grace to you and peace from God our Father and the Lord Jesus Christ.

3 Blessed be the God and Father of our Lord Jesus Christ, the Father of mercies and the God of all consolation, 4 who consoles us in all our affliction, so that we may be able to console those who are in any affliction with the consolation with which we ourselves are consoled by God. 5 For just as the sufferings of Christ are abundant for us, so also our consolation is abundant through Christ. 6 If we are being afflicted, it is for your consolation and salvation; if we are being consoled, it is for your consolation, which you experience when you patiently endure the same sufferings that we are also suffering. 7 Our hope for you is unshaken; for we know that as you share in our sufferings, so also you share in our consolation.

8 We do not want you to be unaware, brothers and sisters,[a] of the affliction we experienced in Asia; for we were so utterly, unbearably crushed that we despaired of life itself. 9 Indeed, we felt that we had received the sentence of death so that we would rely not on ourselves but on God who raises the dead. 10 He who rescued us from so deadly a peril will continue to rescue us; on him we have set our hope that he will rescue us again, 11 as you also join in helping us by your prayers, so that many will give thanks on our[b] behalf for the blessing granted us through the prayers of many.

12 Indeed, this is our boast, the testimony of our conscience: we have behaved in the world with frankness[c] and godly sincerity, not by earthly wisdom but by the grace of God — and all the more toward you. 13 For we write you nothing other than what you can read and also understand; I hope you will understand until the end — 14 as you have already understood us in part — that on the day of the Lord Jesus we are your boast even as you are our boast.

15 Since I was sure of this, I wanted to come to you first, so that you might have a double favor;[d] 16 I wanted to visit you on my way to Macedonia, and to come back to you from Macedonia and have you send me on to Judea. 17 Was I vacillating when I wanted to do this? Do I make my plans according to ordinary human standards,[e] ready to say "Yes, yes" and "No, no" at the same time? 18 As surely as God is faithful, our word to you has not been "Yes and No." 19 For the Son of God, Jesus Christ, whom we proclaimed among you, Silvanus and Timothy and I, was not "Yes and No"; but in him it is always "Yes." 20 For in him every one of God's promises is a "Yes." For this reason it is through him that we say the "Amen," to the glory of God. 21 But it is God who establishes us with you in Christ and has

THE SECOND LETTER OF PAUL TO THE
Corinthians

1 FROM Paul, apostle of Christ Jesus by God's will, and our colleague Timothy, to God's church at Corinth, together with all God's people throughout the whole of Achaia.

2 Grace and peace to you from God our Father and the Lord Jesus Christ.

3 Praise be to the God and Father of our Lord Jesus Christ, the all-merciful Father, the God whose consolation never fails us! 4 He consoles us in all our troubles, so that we in turn may be able to console others in any trouble of theirs and to share with them the consolation we ourselves receive from God. 5 As Christ's suffering exceeds all measure and extends to us, so too it is through Christ that our consolation has no limit. 6 If distress is our lot, it is the price we pay for your consolation and your salvation; if our lot is consolation, it is to help us to bring you consolation, and strength to face with fortitude the same sufferings we now endure. 7 And our hope for you is firmly grounded; for we know that if you share in the suffering, you share also in the consolation.

8 In saying this, my friends, we should like you to know how serious was the trouble that came upon us in the province of Asia. The burden of it was far too heavy for us to bear, so heavy that we even despaired of life. 9 Indeed, we felt in our hearts that we had received a death sentence. This was meant to teach us to place reliance not on ourselves, but on God who raises the dead. 10 From such mortal peril God delivered us; and he will deliver us again, he on whom our hope is fixed. Yes, he will continue to deliver us, 11 while you co-operate by praying for us. Then, with so many people praying for our deliverance, there will be many to give thanks on our behalf for God's gracious favour towards us.

12 THERE is one thing we are proud of: our conscience shows us that in our dealings with others, and above all in our dealings with you, our conduct has been governed by a devout and godly sincerity, by the grace of God and not by worldly wisdom. 13–14 There is nothing in our letters to you but what you can read and understand. You do understand us in some measure, but I hope you will come to understand fully that you have as much reason to be proud of us, as we of you, on the day of our Lord Jesus.

15 It was because I felt so confident about all this that I had intended to come first of all to you and give you the benefit of a double visit: 16 I meant to visit you on my way to Macedonia and, after leaving Macedonia, to return to you, and you could then have sent me on my way to Judaea. 17 That was my intention; did I lightly change my mind? Or do I, when framing my plans, frame them as a worldly man might, first saying 'Yes, yes' and then 'No, no'? 18 God is to be trusted, and therefore what we tell you is not a mixture of Yes and No. 19 The Son of God, Christ Jesus, proclaimed among you by us (by Silvanus and Timothy, I mean, as well as myself), was not a mixture of Yes and No. With him it is always Yes; 20 for all the promises of God have their Yes in him. That is why, when we give glory to God, it is through Christ Jesus that we say 'Amen'. 21 And if you and we belong to Christ, guaranteed as his and anointed, it is all

a Gk brothers   b Other ancient authorities read your   c Other ancient authorities read holiness   d Other ancient authorities read pleasure   e Gk according to the flesh

1:12 devout: some witnesses read frank.   1:17 That was ... mind?: or In forming this intention, did I act irresponsibly?

The Second Letter to the Corinthians

2 Corinthians

THE SECOND LETTER OF PAUL TO THE CHURCH AT CORINTH

1 Paul, an apostle of Christ Jesus by the will of God, and Timothy our brother, to the church of God that is in Corinth, with all the holy ones throughout Achaia: ²grace to you and peace from God our Father and the Lord Jesus Christ.

³Blessed be the God and Father of our Lord Jesus Christ, the Father of compassion and God of all encouragement, ⁴who encourages us in our every affliction, so that we may be able to encourage those who are in any affliction with the encouragement with which we ourselves are encouraged by God. ⁵For as Christ's sufferings overflow to us, so through Christ does our encouragement also overflow. ⁶If we are afflicted, it is for your encouragement and salvation; if we are encouraged, it is for your encouragement, which enables you to endure the same sufferings that we suffer. ⁷Our hope for you is firm, for we know that as you share in the sufferings, you also share in the encouragement.

⁸We do not want you to be unaware, brothers, of the affliction that came to us in the province of Asia; we were utterly weighed down beyond our strength, so that we despaired even of life. ⁹Indeed, we had accepted within ourselves the sentence of death, that we might trust not in ourselves but in God who raises the dead. ¹⁰He rescued us from such great danger of death, and he will continue to rescue us; in him we have put our hope [that] he will also rescue us again, ¹¹as you help us with prayer, so that thanks may be given by many on our behalf for the gift granted us through the prayers of many.

¹²For our boast is this, the testimony of our conscience that we have conducted ourselves in the world, and especially toward you, with the simplicity and sincerity of God, [and] not by human wisdom but by the grace of God. ¹³For we write you nothing but what you can read and understand, and I hope that you will understand completely, ¹⁴as you have come to understand us partially, that we are your boast as you also are ours, on the day of [our] Lord Jesus.

¹⁵With this confidence I formerly intended to come to you so that you might receive a double favor, ¹⁶namely, to go by way of you to Macedonia, and then to come to you again on my return from Macedonia, and have you send me on my way to Judea. ¹⁷So when I intended this, did I act lightly? Or do I make my plans according to human considerations, so that with me it is "yes, yes" and "no, no"? ¹⁸As God is faithful, our word to you is not "yes" and "no." ¹⁹For the Son of God, Jesus Christ, who was proclaimed to you by us, Silvanus and Timothy and me, was not "yes" and "no," but "yes" has been in him. ²⁰For however many are the promises of God, their Yes is in him; therefore, the Amen from us also goes through him to God for glory. ²¹But the one who gives us security with you in Christ and

1 Paul, by the will of God an apostle of Christ Jesus, and Timothy, our brother, to the church of God in Corinth and to all God's holy people in the whole of Achaia. ²Grace to you and peace from God our Father and the Lord Jesus Christ.

³Blessed be the God and Father of our Lord Jesus Christ, the merciful Father and the God who gives every possible encouragement; ⁴he supports us in every hardship, so that we are able to come to the support of others, in every hardship of theirs because of the encouragement that we ourselves receive from God. ⁵For just as the sufferings of Christ overflow into our lives; so too does the encouragement we receive through Christ. ⁶So if we have hardships to undergo, this will contribute to your encouragement and your salvation; if we receive encouragement, this is to gain for you the encouragement which enables you to bear with perseverance the same sufferings as we do. ⁷So our hope for you is secure in the knowledge that you share the encouragement we receive, no less than the sufferings we bear.

⁸So in the hardships we underwent in Asia, we want you to be quite certain, brothers, that we were under extraordinary pressure, beyond our powers of endurance, so that we gave up all hope even of surviving. ⁹In fact we were carrying the sentence of death within our own selves, so that we should be forced to trust not in ourselves but in God, who raises the dead. ¹⁰He did save us from such a death and will save us — we are relying on him to do so. ¹¹Your prayer for us will contribute to this, so that, for God's favour shown to us as the result of the prayers of so many, thanks too may be given by many on our behalf.

¹²There is one thing that we are proud of, namely our conscientious conviction that we have always behaved towards everyone, and especially towards you, with that unalloyed holiness that comes from God, relying not on human reasoning but on the grace of God. ¹³In our writing, there is nothing that you cannot read clearly and understand; ¹⁴and it is my hope that, just as you have already understood us partially, so you will understand fully that you can be as proud of us as we shall be of you when the Day of our Lord Jesus comes.

¹⁵It was with this assurance that I had been meaning to come to you first, so that you would benefit doubly; ¹⁶both to visit you on my way to Macedonia, and then to return to you again from Macedonia, so that you could set me on my way to Judaea. ¹⁷Since that was my purpose, do you think I lightly changed my mind? Or that my plans are based on ordinary human promptings and I have in my mind Yes, yes*a* at the same time as No, no? ¹⁸As surely as God is trustworthy, what we say to you is not both Yes and No. ¹⁹The Son of God, Jesus Christ, who was proclaimed to you by us, that is, by me and by Silvanus and Timothy, was never Yes-and-No; his nature is all Yes. ²⁰For in him is found the Yes to all God's promises and therefore it is 'through him' that we answer 'Amen' to give praise to God. ²¹It is God who gives us, with you, a sure place in Christ

---

a 1 The argument is based on the Hebr. word *Amen* = Yes. The root meaning is 'faithful', 'solid'.

anointed us, 22 by putting his seal on us and giving us his Spirit in our hearts as a first installment.

23 But I call on God as witness against me: it was to spare you that I did not come again to Corinth. 24 I do not mean to imply that we lord it over your faith; rather, we are workers with you for your joy, because you stand firm in the faith. 1 So I made up my mind not to make you another painful visit. 2 For if I cause you pain, who is there to make me glad but the one whom I have pained? 3 And I wrote as I did, so that when I came, I might not suffer pain from those who should have made me rejoice; for I am confident about all of you, that my joy would be the joy of all of you. 4 For I wrote you out of much distress and anguish of heart and with many tears, not to cause you pain, but to let you know the abundant love that I have for you.

5 But if anyone has caused pain, he has caused it not to me, but to some extent—not to exaggerate it—to all of you. 6 This punishment by the majority is enough for such a person; 7 so now instead you should forgive and console him, so that he may not be overwhelmed by excessive sorrow. 8 So I urge you to reaffirm your love for him. 9 I wrote for this reason: to test you and to know whether you are obedient in everything. 10 Anyone whom you forgive, I also forgive. What I have forgiven, if I have forgiven anything, has been for your sake in the presence of Christ. 11 And we do this so that we may not be outwitted by Satan; for we are not ignorant of his designs.

12 When I came to Troas to proclaim the good news of Christ, a door was opened for me in the Lord; 13 but my mind could not rest because I did not find my brother Titus there. So I said farewell to them and went on to Macedonia.

14 But thanks be to God, who in Christ always leads us in triumphal procession, and through us spreads in every place the fragrance that comes from knowing him. 15 For we are the aroma of Christ to God among those who are being saved and among those who are perishing; 16 to the one a fragrance from death to death, to the other a fragrance from life to life. Who is sufficient for these things? 17 For we are not peddlers of God's word like so many;f but in Christ we speak as persons of sincerity, as persons sent from God and standing in his presence.

3 Are we beginning to commend ourselves again? Surely we do not need, as some do, letters of recommendation to you or from you, do we? 2 You yourselves are our letter, written on ourg hearts, to be known and read by all; 3 and you show that you are a letter of Christ, prepared by us, written not with ink but with the Spirit of the living God, not on tablets of stone but on tablets of human hearts.

4 Such is the confidence that we have through Christ toward God. 5 Not that we are competent of ourselves to claim anything as coming from us; our competence is from God, 6 who has made us competent to be ministers of a new covenant, not of letter but of spirit; for the letter kills, but the Spirit gives life.

God's doing; 22 it is God also who has set his seal upon us and, as a pledge of what is to come, has given the Spirit to dwell in our hearts.

23 I appeal to God as my witness and stake my life upon it: it was out of consideration for you that I did not after all come to Corinth. 24 It is not that we have control of your faith; rather we are working with you for your happiness. For it is by that faith that you stand. 1 So I made up my mind that my next visit to you must not be another painful one. 2 If I cause pain to you, who is left to cheer me up, except you whom I have offended? 3 This is precisely the point I made in my letter: I did not want, I said, to come and be made miserable by the very people who ought to have made me happy; and I had sufficient confidence in you all to know that for me to be happy is for all of you to be happy. 4 That letter I sent you came out of great distress and anxiety; how many tears I shed as I wrote it! Not because I wanted to cause you pain; rather I wanted you to know the love, the more than ordinary love, that I have for you.

5 Any injury that has been done has not been done to me; to some extent (I do not want to make too much of it) it has been done to you all. 6 The penalty on which the general meeting has agreed has met the offence well enough. 7 Something very different is called for now: you must forgive the offender and put heart into him; the man's distress must not be made so severe as to overwhelm him. 8 I urge you therefore to reassure him of your love for him. 9 I wrote, I may say, to see how you stood the test, whether you fully accepted my authority. 10 But anyone who has your forgiveness has mine too; and when I speak of forgiving (so far as there is anything for me to forgive), I mean that as the representative of Christ I have forgiven him for your sake. 11 For Satan must not be allowed to get the better of us; we know his wiles all too well.

12 When I came to Troas, where I was to preach the gospel of Christ, and where an opening awaited me for serving the Lord, 13 I still found no relief of mind, for my colleague Titus was not there to meet me; so I took leave of the people and went off to Macedonia. 14 But thanks be to God, who continually leads us as captives in Christ's triumphal procession, and uses us to spread abroad the fragrance of the knowledge of himself! 15 We are indeed the incense offered by Christ to God, both among those who are on the way to salvation, and among those who are on the way to destruction: 16 to the latter it is a deadly fume that kills, to the former a vital fragrance that brings life. Who is equal to such a calling? 17 We are not adulterating the word of God for profit as so many do; when we declare the word we do it in sincerity, as from God and in God's sight, as members of Christ.

3 ARE we beginning all over again to produce our credentials? Do we, like some people, need letters of introduction to you, or from you? 2 No, you are all the letter we need, a letter written on our heart; anyone can see it for what it is and read it for himself. 3 And as for you, it is plain that you are a letter that has come from Christ, given to us to deliver; a letter written not with ink but with the Spirit of the living God, written not on stone tablets but on the pages of the human heart.

4 It is in full reliance upon God, through Christ, that we make such claims. 5 There is no question of our having sufficient power in ourselves: we cannot claim anything as our own. The power we have comes from God; 6 it is he who has empowered us as ministers of a new covenant, not written but spiritual; for the written law condemns to death, but the Spirit gives life.

---

fOther ancient authorities read *like the others*   gOther ancient authorities read *your*

2:10 **as the representative:** *or* in the presence.

who anointed us is God; 22 he has also put his seal upon us and given the Spirit in our hearts as a first installment. 23 But I call upon God as witness, on my life, that it is to spare you that I have not yet gone to Corinth. 24 Not that we lord it over your faith; rather, we work together for your joy, for you stand firm in the faith.

2 For I decided not to come to you again in painful circumstances. 2 For if I inflict pain upon you, then who is there to cheer me except the one pained by me? 3 And I wrote as I did so that when I came I might not be pained by those in whom I should have rejoiced, confident about all of you that my joy is that of all of you. 4 For out of much affliction and anguish of heart I wrote to you with many tears, not that you might be pained but that you might know the abundant love I have for you.

5 If anyone has caused pain, he has caused it not to me, but in some measure (not to exaggerate) to all of you. 6 This punishment by the majority is enough for such a person, 7 so that on the contrary you should forgive and encourage him instead, or else the person may be overwhelmed by excessive pain. 8 Therefore, I urge you to reaffirm your love for him. 9 For this is why I wrote, to know your proven character, whether you were obedient in everything. 10 Whomever you forgive anything, so do I. For indeed what I have forgiven, if I have forgiven anything, has been for you in the presence of Christ, 11 so that we might not be taken advantage of by Satan, for we are not unaware of his purposes.

12 When I went to Troas for the gospel of Christ, although a door was opened for me in the Lord, 13 I had no relief in my spirit because I did not find my brother Titus. So I took leave of them and went on to Macedonia.

14 But thanks be to God, who always leads us in triumph in Christ and manifests through us the odor of the knowledge of him in every place. 15 For we are the aroma of Christ for God among those who are being saved and among those who are perishing, 16 to the latter an odor of death that leads to death, to the former an odor of life that leads to life. Who is qualified for this? 17 For we are not like the many who trade on the word of God; but as out of sincerity, indeed as from God and in the presence of God, we speak in Christ.

3 Are we beginning to commend ourselves again? Or do we need, as some do, letters of recommendation to you or from you? 2 You are our letter, written on our hearts, known and read by all, 3 shown to be a letter of Christ administered by us, written not in ink but by the Spirit of the living God, not on tablets of stone but on tablets that are hearts of flesh.

4 Such confidence we have through Christ toward God. 5 Not that of ourselves we are qualified to take credit for anything as coming from us; rather, our qualification comes from God, 6 who has indeed qualified us as ministers of a new covenant, not of letter but of spirit; for the letter brings death, but the Spirit gives life.

22 and has both anointed us and marked us with his seal, giving us as pledge the Spirit in our hearts. 23 By my life I call on God to be my witness that it was only to spare you that I did not come to Corinth again. b 24 We have no wish to lord it over your faith, but to work with you for your joy; for your stand in the faith is firm.

2 I made up my mind, then, that my next visit to you would not be a painful one, 2 for if I cause you distress I am causing distress to my only possible source of joy. 3 Indeed, I wrote as I did precisely to spare myself distress when I visited you, from the very people who should have given me joy, in the conviction that for all of you my joy was yours too. 4 I wrote to you in agony of mind, not meaning to cause you distress but to show you how very much love I have for you.

5 If anyone did cause distress, he caused it not to me, but — not to exaggerate — in some degree to all of you. 6 The punishment already imposed by the majority was quite enough for such a person; 7 and now by contrast you should forgive and encourage him all the more, or he may be overwhelmed by the extent of his distress. 8 That is why I urge you to give your love towards him definite expression. 9 This was in fact my reason for writing, to test your quality and whether you are completely obedient. 10 But if you forgive anybody, then I too forgive that person; and whatever I have forgiven, if there is anything I have forgiven, I have done it for your sake in Christ's presence, 11 to avoid being outwitted by Satan, whose scheming we know only too well.

12 When I came to Troas for the sake of the gospel of Christ and a door was opened for me there in the Lord, 13 I had no relief from anxiety, not finding my brother Titus there, and I said goodbye to them and went on to Macedonia. 14 But, thanks be to God who always gives us in Christ a part in his triumphal procession, and through us is spreading everywhere the fragrance of the knowledge of himself. 15 To God we are the fragrance of Christ, both among those who are being saved and among those who are on the way to destruction; 16 for these last, the smell of death leading to death, but for the first, the smell of life leading to life. Who is equal to such a task? 17 At least we do not adulterate the word of God, as so many do, but it is in all purity, as envoys of God and in God's presence, that we speak in Christ.

3 Are we beginning to commend ourselves to you afresh — as though we needed, like some others, to have letters of commendation either to you or from you? 2 You yourselves are our letter, written in our hearts, that everyone can read and understand; 3 and it is plain that you are a letter from Christ, entrusted to our care, written not with ink but with the Spirit of the living God; not on stone tablets but on the tablets of human hearts.

4 Such is the confidence we have through Christ in facing God; 5 it is not that we are so competent that we can claim any credit for ourselves; all our competence comes from God. 6 He has given us the competence to be ministers of a new covenant, a covenant which is not of written letters, but of the Spirit; for the written letters kill, but the Spirit gives

b 1 After writing 1 Co Paul 1 paid a brief, stern visit to Corinth and promised to return, 2 sent a messenger who was insulted, 3 sent a severe reprimand which was effective, and 4 wrote this letter.

NEW REVISED STANDARD VERSION

7 Now if the ministry of death, chiseled in letters on stone tablets,*h* came in glory so that the people of Israel could not gaze at Moses' face because of the glory of his face, a glory now set aside, 8 how much more will the ministry of the Spirit come in glory? 9 For if there was glory in the ministry of condemnation, much more does the ministry of justification abound in glory! 10 Indeed, what once had glory has lost its glory because of the greater glory; 11 for if what was set aside came through glory, much more has the permanent come in glory!

12 Since, then, we have such a hope, we act with great boldness, 13 not like Moses, who put a veil over his face to keep the people of Israel from gazing at the end of the glory that*i* was being set aside. 14 But their minds were hardened. Indeed, to this very day, when they hear the reading of the old covenant, that same veil is still there, since only in Christ is it set aside. 15 Indeed, to this very day whenever Moses is read, a veil lies over their minds; 16 but when one turns to the Lord, the veil is removed. 17 Now the Lord is the Spirit, and where the Spirit of the Lord is, there is freedom. 18 And all of us, with unveiled faces, seeing the glory of the Lord as though reflected in a mirror, are being transformed into the same image from one degree of glory to another; for this comes from the Lord, the Spirit.

4 Therefore, since it is by God's mercy that we are engaged in this ministry, we do not lose heart. 2 We have renounced the shameful things that one hides; we refuse to practice cunning or to falsify God's word; but by the open statement of the truth we commend ourselves to the conscience of everyone in the sight of God. 3 And even if our gospel is veiled, it is veiled to those who are perishing. 4 In their case the god of this world has blinded the minds of the unbelievers, to keep them from seeing the light of the gospel of the glory of Christ, who is the image of God. 5 For we do not proclaim ourselves; we proclaim Jesus Christ as Lord and ourselves as your slaves for Jesus' sake. 6 For it is the God who said, "Let light shine out of darkness," who has shone in our hearts to give the light of the knowledge of the glory of God in the face of Jesus Christ.

7 But we have this treasure in clay jars, so that it may be made clear that this extraordinary power belongs to God and does not come from us. 8 We are afflicted in every way, but not crushed; perplexed, but not driven to despair; 9 persecuted, but not forsaken; struck down, but not destroyed; 10 always carrying in the body the death of Jesus, so that the life of Jesus may also be made visible in our bodies. 11 For while we live, we are always being given up to death for Jesus' sake, so that the life of Jesus may be made visible in our mortal flesh. 12 So death is at work in us, but life in you.

13 But just as we have the same spirit of faith that is in accordance with scripture—"I believed, and so I spoke"—we also believe, and so we speak, 14 because we know that the one who raised the Lord Jesus will raise us also with Jesus, and will bring us with you into his presence. 15 Yes, everything is for your sake, so that grace, as it extends to more and more people, may increase thanksgiving, to the glory of God.

16 So we do not lose heart. Even though our outer nature is wasting away, our inner nature is being renewed day by day. 17 For this slight momentary affliction is preparing us for an eternal weight of glory beyond all measure, 18 because we look not at what can be seen but at what cannot be seen; for what can be seen is temporary, but what cannot be seen is eternal.

REVISED ENGLISH BIBLE

7 The ministry that brought death, and that was engraved in written form on stone, was inaugurated with such glory that the Israelites could not keep their eyes on Moses, even though the glory on his face was soon to fade. 8 How much greater, then, must be the glory of the ministry of the Spirit! 9 If glory accompanied the ministry that brought condemnation, how much richer in glory must be the ministry that brings acquittal! 10 Indeed, the glory that once was is now no glory at all; it is outshone by a still greater glory. 11 For if what was to fade away had its glory, how much greater is the glory of what endures!

12 With such a hope as this we speak out boldly; 13 it is not for us to do as Moses did: he put a veil over his face to keep the Israelites from gazing at the end of what was fading away. 14 In any case their minds had become closed, for that same veil is there to this very day when the lesson is read from the old covenant; and it is never lifted, because only in Christ is it taken away. 15 Indeed to this very day, every time the law of Moses is read, a veil lies over the mind of the hearer. 16 But (as scripture says) 'Whenever he turns to the Lord the veil is removed.' 17 Now the Lord of whom this passage speaks is the Spirit; and where the Spirit of the Lord is, there is liberty. 18 And because for us there is no veil over the face, we all see as in a mirror the glory of the Lord, and we are being transformed into his likeness with ever-increasing glory, through the power of the Lord who is the Spirit.

4 SINCE God in his mercy has given us this ministry, we never lose heart. 2 We have renounced the deeds that people hide for very shame; we do not practise cunning or distort the word of God. It is by declaring the truth openly that we recommend ourselves to the conscience of our fellow-men in the sight of God. 3 If our gospel is veiled at all, it is veiled only for those on the way to destruction; 4 their unbelieving minds are so blinded by the god of this passing age that the gospel of the glory of Christ, who is the image of God, cannot dawn upon them and bring them light. 5 It is not ourselves that we proclaim; we proclaim Christ Jesus as Lord, and ourselves as your servants for Jesus's sake. 6 For the God who said, 'Out of darkness light shall shine,' has caused his light to shine in our hearts, the light which is knowledge of the glory of God in the face of Jesus Christ.

7 But we have only earthenware jars to hold this treasure, and this proves that such transcendent power does not come from us; it is God's alone. 8 We are hard pressed, but never cornered; bewildered, but never at our wits' end; 9 hunted, but never abandoned to our fate; struck down, but never killed. 10 Wherever we go we carry with us in our body the death that Jesus died, so that in this body also the life that Jesus lives may be revealed. 11 For Jesus's sake we are all our life being handed over to death, so that the life of Jesus may be revealed in this mortal body of ours. 12 Thus death is at work in us, but life in you.

13 But scripture says, 'I believed, and therefore I spoke out,' and we too, in the same spirit of faith, believe and therefore speak out; 14 for we know that he who raised the Lord Jesus to life will with Jesus raise us too, and bring us to his presence, and you with us. 15 Indeed, all this is for your sake, so that, as the abounding grace of God is shared by more and more, the greater may be the chorus of thanksgiving that rises to the glory of God.

16 No wonder we do not lose heart! Though our outward humanity is in decay, yet day by day we are inwardly renewed. 17 Our troubles are slight and short-lived, and their outcome is an eternal glory which far outweighs them, 18 provided our eyes are fixed, not on the things that are seen, but on the things that are unseen; for what is seen is transient, what is unseen is eternal.

---

h Gk on stones   *i* Gk of what   3:18 **see . . . mirror:** *or* reflect like a mirror.

7 Now if the ministry of death, carved in letters on stone, was so glorious that the Israelites could not look intently at the face of Moses because of its glory that was going to fade, 8 how much more will the ministry of the Spirit be glorious? 9 For if the ministry of condemnation was glorious, the ministry of righteousness will abound much more in glory. 10 Indeed, what was endowed with glory has come to have no glory in this respect because of the glory that surpasses it. 11 For if what was going to fade was glorious, how much more will what endures be glorious.

12 Therefore, since we have such hope, we act very boldly 13 and not like Moses, who put a veil over his face so that the Israelites could not look intently at the cessation of what was fading. 14 Rather, their thoughts were rendered dull, for to this present day the same veil remains unlifted when they read the old covenant, because through Christ it is taken away. 15 To this day, in fact, whenever Moses is read, a veil lies over their hearts, 16 but whenever a person turns to the Lord the veil is removed. 17 Now the Lord is the Spirit, and where the Spirit of the Lord is, there is freedom. 18 All of us, gazing with unveiled face on the glory of the Lord, are being transformed into the same image from glory to glory, as from the Lord who is the Spirit.

4 Therefore, since we have this ministry through the mercy shown us, we are not discouraged. 2 Rather, we have renounced shameful, hidden things; not acting deceitfully or falsifying the word of God, but by the open declaration of the truth we commend ourselves to everyone's conscience in the sight of God. 3 And even though our gospel is veiled, it is veiled for those who are perishing, 4 in whose case the god of this age has blinded the minds of the unbelievers, so that they may not see the light of the gospel of the glory of Christ, who is the image of God. 5 For we do not preach ourselves but Jesus Christ as Lord, and ourselves as your slaves for the sake of Jesus. 6 For God who said, "Let light shine out of darkness," has shone in our hearts to bring to light the knowledge of the glory of God on the face of [Jesus] Christ.

7 But we hold this treasure in earthen vessels, that the surpassing power may be of God and not from us. 8 We are afflicted in every way, but not constrained; perplexed, but not driven to despair; 9 persecuted, but not abandoned; struck down, but not destroyed; 10 always carrying about in the body the dying of Jesus, so that the life of Jesus may also be manifested in our body. 11 For we who live are constantly being given up to death for the sake of Jesus, so that the life of Jesus may be manifested in our mortal flesh. 12 So death is at work in us, but life in you. 13 Since, then, we have the same spirit of faith, according to what is written, "I believed, therefore I spoke," we too believe and therefore speak, 14 knowing that the one who raised the Lord Jesus will raise us also with Jesus and place us with you in his presence. 15 Everything indeed is for you, so that the grace bestowed in abundance on more and more people may cause the thanksgiving to overflow for the glory of God.

16 Therefore, we are not discouraged; rather, although our outer self is wasting away, our inner self is being renewed day by day. 17 For this momentary light affliction is producing for us an eternal weight of glory beyond all comparison, 18 as we look not to what is seen but to what is unseen; for what is seen is transitory, but what is unseen is eternal.

life. 7 Now if the administering of death, engraved in letters on stone, occurred in such glory that the Israelites could not look Moses steadily in the face,c because of its glory, transitory though this glory was, 8 how much more will the ministry of the Spirit occur in glory! 9 For if it is glorious to administer condemnation, to administer saving justice is far richer in glory. 10 Indeed, what was once considered glorious has lost all claim to glory, by contrast with the glory which transcends it. 11 For if what was transitory had any glory, how much greater is the glory of that which lasts for ever.

12 With a hope like this, we can speak with complete fearlessness; 13 not like Moses who put a veil over his face so that the Israelites should not watch the end of what was transitory. 14 But their minds were closed; indeed, until this very day, the same veil remains over the reading of the Old Testament: it is not lifted, for only in Christ is it done away with. 15 As it is, to this day, whenever Moses is read, their hearts are covered with a veil, 16 and this veil will not be taken away till they turn to the Lord. 17 Now this Lord is the Spirit and where the Spirit of the Lord is, there is freedom. 18 And all of us, with our unveiled faces like mirrors reflecting the glory of the Lord, are being transformed into the image that we reflect in brighter and brighter glory; this is the working of the Lord who is the Spirit.

4 Such by God's mercy is our ministry, and therefore we do not waver 2 but have renounced all shameful secrecy. It is not our way to be devious, or to falsify the word of God; instead, in God's sight we commend ourselves to every human being with a conscience by showing the truth openly. 3 If our gospel seems to be veiled at all, it is so to those who are on the way to destruction, 4 the unbelievers whose minds have been blinded by the god of this world, so that they cannot see shining the light of the gospel of the glory of Christ, who is the image of God. 5 It is not ourselves that we are proclaiming, but Christ Jesus as the Lord, and ourselves as your servants for Jesus' sake. 6 It is God who said, 'Let light shine out of darkness,' that has shone into our hearts to enlighten them with the knowledge of God's glory, the glory on the face of Christ.

7 But we hold this treasure in pots of earthenware, so that the immensity of the power is God's and not our own. 8 We are subjected to every kind of hardship, but never distressed; we see no way out but we never despair; 9 we are pursued but never cut off; knocked down, but still have some life in us; 10 always we carry with us in our body the death of Jesus, so that the life of Jesus, too, may be visible in our body. 11 Indeed, while we are still alive, we are continually being handed over to death, for the sake of Jesus, so that the life of Jesus, too, may be visible in our mortal flesh. In us, then, death is at work; in you, life.

13 But as we have the same spirit of faith as is described in scripture — I believed and therefore I spoked — we, too, believe and therefore we, too, speak, 14 realising that he who raised up the Lord Jesus will raise us up with Jesus in our turn, and bring us to himself — and you as well. 15 You see, everything is for your benefit, so that as grace spreads, so, to the glory of God, thanksgiving may also overflow among more and more people.

16 That is why we do not waver; indeed, though this outer human nature of ours may be falling into decay, at the same time our inner human nature is renewed day by day. 17 The temporary, light burden of our hardships is earning us for ever an utterly incomparable, eternal weight of glory, 18 since what we aim for is not visible but invisible. Visible things are transitory, but invisible things eternal.

c 3 cf. Ex 34:29–35.   d 4 Ps 116:10.

5 For we know that if the earthly tent we live in is destroyed, we have a building from God, a house not made with hands, eternal in the heavens. 2 For in this tent we groan, longing to be clothed with our heavenly dwelling — 3 if indeed, when we have taken it off[j] we will not be found naked. 4 For while we are still in this tent, we groan under our burden, because we wish not to be unclothed but to be further clothed, so that what is mortal may be swallowed up by life. 5 He who has prepared us for this very thing is God, who has given us the Spirit as a guarantee.

6 So we are always confident; even though we know that while we are at home in the body we are away from the Lord — 7 for we walk by faith, not by sight. 8 Yes, we do have confidence, and we would rather be away from the body and at home with the Lord. 9 So whether we are at home or away, we make it our aim to please him. 10 For all of us must appear before the judgment seat of Christ, so that each may receive recompense for what has been done in the body, whether good or evil.

11 Therefore, knowing the fear of the Lord, we try to persuade others; but we ourselves are well known to God, and I hope that we are also well known to your consciences. 12 We are not commending ourselves to you again, but giving you an opportunity to boast about us, so that you may be able to answer those who boast in outward appearance and not in the heart. 13 For if we are beside ourselves, it is for God; if we are in our right mind, it is for you. 14 For the love of Christ urges us on, because we are convinced that one has died for all; therefore all have died. 15 And he died for all, so that those who live might live no longer for themselves, but for him who died and was raised for them.

16 From now on, therefore, we regard no one from a human point of view;[k] even though we once knew Christ from a human point of view,[k] we know him no longer in that way. 17 So if anyone is in Christ, there is a new creation: everything old has passed away; see, everything has become new! 18 All this is from God, who reconciled us to himself through Christ, and has given us the ministry of reconciliation; 19 that is, in Christ God was reconciling the world to himself,[l] not counting their trespasses against them, and entrusting the message of reconciliation to us. 20 So we are ambassadors for Christ, since God is making his appeal through us; we entreat you on behalf of Christ, be reconciled to God. 21 For our sake he made him to be sin who knew no sin, so that in him we might become the righteousness of God.

6 As we work together with him,[m] we urge you also not to accept the grace of God in vain. 2 For he says,
"At an acceptable time I have listened to you,
and on a day of salvation I have helped you."
See, now is the acceptable time; see, now is the day of salvation! 3 We are putting no obstacle in anyone's way, so that no fault may be found with our ministry, 4 but as servants of God we have commended ourselves in every way: through great endurance, in afflictions, hardships, calami-

5 1 We know that if the earthly frame that houses us today is demolished, we possess a building which God has provided — a house not made by human hands, eternal and in heaven. 2 In this present body we groan, yearning to be covered by our heavenly habitation put on over this one, 3 in the hope that, being thus clothed, we shall not find ourselves naked. 4 We groan indeed, we who are enclosed within this earthly frame; we are oppressed because we do not want to have the old body stripped off. What we want is to be covered by the new body put on over it, so that our mortality may be absorbed into life immortal. 5 It is for this destiny that God himself has been shaping us; and as a pledge of it he has given us the Spirit.

6 Therefore we never cease to be confident. We know that so long as we are at home in the body we are exiles from the Lord; 7 faith is our guide, not sight. 8 We are confident, I say, and would rather be exiled from the body and make our home with the Lord. 9 That is why it is our ambition, wherever we are, at home or in exile, to be acceptable to him. 10 For we must all have our lives laid open before the tribunal of Christ, where each must receive what is due to him for his conduct in the body, good or bad.

11 WITH this fear of the Lord before our eyes we address our appeal to men and women. To God our lives lie open, and I hope that in your heart of hearts they lie open to you also. 12 This is not another attempt to recommend ourselves to you: we are rather giving you a chance to show yourselves proud of us; then you will have something to say to those whose pride is all in outward show and not in inward worth. 13 If these are mad words, take them as addressed to God; if sound sense, as addressed to you. 14 For the love of Christ controls us once we have reached the conclusion that one man died for all and therefore all mankind has died. 15 He died for all so that those who live should cease to live for themselves, and should live for him who for their sake died and was raised to life. 16 With us therefore worldly standards have ceased to count in our estimate of anyone; even if once they counted in our understanding of Christ, they do so now no longer. 17 For anyone united to Christ, there is a new creation: the old order has gone; a new order has already begun.

18 All this has been the work of God. He has reconciled us to himself through Christ, and has enlisted us in this ministry of reconciliation: 19 God was in Christ reconciling the world to himself, no longer holding people's misdeeds against them, and has entrusted us with the message of reconciliation. 20 We are therefore Christ's ambassadors. It is as if God were appealing to you through us: we implore you in Christ's name, be reconciled to God! 21 Christ was innocent of sin, and yet for our sake God made him one with human sinfulness, so that in him we might be made one with the righteousness of God. **6** 1 Sharing in God's work, we make this appeal: you have received the grace of God; do not let it come to nothing. 2 He has said:

In the hour of my favour I answered you;
on the day of deliverance I came to your aid.

This is the hour of favour, this the day of deliverance. 3 Lest our ministry be brought into discredit, we avoid giving any offence in anything. 4 As God's ministers, we try to recommend ourselves in all circumstances by our steadfast endurance: in affliction, hardship, and distress; 5 when

5:13 **If these . . . to you:** *or* If we speak in ecstasy, it is to God's glory; if we speak sober sense, it is to your advantage.   5:17 **For anyone . . . begun:** *or* When anyone is united to Christ he is a new creature: his old life is over; a new life has already begun.
5:19 **God . . . himself:** *or* God was reconciling the world to himself by Christ.

j Other ancient authorities read *put it on*   k Gk *according to the flesh*   l Or *God was in Christ reconciling the world to himself*   m Gk *As we work together*

NEW AMERICAN BIBLE

NEW JERUSALEM BIBLE

5 For we know that if our earthly dwelling, a tent, should be destroyed, we have a building from God, a dwelling not made with hands, eternal in heaven. 2 For in this tent we groan, longing to be further clothed with our heavenly habitation 3 if indeed, when we have taken it off, we shall not be found naked. 4 For while we are in this tent we groan and are weighed down, because we do not wish to be unclothed but to be further clothed, so that what is mortal may be swallowed up by life. 5 Now the one who has prepared us for this very thing is God, who has given us the Spirit as a first installment.

6 So we are always courageous, although we know that while we are at home in the body we are away from the Lord, 7 for we walk by faith, not by sight. 8 Yet we are courageous, and we would rather leave the body and go home to the Lord. 9 Therefore, we aspire to please him, whether we are at home or away. 10 For we must all appear before the judgment seat of Christ, so that each one may receive recompense, according to what he did in the body, whether good or evil.

11 Therefore, since we know the fear of the Lord, we try to persuade others; but we are clearly apparent to God, and I hope we are also apparent to your consciousness. 12 We are not commending ourselves to you again but giving you an opportunity to boast of us, so that you may have something to say to those who boast of external appearance rather than of the heart. 13 For if we are out of our minds, it is for God; if we are rational, it is for you. 14 For the love of Christ impels us, once we have come to the conviction that one died for all; therefore, all have died. 15 He indeed died for all, so that those who live might no longer live for themselves but for him who for their sake died and was raised.

16 Consequently, from now on we regard no one according to the flesh; even if we once knew Christ according to the flesh, yet now we know him so no longer. 17 So whoever is in Christ is a new creation: the old things have passed away; behold, new things have come. 18 And all this is from God, who has reconciled us to himself through Christ and given us the ministry of reconciliation, 19 namely, God was reconciling the world to himself in Christ, not counting their trespasses against them and entrusting to us the message of reconciliation. 20 So we are ambassadors for Christ, as if God were appealing through us. We implore you on behalf of Christ, be reconciled to God. 21 For our sake he made him to be sin who did not know sin, so that we might become the righteousness of God in him.

6 Working together, then, we appeal to you not to receive the grace of God in vain. 2 For he says:

"In an acceptable time I heard you,
and on the day of salvation I helped you."

Behold, now is a very acceptable time; behold, now is the day of salvation. 3 We cause no one to stumble in anything, in order that no fault may be found with our ministry; 4 on the contrary, in everything we commend ourselves as ministers of God, through much endurance, in afflictions, hard-

5 For we are well aware that when the tent that houses us on earth is folded up, there is a house for us from God, not made by human hands but everlasting, in the heavens. 2 And in this earthly state we do indeed groan, 3 longing to put on our heavenly home over the present one; if indeed we are to be found clothed rather than stripped bare. 4 Yes, indeed, in this present tent, we groan under the burden, not that we want to be stripped of our covering, but because we want to be covered with a second garment on top, so that what is mortal in us may be swallowed up by life. 5 It is God who designed us for this very purpose, and he has given us the Spirit as a pledge.

6 We are always full of confidence, then, realising that as long as we are at home in the body we are exiled from the Lord, 7 guided by faith and not yet by sight; 8 we are full of confidence, then, and long instead to be exiled from the body and to be at home with the Lord. 9 And so whether at home or exiled, we make it our ambition to please him. 10 For at the judgement seat of Christ we are all to be seen for what we are, so that each of us may receive what he has deserved in the body, matched to whatever he has done, good or bad.

11 And so it is with the fear of the Lord always in mind that we try to win people over. But God sees us for what we are, and I hope your consciences do too. 12 Again we are saying this not to commend ourselves to you, but simply to give you the opportunity to take pride in us, so that you may have an answer for those who take pride in appearances and not inner reality. 13 If we have been unreasonable, it was for God; if reasonable, for you. 14 For the love of Christ overwhelms us when we consider that if one man died for all, then all have died; 15 his purpose in dying for all humanity was that those who live should live not any more for themselves, but for him who died and was raised to life.

16 From now onwards, then, we will not consider anyone by human standards: even if we were once familiar with Christ according to human standards, we do not know him in that way any longer. 17 So for anyone who is in Christ, there is a new creation: the old order is gone and a new being is there to see. 18 It is all God's work; he reconciled us to himself through Christ and he gave us the ministry of reconciliation. 19 I mean, God was in Christ reconciling the world to himself, not holding anyone's faults against them, but entrusting to us the message of reconciliation.

20 So we are ambassadors for Christ; it is as though God were urging you through us, and in the name of Christ we appeal to you to be reconciled to God. 21 For our sake he made the sinless one a victim for sin, so that in him we might become the uprightness of God.

6 As his fellow-workers, we urge you not to let your acceptance of his grace come to nothing. 2 As he said, 'At the time of my favour I have answered you; on the day of salvation I have helped you';e well, now is the real time of favour, now the day of salvation is here. 3 We avoid putting obstacles in anyone's way, so that no blame may attach to our work of service; 4 but in everything we prove ourselves authentic servants of God; by resolute perseverance in times of hardships, difficulties and distress; 5 when

e 6 Is 49:8.

ties, 5beatings, imprisonments, riots, labors, sleepless nights, hunger; 6by purity, knowledge, patience, kindness, holiness of spirit, genuine love, 7truthful speech, and the power of God; with the weapons of righteousness for the right hand and for the left; 8in honor and dishonor, in ill repute and good repute. We are treated as impostors, and yet are true; 9as unknown, and yet are well known; as dying, and see—we are alive; as punished, and yet not killed; 10as sorrowful, yet always rejoicing; as poor, yet making many rich; as having nothing, and yet possessing everything.

11 We have spoken frankly to you Corinthians; our heart is wide open to you. 12There is no restriction in our affections, but only in yours. 13In return—I speak as to children—open wide your hearts also.

14 Do not be mismatched with unbelievers. For what partnership is there between righteousness and lawlessness? Or what fellowship is there between light and darkness? 15What agreement does Christ have with Beliar? Or what does a believer share with an unbeliever? 16What agreement has the temple of God with idols? For we*n* are the temple of the living God; as God said,

> "I will live in them and walk among them,
>   and I will be their God,
>   and they shall be my people.
> 17 Therefore come out from them,
>   and be separate from them, says the Lord,
>   and touch nothing unclean;
>   then I will welcome you,
> 18   and I will be your father,
>   and you shall be my sons and daughters,
>   says the Lord Almighty."

7 Since we have these promises, beloved, let us cleanse ourselves from every defilement of body and of spirit, making holiness perfect in the fear of God.

2 Make room in your hearts*o* for us; we have wronged no one, we have corrupted no one, we have taken advantage of no one. 3I do not say this to condemn you, for I said before that you are in our hearts, to die together and to live together. 4I often boast about you; I have great pride in you; I am filled with consolation; I am overjoyed in all our affliction.

5 For even when we came into Macedonia, our bodies had no rest, but we were afflicted in every way—disputes without and fears within. 6But God, who consoles the downcast, consoled us by the arrival of Titus, 7and not only by his coming, but also by the consolation with which he was consoled about you, as he told us of your longing, your mourning, your zeal for me, so that I rejoiced still more. 8For even if I made you sorry with my letter, I do not regret it (though I did regret it, for I see that I grieved you with that letter, though only briefly). 9Now I rejoice, not because you were grieved, but because your grief led to repentance; for you felt a godly grief, so that you were not harmed in any way by us. 10For godly grief produces a repentance that leads to salvation and brings no regret, but worldly grief produces death. 11For see what earnestness this godly grief has produced in you, what eagerness to clear yourselves, what indignation, what alarm, what longing, what zeal, what punishment! At every point you have proved yourselves guiltless in the matter. 12So although I wrote to you,

flogged, imprisoned, mobbed; overworked, sleepless, starving. 6We recommend ourselves by innocent behaviour and grasp of truth, by patience and kindliness, by gifts of the Holy Spirit, by unaffected love, by declaring the truth, by the power of God. We wield the weapons of righteousness in right hand and left. 8Honour and dishonour, praise and blame, are alike our lot: we are the impostors who speak the truth, 9the unknown men whom all men know; dying we still live on; disciplined by suffering, we are not done to death; 10in our sorrows we have always cause for joy; poor ourselves, we bring wealth to many; penniless, we own the world.

11We have spoken very frankly to you, friends in Corinth; we have opened our heart to you. 12There is no constraint on our part; any constraint there may be is in you. 13In fair exchange then (if I may speak to you like a father) open your hearts to us.

14Do NOT team up with unbelievers. What partnership can righteousness have with wickedness? Can light associate with darkness? 15Can Christ agree with Belial, or a believer join with an unbeliever? 16Can there be a compact between the temple of God and idols? And the temple of the living God is what we are. God's own words are: 'I will live and move about among them; I will be their God, and they shall be my people.' 17And therefore, 'Come away and leave them, separate yourselves, says the Lord; touch nothing unclean. Then I will accept you, 18says the Lord Almighty; I will be a father to you, and you shall be my sons and 7 daughters.' 1Such are the promises that have been made to us, dear friends. Let us therefore cleanse ourselves from all that can defile flesh or spirit and, in the fear of God, let us complete our consecration.

2MAKE a place for us in your hearts! We have wronged no one, ruined no one, exploited no one. 3My words are no reflection on you. I have told you before that, come death, come life, your place in our hearts is secure. 4I am speaking to you with great frankness, but my pride in you is just as great. In all our many troubles my cup is full of consolation and overflows with joy.

5Even when we reached Macedonia we still found no relief; instead trouble met us at every turn, fights without and fears within. 6But God, who brings comfort to the downcast, has comforted us by the arrival of Titus, 7and not merely by his arrival, but by his being so greatly encouraged about you. He has told us how you long for me, how sorry you are, and how eager to take my side; and that has made me happier still.

8Even if I did hurt you by the letter I sent, I do not now regret it. I did regret it; but now that I see the letter gave you pain, though only for a time, 9I am happy—not because of the pain but because the pain led to a change of heart. You bore the pain as God would have you bear it, and so you came to no harm from what we did. 10Pain borne in God's way brings no regrets but a change of heart leading to salvation; pain borne in the world's way brings death. 11You bore your pain in God's way, and just look at the results: it made you take the matter seriously and vindicate yourselves; it made you indignant and apprehensive; it aroused your longing for me, your devotion, and your eagerness to see justice done! At every point you have cleared yourselves of blame. 12And so, although I did send you that

---

n Other ancient authorities read *you*   *o* Gk lacks *in your hearts*

ships, constraints, 5 beatings, imprisonments, riots, labors, vigils, fasts; 6 by purity, knowledge, patience, kindness, in a holy spirit, in unfeigned love, 7 in truthful speech, in the power of God; with weapons of righteousness at the right and at the left; 8 through glory and dishonor, insult and praise. We are treated as deceivers and yet are truthful; 9 as unrecognized and yet acknowledged; as dying and behold we live; as chastised and yet not put to death; 10 as sorrowful yet always rejoicing; as poor yet enriching many; as having nothing and yet possessing all things.

11 We have spoken frankly to you, Corinthians; our heart is open wide. 12 You are not constrained by us; you are constrained by your own affections. 13 As recompense in kind (I speak as to my children), be open yourselves.

14 Do not be yoked with those who are different, with unbelievers. For what partnership do righteousness and lawlessness have? Or what fellowship does light have with darkness? 15 What accord has Christ with Beliar? Or what has a believer in common with an unbeliever? 16 What agreement has the temple of God with idols? For we are the temple of the living God; as God said:

"I will live with them and move among them,
    and I will be their God
    and they shall be my people.
17 Therefore, come forth from them
    and be separate," says the Lord,
"and touch nothing unclean;
    then I will receive you
18 and I will be a father to you,
    and you shall be sons and daughters to me,
    says the Lord Almighty."

7 Since we have these promises, beloved, let us cleanse ourselves from every defilement of flesh and spirit, making holiness perfect in the fear of God.

2 Make room for us; we have not wronged anyone, or ruined anyone, or taken advantage of anyone. 3 I do not say this in condemnation, for I have already said that you are in our hearts, that we may die together and live together. 4 I have great confidence in you, I have great pride in you; I am filled with encouragement, I am overflowing with joy all the more because of all our affliction.

5 For even when we came into Macedonia, our flesh had no rest, but we were afflicted in every way — external conflicts, internal fears. 6 But God, who encourages the downcast, encouraged us by the arrival of Titus, 7 and not only by his arrival but also by the encouragement with which he was encouraged in regard to you, as he told us of your yearning, your lament, your zeal for me, so that I rejoiced even more. 8 For even if I saddened you by my letter, I do not regret it; and if I did regret it ([for] I see that that letter saddened you, if only for a while), 9 I rejoice now, not because you were saddened, but because you were saddened into repentance; for you were saddened in a godly way, so that you did not suffer loss in anything because of us. 10 For godly sorrow produces a salutary repentance without regret, but worldly sorrow produces death. 11 For behold what earnestness this godly sorrow has produced for you, as well as readiness for a defense, and indignation, and fear, and yearning, and zeal, and punishment. In every way you have shown yourselves to be innocent in the matter. 12 So then even though

we are flogged or sent to prison or mobbed; labouring, sleepless, starving; 6 in purity, in knowledge, in patience, in kindness; in the Holy Spirit; in a love free of affectation; 7 in the word of truth and in the power of God; by using the weapons of uprightness for attack and for defence: 8 in times of honour or disgrace, blame or praise; taken for impostors and yet we are genuine; 9 unknown and yet we are acknowledged; dying, and yet here we are, alive; scourged but not executed; 10 in pain yet always full of joy; poor and yet making many people rich; having nothing, and yet owning everything.

11 People of Corinth, we have spoken frankly and opened our heart to you. 12 Any distress you feel is not on our side; the distress is in your own selves. 13 In fair exchange — I speak as though to children of mine — you must open your hearts too.

14 Do *f* not harness yourselves in an uneven team with unbelievers; how can uprightness and law-breaking be partners, or what can light and darkness have in common? 15 How can Christ come to an agreement with Beliar and what sharing can there be between a believer and an unbeliever? 16 The temple of God cannot compromise with false gods, and that is what we are — the temple of the living God. We have God's word for it: *I shall fix my home among them and live among them; I will be their God and they will be my people.* 17 *Get away from them, purify yourselves,* says the Lord. *Do not touch anything unclean, and then I shall welcome you.* 18 *I shall be father to you, and you will be sons* and daughters *to me, g* says the almighty Lord.

7 Since these promises have been made to us, my dear friends, we should wash ourselves clean of everything that pollutes either body or spirit, bringing our sanctification to completion in the fear of God.

2 Keep a place for us in your hearts. We have not injured anyone, or ruined anyone, or taken advantage of anyone. 3 I am not saying this to condemn anybody; as I have already told you, you are in our hearts — so that together we live and together we die. 4 I can speak with the greatest frankness to you; and I can speak with the greatest pride about you: in all our hardship, I am filled with encouragement and overflowing with joy.

5 Even after we had come to Macedonia, there was no rest for this body of ours. Far from it; we were beset by hardship on all sides, there were quarrels all around us and misgivings within us. 6 But God, who encourages all those who are distressed, encouraged us through the arrival of Titus; 7 and not simply by his arrival only, but also by means of the encouragement that you had given him, as he told us of your desire to see us, how sorry you were and how concerned for us; so that I was all the more joyful.

8 So now, though I did distress you with my letter, I do not regret it. Even if I did regret it — and I realise that the letter distressed you, even though not for long — 9 I am glad now, not because you were made to feel distress, but because the distress that you were caused led to repentance; your distress was the kind that God approves and so you have come to no kind of harm through us. 10 For to be distressed in a way that God approves leads to repentance and then to salvation with no regrets; it is the world's kind of distress that ends in death. 11 Just look at this present case: at what the result has been of your being made to feel distress in the way that God approves — what concern, what defence, what indignation and what alarm; what yearning, and what enthusiasm, and what justice done. In every way you have cleared yourselves of blame in this matter. 12 So

f 6 6:14 — 7:1 may be a fragment on its own, a warning against infiltration of gentile ways.   *g* 6 Lv 26:11–12; Is 52:11; 2 S 7:14.

NEW REVISED STANDARD VERSION

REVISED ENGLISH BIBLE

it was not on account of the one who did the wrong, nor on account of the one who was wronged, but in order that your zeal for us might be made known to you before God. 13 In this we find comfort.

In addition to our own consolation, we rejoiced still more at the joy of Titus, because his mind has been set at rest by all of you. 14 For if I have been somewhat boastful about you to him, I was not disgraced; but just as everything we said to you was true, so our boasting to Titus has proved true as well. 15 And his heart goes out all the more to you, as he remembers the obedience of all of you, and how you welcomed him with fear and trembling. 16 I rejoice, because I have complete confidence in you.

8 We want you to know, brothers and sisters, *p* about the grace of God that has been granted to the churches of Macedonia; 2 for during a severe ordeal of affliction, their abundant joy and their extreme poverty have overflowed in a wealth of generosity on their part. 3 For, as I can testify, they voluntarily gave according to their means, and even beyond their means, 4 begging us earnestly for the privilege*q* of sharing in this ministry to the saints — 5 and this, not merely as we expected; they gave themselves first to the Lord and, by the will of God, to us, 6 so that we might urge Titus that, as he had already made a beginning, so he should also complete this generous undertaking*r* among you. 7 Now as you excel in everything — in faith, in speech, in knowledge, in utmost eagerness, and in our love for you*s* — so we want you to excel also in this generous undertaking.*r*

8 I do not say this as a command, but I am testing the genuineness of your love against the earnestness of others. 9 For you know the generous act*t* of our Lord Jesus Christ, that though he was rich, yet for your sakes he became poor, so that by his poverty you might become rich. 10 And in this matter I am giving my advice: it is appropriate for you who began last year not only to do something but even to desire to do something — 11 now finish doing it, so that your eagerness may be matched by completing it according to your means. 12 For if the eagerness is there, the gift is acceptable according to what one has — not according to what one does not have. 13 I do not mean that there should be relief for others and pressure on you, but it is a question of a fair balance between 14 your present abundance and their need, so that their abundance may be for your need, in order that there may be a fair balance. 15 As it is written,

"The one who had much did not have too much,
and the one who had little did not have too
little."

16 But thanks be to God who put in the heart of Titus the same eagerness for you that I myself have. 17 For he not only accepted our appeal, but since he is more eager than ever, he is going to you of his own accord. 18 With him we are sending the brother who is famous among all the churches for his proclaiming the good news;*u* 19 and not only that, but he has also been appointed by the churches to travel with us while we are administering this generous undertaking*r* for the glory of the Lord himself*v* and to show our goodwill. 20 We intend that no one should blame us about this generous gift that we are administering, 21 for we intend to do what is right not only in the Lord's sight but also in the sight of others. 22 And with them we are sending our brother whom we have often tested and found eager in many matters, but who is now more eager than ever because of his great confidence in you. 23 As for Titus, he is my

letter, it was not the offender or his victim that most concerned me. My aim in writing was to help to make plain to you, in the sight of God, how truly you are devoted to us. 13 That is why we have been so encouraged.

But besides being encouraged ourselves, we have also been delighted beyond everything by seeing how happy Titus is: you have all helped to set his mind completely at rest. 14 Anything I may have said to him to show my pride in you has been justified. Every word we addressed to you bore the mark of truth, and the same holds of the proud boast we made in the presence of Titus; that also has proved true. 15 His heart warms all the more to you as he recalls how ready you all were to do what he asked, meeting him as you did in fear and trembling. 16 How happy I am now to have complete confidence in you!

8 WE must tell you, friends, about the grace that God has given to the churches in Macedonia. 2 The troubles they have been through have tried them hard, yet in all this they have been so exuberantly happy that from the depths of their poverty they have shown themselves lavishly openhanded. 3 Going to the limit of their resources, as I can testify, and even beyond that limit, 4 they begged us most insistently, and on their own initiative, to be allowed to share in this generous service to their fellow-Christians. 5 And their giving surpassed our expectations; for first of all they gave themselves to the Lord and, under God, to us. 6 The upshot is that we have asked Titus, since he has already made a beginning, to bring your share in this further work of generosity also to completion. 7 You are so rich in everything — in faith, speech, knowledge, and diligence of every kind, as well as in the love you have for us — that you should surely show yourselves equally lavish in this generous service! 8 This is not meant as an order; by telling you how keen others are I am putting your love to the test. 9 You know the generosity of our Lord Jesus Christ: he was rich, yet for your sake he became poor, so that through his poverty you might become rich.

10 Here is my advice, and I have your interests at heart. You made a good beginning last year both in what you did and in your willingness to do it. 11 Now go on and finish it. Be as eager to complete the scheme as you were to adopt it, and give according to your means. 12 If we give eagerly according to our means, that is acceptable to God; he does not ask for what we do not have. 13 There is no question of relieving others at the cost of hardship to yourselves; 14 it is a question of equality. At the moment your surplus meets their need, but one day your need may be met from their surplus. The aim is equality; 15 as scripture has it, 'Those who gathered more did not have too much, and those who gathered less did not have too little.'

16 I thank God that he has made Titus as keen on your behalf as we are! 17 So keen is he that he not only welcomed our request; it is by his own choice he is now leaving to come to you. 18 With him we are sending one of our company whose reputation for his services to the gospel among all the churches is high. 19 Moreover they have duly appointed him to travel with us and help in this beneficent work, by which we do honour to the Lord himself and show our own eagerness to serve. 20 We want to guard against any criticism of our handling of these large sums; 21 for our aims are entirely honourable, not only in the Lord's eyes, but also in the eyes of men and women.

22 We are sending with them another of our company whose enthusiasm we have had repeated opportunities of testing, and who is now all the more keen because of the great confidence he has in you. 23 If there is any question

---

p Gk *brothers*   *q* Gk *grace*   *r* Gk *this grace*   *s* Other ancient
authorities read *your love for us*   *t* Gk *the grace*   *u* Or *the gospel*
v Other ancient authorities lack *himself*

8:7 **the love . . . us:** *some witnesses read* the love we have for you,
or the love which we have kindled in your hearts.

NEW AMERICAN BIBLE

I wrote to you, it was not on account of the one who did the wrong, or on account of the one who suffered the wrong, but in order that your concern for us might be made plain to you in the sight of God. 13 For this reason we are encouraged.

And besides our encouragement, we rejoice even more because of the joy of Titus, since his spirit has been refreshed by all of you. 14 For if I have boasted to him about you, I was not put to shame. No, just as everything we said to you was true, so our boasting before Titus proved to be the truth. 15 And his heart goes out to you all the more, as he remembers the obedience of all of you, when you received him with fear and trembling. 16 I rejoice, because I have confidence in you in every respect.

8 We want you to know, brothers, of the grace of God that has been given to the churches of Macedonia, 2 for in a severe test of affliction, the abundance of their joy and their profound poverty overflowed in a wealth of generosity on their part. 3 For according to their means, I can testify, and beyond their means, spontaneously, 4 they begged us insistently for the favor of taking part in the service to the holy ones, 5 and this, not as we expected, but they gave themselves first to the Lord and to us through the will of God, 6 so that we urged Titus that, as he had already begun, he should also complete for you this gracious act also. 7 Now as you excel in every respect, in faith, discourse, knowledge, all earnestness, and in the love we have for you, may you excel in this gracious act also.

8 I say this not by way of command, but to test the genuineness of your love by your concern for others. 9 For you know the gracious act of our Lord Jesus Christ, that for your sake he became poor although he was rich, so that by his poverty you might become rich. 10 And I am giving counsel in this matter, for it is appropriate for you who began not only to act but to act willingly last year: 11 complete it now, so that your eager willingness may be matched by your completion of it out of what you have. 12 For if the eagerness is there, it is acceptable according to what one has, not according to what one does not have; 13 not that others should have relief while you are burdened, but that as a matter of equality 14 your surplus at the present time should supply their needs, so that their surplus may also supply your needs, that there may be equality. 15 As it is written:

"Whoever had much did not have more,
and whoever had little did not have less."

16 But thanks be to God who put the same concern for you into the heart of Titus, 17 for he not only welcomed our appeal but, since he is very concerned, he has gone to you of his own accord. 18 With him we have sent the brother who is praised in all the churches for his preaching of the gospel. 19 And not only that, but he has also been appointed our traveling companion by the churches in this gracious work administered by us for the glory of the Lord [himself] and for the expression of our eagerness. 20 This we desire to avoid, that anyone blame us about this lavish gift administered by us, 21 for we are concerned for what is honorable not only in the sight of the Lord but also in the sight of others. 22 And with them we have sent our brother whom we often tested in many ways and found earnest, but who is now much more earnest because of his great confidence in you. 23 As for Titus, he is my partner and co-worker for

NEW JERUSALEM BIBLE

although I wrote a letter to you, it was not for the sake of the offender, nor for the one offended, but only so that you yourselves should fully realise in the sight of God what concern you have for us. 13 That is what I have found encouraging.

In addition to all this to encourage us, we were made all the more joyful by Titus' joy, now that his spirit has been refreshed by you all. 14 And if I boasted about you to him in any way, then I have not been made to look foolish; indeed, our boast to Titus has been proved to be as true as anything we said to you. 15 His personal affection for you is all the stronger when he remembers how obedient you have all been, and how you welcomed him with fear and trembling. 16 I am glad that I have every confidence in you.

8 Next, brothers, we will tell you of the grace of God which has been granted to the churches of Macedonia, 2 and how, throughout continual ordeals of hardship, their unfailing joy and their intense poverty have overflowed in a wealth of generosity on their part. 3 I can testify that it was of their own accord that they made their gift, which was not merely as far as their resources would allow, but well beyond their resources; 4 and they had kept imploring us most insistently for the privilege of a share in the fellowship of service to God's holy people — 5 it was not something that we expected of them, but it began by their offering themselves to the Lord and to us at the prompting of the will of God. 6 In the end we urged Titus, since he had already made a beginning, also to bring this work of generosity to completion among you. 7 More, as you are rich in everything — faith, eloquence, understanding, concern for everything, and love for us too — then make sure that you excel in this work of generosity too. 8 I am not saying this as an order, but testing the genuineness of your love against the concern of others. 9 You are well aware of the generosity which our Lord Jesus Christ had, that, although he was rich, he became poor for your sake, so that you should become rich through his poverty. 10 I will give you my considered opinion in the matter; this will be the right course for you as you were the first, a year ago, not only to take any action but also even to conceive the project. 11 Now, then, complete the action as well, so that the fulfilment may — so far as your resources permit — be proportionate to your enthusiasm for the project. 12 As long as the enthusiasm is there, the basis on which it is acceptable is what someone has, not what someone does not have. 13 It is not that you ought to relieve other people's needs and leave yourselves in hardship; but there should be a fair balance — 14 your surplus at present may fill their deficit, and another time their surplus may fill your deficit. So there may be a fair balance; 15 as scripture says: *No one who had collected more had too much, no one who collected less had too little.*[h]

16 Thank God for putting into Titus' heart the same sincere concern for you. 17 He certainly took our urging to heart; but greater still was his own enthusiasm, and he went off to you of his own accord. 18 We have sent with him the brother who is praised as an evangelist in all the churches 19 and who, what is more, was elected by the churches to be our travelling companion in this work of generosity, a work to be administered by us for the glory of the Lord and our complete satisfaction. 20 We arranged it this way so that no one should be able to make any accusation against us about this large sum we are administering. 21 And so *we have been careful to do right* not only *in the sight of the Lord* but also *in the sight of people.*[i] 22 Along with these, we have sent a brother of ours whose eagerness we have tested over and over again in many ways and who is now all the more eager because he has so much faith in you. 23 If Titus is in

h 8 Ex 16:18.   i 8 Pr 3:4 LXX.

NEW REVISED STANDARD VERSION

REVISED ENGLISH BIBLE

partner and co-worker in your service; as for our brothers, they are messengers*w* of the churches, the glory of Christ. 24 Therefore openly before the churches, show them the proof of your love and of our reason for boasting about you.

9 Now it is not necessary for me to write you about the ministry to the saints, 2 for I know your eagerness, which is the subject of my boasting about you to the people of Macedonia, saying that Achaia has been ready since last year; and your zeal has stirred up most of them. 3 But I am sending the brothers in order that our boasting about you may not prove to have been empty in this case, so that you may be ready, as I said you would be; 4 otherwise, if some Macedonians come with me and find that you are not ready, we would be humiliated — to say nothing of you — in this undertaking.*x* 5 So I thought it necessary to urge the brothers to go on ahead to you, and arrange in advance for this bountiful gift that you have promised, so that it may be ready as a voluntary gift and not as an extortion.

6 The point is this: the one who sows sparingly will also reap sparingly, and the one who sows bountifully will also reap bountifully. 7 Each of you must give as you have made up your mind, not reluctantly or under compulsion, for God loves a cheerful giver. 8 And God is able to provide you with every blessing in abundance, so that by always having enough of everything, you may share abundantly in every good work. 9 As it is written,

"He scatters abroad, he gives to the poor;
his righteousness*y* endures forever."

10 He who supplies seed to the sower and bread for food will supply and multiply your seed for sowing and increase the harvest of your righteousness.*y* 11 You will be enriched in every way for your great generosity, which will produce thanksgiving to God through us; 12 for the rendering of this ministry not only supplies the needs of the saints but also overflows with many thanksgivings to God. 13 Through the testing of this ministry you glorify God by your obedience to the confession of the gospel of Christ and by the generosity of your sharing with them and with all others, 14 while they long for you and pray for you because of the surpassing grace of God that he has given you. 15 Thanks be to God for his indescribable gift!

10 I myself, Paul, appeal to you by the meekness and gentleness of Christ — I who am humble when face to face with you, but bold toward you when I am away! — 2 I ask that when I am present I need not show boldness by daring to oppose those who think we are acting according to human standards.*z* 3 Indeed, we live as human beings,*a* but we do not wage war according to human standards;*z* 4 for the weapons of our warfare are not merely human,*b* but they have divine power to destroy strongholds. We destroy arguments 5 and every proud obstacle raised up against the knowledge of God, and we take every thought captive to obey Christ. 6 We are ready to punish every disobedience when your obedience is complete.

7 Look at what is before your eyes. If you are confident that you belong to Christ, remind yourself of this, that just as you belong to Christ, so also do we. 8 Now, even if I boast a little too much of our authority, which the Lord gave for building you up and not for tearing you down, I will not be ashamed of it. 9 I do not want to seem as though I am

about Titus, he is my partner and my fellow-worker in dealings with you; as for the others, they are delegates of the churches and bring honour to Christ. 24 So give them, and through them the churches, clear evidence of your love and justify our pride in you.

9 About this aid for God's people, it is superfluous for me to write to you. 2 I know how eager you are to help and I speak of it with pride to the Macedonians, telling them that Achaia had everything ready last year; and most of them have been fired by your zeal. 3 My purpose in sending these friends is to ensure that what we have said about you in this matter should not prove to be an empty boast. I want you to be prepared, as I told them you were; 4 for if I bring men from Macedonia with me and they find you are not prepared, what a disgrace it will be to us, let alone to you, after all the confidence we have shown! 5 I have accordingly thought it necessary to ask these friends to go on ahead to Corinth, to see that your promised bounty is in order before I come; it will then be awaiting me as genuine bounty, and not as an extortion.

6 Remember: sow sparingly, and you will reap sparingly; sow bountifully, and you will reap bountifully. 7 Each person should give as he has decided for himself; there should be no reluctance, no sense of compulsion; God loves a cheerful giver. 8 And it is in God's power to provide you with all good gifts in abundance, so that, with every need always met to the full, you may have something to spare for every good cause; 9 as scripture says: 'He lavishes his gifts on the needy; his benevolence lasts for ever.' 10 Now he who provides seed for sowing and bread for food will provide the seed for you to sow; he will multiply it and swell the harvest of your benevolence, 11 and you will always be rich enough to be generous. Through our action such generosity will issue in thanksgiving to God, 12 for as a piece of willing service this is not only a contribution towards the needs of God's people; more than that, it overflows in a flood of thanksgiving to God. 13 For with the proof which this aid affords, those who receive it will give honour to God when they see how humbly you obey him and how faithfully you confess the gospel of Christ; and they will thank him for your liberal contribution to their need and to the general good. 14 And as they join in prayer on your behalf, their hearts will go out to you because of the richness of the grace which God has given you. 15 Thanks be to God for his gift which is beyond all praise!

10 I, PAUL, appeal to you by the gentleness and magnanimity of Christ — I who am so timid (you say) when face to face with you, so courageous when I am away from you. 2 Spare me when I come, I beg you, the need for that courage and self-assurance, which I reckon I could confidently display against those who assume my behaviour to be dictated by human weakness. 3 Weak and human we may be, but that does not dictate the way we fight our battles. 4 The weapons we wield are not merely human; they are strong enough with God's help to demolish strongholds. 5 We demolish sophistries and all that rears its proud head against the knowledge of God; we compel every human thought to surrender in obedience to Christ; 6 and we are prepared to punish any disobedience once your own obedience is complete.

7 Look facts in the face. Is someone convinced that he belongs to Christ? Let him think again and reflect that we belong to Christ as much as he does. 8 Indeed, if I am boasting too much about our authority — an authority given by the Lord to build your faith, not pull it down — I shall make good my boast. 9 So you must not think of me as one

w Gk apostles   *x* Other ancient authorities add of boasting
y Or benevolence   *z* Gk according to the flesh   *a* Gk in the flesh
b Gk fleshly

you; as for our brothers, they are apostles of the churches, the glory of Christ. 24 So give proof before the churches of your love and of our boasting about you to them.

9 Now about the service to the holy ones, it is superfluous for me to write to you, 2 for I know your eagerness, about which I boast of you to the Macedonians, that Achaia has been ready since last year; and your zeal has stirred up most of them. 3 Nonetheless, I sent the brothers so that our boast about you might not prove empty in this case, so that you might be ready, as I said, 4 for fear that if any Macedonians come with me and find you not ready we might be put to shame (to say nothing of you) in this conviction. 5 So I thought it necessary to encourage the brothers to go on ahead to you and arrange in advance for your promised gift, so that in this way it might be ready as a bountiful gift and not as an exaction.

6 Consider this: whoever sows sparingly will also reap sparingly, and whoever sows bountifully will also reap bountifully. 7 Each must do as already determined, without sadness or compulsion, for God loves a cheerful giver. 8 Moreover, God is able to make every grace abundant for you, so that in all things, always having all you need, you may have an abundance for every good work. 9 As it is written:

"He scatters abroad, he gives to the poor;
his righteousness endures forever."

10 The one who supplies seed to the sower and bread for food will supply and multiply your seed and increase the harvest of your righteousness. 11 You are being enriched in every way for all generosity, which through us produces thanksgiving to God, 12 for the administration of this public service is not only supplying the needs of the holy ones but is also overflowing in many acts of thanksgiving to God. 13 Through the evidence of this service, you are glorifying God for your obedient confession of the gospel of Christ and the generosity of your contribution to them and to all others, 14 while in prayer on your behalf they long for you, because of the surpassing grace of God upon you. 15 Thanks be to God for his indescribable gift!

10 Now I myself, Paul, urge you through the gentleness and clemency of Christ, I who am humble when face to face with you, but brave toward you when absent, 2 I beg you that, when present, I may not have to be brave with that confidence with which I intend to act boldly against some who consider us as acting according to the flesh. 3 For, although we are in the flesh, we do not battle according to the flesh, 4 for the weapons of our battle are not of flesh but are enormously powerful, capable of destroying fortresses. We destroy arguments 5 and every pretension raising itself against the knowledge of God, and take every thought captive in obedience to Christ, 6 and we are ready to punish every disobedience, once your obedience is complete.

7 Look at what confronts you. Whoever is confident of belonging to Christ should consider that as he belongs to Christ, so do we. 8 And even if I should boast a little too much of our authority, which the Lord gave for building you up and not for tearing you down, I shall not be put to shame. 9 May I not seem as one frightening you through

question—he is my own partner and fellow-worker in your interests; and if our brothers—they are the emissaries of the churches and the glory of Christ. 24 So then, in full view of all the churches, give proof that you love them, and that we were right to boast of you to them.

9 About the help to God's holy people, there is really no need for me to write to you; j 2 for I am well aware of your enthusiasm, and I have been boasting of it to the Macedonians that 'Achaia has been ready for a year'; your enthusiasm has been a spur to many others. 3 All the same, I have sent the brothers, to make sure that our boast about you may not prove hollow in this respect and that you may be ready, as I said you would be; 4 so that if by chance some of the Macedonians came with me and found you unprepared we—to say nothing of yourselves—would not be put to shame by our confidence in you. 5 So I have thought it necessary to encourage the brothers to go to you ahead of us and make sure in advance of the gift that you have already promised, so that it is all at hand as a real gift and not an imposition.

6 But remember: anyone who sows sparsely will reap sparsely as well—and anyone who sows generously will reap generously as well. 7 Each one should give as much as he has decided on his own initiative, not reluctantly or under compulsion, for *God loves a cheerful giver*. k 8 God is perfectly able to enrich you with every grace, so that you always have enough for every conceivable need, and your resources overflow in all kinds of good work. 9 As scripture says: *To the needy he gave without stint, his uprightness stands firm for ever.*l

10 The one who so freely provides *seed for the sower and food to eat*m will provide you with ample store of seed for sowing and make *the harvest of your uprightness*n a bigger one: 11 you will be rich enough in every way for every kind of generosity that makes people thank God for what we have done. 12 For the help provided by this contribution not only satisfies the needs of God's holy people, but also overflows into widespread thanksgiving to God; 13 because when you have proved your quality by this help, they will give glory to God for the obedience which you show in professing the gospel of Christ, as well as for the generosity of your fellowship towards them and towards all. 14 At the same time, their prayer for you will express the affection they feel for you because of the unbounded grace God has given you. 15 Thanks be to God for his gift that is beyond all telling!

10 I urge you by the gentleness and forbearance of Christ—this is Paul now speaking personally—I, the one who is so humble when he is facing you but full of boldness at a distance. 2 Yes, my appeal to you is that I should not have to be bold when I am actually with you, or show the same self-assurance as I reckon to use when I am challenging those who reckon that we are guided by human motives. 3 For although we are human, it is not by human methods that we do battle. 4 The weapons with which we do battle are not those of human nature, but they have the power, in God's cause, to demolish fortresses. It is ideas that we demolish, 5 every presumptuous notion that is set up against the knowledge of God, and we bring every thought into captivity and obedience to Christ; 6 once you have given your complete obedience, we are prepared to punish any disobedience. 7 Look at the evidence of your eyes. Anybody who is convinced that he belongs to Christ should go on to reflect that we belong to Christ no less than he does. 8 Maybe I have taken rather too much pride in our authority, but the Lord gave us that for building you up, not for knocking you down, and I am not going to be shamed 9 into

j 9 As he has just done so, this chapter may be a separate note.
k 9 Pr 22:8 LXX.   l 9 Ps 112:9.   m 9 Is 55:10.   n 9 Ho 12:12.

trying to frighten you with my letters. 10 For they say, "His letters are weighty and strong, but his bodily presence is weak, and his speech contemptible." 11 Let such people understand that what we say by letter when absent, we will also do when present.

12 We do not dare to classify or compare ourselves with some of those who commend themselves. But when they measure themselves by one another, and compare themselves with one another, they do not show good sense. 13 We, however, will not boast beyond limits, but will keep within the field that God has assigned to us, to reach out even as far as you. 14 For we were not overstepping our limits when we reached you; we were the first to come all the way to you with the good news[c] of Christ. 15 We do not boast beyond limits, that is, in the labors of others; but our hope is that, as your faith increases, our sphere of action among you may be greatly enlarged, 16 so that we may proclaim the good news[c] in lands beyond you, without boasting of work already done in someone else's sphere of action. 17 "Let the one who boasts, boast in the Lord." 18 For it is not those who commend themselves that are approved, but those whom the Lord commends.

11 I wish you would bear with me in a little foolishness. Do bear with me! 2 I feel a divine jealousy for you, for I promised you in marriage to one husband, to present you as a chaste virgin to Christ. 3 But I am afraid that as the serpent deceived Eve by its cunning, your thoughts will be led astray from a sincere and pure[d] devotion to Christ. 4 For if someone comes and proclaims another Jesus than the one we proclaimed, or if you receive a different spirit from the one you received, or a different gospel from the one you accepted, you submit to it readily enough. 5 I think that I am not in the least inferior to these super-apostles. 6 I may be untrained in speech, but not in knowledge; certainly in every way and in all things we have made this evident to you.

7 Did I commit a sin by humbling myself so that you might be exalted, because I proclaimed God's good news[e] to you free of charge? 8 I robbed other churches by accepting support from them in order to serve you. 9 And when I was with you and was in need, I did not burden anyone, for my needs were supplied by the friends[f] who came from Macedonia. So I refrained and will continue to refrain from burdening you in any way. 10 As the truth of Christ is in me, this boast of mine will not be silenced in the regions of Achaia. 11 And why? Because I do not love you? God knows I do!

12 And what I do I will also continue to do, in order to deny an opportunity to those who want an opportunity to be recognized as our equals in what they boast about. 13 For such boasters are false apostles, deceitful workers, disguising themselves as apostles of Christ. 14 And no wonder! Even Satan disguises himself as an angel of light. 15 So it is not strange if his ministers also disguise themselves as ministers of righteousness. Their end will match their deeds.

16 I repeat, let no one think that I am a fool; but if you do, then accept me as a fool, so that I too may boast a little. 17 What I am saying in regard to this boastful confidence, I am saying not with the Lord's authority, but as a fool; 18 since many boast according to human standards,[g] I will

who tries to scare you by the letters he writes. 10 'His letters', so it is said, 'are weighty and powerful; but when he is present he is unimpressive, and as a speaker he is beneath contempt.' 11 People who talk in that way should reckon with this: my actions when I come will show the same man as my letters showed while I was absent.

12 We should not dare to class ourselves or compare ourselves with any of those who commend themselves. What fools they are to measure themselves on their own, to find in themselves their standard of comparison! 13 As for us, our boasting will not go beyond the proper limits; and our sphere is determined by the limit God laid down for us, which permitted us to come as far as Corinth. 14 We are not overstretching our commission, as we would be if we had never come to you; but we were the first to reach as far as Corinth in the work of the gospel of Christ. 15 And we do not boast of work done where others have laboured, work beyond our proper sphere. Our hope is rather that, as your faith grows, we may attain a position among you greater than ever before, but still within the limits of our sphere. 16 Then we can carry the gospel to lands that lie beyond you, never priding ourselves on work already done in anyone else's sphere. 17 If anyone would boast, let him boast of the Lord. 18 For it is not the one who recommends himself, but the one whom the Lord recommends, who is to be accepted.

11 I SHOULD like you to bear with me in a little foolishness; please bear with me. 2 I am jealous for you, with the jealousy of God; for I betrothed you to Christ, thinking to present you as a chaste virgin to her true and only husband. 3 Now I am afraid that, as the serpent in his cunning seduced Eve, your thoughts may be corrupted and you may lose your single-hearted devotion to Christ. 4 For if some newcomer proclaims another Jesus, not the Jesus whom we proclaimed, or if you receive a spirit different from the Spirit already given to you, or a gospel different from the gospel you have already accepted, you put up with that well enough. 5 I am not aware of being in any way inferior to those super-apostles. 6 I may be no speaker, but knowledge I do have; at all times we have made known to you the full truth.

7 Or was this my offence, that I made no charge for preaching the gospel of God, humbling myself in order to exalt you? 8 I robbed other churches — by accepting support from them to serve you. 9 If I ran short while I was with you, I did not become a charge on anyone; my needs were fully met by friends from Macedonia; I made it a rule, as I always shall, never to be a burden to you. 10 As surely as the truth of Christ is in me, nothing shall bar me from boasting about this throughout Achaia. 11 Why? Because I do not love you? God knows I do.

12 And I shall go on doing as I am doing now, to cut the ground from under those who would seize any chance to put their vaunted apostleship on the same level as ours. 13 Such people are sham apostles, confidence tricksters masquerading as apostles of Christ. 14 And no wonder! Satan himself masquerades as an angel of light, 15 so it is easy enough for his agents to masquerade as agents of good. But their fate will match their deeds.

16 I repeat: let no one take me for a fool; but if you must, then give me the privilege of a fool, and let me have my little boast like others. 17 In boasting so confidently I am not speaking like a Christian, but like a fool. 18 So many people brag of their earthly distinctions that I shall do so too.

11:3 lose . . . devotion: some witnesses read lose your purity and single-hearted devotion.

letters. 10 For someone will say, "His letters are severe and forceful, but his bodily presence is weak, and his speech contemptible." 11 Such a person must understand that what we are in word through letters when absent, that we also are in action when present.

12 Not that we dare to class or compare ourselves with some of those who recommend themselves. But when they measure themselves by one another and compare themselves with one another, they are without understanding. 13 But we will not boast beyond measure but will keep to the limits God has apportioned us, namely, to reach even to you. 14 For we are not overreaching ourselves, as though we did not reach you; we indeed first came to you with the gospel of Christ. 15 We are not boasting beyond measure, in other people's labors; yet our hope is that, as your faith increases, our influence among you may be greatly enlarged, within our proper limits, 16 so that we may preach the gospel even beyond you, not boasting of work already done in another's sphere. 17 "Whoever boasts, should boast in the Lord." 18 For it is not the one who recommends himself who is approved, but the one whom the Lord recommends.

11 If only you would put up with a little foolishness from me! Please put up with me. 2 For I am jealous of you with the jealousy of God, since I betrothed you to one husband to present you as a chaste virgin to Christ. 3 But I am afraid that, as the serpent deceived Eve by his cunning, your thoughts may be corrupted from a sincere [and pure] commitment to Christ. 4 For if someone comes and preaches another Jesus than the one we preached, or if you receive a different spirit from the one you received or a different gospel from the one you accepted, you put up with it well enough. 5 For I think that I am not in any way inferior to these "superapostles." 6 Even if I am untrained in speaking, I am not so in knowledge; in every way we have made this plain to you in all things.

7 Did I make a mistake when I humbled myself so that you might be exalted, because I preached the gospel of God to you without charge? 8 I plundered other churches by accepting from them in order to minister to you. 9 And when I was with you and in need, I did not burden anyone, for the brothers who came from Macedonia supplied my needs. So I refrained and will refrain from burdening you in any way. 10 By the truth of Christ in me, this boast of mine shall not be silenced in the regions of Achaia. 11 And why? Because I do not love you? God knows I do!

12 And what I do I will continue to do, in order to end this pretext of those who seek a pretext for being regarded as we are in the mission of which they boast. 13 For such people are false apostles, deceitful workers, who masquerade as apostles of Christ. 14 And no wonder, for even Satan masquerades as an angel of light. 15 So it is not strange that his ministers also masquerade as ministers of righteousness. Their end will correspond to their deeds.

16 I repeat, no one should consider me foolish; but if you do, accept me as a fool, so that I too may boast a little. 17 What I am saying I am not saying according to the Lord but as in foolishness, in this boastful state. 18 Since many boast according to the flesh, I too will boast. 19 For you

letting you think that I can put fear into you only by letter. 10 Someone said, 'His letters are weighty enough, and full of strength, but when you see him in person, he makes no impression and his powers of speaking are negligible.' 11 I should like that sort of person to take note that our deeds when we are present will show the same qualities as our letters when we were at a distance.

12 We are not venturing to rank ourselves, or even to compare ourselves with certain people who provide their own commendations. By measuring themselves by themselves and comparing themselves to themselves, they only show their folly. 13 By contrast we do not intend to boast beyond measure, but will measure ourselves by the standard which God laid down for us, namely that of having come all the way to you. 14 We are not overreaching ourselves as we would be if we had not come all the way to you; in fact we were the first to come as far as you with the good news of Christ. 15 So we are not boasting beyond measure, about other men's work; in fact, we hope, as your faith increases, to grow greater and greater by this standard of ours, 16 by preaching the gospel to regions beyond you, rather than boasting about work already done in someone else's province. 17 *Let anyone who wants to boast, boast of the Lord.o* 18 For it is not through self-commendation that recognition is won, but through commendation.

11 I wish you would put up with a little foolishness from me — not that you don't do this already. 2 The jealousy that I feel for you is, you see, God's own jealousy: I gave you all in marriage to a single husband, a virgin pure for presentation to Christ. 3 But I am afraid that, just as the snake with his cunning seduced Eve, your minds may be led astray from single-minded devotion to Christ. 4 Because any chance comer has only to preach a Jesus other than the one we preached, or you have only to receive a spirit different from the one you received, or a gospel different from the one you accepted — and you put up with that only too willingly. 5 Now, I consider that I am not in the least inferior to the super-apostles. 6 Even if there is something lacking in my public speaking, this is not the case with my knowledge, as we have openly shown to you at all times and before everyone.

7 Have I done wrong, then, humbling myself so that you might be raised up, by preaching the gospel of God to you for nothing? 8 I was robbing other churches, taking wages from them in order to work for you. 9 When I was with you and needed money, I was no burden to anybody, for the brothers from Macedonia brought me as much as I needed when they came; I have always been careful not to let myself be a burden to you in any way, and I shall continue to be so. 10 And as Christ's truth is in me, this boast of mine is not going to be silenced in the regions of Achaia. 11 Why should it be? Because I do not love you? God knows that I do. 12 I will go on acting as I do at present, to cut the ground from under the feet of those who are looking for a chance to be proved my equals in grounds for boasting. 13 These people are counterfeit apostles, dishonest workers disguising themselves as apostles of Christ. 14 There is nothing astonishing in this; even Satan disguises himself as an angel of light. 15 It is nothing extraordinary, then, when his servants disguise themselves as the servants of uprightness. They will come to the end appropriate to what they have done.

16 To repeat: let no one take me for a fool, but if you do, then treat me as a fool, so that I, too, can do a little boasting. 17 I shall not be following the Lord's way in what I say now, but will be speaking out of foolishness in the conviction that I have something to boast about. 18 So many people boast on merely human grounds that I shall too. 19 I know

also boast. 19 For you gladly put up with fools, being wise yourselves! 20 For you put up with it when someone makes slaves of you, or preys upon you, or takes advantage of you, or puts on airs, or gives you a slap in the face. 21 To my shame, I must say, we were too weak for that!

But whatever anyone dares to boast of — I am speaking as a fool — I also dare to boast of that. 22 Are they Hebrews? So am I. Are they Israelites? So am I. Are they descendants of Abraham? So am I. 23 Are they ministers of Christ? I am talking like a madman — I am a better one: with far greater labors, far more imprisonments, with countless floggings, and often near death. 24 Five times I have received from the Jews the forty lashes minus one. 25 Three times I was beaten with rods. Once I received a stoning. Three times I was shipwrecked; for a night and a day I was adrift at sea; 26 on frequent journeys, in danger from rivers, danger from bandits, danger from my own people, danger from Gentiles, danger in the city, danger in the wilderness, danger at sea, danger from false brothers and sisters;*h* 27 in toil and hardship, through many a sleepless night, hungry and thirsty, often without food, cold and naked. 28 And, besides other things, I am under daily pressure because of my anxiety for all the churches. 29 Who is weak, and I am not weak? Who is made to stumble, and I am not indignant?

30 If I must boast, I will boast of the things that show my weakness. 31 The God and Father of the Lord Jesus (blessed be he forever!) knows that I do not lie. 32 In Damascus, the governor*i* under King Aretas guarded the city of Damascus in order to*j* seize me, 33 but I was let down in a basket through a window in the wall,*k* and escaped from his hands.

12 It is necessary to boast; nothing is to be gained by it, but I will go on to visions and revelations of the Lord. 2 I know a person in Christ who fourteen years ago was caught up to the third heaven — whether in the body or out of the body I do not know; God knows. 3 And I know that such a person — whether in the body or out of the body I do not know; God knows — 4 was caught up into Paradise and heard things that are not to be told, that no mortal is permitted to repeat. 5 On behalf of such a one I will boast, but on my own behalf I will not boast, except of my weaknesses. 6 But if I wish to boast, I will not be a fool, for I will be speaking the truth. But I refrain from it, so that no one may think better of me than what is seen in me or heard from me, 7 even considering the exceptional character of the revelations. Therefore, to keep*l* me from being too elated, a thorn was given me in the flesh, a messenger of Satan to torment me, to keep me from being too elated.*m* 8 Three times I appealed to the Lord about this, that it would leave me, 9 but he said to me, "My grace is sufficient for you, for power*n* is made perfect in weakness." So, I will boast all the more gladly of my weaknesses, so that the power of Christ may dwell in me. 10 Therefore I am content with weaknesses, insults, hardships, persecutions, and calamities for the sake of Christ; for whenever I am weak, then I am strong.

11 I have been a fool! You forced me to it. Indeed you should have been the ones commending me, for I am not at all inferior to these super-apostles, even though I am nothing. 12 The signs of a true apostle were performed among

19 How gladly you put up with fools, being yourselves so wise! 20 If someone tyrannizes over you, exploits you, gets you in his clutches, puts on airs, and hits you in the face, you put up with it. 21 And you call me a weakling! I admit the reproach.

But if there is to be bravado (and I am still speaking as a fool), I can indulge in it too. 22 Are they Hebrews? So am I. Israelites? So am I. Abraham's descendants? So am I. 23 Are they servants of Christ? I am mad to speak like this, but I can outdo them: more often overworked, more often imprisoned, scourged more severely, many a time face to face with death. 24 Five times the Jews have given me the thirty-nine strokes; 25 three times I have been beaten with rods; once I was stoned; three times I have been shipwrecked, and for twenty-four hours I was adrift on the open sea. 26 I have been constantly on the road; I have met dangers from rivers, dangers from robbers, dangers from my fellow-countrymen, dangers from foreigners, dangers in the town, dangers in the wilderness, dangers at sea, dangers from false Christians. 27 I have toiled and drudged and often gone without sleep; I have been hungry and thirsty and have often gone without food; I have suffered from cold and exposure.

28 Apart from these external things, there is the responsibility that weighs on me every day, my anxious concern for all the churches. 29 Is anyone weak? I share his weakness. If anyone brings about the downfall of another, does my heart not burn with anger? 30 If boasting there must be, I will boast of the things that show up my weakness. 31 He who is blessed for ever, the God and Father of the Lord Jesus, knows that what I say is true. 32 When I was in Damascus, the commissioner of King Aretas kept the city under observation to have me arrested; 33 and I was let down in a basket, through a window in the wall, and so escaped his clutches.

12 It may do no good, but I must go on with my boasting; I come now to visions and revelations granted by the Lord. 2 I know a Christian man who fourteen years ago (whether in the body or out of the body, I do not know — God knows) was caught up as far as the third heaven. 3 And I know that this same man (whether in the body or apart from the body, I do not know — God knows) 4 was caught up into paradise, and heard words so secret that human lips may not repeat them. 5 About such a man I am ready to boast; but I will not boast on my own account, except of my weaknesses. 6 If I chose to boast, it would not be the boast of a fool, for I should be speaking the truth. But I refrain, because I do not want anyone to form an estimate of me which goes beyond the evidence of his own eyes and ears. 7 To keep me from being unduly elated by the magnificence of such revelations, I was given a thorn in my flesh, a messenger of Satan sent to buffet me; this was to save me from being unduly elated. 8 Three times I begged the Lord to rid me of it, 9 but his answer was: 'My grace is all you need; power is most fully seen in weakness.' I am therefore happy to boast of my weaknesses, because then the power of Christ will rest upon me. 10 So I am content with a life of weakness, insult, hardship, persecution, and distress, all for Christ's sake; for when I am weak, then I am strong.

11 I AM being very foolish, but it was you who drove me to it; my credentials should have come from you. In nothing did I prove inferior to those super-apostles, even if I am a nobody. 12 The signs of an apostle were there in the work I

---

h Gk brothers   *i* Gk ethnarch   *j* Other ancient authorities read *and wanted to*   *k* Gk *through the wall*   *l* Other ancient authorities read *To keep*   *m* Other ancient authorities lack *to keep me from being too elated*   *n* Other ancient authorities read *my power*

12:6–7 **ears . . . given:** *some witnesses read* ears, 7and because of the magnificence of the revelations themselves. Therefore to keep me from being unduly elated I was given.

NEW AMERICAN BIBLE

gladly put up with fools, since you are wise yourselves. 20 For you put up with it if someone enslaves you, or devours you, or gets the better of you, or puts on airs, or slaps you in the face. 21 To my shame I say that we were too weak!

But what anyone dares to boast of (I am speaking in foolishness) I also dare. 22 Are they Hebrews? So am I. Are they Israelites? So am I. Are they descendants of Abraham? So am I. 23 Are they ministers of Christ? (I am talking like an insane person.) I am still more, with far greater labors, far more imprisonments, far worse beatings, and numerous brushes with death. 24 Five times at the hands of the Jews I received forty lashes minus one. 25 Three times I was beaten with rods, once I was stoned, three times I was shipwrecked, I passed a night and a day on the deep; 26 on frequent journeys, in dangers from rivers, dangers from robbers, dangers from my own race, dangers from Gentiles, dangers in the city, dangers in the wilderness, dangers at sea, dangers among false brothers; 27 in toil and hardship, through many sleepless nights, through hunger and thirst, through frequent fastings, through cold and exposure. 28 And apart from these things, there is the daily pressure upon me of my anxiety for all the churches. 29 Who is weak, and I am not weak? Who is led to sin, and I am not indignant?

30 If I must boast, I will boast of the things that show my weakness. 31 The God and Father of the Lord Jesus knows, he who is blessed forever, that I do not lie. 32 At Damascus, the governor under King Aretas guarded the city of Damascus, in order to seize me, 33 but I was lowered in a basket through a window in the wall and escaped his hands.

12 I must boast; not that it is profitable, but I will go on to visions and revelations of the Lord. 2 I know someone in Christ who, fourteen years ago (whether in the body or out of the body I do not know, God knows), was caught up to the third heaven. 3 And I know that this person (whether in the body or out of the body I do not know, God knows) 4 was caught up into Paradise and heard ineffable things, which no one may utter. 5 About this person I will boast, but about myself I will not boast, except about my weaknesses. 6 Although if I should wish to boast, I would not be foolish, for I would be telling the truth. But I refrain, so that no one may think more of me than what he sees in me or hears from me 7 because of the abundance of the revelations. Therefore, that I might not become too elated, a thorn in the flesh was given to me, an angel of Satan, to beat me, to keep me from being too elated. 8 Three times I begged the Lord about this, that it might leave me, 9 but he said to me, "My grace is sufficient for you, for power is made perfect in weakness." I will rather boast most gladly of my weaknesses, in order that the power of Christ may dwell with me. 10 Therefore, I am content with weaknesses, insults, hardships, persecutions, and constraints, for the sake of Christ; for when I am weak, then I am strong.

11 I have been foolish. You compelled me, for I ought to have been commended by you. For I am in no way inferior to these "superapostles," even though I am nothing. 12 The

NEW JERUSALEM BIBLE

how happy you are to put up with fools, being so wise yourselves; 20 and how you will still go on putting up with a man who enslaves you, eats up all you possess, keeps you under his orders and sets himself above you, or even slaps you in the face. 21 I say it to your shame; perhaps we have been too weak.

Whatever bold claims anyone makes—now I am talking as a fool—I can make them too. 22 Are they Hebrews? So am I. Are they Israelites? So am I. Are they descendants of Abraham? So am I. 23 Are they servants of Christ? I speak in utter folly—I am too, and more than they are: I have done more work, I have been in prison more, I have been flogged more severely, many times exposed to death. 24 Five times I have been given the thirty-nine lashes by the Jews; 25 three times I have been beaten with sticks; once I was stoned; three times I have been shipwrecked, and once I have been in the open sea for a night and a day; 26 continually travelling, I have been in danger from rivers, in danger from brigands, in danger from my own people and in danger from the gentiles, in danger in the towns and in danger in the open country, in danger at sea and in danger from people masquerading as brothers; 27 I have worked with unsparing energy, for many nights without sleep; I have been hungry and thirsty, and often altogether without food or drink; I have been cold and lacked clothing. 28 And, besides all the external things, there is, day in day out, the pressure on me of my anxiety for all the churches. 29 If anyone weakens, I am weakened as well; and when anyone is made to fall, I burn in agony myself.

30 If I have to boast, I will boast of all the ways in which I am weak. 31 The God and Father of the Lord Jesus—who is for ever to be blessed—knows that I am not lying. 32 When I was in Damascus, the governor who was under King Aretas put guards round Damascus city to catch me, 33 and I was let down in a basket through a window in the wall, and that was how I escaped from his hands.

12 I am boasting because I have to. Not that it does any good, but I will move on to visions and revelations from the Lord. 2 I know a man in Christ who fourteen years ago—still in the body? I do not know; or out of the body? I do not know: God knows—was caught up right into the third heaven. 3 And I know that this man—still in the body? or outside the body? I do not know, God knows— 4 was caught up into Paradise and heard words said that cannot and may not be spoken by any human being. 5 On behalf of someone like that I am willing to boast, but I am not going to boast on my own behalf except of my weaknesses; 6 and then, if I do choose to boast I shall not be talking like a fool because I shall be speaking the truth. But I will not go on in case anybody should rate me higher than he sees and hears me to be, because of the exceptional greatness of the revelations.

7 Wherefore, so that I should not get above myself, I was given a thorn in the flesh, a messenger from Satan to batter me and prevent me from getting above myself. 8 About this, I have three times pleaded with the Lord that it might leave me; 9 but he has answered me, 'My grace is enough for you: for power is at full stretch in weakness.' It is, then, about my weaknesses that I am happiest of all to boast, so that the power of Christ may rest upon me; 10 and that is why I am glad of weaknesses, insults, constraints, persecutions and distress for Christ's sake. For it is when I am weak that I am strong.

11 I have turned into a fool, but you forced me to it. It is you that should have been commending me; those superapostles had no advantage over me, even if I am nothing at all. 12 All the marks characteristic of a true apostle have

you with utmost patience, signs and wonders and mighty works. 13 How have you been worse off than the other churches, except that I myself did not burden you? Forgive me this wrong!

14 Here I am, ready to come to you this third time. And I will not be a burden, because I do not want what is yours but you; for children ought not to lay up for their parents, but parents for their children. 15 I will most gladly spend and be spent for you. If I love you more, am I to be loved less? 16 Let it be assumed that I did not burden you. Nevertheless (you say) since I was crafty, I took you in by deceit. 17 Did I take advantage of you through any of those whom I sent to you? 18 I urged Titus to go, and sent the brother with him. Titus did not take advantage of you, did he? Did we not conduct ourselves with the same spirit? Did we not take the same steps?

19 Have you been thinking all along that we have been defending ourselves before you? We are speaking in Christ before God. Everything we do, beloved, is for the sake of building you up. 20 For I fear that when I come, I may find you not as I wish, and that you may find me not as you wish; I fear that there may perhaps be quarreling, jealousy, anger, selfishness, slander, gossip, conceit, and disorder. 21 I fear that when I come again, my God may humble me before you, and that I may have to mourn over many who previously sinned and have not repented of the impurity, sexual immorality, and licentiousness that they have practiced.

13 This is the third time I am coming to you. "Any charge must be sustained by the evidence of two or three witnesses." 2 I warned those who sinned previously and all the others, and I warn them now while absent, as I did when present on my second visit, that if I come again, I will not be lenient— 3 since you desire proof that Christ is speaking in me. He is not weak in dealing with you, but is powerful in you. 4 For he was crucified in weakness, but lives by the power of God. For we are weak in him,*o* but in dealing with you we will live with him by the power of God.

5 Examine yourselves to see whether you are living in the faith. Test yourselves. Do you not realize that Jesus Christ is in you?—unless, indeed, you fail to meet the test! 6 I hope you will find out that we have not failed. 7 But we pray to God that you may not do anything wrong—not that we may appear to have met the test, but that you may do what is right, though we may seem to have failed. 8 For we cannot do anything against the truth, but only for the truth. 9 For we rejoice when we are weak and you are strong. This is what we pray for, that you may become perfect. 10 So I write these things while I am away from you, so that when I come, I may not have to be severe in using the authority that the Lord has given me for building up and not for tearing down.

11 Finally, brothers and sisters,*p* farewell.*q* Put things in order, listen to my appeal,*r* agree with one another, live in peace; and the God of love and peace will be with you. 12 Greet one another with a holy kiss. All the saints greet you.

13 The grace of the Lord Jesus Christ, the love of God, and the communion of*s* the Holy Spirit be with all of you.

did among you, marked by unfailing endurance, by signs, portents, and miracles. 13 Is there any way in which you were treated worse than the other churches—except this, that I was never a charge on you? Forgive me for being so unfair!

14 I am now getting ready to pay you a third visit; and I am not going to be a charge on you. It is you I want, not your money; parents should make provision for their children, not children for their parents. 15 I would gladly spend everything for you—yes, and spend myself to the limit. If I love you overmuch, am I to be loved the less? 16 All very well, you say; I did not myself prove a burden to you, but I did use a confidence trick to take you in. 17 Was it one of the men I sent to you that I used to exploit you? 18 I begged Titus to visit you, and I sent our friend with him. Did Titus exploit you? Have we not both been guided by the same Spirit, and followed the same course?

19 Perhaps you have been thinking all this time that it is to you we are addressing our defence. No; we are speaking in God's sight, and as Christians. Our whole aim, dear friends, is to build you up. 20 I fear that when I come I may find you different from what I wish, and you may find me to be what you do not wish. I fear I may find quarrelling and jealousy, angry tempers and personal rivalries, backbiting and gossip, arrogance and general disorder. 21 I am afraid that when I come my God may humiliate me again in your presence, that I may have cause to grieve over many who were sinning before and have not repented of their unclean lives, their fornication and sensuality.

13 This will be my third visit to you. As scripture says, 'Every charge must be established on the evidence of two or three witnesses': 2 to those who sinned before, and to everyone else, I repeat the warning I gave last time; on my second visit I gave it in person, and now I give it while absent. It is that when I come this time, I will show no leniency. 3 Then you will have the proof you seek of the Christ who speaks through me, the Christ who, far from being weak with you, makes his power felt among you. 4 True, he died on the cross in weakness, but he lives by the power of God; so you will find that we who share his weakness shall live with him by the power of God.

5 Examine yourselves: are you living the life of faith? Put yourselves to the test. Surely you recognize that Jesus Christ is among you? If not, you have failed the test. 6 I hope you will come to see that we have not failed. 7 Our prayer to God is that you may do no wrong, not that we should win approval; we want you to do what is right, even if we should seem failures. 8 We have no power to act against the truth, but only for it. 9 We are happy to be weak at any time if only you are strong. Our prayer, then, is for your amendment. 10 In writing this letter before I come, my aim is to spare myself, when I do come, any sharp exercise of authority—authority which the Lord gave me for building up and not for pulling down.

11 And now, my friends, farewell. Mend your ways; take our appeal to heart; agree with one another; live in peace; and the God of love and peace will be with you. 12 Greet one another with the kiss of peace. 13 All God's people send you greetings.

14 The grace of the Lord Jesus Christ, and the love of God, and the fellowship of the Holy Spirit, be with you all.

NEW AMERICAN BIBLE

NEW JERUSALEM BIBLE

signs of an apostle were performed among you with all endurance, signs and wonders, and mighty deeds. 13 In what way were you less privileged than the rest of the churches, except that on my part I did not burden you? Forgive me this wrong!

14 Now I am ready to come to you this third time. And I will not be a burden, for I want not what is yours, but you. Children ought not to save for their parents, but parents for their children. 15 I will most gladly spend and be utterly spent for your sakes. If I love you more, am I to be loved less? 16 But granted that I myself did not burden you, yet I was crafty and got the better of you by deceit. 17 Did I take advantage of you through any of those I sent to you? 18 I urged Titus to go and sent the brother with him. Did Titus take advantage of you? Did we not walk in the same spirit? And in the same steps?

19 Have you been thinking all along that we are defending ourselves before you? In the sight of God we are speaking in Christ, and all for building you up, beloved. 20 For I fear that when I come I may find you not such as I wish, and that you may find me not as you wish; that there may be rivalry, jealousy, fury, selfishness, slander, gossip, conceit, and disorder. 21 I fear that when I come again my God may humiliate me before you, and I may have to mourn over many of those who sinned earlier and have not repented of the impurity, immorality, and licentiousness they practiced.

13 This third time I am coming to you. "On the testimony of two or three witnesses a fact shall be established." 2 I warned those who sinned earlier and all the others, and I warn them now while absent, as I did when present on my second visit, that if I come again I will not be lenient, 3 since you are looking for proof of Christ speaking in me. He is not weak toward you but powerful in you. 4 For indeed he was crucified out of weakness, but he lives by the power of God. So also we are weak in him, but toward you we shall live with him by the power of God. 5 Examine yourselves to see whether you are living in faith. Test yourselves. Do you not realize that Jesus Christ is in you? — unless, of course, you fail the test. 6 I hope you will discover that we have not failed. 7 But we pray to God that you may not do evil, not that we may appear to have passed the test but that you may do what is right, even though we may seem to have failed. 8 For we cannot do anything against the truth, but only for the truth. 9 For we rejoice when we are weak but you are strong. What we pray for is your improvement.

10 I am writing this while I am away, so that when I come I may not have to be severe in virtue of the authority that the Lord has given me to build up and not to tear down.

11 Finally, brothers, rejoice. Mend your ways, encourage one another, agree with one another, live in peace, and the God of love and peace will be with you. 12 Greet one another with a holy kiss. All the holy ones greet you.

13 The grace of the Lord Jesus Christ and the love of God and the fellowship of the holy Spirit be with all of you.

been at work among you: complete perseverance, signs, marvels, demonstrations of power. 13 Is there any way in which you have been given less than the rest of the churches, except that I did not make myself a burden to you? Forgive me for this unfairness!

14 Here I am, ready to come to you for the third time and I am not going to be a burden on you: it is not your possessions that I want, but yourselves. Children are not expected to save up for their parents, but parents for their children, 15 and I am more than glad to spend what I have and to be spent for the sake of your souls. Is it because I love you so much more, that I am loved the less?

16 All right, then; I did not make myself a burden to you, but, trickster that I am, I caught you by trickery. 17 Have I taken advantage of you through any of the people I have sent to you? 18 Titus came at my urging, and I sent his companion with him. Did Titus take advantage of you? Can you deny that he and I were following the guidance of the same Spirit and were on the same tracks?

19 All this time you have been thinking that we have been pleading our own cause before you; no, we have been speaking in Christ and in the presence of God — and all, dear friends, to build you up. 20 I am afraid that in one way or another, when I come, I may find you different from what I should like you to be, and you may find me what you would not like me to be; so that in one way or the other there will be rivalry, jealousy, bad temper, quarrels, slander, gossip, arrogance and disorders; 21 and when I come again, my God may humiliate me in front of you and I shall be grieved by all those who sinned in the past and have still not repented of the impurities and sexual immorality and debauchery that they have committed.

13 This will be the third time I have confronted you. *Whatever the misdemeanour, the evidence of two or three witnesses is required to sustain a charge.p* 2 I gave you notice once and now, though I am not with you, I give notice again, just as when I was with you for a second time, to those who sinned before, and to all others; and it is to this effect, that when I do come next time, I shall have no mercy. 3 Since you are asking for a proof that it is Christ who speaks in me; he is not weak with you but his power is at work among you; 4 for, though it was out of weakness that he was crucified, he is alive now with the power of God. We, too, are weak in him, but with regard to you we shall live with him by the power of God.

5 Put yourselves to the test to make sure you are in the faith. Examine yourselves. Do you not recognise yourselves as people in whom Jesus Christ is present? — unless, that is, you fail the test. 6 But we, as I hope you will come to recognise, do not fail the test. 7 It is our prayer to God that you may do nothing wrong — not so that we have the credit of passing a test, but because you will be doing what is right, even if we do not pass the test. 8 We have no power to resist the truth; only to further the truth; 9 and we are delighted to be weak if only you are strong. What we ask in our prayers is that you should be made perfect. 10 That is why I am writing this while still far away, so that when I am with you I shall not have to be harsh, with the authority that the Lord has given me, an authority that is for building up and not for breaking down.

11 To end then, brothers, we wish you joy; try to grow perfect; encourage one another; have a common mind and live in peace, and the God of love and peace will be with you.

12 Greet one another with the holy kiss. All God's holy people send you their greetings.

13 The grace of the Lord Jesus Christ, the love of God and the fellowship of the Holy Spirit be with you all.

p 13 Dt 19:15.

THE LETTER OF PAUL TO THE
Galatians

1 Paul an apostle — sent neither by human commission nor from human authorities, but through Jesus Christ and God the Father, who raised him from the dead — 2 and all the members of God's family*a* who are with me,

To the churches of Galatia:

3 Grace to you and peace from God our Father and the Lord Jesus Christ, 4 who gave himself for our sins to set us free from the present evil age, according to the will of our God and Father, 5 to whom be the glory forever and ever. Amen.

6 I am astonished that you are so quickly deserting the one who called you in the grace of Christ and are turning to a different gospel — 7 not that there is another gospel, but there are some who are confusing you and want to pervert the gospel of Christ. 8 But even if we or an angel*b* from heaven should proclaim to you a gospel contrary to what we proclaimed to you, let that one be accursed! 9 As we have said before, so now I repeat, if anyone proclaims to you a gospel contrary to what you received, let that one be accursed!

10 Am I now seeking human approval, or God's approval? Or am I trying to please people? If I were still pleasing people, I would not be a servant*c* of Christ.

11 For I want you to know, brothers and sisters,*d* that the gospel that was proclaimed by me is not of human origin; 12 for I did not receive it from a human source, nor was I taught it, but I received it through a revelation of Jesus Christ.

13 You have heard, no doubt, of my earlier life in Judaism. I was violently persecuting the church of God and was trying to destroy it. 14 I advanced in Judaism beyond many among my people of the same age, for I was far more zealous for the traditions of my ancestors. 15 But when God, who had set me apart before I was born and called me through his grace, was pleased 16 to reveal his Son to me,*e* so that I might proclaim him among the Gentiles, I did not confer with any human being, 17 nor did I go up to Jerusalem to those who were already apostles before me, but I went away at once into Arabia, and afterwards I returned to Damascus.

18 Then after three years I did go up to Jerusalem to visit Cephas and stayed with him fifteen days; 19 but I did not see any other apostle except James the Lord's brother. 20 In what I am writing to you, before God, I do not lie! 21 Then I went into the regions of Syria and Cilicia, 22 and I was still unknown by sight to the churches of Judea that are in Christ; 23 they only heard it said, "The one who formerly was persecuting us is now proclaiming the faith he once tried to destroy." 24 And they glorified God because of me.

2 Then after fourteen years I went up again to Jerusalem with Barnabas, taking Titus along with me. 2 I went up in response to a revelation. Then I laid before them (though only in a private meeting with the acknowledged leaders) the gospel that I proclaim among the Gentiles, in order to make sure that I was not running, or had not run, in vain.

THE LETTER OF PAUL TO THE
Galatians

1 FROM Paul, an apostle commissioned not by any human authority or human act, but by Jesus Christ and God the Father who raised him from the dead. 2 I and all the friends now with me send greetings to the churches of Galatia.

3 Grace to you and peace from God the Father and our Lord Jesus Christ, 4 who gave himself for our sins, to rescue us out of the present wicked age as our God and Father willed; 5 to him be glory for ever and ever! Amen.

6 I AM astonished to find you turning away so quickly from him who called you by grace, and following a different gospel. 7 Not that it is in fact another gospel; only there are some who unsettle your minds by trying to distort the gospel of Christ. 8 But should anyone, even I myself or an angel from heaven, preach a gospel other than the gospel I preached to you, let him be banned! 9 I warned you in the past and now I warn you again: if anyone preaches a gospel other than the gospel you received, let him be banned!

10 Now do I sound as if I were asking for human approval and not for God's alone? Am I currying favour with men? If I were still seeking human favour, I should be no servant of Christ.

11 I must make it clear to you, my friends, that the gospel you heard me preach is not of human origin. 12 I did not take it over from anyone; no one taught it me; I received it through a revelation of Jesus Christ.

13 You have heard what my manner of life was when I was still a practising Jew: how savagely I persecuted the church of God and tried to destroy it; 14 and how in the practice of our national religion I outstripped most of my Jewish contemporaries by my boundless devotion to the traditions of my ancestors. 15 But then in his good pleasure God, who from my birth had set me apart, and who had called me through his grace, chose 16 to reveal his Son in and through me, in order that I might proclaim him among the Gentiles. Immediately, without consulting a single person, 17 without going up to Jerusalem to see those who were apostles before me, I went off to Arabia, and afterwards returned to Damascus.

18 Three years later I did go up to Jerusalem to get to know Cephas, and I stayed two weeks with him. 19 I saw none of the other apostles, except James, the Lord's brother. 20 What I write is plain truth; God knows I am not lying!

21 Then I left for the regions of Syria and Cilicia. 22 I was still unknown by sight to the Christian congregations in Judaea; 23 they had simply heard it said, 'Our former persecutor is preaching the good news of the faith which once he tried to destroy,' 24 and they praised God for what had happened to me.

2 Fourteen years later, I went up again to Jerusalem with Barnabas, and we took Titus with us. 2 I went in response to a revelation from God; I explained, at a private interview with those of repute, the gospel which I preach to the Gentiles, to make sure that the race I had run and was running should not be in vain. 3 Not even my companion

---

1:3 **God . . . Christ:** *some witnesses read* God our Father and the Lord Jesus Christ.   1:6 **from him . . . grace:** *some witnesses read* from Christ who called you by grace, *or* from him who called you by the grace of Christ.

---

a Gk all the brothers   *b* Or a messenger   *c* Gk slave
d Gk brothers   *e* Gk in me

The Letter
to the Galatians

1 Paul, an apostle not from human beings nor through a human being but through Jesus Christ and God the Father who raised him from the dead, 2 and all the brothers who are with me, to the churches of Galatia: 3 grace to you and peace from God our Father and the Lord Jesus Christ, 4 who gave himself for our sins that he might rescue us from the present evil age in accord with the will of our God and Father, 5 to whom be glory forever and ever. Amen.

6 I am amazed that you are so quickly forsaking the one who called you by [the] grace [of Christ] for a different gospel 7 (not that there is another). But there are some who are disturbing you and wish to pervert the gospel of Christ. 8 But even if we or an angel from heaven should preach [to you] a gospel other than the one that we preached to you, let that one be accursed! 9 As we have said before, and now I say again, if anyone preaches to you a gospel other than the one that you received, let that one be accursed!

10 Am I now currying favor with human beings or God? Or am I seeking to please people? If I were still trying to please people, I would not be a slave of Christ.

11 Now I want you to know, brothers, that the gospel preached by me is not of human origin. 12 For I did not receive it from a human being, nor was I taught it, but it came through a revelation of Jesus Christ.

13 For you heard of my former way of life in Judaism, how I persecuted the church of God beyond measure and tried to destroy it, 14 and progressed in Judaism beyond many of my contemporaries among my race, since I was even more a zealot for my ancestral traditions. 15 But when [God], who from my mother's womb had set me apart and called me through his grace, was pleased 16 to reveal his Son to me, so that I might proclaim him to the Gentiles, I did not immediately consult flesh and blood, 17 nor did I go up to Jerusalem to those who were apostles before me; rather, I went into Arabia and then returned to Damascus.

18 Then after three years I went up to Jerusalem to confer with Kephas and remained with him for fifteen days. 19 But I did not see any other of the apostles, only James the brother of the Lord. 20 (As to what I am writing to you, behold, before God, I am not lying.) 21 Then I went into the regions of Syria and Cilicia. 22 And I was unknown personally to the churches of Judea that are in Christ; 23 they only kept hearing that "the one who once was persecuting us is now preaching the faith he once tried to destroy." 24 So they glorified God because of me.

2 Then after fourteen years I again went up to Jerusalem with Barnabas, taking Titus along also. 2 I went up in accord with a revelation, and I presented to them the gospel that I preach to the Gentiles — but privately to those of repute — so that I might not be running, or have run, in vain. 3 Moreover, not even Titus, who was with me, al-

Galatians

THE LETTER OF PAUL
TO THE CHURCH IN GALATIA

1 From Paul, an apostle appointed not by human beings nor through any human being but by Jesus Christ and God the Father who raised him from the dead, 2 and all the brothers who are with me, to the churches of Galatia. 3 Grace and peace from God the Father and our Lord Jesus Christ 4 who gave himself for our sins to liberate us from this present wicked world, in accordance with the will of our God and Father, 5 to whom be glory for ever and ever. Amen. a

6 I am astonished that you are so promptly turning away from the one who called you in the grace of Christ and are going over to a different gospel — 7 not that it is another gospel; except that there are trouble-makers among you who are seeking to pervert the gospel of Christ. 8 But even if we ourselves or an angel from heaven preaches to you a gospel other than the one we preached to you, let God's curse be on him. 9 I repeat again what we declared before: anyone who preaches to you a gospel other than the one you were first given is to be under God's curse. 10 Whom am I trying to convince now, human beings or God? Am I trying to please human beings? If I were still doing that I should not be a servant of Christ.

11 Now I want to make it quite clear to you, brothers, about the gospel that was preached by me, that it was no human message. 12 It was not from any human being that I received it, and I was not taught it, but it came to me through a revelation of Jesus Christ. 13 You have surely heard how I lived in the past, within Judaism, and how there was simply no limit to the way I persecuted the Church of God in my attempts to destroy it; 14 and how, in Judaism, I outstripped most of my Jewish contemporaries in my limitless enthusiasm for the traditions of my ancestors. 15 But when God, who had set me apart from the time when I was *in my mother's womb, called* b me through his grace and chose 16 to reveal his Son in me, so that I should preach him to the gentiles, I was in no hurry to confer with any human being, 17 or to go up to Jerusalem to see those who were already apostles before me. Instead, I went off to Arabia, and later I came back to Damascus. 18 Only after three years did I go up to Jerusalem to meet Cephas. I stayed fifteen days with him 19 but did not set eyes on any of the rest of the apostles, only James, the Lord's brother. 20 I swear before God that what I have written is the truth. 21 After that I went to places in Syria and Cilicia, 22 and was still unknown by sight to the churches of Judaea which are in Christ, 23 they simply kept hearing it said, 'The man once so eager to persecute us is now preaching the faith that he used to try to destroy,' 24 and they gave glory to God for me.

2 It was not until fourteen years had gone by that I travelled up to Jerusalem again, with Barnabas, and I took Titus with me too. 2 My journey was inspired by a revelation and there, in a private session with the recognised leaders, I expounded the whole gospel that I preach to the gentiles, to make quite sure that the efforts I was making and had already made should not be fruitless. 3 Even then,

---

a 1 Unusually, this address contains no thanks or praise.   *b* 1 Jr 1:5.

3 But even Titus, who was with me, was not compelled to be circumcised, though he was a Greek. 4 But because of false believers f secretly brought in, who slipped in to spy on the freedom we have in Christ Jesus, so that they might enslave us— 5 we did not submit to them even for a moment, so that the truth of the gospel might always remain with you. 6 And from those who were supposed to be acknowledged leaders (what they actually were makes no difference to me; God shows no partiality)—those leaders contributed nothing to me. 7 On the contrary, when they saw that I had been entrusted with the gospel for the uncircumcised, just as Peter had been entrusted with the gospel for the circumcised 8 (for he who worked through Peter making him an apostle to the circumcised also worked through me in sending me to the Gentiles), 9 and when James and Cephas and John, who were acknowledged pillars, recognized the grace that had been given to me, they gave to Barnabas and me the right hand of fellowship, agreeing that we should go to the Gentiles and they to the circumcised. 10 They asked only one thing, that we remember the poor, which was actually what I was g eager to do.

11 But when Cephas came to Antioch, I opposed him to his face, because he stood self-condemned; 12 for until certain people came from James, he used to eat with the Gentiles. But after they came, he drew back and kept himself separate for fear of the circumcision faction. 13 And the other Jews joined him in this hypocrisy, so that even Barnabas was led astray by their hypocrisy. 14 But when I saw that they were not acting consistently with the truth of the gospel, I said to Cephas before them all, "If you, though a Jew, live like a Gentile and not like a Jew, how can you compel the Gentiles to live like Jews?" h

15 We ourselves are Jews by birth and not Gentile sinners; 16 yet we know that a person is justified i not by the works of the law but through faith in Jesus Christ. j And we have come to believe in Christ Jesus, so that we might be justified by faith in Christ, k and not by doing the works of the law, because no one will be justified by the works of the law. 17 But if, in our effort to be justified in Christ, we ourselves have been found to be sinners, is Christ then a servant of sin? Certainly not! 18 But if I build up again the very things that I once tore down, then I demonstrate that I am a transgressor. 19 For through the law I died to the law, so that I might live to God. I have been crucified with Christ; 20 and it is no longer I who live, but it is Christ who lives in me. And the life I now live in the flesh I live by faith in the Son of God, l who loved me and gave himself for me. 21 I do not nullify the grace of God; for if justification m comes through the law, then Christ died for nothing.

3 You foolish Galatians! Who has bewitched you? It was before your eyes that Jesus Christ was publicly exhibited as crucified! 2 The only thing I want to learn from you is this: Did you receive the Spirit by doing the works of the law or by believing what you heard? 3 Are you so foolish? Having started with the Spirit, are you now ending with the flesh? 4 Did you experience so much for nothing?—if it really was for nothing. 5 Well then, does God n supply you with the Spirit and work miracles among you by your doing the works of the law, or by your believing what you heard?

Titus, Greek though he is, was compelled to be circumcised. 4 That course was urged only as a concession to certain sham Christians, intruders who had sneaked in to spy on the liberty we enjoy in the fellowship of Christ Jesus. These men wanted to bring us into bondage, 5 but not for one moment did I yield to their dictation; I was determined that the full truth of the gospel should be maintained for you.

6 As for those reputed to be something (not that their importance matters to me: God does not recognize these personal distinctions)—these men of repute, I say, imparted nothing further to me. 7 On the contrary, they saw that I had been entrusted to take the gospel to the Gentiles as surely as Peter had been entrusted to take it to the Jews; 8 for the same God who was at work in Peter's mission to the Jews was also at work in mine to the Gentiles.

9 Recognizing, then, the privilege bestowed on me, those who are reputed to be pillars of the community, James, Cephas, and John, accepted Barnabas and myself as partners and shook hands on it: the agreement was that we should go to the Gentiles, while they went to the Jews. 10 All they asked was that we should keep in mind the poor, the very thing I have always made it my business to do.

11 But when Cephas came to Antioch, I opposed him to his face, because he was clearly in the wrong. 12 For until some messengers came from James, he was taking his meals with gentile Christians; but after they came he drew back and began to hold aloof, because he was afraid of the Jews. 13 The other Jewish Christians showed the same lack of principle; even Barnabas was carried away and played false like the rest. 14 But when I saw that their conduct did not square with the truth of the gospel, I said to Cephas in front of the whole congregation, 'If you, a Jew born and bred, live like a Gentile, and not like a Jew, how can you insist that Gentiles must live like Jews?'

15 We ourselves are Jews by birth, not gentile sinners; 16 yet we know that no one is ever justified by doing what the law requires, but only through faith in Christ Jesus. So we too have put our faith in Jesus Christ, in order that we might be justified through this faith, and not through actions dictated by law; for no human being can be justified by keeping the law.

17 If then, in seeking to be justified in Christ, we ourselves no less than the Gentiles turn out to be sinners, does that mean that Christ is a promoter of sin? Of course not! 18 On the contrary, it is only if I start building up again all I have pulled down that I prove to be one who breaks the law. 19 For through the law I died to law—to live for God. 20 I have been crucified with Christ: the life I now live is not my life, but the life which Christ lives in me; and my present mortal life is lived by faith in the Son of God, who loved me and gave himself up for me. 21 I will not nullify the grace of God; if righteousness comes by law, then Christ died for nothing.

3 You stupid Galatians! You must have been bewitched—you before whose eyes Jesus Christ was openly displayed on the cross! 2 Answer me one question: did you receive the Spirit by keeping the law or by believing the gospel message? 3 Can you really be so stupid? You started with the spiritual; do you now look to the material to make you perfect? 4 Is all you have experienced to come to nothing—surely not! 5 When God gives you the Spirit and works miracles among you, is it because you keep the law, or is it because you have faith in the gospel message?

---

f Gk false brothers   g Or had been   h Some interpreters hold that the quotation extends into the following paragraph   i Or reckoned as righteous; and so elsewhere   j Or the faith of Jesus Christ   k Or the faith of Christ   l Or by the faith of the Son of God   m Or righteousness   n Gk he

2:4–5 bondage . . . for you: or, following some witnesses, bondage; 5 I yielded to their demand for the moment, to ensure that gospel truth should not be prevented from reaching you.   2:12 the Jews: or the advocates of circumcision.

NEW AMERICAN BIBLE

NEW JERUSALEM BIBLE

though he was a Greek, was compelled to be circumcised, 4 but because of the false brothers secretly brought in, who slipped in to spy on our freedom that we have in Christ Jesus, that they might enslave us— 5 to them we did not submit even for a moment, so that the truth of the gospel might remain intact for you. 6 But from those who were reputed to be important (what they once were makes no difference to me; God shows no partiality)— those of repute made me add nothing. 7 On the contrary, when they saw that I had been entrusted with the gospel to the uncircumcised, just as Peter to the circumcised, 8 for the one who worked in Peter for an apostolate to the circumcised worked also in me for the Gentiles, 9 and when they recognized the grace bestowed upon me, James and Kephas and John, who were reputed to be pillars, gave me and Barnabas their right hands in partnership, that we should go to the Gentiles and they to the circumcised. 10 Only, we were to be mindful of the poor, which is the very thing I was eager to do.

11 And when Kephas came to Antioch, I opposed him to his face because he clearly was wrong. 12 For, until some people came from James, he used to eat with the Gentiles; but when they came, he began to draw back and separated himself, because he was afraid of the circumcised. 13 And the rest of the Jews [also] acted hypocritically along with him, with the result that even Barnabas was carried away by their hypocrisy. 14 But when I saw that they were not on the right road in line with the truth of the gospel, I said to Kephas in front of all, "If you, though a Jew, are living like a Gentile and not like a Jew, how can you compel the Gentiles to live like Jews?"

15 We, who are Jews by nature and not sinners from among the Gentiles, 16 [yet] who know that a person is not justified by works of the law but through faith in Jesus Christ, even we have believed in Christ Jesus that we may be justified by faith in Christ and not by works of the law, because by works of the law no one will be justified. 17 But if, in seeking to be justified in Christ, we ourselves are found to be sinners, is Christ then a minister of sin? Of course not! 18 But if I am building up again those things that I tore down, then I show myself to be a transgressor. 19 For through the law I died to the law, that I might live for God. I have been crucified with Christ; 20 yet I live, no longer I, but Christ lives in me; insofar as I now live in the flesh, I live by faith in the Son of God who has loved me and given himself up for me. 21 I do not nullify the grace of God; for if justification comes through the law, then Christ died for nothing.

3 O stupid Galatians! Who has bewitched you, before whose eyes Jesus Christ was publicly portrayed as crucified? 2 I want to learn only this from you: did you receive the Spirit from works of the law, or from faith in what you heard? 3 Are you so stupid? After beginning with the Spirit, are you now ending with the flesh? 4 Did you experience so many things in vain?— if indeed it was in vain. 5 Does, then, the one who supplies the Spirit to you and works mighty deeds among you do so from works of the law or

and although Titus, a Greek, was with me, there was no demand that he should be circumcised; 4 but because of some false brothers who had secretly insinuated themselves to spy on the freedom that we have in Christ Jesus, intending to reduce us to slavery— 5 people we did not defer to for one moment, or the truth of the gospel preached to you might have been compromised. . . 6 but those who were recognised as important people— whether they actually were important or not: *There is no favouritism with God*[c] — those recognised leaders, I am saying, had nothing to add to my message. 7 On the contrary, once they saw that the gospel for the uncircumcised had been entrusted to me, just as to Peter the gospel for the circumcised 8 (for he who empowered Peter's apostolate to the circumcision also empowered mine to the gentiles), 9 and when they acknowledged the grace that had been given to me, then James and Cephas and John, who were the ones recognised as pillars, offered their right hands to Barnabas and to me as a sign of partnership: we were to go to the gentiles and they to the circumcised. 10 They asked nothing more than that we should remember to help the poor, as indeed I was anxious to do in any case.

11 However, when Cephas came to Antioch,[d] then I did oppose him to his face since he was manifestly in the wrong. 12 Before certain people from James came, he used to eat with gentiles; but as soon as these came, he backed out and kept apart from them, out of fear of the circumcised. 13 And the rest of the Jews put on the same act as he did, so that even Barnabas was carried away by their insincerity.

14 When I saw, though, that their behaviour was not true to the gospel, I said to Cephas in front of all of them, 'Since you, though you are a Jew, live like the gentiles and not like the Jews, how can you compel the gentiles to live like the Jews?'

15 We who were born Jews and not gentile sinners 16 have nevertheless learnt that someone is reckoned as upright not by practising the Law but by faith in Jesus Christ; and we too came to believe in Christ Jesus so as to be reckoned as upright by faith in Christ and not by practising the Law: since no human being *can be found upright*[e] by keeping the Law. 17 Now if we too are found to be sinners on the grounds that we seek our justification in Christ, it would surely follow that Christ was at the service of sin. Out of the question! 18 If I now rebuild everything I once demolished, I prove that I was wrong before. 19 In fact, through the Law I am dead to the Law so that I can be alive to God. I have been crucified with Christ 20 and yet I am alive; yet it is no longer I, but Christ living in me. The life that I am now living, subject to the limitation of human nature, I am living in faith, faith in the Son of God who loved me and gave himself for me. 21 I am not setting aside God's grace as of no value; it is merely that if saving justice comes through the Law, Christ died needlessly.

3 You stupid people in Galatia! After you have had a clear picture of Jesus Christ crucified, right in front of your eyes, who has put a spell on you? 2 There is only one thing I should like you to tell me: How was it that you received the Spirit— was it by the practice of the Law, or by believing in the message you heard? 3 Having begun in the Spirit, can you be so stupid as to end in the flesh? 4 Can all the favours you have received have had no effect at all— if there really has been no effect? 5 Would you say, then, that he who so lavishly sends the Spirit to you, and causes the miracles among you, is doing this through your practice of the Law or because you believed the message you heard?

c 2 Dt 10:17.   *d* 2 cf. Ac 15:19–29.   *e* 2 Ps 143:2.

NEW REVISED STANDARD VERSION

6 Just as Abraham "believed God, and it was reckoned to him as righteousness," 7 so, you see, those who believe are the descendants of Abraham. 8 And the scripture, foreseeing that God would justify the Gentiles by faith, declared the gospel beforehand to Abraham, saying, "All the Gentiles shall be blessed in you." 9 For this reason, those who believe are blessed with Abraham who believed.

10 For all who rely on the works of the law are under a curse; for it is written, "Cursed is everyone who does not observe and obey all the things written in the book of the law." 11 Now it is evident that no one is justified before God by the law; for "The one who is righteous will live by faith."*o* 12 But the law does not rest on faith; on the contrary, "Whoever does the works of the law*p* will live by them." 13 Christ redeemed us from the curse of the law by becoming a curse for us—for it is written, "Cursed is everyone who hangs on a tree"— 14 in order that in Christ Jesus the blessing of Abraham might come to the Gentiles, so that we might receive the promise of the Spirit through faith.

15 Brothers and sisters,*q* I give an example from daily life: once a person's will*r* has been ratified, no one adds to it or annuls it. 16 Now the promises were made to Abraham and to his offspring;*s* it does not say, "And to offsprings,"*t* as of many; but it says, "And to your offspring,"*s* that is, to one person, who is Christ. 17 My point is this: the law, which came four hundred thirty years later, does not annul a covenant previously ratified by God, so as to nullify the promise. 18 For if the inheritance comes from the law, it no longer comes from the promise; but God granted it to Abraham through the promise.

19 Why then the law? It was added because of transgressions, until the offspring*s* would come to whom the promise had been made; and it was ordained through angels by a mediator. 20 Now a mediator involves more than one party; but God is one.

21 Is the law then opposed to the promises of God? Certainly not! For if a law had been given that could make alive, then righteousness would indeed come through the law. 22 But the scripture has imprisoned all things under the power of sin, so that what was promised through faith in Jesus Christ*u* might be given to those who believe.

23 Now before faith came, we were imprisoned and guarded under the law until faith would be revealed. 24 Therefore the law was our disciplinarian until Christ came, so that we might be justified by faith. 25 But now that faith has come, we are no longer subject to a disciplinarian, 26 for in Christ Jesus you are all children of God through faith. 27 As many of you as were baptized into Christ have clothed yourselves with Christ. 28 There is no longer Jew or Greek, there is no longer slave or free, there is no longer male and female; for all of you are one in Christ Jesus. 29 And if you belong to Christ, then you are Abraham's offspring,*s* heirs according to the promise.

4 My point is this: heirs, as long as they are minors, are no better than slaves, though they are the owners of all the property; 2 but they remain under guardians and trustees until the date set by the father. 3 So with us; while we were minors, we were enslaved to the elemental spirits*v* of the world. 4 But when the fullness of time had come, God sent

REVISED ENGLISH BIBLE

6 Look at Abraham: he put his faith in God, and that faith was counted to him as righteousness. 7 You may take it, then, that it is those who have faith who are Abraham's sons. 8 And scripture, foreseeing that God would justify the Gentiles through faith, declared the gospel to Abraham beforehand: 'In you all nations shall find blessing.' 9 Thus it is those with faith who share the blessing with faithful Abraham.

10 On the other hand, those who rely on obedience to the law are under a curse; for scripture says, 'Cursed is everyone who does not persevere in doing everything that is written in the book of the law.' 11 It is evident that no one is ever justified before God by means of the law, because we read, 'He shall gain life who is justified through faith.' 12 Now the law does not operate on the basis of faith, for we read, 'He who does this shall gain life by what he does.' 13 Christ bought us freedom from the curse of the law by coming under the curse for our sake; for scripture says, 'Cursed is everyone who is hanged on a gibbet.' 14 The purpose of this was that the blessing of Abraham should in Jesus Christ be extended to the Gentiles, so that we might receive the promised Spirit through faith.

15 My friends, let me give you an illustration. When a man's will and testament has been duly executed, no one else can set it aside or add a codicil. 16 Now, the promises were pronounced to Abraham and to his 'issue'. It does not say 'issues' in the plural, but 'your issue' in the singular; and by 'issue' is meant Christ. 17 My point is this: a testament, or covenant, had already been validated by God; a law made four hundred and thirty years later cannot invalidate it and so render its promises ineffective. 18 If the inheritance is by legal right, then it is not by promise; but it was by promise that God bestowed it as a free gift on Abraham.

19 Then what of the law? It was added to make wrongdoing a legal offence; it was an interim measure pending the arrival of the 'issue' to whom the promise was made. It was promulgated through angels, and there was an intermediary; 20 but an intermediary is not needed for one party acting alone, and God is one.

21 Does the law, then, contradict the promises? Of course not! If a law had been given which had power to bestow life, then righteousness would indeed have come from keeping the law. 22 But scripture has declared the whole world to be prisoners in subjection to sin, so that faith in Jesus Christ should be the ground on which the promised blessing is given to those who believe.

23 Before this faith came, we were close prisoners in the custody of law, pending the revelation of faith. 24 The law was thus put in charge of us until Christ should come, when we should be justified through faith; 25 and now that faith has come, its charge is at an end.

26 It is through faith that you are all sons of God in union with Christ Jesus. 27 Baptized into union with him, you have all put on Christ like a garment. 28 There is no such thing as Jew and Greek, slave and freeman, male and female; for you are all one person in Christ Jesus. 29 So if you belong to Christ, you are the 'issue' of Abraham and heirs by virtue of the promise.

4 This is what I mean: so long as the heir is a minor, he is no better off than a slave, even though the whole estate is his; 2 he is subject to guardians and trustees until the date set by his father. 3 So it was with us: during our minority we were slaves, subject to the elemental spirits of the universe, 4 but when the appointed time came, God sent his

---

o Or *The one who is righteous through faith will live*   *p* Gk *does them*   *q* Gk *Brothers*   *r* Or *covenant* (as in verse 17)   *s* Gk *seed*
t Gk *seeds*   *u* Or *through the faith of Jesus Christ*   *v* Or *the rudiments*

3:19 **added ... offence:** *or* added to restrain offences.   4:3 **to ... universe:** *or* to elementary notions belonging to this world.

NEW AMERICAN BIBLE

NEW JERUSALEM BIBLE

from faith in what you heard? 6 Thus Abraham "believed God, and it was credited to him as righteousness." 7 Realize then that it is those who have faith who are children of Abraham. 8 Scripture, which saw in advance that God would justify the Gentiles by faith, foretold the good news to Abraham, saying, "Through you shall all the nations be blessed." 9 Consequently, those who have faith are blessed along with Abraham who had faith. 10 For all who depend on works of the law are under a curse; for it is written, "Cursed be everyone who does not persevere in doing all the things written in the book of the law." 11 And that no one is justified before God by the law is clear, for "the one who is righteous by faith will live." 12 But the law does not depend on faith; rather, "the one who does these things will live by them." 13 Christ ransomed us from the curse of the law by becoming a curse for us, for it is written, "Cursed be everyone who hangs on a tree," 14 that the blessing of Abraham might be extended to the Gentiles through Christ Jesus, so that we might receive the promise of the Spirit through faith.

15 Brothers, in human terms I say that no one can annul or amend even a human will once ratified. 16 Now the promises were made to Abraham and to his descendant. It does not say, "And to descendants," as referring to many, but as referring to one, "And to your descendant," who is Christ. 17 This is what I mean: the law, which came four hundred and thirty years afterward, does not annul a covenant previously ratified by God, so as to cancel the promise. 18 For if the inheritance comes from the law, it is no longer from a promise; but God bestowed it on Abraham through a promise.

19 Why, then, the law? It was added for transgressions, until the descendant came to whom the promise had been made; it was promulgated by angels at the hand of a mediator. 20 Now there is no mediator when only one party is involved, and God is one. 21 Is the law then opposed to the promises [of God]? Of course not! For if a law had been given that could bring life, then righteousness would in reality come from the law. 22 But scripture confined all things under the power of sin, that through faith in Jesus Christ the promise might be given to those who believe.

23 Before faith came, we were held in custody under law, confined for the faith that was to be revealed. 24 Consequently, the law was our disciplinarian for Christ, that we might be justified by faith. 25 But now that faith has come, we are no longer under a disciplinarian. 26 For through faith you are all children of God in Christ Jesus. 27 For all of you who were baptized into Christ have clothed yourselves with Christ. 28 There is neither Jew nor Greek, there is neither slave nor free person, there is not male and female; for you are all one in Christ Jesus. 29 And if you belong to Christ, then you are Abraham's descendant, heirs according to the promise.

4 I mean that as long as the heir is not of age, he is no different from a slave, although he is the owner of everything, 2 but he is under the supervision of guardians and administrators until the date set by his father. 3 In the same way we also, when we were not of age, were enslaved to the elemental powers of the world. 4 But when the fullness of time had come, God sent his Son, born of a woman,

6 Abraham, you remember, *put his faith in God,* f and this was reckoned to him as uprightness. 7 Be sure, then, that it is people of faith who are the children of Abraham. 8 And it was because scripture foresaw that God would give saving justice to the gentiles through faith, that it announced the future gospel to Abraham in the words: *All nations will be blessed in you.* g 9 So it is people of faith who receive the same blessing as Abraham, the man of faith.

10 On the other hand, all those who depend on the works of the Law are under a curse, since scripture says: *Accursed be he who does not make what is written in the book of the Law effective, by putting it into practice.* h 11 Now it is obvious that nobody is reckoned as upright in God's sight by the Law, since *the upright will live through faith;* 12 and the Law is based not on faith but on the principle, *whoever complies with it will find life in it.* 13 Christ redeemed us from the curse of the Law by being cursed for our sake since scripture says: *Anyone hanged is accursed,* 14 so that the blessing of Abraham might come to the gentiles in Christ Jesus, and so that we might receive the promised Spirit through faith.

15 To put it in human terms, my brothers: even when a will is only a human one, once it has been ratified nobody can cancel it or add more provisions to it. 16 Now the promises were addressed to Abraham *and to his progeny.* The words were not *and to his progenies* in the plural, but in the singular; *and to your progeny,* which means Christ. 17 What I am saying is this: once a will had been long ago ratified by God, the Law, coming four hundred and thirty years later, could not abolish it and so nullify its promise. 18 You see, if the inheritance comes by the Law, it no longer comes through a promise; but it was by a promise that God made his gift to Abraham.

19 Then what is the purpose of the Law? It was added to deal with crimes until the '*progeny*' to whom the promise had been made should come; and it was promulgated through angels, i by the agency of an intermediary. 20 Now there can be an intermediary only between two parties, yet God is one. 21 Is the Law contrary, then, to God's promises? Out of the question! If the Law that was given had been capable of giving life, then certainly saving justice would have come from the Law. 22 As it is, scripture makes no exception when it says that sin is master everywhere; so the promise can be given only by faith in Jesus Christ to those who have this faith.

23 But before faith came, we were kept under guard by the Law, locked up to wait for the faith which would eventually be revealed to us. 24 So the Law was serving as a slave to look after us, to lead us to Christ, so that we could be justified by faith. 25 But now that faith has come we are no longer under a slave looking after us; 26 for all of you are the children of God, through faith, in Christ Jesus, 27 since every one of you that has been baptised has been clothed in Christ. 28 There can be neither Jew nor Greek, there can be neither slave nor freeman, there can be neither male nor female — for you are all one in Christ Jesus. 29 And simply by being Christ's, you are that *progeny* of Abraham, the heirs named in the promise.

4 What I am saying is this: an heir, during the time while he is still under age, is no different from a slave, even though he is the owner of all the property; 2 he is under the control of guardians and administrators until the time fixed by his father. 3 So too with us, as long as we were still under age, were enslaved to the elemental principles of this world; 4 but when the completion of the time came, God sent his Son, born of a woman, born a subject of the Law,

f 3 Gn 15:6. g 3 Gn 12:3. h 3 Dt 27:26; Hab 2:4; Lv 18:5; Dt 21:23. i 3 A rabbinic tradition. The intermediary is Moses.

his Son, born of a woman, born under the law, 5 in order to redeem those who were under the law, so that we might receive adoption as children. 6 And because you are children, God has sent the Spirit of his Son into our*w* hearts, crying, "Abba!*x* Father!" 7 So you are no longer a slave but a child, and if a child then also an heir, through God.*y*

8 Formerly, when you did not know God, you were enslaved to beings that by nature are not gods. 9 Now, however, that you have come to know God, or rather to be known by God, how can you turn back again to the weak and beggarly elemental spirits?*z* How can you want to be enslaved to them again? 10 You are observing special days, and months, and seasons, and years. 11 I am afraid that my work for you may have been wasted.

12 Friends,*a* I beg you, become as I am, for I also have become as you are. You have done me no wrong. 13 You know that it was because of a physical infirmity that I first announced the gospel to you; 14 though my condition put you to the test, you did not scorn or despise me, but welcomed me as an angel of God, as Christ Jesus. 15 What has become of the goodwill you felt? For I testify that, had it been possible, you would have torn out your eyes and given them to me. 16 Have I now become your enemy by telling you the truth? 17 They make much of you, but for no good purpose; they want to exclude you, so that you may make much of them. 18 It is good to be made much of for a good purpose at all times, and not only when I am present with you. 19 My little children, for whom I am again in the pain of childbirth until Christ is formed in you, 20 I wish I were present with you now and could change my tone, for I am perplexed about you.

21 Tell me, you who desire to be subject to the law, will you not listen to the law? 22 For it is written that Abraham had two sons, one by a slave woman and the other by a free woman. 23 One, the child of the slave, was born according to the flesh; the other, the child of the free woman, was born through the promise. 24 Now this is an allegory: these women are two covenants. One woman, in fact, is Hagar, from Mount Sinai, bearing children for slavery. 25 Now Hagar is Mount Sinai in Arabia*b* and corresponds to the present Jerusalem, for she is in slavery with her children. 26 But the other woman corresponds to the Jerusalem above; she is free, and she is our mother. 27 For it is written,

"Rejoice, you childless one, you who bear no children;
burst into song and shout, you who endure no birth pangs;
for the children of the desolate woman are more numerous
than the children of the one who is married."

28 Now you,*c* my friends,*d* are children of the promise, like Isaac. 29 But just as at that time the child who was born according to the flesh persecuted the child who was born according to the Spirit, so it is now also. 30 But what does the scripture say? "Drive out the slave and her child; for the child of the slave will not share the inheritance with the child of the free woman." 31 So then, friends,*d* we are children, not of the slave but of the free woman.

5 1 For freedom Christ has set us free. Stand firm, therefore, and do not submit again to a yoke of slavery.

2 Listen! I, Paul, am telling you that if you let yourselves be circumcised, Christ will be of no benefit to you. 3 Once again I testify to every man who lets himself be circumcised that he is obliged to obey the entire law. 4 You

Son, born of a woman, born under the law, 5 to buy freedom for those who were under the law, in order that we might attain the status of sons.

6 To prove that you are sons, God has sent into our hearts the Spirit of his Son, crying 'Abba, Father!' 7 You are therefore no longer a slave but a son, and if a son, an heir by God's own act.

8 Formerly, when you did not know God, you were slaves to gods who are not gods at all. 9 But now that you do acknowledge God—or rather, now that he has acknowledged you—how can you turn back to those feeble and bankrupt elemental spirits? Why do you propose to enter their service all over again? 10 You keep special days and months and seasons and years. 11 I am afraid that all my hard work on you may have been wasted.

12 Put yourselves in my place, my friends, I beg you, as I put myself in yours. You never did me any wrong: 13 it was bodily illness, as you will remember, that originally led to my bringing you the gospel, 14 and you resisted any temptation to show scorn or disgust at my physical condition; on the contrary you welcomed me as if I were an angel of God, as you might have welcomed Christ Jesus himself. 15 What has become of the happiness you felt then? I believe you would have torn out your eyes and given them to me, had that been possible! 16 Have I now made myself your enemy by being frank with you?

17 Others are lavishing attention on you, but without sincerity: what they really want is to isolate you so that you may lavish attention on them. 18 To be the object of sincere attentions is always good, and not just when I am with you. 19 You are my own children, and I am in labour with you all over again until you come to have the form of Christ. 20 How I wish I could be with you now, for then I could modify my tone; as it is, I am at my wits' end about you.

21 Tell me now, you that are so anxious to be under law, will you not listen to what the law says? 22 It is written there that Abraham had two sons, the one by a slave, the other by a free-born woman. 23 The slave's son was born in the ordinary course of nature, but the free woman's through God's promise. 24 This is an allegory: the two women stand for two covenants. The one covenant comes from Mount Sinai; that is Hagar, and her children are born into slavery. 25 Sinai is a mountain in Arabia and represents the Jerusalem of today, for she and her children are in slavery. 26 But the heavenly Jerusalem is the free woman; she is our mother. 27 For scripture says, 'Rejoice, O barren woman who never bore a child; break into a shout of joy, you who have never been in labour; for the deserted wife will have more children than she who lives with her husband.'

28 Now you, my friends, like Isaac, are children of God's promise, 29 but just as in those days the natural-born son persecuted the spiritual son, so it is today. 30 Yet what does scripture say? 'Drive out the slave and her son, for the son of the slave shall not share the inheritance with the son of the free woman.' 31 You see, then, my friends, we are no slave's children; our mother is the free woman.

5 1 It is for freedom that Christ set us free. Stand firm, therefore, and refuse to submit again to the yoke of slavery.

2 Mark my words: I, Paul, say to you that if you get yourself circumcised Christ will benefit you no more. 3 I impress on you once again that every man who accepts circumcision is under obligation to keep the entire law.

w Other ancient authorities read *your*   *x* Aramaic for *Father*
y Other ancient authorities read *an heir of God through Christ*
z Or *beggarly rudiments*   *a* Gk *Brothers*   *b* Other ancient
authorities read *For Sinai is a mountain in Arabia*   *c* Other ancient
authorities read *we*   *d* Gk *brothers*

4:9 **bankrupt . . . spirits:** *or* threadbare elementary notions.

born under the law, 5 to ransom those under the law, so that we might receive adoption. 6 As proof that you are children, God sent the spirit of his Son into our hearts, crying out, "Abba, Father!" 7 So you are no longer a slave but a child, and if a child then also an heir, through God.

8 At a time when you did not know God, you became slaves to things that by nature are not gods; 9 but now that you have come to know God, or rather to be known by God, how can you turn back again to the weak and destitute elemental powers? Do you want to be slaves to them all over again? 10 You are observing days, months, seasons, and years. 11 I am afraid on your account that perhaps I have labored for you in vain.

12 I implore you, brothers, be as I am, because I have also become as you are. You did me no wrong; 13 you know that it was because of a physical illness that I originally preached the gospel to you, 14 and you did not show disdain or contempt because of the trial caused you by my physical condition, but rather you received me as an angel of God, as Christ Jesus. 15 Where now is that blessedness of yours? Indeed, I can testify to you that, if it had been possible, you would have torn out your eyes and given them to me. 16 So now have I become your enemy by telling you the truth? 17 They show interest in you, but not in a good way; they want to isolate you, so that you may show interest in them. 18 Now it is good to be shown interest for good reason at all times, and not only when I am with you. 19 My children, for whom I am again in labor until Christ be formed in you! 20 I would like to be with you now and to change my tone, for I am perplexed because of you.

21 Tell me, you who want to be under the law, do you not listen to the law? 22 For it is written that Abraham had two sons, one by the slave woman and the other by the freeborn woman. 23 The son of the slave woman was born naturally, the son of the freeborn through a promise. 24 Now this is an allegory. These women represent two covenants. One was from Mount Sinai, bearing children for slavery; this is Hagar. 25 Hagar represents Sinai, a mountain in Arabia; it corresponds to the present Jerusalem, for she is in slavery along with her children. 26 But the Jerusalem above is freeborn, and she is our mother. 27 For it is written:

"Rejoice, you barren one who bore no children;
    break forth and shout, you who were not
      in labor;
for more numerous are the children of the
      deserted one
    than of her who has a husband."

28 Now you, brothers, like Isaac, are children of the promise. 29 But just as then the child of the flesh persecuted the child of the spirit, it is the same now. 30 But what does the scripture say?

"Drive out the slave woman and her son!
For the son of the slave woman shall not share
    the inheritance with the son"

of the freeborn. 31 Therefore, brothers, we are children not of the slave woman but of the freeborn woman.

5 For freedom Christ set us free; so stand firm and do not submit again to the yoke of slavery.

2 It is I, Paul, who am telling you that if you have yourselves circumcised, Christ will be of no benefit to you. 3 Once again I declare to every man who has himself circumcised that he is bound to observe the entire law. 4 You

5 to redeem the subjects of the Law, so that we could receive adoption as sons. 6 As you are sons, God has sent into our hearts the Spirit of his Son crying, 'Abba, Father'; *j* 7 and so you are no longer a slave, but a son; and if a son, then an heir, by God's own act.

8 But formerly when you did not know God, you were kept in slavery to things which are not really gods at all, 9 whereas now that you have come to recognise God — or rather, be recognised by God — how can you now turn back again to those powerless and bankrupt elements whose slaves you now want to be all over again? 10 You are keeping special days, and months, and seasons and years — 11 I am beginning to be afraid that I may, after all, have wasted my efforts on you.

12 I urge you, brothers, — be like me, as I have become like you. You have never been unfair to me; 13 indeed you remember that it was an illness that first gave me the opportunity to preach the gospel to you, 14 but though my illness was a trial to you, you did not show any distaste or revulsion; instead, you welcomed me as a messenger of God, as if I were Christ Jesus himself. 15 What has happened to the utter contentment you had then? For I can testify to you that you would have plucked your eyes out, were that possible, and given them to me. 16 Then have I turned into your enemy simply by being truthful with you? 17 Their devotion to you has no praiseworthy motive; they simply want to cut you off from me, so that you may centre your devotion on them. 18 Devotion to a praiseworthy cause is praiseworthy at any time, not only when I am there with you. 19 My children, I am going through the pain of giving birth to you all over again, until Christ is formed in you; 20 and how I wish I could be there with you at this moment and find the right way of talking to you: I am quite at a loss with you.

21 Tell me then, you are so eager to be subject to the Law, have you listened to what the Law says? 22 Scripture says that Abraham had two sons, one by the slave girl and one by the freewoman. 23 The son of the slave girl came to be born in the way of human nature; but the son of the freewoman came to be born through a promise. 24 There is an allegory here: these women stand for the two covenants. The one given on Mount Sinai — that is Hagar, whose children are born into slavery; 25 now Sinai is a mountain in Arabia and represents Jerusalem in its present state, for she is in slavery together with her children. 26 But the Jerusalem above is free, and that is the one that is our mother; 27 as scripture says: *Shout for joy, you barren woman who has borne no children! Break into shouts of joy, you who were never in labour. For the sons of the forsaken one are more in number than the sons of the wedded wife.k* 28 Now you, brothers, are like Isaac, children of the promise; 29 just as at that time, the child born in the way of human nature persecuted the child born through the Spirit, so now. 30 But what is it that scripture says? *Drive away that slave girl and her son; the slave girl's son is not to share the inheritance with the son*l *of the freewoman.* 31 So, brothers, we are the children not of the slave girl but of the freewoman.

5 Christ set us free, so that we should remain free. Stand firm, then, and do not let yourselves be fastened again to the yoke of slavery.

2 I, Paul, give you my word that if you accept circumcision, Christ will be of no benefit to you at all. 3 I give my assurance once again to every man who accepts circumcision that he is under obligation to keep the whole Law;

j 4 cf. Rom 8:15.   *k* 4 Is 54:1.   *l* 4 Gn 21:10.

3071

who want to be justified by the law have cut yourselves off from Christ; you have fallen away from grace. 5 For through the Spirit, by faith, we eagerly wait for the hope of righteousness. 6 For in Christ Jesus neither circumcision nor uncircumcision counts for anything; the only thing that counts is faith working*e* through love.

7 You were running well; who prevented you from obeying the truth? 8 Such persuasion does not come from the one who calls you. 9 A little yeast leavens the whole batch of dough. 10 I am confident about you in the Lord that you will not think otherwise. But whoever it is that is confusing you will pay the penalty. 11 But my friends, *f* why am I still being persecuted if I am still preaching circumcision? In that case the offense of the cross has been removed. 12 I wish those who unsettle you would castrate themselves!

13 For you were called to freedom, brothers and sisters;*f* only do not use your freedom as an opportunity for self-indulgence,*g* but through love become slaves to one another. 14 For the whole law is summed up in a single commandment, "You shall love your neighbor as yourself." 15 If, however, you bite and devour one another, take care that you are not consumed by one another.

16 Live by the Spirit, I say, and do not gratify the desires of the flesh. 17 For what the flesh desires is opposed to the Spirit, and what the Spirit desires is opposed to the flesh; for these are opposed to each other, to prevent you from doing what you want. 18 But if you are led by the Spirit, you are not subject to the law. 19 Now the works of the flesh are obvious: fornication, impurity, licentiousness, 20 idolatry, sorcery, enmities, strife, jealousy, anger, quarrels, dissensions, factions, 21 envy, *h* drunkenness, carousing, and things like these. I am warning you, as I warned you before: those who do such things will not inherit the kingdom of God.

22 By contrast, the fruit of the Spirit is love, joy, peace, patience, kindness, generosity, faithfulness, 23 gentleness, and self-control. There is no law against such things. 24 And those who belong to Christ Jesus have crucified the flesh with its passions and desires. 25 If we live by the Spirit, let us also be guided by the Spirit. 26 Let us not become conceited, competing against one another, envying one another.

6 My friends,*i* if anyone is detected in a transgression, you who have received the Spirit should restore such a one in a spirit of gentleness. Take care that you yourselves are not tempted. 2 Bear one another's burdens, and in this way you will fulfill *j* the law of Christ. 3 For if those who are nothing think they are something, they deceive themselves. 4 All must test their own work; then that work, rather than their neighbor's work, will become a cause for pride. 5 For all must carry their own loads.

6 Those who are taught the word must share in all good things with their teacher.

7 Do not be deceived; God is not mocked, for you reap whatever you sow. 8 If you sow to your own flesh, you will reap corruption from the flesh; but if you sow to the Spirit, you will reap eternal life from the Spirit. 9 So let us not grow weary in doing what is right, for we will reap at harvest time, if we do not give up. 10 So then, whenever we have

4 When you seek to be justified by way of law, you are cut off from Christ: you have put yourselves outside God's grace. 5 For it is by the Spirit and through faith that we hope to attain that righteousness which we eagerly await. 6 If we are in union with Christ Jesus, circumcision makes no difference at all, nor does the lack of it; the only thing that counts is faith expressing itself through love.

7 You were running well; who was it hindered you from following the truth? 8 Whatever persuasion was used, it did not come from God who called you. 9 'A little leaven', remember, 'leavens all the dough.' 10 The Lord gives me confidence that you will not adopt the wrong view; but whoever it is who is unsettling your minds must bear God's judgement. 11 As for me, my friends, if I am still advocating circumcision, then why am I still being persecuted? To do that would be to strip the cross of all offence. 12 Those agitators had better go the whole way and make eunuchs of themselves!

13 You, my friends, were called to be free; only beware of turning your freedom into licence for your unspiritual nature. Instead, serve one another in love; 14 for the whole law is summed up in a single commandment: 'Love your neighbour as yourself.' 15 But if you go on fighting one another, tooth and nail, all you can expect is mutual destruction.

16 What I mean is this: be guided by the Spirit and you will not gratify the desires of your unspiritual nature. 17 That nature sets its desires against the Spirit, while the Spirit fights against it. They are in conflict with one another so that you cannot do what you want. 18 But if you are led by the Spirit, you are not subject to law. 19 Anyone can see the behaviour that belongs to the unspiritual nature: fornication, indecency, and debauchery; 20 idolatry and sorcery; quarrels, a contentious temper, envy, fits of rage, selfish ambitions, dissensions, party intrigues, 21 and jealousies; drinking bouts, orgies, and the like. I warn you, as I warned you before, that no one who behaves like that will ever inherit the kingdom of God.

22 But the harvest of the Spirit is love, joy, peace, patience, kindness, goodness, fidelity, 23 gentleness, and self-control. Against such things there is no law. 24 Those who belong to Christ Jesus have crucified the old nature with its passions and desires. 25 If the Spirit is the source of our life, let the Spirit also direct its course.

26 We must not be conceited, inciting one another to rivalry, jealous of one another. 1 If anyone is caught 6 doing something wrong, you, my friends, who live by the Spirit must gently set him right. Look to yourself, each one of you: you also may be tempted. 2 Carry one another's burdens, and in this way you will fulfil the law of Christ.

3 If anyone imagines himself to be somebody when he is nothing, he is deluding himself. 4 Each of you should examine his own conduct, and then he can measure his achievement by comparing himself with himself and not with anyone else; 5 for everyone has his own burden to bear.

6 When anyone is under instruction in the faith, he should give his teacher a share of whatever good things he has.

7 Make no mistake about this: God is not to be fooled; everyone reaps what he sows. 8 If he sows in the field of his unspiritual nature, he will reap from it a harvest of corruption; but if he sows in the field of the Spirit, he will reap from it a harvest of eternal life. 9 Let us never tire of doing good, for if we do not slacken our efforts we shall in due time reap our harvest. 10 Therefore, as opportunity offers,

---

e Or *made effective*   *f* Gk *brothers*   *g* Gk *the flesh*   *h* Other ancient authorities add *murder*   *i* Gk *Brothers*   *j* Other ancient authorities read *in this way fulfill*

NEW AMERICAN BIBLE

NEW JERUSALEM BIBLE

are separated from Christ, you who are trying to be justified by law; you have fallen from grace. 5 For through the Spirit, by faith, we await the hope of righteousness. 6 For in Christ Jesus, neither circumcision nor uncircumcision counts for anything, but only faith working through love.

7 You were running well; who hindered you from following [the] truth? 8 That enticement does not come from the one who called you. 9 A little yeast leavens the whole batch of dough. 10 I am confident of you in the Lord that you will not take a different view, and that the one who is troubling you will bear the condemnation, whoever he may be. 11 As for me, brothers, if I am still preaching circumcision, why am I still being persecuted? In that case, the stumbling block of the cross has been abolished. 12 Would that those who are upsetting you might also castrate themselves!

13 For you were called for freedom, brothers. But do not use this freedom as an opportunity for the flesh; rather, serve one another through love. 14 For the whole law is fulfilled in one statement, namely, "You shall love your neighbor as yourself." 15 But if you go on biting and devouring one another, beware that you are not consumed by one another.

16 I say, then: live by the Spirit and you will certainly not gratify the desire of the flesh. 17 For the flesh has desires against the Spirit, and the Spirit against the flesh; these are opposed to each other, so that you may not do what you want. 18 But if you are guided by the Spirit, you are not under the law. 19 Now the works of the flesh are obvious: immorality, impurity, licentiousness, 20 idolatry, sorcery, hatreds, rivalry, jealousy, outbursts of fury, acts of selfishness, dissensions, factions, 21 occasions of envy, drinking bouts, orgies, and the like. I warn you, as I warned you before, that those who do such things will not inherit the kingdom of God. 22 In contrast, the fruit of the Spirit is love, joy, peace, patience, kindness, generosity, faithfulness, 23 gentleness, self-control. Against such there is no law. 24 Now those who belong to Christ [Jesus] have crucified their flesh with its passions and desires. 25 If we live in the Spirit, let us also follow the Spirit. 26 Let us not be conceited, provoking one another, envious of one another.

6 Brothers, even if a person is caught in some transgression, you who are spiritual should correct that one in a gentle spirit, looking to yourself, so that you also may not be tempted. 2 Bear one another's burdens, and so you will fulfill the law of Christ. 3 For if anyone thinks he is something when he is nothing, he is deluding himself. 4 Each one must examine his own work, and then he will have reason to boast with regard to himself alone, and not with regard to someone else; 5 for each will bear his own load.

6 One who is being instructed in the word should share all good things with his instructor. 7 Make no mistake: God is not mocked, for a person will reap only what he sows, 8 because the one who sows for his flesh will reap corruption from the flesh, but the one who sows for the spirit will reap eternal life from the spirit. 9 Let us not grow tired of doing good, for in due time we shall reap our harvest, if we do not give up. 10 So then, while we have the opportunity, let us do

4 once you seek to be reckoned as upright through the Law, then you have separated yourself from Christ, you have fallen away from grace. 5 We are led by the Spirit to wait in the confident hope of saving justice through faith, 6 since in Christ Jesus it is not being circumcised or being uncircumcised that can effect anything — only faith working through love.

7 You began your race well; who came to obstruct you and stop you obeying the truth? 8 It was certainly not any prompting from him who called you! 9 A pinch of yeast ferments the whole batch. 10 But I feel sure that, united in the Lord, you will not be led astray, and that anyone who makes trouble with you will be condemned, no matter who he is. 11 And I, brothers — if I were still preaching circumcision, why should I still be persecuted? For then the obstacle which is the cross would have no point any more. 12 I could wish that those who are unsettling you would go further and mutilate themselves.*m*

13 After all, brothers, you were called to be free; do not use your freedom as an opening for self-indulgence, but be servants to one another in love, 14 since the whole of the Law is summarised in the one commandment: *You must love your neighbour as yourself.*n 15 If you go snapping at one another and tearing one another to pieces, take care: you will be eaten up by one another.

16 Instead, I tell you, be guided by the Spirit, and you will no longer yield to self-indulgence. 17 The desires of self-indulgence are always in opposition to the Spirit, and the desires of the Spirit are in opposition to self-indulgence: they are opposites, one against the other; that is how you are prevented from doing the things that you want to. 18 But when you are led by the Spirit, you are not under the Law. 19 When self-indulgence is at work the results are obvious: sexual vice, impurity, and sensuality, 20 the worship of false gods and sorcery; antagonisms and rivalry, jealousy, bad temper and quarrels, disagreements, 21 factions and malice, drunkenness, orgies and all such things. And about these, I tell you now as I have told you in the past, that people who behave in these ways will not inherit the kingdom of God. 22 On the other hand the fruit of the Spirit is love, joy, peace, patience, kindness, goodness, trustfulness, 23 gentleness and self-control; no law can touch such things as these. 24 All who belong to Christ Jesus have crucified self with all its passions and desires.

25 Since we are living by the Spirit, let our behaviour be guided by the Spirit 26 and let us not be conceited or provocative and envious of one another.

6 Brothers, even if one of you is caught doing something wrong, those of you who are spiritual should set that person right in a spirit of gentleness; and watch yourselves that you are not put to the test in the same way. 2 Carry each other's burdens; that is how to keep the law of Christ. 3 Someone who thinks himself important, when he is not, only deceives himself; 4 but everyone is to examine his own achievements, and then he will confine his boasting to his own achievements, not comparing them with anybody else's. 5 Each one has his own load to carry.

6 When someone is under instruction in doctrine, he should give his teacher a share in all his possessions. 7 Don't delude yourself: God is not to be fooled; whatever someone sows, that is what he will reap. 8 If his sowing is in the field of self-indulgence, then his harvest from it will be corruption; if his sowing is in the Spirit, then his harvest from the Spirit will be eternal life. 9 And let us never slacken in doing good; for if we do not give up, we shall have our harvest in due time. 10 So then, as long as we have the opportunity let

m 5 Perhaps a reference to the castration practised by the priests of Cybele. *n* 5 Lv 19:18.

an opportunity, let us work for the good of all, and especially for those of the family of faith.

11 See what large letters I make when I am writing in my own hand! 12 It is those who want to make a good showing in the flesh that try to compel you to be circumcised — only that they may not be persecuted for the cross of Christ. 13 Even the circumcised do not themselves obey the law, but they want you to be circumcised so that they may boast about your flesh. 14 May I never boast of anything except the cross of our Lord Jesus Christ, by which[k] the world has been crucified to me, and I to the world. 15 For[l] neither circumcision nor uncircumcision is anything; but a new creation is everything! 16 As for those who will follow this rule — peace be upon them, and mercy, and upon the Israel of God.

17 From now on, let no one make trouble for me; for I carry the marks of Jesus branded on my body.

18 May the grace of our Lord Jesus Christ be with your spirit, brothers and sisters.[m] Amen.

[k] Or *through whom*   [l] Other ancient authorities add *in Christ Jesus*
[m] Gk *brothers*

let us work for the good of all, especially members of the household of the faith.

11 LOOK how big the letters are, now that I am writing to you in my own hand. 12 It is those who want to be outwardly in good standing who are trying to force circumcision on you; their sole object is to escape persecution for the cross of Christ. 13 Even those who do accept circumcision are not thoroughgoing observers of the law; they want you to be circumcised just in order to boast of your submission to that outward rite. 14 God forbid that I should boast of anything but the cross of our Lord Jesus Christ, through which the world is crucified to me and I to the world! 15 Circumcision is nothing; uncircumcision is nothing; the only thing that counts is new creation! 16 All who take this principle for their guide, peace and mercy be upon them, the Israel of God!

17 In future let no one make trouble for me, for I bear the marks of Jesus branded on my body.

18 The grace of our Lord Jesus Christ be with you, my friends. Amen.

6:14 **which:** *or* whom.   6:16 **the . . . God:** *or* and upon the whole Israel of God.

good to all, but especially to those who belong to the family of the faith.

11 See with what large letters I am writing to you in my own hand! 12 It is those who want to make a good appearance in the flesh who are trying to compel you to have yourselves circumcised, only that they may not be persecuted for the cross of Christ. 13 Not even those having themselves circumcised observe the law themselves; they only want you to be circumcised so that they may boast of your flesh. 14 But may I never boast except in the cross of our Lord Jesus Christ, through which the world has been crucified to me, and I to the world. 15 For neither does circumcision mean anything, nor does uncircumcision, but only a new creation. 16 Peace and mercy be to all who follow this rule and to the Israel of God.

17 From now on, let no one make troubles for me; for I bear the marks of Jesus on my body.

18 The grace of our Lord Jesus Christ be with your spirit, brothers. Amen.

all our actions be for the good of everybody, and especially of those who belong to the household of the faith.

11 Notice what large letters I have used in writing to you with my own hand. 12 It is those who want to cut a figure by human standards who force circumcision on you, simply so that they will not be persecuted for the cross of Christ. 13 Even though they are circumcised they still do not keep the Law themselves; they want you to be circumcised only so that they can boast of your outward appearance. 14 But as for me, it is out of the question that I should boast at all, except of the cross of our Lord Jesus Christ, through whom the world has been crucified to me, and I to the world. 15 It is not being circumcised or uncircumcised that matters; but what matters is a new creation. 16 Peace and mercy to all who follow this as their rule and to the Israel of God.

17 After this, let no one trouble me; I carry branded on my body the marks of Jesus.

18 The grace of our Lord Jesus Christ be with your spirit, my brothers. Amen.

THE LETTER OF PAUL TO THE
Ephesians

1 Paul, an apostle of Christ Jesus by the will of God, To the saints who are in Ephesus and are faithful*a* in Christ Jesus:

2 Grace to you and peace from God our Father and the Lord Jesus Christ.

3 Blessed be the God and Father of our Lord Jesus Christ, who has blessed us in Christ with every spiritual blessing in the heavenly places, 4 just as he chose us in Christ*b* before the foundation of the world to be holy and blameless before him in love. 5 He destined us for adoption as his children through Jesus Christ, according to the good pleasure of his will, 6 to the praise of his glorious grace that he freely bestowed on us in the Beloved. 7 In him we have redemption through his blood, the forgiveness of our trespasses, according to the riches of his grace 8 that he lavished on us. With all wisdom and insight 9 he has made known to us the mystery of his will, according to his good pleasure that he set forth in Christ, 10 as a plan for the fullness of time, to gather up all things in him, things in heaven and things on earth. 11 In Christ we have also obtained an inheritance,*c* having been destined according to the purpose of him who accomplishes all things according to his counsel and will, 12 so that we, who were the first to set our hope on Christ, might live for the praise of his glory. 13 In him you also, when you had heard the word of truth, the gospel of your salvation, and had believed in him, were marked with the seal of the promised Holy Spirit; 14 this*d* is the pledge of our inheritance toward redemption as God's own people, to the praise of his glory.

15 I have heard of your faith in the Lord Jesus and your love*e* toward all the saints, and for this reason 16 I do not cease to give thanks for you as I remember you in my prayers. 17 I pray that the God of our Lord Jesus Christ, the Father of glory, may give you a spirit of wisdom and revelation as you come to know him, 18 so that, with the eyes of your heart enlightened, you may know what is the hope to which he has called you, what are the riches of his glorious inheritance among the saints, 19 and what is the immeasur-

THE LETTER OF PAUL TO THE
Ephesians

1 FROM Paul, by the will of God apostle of Christ Jesus, to God's people at Ephesus, to the faithful, incorporate in Christ Jesus.

2 Grace to you and peace from God our Father and the Lord Jesus Christ.

3 BLESSED be the God and Father of our Lord Jesus Christ, who has conferred on us in Christ every spiritual blessing in the heavenly realms. 4 Before the foundation of the world he chose us in Christ to be his people, to be without blemish in his sight, to be full of love; 5 and he predestined us to be adopted as his children through Jesus Christ. This was his will and pleasure 6 in order that the glory of his gracious gift, so graciously conferred on us in his Beloved, might redound to his praise. 7 In Christ our release is secured and our sins forgiven through the shedding of his blood. In the richness of his grace 8 God has lavished on us all wisdom and insight. 9 He has made known to us his secret purpose, in accordance with the plan which he determined beforehand in Christ, 10 to be put into effect when the time was ripe: namely, that the universe, everything in heaven and on earth, might be brought into a unity in Christ.

11 In Christ indeed we have been given our share in the heritage, as was decreed in his design whose purpose is everywhere at work; for it was his will 12 that we, who were the first to set our hope on Christ, should cause his glory to be praised. 13 And in Christ you also — once you had heard the message of the truth, the good news of your salvation, and had believed it — in him you were stamped with the seal of the promised Holy Spirit; 14 and that Spirit is a pledge of the inheritance which will be ours when God has redeemed what is his own, to his glory and praise.

15 Because of all this, now that I have heard of your faith in the Lord Jesus and the love you bear towards all God's people, 16 I never cease to give thanks for you when I mention you in my prayers. 17 I pray that the God of our Lord Jesus Christ, the all-glorious Father, may confer on you the spiritual gifts of wisdom and vision, with the knowledge of him that they bring. 18 I pray that your inward eyes may be enlightened, so that you may know what is the hope to which he calls you, how rich and glorious is the share he offers you among his people in their inheritance, 19 and how

---

a Other ancient authorities lack *in Ephesus*, reading *saints who are also faithful*   *b* Gk *in him*   *c* Or *been made a heritage*   *d* Other ancient authorities read *who*   *e* Other ancient authorities lack *and your love*

1:1 **at Ephesus**: *some witnesses omit.*   1:4–5 **sight . . . he**: *or* sight. In his love 5he.   1:12 **who . . . Christ**: *or* who already looked forward in hope to Christ.

The Letter
to the Ephesians

1 Paul, an apostle of Christ Jesus by the will of God, to the holy ones who are [in Ephesus] faithful in Christ Jesus: ² grace to you and peace from God our Father and the Lord Jesus Christ.

³ Blessed be the God and Father of our Lord Jesus Christ, who has blessed us in Christ with every spiritual blessing in the heavens, ⁴ as he chose us in him, before the foundation of the world, to be holy and without blemish before him. In love ⁵ he destined us for adoption to himself through Jesus Christ, in accord with the favor of his will, ⁶ for the praise of the glory of his grace that he granted us in the beloved. ⁷ In him we have redemption by his blood, the forgiveness of transgressions, in accord with the riches of his grace ⁸ that he lavished upon us. In all wisdom and insight, ⁹ he has made known to us the mystery of his will in accord with his favor that he set forth in him ¹⁰ as a plan for the fullness of times, to sum up all things in Christ, in heaven and on earth.

¹¹ In him we were also chosen, destined in accord with the purpose of the One who accomplishes all things according to the intention of his will, ¹² so that we might exist for the praise of his glory, we who first hoped in Christ. ¹³ In him you also, who have heard the word of truth, the gospel of your salvation, and have believed in him, were sealed with the promised holy Spirit, ¹⁴ which is the first installment of our inheritance toward redemption as God's possession, to the praise of his glory.

¹⁵ Therefore, I, too, hearing of your faith in the Lord Jesus and of your love for all the holy ones, ¹⁶ do not cease giving thanks for you, remembering you in my prayers, ¹⁷ that the God of our Lord Jesus Christ, the Father of glory, may give you a spirit of wisdom and revelation resulting in knowledge of him. ¹⁸ May the eyes of [your] hearts be enlightened, that you may know what is the hope that belongs to his call, what are the riches of glory in his inheritance among the holy ones, ¹⁹ and what is the surpassing greatness

Ephesians

THE LETTER OF PAUL
TO THE CHURCH AT EPHESUS

1 Paul, by the will of God an apostle of Christ Jesus, to God's holy people,*a* faithful in Christ Jesus. ² Grace and peace to you from God our Father and from the Lord Jesus Christ.

³ Blessed be God the Father of our Lord Jesus Christ,

who has blessed us with all the spiritual blessings
of heaven in Christ.

⁴ Thus he chose us in Christ before the world was made

to be holy and faultless before him in love,

⁵ marking us out for himself beforehand, to be adopted sons, through Jesus Christ.

Such was his purpose and good pleasure,

⁶ to the praise of the glory of his grace,

his free gift to us in the Beloved,

⁷ in whom, through his blood, we gain our freedom, the forgiveness of our sins.

Such is the richness of the grace

⁸ which he has showered on us
in all wisdom and insight.

⁹ He has let us know the mystery of his purpose,

according to his good pleasure which he determined beforehand in Christ,

¹⁰ for him to act upon when the times had run their course:

that he would bring everything together under Christ, as head,

everything in the heavens and everything on earth.

¹¹ And it is in him that we have received our heritage,

marked out beforehand as we were,

under the plan of the One who guides all things as he decides by his own will,

¹² chosen to be,

for the praise of his glory,

the people who would put their hopes in Christ before he came.

¹³ Now you too, in him,

have heard the message of the truth and the gospel of your salvation,

and having put your trust in it

you have been stamped with the seal of the Holy Spirit of the Promise,

¹⁴ who is the pledge of our inheritance,

for the freedom of the people whom God has taken for his own,

for the praise of his glory.

¹⁵ That is why I, having once heard about your faith in the Lord Jesus, and your love for all God's holy people, ¹⁶ have never failed to thank God for you and to remember you in my prayers. ¹⁷ May the God of our Lord Jesus Christ, the Father of glory, give you a spirit of wisdom and perception of what is revealed, to bring you to full knowledge of him. ¹⁸ May he enlighten the eyes of your mind so that you can see what hope his call holds for you, how rich is the glory of the heritage he offers among his holy people, ¹⁹ and how

---

1, 1: *[In Ephesus]:* the phrase is lacking in important early witnesses such as P46 (3rd cent.), and Sinaiticus and Vaticanus (4th cent.), appearing in the latter two as a fifth-century addition. Basil and Origen mention its absence from manuscripts.

a 1 Some authorities add 'who are at Ephesus' or 'who are . . . ', leaving a gap for a place-name to be filled in.

able greatness of his power for us who believe, according to the working of his great power. 20 God *f* put this power to work in Christ when he raised him from the dead and seated him at his right hand in the heavenly places, 21 far above all rule and authority and power and dominion, and above every name that is named, not only in this age but also in the age to come. 22 And he has put all things under his feet and has made him the head over all things for the church, 23 which is his body, the fullness of him who fills all in all.

2 You were dead through the trespasses and sins 2 in which you once lived, following the course of this world, following the ruler of the power of the air, the spirit that is now at work among those who are disobedient. 3 All of us once lived among them in the passions of our flesh, following the desires of flesh and senses, and we were by nature children of wrath, like everyone else. 4 But God, who is rich in mercy, out of the great love with which he loved us 5 even when we were dead through our trespasses, made us alive together with Christ *g* — by grace you have been saved — 6 and raised us up with him and seated us with him in the heavenly places in Christ Jesus, 7 so that in the ages to come he might show the immeasurable riches of his grace in kindness toward us in Christ Jesus. 8 For by grace you have been saved through faith, and this is not your own doing; it is the gift of God — 9 not the result of works, so that no one may boast. 10 For we are what he has made us, created in Christ Jesus for good works, which God prepared beforehand to be our way of life.

11 So then, remember that at one time you Gentiles by birth, *h* called "the uncircumcision" by those who are called "the circumcision" — a physical circumcision made in the flesh by human hands — 12 remember that you were at that time without Christ, being aliens from the commonwealth of Israel, and strangers to the covenants of promise, having no hope and without God in the world. 13 But now in Christ Jesus you who once were far off have been brought near by the blood of Christ. 14 For he is our peace; in his flesh he has made both groups into one and has broken down the dividing wall, that is, the hostility between us. 15 He has abolished the law with its commandments and ordinances, that he might create in himself one new humanity in place of the two, thus making peace, 16 and might reconcile both groups to God in one body *i* through the cross, thus putting to death that hostility through it. *j* 17 So he came and proclaimed peace to you who were far off and peace to those who were near; 18 for through him both of us have access in one Spirit to the Father. 19 So then you are no longer strangers and aliens, but you are citizens with the saints and also members of the household of God, 20 built upon the foundation of the apostles and prophets, with Christ Jesus himself as the cornerstone. *k* 21 In him the whole structure is joined together and grows into a holy temple in the Lord; 22 in whom you also are built together spiritually *l* into a dwelling place for God.

3 This is the reason that I Paul am a prisoner for *m* Christ Jesus for the sake of you Gentiles — 2 for surely you have already heard of the commission of God's grace that was given me for you, 3 and how the mystery was made known to me by revelation, as I wrote above in a few words, 4 a reading of which will enable you to perceive my understanding of the mystery of Christ. 5 In former genera-

vast are the resources of his power open to us who have faith. His mighty strength was seen at work 20 when he raised Christ from the dead, and enthroned him at his right hand in the heavenly realms, 21 far above all government and authority, all power and dominion, and any title of sovereignty that commands allegiance, not only in this age but also in the age to come. 22 He put all things in subjection beneath his feet, and gave him as head over all things to the church 23 which is his body, the fullness of him who is filling the universe in all its parts.

2 YOU ONCE were dead because of your sins and wickedness; 2 you followed the ways of this present world order, obeying the commander of the spiritual powers of the air, the spirit now at work among God's rebel subjects. 3 We too were once of their number: we were ruled by our physical desires, and did what instinct and evil imagination suggested. In our natural condition we lay under the condemnation of God like the rest of mankind. 4 But God is rich in mercy, and because of his great love for us, 5 he brought us to life with Christ when we were dead because of our sins; it is by grace you are saved. 6 And he raised us up in union with Christ Jesus and enthroned us with him in the heavenly realms, 7 so that he might display in the ages to come how immense are the resources of his grace, how great his kindness to us in Christ Jesus. 8 For it is by grace you are saved through faith; it is not your own doing. It is God's gift, 9 not a reward for work done. There is nothing for anyone to boast of; 10 we are God's handiwork, created in Christ Jesus for the life of good deeds which God designed for us.

11 Remember then your former condition, Gentiles as you are by birth, 'the uncircumcised' as you are called by those who call themselves 'the circumcised' because of a physical rite. 12 You were at that time separate from Christ, excluded from the community of Israel, strangers to God's covenants and the promise that goes with them. Yours was a world without hope and without God. 13 Once you were far off, but now in union with Christ Jesus you have been brought near through the shedding of Christ's blood. 14 For he is himself our peace. Gentiles and Jews, he has made the two one, and in his own body of flesh and blood has broken down the barrier of enmity which separated them; 15 for he annulled the law with its rules and regulations, so as to create out of the two a single new humanity in himself, thereby making peace. 16 This was his purpose, to reconcile the two in a single body to God through the cross, by which he killed the enmity. 17 So he came and proclaimed the good news: peace to you who were far off, and peace to those who were near; 18 for through him we both alike have access to the Father in the one Spirit.

19 Thus you are no longer aliens in a foreign land, but fellow-citizens with God's people, members of God's household. 20 You are built on the foundation of the apostles and prophets, with Christ Jesus himself as the corner-stone. 21 In him the whole building is bonded together and grows into a holy temple in the Lord. 22 In him you also are being built with all the others into a spiritual dwelling for God.

3 WITH this in mind I pray for you, I, Paul, who for the sake of you Gentiles am now the prisoner of Christ Jesus — 2 for surely you have heard how God's gift of grace to me was designed for your benefit. 3 It was by a revelation that his secret purpose was made known to me. I have already written you a brief account of this, 4 and by reading it you can see that I understand the secret purpose of Christ.

---

f Gk *He*   *g* Other ancient authorities read *in Christ*   *h* Gk *in the flesh*   *i* Or *reconcile both of us in one body for God*   *j* Or *in him, or in himself*   *k* Or *keystone*   *l* Gk *in the Spirit*   *m* Or *of*

1:23 **body . . . parts:** *or* body, filled as he is with the full being of God, who is imparting to all things that same fullness.   2:16 **cross . . . enmity:** *or* cross. Thus in his own person he put to death the enmity.

NEW AMERICAN BIBLE

NEW JERUSALEM BIBLE

of his power for us who believe, in accord with the exercise of his great might, 20 which he worked in Christ, raising him from the dead and seating him at his right hand in the heavens, 21 far above every principality, authority, power, and dominion, and every name that is named not only in this age but also in the one to come. 22 And he put all things beneath his feet and gave him as head over all things to the church, 23 which is his body, the fullness of the one who fills all things in every way.

2 You were dead in your transgressions and sins 2 in which you once lived following the age of this world, following the ruler of the power of the air, the spirit that is now at work in the disobedient. 3 All of us once lived among them in the desires of our flesh, following the wishes of the flesh and the impulses, and we were by nature children of wrath, like the rest. 4 But God, who is rich in mercy, because of the great love he had for us, 5 even when we were dead in our transgressions, brought us to life with Christ (by grace you have been saved), 6 raised us up with him, and seated us with him in the heavens in Christ Jesus, 7 that in the ages to come he might show the immeasurable riches of his grace in his kindness to us in Christ Jesus. 8 For by grace you have been saved through faith, and this is not from you; it is the gift of God; 9 it is not from works, so no one may boast. 10 For we are his handiwork, created in Christ Jesus for the good works that God has prepared in advance, that we should live in them.

11 Therefore, remember that at one time you, Gentiles in the flesh, called the uncircumcision by those called the circumcision, which is done in the flesh by human hands, 12 were at that time without Christ, alienated from the community of Israel and strangers to the covenants of promise, without hope and without God in the world. 13 But now in Christ Jesus you who once were far off have become near by the blood of Christ.

14 For he is our peace, he who made both one and broke down the dividing wall of enmity, through his flesh, 15 abolishing the law with its commandments and legal claims, that he might create in himself one new person in place of the two, thus establishing peace, 16 and might reconcile both with God, in one body, through the cross, putting that enmity to death by it. 17 He came and preached peace to you who were far off and peace to those who were near, 18 for through him we both have access in one Spirit to the Father.

19 So then you are no longer strangers and sojourners, but you are fellow citizens with the holy ones and members of the household of God, 20 built upon the foundation of the apostles and prophets, with Christ Jesus himself as the capstone. 21 Through him the whole structure is held together and grows into a temple sacred in the Lord; 22 in him you also are being built together into a dwelling place of God in the Spirit.

3 Because of this, I, Paul, a prisoner of Christ [Jesus] for you Gentiles — 2 if, as I suppose, you have heard of the stewardship of God's grace that was given to me for your benefit, 3 [namely, that] the mystery was made known to me by revelation, as I have written briefly earlier. 4 When you read this you can understand my insight into the mystery of Christ, 5 which was not made known to human be-

extraordinarily great is the power that he has exercised for us believers; this accords with the strength of his power 20 at work in Christ, the power which he exercised in raising him from the dead and enthroning him at his right hand, in heaven, 21 far above every principality, ruling force, power or sovereignty,b or any other name that can be named, not only in this age but also in the age to come. 22 *He has put all things under his feet,c* and made him, as he is above all things, the head of the Church; 23 which is his Body, the fullness of him who is filled, all in all.

2 And you were dead, through the crimes and the sins 2 which used to make up your way of life when you were living by the principles of this world, obeying the ruler who dominates the air, the spirit who is at work in those who rebel. 3 We too were all among them once, living only by our natural inclinations, obeying the demands of human self-indulgence and our own whim; our nature made us no less liable to God's retribution than the rest of the world. 4 But God, being rich in faithful love, through the great love with which he loved us, 5 even when we were dead in our sins, brought us to life with Christ — it is through grace that you have been saved — 6 and raised us up with him and gave us a place with him in heaven, in Christ Jesus.

7 This was to show for all ages to come, through his goodness towards us in Christ Jesus, how extraordinarily rich he is in grace. 8 Because it is by grace that you have been saved, through faith; not by anything of your own, but by a gift from God; 9 not by anything that you have done, so that nobody can claim the credit. 10 We are God's work of art, created in Christ Jesus for the good works which God has already designated to make up our way of life.

11 Do not forget, then, that there was a time when you who were gentiles by physical descent, termed the uncircumcised by those who speak of themselves as the circumcised by reason of a physical operation, 12 do not forget, I say, that you were at that time separate from Christ and excluded from membership of Israel, aliens with no part in the covenants of the Promise, limited to this world, without hope and without God. 13 But now in Christ Jesus, you that used to be so far off have been brought close, by the blood of Christ. 14 For he is the peace between us, and has made the two into one entity and broken down the barrier which used to keep them apart, by destroying in his own person the hostility, 15 that is, the Law of commandments with its decrees. His purpose in this was, by restoring peace, to create a single New Man out of the two of them, 16 and through the cross, to reconcile them both to God in one Body; in his own person he killed the hostility. 17 He came to bring the good news of *peace to you who were far off and peace to those who were near.d* 18 Through him, then, we both in the one Spirit have free access to the Father.

19 So you are no longer aliens or foreign visitors; you are fellow-citizens with the holy people of God and part of God's household. 20 You are built upon the foundations of the apostles and prophets, and Christ Jesus himself is the cornerstone. 21 Every structure knit together in him grows into a holy temple in the Lord; 22 and you too, in him, are being built up into a dwelling-place of God in the Spirit.

3 It is because of this that I, Paul, a prisoner of the Lord Jesus on behalf of you gentiles. . . 2 You have surely heard the way in which God entrusted me with the grace he gave me for your sake; 3 he made known to me by a revelation the mystery I have just described briefly — 4 a reading of it will enable you to perceive my understanding of the mystery of Christ. 5 This mystery, as it is now revealed in

b 1 Names for cosmic powers.   c 1 Ps 8:6.   d 2 Is 57:19.

tions this mystery[n] was not made known to humankind, as it has now been revealed to his holy apostles and prophets by the Spirit: 6 that is, the Gentiles have become fellow heirs, members of the same body, and sharers in the promise in Christ Jesus through the gospel.

7 Of this gospel I have become a servant according to the gift of God's grace that was given me by the working of his power. 8 Although I am the very least of all the saints, this grace was given to me to bring to the Gentiles the news of the boundless riches of Christ, 9 and to make everyone see[o] what is the plan of the mystery hidden for ages in[p] God who created all things; 10 so that through the church the wisdom of God in its rich variety might now be made known to the rulers and authorities in the heavenly places. 11 This was in accordance with the eternal purpose that he has carried out in Christ Jesus our Lord, 12 in whom we have access to God in boldness and confidence through faith in him.[q] 13 I pray therefore that you[r] may not lose heart over my sufferings for you; they are your glory.

14 For this reason I bow my knees before the Father,[s] 15 from whom every family[t] in heaven and on earth takes its name. 16 I pray that, according to the riches of his glory, he may grant that you may be strengthened in your inner being with power through his Spirit, 17 and that Christ may dwell in your hearts through faith, as you are being rooted and grounded in love. 18 I pray that you may have the power to comprehend, with all the saints, what is the breadth and length and height and depth, 19 and to know the love of Christ that surpasses knowledge, so that you may be filled with all the fullness of God.

20 Now to him who by the power at work within us is able to accomplish abundantly far more than all we can ask or imagine, 21 to him be glory in the church and in Christ Jesus to all generations, forever and ever. Amen.

4 I therefore, the prisoner in the Lord, beg you to lead a life worthy of the calling to which you have been called, 2 with all humility and gentleness, with patience, bearing with one another in love, 3 making every effort to maintain the unity of the Spirit in the bond of peace. 4 There is one body and one Spirit, just as you were called to the one hope of your calling, 5 one Lord, one faith, one baptism, 6 one God and Father of all, who is above all and through all and in all.

7 But each of us was given grace according to the measure of Christ's gift. 8 Therefore it is said,

"When he ascended on high he made captivity
    itself a captive;
  he gave gifts to his people."

9 (When it says, "He ascended," what does it mean but that he had also descended[u] into the lower parts of the earth? 10 He who descended is the same one who ascended far above all the heavens, so that he might fill all things.) 11 The gifts he gave were that some would be apostles, some prophets, some evangelists, some pastors and teachers, 12 to equip the saints for the work of ministry, for building up the body of Christ, 13 until all of us come to the unity of the faith and of the knowledge of the Son of God, to maturity, to the measure of the full stature of Christ. 14 We must no longer be children, tossed to and fro and blown about by every wind of doctrine, by people's trickery, by their craftiness in deceitful scheming. 15 But speaking the truth in love, we must grow up in every way into him who is the head, into Christ, 16 from whom the whole body, joined and knit

5 In former generations that secret was not disclosed to mankind; but now by inspiration it has been revealed to his holy apostles and prophets, 6 that through the gospel the Gentiles are joint heirs with the Jews, part of the same body, sharers together in the promise made in Christ Jesus. 7 Such is the gospel of which I was made a minister by God's unmerited gift, so powerfully at work in me. 8 To me, who am less than the least of all God's people, he has granted the privilege of proclaiming to the Gentiles the good news of the unfathomable riches of Christ, 9 and of bringing to light how this hidden purpose was to be put into effect. It lay concealed for long ages with God the Creator of the universe, 10 in order that now, through the church, the wisdom of God in its infinite variety might be made known to the rulers and authorities in the heavenly realms. 11 This accords with his age-long purpose, which he accomplished in Christ Jesus our Lord, 12 in whom we have freedom of access to God, with the confidence born of trust in him. 13 I beg you, then, not to lose heart over my sufferings for you; indeed, they are your glory.

14 With this in mind, then, I kneel in prayer to the Father, 15 from whom every family in heaven and on earth takes its name, 16 that out of the treasures of his glory he may grant you inward strength and power through his Spirit, 17 that through faith Christ may dwell in your hearts in love. With deep roots and firm foundations 18 may you, in company with all God's people, be strong to grasp what is the breadth and length and height and depth 19 of Christ's love, and to know it, though it is beyond knowledge. So may you be filled with the very fullness of God.

20 Now to him who is able through the power which is at work among us to do immeasurably more than all we can ask or conceive, 21 to him be glory in the church and in Christ Jesus from generation to generation for evermore! Amen.

4 I IMPLORE you then—I, a prisoner for the Lord's sake: as God has called you, live up to your calling. 2 Be humble always and gentle, and patient too, putting up with one another's failings in the spirit of love. 3 Spare no effort to make fast with bonds of peace the unity which the Spirit gives. 4 There is one body and one Spirit, just as there is one hope held out in God's call to you; 5 one Lord, one faith, one baptism; 6 one God and Father of all, who is over all and through all and in all.

7 But each of us has been given a special gift, a particular share in the bounty of Christ. 8 That is why scripture says:

He ascended into the heights;
  he took captives into captivity;
  he gave gifts to men.

9 Now, the word 'ascended' implies that he also descended to the lowest level, down to the very earth. 10 He who descended is none other than he who ascended far above all heavens, so that he might fill the universe. 11 And it is he who has given some to be apostles, some prophets, some evangelists, some pastors and teachers, 12 to equip God's people for work in his service, for the building up of the body of Christ, 13 until we all attain to the unity inherent in our faith and in our knowledge of the Son of God—to mature manhood, measured by nothing less than the full stature of Christ. 14 We are no longer to be children, tossed about by the waves and whirled around by every fresh gust of teaching, dupes of cunning rogues and their deceitful schemes. 15 Rather we are to maintain the truth in a spirit of love; so shall we fully grow up into Christ. He is the head,

---

n Gk it   o Other ancient authorities read *to bring to light*   p Or *by*
q Or *the faith of him*   r Or *I*   s Other ancient authorities add *of
our Lord Jesus Christ*   t Gk *fatherhood*   u Other ancient
authorities add *first*

4:9 **descended . . . earth:** *or* descended to the regions beneath the earth.

ings in other generations as it has now been revealed to his holy apostles and prophets by the Spirit, 6 that the Gentiles are coheirs, members of the same body, and copartners in the promise in Christ Jesus through the gospel.

7 Of this I became a minister by the gift of God's grace that was granted me in accord with the exercise of his power. 8 To me, the very least of all the holy ones, this grace was given, to preach to the Gentiles the inscrutable riches of Christ, 9 and to bring to light [for all] what is the plan of the mystery hidden from ages past in God who created all things, 10 so that the manifold wisdom of God might now be made known through the church to the principalities and authorities in the heavens. 11 This was according to the eternal purpose that he accomplished in Christ Jesus our Lord, 12 in whom we have boldness of speech and confidence of access through faith in him. 13 So I ask you not to lose heart over my afflictions for you; this is your glory.

14 For this reason I kneel before the Father, 15 from whom every family in heaven and on earth is named, 16 that he may grant you in accord with the riches of his glory to be strengthened with power through his Spirit in the inner self, 17 and that Christ may dwell in your hearts through faith; that you, rooted and grounded in love, 18 may have strength to comprehend with all the holy ones what is the breadth and length and height and depth, 19 and to know the love of Christ that surpasses knowledge, so that you may be filled with all the fullness of God.

20 Now to him who is able to accomplish far more than all we ask or imagine, by the power at work within us, 21 to him be glory in the church and in Christ Jesus to all generations, forever and ever. Amen.

4 I, then, a prisoner for the Lord, urge you to live in a manner worthy of the call you have received, 2 with all humility and gentleness, with patience, bearing with one another through love, 3 striving to preserve the unity of the spirit through the bond of peace: 4 one body and one Spirit, as you were also called to the one hope of your call; 5 one Lord, one faith, one baptism; 6 one God and Father of all, who is over all and through all and in all.

7 But grace was given to each of us according to the measure of Christ's gift. 8 Therefore, it says:

"He ascended on high and took prisoners captive;
he gave gifts to men."

9 What does "he ascended" mean except that he also descended into the lower [regions] of the earth? 10 The one who descended is also the one who ascended far above all the heavens, that he might fill all things. 11 And he gave some as apostles, others as prophets, others as evangelists, others as pastors and teachers, 12 to equip the holy ones for the work of ministry, for building up the body of Christ, 13 until we all attain to the unity of faith and knowledge of the Son of God, to mature manhood, to the extent of the full stature of Christ, 14 so that we may no longer be infants, tossed by waves and swept along by every wind of teaching arising from human trickery, from their cunning in the interests of deceitful scheming. 15 Rather, living the truth in love, we should grow in every way into him who is the head, Christ, 16 from whom the whole body,

the Spirit to his holy apostles and prophets, was unknown to humanity in previous generations: 6 that the gentiles now have the same inheritance and form the same Body and enjoy the same promise in Christ Jesus through the gospel. 7 I have been made the servant of that gospel by a gift of grace from God who gave it to me by the workings of his power. 8 I, who am less than the least of all God's holy people, have been entrusted with this special grace, of proclaiming to the gentiles the unfathomable treasure of Christ 9 and of throwing light on the inner workings of the mystery kept hidden through all the ages in God, the Creator of everything. 10 The purpose of this was, that now, through the Church, the principalities and ruling forces should learn how many-sided God's wisdom is, 11 according to the plan which he had formed from all eternity in Christ Jesus our Lord. 12 In him we are bold enough to approach God in complete confidence, through our faith in him; 13 so, I beg you, do not let the hardships I go through on your account make you waver; they are your glory.

14 This, then, is what I pray, kneeling before the Father, 15 from whom every fatherhood, in heaven or on earth, takes its name. 16 In the abundance of his glory may he, through his Spirit, enable you to grow firm in power with regard to your inner self, 17 so that Christ may live in your hearts through faith, and then, planted in love and built on love, 18 with all God's holy people you will have the strength to grasp the breadth and the length, the height and the depth; 19 so that, knowing the love of Christ, which is beyond knowledge, you may be filled with the utter fullness of God.

20 Glory be to him whose power, working in us, can do infinitely more than we can ask or imagine; 21 glory be to him from generation to generation in the Church and in Christ Jesus for ever and ever. Amen.

4 I, the prisoner in the Lord, urge you therefore to lead a life worthy of the vocation to which you were called. 2 With all humility and gentleness, and with patience, support each other in love. 3 Take every care to preserve the unity of the Spirit by the peace that binds you together. 4 There is one Body, one Spirit, just as one hope is the goal of your calling by God. 5 There is one Lord, one faith, one baptism, 6 and one God and Father of all, over all, through all and within all.

7 On each one of us God's favour has been bestowed in whatever way Christ allotted it. 8 That is why it says:

*He went up to the heights, took captives,
he gave gifts to humanity.e*

9 When it says, 'he went up', it must mean that he had gone down to the deepest levels of the earth. 10 The one who went down is none other than the one who went up above all the heavens to fill all things. 11 And to some, his 'gift' was that they should be apostles; to some prophets; to some, evangelists; to some, pastors and teachers; 12 to knit God's holy people together for the work of service to build up the Body of Christ, 13 until we all reach unity in faith and knowledge of the Son of God and form the perfect Man, fully mature with the fullness of Christ himself.

14 Then we shall no longer be children, or tossed one way and another, and carried hither and thither by every new gust of teaching, at the mercy of all the tricks people play and their unscrupulousness in deliberate deception. 15 If we live by the truth and in love, we shall grow completely into Christ, who is the head 16 by whom the whole Body is fitted

---

3, 9: *[For all]:* while some think this phrase was added so as to yield the sense "to enlighten all about the plan . . . ," it is more likely that some manuscripts and Fathers omitted it accidentally or to avoid the idea that *all* conflicted with Paul's assignment to preach to *the Gentiles* (8) specifically.

e 4 Ps 68:18.

| NEW REVISED STANDARD VERSION | REVISED ENGLISH BIBLE |

together by every ligament with which it is equipped, as each part is working properly, promotes the body's growth in building itself up in love.

17 Now this I affirm and insist on in the Lord: you must no longer live as the Gentiles live, in the futility of their minds. 18 They are darkened in their understanding, alienated from the life of God because of their ignorance and hardness of heart. 19 They have lost all sensitivity and have abandoned themselves to licentiousness, greedy to practice every kind of impurity. 20 That is not the way you learned Christ! 21 For surely you have heard about him and were taught in him, as truth is in Jesus. 22 You were taught to put away your former way of life, your old self, corrupt and deluded by its lusts, 23 and to be renewed in the spirit of your minds, 24 and to clothe yourselves with the new self, created according to the likeness of God in true righteousness and holiness.

25 So then, putting away falsehood, let all of us speak the truth to our neighbors, for we are members of one another. 26 Be angry but do not sin; do not let the sun go down on your anger, 27 and do not make room for the devil. 28 Thieves must give up stealing; rather let them labor and work honestly with their own hands, so as to have something to share with the needy. 29 Let no evil talk come out of your mouths, but only what is useful for building up,^{v} as there is need, so that your words may give grace to those who hear. 30 And do not grieve the Holy Spirit of God, with which you were marked with a seal for the day of redemption. 31 Put away from you all bitterness and wrath and anger and wrangling and slander, together with all malice, 32 and be kind to one another, tenderhearted, forgiving one another, as God in Christ has forgiven you. ^{w}

5 1 Therefore be imitators of God, as beloved children, 2 and live in love, as Christ loved us^x and gave himself up for us, a fragrant offering and sacrifice to God.

3 But fornication and impurity of any kind, or greed, must not even be mentioned among you, as is proper among saints. 4 Entirely out of place is obscene, silly, and vulgar talk; but instead, let there be thanksgiving. 5 Be sure of this, that no fornicator or impure person, or one who is greedy (that is, an idolater), has any inheritance in the kingdom of Christ and of God.

6 Let no one deceive you with empty words, for because of these things the wrath of God comes on those who are disobedient. 7 Therefore do not be associated with them. 8 For once you were darkness, but now in the Lord you are light. Live as children of light— 9 for the fruit of the light is found in all that is good and right and true. 10 Try to find out what is pleasing to the Lord. 11 Take no part in the unfruitful works of darkness, but instead expose them. 12 For it is shameful even to mention what such people do secretly; 13 but everything exposed by the light becomes visible, 14 for everything that becomes visible is light. Therefore it says,

> "Sleeper, awake!
> Rise from the dead,
> and Christ will shine on you."

15 Be careful then how you live, not as unwise people but as wise, 16 making the most of the time, because the days are evil. 17 So do not be foolish, but understand what the will of the Lord is. 18 Do not get drunk with wine, for

16 and on him the whole body depends. Bonded and held together by every constituent joint, the whole frame grows through the proper functioning of each part, and builds itself up in love.

17 Here then is my word to you, and I urge it on you in the Lord's name: give up living as pagans do with their futile notions. 18 Their minds are closed, they are alienated from the life that is in God, because ignorance prevails among them and their hearts have grown hard as stone. 19 Dead to all feeling, they have abandoned themselves to vice, and there is no indecency that they do not practise. 20 But that is not how you learned Christ. 21 For were you not told about him, were you not as Christians taught the truth as it is in Jesus? 22 Renouncing your former way of life, you must lay aside the old human nature which, deluded by its desires, is in process of decay: 23 you must be renewed in mind and spirit, 24 and put on the new nature created in God's likeness, which shows itself in the upright and devout life called for by the truth.

25 Then have done with falsehood and speak the truth to each other, for we belong to one another as parts of one body. 26 If you are angry, do not be led into sin; do not let sunset find you nursing your anger; 27 and give no foothold to the devil. 28 The thief must give up stealing, and work hard with his hands to earn an honest living, so that he may have something to share with the needy. 29 Let no offensive talk pass your lips, only what is good and helpful to the occasion, so that it brings a blessing to those who hear it. 30 Do not grieve the Holy Spirit of God, for that Spirit is the seal with which you were marked for the day of final liberation. 31 Have done with all spite and bad temper, with rage, insults, and slander, with evil of any kind. 32 Be generous to one another, tender-hearted, forgiving one another as God in Christ forgave you.

5 In a word, as God's dear children, you must be like him. 2 Live in love as Christ loved you and gave himself up on your behalf, an offering and sacrifice whose fragrance is pleasing to God.

3 Fornication and indecency of any kind, or ruthless greed, must not be so much as mentioned among you, as befits the people of God. 4 No coarse, stupid, or flippant talk: these things are out of place; you should rather be thanking God. 5 For be very sure of this: no one given to fornication or vice, or the greed which makes an idol of gain, has any share in the kingdom of Christ and of God. 6 Let no one deceive you with shallow arguments; it is for these things that divine retribution falls on God's rebel subjects. 7 Have nothing to do with them. 8 Though you once were darkness, now as Christians you are light. Prove yourselves at home in the light, 9 for where light is, there is a harvest of goodness, righteousness, and truth. 10 Learn to judge for yourselves what is pleasing to the Lord; 11 take no part in the barren deeds of darkness, but show them up for what they are. 12 It would be shameful even to mention what is done in secret. 13 But everything is shown up by being exposed to the light, and whatever is exposed to the light itself becomes light. 14 That is why it is said:

> Awake, sleeper,
> rise from the dead,
> and Christ will shine upon you.

15 Take great care, then, how you behave: act sensibly, not like simpletons. 16 Use the present opportunity to the full, for these are evil days. 17 Do not be foolish, but understand what the will of the Lord is. 18 Do not give way to drunken-

---

^{v} Other ancient authorities read *building up faith* ^{w} Other ancient authorities read *us* ^{x} Other ancient authorities read *you*

NEW AMERICAN BIBLE

joined and held together by every supporting ligament, with the proper functioning of each part, brings about the body's growth and builds itself up in love.

17 So I declare and testify in the Lord that you must no longer live as the Gentiles do, in the futility of their minds; 18 darkened in understanding, alienated from the life of God because of their ignorance, because of their hardness of heart, 19 they have become callous and have handed themselves over to licentiousness for the practice of every kind of impurity to excess. 20 That is not how you learned Christ, 21 assuming that you have heard of him and were taught in him, as truth is in Jesus, 22 that you should put away the old self of your former way of life, corrupted through deceitful desires, 23 and be renewed in the spirit of your minds, 24 and put on the new self, created in God's way in righteousness and holiness of truth.

25 Therefore, putting away falsehood, speak the truth, each one to his neighbor, for we are members one of another. 26 Be angry but do not sin; do not let the sun set on your anger, 27 and do not leave room for the devil. 28 The thief must no longer steal, but rather labor, doing honest work with his [own] hands, so that he may have something to share with one in need. 29 No foul language should come out of your mouths, but only such as is good for needed edification, that it may impart grace to those who hear. 30 And do not grieve the holy Spirit of God, with which you were sealed for the day of redemption. 31 All bitterness, fury, anger, shouting, and reviling must be removed from you, along with all malice. 32 [And] be kind to one another, compassionate, forgiving one another as God has forgiven you in Christ.

5 So be imitators of God, as beloved children, 2 and live in love, as Christ loved us and handed himself over for us as a sacrificial offering to God for a fragrant aroma. 3 Immorality or any impurity or greed must not even be mentioned among you, as is fitting among holy ones, 4 no obscenity or silly or suggestive talk, which is out of place, but instead, thanksgiving. 5 Be sure of this, that no immoral or impure or greedy person, that is, an idolater, has any inheritance in the kingdom of Christ and of God.

6 Let no one deceive you with empty arguments, for because of these things the wrath of God is coming upon the disobedient. 7 So do not be associated with them. 8 For you were once darkness, but now you are light in the Lord. Live as children of light, 9 for light produces every kind of goodness and righteousness and truth. 10 Try to learn what is pleasing to the Lord. 11 Take no part in the fruitless works of darkness; rather expose them, 12 for it is shameful even to mention the things done by them in secret; 13 but everything exposed by the light becomes visible, 14 for everything that becomes visible is light. Therefore, it says:

"Awake, O sleeper,
and arise from the dead,
and Christ will give you light."

15 Watch carefully then how you live, not as foolish persons but as wise, 16 making the most of the opportunity, because the days are evil. 17 Therefore, do not continue in ignorance, but try to understand what is the will of the Lord. 18 And do not get drunk on wine, in which lies debauchery,

NEW JERUSALEM BIBLE

and joined together, every joint adding its own strength, for each individual part to work according to its function. So the body grows until it has built itself up in love.

17 So this I say to you and attest to you in the Lord, do not go on living the empty-headed life that the gentiles live. 18 Intellectually they are in the dark, and they are estranged from the life of God, because of the ignorance which is the consequence of closed minds. 19 Their sense of right and wrong once dulled, they have abandoned all self-control and pursue to excess every kind of uncleanness. 20 Now that is hardly the way you have learnt Christ, 21 unless you failed to hear him properly when you were taught what the truth is in Jesus. 22 You were to put aside your old self, which belongs to your old way of life and is corrupted by following illusory desires. 23 Your mind was to be renewed in spirit 24 so that you could put on the New Man that has been created on God's principles, in the uprightness and holiness of the truth.

25 So from now on, there must be no more lies. *Speak the truth to one another, f* since we are all parts of one another. 26 *Even if you are angry, do not sin:g* never let the sun set on your anger 27 or else you will give the devil a foothold. 28 Anyone who was a thief must stop stealing; instead he should exert himself at some honest job with his own hands so that he may have something to share with those in need. 29 No foul word should ever cross your lips; let your words be for the improvement of others, as occasion offers, and do good to your listeners; 30 do not grieve the Holy Spirit of God who has marked you with his seal, ready for the day when we shall be set free. 31 Any bitterness or bad temper or anger or shouting or abuse must be far removed from you — as must every kind of malice. 32 Be generous to one another, sympathetic, forgiving each other as readily as God forgave you in Christ.

5 As God's dear children, then, take him as your pattern, 2 and follow Christ by loving as he loved you, giving himself up for us as *an offering and a sweet-smelling sacrifice to God.h* 3 Among you there must be not even a mention of sexual vice or impurity in any of its forms, or greed: this would scarcely become the holy people of God! 4 There must be no foul or salacious talk or coarse jokes — all this is wrong for you; there should rather be thanksgiving. 5 For you can be quite certain that nobody who indulges in sexual immorality or impurity or greed — which is worshipping a false god — can inherit the kingdom of God. 6 Do not let anyone deceive you with empty arguments: it is such behaviour that draws down God's retribution on those who rebel against him. 7 Make sure that you do not throw in your lot with them. 8 You were darkness once, but now you are light in the Lord; behave as children of light, 9 for the effects of the light are seen in complete goodness and uprightness and truth. 10 Try to discover what the Lord wants of you, 11 take no part in the futile works of darkness but, on the contrary, show them up for what they are. 12 The things which are done in secret are shameful even to speak of; 13 but anything shown up by the light will be illuminated 14 and anything illuminated is itself a light. That is why it is said:

Wake up, sleeper,
rise from the dead,
and Christ will shine on you.

15 So be very careful about the sort of lives you lead, like intelligent and not like senseless people. 16 Make the best of the present time, for it is a wicked age. 17 This is why you must not be thoughtless but must recognise what is the will of the Lord. 18 *Do not get drunk with wine;i* this is simply

f 4 Zc 8:16.   g 4 Ps 4:4.   h 5 Ex 29:18.   i 5 Pr 23:31.

NEW REVISED STANDARD VERSION	REVISED ENGLISH BIBLE

that is debauchery; but be filled with the Spirit, 19 as you sing psalms and hymns and spiritual songs among yourselves, singing and making melody to the Lord in your hearts, 20 giving thanks to God the Father at all times and for everything in the name of our Lord Jesus Christ.

21 Be subject to one another out of reverence for Christ.

22 Wives, be subject to your husbands as you are to the Lord. 23 For the husband is the head of the wife just as Christ is the head of the church, the body of which he is the Savior. 24 Just as the church is subject to Christ, so also wives ought to be, in everything, to their husbands.

25 Husbands, love your wives, just as Christ loved the church and gave himself up for her, 26 in order to make her holy by cleansing her with the washing of water by the word, 27 so as to present the church to himself in splendor, without a spot or wrinkle or anything of the kind—yes, so that she may be holy and without blemish. 28 In the same way, husbands should love their wives as they do their own bodies. He who loves his wife loves himself. 29 For no one ever hates his own body, but he nourishes and tenderly cares for it, just as Christ does for the church, 30 because we are members of his body.*y* 31 "For this reason a man will leave his father and mother and be joined to his wife, and the two will become one flesh." 32 This is a great mystery, and I am applying it to Christ and the church. 33 Each of you, however, should love his wife as himself, and a wife should respect her husband.

6 Children, obey your parents in the Lord,*z* for this is right. 2 "Honor your father and mother"—this is the first commandment with a promise: 3 "so that it may be well with you and you may live long on the earth."

4 And, fathers, do not provoke your children to anger, but bring them up in the discipline and instruction of the Lord.

5 Slaves, obey your earthly masters with fear and trembling, in singleness of heart, as you obey Christ; 6 not only while being watched, and in order to please them, but as slaves of Christ, doing the will of God from the heart. 7 Render service with enthusiasm, as to the Lord and not to men and women, 8 knowing that whatever good we do, we will receive the same again from the Lord, whether we are slaves or free.

9 And, masters, do the same to them. Stop threatening them, for you know that both of you have the same Master in heaven, and with him there is no partiality.

10 Finally, be strong in the Lord and in the strength of his power. 11 Put on the whole armor of God, so that you may be able to stand against the wiles of the devil. 12 For our*a* struggle is not against enemies of blood and flesh, but against the rulers, against the authorities, against the cosmic powers of this present darkness, against the spiritual forces of evil in the heavenly places. 13 Therefore take up the whole armor of God, so that you may be able to withstand on that evil day, and having done everything, to stand firm. 14 Stand therefore, and fasten the belt of truth around your waist, and put on the breastplate of righteousness. 15 As shoes for your feet put on whatever will make you ready to proclaim the gospel of peace. 16 With all of these,*b* take the shield of faith, with which you will be able to quench all the flaming arrows of the evil one. 17 Take the helmet of salvation, and the sword of the Spirit, which is the word of God.

ness and the ruin that goes with it, but let the Holy Spirit fill you: 19 speak to one another in psalms, hymns, and songs; sing and make music from your heart to the Lord; 20 and in the name of our Lord Jesus Christ give thanks every day for everything to our God and Father.

21 BE subject to one another out of reverence for Christ. 22 Wives, be subject to your husbands as though to the Lord; 23 for the man is the head of the woman, just as Christ is the head of the church. Christ is, indeed, the saviour of that body; 24 but just as the church is subject to Christ, so must women be subject to their husbands in everything.

25 Husbands, love your wives, as Christ loved the church and gave himself up for it, 26 to consecrate and cleanse it by water and word, 27 so that he might present the church to himself all glorious, with no stain or wrinkle or anything of the sort, but holy and without blemish. 28 In the same way men ought to love their wives, as they love their own bodies. In loving his wife a man loves himself. 29 For no one ever hated his own body; on the contrary, he keeps it nourished and warm, and that is how Christ treats the church, 30 because it is his body, of which we are living parts. 31 'This is why' (in the words of scripture) 'a man shall leave his father and mother and be united to his wife, and the two shall become one flesh.' 32 There is hidden here a great truth, which I take to refer to Christ and to the church. 33 But it applies also to each one of you: the husband must love his wife as his very self, and the wife must show reverence for her husband.

6 Children, obey your parents; for it is only right that you should. 2 'Honour your father and your mother' is the first commandment to carry a promise with it: 3 'that it may be well with you and that you may live long on the earth.'

4 Fathers, do not goad your children to resentment, but bring them up in the discipline and instruction of the Lord.

5 Slaves, give single-minded obedience to your earthly masters with fear and trembling, as if to Christ. 6 Do it not merely to catch their eye or curry favour with them, but as slaves of Christ do the will of God wholeheartedly. 7 Give cheerful service, as slaves of the Lord rather than of men. 8 You know that whatever good anyone may do, slave or free, will be repaid by the Lord.

9 Masters, treat your slaves in the same spirit: give up using threats, and remember that you both have the same Master in heaven; there is no favouritism with him.

10 FINALLY, find your strength in the Lord, in his mighty power. 11 Put on the full armour provided by God, so that you may be able to stand firm against the stratagems of the devil. 12 For our struggle is not against human foes, but against cosmic powers, against the authorities and potentates of this dark age, against the superhuman forces of evil in the heavenly realms. 13 Therefore, take up the armour of God; then you will be able to withstand them on the evil day and, after doing your utmost, to stand your ground. 14 Stand fast, I say. Fasten on the belt of truth; for a breastplate put on integrity; 15 let the shoes on your feet be the gospel of peace, to give you firm footing; 16 and, with all these, take up the great shield of faith, with which you will be able to quench all the burning arrows of the evil one. 17 Accept salvation as your helmet, and the sword which the Spirit gives you, the word of God. 18 Constantly ask God's help in

y Other ancient authorities add *of his flesh and of his bones* *z* Other ancient authorities lack *in the Lord* *a* Other ancient authorities read *your* *b* Or *In all circumstances*

5:19 **hymns, and:** *some witnesses add* spiritual.

NEW AMERICAN BIBLE

NEW JERUSALEM BIBLE

but be filled with the Spirit, 19 addressing one another [in] psalms and hymns and spiritual songs, singing and playing to the Lord in your hearts, 20 giving thanks always and for everything in the name of our Lord Jesus Christ to God the Father.

21 Be subordinate to one another out of reverence for Christ. 22 Wives should be subordinate to their husbands as to the Lord. 23 For the husband is head of his wife just as Christ is head of the church, he himself the savior of the body. 24 As the church is subordinate to Christ, so wives should be subordinate to their husbands in everything. 25 Husbands, love your wives, even as Christ loved the church and handed himself over for her 26 to sanctify her, cleansing her by the bath of water with the word, 27 that he might present to himself the church in splendor, without spot or wrinkle or any such thing, that she might be holy and without blemish. 28 So [also] husbands should love their wives as their own bodies. He who loves his wife loves himself. 29 For no one hates his own flesh but rather nourishes and cherishes it, even as Christ does the church, 30 because we are members of his body.

31 "For this reason a man shall leave [his] father and [his] mother
and be joined to his wife,
and the two shall become one flesh."

32 This is a great mystery, but I speak in reference to Christ and the church. 33 In any case, each one of you should love his wife as himself, and the wife should respect her husband.

6 Children, obey your parents [in the Lord], for this is right. 2 "Honor your father and mother." This is the first commandment with a promise, 3 "that it may go well with you and that you may have a long life on earth." 4 Fathers, do not provoke your children to anger, but bring them up with the training and instruction of the Lord.

5 Slaves, be obedient to your human masters with fear and trembling, in sincerity of heart, as to Christ, 6 not only when being watched, as currying favor, but as slaves of Christ, doing the will of God from the heart, 7 willingly serving the Lord and not human beings, 8 knowing that each will be requited from the Lord for whatever good he does, whether he is slave or free. 9 Masters, act in the same way toward them, and stop bullying, knowing that both they and you have a Master in heaven and that with him there is no partiality.

10 Finally, draw your strength from the Lord and from his mighty power. 11 Put on the armor of God so that you may be able to stand firm against the tactics of the devil. 12 For our struggle is not with flesh and blood but with the principalities, with the powers, with the world rulers of this present darkness, with the evil spirits in the heavens. 13 Therefore, put on the armor of God, that you may be able to resist on the evil day and, having done everything, to hold your ground. 14 So stand fast with your loins girded in truth, clothed with righteousness as a breastplate, 15 and your feet shod in readiness for the gospel of peace. 16 In all circumstances, hold faith as a shield, to quench all [the] flaming arrows of the evil one. 17 And take the helmet of salvation and the sword of the Spirit, which is the word of God.

dissipation; be filled with the Spirit. 19 Sing psalms and hymns and inspired songs among yourselves, singing and chanting to the Lord in your hearts, 20 always and everywhere giving thanks to God who is our Father in the name of our Lord Jesus Christ.

21 Be subject to one another out of reverence for Christ. 22 Wives should be subject to their husbands as to the Lord, 23 since, as Christ is head of the Church and saves the whole body, so is a husband the head of his wife; 24 and as the Church is subject to Christ, so should wives be to their husbands, in everything. 25 Husbands should love their wives, just as Christ loved the Church and sacrificed himself for her 26 to make her holy by washing her in cleansing water with a form of words, 27 so that when he took the Church to himself she would be glorious, with no speck or wrinkle or anything like that, but holy and faultless. 28 In the same way, husbands must love their wives as they love their own bodies; for a man to love his wife is for him to love himself. 29 A man never hates his own body, but he feeds it and looks after it; and that is the way Christ treats the Church, 30 because we are parts of his Body. 31 This is why a man leaves his father and mother and becomes attached to his wife, and the two become one flesh. j 32 This mystery has great significance, but I am applying it to Christ and the Church. 33 To sum up: you also, each one of you, must love his wife as he loves himself; and let every wife respect her husband.

6 Children, be obedient to your parents in the Lord — that is what uprightness demands. 2 The first commandment that has a promise attached to it is: Honour your father and your mother, 3 and the promise is: so that you may have long life and prosper in the land. k 4 And parents, never drive your children to resentment but bring them up with correction and advice inspired by the Lord.

5 Slaves, be obedient to those who are, according to human reckoning, your masters, with deep respect and sincere loyalty, as you are obedient to Christ: 6 not only when you are under their eye, as if you had only to please human beings, but as slaves of Christ who wholeheartedly do the will of God. 7 Work willingly for the sake of the Lord and not for the sake of human beings. 8 Never forget that everyone, whether a slave or a freeman, will be rewarded by the Lord for whatever work he has done well. 9 And those of you who are employers, treat your slaves in the same spirit; do without threats, and never forget that they and you have the same Master in heaven and there is no favouritism with him.

10 Finally, grow strong in the Lord, with the strength of his power. 11 Put on the full armour of God so as to be able to resist the devil's tactics. 12 For it is not against human enemies that we have to struggle, but against the principalities and the ruling forces who are masters of the darkness in this world, the spirits of evil in the heavens. 13 That is why you must take up all God's armour, or you will not be able to put up any resistance on the evil day, or stand your ground even though you exert yourselves to the full.

14 So stand your ground, with truth a belt round your waist, and uprightness a breastplate, 15 wearing for shoes on your feet the eagerness to spread the gospel of peace l 16 and always carrying the shield of faith so that you can use it to quench the burning arrows of the Evil One. 17 And then you must take salvation as your helmet and the sword of the Spirit, that is, the word of God.

---

j 5 Gn 2:24.   k 6 Ex 20:12.   l 6 Is 59:17; 40:9.

NEW REVISED STANDARD VERSION

18 Pray in the Spirit at all times in every prayer and supplication. To that end keep alert and always persevere in supplication for all the saints. 19 Pray also for me, so that when I speak, a message may be given to me to make known with boldness the mystery of the gospel,*c* 20 for which I am an ambassador in chains. Pray that I may declare it boldly, as I must speak.

21 So that you also may know how I am and what I am doing, Tychicus will tell you everything. He is a dear brother and a faithful minister in the Lord. 22 I am sending him to you for this very purpose, to let you know how we are, and to encourage your hearts.

23 Peace be to the whole community,*d* and love with faith, from God the Father and the Lord Jesus Christ. 24 Grace be with all who have an undying love for our Lord Jesus Christ.*e*

c Other ancient authorities lack *of the gospel* *d* Gk *to the brothers*
e Other ancient authorities add *Amen*

REVISED ENGLISH BIBLE

prayer, and pray always in the power of the Spirit. To this end keep watch and persevere, always interceding for all God's people. 19 Pray also for me, that I may be granted the right words when I speak, and may boldly and freely make known the hidden purpose of the gospel, 20 for which I am an ambassador — in chains. Pray that I may speak of it boldly, as is my duty.

21 YOU WILL want to know how I am and what I am doing; Tychicus will give you all the news. He is our dear brother and trustworthy helper in the Lord's work. 22 I am sending him to you on purpose to let you have news of us and to put fresh heart into you.

23 Peace to the community and love with faith, from God the Father and the Lord Jesus Christ. 24 God's grace be with all who love our Lord Jesus Christ with undying love.

6:24 **Christ . . . love:** *or* Christ, grace and immortality.

18 With all prayer and supplication, pray at every opportunity in the Spirit. To that end, be watchful with all perseverance and supplication for all the holy ones 19 and also for me, that speech may be given me to open my mouth, to make known with boldness the mystery of the gospel 20 for which I am an ambassador in chains, so that I may have the courage to speak as I must.

21 So that you also may have news of me and of what I am doing, Tychicus, my beloved brother and trustworthy minister in the Lord, will tell you everything. 22 I am sending him to you for this very purpose, so that you may know about us and that he may encourage your hearts.

23 Peace be to the brothers, and love with faith, from God the Father and the Lord Jesus Christ. 24 Grace be with all who love our Lord Jesus Christ in immortality.

18 In all your prayer and entreaty keep praying in the Spirit on every possible occasion. Never get tired of staying awake to pray for all God's holy people, 19 and pray for me to be given an opportunity to open my mouth and fearlessly make known the mystery of the gospel 20 of which I am an ambassador in chains; pray that in proclaiming it I may speak as fearlessly as I ought to.

21 So that you know, as well, what is happening to me and what I am doing, my dear friend Tychicus, my trustworthy helper in the Lord, will tell you everything. 22 I am sending him to you precisely for this purpose, to give you news about us and encourage you thoroughly.

23 May God the Father and the Lord Jesus Christ grant peace, love and faith to all the brothers. 24 May grace be with all who love our Lord Jesus Christ, in life imperishable.

THE LETTER OF PAUL TO THE
Philippians

1 Paul and Timothy, servants*a* of Christ Jesus,
To all the saints in Christ Jesus who are in Philippi, with the bishops*b* and deacons:*c*
2 Grace to you and peace from God our Father and the Lord Jesus Christ.

3 I thank my God every time I remember you, 4 constantly praying with joy in every one of my prayers for all of you, 5 because of your sharing in the gospel from the first day until now. 6 I am confident of this, that the one who began a good work among you will bring it to completion by the day of Jesus Christ. 7 It is right for me to think this way about all of you, because you hold me in your heart,*d* for all of you share in God's grace*e* with me, both in my imprisonment and in the defense and confirmation of the gospel. 8 For God is my witness, how I long for all of you with the compassion of Christ Jesus. 9 And this is my prayer, that your love may overflow more and more with knowledge and full insight 10 to help you to determine what is best, so that in the day of Christ you may be pure and blameless, 11 having produced the harvest of righteousness that comes through Jesus Christ for the glory and praise of God.

12 I want you to know, beloved,*f* that what has happened to me has actually helped to spread the gospel, 13 so that it has become known throughout the whole imperial guard*g* and to everyone else that my imprisonment is for Christ; 14 and most of the brothers and sisters,*f* having been made confident in the Lord by my imprisonment, dare to speak the word*h* with greater boldness and without fear. 15 Some proclaim Christ from envy and rivalry, but others from goodwill. 16 These proclaim Christ out of love, knowing that I have been put here for the defense of the gospel; 17 the others proclaim Christ out of selfish ambition, not sincerely but intending to increase my suffering in my imprisonment. 18 What does it matter? Just this, that Christ is proclaimed in every way, whether out of false motives or true; and in that I rejoice.

Yes, and I will continue to rejoice, 19 for I know that through your prayers and the help of the Spirit of Jesus Christ this will turn out for my deliverance. 20 It is my eager expectation and hope that I will not be put to shame in any way, but that by my speaking with all boldness, Christ will be exalted now as always in my body, whether by life or by death. 21 For to me, living is Christ and dying is gain. 22 If I am to live in the flesh, that means fruitful labor for me; and I do not know which I prefer. 23 I am hard pressed between the two: my desire is to depart and be with Christ, for that is far better; 24 but to remain in the flesh is more necessary for you. 25 Since I am convinced of this, I know that I will remain and continue with all of you for your progress and joy in faith, 26 so that I may share abundantly in your boasting in Christ Jesus when I come to you again.

THE LETTER OF PAUL TO THE
Philippians

1 FROM Paul and Timothy, servants of Christ Jesus, to all God's people at Philippi, who are incorporate in Christ Jesus, with the bishops and deacons.
2 Grace to you and peace from God our Father and the Lord Jesus Christ.

3 I thank my God every time I think of you; 4 whenever I pray for you all, my prayers are always joyful, 5 because of the part you have taken in the work of the gospel from the first day until now. 6 Of this I am confident, that he who started the good work in you will bring it to completion by the day of Christ Jesus. 7 It is only natural that I should feel like this about you all, because I have great affection for you, knowing that, both while I am kept in prison and when I am called on to defend the truth of the gospel, you all share in this privilege of mine. 8 God knows how I long for you all with the deep yearning of Christ Jesus himself. 9 And this is my prayer, that your love may grow ever richer in knowledge and insight of every kind, 10 enabling you to learn by experience what things really matter. Then on the day of Christ you will be flawless and without blame, 11 yielding the full harvest of righteousness that comes through Jesus Christ, to the glory and praise of God.

12 My friends, I want you to understand that the progress of the gospel has actually been helped by what has happened to me. 13 It has become common knowledge throughout the imperial guard, and indeed among the public at large, that my imprisonment is in Christ's cause; 14 and my being in prison has given most of our fellow-Christians confidence to speak the word of God fearlessly and with extraordinary courage. 15 Some, it is true, proclaim Christ in a jealous and quarrelsome spirit, but some do it in goodwill. 16 These are moved by love, knowing that it is to defend the gospel that I am where I am; 17 the others are moved by selfish ambition and present Christ from mixed motives, meaning to cause me distress as I lie in prison. 18 What does it matter? One way or another, whether sincerely or not, Christ is proclaimed; and for that I rejoice.

Yes, and I shall go on rejoicing; 19 for I know well that the issue will be my deliverance, because you are praying for me and the Spirit of Jesus Christ is given me for support. 20 It is my confident hope that nothing will daunt me or prevent me from speaking boldly; and that now as always Christ will display his greatness in me, whether the verdict be life or death. 21 For to me life is Christ, and death is gain. 22 If I am to go on living in the body there is fruitful work for me to do. Which then am I to choose? I cannot tell. 23 I am pulled two ways: my own desire is to depart and be with Christ — that is better by far; 24 but for your sake the greater need is for me to remain in the body. 25 This convinces me: I am sure I shall remain, and stand by you all to ensure your progress and joy in the faith, 26 so that on my account you may have even more cause for pride in Christ Jesus — through seeing me restored to you.

The Letter
to the Philippians

Philippians

THE LETTER OF PAUL
TO THE CHURCH AT PHILIPPI

1 Paul and Timothy, slaves of Christ Jesus, to all the holy ones in Christ Jesus who are in Philippi, with the overseers and ministers: 2 grace to you and peace from God our Father and the Lord Jesus Christ.

3 I give thanks to my God at every remembrance of you, 4 praying always with joy in my every prayer for all of you, 5 because of your partnership for the gospel from the first day until now. 6 I am confident of this, that the one who began a good work in you will continue to complete it until the day of Christ Jesus. 7 It is right that I should think this way about all of you, because I hold you in my heart, you who are all partners with me in grace, both in my imprisonment and in the defense and confirmation of the gospel. 8 For God is my witness, how I long for all of you with the affection of Christ Jesus. 9 And this is my prayer: that your love may increase ever more and more in knowledge and every kind of perception, 10 to discern what is of value, so that you may be pure and blameless for the day of Christ, 11 filled with the fruit of righteousness that comes through Jesus Christ for the glory and praise of God.

12 I want you to know, brothers, that my situation has turned out rather to advance the gospel, 13 so that my imprisonment has become well known in Christ throughout the whole praetorium and to all the rest, 14 and so that the majority of the brothers, having taken encouragement in the Lord from my imprisonment, dare more than ever to proclaim the word fearlessly.

15 Of course, some preach Christ from envy and rivalry, others from good will. 16 The latter act out of love, aware that I am here for the defense of the gospel; 17 the former proclaim Christ out of selfish ambition, not from pure motives, thinking that they will cause me trouble in my imprisonment. 18 What difference does it make, as long as in every way, whether in pretense or in truth, Christ is being proclaimed? And in that I rejoice.

Indeed I shall continue to rejoice, 19 for I know that this will result in deliverance for me through your prayers and support from the Spirit of Jesus Christ. 20 My eager expectation and hope is that I shall not be put to shame in any way, but that with all boldness, now as always, Christ will be magnified in my body, whether by life or by death. 21 For to me life is Christ, and death is gain. 22 If I go on living in the flesh, that means fruitful labor for me. And I do not know which I shall choose. 23 I am caught between the two. I long to depart this life and be with Christ, [for] that is far better. 24 Yet that I remain [in] the flesh is more necessary for your benefit. 25 And this I know with confidence, that I shall remain and continue in the service of all of you for your progress and joy in the faith, 26 so that your boasting in Christ Jesus may abound on account of me when I come to you again.

1 Paul and Timothy, servants of Christ Jesus, to all God's holy people in Christ Jesus at Philippi, together with their presiding elders and the deacons. 2 Grace and peace to you from God our Father and the Lord Jesus Christ.

3 I thank my God whenever I think of you, 4 and every time I pray for you all, I always pray with joy 5 for your partnership in the gospel from the very first day up to the present. 6 I am quite confident that the One who began a good work in you will go on completing it until the Day of Jesus Christ comes. 7 It is only right that I should feel like this towards you all, because you have a place in my heart, since you have all shared together in the grace that has been mine, both my chains and my work defending and establishing the gospel. 8 For God will testify for me how much I long for you all with the warm longing of Christ Jesus; 9 it is my prayer that your love for one another may grow more and more with the knowledge and complete understanding 10 that will help you to come to true discernment, so that you will be innocent and free of any trace of guilt when the Day of Christ comes, 11 entirely filled with the fruits of uprightness through Jesus Christ, for the glory and praise of God.

12 Now I want you to realise, brothers, that the circumstances of my present life are helping rather than hindering the advance of the gospel. 13 My chains in Christ have become well known not only to all the Praetorium,[a] but to everybody else, 14 and so most of the brothers in the Lord have gained confidence from my chains and are getting more and more daring in announcing the Message without any fear. 15 It is true that some of them are preaching Christ out of malice and rivalry; but there are many as well whose intentions are good; 16 some are doing it out of love, knowing that I remain firm in my defence of the gospel. 17 There are others who are proclaiming Christ out of jealousy, not in sincerity but meaning to add to the weight of my chains. 18 But what does it matter? Only that in both ways, whether with false motives or true, Christ is proclaimed, and for that I am happy; 19 and I shall go on being happy, too, because I know that *this is what will save me*,[b] with your prayers and with the support of the Spirit of Jesus Christ; 20 all in accordance with my most confident hope and trust that I shall never have to admit defeat, but with complete fearlessness I shall go on, so that now, as always, Christ will be glorified in my body, whether by my life or my death. 21 Life to me, of course, is Christ, but then death would be a positive gain. 22 On the other hand again, if to be alive in the body gives me an opportunity for fruitful work, I do not know which I should choose. 23 I am caught in this dilemma: I want to be gone and to be with Christ, and this is by far the stronger desire — 24 and yet for your sake to stay alive in this body is a more urgent need. 25 This much I know for certain, that I shall stay and stand by you all, to encourage your advance and your joy in the faith, 26 so that my return to be among you may increase to overflowing your pride in Jesus Christ on my account.

---

a 1 The headquarters of the Praetorian guard wherever Paul is captive (Ephesus, Caesarea, Rome?). b 1 Jb 13:16.

27 Only, live your life in a manner worthy of the gospel of Christ, so that, whether I come and see you or am absent and hear about you, I will know that you are standing firm in one spirit, striving side by side with one mind for the faith of the gospel, 28 and are in no way intimidated by your opponents. For them this is evidence of their destruction, but of your salvation. And this is God's doing. 29 For he has graciously granted you the privilege not only of believing in Christ, but of suffering for him as well — 30 since you are having the same struggle that you saw I had and now hear that I still have.

2 If then there is any encouragement in Christ, any consolation from love, any sharing in the Spirit, any compassion and sympathy, 2 make my joy complete: be of the same mind, having the same love, being in full accord and of one mind. 3 Do nothing from selfish ambition or conceit, but in humility regard others as better than yourselves. 4 Let each of you look not to your own interests, but to the interests of others. 5 Let the same mind be in you that was*i* in Christ Jesus,

6   who, though he was in the form of God,
      did not regard equality with God
      as something to be exploited,
7   but emptied himself,
      taking the form of a slave,
      being born in human likeness.
  And being found in human form,
8   he humbled himself
      and became obedient to the point of death —
      even death on a cross.
9   Therefore God also highly exalted him
      and gave him the name
      that is above every name,
10   so that at the name of Jesus
      every knee should bend,
      in heaven and on earth and under the earth,
11   and every tongue should confess
      that Jesus Christ is Lord,
      to the glory of God the Father.

12 Therefore, my beloved, just as you have always obeyed me, not only in my presence, but much more now in my absence, work out your own salvation with fear and trembling; 13 for it is God who is at work in you, enabling you both to will and to work for his good pleasure.

14 Do all things without murmuring and arguing, 15 so that you may be blameless and innocent, children of God without blemish in the midst of a crooked and perverse generation, in which you shine like stars in the world. 16 It is by your holding fast to the word of life that I can boast on the day of Christ that I did not run in vain or labor in vain. 17 But even if I am being poured out as a libation over the sacrifice and the offering of your faith, I am glad and rejoice with all of you — 18 and in the same way you also must be glad and rejoice with me.

19 I hope in the Lord Jesus to send Timothy to you soon, so that I may be cheered by news of you. 20 I have no one like him who will be genuinely concerned for your welfare. 21 All of them are seeking their own interests, not those of Jesus Christ. 22 But Timothy's *j* worth you know, how like a son with a father he has served with me in the work of the gospel. 23 I hope therefore to send him as soon

27 WHATEVER happens, let your conduct be worthy of the gospel of Christ, so that whether or not I come and see you for myself I may hear that you are standing firm, united in spirit and in mind, side by side in the struggle to advance the gospel faith, 28 meeting your opponents without so much as a tremor. This is a sure sign to them that destruction is in store for them and salvation for you, a sign from God himself; 29 for you have been granted the privilege not only of believing in Christ but also of suffering for him. 30 Your conflict is the same as mine; once you saw me in it, and now you hear I am in it still.

2 If then our common life in Christ yields anything to stir the heart, any consolation of love, any participation in the Spirit, any warmth of affection or compassion, 2 fill up my cup of happiness by thinking and feeling alike, with the same love for one another and a common attitude of mind. 3 Leave no room for selfish ambition and vanity, but humbly reckon others better than yourselves. 4 Look to each other's interests and not merely to your own.

5 Take to heart among yourselves what you find in Christ Jesus: 6 'He was in the form of God; yet he laid no claim to equality with God, 7 but made himself nothing, assuming the form of a slave. Bearing the human likeness, 8 sharing the human lot, he humbled himself, and was obedient, even to the point of death, death on a cross! 9 Therefore God raised him to the heights and bestowed on him the name above all names, 10 that at the name of Jesus every knee should bow — in heaven, on earth, and in the depths — 11 and every tongue acclaim, "Jesus Christ is Lord," to the glory of God the Father.'

12 So you too, my friends, must be obedient, as always; even more, now that I am absent, than when I was with you. You must work out your own salvation in fear and trembling; 13 for it is God who works in you, inspiring both the will and the deed, for his own chosen purpose.

14 Do everything without grumbling or argument. 15 Show yourselves innocent and above reproach, faultless children of God in a crooked and depraved generation, in which you shine like stars in a dark world 16 and proffer the word of life. Then you will be my pride on the day of Christ, proof that I did not run my race in vain or labour in vain. 17 But if my life-blood is to be poured out to complete the sacrifice and offering up of your faith, I rejoice and share my joy with you all. 18 You too must rejoice and share your joy with me.

19 I HOPE, in the Lord Jesus, to send Timothy to you soon; it will cheer me up to have news of you. 20 I have no one else here like him, who has a genuine concern for your affairs; 21 they are all bent on their own interests, not on those of Christ Jesus. 22 But Timothy's record is known to you: you know that he has been at my side in the service of the gospel like a son working under his father. 23 So he is the one I mean to send as soon as I see how things go with

---

i Or *that you have*   *j* Gk *his*

2:20 **no one . . . who has:** *or* no one else here who sees things as I do, and has.

NEW AMERICAN BIBLE | NEW JERUSALEM BIBLE

27 Only, conduct yourselves in a way worthy of the gospel of Christ, so that, whether I come and see you or am absent, I may hear news of you, that you are standing firm in one spirit, with one mind struggling together for the faith of the gospel, 28 not intimidated in any way by your opponents. This is proof to them of destruction, but of your salvation. And this is God's doing. 29 For to you has been granted, for the sake of Christ, not only to believe in him but also to suffer for him. 30 Yours is the same struggle as you saw in me and now hear about me.

2 If there is any encouragement in Christ, any solace in love, any participation in the Spirit, any compassion and mercy, 2 complete my joy by being of the same mind, with the same love, united in heart, thinking one thing. 3 Do nothing out of selfishness or out of vainglory; rather, humbly regard others as more important than yourselves, 4 each looking out not for his own interests, but [also] everyone for those of others.

5 Have among yourselves the same attitude that is also yours in Christ Jesus,

6 Who, though he was in the form of God,
did not regard equality with God something to
be grasped.
7 Rather, he emptied himself,
taking the form of a slave,
coming in human likeness;
and found human in appearance,
8 he humbled himself,
becoming obedient to death,
even death on a cross.
9 Because of this, God greatly exalted him
and bestowed on him the name
that is above every name,
10 that at the name of Jesus
every knee should bend,
of those in heaven and on earth and under
the earth,
11 and every tongue confess that
Jesus Christ is Lord,
to the glory of God the Father.

12 So then, my beloved, obedient as you have always been, not only when I am present but all the more now when I am absent, work out your salvation with fear and trembling. 13 For God is the one who, for his good purpose, works in you both to desire and to work. 14 Do everything without grumbling or questioning, 15 that you may be blameless and innocent, children of God without blemish in the midst of a crooked and perverse generation, among whom you shine like lights in the world, 16 as you hold on to the word of life, so that my boast for the day of Christ may be that I did not run in vain or labor in vain. 17 But, even if I am poured out as a libation upon the sacrificial service of your faith, I rejoice and share my joy with all of you. 18 In the same way you also should rejoice and share your joy with me.

19 I hope, in the Lord Jesus, to send Timothy to you soon, so that I too may be heartened by hearing news of you. 20 For I have no one comparable to him for genuine interest in whatever concerns you. 21 For they all seek their own interests, not those of Jesus Christ. 22 But you know his worth, how as a child with a father he served along with me in the cause of the gospel. 23 He it is, then, whom I hope to send as soon as I see how things go with me, 24 but I am

27 But you must always behave in a way that is worthy of the gospel of Christ, so that whether I come to you and see for myself or whether I only hear all about you from a distance, I shall find that you are standing firm and united in spirit, battling, as a team with a single aim, for the faith of the gospel, 28 undismayed by any of your opponents. This will be a clear sign, for them that they are to be lost, and for you that you are to be saved. 29 This comes from God, for you have been granted the privilege for Christ's sake not only of believing in him but of suffering for him as well; 30 you are fighting the same battle which you saw me fighting for him and which you hear I am fighting still.

2 So if in Christ there is anything that will move you, any incentive in love, any fellowship in the Spirit, any warmth or sympathy—I appeal to you, 2 make my joy complete by being of a single mind, one in love, one in heart and one in mind. 3 Nothing is to be done out of jealousy or vanity; instead, out of humility of mind everyone should give preference to others, 4 everyone pursuing not selfish interests but those of others. 5 Make your own the mind of Christ Jesus:

6 Who, being in the form of God,
did not count equality with God
something to be grasped.
7 But he emptied himself,
taking the form of a slave,
becoming as human beings are;
and being in every way like a human being,
8 he was humbler yet,
even to accepting death, death on a cross.
9 And for this God raised him high,
and gave him the name
which is above all other names;
10 so that all beings
in the heavens, on earth and in the underworld,
should bend the knee at the name of Jesus
11 and that every tongue should acknowledge c
Jesus Christ as Lord,
to the glory of God the Father.

12 So, my dear friends, you have always been obedient; your obedience must not be limited to times when I am present. Now that I am absent it must be more in evidence, so work out your salvation in fear and trembling. 13 It is God who, for his own generous purpose, gives you the intention and the powers to act. 14 Let your behaviour be free of murmuring and complaining 15 so that you remain faultless and pure, unspoilt children of God surrounded by a deceitful and underhand brood, d shining out among them like bright stars in the world, 16 proffering to it the Word of life. Then I shall have reason to be proud on the Day of Christ, for it will not be for nothing that I have run the race and toiled so hard. 17 Indeed, even if my blood has to be poured as a libation over your sacrifice and the offering of your faith, then I shall be glad and join in your rejoicing — 18 and in the same way, you must be glad and join in my rejoicing.

19 I hope, in the Lord Jesus, to send Timothy to you soon, so that my mind may be set at rest when I hear how you are. 20 There is nobody else that I can send who is like him and cares as sincerely for your well-being; 21 they all want to work for themselves, not for Jesus Christ. 22 But you know what sort of person he has proved himself, working with me for the sake of the gospel like a son with his father. 23 That is the man, then, that I am hoping to send to you immediately I can make out what is going to happen to me; 24 but

c 2 Is 45:23.   d 2 Dt 32:5.

NEW REVISED STANDARD VERSION	REVISED ENGLISH BIBLE

as I see how things go with me; 24 and I trust in the Lord that I will also come soon.

25 Still, I think it necessary to send to you Epaphroditus — my brother and co-worker and fellow soldier, your messenger[k] and minister to my need; 26 for he has been longing for[l] all of you, and has been distressed because you heard that he was ill. 27 He was indeed so ill that he nearly died. But God had mercy on him, and not only on him but on me also, so that I would not have one sorrow after another. 28 I am the more eager to send him, therefore, in order that you may rejoice at seeing him again, and that I may be less anxious. 29 Welcome him then in the Lord with all joy, and honor such people, 30 because he came close to death for the work of Christ,[m] risking his life to make up for those services that you could not give me.

3 Finally, my brothers and sisters,[n] rejoice[o] in the Lord.

To write the same things to you is not troublesome to me, and for you it is a safeguard.
2 Beware of the dogs, beware of the evil workers, beware of those who mutilate the flesh![p] 3 For it is we who are the circumcision, who worship in the Spirit of God[q] and boast in Christ Jesus and have no confidence in the flesh — 4 even though I, too, have reason for confidence in the flesh.

If anyone else has reason to be confident in the flesh, I have more: 5 circumcised on the eighth day, a member of the people of Israel, of the tribe of Benjamin, a Hebrew born of Hebrews; as to the law, a Pharisee; 6 as to zeal, a persecutor of the church; as to righteousness under the law, blameless.

7 Yet whatever gains I had, these I have come to regard as loss because of Christ. 8 More than that, I regard everything as loss because of the surpassing value of knowing Christ Jesus my Lord. For his sake I have suffered the loss of all things, and I regard them as rubbish, in order that I may gain Christ 9 and be found in him, not having a righteousness of my own that comes from the law, but one that comes through faith in Christ,[r] the righteousness from God based on faith. 10 I want to know Christ[s] and the power of his resurrection and the sharing of his sufferings by becoming like him in his death, 11 if somehow I may attain the resurrection from the dead.

12 Not that I have already obtained this or have already reached the goal;[t] but I press on to make it my own, because Christ Jesus has made me his own. 13 Beloved,[u] I do not consider that I have made it my own;[v] but this one thing I do: forgetting what lies behind and straining forward to what lies ahead, 14 I press on toward the goal for the prize of the heavenly[w] call of God in Christ Jesus. 15 Let those of us then who are mature be of the same mind; and if you think differently about anything, this too God will reveal to you. 16 Only let us hold fast to what we have attained.

17 Brothers and sisters,[u] join in imitating me, and observe those who live according to the example you have in us. 18 For many live as enemies of the cross of Christ; I have often told you of them, and now I tell you even with tears. 19 Their end is destruction; their god is the belly; and their glory is in their shame; their minds are set on earthly things. 20 But our citizenship[x] is in heaven, and it is from there that we are expecting a Savior, the Lord Jesus Christ. 21 He will

me; 24 and I am confident, in the Lord, that I shall be coming myself before long.

25 I have decided I must also send our brother Epaphroditus, my fellow-worker and comrade, whom you commissioned to attend to my needs. 26 He has been missing you all, and was upset because you heard he was ill. 27 Indeed he was dangerously ill, but God was merciful to him; and not only to him but to me, to spare me one sorrow on top of another. 28 For this reason I am all the more eager to send him and give you the happiness of seeing him again; that will relieve my anxiety as well. 29 Welcome him then in the fellowship of the Lord with wholehearted delight. You should honour people like him; 30 in Christ's cause he came near to death, risking his life to render me the service you could not give. **3** 1 And now, my friends, I wish you joy in the Lord.

TO REPEAT what I have written to you before is no trouble to me, and it is a safeguard for you. 2 Be on your guard against those dogs, those who do nothing but harm and who insist on mutilation — 'circumcision' I will not call it; 3 we are the circumcision, we who worship by the Spirit of God, whose pride is in Christ Jesus, and who put no confidence in the physical. 4 It is not that I am myself without grounds for such confidence. If anyone makes claims of that kind, I can make a stronger case for myself: 5 circumcised on my eighth day, Israelite by race, of the tribe of Benjamin, a Hebrew born and bred; in my practice of the law a Pharisee, 6 in zeal for religion a persecutor of the church, by the law's standard of righteousness without fault. 7 But all such assets I have written off because of Christ. 8 More than that, I count everything sheer loss, far outweighed by the gain of knowing Christ Jesus my Lord, for whose sake I did in fact forfeit everything. I count it so much rubbish, for the sake of gaining Christ 9 and finding myself in union with him, with no righteousness of my own based on the law, nothing but the righteousness which comes from faith in Christ, given by God in response to faith. 10 My one desire is to know Christ and the power of his resurrection, and to share his sufferings in growing conformity with his death, 11 in hope of somehow attaining the resurrection from the dead.

12 It is not that I have already achieved this. I have not yet reached perfection, but I press on, hoping to take hold of that for which Christ once took hold of me. 13 My friends, I do not claim to have hold of it yet. What I do say is this: forgetting what is behind and straining towards what lies ahead, 14 I press towards the finishing line, to win the heavenly prize to which God has called me in Christ Jesus.

15 We who are mature should keep to this way of thinking. If on any point you think differently, this also God will make plain to you. 16 Only let our conduct be consistent with what we have already attained.

17 Join together, my friends, in following my example. You have us for a model; imitate those whose way of life conforms to it. 18 As I have often told you, and now tell you with tears, there are many whose way of life makes them enemies of the cross of Christ. 19 They are heading for destruction, they make appetite their god, they take pride in what should bring shame; their minds are set on earthly things. 20 We, by contrast, are citizens of heaven, and from heaven we expect our deliverer to come, the Lord Jesus Christ. 21 He will transfigure our humble bodies, and give

---

[k] Gk apostle [l] Other ancient authorities read longing to see
[m] Other ancient authorities read of the Lord [n] Gk my brothers
[o] Or farewell [p] Gk the mutilation [q] Other ancient authorities
read worship God in spirit [r] Or through the faith of Christ
[s] Gk him [t] Or have already been made perfect [u] Gk Brothers
[v] Other ancient authorities read my own yet [w] Gk upward
[x] Or commonwealth

3:3 who worship . . . God: some witnesses read who worship God
in the spirit; one reads whose worship is spiritual.

confident in the Lord that I myself will also come soon. 25 With regard to Epaphroditus, my brother and co-worker and fellow soldier, your messenger and minister in my need, I consider it necessary to send him to you. 26 For he has been longing for all of you and was distressed because you heard that he was ill. 27 He was indeed ill, close to death; but God had mercy on him, not just on him but also on me, so that I might not have sorrow upon sorrow. 28 I send him therefore with the greater eagerness, so that, on seeing him, you may rejoice again, and I may have less anxiety. 29 Welcome him then in the Lord with all joy and hold such people in esteem, 30 because for the sake of the work of Christ he came close to death, risking his life to make up for those services to me that you could not perform.

3 Finally, my brothers, rejoice in the Lord. Writing the same things to you is no burden for me but is a safeguard for you.

2 Beware of the dogs! Beware of the evil-workers! Beware of the mutilation! 3 For we are the circumcision, we who worship through the Spirit of God, who boast in Christ Jesus and do not put our confidence in flesh, 4 although I myself have grounds for confidence even in the flesh.

If anyone else thinks he can be confident in flesh, all the more can I. 5 Circumcised on the eighth day, of the race of Israel, of the tribe of Benjamin, a Hebrew of Hebrew parentage, in observance of the law a Pharisee, 6 in zeal I persecuted the church, in righteousness based on the law I was blameless.

7 [But] whatever gains I had, these I have come to consider a loss because of Christ. 8 More than that, I even consider everything as a loss because of the supreme good of knowing Christ Jesus my Lord. For his sake I have accepted the loss of all things and I consider them so much rubbish, that I may gain Christ 9 and be found in him, not having any righteousness of my own based on the law but that which comes through faith in Christ, the righteousness from God, depending on faith 10 to know him and the power of his resurrection and [the] sharing of his sufferings by being conformed to his death, 11 if somehow I may attain the resurrection from the dead.

12 It is not that I have already taken hold of it or have already attained perfect maturity, but I continue my pursuit in hope that I may possess it, since I have indeed been taken possession of by Christ [Jesus]. 13 Brothers, I for my part do not consider myself to have taken possession. Just one thing: forgetting what lies behind but straining forward to what lies ahead, 14 I continue my pursuit toward the goal, the prize of God's upward calling, in Christ Jesus. 15 Let us, then, who are "perfectly mature" adopt this attitude. And if you have a different attitude, this too God will reveal to you. 16 Only, with regard to what we have attained, continue on the same course.

17 Join with others in being imitators of me, brothers, and observe those who thus conduct themselves according to the model you have in us. 18 For many, as I have often told you and now tell you even in tears, conduct themselves as enemies of the cross of Christ. 19 Their end is destruction. Their God is their stomach; their glory is in their "shame." Their minds are occupied with earthly things. 20 But our citizenship is in heaven, and from it we also await a savior, the Lord Jesus Christ. 21 He will change our lowly body to

I am confident in the Lord that I shall come myself, too, before long. 25 Nevertheless I thought it essential to send to you Epaphroditus, my brother and fellow-worker and companion-in-arms since he came as your representative to look after my needs; 26 because he was missing you all and was worrying because you had heard that he was ill. 27 Indeed he was seriously ill, and nearly died; but God took pity on him — and not only on him but also on me, to spare me one grief on top of another. 28 So I am sending him back as promptly as I can so that you will have the joy of seeing him again, and that will be some comfort to me in my distress. 29 Welcome him in the Lord, then, with all joy; hold people like him in honour, 30 because it was for Christ's work that he came so near to dying, risking his life to do the duty to me which you could not do yourselves.

3 Finally, brothers, I wish you joy in the Lord.

To write to you what I have already written before is no trouble to me and to you will be a protection. 2 Beware of dogs! Beware of evil workmen! Beware of self-mutilators! 3 We are the true people of the circumcision since we worship by the Spirit of God and make Christ Jesus our only boast, not relying on physical qualifications, 4 although, I myself could rely on these too. If anyone does claim to rely on them, my claim is better. 5 Circumcised on the eighth day of my life, I was born of the race of Israel, of the tribe of Benjamin, a Hebrew born of Hebrew parents. In the matter of the Law, I was a Pharisee; 6 as for religious fervour, I was a persecutor of the Church; as for the uprightness embodied in the Law, I was faultless. 7 But what were once my assets I now through Christ Jesus count as losses. 8 Yes, I will go further: because of the supreme advantage of knowing Christ Jesus my Lord, I count everything else as loss. For him I have accepted the loss of all other things, and look on them all as filth if only I can gain Christ 9 and be given a place in him, with the uprightness I have gained not from the Law, but through faith in Christ, an uprightness from God, based on faith, 10 that I may come to know him and the power of his resurrection, and partake of his sufferings by being moulded to the pattern of his death, 11 striving towards the goal of resurrection from the dead. 12 Not that I have secured it already, nor yet reached my goal, but I am still pursuing it in the attempt to take hold of the prize for which Christ Jesus took hold of me. 13 Brothers, I do not reckon myself as having taken hold of it; I can only say that forgetting all that lies behind me, and straining forward to what lies in front, 14 I am racing towards the finishing-point to win the prize of God's heavenly call in Christ Jesus. 15 So this is the way in which all of us who are mature should be thinking, and if you are still thinking differently in any way, then God has yet to make this matter clear to you. 16 Meanwhile, let us go forward from the point we have each attained.

17 Brothers, be united in imitating me. Keep your eyes fixed on those who act according to the example you have from me. 18 For there are so many people of whom I have often warned you, and now I warn you again with tears in my eyes, who behave like the enemies of Christ's cross. 19 They are destined to be lost; their god is the stomach; they glory in what they should think shameful, since their minds are set on earthly things. 20 But our homeland is in heaven and it is from there that we are expecting a Saviour, the Lord Jesus Christ, 21 who will transfigure the wretched body

NEW REVISED STANDARD VERSION	REVISED ENGLISH BIBLE

transform the body of our humiliation*y* that it may be conformed to the body of his glory,*z* by the power that also enables him to make all things subject to himself.

4 [1] Therefore, my brothers and sisters,*a* whom I love and long for, my joy and crown, stand firm in the Lord in this way, my beloved.

[2] I urge Euodia and I urge Syntyche to be of the same mind in the Lord. [3] Yes, and I ask you also, my loyal companion,*b* help these women, for they have struggled beside me in the work of the gospel, together with Clement and the rest of my co-workers, whose names are in the book of life.

[4] Rejoice*c* in the Lord always; again I will say, Rejoice.*c* [5] Let your gentleness be known to everyone. The Lord is near. [6] Do not worry about anything, but in everything by prayer and supplication with thanksgiving let your requests be made known to God. [7] And the peace of God, which surpasses all understanding, will guard your hearts and your minds in Christ Jesus.

[8] Finally, beloved,*d* whatever is true, whatever is honorable, whatever is just, whatever is pure, whatever is pleasing, whatever is commendable, if there is any excellence and if there is anything worthy of praise, think about*e* these things. [9] Keep on doing the things that you have learned and received and heard and seen in me, and the God of peace will be with you.

[10] I rejoice*f* in the Lord greatly that now at last you have revived your concern for me; indeed, you were concerned for me, but had no opportunity to show it.*g* [11] Not that I am referring to being in need; for I have learned to be content with whatever I have. [12] I know what it is to have little, and I know what it is to have plenty. In any and all circumstances I have learned the secret of being well-fed and of going hungry, of having plenty and of being in need. [13] I can do all things through him who strengthens me. [14] In any case, it was kind of you to share my distress.

[15] You Philippians indeed know that in the early days of the gospel, when I left Macedonia, no church shared with me in the matter of giving and receiving, except you alone. [16] For even when I was in Thessalonica, you sent me help for my needs more than once. [17] Not that I seek the gift, but I seek the profit that accumulates to your account. [18] I have been paid in full and have more than enough; I am fully satisfied, now that I have received from Epaphroditus the gifts you sent, a fragrant offering, a sacrifice acceptable and pleasing to God. [19] And my God will fully satisfy every need of yours according to his riches in glory in Christ Jesus. [20] To our God and Father be glory forever and ever. Amen.

[21] Greet every saint in Christ Jesus. The friends*d* who are with me greet you. [22] All the saints greet you, especially those of the emperor's household.

[23] The grace of the Lord Jesus Christ be with your spirit.*h*

them a form like that of his own glorious body, by that power which enables him to make all things subject to

4 himself. [1] This, my dear friends, whom I love and long for, my joy and crown, this is what it means to stand firm in the Lord.

[2] Euodia and Syntyche, I appeal to you both: agree together in the Lord. [3] Yes, and you too, my loyal comrade, I ask you to help these women, who shared my struggles in the cause of the gospel, with Clement and my other fellow-workers, who are enrolled in the book of life.

[4] I wish you joy in the Lord always. Again I say: all joy be yours.

[5] Be known to everyone for your consideration of others.

The Lord is near; [6] do not be anxious, but in everything make your requests known to God in prayer and petition with thanksgiving. [7] Then the peace of God, which is beyond all understanding, will guard your hearts and your thoughts in Christ Jesus.

[8] And now, my friends, all that is true, all that is noble, all that is just and pure, all that is lovable and attractive, whatever is excellent and admirable—fill your thoughts with these things.

[9] Put into practice the lessons I taught you, the tradition I have passed on, all that you heard me say or saw me do; and the God of peace will be with you.

[10] It is a great joy to me in the Lord that after so long your care for me has now revived. I know you always cared; it was opportunity you lacked. [11] Not that I am speaking of want, for I have learned to be self-sufficient whatever my circumstances. [12] I know what it is to have nothing, and I know what it is to have plenty. I have been thoroughly initiated into fullness and hunger, plenty and poverty. [13] I am able to face anything through him who gives me strength. [14] All the same, it was kind of you to share the burden of my troubles.

[15] You Philippians are aware that, when I set out from Macedonia in the early days of my mission, yours was the only church to share with me in the giving and receiving; [16] more than once you contributed to my needs, even at Thessalonica. [17] Do not think I set my heart on the gift; all I care for is the interest mounting up in your account. [18] I have been paid in full; I have all I need and more, now that I have received from Epaphroditus what you sent. It is a fragrant offering, an acceptable sacrifice, pleasing to God. [19] And my God will supply all your needs out of the magnificence of his riches in Christ Jesus. [20] To our God and Father be glory for ever and ever! Amen.

[21] Give my greetings, in the fellowship of Christ Jesus, to each one of God's people. My colleagues send their greetings to you, [22] and so do all God's people here, particularly those in the emperor's service.

[23] The grace of our Lord Jesus Christ be with your spirit.

---

y Or *our humble bodies*   *z* Or *his glorious body*   *a* Gk *my brothers*   *b* Or *loyal Syzygus*   *c* Or *Farewell*   *d* Gk *brothers*   *e* Gk *take account of*   *f* Gk *I rejoiced*   *g* Gk lacks *to show it*   *h* Other ancient authorities add *Amen*

NEW AMERICAN BIBLE

NEW JERUSALEM BIBLE

conform with his glorified body by the power that enables him also to bring all things into subjection to himself.

4 Therefore, my brothers, whom I love and long for, my joy and crown, in this way stand firm in the Lord, beloved.

2 I urge Euodia and I urge Syntyche to come to a mutual understanding in the Lord. 3 Yes, and I ask you also, my true yokemate, to help them, for they have struggled at my side in promoting the gospel, along with Clement and my other co-workers, whose names are in the book of life.

4 Rejoice in the Lord always. I shall say it again: rejoice! 5 Your kindness should be known to all. The Lord is near. 6 Have no anxiety at all, but in everything, by prayer and petition, with thanksgiving, make your requests known to God. 7 Then the peace of God that surpasses all understanding will guard your hearts and minds in Christ Jesus.

8 Finally, brothers, whatever is true, whatever is honorable, whatever is just, whatever is pure, whatever is lovely, whatever is gracious, if there is any excellence and if there is anything worthy of praise, think about these things. 9 Keep on doing what you have learned and received and heard and seen in me. Then the God of peace will be with you.

10 I rejoice greatly in the Lord that now at last you revived your concern for me. You were, of course, concerned about me but lacked an opportunity. 11 Not that I say this because of need, for I have learned, in whatever situation I find myself, to be self-sufficient. 12 I know indeed how to live in humble circumstances; I know also how to live with abundance. In every circumstance and in all things I have learned the secret of being well fed and of going hungry, of living in abundance and of being in need. 13 I have the strength for everything through him who empowers me. 14 Still, it was kind of you to share in my distress.

15 You Philippians indeed know that at the beginning of the gospel, when I left Macedonia, not a single church shared with me in an account of giving and receiving, except you alone. 16 For even when I was at Thessalonica you sent me something for my needs, not only once but more than once. 17 It is not that I am eager for the gift; rather, I am eager for the profit that accrues to your account. 18 I have received full payment and I abound. I am very well supplied because of what I received from you through Epaphroditus, "a fragrant aroma," an acceptable sacrifice, pleasing to God. 19 My God will fully supply whatever you need, in accord with his glorious riches in Christ Jesus. 20 To our God and Father, glory for ever and ever. Amen.

21 Give my greetings to every holy one in Christ Jesus. The brothers who are with me send you their greetings; 22 all the holy ones send you their greetings, especially those of Caesar's household. 23 The grace of the Lord Jesus Christ be with your spirit.

of ours into the mould of his glorious body, through the working of the power which he has, even to bring all things under his mastery.

4 So then, my brothers and dear friends whom I miss so much, my joy and my crown, hold firm in the Lord, dear friends.

2 I urge Euodia, and I urge Syntyche to come to agreement with each other in the Lord; 3 and I ask you, Syzygus, really to be a 'partner' *e* and help them. These women have struggled hard for the gospel with me, along with Clement and all my other fellow-workers, whose names are written in the book of life.

4 Always be joyful, then, in the Lord; I repeat, be joyful. 5 Let your good sense be obvious to everybody. The Lord is near. 6 Never worry about anything; but tell God all your desires of every kind in prayer and petition shot through with gratitude, 7 and the peace of God which is beyond our understanding will guard your hearts and your thoughts in Christ Jesus. 8 Finally, brothers, let your minds be filled with everything that is true, everything that is honourable, everything that is upright and pure, everything that we love and admire — with whatever is good and praiseworthy. 9 Keep doing everything you learnt from me and were told by me and have heard or seen me doing. Then the God of peace will be with you.

10 As for me, I am full of joy in the Lord, now that at last your consideration for me has blossomed again; though I recognise that you really did have consideration before, but had no opportunity to show it. 11 I do not say this because I have lacked anything; I have learnt to manage with whatever I have. 12 I know how to live modestly, and I know how to live luxuriously too: in every way now I have mastered the secret of all conditions: full stomach and empty stomach, plenty and poverty. 13 There is nothing I cannot do in the One who strengthens me. 14 All the same, it was good of you to share with me in my hardships. 15 In the early days of the gospel, as you of Philippi well know, when I left Macedonia, no church other than yourselves made common account with me in the matter of expenditure and receipts. You were the only ones; 16 and what is more, you have twice sent me what I needed in Thessalonica. 17 It is not the gift that I value most; what I value is the interest that is mounting up in your account. 18 I have all that I need and more: I am fully provided, now that I have received from Epaphroditus the offering that you sent, *a pleasing smell,f* the sacrifice which is acceptable and pleasing to God. 19 And my God will fulfil all your needs out of the riches of his glory in Christ Jesus. 20 And so glory be to God our Father, for ever and ever. Amen.

21 My greetings to every one of God's holy people in Christ Jesus. The brothers who are with me send you their greetings. 22 All God's holy people send you their greetings, especially those of Caesar's household.

23 May the grace of the Lord Jesus Christ be with your spirit.

e **4** Syzygus means 'yoke-fellow' or 'partner'.   *f* **4** Gn 8:21.

THE LETTER OF PAUL TO THE
Colossians

THE LETTER OF PAUL TO THE
Colossians

1 Paul, an apostle of Christ Jesus by the will of God, and Timothy our brother,

2 To the saints and faithful brothers and sisters*a* in Christ in Colossae:

Grace to you and peace from God our Father.

3 In our prayers for you we always thank God, the Father of our Lord Jesus Christ, 4 for we have heard of your faith in Christ Jesus and of the love that you have for all the saints, 5 because of the hope laid up for you in heaven. You have heard of this hope before in the word of the truth, the gospel 6 that has come to you. Just as it is bearing fruit and growing in the whole world, so it has been bearing fruit among yourselves from the day you heard it and truly comprehended the grace of God. 7 This you learned from Epaphras, our beloved fellow servant.*b* He is a faithful minister of Christ on your*c* behalf, 8 and he has made known to us your love in the Spirit.

9 For this reason, since the day we heard it, we have not ceased praying for you and asking that you may be filled with the knowledge of God's*d* will in all spiritual wisdom and understanding, 10 so that you may lead lives worthy of the Lord, fully pleasing to him, as you bear fruit in every good work and as you grow in the knowledge of God. 11 May you be made strong with all the strength that comes from his glorious power, and may you be prepared to endure everything with patience, while joyfully 12 giving thanks to the Father, who has enabled*e* you*f* to share in the inheritance of the saints in the light. 13 He has rescued us from the power of darkness and transferred us into the kingdom of his beloved Son, 14 in whom we have redemption, the forgiveness of sins.*g*

15 He is the image of the invisible God, the firstborn of all creation; 16 for in*h* him all things in heaven and on earth were created, things visible and invisible, whether thrones or dominions or rulers or powers—all things have been created through him and for him. 17 He himself is before all things, and in*h* him all things hold together. 18 He is the head of the body, the church; he is the beginning, the firstborn from the dead, so that he might come to have first place in everything. 19 For in him all the fullness of God was pleased to dwell, 20 and through him God was pleased to reconcile to himself all things, whether on earth or in heaven, by making peace through the blood of his cross. 21 And you who were once estranged and hostile in mind, doing evil deeds, 22 he has now reconciled*i* in his

1 FROM Paul, by the will of God apostle of Christ Jesus, and our colleague Timothy, 2 to God's people at Colossae, our fellow-believers in Christ.

Grace to you and peace from God our Father.

3 In all our prayers to God, the Father of our Lord Jesus Christ, we thank him for you, 4 because we have heard of your faith in Christ Jesus and the love you bear towards all God's people; 5 both spring from that hope stored up for you in heaven of which you learned when the message of the true gospel first 6 came to you. That same gospel is bearing fruit and making new growth the whole world over, as it does among you and has done since the day when you heard of God's grace and learned what it truly is. 7 It was Epaphras, our dear fellow-servant and a trusted worker for Christ on our behalf, who taught you this, 8 and it is he who has brought us news of the love the Spirit has awakened in you.

9 THIS is why, ever since we first heard about you, we have not ceased to pray for you. We ask God that you may receive from him full insight into his will, all wisdom and spiritual understanding, 10 so that your manner of life may be worthy of the Lord and entirely pleasing to him. We pray that you may bear fruit in active goodness of every kind, and grow in knowledge of God. 11 In his glorious might may he give you ample strength to meet with fortitude and patience whatever comes; 12 and to give joyful thanks to the Father who has made you fit to share the heritage of God's people in the realm of light.

13 He rescued us from the domain of darkness and brought us into the kingdom of his dear Son, 14 through whom our release is secured and our sins are forgiven. 15 He is the image of the invisible God; his is the primacy over all creation. 16 In him everything in heaven and on earth was created, not only things visible but also the invisible orders of thrones, sovereignties, authorities, and powers: the whole universe has been created through him and for him. 17 He exists before all things, and all things are held together in him. 18 He is the head of the body, the church. He is its origin, the first to return from the dead, to become in all things supreme. 19 For in him God in all his fullness chose to dwell, 20 and through him to reconcile all things to himself, making peace through the shedding of his blood on the cross—all things, whether on earth or in heaven.

21-22 Formerly you yourselves were alienated from God, his enemies in heart and mind, as your evil deeds showed. But now by Christ's death in his body of flesh and blood

---

a Gk *brothers*   *b* Gk *slave*   *c* Other ancient authorities read *our*   *d* Gk *his*   *e* Other ancient authorities read *called*   *f* Other ancient authorities read *us*   *g* Other ancient authorities add *through his blood*   *h* Or *by*   *i* Other ancient authorities read *you have now been reconciled*

1:7 **our behalf:** *some witnesses read* your behalf.
1:11–12 **patience . . . thanks:** *or* patience, and joy whatever comes;
12 and to give thanks.   1:16 **for him:** *or* with him as its goal.
1:20 **to himself:** *or* to their goal in him.

The Letter to the Colossians

1 Paul, an apostle of Christ Jesus by the will of God, and Timothy our brother, ²to the holy ones and faithful brothers in Christ in Colossae: grace to you and peace from God our Father.

³We always give thanks to God, the Father of our Lord Jesus Christ, when we pray for you, ⁴for we have heard of your faith in Christ Jesus and the love that you have for all the holy ones ⁵because of the hope reserved for you in heaven. Of this you have already heard through the word of truth, the gospel, ⁶that has come to you. Just as in the whole world it is bearing fruit and growing, so also among you, from the day you heard it and came to know the grace of God in truth, ⁷as you learned it from Epaphras our beloved fellow slave, who is a trustworthy minister of Christ on your behalf ⁸and who also told us of your love in the Spirit.

⁹Therefore, from the day we heard this, we do not cease praying for you and asking that you may be filled with the knowledge of his will through all spiritual wisdom and understanding ¹⁰to live in a manner worthy of the Lord, so as to be fully pleasing, in every good work bearing fruit and growing in the knowledge of God, ¹¹strengthened with every power, in accord with his glorious might, for all endurance and patience, with joy ¹²giving thanks to the Father, who has made you fit to share in the inheritance of the holy ones in light. ¹³He delivered us from the power of darkness and transferred us to the kingdom of his beloved Son, ¹⁴in whom we have redemption, the forgiveness of sins.

¹⁵He is the image of the invisible God,
  the firstborn of all creation.
¹⁶For in him were created all things in heaven and
    on earth,
  the visible and the invisible,
  whether thrones or dominions or principalities
    or powers;
  all things were created through him and for him.
¹⁷He is before all things,
  and in him all things hold together.
¹⁸He is the head of the body, the church.
He is the beginning, the firstborn from the dead,
  that in all things he himself might
    be preeminent.
¹⁹For in him all the fullness was pleased to dwell,
²⁰ and through him to reconcile all things for him,
  making peace by the blood of his cross
  [through him], whether those on earth or those
    in heaven.

²¹And you who once were alienated and hostile in mind because of evil deeds ²²he has now reconciled in his fleshly

Colossians

THE LETTER OF PAUL
TO THE CHURCH AT COLOSSAE

1 From Paul, by the will of God an apostle of Christ Jesus, and from our brother Timothy ²to God's holy people in Colossae, our faithful brothers in Christ. Grace and peace to you from God our Father.

³We give thanks for you to God, the Father of our Lord Jesus Christ, continually in our prayers, ⁴ever since we heard about your faith in Christ Jesus and the love that you show towards all God's holy people ⁵because of the hope which is stored up for you in heaven. News of this hope reached you not long ago through the word of truth, the gospel ⁶that came to you in the same way as it is bearing fruit and growing throughout the world. It has had the same effect among you, ever since you heard about the grace of God and recognised it for what it truly is. ⁷This you learnt from Epaphras, our very dear fellow-worker and a trustworthy deputy for us as Christ's servant, ⁸and it was he who also told us all about your love in the Spirit.

⁹That is why, ever since the day he told us, we have never failed to remember you in our prayers and ask that through perfect wisdom and spiritual understanding you should reach the fullest knowledge of his will ¹⁰and so be able to lead a life worthy of the Lord, a life acceptable to him in all its aspects, bearing fruit in every kind of good work and growing in knowledge of God, ¹¹fortified, in accordance with his glorious strength, with all power always to persevere and endure, ¹²giving thanks with joy to the Father who has made you able to share the lot of God's holy people and with them to inherit the light.

¹³Because that is what he has done. It is he who has rescued us from the ruling force of darkness and transferred us to the kingdom of the Son that he loves, ¹⁴and in him we enjoy our freedom, the forgiveness of sin.

¹⁵He is the image of the unseen God,
  the first-born of all creation,[a]
¹⁶for in him were created all things
  in heaven and on earth:
  everything visible and everything invisible,
  thrones, ruling forces, sovereignties, powers –
  all things were created through him and for him.
¹⁷He exists before all things
  and in him all things hold together,
¹⁸and he is the Head of the Body,
  that is, the Church.

He is the Beginning,
  the first-born from the dead,
  so that he should be supreme in every way;
¹⁹because God wanted all fullness to be found in him
²⁰and through him to reconcile all things to him,
  everything in heaven and everything on earth,
  by making peace through his death on the cross.
²¹You were once estranged and of hostile intent through your evil behaviour; ²²now he has reconciled you, by his

---

1, 20: *[Through him]*: the phrase, lacking in some manuscripts, seems superfluous but parallels the reference to reconciliation through Christ earlier in the verse.

a **1** cf. Ws 7:26.

NEW REVISED STANDARD VERSION	REVISED ENGLISH BIBLE

fleshly body*j* through death, so as to present you holy and blameless and irreproachable before him— 23 provided that you continue securely established and steadfast in the faith, without shifting from the hope promised by the gospel that you heard, which has been proclaimed to every creature under heaven. I, Paul, became a servant of this gospel.

24 I am now rejoicing in my sufferings for your sake, and in my flesh I am completing what is lacking in Christ's afflictions for the sake of his body, that is, the church. 25 I became its servant according to God's commission that was given to me for you, to make the word of God fully known, 26 the mystery that has been hidden throughout the ages and generations but has now been revealed to his saints. 27 To them God chose to make known how great among the Gentiles are the riches of the glory of this mystery, which is Christ in you, the hope of glory. 28 It is he whom we proclaim, warning everyone and teaching everyone in all wisdom, so that we may present everyone mature in Christ. 29 For this I toil and struggle with all the energy that he powerfully inspires within me.

2 For I want you to know how much I am struggling for you, and for those in Laodicea, and for all who have not seen me face to face. 2 I want their hearts to be encouraged and united in love, so that they may have all the riches of assured understanding and have the knowledge of God's mystery, that is, Christ himself,*k* 3 in whom are hidden all the treasures of wisdom and knowledge. 4 I am saying this so that no one may deceive you with plausible arguments. 5 For though I am absent in body, yet I am with you in spirit, and I rejoice to see your morale and the firmness of your faith in Christ.

6 As you therefore have received Christ Jesus the Lord, continue to live your lives*l* in him, 7 rooted and built up in him and established in the faith, just as you were taught, abounding in thanksgiving.

8 See to it that no one takes you captive through philosophy and empty deceit, according to human tradition, according to the elemental spirits of the universe,*m* and not according to Christ. 9 For in him the whole fullness of deity dwells bodily, 10 and you have come to fullness in him, who is the head of every ruler and authority. 11 In him also you were circumcised with a spiritual circumcision,*n* by putting off the body of the flesh in the circumcision of Christ; 12 when you were buried with him in baptism, you were also raised with him through faith in the power of God, who raised him from the dead. 13 And when you were dead in trespasses and the uncircumcision of your flesh, God*o* made you*p* alive together with him, when he forgave us all our trespasses, 14 erasing the record that stood against us with its legal demands. He set this aside, nailing it to the cross. 15 He disarmed*q* the rulers and authorities and made a public example of them, triumphing over them in it.

16 Therefore do not let anyone condemn you in matters of food and drink or of observing festivals, new moons, or sabbaths. 17 These are only a shadow of what is to come, but the substance belongs to Christ. 18 Do not let anyone disqualify you, insisting on self-abasement and worship of angels, dwelling*r* on visions,*s* puffed up without cause by a human way of thinking,*t* 19 and not holding fast to the

God has reconciled you to himself, so that he may bring you into his own presence, holy and without blame or blemish. 23 Yet you must persevere in faith, firm on your foundations and never to be dislodged from the hope offered in the gospel you accepted. This is the gospel which has been proclaimed in the whole creation under heaven, the gospel of which I, Paul, became a minister.

24 It is now my joy to suffer for you; for the sake of Christ's body, the church, I am completing what still remains for Christ to suffer in my own person. 25 I became a servant of the church by virtue of the task assigned to me by God for your benefit: to put God's word into full effect, 26 that secret purpose hidden for long ages and through many generations, but now disclosed to God's people. 27 To them he chose to make known what a wealth of glory is offered to the Gentiles in this secret purpose: Christ in you, the hope of glory.

28 He it is whom we proclaim. We teach everyone and instruct everyone in all the ways of wisdom, so as to present each one of you as a mature member of Christ's body. 29 To this end I am toiling strenuously with all the energy and power of Christ at work in me. 1 I want you to know how strenuous are my exertions for you and the Laodiceans, and for all who have never set eyes on me. 2 My aim is to keep them in good heart and united in love, so that they may come to the full wealth of conviction which understanding brings, and grasp God's secret, which is Christ himself, 3 in whom lie hidden all the treasures of wisdom and knowledge. 4 I tell you this to make sure no one talks you into error by specious arguments. 5 I may be absent in body, but in spirit I am with you, and rejoice to see your unbroken ranks and the solid front which your faith in Christ presents.

6 THEREFORE, since you have accepted Christ Jesus as Lord, live in union with him. 7 Be rooted in him, be built in him, grow strong in the faith as you were taught; let your hearts overflow with thankfulness. 8 Be on your guard; let no one capture your minds with hollow and delusive speculations, based on traditions of human teaching and centred on the elemental spirits of the universe and not on Christ.

9 For it is in Christ that the Godhead in all its fullness dwells embodied, 10 it is in him you have been brought to fulfilment. Every power and authority in the universe is subject to him as head. 11 In him also you were circumcised, not in a physical sense, but by the stripping away of the old nature, which is Christ's way of circumcision. 12 For you were buried with him in baptism, and in that baptism you were also raised to life with him through your faith in the active power of God, who raised him from the dead. 13 And although you were dead because of your sins and your uncircumcision, he has brought you to life with Christ. For he has forgiven us all our sins; 14 he has cancelled the bond which was outstanding against us with its legal demands; he has set it aside, nailing it to the cross. 15 There he disarmed the cosmic powers and authorities and made a public spectacle of them, leading them as captives in his triumphal procession.

16 ALLOW no one, therefore, to take you to task about what you eat or drink, or over the observance of festival, new moon, or sabbath. 17 These are no more than a shadow of what was to come; the reality is Christ's. 18 You are not to be disqualified by the decision of people who go in for self-mortification and angel-worship and access to some visionary world. Such people, bursting with the futile conceit of worldly minds, 19 lose their hold upon the head; yet

---

j Gk *in the body of his flesh* *k* Other ancient authorities read *of the mystery of God, both of the Father and of Christ* *l* Gk *to walk* *m* Or *the rudiments of the world* *n* Gk *a circumcision made without hands* *o* Gk *he* *p* Other ancient authorities read *made us*; others, made *q* Or *divested himself of* *r* Other ancient authorities read *not dwelling* *s* Meaning of Gk uncertain *t* Gk *by the mind of his flesh*

2:8 **and centred . . . universe:** *or* and elementary ideas belonging to this world. 2:15 **he disarmed . . . of them:** *or* he stripped himself of his physical body, and thereby made a public spectacle of the cosmic powers and authorities.

body through his death, to present you holy, without blemish, and irreproachable before him, 23 provided that you persevere in the faith, firmly grounded, stable, and not shifting from the hope of the gospel that you heard, which has been preached to every creature under heaven, of which I, Paul, am a minister.

24 Now I rejoice in my sufferings for your sake, and in my flesh I am filling up what is lacking in the afflictions of Christ on behalf of his body, which is the church, 25 of which I am a minister in accordance with God's stewardship given to me to bring to completion for you the word of God, 26 the mystery hidden from ages and from generations past. But now it has been manifested to his holy ones, 27 to whom God chose to make known the riches of the glory of this mystery among the Gentiles; it is Christ in you, the hope for glory. 28 It is he whom we proclaim, admonishing everyone and teaching everyone with all wisdom, that we may present everyone perfect in Christ. 29 For this I labor and struggle, in accord with the exercise of his power working within me.

2 For I want you to know how great a struggle I am having for you and for those in Laodicea and all who have not seen me face to face, 2 that their hearts may be encouraged as they are brought together in love, to have all the richness of fully assured understanding, for the knowledge of the mystery of God, Christ, 3 in whom are hidden all the treasures of wisdom and knowledge.

4 I say this so that no one may deceive you by specious arguments. 5 For even if I am absent in the flesh, yet I am with you in spirit, rejoicing as I observe your good order and the firmness of your faith in Christ. 6 So, as you received Christ Jesus the Lord, walk in him, 7 rooted in him and built upon him and established in the faith as you were taught, abounding in thanksgiving. 8 See to it that no one captivate you with an empty, seductive philosophy according to human tradition, according to the elemental powers of the world and not according to Christ.

9 For in him dwells the whole fullness of the deity bodily, 10 and you share in this fullness in him, who is the head of every principality and power. 11 In him you were also circumcised with a circumcision not administered by hand, by stripping off the carnal body, with the circumcision of Christ. 12 You were buried with him in baptism, in which you were also raised with him through faith in the power of God, who raised him from the dead. 13 And even when you were dead [in] transgressions and the uncircumcision of your flesh, he brought you to life along with him, having forgiven us all our transgressions; 14 obliterating the bond against us, with its legal claims, which was opposed to us, he also removed it from our midst, nailing it to the cross; 15 despoiling the principalities and the powers, he made a public spectacle of them, leading them away in triumph by it.

16 Let no one, then, pass judgment on you in matters of food and drink or with regard to a festival or new moon or sabbath. 17 These are shadows of things to come; the reality belongs to Christ. 18 Let no one disqualify you, delighting in self-abasement and worship of angels, taking his stand on visions, inflated without reason by his fleshly mind, 19 and

death and in that mortal body, to bring you before himself holy, faultless and irreproachable — 23 as long as you persevere and stand firm on the solid base of the faith, never letting yourselves drift away from the hope promised by the gospel, which you have heard, which has been preached to every creature under heaven, and of which I, Paul, have become the servant.

24 It makes me happy to be suffering for you now, and in my own body to make up all the hardships that still have to be undergone by Christ for the sake of his body, the Church, 25 of which I was made a servant with the responsibility towards you that God gave to me, that of completing God's message, 26 the message which was a mystery hidden for generations and centuries and has now been revealed to his holy people. 27 It was God's purpose to reveal to them how rich is the glory of this mystery among the gentiles; it is Christ among you, your hope of glory: 28 this is the Christ we are proclaiming, admonishing and instructing everyone in all wisdom, to make everyone perfect in Christ. 29 And it is for this reason that I labour, striving with his energy which works in me mightily.

2 I want you to know, then, what a struggle I am having on your behalf and on behalf of those in Laodicea, and on behalf of so many others who have never seen me face to face. 2 It is all to bind them together in love and to encourage their resolution until they are rich in the assurance of their complete understanding and have knowledge of the mystery of God 3 in which all the jewels of wisdom and knowledge are hidden.

4 I say this to make sure that no one deceives you with specious arguments. 5 I may be absent in body, but in spirit I am there among you, delighted to find how well-ordered you are and to see how firm your faith in Christ is.

6 So then, as you received Jesus as Lord and Christ, now live your lives in him, 7 be rooted in him and built up on him, held firm by the faith you have been taught, and overflowing with thanksgiving.

8 Make sure that no one captivates you with the empty lure of a 'philosophy' of the kind that human beings hand on, based on the principles of this world and not on Christ.

9 In him, in bodily form, lives divinity in all its fullness, 10 and in him you too find your own fulfilment, in the one who is the head of every sovereignty and ruling force. 11 In him you have been circumcised, with a circumcision performed, not by human hand, but by the complete stripping of your natural self. This is circumcision according to Christ. 12 You have been buried with him by your baptism; by which, too, you have been raised up with him through your belief in the power of God who raised him from the dead. 13 You were dead, because you were sinners and uncircumcised in body: he has brought you to life with him, he has forgiven us every one of our sins.

14 He has wiped out the record of our debt to the Law, which stood against us; he has destroyed it by nailing it to the cross; 15 and he has stripped the sovereignties and the ruling forces, and paraded them in public, behind him in his triumphal procession.

16 Then never let anyone criticise you for what you eat or drink, or about observance of annual festivals, New Moons or Sabbaths. 17 These are only a shadow of what was coming: the reality is the body of Christ. 18 Do not be cheated of your prize by anyone who chooses to grovel to angels and worship them, pinning every hope on visions received, vainly puffed up by a human way of thinking; 19 such a

NEW REVISED STANDARD VERSION

head, from whom the whole body, nourished and held together by its ligaments and sinews, grows with a growth that is from God.

20 If with Christ you died to the elemental spirits of the universe,^{u} why do you live as if you still belonged to the world? Why do you submit to regulations, 21 "Do not handle, Do not taste, Do not touch"? 22 All these regulations refer to things that perish with use; they are simply human commands and teachings. 23 These have indeed an appearance of wisdom in promoting self-imposed piety, humility, and severe treatment of the body, but they are of no value in checking self-indulgence.^{v}

3 So if you have been raised with Christ, seek the things that are above, where Christ is, seated at the right hand of God. 2 Set your minds on things that are above, not on things that are on earth, 3 for you have died, and your life is hidden with Christ in God. 4 When Christ who is your^w life is revealed, then you also will be revealed with him in glory.

5 Put to death, therefore, whatever in you is earthly: fornication, impurity, passion, evil desire, and greed (which is idolatry). 6 On account of these the wrath of God is coming on those who are disobedient.^{x} 7 These are the ways you also once followed, when you were living that life.^{y} 8 But now you must get rid of all such things — anger, wrath, malice, slander, and abusive^z language from your mouth. 9 Do not lie to one another, seeing that you have stripped off the old self with its practices 10 and have clothed yourselves with the new self, which is being renewed in knowledge according to the image of its creator. 11 In that renewal^a there is no longer Greek and Jew, circumcised and uncircumcised, barbarian, Scythian, slave and free; but Christ is all and in all!

12 As God's chosen ones, holy and beloved, clothe yourselves with compassion, kindness, humility, meekness, and patience. 13 Bear with one another and, if anyone has a complaint against another, forgive each other; just as the Lord^b has forgiven you, so you also must forgive. 14 Above all, clothe yourselves with love, which binds everything together in perfect harmony. 15 And let the peace of Christ rule in your hearts, to which indeed you were called in the one body. And be thankful. 16 Let the word of Christ^c dwell in you richly; teach and admonish one another in all wisdom; and with gratitude in your hearts sing psalms, hymns, and spiritual songs to God.^{d} 17 And whatever you do, in word or deed, do everything in the name of the Lord Jesus, giving thanks to God the Father through him.

18 Wives, be subject to your husbands, as is fitting in the Lord. 19 Husbands, love your wives and never treat them harshly.

20 Children, obey your parents in everything, for this is your acceptable duty in the Lord. 21 Fathers, do not provoke your children, or they may lose heart. 22 Slaves, obey your earthly masters^e in everything, not only while being watched and in order to please them, but wholeheartedly, fearing the Lord.^{e} 23 Whatever your task, put yourselves into it, as done for the Lord and not for your masters,^{f} 24 since you know that from the Lord you will receive the

REVISED ENGLISH BIBLE

it is from the head that the whole body, with all its joints and ligaments, has its needs supplied, and thus knit together grows according to God's design.

20 Did you not die with Christ and pass beyond reach of the elemental spirits of the universe? Then why behave as though you were still living the life of the world? Why let people dictate to you: 21 'Do not handle this, do not taste that, do not touch the other' — 22 referring to things that must all perish as they are used? That is to follow human rules and regulations. 23 Such conduct may have an air of wisdom, with its forced piety, its self-mortification, and its severity to the body; but it is of no use at all in combating sensuality.

3 Were you not raised to life with Christ? Then aspire to the realm above, where Christ is, seated at God's right hand, 2 and fix your thoughts on that higher realm, not on this earthly life. 3 You died; and now your life lies hidden with Christ in God. 4 When Christ, who is our life, is revealed, then you too will be revealed with him in glory.

5 So PUT to death those parts of you which belong to the earth — fornication, indecency, lust, evil desires, and the ruthless greed which is nothing less than idolatry; 6 on these divine retribution falls. 7 This is the way you yourselves once lived; 8 but now have done with rage, bad temper, malice, slander, filthy talk — banish them all from your lips! 9 Do not lie to one another, now that you have discarded the old human nature and the conduct that goes with it, 10 and have put on the new nature which is constantly being renewed in the image of its Creator and brought to know God. 11 There is no question here of Greek and Jew, circumcised and uncircumcised, barbarian, Scythian, slave and freeman; but Christ is all, and is in all.

12 Put on, then, garments that suit God's chosen and beloved people: compassion, kindness, humility, gentleness, patience. 13 Be tolerant with one another and forgiving, if any of you has cause for complaint: you must forgive as the Lord forgave you. 14 Finally, to bind everything together and complete the whole, there must be love. 15 Let Christ's peace be arbiter in your decisions, the peace to which you were called as members of a single body. Always be thankful. 16 Let the gospel of Christ dwell among you in all its richness; teach and instruct one another with all the wisdom it gives you. With psalms and hymns and spiritual songs, sing from the heart in gratitude to God. 17 Let every word and action, everything you do, be in the name of the Lord Jesus, and give thanks through him to God the Father.

18 WIVES, be subject to your husbands; that is your Christian duty. 19 Husbands, love your wives and do not be harsh with them. 20 Children, obey your parents in everything, for that is pleasing to God and is the Christian way. 21 Fathers, do not exasperate your children, in case they lose heart. 22 Slaves, give entire obedience to your earthly masters, not merely to catch their eye or curry favour with them, but with single-mindedness, out of reverence for the Lord. 23 Whatever you are doing, put your whole heart into it, as if you were doing it for the Lord and not for men, 24 knowing that there is a master who will give you an inheritance

---

^{u} Or the rudiments of the world ^{v} Or are of no value, serving only to indulge the flesh ^{w} Other authorities read our ^{x} Other ancient authorities lack on those who are disobedient (Gk the children of disobedience) ^{y} Or living among such people ^{z} Or filthy ^{a} Gk its creator, ^{11}where ^{b} Other ancient authorities read just as Christ ^{c} Other ancient authorities read of God, or of the Lord ^{d} Other ancient authorities read to the Lord ^{e} In Greek the same word is used for master and Lord ^{f} Gk not for men

2:20 elemental . . . universe: or elementary ideas belonging to this world.

not holding closely to the head, from whom the whole body, supported and held together by its ligaments and bonds, achieves the growth that comes from God. 20 If you died with Christ to the elemental powers of the world, why do you submit to regulations as if you were still living in the world? 21 "Do not handle! Do not taste! Do not touch!" 22 These are all things destined to perish with use; they accord with human precepts and teachings. 23 While they have a semblance of wisdom in rigor of devotion and self-abasement [and] severity to the body, they are of no value against gratification of the flesh.

3 If then you were raised with Christ, seek what is above, where Christ is seated at the right hand of God. 2 Think of what is above, not of what is on earth. 3 For you have died, and your life is hidden with Christ in God. 4 When Christ your life appears, then you too will appear with him in glory.

5 Put to death, then, the parts of you that are earthly: immorality, impurity, passion, evil desire, and the greed that is idolatry. 6 Because of these the wrath of God is coming [upon the disobedient]. 7 By these you too once conducted yourselves, when you lived in that way. 8 But now you must put them all away: anger, fury, malice, slander, and obscene language out of your mouths. 9 Stop lying to one another, since you have taken off the old self with its practices 10 and have put on the new self, which is being renewed, for knowledge, in the image of its creator. 11 Here there is not Greek and Jew, circumcision and uncircumcision, barbarian, Scythian, slave, free; but Christ is all and in all.

12 Put on then, as God's chosen ones, holy and beloved, heartfelt compassion, kindness, humility, gentleness, and patience, 13 bearing with one another and forgiving one another, if one has a grievance against another; as the Lord has forgiven you, so must you also do. 14 And over all these put on love, that is, the bond of perfection. 15 And let the peace of Christ control your hearts, the peace into which you were also called in one body. And be thankful. 16 Let the word of Christ dwell in you richly, as in all wisdom you teach and admonish one another, singing psalms, hymns, and spiritual songs with gratitude in your hearts to God. 17 And whatever you do, in word or in deed, do everything in the name of the Lord Jesus, giving thanks to God the Father through him.

18 Wives, be subordinate to your husbands, as is proper in the Lord. 19 Husbands, love your wives, and avoid any bitterness toward them. 20 Children, obey your parents in everything, for this is pleasing to the Lord. 21 Fathers, do not provoke your children, so they may not become discouraged.

22 Slaves, obey your human masters in everything, not only when being watched, as currying favor, but in simplicity of heart, fearing the Lord. 23 Whatever you do, do from the heart, as for the Lord and not for others, 24 knowing that you will receive from the Lord the due payment of the inheritance; be slaves of the Lord Christ. 25 For the

person has no connection to the Head, by which the whole body, given all that it needs and held together by its joints and sinews, grows with the growth given by God. 20 If you have really died with Christ to the principles of this world, why do you still let rules dictate to you, as though you were still living in the world? 21 — 'Do not pick up this, do not eat that, do not touch the other,' 22 and all about things which perish even while they are being used— according to merely *human commandments and doctrines*! *b* 23 In these rules you can indeed find what seems to be good sense— the cultivation of the will, and a humility which takes no account of the body; but in fact they have no value against self-indulgence.

3 Since you have been raised up to be with Christ, you must look for the things that are above, where Christ is, sitting at God's right hand. 2 Let your thoughts be on things above, not on the things that are on the earth, 3 because you have died, and now the life you have is hidden with Christ in God. 4 But when Christ is revealed— and he is your life— you, too, will be revealed with him in glory.

5 That is why you must kill everything in you that is earthly: sexual vice, impurity, uncontrolled passion, evil desires and especially greed, which is the same thing as worshipping a false god; 6 it is precisely these things which draw God's retribution upon those who resist. 7 And these things made up your way of life when you were living among such people, 8 but now you also must give up all these things: human anger, hot temper, malice, abusive language and dirty talk; 9 and do not lie to each other. You have stripped off your old behaviour with your old self, 10 and you have put on a new self which will progress towards true knowledge the more it is renewed in the image of its Creator; 11 and in that image there is no room for distinction between Greek and Jew, between the circumcised and uncircumcised, or between barbarian and Scythian, slave and free. There is only Christ: he is everything and he is in everything.

12 As the chosen of God, then, the holy people whom he loves, you are to be clothed in heartfelt compassion, in generosity and humility, gentleness and patience. 13 Bear with one another; forgive each other if one of you has a complaint against another. The Lord has forgiven you; now you must do the same. 14 Over all these clothes, put on love, the perfect bond. 15 And may the peace of Christ reign in your hearts, because it is for this that you were called together in one body. Always be thankful.

16 Let the Word of Christ, in all its richness, find a home with you. Teach each other, and advise each other, in all wisdom. With gratitude in your hearts sing psalms and hymns and inspired songs to God; 17 and whatever you say or do, let it be in the name of the Lord Jesus, in thanksgiving to God the Father through him.

18 Wives, be subject to your husbands, as you should in the Lord. 19 Husbands, love your wives and do not be sharp with them. 20 Children, be obedient to your parents always, because that is what will please the Lord. 21 Parents, do not irritate your children or they will lose heart.

22 Slaves, be obedient in every way to the people who, according to human reckoning, are your masters; not only when you are under their eye, as if you had only to please human beings, but wholeheartedly, out of respect for the Master. 23 Whatever your work is, put your heart into it as done for the Lord and not for human beings, 24 knowing that the Lord will repay you by making you his heirs. It is Christ

---

3, 6: Many manuscripts add, as at Eph 5, 6, "upon the disobedient."   *b* **2** Is 29:13.

NEW REVISED STANDARD VERSION

inheritance as your reward; you serve*g* the Lord Christ. 25 For the wrongdoer will be paid back for whatever wrong

4 has been done, and there is no partiality. 1 Masters, treat your slaves justly and fairly, for you know that you also have a Master in heaven.

2 Devote yourselves to prayer, keeping alert in it with thanksgiving. 3 At the same time pray for us as well that God will open to us a door for the word, that we may declare the mystery of Christ, for which I am in prison, 4 so that I may reveal it clearly, as I should.

5 Conduct yourselves wisely toward outsiders, making the most of the time.*h* 6 Let your speech always be gracious, seasoned with salt, so that you may know how you ought to answer everyone.

7 Tychicus will tell you all the news about me; he is a beloved brother, a faithful minister, and a fellow servant*i* in the Lord. 8 I have sent him to you for this very purpose, so that you may know how we are*j* and that he may encourage your hearts; 9 he is coming with Onesimus, the faithful and beloved brother, who is one of you. They will tell you about everything here.

10 Aristarchus my fellow prisoner greets you, as does Mark the cousin of Barnabas, concerning whom you have received instructions—if he comes to you, welcome him. 11 And Jesus who is called Justus greets you. These are the only ones of the circumcision among my co-workers for the kingdom of God, and they have been a comfort to me. 12 Epaphras, who is one of you, a servant*i* of Christ Jesus, greets you. He is always wrestling in his prayers on your behalf, so that you may stand mature and fully assured in everything that God wills. 13 For I testify for him that he has worked hard for you and for those in Laodicea and in Hierapolis. 14 Luke, the beloved physician, and Demas greet you. 15 Give my greetings to the brothers and sisters*k* in Laodicea, and to Nympha and the church in her house. 16 And when this letter has been read among you, have it read also in the church of the Laodiceans; and see that you read also the letter from Laodicea. 17 And say to Archippus, "See that you complete the task that you have received in the Lord."

18 I, Paul, write this greeting with my own hand. Remember my chains. Grace be with you.*l*

g Or *you are slaves of*, or *be slaves of*   *h* Or *opportunity*
i Gk *slave*   *j* Other authorities read *that I may know how you are*
k Gk *brothers*   *l* Other ancient authorities add *Amen*

REVISED ENGLISH BIBLE

as a reward for your service. Christ is the master you must serve. 25 Wrongdoers will pay for the wrong they do; there

4 will be no favouritism. 1 Masters, be just and fair to your slaves, knowing that you too have a master in heaven.

2 Persevere in prayer, with minds alert and with thankful hearts; 3 and include us in your prayers, asking God to provide an opening for the gospel, that we may proclaim the secret of Christ, for which indeed I am in prison. 4 Pray that I may make the secret plain, as it is my duty to do.

5 Be wise in your dealings with outsiders, but use your opportunities to the full. 6 Let your words always be gracious, never insipid; learn how best to respond to each person you meet.

7 YOU WILL hear all my news from Tychicus, our dear brother and trustworthy helper and fellow-servant in the Lord's work. 8 I am sending him to you for this purpose, to let you know how we are and to put fresh heart into you. 9 With him comes Onesimus, our trustworthy and dear brother, who is one of yourselves. They will tell you all that has happened here.

10 Aristarchus, Christ's captive like myself, sends his greetings; so does Mark, the cousin of Barnabas (you have had instructions about him; if he comes, make him welcome), 11 and Jesus Justus. Of the Jewish Christians, these are the only ones working with me for the kingdom of God, and they have been a great comfort to me. 12 Greetings from Epaphras, servant of Christ, who is one of yourselves. He prays hard for you all the time, that you may stand fast, as mature Christians, fully determined to do the will of God. 13 I can vouch for him, that he works tirelessly for you and the people at Laodicea and Hierapolis. 14 Greetings to you from our dear friend Luke, the doctor, and from Demas. 15 Give our greetings to the Christians at Laodicea, and to Nympha and the congregation that meets at her house. 16 Once this letter has been read among you, see that it is read also to the church at Laodicea, and that you in turn read my letter to Laodicea. 17 Give Archippus this message: 'See that you carry out fully the duty entrusted to you in the Lord's service.'

18 I add this greeting in my own hand—Paul. Remember I am in prison. Grace be with you.

4:15 **Nympha . . . her house:** *some witnesses read* Nymphas . . . his house.

| NEW AMERICAN BIBLE | NEW JERUSALEM BIBLE |

wrongdoer will receive recompense for the wrong he committed, and there is no partiality.

4 Masters, treat your slaves justly and fairly, realizing that you too have a Master in heaven.

2 Persevere in prayer, being watchful in it with thanksgiving; 3 at the same time, pray for us, too, that God may open a door to us for the word, to speak of the mystery of Christ, for which I am in prison, 4 that I may make it clear, as I must speak. 5 Conduct yourselves wisely toward outsiders, making the most of the opportunity. 6 Let your speech always be gracious, seasoned with salt, so that you know how you should respond to each one.

7 Tychicus, my beloved brother, trustworthy minister, and fellow slave in the Lord, will tell you all the news of me. 8 I am sending him to you for this very purpose, so that you may know about us and that he may encourage your hearts, 9 together with Onesimus, a trustworthy and beloved brother, who is one of you. They will tell you about everything here.

10 Aristarchus, my fellow prisoner, sends you greetings, as does Mark the cousin of Barnabas (concerning whom you have received instructions; if he comes to you, receive him), 11 and Jesus, who is called Justus, who are of the circumcision; these alone are my co-workers for the kingdom of God, and they have been a comfort to me. 12 Epaphras sends you greetings; he is one of you, a slave of Christ [Jesus], always striving for you in his prayers so that you may be perfect and fully assured in all the will of God. 13 For I can testify that he works very hard for you and for those in Laodicea and those in Hierapolis. 14 Luke the beloved physician sends greetings, as does Demas.

15 Give greetings to the brothers in Laodicea and to Nympha and to the church in her house. 16 And when this letter is read before you, have it read also in the church of the Laodiceans, and you yourselves read the one from Laodicea. 17 And tell Archippus, "See that you fulfill the ministry that you received in the Lord."

18 The greeting is in my own hand, Paul's. Remember my chains. Grace be with you.

the Lord that you are serving. 25 Anyone who does wrong will be repaid in kind. For there is no favouritism.

4 Masters, make sure that your slaves are given what is upright and fair, knowing that you too have a Master in heaven.

2 Be persevering in your prayers and be thankful as you stay awake to pray. 3 Pray for us especially, asking God to throw open a door for us to announce the message and proclaim the mystery of Christ, for the sake of which I am in chains; 4 pray that I may proclaim it as clearly as I ought.

5 Act wisely with outsiders, making the best of the present time. 6 Always talk pleasantly and with a flavour of wit but be sensitive to the kind of answer each one requires.

7 Tychicus will tell you all the news about me. He is a very dear brother, and a trustworthy helper and companion in the service of the Lord. 8 I am sending him to you precisely for this purpose: to give you news about us and to encourage you thoroughly. 9 With him I am sending Onesimus,c that dear and trustworthy brother who is a fellow-citizen of yours. They will tell you everything that is happening here.

10 Aristarchus, who is here in prison with me, sends his greetings, and so does Mark, the cousin of Barnabas — you were sent some instructions about him; if he comes to you, give him a warm welcome — 11 and Jesus Justus adds his greetings. Of all those who have come over from the circumcision, these are the only ones actually working with me for the kingdom of God. They have been a great comfort to me. 12 Epaphras, your fellow-citizen, sends his greetings; this servant of Christ Jesus never stops battling for you, praying that you will never lapse but always hold perfectly and securely to the will of God. 13 I can testify for him that he works hard for you, as well as for those at Laodicea and Hierapolis. 14 Greetings from my dear friend Luke, the doctor, and also from Demas.

15 Please give my greetings to the brothers at Laodicea and to Nympha and the church which meets in her house. 16 After this letter has been read among you, send it on to be read in the church of the Laodiceans; and get the letter from Laodicead for you to read yourselves. 17 Give Archippus this message, 'Remember the service that the Lord assigned to you, and try to carry it out.'

18 This greeting is in my own hand — PAUL. Remember the chains I wear. Grace be with you.

c 4 cf. Phm 10.   d 4 Possibly this letter is Ep.

THE FIRST LETTER OF PAUL TO THE
Thessalonians

1 Paul, Silvanus, and Timothy,
To the church of the Thessalonians in God the Father and the Lord Jesus Christ:
Grace to you and peace.

2 We always give thanks to God for all of you and mention you in our prayers, constantly 3 remembering before our God and Father your work of faith and labor of love and steadfastness of hope in our Lord Jesus Christ. 4 For we know, brothers and sisters*a* beloved by God, that he has chosen you, 5 because our message of the gospel came to you not in word only, but also in power and in the Holy Spirit and with full conviction; just as you know what kind of persons we proved to be among you for your sake. 6 And you became imitators of us and of the Lord, for in spite of persecution you received the word with joy inspired by the Holy Spirit, 7 so that you became an example to all the believers in Macedonia and in Achaia. 8 For the word of the Lord has sounded forth from you not only in Macedonia and Achaia, but in every place your faith in God has become known, so that we have no need to speak about it. 9 For the people of those regions*b* report about us what kind of welcome we had among you, and how you turned to God from idols, to serve a living and true God, 10 and to wait for his Son from heaven, whom he raised from the dead — Jesus, who rescues us from the wrath that is coming.

2 You yourselves know, brothers and sisters,*a* that our coming to you was not in vain, 2 but though we had already suffered and been shamefully mistreated at Philippi, as you know, we had courage in our God to declare to you the gospel of God in spite of great opposition. 3 For our appeal does not spring from deceit or impure motives or trickery, 4 but just as we have been approved by God to be entrusted with the message of the gospel, even so we speak, not to please mortals, but to please God who tests our hearts. 5 As you know and as God is our witness, we never came with words of flattery or with a pretext for greed; 6 nor did we seek praise from mortals, whether from you or from others, 7 though we might have made demands as apostles of Christ. But we were gentle*c* among you, like a nurse tenderly caring for her own children. 8 So deeply do we care for you that we are determined to share with you not only the gospel of God but also our own selves, because you have become very dear to us.

9 You remember our labor and toil, brothers and sisters;*a* we worked night and day, so that we might not burden any of you while we proclaimed to you the gospel of God. 10 You are witnesses, and God also, how pure, upright, and blameless our conduct was toward you believers. 11 As you know, we dealt with each one of you like a father with his children, 12 urging and encouraging you and pleading that you lead a life worthy of God, who calls you into his own kingdom and glory.

1 From Paul, Silvanus, and Timothy to the church of the Thessalonians who belong to God the Father and the Lord Jesus Christ.
Grace to you and peace.

2 We always thank God for you all, and mention you in our prayers. 3 We continually call to mind, before our God and Father, how your faith has shown itself in action, your love in labour, and your hope of our Lord Jesus Christ in perseverance. 4 My dear friends, beloved by God, we are certain that he has chosen you, 5 because when we brought you the gospel we did not bring it in mere words but in the power of the Holy Spirit and with strong conviction. You know what we were like for your sake when we were with you.

6 You, in turn, followed the example set by us and by the Lord; the welcome you gave the message meant grave suffering for you, yet you rejoiced in the Holy Spirit; 7 and so you have become a model for all believers in Macedonia and in Achaia. 8 From you the word of the Lord rang out; and not in Macedonia and Achaia alone, but everywhere your faith in God has become common knowledge. No words of ours are needed; 9 everyone is spreading the story of our visit to you: how you turned from idols to be servants of the true and living God, 10 and to wait expectantly for his Son from heaven, whom he raised from the dead, Jesus our deliverer from the retribution to come.

2 You know for yourselves, my friends, that our visit to you was not fruitless. 2 Far from it! After all the injury and outrage which as you know we had suffered at Philippi, by the help of our God we declared the gospel of God to you frankly and fearlessly in face of great opposition. 3 The appeal we make does not spring from delusion or sordid motive or from any attempt to deceive; 4 but God has approved us as fit to be entrusted with the gospel. So when we preach, we do not curry favour with men; we seek only the favour of God, who is continually testing our hearts. 5 We have never resorted to flattery, as you have cause to know; nor, as God is our witness, have our words ever been a cloak for greed. 6 We have never sought honour from men, not from you or from anyone else, 7 although as Christ's own envoys we might have made our weight felt; but we were as gentle with you as a nurse caring for her children. 8 Our affection was so deep that we were determined to share with you not only the gospel of God but our very selves; that is how dear you had become to us! 9 You remember, my friends, our toil and drudgery; night and day we worked for a living, rather than be a burden to any of you while we proclaimed to you the good news of God.

10 We call you to witness, yes and God himself, how devout and just and blameless was our conduct towards you who are believers. 11 As you well know, we dealt with each one of you as a father deals with his children; 12 we appealed to you, we encouraged you, we urged you, to live lives worthy of the God who calls you into his kingdom and glory.

---

a Gk *brothers* *b* Gk *For they* *c* Other ancient authorities read *infants*

The First Letter
to the Thessalonians

1 Paul, Silvanus, and Timothy to the church of the Thessalonians in God the Father and the Lord Jesus Christ: grace to you and peace.

2 We give thanks to God always for all of you, remembering you in our prayers, unceasingly 3 calling to mind your work of faith and labor of love and endurance in hope of our Lord Jesus Christ, before our God and Father, 4 knowing, brothers loved by God, how you were chosen. 5 For our gospel did not come to you in word alone, but also in power and in the holy Spirit and [with] much conviction. You know what sort of people we were [among] you for your sake. 6 And you became imitators of us and of the Lord, receiving the word in great affliction, with joy from the holy Spirit, 7 so that you became a model for all the believers in Macedonia and in Achaia. 8 For from you the word of the Lord has sounded forth not only in Macedonia and [in] Achaia, but in every place your faith in God has gone forth, so that we have no need to say anything. 9 For they themselves openly declare about us what sort of reception we had among you, and how you turned to God from idols to serve the living and true God 10 and to await his Son from heaven, whom he raised from [the] dead, Jesus, who delivers us from the coming wrath.

2 For you yourselves know, brothers, that our reception among you was not without effect. 2 Rather, after we had suffered and been insolently treated, as you know, in Philippi, we drew courage through our God to speak to you the gospel of God with much struggle. 3 Our exhortation was not from delusion or impure motives, nor did it work through deception. 4 But as we were judged worthy by God to be entrusted with the gospel, that is how we speak, not as trying to please human beings, but rather God, who judges our hearts. 5 Nor, indeed, did we ever appear with flattering speech, as you know, or with a pretext for greed — God is witness — 6 nor did we seek praise from human beings, either from you or from others, 7 although we were able to impose our weight as apostles of Christ. Rather, we were gentle among you, as a nursing mother cares for her children. 8 With such affection for you, we were determined to share with you not only the gospel of God, but our very selves as well, so dearly beloved had you become to us. 9 You recall, brothers, our toil and drudgery. Working night and day in order not to burden any of you, we proclaimed to you the gospel of God. 10 You are witnesses, and so is God, how devoutly and justly and blamelessly we behaved toward you believers. 11 As you know, we treated each one of you as a father treats his children, 12 exhorting and encouraging you and insisting that you conduct yourselves as worthy of the God who calls you into his kingdom and glory.

1 Thessalonians

THE FIRST LETTER OF PAUL
TO THE CHURCH IN THESSALONICA

1 Paul, Silvanus and Timothy, to the Church in Thessalonica which is in God the Father and the Lord Jesus Christ. Grace to you and peace.

2 We always thank God for you all, mentioning you in our prayers continually. 3 We remember before our God and Father how active is the faith, how unsparing the love, how persevering the hope which you have from our Lord Jesus Christ.

4 We know, brothers loved by God, that you have been chosen, 5 because our gospel came to you not only in words, but also in power and in the Holy Spirit and with great effect. And you observed the sort of life we lived when we were with you, which was for your sake. 6 You took us and the Lord as your model, welcoming the word with the joy of the Holy Spirit in spite of great hardship. 7 And so you became an example to all believers in Macedonia and Achaia 8 since it was from you that the word of the Lord rang out — and not only throughout Macedonia and Achaia, for your faith in God has spread everywhere. We do not need to tell other people about it: 9 other people tell us how we started the work among you, how you broke with the worship of false gods when you were converted to God and became servants of the living and true God; 10 and how you are now waiting for Jesus, his Son, whom he raised from the dead, to come from heaven. It is he who saves us from the Retribution which is coming.

2 You know yourselves, my brothers, that our visit to you has not been pointless. 2 Although, as you know, we had received rough treatment and insults at Philippi, God gave us the courage to speak his gospel to you fearlessly, in spite of great opposition. 3 Our encouragement to you does not come from any delusion or impure motives or trickery. 4 No, God has approved us to be entrusted with the gospel, and this is how we preach, seeking to please not human beings but God who *tests* our *hearts*.ᵃ 5 Indeed, we have never acted with the thought of flattering anyone, as you know, nor as an excuse for greed, God is our witness; 6 nor have we ever looked for honour from human beings, either from you or anybody else, 7 when we could have imposed ourselves on you with full weight, as apostles of Christ.

Instead, we lived unassumingly among you. Like a mother feeding and looking after her children, 8 we felt so devoted to you, that we would have been happy to share with you not only the gospel of God, but also our own lives, so dear had you become. 9 You remember, brothers, with what unsparing energy we used to work, slaving night and day so as not to be a burden on any one of you while we were proclaiming the gospel of God to you. 10 You are witnesses, and so is God, that our treatment of you, since you believed, has been impeccably fair and upright. 11 As you know, we treated every one of you as a father treats his children, 12 urging you, encouraging you and appealing to you to live a life worthy of God, who calls you into his kingdom and his glory.

a 2 Jr 11.20.

NEW REVISED STANDARD VERSION	REVISED ENGLISH BIBLE

13 We also constantly give thanks to God for this, that when you received the word of God that you heard from us, you accepted it not as a human word but as what it really is, God's word, which is also at work in you believers. 14 For you, brothers and sisters,*d* became imitators of the churches of God in Christ Jesus that are in Judea, for you suffered the same things from your own compatriots as they did from the Jews, 15 who killed both the Lord Jesus and the prophets,*e* and drove us out; they displease God and oppose everyone 16 by hindering us from speaking to the Gentiles so that they may be saved. Thus they have constantly been filling up the measure of their sins; but God's wrath has overtaken them at last.*f*

17 As for us, brothers and sisters,*d* when, for a short time, we were made orphans by being separated from you —in person, not in heart—we longed with great eagerness to see you face to face. 18 For we wanted to come to you— certainly I, Paul, wanted to again and again—but Satan blocked our way. 19 For what is our hope or joy or crown of boasting before our Lord Jesus at his coming? Is it not you? 20 Yes, you are our glory and joy!

3 Therefore when we could bear it no longer, we decided to be left alone in Athens; 2 and we sent Timothy, our brother and co-worker for God in proclaiming*g* the gospel of Christ, to strengthen and encourage you for the sake of your faith, 3 so that no one would be shaken by these persecutions. Indeed, you yourselves know that this is what we are destined for. 4 In fact, when we were with you, we told you beforehand that we were to suffer persecution; so it turned out, as you know. 5 For this reason, when I could bear it no longer, I sent to find out about your faith; I was afraid that somehow the tempter had tempted you and that our labor had been in vain.

6 But Timothy has just now come to us from you, and has brought us the good news of your faith and love. He has told us also that you always remember us kindly and long to see us—just as we long to see you. 7 For this reason, brothers and sisters,*d* during all our distress and persecution we have been encouraged about you through your faith. 8 For we now live, if you continue to stand firm in the Lord. 9 How can we thank God enough for you in return for all the joy that we feel before our God because of you? 10 Night and day we pray most earnestly that we may see you face to face and restore whatever is lacking in your faith.

11 Now may our God and Father himself and our Lord Jesus direct our way to you. 12 And may the Lord make you increase and abound in love for one another and for all, just as we abound in love for you. 13 And may he so strengthen your hearts in holiness that you may be blameless before our God and Father at the coming of our Lord Jesus with all his saints.

4 Finally, brothers and sisters,*d* we ask and urge you in the Lord Jesus that, as you learned from us how you ought to live and to please God (as, in fact, you are doing), you should do so more and more. 2 For you know what instructions we gave you through the Lord Jesus. 3 For this is the will of God, your sanctification: that you abstain from fornication; 4 that each one of you know how to control your own body*h* in holiness and honor, 5 not with lustful passion, like the Gentiles who do not know God; 6 that no one

13 We have reason to thank God continually because, when we handed on God's message, you accepted it, not as the word of men, but as what it truly is, the very word of God at work in you who are believers. 14 You, my friends, have followed the example of the Christians in the churches of God in Judaea: you have been treated by your own countrymen as they were treated by the Jews, 15 who killed the Lord Jesus and the prophets and drove us out, and are so heedless of God's will and such enemies of their fellowmen 16 that they hinder us from telling the Gentiles how they may be saved. All this time they have been making up the full measure of their guilt. But now retribution has overtaken them for good and all!

17 My friends, when for a short spell you were lost to us— out of sight but not out of mind—we were exceedingly anxious to see you again. 18 So we made up our minds to visit you—I, Paul, more than once—but Satan thwarted us. 19 For what hope or joy or triumphal crown is there for us when we stand before our Lord Jesus at his coming? What indeed but you? 20 You are our glory and our joy.

3 So when we could bear it no longer, we decided to stay on alone at Athens, 2 and sent Timothy, our colleague and a fellow-worker with God in the service of the gospel of Christ, to encourage you to stand firm for the faith 3 and under all these hardships remain unshaken. You know that this is our appointed lot, 4 for when we were with you we warned you that we were bound to suffer hardship; and so it has turned out, as you have found. 5 This was why I could bear it no longer and sent to find out about your faith; I was afraid that the tempter might have tempted you and our labour might be wasted.

6 But now Timothy has just returned from his visit to you, bringing good news of your faith and love. He tells us that you always think kindly of us, and are as anxious to see us as we are to see you. 7 So amid all our difficulties and hardships we are reassured, my friends, by the news of your faith. 8 It is the breath of life to us to know that you stand firm in the Lord. 9 What thanks can we give to God in return for you? What thanks for all the joy you have brought us, making us rejoice before our God 10 while we pray most earnestly night and day to be allowed to see you again and to make good whatever is lacking in your faith?

11 May our God and Father himself, and our Lord Jesus, open the way for us to come to you; 12 and may the Lord make your love increase and overflow to one another and to everyone, as our love does to you. 13 May he make your hearts firm, so that you may stand before our God and Father holy and faultless when our Lord Jesus comes with all those who are his own.

4 And now, friends, we have one thing to ask of you, as fellow-Christians. We passed on to you the tradition of the way we must live if we are to please God; you are indeed already following it, but we beg you to do so yet more thoroughly. 2 You know the rules we gave you in the name of the Lord Jesus. 3 This is the will of God, that you should be holy: you must abstain from fornication; 4 each one of you must learn to gain mastery over his body, to hallow and honour it, 5 not giving way to lust like the pagans who know nothing of God; 6 no one must do his fel-

---

d Gk *brothers*   *e* Other ancient authorities read *their own prophets*
f Or *completely* or *forever*   *g* Gk lacks *proclaiming*   *h* Or *how to take a wife for himself*

NEW AMERICAN BIBLE

NEW JERUSALEM BIBLE

13 And for this reason we too give thanks to God unceasingly, that, in receiving the word of God from hearing us, you received not a human word but, as it truly is, the word of God, which is now at work in you who believe. 14 For you, brothers, have become imitators of the churches of God that are in Judea in Christ Jesus. For you suffer the same things from your compatriots as they did from the Jews, 15 who killed both the Lord Jesus and the prophets and persecuted us; they do not please God, and are opposed to everyone, 16 trying to prevent us from speaking to the Gentiles that they may be saved, thus constantly filling up the measure of their sins. But the wrath of God has finally begun to come upon them.

17 Brothers, when we were bereft of you for a short time, in person, not in heart, we were all the more eager in our great desire to see you in person. 18 We decided to go to you — I, Paul, not only once but more than once — yet Satan thwarted us. 19 For what is our hope or joy or crown to boast of in the presence of our Lord Jesus at his coming if not you yourselves? 20 For you are our glory and joy.

3 That is why, when we could bear it no longer, we decided to remain alone in Athens 2 and sent Timothy, our brother and co-worker for God in the gospel of Christ, to strengthen and encourage you in your faith, 3 so that no one be disturbed in these afflictions. For you yourselves know that we are destined for this. 4 For even when we were among you, we used to warn you in advance that we would undergo affliction, just as has happened, as you know. 5 For this reason, when I too could bear it no longer, I sent to learn about your faith, for fear that somehow the tempter had put you to the test and our toil might come to nothing. 6 But just now Timothy has returned to us from you, bringing us the good news of your faith and love, and that you always think kindly of us and long to see us as we long to see you. 7 Because of this, we have been reassured about you, brothers, in our every distress and affliction, through your faith. 8 For we now live, if you stand firm in the Lord.

9 What thanksgiving, then, can we render to God for you, for all the joy we feel on your account before our God? 10 Night and day we pray beyond measure to see you in person and to remedy the deficiencies of your faith. 11 Now may God himself, our Father, and our Lord Jesus direct our way to you, 12 and may the Lord make you increase and abound in love for one another and for all, just as we have for you, 13 so as to strengthen your hearts, to be blameless in holiness before our God and Father at the coming of our Lord Jesus with all his holy ones. [Amen.]

4 Finally, brothers, we earnestly ask and exhort you in the Lord Jesus that, as you received from us how you should conduct yourselves to please God — and as you are conducting yourselves — you do so even more. 2 For you know what instructions we gave you through the Lord Jesus.

3 This is the will of God, your holiness: that you refrain from immorality, 4 that each of you know how to acquire a wife for himself in holiness and honor, 5 not in lustful passion as do the Gentiles who do not know God; 6 not to take

13 Another reason why we continually thank God for you is that as soon as you heard the word that we brought you as God's message, you welcomed it for what it really is, not the word of any human being, but God's word, a power that is working among you believers. 14 For you, my brothers, have modelled yourselves on the churches of God in Christ Jesus which are in Judaea, in that you have suffered the same treatment from your own countrymen as they have had from the Jews, 15 who put the Lord Jesus to death, and the prophets too, and persecuted us also. Their conduct does not please God, and makes them the enemies of the whole human race, 16 because they are hindering us from preaching to gentiles to save them. Thus all the time they are *reaching the full extent of* their *iniquity*,[b] but retribution has finally overtaken them.

17 Although we had been deprived of you for only a short time in body but never in affection, brothers, we had an especially strong desire and longing to see you face to face again, 18 and we tried hard to come and visit you; I, Paul, tried more than once, but Satan prevented us. 19 What do you think is our hope and our joy, and what *our crown of honour*[c] in the presence of our Lord Jesus when he comes? 20 You are, for you are our pride and joy.

3 When we could not bear it any longer, we decided it would be best to be left without a companion at Athens, 2 and sent our brother Timothy, who is God's helper in spreading the gospel of Christ, to keep you firm and encourage you about your faith 3 and prevent any of you from being unsettled by the present hardships. As you know, these are bound to come our way: 4 indeed, when we were with you, we warned you that we are certain to have hardships to bear, and that is what has happened now, as you have found out. 5 That is why, when I could not bear it any longer, I sent to assure myself of your faith: I was afraid the Tester might have put you to the test, and all our work might have been pointless.

6 However, Timothy has returned from you and has given us good news of your faith and your love, telling us that you always remember us with pleasure and want to see us quite as much as we want to see you. 7 And so, brothers, your faith has been a great encouragement to us in the middle of our own distress and hardship; 8 now we can breathe again, as you are holding firm in the Lord. 9 How can we thank God enough for you, for all the joy we feel before our God on your account? 10 We are earnestly praying night and day to be able to see you face to face again and make up any shortcomings in your faith.

11 May God our Father himself, and our Lord Jesus, ease our path to you. 12 May the Lord increase and enrich your love for each other and for all, so that it matches ours for you. 13 And may he so confirm your hearts in holiness that you may be blameless in the sight of our God and Father when our Lord Jesus comes *with all his holy ones*.[d]

4 Finally, brothers, we urge you and appeal to you in the Lord Jesus; we instructed you how to live in the way that pleases God, and you are so living; but make more progress still. 2 You are well aware of the instructions we gave you on the authority of the Lord Jesus.

3 God wills you all to be holy. He wants you to keep away from sexual immorality, 4 and each one of you to know how to control his body in a way that is holy and honourable, 5 not giving way to selfish lust like *the nations who do not acknowledge God*.[e] 6 He wants nobody at all ever to sin by

wrong or exploit a brother or sister[i] in this matter, because the Lord is an avenger in all these things, just as we have already told you beforehand and solemnly warned you. [7]For God did not call us to impurity but in holiness. [8]Therefore whoever rejects this rejects not human authority but God, who also gives his Holy Spirit to you.

[9] Now concerning love of the brothers and sisters,[j] you do not need to have anyone write to you, for you yourselves have been taught by God to love one another; [10]and indeed you do love all the brothers and sisters[j] throughout Macedonia. But we urge you, beloved,[j] to do so more and more, [11]to aspire to live quietly, to mind your own affairs, and to work with your hands, as we directed you, [12]so that you may behave properly toward outsiders and be dependent on no one.

[13] But we do not want you to be uninformed, brothers and sisters,[j] about those who have died,[k] so that you may not grieve as others do who have no hope. [14]For since we believe that Jesus died and rose again, even so, through Jesus, God will bring with him those who have died.[k] [15]For this we declare to you by the word of the Lord, that we who are alive, who are left until the coming of the Lord, will by no means precede those who have died.[k] [16]For the Lord himself, with a cry of command, with the archangel's call and with the sound of God's trumpet, will descend from heaven, and the dead in Christ will rise first. [17]Then we who are alive, who are left, will be caught up in the clouds together with them to meet the Lord in the air; and so we will be with the Lord forever. [18]Therefore encourage one another with these words.

5 Now concerning the times and the seasons, brothers and sisters,[j] you do not need to have anything written to you. [2]For you yourselves know very well that the day of the Lord will come like a thief in the night. [3]When they say, "There is peace and security," then sudden destruction will come upon them, as labor pains come upon a pregnant woman, and there will be no escape! [4]But you, beloved,[j] are not in darkness, for that day to surprise you like a thief; [5]for you are all children of light and children of the day; we are not of the night or of darkness. [6]So then let us not fall asleep as others do, but let us keep awake and be sober; [7]for those who sleep sleep at night, and those who are drunk get drunk at night. [8]But since we belong to the day, let us be sober, and put on the breastplate of faith and love, and for a helmet the hope of salvation. [9]For God has destined us not for wrath but for obtaining salvation through our Lord Jesus Christ, [10]who died for us, so that whether we are awake or asleep we may live with him. [11]Therefore encourage one another and build up each other, as indeed you are doing.

[12] But we appeal to you, brothers and sisters,[j] to respect those who labor among you, and have charge of you in the Lord and admonish you; [13]esteem them very highly in love because of their work. Be at peace among yourselves. [14]And we urge you, beloved,[j] to admonish the idlers, encourage the faint hearted, help the weak, be patient with all of them. [15]See that none of you repays evil for evil, but always seek to do good to one another and to all. [16]Rejoice always, [17]pray without ceasing, [18]give thanks in all circumstances; for this is the will of God in Christ Jesus for you. [19]Do not quench the Spirit. [20]Do not despise the words of prophets,[l] [21]but test everything; hold fast to what is good; [22]abstain from every form of evil.

[23] May the God of peace himself sanctify you entirely; and may your spirit and soul and body be kept sound[m] and

low-Christian wrong in this matter, or infringe his rights. As we impressed on you before, the Lord punishes all such offences. [7]For God called us to holiness, not to impurity. [8]Anyone therefore who flouts these rules is flouting not man but the God who bestows on you his Holy Spirit.

[9]About love of the brotherhood you need no words of mine, for you are yourselves taught by God to love one another, [10]and you are in fact practising this rule of love towards all your fellow-Christians throughout Macedonia. Yet we appeal to you, friends, to do better still. [11]Let it be your ambition to live quietly and attend to your own business; and to work with your hands, as we told you, [12]so that you may command the respect of those outside your own number, and at the same time never be in want.

[13]WE wish you not to remain in ignorance, friends, about those who sleep in death; you should not grieve like the rest of mankind, who have no hope. [14]We believe that Jesus died and rose again; so too will God bring those who died as Christians to be with Jesus. [15]This we tell you as a word from the Lord: those of us who are still alive when the Lord comes will have no advantage over those who have died; [16]when the command is given, when the archangel's voice is heard, when God's trumpet sounds, then the Lord himself will descend from heaven; first the Christian dead will rise, [17]then we who are still alive shall join them, caught up in clouds to meet the Lord in the air. Thus we shall always be with the Lord. [18]Console one another, then, with these words.

5 About dates and times, my friends, there is no need to write to you, [2]for you yourselves know perfectly well that the day of the Lord comes like a thief in the night. [3]While they are saying, 'All is peaceful, all secure,' destruction is upon them, sudden as the pangs that come on a woman in childbirth; and there will be no escape. [4]But you, friends, are not in the dark; the day will not come upon you like a thief. [5]You are all children of light, children of day. We do not belong to night and darkness, [6]and we must not sleep like the rest, but keep awake and sober. [7]Sleepers sleep at night, and drunkards get drunk at night, [8]but we, who belong to the daylight, must keep sober, armed with the breastplate of faith and love, and the hope of salvation for a helmet. [9]God has not destined us for retribution, but for the full attainment of salvation through our Lord Jesus Christ. [10]He died for us so that awake or asleep we might live in company with him. [11]Therefore encourage one another, build one another up—as indeed you do.

[12]WE beg you, friends, to acknowledge those who are working so hard among you, and are your leaders and counsellors in the Lord's fellowship. [13]Hold them in the highest esteem and affection for the work they do.

Live at peace among yourselves. [14]We urge you, friends, to rebuke the idle, encourage the faint-hearted, support the weak, and be patient with everyone.

[15]See to it that no one pays back wrong for wrong, but always aim at what is best for each other and for all.

[16]Always be joyful; [17]pray continually; [18]give thanks whatever happens; for this is what God wills for you in Christ Jesus.

[19]Do not stifle inspiration [20]or despise prophetic utterances, [21]but test them all; keep hold of what is good [22]and avoid all forms of evil.

[23]May God himself, the God of peace, make you holy through and through, and keep you sound in spirit, soul,

---

[i]Gk brother   [j]Gk brothers   [k]Gk fallen asleep
[l]Gk despise prophecies   [m]Or complete

advantage of or exploit a brother in this matter, for the Lord is an avenger in all these things, as we told you before and solemnly affirmed. 7 For God did not call us to impurity but to holiness. 8 Therefore, whoever disregards this, disregards not a human being but God, who [also] gives his holy Spirit to you.

9 On the subject of mutual charity you have no need for anyone to write you, for you yourselves have been taught by God to love one another. 10 Indeed, you do this for all the brothers throughout Macedonia. Nevertheless we urge you, brothers, to progress even more, 11 and to aspire to live a tranquil life, to mind your own affairs, and to work with your [own] hands, as we instructed you, 12 that you may conduct yourselves properly toward outsiders and not depend on anyone.

13 We do not want you to be unaware, brothers, about those who have fallen asleep, so that you may not grieve like the rest, who have no hope. 14 For if we believe that Jesus died and rose, so too will God, through Jesus, bring with him those who have fallen asleep. 15 Indeed, we tell you this, on the word of the Lord, that we who are alive, who are left until the coming of the Lord, will surely not precede those who have fallen asleep. 16 For the Lord himself, with a word of command, with the voice of an archangel and with the trumpet of God, will come down from heaven, and the dead in Christ will rise first. 17 Then we who are alive, who are left, will be caught up together with them in the clouds to meet the Lord in the air. Thus we shall always be with the Lord. 18 Therefore, console one another with these words.

5 Concerning times and seasons, brothers, you have no need for anything to be written to you. 2 For you yourselves know very well that the day of the Lord will come like a thief at night. 3 When people are saying, "Peace and security," then sudden disaster comes upon them, like labor pains upon a pregnant woman, and they will not escape. 4 But you, brothers, are not in darkness, for that day to overtake you like a thief. 5 For all of you are children of the light and children of the day. We are not of the night or of darkness. 6 Therefore, let us not sleep as the rest do, but let us stay alert and sober. 7 Those who sleep go to sleep at night, and those who are drunk get drunk at night. 8 But since we are of the day, let us be sober, putting on the breastplate of faith and love and the helmet that is hope for salvation. 9 For God did not destine us for wrath, but to gain salvation through our Lord Jesus Christ, 10 who died for us, so that whether we are awake or asleep we may live together with him. 11 Therefore, encourage one another and build one another up, as indeed you do.

12 We ask you, brothers, to respect those who are laboring among you and who are over you in the Lord and who admonish you, 13 and to show esteem for them with special love on account of their work. Be at peace among yourselves.

14 We urge you, brothers, admonish the idle, cheer the fainthearted, support the weak, be patient with all. 15 See that no one returns evil for evil; rather, always seek what is good [both] for each other and for all. 16 Rejoice always. 17 Pray without ceasing. 18 In all circumstances give thanks, for this is the will of God for you in Christ Jesus. 19 Do not quench the Spirit. 20 Do not despise prophetic utterances. 21 Test everything; retain what is good. 22 Refrain from every kind of evil.

23 May the God of peace himself make you perfectly holy and may you entirely, spirit, soul, and body, be preserved

taking advantage of a brother in these matters; the Lord always *pays back ƒ* sins of that sort, as we told you before emphatically. 7 God called us to be holy, not to be immoral; 8 in other words, anyone who rejects this is rejecting not human authority, but God, *who gives you his Holy Spirit.ᵍ*

9 As for brotherly love, there is no need to write to you about that, since you have yourselves learnt from God to love one another, 10 and in fact this is how you treat all the brothers throughout the whole of Macedonia. However, we do urge you, brothers, to go on making even greater progress 11 and to make a point of living quietly, attending to your own business and earning your living, just as we told you to, 12 so that you may earn the respect of outsiders and not be dependent on anyone.

13 We want you to be quite certain, brothers, about those who have fallen asleep, to make sure that you do not grieve for them, as others do who have no hope. 14 We believe that Jesus died and rose again, and that in the same way God will bring with him those who have fallen asleep in Jesus. 15 We can tell you this from the Lord's own teaching, that we who are still alive for the Lord's coming will not have any advantage over those who have fallen asleep. 16 At the signal given by the voice of the Archangel and the trumpet of God, the Lord himself will come down from heaven; those who have died in Christ will be the first to rise, 17 and only after that shall we who remain alive be taken up in the clouds, together with them, to meet the Lord in the air. This is the way we shall be with the Lord for ever. 18 With such thoughts as these, then, you should encourage one another.

5 About times and dates, brothers, there is no need to write to you 2 for you are well aware in any case that the Day of the Lord is going to come like a thief in the night. 3 It is when people are saying, 'How quiet and peaceful it is' that sudden destruction falls on them, as suddenly as labour pains come on a pregnant woman; and there is no escape. 4 But you, brothers, do not live in the dark, that the Day should take you unawares like a thief. 5 No, you are all children of light and children of the day: we do not belong to the night or to darkness, 6 so we should not go on sleeping, as everyone else does, but stay wide awake and sober. 7 Night is the time for sleepers to sleep and night the time for drunkards to be drunk, 8 but we belong to the day and we should be sober; let us put on faith and love for a *breastplate*, and the hope of *salvation* for a *helmet.ʰ* 9 God destined us not for his retribution, but to win salvation through our Lord Jesus Christ, 10 who died for us so that, awake or asleep, we should still live united to him. 11 So give encouragement to each other, and keep strengthening one another, as you do already.

12 We appeal to you, my brothers, to be considerate to those who work so hard among you as your leaders in the Lord and those who admonish you. 13 Have the greatest respect and affection for them because of their work.

Be at peace among yourselves. 14 We urge you, brothers, to admonish those who are undisciplined, encourage the apprehensive, support the weak and be patient with everyone. 15 Make sure that people do not try to repay evil for evil; always aim at what is best for each other and for everyone. 16 Always be joyful; 17 pray constantly; 18 and for all things give thanks; this is the will of God for you in Christ Jesus.

19 Do not stifle the Spirit 20 or despise the gift of prophecy with contempt; 21 test everything and hold on to what is good 22 and *shun every* form of *evil.ⁱ*

23 May the God of peace make you perfect and holy; and may your spirit, life and body be kept blameless for the

ƒ 4 Dt 32:35.   ᵍ 4 Ezk 37:14.   ʰ 5 Is 59:17.   ⁱ 5 Jb 1:8.

NEW REVISED STANDARD VERSION

blameless at the coming of our Lord Jesus Christ. 24 The one who calls you is faithful, and he will do this.

25 Beloved,[n] pray for us.

26 Greet all the brothers and sisters[o] with a holy kiss. 27 I solemnly command you by the Lord that this letter be read to all of them.[p]

28 The grace of our Lord Jesus Christ be with you.[q]

[n] Gk Brothers [o] Gk brothers [p] Gk to all the brothers [q] Other ancient authorities add Amen

REVISED ENGLISH BIBLE

and body, free of any fault when our Lord Jesus Christ comes. 24 He who calls you keeps faith; he will do it.

25 Friends, pray for us also.

26 Greet all our fellow-Christians with the kiss of peace. 27 I adjure you by the Lord to have this letter read to them all.

28 The grace of our Lord Jesus Christ be with you!

blameless for the coming of our Lord Jesus Christ. 24 The one who calls you is faithful, and he will also accomplish it. 25 Brothers, pray for us [too].

26 Greet all the brothers with a holy kiss. 27 I adjure you by the Lord that this letter be read to all the brothers. 28 The grace of our Lord Jesus Christ be with you.

coming of our Lord Jesus Christ. 24 He who has called you is trustworthy and will carry it out.

25 Pray for us, my brothers.

26 Greet all the brothers with a holy kiss. 27 My orders, in the Lord's name, are that this letter is to be read to all the brothers.

28 The grace of our Lord Jesus Christ be with you.

THE SECOND LETTER OF PAUL TO THE

Thessalonians

1 Paul, Silvanus, and Timothy,
To the church of the Thessalonians in God our Father and the Lord Jesus Christ:
2 Grace to you and peace from God our[a] Father and the Lord Jesus Christ.

3 We must always give thanks to God for you, brothers and sisters,[b] as is right, because your faith is growing abundantly, and the love of everyone of you for one another is increasing. 4 Therefore we ourselves boast of you among the churches of God for your steadfastness and faith during all your persecutions and the afflictions that you are enduring.

5 This is evidence of the righteous judgment of God, and is intended to make you worthy of the kingdom of God, for which you are also suffering. 6 For it is indeed just of God to repay with affliction those who afflict you, 7 and to give relief to the afflicted as well as to us, when the Lord Jesus is revealed from heaven with his mighty angels 8 in flaming fire, inflicting vengeance on those who do not know God and on those who do not obey the gospel of our Lord Jesus. 9 These will suffer the punishment of eternal destruction, separated from the presence of the Lord and from the glory of his might, 10 when he comes to be glorified by his saints and to be marveled at on that day among all who have believed, because our testimony to you was believed. 11 To this end we always pray for you, asking that our God will make you worthy of his call and will fulfill by his power every good resolve and work of faith, 12 so that the name of our Lord Jesus may be glorified in you, and you in him, according to the grace of our God and the Lord Jesus Christ.

2 As to the coming of our Lord Jesus Christ and our being gathered together to him, we beg you, brothers and sisters,[b] 2 not to be quickly shaken in mind or alarmed, either by spirit or by word or by letter, as though from us, to the effect that the day of the Lord is already here. 3 Let no one deceive you in any way; for that day will not come unless the rebellion comes first and the lawless one[c] is revealed, the one destined for destruction.[d] 4 He opposes and exalts himself above every so-called god or object of worship, so that he takes his seat in the temple of God, declaring himself to be God. 5 Do you not remember that I told you these things when I was still with you? 6 And you know what is now restraining him, so that he may be revealed when his time comes. 7 For the mystery of lawlessness is already at work, but only until the one who now restrains it is removed. 8 And then the lawless one will be revealed, whom the Lord Jesus[e] will destroy[f] with the breath of his mouth, annihilating him by the manifestation of his coming. 9 The coming of the lawless one is apparent in the working of Satan, who uses all power, signs, lying wonders, 10 and every kind of wicked deception for those who are perishing, because they refused to love the truth and so be saved. 11 For this reason God sends them a powerful delusion, leading them to believe what is false, 12 so that

---

THE SECOND LETTER OF PAUL TO THE

Thessalonians

1 FROM Paul, Silvanus, and Timothy to the church of the Thessalonians who belong to God our Father and the Lord Jesus Christ.
2 Grace to you and peace from God the Father and the Lord Jesus Christ.

3 Friends, we are always bound to thank God for you, and it is right that we should, because your faith keeps on increasing and the love you all have for each other grows ever greater. 4 Indeed we boast about you among the churches of God, because your faith remains so steadfast under all the persecutions and troubles you endure. 5 This points to the justice of God's judgement; you will be proved worthy of the kingdom of God, for which indeed you are suffering. 6 It is just that God should balance the account by sending affliction to those who afflict you, 7 and relief to you who are afflicted, and to us as well, when the Lord Jesus is revealed from heaven with his mighty angels 8 in blazing fire. Then he will mete out punishment to those who refuse to acknowledge God and who will not obey the gospel of our Lord Jesus. 9 They will suffer the penalty of eternal destruction, cut off from the presence of the Lord and the splendour of his might, 10 when on the great day he comes to reveal his glory among his own and his majesty among all believers; and therefore among you, since you believed the testimony we brought you.

11 With this in mind we pray for you always, that our God may count you worthy of your calling, and that his power may bring to fulfilment every good purpose and every act inspired by faith, 12 so that the name of our Lord Jesus may be glorified in you, and you in him, according to the grace of our God and the Lord Jesus Christ.

2 Now ABOUT the coming of our Lord Jesus Christ, when he is to gather us to himself: I beg you, my friends, 2 do not suddenly lose your heads, do not be alarmed by any prophetic utterance, any pronouncement, or any letter purporting to come from us, alleging that the day of the Lord is already here. 3 Let no one deceive you in any way. That day cannot come before the final rebellion against God, when wickedness will be revealed in human form, the man doomed to destruction. 4 He is the adversary who raises himself up against every so-called god or object of worship, and even enthrones himself in God's temple claiming to be God. 5 Do you not remember that I told you this while I was still with you? 6 You know, too, about the restraining power which ensures that he will be revealed only at his appointed time; 7 for already the secret forces of wickedness are at work, secret only for the present until the restraining hand is removed from the scene. 8 Then he will be revealed, the wicked one whom the Lord Jesus will destroy with the breath of his mouth and annihilate by the radiance of his presence. 9 The coming of the wicked one is the work of Satan; it will be attended by all the powerful signs and miracles that falsehood can devise, 10 all the deception that sinfulness can impose on those doomed to destruction, because they did not open their minds to love of the truth and so find salvation. 11 That is why God puts them under a compelling delusion, which makes them believe what is false, 12 so that all who have not believed the truth

---

[a] Other ancient authorities read *the*   [b] Gk *brothers*   [c] Gk *the man of lawlessness*; other ancient authorities read *the man of sin*
[d] Gk *the son of destruction*   [e] Other ancient authorities lack *Jesus*
[f] Other ancient authorities read *consume*

The Second Letter to the Thessalonians

2 Thessalonians

THE SECOND LETTER OF PAUL TO THE CHURCH IN THESSALONICA

1 Paul, Silvanus, and Timothy to the church of the Thessalonians in God our Father and the Lord Jesus Christ: 2 grace to you and peace from God [our] Father and the Lord Jesus Christ.

3 We ought to thank God always for you, brothers, as is fitting, because your faith flourishes ever more, and the love of every one of you for one another grows ever greater. 4 Accordingly, we ourselves boast of you in the churches of God regarding your endurance and faith in all your persecutions and the afflictions you endure.

5 This is evidence of the just judgment of God, so that you may be considered worthy of the kingdom of God for which you are suffering. 6 For it is surely just on God's part to repay with afflictions those who are afflicting you, 7 and to grant rest along with us to you who are undergoing afflictions, at the revelation of the Lord Jesus from heaven with his mighty angels, 8 in blazing fire, inflicting punishment on those who do not acknowledge God and on those who do not obey the gospel of our Lord Jesus. 9 These will pay the penalty of eternal ruin, separated from the presence of the Lord and from the glory of his power, 10 when he comes to be glorified among his holy ones and to be marveled at on that day among all who have believed, for our testimony to you was believed.

11 To this end, we always pray for you, that our God may make you worthy of his calling and powerfully bring to fulfillment every good purpose and every effort of faith, 12 that the name of our Lord Jesus may be glorified in you, and you in him, in accord with the grace of our God and Lord Jesus Christ.

2 We ask you, brothers, with regard to the coming of our Lord Jesus Christ and our assembling with him, 2 not to be shaken out of your minds suddenly, or to be alarmed either by a "spirit," or by an oral statement, or by a letter allegedly from us to the effect that the day of the Lord is at hand. 3 Let no one deceive you in any way. For unless the apostasy comes first and the lawless one is revealed, the one doomed to perdition, 4 who opposes and exalts himself above every so-called god and object of worship, so as to seat himself in the temple of God, claiming that he is a god — 5 do you not recall that while I was still with you I told you these things? 6 And now you know what is restraining, that he may be revealed in his time. 7 For the mystery of lawlessness is already at work. But the one who restrains is to do so only for the present, until he is removed from the scene. 8 And then the lawless one will be revealed, whom the Lord [Jesus] will kill with the breath of his mouth and render powerless by the manifestation of his coming, 9 the one whose coming springs from the power of Satan in every mighty deed and in signs and wonders that lie, 10 and in every wicked deceit for those who are perishing because they have not accepted the love of truth so that they may be saved. 11 Therefore, God is sending them a deceiving power so that they may believe the lie, 12 that all who have not

1 Paul, Silvanus and Timothy, to the Church in Thessalonica which is in God our Father and the Lord Jesus Christ. 2 Grace to you and peace from God the Father and the Lord Jesus Christ.

3 We must always thank God for you, brothers; quite rightly, because your faith is growing so wonderfully and the mutual love that each one of you has for all never stops increasing. 4 Among the churches of God we take special pride in you for your perseverance and faith under all the persecutions and hardships you have to bear. 5 It all shows that God's judgement is just, so that you may be found worthy of the kingdom of God; it is for the sake of this that you are suffering now.

6 For God's justice will surely mean hardship being inflicted on those who are now inflicting hardship on you, 7 and for you who are now suffering hardship, relief with us, when the Lord Jesus appears from heaven with the angels of his power. 8 He will come *amid flaming fire*; *he will impose a penalty*[a] on those who *do not acknowledge God* and *refuse to accept* the gospel of our Lord Jesus. 9 Their punishment is to be lost eternally, excluded *from the presence of the Lord and from the glory of his strength* 10 *on that day* when he comes *to be glorified among his holy ones* and *marvelled at* by all who believe in him; and you are among those who believed our witness.

11 In view of this we also pray continually that our God will make you worthy of his call, and by his power fulfil all your desires for goodness, and complete all that you have been doing through faith; 12 so that the *name* of our Lord Jesus Christ *may be glorified* in you and you in him, by the grace of our God and the Lord Jesus Christ.

2 About the coming of our Lord Jesus Christ, brothers, and our being gathered to him: 2 please do not be too easily thrown into confusion or alarmed by any manifestation of the Spirit or any statement or any letter claiming to come from us, suggesting that the Day of the Lord has already arrived. 3 Never let anyone deceive you in any way.

It cannot happen until the Great Revolt[b] has taken place and there has appeared the wicked One, the lost One, 4 the Enemy, who *raises himself above every* so-called *God* or object of worship, to *enthrone himself in God's* sanctuary and flaunts the claim that he is God. 5 Surely you remember my telling you about this when I was with you? 6 And you know, too, what is still holding him back from appearing before his appointed time. 7 The mystery of wickedness is already at work, but let him who is restraining it once be removed, 8 and the wicked One will appear openly. The Lord *will destroy him with the breath of his mouth* and will annihilate him with his glorious appearance at his coming.

9 But the coming of the wicked One will be marked by Satan being at work in all kinds of counterfeit miracles and signs and wonders, 10 and every wicked deception aimed at those who are on the way to destruction because they would not accept the love of the truth and so be saved. 11 And therefore God sends on them a power that deludes people so that they believe what is false, 12 and so that those who do

---

a 1 This threatening imagery of the Day of the Lord uses Is 66:15; Jr 10:25; Is 2:10–17; 49:3; 66:5.　　*b* 2 Paul uses biblical symbolism: Is 11:4; 14:13; Ezk 28:2; Ps 33:6.

all who have not believed the truth but took pleasure in unrighteousness will be condemned.

13 But we must always give thanks to God for you, brothers and sisters[g] beloved by the Lord, because God chose you as the first fruits[h] for salvation through sanctification by the Spirit and through belief in the truth. 14 For this purpose he called you through our proclamation of the good news,[i] so that you may obtain the glory of our Lord Jesus Christ. 15 So then, brothers and sisters,[g] stand firm and hold fast to the traditions that you were taught by us, either by word of mouth or by our letter.

16 Now may our Lord Jesus Christ himself and God our Father, who loved us and through grace gave us eternal comfort and good hope, 17 comfort your hearts and strengthen them in every good work and word.

3 Finally, brothers and sisters,[g] pray for us, so that the word of the Lord may spread rapidly and be glorified everywhere, just as it is among you, 2 and that we may be rescued from wicked and evil people; for not all have faith. 3 But the Lord is faithful; he will strengthen you and guard you from the evil one.[j] 4 And we have confidence in the Lord concerning you, that you are doing and will go on doing the things that we command. 5 May the Lord direct your hearts to the love of God and to the steadfastness of Christ.

6 Now we command you, beloved,[g] in the name of our Lord Jesus Christ, to keep away from believers who are[k] living in idleness and not according to the tradition that they[l] received from us. 7 For you yourselves know how you ought to imitate us; we were not idle when we were with you, 8 and we did not eat anyone's bread without paying for it; but with toil and labor we worked night and day, so that we might not burden any of you. 9 This was not because we do not have that right, but in order to give you an example to imitate. 10 For even when we were with you, we gave you this command: Anyone unwilling to work should not eat. 11 For we hear that some of you are living in idleness, mere busybodies, not doing any work. 12 Now such persons we command and exhort in the Lord Jesus Christ to do their work quietly and to earn their own living. 13 Brothers and sisters,[m] do not be weary in doing what is right.

14 Take note of those who do not obey what we say in this letter; have nothing to do with them, so that they may be ashamed. 15 Do not regard them as enemies, but warn them as believers.[n]

16 Now may the Lord of peace himself give you peace at all times in all ways. The Lord be with all of you.

17 I, Paul, write this greeting with my own hand. This is the mark in every letter of mine; it is the way I write. 18 The grace of our Lord Jesus Christ be with all of you.[o]

g Gk brothers   h Other ancient authorities read from the beginning
i Or through our gospel   j Or from evil   k Gk from every brother
who is   l Other ancient authorities read you   m Gk Brothers
n Gk a brother   o Other ancient authorities add Amen

but made sinfulness their choice may be brought to judgement.

13 WE are always bound to thank God for you, my friends beloved by the Lord. From the beginning of time God chose you to find salvation in the Spirit who consecrates you and in the truth you believe. 14 It was for this that he called you through the gospel we brought, so that you might come to possess the splendour of our Lord Jesus Christ.

15 Stand firm then, my friends, and hold fast to the traditions which you have learned from us by word or by letter. 16 And may our Lord Jesus Christ himself and God our Father, who has shown us such love, and in his grace has given us such unfailing encouragement and so sure a hope, 17 still encourage and strengthen you in every good deed and word.

3 AND now, friends, pray for us, that the word of the Lord may have everywhere the swift and glorious success it has had among you, 2 and that we may be rescued from wrong-headed and wicked people; for not all have faith. 3 But the Lord keeps faith, and he will strengthen you and guard you from the evil one; 4 and in the Lord we have confidence about you, that you are doing and will continue to do what we tell you. 5 May the Lord direct your hearts towards God's love and the steadfastness of Christ.

6 These are our instructions to you, friends, in the name of our Lord Jesus Christ: hold aloof from every Christian who falls into idle habits, and disregards the tradition you received from us. 7 You yourselves know how you ought to follow our example: you never saw us idling; 8 we did not accept free hospitality from anyone; night and day in toil and drudgery we worked for a living, rather than be a burden to any of you — 9 not because we do not have the right to maintenance, but to set an example for you to follow. 10 Already during our stay with you we laid down this rule: anyone who will not work shall not eat. 11 We mention this because we hear that some of you are idling their time away, minding everybody's business but their own. 12 We instruct and urge such people in the name of the Lord Jesus Christ to settle down to work and earn a living.

13 My friends, you must never tire of doing right. 14 If anyone disobeys the instructions given in my letter, single him out, and have nothing to do with him until he is ashamed of himself. 15 I do not mean treat him as an enemy, but admonish him as one of the family.

16 May the Lord of peace himself give you peace at all times and in all ways. The Lord be with you all.

17 This greeting is in my own handwriting; all genuine letters of mine bear the same signature — Paul.

18 The grace of our Lord Jesus Christ be with you all.

2:13 From . . . chose you: some witnesses read God chose you as his firstfruits.

believed the truth but have approved wrongdoing may be condemned.

13 But we ought to give thanks to God for you always, brothers loved by the Lord, because God chose you as the firstfruits for salvation through sanctification by the Spirit and belief in truth. 14 To this end he has [also] called you through our gospel to possess the glory of our Lord Jesus Christ. 15 Therefore, brothers, stand firm and hold fast to the traditions that you were taught, either by an oral statement or by a letter of ours.

16 May our Lord Jesus Christ himself and God our Father, who has loved us and given us everlasting encouragement and good hope through his grace, 17 encourage your hearts and strengthen them in every good deed and word.

3 Finally, brothers, pray for us, so that the word of the Lord may speed forward and be glorified, as it did among you, 2 and that we may be delivered from perverse and wicked people, for not all have faith. 3 But the Lord is faithful; he will strengthen you and guard you from the evil one. 4 We are confident of you in the Lord that what we instruct you, you [both] are doing and will continue to do. 5 May the Lord direct your hearts to the love of God and to the endurance of Christ.

6 We instruct you, brothers, in the name of [our] Lord Jesus Christ, to shun any brother who conducts himself in a disorderly way and not according to the tradition they received from us. 7 For you know how one must imitate us. For we did not act in a disorderly way among you, 8 nor did we eat food received free from anyone. On the contrary, in toil and drudgery, night and day we worked, so as not to burden any of you. 9 Not that we do not have the right. Rather, we wanted to present ourselves as a model for you, so that you might imitate us. 10 In fact, when we were with you, we instructed you that if anyone was unwilling to work, neither should that one eat. 11 We hear that some are conducting themselves among you in a disorderly way, by not keeping busy but minding the business of others. 12 Such people we instruct and urge in the Lord Jesus Christ to work quietly and to eat their own food. 13 But you, brothers, do not be remiss in doing good. 14 If anyone does not obey our word as expressed in this letter, take note of this person not to associate with him, that he may be put to shame. 15 Do not regard him as an enemy but admonish him as a brother. 16 May the Lord of peace himself give you peace at all times and in every way. The Lord be with all of you.

17 This greeting is in my own hand, Paul's. This is the sign in every letter; this is how I write. 18 The grace of our Lord Jesus Christ be with all of you.

not believe the truth and take their pleasure in wickedness may all be condemned.

13 But we must always thank God for you, brothers whom the Lord loves, because God chose you from the beginning to be saved by the Spirit who makes us holy and by faith in the truth. 14 Through our gospel he called you to this so that you should claim as your own the glory of our Lord Jesus Christ. 15 Stand firm, then, brothers, and keep the traditions that we taught you, whether by word of mouth or by letter. 16 May our Lord Jesus Christ himself, and God our Father who has given us his love and, through his grace, such ceaseless encouragement and such sure hope, 17 encourage you and strengthen you in every good word and deed.

3 Finally, brothers, pray for us that the Lord's message may spread quickly, and be received with honour as it was among you; 2 and pray that we may be preserved from bigoted and evil people, for not everyone has faith. 3 You can rely on the Lord, who will give you strength and guard you from the evil One, 4 and we, in the Lord, have every confidence in you, that you are doing and will go on doing all that we tell you. 5 May the Lord turn your hearts towards the love of God and the perseverance of Christ.

6 In the name of the Lord Jesus Christ, we urge you, brothers, to keep away from any of the brothers who lives an undisciplined life, not in accordance with the tradition you received from us.

7 You know how you should take us as your model: we were not undisciplined when we were with you, 8 nor did we ever accept food from anyone without paying for it; no, we worked with unsparing energy, night and day, so as not to be a burden on any of you. 9 This was not because we had no right to be, but in order to make ourselves a model for you to imitate.

10 We urged you when we were with you not to let anyone eat who refused to work. 11 Now we hear that there are some of you who are living lives without any discipline, doing no work themselves but interfering with other people's. 12 In the Lord Jesus Christ, we urge and call on people of this kind to go on quietly working and earning the food that they eat.

13 My brothers, never slacken in doing what is right. 14 If anyone refuses to obey what I have written in this letter, take note of him and have nothing to do with him, so that he will be ashamed of himself, 15 though you are not to treat him as an enemy, but to correct him as a brother.

16 May the Lord of peace himself give you peace at all times and in every way. The Lord be with you all.

17 This greeting is in my own hand — PAUL. It is the mark of genuineness in every letter; this is my own writing. 18 May the grace of our Lord Jesus Christ be with you all.

THE FIRST LETTER OF PAUL TO
Timothy

1 Paul, an apostle of Christ Jesus by the command of God our Savior and of Christ Jesus our hope, 2 To Timothy, my loyal child in the faith:

Grace, mercy, and peace from God the Father and Christ Jesus our Lord.

3 I urge you, as I did when I was on my way to Macedonia, to remain in Ephesus so that you may instruct certain people not to teach any different doctrine, 4 and not to occupy themselves with myths and endless genealogies that promote speculations rather than the divine training^a that is known by faith. 5 But the aim of such instruction is love that comes from a pure heart, a good conscience, and sincere faith. 6 Some people have deviated from these and turned to meaningless talk, 7 desiring to be teachers of the law, without understanding either what they are saying or the things about which they make assertions.

8 Now we know that the law is good, if one uses it legitimately. 9 This means understanding that the law is laid down not for the innocent but for the lawless and disobedient, for the godless and sinful, for the unholy and profane, for those who kill their father or mother, for murderers, 10 fornicators, sodomites, slave traders, liars, perjurers, and whatever else is contrary to the sound teaching 11 that conforms to the glorious gospel of the blessed God, which he entrusted to me.

12 I am grateful to Christ Jesus our Lord, who has strengthened me, because he judged me faithful and appointed me to his service, 13 even though I was formerly a blasphemer, a persecutor, and a man of violence. But I received mercy because I had acted ignorantly in unbelief, 14 and the grace of our Lord overflowed for me with the faith and love that are in Christ Jesus. 15 The saying is sure and worthy of full acceptance, that Christ Jesus came into the world to save sinners—of whom I am the foremost. 16 But for that very reason I received mercy, so that in me, as the foremost, Jesus Christ might display the utmost patience, making me an example to those who would come to believe in him for eternal life. 17 To the King of the ages, immortal, invisible, the only God, be honor and glory forever and ever.^b Amen.

18 I am giving you these instructions, Timothy, my child, in accordance with the prophecies made earlier about you, so that by following them you may fight the good fight, 19 having faith and a good conscience. By rejecting conscience, certain persons have suffered shipwreck in the faith; 20 among them are Hymenaeus and Alexander, whom I have turned over to Satan, so that they may learn not to blaspheme.

2 First of all, then, I urge that supplications, prayers, intercessions, and thanksgivings be made for everyone, 2 for kings and all who are in high positions, so that we may lead a quiet and peaceable life in all godliness and dignity. 3 This is right and is acceptable in the sight of God our Savior, 4 who desires everyone to be saved and to come to the knowledge of the truth. 5 For

THE FIRST LETTER OF PAUL TO
Timothy

1 From Paul, apostle of Christ Jesus by command of God our Saviour and Christ Jesus our hope, 2 to Timothy his true-born son in the faith.

Grace, mercy, and peace to you from God the Father and Christ Jesus our Lord.

3 When I was starting for Macedonia, I urged you to stay on at Ephesus. You were to instruct certain people to give up teaching erroneous doctrines 4 and devoting themselves to interminable myths and genealogies, which give rise to mere speculation, and do not further God's plan for us, which works through faith.

5 This instruction has love as its goal, the love which springs from a pure heart, a good conscience, and a genuine faith. 6 Through lack of these some people have gone astray into a wilderness of words. 7 They set out to be teachers of the law, although they do not understand either the words they use or the subjects about which they are so dogmatic.

8 We all know that the law is an admirable thing, provided we treat it as law, 9 recognizing that it is designed not for good citizens, but for the lawless and unruly, the impious and sinful, the irreligious and worldly, for parricides and matricides, murderers 10 and fornicators, perverts, kidnappers, liars, perjurers—in fact all whose behaviour flouts the sound teaching 11 which conforms with the gospel entrusted to me, the gospel which tells of the glory of the ever-blessed God.

12 I give thanks to Christ Jesus our Lord, who has made me equal to the task; I thank him for judging me worthy of trust and appointing me to his service—13 although in the past I had met him with abuse and persecution and outrage. But because I acted in the ignorance of unbelief I was dealt with mercifully; 14 the grace of our Lord was lavished upon me, along with the faith and love which are ours in Christ Jesus.

15 Here is a saying you may trust, one that merits full acceptance: 'Christ Jesus came into the world to save sinners'; and among them I stand first. 16 But I was mercifully dealt with for this very purpose, that Jesus Christ might find in me the first occasion for displaying his inexhaustible patience, and that I might be typical of all who were in future to have faith in him and gain eternal life. 17 To the King eternal, immortal, invisible, the only God, be honour and glory for ever and ever! Amen.

18 In laying this charge upon you, Timothy my son, I am guided by those prophetic utterances which first directed me to you. Encouraged by them, fight the good fight 19 with faith and a clear conscience. It was through spurning conscience that certain persons made shipwreck of their faith, 20 among them Hymenaeus and Alexander, whom I consigned to Satan, in the hope that through this discipline they might learn not to be blasphemous.

2 First of all, then, I urge that petitions, prayers, intercessions, and thanksgivings be offered for everyone, 2 for sovereigns and for all in high office so that we may lead a tranquil and quiet life, free to practise our religion with dignity. 3 Such prayer is right, and approved by God our Saviour, 4 whose will it is that all should find salvation

---

1:4 **do not . . . faith:** *or* do not promote the faithful discharge of God's stewardship.

^a Or *plan*   ^b Gk *to the ages of the ages*

The First Letter to Timothy

1 Timothy

THE FIRST LETTER
FROM PAUL TO TIMOTHY

1 Paul, an apostle of Christ Jesus by command of God our savior and of Christ Jesus our hope, 2 to Timothy, my true child in faith: grace, mercy, and peace from God the Father and Christ Jesus our Lord.

3 I repeat the request I made of you when I was on my way to Macedonia, that you stay in Ephesus to instruct certain people not to teach false doctrines 4 or to concern themselves with myths and endless genealogies, which promote speculations rather than the plan of God that is to be received by faith. 5 The aim of this instruction is love from a pure heart, a good conscience, and a sincere faith. 6 Some people have deviated from these and turned to meaningless talk, 7 wanting to be teachers of the law, but without understanding either what they are saying or what they assert with such assurance.

8 We know that the law is good, provided that one uses it as law, 9 with the understanding that law is meant not for a righteous person but for the lawless and unruly, the godless and sinful, the unholy and profane, those who kill their fathers or mothers, murderers, 10 the unchaste, practicing homosexuals, kidnappers, liars, perjurers, and whatever else is opposed to sound teaching, 11 according to the glorious gospel of the blessed God, with which I have been entrusted.

12 I am grateful to him who has strengthened me, Christ Jesus our Lord, because he considered me trustworthy in appointing me to the ministry. 13 I was once a blasphemer and a persecutor and an arrogant man, but I have been mercifully treated because I acted out of ignorance in my unbelief. 14 Indeed, the grace of our Lord has been abundant, along with the faith and love that are in Christ Jesus. 15 This saying is trustworthy and deserves full acceptance: Christ Jesus came into the world to save sinners. Of these I am the foremost. 16 But for that reason I was mercifully treated, so that in me, as the foremost, Christ Jesus might display all his patience as an example for those who would come to believe in him for everlasting life. 17 To the king of ages, incorruptible, invisible, the only God, honor and glory forever and ever. Amen.

18 I entrust this charge to you, Timothy, my child, in accordance with the prophetic words once spoken about you. Through them may you fight a good fight 19 by having faith and a good conscience. Some, by rejecting conscience, have made a shipwreck of their faith, 20 among them Hymenaeus and Alexander, whom I have handed over to Satan to be taught not to blaspheme.

2 First of all, then, I ask that supplications, prayers, petitions, and thanksgivings be offered for everyone, 2 for kings and for all in authority, that we may lead a quiet and tranquil life in all devotion and dignity. 3 This is good and pleasing to God our savior, 4 who wills everyone to be saved and to come to knowledge of the truth.

1 Paul, apostle of Christ Jesus appointed by the command of God our Saviour and of Christ Jesus our hope, 2 to Timothy, true child of mine in the faith. Grace, mercy and peace from God the Father and from Christ Jesus our Lord.

3 When I was setting out for Macedonia I urged you to stay on in Ephesus to instruct certain people not to spread wrong teaching 4 or to give attention to myths and unending genealogies; these things only foster doubts instead of furthering God's plan which is founded on faith. 5 The final goal at which this instruction aims is love, issuing from a pure heart, a clear conscience and a sincere faith. 6 Some people have missed the way to these things and turned to empty speculation, 7 trying to be teachers of the Law; but they understand neither the words they use nor the matters about which they make such strong assertions.

8 We are well aware that the Law is good, but only provided it is used legitimately, 9 on the understanding that laws are not framed for people who are upright. On the contrary, they are for criminals and the insubordinate, for the irreligious and the wicked, for the sacrilegious and the godless; they are for people who kill their fathers or mothers and for murderers, 10 for the promiscuous, homosexuals, kidnappers, for liars and for perjurers — and for everything else that is contrary to the sound teaching 11 that accords with the gospel of the glory of the blessed God, the gospel that was entrusted to me.

12 I thank Christ Jesus our Lord, who has given me strength. By calling me into his service he has judged me trustworthy, 13 even though I used to be a blasphemer and a persecutor and contemptuous. Mercy, however, was shown me, because while I lacked faith I acted in ignorance; 14 but the grace of our Lord filled me with faith and with the love that is in Christ Jesus. 15 Here is a saying that you can rely on and nobody should doubt: that Christ Jesus came into the world to save sinners. I myself am the greatest of them; 16 and if mercy has been shown to me, it is because Jesus Christ meant to make me the leading example of his inexhaustible patience for all the other people who were later to trust in him for eternal life. 17 To the eternal King, the undying, invisible and only God, be honour and glory for ever and ever. Amen.

18 Timothy, my son, these are the instructions that I am giving you, in accordance with the words once spoken over you by the prophets, so that in their light you may fight like a good soldier 19 with faith and a good conscience for your weapons. Some people have put conscience aside and wrecked their faith in consequence. 20 I mean men like Hymenaeus and Alexander, whom I have handed over to Satan so that they may learn not to be blasphemous.

2 I urge then, first of all that petitions, prayers, intercessions and thanksgiving should be offered for everyone, 2 for kings and others in authority, so that we may be able to live peaceful and quiet lives with all devotion and propriety. 3 To do this is right, and acceptable to God our Saviour: 4 he wants everyone to be saved and reach full knowledge of

NEW REVISED STANDARD VERSION	REVISED ENGLISH BIBLE

there is one God;
> there is also one mediator between God and
> humankind,
> Christ Jesus, himself human,
6   who gave himself a ransom for all
—this was attested at the right time. 7For this I was appointed a herald and an apostle (I am telling the truth,c I am not lying), a teacher of the Gentiles in faith and truth.

8 I desire, then, that in every place the men should pray, lifting up holy hands without anger or argument; 9also that the women should dress themselves modestly and decently in suitable clothing, not with their hair braided, or with gold, pearls, or expensive clothes, 10but with good works, as is proper for women who profess reverence for God. 11Let a womand learn in silence with full submission. 12I permit no womand to teach or to have authority over a man;e she is to keep silent. 13For Adam was formed first, then Eve; 14and Adam was not deceived, but the woman was deceived and became a transgressor. 15Yet she will be saved through childbearing, provided they continue in faith and love and holiness, with modesty.

3 The saying is sure:f whoever aspires to the office of bishopg desires a noble task. 2Now a bishoph must be above reproach, married only once,i temperate, sensible, respectable, hospitable, an apt teacher, 3not a drunkard, not violent but gentle, not quarrelsome, and not a lover of money. 4He must manage his own household well, keeping his children submissive and respectful in every way — 5for if someone does not know how to manage his own household, how can he take care of God's church? 6He must not be a recent convert, or he may be puffed up with conceit and fall into the condemnation of the devil. 7Moreover, he must be well thought of by outsiders, so that he may not fall into disgrace and the snare of the devil.

8 Deacons likewise must be serious, not double-tongued, not indulging in much wine, not greedy for money; 9they must hold fast to the mystery of the faith with a clear conscience. 10And let them first be tested; then, if they prove themselves blameless, let them serve as deacons. 11Womenj likewise must be serious, not slanderers, but temperate, faithful in all things. 12Let deacons be married only once,k and let them manage their children and their households well; 13for those who serve well as deacons gain a good standing for themselves and great boldness in the faith that is in Christ Jesus.

14 I hope to come to you soon, but I am writing these instructions to you so that, 15if I am delayed, you may know how one ought to behave in the household of God, which is the church of the living God, the pillar and bulwark of the truth. 16Without any doubt, the mystery of our religion is great:
> Hel was revealed in flesh,
> > vindicatedm in spirit,n
> > > seen by angels,
> > proclaimed among Gentiles,
> > believed in throughout the world,
> > · taken up in glory.

and come to know the truth. 5For there is one God, and there is one mediator between God and man, Christ Jesus, himself man, 6who sacrificed himself to win freedom for all mankind, revealing God's purpose at God's good time; 7of this I was appointed herald and apostle (this is no lie, it is the truth), to instruct the Gentiles in the true faith.

8It is my desire, therefore, that everywhere prayers be said by the men of the congregation, who shall lift up their hands with a pure intention, without anger or argument. 9Women must dress in becoming manner, modestly and soberly, not with elaborate hair-styles, not adorned with gold or pearls or expensive clothes, 10but with good deeds, as befits women who claim to be religious. 11Their role is to learn, listening quietly and with due submission. 12I do not permit women to teach or dictate to the men; they should keep quiet. 13For Adam was created first, and Eve afterwards; 14moreover it was not Adam who was deceived; it was the woman who, yielding to deception, fell into sin. 15But salvation for the woman will be in the bearing of children, provided she continues in faith, love, and holiness, with modesty.

3 Here is a saying you may trust: 'To aspire to leadership is an honourable ambition.' 2A bishop, therefore, must be above reproach, husband of one wife, sober, temperate, courteous, hospitable, and a good teacher; 3he must not be given to drink or brawling, but be of a forbearing disposition, avoiding quarrels, and not avaricious. 4He must be one who manages his own household well and controls his children without losing his dignity, 5for if a man does not know how to manage his own family, how can he take charge of a congregation of God's people? 6He should not be a recent convert; conceit might bring on him the devil's punishment. 7He must moreover have a good reputation with the outside world, so that he may not be exposed to scandal and be caught in the devil's snare.

8Deacons, likewise, must be dignified, not indulging in double talk, given neither to excessive drinking nor to money-grubbing. 9They must be men who combine a clear conscience with a firm hold on the mystery of the faith. 10And they too must first undergo scrutiny, and only if they are of unimpeachable character may they serve as deacons. 11Women in this office must likewise be dignified, not scandalmongers, but sober, and trustworthy in every way. 12A deacon must be the husband of one wife, and good at managing his children and his own household. 13For deacons with a good record of service are entitled to high standing and the right to be heard on matters of the Christian faith.

14I am hoping to come to you before long, but I write this 15in case I am delayed, to let you know what is proper conduct in God's household, that is, the church of the living God, the pillar and bulwark of the truth. 16And great beyond all question is the mystery of our religion:

> He was manifested in flesh,
> vindicated in spirit,
> seen by angels;
> he was proclaimed among the nations,
> believed in throughout the world,
> raised to heavenly glory.

---

cOther ancient authorities add in Christ   dOr wife   eOr her husband   fSome interpreters place these words at the end of the previous paragraph. Other ancient authorities read The saying is commonly accepted   gOr overseer   hOr an overseer   iGk the husband of one wife   jOr Their wives, or Women deacons kGk be husbands of one wife   lGk Who; other ancient authorities read God; others, Which   mOr justified   nOr by the Spirit

3:1 **Here . . . trust:** some witnesses read There is a popular saying.
3:11 **Women . . . office:** or Their wives.

5 For there is one God.
There is also one mediator between God and the
    human race,
Christ Jesus, himself human,
6 who gave himself as ransom for all.

This was the testimony at the proper time. 7 For this I was appointed preacher and apostle (I am speaking the truth, I am not lying), teacher of the Gentiles in faith and truth.

8 It is my wish, then, that in every place the men should pray, lifting up holy hands, without anger or argument. 9 Similarly, [too,] women should adorn themselves with proper conduct, with modesty and self-control, not with braided hairstyles and gold ornaments, or pearls, or expensive clothes, 10 but rather, as befits women who profess reverence for God, with good deeds. 11 A woman must receive instruction silently and under complete control. 12 I do not permit a woman to teach or to have authority over a man. She must be quiet. 13 For Adam was formed first, then Eve. 14 Further, Adam was not deceived, but the woman was deceived and transgressed. 15 But she will be saved through motherhood, provided women persevere in faith and love and holiness, with self-control.

3 This saying is trustworthy: whoever aspires to the office of bishop desires a noble task. 2 Therefore, a bishop must be irreproachable, married only once, temperate, self-controlled, decent, hospitable, able to teach, 3 not a drunkard, not aggressive, but gentle, not contentious, not a lover of money. 4 He must manage his own household well, keeping his children under control with perfect dignity; 5 for if a man does not know how to manage his own household, how can he take care of the church of God? 6 He should not be a recent convert, so that he may not become conceited and thus incur the devil's punishment. 7 He must also have a good reputation among outsiders, so that he may not fall into disgrace, the devil's trap.

8 Similarly, deacons must be dignified, not deceitful, not addicted to drink, not greedy for sordid gain, 9 holding fast to the mystery of the faith with a clear conscience. 10 Moreover, they should be tested first; then, if there is nothing against them, let them serve as deacons. 11 Women, similarly, should be dignified, not slanderers, but temperate and faithful in everything. 12 Deacons may be married only once and must manage their children and their households well. 13 Thus those who serve well as deacons gain good standing and much confidence in their faith in Christ Jesus.

14 I am writing you about these matters, although I hope to visit you soon. 15 But if I should be delayed, you should know how to behave in the household of God, which is the church of the living God, the pillar and foundation of truth. 16 Undeniably great is the mystery of devotion,

Who was manifested in the flesh,
    vindicated in the spirit,
    seen by angels,
proclaimed to the Gentiles,
believed in throughout the world,
    taken up in glory.

the truth. 5 For there is only one God, and there is only one mediator between God and humanity, himself a human being, Christ Jesus, 6 who offered himself as a ransom for all. This was the witness given at the appointed time, 7 of which I was appointed herald and apostle and — I am telling the truth and no lie — a teacher of the gentiles in faith and truth.

8 In every place, then, I want the men to lift their hands up reverently in prayer, with no anger or argument.

9 Similarly, women are to wear suitable clothes and to be dressed quietly and modestly, without braided hair or gold and jewellery or expensive clothes; 10 their adornment is to do the good works that are proper for women who claim to be religious. 11 During instruction, a woman should be quiet and respectful. 12 I give no permission for a woman to teach or to have authority over a man. A woman ought to be quiet, 13 because Adam was formed first and Eve afterwards, 14 and it was not Adam who was led astray but the woman who was led astray and fell into sin. 15 Nevertheless, she will be saved by child-bearing, provided she lives a sensible life and is constant in faith and love and holiness.

3 Here is a saying that you can rely on: to want to be a presiding elder is to desire a noble task. 2 That is why the presiding elder must have an impeccable character. Husband of one wife, he must be temperate, discreet and courteous, hospitable and a good teacher; 3 not a heavy drinker, nor hot-tempered, but gentle and peaceable, not avaricious, 4 a man who manages his own household well and brings his children up to obey him and be well-behaved: 5 how can any man who does not understand how to manage his own household take care of the Church of God? 6 He should not be a new convert, in case pride should turn his head and he incur the same condemnation as the devil. 7 It is also necessary that he be held in good repute by outsiders, so that he never falls into disrepute and into the devil's trap.

8 Similarly, deacons must be respectable, not double-tongued, moderate in the amount of wine they drink and with no squalid greed for money. 9 They must hold to the mystery of the faith with a clear conscience. 10 They are first to be examined, and admitted to serve as deacons only if there is nothing against them. 11 Similarly, women must be respectable, not gossips, but sober and wholly reliable. 12 Deacons must be husbands of one wife and must be people who manage their children and households well. 13 Those of them who carry out their duties well as deacons will earn a high standing for themselves and an authoritative voice in matters concerning faith in Christ Jesus.

14 I write this to you in the hope that I may be able to come to you soon; 15 but in case I should be delayed, I want you to know how people ought to behave in God's household — that is, in the Church of the living God, pillar and support of the truth. 16 Without any doubt, the mystery of our religion is very deep indeed:

He was made visible in the flesh,
    justified in the Spirit,
    seen by angels,
proclaimed to the gentiles,
believed in throughout the world,
    taken up in glory.

NEW REVISED STANDARD VERSION

4 Now the Spirit expressly says that in later° times some will renounce the faith by paying attention to deceitful spirits and teachings of demons, 2 through the hypocrisy of liars whose consciences are seared with a hot iron. 3 They forbid marriage and demand abstinence from foods, which God created to be received with thanksgiving by those who believe and know the truth. 4 For everything created by God is good, and nothing is to be rejected, provided it is received with thanksgiving; 5 for it is sanctified by God's word and by prayer.

6 If you put these instructions before the brothers and sisters, P you will be a good servant q of Christ Jesus, nourished on the words of the faith and of the sound teaching that you have followed. 7 Have nothing to do with profane myths and old wives' tales. Train yourself in godliness, 8 for, while physical training is of some value, godliness is valuable in every way, holding promise for both the present life and the life to come. 9 The saying is sure and worthy of full acceptance. 10 For to this end we toil and struggle, r because we have our hope set on the living God, who is the Savior of all people, especially of those who believe.

11 These are the things that you must insist on and teach. 12 Let no one despise your youth, but set the believers an example in speech and conduct, in love, in faith, in purity. 13 Until I arrive, give attention to the public reading of scripture, s to exhorting, to teaching. 14 Do not neglect the gift that is in you, which was given to you through prophecy with the laying on of hands by the council of elders. t 15 Put these things into practice, devote yourself to them, so that all may see your progress. 16 Pay close attention to yourself and to your teaching; continue in these things, for in doing this you will save both yourself and your hearers.

5 Do not speak harshly to an older man, u but speak to him as to a father, to younger men as brothers, 2 to older women as mothers, to younger women as sisters — with absolute purity.

3 Honor widows who are really widows. 4 If a widow has children or grandchildren, they should first learn their religious duty to their own family and make some repayment to their parents; for this is pleasing in God's sight. 5 The real widow, left alone, has set her hope on God and continues in supplications and prayers night and day; 6 but the widow v who lives for pleasure is dead even while she lives. 7 Give these commands as well, so that they may be above reproach. 8 And whoever does not provide for relatives, and especially for family members, has denied the faith and is worse than an unbeliever.

9 Let a widow be put on the list if she is not less than sixty years old and has been married only once; w 10 she must be well attested for her good works, as one who has brought up children, shown hospitality, washed the saints' feet, helped the afflicted, and devoted herself to doing good

REVISED ENGLISH BIBLE

4 THE Spirit explicitly warns us that in time to come some will forsake the faith and surrender their minds to subversive spirits and demon-inspired doctrines, 2 through the plausible falsehoods of those whose consciences have been permanently branded. 3 They will forbid marriage, and insist on abstinence from foods which God created to be enjoyed with thanksgiving by believers who have come to knowledge of the truth. 4 Everything that God has created is good, and nothing is to be rejected provided it is accepted with thanksgiving, 5 for it is then made holy by God's word and by prayer.

6 By offering such advice as this to the brotherhood you will prove to be a good servant of Christ Jesus, nurtured in the precepts of our faith and the sound instruction which you have followed. 7 Have nothing to do with superstitious myths, mere old wives' tales. Keep yourself in training for the practice of religion; 8 for while the training of the body brings limited benefit, the benefits of religion are without limit, since it holds out promise not only for this life but also for the life to come. 9 Here is a saying you may trust, one that merits full acceptance. 10 'This is why we labour and struggle, because we have set our hope on the living God, who is the Saviour of all' — the Saviour, above all, of believers.

11 Insist on these things in your teaching. 12 Let no one underrate you because you are young, but be to believers an example in speech and behaviour, in love, fidelity, and purity. 13 Until I arrive devote yourself to the public reading of the scriptures, to exhortation, and to teaching. 14 Do not neglect the spiritual endowment given you when, under the guidance of prophecy, the elders laid their hands on you.

15 Make these matters your business, make them your absorbing interest, so that your progress may be plain to all. 16 Persevere in them, keeping close watch on yourself and on your teaching; by doing so you will save both yourself and your hearers.

5 NEVER be harsh with an older man; appeal to him as if he were your father. Treat the younger men as brothers, 2 the older women as mothers, and the younger as your sisters, in all purity.

3 Enrol as widows only those who are widows in the fullest sense. 4 If a widow has children or grandchildren, they should learn as their first duty to show loyalty to the family and so repay what they owe to their parents and grandparents; for that has God's approval. 5 But a widow in the full sense, one who is alone in the world, puts all her trust in God, and regularly, night and day, attends the meetings for prayer and worship. 6 A widow given to self-indulgence, however, is as good as dead. 7 Add these instructions to the rest, so that the widows may be above reproach. 8 And if anyone does not make provision for his relations, and especially for members of his own household, he has denied the faith and is worse than an unbeliever.

9 A widow under sixty years of age should not be put on the roll. An enrolled widow must have been the wife of one husband, 10 and must have gained a reputation for good deeds, by taking care of children, by showing hospitality, by washing the feet of God's people, by supporting those in distress — in short, by doing good at every opportunity.

4:1 **in time to come:** *or* in the last times. 4:2 **branded:** *or* seared. 4:8–10 **for while . . . Saviour of all':** *or* for 'While the training of the body brings limited benefit, the benefits of religion are without limit, since it holds out promise not only for this life but also for the life to come.' 9 That is a saying you may trust, one that merits full acceptance. 10 This is why we labour and struggle, because we have set our hope on the living God, who is the Saviour of all. 4:14 **prophecy . . . on you:** *or* prophecy, you were ordained as an elder.

° Or *the last* p Gk *brothers* q Or *deacon* r Other ancient authorities read *suffer reproach* s Gk *to the reading* t Gk *by the presbytery* u Or *an elder*, or *a presbyter* v Gk *she* w Gk *the wife of one husband*

4 Now the Spirit explicitly says that in the last times some will turn away from the faith by paying attention to deceitful spirits and demonic instructions ²through the hypocrisy of liars with branded consciences. ³They forbid marriage and require abstinence from foods that God created to be received with thanksgiving by those who believe and know the truth. ⁴For everything created by God is good, and nothing is to be rejected when received with thanksgiving, ⁵for it is made holy by the invocation of God in prayer.

⁶If you will give these instructions to the brothers, you will be a good minister of Christ Jesus, nourished on the words of the faith and of the sound teaching you have followed. ⁷Avoid profane and silly myths. Train yourself for devotion, ⁸for, while physical training is of limited value, devotion is valuable in every respect, since it holds a promise of life both for the present and for the future. ⁹This saying is trustworthy and deserves full acceptance. ¹⁰For this we toil and struggle, because we have set our hope on the living God, who is the savior of all, especially of those who believe.

¹¹Command and teach these things. ¹²Let no one have contempt for your youth, but set an example for those who believe, in speech, conduct, love, faith, and purity. ¹³Until I arrive, attend to the reading, exhortation, and teaching. ¹⁴Do not neglect the gift you have, which was conferred on you through the prophetic word with the imposition of hands of the presbyterate. ¹⁵Be diligent in these matters, be absorbed in them, so that your progress may be evident to everyone. ¹⁶Attend to yourself and to your teaching; persevere in both tasks, for by doing so you will save both yourself and those who listen to you.

5 Do not rebuke an older man, but appeal to him as a father. Treat younger men as brothers, ²older women as mothers, and younger women as sisters with complete purity.

³Honor widows who are truly widows. ⁴But if a widow has children or grandchildren, let these first learn to perform their religious duty to their own family and to make recompense to their parents, for this is pleasing to God. ⁵The real widow, who is all alone, has set her hope on God and continues in supplications and prayers night and day. ⁶But the one who is self-indulgent is dead while she lives. ⁷Command this, so that they may be irreproachable. ⁸And whoever does not provide for relatives and especially family members has denied the faith and is worse than an unbeliever.

⁹Let a widow be enrolled if she is not less than sixty years old, married only once, ¹⁰with a reputation for good works, namely, that she has raised children, practiced hospitality, washed the feet of the holy ones, helped those in distress, involved herself in every good work. ¹¹But ex-

4 The Spirit has explicitly said that during the last times some will desert the faith and pay attention to deceitful spirits and doctrines that come from devils, ²seduced by the hypocrisy of liars whose consciences are branded as though with a red-hot iron: ³they forbid marriage and prohibit foods which God created to be accepted with thanksgiving by all who believe and who know the truth. ⁴Everything God has created is good, and no food is to be rejected, provided it is received with thanksgiving: ⁵the word of God and prayer make it holy. ⁶If you put all this to the brothers, you will be a good servant of Christ Jesus and show that you have really digested the teaching of the faith and the good doctrine which you have always followed. ⁷Have nothing to do with godless myths and old wives' tales. Train yourself for religion. ⁸Physical exercise is useful enough, but the usefulness of religion is unlimited, since it holds out promise both for life here and now and for the life to come; ⁹that is a saying that you can rely on and nobody should doubt it. ¹⁰I mean that the point of all our toiling and battling is that we have put our trust in the living God and he is the Saviour of the whole human race but particularly of all believers. ¹¹This is what you are to instruct and teach.

¹²Let no one disregard you because you are young, but be an example to all the believers in the way you speak and behave, and in your love, your faith and your purity. ¹³Until I arrive, devote yourself to reading to the people, encouraging and teaching. ¹⁴You have in you a spiritual gift which was given to you when the prophets spoke and the body of elders laid their hands on you; do not neglect it. ¹⁵Let this be your care and your occupation, and everyone will be able to see your progress. ¹⁶Be conscientious about what you do and what you teach; persevere in this, and in this way you will save both yourself and those who listen to you.

5 Never speak sharply to a man older than yourself, but appeal to him as you would to your own father; treat younger men as brothers, ²older women as mothers and young women as sisters with all propriety.

³Be considerate to widows — if they really are widowed. ⁴If a widow has children or grandchildren, they are to learn first of all to do their duty to their own families and repay their debt to their parents, because this is what pleases God. ⁵But a woman who is really widowed and left on her own has set her hope on God and perseveres night and day in petitions and prayer. ⁶The one who thinks only of pleasure is already dead while she is still alive: ⁷instruct them in this, too, so that their lives may be blameless. ⁸Anyone who does not look after his own relations, especially if they are living with him, has rejected the faith and is worse than an unbeliever.

⁹Enrolment as a widow is permissible only for a woman at least sixty years old who has had only one husband. ¹⁰She must be a woman known for her good works — whether she has brought up her children, been hospitable to strangers and washed the feet of God's holy people, helped people in hardship or been active in all kinds of good work.

in every way. 11 But refuse to put younger widows on the list; for when their sensual desires alienate them from Christ, they want to marry, 12 and so they incur condemnation for having violated their first pledge. 13 Besides that, they learn to be idle, gadding about from house to house; and they are not merely idle, but also gossips and busybodies, saying what they should not say. 14 So I would have younger widows marry, bear children, and manage their households, so as to give the adversary no occasion to revile us. 15 For some have already turned away to follow Satan. 16 If any believing woman*x* has relatives who are really widows, let her assist them; let the church not be burdened, so that it can assist those who are real widows.

17 Let the elders who rule well be considered worthy of double honor,*y* especially those who labor in preaching and teaching; 18 for the scripture says, "You shall not muzzle an ox while it is treading out the grain," and, "The laborer deserves to be paid." 19 Never accept any accusation against an elder except on the evidence of two or three witnesses. 20 As for those who persist in sin, rebuke them in the presence of all, so that the rest also may stand in fear. 21 In the presence of God and of Christ Jesus and of the elect angels, I warn you to keep these instructions without prejudice, doing nothing on the basis of partiality. 22 Do not ordain*z* anyone hastily, and do not participate in the sins of others; keep yourself pure.

23 No longer drink only water, but take a little wine for the sake of your stomach and your frequent ailments.

24 The sins of some people are conspicuous and precede them to judgment, while the sins of others follow them there. 25 So also good works are conspicuous; and even when they are not, they cannot remain hidden.

6 Let all who are under the yoke of slavery regard their masters as worthy of all honor, so that the name of God and the teaching may not be blasphemed. 2 Those who have believing masters must not be disrespectful to them on the ground that they are members of the church;*a* rather they must serve them all the more, since those who benefit by their service are believers and beloved.*b*

Teach and urge these duties. 3 Whoever teaches otherwise and does not agree with the sound words of our Lord Jesus Christ and the teaching that is in accordance with godliness, 4 is conceited, understanding nothing, and has a morbid craving for controversy and for disputes about words. From these come envy, dissension, slander, base suspicions, 5 and wrangling among those who are depraved in mind and bereft of the truth, imagining that godliness is a means of gain.*c* 6 Of course, there is great gain in godliness combined with contentment; 7 for we brought nothing into the world, so that*d* we can take nothing out of it; 8 but if we have food and clothing, we will be content with these. 9 But those who want to be rich fall into temptation and are trapped by many senseless and harmful desires that plunge people into ruin and destruction. 10 For the love of money is a root of all kinds of evil, and in their eagerness to be rich some have wandered away from the faith and pierced themselves with many pains.

11 Do not admit younger widows to the roll; for if they let their passions distract them from Christ's service they will want to marry again, 12 and so be guilty of breaking their earlier vow to him. 13 Besides, in going round from house to house they would learn to be idle, indeed worse than idle, gossips and busybodies, speaking of things better left unspoken. 14 For that reason it is my wish that young widows should marry again, have children, and manage a household; then they will give the enemy no occasion for scandal. 15 For there have in fact been some who have taken the wrong turning and gone over to Satan. 16 If a Christian woman has widows in her family, she must support them; the congregation must be relieved of the burden, so that it may be free to support those who are widows in the full sense.

17 Elders who give good service as leaders should be reckoned worthy of a double stipend, in particular those who work hard at preaching and teaching. 18 For scripture says, 'You shall not muzzle an ox while it is treading out the grain'; besides, 'The worker earns his pay.' 19 Do not entertain a charge against an elder unless it is supported by two or three witnesses. 20 Those who do commit sins you must rebuke in public, to put fear into the others. 21 Before God and Christ Jesus and the angels who are his chosen, I solemnly charge you: maintain these rules, never prejudging the issue, but acting with strict impartiality. 22 Do not be over-hasty in the laying on of hands, or you may find yourself implicated in other people's misdeeds; keep yourself above reproach.

23 Stop drinking only water; in view of your frequent ailments take a little wine to help your digestion.

24 There are people whose offences are so obvious that they precede them into court, and others whose offences have not yet caught up with them. 25 So too with good deeds; they may be obvious, but, even if they are not, they cannot be concealed for ever.

6 All who wear the yoke of slavery must consider their masters worthy of all respect, so that the name of God and the Christian teaching are not brought into disrepute. 2 Slaves of Christian masters must not take liberties with them just because they are their brothers. Quite the contrary: they must do their work all the better because those who receive the benefit of their service are one with them in faith and love.

THIS is what you are to teach and preach. 3 Anyone who teaches otherwise, and does not devote himself to sound precepts — that is, those of our Lord Jesus Christ — and to good religious teaching, 4 is a pompous ignoramus with a morbid enthusiasm for mere speculations and quibbles. These give rise to jealousy, quarrelling, slander, base suspicions, 5 and endless wrangles — all typical of those whose minds are corrupted and who have lost their grip of the truth. They think religion should yield dividends; 6 and of course religion does yield high dividends, but only to those who are content with what they have. 7 We brought nothing into this world, and we can take nothing out; 8 if we have food and clothing let us rest content. 9 Those who want to be rich fall into temptations and snares and into many foolish and harmful desires which plunge people into ruin and destruction. 10 The love of money is the root of all evil, and in pursuit of it some have wandered from the faith and spiked themselves on many a painful thorn.

---

x Other ancient authorities read *believing man or woman*; others, *believing man*   *y* Or *compensation*   *z* Gk *Do not lay hands on*   *a* Gk *are brothers*   *b* Or *since they are believers and beloved, who devote themselves to good deeds*   *c* Other ancient authorities add *Withdraw yourself from such people*   *d* Other ancient authorities read *world—it is certain that*

clude younger widows, for when their sensuality estranges them from Christ, they want to marry 12 and will incur condemnation for breaking their first pledge. 13 And furthermore, they learn to be idlers, going about from house to house, and not only idlers but gossips and busybodies as well, talking about things that ought not to be mentioned. 14 So I would like younger widows to marry, have children, and manage a home, so as to give the adversary no pretext for maligning us. 15 For some have already turned away to follow Satan. 16 If any woman believer has widowed relatives, she must assist them; the church is not to be burdened, so that it will be able to help those who are truly widows.

17 Presbyters who preside well deserve double honor, especially those who toil in preaching and teaching. 18 For the scripture says, "You shall not muzzle an ox when it is threshing," and, "A worker deserves his pay." 19 Do not accept an accusation against a presbyter unless it is supported by two or three witnesses. 20 Reprimand publicly those who do sin, so that the rest also will be afraid. 21 I charge you before God and Christ Jesus and the elect angels to keep these rules without prejudice, doing nothing out of favoritism. 22 Do not lay hands too readily on anyone, and do not share in another's sins. Keep yourself pure. 23 Stop drinking only water, but have a little wine for the sake of your stomach and your frequent illnesses.

24 Some people's sins are public, preceding them to judgment; but other people are followed by their sins. 25 Similarly, good works are also public; and even those that are not cannot remain hidden.

6 Those who are under the yoke of slavery must regard their masters as worthy of full respect, so that the name of God and our teaching may not suffer abuse. 2 Those whose masters are believers must not take advantage of them because they are brothers but must give better service because those who will profit from their work are believers and are beloved.

Teach and urge these things. 3 Whoever teaches something different and does not agree with the sound words of our Lord Jesus Christ and the religious teaching 4 is conceited, understanding nothing, and has a morbid disposition for arguments and verbal disputes. From these come envy, rivalry, insults, evil suspicions, 5 and mutual friction among people with corrupted minds, who are deprived of the truth, supposing religion to be a means of gain. 6 Indeed, religion with contentment is a great gain. 7 For we brought nothing into the world, just as we shall not be able to take anything out of it. 8 If we have food and clothing, we shall be content with that. 9 Those who want to be rich are falling into temptation and into a trap and into many foolish and harmful desires, which plunge them into ruin and destruction. 10 For the love of money is the root of all evils, and some people in their desire for it have strayed from the faith and have pierced themselves with many pains.

11 Do not accept young widows because if their natural desires distract them from Christ, they want to marry again, 12 and then people condemn them for being unfaithful to their original promise. 13 Besides, they learn how to be idle and go round from house to house; and then, not merely idle, they learn to be gossips and meddlers in other people's affairs and to say what should remain unsaid. 14 I think it is best for young widows to marry again and have children and a household to look after, and not give the enemy any chance to raise a scandal about them; 15 there are already some who have turned aside to follow Satan. 16 If a woman believer has widowed relatives, she should support them and not make the Church bear the expense but enable it to support those who are really widowed.

17 Elders who do their work well while they are in charge earn double reward, especially those who work hard at preaching and teaching. 18 As scripture says: *You must not muzzle an ox when it is treading out the corn;a* and again: *The worker deserves his wages.* 19 Never accept any accusation brought against an elder unless it is supported *by two or three witnesses.* 20 If anyone is at fault, reprimand him publicly, as a warning to the rest. 21 Before God, and before Jesus Christ and the angels he has chosen, I charge you to keep these rules impartially and never to be influenced by favouritism. 22 Do not be too quick to lay hands on anyone, and never make yourself an accomplice in anybody else's sin; keep yourself pure.

23 You should give up drinking only water and have a little wine for the sake of your digestion and the frequent bouts of illness that you have.

24 The faults of some people are obvious long before they come to the reckoning, while others have faults that are not discovered until later. 25 Similarly, the good that people do can be obvious; but even when it is not, it cannot remain hidden.

6 All those under the yoke of slavery must have unqualified respect for their masters, so that the name of God and our teaching are not brought into disrepute. 2 Those whose masters are believers are not to respect them less because they are brothers; on the contrary, they should serve them all the better, since those who have the benefit of their services are believers and dear to God.

This is what you are to teach and urge. 3 Anyone who teaches anything different and does not keep to the sound teaching which is that of our Lord Jesus Christ, the doctrine which is in accordance with true religion, 4 is proud and has no understanding, but rather a weakness for questioning everything and arguing about words. All that can come of this is jealousy, contention, abuse and evil mistrust; 5 and unending disputes by people who are depraved in mind and deprived of truth, and imagine that religion is a way of making a profit. 6 Religion, of course, does bring large profits, but only to those who are content with what they have. 7 We brought nothing into the world, and we can take nothing out of it; 8 but as long as we have food and clothing, we shall be content with that. 9 People who long to be rich are a prey to trial; they get trapped into all sorts of foolish and harmful ambitions which plunge people into ruin and destruction. 10 'The love of money is the root of all evils' and there are some who, pursuing it, have wandered away from the faith and so given their souls any number of fatal wounds.

a 5 Dt 25:4 followed by Lk 10:7; Dt 19:15.

NEW REVISED STANDARD VERSION	REVISED ENGLISH BIBLE

NEW REVISED STANDARD VERSION

11 But as for you, man of God, shun all this; pursue righteousness, godliness, faith, love, endurance, gentleness. 12 Fight the good fight of the faith; take hold of the eternal life, to which you were called and for which you made*e* the good confession in the presence of many witnesses. 13 In the presence of God, who gives life to all things, and of Christ Jesus, who in his testimony before Pontius Pilate made the good confession, I charge you 14 to keep the commandment without spot or blame until the manifestation of our Lord Jesus Christ, 15 which he will bring about at the right time — he who is the blessed and only Sovereign, the King of kings and Lord of lords. 16 It is he alone who has immortality and dwells in unapproachable light, whom no one has ever seen or can see; to him be honor and eternal dominion. Amen.

17 As for those who in the present age are rich, command them not to be haughty, or to set their hopes on the uncertainty of riches, but rather on God who richly provides us with everything for our enjoyment. 18 They are to do good, to be rich in good works, generous, and ready to share, 19 thus storing up for themselves the treasure of a good foundation for the future, so that they may take hold of the life that really is life.

20 Timothy, guard what has been entrusted to you. Avoid the profane chatter and contradictions of what is falsely called knowledge; 21 by professing it some have missed the mark as regards the faith.

Grace be with you.*f*

e Gk *confessed* *f* The Greek word for *you* here is plural; in other ancient authorities it is singular. Other ancient authorities add *Amen*

REVISED ENGLISH BIBLE

11 But you, man of God, must shun all that, and pursue justice, piety, integrity, love, fortitude, and gentleness. 12 Run the great race of faith and take hold of eternal life, for to this you were called, when you confessed your faith nobly before many witnesses. 13 Now in the presence of God, who gives life to all things, and of Jesus Christ, who himself made that noble confession in his testimony before Pontius Pilate, I charge you 14 to obey your orders without fault or failure until the appearance of our Lord Jesus Christ 15 which God will bring about in his own good time. He is the blessed and only Sovereign, King of kings and Lord of lords; 16 he alone possesses immortality, dwelling in unapproachable light; him no one has ever seen or can ever see; to him be honour and dominion for ever! Amen.

17 Instruct those who are rich in this world's goods not to be proud, and to fix their hopes not on so uncertain a thing as money, but on God, who richly provides all things for us to enjoy. 18 They are to do good and to be rich in well-doing, to be ready to give generously and to share with others, 19 and so acquire a treasure which will form a good foundation for the future. Then they will grasp the life that is life indeed.

20 Timothy, keep safe what has been entrusted to you. Turn a deaf ear to empty and irreligious chatter, and the contradictions of 'knowledge' so-called, 21 for by laying claim to it some have strayed far from the faith.

Grace be with you all!

NEW AMERICAN BIBLE

11 But you, man of God, avoid all this. Instead, pursue righteousness, devotion, faith, love, patience, and gentleness. 12 Compete well for the faith. Lay hold of eternal life, to which you were called when you made the noble confession in the presence of many witnesses. 13 I charge [you] before God, who gives life to all things, and before Christ Jesus, who gave testimony under Pontius Pilate for the noble confession, 14 to keep the commandment without stain or reproach until the appearance of our Lord Jesus Christ 15 that the blessed and only ruler will make manifest at the proper time, the King of kings and Lord of lords, 16 who alone has immortality, who dwells in unapproachable light, and whom no human being has seen or can see. To him be honor and eternal power. Amen.

17 Tell the rich in the present age not to be proud and not to rely on so uncertain a thing as wealth but rather on God, who richly provides us with all things for our enjoyment. 18 Tell them to do good, to be rich in good works, to be generous, ready to share, 19 thus accumulating as treasure a good foundation for the future, so as to win the life that is true life.

20 O Timothy, guard what has been entrusted to you. Avoid profane babbling and the absurdities of so-called knowledge. 21 By professing it, some people have deviated from the faith.

Grace be with all of you.

NEW JERUSALEM BIBLE

11 But, as someone dedicated to God, avoid all that. You must aim to be upright and religious, filled with faith and love, perseverance and gentleness. 12 Fight the good fight of faith and win the eternal life to which you were called and for which you made your noble profession of faith before many witnesses. 13 Now, before God, the source of all life, and before Jesus Christ, who witnessed to his noble profession of faith before Pontius Pilate, I charge you 14 to do all that you have been told, with no faults or failures, until the appearing of our Lord Jesus Christ,

15 who at the due time will be revealed
by God, the blessed and only Ruler of all,
the King of kings and the Lord of lords,
16 who alone is immortal,
whose home is in inaccessible light,
whom no human being has seen
or is able to see:
to him be honour and everlasting power.
Amen.

17 Instruct those who are rich in this world's goods that they should not be proud and should set their hopes not on money, which is untrustworthy, but on God who gives us richly all that we need for our happiness. 18 They are to do good and be rich in good works, generous in giving and always ready to share — 19 this is the way they can amass a good capital sum for the future if they want to possess the only life that is real.

20 My dear Timothy, take great care of all that has been entrusted to you. Turn away from godless philosophical discussions and the contradictions of the 'knowledge' which is not knowledge at all; 21 by adopting this, some have missed the goal of faith. Grace be with you.

THE SECOND LETTER OF PAUL TO
Timothy

1 Paul, an apostle of Christ Jesus by the will of God, for the sake of the promise of life that is in Christ Jesus, 2 To Timothy, my beloved child:

Grace, mercy, and peace from God the Father and Christ Jesus our Lord.

3 I am grateful to God — whom I worship with a clear conscience, as my ancestors did — when I remember you constantly in my prayers night and day. 4 Recalling your tears, I long to see you so that I may be filled with joy. 5 I am reminded of your sincere faith, a faith that lived first in your grandmother Lois and your mother Eunice and now, I am sure, lives in you. 6 For this reason I remind you to rekindle the gift of God that is within you through the laying on of my hands; 7 for God did not give us a spirit of cowardice, but rather a spirit of power and of love and of self-discipline.

8 Do not be ashamed, then, of the testimony about our Lord or of me his prisoner, but join with me in suffering for the gospel, relying on the power of God, 9 who saved us and called us with a holy calling, not according to our works but according to his own purpose and grace. This grace was given to us in Christ Jesus before the ages began, 10 but it has now been revealed through the appearing of our Savior Christ Jesus, who abolished death and brought life and immortality to light through the gospel. 11 For this gospel I was appointed a herald and an apostle and a teacher, *a* 12 and for this reason I suffer as I do. But I am not ashamed, for I know the one in whom I have put my trust, and I am sure that he is able to guard until that day what I have entrusted to him. *b* 13 Hold to the standard of sound teaching that you have heard from me, in the faith and love that are in Christ Jesus. 14 Guard the good treasure entrusted to you, with the help of the Holy Spirit living in us.

15 You are aware that all who are in Asia have turned away from me, including Phygelus and Hermogenes. 16 May the Lord grant mercy to the household of Onesiphorus, because he often refreshed me and was not ashamed of my chain; 17 when he arrived in Rome, he eagerly *c* searched for me and found me 18 — may the Lord grant that he will find mercy from the Lord on that day! And you know very well how much service he rendered in Ephesus.

2 You then, my child, be strong in the grace that is in Christ Jesus; 2 and what you have heard from me through many witnesses entrust to faithful people who will be able to teach others as well. 3 Share in suffering like a good soldier of Christ Jesus. 4 No one serving in the army gets entangled in everyday affairs; the soldier's aim is to please the enlisting officer. 5 And in the case of an athlete, no one is crowned without competing according to the rules. 6 It is the farmer who does the work who ought to have the first share of the crops. 7 Think over what I say, for the Lord will give you understanding in all things.

THE SECOND LETTER OF PAUL TO
Timothy

1 FROM Paul, apostle of Christ Jesus by the will of God, whose promise of life is fulfilled in Christ Jesus, 2 to Timothy his dear son.

Grace, mercy, and peace to you from God the Father and Christ Jesus our Lord.

3 I give thanks to the God of my forefathers, whom I worship with a clear conscience, when I mention you in my prayers as I do constantly night and day; 4 when I remember the tears you shed, I long to see you again and so make my happiness complete. 5 I am reminded of the sincerity of your faith, a faith which was alive in Lois your grandmother and Eunice your mother before you, and which, I am confident, now lives in you.

6 THAT is why I remind you to stir into flame the gift from God which is yours through the laying on of my hands. 7 For the spirit that God gave us is no cowardly spirit, but one to inspire power, love, and self-discipline. 8 So never be ashamed of your testimony to our Lord, nor of me imprisoned for his sake, but through the power that comes from God accept your share of suffering for the sake of the gospel. 9 It is he who has brought us salvation and called us to a dedicated life, not for any merit of ours but for his own purpose and of his own grace, granted to us in Christ Jesus from all eternity, 10 and now at length disclosed by the appearance on earth of our Saviour Jesus Christ. He has broken the power of death and brought life and immortality to light through the gospel.

11 Of this gospel I have been appointed herald, apostle, and teacher. 12 That is the reason for my present plight; but I am not ashamed of it, because I know whom I have trusted, and am confident of his power to keep safe what he has put into my charge until the great day. 13 Hold to the outline of sound teaching which you heard from me, living by the faith and love which are ours in Christ Jesus. 14 Keep safe the treasure put into our charge, with the help of the Holy Spirit dwelling within us.

15 As you are aware, everyone in the province of Asia deserted me, including Phygelus and Hermogenes. 16 But may the Lord's mercy rest on the house of Onesiphorus! He has often relieved me in my troubles; he was not ashamed to visit a prisoner, 17 but when he came to Rome took pains to search me out until he found me. 18 The Lord grant that he find mercy from the Lord on the great day! You know as well as anyone the many services he rendered at Ephesus.

2 TAKE strength, my son, from the grace of God which is ours in Christ Jesus. 2 You heard my teaching in the presence of many witnesses; hand on that teaching to reliable men who in turn will be qualified to teach others. 3 Take your share of hardship, like a good soldier of Christ Jesus. 4 A soldier on active service must not let himself be involved in the affairs of everyday life if he is to give satisfaction to his commanding officer. 5 Again, no athlete wins a prize unless he abides by the rules. 6 The farmer who does the work has first claim on the crop. 7 Reflect on what I am saying, and the Lord will help you to full understanding.

---

a Other ancient authorities add *of the Gentiles*   *b* Or *what has been entrusted to me*   *c* Or *promptly*

1:12 **what . . . charge:** *or* what I have put into his charge.
1:13 **Hold . . . teaching:** *or* Take as your model the sound teaching.

The Second Letter to Timothy

2 Timothy

THE SECOND LETTER FROM PAUL TO TIMOTHY

1 Paul, an apostle of Christ Jesus by the will of God for the promise of life in Christ Jesus, ²to Timothy, my dear child: grace, mercy, and peace from God the Father and Christ Jesus our Lord.

³I am grateful to God, whom I worship with a clear conscience as my ancestors did, as I remember you constantly in my prayers, night and day. ⁴I yearn to see you again, recalling your tears, so that I may be filled with joy, ⁵as I recall your sincere faith that first lived in your grandmother Lois and in your mother Eunice and that I am confident lives also in you.

⁶For this reason, I remind you to stir into flame the gift of God that you have through the imposition of my hands. ⁷For God did not give us a spirit of cowardice but rather of power and love and self-control. ⁸So do not be ashamed of your testimony to our Lord, nor of me, a prisoner for his sake; but bear your share of hardship for the gospel with the strength that comes from God.

⁹He saved us and called us to a holy life, not according to our works but according to his own design and the grace bestowed on us in Christ Jesus before time began, ¹⁰but now made manifest through the appearance of our savior Christ Jesus, who destroyed death and brought life and immortality to light through the gospel, ¹¹for which I was appointed preacher and apostle and teacher. ¹²On this account I am suffering these things; but I am not ashamed, for I know him in whom I have believed and am confident that he is able to guard what has been entrusted to me until that day. ¹³Take as your norm the sound words that you heard from me, in the faith and love that are in Christ Jesus. ¹⁴Guard this rich trust with the help of the holy Spirit that dwells within us.

¹⁵You know that everyone in Asia deserted me, including Phygelus and Hermogenes. ¹⁶May the Lord grant mercy to the family of Onesiphorus because he often gave me new heart and was not ashamed of my chains. ¹⁷But when he came to Rome, he promptly searched for me and found me. ¹⁸May the Lord grant him to find mercy from the Lord on that day. And you know very well the services he rendered in Ephesus.

2 So you, my child, be strong in the grace that is in Christ Jesus. ²And what you heard from me through many witnesses entrust to faithful people who will have the ability to teach others as well. ³Bear your share of hardship along with me like a good soldier of Christ Jesus. ⁴To satisfy the one who recruited him, a soldier does not become entangled in the business affairs of life. ⁵Similarly, an athlete cannot receive the winner's crown except by competing according to the rules. ⁶The hardworking farmer ought to have the first share of the crop. ⁷Reflect on what I am saying, for the Lord will give you understanding in everything.

1 From Paul, apostle of Christ Jesus through the will of God in accordance with his promise of life in Christ Jesus, ²to Timothy, dear son of mine. Grace, mercy and peace from God the Father and from Christ Jesus our Lord.

³Night and day I thank God whom I serve with a pure conscience as my ancestors did. I remember you in my prayers constantly night and day; ⁴I remember your tears and long to see you again to complete my joy. ⁵I also remember your sincere faith, a faith which first dwelt in your grandmother Lois, and your mother Eunice, and I am sure dwells also in you.

⁶That is why I am reminding you now to fan into a flame the gift of God that you possess through the laying on of my hands. ⁷God did not give us a spirit of timidity, but the Spirit of power and love and self-control. ⁸So you are never to be ashamed of witnessing to our Lord, or ashamed of me for being his prisoner; but share in my hardships for the sake of the gospel, relying on the power of God ⁹who has saved us and called us to be holy—not because of anything we ourselves had done but for his own purpose and by his own grace. This grace had already been granted to us, in Christ Jesus, before the beginning of time, ¹⁰but it has been revealed only by the appearing of our Saviour Christ Jesus. He has abolished death, and he has brought to light immortality and life through the gospel, ¹¹in whose service I have been made herald, apostle and teacher.

¹²That is why I am experiencing my present sufferings; but I am not ashamed, because I know in whom I have put my trust, and I have no doubt at all that he is able to safeguard until that Day what I have entrusted to him. ¹³Keep as your pattern the sound teaching you have heard from me, in the faith and love that are in Christ Jesus. ¹⁴With the help of the Holy Spirit who dwells in us, look after that precious thing given in trust.

¹⁵As you know, Phygelus and Hermogenes and all the others in Asia have deserted me. ¹⁶I hope the Lord will be kind to all the family of Onesiphorus, because he has often been a comfort to me and has never been ashamed of my chains. ¹⁷On the contrary, as soon as he reached Rome, he searched hard for me and found me. ¹⁸May the Lord grant him to find the Lord's mercy on that Day. You know better than anyone else how much he helped me at Ephesus.

2 As for you, my dear son, take strength from the grace which is in Christ Jesus. ²Pass on to reliable people what you have heard from me through many witnesses so that they in turn will be able to teach others.

³Bear with your share of difficulties, like a good soldier of Christ Jesus. ⁴No one on active service involves himself in the affairs of civilian life, because he must win the approval of the man who enlisted him; ⁵or again someone who enters an athletic contest wins only by competing in the sports—a prize can be won only by competing according to the rules; ⁶and again, it is the farmer who works hard that has the first claim on any crop that is harvested. ⁷Think over what I have said, and the Lord will give you full understanding.

NEW REVISED STANDARD VERSION

8 Remember Jesus Christ, raised from the dead, a descendant of David—that is my gospel, 9 for which I suffer hardship, even to the point of being chained like a criminal. But the word of God is not chained. 10 Therefore I endure everything for the sake of the elect, so that they may also obtain the salvation that is in Christ Jesus, with eternal glory. 11 The saying is sure:
> If we have died with him, we will also live with
>   him;
> 12 if we endure, we will also reign with him;
>   if we deny him, he will also deny us;
> 13 if we are faithless, he remains faithful—
>   for he cannot deny himself.

14 Remind them of this, and warn them before God*d* that they are to avoid wrangling over words, which does no good but only ruins those who are listening. 15 Do your best to present yourself to God as one approved by him, a worker who has no need to be ashamed, rightly explaining the word of truth. 16 Avoid profane chatter, for it will lead people into more and more impiety, 17 and their talk will spread like gangrene. Among them are Hymenaeus and Philetus, 18 who have swerved from the truth by claiming that the resurrection has already taken place. They are upsetting the faith of some. 19 But God's firm foundation stands, bearing this inscription: "The Lord knows those who are his," and, "Let everyone who calls on the name of the Lord turn away from wickedness."

20 In a large house there are utensils not only of gold and silver but also of wood and clay, some for special use, some for ordinary. 21 All who cleanse themselves of the things I have mentioned*e* will become special utensils, dedicated and useful to the owner of the house, ready for every good work. 22 Shun youthful passions and pursue righteousness, faith, love, and peace, along with those who call on the Lord from a pure heart. 23 Have nothing to do with stupid and senseless controversies; you know that they breed quarrels. 24 And the Lord's servant*f* must not be quarrelsome but kindly to everyone, an apt teacher, patient, 25 correcting opponents with gentleness. God may perhaps grant that they will repent and come to know the truth, 26 and that they may escape from the snare of the devil, having been held captive by him to do his will.*g*

3 You must understand this, that in the last days distressing times will come. 2 For people will be lovers of themselves, lovers of money, boasters, arrogant, abusive, disobedient to their parents, ungrateful, unholy, 3 inhuman, implacable, slanderers, profligates, brutes, haters of good, 4 treacherous, reckless, swollen with conceit, lovers of pleasure rather than lovers of God, 5 holding to the outward form of godliness but denying its power. Avoid them! 6 For among them are those who make their way into households and captivate silly women, overwhelmed by their sins and swayed by all kinds of desires, 7 who are always being instructed and can never arrive at a knowledge of the truth. 8 As Jannes and Jambres opposed Moses, so these people, of corrupt mind and counterfeit faith, also oppose the truth. 9 But they will not make much progress, because, as in the case of those two men,*h* their folly will become plain to everyone.

d Other ancient authorities read *the Lord*   *e* Gk *of these things*
f Gk *slave*   *g* Or *by him, to do his* (that is, God's) *will*
h Gk lacks *two men*

REVISED ENGLISH BIBLE

8 Remember the theme of my gospel: Jesus Christ, risen from the dead, born of David's line. 9 For preaching this I am exposed to hardship, even to the point of being fettered like a criminal; but the word of God is not fettered. 10 All this I endure for the sake of God's chosen ones, in the hope that they too may attain the glorious and eternal salvation which is in Christ Jesus.
11 Here is a saying you may trust:
> If we died with him, we shall live with him;
> 12 if we endure, we shall reign with him;
>   if we disown him, he will disown us;
> 13 if we are faithless, he remains faithful,
>   for he cannot disown himself.

14 Keep on reminding people of this, and charge them solemnly before God to stop disputing about mere words; it does no good, and only ruins those who listen. 15 Try hard to show yourself worthy of God's approval, as a worker with no cause for shame; keep strictly to the true gospel, 16 avoiding empty and irreligious chatter; those who indulge in it will stray farther and farther into godless ways, 17 and the infection of their teaching will spread like gangrene. Such are Hymenaeus and Philetus; 18 in saying that our resurrection has already taken place they are wide of the truth and undermine people's faith. 19 But God has laid a foundation-stone, and it stands firm, bearing this inscription: 'The Lord knows his own' and 'Everyone who takes the Lord's name upon his lips must forsake wickedness.' 20 Now in any great house there are not only utensils of gold and silver, but also others of wood and earthenware; the former are valued, the latter held cheap. 21 Anyone who cleanses himself from all this wickedness will be a vessel valued and dedicated, a thing useful to the master of the house, and fit for any honourable purpose.

22 Turn from the wayward passions of youth, and pursue justice, integrity, love, and peace together with all who worship the Lord in singleness of mind; 23 have nothing to do with foolish and wild speculations. You know they breed quarrels, 24 and a servant of the Lord must not be quarrelsome; he must be kindly towards all. He should be a good teacher, tolerant, 25 and gentle when he must discipline those who oppose him. God may then grant them a change of heart and lead them to recognize the truth; 26 thus they may come to their senses and escape from the devil's snare in which they have been trapped and held at his will.

3 Remember, the final age of this world is to be a time of turmoil! 2 People will love nothing but self and money; they will be boastful, arrogant, and abusive; disobedient to parents, devoid of gratitude, piety, 3 and natural affection; they will be implacable in their hatreds, scandalmongers, uncontrolled and violent, hostile to all goodness, 4 perfidious, foolhardy, swollen with self-importance. They will love their pleasures more than their God. 5 While preserving the outward form of religion, they are a standing denial of its power. Keep clear of them. 6 They are the sort that insinuate themselves into private houses and there get silly women into their clutches, women burdened with sins and carried away by all kinds of desires, 7 always wanting to be taught but incapable of attaining to a knowledge of the truth. 8 As Jannes and Jambres opposed Moses, so these men oppose the truth; their warped minds disqualify them from grasping the faith. 9 Their successes will be shortlived; like those opponents of Moses, they will come to be recognized by everyone for the fools they are.

2:26 **trapped . . . will:** or trapped, and be made subject to God's will.

8 Remember Jesus Christ, raised from the dead, a descendant of David: such is my gospel, 9 for which I am suffering, even to the point of chains, like a criminal. But the word of God is not chained. 10 Therefore, I bear with everything for the sake of those who are chosen, so that they too may obtain the salvation that is in Christ Jesus, together with eternal glory. 11 This saying is trustworthy:

If we have died with him
  we shall also live with him;
12 if we persevere
  we shall also reign with him.
But if we deny him
  he will deny us.
13 If we are unfaithful
  he remains faithful,
  for he cannot deny himself.

14 Remind people of these things and charge them before God to stop disputing about words. This serves no useful purpose since it harms those who listen. 15 Be eager to present yourself as acceptable to God, a workman who causes no disgrace, imparting the word of truth without deviation. 16 Avoid profane, idle talk, for such people will become more and more godless, 17 and their teaching will spread like gangrene. Among them are Hymenaeus and Philetus, 18 who have deviated from the truth by saying that [the] resurrection has already taken place and are upsetting the faith of some. 19 Nevertheless, God's solid foundation stands, bearing this inscription, "The Lord knows those who are his"; and, "Let everyone who calls upon the name of the Lord avoid evil."

20 In a large household there are vessels not only of gold and silver but also of wood and clay, some for lofty and others for humble use. 21 If anyone cleanses himself of these things, he will be a vessel for lofty use, dedicated, beneficial to the master of the house, ready for every good work. 22 So turn from youthful desires and pursue righteousness, faith, love, and peace, along with those who call on the Lord with purity of heart. 23 Avoid foolish and ignorant debates, for you know that they breed quarrels. 24 A slave of the Lord should not quarrel, but should be gentle with everyone, able to teach, tolerant, 25 correcting opponents with kindness. It may be that God will grant them repentance that leads to knowledge of the truth, 26 and that they may return to their senses out of the devil's snare, where they are entrapped by him, for his will.

3 But understand this: there will be terrifying times in the last days. 2 People will be self-centered and lovers of money, proud, haughty, abusive, disobedient to their parents, ungrateful, irreligious, 3 callous, implacable, slanderous, licentious, brutal, hating what is good, 4 traitors, reckless, conceited, lovers of pleasure rather than lovers of God, 5 as they make a pretense of religion but deny its power. Reject them. 6 For some of these slip into homes and make captives of women weighed down by sins, led by various desires, 7 always trying to learn but never able to reach a knowledge of the truth. 8 Just as Jannes and Jambres opposed Moses, so they also oppose the truth — people of depraved mind, unqualified in the faith. 9 But they will not make further progress, for their foolishness will be plain to all, as it was with those two.

8 Remember the gospel that I carry, 'Jesus Christ risen from the dead, sprung from the race of David'; 9 it is on account of this that I have to put up with suffering, even to being chained like a criminal. But God's message cannot be chained up. 10 So I persevere for the sake of those who are chosen, so that they, too, may obtain the salvation that is in Christ Jesus with eternal glory. 11 Here is a saying that you can rely on:

If we have died with him,
  then we shall live with him.
12 If we persevere,
  then we shall reign with him.
If we disown him, then he will disown us.
13 If we are faithless, he is faithful still,
  for he cannot disown his own self.

14 Remind them of this; and tell them in the name of God that there must be no wrangling about words: all that this ever achieves is the destruction of those who are listening. 15 Make every effort to present yourself before God as a proven worker who has no need to be ashamed, but who keeps the message of truth on a straight path. 16 Have nothing to do with godless philosophical discussions — they only lead further and further away from true religion. 17 Talk of this kind spreads corruption like gangrene, as in the case of Hymenaeus and Philetus, 18 the men who have gone astray from the truth, claiming that the resurrection has already taken place. They are upsetting some people's faith.

19 However, God's solid foundation-stone stands firm, and this is the seal on it: '*The Lord knows those who are his own*' and 'All who *call on the name of the Lord*a must avoid evil.'

20 Not all the dishes in a large house are made of gold and silver; some are made of wood or earthenware: the former are held in honour, the latter held cheap. 21 If someone holds himself aloof from these faults I speak of, he will be a vessel held in honour, dedicated and fit for the Master, ready for any good work. 22 Turn away from the passions of youth, concentrate on uprightness, faith, love and peace, in union with all those who call on the Lord with a pure heart. 23 Avoid these foolish and undisciplined speculations, understanding that they only give rise to quarrels; 24 and a servant of the Lord must not engage in quarrels, but must be kind to everyone, a good teacher, and patient. 25 He must be gentle when he corrects people who oppose him, in the hope that God may give them a change of mind so that they recognise the truth 26 and come to their senses, escaping the trap of the devil who made them his captives and subjected them to his will.

3 You may be quite sure that in the last days there will be some difficult times. 2 People will be self-centred and avaricious, boastful, arrogant and rude; disobedient to their parents, ungrateful, irreligious; 3 heartless and intractable; they will be slanderers, profligates, savages and enemies of everything that is good; 4 they will be treacherous and reckless and demented by pride, preferring their own pleasure to God. 5 They will keep up the outward appearance of religion but will have rejected the inner power of it. Keep away from people like that. 6 Of the same kind, too, are those men who insinuate themselves into families in order to get influence over silly women who are obsessed with their sins and follow one craze after another, 7 always seeking learning, but unable ever to come to knowledge of the truth. 8 Just as Jannes and Jambres defied Moses,b so these men defy the truth, their minds corrupt and their faith spurious. 9 But they will not be able to go on much longer: their folly, like that of the other two, must become obvious to everybody.

a **2** Nb 16:5; Is 26:13.   *b* **3** In Jewish tradition (but not the Bible) the leaders of the Egyptian magicians, cf. Ex 7:11.

NEW REVISED STANDARD VERSION

10 Now you have observed my teaching, my conduct, my aim in life, my faith, my patience, my love, my steadfastness, 11 my persecutions and suffering the things that happened to me in Antioch, Iconium, and Lystra. What persecutions I endured! Yet the Lord rescued me from all of them. 12 Indeed, all who want to live a godly life in Christ Jesus will be persecuted. 13 But wicked people and impostors will go from bad to worse, deceiving others and being deceived. 14 But as for you, continue in what you have learned and firmly believed, knowing from whom you learned it, 15 and how from childhood you have known the sacred writings that are able to instruct you for salvation through faith in Christ Jesus. 16 All scripture is inspired by God and is*i* useful for teaching, for reproof, for correction, and for training in righteousness, 17 so that everyone who belongs to God may be proficient, equipped for every good work.

4 In the presence of God and of Christ Jesus, who is to judge the living and the dead, and in view of his appearing and his kingdom, I solemnly urge you: 2 proclaim the message; be persistent whether the time is favorable or unfavorable; convince, rebuke, and encourage, with the utmost patience in teaching. 3 For the time is coming when people will not put up with sound doctrine, but having itching ears, they will accumulate for themselves teachers to suit their own desires, 4 and will turn away from listening to the truth and wander away to myths. 5 As for you, always be sober, endure suffering, do the work of an evangelist, carry out your ministry fully.

6 As for me, I am already being poured out as a libation, and the time of my departure has come. 7 I have fought the good fight, I have finished the race, I have kept the faith. 8 From now on there is reserved for me the crown of righteousness, which the Lord, the righteous judge, will give me on that day, and not only to me but also to all who have longed for his appearing.

9 Do your best to come to me soon, 10 for Demas, in love with this present world, has deserted me and gone to Thessalonica; Crescens has gone to Galatia,*j* Titus to Dalmatia. 11 Only Luke is with me. Get Mark and bring him with you, for he is useful in my ministry. 12 I have sent Tychicus to Ephesus. 13 When you come, bring the cloak that I left with Carpus at Troas, also the books, and above all the parchments. 14 Alexander the coppersmith did me great harm; the Lord will pay him back for his deeds. 15 You also must beware of him, for he strongly opposed our message.

16 At my first defense no one came to my support, but all deserted me. May it not be counted against them! 17 But the Lord stood by me and gave me strength, so that through me the message might be fully proclaimed and all the Gentiles might hear it. So I was rescued from the lion's mouth. 18 The Lord will rescue me from every evil attack and save me for his heavenly kingdom. To him be the glory forever and ever. Amen.

19 Greet Prisca and Aquila, and the household of Onesiphorus. 20 Erastus remained in Corinth; Trophimus I left ill in Miletus. 21 Do your best to come before winter. Eubulus sends greetings to you, as do Pudens and Linus and Claudia and all the brothers and sisters.*k*

22 The Lord be with your spirit. Grace be with you.*l*

REVISED ENGLISH BIBLE

10 But you, my son, have observed closely my teaching and manner of life, my resolution, my faithfulness, patience, and spirit of love, and my fortitude 11 under persecution and suffering—all I went through at Antioch, at Iconium, at Lystra, and the persecutions I endured; and from all of them the Lord rescued me. 12 Persecution will indeed come to everyone who wants to live a godly life as a follower of Christ Jesus, 13 whereas evildoers and charlatans will progress from bad to worse, deceiving and deceived. 14 But for your part, stand by the truths you have learned and are assured of. Remember from whom you learned them; 15 remember that from early childhood you have been familiar with the sacred writings which have power to make you wise and lead you to salvation through faith in Christ Jesus. 16 All inspired scripture has its use for teaching the truth and refuting error, or for reformation of manners and discipline in right living, 17 so that the man of God may be capable and equipped for good work of every kind.

4 Before God, and before Christ Jesus who is to judge the living and the dead, I charge you solemnly by his coming appearance and his reign, 2 proclaim the message, press it home in season and out of season, use argument, reproof, and appeal, with all the patience that teaching requires. 3 For the time will come when people will not stand sound teaching, but each will follow his own whim and gather a crowd of teachers to tickle his fancy. 4 They will stop their ears to the truth and turn to fables. 5 But you must keep your head whatever happens; put up with hardship, work to spread the gospel, discharge all the duties of your calling.

6 As for me, my life is already being poured out on the altar, and the hour for my departure is upon me. 7 I have run the great race, I have finished the course, I have kept the faith. 8 And now there awaits me the garland of righteousness which the Lord, the righteous Judge, will award to me on the great day, and not to me alone, but to all who have set their hearts on his coming appearance.

9 Do your best to join me soon. 10 Demas, his heart set on this present world, has deserted me and gone to Thessalonica; Crescens is away in Galatia, Titus in Dalmatia; apart from Luke 11 I have no one with me. Get hold of Mark and bring him with you; he is a great help to me. 12 Tychicus I have sent to Ephesus. 13 When you come, bring the cloak I left with Carpus at Troas, and the books, particularly my notebooks.

14 Alexander the coppersmith did me a great deal of harm. The Lord will deal with him as he deserves, 15 but you had better be on your guard against him, for he is bitterly opposed to everything we teach. 16 At the first hearing of my case no one came into court to support me; they all left me in the lurch; I pray that it may not be counted against them. 17 But the Lord stood by me and lent me strength, so that I might be his instrument in making the full proclamation of the gospel for the whole pagan world to hear; and thus I was rescued from the lion's jaws. 18 The Lord will rescue me from every attempt to do me harm, and bring me safely into his heavenly kingdom. Glory to him for ever and ever! Amen.

19 Greetings to Prisca and Aquila, and the household of Onesiphorus.

20 Erastus stayed behind at Corinth, and Trophimus I left ill at Miletus. 21 Do try to get here before winter.

Greetings from Eubulus, Pudens, Linus, and Claudia, and from all the brotherhood here.

22 The Lord be with your spirit. Grace be with you all!

---

i Or *Every scripture inspired by God is also*   *j* Other ancient authorities read *Gaul*   *k* Gk *all the brothers*   *l* The Greek word for *you* here is plural. Other ancient authorities add *Amen*

4:10 **Galatia:** or Gaul.

NEW AMERICAN BIBLE

10 You have followed my teaching, way of life, purpose, faith, patience, love, endurance, 11 persecutions, and sufferings, such as happened to me in Antioch, Iconium, and Lystra, persecutions that I endured. Yet from all these things the Lord delivered me. 12 In fact, all who want to live religiously in Christ Jesus will be persecuted. 13 But wicked people and charlatans will go from bad to worse, deceivers and deceived. 14 But you, remain faithful to what you have learned and believed, because you know from whom you learned it, 15 and that from infancy you have known [the] sacred scriptures, which are capable of giving you wisdom for salvation through faith in Christ Jesus. 16 All scripture is inspired by God and is useful for teaching, for refutation, for correction, and for training in righteousness, 17 so that one who belongs to God may be competent, equipped for every good work.

4 I charge you in the presence of God and of Christ Jesus, who will judge the living and the dead, and by his appearing and his kingly power: 2 proclaim the word; be persistent whether it is convenient or inconvenient; convince, reprimand, encourage through all patience and teaching. 3 For the time will come when people will not tolerate sound doctrine but, following their own desires and insatiable curiosity, will accumulate teachers 4 and will stop listening to the truth and will be diverted to myths. 5 But you, be self-possessed in all circumstances; put up with hardship; perform the work of an evangelist; fulfill your ministry.

6 For I am already being poured out like a libation, and the time of my departure is at hand. 7 I have competed well; I have finished the race; I have kept the faith. 8 From now on the crown of righteousness awaits me, which the Lord, the just judge, will award to me on that day, and not only to me, but to all who have longed for his appearance.

9 Try to join me soon, 10 for Demas, enamored of the present world, deserted me and went to Thessalonica, Crescens to Galatia, and Titus to Dalmatia. 11 Luke is the only one with me. Get Mark and bring him with you, for he is helpful to me in the ministry. 12 I have sent Tychicus to Ephesus. 13 When you come, bring the cloak I left with Carpus in Troas, the papyrus rolls, and especially the parchments.

14 Alexander the coppersmith did me a great deal of harm; the Lord will repay him according to his deeds. 15 You too be on guard against him, for he has strongly resisted our preaching.

16 At my first defense no one appeared on my behalf, but everyone deserted me. May it not be held against them! 17 But the Lord stood by me and gave me strength, so that through me the proclamation might be completed and all the Gentiles might hear it. And I was rescued from the lion's mouth. 18 The Lord will rescue me from every evil threat and will bring me safe to his heavenly kingdom. To him be glory forever and ever. Amen.

19 Greet Prisca and Aquila and the family of Onesiphorus. 20 Erastus remained in Corinth, while I left Trophimus sick at Miletus. 21 Try to get here before winter. Eubulus, Pudens, Linus, Claudia, and all the brothers send greetings. 22 The Lord be with your spirit. Grace be with all of you.

NEW JERUSALEM BIBLE

10 You, though, have followed my teaching, my way of life, my aims, my faith, my patience and my love, my perseverance 11 and the persecutions and sufferings that came to me in places like Antioch, Iconium and Lystra — all the persecutions I have endured; and the Lord has rescued me from every one of them. 12 But anybody who tries to live in devotion to Christ is certain to be persecuted; 13 while these wicked impostors will go from bad to worse, deceiving others, and themselves deceived.

14 You must keep to what you have been taught and know to be true; remember who your teachers were, 15 and how, ever since you were a child, you have known the holy scriptures c — from these you can learn the wisdom that leads to salvation through faith in Christ Jesus. 16 All scripture is inspired by God and useful for refuting error, for guiding people's lives and teaching them to be upright. 17 This is how someone who is dedicated to God becomes fully equipped and ready for any good work.

4 Before God and before Christ Jesus who is to be judge of the living and the dead, I charge you, in the name of his appearing and of his kingdom: 2 proclaim the message and, welcome or unwelcome, insist on it. Refute falsehood, correct error, give encouragement — but do all with patience and with care to instruct. 3 The time is sure to come when people will not accept sound teaching, but their ears will be itching for anything new and they will collect themselves a whole series of teachers according to their own tastes; 4 and then they will shut their ears to the truth and will turn to myths. 5 But you must keep steady all the time; put up with suffering; do the work of preaching the gospel; fulfil the service asked of you.

6 As for me, my life is already being poured away as a libation, and the time has come for me to depart. 7 I have fought the good fight to the end; I have run the race to the finish; I have kept the faith; 8 all there is to come for me now is the crown of uprightness which the Lord, the upright judge, will give to me on that Day; and not only to me but to all those who have longed for his appearing.

9 Make every effort to come and see me as soon as you can. 10 As it is, Demas has deserted me for love of this life and gone to Thessalonica, Crescens has gone to Galatia and Titus to Dalmatia; 11 only Luke is with me. Bring Mark with you; I find him a useful helper in my work. 12 I have sent Tychicus to Ephesus. 13 When you come, bring the cloak I left with Carpus in Troas, and the scrolls, especially the parchment ones. 14 Alexander the coppersmith has done me a lot of harm; *the Lord will repay him as his deeds deserve*. d 15 Be on your guard against him yourself, because he has been bitterly contesting everything that we say.

16 The first time I had to present my defence, no one came into court to support me. Every one of them deserted me — may they not be held accountable for it. 17 But the Lord stood by me and gave me power, so that through me the message might be fully proclaimed for all the gentiles to hear; and so I was *saved from the lion's mouth*. e 18 The Lord will rescue me from all evil attempts on me, and bring me safely to his heavenly kingdom. To him be glory for ever and ever. Amen.

19 Greetings to Prisca and Aquila, and the family of Onesiphorus. 20 Erastus stayed behind at Corinth, and I left Trophimus ill at Miletus. 21 Make every effort to come before the winter.

Greetings to you from Eubulus, Pudens, Linus, Claudia and all the brothers. 22 The Lord be with your spirit. Grace be with you.

c 3 Probably the OT. There is no sign that the NT writings were yet set on the same level. d 4 Ps 28:4. e 4 Ps 22:21.

THE LETTER OF PAUL TO
Titus

1 Paul, a servant*a* of God and an apostle of Jesus Christ, for the sake of the faith of God's elect and the knowledge of the truth that is in accordance with godliness, 2 in the hope of eternal life that God, who never lies, promised before the ages began — 3 in due time he revealed his word through the proclamation with which I have been entrusted by the command of God our Savior,

4 To Titus, my loyal child in the faith we share:
Grace*b* and peace from God the Father and Christ Jesus our Savior.

5 I left you behind in Crete for this reason, so that you should put in order what remained to be done, and should appoint elders in every town, as I directed you: 6 someone who is blameless, married only once,*c* whose children are believers, not accused of debauchery and not rebellious. 7 For a bishop,*d* as God's steward, must be blameless; he must not be arrogant or quick-tempered or addicted to wine or violent or greedy for gain; 8 but he must be hospitable, a lover of goodness, prudent, upright, devout, and self-controlled. 9 He must have a firm grasp of the word that is trustworthy in accordance with the teaching, so that he may be able both to preach with sound doctrine and to refute those who contradict it.

10 There are also many rebellious people, idle talkers and deceivers, especially those of the circumcision; 11 they must be silenced, since they are upsetting whole families by teaching for sordid gain what it is not right to teach. 12 It was one of them, their very own prophet, who said,
> "Cretans are always liars, vicious brutes, lazy gluttons."

13 That testimony is true. For this reason rebuke them sharply, so that they may become sound in the faith, 14 not paying attention to Jewish myths or to commandments of those who reject the truth. 15 To the pure all things are pure, but to the corrupt and unbelieving nothing is pure. Their very minds and consciences are corrupted. 16 They profess to know God, but they deny him by their actions. They are detestable, disobedient, unfit for any good work.

2 But as for you, teach what is consistent with sound doctrine. 2 Tell the older men to be temperate, serious, prudent, and sound in faith, in love, and in endurance.

3 Likewise, tell the older women to be reverent in behavior, not to be slanderers or slaves to drink; they are to teach what is good, 4 so that they may encourage the young women to love their husbands, to love their children, 5 to be self-controlled, chaste, good managers of the household, kind, being submissive to their husbands, so that the word of God may not be discredited.

6 Likewise, urge the younger men to be self-controlled. 7 Show yourself in all respects a model of good works, and in your teaching show integrity, gravity, 8 and sound speech that cannot be censured; then any opponent will be put to shame, having nothing evil to say of us.

THE LETTER OF PAUL TO
Titus

1 FROM Paul, servant of God and apostle of Jesus Christ, marked as such by the faith of God's chosen people and the knowledge of the truth enshrined in our religion 2 with its hope of eternal life, which God, who does not lie, promised long ages ago, 3 and now in his own good time has openly declared in the proclamation entrusted to me by command of God our Saviour.

4 To Titus, my true-born son in the faith which we share. Grace and peace to you from God the Father and Jesus Christ our Saviour.

5 My intention in leaving you behind in Crete was that you should deal with any outstanding matters, and in particular should appoint elders in each town in accordance with the principles I have laid down: 6 Are they men of unimpeachable character? Is each the husband of one wife? Are their children believers, not open to any charge of dissipation or indiscipline? 7 For as God's steward a bishop must be a man of unimpeachable character. He must not be overbearing or short-tempered or given to drink; no brawler, no money-grubber, 8 but hospitable, right-minded, temperate, just, devout, and self-controlled. 9 He must keep firm hold of the true doctrine, so that he may be well able both to appeal to his hearers with sound teaching and to refute those who raise objections.

10 There are many, especially among Jewish converts, who are undisciplined, who talk wildly and lead others astray. 11 Such men must be muzzled, because they are ruining whole families by teaching what they should not, and all for sordid gain. 12 It was a Cretan prophet, one of their own countrymen, who said, 'Cretans were ever liars, vicious brutes, lazy gluttons' — 13 and how truly he spoke! All the more reason why you should rebuke them sharply, so that they may be restored to a sound faith, 14 instead of paying heed to Jewish myths and to human commandments, the work of those who turn their backs on the truth.

15 To the pure all things are pure; but nothing is pure to tainted disbelievers, tainted both in reason and in conscience. 16 They profess to know God but by their actions deny him; they are detestable and disobedient, disqualified for any good work.

2 For your part, what you say must be in keeping with sound doctrine. 2 The older men should be sober, dignified, and temperate, sound in faith, love, and fortitude. 3 The older women, similarly, should be reverent in their demeanour, not scandalmongers or slaves to excessive drinking; they must set a high standard, 4 and so teach the younger women to be loving wives and mothers, 5 to be temperate, chaste, busy at home, and kind, respecting the authority of their husbands. Then the gospel will not be brought into disrepute.

6 Urge the younger men, similarly, to be temperate 7 in all things, and set them an example of good conduct yourself. In your teaching you must show integrity and seriousness, 8 and offer sound instruction to which none can take exception. Any opponent will be at a loss when he finds nothing to say to our discredit.

---

a Gk *slave*   *b* Other ancient authorities read *Grace, mercy,*
c Gk *husband of one wife*   *d* Or *an overseer*

1:1 **apostle . . . knowledge:** *or* apostle of Jesus Christ, to bring God's chosen people to faith and to knowledge.

The Letter to Titus

1 Paul, a slave of God and apostle of Jesus Christ for the sake of the faith of God's chosen ones and the recognition of religious truth, 2 in the hope of eternal life that God, who does not lie, promised before time began, 3 who indeed at the proper time revealed his word in the proclamation with which I was entrusted by the command of God our savior, 4 to Titus, my true child in our common faith: grace and peace from God the Father and Christ Jesus our savior.

5 For this reason I left you in Crete so that you might set right what remains to be done and appoint presbyters in every town, as I directed you, 6 on condition that a man be blameless, married only once, with believing children who are not accused of licentiousness or rebellious. 7 For a bishop as God's steward must be blameless, not arrogant, not irritable, not a drunkard, not aggressive, not greedy for sordid gain, 8 but hospitable, a lover of goodness, temperate, just, holy, and self-controlled, 9 holding fast to the true message as taught so that he will be able both to exhort with sound doctrine and to refute opponents. 10 For there are also many rebels, idle talkers and deceivers, especially the Jewish Christians. 11 It is imperative to silence them, as they are upsetting whole families by teaching for sordid gain what they should not. 12 One of them, a prophet of their own, once said, "Cretans have always been liars, vicious beasts, and lazy gluttons." 13 That testimony is true. Therefore, admonish them sharply, so that they may be sound in the faith, 14 instead of paying attention to Jewish myths and regulations of people who have repudiated the truth. 15 To the clean all things are clean, but to those who are defiled and unbelieving nothing is clean; in fact, both their minds and their consciences are tainted. 16 They claim to know God, but by their deeds they deny him. They are vile and disobedient and unqualified for any good deed.

2 As for yourself, you must say what is consistent with sound doctrine, namely, 2 that older men should be temperate, dignified, self-controlled, sound in faith, love, and endurance. 3 Similarly, older women should be reverent in their behavior, not slanderers, not addicted to drink, teaching what is good, 4 so that they may train younger women to love their husbands and children, 5 to be self-controlled, chaste, good homemakers, under the control of their husbands, so that the word of God may not be discredited.

6 Urge the younger men, similarly, to control themselves, 7 showing yourself as a model of good deeds in every respect, with integrity in your teaching, dignity, 8 and sound speech that cannot be criticized, so that the opponent will be put to shame without anything bad to say about us.

Titus

THE LETTER FROM PAUL TO TITUS

1 From Paul, servant of God, an apostle of Jesus Christ to bring those whom God has chosen to faith and to the knowledge of the truth that leads to true religion, 2 and to give them the hope of the eternal life that was promised so long ago by God. He does not lie 3 and so, in due time, he made known his message by a proclamation which was entrusted to me by the command of God our Saviour. 4 To Titus, true child of mine in the faith that we share. Grace and peace from God the Father and from Christ Jesus our Saviour.

5 The reason I left you behind in Crete was for you to organise everything that still had to be done and appoint elders in every town, in the way that I told you, 6 that is, each of them must be a man of irreproachable character, husband of one wife, and his children must be believers and not liable to be charged with disorderly conduct or insubordination. 7 The presiding elder has to be irreproachable since he is God's representative: never arrogant or hot-tempered, nor a heavy drinker or violent, nor avaricious; 8 but hospitable and a lover of goodness; sensible, upright, devout and self-controlled; 9 and he must have a firm grasp of the unchanging message of the tradition, so that he can be counted on both for giving encouragement in sound doctrine and for refuting those who argue against it.

10 And in fact there are many people who are insubordinate, who talk nonsense and try to make others believe it, particularly among those of the circumcision. 11 They must be silenced: people of this kind upset whole families, by teaching things that they ought not to, and doing it for the sake of sordid gain. 12 It was one of themselves, one of their own prophets, who said,[a] 'Cretans were never anything but liars, dangerous animals, all greed and laziness'; 13 and that is a true statement. So be severe in correcting them, and make them sound in the faith 14 so that they stop taking notice of Jewish myths and the orders of people who turn away from the truth.

15 To those who are pure themselves, everything is pure; but to those who have been corrupted and lack faith, nothing can be pure — the corruption is both in their minds and in their consciences. 16 They claim to know God but by their works they deny him; they are outrageously rebellious and quite untrustworthy for any good work.

2 It is for you, then, to preach the behaviour which goes with healthy doctrine. 2 Older men should be reserved, dignified, moderate, sound in faith and love and perseverance. 3 Similarly, older women should behave as befits religious people, with no scandal-mongering and no addiction to wine — they must be the teachers of right behaviour 4 and show younger women how they should love their husbands and love their children, 5 how they must be sensible and chaste, and how to work in their homes, and be gentle, and obey their husbands, so that the message of God is not disgraced. 6 Similarly, urge younger men to be moderate in everything that they do, 7 and you yourself set an example of good works, by sincerity and earnestness, when you are teaching, and by a message sound and irreproachable 8 so that any opponent will be at a loss, with no accusation to

NEW REVISED STANDARD VERSION

9 Tell slaves to be submissive to their masters and to give satisfaction in every respect; they are not to talk back, 10 not to pilfer, but to show complete and perfect fidelity, so that in everything they may be an ornament to the doctrine of God our Savior.

11 For the grace of God has appeared, bringing salvation to all, *e* 12 training us to renounce impiety and worldly passions, and in the present age to live lives that are self-controlled, upright, and godly, 13 while we wait for the blessed hope and the manifestation of the glory of our great God and Savior, *f* Jesus Christ. 14 He it is who gave himself for us that he might redeem us from all iniquity and purify for himself a people of his own who are zealous for good deeds.

15 Declare these things; exhort and reprove with all authority. *g* Let no one look down on you.

3 Remind them to be subject to rulers and authorities, to be obedient, to be ready for every good work, 2 to speak evil of no one, to avoid quarreling, to be gentle, and to show every courtesy to everyone. 3 For we ourselves were once foolish, disobedient, led astray, slaves to various passions and pleasures, passing our days in malice and envy, despicable, hating one another. 4 But when the goodness and loving kindness of God our Savior appeared, 5 he saved us, not because of any works of righteousness that we had done, but according to his mercy, through the water *h* of rebirth and renewal by the Holy Spirit. 6 This Spirit he poured out on us richly through Jesus Christ our Savior, 7 so that, having been justified by his grace, we might become heirs according to the hope of eternal life. 8 The saying is sure.

I desire that you insist on these things, so that those who have come to believe in God may be careful to devote themselves to good works; these things are excellent and profitable to everyone. 9 But avoid stupid controversies, genealogies, dissensions, and quarrels about the law, for they are unprofitable and worthless. 10 After a first and second admonition, have nothing more to do with anyone who causes divisions, 11 since you know that such a person is perverted and sinful, being self-condemned.

12 When I send Artemas to you, or Tychicus, do your best to come to me at Nicopolis, for I have decided to spend the winter there. 13 Make every effort to send Zenas the lawyer and Apollos on their way, and see that they lack nothing. 14 And let people learn to devote themselves to good works in order to meet urgent needs, so that they may not be unproductive.

15 All who are with me send greetings to you. Greet those who love us in the faith.

Grace be with all of you. *i*

REVISED ENGLISH BIBLE

9 Slaves are to respect their masters' authority in everything and to give them satisfaction; they are not to answer back, 10 nor to pilfer, but are to show themselves absolutely trustworthy. In all this they will add lustre to the doctrine of God our Saviour.

11 For the grace of God has dawned upon the world with healing for all mankind; 12 and by it we are disciplined to renounce godless ways and worldly desires, and to live a life of temperance, honesty, and godliness in the present age, 13 looking forward to the happy fulfilment of our hope when the splendour of our great God and Saviour Christ Jesus will appear. 14 He it is who sacrificed himself for us, to set us free from all wickedness and to make us his own people, pure and eager to do good.

15 These are your themes; urge them and argue them with an authority which no one can disregard.

3 Remind everyone to be submissive to the government and the authorities, and to obey them; to be ready for any honourable work; 2 to slander no one, to avoid quarrels, and always to show forbearance and a gentle disposition to all.

3 There was a time when we too were lost in folly and disobedience and were slaves to passions and pleasures of every kind. Our days were passed in malice and envy; hateful ourselves, we loathed one another. 4 'But when the kindness and generosity of God our Saviour dawned upon the world, 5 then, not for any good deeds of our own, but because he was merciful, he saved us through the water of rebirth and the renewing power of the Holy Spirit, 6 which he lavished upon us through Jesus Christ our Saviour, 7 so that, justified by his grace, we might in hope become heirs to eternal life.' 8 That is a saying you may trust.

SUCH are the points I want you to insist on, so that those who have come to believe in God may be sure to devote themselves to good works. These precepts are good in themselves and also useful to society. 9 But avoid foolish speculations, genealogies, quarrels, and controversies over the law; they are unprofitable and futile.

10 If someone is contentious, he should be allowed a second warning; after that, have nothing more to do with him, 11 recognizing that anyone like that has a distorted mind and stands self-condemned in his sin.

12 Once I have sent Artemas or Tychicus to you, join me at Nicopolis as soon as you can, for that is where I have decided to spend the winter. 13 Do your utmost to help Zenas the lawyer and Apollos on their travels, and see that they are not short of anything. 14 And our own people must be taught to devote themselves to good works to meet urgent needs; they must not be unproductive.

15 All who are with me send you my greetings. My greetings to our friends in the faith. Grace be with you all!

2:13 **of our great . . . Saviour:** *or* of the great God and our Saviour.
3:5 **water . . . power of:** *or* water of rebirth and of renewal by.
3:8 **devote . . . good in themselves:** *or* engage in honest employment. This is good in itself.   3:14 **devote . . . needs:** *or* engage in honest employment to produce the necessities of life.

e Or *has appeared to all, bringing salvation*   *f* Or *of the great God and our Savior*   *g* Gk *commandment*   *h* Gk *washing*   *i* Other ancient authorities add *Amen*

NEW AMERICAN BIBLE

9 Slaves are to be under the control of their masters in all respects, giving them satisfaction, not talking back to them 10 or stealing from them, but exhibiting complete good faith, so as to adorn the doctrine of God our savior in every way.

11 For the grace of God has appeared, saving all 12 and training us to reject godless ways and worldly desires and to live temperately, justly, and devoutly in this age, 13 as we await the blessed hope, the appearance of the glory of the great God and of our savior Jesus Christ, 14 who gave himself for us to deliver us from all lawlessness and to cleanse for himself a people as his own, eager to do what is good.

15 Say these things. Exhort and correct with all authority. Let no one look down on you.

3 Remind them to be under the control of magistrates and authorities, to be obedient, to be open to every good enterprise. 2 They are to slander no one, to be peaceable, considerate, exercising all graciousness toward everyone. 3 For we ourselves were once foolish, disobedient, deluded, slaves to various desires and pleasures, living in malice and envy, hateful ourselves and hating one another.

4 But when the kindness and generous love
    of God our savior appeared,
5 not because of any righteous deeds we had done
    but because of his mercy,
he saved us through the bath of rebirth
    and renewal by the holy Spirit,
6 whom he richly poured out on us
    through Jesus Christ our savior,
7 so that we might be justified by his grace
    and become heirs in hope of eternal life.

8 This saying is trustworthy.

I want you to insist on these points, that those who have believed in God be careful to devote themselves to good works; these are excellent and beneficial to others. 9 Avoid foolish arguments, genealogies, rivalries, and quarrels about the law, for they are useless and futile. 10 After a first and second warning, break off contact with a heretic, 11 realizing that such a person is perverted and sinful and stands self-condemned.

12 When I send Artemas to you, or Tychicus, try to join me at Nicopolis, where I have decided to spend the winter. 13 Send Zenas the lawyer and Apollos on their journey soon, and see to it that they have everything they need. 14 But let our people, too, learn to devote themselves to good works to supply urgent needs, so that they may not be unproductive.

15 All who are with me send you greetings. Greet those who love us in the faith.

Grace be with all of you.

NEW JERUSALEM BIBLE

make against us. 9 Slaves must be obedient to their masters in everything, and do what is wanted without argument; 10 and there must be no pilfering — they must show complete honesty at all times, so that they are in every way a credit to the teaching of God our Saviour.

11 You see, God's grace has been revealed to save the whole human race; 12 it has taught us that we should give up everything contrary to true religion and all our worldly passions; we must be self-restrained and live upright and religious lives in this present world, 13 waiting in hope for the blessing which will come with the appearing of the glory of our great God and Saviour Christ Jesus. 14 He offered himself for us in order to ransom us from all our *faults* and *to purify a people to be his very own*b and eager to do good.

15 This is what you must say, encouraging or arguing with full authority; no one should despise you.

3 Remind them to be obedient to the officials in authority; to be ready to do good at every opportunity; 2 not to go slandering other people but to be peaceable and gentle, and always polite to people of all kinds. 3 There was a time when we too were ignorant, disobedient and misled and enslaved by different passions and dissipations; we lived then in wickedness and malice, hating each other and hateful ourselves.

4 But when the kindness and love of God our Saviour for humanity were revealed, 5 it was not because of any upright actions we had done ourselves; it was for no reason except his own faithful love that he saved us, by means of the cleansing water of rebirth and renewal in the Holy Spirit 6 which he has so generously poured over us through Jesus Christ our Saviour; 7 so that, justified by his grace, we should become heirs in hope of eternal life. 8 This is doctrine that you can rely on.

I want you to be quite uncompromising in teaching all this, so that those who now believe in God may keep their minds constantly occupied in doing good works. All this is good, and useful for everybody. 9 But avoid foolish speculations, and those genealogies, and the quibbles and disputes about the Law — they are useless and futile. 10 If someone disputes what you teach, then after a first and a second warning, have no more to do with him: 11 you will know that anyone of that sort is warped and is self-condemned as a sinner.

12 As soon as I have sent Artemas or Tychicus to you, do your best to join me at Nicopolis, where I have decided to spend the winter. 13 Help eagerly on their way Zenas the lawyer and Apollos, and make sure they have everything they need. 14 All our people must also learn to occupy themselves in doing good works for their practical needs, and not to be unproductive.

15 All those who are with me send their greetings. Greetings to those who love us in the faith. Grace be with you all.

b 2 Ex 19:5.

THE LETTER OF PAUL TO
Philemon

THE LETTER OF PAUL TO
Philemon

1 Paul, a prisoner of Christ Jesus, and Timothy our brother,*a*

To Philemon our dear friend and co-worker, 2 to Apphia our sister,*b* to Archippus our fellow soldier, and to the church in your house:

3 Grace to you and peace from God our Father and the Lord Jesus Christ.

4 When I remember you*c* in my prayers, I always thank my God 5 because I hear of your love for all the saints and your faith toward the Lord Jesus. 6 I pray that the sharing of your faith may become effective when you perceive all the good that we*d* may do for Christ. 7 I have indeed received much joy and encouragement from your love, because the hearts of the saints have been refreshed through you, my brother.

8 For this reason, though I am bold enough in Christ to command you to do your duty, 9 yet I would rather appeal to you on the basis of love — and I, Paul, do this as an old man, and now also as a prisoner of Christ Jesus.*e* 10 I am appealing to you for my child, Onesimus, whose father I have become during my imprisonment. 11 Formerly he was useless to you, but now he is indeed useful*f* both to you and to me. 12 I am sending him, that is, my own heart, back to you. 13 I wanted to keep him with me, so that he might be of service to me in your place during my imprisonment for the gospel; 14 but I preferred to do nothing without your consent, in order that your good deed might be voluntary and not something forced. 15 Perhaps this is the reason he was separated from you for a while, so that you might have him back forever, 16 no longer as a slave but more than a slave, a beloved brother — especially to me but how much more to you, both in the flesh and in the Lord.

17 So if you consider me your partner, welcome him as you would welcome me. 18 If he has wronged you in any way, or owes you anything, charge that to my account. 19 I, Paul, am writing this with my own hand: I will repay it. I say nothing about your owing me even your own self. 20 Yes, brother, let me have this benefit from you in the Lord! Refresh my heart in Christ. 21 Confident of your obedience, I am writing to you, knowing that you will do even more than I say.

22 One thing more — prepare a guest room for me, for I am hoping through your prayers to be restored to you.

23 Epaphras, my fellow prisoner in Christ Jesus, sends greetings to you,*g* 24 and so do Mark, Aristarchus, Demas, and Luke, my fellow workers.

25 The grace of the Lord Jesus Christ be with your spirit.*h*

FROM Paul, a prisoner of Christ Jesus, and our colleague Timothy, to Philemon our dear friend and fellow-worker, 2 together with Apphia our sister, and Archippus our comrade-in-arms, and the church that meets at your house.

3 Grace to you and peace from God our Father and the Lord Jesus Christ.

4 I thank my God always when I mention you in my prayers, 5 for I hear of your love and faith towards the Lord Jesus and for all God's people. 6 My prayer is that the faith you hold in common with us may deepen your understanding of all the blessings which belong to us as we are brought closer to Christ. 7 Your love has brought me much joy and encouragement; through you God's people have been much refreshed.

8 ACCORDINGLY, although in Christ I might feel free to dictate where your duty lies, 9 yet, because of that same love, I would rather appeal to you. Ambassador as I am of Christ Jesus, and now his prisoner, 10 I, Paul, appeal to you about my child, whose father I have become in this prison. I mean Onesimus, 11 once so useless to you, but now useful indeed, both to you and to me. 12 In sending him back to you I am sending my heart. 13 I should have liked to keep him with me, to look after me on your behalf, here in prison for the gospel, 14 but I did not want to do anything without your consent, so that your kindness might be a matter not of compulsion, but of your own free will. 15 Perhaps this is why you lost him for a time to receive him back for good — 16 no longer as a slave, but as more than a slave: as a dear brother, very dear to me, and still dearer to you, both as a man and as a Christian.

17 If, then, you think of me as your partner in the faith, welcome him as you would welcome me. 18 If he did you any wrong and owes you anything, put it down to my account. 19 Here is my signature: Paul. I will repay you — not to mention that you owe me your very self. 20 Yes, brother, I am asking this favour of you as a fellow-Christian; set my mind at rest.

21 I write to you confident that you will meet my wishes; I know that you will in fact do more than I ask. 22 And one last thing: have a room ready for me, for I hope through the prayers of you all to be restored to you.

23 Epaphras, a captive of Christ Jesus like myself, sends you greetings. 24 So do my fellow-workers Mark, Aristarchus, Demas, and Luke.

25 The grace of the Lord Jesus Christ be with your spirit!

---

a Gk *the brother*   *b* Gk *the sister*   *c* From verse 4 through verse 21, *you* is singular   *d* Other ancient authorities read *you* (plural)   *e* Or *as an ambassador of Christ Jesus, and now also his prisoner*   *f* The name Onesimus means *useful* or (compare verse 20) *beneficial*   *g* Here *you* is singular   *h* Other ancient authorities add *Amen*

The Letter to Philemon

1 Paul, a prisoner for Christ Jesus, and Timothy our brother, to Philemon, our beloved and our co-worker, 2 to Apphia our sister, to Archippus our fellow soldier, and to the church at your house. 3 Grace to you and peace from God our Father and the Lord Jesus Christ.

4 I give thanks to my God always, remembering you in my prayers, 5 as I hear of the love and the faith you have in the Lord Jesus and for all the holy ones, 6 so that your partnership in the faith may become effective in recognizing every good there is in us that leads to Christ.

7 For I have experienced much joy and encouragement from your love, because the hearts of the holy ones have been refreshed by you, brother. 8 Therefore, although I have the full right in Christ to order you to do what is proper, 9 I rather urge you out of love, being as I am, Paul, an old man, and now also a prisoner for Christ Jesus. 10 I urge you on behalf of my child Onesimus, whose father I have become in my imprisonment, 11 who was once useless to you but is now useful to [both] you and me. 12 I am sending him, that is, my own heart, back to you. 13 I should have liked to retain him for myself, so that he might serve me on your behalf in my imprisonment for the gospel, 14 but I did not want to do anything without your consent, so that the good you do might not be forced but voluntary. 15 Perhaps this is why he was away from you for a while, that you might have him back forever, 16 no longer as a slave but more than a slave, a brother, beloved especially to me, but even more so to you, as a man and in the Lord. 17 So if you regard me as a partner, welcome him as you would me. 18 And if he has done you any injustice or owes you anything, charge it to me. 19 I, Paul, write this in my own hand: I will pay. May I not tell you that you owe me your very self. 20 Yes, brother, may I profit from you in the Lord. Refresh my heart in Christ.

21 With trust in your compliance I write to you, knowing that you will do even more than I say. 22 At the same time prepare a guest room for me, for I hope to be granted to you through your prayers.

23 Epaphras, my fellow prisoner in Christ Jesus, greets you, 24 as well as Mark, Aristarchus, Demas, and Luke, my co-workers. 25 The grace of the Lord Jesus Christ be with your spirit.

Philemon

THE LETTER FROM PAUL TO PHILEMON

From Paul, a prisoner of Christ Jesus and from our brother Timothy; to our dear fellow worker Philemon, 2 our sister Apphia, our fellow soldier Archippus and the church that meets in your house. 3 Grace and the peace of God our Father and the Lord Jesus Christ.

4 I always thank my God, mentioning you in my prayers, 5 because I hear of the love and the faith which you have for the Lord Jesus and for all God's holy people. 6 I pray that your fellowship in faith may come to expression in full knowledge of all the good we can do for Christ. 7 I have received much joy and encouragement by your love; you have set the hearts of God's holy people at rest.

8 Therefore, although in Christ I have no hesitations about telling you what your duty is, 9 I am rather appealing to your love, being what I am, Paul, an old man, and now also a prisoner of Christ Jesus. 10 I am appealing to you for a child of mine, whose father I became while wearing these chains: I mean Onesimus.a 11 He was of no use to you before, but now he is useful both to you and to me. 12 I am sending him back to you — that is to say, sending you my own heart. 13 I should have liked to keep him with me; he could have been a substitute for you, to help me while I am in the chains that the gospel has brought me. 14 However, I did not want to do anything without your consent; it would have been forcing your act of kindness, which should be spontaneous. 15 I suppose you have been deprived of Onesimus for a time, merely so that you could have him back for ever, 16 no longer as a slave, but something much better than a slave, a dear brother; especially dear to me, but how much more to you, both on the natural plane and in the Lord. 17 So if you grant me any fellowship with yourself, welcome him as you would me; 18 if he has wronged you in any way or owes you anything, put it down to my account. 19 I am writing this in my own hand: I, Paul, shall pay it back — I make no mention of a further debt, that you owe me your very self to me! 20 Well then, brother, I am counting on you, in the Lord; set my heart at rest, in Christ. 21 I am writing with complete confidence in your compliance, sure that you will do even more than I ask.

22 There is another thing: will you get a place ready for me to stay in? I am hoping through your prayers to be restored to you.

23 Epaphras, a prisoner with me in Christ Jesus, sends his greetings; 24 so do my fellow-workers Mark, Aristarchus, Demas and Luke.

25 May the grace of our Lord Jesus Christ be with your spirit.

a A pun: Onesimus means 'useful'.

THE LETTER TO THE
Hebrews

1 Long ago God spoke to our ancestors in many and various ways by the prophets, 2 but in these last days he has spoken to us by a Son,*a* whom he appointed heir of all things, through whom he also created the worlds. 3 He is the reflection of God's glory and the exact imprint of God's very being, and he sustains*b* all things by his powerful word. When he had made purification for sins, he sat down at the right hand of the Majesty on high, 4 having become as much superior to angels as the name he has inherited is more excellent than theirs.

5 For to which of the angels did God ever say,
"You are my Son;
    today I have begotten you"?
Or again,
"I will be his Father,
    and he will be my Son"?
6 And again, when he brings the firstborn into the world, he says,
"Let all God's angels worship him."
7 Of the angels he says,
"He makes his angels winds,
    and his servants flames of fire."
8 But of the Son he says,
"Your throne, O God,*c* is forever and ever,
    and the righteous scepter is the scepter of
        your*d* kingdom.
9 You have loved righteousness and hated
        wickedness;
    therefore God, your God, has anointed you
        with the oil of gladness beyond your
            companions."
10 And,
"In the beginning, Lord, you founded the earth,
    and the heavens are the work of your hands;
11 they will perish, but you remain;
    they will all wear out like clothing;
12 like a cloak you will roll them up,
    and like clothing*e* they will be changed.
But you are the same,
    and your years will never end."
13 But to which of the angels has he ever said,
"Sit at my right hand
    until I make your enemies a footstool for your
        feet"?
14 Are not all angels*f* spirits in the divine service, sent to serve for the sake of those who are to inherit salvation?

2 Therefore we must pay greater attention to what we have heard, so that we do not drift away from it. 2 For if the message declared through angels was valid, and every transgression or disobedience received a just penalty, 3 how can we escape if we neglect so great a salvation? It was declared at first through the Lord, and it was attested to us by those who heard him, 4 while God added his testimony

A LETTER TO
Hebrews

1 When in times past God spoke to our forefathers, he spoke in many and varied ways through the prophets. 2 But in this the final age he has spoken to us in his Son, whom he has appointed heir of all things; and through him he created the universe. 3 He is the radiance of God's glory, the stamp of God's very being, and he sustains the universe by his word of power. When he had brought about purification from sins, he took his seat at the right hand of God's Majesty on high, 4 raised as far above the angels as the title he has inherited is superior to theirs.

5 To which of the angels did God ever say, 'You are my son; today I have become your father,' or again, 'I shall be his father, and he will be my son'? 6 Again, when he presents the firstborn to the world, he says, 'Let all God's angels pay him homage.' 7 Of the angels he says:

He makes his angels winds,
    and his ministers flames of fire;
8 but of the Son:

Your throne, O God, is for ever and ever,
    and the sceptre of his kingdom is the sceptre of
        justice.
9 You have loved right and hated wrong;
    therefore, O God, your God has set you above
        your fellows
    by anointing you with oil, the token of joy.
10 And again:

By you, Lord, were earth's foundations laid of old,
    and the heavens are the work of your hands.
11 They will perish, but you remain;
    like clothes they will all wear out.
12 You will fold them up like a cloak,
    they will be changed like any garment.
But you are the same, and your years will have no
        end.

13 To which of the angels has he ever said, 'Sit at my right hand until I make your enemies your footstool'? 14 Are they not all ministering spirits sent out in God's service, for the sake of those destined to receive salvation?

2 That is why we are bound to pay all the more heed to what we have been told, for fear of drifting from our course. 2 For if God's word spoken through angels had such force that any violation of it, or any disobedience, met with its proper penalty, 3 what escape can there be for us if we ignore so great a deliverance? This deliverance was first announced through the Lord, and those who heard him confirmed it to us, 4 God himself adding his testimony by

---

a Or *the Son*   *b* Or *bears along*   *c* Or *God is your throne*
d Other ancient authorities read *his*   *e* Other ancient authorities lack
like clothing   *f* Gk *all of them*

1:6 **Again . . . presents:** *or* And when he again presents.
1:9 **therefore . . . your God:** *or* therefore God who is your God.

The Letter to the Hebrews

1 In times past, God spoke in partial and various ways to our ancestors through the prophets; 2 in these last days, he spoke to us through a son, whom he made heir of all things and through whom he created the universe,
3 who is the refulgence of his glory,
the very imprint of his being,
and who sustains all things by his mighty word.
When he had accomplished purification from sins,
he took his seat at the right hand of the Majesty on high,
4 as far superior to the angels
as the name he has inherited is more excellent than theirs.

5 For to which of the angels did God ever say:
"You are my son; this day I have begotten you"?
Or again:
"I will be a father to him, and he shall be a son to me"?
6 And again, when he leads the firstborn into the world, he says:
"Let all the angels of God worship him."
7 Of the angels he says:
"He makes his angels winds
and his ministers a fiery flame";
8 but of the Son:
"Your throne, O God, stands forever and ever;
and a righteous scepter is the scepter of your kingdom.
9 You loved justice and hated wickedness;
therefore God, your God, anointed you
with the oil of gladness above your companions";
10 and:
"At the beginning, O Lord, you established the earth,
and the heavens are the works of your hands.
11 They will perish, but you remain;
and they will all grow old like a garment.
12 You will roll them up like a cloak,
and like a garment they will be changed.
But you are the same, and your years will have no end."
13 But to which of the angels has he ever said:
"Sit at my right hand
until I make your enemies your footstool"?
14 Are they not all ministering spirits sent to serve, for the sake of those who are to inherit salvation?

2 Therefore, we must attend all the more to what we have heard, so that we may not be carried away. 2 For if the word announced through angels proved firm, and every transgression and disobedience received its just recompense, 3 how shall we escape if we ignore so great a salvation? Announced originally through the Lord, it was confirmed for us by those who had heard. 4 God added his

THE LETTER TO THE Hebrews

1 At many moments in the past and by many means, God spoke to our ancestors through the prophets; but 2 in our time, the final days, he has spoken to us in the person of his Son, whom he appointed heir of all things and through whom he made the ages. 3 He is the reflection of God's glory and bears the impress of God's own being, *a* sustaining all things by his powerful command; and now that he has purged sins away, he has taken his seat at the right hand of the divine Majesty on high. 4 So he is now as far above the angels as the title which he has inherited is higher than their own name.

5 *b* To which of the angels, then, has God ever said:

You are my Son, today I have fathered you,

or:

I shall be a father to him and he a son to me?

6 Again, when he brings the First-born into the world, he says:

Let all the angels of God pay him homage.

7 To the angels, he says:

appointing the winds his messengers and flames of fire his servants,

8 but to the Son he says:

Your throne, God, is for ever and ever;

and:

the *sceptre* of his *kingdom* is *a sceptre of justice;*
9 *you love uprightness and detest evil.*
This is why God, your God, has anointed you
with the oil of gladness, as none of your rivals.

10 And again:

Long ago, Lord, you laid earth's foundations,
the heavens are the work of your hands.
11 *They pass away but you remain,*
they all wear out like a garment.
12 *Like a cloak you will roll them up,* like a garment,
and they will be changed.
But you never alter and your years are unending.

13 To which of the angels has God ever said:

Take your seat at my right hand
till I have made your enemies your footstool?

14 Are they not all ministering spirits, sent to serve for the sake of those who are to inherit salvation?

2 We ought, then, to turn our minds more attentively than before to what we have been taught, so that we do not drift away. 2 If a message that was spoken through angels proved to be so reliable that every infringement and disobedience brought its own proper punishment, 3 then we shall certainly not go unpunished if we neglect such a great salvation. It was first announced by the Lord himself, and is guaranteed to us by those who heard him; 4 God himself

a **1** cf. Ws 7:25–26. *b* **1** Texts used in v. 5 seq.: Ps 2:7; 2 S 7:14; Ps 97:7; 104:4; 45:6–7; 102:25–27; 110:1.

by signs and wonders and various miracles, and by gifts of the Holy Spirit, distributed according to his will.

5 Now God *g* did not subject the coming world, about which we are speaking, to angels. 6 But someone has testified somewhere,

"What are human beings that you are mindful of them, *h*
or mortals, that you care for them? *i*
7 You have made them for a little while lower *j* than the angels;
you have crowned them with glory and honor, *k*
8 subjecting all things under their feet."

Now in subjecting all things to them, God *g* left nothing outside their control. As it is, we do not yet see everything in subjection to them, 9 but we do see Jesus, who for a little while was made lower *l* than the angels, now crowned with glory and honor because of the suffering of death, so that by the grace of God *m* he might taste death for everyone. 10 It was fitting that God, *g* for whom and through whom all things exist, in bringing many children to glory, should make the pioneer of their salvation perfect through sufferings. 11 For the one who sanctifies and those who are sanctified all have one Father. *n* For this reason Jesus *g* is not ashamed to call them brothers and sisters, *o* 12 saying,

"I will proclaim your name to my brothers and sisters, *o*
in the midst of the congregation I will praise you."

13 And again,

"I will put my trust in him."

And again,

"Here am I and the children whom God has given me."

14 Since, therefore, the children share flesh and blood, he himself likewise shared the same things, so that through death he might destroy the one who has the power of death, that is, the devil, 15 and free those who all their lives were held in slavery by the fear of death. 16 For it is clear that he did not come to help angels, but the descendants of Abraham. 17 Therefore he had to become like his brothers and sisters *o* in every respect, so that he might be a merciful and faithful high priest in the service of God, to make a sacrifice of atonement for the sins of the people. 18 Because he himself was tested by what he suffered, he is able to help those who are being tested.

3 Therefore, brothers and sisters, *o* holy partners in a heavenly calling, consider that Jesus, the apostle and high priest of our confession, 2 was faithful to the one who appointed him, just as Moses also "was faithful in all *p* God's *q* house." 3 Yet Jesus *r* is worthy of more glory than Moses, just as the builder of a house has more honor than the house itself. 4 (For every house is built by someone, but the builder of all things is God.) 5 Now Moses was faithful in all God's *q* house as a servant, to testify to the things that would be spoken later. 6 Christ, however, was faithful over God's *q* house as a son, and we are his house if we hold firm *s* the confidence and the pride that belong to hope.

7 Therefore, as the Holy Spirit says,

"Today, if you hear his voice,

signs and wonders, by miracles of many kinds, and by gifts of the Holy Spirit distributed at his own will.

5 For it is not to angels that he has subjected the world to come, which is our theme. 6 There is somewhere this solemn assurance:

What is man, that you should remember him,
a man, that you should care for him?
7 You made him for a short while subordinate to the angels;
with glory and honour you crowned him;
8 you put everything in subjection beneath his feet.

For in subjecting everything to him, God left nothing that is not made subject. But in fact we do not yet see everything in subjection to man. 9 What we do see is Jesus, who for a short while was made subordinate to the angels, crowned now with glory and honour because he suffered death, so that, by God's gracious will, he should experience death for all mankind.

10 In bringing many sons to glory it was fitting that God, for whom and through whom all things exist, should make the pioneer of their salvation perfect through sufferings; 11 for he who consecrates and those who are consecrated are all of one stock. That is why he does not shrink from calling men his brothers, 12 when he says, 'I will make your fame known to my brothers; in the midst of the assembly I will praise you'; 13 and again, 'I will keep my trust fixed on him'; and again, 'Here am I, and the children whom God has given me.' 14 Since the children share in flesh and blood, he too shared in them, so that by dying he might break the power of him who had death at his command, that is, the devil, 15 and might liberate those who all their life had been in servitude through fear of death. 16 Clearly they are not angels whom he helps, but the descendants of Abraham. 17 Therefore he had to be made like his brothers in every way, so that he might be merciful and faithful as their high priest before God, to make expiation for the sins of the people. 18 Because he himself has passed through the test of suffering, he is able to help those who are in the midst of their test.

3 THEREFORE, brothers in the family of God, partners in a heavenly calling, think of Jesus, the apostle and high priest of the faith we profess: 2 he was faithful to God who appointed him, as Moses also was faithful in God's household; 3 but Jesus has been counted worthy of greater honour than Moses, as the founder of a house enjoys more honour than his household. 4 Every house has its founder; and the founder of all is God. 5 Moses indeed was faithful as a servant in God's whole household; his task was to bear witness to the words that God would speak; 6 but Christ is faithful as a son, set over the household. And we are that household, if only we are fearless and keep our hope high.

7 'TODAY', therefore, as the Holy Spirit says—

Today if you hear his voice,

---

g Gk *he*   *h* Gk *What is man that you are mindful of him?*   *i* Gk *or the son of man that you care for him?* In the Hebrew of Psalm 8.4-6 both *man* and *son of man* refer to all humankind   *j* Or *them only a little lower*   *k* Other ancient authorities add *and set them over the works of your hands*   *l* Or *who was made a little lower*   *m* Other ancient authorities read *apart from God*   *n* Gk *are all of one*   *o* Gk *brothers*   *p* Other ancient authorities lack *all*   *q* Gk *his*   *r* Gk *this one*   *s* Other ancient authorities add *to the end*

2:9 so that ... will: *some witnesses read* so that, apart from God.

testimony by signs, wonders, various acts of power, and distribution of the gifts of the holy Spirit according to his will.

5 For it was not to angels that he subjected the world to come, of which we are speaking. 6 Instead, someone has testified somewhere:

> "What is man that you are mindful of him,
> or the son of man that you care for him?
> 7 You made him for a little while lower than
> the angels;
> you crowned him with glory and honor,
> 8 subjecting all things under his feet."

In "subjecting" all things [to him], he left nothing not "subject to him." Yet at present we do not see "all things subject to him," 9 but we do see Jesus "crowned with glory and honor" because he suffered death, he who "for a little while" was made "lower than the angels," that by the grace of God he might taste death for everyone.

10 For it was fitting that he, for whom and through whom all things exist, in bringing many children to glory, should make the leader to their salvation perfect through suffering. 11 He who consecrates and those who are being consecrated all have one origin. Therefore, he is not ashamed to call them "brothers," 12 saying:

> "I will proclaim your name to my brothers,
> in the midst of the assembly I will praise you";

13 and again:

> "I will put my trust in him";

and again:

> "Behold, I and the children God has given me."

14 Now since the children share in blood and flesh, he likewise shared in them, that through death he might destroy the one who has the power of death, that is, the devil, 15 and free those who through fear of death had been subject to slavery all their life. 16 Surely he did not help angels but rather the descendants of Abraham; 17 therefore, he had to become like his brothers in every way, that he might be a merciful and faithful high priest before God to expiate the sins of the people. 18 Because he himself was tested through what he suffered, he is able to help those who are being tested.

3 Therefore, holy "brothers," sharing in a heavenly calling, reflect on Jesus, the apostle and high priest of our confession, 2 who was faithful to the one who appointed him, just as Moses was "faithful in [all] his house." 3 But he is worthy of more "glory" than Moses, as the founder of a house has more "honor" than the house itself. 4 Every house is founded by someone, but the founder of all is God. 5 Moses was "faithful in all his house" as a "servant" to testify to what would be spoken, 6 but Christ was faithful as a son placed over his house. We are his house, if [only] we hold fast to our confidence and pride in our hope.

7 Therefore, as the holy Spirit says:

> "Oh, that today you would hear his voice,

confirmed their witness with signs and marvels and miracles of all kinds, and by distributing the gifts of the Holy Spirit in the various ways he wills.

5 It was not under angels that he put the world to come, about which we are speaking. 6 Someone witnesses to this somewhere with the words:

> *What are human beings that you spare a thought
> for them,*
> *a child of Adam that you care for him?*
> 7 *For a short while you have made him less than the*
> *angels;*
> *you have crowned him with glory and honour,*
> 8 *put all things under his feet.* c

For in *putting all things under* him he made no exceptions. At present, it is true, we are not able to see that *all things are under him*, 9 but we do see Jesus, who was *for a short while made less than the angels*, now *crowned with glory and honour* because he submitted to death; so that by God's grace his experience of death should benefit all humanity.

10 It was fitting that God, for whom and through whom everything exists, should, in bringing many sons to glory, make perfect through suffering the leader of their salvation. 11 For consecrator and consecrated are all of the same stock; that is why he is not ashamed to call them *brothers* 12 in the text: *I shall proclaim your name to my brothers, praise you in full assembly*; or in the text: 13 *I shall put my hope in him*; followed by *Look, I and the children whom God has given me.* d

14 Since all the *children* share the same human nature, he too shared equally in it, so that by his death he could set aside him who held the power of death, namely the devil, 15 and set free all those who had been held in slavery all their lives by the fear of death. 16 For it was not the angels that he took to himself; he took to himself *the line of Abraham*. 17 It was essential that he should in this way be made completely like his brothers so that he could become a compassionate and trustworthy high priest for their relationship to God, able to expiate the sins of the people. 18 For the suffering he himself passed through while being put to the test enables him to help others when they are being put to the test.

3 That is why all you who are holy brothers and share the same heavenly call should turn your minds to Jesus, the apostle and the high priest of our profession of faith. 2 He was *trustworthy* to the one who appointed him, just like Moses, who remained trustworthy *in all his household*; e 3 but he deserves a greater glory than Moses, just as the builder of a house is more honoured than the house itself. 4 Every house is built by someone, of course; but God built everything that exists. 5 It is true that Moses was *trustworthy in the household* of God, as a *servant* is, acting as witness to the things which were yet to be revealed, 6 but Christ is trustworthy as a son is, over his household. And we are his household, as long as we fearlessly maintain the hope in which we glory.

7 That is why, as the Holy Spirit says:

> f *If only you would listen to him today!*

c 2 Ps 8:4–6.   d 2 Ps 22:22; Is 8:17, 18.   e 3 Nb 12:7.
f 3 An elaboration on Ps 95:7–11.

8 do not harden your hearts as in the rebellion,
  as on the day of testing in the wilderness,
9 where your ancestors put me to the test,
  though they had seen my works 10 for forty
    years.
  Therefore I was angry with that generation,
  and I said, 'They always go astray in their hearts,
    and they have not known my ways.'
11 As in my anger I swore,
  'They will not enter my rest.' "

12 Take care, brothers and sisters,*t* that none of you may have an evil, unbelieving heart that turns away from the living God. 13 But exhort one another every day, as long as it is called "today," so that none of you may be hardened by the deceitfulness of sin. 14 For we have become partners of Christ, if only we hold our first confidence firm to the end. 15 As it is said,
  "Today, if you hear his voice,
  do not harden your hearts as in the rebellion."
16 Now who were they who heard and yet were rebellious? Was it not all those who left Egypt under the leadership of Moses? 17 But with whom was he angry forty years? Was it not those who sinned, whose bodies fell in the wilderness? 18 And to whom did he swear that they would not enter his rest, if not to those who were disobedient? 19 So we see that they were unable to enter because of unbelief.

4 Therefore, while the promise of entering his rest is still open, let us take care that none of you should seem to have failed to reach it. 2 For indeed the good news came to us just as to them; but the message they heard did not benefit them, because they were not united by faith with those who listened.*u* 3 For we who have believed enter that rest, just as God*v* has said,
  "As in my anger I swore,
  'They shall not enter my rest,' "
though his works were finished at the foundation of the world. 4 For in one place it speaks about the seventh day as follows, "And God rested on the seventh day from all his works." 5 And again in this place it says, "They shall not enter my rest." 6 Since therefore it remains open for some to enter it, and those who formerly received the good news failed to enter because of disobedience, 7 again he sets a certain day—"today"—saying through David much later, in the words already quoted,
  "Today, if you hear his voice,
  do not harden your hearts."
8 For if Joshua had given them rest, God*v* would not speak later about another day. 9 So then, a sabbath rest still remains for the people of God; 10 for those who enter God's rest also cease from their labors as God did from his. 11 Let us therefore make every effort to enter that rest, so that no one may fall through such disobedience as theirs.

12 Indeed, the word of God is living and active, sharper than any two-edged sword, piercing until it divides soul from spirit, joints from marrow; it is able to judge the thoughts and intentions of the heart. 13 And before him no creature is hidden, but all are naked and laid bare to the eyes of the one to whom we must render an account.

14 Since, then, we have a great high priest who has passed through the heavens, Jesus, the Son of God, let us hold fast to our confession. 15 For we do not have a high priest who is unable to sympathize with our weaknesses, but we have one who in every respect has been tested*w* as we are, yet without sin. 16 Let us therefore approach the throne

8 do not grow stubborn as in the rebellion,
  at the time of testing in the desert,
9 where your forefathers tried me and tested me,
  though for forty years they saw the things I did.
10 Therefore I was incensed with that generation
  and said, Their hearts are for ever astray;
  they would not discern my ways;
11 so I vowed in my anger,
  they shall never enter my rest.

12 See to it, my friends, that no one among you has the wicked and faithless heart of a deserter from the living God. 13 Rather, day by day, as long as that word 'today' sounds in your ears, encourage one another, so that no one of you is made stubborn by the wiles of sin. 14 For we have become partners with Christ, if only we keep our initial confidence firm to the end. 15 When scripture says, 'Today if you hear his voice, do not grow stubborn as in the rebellion,' 16 who was it that heard and yet rebelled? All those, surely, whom Moses had led out of Egypt. 17 And with whom was God indignant for forty years? With those, surely, who had sinned, whose bodies lay where they fell in the desert. 18 And to whom did he vow that they should not enter his rest, if not to those who had refused to believe? 19 We see, then, it was unbelief that prevented their entering.

4 What we must fear, therefore, is that, while the promise of entering his rest remains open, any one of you should be found to have missed his opportunity. 2 For indeed we have had the good news preached to us, just as they had. But the message they heard did them no good, for it was not combined with faith in those who heard it. 3 Because we have faith, it is we who enter that rest of which he has said: 'As I vowed in my anger, they shall never enter my rest.' Yet God's work had been finished ever since the world was created. 4 Scripture somewhere says of the seventh day: 'God rested from all his work on the seventh day'—5 and in the passage above we read: 'They shall never enter my rest.' 6 This implies that some are to enter it, and since those who first heard the good news failed to enter through unbelief, 7 once more God sets a day. 'Today', he says, speaking so many years later in the words already quoted from the Psalms: 'Today if you hear his voice, do not grow stubborn.' 8 If Joshua had given them rest, God would not have spoken afterwards of another day. 9 Therefore, a sabbath rest still awaits the people of God; 10 anyone who enters God's rest, rests from his own work, as God did from his. 11 Let us, then, make every effort to enter that rest, so that no one may fall by following the old example of unbelief.

12 The word of God is alive and active. It cuts more keenly than any two-edged sword, piercing so deeply that it divides soul and spirit, joints and marrow; it discriminates among the purposes and thoughts of the heart. 13 Nothing in creation can hide from him; everything lies bare and exposed to the eyes of him to whom we must render account.

14 Since therefore we have a great high priest who has passed through the heavens, Jesus the Son of God, let us hold fast to the faith we profess. 15 Ours is not a high priest unable to sympathize with our weaknesses, but one who has been tested in every way as we are, only without sinning.

---

t Gk *brothers*   *u* Other ancient authorities read *it did not meet with faith in those who listened*   *v* Gk *he*   *w* Or *tempted*

8 'Harden not your hearts as at the rebellion
   in the day of testing in the desert,
9 where your ancestors tested and tried me
   and saw my works 10 for forty years.
Because of this I was provoked with
       that generation
   and I said, "They have always been of
       erring heart,
   and they do not know my ways."
11 As I swore in my wrath,
   "They shall not enter into my rest." ' "

12 Take care, brothers, that none of you may have an evil
and unfaithful heart, so as to forsake the living God. 13 Encourage yourselves daily while it is still "today," so that
none of you may grow hardened by the deceit of sin. 14 We
have become partners of Christ if only we hold the beginning of the reality firm until the end, 15 for it is said:
   "Oh, that today you would hear his voice:
   'Harden not your hearts as at the rebellion.' "
16 Who were those who rebelled when they heard? Was it
not all those who came out of Egypt under Moses? 17 With
whom was he "provoked for forty years"? Was it not those
who had sinned, whose corpses fell in the desert? 18 And to
whom did he "swear that they should not enter into his
rest," if not to those who were disobedient? 19 And we see
that they could not enter for lack of faith.

4 Therefore, let us be on our guard while the promise of
   entering into his rest remains, that none of you seem to
have failed. 2 For in fact we have received the good news
just as they did. But the word that they heard did not profit
them, for they were not united in faith with those who
listened. 3 For we who believed enter into [that] rest, just as
he has said:
   "As I swore in my wrath,
   'They shall not enter into my rest,' "
and yet his works were accomplished at the foundation of
the world. 4 For he has spoken somewhere about the seventh
day in this manner, "And God rested on the seventh day
from all his works"; 5 and again, in the previously mentioned place, "They shall not enter into my rest." 6 Therefore, since it remains that some will enter into it, and those
who formerly received the good news did not enter because
of disobedience, 7 he once more set a day, "today," when
long afterwards he spoke through David, as already quoted:
   "Oh, that today you would hear his voice:
   'Harden not your hearts.' "
8 Now if Joshua had given them rest, he would not have
spoken afterwards of another day. 9 Therefore, a sabbath
rest still remains for the people of God. 10 And whoever
enters into God's rest, rests from his own works as God did
from his. 11 Therefore, let us strive to enter into that rest, so
that no one may fall after the same example of disobedience.
12 Indeed, the word of God is living and effective, sharper
than any two-edged sword, penetrating even between soul
and spirit, joints and marrow, and able to discern reflections
and thoughts of the heart. 13 No creature is concealed from
him, but everything is naked and exposed to the eyes of him
to whom we must render an account.
14 Therefore, since we have a great high priest who has
passed through the heavens, Jesus, the Son of God, let us
hold fast to our confession. 15 For we do not have a high
priest who is unable to sympathize with our weaknesses, but
one who has similarly been tested in every way, yet without

8 Do not harden your hearts, as at the rebellion,
   as at the time of testing in the desert,
9 when your ancestors challenged me,
   and put me to the test, and saw what I could do
10 for forty years.

That was why

   that generation sickened me
   and I said, 'Always fickle hearts,
   that cannot grasp my ways!'
11 And then in my anger I swore
   that they would never enter my place of rest.

12 Take care, brothers, that none of you ever has a wicked
heart, so unbelieving as to turn away from the living God.
13 Every day, as long as this today lasts, keep encouraging
one another so that none of you is hardened by the lure of
sin, 14 because we have been granted a share with Christ
only if we keep the grasp of our first confidence firm to the
end. 15 In this saying: If only you would listen to him today;
do not harden your hearts, as at the Rebellion, 16 who was
it who listened and rebelled? Surely all those whom
Moses led out of Egypt. 17 And with whom was he angry for
forty years? Surely with those who sinned and whose dead
bodies fell in the desert. 18 To whom did he swear they
would never enter his place of rest? Surely those who would
not believe. 19 So we see that it was their refusal to believe
which prevented them from entering.

4 Let us beware, then: since the promise never lapses,
   none of you must think that he has come too late for the
promise of entering his place of rest. 2 We received the
gospel exactly as they did; but hearing the message did them
no good because they did not share the faith of those who
did listen. 3 We, however, who have faith, are entering a
place of rest, as in the text: And then in my anger I swore
that they would never enter my place of rest. Now God's
work was all finished at the beginning of the world; 4 as one
text says, referring to the seventh day: And God rested on
the seventh day after all the work he had been doing. 5 And,
again, the passage above says: They will never reach my
place of rest. 6 It remains the case, then, that there would be
some people who would reach it, and since those who first
heard the good news were prevented from entering by their
refusal to believe, 7 God fixed another day, a Today, when
he said through David in the text already quoted: If only you
would listen to him today; do not harden your hearts. 8 If
Joshua had led them into this place of rest, God would not
later have spoken of another day. 9 There must still be,
therefore, a seventh-day rest reserved for God's people,
10 since to enter the place of rest is to rest after your work,
as God did after his. 11 Let us, then, press forward to enter
this place of rest, or some of you might copy this example
of refusal to believe and be lost.
12 The word of God is something alive and active: it cuts
more incisively than any two-edged sword: it can seek out
the place where soul is divided from spirit, or joints from
marrow; it can pass judgement on secret emotions and
thoughts. 13 No created thing is hidden from him; everything is uncovered and stretched fully open to the eyes of
the one to whom we must give account of ourselves.

14 Since in Jesus, the Son of God, we have the supreme
high priest who has gone through to the highest heaven, we
must hold firm to our profession of faith. 15 For the high
priest we have is not incapable of feeling our weaknesses
with us, but has been put to the test in exactly the same way
as ourselves, apart from sin. 16 Let us, then, have no fear in

of grace with boldness, so that we may receive mercy and find grace to help in time of need.

5 Every high priest chosen from among mortals is put in charge of things pertaining to God on their behalf, to offer gifts and sacrifices for sins. 2 He is able to deal gently with the ignorant and wayward, since he himself is subject to weakness; 3 and because of this he must offer sacrifice for his own sins as well as for those of the people. 4 And one does not presume to take this honor, but takes it only when called by God, just as Aaron was.

5 So also Christ did not glorify himself in becoming a high priest, but was appointed by the one who said to him,
"You are my Son,
today I have begotten you";
6 as he says also in another place,
"You are a priest forever,
according to the order of Melchizedek."

7 In the days of his flesh, Jesus[x] offered up prayers and supplications, with loud cries and tears, to the one who was able to save him from death, and he was heard because of his reverent submission. 8 Although he was a Son, he learned obedience through what he suffered; 9 and having been made perfect, he became the source of eternal salvation for all who obey him, 10 having been designated by God a high priest according to the order of Melchizedek.

11 About this[y] we have much to say that is hard to explain, since you have become dull in understanding. 12 For though by this time you ought to be teachers, you need someone to teach you again the basic elements of the oracles of God. You need milk, not solid food; 13 for everyone who lives on milk, being still an infant, is unskilled in the word of righteousness. 14 But solid food is for the mature, for those whose faculties have been trained by practice to distinguish good from evil.

6 Therefore let us go on toward perfection,[z] leaving behind the basic teaching about Christ, and not laying again the foundation: repentance from dead works and faith toward God, 2 instruction about baptisms, laying on of hands, resurrection of the dead, and eternal judgment. 3 And we will do[a] this, if God permits. 4 For it is impossible to restore again to repentance those who have once been enlightened, and have tasted the heavenly gift, and have shared in the Holy Spirit, 5 and have tasted the goodness of the word of God and the powers of the age to come, 6 and then have fallen away, since on their own they are crucifying again the Son of God and are holding him up to contempt. 7 Ground that drinks up the rain falling on it repeatedly, and that produces a crop useful to those for whom it is cultivated, receives a blessing from God. 8 But if it produces thorns and thistles, it is worthless and on the verge of being cursed; its end is to be burned over.

9 Even though we speak in this way, beloved, we are confident of better things in your case, things that belong to salvation. 10 For God is not unjust; he will not overlook your work and the love that you showed for his sake[b] in serving the saints, as you still do. 11 And we want each one of you to show the same diligence so as to realize the full assurance of hope to the very end, 12 so that you may not become sluggish, but imitators of those who through faith and patience inherit the promises.

13 When God made a promise to Abraham, because he had no one greater by whom to swear, he swore by himself,

16 Let us therefore boldly approach the throne of grace, in order that we may receive mercy and find grace to give us timely help.

5 For every high priest is taken from among men and appointed their representative before God, to offer gifts and sacrifices for sins. 2 He is able to bear patiently with the ignorant and erring, since he too is beset by weakness; 3 and because of this he is bound to make sin-offerings for himself as well as for the people. 4 Moreover nobody assumes the office on his own authority: he is called by God, just as Aaron was. 5 So it is with Christ: he did not confer on himself the glory of becoming high priest; it was granted by God, who said to him, 'You are my son; today I have become your father'; 6 as also in another place he says, 'You are a priest for ever, in the order of Melchizedek.' 7 In the course of his earthly life he offered up prayers and petitions, with loud cries and tears, to God who was able to deliver him from death. Because of his devotion his prayer was heard: 8 son though he was, he learned obedience through his sufferings, 9 and, once perfected, he became the source of eternal salvation for all who obey him, 10 and by God he was designated high priest in the order of Melchizedek.

11 About Melchizedek we have much to say, much that is difficult to explain to you, now that you have proved so slow to learn. 12 By this time you ought to be teachers, but instead you need someone to teach you the ABC of God's oracles over again. It comes to this: you need milk instead of solid food. 13 Anyone who lives on milk is still an infant, with no experience of what is right. 14 Solid food is for adults, whose perceptions have been trained by long use to discriminate between good and evil.

6 1–2 Let us stop discussing the rudiments of Christianity. We ought not to be laying the foundation all over again: repentance from the deadness of our former ways and faith in God, by means of instruction about cleansing rites and the laying on of hands, the resurrection of the dead and eternal judgement. Instead, let us advance towards maturity; 3 and so we shall, if God permits. 4 For when people have once been enlightened, when they have tasted the heavenly gift and have shared in the Holy Spirit, 5 when they have experienced the goodness of God's word and the spiritual power of the age to come, 6 and then after all this have fallen away, it is impossible to bring them afresh to repentance; for they are crucifying to their own hurt the Son of God and holding him up to mockery. 7 When the soil drinks in the rain that falls often upon it, and yields a crop for the use of those who cultivate it, it receives its blessing from God; 8 but if it bears thorns and thistles, it is worthless and a curse hangs over it; it ends by being burnt.

9 Yet although we speak as we do, we are convinced that you, dear friends, are in a better state, which makes for your salvation. 10 For God is not so unjust as to forget what you have done for love of his name in rendering service to his people, as you still do. 11 But we should dearly like each one of you to show the same keenness to the end, until your hope is fully realized. 12 We want you not to be lax, but to imitate those who, through faith and patience, receive the promised inheritance.

13 When God made his promise to Abraham, because he had no one greater to swear by he swore by himself: 14 'I

---

[x] Gk *he*   [y] Or *him*   [z] Or *toward maturity*   [a] Other ancient
authorities read *let us do*   [b] Gk *for his name*

6:6 **crucifying:** *or* crucifying again.

sin. 16 So let us confidently approach the throne of grace to receive mercy and to find grace for timely help.

5 Every high priest is taken from among men and made their representative before God, to offer gifts and sacrifices for sins. 2 He is able to deal patiently with the ignorant and erring, for he himself is beset by weakness 3 and so, for this reason, must make sin offerings for himself as well as for the people. 4 No one takes this honor upon himself but only when called by God, just as Aaron was. 5 In the same way, it was not Christ who glorified himself in becoming high priest, but rather the one who said to him:

"You are my son;
    this day I have begotten you";

6 just as he says in another place:

"You are a priest forever
    according to the order of Melchizedek."

7 In the days when he was in the flesh, he offered prayers and supplications with loud cries and tears to the one who was able to save him from death, and he was heard because of his reverence. 8 Son though he was, he learned obedience from what he suffered; 9 and when he was made perfect, he became the source of eternal salvation for all who obey him, 10 declared by God high priest according to the order of Melchizedek.

11 About this we have much to say, and it is difficult to explain, for you have become sluggish in hearing. 12 Although you should be teachers by this time, you need to have someone teach you again the basic elements of the utterances of God. You need milk, [and] not solid food. 13 Everyone who lives on milk lacks experience of the word of righteousness, for he is a child. 14 But solid food is for the mature, for those whose faculties are trained by practice to discern good and evil.

6 Therefore, let us leave behind the basic teaching about Christ and advance to maturity, without laying the foundation all over again: repentance from dead works and faith in God, 2 instruction about baptisms and laying on of hands, resurrection of the dead and eternal judgment. 3 And we shall do this, if only God permits. 4 For it is impossible in the case of those who have once been enlightened and tasted the heavenly gift and shared in the holy Spirit 5 and tasted the good word of God and the powers of the age to come, 6 and then have fallen away, to bring them to repentance again, since they are recrucifying the Son of God for themselves and holding him up to contempt. 7 Ground that has absorbed the rain falling upon it repeatedly and brings forth crops useful to those for whom it is cultivated receives a blessing from God. 8 But if it produces thorns and thistles, it is rejected; it will soon be cursed and finally burned.

9 But we are sure in your regard, beloved, of better things related to salvation, even though we speak in this way. 10 For God is not unjust so as to overlook your work and the love you have demonstrated for his name by having served and continuing to serve the holy ones. 11 We earnestly desire each of you to demonstrate the same eagerness for the fulfillment of hope until the end, 12 so that you may not become sluggish, but imitators of those who, through faith and patience, are inheriting the promises.

13 When God made the promise to Abraham, since he had no one greater by whom to swear, "he swore by himself,"

approaching the throne of grace to receive mercy and to find grace when we are in need of help.

5 Every high priest is taken from among human beings and is appointed to act on their behalf in relationships with God, to offer gifts and sacrifices for sins; 2 he can sympathise with those who are ignorant or who have gone astray, because he too is subject to the limitations of weakness. 3 That is why he has to make sin offerings for himself as well as for the people. 4 No one takes this honour on himself; it needs a call from God, as in Aaron's case. 5 And so it was not Christ who gave himself the glory of becoming high priest, but the one who said to him: *You are my Son, today I have fathered you,*g 6 and in another text: *You are a priest for ever, of the order of Melchizedek.* 7 During his life on earth, he offered up prayer and entreaty, with loud cries and with tears, to the one who had the power to save him from death, and, winning a hearing by his reverence, 8 he learnt obedience, Son though he was, through his sufferings; 9 when he had been perfected, he became for all who obey him the source of eternal salvation 10 and was acclaimed by God with the title of high *priest of the order of Melchizedek.*

11 On this subject we have many things to say, and they are difficult to explain because you have grown so slow at understanding. 12 Indeed, when you should by this time have become masters, you need someone to teach you all over again the elements of the principles of God's sayings; you have gone back to needing milk, and not solid food. 13 Truly, no one who is still living on milk can digest the doctrine of saving justice, being still a baby. 14 Solid food is for adults with minds trained by practice to distinguish between good and bad.

6 Let us leave behind us then all the elementary teaching about Christ and go on to its completion, without going over the fundamental doctrines again: the turning away from dead actions, faith in God, 2 the teaching about baptisms and the laying-on of hands, the resurrection of the dead and eternal judgement. 3 This, God willing, is what we propose to do.

4 As for those people who were once brought into the light, and tasted the gift from heaven, and received a share of the Holy Spirit, 5 and tasted the goodness of God's message and the powers of the world to come 6 and yet in spite of this have fallen away — it is impossible for them to be brought to the freshness of repentance a second time, since they are crucifying the Son of God again for themselves, and making a public exhibition of him. 7 A field that drinks up the rain that has fallen frequently on it, and yields the crops that are wanted by the owners who grew them, receives God's blessing; 8 but one that grows brambles and thistles is worthless, and near to being cursed. It will end by being burnt.

9 But you, my dear friends — in spite of what we have just said, we are sure you are in a better state and on the way to salvation. 10 God would not be so unjust as to forget all you have done, the love that you have for his name or the services you have done, and are still doing, for the holy people of God. 11 Our desire is that every one of you should go on showing the same enthusiasm till the ultimate fulfilment of your hope, 12 never growing careless, but taking as your model those who by their faith and perseverance are heirs of the promises.

13 When God made the promise to Abraham, he *swore by his own self*, since there was no one greater he could swear

g 5 Ps 2:7 followed by Ps 110:4.

NEW REVISED STANDARD VERSION

14 saying, "I will surely bless you and multiply you." 15 And thus Abraham,*c* having patiently endured, obtained the promise. 16 Human beings, of course, swear by someone greater than themselves, and an oath given as confirmation puts an end to all dispute. 17 In the same way, when God desired to show even more clearly to the heirs of the promise the unchangeable character of his purpose, he guaranteed it by an oath, 18 so that through two unchangeable things, in which it is impossible that God would prove false, we who have taken refuge might be strongly encouraged to seize the hope set before us. 19 We have this hope, a sure and steadfast anchor of the soul, a hope that enters the inner shrine behind the curtain, 20 where Jesus, a forerunner on our behalf, has entered, having become a high priest forever according to the order of Melchizedek.

7 This "King Melchizedek of Salem, priest of the Most High God, met Abraham as he was returning from defeating the kings and blessed him"; 2 and to him Abraham apportioned "one-tenth of everything." His name, in the first place, means "king of righteousness"; next he is also king of Salem, that is, "king of peace." 3 Without father, without mother, without genealogy, having neither beginning of days nor end of life, but resembling the Son of God, he remains a priest forever.

4 See how great he is! Even*d* Abraham the patriarch gave him a tenth of the spoils. 5 And those descendants of Levi who receive the priestly office have a commandment in the law to collect tithes*e* from the people, that is, from their kindred,*f* though these also are descended from Abraham. 6 But this man, who does not belong to their ancestry, collected tithes*e* from Abraham and blessed him who had received the promises. 7 It is beyond dispute that the inferior is blessed by the superior. 8 In the one case, tithes are received by those who are mortal; in the other, by one of whom it is testified that he lives. 9 One might even say that Levi himself, who receives tithes, paid tithes through Abraham, 10 for he was still in the loins of his ancestor when Melchizedek met him.

11 Now if perfection had been attainable through the levitical priesthood — for the people received the law under this priesthood — what further need would there have been to speak of another priest arising according to the order of Melchizedek, rather than one according to the order of Aaron? 12 For when there is a change in the priesthood, there is necessarily a change in the law as well. 13 Now the one of whom these things are spoken belonged to another tribe, from which no one has ever served at the altar. 14 For it is evident that our Lord was descended from Judah, and in connection with that tribe Moses said nothing about priests.

15 It is even more obvious when another priest arises, resembling Melchizedek, 16 one who has become a priest, not through a legal requirement concerning physical descent, but through the power of an indestructible life. 17 For it is attested of him,

"You are a priest forever,
    according to the order of Melchizedek."

18 There is, on the one hand, the abrogation of an earlier commandment because it was weak and ineffectual 19 (for the law made nothing perfect); there is, on the other hand, the introduction of a better hope, through which we approach God.

20 This was confirmed with an oath; for others who became priests took their office without an oath, 21 but this

REVISED ENGLISH BIBLE

vow that I will bless you abundantly and multiply your descendants.' 15 Thus it was that Abraham, after patient waiting, obtained the promise. 16 People swear by what is greater than themselves, and making a statement on oath sets a limit to what can be called in question; 17 and so, since God desired to show even more clearly to the heirs of his promise how immutable was his purpose, he guaranteed it by an oath. 18 Here, then, are two irrevocable acts in which God could not possibly play us false. They give powerful encouragement to us, who have laid claim to his protection by grasping the hope set before us. 19 We have that hope as an anchor for our lives, safe and secure. It enters the sanctuary behind the curtain, 20 where Jesus has entered on our behalf as forerunner, having become high priest for ever in the order of Melchizedek.

7 THIS Melchizedek, king of Salem, priest of God Most High, met Abraham returning from the defeat of the kings and blessed him; 2 and Abraham gave him a tithe of everything as his share. His name, in the first place, means 'king of righteousness'; next he is king of Salem, that is, 'king of peace'. 3 He has no father, no mother, no ancestors; his life has no beginning and no end. Bearing the likeness of the Son of God, he remains a priest for all time.

4 Consider now how great he must be for the patriarch Abraham to give him his tithe from the finest of the spoil. 5 The descendants of Levi who succeed to the priestly office are required by the law to tithe the people, that is, their fellow-countrymen, although they too are descendants of Abraham. 6 But Melchizedek, though he does not share their ancestry, tithed Abraham himself and gave his blessing to the man who had been given the promises; 7 and, beyond all dispute, it is always the lesser who is blessed by the greater. 8 Moreover, in the one instance tithes are received by men who must die; but in the other, by one whom scripture affirms to be alive. 9 It might even be said that Levi, the receiver of tithes, was himself tithed through Abraham; 10 for he was still in his ancestor's loins when Melchizedek met him.

11 Now if perfection had been attainable through the levitical priesthood (on the basis of which the people were given the law), there would have been no need for another kind of priest to arise, described as being in the order of Melchizedek, instead of in the order of Aaron. 12 But a change of priesthood must mean a change of law; 13 for he who is spoken of here belongs to a different tribe, no member of which has ever served at the altar. 14 It is beyond all doubt that our Lord is sprung from Judah, a tribe to which Moses made no reference in speaking of priests.

15 What makes this still clearer is that a new priest has arisen, one like Melchizedek; 16 he owes his priesthood not to a system of rules relating to descent but to the power of a life that cannot be destroyed. 17 For here is the testimony: 'You are a priest for ever, in the order of Melchizedek.' 18 The earlier rules are repealed as ineffective and useless, 19 since the law brought nothing to perfection; and a better hope is introduced, through which we draw near to God.

20-22 Notice also that no oath was sworn when the other men were made priests; but for this priest an oath was sworn

c Gk *he*   *d* Other ancient authorities lack *Even*   *e* Or *a tenth*
f Gk *brothers*

6:18 **They give . . . grasping:** *or* They give to us, who have laid claim to his protection, a powerful encouragement to grasp.

14 and said, "I will indeed bless you and multiply" you. 15 And so, after patient waiting, he obtained the promise. 16 Human beings swear by someone greater than themselves; for them an oath serves as a guarantee and puts an end to all argument. 17 So when God wanted to give the heirs of his promise an even clearer demonstration of the immutability of his purpose, he intervened with an oath, 18 so that by two immutable things, in which it was impossible for God to lie, we who have taken refuge might be strongly encouraged to hold fast to the hope that lies before us. 19 This we have as an anchor of the soul, sure and firm, which reaches into the interior behind the veil, 20 where Jesus has entered on our behalf as forerunner, becoming high priest forever according to the order of Melchizedek.

7 This "Melchizedek, king of Salem and priest of God Most High," "met Abraham as he returned from his defeat of the kings" and "blessed him." 2 And Abraham apportioned to him "a tenth of everything." His name first means righteous king, and he was also "king of Salem," that is, king of peace. 3 Without father, mother, or ancestry, without beginning of days or end of life, thus made to resemble the Son of God, he remains a priest forever.

4 See how great he is to whom the patriarch "Abraham [indeed] gave a tenth" of his spoils. 5 The descendants of Levi who receive the office of priesthood have a commandment according to the law to exact tithes from the people, that is, from their brothers, although they also have come from the loins of Abraham. 6 But he who was not of their ancestry received tithes from Abraham and blessed him who had received the promises. 7 Unquestionably, a lesser person is blessed by a greater. 8 In the one case, mortal men receive tithes; in the other, a man of whom it is testified that he lives on. 9 One might even say that Levi himself, who receives tithes, was tithed through Abraham, 10 for he was still in his father's loins when Melchizedek met him.

11 If, then, perfection came through the levitical priesthood, on the basis of which the people received the law, what need would there still have been for another priest to arise according to the order of Melchizedek, and not reckoned according to the order of Aaron? 12 When there is a change of priesthood, there is necessarily a change of law as well. 13 Now he of whom these things are said belonged to a different tribe, of which no member ever officiated at the altar. 14 It is clear that our Lord arose from Judah, and in regard to that tribe Moses said nothing about priests. 15 It is even more obvious if another priest is raised up after the likeness of Melchizedek, 16 who has become so, not by a law expressed in a commandment concerning physical descent but by the power of a life that cannot be destroyed. 17 For it is testified:

"You are a priest forever
according to the order of Melchizedek."

18 On the one hand, a former commandment is annulled because of its weakness and uselessness, 19 for the law brought nothing to perfection; on the other hand, a better hope is introduced, through which we draw near to God. 20 And to the degree that this happened not without the taking of an oath — for others became priests without an

by: 14 *I will shower blessings on you and give you many descendants.* [h] 15 Because of that, Abraham persevered and received fulfilment of the promise. 16 Human beings, of course, swear an oath by something greater than themselves, and between them, confirmation by an oath puts an end to all dispute. 17 In the same way, when God wanted to show the heirs of the promise even more clearly how unalterable his plan was, he conveyed it by an oath 18 so that through two unalterable factors in which God could not be lying, we who have fled to him might have a vigorous encouragement to grasp the hope held out to us. 19 This is the anchor our souls have, reaching right through *inside the curtain* 20 where Jesus has entered as a forerunner on our behalf, having become a high *priest for ever, of the order of Melchizedek.*

7 [i] *Melchizedek, king of Salem, a priest of God Most High, came to meet Abraham when he returned from defeating the kings,* and *blessed him*; 2 and Abraham gave him *a tenth of everything.* By the interpretation of his name, he is, first, 'king of saving justice' and also *king of Salem,* that is, 'king of peace'; 3 he has no father, mother or ancestry, and his life has no beginning or ending; he is like the Son of God. He remains a priest for ever.

4 Now think how great this man must have been, if the patriarch *Abraham gave him a tenth* of the finest plunder. 5 We know that any of the descendants of Levi who are admitted to the priesthood are obliged by the Law to take tithes from the people, that is, from their own brothers although they too are descended from Abraham. 6 But this man, who was not of the same descent, took his tithe from Abraham, and he gave his blessing to the holder of the promises. 7 Now it is indisputable that a blessing is given by a superior to an inferior. 8 Further, in the normal case it is ordinary mortal men who receive the tithes, whereas in that case it was one who is attested as being alive. It could be said that Levi himself, who receives tithes, actually paid tithes, in the person of Abraham, 10 because he was still in the loins of his ancestor when *Melchizedek came to meet him.*

11 Now if perfection had been reached through the levitical priesthood — and this was the basis of the Law given to the people — why was it necessary for a different kind of priest to arise, spoken of as being *of the order of Melchizedek* rather than of the order of Aaron? 12 Any change in the priesthood must mean a change in the Law as well.

13 So our Lord, of whom these things were said, belonged to a different tribe, the members of which have never done service at the altar; 14 everyone knows he came from Judah, a tribe which Moses did not mention at all when dealing with priests.

15 This becomes even more clearly evident if another priest, of the type of Melchizedek, arises who is a priest 16 not in virtue of a law of physical descent, but in virtue of the power of an indestructible life. 17 For he is attested by the prophecy: *You are a priest for ever of the order of Melchizedek.* 18 The earlier commandment is thus abolished, because of its weakness and ineffectiveness 19 since the Law could not make anything perfect; but now this commandment is replaced by something better — the hope that brings us close to God.

20 Now the former priests became priests without any

h 6 Gn 22:16.   i 7 A commentary on Gn 14:17–20.

one became a priest with an oath, because of the one who said to him,

"The Lord has sworn
    and will not change his mind,
'You are a priest forever' " —

22 accordingly Jesus has also become the guarantee of a better covenant.

23 Furthermore, the former priests were many in number, because they were prevented by death from continuing in office; 24 but he holds his priesthood permanently, because he continues forever. 25 Consequently he is able for all time to save*g* those who approach God through him, since he always lives to make intercession for them.

26 For it was fitting that we should have such a high priest, holy, blameless, undefiled, separated from sinners, and exalted above the heavens. 27 Unlike the other*h* high priests, he has no need to offer sacrifices day after day, first for his own sins, and then for those of the people; this he did once for all when he offered himself. 28 For the law appoints as high priests those who are subject to weakness, but the word of the oath, which came later than the law, appoints a Son who has been made perfect forever.

8 Now the main point in what we are saying is this: we have such a high priest, one who is seated at the right hand of the throne of the Majesty in the heavens, 2 a minister in the sanctuary and the true tent*i* that the Lord, and not any mortal, has set up. 3 For every high priest is appointed to offer gifts and sacrifices; hence it is necessary for this priest also to have something to offer. 4 Now if he were on earth, he would not be a priest at all, since there are priests who offer gifts according to the law. 5 They offer worship in a sanctuary that is a sketch and shadow of the heavenly one; for Moses, when he was about to erect the tent,*i* was warned, "See that you make everything according to the pattern that was shown you on the mountain." 6 But Jesus*j* has now obtained a more excellent ministry, and to that degree he is the mediator of a better covenant, which has been enacted through better promises. 7 For if that first covenant had been faultless, there would have been no need to look for a second one.

8 God*k* finds fault with them when he says:
"The days are surely coming, says the Lord,
    when I will establish a new covenant with the
        house of Israel
    and with the house of Judah;
9   not like the covenant that I made with their
        ancestors,
    on the day when I took them by the hand to
        lead them out of the land of Egypt;
    for they did not continue in my covenant,
    and so I had no concern for them, says the
        Lord.
10 This is the covenant that I will make with the
        house of Israel
    after those days, says the Lord:
I will put my laws in their minds,
    and write them on their hearts,
and I will be their God,
    and they shall be my people.
11 And they shall not teach one another
    or say to each other, 'Know the Lord,'
    for they shall all know me,
    from the least of them to the greatest.
12 For I will be merciful toward their iniquities,
    and I will remember their sins no more."

in the words addressed to him: 'The Lord has sworn and will not go back on his word, "You are a priest for ever." ' In the same way, God's oath shows how superior is the covenant which Jesus guarantees. 23 There have been many levitical priests, because death prevents them from continuing in office; 24 but Jesus holds a perpetual priesthood, because he remains for ever. 25 That is why he is able to save completely those who approach God through him, since he is always alive to plead on their behalf.

26 Such a high priest is indeed suited to our need: he is holy, innocent, undefiled, set apart from sinners, and raised high above the heavens. 27 He has no need to offer sacrifices daily, as the high priests do, first for their own sins and then for those of the people; he did this once for all when he offered up himself. 28 The high priests appointed by the law are men in all their weakness; but the priest appointed by the words of the oath which supersedes the law is the Son, who has been made perfect for ever.

8 My main point is: this is the kind of high priest we have, and he has taken his seat at the right hand of the throne of Majesty in heaven, 2 a minister in the real sanctuary, the tent set up by the Lord, not by man. 3 Every high priest is appointed to offer gifts and sacrifices; hence, of necessity, this one too had something to offer. 4 If he were on earth, he would not be a priest at all, since there are already priests to offer the gifts prescribed by the law, 5 although the sanctuary in which they minister is only a shadowy symbol of the heavenly one. This is why Moses, when he was about to put up the tent, was instructed by God: 'See to it that you make everything according to the pattern shown you on the mountain.' 6 But in fact the ministry which Jesus has been given is superior to theirs, for he is the mediator of a better covenant, established on better promises.

7 Had that first covenant been faultless, there would have been no occasion to look for a second to replace it. 8 But God finds fault with his people when he says, 'The time is coming, says the Lord, when I shall conclude a new covenant with the house of Israel and the house of Judah. 9 It will not be like the covenant I made with their forefathers when I took them by the hand to lead them out of Egypt; because they did not abide by the terms of that covenant, and so I abandoned them, says the Lord. 10 For this is the covenant I shall make with Israel after those days, says the Lord: I shall set my laws in their understanding and write them on their hearts; I shall be their God, and they will be my people. 11 They will not teach one another, each saying to his fellow-citizen and his brother, "Know the Lord!" For all of them will know me, high and low alike; 12 I shall pardon their wicked deeds, and their sins I shall remember no more.' 13 By speaking of a new covenant, he has pro-

---

g Or *able to save completely*   *h* Gk lacks *other*   *i* Or *tabernacle*
j Gk *he*   *k* Gk *He*

7:25 **completely:** *or* for all time.

oath, 21 but he with an oath, through the one who said to him:

"The Lord has sworn, and he will not repent:
'You are a priest forever' " —

22 to that same degree has Jesus [also] become the guarantee of an [even] better covenant. 23 Those priests were many because they were prevented by death from remaining in office, 24 but he, because he remains forever, has a priesthood that does not pass away. 25 Therefore, he is always able to save those who approach God through him, since he lives forever to make intercession for them.

26 It was fitting that we should have such a high priest: holy, innocent, undefiled, separated from sinners, higher than the heavens. 27 He has no need, as did the high priests, to offer sacrifice day after day, first for his own sins and then for those of the people; he did that once for all when he offered himself. 28 For the law appoints men subject to weakness to be high priests, but the word of the oath, which was taken after the law, appoints a son, who has been made perfect forever.

8 The main point of what has been said is this: we have such a high priest, who has taken his seat at the right hand of the throne of the Majesty in heaven, 2 a minister of the sanctuary and of the true tabernacle that the Lord, not man, set up. 3 Now every high priest is appointed to offer gifts and sacrifices; thus the necessity for this one also to have something to offer. 4 If then he were on earth, he would not be a priest, since there are those who offer gifts according to the law. 5 They worship in a copy and shadow of the heavenly sanctuary, as Moses was warned when he was about to erect the tabernacle. For he says, "See that you make everything according to the pattern shown you on the mountain." 6 Now he has obtained so much more excellent a ministry as he is mediator of a better covenant, enacted on better promises.

7 For if that first covenant had been faultless, no place would have been sought for a second one. 8 But he finds fault with them and says:

"Behold, the days are coming, says the Lord,
when I will conclude a new covenant with the
house of Israel and the house of Judah.
9 It will not be like the covenant I made with
their fathers
the day I took them by the hand to lead them
forth from the land of Egypt;
for they did not stand by my covenant
and I ignored them, says the Lord.
10 But this is the covenant I will establish with the
house of Israel
after those days, says the Lord:
I will put my laws in their minds
and I will write them upon their hearts.
I will be their God,
and they shall be my people.
11 And they shall not teach, each one his
fellow citizen
and kinsman, saying, 'Know the Lord,'
for all shall know me,
from least to greatest.
12 For I will forgive their evildoing
and remember their sins no more."

oath being sworn, 21 but this one with the swearing of an oath by him who said to him, *The Lord has sworn an oath he will never retract: you are a priest for ever*; 22 the very fact that it occurred with the swearing of an oath makes the covenant of which Jesus is the guarantee all the greater. 23 Further, the former priests were many in number, because death put an end to each one of them; 24 but this one, because he remains *for ever*, has a perpetual priesthood. 25 It follows, then, that his power to save those who come to God through him is absolute, since he lives for ever to intercede for them.

26 Such is the high priest that met our need, holy, innocent and uncontaminated, set apart from sinners, and raised up above the heavens; 27 he has no need to offer sacrifices every day, as the high priests do, first for their own sins and only then for those of the people; this he did once and for all by offering himself. 28 The Law appoints high priests who are men subject to weakness; but the promise on oath, which came after the Law, appointed the Son who is made perfect *for ever*.

8 The principal point of all that we have said is that we have a high priest of exactly this kind. He *has taken his seat at the right*[j] of the throne of divine Majesty in the heavens, 2 and he is the minister of the sanctuary and of the true *Tent* which *the Lord*, and not any man, *set up.*[k] 3 Every high priest is constituted to offer gifts and sacrifices, and so this one too must have something to offer. 4 In fact, if he were on earth, he would not be a priest at all, since there are others who make the offerings laid down by the Law, 5 though these maintain the service only of a model or a reflection of the heavenly realities; just as Moses, when he had the Tent to build, was warned by God who said: *See that you work to the design that was shown you on the mountain.*[l]

6 As it is, he has been given a ministry as far superior as is the covenant of which he is the mediator, which is founded on better promises. 7 If that first covenant had been faultless, there would have been no room for a second one to replace it. 8 And in fact God does find fault with them; he says:

*Look, the days are coming, the Lord declares,
when I will make a new covenant
with the House of Israel and the House of Judah,
9 but not a covenant like the one I made with their
ancestors,
the day I took them by the hand to bring them out
of Egypt,
which covenant of mine they broke,
and I too abandoned them, the Lord declares.
10 No, this is the covenant I will make with the House
of Israel,
when those days have come, the Lord declares:
In their minds I shall plant my laws
writing them on their hearts.
Then I shall be their God,
and they shall be my people.
11 There will be no further need for each to teach his
neighbour,
and each his brother, saying 'Learn to know the
Lord!'
No, they will all know me,
from the least to the greatest,
12 since I shall forgive their guilt
and never more call their sins to mind.*[m]

j 8 Ps 110:1.   *k* 8 Nb 24:6.   *l* 8 Ex 25:40.   *m* 8 Jr 31:31–34.

13 In speaking of "a new covenant," he has made the first one obsolete. And what is obsolete and growing old will soon disappear.

9 Now even the first covenant had regulations for worship and an earthly sanctuary. 2 For a tent*l* was constructed, the first one, in which were the lampstand, the table, and the bread of the Presence;*m* this is called the Holy Place. 3 Behind the second curtain was a tent*l* called the Holy of Holies. 4 In it stood the golden altar of incense and the ark of the covenant overlaid on all sides with gold, in which there were a golden urn holding the manna, and Aaron's rod that budded, and the tablets of the covenant; 5 above it were the cherubim of glory overshadowing the mercy seat.*n* Of these things we cannot speak now in detail.

6 Such preparations having been made, the priests go continually into the first tent*l* to carry out their ritual duties; 7 but only the high priest goes into the second, and he but once a year, and not without taking the blood that he offers for himself and for the sins committed unintentionally by the people. 8 By this the Holy Spirit indicates that the way into the sanctuary has not yet been disclosed as long as the first tent*l* is still standing. 9 This is a symbol*o* of the present time, during which gifts and sacrifices are offered that cannot perfect the conscience of the worshiper, 10 but deal only with food and drink and various baptisms, regulations for the body imposed until the time comes to set things right.

11 But when Christ came as a high priest of the good things that have come,*p* then through the greater and perfect*q* tent*l* (not made with hands, that is, not of this creation), 12 he entered once for all into the Holy Place, not with the blood of goats and calves, but with his own blood, thus obtaining eternal redemption. 13 For if the blood of goats and bulls, with the sprinkling of the ashes of a heifer, sanctifies those who have been defiled so that their flesh is purified, 14 how much more will the blood of Christ, who through the eternal Spirit*r* offered himself without blemish to God, purify our*s* conscience from dead works to worship the living God!

15 For this reason he is the mediator of a new covenant, so that those who are called may receive the promised eternal inheritance, because a death has occurred that redeems them from the transgressions under the first covenant.*t* 16 Where a will*t* is involved, the death of the one who made it must be established. 17 For a will*t* takes effect only at death, since it is not in force as long as the one who made it is alive. 18 Hence not even the first covenant was inaugurated without blood. 19 For when every commandment had been told to all the people by Moses in accordance with the law, he took the blood of calves and goats,*u* with water and scarlet wool and hyssop, and sprinkled both the scroll itself and all the people, 20 saying, "This is the blood of the covenant that God has ordained for you." 21 And in the same way he sprinkled with the blood both the tent*l* and all the vessels used in worship. 22 Indeed, under the law almost everything is purified with blood, and without the shedding of blood there is no forgiveness of sins.

23 Thus it was necessary for the sketches of the heavenly things to be purified with these rites, but the heavenly things themselves need better sacrifices than these. 24 For

nounced the first one obsolete; and anything that is becoming obsolete and growing old will shortly disappear.

9 THE first covenant had its ordinances governing divine service and its sanctuary, but it was an earthly sanctuary. 2 An outer tent, called the Holy Place, was set up to contain the lampstand, the table, and the Bread of the Presence. 3 Beyond the second curtain was the tent called the Most Holy Place. 4 Here were a gold incense-altar and the Ark of the Covenant plated all over with gold, in which were kept a gold jar containing the manna, and Aaron's staff which once budded, and the tablets of the covenant; 5 and above the Ark were the cherubim of God's glory, overshadowing the place of expiation. These we need not discuss in detail now.

6 Under this arrangement, the priests are continually entering the first tent in the performance of their duties; 7 but the second tent is entered by the high priest alone, and that only once a year. He takes with him the blood which he offers for himself and for the people's inadvertent sins. 8 By this the Holy Spirit indicates that so long as the outer tent still stands, the way into the sanctuary has not been opened up. 9 All this is symbolic, pointing to the present time. It means that the prescribed offerings and sacrifices cannot give the worshipper a clear conscience and so bring him to perfection; 10 they are concerned only with food and drink and various rites of cleansing—external ordinances in force until the coming of the new order.

11 But now Christ has come, high priest of good things already in being. The tent of his priesthood is a greater and more perfect one, not made by human hands, that is, not belonging to this created world; 12 the blood of his sacrifice is his own blood, not the blood of goats and calves; and thus he has entered the sanctuary once for all and secured an eternal liberation. 13 If sprinkling the blood of goats and bulls and the ashes of a heifer consecrates those who have been defiled and restores their ritual purity, 14 how much greater is the power of the blood of Christ; through the eternal Spirit he offered himself without blemish to God. His blood will cleanse our conscience from the deadness of our former ways to serve the living God.

15 That is why the new covenant or testament of which he is mediator took effect once a death had occurred, to bring liberation from sins committed under the former covenant; its purpose is to enable those whom God has called to receive the eternal inheritance he has promised them. 16 Now where there is a testament it is necessary for the death of the testator to be established; 17 for a testament takes effect only when a death has occurred: it has no force while the testator is still alive. 18 Even the former covenant itself was not inaugurated without blood, 19 for when Moses had told the assembled people all the commandments as set forth in the law, he took the blood of calves, with water, scarlet wool, and marjoram, and sprinkled the law book itself and all the people, 20 saying, 'This is the blood of the covenant which God commanded you to keep.' 21 In the same way he sprinkled the blood over the tent and all the vessels of divine service. 22 Indeed, under the law, it might almost be said that everything is cleansed by blood, and without the shedding of blood there is no forgiveness.

23 IF, then, the symbols of heavenly things required those sacrifices to cleanse them, the heavenly things themselves required still better sacrifices; 24 for Christ has not entered

---

l Or *tabernacle*   *m* Gk *the presentation of the loaves*   *n* Or *the place of atonement*   *o* Gk *parable*   *p* Other ancient authorities read *good things to come*   *q* Gk *more perfect*   *r* Other ancient authorities read *Holy Spirit*   *s* Other ancient authorities read *your*   *t* The Greek word used here means both *covenant* and *will*   *u* Other ancient authorities lack *and goats*

9:11 **things . . . being:** *some witnesses read* things to be.

13 When he speaks of a "new" covenant, he declares the first one obsolete. And what has become obsolete and has grown old is close to disappearing.

9 Now [even] the first covenant had regulations for worship and an earthly sanctuary. 2 For a tabernacle was constructed, the outer one, in which were the lampstand, the table, and the bread of offering; this is called the Holy Place. 3 Behind the second veil was the tabernacle called the Holy of Holies, 4 in which were the gold altar of incense and the ark of the covenant entirely covered with gold. In it were the gold jar containing the manna, the staff of Aaron that had sprouted, and the tablets of the covenant. 5 Above it were the cherubim of glory overshadowing the place of expiation. Now is not the time to speak of these in detail.

6 With these arrangements for worship, the priests, in performing their service, go into the outer tabernacle repeatedly, 7 but the high priest alone goes into the inner one once a year, not without blood that he offers for himself and for the sins of the people. 8 In this way the holy Spirit shows that the way into the sanctuary had not yet been revealed while the outer tabernacle still had its place. 9 This is a symbol of the present time, in which gifts and sacrifices are offered that cannot perfect the worshiper in conscience 10 but only in matters of food and drink and various ritual washings: regulations concerning the flesh, imposed until the time of the new order.

11 But when Christ came as high priest of the good things that have come to be, passing through the greater and more perfect tabernacle not made by hands, that is, not belonging to this creation, 12 he entered once for all into the sanctuary, not with the blood of goats and calves but with his own blood, thus obtaining eternal redemption. 13 For if the blood of goats and bulls and the sprinkling of a heifer's ashes can sanctify those who are defiled so that their flesh is cleansed, 14 how much more will the blood of Christ, who through the eternal spirit offered himself unblemished to God, cleanse our consciences from dead works to worship the living God.

15 For this reason he is mediator of a new covenant: since a death has taken place for deliverance from transgressions under the first covenant, those who are called may receive the promised eternal inheritance. 16 Now where there is a will, the death of the testator must be established. 17 For a will takes effect only at death; it has no force while the testator is alive. 18 Thus not even the first covenant was inaugurated without blood. 19 When every commandment had been proclaimed by Moses to all the people according to the law, he took the blood of calves [and goats], together with water and crimson wool and hyssop, and sprinkled both the book itself and all the people, 20 saying, "This is 'the blood of the covenant which God has enjoined upon you.' " 21 In the same way, he sprinkled also the tabernacle and all the vessels of worship with blood. 22 According to the law almost everything is purified by blood, and without the shedding of blood there is no forgiveness.

23 Therefore, it was necessary for the copies of the heavenly things to be purified by these rites, but the heavenly things themselves by better sacrifices than these. 24 For

13 By speaking of a *new* covenant, he implies that the first one is old. And anything old and ageing is ready to disappear.

9 The first covenant also had its laws governing worship and its sanctuary, a sanctuary on this earth. 2 There was a tent which comprised two compartments: the first, in which the lamp-stand, the table and the loaves of permanent offering were kept, was called the Holy Place; 3 then beyond the second veil, a second compartment which was called the Holy of Holies 4 to which belonged the gold altar of incense, and the ark of the covenant, plated all over with gold. In this were kept the gold jar containing the manna, Aaron's branch that grew the buds, and the tables of the covenant. 5 On top of it were the glorious winged creatures, overshadowing the throne of mercy. This is not the time to go into detail about this.

6 Under these provisions, priests go regularly into the outer tent to carry out their acts of worship, 7 but the second tent is entered only once a year, and then only by the high priest who takes in the blood to make an offering for his own and the people's faults of inadvertence. 8 By this, the Holy Spirit means us to see that as long as the old tent stands, the way into the holy place is not opened up; 9 it is a symbol for this present time. None of the gifts and sacrifices offered under these regulations can possibly bring any worshipper to perfection in his conscience; 10 they are rules about outward life, connected with food and drink and washing at various times, which are in force only until the time comes to set things right.

11 But now Christ has come, as the high priest of all the blessings which were to come. He has passed through the greater, the more perfect tent, not made by human hands, that is, not of this created order; 12 and he has entered the sanctuary once and for all, taking with him not the blood of goats and bull calves, but his own blood, having won an eternal redemption. 13 The blood of goats and bulls and the ashes of a heifer, sprinkled on those who have incurred defilement, may restore their bodily purity. 14 How much more will the blood of Christ, who offered himself, blameless as he was, to God through the eternal Spirit, purify our conscience from dead actions so that we can worship the living God.

15 This makes him the mediator of a new covenant, so that, now that a death has occurred to redeem the sins committed under an earlier covenant, those who have been called to an eternal inheritance may receive the promise. 16 Now wherever a will is in question, the death of the testator must be established; 17 a testament comes into effect only after a death, since it has no force while the testator is still alive. 18 That is why even the earlier covenant was inaugurated with blood, 19 and why, after Moses had promulgated all the commandments of the Law to the people, he took the calves' blood, the goats' blood and some water, and with these he sprinkled the book itself and all the people, 20 saying as he did so: *This is the blood of the covenant that God has made with you.* n 21 And he sprinkled both the tent and all the liturgical vessels with blood in the same way. 22 In fact, according to the Law, practically every purification takes place by means of blood; and if there is no shedding of blood, there is no remission. 23 Only the copies of heavenly things are purified in this way; the heavenly things themselves have to be purified by a higher sort of sacrifice than this. 24 It is not as

n 9 Ex 24:8.

NEW REVISED STANDARD VERSION

Christ did not enter a sanctuary made by human hands, a mere copy of the true one, but he entered into heaven itself, now to appear in the presence of God on our behalf. 25 Nor was it to offer himself again and again, as the high priest enters the Holy Place year after year with blood that is not his own; 26 for then he would have had to suffer again and again since the foundation of the world. But as it is, he has appeared once for all at the end of the age to remove sin by the sacrifice of himself. 27 And just as it is appointed for mortals to die once, and after that the judgment, 28 so Christ, having been offered once to bear the sins of many, will appear a second time, not to deal with sin, but to save those who are eagerly waiting for him.

10 Since the law has only a shadow of the good things to come and not the true form of these realities, it[v] can never, by the same sacrifices that are continually offered year after year, make perfect those who approach. 2 Otherwise, would they not have ceased being offered, since the worshipers, cleansed once for all, would no longer have any consciousness of sin? 3 But in these sacrifices there is a reminder of sin year after year. 4 For it is impossible for the blood of bulls and goats to take away sins. 5 Consequently, when Christ[w] came into the world, he said,

"Sacrifices and offerings you have not desired,
  but a body you have prepared for me;
6 in burnt offerings and sin offerings
  you have taken no pleasure.
7 Then I said, 'See, God, I have come to do your
  will, O God'
  (in the scroll of the book[x] it is written of
  me)."

8 When he said above, "You have neither desired nor taken pleasure in sacrifices and offerings and burnt offerings and sin offerings" (these are offered according to the law), 9 then he added, "See, I have come to do your will." He abolishes the first in order to establish the second. 10 And it is by God's will[y] that we have been sanctified through the offering of the body of Jesus Christ once for all.

11 And every priest stands day after day at his service, offering again and again the same sacrifices that can never take away sins. 12 But when Christ[z] had offered for all time a single sacrifice for sins, "he sat down at the right hand of God," 13 and since then has been waiting "until his enemies would be made a footstool for his feet." 14 For by a single offering he has perfected for all time those who are sanctified. 15 And the Holy Spirit also testifies to us, for after saying,

16 "This is the covenant that I will make with them
  after those days, says the Lord:
I will put my laws in their hearts,
  and I will write them on their minds,"
17 he also adds,

"I will remember[a] their sins and their lawless
  deeds no more."

18 Where there is forgiveness of these, there is no longer any offering for sin.

19 Therefore, my friends,[b] since we have confidence to enter the sanctuary by the blood of Jesus, 20 by the new and living way that he opened for us through the curtain (that is, through his flesh), 21 and since we have a great priest over the house of God, 22 let us approach with a true heart in full

REVISED ENGLISH BIBLE

a sanctuary made by human hands which is only a pointer to the reality; he has entered heaven itself, to appear now before God on our behalf. 25 It was not his purpose to offer himself again and again, as the high priest enters the sanctuary year after year with blood not his own; 26 for then he would have had to suffer repeatedly since the world was created. But as it is, he has appeared once for all at the climax of history to abolish sin by the sacrifice of himself. 27 Just as it is our human lot to die once, with judgement to follow, 28 so Christ was offered once to bear the sins of mankind, and will appear a second time, not to deal with sin, but to bring salvation to those who eagerly await him.

10 THE law contains but a shadow of the good things to come, not the true picture. With the same sacrifices offered year after year for all time, it can never bring the worshippers to perfection. 2 If it could, these sacrifices would surely have ceased to be offered, because the worshippers, cleansed once for all, would no longer have any sense of sin. 3 Instead, by these sacrifices sins are brought to mind year after year, 4 because they can never be removed by the blood of bulls and goats.

5 That is why, at Christ's coming into the world, he says:

Sacrifice and offering you did not desire,
  but you have prepared a body for me.
6 Whole-offerings and sin-offerings you did not
  delight in.
7 Then I said, 'Here I am: as it is written of me in
  the scroll,
  I have come, O God, to do your will.'

8 First he says, 'Sacrifices and offerings, whole-offerings and sin-offerings, you did not desire or delight in,' although the law prescribes them. 9 Then he adds, 'Here I am: I have come to do your will.' He thus abolishes the former to establish the latter. 10 And it is by the will of God that we have been consecrated, through the offering of the body of Jesus Christ once for all.

11 Daily every priest stands performing his service and time after time offering the same sacrifices, which can never remove sins. 12 Christ, having offered for all time a single sacrifice for sins, took his seat at God's right hand, 13 where he now waits until his enemies are made his footstool. 14 So by one offering he has perfected for ever those who are consecrated by it. 15 To this the Holy Spirit also adds his witness. First he says, 16 'This is the covenant which I will make with them after those days, says the Lord: I will set my laws in their hearts and write them on their understanding'; 17 then he adds, 'and their sins and wicked deeds I will remember no more.' 18 And where these have been forgiven, there are no further offerings for sin.

19 SO NOW, my friends, the blood of Jesus makes us free to enter the sanctuary with confidence 20 by the new and living way which he has opened for us through the curtain, the way of his flesh. 21 We have a great priest set over the household of God; 22 so let us make our approach in sinceri-

---

[v]Other ancient authorities read they   [w]Gk he   [x]Meaning of Gk uncertain   [y]Gk by that will   [z]Gk this one   [a]Gk on their minds and I will remember   [b]Gk Therefore, brothers

Christ did not enter into a sanctuary made by hands, a copy of the true one, but heaven itself, that he might now appear before God on our behalf. 25 Not that he might offer himself repeatedly, as the high priest enters each year into the sanctuary with blood that is not his own; 26 if that were so, he would have had to suffer repeatedly from the foundation of the world. But now once for all he has appeared at the end of the ages to take away sin by his sacrifice. 27 Just as it is appointed that human beings die once, and after this the judgment, 28 so also Christ, offered once to take away the sins of many, will appear a second time, not to take away sin but to bring salvation to those who eagerly await him.

10 Since the law has only a shadow of the good things to come, and not the very image of them, it can never make perfect those who come to worship by the same sacrifices that they offer continually each year. 2 Otherwise, would not the sacrifices have ceased to be offered, since the worshipers, once cleansed, would no longer have had any consciousness of sins? 3 But in those sacrifices there is only a yearly remembrance of sins, 4 for it is impossible that the blood of bulls and goats take away sins. 5 For this reason, when he came into the world, he said:

"Sacrifice and offering you did not desire,
but a body you prepared for me;
6 holocausts and sin offerings you took no delight in.
7 Then I said, 'As is written of me in the scroll,
Behold, I come to do your will, O God.' "

8 First he says, "Sacrifices and offerings, holocausts and sin offerings, you neither desired nor delighted in." These are offered according to the law. 9 Then he says, "Behold, I come to do your will." He takes away the first to establish the second. 10 By this "will," we have been consecrated through the offering of the body of Jesus Christ once for all.

11 Every priest stands daily at his ministry, offering frequently those same sacrifices that can never take away sins. 12 But this one offered one sacrifice for sins, and took his seat forever at the right hand of God; 13 now he waits until his enemies are made his footstool. 14 For by one offering he has made perfect forever those who are being consecrated. 15 The holy Spirit also testifies to us, for after saying:

16 "This is the covenant I will establish with them
after those days, says the Lord:
'I will put my laws in their hearts,
and I will write them upon their minds,' "

17 he also says:

"Their sins and their evildoing
I will remember no more."

18 Where there is forgiveness of these, there is no longer offering for sin.

19 Therefore, brothers, since through the blood of Jesus we have confidence of entrance into the sanctuary 20 by the new and living way he opened for us through the veil, that is, his flesh, 21 and since we have "a great priest over the house of God," 22 let us approach with a sincere heart and

though Christ had entered a man-made sanctuary which was merely a model of the real one; he entered heaven itself, so that he now appears in the presence of God on our behalf. 25 And he does not have to offer himself again and again, as the high priest goes into the sanctuary year after year with the blood that is not his own, 26 or else he would have had to suffer over and over again since the world began. As it is, he has made his appearance once and for all, at the end of the last age, to do away with sin by sacrificing himself. 27 Since human beings die only once, after which comes judgement, 28 so Christ too, having offered himself only once *to bear the sin of many,o* will manifest himself a second time, sin being no more, to those who are waiting for him, to bring them salvation.

10 So, since the Law contains no more than a reflection of the good things which were still to come, and no true image of them, it is quite incapable of bringing the worshippers to perfection, by means of the same sacrifices repeatedly offered year after year. 2 Otherwise, surely the offering of them would have stopped, because the worshippers, when they had been purified once, would have no awareness of sins. 3 But in fact the sins are recalled year after year in the sacrifices. 4 Bulls' blood and goats' blood are incapable of taking away sins, 5 and that is why he said, on coming into the world:

*You wanted no sacrifice or cereal offering,
but you gave me a body.*
6 *You took no pleasure in burnt offering or sacrifice
for sin;*
7 *then I said, 'Here I am, I am coming,'
in the scroll of the book it is written of me,
to do your will, God.p*

8 He says first *You did not want* what the Law lays down as the things to be offered, that is: *the sacrifices, the cereal offerings, the burnt offerings and the sacrifices for sin,* and *you took no pleasure* in them; 9 and then he says: *Here I am! I am coming to do your will.* He is abolishing the first sort to establish the second. 10 And this *will* was for us to be made holy by the *offering* of the *body* of Jesus Christ made once and for all.

11 Every priest stands at his duties every day, offering over and over again the same sacrifices which are quite incapable of taking away sins. 12 He, on the other hand, has offered one single sacrifice for sins, and then *taken his seat for ever, at the right hand of God,* 13 where he is now waiting *till his enemies are made his footstool.q* 14 By virtue of that one single offering, he has achieved the eternal perfection of all who are sanctified. 15 The Holy Spirit attests this to us, for after saying:

16 *No, this is the covenant I will make with them,
when those days have come.*

the Lord says:

*In their minds I will plant my Laws
writing them on their hearts,*
17 *and I shall never more call their sins to mind,r
or their offences.*

18 When these have been forgiven, there can be no more sin offerings.

19 We have then, brothers, complete confidence through the blood of Jesus in entering the sanctuary, 20 by a new way which he has opened for us, a living opening through the curtain, that is to say, his flesh. 21 And we have the *high priest* over all *the sanctuary of God.s* 22 So as we go in, let

o 9 Is 53:12.   p 10 Ps 40:6–8.   q 10 Ps 110:1.
r 10 Jr 31:33–34.   s 10 Zc 6:11–12.

NEW REVISED STANDARD VERSION

assurance of faith, with our hearts sprinkled clean from an evil conscience and our bodies washed with pure water. 23 Let us hold fast to the confession of our hope without wavering, for he who has promised is faithful. 24 And let us consider how to provoke one another to love and good deeds, 25 not neglecting to meet together, as is the habit of some, but encouraging one another, and all the more as you see the Day approaching.

26 For if we willfully persist in sin after having received the knowledge of the truth, there no longer remains a sacrifice for sins, 27 but a fearful prospect of judgment, and a fury of fire that will consume the adversaries. 28 Anyone who has violated the law of Moses dies without mercy "on the testimony of two or three witnesses." 29 How much worse punishment do you think will be deserved by those who have spurned the Son of God, profaned the blood of the covenant by which they were sanctified, and outraged the Spirit of grace? 30 For we know the one who said, "Vengeance is mine, I will repay." And again, "The Lord will judge his people." 31 It is a fearful thing to fall into the hands of the living God.

32 But recall those earlier days when, after you had been enlightened, you endured a hard struggle with sufferings, 33 sometimes being publicly exposed to abuse and persecution, and sometimes being partners with those so treated. 34 For you had compassion for those who were in prison, and you cheerfully accepted the plundering of your possessions, knowing that you yourselves possessed something better and more lasting. 35 Do not, therefore, abandon that confidence of yours; it brings a great reward. 36 For you need endurance, so that when you have done the will of God, you may receive what was promised.

37 For yet "in a very little while,
the one who is coming will come and will not delay;
38 but my righteous one will live by faith.
My soul takes no pleasure in anyone who shrinks back."

39 But we are not among those who shrink back and so are lost, but among those who have faith and so are saved.

11 Now faith is the assurance of things hoped for, the conviction of things not seen. 2 Indeed, by faith[c] our ancestors received approval. 3 By faith we understand that the worlds were prepared by the word of God, so that what is seen was made from things that are not visible.[d]

4 By faith Abel offered to God a more acceptable[e] sacrifice than Cain's. Through this he received approval as righteous, God himself giving approval to his gifts; he died, but through his faith[f] he still speaks. 5 By faith Enoch was taken so that he did not experience death; and "he was not found, because God had taken him." For it was attested before he was taken away that "he had pleased God." 6 And without faith it is impossible to please God, for whoever would approach him must believe that he exists and that he rewards those who seek him. 7 By faith Noah, warned by God about events as yet unseen, respected the warning and built an ark to save his household; by this he condemned the world and became an heir to the righteousness that is in accordance with faith.

REVISED ENGLISH BIBLE

ty of heart and the full assurance of faith, inwardly cleansed from a guilty conscience, and outwardly washed with pure water. 23 Let us be firm and unswerving in the confession of our hope, for the giver of the promise is to be trusted. 24 We ought to see how each of us may best arouse others to love and active goodness. 25 We should not stay away from our meetings, as some do, but rather encourage one another, all the more because we see the day of the Lord drawing near.

26 For if we deliberately persist in sin after receiving the knowledge of the truth, there can be no further sacrifice for sins; there remains 27 only a terrifying expectation of judgement, of a fierce fire which will consume God's enemies. 28 Anyone who flouts the law of Moses is put to death without mercy on the evidence of two or three witnesses. 29 Think how much more severe a penalty will be deserved by anyone who has trampled underfoot the Son of God, profaned the blood of the covenant by which he was consecrated, and insulted God's gracious Spirit! 30 For we know who it is that said, 'Justice is mine: I will repay'; and again, 'The Lord will judge his people.' 31 It is a terrifying thing to fall into the hands of the living God.

32 Remember those early days when, newly enlightened, you met the test of great suffering and held firm. 33 Some of you were publicly exposed to abuse and tormented, while others stood loyally by those who were so treated. 34 For indeed you shared the sufferings of those who were in prison, and you cheerfully accepted the seizure of your possessions, knowing that you had a better, more lasting possession. 35 Do not, therefore, throw away your confidence, for it carries a great reward. 36 You need endurance in order to do God's will and win what he has promised. 37 For, in the words of scripture,

very soon he who is to come will come;
he will not delay;
38 and by faith my righteous servant shall find life;
but if anyone shrinks back,
I take no pleasure in him.

39 But we are not among those who shrink back and are lost; we have the faith to preserve our life.

11 FAITH gives substance to our hopes and convinces us of realities we do not see.

2 It was for their faith that the people of old won God's approval.

3 By faith we understand that the universe was formed by God's command, so that the visible came forth from the invisible.

4 By faith Abel offered a greater sacrifice than Cain's; because of his faith God approved his offerings and attested his goodness; and through his faith, though he is dead, he continues to speak.

5 By faith Enoch was taken up to another life without passing through death; he was not to be found, because God had taken him, and it is the testimony of scripture that before he was taken he had pleased God. 6 But without faith it is impossible to please him, for whoever comes to God must believe that he exists and rewards those who seek him.

7 By faith Noah took good heed of the divine warning about the unseen future, and built an ark to save his household. Through his faith he put the whole world in the wrong, and made good his own claim to the righteousness which comes of faith.

---

c Gk by this   d Or was not made out of visible things
e Gk greater   f Gk through it

11:1 **substance:** or assurance.

in absolute trust, with our hearts sprinkled clean from an evil conscience and our bodies washed in pure water. 23 Let us hold unwaveringly to our confession that gives us hope, for he who made the promise is trustworthy. 24 We must consider how to rouse one another to love and good works. 25 We should not stay away from our assembly, as is the custom of some, but encourage one another, and this all the more as you see the day drawing near.

26 If we sin deliberately after receiving knowledge of the truth, there no longer remains sacrifice for sins 27 but a fearful prospect of judgment and a flaming fire that is going to consume the adversaries. 28 Anyone who rejects the law of Moses is put to death without pity on the testimony of two or three witnesses. 29 Do you not think that a much worse punishment is due the one who has contempt for the Son of God, considers unclean the covenant-blood by which he was consecrated, and insults the spirit of grace? 30 We know the one who said:

"Vengeance is mine; I will repay,"

and again:

"The Lord will judge his people."

31 It is a fearful thing to fall into the hands of the living God.

32 Remember the days past when, after you had been enlightened, you endured a great contest of suffering. 33 At times you were publicly exposed to abuse and affliction; at other times you associated yourselves with those so treated. 34 You even joined in the sufferings of those in prison and joyfully accepted the confiscation of your property, knowing that you had a better and lasting possession. 35 Therefore, do not throw away your confidence; it will have great recompense. 36 You need endurance to do the will of God and receive what he has promised.

37 "For, after just a brief moment,
 he who is to come shall come;
 he shall not delay.
38 But my just one shall live by faith,
 and if he draws back I take no pleasure in him."

39 We are not among those who draw back and perish, but among those who have faith and will possess life.

11 Faith is the realization of what is hoped for and evidence of things not seen. 2 Because of it the ancients were well attested. 3 By faith we understand that the universe was ordered by the word of God, so that what is visible came into being through the invisible. 4 By faith Abel offered to God a sacrifice greater than Cain's. Through this he was attested to be righteous, God bearing witness to his gifts, and through this, though dead, he still speaks. 5 By faith Enoch was taken up so that he should not see death, and "he was found no more because God had taken him." Before he was taken up, he was attested to have pleased God. 6 But without faith it is impossible to please him, for anyone who approaches God must believe that he exists and that he rewards those who seek him. 7 By faith Noah, warned about what was not yet seen, with reverence built an ark for the salvation of his household. Through this he condemned the world and inherited the righteousness that comes through faith.

us be sincere in heart and filled with faith, our hearts sprinkled and free from any trace of bad conscience, and our bodies washed with pure water. 23 Let us keep firm in the hope we profess, because the one who made the promise is trustworthy. 24 Let us be concerned for each other, to stir a response in love and good works. 25 Do not absent yourself from your own assemblies, as some do, but encourage each other; the more so as you see the Day drawing near.

26 If, after we have been given knowledge of the truth, we should deliberately commit any sins, then there is no longer any sacrifice for them. 27 There is only the dreadful prospect of judgement and of *the fiery wrath* that is to *devour your enemies.*[t] 28 Anyone who disregards the Law of Moses is ruthlessly *put to death on the word of two witnesses or three;*[u] 29 and you may be sure that anyone who tramples on the Son of God, and who treats *the blood of the covenant* which sanctified him as if it were not holy, and who insults the Spirit of grace, will be condemned to a far severer punishment. 30 We are all aware who it was that said: *Vengeance is mine; I will pay them back.*[v] And again: *The Lord will vindicate his people.* 31 It is a dreadful thing to fall into the hands of the living God.

32 Remember the great challenge of the sufferings that you had to meet after you received the light, in earlier days; 33 sometimes by being yourselves publicly exposed to humiliations and violence, and sometimes as associates of others who were treated in the same way. 34 For you not only shared in the sufferings of those who were in prison, but you accepted with joy being stripped of your belongings, knowing that you owned something that was better and lasting. 35 Do not lose your fearlessness now, then, since the reward is so great. 36 You will need perseverance if you are to do God's will and gain what he has promised.

37 Only *a little while now, a very little while,*
 for come he certainly will before too long.[w]
38 *My upright person will live through faith*
 but if he draws back, my soul will take no pleasure
 in him.[x]

39 We are not the sort of people who *draw back*, and are lost by it; we are the sort who keep *faith* until our souls are saved.

11 Only faith can guarantee the blessings that we hope for, or prove the existence of realities that are unseen. 2 It is for their faith that our ancestors are acknowledged.

3 It is by faith that we understand that the ages were created by a word from God, so that from the invisible the visible world came to be.

4 It was because of his faith that Abel offered God a better sacrifice than Cain, and for that he was acknowledged as upright when *God* himself made acknowledgement of *his offerings*. Though he is dead, he still speaks by faith.

5 It was because of his faith that Enoch was taken up and did not experience death: *he was no more, because God took him;*[y] because before his assumption he was acknowledged to *have pleased God*. 6 Now it is impossible to please God without faith, since anyone who comes to him must believe that he exists and rewards those who seek him.

7 It was through his faith that Noah, when he had been warned by God of something that had never been seen before, took care to build an ark to save his family. His faith was a judgement on the world, and he was able to claim the uprightness which comes from faith.

t **10** Is 26:11.   *u* **10** Dt 17:6.   *v* **10** Dt 32:35–36.   *w* **10** Is 26:20.   *x* **10** Hab 2:3–4.   *y* **11** Gn 5:24.

NEW REVISED STANDARD VERSION	REVISED ENGLISH BIBLE

NEW REVISED STANDARD VERSION

8 By faith Abraham obeyed when he was called to set out for a place that he was to receive as an inheritance; and he set out, not knowing where he was going. 9 By faith he stayed for a time in the land he had been promised, as in a foreign land, living in tents, as did Isaac and Jacob, who were heirs with him of the same promise. 10 For he looked forward to the city that has foundations, whose architect and builder is God. 11 By faith he received power of procreation, even though he was too old — and Sarah herself was barren — because he considered him faithful who had promised.^g 12 Therefore from one person, and this one as good as dead, descendants were born, "as many as the stars of heaven and as the innumerable grains of sand by the seashore."

13 All of these died in faith without having received the promises, but from a distance they saw and greeted them. They confessed that they were strangers and foreigners on the earth, 14 for people who speak in this way make it clear that they are seeking a homeland. 15 If they had been thinking of the land that they had left behind, they would have had opportunity to return. 16 But as it is, they desire a better country, that is, a heavenly one. Therefore God is not ashamed to be called their God; indeed, he has prepared a city for them.

17 By faith Abraham, when put to the test, offered up Isaac. He who had received the promises was ready to offer up his only son, 18 of whom he had been told, "It is through Isaac that descendants shall be named for you." 19 He considered the fact that God is able even to raise someone from the dead — and figuratively speaking, he did receive him back. 20 By faith Isaac invoked blessings for the future on Jacob and Esau. 21 By faith Jacob, when dying, blessed each of the sons of Joseph, "bowing in worship over the top of his staff." 22 By faith Joseph, at the end of his life, made mention of the exodus of the Israelites and gave instructions about his burial.^h

23 By faith Moses was hidden by his parents for three months after his birth, because they saw that the child was beautiful; and they were not afraid of the king's edict.ⁱ 24 By faith Moses, when he was grown up, refused to be called a son of Pharaoh's daughter, 25 choosing rather to share ill-treatment with the people of God than to enjoy the fleeting pleasures of sin. 26 He considered abuse suffered for the Christ^j to be greater wealth than the treasures of Egypt, for he was looking ahead to the reward. 27 By faith he left Egypt, unafraid of the king's anger; for he persevered as though^k he saw him who is invisible. 28 By faith he kept the Passover and the sprinkling of blood, so that the destroyer of the firstborn would not touch the firstborn of Israel.^l

29 By faith the people passed through the Red Sea as if it were dry land, but when the Egyptians attempted to do so they were drowned. 30 By faith the walls of Jericho fell after they had been encircled for seven days. 31 By faith Rahab the prostitute did not perish with those who were disobedient,^m because she had received the spies in peace.

32 And what more should I say? For time would fail me to tell of Gideon, Barak, Samson, Jephthah, of David and Samuel and the prophets — 33 who through faith conquered kingdoms, administered justice, obtained promises, shut the mouths of lions, 34 quenched raging fire, escaped the edge

REVISED ENGLISH BIBLE

8 By faith Abraham obeyed the call to leave his home for a land which he was to receive as a possession; he went away without knowing where he was to go. 9 By faith he settled as an alien in the land which had been promised him, living in tents with Isaac and Jacob, who were heirs with him to the same promise. 10 For he was looking forward to a city with firm foundations, whose architect and builder is God.

11 By faith even Sarah herself was enabled to conceive, though she was past the age, because she judged that God who had promised would keep faith. 12 Therefore from one man, a man as good as dead, there sprang descendants as numerous as the stars in the heavens or the countless grains of sand on the seashore.

13 All these died in faith. Although they had not received the things promised, yet they had seen them far ahead and welcomed them, and acknowledged themselves to be strangers and aliens without fixed abode on earth. 14 Those who speak in that way show plainly that they are looking for a country of their own. 15 If their thoughts had been with the country they had left, they could have found opportunity to return. 16 Instead, we find them longing for a better country, a heavenly one. That is why God is not ashamed to be called their God; for he has a city ready for them.

17 By faith Abraham, when put to the test, offered up Isaac: he had received the promises, and yet he was ready to offer his only son, 18 of whom he had been told, 'Through the line of Isaac your descendants shall be traced.' 19 For he reckoned that God had power even to raise from the dead — and it was from the dead, in a sense, that he received him back.

20 By faith Isaac blessed Jacob and Esau and spoke of things to come. 21 By faith Jacob, as he was dying, blessed each of Joseph's sons, and bowed in worship over the top of his staff.

22 By faith Joseph, at the end of his life, spoke of the departure of Israel from Egypt, and gave instructions about his burial.

23 By faith, when Moses was born, his parents hid him for three months, because they saw what a fine child he was; they were not intimidated by the king's edict. 24 By faith Moses, when he grew up, refused to be called a son of Pharaoh's daughter, 25 preferring to share hardship with God's people rather than enjoy the transient pleasures of sin. 26 He considered the stigma that rests on God's Anointed greater wealth than the treasures of Egypt, for his eyes were fixed on the coming reward. 27 By faith he left Egypt, with no fear of the king's anger; for he was resolute, as one who saw the invisible God.

28 By faith he celebrated the Passover and the sprinkling of blood, so that the destroying angel might not touch the firstborn of Israel. 29 By faith they crossed the Red Sea as though it were dry land, whereas the Egyptians, when they attempted the crossing, were engulfed.

30 By faith the walls of Jericho were made to fall after they had been encircled on seven successive days. 31 By faith the prostitute Rahab escaped the fate of the unbelievers, because she had given the spies a kindly welcome.

32 Need I say more? Time is too short for me to tell the stories of Gideon, Barak, Samson, and Jephthah, of David and Samuel and the prophets. 33 Through faith they overthrew kingdoms, established justice, saw God's promises fulfilled. They shut the mouths of lions, 34 quenched the

g Other ancient authorities read *By faith Sarah herself, though barren, received power to conceive, even when she was too old, because she considered him faithful who had promised.* h Gk *his bones* i Other ancient authorities add *By faith Moses, when he was grown up, killed the Egyptian, because he observed the humiliation of his people* (Gk *brothers*) j Or *the Messiah* k Or *because* l Gk *would not touch them* m Or *unbelieving*

11:11 **though she was:** *some witnesses add* barren and.

8 By faith Abraham obeyed when he was called to go out to a place that he was to receive as an inheritance; he went out, not knowing where he was to go. 9 By faith he sojourned in the promised land as in a foreign country, dwelling in tents with Isaac and Jacob, heirs of the same promise; 10 for he was looking forward to the city with foundations, whose architect and maker is God. 11 By faith he received power to generate, even though he was past the normal age — and Sarah herself was sterile — for he thought that the one who had made the promise was trustworthy. 12 So it was that there came forth from one man, himself as good as dead, descendants as numerous as the stars in the sky and as countless as the sands on the seashore.

13 All these died in faith. They did not receive what had been promised but saw it and greeted it from afar and acknowledged themselves to be strangers and aliens on earth, 14 for those who speak thus show that they are seeking a homeland. 15 If they had been thinking of the land from which they had come, they would have had opportunity to return. 16 But now they desire a better homeland, a heavenly one. Therefore, God is not ashamed to be called their God, for he has prepared a city for them.

17 By faith Abraham, when put to the test, offered up Isaac, and he who had received the promises was ready to offer his only son, 18 of whom it was said, "Through Isaac descendants shall bear your name." 19 He reasoned that God was able to raise even from the dead, and he received Isaac back as a symbol. 20 By faith regarding things still to come Isaac blessed Jacob and Esau. 21 By faith Jacob, when dying, blessed each of the sons of Joseph and "bowed in worship, leaning on the top of his staff." 22 By faith Joseph, near the end of his life, spoke of the Exodus of the Israelites and gave instructions about his bones.

23 By faith Moses was hidden by his parents for three months after his birth, because they saw that he was a beautiful child, and they were not afraid of the king's edict. 24 By faith Moses, when he had grown up, refused to be known as the son of Pharaoh's daughter; 25 he chose to be ill-treated along with the people of God rather than enjoy the fleeting pleasure of sin. 26 He considered the reproach of the Anointed greater wealth than the treasures of Egypt, for he was looking to the recompense. 27 By faith he left Egypt, not fearing the king's fury, for he persevered as if seeing the one who is invisible. 28 By faith he kept the Passover and sprinkled the blood, that the Destroyer of the firstborn might not touch them. 29 By faith they crossed the Red Sea as if it were dry land, but when the Egyptians attempted it they were drowned. 30 By faith the walls of Jericho fell after being encircled for seven days. 31 By faith Rahab the harlot did not perish with the disobedient, for she had received the spies in peace.

32 What more shall I say? I have not time to tell of Gideon, Barak, Samson, Jephthah, of David and Samuel and the prophets, 33 who by faith conquered kingdoms, did what was righteous, obtained the promises; they closed the mouths of lions, 34 put out raging fires, escaped the devour-

8 It was by faith that Abraham obeyed the call to *set out* for a country that was the inheritance given to him and his descendants, and that *he set out* without knowing where he was going. 9 By faith he *sojourned* in the Promised Land as though it were not his, living in tents with Isaac and Jacob, who were heirs with him of the same promise. 10 He looked forward to the well-founded city, designed and built by God.

11 It was equally by faith that Sarah, in spite of being past the age, was made able to conceive, because she believed that he who had made the promise was faithful to it. 12 Because of this, there came from one man, and one who already had the mark of death on him, descendants *as numerous as the stars of heaven and the grains of sand on the seashore which cannot be counted.* z

13 All these died in faith, before receiving any of the things that had been promised, but they saw them in the far distance and welcomed them, recognising that they were only *strangers and nomads on earth.* 14 People who use such terms about themselves make it quite plain that they are in search of a homeland. 15 If they had meant the country they came from, they would have had the opportunity to return to it; 16 but in fact they were longing for a better homeland, their heavenly homeland. That is why God is not ashamed to be called their God, since he has founded the city for them.

17 It was by faith that Abraham, *when put to the test, offered up Isaac.* a He offered to sacrifice *his only son* even though he had yet to receive what had been promised, 18 and he had been told: *Isaac is the one through whom your name will be carried on.* b 19 He was confident that God had the power even to raise the dead; and so, figuratively speaking, he was given back Isaac from the dead.

20 It was by faith that this same Isaac gave his blessing to Jacob and Esau for the still distant future. 21 By faith Jacob, when he was dying, blessed each of Joseph's sons, *bowed in reverence, as he leant on his staff.* c 22 It was by faith that, when he was about to die, Joseph mentioned the Exodus of the Israelites and gave instructions about his own remains.

23 It was by faith that Moses, when he was born, *was kept hidden by his parents for three months;* d because they *saw* that he was a *fine* child; they were not afraid of the royal edict. 24 It was by faith that, *when he was grown up*, Moses refused to be known as the son of Pharaoh's daughter 25 and chose to be ill-treated in company with God's people rather than to enjoy the transitory pleasures of sin. 26 He considered that the humiliations offered to the Anointed were something more precious than all the treasures of Egypt, because he had his eyes fixed on the reward. 27 It was by faith that he left Egypt without fear of the king's anger; he held to his purpose like someone *who could see the Invisible.* 28 It was by faith that he kept *the Passover* and sprinkled *the blood* to prevent *the Destroyer* from touching any of their first-born sons. 29 It was by faith they crossed the Red Sea as easily as dry land, while the Egyptians, trying to do the same, were drowned.

30 It was through faith that the walls of Jericho fell down when the people had marched round them for seven days. 31 It was by faith that Rahab the prostitute welcomed the spies and so was not killed with the unbelievers.

32 What more shall I say? There is not time for me to give an account of Gideon, Barak, Samson, Jephthah, or of David, Samuel and the prophets. 33 These were men who through faith conquered kingdoms, did what was upright and earned the promises. They could keep a lion's mouth shut, 34 put out blazing fires and emerge unscathed from

z 11 Gn 22:17. a 11 Gn 22:1–14. b 11 Gn 21:12. c 11 Gn 47:31. d 11 Ex 2:2, 11.

NEW REVISED STANDARD VERSION

REVISED ENGLISH BIBLE

of the sword, won strength out of weakness, became mighty in war, put foreign armies to flight. 35 Women received their dead by resurrection. Others were tortured, refusing to accept release, in order to obtain a better resurrection. 36 Others suffered mocking and flogging, and even chains and imprisonment. 37 They were stoned to death, they were sawn in two,n they were killed by the sword; they went about in skins of sheep and goats, destitute, persecuted, tormented— 38 of whom the world was not worthy. They wandered in deserts and mountains, and in caves and holes in the ground.

39 Yet all these, though they were commended for their faith, did not receive what was promised, 40 since God had provided something better so that they would not, apart from us, be made perfect.

12 Therefore, since we are surrounded by so great a cloud of witnesses, let us also lay aside every weight and the sin that clings so closely,o and let us run with perseverance the race that is set before us, 2 looking to Jesus the pioneer and perfecter of our faith, who for the sake of p the joy that was set before him endured the cross, disregarding its shame, and has taken his seat at the right hand of the throne of God.

3 Consider him who endured such hostility against himself from sinners,q so that you may not grow weary or lose heart. 4 In your struggle against sin you have not yet resisted to the point of shedding your blood. 5 And you have forgotten the exhortation that addresses you as children—

"My child, do not regard lightly the discipline of
the Lord,
or lose heart when you are punished by him;
6 for the Lord disciplines those whom he loves,
and chastises every child whom he accepts."

7 Endure trials for the sake of discipline. God is treating you as children; for what child is there whom a parent does not discipline? 8 If you do not have that discipline in which all children share, then you are illegitimate and not his children. 9 Moreover, we had human parents to discipline us, and we respected them. Should we not be even more willing to be subject to the Father of spirits and live? 10 For they disciplined us for a short time as seemed best to them, but he disciplines us for our good, in order that we may share his holiness. 11 Now, discipline always seems painful rather than pleasant at the time, but later it yields the peaceful fruit of righteousness to those who have been trained by it.

12 Therefore lift your drooping hands and strengthen your weak knees, 13 and make straight paths for your feet, so that what is lame may not be put out of joint, but rather be healed.

14 Pursue peace with everyone, and the holiness without which no one will see the Lord. 15 See to it that no one fails to obtain the grace of God; that no root of bitterness springs up and causes trouble, and through it many become defiled. 16 See to it that no one becomes like Esau, an immoral and godless person, who sold his birthright for a single meal. 17 You know that later, when he wanted to inherit the blessing, he was rejected, for he found no chance to repent,r even though he sought the blessings with tears.

18 You have not come to somethingt that can be touched, a blazing fire, and darkness, and gloom, and a tempest, 19 and the sound of a trumpet, and a voice whose words made the hearers beg that not another word be spoken to them. 20 (For they could not endure the order that was

fury of fire, escaped death by the sword. Their weakness was turned to strength, they grew powerful in war, they put foreign armies to rout. 35 Women received back their dead raised to life. Others were tortured to death, refusing release, to win resurrection to a better life. 36 Others, again, had to face jeers and flogging, even fetters and prison bars. 37 They were stoned to death, they were sawn in two, they were put to the sword, they went about clothed in skins of sheep or goats, deprived, oppressed, ill-treated. 38 The world was not worthy of them. They were refugees in deserts and on the mountains, hiding in caves and holes in the ground. 39 All these won God's approval because of their faith; and yet they did not receive what was promised, 40 because, with us in mind, God had made a better plan, that only with us should they reach perfection.

12 WITH this great cloud of witnesses around us, therefore, we too must throw off every encumbrance and the sin that all too readily restricts us, and run with resolution the race which lies ahead of us, 2 our eyes fixed on Jesus, the pioneer and perfecter of faith. For the sake of the joy that lay ahead of him, he endured the cross, ignoring its disgrace, and has taken his seat at the right hand of the throne of God.

3 Think of him who submitted to such opposition from sinners: that will help you not to lose heart and grow faint. 4 In the struggle against sin, you have not yet resisted to the point of shedding your blood. 5 You have forgotten the exhortation which addresses you as sons:

My son, do not think lightly of the Lord's
discipline,
or be discouraged when he corrects you;
6 for whom the Lord loves he disciplines;
he chastises every son whom he acknowledges.

7 You must endure it as discipline: God is treating you as sons. Can anyone be a son and not be disciplined by his father? 8 If you escape the discipline in which all sons share, you must be illegitimate and not true sons. 9 Again, we paid due respect to our human fathers who disciplined us; should we not submit even more readily to our spiritual Father, and so attain life? 10 They disciplined us for a short time as they thought best; but he does so for our true welfare, so that we may share his holiness. 11 Discipline, to be sure, is never pleasant; at the time it seems painful, but afterwards those who have been trained by it reap the harvest of a peaceful and upright life. 12 So brace up your drooping arms and shaking knees, 13 and keep to a straight path; then the weakened limb will not be put out of joint, but will regain its former powers.

14 AIM at peace with everyone and a holy life, for without that no one will see the Lord. 15 Take heed that there is no one among you who forfeits the grace of God, no bitter, noxious weed growing up to contaminate the rest, 16 no immoral person, no one worldly-minded like Esau. He sold his birthright for a single meal, 17 and you know that afterwards, although he wanted to claim the blessing, he was rejected; though he begged for it to the point of tears, he found no way open for a change of mind.

18 IT is not to the tangible, blazing fire of Sinai that you have come, with its darkness, gloom, and whirlwind, 19 its trumpet-blast and oracular voice, which the people heard and begged to hear no more; 20 for they could not bear the com-

---

n Other ancient authorities add they were tempted   o Other ancient authorities read sin that easily distracts   p Or who instead of
q Other ancient authorities read such hostility from sinners against themselves   r Or no chance to change his father's mind   s Gk it
t Other ancient authorities read a mountain

11:37 stoned to death: some witnesses add they were tested.
12:1 restricts: some witnesses read distracts.   12:2 For the sake
. . . him: or In place of the joy that was open to him.

ing sword; out of weakness they were made powerful, became strong in battle, and turned back foreign invaders. 35 Women received back their dead through resurrection. Some were tortured and would not accept deliverance, in order to obtain a better resurrection. 36 Others endured mockery, scourging, even chains and imprisonment. 37 They were stoned, sawed in two, put to death at sword's point; they went about in skins of sheep or goats, needy, afflicted, tormented. 38 The world was not worthy of them. They wandered about in deserts and on mountains, in caves and in crevices in the earth.

39 Yet all these, though approved because of their faith, did not receive what had been promised. 40 God had foreseen something better for us, so that without us they should not be made perfect.

12 Therefore, since we are surrounded by so great a cloud of witnesses, let us rid ourselves of every burden and sin that clings to us and persevere in running the race that lies before us 2 while keeping our eyes fixed on Jesus, the leader and perfecter of faith. For the sake of the joy that lay before him he endured the cross, despising its shame, and has taken his seat at the right of the throne of God. 3 Consider how he endured such opposition from sinners, in order that you may not grow weary and lose heart. 4 In your struggle against sin you have not yet resisted to the point of shedding blood. 5 You have also forgotten the exhortation addressed to you as sons:

"My son, do not disdain the discipline of the Lord
    or lose heart when reproved by him;
6 for whom the Lord loves, he disciplines;
    he scourges every son he acknowledges."

7 Endure your trials as "discipline"; God treats you as sons. For what "son" is there whom his father does not discipline? 8 If you are without discipline, in which all have shared, you are not sons but bastards. 9 Besides this, we have had our earthly fathers to discipline us, and we respected them. Should we not [then] submit all the more to the Father of spirits and live? 10 They disciplined us for a short time as seemed right to them, but he does so for our benefit, in order that we may share his holiness. 11 At the time, all discipline seems a cause not for joy but for pain, yet later it brings the peaceful fruit of righteousness to those who are trained by it.

12 So strengthen your drooping hands and your weak knees. 13 Make straight paths for your feet, that what is lame may not be dislocated but healed.

14 Strive for peace with everyone, and for that holiness without which no one will see the Lord. 15 See to it that no one be deprived of the grace of God, that no bitter root spring up and cause trouble, through which many may become defiled, 16 that no one be an immoral or profane person like Esau, who sold his birthright for a single meal. 17 For you know that later, when he wanted to inherit his father's blessing, he was rejected because he found no opportunity to change his mind, even though he sought the blessing with tears.

18 You have not approached that which could be touched and a blazing fire and gloomy darkness and storm 19 and a trumpet blast and a voice speaking words such that those who heard begged that no message be further addressed to them, 20 for they could not bear to hear the command: "If

battle. They were weak people who were given strength to be brave in war and drive back foreign invaders. 35 Some returned to their wives from the dead by resurrection; and others submitted to torture, refusing release so that they would rise again to a better life. 36 Some had to bear being pilloried and flogged, or even chained up in prison. 37 They were stoned, or sawn in half,*e* or killed by the sword; they were homeless, and wore only the skins of sheep and goats; they were in want and hardship, and maltreated. 38 They were too good for the world and they wandered in deserts and mountains and in caves and ravines. 39 These all won acknowledgement through their faith, but they did not receive what was promised, 40 since God had made provision for us to have something better, and they were not to reach perfection except with us.

12 With so many witnesses in a great cloud all around us, we too, then, should throw off everything that weighs us down and the sin that clings so closely, and with perseverance keep running in the race which lies ahead of us. 2 Let us keep our eyes fixed on Jesus, who leads us in our faith and brings it to perfection: for the sake of the joy which lay ahead of him, he endured the cross, disregarding the shame of it, and *has taken his seat at the right* of God's throne. 3 Think of the way he persevered against such opposition from sinners and then you will not lose heart and come to grief. 4 In the fight against sin, you have not yet had to keep fighting to the point of bloodshed.

5 Have you forgotten that encouraging text in which you are addressed as sons?

My son, do not scorn correction from the Lord,
    do not resent his training,
6 *for the Lord trains those he loves,*
    and chastises every son he accepts. f

7 Perseverance is part of your *training*; God is treating you as his *sons*. Has there ever been any *son* whose father did not *train* him? 8 If you were not getting this training, as all of you are, then you would be not *sons* but bastards. 9 Besides, we have all had our human fathers who punished us, and we respected them for it; all the more readily ought we to submit to the Father of spirits, and so earn life. 10 Our human fathers were training us for a short life and according to their own lights; but he does it all for our own good, so that we may share his own holiness. 11 Of course, any discipline is at the time a matter for grief, not joy; but later, in those who have undergone it, it bears fruit in peace and uprightness. 12 So *steady all weary hands and trembling kneesg* 13 and make your crooked paths straight; then the injured limb will not be maimed, it will get better instead.

14 *Seek peaceh* with all people, and the holiness without which no one can ever see the Lord. 15 Be careful that no one is deprived of the grace of God and that no *root of bitterness should begin to grow and make trouble*;*i* this can poison a large number. 16 And be careful that there is no immoral person, or anyone worldly minded like Esau, *who sold his birthright j* for one single meal. 17 As you know, when he wanted to obtain the blessing afterwards, he was rejected and, though he pleaded for it with tears, he could find no way of reversing the decision.

18 What you have come to is nothing known to the senses: not a *blazing fire,k* or *gloom* or *total darkness*, or a *storm*; 19 or *trumpet-blast* or the *sound of a voice speaking* which made everyone that heard it beg that no more should be said to them. 20 They could not bear the order that was given: *If*

---

e **11** Some apocryphal texts say that Isaiah was executed in this way by King Manasseh.   *f* **12** Pr 3:11–12.   *g* **12** Is 35:3.
h **12** Ps 34:14.   *i* **12** Dt 29:17.   *j* **12** Gn 25:33.
k **12** Ex 19–20, followed by Dt 9:19; Hg 2:6; Dt 4:24.

given, "If even an animal touches the mountain, it shall be stoned to death." 21 Indeed, so terrifying was the sight that Moses said, "I tremble with fear.") 22 But you have come to Mount Zion and to the city of the living God, the heavenly Jerusalem, and to innumerable angels in festal gathering, 23 and to the assembly*u* of the firstborn who are enrolled in heaven, and to God the judge of all, and to the spirits of the righteous made perfect, 24 and to Jesus, the mediator of a new covenant, and to the sprinkled blood that speaks a better word than the blood of Abel.

25 See that you do not refuse the one who is speaking; for if they did not escape when they refused the one who warned them on earth, how much less will we escape if we reject the one who warns from heaven! 26 At that time his voice shook the earth; but now he has promised, "Yet once more I will shake not only the earth but also the heaven." 27 This phrase, "Yet once more," indicates the removal of what is shaken — that is, created things — so that what cannot be shaken may remain. 28 Therefore, since we are receiving a kingdom that cannot be shaken, let us give thanks, by which we offer to God an acceptable worship with reverence and awe; 29 for indeed our God is a consuming fire.

13 Let mutual love continue. 2 Do not neglect to show hospitality to strangers, for by doing that some have entertained angels without knowing it. 3 Remember those who are in prison, as though you were in prison with them; those who are being tortured, as though you yourselves were being tortured.*v* 4 Let marriage be held in honor by all, and let the marriage bed be kept undefiled; for God will judge fornicators and adulterers. 5 Keep your lives free from the love of money, and be content with what you have; for he has said, "I will never leave you or forsake you." 6 So we can say with confidence,

"The Lord is my helper;
    I will not be afraid.
What can anyone do to me?"

7 Remember your leaders, those who spoke the word of God to you; consider the outcome of their way of life, and imitate their faith. 8 Jesus Christ is the same yesterday and today and forever. 9 Do not be carried away by all kinds of strange teachings; for it is well for the heart to be strengthened by grace, not by regulations about food,*w* which have not benefited those who observe them. 10 We have an altar from which those who officiate in the tent*x* have no right to eat. 11 For the bodies of those animals whose blood is brought into the sanctuary by the high priest as a sacrifice for sin are burned outside the camp. 12 Therefore Jesus also suffered outside the city gate in order to sanctify the people by his own blood. 13 Let us then go to him outside the camp and bear the abuse he endured. 14 For here we have no lasting city, but we are looking for the city that is to come. 15 Through him, then, let us continually offer a sacrifice of praise to God, that is, the fruit of lips that confess his name. 16 Do not neglect to do good and to share what you have, for such sacrifices are pleasing to God.

17 Obey your leaders and submit to them, for they are keeping watch over your souls and will give an account. Let them do this with joy and not with sighing — for that would be harmful to you.

18 Pray for us; we are sure that we have a clear conscience, desiring to act honorably in all things. 19 I urge you all the more to do this, so that I may be restored to you very soon.

mand, 'If even an animal touches the mountain, it must be stoned to death.' 21 So appalling was the sight that Moses said, 'I shudder with fear.'

22 No, you have come to Mount Zion, the city of the living God, the heavenly Jerusalem, to myriads of angels, 23 to the full concourse and assembly of the firstborn who are enrolled in heaven, and to God the judge of all, and to the spirits of good men made perfect, 24 and to Jesus the mediator of a new covenant, whose sprinkled blood has better things to say than the blood of Abel. 25 See that you do not refuse to hear the voice that speaks. Those who refused to hear the oracle speaking on earth found no escape; still less shall we escape if we reject him who speaks from heaven. 26 Then indeed his voice shook the earth, but now he has promised, 'Once again I will shake not only the earth, but the heavens also.' 27 The words 'once again' point to the removal of all created things, of all that is shaken, so that what cannot be shaken may remain. 28 The kingdom we are given is unshakeable; let us therefore give thanks to God for it, and so worship God as he would be worshipped, with reverence and awe; 29 for our God is a devouring fire.

13 NEVER cease to love your fellow-Christians. 2 Do not neglect to show hospitality; by doing this, some have entertained angels unawares. 3 Remember those in prison, as if you were there with them, and those who are being maltreated, for you are vulnerable too.

4 Marriage must be honoured by all, and the marriage bond be kept inviolate; for God's judgement will fall on fornicators and adulterers.

5 Do not live for money; be content with what you have, for God has said, 'I will never leave you or desert you.' 6 So we can take courage and say, 'The Lord is my helper, I will not fear; what can man do to me?'

7 Remember your leaders, who spoke God's message to you. Keep before you the outcome of their life and follow the example of their faith.

8 Jesus Christ is the same yesterday, today, and for ever. 9 So do not be swept off your course by all sorts of outlandish teachings; it is good that we should gain inner strength from the grace of God, and not from rules about food, which have never benefited those who observed them.

10 Our altar is one from which the priests of the sacred tent have no right to eat. 11 As you know, the animals whose blood is brought by the high priest into the sanctuary as a sin-offering have their bodies burnt outside the camp. 12 Therefore, to consecrate the people by his own blood, Jesus also suffered outside the gate. 13 Let us then go to him outside the camp, bearing the stigma that he bore. 14 For here we have no lasting city, but we are seekers after the city which is to come. 15 Through Jesus let us continually offer up to God a sacrifice of praise, that is, the tribute of lips which acknowledge his name.

16 Never neglect to show kindness and to share what you have with others; for such are the sacrifices which God approves.

17 Obey your leaders and submit to their authority; for they are tireless in their care for you, as those who must render an account. See that their work brings them happiness, not pain and grief, for that would be no advantage to you.

18 Pray for us. We are sure that our conscience is clear, and our desire is always to do what is right. 19 I specially ask for your prayers, so that I may be restored to you the sooner.

---

u Or angels, and to the festal gathering 23and assembly   v Gk were in the body   w Gk not by foods   x Or tabernacle

NEW AMERICAN BIBLE

even an animal touches the mountain, it shall be stoned."
21 Indeed, so fearful was the spectacle that Moses said, "I
am terrified and trembling." 22 No, you have approached
Mount Zion and the city of the living God, the heavenly
Jerusalem, and countless angels in festal gathering, 23 and
the assembly of the firstborn enrolled in heaven, and God
the judge of all, and the spirits of the just made perfect,
24 and Jesus, the mediator of a new covenant, and the sprinkled blood that speaks more eloquently than that of Abel.
25 See that you do not reject the one who speaks. For if
they did not escape when they refused the one who warned
them on earth, how much more in our case if we turn away
from the one who warns from heaven. 26 His voice shook
the earth at that time, but now he has promised, "I will once
more shake not only earth but heaven." 27 That phrase,
"once more," points to [the] removal of shaken, created
things, so that what is unshaken may remain. 28 Therefore,
we who are receiving the unshakable kingdom should have
gratitude, with which we should offer worship pleasing to
God in reverence and awe. 29 For our God is a consuming
fire.

13 Let mutual love continue. 2 Do not neglect hospitality, for through it some have unknowingly entertained angels. 3 Be mindful of prisoners as if sharing their
imprisonment, and of the ill-treated as of yourselves, for
you also are in the body. 4 Let marriage be honored among
all and the marriage bed be kept undefiled, for God will
judge the immoral and adulterers. 5 Let your life be free
from love of money but be content with what you have, for
he has said, "I will never forsake you or abandon you."
6 Thus we may say with confidence:

> "The Lord is my helper,
> [and] I will not be afraid.
> What can anyone do to me?"

7 Remember your leaders who spoke the word of God to
you. Consider the outcome of their way of life and imitate
their faith. 8 Jesus Christ is the same yesterday, today, and
forever.
9 Do not be carried away by all kinds of strange teaching.
It is good to have our hearts strengthened by grace and not
by foods, which do not benefit those who live by them.
10 We have an altar from which those who serve the tabernacle have no right to eat. 11 The bodies of the animals whose
blood the high priest brings into the sanctuary as a sin
offering are burned outside the camp. 12 Therefore, Jesus
also suffered outside the gate, to consecrate the people by
his own blood. 13 Let us then go to him outside the camp,
bearing the reproach that he bore. 14 For here we have no
lasting city, but we seek the one that is to come. 15 Through
him [then] let us continually offer God a sacrifice of praise,
that is, the fruit of lips that confess his name. 16 Do not
neglect to do good and to share what you have; God is
pleased by sacrifices of that kind.
17 Obey your leaders and defer to them, for they keep
watch over you and will have to give an account, that they
may fulfill their task with joy and not with sorrow, for that
would be of no advantage to you.
18 Pray for us, for we are confident that we have a clear
conscience, wishing to act rightly in every respect. 19 I especially ask for your prayers that I may be restored to you very
soon.

NEW JERUSALEM BIBLE

even a beast touches the mountain, it must be stoned.[l]
21 The whole scene was so terrible that Moses said, 'I am
afraid and trembling.' 22 But what you have come to is
Mount Zion and the city of the living God, the heavenly
Jerusalem where the millions of angels have gathered for
the festival, 23 with the whole Church of first-born sons,
enrolled as citizens of heaven. You have come to God himself, the supreme Judge, and to the spirits of the upright
who have been made perfect; 24 and to Jesus, the mediator
of a new covenant, and to purifying blood which pleads
more insistently than Abel's. 25 Make sure that you never
refuse to listen when he speaks. If the people who on earth
refused to listen to a warning could not escape their punishment, how shall we possibly escape if we turn away from
a voice that warns us from heaven? 26 That time his voice
made the earth shake, but now he has given us this promise:
I am going to shake the earth once more and not only the
earth but *heaven as well.*[m] 27 The words *once more* indicate
the removal of what is shaken, since these are created
things, so that what is not shaken remains. 28 We have been
given possession of an unshakeable kingdom. Let us therefore be grateful and use our gratitude to worship God in the
way that pleases him, in reverence and fear. 29 For our *God*
is a *consuming fire.*[n]

13 Continue to love each other like brothers, 2 and remember always to welcome strangers, for by doing
this, some people have entertained angels without knowing
it. 3 Keep in mind those who are in prison, as though you
were in prison with them; and those who are being badly
treated, since you too are in the body. 4 Marriage must be
honoured by all, and marriages must be kept undefiled,
because the sexually immoral and adulterers will come under God's judgement. 5 Put avarice out of your lives and be
content with whatever you have; God himself has said: *I
shall not fail you or desert you,*[o] 6 and so we can say with
confidence: *With the Lord on my side, I fear nothing: what
can human beings do to me?*[p]
7 Remember your leaders, who preached the word of God
to you, and as you reflect on the outcome of their lives, take
their faith as your model. 8 Jesus Christ is the same today as
he was yesterday and as he will be for ever. 9 Do not be led
astray by all sorts of strange doctrines: it is better to rely on
grace for inner strength than on food, which has done no
good to those who concentrate on it. 10 We have our own
altar from which those who serve the Tent have no right to
eat. 11 The bodies of the animals *whose blood is taken into
the sanctuary* by the high priest *for the rite of expiation are
burnt outside the camp,*[q] 12 and so Jesus too suffered outside the gate to sanctify the people with his own blood.
13 Let us go to him, then, *outside the camp*, and bear his
humiliation. 14 There is no permanent city for us here; we
are looking for the one which is yet to be. 15 Through him,
let us offer God an unending *sacrifice* of praise, the fruit of
the lips of those who acknowledge his name. 16 Keep doing
good works and sharing your resources, for these are the
kinds of sacrifice that please God.
17 Obey your leaders and give way to them; they watch
over your souls because they must give an account of them;
make this a joy for them to do, and not a grief—you yourselves would be the losers. 18 Pray for us; we are sure that
our own conscience is clear and we are certainly determined
to behave honourably in everything we do. 19 I ask you very
particularly to pray that I may come back to you all the
sooner.

[l] **12** Ex 19:12seq. [m] **12** Hg 2:6. [n] **12** Dt 4:24. [o] **13** Dt 31:6.
[p] **13** Ps 118:6 . [q] **13** Lv 16:27.

20 Now may the God of peace, who brought back from the dead our Lord Jesus, the great shepherd of the sheep, by the blood of the eternal covenant, 21 make you complete in everything good so that you may do his will, working among us *y* that which is pleasing in his sight, through Jesus Christ, to whom be the glory forever and ever. Amen.

22 I appeal to you, brothers and sisters,*z* bear with my word of exhortation, for I have written to you briefly. 23 I want you to know that our brother Timothy has been set free; and if he comes in time, he will be with me when I see you. 24 Greet all your leaders and all the saints. Those from Italy send you greetings. 25 Grace be with all of you.*a*

y Other ancient authorities read *you*   *z* Gk *brothers*   *a* Other ancient authorities add *Amen*

20 May the God of peace, who brought back from the dead our Lord Jesus, the great Shepherd of the sheep, through the blood of an eternal covenant, 21 make you perfect in all goodness so that you may do his will; and may he create in us what is pleasing to him, through Jesus Christ, to whom be glory for ever and ever! Amen.

22 I beg you, friends, bear with my appeal; for this is after all a short letter. 23 I have news for you: our friend Timothy has been released; and if he comes in time he will be with me when I see you.

24 Greet all your leaders and all God's people. Greetings to you from our Italian friends.

25 God's grace be with you all!

NEW AMERICAN BIBLE

20 May the God of peace, who brought up from the dead the great shepherd of the sheep by the blood of the eternal covenant, Jesus our Lord, 21 furnish you with all that is good, that you may do his will. May he carry out in you what is pleasing to him through Jesus Christ, to whom be glory forever [and ever]. Amen.

22 Brothers, I ask you to bear with this message of encouragement, for I have written to you rather briefly. 23 I must let you know that our brother Timothy has been set free. If he comes soon, I shall see you together with him. 24 Greetings to all your leaders and to all the holy ones. Those from Italy send you greetings. 25 Grace be with all of you.

NEW JERUSALEM BIBLE

20 I pray that the God of peace, *who brought back* from the dead our Lord Jesus, the great *Shepherd of the sheep, by the blood that sealed an eternal covenant,*r 21 may prepare you to do his will in every kind of good action; effecting in us all whatever is acceptable to himself through Jesus Christ, to whom be glory for ever and ever. Amen.

22 I urge you, brothers, to take these words of encouragement kindly; that is why I have written to you briefly.

23 I want you to know that our brother Timothy has been set free. If he arrives in time, he will be with me when I see you. 24 Greetings to all your leaders and to all God's holy people. God's holy people in Italy send you greetings. 25 Grace be with you all.

r 13 A combination of Is 63:11 with Ezk 34:23; 37:26.

THE LETTER OF
James

1 James, a servant*a* of God and of the Lord Jesus Christ,
To the twelve tribes in the Dispersion:
Greetings.

2 My brothers and sisters,*b* whenever you face trials of any kind, consider it nothing but joy, 3 because you know that the testing of your faith produces endurance; 4 and let endurance have its full effect, so that you may be mature and complete, lacking in nothing.

5 If any of you is lacking in wisdom, ask God, who gives to all generously and ungrudgingly, and it will be given you. 6 But ask in faith, never doubting, for the one who doubts is like a wave of the sea, driven and tossed by the wind; 7, 8 for the doubter, being double-minded and unstable in every way, must not expect to receive anything from the Lord.

9 Let the believer*c* who is lowly boast in being raised up, 10 and the rich in being brought low, because the rich will disappear like a flower in the field. 11 For the sun rises with its scorching heat and withers the field; its flower falls, and its beauty perishes. It is the same way with the rich; in the midst of a busy life, they will wither away.

12 Blessed is anyone who endures temptation. Such a one has stood the test and will receive the crown of life that the Lord*d* has promised to those who love him. 13 No one, when tempted, should say, "I am being tempted by God"; for God cannot be tempted by evil and he himself tempts no one. 14 But one is tempted by one's own desire, being lured and enticed by it; 15 then, when that desire has conceived, it gives birth to sin, and that sin, when it is fully grown, gives birth to death. 16 Do not be deceived, my beloved.*e*

17 Every generous act of giving, with every perfect gift, is from above, coming down from the Father of lights, with whom there is no variation or shadow due to change.*f* 18 In fulfillment of his own purpose he gave us birth by the word of truth, so that we would become a kind of first fruits of his creatures.

19 You must understand this, my beloved:*e* let everyone be quick to listen, slow to speak, slow to anger; 20 for your anger does not produce God's righteousness. 21 Therefore rid yourselves of all sordidness and rank growth of wickedness, and welcome with meekness the implanted word that has the power to save your souls.

22 But be doers of the word, and not merely hearers who deceive themselves. 23 For if any are hearers of the word and not doers, they are like those who look at themselves*g* in a mirror; 24 for they look at themselves and, on going away, immediately forget what they were like. 25 But those who look into the perfect law, the law of liberty, and persevere, being not hearers who forget but doers who act — they will be blessed in their doing.

26 If any think they are religious, and do not bridle their tongues but deceive their hearts, their religion is worthless. 27 Religion that is pure and undefiled before God, the Fa-

A LETTER OF
James

1 FROM James, a servant of God and the Lord Jesus Christ. Greetings to the twelve tribes dispersed throughout the world.

2 MY friends, whenever you have to face all sorts of trials, count yourselves supremely happy 3 in the knowledge that such testing of your faith makes for strength to endure. 4 Let endurance perfect its work in you that you may become perfected, sound throughout, lacking in nothing. 5 If any of you lacks wisdom, he should ask God and it will be given him, for God is a generous giver who neither grudges nor reproaches anyone. 6 But he who asks must ask in faith, with never a doubt in his mind; for the doubter is like a wave of the sea tossed hither and thither by the wind. 7 A man like that should not think he will receive anything from the Lord. 8 He is always in two minds and unstable in all he does.

9 The church member in humble circumstances does well to take pride in being exalted; 10 the wealthy member must find his pride in being brought low, for the rich man will disappear like a wild flower; 11 once the sun is up with its scorching heat, it parches the plant, its flower withers, and what was lovely to look at is lost for ever. So shall the rich man fade away as he goes about his business.

12 Happy is the man who stands up to trial! Having passed that test he will receive in reward the life which God has promised to those who love him. 13 No one when tempted should say, 'I am being tempted by God'; for God cannot be tempted by evil and does not himself tempt anyone. 14 Temptation comes when anyone is lured and dragged away by his own desires; 15 then desire conceives and gives birth to sin, and sin when it is full-grown breeds death.

16 Make no mistake, my dear friends. 17 Every good and generous action and every perfect gift come from above, from the Father who created the lights of heaven. With him there is no variation, no play of passing shadows. 18 Of his own choice, he brought us to birth by the word of truth to be a kind of firstfruits of his creation.

19 Of that you may be certain, my dear friends. But everyone should be quick to listen, slow to speak, and slow to be angry. 20 For human anger does not promote God's justice. 21 Then discard everything sordid, and every wicked excess, and meekly accept the message planted in your hearts, with its power to save you.

22 Only be sure you act on the message, and do not merely listen and so deceive yourselves. 23 Anyone who listens to the message but does not act on it is like somebody looking in a mirror at the face nature gave him; 24 he glances at himself and goes his way, and promptly forgets what he looked like. 25 But he who looks into the perfect law, the law that makes us free, and does not turn away, remembers what he hears; he acts on it, and by so acting he will find happiness.

26 If anyone thinks he is religious but does not bridle his tongue, he is deceiving himself; that man's religion is futile. 27 A pure and faultless religion in the sight of God the Father

---

a Gk *slave*   *b* Gk *brothers*   *c* Gk *brother*   *d* Gk *he; other ancient authorities read God*   *e* Gk *my beloved brothers*   *f* Other ancient authorities read *variation due to a shadow of turning*   *g* Gk *at the face of his birth*

1:17 **no variation . . . shadows:** *some witnesses read* no variation, or shadow caused by change.   1:21 **Then discard . . . and meekly accept:** *or* Then meekly discard . . . and accept.

The Letter of James

THE LETTER OF James

1 James, a slave of God and of the Lord Jesus Christ, to the twelve tribes in the dispersion, greetings.

2 Consider it all joy, my brothers, when you encounter various trials, 3 for you know that the testing of your faith produces perseverance. 4 And let perseverance be perfect, so that you may be perfect and complete, lacking in nothing. 5 But if any of you lacks wisdom, he should ask God who gives to all generously and ungrudgingly, and he will be given it. 6 But he should ask in faith, not doubting, for the one who doubts is like a wave of the sea that is driven and tossed about by the wind. 7 For that person must not suppose that he will receive anything from the Lord, 8 since he is a man of two minds, unstable in all his ways.

9 The brother in lowly circumstances should take pride in his high standing, 10 and the rich one in his lowliness, for he will pass away "like the flower of the field." 11 For the sun comes up with its scorching heat and dries up the grass, its flower droops, and the beauty of its appearance vanishes. So will the rich person fade away in the midst of his pursuits.

12 Blessed is the man who perseveres in temptation, for when he has been proved he will receive the crown of life that he promised to those who love him. 13 No one experiencing temptation should say, "I am being tempted by God"; for God is not subject to temptation to evil, and he himself tempts no one. 14 Rather, each person is tempted when he is lured and enticed by his own desire. 15 Then desire conceives and brings forth sin, and when sin reaches maturity it gives birth to death.

16 Do not be deceived, my beloved brothers: 17 all good giving and every perfect gift is from above, coming down from the Father of lights, with whom there is no alteration or shadow caused by change. 18 He willed to give us birth by the word of truth that we may be a kind of firstfruits of his creatures.

19 Know this, my dear brothers: everyone should be quick to hear, slow to speak, slow to wrath, 20 for the wrath of a man does not accomplish the righteousness of God. 21 Therefore, put away all filth and evil excess and humbly welcome the word that has been planted in you and is able to save your souls.

22 Be doers of the word and not hearers only, deluding yourselves. 23 For if anyone is a hearer of the word and not a doer, he is like a man who looks at his own face in a mirror. 24 He sees himself, then goes off and promptly forgets what he looked like. 25 But the one who peers into the perfect law of freedom and perseveres, and is not a hearer who forgets but a doer who acts, such a one shall be blessed in what he does.

26 If anyone thinks he is religious and does not bridle his tongue but deceives his heart, his religion is vain. 27 Religion that is pure and undefiled before God and the Father is

1 From James, servant of God and of the Lord Jesus Christ. Greetings to the twelve tribes of the Dispersion. *a*

2 My brothers, consider it a great joy when trials of many kinds come upon you, 3 for you well know that the testing of your faith produces perseverance, and 4 perseverance must complete its work so that you will become fully developed, complete, not deficient in any way.

5 Any of you who lacks wisdom must ask God, who gives to all generously and without scolding; it will be given. 6 But the prayer must be made with faith, and no trace of doubt, because a person who has doubts is like the waves thrown up in the sea by the buffeting of the wind. 7 That sort of person, in two minds, 8 inconsistent in every activity, must not expect to receive anything from the Lord.

9 It is right that the brother in humble circumstances should glory in being lifted up, 10 and the rich in being brought low. For the rich will last no longer than *the wild flower*; 11 the scorching sun comes up, and the *grass withers*, its *flower falls*, *b* its beauty is lost. It is the same with the rich: in the middle of a busy life, the rich will wither.

12 *Blessed is anyone who perseveres* *c* when trials come. Such a person is of proven worth and will win the prize of life, the crown that the Lord has promised to those who love him.

13 Never, when you are being put to the test, say, 'God is tempting me'; God cannot be tempted by evil, and he does not put anybody to the test. 14 Everyone is put to the test by being attracted and seduced by that person's own wrong desire. 15 Then the desire conceives and gives birth to sin, and when sin reaches full growth, it gives birth to death.

16 Make no mistake about this, my dear brothers: 17 all that is good, all that is perfect, is given us from above; it comes down from the Father of all light; with him there is no such thing as alteration, no shadow caused by change. 18 By his own choice he gave birth to us by the message of the truth so that we should be a sort of first-fruits of all his creation.

19 Remember this, my dear brothers: everyone should be *quick to listen* *d* but *slow* to speak and slow to human anger; 20 God's saving justice is never served by human anger; 21 so do away with all impurities and remnants of evil. Humbly welcome the Word which has been planted in you and can save your souls.

22 But you must do what the Word tells you and not just listen to it and deceive yourselves. 23 Anyone who listens to the Word and takes no action is like someone who looks at his own features in a mirror and, 24 once he has seen what he looks like, goes off and immediately forgets it. 25 But anyone who looks steadily at the perfect law of freedom and keeps to it — not listening and forgetting, but putting it into practice — will be blessed in every undertaking.

26 Nobody who fails to keep a tight rein on the tongue can claim to be religious; this is mere self-deception; that person's religion is worthless. 27 Pure, unspoilt religion, in the eyes of God our Father, is this: coming to the help of

---

a 1 Properly, Jews scattered in the gentile world, successors of the twelve tribes. *b* 1 Is 40:6–7. *c* 1 Dn 12:2. *d* 1 Si 5:11.

NEW REVISED STANDARD VERSION

REVISED ENGLISH BIBLE

ther, is this: to care for orphans and widows in their distress, and to keep oneself unstained by the world.

2 My brothers and sisters,[h] do you with your acts of favoritism really believe in our glorious Lord Jesus Christ?[i] 2 For if a person with gold rings and in fine clothes comes into your assembly, and if a poor person in dirty clothes also comes in, 3 and if you take notice of the one wearing the fine clothes and say, "Have a seat here, please," while to the one who is poor you say, "Stand there," or, "Sit at my feet,"[j] 4 have you not made distinctions among yourselves, and become judges with evil thoughts? 5 Listen, my beloved brothers and sisters.[k] Has not God chosen the poor in the world to be rich in faith and to be heirs of the kingdom that he has promised to those who love him? 6 But you have dishonored the poor. Is it not the rich who oppress you? Is it not they who drag you into court? 7 Is it not they who blaspheme the excellent name that was invoked over you?

8 You do well if you really fulfill the royal law according to the scripture, "You shall love your neighbor as yourself." 9 But if you show partiality, you commit sin and are convicted by the law as transgressors. 10 For whoever keeps the whole law but fails in one point has become accountable for all of it. 11 For the one who said, "You shall not commit adultery," also said, "You shall not murder." Now if you do not commit adultery but if you murder, you have become a transgressor of the law. 12 So speak and so act as those who are to be judged by the law of liberty. 13 For judgment will be without mercy to anyone who has shown no mercy; mercy triumphs over judgment.

14 What good is it, my brothers and sisters,[k] if you say you have faith but do not have works? Can faith save you? 15 If a brother or sister is naked and lacks daily food, 16 and one of you says to them, "Go in peace; keep warm and eat your fill," and yet you do not supply their bodily needs, what is the good of that? 17 So faith by itself, if it has no works, is dead.

18 But someone will say, "You have faith and I have works." Show me your faith apart from your works, and I by my works will show you my faith. 19 You believe that God is one; you do well. Even the demons believe — and shudder. 20 Do you want to be shown, you senseless person, that faith apart from works is barren? 21 Was not our ancestor Abraham justified by works when he offered his son Isaac on the altar? 22 You see that faith was active along with his works, and faith was brought to completion by the works. 23 Thus the scripture was fulfilled that says, "Abraham believed God, and it was reckoned to him as righteousness," and he was called the friend of God. 24 You see that a person is justified by works and not by faith alone. 25 Likewise, was not Rahab the prostitute also justified by works when she welcomed the messengers and sent them out by another road? 26 For just as the body without the spirit is dead, so faith without works is also dead.

3 Not many of you should become teachers, my brothers and sisters,[k] for you know that we who teach will be judged with greater strictness. 2 For all of us make many mistakes. Anyone who makes no mistakes in speaking is perfect, able to keep the whole body in check with a bridle. 3 If we put bits into the mouths of horses to make them obey us, we guide their whole bodies. 4 Or look at ships: though

is this: to look after orphans and widows in trouble and to keep oneself untarnished by the world.

2 My friends, you believe in our Lord Jesus Christ who reigns in glory and you must always be impartial. 2 For instance, two visitors may enter your meeting, one a well-dressed man with gold rings, and the other a poor man in grimy clothes. 3 Suppose you pay special attention to the well-dressed man and say to him, 'Please take this seat,' while to the poor man you say, 'You stand over there, or sit here on the floor by my footstool,' 4 do you not see that you are discriminating among your members and judging by wrong standards? 5 Listen, my dear friends: has not God chosen those who are poor in the eyes of the world to be rich in faith and to possess the kingdom he has promised to those who love him? 6 And yet you have humiliated the poor man. Moreover, are not the rich your oppressors? Is it not they who drag you into court 7 and pour contempt on the honoured name by which God has claimed you?

8 If, however, you are observing the sovereign law laid down in scripture, 'Love your neighbour as yourself,' that is excellent. 9 But if you show partiality, you are committing a sin and you stand convicted by the law as offenders. 10 For if a man breaks just one commandment and keeps all the others, he is guilty of breaking all of them. 11 For he who said, 'You shall not commit adultery,' said also, 'You shall not commit murder.' If you commit murder you are a breaker of the law, even if you do not commit adultery as well. 12 Always speak and act as men who are to be judged under a law which makes them free. 13 In that judgement there will be no mercy for the man who has shown none. Mercy triumphs over judgement.

14 What good is it, my friends, for someone to say he has faith when his actions do nothing to show it? Can that faith save him? 15 Suppose a fellow-Christian, whether man or woman, is in rags with not enough food for the day, 16 and one of you says, 'Goodbye, keep warm, and have a good meal,' but does nothing to supply their bodily needs, what good is that? 17 So with faith; if it does not lead to action, it is by itself a lifeless thing.

18 But someone may say: 'One chooses faith, another action.' To which I reply: 'Show me this faith you speak of with no actions to prove it, while I by my actions will prove to you my faith.' 19 You have faith and believe that there is one God. Excellent! Even demons have faith like that, and it makes them tremble. 20 Do you have to be told, you fool, that faith divorced from action is futile? 21 Was it not by his action, in offering his son Isaac upon the altar, that our father Abraham was justified? 22 Surely you can see faith was at work in his actions, and by these actions his faith was perfected? 23 Here was fulfilment of the words of scripture: 'Abraham put his faith in God, and that faith was counted to him as righteousness,' and he was called 'God's friend'. 24 You see then it is by action and not by faith alone that a man is justified. 25 The same is true also of the prostitute Rahab. Was she not justified by her action in welcoming the messengers into her house and sending them away by a different route? 26 As the body is dead when there is no breath left in it, so faith divorced from action is dead.

3 My friends, not many of you should become teachers, for you may be certain that we who teach will ourselves face severer judgement. 2 All of us go wrong again and again; a man who never says anything wrong is perfect and is capable of controlling every part of his body. 3 When we put a bit into a horse's mouth to make it obey our will, we can direct the whole animal. 4 Or think of a ship: large

---

[h] Gk My brothers [i] Or hold the faith of our glorious Lord Jesus Christ without acts of favoritism [j] Gk Sit under my footstool
[k] Gk brothers

2:3 Please . . . seat: or Do take this comfortable seat.

this: to care for orphans and widows in their affliction and to keep oneself unstained by the world.

2 My brothers, show no partiality as you adhere to the faith in our glorious Lord Jesus Christ. 2 For if a man with gold rings on his fingers and in fine clothes comes into your assembly, and a poor person in shabby clothes also comes in, 3 and you pay attention to the one wearing the fine clothes and say, "Sit here, please," while you say to the poor one, "Stand there," or "Sit at my feet," 4 have you not made distinctions among yourselves and become judges with evil designs?

5 Listen, my beloved brothers. Did not God choose those who are poor in the world to be rich in faith and heirs of the kingdom that he promised to those who love him? 6 But you dishonored the poor person. Are not the rich oppressing you? And do they themselves not haul you off to court? 7 Is it not they who blaspheme the noble name that was invoked over you? 8 However, if you fulfill the royal law according to the scripture, "You shall love your neighbor as yourself," you are doing well. 9 But if you show partiality, you commit sin, and are convicted by the law as transgressors. 10 For whoever keeps the whole law, but falls short in one particular, has become guilty in respect to all of it. 11 For he who said, "You shall not commit adultery," also said, "You shall not kill." Even if you do not commit adultery but kill, you have become a transgressor of the law. 12 So speak and so act as people who will be judged by the law of freedom. 13 For the judgment is merciless to one who has not shown mercy; mercy triumphs over judgment.

14 What good is it, my brothers, if someone says he has faith but does not have works? Can that faith save him? 15 If a brother or sister has nothing to wear and has no food for the day, 16 and one of you says to them, "Go in peace, keep warm, and eat well," but you do not give them the necessities of the body, what good is it? 17 So also faith of itself, if it does not have works, is dead.

18 Indeed someone might say, "You have faith and I have works." Demonstrate your faith to me without works, and I will demonstrate my faith to you from my works. 19 You believe that God is one. You do well. Even the demons believe that and tremble. 20 Do you want proof, you ignoramus, that faith without works is useless? 21 Was not Abraham our father justified by works when he offered his son Isaac upon the altar? 22 You see that faith was active along with his works, and faith was completed by the works. 23 Thus the scripture was fulfilled that says, "Abraham believed God, and it was credited to him as righteousness," and he was called "the friend of God." 24 See how a person is justified by works and not by faith alone. 25 And in the same way, was not Rahab the harlot also justified by works when she welcomed the messengers and sent them out by a different route? 26 For just as a body without a spirit is dead, so also faith without works is dead.

3 Not many of you should become teachers, my brothers, for you realize that we will be judged more strictly, 2 for we all fall short in many respects. If anyone does not fall short in speech, he is a perfect man, able to bridle his whole body also. 3 If we put bits into the mouths of horses to make them obey us, we also guide their whole bodies. 4 It is the same with ships: even though they are so

orphans and widows in their hardships, and keeping oneself uncontaminated by the world.

2 My brothers, do not let class distinction enter into your faith in Jesus Christ, our glorified Lord. 2 Now suppose a man comes into your synagogue, well-dressed and with a gold ring on, and at the same time a poor man comes in, in shabby clothes, 3 and you take notice of the well-dressed man, and say, 'Come this way to the best seats'; then you tell the poor man, 'Stand over there' or 'You can sit on the floor by my foot-rest.' 4 In making this distinction among yourselves have you not used a corrupt standard?

5 Listen, my dear brothers: it was those who were poor according to the world that God chose, to be rich in faith and to be the heirs to the kingdom which he promised to those who love him. 6 You, on the other hand, have dishonoured the poor. Is it not the rich who lord it over you? 7 Are not they the ones who drag you into court, who insult the honourable name which has been pronounced over you? 8 Well, the right thing to do is to keep the supreme Law of scripture: *you will love your neighbour as yourself;e* 9 but as soon as you make class distinctions, you are committing sin and under condemnation for breaking the Law.

10 You see, anyone who keeps the whole of the Law but trips up on a single point, is still guilty of breaking it all. 11 He who said, '*You must not commit adultery*' said also, '*You must not kill.'f* Now if you commit murder, you need not commit adultery as well to become a breaker of the Law. 12 Talk and behave like people who are going to be judged by the law of freedom. 13 Whoever acts without mercy will be judged without mercy but mercy can afford to laugh at judgement.

14 How does it help, my brothers, when someone who has never done a single good act claims to have faith? Will that faith bring salvation? 15 If one of the brothers or one of the sisters is in need of clothes and has not enough food to live on, 16 and one of you says to them, 'I wish you well; keep yourself warm and eat plenty,' without giving them these bare necessities of life, then what good is that? 17 In the same way faith, if good deeds do not go with it, is quite dead.

18 But someone may say: So you have faith and I have good deeds? Show me this faith of yours without deeds, then! It is by my deeds that I will show you my faith. 19 You believe in the one God — that is creditable enough, but even the demons have the same belief, and they tremble with fear. 20 Fool! Would you not like to know that faith without deeds is useless? 21 Was not Abraham our father justified by his deed, because he *offered his son Isaac on the altar?g* 22 So you can see that his faith was working together with his deeds; his faith became perfect by what he did. 23 In this way the scripture was fulfilled: *Abraham put his faith in God, and this was considered as making him upright;h* and he received the name 'friend of God'.

24 You see now that it is by deeds, and not only by believing, that someone is justified. 25 There is another example of the same kind: Rahab the prostitute,*i* was she not justified by her deeds because she welcomed the messengers and showed them a different way to leave? 26 As a body without a spirit is dead, so is faith without deeds.

3 Only a few of you, my brothers, should be teachers, bearing in mind that we shall receive a stricter judgement. 2 For we all trip up in many ways.

Someone who does not trip up in speech has reached perfection and is able to keep the whole body on a tight rein. 3 Once we put a bit in the horse's mouth, to make it do what we want, we have the whole animal under our control. 4 Or

e **2** Lv 19:18.   *f* **2** Ex 20:3, 14.   *g* **2** Gn 22:9.   *h* **2** Gn 15:6.
i **2** Jos 2:1seq.

they are so large that it takes strong winds to drive them, yet they are guided by a very small rudder wherever the will of the pilot directs. 5 So also the tongue is a small member, yet it boasts of great exploits.

How great a forest is set ablaze by a small fire! 6 And the tongue is a fire. The tongue is placed among our members as a world of iniquity; it stains the whole body, sets on fire the cycle of nature,*l* and is itself set on fire by hell.*m* 7 For every species of beast and bird, of reptile and sea creature, can be tamed and has been tamed by the human species, 8 but no one can tame the tongue — a restless evil, full of deadly poison. 9 With it we bless the Lord and Father, and with it we curse those who are made in the likeness of God. 10 From the same mouth come blessing and cursing. My brothers and sisters,*n* this ought not to be so. 11 Does a spring pour forth from the same opening both fresh and brackish water? 12 Can a fig tree, my brothers and sisters,*o* yield olives, or a grapevine figs? No more can salt water yield fresh.

13 Who is wise and understanding among you? Show by your good life that your works are done with gentleness born of wisdom. 14 But if you have bitter envy and selfish ambition in your hearts, do not be boastful and false to the truth. 15 Such wisdom does not come down from above, but is earthly, unspiritual, devilish. 16 For where there is envy and selfish ambition, there will also be disorder and wickedness of every kind. 17 But the wisdom from above is first pure, then peaceable, gentle, willing to yield, full of mercy and good fruits, without a trace of partiality or hypocrisy. 18 And a harvest of righteousness is sown in peace for*p* those who make peace.

4 Those conflicts and disputes among you, where do they come from? Do they not come from your cravings that are at war within you? 2 You want something and do not have it; so you commit murder. And you covet*q* something and cannot obtain it; so you engage in disputes and conflicts. You do not have, because you do not ask. 3 You ask and do not receive, because you ask wrongly, in order to spend what you get on your pleasures. 4 Adulterers! Do you not know that friendship with the world is enmity with God? Therefore whoever wishes to be a friend of the world becomes an enemy of God. 5 Or do you suppose that it is for nothing that the scripture says, "God*r* yearns jealously for the spirit that he has made to dwell in us"? 6 But he gives all the more grace; therefore it says,

"God opposes the proud,
    but gives grace to the humble."
7 Submit yourselves therefore to God. Resist the devil, and he will flee from you. 8 Draw near to God, and he will draw near to you. Cleanse your hands, you sinners, and purify your hearts, you double-minded. 9 Lament and mourn and weep. Let your laughter be turned into mourning and your joy into dejection. 10 Humble yourselves before the Lord, and he will exalt you.

11 Do not speak evil against one another, brothers and sisters.*s* Whoever speaks evil against another or judges another, speaks evil against the law and judges the law; but if you judge the law, you are not a doer of the law but a judge. 12 There is one lawgiver and judge who is able to save and to destroy. So who, then, are you to judge your neighbor?

13 Come now, you who say, "Today or tomorrow we will go to such and such a town and spend a year there, doing business and making money." 14 Yet you do not even

though it may be and driven by gales, it can be steered by a very small rudder on whatever course the helmsman chooses. 5 So with the tongue; it is small, but its pretensions are great.

What a vast amount of timber can be set ablaze by the tiniest spark! 6 And the tongue is a fire, representing in our body the whole wicked world. It pollutes our whole being, it sets the whole course of our existence alight, and its flames are fed by hell. 7 Beasts and birds of every kind, creatures that crawl on the ground or swim in the sea, can be subdued and have been subdued by man; 8 but no one can subdue the tongue. It is an evil thing, restless and charged with deadly venom. 9 We use it to praise our Lord and Father; then we use it to invoke curses on our fellow-men, though they are made in God's likeness. 10 Out of the same mouth come praise and curses. This should not be so, my friends. 11 Does a fountain flow with both fresh and brackish water from the same outlet? 12 My friends, can a fig tree produce olives, or a grape vine produce figs? No more can salt water produce fresh.

13 Which of you is wise or learned? Let him give practical proof of it by his right conduct, with the modesty that comes of wisdom. 14 But if you are harbouring bitter jealousy and the spirit of rivalry in your hearts, stop making false claims in defiance of the truth. 15 This is not the wisdom that comes from above; it is earth-bound, sensual, demonic. 16 For with jealousy and rivalry come disorder and the practice of every kind of evil. 17 But the wisdom from above is in the first place pure; and then peace-loving, considerate, and open-minded; it is straightforward and sincere, rich in compassion and in deeds of kindness that are its fruit. 18 Peace is the seed-bed of righteousness, and the peacemakers will reap its harvest.

4 What causes fighting and quarrels among you? Is not their origin the appetites that war in your bodies? 2 You want what you cannot have, so you murder; you are envious, and cannot attain your ambition, so you quarrel and fight. You do not get what you want, because you do not pray for it. 3 Or, if you do, your requests are not granted, because you pray from wrong motives, in order to squander what you get on your pleasures. 4 Unfaithful creatures! Surely you know that love of the world means enmity to God? Whoever chooses to be the world's friend makes himself God's enemy. 5 Or do you suppose that scripture has no point when it says that the spirit which God implanted in us is filled with envious longings? 6 But the grace he gives is stronger; thus scripture says, 'God opposes the arrogant and gives grace to the humble.' 7 Submit then to God. Stand up to the devil, and he will turn and run. 8 Come close to God, and he will draw close to you. Sinners, make your hands clean; you whose motives are mixed, see that your hearts are pure. 9 Be sorrowful, mourn, and weep. Turn your laughter into mourning and your gaiety into gloom. 10 Humble yourselves before the Lord, and he will exalt you.

11 Friends, you must never speak ill of one another. He who speaks ill of a brother or passes judgement on him speaks ill of the law and judges the law. But if you judge the law, you are not keeping it but sitting in judgement upon it. 12 There is only one lawgiver and judge: he who is able to save life or destroy it. So who are you to judge your neighbour?

13 Now a word with all who say, 'Today or the next day we will go off to such and such a town and spend a year there trading and making money.' 14 Yet you have no idea what

l Or wheel of birth   *m* Gk Gehenna   *n* Gk My brothers
o Gk my brothers   *p* Or by   *q* Or you murder and you covet
r Gk He   *s* Gk brothers

large and driven by fierce winds, they are steered by a very small rudder wherever the pilot's inclination wishes. 5 In the same way the tongue is a small member and yet has great pretensions.

Consider how small a fire can set a huge forest ablaze. 6 The tongue is also a fire. It exists among our members as a world of malice, defiling the whole body and setting the entire course of our lives on fire, itself set on fire by Gehenna. 7 For every kind of beast and bird, of reptile and sea creature, can be tamed and has been tamed by the human species, 8 but no human being can tame the tongue. It is a restless evil, full of deadly poison. 9 With it we bless the Lord and Father, and with it we curse human beings who are made in the likeness of God. 10 From the same mouth come blessing and cursing. This need not be so, my brothers. 11 Does a spring gush forth from the same opening both pure and brackish water? 12 Can a fig tree, my brothers, produce olives, or a grapevine figs? Neither can salt water yield fresh.

13 Who among you is wise and understanding? Let him show his works by a good life in the humility that comes from wisdom. 14 But if you have bitter jealousy and selfish ambition in your hearts, do not boast and be false to the truth. 15 Wisdom of this kind does not come down from above but is earthly, unspiritual, demonic. 16 For where jealousy and selfish ambition exist, there is disorder and every foul practice. 17 But the wisdom from above is first of all pure, then peaceable, gentle, compliant, full of mercy and good fruits, without inconstancy or insincerity. 18 And the fruit of righteousness is sown in peace for those who cultivate peace.

4 Where do the wars and where do the conflicts among you come from? Is it not from your passions that make war within your members? 2 You covet but do not possess. You kill and envy but you cannot obtain; you fight and wage war. You do not possess because you do not ask. 3 You ask but do not receive, because you ask wrongly, to spend it on your passions. 4 Adulterers! Do you not know that to be a lover of the world means enmity with God? Therefore, whoever wants to be a lover of the world makes himself an enemy of God. 5 Or do you suppose that the scripture speaks without meaning when it says, "The spirit that he has made to dwell in us tends toward jealousy"? 6 But he bestows a greater grace; therefore, it says:

"God resists the proud,
but gives grace to the humble."

7 So submit yourselves to God. Resist the devil, and he will flee from you. 8 Draw near to God, and he will draw near to you. Cleanse your hands, you sinners, and purify your hearts, you of two minds. 9 Begin to lament, to mourn, to weep. Let your laughter be turned into mourning and your joy into dejection. 10 Humble yourselves before the Lord and he will exalt you.

11 Do not speak evil of one another, brothers. Whoever speaks evil of a brother or judges his brother speaks evil of the law and judges the law. If you judge the law, you are not a doer of the law but a judge. 12 There is one lawgiver and judge who is able to save or to destroy. Who then are you to judge your neighbor?

13 Come now, you who say, "Today or tomorrow we shall go into such and such a town, spend a year there doing business, and make a profit" — 14 you have no idea what

think of ships: no matter how big they are, even if a gale is driving them, they are directed by a tiny rudder wherever the whim of the helmsman decides. 5 So the tongue is only a tiny part of the body, but its boasts are great. Think how small a flame can set fire to a huge forest; 6 The tongue is a flame too. Among all the parts of the body, the tongue is a whole wicked world: it infects the whole body; catching fire itself from hell, it sets fire to the whole wheel of creation. 7 Wild animals and birds, reptiles and fish of every kind can all be tamed, and have been tamed, by humans; 8 but nobody can tame the tongue — it is a pest that will not keep still, full of deadly poison. 9 We use it to bless the Lord and Father, but we also use it to curse people who are made in God's image: 10 the blessing and curse come out of the same mouth. My brothers, this must be wrong — 11 does any water supply give a flow of fresh water and salt water out of the same pipe? 12 Can a fig tree yield olives, my brothers, or a vine yield figs? No more can sea water yield fresh water.

13 Anyone who is wise or understanding among you should from a good life give evidence of deeds done in the gentleness of wisdom. 14 But if at heart you have the bitterness of jealousy, or selfish ambition, do not be boastful or hide the truth with lies; 15 this is not the wisdom that comes from above, but earthly, human and devilish. 16 Wherever there are jealousy and ambition, there are also disharmony and wickedness of every kind; 17 whereas the wisdom that comes down from above is essentially something pure; it is also peaceable, kindly and considerate; it is full of mercy and shows itself by doing good; nor is there any trace of partiality or hypocrisy in it. 18 The peace sown by peacemakers brings a harvest of justice.

4 Where do these wars and battles between yourselves first start? Is it not precisely in the desires fighting inside your own selves? 2 You want something and you lack it; so you kill. You have an ambition that you cannot satisfy; so you fight to get your way by force. It is because you do not pray that you do not receive; 3 when you do pray and do not receive, it is because you prayed wrongly, wanting to indulge your passions.

4 Adulterers! Do you not realise that love for the world is hatred for God? Anyone who chooses the world for a friend is constituted an enemy of God. 5 Can you not see the point of the saying in scripture, 'The longing of the spirit he sent to dwell in us is a jealous longing.'? 6 But he has given us an even greater grace, as scripture says: j God opposes the proud but he accords his favour to the humble. 7 Give in to God, then; resist the devil, and he will run away from you. 8 The nearer you go to God, the nearer God will come to you. Clean your hands, you sinners, and clear your minds, you waverers. 9 Appreciate your wretchedness, and weep for it in misery. Your laughter must be turned to grief, your happiness to gloom. 10 Humble yourselves before the Lord and he will lift you up.

11 Brothers, do not slander one another. Anyone who slanders a brother, or condemns one, is speaking against the Law and condemning the Law. But if you condemn the Law, you have ceased to be subject to it and become a judge over it.

12 There is only one lawgiver and he is the only judge and has the power to save or to destroy. Who are you to give a verdict on your neighbour?

13 Well now, you who say, 'Today or tomorrow we are off to this or that town; we are going to spend a year there, trading, and make some money.' 14 You never know what

j 4 Pr 3:34. The saying in v. 5 is not in the OT.

NEW REVISED STANDARD VERSION

know what tomorrow will bring. What is your life? For you are a mist that appears for a little while and then vanishes. 15 Instead you ought to say, "If the Lord wishes, we will live and do this or that." 16 As it is, you boast in your arrogance; all such boasting is evil. 17 Anyone, then, who knows the right thing to do and fails to do it, commits sin.

5 Come now, you rich people, weep and wail for the miseries that are coming to you. 2 Your riches have rotted, and your clothes are moth-eaten. 3 Your gold and silver have rusted, and their rust will be evidence against you, and it will eat your flesh like fire. You have laid up treasure*t* for the last days. 4 Listen! The wages of the laborers who mowed your fields, which you kept back by fraud, cry out, and the cries of the harvesters have reached the ears of the Lord of hosts. 5 You have lived on the earth in luxury and in pleasure; you have fattened your hearts in a day of slaughter. 6 You have condemned and murdered the righteous one, who does not resist you.

7 Be patient, therefore, beloved,*u* until the coming of the Lord. The farmer waits for the precious crop from the earth, being patient with it until it receives the early and the late rains. 8 You also must be patient. Strengthen your hearts, for the coming of the Lord is near.*v* 9 Beloved,*w* do not grumble against one another, so that you may not be judged. See, the Judge is standing at the doors! 10 As an example of suffering and patience, beloved,*u* take the prophets who spoke in the name of the Lord. 11 Indeed we call blessed those who showed endurance. You have heard of the endurance of Job, and you have seen the purpose of the Lord, how the Lord is compassionate and merciful.

12 Above all, my beloved,*u* do not swear, either by heaven or by earth or by any other oath, but let your "Yes" be yes and your "No" be no, so that you may not fall under condemnation.

13 Are any among you suffering? They should pray. Are any cheerful? They should sing songs of praise. 14 Are any among you sick? They should call for the elders of the church and have them pray over them, anointing them with oil in the name of the Lord. 15 The prayer of faith will save the sick, and the Lord will raise them up; and anyone who has committed sins will be forgiven. 16 Therefore confess your sins to one another, and pray for one another, so that you may be healed. The prayer of the righteous is powerful and effective. 17 Elijah was a human being like us, and he prayed fervently that it might not rain, and for three years and six months it did not rain on the earth. 18 Then he prayed again, and the heaven gave rain and the earth yielded its harvest.

19 My brothers and sisters,*x* if anyone among you wanders from the truth and is brought back by another, 20 you should know that whoever brings back a sinner from wandering will save the sinner's*y* soul from death and will cover a multitude of sins.

t Or will eat your flesh, since you have stored up fire
u Gk brothers   v Or is at hand   w Gk Brothers   x Gk My
brothers   y Gk his

REVISED ENGLISH BIBLE

tomorrow will bring. What is your life after all? You are no more than a mist, seen for a little while and then disappearing. 15 What you ought to say is: 'If it be the Lord's will, we shall live to do so and so.' 16 But instead, you boast and brag, and all such boasting is wrong. 17 What it comes to is that anyone who knows the right thing to do and does not do it is a sinner.

5 Next a word to you who are rich. Weep and wail over the miserable fate overtaking you: 2 your riches have rotted away; your fine clothes are moth-eaten; 3 your silver and gold have corroded, and their corrosion will be evidence against you and consume your flesh like fire. You have piled up wealth in an age that is near its close. 4 The wages you never paid to the men who mowed your fields are crying aloud against you, and the outcry of the reapers has reached the ears of the Lord of Hosts. 5 You have lived on the land in wanton luxury, gorging yourselves—and that on the day appointed for your slaughter. 6 You have condemned and murdered the innocent one, who offers no resistance.

7 YOU MUST be patient, my friends, until the Lord comes. Consider: the farmer looking for the precious crop from his land can only wait in patience until the early and late rains have fallen. 8 You too must be patient and stout-hearted, for the coming of the Lord is near. 9 My friends, do not blame your troubles on one another, or you will fall under judgement; and there at the door stands the Judge. 10 As a pattern of patience under ill-treatment, take the prophets who spoke in the name of the Lord. 11 We count those happy who stood firm. You have heard how Job stood firm, and you have seen how the Lord treated him in the end, for the Lord is merciful and compassionate.

12 ABOVE all things, my friends, do not use oaths, whether 'by heaven' or 'by earth' or by anything else. When you say 'Yes' or 'No', let it be plain Yes or No, for fear you draw down judgement on yourselves.

13 Is anyone among you in trouble? Let him pray. Is anyone in good heart? Let him sing praises. 14 Is one of you ill? Let him send for the elders of the church to pray over him and anoint him with oil in the name of the Lord; 15 the prayer offered in faith will heal the sick man, the Lord will restore him to health, and if he has committed sins they will be forgiven. 16 Therefore confess your sins to one another, and pray for one another, that you may be healed. A good man's prayer is very powerful and effective. 17 Elijah was a man just like us; yet when he prayed fervently that there should be no rain, the land had no rain for three and a half years; 18 when he prayed again, the rain poured down and the land bore crops once more.

19 My friends, if one of you strays from the truth and another succeeds in bringing him back, 20 you may be sure of this: the one who brings a sinner back from his erring ways will be rescuing a soul from death and cancelling a multitude of sins.

your life will be like tomorrow. You are a puff of smoke that appears briefly and then disappears. 15 Instead you should say, "If the Lord wills it, we shall live to do this or that." 16 But now you are boasting in your arrogance. All such boasting is evil. 17 So for one who knows the right thing to do and does not do it, it is a sin.

5 Come now, you rich, weep and wail over your impending miseries. 2 Your wealth has rotted away, your clothes have become moth-eaten, 3 your gold and silver have corroded, and that corrosion will be a testimony against you; it will devour your flesh like a fire. You have stored up treasure for the last days. 4 Behold, the wages you withheld from the workers who harvested your fields are crying aloud, and the cries of the harvesters have reached the ears of the Lord of hosts. 5 You have lived on earth in luxury and pleasure; you have fattened your hearts for the day of slaughter. 6 You have condemned; you have murdered the righteous one; he offers you no resistance.

7 Be patient, therefore, brothers, until the coming of the Lord. See how the farmer waits for the precious fruit of the earth, being patient with it until it receives the early and the late rains. 8 You too must be patient. Make your hearts firm, because the coming of the Lord is at hand. 9 Do not complain, brothers, about one another, that you may not be judged. Behold, the Judge is standing before the gates. 10 Take as an example of hardship and patience, brothers, the prophets who spoke in the name of the Lord. 11 Indeed we call blessed those who have persevered. You have heard of the perseverance of Job, and you have seen the purpose of the Lord, because "the Lord is compassionate and merciful."

12 But above all, my brothers, do not swear, either by heaven or by earth or with any other oath, but let your "Yes" mean "Yes" and your "No" mean "No," that you may not incur condemnation.

13 Is anyone among you suffering? He should pray. Is anyone in good spirits? He should sing praise. 14 Is anyone among you sick? He should summon the presbyters of the church, and they should pray over him and anoint [him] with oil in the name of the Lord, 15 and the prayer of faith will save the sick person, and the Lord will raise him up. If he has committed any sins, he will be forgiven.

16 Therefore, confess your sins to one another and pray for one another, that you may be healed. The fervent prayer of a righteous person is very powerful. 17 Elijah was a human being like us; yet he prayed earnestly that it might not rain, and for three years and six months it did not rain upon the land. 18 Then he prayed again, and the sky gave rain and the earth produced its fruit.

19 My brothers, if anyone among you should stray from the truth and someone bring him back, 20 he should know that whoever brings back a sinner from the error of his way will save his soul from death and will cover a multitude of sins.

will happen tomorrow: you are no more than a mist that appears for a little while and then disappears. 15 Instead of this, you should say, 'If it is the Lord's will, we shall still be alive to do this or that.' 16 But as it is, how boastful and loud-mouthed you are! Boasting of this kind is always wrong. 17 Everyone who knows what is the right thing to do and does not do it commits a sin.

5 Well now, you rich! Lament, weep for the miseries that are coming to you. 2 Your wealth is rotting, your clothes are all moth-eaten. 3 All your gold and your silver are corroding away, and the same corrosion will be a witness against you and eat into your body. It is like a fire which you have stored up for the final days. 4 Can you hear crying out against you the wages which you kept back from the labourers mowing your fields? The cries of the reapers have reached the ears of the Lord Sabaoth. 5 On earth you have had a life of comfort and luxury; in the time of slaughter you went on eating to your heart's content. 6 It was you who condemned the upright and killed them; they offered you no resistance.

7 Now be patient, brothers, until the Lord's coming. Think of a farmer: how patiently he waits for the precious fruit of the ground until it has had the autumn rains and the spring rains! 8 You too must be patient; do not lose heart, because the Lord's coming will be soon. 9 Do not make complaints against one another, brothers, so as not to be brought to judgement yourselves; the Judge is already to be seen waiting at the gates. 10 For your example, brothers, in patiently putting up with persecution, take the prophets who spoke in the Lord's name; 11 remember it is those who had perseverance that we say are the blessed ones. You have heard of the perseverance of Job and understood the Lord's purpose, realising that *the Lord is kind and compassionate.k*

12 Above all, my brothers, do not swear by heaven or by the earth or use any oaths at all. If you mean 'yes', you must say 'yes'; if you mean 'no', say 'no'. Otherwise you make yourselves liable to judgement.

13 Any one of you who is in trouble should pray; anyone in good spirits should sing a psalm. 14 Any one of you who is ill should send for the elders of the church, and they must anoint the sick person with oil in the name of the Lord and pray over him. 15 The prayer of faith will save the sick person and the Lord will raise him up again; and if he has committed any sins, he will be forgiven. 16 So confess your sins to one another, and pray for one another to be cured; the heartfelt prayer of someone upright works very powerfully. 17 Elijah was a human being as frail as ourselves — he prayed earnestly for it not to rain, and no rain fell for three and a half years; 18 then he prayed again and the sky gave rain and the earth gave crops.

19 My brothers, if one of you strays away from the truth, and another brings him back to it, 20 he may be sure that anyone who can bring back a sinner from his erring ways will be saving his soul from death and *covering over many a sin.l*

k 5 Ps 103:8.   l 5 Pr 10:12; Tb 12:9.

THE FIRST LETTER OF
Peter

1 Peter, an apostle of Jesus Christ,
To the exiles of the Dispersion in Pontus, Galatia, Cappadocia, Asia, and Bithynia, 2 who have been chosen and destined by God the Father and sanctified by the Spirit to be obedient to Jesus Christ and to be sprinkled with his blood:

May grace and peace be yours in abundance.

3 Blessed be the God and Father of our Lord Jesus Christ! By his great mercy he has given us a new birth into a living hope through the resurrection of Jesus Christ from the dead, 4 and into an inheritance that is imperishable, undefiled, and unfading, kept in heaven for you, 5 who are being protected by the power of God through faith for a salvation ready to be revealed in the last time. 6 In this you rejoice,*a* even if now for a little while you have had to suffer various trials, 7 so that the genuineness of your faith — being more precious than gold that, though perishable, is tested by fire — may be found to result in praise and glory and honor when Jesus Christ is revealed. 8 Although you have not seen*b* him, you love him; and even though you do not see him now, you believe in him and rejoice with an indescribable and glorious joy, 9 for you are receiving the outcome of your faith, the salvation of your souls.

10 Concerning this salvation, the prophets who prophesied of the grace that was to be yours made careful search and inquiry, 11 inquiring about the person or time that the Spirit of Christ within them indicated when it testified in advance to the sufferings destined for Christ and the subsequent glory. 12 It was revealed to them that they were serving not themselves but you, in regard to the things that have now been announced to you through those who brought you good news by the Holy Spirit sent from heaven — things into which angels long to look!

13 Therefore prepare your minds for action;*c* discipline yourselves; set all your hope on the grace that Jesus Christ will bring you when he is revealed. 14 Like obedient children, do not be conformed to the desires that you formerly had in ignorance. 15 Instead, as he who called you is holy, be holy yourselves in all your conduct; 16 for it is written, "You shall be holy, for I am holy."

17 If you invoke as Father the one who judges all people impartially according to their deeds, live in reverent fear during the time of your exile. 18 You know that you were ransomed from the futile ways inherited from your ancestors, not with perishable things like silver or gold, 19 but with the precious blood of Christ, like that of a lamb without defect or blemish. 20 He was destined before the foundation of the world, but was revealed at the end of the ages for your sake. 21 Through him you have come to trust in God, who raised him from the dead and gave him glory, so that your faith and hope are set on God.

22 Now that you have purified your souls by your obedience to the truth*d* so that you have genuine mutual love, love one another deeply*e* from the heart.*f* 23 You have been born anew, not of perishable but of imperishable seed, through the living and enduring word of God.*g* 24 For

THE FIRST LETTER OF
Peter

1 FROM Peter, apostle of Jesus Christ, to the scattered people of God now living as aliens in Pontus, Galatia, Cappadocia, Asia, and Bithynia, 2 chosen in the foreknowledge of God the Father, by the consecrating work of the Holy Spirit, for obedience to Jesus Christ and sprinkling with his blood.

Grace and peace to you in fullest measure.

3 PRAISED be the God and Father of our Lord Jesus Christ! In his great mercy by the resurrection of Jesus Christ from the dead, he gave us new birth into a living hope, 4 the hope of an inheritance, reserved in heaven for you, which nothing can destroy or spoil or wither. 5 Because you put your faith in God, you are under the protection of his power until the salvation now in readiness is revealed at the end of time.

6 This is cause for great joy, even though for a little while you may have had to suffer trials of many kinds. 7 Even gold passes through the assayer's fire, and much more precious than perishable gold is faith which stands the test. These trials come so that your faith may prove itself worthy of all praise, glory, and honour when Jesus Christ is revealed.

8 You have not seen him, yet you love him; and trusting in him now without seeing him, you are filled with a glorious joy too great for words, 9 while you are reaping the harvest of your faith, that is, salvation for your souls.

10 THIS salvation was the subject of intense search by the prophets who prophesied about the grace of God awaiting you. 11 They tried to find out the time and the circumstances to which the spirit of Christ in them pointed, when it foretold the sufferings in Christ's cause and the glories to follow. 12 It was disclosed to them that these matters were not for their benefit but for yours. Now they have been openly announced to you through preachers who have brought you the gospel in the power of the Holy Spirit sent from heaven. These are things that angels long to glimpse.

13 Your minds must therefore be stripped for action and fully alert. Fix your hopes on the grace which is to be yours when Jesus Christ is revealed. 14 Be obedient to God your Father, and do not let your characters be shaped any longer by the desires you cherished in your days of ignorance. 15 He who called you is holy; like him, be holy in all your conduct. 16 Does not scripture say, 'You shall be holy, for I am holy'?

17 If you say 'Father' to him who judges everyone impartially on the basis of what they have done, you must live in awe of him during your time on earth. 18 You know well that it was nothing of passing value, like silver or gold, that bought your freedom from the futility of your traditional ways. 19 You were set free by Christ's precious blood, blood like that of a lamb without mark or blemish. 20 He was predestined before the foundation of the world, but in this last period of time he has been revealed for your sake. 21 Through him you have come to trust in God who raised him from the dead and gave him glory, and so your faith and hope are fixed on God.

22 Now that you have purified your souls by obedience to the truth until you feel sincere affection towards your fellow-Christians, love one another wholeheartedly with all your strength. 23 You have been born again, not of mortal but of immortal parentage, through the living and enduring word of God. 24 As scripture says:

---

a Or *Rejoice in this*   *b* Other ancient authorities read *known*
c Gk *gird up the loins of your mind*   *d* Other ancient authorities add
through the Spirit   *e* Or *constantly*   *f* Other ancient authorities
read *a pure heart*   *g* Or *through the word of the living and
enduring God*

1:11 **the time:** *or* the person.

The First Letter
of Peter

1 Peter, an apostle of Jesus Christ, to the chosen sojourners of the dispersion in Pontus, Galatia, Cappadocia, Asia, and Bithynia, 2 in the foreknowledge of God the Father, through sanctification by the Spirit, for obedience and sprinkling with the blood of Jesus Christ: may grace and peace be yours in abundance.

3 Blessed be the God and Father of our Lord Jesus Christ, who in his great mercy gave us a new birth to a living hope through the resurrection of Jesus Christ from the dead, 4 to an inheritance that is imperishable, undefiled, and unfading, kept in heaven for you 5 who by the power of God are safeguarded through faith, to a salvation that is ready to be revealed in the final time. 6 In this you rejoice, although now for a little while you may have to suffer through various trials, 7 so that the genuineness of your faith, more precious than gold that is perishable even though tested by fire, may prove to be for praise, glory, and honor at the revelation of Jesus Christ. 8 Although you have not seen him you love him; even though you do not see him now yet believe in him, you rejoice with an indescribable and glorious joy, 9 as you attain the goal of [your] faith, the salvation of your souls.

10 Concerning this salvation, prophets who prophesied about the grace that was to be yours searched and investigated it, 11 investigating the time and circumstances that the Spirit of Christ within them indicated when it testified in advance to the sufferings destined for Christ and the glories to follow them. 12 It was revealed to them that they were serving not themselves but you with regard to the things that have now been announced to you by those who preached the good news to you [through] the holy Spirit sent from heaven, things into which angels longed to look.

13 Therefore, gird up the loins of your mind, live soberly, and set your hopes completely on the grace to be brought to you at the revelation of Jesus Christ. 14 Like obedient children, do not act in compliance with the desires of your former ignorance 15 but, as he who called you is holy, be holy yourselves in every aspect of your conduct, 16 for it is written, "Be holy because I [am] holy."

17 Now if you invoke as Father him who judges impartially according to each one's works, conduct yourselves with reverence during the time of your sojourning, 18 realizing that you were ransomed from your futile conduct, handed on by your ancestors, not with perishable things like silver or gold 19 but with the precious blood of Christ as of a spotless unblemished lamb. 20 He was known before the foundation of the world but revealed in the final time for you, 21 who through him believe in God who raised him from the dead and gave him glory, so that your faith and hope are in God.

22 Since you have purified yourselves by obedience to the truth for sincere mutual love, love one another intensely from a [pure] heart. 23 You have been born anew, not from perishable but from imperishable seed, through the living and abiding word of God, 24 for:

1 Peter

THE FIRST LETTER OF PETER

1 Peter, apostle of Jesus Christ, to all those living as aliens in the Dispersion*a* of Pontus, Galatia, Cappadocia, Asia and Bithynia, who have been chosen, 2 in the foresight of God the Father, to be made holy by the Spirit, obedient to Jesus Christ and sprinkled with his blood: Grace and peace be yours in abundance.

3 Blessed be God the Father of our Lord Jesus Christ, who in his great mercy has given us a new birth into a living hope through the resurrection of Jesus Christ from the dead 4 and into a heritage that can never be spoilt or soiled and never fade away. It is reserved in heaven for you 5 who are being kept safe by God's power through faith until the salvation which has been prepared is revealed at the final point of time.

6 This is a great joy to you, even though for a short time yet you must bear all sorts of trials; 7 so that the worth of your faith, more valuable than gold, which is perishable even if it has been tested by fire, may be proved — to your praise and honour when Jesus Christ is revealed. 8 You have not seen him, yet you love him; and still without seeing him you believe in him and so are already filled with a joy so glorious that it cannot be described; 9 and you are sure of the goal of your faith, that is, the salvation of your souls.

10 This salvation was the subject of the search and investigation of the prophets who spoke of the grace you were to receive, 11 searching out the time and circumstances for which the Spirit of Christ, bearing witness in them, was revealing the sufferings of Christ and the glories to follow them. 12 It was revealed to them that it was for your sake and not their own that they were acting as servants delivering the message which has now been announced to you by those who preached to you the gospel through the Holy Spirit sent from heaven. Even the angels long to catch a glimpse of these things.

13 Your minds, then, must be sober and ready for action; put all your hope in the grace brought to you by the revelation of Jesus Christ. 14 Do not allow yourselves to be shaped by the passions of your old ignorance, 15 but as obedient children, be yourselves holy in all your activity, after the model of the Holy One who calls us, 16 since scripture says, '*Be holy, for I am holy.'b* 17 And if you address as Father him who judges without favouritism according to each individual's deeds, live out the time of your exile here in reverent awe. 18 For you know that the price of your ransom from the futile way of life handed down from your ancestors was paid, not in anything perishable like silver or gold,*c* 19 but in precious blood as of a blameless and spotless lamb, Christ. 20 He was marked out before the world was made, and was revealed at the final point of time for your sake. 21 Through him you now have faith in God, who raised him from the dead and gave him glory for this very purpose — that your faith and hope should be in God.

22 Since by your obedience to the truth you have purified yourselves so that you can experience the genuine love of brothers, love each other intensely from the heart; 23 for your new birth was not from any perishable seed but from imperishable seed, the living and enduring Word of God.

---

a **1** See Jm *a*1 note.   *b* **1** Lv 19:2.   *c* **1** Is 52:3.

"All flesh is like grass
and all its glory like the flower of grass.
The grass withers,
and the flower falls,
25 but the word of the Lord endures forever."
That word is the good news that was announced to you.

2 Rid yourselves, therefore, of all malice, and all guile, insincerity, envy, and all slander. 2 Like newborn infants, long for the pure, spiritual milk, so that by it you may grow into salvation— 3 if indeed you have tasted that the Lord is good.

4 Come to him, a living stone, though rejected by mortals yet chosen and precious in God's sight, and 5 like living stones, let yourselves be built*h* into a spiritual house, to be a holy priesthood, to offer spiritual sacrifices acceptable to God through Jesus Christ. 6 For it stands in scripture:
"See, I am laying in Zion a stone,
a cornerstone chosen and precious;
and whoever believes in him*i* will not be put to shame."
7 To you then who believe, he is precious; but for those who do not believe,
"The stone that the builders rejected
has become the very head of the corner,"
8 and
"A stone that makes them stumble,
and a rock that makes them fall."
They stumble because they disobey the word, as they were destined to do.

9 But you are a chosen race, a royal priesthood, a holy nation, God's own people,*j* in order that you may proclaim the mighty acts of him who called you out of darkness into his marvelous light.
10 Once you were not a people,
but now you are God's people;
once you had not received mercy,
but now you have received mercy.

11 Beloved, I urge you as aliens and exiles to abstain from the desires of the flesh that wage war against the soul. 12 Conduct yourselves honorably among the Gentiles, so that, though they malign you as evildoers, they may see your honorable deeds and glorify God when he comes to judge.*k*

13 For the Lord's sake accept the authority of every human institution,*l* whether of the emperor as supreme, 14 or of governors, as sent by him to punish those who do wrong and to praise those who do right. 15 For it is God's will that by doing right you should silence the ignorance of the foolish. 16 As servants*m* of God, live as free people, yet do not use your freedom as a pretext for evil. 17 Honor everyone. Love the family of believers.*n* Fear God. Honor the emperor.

18 Slaves, accept the authority of your masters with all deference, not only those who are kind and gentle but also those who are harsh. 19 For it is a credit to you if, being aware of God, you endure pain while suffering unjustly. 20 If you endure when you are beaten for doing wrong, what credit is that? But if you endure when you do right and suffer for it, you have God's approval. 21 For to this you have been called, because Christ also suffered for you, leaving you an example, so that you should follow in his steps.
22 "He committed no sin,
and no deceit was found in his mouth."

All mortals are like grass;
all their glory like the flower of the field;
the grass withers, the flower falls;
25 but the word of the Lord endures for evermore.
And this 'word' is the gospel which was preached to you.

2 Then away with all wickedness and deceit, hypocrisy and jealousy and malicious talk of any kind! 2 Like the newborn infants you are, you should be craving for pure spiritual milk so that you may thrive on it and be saved; for 3 surely you have tasted that the Lord is good.

4 So come to him, to the living stone which was rejected by men but chosen by God and of great worth to him. 5 You also, as living stones, must be built up into a spiritual temple, and form a holy priesthood to offer spiritual sacrifices acceptable to God through Jesus Christ. 6 For you will find in scripture:
I am laying in Zion a chosen corner-stone of great worth.
Whoever has faith in it will not be put to shame.
7 So for you who have faith it has great worth; but for those who have no faith 'the stone which the builders rejected has become the corner-stone', 8 and also 'a stone to trip over, a rock to stumble against'. They trip because they refuse to believe the word; this is the fate appointed for them.

9 But you are a chosen race, a royal priesthood, a dedicated nation, a people claimed by God for his own, to proclaim the glorious deeds of him who has called you out of darkness into his marvellous light. 10 Once you were not a people at all; but now you are God's people. Once you were outside his mercy; but now you are outside no longer.

11 DEAR friends, I appeal to you, as aliens in a foreign land, to avoid bodily desires which make war on the soul. 12 Let your conduct among unbelievers be so good that, although they now malign you as wrongdoers, reflection on your good deeds will lead them to give glory to God on the day when he comes in judgement.

13 Submit yourselves for the sake of the Lord to every human authority, whether to the emperor as supreme, 14 or to governors as his deputies for the punishment of those who do wrong and the commendation of those who do right. 15 For it is God's will that by doing right you should silence ignorance and stupidity.

16 Live as those who are free; not however as though your freedom provided a cloak for wrongdoing, but as slaves in God's service. 17 Give due honour to everyone: love your fellow-Christians, reverence God, honour the emperor.

18 Servants, submit to your masters with all due respect, not only to those who are kind and forbearing, but even to those who are unjust. 19 It is a sign of grace if, because God is in his thoughts, someone endures the pain of undeserved suffering. 20 What credit is there in enduring the beating you deserve when you have done wrong? On the other hand, when you have behaved well and endured suffering for it, that is a sign of grace in the sight of God. 21 It is your vocation because Christ himself suffered on your behalf, and left you an example in order that you should follow in his steps. 22 'He committed no sin, he was guilty of no falsehood.' 23 When he was abused he did not retaliate,

---

h Or you yourselves are being built i Or it j Gk a people for his possession k Gk God on the day of visitation l Or every institution ordained for human beings m Gk slaves n Gk Love the brotherhood

2:19,20 a sign of grace: or creditable. 2:21 suffered: some witnesses read died.

NEW AMERICAN BIBLE

"All flesh is like grass,
    and all its glory like the flower of the field;
the grass withers,
    and the flower wilts;
25 but the word of the Lord remains forever."

This is the word that has been proclaimed to you.

2 Rid yourselves of all malice and all deceit, insincerity, envy, and all slander; 2 like newborn infants, long for pure spiritual milk so that through it you may grow into salvation, 3 for you have tasted that the Lord is good. 4 Come to him, a living stone, rejected by human beings but chosen and precious in the sight of God, 5 and, like living stones, let yourselves be built into a spiritual house to be a holy priesthood to offer spiritual sacrifices acceptable to God through Jesus Christ. 6 For it says in scripture:

"Behold, I am laying a stone in Zion,
    a cornerstone, chosen and precious,
and whoever believes in it shall not be put
      to shame."

7 Therefore, its value is for you who have faith, but for those without faith:

"The stone which the builders rejected
    has become the cornerstone,"

8 and

"A stone that will make people stumble,
    and a rock that will make them fall."

They stumble by disobeying the word, as is their destiny.
9 But you are "a chosen race, a royal priesthood, a holy nation, a people of his own, so that you may announce the praises" of him who called you out of darkness into his wonderful light.

10 Once you were "no people"
    but now you are God's people;
you "had not received mercy"
    but now you have received mercy.

11 Beloved, I urge you as aliens and sojourners to keep away from worldly desires that wage war against the soul. 12 Maintain good conduct among the Gentiles, so that if they speak of you as evildoers, they may observe your good works and glorify God on the day of visitation.

13 Be subject to every human institution for the Lord's sake, whether it be to the king as supreme 14 or to governors as sent by him for the punishment of evildoers and the approval of those who do good. 15 For it is the will of God that by doing good you may silence the ignorance of foolish people. 16 Be free, yet without using freedom as a pretext for evil, but as slaves of God. 17 Give honor to all, love the community, fear God, honor the king.

18 Slaves, be subject to your masters with all reverence, not only to those who are good and equitable but also to those who are perverse. 19 For whenever anyone bears the pain of unjust suffering because of consciousness of God, that is a grace. 20 But what credit is there if you are patient when beaten for doing wrong? But if you are patient when you suffer for doing what is good, this is a grace before God. 21 For to this you have been called, because Christ also suffered for you, leaving you an example that you should follow in his footsteps.

22 "He committed no sin,
    and no deceit was found in his mouth."

NEW JERUSALEM BIBLE

24 For *all humanity is grass, and all its beauty like the wild flower's. As grass withers, the flower fades,* 25 *but the Word of the Lord remains for ever.*[d] And this Word is the Good News that has been brought to you.

2 Rid yourselves, then, of all spite, deceit, hypocrisy, envy and carping criticism. 2 Like new-born babies all your longing should be for milk — the unadulterated spiritual milk — which will help you to grow up to salvation, 3 at any rate if *you have tasted that the Lord is good*[e].

4 He is the living stone, rejected by human beings but chosen by God and precious to him; set yourselves close to him 5 so that you, too, may be living stones making a spiritual house as a holy priesthood to offer the spiritual sacrifices made acceptable to God through Jesus Christ. 6 As scripture says: *Now I am laying a stone in Zion, a chosen, precious cornerstone* and *no one who relies on this will be brought to disgrace.*[f] 7 To you believers it brings honour. But for unbelievers, it is rather a *stone which the builders rejected that became a cornerstone,*[g] 8 *a stumbling stone, a rock to trip people up.*[h] They stumble over it because they do not believe in the Word; it was the fate in store for them.

9 But you are *a chosen race, a kingdom of priests, a holy nation, a people to be a personal possession*[i] to sing the praises of God who called you out of the darkness into his wonderful light. 10 Once you were *a non-people* and now you are the People of God; once you were *outside his pity;* now you *have received pity.*[j]

11 I urge you, my dear friends, as *strangers and nomads,*[k] to keep yourselves free from the disordered natural inclinations that attack the soul. 12 Always behave honourably among gentiles so that they can see for themselves what moral lives you lead, and when the day of reckoning comes, give thanks to God for the things which now make them denounce you as criminals.

13 For the sake of the Lord, accept the authority of every human institution: the emperor, as the supreme authority, 14 and the governors as commissioned by him to punish criminals and praise those who do good. 15 It is God's will that by your good deeds you should silence the ignorant talk of fools. 16 You are slaves of no one except God, so behave like free people, and never use your freedom as a cover for wickedness. 17 Have respect for everyone and love for your fellow-believers; fear God and honour the emperor.

18 Slaves, you should obey your masters respectfully, not only those who are kind and reasonable but also those who are difficult to please. 19 You see, there is merit if, in awareness of God, you put up with the pains of undeserved punishment; 20 but what glory is there in putting up with a beating after you have done something wrong? The merit in the sight of God is in putting up with it patiently when you are punished for doing your duty.

21 This, in fact, is what you were called to do, because Christ suffered for you and left an example for you to follow in his steps. 22 He had done nothing wrong, and *had spoken no deceit.*[l] 23 He was insulted and did not retaliate with

d 1 Is 40:6–8.   *e* 2 Ps 34:8.   *f* 2 Is 28:16.   *g* 2 Ps 118:22.
h 2 Is 8:14.   *i* 2 Is 43:20–21.   *j* 2 Ho 1:9 and allusions to Ho 2.
k 2 Ps 39:12.   *l* 2 Several quotations from Is 53:5–9.

NEW REVISED STANDARD VERSION

23 When he was abused, he did not return abuse; when he suffered, he did not threaten; but he entrusted himself to the one who judges justly. 24 He himself bore our sins in his body on the cross,*o* so that, free from sins, we might live for righteousness; by his wounds*p* you have been healed. 25 For you were going astray like sheep, but now you have returned to the shepherd and guardian of your souls.

3 Wives, in the same way, accept the authority of your husbands, so that, even if some of them do not obey the word, they may be won over without a word by their wives' conduct, 2 when they see the purity and reverence of your lives. 3 Do not adorn yourselves outwardly by braiding your hair, and by wearing gold ornaments or fine clothing; 4 rather, let your adornment be the inner self with the lasting beauty of a gentle and quiet spirit, which is very precious in God's sight. 5 It was in this way long ago that the holy women who hoped in God used to adorn themselves by accepting the authority of their husbands. 6 Thus Sarah obeyed Abraham and called him lord. You have become her daughters as long as you do what is good and never let fears alarm you.

7 Husbands, in the same way, show consideration for your wives in your life together, paying honor to the woman as the weaker sex,*q* since they too are also heirs of the gracious gift of life — so that nothing may hinder your prayers.

8 Finally, all of you, have unity of spirit, sympathy, love for one another, a tender heart, and a humble mind. 9 Do not repay evil for evil or abuse for abuse; but, on the contrary, repay with a blessing. It is for this that you were called — that you might inherit a blessing. 10 For

"Those who desire life
    and desire to see good days,
let them keep their tongues from evil
    and their lips from speaking deceit;
11 let them turn away from evil and do good;
    let them seek peace and pursue it.
12 For the eyes of the Lord are on the righteous,
    and his ears are open to their prayer.
But the face of the Lord is against those who do evil."

13 Now who will harm you if you are eager to do what is good? 14 But even if you do suffer for doing what is right, you are blessed. Do not fear what they fear,*r* and do not be intimidated, 15 but in your hearts sanctify Christ as Lord. Always be ready to make your defense to anyone who demands from you an accounting for the hope that is in you; 16 yet do it with gentleness and reverence.*s* Keep your conscience clear, so that, when you are maligned, those who abuse you for your good conduct in Christ may be put to shame. 17 For it is better to suffer for doing good, if suffering should be God's will, than to suffer for doing evil. 18 For Christ also suffered*t* for sins once for all, the righteous for the unrighteous, in order to bring you*u* to God. He was put to death in the flesh, but made alive in the spirit, 19 in which also he went and made a proclamation to the spirits in prison, 20 who in former times did not obey, when God waited patiently in the days of Noah, during the building of the ark, in which a few, that is, eight persons, were saved through water. 21 And baptism, which this prefigured, now saves you — not as a removal of dirt from the body, but as an appeal to God for*v* a good conscience, through the resurrection of Jesus Christ, 22 who has gone into heaven

REVISED ENGLISH BIBLE

when he suffered he uttered no threats, but delivered himself up to him who judges justly. 24 He carried our sins in his own person on the gibbet, so that we might cease to live for sin and begin to live for righteousness. By his wounds you have been healed. 25 You were straying like sheep, but now you have turned towards the Shepherd and Guardian of your souls.

3 In the same way you women must submit to your husbands, so that if there are any of them who disbelieve the gospel they may be won over without a word being said, 2 by observing your chaste and respectful behaviour. 3 Your beauty should lie, not in outward adornment — braiding the hair, wearing gold ornaments, or dressing up in fine clothes — 4 but in the inmost self, with its imperishable quality of a gentle, quiet spirit, which is of high value in the sight of God. 5 This is how in past days the women of God's people, whose hope was in him, used to make themselves attractive, submitting to their husbands. 6 Such was Sarah, who obeyed Abraham and called him master. By doing good and showing no fear, you have become her daughters.

7 In the same way, you husbands must show understanding in your married life: treat your wives with respect, not only because they are physically weaker, but also because God's gift of life is something you share together. Then your prayers will not be impeded.

8 Finally, be united, all of you, in thought and feeling; be full of brotherly affection, kindly and humble. 9 Do not repay wrong with wrong, or abuse with abuse; on the contrary, respond with blessing, for a blessing is what God intends you to receive. As scripture says:

10 If anyone wants to love life
    and see good days
    he must restrain his tongue from evil
    and his lips from deceit;
11 he must turn from wrong and do good,
    seek peace and pursue it.
12 The Lord has eyes for the righteous,
    and ears open to their prayers;
    but the face of the Lord is set against wrongdoers.

13 Who is going to do you harm if you are devoted to what is good? 14 Yet if you should suffer for doing right you may count yourselves happy. Have no fear of other people: do not be perturbed, 15 but hold Christ in your hearts in reverence as Lord. Always be ready to make your defence when anyone challenges you to justify the hope which is in you. But do so with courtesy and respect, 16 keeping your conscience clear, so that when you are abused, those who malign your Christian conduct may be put to shame. 17 It is better to suffer for doing right, if such should be the will of God, than for doing wrong.

18 Christ too suffered for our sins once and for all, the just for the unjust, that he might bring us to God; put to death in the body, he was brought to life in the spirit. 19 In the spirit also he went and made his proclamation to the imprisoned spirits, 20 those who had refused to obey in the past, while God waited patiently in the days when Noah was building the ark; in it a few people, eight in all, were brought to safety through the water. 21 This water symbolized baptism, through which you are now brought to safety. Baptism is not the washing away of bodily impurities but the appeal made to God from a good conscience; and it brings salvation through the resurrection of Jesus Christ,

---

o Or *carried up our sins in his body to the tree*   *p* Gk *bruise*
q Gk *vessel*   *r* Gk *their fear*   *s* Or *respect*   *t* Other ancient
authorities read *died*   *u* Other ancient authorities read *us*   *v* Or *a pledge to God from*

2:24 **on the gibbet:** *or* to the gibbet.   3:14 **Have . . . people:** *or*
Do not fear what other people fear.   3:18 **suffered:** *some*
witnesses read died. **for our sins:** *some witnesses read* for sins.
3:21 **from a good conscience:** *or* for a good conscience.

23 When he was insulted, he returned no insult; when he suffered, he did not threaten; instead, he handed himself over to the one who judges justly. 24 He himself bore our sins in his body upon the cross, so that, free from sin, we might live for righteousness. By his wounds you have been healed. 25 For you had gone astray like sheep, but you have now returned to the shepherd and guardian of your souls.

3 Likewise, you wives should be subordinate to your husbands so that, even if some disobey the word, they may be won over without a word by their wives' conduct 2 when they observe your reverent and chaste behavior. 3 Your adornment should not be an external one: braiding the hair, wearing gold jewelry, or dressing in fine clothes, 4 but rather the hidden character of the heart, expressed in the imperishable beauty of a gentle and calm disposition, which is precious in the sight of God. 5 For this is also how the holy women who hoped in God once used to adorn themselves and were subordinate to their husbands; 6 thus Sarah obeyed Abraham, calling him "lord." You are her children when you do what is good and fear no intimidation.

7 Likewise, you husbands should live with your wives in understanding, showing honor to the weaker female sex, since we are joint heirs of the gift of life, so that your prayers may not be hindered.

8 Finally, all of you, be of one mind, sympathetic, loving toward one another, compassionate, humble. 9 Do not return evil for evil, or insult for insult; but, on the contrary, a blessing, because to this you were called, that you might inherit a blessing. 10 For:

"Whoever would love life
  and see good days
must keep the tongue from evil
  and the lips from speaking deceit,
11 must turn from evil and do good,
  seek peace and follow after it.
12 For the eyes of the Lord are on the righteous
  and his ears turned to their prayer,
but the face of the Lord is against evildoers."

13 Now who is going to harm you if you are enthusiastic for what is good? 14 But even if you should suffer because of righteousness, blessed are you. Do not be afraid or terrified with fear of them, 15 but sanctify Christ as Lord in your hearts. Always be ready to give an explanation to anyone who asks you for a reason for your hope, 16 but do it with gentleness and reverence, keeping your conscience clear, so that, when you are maligned, those who defame your good conduct in Christ may be put to shame. 17 For it is better to suffer for doing good, if that be the will of God, than for doing evil.

18 For Christ also suffered for sins once, the righteous for the sake of the unrighteous, that he might lead you to God. Put to death in the flesh, he was brought to life in the spirit. 19 In it he also went to preach to the spirits in prison, 20 who had once been disobedient while God patiently waited in the days of Noah during the building of the ark, in which a few persons, eight in all, were saved through water. 21 This prefigured baptism, which saves you now. It is not a removal of dirt from the body but an appeal to God for a clear conscience, through the resurrection of Jesus Christ, 22 who

insults; when he was suffering he made no threats but put his trust in the upright judge. 24 He was *bearing our sins* in his own body on the cross, so that we might die to our sins and live for uprightness; *through his bruises you have been healed.* 25 You had *gone astray like sheep* but now you have returned to the shepherd and guardian of your souls.

3 In the same way, you wives should be obedient to your husbands. Then if there are some husbands who do not believe the Word, they may find themselves won over, without a word spoken, by the way their wives behave, 2 when they see the reverence and purity of your way of life. 3 Your adornment should be not an exterior one, consisting of braided hair or gold jewellery or fine clothing, 4 but the interior disposition of the heart, consisting in the imperishable quality of a gentle and peaceful spirit, so precious in the sight of God. 5 That was how the holy women of the past dressed themselves attractively — they hoped in God and were submissive to their husbands; 6 like Sarah, who was obedient to Abraham, and called him her *lord.* m You are now her children, as long as you live good lives free from fear and worry.

7 In the same way, husbands must always treat their wives with consideration in their life together, respecting a woman as one who, though she may be the weaker partner, is equally an heir to the generous gift of life. This will prevent anything from coming in the way of your prayers.

8 Finally: you should all agree among yourselves and be sympathetic; love the brothers, have compassion and be self-effacing. 9 Never repay one wrong with another, or one abusive word with another; instead, repay with a blessing. That is what you are called to do, so that you inherit a blessing. 10 For

Who among you delights in life,
  longs for time to enjoy prosperity?
Guard your tongue from evil,
  your lips from any breath of deceit.
11 *Turn away from evil and do good, seek peace and*
  pursue it.
12 *For the eyes of the Lord are on the upright,*
  his ear turned to their cry.
But the Lord's face is set against those who do evil. n

13 No one can hurt you if you are determined to do only what is right; 14 and blessed are you if you have to suffer for being upright. *Have no dread of them; have no fear.* o 15 Simply *proclaim the Lord* Christ *holy* in your hearts, and always have your answer ready for people who ask you the reason for the hope that you have. 16 But give it with courtesy and respect and with a clear conscience, so that those who slander your good behaviour in Christ may be ashamed of their accusations. 17 And if it is the will of God that you should suffer, it is better to suffer for doing right than for doing wrong.

18 Christ himself died once and for all for sins, the upright for the sake of the guilty, to lead us to God. In the body he was put to death, in the spirit he was raised to life, 19 and, in the spirit, he went to preach to the spirits in prison. 20 They refused to believe long ago, while God patiently waited to receive them, in Noah's time when the ark was being built. In it only a few, that is eight souls, were saved through water. 21 It is the baptism corresponding to this water which saves you now — not the washing off of physical dirt but the pledge of a good conscience given to God through the resurrection of Jesus Christ, 22 who has entered

m 3 Gn 18:12.   n 3 Ps 34:12–16.   o 3 Is 8:12–13.

| NEW REVISED STANDARD VERSION | REVISED ENGLISH BIBLE |

and is at the right hand of God, with angels, authorities, and powers made subject to him.

4 Since therefore Christ suffered in the flesh,[w] arm yourselves also with the same intention (for whoever has suffered in the flesh has finished with sin), [2] so as to live for the rest of your earthly life[x] no longer by human desires but by the will of God. [3] You have already spent enough time in doing what the Gentiles like to do, living in licentiousness, passions, drunkenness, revels, carousing, and lawless idolatry. [4] They are surprised that you no longer join them in the same excesses of dissipation, and so they blaspheme.[y] [5] But they will have to give an accounting to him who stands ready to judge the living and the dead. [6] For this is the reason the gospel was proclaimed even to the dead, so that, though they had been judged in the flesh as everyone is judged, they might live in the spirit as God does.

[7] The end of all things is near;[z] therefore be serious and discipline yourselves for the sake of your prayers. [8] Above all, maintain constant love for one another, for love covers a multitude of sins. [9] Be hospitable to one another without complaining. [10] Like good stewards of the manifold grace of God, serve one another with whatever gift each of you has received. [11] Whoever speaks must do so as one speaking the very words of God; whoever serves must do so with the strength that God supplies, so that God may be glorified in all things through Jesus Christ. To him belong the glory and the power forever and ever. Amen.

[12] Beloved, do not be surprised at the fiery ordeal that is taking place among you to test you, as though something strange were happening to you. [13] But rejoice insofar as you are sharing Christ's sufferings, so that you may also be glad and shout for joy when his glory is revealed. [14] If you are reviled for the name of Christ, you are blessed, because the spirit of glory,[a] which is the Spirit of God, is resting on you.[b] [15] But let none of you suffer as a murderer, a thief, a criminal, or even as a mischief maker. [16] Yet if any of you suffers as a Christian, do not consider it a disgrace, but glorify God because you bear this name. [17] For the time has come for judgment to begin with the household of God; if it begins with us, what will be the end for those who do not obey the gospel of God? [18] And

"If it is hard for the righteous to be saved,
    what will become of the ungodly and the
        sinners?"
[19] Therefore, let those suffering in accordance with God's will entrust themselves to a faithful Creator, while continuing to do good.

5 Now as an elder myself and a witness of the sufferings of Christ, as well as one who shares in the glory to be revealed, I exhort the elders among you [2] to tend the flock of God that is in your charge, exercising the oversight,[c] not under compulsion but willingly, as God would have you do it[d]—not for sordid gain but eagerly. [3] Do not lord it over those in your charge, but be examples to the flock. [4] And when the chief shepherd appears, you will win the crown of glory that never fades away. [5] In the same way, you who are

[22] who is now at the right hand of God, having entered heaven and received the submission of angels, authorities, and powers.

4 SINCE Christ endured bodily suffering, you also must arm yourselves with the same disposition. When anyone has endured bodily suffering he has finished with sin, [2] so that for the rest of his days on earth he may live, not to satisfy human appetites, but to do what God wills. [3] You have spent time enough in the past doing what pagans like to do. You lived then in licence and debauchery, drunkenness, orgies and carousal, and the forbidden worship of idols. [4] Now, when you no longer plunge with the pagans into all this reckless dissipation, they cannot understand it and start abusing you; [5] but they will have to give account of themselves to him who is ready to pass judgement on the living and the dead. [6] That was why the gospel was preached even to the dead: in order that, although in the body they were condemned to die as everyone dies, yet in the spirit they might live as God lives.

[7] The end of all things is upon us; therefore to help you to pray you must lead self-controlled and sober lives. [8] Above all, maintain the fervour of your love for one another, because love cancels a host of sins. [9] Be hospitable to one another without grumbling. [10] As good stewards of the varied gifts given you by God, let each use the gift he has received in service to others. [11] Are you a speaker? Speak as one who utters God's oracles. Do you give service? Give it in the strength which God supplies. In all things let God be glorified through Jesus Christ; to him belong glory and power for ever and ever. Amen.

[12] DEAR friends, do not be taken aback by the fiery ordeal which has come to test you, as though it were something extraordinary. [13] On the contrary, in so far as it gives you a share in Christ's sufferings, you should rejoice; and then when his glory is revealed, your joy will be unbounded. [14] If you are reviled for being Christians, count yourselves happy, because the Spirit of God in all his glory rests upon you. [15] If you do suffer, it must not be for murder, theft, or any other crime, nor should it be for meddling in other people's business. [16] But if anyone suffers as a Christian, he should feel it no disgrace, but confess that name to the honour of God.

[17] The time has come for the judgement to begin; it is beginning with God's own household. And if it is starting with us, how will it end for those who refuse to obey the gospel of God? [18] Scripture says: 'It is hard enough for the righteous to be saved; what then will become of the impious and sinful?' [19] So let those who suffer according to God's will entrust their souls to him while continuing to do good; their Maker will not fail them.

5 NOW I APPEAL to the elders of your community, as a fellow-elder and a witness to Christ's sufferings, and as one who has shared in the glory to be revealed: [2] look after the flock of God whose shepherds you are; do it, not under compulsion, but willingly, as God would have it; not for gain but out of sheer devotion; [3] not lording it over your charges, but setting an example to the flock. [4] So when the chief shepherd appears, you will receive glory, a crown that never fades.

---

[w] Other ancient authorities add *for us*; others, *for you*   [x] Gk *rest of the time in the flesh*   [y] Or *they malign you*   [z] Or *is at hand*   [a] Other ancient authorities add *and of power*   [b] Other ancient authorities add *On their part he is blasphemed, but on your part he is glorified*   [c] Other ancient authorities lack *exercising the oversight*   [d] Other ancient authorities lack *as God would have you do it*

4:6 **although . . . lives**: *or although in the body they suffered judgement by human standards, in the spirit they might be given life in accordance with God's purpose.*

has gone into heaven and is at the right hand of God, with angels, authorities, and powers subject to him.

4 Therefore, since Christ suffered in the flesh, arm yourselves also with the same attitude (for whoever suffers in the flesh has broken with sin), 2 so as not to spend what remains of one's life in the flesh on human desires, but on the will of God. 3 For the time that has passed is sufficient for doing what the Gentiles like to do: living in debauchery, evil desires, drunkenness, orgies, carousing, and wanton idolatry. 4 They are surprised that you do not plunge into the same swamp of profligacy, and they vilify you; 5 but they will give an account to him who stands ready to judge the living and the dead. 6 For this is why the gospel was preached even to the dead that, though condemned in the flesh in human estimation, they might live in the spirit in the estimation of God.

7 The end of all things is at hand. Therefore, be serious and sober for prayers. 8 Above all, let your love for one another be intense, because love covers a multitude of sins. 9 Be hospitable to one another without complaining. 10 As each one has received a gift, use it to serve one another as good stewards of God's varied grace. 11 Whoever preaches, let it be with the words of God; whoever serves, let it be with the strength that God supplies, so that in all things God may be glorified through Jesus Christ, to whom belong glory and dominion forever and ever. Amen.

12 Beloved, do not be surprised that a trial by fire is occurring among you, as if something strange were happening to you. 13 But rejoice to the extent that you share in the sufferings of Christ, so that when his glory is revealed you may also rejoice exultantly. 14 If you are insulted for the name of Christ, blessed are you, for the Spirit of glory and of God rests upon you. 15 But let no one among you be made to suffer as a murderer, a thief, an evildoer, or as an intriguer. 16 But whoever is made to suffer as a Christian should not be ashamed but glorify God because of the name. 17 For it is time for the judgment to begin with the household of God; if it begins with us, how will it end for those who fail to obey the gospel of God?

18 "And if the righteous one is barely saved,
    where will the godless and the sinner appear?"

19 As a result, those who suffer in accord with God's will hand their souls over to a faithful creator as they do good.

5 So I exhort the presbyters among you, as a fellow presbyter and witness to the sufferings of Christ and one who has a share in the glory to be revealed. 2 Tend the flock of God in your midst, [overseeing] not by constraint but willingly, as God would have it, not for shameful profit but eagerly. 3 Do not lord it over those assigned to you, but be examples to the flock. 4 And when the chief Shepherd is revealed, you will receive the unfading crown of glory.

heaven and is at God's right hand, with angels, ruling forces and powers subject to him.

4 As Christ has undergone bodily suffering, you too should arm yourselves with the same conviction, that anyone who has undergone bodily suffering has broken with sin, 2 because for the rest of life on earth that person is ruled not by human passions but only by the will of God. 3 You spent quite long enough in the past living the sort of life that gentiles choose to live, behaving in a debauched way, giving way to your passions, drinking to excess, having wild parties and drunken orgies and sacrilegiously worshipping false gods. 4 So people are taken aback that you no longer hurry off with them to join this flood which is rushing down to ruin, and then abuse you for it. 5 They will have to answer for it before the judge who is to judge the living and the dead. 6 And this was why the gospel was brought to the dead as well, so that, though in their bodies they had undergone the judgement that faces all humanity, in their spirit they might enjoy the life of God.

7 The end of all things is near, so keep your minds calm and sober for prayer. 8 Above all preserve an intense love for each other, since *love covers over many a sin.p* 9 Welcome each other into your houses without grumbling. 10 Each one of you has received a special grace, so, like good stewards responsible for all these varied graces of God, put it at the service of others. 11 If anyone is a speaker, let it be as the words of God, if anyone serves, let it be as in strength granted by God; so that in everything God may receive the glory, through Jesus Christ, since to him alone belong all glory and power for ever and ever. Amen.

12 My dear friends, do not be taken aback at the testing by fire which is taking place among you, as though something strange were happening to you; 13 but in so far as you share in the sufferings of Christ, be glad, so that you may enjoy a much greater gladness when his glory is revealed. 14 If you are insulted for bearing Christ's name, blessed are you, for *on you rests the Spirit of God,q* the Spirit of glory. 15 None of you should ever deserve to suffer for being a murderer, a thief, a criminal or an informer; 16 but if any one of you should suffer for being a Christian, then there must be no shame but thanksgiving to God for bearing this name. 17 The time has come for the judgement to begin at the household of God; and if it begins with us, what will be the end for those who refuse to believe God's gospel? 18 *If it is hard for the upright to be saved, what will happen to the wicked and to sinners?r* 19 So even those whom God allows to suffer should commit themselves to a Creator who is trustworthy, and go on doing good.

5 I urge the elders among you, as a fellow-elder myself and a witness to the sufferings of Christ, and as one who is to have a share in the glory that is to be revealed: 2 give a shepherd's care to the flock of God that is entrusted to you: watch over it, not simply as a duty but gladly, as God wants; not for sordid money, but because you are eager to do it. 3 Do not lord it over the group which is in your charge, but be an example for the flock. 4 When the chief shepherd appears, you will be given the unfading crown of glory.

p 4 Pr 10:12; Tb 12:9.   q 4 Is 11:2.   r 4 Pr 11:31 LXX.

younger must accept the authority of the elders.*e* And all of you must clothe yourselves with humility in your dealings with one another, for

> "God opposes the proud,
> but gives grace to the humble."

6 Humble yourselves therefore under the mighty hand of God, so that he may exalt you in due time. 7 Cast all your anxiety on him, because he cares for you. 8 Discipline yourselves, keep alert.*f* Like a roaring lion your adversary the devil prowls around, looking for someone to devour. 9 Resist him, steadfast in your faith, for you know that your brothers and sisters*g* in all the world are undergoing the same kinds of suffering. 10 And after you have suffered for a little while, the God of all grace, who has called you to his eternal glory in Christ, will himself restore, support, strengthen, and establish you. 11 To him be the power forever and ever. Amen.

12 Through Silvanus, whom I consider a faithful brother, I have written this short letter to encourage you and to testify that this is the true grace of God. Stand fast in it. 13 Your sister church*h* in Babylon, chosen together with you, sends you greetings; and so does my son Mark. 14 Greet one another with a kiss of love.

Peace to all of you who are in Christ.*i*

e Or of those who are older   f Or be vigilant   g Gk your brotherhood   h Gk She who is   i Other ancient authorities add Amen

5 In the same way the younger men should submit to the older. You should all clothe yourselves with humility towards one another, because 'God sets his face against the arrogant but shows favour to the humble.' 6 Humble yourselves, then, under God's mighty hand, and in due time he will lift you up. 7 He cares for you, so cast all your anxiety on him.

8 Be on the alert! Wake up! Your enemy the devil, like a roaring lion, prowls around looking for someone to devour. 9 Stand up to him, firm in your faith, and remember that your fellow-Christians in this world are going through the same kinds of suffering. 10 After your brief suffering, the God of all grace, who called you to his eternal glory in Christ, will himself restore, establish, and strengthen you on a firm foundation. 11 All power belongs to him for ever and ever! Amen.

12 I WRITE you this brief letter through Silvanus, whom I know to be a trustworthy colleague, to encourage you and to testify that this is the true grace of God; in this stand fast.

13 Greetings from your sister church in Babylon, and from my son Mark. 14 Greet one another with a loving kiss. Peace to you all who belong to Christ!

NEW AMERICAN BIBLE

NEW JERUSALEM BIBLE

5 Likewise, you younger members, be subject to the presbyters. And all of you, clothe yourselves with humility in your dealings with one another, for:

"God opposes the proud
but bestows favor on the humble."

6 So humble yourselves under the mighty hand of God, that he may exalt you in due time. 7 Cast all your worries upon him because he cares for you.

8 Be sober and vigilant. Your opponent the devil is prowling around like a roaring lion looking for [someone] to devour. 9 Resist him, steadfast in faith, knowing that your fellow believers throughout the world undergo the same sufferings. 10 The God of all grace who called you to his eternal glory through Christ [Jesus] will himself restore, confirm, strengthen, and establish you after you have suffered a little. 11 To him be dominion forever. Amen.

12 I write you this briefly through Silvanus, whom I consider a faithful brother, exhorting you and testifying that this is the true grace of God. Remain firm in it. 13 The chosen one at Babylon sends you greeting, as does Mark, my son. 14 Greet one another with a loving kiss. Peace to all of you who are in Christ.

5 In the same way, younger people, be subject to the elders. Humility towards one another must be the garment you all wear constantly, because *God opposes the proud but accords his favour to the humble.*[s] 6 Bow down, then, before the power of God now, so that he may raise you up in due time; 7 *unload all your burden on to him,*[t] since he is concerned about you. 8 Keep sober and alert, because your enemy the devil is on the prowl like a *roaring lion,*[u] looking for someone to devour. 9 Stand up to him, strong in faith and in the knowledge that it is the same kind of suffering that the community of your brothers throughout the world is undergoing. 10 You will have to suffer only for a little while: the God of all grace who called you to eternal glory in Christ will restore you, he will confirm, strengthen and support you. 11 His power lasts for ever and ever. Amen.

12 I write these few words to you through Silvanus, who is a trustworthy brother, to encourage you and attest that this is the true grace of God. Stand firm in it!

13 Your sister in Babylon, who is with you among the chosen, sends you greetings; so does my son, Mark.

14 Greet one another with a kiss of love.
Peace to you all who are in Christ.

---

s 5 Pr 3:34 LXX. *t* 5 Ps 55:22. *u* 5 Ps 22:13.

THE SECOND LETTER OF
Peter

1 Simeon*a* Peter, a servant*b* and apostle of Jesus Christ,

To those who have received a faith as precious as ours through the righteousness of our God and Savior Jesus Christ:*c*

2 May grace and peace be yours in abundance in the knowledge of God and of Jesus our Lord.

3 His divine power has given us everything needed for life and godliness, through the knowledge of him who called us by*d* his own glory and goodness. 4 Thus he has given us, through these things, his precious and very great promises, so that through them you may escape from the corruption that is in the world because of lust, and may become participants of the divine nature. 5 For this very reason, you must make every effort to support your faith with goodness, and goodness with knowledge, 6 and knowledge with self-control, and self-control with endurance, and endurance with godliness, 7 and godliness with mutual*e* affection, and mutual*e* affection with love. 8 For if these things are yours and are increasing among you, they keep you from being ineffective and unfruitful in the knowledge of our Lord Jesus Christ. 9 For anyone who lacks these things is nearsighted and blind, and is forgetful of the cleansing of past sins. 10 Therefore, brothers and sisters,*f* be all the more eager to confirm your call and election, for if you do this, you will never stumble. 11 For in this way, entry into the eternal kingdom of our Lord and Savior Jesus Christ will be richly provided for you.

12 Therefore I intend to keep on reminding you of these things, though you know them already and are established in the truth that has come to you. 13 I think it right, as long as I am in this body,*g* to refresh your memory, 14 since I know that my death*h* will come soon, as indeed our Lord Jesus Christ has made clear to me. 15 And I will make every effort so that after my departure you may be able at any time to recall these things.

16 For we did not follow cleverly devised myths when we made known to you the power and coming of our Lord Jesus Christ, but we had been eyewitnesses of his majesty. 17 For he received honor and glory from God the Father when that voice was conveyed to him by the Majestic Glory, saying, "This is my Son, my Beloved,*i* with whom I am well pleased." 18 We ourselves heard this voice come from heaven, while we were with him on the holy mountain.

19 So we have the prophetic message more fully confirmed. You will do well to be attentive to this as to a lamp shining in a dark place, until the day dawns and the morning star rises in your hearts. 20 First of all you must understand this, that no prophecy of scripture is a matter of one's own interpretation, 21 because no prophecy ever came by human will, but men and women moved by the Holy Spirit spoke from God.*j*

THE SECOND LETTER OF
Peter

1 FROM Simeon Peter, servant and apostle of Jesus Christ, to those who share equally with us in the privileges of faith through the righteousness of our God and Saviour Jesus Christ.

2 Grace and peace be yours in fullest measure, through knowledge of God and of Jesus our Lord.

3 GOD's divine power has bestowed on us everything that makes for life and true religion, through our knowledge of him who called us by his own glory and goodness. 4 In this way he has given us his promises, great beyond all price, so that through them you may escape the corruption with which lust has infected the world, and may come to share in the very being of God.

5 With all this in view, you should make every effort to add virtue to your faith, knowledge to virtue, 6 self-control to knowledge, fortitude to self-control, piety to fortitude, 7 brotherly affection to piety, and love to brotherly affection.

8 If you possess and develop these gifts, you will grow actively and effectively in knowledge of our Lord Jesus Christ. 9 Whoever lacks them is wilfully blind; he has forgotten that his past sins were washed away. 10 All the more then, my friends, do your utmost to establish that God has called and chosen you. If you do this, you will never stumble, 11 and there will be rich provision for your entry into the eternal kingdom of our Lord and Saviour Jesus Christ.

12 I shall keep reminding you of all this, although you know it and are well grounded in the truth you possess; 13 yet I think it right to keep on reminding you as long as I still lodge in this body. 14 I know I must soon leave it, as our Lord Jesus Christ told me. 15 But I will do my utmost to ensure that after I am gone you will always be able to call these things to mind.

16 It was not on tales, however cleverly concocted, that we relied when we told you about the power of our Lord Jesus Christ and his coming; rather with our own eyes we had witnessed his majesty. 17 He was invested with honour and glory by God the Father, and there came to him from the sublime Presence a voice which said: 'This is my Son, my Beloved, on whom my favour rests.' 18 We ourselves heard this voice when it came from heaven, for we were with him on the sacred mountain.

19 All this confirms for us the message of the prophets, to which you will do well to attend; it will go on shining like a lamp in a murky place, until day breaks and the morning star rises to illuminate your minds.

20 BUT first note this: no prophetic writing is a matter for private interpretation. 21 It was not on any human initiative that prophecy came; rather, it was under the compulsion of the Holy Spirit that people spoke as messengers of God.

---

a Other ancient authorities read *Simon*   *b* Gk *slave*   *c* Or *of our God and the Savior Jesus Christ*   *d* Other ancient authorities read *through*   *e* Gk *brotherly*   *f* Gk *brothers*   *g* Gk *the putting off of my tent*   *h* Gk *my beloved Son*   *i* Other ancient authorities read *my beloved Son*   *j* Other ancient authorities read *but moved by the Holy Spirit saints of God spoke*

1:17 **This . . . Beloved:** *or* This is my only Son.

The Second Letter of Peter

1 Symeon Peter, a slave and apostle of Jesus Christ, to those who have received a faith of equal value to ours through the righteousness of our God and savior Jesus Christ: 2 may grace and peace be yours in abundance through knowledge of God and of Jesus our Lord.

3 His divine power has bestowed on us everything that makes for life and devotion, through the knowledge of him who called us by his own glory and power. 4 Through these, he has bestowed on us the precious and very great promises, so that through them you may come to share in the divine nature, after escaping from the corruption that is in the world because of evil desire. 5 For this very reason, make every effort to supplement your faith with virtue, virtue with knowledge, 6 knowledge with self-control, self-control with endurance, endurance with devotion, 7 devotion with mutual affection, mutual affection with love. 8 If these are yours and increase in abundance, they will keep you from being idle or unfruitful in the knowledge of our Lord Jesus Christ. 9 Anyone who lacks them is blind and shortsighted, forgetful of the cleansing of his past sins. 10 Therefore, brothers, be all the more eager to make your call and election firm, for, in doing so, you will never stumble. 11 For, in this way, entry into the eternal kingdom of our Lord and savior Jesus Christ will be richly provided for you.

12 Therefore, I will always remind you of these things, even though you already know them and are established in the truth you have. 13 I think it right, as long as I am in this "tent," to stir you up by a reminder, 14 since I know that I will soon have to put it aside, as indeed our Lord Jesus Christ has shown me. 15 I shall also make every effort to enable you always to remember these things after my departure.

16 We did not follow cleverly devised myths when we made known to you the power and coming of our Lord Jesus Christ, but we had been eyewitnesses of his majesty. 17 For he received honor and glory from God the Father when that unique declaration came to him from the majestic glory, "This is my Son, my beloved, with whom I am well pleased." 18 We ourselves heard this voice come from heaven while we were with him on the holy mountain. 19 Moreover, we possess the prophetic message that is altogether reliable. You will do well to be attentive to it, as to a lamp shining in a dark place, until day dawns and the morning star rises in your hearts. 20 Know this first of all, that there is no prophecy of scripture that is a matter of personal interpretation, 21 for no prophecy ever came through human will; but rather human beings moved by the holy Spirit spoke under the influence of God.

2 Peter

THE SECOND LETTER OF PETER

1 Simon Peter, servant and apostle of Jesus Christ, to those who have received a faith as precious as our own, given through the saving justice of our God and Saviour Jesus Christ. 2 Grace and peace be yours in abundance through the knowledge of our Lord.

3 By his divine power, he has lavished on us all the things we need for life and for true devotion, through the knowledge of him who has called us by his own glory and goodness. 4 Through these, the greatest and priceless promises have been lavished on us, that through them you should share the divine nature and escape the corruption rife in the world through disordered passion. 5 With this in view, do your utmost to support your faith with goodness, goodness with understanding, 6 understanding with self-control, self-control with perseverance, perseverance with devotion, 7 devotion with kindness to the brothers, and kindness to the brothers with love. 8 The possession and growth of these qualities will prevent your knowledge of our Lord Jesus Christ from being ineffectual or unproductive. 9 But without them, a person is blind or short-sighted, forgetting how the sins of the past were washed away. 10 Instead of this, brothers, never allow your choice or calling to waver; then there will be no danger of your stumbling, 11 for in this way you will be given the generous gift of entry to the eternal kingdom of our Lord and Saviour Jesus Christ.

12 That is why I will always go on recalling the same truths to you, even though you already know them and are firmly fixed in these truths. 13 I am sure it is my duty, as long as I am in this tent, to keep stirring you up with reminders, 14 since I know the time for me to lay aside this tent is coming soon, as our Lord Jesus Christ made clear to me. 15 And I shall take great care that after my own departure you will still have a means to recall these things to mind.

16 When we told you about the power and the coming of our Lord Jesus Christ, we were not slavishly repeating cleverly invented myths; no, we had seen his majesty with our own eyes. 17 He was honoured and glorified by God the Father, when a voice came to him from the transcendent Glory, *This is my Son, the Beloved; he enjoys my favour.* a 18 We ourselves heard this voice from heaven, when we were with him on the holy mountain. 19 So we have confirmation of the words of the prophets; and you will be right to pay attention to it as to a lamp for lighting a way through the dark, until the dawn comes and the morning star rises in your minds. 20 At the same time, we must recognise that the interpretation of scriptural prophecy is never a matter for the individual. 21 For no prophecy ever came from human initiative. When people spoke for God it was the Holy Spirit that moved them.

2 But false prophets also arose among the people, just as there will be false teachers among you, who will secretly bring in destructive opinions. They will even deny the Master who bought them—bringing swift destruction on themselves. [2] Even so, many will follow their licentious ways, and because of these teachers[k] the way of truth will be maligned. [3] And in their greed they will exploit you with deceptive words. Their condemnation, pronounced against them long ago, has not been idle, and their destruction is not asleep.

[4] For if God did not spare the angels when they sinned, but cast them into hell[l] and committed them to chains[m] of deepest darkness to be kept until the judgment; [5] and if he did not spare the ancient world, even though he saved Noah, a herald of righteousness, with seven others, when he brought a flood on a world of the ungodly; [6] and if by turning the cities of Sodom and Gomorrah to ashes he condemned them to extinction[n] and made them an example of what is coming to the ungodly;[o] [7] and if he rescued Lot, a righteous man greatly distressed by the licentiousness of the lawless [8] (for that righteous man, living among them day after day, was tormented in his righteous soul by their lawless deeds that he saw and heard), [9] then the Lord knows how to rescue the godly from trial, and to keep the unrighteous under punishment until the day of judgment [10] —especially those who indulge their flesh in depraved lust, and who despise authority.

Bold and willful, they are not afraid to slander the glorious ones,[p] [11] whereas angels, though greater in might and power, do not bring against them a slanderous judgment from the Lord.[q] [12] These people, however, are like irrational animals, mere creatures of instinct, born to be caught and killed. They slander what they do not understand, and when those creatures are destroyed,[r] they also will be destroyed, [13] suffering[s] the penalty for doing wrong. They count it a pleasure to revel in the daytime. They are blots and blemishes, reveling in their dissipation[t] while they feast with you. [14] They have eyes full of adultery, insatiable for sin. They entice unsteady souls. They have hearts trained in greed. Accursed children! [15] They have left the straight road and have gone astray, following the road of Balaam son of Bosor,[u] who loved the wages of doing wrong, [16] but was rebuked for his own transgression; a speechless donkey spoke with a human voice and restrained the prophet's madness.

[17] These are waterless springs and mists driven by a storm; for them the deepest darkness has been reserved. [18] For they speak bombastic nonsense, and with licentious desires of the flesh they entice people who have just[v] escaped from those who live in error. [19] They promise them freedom, but they themselves are slaves of corruption; for people are slaves to whatever masters them. [20] For if, after they have escaped the defilements of the world through the knowledge of our Lord and Savior Jesus Christ, they are again entangled in them and overpowered, the last state has become worse for them than the first. [21] For it would have been better for them never to have known the way of righteousness than, after knowing it, to turn back from the holy commandment that was passed on to them. [22] It has hap-

2 IN the past there were also false prophets among the people, just as you also will have false teachers among you. They will introduce their destructive views, disowning the very Master who redeemed them, and bringing swift destruction on their own heads. [2] They will gain many adherents to their dissolute practices, through whom the way of truth will be brought into disrepute. [3] In their greed for money they will trade on your credulity with sheer fabrications.

But judgement has long been in preparation for them; destruction waits for them with unsleeping eyes. [4] God did not spare the angels who sinned, but consigned them to the dark pits of hell, where they are held for judgement. [5] Nor did he spare the world in ancient times (except for Noah, who proclaimed righteousness, and was preserved with seven others), but brought the flood upon that world with its godless people. [6] God reduced the cities of Sodom and Gomorrah to ashes, condemning them to total ruin as an object-lesson for the ungodly in future days. [7] But he rescued Lot, a good man distressed by the dissolute habits of the lawless society in which he lived; [8] day after day every sight and sound of their evil ways tortured that good man's heart. [9] The Lord knows how to rescue the godly from their trials, and to keep the wicked under punishment until the day of judgement.

[10] Above all he will punish those who follow their abominable lusts and flout authority. Reckless and headstrong, they are not afraid to insult celestial beings, [11] whereas angels, for all their superior strength and power, employ no insults in seeking judgement against them before the Lord.

[12] These men are like brute beasts, mere creatures of instinct, born to be caught and killed. They pour abuse upon things they do not understand; they will perish like the beasts, [13] suffering hurt for the hurt they have inflicted. To carouse in broad daylight is their idea of pleasure; while they sit with you at table they are an ugly blot on your company, because they revel in their deceits. [14] They have eyes for nothing but loose women, eyes never resting from sin. They lure the unstable to their ruin; experts in mercenary greed, God's curse is on them! [15] They have abandoned the straight road and gone astray. They have followed in the steps of Balaam son of Bosor, who eagerly accepted payment for doing wrong, [16] but had his offence brought home to him when a dumb beast spoke with a human voice and checked the prophet's madness.

[17] These men are springs that give no water, mists driven by a storm; the place reserved for them is blackest darkness. [18] They utter empty bombast; they use sensual lusts and debauchery as a bait to catch people who have only just begun to escape from their pagan associates. [19] They promise them freedom, but are themselves slaves of corruption; for people are the slaves of whatever has mastered them. [20] If they escaped the world's defilements through coming to know our Lord and Saviour Jesus Christ and entangled themselves in them again, and were mastered by them, their last state was worse than the first. [21] Better for them never to have known the right way, than, having known it, to turn back and abandon the sacred commandment entrusted to them! [22] In their case the proverb has proved true: 'The

---

[k] Gk *because of them*   [l] Gk *Tartaros*   [m] Other ancient authorities read *pits*   [n] Other ancient authorities lack *to extinction*   [o] Other ancient authorities read *an example to those who were to be ungodly*   [p] Or *angels*; Gk *glories*   [q] Other ancient authorities read *before the Lord*; others lack the phrase   [r] Gk *in their destruction*   [s] Other ancient authorities read *receiving*   [t] Other ancient authorities read *love feasts*   [u] Other ancient authorities read *Beor*   [v] Other ancient authorities read *actually*

2:4 **consigned . . . hell:** *some witnesses read* consigned them to darkness and chains in hell.   2:15 **Bosor:** *some witnesses read* Beor.

NEW AMERICAN BIBLE

NEW JERUSALEM BIBLE

2 There were also false prophets among the people, just as there will be false teachers among you, who will introduce destructive heresies and even deny the Master who ransomed them, bringing swift destruction on themselves. 2 Many will follow their licentious ways, and because of them the way of truth will be reviled. 3 In their greed they will exploit you with fabrications, but from of old their condemnation has not been idle and their destruction does not sleep.

4 For if God did not spare the angels when they sinned, but condemned them to the chains of Tartarus and handed them over to be kept for judgment; 5 and if he did not spare the ancient world, even though he preserved Noah, a herald of righteousness, together with seven others, when he brought a flood upon the godless world; 6 and if he condemned the cities of Sodom and Gomorrah [to destruction], reducing them to ashes, making them an example for the godless [people] of what is coming; 7 and if he rescued Lot, a righteous man oppressed by the licentious conduct of unprincipled people 8 (for day after day that righteous man living among them was tormented in his righteous soul at the lawless deeds that he saw and heard), 9 then the Lord knows how to rescue the devout from trial and to keep the unrighteous under punishment for the day of judgment, 10 and especially those who follow the flesh with its depraved desire and show contempt for lordship.

Bold and arrogant, they are not afraid to revile glorious beings, 11 whereas angels, despite their superior strength and power, do not bring a reviling judgment against them from the Lord. 12 But these people, like irrational animals born by nature for capture and destruction, revile things that they do not understand, and in their destruction they will also be destroyed, 13 suffering wrong as payment for wrongdoing. Thinking daytime revelry a delight, they are stains and defilements as they revel in their deceits while carousing with you. 14 Their eyes are full of adultery and insatiable for sin. They seduce unstable people, and their hearts are trained in greed. Accursed children! 15 Abandoning the straight road, they have gone astray, following the road of Balaam, the son of Bosor, who loved payment for wrongdoing, 16 but he received a rebuke for his own crime: a mute beast spoke with a human voice and restrained the prophet's madness.

17 These people are waterless springs and mists driven by a gale; for them the gloom of darkness has been reserved. 18 For, talking empty bombast, they seduce with licentious desires of the flesh those who have barely escaped from people who live in error. 19 They promise them freedom, though they themselves are slaves of corruption, for a person is a slave of whatever overcomes him. 20 For if they, having escaped the defilements of the world through the knowledge of [our] Lord and savior Jesus Christ, again become entangled and overcome by them, their last condition is worse than their first. 21 For it would have been better for them not to have known the way of righteousness than after knowing it to turn back from the holy commandment handed down to them. 22 What is expressed in the true prov-

2 As there were false prophets in the past history of our people, so you too will have your false teachers, who will insinuate their own disruptive views and, by disowning the Lord who bought them freedom, will bring upon themselves speedy destruction. 2 Many will copy their debauched behaviour, and the Way of Truth will be brought into disrepute on their account. 3 In their greed they will try to make a profit out of you with untrue tales. But the judgement made upon them long ago is not idle, and the destruction awaiting them is for ever on the watch.

4 When angels sinned, God did not spare them: he sent them down into the underworld and consigned them to the dark abyss to be held there until the Judgement. 5 He did not spare the world in ancient times: he saved only Noah, the preacher of uprightness, along with seven others, when he sent the Flood over a world of sinners. 6 He condemned the cities of Sodom and Gomorrah by reducing them to ashes as a warning to future sinners; 7 but rescued Lot, an upright man who had been sickened by the debauched way in which these vile people behaved— 8 for that upright man, living among them, was outraged in his upright soul by the crimes that he saw and heard every day. 9 All this shows that the Lord is well able to rescue the good from their trials, and hold the wicked for their punishment until the Day of Judgement, 10 especially those who follow the desires of their corrupt human nature and have no respect for the Lord's authority.

Such self-willed people with no reverence are not afraid of offending against the glorious ones, 11 but the angels in their greater strength and power make no complaint or accusation against them in the Lord's presence. 12 But these people speak evil of what they do not understand; they are like brute beasts, born only to be caught and killed, and like beasts they will be destroyed, being injured in return for the injuries they have inflicted. 13 Debauchery even by day they make their pleasure; they are unsightly blots, and amuse themselves by their trickery even when they are sharing your table; 14 with their eyes always looking for adultery, people with an insatiable capacity for sinning, they will seduce any but the most stable soul. Where greed is concerned they are at their peak of fitness. They are under a curse. 15 They have left the right path and wandered off to follow the path of Balaam son of Bosor, who set his heart on a dishonest reward, but soon had his fault pointed out to him: 16 a dumb beast of burden, speaking with a human voice, put a stop to the madness of the prophet.

17 People like this are dried-up springs, fogs swirling in the wind, and the gloom of darkness is stored up for them. 18 With their high-sounding but empty talk they tempt back people who have scarcely escaped from those who live in error, by playing on the disordered desires of their human nature and by debaucheries. 19 They may promise freedom but are themselves slaves to corruption; because if anyone lets himself be dominated by anything, then he is a slave to it; 20 and anyone who has escaped the pollution of the world by coming to know our Lord and Saviour Jesus Christ, and who then allows himself to be entangled and mastered by it a second time, ends up by being worse than he was before. 21 It would have been better for them never to have learnt the way of uprightness, than to learn it and then desert the holy commandment that was entrusted to them. 22 What

pened to them according to the true proverb,

"The dog turns back to its own vomit,"

and,

"The sow is washed only to wallow in the mud."

3 This is now, beloved, the second letter I am writing to you; in them I am trying to arouse your sincere intention by reminding you 2 that you should remember the words spoken in the past by the holy prophets, and the commandment of the Lord and Savior spoken through your apostles. 3 First of all you must understand this, that in the last days scoffers will come, scoffing and indulging their own lusts 4 and saying, "Where is the promise of his coming? For ever since our ancestors died,^{w} all things continue as they were from the beginning of creation!" 5 They deliberately ignore this fact, that by the word of God heavens existed long ago and an earth was formed out of water and by means of water, 6 through which the world of that time was deluged with water and perished. 7 But by the same word the present heavens and earth have been reserved for fire, being kept until the day of judgment and destruction of the godless.

8 But do not ignore this one fact, beloved, that with the Lord one day is like a thousand years, and a thousand years are like one day. 9 The Lord is not slow about his promise, as some think of slowness, but is patient with you,^{x} not wanting any to perish, but all to come to repentance. 10 But the day of the Lord will come like a thief, and then the heavens will pass away with a loud noise, and the elements will be dissolved with fire, and the earth and everything that is done on it will be disclosed.^{y}

11 Since all these things are to be dissolved in this way, what sort of persons ought you to be in leading lives of holiness and godliness, 12 waiting for and hastening^z the coming of the day of God, because of which the heavens will be set ablaze and dissolved, and the elements will melt with fire? 13 But, in accordance with his promise, we wait for new heavens and a new earth, where righteousness is at home.

14 Therefore, beloved, while you are waiting for these things, strive to be found by him at peace, without spot or blemish; 15 and regard the patience of our Lord as salvation. So also our beloved brother Paul wrote to you according to the wisdom given him, 16 speaking of this as he does in all his letters. There are some things in them hard to understand, which the ignorant and unstable twist to their own destruction, as they do the other scriptures. 17 You therefore, beloved, since you are forewarned, beware that you are not carried away with the error of the lawless and lose your own stability. 18 But grow in the grace and knowledge of our Lord and Savior Jesus Christ. To him be the glory both now and to the day of eternity. Amen.^{a}

^{w} Gk our fathers fell asleep ^{x} Other ancient authorities read on your account ^{y} Other ancient authorities read will be burned up ^{z} Or earnestly desiring ^{a} Other ancient authorities lack Amen

dog returns to its vomit,' and 'The washed sow wallows in the mud again.'

3 THIS, dear friends, is now my second letter to you. In both I have been recalling to you what you already know, to rouse you to honest thought. 2 Remember the predictions made by God's own prophets, and the commandment given by the Lord and Saviour through your apostles.

3 First of all, note this: in the last days there will come scoffers who live self-indulgent lives; they will mock you and say: 4 'What has happened to his promised coming? Our fathers have been laid to rest, but still everything goes on exactly as it always has done since the world began.'

5 In maintaining this they forget that there were heavens and earth long ago, created by God's word out of water and with water; 6 and that the first world was destroyed by water, the water of the flood. 7 By God's word the present heavens and earth are being reserved for burning; they are being kept until the day of judgement when the godless will be destroyed.

8 Here is something, dear friends, which you must not forget: in the Lord's sight one day is like a thousand years and a thousand years like one day. 9 It is not that the Lord is slow in keeping his promise, as some suppose, but that he is patient with you. It is not his will that any should be lost, but that all should come to repentance.

10 But the day of the Lord will come like a thief. On that day the heavens will disappear with a great rushing sound, the elements will be dissolved in flames, and the earth with all that is in it will be brought to judgement.

11 Since the whole universe is to dissolve in this way, think what sort of people you ought to be, what devout and dedicated lives you should live! 12 Look forward to the coming of the day of God, and work to hasten it on; that day will set the heavens ablaze until they fall apart, and will melt the elements in flames. 13 Relying on his promise we look forward to new heavens and a new earth, in which justice will be established.

14 In expectation of all this, my friends, do your utmost to be found at peace with him, unblemished and above reproach. 15 Bear in mind that our Lord's patience is an opportunity for salvation, as Paul, our dear friend and brother, said when he wrote to you with the wisdom God gave him. 16 He does the same in all his other letters, wherever he speaks about this, though they contain some obscure passages, which the ignorant and unstable misinterpret to their own ruin, as they do the other scriptures.

17 So, dear friends, you have been forewarned. Take care not to let these unprincipled people seduce you with their errors; do not lose your own safe foothold. 18 But grow in grace and in the knowledge of our Lord and Saviour Jesus Christ. To him be glory both now and for all eternity!

3:10 will be brought to judgement: lit. will be found.

erb has happened to them, "The dog returns to its own vomit," and "A bathed sow returns to wallowing in the mire."

3 This is now, beloved, the second letter I am writing to you; through them by way of reminder I am trying to stir up your sincere disposition, 2 to recall the words previously spoken by the holy prophets and the commandment of the Lord and savior through your apostles. 3 Know this first of all, that in the last days scoffers will come [to] scoff, living according to their own desires 4 and saying, "Where is the promise of his coming? From the time when our ancestors fell asleep, everything has remained as it was from the beginning of creation." 5 They deliberately ignore the fact that the heavens existed of old and earth was formed out of water and through water by the word of God; 6 through these the world that then existed was destroyed, deluged with water. 7 The present heavens and earth have been reserved by the same word for fire, kept for the day of judgment and of destruction of the godless.

8 But do not ignore this one fact, beloved, that with the Lord one day is like a thousand years and a thousand years like one day. 9 The Lord does not delay his promise, as some regard "delay," but he is patient with you, not wishing that any should perish but that all should come to repentance. 10 But the day of the Lord will come like a thief, and then the heavens will pass away with a mighty roar and the elements will be dissolved by fire, and the earth and everything done on it will be found out.

11 Since everything is to be dissolved in this way, what sort of persons ought [you] to be, conducting yourselves in holiness and devotion, 12 waiting for and hastening the coming of the day of God, because of which the heavens will be dissolved in flames and the elements melted by fire. 13 But according to his promise we await new heavens and a new earth in which righteousness dwells.

14 Therefore, beloved, since you await these things, be eager to be found without spot or blemish before him, at peace. 15 And consider the patience of our Lord as salvation, as our beloved brother Paul, according to the wisdom given to him, also wrote to you, 16 speaking of these things as he does in all his letters. In them there are some things hard to understand that the ignorant and unstable distort to their own destruction, just as they do the other scriptures.

17 Therefore, beloved, since you are forewarned, be on your guard not to be led into the error of the unprincipled and to fall from your own stability. 18 But grow in grace and in the knowledge of our Lord and savior Jesus Christ. To him be glory now and to the day of eternity. [Amen.]

they have done is exactly as the proverb rightly says: *The dog goes back to its vomit*[b] and: As soon as the sow has been washed, it wallows in the mud.

3 My dear friends, this is the second letter I have written to you, trying to awaken in you by my reminders an unclouded understanding. 2 Remember what was said in the past by the holy prophets and the command of the Lord and Saviour given by your apostles.

3 First of all, do not forget that in the final days there will come sarcastic scoffers whose life is ruled by their passions. 4 'What has happened to the promise of his coming?' they will say, 'Since our Fathers died everything has gone on just as it has since the beginning of creation!' 5 They deliberately ignore the fact that long ago there were the heavens and the earth, formed out of water and through water by the Word of God, 6 and that it was through these same factors that the world of those days was destroyed by the floodwaters. 7 It is the same Word which is reserving the present heavens and earth for fire, keeping them till the Day of Judgement and of the destruction of sinners.

8 But there is one thing, my dear friends, that you must never forget: that with the Lord, a day is like a thousand years, and *a thousand years are like a day*.[c] 9 The Lord is not being slow in carrying out his promises, as some people think he is; rather is he being patient with you, wanting nobody to be lost and everybody to be brought to repentance. 10 The Day of the Lord will come like a thief, and then with a roar the sky will vanish, the elements will catch fire and melt away, the earth and all that it contains will be burned up.

11 Since everything is coming to an end like this, what holy and saintly lives you should be living 12 while you wait for the Day of God to come, and try to hasten its coming: on that Day the sky will dissolve in flames and the elements melt in the heat. 13 What we are waiting for, relying on his promises, is the new heavens and new earth, where uprightness will be at home. 14 So then, my dear friends, while you are waiting, do your best to live blameless and unsullied lives so that he will find you at peace. 15 Think of our Lord's patience as your opportunity to be saved; our brother Paul, who is so dear to us, told you this when he wrote to you with the wisdom that he was given. 16 He makes this point too in his letters as a whole wherever he touches on these things. In all his letters there are of course some passages which are hard to understand, and these are the ones that uneducated and unbalanced people distort, in the same way as they distort the rest of scripture[d] — to their own destruction. 17 Since you have been forewarned about this, my dear friends, be careful that you do not come to the point of losing the firm ground that you are standing on, carried away by the errors of unprincipled people. 18 Instead, continue to grow in the grace and in the knowledge of our Lord and Saviour Jesus Christ. To him be glory, in time and eternity. Amen.

[b] 2 Pr 26:11.   [c] 3 Ps 90:4.   [d] 3 Paul's letters seemingly already exist as a collection, and are put on the same level as the OT.

THE FIRST LETTER OF
John

1 We declare to you what was from the beginning, what we have heard, what we have seen with our eyes, what we have looked at and touched with our hands, concerning the word of life — 2 this life was revealed, and we have seen it and testify to it, and declare to you the eternal life that was with the Father and was revealed to us — 3 we declare to you what we have seen and heard so that you also may have fellowship with us; and truly our fellowship is with the Father and with his Son Jesus Christ. 4 We are writing these things so that our*a* joy may be complete.

5 This is the message we have heard from him and proclaim to you, that God is light and in him there is no darkness at all. 6 If we say that we have fellowship with him while we are walking in darkness, we lie and do not do what is true; 7 but if we walk in the light as he himself is in the light, we have fellowship with one another, and the blood of Jesus his Son cleanses us from all sin. 8 If we say that we have no sin, we deceive ourselves, and the truth is not in us. 9 If we confess our sins, he who is faithful and just will forgive us our sins and cleanse us from all unrighteousness. 10 If we say that we have not sinned, we make him a liar, and his word is not in us.

2 My little children, I am writing these things to you so that you may not sin. But if anyone does sin, we have an advocate with the Father, Jesus Christ the righteous; 2 and he is the atoning sacrifice for our sins, and not for ours only but also for the sins of the whole world.

3 Now by this we may be sure that we know him, if we obey his commandments. 4 Whoever says, "I have come to know him," but does not obey his commandments, is a liar, and in such a person the truth does not exist; 5 but whoever obeys his word, truly in this person the love of God has reached perfection. By this we may be sure that we are in

THE FIRST LETTER OF
John

1 IT was there from the beginning; we have heard it; we have seen it with our own eyes; we looked upon it, and felt it with our own hands: our theme is the Word which gives life. 2 This life was made visible; we have seen it and bear our testimony; we declare to you the eternal life which was with the Father and was made visible to us. 3 It is this which we have seen and heard that we declare to you also, in order that you may share with us in a common life, that life which we share with the Father and his Son Jesus Christ. 4 We are writing this in order that our joy may be complete.

5 HERE is the message we have heard from him and pass on to you: God is light, and in him there is no darkness at all. 6 If we claim to be sharing in his life while we go on living in darkness, our words and our lives are a lie. 7 But if we live in the light as he himself is in the light, then we share a common life, and the blood of Jesus his Son cleanses us from all sin.

8 If we claim to be sinless, we are self-deceived and the truth is not in us. 9 If we confess our sins, he is just and may be trusted to forgive our sins and cleanse us from every kind of wrongdoing. 10 If we say we have committed no sin, we make him out to be a liar and his word has no place in us.

2 My children, I am writing this to you so that you should not commit sin. But if anybody does, we have in Jesus Christ one who is acceptable to God and will plead our cause with the Father. 2 He is himself a sacrifice to atone for our sins, and not ours only but the sins of the whole world.

3 It is by keeping God's commands that we can be sure we know him. 4 Whoever says, 'I know him,' but does not obey his commands, is a liar and the truth is not in him; 5 but whoever is obedient to his word, in him the love of God is truly made perfect. This is how we can be sure that we are

a Other ancient authorities read *your*

The First Letter of John

1 What was from the beginning,
    what we have heard,
    what we have seen with our eyes,
    what we looked upon
    and touched with our hands
    concerns the Word of life —
² for the life was made visible;
    we have seen it and testify to it
    and proclaim to you the eternal life
    that was with the Father and was made visible
        to us —
³ what we have seen and heard
    we proclaim now to you,
    so that you too may have fellowship with us;
    for our fellowship is with the Father
    and with his Son, Jesus Christ.
⁴ We are writing this so that our joy may
    be complete.

⁵ Now this is the message that we have heard from him and proclaim to you: God is light, and in him there is no darkness at all. ⁶ If we say, "We have fellowship with him," while we continue to walk in darkness, we lie and do not act in truth. ⁷ But if we walk in the light as he is in the light, then we have fellowship with one another, and the blood of his Son Jesus cleanses us from all sin. ⁸ If we say, "We are without sin," we deceive ourselves, and the truth is not in us. ⁹ If we acknowledge our sins, he is faithful and just and will forgive our sins and cleanse us from every wrongdoing. ¹⁰ If we say, "We have not sinned," we make him a liar, and his word is not in us.

2 My children, I am writing this to you so that you may not commit sin. But if anyone does sin, we have an Advocate with the Father, Jesus Christ the righteous one. ² He is expiation for our sins, and not for our sins only but for those of the whole world. ³ The way we may be sure that we know him is to keep his commandments. ⁴ Whoever says, "I know him," but does not keep his commandments is a liar, and the truth is not in him. ⁵ But whoever keeps his word, the love of God is truly perfected in him. This is the way we may know that we are in union with him: ⁶ whoever

1 John

THE FIRST LETTER OF JOHN

1 Something which has existed since the beginning,
    which we have heard,
    which we have seen with our own eyes,
    which we have watched
    and touched with our own hands,
    the Word of life —
    this is our theme.
² That life was made visible;
    we saw it and are giving our testimony,
    declaring to you the eternal life,
    which was present to the Father
    and has been revealed to us.
³ We are declaring to you
    what we have seen and heard,
    so that you too may share our life.
    Our life is shared with the Father
    and with his Son Jesus Christ.
⁴ We are writing this to you so that our joy may be
    complete.

⁵ This is what we have heard from him
    and are declaring to you:
    God is light, and there is no darkness in him at all.
⁶ If we say that we share in God's life
    while we are living in darkness,
    we are lying, because we are not living the truth.
⁷ But if we live in light,
    as he is in light,
    we have a share in another's life,
    and the blood of Jesus, his Son,
    cleanses us from all sin.
⁸ If we say, 'We have no sin,'
    we are deceiving ourselves,
    and truth has no place in us;
⁹ if we acknowledge our sins,
    he is trustworthy and upright,
    so that he will forgive our sins
    and will cleanse us from all evil.
¹⁰ If we say, 'We have never sinned,'
    we make him a liar,
    and his word has no place in us.

2 My children, I am writing this to prevent you from
    sinning;
    but if anyone does sin,
    we have an advocate with the Father,
    Jesus Christ, the upright.
² He is the sacrifice to expiate our sins,
    and not only ours,
    but also those of the whole world.
³ In this way we know
    that we have come to know him,
    if we keep his commandments.
⁴ Whoever says, 'I know him'
    without keeping his commandments,
    is a liar,
    and truth has no place in him.
⁵ But anyone who does keep his word,
    in such a one God's love truly reaches its
        perfection.
    This is the proof
    that we are in God.

him: 6 whoever says, "I abide in him," ought to walk just as he walked.

7 Beloved, I am writing you no new commandment, but an old commandment that you have had from the beginning; the old commandment is the word that you have heard. 8 Yet I am writing you a new commandment that is true in him and in you, because*b* the darkness is passing away and the true light is already shining. 9 Whoever says, "I am in the light," while hating a brother or sister,*c* is still in the darkness. 10 Whoever loves a brother or sister*d* lives in the light, and in such a person*e* there is no cause for stumbling. 11 But whoever hates another believer*f* is in the darkness, walks in the darkness, and does not know the way to go, because the darkness has brought on blindness.

12 I am writing to you, little children,
    because your sins are forgiven on account of
        his name.
13 I am writing to you, fathers,
    because you know him who is from the
        beginning.
I am writing to you, young people,
    because you have conquered the evil one.
14 I write to you, children,
    because you know the Father.
I write to you, fathers,
    because you know him who is from the
        beginning.
I write to you, young people,
    because you are strong
    and the word of God abides in you,
    and you have overcome the evil one.

15 Do not love the world or the things in the world. The love of the Father is not in those who love the world; 16 for all that is in the world — the desire of the flesh, the desire of the eyes, the pride in riches — comes not from the Father but from the world. 17 And the world and its desire*g* are passing away, but those who do the will of God live forever.

18 Children, it is the last hour! As you have heard that antichrist is coming, so now many antichrists have come. From this we know that it is the last hour. 19 They went out from us, but they did not belong to us; for if they had belonged to us, they would have remained with us. But by going out they made it plain that none of them belongs to us. 20 But you have been anointed by the Holy One, and all of you have knowledge.*h* 21 I write to you, not because you

in him: 6 whoever claims to be dwelling in him must live as Christ himself lived.

7 Dear friends, it is no new command that I am sending you, but an old command which you have had from the beginning; the old command is the instruction which you have already received. 8 Yet because the darkness is passing away and the true light already shining, it is a new command that I write and it is true in Christ's life and in yours.

9 Whoever says, 'I am in the light,' but hates his fellow-Christian, is still in darkness. 10 He who loves his fellow-Christian dwells in light: there is no cause of stumbling in him. 11 But anyone who hates his fellow is in darkness; he walks in the dark and has no idea where he is going, because the darkness has made him blind.

12 I write to you, children, because your sins have
        been forgiven for his sake.
13 I write to you, fathers, because you know him who
        is and has been from the beginning.
I write to you, young men, because you have
        conquered the evil one.

I have written to you, children, because you know
        the Father.
14 I have written to you, fathers, because you know
        him who is and has been from the
        beginning.

I have written to you, young men, because you are
        strong; God's word remains in you, and you
        have conquered the evil one.

15 Do not set your hearts on the world or what is in it. Anyone who loves the world does not love the Father. 16 Everything in the world, all that panders to the appetites or entices the eyes, all the arrogance based on wealth, these spring not from the Father but from the world. 17 That world with all its allurements is passing away, but those who do God's will remain for ever.

18 CHILDREN, this is the last hour! You were told that an antichrist was to come. Well, many antichrists have already appeared, proof to us that this is indeed the last hour. 19 They left our ranks, but never really belonged to us; if they had, they would have stayed with us. They left so that it might be clear that none of them belong to us. 20 What is more, you have been anointed by the Holy One, and so you all have knowledge. 21 It is not because you

---

b Or that   *c* Gk hating a brother   *d* Gk loves a brother   *e* Or in it   *f* Gk hates a brother   *g* Or the desire for it   *h* Other ancient authorities read *you know all things*

2:9 **fellow-Christian**: *lit.* brother.   2:19 **none of them**: *or* not all of them.   2:20 **you all have knowledge**: *some witnesses read* you have all knowledge.

claims to abide in him ought to live [just] as he lived. 7 Beloved, I am writing no new commandment to you but an old commandment that you had from the beginning. The old commandment is the word that you have heard. 8 And yet I do write a new commandment to you, which holds true in him and among you, for the darkness is passing away, and the true light is already shining. 9 Whoever says he is in the light, yet hates his brother, is still in the darkness. 10 Whoever loves his brother remains in the light, and there is nothing in him to cause a fall. 11 Whoever hates his brother is in darkness; he walks in darkness and does not know where he is going because the darkness has blinded his eyes.

12 I am writing to you, children, because your sins have been forgiven for his name's sake.

13 I am writing to you, fathers, because you know him who is from the beginning.

I am writing to you, young men, because you have conquered the evil one.

14 I write to you, children, because you know the Father.

I write to you, fathers, because you know him who is from the beginning.

I write to you, young men, because you are strong and the word of God remains in you, and you have conquered the evil one.

15 Do not love the world or the things of the world. If anyone loves the world, the love of the Father is not in him. 16 For all that is in the world, sensual lust, enticement for the eyes, and a pretentious life, is not from the Father but is from the world. 17 Yet the world and its enticement are passing away. But whoever does the will of God remains forever.

18 Children, it is the last hour; and just as you heard that the antichrist was coming, so now many antichrists have appeared. Thus we know this is the last hour. 19 They went out from us, but they were not really of our number; if they had been, they would have remained with us. Their desertion shows that none of them was of our number. 20 But you have the anointing that comes from the holy one, and you all have knowledge. 21 I write to you not because you do not

6 Whoever claims to remain in him
must act as he acted.
7 My dear friends,
this is not a new commandment I am writing for
you,
but an old commandment
that you have had from the beginning;
the old commandment is the message you have
heard.
8 Yet in another way, I am writing a new
commandment for you
— and this is true for you, just as much as for
him —
for darkness is passing away
and the true light is already shining.
9 Whoever claims to be in light
but hates his brother
is still in darkness.
10 Anyone who loves his brother remains in light
and there is in him nothing to make him fall away.
11 But whoever hates his brother is in darkness
and is walking about in darkness
not knowing where he is going,
because darkness has blinded him.
12 I am writing to you, children,
because your sins have been forgiven through his
name.
13 I am writing to you, fathers,
because you have come to know the One who has
existed since the beginning.
I am writing to you, young people,
because you have overcome the Evil One.
14 I have written to you, children,
because you have come to know the Father.
I have written to you, parents,
because you have come to know the One who has
existed since the beginning.
I have written to you, young people,
because you are strong,
and God's word remains in you,
and you have overcome the Evil One.
15 Do not love the world
or what is in the world.
If anyone does love the world,
the love of the Father finds no place in him,
16 because everything there is in the world —
disordered bodily desires,
disordered desires of the eyes,
pride in possession —
is not from the Father
but is from the world.
17 And the world, with all its disordered desires,
is passing away.
But whoever does the will of God
remains for ever.
18 Children, this is the final hour;
you have heard that the Antichrist[a] is coming,
and now many Antichrists have already come;
from this we know that it is the final hour.
19 They have gone from among us,
but they never really belonged to us;
if they had belonged to us, they would have stayed
with us.
But this was to prove
that not one of them belonged to us.
20 But you have been anointed by the Holy One,
and have all received knowledge.

a 2 cf. 2 Th 2:3–4.

NEW REVISED STANDARD VERSION

do not know the truth, but because you know it, and you know that no lie comes from the truth. 22 Who is the liar but the one who denies that Jesus is the Christ?[i] This is the antichrist, the one who denies the Father and the Son. 23 No one who denies the Son has the Father; everyone who confesses the Son has the Father also. 24 Let what you heard from the beginning abide in you. If what you heard from the beginning abides in you, then you will abide in the Son and in the Father. 25 And this is what he has promised us,[j] eternal life.

26 I write these things to you concerning those who would deceive you. 27 As for you, the anointing that you received from him abides in you, and so you do not need anyone to teach you. But as his anointing teaches you about all things, and is true and is not a lie, and just as it has taught you, abide in him.[k]

28 And now, little children, abide in him, so that when he is revealed we may have confidence and not be put to shame before him at his coming.

29 If you know that he is righteous, you may be sure that everyone who does right has been born of him.

3 1 See what love the Father has given us, that we should be called children of God; and that is what we are. The reason the world does not know us is that it did not know him. 2 Beloved, we are God's children now; what we will be has not yet been revealed. What we do know is this: when he[k] is revealed, we will be like him, for we will see him as he is. 3 And all who have this hope in him purify themselves, just as he is pure.

4 Everyone who commits sin is guilty of lawlessness; sin is lawlessness. 5 You know that he was revealed to take away sins, and in him there is no sin. 6 No one who abides in him sins; no one who sins has either seen him or known him. 7 Little children, let no one deceive you. Everyone who does what is right is righteous, just as he is righteous. 8 Everyone who commits sin is a child of the devil; for the devil has been sinning from the beginning. The Son of God was revealed for this purpose, to destroy the works of the devil. 9 Those who have been born of God do not sin, be-

REVISED ENGLISH BIBLE

are ignorant of the truth that I have written to you, but because you do know it, and know that lies never come from the truth.

22 Anyone who denies that Jesus is the Christ is nothing but a liar. He is the antichrist, for he denies both the Father and the Son: 23 to deny the Son is to be without the Father; to acknowledge the Son is to have the Father too. 24 You must therefore keep hold of what you heard at the beginning; if what you heard then still dwells in you, you will yourselves dwell both in the Son and in the Father. 25 And this is the promise that he himself gave us, the promise of eternal life.

26 So much for those who would mislead you. 27 But as for you, the anointing which you received from him remains with you; you need no other teacher, but you learn all you need to know from his anointing, which is true and no lie. Dwell in him as he taught you to do.

28 Even now, children, dwell in him, so that when he appears we may be confident and unashamed before him at his coming. 29 You know that God is righteous; then recognize that everyone who does what is right is his child.

3 CONSIDER how great is the love which the Father has bestowed on us in calling us his children! For that is what we are. The reason why the world does not recognize us is that it has not known him. 2 Dear friends, we are now God's children; what we shall be has not yet been disclosed, but we know that when Christ appears we shall be like him, because we shall see him as he is. 3 As he is pure, everyone who has grasped this hope makes himself pure.

4 To commit sin is to break God's law: for sin is lawlessness. 5 You know that Christ appeared in order to take away sins, and in him there is no sin. 6 No one who dwells in him sins any more; the sinner has neither seen him nor known him.

7 Children, do not be misled: anyone who does what is right is righteous, just as Christ is righteous; 8 anyone who sins is a child of the devil, for the devil has been a sinner from the first; and the Son of God appeared for the very purpose of undoing the devil's work. 9 No child of God

i Or *the Messiah*   *j* Other ancient authorities read *you*   *k* Or *it*

know the truth but because you do, and because every lie is alien to the truth. 22 Who is the liar? Whoever denies that Jesus is the Christ. Whoever denies the Father and the Son, this is the antichrist. 23 No one who denies the Son has the Father, but whoever confesses the Son has the Father as well.

24 Let what you heard from the beginning remain in you. If what you heard from the beginning remains in you, then you will remain in the Son and in the Father. 25 And this is the promise that he made us: eternal life. 26 I write you these things about those who would deceive you. 27 As for you, the anointing that you received from him remains in you, so that you do not need anyone to teach you. But his anointing teaches you about everything and is true and not false; just as it taught you, remain in him.

28 And now, children, remain in him, so that when he appears we may have confidence and not be put to shame by him at his coming. 29 If you consider that he is righteous, you also know that everyone who acts in righteousness is begotten by him.

3 See what love the Father has bestowed on us that we may be called the children of God. Yet so we are. The reason the world does not know us is that it did not know him. 2 Beloved, we are God's children now; what we shall be has not yet been revealed. We do know that when it is revealed we shall be like him, for we shall see him as he is. 3 Everyone who has this hope based on him makes himself pure, as he is pure.

4 Everyone who commits sin commits lawlessness, for sin is lawlessness. 5 You know that he was revealed to take away sins, and in him there is no sin. 6 No one who remains in him sins; no one who sins has seen him or known him. 7 Children, let no one deceive you. The person who acts in righteousness is righteous, just as he is righteous. 8 Whoever sins belongs to the devil, because the devil has sinned from the beginning. Indeed, the Son of God was revealed to destroy the works of the devil. 9 No one who is begotten by

21 I have written to you
not because you are ignorant of the truth,
but because you are well aware of it,
and because no lie can come from the truth.
22 Who is the liar,
if not one who claims that Jesus is not the Christ?
This is the Antichrist,
who denies both the Father and the Son.
23 Whoever denies the Son cannot have the Father either;
whoever acknowledges the Son has the Father too.
24 Let what you heard in the beginning remain in you;
as long as what you heard in the beginning remains in you,
you will remain in the Son
and in the Father.
25 And the promise he made you himself
is eternal life.
26 So much have I written to you
about those who are trying to lead you astray.
27 But as for you, the anointing you received from him
remains in you,
and you do not need anyone to teach you;
since the anointing he gave you teaches you everything,
and since it is true, not false,
remain in him just as he has taught you.
28 Therefore remain in him now, children,
so that when he appears we may be fearless,
and not shrink from him in shame
at his coming.
29 If you know that he is upright
you must recognise that everyone whose life is upright
is a child of his.

3 You must see what great love the Father has lavished on us
by letting us be called God's children —
which is what we are!
The reason why the world does not acknowledge us
is that it did not acknowledge him.
2 My dear friends, we are already God's children,
but what we shall be in the future has not yet been revealed.
We are well aware that when he appears
we shall be like him,
because we shall see him as he really is.
3 Whoever treasures this hope of him
purifies himself, to be as pure as he is.
4 Whoever sins, acts wickedly,
because all sin is wickedness.
5 Now you are well aware that he has appeared in order to take sins away,
and that in him there is no sin.
6 No one who remains in him sins,
and whoever sins
has neither seen him nor recognised him.
7 Children, do not let anyone lead you astray.
Whoever acts uprightly is upright,
just as he is upright.
8 Whoever lives sinfully belongs to the devil,
since the devil has been a sinner from the beginning.
This was the purpose of the appearing of the Son of God,
to undo the work of the devil.

NEW REVISED STANDARD VERSION

cause God's seed abides in them;*l* they cannot sin, because they have been born of God. 10 The children of God and the children of the devil are revealed in this way: all who do not do what is right are not from God, nor are those who do not love their brothers and sisters.*m*

11 For this is the message you have heard from the beginning, that we should love one another. 12 We must not be like Cain who was from the evil one and murdered his brother. And why did he murder him? Because his own deeds were evil and his brother's righteous. 13 Do not be astonished, brothers and sisters,*n* that the world hates you. 14 We know that we have passed from death to life because we love one another. Whoever does not love abides in death. 15 All who hate a brother or sister*m* are murderers, and you know that murderers do not have eternal life abiding in them. 16 We know love by this, that he laid down his life for us—and we ought to lay down our lives for one another. 17 How does God's love abide in anyone who has the world's goods and sees a brother or sister*o* in need and yet refuses help?

18 Little children, let us love, not in word or speech, but in truth and action. 19 And by this we will know that we are from the truth and will reassure our hearts before him 20 whenever our hearts condemn us; for God is greater than our hearts, and he knows everything. 21 Beloved, if our hearts do not condemn us, we have boldness before God; 22 and we receive from him whatever we ask, because we obey his commandments and do what pleases him.

23 And this is his commandment, that we should believe in the name of his Son Jesus Christ and love one another, just as he has commanded us. 24 All who obey his commandments abide in him, and he abides in them. And by this we know that he abides in us, by the Spirit that he has given us.

4 Beloved, do not believe every spirit, but test the spirits to see whether they are from God; for many false prophets have gone out into the world. 2 By this you know the Spirit of God: every spirit that confesses that Jesus Christ has come in the flesh is from God, 3 and every spirit

REVISED ENGLISH BIBLE

commits sin, because the divine seed remains in him; indeed because he is God's child he cannot sin. 10 This is what shows who are God's children and who are the devil's: anyone who fails to do what is right or love his fellow-Christians is not a child of God.

11 The message you have heard from the beginning is that we should love one another. 12 Do not be like Cain, who was a child of the evil one and murdered his brother. And why did he murder him? Because his own actions were wrong, and his brother's were right.

13 Friends, do not be surprised if the world hates you. 14 We know we have crossed over from death to life, because we love our fellow-Christians. Anyone who does not love is still in the realm of death, 15 for everyone who hates a fellow-Christian is a murderer, and murderers, as you know, do not have eternal life dwelling within them. 16 This is how we know what love is: Christ gave his life for us. And we in our turn must give our lives for our fellow-Christians. 17 But if someone who possesses the good things of this world sees a fellow-Christian in need and withholds compassion from him, how can it be said that the love of God dwells in him?

18 Children, love must not be a matter of theory or talk; it must be true love which shows itself in action. 19 This is how we shall know that we belong to the realm of truth, and reassure ourselves in his sight 20 where conscience condemns us; for God is greater than our conscience and knows all.

21 My dear friends, if our conscience does not condemn us, then we can approach God with confidence, 22 and obtain from him whatever we ask, because we are keeping his commands and doing what he approves. 23 His command is that we should give our allegiance to his Son Jesus Christ and love one another, as Christ commanded us. 24 Those who keep his commands dwell in him and he dwells in them. And our certainty that he dwells in us comes from the Spirit he has given us.

4 My dear friends, do not trust every spirit, but test the spirits, to see whether they are from God; for there are many false prophets about in the world. 2 The way to recognize the Spirit of God is this: every spirit which acknowledges that Jesus Christ has come in the flesh is from God,

---

l Or *because the children of God abide in him*   *m* Gk *his brother*
n Gk *brothers*   *o* Gk *brother*

3:19–20 **reassure . . . than our conscience:** *or* convince ourselves in his sight that even if our conscience condemns us, God is greater than our conscience.

God commits sin, because God's seed remains in him; he cannot sin because he is begotten by God. 10 In this way, the children of God and the children of the devil are made plain; no one who fails to act in righteousness belongs to God, nor anyone who does not love his brother.

11 For this is the message you have heard from the beginning: we should love one another, 12 unlike Cain who belonged to the evil one and slaughtered his brother. Why did he slaughter him? Because his own works were evil, and those of his brother righteous. 13 Do not be amazed, [then,] brothers, if the world hates you. 14 We know that we have passed from death to life because we love our brothers. Whoever does not love remains in death. 15 Everyone who hates his brother is a murderer, and you know that no murderer has eternal life remaining in him. 16 The way we came to know love was that he laid down his life for us; so we ought to lay down our lives for our brothers. 17 If someone who has worldly means sees a brother in need and refuses him compassion, how can the love of God remain in him? 18 Children, let us love not in word or speech but in deed and truth.

19 [Now] this is how we shall know that we belong to the truth and reassure our hearts before him 20 in whatever our hearts condemn, for God is greater than our hearts and knows everything. 21 Beloved, if [our] hearts do not condemn us, we have confidence in God 22 and receive from him whatever we ask, because we keep his commandments and do what pleases him. 23 And his commandment is this: we should believe in the name of his Son, Jesus Christ, and love one another just as he commanded us. 24 Those who keep his commandments remain in him, and he in them, and the way we know that he remains in us is from the Spirit that he gave us.

4 Beloved, do not trust every spirit but test the spirits to see whether they belong to God, because many false prophets have gone out into the world. 2 This is how you can know the Spirit of God: every spirit that acknowledges Jesus Christ come in the flesh belongs to God, 3 and every

9 No one who is a child of God sins
because God's seed remains in him.
Nor can he sin, because he is a child of God.
10 This is what distinguishes
the children of God from the children of the devil:
whoever does not live uprightly
and does not love his brother
is not from God.
11 This is the message
which you heard from the beginning,
that we must love one another,
12 not to be like Cain, who was from the Evil One
and murdered his brother.
And why did he murder his brother?
Because his own actions were evil and his
brother's upright.
13 Do not be surprised, brothers,
if the world hates you.
14 We are well aware that we have passed over from
death to life
because we love our brothers.
Whoever does not love, remains in death.
15 Anyone who hates his brother is a murderer,
and you are well aware that no murderer
has eternal life remaining in him.
16 This is the proof of love,
that he laid down his life for us,
and we too ought to lay down our lives for our
brothers.
17 If anyone is well-off in worldly possessions
and sees his brother in need
but closes his heart to him,
how can the love of God be remaining in him?
18 Children,
our love must be not just words or mere talk,
but something active and genuine.
19 This will be the proof that we belong to the truth,
and it will convince us in his presence,
20 even if our own feelings condemn us,
that God is greater than our feelings and knows all
things.
21 My dear friends,
if our own feelings do not condemn us,
we can be fearless before God,
22 and whatever we ask
we shall receive from him,
because we keep his commandments
and do what is acceptable to him.
23 His commandment is this,
that we should believe in the name of his Son
Jesus Christ
and that we should love one another
as he commanded us.
24 Whoever keeps his commandments
remains in God, and God in him.
And this is the proof that he remains in us:
the Spirit that he has given us.

4 My dear friends,
not every spirit is to be trusted,
but test the spirits to see whether they are from
God,
for many false prophets are at large in the world.
2 This is the proof of the spirit of God:
any spirit which acknowledges Jesus Christ, come
in human nature,
is from God,

NEW REVISED STANDARD VERSION

that does not confess Jesus*p* is not from God. And this is the spirit of the antichrist, of which you have heard that it is coming; and now it is already in the world. 4 Little children, you are from God, and have conquered them; for the one who is in you is greater than the one who is in the world. 5 They are from the world; therefore what they say is from the world, and the world listens to them. 6 We are from God. Whoever knows God listens to us, and whoever is not from God does not listen to us. From this we know the spirit of truth and the spirit of error.

7 Beloved, let us love one another, because love is from God; everyone who loves is born of God and knows God. 8 Whoever does not love does not know God, for God is love. 9 God's love was revealed among us in this way: God sent his only Son into the world so that we might live through him. 10 In this is love, not that we loved God but that he loved us and sent his Son to be the atoning sacrifice for our sins. 11 Beloved, since God loved us so much, we also ought to love one another. 12 No one has ever seen God; if we love one another, God lives in us, and his love is perfected in us.

13 By this we know that we abide in him and he in us, because he has given us of his Spirit. 14 And we have seen and do testify that the Father has sent his Son as the Savior of the world. 15 God abides in those who confess that Jesus is the Son of God, and they abide in God. 16 So we have known and believe the love that God has for us.

God is love, and those who abide in love abide in God, and God abides in them. 17 Love has been perfected among us in this: that we may have boldness on the day of judgment, because as he is, so are we in this world. 18 There is no fear in love, but perfect love casts out fear; for fear has to do with punishment, and whoever fears has not reached perfection in love. 19 We love*q* because he first loved us.

REVISED ENGLISH BIBLE

3 and no spirit is from God which does not acknowledge Jesus. This is the spirit of antichrist; you have been warned that it was to come, and now here it is, in the world already!

4 Children, you belong to God's family, and you have the mastery over these false prophets, because God who inspires you is greater than the one who inspires the world. 5 They belong to that world, and so does their teaching; that is why the world listens to them. 6 But we belong to God and whoever knows God listens to us, while whoever does not belong to God refuses to listen to us. That is how we can distinguish the spirit of truth from the spirit of error.

7 My dear friends, let us love one another, because the source of love is God. Everyone who loves is a child of God and knows God, 8 but the unloving know nothing of God, for God is love. 9 This is how he showed his love among us: he sent his only Son into the world that we might have life through him. 10 This is what love really is: not that we have loved God, but that he loved us and sent his Son as a sacrifice to atone for our sins. 11 If God thus loved us, my dear friends, we also must love one another. 12 God has never been seen by anyone, but if we love one another, he himself dwells in us; his love is brought to perfection within us.

13 This is how we know that we dwell in him and he dwells in us: he has imparted his Spirit to us. 14 Moreover, we have seen for ourselves, and we are witnesses, that the Father has sent the Son to be the Saviour of the world. 15 If anyone acknowledges that Jesus is God's Son, God dwells in him and he in God. 16 Thus we have come to know and believe in the love which God has for us.

God is love; he who dwells in love is dwelling in God, and God in him. 17 This is how love has reached its perfection among us, so that we may have confidence on the day of judgement; and this we can have, because in this world we are as he is. 18 In love there is no room for fear; indeed perfect love banishes fear. For fear has to do with punishment, and anyone who is afraid has not attained to love in its perfection. 19 We love because he loved us first. 20 But if

p Other ancient authorities read *does away with Jesus* (Gk *dissolves Jesus*)   *q* Other ancient authorities add *him*; others add *God*

spirit that does not acknowledge Jesus does not belong to God. This is the spirit of the antichrist that, as you heard, is to come, but in fact is already in the world. 4 You belong to God, children, and you have conquered them, for the one who is in you is greater than the one who is in the world. 5 They belong to the world; accordingly, their teaching belongs to the world, and the world listens to them. 6 We belong to God, and anyone who knows God listens to us, while anyone who does not belong to God refuses to hear us. This is how we know the spirit of truth and the spirit of deceit.

7 Beloved, let us love one another, because love is of God; everyone who loves is begotten by God and knows God. 8 Whoever is without love does not know God, for God is love. 9 In this way the love of God was revealed to us: God sent his only Son into the world so that we might have life through him. 10 In this is love: not that we have loved God, but that he loved us and sent his Son as expiation for our sins. 11 Beloved, if God so loved us, we also must love one another. 12 No one has ever seen God. Yet, if we love one another, God remains in us, and his love is brought to perfection in us.

13 This is how we know that we remain in him and he in us, that he has given us of his Spirit. 14 Moreover, we have seen and testify that the Father sent his Son as savior of the world. 15 Whoever acknowledges that Jesus is the Son of God, God remains in him and he in God. 16 We have come to know and to believe in the love God has for us.

God is love, and whoever remains in love remains in God and God in him. 17 In this is love brought to perfection among us, that we have confidence on the day of judgment because as he is, so are we in this world. 18 There is no fear in love, but perfect love drives out fear because fear has to do with punishment, and so one who fears is not yet perfect in love. 19 We love because he first loved us. 20 If anyone

3 and no spirit which fails to acknowledge Jesus
is from God;
it is the spirit of Antichrist,
whose coming you have heard of;
he is already at large in the world.
4 Children, you are from God
and have overcome them,
because he who is in you
is greater than he who is in the world.
5 They are from the world,
and therefore the world inspires what they say,
and listens to them.
6 We are from God;
whoever recognises God listens to us;
anyone who is not from God refuses to listen to
us.
This is how we can distinguish
the spirit of truth from the spirit of falsehood.
7 My dear friends,
let us love one another,
since love is from God
and everyone who loves is a child of God and
knows God.
8 Whoever fails to love does not know God,
because God is love.
9 This is the revelation of God's love for us,
that God sent his only Son into the world
that we might have life through him.
10 Love consists in this:
it is not we who loved God,
but God loved us and sent his Son
to expiate our sins.
11 My dear friends,
if God loved us so much,
we too should love one another.
12 No one has ever seen God,
but as long as we love one another
God remains in us
and his love comes to its perfection in us.
13 This is the proof that we remain in him
and he in us,
that he has given us a share in his Spirit.
14 We ourselves have seen and testify
that the Father sent his Son
as Saviour of the world.
15 Anyone who acknowledges that Jesus is the Son of
God,
God remains in him and he in God.
16 We have recognised for ourselves,
and put our faith in, the love God has for us.
God is love,
and whoever remains in love remains in God
and God in him.
17 Love comes to its perfection in us
when we can face the Day of Judgement fearlessly,
because even in this world
we have become as he is.
18 In love there is no room for fear,
but perfect love drives out fear,
because fear implies punishment
and no one who is afraid has come to perfection in
love.
19 Let us love, then,
because he first loved us.

NEW REVISED STANDARD VERSION	REVISED ENGLISH BIBLE

20 Those who say, "I love God," and hate their brothers or sisters,*r* are liars; for those who do not love a brother or sister*s* whom they have seen, cannot love God whom they have not seen. 21 The commandment we have from him is this: those who love God must love their brothers and sisters*r* also.

5 Everyone who believes that Jesus is the Christ*t* has been born of God, and everyone who loves the parent loves the child. 2 By this we know that we love the children of God, when we love God and obey his commandments. 3 For the love of God is this, that we obey his commandments. And his commandments are not burdensome, 4 for whatever is born of God conquers the world. And this is the victory that conquers the world, our faith. 5 Who is it that conquers the world but the one who believes that Jesus is the Son of God?

6 This is the one who came by water and blood, Jesus Christ, not with the water only but with the water and the blood. And the Spirit is the one that testifies, for the Spirit is the truth. 7 There are three that testify:*u* 8 the Spirit and the water and the blood, and these three agree. 9 If we receive human testimony, the testimony of God is greater; for this is the testimony of God that he has testified to his Son. 10 Those who believe in the Son of God have the testimony in their hearts. Those who do not believe in God*v* have made him a liar by not believing in the testimony that God has given concerning his Son. 11 And this is the testimony: God gave us eternal life, and this life is in his Son. 12 Whoever has the Son has life; whoever does not have the Son of God does not have life.

13 I write these things to you who believe in the name of the Son of God, so that you may know that you have eternal life.

14 And this is the boldness we have in him, that if we ask anything according to his will, he hears us. 15 And if we know that he hears us in whatever we ask, we know that we have obtained the requests made of him. 16 If you see your brother or sister*w* committing what is not a mortal sin, you will ask, and God*x* will give life to such a one—to those whose sin is not mortal. There is sin that is mortal; I do not

someone says, 'I love God,' while at the same time hating his fellow-Christian, he is a liar. If he does not love a fellow-Christian whom he has seen, he is incapable of loving God whom he has not seen. 21 We have this command from Christ: whoever loves God must love his fellow-Christian too.

5 EVERYONE who believes that Jesus is the Christ is a child of God. To love the parent means to love his child. 2 It follows that when we love God and obey his commands we love his children too. 3 For to love God is to keep his commands; and these are not burdensome, 4 because every child of God overcomes the world. Now, the victory by which the world is overcome is our faith, 5 for who is victor over the world but he who believes that Jesus is the Son of God?

6 This is he whose coming was with water and blood: Jesus Christ. He came, not by the water alone, but both by the water and by the blood; and to this the Spirit bears witness, because the Spirit is truth. 7-8 In fact there are three witnesses, the Spirit, the water, and the blood, and these three are in agreement. 9 We accept human testimony, but surely the testimony of God is stronger, and the testimony of God is the witness he has borne to his Son. 10 He who believes in the Son of God has the testimony in his own heart, but he who does not believe God makes him out to be a liar by refusing to accept God's witness to his Son. 11 This is the witness: God has given us eternal life, and this life is found in his Son. 12 He who possesses the Son possesses life; he who does not possess the Son of God does not possess life.

13 YOU HAVE given your allegiance to the Son of God; this letter is to assure you that you have eternal life.

14 We can approach God with this confidence: if we make requests which accord with his will, he listens to us; 15 and if we know that our requests are heard, we also know that all we ask of him is ours.

16 If anyone sees a fellow-Christian committing a sin which is not a deadly sin, he should intercede for him, and God will grant him life—that is, to those who are not guilty of deadly sin. There is such a thing as deadly sin, and I do

---

r Gk *brothers*   *s* Gk *brother*   *t* Or *the Messiah*   *u* A few other authorities read (with variations) *7There are three that testify in heaven, the Father, the Word, and the Holy Spirit, and these three are one. 8And there are three that testify on earth:*   *v* Other ancient authorities read *in the Son*   *w* Gk *your brother*   *x* Gk *he*

NEW AMERICAN BIBLE

NEW JERUSALEM BIBLE

says, "I love God," but hates his brother, he is a liar; for whoever does not love a brother whom he has seen cannot love God whom he has not seen. 21 This is the commandment we have from him: whoever loves God must also love his brother.

5 Everyone who believes that Jesus is the Christ is begotten by God, and everyone who loves the father loves [also] the one begotten by him. 2 In this way we know that we love the children of God when we love God and obey his commandments. 3 For the love of God is this, that we keep his commandments. And his commandments are not burdensome, 4 for whoever is begotten by God conquers the world. And the victory that conquers the world is our faith. 5 Who [indeed] is the victor over the world but the one who believes that Jesus is the Son of God?

6 This is the one who came through water and blood, Jesus Christ, not by water alone, but by water and blood. The Spirit is the one that testifies, and the Spirit is truth. 7 So there are three that testify, 8 the Spirit, the water, and the blood, and the three are of one accord. 9 If we accept human testimony, the testimony of God is surely greater. Now the testimony of God is this, that he has testified on behalf of his Son. 10 Whoever believes in the Son of God has this testimony within himself. Whoever does not believe God has made him a liar by not believing the testimony God has given about his Son. 11 And this is the testimony: God gave us eternal life, and this life is in his Son. 12 Whoever possesses the Son has life; whoever does not possess the Son of God does not have life.

13 I write these things to you so that you may know that you have eternal life, you who believe in the name of the Son of God. 14 And we have this confidence in him, that if we ask anything according to his will, he hears us. 15 And if we know that he hears us in regard to whatever we ask, we know that what we have asked him for is ours. 16 If anyone sees his brother sinning, if the sin is not deadly, he should pray to God and he will give him life. This is only for those whose sin is not deadly. There is such a thing as deadly sin, about which I do not say that you should pray.

20 Anyone who says 'I love God'
and hates his brother,
is a liar,
since whoever does not love the brother whom he can see
cannot love God whom he has not seen.
21 Indeed this is the commandment we have received from him,
that whoever loves God, must also love his brother.

5 Whoever believes that Jesus is the Christ
is a child of God,
and whoever loves the father
loves the son.
2 In this way we know that we love God's children,
when we love God and keep his commandments.
3 This is what the love of God is:
keeping his commandments.
Nor are his commandments burdensome,
4 because every child of God
overcomes the world.
And this is the victory that has overcome the world —
our faith.
5 Who can overcome the world
but the one who believes that Jesus is the Son of God?
6 He it is who came by water and blood, b
Jesus Christ,
not with water alone
but with water and blood,
and it is the Spirit that bears witness,
for the Spirit is Truth.
7 So there are three witnesses,
8 the Spirit, water and blood;
and the three of them coincide.
9 If we accept the testimony of human witnesses,
God's testimony is greater,
for this is God's testimony
which he gave about his Son.
10 Whoever believes in the Son of God
has this testimony within him,
and whoever does not believe
is making God a liar,
because he has not believed
the testimony God has given about his Son.
11 This is the testimony:
God has given us eternal life,
and this life is in his Son.
12 Whoever has the Son has life,
and whoever has not the Son of God has not life.
13 I have written this to you
who believe in the name of the Son of God
so that you may know that you have eternal life.
14 Our fearlessness towards him consists in this,
that if we ask anything in accordance with his will
he hears us.
15 And if we know that he listens to whatever we ask him,
we know that we already possess whatever we have asked of him.
16 If anyone sees his brother commit a sin
that is not a deadly sin,
he has only to pray, and God will give life to this brother
—provided that it is not a deadly sin.
There is sin that leads to death
and I am not saying you must pray about that.

b 5 cf. Jn 19:34.

NEW REVISED STANDARD VERSION

say that you should pray about that. 17 All wrongdoing is sin, but there is sin that is not mortal.

18 We know that those who are born of God do not sin, but the one who was born of God protects them, and the evil one does not touch them. 19 We know that we are God's children, and that the whole world lies under the power of the evil one. 20 And we know that the Son of God has come and has given us understanding so that we may know him who is true;y and we are in him who is true, in his Son Jesus Christ. He is the true God and eternal life.

21 Littel children, keep yourselves from idols. z

y Other ancient authorities read *know the true God* z Other ancient authorities add *Amen*

REVISED ENGLISH BIBLE

not suggest that he should pray about that. 17 Although all wrongdoing is sin, not all sin is deadly sin.

18 We know that no child of God commits sin; he is kept safe by the Son of God, and the evil one cannot touch him.

19 We know that we are of God's family, but that the whole world lies in the power of the evil one.

20 We know that the Son of God has come and given us understanding to know the true God; indeed we are in him who is true, since we are in his Son Jesus Christ. He is the true God and eternal life. 21 Children, be on your guard against idols.

NEW AMERICAN BIBLE

17 All wrongdoing is sin, but there is sin that is not deadly. 18 We know that no one begotten by God sins; but the one begotten by God he protects, and the evil one cannot touch him. 19 We know that we belong to God, and the whole world is under the power of the evil one. 20 We also know that the Son of God has come and has given us discernment to know the one who is true. And we are in the one who is true, in his Son Jesus Christ. He is the true God and eternal life. 21 Children, be on your guard against idols.

NEW JERUSALEM BIBLE

17 Every kind of wickedness is sin,
but not all sin leads to death.
18 We are well aware that no one who is a child of
God sins,
because he who was born from God protects him,
and the Evil One has no hold over him.
19 We are well aware that we are from God,
and the whole world is in the power of the Evil
One.
20 We are well aware also that the Son of God has
come,
and has given us understanding
so that we may know the One who is true.
We are in the One who is true
as we are in his Son, Jesus Christ.
He is the true God
and this is eternal life.
Children, be on your guard against false gods.

THE SECOND LETTER OF
John

1 The elder to the elect lady and her children, whom I love in the truth, and not only I but also all who know the truth, 2 because of the truth that abides in us and will be with us forever:

3 Grace, mercy, and peace will be with us from God the Father and from*a* Jesus Christ, the Father's Son, in truth and love.

4 I was overjoyed to find some of your children walking in the truth, just as we have been commanded by the Father. 5 But now, dear lady, I ask you, not as though I were writing you a new commandment, but one we have had from the beginning, let us love one another. 6 And this is love, that we walk according to his commandments; this is the commandment just as you have heard it from the beginning — you must walk in it.

7 Many deceivers have gone out into the world, those who do not confess that Jesus Christ has come in the flesh; any such person is the deceiver and the antichrist! 8 Be on your guard, so that you do not lose what we*b* have worked for, but may receive a full reward. 9 Everyone who does not abide in the teaching of Christ, but goes beyond it, does not have God; whoever abides in the teaching has both the Father and the Son. 10 Do not receive into the house or welcome anyone who comes to you and does not bring this teaching; 11 for to welcome is to participate in the evil deeds of such a person.

12 Although I have much to write to you, I would rather not use paper and ink; instead I hope to come to you and talk with you face to face, so that our joy may be complete.

13 The children of your elect sister send you their greetings.*c*

THE SECOND LETTER OF
John

THE Elder to the Lady chosen by God and to her children whom I love in the truth, and not I alone but all who know the truth. 2 We love you for the sake of the truth that dwells among us and will be with us for ever.

3 Grace, mercy, and peace will be with us from God the Father and from Jesus Christ the Son of the Father, in truth and love.

4 I was very glad to find that some of your children are living by the truth, in accordance with the command we have received from the Father. 5 And now, Lady, I have a request to make of you. Do not think I am sending a new command; I am recalling the one we have had from the beginning: I ask that we love one another. 6 What love means is to live according to the commands of God. This is the command that was given you from the beginning, to be your rule of life.

7 Many deceivers have gone out into the world, people who do not acknowledge Jesus Christ as coming in the flesh. Any such person is the deceiver and antichrist. 8 See to it that you do not lose what we have worked for, but receive your reward in full.

9 Anyone who does not stand by the teaching about Christ, but goes beyond it, does not possess God; he who stands by it possesses both the Father and the Son. 10 If anyone comes to you who does not bring this teaching, do not admit him to your house or give him any greeting; 11 for he who greets him becomes an accomplice in his evil deeds.

12 I have much to write to you, but I do not care to put it down on paper. Rather, I hope to visit you and talk with you face to face, so that our joy may be complete. 13 The children of your Sister, chosen by God, send you greetings.

---

a Other ancient authorities add *the Lord*   *b* Other ancient authorities read *you*   *c* Other ancient authorities add *Amen*

The Second Letter of John

2 John

THE SECOND LETTER OF JOHN

[1] The Presbyter to the chosen Lady and to her children whom I love in truth — and not only I but also all who know the truth — [2] because of the truth that dwells in us and will be with us forever. [3] Grace, mercy, and peace will be with us from God the Father and from Jesus Christ the Father's Son in truth and love.

[4] I rejoiced greatly to find some of your children walking in the truth just as we were commanded by the Father. [5] But now, Lady, I ask you, not as though I were writing a new commandment but the one we have had from the beginning: let us love one another. [6] For this is love, that we walk according to his commandments; this is the commandment, as you heard from the beginning, in which you should walk.

[7] Many deceivers have gone out into the world, those who do not acknowledge Jesus Christ as coming in the flesh; such is the deceitful one and the antichrist. [8] Look to yourselves that you do not lose what we worked for but may receive a full recompense. [9] Anyone who is so "progressive" as not to remain in the teaching of the Christ does not have God; whoever remains in the teaching has the Father and the Son. [10] If anyone comes to you and does not bring this doctrine, do not receive him in your house or even greet him; [11] for whoever greets him shares in his evil works.

[12] Although I have much to write to you, I do not intend to use paper and ink. Instead, I hope to visit you and to speak face to face so that our joy may be complete. [13] The children of your chosen sister send you greetings.

From the Elder:[a] my greetings to the Lady, the chosen one,[b] and to her children, whom I love in truth — and I am not the only one, for so do all who have come to know the Truth — [2] because of the truth that remains in us and will be with us for ever. [3] In our life of truth and love, we shall have grace, faithful love and peace from God the Father and from Jesus Christ, the Son of the Father.

[4] It has given me great joy to find that children of yours have been living the life of truth as we were commanded by the Father. [5] And now I am asking you — dear lady, not as though I were writing you a new commandment, but only the one which we have had from the beginning — that we should love one another.

[6] To love is to live according to his commandments: this is the commandment which you have heard since the beginning, to live a life of love.

[7] There are many deceivers at large in the world, refusing to acknowledge Jesus Christ as coming in human nature. They are the Deceiver; they are the Antichrist. [8] Watch yourselves, or all our work will be lost and you will forfeit your full reward. [9] If anybody does not remain in the teaching of Christ but goes beyond it, he does not have God with him: only those who remain in what he taught can have the Father and the Son with them. [10] If anyone comes to you bringing a different doctrine, you must not receive him into your house or even give him a greeting. [11] Whoever greets him has a share in his wicked activities.

[12] There are several things I have to tell you, but I have thought it best not to trust them to paper and ink. I hope instead to visit you and talk to you in person, so that our joy may be complete.

[13] Greetings to you from the children of your sister,[c] the chosen one.

[a] The elders were the leaders in each community; 'the Elder' must indicate a special leadership.   [b] i.e. one of the local churches.   [c] A neighbouring church.

THE THIRD LETTER OF
John

1 The elder to the beloved Gaius, whom I love in truth. 2 Beloved, I pray that all may go well with you and that you may be in good health, just as it is well with your soul. 3 I was overjoyed when some of the friends*a* arrived and testified to your faithfulness to the truth, namely how you walk in the truth. 4 I have no greater joy than this, to hear that my children are walking in the truth.

5 Beloved, you do faithfully whatever you do for the friends,*a* even though they are strangers to you; 6 they have testified to your love before the church. You will do well to send them on in a manner worthy of God; 7 for they began their journey for the sake of Christ,*b* accepting no support from non-believers.*c* 8 Therefore we ought to support such people, so that we may become co-workers with the truth.

9 I have written something to the church; but Diotrephes, who likes to put himself first, does not acknowledge our authority. 10 So if I come, I will call attention to what he is doing in spreading false charges against us. And not content with those charges, he refuses to welcome the friends,*a* and even prevents those who want to do so and expels them from the church.

11 Beloved, do not imitate what is evil but imitate what is good. Whoever does good is from God; whoever does evil has not seen God. 12 Everyone has testified favorably about Demetrius, and so has the truth itself. We also testify for him,*d* and you know that our testimony is true.

13 I have much to write to you, but I would rather not write with pen and ink; 14 instead I hope to see you soon, and we will talk together face to face.

15 Peace to you. The friends send you their greetings. Greet the friends there, each by name.

a Gk *brothers*   *b* Gk *for the sake of the name*   *c* Gk *the Gentiles*
d Gk lacks *for him*

THE THIRD LETTER OF
John

THE Elder to dear Gaius, whom I love in the truth. 2 Dear friend, above all I pray that things go well with you, and that you may enjoy good health: I know it is well with your soul. 3 I was very glad when some fellow-Christians arrived and told me of your faithfulness to the truth; indeed you live by the truth. 4 Nothing gives me greater joy than to hear that my children are living by the truth.

5 Dear friend, you show a fine loyalty in what you do for our fellow-Christians, though they are strangers to you. 6 They have testified to your kindness before the congregation here. Please help them on their journey in a manner worthy of the God we serve. 7 It was for love of Christ's name that they went out; and they would accept nothing from unbelievers. 8 Therefore we ought to support such people, and so play our part in spreading the truth.

9 I wrote to the congregation, but Diotrephes, who enjoys taking the lead, will have nothing to do with us. 10 So when I come, I will draw attention to the things he is doing: he lays nonsensical and spiteful charges against us; not content with that, he refuses to receive fellow-Christians himself, and interferes with those who would receive them, and tries to expel them from the congregation.

11 Dear friend, follow good examples, not bad ones. The well-doer is a child of God; the evildoer has never seen God.

12 Demetrius is well spoken of by everyone, and even by the truth itself. I add my testimony, and you know that my testimony is true.

13 I had much to write to you, but I do not care to set it down with pen and ink. 14 I hope to see you very soon, when we will talk face to face. Peace be with you. Your friends here send you greetings. Greet each of our friends by name.

The Third Letter of John

[1] The Presbyter to the beloved Gaius whom I love in truth.

[2] Beloved, I hope you are prospering in every respect and are in good health, just as your soul is prospering. [3] I rejoiced greatly when some of the brothers came and testified to how truly you walk in the truth. [4] Nothing gives me greater joy than to hear that my children are walking in the truth.

[5] Beloved, you are faithful in all you do for the brothers, especially for strangers; [6] they have testified to your love before the church. Please help them in a way worthy of God to continue their journey. [7] For they have set out for the sake of the Name and are accepting nothing from the pagans. [8] Therefore, we ought to support such persons, so that we may be co-workers in the truth.

[9] I wrote to the church, but Diotrephes, who loves to dominate, does not acknowledge us. [10] Therefore, if I come, I will draw attention to what he is doing, spreading evil nonsense about us. And not content with that, he will not receive the brothers, hindering those who wish to do so and expelling them from the church.

[11] Beloved, do not imitate evil but imitate good. Whoever does what is good is of God; whoever does what is evil has never seen God. [12] Demetrius receives a good report from all, even from the truth itself. We give our testimonial as well, and you know our testimony is true.

[13] I have much to write to you, but I do not wish to write with pen and ink. [14] Instead, I hope to see you soon, when we can talk face to face. [15] Peace be with you. The friends greet you; greet the friends there each by name.

3 John

THE THIRD LETTER OF JOHN

From the Elder: greetings to my dear friend Gaius, whom I love in truth. [2] My dear friend, I hope everything is going happily with you and that you are as well physically as you are spiritually. [3] It was a great joy to me when some brothers came and told of your faithfulness to the truth, and of your life in the truth. [4] It is always my greatest joy to hear that my children are living according to the truth.

[5] My dear friend, you have done loyal work in helping these brothers, even though they were strangers to you. [6] They are a proof to the whole Church of your love and it would be a kindness if you could help them on their journey as God would approve. [7] It was entirely for the sake of the name that they set out, without depending on the non-believers for anything; [8] it is our duty to welcome people of this sort and contribute our share to their work for the truth.

[9] I have written a note for the members of the church, but Diotrephes, who enjoys being in charge of it, refuses to accept us. [10] So if I come, I shall tell everyone how he has behaved, and about the wicked accusations he has been circulating against us. As if that were not enough, he not only refuses to welcome our brothers, but prevents from doing so other people who would have liked to, and expels them from the church. [11] My dear friend, never follow a bad example, but keep following the good one; whoever does what is right is from God, but no one who does what is wrong has ever seen God.

[12] Demetrius has been approved by everyone, and indeed by Truth itself. We too will vouch for him and you know that our testimony is true.

[13] There were several things I had to tell you but I would rather not trust them to pen and ink. [14] However, I hope to see you soon and talk to you in person. [15] Peace be with you; greetings from your friends; greet each of our friends by name.

THE LETTER OF
Jude

1 Jude,*a* a servant*b* of Jesus Christ and brother of James,

To those who are called, who are beloved*c* in*d* God the Father and kept safe for*d* Jesus Christ:

2 May mercy, peace, and love be yours in abundance.

3 Beloved, while eagerly preparing to write to you about the salvation we share, I find it necessary to write and appeal to you to contend for the faith that was once for all entrusted to the saints. 4 For certain intruders have stolen in among you, people who long ago were designated for this condemnation as ungodly, who pervert the grace of our God into licentiousness and deny our only Master and Lord, Jesus Christ.*e*

5 Now I desire to remind you, though you are fully informed, that the Lord, who once for all saved*f* a people out of the land of Egypt, afterward destroyed those who did not believe. 6 And the angels who did not keep their own position, but left their proper dwelling, he has kept in eternal chains in deepest darkness for the judgment of the great Day. 7 Likewise, Sodom and Gomorrah and the surrounding cities, which, in the same manner as they, indulged in sexual immorality and pursued unnatural lust,*g* serve as an example by undergoing a punishment of eternal fire.

8 Yet in the same way these dreamers also defile the flesh, reject authority, and slander the glorious ones.*h* 9 But when the archangel Michael contended with the devil and disputed about the body of Moses, he did not dare to bring a condemnation of slander*i* against him, but said, "The Lord rebuke you!" 10 But these people slander whatever they do not understand, and they are destroyed by those things that, like irrational animals, they know by instinct. 11 Woe to them! For they go the way of Cain, and abandon themselves to Balaam's error for the sake of gain, and perish in Korah's rebellion. 12 These are blemishes*j* on your love-feasts, while they feast with you without fear, feeding themselves.*k* They are waterless clouds carried along by the winds; autumn trees without fruit, twice dead, uprooted; 13 wild waves of the sea, casting up the foam of their own shame; wandering stars, for whom the deepest darkness has been reserved forever.

14 It was also about these that Enoch, in the seventh generation from Adam, prophesied, saying, "See, the Lord is coming*l* with ten thousands of his holy ones, 15 to execute judgment on all, and to convict everyone of all the deeds of ungodliness that they have committed in such an ungodly way, and of all the harsh things that ungodly sinners have spoken against him." 16 These are grumblers and malcontents; they indulge their own lusts; they are bombastic in speech, flattering people to their own advantage.

A LETTER OF
Jude

FROM Jude, servant of Jesus Christ and brother of James, to those whom God has called, who live in the love of God the Father and are kept safe for the coming of Jesus Christ.

2 Mercy, peace, and love be yours in fullest measure.

3 My friends, I was fully intending to write to you about the salvation we share, when I found it necessary to take up my pen and urge you to join in the struggle for that faith which God entrusted to his people once for all. 4 Certain individuals have wormed their way in, the very people whom scripture long ago marked down for the sentence they are now incurring. They are enemies of religion; they pervert the free favour of our God into licentiousness, disowning Jesus Christ, our only Master and Lord.

5 You already know all this, but let me remind you how the Lord, having once for all delivered his people out of Egypt, later destroyed those who did not believe. 6 Remember too those angels who were not content to maintain the dominion assigned to them, but abandoned their proper dwelling-place; God is holding them, bound in darkness with everlasting chains, for judgement on the great day. 7 Remember Sodom and Gomorrah and the neighbouring towns; like the angels, they committed fornication and indulged in unnatural lusts; and in eternal fire they paid the penalty, a warning for all.

8 In the same way these deluded dreamers continue to defile their bodies, flout authority, and insult celestial beings. 9 Not even the archangel Michael, when he was disputing with the devil for possession of Moses' body, presumed to condemn him in insulting words, but said, 'May the Lord rebuke you!'

10 But these people abuse on whatever they do not understand; the things that, like brute beasts, they understand by their senses prove their undoing. 11 Alas for them! They have followed the way of Cain; for profit they have plunged into Balaam's error; they have rebelled like Korah, and they share his fate.

12 These people are a danger at your love-feasts with their shameless carousals. They are shepherds who take care only of themselves. They are clouds carried along by a wind without giving rain, trees fruitless in autumn, dead twice over and pulled up by the roots. 13 They are wild sea waves, foaming with disgraceful deeds; they are stars that have wandered from their courses, and the place reserved for them is an eternity of blackest darkness.

14 It was against them that Enoch, the seventh in descent from Adam, prophesied when he said: 'I saw the Lord come with his myriads of angels, 15 to bring all mankind to judgement and to convict all the godless of every godless deed they had committed, and of every defiant word they had spoken against him, godless sinners that they are.'

16 They are a set of grumblers and malcontents. They follow their lusts. Bombast comes rolling from their lips, and they court favour to gain their ends. 17 But you, my

---

a Gk *Judas*   *b* Gk *slave*   *c* Other ancient authorities read *sanctified*   *d* Or *by*   *e* Or *the only Master and our Lord Jesus Christ*   *f* Other ancient authorities read *though you were once for all fully informed, that Jesus* (or *Joshua*) *who saved*   *g* Gk *went after other flesh*   *h* Or *angels;* Gk *glories*   *i* Or *condemnation for blasphemy*   *j* Or *reefs*   *k* Or *without fear. They are shepherds who care only for themselves*   *l* Gk *came*

---

1 **kept . . . coming:** *or* in the safe keeping.   4 **disowning . . . Lord:** *or* disowning our one and only Master, and Jesus Christ our Lord.   5 **the Lord:** *some witnesses read* Jesus; *others read* God.   9 **to condemn . . . words:** *or* to charge him with blasphemy.

The Letter of Jude

THE LETTER OF Jude

¹ Jude, a slave of Jesus Christ and brother of James, to those who are called, beloved in God the Father and kept safe for Jesus Christ: ² may mercy, peace, and love be yours in abundance.

³ Beloved, although I was making every effort to write to you about our common salvation, I now feel a need to write to encourage you to contend for the faith that was once for all handed down to the holy ones. ⁴ For there have been some intruders, who long ago were designated for this condemnation, godless persons, who pervert the grace of our God into licentiousness and who deny our only Master and Lord, Jesus Christ.

⁵ I wish to remind you, although you know all things, that [the] Lord who once saved a people from the land of Egypt later destroyed those who did not believe. ⁶ The angels too, who did not keep to their own domain but deserted their proper dwelling, he has kept in eternal chains, in gloom, for the judgment of the great day. ⁷ Likewise, Sodom, Gomorrah, and the surrounding towns, which, in the same manner as they, indulged in sexual promiscuity and practiced unnatural vice, serve as an example by undergoing a punishment of eternal fire.

⁸ Similarly, these dreamers nevertheless also defile the flesh, scorn lordship, and revile glorious beings. ⁹ Yet the archangel Michael, when he argued with the devil in a dispute over the body of Moses, did not venture to pronounce a reviling judgment upon him but said, "May the Lord rebuke you!" ¹⁰ But these people revile what they do not understand and are destroyed by what they know by nature like irrational animals. ¹¹ Woe to them! They followed the way of Cain, abandoned themselves to Balaam's error for the sake of gain, and perished in the rebellion of Korah. ¹² These are blemishes on your love feasts, as they carouse fearlessly and look after themselves. They are waterless clouds blown about by winds, fruitless trees in late autumn, twice dead and uprooted. ¹³ They are like wild waves of the sea, foaming up their shameless deeds, wandering stars for whom the gloom of darkness has been reserved forever.

¹⁴ Enoch, of the seventh generation from Adam, prophesied also about them when he said, "Behold, the Lord has come with his countless holy ones ¹⁵ to execute judgment on all and to convict everyone for all the godless deeds that they committed and for all the harsh words godless sinners have uttered against him." ¹⁶ These people are complainers, disgruntled ones who live by their desires; their mouths utter bombast as they fawn over people to gain advantage.

From Jude, servant of Jesus Christ and brother of James; to those who are called, to those who are dear to God the Father and kept safe for Jesus Christ, ² mercy, peace and love be yours in abundance.

³ My dear friends, at a time when I was eagerly looking forward to writing to you about the salvation that we all share, I felt that I must write to you encouraging you to fight hard for the faith which has been once and for all entrusted to God's holy people. ⁴ Certain people have infiltrated among you, who were long ago marked down for condemnation on this account; without any reverence they pervert the grace of our God to debauchery and deny all religion, rejecting our only Master and Lord, Jesus Christ.

⁵ I should like to remind you — though you have already learnt it once and for all — that the Lord rescued the nation from Egypt, but afterwards he still destroyed the people who refused to believe him; ⁶ and the angels who did not keep to the authority they had, but left their appointed sphere, ᵃ he has kept in darkness in eternal bonds until the judgement of the great Day. ⁷ Sodom and Gomorrah, too, and the neighbouring towns, who with the same sexual immorality pursued unnatural lusts, ᵇ are put before us as an example since they are paying the penalty of eternal fire.

⁸ Nevertheless, these people are doing the same: in their delusions they not only defile their bodies and disregard Authority, but abuse the Glories as well. ⁹ Not even the archangel Michael, when he was engaged in argument with the devil about the corpse of Moses, ᶜ dared to denounce him in the language of abuse; all he said was, *'May the Lord rebuke you.'* ᵈ ¹⁰ But these people abuse anything they do not understand; and the only things they do understand — merely by nature like unreasoning animals — will turn out to be fatal to them.

¹¹ Alas for them, because they have followed Cain; ᵉ they have thrown themselves into the same delusion as Balaam ᶠ for a reward; they have been ruined by the same rebellion as Korah ᵍ — and share the same fate. ¹² They are a dangerous hazard at your community meals, coming for the food and quite shamelessly only looking after themselves. They are like the clouds blown about by the winds and bringing no rain, or like autumn trees, barren and uprooted and so twice dead; ¹³ like wild sea waves with their own shame for foam; or like wandering stars for whom the gloom of darkness is stored up for ever. ¹⁴ It was with them in mind that Enoch, the seventh patriarch from Adam, made his prophecy when he said, 'I tell you, the Lord will come with his holy ones in their tens of thousands, ¹⁵ to pronounce judgement on all humanity and to sentence the godless for all the godless things they have done, and for all the defiant things said against him by godless sinners.' ʰ ¹⁶ They are mischief-makers, grumblers governed only by their own desires, with *mouths full of boastful talk,* ⁱ ready to flatter others for gain.

ᵃ Gn 6:1–2, elaborated in *The Book of Enoch*.   ᵇ Gn 19:1–11, elaborated in *The Testament of the Twelve Patriarchs*.
ᶜ *See* the apocryphal *Assumption of Moses*.   ᵈ Zc 3:2.   ᵉ Gn 4:8.
ᶠ Nb 22:2.   ᵍ Nb 16.   ʰ *Enoch* 1:9.   ⁱ Lv 19:15.

NEW REVISED STANDARD VERSION

17 But you, beloved, must remember the predictions of the apostles of our Lord Jesus Christ; 18 for they said to you, "In the last time there will be scoffers, indulging their own ungodly lusts." 19 It is these worldly people, devoid of the Spirit, who are causing divisions. 20 But you, beloved, build yourselves up on your most holy faith; pray in the Holy Spirit; 21 keep yourselves in the love of God; look forward to the mercy of our Lord Jesus Christ that leads to*m* eternal life. 22 And have mercy on some who are wavering; 23 save others by snatching them out of the fire; and have mercy on still others with fear, hating even the tunic defiled by their bodies.*n*

24 Now to him who is able to keep you from falling, and to make you stand without blemish in the presence of his glory with rejoicing, 25 to the only God our Savior, through Jesus Christ our Lord, be glory, majesty, power, and authority, before all time and now and forever. Amen.

m Gk *Christ to*   *n* Gk *by the flesh.* The Greek text of verses 22-23 is uncertain at several points

REVISED ENGLISH BIBLE

friends, should remember the predictions made by the apostles of our Lord Jesus Christ. 18 They said to you: 'In the final age there will be those who mock at religion and follow their own ungodly lusts.'

19 These people create divisions; they are worldly and unspiritual. 20 But you, my friends, must make your most sacred faith the foundation of your lives. Continue to pray in the power of the Holy Spirit. 21 Keep yourselves in the love of God, and look forward to the day when our Lord Jesus Christ in his mercy will give eternal life.

22 There are some doubting souls who need your pity. 23 Others you should save by snatching them from the flames. For others your pity must be mixed with fear; hate the very clothing that is contaminated with sensuality.

24 Now to the One who can keep you from falling and set you in the presence of his glory, jubilant and above reproach, 25 to the only God our Saviour, be glory and majesty, power and authority, through Jesus Christ our Lord, before all time, now, and for evermore. Amen.

19 **These ... unspiritual:** *or* These people draw a line between spiritual and unspiritual persons, although they themselves are unspiritual, not spiritual.   23 **Others you ... fear:** *some witnesses read* There are some whom you should snatch from the flames. Show pity to doubting souls with fear.

17But you, beloved, remember the words spoken beforehand by the apostles of our Lord Jesus Christ, 18for they told you, "In [the] last time there will be scoffers who will live according to their own godless desires." 19These are the ones who cause divisions; they live on the natural plane, devoid of the Spirit. 20But you, beloved, build yourselves up in your most holy faith; pray in the holy Spirit. 21Keep yourselves in the love of God and wait for the mercy of our Lord Jesus Christ that leads to eternal life. 22On those who waver, have mercy; 23save others by snatching them out of the fire; on others have mercy with fear, abhorring even the outer garment stained by the flesh.

24To the one who is able to keep you from stumbling and to present you unblemished and exultant, in the presence of his glory, 25to the only God, our savior, through Jesus Christ our Lord be glory, majesty, power, and authority from ages past, now, and for ages to come. Amen.

17But remember, my dear friends, what the apostles of our Lord Jesus Christ foretold. 18'At the final point of time', they told you, 'there will be mockers who follow nothing but their own godless desires.' 19It is they who cause division, who live according to nature and do not possess the Spirit.

20But you, my dear friends, must build yourselves up on the foundation of your most holy faith, praying in the Holy Spirit; 21keep yourselves within the love of God and wait for the mercy of our Lord Jesus Christ to give you eternal life. 22To some you must be compassionate because they are wavering; 23others you must save by snatching them from the fire; to others again you must be compassionate but wary, hating even the tunic stained by their bodies.

24To him who can keep you from falling and bring you safe to his glorious presence, innocent and joyful, 25to the only God, our Saviour, through Jesus Christ our Lord, be glory, majesty, authority and power, before all ages, now and for ever. Amen.

The Revelation

TO JOHN

1 The revelation of Jesus Christ, which God gave him to show his servants*a* what must soon take place; he made*b* it known by sending his angel to his servant*c* John, 2 who testified to the word of God and to the testimony of Jesus Christ, even to all that he saw.

3 Blessed is the one who reads aloud the words of the prophecy, and blessed are those who hear and who keep what is written in it; for the time is near.

4 John to the seven churches that are in Asia:

Grace to you and peace from him who is and who was and who is to come, and from the seven spirits who are before his throne, 5 and from Jesus Christ, the faithful witness, the firstborn of the dead, and the ruler of the kings of the earth.

To him who loves us and freed*d* us from our sins by his blood, 6 and made*b* us to be a kingdom, priests serving*e* his God and Father, to him be glory and dominion forever and ever. Amen.

7 Look! He is coming with the clouds;
every eye will see him,
even those who pierced him;
and on his account all the tribes of the earth
will wail.
So it is to be. Amen.

8 "I am the Alpha and the Omega," says the Lord God, who is and who was and who is to come, the Almighty.

9 I, John, your brother who share with you in Jesus the persecution and the kingdom and the patient endurance, was on the island called Patmos because of the word of God and the testimony of Jesus.*f* 10 I was in the spirit*g* on the Lord's day, and I heard behind me a loud voice like a trumpet 11 saying, "Write in a book what you see and send it to the seven churches, to Ephesus, to Smyrna, to Pergamum, to Thyatira, to Sardis, to Philadelphia, and to Laodicea."

12 Then I turned to see whose voice it was that spoke to me, and on turning I saw seven golden lampstands, 13 and in the midst of the lampstands I saw one like the Son of Man, clothed with a long robe and with a golden sash across his chest. 14 His head and his hair were white as white wool, white as snow; his eyes were like a flame of fire, 15 his feet were like burnished bronze, refined as in a furnace, and his voice was like the sound of many waters. 16 In his right hand he held seven stars, and from his mouth came a sharp, two-edged sword, and his face was like the sun shining with full force.

17 When I saw him, I fell at his feet as though dead. But he placed his right hand on me, saying, "Do not be afraid; I am the first and the last, 18 and the living one. I was dead, and see, I am alive forever and ever; and I have the keys of Death and of Hades. 19 Now write what you have seen, what is, and what is to take place after this. 20 As for the mystery of the seven stars that you saw in my right hand, and the seven golden lampstands: the seven stars are the angels of the seven churches, and the seven lampstands are the seven churches.

The Revelation

OF JOHN

1 THIS is the revelation of Jesus Christ, which God gave him so that he might show his servants what must soon take place. He made it known by sending his angel to his servant John, 2 who in telling all that he saw has borne witness to the word of God and to the testimony of Jesus Christ.

3 Happy is the one who reads aloud the words of this prophecy, and happy those who listen if they take to heart what is here written; for the time of fulfilment is near.

4 JOHN, to the seven churches in the province of Asia.

Grace be to you and peace, from him who is, who was, and who is to come, from the seven spirits before his throne, 5 and from Jesus Christ, the faithful witness, the firstborn from the dead and ruler of the kings of the earth.

To him who loves us and has set us free from our sins with his blood, 6 who has made of us a royal house to serve as the priests of his God and Father—to him be glory and dominion for ever! Amen.

7 Look, he is coming with the clouds; everyone shall see him, including those who pierced him; and all the peoples of the world shall lament in remorse. So it shall be. Amen.

8 'I am the Alpha and the Omega,' says the Lord God, who is, who was, and who is to come, the sovereign Lord of all.

9 I, John, your brother, who share with you in the suffering, the sovereignty, and the endurance which are ours in Jesus, was on the island called Patmos because I had preached God's word and borne my testimony to Jesus. 10 On the Lord's day the Spirit came upon me; and I heard behind me a loud voice, like the sound of a trumpet, 11 which said, 'Write down in a book what you see and send it to the seven churches: to Ephesus, Smyrna, Pergamum, Thyatira, Sardis, Philadelphia, and Laodicea.' 12 I turned to see whose voice it was that spoke to me; and when I turned I saw seven lampstands of gold. 13 Among the lamps was a figure like a man, in a robe that came to his feet, with a golden girdle round his breast. 14 His hair was as white as snow-white wool, and his eyes flamed like fire; 15 his feet were like burnished bronze refined in a furnace, and his voice was like the sound of a mighty torrent. 16 In his right hand he held seven stars, and from his mouth came a sharp, two-edged sword; his face shone like the sun in full strength.

17 When I saw him, I fell at his feet as though I were dead. But he laid his right hand on me and said, 'Do not be afraid. I am the first and the last, 18 and I am the living One; I was dead and now I am alive for evermore, and I hold the keys of death and Hades. 19 Write down therefore what you have seen, what is now, and what is to take place hereafter.

20 'This is the secret meaning of the seven stars you saw in my right hand, and of the seven gold lamps: the seven stars are the angels of the seven churches, and the seven lamps are the seven churches themselves.

The Revelation to John

1 The revelation of Jesus Christ, which God gave to him, to show his servants what must happen soon. He made it known by sending his angel to his servant John, 2 who gives witness to the word of God and to the testimony of Jesus Christ by reporting what he saw. 3 Blessed is the one who reads aloud and blessed are those who listen to this prophetic message and heed what is written in it, for the appointed time is near.

4 John, to the seven churches in Asia: grace to you and peace from him who is and who was and who is to come, and from the seven spirits before his throne, 5 and from Jesus Christ, the faithful witness, the firstborn of the dead and ruler of the kings of the earth. To him who loves us and has freed us from our sins by his blood, 6 who has made us into a kingdom, priests for his God and Father, to him be glory and power forever [and ever]. Amen.

7 Behold, he is coming amid the clouds,
    and every eye will see him,
    even those who pierced him.
All the peoples of the earth will lament him.
    Yes. Amen.

8 "I am the Alpha and the Omega," says the Lord God, "the one who is and who was and who is to come, the almighty."
9 I, John, your brother, who share with you the distress, the kingdom, and the endurance we have in Jesus, found myself on the island called Patmos because I proclaimed God's word and gave testimony to Jesus. 10 I was caught up in spirit on the Lord's day and heard behind me a voice as loud as a trumpet, 11 which said, "Write on a scroll what you see and send it to the seven churches: to Ephesus, Smyrna, Pergamum, Thyatira, Sardis, Philadelphia, and Laodicea." 12 Then I turned to see whose voice it was that spoke to me, and when I turned, I saw seven gold lamp-stands 13 and in the midst of the lampstands one like a son of man, wearing an ankle-length robe, with a gold sash around his chest. 14 The hair of his head was as white as white wool or as snow, and his eyes were like a fiery flame. 15 His feet were like polished brass refined in a furnace, and his voice was like the sound of rushing water. 16 In his right hand he held seven stars. A sharp two-edged sword came out of his mouth, and his face shone like the sun at its brightest.

17 When I caught sight of him, I fell down at his feet as though dead. He touched me with his right hand and said, "Do not be afraid. I am the first and the last, 18 the one who lives. Once I was dead, but now I am alive forever and ever. I hold the keys to death and the netherworld. 19 Write down, therefore, what you have seen, and what is happening, and what will happen afterwards. 20 This is the secret meaning of the seven stars you saw in my right hand, and of the seven gold lampstands: the seven stars are the angels of the seven churches, and the seven lampstands are the seven churches.

The Revelation to John

1 A revelation of Jesus Christ, which God gave him so that he could tell his servants *what is* now *to take place*[a] very soon; he sent his angel to make it known to his servant John, 2 and John has borne witness to the Word of God and to the witness of Jesus Christ, everything that he saw. 3 Blessed is anyone who reads the words of this prophecy, and blessed those who hear them, if they treasure the content, because the Time is near.

4 [b] John, to the seven churches of Asia: grace and peace to you from him who is, who was, and who is to come, from the seven spirits who are before his throne, 5 and from Jesus Christ, *the faithful witness, the First-born* from the dead, *the highest of earthly kings*. He loves us and has washed away our sins with his blood, 6 and made us a *Kingdom of Priests* to serve his God and Father; to him, then, be glory and power for ever and ever. Amen. 7 Look, he *is coming on the clouds*; everyone will see him, even *those who pierced him*, and *all the races of the earth will mourn over him*. Indeed this shall be so. Amen. 8 'I am the Alpha and the Omega,' says the Lord God, who is, who was, and who is to come, the Almighty.

9 I, John, your brother and partner in hardships, in the kingdom and in perseverance in Jesus, was on the island of Patmos on account of the Word of God and of witness to Jesus; 10 it was the Lord's Day and I was in ecstasy, and I heard a loud voice behind me, like the sound of a trumpet, saying, 11 'Write down in a book all that you see, and send it to the seven churches of Ephesus, Smyrna, Pergamum, Thyatira, Sardis, Philadelphia and Laodicea.' 12 I turned round to see who was speaking to me, and when I turned I saw seven golden lamp-stands 13 and, in the middle of them, one *like a Son of man*,[c] dressed in a long robe tied at the waist with a *belt of gold*. 14 *His head and his hair were white with the whiteness of wool, like snow, his eyes* like a *burning* flame, 15 *his feet like burnished bronze* when it has been refined in a furnace, and *his voice like the sound of the ocean.* 16 In his right hand he was holding seven stars, out of his mouth came a sharp sword, double-edged, and his face was like the sun shining with all its force.

17 When I saw him, I fell at his feet as though dead, but he laid his right hand on me and said, 'Do not be afraid; it is I, *the First* and the *Last*; I am the Living One, 18 I was dead and look—I am alive for ever and ever, and I hold the keys of death and of Hades. 19 Now write down all that you see of present happenings and *what is still to come*.[d] 20 The secret of the seven stars you have seen in my right hand, and of the seven golden lamp-stands, is this: the seven stars are the angels of the seven churches, and the seven lamp-stands are the seven churches themselves.'

---

a 1 Dn 2:28.   *b* 1 The quotations point to the glorious Messiah: Ps 89:37, 27; Is 55:4; Ex 19:6; Dn 7:13; Zc 12:10, 44.
c 1 Allusions to Dn 7 and 10 and Ezk 43:2.   *d* 1 Dn 2:28.

2 "To the angel of the church in Ephesus write: These are the words of him who holds the seven stars in his right hand, who walks among the seven golden lampstands:

2 "I know your works, your toil and your patient endurance. I know that you cannot tolerate evildoers; you have tested those who claim to be apostles but are not, and have found them to be false. 3 I also know that you are enduring patiently and bearing up for the sake of my name, and that you have not grown weary. 4 But I have this against you, that you have abandoned the love you had at first. 5 Remember then from what you have fallen; repent, and do the works you did at first. If not, I will come to you and remove your lampstand from its place, unless you repent. 6 Yet this is to your credit: you hate the works of the Nicolaitans, which I also hate. 7 Let anyone who has an ear listen to what the Spirit is saying to the churches. To everyone who conquers, I will give permission to eat from the tree of life that is in the paradise of God.

8 "And to the angel of the church in Smyrna write: These are the words of the first and the last, who was dead and came to life:

9 "I know your affliction and your poverty, even though you are rich. I know the slander on the part of those who say that they are Jews and are not, but are a synagogue of Satan. 10 Do not fear what you are about to suffer. Beware, the devil is about to throw some of you into prison so that you may be tested, and for ten days you will have affliction. Be faithful until death, and I will give you the crown of life. 11 Let anyone who has an ear listen to what the Spirit is saying to the churches. Whoever conquers will not be harmed by the second death.

12 "And to the angel of the church in Pergamum write: These are the words of him who has the sharp two-edged sword:

13 "I know where you are living, where Satan's throne is. Yet you are holding fast to my name, and you did not deny your faith in me[h] even in the days of Antipas my witness, my faithful one, who was killed among you, where Satan lives. 14 But I have a few things against you: you have some there who hold to the teaching of Balaam, who taught Balak to put a stumbling block before the people of Israel, so that they would eat food sacrificed to idols and practice fornication. 15 So you also have some who hold to the teaching of the Nicolaitans. 16 Repent then. If not, I will come to you soon and make war against them with the sword of my mouth. 17 Let anyone who has an ear listen to what the Spirit is saying to the churches. To everyone who conquers I will give some of the hidden manna, and I will give a white stone, and on the white stone is written a new name that no one knows except the one who receives it.

18 "And to the angel of the church in Thyatira write: These are the words of the Son of God, who has eyes like a flame of fire, and whose feet are like burnished bronze:

19 "I know your works — your love, faith, service, and patient endurance. I know that your last works are greater than the first. 20 But I have this against you: you tolerate that woman Jezebel, who calls herself a prophet and is teaching and beguiling my servants[i] to practice fornication and to eat food sacrificed to idols. 21 I gave her time to repent, but she refuses to repent of her fornication. 22 Beware, I am throwing her on a bed, and those who commit adultery with her I am throwing into great distress, unless they repent of her doings; 23 and I will strike her children dead. And all the churches will know that I am the one who searches minds and hearts, and I will give to each of you as your works deserve. 24 But to the rest of you in Thyatira, who do not

2 'To THE angel of the church at Ephesus write:
' "These are the words of the One who holds the seven stars in his right hand, who walks among the seven gold lamps: 2 I know what you are doing, how you toil and endure. I know you cannot abide wicked people; you have put to the test those who claim to be apostles but are not, and you have found them to be false. 3 Endurance you have; you have borne up in my cause and have never become weary. 4 However, I have this against you: the love you felt at first you have now lost. 5 Think from what a height you have fallen; repent, and do as once you did. If you do not, I will come to you and remove your lamp from its place. 6 Yet you have this much in your favour: you detest as I do the practices of the Nicolaitans. 7 You have ears, so hear what the Spirit says to the churches! To those who are victorious I will give the right to eat from the tree of life that stands in the garden of God."

8 'To the angel of the church at Smyrna write:
' "These are the words of the First and the Last, who was dead and came to life again: 9 I know how hard pressed and poor you are, but in reality you are rich. I know how you are slandered by those who claim to be Jews but are not; they are really a synagogue of Satan. 10 Do not be afraid of the sufferings to come. The devil will throw some of you into prison, to be put to the test, and for ten days you will be hard pressed. Be faithful till death, and I will give you the crown of life. 11 You have ears, so hear what the Spirit says to the churches! Those who are victorious cannot be harmed by the second death."

12 'To the angel of the church at Pergamum write:
' "These are the words of the One who has the sharp, two-edged sword: 13 I know where you live; it is where Satan is enthroned. Yet you are holding fast to my cause, and did not deny your faith in me even at the time when Antipas, my faithful witness, was put to death in your city, where Satan has his home. 14 But I have a few matters to bring against you. You have in Pergamum some that hold to the teaching of Balaam, who taught Balak to put temptation in the way of the Israelites; he encouraged them to eat food sacrificed to idols and to commit fornication. 15 In the same way you also have some who hold to the teaching of the Nicolaitans. 16 So repent! If you do not, I will come to you quickly and make war on them with the sword that comes out of my mouth. 17 You have ears, so hear what the Spirit says to the churches! To anyone who is victorious I will give some of the hidden manna; I will also give him a white stone, and on it will be written a new name, known only to him who receives it."

18 'To the angel of the church at Thyatira write:
' "These are the words of the Son of God, whose eyes flame like fire, and whose feet are like burnished bronze: 19 I know what you are doing, your love and faithfulness, your service and your endurance; indeed of late you have done even better than you did at first. 20 But I have this against you: you tolerate that Jezebel, the woman who claims to be a prophetess, whose teaching lures my servants into fornication and into eating food sacrificed to idols. 21 I have given her time to repent, but she refuses to repent of her fornication. 22 So I will throw her on a bed of pain, and I will plunge her lovers into terrible suffering, unless they renounce what she is doing; 23 and her children I will kill with pestilence. This will teach all the churches that I am the searcher of men's hearts and minds, and that I will give to each of you what his deeds deserve. 24 And now I speak

h Or deny my faith   *i Gk slaves*

NEW AMERICAN BIBLE

2 "To the angel of the church in Ephesus, write this: " 'The one who holds the seven stars in his right hand and walks in the midst of the seven gold lampstands says this: 2 "I know your works, your labor, and your endurance, and that you cannot tolerate the wicked; you have tested those who call themselves apostles but are not, and discovered that they are impostors. 3 Moreover, you have endurance and have suffered for my name, and you have not grown weary. 4 Yet I hold this against you: you have lost the love you had at first. 5 Realize how far you have fallen. Repent, and do the works you did at first. Otherwise, I will come to you and remove your lampstand from its place, unless you repent. 6 But you have this in your favor: you hate the works of the Nicolaitans, which I also hate.

7 " ' "Whoever has ears ought to hear what the Spirit says to the churches. To the victor I will give the right to eat from the tree of life that is in the garden of God." '

8 "To the angel of the church in Smyrna, write this: " 'The first and the last, who once died but came to life, says this: 9 "I know your tribulation and poverty, but you are rich. I know the slander of those who claim to be Jews and are not, but rather are members of the assembly of Satan. 10 Do not be afraid of anything that you are going to suffer. Indeed, the devil will throw some of you into prison, that you may be tested, and you will face an ordeal for ten days. Remain faithful until death, and I will give you the crown of life.

11 " ' "Whoever has ears ought to hear what the Spirit says to the churches. The victor shall not be harmed by the second death." ' "

12 "To the angel of the church in Pergamum, write this: " 'The one with the sharp two-edged sword says this: 13 "I know that you live where Satan's throne is, and yet you hold fast to my name and have not denied your faith in me, not even in the days of Antipas, my faithful witness, who was martyred among you, where Satan lives. 14 Yet I have a few things against you. You have some people there who hold to the teaching of Balaam, who instructed Balak to put a stumbling block before the Israelites: to eat food sacrificed to idols and to play the harlot. 15 Likewise, you also have some people who hold to the teaching of [the] Nicolaitans. 16 Therefore, repent. Otherwise, I will come to you quickly and wage war against them with the sword of my mouth.

17 " ' "Whoever has ears ought to hear what the Spirit says to the churches. To the victor I shall give some of the hidden manna; I shall also give a white amulet upon which is inscribed a new name, which no one knows except the one who receives it." ' "

18 "To the angel of the church in Thyatira, write this: " 'The Son of God, whose eyes are like a fiery flame and whose feet are like polished brass, says this: 19 "I know your works, your love, faith, service, and endurance, and that your last works are greater than the first. 20 Yet I hold this against you, that you tolerate the woman Jezebel, who calls herself a prophetess, who teaches and misleads my servants to play the harlot and to eat food sacrificed to idols. 21 I have given her time to repent, but she refuses to repent of her harlotry. 22 So I will cast her on a sickbed and plunge those who commit adultery with her into intense suffering unless they repent of her works. 23 I will also put her children to death. Thus shall all the churches come to know that I am the searcher of hearts and minds and that I will give each of you what your works deserve. 24 But I say to the rest of you

NEW JERUSALEM BIBLE

2 'Write to the angel of the church in Ephesus and say, "Here is the message of the one who holds the seven stars in his right hand and who lives among the seven golden lamp-stands: 2 I know your activities, your hard work and your perseverance. I know you cannot stand wicked people, and how you put to the test those who were self-styled apostles, and found them false. 3 I know too that you have perseverance, and have suffered for my name without growing tired. 4 Nevertheless, I have this complaint to make: you have less love now than formerly. 5 Think where you were before you fell; repent, and behave as you did at first, or else, if you will not repent, I shall come to you and take your lamp-stand from its place. 6 It is in your favour, nevertheless, that you loathe as I do the way the Nicolaitans are behaving. 7 Let anyone who can hear, listen to what the Spirit is saying to the churches: those who prove victorious I will feed *from the tree of life* set *in* God's *paradise*." *e*

8 'Write to the angel of the church in Smyrna and say, "Here is the message of *the First* and *the Last*, who was dead and has come to life again: 9 I know your hardships and your poverty, and — though you are rich — the slander of the people who falsely claim to be Jews but are really members of the synagogue of Satan. 10 Do not be afraid of the sufferings that are coming to you. Look, the devil will send some of you to prison *to put you to the test*, and you must face hardship for *ten days*. *f* Even if you have to die, keep faithful, and I will give you the crown of life for your prize. 11 Let anyone who can hear, listen to what the Spirit is saying to the churches: for those who prove victorious will come to no harm from the second death."

12 'Write to the angel of the church in Pergamum and say, "Here is the message of the one who has the sharp sword, double-edged: 13 I know where you live, in the place where Satan is enthroned, and that you still hold firmly to my name, and did not disown your faith in me even when my faithful witness, Antipas, was killed among you, where Satan lives. 14 "Nevertheless, I have one or two charges against you: some of you are followers of Balaam, who taught Balak to set a trap for the Israelites so that they committed adultery by eating food that had been sacrificed to idols; 15 and among you too there are some also who follow the teaching of the Nicolaitans. 16 So repent, or I shall soon come to you and attack these people with the sword out of my mouth. 17 Let anyone who can hear, listen to what the Spirit is saying to the churches: to those who prove victorious I will give some hidden manna and a white stone, with *a new name* written on it, known only to the person who receives it."

18 'Write to the angel of the church in Thyatira and say, "Here is the message of the Son of God who has eyes like a burning flame and feet like burnished bronze: 19 I know your activities, your love, your faith, your service and your perseverance, and I know how you are still making progress. 20 Nevertheless, I have a complaint to make: you tolerate the woman Jezebel *g* who claims to be a prophetess, and by her teaching she is luring my servants away to commit the adultery of eating food which has been sacrificed to idols. 21 I have given her time to repent but she is not willing to repent of her adulterous life. 22 Look, I am consigning her to a bed of pain, and all her partners in adultery to great hardship, unless they repent of their practices; 23 and I will see that her children die, so that all the churches realise that it is I who *test motives and thoughts and repay* you *as your deeds deserve*. *h* 24 But on the rest of you in Thyatira, all of

e 2 Gn 2:9.　　*f* 2 Dn 1:12.　　*g* 2 cf. 2 K 9:22.　　*h* 2 Jr 11:20; 17:10.

hold this teaching, who have not learned what some call 'the deep things of Satan,' to you I say, I do not lay on you any other burden; 25 only hold fast to what you have until I come. 26 To everyone who conquers and continues to do my works to the end,

I will give authority over the nations;
   27 to rule *j* them with an iron rod,
     as when clay pots are shattered —
28 even as I also received authority from my Father. To the one who conquers I will also give the morning star. 29 Let anyone who has an ear listen to what the Spirit is saying to the churches.

3 "And to the angel of the church in Sardis write: These are the words of him who has the seven spirits of God and the seven stars:

"I know your works; you have a name of being alive, but you are dead. 2 Wake up, and strengthen what remains and is on the point of death, for I have not found your works perfect in the sight of my God. 3 Remember then what you received and heard; obey it, and repent. If you do not wake up, I will come like a thief, and you will not know at what hour I will come to you. 4 Yet you have still a few persons in Sardis who have not soiled their clothes; they will walk with me, dressed in white, for they are worthy. 5 If you conquer, you will be clothed like them in white robes, and I will not blot your name out of the book of life; I will confess your name before my Father and before his angels. 6 Let anyone who has an ear listen to what the Spirit is saying to the churches.

7 "And to the angel of the church in Philadelphia write: These are the words of the holy one, the true one,

  who has the key of David,
  who opens and no one will shut,
  who shuts and no one opens:

8 "I know your works. Look, I have set before you an open door, which no one is able to shut. I know that you have but little power, and yet you have kept my word and have not denied my name. 9 I will make those of the synagogue of Satan who say that they are Jews and are not, but are lying — I will make them come and bow down before your feet, and they will learn that I have loved you. 10 Because you have kept my word of patient endurance, I will keep you from the hour of trial that is coming on the whole world to test the inhabitants of the earth. 11 I am coming soon; hold fast to what you have, so that no one may seize your crown. 12 If you conquer, I will make you a pillar in the temple of my God; you will never go out of it. I will write on you the name of my God, and the name of the city of my God, the new Jerusalem that comes down from my God out of heaven, and my own new name. 13 Let anyone who has an ear listen to what the Spirit is saying to the churches.

14 "And to the angel of the church in Laodicea write: The words of the Amen, the faithful and true witness, the origin *k* of God's creation:

15 "I know your works; you are neither cold nor hot. I wish that you were either cold or hot. 16 So, because you are lukewarm, and neither cold nor hot, I am about to spit you out of my mouth. 17 For you say, 'I am rich, I have prospered, and I need nothing.' You do not realize that you are wretched, pitiable, poor, blind, and naked. 18 Therefore I counsel you to buy from me gold refined by fire so that you may be rich; and white robes to clothe you and to keep the shame of your nakedness from being seen; and salve to anoint your eyes so that you may see. 19 I reprove and

to the rest of you in Thyatira, all who do not accept this teaching and have had no experience of what they call the deep secrets of Satan. On you I impose no further burden; 25 only hold fast to what you have, until I come. 26 To him who is victorious, to him who perseveres in doing my will to the end, I will give authority over the nations — 27 that same authority which I received from my Father — and he will rule them with a rod of iron, smashing them to pieces like earthenware; 28 and I will give him the star of dawn. 29 You have ears, so hear what the Spirit says to the churches!"

3 'To the angel of the church at Sardis write: ' "These are the words of the One who has the seven spirits of God and the seven stars: I know what you are doing; people say you are alive, but in fact you are dead. 2 Wake up, and put some strength into what you still have, because otherwise it must die! For I have not found any work of yours brought to completion in the sight of my God. 3 Remember therefore the teaching you received; observe it, and repent. If you do not wake up, I will come upon you like a thief, and you will not know the moment of my coming. 4 Yet you have a few people in Sardis who have not polluted their clothing, and they will walk with me in white, for so they deserve. 5 Anyone who is victorious will be robed in white like them, and I shall never strike his name off the roll of the living; in the presence of my Father and his angels I shall acknowledge him as mine. 6 You have ears, so hear what the Spirit says to the churches!"

7 'To the angel of the church at Philadelphia write: ' "These are the words of the Holy One, the True One, who has David's key, so that when he opens the door, no one can shut it, and when he shuts it, no one can open it: 8 I know what you are doing. I have set before you an open door which no one can shut. I know your strength is small, yet you have observed my command and have not disowned my name. 9 As for those of Satan's synagogue, who falsely claim to be Jews, I will make them come and fall at your feet; and they will know that you are my beloved people. 10 Because you have kept my command to stand firm, I will also keep you from the ordeal that is to fall upon the whole world to test its inhabitants. 11 I am coming soon; hold fast to what you have, and let no one rob you of your crown. 12 Those who are victorious I shall make pillars in the temple of my God; they will remain there for ever. I shall write on them the name of my God, and the name of the city of my God, that new Jerusalem which is coming down out of heaven from my God, and my own new name. 13 You have ears, so hear what the Spirit says to the churches!"

14 'To the angel of the church at Laodicea write: ' "These are the words of the Amen, the faithful and true witness, the source of God's creation: 15 I know what you are doing; you are neither cold nor hot. How I wish you were either cold or hot! 16 Because you are neither one nor the other, but just lukewarm, I will spit you out of my mouth. 17 You say, 'How rich I am! What a fortune I have made! I have everything I want.' In fact, though you do not realize it, you are a pitiful wretch, poor, blind, and naked. 18 I advise you to buy from me gold refined in the fire to make you truly rich, and white robes to put on to hide the shame of your nakedness, and ointment for your eyes so that you may see. 19 All whom I love I reprove and disci-

in Thyatira, who do not uphold this teaching and know nothing of the so-called deep secrets of Satan: on you I will place no further burden, 25 except that you must hold fast to what you have until I come. 26 " ' "To the victor, who keeps to my ways until the end,

I will give authority over the nations.
27 He will rule them with an iron rod.

Like clay vessels will they be smashed,
28 just as I received authority from my Father. And to him I will give the morning star.
29 " ' "Whoever has ears ought to hear what the Spirit says to the churches." '

3 "To the angel of the church in Sardis, write this:
" 'The one who has the seven spirits of God and the seven stars says this: "I know your works, that you have the reputation of being alive, but you are dead. 2 Be watchful and strengthen what is left, which is going to die, for I have not found your works complete in the sight of my God. 3 Remember then how you accepted and heard; keep it, and repent. If you are not watchful, I will come like a thief, and you will never know at what hour I will come upon you. 4 However, you have a few people in Sardis who have not soiled their garments; they will walk with me dressed in white, because they are worthy.

5 " ' "The victor will thus be dressed in white, and I will never erase his name from the book of life but will acknowledge his name in the presence of my Father and of his angels.
6 " ' "Whoever has ears ought to hear what the Spirit says to the churches." '

7 "To the angel of the church in Philadelphia, write this:
" 'The holy one, the true,

who holds the key of David,

who opens and no one shall close,

who closes and no one shall open,
says this:
8 " ' "I know your works (behold, I have left an open door before you, which no one can close). You have limited strength, and yet you have kept my word and have not denied my name. 9 Behold, I will make those of the assembly of Satan who claim to be Jews and are not, but are lying, behold I will make them come and fall prostrate at your feet, and they will realize that I love you. 10 Because you have kept my message of endurance, I will keep you safe in the time of trial that is going to come to the whole world to test the inhabitants of the earth. 11 I am coming quickly. Hold fast to what you have, so that no one may take your crown.

12 " ' "The victor I will make into a pillar in the temple of my God, and he will never leave it again. On him I will inscribe the name of my God and the name of the city of my God, the new Jerusalem, which comes down out of heaven from my God, as well as my new name.
13 " ' "Whoever has ears ought to hear what the Spirit says to the churches." '

14 "To the angel of the church in Laodicea, write this:
" 'The Amen, the faithful and true witness, the source of God's creation, says this: 15 "I know your works; I know that you are neither cold nor hot. I wish you were either cold or hot. 16 So, because you are lukewarm, neither hot nor cold, I will spit you out of my mouth. 17 For you say, 'I am rich and affluent and have no need of anything," and yet do not realize that you are wretched, pitiable, poor, blind, and naked. 18 I advise you to buy from me gold refined by fire so that you may be rich, and white garments to put on so that your shameful nakedness may not be exposed, and buy ointment to smear on your eyes so that you may see.

you who have not accepted this teaching or learnt the deep secrets of Satan, as they are called, I am not laying any other burden; 25 but hold on firmly to what you already have until I come. 26 To anyone who proves victorious, and keeps working for me until the end, *I will give the authority over the nations* 27 which I myself have been given by my Father, *to rule them with an iron sceptre and shatter them like so many pots.i* 28 And I will give such a person the Morning Star. 29 Let anyone who can hear, listen to what the Spirit is saying to the churches."

3 'Write to the angel of the church in Sardis and say, "Here is the message of the one who holds the seven spirits of God and the seven stars: I know about your behaviour: how you are reputed to be alive and yet are dead. 2 Wake up; put some resolve into what little vigour you have left: it is dying fast. So far I have failed to notice anything in your behaviour that my God could possibly call perfect; 3 remember how you first heard the message. Hold on to that. Repent! If you do not wake up, I shall come to you like a thief, and you will have no idea at what hour I shall come upon you. 4 There are a few in Sardis, it is true, who have kept their robes unstained, and they are fit to come with me, dressed in white. 5 Anyone who proves victorious will be dressed, like these, in white robes; I shall not blot that name out of the book of life, but acknowledge it in the presence of my Father and his angels. 6 Let anyone who can hear, listen to what the Spirit is saying to the churches."

7 'Write to the angel of the church in Philadelphia and say, "Here is the message of the holy and true one who has *the key of David,* so that *when he opens, no one will close, and when he closes, no one will open:j* 8 I know about your activities. Look, I have opened in front of you a door that no one will be able to close — and I know that though you are not very strong, you have kept my commandments and not disowned my name. 9 Look, I am going to make the synagogue of Satan — those who falsely claim to be Jews, but are liars, because they are no such thing — I will make them *come and fall at your feet* and recognize that *I have loved you.k* 10 Because you have kept my commandment to persevere, I will keep you safe in the time of trial which is coming for the whole world, to put the people of the world to the test. 11 I am coming soon: hold firmly to what you already have, and let no one take your victor's crown away from you. 12 Anyone who proves victorious I will make into a pillar in the sanctuary of my God, and it will stay there for ever; I will inscribe on it the name of my God and the name of the city of my God, the new Jerusalem which is coming down from my God in heaven, and my own new name as well. 13 Let anyone who can hear, listen to what the Spirit is saying to the churches."

14 'Write to the angel of the church in Laodicea and say, "Here is the message of the Amen,l the trustworthy, the true witness, the Principle of God's creation: 15 I know about your activities: how you are neither cold nor hot. I wish you were one or the other, 16 but since you are neither hot nor cold, but only lukewarm, I will spit you out of my mouth. 17 You say to yourself: I am rich, I have made a fortune and have everything I want, never realising that you are wretchedly and pitiably poor, and blind and naked too. 18 I warn you, buy from me the gold that has been tested in the fire to make you truly rich, and white robes to clothe you and hide your shameful nakedness, and ointment to put on your eyes to enable you to see. 19 I *reprove and train*

---

i 2 Ps 2:8–9.   *j* 3 Is 22:22.   *k* 3 Is 43:3.   *l* 3 *Amen* is Hebr. for truth, firmness.

discipline those whom I love. Be earnest, therefore, and repent. 20 Listen! I am standing at the door, knocking; if you hear my voice and open the door, I will come in to you and eat with you, and you with me. 21 To the one who conquers I will give a place with me on my throne, just as I myself conquered and sat down with my Father on his throne. 22 Let anyone who has an ear listen to what the Spirit is saying to the churches."

4 After this I looked, and there in heaven a door stood open! And the first voice, which I had heard speaking to me like a trumpet, said, "Come up here, and I will show you what must take place after this." 2 At once I was in the spirit,¹ and there in heaven stood a throne, with one seated on the throne! 3 And the one seated there looks like jasper and carnelian, and around the throne is a rainbow that looks like an emerald. 4 Around the throne are twenty-four thrones, and seated on the thrones are twenty-four elders, dressed in white robes, with golden crowns on their heads. 5 Coming from the throne are flashes of lightning, and rumblings and peals of thunder, and in front of the throne burn seven flaming torches, which are the seven spirits of God; 6 and in front of the throne there is something like a sea of glass, like crystal.

Around the throne, and on each side of the throne, are four living creatures, full of eyes in front and behind: 7 the first living creature like a lion, the second living creature like an ox, the third living creature with a face like a human face, and the fourth living creature like a flying eagle. 8 And the four living creatures, each of them with six wings, are full of eyes all around and inside. Day and night without ceasing they sing,

"Holy, holy, holy,
 the Lord God the Almighty,
  who was and is and is to come."

9 And whenever the living creatures give glory and honor and thanks to the one who is seated on the throne, who lives forever and ever, 10 the twenty-four elders fall before the one who is seated on the throne and worship the one who lives forever and ever; they cast their crowns before the throne, singing,

11 "You are worthy, our Lord and God,
   to receive glory and honor and power,
  for you created all things,
   and by your will they existed and were
    created."

5 Then I saw in the right hand of the one seated on the throne a scroll written on the inside and on the back, sealed^m with seven seals; 2 and I saw a mighty angel proclaiming with a loud voice, "Who is worthy to open the scroll and break its seals?" 3 And no one in heaven or on earth or under the earth was able to open the scroll or to look into it. 4 And I began to weep bitterly because no one was found worthy to open the scroll or to look into it. 5 Then one of the elders said to me, "Do not weep. See, the Lion of the tribe of Judah, the Root of David, has conquered, so that he can open the scroll and its seven seals."

6 Then I saw between the throne and the four living creatures and among the elders a Lamb standing as if it had been slaughtered, having seven horns and seven eyes, which are the seven spirits of God sent out into all the earth. 7 He went and took the scroll from the right hand of the one who was seated on the throne. 8 When he had taken the

pline. Be wholehearted therefore in your repentance. 20 Here I stand knocking at the door; if anyone hears my voice and opens the door, I will come in and he and I will eat together. 21 To anyone who is victorious I will grant a place beside me on my throne, as I myself was victorious and sat down with my Father on his throne. 22 You have ears, so hear what the Spirit says to the churches!" '

4 AFTER this I had a vision: a door stood open in heaven, and the voice that I had first heard speaking to me like a trumpet said, 'Come up here, and I will show you what must take place hereafter.' 2 At once the Spirit came upon me. There in heaven stood a throne. On it sat One ³ whose appearance was like jasper or cornelian, and round it was a rainbow, bright as an emerald. 4 In a circle about this throne were twenty-four other thrones, and on them were seated twenty-four elders, robed in white and wearing gold crowns. 5 From the throne came flashes of lightning and peals of thunder. Burning before the throne were seven flaming torches, the seven spirits of God, 6 and in front of it stretched what looked like a sea of glass or a sheet of ice.

In the centre, round the throne itself, were four living creatures, covered with eyes in front and behind. 7 The first creature was like a lion, the second like an ox, the third had a human face, and the fourth was like an eagle in flight. 8 Each of the four living creatures had six wings, and eyes all round and inside them. Day and night unceasingly they sing:

'Holy, holy, holy is God the sovereign Lord of all, who was, and is, and is to come!'

9 Whenever the living creatures give glory and honour and thanks to the One who sits on the throne, who lives for ever and ever, 10 the twenty-four elders prostrate themselves before the One who sits on the throne and they worship him who lives for ever and ever. As they lay their crowns before the throne they cry:

11 'You are worthy, O Lord our God, to receive glory and honour and power, because you created all things; by your will they were created and have their being!'

5 I saw in the right hand of the One who sat on the throne a scroll with writing on both sides, and sealed with seven seals. 2 And I saw a mighty angel proclaiming in a loud voice, 'Who is worthy to break the seals and open the scroll?' 3 But there was no one in heaven or on earth or under the earth able to open the scroll or to look inside it. 4 And because no one was found worthy to open the scroll and look inside, I wept bitterly. 5 One of the elders said to me: 'Do not weep; the Lion from the tribe of Judah, the shoot growing from David's stock, has won the right to open the scroll and its seven seals.'

6 Then I saw a Lamb with the marks of sacrifice on him, standing with the four living creatures between the throne and the elders. He had seven horns and seven eyes, the eyes which are the seven spirits of God sent to every part of the world. 7 The Lamb came and received the scroll from the right hand of the One who sat on the throne. 8 As he did so,

---

¹ Or *in the Spirit*   ^m Or *written on the inside, and sealed on the back*

5:6 **standing . . . elders:** *or* standing in the middle of the throne, inside the circle of living creatures and the circle of elders.

19 Those whom I love, I reprove and chastise. Be earnest, therefore, and repent.

20 " ' "Behold, I stand at the door and knock. If anyone hears my voice and opens the door, [then] I will enter his house and dine with him, and he with me. 21 I will give the victor the right to sit with me on my throne, as I myself first won the victory and sit with my Father on his throne.

22 " ' "Whoever has ears ought to hear what the Spirit says to the churches." ' "

4 After this I had a vision of an open door to heaven, and I heard the trumpetlike voice that had spoken to me before, saying, "Come up here and I will show you what must happen afterwards." 2 At once I was caught up in spirit. A throne was there in heaven, and on the throne sat 3 one whose appearance sparkled like jasper and carnelian. Around the throne was a halo as brilliant as an emerald. 4 Surrounding the throne I saw twenty-four other thrones on which twenty-four elders sat, dressed in white garments and with gold crowns on their heads. 5 From the throne came flashes of lightning, rumblings, and peals of thunder. Seven flaming torches burned in front of the throne, which are the seven spirits of God. 6 In front of the throne was something that resembled a sea of glass like crystal.

In the center and around the throne, there were four living creatures covered with eyes in front and in back. 7 The first creature resembled a lion, the second was like a calf, the third had a face like that of a human being, and the fourth looked like an eagle in flight. 8 The four living creatures, each of them with six wings, were covered with eyes inside and out. Day and night they do not stop exclaiming:

> "Holy, holy, holy is the Lord God almighty,
>   who was, and who is, and who is to come."

9 Whenever the living creatures give glory and honor and thanks to the one who sits on the throne, who lives forever and ever, 10 the twenty-four elders fall down before the one who sits on the throne and worship him, who lives forever and ever. They throw down their crowns before the throne, exclaiming:

> 11 "Worthy are you, Lord our God,
>   to receive glory and honor and power,
>   for you created all things;
>   because of your will they came to be and
>   were created."

5 I saw a scroll in the right hand of the one who sat on the throne. It had writing on both sides and was sealed with seven seals. 2 Then I saw a mighty angel who proclaimed in a loud voice, "Who is worthy to open the scroll and break its seals?" 3 But no one in heaven or on earth or under the earth was able to open the scroll or to examine it. 4 I shed many tears because no one was found worthy to open the scroll or to examine it. 5 One of the elders said to me, "Do not weep. The lion of the tribe of Judah, the root of David, has triumphed, enabling him to open the scroll with its seven seals."

6 Then I saw standing in the midst of the throne and the four living creatures and the elders a Lamb that seemed to have been slain. He had seven horns and seven eyes; these are the [seven] spirits of God sent out into the whole world. 7 He came and received the scroll from the right hand of the one who sat on the throne. 8 When he took it, the four living

those whom I love:m so repent in real earnest. 20 Look, I am standing at the door, knocking. If one of you hears me calling and opens the door, I will come in to share a meal at that person's side. 21 Anyone who proves victorious I will allow to share my throne, just as I have myself overcome and have taken my seat with my Father on his throne. 22 Let anyone who can hear, listen to what the Spirit is saying to the churches.' '

4 n Then, in my vision, I saw a door open in heaven and heard the same voice speaking to me, the voice like a trumpet, saying, 'Come up here: I will show you what is to take place in the future.' 2 With that, I fell into ecstasy and I saw a throne standing in heaven, and the One who was sitting on the throne, 3 and the One sitting there looked like a diamond and a ruby. There was a rainbow encircling the throne, and this looked like an emerald. 4 Round the throne in a circle were twenty-four thrones, and on them twenty-four elders sitting, dressed in white robes with golden crowns on their heads. 5 Flashes of lightning were coming from the throne, and the sound of peals of thunder, and in front of the throne there were seven flaming lamps burning, the seven Spirits of God. 6 In front of the throne was a sea as transparent as crystal. In the middle of the throne and around it, were four living creatures all studded with eyes, in front and behind. 7 The first living creature was like a lion, the second like a bull, the third living creature had a human face, and the fourth living creature was like a flying eagle. 8 Each of the four living creatures had six wings and was studded with eyes all the way round as well as inside; and day and night they never stopped singing:

> Holy, Holy, Holy
> is the Lord God, the Almighty;
> who was, and is and is to come.'

9 Every time the living creatures glorified and honoured and gave thanks to the One sitting on the throne, who lives for ever and ever, 10 the twenty-four elders prostrated themselves before him to worship the One who lives for ever and ever, and threw down their crowns in front of the throne, saying:

> 11 You are worthy, our Lord and God,
> to receive glory and honour and power,
> for you made the whole universe;
> by your will, when it did not exist, it was created.

5 I saw that in the right hand of the One sitting on the throne there was a scroll that was written on back and fronto and was sealed with seven seals. 2 Then I saw a powerful angel who called with a loud voice, 'Who is worthy to open the scroll and break its seals?' 3 But there was no one, in heaven or on the earth or under the earth, who was able to open the scroll and read it. 4 I wept bitterly because nobody could be found to open the scroll and read it, 5 but one of the elders said to me, 'Do not weep. Look, the Lion of the tribe of Judah, the RootP of David, has triumphed, and so he will open the scroll and its seven seals.'

6 Then I saw, in the middle of the throne with its four living creatures and the circle of the elders, a Lamb standing that seemed to have been sacrificed; it had seven horns, and it had seven eyes, which are the seven Spirits that God has sent out over the whole world.q 7 The Lamb came forward to take the scroll from the right hand of the One sitting on the throne, 8 and when he took it, the four living creatures

---

m 3 Pr 3:12.   n 4 The scene draws on Ezk 1; 10 and Is 6.
o 5 Ezk 2:9.   p 5 Gn 49:9; Is 11:10.   q 5 Zc 4:10.

NEW REVISED STANDARD VERSION

scroll, the four living creatures and the twenty-four elders fell before the Lamb, each holding a harp and golden bowls full of incense, which are the prayers of the saints. 9 They sing a new song:

> "You are worthy to take the scroll
> and to open its seals,
> for you were slaughtered and by your blood you
> ransomed for God
> saints from[n] every tribe and language and
> people and nation;
> 10 you have made them to be a kingdom and priests
> serving[o] our God,
> and they will reign on earth."

11 Then I looked, and I heard the voice of many angels surrounding the throne and the living creatures and the elders; they numbered myriads of myriads and thousands of thousands, 12 singing with full voice,

> "Worthy is the Lamb that was slaughtered
> to receive power and wealth and wisdom and
> might
> and honor and glory and blessing!"

13 Then I heard every creature in heaven and on earth and under the earth and in the sea, and all that is in them, singing,

> "To the one seated on the throne and to the Lamb
> be blessing and honor and glory and might
> forever and ever!"

14 And the four living creatures said, "Amen!" And the elders fell down and worshiped.

6 Then I saw the Lamb open one of the seven seals, and I heard one of the four living creatures call out, as with a voice of thunder, "Come!"[p] 2 I looked, and there was a white horse! Its rider had a bow; a crown was given to him, and he came out conquering and to conquer.

3 When he opened the second seal, I heard the second living creature call out, "Come!"[p] 4 And out came[q] another horse, bright red; its rider was permitted to take peace from the earth, so that people would slaughter one another; and he was given a great sword.

5 When he opened the third seal, I heard the third living creature call out, "Come!"[p] I looked, and there was a black horse! Its rider held a pair of scales in his hand, 6 and I heard what seemed to be a voice in the midst of the four living creatures saying, "A quart of wheat for a day's pay,[r] and three quarts of barley for a day's pay,[r] but do not damage the olive oil and the wine!"

7 When he opened the fourth seal, I heard the voice of the fourth living creature call out, "Come!"[p] 8 I looked and there was a pale green horse! Its rider's name was Death, and Hades followed with him; they were given authority over a fourth of the earth, to kill with sword, famine, and pestilence, and by the wild animals of the earth.

9 When he opened the fifth seal, I saw under the altar the souls of those who had been slaughtered for the word of God and for the testimony they had given; 10 they cried out with a loud voice, "Sovereign Lord, holy and true, how long will it be before you judge and avenge our blood on the inhabitants of the earth?" 11 They were each given a white robe and told to rest a little longer, until the number would be complete both of their fellow servants[s] and of their brothers and sisters,[t] who were soon to be killed as they themselves had been killed.

REVISED ENGLISH BIBLE

the four living creatures and the twenty-four elders prostrated themselves before the Lamb. Each of the elders had a harp; they held golden bowls full of incense, the prayers of God's people, 9 and they were singing a new song:

> 'You are worthy to receive the scroll and break its seals,
> for you were slain and by your blood you bought for God
> people of every tribe and language, nation and race.
> 10 You have made them a royal house of priests for our
> God, and they shall reign on earth.'

11 As I looked I heard, all round the throne and the living creatures and the elders, the voices of many angels, thousands on thousands, myriads on myriads. 12 They proclaimed with loud voices:

> 'Worthy is the Lamb who was slain, to receive power and
> wealth, wisdom and might, honour and glory and praise!'

13 Then I heard all created things, in heaven, on earth, under the earth, and in the sea, crying:

> 'Praise and honour, glory and might, to him who sits on
> the throne and to the Lamb for ever!'

14 The four living creatures said, 'Amen,' and the elders prostrated themselves in worship.

6 I WATCHED as the Lamb broke the first of the seven seals, and I heard one of the four living creatures say in a voice like thunder, 'Come!' 2 There before my eyes was a white horse, and its rider held a bow. He was given a crown, and he rode forth, conquering and to conquer.

3 The Lamb broke the second seal, and I heard the second creature say, 'Come!' 4 Out came another horse, which was red. Its rider was given power to take away peace from the earth that men might slaughter one another; and he was given a great sword.

5 He broke the third seal, and I heard the third creature say, 'Come!' There, as I looked, was a black horse, and its rider was holding in his hand a pair of scales. 6 I heard what sounded like a voice from among the four living creatures; it said, 'A day's wage for a quart of flour, a day's wage for three quarts of barley-meal! But do not damage the olive and the vine!'

7 He broke the fourth seal, and I heard the fourth creature say, 'Come!' 8 There, as I looked, was another horse, sickly pale; its rider's name was Death, and Hades followed close behind. To them was given power over a quarter of the earth, power to kill by sword and famine, by pestilence and wild beasts.

9 He broke the fifth seal, and I saw beneath the altar the souls of those who had been slaughtered for God's word and for the testimony they bore. 10 They gave a great cry: 'How long, sovereign Lord, holy and true, must it be before you will vindicate us and avenge our death on the inhabitants of the earth?' 11 They were each given a white robe, and told to rest a little longer, until the number should be complete of all their brothers in Christ's service who were to be put to death, as they themselves had been.

---

[n] Gk ransomed for God from   [o] Gk priests to   [p] Or "Go!"
[q] Or went   [r] Gk a denarius   [s] Gk slaves   [t] Gk brothers   6:9 **beneath:** or at the foot of.

NEW AMERICAN BIBLE

NEW JERUSALEM BIBLE

creatures and the twenty-four elders fell down before the Lamb. Each of the elders held a harp and gold bowls filled with incense, which are the prayers of the holy ones. 9 They sang a new hymn:

"Worthy are you to receive the scroll
and to break open its seals,
for you were slain and with your blood you
purchased for God
those from every tribe and tongue, people
and nation.
10 You made them a kingdom and priests for
our God,
and they will reign on earth."

11 I looked again and heard the voices of many angels who surrounded the throne and the living creatures and the elders. They were countless in number, 12 and they cried out in a loud voice:

"Worthy is the Lamb that was slain
to receive power and riches, wisdom
and strength,
honor and glory and blessing."

13 Then I heard every creature in heaven and on earth and under the earth and in the sea, everything in the universe, cry out:

"To the one who sits on the throne and to
the Lamb
be blessing and honor, glory and might,
forever and ever."

14 The four living creatures answered, "Amen," and the elders fell down and worshiped.

6 Then I watched while the Lamb broke open the first of the seven seals, and I heard one of the four living creatures cry out in a voice like thunder, "Come forward." 2 I looked, and there was a white horse, and its rider had a bow. He was given a crown, and he rode forth victorious to further his victories.

3 When he broke open the second seal, I heard the second living creature cry out, "Come forward." 4 Another horse came out, a red one. Its rider was given power to take peace away from the earth, so that people would slaughter one another. And he was given a huge sword.

5 When he broke open the third seal, I heard the third living creature cry out, "Come forward." I looked, and there was a black horse, and its rider held a scale in his hand. 6 I heard what seemed to be a voice in the midst of the four living creatures. It said, "A ration of wheat costs a day's pay, and three rations of barley cost a day's pay. But do not damage the olive oil or the wine."

7 When he broke open the fourth seal, I heard the voice of the fourth living creature cry out, "Come forward." 8 I looked, and there was a pale green horse. Its rider was named Death, and Hades accompanied him. They were given authority over a quarter of the earth, to kill with sword, famine, and plague, and by means of the beasts of the earth.

9 When he broke open the fifth seal, I saw underneath the altar the souls of those who had been slaughtered because of the witness they bore to the word of God. 10 They cried out in a loud voice, "How long will it be, holy and true master, before you sit in judgment and avenge our blood on the inhabitants of the earth?" 11 Each of them was given a white robe, and they were told to be patient a little while longer until the number was filled of their fellow servants and brothers who were going to be killed as they had been.

prostrated themselves before him and with them the twenty-four elders; each one of them was holding a harp and had a golden bowl full of incense which are the prayers of the saints. 9 They sang a new hymn:

You are worthy to take the scroll
and to break its seals,
because you were sacrificed, and with your blood
you bought people for God
of every race, language, people and nation
10 and made them *a line of kings and priests*r for God,
to rule the world.

11 In my vision, I heard the sound of an immense number of angels gathered round the throne and the living creatures and the elders; there were *ten thousand times ten thousand of them* and *thousands upon thousands*,s 12 loudly chanting:

Worthy is the Lamb that was sacrificed
to receive power, riches, wisdom,
strength, honour, glory and blessing.

13 Then I heard all the living things in creation — everything that lives in heaven, and on earth, and under the earth, and in the sea, crying:

To the One seated on the throne and to the Lamb,
be all praise, honour, glory and power,
for ever and ever.

14 And the four living creatures said, 'Amen'; and the elders prostrated themselves to worship.

6 Then, in my vision, I saw the Lamb break one of the seven seals, and I heard one of the four living creatures shout in a voice like thunder, 'Come!' 2 Immediately I saw a white horset appear, and its rider was holding a bow; he was given a victor's crown and he went away, to go from victory to victory.

3 When he broke the second seal, I heard the second living creature shout, 'Come!' 4 And out came another horse, bright red, and its rider was given this duty: to take away peace from the earth and set people killing each other. He was given a huge sword.

5 When he broke the third seal, I heard the third living creature shout, 'Come!' Immediately I saw a black horse appear, and its rider was holding a pair of scales; 6 and I seemed to hear a voice shout from among the four living creatures and say, 'A day's wages for a quart of corn, and a day's wages for three quarts of barley, but do not tamper with the oil or the wine.'

7 When he broke the fourth seal, I heard the voice of the fourth living creature shout, 'Come!' 8 Immediately I saw another horse appear, deathly pale, and its rider was called Death, and Hades followed at its heels.

They were given authority over a quarter of the earth, *to kill by the sword, by famine, by plague and through wild beasts.*u

9 When he broke the fifth seal, I saw underneath the altar the souls of all the people who had been killed on account of the Word of God, for witnessing to it. 10 They shouted in a loud voice, 'Holy, true Master, how much longer will you wait before you pass sentence and take vengeance for our death on the inhabitants of the earth?' 11 Each of them was given a white robe, and they were told to be patient a little longer, until the roll was completed of their fellow-servants and brothers who were still to be killed as they had been.

r 5 Is 61:6. s 5 Dn 7:10. t 6 The horsemen echo Zc 1:8–10; 6:1–3. u 6 Ezk 14:21.

12 When he opened the sixth seal, I looked, and there came a great earthquake; the sun became black as sackcloth, the full moon became like blood, 13 and the stars of the sky fell to the earth as the fig tree drops its winter fruit when shaken by a gale. 14 The sky vanished like a scroll rolling itself up, and every mountain and island was removed from its place. 15 Then the kings of the earth and the magnates and the generals and the rich and the powerful, and everyone, slave and free, hid in the caves and among the rocks of the mountains, 16 calling to the mountains and rocks, "Fall on us and hide us from the face of the one seated on the throne and from the wrath of the Lamb; 17 for the great day of their wrath has come, and who is able to stand?"

7 After this I saw four angels standing at the four corners of the earth, holding back the four winds of the earth so that no wind could blow on earth or sea or against any tree. 2 I saw another angel ascending from the rising of the sun, having the seal of the living God, and he called with a loud voice to the four angels who had been given power to damage earth and sea, 3 saying, "Do not damage the earth or the sea or the trees, until we have marked the servants*u* of our God with a seal on their foreheads."

4 And I heard the number of those who were sealed, one hundred forty-four thousand, sealed out of every tribe of the people of Israel:

5 From the tribe of Judah twelve thousand sealed,
from the tribe of Reuben twelve thousand,
from the tribe of Gad twelve thousand,
6 from the tribe of Asher twelve thousand,
from the tribe of Naphtali twelve thousand,
from the tribe of Manasseh twelve thousand,
7 from the tribe of Simeon twelve thousand,
from the tribe of Levi twelve thousand,
from the tribe of Issachar twelve thousand,
8 from the tribe of Zebulun twelve thousand,
from the tribe of Joseph twelve thousand,
from the tribe of Benjamin twelve thousand sealed.

9 After this I looked, and there was a great multitude that no one could count, from every nation, from all tribes and peoples and languages, standing before the throne and before the Lamb, robed in white, with palm branches in their hands. 10 They cried out in a loud voice, saying,

"Salvation belongs to our God who is seated on the throne, and to the Lamb!"

11 And all the angels stood around the throne and around the elders and the four living creatures, and they fell on their faces before the throne and worshiped God, 12 singing,

"Amen! Blessing and glory and wisdom
and thanksgiving and honor
and power and might
be to our God forever and ever! Amen."

13 Then one of the elders addressed me, saying, "Who are these, robed in white, and where have they come from?" 14 I said to him, "Sir, you are the one that knows." Then he said to me, "These are they who have come out of the great ordeal; they have washed their robes and made them white in the blood of the Lamb.

15 For this reason they are before the throne of God,
and worship him day and night within his temple,
and the one who is seated on the throne will shelter them.
16 They will hunger no more, and thirst no more;
the sun will not strike them,
nor any scorching heat;

12 I watched as the Lamb broke the sixth seal. There was a violent earthquake; the sun turned black as a funeral pall and the moon all red as blood; 13 the stars in the sky fell to the earth, like figs blown off a tree in a gale; 14 the sky vanished like a scroll being rolled up, and every mountain and island was dislodged from its place. 15 The kings of the earth, the nobles and the commanders, the rich and the powerful, and all men, slave or free, hid themselves in caves and under mountain crags; 16 and they called out to the mountains and the crags, 'Fall on us, hide us from the One who sits on the throne and from the wrath of the Lamb, 17 for the great day of their wrath has come, and who can stand?'

7 After that I saw four angels stationed at the four corners of the earth, holding back its four winds so that no wind should blow on land or sea or on any tree. 2 I saw another angel rising from the east, bearing the seal of the living God. To the four angels who had been given the power to ravage land and sea, he cried out: 3 'Do no damage to land or sea or to the trees until we have set the seal of our God upon the foreheads of his servants.' 4 I heard how many had been marked with the seal—a hundred and forty-four thousand from all the tribes of Israel: 5 twelve thousand from the tribe of Judah, twelve thousand from the tribe of Reuben, twelve thousand from the tribe of Gad, 6 twelve thousand from the tribe of Asher, twelve thousand from the tribe of Naphtali, twelve thousand from the tribe of Manasseh, 7 twelve thousand from the tribe of Simeon, twelve thousand from the tribe of Levi, twelve thousand from the tribe of Issachar, 8 twelve thousand from the tribe of Zebulun, twelve thousand from the tribe of Joseph, and twelve thousand from the tribe of Benjamin.

9 After that I looked and saw a vast throng, which no one could count, from all races and tribes, nations and languages, standing before the throne and the Lamb. They were robed in white and had palm branches in their hands, 10 and they shouted aloud:

'Victory to our God who sits on the throne, and to the Lamb!'

11 All the angels who stood round the throne and round the elders and the four living creatures prostrated themselves before the throne and worshipped God, 12 crying:

'Amen! Praise and glory and wisdom, thanksgiving and honour, power and might, be to our God for ever! Amen.'

13 One of the elders turned to me and asked, 'Who are these all robed in white, and where do they come from?' 14 I answered, 'My lord, it is you who know.' He said to me, 'They are those who have passed through the great ordeal; they have washed their robes and made them white in the blood of the Lamb. 15 That is why they stand before the throne of God and worship him day and night in his temple; and he who sits on the throne will protect them with his presence. 16 Never again shall they feel hunger or thirst; never again shall the sun beat on them or any scorching

---

u Gk slaves

12 Then I watched while he broke open the sixth seal, and there was a great earthquake; the sun turned as black as dark sackcloth and the whole moon became like blood. 13 The stars in the sky fell to the earth like unripe figs shaken loose from the tree in a strong wind. 14 Then the sky was divided like a torn scroll curling up, and every mountain and island was moved from its place. 15 The kings of the earth, the nobles, the military officers, the rich, the powerful, and every slave and free person hid themselves in caves and among mountain crags. 16 They cried out to the mountains and the rocks, "Fall on us and hide us from the face of the one who sits on the throne and from the wrath of the Lamb, 17 because the great day of their wrath has come and who can withstand it?"

7 After this I saw four angels standing at the four corners of the earth, holding back the four winds of the earth so that no wind could blow on land or sea or against any tree. 2 Then I saw another angel come up from the East, holding the seal of the living God. He cried out in a loud voice to the four angels who were given power to damage the land and the sea, 3 "Do not damage the land or the sea or the trees until we put the seal on the foreheads of the servants of our God." 4 I heard the number of those who had been marked with the seal, one hundred and forty-four thousand marked from every tribe of the Israelites: 5 twelve thousand were marked from the tribe of Judah, twelve thousand from the tribe of Reuben, twelve thousand from the tribe of Gad, 6 twelve thousand from the tribe of Asher, twelve thousand from the tribe of Naphtali, twelve thousand from the tribe of Manasseh, 7 twelve thousand from the tribe of Simeon, twelve thousand from the tribe of Levi, twelve thousand from the tribe of Issachar, 8 twelve thousand from the tribe of Zebulun, twelve thousand from the tribe of Joseph, and twelve thousand were marked from the tribe of Benjamin.

9 After this I had a vision of a great multitude, which no one could count, from every nation, race, people, and tongue. They stood before the throne and before the Lamb, wearing white robes and holding palm branches in their hands. 10 They cried out in a loud voice:

"Salvation comes from our God, who is seated on the throne,
and from the Lamb."

11 All the angels stood around the throne and around the elders and the four living creatures. They prostrated themselves before the throne, worshiped God, 12 and exclaimed:

"Amen. Blessing and glory, wisdom
and thanksgiving,
honor, power, and might
be to our God forever and ever. Amen."

13 Then one of the elders spoke up and said to me, "Who are these wearing white robes, and where did they come from?" 14 I said to him, "My lord, you are the one who knows." He said to me, "These are the ones who have survived the time of great distress; they have washed their robes and made them white in the blood of the Lamb.

15 "For this reason they stand before God's throne
and worship him day and night in his temple.
The one who sits on the throne will
shelter them.
16 They will not hunger or thirst anymore,
nor will the sun or any heat strike them.

12 In my vision, when he broke the sixth seal, there was a violent earthquake and the sun went as black as coarse sackcloth; the moon turned red as blood all over, 13 and *the stars of the sky fell* v onto the earth *like figs* dropping from a fig tree when a high wind shakes it; 14 the *sky disappeared like a scroll rolling up* and all the mountains and islands were shaken from their places. 15 Then all the kings of the earth, the governors and the commanders, the rich people and the men of influence, the whole population, slaves and citizens, *hid in caverns and among the rocks of the mountains.* w 16 *They said to the mountains* x and the rocks, 'Fall on us and hide us away from the One who sits on the throne and from the retribution of the Lamb. 17 For *the Great Day of his retribution* has come, *and who can face it?'* y

7 z Next I saw four angels, standing at *the four corners of the earth,* a holding back the four winds of the world to keep them from blowing over the land or the sea or any tree. 2 Then I saw another angel rising where the sun rises, carrying the seal of the living God; he called in a powerful voice to the four angels whose duty was to devastate land and sea, 3 'Wait before you do any damage on land or at sea or to the trees, until we have put the *seal on the foreheads* b of the servants of our God.' 4 And I heard how many had been sealed: a hundred and forty-four thousand, c out of all the tribes of Israel.

5 From the tribe of Judah, twelve thousand had been sealed;
from the tribe of Reuben, twelve thousand;
from the tribe of Gad, twelve thousand;
6 from the tribe of Asher, twelve thousand;
from the tribe of Naphtali, twelve thousand;
from the tribe of Manasseh, twelve thousand;
7 from the tribe of Simeon, twelve thousand;
from the tribe of Levi, twelve thousand;
from the tribe of Issachar, twelve thousand;
8 from the tribe of Zebulun, twelve thousand;
from the tribe of Joseph, twelve thousand;
and from the tribe of Benjamin, twelve thousand had been sealed.

9 d After that I saw that there was a huge number, impossible for anyone to count, of people from every nation, race, tribe and language; they were standing in front of the throne and in front of the Lamb, dressed in white robes and holding palms in their hands. 10 They shouted in a loud voice, 'Salvation to our God, who sits on the throne, and to the Lamb!' 11 And all the angels who were standing in a circle round the throne, surrounding the elders and the four living creatures, prostrated themselves before the throne, and touched the ground with their foreheads, worshipping God 12 with these words:

Amen. Praise and glory and wisdom,
thanksgiving and honour and power and strength
to our God for ever and ever. Amen.

13 One of the elders then spoke and asked me, 'Who are these people, dressed in white robes, and where have they come from?' 14 I answered him, 'You can tell me, sir.' Then he said, 'These are the people who have been through the great trial; they have washed their robes white again in the blood of the Lamb. 15 That is why they are standing in front of God's throne and serving him day and night in his sanctuary; and the One who sits on the throne will spread his tent over them. 16 *They will never hunger or thirst* again; *sun and scorching wind will never plague them,* 17 because the

---

v **6** Is 34:4.　w **6** Ho 10:8.　x **6** Is 2:10, 18, 19.　y **6** Jl 2:11; 3:4.
z **7** vv. 1–8 = 14:1–5.　a **7** Ezk 7:2.　b **7** Ezk 9:4.
c **7** The sacred number 12 squared and multiplied by 1000 indicates the totality of the saved.　d **7** = 15:2–5.

NEW REVISED STANDARD VERSION	REVISED ENGLISH BIBLE

17 for the Lamb at the center of the throne will be
their shepherd,
and he will guide them to springs of the water
of life,
and God will wipe away every tear from their
eyes."

8 When the Lamb opened the seventh seal, there was silence in heaven for about half an hour. 2 And I saw the seven angels who stand before God, and seven trumpets were given to them.

3 Another angel with a golden censer came and stood at the altar; he was given a great quantity of incense to offer with the prayers of all the saints on the golden altar that is before the throne. 4 And the smoke of the incense, with the prayers of the saints, rose before God from the hand of the angel. 5 Then the angel took the censer and filled it with fire from the altar and threw it on the earth; and there were peals of thunder, rumblings, flashes of lightning, and an earthquake.

6 Now the seven angels who had the seven trumpets made ready to blow them.

7 The first angel blew his trumpet, and there came hail and fire, mixed with blood, and they were hurled to the earth; and a third of the earth was burned up, and a third of the trees were burned up, and all green grass was burned up.

8 The second angel blew his trumpet, and something like a great mountain, burning with fire, was thrown into the sea. 9 A third of the sea became blood, a third of the living creatures in the sea died, and a third of the ships were destroyed.

10 The third angel blew his trumpet, and a great star fell from heaven, blazing like a torch, and it fell on a third of the rivers and on the springs of water. 11 The name of the star is Wormwood. A third of the waters became wormwood, and many died from the water, because it was made bitter.

12 The fourth angel blew his trumpet, and a third of the sun was struck, and a third of the moon, and a third of the stars, so that a third of their light was darkened; a third of the day was kept from shining, and likewise the night.

13 Then I looked, and I heard an eagle crying with a loud voice as it flew in midheaven, "Woe, woe, woe to the inhabitants of the earth, at the blasts of the other trumpets that the three angels are about to blow!"

9 And the fifth angel blew his trumpet, and I saw a star that had fallen from heaven to earth, and he was given the key to the shaft of the bottomless pit; 2 he opened the shaft of the bottomless pit, and from the shaft rose smoke like the smoke of a great furnace, and the sun and the air were darkened with the smoke from the shaft. 3 Then from the smoke came locusts on the earth, and they were given authority like the authority of scorpions of the earth. 4 They were told not to damage the grass of the earth or any green growth or any tree, but only those people who do not have the seal of God on their foreheads. 5 They were allowed to torture them for five months, but not to kill them, and their torture was like the torture of a scorpion when it stings someone. 6 And in those days people will seek death but will not find it; they will long to die, but death will flee from them.

7 In appearance the locusts were like horses equipped for battle. On their heads were what looked like crowns of gold; their faces were like human faces, 8 their hair like women's hair, and their teeth like lions' teeth; 9 they had scales like iron breastplates, and the noise of their wings was like the noise of many chariots with horses rushing into battle. 10 They have tails like scorpions, with stingers, and

heat, 17 because the Lamb who is at the centre of the throne will be their shepherd and will guide them to springs of the water of life; and God will wipe every tear from their eyes.'

8 Now when the Lamb broke the seventh seal, there was silence in heaven for about half an hour.

2 I saw the seven angels who stand in the presence of God: they were given seven trumpets.

3 Another angel came and stood at the altar, holding a golden censer. He was given much incense to offer with the prayers of all God's people on the golden altar in front of the throne, 4 and the smoke of the incense from the angel's hand went up before God with his people's prayers. 5 The angel took the censer, filled it with fire from the altar, and threw it down on the earth; and there came peals of thunder, lightning-flashes, and an earthquake.

6 THE seven angels who held the seven trumpets prepared to blow them.

7 The first angel blew his trumpet. There came hail and fire mingled with blood, and this was hurled upon the earth; a third of the earth was burnt, a third of the trees, and all the green grass.

8 The second angel blew his trumpet. What looked like a great mountain flaming with fire was hurled into the sea; a third of the sea was turned to blood, 9 a third of the living creatures in it died, and a third of the ships on it were destroyed.

10 The third angel blew his trumpet. A great star shot from the sky, flaming like a torch, and fell on a third of the rivers and springs; 11 the name of the star was Wormwood. A third of the water turned to wormwood, and great numbers of people died from drinking the water because it had been made bitter.

12 The fourth angel blew his trumpet. A third part of the sun was struck, a third of the moon, and a third of the stars, so that a third part of them turned dark and a third of the light failed to appear by day or by night.

13 As I looked, I heard an eagle calling with a loud cry as it flew in mid-heaven: 'Woe, woe, woe to the inhabitants of the earth at the sound of the other trumpets which the next three angels must now blow!'

9 The fifth angel blew his trumpet. I saw a star that had fallen from heaven to earth, and the star was given the key to the shaft of the abyss. 2 He opened it, and smoke came up from it like smoke from a great furnace and darkened the sun and the air. 3 Out of the smoke came locusts over the earth, and they were given the powers of scorpions. 4 They were told not to do damage to the grass or to any plant or tree, but only to those people who had not received God's seal on their foreheads. 5 They were given permission to torment them for five months with torment like a scorpion's sting; but they were not to kill them. 6 During that time people will seek death, but will not find it; they will long to die, but death will elude them.

7 In appearance the locusts were like horses equipped for battle. On their heads were what looked like gold crowns; their faces were like human faces 8 and their hair like women's hair; they had teeth like lions' teeth 9 and chests like iron breastplates; the sound of their wings was like the noise of many horses and chariots charging into battle; 10 they had

17 For the Lamb who is in the center of the throne
will shepherd them
and lead them to springs of life-giving water,
and God will wipe away every tear from
their eyes."

8 When he broke open the seventh seal, there was silence in heaven for about half an hour. 2 And I saw
the seven angels who stood before God were given seven
trumpets.
3 Another angel came and stood at the altar, holding a
gold censer. He was given a great quantity of incense to
offer, along with the prayers of all the holy ones, on the
gold altar that was before the throne. 4 The smoke of the
incense along with the prayers of the holy ones went up
before God from the hand of the angel. 5 Then the angel
took the censer, filled it with burning coals from the altar,
and hurled it down to the earth. There were peals of thunder, rumblings, flashes of lightning, and an earthquake.
6 The seven angels who were holding the seven trumpets
prepared to blow them.
7 When the first one blew his trumpet, there came hail and
fire mixed with blood, which was hurled down to the earth.
A third of the land was burned up, along with a third of the
trees and all green grass.
8 When the second angel blew his trumpet, something
like a large burning mountain was hurled into the sea. A
third of the sea turned to blood, 9 a third of the creatures
living in the sea died, and a third of the ships were wrecked.
10 When the third angel blew his trumpet, a large star
burning like a torch fell from the sky. It fell on a third of
the rivers and on the springs of water. 11 The star was called
"Wormwood," and a third of all the water turned to wormwood. Many people died from this water, because it was
made bitter.
12 When the fourth angel blew his trumpet, a third of the
sun, a third of the moon, and a third of the stars were struck,
so that a third of them became dark. The day lost its light
for a third of the time, as did the night.
13 Then I looked again and heard an eagle flying high
overhead cry out in a loud voice, "Woe! Woe! Woe to the
inhabitants of the earth from the rest of the trumpet blasts
that the three angels are about to blow!"

9 Then the fifth angel blew his trumpet, and I saw a star
that had fallen from the sky to the earth. It was given
the key for the passage to the abyss. 2 It opened the passage
to the abyss, and smoke came up out of the passage like
smoke from a huge furnace. The sun and the air were darkened by the smoke from the passage. 3 Locusts came out of
the smoke onto the land, and they were given the same
power as scorpions of the earth. 4 They were told not to
harm the grass of the earth or any plant or any tree, but only
those people who did not have the seal of God on their
foreheads. 5 They were not allowed to kill them but only to
torment them for five months; the torment they inflicted was
like that of a scorpion when it stings a person. 6 During that
time these people will seek death but will not find it, and
they will long to die but death will escape them.
7 The appearance of the locusts was like that of horses
ready for battle. On their heads they wore what looked like
crowns of gold; their faces were like human faces, 8 and
they had hair like women's hair. Their teeth were like lions'
teeth, 9 and they had chests like iron breastplates. The sound
of their wings was like the sound of many horse-drawn
chariots racing into battle. 10 They had tails like scorpions,

Lamb who is at the heart of the throne *will be their shepherd
and will guide them to springs of living water;e* and God
will wipe away all tears from their eyes.'f

8 The Lamb then broke the seventh seal, and there was
silence in heaven for about half an hour.
2 Next I saw seven trumpets being given to the seven
angels who stand in the presence of God. 3 Another angel,
who had a golden censer, came and stood at the altar. A
large quantity of incense was given to him to offer with the
prayers of all the saints on the golden altar that stood in
front of the throne; 4 and so from the angel's hand the smoke
of the incense went up in the presence of God and with it
the prayers of the saints. 5 Then the angel took the censer
and *filled it from the fire of the altar,g* which he then hurled
down onto the earth; immediately there came peals of thunder and flashes of lightning, and the earth shook.
6 h The seven angels that had the seven trumpets now
made ready to sound them. 7 The first blew his trumpet and,
with that, hail and fire, mixed with blood, were hurled on
the earth: a third of the earth was burnt up, and a third of
all trees, and every blade of grass was burnt. 8 The second
angel blew his trumpet, and it was as though a great mountain blazing with fire was hurled into the sea: a third of the
sea turned into blood, 9 a third of all the living things in the
sea were killed, and a third of all ships were destroyed.
10 The third angel blew his trumpet, and a huge star fell
from the sky, burning like a ball of fire, and it fell on a third
of all rivers and on the springs of water; 11 this was the star
called Wormwood, and a third of all water turned to wormwood, so that many people died; the water had become so
bitter. 12 The fourth angel blew his trumpet, and a third of
the sun and a third of the moon and a third of the stars were
blasted, so that the light went out of a third of them and the
day lost a third of its illumination, and likewise the night.
13 In my vision, I heard an eagle, calling aloud as it flew
high overhead, 'Disaster, disaster, disaster, on all the people on earth at the sound of the other three trumpets which
the three angels have yet to blow!'

9 Then the fifth angel blew his trumpet, and I saw a star
that had fallen from heaven onto the earth, and the
angel was given the key to the shaft leading down to the
Abyss. 2 When he unlocked the shaft of the Abyss, *smoke
rose* out of the Abyss *like the smoke from a* huge *furnacei*
so that the sun and the sky were darkened by the smoke
from the Abyss, 3 and out of the smoke dropped locusts onto
the earth: they were given the powers that scorpions have on
the earth: 4 they were forbidden to harm any fields or crops
or trees and told to attack only those people who were
without God's seal on their foreheads. 5 They were not to
kill them, but to give them anguish for five months, and the
anguish was to be the anguish of a scorpion's sting. 6 When
this happens, *people will long for death and not find it
anywhere;j* they will want to die and death will evade
them.
7 These locusts *looked like horsesk* armoured *for battle*;
they had what looked like gold crowns on their heads, and
their faces looked human, 8 and their hair was like women's
hair, and *teeth like lion's teeth.* 9 They had body-armour like
iron breastplates, and the noise of their wings sounded like
the racket of chariots with many horses charging. 10 Their

e 7 Is 49:10.   f 7 = 21:4; Is 25:8.   g 8 Lv 16:12; Ezk 10:2.
h 8 = 16:1–9.   i 9 Ex 19:18.   j 9 Jb 3:21.   k 9 The details of vv.
7–9 echo Jl 1 and 2.

NEW REVISED STANDARD VERSION	REVISED ENGLISH BIBLE

in their tails is their power to harm people for five months. 11 They have as king over them the angel of the bottomless pit; his name in Hebrew is Abaddon,ᵛ and in Greek he is called Apollyon. ʷ

12 The first woe has passed. There are still two woes to come.

13 Then the sixth angel blew his trumpet, and I heard a voice from the fourˣ horns of the golden altar before God, 14 saying to the sixth angel who had the trumpet, "Release the four angels who are bound at the great river Euphrates." 15 So the four angels were released, who had been held ready for the hour, the day, the month, and the year, to kill a third of humankind. 16 The number of the troops of cavalry was two hundred million; I heard their number. 17 And this was how I saw the horses in my vision: the riders wore breastplates the color of fire and of sapphireʸ and of sulfur; the heads of the horses were like lions' heads, and fire and smoke and sulfur came out of their mouths. 18 By these three plagues a third of humankind was killed, by the fire and smoke and sulfur coming out of their mouths. 19 For the power of the horses is in their mouths and in their tails; their tails are like serpents, having heads; and with them they inflict harm.

20 The rest of humankind, who were not killed by these plagues, did not repent of the works of their hands or give up worshiping demons and idols of gold and silver and bronze and stone and wood, which cannot see or hear or walk. 21 And they did not repent of their murders or their sorceries or their fornication or their thefts.

10 And I saw another mighty angel coming down from heaven, wrapped in a cloud, with a rainbow over his head; his face was like the sun, and his legs like pillars of fire. 2 He held a little scroll open in his hand. Setting his right foot on the sea and his left foot on the land, 3 he gave a great shout, like a lion roaring. And when he shouted, the seven thunders sounded. 4 And when the seven thunders had sounded, I was about to write, but I heard a voice from heaven saying, "Seal up what the seven thunders have said, and do not write it down." 5 Then the angel whom I saw standing on the sea and the land

raised his right hand to heaven

6 and swore by him who lives forever and ever, who created heaven and what is in it, the earth and what is in it, and the sea and what is in it: "There will be no more delay, 7 but in the days when the seventh angel is to blow his trumpet, the mystery of God will be fulfilled, as he announced to his servantsᶻ the prophets."

8 Then the voice that I had heard from heaven spoke to me again, saying, "Go, take the scroll that is open in the hand of the angel who is standing on the sea and on the land." 9 So I went to the angel and told him to give me the little scroll; and he said to me, "Take it, and eat; it will be bitter to your stomach, but sweet as honey in your mouth." 10 So I took the little scroll from the hand of the angel and ate it; it was sweet as honey in my mouth, but when I had eaten it, my stomach was made bitter.

11 Then they said to me, "You must prophesy again about many peoples and nations and languages and kings."

11 Then I was given a measuring rod like a staff, and I was told, "Come and measure the temple of God and the altar and those who worship there; 2 but do not measure the court outside the temple; leave that out, for it is given over to the nations, and they will trample over the holy city for forty-two months. 3 And I will grant my two

tails like scorpions, with stings in them, and in their tails lay their power to injure people for five months. 11 They had for their king the angel of the abyss, whose name in Hebrew is Abaddon, and in Greek Apollyon, the Destroyer.

12 The first woe has now passed; but there are still two more to come.

13 The sixth angel blew his trumpet. I heard a voice coming from the horns of the golden altar that stood in the presence of God. 14 To the sixth angel, who held the trumpet, the voice said: 'Release the four angels held bound at the Great River, the Euphrates!' 15 So the four angels were let loose, to kill a third of mankind; they had been held in readiness for this very year, month, day, and hour. 16 And their squadrons of cavalry numbered twice ten thousand times ten thousand; this was the number I heard. 17 This was how I saw the horses and their riders in my vision: they wore breastplates, fiery red, turquoise, and sulphur-yellow; the horses had heads like lions' heads, and from their mouths issued fire, smoke, and sulphur. 18 By these three plagues, the fire, the smoke, and the sulphur that came from their mouths, a third of mankind was killed. 19 The power of the horses lay in their mouths and in their tails; for their tails had heads like serpents, and with them they inflicted injuries.

20 The rest of mankind who survived these plagues still did not renounce the gods their hands had made, or cease their worship of demons and of idols fashioned from gold, silver, bronze, stone, and wood, which cannot see or hear or walk; 21 nor did they repent of their murders, their sorcery, their fornication, or their robberies.

10 I SAW another mighty angel coming down from heaven. He was wrapped in cloud, with a rainbow over his head; his face shone like the sun and his legs were like pillars of fire. 2 In his hand he held a little scroll which had been opened. He planted his right foot on the sea and his left on the land, 3 and gave a great shout like the roar of a lion; when he shouted, the seven thunders spoke. 4 I was about to write down what the seven thunders had said, but I heard a voice from heaven saying, 'Put under seal what the seven thunders have said; do not write it down.' 5 Then the angel whom I saw standing on the sea and the land raised his right hand towards heaven 6 and swore by him who lives for ever, who created heaven and earth and the sea and everything in them: 'There shall be no more delay; 7 when the time comes for the seventh angel to sound his trumpet, the hidden purpose of God will have been fulfilled, as he promised to his servants the prophets.'

8 The voice which I had heard from heaven began speaking to me again; it said, 'Go and take the scroll which is open in the hand of the angel who stands on the sea and the land.' 9 I went to the angel and asked him to give me the little scroll. He answered, 'Take it, and eat it. It will turn your stomach sour, but in your mouth it will taste as sweet as honey.' 10 I took the scroll from the angel's hand and ate it, and in my mouth it did taste as sweet as honey, but when I swallowed it my stomach turned sour.

11 Then I was told, 'Once again you must utter prophecies over many nations, races, languages, and kings.'

11 I was given a long cane to use as a measuring rod, and was told: 'Go and measure the temple of God and the altar, and count the worshippers. 2 But leave the outer court of the temple out of your measurements; it has been given over to the Gentiles, and for forty-two months they will trample the Holy City underfoot. 3 I will give my

---

ᵛ That is, *Destruction* ʷ That is, *Destroyer* ˣ Other ancient authorities lack *four* ʸ Gk *hyacinth* ᶻ Gk *slaves*

with stingers; with their tails they had power to harm people for five months. 11 They had as their king the angel of the abyss, whose name in Hebrew is Abaddon and in Greek Apollyon.

12 The first woe has passed, but there are two more to come.

13 Then the sixth angel blew his trumpet, and I heard a voice coming from the [four] horns of the gold altar before God, 14 telling the sixth angel who held the trumpet, "Release the four angels who are bound at the banks of the great river Euphrates." 15 So the four angels were released, who were prepared for this hour, day, month, and year to kill a third of the human race. 16 The number of cavalry troops was two hundred million; I heard their number. 17 Now in my vision this is how I saw the horses and their riders. They wore red, blue, and yellow breastplates, and the horses' heads were like heads of lions, and out of their mouths came fire, smoke, and sulfur. 18 By these three plagues of fire, smoke, and sulfur that came out of their mouths a third of the human race was killed. 19 For the power of the horses is in their mouths and in their tails; for their tails are like snakes, with heads that inflict harm.

20 The rest of the human race, who were not killed by these plagues, did not repent of the works of their hands, to give up the worship of demons and idols made from gold, silver, bronze, stone, and wood, which cannot see or hear or walk. 21 Nor did they repent of their murders, their magic potions, their unchastity, or their robberies.

10 Then I saw another mighty angel come down from heaven wrapped in a cloud, with a halo around his head; his face was like the sun and his feet were like pillars of fire. 2 In his hand he held a small scroll that had been opened. He placed his right foot on the sea and his left foot on the land, 3 and then he cried out in a loud voice as a lion roars. When he cried out, the seven thunders raised their voices, too. 4 When the seven thunders had spoken, I was about to write it down; but I heard a voice from heaven say, "Seal up what the seven thunders have spoken, but do not write it down." 5 Then the angel I saw standing on the sea and on the land raised his right hand to heaven 6 and swore by the one who lives forever and ever, who created heaven and earth and sea and all that is in them, "There shall be no more delay. 7 At the time when you hear the seventh angel blow his trumpet, the mysterious plan of God shall be fulfilled, as he promised to his servants the prophets."

8 Then the voice that I had heard from heaven spoke to me again and said, "Go, take the scroll that lies open in the hand of the angel who is standing on the sea and on the land." 9 So I went up to the angel and told him to give me the small scroll. He said to me, "Take and swallow it. It will turn your stomach sour, but in your mouth it will taste as sweet as honey." 10 I took the small scroll from the angel's hand and swallowed it. In my mouth it was like sweet honey, but when I had eaten it, my stomach turned sour. 11 Then someone said to me, "You must prophesy again about many peoples, nations, tongues, and kings."

11 Then I was given a measuring rod like a staff and I was told, "Come and measure the temple of God and the altar, and count those who are worshiping in it. 2 But exclude the outer court of the temple; do not measure it, for it has been handed over to the Gentiles, who will trample the holy city for forty-two months. 3 I will commis-

tails were like scorpions' tails, with stings, and with their tails they were able to torture people for five months. 11 As their leader they had their emperor, the angel of the Abyss, whose name in Hebrew is Abaddon, and in Greek Apollyon.*l*

12 That was the first of the disasters; there are still two more to come.

13 The sixth angel blew his trumpet, and I heard a single voice issuing from the four horns of the golden altar in God's presence. 14 It spoke to the sixth angel with the trumpet, and said, 'Release the four angels that are chained up at the great river Euphrates.' 15 These four angels had been ready for this hour of this day of this month of this year, and ready to destroy a third of the human race. 16 I learnt how many there were in their army: twice ten thousand times ten thousand mounted men. 17 In my vision I saw the horses, and the riders with their breastplates of flame colour, hyacinth-blue and sulphur-yellow; the horses had lions' heads, and fire, smoke and sulphur were coming from their mouths. 18 It was by these three plagues, the fire, the smoke and the sulphur coming from their mouths, that the one third of the human race was killed. 19 All the horses' power was in their mouths and their tails: their tails were like snakes, and had heads which inflicted wounds. 20 But the rest of the human race, who escaped death by these plagues, refused either to abandon *their own handiwork*[m] or to stop worshipping devils, the *idols made of gold, silver, bronze, stone and wood*[n] that can neither see nor hear nor move. 21 Nor did they give up their murdering, or witchcraft, or fornication or stealing.

10 Then I saw another powerful angel coming down from heaven, wrapped in cloud, with a rainbow over his head; his face was like the sun, and his legs were pillars of fire. 2 In his hand he had a small scroll, unrolled; he put his right foot in the sea and his left foot on the land 3 and he shouted so loud, it was *like a lion roaring.*[o] At this, the seven claps of thunder made themselves heard 4 and when the seven thunderclaps had sounded, I was preparing to write, when I heard a voice from heaven say to me, 'Keep the words of the seven thunderclaps secret and do not write them down.' 5 Then the angel that I had seen, standing on the sea and the land, *raised his right hand to heaven,*[p] 6 and *swore by him who lives for ever* and ever, *and made heaven and all that it contains,*[q] and *earth and all it contains,* and *the sea and all it contains,* 'The time of waiting is over; 7 at the time when the seventh angel is heard sounding his trumpet, the mystery of God will be fulfilled, just as he announced in the gospel to *his servants the prophets.'*

8 Then I heard the voice I had heard from heaven speaking to me again. 'Go', it said, 'and take that open scroll from the hand of the angel standing on sea and land.' 9 I went to the angel and asked him to give me the small scroll, and he said, 'Take it and eat it; it will turn your stomach sour, but it will taste as sweet as honey.' 10 So I took it out of the angel's hand, and *I ate it and it tasted sweet as honey,*[r] but when I had eaten it my stomach turned sour. 11 Then I was told, 'You are to prophesy again, this time against many different nations and countries and languages and kings.'

11 Then I was given a long cane like a measuring rod, and I was told, 'Get up and measure God's sanctuary, and the altar, and the people who worship there; 2 but exclude the outer court and do not measure it, because it has been handed over to gentiles — they will trample on the holy city for forty-two months.*s* 3 But I shall send my two wit-

l 9 Both names mean 'Destroyer'.   *m* 9 Is 17:8.   *n* 9 Dn 5:4.
o 10 Am 1:2; 3:8.   *p* 10 Dt 32:40.   *q* 10 Ne 9:6.
r 10 Ezk 3:1–13.   *s* 11 Cf. Dn 7:25. Half seven years, so the opposite of completion, a short and incomplete time of persecution.

9, 13: [Four]: many Greek manuscripts and versions omit the word.

| NEW REVISED STANDARD VERSION | REVISED ENGLISH BIBLE |

witnesses authority to prophesy for one thousand two hundred sixty days, wearing sackcloth."

4 These are the two olive trees and the two lampstands that stand before the Lord of the earth. 5 And if anyone wants to harm them, fire pours from their mouth and consumes their foes; anyone who wants to harm them must be killed in this manner. 6 They have authority to shut the sky, so that no rain may fall during the days of their prophesying, and they have authority over the waters to turn them into blood, and to strike the earth with every kind of plague, as often as they desire.

7 When they have finished their testimony, the beast that comes up from the bottomless pit will make war on them and conquer them and kill them, 8 and their dead bodies will lie in the street of the great city that is prophetically[a] called Sodom and Egypt, where also their Lord was crucified. 9 For three and a half days members of the peoples and tribes and languages and nations will gaze at their dead bodies and refuse to let them be placed in a tomb; 10 and the inhabitants of the earth will gloat over them and celebrate and exchange presents, because these two prophets had been a torment to the inhabitants of the earth.

11 But after the three and a half days, the breath[b] of life from God entered them, and they stood on their feet, and those who saw them were terrified. 12 Then they[c] heard a loud voice from heaven saying to them, "Come up here!" And they went up to heaven in a cloud while their enemies watched them. 13 At that moment there was a great earthquake, and a tenth of the city fell; seven thousand people were killed in the earthquake, and the rest were terrified and gave glory to the God of heaven.

14 The second woe has passed. The third woe is coming very soon.

15 Then the seventh angel blew his trumpet, and there were loud voices in heaven, saying,

"The kingdom of the world has become the
    kingdom of our Lord
    and of his Messiah,[d]
and he will reign forever and ever."

16 Then the twenty-four elders who sit on their thrones before God fell on their faces and worshiped God, 17 singing,

"We give you thanks, Lord God Almighty,
    who are and who were,
for you have taken your great power
    and begun to reign.
18 The nations raged,
    but your wrath has come,
    and the time for judging the dead,
for rewarding your servants,[e] the prophets
    and saints and all who fear your name,
    both small and great,
and for destroying those who destroy the earth."

19 Then God's temple in heaven was opened, and the ark of his covenant was seen within his temple; and there were flashes of lightning, rumblings, peals of thunder, an earthquake, and heavy hail.

12 A great portent appeared in heaven: a woman clothed with the sun, with the moon under her feet, and on her head a crown of twelve stars. 2 She was pregnant and was crying out in birth pangs, in the agony of giving birth. 3 Then another portent appeared in heaven: a great red dragon, with seven heads and ten horns, and seven diadems on his heads. 4 His tail swept down a third of the stars of

two witnesses authority to prophesy, dressed in sackcloth, for those twelve hundred and sixty days.' 4 They are the two olive trees and the two lamps that stand in the presence of the Lord of the earth. 5 If anyone tries to injure them, fire issues from their mouths and consumes their enemies; so shall anyone die who tries to do them injury. 6 These two have the power to shut up the sky, so that no rain falls during the time of their prophesying; and they have power to turn water into blood and to afflict the earth with every kind of plague whenever they like. 7 But when they have completed their testimony, the beast that comes up from the abyss will wage war on them and will overcome and kill them. 8 Their bodies will lie in the street of the great city, whose name in prophetic language is Sodom, or Egypt, where also their Lord was crucified. 9 For three and a half days people from every nation and tribe, language, and race, gaze on their corpses and refuse them burial. 10 The earth's inhabitants gloat over them; they celebrate and exchange presents, for these two prophets were a torment to them. 11 But at the end of the three and a half days the breath of life from God came into their bodies, and they rose to their feet, to the terror of those who saw them. 12 A loud voice from heaven was heard saying to them, 'Come up here!' and they ascended to heaven in a cloud, in full view of their enemies. 13 At that moment there was a violent earthquake, and a tenth of the city collapsed. Seven thousand people were killed in the earthquake; the rest, filled with fear, did homage to the God of heaven.

14 The second woe has now passed; but the third is soon to come.

15 Then the seventh angel blew his trumpet. Voices in heaven were heard crying aloud:

'Sovereignty over the world has passed to our Lord and his Christ, and he shall reign for ever!'

16 The twenty-four elders, who sit on their thrones before God, prostrated themselves before him in adoration, 17 saying:

'O Lord God, sovereign over all, you are and you were; we give you thanks because you have assumed full power and entered upon your reign. 18 The nations rose in wrath, but your day of wrath has come. Now is the time for the dead to be judged; now is the time for rewards to be given to your servants the prophets, to your own people, and to all who honour your name, both small and great; now is the time to destroy those who destroy the earth.'

19 God's sanctuary in heaven was opened, and within his sanctuary was seen the ark of his covenant. There came flashes of lightning and peals of thunder, an earthquake, and a violent hailstorm.

12 AFTER that there appeared a great sign in heaven: a woman robed with the sun, beneath her feet the moon, and on her head a crown of twelve stars. 2 She was about to bear a child, and in the anguish of her labour she cried out to be delivered. 3 Then a second sign appeared in heaven: a great, fiery red dragon with seven heads and ten horns. On his heads were seven diadems, 4 and with his tail

---

[a] Or allegorically; Gk spiritually   [b] Or the spirit   [c] Other ancient authorities read I   [d] Gk Christ   [e] Gk slaves

NEW AMERICAN BIBLE | NEW JERUSALEM BIBLE

sion my two witnesses to prophesy for those twelve hundred and sixty days, wearing sackcloth." 4 These are the two olive trees and the two lampstands that stand before the Lord of the earth. 5 If anyone wants to harm them, fire comes out of their mouths and devours their enemies. In this way, anyone wanting to harm them is sure to be slain. 6 They have the power to close up the sky so that no rain can fall during the time of their prophesying. They also have power to turn water into blood and to afflict the earth with any plague as often as they wish.

7 When they have finished their testimony, the beast that comes up from the abyss will wage war against them and conquer them and kill them. 8 Their corpses will lie in the main street of the great city, which has the symbolic names "Sodom" and "Egypt," where indeed their Lord was crucified. 9 Those from every people, tribe, tongue, and nation will gaze on their corpses for three and a half days, and they will not allow their corpses to be buried. 10 The inhabitants of the earth will gloat over them and be glad and exchange gifts because these two prophets tormented the inhabitants of the earth. 11 But after the three and a half days, a breath of life from God entered them. When they stood on their feet, great fear fell on those who saw them. 12 Then they heard a loud voice from heaven say to them, "Come up here." So they went up to heaven in a cloud as their enemies looked on. 13 At that moment there was a great earthquake, and a tenth of the city fell in ruins. Seven thousand people were killed during the earthquake; the rest were terrified and gave glory to the God of heaven.

14 The second woe has passed, but the third is coming soon.

15 Then the seventh angel blew his trumpet. There were loud voices in heaven, saying, "The kingdom of the world now belongs to our Lord and to his Anointed, and he will reign forever and ever." 16 The twenty-four elders who sat on their thrones before God prostrated themselves and worshiped God 17 and said:

"We give thanks to you, Lord God almighty,
 who are and who were.
For you have assumed your great power
 and have established your reign.
18 The nations raged,
 but your wrath has come,
 and the time for the dead to be judged,
and to recompense your servants, the prophets,
 and the holy ones and those who fear
  your name,
 the small and the great alike,
 and to destroy those who destroy the earth."

19 Then God's temple in heaven was opened, and the ark of his covenant could be seen in the temple. There were flashes of lightning, rumblings, and peals of thunder, an earthquake, and a violent hailstorm.

12 A great sign appeared in the sky, a woman clothed with the sun, with the moon under her feet, and on her head a crown of twelve stars. 2 She was with child and wailed aloud in pain as she labored to give birth. 3 Then another sign appeared in the sky; it was a huge red dragon, with seven heads and ten horns, and on its heads were seven diadems. 4 Its tail swept away a third of the stars in the sky

nesses to prophesy for twelve hundred and sixty days, wearing sackcloth. 4 These are the *two olive trees*[t] and the two lamps *in attendance on the Lord of the world*.[u] 5 Fire comes from their mouths and consumes their enemies if anyone tries to harm them; and anyone who tries to harm them will certainly be killed in this way. 6 They have the power to lock up the sky so that it does not rain as long as they are prophesying; they have the power to turn water into blood and strike the whole world with any plague as often as they like. 7 When they have completed their witnessing, the beast that comes out of the Abyss *is going to make war on them and overcome them*[v] and kill them. 8 Their corpses lie in the main street of the great city[w] known by the symbolic names Sodom and Egypt, in which their Lord was crucified. 9 People of every race, tribe, language and nation stare at their corpses, for three-and-a-half days, not letting them be buried, 10 and the people of the world are glad about it and celebrate the event by giving presents to each other, because these two prophets have been a plague to the people of the world.'

11 After the three-and-a-half days, *God breathed life into them and they stood up on their feet*,[x] and everybody who saw it happen was terrified; 12 then I heard a loud voice from heaven say to them, 'Come up here,' and while their enemies were watching, they went up to heaven in a cloud. 13 Immediately, there was a violent earthquake, and a tenth of the city collapsed; seven thousand persons were killed in the earthquake, and the survivors, overcome with fear, could only praise the God of heaven.

14 That was the second of the disasters; the third is to come quickly after it.

15 Then the seventh angel blew his trumpet, and voices could be heard shouting in heaven, calling, 'The kingdom of the world has become the kingdom of our Lord and his Christ, and he will reign for ever and ever.' 16 The twenty-four elders, enthroned in the presence of God, prostrated themselves and touched the ground with their foreheads worshipping God 17 with these words, 'We give thanks to you, Almighty Lord God, He who is, He who was, for assuming your great power and beginning your reign. 18 *The nations were in uproar*[y] and now the time has come for your retribution, and for the dead to be judged, and for *your servants the prophets*, for the saints and for *those who fear* your name, *small and great alike*, to be rewarded. The time has come to destroy those who are destroying the earth.'

19 Then the sanctuary of God in heaven opened, and the ark of the covenant could be seen inside it. Then came flashes of lightning, peals of thunder and an earthquake and violent hail.

12 Now a great sign appeared in heaven: a woman, robed with the sun, standing on the moon, and on her head a crown of twelve stars. 2 She was pregnant, and in labour, crying aloud in the pangs of childbirth. 3 Then a second sign appeared in the sky: there was a huge red dragon with seven heads and ten horns, and each of the seven heads crowned with a coronet. 4 Its tail swept a third

---

t **11** Zc 4:3, 14. *u* **11** 2 K 1:10. *v* **11** Dn 7:21.
w **11** Also called Babylon. It is the centre of evil and persecution, possibly Rome. *x* **11** Ezk 37:5, 10. *y* **11** Ps 2:1, 5, followed by Am 3:7; Ps 115:13.

heaven and threw them to the earth. Then the dragon stood before the woman who was about to bear a child, so that he might devour her child as soon as it was born. 5 And she gave birth to a son, a male child, who is to rule*f* all the nations with a rod of iron. But her child was snatched away and taken to God and to his throne; 6 and the woman fled into the wilderness, where she has a place prepared by God, so that there she can be nourished for one thousand two hundred sixty days.

7 And war broke out in heaven; Michael and his angels fought against the dragon. The dragon and his angels fought back, 8 but they were defeated, and there was no longer any place for them in heaven. 9 The great dragon was thrown down, that ancient serpent, who is called the Devil and Satan, the deceiver of the whole world — he was thrown down to the earth, and his angels were thrown down with him.

10 Then I heard a loud voice in heaven, proclaiming,
"Now have come the salvation and the power
    and the kingdom of our God
    and the authority of his Messiah,*g*
for the accuser of our comrades*h* has been
    thrown down,
    who accuses them day and night before our
      God.
11 But they have conquered him by the blood of the
    Lamb
    and by the word of their testimony,
for they did not cling to life even in the face of
    death.
12 Rejoice then, you heavens
    and those who dwell in them!
But woe to the earth and the sea,
    for the devil has come down to you
    with great wrath,
    because he knows that his time is short!"

13 So when the dragon saw that he had been thrown down to the earth, he pursued*i* the woman who had given birth to the male child. 14 But the woman was given the two wings of the great eagle, so that she could fly from the serpent into the wilderness, to her place where she is nourished for a time, and times, and half a time. 15 Then from his mouth the serpent poured water like a river after the woman, to sweep her away with the flood. 16 But the earth came to the help of the woman; it opened its mouth and swallowed the river that the dragon had poured from his mouth. 17 Then the dragon was angry with the woman, and went off to make war on the rest of her children, those who keep the commandments of God and hold the testimony of Jesus.

18 Then the dragon*j* took his stand on the sand of the seashore.

13 1 And I saw a beast rising out of the sea, having ten horns and seven heads; and on its horns were ten diadems, and on its heads were blasphemous names. 2 And the beast that I saw was like a leopard, its feet were like a bear's, and its mouth was like a lion's mouth. And the dragon gave it his power and his throne and great authority. 3 One of its heads seemed to have received a death-blow, but its mortal wound*k* had been healed. In amazement the whole earth followed the beast. 4 They worshiped the dragon, for he had given his authority to the beast, and they worshiped the beast, saying, "Who is like the beast, and who can fight against it?"

he swept down a third of the stars in the sky and hurled them to the earth. The dragon stood in front of the woman who was about to give birth, so that when her child was born he might devour it. 5 But when she gave birth to a male child, who is destined to rule all nations with a rod of iron, the child was snatched up to God and to his throne. 6 The woman herself fled into the wilderness, where she was to be looked after for twelve hundred and sixty days in a place prepared for her by God.

7 Then war broke out in heaven; Michael and his angels fought against the dragon. The dragon with his angels fought back, 8 but he was too weak, and they lost their place in heaven. 9 The great dragon was thrown down, that ancient serpent who led the whole world astray, whose name is the Devil, or Satan; he was thrown down to the earth, and his angels with him.

10 I heard a loud voice in heaven proclaim: 'This is the time of victory for our God, the time of his power and sovereignty, when his Christ comes to his rightful rule! For the accuser of our brothers, he who day and night accused them before our God, is overthrown. 11 By the sacrifice of the Lamb and by the witness they bore, they have conquered him; faced with death they did not cling to life. 12 Therefore rejoice, you heavens and you that dwell in them! But woe to you, earth and sea, for the Devil has come down to you in great fury, knowing that his time is short!'

13 When the dragon saw that he had been thrown down to the earth, he went in pursuit of the woman who had given birth to the male child. 14 But she was given the wings of a mighty eagle, so that she could fly to her place in the wilderness where she was to be looked after for three and a half years, out of reach of the serpent. 15 From his mouth the serpent spewed a flood of water after the woman to sweep her away with its spate. 16 But the earth came to her rescue: it opened its mouth and drank up the river which the dragon spewed from his mouth. 17 Furious with the woman, the dragon went off to wage war on the rest of her offspring, those who keep God's commandments and maintain their witness to Jesus.

13 1 He took his stand on the seashore.
Then I saw a beast rising out of the sea. It had ten horns and seven heads; on the horns were ten diadems, and on each head was a blasphemous name. 2 The beast I saw resembled a leopard, but its feet were like a bear's and its mouth like a lion's. The dragon conferred on it his own power, his throne, and great authority. 3 One of the heads seemed to have been given a death blow, yet its mortal wound was healed. The whole world went after the beast in wondering admiration, 4 and worshipped the dragon because he had conferred his authority on the beast; they worshipped the beast also. 'Who is like the beast?' they said. 'Who can fight against it?'

---

f Or *to shepherd*   *g* Gk *Christ*   *h* Gk *brothers*   *i* Or *persecuted*
j Gk *Then he;* other ancient authorities read *Then I stood*   *k* Gk *the plague of its death*

12:11 **the witness they bore:** or *the word of God to which they bore witness.*

and hurled them down to the earth. Then the dragon stood before the woman about to give birth, to devour her child when she gave birth. 5 She gave birth to a son, a male child, destined to rule all the nations with an iron rod. Her child was caught up to God and his throne. 6 The woman herself fled into the desert where she had a place prepared by God, that there she might be taken care of for twelve hundred and sixty days.

7 Then war broke out in heaven; Michael and his angels battled against the dragon. The dragon and its angels fought back, 8 but they did not prevail and there was no longer any place for them in heaven. 9 The huge dragon, the ancient serpent, who is called the Devil and Satan, who deceived the whole world, was thrown down to earth, and its angels were thrown down with it.

10 Then I heard a loud voice in heaven say:

"Now have salvation and power come,
and the kingdom of our God
and the authority of his Anointed.
For the accuser of our brothers is cast out,
who accuses them before our God day and night.
11 They conquered him by the blood of the Lamb
and by the word of their testimony;
love for life did not deter them from death.
12 Therefore, rejoice, you heavens,
and you who dwell in them.
But woe to you, earth and sea,
for the Devil has come down to you in
great fury,
for he knows he has but a short time."

13 When the dragon saw that it had been thrown down to the earth, it pursued the woman who had given birth to the male child. 14 But the woman was given the two wings of the great eagle, so that she could fly to her place in the desert, where, far from the serpent, she was taken care of for a year, two years, and a half-year. 15 The serpent, however, spewed a torrent of water out of his mouth after the woman to sweep her away with the current. 16 But the earth helped the woman and opened its mouth and swallowed the flood that the dragon spewed out of its mouth. 17 Then the dragon became angry with the woman and went off to wage war against the rest of her offspring, those who keep God's commandments and bear witness to Jesus. 18 It took its position on the sand of the sea.

13 Then I saw a beast come out of the sea with ten horns and seven heads; on its horns were ten diadems, and on its heads blasphemous name[s]. 2 The beast I saw was like a leopard, but it had feet like a bear's, and its mouth was like the mouth of a lion. To it the dragon gave its own power and throne, along with great authority. 3 I saw that one of its heads seemed to have been mortally wounded, but this mortal wound was healed. Fascinated, the whole world followed after the beast. 4 They worshiped the dragon because it gave its authority to the beast; they also worshiped the beast and said, "Who can compare with the beast or who can fight against it?"

of *the stars from the sky and hurled them to the ground,*z and the dragon stopped in front of the woman as she was at the point of giving birth, so that it could eat the child as soon as it was born. 5 The woman *was delivered of a boy,*a the son who was *to rule all the nations with an iron sceptre*, and the child was taken straight up to God and to his throne, 6 while the woman escaped into the desert, where God had prepared a place for her to be looked after for twelve hundred and sixty days.

7 And now war broke out in heaven, when *Michael*b with his angels attacked the dragon. The dragon fought back with his angels, 8 but they were defeated and driven out of heaven. 9 The great dragon, the primeval serpent, known as the devil or Satan, who had led all the world astray, was hurled down to the earth and his angels were hurled down with him. 10 Then I heard a voice shout from heaven, 'Salvation and power and empire for ever have been won by our God, and all authority for his Christ, now that the accuser, who accused our brothers day and night before our God, has been brought down. 11 They have triumphed over him by the blood of the Lamb and by the word to which they bore witness, because even in the face of death they did not cling to life. 12 So let the heavens rejoice and all who live there; but for you, earth and sea, disaster is coming—because the devil has gone down to you in a rage, knowing that he has little time left.'

13 As soon as the dragon found himself hurled down to the earth, he sprang in pursuit of the woman, the mother of the male child, 14 but she was given a pair of the great eagle's wings to fly away from the serpent into the desert, to the place where she was to be looked after for *a time, two times and half a time*.c 15 So the serpent vomited water from his mouth, like a river, after the woman, to sweep her away in the current, 16 but the earth came to her rescue; it opened its mouth and swallowed the river spewed from the dragon's mouth. 17 Then the dragon was enraged with the woman and went away to make war on the rest of her children, who obey God's commandments and have in themselves the witness of Jesus.

18 And I took my stand on the seashore.

13 Then I saw *a beast*d *emerge from the sea*: it had seven heads and ten horns, with a coronet on each of its ten horns, and its heads were marked with blasphemous titles. 2 I saw that the beast *was like a leopard*, with paws like *a bear* and a mouth like *a lion*; the dragon had handed over to it his own power and his throne and his immense authority. 3 I saw that one of its heads seemed to have had a fatal wound but that this deadly injury had healed and the whole world had marvelled and followed the beast. 4 They prostrated themselves in front of the dragon because he had given the beast his authority; and they prostrated themselves in front of the beast, saying, 'Who can compare with the beast? Who can fight against it?' 5 The

---

12, 18: *It took its position:* many later manuscripts and versions read "I took my position," thus connecting the sentence to the following paragraph.

z **12** Dn 8:10. a **12** Is 66:7, followed by Ps 2:9. The woman is the people of God, and the boy is the Messiah. b **12** God's champion in Dn 10:13; 12:1. c **12** See a11 note. d **13** The vision draws on Dn 7.

NEW REVISED STANDARD VERSION

5 The beast was given a mouth uttering haughty and blasphemous words, and it was allowed to exercise authority for forty-two months. 6 It opened its mouth to utter blasphemies against God, blaspheming his name and his dwelling, that is, those who dwell in heaven. 7 Also it was allowed to make war on the saints and to conquer them.*l* It was given authority over every tribe and people and language and nation, 8 and all the inhabitants of the earth will worship it, everyone whose name has not been written from the foundation of the world in the book of life of the Lamb that was slaughtered.*m*

9 Let anyone who has an ear listen:

10 If you are to be taken captive,
into captivity you go;
if you kill with the sword,
with the sword you must be killed.

Here is a call for the endurance and faith of the saints.

11 Then I saw another beast that rose out of the earth; it had two horns like a lamb and it spoke like a dragon. 12 It exercises all the authority of the first beast on its behalf, and it makes the earth and its inhabitants worship the first beast, whose mortal wound*n* had been healed. 13 It performs great signs, even making fire come down from heaven to earth in the sight of all; 14 and by the signs that it is allowed to perform on behalf of the beast, it deceives the inhabitants of earth, telling them to make an image for the beast that had been wounded by the sword*o* and yet lived; 15 and it was allowed to give breath*p* to the image of the beast so that the image of the beast could even speak and cause those who would not worship the image of the beast to be killed. 16 Also it causes all, both small and great, both rich and poor, both free and slave, to be marked on the right hand or the forehead, 17 so that no one can buy or sell who does not have the mark, that is, the name of the beast or the number of its name. 18 This calls for wisdom: let anyone with understanding calculate the number of the beast, for it is the number of a person. Its number is six hundred sixty-six.*q*

14 Then I looked, and there was the Lamb, standing on Mount Zion! And with him were one hundred forty-four thousand who had his name and his Father's name written on their foreheads. 2 And I heard a voice from heaven like the sound of many waters and like the sound of loud thunder; the voice I heard was like the sound of harpists playing on their harps, 3 and they sing a new song before the throne and before the four living creatures and before the elders. No one could learn that song except the one hundred forty-four thousand who have been redeemed from the earth. 4 It is these who have not defiled themselves with women, for they are virgins; these follow the Lamb wherever he goes. They have been redeemed from humankind as first fruits for God and the Lamb, 5 and in their mouth no lie was found; they are blameless.

6 Then I saw another angel flying in midheaven, with an eternal gospel to proclaim to those who live*r* on the earth —to every nation and tribe and language and people. 7 He said in a loud voice, "Fear God and give him glory, for the hour of his judgment has come; and worship him who made heaven and earth, the sea and the springs of water."

8 Then another angel, a second, followed, saying, "Fallen, fallen is Babylon the great! She has made all nations drink of the wine of the wrath of her fornication."

REVISED ENGLISH BIBLE

5 The beast was allowed to mouth bombast and blasphemy, and was granted permission to continue for forty-two months. 6 It uttered blasphemies against God, reviling his name and his dwelling-place, that is, those who dwell in heaven. 7 It was also allowed to wage war on God's people and to defeat them, and it was granted authority over every tribe, nation, language, and race. 8 All the inhabitants of the earth will worship it, all whose names have not been written in the book of life of the Lamb, slain since the foundation of the world.

9 You have ears, so hear! 10 Whoever is to be made prisoner, to prison he shall go; whoever is to be slain by the sword, by the sword he must be slain. This calls for the endurance and faithfulness of God's people.

11 Then I saw another beast; it came up out of the earth, and had two horns like a lamb's, but spoke like a dragon. 12 It wielded all the authority of the first beast in its presence, and made the earth and its inhabitants worship this first beast, whose mortal wound had been healed. 13 It worked great miracles, even making fire come down from heaven to earth, where people could see it. 14 By the miracles it was allowed to perform in the presence of the beast it deluded the inhabitants of the earth, and persuaded them to erect an image in honour of the beast which had been wounded by the sword and yet lived. 15 It was allowed to give breath to the image of the beast, so that it could even speak and cause all who would not worship the image to be put to death. 16 It caused everyone, small and great, rich and poor, free man and slave, to have a mark put on his right hand or his forehead, 17 and no one was allowed to buy or sell unless he bore this beast's mark, either name or number. 18 (This calls for skill; let anyone who has intelligence work out the number of the beast, for the number represents a man's name, and the numerical value of its letters is six hundred and sixty-six.)

14 I LOOKED, and there on Mount Zion stood the Lamb, and with him were a hundred and forty-four thousand who had his name and the name of his Father written on their foreheads. 2 I heard a sound from heaven like a mighty torrent or a great peal of thunder; what I heard was like harpists playing on their harps. 3 They were singing a new song before the throne and the four living creatures and the elders, and no one could learn it except the hundred and forty-four thousand ransomed from the earth. 4 These are men who have kept themselves chaste and have not defiled themselves with women; these follow the Lamb wherever he goes. They have been ransomed as the first-fruits of mankind for God and the Lamb. 5 No lie was found on their lips; they are without fault.

6 Then I saw an angel flying in mid-heaven, with an eternal gospel to proclaim to those on earth, to every race, tribe, language, and nation. 7 He spoke in a loud voice: 'Fear God and pay him homage, for the hour of his judgement has come! Worship him who made heaven and earth, the sea and the springs of water!'

8 A second angel followed, saying, 'Fallen, fallen is Babylon the great, who has made all nations drink the wine of God's anger roused by her fornication!'

---

l Other ancient authorities lack this sentence   *m* Or *written in the book of life of the Lamb that was slaughtered from the foundation of the world*   *n* Gk *whose plague of its death*   *o* Or *that had received the plague of the sword*   *p* Or *spirit*   *q* Other ancient authorities read *six hundred sixteen*   *r* Gk *sit*

13:8 **written . . . world:** *or* written, since the foundation of the world, in the book of life of the slain Lamb.   13:10 **whoever . . . slain by the sword:** *or* whoever takes the sword to slay.   13:18 **the numerical . . . letters:** *lit.* his number.

5 The beast was given a mouth uttering proud boasts and blasphemies, and it was given authority to act for forty-two months. 6 It opened its mouth to utter blasphemies against God, blaspheming his name and his dwelling and those who dwell in heaven. 7 It was also allowed to wage war against the holy ones and conquer them, and it was granted authority over every tribe, people, tongue, and nation. 8 All the inhabitants of the earth will worship it, all whose names were not written from the foundation of the world in the book of life, which belongs to the Lamb who was slain.

9 Whoever has ears ought to hear these words.
10 Anyone destined for captivity goes into captivity.
   Anyone destined to be slain by the sword shall
      be slain by the sword.

Such is the faithful endurance of the holy ones.

11 Then I saw another beast come up out of the earth; it had two horns like a lamb's but spoke like a dragon. 12 It wielded all the authority of the first beast in its sight and made the earth and its inhabitants worship the first beast, whose mortal wound had been healed. 13 It performed great signs, even making fire come down from heaven to earth in the sight of everyone. 14 It deceived the inhabitants of the earth with the signs it was allowed to perform in the sight of the first beast, telling them to make an image for the beast who had been wounded by the sword and revived. 15 It was then permitted to breathe life into the beast's image, so that the beast's image could speak and [could] have anyone who did not worship it put to death. 16 It forced all the people, small and great, rich and poor, free and slave, to be given a stamped image on their right hands or their foreheads, 17 so that no one could buy or sell except one who had the stamped image of the beast's name or the number that stood for its name.

18 Wisdom is needed; one who understands can calculate the number of the beast, for it is a number that stands for a person. His number is six hundred and sixty-six.

14 Then I looked and there was the Lamb standing on Mount Zion, and with him a hundred and forty-four thousand who had his name and his Father's name written on their foreheads. 2 I heard a sound from heaven like the sound of rushing water or a loud peal of thunder. The sound I heard was like that of harpists playing their harps. 3 They were singing [what seemed to be] a new hymn before the throne, before the four living creatures and the elders. No one could learn this hymn except the hundred and forty-four thousand who had been ransomed from the earth. 4 These are they who were not defiled with women; they are virgins and these are the ones who follow the Lamb wherever he goes. They have been ransomed as the firstfruits of the human race for God and the Lamb. 5 On their lips no deceit has been found; they are unblemished.

6 Then I saw another angel flying high overhead, with everlasting good news to announce to those who dwell on earth, to every nation, tribe, tongue, and people. 7 He said in a loud voice, "Fear God and give him glory, for his time has come to sit in judgment. Worship him who made heaven and earth and sea and springs of water."

8 A second angel followed, saying:

"Fallen, fallen is Babylon the great,
   that made all the nations drink
   the wine of her licentious passion."

beast was allowed *to mouth its boasts* and blasphemies and to be active for forty-two months; 6 and it mouthed its blasphemies against God, against his name, his heavenly Tent and all those who are sheltered there. 7 It was allowed *to make war against the saints and conquer them, and given power* over every race, people, language and nation; 8 and all people of the world will worship it, that is, everybody whose name has not been written down since the foundation of the world in the sacrificial Lamb's book of life. 9 Let anyone who can hear, listen: 10 *Those for captivity to captivity; those for* death by *the sword to* death by *the sword.*e This is why the saints must have perseverance and faith.

11 Then I saw a second beast, emerging from the ground; it had two horns like a lamb, but made a noise like a dragon. 12 This second beast exercised all the power of the first beast, on its behalf making the world and all its people worship the first beast, whose deadly injury had healed. 13 And it worked great miracles, even to calling down fire from heaven onto the earth while people watched. 14 Through the miracles which it was allowed to do on behalf of the first beast, it was able to lead astray the people of the world and persuade them to put up a statue in honour of the beast that had been wounded by the sword and still lived. 15 It was allowed to breathe life into this statue, so that the statue of the beast was able to speak, and to have *anyone who refused to worship the statue* f of the beast put to death. 16 It compelled everyone — small and great alike, rich and poor, slave and citizen — to be branded on the right hand or on the forehead, 17 and made it illegal for anyone to buy or sell anything unless he had been branded with the name of the beast or with the number of its name.

18 There is need for shrewdness here: anyone clever may interpret the number of the beast: it is the number of a human being, the number 666.g

14 hNext in my vision I saw Mount Zion, and standing on it the Lamb who had with him a hundred and forty-four thousand people, all with his name and his Father's name written on their foreheads. 2 I heard a sound coming out of heaven like the sound of the ocean or the roar of thunder; it was like the sound of harpists playing their harps. 3 There before the throne they were singing a new hymn in the presence of the four living creatures and the elders, a hymn that could be learnt only by the hundred and forty-four thousand who had been redeemed from the world. 4 These are the sons who have kept their virginity and not been defiled with women; they *follow* the Lamb wherever he goes; they, out of all people, have been redeemed to be *the first-fruits for God*i and for the Lamb. 5 *No lie*j was found in their mouths and no fault can be found in them.

6 Then I saw another angel, flying high overhead, sent to announce the gospel of eternity to all who live on the earth, every nation, race, language and tribe. 7 He was calling, 'Fear God and glorify him, because the time has come for him to sit in judgement; worship *the maker of heaven and earth and sea*k and the springs of water.'

8 A second angel followed him, calling, '*Babylon has fallen, Babylon the Great has fallen,* Babylon which gave the whole world *the wine of retribution* to drink.'l

e **13** Jr 15:2.   *f* **13** Dn 3:5−7, 15.   *g* **13** 6 = 7−1, so 666 = triple imperfection. It may also symbolise a name.   *h* **14** = 7:1−8.   *i* **14** Jr 2:2−3.   *j* **14** Zp 3:13.   *k* **14** Ex 20:11.   *l* **14** = 18:2−3; cf. Is 21:9; 51:17.

NEW REVISED STANDARD VERSION	REVISED ENGLISH BIBLE

NEW REVISED STANDARD VERSION

9 Then another angel, a third, followed them, crying with a loud voice, "Those who worship the beast and its image, and receive a mark on their foreheads or on their hands, 10 they will also drink the wine of God's wrath, poured unmixed into the cup of his anger, and they will be tormented with fire and sulfur in the presence of the holy angels and in the presence of the Lamb. 11 And the smoke of their torment goes up forever and ever. There is no rest day or night for those who worship the beast and its image and for anyone who receives the mark of its name."

12 Here is a call for the endurance of the saints, those who keep the commandments of God and hold fast to the faith of[s] Jesus.

13 And I heard a voice from heaven say, "Write this: Blessed are the dead who from now on die in the Lord." "Yes," says the Spirit, "they will rest from their labors, for their deeds follow them."

14 Then I looked, and there was a white cloud, and seated on the cloud was one like the Son of Man, with a golden crown on his head, and a sharp sickle in his hand! 15 Another angel came out of the temple, calling with a loud voice to the one who sat on the cloud, "Use your sickle and reap, for the hour to reap has come, because the harvest of the earth is fully ripe." 16 So the one who sat on the cloud swung his sickle over the earth, and the earth was reaped.

17 Then another angel came out of the temple in heaven, and he too had a sharp sickle. 18 Then another angel came out from the altar, the angel who has authority over fire, and he called with a loud voice to him who had the sharp sickle, "Use your sharp sickle and gather the clusters of the vine of the earth, for its grapes are ripe." 19 So the angel swung his sickle over the earth and gathered the vintage of the earth, and he threw it into the great wine press of the wrath of God. 20 And the wine press was trodden outside the city, and blood flowed from the wine press, as high as a horse's bridle, for a distance of about two hundred miles.[t]

15 Then I saw another portent in heaven, great and amazing: seven angels with seven plagues, which are the last, for with them the wrath of God is ended.

2 And I saw what appeared to be a sea of glass mixed with fire, and those who had conquered the beast and its image and the number of its name, standing beside the sea of glass with harps of God in their hands. 3 And they sing the song of Moses, the servant[u] of God, and the song of the Lamb:

"Great and amazing are your deeds,
Lord God the Almighty!
Just and true are your ways,
King of the nations![v]
4 Lord, who will not fear
and glorify your name?
For you alone are holy.
All nations will come
and worship before you,
for your judgments have been revealed."

5 After this I looked, and the temple of the tent[w] of witness in heaven was opened, 6 and out of the temple came the seven angels with the seven plagues, robed in pure bright linen,[x] with golden sashes across their chests. 7 Then one of the four living creatures gave the seven angels seven golden bowls full of the wrath of God, who lives forever and ever; 8 and the temple was filled with smoke from the glory of God and from his power, and no one could enter the temple until the seven plagues of the seven angels were ended.

REVISED ENGLISH BIBLE

9 A third angel followed, saying in a loud voice, 'Whoever worships the beast and its image and receives its mark on his forehead or hand, 10 he too shall drink the wine of God's anger, poured undiluted into the cup of his wrath. He shall be tormented in sulphurous flames in the sight of the holy angels and the Lamb. 11 The smoke of their torment will rise for ever; there is no respite day or night for those who worship the beast and its image, or for anyone who receives the mark of its name.' 12 This calls for the endurance of God's people, all those who keep his commands and remain loyal to Jesus.

13 I heard a voice from heaven say, 'Write this: "Happy are the dead who henceforth die in the faith of the Lord!" "Yes," says the Spirit, "let them rest from their labours, for the record of their deeds goes with them." '

14 As I looked there appeared a white cloud, on which was seated a figure like a man; he had a gold crown on his head and a sharp sickle in his hand. 15 Another angel came out of the temple and called in a loud voice to him who sat on the cloud: 'Put in your sickle and reap, for harvest time has come and earth's crop is fully ripe.' 16 So the one who sat on the cloud swept over the earth with his sickle and the harvest was reaped.

17 Another angel came out of the heavenly sanctuary, and he also had a sharp sickle. 18 Then from the altar came yet another, the angel who has authority over fire, and he called aloud to the one with the sharp sickle: 'Put in your sharp sickle, and gather in earth's grape harvest, for its clusters are ripe.' 19 So the angel swept over the earth with his sickle and gathered in its grapes, and threw them into the great winepress of God's wrath. 20 The winepress was trodden outside the city, and for a distance of two hundred miles blood flowed from the press to the height of horses' bridles.

15 THEN I saw in heaven another great and astonishing sign: seven angels with seven plagues, the last plagues of all, for with them the wrath of God was completed.

2 I saw what looked like a sea of glass shot through with fire. Standing beside it and holding the harps which God had given them were those who had been victorious against the beast, its image, and the number of its name. 3 They were singing the song of Moses, the servant of God, and the song of the Lamb:

'Great and marvellous are your deeds,
O Lord God, sovereign over all;
just and true are your ways,
O King of the ages.
4 Who shall not fear you, Lord,
and do homage to your name?
For you alone are holy.
All nations shall come and worship before you,
for your just decrees stand revealed.'

5 After this, as I looked, the sanctuary of the heavenly Tent of Testimony was opened, 6 and from it came the seven angels with the seven plagues. They were robed in fine linen, pure and shining, and had golden girdles round their breasts. 7 One of the four living creatures gave to the seven angels seven golden bowls full of the wrath of God who lives for ever. 8 The sanctuary was filled with smoke from the glory of God and from his power, so that no one could enter it until the seven plagues of the seven angels were completed.

---

[s] Or to their faith in   [t] Gk one thousand six hundred stadia
[u] Gk slave   [v] Other ancient authorities read the ages
[w] Or tabernacle   [x] Other ancient authorities read stone

14:13 the dead . . . the Spirit: some witnesses read the dead who die trusting in the Lord! Henceforth", says the Spirit.

9 A third angel followed them and said in a loud voice, "Anyone who worships the beast or its image, or accepts its mark on forehead or hand, 10 will also drink the wine of God's fury, poured full strength into the cup of his wrath, and will be tormented in burning sulfur before the holy angels and before the Lamb. 11 The smoke of the fire that torments them will rise forever and ever, and there will be no relief day or night for those who worship the beast or its image or accept the mark of its name." 12 Here is what sustains the holy ones who keep God's commandments and their faith in Jesus.

13 I heard a voice from heaven say, "Write this: Blessed are the dead who die in the Lord from now on." "Yes," said the Spirit, "let them find rest from their labors, for their works accompany them."

14 Then I looked and there was a white cloud, and sitting on the cloud one who looked like a son of man, with a gold crown on his head and a sharp sickle in his hand. 15 Another angel came out of the temple, crying out in a loud voice to the one sitting on the cloud, "Use your sickle and reap the harvest, for the time to reap has come, because the earth's harvest is fully ripe." 16 So the one who was sitting on the cloud swung his sickle over the earth, and the earth was harvested.

17 Then another angel came out of the temple in heaven who also had a sharp sickle. 18 Then another angel [came] from the altar, [who] was in charge of the fire, and cried out in a loud voice to the one who had the sharp sickle, "Use your sharp sickle and cut the clusters from the earth's vines, for its grapes are ripe." 19 So the angel swung his sickle over the earth and cut the earth's vintage. He threw it into the great wine press of God's fury. 20 The wine press was trodden outside the city and blood poured out of the wine press to the height of a horse's bridle for two hundred miles.

15 Then I saw in heaven another sign, great and awe-inspiring: seven angels with the seven last plagues, for through them God's fury is accomplished.

2 Then I saw something like a sea of glass mingled with fire. On the sea of glass were standing those who had won the victory over the beast and its image and the number that signified its name. They were holding God's harps, 3 and they sang the song of Moses, the servant of God, and the song of the Lamb:

"Great and wonderful are your works,
    Lord God almighty.
Just and true are your ways,
    O king of the nations.
4 Who will not fear you, Lord,
    or glorify your name?
For you alone are holy.
All the nations will come
    and worship before you,
for your righteous acts have been revealed."

5 After this I had another vision. The temple that is the heavenly tent of testimony opened, 6 and the seven angels with the seven plagues came out of the temple. They were dressed in clean white linen, with a gold sash around their chests. 7 One of the four living creatures gave the seven angels seven gold bowls filled with the fury of God, who lives forever and ever. 8 Then the temple became so filled with the smoke from God's glory and might that no one could enter it until the seven plagues of the seven angels had been accomplished.

9 A third angel followed, shouting aloud, 'All those who worship the beast and his statue, or have had themselves branded on the hand or forehead, 10 will be made to drink the wine of God's fury which is ready, undiluted, in his cup of retribution; in *fire and brimstone* [m] they will be tortured in the presence of the holy angels and the Lamb 11 and *the smoke* of their torture will *rise for ever and ever*. [n] There will be no respite, *night or day*, for those who worship the beast or its statue or accept branding with its name.' 12 This is why there must be perseverance in the saints who keep the commandments of God and faith in Jesus. 13 Then I heard a voice from heaven say to me, 'Write down: Blessed are those who die in the Lord! Blessed indeed, the Spirit says; now they can rest for ever after their work, since their good deeds go with them.'

14 o Now in my vision I saw a white *cloud* and, *sitting on it, one like a son of man* with a gold crown on his head and a sharp sickle in his hand. 15 Then another angel came out of the sanctuary and shouted at the top of his voice to the one sitting on the cloud, '*Ply* your *sickle* and reap: harvest time has come and *the harvest* of the earth *is ripe*.' 16 Then the one sitting on the cloud set his sickle to work on the earth, and the harvest of earth was reaped.

17 Another angel, who also carried a sharp sickle, came out of the temple in heaven, 18 and the angel in charge of the fire left the altar and shouted at the top of his voice to the one with the sharp sickle, 'Put your sickle in, and harvest the bunches from the vine of the earth; all its grapes are ripe.' 19 So the angel set his sickle to work on the earth and harvested the whole vintage of the earth and put it into a huge winepress, the winepress of God's anger, 20 outside the city, where it was trodden until the blood that came out of the winepress was up to the horses' bridles as far away as sixteen hundred furlongs.

15 p And I saw in heaven another sign, great and wonderful: seven angels were bringing the seven plagues that are the last of all, because they exhaust the anger of God. 2 I seemed to be looking at a sea of crystal suffused with fire, and standing by the lake of glass, those who had fought against the beast and won, and against his statue and the number which is his name. They all had harps from God, 3 and they were singing the hymn of Moses, q the servant of God, and the hymn of the Lamb:

How great and wonderful are all your works,
    Lord God Almighty;
upright and true are all your ways,
    King of nations.
4 *Who does not revere* and *glorify your name*,
    O Lord?
For you alone are holy,
and all nations will come and adore you
for the many acts of saving justice you have
    shown.

5 After this, in my vision, the sanctuary, the tent of the Testimony, opened in heaven, 6 and out came the seven angels with the seven plagues, wearing pure white linen, fastened round their waists with belts of gold. 7 One of the four living creatures gave the seven angels seven golden bowls filled with the anger of God who lives for ever and ever. 8 *The smoke from the glory* and the power *of God* filled the temple r so that no one could go into it until the seven plagues of the seven angels were completed.

m 14 Gn 19:24.   n 14 Is 34:9–10.   o 14 Dn 7:13; Jl 4:12–13.
p 15 = 7:1–8.   q 15 Ex 15; in fact the hymn uses Jr 10:7; Ps 86:9.
r 15 1 K 8:10.

16

Then I heard a loud voice from the temple telling the seven angels, "Go and pour out on the earth the seven bowls of the wrath of God."

2 So the first angel went and poured his bowl on the earth, and a foul and painful sore came on those who had the mark of the beast and who worshiped its image.

3 The second angel poured his bowl into the sea, and it became like the blood of a corpse, and every living thing in the sea died.

4 The third angel poured his bowl into the rivers and the springs of water, and they became blood. 5 And I heard the angel of the waters say,

"You are just, O Holy One, who are and were,
for you have judged these things;
6 because they shed the blood of saints and
prophets,
you have given them blood to drink.
It is what they deserve!"
7 And I heard the altar respond,
"Yes, O Lord God, the Almighty,
your judgments are true and just!"

8 The fourth angel poured his bowl on the sun, and it was allowed to scorch them with fire; 9 they were scorched by the fierce heat, but they cursed the name of God, who had authority over these plagues, and they did not repent and give him glory.

10 The fifth angel poured his bowl on the throne of the beast, and its kingdom was plunged into darkness; people gnawed their tongues in agony, 11 and cursed the God of heaven because of their pains and sores, and they did not repent of their deeds.

12 The sixth angel poured his bowl on the great river Euphrates, and its water was dried up in order to prepare the way for the kings from the east. 13 And I saw three foul spirits like frogs coming from the mouth of the dragon, from the mouth of the beast, and from the mouth of the false prophet. 14 These are demonic spirits, performing signs, who go abroad to the kings of the whole world, to assemble them for battle on the great day of God the Almighty. 15 ("See, I am coming like a thief! Blessed is the one who stays awake and is clothed,*y* not going about naked and exposed to shame.") 16 And they assembled them at the place that in Hebrew is called Harmagedon.

17 The seventh angel poured his bowl into the air, and a loud voice came out of the temple, from the throne, saying, "It is done!" 18 And there came flashes of lightning, rumblings, peals of thunder, and a violent earthquake, such as had not occurred since people were upon the earth, so violent was that earthquake. 19 The great city was split into three parts, and the cities of the nations fell. God remembered great Babylon and gave her the wine-cup of the fury of his wrath. 20 And every island fled away, and no mountains were to be found; 21 and huge hailstones, each weighing about a hundred pounds,*z* dropped from heaven on people, until they cursed God for the plague of the hail, so fearful was that plague.

17

Then one of the seven angels who had the seven bowls came and said to me, "Come, I will show you the judgment of the great whore who is seated on many waters, 2 with whom the kings of the earth have committed fornication, and with the wine of whose fornication the inhabitants of the earth have become drunk." 3 So he carried

16

I heard a loud voice from the sanctuary say to the seven angels, 'Go and pour out the seven bowls of God's wrath on the earth.'

2 The first angel went and poured out his bowl on the earth; and foul malignant sores appeared on the men that wore the mark of the beast and worshipped its image.

3 The second angel poured out his bowl on the sea; and the sea turned to blood like the blood from a dead body; and every living thing in it died.

4 The third angel poured out his bowl on the rivers and springs, and they turned to blood.

5 And I heard the angel of the waters say, 'You are just in these your judgements, you who are, and were, O Holy One; 6 for they shed the blood of your people and your prophets, and blood you have given them to drink. They have what they deserve!' 7 I heard a voice from the altar cry, 'Yes, Lord God, sovereign over all, true and just are your judgements!'

8 The fourth angel poured out his bowl on the sun; and it was allowed to burn people with its flames. 9 They were severely burned, and cursed the name of God who had the power to inflict such plagues, but they did not repent and do him homage.

10 The fifth angel poured out his bowl on the throne of the beast; and its kingdom was plunged into darkness. Men gnawed their tongues in agony, 11 and cursed the God of heaven for their pain and sores, but they would not repent of what they had done.

12 The sixth angel poured out his bowl on the Great River, the Euphrates; and its water was dried up to prepare a way for the kings from the east.

13 I saw three foul spirits like frogs coming from the mouths of the dragon, the beast, and the false prophet. 14 These are demonic spirits with power to work miracles, sent out to muster all the kings of the world for the battle on the great day of God the sovereign Lord. 15 ('See, I am coming like a thief! Happy the man who stays awake, and keeps his clothes at hand so that he will not have to go naked and ashamed for all to see!') 16 These spirits assembled the kings at the place called in Hebrew Armageddon.

17 The seventh angel poured out his bowl on the air; and out of the sanctuary came a loud voice from the throne, which said, 'It is over!' 18 There followed flashes of lightning and peals of thunder, and a violent earthquake, so violent that nothing like it had ever happened in human history.

19 THE great city was split in three, and the cities of the nations collapsed in ruin. God did not forget Babylon the great, but made her drink the cup which was filled with the fierce wine of his wrath. 20 Every island vanished, and not a mountain was to be seen. 21 Huge hailstones, weighing as much as a hundredweight, crashed down from the sky on the people; and they cursed God because the plague of hail was so severe.

17

ONE of the seven angels who held the seven bowls came and spoke to me; 'Come,' he said, 'I will show you the verdict on the great whore, she who is enthroned over many waters. 2 The kings of the earth have committed fornication with her, and people the world over have made themselves drunk on the wine of her fornication.' 3 He carried me in spirit into the wilderness, and I saw

---

y Gk *and keeps his robes*   *z* Gk *weighing about a talent*

16 I heard a loud voice speaking from the temple to the seven angels, "Go and pour out the seven bowls of God's fury upon the earth."

2 The first angel went and poured out his bowl on the earth. Festering and ugly sores broke out on those who had the mark of the beast or worshiped its image.

3 The second angel poured out his bowl on the sea. The sea turned to blood like that from a corpse; every creature living in the sea died.

4 The third angel poured out his bowl on the rivers and springs of water. These also turned to blood. 5 Then I heard the angel in charge of the waters say:

"You are just, O Holy One,
who are and who were,
in passing this sentence.

6 For they have shed the blood of the holy ones and the prophets,
and you [have] given them blood to drink;
it is what they deserve."

7 Then I heard the altar cry out,
"Yes, Lord God almighty,
your judgments are true and just."

8 The fourth angel poured out his bowl on the sun. It was given the power to burn people with fire. 9 People were burned by the scorching heat and blasphemed the name of God who had power over these plagues, but they did not repent or give him glory.

10 The fifth angel poured out his bowl on the throne of the beast. Its kingdom was plunged into darkness, and people bit their tongues in pain 11 and blasphemed the God of heaven because of their pains and sores. But they did not repent of their works.

12 The sixth angel emptied his bowl on the great river Euphrates. Its water was dried up to prepare the way for the kings of the East. 13 I saw three unclean spirits like frogs come from the mouth of the dragon, from the mouth of the beast, and from the mouth of the false prophet. 14 These were demonic spirits who performed signs. They went out to the kings of the whole world to assemble them for the battle on the great day of God the almighty. 15 ("Behold, I am coming like a thief." Blessed is the one who watches and keeps his clothes ready, so that he may not go naked and people see him exposed.) 16 They then assembled the kings in the place that is named Armageddon in Hebrew.

17 The seventh angel poured out his bowl into the air. A loud voice came out of the temple from the throne, saying, "It is done." 18 Then there were lightning flashes, rumblings, and peals of thunder, and a great earthquake. It was such a violent earthquake that there has never been one like it since the human race began on earth. 19 The great city was split into three parts, and the gentile cities fell. But God remembered great Babylon, giving it the cup filled with the wine of his fury and wrath. 20 Every island fled, and mountains disappeared. 21 Large hailstones like huge weights came down from the sky on people, and they blasphemed God for the plague of hail because this plague was so severe.

17 Then one of the seven angels who were holding the seven bowls came and said to me, "Come here. I will show you the judgment on the great harlot who lives near the many waters. 2 The kings of the earth have had intercourse with her, and the inhabitants of the earth became drunk on the wine of her harlotry." 3 Then he carried me

16 Then I heard a loud voice from the sanctuary calling to the seven angels, 'Go, and empty the seven bowls of God's anger over the earth.'

2 The first angel went and emptied his bowl over the earth; at once, on all the people who had been branded with the mark of the beast and had worshipped its statue, there came disgusting and virulent sores.

3 The second angel emptied his bowl over the sea, and it turned to blood, like the blood of a corpse, and every living creature in the sea died.

4 The third angel emptied his bowl into the rivers and springs of water and they turned into blood. 5 Then I heard the angel of water say, 'You are the Upright One, He who is, He who was, the Holy One, for giving this verdict: 6 they spilt the blood of the saints and the prophets, and blood is what you have given them to drink; it is what they deserve.' 7 And I heard the altar itself say, 'Truly, Lord God Almighty, the punishments you give are true and just.'

8 The fourth angel emptied his bowl over the sun and it was made to scorch people with its flames; 9 but though people were scorched by the fierce heat of it, they cursed the name of God who had the power to cause such plagues, and they would not repent and glorify him.

10 The fifth angel emptied his bowl over the throne of the beast and its whole empire was plunged into darkness. People were biting their tongues for pain, 11 but instead of repenting for what they had done, they cursed the God of heaven because of their pains and sores.

12 The sixth angel emptied his bowl over the great river Euphrates; all the water dried up so that a way was made for the kings of the East to come in. 13 Then from the jaws of dragon and beast and false prophet I saw three foul spirits come; they looked like frogs 14 and in fact were demon spirits, able to work miracles, going out to all the kings of the world to call them together for the war of the Great Day of God the Almighty. — 15 Look, I shall come like a thief. Blessed is anyone who has kept watch, and has kept his clothes on, so that he does not go out naked and expose his shame. — 16 They called the kings together at the place called, in Hebrew, Armageddon. *t*

17 The seventh angel emptied his bowl into the air, and a great voice boomed out from the sanctuary, 'The end has come.' 18 Then there were flashes of lightning and peals of thunder and a violent earthquake, *unparalleled since* humanity *first came into existence.u* 19 The Great City was split into three parts and the cities of the world collapsed; Babylon the Great was not forgotten: God made her drink the full winecup of his retribution. 20 Every island vanished and the mountains disappeared; 21 and hail, with great hailstones weighing a talent each, fell from the sky on the people. They cursed God for sending a plague of hail; it was the most terrible plague.

17 One of the seven angels that had the seven bowls came to speak to me, and said, 'Come here and I will show you the punishment of the great prostitute *who* is *enthroned beside abundant waters,v* 2 with whom all the kings of the earth have prostituted themselves, and who has made all the population of the world drunk with the wine of her adultery.' 3 He took me in spirit to a desert, and there I

s **16** = 8:6–12.   t **16** i.e. the mountains of Megiddo, symbol of disaster since King Josiah was killed there, 2 K 23:29.
u **16** Dn 12:1.   v **17** Jr 51:13. The seven heads are the seven hills of Rome.

me away in the spirit[a] into a wilderness, and I saw a woman sitting on a scarlet beast that was full of blasphemous names, and it had seven heads and ten horns. 4 The woman was clothed in purple and scarlet, and adorned with gold and jewels and pearls, holding in her hand a golden cup full of abominations and the impurities of her fornication; 5 and on her forehead was written a name, a mystery: "Babylon the great, mother of whores and of earth's abominations." 6 And I saw that the woman was drunk with the blood of the saints and the blood of the witnesses to Jesus.

When I saw her, I was greatly amazed. 7 But the angel said to me, "Why are you so amazed? I will tell you the mystery of the woman, and of the beast with seven heads and ten horns that carries her. 8 The beast that you saw was, and is not, and is about to ascend from the bottomless pit and go to destruction. And the inhabitants of the earth, whose names have not been written in the book of life from the foundation of the world, will be amazed when they see the beast, because it was and is not and is to come.

9 "This calls for a mind that has wisdom: the seven heads are seven mountains on which the woman is seated; also, they are seven kings, 10 of whom five have fallen, one is living, and the other has not yet come; and when he comes, he must remain only a little while. 11 As for the beast that was and is not, it is an eighth but it belongs to the seven, and it goes to destruction. 12 And the ten horns that you saw are ten kings who have not yet received a kingdom, but they are to receive authority as kings for one hour, together with the beast. 13 These are united in yielding their power and authority to the beast; 14 they will make war on the Lamb, and the Lamb will conquer them, for he is Lord of lords and King of kings, and those with him are called and chosen and faithful."

15 And he said to me, "The waters that you saw, where the whore is seated, are peoples and multitudes and nations and languages. 16 And the ten horns that you saw, they and the beast will hate the whore; they will make her desolate and naked; they will devour her flesh and burn her up with fire. 17 For God has put it into their hearts to carry out his purpose by agreeing to give their kingdom to the beast, until the words of God will be fulfilled. 18 The woman you saw is the great city that rules over the kings of the earth."

a woman mounted on a scarlet beast which was covered with blasphemous names and had seven heads and ten horns. 4 The woman was clothed in purple and scarlet, and decked out with gold and precious stones and pearls. In her hand she held a gold cup full of obscenities and the foulness of her fornication. 5 Written on her forehead was a name with a secret meaning: 'Babylon the great, the mother of whores and of every obscenity on earth.' 6 I saw that the woman was drunk with the blood of God's people, and with the blood of those who had borne their testimony to Jesus.

At the sight of her I was greatly astonished. 7 But the angel said to me, 'Why are you astonished? I will tell you the secret of the woman and of the beast she rides, with the seven heads and the ten horns. 8 The beast you saw was once alive, and is alive no longer, but has yet to ascend out of the abyss before going to be destroyed. All the inhabitants of the earth whose names have not been written in the book of life since the foundation of the world will be astonished to see the beast, which once was alive, and is alive no longer, and has still to appear.

9 'This calls for a mind with insight. The seven heads are seven hills on which the woman sits enthroned. 10 They also represent seven kings: five have already fallen, one is now reigning, and the other has yet to come. When he does come, he is to last for only a little while. 11 As for the beast that once was alive and is alive no longer, he is an eighth— and yet he is one of the seven, and he is going to destruction. 12 The ten horns you saw are ten kings who have not yet begun to reign, but who for a brief hour will share royal authority with the beast. 13 They have a single purpose and will confer their power and authority on the beast. 14 They will wage war on the Lamb, but the Lamb will conquer them, for he is Lord of lords and King of kings, and those who are with him are called and chosen and faithful.'

15 He continued: 'The waters you saw, where the great whore sat enthroned, represent nations, populations, races, and languages. 16 As for the ten horns you saw, and the beast, they will come to hate the whore. They will strip her naked and leave her destitute; they will devour her flesh and burn her up. 17 For God has put it into their minds to carry out his purpose, by making common cause and conferring their sovereignty on the beast until God's words are fulfilled. 18 The woman you saw is the great city that holds sway over the kings of the earth.'

18 After this I saw another angel coming down from heaven, having great authority; and the earth was made bright with his splendor. 2 He called out with a mighty voice,

"Fallen, fallen is Babylon the great!
It has become a dwelling place of demons,
a haunt of every foul spirit,
a haunt of every foul bird,
a haunt of every foul and hateful beast.[b]
3 For all the nations have drunk[c]
of the wine of the wrath of her fornication,
and the kings of the earth have committed
fornication with her,
and the merchants of the earth have grown rich
from the power[d] of her luxury."

18 After this I saw another angel coming down from heaven; he possessed great authority and the earth shone with his splendour. 2 In a mighty voice he proclaimed, 'Fallen, fallen is Babylon the great! She has become a dwelling for demons, a haunt for every unclean spirit, for every unclean and loathsome bird. 3 All the nations have drunk the wine of God's anger roused by her fornication; the kings of the earth have committed fornication with her, and merchants the world over have grown rich on her wealth and luxury.'

17:10 **kings:** or emperors.

|

away in spirit to a deserted place where I saw a woman seated on a scarlet beast that was covered with blasphemous names, with seven heads and ten horns. 4 The woman was wearing purple and scarlet and adorned with gold, precious stones, and pearls. She held in her hand a gold cup that was filled with the abominable and sordid deeds of her harlotry. 5 On her forehead was written a name, which is a mystery, "Babylon the great, the mother of harlots and of the abominations of the earth." 6 I saw that the woman was drunk on the blood of the holy ones and on the blood of the witnesses to Jesus.

When I saw her I was greatly amazed. 7 The angel said to me, "Why are you amazed? I will explain to you the mystery of the woman and of the beast that carries her, the beast with the seven heads and ten horns. 8 The beast that you saw existed once but now exists no longer. It will come up from the abyss and is headed for destruction. The inhabitants of the earth whose names have not been written in the book of life from the foundation of the world shall be amazed when they see the beast, because it existed once but exists no longer, and yet it will come again. 9 Here is a clue for one who has wisdom. The seven heads represent seven hills upon which the woman sits. They also represent seven kings: 10 five have already fallen, one still lives, and the last has not yet come, and when he comes he must remain only a short while. 11 The beast that existed once but exists no longer is an eighth king, but really belongs to the seven and is headed for destruction. 12 The ten horns that you saw represent ten kings who have not yet been crowned; they will receive royal authority along with the beast for one hour. 13 They are of one mind and will give their power and authority to the beast. 14 They will fight with the Lamb, but the Lamb will conquer them, for he is Lord of lords and king of kings, and those with him are called, chosen, and faithful."

15 Then he said to me, "The waters that you saw where the harlot lives represent large numbers of peoples, nations, and tongues. 16 The ten horns that you saw and the beast will hate the harlot; they will leave her desolate and naked; they will eat her flesh and consume her with fire. 17 For God has put it into their minds to carry out his purpose and to make them come to an agreement to give their kingdom to the beast until the words of God are accomplished. 18 The woman whom you saw represents the great city that has sovereignty over the kings of the earth."

18 After this I saw another angel coming down from heaven, having great authority, and the earth became illumined by his splendor. 2 He cried out in a mighty voice:

"Fallen, fallen is Babylon the great.
    She has become a haunt for demons.
She is a cage for every unclean spirit,
    a cage for every unclean bird,
    [a cage for every unclean] and
        disgusting [beast].
3 For all the nations have drunk
    the wine of her licentious passion.
The kings of the earth had intercourse with her,
    and the merchants of the earth grew rich from
        her drive for luxury."

saw a woman riding a scarlet beast which had seven heads and ten horns and had blasphemous titles written all over it. 4 The woman was dressed in purple and scarlet and glittered with gold and jewels and pearls, and she was holding a gold winecup filled with the disgusting filth of her prostitution; 5 on her forehead was written a name, a cryptic name: 'Babylon the Great, the mother of all the prostitutes and all the filthy practices on the earth.' 6 I saw that she was drunk, drunk with the blood of the saints, and the blood of the martyrs of Jesus; and when I saw her, I was completely mystified. 7 The angel said to me, 'Do you not understand? I will tell you the meaning of this woman, and of the beast she is riding, with the seven heads and the ten horns.

8 'The beast you have seen was once alive and is alive no longer; it is yet to come up from the Abyss, but only to go to its destruction. And the people of the world, whose names have not been written since the beginning of the world in the book of life, will be astonished when they see how the beast was once alive and is alive no longer, and is still to come.

9 'This calls for shrewdness. The seven heads are the seven hills, on which the woman is sitting. 10 The seven heads are also seven emperors. Five of them have already gone, one is here now, and one is yet to come; once here, he must stay for a short while. 11 The beast, who was alive and is alive no longer, is at the same time the eighth and one of the seven, and he is going to his destruction.

12 'The ten horns which you saw are ten kings[w] who have not yet been given their royal power but will have royal authority only for a single hour and in association with the beast. 13 They are all of one mind in putting their strength and their powers at the beast's disposal, 14 and they will go to war against the Lamb; but because the Lamb is Lord of lords and King of kings,[x] he will defeat them, he and his followers, the called, the chosen, the trustworthy.'

15 The angel continued, 'The waters you saw, beside which the prostitute was sitting, are all the peoples, the populations, the nations and the languages. 16 But the ten horns and the beast will turn against the prostitute, and tear off her clothes and leave her stark naked;[y] then they will eat her flesh and burn the remains in the fire. 17 In fact, God has influenced their minds to do what he intends, to agree together to put their royal powers at the beast's disposal until the time when God's words shall be fulfilled. 18 The woman you saw is the great city which has authority over all the rulers on earth.'

18 [z] After this, I saw another angel come down from heaven, with great authority given to him; the earth shone with his glory. 2 At the top of his voice he shouted,[a] 'Babylon has fallen, Babylon the Great has fallen, and has become the haunt of devils and a lodging for every foul spirit and dirty, loathsome bird. 3 All the nations have drunk deep of the wine of her prostitution; every king on the earth has prostituted himself with her, and every merchant grown rich through her debauchery.'

---

w **17** Dn 7:24.   x **17** Dn 10:17.   y **17** Ezk 16:39.
z **18** The songs of doom in ch. 18 draw on OT threats to a proud city, especially Jr 50—51; Ezk 26—28; Is 47.   a **18** = 14:8.

4 Then I heard another voice from heaven saying,
 "Come out of her, my people,
  so that you do not take part in her sins,
 and so that you do not share
  in her plagues;
5   for her sins are heaped high as heaven,
  and God has remembered her iniquities.
6 Render to her as she herself has rendered,
  and repay her double for her deeds;
 mix a double draught for her in the cup she
  mixed.
7   As she glorified herself and lived luxuriously,
 so give her a like measure of torment and
  grief.
Since in her heart she says,
 'I rule as a queen;
I am no widow,
 and I will never see grief,'
8   therefore her plagues will come in a single day —
 pestilence and mourning and famine —
 and she will be burned with fire;
 for mighty is the Lord God who judges her."

9 And the kings of the earth, who committed fornication
and lived in luxury with her, will weep and wail over her
when they see the smoke of her burning; 10 they will stand
far off, in fear of her torment, and say,
 "Alas, alas, the great city,
  Babylon, the mighty city!
 For in one hour your judgment has come."

11 And the merchants of the earth weep and mourn for
her, since no one buys their cargo anymore, 12 cargo of
gold, silver, jewels and pearls, fine linen, purple, silk and
scarlet, all kinds of scented wood, all articles of ivory, all
articles of costly wood, bronze, iron, and marble, 13 cinnamon, spice, incense, myrrh, frankincense, wine, olive oil,
choice flour and wheat, cattle and sheep, horses and chariots, slaves — and human lives.[e]
14   "The fruit for which your soul longed
  has gone from you,
 and all your dainties and your splendor
  are lost to you,
  never to be found again!"
15 The merchants of these wares, who gained wealth from
her, will stand far off, in fear of her torment, weeping and
mourning aloud,
16   "Alas, alas, the great city,
  clothed in fine linen,
  in purple and scarlet,
  adorned with gold,
  with jewels, and with pearls!
17 For in one hour all this wealth has been laid
  waste!"
And all shipmasters and seafarers, sailors and all whose
trade is on the sea, stood far off 18 and cried out as they saw
the smoke of her burning,
 "What city was like the great city?"
19 And they threw dust on their heads, as they wept and
mourned, crying out,
 "Alas, alas, the great city,
  where all who had ships at sea
  grew rich by her wealth!
 For in one hour she has been laid waste.
20   Rejoice over her, O heaven,
  you saints and apostles and prophets!
 For God has given judgment for you against her."

4 I heard another voice from heaven saying: 'Come out
from her, my people, lest you have any part in her sins and
you share in her plagues, 5 for her sins are piled high as
heaven, and God has not forgotten her crimes. 6 Pay her
back in her own coin, repay her twice over for her deeds!
Give her a potion twice as strong as the one she mixed!
7 Measure out torment and grief to match her pomp and
luxury! "I am a queen on my throne!" she says to herself.
"No widow's weeds for me, no mourning!" 8 That is why
plagues shall strike her in a single day, pestilence, bereavement, and famine, and she shall perish in flames; for mighty
is the Lord God who has pronounced her doom!'

9 The kings of the earth who committed fornication with
her and wallowed in her luxury will weep and wail over her,
as they see the smoke of her burning. 10 In terror at her
torment they will keep their distance and say, 'Alas, alas for
you great city, mighty city of Babylon! In a moment your
doom has come upon you!'

11 The merchants of the world will weep and mourn for
her, because no one buys their cargoes any more, 12 cargoes
of gold and silver, precious stones and pearls, purple and
scarlet cloth, silks and fine linens; all sorts of fragrant
wood, and all kinds of objects made of ivory or of costly
woods, bronze, iron, or marble; 13 cinnamon and spice, incense, perfumes, and frankincense; wine, oil, flour and
wheat, cattle and sheep, horses, chariots, slaves, and human lives. 14 'The harvest you longed for', they will say, 'is
gone from you; all the glitter and glamour are lost, never to
be found again!' 15 The traders in all these goods, who grew
rich on her, will keep their distance in terror at her torment;
weeping and mourning 16 they will say: 'Alas, alas for the
great city that was clothed in fine linen and purple and
scarlet, decked out with gold and precious stones and
pearls! 17 So much wealth laid waste in a moment!'

All the sea-captains and voyagers, the sailors and those
who made a living on the sea, stayed at a distance; 18 as they
saw the smoke of her burning, they cried out, 'Was there
ever a city like the great city?' 19 They threw dust on their
heads and, weeping and mourning, they cried aloud: 'Alas,
alas for the great city, where all who had ships at sea grew
rich from her prosperity! In a single hour she has been laid
waste!'

20 But let heaven exult over her; exult, God's people,
apostles and prophets, for he has imposed on her the sentence she passed on you!'

---

[e] Or chariots, and human bodies and souls

4 Then I heard another voice from heaven say:

> "Depart from her, my people,
>> so as not to take part in her sins
>> and receive a share in her plagues,
> 5 for her sins are piled up to the sky,
>> and God remembers her crimes.
> 6 Pay her back as she has paid others.
>> Pay her back double for her deeds.
>> Into her cup pour double what she poured.
> 7 To the measure of her boasting and wantonness
>> repay her in torment and grief;
>> for she said to herself,
>> 'I sit enthroned as queen;
> I am no widow,
>> and I will never know grief.'
> 8 Therefore, her plagues will come in one day,
>> pestilence, grief, and famine;
>> she will be consumed by fire.
> For mighty is the Lord God who judges her."

9 The kings of the earth who had intercourse with her in their wantonness will weep and mourn over her when they see the smoke of her pyre. 10 They will keep their distance for fear of the torment inflicted on her, and they will say:

> "Alas, alas, great city,
>> Babylon, mighty city.
>> In one hour your judgment has come."

11 The merchants of the earth will weep and mourn for her, because there will be no more markets for their cargo: 12 their cargo of gold, silver, precious stones, and pearls; fine linen, purple silk, and scarlet cloth; fragrant wood of every kind, all articles of ivory and all articles of the most expensive wood, bronze, iron, and marble; 13 cinnamon, spice, incense, myrrh, and frankincense; wine, olive oil, fine flour, and wheat; cattle and sheep, horses and chariots, and slaves, that is, human beings.

14 "The fruit you craved
> has left you.
> All your luxury and splendor are gone,
>> never again will one find them."

15 The merchants who deal in these goods, who grew rich from her, will keep their distance for fear of the torment inflicted on her. Weeping and mourning, 16 they cry out:

> "Alas, alas, great city,
>> wearing fine linen, purple and scarlet,
>> adorned [in] gold, precious stones, and pearls.
> 17 In one hour this great wealth has been ruined."

Every captain of a ship, every traveler at sea, sailors, and seafaring merchants stood at a distance 18 and cried out when they saw the smoke of her pyre, "What city could compare with the great city?" 19 They threw dust on their heads and cried out, weeping and mourning:

> "Alas, alas, great city,
>> in which all who had ships at sea
>> grew rich from her wealth.
> In one hour she has been ruined.
> 20 Rejoice over her, heaven,
>> you holy ones, apostles, and prophets.
> For God has judged your case against her."

4 Another voice spoke from heaven; I heard it say, 'Come out, my people, away from her, so that you do not share in her crimes and have the same plagues to bear. 5 *Her sins have reached up to the sky*, and God has her crimes in mind: *treat her as she has treated others.* 6 She must be paid double the amount she exacted. She is to have a doubly strong cup of her own mixture. 7 Every one of her pomps and orgies is to be matched by a torture or an agony. *I am enthroned as queen, she thinks; I am no widow and will never know bereavement.* 8 For that, *in one day*, the plagues will fall on her: disease and mourning and famine. She will be burned to the ground. The Lord God who has condemned her is mighty.'

9 'There will be mourning and weeping for her by the kings of the earth who have prostituted themselves with her and held orgies with her. They see the smoke as she burns, 10 while they keep at a safe distance through fear of her anguish. They will say:

> Mourn, mourn for this great city,
> Babylon, so powerful a city,
> in one short hour your doom has come upon you.

11 'There will be weeping and distress over her among all the traders of the earth when no one is left to buy their cargoes of goods; 12 their stocks of gold and silver, jewels and pearls, linen and purple and silks and scarlet; all the sandalwood, every piece in ivory or fine wood, in bronze or iron or marble; 13 the cinnamon and spices, the myrrh and ointment and incense; wine, oil, flour and corn; their stocks of cattle, sheep, horses and chariots, their slaves and their human cargo.

14 'All the fruits you had set your hearts on have failed you; gone for ever, never to return again, is your life of magnificence and ease.

15 'The traders who had made a fortune out of her will be standing at a safe distance through fear of her anguish, mourning and weeping. 16 They will be saying:

> Mourn, mourn for this great city;
> for all the linen and purple and scarlet that you wore,
> for all your finery of gold and jewels and pearls;
> 17 your huge riches are all destroyed within a single hour.'

All the captains and seafaring men, sailors and all those who make a living from the sea kept a safe distance, 18 watching the smoke as she burned, and crying out, 'Has there ever been a city as great as this!' 19 They threw dust on their heads and said, with tears and groans:

> 'Mourn, mourn for this great city
> whose lavish living has made a fortune
> for every owner of a sea-going ship,
> ruined within a single hour.

20 'Now heaven, celebrate her downfall, and all you saints, apostles and prophets: God has given judgement for you against her.'

NEW REVISED STANDARD VERSION	REVISED ENGLISH BIBLE

NEW REVISED STANDARD VERSION

21 Then a mighty angel took up a stone like a great millstone and threw it into the sea, saying,

"With such violence Babylon the great city
will be thrown down,
and will be found no more;
22 and the sound of harpists and minstrels and of
flutists and trumpeters
will be heard in you no more;
and an artisan of any trade
will be found in you no more;
and the sound of the millstone
will be heard in you no more;
23 and the light of a lamp
will shine in you no more;
and the voice of bridegroom and bride
will be heard in you no more;
for your merchants were the magnates of the
earth,
and all nations were deceived by your sorcery.
24 And in you*f* was found the blood of prophets
and of saints,
and of all who have been slaughtered on
earth."

19 After this I heard what seemed to be the loud voice of a great multitude in heaven, saying,
"Hallelujah!
Salvation and glory and power to our God,
2 for his judgments are true and just;
he has judged the great whore
who corrupted the earth with her fornication,
and he has avenged on her the blood of his
servants."*g*
3 Once more they said,
"Hallelujah!
The smoke goes up from her forever and ever."
4 And the twenty-four elders and the four living creatures fell down and worshiped God who is seated on the throne, saying,
"Amen. Hallelujah!"
5 And from the throne came a voice saying,
"Praise our God,
all you his servants,*g*
and all who fear him,
small and great."
6 Then I heard what seemed to be the voice of a great multitude, like the sound of many waters and like the sound of mighty thunderpeals, crying out,
"Hallelujah!
For the Lord our God
the Almighty reigns.
7 Let us rejoice and exult
and give him the glory,
for the marriage of the Lamb has come,
and his bride has made herself ready;
8 to her it has been granted to be clothed
with fine linen, bright and pure"*
for the fine linen is the righteous deeds of the saints.
9 And the angel said *h* to me, "Write this: Blessed are those who are invited to the marriage supper of the Lamb." And he said to me, "These are true words of God." 10 Then I fell down at his feet to worship him, but he said to me, "You must not do that! I am a fellow servant *i* with you and your comrades*j* who hold the testimony of Jesus.*k* Worship God! For the testimony of Jesus*k* is the spirit of prophecy."

REVISED ENGLISH BIBLE

21 Then a mighty angel picked up a stone like a great millstone and hurled it into the sea, saying, 'Thus shall Babylon, the great city, be sent hurtling down, never to be seen again! 22 The sound of harpists and minstrels, flute-players and trumpeters, shall no more be heard in you; no more shall craftsmen of any trade be found in you, or the sound of the mill be heard in you; 23 no more shall the light of the lamp appear in you, no more the voices of the bridegroom and bride be heard in you! Your traders were once the merchant princes of the world, and with your sorcery you deceived all the nations.' 24 The blood of the prophets and of God's people was found in her, the blood of all who had been slain on earth.

19 After this I heard what sounded like a vast throng in heaven shouting:
'Hallelujah! Victory and glory and power belong to our God, 2 for true and just are his judgements! He has condemned the great whore who corrupted the earth with her fornication; he has taken vengeance on her for the blood of his servants.'
3 Once more they shouted:
'Hallelujah! The smoke from her burning will rise for ever!'
4 The twenty-four elders and the four living creatures bowed down and worshipped God who sits on the throne; they cried: 'Amen! Hallelujah!'

5 THERE came a voice from the throne saying: 'Praise our God, all you his servants, you that fear him, both small and great!' 6 And I heard what sounded like a vast throng, like the sound of a mighty torrent or of great peals of thunder, and they cried:
'Hallelujah! The Lord our God, sovereign over all, has entered on his reign! 7 Let us rejoice and shout for joy and pay homage to him, for the wedding day of the Lamb has come! His bride has made herself ready, 8 and she has been given fine linen, shining and clean, to wear.'
(The fine linen signifies the righteous deeds of God's people.)

9 THE angel said to me, 'Write this: "Happy are those who are invited to the wedding banquet of the Lamb!" ' He added, 'These are the very words of God.' 10 I prostrated myself to worship him, but he said, 'You must not do that! I am a fellow-servant with you and your brothers who bear their witness to Jesus. It is God you must worship. For those who bear witness to Jesus have the spirit of prophecy.'

f Gk *her*   *g* Gk *slaves*   *h* Gk *he said*   *i* Gk *slave*
j Gk *brothers*   *k* Or *to Jesus*

NEW AMERICAN BIBLE

21 A mighty angel picked up a stone like a huge millstone and threw it into the sea and said:

"With such force will Babylon the great city be
thrown down,
and will never be found again.
22 No melodies of harpists and musicians,
flutists and trumpeters,
will ever be heard in you again.
No craftsmen in any trade
will ever be found in you again.
No sound of the millstone
will ever be heard in you again.
23 No light from a lamp
will ever be seen in you again.
No voices of bride and groom
will ever be heard in you again.
Because your merchants were the great ones of
the world,
all nations were led astray by your magic potion.
24 In her was found the blood of prophets and
holy ones
and all who have been slain on the earth."

19

After this I heard what sounded like the loud voice of a great multitude in heaven, saying:

"Alleluia!
Salvation, glory, and might belong to our God,
2 for true and just are his judgments.
He has condemned the great harlot
who corrupted the earth with her harlotry.
He has avenged on her the blood of his servants."

3 They said a second time:

"Alleluia! Smoke will rise from her forever
and ever."

4 The twenty-four elders and the four living creatures fell down and worshiped God who sat on the throne, saying, "Amen. Alleluia."

5 A voice coming from the throne said:

"Praise our God, all you his servants,
[and] you who revere him, small and great."

6 Then I heard something like the sound of a great multitude or the sound of rushing water or mighty peals of thunder, as they said:

"Alleluia!
The Lord has established his reign,
[our] God, the almighty.
7 Let us rejoice and be glad
and give him glory.
For the wedding day of the Lamb has come,
his bride has made herself ready.
8 She was allowed to wear
a bright, clean linen garment."

(The linen represents the righteous deeds of the holy ones.)
9 Then the angel said to me, "Write this: Blessed are those who have been called to the wedding feast of the Lamb." And he said to me, "These words are true; they come from God." **10** I fell at his feet to worship him. But he said to me, "Don't! I am a fellow servant of yours and of your brothers who bear witness to Jesus. Worship God. Witness to Jesus is the spirit of prophecy."

NEW JERUSALEM BIBLE

21 Then a powerful angel picked up a boulder like a great millstone, and as he hurled it into the sea, he said, 'That is how the great city of Babylon is going to be hurled down, never to be seen again.

22 Never again in you
will be heard the song of harpists and minstrels,
the music of flute and trumpet;
never again will craftsmen of every skill be found
in you
or *the sound of the handmill* b be heard;
23 never again will shine *the light of the lamp* in you,
never again will be heard in you
the voices of bridegroom and bride.
Your traders were the princes of the earth,
all the nations were led astray by your sorcery.

24 In her was found the blood of prophets and saints, and all the blood that was ever shed on earth.'

19

After this I heard what seemed to be the great sound of a huge crowd in heaven, singing, 'Alleluia! Salvation and glory and power to our God! **2** He judges fairly, he punishes justly, and he has condemned the great prostitute who corrupted the earth with her prostitution; he has avenged the blood of his servants which she shed.' **3** And again they sang, 'Alleluia! *The smoke* of her *will rise for ever and ever.*' c **4** Then the twenty-four elders and the four living creatures threw themselves down and worshipped God seated on his throne, and they cried, 'Amen, Alleluia.'

5 Then a voice came from the throne; it said, 'Praise our God, you servants of his and *those who fear him, small and great alike.*' d **6** And I heard what seemed to be the voices of a huge crowd, like the sound of the ocean or the great roar of thunder, answering, 'Alleluia! The reign of the Lord our God Almighty has begun; **7** let us be glad and joyful and give glory to God, because this is the time for the marriage of the Lamb. **8** His bride is ready, and she has been able to dress herself in dazzling white linen, because her linen is made of the good deeds of the saints.' **9** The angel said, 'Write this, "Blessed are those who are invited to the wedding feast of the Lamb," ' and he added, 'These words of God are true.' **10** Then I knelt at his feet to worship him, but he said to me, 'Never do that: I am your fellow-servant and the fellow-servant of all your brothers who have in themselves the witness of Jesus. God alone you must worship.' The witness of Jesus is the spirit of prophecy.

---

b **18** Jr 25:10, followed by Jr 7:34; Is 23:8.   c **19** Is 34:10.
d **19** Ps 115:13.

11   Then I saw heaven opened, and there was a white horse! Its rider is called Faithful and True, and in righteousness he judges and makes war. 12 His eyes are like a flame of fire, and on his head are many diadems; and he has a name inscribed that no one knows but himself. 13 He is clothed in a robe dipped in *l* blood, and his name is called The Word of God. 14 And the armies of heaven, wearing fine linen, white and pure, were following him on white horses. 15 From his mouth comes a sharp sword with which to strike down the nations, and he will rule *m* them with a rod of iron; he will tread the wine press of the fury of the wrath of God the Almighty. 16 On his robe and on his thigh he has a name inscribed, "King of kings and Lord of lords."

17   Then I saw an angel standing in the sun, and with a loud voice he called to all the birds that fly in midheaven, "Come, gather for the great supper of God, 18 to eat the flesh of kings, the flesh of captains, the flesh of the mighty, the flesh of horses and their riders — flesh of all, both free and slave, both small and great." 19 Then I saw the beast and the kings of the earth with their armies gathered to make war against the rider on the horse and against his army. 20 And the beast was captured, and with it the false prophet who had performed in its presence the signs by which he deceived those who had received the mark of the beast and those who worshiped its image. These two were thrown alive into the lake of fire that burns with sulfur. 21 And the rest were killed by the sword of the rider on the horse, the sword that came from his mouth; and all the birds were gorged with their flesh.

20   Then I saw an angel coming down from heaven, holding in his hand the key to the bottomless pit and a great chain. 2 He seized the dragon, that ancient serpent, who is the Devil and Satan, and bound him for a thousand years, 3 and threw him into the pit, and locked and sealed it over him, so that he would deceive the nations no more, until the thousand years were ended. After that he must be let out for a little while.

4   Then I saw thrones, and those seated on them were given authority to judge. I also saw the souls of those who had been beheaded for their testimony to Jesus *n* and for the word of God. They had not worshiped the beast or its image and had not received its mark on their foreheads or their hands. They came to life and reigned with Christ a thousand years. 5 (The rest of the dead did not come to life until the thousand years were ended.) This is the first resurrection. 6 Blessed and holy are those who share in the first resurrection. Over these the second death has no power, but they will be priests of God and of Christ, and they will reign with him a thousand years.

7   When the thousand years are ended, Satan will be released from his prison 8 and will come out to deceive the nations at the four corners of the earth, Gog and Magog, in order to gather them for battle; they are as numerous as the sands of the sea. 9 They marched up over the breadth of the earth and surrounded the camp of the saints and the beloved city. And fire came down from heaven *o* and consumed them. 10 And the devil who had deceived them was thrown into the lake of fire and sulfur, where the beast and the false prophet were, and they will be tormented day and night forever and ever.

11 I SAW heaven wide open, and a white horse appeared; its rider's name was Faithful and True, for he is just in judgement and just in war. 12 His eyes flamed like fire, and on his head were many diadems. Written on him was a name known to none but himself; 13 he was robed in a garment dyed in blood, and he was called the Word of God. 14 The armies of heaven followed him, riding on white horses and clothed in fine linen, white and clean. 15 Out of his mouth came a sharp sword to smite the nations; for it is he who will rule them with a rod of iron, and tread the winepress of the fierce wrath of God the sovereign Lord. 16 On his robe and on his thigh was written the title: 'King of kings and Lord of lords'.

17 I saw an angel standing in the sun. He cried aloud to all the birds flying in mid-heaven: 'Come, gather together for God's great banquet, 18 to eat the flesh of kings, commanders, and warriors, the flesh of horses and their riders, the flesh of all, the free and the slave, the small and the great!' 19 I saw the beast and the kings of the earth with their armies mustered to do battle against the rider and his army. 20 The beast was taken prisoner, along with the false prophet who had worked miracles in its presence and deluded those who had received the mark of the beast and worshipped its image. The two of them were thrown alive into the lake of fire with its sulphurous flames. 21 The rest were killed by the sword which came out of the rider's mouth, and the birds all gorged themselves on their flesh.

20   I saw an angel coming down from heaven with the key to the abyss and a great chain in his hand. 2 He seized the dragon, that ancient serpent who is the Devil, or Satan, and chained him up for a thousand years; 3 he threw him into the abyss, shutting and sealing it over him, so that he might not seduce the nations again till the thousand years were ended. After that he must be let loose for a little while.

4 I saw thrones, and on them sat those to whom judgement was committed. I saw the souls of those who, for the sake of God's word and their witness to Jesus, had been beheaded, those who had not worshipped the beast and its image or received its mark on forehead or hand. They came to life again and reigned with Christ for a thousand years, 5 though the rest of the dead did not come to life until the thousand years were ended. This is the first resurrection. 6 Blessed and holy are those who share in this first resurrection! Over them the second death has no power; but they shall be priests of God and of Christ, and shall reign with him for the thousand years.

7 When the thousand years are ended, Satan will be let loose from his prison, 8 and he will come out to seduce the nations in the four quarters of the earth. He will muster them for war, the hosts of Gog and Magog, countless as the sands of the sea. 9 They marched over the breadth of the land and laid siege to the camp of God's people and the city that he loves. But fire came down from heaven and consumed them. 10 Their seducer, the Devil, was flung into the lake of fire and sulphur, where the beast and the false prophet had been flung to be tormented day and night for ever.

---

l Other ancient authorities read *sprinkled with*   *m* Or *will shepherd*
n Or *for the testimony of Jesus*   *o* Other ancient authorities read *from God, out of heaven,* or *out of heaven from God*

11 Then I saw the heavens opened, and there was a white horse; its rider was [called] "Faithful and True." He judges and wages war in righteousness. 12 His eyes were [like] a fiery flame, and on his head were many diadems. He had a name inscribed that no one knows except himself. 13 He wore a cloak that had been dipped in blood, and his name was called the Word of God. 14 The armies of heaven followed him, mounted on white horses and wearing clean white linen. 15 Out of his mouth came a sharp sword to strike the nations. He will rule them with an iron rod, and he himself will tread out in the wine press the wine of the fury and wrath of God the almighty. 16 He has a name written on his cloak and on his thigh, "King of kings and Lord of lords."

17 Then I saw an angel standing on the sun. He cried out [in] a loud voice to all the birds flying high overhead, "Come here. Gather for God's great feast, 18 to eat the flesh of kings, the flesh of military officers, and the flesh of warriors, the flesh of horses and of their riders, and the flesh of all, free and slave, small and great." 19 Then I saw the beast and the kings of the earth and their armies gathered to fight against the one riding the horse and against his army. 20 The beast was caught and with it the false prophet who had performed in its sight the signs by which he led astray those who had accepted the mark of the beast and those who had worshiped its image. The two were thrown alive into the fiery pool burning with sulfur. 21 The rest were killed by the sword that came out of the mouth of the one riding the horse, and all the birds gorged themselves on their flesh.

20 Then I saw an angel come down from heaven, holding in his hand the key to the abyss and a heavy chain. 2 He seized the dragon, the ancient serpent, which is the Devil or Satan, and tied it up for a thousand years 3 and threw it into the abyss, which he locked over it and sealed, so that it could no longer lead the nations astray until the thousand years are completed. After this, it is to be released for a short time.

4 Then I saw thrones; those who sat on them were entrusted with judgment. I also saw the souls of those who had been beheaded for their witness to Jesus and for the word of God, and who had not worshiped the beast or its image nor had accepted its mark on their foreheads or hands. They came to life and they reigned with Christ for a thousand years. 5 The rest of the dead did not come to life until the thousand years were over. This is the first resurrection. 6 Blessed and holy is the one who shares in the first resurrection. The second death has no power over these; they will be priests of God and of Christ, and they will reign with him for [the] thousand years.

7 When the thousand years are completed, Satan will be released from his prison. 8 He will go out to deceive the nations at the four corners of the earth, Gog and Magog, to gather them for battle; their number is like the sand of the sea. 9 They invaded the breadth of the earth and surrounded the camp of the holy ones and the beloved city. But fire came down from heaven and consumed them. 10 The Devil who had led them astray was thrown into the pool of fire and sulfur, where the beast and the false prophet were. There they will be tormented day and night forever and ever.

11 e And now I saw heaven open, and a white horse appear; its rider was called Trustworthy and True; in uprightness he judges and makes war. 12 His eyes were flames of fire, and he was crowned with many coronets; the name written on him was known only to himself, 13 his cloak was soaked in blood. He is known by the name, The Word of God. 14 Behind him, dressed in linen of dazzling white, rode the armies of heaven on white horses. 15 From his mouth came a sharp sword with which to strike the unbelievers; he is the one who will rule them with an iron sceptre, and tread out the wine of Almighty God's fierce retribution. 16 On his cloak and on his thigh a name was written: King of kings and Lord of lords.

17 I saw an angel standing in the sun, and he shouted aloud to all the birds that were flying high overhead in the sky, 'Come here. Gather together at God's great feast. 18 You will eat the flesh of kings, and the flesh of great generals and heroes, the flesh of horses and their riders and of all kinds of people, citizens and slaves, small and great alike.'

19 Then I saw the beast, with all the kings of the earth and their armies, gathered together to fight the Rider and his army. 20 But the beast was taken prisoner, together with the false prophet who had worked miracles on the beast's behalf and by them had deceived those who had accepted branding with the mark of the beast and those who had worshipped his statue. These two were hurled alive into the fiery lake of burning sulphur. 21 All the rest were killed by the sword of the Rider, which came out of his mouth, and all the birds glutted themselves with their flesh.

20 Then I saw an angel come down from heaven with the key of the Abyss in his hand and an enormous chain. 2 He overpowered the dragon, that primeval serpent which is the devil and Satan, and chained him up for a thousand years. 3 He hurled him into the Abyss and shut the entrance and sealed it over him, to make sure he would not lead the nations astray again until the thousand years had passed. At the end of that time he must be released, but only for a short while.

4 Then I saw thrones, where they took their seats, and on them was conferred the power to give judgement. f I saw the souls of all who had been beheaded for having witnessed for Jesus and for having preached God's word, and those who refused to worship the beast or his statue and would not accept the brand-mark on their foreheads or hands; they came to life, and reigned with Christ for a thousand years. g 5 The rest of the dead did not come to life until the thousand years were over; this is the first resurrection. 6 Blessed and holy are those who share in the first resurrection; the second death has no power over them but they will be priests of God and of Christ and reign with him for a thousand years.

7 When the thousand years are over, h Satan will be released from his prison 8 and will come out to lead astray all the nations in the four quarters of the earth, Gog and Magog, i and mobilise them for war, his armies being as many as the sands of the sea. 9 They came swarming over the entire country and besieged the camp of the saints, which is the beloved City. But fire rained down on them from heaven j and consumed them. 10 Then the devil, who led them astray, was hurled into the lake of fire and sulphur, where the beast and the false prophet are, and their torture will not come to an end, day or night, for ever and ever.

e 19 = 20:7–10. The OT allusions show this avenger to be the Messiah: Is 11:4; 63:1; Ps 2:9; Ezk 39:17, 20. f 20 Dn 7:22.
g 20 The time of the Church after the end of the persecution, not a reign of a returned Christ. h 20 = 19:11–21. i 20 Ezk 38:2.
j 20 Ezk 38:22.

11 Then I saw a great white throne and the one who sat on it; the earth and the heaven fled from his presence, and no place was found for them. 12 And I saw the dead, great and small, standing before the throne, and books were opened. Also another book was opened, the book of life. And the dead were judged according to their works, as recorded in the books. 13 And the sea gave up the dead that were in it, Death and Hades gave up the dead that were in them, and all were judged according to what they had done. 14 Then Death and Hades were thrown into the lake of fire. This is the second death, the lake of fire; 15 and anyone whose name was not found written in the book of life was thrown into the lake of fire.

21 Then I saw a new heaven and a new earth; for the first heaven and the first earth had passed away, and the sea was no more. 2 And I saw the holy city, the new Jerusalem, coming down out of heaven from God, prepared as a bride adorned for her husband. 3 And I heard a loud voice from the throne saying,

"See, the home *p* of God is among mortals.
He will dwell *p* with them as their God; *q*
they will be his peoples, *r*
and God himself will be with them; *s*
4 he will wipe every tear from their eyes.
Death will be no more;
mourning and crying and pain will be no more,
for the first things have passed away."

5 And the one who was seated on the throne said, "See, I am making all things new." Also he said, "Write this, for these words are trustworthy and true." 6 Then he said to me, "It is done! I am the Alpha and the Omega, the beginning and the end. To the thirsty I will give water as a gift from the spring of the water of life. 7 Those who conquer will inherit these things, and I will be their God and they will be my children. 8 But as for the cowardly, the faithless, *t* the polluted, the murderers, the fornicators, the sorcerers, the idolaters, and all liars, their place will be in the lake that burns with fire and sulfur, which is the second death."

9 Then one of the seven angels who had the seven bowls full of the seven last plagues came and said to me, "Come, I will show you the bride, the wife of the Lamb." 10 And in the spirit *u* he carried me away to a great, high mountain and showed me the holy city Jerusalem coming down out of heaven from God. 11 It has the glory of God and a radiance like a very rare jewel, like jasper, clear as crystal. 12 It has a great, high wall with twelve gates, and at the gates twelve angels, and on the gates are inscribed the names of the twelve tribes of the Israelites; 13 on the east three gates, on the north three gates, on the south three gates, and on the west three gates. 14 And the wall of the city has twelve foundations, and on them are the twelve names of the twelve apostles of the Lamb.

15 The angel *v* who talked to me had a measuring rod of gold to measure the city and its gates and walls. 16 The city lies foursquare, its length the same as its width; and he measured the city with his rod, fifteen hundred miles; *w* its length and width and height are equal. 17 He also measured its wall, one hundred forty-four cubits *x* by human measurement, which the angel was using. 18 The wall is built of jasper, while the city is pure gold, clear as glass. 19 The foundations of the wall of the city are adorned with every jewel; the first was jasper, the second sapphire, the third agate, the fourth emerald, 20 the fifth onyx, the sixth carne-

11 I saw a great, white throne, and the One who sits upon it. From his presence earth and heaven fled away, and there was no room for them any more. 12 I saw the dead, great and small, standing before the throne; and books were opened. Then another book, the book of life, was opened. The dead were judged by what they had done, as recorded in these books. 13 The sea gave up the dead that were in it, and Death and Hades gave up the dead in their keeping. Everyone was judged on the record of his deeds. 14 Then Death and Hades were flung into the lake of fire. This lake of fire is the second death; 15 into it were flung any whose names were not to be found in the book of life.

21 I saw a new heaven and a new earth, for the first heaven and the first earth had vanished, and there was no longer any sea. 2 I saw the Holy City, new Jerusalem, coming down out of heaven from God, made ready like a bride adorned for her husband. 3 I heard a loud voice proclaiming from the throne: 'Now God has his dwelling with mankind! He will dwell among them and they shall be his people, and God himself will be with them. 4 He will wipe every tear from their eyes. There shall be an end to death, and to mourning and crying and pain, for the old order has passed away!'

5 The One who sat on the throne said, 'I am making all things new!' ('Write this down,' he said, 'for these words are trustworthy and true.') 6 Then he said to me, 'It is done! I am the Alpha and the Omega, the beginning and the end. To the thirsty I will give water from the spring of life as a gift. 7 This is the victors' heritage; and I will be their God and they will be my children. 8 But as for the cowardly, the faithless, and the obscene, the murderers, fornicators, sorcerers, idolaters, and liars of every kind, the lake that burns with sulphurous flames will be their portion, and that is the second death.'

9 ONE of the seven angels who held the seven bowls full of the seven last plagues came and spoke to me. 'Come,' he said, 'and I will show you the bride, the wife of the Lamb.' 10 So in the spirit he carried me away to a great and lofty mountain, and showed me Jerusalem, the Holy City, coming down out of heaven from God. 11 It shone with the glory of God; it had the radiance of some priceless jewel, like a jasper, clear as crystal. 12 It had a great and lofty wall with twelve gates, at which were stationed twelve angels; on the gates were inscribed the names of the twelve tribes of Israel. 13 There were three gates to the east, three to the north, three to the south, and three to the west. 14 The city wall had twelve foundation-stones, and on them were the names of the twelve apostles of the Lamb.

15 The angel who spoke with me carried a gold measuring rod to measure the city, its gates, and its wall. 16 The city had four sides, and it was as wide as it was long. Measured by his rod, it was twelve thousand furlongs, its length and breadth and height being equal. 17 Its wall was one hundred and forty-four cubits high, by human measurements, which the angel used. 18 The wall was built of jasper, while the city itself was of pure gold, bright as clear glass. 19 The foundations of the city wall were adorned with precious stones of every kind, the first of the foundation-stones being jasper, the second lapis lazuli, the third chalcedony, the fourth emerald, 20 the fifth sardonyx, the sixth cornelian,

---

p Gk *tabernacle*   *q* Other ancient authorities lack *as their God*
r Other ancient authorities read *people*   *s* Other ancient authorities add *and be their God*   *t* Or *the unbelieving*   *u* Or *in the Spirit*
v Gk *He*   *w* Gk *twelve thousand stadia*   *x* That is, almost seventy-five yards

NEW AMERICAN BIBLE

11 Next I saw a large white throne and the one who was sitting on it. The earth and the sky fled from his presence and there was no place for them. 12 I saw the dead, the great and the lowly, standing before the throne, and scrolls were opened. Then another scroll was opened, the book of life. The dead were judged according to their deeds, by what was written in the scrolls. 13 The sea gave up its dead; then Death and Hades gave up their dead. All the dead were judged according to their deeds. 14 Then Death and Hades were thrown into the pool of fire. (This pool of fire is the second death.) 15 Anyone whose name was not found written in the book of life was thrown into the pool of fire.

21 Then I saw a new heaven and a new earth. The former heaven and the former earth had passed away, and the sea was no more. 2 I also saw the holy city, a new Jerusalem, coming down out of heaven from God, prepared as a bride adorned for her husband. 3 I heard a loud voice from the throne saying, "Behold, God's dwelling is with the human race. He will dwell with them and they will be his people and God himself will always be with them [as their God]. 4 He will wipe every tear from their eyes, and there shall be no more death or mourning, wailing or pain, [for] the old order has passed away."

5 The one who sat on the throne said, "Behold, I make all things new." Then he said, "Write these words down, for they are trustworthy and true." 6 He said to me, "They are accomplished. I [am] the Alpha and the Omega, the beginning and the end. To the thirsty I will give a gift from the spring of life-giving water. 7 The victor will inherit these gifts, and I shall be his God, and he will be my son. 8 But as for cowards, the unfaithful, the depraved, murderers, the unchaste, sorcerers, idol-worshipers, and deceivers of every sort, their lot is like in the burning pool of fire and sulfur, which is the second death."

9 One of the seven angels who held the seven bowls filled with the seven last plagues came and said to me, "Come here. I will show you the bride, the wife of the Lamb." 10 He took me in spirit to a great, high mountain and showed me the holy city Jerusalem coming down out of heaven from God. 11 It gleamed with the splendor of God. Its radiance was like that of a precious stone, like jasper, clear as crystal. 12 It had a massive, high wall, with twelve gates where twelve angels were stationed and on which names were inscribed, [the names] of the twelve tribes of the Israelites. 13 There were three gates facing east, three north, three south, and three west. 14 The wall of the city had twelve courses of stones as its foundation, on which were inscribed the twelve names of the twelve apostles of the Lamb.

15 The one who spoke to me held a gold measuring rod to measure the city, its gates, and its wall. 16 The city was square, its length the same as [also] its width. He measured the city with the rod and found it fifteen hundred miles in length and width and height. 17 He also measured its wall: one hundred and forty-four cubits according to the standard unit of measurement the angel used. 18 The wall was constructed of jasper, while the city was pure gold, clear as glass. 19 The foundations of the city wall were decorated with every precious stone; the first course of stones was jasper, the second sapphire, the third chalcedony, the fourth emerald, 20 the fifth sardonyx, the sixth carnelian, the sev-

NEW JERUSALEM BIBLE

11 Then I saw a great white throne and the One who was sitting on it. In his presence, earth and sky vanished, leaving no trace. 12 I saw the dead, great and small alike, standing in front of his throne while *the books lay open.*k And another book was opened, which is the book of life, and the dead were judged from what was written in the books, as their deeds deserved.

13 The sea gave up all the dead who were in it; 14 Death and Hades were emptied of the dead that were in them; and every one was judged as his deeds deserved. Then Death and Hades were hurled into the burning lake. This burning lake is the second death; 15 and anybody whose name could not be found written in the book of life was hurled into the burning lake.

21 Then I saw *a new heaven and a new earth;*l the first heaven and the first earth had disappeared now, and there was no longer any sea. 2 I saw the holy city, the new Jerusalem, coming down out of heaven from God, prepared as a bride dressed for her husband. 3 Then I heard a loud voice call from the throne, 'Look, here God lives among human beings. He will make *his home among them; they will be his people,*m and he will be their God, *God-with-them.* 4 *He will wipe* away all *tears from their eyes;*n there will be no more death, and no more mourning or sadness or pain. The world of the past has gone.'

5 Then the One sitting on the throne spoke. 'Look, I am making the whole of creation new. Write this, "What I am saying is trustworthy and will come true." ' 6 Then he said to me, 'It has already happened. I am the Alpha and the Omega, the Beginning and the End. I will give water from the well of life free to anybody who is thirsty; 7 anyone who proves victorious will inherit these things; and *I will be his* God and *he will be my son.*o 8 But the legacy for cowards, for those who break their word, or worship obscenities, for murderers and the sexually immoral, and for sorcerers, worshippers of false gods or any other sort of liars, is the second death in the burning lake of sulphur.'

9 One of the seven angels that had the seven bowls full of the seven final plagues came to speak to me and said, 'Come here and I will show you the bride that the Lamb has married.' 10 *In the spirit, he carried me to the top of a very high mountain,*p and showed me Jerusalem, the holy city, coming down out of heaven from God. 11 It had *all the glory of God*q and glittered like some precious jewel of crystal-clear diamond. 12 Its wall was of a great height and had twelve gates; at each of the twelve gates there was an angel, and over the gates were written the names *of the twelve tribes of Israel;* 13 *on the east there were three gates, on the north three gates, on the south three gates, and on the west three gates.*r 14 The city walls stood on twelve foundation stones, each one of which bore the name of one of the twelve apostles of the Lamb.

15 The angel that was speaking to me was carrying a gold measuring rod to measure the city and its gates and wall. 16 The plan of the city is perfectly square, its length the same as its breadth. He measured the city with his rod and it was twelve thousand furlongs, equal in length and in breadth, and equal in height. 17 He measured its wall, and this was a hundred and forty-four cubits high — by human measurements. 18 The wall was built of diamond, and the city of pure gold, like clear glass. 19 The foundations of the city wall were faced with all kinds of precious stone: the first with diamond, the second lapis lazuli, the third turquoise, the fourth crystal, 20 the fifth agate, the sixth ruby,

k **20** Dn 7:10. A register of human deeds and a list of the predestined. l **21** Is 65:17. m **21** Ezk 37:27. n **21** Is 8:8; 25:8. o **21** 2 S 7:14. p **21** Ezk 40:2. q **21** Is 60:1–2. r **21** Ezk 48:31–35.

NEW REVISED STANDARD VERSION

lian, the seventh chrysolite, the eighth beryl, the ninth topaz, the tenth chrysoprase, the eleventh jacinth, the twelfth amethyst. 21 And the twelve gates are twelve pearls, each of the gates is a single pearl, and the street of the city is pure gold, transparent as glass.

22 I saw no temple in the city, for its temple is the Lord God the Almighty and the Lamb. 23 And the city has no need of sun or moon to shine on it, for the glory of God is its light, and its lamp is the Lamb. 24 The nations will walk by its light, and the kings of the earth will bring their glory into it. 25 Its gates will never be shut by day — and there will be no night there. 26 People will bring into it the glory and the honor of the nations. 27 But nothing unclean will enter it, nor anyone who practices abomination or falsehood, but only those who are written in the Lamb's book of life.

22 Then the angel *y* showed me the river of the water of life, bright as crystal, flowing from the throne of God and of the Lamb 2 through the middle of the street of the city. On either side of the river is the tree of life *z* with its twelve kinds of fruit, producing its fruit each month; and the leaves of the tree are for the healing of the nations. 3 Nothing accursed will be found there any more. But the throne of God and of the Lamb will be in it, and his servants *a* will worship him; 4 they will see his face, and his name will be on their foreheads. 5 And there will be no more night; they need no light of lamp or sun, for the Lord God will be their light, and they will reign forever and ever.

6 And he said to me, "These words are trustworthy and true, for the Lord, the God of the spirits of the prophets, has sent his angel to show his servants *a* what must soon take place."

7 "See, I am coming soon! Blessed is the one who keeps the words of the prophecy of this book."

8 I, John, am the one who heard and saw these things. And when I heard and saw them, I fell down to worship at the feet of the angel who showed them to me; 9 but he said to me, "You must not do that! I am a fellow servant *b* with you and your comrades *c* the prophets, and with those who keep the words of this book. Worship God!"

10 And he said to me, "Do not seal up the words of the prophecy of this book, for the time is near. 11 Let the evildoer still do evil, and the filthy still be filthy, and the righteous still do right, and the holy still be holy."

12 "See, I am coming soon; my reward is with me, to repay according to everyone's work. 13 I am the Alpha and the Omega, the first and the last, the beginning and the end."

14 Blessed are those who wash their robes, *d* so that they will have the right to the tree of life and may enter the city by the gates. 15 Outside are the dogs and sorcerers and fornicators and murderers and idolaters, and everyone who loves and practices falsehood.

16 "It is I, Jesus, who sent my angel to you with this testimony for the churches. I am the root and the descendant of David, the bright morning star."

17 The Spirit and the bride say, "Come."
And let everyone who hears say, "Come."
And let everyone who is thirsty come.
Let anyone who wishes take the water of life as a gift.

18 I warn everyone who hears the words of the prophecy of this book: if anyone adds to them, God will add to that person the plagues described in this book; 19 if anyone

REVISED ENGLISH BIBLE

the seventh chrysolite, the ninth topaz, the tenth chrysoprase, the eleventh turquoise, and the twelfth amethyst. 21 The twelve gates were twelve pearls, each gate fashioned from a single pearl. The great street of the city was of pure gold, like translucent glass.

22 I saw no temple in the city, for its temple was the sovereign Lord God and the Lamb. 23 The city did not need the sun or the moon to shine on it, for the glory of God gave it light, and its lamp was the Lamb. 24 By its light shall the nations walk, and to it the kings of the earth shall bring their splendour. 25 The gates of the city shall never be shut by day, nor will there be any night there. 26 The splendour and wealth of the nations shall be brought into it, 27 but nothing unclean shall enter, nor anyone whose ways are foul or false; only those shall enter whose names are inscribed in the Lamb's book of life.

22 Then the angel showed me the river of the water of life, sparkling like crystal, flowing from the throne of God and of the Lamb 2 down the middle of the city's street. On either side of the river stood a tree of life, which yields twelve crops of fruit, one for each month of the year. The leaves of the trees are for the healing of the nations. 3 Every accursed thing shall disappear. The throne of God and of the Lamb will be there, and his servants shall worship him; 4 they shall see him face to face and bear his name on their foreheads. 5 There shall be no more night, nor will they need the light of lamp or sun, for the Lord God will give them light; and they shall reign for ever.

6 HE said to me, 'These words are trustworthy and true. The Lord God who inspires the prophets has sent his angel to show his servants what must soon take place. 7 And remember, I am coming soon!'

Happy is the man who takes to heart the words of prophecy contained in this book! 8 It was I, John, who heard and saw these things. When I had heard and seen them, I prostrated myself to worship the angel who had shown them to me. 9 But he said, 'You must not do that! I am a fellow-servant with you and your brothers the prophets and with those who take to heart the words of this book. It is God you must worship.' 10 He told me, 'Do not seal up the words of the prophecy that are in this book, for the time of fulfilment is near. 11 Meanwhile, let the evildoers persist in doing evil and the filthy-minded continue in their filth, but let the good persevere in their goodness and the holy continue in holiness.'

12 'I am coming soon, and bringing with me my recompense to repay everyone according to what he has done! 13 I am the Alpha and the Omega, the first and the last, the beginning and the end.'

14 Happy are those who wash their robes clean! They shall be free to eat from the tree of life and may enter the city by the gates. 15 Outside are the perverts, the sorcerers and fornicators, the murderers and idolaters, and all who love and practise deceit.

16 'I, Jesus, have sent my angel to you with this testimony for the churches. I am the offspring of David, the shoot growing from his stock, the bright star of dawn.'

17 'Come!' say the Spirit and the bride.
'Come!' let each hearer reply.
Let the thirsty come; let whoever wishes accept the water of life as a gift.

18 I, John, give this warning to everyone who is listening to the words of prophecy in this book: if anyone adds to them, God will add to him the plagues described in this book; 19 if anyone takes away from the words in this book

---

y Gk he   *z* Or the Lamb.   2 In the middle of the street of the city, and on either side of the river, is the tree of life   *a* Gk slaves
b Gk slave   *c* Gk brothers   *d* Other ancient authorities read *do his commandments*

22:15 **perverts:** *lit.* dogs.

enth chrysolite, the eighth beryl, the ninth topaz, the tenth chrysoprase, the eleventh hyacinth, and the twelfth amethyst. 21 The twelve gates were twelve pearls, each of the gates made from a single pearl; and the street of the city was of pure gold, transparent as glass.

22 I saw no temple in the city, for its temple is the Lord God almighty and the Lamb. 23 The city had no need of sun or moon to shine on it, for the glory of God gave it light, and its lamp was the Lamb. 24 The nations will walk by its light, and to it the kings of the earth will bring their treasure. 25 During the day its gates will never be shut, and there will be no night there. 26 The treasure and wealth of the nations will be brought there, 27 but nothing unclean will enter it, nor any[one] who does abominable things or tells lies. Only those will enter whose names are written in the Lamb's book of life.

22 Then the angel showed me the river of life-giving water, sparkling like crystal, flowing from the throne of God and of the Lamb 2 down the middle of its street. On either side of the river grew the tree of life that produces fruit twelve times a year, once each month; the leaves of the trees serve as medicine for the nations. 3 Nothing accursed will be found there anymore. The throne of God and of the Lamb will be in it, and his servants will worship him. 4 They will look upon his face, and his name will be on their foreheads. 5 Night will be no more, nor will they need light from lamp or sun, for the Lord God shall give them light, and they shall reign forever and ever.

6 And he said to me, "These words are trustworthy and true, and the Lord, the God of prophetic spirits, sent his angel to show his servants what must happen soon." 7 "Behold, I am coming soon." Blessed is the one who keeps the prophetic message of this book.

8 It is I, John, who heard and saw these things, and when I heard and saw them I fell down to worship at the feet of the angel who showed them to me. 9 But he said to me, "Don't! I am a fellow servant of yours and of your brothers the prophets and of those who keep the message of this book. Worship God."

10 Then he said to me, "Do not seal up the prophetic words of this book, for the appointed time is near. 11 Let the wicked still act wickedly, and the filthy still be filthy. The righteous must still do right, and the holy still be holy."

12 "Behold, I am coming soon. I bring with me the recompense I will give to each according to his deeds. 13 I am the Alpha and the Omega, the first and the last, the beginning and the end."

14 Blessed are they who wash their robes so as to have the right to the tree of life and enter the city through its gates. 15 Outside are the dogs, the sorcerers, the unchaste, the murderers, the idol-worshipers, and all who love and practice deceit.

16 "I, Jesus, sent my angel to give you this testimony for the churches. I am the root and offspring of David, the bright morning star."

17 The Spirit and the bride say, "Come." Let the hearer say, "Come." Let the one who thirsts come forward, and the one who wants it receive the gift of life-giving water.

18 I warn everyone who hears the prophetic words in this book: if anyone adds to them, God will add to him the plagues described in this book, 19 and if anyone takes away

the seventh gold quartz, the eighth malachite, the ninth topaz, the tenth emerald, the eleventh sapphire and the twelfth amethyst. 21 The twelve gates were twelve pearls, each gate being made of a single pearl, and the main street of the city was pure gold, transparent as glass. 22 I could not see any temple in the city since the Lord God Almighty and the Lamb were themselves the temple, 23 and the city did not need the sun or the moon for light, since it was lit by the radiant glory of God, and the Lamb was a lighted torch for it. 24 *The nations will come to its lights* and the kings of the earth will bring it their treasures. 25 Its *gates will never be closed by day* — and there will be no night there — 26 and *the nations will come, bringing their treasure* and their wealth. 27 Nothing unclean may come into it: no one who does what is loathsome or false, but only those who are listed in the Lamb's book of life.

22 Then the angel showed me the river of life, rising from the throne of God and of the Lamb and flowing crystal-clear. 2 Down the middle of the city street, *on either bank of the river were the trees of life, which bear twelve crops of fruit in a year, one in each month, and the leaves of which are the cure for the nations.*[t]

3 *The curse of destruction will be abolished.*[u] The throne of God and of the Lamb will be in the city; his servants will worship him, 4 they will see him face to face, and his name will be written on their foreheads. 5 And night will be abolished; they will not need lamplight or sunlight, because the Lord God will be shining on them. They will reign for ever and ever.

6 The angel said to me, 'All that you have written is sure and will come true: the Lord God who inspires the prophets has sent his angel to reveal to his servants *what is soon to take place.* 7 I am coming soon!' Blessed are those who keep the prophetic message of this book.

8 I, John, am the one who heard and saw these things. When I had heard and seen them all, I knelt at the feet of the angel who had shown them to me, to worship him; 9 but he said, 'Do no such thing: I am your fellow-servant and the fellow-servant of your brothers the prophets and those who keep the message of this book. God alone you must worship.'

10 This, too, he said to me, 'Do not keep the prophecies in this book a secret, because the Time is close. 11 Meanwhile let the sinner continue sinning, and the unclean continue to be unclean; let the upright continue in his uprightness, and those who are holy continue to be holy. 12 *Look, I am coming soon,* and my *reward is with* me, *to repay everyone as their deeds deserve.*[v] 13 I am the Alpha and the Omega, *the First and the Last,* the Beginning and the End. 14 Blessed are those who will have washed their robes clean, so that they will have the right to feed on the tree of life and can come through the gates into the city. 15 Others must stay outside: dogs, fortune-tellers, and the sexually immoral, murderers, idolaters, and everyone of false speech and false life.'

16 I, Jesus, have sent my angel to attest these things to you for the sake of the churches. I am the sprig from the root of David and the bright star of the morning.

17 The Spirit and the Bride say, 'Come!' Let everyone who listens answer, 'Come!' Then *let all who are thirsty come:*[w] all who want it may *have the water* of life, and have it *free.*

18 This is my solemn attestation to all who hear the prophecies in this book: if anyone adds anything to them, God will add to him every plague mentioned in the book; 19 if

---

s 21 Is 60:3. t 22 Ezk 47:12. u 22 Zc 14:11. v 22 Ps 62:12.
w 22 Is 55:1.

takes away from the words of the book of this prophecy, God will take away that person's share in the tree of life and in the holy city, which are described in this book.

20 The one who testifies to these things says, "Surely I am coming soon."

Amen. Come, Lord Jesus!

21 The grace of the Lord Jesus be with all the saints. Amen.*e*

e Other ancient authorities lack *all*; others lack *the saints*; others lack *Amen*

of prophecy, God will take away from him his share in the tree of life and in the Holy City, which are described in this book.

20 He who gives this testimony says: 'Yes, I am coming soon!'

Amen. Come, Lord Jesus!

21 The grace of the Lord Jesus be with all.

from the words in this prophetic book, God will take away his share in the tree of life and in the holy city described in this book.

20 The one who gives this testimony says, "Yes, I am coming soon." Amen! Come, Lord Jesus!

21 The grace of the Lord Jesus be with all.

anyone cuts anything out of the prophecies in this book, God will cut off his share of the tree of life and of the holy city, which are described in the book.

20 The one who attests these things says: I am indeed coming soon.

Amen; come, Lord Jesus.

21 May the grace of the Lord Jesus be with you all. Amen.